Features Index to Children's Books Awards 1983-1993

Children's Books in Print® 1994

An Author, Title, and Illustrator
Index to Books for Children and Young Adults

This edition of CHILDREN'S BOOKS IN PRINT
was prepared by the R.R. Bowker Bibliographic Group in collaboration
with the Publication Systems Department.

Peter Simon, Senior Vice President, Database Publishing

Albert Simmonds, Managing Director
June M. Hillis, Office Coordinator

Data Processing
Brenda McElroy, Senior Managing Editor
Beverley Lamar, Managing Editor,
Children's Book Awards and Selected Listings
Doret Dixon, Senior Editor
Lynda Romeo, Associate Editor
Margaret Allen, Edward Han, Ila Joseph,
George Krubski, David Widmer, Assistant Editors
Dorothy Perry-Gilchrist, Coordinator

Quality Control
Michael Olenick, Managing Editor
Raymond Padilla, Senior Editor
Daniel Dickholtz, Senior Associate Editor

Editorial Production
Doreen Gravesande, Production Director
Myriam Nunez, Managing Editor
Barbara Holton, Senior Editor
Megan Roxberry and Suzette Lawler, Senior Associate Editors
Clarice D. Isaacs, Assistant Editor

Electronic Data Transfer Group
Frank Accurso, Managing Editor
Mary Craig Daley, Senior Editor
William Zavorskas, Senior Associate Editor

Publishers Authority Database
&
International Standard Book Number Agency
Don Riseborough, Senior Managing Editor
Lynn DeVita, Sennior Editor
William D. McCahery, Senior Associate Editor
Diane Fumando, Coordinator
Janet Weiss, Assistant Editor

Data Collection & Processing Group
Bonnie Walton, Manager
Cheryl Patrick and Rhonda McKendrick, Coordinators
Leslie Fisher and Cynthia Werry, Assistant Coordinators

Computer Operations Group
Max Kobrinsky, Manager
Jack Murphy, Computer Operations

Features Index to Children's Books Awards 1983-1993

Children's Books in Print
1994

Vol. 1
Awards
Authors
Illustrators

An Author, Title, and Illustrator
Index to Books for Children and Young Adults

R. R. BOWKER
A Reed Reference Publishing Company
New Providence, New Jersey

Published by R. R. Bowker, A Reed Reference Publishing Company
121 Chanlon Road, New Providence, NJ 07974.
Copyright © 1994 by Reed Elsevier Inc.
All rights reserved.

International Standard Book Number: 0-8352-3451-7
Vol. 1 0-8352-3452-5 Vol. 2 0-8352-3453-3
International Standard Serial Number 0069-3480
Library of Congress Catalog Number 70-101705
Printed and bound in the United States of America

2 Volume Set

ISBN 0 - 8352 - 3451 - 7

9 780835 234511

FOREWORD

v

WHAT'S IN A NAME?

The twenty-fifth edition of *Children's Books in Print* is a two-volume author, illustrator, and title index to 88,153 books published in the United States for children and currently available for purchase. Since the publication of the first edition in 1969, *Children's Books in Print* has become an essential bibliography among R. R. Bowker's *In Print* book finding tools; the parent *Books in Print* and *Subject Guide to Books in Print*, which were its models. *Children's Books in Print* employs the same methods of collecting all author, title, and pricing information from the books' publishers; it follows the same up-to-date revision schedule that provides annually corrected and expanded book ordering information for librarians and booksellers.

HOW IT BEGAN

From 1962 to 1965 Bowker published *Publisher's Library Bindings in Print*, a catalog of the titles available in publishers' guaranteed library bindings. This list became the nucleus of *Children's Books for Schools and Libraries*, an expanded list that included trade books as well as library bindings and was the first bibliography we produced from computer-stored information. We published three annual editions of *Children's Books for Schools and Libraries*, from 1966 through 1968. The last edition was a title and author index of some 24,000 titles, of which 15,000 were in library bindings; 9,000 were trade editions of titles also available in library bindings and trade editions on standard recommendation lists and books reviewed during the previous three years in *School Library Journal*. Before undertaking the compilation of the book ordering data on all the titles that were not included in *Children's Books for Schools and Libraries*, the following questions (that have been without officially agreed-upon answers since books began) had to be settled in order to give us working boundaries for *Children's Books in Print:*

What is a book?
What is a children's book?
When is a children's book *in print?*

THE PRACTICAL ANSWERS

The answer to the first question seriously affects the United States title count in the statistics gathered by the United Nations, which considers anything under 49 pages in length a pamphlet. This definition denies book status to nearly 25 per cent of what specialists in the children's book field consider to be essential titles—so this definition of a book was not employed. (The error in this definition has been recognized and corrected by the American National Standards for compiling book publishing statistics.) Instead, Bowker supplied its own boundaries—no textbooks, no toybooks, and no workbooks for children were considered eligible for listing, and books in all bindings—paper, library or general trade—which are in print, are included here.

The second question was much more difficult to resolve. Because any books children can read could be called "children's books" (even though many books such as *Huckleberry Finn, Gulliver's Travels* and many others were originally for an adult readership), Bowker decided to forego a purist approach to this question and instead let the publishers be the authority. If the publishers' catalogs listed such titles as children's books, so be it. This is also true of variant titles among literary classics and of variations in authors' and illustrators' names. Individual decisions for each title variation or the establishment of authority for each author or illustrator entry would prohibit the annual appearance of *Children's Books in Print*. It would also retard work on its annual companion volume, *Subject Guide to Children's Books in Print*. Such checking would seriously increase the necessary staff and costs required for gathering the data and thus more than double the price of the bibliography. Therefore, all the information on authors, illustrators, editions and prices is printed here as the publishers supply it.

The answer to the third question rests with the publishers. *Children's Books In Print* is annually updated by the publishers themselves, who receive computer printouts of all their titles listed. Those titles no longer available for sale are removed and new titles are inserted. Thus, it is the publishers who promise that the books listed herein are obtainable.

The solutions we have chosen for these serious considerations are not perfect. R. R. Bowker does not claim that this bibliography is complete. But these working decisions provide the foundation for the most complete list of currently available children's books. Future editions will involve continuous revision to make this reference tool as complete as possible.

Lillian N. Gerhardt
Editor-in-Chief
SCHOOL LIBRARY JOURNAL

How to Use
CHILDREN'S
BOOKS IN PRINT

The twenty-fifth edition of *Children's Books in Print* is produced from records stored on magnetic tape, edited by computer programs, and set in type by computer-controlled photo-composition. This volume includes 88,153 titles, available from some 5,430 United States publishers. It provides an awards list arranged alphabetically by award or prize, an author index, arranged alphabetically by author, an alphabetically-arranged title index, and an alphabetically-arranged index of illustrators. A list of the publishers of the books listed in this volume appears at the end of the book.

NEW FEATURE: PUBLISHER PROVIDED ANNOTATIONS

Appearing for the second time this year are annotated entries, using information provided by participating publishers. This feature allows publishers to purchase space to highlight and describe their titles, and provides the reader with extra book information which he or she will find valuable for reference and acquisition decisions. If you wish to participate in this program, please contact Bowker at 908-464-6800.

CHILDREN'S BOOK AWARDS AND SELECTED LISTINGS

This list includes 57 major awards & selected listings, prizes or "best book" selections given to children's books since 1983. The awards are arranged alphabetically and the titles listed in alphabetical order under descending award years. Title entries are abridged, and consist of only title, author, editor, illustrator, publication date, and publisher.

ALPHABETICAL ARRANGEMENT OF AUTHOR, TITLE AND ILLUSTRATOR INDEXES

Within each index entries are filed *alphabetically by word*, with the following exceptions:

Initial articles of titles in English, French, German, Italian and Spanish are deleted from both author and title entries.

M', Mc and *Mac* are filed as if they were written *Mac* and are interfiled with other names beginning with *Mac*; for example, Macan, McAnally, Macardle, McAree, McArthur, Macarthur, Macartney, M'Aulay, Macaulay, McAuley. Within a specific name grouping *Mc* and *Mac* are interfiled according to the given name of the author; for example, Macdonald, Agnes; MacDonald, Alexander; McDonald, Annie L.; MacDonald, Austin F.; MacDonald, Betty. Compound names are listed under the first part of the name, and cross-references appear under the last part of the name.

Entries beginning with initial letters (whether authors' given names, or titles) are filed first, e.g., Smith, H.C., comes before Smith, Harold A.; B is for Betsy comes before Baba, Babar, etc.

Numerals, including year dates, are written out in most cases and are filed alphabetically.

U.S., UN, Dr., Mr., and St. are filed as though they were spelled out. In the author index, however, "Dr." remains abbreviated and files with the first letter of the personal name that follows it. For example, "Dr. Seuss" files as "Drs" and appears after an entry such as "Drowner, Margaret S."

SPECIAL NOTE ON HOW TO FIND AN AUTHOR'S OR ILLUSTRATOR'S COMPLETE LISTING

In sorting author and illustrator listings by computer it is not possible to group the entire listing for an individual together unless a standard spelling and format for each name is used. The information in *Children's Books in Print 1994* comes from data received from the publishers. If a name appears in various forms in this data, the listings in the index may be divided into several groups.

INFORMATION INCLUDED IN AUTHOR, TITLE AND ILLUSTRATOR ENTRIES

Entries include the following bibliographic information, when available: author, co-author, editor, co-editor, translator, co-translator, illustrator, co-illustrator, photographer, co-photographer, title, number of volumes, edition, Library of Congress number, series information, language if other than English, whether or not illustrated, grade range, year of publication, type of binding if other than cloth over boards, price, International Standard Book Number, publisher's order number, imprint, and publisher abbreviation. When an entry includes the prices for both the hardcover and paperback editions, the publication date within the entry refers to the hardcover binding; however, when the paperback binding is the only one included in the entry, the publication date is the paperback publication date. (Information on the International Standard Book Numbering System is available from R. R. Bowker.)

The prices cited are those provided by the publishers and generally refer to either the trade edition or the Publisher's Library Bound edition (PLB). The abbreviation PLB is used whenever the price cited is for a publisher's library bound edition.

Since some trade editions are bound to the same standards as some library editions, the symbol "g" is used *after* a price to indicate that the edition is guaranteed by the publisher to give satisfaction in normal library use.

If the price is merely tentatively suggested, a lower case "t" follows the anticipated price, e.g., 3.87t; "x" indicates a short discount—20%, or less. Short discount (20% or less) information is generally supplied by publishers to Bowker for each publication. However, all publishers do not uniformly supply this information, and Bowker can only make its best efforts to transmit this information when it is provided. PLB indicates a publishers' library binding.

The symbol "a" *after* a price indicates that a library binding is available at a special price.

An "i" following the price indicates an invoice price. Specific policies for such titles should be obtained from individual publishers.

KEY TO PUBLISHERS' AND DISTRIBUTORS' ABBREVIATIONS

Publishers' and distributors' names are abbreviated in the listings of *Children's Books in Print*. A key to these abbreviations will be found in *Key to Publishers' & Distributors' Abbreviations* at the end of this volume. Entries in this "Key" are arranged alphabetically by the abbreviations used in the bibliographic entries. The full name, ISBN prefix, editorial address, telephone number, ordering address (if different from the editorial address), and imprints follow the abbreviation. SAN (Standard Address Number) is a unique identification code for each address of each organization in or served by the book industry.

For example:

Bowker, (Bowker, R. R.; 0-8352), A Reed Reference Publishing Company, 121 Chanlon Rd., New Providence, NJ 07974 (SAN 214-1191) Tel 908-464-6800; Toll free: 800-521-8110, 800-537-8416 (in Canada).

If an entry contains a "Pub. by" note after the price the title should be ordered from the distributor whose abbreviation appears at the end of the entry. Entries which include the note "Dist. by" should also be ordered from the distributor, not the publisher.

The information in this bibliography has been obtained from publishers' catalogs and from other information submitted by publishers for *Books in Print 1993-94*.

LIST OF ABBREVIATIONS

a	after price, specially priced library edition available
abr.	abridged
adpt.	adapted
Amer.	American
annot.	annotation(s), annotated
ans.	answer(s)
app.	appendix
approx.	approximately
assn.	association
auth.	author
bd.	bound
bdg.	binding
bds.	boards
bibl(s).	bibliography(ies)
bk(s).	book, books
bklet(s)	booklets
Bro.	Brother
coll.	college
comm.	commission, committee
co.	company
cond.	condensed
comp(s).	compiler(s)
corp.	corporation
dept.	department
diag(s).	diagram(s)
dir.	director
disk	software disk or diskette
dist.	distributed
Div.	Division
doz.	dozen
ea.	each
ed.	editor, edited, edition
eds.	editions, editors
educ.	education
elem.	elementary
ency.	encyclopedia
ENG	English
enl.	enlarged
exp.	expurgated
fac.	facsimile
fasc.	fascicule
fict.	fiction
fig(s).	figure(s)
for.	foreign
FRE	French
frwd.	foreword
g	after price, guaranteed juvenile binding
gen.	general
GER	German
GRE	Greek
gr.	grade, grades
hdbk.	handbook
HEB	Hebrew
i	invoice price—see publisher for specific pricing policies
ISBN	International Standard Book Number
i.t.a.	initial teaching alphabet
Illus.	illustrated, illustration(s), illustrator(s)
in prep.	in preparation
incl.	includes, including
inst.	institute
intro.	introduction
ITA	Italian
Jr.	Junior
jt. auth.	joint author
jt. ed.	joint editor
k	kindergarten audience level
l.p.	long playing
ltd. ed.	limited edition
lab.	laboratory
lang(s).	language(s)
LAT	Latin
lea.	leather
lib.	library
lit.	literature, literary
math.	mathematics
mod.	modern
mor.	morocco
MS, MSS	manuscript, manuscripts
natl.	national
no., nos.	number, numbers
o.p.	out of print
orig.	original text, not a reprint
o.s.i.	out of stock indefinitely
pap.	paper
photos	photographs, photographer
PLB	publisher's library binding
POL	Polish
pop. ed.	popular edition
POR	Portuguese
prep.	preparation
probs.	problems
prog. bk.	programmed book
ps	preschool audience level
pseud.	pseudonym
pt(s).	part, parts
pub.	published, publisher, publishing
pubn.	publication
ref(s).	reference(s)
repr.	reprint
reprod(s).	reproduction(s)
rev.	revised
rpm.	revolution per minute (phono records)
RUS	Russian
SAN	Standard Address Number
S&L	Signed and Limited
s.p.	school price
scp	single copy Direct to the Consumer Price
sec.	section
sel.	selected
ser.	series
Soc.	Society
sols.	solutions
SPA	Spanish
Sr. (after given name)	Senior
Sr. (before given name)	Sister
St.	Saint
subs.	subsidiary
subsc.	subscription
suppl.	supplement
t	after price, tentative price
tech.	technical
text ed.	text edition
tr.	translator, translated, translation
univ.	university
vol(s).	volume, volumes
wkbk.	workbook
x	after price, short discount (20% or less)
YA	young adult audience level
yrbk.	yearbook

INTERNATIONAL STANDARD
BOOK NUMBER

The 1994 CHILDREN'S BOOKS IN PRINT lists each title or edition of a title with an ISBN. All publishers were notified and requested to submit a valid ISBN for their titles.

During the past decade, the majority of the publishers complied with requirements of the standard and implemented the ISBN. At present, approximately 97% of all new titles and all new editions are submitted for listing with a valid ISBN.

To fulfill the responsibility of accomplishing total book numbering, the ISBN Agency allocated the ISBN prefixes 0-317, 0-318, 0-685 and 0-686 to number their titles in the BOOKS IN PRINT database without an ISBN. Titles not having an ISBN at the closing date of this publication were assigned an ISBN with one of these prefixes by the International Standard Book Numbering Agency.

Titles numbered within the prefixes 0-317, 0-318, 0-685 and 0-686 are:
—Publishers who did not assign ISBNs to their titles.
—Distributors with titles published and imported from countries not in the ISBN system, or not receiving the ISBN from the originating publisher.
—Errors from transposition and transcription which occurred in transmitting the ISBN to the BOOKS IN PRINT database.

All the ISBNs listed in BOOKS IN PRINT are validated by using the check digit control, and only valid ISBNs are listed in the BIP database.

All publishers participating in the ISBN system having titles numbered within the prefixes 0-317, 0-318, 0-685 and 0-686 will receive a computer printout, requesting them to submit the correct ISBN.

Publishers not participating in the ISBN system may request from the ISBN Agency the assignment of an ISBN Publisher Prefix, and start numbering their titles.

The Book Industry System Advisory Committee (BISAC) has developed a standard format for data transmission, and many companies are already accepting orders transmitted on magnetic tape using the ISBN.

BISAC has also developed several other formats, also using the ISBN, including the title status format from which it is possible to update bibliographic information by magnetic tape exchange. Books in Print has been participating in such an exchange with many publishers, and welcomes inquiries from prospective participants.

The ISBN Agency and the Database Publishing Group of R. R. Bowker wish to express their appreciation to all publishers who collaborated in making the ISBN system the standard of the publishing industry.

SAN, an acronym of Standard Address Number, is a unique identification code for each address of each organization in or served by the book industry.

SANs are assigned to publishers, distributors, wholesalers, associations, software producers and manufacturers in the U.S.

The SAN itself merely defines an address. It becomes functional only in its application to activities such as purchasing, invoicing, billing, shipping, receiving, paying, crediting and refunding.

For additional information related to the ISBN total numbering, please refer to Emery Koltay, Director of the ISBN/SAN Agency, c/o R.R. Bowker.

CHILDREN'S BOOK AWARDS
AND SELECTED LISTINGS
1983–1993

We at Bowker cannot fail to recognize the phenomenal growth in the publication of children's books from the late nineteenth century to the present. This increased attention to children's literature and the greater emphasis on excellence by both authors and illustrators have been reflected by the growth in the number of prizes, awards and selected listings, that are sponsored or compiled annually by such prestigious groups as the American Library Association and the British Library Association.

The 1987-88 edition of *Children's Books in Print* was the first edition to include a selective list of Children's Book Awards. The list covered the period 1980-1986 and included the most popular United States awards such as the Newbery and Caldecott Medals, the most significant awards given in Canada, as well as awards and recognition given to authors and illustrators who have made a significant contribution to children's literature.

For this edition of *Children's Books In Print*, the list includes 57 awards and listings covering the years 1983-1993 seventeen of which have been discontinued. The Children's Books Awards and Selected Listings Index includes major awards and prizes given to children's books, authors and illustrators from the United States, United Kingdom, Canada, Australia and New Zealand. Excluded are those awards and listings that are restricted to specific geographical regions. We have, however, included foreign publications (preceded by double daggers (††)), and out of print titles (which are indicated by the notation "o.p." at the end of the entry).

The listing is alphabetical according to the name of the award or listing. Within these listings, entries are arranged alphabetically by title in descending order of the year the award was received or the listing compiled. Elements included are: title, author, editor and/or illustrator, publication date and publisher. When appropriate, specific abbreviated descriptions pertaining to age groups—(Younger and Older), and categories—text, illustrations (Text, Illus.) are included. In most cases, awards were given one year after the publication date of the book. Runners-up and honor books have been excluded. However, honor lists like International Board on Books for Young People (IBBY) and commended listings like the American Library Association Notable Books for Children, New York Times Best Illustrated Children's Books of the year, and School Library Journal's "Best Books of the Year" are included.

The Body of Work Awards listing includes the names of people who have received awards and commendation for their contributions to children's literature over a number of years. These are also in alphabetical order according to the name of the award.

In preparing this list, Bowker's editors have either contacted the award societies or researched independently published lists. Occasionally there are inconsistencies relating to publication dates or the years some awards were given; whenever this occurred, the dates indicated by award societies have been cited.

The editors acknowledge with thanks the personnel from the many award societies who co-operated by responding to requests for lists and information on these awards. Particularly invaluable tools in our research were *Children's Books: Awards & Prizes* by the Children's Book Council (1986) and *Children's Literature Awards & Winners* by Dolores Blythe Jones (Gale Research, 1983).

CHILDREN'S BOOK AWARDS AND SELECTED LISTINGS 1983-1993

Jane Addams Children's Book Award

Sponsored by the Women's International League for Peace and Freedom, and the Jane Addams Peace Association, this award has been presented annually since 1953 for the children's book which best promotes peace, equality and social justice. The recipient of this award receives a hand-illuminated scroll. A silver seal is placed on the jacket of the winning book by the publisher.

1993

Taste of Salt: Story of Modern Haiti. Frances Temple. 1992. Orchard Bks Watts.

1992

Journey of the Sparrows. Fran L Buss. Ed. by Daisy Cubias. 1991. (Lodestar Bks). Dutton Child Bks.

1991

Big Book for Peace. Ann Durell & Marilyn Sachs. 1990. Dutton Child Bks.

1990

Long Hard Journey: The Story of the Pullman Porter. Patricia McKissack. Illus. by Fredrick McKissack. 1990. Walker & Co.

1989

Anthony Burns: The Defeat & Triumph of a Fugitive Slave. Virginia Hamilton. 1988. Knopf.

Looking Out. Victoria Boutis. 1988. (Four Winds). Macmillan.

1988

Waiting for the Rain: A Novel of South Africa. Sheila Gordon. 1987. Orchard Bks Watts.

1987

Nobody Wants a Nuclear War. Judith Vigna. Ed. by Kathleen Tucker. Illus. by Judith Vigna. 1986. A Whitman.

1986

Ain't Gonna Study War No More: The Story of America's Peace Seekers. Milton Meltzer. 1985. (HarpJ). Har-Row.

1985

Short Life of Sophie Scholl. Herman Vinke. Tr. by Hedwig Pachter from Ger. 1984. HarpJ.

1984

Rain of Fire. Marion Bauer. 1983. (Clarion). HM.

1983

Hiroshima No Pika. Toshi Maruki. Illus. by Toshi Maruki. 1982. Lothrop.

American Book Award

Established in 1980 by the Association of American Publishers, this annual award replaced the discontinued National Book award. Two of its four purposes are to "recognize & reward books of literary and artistict merit," and to "generate public awareness of books." Seventeen categories are represented, including: children's paperback fiction (Pbk/F), children's hardcover fiction (H/F), children's hardcover picture books (H/Pic), children's paperback picture books (Pbk/Pic), and children's nonfiction (N/F). There are also "six categories" pertaining to "graphics" in children's books which are given special consideration. The recipient of this award must be a United States citizen who has written, translated or designed the book during the preceding year. Prizes include $1,000 for literary works, and a Louise Nevelson wall sculpture for graphic works. Since 1984 the children's book section of the American Book Award has been discontinued.

1983

Chimney Sweeps. James C. Giblin. Illus. by Margot Tomes. 1982. Crowell Jr Bks. (N/F).

Doctor De Soto. William Steig. 1982. FS&G. (H/Pic).

Homesick: My Own Story. Jean Fritz. Illus. by Margot Tomes. 1982. (Putnam). Putnam Pub Group. (H/F).

House is a House for Me. Mary A. Hoberman. Illus. by Betty Fraser. 1982. Viking. (Pbk/Pic).

Marked by Fire. Joyce C. Thomas. 1982. (Flare). Avon. (Pbk/F).

Miss Rumphius. Barbara Cooney. Illus. by Barbara Cooney. 1982. Viking. (H/Pic).

Place Apart. Paula Fox. 1982. (XSig). NAL-Dutton. (Pbk/F).

American Library Association Notable Books for Children

Since its inception in 1940, this listing is compiled annually by the Notable Children's Books Committee of the Association for Library Service to Children (ALSC), a division of the American Library Association. Included are books of commendable quality that encourage and reflect children's interests. In making the selections, the Committee considers "literary quality," "originality of text and illustration," "clarity and style of language," "excellence of illustration, design and format," "subject matter of interest and value to children," and "likelihood of acceptance by children." (Whereas previous listings were for publications of that same year, the 1989 publications are listed in the 1990 list.)

1993

Against the Storm. Gaye Hicyilmaz. 1992. (Joy Street Bks). Little. (Older).

Ajeemah & His Son. James Berry. 1992. HarpC Child Bks. (Older).

All But Alice. Phyllis R. Naylor. 1992. Atheneum. (Middle).

Amazing Potato: A Story in Which the Incas, Conquistadors, Marie Antoinette, Thomas Jefferson, Wars, Famines, Immigrants, & French Fries All Play a Part. Milton Meltzer. 1992. HarpC Child Bks. (Middle).

And the Green Grass Grew All Around: Folk Poetry from Everyone. Alvin Schwartz. Illus. by Sue Truesdell. 1992. HarpC Child Bks. (Middle).

Angel for Solomon Singer. Cynthia Rylant. Illus. by Peter Catalantto. 1992. Orchard Bks Watts. (All).

Antarctica: The Last Unspoiled Continent. Laurence Pringle. Illus. by Laurence Pringle. 1992. Simon & Schuster. (Middle).

Back Home. Gloria J. Pinkney. Illus. by Jerry Pinkney. 1992. Dial Bks Young. (Younger).

Bard of Avon: The Story of William Shakespeare. Diane Stanley & Peter Vennema. Illus. by Diane Stanley. 1992. Morrow. (Middle)..

Beggar's Ride. Theresa Nelson. 1992. Orchard Bks Watts. (Older).

Bently & Egg. William Joyce. Illus. by Laura Geringer. 1992. HarpC Child Bks. (Younger).

Charlie Parker Played Be Bop. Chris Raschka. Illus. by Chris Raschka. 1992. Orchard Bks Watts. (All).

Chicken Sunday. Patricia Polacco. 1992. (Philomel Bks). Putnam Pub Group. (Younger).

Children of the Dust Bowl: The True Story of the School at Weedpatch Camp. Jerry Stanley. Illus. by Jerry Stanley. 1992. Crown Bks Yng Read. (Older).

Dark-Thirty: Southern Tales of the Supernatural. Patricia McKissack. Illus. by Brian Pinkney. 1992. Knopf Bks Yng Read. (Middle).

Don't You Know There's a War On? James Stevenson. 1992. Greenwillow. (Younger).

Emily. Michael Bedard. Illus. by Barbara Cooney. 1992. Doubleday. (Younger).

Farmer Duck. Martin Waddell. Illus. by Helen Oxenbury. 1992. Candlewick Pr. (Younger).

Fortune-Tellers. Lloyd Alexander. Illus. by Trina Schart-Hyman. 1992. (DCB). Dutton Child Bks. (Younger).

Gonna Sing My Head Off! American Folk Songs for Children. Ed. by Kathleen Krull. Illus. by Allen Garns. 1992. Knopf Bks Yng Read. (All).

Harmony Arms. Ron Koertge. 1992. (Joy Street Bks). Little. (Older).

Hugh Can Do. Jennifer Armstrong. Illus. by Kimberly B. Root. 1992. Crown Bks Yng Read. (Younger).

I Saw Esau: The Schoolchild's Pocket Book. Ed. by Iona Opie & Peter Opie. Illus. by Maurice Sendak. 1992. Candlewick Pr. (All).

Indian Winter. Russell Freedman. Illus. by Karl Bodmer. 1992. Holiday Hse. (Older).

Jim Ugly. Sid Fleischman. Illus. by Jos A. Smith. 1992. Greenwillow. (Middle).

June 29, 1999. David Wiesner. 1992. (Clarion Bks). HM. (Younger).

Leaving. Budge Wilson. 1992. (Philomel Bks). Putnam Pub Group. (Older).

Letters from a Slave Girl: The Story of Harriet Jacobs. Mary E. Lyons. 1992. (Scribners Young Read). Macmillan Child Grp. (Older).

Letters from Rifka. Karen Hesse. 1992. (Bks Young Re ad). H Holt & Co. (Older).

Letting Swift River Go. Jane Yolen. Illus. by Barbara Cooney. 1992. Little. (Younger).

Life & Times of the Apple. Charles Micicci. 1992. Orchard Bks Watts. (Younger).

Life's a Funny Proposition, Horatio. Barbara G. Polikoff. 1992. (Bks Young Read). H Holt & Co. (Middle).

Li'l Sis & Uncle Willie: A Story Based on the Life & Paintings of William H. Johnson. Gwen Everett. 1992. Rizzoli. (Middle).

Loop the Loop. Barbara Dugan. Illus. by James Stevenson. 1992. Greenwillow. (Middle).

Love Flute. Paul Goble. 1992. Bradbury Pr. (Middle).

Lunch. Denise Fleming. Illus. by Denise Fleming. 1992. H Holt & Co. (Younger)..

Martha Speaks. Susan Meddaugh. 1992. HM. (Younger).

Mirette on the High Wire. Emily A. McCully. 1992. Putnam Pub Group. (Younger).

Missing May. Cynthia Rylant. 1992. Orchard Bks Watts. (Older).

Moon & I. Betsy Byars. 1992. Messner. (Middle).

Moon Rope: A Peruvian Folktale. Lois Ehlert. Tr. by Amy Prince. 1992. (HB Juv Bks). Harbrace. (Younger)..

Moonbow of Mr. B. Bones. J. Patrick Lewis. Illus. by Dirk Zimmer. 1992. Knopf Bks Yng Read. (Younger).

My Great-Aunt Arizona. Gloria Houston. Illus. by Susan C. Lamb. 1992. HarpC Child Bks. (Younger).

No Place to Be: Voices of Homeless Children. Judith Berck. 1992. HM. (Older).

Old Black Fly. Jim Avlesworth. Illus. by Stephen Gammell. 1992. (Bks Young Read). H Holt & Co. (Younger).

Our Solar System. Seymour Simon. Illus. by Seymour Simon. 1992. Morrow. (Middle).

Pigman & Me. Paul Zindel. Illus. by Paul Zindel. 1992. HarpC Child Bks. (Older).

Red Dragonfly on My Shoulder. Sylvia Cassedy. Illus. by Molly Bang. 1992. HarpC Child Bks. (All).

Rosa Parks: My Story. Rosa Parks & Jim Haskins. 1992. Dial Bks Young. (Older).

Seven Blind Mice. Ed. Young. 1992. (Philomel Bks). Putnam Pub Group. (Younger).

Snakes. Seymour Simon. Illus. by Seymour Simon. 1992. HarpC Child Bks. (Middle).

Soap Soup & Other Verses. Karla Kuskin. Illus. by Charlotte Zolotow. 1992. HarpC Child Bks. (Younger).

Somewhere in the Darkness. Walter D. Myers. 1992. Scholastic Inc. (Older).

Soujourner Truth: Ain't I a Woman? Patricia C. McKissack & Fredrick McKissack. 1992. Scholastic Inc. (Older).

Steal Away. Jennifer Armstrong. 1992. Orchard Bks Watts. (Older).

Stinky Cheese Man & Other Fairly Stupid Tales. Jon Scieszka. Illus. by Lane Smith. 1992. (Penguin Bks). Viking. (All).

Sukey & the Mermaid. Robert D. San Souci. 1992. (Four Winds). Macmillan Child Grp. (Middle).

Sundiata. David Wisniewski. Illus. by David Wisniewski. 1992. (Clarion Bks). HM. (Middle).

Surtsey: The Newest Place on Earth. Kathryn Lasky. Illus. by Christopher G. Knight. 1992. Hyprn Child Bks. (Middle).

Talking Like the Rain: A First Book of Poems. Ed. by X. J. Kennedy & Dorothy M. Kennedy. Illus. by Jane Dyer. 1992. Little. (Younger)..

Talking with Artists. Ed. by Pat Cummings. Illus. by Pat Cummings. 1992. (Bradbury Pr). Macmillan Child Grp. (All).

This Same Sky: A Collection of Poems from Around the World. Ed. by Naomi S. Nye. 1992. Four Winds. (Older).

Twilight Struggle: The Life of John Fitzgerald Kennedy. Barbara Harrison & Daniel Terris. 1992. Lothrop. (Older).

Underrunners. Margaret Mahy. 1992. Viking Child Bks. (Middle).

What Hearts. Bruce Brooks. 1992. HarpC Child Bks. (Older).

What's Your Story? A Young Person's Guide to Writing Fiction. Marion D. Bauer. 1992. (Clarion Bks). HM. (Older).

When the Road Ends. Jean Thesman. 1992. HM. (Older).

Who Shrank My Grandmother's House? Poems of Discovery. Barbara Esbensen. Illus. by Eric Beddows. 1992. HarpC Child Bks. (Middle).

Who Was That Masked Ma, Anyway? Avi. 1992. Orchard Bks Watts. (Middle).

Widow's Broom. Chris Van Allsburg. Illus. by Chris Van Allsburg. 1992. HM. (All).

Wings Along the Waterway. Mary B. Brown. 1992. Orchard Bks Watts. (Middle).

Words of Stone. Kevin Henkes. 1992. Greenwillow. (Middle).

Working Cotton. Sherley A. Williams. Illus. by Carole Byard. 1992. (HB Juv Bks). Harbrace. (Younger).

World in 1492. Jean Fritz. Illus. by Stefano Vitale. 1992. (Bks Yng Read). H Holt & Co. (All).

1992

Abuela. Arthur Dorros. Illus. by Elisa Kleven. 1991. Dutton Child Bks. (Younger).

Adventures of Isabel. Ogden Nash. Illus. by James Marshall. 1991. (Joy Street). Little. (Younger).

Albert's Alphabet. Leslie Tryon. Illus. by Leslie Tryon. 1991. (Atheneum Child Bk). Macmillan Child Grp. (Younger).

All of You Was Singing. Richard Lewis. Illus. by Ed Young. 1991. Atheneum. (All).

Along the Tracks. Tamar Bergman. Tr. by Michael Swirsky. 1991. HM. (Older).

Amazing Grace. Mary Hoffman. Illus. by Caroline Binch. 1991. Dial Bks Young. (Younger).

Amazing Grace. Mary Hoffman. Illus. by Caroline Binch. 1991. Dial Bks Young. (Younger).

Animal Fables from Aesop. Aesop. Illus. by Barbara McClintock. Adapted by Barbara McClintock. 1991. Godine. (All).

Anno's Math Games III. Mitsumasa Anno. 1991. (Philomel Bks). Putnam Pub Group. (All).

Appalachia. Cynthia Rylant. Illus. by Barry Moser. 1991. HarBraceJ. (All).

At the Crossroads. Rachel Isadora. 1991. Greemwillow. (Younger).

Bigmama's. Donald Crews. 1991. Greenwillow. (Younger).

Borning Room. Paul Fleischman. 1991. (Charlotte Zolotow Bks). HarpC Child Bks. (Older).

Bully for You, Teddy Roosevelt! Jean Fritz. Illus. by Mike Wimmer. 1991. Putnam Pub Group. (Middle).

Castle in the Air. Diana Wynne Jones. 1991. Greenwillow. (Older).

Chameleons: Dragons in the Trees. James Martin. Photos by Art Wolfe. 1991. Crown. (Middle).

Changes. Anthony Browne. 1991. Knopf. (Younger).

Chrysanthemun. Kevin Henkes. 1991. Greenwillow. (Younger).

Diamond Tree: Jewish Tales from Around the World. Howard Schwartz & Barbara Rush. Illus. by Uri Shulevitz. 1991. HarpC Child Bks. (Middle).

Discovering Christopher Columbus: How History Is Invented. Kathy Pelta. 1991. Lerner Pubns. (Older).

Discovery of the Americas. Betsy Maestro. Illus. by Giulio Maestro. 1991. Lothrop. (Middle).

Eating Fractions. Bruce Mcmillan. 1991. Scholastic Inc. (Younger).

Flight: The Journey of Charles Lindbergh. Robert Burleigh. Illus. by Mike Wimmer. 1991. (Philomel Bks). Putnam Pub Group. (Middle).

Fly Away Home. Eve Bunting. Illus. by Ronald Himler. 1991. (Clarion Bks). HM. (Younger).

Frog Prince, Continued. Jon Scieszka. Illus. by Steve Jonson. 1991. Viking Child Bks. (Middle).

Glasses--Who Needs 'Em. Lane Smith. 1991. Viking Child Bks. (Middle).

Handmade Alphabet. Laura Rankin. 1991. Dial BBks Young. (All).

In the Tall, Tall Grass. Denise Fleming. Illus. by Denise Fleming. 1991. H. Holt & Co. (Younger).

Jack and the Beanstalk. Retold by Steven Kellogg. Illus. by Steven Kellogg. 1991. Morrow Jr Bks. (Younger).

Journey. Patricia MacLachlan. 1991. Delacorte. (Middle).

Last Princess: The Story of Princess Ka'iolani of Hawaii. Fay Stanley. Illus. by Diane Stanley. 1991. (Four Winds Bks). Macmillan Child Grp. (Middle).

Living with Dinosaurs. Patricia Lauber. Illus. by Douglas Henderson. 1991. (Bradbury). Macmillan Child Grp. (Middle).

Lyddie. Katherine Paterson. 1991. (Lodestar Bks). Dutton Child Bks. (Older).

Man from the Other Side. Uri Orlev. 1991. HM. (Older).

Max's Dragon Shirt. Rosemary Wells. 1991. Dial. (Younger).

Michael Foreman's Mother Goose. Mother Goose. 1991. HarbraceJ.

Monkey Island. Paula Fox. 1991. Orchard Bks Watts. (Older).

Moon Rope: A Peruvian Folktale. Lois Ehlert. Tr. by Amy Prince. 1992. (HB Juv Bks). Harbrace. (Younger).

Mouse Count. Ellen S Walsh. Ed. by Diane D'Andrade. Illus. by Ellen S Walsh. 1991. HarBracJ. (Younger).

Mozart Season. Virginia Euwer Wolff. 1991. H Holt & Co. (Older).

Nekomah Creek. Linda Crew. Illus. by Charles Robinson. 1991. Delacorte. (Middle).

Night on Neighborhood Street. Eloise Greenfield. Illus. by Jan Spivey Gilchrist. 1991. Dial Bks Young. (All).

Nothing But the Truth : A Documentary Novel. Avi. 1991. Orchard Bks Watts. (Older).

Now Is Your Time! The African-American Struggle for Freedom. Walter Dean Myers. 1991. HarpC Child Bks. (Older).

Old Mother Hubbard & Her Wonderful Dog. James Marshall. Illus. by James Marshall. 1991. FS&G. (Younger).

Orphan Boy: A Maasai Story. Tololwa M Mollel. Illus. by Paul Morin. 1991. (Clarion Bks). HM. (Middle).

Owl and the Pussycat. Edward Lear. Illus. by Jan Brett. 1991. Putnam Pub Group. (Younger).

Painter's Eye: Learning to Look at Contemporary American Art. Jan Greenberg & Sandra Jordan. 1991. Delacorte. (Older).

Pennywhistle Tree. Doris B Smith. Illus. by Leslie Bowman. 1991. Putnam Pub Group. (Middle).

Piggies. Audrey Wood & Don Wood. Illus. by Don Wood. 1991. HarBraceJ. (Younger).

Pish, Posh, Said Hieronymus Bosch. Nancy Willard. Illus. by L. D Dillons. 1991. HarBraceJ. (All).

Place Where Nobody Stopped. Jerry Segal. Illus. by Dav Pilkey. 1991. Orchard Bks Watts. (Older).

Poem-Making: Ways to Begin Writing Poetry. Myra Cohn Livingston. 1991. (Charlotte Zolotow Bks). HarpC Child Bks. (Older).

Rats on the Roof & Other Stories. James Marshall. Illus. by James Marshall. 1991. Dial Bks Young. (Middle).

Remarkable Voyages of Captain Cook. Rhoda Blumberg. Ed. by Barbara Lalicki. 1991. (Bradbury Bks). Macmillan Child Grp. (Older).

Saint Jerome & the Lion. Illus. by Barry Moser. Retold by Margaret Hodges. 1991. Orchard Bks Watts. (All).

Searching for Dragons: The Enchanted Forest Chronicles. Patricia C Wrede. 1991. HarBraceJ. (Older).

Separate Battle: Women & the Civil War. Ina Chang. 1991. (Lodestar Bks). Dutton Child Bks. (Older).

Shiloh. Phyllis Naylor. 1991. (Atheneum Child Bk). Macmillan Child Grp. (Middle).

Songs of the Wild West. Metropolitan Museum of Art. Commentary by Alan Axelrod. 1991. S&S Trade. (All).

Stars Come Out Within. Jean Little. 1991. Viking Child Bks. (Older).

Stepping on the Cracks. Mary Downing Hahn. 1991. (Clarion Bks). HM. (Older).

Story of Christmas: Word from the Gospels of Matthews. Bible. Illus. by Jane Ray. 1991. Dutton Child Bks. (All).

Summer of Fire: Yellowstone 1988. Patricia Lauber. 1991. Orchard Bks Watts. (Middle).

Tales of the Early World. Ted Hughes. Illus. by Andrew Davidson. 1991. FS&G. (Older).

Tar Beach. Faith Ringgold. Illus. by Faith Ringgold. 1991. Crown. (Younger).

Thomas Jefferson: The Revolutionary Aristocrat. Milton Meltzer. 1991. Orchard Bks Watts. (Older).

Tiger with Wings: The Great Horned Owl. Barbara J Esbensen. Illus. by Mary B Brown. 1991. Orchard Bks Watts. (Middle).

Traveling to Tondo: A Tale of the Nkundo of Zaire. Verna Aardema. Illus. by Will Hillenbrand. 1991. Knopf. (Younger).

Tree of Cranes. Allen Say. 1991. (Sandpiper). HM. (Younger).

Truth about Unicorns. James Cross Giblin. Illus. by Michael McDermott. 1991. HarpC Child Bks. (Older).

Tuesday. David Wiesner. 1991. (Clarion Bks). HM. (All).

Wanted...Mud Blossom. Betsy Byars. Illus. by Jacqueline Rogers. 1991. Delacorte. (Middle).

Wave in Her Pocket: Stories from Trinidad. Lynn Joseph. Illus. by Brian Pinkney. 1991. (Clarion Bks). HM. (Middle).

Wright Brothers: How They Invented the Airplane. Russell Freedman. Photos by Wilbur Wright & Orville Wright. 1991. Holiday. (Older).

Year of Impossible Goodbyes. Sook Nyul Choi. 1991. (Sandpiper). HM. (Older).

Young Painter. Zheng Zhensun & Alice Low. 1991. Scholastic Inc. (Older).

1991

Aardvarks, Disembark! Ann Jonas. 1990. Greenwillow.

Aida. Leontyne Price. Illus. by Leo Dillon & Diane Dillon. 1990. HarcBraceJ.

Big Book for Peace. Ann Durell & Marilyn Sachs. 1990. Dutton.

Bingo Brown, Gypsy Lover. Betsy Byars. 1990. Viking Penguin.

Bird Watch. Jane Yolen. Illus. by Ted Lewin. 1990. (Philomel Bks). Putnam.

Black & White. David Macaulay. 1990. HM.

Christopher Columbus: Voyager to the Unknown. Nancy Smiler Levinson. 1990. (Lodestar Bks). Dutton.

Columbus and the World Around Him. Milton Meltzer. 1990. Watts.

Come a Tide. George Ella Lyon. Illus. by Stephen Gammell. 1990. Orchard Bks Watts.

Cousins. Virginia Hamilton. 1990. (Philomel Bks). Putnam.

Cowboy Dreams. Dayal Kaur Khalsa. 1990. Crown.

Day of Ahmed's Secret. Florence Parry Heide & Judith Heide Gilliland. Illus. by Ted Lewin. 1990. Lothrop.

Dixie Storms. Barbara Hall. 1990. HBJ.

Everywhere. Bruce Brooks. 1990. HarperJ.

Family Pictures. Garza Lomas. Illus. by Garza Lomas. 1990. Children's Book Pr.

Fox Be Nimble. James Marshall. 1990. Dial Bks Young.

Franklin Delano Roosevelt. Russell Freedman. Illus. by Russell Freedman. 1990. (Clarion Bks). HM.

Further Tales of Uncle Remus: The Misadventures of Brer Rabbit, Brer Fox, Brer Wolf, the Doodang and other creatures. Julius Lester. Illus. by Jerry Pinkney. 1990. (Dial). Doubleday.

Giraffes, the Sentinels of the Savannas. Helen Roney Sattler. Illus. by Christopher Santoro. 1990. Lothrop.

Good Queen Bess: The Story of Elizabeth I of England. Diane Stanley & Peter Vennema. 1990. (Four Winds). Macmillan.

Hand Full of Stars. Rafik Schami. Tr. by Rika Lesser. 1990. Dutton.

Henry and Mudge and the Happy Cat. Cynthia Rylant. Illus. by Sucie Stevenson. 1990. Bradbury Pr.

I Went Walking. Sue Williams. Illus. by Julie Vivas. 1990. (Gulliver Bks). HarBraceJ.

Insect Metamorphosis: From Egg to Adult. Ron Goor & Nancy Goor. 1990. (Atheneum Childrens Bks). Macmillan.

Julius: The Baby of the World. Kevin Henkes. 1990. Greenwillow.

July. James Stevenson. 1990. Greenwillow.

Little Dog Laughed. Lucy Cousins. Illus. by Lucy Cousins. 1990. Dutton Child Bks.

Little Tricker the Squirrel Meets Big Double the Bear. Ken Kesey. Illus. by Barry Moser. 1990. Viking Penguin.

Maniac Magee. Jerry Spinelli. 1990. Little.

Mice Are Nice. Ed. by Nancy Larrick. Illus. by Ed Young. 1990. (Philomel Bks). Putnam.

Midnight Horse. Sid Fleischman. Illus. by Peter Sis. 1990. Greenwillow.

More More More, Said the Baby: 3 Love Stories. Vera B. Williams. 1990. Greenwillow.

Mousehole Cat. Barber Antonia. Illus. by Nicola Bayley. 1990. Macmillan.

Old John. Peter Hartling. Tr. by Elizabeth D. Crawford. 1990. Lothrop.

One Sun: A Book of Terse Verse. Bruce McMillan. 1990. Holiday.

Quest for a Maid. Frances Mary Hendry. 1990. Farrar.

Rachel Chance. Jean Thesman. 1990. HM.

Riddle of the Rosetta Stone: Key to Ancient Egypt. James Cross Giblin. 1990. (Crowell Jr Bks). HarpJ.

Ruby. Michael Emberley. 1990. Little.

Saturnalia. Paul Fleischman. 1990. HarpJ.

Seeing Earth from Space. Patricia Lauber. 1990. Orchard Bks Watts.

Seven Chinese Brothers. Margaret Mahy. Illus. by Jean Tseng. 1990. Scholastic.

Shadows and Reflections. Tana Hoban. 1990. Greenwillow.

Shake It to the One That You Love the Best: Play Songs and Lullabies from Black Musical Traditions. Ed. by Cheryl Warren Mattox. Illus. by Varnette P. Honeywood. 1990. Warren-Mattox.

Shining Company. Rosemary Sutcliff. 1990. Farrar.

Sister. Ellen Howard. 1990. (Atheneum). Macmillan.

Sky Dogs. Jane Yolen. Illus. by Barry Moser. 1990. HarBraceJ.

Something Big Has Been Here. Jack Prelutsky. Illus. by James Stevenson. 1990. Greenwillow.

Tale of the Mandarin Ducks. Katherine Paterson. Illus. by Leo Dillon & Diane Dillon. 1990. (Lodestar Bks). Dutton.

Telling of the Tales: Five Stories. William J Brooke. Illus. by Richard Egielski. 1990. HarperJ.

Train Song. Diane Siebert. Illus. by Mike Wimmer. 1990. (Crowell). HarpJ.

True Confessions of Charlotte Doyle. Avi. 1990. Orchards Bks Watts.

Two Short and One Long. Nina Ring Aamundsen. 1990. HM.

Very Best of Friends. Margaret Wild. Illus. by Julie Vivas. 1990. (Gulliver Bks). HarBraceJ.

Wall. Eve Bunting. Illus. by Eve Bunting. 1990. (Clarion Bks). HM.

Weasel. Cynthia DeFelice. 1990. Macmillan.

Wheels on the Bus: A Book with Parts That Move. Paul O Zelinsky. 1990. Dutton.

When I Am Old with You. Angela Johnson. Illus. by David Soman. 1990. Orchard Bks Watts.

White Peak Farm. Berlie Doherty. 1990. Orchard Bks Watts.

Woodsong. Gary Paulsen. 1990. Bradbury Pr.

1990

Adventures of High John the Conqueror. Steve Sanfield. Illus. by John Ward. 1989. Orchard Bks Watts.

Afternoon of the Elves. Janet T. Lisle. Ed. by Richard Jackson. 1989. Watts.

Ali Baba and the Forty Thieves. Illus. by Margaret Early. Retold by Walter McVitty. 1989. Abrams.

American Family Farm. Joan Anderson. Illus. by George Ancona. 1989. HarBraceJ.

And One For All. Theresa Nelson. 1989. Orchard Bks Watts.

Animals, Animals. Laura Whipple. Illus. by Eric Carle. 1989. (Philomel Bks). Putnam Pub Group.

Bells of Christmas. Virginia Hamilton. Illus. by Lambert Davis. 1989. HarbraceJ.

Big Alfie and Annie Rose Storybook. Shirley Hughes. 1989. Lothrop.

Bill Peet: An Autobiography. Bill Peet. Illus. by Bill Peet. 1989. HM.

Birdy and the Ghosties. Jill Paton Walsh. Illus. by Alan Marks. 1989. FS&G.

Book of Eagles. Helen R. Sattler. Illus. by Jean D. Zallinger. 1989. Lothrop.

Broccoli Tapes. Jan Sleplan. 1989. (Philomel Bks). Putnam Pub Group.

Buffalo Brenda. Jill Pinkwater. 1989. Macmillan.

Buster's World. Bjarne Reuter. Tr. by Anthea Bell. 1989. Dutton.

Canada Geese Quilt. Natalie Kinsey-Warnock. Illus. by Leslie W. Bowman. 1989. (Cobblehill). Dutton.

Chicka Chicka Boom Boom. Bill Martin & John Archambault. Illus. by Lois Ehlert. 1989. S & S Trade.

Children and the AIDS Virus: A Book for Children, Parents and Teachers. Rosmarie Hausherr. Illus. by Rosmarie Hausherr. 1989. (Pub by Clarion). HM.

Chimpanzee Family Book. Jane Goodall. Illus. by Michael Neugebauer. 1989. Picture Bk Studio.

Chita's Christmas Tree. Elizabeth Fitzgerald Howard. Illus. by Floyd Cooper. 1989. Bradbury Pr.

Color Zoo. Lois Ehlert. Illus. by Lois Ehlert. 1989. (Lipp Jr Bks). HarpJ.

Dance, Tanya. Patricia L. Gauch. Illus. by Satomi Ichikawa. 1989. (Philomel Bks). Putnam Pub Group.

Dancing Teepees: Poems of American Indian Youth. Ed. by Virginia D. H. Sneve. Illus. by Stephen Gammell. 1989. Holiday.

Dinosaur Mountain: Graveyard of the Past. Caroline Arnold. Illus. by Richard Hewett. 1989. (Clarion Bks.). HM.

Eva. Peter Dickinson. 1989. Delacorte.

Great American Gold Rush. Rhoda Blumberg. 1989. Bradbury Pr.

Great Little Madison. Jean Fritz. 1989. (Putnam). Putnam Pub Group.

Harry in Trouble. Barbara A. Porte. Illus. by Yossi Abolafia. 1989. Grenwillow.

Hershel and the Hanukkah Goblins. Eric Kimmel. Illus. by Trina Hyman. 1989. Holiday.

Hey World, Here I Am! Jean Little. Illus. by Sue Truesdell. 1989. Har-Row.

How Many Spots Does a Leopard Have? and Other Tales. Julius Lester. Illus. by David Shannon. 1989. Scholastic Inc.

I Hate English! Ellen Levine. Illus. by Steve Bjorkman. 1989. Scholastic Inc.

If You Made a Million. David M Schwartz. Illus. by Steven Kellogg. 1989. Lothrop.

Inspirations: Stories about Women Artists. Leslie Sills. Illus. by Ann Fay. 1989. Whitman.

It's an Armadillo. Bianca Lavics. 1989. Dutton.

Lon Po Po: A Red-Riding Hood Story from China. Tr. by Ed Young. Illus. by Ed Young. 1989. (Philomel Bks). Putnam Pub Group.

Long Hard Journey: The Story of the Pullman Porter. Patricia McKissack & Frederick McKissack. 1989. Walker.

Martin's Mice. Dick King-Smith. Illus. by Jez Alborough. 1989. Crown.

Max's Chocolate Chicken. Rosemary Wells. Illus. by Rosemary Wells. 1989. Dial Bks Young.

Melisande. E Nesbit. Illus. by Patrick Lynch. 1989. HarBraceJ.

My War with Goggle-Eyes. Anne Fine. 1989. (Joy St Bks). Little.

Nathaniel Talking. Eloise Greenfield. Illus. by Jan Gilchrist. 1989. Black Butterfly Children's Book Pr.

Nine-in-One Grr! Grr! Bila Xiong. Adapted by Cathy Spagnoli. Illus. by Nancy Hom. 1989. Children's Book Pr.

No Star Nights. Anna Egan Smucker. Illus. by Steve Johnson. 1989. Knopf.

Number the Stars. Lois Lowry. 1989. HM.

Of Colors and Things. Tana Hoban. 1989. Greenwillow.

On Our Own Terms: Children Living With Physical Disabilities. Thomas Bergman. 1989. Gareth Stevens Inc.

Once Upon a Horse: A History of Horses and How They Shaped Our History. Suzanne Jurmain. 1989. Lothrop.

Outside Child. Nina Bawden. Ed. by Dorothy Briley. 1989. Lothrop.

Panama Canal: Gateway to the World. Judith St. George. 1989. Putnam Pub Group.

Poems of A. Nonny Mouse. Jack Prelutsky. Illus. by Henrik Drescher. 1989. Knopf.

Ragtime Tumpie. Alan Schroeder. Illus. by Bernie Fuchs. 1989. (Joy St Bks). Little.

Rainbow People. Laurence Yep. Illus. by David Wiesner. 1989. HarpJ.

Shabanu: Daughter of the Wind. Suzanne Fischer Staples. 1989. Knopf.

Shades of Gray. Carolyn Reeder. 1989. Macmillan.

Story of Hanukkah. Amy Ehrlich. Illus. by Ori Sherman. 1989. (Dial). Doubleday.

Swan Lake. Margot Fonteyn. Illus. by Trina Schart Hyman. 1989. (Gulliver Bks). HarBraceJ.

Sweetgrass. Jan Hudson. 1989. (Philomel Bks). Putnam Pub Group.

Talking Eggs: A Folktale from the American South. Robert San Souci. Illus. by Jerry Pinkney. 1989. (Doubleday). Dial.

Three Little Pigs and the Fox. William Hooks. Illus. by S. D. Schindler. 1989. Macmillan.

True Story of the Three Little Pigs. Jon Scicszka. Illus. by Lane Smith. 1989. Viking.

Tub People. Pam Conrad. Illus. by Richard Egielski. 1989. HarpJ.

Valentine and Orson. Nancy E. Burkert. Illus. by Nancy E. Burkert. 1989. FS&G.

Voyage of the Frog. Gary Paulsen. 1989. Orhard Bks Watts.

Wednesday Surprise. Eve Bunting. Illus. by Donald Carrick. 1989. (Pub. by Clarion). Ticknor & Fields.

Where Does the Brown Bear Go? Nicki Weiss. 1989. Greenwillow.

Will's Mammoth. Rafe Martin. Illus. by Stephen Gammell. 1989. (Putnam). Putnman Pub Group.

Winter Room. Gary Paulsen. 1989. Orchard Bks Watts.

1988

Always to Remember: The Story of the Vietnam Veterans Memorial. Brent Ashabranner. Photos by Jennifer Ashabranner. 1988. Putnam Pub Group.

Annabelle Swift, Kindergartner. Amy Schwartz. Illus. by Amy Schwartz. 1988. Ochard Bks Watts.

Anthony Burns: The Defeat & Triumph of a Fugitive Slave. Virginia Hamilton. 1988. Knopf.

Benjamin Franklin: The New American. Ed. by Milton Meltzer. 1988. Watts.

Big Beast Book: Dinosaurs & How They Got That Way. Jerry Booth. Illus. by Martha Weston. 1988. Little.

Boy of the Three-Year Nap. Adapted by Dianne Snyder. Illus. by Allen Say. 1988. HM.

Buffalo Hunt. Russell Freedman. 1988. Holiday.

Caribou Alphabet. Mary B. Owens. 1988. Dog Ear.

Cats Are Cats. Compiled by Nancy Larrick. Illus. by Ed Young. 1988. (Philomel Bks). Putnam Pub Group.

Chester's Way. Kevin Henkes. 1988. Greenwillow.

China's Long March. Jean Fritz. Illus. by Yang Zhr Cheng. 1988. Putnam Pub Group.

Company's Coming. Authur Yorinks. Illus. by David Small. 1988. Crown.

Crutches. Peter Hartling. Tr. by Elizabeth D. Crawford. 1988. Lothrop.

Facts & Fictions of Minna Pratt. Patricia MacLachlan. 1988. HarpJ.

Family Project. Sarah Ellis. 1988. (M K McElderry). Macmillan.

Farmer Schulz's Duck. Colin Thiele. Illus. by Mary Milton. 1988. HarpJ.

Free Fall. David Wiesner. 1988. Lothrop.

Girl from Yamhill: A Memoir. Beverly Cleary. 1988. (Morrow Junior Books). Morrow.

Goldilocks & the Three Bears. James Marshall. Illus. by James Marshall. 1988. Dial Bks Young.

Grandpa's Face. Eloise Greenfield. Illus. by Floyd Cooper. 1988. (Philomel Bks). Putnam Pub Group.

Henry. Nina Bawden. Illus. by Joyce Powzyk. 1988. Lothrop.

Hominids: A Look at Our Ancestors. Helen R. Sattler. Illus. by Christopher Santoro. 1988. Lothrop.

I Want to Be an Astronaut. Byron Barton. Illus. by Byron Barton. 1988. (Crowell Jr Bks). HarpJ.

Iktomi & the Boulder: A Plains Indian Story. Retold by Paul Goble. Illus. by Paul Goble. 1988. Orchard Bks Watts.

In the Beginning: Creation Stories From Around the World. Virginia Hamilton. Illus. by Barry Moser. 1988. HarBraceJ.

Incredible Painting of Felix Clousseau. Jon Agee. 1988. FS&G.

Joyful Noise: Poems for Two Voices. Paul Fleischman. Illus. by Eric Beddows. 1988. HarpJ.

Let There Be Light: A Book About Windows. James C. Giblin. 1988. (Crowell Jr Bks). HarpJ.

Linnea's Windowsill Garden. Christina Bjork. Illus. by Lena Anderson. Tr. by Joan Sandin. 1988. (R & S Bks). FS&G.

Little by Little: A Writers's Education. Jean Little. 1988. Viking.

Lives of Christopher Chant. Diana W. Jones. 1988. Greenwillow.

Me, Mop, and the Moondance Kid. Walter D. Myers. Illus. by Rodney Pate. 1988. Delacorte.

Merlin Dreams. Peter Dickinson. Illus. by Allan Lee. 1988. Delacorte.

Mirandy & Brother Wind. Patricia C. McKissack. Illus. by Jerry Pinkney. 1988. Knopf.

Monster Garden. Vivien Alcock. 1988. Delacorte.

More Tales of Uncle Remus: Further Adventures of Brer Rabbit, His Friends, Enemies & Others. As told by Julius Lester. Illus. by Jerry Pinkney. 1988. Dial Bks Young.

Nativity. Julie Vivas. Illus. by Julie Vivas. 1988. (Gulliver Bks). HarBraceJ.

Out & About. Shirley Hughes. 1988. Lothrop.

Outlaws of Sherwood. Robin McKinley. 1988. Greenwillow.

Painting Faces. Suzanne Haldane. 1988. Dutton.

Ramona: Behind the Scenes of a Television show. Elaine Scott. Photos by Margaret Miller. 1988. Morrow.

Rescue: The Story of How Gentiles Saved Jews in the Holocaust. Milton Meltzer. 1988. HarpJ.

Rhythm Road: Poems to Move To. Lillian Morrison. 1988. Lothrop.

Saying Good-bye to Grandma. Jane R. Thomas. Illus. by Marcia Sewall. 1988. (Pub. by Clarion). Ticknor & Fields.

Scorpions. Walter D. Myers. 1988. HarpJ.

Shadow Shark. Colin Thiele. 1988. HarpJ.

Sing a Song of Popcorn: Every Child's Book of Poems. Ed. by Beatrice S. De Regniers. 1988. (Scholastic Hardcovers). Scholastic Inc.

Skeleton. Steve Parker. 1988. Knopf.

Sketching Outdoors in Winter. Jim Arnosky. 1988. Lothrop.

Smoke & Ashes: The Story of the Holocaust. Barbara Rogasky. 1988. Holiday.

Song & Dance Man. Karen Ackerman. Illus. by Stephen Gammell. 1988. Knopf.

Spinky Sulks. William Steig. 1988. FS&G.

Stringbean's Trip to the Shining Sea. Vera B. Williams. Illus. by Jennifer Williams. 1988. Greenwillow.

Sweet Creek Holler. Ruth White. 1988. FS&G.

Tail Feathers from Mother Goose: The Opie Rhyme Book. Ed. by Peter Opie & Iona Opie. 1988. Little.

Thief in the Village & Other Stories. James Berry. 1988. Orchard Bks Watts.

Touch Wood: A Girlhood in Occupied France. Renee Roth-Hano. 1988. (Four Winds). Macmillan.

Tucking Mommy In. Morag Loh. Illus. by Donna Rawlins. 1988. Orchard Bks Watts.

Under the Sunday Tree. Eloise Greenfield. Illus. by Amos Ferguson. 1988. HarpJ.

Village by the Sea. Paula Fox. 1988. Orchard Bks Watts.

1987

Actors's Life for Me! Lillian Gish. Ed. by Selma G. Lanes. Illus. by Patricia H. Lincoln. 1987. Viking.

African Journey. John Chiasson. Illus. by John Chiasson. 1987. Bradbury Pr.

After the Rain. Norma F. Mazer. 1987. (Morrow Jr Bks). Morrow.

All Fall Down. Helen Oxenbury. Illus. by Helen Oxenbury. 1987. (Aladdin Bks). Macmillan.

Anno's Math Games. Mitsumasa Anno. 1987. (Philomel Bks). Putnam Pub Group.

Blossoms and the Green Phantom. Betsy Byars. Illus. by Jacqueline Rogers. 1987. Delacorte.

British Folk Tales: New Versions. Retold by Kevin Crossley-Holland. 1987. (Orchard Bks). Watts.

Cat Poems. Ed. by Myra C. Livingston. Illus. by Trina S. Hyman. 1987. Holiday.

Clap Hands. Helen Oxenbury. Illus. by Helen Oxenbury. 1987. (Aladdin Bks). Macmillan.

Convention of Delegates: The Creation of the Constitution. Denis J. Hauptly. 1987. (Atheneum Childrens Bks). Macmillan.

Cremation of Sam McGhee. Robert W. Service. Illus. by Ted Harrison. 1987. Greenwillow.

Dinosaurs Walked Here and Other Stories Fossils Tell. Patricia Lauber. 1987. Bradbury Pr.

Enchanted Hair Tale. Alexis DeVeaux. Illus. by Cheryl Hanna. 1987. HarpJ.

Fox's Dream. Tejima. Illus. by Tejima. 1987. (Philomel Bks). Putnam Pub Group.

Fran Ellen's House. Marilyn Sachs. 1987. Dutton.

Friendship. Mildred D. Taylor. Illus. by Max Ginsburg. 1987. Dial Bks Young.

From Hand to Mouth: Or, How We Invented Knives, Forks, Spoons, and Chopsticks & the Table Manners to Go With Them. James Giblin. 1987. (Crowell Jr Bks). HarpJ.

Go In and Out the Window: An Illustrated Songbook for Young People. Compiled by Dan Fox. 1987. (Co-Pub. with Metropolitan Museum of Art). H Holt & Co.

Goats. Brock Cole. Illus. by Brock Cole. 1987. FS&G.

Grandaddy's Place. Helen Griffith. Illus. by James Stevenson. 1987. Greenwillow.

Harry's Mad. Dick King-Smith. Illus. by Jill Bennet. 1987. Crown.

Hatchet. Gary Paulsen. 1987. Bradbury Pr.

Henry and Mudge Under the Yellow Moon. Cynthia Rylant. Illus. by Sucie Stevenson. 1987. Bradbury Pr.

House on the Hill. Eileen Dunlop. 1987. Holiday.

I Want a Dog. Dayal K. Khalsa. Illus. by Dayal K. Khalsa. 1987. Tundra Bks.

If You Didn't Have Me. Ulf Nilsson. Illus. by Eva Eriksson. Tr. by Lone T. Blecher & George Blecher. 1987. (McElderry). Macmillan.

In Coal Country. Judith Hendershot. Ed. by Frances Foster. Illus. by Thomas B. Allen. 1987. Knopf.

Incredible Journey of Lewis and Clark. Rhoda Blumberg. 1987. Lothrop.

Indian Chiefs. Russell Freedman. Illus. by Russell Freedman. 1987. Holiday.

Into a Strange Land: Unaccompanied Refugee Youth in America. Brent Ashabranner & Melissa Ashabranner. 1987. Dodd.

Invisible Hunters. Harriet Rohmer. Illus. by Joe Sam. 1987. Children's Book Pr.

Jump Again! More Adventures of Brer Rabbit. Van Dyke Parks. Illus. by Barry Moser. 1987. (HJ). HarBraceJ.

Lincoln: A Photobiography. Russell Freedman. 1987. (Pub. by Clarion). Ticknor & Fields.

M. E. and Morton. Sylvia Cassedy. 1987. (Crowell Jr Bks). HarpJ.

Maggie By My Side. Beverly Butler. 1987. Dodd.

Making Friends. Jan Omerod. 1987. Lothrop.

Mars. Simon Seymour. 1987. (Morrow Jr Bks). Morrow.

Mom's Home. Jan Omerod. 1987. Lothrop.

More Perfect Union. Betsy Maestro. Illus. by Giulio Maestro. 1987. Lothrop.

Mufaro's Beautiful Daughters: An African Tale. John Steptoe. Illus. by John Steptoe. 1987. Lothrop.

Naked Bear: Folktales of the Iroquois. Ed. by John Bierhorst. Illus. by Dirk Zimmer. 1987. (Morrow Jr Bks). Morrow.

Nightmare in History: The Holocaust 1933-1945. Miriam Chaikin. 1987. (Pub. by Clarion). Ticknor & Fields.

Oma & Bobo. Amy Schwartz. 1987. Bradbury Pr.

Owl Lake. Tejima. Illus. by Tejima. 1987. (Philomel bks). Putnam Pub Group.

Owl Moon. Jane Yolem. Illus. by John Schoenherr. 1987. (Philomel Bks). Putnam Pub Group.

Return. Sonia Levitin. 1987. (Atheneum Childrens Bks). Macmillan.

Roscoe's Leap. Gillian Cross. 1987. Holiday.

Say Goodnight. Helen Oxenbury. Illus. by Helen Oxenbury. 1987. (Aladdin Bks). Macmillan.

Shh! We're Writing the Constitution. Jean Fritz. Illus. by Tomie De Paola. 1987. Putnam Pub Group.

Sketching Outdoors in Spring. Jim Arnosky. 1987. Lothrop.

Tales of Uncle Remus: The Adventures of Brer Rabbit. Ed. by Julius Lester. Illus. by Jerry Pinkney. 1987. Dial Bks Young.

Tasmania: A Wildlife Journey. Joyce Powzyk. 1987. Lothrop.

These Small Stones. Ed. by Norma Farber & Myra C. Livingston. 1987. HarpJ.

This Little Nose. Jan Omerod. 1987. Lothrop.

Tickle, Tickle. Helen Oxenbury. Illus. by Helen Oxenbury. 1987. (Aladdin Bks). Macmillan.

Turtle Watch. George Ancona. Photos by George Ancona. 1987. Macmillan.

Waiting For the Rain: A Novel of South Africa. Sheila Gordon. 1987. (Orchard Bks). Watts.

Whales, The Nomads of the Sea. Helen R. Sattler. Illus. by Jean D. Zallinger. 1987. Lothrop.

What a Morning! The Christmas Story in Black Spirituals. Ed. by John Langstaff. Illus. by Ashley Bryan. 1987. (McElderry Bks). Macmillan.

Wise Child. Monica Furlong. 1987. Knopf.

Wolf's Chicken Stew. Keiko Kasza. Illus. by Keiko Kasza. 1987. (Putnam). Putnam Pub Group.

Za Was Zapped. Chris Van Allsburg. 1987. HM.

1986

Afraid to Ask: A Book for Families to Share about Cancer. Judylaine Fine. 1986. Lothrop.

After the Dancing Days. Margaret I. Rostkowski. 1986. HarpJ.

Alphabatics. Suse MacDonald. 1986. Bradbury Pr.

Amahl & the Night Visitors. Gian-Carlo Menotti. Illus. by Michele Lemieux. 1986. (Morrow Jr Bks). Morrow.

Bag of Moonshine. Alan Garner. 1986. Delacorte.

Being Born. Sheila Kitzinger. Illus. by Lennart Nilsson. 1986. (Pub by G&D). Putnam Pub Group.

Cherries & Cherry Pits. Vera B. Williams. Illus. by Vera B. Williams. 1986. Greenwillow.

Children of the Maya: A Guatemalan Indian Odyssey. Brent Ashabranner. Photos by Paul Conklin. 1986. Dodd.

Counting Wildflowers. Bruce McMillan. 1986. Lothrop.

Don't Say a Word. Barbara Gehrts. Ed. by Margaret k. McElderry. Tr. by Elizabeth D. Crawford. 1986. (McElderry Bk). Macmillan.

Doorbell Rang. Pat Hutchins. Illus. by Pat Hutchins. 1986. Greenwillow.

Earthworms, Dirt & Rotten Leaves: An Exploration in Ecology. Molly McLaughlin. Illus. by Robert Shetterly. 1986. (Childrens Bk). Macmillan.

Fine White Dust. Cynthia Rylant. 1986. Bradbury Pr.

Flies in the Water, Fish in the Air: A Personal Introduction to Fly Fishing. Jim Arnosky. 1986. Lothrop.

Georgia Music. Helen Griffith. Illus. by James Stevenson. 1986. Greenwillow.

Hey, Al. Arthur Yorinks. Illus. by Richard Egielski. 1986. FS&G.

Howl's Moving Castle. Diana W. Jones. 1986. Greenwillow.

Illyrian Adventure. Lloyd Alexander. 1986. Dutton.

Josie Gambit. Mary F. Shura. 1986. Dodd.

Jump: The Adventures of Brer Rabbit. Van D. Parks & Malcolm Jones. Illus. by Barry Moser. 1986. (HJ). HarBraceJ.

Keeper. Phyliss Naylor. 1986. (Childrens Bk). Macmillan.

Make Way for Sam Houston. Jean Fritz. Illus. by Elise Primavera. 1986. Putnam Pub Group.

Max's Christmas. Rosemary Wells. Illus. by Rosemary Wells. 1986. Dial Bks Young.

Milk: The Fight for Purity. James Giblin. 1986. Crowell Jr Bks.

Moonlight Man. Paula Fox. 1986. Bradbury Pr.

More Stories Julian Tells. Ann Cameron. Illus. by Ann Strugnell. 1986. Knopf.

Moses in the Bulrushes. Warwick Hutton. Illus. by Warwick Hutton. 1986. (McElderry Bk). Macmillan.

My Prairie Year: Based on the Diary of Elenore Plaisted. Brett Harvey. Illus. by Deborah K. Ray. 1986. Holiday.

New Coat for Anna. Harriet Ziefert. Illus. by Anita Lobel. 1986. Knopf.

No Hero for the Kaiser. Rudolf Frank. Tr. by Patricia Crampton from Ger. Illus. by Klaus Steffans. 1986. Lothrop.

On My Honor. Marion D. Bauer. 1986. (Clarion). Ticknor & Fields.

Peeping in the Shell: A Whooping Crane is Hatched. Faith McNulty. Illus. by Irene Brady. 1986. HarpJ.

Peter the Great. Diane Stanley. Illus. by Diane Stanley. 1986. (Four Winds). Macmillan.

Purple Coat. Amy Hest. Illus. by Amy Schwartz. 1986. (Four Winds Pr). Macmillan.

Random House Book of Mother Goose: A Treasury of Three Hundred & Six Timeless Nursery Rhymes. Selected by Arnold Lobel. Illus. by Arnold Lobel. 1986. (BYR). Random.

Return to Bitter Creek. Doris B. Smith. 1986. (Viking Kestrel). Viking.

Rumor of Otters. Deborah Savage. 1986. HM.

Rumpelstiltskin. Retold by Paul O. Zelinsky. Illus. by Paul O. Zelinsky. 1986. Dutton.

Small Poems Again. Valerie Worth. Illus. by Natalie Babbitt. 1986. FS&G.

So Far from the Bamboo Grove. Yoko K. Watkins. Intro. by Jean Fritz. 1986. Lothrop.

Story of Chicken Licken. Jan Ormerod. Illus. by Jan Ormerod. 1986. Lothrop.

Tales of a Gambling Grandma. Dayal K. Khalsa. Illus. by Dayal K. Khalsa. 1986. (C. N. Potter Bks). Crown.

To Space & Back. Sally Ride & Susan Okie. 1986. Lothrop.

Up from Jericho Tel. E. L. Konigsburg. 1986. (Childrens Bk). Macmillan.
Very Last Time. Jan Andrews. Illus. by Ian Wallace. 1986. (McElderry Bk). Macmillan.
Village of Round & Square Houses. Ann Grifalconi. Illus. by Ann Grifalconi. 1986. Little.
Volcano: The Eruption & Heating of Mount St. Helens. Patricia Lauber. 1986. Bradbury Pr.
What Happened to Patrick's Dinosaurs? Carol Carrick. Illus. by Donald Carrick. 1986. (Clarion). Ticknor & Fields.
When I Was Nine. James Stevenson. Illus. by James Stevenson. 1986. Greenwillow.
Whipping Boy. Sid Fleischman. Illus. by Peter Sis. 1986. Greenwillow.

1985
Agony of Alice. Phyllis R. Naylor. 1985. (Childrens Bk). Macmillan.
Ain't Gonna Study War No More: The Story of America's Peace Seekers. Milton Meltzer. 1985. Har-Row.
Amy's Eyes. Richard Kennedy. Illus. by Richard Egielski. 1985. HarpJ.
Auks, Rocks & the Odd Dinosaur: Inside Stories from the Smithsonian's Museum of Natural History. Peggy Thomson. 1985. Crowell Jr Bks.
Babe: The Gallant Pig. Dick King-Smith. Illus. by Mary Rayner. 1985. Crown.
Bathwater's Hot. Shirley Hughes. 1985. Lothrop.
Blackberries in the Dark. Mavis Jukes. Illus. by Thomas B. Allen. 1985. Knopf.
Blue-Eyed Daisy. Cynthia Rylant. 1985. Bradbury Pr.
Cat's Purr. Ashley Bryan. 1985. (Childrens Bk). Macmillan.
Child's Christmas in Wales. Dylan Thomas. Illus. by Trina S. Hyman. 1985. Holiday.
China Homecoming. Jean Fritz. 1985. (Putnam). Putnam Pub Group.
Come Sing, Jimmy Jo. Katherine Patterson. 1985. Lodestar Bks.
Commodore Perry in the Land of the Shogun. Rhoda Blumberg. 1985. Lothrop.
Cowboys of the Wild West. Russell Freedman. 1985. (Clarion). Ticknor & Fields.
Cracker Jackson. Betsy C. Byars. 1985. Viking.
Dad's Back. Jan Ormerod. 1985. Lothrop.
Dakota Dugout. Ann Turner. Illus. by Ronald Himler. 1985. Macmillan.
Dark Harvest: Migrant Farmworkers in America. Brent Ashabranner. Photos by Paul Conklin. 1985. Dodd.
Dogsong. Gary Paulsen. 1985. Bradbury Pr.
Enchanted Caribou. Elizabeth Cleaver. 1985. (Childrens Bk). Macmillan.
Evening at Alfie's. Shirley Hughes. Illus. by Shirley Hughes. 1985. Lothrop.
Foolish Rabbit's Big Mistake. Rev. by Rafe Martin. Illus. by Ed Young. 1985. Putnam Pub Group.
Forgetful Wishing Well: Poems for Young People. X. J. Kennedy. Illus. by Monica Incisa. 1985. (Mcelderry Bk). Macmillan.
Four on the Shore. Edward Marshall. Illus. by James Marshall. 1985. Dial Bks Young.
Handles. Jan Mark. 1985. Atheneum.
Hit & Run. Joan Phipson. 1985. Macmillan.
How Much is a Million? David M. Schwartz. Illus. by Steven Kellogg. 1985. Lothrop.
In Summer Light. Zibby O'Neal. 1985. Viking.
King Bidgood's in the Bathtub. Audrey Wood. Illus. by Don Wood. 1985. (HJ). HarBraceJ.
Man Named Thoreau. Robert Burleigh. Illus. by Lloyd Bloom. 1985. (Children's Bk). Macmillan.
Max's Breakfast. Rosemary Wells. Illus. by Rosemary Wells. 1985. Dial Bks Young.
Messy Baby. Jan Ormerod. 1985. Lothrop.
Milk Makers. Gail Gibbons. 1985. Macmillan.
Mount Rushmore Story. Judith Saint-George. 1985. Putnam Pub Group.
Nature of the Beast. Janni Howker. 1985. Greenwillow.
Night Outside. Patricia Wrightson. Illus. by Beth Peck. 1985. (McElderry Bk). Macmillan.
Noisy. Shirley Hughes. 1985. Lothrop.
Nova Space Explorer's Guide: Where to Go & What to See. Richard Maurer. 1985. (C. N. Potter). Crown.
On the Edge. Gillian Cross. 1985. Holiday.
One, Two, Three. Tana Hoban. Illus. by Tana Hoban. 1985. Greenwillow.
Paper Crane. Molly Bang. Illus. by Molly Bang. 1985. Greenwillow.
Patchwork Quilt. Valerie Flournoy. Illus. by Jerry Pinkney. 1985. Dial Bks Young.
People Could Fly. Virginia Hamilton. Illus. by Leo Dillon & Diane Dillon. 1985. Knopf.
Polar Express. Chris Van Allsburg. Illus. by Chris Van Allsburg. 1985. HM.
Puppeteer. Kathryn Lasky. Illus. by Christopher G. Knight. 1985. Macmillan.
Reading. Jan Ormerod. 1985. Lothrop.

Relatives Came. Cynthia Rylant. Illus. by Stephen Gammell. 1985. Bradbury Pr.
Remembering the Good Times. Richard Peck. 1985. Delacorte.
Rose Blanche: Based on the Original Idea of Roberto Innocenti. Christophe Gallaz. Ed. by Etienne Delessert & Ann Redpath. Tr. by Martha Coventry. 1985. Creative Ed.
Sarah, Plain & Tall. Patricia MacLachlan. 1985. HarpJ.
Saturn. Seymour Simon. 1985. Morrow.
Sheep Dog. George Ancona. 1985. Lothrop.
Sign in Mendel's Window. Mildred Phillips. Illus. by Margot Zemach. 1985. Macmillan.
Sir Gawain & the Loathly Lady. Selina Hastings. Illus. by Juan Wijngaard. 1985. Lothrop.
Sirens & Spies. Janet T. Lisle. 1985. Bradbury Pr.
Statue of Liberty. Leonard E. Fisher. Illus. by Leonard E. Fisher. 1985. Holiday.
Tales Mummies Tell. Patricia Lauber. 1985. Crowell Jr Bks.
Three Hat Day. Laura Geringer. Illus. by Arnold Lobel. 1985. HarpJ.
Tog the Ribber: Or Granny's Tales. Paul Coltman. Illus. by Gillian McClure. 1985. FS&G.
Tomie De Paola's "Mother Goose" 1985. (Putnam). Putnam Pub Group.
Travellers by Night. Vivien Alcock. 1985. Delacorte.
Trek. Ann Jonas. Illus. by Ann Jonas. 1985. Greenwillow.
Truth about Santa Claus. James C. Giblin. 1985. Crowell Jr Bks.
Very Busy Spider. Eric Carle. Illus. by Eric Carle. 1985. Putnam Pub Group.
Wallaby Creek. Joyce Powzyk. 1985. Lothrop.
Watch the Stars Come Out. Riki Levinson. Illus. by Diane Goode. 1985. Dutton.
When We Went to the Park. Shirley Hughes. 1985. Lothrop.
Wilfred Gordon McDonald Partridge. Mem Fox. Illus. by Julie Vivas. 1985. Kane Miller Bk.
Wolf Pack: Tracking Wolves in the Wild. Sylvia Johnson & Alice Aamodt. 1985. Lerner Pubns.

1984
Alfie Gives a Hand. Shirley Hughes. Illus. by Shirley Hughes. 1984. Lothrop.
Animal Alphabet. Bert Kitchen. Illus. by Bert Kitchen. 1984. Dial Bks Young.
Archer's Goon. Diana W. Jones. 1984. Greenwillow.
Being Adopted. Maxine B. Rosenberg. Photos by George Ancona. 1984. Lothrop.
Bionic Bunny Show. Marc Brown & Lauren K. Krasny. Illus. by Marc Brown. 1984. (Pub by Atlantic Monthly Pr). Little.
Black Americans: A History in Their Own Words, 1619-1983. Milton Meltzer. 1984. Crowell Jr Bks.
Buffalo Woman. Paul Goble. 1984. Bradbury Pr.
Changeover: A Supernatural Romance. Margaret Mahy. 1984. (McElderry Bk). Macmillan.
Christmas Poems. Selected by Myra L. Cohn. Illus. by Trina S. Hyman. 1984. Holiday.
Drawing Life in Motion. Jim Arnosky. 1984. Lothrop.
Facts of Life. Jonathan Miller & David Pelham. Illus. by Harry Willock. 1984. Viking.
Fighting Ground. Avi. Illus. by Ellen Thompson. 1984. Lipp Jr Bks.
Gaffer Samson's Luck. Jill P. Walsh. Illus. by Brock Cole. 1984. FS&G.
Gavriel & Jamal: Two Boys of Jerusalem. Brent Ashabranner. Photos by Paul Conklin. 1984. Dodd.
Hansel & Gretel. Retold by Rika Lesser. Illus. by Paul O. Zelinsky. 1984. Dodd.
Harry's Dog. Barbara A. Porte. Illus. by Yossi Abolafia. 1984. Greenwillow.
Have You Seen My Duckling? Nancy Tafuri. Illus. by Nancy Tafuri. 1984. Greenwillow.
Hero & the Crown. Robin Mckinley. 1984. Greenwillow.
Holes & Peeks. Ann Jonas. Illus. by Ann Jonas. 1984. Greenwillow.
Home in the Sky. Jeannie Baker. Illus. by Jeannie Baker. 1984. Greenwillow.
How It Feels When Parents Divorce. Jill Krementz. 1984. Knopf.
How My Parents Learned to Eat. Ina Friedman. Illus. by Allen Say. 1984. HM.
How You Were Born. Joanna Cole. 1984. (Morrow Jr Bks). Morrow.
In a Dark, Dark Room & Other Scary Stories. Alvin Schwartz. Illus. by Dirk Zimmer. 1984. HarpJ.
In the Year of the Boar & Jackie Robinson. Bette B. Lord. Illus. by Marc Simont. 1984. HarpJ.
Interstellar Pig. William Sleator. 1984. Dutton.
Island on Bird Street. Uri Orlev. Tr. by Hillel Halkin from Hebrew. 1984. HM.
Legend Days. Jamake Highwater. 1984. HarpJ.
Like Jake & Me. Mavis Jukes. Illus. by Lloyd Bloom. 1984. Knopf.

Mary Had a Little Lamb. Sarah J. Hale. Illus. by Tomie De Paola. 1984. Holiday.
Moon. Seymour Simon. 1984. (Four Winds). Macmillan.
Moves Make the Man. Bruce Brooks. 1984. HarpJ.
Music, Music for Everyone. Vera B. Williams. Illus. by Vera B. Williams. 1984. Greenwillow.
Mysteries of Harris Burdick. Chris Van Allsburg. Illus. by Chris Van Allsburg. 1984. HM.
Napping House. Audrey Wood. Illus. by Don Wood. 1984. HarpJ.
New Kid on the Block. Jack Prelutsky. Illus. by James Stevenson. 1984. Greenwillow.
One-Eyed Cat. Paula Fox. Illus. by Irene Trivas. 1984. Bradbury Pr.
Picnic. Emily A. McCully. 1984. HarpJ.
Quilt. Ann Jonas. Illus. by Ann Jonas. 1984. Greenwillow.
Ramona, Forever. Beverly Cleary. Illus. by Alan Tiegreen. 1984. Morrow.
Saint George & the Dragon. Adapted by Margaret Hodges. Illus. by Trina S. Hyman. 1984. Little.
Samurai's Tale. Erik C. Haugaard. 1984. HM.
Secret Language of Snow. Terry T. Williams & Ted Major. Illus. by Jennifer Dewey. 1984. Pantheon.
Secret World of Polly Flint. Helen Cresswell. Illus. by Shirley Felts. 1984. Macmillan.
Spirit Child: A Story of the Nativity. Tr. by John Bierhorst. 1984. Morrow.
Stories for Children. Isaac B. Singer. 1984. FS&G.
Story of Jumping Mouse. John Steptoe. Illus. by John Steptoe. 1984. Lothrop.
Surprises. Ed. by Lee B. Hopkins. 1984. HarpJ.
Tipi: A Center of Native American Life. Charlotte Yue. Illus. by David Yue. 1984. Knopf.
Tree Flowers. Millicent Selsam. Illus. by Carol Lerner. 1984. Morrow.
Truck Song. Diane Siebert. Illus. by Byron Barton. 1984. Crowell Jr Bks.
Unclaimed Treasures. Patricia MacLachlan. 1984. HarpJ.
Waiting to Waltz: A Childhood. Cynthia Rylant. Illus. by Stephen Gammell. 1984. Bradbury Pr.
Way to Satin Shore. Philippa Pearce. Illus. by Charlotte Voake. 1984. Greenwillow.
Year of Birds. Ashley Wolff. Illus. by Ashley Wolff. 1984. Dodd.
Young Writer's Handbook. Susan Tchudi & Stephen Tchudi. 1984. (ScribT). Scribner.

1983
Alfie's Feet. Shirley Hughes. Illus. by Shirley Hughes. 1983. Lothrop.
Anno's Mysterious Multiplying Jar. Mitsumasa Anno & Mitsumasa Anno. 1983. (Philomel). Putnam Pub Group.
Baby's Catalogue. Janet Ahlberg & Allan Ahlberg. 1983. (Atlantic Monthly Pr). Little.
Behind the Attic Wall. Sylvia Cassedy. 1983. Crowell Jr Bks.
Best Bad Thing. Yoshiko Uchida. 1983. (McElderry Bk). Macmillan.
Bony-Legs. Joanna Cole. Illus. by Dirk Zimmer. 1983. (Four Winds). Macmillan.
Book of Pigericks: Pig Limericks. Arnold Lobel. Illus. by Arnold Lobel. 1983. HarpJ.
Cars & How They Go. Joanna Cole. Illus. by Gail Gibbons. 1983. Crowell Jr Bks.
Children of the Wild West. Russell Freedman. 1983. (Clarion). HM.
Dancing Class. Helen Oxenbury. Illus. by Helen Oxenbury. 1983. Dial Bks Young.
Dear Mr. Henshaw. Beverly Cleary. Illus. by Paul O. Zelinsky. 1983. Morrow.
Double Life of Pocahontas. Jean Fritz. Illus. by Ed Young. 1983. (Putnam). Putnam Pub Group.
Esteban & the Ghost. Sibyl Hancock. Illus. by Dirk Zimmer. 1983. Dial Bks Young.
First Hard Times. Doris B. Smith. 1983. Viking.
Glorious Flight: Across the Channel with Louis Bleriot. Alice Provensen. Illus. by Martin Provensen. 1983. (Viking Kestrel). Viking.
Harry's Visit. Barbara A. Porte. Illus. by Yossi Abolafia. 1983. Greenwillow.
Hazel Rye. Vera Cleaver. Illus. by Bill Cleaver. 1983. Lipp Jr Bks.
Hide Crawford Quick. Margaret W. Froehlich. 1983. HM.
Human Body. Johnathan Miller. Ed. by David Pelham. Illus. by Harry Willock. 1983. (Studio). Viking.
Little Fear. Patricia Wrightson. 1983. (McElderry Bk). Macmillan.
Luttrell Village: Country Life in the Middle Ages. Sheila Sancha. Illus. by Sheila Sancha. 1983. Crowell Jr Bks.
Magical Adventures of Pretty Pearl. Virginia Hamilton. 1983. HarpJ.
Mill. David Macaulay. Illus. by David Macaulay. 1983. HM.

My Friend Leslie: The Story of a Handicapped Child. Maxine B. Rosenberg. Illus. by George Ancona. 1983. Lothrop.
New Americans: Changing Patterns in U. S. Immigration. Brent Ashabranner. Illus. by Paul Conkin. 1983. Dodd.
One Hundredth Thing about Caroline. Lois Lowry. 1983. HM.
Queen Eleanor: Independent Spirit of the Medieval World: A Biography of Eleanor of Aquitane. Polly S. Brooks. 1983. Lipp Jr Bks.
Random House Book of Poetry for Children. Jack Prelutsky. Illus. by Arnold Lobel. 1983. Random.
Rip-Roaring Russell. Johanna Hurwitz. Illus. by Lillian Hoban. 1983. Morrow.
Root Cellar. Janet Lunn. 1983. (Pub. by Scribner). Macmillan.
Round & Round & Round. Tana Hoban. Illus. by Tana Hoban. 1983. Greenwillow.
Round Trip. Ann Jonas. Illus. by Ann Jonas. 1983. Greenwillow.
Sacred Path: Spells, Prayers & Power Songs of the American Indians. Ed. by John Bierhorst. 1983. Morrow.
Sam's Bath. Barbro Lindgren. Illus. by Eva Eriksson. 1983. Morrow.
Secrets of a Wildlife Watcher. Jim Arnosky. 1983. Lothrop.
Sign of the Beaver. Elizabeth G. Speare. 1983. HM.
Silver Cow: A Welsh Tale. Susan Cooper. Illus. by Warwick Hutton. 1983. (McElderry Bk). Macmillan.
Something Special for Me. Vera B. Williams. Illus. by Vera B. Williams. 1983. Greenwillow.
Song in Stone: City Poems. Ed. by Lee B. Hopkins. Photos by Anna H. Audette. 1983. Crowell Jr Bks.
Storm Without Rain: A Novel in Time. Jan Adkins. 1983. Little.
Sugaring Time. Kathryn Lasky. Illus. by Christopher G. Knight. 1983. Macmillan.
Tales of Amanda Pig. Jean Van Leeuwen. Illus. by Ann Schweninger. 1983. Dial Bks Young.
Ten, Nine, Eight. Molly G. Bang. Illus. by Molly G. Bang. 1983. Greenwillow.
Unriddling. Alvin Schwartz. Illus. by Susan Truesdell. 1983. Lipp Jr Bks.
What's under My Bed? James Stevenson. Illus. by James Stevenson. 1983. Greenwillow.
When the Dark Comes Dancing: A Bedtime Poetry Book. Nancy Larrick. Illus. by John Wallner. 1983. (Philomel). Putnam Pub Group.
Willie Bee & the Time the Martians Landed. Virginia Hamilton. 1983. Greenwillow.
Wish Giver: Three Tales of Coven Tree. Bill Brittain. Illus. by Andrew Glass. 1983. HarpJ.
Witches. Roald Dahl. Photos by Quentin Blake. 1983. FS&G.
Wreck of the Zephyr. Chris Van Allsburg. Illus. by Chris Van Allsburg. 1983. HM.

Luncj. Denise Fleming. (Bks Young Read). H H Holt Co. (Younger).
True Story of the Three Little Pigs. Jon Scieszka. Illus. by Steven Kellog. (Viking Penguin). Viking Kestrel.
Woman Who Outshone the Sun: The Legend of Lucia Zentano. Alejandro Cruz Martinez. Illus. by Fernando Olivera. Rosalma Zubizarreta. Childrens Bk Pr. (All).

Association of Jewish Libraries Children's Book Award

This award is given annually, and was established in 1968 as the Shirley Kravitz Award by the Association of Jewish Libraries, School and Center Division. The recipient is an author or illustrator whose work must have made the most outstanding contribution in the field of Jewish Literature for children and young people during the past year. In 1975 the entire organization of the Association of Jewish Libraries became the sponsor, and the award was given its present name. Since 1982, the award has been given to two titles, one published for younger readers, and one for older readers. The winner receives a plaque. (Please refer to the "Body of Work Awards" at the end of this index for winners in that category.)

1991
Chanukkah Guest. Eric A Kimmel. Illus. by Carmi Giora. 1990. Holiday. (Younger).
My Grandmother's Stories: A Collection of Jewish Folktales. Adele Geras. Illus. by Jael Jordon. 1990. Knopf. (Older).
1990
Berchick, My Mother's Horse. Esther S. Blanc. Illus. by Tennessee Dixon. 1989. Volcano Pr. (Younger).
Number the Stars. Lois Lowry. 1989. HM. (Older).

1989
Devil's Arithmetic. Jane Yolen. 1988. (Viking Kestrel). Penguin USA. (Older).
Keeping Quilt. Patricia Polacco. Illus. by Patricia Polacco. 1988. S&S. (Younger).
1988
Number on My Grandfather's Arm. David A. Adler. 1987. UAHC. (Younger).
Return. Sonia Levitin. 1987. (Atheneum Children's Books). Macmillan. (Older).
1987
Beyond the High White Wall. Nancy Pitt. 1986. (Pub. by Scribner). Macmillan. (Older).
Poems for Jewish Holidays. Ed. by Myra C. Livingston. Illus. by Lloyd Bloom. 1986. Holiday. (Younger).
1985
Island on Bird Street. Uri Orlev. Tr. by Hillel Halkin from Hebrew. 1984. HM. (Older).
Mrs. Moskowitz and the Sabbath Candlesticks. Amy Schwartz. 1984. JPS Phila. (Younger).
1984
Bubbie, Me and Memories. Barbara Pomerantz. 1983. UAHC. (Younger).
In the Mouth of the Wolf. Rose Zar. 1983. JPS Phila. (Older).
1983
Castle on Hester Street. Linda Heller. 1982. JPS Phila. (Younger).

Australian Children's Book Awards

Established in 1946, the Australian Children's Book Award was administered by various state agencies which presented the first Picture Book of the Year Award (PBY) in 1956. Later when the Australian Children's Book Council was formed in 1959, they assumed the responsibilities of the agencies and established the all-Australian Book of the Year Award (BY). In 1982 the Junior Book of the Year Award (JBY) was added. Winners receive medals and various stipends.

1991
†† House Guest. Eleanor Nilsson. 1990. Viking. (BY).
Magnificent Nose & Other Marvels. Anna Fienberg. Illus. by Kim Gamble. 1990. Allen & Unwin. (Younger).
†† Window. Jeannie Baker. 1990. Julia MacRae Bks. (PBY).
1990
†† Come Back to Show You I Could Fly. Robin Klein. 1989. Viking Kestrel. (BY).
†† Pigs and Honey. Jeanne Baker. Illus. by Jeanne Baker. 1989. Omnibus Bks.
†† Very Best of Friends. Margaret Wild. Illus. by Mem Fox. 1989. Margaret Hamilton. (PBY).
1989
†† Best-Kept Secret. Emily Rodda. Angus & Robertson. (JBY).
†† Beyond the Labyrinth. Gillian Rubinstein. Hayland House. (BY).
†† Drac & the Gremlin. Allan Baillie. Illus. by Jane Tanner. Viking Kestrel. (PBY).
†† Eleventh Hour. Graeme Base. Illus. by Graeme Base. Viking Kestrel. (PBY).
1988
†† Crusher is Coming. Bob Graham. Lothian. (PBY).
†† My Place. Nadia Wheatley & Donna Rawlins. Collins Dove. (JBY).
†† So Much to Tell You... John Marsden. Walter McVitty. (BY).
1987
†† All We Know. Simon French. Angus & Robertson. (BY).
†† Kojuro and the Bears. Junko Morimoto. Collins. (BPY).
†† Pigs Might Fly. Emily Rodda. Illus. by Noela Young. Angus & Robertson. (JBY).
1986
†† Akwright. Mary Steele. Hyland. (JBY).
†† Felix & Alexander. Terry Denton. Oxford Univ Pr. (PBY).
†† Green Wind. Thurley Fowler. Rigby. (BY).
1985
†† Something Special. Emily Rodda. Illus. by Noela Young. Angus & Robertson. (JBY).
†† True Story of Lilli Stubeck. James Aldridge. 1987. Hyland House. (BY).
1984
†† Bernice Knows Best. Max Dann. Illus. by Ann James. Oxford Univ Pr. (JBY).
†† Little Fear. Patricia Wrightson. Hutchinson. (BY).
1983
†† Master of the Grove. Victor Kelleher. Penguin. (BY).
†† Who Sank the Boat? Pamela Allen. Nelson. (PBY).

Mildred L. Batchelder Award

This award honoring Mildred L. Batchelder was established in 1966 by the Children's Services Division (now Association for Library Service to Children) of the American Library Association. Its purpose is to "encourage international exchange of quality children's books by recognizing U.S. publishers of such books, in translation." It is presented annually to an American publisher for the "most outstanding English translation of a children's book originally published in a foreign language and foreign country during the preceding year." The winning publisher receives a citation.

1993
Letters from Rifka. Karen Hesse. 1992. (Bks Young Read). H Holt & Co.
Old Turtle. Douglas Wood. Illus. by Cheng-Khee Chee. 1991. Pfeifer-Hamilton.
1992
Man from the Other Side. Uri Orlev. Tr. by Hillel Halkin. 1991. HM.
1991
Hand Full of Stars. Rafik Schami. Tr. by Rika Lesser. 1990. Dutton.
1990
Buster's World. Bjarne Reuter. 1989. Dutton.
1989
Crutches. Peter Hartling. Tr. by Elizabeth D. Crawford. 1988. Lothrop.
1988
If You Didn't Have Me. Ulf Nilsson. Illus. by Eva Eriksson. Tr. by Lone T. Blecher & George Blecher. 1987. (McElderry Bks). Macmillan.
1987
No Hero for the Kaiser. Rudolf Frank. Tr. by Patricia Crampton from Ger. Illus. by Klaus Steffans. 1986. Lothrop.
1986
Rose Blanche: Based on the Original Idea of Roberto Innocenti. Christophe Gallaz. Ed. by Etienne Delessert & Ann Redpath. Tr. by Martha Coventry from Fr. 1985. Creative Ed.
1985
Island on Bird Street. Uri Orlev. Tr. by Hillel Halkin from Hebrew. 1984. HM.
1984
Ronia, the Robber's Daughter. Astrid Lingren. Tr. by Patricia Crampton from Swedish. 1983. Viking.
1983
Hiroshima No Pika. Toshi Maruki. 1982. Lothrop.

Irma Simonton Black Award

Irma Simonton Black (1906-1972) was a faculty member of the Bank Street College of Education and an author of children's books. This award has been presented annually since 1973 in her memory, and is sponsored by the Bank Street College of Education, Book Award Committee. Eligibility is based on "excellence in text and illustration" in a book published for children. Winners are presented with scrolls.

1992
Enchanted Wood. Ruth Sanderson. Illus. by Ruth Sanderson. 1991. Little Brown.
1991
Charlie Anderson. Barbara Abercrombie. Illus. by Mark Graham. 1990. (M K McElderry Books). MacMillan Child Grp.
1990
Talking Eggs. Robert D. San Souci. Illus. by Jerry Pinkney. 1989. Dial Bks Young.
1989
Porcupine Mouse. Bonnie Pryor. Illus. by Maryjane Begin. 1988. Morrow.
1988
Heckedy Peg. Audrey Wood. Illus. by Don Wood. 1987. (HJ). HarBraceJ.
1987
Doctor Change. Joanna Cole. Illus. by Donald Carrick. 1986. Morrow.
1986
Chloe & Maud. Sandra Boynton. Illus. by Sandra Boynton. 1985. Little.
1985
Mysteries of Harris Burdick. Chris Van Allsburg. Illus. by Chris Van Allsburg. 1984. HM.

Boston Globe - Horn Book Awards

The Boston Globe and the Horn Book Magazine are co-sponsors of this award, which was established in 1967. Initially, awards were given for text and illustration; however, these categories were changed in 1976 to outstanding fiction (Fic) and non-fiction (N/F), as well as illustration (illus). Among some of the prizes the winners receive are "$200 and an engraved pewter bowl." The recipients of these awards need not be American citizens, however the books must have been published in the United States.

1992

Missing May. Cynthia Rylant. 1991. Orchard Bks Watts. Fic/Poetry.

Seven Blind Mice. Ed Young. Illus. by Ed Young. 1992. (Philomel). Putnam Pub Group. Picture Book.

Talking With Artists. Ed. by Pat Cummings. Compiled by Pat Cummings. 1992. (Bradbury Press). Macmillan Child Grp. Nonfiction.

1991

Appalachia: The Voices of Sleeping Birds. Cynthia Rylant. Illus. by Barry Moser. 1991. HBJ. (N/Fic).

Tale of the Mandarin Ducks. Katherine Paterson. Illus. by Leo Dillon & Diane Dillon. 1990. Lodestar Bks. (Illus).

True Confessions of Charlotte Doyle. Avi. Illus. by Ruth E Murray. 1990. Orchard Bks Watts. (Fic).

1990

Great Little Madison. Jean Fritz. 1989. Putnam Pub Group. (N/Fic).

Lon Po Po: A Red Riding Hood Story from China. Ed Young. 1989. (Philomel Bks). Putnam Pub Group. (Illus).

Maniac Magee. Jerry Spinelli. 1990. Little. (Fic).

1989

Shy Charles. Rosemary Wells. Illus. by Rosemary Wells. 1988. Dial Bks Young. (Illus).

Village by the Sea. Paula Fox. 1988. Orchard Bks Watts. (Fic).

Way Things Work. David Macaulay. Illus. by David Macaulay. 1988. HM. (N/Fic).

1988

Anthony Burns: The Defeat & Triumph of a Fugitive Slave. Virginia Hamilton. 1988. Knopf. (N/Fic).

Boy of the Three-Year Nap. Retold by Dianne Snyder. Illus. by Allen Say. 1988. HM. (Illus).

Friendship. Mildred D. Taylor. Illus. by Max Ginsburg. 1987. Dial Bks Young. (Fic).

1987

Mufaro's Beautiful Daughters: An African Tale. John Steptoe. Illus. by John Steptoe. 1987. Lothrop. (Illus).

Pilgrims of Plimoth. Marcia Sewall. Illus. by Marcia Sewall. 1986. (Atheneum Children's Bks). Macmillan. (N/Fic).

Rabble Starkey. Lois Lowry. 1987. HM. (Fic).

1986

Auks, Rocks & the Odd Dinosaur: Inside Stories from the Smithsonian Museum of History. Peggy Thomson. 1985. Crowell Jr Bks. (N/Fic).

In Summer Light. Zibby O'Neal. 1985. Viking. (Fic).

Paper Crane. Molly Bang. Illus. by Molly Bang. 1985. Greenwillow. (Illus).

1985

Commodore Perry in the Land of the Shogun. Rhoda Blumberg. 1984. Lothrop. (N/Fic).

Mama Don't Allow. Thacher Hurd. 1984. HarpJ. (Illus).

Moves Make the Man. Bruce Brooks. 1984. HarpJ. (Fic).

1984

Double Life of Pocahontas. Jean Fritz. Illus. by Ed Young. 1983. (Putnam). Putnam Pub Group. (N/Fic).

Jonah & the Great Fish. Warwick Hutton. 1983. (McElderry Bk). Atheneum. (Illus).

Little Fear. Patricia Wrightson. 1983. (McElderry Bk). Macmillan. (Fic).

1983

Behind Barbed Wire: The Imprisonment of Japanese Americans During World War II. Daniel S. Davis. 1982. Dutton. (N/Fic).

Chair for My Mother. Vera B. Williams. Illus. by Vera B. Williams. 1982. Greenwillow. (Illus).

Sweet Whispers, Brother Rush. Virginia Hamilton. 1982. (Philomel). Putnam Pub Group. (Fic).

Randolph Caldecott Medal

The Randolph Caldecott Medal is an award given to an illustrator(s) of the most outstanding picture book. The late Frederic G. Melcher established this award in 1937, because he considered Randolph Caldecott one of the most distinguished English illustrators. This medal is presented annually by the awards committee of the Children's Services Division of the American Library Association, to a citizen or resident of the United States whose books were published in the United States during the preceding year.

1993

Mirette on the High Wire. Illus. by Emily A. McCully. 1993. (Philomel Bks). Putnam Pub Group.

1992

Tuesday. David Wiesner. Ed. by Dorothy Briley. Illus. by David Wiesner. 1991. (XClarion Bks). HM.

1991

Black & White. David Macaulay. 1990. HM.

1990

Lon Po Po: A Red Riding-Hood Story from China. Tr. by Ed Young from Chinese. Illus. by Ed Young. 1989. (Philomel Bks). Putnam Pub Group.

1989

Song & Dance Man. Karen Ackerman. Illus. by Stephen Gammell. 1988. Knopf.

1988

Owl Moon. Jane Yolen. Illus. by John Schoenherr. 1987. (Philomel Bks). Putnam Pub Group.

1987

Hey, Al. Arthur Yorinks. Illus. by Richard Egielski. 1986. FS&G.

1986

Polar Express. Chris Van Allsburg. Illus. by Chris Van Allsburg. 1985. HM.

1985

Saint George & the Dragon. Adapted by Margaret Hodges. Illus. by Trina S. Hyman. 1984. Little.

1984

Glorious Flight Across the Channel with Louis Bleriot. Alice Provensen & Martin Provensen. 1983. (Viking Kestrel). Viking.

1983

Shadow. Blaise Cendrars. Tr. by Marcia Brown. Illus. by Marcia Brown. 1982. (Scribner). Macmillan.

Canada Council Children's Literature Prizes

Established in 1976 by the Canada Council, this award is given annually to a Canadian or a "landed" immigrant with a least five years residence, whose books portray excellence in text or illustration (Illus). Books are judged in two categories -- English-language and French-language, and must have been published during the preceding year, either abroad or in Canada. Winners receive a monetary award of $2,500.

1991

Deux heures et demie avant Jasmine. Francois Gravel. 1992. Editions du Boreal. Text.

Doctor Kiss Says Yes. Joanne Fitzgerald. 1992. Groundwood Bks.

†† Fantaisies de l'oncle Henri. Benedicte Froissart. Illus. by Pierre Pratt. 1990. Annick Pr. (Illus).

†† Orphan Boy. Tololwa M. Mollel. Illus. by Paul Morin. 1990. Oxford University Pr. (Illus).

Pick-Up Sticks. Sarah Ellis. 1992. Groundwood Bks.

†† Redwork. Bedard Michael. 1990. Lester & Orpen Dennys. (Text).

Un Champion. Sheldon Cohen. 1992. Livres Toundra Grandir.

†† Vraie Histoire du chien de Clara Vic. Christiane Duchesne. 1990. Quebec Amerique. (Text).

1990

†† Bad Boy. Diana Wieler. 1989. (A Groundwood Book). Douglas & McIntyre. (Text).

†† Magic Paintbrush. Robin Muller. 1989. Doubleday Canada. (Illus).

1989

†† Amos's Sweater. Janet Lunn. Illus. by Kim LaSave. 1988. (Groundwood Bks). Douglas & McIntyre. (Illus).

†† Third Magic. Welwyn W. Katz. 1989. (Groundwood Bks). Douglas & McIntyre. (Text).

1988

†† Galahad Schwartz and the Cockroach Army. Morgan Nyberg. 1987. Douglas & McIntyre. (Text).

†† Rainy Day Magic. Marie-Louise Gay. 1987. Stoddart. (Illus).

1987

†† Have You Seen Birds? Joanne Oppenheim. Illus. by Barbara Reid. 1986. North Winds. (Illus).

†† Shadow in Hawthorn Bay. Janet Lunn. 1986. Lester & Orpen Dennys. (Text).

1986

†† Julie. Cora Taylor. 1985. Western Producer Prairie. (Text).

†† Murdo's Story. Murdo Scribe. Illus. by Terry Gallagher. 1985. Pemmican. (Illus).

1985

†† Lizzy's Lion. Dennis Lee. Illus. by Marie-Louise Gay. 1984. Stoddart. (Illus).

†† Sweetgrass. Jan Hudson. 1984. Tree Frog Pr. (Text).

1984

†† Ghost Horse of the Mounties. Sean Ohuigin. 1983. BlacK Moss. (Text).

†† Little Mermaid. Margaret C. Maloney. Illus. by Laszlo Gal. 1983. Methuen. (Illus).

1983

†† ABC-123: The Canadian Alphabet and Counting Book. Vlasta Van Kempen. Illus. by Vlasta Van Kempen. 1982. Hurtig. (Illus).

†† Hunter in the Dark. Monica Hughes. 1982. Clarke, Irwin. (Text).

Canada

1992

Gilles Tibo. Simon A. Lavillecanton. 1992. Livres Toundra. (Illus).

Hero of Lesser Cause. Julie Johnston. 1992. Lester Pubns. (Text).

Victor. Christiane Duchesne. 1992. Du Quebec Amerique. (Text).

Waiting for the Whales. Ron Rightburn. 1991. Orca Bks. (Illus).

Canadian Library Association Book-of-the-Year for Children Award

This award established in 1946 by the Canadian Association of Children's Librarians, a section of the Canadian Library Association, was first presented in 1947. It is given annually for a children's book of outstanding literary merit. The recipient must be a citizen or resident of Canada, and he receives a bronze medal "bearing Albert Laliberte's figure of Marie Rollet Herbert reading with her children."

1992

†† Eating Between the Line. Kevin Major. 1991. Doubleday Canada.

1991

†† Redwork. Bedard Michael. 1990. Lester & Orpen Dennys. (Text).

1990

†† Sky Is Falling. Kit Pearson. 1990. Viking Penguin.

1989

†† Easy Avenue. Brian Doyle. 1988. Groundwood Bks.

1988

†† Handful of Time. Kit Pearson. 1987. Penguin.

1987

†† Shadow in Hawthorn Bay. Janet Lunn. 1986. Lester & Orpen Dennys.

1986

†† Julie. Cora Taylor. 1985. Western Producer Prairie.

1985

†† Mama's Going to Buy You a Mockingbird. Jean Little. 1984. Viking Kestrel.

1984

†† Sweetgrass. Jan Hudson. 1984. Tree Frog Pr.

1983

†† Up to Low. Brian Doyle. 1982. Groundwood.

Carnegie Medal

This award has been presented annually since 1937 by the British Library Association to mark the centenary of Andrew Carnegie's birth, and to encourage writers of outstanding children's books. In order to be eligible, these books must be written in English and first published in the United Kingdom during the preceding year. The winner receives a medal.

1993

Zoo. Anthony Browne. 1993. (Umbrella Books). Knopf Bks Yng Read.

1992

Dear Nobody. Berlie Doherty. 1991. Orchard Bks Watts.

1991

†† Wolf. Gillian Cross. 1990. Oxford Univ Pr.

1990

†† Goggle-Eyes. Anne Fine. 1989. Hamish Hamilton.

1989

†† Pack of Lies. Geraldine McCaughrean. 1988. Oxford U Pr.

1988

†† Ghost Drum. Susan Price. 1987. Faber.

1987

†† Granny Was a Buffer Girl. Berlie Doherty. 1986. Methuen.

1986

†† Storm. Kevin Crossley-Holland. 1985. Heinemann.

1985

†† Changeover: A Supernatural Romance. Margaret Mahy. 1984. Dent.

1984

Handles. Jan Mark. 1983. (Viking Kestrel). Viking.

1983

†† Haunting. Margaret Mahy. 1982. Dent.

Catholic Book Awards

The Catholic Book Awards are sponsored by the Catholic Press of the United States ans Canada. For the children's category, the contents of the book must reflect "sound Christian and psychological values." The age groups covered are Children's Books (C: up to age 12), and Youth Books (Y: 12 years and older). Winners receive certificates. There were no awards presentations in the children's category in 1987 and 1988, and have since 1989 been cancelled.

1986

Back-Back and the Lima Bear. Thomas L. Weck. 1985. Winston-Derek. (C).

Hang Toughf. Matthew Lancaster. 1985. Paulist Pr. (Y).

1985

Mother Teresa of Calcutta. David Michelinie & Roy M. Gasnick. 1984. (Co-Pub with Marvel Comics and Paulist Pr). Franciscan Communications Office. (Y).

1984

No Strangers to Violence, No Strangers to Love. Biniface Hanley. 1983. Ave Maria Pr. (Y).

Story of Brother Francis. Lene Mayer-Skumanz. Illus. by Alicia Sancha. Tr. by Hildegard Bomer. 1983. Ave Maria Pr. (C).

Child Study Children's Book Award

Given annually since 1943 by Child Study Children's Book Committee at Bank Street College of Education, this award is for a book, fiction or non-fiction, which deals "realistically" with the problems of the world. The award includes a framed scroll and a small monetary prize.

1991

Secret City, U.S.A. Felice Holman. 1990. (Scribner's). Macmillan.

1990

Shades of Gray. Carolyn Reeder. 1989. Macmillan.

1989

December Stillness. Mary D. Hahn. 1988. (Clarion). Ticknor & Field.

Most Beautiful Place in the World. Ann Cameron. Tr. by Thomas B. Allen. 1988. Knopf.

1988

Rabble Starkey. Lois Lowry. 1987. HM.

1987

Journey to Jo'burg: A South African Story. Beverly Naidoo. Illus. by Eric Velasquez. 1986. Lipp Jr Bks.

1986

Ain't Gonna Study War No More: The Story of America's Peace Seekers. Milton Meltzer. 1985. Har-Row.

1985

One-Eyed Cat. Paula Fox. Illus. by Irene Trivas. 1984. Bradbury Pr.

With Westie & the Tin Man. C. S. Adler. 1984. Macmillan.

1984

Sign of the Beaver. Elizabeth G. Speare. 1983. HM.

Solomon System. Phyllis R. Naylor. 1983. (Atheneum Children's Bk). Macmillan.

1983

Homesick: My Own Story. Jean Fritz. Illus. by Margot Tomes. 1982. (Putnam). Putnam Pub Group.

Children's Book Award

This award is sponsored by the Federation of Children's Book Groups, Essex, England. It is given to the year's best fictional work suitable for children up to fourteen years, and is selected by children and adults. The prize awarded is a certificate.

1985

†† Brother in the Land. Robert Swindells. 1984. Oxford.

1984

†† Saga of Erik the Viking. Terry Jones. Illus. by Michael Foreman. 1983. Pavilion.

1983

†† BFG. Roald Dahl. 1982. Cape.

Christopher Award

Although this award was established in 1949, it was not until 1969 that children's books were included. It is presented annually by "The Christophers" to authors and illustrators whose works have achieved "artistic excellence .... affirming the highest values of the human spirit," and have been widely accepted by the public. Award winners receive bronze medallions.

1993

Letters from Rifka. Karen Hesse. 1992. (Bks Young Read). H Holt & Co.

Mississippi Challenge. Mildred P. Walter. 1992. (Bradbury Press). Macmillan Child Grp.

Rainbow Fish. Marcus Pfister. Tr. by J. Alison James. 1992. North-South Bks.

Rosie & the Yellow Ribbon. Paula DePaolo. Illus. by Janet Wolf. 1992. Little.

1992

Gold Coin. Alma F Ada. Illus. by Neil Waldman. Tr. by Bernice Randall. 1991. (Atheneum). Macmillan.

Somebody Loves You, Mr. Hatch. Eileen Spinelli. Illus. by Paul Yalowitz. 1992. (Bradbury). Macmillan Child Grp.

Star Fisher. Laurence Yep. 1991. Morrow Jr Bks.

Stephen's Feast. Jean Richardson. Illus. by Alice Englander. 1991. Little Brown.

Where Does God Live? Questions & Answers for Parents & Children. Rabbi Marc Gellman & Monsignor Thomas Hartman. Illus. by William Zdinak. 1991. (Triumph Bks). Gleneida Pub.

1991

Anton the Dove Fancier: And Other Tales of the Holocaust. Bernard Gotfryd. Ed. by Jane Roseman. 1990. (Washington Square Pr). PB.

Mississippi Bridge. Mildred D Taylor. Illus. by Max Ginsburg. 1990. Dial Bks Young.

Paul Revere's Ride. Henry Wadsworth Longfellow. Illus. by Ted Rand. 1990. Dutton.

1990

Can the Whales Be Saved? Philip Whitfield. 1989. (Viking Kestrel). Penguin USA.

Keeping a Christmas Secret. Phyllis R. Naylor. Illus. by Lena Shiffman. 1989. (Atheneum Childrens Bks). Macmillan.

So Much to Tell You... John Marsden. 1989. (Joy Street Bks). Little.

William and Grandpa. Alice Schertle. Ed. by D. Stevenson. Illus. by Lydia Dabcovich. 1988. Lothrop.

1989

Family Farm. Thomas Locker. Illus. by Thomas Locker. 1988. Dial Bks Young.

Good-bye Book. Judith Viorst. Illus. by Kay Chorao. 1988. (Atheneum Childrens Bks). Macmillan.

Lies, Deception & Truth. Ann E. Weiss. 1988. HM.

Looking the Tiger in the Eye: Confronting the Nuclear Threat. Carl B. Feldbaum & Ronald J. Bee. 1988. HarpJ.

1988

Gold Cadillac. Mildred D. Taylor. Illus. by Michael Hays. 1987. Dial Young Bks.

Heckedy Peg. Audrey Wood. Illus. by Don Wood. 1987. HarBraceJ.

Humphrey's Bear. Jan Wahl. Illus. by William Joyce. 1987. H Holt & Co.

Into a Strange Land: Unaccompanied Refugee Youth in America. Brent Ashabranner & Melissa Ashabranner. 1987. Dodd.

1987

Class Dismissed: More High School Poems, No. II. Mel Glenn. Illus. by Michael J. Bernstein. 1986. (Clarion Bks). Ticknor & Fields.

Duncan & Dolores. Barbara Samuels. Illus. by Barbara Samuels. 1986. Bradbury Pr.

Purple Coat. Amy Hest. Illus. by Amy Schwartz. 1986. (Four Winds Pr). Macmillan.

1986

Mount Rushmore Story. Judith Saint-George. 1985. Putnam Pub Group.

Patchwork Quilt. Valerie Flournoy. Illus. by Jerry Pinkey. 1985. Dial Bks Young.

Promise Not to Tell. Carolyn Polese. Illus. by Jennifer Barrett. 1985. (Dist. by Independent Pub. Group). Human Sci Pr.

Sarah, Plain & Tall. Patricia MacLachlan. 1985. HarpJ.

1985

How My Parents Learned to Eat. Ina Friedman. Illus. by Allen Say. 1984. HM.

Imagine That!!! Exploring Make-Believe. Joyce Strauss. Illus. by Jennifer Barrett. 1984. Human Sci Pr.

One-Eyed Cat. Paula Fox. Illus. by Irene Trivas. 1984. Bradbury Pr.

Picnic. Emily A. McCully. 1984. HarpJ.

Secrets of a Small Brother. Richard J. Margolis. Illus. by Donald Carrick. 1984. Macmillan.

1984

Dear Mr. Henshaw. Beverly Cleary. Illus. by Paul O. Zelinsky. 1983. Morrow.

Nuclear Arms Race: Can We Survive It? Ann E. Weiss. 1983. HM.

Sign of the Beaver. Elizabeth G. Speare. 1983. HM.

1983

Drawing from Nature. Jim Arnosky. Illus. by Jim Arnosky. 1982. Lothrop.

Formal Feeling. Zibby Oneal. 1982. Viking.

Homesick: My Own Story. Jean Fritz. Illus. by Margot Tomes. 1982. (Putnam). Putnam Pub Group.

We Can't Sleep. James Stevenson. 1982. Greenwillow.

Carolyn W. Field Award

Sponsored by the Youth Services Division of the Pennsylvania Library Association, this award is named after the former co-ordinator of Children's Services at the Free Library of Philadelphia. It was first presented in 1984, and has subsequently been given annually to a Pennsylvanian author or illustrator of a distinguished children's book published during the preceding year. The prize is a medal.

1992

Great Pumpkin Switch. Megan McDonald. Illus. by Ted Lewin. 1992. Orchard Bks Watts.

I Am Regina. Sally Keehn. 1991. (Philomel Bks). Putnam Pub Group.

1991

Maniac Magee. Jerry Spinelli. 1990. Little. (Author).

1990

Box Turtle at Long Pond. William T. George. Illus. by George Lindsay Barrett. 1989. Greenwillow. (Illus).

1989

Catwings. Ursula K. Le Guin. Illus. by S. D. Schindler. 1988. Orchard Bks Watts. (Illus).

1988

Little Tree. E. E. Cummings. Illus. by Deborah K. Ray. 1987. Crown. (Illus).

1987

Illyrian Adventure. Lloyd Alexander. 1986. Dutton. (Author).

1986

New Baby. Fred Rogers. Photos by Jim Judkis. 1985. (Putnam). Putnam Pub Group. (Author).

1985

Saint George and the Dragon. Retold by Margaret Hodges. Illus. by Trina S. Hyman. 1984. Little. (Author).

1984

Some Things Go Together. Charlotte Zolotow. Illus. by Karen Gundersheimer. 1983. (Crowell Jr Bks). HarpJ. (Illus).

Dorothy Canfield Fisher Children's Book Award

Co-sponsored by the Vermont Department of Libraries and the Vermont Congress of Parents and Teachers, this award was first presented in 1957 in honor of Dorothy Canfield Fisher, a distinguished Vermont author. Its purpose is to encourage the children of Vermont to read. Winners are selected from a list of books published two years prior to the award year. The prize is an illuminated scroll.

1993

Shiloh. Phyllis R. Naylor. 1991. (Atheneum). Macmillan.

1991

Maniac Magee. Jerry Spinelli. 1990. Little Brown.

1990

Where It Stops, Nobody Knows. Amy Ehrlich. 1988. Dial Bks Young.

1989

Hatchet. Gary Paulsen. 1987. Bradbury Pr.

Number the Stars. Lois Lowry. 1991. HM.

1988

Wait Till Helen Comes. Mary D. Hahn. 1986. (Clarion Bks). HM.

1987

Castle in the Attic. Elizabeth Winthrop. Illus. by Trina S. Hyman. 1985. Holiday.

1986

War with Grandpa. Robert K. Smith. Illus. by Richard Lauter. 1984. Delacorte.

1985

Dear Mr. Henshaw. Beverly Cleary. Illus. by Paul O. Zelinsky. 1983. Morrow.

1984

Bundle of Sticks. Patricia R. Mauser. Illus. by Gail Owens. 1982. (Childrens Bk). Atheneum.

1983

Tiger Eyes. Judy Blume. 1981. Bradbury Pr.

Friends of American Writers Juvenile Book Merit Award

These annual awards were first given in 1960, and are sponsored by the Friends of American Writers. "The categories represented are young adult, middle ages, beginning reader and author/illustrator." The contents of thr winning book must reflect the following ten criteria: appearance, well written, plot, setting theme, characterizations, style, illustration, will children read this book? and other considerations. "This winner must be a native or resident of one of the 16 Mid-western states for at least five years, or one of those states must be the location of the winning book." The prize, a certificate of merit and cash in the sum of $400 or more is given to each winning author.

1992
Children of the Fire. Harriette Gillem Robinet. 1991. (Atheneum). Macmillan Child Grp.
Place to Claim as Home. Patricia Willis. 1991. (Clarion Bks). HM.

1991
Boy in the Moon. Ron Koertge. 1990. Little.
Night Owls. Sharon Phillips Denslow. 1990. Macmillan.

1990
Dying Sun. Gary L. Blackwood. 1989. (Atheneum Children's Bks). Macmillan.
Unlived Affections. George Shannon. 1989. (Zolotow Bks). HarpJ.

1989
Secret Friendship. Virginia Brosseit. 1988. Winston-Derek.
Tonia the Tree. Sandy Stryker. 1988. Advocacy Pr.

1988
Island of Peril. Raboo Rodgers. 1987. HM.
Lighthouse Keeper's Daughter. Arielle N. Olson. Illus. by Elaine Wentworth. 1987. Little.

1987
Rover and Coo Coo. John Hay. Illus. by Tim Solliday. 1986. Green Tiger Pr.

1986
Where the Pirates are. Tom Townsend. 1985. Eakin.
Wolf of Shadows. Whitley Streiber. 1985. Knopf.

1985
Rodeo Summer. Judie Gulley. 1984. HM.

1984
Raspberry One. Charles Ferry. 1983. HM.

1983
Land I Lost. Huynh Quang Nhuong. 1982. HarpJ.

Garden State Children's Book Awards

The Garden State Children's Book Award was established in 1977, and is given annually by the Children's Services section of the New Jersey Library Association. "The purpose of the award is to show recognition for early and middle-grade books and to encourage, stimulate, and captivate the potential reader through the printed word and good illustrations." Three categories are presented: easy-to-read (ER), as determined by publishers, younger fiction (YF: grades 2 through 5) and younger non-fiction (Y/NF: grades 2 through 5). The eligible books are new American hardcover titles. Reprints, re-issues, and newly illustrated versions of older titles are not considered. "Titles that are considered must have been published three years earlier, and have literary and artistic merit as well as popularity with the readers." The winners receive framed certificates.

1993
Henry and Mudge and the Happy Cat. Cynthia Rylant. Illus. by Sucie Stevenson. 1990. (Bradbury Pr). Macmillan Child Grp. (ER)..
Magic School Bus Lost in the Solar System. Joanna Cole. Illus. by Bruce Degen. 1990. (Scholastic Hardcover). Scholastic Inc. (Y.NF)..
Muggie Maggie. Beverly Cleary. Illus. by Kay Life Morrow. 1990. (Camelot). Avon. (YF)..

1992
Henry & Mudge Get the Cold Shivers. Cynthia Rylant. Illus. by Sucie Stevenson. 1989. (Bradbury). Macmillan Child Grp.
Magic School Bus: Inside The Human Body. Joanna Cole. Illus. by Bruce Degen. 1989. Scholastic, Inc.
Wayside School is Falling Down. Louis Sachar. Illus. by Joel Schick. 1989. Lothrop, Lee & Shepard.

1991
Burning Questions of Bingo Brown. Betsy Byars & Cathy Bobak. 1989. (Kestrel). Viking. (YF).
Fox on the Job. James Marshall. Illus. by James Marshall. 1989. Dial Bks Young. (ER).
Teacher's Pet. Johanna Hurwitz. Illus. by Sheila Hamanaka. 1989. (Morrow Jr Bks). Morrow. (YF).
Volcanoes. Seymour Simon. 1989. (Morrow Jr Bks). Morrow. (Y/NF).

1990
Henry & Mudge in Puddle Trouble: The Second Book of Their Adventures. Cynthia Rylant. Illus. by Sucie Stevenson. 1987. Bradbury Pr. (ER).
Koko's Story. Francine Patterson. Illus. by Ronald H. Cohn. 1988. Scholastic Inc. (Y/NF).
Nighty-Nightmare. James Howe. Illus. by Leslie Morrill. 1987. (Atheneum Childrens Bks). Macmillan. (Y/F).

1989
Anastasia Has the Answers. Lois Lowry. 1985. HM. (Y/F).
Merry Christmas, Amelia Bedelia. Peggy Parish. Illus. by Lynn Sweat. 1986. Greenwillow. (ER).
To Space & Back. Sally Ride & Susan Okie. 1986. Lothrop. (Y/NF).

1988
Amelia Bedelia Goes Camping. Peggy Parrish. 1985. Greenwillow. (ER).
How They Built the Statue of Liberty. Mary J. Shapiro. Illus. by Huck Scarry. 1985. Random. (Y/NF).
Sarah, Plain and Tall. Patricia MacLachlan. 1985. (Trophy). HarpJ. (Y/F).

1987
Anastasia, Ask Your Analyst. Lois Lowry. 1984. HM. (Y/F).
In a Dark, Dark Room & Other Scary Stories. Alvin Schwartz. Illus. by Dirk Zimmer. 1984. HarpJ. (ER).
New Kid on the Block. Jack Prelutsky. Illus. by James Stevenson. 1984. Greenwillow. (Y/NF).

1986
Dear Mr. Hinshaw. Beverly Cleary. Illus. by Paul Zelinsky. 1983. Morrow. (Y/F).
Draw Fifty Monsters, Creepy Creatures, Superheroes, Demons, Dragons, Nerds, Dirts, Ghouls, Giants, Vampires, Zombies & Other Curiosa. Lee J. Ames. 1983. Doubleday. (Y/NF).
M & M and the Bad News Babies. Pat Moss. Illus. by Marilyn Hafner. 1983. Knopf. (ER).

1985
Nate the Great & The Snowy Trail. Marjorie Sharmat. Illus. by Marc Simont. 1982. (Coward). Putnam Pub Group. (ER).
Ralph S. Mouse. Beverly Cleary. Illus. by Paul Zelinsky. 1982. Morrow. (Y/F).

1984
Light in the Attic. Shel Silverstein. 1981. HarpJ. (Y/NF).
Nate the Great & the Missing Key. Marjorie Sharmat. Illus. by Marc Simont. 1981. (Coward). Putnam Pub Group. (ER).
Ramona Quimbly, Age 8. Beverly Cleary. Illus. by Alan Tiegreen. 1981. Morrow. (Y/F).

1983
Commander Toad in Space. Jane Yolen. Illus. by Bruce Degen. 1980. (Coward). Putnam Pub Group. (ER).
Show of Hands: Say it in Sign Language. MaryBeth Sullivan. Illus. by Linda Bourke. 1980. Addison-Wesley. (Y/NF).
Superfudge. Judy Blume. 1980. Dutton. (Y/F).

Esther Glen Award

The Esther Glen Award was established in 1945 in honor of Esther Glen, a New Zealand journalist, children's book editor and author. Offered annually when merited, it is administered by the New Zealand Library Association. The recipient must be a children's book author, and a citizen or resident of New Zealand whose work is "considered to be the most distinguished of the year" in New Zealand. The award winner receives a medal an NZ$50.

1984
†† Elephant Rock. Caroline Macdonald. 1983. Hodder.

1983
†† Jacky Nobody. Anne De Roo. 1982. Methuen.

Golden Kite Awards

The award, first presented in 1973 for fictional works (F), is sponsored and administered by the Society of Children's Book Writers. In 1977 a non-fiction (NF) category was added, and in 1982 a picture-illustration (PI) category. "The winning titles are those which exhibit excellence in writing and genuinely appeal to the interest and concerns of children." Each winner is awarded a Golden Kite statuette.

1993
Letters from a Slave Girl. M. E. Lyons. 1992. Scribners. F.
Steal away. Jennifer Armstrong. 1992. Orchard Bks Watts. F.

1992
Chicken Sunday. Illus. by Patricia Polacco. 1992. (XPhilomel Bks). Putnam Pub Group. Illus..
Fortuneteller. Illus. by Triva Schut. 1992. Unwin Hyman. Illus..
Indian Winter. Freedman Russel. 1992. Holiday. NF.
Long Road to Gettysburg. Jim Murray. 1992. (Clarion Bks). HM. NF.

1991
Boy's War. Jim Murphy. 1990. (Clarion Bks). HM. (NF).
Home Place. Jerry Pinkey. 1990. MacMillan. (PI).
Rain Catchers. Jean Thesman. 1991. HM.
True Confessions of Charlotte Doyle. Avi. Illus. by Ruth E. Murray. 1990. Orchard Bks Watts. (F).

1990
Jenny of the Tetons. Kristiana Gregory. 1989. HarBraceJ. (F).
Panama Canal: Gateway to the World. Judith St. George. 1989. (Putnam). Putnam Pub Group. (NF).
Tom Thumb. Richard J. Watson. 1989. HarBraceJ. (PI).

1989
Borrowed Children. Georgella Lyon. 1988. Orchard Bks Watts. (F).
Forest of Dreams. Rosemary Wells & Susan Jeffers. 1988. Dial Bks Young. (PI).
Let There Be Light: A Book About Windows. James C. Giblin. 1988. (Crowell Jr Bks). HarpJ. (NF).

1988
Devil and Mother Crump. Valerie S. Carey. 1987. HarpJ. (PI).
Incredible Journey of Lewis and Clark. Rhoda Blumberg. 1987. Lothrop. (NF).
Rabble Starkey. Lois Lowry. 1987. HM. (F).

1987
After the Dancing Days. Margaret Rostkowski. 1986. HarpJ. (F).
Alphabatics. Suse MacDonald. 1986. Bradbury Pr. (PI).
Poverty in America. Milton Meltzer. 1986. (Morrow Jr Bks). Morrow. (NF).

1986
Commodore Perry in the Land of the Shogun. Rhoda Blumberg. 1985. Lothrop. (NF).
Donkey's Dream. Barbara H. Berger. 1985. (Philomel Bks). Putnam Pub Group. (PI).
Sara, Plain and Tall. Patricia MacLachlan. 1985. HarpJ. (F).

1985
Napping House. Audrey Wood. Illus. by Don Wood. 1984. HarBraceJ. (PI).
Tancy. Belinda Hurmence. 1984. (Clarion). HM. (F).
Walls: Defenses Throughout History. James C. Giblin. 1984. Little. (NF).

1984
Illustrated Dinosaur Dictionary. Helen R. Satler. 1983. Lothrop. (NF).
Little Red Riding Hood. Trina S. Hyman. 1983. Holiday. (PI).
Tempering. Gloria Skurzynski. 1983. (Clarion). HM. (F).

1983
Chimney Sweeps. James Giblin Cross. Illus. by Margot Tomes. 1982. (Crowell Jr Bks). HarpJ. (NF).
Giorgio's Village. Tomie DePaola. 1982. (Putnam). Putnam Pub Group. (PI).
Ralph S. Mouse. Beverly Cleary. Illus. by Paul O. Zelinsky. 1982. Morrow. (F).

Letters from a Slave Girl. M. E. Lyons. Orchard Bks.
Letters from a Slave Girl. M. E. Lyons. Scribners. F.

Kate Greenaway Medal

This award has been administered by the British Library Association since 1955, and is presented annually to an illustrator with the most outstanding illustrations in children's books published in the United Kingdom during the preceding year. Winners receive a medal.

1993
Flour Babies. Anne Fine. 1992. Hamish Hamilton.
Zoo. Illus. by Anthony Browne. 1992. (XUmbrella Bks). Knopf Bks Yng Read.

1992
Jolly Postman. Janet Ahlberg. Illus. by Janet Ahlberg. 1991. Little.

1991
†† Whales' Song. Dyan Sheldon. Illus. by Gary Blythe. 1990. Hutchinson.

1990
†† War Boy: A Country Childhood. Michael Foreman. 1989. Pavilion Bks.

1989
†† Can't You Sleep Little Bear? Martin Waddell & Barbara Firth. 1988. Walker Bks.

1988

†† Crafty Chameleon. Mwenye Hadithi. Illus. by Adrienne Kennaway. 1987. Hodder & Stoughton.

1987

Snow White in New York. Fiona French. 1986. Oxford Univ Pr.

1986

†† Sir Gawain & the Loathly Lady. Selina Hastings. Illus. by Juan Wijngaard. 1985. Walker.

1985

†† Hiawatha's Childhood. Henry W. Longfellow. Illus. by Errol Le Cain. 1984. Faber.

1984

Gorilla. Anthony Browne. Illus. by Anthony Browne. 1983. (Julia McCrea Bks). Watts.

1983

†† Long Neck and Thunder Foot. Helen Piers. Illus. by Michael Foreman. 1982. Kestrel.

†† Sleeping Beauty and other Favourite Fairy Tales. Selected by Angela Carter. Illus. by Michael Foreman. 1982. Gollancz.

Guardian Award for Children's Fiction

This award was established in 1967 by the staff of The Guardian (London, England). It is presented annually to a British or Commonwealth author, for an outstanding work of fiction which was published during the preceding year. The winner receives a monetary prize of 50 English pounds.

1992

Exiles. Hilary McKay. 1991. Gollancz.

Paper Faces. Rachel Anderson. 1991. Oxford U Pr.

1991

†† Kingdom By the Sea. Robert Westall. 1990. Methuen.

1990

†† Goggle-Eyes. Anne Fine. 1989. Hamish Hamilton.

1989

Pack of Lies. Geraldine McCaughrean. 1988. Oxford Univ Pr.

1988

†† Runaways. Ruth Thomas. 1987. Hutchinson.

1987

True Story of Spit MacPhee. James Aldridge. 1986. (Viking Kestrel). Viking.

1986

Henry's Leg. Ann Pilling. 1985. (Viking Kestrel). Viking.

1985

†† What Is the Truth? Ted Hughes. 1984. Faber.

1984

†† Sheep-Pig. Dick King-Smith. 1983. Gollancz.

1983

†† Village By the Sea. Anita Desai. 1982. Heinemann.

Amelia Frances Howard-Gibbon Illustrator's Award

This award, established in 1969 by the Canadian Association of Children's Literature, is presented annually to the most outstanding Canadian illustrator whose work is published in Canada. Included are picture books, fiction and non-fiction. Nominations are made by members of CACL, although final selections are entirely up to the five-member committee of children's librarians. The recipient of this award receives a monetary prize, a citation, and a medal designed by James Houston (Canadian author and illustrator).

1993

Dragon's Pearl. Illus. by Paul Morin. 1993. Oxford Univ Pr.

1992

†† Waiting for the Whales. Sheryl McFarlane. Illus. by Ron Lightbourne. 1991. Orca Bk Publishers.

1991

†† Orphan Boy. Tololwa M Mollel. Illus. by Paul Morin. 1990. Oxford Univ Pr.

1990

†† Til All the Stars Have Fallen: Canadian Poems for Children. Selected by David Booth. Illus. by Kady McDonald Denton. 1989. Kids Can Pr.

1989

†† Easy Avenue. Brian Doyle. 1988. Groundwood Bks.

1988

†† Rainy Day Magic. Mary L. Gay. 1987. Stoddart.

1986

†† Zoom Away. Tim Wynne-Jones. Illus. by Ken Nutt. 1985. Groundwood Bks.

1985

†† Chin Chiang & the Dragon's Dance. Ian Wallace. 1984. Groundwood Bks.

1984

†† Zoom at Sea. Tim Wynne-Jones. Illus. by Ken Nutt. 1983. Groundwood Bks.

1983

†† Chester's Barn. Lindee Climo. Illus. by Lindee Climo. 1982. Tundra Bks.

International Board on Books for Young People (Honor List)

Established in 1956, this list is compiled biennially to internationally represent the best literature for children. Books for excellence in writing (Text), illustration (Illus), and translation (Trans) are recognised by the same jury that selects the Hans Christian Andersen Awards. Criteria for the books considered are that they be "representative of the children's literature from each country" and that "the books are recommended as suitable for publication throughout the world." Winners are presented with diplomas. (The following list does not include foreign language titles which might also have been honored for either text, illustration or translation).

Australia

1992

†† AESOP"S Fables. Rodney McRae. 1990. Margaret Hamilton Bks PTY. (Illus).

†† Dodger. Libby Gleeson. 1990. Turton & Chambers Ltd. (Text).

1990

†† My Place. Nadia Wheatley & Donna Rawlins. Illus. by Donna Rawlins. 1987. Collins Dove. (Text).

†† Where the Forest Meets the Sea. Jeannie Baker. 1987. Julie MacRae Books. (Illus).

1988

†† First There was Frances. Bob Graham. Illus. by Bob Graham. 1985. Lothian Pub Co. (Illus).

†† Riverman. Allan Baillie. Illus. by Mark O'Neill. 1986. Thomas Nelson Pub. (Text).

1986

†† Dancing in the Anzac Deli. Nadia Wheatley. Illus. by Neil Phillips & Waldemar Buczynski. Oxford Univ Pr. (Text).

†† Possum Magic. Mem Fox. Illus. by Julie Vivas. Omnibus Bks. (Illus).

1984

†† Watcher in the Garden. Joan Phipson. Methuen. (Text).

†† Who Sank the Boat? Pamela Allen. Nelson. (Illus).

Canada

1992

†† Bibitsa ou L'etrange Voyage de Clara Vic. Christiane Duchesne. 1991. Quebec Amerique. (Text).

†† Orphan Boy. Tololwa M Mollel. Illus. by Paul Morin. 1990. Oxford University Pr., Toronto. (Illus).

†† Redwork. Michael Bedard. 1990. Lester & Orpen Dennys Ltd. (Text).

1990

†† Bad Boy. Diana J. Wieler. 1989. Groundwood Books Douglas and McIntyre. (Text).

†† Could You Stop Josephine? Stephane Poulin. 1988. Tundra. (Illus).

1988

†† Shadow in Hawthorn Bay. Janet Lunn. Illus. by Amanda Duff. 1986. Lester & Orpen Dennys. (Text).

†† The Emperor's Panda. David Day. Illus. by Eric Beddows. 1986. McClelland & Stewart. (Illus).

1986

†† Chin Chiang and the Dragon's Dance. Ian Wallace. Illus. by Ian Wallace. Groundwood. (Illus).

†† Emily of New Moon. Lucy Montgomery. Tr. by Paule Daveluy. Pierre Tisseyre. (Trans).

†† Sweetgrass. Jan Hudson. Tree Frog Pr. (Text).

1984

†† Northern Alphabet. Ted Harrison. Tundra. (Illus).

†† Root Cellar. Janet Lunn. Dennys. (Text).

Great Britain

1990

†† Easter. Jan Pienkowski. 1989. William Heinemann Ltd. (Illus).

†† Slambash Wangs of a Compo Gormer. Robert Leeson. Illus. by Steve Crisp. 1987. Collins. (Text).

1988

†† Jolly Postman or Other People's Letters. Janet Ahlberg & Allan Ahlberg. Illus. by Janet Ahlberg & Allan Ahlberg. 1986. William Heinemann. (Illus).

†† Woof! Allan Ahlberg. Illus. by Fritz Wegner. 1986. Viking Kestrel. (Text).

1986

†† Changeover. Margaret Mahy. J M Dent. (Text).

†† Fifth Corner. Tr. by Patricia Crampton. Methuen. (Trans).

---

†† Hiawatha's Childhood. Henry W. Longfellow. Illus. by Errol Le Cain. Faber & Faber. (Illus).

1984

†† All the King's Men. William Mayne. Jonathan Cape. (Text).

†† Hansel and Gretel. Wilhelm Grimm & Jacob Grimm. Illus. by Anthony Browne. Julia Macrae. (Illus).

†† Magic Inkstand and Other Stories. Heinrich Seidel. Tr. by Elizabeth W. Taylor. Jonathan Cape. (Trans).

United States

1992

†† Little Tricker the Squirrel Meets Big Double the Bear. Ken Kesey. Illus. by Barry Moser. 1990. Penguin. (Text).

†† Shabanu: Daughter of the Wind. Suzanne Fisher-Staples. 1989. Knopf. (Text).

†† We Were Not Like Other People. Ephraim Sevela. Tr. by Antonina W Bouis. 1989. HarpC Child Bks. (Trans).

1990

†† Lincoln: A Photobiography. Russell Freedman. 1987. (Clarion Bks). HM. (Text).

Owl Moon. Jane Yolen. Illus. by John Schoenherr. 1987. (Philomel Bks). Putnam Pub Group. (Illus).

1988

Don't Say a Word. Barbara Gehrts. Tr. by Elizabeth D. Crawford. 1986. (McElderry Bks). Macmillan. (Trans).

Paper Crane. Molly Bang. Illus. by Molly Bang. 1985. Greenwillow Bks. (Illus).

Sarah, Plain & Tall. Patricia MacLachlan. Illus. by Constance Fogler. 1985. HarpJ. (Text).

1986

One-Eyed Cat. Paula Fox. Illus. by Irene Trivas. 1984. Bradbury Pr. (Text).

People Could Fly: American Black Folktales. Virginia Hamilton. Illus. by Leo Dillon & Diane Dillon. 1985. Knopf. (Illus).

1984

Battle Horse. Harry Kullman. Tr. by George Blecher & Lone T. Blecher. 1981. Bradbury Pr. (Trans).

Doctor De Soto. William Steig. 1982. FS&G. (Illus).

Sweet Whispers, Brother Rush. Virginia Hamilton. 1982. (Philomel). Putnam Pub Group. (Text).

International Reading Association Children's Books Award

First presented in 1975, this award is given annually to an author's first or second title published in the preceding year for a juvenile audience. Selections are made from fiction and non-fiction, as well as young adult books written in any language, and since 1987 a prize is given in the Older as well as the Younger category. Some of the criteria for selection stipulated by the International Reading Association are: the winning book should serve as a "literary standard by which readers can measure other books" where appropriate, they should "provide believable and intriguing characters growing naturally out of the events of the story", be "non-racist and non-sexist", and should "encourage young readers to read by providing them with something they will delight in and profit from." The winning author receives a plaque and a monetary prize of $1,000.

1993

Letters from Rifka. Karen Hesse. 1992. (XBks Young Read). H Holt & Co.

Old Turtle. Douglas Wood. Illus. by Cheng-Khee Chee. 1991. Pfeiffer-Hamilton.

1992

Five Words. Pnina Kass. 1991. Cricket Magazine.

Rescue Josh McGuire. Ben Mikaelsen. 1991. (Hyperion Bks). W Disney Bk Pub.

Ten Little Rabbits. Virginia Grossman. Illus. by Sylvia Long. 1991. Chronicle Bks.

1991

Is This a House for Hermit Crab? Megan McDonald. Illus. by F. D. Schindler. 1990. Orchard Bks Watts. (Younger).

Under the Hawthorn Tree. Mariata Conlon-McKenna. Illus. by Donald Teskey. 1990. Holiday. (Older).

1990

Children of the River. Linda Crew. 1989. Delacorte. (Older).

No Star Nights. Anna E. Smucker. Illus. by Steve Johnson. 1989. Knopf. (Younger).

1989

Probably Still Nick Swansen. Virginia E. Wolff. 1988. H Holt & Co. (Older).

Rechenka's Eggs. Patricia Polacco. Illus. by Patricia Polacco. 1988. (Philomel Bks). Putnam Pub Group. (Younger).

1988

Ruby in the Smoke. Philip Pullman. 1987. Knopf.

Third Story Cat. Leslie Baker. Illus. by Leslie Baker. 1987. Little. (Younger).

1987
After the Dancing Days. Margaret I. Rostkowski. 1986. HarpJ. (Older).
Line Up Book. Marisabina Russo. Illus. by Marisabina Russo. 1986. Greenwillow. (Younger).

1986
Prairie Songs. Pamela Conrad. Illus. by Darryl Zudeck. 1985. HarpJ.

1985
†† Badger on the Barge & Other Stories. Janni Howker. 1984. Julia MacRae.

1984
Ratha's Creature. Clare Bell. 1983. Macmillan.

1983
Darkangel. Meredith Pierce. 1982. (Pub. by Atlantic Monthly Pr). Little.

Jefferson Cup Award

Established in 1983 and named for the third President of the United States, this award is administered by the Children's and Young Adult Round Table of the Virginia Library Association. It is presented annually to "encourage the writing of quality books on history, biography and historical fiction" published during the preceding year, and to promote the reading of books which illustrate America's past. A pewter inscribed Jefferson Cup and a small honorarium are presented to the winner.

1991
Franklin Delano Roosevelt. Russell Freedman. 1990. (Clarion Bks). HM.

1990
Shades of Gray. Carolyn Reeder. 1989. Macmillan.

1989
Anthony Burns: The Defeat & Triumph of a Fugitive Slave. Virginia Hamilton. 1988. Knopf.

1988
Lincoln: A Photobiography. Russell Freedman. 1987. (Clarion). Ticknor & Fields.

1987
After the Dancing Days. Margaret Rostkowski. 1986. HarpJ.

1986
Sarah, Plain and Tall. Patricia MacLachlan. 1985. HarpJ.

1985
In the Year of the Boar and Jackie Robinson. Bette B. Lord. 1984. HarpJ.

1984
Who Speaks for Wolf? Paula U. Spencer. 1983. Tribe of Two Pr.

1983
Jewish Americans: A History in Their Own Words, 1650-1950. Milton Meltzer. 1982. (Crowell Jr Bks). HarpJ.

Coretta Scott King Award

Established in 1969, this award commemorates the life and work of the late Dr. Martin Luther King, Jr., and honors Mrs. King "for her courage and determination to continue the work for peace and world brotherhood." It is presented annually at the American Library Association, to a black author (A) and illustrator (I) whose works "encourage and promote" world unity and peace, and serve as an inspiration to young people in the achievement of their goals. A plaque honorarium and an encyclopedia are presented as gifts.

1992
Now Is Your Time: The African American Struggle for Freedom. Walter D Myers. 1991. HarperC Child Bks. (A).
Tar Beach. Faith Ringgold. Illus. by Faith Ringgold. 1991. Crown Bks Yng Read. (I).

1991
Aida. Leontyne Price. Illus. by Leo Dillon & Diane Dillon. 1990. HBJ. (I).
Road to Memphis. Mildred D Taylor. Ed. by Phyllis Fogelman. 1990. Dial Bks Young. (A).

1990
Long Hard Journey. Patricia McKissack & Frederick McKissack. 1989. Walker & Co. (A).
Nathaniel Talking. Eloise Greenfield. Illus. by Jan S. Gilchrist. 1989. Black Butterfly Children's Pr. (I).

1989
Fallen Angels. Walter D. Myers. 1988. Scholastic Inc. (A).
Mirandy & Brother Wind. Patricia C. Mckissack. Illus. by Jerry Pinkney. 1988. Knopf. (I).

1988
Friendship. Mildred D. Taylor. Illus. by Max Ginsburg. 1987. Dial Bks Young. (A).
Mufaro's Beautiful Daughter: An African Tale. Ed. by John Steptoe. Illus. by John Steptoe. 1987. Lothrop. (I).

1987
Half a Moon & One Whole Star. Crescent Dragonwagon. Illus. by Jerry Pinkney. 1986. Macmillan. (I).
Justin & the Best Biscuits in the World. Mildred P. Walter. Illus. by Catherine Stock. 1986. Lothrop. (A).

1986
Patchwork Quilt. Valerie Flournoy. Illus. by Jerry Pinkey. 1985. Dial Bks Young. (I).
People Could Fly. Virginia Hamilton. Illus. by Leo Dillon & Diane Dillon. 1985. Knopf. (A).

1985
Motown & Didi: A Love Story. Walter D. Myers. 1984. (Viking Kestrel). Viking. (A).

1984
Everett Anderson's Goodbye. Lucille Clifton et al. Illus. by Ann Grifalconi. 1983. H Holt & Co. (A).
My Mama Needs Me. Mildred P. Walter. Illus. by Pat Cummings. 1983. Lothrop. (I).

1983
Black Child. Peter Magubane. 1982. Knopf. (I).
Sweet Whispers, Brother Rush. Virginia Hamilton. 1982. (Philomel). Putnam Pub Group. (A).

Janusz Korczak Literary Competition (Anti-Defamation League of B'nai B'rith)

The Janusz Korczak Literary Competition was inspired by the life and death of Korczak (1879-1942), a brilliant Polish pediatrician who founded two Warsaw orphanages, one housing Jewish children and the other Catholic. This biennial award was first presented in 1981 for books "exemplifying the principles of selflessness and human dignity." In the children's category, the winning books are those judged as the best fiction or non-fiction suitable for use at either the elementary or secondary school level. Books published in any language, anywhere in the world, are eligible. A prize of $1,000 is awarded to the winner.

1991
Shadow of the Wall. Christa Laird. 1990. Greenwillow Books.

1986
Days of Honey: The Tunisian Boyhood of Rafael Uzan. Irene Awret. 1984. Schocken Bks.

1984
Seaward. Susan Cooper. 1983. (Atheneum). Macmillan.

Before Their Time: Four Generations of Teenage Mothers. Joelle Sander. HarBraceJ.

Kurt Maschler ('Emil') Award

The award was established by the founder of Atrium Press in Zurich in honor of Erich Kastner's "Emil und die Detektive," and is administered by the National Book League, London, England. It is presented for a "work of imagination" in children's literature in which text and illustration are so presented, and are of such excellence that each "enhances yet balances the other." A monetary prize of 1,000 English pounds and a bronze statuette are given to the winner.

1991
Have You Seen Who's Just Moved In Next Door To Us? Colin McNaughton. 1991. Walker Bks.

1990
†† All Join In. Quentin Blake. Illus. by Quentin Blake. 1990. Cape.

1989
†† Park in the Dark. Martin Waddell. Illus. by Barbara Firth. 1989. Walker Bk.

1987
†† Jack the Treacle Eater. Charles Causley. Illus. by Charles Keeping. 1986. Macmillan.

1986
†† Jolly Postman. Allan Ahlberg & Janet Ahlberg. Illus. by Allan Ahlberg & Janet Ahlberg. 1985. Collins.

1985
†† Iron Man. Ted Hughes. Illus. by Andrew Davidson. 1984. Faber.

1984
†† Grandpa. John Burningham. 1983. Cape.

1983
†† Gorilla. Anthony Browne. 1982. Julia MacRae.

Vicky Metcalf Short Story Award

The Vicky Metcalf Short Story Award was first given in 1979 to a Canadian author, for the best children's short story first published in English in a Canadian periodical, or anthology during the calendar year. In 1988, for the first time the editor of the winning short story was also awarded a matching prize of $1,000. Winners must be Canadian citizens and they receive prizes of $1,000 each.

1992
Adventure on Thunder Island. Edna King. James Lorimer.

1990
†† Choose Your Grandma. Patricia Armstrong. 1989. Cateau Bks.

1989
†† Paradise Cafe & Other Stories. Martha Brooks. 1988. Thistledown Pr.

1988
†† Marvin & Me & the Flies. Claire Mackay. Ed. by Brian Cross. 1987. (Canadian Children's Annual). Grollier.

1987
†† Viking Dagger. Isabel Reimer. 1986. (Of the Jigsaw). Peguis.

1986
†† Boy Who Walked Backwards. Diana J. Weiler. 1985. Western Producer Prairie.

1985
†† Here She is, Ms. Teeny-Wonderful! Martyn Godfrey. 1984. Crackers Magazine. Number 12, Spring.

1984
†† Dog Who Wanted to Die. P. C. Archer. 1983. Jam Magazine. Vol. 4, Number 1 (Sept/Oct).

1983
†† Iron Barred Door. Monica Hughes. 1982. (Anthology Two). Nelson.

Mother Goose Award

Established by booksellers Clodagh and Chris Alborough in 1979, the Mother Goose Award is presented annually and is administered by Books for, London, England. The award encourages new talent by giving recognition to "the most exciting newcomer to the field of illustration of children's books in Great Britain" published during the preceding year. The winner receives a bronze egg, a scroll, and a monetary award of 200 English pounds. No award was presented in this category in 1986.

1993
Seashell Song. Clare Fletcher. 1993. Bodley Head.

1992
Inside The Whale. Steve Parker. Illus. by Ted Dewan. 1991. Darling Kindersley.

1991
Close Call. Amanda Harvey. 1990. Macmillan.

1990
Strat and Chatto. Jan Mark. Illus. by David Hughes. 1989. Walker Bks.

1989
†† Bush Vark's First Day Out. Charles Fuge. Illus. by Charles Fuge. 1988. Macmillan.

1988
†† Listen to This. Compiled by Laura Cecil. Illus. by Emma Chichester-Clark. 1987. Bodley Head.

1987
†† Bag Of Moonshine. Alan Garner. Illus. by Patrick J. Lynch. 1986. Collins.

1985
†† Badger's Parting Gifts. Susan Varley. 1984. Andersen.

1984
†† Hob Stories. William Mayne. Illus. by Patrick Benson. 1983. Walker.

1983
†† Angry Arthur. Satoshi Kitamura. 1982. Andersen.

Close Call. Amanda Harvey. Illus. by Amanda Harvey. Macmillan.

National Jewish Book Awards

The Jewish Welfare Board/Jewish Book Council sponsors several categories of the National Jewish Book Awards, and recognizes and honors authors and illustrators who have made outstanding contributions to Jewish Literature for children. Among them are the Children's Literature category (Lit), which was established in 1952 to encourage and award the author of an original, English publication for children, which embraces a Jewish theme, or to recognize the cumulative works of an author's contribution to Jewish juvenile literature. The Children's Illustrated Book category (Illus), which was established in 1982, honors the author and illustrator of a book which has "Jewish themes in which the illustrations are an intrinsic part of the text." Candidates for both categories must be United States or Canadian citizens and each winner receives a monetary award of $750. The publishers are also awarded citations.

1992
Chicken Man. Michelle Edwards. 1991. Lothrop, Lee & Shepard Bks.
The Man From the Other Side. Uri Orlev. Tr. by Hillel Halkin. 1991. HM.

1991

Becoming Gershona. Nava Semel. Tr. by Seymour Simckes. 1990. Viking Child Bks. (Lit).

Hannukkah. Roni Schotter. Illus. by Marylin Hafner. 1990. (Joy St Bks). Little. (Illus).

1990

Berchick, My Mother's Horse. Esther S. Blanc. Illus. by Tennessee Dixon. 1989. Volcano Pr. (Illus).

Number the Stars. Lois Lowry. 1989. HM. (Lit).

1989

Devil's Arithmetic. Jane Yolen. 1988. (Viking Kestrel). Penguin USA. (Lit).

Just enough is Plenty: A Hanukkah Tale. Barbara D. Goldin. Illus. by Seymour Chwast. 1988. (Viking Kestrel). Penguin USA. (Illus).

1988

Exodus. Adapted by Miriam Chaikin. Illus. by Charles Mikolaycak. 1987. Holiday. (Illus).

Return. Sonia Levitin. 1987. (Atheneum Children's Bk). Macmillan. (Lit).

1987

Monday in Odessa. Eileen B. Sherman. 1986. JPS Phila. (Lit).

Poems for Jewish Holidays. Myra C. Livingston. Illus. by Lloyd Bloom. 1986. Holiday House. (Illus).

1986

Brothers. Florence B. Freedman. Illus. by Robert A. Parker. 1985. HarpJ. (Illus).

In Kindling Flame: The Story of Hannah Senesh, 1921-1944. Linda Atkinson. 1985. Lothrop. (Lit).

1985

Good If It Goes. Gail Provost & Gail Levine-Freidus. 1984. Bradbury Pr. (Lit).

Mrs. Moskowitz & the Sabbath Candlesticks. Amy Schwartz. 1984. JPS Phila. (Illus).

1984

Jewish Kids Catalog. Chaya M. Burstein. Illus. by Chaya M. Burstein. 1983. JPS Phila. (Lit).

1983

King of the Seventh Grade. Barbara Cohen. 1982. Lothrop. (Lit).

Yussel's Prayer: A Yom Kippur Story. Barbara Cohen. Illus. by Michael Deraney. 1982. Lothrop. (Illus).

New York Academy of Sciences, Children's Science Book Award

This award was established in 1970 to encourage and promote a high standard in the writing and publication of children's science books. Prizes were given to authors in two categories, Younger (Y) and Older (O), but since 1975 has also been given to a "book's illustrator if he/she is not also the author." In 1983 a third award was added -- the Elliott Montroll Special Award (EM); named for the illustrious professor of Mathematics at the University of Maryland. The Montroll Award is presented for a "science book that provides unusual historical data or background material on a science subject." The recipients either receive or share citations and a monetary award.

1989

Digging Dinosaurs. John R. Horner & James Gorman. Illus. by Donna Braginetz & Kris Ellingsen. 1988. Workman Pub. (O).

Log of Christopher Columbus. Tr. by Robert H. Fuson. 1987. Int Marine Pub. (EM).

Sierra Club Wayfinding Book. Vicki McVey. Illus. by Martha Weston. 1989. (Sierra Club Bks). Little. (Y).

1988

Exploring the Night Sky. Terence Dickinson. Illus. by Terence Dickinson. 1987. Camden House Pub. (O).

Icebergs and Glaciers. Seymour Simon. 1987. (Morrow Jr Bks). Morrow. (Y).

Media Lab: Inventing 'The Future at MIT' Stewart Brand. 1987. (Viking Kestrel). Viking. (EM).

1987

Exploring the Night Sky. Terence Dickinson. Illus. by John Bianchi. 1986. Camden House Pub. (O).

Icebergs and Glaciers. Seymour Simon. 1986. (Morrow Jr Bks). Morrow. (Y).

Media Lab: Inventing the Future at MIT. Stewart Brand. 1986. Viking. (EM).

1986

Atlas of North America. Ed. by Wilbur E. Garret. 1985. National Geographic. (EM).

Evolution Book: The Story of 4000 Million Years of Life on Earth. Sara Stein. Illus. by Sara Stein. 1985. Workman Pub. (O).

When Sheep Cannot Sleep. Satoshi Kitamura. 1985. FS&G. (Y).

1985

Big Stretch: The Complete Book of the Amazing Rubber Band. Ada Graham & Frank Graham. Illus. by Richard Rosenblum. 1984. Knopf. (Y).

Comet Halley: Once in a Lifetime. Mark Littman & Donald K. Yeomans. 1985. American Chemical Soc. (EM).

1984

Daywatchers. Peter Parnall. Illus. by Peter Parnall. 1984. Macmillan. (O).

Dreamers & Doers. Norman Richards. 1984. (Atheneum). Macmillan. (EM).

Secret Language of Snow. Terry T. Williams & Ted Major. Illus. by Jennifer Dewey. 1984. Pantheon. (Y).

1983

From Hand Ax to Laser. John Purcell. Illus. by Judy Skorpil. 1983. Vanguard. (EM).

Oak & Company. Richard Mabey. Illus. by Clare Roberts. 1983. Greenwillow. (Y).

Volcano Weather: The Story of 1816, the Year Without a Summer. Henry Strommel & Elizabeth Strommel. 1983. Seven Seas. (O).

New York Times Choice of Best Illustrated Children's Books of the Year

Sponsored by The New York Times and first compiled in 1952, this list honors the highest quality illustrations in children's books published in the United States during that year. Winners are announced annually in The New York Times Book Review in mid-November.

1990

Beach Ball. Peter Sis. Illus. by Peter Sis. 1990. Greenwillow.

Beneath a Blue Umbrella. Jack Prelutsky. Illus. by Garth Williams. 1990. Greenwillow.

Christmas Carol. Charles Dickens. Illus. by Roberto Innocenti. Stewart, Tabori & Chang.

Dancing Palm Tree: And Other Nigerian Folktales. Barbara K. Walker. Illus. by Helen Siegl. 1990. Texas Tech Univ Pr.

Fish Eyes: A Book You Can Count On. Lois Ehlert. Illus. by Lois Ehlert. 1990. HBJ.

Fool and the Fish: A Tale From Russia. Alexander Nikolayevich Afanasyev & Lenny Hort. Illus. by Gennady Spirin. 1990. Dial Bk Young.

I'm Flying! Alan Wade. Illus. by Petra Mathers. 1990. Knopf.

One Gorilla: A Counting Book. Atsuko Morozumi. Illus. by Atsuko Morozumi. 1990. FS&G.

Tale of the Madarin Ducks. Katherine Paterson. Illus. by Leo Dillon & Diane Dillon. 1990. Lodestar Bks.

War Boy: A Country Childhood. Michael Foreman. Illus. by Michael Foreman. 1990. Arcade Pub Inc.

1989

Dancing Skeleton. Cynthia C. DeFelice. Illus. by Robert A. Parker. 1989. Macmillan.

Does God Have a Big Toe? Stories About Stories in the Bible. Marc Gellman. Illus. by Oscar De Mejo. 1989. HarpJ.

Heartaches of a French Cat. Barbara McClintock. Illus. by Barbara McClintock. 1989. Godine.

How Pizza Came to Queens. Dayal K. Khalsa. Illus. by Dayal K. Khalsa. 1989. (C N Potter Bks). Crown.

Nicholas Cricket. Joyce Maxner. Illus. by William Joyce. 1989. HarpJ.

Olson's Meat Pies. Peter Cohen. Tr. by Richard E. Fisher. Illus. by Olof Landstrom. 1989. (Pub by R & S Bks). FS&G.

Peacock Pie: A Book of Rhymes. Walter De la Mare. Illus. by Louise Brierley. 1989. H Holt & Co.

Theseus and the Minotaur. Retold by Warwick Hutton. Illus. by Warwick Hutton. 1989. (M K McElderry). Macmillan.

Turtle in July. Marilyn Singer. Illus. by Jerry Pinkney. 1989. Macmillan.

Whales. Seymour Simon. 1989. (Crowell Jr Bks). HarpJ.

1988

Cats Are Cats: Poems. Compiled by Nancy Larrick. Illus. by Ed Young. 1988. (Philomel Bks). Putnam Pub Group.

Fire Came to the Earth People. Susan L. Roth. 1988. St Martin.

I Want to Be an Astronaut. Byron Barton. Illus. by Byron Barton. 1988. (Crowell Jr Bks). HarpJ.

Look! Look! Look! Tana Hoban. 1988. Greenwillow.

River Dream. Allen Say. Illus. by Allen Say. 1988. HM.

Shaka: King of the Zulus. Diane Stanley & Peter Vennema. 1988. Morrow.

Sir Francis Drake: His Daring Deeds. Roy Gerrard. 1988. FS&G.

Stringbean's Trip to the Shining Sea. Vera B. Williams. Illus. by Jennifer Williams & Vera B. Williams. 1988. Greenwillow.

Theodor & Mr. Balbini. Petra Mathers. Illus. by Petra Mathers. 1988. HarpJ.

1987

Cremation of Sam McGee. Robert W. Service. Illus. by Ted Harrison. 1987. Greenwillow.

Fox's Dream. Tejima. Illus. by Tejima. 1987. (Philomel Bks). Putnam Pub Group.

Halloween ABC. Eve Merriam. Illus. by Lane Smith. 1987. Macmillan.

Handtalk Birthday: A Number and Story Book in Sign Language. Remy Charlip & Mary B. Miller. Illus. by George Ancona. 1987. (Four Winds). Macmillan.

In Coal Country. Judith Hendershot. Illus. by Thomas B. Allen. 1987. Knopf.

Jump Again! More Adventures of Brer Rabbit. Joel C. Harris. Adapted by Van Dyke Parks. Illus. by Barry Moser. 1987. HarBraceJ.

Mountains of Tibet. Mordicai Gerstein. Illus. by Mordicai Gerstein. 1987. HarpJ.

Rainbow Rhino. Peter Sis. Illus. by Peter Sis. 1987. Knopf.

Seventeen Kings & Forty-Two Elephants. Margaret Mahy. Illus. by Patricia MacCarthy. 1987. Dial Bks Young.

Yellow Umbrella. Henrik Drescher. Illus. by Henrik Drescher. 1987. Bradbury Pr.

1986

Brave Irene. William Steig. 1986. FS&G.

Cherries & Cherry Pits. Vera B. Williams. Illus. by Vera B. Williams. 1986. Greenwillow.

Flying. Donald Crews. Illus. by Donald Crews. 1986. Greenwillow.

Molly's New Washing Machine. Laura Geringer. Illus. by Petra Mathers. 1986. HarpJ.

One Morning. Canna Funakoshi. Tr. by Yohiji Izawa from Japanese. 1986. Picture Bk Studio USA.

Owl Scatterer. Norman Howard. Illus. by Michael McCurdy. 1986. (Atlantic Monthly Pr). Little.

Pigs from A to Z. Arthur Geisert. Illus. by Arthur Geisert. 1986. HM.

Rembrandt Takes a Walk. Mark Strand. Illus. by Red Grooms. 1986. Crown.

Stranger. Chris Van Allsburg. Illus. by Chris Van Allsburg. 1986. HM.

1985

Gorilla. Anthony Browne. Illus. by Anthony Browne. 1985. Knopf.

Grandpa. John Burningham. Illus. by John Burningham. 1985. Crown.

Hazel's Amazing Mother. Rosemary Wells. Illus. by Rosemary Wells. 1985. Dial Bks Young.

Inside-Outside Book of New York City. Roxie Munro. Illus. by Roxie Munro. 1985. Dodd.

Legend of Rosepetal. Clemens Brentano. Illus. by Lisbeth Zwerger. 1985. Picture Bk Studio USA.

People Could Fly. Virginia Hamilton. Illus. by Leo Dillon & Diane Dillon. 1985. Knopf.

Polar Express. Chris Van Allsburg. Illus. by Chris Van Allsburg. 1985. HM.

Relatives Came. Cynthia Rylant. Illus. by Stephen Gammell. 1985. Bradbury Pr.

Story of Mr. Loveright & Purrless Her Cat. Lore Segal. Illus. by Paul O. Zelinsky. 1985. Knopf.

1984

Animal Alphabet. Bert Kitchen. Illus. by Bert Kitchen. 1984. Dial Bks Young.

Babushka: An Old Russian Folktale. Charles Mikolaycak. Illus. by Charles Mikolaycak. 1984. Holiday.

If There Were Dreams to Sell. Barbara Lalicki. Illus. by Margot Tomes. 1984. Lothrop.

Jonah & the Great Fish. Warwick Hutton. 1984. (McElderry Bk). Macmillan.

Mysteries of Harris Burdick. Chris Van Allsburg. Illus. by Chris Van Allsburg. 1984. HM.

Napping House. Audrey Wood. Illus. by Don Wood. 1984. HarBraceJ.

Nutcracker. E. T. Hoffman. Tr. by Ralph Manheim. Illus. by Maurice Sendak. 1984. Crown.

Saint George & the Dragon. Adapted by Margaret Hodges. Illus. by Trina S. Hyman. 1984. Little.

Sir Cedric. Roy Gerrard. 1984. FS&G.

Where the River Begins. Thomas Locker. 1984. Dial Bks Young.

1983

Favershams. Roy Gerrard. 1983. FS&G.

Little Red Cap. Jacob Grimm & Wilhelm K. Grimm. Tr. by Elizabeth D. Crawford from Ger. Illus. by Lisbeth Zwerger. 1983. Morrow.

Round Trip. Ann Jonas. Illus. by Ann Jonas. 1983. Greenwillow.

Simon's Book. Henrik Drescher. 1983. Lothrop.

Tools. Ken Robbins. 1983. (Four Winds). Macmillan.

Twelve Cats for Christmas. Martin Leman. 1983. Merrimack Pub Cir.

Up a Tree. Ed Young. Illus. by Ed Young. 1983. HarpJ.

Wreck of the Zephyr. Chris Van Allsburg. Illus. by Chris Van Allsburg. 1983. HM.

John Newbery Medal

Since 1922 the Newbery Medal has been presented annually by an award committee of the Children's Services Division of the American Library Association, to the author with the most outstanding contribution to children's literature. The award was donated by the late Frederic G. Melcher and named in honor of John Newbery (1713-1767), British bookseller and the first publisher of children's periodicals, to encourage "original and creative work" in children's books. These books must be written by a United States citizen or resident, and published during the preceding year. The recipient receives a medal donated by the Melcher family.

1992
Shiloh. Phyllis Reynolds. 1991. (Atheneum). Macmillan.
1991
Maniac Magee. Jerry Spinelli. 1990. Little.
1990
Number the Stars. Lois Lowry. 1989. HM.
1989
Joyful Noise: Poems for Two Voices. Paul Fleischman. Illus. by Eric Beddows. 1988. HarpJ.
1988
Lincoln: A Photobiography. Russell Freedman. 1987. (Pub. by Clarion). Ticknor & Fields.
1987
Whipping Boy. Sid Fleischman. Illus. by Peter Sis. 1986. Greenwillow.
1986
Sarah, Plain & Tall. Patricia Maclachlan. 1985. HarpJ.
1985
Hero & the Crown. Robin McKinley. 1984. Greenwillow.
1984
Dear Mr. Henshaw. Beverly Cleary. Illus. by Paul O. Zelinsky. 1983. Morrow.
1983
Dicey's Song. Cynthia Voigt. 1982. (Childrens Bk). Macmillan.

Scott O'Dell Award for Historical Fiction

Administered by the Advisory Committee of the Bulletin of the Center for Children's Books, this annual award was established in 1981 by Scott O'Dell, a noted author. The book content must be historical fiction set in the new world and has literary merit. It must also have been published in the previous year by a United States publisher. The award is primarily given to juvenile literature, but includes young adults also. A monetary award of $5,000 is given to the winner.

1993
Morning Girl. Michael Dorris. 1992. Hyprn Child.
1992
Stepping on the Cracks. Mary D Hahn. 1991. (Clarion Bks). Macmillan.
1991
Time of Troubles. Pieter Van Raven. 1990. (Scribner's). Macmillan.
1990
Shades of Gray. Carolyn Reeder. 1989. Macmillan.
1989
Honorable Prison. Lyll B. De Jenkins. 1988. Lodestar Bks.
1988
Charley Skedaddle. Patricia Beatty. 1987. (Morrow Jr Bks). Morrow.
1987
Streams to the River, River to the Sea: A Novel of Sacagawea. Scott O'Dell. 1986. HM.
1986
Sarah, Plain & Tall. Patricia MacLachlan. 1985. HarpJ.
1985
Fighting Ground. Avi. Illus. by Ellen Thompson. 1984. Lipp Jr Bks.
1984
Sign of the Beaver. Elizabeth G. Speare. 1983. HM.

Other Award

Established in 1975 and sponsored by the Children's Book Bulletin (London, England), the Other Award was given to writers and illustrators whose works were considered "progressive in their treatment of ethnic minorities, the sex roles, and social differences." Winners received commendations. However, this award was discontinued in 1988.

1987
†† My Love, My Love. Rosa Guy. Upstarts.
†† "Next Door" Books. Peter Heaslip. Methuen Educational.
†† Palestinians. David McDowall. Watts.
†† Push Me, Pull Me. Sandra Chick. Livewires.

1986
†† Bus Driver. Anne Stewart. Hamish Hamilton "Cherrystones"
People Could Fly. Virginia Hamilton. (Pub. by Walker). Knopf.
†† Say It Again, Granny! John Agard. Bodley Head.
†† Starry Night. Catherine Sefton. Hamish Hamilton.
1985
†† Coal-Mining Women. Angela V. John. Cambridge Educational.
†† Comfort Herself. Geraldine Kaye. (Co-Published with Magnet). Deutch.
†† Journey to Jo'burg. Beverley Naidoo. (Co-Pub with Lions). Longman "Knockouts"
†† Motherland. Elyse Dodgson. Heinemann Educational.
†† Our Kids. Millie et al. Peckham Pub Project.
†† Vila. Sarah Baylis. Brilliance.
1984
†† Brother in the Land. Robert Swindells. Oxford.
†† Chair for My Mother. Julia MacRae.
†† Wheel Around the World. Ed. by Chris Searle. MacDonald.
†† Who Lies Inside. Timothy Ireland. Gay Men's Pr.
1983
†† Everybody Here! Compiled by Michael Rosen. Bodley Head.
†† Nowhere to Play. Karusa. A & C Black.
†† Talking in Whispers. James Watson. Gollancz.
†† Will of Iron. Gerard Melia. Longmans.

Parents' Choice Award for Illustration in Children's Books

Established in 1980 and sponsored by the Parents' Choice Foundation, this award is given to "recognise children's books with illustrations of more than remarkable charm." The winners are selected by children's books artists working in the field. Final choices are made by an outstanding critic or artist.

1992
Africa Dream. Eloise Greenfield. 1992. (Trophy). HarpC Child Bks.
Amos & Boris. William Steig. 1992. FS&G.
Back Home. Gloria J. Pinkney. Illus. by Jerry Pinkney. 1992. Dial Bks Young. Picture.
Blue Skin of the Sea. Graham Salisbury. 1992. Delacorte.
Boy and the Ghost. Robert D. San Souci. 1192. (S&S BFYR). S&S Trade.
Cats. Peggy Roalf. 1992. Hyprn Child.
Don't You Know There's a War On? James Stevenson. 1992. Greenwillow. Picture.
Fish Eyes: A Book You Can Count On. Lois Ehlert. 1992. (Voyager Bks). HarBrace.
Fortune Tellers. LLoyd Alexander. 1992. (DCB). Dutton Child Bks.
Golden Locket. C. Green. Illus. by M. Sewall. 1992. (HB Juv Bks). HarBrace. Picture.
Humbug. Nina Bawden. 1992. (Clarion). HM.
I hear a Noise. Diane Goode. Illus. by Diane Goode. 1992. (DCB). Dutton Child Bks.
I Saw Esau: The Schoolchild's Pocketbook. Ed. by Peter Opie & Iona Opie. Illus. by Maurice Sendak. 1992. Candlewick Pr. Picture.
I Spy: An Allphabet in Art. Lucy Micklethwait. 1992. Greenwillow. Picture.
Jim Ugly. Sid Fleischman. Illus. by Marcia Sewall. 1992. Greenwillow.
June 29, 1999. David Wiesner. Illus. by David Wiesner. 1992. (Clarion Bks). HM. Picture.
Klara's New World. Jeanette Winter. Illus. by Jeanette Winter. 1992. Knopf Bks Yng Read. Picture.
Maria Theresa. Petra Mathers. Illus. by Petra Mathers. 1992. (Trophy). HarpC Child Bks.
Missing May. Cynthia Ryland. 1992. Orchard Bks Watts.
Mojave. Diane Siebert. 1992. (Trophy). HarpC Child Bks.
My Little Red Car. Chris L. Demarest. Illus. by Chris L. Demarest. 1992. Boyds Mills Pr. Picture.
My Place in Space. Robin Hirst & Sally Hirst. Illus. by Roland Harvey. 1992. Orchard Bks Watts.
Our Home is the Sea. Riki Levinson. Illus. by Dennis Luzak. 1992. (Puffin Unicorn). Puffin Bks.
Our Home is the Sea. Riki Levinson. Illus. by Dennis Luzak. 1992. (Puffin Unicorn). Puffin Bks.
Quetzalcoatl Tale of the Ballgame. Marilyn Parke & Sharon Panik. 1992. Fearon Teach Aids.
Return of Freddy LeGrand. Jon Agee. 1992. FS&G. Picture.
Ride on the Red Mare's Back. Ursula K. Le Guin. Illus. by Julie Downing. 1992. Orchard Bks Watts.
Righteous Revenge of Artemis Bonner. Walter D. Myers. 1992. HarpC Child Bks.
Rosa Parks: My Story. Rosa Parks. 1992. Dial Bks Young.
Ruby. Michael Emberlry. 1992. Little.

Sam Johnson and the Blue Ribbon Quilt. Lisa C. Ernst. 1992. (Mulberry). Morrow.
Shortcut. Donald Crews. 1992. Greenwillow. Picture.
Slither McCreep and his Brother, Joe. T. Johnston. Illus. by I. Chess. 1992. (HB Juv Bks). HarBrace.
Soap Soup and other Verses. Karla Kuskin. 1992. HarpC Child Bks.
Steadfast Tin Soldier. Hans Christhia Andersen. Ed. by Tor Seidler. 1992. HarpC Child Bks. Picture.
Talk, Talk: An Ashanti Legend. Deborah M. Chocolate. Illus. by Dave Albers. 1992. Troll Assocs.
Through the Mickle Woods. Valiska Gregory. 1992. Little.
Tricky Tortoise. Mwenye Hadithi. 1992. Little.
Twilight Struggle: The Life of John Fitzgerald Kennedy. Barbara Harrison & Daniel Terris. 1992. Lothrop.
Whales. Seymour Simon. 1992. (Trophy). HarpC Child Bk.
When Jeremiah Found Mrs. Ming. Sharon Jennings. Illus. by Mireille Levert. 1992. (Annick Pr). Firefly Bks Ltd.
Widow's Broom. Chris Van Allsburg. 1992. HM. Picture.
Will's New Cap. Olof Landstrom & Lena Landstrom. 1992. (Pub by R & S Bks). FS&F.

1991
Abuela. Arthur Dirris. Illus. by Elisa Kleven. 1991. Dutton Child Bks. Picture.
Adventures of Israel. James Marshall. 1991. Little. Picture.
Alphabet Parade. Seymour Chwast. 1991. Gulliver-HarBraceJ. Picture.
Anancy & Mr. Dry-Bone. Fiona French. 1991. Little. Picture.
Anno's Math Games III. Mitsumasa Anno. 1991. (Philomel Bks). Putnam Pub Group. Picture.
Antler, Bear, Canoe. Betsy Bowen. 1991. (Joy Street Books). Little. Picture.
Appalachia, The Voices of Sleeping Birds. Cynthia Rylant. Illus. by Barry Moser. 1991. HarBraceJ. Picture.
At The Crossroads. Rachel Isadora. 1991. Greenwillow. Story.
Aunt Flossie's Hats. Elizabeth F Howard. Illus. by James Ransome. 1991. (Clarion Bks). HM. Picture.
Auto Mechanic. Douglas Florian. 1991. Greenwillow. Picture.
Boy & The Samurai. Eric C Haugaard. 1991. HM. Story.
Bridges. Ken Robbins. 1991. Dial Books for Young. Picture.
Brother Eagle, Sister Sky. Illus. by Susan Jeffers. 1991. Dial Books. Picture.
Cactus Hotel. Brenda Guiberson. Illus. by Megan Lloyd. 1991. H Holt & Co. Picture.
Dakota of The White Flats. Philip Ridley. 1991. Knopf. Story.
Day With Wilbur Robinson. William Joyce. 1990. Harper Collins. Picture.
Diego. Jonah Winter. Illus. by Jeanette Winter. 1991. Knopf. Picture.
Dogs Don't Tell Jokes. Louis Sachar. 1991. Knopf. Story.
Dwarf Giant. Illus. by Anita Lobel. 1991. Holiday. Picture.
Fat Glenda Turns Fourteen. Lila Perl. 1991. (Clarion Bks). HM. Story.
Feather Merchants & Other Tales of The Fools Chelm. Illus. by M Magaril. 1991. (Orchard Bks). Watts. Picture.
Garden Alphabet. Isabel Wilner. Illus. by Ashely Wolff. 1991. Dutton Child Bks. Picture.
Glasses, Who Needs 'Em? Lane Smith. 1991. Viking Child Bks. Picture.
Gretchen's ABC. Illus. by Gretchen D Simpson. 1991. Harper Child Bks. Picture.
How The Ox Star Fell From Heaven. Lily T Hong. Ed. by Ann Fay. 1991. Al Whitman. Picture.
If You Give A Moose A Muffin. Laura J Nuneroff. Illus. by Felicia Bond. 1991. Harper Child Bks. Story.
Just So Stories. Rudyard Kipling. Illus. by David Frampton. 1991. Harper Child Bks. Picture.
Little Red Riding Hood. Beni Montresor. 1991. Doubleday. Story.
Long Is A Dragon: Chinese Writing For Children. Peggy Goldstein. 1990. China Books. Story.
Magic Carpet. Amy Schwartz & Pat Brisson. 1991. (Bradbury Pr). Macmillan Child Grp. Picture.
Mr. Mistoffelees With Mungojerrie & Rumpelteazer. T S Eliot. Ed. by Louise Howton. Illus. by Errol Lecain. 1991. FS & G. Picture.
Mozart Season. Virginia Euwerwolff. 1991. Holt & CO. Story.
New Creatures. Illus. by Mordecai Gerstein. 1991. Harper Child Bks. Picture.
Night Ones. Patricia Grossman. Illus. by Lydia Dabcovich. 1991. HarBraceJ. Picture.

On The Day You Were Born. Debra Frase. 1991. HarBraceJ. Picture.

On the Pampas. Maria C Brusca. 1991. H Holt & Co. Picture.

One Stuck Drawer. Laura N Montenegro. 1991. HM. Picture.

Pedro & The Padre. Verna Aardema. Illus. by Friso Henstra. 1991. Dial Bks for Young. Story.

Pish, Posh, Hieronymous Bosch. Illus. by Leo Dillon & Diane Dillon. 1991. HarBraceJ. Picture.

Rats On The Roof & Other Stories. James Marshall. 1991. Dial Bks for Young. Story.

Reluctantly Alice. Phyllis R Naylor. 1991. (Atheneum Child Bks). Macmillan Child Grp. Story.

Remarkable Journey of Prince Jen. Lloyd Alexander. 1991. Dutton Child Bks. Story.

Rosie Swanson: Fourth Grade Geek For President. Barbara Park. 1991. Knopf.

Short Short Stories. William Accorsi. 1991. Greenwillow. Picture.

Some Birthday. Patricia Polacco. 1991. S & S Trade. Picture.

Sophie & Lou. Illus. by Petra Mathers. 1991. Harper Child Bks. Picture.

Tar Beach. Illus. by Faith Ringgold. 1991. Crown. Picture.

Tigress. Helen Coucher. 1991. FS & G. Picture.

Wave In Her Pocket: Stories From Trinidad. Lynn Joseph. Illus. by Brian Pinkney. 1991. (Clarion Bks). HM. Story.

Whisper From The Woods. Illus. by A. Scott Banfill. 1991. Green Tiger Press. Picture.

Witch Hazel. Alice Schertle. Illus. by Margot Tomes. 1991. Harper Child Bks. Picture.

Wolf. Gillian Cross. 1991. Holiday. Story.

Wright Brothers: How They Invented The Airplane. Russell Freedman. Illus. by Wilbur Wright & Orville Wright. 1991. Holiday. Story.

1990

Adventures of Taxi Dog. Debra Barracca & Sal Barracca. Illus. by Mark Buehner. 1990. Dial Bks Young.

Bingo Brown Gypsy Lover. Betsy Byars. 1990. Viking Penguin.

Box and Cow. Grace Chetwin. Illus. by David Small. 1990. Bradbury.

Boy Who owned the School. Gary Paulsen. 1990. (Orchard Bks). Watts.

Crow and Weasel. Barry Lopez. Illus. by Tom Pohrt. 1990. North Point. I.

Ducks Fly. Lydia Dabocvich. 1990. Dutton.

Elizabeth and Larry. Marilyn Sadler. Illus. by Roger Bollen. 1990. S&S.

Further Tales of Uncle Remus. Julius Lester. Illus. by Jerry Pinkney. 1990. Dial Bks Young.

Hey! Get Off Our Train. John Burningham. Illus. by John Burningham. 1990. Crown.

I Hate English. Ellen Levine. Illus. by Steve Bjorkman. 1990. Scholastic.

Laura Charlotte. Katherine Galbraith. Illus. by Floyd Cooper. 1990. (Philomel). Putnam Pub Group.

Maxie, Rosie, and Earl - Partners in Crime. Barbara Park. 1990. Knopf.

Midnight Horse. Sid Fleischman. Illus. by Peter Sis. 1990. (Greenwillow). Morrow.

More Bugs in Boxes. David A Carter. 1990. S&S.

Mouse Rap. Walter Dean Myers. 1990. HarpJ.

My Daddy was a Soldier: A World War II Story. Deborah Kogan Ray. 1990. Holiday.

Nessa's Fish. Nancy Luenn. Illus. by Neil Waldman. 1990. (Atheneum). Macmillan.

Possum Come A-Knockin' Nancy Van Laan. Illus. by George Booth. 1990. Knopf.

Puss in Boots. Charles Perrault. Illus. by Fred Marcellino. 1990. FS&G.

Rice without Rain. Minfong Ho. 1990. Lothrop.

Shadows and Reflections. Illus. by Tana Hoban. 1990. Greenwillow.

Shrek. William Steig. 1990. FS&G.

Squeaky Wheel. Robert Kimmel Smith. 1990. Delacorte.

Stonewords. Pam Conrad. 1990. HarperJ.

Uncle Wizzmo's New Used Car. Rodney A. Greenblat. 1990. HarpJ.

Wheels on the Bus. Paul O Zelinsky. 1990. Dutton Child Bks.

1989

Aesop's Fables. Illus. by Lizbeth Zwerger. 1989. Picture Bk Studio.

Anno's Math Game II. Mitsumasa Anno. 1989. (Philomel Bks). Putnan Pub Group.

AS: A Surfeit of Similes. Norton Juster. Illus. by David Small. 1989. Morrow.

Hey Willy, See the Pyramids. Maira Kalman. 1989. Viking Child Bks.

Lady Who Put Salt in Her Coffee. Lucetia Hale. Ed. by Amy Schwartz. Illus. by Amy Schwartz. 1989. HarBraceJ.

Ragtime Tumpie. Alan Schroeder. Illus. by Bernie Fuchs. 1989. (XJoy St Bks). Little.

Rosie and the Rustlers. Roy Gerrard. 1989. FS&G.

Talking Eggs. Robert D. San Souci. Illus. by Jerry Pinkney. 1989. Dial Bks Young.

Tub People. Pam Conrad. Illus. by Richard Egielski. 1989. HarpJ.

Valentine & Orson. Nancy E. Burkert. Illus. by Nancy E. Burkert. 1989. FS&G.

We're Going on a Bear Hunt. Retold by Michael Rosen. Illus. by Helen Oxenbury. 1989. (M K McElderry). Macmillan.

William and Grandpa. Alice Schertle. Ed. by D. Stevenson. Illus. by Lydia Dabcovich. 1988. Lothrop.

1988

Dove's Letter. Keith Baker. Illus. by Keith Baker. 1988. HarBraceJ.

Enchanter's Daughter. Antonia Barber. Illus. by Errol Le Cain. 1988. FS&S.

Flamboyan. Arnold Adoff. Illus. by Karen Barbour. 1988. (HJ). HarBraceJ.

Goldilocks & the Three Bears. James Marshall. Illus. by James Marshall. 1988. Dial Bks Young.

John Patrick Norman McHennessey: The Boy Who Was Always Late. John Burningham. 1988. Crown.

Just Enough Is Plenty: A Hanukkah Tale. Barbara D. Goldin. Illus. by Seymour Chwast. 1988. (Viking Kestrel). Viking.

Rumor of Pavel Paali: A Ukranian Folktale. Carole Kismaric. Illus. by Charles Mikolaycak. 1988. HarpJ.

Secret in the Matchbox. Val Willis. Illus. by John Shelley. 1988. FS&G.

Seven Wild Pigs. Helme Heine. 1988. (M K McElderry). Macmillan.

Sleepers. Dayal K. Khalsa. 1988. (C N Potter Bks). Crown.

Step into the Night. Joanne Ryder. Illus. by Dennis Nolan. 1988. (Four Winds). Macmillan.

1987

Adam & Eve: The Bible Story. Warwick Hutton. 1987. (M. K. McElderry). Macmillan.

Bossyboots. David Cox. 1987. Crown.

Cremation of Sam McGee. Robert W. Service. Illus. by Ted Harrison. 1987. Greenwillow.

Devil and Mother Crump. Valerie S. Carey. Illus. by Arnold Lobel. 1987. HarpJ.

Eyes of the Dragon. Margaret Leaf. Illus. by Ed Young. 1987. Lothrop.

Gunga Din. Rudyard Kipling. Illus. by Robert A. Parker. 1987. (Gulliver Bks). HarBraceJ.

Higher on the Door. James Stevenson. 1987. Greenwillow.

I Have a Friend. Keiko Harahashi. 1987. (M. K. McElderry). Macmillan.

Peter and the Wolf. Retold by Selina Hastings. Illus. by Reg Cartwright. 1987. H Holt & Co.

Piggybook. Anthony Browne. 1987. Knopf.

Random House Book of Mother Goose. Selected by Arnold Lobel. Illus. by Arnold Lobel. 1987. Random.

Tongue-Cut Sparrow. Retold by Momoko Ishii. Illus. by Suekichi Akaba. Tr. by Katherine Paterson. 1987. (Lodestar Bks). Dutton.

Why the Chicken Crossed the Road. David Macaulay. 1987. HM.

Za Was Zapped. Chris Van Allsburg. Illus. by Chris Van Allsburg. 1987. HM.

Zabajaba Jungle. William Steig. 1987. (Di Capua). FS&G.

1986

Bronwen, the Traw, & the Shape-Shifter. James Dickey. Illus. by Richard J. Watson. 1986. (HJ). HarBraceJ.

Come Out to Play. 1986. Knopf.

Doctor Change. Joanna Cole. Illus. by Donald Carrick. 1986. (Morrow Jr Bks). Morrow.

I Go With My Family to Grandma's. Riki Levinson. Illus. by Diane Goode. 1986. Dutton.

Lady & the Spider. Faith McNulty. Illus. by Bob Marstall. 1986. HarpJ.

Molly's New Washing Machine. Laura Geringer. Illus. by Petra Mathers. 1986. HarpJ.

Pecos Bill. Steven Kellogg. Illus. by Steven Kellogg. 1986. Morrow.

Ring of Earth: A Child's Book of Seasons. Jane Yolen. Illus. by John Wallner. 1986. (HJ). HarBraceJ.

Rumpelstiltskin. Retold by Paul O. Zelinsky. Illus. by Paul O. Zelinsky. 1986. Dutton.

Stranger. Chris Van Allsburg. 1986. HM.

Up & Up. Shirley Hughes. 1986. Lothrop.

When Sheep Cannot Sleep. Satoshi Kitamura. 1986. FS&G.

Where Are You, Ernest & Celestine? Gabrielle Vincent. Illus. by Gabrielle Vincent. 1986. Greenwillow.

1985

Beauty & the Beast. Warwick Hutton. Illus. by Warwick Hutton. 1985. (McElderry Bk). Macmillan.

Bells of London. Ashley Wolff. Illus. by Ashley Wolff. 1985. Dodd.

Grandpa. John Burningham. Illus. by John Burningham. 1985. Crown.

King Bidgood's in the Bathtub. Audrey Wood. Illus. by Don Wood. 1985. (HJ). HarBraceJ.

Leonardo Da Vinci: The Artist, Inventor, Scientist in Three-Dimensional Movable Pictures. Alice Provensen & Martin Provensen. 1984. (Viking Kestrel). Viking.

Magic Island. Janet Marsh. 1985. Merrimack.

Maria Theresa. Petra Mathers. 1985. HarpJ.

Mrs. Huggins & Her Hen Hannah. Lydia Dabcovich. Illus. by Lydia Dabcovich. 1985. Dutton.

Nightingale. Hans C. Andersen. Illus. by Demi. 1985. (HJ). HarBraceJ.

Polar Express. Chris Van Allsburg. Illus. by Chris Van Allsburg. 1985. HM.

Riding That Strawberry Roan. Marcia Sewall. 1985. Viking.

Sing a Song of Sixpence. Illus. by Tracey C. Pearson. 1985. Dial Bks Young.

Story of the Dancing Frog. Quentin Blake. Illus. by Quentin Blake. 1985. Knopf.

Three Hat Day. Laura Geringer. Illus. by Arnold Lobel. 1985. HarpJ.

1984

A, My Name is Alice. Jane Bayer. Illus. by Steven Kellogg. 1984. Dial Bks Young.

Animal Alphabet. Bert Kitchen. Illus. by Bert Kitchen. 1984. Dial Bks Young.

Baa, Baa, Black Sheep: A Nursery Rhyme Press-Out Book. 1984. (Bedrick Blackie). P Bedrick Bks.

Blue Faience Hippopotamus. Joan Grant. Illus. by Alexander Day. 1984. (Star & Elephant Bks). Green Tiger Pr.

Grandfather Twilight. Barbara Berger. Illus. by Barbara Berger. 1984. (Philomel). Putnam Pub Group.

If There Were Dreams to Sell. Ed. by Barbara Lalicki. Illus. by Margot Tomes. 1984. Lothrop.

Jonah & the Great Fish. Warwick Hutton. 1984. (McElderry Bk). Macmillan.

Lion & the Stoat. Paul O. Zelinsky. 1984. Greenwillow.

Mysteries of Harris Burdick. Chris Van Allsburg. 1984. HM.

Rose in My Garden. Arnold Lobel. Illus. by Anita Lobel. 1984. Greenwillow.

Where the River Begins. Thomas Locker. 1984. Dial Young Bks.

1983

Anno's Mysterious Multiplying Jar. Mitsumasa Anno. Illus. by Mitsumasa Anno. 1983. (Philomel). Putnam Pub Group.

Doctor De Soto. William Steig. 1982. FS&G.

Favershams. Roy Gerrard. 1983. FS&G.

Glorious Flight Across the Channel with Louis Bleriot. Alice Provensen & Martin Provensen. 1983. (Viking Kestrel). Viking.

If You Take a Pencil. Fulvio Testa. Illus. by Fulvio Testa. 1982. Dial Bks Young.

Leonard Baskin's Miniature Natural History. Leonard Baskin. Illus. by Leonard Baskin. 1983. Pantheon.

Little Red Riding Hood. Jacob Grimm & Wilhelm K. Grimm. Retold by Trina S. Hyman. Illus. by Trina S. Hyman. 1982. Holiday.

Magnificent Moo. Victoria Forrester. 1983. (Children's Bk). Macmillan.

Mill. David Macaulay. Illus. by David Macaulay. 1983. HM.

Pelican. Brian Wildsmith. Illus. by Brian Wildsmith. 1983. Pantheon.

Pigs in Hiding. Arlene Dubanevich. Illus. by Arlene Dubanevich. 1983. (Four Winds). Macmillan.

Silver Cow: A Welsh Tale. Susan Cooper. Illus. by Warwick Hutton. 1983. (McElderry Bk). Macmillan.

Simon's Book. Henrik Drescher. 1983. Lothrop.

Tale of John Barleycorn: Or From Barley to Beer. Mary Azarian. Illus. by Mary Azarian. 1983. Godine.

Up a Tree. Ed Young. Illus. by Ed Young. 1983. HarpJ.

1992

Indian Winter. Russell Freedman. Illus. by Karl Bodmer. 1992. Holiday House.

Sing to the Sun. Ashley Bryan. 1992. HarpC Child Bks.

Edgar Allan Poe Award/Mystery Writers of America

This annual award was established in 1945 and is sponsored by the Mystery Writers of America. Although given for numerous categories since its inception, the award for juvenile mystery was first presented in 1961. The winning author receives a ceramic bust of Poe (known as an "Edgar"). There were no presentations in this category in 1990.

1993
Coffin on a Case. Eve Bunting. 1992. HarpC Child Bks.
Little Bit Dead. Chap Reaver. 1992. Delacorte.

1992
Ghost Cave. Barbara Steiner. 1990. Harcourt, Brace, Jovanovich.
Guilt Trip. Stephen Schwandt. 1990. (Atheneum). Macmillan Child Grp.
Midnight Horse. Sid Fleischman. 1990. Greenwillow.
Secret Keeper. Gloria Whelan. 1991. Knopf.
Tormentors. Lynn Hall. 1990. HArcourt, Brace Jovanovich.
Wanted...Mud Blossom. Betsy Byars. 1991. Delacorte.
Zachary. Ernest Pintoff. 1990. Eriksson.

1991
Mote. Chap Rearer. 1990. Delacorte.
Stonewords: A Ghost Story. Pam Conrad. 1990. HarpC Child Bks.
To Grandmother's House We Go. Willow D Roberts. 1990. (Atheneum). Macmillan.

1989
Megan's Island. Willo D. Roberts. 1988. (Atheneum Childrens Bks). Macmillan.

1988
Lucy Forever & Miss Rose Tree, Shrinks. Susan Shreve. 1987. H Holt & Co.

1985
Night Cry. Phyllis R. Naylor. 1984. (Childrens Bk). Macmillan.

1984
Callender Papers. Cynthia Voigt. 1983. (Childrens Bks). Macmillan.

Raintree's Heritage Publish-A-Book Contest

Established in 1984 and sponsored by Raintree Publishers, this award is presented annually. The award winning work must be "700-800 words long, written by a young person in grades 4, 5, or 6... about a person in the child's family, or something that happened in the child's family past." The winning story is published by Raintree, and the winners receive $500 each.

1993
Birth of a New Tradition. Ramsey Asmar. 1992. Raintree Pubs.
Faster Than the Bull. Lutz Braum. 1992. Raintree Pubs.
Friends Afloat. Eliza Rosenbaum. 1992. Raintree Pubs.
Old Barn. Rose Miller. 1992. Raintree Pubs.
Treasure in the Attic. Christina Chapman. 1992. Raintree Pubs.

1991
Going To Grandmas. Marriesa Oxford. 1991. Raintree Pubs.
Old Slippery Mark. Mark Belanger. 1991. Raintree Pubs.
Second Thought. Michael Cormier. 1991. Raintree Pubs.
Story About Courage. Joel Vecere. 1991. Raintree Pubs.
The Pegasus Club & Me. Amanda Back. 1991. Raintree Pubs.

1990
Ball, the Book, and the Drum. Morgan Troll. 1990. Raintree Pubs.
China Shelf Luxury. Lily Troia. 1990. Raintree Pubs.
How Honu the Turtle Got His Shell. Casey A. Turcotte McQuire. 1990. Raintree Pubs.
Miloli's Orchids. Alisandra Jezeka. 1990. Raintree Pubs.

1989
Long Green Pencil. Sara Werner. 1989. Raintree Pubs.
Magic Donkey. Adam Pio. 1989. Raintree Pubs.
Salcott, the Indian Boy. Melinda Eldridge. 1989. Raintree Pubs.
Snowman Who Wanted to See July. Nicole E. Estvanik. 1989. Raintree Pubs.

1988
Haun Ching and the Golden Fish. Michael Reeser. 1988. Raintree Pubs.
Luck of the Irish. Brendan P. Paulsen. 1988. Raintree Pubs.
Only at Children's Table. Daria Baron-Hall. 1988. Raintree Pubs.

Very Scraggly Christmas Tree. Christie Pippen. 1988. Raintree Pubs.

1987
Erwin the Sock. David J. Klein. 1987. Raintree.

1986
To See or Not to See. Steve Strubble. 1986. Raintree.

1985
Mountain Boy. Anna C. Josephs. Illus. by Bill Ersland. 1985. Raintree.

1984
Jamie's Turn. Jamie De Witt. Illus. by Julie Brinckloe. 1984. Raintree Pubs.

School Library Journal "Best Books of the Year"

Established in 1966 and published yearly in its December issue of School Library Journal, "Best Books of the Year" ranks among the prestigious and renowned listing in the United States. Books are selected by the book review editors of the magazine. The criteria for selection are based on "clarity," "excellence in text and illustration," and a book's "potential to attract readership among children and young adults."

1992
Ajeemah & His Son. James Berry. 1992. HarpC Child Bks.
Alpha Beta Chowder. Jeanne Steig. Illus. by William Steig. 1992. HarpC Child Bks.
Amazing Potato: A Story in Which the Inca, Conquistadors, Marie Antoinette, Thomas Jefferson, Wars, Famines, Immigrants, & French Fries All Play a Part. Milton Meltzer. 1992. HarpC Child Bks.
Amos Camps Out: A Couch Adventure in the Woods. Susan Seligson & Howie Schneider. Illus. by Howie Schneider. 1992. Little.
Ancient Cliff Dwellers of Mesa Verde. Caroline Arnold. Photos by Richard Hewett. 1992. (Clarion Bks). Macmillan Child Grp.
Annie's Promise. Sonia Levitin. 1993. (Atheneum Child Bks.). Macmillan Child Grp.
Antics. Cathi Hepworth. Illus. by Cathi Hepworth. 1992. (Putnam). Putnam Pub Group.
Arthur's Family Vacation. Marc Brown. Illus. by Marc Brown. 1992. Little.
Artic Hunter. Diane Hoyt-Goldsmith. Illus. by Lawrence Migdale. 1992. Holiday.
Aunt Harriet's Underground Railroad in the Sky. Faith Ringgold. Illus. by Faith Ringgold. 1992. Crown Bks Yng Read.
Bard of Avon: The Story of William Shakespeare. Diane Stanley & Peter Vennema. Illus. by Diane Stanley. 1992. Morrow Jr Bks.
Beauty & the Beast. Nancy Willard. Illus. by Barry Moser. 1992. (HB Juv Bks). Harbrace.
Becca's Story. James D. Forman. 1992. (Scribners Yng Read). Macmillan Child Grp.
Bee Tree. Patricia Polacco. Illus. by Patricia Polacco. 1993. (Philomel Bks). Putnam Pub Group.
Beggar's Ride. Theresa Nelson. 1992. Orchard Bks Watts.
Best Girl. Doris Buchanan Smith. 1992. Viking Child Bks.
Big Alfie Out of Doors Storybook. Shirley Hughes. Illus. by Shirley Hughes. 1992. Lothrop.
Big Pumpkin. Erica Silverman. Illus. by S. D. Schindler. 1992. Macmillan Child Grp.
Boggart. Susan Cooper. 1992. (M K McElderry). Macmillan Child Grp.
Bone from a Dry Sea. Peter Dickinson. 1992. Delacorte.
Bootsie Barker Bites. Barbara Bottner. Illus. by Peggy Rathmann. 1992. Putnam Pub Group.
Breaking the Chains: The Crusade of Dorthea Lynde Dix. Penny Colman. 1992. (Shoe Tree Pr). Betterway.
Bull Run. Paul Fleischman. 1992. (HarpT). HarpC Child Bks.
Bury My Bones but Keep My Words: African Tales for Retelling. Retold by Tony Fairman. Illus. by Meshack Asare. 1992. (Books Young Read). H Holt & Co.
Bus People. Rachel Anderson. 1992. (Bks Young Read). H Holt & Co.
Carmen Prayers from the Ark. Bernos De Gasztold. 1992. Viking Child Bks.
Chi-Hoon: A Korean Girl. Patricia McMahon. Photos by Michael O'Brien. 1992. Boyds Mills Pr.
Children of the Dust Bowl: The True Story of the School at Weedpatch Camp. Jerry Stanley. 1992. Crown Bks Yng Read.
Cow Who Wouldn't Come Down. Paul B. Johnson. Illus. by Paul B. Johnson. 1993. Orchard Bks Watts.
Coyote Steals the Blanket: A Ute Tale. Retold by Janet Stevens. 1992. Holiday House.
Crazy Lady! Jane L. Conly. 1992. HarpC Child Bks.
Cuckoo Child. Dick King-Smith. Illus. by Leslie Bowman. 1992. Hyprn Child.

Dark Thirty: Tales of the Supernatural. Patricia C. McKissack. Illus. by Brian Pinkney. 1992. Knopf Bks Yng Read.
Dead Water Zone. Kenneth Oppel. 1992. (Joy St Bks). Little.
Dear Nobody. Berlie Doherty. 1992. Orchard Bks Watts.
Down Came a Blackbird. Nicholas Wilde. 1992. (Bks Young Read). H Holt & Co.
Dreadful Sorry. Kathryn Reiss. 1992. (HB Juv Bks). HarBrace.
Dreamplace. George E. Lyon. Illus. by Peter Catalanotto. 1993. Orchard Bks Watts.
Earliest Americans. Helen R. Sattler. Illus. by Jean D. Zallinger. 1992. (Clarion Bks). HM.
Feathers. Dorothy H. Patent. Illus. by William Munoz. 1992. (DCB). Dutton Child Bks.
Feathers & Tails: Animal Fables from around the World. David Kherdian. Illus. by Nonny Hogrogian. 1992. (Philomel Bks). Putnam Pub Grp.
First Song Ever Sung. Laura K. Melmed. Illus. by Ed Young. 1993. Lothrop.
Fish & Bones. Ray Prather. 1992. HarpC Child Bks.
Five Bad Boys, Billy Que & the Dustdobbin. Susan Patron. Illus. by Mike Shenon. 1992. Orchard Bks Watts.
For the Love of Pete. Jan Marino. 1992. Little.
Fortune-Tellers. Lloyd Alexander. Illus. by Trina S. Hyman. 1992. (DCB). Dutton Child Bks.
Freedom's Children: Young Civil Rights Activists Tell Their Own Stories. Ellen Levine. 1992. Putnam Pub Group.
Gingerbread Man. Retold by Eric A. Kimmel. Illus. by Megan Lloyd. 1992. Holiday House.
Giver. Lois Lowry. 1992. (Clarion Bks). HM.
Gonna Sing My Head Off! Kathleen Krull. Illus. by Allen Garns. 1992. Knopf Bks Yng Read.
Good-bye, Billy Radish. Gloria Skurzynski. 1992. (Bradbury Bks). Macmillan Child Grp.
Good Fortunes Gang. Margaret Mahy. Illus. by Marion Young. 1992. Delacorte.
Gorillas. Paul H. Burgel & Manfred Hartwig. 1992. Carolrhoda Bks.
Grab Hands & Run. Frances Temple. 1992. Orchard Bks Watts.
Grace. Jill Paton Walsh. 1992. FS&G.
Grandaddy & Janetta. Helen V. Griffith. Illus. by James Stevenson. 1993. Greenwillow.
Great American Elephant Chase. Gillian Cross. 1992. Holiday Hse.
Great Pumpkin Switch. Megan McDonald. Illus. by Ted Lewin. 1992. Orchard Bks Watts.
Harmony Arms. Ron Koertge. 1992. Little.
Hero of Lesser Causes. Julie Johnston. 1992. (XJoy St Bks). Little.
Hiawatha: Messenger of Peace. Dennis B. Fradin. 1992. (M K McElderry). Macmillan Child Grp.
Honest Abe. Edith Kunhardt. Illus. by Malcah Zeldis. 1992. Greenwillow.
How to Make Super Pop-Ups. Joan Irvine. Illus. by Linda Hendry. 1992. Morrow Jr Bks.
How You Were Born. Joanna Cole. 1992. (Mulberry). Morrow.
Hugh Can Do. Jennifer Armstrong. Illus. by Kimberly B. Root. 1992. Crown Bks Young Read.
I Have a Dream: The Life & Words of Martin Luther King, Jr. Jim Haskins. 1992. Millbrook Pr.
Ice Cream Store. Dennis Lee. Illus. by David McPhail. 1992. Scholastic.
I'll See You in My Dreams. Mavis Jukes. Illus. by Stacey Schuett. 1993. Knopf Bks Yng Read.
Inside the Zoo Nursery. Roland Smith. Photos by William Munoz. 1992. (Cobblehill Bks). Dutton Child Bks.
Into the Mummy's Tomb: The Real-Life Discovery of Tutankhamun's Treasures. Nicholas Reeves. 1992. Scholastic Inc.
Island Baby. Holly Keller. Illus. by Holly Keller. 1992. Greenwillow.
Jocasta Carr, Movie Star. Roy Gerrard. Illus. by Roy Gerrard. 1992. FS&G.
Juliet Fisher & the Foolproof Plan. Natalie Honeycutt. 1992. (Bradbury). Macmillan Child Grp.
Julius. Angela Johnson. Illus. by Daw Pilkey. 1993. Orchard Bks Watts.
Jump at de Sun: The Story of Zora Neale Hurston. A. P. Porter. 1992. Carolrhoda Bks.
June 29, 1999. David Wiesner. Illus. by David Wiesner. 1992. (Clarion Bks). HM.
King's Equal. Katherine Paterson. Illus. by Vladimir Vagin. 1992. HarpC Child Bks.
Land & People of Pakistan. Mark Weston. 1992. HarpC Child Bks.
Letters from a Slave Girl: The Story of Harriet Jacobs. Mary E. Lyons. 1992. (Scribners Young Read). Macmillan Child Grp.
Letters from Rifka. Karen Hesse. 1992. (Bks Young Read). H Holt & Co.

Letting Swift River Go. Jane Yolen. Illus. by Barbara Cooney. 1992. Little.

Life's a Funny Proposition, Horatio. Barbara G. Polikoff. 1992. (Bks Young Read). H Holt & Co.

Lightning. Stephen Kramer. Photos by Warren Faidley. 1992. Carolrhoda Bks.

Lion & the Little Red Bird. Elisa Kleven. Illus. by Elisa Kleven. 1992. (DCB). Dutton Child Bks.

Lives of the Musicians: Good Times, Bad Times (And What the Neighbors Thought) Kathleen Krull. Illus. by Kathryn Hewitt. 1992. (HB Juv Bks). HarBrace.

Looking for Your Name: A Collection of Contemporary Poems. Paul B. Janeczko. 1992. Orchard Bks Watts.

Lunch. Denise Fleming. Illus. by Denise Fleming. 1992. (Bks Young Read). H Holt & Co.

Magic School Bus on the Ocean Floor. Joanna Cole. Illus. by Bruce Degen. 1992. Scholastic Inc.

Magic Wood. Henry Treece. Illus. by Barry Moser. 1992. HarpC Child Bks.

Man Who Loved Clowns. June R. Wood. 1992. Putnam Pub Group.

Many Thousand Gone: African Americans from Slavery to Freedom. Virginia Hamilton. Illus. by Leo Dillon & Diane Dillon. 1992. (Umbrella Bks). Knopf Bks Young Read.

Maybe Yes, Maybe No, Maybe Maybe. Susan Patron. Illus. by Dorothy Donahue. 1993. Orchard Bks Watts.

Me First. Helen Lester. Illus. by Lynn Munsinger. 1992. HM.

Messiah: The Workbook for the Oratorio. George F. Handel. Illus. by Barry Moser. 1992. HarpC Child Bks.

Minstrel & The Dragon Pup. Rosemary Sutcliff. Illus. by Emma C. Clark. 1993. Candlewick Pr.

Mirette on the High Wire. Emily A. McCully. Illus. by Emily A. McCully. 1992. (Putnam). Putnam Pub Group.

Monarch Butterflies: Mysterious Travelers. Bianca Lavies. 1992. (DCB). Dutton Child Bks.

Moon Rope: A Peruvian Folktale. Lois Ehlert. Illus. by Lois Ehlert. 1992. (HB Juv Bks). Harbrace.

Morning Girl. Michael Dorris. 1992. Hyprn Child Bks.

Nightjohn. Gary Paulsen. 1992. Delacourte.

No Milk! Jennifer A. Ericsson. Illus. by Ora Eitan. 1993. (Tambourine Bks). Morrow.

On the Brink of Extinction: The California Condot. Caroline Arnold. Photos by Michael Wallace. 1992. (HBJ Juv Bks). HarBrace.

One Hundred Questions & Answers about AIDS: A Guide for Young People. Michael T. Ford. 1992. Macmillan.

Operation Siberian Crane: The Story Behind the International Effort to Save an Amazing Bird. Judi Friedman. 1992. (Dillon). Macmillan Child Grp.

Original Freddie Ackerman. Hadley Irwin. 1992. (M K McElderry). Macmillan Child Grp.

Otters under Water. Jim Arnosky. Illus. by Jim Arnosky. 1992. (Putnam). Putnam Pub Group.

Out of Control. Norma F. Mazer. 1992. Morrow Jr Bks.

Owl Who Became the Moon. Jonathan London. Illus. by Ted Rand. 1993. (DCB). Dutton Child Bks.

Peeping Beauty. Mary J. Auch. 1992. Holiday Hse.

Picnic. Ruth Brown. 1993. Dutton Child Bks.

Pigman & Me. Paul Zindel. 1992. HarpC Child Bks.

Powwow. George Ancona. 1992. (HB Juv Bks). HarBrace.

Raven: A Trickster Tale from the Pacific Northwest. Gerald McDermott. Illus. by Gerald McDermott. 1992. (HB Juv Bks). HarBrace.

Red-Dirt Jessie. Anna Myers. 1992. Walker & Co.

Return of Freddy LeGrand. Jon Agee. Illus. by Jon Agee. 1992. FS&G.

Return of the Shadows. Norma Farber. Illus. by Andrea Baruffi. 1992. HarpC Child Bks.

Revolutions of the Heart. Marsha Qualey. 1992. (Clarion Bks). HM.

Ride on the Red Mare's Back. Ursula K. Le Guin. Illus. by Julie Downing. 1992. Orchard Bks Watts.

Rising Voices: Writings of Young Native Americans. Arlene B. Hirschfelder & Beverly R. Singer. 1992. (Scribners Yng Read). Macmillan Child Grp.

Screen of Frogs. Retold by Sheila Hamanaka. 1992. Orchard Bks Watts.

Shadows of Night: The Hidden World of the Little Brown Bat. Barbara Bash. Illus. by Barbara Bash. 1992. Sierra.

Sharks: Challengers of the Deep. Mary Cerullo. Photos by Jeffrey L. Rotman. 1992. (DCB). Dutton Child Bks.

Sheep Out to Eat. Nancy Shaw. Illus. by Margot Apple. 1992. HM.

Sofie's Role. Amy Heath. Illus. by Sheila Hamanaka. 1992. (Four Winds). Macmillan Child Grp.

Spotted Pony: A Collection of Hanukkah Stories. Eric A. Kimmel. Illus. by Leonard E. Fisher. 1992. Holiday.

Squashed. Joan Bauer. 1992. Delacorte.

Staying Fat for Sarah Byrnes. Chris Crutcher. 1992. Greenwillow.

Stealing Home. Mary Stolz. 1992. HarpC Child Bks.

Stegosaurs: The Solar-Powered Dinosaurs. Helen R. Sattler. Illus. by Turi MacCombie. 1992. Lothrop.

Stephen Crane. Mark Sufrin. 1992. (Atheneum Child Bks). Macmillan Child Grp.

Stinky Cheese Man & Other Fairly Stupid Tales. Jon Scieszka. Illus. by Lane Smith. 1992. Viking Child Bks.

Story of May. Mordicai Gerstein. Illus. by Mordicai Gerstein. 1993. HarpC Child Bks.

Story of Money. Betsy Maestro. Illus. by Giulio Maestro. 1992. (Clarion Bks). HM.

Story of the Creation: Words from Genesis. Illus. by Jane Ray. 1992. (XDCP). Dutton Child Bks.

Sundiata: Lion King of Mali. David Wisniewski. Illus. by David Wisniewski. 1992. (Clarion Bks). HM.

Surtsey: The Newest Place on Earth. Kathryn Lasky. Photos by Christopher G. Knight. 1992. Hyprn Child.

Switching Well. Peni R. Griffin. 1992. (M K McElderry). Macmillan Child Grp.

Take Me Out to the Ballgame. Jack Norworth. Illus. by Alec Gillman. 1992. (Four Winds). Macmillan Child Grp.

Taste of Salt. Frances Temple. 1992. Orchard Bks Watts.

Theodore Roosevelt Takes Charge. Nancy Whitelaw. 1992. A Whitman.

Thirteenth Clue. Ann Jonas. Illus. by Ann Jonas. 1992. Greenwillow.

Three Billy Goats Gruff. Glen Rounds. Illus. by Glen Rounds. 1992. Holiday.

Toning the Sweep. Angela Johnson. 1992. Orchard Bks Watts.

Turnip. Walter De La Mare. Illus. by Kevin Hawkes. 1992. Godine.

Twelve Days in August. Liza K. Murrow. 1992. Holiday.

Twelve Days of Christmas. Dorothee Duntze. 1992. North-South Bks NYC.

Two of Everything. Retold by Lily Toy Hong. Illus. by Lily Toy Hong. 1992. A Whitman.

Visions: Stories about Women Artists. Leslie Sills. 1992. A Whitman.

Welcome to the Green House. Jane Yolen. Illus. by Laura Regan. 1992. (Putnam). Putnam.

Whaling Days. Carol Carrick. Illus. by David Frampton. 1992. (Clarion Bks). HM.

When Cats Dream. Dav. Pilkey. Illus. by Dav. Pilkey. 1992. Orchard Bks Watts.

Who Do You Think You Are? Stories of Friends & Enemies. Hazel Rochman & Darlene Z. McCampbell. 1992. (Joy St Bks). Little.

Who Was That Masked Man, Anyway? Avi. 1992. Orchard Bks Watts.

Whole New Ball Game: The Story of the All-American Girls Professional Baseball League. Sue Macy. 1992. (Bks Young Read). H Holt & Co.

Why the Sky Is Far Away. Mary-Joan Gerson. Illus. by Carla Golembe. 1992. (Joy St Bks). Little.

Widow's Broom. Chris Van Allsburg. Illus. by Chris Van Allsburg. 1992. HM.

Women in American Indian Society. Rayna Green. 1992. Chelsea Hse.

Woody's Twenty Grow Big Songs. Woody Guthrie. Illus. by Woody Guthrie. 1992. HarpC Child Bks.

Words of Stone. Kevin Henkes. 1992. Greenwillow.

World in 1492. Illus. by Stefano Vitale. 1992. (Bks Young Read). H Holt & Co. Illus.

World Water Watch. Michelle Koch. Photos by Michelle Koch. 1992. Greenwillow.

Yang the Youngest & His Terrible Ear. Lensey Namioka. Illus. by Kees De Kiefte. 1992. Little.

Yo! Yes? Chris Raschka. Illus. by Chris Raschka. 1993. Orchard Bks Watts.

Zinnia & Dot. Lisa C. Ernst. Illus. by Lisa C. Ernst. 1992. Viking Child Bks.

Zomo the Rabbit: A Trickster Tale from West Africa. Gerald McDermott. 1992. (HB Juv Bks). HarBrace.

Zoo. Anthony Browne. Illus. by Anthony Browne. 1992. Knopf Bks Yng Read.

Zoomrimes: Poems about Things that Go. Sylvia Cassedy. Illus. by Michele Chessare. 1992. HarpC Child Bks.

1991

Adventures of Isabel. Ogden Nash. Illus. by James Marshall. 1991. (Joy Bks). Little.

All about Where. Tana Hoban. Photos by Tana Hoban. 1991. Greenwillow.

Almost the Real Thing: Simulation in Your High-Tech World. Gloria Skurzynski. 1991. (Bradbury Pr). Macmillan Child Grp.

Alpha & the Dirty Baby. Brock Cole. Illus. by Brock Cole. 1991. FS&G.

Amazing Grace. Mary Hoffman. Illus. by Caroline Binch. 1991. Dial Bks Young.

Amazing Gracie. A. E Cannon. 1991. Delacorte.

American Tall Tales. Mary Pope Osborne. Illus. by Michael McCurdy. 1991. Knopf.

Andrew Wyeth. Richard Meryman. 1991. Abrams.

Appalachia: The Voices of Sleeping Birds. Cynthia Rylant. Illus. by Barry Moser. 1991. HarBraceJ.

Appelemando's Dreams. Patricia Polacco. Illus. by Patricia Polacco. 1991. (Philomel Bks). Putnam Pub Grp.

Aren't You Lucky! Catherine Anholt. Illus. by Catherine Anholt. 1991. (Joy Street Bks). Little.

At the Crossroads. Rachel Isadora. Illus. by Rachel Isadora. 1991. Greenwillow.

Athletic Shorts: Six Short Stories. Chris Crutcher. 1991. Greenwillow.

Bear. John Schoenherr. Illus. by John Schoenherr. 1991. (Philomel Bks). Putnam Pub Grp.

Bear. Juan Wijngaard. Illus. by Juan Wijngaard. 1991. Crown.

Behind the Blue & the Gray: The Soldier's Life in the Civil War. Delia Ray. 1991. (Lodestar Bks). Dutton Child Bks.

Berlioz the Bear. Jan Brett. Illus. by Jan Brett. 1991. Putnam Pub Grp.

Best of Aesop's Fables. Retold by Margaret Clark. Illus. by Charlotte Voake. 1990. (Joy Street Bks). Little.

Bill of Rights: How We Got It & What It Means. Milton Meltzer. 1990. (Crowell Jr Bks). HarpC Child Bks.

Birds, Beasts & Fishes: A Selection of Animal Poems. Compiled by Anne Carter. Illus. by Reg Cartwright. 1991. Macmillan Child Grp.

Book of the Banshee. Anne Fine. 1991. Little.

Borning Room. Paul Fleischman. 1991. (Charlotte Zolotow Bks). HarpC Child Bks.

Borreguita & the Coyote: A tale from Ayutla, Mexico. Verna Aardema. Illus. by Petra Mathers. 1991. Knopf.

Boy's War: Confederate & Union Soldiers Talk about the Civil War. Jim Murphy. 1990. (Clarion Bks). HM.

Brave. Robert Lipsyte. 1991. (Charlotte Zolotow Bks). HarC Child Bks.

Bully for You, Teddy Roosevelt! Jean Fritz. Illus. by Mike Wimmer. 1991. Putnam Pub Group.

Cakes & Miracles: A Purim Tale. Barbara D Goldin. Illus. by Erika Weihs. 1991. Viking Child Bks.

Castle in the Air. Diana W Jones. 1991. Greenwillow.

Cat. Juan Wijngaard. Illus. by Juan Wijngaard. 1991. Crown.

Cecil's Story. George E Lyon. Illus. by Peter Catalanotto. 1991. Orchard Bks Watts.

Checking on the Moon. Jenny Davis. 1991. (Richard Jackson Bks). Orchard Bks Watts.

Chrysanthemum. Kevin Henkes. Illus. by Kevin Henkes. 1991. Greenwillow.

Circles. Marilyn Sachs. 1991. Dutton Child Bks.

Colors. Philip Yenawine. 1991. Delacorte.

Cookcamp. Gary Paulsen. 1991. Orchard Bks Watts.

Country Crossing. Jim Aylesworth. 1991. (Atheneum Child Bk). Macmillam Child Grp.

Cowboys. Glen Rounds. Illus. by Glen Rounds. 1991. Holiday.

Daisy's Taxi. Ruth Young. Illus. by Marcia Sewall. 1991. Orchard Bks Watts.

Dangerous Spaces. Margaret Mahy. 1991. Viking Child Bks.

Day That Elvis Came to Town. Jan Marino. 1991. Little.

Dial-a-Croc. Mike Dumbleton. Illus. by Ann James. 1991. Orchard Bks Watts.

Discovering Christopher Columbus: How History Is Invented. Kathy Pelta. 1991. Lerner.

Discovery of the Americas. Betsy Maestro. Illus. by Giulio Maestro. 1991. Lothrop.

Dog. Juan Wijngaard. Illus. by Juan Wijngaard. 1991. Crown.

Duck. Juan Wijngaard. Illus. by Juan Wijngaard. 1991. Crown.

Earth Verses & Water Rhymes. J. Patrick Lewis. Illus. by Robert Sabuda. 1991. (Atheneum Child Bk). Macmillian Child Grp.

Eating Fractions. Bruce Mcmillan. Photos by Bruce McMillan. 1991. Scholastic Inc.

Eric Carle's Dragons & Other Creatures That Never Were. Compiled by Laura Whipple. Illus. by Eric Carle. 1991. (Philomel). Putnam.

Evan's Corner. Elizabeth S Hill. Illus. by Sandra Speidel. 1991. Viking Child Bks.

Everybody's Daughter. Marsha Qualey. 1991. HM.

Family Read-Aloud Holiday Treasury. Alice Low. Illus. by Marc Brown. 1991. (Joy Street Bks). Little.

Fast Talk on a Slow Track. Rita Williams-Garcia. 1991. (Lodestar). Dutton Child Bks.

Fat Fanny, Beanpole Bertha, & the Boys. Barbara A Porte. Illus. by Maxie Chambliss. 1991. Orchard Bks Watts.

Fishing at Long Pond. William T George. Illus. by Lindsay B George. 1991. Greenwillow.

Flawed Glass. Ian Strachan. 1990. Little.

Fly Away Home. Eve Bunting. Ed. by James Giblin. Illus. by Ronald Himler. 1991. (Clarion Bks). HM.

Follow the Dream: The Story of Christopher Columbus. Peter Sis. Illus. by Peter Sis. 1991. Knopf.

For Laughing Out Loud: Poems to Tickle Your Funnybone. Compiled by Jack Prelutsky. Illus. by Majorie Priceman. 1991. Knopf.

Frances Hodgson Burnett: Beyond the Secret Garden. Angelica S Carpenter & Jean Shirley. 1990. Lerner.

Frog Prince Continued. Jon Scieszka. Illus. by Steve Johnson. 1991. Viking Child Bks.

From the Beginning: The Story of Human Evolution. David Peters. Illus. by David Peters. 1991. Morrow Jr Bks.

George Washington: Leader of a New Nation. Mary Pope Osborne. 1991. Dial Bks Young.

Georgia O'Keeffe. Robyn Montana Turner. 1991. Little.

Gift of the Girl Who Couldn't Hear. Susan Shreve. 1991. (Tambourine Bks). Morrow.

Go Fish. Mary Stolz. Illus. by Pat Cummings. 1991. HarpC Child Bks.

Golden Days. Gail Radley. 1991. Macmillan.

Grandpa Jake & the Grand Christmas. Mildred Ames. 1990. Scribners.

Grandpa's Song. Tony Johnston. Illus. by Brad Sneed. 1991. Dial Bks Young.

Half Child. Kathleen Hersom. 1991. S&S.

Handmade Alphabet. Laura Rankin. Illus. by Laura Rankin. 1991. Dial Bks Young.

Hark! a Christmas Sampler. Jane Yolen. Illus. by Tomie DePaola. 1991. Putnam Pub Group.

Henry & Mudge & the Bedtime Thumps. Cynthia Rylant. Illus. by Sucie Stevenson. 1991. (Bradbury Pr). Macmillan Child Grp.

Hide & Snake. Keith Baker. Illus. by Keith Baker. 1991. HarBraceJ.

High-Wire Henry. Mary Calhoun. Illus. by Erick Ingraham. 1991. Morrow Jr Bks.

How Nature Works: One Hundred Ways Parents & Kids Can Share the Secrets of Nature. David Burnie. 1991. (Dist. by Random). RD Assn.

How the Ox Star Fell from Heaven. Lily Toy Hong. Ed. by Ann Fay. Illus. by Lily Hong. 1991. Whitman.

I Wonder If I'll See a Whale. Frances Weller. Illus. by Ted Lewin. 1991. (Philomel Bks). Putnam Pub Group.

If You Give a Moose a Muffin. Laura J Numeroff. Illus. by Felicia Bond. 1991. HarpC Child Bks.

In the Tall, Tall Grass. Denise Fleming. 1991. H Holt & Co.

Invitation to the Game. Monica Hughes. 1991. S&S.

Jack & the Beanstalk. Retold by Steven Kellogg. Illus. by Steven Kellogg. 1991. Morrow Jr Bks.

Jayhawker. Patricia Beatty. 1991. Morrow Jr Bks.

Journey. Patricia MacLachlan. Illus. by Barry Moser. 1991. Delacorte.

Journey Home. Alison Lester. Illus. by Alison Lester. 1991. Knopf.

Keep Laughing. Cynthia D Grant. 1991. (Atheneum Child Bk). Macmillan Child Grp.

Kid's Guide to Social Action: How to Solve the Social Problems You Choose - & Turn Creative Thinking into Positive Action. Barbara A Lewis. Ed. by Pamela Espeland. 1991. Free Spirit Pub.

Knights of the Kitchen Table. Jon Scieszka. Illus. by Lane Smith. 1991. Viking Child Bks.

Kool Ada. Sheila Solomon Klass. 1991. Scholastic Inc.

Lampfish of Twill. Janet Taylor Lisle. Illus. by Wendy Anderson Halperin. 1991. Orchard Bks Watts.

Land and People of Cambodia. David P Chandler. 1991. HarpC Child Bks.

Land & People of Korea. S. E Solberg. 1991. HarpC Child Bks.

Last Princess: The Story of Princess Kaiulani of Hawaii. Fay Stanley. Illus. by Diane Stanley. 1991. (Four Winds). Macmillan Child Grp.

Leonardo da Vinci. Richard McLanathan. 1990. Abrams.

Lines. Philip Yenawine. 1991. Delacorte.

Little Penguin. Patrick Benson. Illus. by Patrick Benson. 1991. (Philomel Child Bks). Putnam Pub Grp.

Living with Dinosaurs. Patricia Lauber. Illus. by Douglas Henderson. 1991. (Bradbury). Macmillan Child Grp.

Lost Garden. Laurence Yep. 1991. Messner.

Lyddie. Katherine Paterson. 1991. (Lodestar Bks). Dutton Child Bks.

Make Your Own Animated Movies & Videotapes. Yvonne Andersen & Andersen, Yvonne. 1991. Little.

Mama Do You Love Me? Barbara M Joosse. Illus. by Barbara Lavallee. 1991. Chronicle Bks.

Mama, Let's Dance. Patricia Hermes. 1991. Little.

Man from the Other Side. Uri Orlev. Tr. by Hillel Halkin. 1991. HM.

Many Moons. James Thurber. Illus. by Marc Simont. 1990. HarBraceJ.

Matepo. Angela McAllister. Illus. by Jill Newton. 1991. Dial.

Matthew's Dream. Leo Lionni. Illus. by Leo Lionni. 1991. Knopf.

Max's Dragon Shirt. Rosemary Wells. Illus. by Rosemary Wells. 1991. Dial.

Messages in the Mailbox: How to Write a Letter. Loreen Leedy. Illus. by Loreen Leedy. 1991. Holiday.

Michael Foreman's Mother Goose. Michael Foreman. Illus. by Michael Foreman. 1991. HarBraceJ.

Mr. Mistoffelees with Mungojerrie & Rumpelteazer. T. S Eliot. Illus. by Errol LeCain. 1991. HarBraceJ.

Monument. Gary Paulsen. 1991. Delacorte.

Mouse Count. Ellen S Walsh. Illus. by Ellen S Walsh. 1991. HarBraceJ.

My Name Is Sus5an Smith: The 5 Is Silent. Louise Plummer. 1991. Delacorte.

My Shadow. Robert Louis Stevenson. Illus. by Ted Rand. 1991. Putnam Pub Group.

My Sister Sif. Ruth Park. 1991. Viking Child Bks.

Napoleon & the Napoleonic Wars. Albert Marrin. 1991. Viking Child Bks.

Newbery Christmas. Ed. by Martin Greenberg & Charles G Waugh. 1991. Delacorte.

Next Thing to Strangers. Sheri Cooper Sinykin. 1991. Lothrop.

Night on Neighborhood Street. Eloise Greenfield. Illus. by Jan S Gilchrist. 1991. Dial Bks Young.

Night Tree. Eve Bunting. Illus. by Ted Rand. 1991. HarBraceJ.

Not the Piano, Mrs. Medley! Evan Levine. Illus. by S. D Schindler. 1991. Orchard Bks Watts.

Nothing But the Truth: A Documentary Novel. Avi. 1991. Orchard Bks Watts.

Old Mother Hubbard & Her Wonderful Dog. Illus. by James Marshall. 1991. FS&G.

On the Day You Were Born. Debra Frasier. Illus. by Debra Frasier. 1991. HarbraceJ.

On the Pampas. Maria C Brusca. Illus. by Maria C Brusca. 1991. H Holt & Co.

Orphan Boy. Tololwa M Mollel. Illus. by Paul Morin. 1991. (Clarion Bks). HM.

Our Vanishing Farm Animals: Saving America's Rare Breeds. Catherine Paladino. Illus. by Catherine Paladino. 1991. (Joy Street Bks). Little.

Owl & the Pussycat. Edward Lear. Illus. by Jan Brett. 1991. Putnam Pub Group.

Pennywhistle Tree. Doris Buchanan Smith. Illus. by Leslie Bowman. 1991. Putnam Pub Group.

People of the Breaking Day. Marcia Sewall. Illus. by Marcia Sewall. 1990. Atheneum.

Piggies. Don Wood & Audrey Wood. Illus. by Don Wood. 1991. HarBraceJ.

Pillow of Clouds. Marc Talbert. 1991. Dial Bks Young.

Pish, Posh, Said Hieronymus Bosch. Nancy Willard. Illus. by L. D Dillon. 1991. HarBraceJ.

Polar Bear, Polar Bear, What Do You Hear? Bill Martin. Illus. by Eric Carle. 1991. H Holt & Co.

Potato Man. Megan McDonald. Illus. by Ted Lewin. 1991. Orchard Bks Watts.

Preposterous: Poems of Youth. Paul Janeczko. 1991. Orchard Bks Watts.

Pueblo Boy: Growing Up in Two Worlds. Marcia Keegan. Photos by Marcia Keegan. 1991. (Cobblehill Bks). Dutton Child Bks.

Puss in Boots. Charles Perrault. Tr. by Malcolm Arthur. Illus. by Fred Marcellino. 1991. FS&G.

Rag Coat. Lauren Mills. Illus. by Lauren Mills. 1991. Little.

Rain Catchers. Jean Thesman. 1991. HM.

Rats on the Roof: And Other Stories. James Marshall. Illus. by James Marshall. 1991. Dial Bks Young.

Raw Head, Bloody Bones: African-American Tales the Supernatural. Selected by Mary E Lyons. 1991. (Scribners Young Read). Macmillan Child Grp.

Reluctantly Alice. Phyllis R Naylor. 1991. Atheneum.

Remarkable Journey of Prince Jen. Lloyd Alexander. 1991. Dutton Child Bks.

Remarkable Voyages of Captain Cook. Rhoda Blumberg. Ed. by Barbara Lalicki. 1991. (Bradbury Press). Macmillan Pub Grp.

Rosa Bonheur. Robyn Montana Turner. 1991. Little.

Rosebud & Red Flannel. Ethel Pochocki. Illus. by Mary B Owens. 1991. H Holt & Co.

Rosemary's Witch. Ann Turner. 1991. (Charlotte Zolotow Bks). HarpC Child Bks.

Roxaboxen. Alice McLerran. Illus. by Barbara Cooney. 1991. Lothrop.

Shapes. Philip Yenawine. 1991. Delacorte.

Sheep in a Shop. Nancy Shaw. Illus. by Margot Apple. 1991. HM.

Sierra. Diane Siebert. Illus. by Wendell Minor. 1991. HarperC Child Bks.

Slippery Babies: Young Frogs, Toads & Salamanders. Ginny Johnston & Judy Cutchins. 1991. Morrow Jr Bks.

Snow Lady. Shirley Hughes. Illus. by Shirley Hughes. 1991. Lothrop.

Sorrow's Kitchen: The Life & Folklore of Zora Neal Hurston. Mary Lyons. 1990. (Scribners Young Read). Macmillan Child Grp.

Speeding Bullet. Neal Shusterman. 1991. Little.

Spill! The Story of the Exxon Valdez. Terry Carr. 1991. Watts.

Spring-Heeled Jack. Philip Pullman. Illus. by David Mostyn. 1991. Knopf.

Stepbrother Sabotage. Sally Wittman. Illus. by Emily A McCully. 1990. HarpC Child Bks.

Stepping on the Cracks. Mary Downing Hahn. 1991. (Clarion Bks). HM.

Stories. Philip Yenawine. 1991. Delacorte.

Story of Christmas: Words from the Gospel of Matthew & Luke. Bible. Illus. by Jane Ray. 1991. Dutton Child Bks.

Tales of the Early World. Ted Hughes. Illus. by Andrew Davidson. 1991. FS&G.

Tar Beach. Faith Ringgold. Illus. by Faith Ringgold. 1991. Crown.

Teenage Soldiers, Adult Wars. Ed. by Roger Rosen & Patra McSharry. 1991. Rosen.

There's a Girl in My Hammerlock. Jerry Spinelli. 1991. S&S.

Thin Air. David Getz. 1990. H Holt & Co.

Thomas Jefferson: The Revolutionary Aristocrat. Milton Meltzer. 1991. Watts.

Three Names. Patricia MacLachlan. Illus. by Alexander Pertzoff. 1991. HarpC Child Bks.

Thunderwith. Libby Hathorn. 1991. Little.

Tiger with Wings: The Great Horned Owl. Barbara J Esbensen. Illus. by Mary B Brown. 1991. Orchard Bks Watts.

Tigress. Helen Cowcher. Illus. by Helen Cowcher. 1991. FS&G.

Time Train. Paul Fleischman. Illus. by Claire Ewart. 1991. HarpC Child Bks.

Traveling to Tondo: A Tale of the Nkundo of Zaire. Verna Aardema. Illus. by Will Hillenbrand. 1991. Knopf.

Tree of Cranes. Allen Say. Illus. by Allen Say. 1991. HM.

Truth about Unicorns. James Cross Giblin. Illus. by Michael McDermott. 1991. HarpC Child Bks.

Tuesday. David Wiesner. Illus. by David Wiesner. 1991. (Clarion Bks). HM.

Two Thousand & Forty-one: Twelve Short Stories about the Future. Ed. by Jane Yolen. 1991. Delacorte.

Unreal! Eight Surprising Stories. Paul Jennings. 1991. Viking.

Waiting for Anya. Michael Morpurgo. 1991. Viking Child Bk.

Wanted...Mud Blossom. Betsy Byars. Illus. by Jacqueline Rogers. 1991. Delacorte.

Wave in Her Pocket: Stories from Trinidad. Lynn Joseph. Illus. by Brian Pinkney. 1991. (Clarion Bks). HM.

Way Home. Judith Richardson. Illus. by Salley Mavor. 1991. (Macmillan Child Bk). Macmillan Child Grp.

We All Fall Down. Robert Cormier. 1991. Delacorte.

Wheels. Shirley Hughes. Illus. by Shirley Hughes. 1991. Lothrop.

Where Are You When I Need You? Suzanne Newton. 1991. Viking Child Bks.

Where's Our Mama? Diane Goode. Illus. by Diane Goode. 1991. Dutton.

Which One Is Whitney? James Stevenson. Illus. by James Stevenson. 1990. Greenwillow.

Window. Jeannie Baker. Illus. by Jeannie Baker. 1991. Greenwillow.

Window. Jeannie Baker. Illus. by Jeannie Baker. 1991. Greenwillow.

Witch Baby. Francesca Lia Block. 1991. (Zolotow Bks). HarpC Child Bks.

Witch Hazel. Alice Schertle. Illus. by Margot Tomes. 1991. HarpC Child Bks.

Wonder. Rachel Vail. 1991. Orchard Bks Watts.

Wright Brothers: How They Invented the Airplane. Russell Freedman. Photos by Orville Wright & Wilbur Wright. 1991. Holiday.

Year of Impossible Goodbyes. Sook Nyul Choi. 1991. HM.

1990

AArdvarks, Disembark! Ann Jonas. Illus. by Ann Jonas. 1990. Greenwillow.

Ace: The Very Important Pig. Dick King-Smith. Illus. by Lynette Hemmant. 1990. Crown.
Agnes Cecilia. Maria Gripe. Tr. by Rika Lesser. 1990. HarpJ.
And Then There Was One: The Mysteries of Extinction. Margery Facklam. Illus. by Pamela Johnson. 1990. (Sierra Club Bks). Little.
Bingo Brown, Gypsy Lover. Betsy Byars. 1990. Viking Penguin.
Breaking the Chains: African-American Slave Resistance. William Loren Katz. 1990. (Atheneum). Macmillan.
Columbus and the World Around Him. Milton Meltzer. 1990. Watts.
Come a Tide. George Ella Lyon. Illus. by Stephen Gammell. 1990. Orchard Bks Watts.
Day of Ahmed's Secret. Florence Parry Heide & Judith Heide Gilliland. Illus. by Ted Lewin. 1990. Lothrop.
Dealing with Dragons. Patricia Wrede. 1990. HBJ.
Dixie Storms. Barbara Hall. 1990. HBJ.
Everywhere. Bruce Brooks. 1990. HarpJ.
Family Pictures. Garza Lomas. Tr. by Rosalma Zubizarreta. 1990. Dutton Child Bk.
Follow Me! Nancy Tafuri. Illus. by Nancy Tafuri. 1990. Greenwillow.
Franklin Delano Roosevelt. Russell Freedman. 1990. (Clarion Bks). HM.
Ginger Jumps. Lisa Campbell Ernst. Illus. by Lisa Campbell Ernst. 1990. Bradbury.
Giraffes, the Sentinels of the Savannahs. Henen Roney Sattler. Illus. by Christopher Santoro. 1990. Lothrop.
Great White Man-Eating Shark: A Cautionary Tale. Margaret Mahy. Illus. by Jonathan Allen. 1990. Dial Bks Young.
Hansel and Gretel. Retold by James Marshall. 1990. Dial Bk Young.
Henry and Mudge and the Happy Cat. Cynthia Rylant. Illus. by Sucie Stevenson. 1990. Bradbury.
Hippopotamusn't. J. Patrick Lewis. Illus. by Victoria Chess. 1990. (Dial Bks Young). Doubleday.
Hurricane. David Wiesner. Illus. by David Wiesner. 1990. (Clarion Bks). HM.
Insect Metamorphosis: From Egg to Adult. Ron Goor. Illus. by Ron Goor. 1990. (Atheneum). Macmillan.
Is This a House for Hermit Crab? Megan McDonald. Illus. by S. D. Schindler. 1990. Orchard Bks Watts.
Journey: Japanese Americans, Racism, and Renewal. Sheila Hamanaka. Illus. by Sheila Hamanaka. 1990. Orchard Bks Watts.
Just Plain Fancy. Patricia Polacco. Illus. by Patricia Polacco. 1990. Bantam.
Land and People of South Africa. 1990. Lippincott.
Laura Charlotte. Kathryn Galbraith. Illus. by Floyd Cooper. 1990. (Philomel Bks). Putnam Pub Group.
Libby on Wednesday. Zilpha Keatley Snyder. 1990. Delacorte.
Little Dog Laughed and Other Nursery Rhymes. Illus. by Lucy Cousins. 1990. Dutton Child Bks.
Magic School Bus Lost in the Solar System. Joanna Cole. Illus. by Bruce Degen. 1990. Scholastic.
Midnight Horse. Sid Fleischman. Illus. by Peter Sis. 1990. Greenwillow.
More, More More, Said the Baby. Vera B. Williams. Illus. by Vera B. Williams. 1990. Greenwillow.
Nation Torn: The Story of How the Civil War Began. Delia Ray. 1990. Lodestar Bks.
Neighbors at Odds: U.S. Policy in Latin America. Elaine Pascoe. 1990. Watts.
Next-Door Neighbors. Sarah Ellis. 1990. (McElderry). Macmillan.
Old John. Peter Hartling. Tr. by Elizabeth D Crawford. 1990. Lothrop.
Orchard Book of Nursery Rhymes. Zena Sutherland. Illus. by Faith Jaques. 1990. Orchard Bks Watts.
Our Sixth-Grade Sugar Babies. Eve Bunting. 1990. Lippincott.
Paradise Cafe and Other Stories. Martha Brooks. 1990. (Joy Street Bks). Little.
Riptide. Frances Ward Weller. Illus. by Robert J Blake. 1990. (Philomel Bks). Putnam Pub Group.
Saturnalia. Paul Fleischman. 1990. HarpJ.
Seeing Earth from Space. Patricia Lauber. 1990. Orchard Bks Watts.
Sherk! Willian Steig. Illus. by William Steig. 1990. FS&G.
Shining Company. Rosemary Sutcliff. 1990. FS&G.
Shoebag. Mary James. 1990. Scholastic.
Silver Kiss. Annette Curtis Klause. 1990. Delacorte.
Something Big Has Been Here. Jack Prelutsky. Illus. by James Stevenson. 1990. Greenwillow.
Tale of the Mandarin Ducks. Katherine Paterson. Illus. by Leo Dillon & Diane Dillon. 1990. Lodestar Bks.
Train Song. Diane Siebert. Illus. by Mike Wimmer. 1990. T Y Crowell.

True Confessions of Charlotte Doyle. Avi. 1990. Orchard Bks Watts.
Wall. Eve Bunting. 1990. (Clarion Bks). HM.
Weasel. Cynthia DeFelice. 1990. Macmillan.
White Peak Farm. Berlie Doherty. 1990. Orchard Bks Watts.
Woodsong. Gary Paulsen. Illus. by Ruth Wright. 1990. Bradbury.

1989

Abduction. Mette Newth. Tr. by Tiina Nunnally & Steve Murray. 1989. FS&G.
Afternoon of the Elves. Janet Taylor Lisle. 1989. Orchard Bks Watts.
Alice in Rapture, Sort Of. Phyllis R. Naylor. 1989. (Atheneum Childrens Bks). Macmillan.
American Family Farm. Joan Anderson. Photos by George Ancona. 1989. HarBraceJ.
And One for All. Theresa Nelson. 1989. Orchard Bks Watts.
Beyond Safe Boundaries. Magaret Sacks. 1989. Lodestar Bks.
Bill Peet: An Autobiography. Bill Peet. Illus. by Bill Peet. 1989. HM.
Bingo Brown and the Language of Love. Betsy Byars. 1989. (Viking Kestrel). Penguin USA.
Book of Eagles. Helen R. Sattler. Illus. by Jean D. Zallinger. 1989. Lothrop.
Broccoli Tapes. Jan Slepian. 1989. (Philomel Bks). Putnam Pub Group.
Captain Snap and the Children of Vinegar Lane. Roni Schotter. Illus. by Marcia Sewall. 1989. Orchard Bks Watts.
Celine. Brock Cole. 1989. FS&G.
Commander Coatrack Returns. Joseph McNair. 1989. HM.
Eric Carle's Animals Animals. Compiled by Laura Whipple. Illus. by Eric Carle. 1989. (Philomel Bks). Putnam Pub Group.
Eva. Peter Dickinson. 1989. Delacorte.
Frog Prince. Alix Berenzy. Illus. by Alix Berenzy. 1989. H Holt & Co.
Great American Gold Rush. Rhoda Blumberg. 1989. Bradbury Pr.
Great Little Madison. Jean Fritz. 1989. (Putnam). Putnam Pub Group.
Heartbeats: And Other Stories. Peter D. Sieruta. 1989. HarpJ.
Hey World, Here I Am! Jean Little. Illus. by Sue Truesdell. 1989. HarpJ.
If You Made a Million. David M. Schwartz. Illus. by Steven Kellogg. Photos by George Ancona. 1989. Lothrop.
Jessica. Kevin Henkes. Illus. by Kevin Henkes. 1989. Greenwillow.
Lon Po Po: A Red-Riding Hood Story from China. Ed Young. 1989. (Philomel Bks). Putnam Pub Group.
Loving Ben. Elizabeth Laird. 1989. Delacorte.
Magic Fan. Keith Baker. Illus. by Keith Baker. 1989. HarBraceJ.
Martin's Mice. Dick King-Smith. Illus. by Jez Alborough. 1989. Crown.
Max's Chocolate Chicken. Rosemary Wells. Illus. by Rosemary Wells. 1989. Dial Bks Young.
Moses' Ark: Stories From the Bible. Alice Bach & Cheryl Exum. Illus. by Leo Dillon & Diane Dillon. 1989. Delacorte.
My War with Goggle-Eyes. Anne Fine. 1989. (Joy St Bks). Little.
News about Dinosaurs. Patricia Lauber. 1989. Bradbury Pr.
Night Riding. Katherine Martin. 1989. Knopf.
No Kidding. Bruce Brooks. 1989. HarpJ.
Number the Stars. Lois Lowry. 1989. HM.
Of Colors and Things. Tana Hoban. Photos by Tana Hoban. 1989. Greenwillow.
Oh, Brother. Arthur Yorinks. Illus. by Richard Egielski. 1989. FS&G.
Panama Canal: Gateway to the World. Judith St. George. 1989. (Putnam). Putnam Pub Group.
Pheonix Rising: Or How to Survive Your Life. Cynthia D. Grant. 1989. (Atheneum Childrens Bks). Macmillan.
Princess Furball. Charlotte Huck. Illus. by Anita Lobel. 1989. Greenwillow.
Salem Witchcraft Trials. Karen Zeinert. 1989. Watts.
Seventeen Against the Dealer. Cynthia Voigt. 1989. (Atheneum Childrens Bks). Macmillan.
Super Super Super-words. Bruce McMillan. Photos by Bruce McMillan. 1989. Lothrop.
Sweetgrass. Jan Hudson. 1989. (Philomel Bks). Putnam Pub Group.
Sydney, Herself. Colby Rodowsky. 1989. FS&G.
Tell Me a Story, Mama. Angela Johnson. Illus. by David Soman. 1989. Orchard Bks Watts.
Theseus and the Minotaur. Retold by Warwick Hutton. Illus. by Warwick Hutton. 1989. (McElderry Bks). Macmillan.
Three Little Pigs. James Marshall. Illus. by James Marshall. 1989. (Dial). Doubleday.

Unlived Affections. George Shannon. 1989. HarpJ.
Voices From the Civil War: A Documentary History of the Great American Conflict. Milton Meltzer. 1989. (Crowell Jr Bks). HarpJ.
Voyage of the Frog. Gary Paulsen. 1989. Orchard Bks Watts.
Wednesday Surprise. Eve Bunting. Illus. by Donald Carrick. 1989. (Pub by Clarion). Ticknor & Fields.
We're Going on a Bear Hunt. Michael Rosen. Illus. by Helen Oxenbury. 1989. (McElderry Bks). Macmillan.
Where Does the Brown Bear Go? Nicki Weiss. Illus. by Nicki Weiss. 1989. Greenwillow.
White House. Leonard E. Fisher. 1989. Holiday.
Will's Mammoth. Rafe Martin. Illus. by Stephen Gammell. 1989. (Putnam). Putnam Pub Group.
Young Lions. Toshi Yoshida. Illus. by Toshi Yoshida. 1989. (Philomel Bks). Putnam Pub Group.

1988

Aesop's Fables. Tom Paxton. Illus. by Richard Rayevsky. 1988. Morrow.
Alice's Adventures in Wonderland. Lewis Carroll. Illus. by Anthony Browne. 1988. Knopf.
All About Sam. Lois Lowry. Illus. by Diane DeGroat. 1988. HM.
Annabelle Swift, Kindergartner. Amy Schwartz. Illus. by Amy Schwartz. 1988. (Orchard Bks). Watts.
Anthony Burns: The Defeat & Triumph of a Fugitive Slave. Virginia Hamilton. 1988. Knopf.
Bone Wars. Kathryn Lasky. 1988. Morrow.
Borrowed Children. Illus. by George E. Lyon. 1988. (Orchard Bks). Watts.
Boy of the Three-Year Nap. Dianne Snyder. Illus. by Allen Say. 1988. HM.
Bravo, Minski. Arthur Yorkinks. Illus. by Richard Egielski. 1988. FS&G.
Buffalo Hunt. Russell Freedman. 1988. Holiday.
Burning Questions of Bingo Brown. Betsy Byars. 1988. Viking.
Canterbury Tales. Geoffrey Chaucer. Tr. by Barbara Cohen from Middle English. Adapted by Barbara Cohen. Illus. by Trina S. Hyman. 1988. Lothrop.
Duplicate. William Sleator. 1988. Dutton.
Empty Sleeve. Leon Garfield. 1988. Delacorte.
Exploring the Titanic. Robert D. Ballard. 1988. Scholastic.
Fallen Angels. Walter D. Myers. 1988. Scholastic.
False Face. Welwyn W. Katz. 1988. (McElderry Bks). Macmillan.
Feel Better, Ernest! Gabrielle Vincent. Illus. by Gabrielle Vincent. 1988. Greenwillow.
Goldilocks & the Three Bears. Retold by James Marshall. Illus. by James Marshall. 1988. Dial.
Good Courage. Stephanie S. Tolan. 1988. Morrow.
Grandpa's Face. Eloise Greenfield. Illus. by Floyd Cooper. 1988. Philomel.
Her Seven Brothers. Paul Goble. Illus. by Paul Goble. 1988. Bradbury.
Hominids: A Look Back at Our Ancestors. Helen R. Sattler. Illus. by Christopher Santoro. 1988. Lothrop.
I'll Meet You at the Cucumbers. Lilian Moore. Illus. by Sharon Wooding. 1988. Atheneum.
Island Boy. Barbara Cooney. Illus. by Barbara Cooney. 1988. Viking.
Kindness. Cynthia Rylant. 1988. (Orchard Bks). Watts.
Lynda Madaras Talks to Teens About AIDS. Lynda Madaras. 1988. Newmarket Pr.
Memory. Margaret Mahy. 1988. (MCElderry Bks). Macmillan.
More Tales of Uncle Remus: Futher Adventures of Brer Rabits, His Friends, Enemies, & Others. Retold by Julius Lester. Illus. by Jerry Pinkney. 1988. Dial.
Music of What Happens: Poems That Tell Stories. Paul B. Janeczko. 1988. (Orchard Bks). Watts.
Nebulae: The Birth & Death of Stars. Necia H. Apfel. 1988. Lothrop.
New Baby. Emily A. McCully. Illus. by Emily . McCully. 1988. HarpJ.
Other Side of the Family. Maureen Pople. 1988. Holt.
Pigs' Picnic. Keiko Kasza. Illus. by Keiko Kasza. 1988. Putnam.
Probably Still Nick Swansen. Virginia E. Wolff. 1988. H Holt & Co.
Rescue: The Story of How Gentiles Saved Jews in the Holocaust. Milton Meltzer. 1988. HarpJ.
Sea Swan. Kathryn Lasky. Illus. by Catherine Stock. 1988. Macmillan.
Sex Education. Jenny Davis. 1988. (Orchard Bks). Watts.
Show-and-Tell War: And Other Stories About Adam Joshua. Janice L. Smith. Illus. by Dick Gackenbach. 1988. HarpJ.
Shy Charles. Rosemary Wells. Illus. by Rosemary Wells. 1988. Dial.
Sing a Song of Popcorn: Every Child's Book of Poems. Selected by Beatrice S. De Regniers et al. Illus. by Marcia Brown et al. 1988. Scholastic.

Smoke & Ashes: The Story of the Holocaust. Barbara Rogasky. 1988. Holiday.
Stalin: Russia's Man of Steel. Albert Marrin. 1988. Viking.
Stringbean's Trip to the Shining Sea. Vera B. Williams. Illus. by Vera B. Williams & Jennifer Williams. 1988. Greenwillow.
Tail Feathers from Mother Goose: The Opie Rhyme Book. Compiled by Peter Opie & Iona Opie. 1988. Little.
Village by the Sea. Paula Fox. 1988. (Orchard Bks). Watts.
War for Independence: The Story of the American Revolution. Albert Marrin. 1988. Atheneum.
Way Things Work. David Macaulay. Illus. by David Macaulay. 1988. HM.
Where's the Baby? Pat Hutchins. Illus. by Pat Hutchins. 1988. Greenwillow.

1987
After the Rain. Norma F. Mazer. 1987. (Morrow Jr Bks). Morrow.
American Revolutionaries: A History in Their Own Words. Milton Meltzer. 1987. (Crowell Jr Bks). HarpJ.
Angel's Mother's Wedding. Judy Delton. Illus. by Margot Apple. 1987. HM.
Arthur's Baby. Marc Brown. Illus. by Marc Brown. 1987. Little.
Blossoms and the Green Phantom. Betsy Byars. Illus. by Jacqueline Rogers. 1987. Delacorte.
Book of Adam to Moses. Tr. by Lore Segal. Illus. by Leonard Baskin. 1987. Knopf.
Chartbreaker. Gillian Cross. 1987. Holiday.
Children of Christmas: Stories for the Season. Cynthia Rylant. Illus. by S. D. Schindler. 1987. (Orchard Bks). Watts.
Class Clown. Johanna Hurwitz. Illus. by Sheila Hamanaka. 1987. Morrow.
Dinosaurs Walked Here & Other Stories Fossils Tell. Patricia Lauber. 1987. Bradbury Pr.
Edith Herself. Ellen Howard. Illus. by Ronald Himler. 1987. Atheneum.
Eyes of the Dragon. Margaret Leaf. Illus. by Ed Young. 1987. Lothrop.
Fish in His Pocket. Denys Cazet. 1987. (Orchard Bks). Watts.
Fox's Dream. Keizaburo Tejima. Tr. by Susan Matsui from Japanese. Illus. by Keizaburo Tejima. 1987. (Philomel Bks). Putnam Pub Group.
Ghost Drum: A Cat's Tale. Susan Price. 1987. FS&G.
Ghost's Hour, Spook's Hour. Eve Bunting. Illus. by Donald Carrick. 1987. (Clarion). Ticknor & Fields.
Gingerbread Boy. Illus. by Scott Cook. 1987. Knopf.
Goats. Brock Cole. 1987. FS&G.
Good-bye and Keep Cold. Jenny Davis. 1987. (Orchard Bks). Watts.
Grandaddy's Place. Helen V. Griffith. Illus. by James Stevenson. 1987. Greenwillow.
Halloween ABC. Eve Merriam. Illus. by Lane Smith. 1987. Macmillan.
Harry's Mad. Dick King-Smith. Illus. by Jill Bennett. 1987. Crown.
Heckedy Peg. Audrey Wood. Illus. by Don Wood. 1987. HarBraceJ.
Hilter. Albert Marrin. 1987. Viking.
Icebrgs and Glaciers. Seymour Simon. 1987. Morrow.
Incredible Journey of Lewis & Clark. Rhoda Blumberg. 1987. Lothrop.
Indian Chiefs. Russell Freedman. 1987. Holiday.
Into a Strange Land: Unaccompanied Refugee Youth in America. Brent Ashabranner & Melissa Ashabrabnner. 1987. Dodd.
Invincible Summer. Jean Ferris. 1987. FS&G.
Jerusalem, Shining Still. Karla Kushkin. Illus. by David Frampton. 1987. HarpJ.
Jump Again! More Adventures of Brer Rabbit. Joel C. Harris. Ed. by Van D. Parks. Illus. by Barry Moser. 1987. HarBraceJ.
Knots on a Counting Rope. Bill Martin, Jr. & John Archambault. Illus. by Ted Rand. 1987. H Holt & Co.
Lincoln: A Photobiography. Russell Freedman. 1987. (Clarion). Ticknor & Fields.
M. E. and Morton. Sylvia Cassedy. 1987. (Crowell Jr Bks). HarpJ.
Making Friends. Fred Rogers. 1987. Putnam Pub Group.
Mrs. Pig Gets Cross: And Other Stories. Mary Rayner. Illus. by Mary Raynor. 1987. Dutton.
Moss Gown. William H. Hooks. Illus. by Donald Carrick. 1987. (Clarion). Ticknor & Fields.
Moving. Fred Rogers. Illus. by Jim Judkis. 1987. (Putnam). Putnam Pub Group.
Mufaro's Beautiful Daughters: An African Tale. John Steptoe. Illus. by John Steptoe. 1987. Lothrop.
Oma and Bobo. Amy Schwartz. Illus. by Amy Schwartz. 1987. Bradbury Pr.
Permanent Connections. Sue Ellen Bridgers. 1987. HarpJ.

Prehistoric Pinkerton. Steven Kellogg. Illus. by Steven Kellogg. 1987. Dial Bks Young.
Red Riding Hood. Retold by James Marshall. Illus. by James Marshall. 1987. Dial Bks Young.
Redwall. Brian Jacques. Illus. by Gary Chalk. 1987. (Philomel Bks). Putnam Pub Group.
Return. Sonia Levitin. 1987. Atheneum.
Ruby in the Smoke. Philip Pullman. 1987. Knopf.
Seventeen Kings and Forty-Two Elephants. Margaret Mahy. Illus. by Patricia MacCarthy. 1987. Dials Bks Young.
Sons From Afar. Cynthia Voigt. 1987. Atheneum.
Tricksters. Margaret Mahy. 1987. (McElderry Bks). MacMillan.
Twenty-Six Letters and Ninety-Nine Cents. Tana Hoban. Photos by Tana Hoban. 1987. Greenwillow.
Under All Silences: Shades of Love. Selected by Ruth Gordon. 1987. HarpJ.
Voyage of the Ludgate Hill: Travels With Robert Louis Stevenson. Nancy Willard. Illus. by Alice Provensen & Martin Provensen. 1987. HarBraceJ.
We the People: The Story of the United States Constitution Since 1787. Doris Faber & Harold Faber. 1987. (Pub. by Scribner). Macmillan.
Year Without Michael. Susan B. Pfeffer. 1987. Bantam.

1986
Alphabatics. Sue MacDonald. 1986. Bradbury Pr.
Amahl & the Night Visitors. Gian-Carlo Menotti. Illus. by Michele Lemieux. 1986. (Morrow Jr Bks). Morrow.
Boy Who Reversed Himself. William Sleator. 1986. Dutton.
Buffalo: The American Bison Today. Dorothy Hinshaw Patent. Photos by William Munoz. 1986. (Clarion). Ticknor & Field.
Children of the Maya: A Guatemalan Indian Odyssey. Brent Ashabranner. Photos by Paul Conklin. 1986. Dodd.
Class Dismissed: More High School Poems, No. II. Mel Glenn. Illus. by Michael J. Bernstein. 1986. (Clarion). Ticknor & Fields.
Come a Stranger. Cynthia Voigt. Ed. by Gail Paris. 1986. (Childrens Bk). Macmillan.
Cuckoo Sister. Vivien Alcock. 1986. Delacorte.
Dinosaurs Divorce: A Guide for Changing Families. Laurence K. Brown & Marc Brown. 1986. Atlantic Monthly.
Ellis Island: Gateway to the New World. Leonard E. Fisher. Illus. by Leonard E. Fisher. 1986. Holiday.
Fine White Dust. Cynthia Rylant. 1986. Bradbury Pr.
Flies in the Water, Fish in the Air: A Personal Introduction to Fly Fishing. Jim Arnosky. 1986. Lothrop.
Flossie & the Fox. Patricia C. McKissack. Illus. by Rachel Isadora. 1986. Dial Bks Young.
Georgia Music. Helen Griffith. Illus. by James Stevenson. 1986. Greenwillow.
Incredible Sixties: The Stormy Years That Changed America. Jules Archer. 1986. (HJ). HarBraceJ.
Jump: The Adventures of Brer Rabbit. Van D. Parks & Malcolm Jones. Illus. by Barry Moser. 1986. (HJ). HarBraceJ.
Make Way for Sam Houston. Jean Fritz. Illus. by Elise Primavera. 1986. Putnam Pub Group.
Max's Christmas. Rosemary Wells. Illus. by Rosemary Wells. 1986. Dial Bks Young.
Midnight Hour Encores. Bruce Brooks. 1986. HarpJ.
Moonlight Man. Paula Fox. 1986. Bradbury Pr.
More Stories Julian Tells. Ann Cameron. Illus. by Ann Strugnell. 1986. Knopf.
Mother's Day Mice. Eve Bunting. Illus. by Jan Brett. 1986. (Clarion). Ticknor & Fields.
Night in the Country. Cynthia Rylant. Illus. by Mary Szilagyi. 1986. Bradbury Pr.
Not So Fast, Songololo. Niki Daly. Illus. by Niki Daly. 1986. (McElderry Bk). Macmillan.
On My Honor. Marion D. Bauer. 1986. (Clarion). Ticknor & Fields.
Pea Patch Jig. Thacher Hurd. 1986. Crown.
Pecos Bill. Steven Kellogg. Illus. by Steven Kellogg. 1986. Morrow.
Piggybook. Anthony Browne. Illus. by Anthony Browne. 1986. Knopf.
Pilgrims of Plimoth. Marcia Sewall. Ed. by Marcia Marshall. Illus. by Marcia Sewall. 1986. (Childrens Bk). Macmillan.
Pompeii: Exploring a Roman Ghost Town. Ron Goor & Nancy Goor. Illus. by Ron Goor & Nancy Goor. 1986. Crowell Jr Bks.
Poverty in America. Milton Meltzer. 1986. (Morrow Jr Bks). Morrow.
Pueblo. David Yue & Charlotte Yue. 1986. HM.
Random House Book of Mother Goose: A Treasury of Three Hundred & Six Timeless Nursery Rhymes. Selected by Arnold Lobel. Illus. by Arnold Lobel. 1986. Random.

Read-Aloud Rhymes for the Very Young. Ed. by Jack Prelutsky. Illus. by Marc Brown. Intro. by Jim Trelease. 1986. Knopf.
Rear-View Mirrors. Paul Fleischman. 1986. HarpJ.
Return to Bitter Creek. Doris B. Smith. 1986. (Viking Kestrel). Viking.
Rumor of Otters. Deborah Savage. 1986. HM.
Rumpelstiltskin. Retold by Paul O. Zelinsky. Illus. by Paul O. Zelinsky. 1986. Dutton.
Shapes, Shapes, Shapes. Tana Hoban. Photos by Tana Hoban. 1986. Greenwillow.
So Far from the Bamboo Grove. Yoko K. Watkins. Intro. by Jean Fritz. 1986. Lothrop.
Thinking Big: The Story of a Young Dwarf. Susan Kuklin. 1986. Lothrop.
To Space & Back. Sally Ride & Susan Okie. 1986. Lothrop.
Twenty-Five Cents Miracle. Theresa Nelson. 1986. Bradbury Pr.
Up to Ten & Down Again. Lisa C. Ernst. 1986. Lothrop.
Village of Round & Square Houses. Ann Grifalconi. Illus. by Ann Grifalconi. 1986. Little.
Volcano: The Eruption & Healing of Mount St. Helens. Patricia Lauber. 1986. Bradbury Pr.
Water of Life. Ed. by Barbara Rogasky. Illus. by Trina S. Hyman. 1986. Holiday.
What Happened to Patrick's Dinosaurs? Carol Carrick. Illus. by Donald Carrick. 1986. (Clarion). Ticknor & Fields.
Whipping Boy. Sid Fleischman. Illus. by Peter Sis. 1986. Greenwillow.
White Dynamite & Curly Kidd. Bill Martin, Jr. & John Archambault. Illus. by Ted Rand. 1986. H Holt & Co.

1985
Ain't Gonna Study War No More: The Story of America's Peace Seekers. Milton Meltzer. 1985. Har-Row.
Alan Garner's Book of British Fairy Tales. Alan Gerner. Illus. by Derek Collard. 1985. Delecorte.
Badger on the Barge & Other Stories. Janni Howker. 1985. Greenwillow.
Blackberries in the Dark. Mavis Jukes. Illus. by Thomas B. Allen. 1985. Knopf.
Breakthrough: The Story of Penicillin. Francine Jacobs. 1985. Dodd.
Chemically Active: Experiments You Can Do at Home. Vicki Cobb. Illus. by Theo Cobb. 1985. Lipp Jr Bks.
China Homecoming. Jean Fritz. 1985. Putnam Pub Group.
Come Sing, Jimmy Jo. Katherine Paterson. 1985. Lodestar Bks.
Commodore Perry in the Land of the Shogun. Rhoda Blumberg. 1985. Lothrop.
Cowboys of the Wild West. Russell Freedman. 1985. (Clarion). Ticknor & Fields.
Cracker Jackson. Betsy C. Byars. 1985. Viking.
Deep Wizardry. Diane Duane. 1985. Delacorte.
Dogsong. Gary Paulsen. 1985. Bradbury Pr.
Every Living Thing. Cynthia Rylant. Illus. by Stephen D. Schindler. 1985. Bradbury Pr.
George Shrinks. William Joyce. Illus. by William Joyce. 1985. HarpJ.
Healer. Peter Dickinson. 1985. Delacorte.
In Kindling Flame: The Story of Hannah Senesh 1921-1944. Linda Atkinson. 1985. Lothrop.
In Summer Light. Zibby O'Neal. 1985. Viking.
Jupiter. Seymour Simon. 1985. Morrow.
Kids' Book About Death & Dying. Fayerweather Street School Staff. Ed. by Eric E. Rofes. 1985. Little.
King Bidgood's in the Bathtub. Audrey Wood. Illus. by Don Wood. 1985. HarBraceJ.
Koko's Kitten. Francine Patterson. Illus. by Ronald H. Cohn. 1985. Scholastic Inc.
Max's Bath. Rosemary Wells. Illus. by Rosemary Wells. 1985. Dial Bks Young.
Max's Bedtime. Rosemary Wells. Illus. by Rosemary Wells. 1985. Dial Bks Young.
Max's Birthday. Rosemary Wells. Illus. by Rosemary Wells. 1985. Dial Bks Young.
Max's Breakfast. Rosemary Wells. Illus. by Rosemary Wells. 1985. Dial Bks Young.
Mystery of the Ancient Maya. Carolyn Meyer & Charles Gallenkamp. 1985. (McElderry Bk). Macmillan.
New Baby. Fred Rogers. Photos by Jim Judkis. 1985. Putnam Pub Group.
Paper Crane. Molly Bang. Illus. by Molly Bang. 1985. Greenwillow.
People Could Fly: American Black Folk Tales. Virginia Hamilton. Illus. by Leo Dillon & Diane Dillon. 1985. Knopf.
Pocket Poems: Selected for a Journey. Ed. by Paul B. Janeczko. 1985. Bradbury Pr.
Polar Express. Chris Van Allsburg. Illus. by Chris Van Allsburg. 1985. HM.

Quentin Corn. Mary Stolz. Illus. by Pamela Johnson. 1985. Godine.
Remembering the Good Times. Richard Peck. 1985. Delacorte.
Sarah, Plain & Tall. Patricia MacLachlan. 1985. HarpJ.
Saturn. Seymour Simon. 1985. Morrow.
Saving the Peregrine Falcon. Caroline Arnold. Photos by Richard P. Hewett. 1985. Carolrhoda Bks.
Sirens & Spies. Janet T. Lisle. 1985. Bradbury Pr.
Stay Away from Simon. Carol Carrick. Illus. by Donald Carrick. 1985. (Clarion). Ticknor & Fields.
Tales Mummies Tell. Patricia Lauber. 1985. Crowell Jr Bks.
Thanksgiving Poems. Ed. by Myra C. Livingston. Illus. by Stephen Gammell. 1985. Holiday.
Trek. Ann Jonas. Illus. by Ann Jonas. 1985. Greenwillow.
Truth about Santa Claus. James C. Giblin. 1985. Crowell Jr Bks.
Very Worst Monster. Pat Hutchins. Illus. by Pat Hutchins. 1985. Greenwillow.
Witch Who Lives Down the Hall. Donna Guthrie. Illus. by Amy Schwartz. 1985. HarBraceJ.
Wolf of Shadows. Whitley Strieber. 1985. Knopf.

1984

Alfie Gives a Hand. Shirley Hughes. Illus. by Shirley Hughes. 1984. Lothrop.
Animal Alphabet. Bert Kitchen. Illus. by Bert Kitchen. 1984. Dial Bks Young.
Archer's Goon. Diana W. Jones. 1984. Greenwillow.
Bionic Bunny Show. Marc Brown & Lauren K. Krasny. 1984. (Atlantic Monthly Pr). Little.
Buffalo Woman. Paul Goble. 1984. Bradbury Pr.
Building Blocks. Cynthia Voigt. 1984. (Childrens Bk). Macmillan.
Changeover: A Supernatural Romance. Margaret Mahy. 1984. (McElderry Bk). Macmillan.
Comets. Franklyn M. Branley. Illus. by Guilio Maestro. 1984. Crowell Jr Bks.
Dark Behind the Curtain. Gillian Cross. Illus. by David Parkins. 1984. Merrimack Pub Cir.
Drawing Life in Motion. Jim Arnosky. 1984. Lothrop.
Fireworks Tonight! Martha Brenner. 1984. Hastings.
Fix-It. David McPhail. Illus. by David McPhail. 1984. Dutton.
Geraldine's Blanket. Holly Keller. Illus. by Holly Keller. 1984. Greenwillow.
Hansel & Gretel. Ed. by Rika Lesser. Illus. by Paul O. Zelinsky. 1984. Dodd.
Have You Seen My Duckling? Nancy Tafuri. Illus. by Nancy Tafuri. 1984. Greenwillow.
Hero & the Crown. Robin McKinley. 1984. Greenwillow.
Holes & Peeks. Ann Jonas. Illus. by Ann Jonas. 1984. Greenwillow.
How You Were Born. Joanna Cole. 1984. Morrow.
In a Dark, Dark, Room & Other Scary Stories. Alvin Schwartz. Illus. by Dirk Zimmer. 1984. HarpJ.
In the Year of the Boar & Jackie Robinson. Bette B. Lord. Illus. by Marc Simont. 1984. HarpJ.
Interstellar Pig. William Sleator. 1984. Dutton.
Invisible World of Infrared. Jack R. White. 1984. Dodd.
Legend Days. Jamake Highwater. 1984. HarpJ.
Like Jake & Me. Mavis Jukes. Illus. by Lloyd Bloom. 1984. Knopf.
Louisville Slugger: The Making of a Baseball Bat. Jan Arnow. Photos by Jan Arnow. 1984. Pantheon.
Love Is Like the Lion's Tooth. Ed. by Frances McCullough. 1984. HarpJ.
Mary Had a Little Lamb. Sarah J. Hale. Illus. by Tomie De Paola. 1984. Holiday.
Merry Christmas, Ernest & Celestine. Gabrielle Vincent. Illus. by Gabrielle Vincent. 1984. Greenwillow.
Moves Make the Man. Bruce Brooks. 1984. HarpJ.
Music, Music for Everyone. Vera B. Williams. Illus. by Vera B. Williams. 1984. Greenwillow.
Mysteries of Harris Burdick. Chris Van Allsburg. Illus. by Chris Van Allsburg. 1984. HM.
New Kid on the Block. Jack Prelutsky. Illus. by James Stevenson. 1984. Greenwillow.
Picnic. Emily A. McCully. 1984. HarpJ.
Ramona, Forever. Beverly Cleary. Illus. by Alan Tiegreen. 1984. Morrow.
Rose In My Garden. Arnold Lobel. Illus. by Anita Lobel. 1984. Greenwillow.
School Bus. Donald Crews. Illus. by Donald Crews. 1984. Greenwillow.
Sixteen: Short Stories by Outstanding Writers for Young Adults. Donald R. Gallo. 1984. Delacorte.
Story of the Jumping Mouse. John Steptoe. Illus. by John Steptoe. 1984. Lothrop.
Surprises. Ed. by Lee B. Hopkins. 1984. HarpJ.
Tipi: A Center of Native American Life. Charlotte Yue. Illus. by David Yue. 1984. Knopf.
Truck Song. Diane Siebert. Illus. by Byron Barton. 1984. Crowell Jr Bks.

Waiting to Waltz: A Childhood. Cynthia Rylant. Illus. by Stephen Gammell. 1984. Bradbury Pr.
Way to Satin Shore. Philippa Pearce. Illus. by Charlotte Voake. 1984. Greenwillow.
Winners & Losers: How Elections Work in America. Jules Archer. 1984. (HJ). HarBraceJ.
Young Writer's Handbook. Susan Tchudi. 1984. (ScribT). Scribner.

1983

Baby's Catalogue. Janet Ahlberg & Allan Ahlberg. 1983. (Atlantic Monthly Pr). Little.
Behind the Attic Wall. Sylvia Cassedy. 1983. Crowell Jr Bks.
Best Bad Thing. Yoshiko Uchida. 1983. (McElderry Bk). Macmillan.
Bony-Legs. Joanna Cole. Illus. by Dirk Zimmer. 1983. (Four Winds). Macmillan.
Bumblebee Flies Anyway. Robert Cormier. 1983. Knopf.
Cars & How They Go. Joanna Cole. Illus. by Gail Gibbons. 1983. Crowell Jr Bks.
Daphne's Book. Mary D. Hahn. 1983. (Clarion). HM.
Dear Mr. Henshaw. Beverly Cleary. Illus. by Paul O. Zelinsky. 1983. Morrow.
Devil With the Three Golden Hairs. Jacob Grimm & Wilhelm K. Grimm. Illus. by Nonny Hogrogian. 1983. Knopf.
Double Life of Pocahontas. Jean Fritz. Illus. by Ed Young. 1983. (Putnam). Putnam Pub Group.
Early Morning in the Barn. Nancy Tafuri. Illus. by Nancy Tafuri. 1983. Greenwillow.
Elephant's Child. Rudyard Kipling. Illus. by Lorinda B. Cauley. 1983. (HJ). HarpJ.
Fingers. William Sleator. 1983. (Childrens Bk). Macmillan.
Glorious Flight Across the Channel with Louis Bleriot. Alice Provensen & Martin Provensen. 1983. (Viking Kestrel). Viking.
Grand Constructions. Gian P. Ceserani. Illus. by Piero Ventura. 1983. (Putnam). Putnam Pub Group.
Hiawatha. Henry W. Longfellow. 1983. Dial Bks Young.
I Unpacked My Grandmother's Trunk. Susan Hoguet. Illus. by Susan Hoguet. 1983. Dutton.
Lenny Kandell, Smart Aleck. Ellen Conford. Illus. by Walter Gaffney-Kessell. 1983. Little.
Luttrell Village: Country Life in the Middle Ages. Sheila Sancha. Illus. by Sheila Sancha. 1983. Crowell Jr Bks.
Magic Wings: A Tale from China. Diane Wolkstein. Illus. by Robert A. Parker. 1983. Dutton.
Max & Me & the Time Machine. Gery Greer & Bob Ruddick. 1983. (HJ). HarBraceJ.
Medieval Feast. Aliki. 1983. Crowell Jr Bks.
Mill. David Macaulay. Illus. by David Macaulay. 1983. HM.
Month-Brothers: A Slavic Tale. Samuel Marshak. Tr. by Thomas P. Whitney from Rus. Illus. by Diane Stanley. 1983. Morrow.
Mummy, the Will, & the Crypt. John Bellairs. Illus. by Edward Gorey. 1983. Dial Bks Young.
Night in Distant Motion. Irina Korschunow. Tr. by Leigh Hafrey from Ger. 1983. Godine.
No One Is Going to Nashville. Mavis Jukes. Illus. by Lloyd Bloom. 1983. Knopf.
Pigs in Hiding. Arlene Dubanevich. Illus. by Arlene Dubanevich. 1983. Macmillan.
Poetspeak: In Their Work, About Their Work. Ed. by Paul B. Janeczko. 1983. Bradbury Pr.
Queen Eleanor: Independent Spirit of the Medieval World--A Biography of Eleanor of Aquitaine. Polly S. Brooks. 1983. Lipp Jr Bks.
Random House Book of Poetry for Children. Jack Prelutsky. Illus. by Arnold Lobel. 1983. Random.
Raspberry One. Charles Ferry. 1983. HM.
Root Cellar. Janet Lunn. 1983. (Scribner). Macmillan.
Saturn. Franklyn M. Branley. Illus. by Leonard Kessler. 1983. Crowell Jr Bks.
Sign of the Beaver. Elizabeth G. Speare. 1983. HM.
Silver Cow: A Welsh Tale. Susan Cooper. Illus. by Warwick Hutton. 1983. (McElderry Bk). Macmillan.
Sing, Pierrot, Sing: A Picture Book in Mime. Tomie De Paola. Illus. by Tomie De Paola. 1983. (HJ). HarBraceJ.
Sky Above & Worlds Beyond. Judith Herbst. Illus. by Richard Rosenblum & George Lovi. 1983. Atheneum.
Sky Is Full of Song. Lee B. Hopkins. Illus. by Dirk Zimmer. 1983. HarpJ.
Something Special for Me. Vera B. Williams. Illus. by Vera B. Williams. 1983. Greenwillow.
Story of Baseball. Lawrence S. Ritter. 1983. Morrow.
Tempering. Gloria Skurzynski. 1983. (Clarion Bks). HM.
Ten, Nine Eight. Molly Bang. Illus. by Molly Bang. 1983. Greenwillow.
Thistle. Walter Wangerin, Jr. Illus. by Marcia Sewall. 1983. HarpJ.

What's Under My Bed. James Stevenson. Illus. by James Stevenson. 1983. Greenwillow.
Wish Giver: Three Tales of Coven Tree. Bill Brittain. Illus. by Andrew Glass. 1983. HarpJ.

Fly Away Home. Eve Bunting. Illus. by Ronald Himler. (Clarion). HM.
Remarkable Journey of Prince Jen. Lloyd Alexander. Dutton Child Bks.
Witch Baby. Francesca L Block. (Charlotte Zolotow Bks). Harper Child Bks.

Ruth Schwartz Children's Book Award

This award founded in 1976 by the Ruth Schwartz Foundation, is presented annually, and administered jointly by the Canadian Booksellers Association and the Ontario Arts Council. Nominees must be either Canadian citizens or landedimmigrants who have produced outstanding work in Canadian children's literature. The nominated books must reflect the best creative effort in children's literature and must be published in Canada during the preceding year. The writer (A) or illustrator (I) of an outstanding work receives a cash award of $2,000.

1993

Something from Nothing. Phoebe Gilman. 1993. Scholastic Inc.

1992

Roses Sing On New Snow. Paul Yee. 1992. Illus. by Harvey Chan. 1992. Groundwood.

1991

†† Forbidden City. William Bell. 1990. Doubleday Canada.

1990

†† Bad Boy. Diana Wieler. 1990. (XGroundwood Bks). Douglas & McIntyre. (A).

1989

†† Amos's Sweater. Janet Lunn. Illus. by Kim Lafave. 1988. Groundwood Bks. (A).

1988

†† Doll. Cora Taylor. 1987. Western Producer Prairie Bks. (A).

1987

†† Have You Seen Birds? Joanne Oppenheim. Illus. by Barbara Reid. 1986. North Winds. (I).

1986

†† Thomas' Snowsuit. Robert Munsch. 1985. Annick. (A).

1985

Mama's Going to Buy You a Mockingbird. Jean Little. 1984. (Viking Kestrel). Viking. (A).

1984

†† Zoom at Sea. Tim Wynne-Jones. 1983. Groundwood. (A).

Signal Poetry Award

The Signal Poetry Award was established in 1979 to "highlight excellence in poetry published for children, and in the work done to promote poetry with children." The award is presented annually for "excellence in any one of the following categories: single-poet collections published for children, body of work for children by a contemporary poet, or educational or critical activity which enhances the cause of poetry for children." This award is not limited to books published in Great Britain, but any book published during the course of the year.

1993

Two's Company. Jackie Kay. Illus. by Shirley Tourret. 1992. Blackie.

1992

Shades of Green. Anne Harvey. Illus. by John Lawrence. 1991. Julia MacRae Bks.

1991

†† This Poem Doesn't Rhyme. Gerard Benson. 1990. Viking.

1990

†† Heard It in the Playground. Allan Ahlberg. Illus. by Fritz Wegner. 1989. Viking Kestrel.

1989

†† When I Dance. James Berry. 1988. Hamish Hamilton.

1988

†† Boo to a Goose. John Mole. 1987. Peterloo Poets.

1986

†† Song of the City. Gareth Owen. 1985. Fontana Young Bks.

1985

†† What is the Truth? Ted Hughes. 1984. Faber.

1984

Sky in the Pie. Roger McGough. 1983. (Viking Kestrel). Viking.

1983

†† Rattle Bag. Ed. by Seamus Heaney & Ted Hughes. 1982. Faber.

George G. Stone Center for Children's Books Recognition of Merit Award

The Recognition of Merit Award is an annual award which was established by Priscilla Neff Fenn and first presented in 1965. It is given to an "author or artist of a children's book, or for a body of work for its power to please and heighten the awareness of the complexity and the beauty of the expanding universe." A hand-lettered scroll is given to the winning author or artist. (Winners of the Body of Work Award can be found at the end of this index.)

1991
Road to Memphis. Mildred D Taylor. Ed. by Jerry Pinkney. 1990. Dial Bks Young.
Roll of Thunder, Hear My Cry. Mildred D Taylor. 1976. Dial.

1990
Honey I Love: And Other Love Poems. Eloise Greenfield. 1978. (Crowell Jr Bks). HarpJ.
Let the Circle Be Unbroken. Mildred D. Taylor. 1981. Dial Bks Young.

1989
Bears' House. Marilyn Sachs. 1987. Dutton.
Fran Ellen House. Marilyn Sachs. 1987. Dutton.

1988
Alexander & the Terrible, Horrible, No-Good, Very Bad Day. Judith Viorst. Illus. by Ray Cruz. 1972. (Atheneum Children's Bk). Macmillan.

1987
Stone Fox. John R. Gardiner. Illus. by Marcia Sewall. 1980. (Crowell Jr Bks). HarpJ.

1984
Light in the Attic. Shel Silverstein. 1983. Harper.
Where the Sidewalk Ends. Shel Silverstein. 1983. Harper.

Times Educational Supplement Information Book Awards

Established in 1972 by the Times Educational Supplement (London, England), this award is limited to non-fiction trade books which originate in the United Kingdom or the Commonwealth countries. The books are selected based on their distinction in content and presentation of information. The categories presented are: Junior (J:up to age 9), and Seniors (S: ages 10-16). The winning author in each category receives a monetary award of 150 English pounds.

1991
After The Bomb: Brother in the Land. 1990. English & Media Centre.
Thin Ice. 1990. Oxford U Pr.

1990
†† New Oxford School Atlas. 1989. Oxford Univ Pr. (S).
†† Tree. Judy Hindey. 1989. ABC BK. (J).

1989
†† Way Things Work. David Macaulay. 1988. Dorling Kindersley. (S).
†† Why Do People Smoke? Pete Sanders. 1988. Watts. (J).

1988
†† Conker. Barrie Watts. 1987. A & C Black. (J).
†† Making a Book. Ruth Thomson. Photos by Chris Fairclough. 1987. Watts. (J).
†† Martin Luther King. Valerie Schloredt & Pam Brown. 1987. Exley. (S).

1987
†† Being Born. Sheila Kitzinger. 1986. Dorling Kindersley. (J).
†† Galaxies and Quasars. Heather Couper & Nigel Henbest. 1986. Watts. (S).
†† Ultimate Alphabet. Mike Wilks. 1986. Pavilion. (S).

1986
†† Legend of Odysseus. Peter Connolly. 1985. Oxford University Pr. (S).
†† Polar Regions. Terry Jennings. 1985. Oxford Univ Pr. (J).

1985
†† Growing Up: Adolescence, Body Changes and Sex. Susan Meredith. 1984. Usborne Pub. (S).
†† KwaZulu South Africa. Nancy D. McKenna. 1984. A & C Black. (J).
†† Sunday Times Countryside Companion. Geoffrey Young. 1984. Country Life Bks. (S).

1984
†† In Deutschland. Rod Nash. 1983. Nelson. (S).

1983
†† Just Imagine. Robert Cumming. 1982. Kestrel. (S).
†† Mum, I Feel Funny. Ann McPherson & Aidan MacFarlane. 1982. Chatto. (J).

Western Heritage Awards

Sponsored by the National Cowboy Hall of Fame since 1961, the children's literature category of these awards was first recognized in 1962. Juvenile books published in the preceding year are eligible, and are judged for their "artistic merit, integrity, and outstanding achievement in portraying the spirit of the pioneers of the developing West." The winner receives a trophy. No award was presented in 1978.

1993
Indian Winter. Russell Freedman. Illus. by Karl Bodmer. 1992. Holiday.

1992
Monster Slayer: A Navajo Folktale. Vee Browne. Illus. by Baje Whitethorne. 1991. Northland AZ.

1991
Bunk House Journal. Diane Johnston Hamm. 1990. Macmillan.

1990
Letters to Oma: A Young German Girl's Account of Her First Year in Texas, 1847. Marj Gurasich. Illus. by Barbara Whitehead. 1989. Tex Christian.

1989
Stay Put, Robbie McAmiss. Frances G. Tunbo. Illus. by Charles Shaw. 1988. Tex Christian.

1988
Covered Wagon & Other Adventures. Lynn Scott. 1987. University of Nebraska Press.

1987
Happily May I Walk: American Indians & Alaska Natives Today. Arlene Hirschfelder. 1986. (Pub. by Scribner). Macmillan.

1986
Prairie Song. Pam Conrad. Illus. by Darryl S. Zudeck. 1985. HarpJ.

1984
Children of the Wild West. Russell Freedman. 1983. (Clarion). HM.

Western Writers of America Spur Awards

The Golden Spur Award has been sponsored by the Western Writers of America since 1953 to "recognize the advancement of meritorious writing in western literature, both fiction and non-fiction." Several categories are recognized -- among them is the Best Western Juvenile Book (fiction or non-fiction). The winner receives a plaque.

1987
Make Way For Sam Houston. Jean Fritz. 1986. (Putnam). Putnam Pub Group.

1986
Prairie Songs. Pam Conrad. Illus. by Darryl Zuedeck. 1985. HarpJ.

1985
Trapped in Sliprock Canyon. Gloria Skurzynski. Illus. by Daniel S. Soucie. 1984. Lothrop.

1984
Thunder on the Tennessee. Gary C. Wisler. 1983. (Loderstar Bks). Dutton.

1983
Before the Lark. Irene B. Brown. 1982. Atheneum.

Whitbread Awards

The Whitbread Awards founded in 1971 by the Whitbread Brewery (London, England), is an annual award intended to promote a high standard of English Literature. In 1972 the children's book category was added to represent children's books for ages 7 and up, published in the United Kingdom or the Republic of Ireland, and written by an author who has lived in the United Kingdom or Ireland for five years. A monetary prize of 3,000 English pounds is awarded the winner.

1991
Harvey Angell. Diana Hendry. 1990. Julia MacRae.

1990
†† AK. Peter Dickinson. Gollancz.

1989
†† Why Weeps the Brogan? Hugh Scott. Walker Bks.

1988
†† Awaiting Developments. Judy Allen. Julia MacRae.

1987
†† Little Lower than the Angels. Geraldine McCaughrean. Oxford Univ.

1986
†† Coal House. Andrew Taylor. Collins.

1985
†† Nature of the Beast. Janni Howker. Julia MacRae.

1984
†† Queen of the Pharisees' Children. Barbara Willard. Julia MacRae.

1983
†† Witches. Roald Dahl. Cape.

Carter G. Woodson Book Award

Established in 1973 in honor of the black historian and educator, Carter G. Woodson, this annual award is sponsored by the National Council for the Social Studies. It is intended to "encourage the writing, publishing and dissemination of outstanding social studies books for young readers, which treat topics related to ethnic minority and race relations sensitively and accurately." Non-fiction books with a United States setting, published in the United States during the preceding year are eligible. The winner receives a plaque.

1990
In Two Worlds: A Yup'ik Eskimo Family. Aylette Jenness & Alice Rivers. 1989. HM.
Paul Robeson: Hero Before His Tme. Rebecca Larsen. 1989. Watts.

1989
Walking the Road to Freedom: A Story about Sojourner Truth. Jeri Ferris. Illus. by Peter E. Hanson. 1988. Carolrhoda Bks.

1988
Black Music in America: A History Through Its People. James Haskins. 1987. (Crowell Jr Bks). HarpJ.

1987
Happily May I Walk. Arlene Hirschfelder. 1986. (Pub. by Scribner). Macmillan.

1986
Dark Harvest: Migrant Farmworkers in America. Brent Ashabranner. Photos by Paul Conklin. 1985. Dodd.

1985
To Live in Two Worlds: American Indian Youth Today. Brent Ashabranner. Photos by Paul Conklin. 1984. Dodd.

1984
Mexico & the United States: Their Linked Destinies. E. B. Fincher. 1983. Crowell Jr Bks.

1983
Morning Star, Black Sun: The Cheyenne Indians & America's Energy Crisis. Brent Ashabranner. Photos by Paul Conklin. 1982. Dodd.

BODY OF WORK AWARDS

Hans Christian Andersen Awards

The Hans Christian Andersen Awards were established in 1956, and "given biennially by the International Board on Books for Young People (IBBY) to one author (since 1956) and one illustrator (since 1966)." It is one of the most distinguished international prizes given in children's literature. The complete works of the author and illustrator are considered and judged according to their artistic and literary contents. For both medals the nominees, selected by each national section of IBBY, must be living at the time of their nomination. Winners receive gold medals. Diplomas are given to the runners-up.

1992
Virginia Hamilton (American : Author)
Kveta Pacovska (Czech : Illustrator)

1991
No Award

1990
Tormod Haugen (Norwegian : Author)
Lisbeth Zwerger (Austrian : Illustrator)

1988
Annie M. G. Schmidt (Holland : Author)
Dusan Kallay (Yugoslavia : Illustrator)

1986
Patricia Wrightson (Australia : Author)
Robert Ingpen (Australia : Illustrator)

1984
Christine Nostlinger (Austria : Author)
Mitsumasa Anno (Japan : Illustrator)

1982
Lygia Bojunga Nunes (Brazil : Author)
Zbigniew Rychlicki (Poland : Illustrator)

1980
Bohumil Riha (Czechoslovakia : Author)
Suekichi Akaba (Japan : Illustrator)

**The Association of Jewish Libraries—
Sydney Taylor Body of Work Award**

First presented in 1978, this annual award honors an author's entire body of work. The recipient is an author whose work must have made the most outstanding contribution in the field of Jewish Literature for children and young people, have withstood time and have had a positive effect on its readers. Each winner receives a plaque. (Please refer to "The Association of Jewish Libraries…" title award in the main section—Children's Book Awards 1979–1989, for additional information.)

1993
No Award

1992
No Award

1991
No Award

1990
Yaffa Ganz

1984
Miriam Chaikin

1983
No Award

1982
No Award

1981
Barbara Cohen

Eva L. Gordon Award for Children's Science Literature

This award was founded by the American Nature Study Society in 1964 and is given annually in the honor of Eva L. Gordon, "author, reviewer and professor of Children's Science Literature at Cornell University." The award honors the body of work of an author or illustrator whose books reflect the high standards of good attitudes, understanding of interrelationships, accuracy, readability, represents new adventure, scientific observations, joyousness and timeliness, while they extend either directly or subtly an invitation to the child to become involved." The winner is awarded a certificate.

1993
Augusta Goldin

1992
Byrd Baylor

1991
Jim Arnosky

1990
Joanne Cole

1989
Ada & Frank Graham

1988
Franklyn Branley

1987
Patricia Lauber

1986
Dorothy H. Patent

1985
Vicki Cobb

1984
Seymour Simon

1983
Lawrence Pringle

1982
Peter Parnall

1981
Herbert Zim

Kerlan Award

Established in 1975 by the Kerlan Collection Twenty-fifth Anniversary Committee, the award is given annually "in recognition of singular attainments in the creation of children's literature, and in appreciation for generous donations of unique resources to the Kerlan Collection for the study of children's literature." The winner is presented with a plaque.

1993
Mary Stolc

1992
Barbara Cooney

1991
Leonard Everett Fisher

1990
Madeleine L'Engle

1989
Gail Haley

1988
Jane Yolen

1987
Charles Mikolaycak

1986
Charlotte Zolotow

1985
Eleanor Cameron

1984
Margaret Wise Brown

1983
Katherine Paterson

1982
Jean Craighead George

1981
Tomie de Paola

Lucky Four-Leaf Clover Award

The Lucky Book Club Four-Leaf Clover Award was established in 1971 "to recognize an author's contribution to the reading pleasures of seven and eight year olds." To be eligible for this award, works by the author "must be familiar to and popular with the readers of the Lucky Book Club Books."
"A photograph of the winning author is sent to teachers for posting on classroom bulletin boards. A copy of this photograph is framed and presented to the winning author." There has been no award since 1983, and only recently (1989) the committee discontinued it.

1983
Betty Polisar Reigot

1982
Arnold Lobel

1981
Nancy K. Robinson

The Vicky Metcalf Award

The Vicky Metcalf Award, founded by Vicky Metcalf in 1963, is administered by the Canadian Authors Association. It is offered annually to a Canadian author (citizen or landed immigrant) who has published a body of work comprising a "minimum of four books—fiction, non-fiction, poetry or picture books inspirational to young people." The winner is announced at the Association's conference, and is presented with a prize of $2,000.

1992
Kevin Major

1991
Brian Doyle

1990
Berneice Thurman Hunter

1989
Stephane Poulin

1988
Barbara Smucker

1987
Robert Munsch

1986
Dennis Lee

1985
Edith Fowke

1984
Bill Freeman

1983
Claire Mackay

1982
Janet Lunn

1981
Monica Hughes

National Council of Teachers of English Award for Excellence in Poetry for Children

First presented by the National Council of Teachers of English in 1977, the award is given annually to a living American poet in recognition of his/her cumulated works in poetry. Since 1982 the award has been presented every three years. The winner receives a plaque.

1991
Valerie Worth

1988
Arnold Adoff

1985
Lilian Moore

1982
John Ciardi

1981
Eve Merriam

Regina Medal

The Regina Medal was established in 1959 by the Catholic Library Association. Its purpose is to "recognize an individual for continued distinguished contributions to children's literature." The recipient receives the Regina Medal, which is an oval shaped silver medal.

1993
Chris Van Allsburg

1992
Jane Yolen

1991
Leonard Everett Fisher

1990
Virginia Hamilton

1989
Stephen Kellogg

1988
Katherine Paterson

1987
Betsy Byars

1986
Lloyd Alexander

1985
Jean Fritz

1984
Madeleine L'Engle

1983
Tomie de Paola

1982
Theodor Seuss Geisel

1981
Augusta Baker

George G. Stone Center for Children's Books—Recognition of Merit Award (Body of Work)

This Recognition of Merit Award is an annual award which was established in 1964 by Priscilla Neff Fenn. It is given to "an author or artist of a children's book, or for a body of work for its power to please and to heighten the awareness of children and teachers as they have shared in the classrooms." The book or body of work should also have the capacity to arouse in children an awareness of the complexity and the beauty of the expanding universe. A hand-lettered scroll is given to the winning author or artist. For the years 1980, 1984, and 1987-1990, awards were not presented in this category. (Please refer to "George G. Stone Center for Children's Books..." Title Award in the main section—Children's Book Awards 1979-1989, for additional information.)

1993
Gary Soto

1992
Mitsumasa A.

1991
No Award

1986
Tanna Hoban

1985
Bill Peet

1983
Beverly Cleary

1982
Mary Stolz

1981
No Award

University of Southern Mississippi Medallion

This award honors an author or illustrator of an entire body of work who has made an outstanding contribution to the field of children's literature. The nominees are received from "publishers, authors, illustrators, professors, and anyone else interested in children's literature." The winner, chosen by a majority vote cast by a committee composed of authors, librarians, and children's literature specialists, receives a silver medallion.

1992
James Marshall

1991
Richard Peck

1990
Charlotte Zolotow

1989
Lee Bennett Hopkins

1988
Jean Fritz

1987
Paula Fox

1986
Jean Craighead George

1985
Arnold Lobel

1984
Peter Spier

1983
Katherine Paterson

1982
Beverly Cleary

1981
Maurice Sendak

Laura Ingalls Wilder Award

First awarded in 1954 and administered by the Association for Library Service to Children, the Laura Ingalls Wilder Award was given every five years from 1960-1980. However, since 1983 the award has been given every three years. It honors an author or illustrator whose books, published in the United States, have made a substantial and lasting contribution to children's literature. The winner receives a bronze medal.

1992
Marsha Brown

1989
Elizabeth George Speare

1986
Jean Fritz

1983
Maurice Sendak

AUTHOR INDEX

A

AAIB Home Economics Workshop Cookbook Committee Staff. Food at Your Fingertips. large type ed. 116p. (gr. 3 up). 1958. loose-leaf bdg. 29.00 (0-317-01887-6, J-06850-00) Am Printing Hse.

Aamodt, Alice, jt. auth. see Johnson, Sylvia A.

Aamundsen, Nina R. Two Short & One Long. 112p. (gr. 4-8). 1990. 13.50 (0-395-52434-2) HM.

Aardema, Verna. Anansi Finds a Fool. Waldman, Bryna, illus. LC 91-21127. 32p. (ps-3). 1992. 14.00 (0-8037-1164-6); PLB 13.89 (0-8037-1165-4) Dial Bks Young.

—Bimwili & the Zimwi. Meddaugh, Susan, illus. LC 85-4449. 32p. (ps-3). 1985. 14.99 (0-8037-0212-4); PLB 12.89 (0-8037-0213-2) Dial Bks Young.

—Bimwili & the Zimwi. Meddaugh, Susan, illus. LC 85-4449. 32p. (Orig.). (ps-3). 1988. pap. 4.95 (0-8037-0553-0) Dial Bks Young.

—Bringing the Rain to Kapiti Plain. Vidal, Beatriz, illus. LC 80-25886. 32p. (ps). 1981. 14.95 (0-8037-0809-2); PLB 13.89 (0-8037-0807-6) Dial Bks Young.

—Bringing the Rain to Kapiti Plain. Vidal, Beatriz, illus. 32p. (ps-2). 1983. pap. 3.95 (0-8037-0904-8, Dial Pied Piper) Puffin Bks.

—Bringing the Rain to Kapiti Plain. (ps-3). 1992. pap. 4.99 (0-14-054616-2) Puffin Bks.

—Bringing the Rain to Kapiti Plain: A Nandi Tale. Vidal, Beatriz, illus. (ps-3). 1993. pap. 6.99 incl. cassette (0-14-095052-4, Puffin) Puffin Bks.

—Oh, Kojo! How Could You? Brown, Marc, illus. LC 84-1710. 32p. (ps-3). 1984. 14.00 (0-8037-0006-7); PLB 12.89 (0-8037-0007-5) Dial Bks Young.

—Oh, Kojo! How Could You! Brown, Marc, illus. LC 84-1710. 32p. (ps-3). 1988. pap. 4.99 (0-8037-0449-6) Dial Bks Young.

—Pedro & the Padre. Henstra, Friso, illus. LC 87-24476. 32p. (ps-3). 1991. 12.95 (0-8037-0522-0); PLB 12.89 (0-8037-0523-9) Dial Bks Young.

—Princess Gorilla & a New Kind of Water. Chase, Victoria, illus. LC 86-32888. 32p. (ps-3). 1988. 10.95 (0-8037-0412-7); PLB 10.89 (0-8037-0413-5) Dial Bks Young.

—Princess Gorilla & a New Kind of Water. Chess, Victoria, illus. LC 86-32888. 32p. (ps-3). 1991. pap. 3.95 (0-8037-0914-5, Dial Pied Piper) Puffin Bks.

—Rabbit Makes a Monkey of Lion. Pinkney, Jerry, illus. LC 86-11523. 32p. (ps-3). 1989. 11.95 (0-8037-0297-3); PLB 11.89 (0-8037-0298-1) Dial Bks Young.

—Sebgugugu the Glutton. Clouse, Nancy, illus. 40p. (gr. k-4). 1993. text ed. 14.99 (0-8028-5073-1) Eerdmans.

—The Vingananee & the Tree Toad. Weiss, Ellen, illus. (gr. 3-8). 1988. pap. 4.99 (0-14-050890-2, Puffin) Puffin Bks.

—What's So Funny, Ketu? Brown, Marc, illus. LC 82-70195. 32p. (ps-3). 1989. pap. 4.95 (0-8037-0646-4) Dial Bks Young.

—What's So Funny Ketu? (ps-3). 1992. pap. 4.99 (0-14-054722-3) Puffin Bks.

—Why Mosquitoes Buzz in People's Ears: A West African Tale. Dillon, Leo & Dillon, Diane, illus. LC 77-71514. (ps-3). 1978. pap. 4.95 (0-8037-6088-4, Dial Pied Piper) Puffin Bks.

—Why Mosquitoes Buzz in People's Ears: A West African Tale. Dillon, Leo & Dillon, Diane, illus. LC 74-2886. 32p. (ps-3). 1975. 15.00 (0-8037-6089-2); PLB 14.89 (0-8037-6087-6) Dial Bks Young.

Aardema, Verna & Clouse, Nancy. Sebugugugu the Glutton: A Bantu Tale from Ruanda, Africa. (Illus.). 32p. (gr. 2-4). 1993. 14.95 (0-86543-377-1) Africa World.

Aardema, Verna, retold by. & tr. Borreguita & the Coyote: A Tale from Ayutla, Mexico. Mathers, Peter, illus. LC 90-39419. 40p. (ps-3). 1991. 15.00 (0-679-80921-X); lib. bdg. 15.99 (0-679-90921-4) Knopf Bks Yng Read.

Aardema, Verna, compiled by. Misoso: Once Upon a Time Tales from Africa. Ruffins, Reynold, illus. LC 92-43288. (gr. 4 up). 1994. 18.00 (0-679-83430-3); lib. bdg. 18.99 (0-679-93430-8) Knopf.

Aardema, Verna, retold by. Rabbit Makes a Monkey of Lion: A Swahili Tale. Pinkney, Jerry, illus. 32p. (ps-3). 1993. pap. 4.99 (0-14-054593-X) Puffin Bks.

—Traveling to Tondo: A Tale of the Nkundo of Zaire. Hillenbrand, Will, illus. LC 90-39419. 40p. (gr. k-4). 1991. 14.00 (0-679-80081-6); PLB 14.99 (0-679-90081-0) Knopf Bks Yng Read.

—Who's in Rabbit's House? Dillon, Leo & Dillon, Diane, illus. LC 77-71514. 32p. (gr. k-3). 1977. PLB 14.89 (0-8037-9551-3) Dial Bks Young.

—Who's in Rabbit's House? Dillon, Leo & Dillon, Diane, illus. LC 77-71514. 32p. (ps-3). 1979. pap. 4.95 (0-8037-9549-1) Dial Bks Young.

—Why Mosquitoes Buzz in People's Ears: A West African Tale. giant ed. Dillon, Leo & Dillon, Diane, illus. 32p. (ps-3). 1993. pap. 17.99 (0-14-054589-1) Puffin Bks.

—Why Mosquitoes Buzz in People's Ears: A West African Tale. Dillon, Leo & Dillon, Diane, illus. 32p. (ps-3). Date not set. pap. 4.99 (0-14-054905-6) Puffin Bks.

—Why Mosquitoes Buzz in People's Ears Read-Aloud Set. Dillon, Leo & Dillon, Diane, illus. (ps-3). 1993. Set incls. 1 Giant copy, 6 paperbacks, giant-sized bookmark & tchr's. guide in a free- standing easel. pap. 47.93 (0-14-778979-6) Puffin Bks.

Aaron, Chester. Alex, Who Won His War. 144p. (gr. 5 up). 1991. 17.95 (0-8027-8098-9) Walker & Co.

—Gideon. large type ed. 200p. (gr. 7-10). 1984. Repr. of 1982 ed. 55.61 (0-317-01893-0, 4-08540-00) Am Printing Hse.

Aaron, Gregory. Weather Tracker's Kit. (Illus.). 64p. (Orig.). (gr. 3 up). 1991. incl. weather station 16.95 (0-89471-998-X) Running Pr.

Aaron, I., et al. Scott, Foresman Reading. large type ed. Incl. Level 2C - Pre-Primer 3 - On Our Own. 88p. (ps). 1982. 15.61 (0-317-04468-0, 4-33640-00); Level 3 - Primer - Hang on to Your Hats. 236p. (ps). 1981. 60.00 (0-317-04469-9, J-33670-00); wkbk., 100p. o.p. 18.98 (0-317-04470-2, 4-33680-00); end-of-bk. test, 20p. 5.24 (0-317-04471-0, 4-33690-00); Level 4 - Kick up Your Heels, 2 vols. 284p. (gr. 1). Text, Vols. 1 & 2. 76.50 (0-317-04472-9, J-33700-00); wkbk., 100p. 18. 98 (0-317-04473-7, 4-33710-00); end-of-bk. test, 20p. 5.24 (0-317-04474-5, 4-33720-00); Level 5 - Rainbow Shower, 2 vols. 304p. (gr. 2). 1982. Vols. 1 & 2. 77.00 (0-317-04475-3, J-33730-00); Vols. Pts. 1 & 2, 236p. wkbk. 41.36 (0-317-04476-1, 4-33740-00); end-of-bk. test 7.00 (0-317-04477-X, 4-33750-00); Level 6 - Crystal Kingdom, 2 vols. 336p. (gr. 2). 1981. Vols. 1 & 2. 96.50 (0-317-04478-8, J-33760-00); Vols. 1 & 2, 234p. wkbk. 41.36 (0-317-04479-6, 4-33770-00); end-of-bk. test o.p. 7.00 (0-317-04480-X, 4-33780-00); Level 7 - Hidden Wonders, 2 vols. 396p. (gr. 3). 1982. (4-33800-00) (4-33810-00); Level 8 - Golden Secrets, 2 vols. 402p. (gr. 3). 1982. Vols. 1 & 2. 106.00 (0-317-04484-2, J-33820-00); Vols. 1 & 2, 232p. wkbk. 41.36 (0-317-04485-0, 4-33830-00); end-of-bk. test o.p. 7.00 (0-317-04486-9, 4-33840-00); Level 9 - Sea Treasures, 3 vols. 590p. (gr. 4). 1982. Vols. 1-3. 147. 50 (0-317-04487-7, J-33850-00); Vols. 1 & 2, 332p. wkbk. 85.00 (0-317-04488-5, J-33860-00); end-of-bk. test o.p. 8.68 (0-317-04489-3, 4-33870-00); Level 10 - Sky Climbers, 3 vols. 652p. (gr. 5). 1982. Vols. 1-3. 151.67 (0-317-04490-7, 4-33880-00); Vols. 1 & 2, 328p. wkbk. 58.72 (0-317-04491-5, 4-33890-00); end-of-bk. test 8.68 (0-317-04492-3, 4-33900-00); Level 11 - Star Flight, 3 vols. 632p. (gr. 6). 1982. Vols. 1-3. 202.50 (0-317-04493-1, J-33910-00); Vols. 1 & 2, 328p. wkbk. 58.72 (0-317-04494-X, 4-33920-00); end-of-bk. test 8.68 (0-317-04495-8, 4-33930-00). (ps-6) Am Printing Hse.

Aaseng, Nathan. Animal Specialists. Dornisch, Alcuin C., illus. 48p. (gr. k-3). 1987. PLB 10.95 (0-8225-1120-7) Lerner Pubns.

—At Left Linebacker, Chip Demory. LC 87-30905. (gr. 3-7). 1988. pap. 4.49 (1-55513-921-3, Chariot Bks) Cook.

—Barry Sanders. LC 93-6173. 1994. write for info. (0-89490-484-1) Enslow Pubs.

—Baseball: It's Your Team. (gr. k-12). 1987. pap. 2.50 (0-440-90507-9, LFL) Dell.

—Baseball: You Are the Manager. LC 82-268. (Illus.). 104p. (gr. 4up). 1983. PLB 14.95 (0-8225-1552-0) Lerner Pubns.

—Baseball's Finest Pitchers. LC 80-12275. (Illus.). 72p. (gr. 4 up). 1980. PLB 11.95 (0-8225-1061-8) Lerner Pubns.

—Baseball's Greatest Teams. (Illus.). 80p. (gr. 4 up). 1985. PLB 15.95 (0-8225-1526-1) Lerner Pubns.

—Basketball's High Flyers. Aaseng, Nathan, photos by. LC 79-17137. (Illus.). 80p. (gr. 4 up) 1980. PLB 11.95 (0-8225-1058-8) Lerner Pubns.

—Basketball's Playmakers. LC 83-1041. (Illus.). 80p. (gr. 4up). 1983. PLB 11.95 (0-8225-1330-7) Lerner Pubns.

—Better Mousetraps: Product Improvements That Led to Success. (Illus.). 80p. (gr. 5 up). 1989. PLB 18.95 (0-8225-0680-7) Lerner Pubns.

—Breaking the Sound Barrier. 1992. lib. bdg. 12.98 (0-671-74212-4, J Messner) S&S Trade.

—Breaking the Sound Barrier. 1992. lib. bdg. 7.95 (0-671-74213-2, J Messner) S&S Trade.

—Carl Lewis: Legend Chaser. LC 84-23348. (Illus.). 56p. (gr. 4-9). 1985. PLB 13.50 (0-8225-0496-0) Lerner Pubns.

—Cerebral Palsy. (Illus.). 112p. (gr. 9-12). 1991. PLB 13.40 (0-531-12529-7) Watts.

—Charles Darwin: Revolutionary Biologist. LC 92-45281. 1993. 21.50 (0-8225-4914-X) Lerner Pubns.

—Close Calls: From the Brink of Ruin to Business Success. (Illus.). 80p. (gr. 5 up). 1990. PLB 18.95 (0-8225-0682-3) Lerner Pubns.

—College Basketball: You Are the Coach. LC 83-19996. (Illus.). 104p. (gr. 4 up). 1984. lib. bdg. 13.50 (0-8225-1555-5) Lerner Pubns.

—College Football: You Are the Coach. LC 83-22193. (Illus.). 104p. (gr. 4 up). 1984. lib. bdg. 13.50 (0-8225-1556-3) Lerner Pubns.

—Comeback Stars of Pro Sports. LC 83-737. (Illus.). 80p. (gr. 4up). 1983. PLB 11.95 (0-8225-1327-7) Lerner Pubns.

—The Common Cold & the Flu. LC 92-15137. (Illus.). 128p. (gr. 9-12). 1992. PLB 13.40 (0-531-12537-8) Watts.

—A Decade of Champions: Super Bowls XVI-XXIV. (Illus.). 64p. (gr. 5 up). 1991. PLB 15.95 (0-8225-1504-0) Lerner Pubns.

—The Disease Fighters: The Nobel Prize in Medicine. (Illus.). 80p. (gr. 5 up). 1987. PLB 17.50 (0-8225-0652-1) Lerner Pubns.

—The Disease Fighters: The Nobel Prize in Medicine. 120p. (gr. 5 up). 1987. 9.60 (0-685-63800-6, BR7856) W A T Braille.

—Dwight Gooden: Strikeout King. (Illus.). 56p. (gr. 4-9). 1988. PLB 13.50 (0-8225-0478-2, First Ave Edns); pap. 4.95 (0-8225-9549-4, First Ave Edns) Lerner Pubns.

—Ending World Hunger. LC 90-46207. (Illus.). 144p. (gr. 9-12). 1991. PLB 13.90 (0-531-11007-9) Watts.

—Florence Griffith Joyner: Dazzling Olympian. (Illus.). 56p. (gr. 4-9). 1989. PLB 13.50 (0-8225-0495-2) Lerner Pubns.

—Florence Griffith Joyner: Dazzling Olympian. 1991. pap. 3.95 (0-8225-9587-7) Lerner Pubns.

—Football: It's Your Team. (Illus.). 104p. (gr. 4 up). 1985. PLB 13.50 (0-8225-1557-1) Lerner Pubns.

—Football: It's Your Team. (gr. k-12). 1987. pap. 2.50 (0-440-92648-3, LFL) Dell.

—Football's Breakaway Backs. LC 80-16691. (Illus.). 72p. (gr. 4 up). 1980. PLB 11.95 (0-8225-1063-4) Lerner Pubns.

—Football's Cunning Coaches. LC 80-29252. (Illus.). 80p. (gr. 4 up). 1981. PLB 11.95 (0-8225-1065-0) Lerner Pubns.

—Football's Fierce Defenses. Aaseng, Nathan, photos by. LC 79-16315. (Illus.). 72p. (gr. 4 up). 1980. PLB 11.95 (0-8225-1057-X) Lerner Pubns.

—Football's Most Controversial Calls. (Illus.). 72p. (gr. 4 up). 1985. PLB 15.95 (0-8225-1528-8) Lerner Pubns.

—Football's Most Shocking Upsets. (Illus.). 80p. (gr. 4 up). 1985. PLB 15.95 (0-8225-1529-6) Lerner Pubns.

—Football's Super Bowl Champions: I-VIII. LC 81-13659. (Illus.). 80p. (gr. 4 up). 1982. PLB 11.95 (0-8225-1072-3) Lerner Pubns.

—Football's Super Bowl Champions: IX-XVI. LC 82-10099. (Illus.). 72p. (gr. 4 up). 1982. PLB 11.95 (0-8225-1333-1) Lerner Pubns.

—Football's Sure-Handed Receivers. LC 80-17762. (Illus.). 72p. (gr. 4 up). 1980. PLB 11.95 (0-8225-1064-2) Lerner Pubns.

—Football's Winning Quarterbacks. LC 80-12074. (Illus.). 80p. (gr. 4 up). 1980. PLB 11.95 (0-8225-1062-6) Lerner Pubns.

—The Fortunate Fortunes: Business Successes That Began with a Lucky Break. (Illus.). 80p. (gr. 5 up). 1989. lib. bdg. 18.95 (0-8225-0678-5) Lerner Pubns.

—From Rags to Riches: People Who Started Businesses from Scratch. (Illus.). 80p. (gr. 5 up). 1990. PLB 18.95 (0-8225-0679-3) Lerner Pubns.

—Great Justices of the Supreme Court. LC 92-18443. 160p. (gr. 5-12). 1992. PLB 14.95 (1-881508-01-3) Oliver Pr MN.

—Great Summer Olympic Moments. (Illus.). 72p. (gr. 4 up). 1990. PLB 14.95 (0-8225-1536-9) Lerner Pubns.

—Great Winter Olympic Moments. (Illus.). 72p. (gr. 4 up). 1990. PLB 14.95 (0-8225-1535-0) Lerner Pubns.

—Hockey: You Are the Coach. LC 82-17170. (Illus.). 104p. (gr. 4up). 1983. PLB 13.50 (0-8225-1554-7) Lerner Pubns.

—Hockey's Fearless Goalies. LC 83-17512. (Illus.). 80p. (gr. 4 up). 1984. PLB 11.95 (0-8225-1341-2) Lerner Pubns.

—Hockey's Super Scorers. LC 83-17511. (Illus.). 80p. (gr. 4up). 1984. PLB 11.95 (0-8225-1340-4) Lerner Pubns.

—Horned Animals. Dornisch, Alcuin C., illus. 48p. (gr. k-3). 1987. PLB 10.95 (0-8225-1119-3) Lerner Pubns.

—I'm Learning, Lord, but I Still Need Help: Story Devotions for Boys. LC 81-65652. 112p. (Orig.). (gr. 3-7). 1981. pap. 5.99 (0-8066-1888-4, 10-3202, Augsburg) Augsburg Fortress.

—I'm Searching, Lord, but I Need Your Light. LC 82-72644. 112p. (gr. 3-6). 1983. pap. 5.99 (0-8066-1950-3, 10-3203, Augsburg) Augsburg Fortress.

—The Inventors: Nobel Prizes in Chemistry, Physics, & Medicine. (Illus.). 80p. (gr. 4 up). 1988. PLB 17.50 (0-8225-0651-3) Lerner Pubns.

—Invertebrates. (Illus.). 112p. (gr. 7-12). 1993. PLB 13.40 (0-531-12550-5) Watts.

—Jerry Rice: Touchdown Talent. LC 93-10010. 1993. 13.50 (0-8225-0521-5) Lerner Pubns.

—Jim Henson: Muppet Master. (Illus.). 40p. (gr. 4-9). 1988. 13.50 (0-8225-1615-2) Lerner Pubns.

—Jose Canseco: Baseball's Forty-Forty Man. (Illus.). 56p. (gr. 4-9). 1989. PLB 13.50 (0-8225-0493-6) Lerner Pubns.

—Jose Canseco: Baseball's Forty-Forty Man. 1991. pap. 4.95 (0-8225-9586-9) Lerner Pubns.

—Little Giants of Pro Sports. LC 80-12031. (Illus.). 64p. (gr. 4 up). 1983. PLB 11.95 (0-8225-1059-6) Lerner Pubns.

—The Locker Room Mirror: How Sports Reflect Society. LC 92-34582. (Illus.). 144p. (gr. 5 up). 1993. 14.95 (0-8027-8217-5); PLB 15.85 (0-8027-8218-3) Walker & Co.

—Meat-Eating Animals. Dornisch, Alcuin C., illus. 48p. (gr. k-3). 1987. PLB 10.95 (0-8225-1118-5) Lerner Pubns.

—Memorable World Series Moments. LC 81-13725. (Illus.). 80p. (gr. 4 up). 1982. PLB 11.95 (0-8225-1073-1) Lerner Pubns.

—Midstream Changes: People Who Started over & Made It Work. (Illus.). 80p. (gr. 5 up). 1990. PLB 18.95 (0-8225-0681-5) Lerner Pubns.

—Navajo Code Talkers. LC 91-11408. 114p. 1992. 14.95 (0-8027-8182-9); PLB 15.85 (0-8027-8183-7) Walker & Co.

—Overpopulation: Crisis or Challenge? (Illus.). 160p. (gr. 9-12). 1991. PLB 13.90 (0-531-11006-0) Watts.

—Paris. LC 92-709. (Illus.). 96p. (gr. 6 up) 1992. RSBE 13.95 (0-02-700010-9, New Discovery) Macmillan Child Grp.

—The Peace Seekers: The Nobel Peace Prize. (Illus.). 80p. (gr. 5 up). 1987. PLB 17.50 (0-8225-0654-8) Lerner Pubns.

—Peace Seekers: The Nobel Peace Prize. (gr. 4-7). 1991. pap. 5.95 (0-8225-9604-0) Lerner Pubns.

—Prey Animals. Dornisch, Alcuin, illus. 48p. (gr. k-3). 1987. PLB 10.95 (0-8225-1121-5) Lerner Pubns.

—The Problem Solvers: People Who Turned Problems into Products. (Illus.). 80p. (gr. 5 up). 1989. lib. bdg. 18.95 (0-8225-0675-0) Lerner Pubns.

—Record Breakers of Pro Sports. (Illus.). 80p. (gr. 4 up). 1987. PLB 14.95 (0-8225-1533-4) Lerner Pubns.

—The Rejects: People & Products That Outsmarted the Experts. (Illus.). 80p. (gr. 5 up). 1989. 18.95 (0-8225-0677-7) Lerner Pubns.

—Robert E. Lee. (Illus.). 112p. (gr. 5 up). 1991. PLB 21.50 (0-8225-4909-3) Lerner Pubns.

—Science or Pseudoscience? ESP, UFOs, & Other Dubious Claims. LC 93-30014. 1994. write for info. (0-531-11182-2) Watts.

—Sports Great David Robinson. LC 91-41532. (Illus.). 64p. (gr. 4-10). 1992. lib. bdg. 15.95 (0-89490-373-X) Enslow Pubs.

—Sports Great Kirby Puckett. (Illus.). 64p. (gr. 4-10). 1993. lib. bdg. 15.95 (0-89490-392-6) Enslow Pubs.

—Sports Great Michael Jordan. LC 91-11607. (Illus.). 64p. (gr. 4-10). 1992. lib. bdg. 15.95 (0-89490-370-5) Enslow Pubs.

—Superstars Stopped Short. LC 81-12431. (Illus.). 80p. (gr. 4 up). 1982. PLB 11.95 (0-8225-1326-9) Lerner Pubns.

—Track's Magnificent Milers. LC 80-27404. (Illus.). (gr. 4 up). 1981. PLB 11.95 (0-8225-1066-9) Lerner Pubns.

—True Champions: Great Athletes & Their Off-the-Field Heroics. LC 92-36942. (Illus.). 128p. (gr. 5 up). 1993. 14.95 (0-8027-8246-9); PLB 15.85 (0-8027-8247-7) Walker & Co.

—Twentieth Century Inventors. (Illus.). 128p. (gr. 7-12). 1991. 16.95x (0-8160-2485-5) Facts on File.

—Ultramarathons: The World's Most Punishing Races. (Illus.). 72p. (gr. 4 up). 1987. PLB 14.95 (0-8225-1534-2) Lerner Pubns.

—The Unsung Heroes: Unheralded People Who Invented Famous Products. (Illus.). 80p. (gr. 5 up). 1989. 18.95 (0-8225-0676-9) Lerner Pubns.

—Vertebrates. LC 93-13391. (Illus.). 112p. (gr. 7-12). 1993. PLB 13.40 (0-531-12551-3) Watts.

—Which Way Are You Leading Me, Lord? Bible Devotions for Boys. LC 84-21562. 112p. (Orig.). (gr. 3-7). 1984. pap. 5.99 (0-8066-2113-3, 10-7099, Augsburg) Augsburg Fortress.

—Winning Men of Tennis. LC 80-28598. (Illus.). 80p. (gr. 4 up). 1981. PLB 11.95 (0-8225-1068-5) Lerner Pubns.

—Winning Season for the Braves. LC 82-72711. (gr. 3-7). 1988. pap. 4.49 (1-55513-950-7, Chariot Bks) Cook.

—Winning Women of Tennis. LC 81-6033. (Illus.). 80p. (gr. 4 up). 1981. PLB 11.95 (0-8225-1067-7) Lerner Pubns.

—World-Class Marathoners. LC 81-13660. (Illus.). 80p. (gr. 4 up). 1982. PLB 11.95 (0-8225-1325-0) Lerner Pubns.

—You Are the Coach: College Football. (gr. 6-12). 1985. pap. 2.25 (0-440-99840-9, LFL) Dell.

—You Are the Coach: Football. (gr. 5 up). 1983. pap. 2.50 (0-440-99136-6, LFL) Dell.

—You Are the General. LC 93-11661. (Illus.). 160p. (gr. 5-12). 1994. PLB 14.95 (1-881508-11-0) Oliver Pr MN.

—You Are the Manager: Baseball. 112p. (gr. 5 up). 1984. pap. 1.95 (0-440-99829-8, LFL) Dell.

—You Are the President. LC 93-5776. (Illus.). 160p. (gr. 5-12). 1994. PLB 14.95 (1-881508-10-2) Oliver Pr MN.

Aba, Adam. The Secret of the Doo Dah House. Nagle, I., illus. LC 91-89270. 192p. (gr. 4-7). 1992. pap. 16.95 (1-878756-51-6) YCP Pubns.

Abajian, Diane. Praying & Doing the Stations of the Cross with Children. Read, Maryann, illus. 24p. (gr. 1-3). 1980. pap. 1.95 (0-89622-118-0) Twenty-Third.

Abbas, Kathleen, jt. auth. see Johnston, Dorothy G.

Abbay, Ellen. Noah Takes Two. LC 85-80406. 1985. 9.95 (0-9615015-0-2) Kudzu.

Abbazia, Patrick. Nathanael Greene: Commander of the American Continental Army in the South. Rahmas, Steve, ed. (gr. 7-12). 1976. lib. bdg. 4.95 incl. catalog cards (0-87157-587-6) SamHar Pr.

Abbe, George. The Larks. (gr. 7 up). 1974. pap. 8.95 (0-87233-033-8) Bauhan.

Abbey, Nancy & Wagman, Ellen. Saying No to Alcohol. Nelson, Mary, ed. (Illus.). 72p. 1987. tchrs. ed. 11.95 (0-941816-37-0) ETR Assocs.

Abbey, Randall. Octahedral: Eight Intermediate Piano Solos. 24p. (gr. 5-8). 1993. 3.95 (0-9636777-6-4) Aplomb Pub.

Abbott, Abbe, jt. auth. see Green, Paul.

Abbott, Donald. How the Wizard Came to Oz. Abbott, Donald, illus. (gr. 3 up). 1991. 19.95 (0-929605-15-2); pap. 9.95 (0-685-59165-4) Books Wonder.

—The Magic Chest of Oz. Abbott, Donald, illus. (gr. 3 up). 1993. 34.95 (0-929605-21-7); pap. 9.95 (0-929605-20-9) Books Wonder.

Abbott, Frank F. The Common People of Ancient Rome: Studies of Roman Life & Literature. LC 65-23487. (gr. 7 up). 1965. Repr. of 1911 ed. 25.00 (0-8196-0157-8) Biblo.

—A History & Description of Roman Political Institutions. 3rd ed. LC 63-10766. 451p. (gr. 7 up). 1910. 24.00 (0-8196-0117-9) Biblo.

—Society & Politics in Ancient Rome: Essays & Sketches. LC 63-10767. 267p. (gr. 7 up). 1909. 24.00 (0-8196-0118-7) Biblo.

Abbott, Jennie. The Boy Who Remembered Everything. Badenhop, Mary, illus. LC 87-14986. 96p. (gr. 5-8). 1988. PLB 9.89 (0-8167-1183-6); pap. text ed. 2.95 (0-8167-1184-4) Troll Assocs.

—Costume Party. Badenhop, Mary, illus. LC 87-14987. 96p. (gr. 5-8). 1988. PLB 9.89 (0-8167-1189-5); pap. text ed. 2.95 (0-8167-1190-9) Troll Assocs.

—The Ghost of Hanover Hill. Badenhop, Mary, illus. LC 87-14983. 96p. (gr. 5-8). 1988. PLB 9.89 (0-8167-1185-2); pap. text ed. 2.95 (0-8167-1186-0) Troll Assocs.

—The Most Beautiful Dog in the World. Badenhop, Mary, illus. LC 87-14985. 96p. (gr. 5-8). 1988. PLB 9.89 (0-8167-1187-9); pap. text ed. 2.95 (0-8167-1188-7) Troll Assocs.

Abbott, Marti & Polk, Betty J. About Me. (gr. k-4). 1991. 10.95 (0-8224-0491-5) Fearon Teach Aids.

—Bunnies, Bears & Birthdays. (gr. k-4). 1991. 10.95 (0-8224-0638-1) Fearon Teach Aids.

—Clouds, Rain, Wind & Snow. (gr. k-4). 1991. 10.95 (0-8224-1351-5) Fearon Teach Aids.

—Families. (gr. k-4). 1991. 10.95 (0-8224-3168-8) Fearon Teach Aids.

Abbott, Phyllis, et al, eds. see Deegan, Paul.

Abbott, R. Tucker. Seashells of North America. Zim, Herbert S., ed. Sandstrom, George F., illus. (gr. 9 up). 1969. (Golden Pr); pap. write for info (0-307-13657-4) Western Pub.

—Seashells of the World. Rev. ed. Zim, Herbert S., ed. Sandstrom, George F. & Sandstrom, Marita, illus. (gr. 9 up). 1985. pap. write for info. (0-307-24410-5, Golden Pr) Western Pub.

Abbott, Tony. Noodle & Zeek Blast Off. Scribner, Joanne, illus. 1994. pap. write for info. (0-06-440520-6, Trophy) HarpC Child Bks.

—Noodle & Zeek, Danger Guys. LC 93-29799. (gr. 4 up). 1994. pap. write for info. (0-06-440519-2, Trophy) HarpC Child Bks.

Abbs, Brian. Longman Picture Wordbook. (Illus.). (ps-2). 1988. 18.95 (0-582-02239-8, 70444) Longman.

Abby Aldrich Rockefeller Folk Art Center Staff & Watson, Amy. The Folk Art Counting Book: From the Abby Aldrich Rockefeller Folk Art Center. (Illus.). 40p. (ps-k). 1992. 9.95 (0-87935-084-9, Co-Pub. by Abrams) Williamsburg.

Abd al-Salam Nadvi. Umar bin Abd al-Aziz. 200p. (gr. 7-12). 1985. pap. 9.95 (1-56744-406-7) Kazi Pubns.

Abdelnoor, R. E. The Silver Burdett Mathematical Dictionary. LC 86-45568. (Illus.). 126p. (gr. 5-12). 12.98 (0-382-09485-9); pap. 7.95 (0-382-09309-7) Silver Burdett Pr.

Abdu'l-Baha. Tablet of the Heart: God & Me. Fisher, Betty J. & Lundberg, Leslie, eds. Ostovar, Terry, illus. Oldziey, Pepper P., contrib. by. (ps-2). 1987. PLB 15.95 (0-87743-207-4) Bahai.

Abdul-Baki, Kathryn K. Fields of Fig & Olive: Ameera & Other Stories of the Middle East. Stone, Ellen, intro. by. 208p. (Orig.). (gr. 10 up). 1991. 18.00 (0-89410-725-9); pap. 10.00 (0-89410-726-7) Three Continents.

Abdullah, jt. auth. see Obaba, Al-Imam.

Abdul Waheed Khan. Beacon Lights, Bks. I-IV: True Tales for Children, 2 vol. set. 32p. (gr. 1-6). 1985. pap. 6.50 (1-56744-222-6) Kazi Pubns.

Abdur Rehman Shad. Uthman ibn Affan: The Third Caliph of Islam. 96p. (gr. 10-12). 1985. pap. 3.50 (1-56744-409-1) Kazi Pubns.

Abel, Ernest L. America's Twenty-Five Top Killers. LC 90-30768. 144p. (gr. 6 up). 1991. lib. bdg. 18.95 (0-89490-279-2) Enslow Pubs.

Abell, ed. & illus. see Abell-Grubbs, J.
Abell, ed. & illus. see Baker.
Abell, ed. & illus. see Grubbs, J.
Abell, ed. see Grubbs, Joan, et al.
Abell, ed. & illus. see Grubbs, Joan, et al.
Abell, ed. & illus. see Grubbs, Joan P.
Abell, ed. & illus. see Joan, et al.
Abell, ed. & illus. see Joan & Gene.
Abell, ed. & illus. see Rebellion, Boxer.
Abell, ed. & illus. see Wolfer, J.
Abell, J., jt. auth. see Grubbs, J.
Abell, J., ed. see Grubbs, J.
Abell, J., ed. see Grubbs, Joan.
Abell, J., ed. & illus. see Grubbs, T.
Abell, Joan. Books for Young Ladies. rev. ed. Abell, Joan, illus. Date not set. 22.00 (*1-56611-028-9*); PLB 22.00 (*0-685-65771-X*); pap. 10.00 (*0-685-65772-8*) Jones.
Abell, Joan P. You Will Be King: Gallantry, Bk. 2: Age Three. rev. ed. Abell, Joan P., illus. 50p. (gr. 5-8). 1993. 22.00 (*1-56611-025-4*); PLB 22.00 (*0-685-65767-1*); pap. 10.00 (*0-685-65768-X*) Jones.
Abell-Grubbs, J. Socks Changes His Mind: (The White House Cat, Bk. II. Abell, ed. & illus. (gr. 1 up). 1993. 23.00 (*1-56611-043-2*); pap. 15.00 (*1-56611-044-0*) Jones.
Abells, Chana B. The Children We Remember. LC 85-24876. (Illus.). 48p. (ps up). 1986. 13.00 (*0-688-06371-3*); PLB 12.93 (*0-688-06372-1*) Greenwillow.
Abels, Harriette S. Bermuda Triangle. LC 87-14029. (Illus.). 48p. (gr. 5-6). 1987. RSBE 12.95 (*0-89686-340-9*, Crestwood Hse) Macmillan Child Grp.
—Killer Bees. LC 87-14085. (Illus.). 48p. (gr. 5-6). 1987. RSBE 12.95 (*0-89686-342-5*, Crestwood Hse) Macmillan Child Grp.
—Loch Ness Monster. LC 87-9027. (Illus.). 48p. (gr. 5-6). 1987. RSBE 12.95 (*0-89686-343-3*, Crestwood Hse) Macmillan Child Grp.
—Lost City of Atlantis. LC 87-13440. (Illus.). 48p. (gr. 5-6). 1987. RSBE 12.95 (*0-89686-344-1*, Crestwood Hse) Macmillan Child Grp.
—The Pyramids. LC 87-15455. (Illus.). 48p. (gr. 5-6). 1987. RSBE 12.95 (*0-89686-345-X*, Crestwood Hse) Macmillan Child Grp.
—Stonehenge. LC 87-13638. (Illus.). 48p. (gr. 5-6). 1987. RSBE 12.95 (*0-89686-346-8*, Crestwood Hse) Macmillan Child Grp.
Abelson, Danny. The Muppets Take Manhattan: The Storybook Based on the Movie. LC 83-19153. (Illus.). 64p. (gr. k-6). 1984. 6.95 (*0-394-86386-0*); lib. bdg. 7.99 (*0-394-96386-5*, BYR) Random Bks Yng Read.
Aber, Linda W. Lost Girls Adrift. 176p. (gr. 3-7). 1991. pap. 2.75 (*0-590-43536-1*, Apple Paperbacks) Scholastic Inc.
—Stuck on Cooking. 96p. (Orig.). (gr. 4 up). 1991. pap. 6.95 (*0-590-43281-8*) Scholastic Inc.
Abercrombie, Barbara. Charlie Anderson. Graham, Mark, illus. LC 89-2449. 32p. (ps-4). 1990. SBE 13.95 (*0-689-50486-1*, M K McElderry) Macmillan Child Grp.
—Michael & the Cats. Graham, Mark, illus. LC 92-23950. 32p. (ps-2). 1993. SBE 13.95 (*0-689-50543-4*, M K McElderry) Macmillan Child Grp.
Abernathy, Susan. Space Machines. LaPadula, Tom, illus. (gr. 3-6). 1991. 8.50 (*0-307-17872-2*, Golden Pr) Western Pub.
Abernethy, Francis E. How the Critters Created Texas. Sargent, Ben, illus. LC 82-80440. 40p. (gr. 4-12). 1982. pap. 8.95 (*0-936650-01-X*) E C Temple.
Abernethy, Jane F. & Tune, Suelyn C. Made in Hawaii. Williams, Julie S., illus. LC 83-4895. 140p. (gr. 3-12). 1983. pap. 7.95 (*0-8248-0870-3*) UH Pr.
Abisch, Roz, et al. Stories from Miss A. Perle, Ruth L., ed. (gr. k-1). 1977. pap. text ed. 2.75 (*0-89796-850-6*) New Dimens Educ.
—Stories from Miss E. Perle, Ruth L., ed. (Illus.). (gr. k-1). 1977. pap. text ed. 2.75 (*0-89796-851-4*) New Dimens Educ.
—Stories from Miss I. Perle, Ruth L., ed. (Illus.). (gr. k-1). 1977. pap. text ed. 2.75 (*0-89796-852-2*) New Dimens Educ.
—Stories from Miss O. Perle, Ruth L., ed. (Illus.). (gr. k-1). 1977. pap. text ed. 2.75 (*0-89796-853-0*) New Dimens Educ.
Abler, David A. & Natti, Susanna. Cam Jansen & Mystery Carnival Prize. LC 84-3617. (Illus.). 64p. (gr. 2-5). 1984. pap. 10.95 (*0-670-20034-4*) Viking Child Bks.
Ables. Mystery on the Delta. (gr. 7 up). PLB 7.19 (*0-8313-0001-9*) Lantern.
Abm, Steven J. The Basket Marker. 32p. (gr. 2). 1992. write for info. (*0-9632943-0-X*) Sleepy Zebra.
Abodaher, David J. Puerto Rico: America's Fifty-First State. LC 92-39474. (Illus.). 112p. (gr. 9-12). 1993. PLB 13.40 (*0-531-13024-X*) Watts.
—Youth in the Middle East: Voices of Despair. (Illus.). 128p. (gr. 9-12). 1990. PLB 13.40 (*0-531-10961-5*) Watts.
Abolafia, Yossi. A Fish for Mrs. Gardenia. LC 87-17907. (Illus.). 32p. (gr. k-3). 1988. 11.95 (*0-688-07467-7*); lib. bdg. 11.88 (*0-688-07468-5*) Greenwillow.
—Fox Tale. LC 89-77501. (Illus.). 32p. (ps up). 1991. 13.95 (*0-688-09541-0*); PLB 13.88 (*0-688-09542-9*) Greenwillow.
—Fox Tale. (ps-3). 1992. 3.99 (*0-440-40667-6*, YB) Dell.

—Yanosh's Island. LC 86-19462. 32p. (gr. k-3). 1987. 11.75 (*0-688-06816-2*); PLB 11.88 (*0-688-06817-0*) Greenwillow.
Abood, Doris M. Lebanon: Bridge Between East & West. Art, Eve, illus. Thomas, Danny, intro. by. LC 73-84565. (Illus.). 40p. (gr. 5-10). 1973. 3.50 (*0-913228-07-9*) Dillon-Liederbach.
Abraham, Angela & Abraham, Ken. The Hosanna Bible. Anderson, Terry, et al, illus. LC 93-593. 448p. (ps-3). 1993. 15.99 (*0-8499-1036-6*) Word Inc.
Abraham, Ken, jt. auth. see Abraham, Angela.
Abraham, Ken, jt. auth. see Boyce, Kim.
Abraham, Norma J. Erik of the Dragon Ships. Steiner, Pat, illus. LC 83-50987. 163p. (Orig.). (gr. 8-11). 1983. pap. 3.95 (*0-912661-00-3*) Woodsong Graph.
Abrahams, Edith, jt. ed. see Tauben, Carol.
Abrahamson, Ruth. The Kingston Castle. Shinan, Devora, illus. 102p. (gr. 3-8). 1991. 10.95 (*0-922613-42-7*); pap. 8.95 (*0-922613-43-5*) Hachai Pubns.
Abramowitz, Jack. American History, 5 vols. 6th, large type ed. 1390p. (gr. 9-12). 1983. Set. 312.50 (*0-317-01867-1*, J-01690-00) Am Printing Hse.
—Readings in American History, Bk. 2. (gr. 4-5). 1987. pap. text ed. 5.25 (*0-89525-862-5*) Ed Activities.
Abramowitz, Jack & Uva, Kenneth. Consumers & the Law. (gr. 7-12). 1987. pap. text ed. 3.50 (*0-89525-871-4*) Ed Activities.
Abramowski, Dwain. Mountain Bikes. (Illus.). 64p. (gr. 5-8). 1990. PLB 12.90 (*0-531-10871-6*) Watts.
Abrams, Jodell. The Enchanted Forest Color & Story Album. (Illus.). 32p. (Orig.). 1981. pap. 3.99 (*0-8431-1712-5*) Troubador Pr.
—Enchanted Kingdom Color & Story Album. (Orig.). (ps up). 1983. pap. 4.50 (*0-8431-1707-9*) Troubador Pr.
Abrams, Judith. Sukkot: A Family Seder. Kahn, Katherine J., illus. 24p. (ps-6). 1993. pap. 3.95 (*0-929371-75-5*) Kar Ben.
Abrams, Judith Z. Rosh Hashanah - A Family Service. Kahn, Katherine J., illus. LC 90-4855. 32p. (Orig.). (ps-4). 1990. pap. 3.95 (*0-929371-16-X*) Kar Ben.
—Selichot - A Family Service. Kahn, Katherine J., illus. LC 90-4863. 24p. (ps-4). 1990. pap. 3.95 (*0-929371-15-1*) Kar Ben.
—Shabbat: A Family Service. Kahn, Katherine J., illus. LC 91-31640. 24p. (Orig.). (gr. k-3). 1992. pap. text ed. 3.95 (*0-929371-29-1*) Kar Ben.
—Yom Kippur - A Family Service. Kahn, Katherine J., illus. LC 90-4862. 22p. (Orig.). (ps-4). 1990. pap. 3.95 (*0-929371-17-8*) Kar Ben.
Abrams, Kathleen S. Guide to Careers Without College. Rasof, Henry, ed. LC 88-5723. (Illus.). 112p. (gr. 7-12). 1988. PLB 13.40 (*0-531-10585-7*) Watts.
Abrams, Rita. Stepping Out. 1991. bds. 12.95 incl. song tape (*0-938971-75-1*) JTG Nashville.
Abramson, Ruth. The Cresta Adventure. (gr. 4-7). 1989. 8.95 (*0-87306-493-3*) Feldheim.
Abranson, Lillian. Hanukkah ABC. (Illus.). (gr. 3-7). 1968. text ed. 5.00 (*0-914080-60-1*) Shulsinger Sales.
Abrashkin, Raymond, jt. auth. see Williams, Jay.
Abrera, Dette L. Handyong. Abrera, Jess, illus. (Orig.). (gr. 7-9). 1985. pap. 5.75 (*971-10-0200-0*, Pub. by New Day Pub PI) Cellar.
Abresch, Richard T. & Kern, Roger G. The Test Taking Advantage Strategy Manual. (Illus.). 181p. (gr. 10-12). 1990. pap. text ed. 35.50 (*0-9627360-0-7*) Test Taking Advan.
Abromowitz, Jack & Uva, Kenneth. The Constitution & the Government of the U. S. (gr. 7-12). 1987. pap. text ed. 3.50 (*0-89525-747-5*) Ed Activities.
Absolon, K. B., ed. & illus. see Absolon, Karel B.
Absolon, Karel B. The Tale of the Bad Macocha & the Fable of the Underground Punkva River. Absolon, K. B., ed. & illus. 40p. (Orig.). (gr. 4). 1984. pap. text ed. 12.00 (*0-930329-02-3*) KABEL Pubs.
Absolon, Mary. A Song at Christmas. Morris, Tony, illus. 64p. (gr. 3-8). 1991. 9.99 (*0-7459-1951-0*) Lion USA.
Accent, Inc. Staff, tr. see Barstow, Robbins.
Accorsi, William. Billy's Button. LC 91-37742. (Illus.). 24p. (ps-3). 1992. 14.00 (*0-688-10686-2*); PLB 13.93 (*0-688-10687-0*) Greenwillow.
—Friendship's First Thanksgiving. Accorsi, William, illus. LC 91-45132. 32p. (ps-3). 1992. reinforced bdg. 14.95 (*0-8234-0963-5*) Holiday.
—My Name Is Pocahontas. Accorsi, William, illus. LC 91-24218. 32p. (ps-3). 1992. reinforced bdg. 14.95 (*0-8234-0932-5*) Holiday.
—Rachel Carson. LC 92-43760. (Illus.). 32p. (ps-3). 1993. reinforced bdg. 15.95 (*0-8234-0994-5*) Holiday.
—Short Short Short Stories. LC 90-48179. (Illus.). 32p. (ps up). 1991. 13.95 (*0-688-10180-1*); PLB 13.88 (*0-688-10181-X*) Greenwillow.
Acevedo, Maria, ed. see Machamer, Gene.
Acey, Mark. Garfield Learns about Conservation: Endangered Odie? Davis, Jim, created by. (Illus.). 36p. (gr. k-3). 1992. write for info. incl. environmental stickers (*0-307-15730-X*, 15730, Golden Pr) Western Pub.
—Garfield Learns about Cooking: Any Cat Can Cook. Davis, Jim, created by. (Illus.). 36p. (gr. k-3). 1992. write for info. incl. recipe cards (*0-307-15728-8*, 15728, Golden Pr) Western Pub.
—Garfield Learns about Fire Safety: Where's the Fire? Davis, Jim, created by. (Illus.). 36p. (gr. k-3). 1992. write for info. incl. fire chief hat (*0-307-15726-1*, 15726, Golden Pr) Western Pub.

—Garfield Learns about Money: Money Madness! Davis, Jim, created by. (Illus.). 36p. (gr. k-3). 1992. write for info. incl. play money (*0-307-15725-3*, 15725, Golden Pr) Western Pub.
—Garfield Learns about Planning: Surprise Party. Davis, Jim, created by. (Illus.). 36p. (gr. k-3). 1992. write for info. incl. party invitations (*0-307-15731-8*, 15731, Golden Pr) Western Pub.
—Garfield Learns about Thoughtfulness: Don't Be Late! Davis, Jim, created by. (Illus.). 36p. (gr. k-3). 1992. write for info. incl. wipe-off calendar (*0-307-15732-6*, 15732, Golden Pr) Western Pub.
Achebe, Chinua & Iroaganachi, John. How the Leopard Got His Claws. Christiansen, Per, illus. LC 72-93381. 32p. (gr. 6 up). 1973. 11.95 (*0-89388-056-6*) Okpaku Communications.
Achu, Kamala. Nigeria. LC 92-6640. (Illus.). 48p. (gr. 5-8). 1992. PLB 13.90 (*0-531-18482-X*, Pub. by Bookwright Pr) Watts.
Acid Rain Foundation, Inc. Staff, compiled by. Acid Rain Curriculum: Grades 6-12. (Illus.). (gr. 6-12). 1986. 59.95 (*0-935577-03-3*) Acid Rain Found.
Acierno, Maria. The Never-Never Children. 80p. (gr. 4-6). 1994. PLB 12.95 (*1-881889-52-1*) Silver Moon.
Acker, Alison. Children of the Volcano. LC 86-93593. 168p. (Orig.). (gr. 9-12). 1987. pap. 7.95 (*0-919946-67-4*) L Hill Bks.
Acker, Toni. Tobey: A Tale of Transition. Verrier, Claude, illus. 40p. (gr. 7-12). 1987. pap. 5.95 (*0-942953-00-2*) Wonder Works Studio.
Ackerly, Salley M., jt. auth. see Riekes, Linda.
Ackerman, Karen. Araminta's Paint Box. Lewin, Betsy, illus. LC 88-35033. 32p. (gr. 1-3). 1990. SBE 13.95 (*0-689-31462-0*, Atheneum Child Bk) Macmillan Child Grp.
—The Banshee. Ray, David, illus. 32p. (ps-3). 1990. 14.95 (*0-399-21924-2*, Philomel Bks) Putnam Pub Group.
—Broken Boy. 160p. 1991. 14.95 (*0-399-22254-5*, Philomel Bks) Putnam Pub Group.
—By the Dawn's Early Light: Al Amanecer. Ada, Alma F., tr. Stock, Catherine, illus. LC 92-35633. (ENG & SPA.). 40p. (ps-3). 1994. English ed. SBE 14.95 (*0-689-31788-3*, Atheneum Child Bk); Spanish ed. SBE 14.95 (*0-689-31917-7*) Macmillan Child Grp.
—I Know a Place. Ray, Deborah K., illus. 32p. (ps-3). 1992. 13.45 (*0-395-53932-3*) HM.
—Just Like Max. Schmidt, George, illus. LC 88-13214. 32p. (ps-3). 1990. PLB 13.99 (*0-394-90176-2*) Knopf Bks Yng Read.
—The Leaves in October. LC 90-550. 128p. (gr. 3-7). 1991. SBE 12.95 (*0-689-31583-X*, Atheneum Child Bk) Macmillan Child Grp.
—Leaves in October. 1993. pap. 3.50 (*0-440-40868-7*) Dell.
—Song & Dance Man. Gammell, Stephen, illus. LC 87-3200. 32p. (ps-2). 1988. 15.00 (*0-394-89330-1*); lib. bdg. 15.99 (*0-394-99330-6*) Knopf Bks Yng Read.
—This Old House. Wickstrom, Sylvie, illus. LC 91-20449. 40p. (ps-1). 1992. SBE 14.95 (*0-689-31741-7*, Atheneum Child Bk) Macmillan Child Grp.
—The Tin Heart. Hays, Michael, illus. LC 89-6528. 32p. (gr. 1-3). 1990. SBE 13.95 (*0-689-31461-2*, Atheneum Child Bk) Macmillan Child Grp.
—Walking with Clara Belle. Mason, Debbie, illus. 40p. (gr. k-3). 1993. 9.95 (*0-8198-8243-7*) St Paul Bks.
—When Mama Retires. Grace, Alexa, illus. LC 91-19139. 40p. (ps-3). 1992. 15.00 (*0-679-80289-4*); PLB 15.99 (*0-679-90289-9*) Knopf Bks Yng Read.
Ackerman, Karen, compiled by see Dickinson, Emily.
Ackerman, Jean. A Pride of Heroes: Candid Celebrations. v, 22p. (Orig.). (gr. 8-12). 1984. pap. 6.00 (*0-9614506-0-6*) Box Four Twenty-Four.
Ackley, Meredith & Weber, Valerie, eds. Children of the World: Japan. LC 89-11493. (Illus.). 64p. (gr. 5-6). 1989. PLB 19.93 (*0-8368-0121-0*) Gareth Stevens Inc.
Ackley, Meredith, et al, eds. Nicaragua. Birmingham, Lucy, et al, photos by. LC 89-43174. (Illus.). (gr. 3-8). PLB 19.93 (*0-8368-0221-7*); PLB 19.93 s.p. (*0-685-61532-4*) Gareth Stevens Inc.
Acocella, Christine, jt. auth. see Taliercio, Carmela.
Acorn, John, jt. auth. see Russell, Dale A.
Actis, Helen. Story of Peety & Patty Ant. (ps-3). 1991. 6.95 (*0-8062-4174-8*) Carlton.

Ada, Alam F. In the Cow's Backyard - La Hamaca De La Vaca. Escriva, Vivi, illus. (SPA & ENG.). 23p. (gr. k-2). 1991. English ed. 6.95 (*1-56014-275-8*); Spanish ed. 6.95 (*1-56014-219-7*) Santillana.
Young readers will be enchanted with the menagerie of animal characters in this whimsical selection. A hospitable cow discovers an ant in her hammock, then a frog, then a chick. a hen, & a goose. But, says the cow, "There's always room for one more friend." This selection makes an enjoyable counting book, while the rhyming text makes for easy reading. English & Spanish versions are available to entertain children in both languages. To order:

Santillana, 901 West Walnut, Compton, CA 90220. Telephone 1-310-763-0455. *Publisher Provided Annotation.*

—A Strange Visitor - Una Extrana Visita. Escriva, Vivi, illus. (SPA & ENG.). 26p. (Orig.). (gr. k-2). 1989. English ed. 3.95 (*0-88272-802-4*); Spanish Ed. 3.95 (*0-88272-793-1*) Santillana.
A delightful collection of animals gather to play various musical instruments: cows with maracas, crickets with fiddles, & mice playing accordions. Days of the week & counting are also introduced in this entertaining book. The story is available in both English & Spanish with rhyming text in both languages. Ingeniously drawn illustrations by Vivi Escriva add to the fun. To order: Santillana, 901 West Walnut, Compton, CA 90220. Telephone 1-310-763-0455. *Publisher Provided Annotation.*

Ada, Alma F. Barquitos de Papel. Torrecilla, Pablo, illus. (SPA.). 24p. (gr. 3-9). 1993. 16.95x (*1-56492-118-2*) Laredo.
—Barrilets. Torrecilla, Pablo, illus. (SPA.). 24p. (gr. 3-9). 1993. 16.95x (*1-56492-126-3*) Laredo.
—Dear Peter Rabbit: Querido Pedrin. Zubizarreta, Rosa, tr. Tryon, Leslie, illus. LC 93-8459. 40p. (ps-3). 1994. English ed. SBE 14.95 (*0-689-31850-2*, Atheneum Child Bk); Spanish ed. SBE 14.95 (*0-689-31915-0*, Atheneum Child Bk) Macmillan Child Grp.
—Dias de Circo. Torrecilla, Pablo, illus. (SPA.). 24p. (gr. 3-9). 1993. 16.95x (*1-56492-127-1*) Laredo.

—Friends - Amigos. Koch, Barry, illus. (SPA & ENG.). 26p. (gr. k-2). 1989. Spanish ed. 5.25 (*0-88272-501-7*); English ed. 5.25 (*0-88272-500-9*) Santillana.
Prejudice & tolerance are treated in a sensitive & easy-to-understand manner in this story. The main characters are geometric shapes who are not allowed to play or talk to each other. Then one day they inadvertently discover that friends can come in many different forms. English & Spanish versions are available of this entertaining & instructive story. To order: Santillana, 901 West Walnut, Compton, CA 90220. Telephone 1-310-763-0455. *Publisher Provided Annotation.*

—The Gold Coin. Waldman, Neil, illus. LC 90-32806. 32p. (gr. k-3). 1991. SBE 13.95 (*0-689-31633-X*, Atheneum Child Bk) Macmillan Child Grp.
—The Gold Coin. Waldman, Neil, illus. Randall, Bernice, tr. from SPA. LC 93-14403. (Illus.). (gr. k-3). 1994. pap. 4.95 (*0-689-71793-8*, Aladdin) Macmillan Child Grp.

—The Kite - El Papalote. Escriva, Vivi, illus. (SPA & ENG.). 23p. (gr. k-2). 1992. English ed. 6.95 (*1-56014-228-6*); Spanish ed. 6.95 (*1-56014-227-8*) Santillana.
A resourceful mother helps her children make & fly a kite in this entertaining selection. A surprise ending adds to the reading experience. Predictable language patterns help young readers to decode the text easily. English & Spanish versions are available to delight children in both languages. To order: Santillana, 901 West Walnut, Compton, CA 90220. Telephone 1-310-763-0455. *Publisher Provided Annotation.*

—Manzano, Manzano! Kalthoff, Sandra C., illus. 24p. (Orig.). (gr. k-3). 1989. Six-Pack Set. pap. text ed. 36.00 (*0-917837-46-0*) Hampton-Brown.

—Manzano, Manzano! (Big Book) Kalthoff, Sandra C., illus. (SPA.). 24p. (Orig.). (gr. k-3). 1989. pap. text ed. 29.95 (*0-917837-09-6*) Hampton-Brown.
—My Name Is Maria Isabel. Cerro, Ana M., tr. from SPA. Thompson, K. Dyble, illus. LC 91-44910. 64p. (gr. 2-5). 1993. SBE 12.95 (*0-689-31517-1*, Atheneum Child Bk) Macmillan Child Grp.
—El Oso Mas Elegante. Kalthoff, Sandra C., illus. 24p. (Orig.). (gr. k-3). 1989. Six-Pack Set. pap. text ed. 36.00 (*0-917837-43-6*) Hampton-Brown.
—El Oso Mas Elegante (Big Book) Kalthoff, Sandra C., illus. 24p. (Orig.). (gr. k-3). 1989. pap. text ed. 29.95 (*0-917837-10-X*) Hampton-Brown.

—El Panuelo de Seda. (SPA., Illus.). 24p. 1993. PLB 16.95x (*1-56492-105-0*) Laredo.
This is the touching story of a young girl, her treasured silk scarf, & her love for watching cranes fly in the sky. Beautiful color illustrations. *Publisher Provided Annotation.*

—El Patio de Mi Casa: Cuento Basado en una Rima Tradicional. Callen, Liz, illus. (SPA.). 24p. (Orig.). (gr. 1-3). 1991. pap. text ed. 29.95 big bk. (*1-56334-018-6*); pap. text ed. 3.50 small bk. (*1-56334-044-5*) Hampton-Brown.
—Pin, Pin, Sarabin. Torrecilla, Pablo, illus. (SPA.). 24p. (gr. 3-9). 1993. 16.95x (*1-56492-130-1*) Laredo.

—Pregones. Torrecilla, Pablo, illus. (SPA.). 24p. (gr. 3-8). 1993. PLB 16.95x (*1-56492-110-7*) Laredo.
The author remembers the everyday sights & sounds of the street vendors who came to her house & the important lesson she learned as a child about the value of being fair & honest. Rich descriptions of "vendor cries" & beautiful color illustrations. Text in Spanish. *Publisher Provided Annotation.*

—Sale El Oso (Big Book) Myers, Amy, illus. (SPA.). 16p. (Orig.). (gr. k-3). 1988. pap. text ed. 29.95 (*0-917837-03-7*) Hampton-Brown.
—Sale el Oso (Small Book) Myers, Amy, illus. (SPA.). 16p. (Orig.). (gr. k-3). 1992. pap. text ed. 6.00 (*1-56334-079-8*) Hampton-Brown.
—Los Seis Deseos de la Jirafa (Big Book) Roy, Doug, illus. (SPA.). 16p. (Orig.). (gr. k-3). 1988. pap. text ed. 29.95 (*0-917837-02-9*) Hampton-Brown.
—Los Seis Deseos de la Jirafa (Small Book) Roy, Doug, illus. (SPA.). 16p. (Orig.). (gr. k-3). 1992. pap. text ed. 6.00 (*1-56334-078-X*) Hampton-Brown.
—Una Semilla Nada Mas (Big Book) Remkiewicz, Frank, illus. (SPA.). 16p. (Orig.). (gr. k-3). 1990. pap. text ed. 29.95 (*0-917837-56-8*) Hampton-Brown.
—Una Semilla Nada Mas (Small Book) Remkiewicz, Frank, illus. (SPA.). 16p. (Orig.). (gr. k-3). 1992. pap. text ed. 6.00 (*1-56334-083-6*) Hampton-Brown.
—Serafina's Birthday. Bates, Louise, illus. LC 91-15389. 32p. (ps-2). 1992. SBE 13.95 (*0-689-31516-3*, Atheneum Child Bk) Macmillan Child Grp.
—The Unicorn of the West: El Unicornio del Oeste. Zubizarreta, Rosa, tr. Pizer, Abigail, illus. LC 92-7425. (ENG & SPA.). 40p. (gr. 1-3). 1994. English ed. SBE 14.95 (*0-689-31778-6*, Atheneum Child Bk); Spanish ed. SBE 14.95 (*0-689-31916-9*, Atheneum Child Bk) Macmillan Child Grp.

—Who's Hatching Here? - Quien Nacera Aqui? Escriva, Vivi, illus. (SPA & ENG.). 24p. (gr. k-2). 1989. English ed. 3.95 (*0-88272-811-3*); Spanish ed. 3.95 (*0-88272-800-8*) Santillana.
Charming story by the incomparable Alma Flor Ada portraying the habitats & birth cycles of numerous animals & insects: chicks, mosquitoes, frogs, turtles, & butterflies are included. Water color illustrations by Vivi Escriva add to young readers' enjoyment. To order: Santillana, 901 West Walnut, Compton, CA 90220. Telephone 1-310-763-0455. *Publisher Provided Annotation.*

Ada, Alma F., jt. auth. see Perl, Lila.
Ada, Alma F., ed. Olmo y la Mariposa Azul. Escriba, Vivi, illus. 24p. (gr. k-3). 1992. pap. 7.50x (*1-56492-095-X*) Laredo.

Ada, Alma F., retold by. The Rooster Who Went to His Uncle's Wedding: A Latin American Folktale. Kuchera, Kathleen, illus. LC 92-14087. 32p. (ps-3). 1992. PLB 14.95 (*0-399-22412-2*, Putnam) Putnam Pub Group.
Ada, Alma F., tr. La Pequena Locomotora Que Si Pudo: The Little Engine That Could. Hauman, George & Hauman, Doris, illus. (SPA.). 48p. (gr-6). 1992. 5.95 (*0-448-41096-6*, Platt & Munk Pubs) Putnam Pub Group.
Ada, Alma F., tr. see Ackerman, Karen.
Ada, Alma F., tr. see Baden, Robert.
Ada, Alma F., tr. see Blume, Judy.
Ada, Alma F., tr. see Franklin, Kristine L.
Ada, Alma F., tr. see Luenn, Nancy.
Ada, Alma F., tr. see Rohmer, Harriet.
Ada, Alma F., tr. see Viorst, Judith.
Ada, Alma F., et al. Choices & Other Stories from the Caribbean. LC 92-43134. 1993. pap. 6.95 (*0-377-00257-7*) Friendship Pr.
Ada, Alma Flor see Rohmer, Harriet.
Adachi, Kelly. The Kids' Handbook. (Illus.). 112p. (gr. 1 up). 1985. 7.95 (*0-8184-0365-5*); pap. 4.95 (*0-8184-0368-3*) Carol Pub Group.
Adair, jt. auth. see Amery.
Adair, Audrey J. Great Composers & Their Music History, Unit 5: Fifty Ready to Use Activities. 112p. (gr. 3-9). 1987. pap. text ed. 18.95 (*0-13-363797-2*, Parker Publishing Co.) P-H.
—Musical Instruments & the Voices: Fifty Ready-to-Use Activities. 112p. (gr. 3-9). 1987. pap. 12.95 (*0-13-606963-0*) P-H.
—Special Days Throughout the Year: Fifty Ready-to-Use Activities, Unit 6. 112p. (gr. 3-9). 1987. pap. 12.95 (*0-13-826421-X*, Parker Publishing Co) P-H.
Adair, Dennis & Rosenstock, Janet. The Journey Begins, No. 1. (gr. 3-7). 1992. pap. 3.99 (*0-553-48027-8*, Skylark) Bantam.
Adair, Dick. Aloha Bear & the Meaning of Aloha. (Illus.). 24p. (ps-k). 1987. 7.95 (*0-89610-077-4*) Island Heritage.
—The Story of Aloha Bear. Adair, Dick, illus. 24p. (ps-k). 1986. 7.95 (*0-89610-049-9*) Island Heritage.
Adair, Gene. George Washington Carver. King, Coretta Scott, intro. by. (Illus.). 112p. (gr. 5 up). 1989. 17.95 (*1-55546-577-3*); pap. 9.95 (*0-7910-0234-9*) Chelsea Hse.
Adair, Lynn, ed. see Busiek, Kurt.
Adair, Peggy. Chance. LC 90-82750. 200p. (Orig.). (gr. 6-12). 1990. pap. 4.95 (*0-9626803-9-7*) Deep Riv Pr.
Adair, R., et al. Brinca de Alegria Hacia la Primavera con las Matematicas y Ciencias. (SPA & ENG.). 94p. (gr. k-1). 1988. pap. text ed. 16.95 (*1-881431-21-5*) AIMS Educ Fnd.
—Caete de Gusto Hacid el Otono con las Matematicas y Ciencias. (SPA & ENG.). 116p. (gr. k-1). 1988. pap. text ed. 16.95 (*1-881431-19-3*) AIMS Educ Fnd.
—Patine al Invierno con Matematicas y Ciencias. (SPA & ENG.). 105p. (gr. k-1). 1988. pap. text ed. 16.95 (*1-881431-20-7*) AIMS Educ Fnd.
Adam, G. Mercer, ed. see Kingsley, Charles.
Adamek, Maurine R. I'll Do Better Tomorrow, I Promise. Schubert, Annalee, illus. LC 92-11169. 32p. 1992. pap. 6.99 (*0-9628579-3-9*) Vision WY.
Adamo, Adam. Babysitters Club Trivia & Puzzle Fun Book. (gr. 4-7). 1992. pap. 3.50 (*0-590-47314-X*) Scholastic Inc.
Adamoli, Vida & Howard, Tom. The Love of Dogs. (Illus.). 96p. 1993. 12.98 (*0-8317-2187-1*) Smithmark.
Adams & Coudert, Allison. Alice Whipple, Fifth Grade Detective. (ps-7). 1987. pap. 2.25 (*0-317-64197-2*, Skylark) Bantam.
Adams, Adrienne. The Christmas Party. Adams, Adrienne, illus. LC 78-16230. 32p. (ps-3). 1978. SBE 13.95 (*0-684-15930-9*, Scribners Young Read) Macmillan Child Grp.
—The Christmas Party. 2nd ed. Adams, Adrienne, illus. LC 91-42159. 32p. (ps-3). 1992. pap. 3.95 (*0-689-71630-3*, Aladdin) Macmillan Child Grp.
—The Easter Egg Artists. Adams, Adrienne, illus. LC 75-39301. 32p. (ps-3). 1976. RSBE 13.95 (*0-684-14652-5*, Scribners Young Read) Macmillan Child Grp.
—The Easter Egg Artists. LC 90-1097. (Illus.). 32p. (gr. k-3). 1981. pap. 2.95 (*0-689-70479-8*, Aladdin) Macmillan Child Grp.
—The Easter Egg Artists. Adams, Adrienne, illus. LC 90-1097. 32p. (ps-3). 1991. pap. 4.95 (*0-689-71481-5*, Aladdin) Macmillan Child Grp.
—The Great Valentine's Day Balloon Race. Adams, Adrienne, illus. LC 80-19527. 32p. (ps-3). 1980. RSBE 14.95 (*0-684-16640-2*, Scribners Young Read) Macmillan Child Grp.
—The Great Valentine's Day Balloon Race. Adams, Adrienne, illus. LC 86-3382. 32p. (ps-3). 1986. pap. 4.95 (*0-689-71085-2*, Aladdin) Macmillan Child Grp.
—A Halloween Happening. Adams, Adrienne, illus. LC 81-8969. 32p. (ps-3). 1981. SBE 13.95 (*0-684-17166-X*, Scribners Young Read) Macmillan Child Grp.
—A Halloween Happening. Adams, Adrienne, illus. LC 91-6907. 32p. (ps-3). 1991. pap. 3.95 (*0-689-71502-1*, Aladdin) Macmillan Child Grp.
—Woggle of Witches. Adams, Adrienne, illus. LC 70-161536. 32p. (ps-3). 1971. RSBE 13.95 (*0-684-12506-4*, Scribners Young Read) Macmillan Child Grp.

—A Woggle of Witches. Adams, Adrienne, illus. LC 87-18703. 32p. (ps-1). 1985. pap. 4.95 (*0-689-71050-X*, Aladdin) Macmillan Child Grp.

Adams, Andy. Log of a Cowboy. (gr. 7 up). 1969. pap. 1.95 (*0-8049-0201-1*, CL-201) Airmont.

Adams, Anne, et al. Success in Kindergarten Reading & Writing. (gr. k). 1980. 16.95 (*0-673-16437-3*) Scott F.

Adams, Anne H. Success in Beginning Reading & Writing: Grade 1. (gr. 1-3). 1984. text ed. 16.95 (*0-673-16551-5*) Scott F.

Adams, Anne H., et al. Success in Reading & Writing. (gr. 5). 1982. 16.95 (*0-673-16546-9*) Scott F.

Adams, Barbara. Can This Telethon Be Saved. (gr. k-6). 1987. pap. 2.50 (*0-440-41427-X*, YB) Dell.

—The Not-Quite-Ready-for-Prime-Time Bandits. (Orig.). (gr. 3-6). 1986. pap. 2.50 (*0-440-49551-2*, YB) Dell.

—On the Air & off the Wall. (Orig.). (gr. 3-6). 1986. pap. 2.50 (*0-440-46771-3*, YB) Dell.

—Rock Video Strikes Again. (Orig.). (gr. 2-6). 1986. pap. 2.50 (*0-440-47170-2*, YB) Dell.

Adams, Barbara J. The Go-Around Dollar. Zarins, Joyce A., illus. LC 90-26269. 32p. (gr. 1-4). 1992. RSBE 13.95 (*0-02-700031-1*, Four Winds) Macmillan Child Grp.

Adams, Barbara Johnston. New York City. LC 88-20245. (Illus.). 60p. (gr. 3 up). 1988. RSBE 13.95 (*0-87518-384-0*, Dillon) Macmillan Child Grp.

Adams, Brian. Medieval Castles. LC 88-83092. (Illus.). 32p. (gr. 5-7). 1989. PLB 12.40 (*0-531-17155-8*, Gloucester Pr) Watts.

Adams, Carolyn. Stars over Texas. rev. ed. (Illus.). 128p. (gr. 1-6). 1983. 9.95 (*0-89015-411-2*, Pub. by Panda Bks) Eakin-Sunbelt.

Adams, David. Life after High School. (Illus.). 48p. (gr. 9-12). 1991. pap. 7.99 (*1-55945-220-X*) Group Pub.

—Movies, Music, TV & Me. (Illus.). 48p. (gr. 9-12). 1991. pap. 7.99 (*1-55945-213-7*) Group Pub.

—The Three Little Pigs Go to Greasy Pete's. Holland, Janet, illus. 40p. (ps-3). 1993. PLB 14.95 (*0-9638421-9-6*); pap. 5.95 (*0-9638421-8-8*) Flatland Tales. SUBJECT - Our story is the tale of the Three Little Pigs before their classical encounter with a big bad wolf. This adventure finds the three young, fun loving, ornery piglets living at home with Mom & Dad. AUTHOR - With his stories, the author David Adams brings children to attentive silence at schools, churches, & family gatherings. His sense of humor & plays on words capture kids' imaginations. Parents are pleased with the way he weaves good manners into this story. ILLUSTRATION - Kids today are becoming more & more experienced working with computers. They will be intrigued to discover the illustrations for this book were created with a computer using the latest technology. Published & distributed by: Flatland Tales Publishing, P.O. Box 887, Ottawa, KS 66067-0887, specializing in quality children's books. *Publisher Provided Annotation.*

—Today's Lessons from Yesterday's Prophets. (Illus.). 48p. (gr. 9-12). 1992. pap. 7.99 (*1-55945-227-7*) Group Pub.

Adams, Edward B. Herdboy & Weaver. Choi, Dong-Ho, illus. 32p. (gr. 3). 1981. 8.95 (*0-8048-1470-8*, Pub by Seoul Intl Publishing House) C E Tuttle.

—Woodcutter & Nymph. Choi, Dong-Ho, illus. 32p. (gr. 3). 1982. 8.95 (*0-8048-1471-6*, Pub by Seoul Intl Publishing House) C E Tuttle.

Adams, Edward B., ed. Blindman's Daughter. Choi, Dong Ho, illus. 32p. (gr. 3). 1981. 8.95 (*0-8048-1472-4*, Pub. by Seoul Intl Tourist SK) C E Tuttle.

—Korean Cinderella. Choi, Dong Ho, illus. 32p. (gr. 3). 1982. 8.95 (*0-8048-1473-2*, Pub. by Seoul Intl Tourist SK) C E Tuttle.

—Two Brothers & Their Magic Gourds. Dong-Ho, Choi, illus. 32p. (gr. 3). 1981. 8.95 (*0-8048-1474-0*, Pub. by Seoul Intl Tourist SK) C E Tuttle.

Adams, Edward B., tr. see Ilyon.

Adams, Faith. El Salvador: Beauty among the Ashes. LC 85-6945. (Illus.). 136p. (gr. 5 up). 1986. RSBE 14.95 (*0-87518-309-3*, Dillon) Macmillan Child Grp.

—Nicaragua: Struggling with Change. LC 86-11608. (Illus.). 152p. (gr. 5 up). 1987. RSBE 14.95 (*0-87518-340-9*, Dillon) Macmillan Child Grp.

Adams, Fern. China's Daughter. 134p. (Orig.). (gr. 7-12). 1991. pap. 4.95 (*0-8474-6623-X*) Back to Bible.

Adams, Florence. Catch a Sunbeam: A Book of Solar Study & Experiments. Komoda, Kiyo, illus. LC 78-52820. (gr. 3-7). 1978. 10.95 (*0-15-215197-4*, HB Juv Bks) HarBrace.

Adams, Georgie. Fish Fish Fish. Willgoss, Brigitte, illus. LC 91-43748. 32p. (ps-2). 1993. 13.00 (*0-8037-1208-1*) Dial Bks Young.

—Nanny Fox. Young, Selina, illus. LC 93-72433. 32p. (ps-2). 1994. SBE 13.95 (*0-689-31920-7*, Atheneum Child Bk) Macmillan Child Grp.

Adams, Henry. Democracy: An American Novel. Andrews, C. A., intro. by. (gr. 9 up). 1968. pap. 1.50 (*0-8049-0164-3*, CL-164) Airmont.

—Handbook of American Paintings in the Nelson - Atkins Museum of Art, Kansas City, Missouri. LC 91-29780. (Illus.). 208p. (Orig.). 1991. pap. 4.00 (*0-942614-17-8*) Nelson-Atkins.

Adams, James T. Album of American History, 3 vols. rev. ed. LC 74-91746. (gr. 5 up). 1981. Set. 290.00 (*0-684-16848-0*, Scribners Young Read) Macmillan Child Grp.

Adams, Jean-Pierre. Mediterranean Civilizations. LC 86-426550. (Illus.). 77p. (gr. 7 up). 1987. 17.98 (*0-382-09215-5*); 13.49s.p. (*0-685-17551-0*) Silver Burdett Pr.

Adams, Jeanie. Going for Oysters. (ps-3). 1993. 14.95 (*0-8075-2978-8*) A Whitman.

Adams, K. J. Crazy in Love. 1993. pap. 3.50 (*0-06-106161-1*, Harp PBks) HarpC.

Adams, Kathleen. Family Homework. (ps-1). 1989. pap. 6.95 (*0-8224-3052-5*) Fearon Teach Aids.

Adams, Ken. When I Was Your Age. Biro, Val, illus. 32p. (ps-2). 1991. incl. dust jacket 12.95 (*0-8120-6249-3*) Barron.

Adams, Laurie. Alice Whipple Shapes Up. (gr. 4-7). 1990. pap. 2.75 (*0-553-15803-1*) Bantam.

Adams, Laurie & Coudert, Allison. Alice Investigates. 96p. (Orig.). 1987. pap. 2.75 (*0-553-15485-0*, Skylark) Bantam.

—Who Wants a Turnip for President, Anyway? 96p. (Orig.). 1990. pap. 2.75 (*0-553-15432-X*) Bantam.

Adams, Lynn, illus. Don Cooper's Musical Games. Cooper, Don, contrib. by. (Illus.). (gr. ps-3). 1991. pap. 6.95 incl. 30-min. cassette (*0-679-81935-5*) Random Bks Yng Read.

Adams, Mary A. Whoopi Goldberg: From Street to Stardom. LC 92-23766. (Illus.). 64p. (gr. 3 up). 1993. RSBE 13.95 (*0-87518-562-2*, Dillon) Macmillan Child Grp.

Adams, Marylou. Brighten up at Breakfast: Helpful Tips for Heavenly Bodies. Adams, Marylou, illus. LC 81-51601. 120p. (gr. 2-7). 1981. plastic comb 7.95 (*0-9606248-0-5*) Starbright.

Adams, Michael, illus. Andersen's Classic Fairy Tales. 48p. (gr. k-5). 1993. 5.95 (*0-88101-276-9*) Unicorn Pub.

—Andersen's Fables & Fairy Tales. 48p. (gr. k-5). 1993. 5.95 (*0-685-63134-6*) Unicorn Pub.

—The Emperor's New Clothes. Ingram, John, ed. Adams, Michael, illus. 48p. (gr. 1-4). 1990. 5.95 (*0-88101-106-1*) Unicorn Pub.

Adams, Nate. Energizers. 192p. 1993. pap. 8.99 (*0-310-37371-9*, Pub. by Youth Spec) Zondervan.

Adams, Nicholas. Final Curtain. 1991. pap. 3.50 (*0-06-106079-8*, Harp PBks) HarpC.

—Heartbreaker. (gr. 9-12). 1991. pap. 3.50 (*0-06-106037-2*, PL) HarpC.

—I. O. U. 1991. pap. 3.50 (*0-06-106106-9*, Harp PBks) HarpC.

—Mr. Popularity. (gr. 9-12). 1990. pap. 3.50 (*0-06-106018-6*, PL) HarpC.

—New Kid on the Block. (gr. 9-12). 1991. pap. 3.50 (*0-06-106061-5*, PL) HarpC.

—Santa Claws. 1991. pap. 3.50 (*0-06-106108-5*, Harp PBks) HarpC.

Adams, P., illus. The Child's Play Museum. LC 90-46592. (ps-2). 1976. 9.95 (*0-85953-094-9*, Pub. by Childs Play England) Childs Play.

Adams, Pam. Alf 'n Bet's Handwriting Book. (ps-3). 1993. pap. 5.95 (*0-85953-168-6*) Childs Play.

—All Kinds: Race & Colour. LC 90-45703. (gr. 4 up). 1990. 7.95 (*0-85953-363-8*); pap. 3.95 (*0-85953-353-0*) Childs Play.

—Baby Bubbles. (gr. 3 up). 1981. 5.95 (*0-85953-265-8*) Childs Play.

—Disabled People. (gr. 4 up). 1990. 7.95 (*0-85953-361-1*); pap. 3.95 (*0-85953-351-4*) Childs Play.

—Dolly Dolphin's Play School. 1981. 4.95 (*0-85953-266-6*) Childs Play.

—Elderly People. LC 90-45702. (gr. 4 up). 1990. 7.95 (*0-85953-362-X*); pap. 3.95 (*0-85953-352-2*) Childs Play.

—The Fairground. (Illus.). 32p. (ps). 1984. 8.95 (*0-85953-194-5*, Child's Play England) Childs Play.

—The Frog. 1985. 4.95 (*0-85953-259-3*) Childs Play.

—Froglet's Bathtime. (gr. 3 up). 1981. 9.95 (*0-85953-329-8*) Childs Play.

—The Green-Eyed Monster. (gr. 4 up). 1985. 8.95 (*0-85953-195-3*) Childs Play.

—Helpful Shoelace. LC 90-49236. 1989. 11.95 (*0-85953-256-X*) Childs Play.

—Law & Order. LC 90-25106. 1990. 7.95 (*0-685-52309-8*); pap. 3.95 (*0-85953-354-9*) Childs Play.

—Mrs. Honey's Dream. Adams, Pam, illus. LC 92-40124. 1993. 7.95 (*0-85953-331-X*); pap. 3.95 (*0-85953-332-8*) Childs Play.

—Mrs. Honey's Dream. (ps-3). 1993. 7.95 (*0-85953-759-5*); pap. 3.95 (*0-85953-760-9*) Childs Play.

—Mrs Honey's Glasses. LC 93-12368. (Illus.). ps-3). 1993. 7.95 (*0-85953-757-9*); pap. 3.95 (*0-85953-758-7*) Childs Play.

—Mrs. Honey's Hat. LC 90-46604. (Illus.). 24p. (ps-2). 1980. 7.95 (*0-85953-099-X*, Pub. by Child's Play England); pap. 3.95 (*0-85953-325-5*) Childs Play.

—Mrs. Honey's Holiday. Adams, Pam, illus. LC 92-41886. 1993. 7.95 (*0-85953-755-2*); pap. 3.95 (*0-85953-756-0*) Childs Play.

—Myst Express. LC 90-45758. 1989. 9.95 (*0-85953-180-5*) Childs Play.

—Noah's Ark. (gr. 3 up). 1981. 5.95 (*0-85953-267-4*) Childs Play.

—The Ocean. 32p. (ps). 1984. 5.95 (*0-85953-193-7*, Child's Play England) Childs Play.

—Oh, Soldier! Soldier! LC 90-48946. (ps-3). 1990. pap. 5.95 (*0-85953-092-2*, Pub. by Child's Play England) Childs Play.

—On a Cold & Frosty Morning. (gr. 4 up). 1990. 4.95 (*0-85953-442-1*) Childs Play.

—Owls Number School. LC 90-48662. 1989. 9.95 (*0-85953-166-X*) Childs Play.

—Playmates. (gr. 3 up). 1991. 5.95 (*0-85953-449-9*) Childs Play.

—The Red-Eyed Monster. (gr. 4 up). 1985. 8.95 (*0-85953-196-1*) Childs Play.

—Six in a Bath. (gr. 4 up). 1990. 4.95 (*0-85953-443-X*) Childs Play.

—Ten Beads Tall. LC 90-1964. 1989. 11.95 (*0-85953-242-9*) Childs Play.

—There Was an Old Lady. LC 90-46921. 1972. 11.95 (*0-85953-076-0*) Childs Play.

—There Was an Old Lady Who Swallowed a Fly. LC 90-46921. (ps-3). 1990. 8.99 (*0-85953-021-3*) Childs Play.

—Tingaling. (gr. 4 up). 1981. 9.95 (*0-85953-328-X*) Childs Play.

—Ups & Downs. (gr. 4 up). 1985. 4.95 (*0-85953-257-7*) Childs Play.

—Wally Whale & Friends. (gr. 4 up). 1981. pap. 5.95 (*0-85953-268-2*) Childs Play.

—What on Earth. LC 90-45581. 1989. 9.95 (*0-85953-165-1*) Childs Play.

Adams, Pam & Jones, Ceri. I Thought I Saw. LC 90-45582. (Illus., Orig.). (ps-2). 1974. (Pub. by Child's Play England); pap. 5.95 (*0-85953-029-9*) Childs Play.

Adams, Pam & Twin, Michael. Rabbits Golden Rule Book. LC 90-2677. 1989. 9.95 (*0-85953-298-4*) Childs Play.

Adams, Pam, jt. auth. see Twinn, Michael.

Adams, Pam, illus. Alf 'N Bet. LC 92-14641. 1992. 5.95 (*0-85953-167-8*) Childs Play.

—Day Dreams. LC 90-45583. 32p. (Orig.). (ps-2). 1978. 11.95 (*0-85953-105-8*, Pub. by Child's Play England); pap. 5.95 (*0-85953-082-5*) Childs Play.

—The Gingerbread Man. LC 90-45757. 24p. (ps-2). 1981. 9.95 (*0-85953-107-4*, Pub. by Child's Play England) Childs Play.

—How Many? 16p. (Orig.). (ps-2). 1975. pap. 3.95 (*0-85953-045-0*, Pub. by Child's Play England) Childs Play.

—If I Weren't Me. LC 90-46184. 24p. (ps-2). 1981. 9.95 (*0-85953-108-2*, Pub. by Child's Play England) Childs Play.

—Letters & Words. 16p. (Orig.). (ps-2). 1975. pap. 3.95 (*0-85953-046-9*, Pub. by Child's Play England) Childs Play.

—Magic. LC 90-46518. 32p. (Orig.). (ps-2). 1978. 11.95 (*0-85953-104-X*, Pub. by Child's Play England); pap. 5.95 (*0-85953-081-7*) Childs Play.

—Oh, Soldier! Soldier! LC 90-48946. 16p. (ps-2). 1978. 11.95 (*0-85953-093-0*, Pub. by Child's Play England) Childs Play.

—Old MacDonald Had a Farm. LC 90-46923. (Orig.). (ps-2). 1975. pap. 5.95 (*0-85953-053-1*, Pub. by Child's Play England) Childs Play.

—Same & Different. 16p. (Orig.). (ps-2). 1975. pap. 3.95 (*0-85953-043-4*, Pub. by Child's Play England) Childs Play.

—There Was an Old Lady Who Swallowed a Fly. LC 90-46921. 16p. (ps-2). 1989. pap. 5.99 (*0-85953-018-3*, Pub. by Child's Play UK) Childs Play.

—There Were Ten in the Bed. LC 90-45580. 24p. (ps-2). 1979. 9.95 (*0-85953-095-7*, Pub. by Childs's Play England) Childs Play.

—This Is the House That Jack Built. LC 90-46922. 16p. (Orig.). (ps-2). 1977. pap. 5.95 (*0-85953-075-2*, Pub. by Child's Play England) Childs Play.

—This Old Man. LC 90-34327. 16p. (Orig.). (ps-2). 1974. (Pub. by Child's Play England); pap. 5.95 (*0-85953-026-4*, Pub. by Child's Play England) Childs Play.

—What Is It? (Orig.). (ps-2). 1975. pap. 3.95 (*0-85953-044-2*, Pub. by Child's Play England) Childs Play.

Adams, Pam & Jones, Ceri, illus. A Book of Ghosts. LC 90-45584. 32p. (Orig.). (ps-2). 1974. (Pub. by Child's Play England); pap. 5.95 (*0-85953-028-0*) Childs Play.

Adams, Patricia & Marzollo, Jean. The Helping Hands Handbook. Moores, Jeff, illus. LC 91-42947. 96p. (Orig.). (gr. 3 up). 1992. PLB 11.99 (*0-679-92816-2*); pap. 4.99 (*0-679-82816-8*) Random Bks Yng Read.

Adams, Peter. Storytelling Time. (gr. 3 up). 1993. 8.50 (*0-8062-4735-5*) Carlton.

Adams, Peter D. Early Loggers & the Sawmill. (Illus.). 64p. (gr. 4-5). 1981. 15.95 (*0-86505-005-8*); pap. 7.95 (*0-86505-006-6*) Crabtree Pub Co.

Adams, Randy L. & Sodaro, Craig. Wyoming: Courage in a Lonesome Land. Lynch, Don, ed. Exact Art Design Staff & Fay, Keith, illus. LC 90-82123. 313p. (ps-6). 1990. Centennial Edition. text ed. 24.95 (*0-913205-12-5*); special price 14.97 Grace Dangberg.

Adams, Raymond S. Video, No. 101. (Illus.). 116p. (gr. 11-12). 1992. pap. text ed. write for info. (*0-935648-39-9*) Halldin Pub.

Adams, Richard. Our Amazing Sun. Boyd, Patti, illus. LC 82-17419. 32p. (gr. 3-6). 1983. PLB 10.59 (*0-89375-890-6*); pap. text ed. 2.95 (*0-89375-891-4*) Troll Assocs.

—Our Wonderful Solar System. Burns, Raymond, illus. LC 82-17413. 32p. (gr. 3-6). 1983. PLB 10.59 (*0-89375-872-8*); pap. text ed. 2.95 (*0-89375-873-6*) Troll Assocs.

Adams, Richard, ed. see Dickens, Charles.

Adams, Richard, ed. see Shakespeare, William.

Adams, Sara, ed. see Farr, J. Michael & Christophersen, Susan.

Adams, Sara, ed. see Lindsay, Norene.

Adams, Simon. Explore the World of Man-Made Wonders. Biesty, Stephan, illus. (gr. 3-7). 1991. 7.95 (*0-685-54426-5*, Golden Pr) Western Pub.

—Explore the World of Man-Made Wonders. (gr. 4-7). 1991. 6.95 (*0-307-15603-6*) Western Pub.

Adams, Simon, et al. Illustrated Atlas of World History. LC 91-16652. (Illus.). 160p. (Orig.). (gr. 5 up). 1992. PLB 16.99 (*0-679-92465-5*); pap. 13.00 (*0-679-82465-0*) Random Bks Yng Read.

Adamson, Joy. Born Free. large type ed. (gr. 10 up). Repr. of 1960 ed. write for info. NAVH.

Adamson, Wendy, jt. auth. see Gadler, Steve.

Addams, Shay, ed. Quest for Clues, No. III. Dee, Jeff, illus. 198p. 1990. 24.99 (*0-685-41032-3*) Origin Syst.

Addeo, Pat. Mrs. Blake's Cakes. 1991. 6.95 (*0-533-08807-0*) Vantage.

Adderholdt-Elliott, Miriam. Perfectionism: What's Bad about Being Too Good? Espeland, Pamela, ed. LC 86-81130. (Illus.). 136p. (gr. 7 up). 1987. pap. 8.95 (*0-915793-07-5*) Free Spirit Pub.

Addison, Harry W. Write That Down for Me Daddy. Schendle, Kathy A., illus. LC 78-9028. 50p. (gr. 6-12). 1978. Repr. of 1974 ed. 4.95 (*0-88289-871-X*) Pelican.

Addison, John, ed. Suleyman & the Ottoman Empire. Yapp, Malcolm & Killingray, Margaret, eds. (Illus.). (gr. 6-10). 1980. pap. text ed. 3.45 (*0-89908-013-8*) Greenhaven.

—Traditional Africa. Yapp, Malcolm, et al, eds. (Illus.). 32p. (gr. 6-11). 1980. pap. text ed. 3.45 (*0-89908-009-X*) Greenhaven.

Addison-Wesley Staff. El Conejo la Tortuga - Big Book. (SPA., Illus.). 16p. (gr. k-3). 1989. pap. text ed. 31.75 (*0-201-19937-8*) Addison-Wesley.

—El Conejo la Tortuga - Little Book. (SPA., Illus.). 16p. (gr. k-3). 1989. pap. text ed. 4.50 (*0-201-19709-X*) Addison-Wesley.

—The Farmer & the Beet. (Illus.). (gr. k-2). 1988. text ed. 31.75 (*0-201-19318-3*); pap. text ed. 12.95 (*0-201-19059-1*) Addison-Wesley.

—The Farmer & the Beet Little Book. (Illus.). 16p. (gr. k-3). 1989. pap. text ed. 4.50 (*0-201-19053-2*) Addison-Wesley.

—La Gallinita Roja Big Book. (SPA., Illus.). 16p. (gr. k-3). 1989. pap. text ed. 31.75 (*0-201-19936-X*) Addison-Wesley.

—La Gallinita Roja, Spanish Little Book. (SPA., Illus.). 16p. (gr. k-3). 1989. pap. text ed. 4.50 (*0-201-19708-1*) Addison-Wesley.

—The Gingerbread Man. (Illus.). 16p. (gr. k-2). 1989. text ed. 31.75 (*0-201-19320-5*); pap. text ed. 12.95 (*0-201-19064-8*) Addison-Wesley.

—The Gingerbread Man Little Book. (Illus.). 16p. (gr. k-3). 1989. pap. text ed. 4.50 (*0-201-19054-0*) Addison-Wesley.

—Goldilocks & the Three Bears. (Illus.). (gr. k-2). 1988. pap. text ed. 31.75 (*0-201-19319-1*) Addison-Wesley.

—Goldilocks & the Three Bears Little Book. (Illus.). 16p. (gr. k-3). 1989. text ed. 12.95 (*0-201-19065-6*); pap. text ed. 4.50 (*0-201-19055-9*) Addison-Wesley.

—The Hare & the Tortoise. (Illus.). 16p. (gr. k-2). 1989. 31.75 (*0-201-19324-8*); pap. text ed. 12.95 (*0-201-19369-8*) Addison-Wesley.

—The Hare & the Tortoise Little Book. (Illus.). 16p. (gr. k-3). 1989. pap. text ed. 4.50 (*0-201-19365-5*) Addison-Wesley.

—How the Moon Got in the Sky. (Illus.). (gr. k-2). 1989. 31.75 (*0-201-19325-6*); pap. text ed. 12.95 (*0-201-19366-3*) Addison-Wesley.

—How the Moon Got in the Sky Little Book. (Illus.). 16p. (gr. k-3). 1989. pap. text ed. 4.50 (*0-201-19359-0*) Addison-Wesley.

—The Little Red Hen. (Illus.). 16p. (gr. k-2). 1989. text ed. 31.75 (*0-201-19323-X*); pap. text ed. 12.95 (*0-201-19368-X*) Addison-Wesley.

—The Little Red Hen Little Book. (Illus.). 16p. (gr. k-3). 1989. pap. 4.50 (*0-201-19364-7*) Addison-Wesley.

—The Rabbit & the Turnip. (Illus.). 16p. (gr. k-2). 1989. 31.75 (*0-201-19326-4*); PLB 12.95 (*0-201-19367-1*); pap. text ed. 4.50 (*0-201-19360-4*) Addison-Wesley.

—Ricitos de Oro - Little Book. (SPA., Illus.). 16p. (gr. k-3). 1989. pap. text ed. 4.50 (*0-201-19707-3*) Addison-Wesley.

—Ricitos de Oro y los Tres Osos Big Book. (SPA., Illus.). 16p. (gr. k-3). 1989. pap. text ed. 31.75 (*0-201-19935-1*) Addison-Wesley.

—The Three Little Pigs. 16p. (gr. k-2). 1988. text ed. 31.75 (*0-201-19322-1*); pap. 12.95 (*0-201-19066-4*) Addison-Wesley.

—The Three Little Pigs Little Book. (Illus.). 16p. (gr. k-3). 1989. pap. text ed. 4.50 (*0-201-19058-3*) Addison-Wesley.

—Los Tres Cerditos - Little Book. (SPA., Illus.). 16p. (gr. k-3). 1989. pap. text ed. 4.50 (*0-201-19710-3*) Addison-Wesley.

—Los Tres Cerditos Big Book. (SPA., Illus.). 16p. (gr. k-3). 1989. pap. text ed. 31.75 (*0-201-19938-6*) Addison-Wesley.

Addo, Peter E. How the Spider Became Bald: African Folk Tales & Legends from Ghana. 128p. (gr. 8-12). 1993. 17.95 (*1-883846-00-5*); pap. 9.95 (*1-883846-01-3*) M Reynolds.

Addy, Sharon. We Didn't Mean to. Blair, Jay, illus. McDermot, Gerald, intro. by. LC 80-24976. (Illus.). 32p. (gr. k-6). 1981. PLB 16.67 (*0-8172-1370-8*) Raintree Pubs Ltd.

Addy, Sharon H. A Visit with Great-Grandma. Fay, Ann, ed. LC 88-20867. (Illus.). 32p. (gr. 1-3). 1989. 13.95g (*0-8075-8497-5*) A Whitman.

Addy-Trout, Elaine, jt. auth. see Marquis, M. Ann.

Adelman, Deborah. The Children of Perestroika Come of Age: Young People of Moscow Talk about Life in the New Russia. LC 90-25104. 280p. 1993. text ed. 29.95 (*1-56324-286-9*) M E Sharpe.

Adelman, Elizabeth, ed. see Rand McNally Staff & Reddy, Francis.

Adelman, Sherri, ed. see Gibson, Litzkah R.

Aderholdt, Kristel. Boredom Rx. (Illus.). 144p. (gr. 1-8). 1991. 27.95 (*0-937857-19-X*, 1583) Speech Bin.

Aderman, James. Is He the One? Fischer, William E., ed. Woodfin, James, illus. 64p. (gr. 9-12). 1985. pap. 3.95 leader's guide (*0-938272-21-7*); pap. 3.25 student's guide (*0-938272-20-9*) WELS Board.

Adinolfi, JoAnn. The Egyptian Polar Bear. Adinolfi, JoAnn, illus. 1994. write for info. (*0-395-68074-3*) HM.

Adkins, Jan. How a House Happens. (Illus.). 32p. (gr. 5 up). 1983. pap. 3.95 (*0-8027-7206-4*) Walker & Co.

—Moving Heavy Things. (Illus.). (gr. 5 up). 1980. 13.45 (*0-395-29206-9*) HM.

—Moving Heavy Things. Adkins, Jan, illus. 48p. (gr. 4-6). 1991. pap. 4.80 (*0-395-60284-X*, Sandpiper) HM.

—Solstice: A Mystery of the Season. Adkins, Jan, illus. 128p. 1990. 12.95 (*0-8027-6970-5*); lib. bdg. 13.85 reinforced (*0-8027-6971-3*) Walker & Co.

—A Storm Without Rain. LC 92-24601. 192p. (gr. 7 up). 1993. pap. 3.95 (*0-688-11852-6*, Pub. by Beech Tree Bks) Morrow.

—String: Tying It up, Tying It Down. Adkins, Jan, illus. LC 91-25786. 48p. (gr. 5 up). 1992. SBE 13.95 (*0-684-18875-9*, Scribners Young Read) Macmillan Child Grp.

Adlard, John, tr. see Karadzic, Vuk.

Adler, Ann. A Family in West Germany. LC 85-6981. (Illus.). 32p. (gr. 2-5). 1985. PLB 13.50 (*0-8225-1658-6*) Lerner Pubns.

Adler, Bill, compiled by. Children's Letters to Santa Claus. LC 93-25377. (Illus.). (ps-3). 1993. 9.95 (*1-55972-196-0*, Birch Ln Pr) Carol Pub Group.

Adler, C. S. Always & Forever Friends. 176p. 1990. pap. 3.99 (*0-380-70687-3*, Camelot) Avon.

—Binding Ties. (gr. k-12). 1989. pap. 2.95 (*0-440-20413-5*, LFL) Dell.

—Daddy's Climbing Tree. 144p. (gr. 4-7). 1993. 13.95 (*0-395-63032-0*, Clarion Bks) HM.

—Eddie's Blue-Winged Dragon. 144p. 1990. pap. 3.50 (*0-380-70768-3*, Camelot) Avon.

—Footsteps on the Stairs. LC 81-15146. 160p. (gr. 4-6). 1982. pap. 12.95 (*0-385-28303-2*) Delacorte.

—Footsteps on the Stairs. 160p. (gr. 5-9). 1984. pap. 2.25 (*0-440-42654-5*, YB) Dell.

—Ghost Brother. 160p. (gr. 4-8). 1990. 13.95 (*0-395-52592-6*) HM.

—Ghost Brother. 144p. 1992. pap. 3.50 (*0-380-71386-1*, Camelot) Avon.

—Good-Bye Pink Pig. 176p. (gr. 3-7). 1986. pap. 2.75 (*0-380-70175-8*, Camelot) Avon.

—If You Need Me. LC 87-36467. 160p. (gr. 4-8). 1988. SBE 13.95 (*0-02-700420-1*, Macmillan Child Bk) Macmillan Child Grp.

—In Our House Scott Is My Brother. LC 79-20693. 144p. (gr. 5-9). 1980. SBE 13.95 (*0-02-700140-7*, Macmillan Child Bk) Macmillan Child Grp.

—The Lump in the Middle. 160p. 1991. pap. 3.50 (*0-380-71176-1*, Camelot) Avon.

—Mismatched Summer. 144p. 1991. 14.95 (*0-399-21776-2*, Putnam) Putnam Pub Group.

—One Sister Too Many. LC 91-15530. 176p. (gr. 3-7). 1991. pap. 3.95 (*0-689-71521-8*, Aladdin) Macmillan Child Grp.

—One Sister Too Many (A Sequel to Split Sisters) LC 88-13144. 176p. (gr. 4-8). 1989. SBE 13.95 (*0-02-700271-3*, Macmillan Child Bk) Macmillan Child Grp.

—The Silver Coach. 112p. (gr. 3-7). 1988. pap. 2.50 (*0-380-75498-3*, Camelot) Avon.

—Some Other Summer. (gr. 3-7). 1988. pap. 2.95 (*0-380-70515-X*, Camelot) Avon.

—Split Sisters. LC 89-18308. 176p. (gr. 4-7). 1990. pap. 3.95 (*0-689-71369-X*, Aladdin) Macmillan Child Grp.

—A Tribe for Lexi. LC 90-6322. 144p. (gr. 3-7). 1991. SBE 13.95 (*0-02-700361-2*, Macmillan Child Bk) Macmillan Child Grp.

—Tuna Fish Thanksgiving. 160p. (gr. 5-9). 1992. 13.45 (*0-395-58829-4*, Clarion Bks) HM.

—Willie, the Frog Prince. LC 92-44113. 1994. write for info. (*0-395-65615-X*, Clarion Bks) HM.

Adler, Carole S. Riding Whiskey. LC 93-30196. 1994. write for info. (*0-395-68185-5*, Clarion Bks) HM.

Adler, David. All about the Moon. Burns, Raymond, illus. LC 82-17422. 32p. (gr. 3-6). 1983. PLB 10.59 (*0-89375-886-8*); pap. text ed. 2.95 (*0-89375-887-6*) Troll Assocs.

—Amazing Magnets. Lawler, Dan, illus. LC 82-17377. 32p. (gr. 3-6). 1983. PLB 10.59 (*0-89375-894-9*); pap. text ed. 2.95 (*0-89375-895-7*) Troll Assocs.

—Cam Jansen & the Mystery at the Monkey House. Natti, Susanna, illus. LC 93-13047. 64p. (gr. 2-5). 1993. pap. 3.99 (*0-14-036023-9*, Puffin) Puffin Bks.

—The Dinosaur Princess & Other Prehistoric Riddles. (gr. k-3). 1992. pap. 2.99 (*0-553-15793-0*, Skylark) Bantam.

—The House on the Roof. Hirsh, Marilyn, illus. LC 84-12555. 32p. (ps-4). 1984. pap. 4.95 (*0-930494-35-0*) Kar-Ben.

—Jewish Holiday Fun. 64p. (Orig.). (gr. 2-6). 1987. pap. 3.95 (*0-930494-72-5*) Kar Ben.

—Our Amazing Ocean. Veno, Joseph, illus. LC 82-17373. 32p. (gr. 3-6). 1983. PLB 10.59 (*0-89375-882-5*); pap. text ed. 2.95 (*0-89375-883-3*) Troll Assocs.

—We Remember the Holocaust. LC 87-21139. (Illus.). 144p. (gr. 6 up). 1989. 17.95 (*0-8050-0434-3*, Bks Young Read) H Holt & Co.

—Wonders of Energy. Johnson, Lewis, illus. LC 82-20042. 32p. (gr. 3-6). 1983. PLB 10.59 (*0-89375-884-1*); pap. text ed. 2.95 (*0-89375-885-X*) Troll Assocs.

—World of Weather. Burns, Raymond, illus. LC 82-17398. 32p. (gr. 3-6). 1983. PLB 10.59 (*0-89375-870-1*); pap. text ed. 2.95 (*0-89375-871-X*) Troll Assocs.

Adler, David A. Benjamin Franklin: Printer, Inventor, Statesman. Miller, Lyle, illus. LC 91-28816. 48p. (gr. 2-5). 1992. reinforced bdg. 14.95 (*0-8234-0929-5*) Holiday.

—Bible Fun Book: Puzzles, Riddles, Magic, & More. (Illus., Orig.). (gr. 1-5). 1979. pap. 3.95 (*0-88482-769-0*) Hebrew Pub.

—Bunny Rabbit Rebus. Linden, Madelaine G., illus. LC 82-45574. 40p. (gr. 1-4). 1983. (Crowell Jr Bks); (Crowell Jr Bks) HarpC Child Bks.

—Bunny Rabbit Rebus. Linden, Madelaine G., illus. (ps-3). 1987. pap. 3.95 (*0-14-050775-2*, Puffin) Puffin Bks.

—Cam Jansen & the Mystery at the Haunted House. Natti, Susanna, illus. 64p. (gr. 2-5). 1992. PLB 11.00 (*0-670-83419-X*) Viking Child Bks.

—Cam Jansen & the Mystery at the Monkey House. Natti, Susanna, illus. LC 85-40443. 56p. (gr. 2-4). 1985. pap. 10.95 (*0-670-80782-6*) Viking Child Bks.

—Cam Jansen & the Mystery Corn Popper. Natti, Susanna, illus. 64p. (gr. 2-5). 1986. pap. 10.95 (*0-670-81118-1*) Viking Child Bks.

—Cam Jansen & the Mystery Monster Movie. Natti, Susanna, illus. LC 83-16693. 64p. (gr. 2-5). 1984. pap. 10.95 (*0-670-20035-2*) Viking Child Bks.

—Cam Jansen & the Mystery of Flight 54. Natti, Susanna, illus. 64p. (gr. 2-5). 1989. pap. 10.95 (*0-670-81841-0*) Viking Child Bks.

—Cam Jansen & the Mystery of Flight 54. Natti, Susanna, illus. 64p. (gr. 2-5). 1992. pap. 3.99 (*0-14-036104-9*, Puffin) Puffin Bks.

—Cam Jansen & the Mystery of the Babe Ruth Baseball. Natti, Susanna, illus. LC 82-2621. 64p. (gr. 2-5). 1982. pap. 11.00 (*0-670-20037-9*) Viking Child Bks.

—Cam Jansen & the Mystery of the Babe Ruth Baseball. Natti, Susanna, illus. 64p. (gr. 1-4). 1984. pap. 2.75 (*0-440-41020-7*, YB) Dell.

—Cam Jansen & the Mystery of the Babe Ruth Baseball. (gr. 4-7). 1991. pap. 3.99 (*0-14-034895-6*, Puffin) Puffin Bks.

—Cam Jansen & the Mystery of the Carnival Prize. (gr. k-6). 1987. pap. 2.99 (*0-440-41202-1*, YB) Dell.

—Cam Jansen & the Mystery of the Carnival Prize. Natti, Susanna, illus. 64p. (gr. 2-5). 1992. pap. 3.99 (*0-14-036022-0*) Puffin Bks.

—Cam Jansen & the Mystery of the Chocolate Fudge Sale. Natti, Susanna, illus. 64p. (gr. 2-5). 1993. reinforced bdg. 11.99 (*0-670-84968-5*) Viking Child Bks.

—Cam Jansen & the Mystery of the Circus Clown. Natti, Susanna, illus. LC 82-50363. 64p. (gr. 2-4). 1983. pap. 10.95 (*0-670-20036-0*) Viking Child Bks.

—Cam Jansen & the Mystery of the Circus Clown. Natti, Susanna, illus. 64p. (gr. 1-4). 1985. pap. 2.75 (*0-440-41021-5*, YB) Dell.

—Cam Jansen & the Mystery of the Circus Clown. (gr. 4-7). 1991. pap. 3.99 (*0-14-034897-2*, Puffin) Puffin Bks.

—Cam Jansen & the Mystery of the Dinosaur Bones. Natti, Susanna, illus. LC 80-25132. 64p. (gr. 2-5). 1981. pap. 11.99 (*0-670-20040-9*) Viking Child Bks.

—Cam Jansen & the Mystery of the Dinosaur Bones. Natti, Susanna, illus. (gr. 1-4). 1983. pap. 2.75 (*0-440-41199-8*, YB) Dell.

—Cam Jansen & the Mystery of the Dinosaur Bones. Natti, Susanna, illus. 64p. (gr. 2-5). 1991. pap. 3.99 (*0-14-034674-0*, Puffin) Puffin Bks.

—Cam Jansen & the Mystery of the Gold Coins. Natti, Susanna, illus. LC 81-16158. 64p. (gr. 2-5). 1982. pap. 10.95 (0-570-20038-7) Viking Child Bks.
—Cam Jansen & the Mystery of the Gold Coins. Natti, Susanna, illus. 64p. (gr. k-6). 1984. pap. 2.75 (0-440-40996-9, YB) Dell.
—Cam Jansen & the Mystery of the Gold Coins. (gr. 4-7). 1991. pap. 3.99 (0-14-034896-4, Puffin) Puffin Bks.
—Cam Jansen & the Mystery of the Haunted House, No. 13. Natti, Susanna, illus. 64p. (gr. 2-5). 1994. pap. 3.99 (0-14-034478-0) Puffin Bks.
—Cam Jansen & the Mystery of the Monster Movie. Natti, Susanna, illus. 64p. (gr. 2-5). 1992. pap. 3.99 (0-14-036021-2) Puffin Bks.
—Cam Jansen & the Mystery of the Stolen Corn Popper. Natti, Susanna, illus. 64p. (gr. 2-5). 1992. pap. 3.99 (0-14-036103-0, Puffin) Puffin Bks.
—Cam Jansen & the Mystery of the Stolen Diamonds. Natti, Susanna, illus. LC 79-20695. 64p. (gr. 2-5). 1980. pap. 10.95 (0-670-20039-5) Viking Child Bks.
—Cam Jansen & the Mystery of the Stolen Diamonds. Natti, Susanna, illus. 64p. (gr. 1-4). 1982. pap. 2.75 (0-440-41111-4, YB) Dell.
—Cam Jansen & the Mystery of the Stolen Diamonds. Natti, Susanna, illus. 64p. (gr. 2-5). 1991. pap. 3.99 (0-14-034670-8) Puffin Bks.
—Cam Jansen & the Mystery of the Television Dog. Natti, Susanna, illus. LC 81-2207. 64p. (gr. 2-5). 1981. pap. 10.95 (0-670-20042-5) Viking Child Bks.
—Cam Jansen & the Mystery of the Television Dog. Natti, Susanna, illus. 64p. (gr. 1-4). 1983. pap. 2.75 (0-440-41196-3, YB) Dell.
—Cam Jansen & the Mystery of the Television Dog. Natti, Susanna, illus. 64p. (gr. 2-5). 1991. pap. 3.99 (0-14-034676-7, Puffin) Puffin Bks.
—Cam Jansen & the Mystery of the U. F. O. Natti, Susanna, illus. LC 80-15580. 64p. (gr. 7-10). 1980. pap. 10.95 (0-670-20041-7) Viking Child Bks.
—Cam Jansen & the Mystery of the U. F. O. Natti, Susanna, illus. 64p. (gr. 2-5). 1991. pap. 3.99 (0-14-034672-4, Puffin) Puffin Bks.
—The Cam Jansen Fun Book. Natti, Susanna, illus. 32p. (gr. 2-5). 1992. pap. 3.99 (0-14-034490-X, Puffin) Puffin Bks.
—The Carsick Zebra & Other Animal Riddles. De Paola, Tomie, illus. LC 82-48750. 64p. (gr. 1-4). 1983. reinforced bdg. 12.95 (0-8234-0479-X) Holiday.
—The Carsick Zebra & Other Animal Riddles. De Paola, Tomie, illus. 64p. (Orig.). (gr. 1). 1985. pap. 2.25 (0-553-15487-7) Bantam.
—The Children's Book of Jewish Holidays. Sears, Dovid, illus. 48p. (gr. k-6). 1987. 11.95 (0-89906-810-3); pap. 7.95 (0-89906-811-1) Mesorah Pubns.
—Christopher Columbus: Great Explorer. Miller, Lyle, illus. LC 90-28668. 48p. (gr. 2-5). 1991. reinforced bdg. 14.95 (0-8234-0895-7) Holiday.
—The Dinosaur Princess & Other Prehistoric Riddles. Leedy, Loreen, illus. LC 87-25121. 64p. (gr. 1-4). 1988. reinforced bdg. 14.95 (0-8234-0686-5) Holiday.
—Eaton Stanley & the Mind Control Experiment. Drescher, Joan, illus. LC 84-21135. 96p. (gr. 2-6). 1985. 11.95 (0-525-44117-4, DCB) Dutton Child Bks.
—The Fourth Floor Twins & the Fish Snitch Mystery. Trivas, Irene, illus. 64p. (gr. 1-4). 1986. pap. 3.99 (0-14-032082-2, Puffin) Puffin Bks.
—The Fourth Floor Twins & the Fortune Cookie Chase. Trivas, Irene, illus. 64p. (gr. 1-4). 1986. pap. 3.95 (0-14-032083-0) Puffin Bks.
—The Fourth Floor Twins & the Sand Castle Contest. Trivas, Irene, illus. (gr. 2-5). 1988. 9.95 (0-318-37432-3) Viking Child Bks.
—The Fourth Floor Twins & the Silver Ghost Express. Trivas, Irene, illus. (gr. 2-5). 1987. pap. 4.99 (0-14-032215-9, Puffin) Puffin Bks.
—George Washington: Father of Our Country. Garrick, Jacqueline, illus. LC 88-4691. 48p. (gr. 2-5). 1988. reinforced bdg. 14.95 (0-8234-0717-9) Holiday.
—Hanukkah Fun Book: Puzzles, Riddles, Magic & More. LC 76-47459. (Illus.). (gr. 3-7). 1976. pap. 3.95 (0-88482-754-2, Bonim Bks) Hebrew Pub.
—Hanukkah Game Book: Games, Riddles, Puzzles & More. (Illus.). (gr. 1-5). 1978. pap. 3.95 (0-88482-764-X, Bonim Bks) Hebrew Pub.
—Happy Hanukkah Rebus. Palmer, Jan, illus. 32p. (ps-3). 1989. pap. 11.95 (0-670-82419-4) Viking Child Bks.
—Happy Hanukkah Rebus. Palmer, Jan, illus. 32p. (ps-3). 1991. 3.99 (0-14-050915-1, Puffin) Puffin Bks.
—Happy Thanksgiving Rebus. (ps-3). 1991. 12.95 (0-670-83388-6) Viking Child Bks.
—I Know I'm a Witch. Stevenson, Sucie, illus. LC 86-33508. 32p. (ps-2). 1990. pap. 4.95 (0-8050-1480-2, Bks Young Read) H Holt & Co.
—Jackie Robinson, He Was the First. LC 88-32394. (Illus.). (gr. 2-5). 1989. reinforced bdg. 14.95 (0-8234-0739-X) Holiday.
—Jackie Robinson: He Was the First. Casilla, Robert, illus. LC 88-32394. 48p. (gr. 2-5). 1990. pap. 4.95 (0-8234-0799-3) Holiday.
—Un Libro Ilustrado sobre Abraham Lincoln. Mlawer, Teresa, tr. from ENG. Wallner, John & Wallner, Alexandra, illus. (SPA.). 32p. (ps-3). 1992. reinforced bdg. 14.95 (0-8234-0980-5); pap. 5.95 (0-8234-0989-9) Holiday.

—Un Libro Ilustrado Sobre Cristobal Colon. Mlawer, Teresa, tr. from ENG. Wallner, John & Wallner, Alexandra, illus. (SPA.). 32p. (ps-3). 1992. reinforced bdg. 14.95 (0-8234-0981-3); pap. 5.95 (0-8234-0990-2) Holiday.
—Un Libro Ilustrado Sobre Martin Luther King, Hijo. Mlawer, Teresa, tr. from ENG. Casilla, Robert, illus. (SPA.). 32p. (ps-3). 1992. reinforced bdg. 14.95 (0-8234-0982-1); pap. 5.95 (0-8234-0991-0) Holiday.
—Malke's Secret Recipe: A Chanukah Story from Chelm. LC 88-32019. (ps-3). 1989. 10.95 (0-930494-88-1); pap. 4.95 (0-930494-89-X) Kar Ben.
—Martin Luther King, Jr. Free at Last. Casilla, Robert, illus. LC 86-4670. 48p. (gr. 2-5). 1986. reinforced bdg. 14.95 (0-8234-0618-0); pap. 4.95 (0-8234-0619-9) Holiday.
—My Dog & the Birthday Mystery. Gackenbach, Dick, illus. LC 86-14269. 32p. (gr. 1-4). 1987. reinforced bdg. 13.95 (0-8234-0632-6); pap. 5.95 (0-8234-0710-1) Holiday.
—My Dog & the Green Sock Mystery. Gackenbach, Dick, illus. LC 85-14145. 32p. (gr. 1-4). 1986. reinforced bdg. 13.95 (0-8234-0590-7) Holiday.
—The Number on My Grandfather's Arm. 28p. (gr. 1-3). 1987. 7.95 (0-8074-0328-8, 103641) UAHC.
—Onion Sundaes. Harms, Heather, illus. LC 93-5878. 1994. PLB write for info. (0-679-94697-7); pap. write for info. (0-679-84697-2) Random.
—Our Golda: The Story of Golda Meir. Ruff, Donna, illus. LC 83-16798. 64p. (gr. 3-7). 1984. pap. 11.95 (0-670-53107-3) Viking Child Bks.
—Our Golda: The Story of Golda Meir. Ruff, Donna, illus. 64p. (gr. 2-6). 1986. pap. 4.50 (0-14-032104-7, Puffin) Puffin Bks.
—Passover Fun Book: Puzzles, Riddles, Magic & More. (Illus.). (gr. k-5). 1978. saddlewire bdg. 3.95 (0-88482-759-3, Bonim Bks) Hebrew Pub.
—Picture Book of Abraham Lincoln. LC 88-16393. (Illus.). 32p. (ps-3). 1989. reinforced bdg. 14.95 (0-8234-0731-4); pap. 5.95 (0-8234-0801-9) Holiday.
—A Picture Book of Anne Frank. Ritz, Karen, illus. LC 92-17283. 32p. (ps-3). 1993. reinforced bdg. 14.95 (0-8234-1003-X) Holiday.
—A Picture Book of Benjamin Franklin. Wallner, John & Wallner, Alexandra, illus. LC 89-20059. 32p. (ps-3). 1990. reinforced bdg. 14.95 (0-8234-0792-6); pap. 5.95 (0-8234-0882-5) Holiday.
—A Picture Book of Christopher Columbus. Wallner, John & Wallner, Alexandra, illus. LC 90-39211. 32p. (ps-3). 1991. reinforced 14.95 (0-8234-0857-4) Holiday.
—A Picture Book of Christopher Columbus. Wallner, John & Wallner, Alexandra, illus. pap. 5.95 (0-8234-0949-X) Holiday.
—A Picture Book of Eleanor Roosevelt. Casilla, Robert, illus. LC 90-39212. 32p. (ps-3). 1991. reinforced 14.95 (0-8234-0856-6) Holiday.
—A Picture Book of Florence Nightingale. Wallner, John & Wallner, Alexandra, illus. LC 91-43388. 32p. (ps-3). 1992. reinforced bdg. 14.95 (0-8234-0965-1) Holiday.
—A Picture Book of Frederick Douglass. Byrd, Samuel, illus. LC 92-17378. 32p. (ps-3). 1993. reinforced bdg. 14.95 (0-8234-1002-1) Holiday.
—A Picture Book of George Washington. Wallner, John & Wallner, Alexandra, illus. LC 88-16384. 32p. (ps-3). 1989. reinforced bdg. 14.95 (0-8234-0732-2); pap. 5.95 (0-8234-0800-0) Holiday.
—A Picture Book of Hanukkah. Heller, Linda, illus. LC 82-2942. 32p. (ps-3). 1982. reinforced bdg. 14.95 (0-8234-0458-7); pap. 5.95 (0-8234-0574-5) Holiday.
—A Picture Book of Harriet Tubman. Byrd, Samuel, illus. LC 91-19628. 32p. (ps-3). 1992. reinforced bdg. 14.95 (0-8234-0926-0) Holiday.
—A Picture Book of Helen Keller. Wallner, John & Wallner, Alexandra, illus. LC 89-77510. 32p. (ps-3). 1990. reinforced 14.95 (0-8234-0818-3) Holiday.
—A Picture Book of Helen Keller. Wallner, John & Wallner, Alexandra, illus. LC 89-77510. pap. 5.95 (0-8234-0950-3) Holiday.
—A Picture Book of Jackie Robinson. Casilla, Robert, illus. LC 93-27224. (gr. 3 up). 1994. write for info. (0-8234-1122-2) Holiday.
—A Picture Book of Jesse Owens. Casilla, Robert, illus. LC 91-44735. 32p. (ps-3). 1992. reinforced bdg. 14.95 (0-8234-0966-X) Holiday.
—A Picture Book of Jewish Holidays. Heller, Linda, illus. LC 81-2765. 32p. (ps-3). 1981. reinforced bdg. 14.95 (0-8234-0396-3); pap. 5.95 (0-8234-0756-X) Holiday.
—A Picture Book of John F. Kennedy. Casilla, Robert, illus. LC 90-23589. 32p. (ps-3). 1991. reinforced 14.95 (0-8234-0884-1); pap. 5.95 (0-8234-0976-7) Holiday.
—A Picture Book of Martin Luther King, Jr. Casilla, Robert, illus. LC 89-9030. 32p. (ps-3). 1989. reinforced bdg. 14.95 (0-8234-0770-5); pap. 5.95 (0-8234-0847-7) Holiday.
—A Picture Book of Passover. Heller, Linda, illus. LC 81-6983. 32p. (ps-3). 1982. reinforced bdg. 14.95 (0-8234-0439-0); pap. 5.95 (0-8234-0609-1) Holiday.
—A Picture Book of Robert E. Lee. Wallner, John & Wallner, Alexandra, illus. LC 93-22998. 32p. (gr. 4-8). 1994. 15.95 (0-8234-1111-7) Holiday.
—A Picture Book of Rosa Parks. Casilla, Robert, illus. LC 92-41826. 32p. (ps-3). 1993. reinforced bdg. 15.95 (0-8234-1041-2) Holiday.
—A Picture Book of Simon Bolivar. Casilla, Robert, illus. LC 91-19419. 32p. (ps-3). 1992. reinforced bdg. 14.95 (0-8234-0927-9) Holiday.

—A Picture Book of Sitting Bull. Byrd, Samuel, illus. LC 92-47119. (ps-3). 1993. reinforced bdg. 15.95 (0-8234-1044-7) Holiday.
—A Picture Book of Sojourner Truth. Griffith, Gershom, illus. LC 93-7478. 32p. (gr. 4-8). 1994. 15.95 (0-8234-1072-2) Holiday.
—A Picture Book of Thomas Jefferson. Wallner, John & Wallner, Alexandra, illus. LC 89-20076. 32p. (ps-3). 1990. reinforced bdg. 14.95 (0-8234-0791-8); pap. 5.95 (0-8234-0881-7) Holiday.
—The Purple Turkey & Other Thanksgiving Riddles. Hafner, Marylin, illus. LC 86-310. 64p. (gr. 1-4). 1986. reinforced bdg. 11.95 (0-8234-0613-X) Holiday.
—Remember Betsy Floss & Other Colonial American Riddles. Wallner, John, illus. LC 87-45333. 64p. (gr. 1-4). 1987. reinforced bdg. 11.95 (0-8234-0664-4) Holiday.
—Roman Numerals. Barton, Byron, illus. LC 77-2270. 40p. (gr. 1-4). 1977. PLB 14.89 (0-690-01302-7, Crowell Jr Bks) HarpC Child Bks.
—T. F. Benson & the Detective Dog Mystery. (gr. 4-7). 1993. pap. 3.25 (0-553-15982-8) Bantam.
—T. F. Benson & the Dinosaur Madness Mystery. (gr. 4-7). 1992. pap. 2.99 (0-553-15980-1) Bantam.
—T. F. Benson & the Eye Spy Mystery. (gr. 4-7). 1993. pap. 3.25 (0-553-15981-X) Bantam.
—T. F. Benson & the Funny Money Mystery. (gr. 4-7). 1992. pap. 2.99 (0-553-15979-8) Bantam.
—A Teacher on Roller Skates & Other School Riddles. Wallner, John, illus. LC 89-1929. 64p. (gr. 1-4). 1989. reinforced bdg. 11.95 (0-8234-0775-6) Holiday.
—Thomas Alva Edison: Great Inventor. Miller, Lyle, illus. LC 89-77507. 48p. (gr. 2-5). 1990. reinforced bdg. 14.95 (0-8234-0820-5) Holiday.
—Thomas Jefferson: Father of Our Democracy. Garrick, Jacqueline, illus. LC 87-45336. 48p. (gr. 2-5). 1987. reinforced bdg. 14.95 (0-8234-0667-9) Holiday.
—The Twisted Witch & Other Spooky Riddles. Chess, Victoria, illus. LC 85-909. 64p. (gr. 1-4). 1985. reinforced bdg. 11.95 (0-8234-0571-0) Holiday.
—The Twisted Witch & Other Spooky Riddles. 64p. 1986. pap. 2.25 (0-553-15447-8) Bantam.
—Wild Pill Hickok & Other Old West Riddles. Rounds, Glen, illus. LC 88-6480. 64p. (gr. 1-4). 1988. reinforced bdg. 11.95 (0-8234-0718-7) Holiday.
—You Breathe In, You Breathe Out: All about Your Lungs. Roxas, Reni, ed. Paterson, Diane, illus. 32p. (gr. 1-4). 1991. PLB 12.90 (0-531-10700-0) Watts.
Adler, Irene. Ballooning: High & Wild. LC 75-23406. (Illus.). 32p. (gr. 5-10). 1976. PLB 10.79 (0-89375-001-8); pap. 2.95 (0-89375-017-4) Troll Assocs.
Adler, Katie & McBride, Rachael. For Sale: One Sister--Cheap! Venezia, Mike, illus. LC 86-11723. 32p. (ps-3). 1986. PLB 13.93 (0-516-03476-6); pap. 3.95 (0-516-43476-4) Childrens.
Adler, Larry. Help Wanted: Riddles about Jobs. Burke, Susan S., illus. 32p. (gr. 1-4). 1989. PLB 11.95 (0-8225-2325-6) Lerner Pubns.
Adler, Robin W., jt. auth. see Halpern-Gold, Julia.
Adler, Susan S. Meet Samantha: An American Girl. Thieme, Jeanne, ed. Niles, Nancy & Lusk, Nancy M, illus. 72p. (gr. 2-5). 1986. 12.95 (0-937295-03-5); PLB 12.95 (0-937295-80-9); pap. 5.95 (0-937295-04-3) Pleasant Co.
—Samantha Learns a Lesson: A School Story. Thieme, Jeanne, ed. Niles, Nancy & Lusk, Nancy N, illus. 72p. (gr. 2-5). 1986. 12.95 (0-937295-12-4); PLB 12.95 (0-937295-83-3); pap. 5.95 (0-937295-13-2) Pleasant Co.
Adler, Susan S, et al. Samantha, 6 bks. Niles, Nancy, et al, illus. 432p. (gr. 2-5). 1991. Boxed Set. 74.95 (1-56247-013-2); Boxed Set. lib. bdg. 74.95 (1-56247-050-7); Boxed Set. pap. 34.95 (0-937295-77-9) Pleasant Co.
Adoff, Arnold. All the Colors of the Race. Steptoe, John, illus. LC 81-11777. 64p. (gr. 5 up). 1982. 13.95 (0-688-00879-8); PLB 13.88 (0-688-00880-1) Lothrop.
—All the Colors of the Race. Steptoe, John, illus. LC 81-11777. 80p. 1992. pap. 4.95 (0-688-11496-2, Pub. by Beech Tree Bks) Morrow.
—Birds. Howell, Troy, illus. LC 81-47753. 64p. (gr. k-5). 1982. (Lipp Jr Bks) HarpC Child Bks.
—Black Is Brown Is Tan. McCully, Emily A., illus. LC 73-9855. 32p. (ps-3). 1973. 15.00i (0-06-020083-9); PLB 14.89 (0-06-020084-7) HarpC Child Bks.
—Black Is Brown Is Tan. McCully, Emily A., illus. LC 73-9855. 32p. (ps-3). 1992. pap. 3.95 (0-06-443269-6, Trophy) HarpC Child Bks.
—The Cabbages Are Chasing the Rabbits. Stevens, Janet, illus. LC 85-893. 32p. (gr. k-3). 1985. 15.95 (0-15-213875-7, HB Juv Bks) HarBrace.
—Chocolate Dreams. MacCombie, Turi, illus. LC 88-27208. 64p. (gr. 3 up). 1989. 13.95 (0-688-06822-7); PLB 13.88 (0-688-06823-5) Lothrop.
—Eats. ALC Staff, ed. Russo, Susan, illus. LC 79-11300. 48p. (gr. 2 up). 1992. pap. 3.95 (0-688-11695-7, Mulberry) Morrow.
—Eats: Poems. Russo, Susan, illus. LC 79-11300. (gr. 4 up). 1979. 13.95 (0-688-41901-1); PLB 12.88 (0-688-51901-6) Lothrop.
—Flamboyan. Barbour, Karen, illus. 32p. (ps-3). 1988. 14.95 (0-15-228404-4, HB Juv Bks) HarBrace.
—Friend Dog. Howell, Troy, illus. LC 80-7773. 48p. (gr. k-5). 1980. PLB 11.89 (0-685-02080-0, Lipp Jr Bks) HarpC Child Bks.

—Greens. Lewin, Betsy, illus. LC 85-16631. (gr. 1-5). 1988. 12.95 (*0-688-04276-7*); lib. bdg. 12.88 (*0-688-04277-5*) Lothrop.
—Hard to Be Six. Hanna, Cheryl, illus. LC 89-45903. 32p. (gr. k-3). 1990. 12.95 (*0-688-09013-3*); lib. bdg. 12.88 (*0-688-09579-8*) Lothrop.
—In for Winter, Out for Spring. Ingber, Bonnie V., ed. Pinkney, Jerry, illus. 43p. (ps-3). 1991. 14.95 (*0-15-238637-8*) HarBrace.
—Malcolm X. Wilson, John, illus. LC 85-42974. 40p. (gr. 2-5). 1985. pap. 5.95 (*0-06-446015-0*, Trophy) HarpC Child Bks.
—Malcolm X. Wilson, John, illus. LC 70-94787. 48p. (gr. 2-5). 1970. PLB 14.89 (*0-690-51414-X*, Crowell Jr Bks) HarpC Child Bks.
—Malcolm X. (gr. 1-4). 1992. 18.00 (*0-8446-6587-8*) Peter Smith.
—Sports Pages. Kuzma, Steve, illus. LC 85-45169. 80p. (gr. 3-7). 1986. (Lipp Jr Bks); PLB 14.89 (*0-397-32103-1*, Lipp Jr Bks) HarpC Child Bks.
—Sports Pages. Kuzma, Steve, illus. LC 85-45169. 80p. (gr. 3 up). 1990. pap. 5.95 (*0-06-446098-3*, Trophy) HarpC Child Bks.
—Street Music: City Poems. Barbour, Karen, illus. LC 92-28539. 1992. 15.00 (*0-06-021522-4*); PLB 14.89 (*0-06-021523-2*) HarpC Child Bks.
Adoff, Arnold, ed. I Am the Darker Brother: An Anthology of Modern Poems by Negro Americans. LC 68-12077. (Illus.). 128p. (gr. 7 up). 1970. pap. 4.95 (*0-02-041120-0*, Collier Young Ad) Macmillan Child Grp.
—My Black Me: A Beginning Book of Black Poetry. LC 73-16445. 96p. (gr. 3 up). 1974. 12.95 (*0-525-35460-3*, DCB) Dutton Child Bks.
—My Black Me: A Beginning Book of Black Poetry. (Illus.). 96p. (gr. 4-7). 1994. 14.99 (*0-525-45216-8*, DCB) Dutton Child Bks.
—The Poetry of Black America: Anthology of the Twentieth Century. Brooks, Gwendolyn, intro. by. LC 72-76518. 576p. (gr. 7 up). 1973. 25.00 (*0-06-020089-8*); PLB 24.89 (*0-06-020090-1*) HarpC Child Bks.
Adorjan, Carol. The Copy Cat Mystery. 128p. 1990. pap. 2.95 (*0-380-75743-5*, Camelot) Avon.
—I Can! Can You? rev. ed. Levine, Abby, ed. Nerlove, Miriam, illus. LC 90-37665. 24p. (ps). 1990. 11.95 (*0-8075-3491-9*) A Whitman.
—That's What Friends Are For. 1990. pap. 2.75 (*0-590-42454-8*) Scholastic Inc.
Adorjan, Carol & Rasovsky, Yuri. WKID: Easy Radio Plays. LC 88-132. (Illus.). 80p. (gr. 3-8). 1988. 9.95 (*0-8075-9155-6*) A Whitman.
Adorjan, Carol M., adapted by see Burnett, Frances H.
Adrian, Mary. The Fireball Mystery. Lonette, Reisie, illus. LC 77-17151. (gr. 2-6). 1977. 8.95 (*0-8038-2325-8*) Hastings.
Adrian-Vallance, D'Arcy, adapted by see Grey, Charlotte.
Adrine-Robinson, Kenyette, ed. see Gaines, Edith M., et al.
Adshead, Paul. The Chicken That Could Swim. LC 90-34358. (ps-3). 1990. 11.95 (*0-85953-294-1*); pap. 5.95 (*0-85953-346-8*) Childs Play.
—Incredible Reversing Peppermints. (ps-3). 1993. 7.95 (*0-85953-514-2*) Childs Play.
—Puzzle Island. LC 91-33416. (Illus.). (gr. k-7). 1991. 11.95 (*0-85953-402-2*); pap. 5.95 (*0-85953-403-0*) Childs Play.
—The Secret Hedgehog. LC 91-38897. (gr. 4 up). 1991. 7.95 (*0-85953-510-X*) Childs Play.
—Trilby. 1990. 7.95 (*0-85953-513-4*) Childs Play.
Advance Cal-Tech Inc. Let's Praise & Play: Children's Christian Mini-Piano Book. Kung, Edward, ed. Mc Kig, Susan, illus. Childe, Laura, intro. by. (Illus.). 36p. (ps-6). text ed. write for info. (*0-943759-00-5*) Advance Cal Tech.
Advantage International, Inc. Staff. My First Computer Book. (Illus.). 18p. 1992. activity bk. 3.00 (*1-56756-002-4*, SAC200) Advant Intl.
Adventure Publications. My Very Own Phone Book. (ps-3). 1993. pap. 7.95 (*0-9635490-0-6*) Just Mom & Me.
Adwry, W. Gordon and the Famous Visitor. Mitton, David & Permane, Terry, photos by. LC 92-45569. (Illus.). 32p. (ps-2). 1993. 3.50 (*0-679-84764-2*) Random Bks Yng Read.
Aerial Photography Services, Inc. Staff. Great Smoky Mtn. National Park. 32p. (ps-12). 2.95 (*0-936672-09-9*) Aerial Photo.
Aero Products Research, Inc., Industries Division Staff. Official CB Crossword Puzzles for Big Dummy's. (Illus.). (gr. 8 up). 1977. pap. 1.98 (*0-912682-18-3*) Aero Products.
Aeschylus. Oresteian Trilogy. Vellacott, Philip, tr. Incl. Agamemnon; Choephori; Eumenides. (Orig.). (gr. 9 up). 1956. pap. 5.95 (*0-14-044067-4*, Penguin Classics) Viking Penguin.
Aeschylus see Lind, Levi R.
Aesop. The Aesop for Children. large type ed. Clauss, J., intro. by. Winter, Nilo, illus. (gr. 1-12). 1976. lib. bdg. 20.95x (*0-88411-991-2*, Pub. by Aeonian Pr) Amereon Ltd.
—Aesop for Children. Winter, Milo, illus. LC 86-73175. 96p. (gr. 2 up). 1984. Repr. of 1919 ed. 12.95 (*1-56288-039-X*) Checkerboard.
—Aesop's Fables. Winder, Blanche, ed. LC 33-31662. (Illus.). (gr. 4 up). 1965. pap. 1.95 (*0-8049-0081-7*, CL-81) Airmont.

—Aesop's Fables. Kredel, Fritz, illus. LC 33-31662. (gr. 4-6). 1963. (G&D); deluxe ed. 12.95 (*0-448-06003-5*); Companion Library. companion lib. o.p. 2.95 (*0-448-05453-1*); pap. ed (IJL) o.p. 4.95 (*0-686-76870-1*) Putnam Pub Group.
—Aesop's Fables. Paxton, Tom, retold by. Rayevsky, Robert, illus. LC 88-1652. 40p. (ps-2). 1988. 13.95 (*0-688-07360-3*); PLB 13.88 (*0-688-07361-1*, Morrow Jr Bks) Morrow Jr Bks.
—Aesop's Fables. LC 89-62860. 80p. (ps up). 1990. 4.95 (*0-89471-795-2*) Running Pr.
—Aesop's Fables. Hejduk, John, illus. LC 90-26710. 32p. 1991. 17.95 (*0-8478-1364-9*) Rizzoli Intl.
—Aesop's Fables. LC 91-2414. (ps-3). 1992. write for info. (*0-15-200350-9*, HB Juv Bks) HarBrace.
—Aesops Fables-Color Book. 1978. pap. 2.95 (*0-486-21040-5*) Dover.
—The City Mouse & the Country Mouse. Wheeler, Jody, illus. LC 85-70290. 18p. (ps). 1985. 3.95 (*0-448-10226-9*, G&D) Putnam Pub Group.
—Fables. Gooden, Stephen, illus. L'Estrange, Roger, tr. LC 92-53179. (Illus.). 224p. 1992. 12.95 (*0-679-41790-7*, Evrymans Lib Childs Class) Knopf.
—Feed Me! An Aesop Fable. (ps-3). 1992. 9.99 (*0-553-08950-1*); pap. 3.50 (*0-553-37023-5*) Bantam.
—The Hare & the Tortoise. Friedman, Arthur, illus. LC 80-28162. 32p. (gr. k-3). 1981. PLB 9.79 (*0-89375-468-4*); pap. text ed. 1.95 (*0-89375-469-2*) Troll Assocs.
—The Lion & the Mouse. Dole, Bob, illus. LC 80-28154. 32p. (gr. k-3). 1981. PLB 9.79 (*0-89375-466-8*); pap. text ed. 1.95 (*0-89375-467-6*) Troll Assocs.
—Little Red Riding Hood. Dyer, Jane, illus. LC 85-70289. 18p. (ps). 1985. 3.95 (*0-448-10227-7*, G&D) Putnam Pub Group.
—The Miller, His Son & Their Donkey. Sopko, Eugen, illus. LC 85-7198. 32p. (gr. k-3). 1988. 14.95 (*1-55858-067-0*) North-South Bks NYC.
—The Tortoise & the Hare. Alchemy II, Inc. Staff, illus. 26p. 1988. incl. cassette 9.95 (*1-55578-902-1*) Worlds Wonder.
—Town Mouse & the Country Mouse. new ed. LC 78-18062. (Illus.). 32p. (gr. k-3). 1979. PLB 9.79 (*0-89375-131-6*); pap. 1.95 (*0-89375-109-X*) Troll Assocs.
—The Wind & the Sun. Watts, Bernadette, illus. LC 92-2653. 32p. (gr. k-3). 1992. 14.95 (*1-55858-162-6*); PLB 14.88 (*1-55858-163-4*) North-South Bks NYC.
Aesop & Holder, Heidi. Aesop's Fables. LC 33-31662. (Illus.). 1981. pap. 16.00 (*0-670-10643-7*) Viking Child Bks.
Aesop, et al. Eric Carle's Treasury of Classic Stories for Children. Carle, Eric, illus. & retold by. LC 87-22072. 160p. (ps-4). 1988. 21.95 (*0-531-05742-9*) Orchard Bks Watts.
AESOP Enterprises, Inc. Staff & Crenshaw, Gwendolyn J. Akhenaton: Torchbearer of Light. 14p. (gr. 3-12). 1991. pap. write for info. incl. cassette (*1-880771-12-8*) AESOP Enter.
—Albert Einstein: Physicist & Peace Seeker. 12p. (gr. 3-12). 1991. pap. write for info. incl. cassette (*1-880771-10-1*) AESOP Enter.
—Aleksandr Sergeyevich Pushkin: Poetic Freedom Fighter for the People. 16p. (gr. 3-12). 1991. pap. write for info. incl. cassette (*1-880771-15-2*) AESOP Enter.
—Charles Richard Drew: A Navigator on the River of Life. 16p. (gr. 3-12). 1991. pap. write for info. incl. cassette (*1-880771-06-3*) AESOP Enter.
—Frederick Douglass: Adventures in Literacy. 20p. (gr. 3-12). 1991. pap. write for info. incl. cassette (*1-880771-03-9*) AESOP Enter.
—George Washington Carver: A Scientist Glorifying the Glories of Nature. 16p. (gr. 3-12). 1991. pap. write for info. incl. cassette (*1-880771-04-7*) AESOP Enter.
—Harriet Tubman: Stand & Deliver. 20p. (gr. 3-12). 1991. pap. write for info. incl. cassette (*1-880771-02-0*) AESOP Enter.
—Imhotep: Developing Your Talents. 14p. (gr. 3-12). 1991. pap. write for info. incl. cassette (*1-880771-07-1*) AESOP Enter.
—Langston Hughes: The Poetic Rebirth of Self-Identity. 32p. (gr. 3-12). 1991. pap. write for info. incl. cassette (*1-880771-05-5*) AESOP Enter.
—Malcolm X: Developing Self-Esteem, Self-Love, & Self-Dignity. 27p. (gr. 3-12). 1991. pap. write for info. incl. cassette (*1-880771-00-4*) AESOP Enter.
—Martin Luther King, Jr. Personalism & the Sacredness of the Human Personality. 14p. (gr. 3-12). 1991. pap. write for info. incl. cassette (*1-880771-01-2*) AESOP Enter.
—Mary McLeod Bethune: We've Come This Far by Faith. 14p. (gr. 3-12). 1991. pap. write for info. incl. cassette (*1-880771-08-X*) AESOP Enter.
—Nzinga: Developing Determination & Persistence. 16p. (gr. 3-12). 1991. pap. write for info. incl. cassette (*1-880771-14-4*) AESOP Enter.
—Queen Hatshepsut: Glorifying the Past for the Present & Future. 14p. (gr. 3-12). 1991. pap. write for info. incl. cassette (*1-880771-11-X*) AESOP Enter.
—Susan B. Anthony: A Crusader for Womanhood. 14p. (gr. 3-12). 1991. pap. write for info. incl. cassette (*1-880771-09-8*) AESOP Enter.
—Thomas Alva Edison: Persistent Dreamer & Doer. 14p. (gr. 3-12). 1991. pap. write for info. incl. cassette (*1-880771-13-6*) AESOP Enter.
Afanasev, Aleksandr. Russian Fairy Tales. LC 44-37884. (gr. 6 up). 1976. pap. 17.00 (*0-394-73090-9*) Pantheon.

Afanasiev, A. N. Ivan Korovavich: The Son of a Cow. Lesch, Christiane, illus. 28p. (gr. k-4). 1990. 14.95 (*0-903540-57-6*, 625, Pub. by Floris Bks UK) Anthroposophic.
Afanasyev, Alexander. Fool & the Fish: A Tale from Russia. Hort, Lenny, retold by. Spirin, Gennady, illus. 32p. (ps-3). 1990. 12.95 (*0-8037-0861-0*) Dial Bks Young.
African Islamic Mission Staff. One Hundred Amazing Facts about the Nubian Man & Woman. Obaba, Al I., ed. (Illus.). 124p. (Orig.). 1991. pap. text ed. 8.95 (*0-916157-87-3*) African Islam Miss Pubns.
Agard, John. The Calypso Alphabet. Bent, Jennifer, illus. LC 89-945617. 32p. (ps-2). 1989. 13.95 (*0-8050-1177-3*, Bks Young Read) H Holt & Co.
—Life Doesn't Frighten Me at All. LC 89-26766. (Illus.). 96p. (gr. 6 up). 1990. 14.95 (*0-8050-1237-0*, Bks Young Read) H Holt & Co.
Agay, Denes. Best Loved Songs of the American People. LC 74-4502. 416p. 1991. 19.00 (*0-385-14006-1*); pap. 15.95 (*0-385-00004-9*) Doubleday.
Agee, James. Death in the Family. 320p. (gr. 10 up). 1971. pap. 3.95 (*0-553-23392-0*) Bantam.
Agee, Joel, tr. see Moser, Erwin.
Agee, Jon. Ellsworth. (Illus.). (ps up). 1989. pap. 3.95 (*0-374-42082-3*, Sunburst) FS&G.
—Flapstick! Agee, Jon, illus. 24p. 1993. 10.99 (*0-525-45124-2*, DCB) Dutton Child Bks.
—Go Hang a Salami! I'm a Lasagna Hog! And Other Palindromes. (Illus.). 80p. 1992. 12.21 (*0-374-33473-0*) FS&G.
—The Incredible Painting of Felix Clousseau. (Illus.). 32p. (ps up). 1988. 15.00 (*0-374-33633-4*) FS&G.
—Incredible Painting of Felix Clousseau. (gr. 4-8). 1990. pap. 4.95 (*0-374-43582-0*, Sunburst) FS&G.
—Return of Freddy LeGrand. (ps-3). 1992. 15.00 (*0-374-36249-1*) FS&G.
Agel, Jerome, jt. auth. see Bernstein, Richard.
Agell, Charlotte. I Wear Long Green Hair in the Summer. Agell, Charlotte, illus. LC 93-33612. 32p. (ps up). 1994. 6.95 (*0-88448-121-2*) Tilbury Hse.
—Mud Makes Me Dance in the Spring. Agell, Charlotte, illus. LC 93-33610. 32p. (ps up). 1994. 6.95 (*0-88448-112-3*) Tilbury Hse.
—The Sailor's Book. Agell, Charlotte, illus. 32p. (gr. 3-6). 1991. PLB 14.95 (*0-920668-90-9*); pap. 4.95 (*0-920668-91-7*) Firefly Bks Ltd.
Agler, Leigh. Liquid Explorations. Bergman, Lincoln & Fairwell, Kay, eds. Klofkorn, Lisa, illus. Hoyt, Richard, photos by. (Illus.). 67p. (Orig.). (gr. 1-3). 1987. pap. 8.50 (*0-912511-51-6*) Lawrence Science.
Agnew, Robin. Rebecca of Grand Hotel. Agnew, Robin, illus. 72p. 1990. text ed. 15.95 (*0-9627301-0-6*) Grand Hotel.
Aguiar, Elithe. Legends of Hawaii As Told By Lani Goose. Aguiar, Elithe & Sakamoto, Dean, illus. 20p. (gr. k up). 1986. pap. 8.95 incl. audio cassette (*0-944264-00-X*) Lani Goose Pubns.
Aguon, Jane M. Mr. Munchkin's Tennis. (gr. 4 up). 1993. 10.75 (*0-8062-4719-3*) Carlton.
Agy, Christine. Zwort's Nature Report: Animal Adventure Game. (Illus.). 20p. (ps-4). 1991. 12.95 (*1-55999-203-4*) LinguiSystems.
—Zwort's Nature Report Think 'n' Do Book: Forest, Ocean, Safari. Anderson, Terri, illus. 100p. (ps-4). 1991. spiral bdg., wkbk. 3.95 (*1-55999-159-3*) LinguiSystems.
Ahbe, Dottie & Pluta, Terry. Safety Always Matters. Saba Designs, Inc. Staff & Ahbe, S., illus. 16p. (gr. 1-3). 1992. wkbk. 0.59 (*0-9620584-1-6*) Safety Always Matters.
—Safety Always Matters. Saba Designs, Inc. Staff & Ahbe, S., illus. 16p. (ps-k). 1992. wkbk. 0.59 (*0-9620584-0-8*) Safety Always Matters.
—Safety Always Matters. Saba Designs, Inc. Staff & Ahbe, S., illus. 16p. (gr. 4-6). 1992. wkbk. 0.59 (*0-9620584-2-4*) Safety Always Matters.
—Safety Always Matters. Saba Designs, Inc. Staff & Ahbe, S., illus. 32p. (ps-k). 1991. wkbk. 2.00 (*0-9620584-3-2*) Safety Always Matters.
—Safety Always Matters. Saba Designs, Inc. Staff & Ahbe, S., illus. 32p. (gr. 1-3). 1988. wkbk. 2.00 (*0-9620584-4-0*) Safety Always Matters.
—Safety Always Matters. Saba Designs, Inc. Staff & Ahbe, S., illus. 32p. (gr. 4-6). 1988. wkbk. 2.00 (*0-9620584-5-9*) Safety Always Matters.
Ahern, Denise. Bread & the Wine, No. Sixteen. (Illus.). (gr. k-4). 1979. 1.89 (*0-570-06127-X*, 59-1245) Concordia.
Ahern, James, jt. auth. see Peternel, Carolyn R.
Ahern, Jerry. Escape. 1989. pap. 3.50 (*0-440-20330-9*) Dell.
Ahern, Jerry & Ahern, Sharon. The Defender, No. 3. (Orig.). 1988. pap. 3.50 (*0-318-33285-X*) Dell.
Ahern, Sharon, jt. auth. see Ahern, Jerry.
Ahlberg, Allan. The Bear Nobody Wanted. Ahlberg, Janet, illus. 144p. (gr. 3-7). 1993. 15.00 (*0-670-83982-5*) Viking Child Bks.
—The Black Cat. Amstutz, Andre, illus. LC 90-2886. 32p. (ps up). 1990. 12.95 (*0-688-09903-3*); PLB 12.88 (*0-688-09904-1*) Greenwillow.
—The Black Cat. Amstutz, Andre, illus. LC 92-45621. 32p. (gr. k up). 1993. pap. text ed. 4.95 (*0-688-12679-0*, Mulberry) Morrow.
—Burglar Bill. Ahlberg, Janet, illus. 1992. pap. 3.99 (*0-14-050301-3*) Viking Child Bks.
—The Cinderella Show. Ahlberg, Janet, illus. (ps-3). 1987. pap. 4.95 (*0-670-81037-1*) Viking Child Bks.

—Dinosaur Dreams. LC 90-2943. (Illus.). 24p. (ps up). 1991. 12.95 (*0-688-09955-6*); PLB 12.88 (*0-688-09956-4*) Greenwillow.

—Funnybones. Ahlberg, Janet, illus. LC 79-24872. 32p. (gr. k-3). 1981. 12.88 (*0-688-80238-9*); PLB 11.88 (*0-688-84238-0*) Greenwillow.

—Funnybones. Ahlberg, Janet, illus. 32p. (gr. k up). 1993. minibook 4.95 (*0-688-12671-5*, Tupelo Bks) Morrow.

—The Ghost Train. Amstutz, Andre, illus. LC 91-39838. 32p. (ps-6). 1992. 14.00 (*0-688-11435-0*) Greenwillow.

—Ghost Train. ALC Staff, ed. Amstutz, Andre, illus. LC 91-39838. 32p. (gr. k up). 1992. pap. 3.95 (*0-688-11659-0*, Mulberry) Morrow.

—It Was a Dark & Stormy Night. Ahlberg, Janet, illus. 32p. (ps-3). 1994. 13.99 (*0-670-85159-0*) Viking Child Bks.

—Mystery Tour. LC 90-2942. (Illus.). 24p. (ps up). 1991. 12.95 (*0-688-09957-2*); PLB 12.88 (*0-688-09958-0*) Greenwillow.

—The Pet Shop. Amstutz, Andre, illus. LC 90-2881. 32p. (ps up). 1990. 12.95 (*0-688-09905-X*); PLB 12.88 (*0-688-09906-8*) Greenwillow.

—The Pet Shop. Amstutz, Andre, illus. LC 92-45657. 32p. (gr. k up). 1993. pap. 4.95 (*0-688-12680-4*, Mulberry) Morrow.

—Skeleton Crew. Amstutz, Andre, illus. LC 91-39161. 32p. (ps-6). 1992. 14.00 (*0-688-11436-9*) Greenwillow.

—Skeleton Crew. ALC Staff, ed. Amstutz, Andre, illus. LC 91-39161. 32p. (gr. k up). 1992. pap. 3.95 (*0-688-11660-4*, Mulberry) Morrow.

—Starting School. Ahlberg, Janet, illus. LC 88-50053. (ps-1). 1988. pap. 11.95 (*0-670-82175-6*) Viking Child Bks.

—Ten in a Bed. Amstutz, Andre, illus. 112p. 1989. pap. 12.95 (*0-670-82042-3*) Viking Child Bks.

—Ten in a Bed. Amstutz, Andre, illus. 112p. (gr. 2-6). 1991. pap. 3.99 (*0-14-032531-X*, Puffin) Puffin Bks.

—Woof! Wegner, Fritz, illus. LC 86-40009. 155p. (gr. 3-7). 1986. pap. 11.95 (*0-670-80832-6*) Viking Child Bks.

—Woof! Wegner, Fritz, illus. (gr. 3-7). 1988. pap. 3.99 (*0-14-031996-4*, Puffin) Puffin Bks.

Ahlberg, Allan & Amstutz, Andre. Ten in a Bed. large type ed. 168p. (gr. 1-7). 1991. 13.95 (*0-7451-1244-7*, Galaxy Child Lrg Print) Chivers N Amer.

Ahlberg, Allan, jt. auth. see Ahlberg, Janet.

Ahlberg, Janet. Bye-Bye, Baby: A Baby Without a Mommy in Search of One, Vol. 1. 1990. 12.95 (*0-316-02034-6*) Little.

—Peek-A-Boo. (ps). 1990. 4.95 (*0-670-83283-9*) Viking Child Bks.

—Starting School. 1990. pap. 4.95 (*0-14-050843-0*, Puffin) Puffin Bks.

Ahlberg, Janet & Ahlberg, Allan. Adios Pequeno - Bye Bye, Baby. Puncel, Maria, tr. (SPA., Illus.). 28p. (gr. k-1). 1990. write for info. (*84-372-6613-0*) Santillana.

—The Baby's Catalogue. LC 82-9928. (Illus.). 32p. (gr. k up). 1986. 15.95i (*0-316-02037-0*, Joy St Bks) Little.

—The Baby's Catalogue. Ahlberg, Janet & Ahlberg, Allan, illus. 32p. (gr. k up). 1986. pap. 5.95 (*0-316-02038-9*) Little.

—The Clothes Horse & Other Stories. (Illus.). 32p. (ps-3). 1992. pap. 4.99 (*0-14-032907-2*) Puffin Bks.

—Each Peach Pear Plum. Ahlberg, Janet & Ahlberg, Allan, illus. 32p. (ps-1). 1986. pap. 3.99 (*0-14-050639-X*, Puffin) Puffin Bks.

—Each Peach Pear Plum. (Illus.). 32p. (ps-k). 1992. miniature ed. 4.95 (*0-670-84018-1*) Viking Child Bks.

—Each Peach Pear Plum: An I-Spy Story. LC 79-16726. (Illus.). 32p. (gr. k-3). 1979. pap. 12.95 (*0-670-28705-9*) Viking Child Bks.

—Funnybones. LC 79-24872. (Illus.). 32p. (ps-2). 1990. pap. 3.95 (*0-688-09927-0*, Mulberry) Morrow.

—The Ha Ha Bonk Bonk Book. (Illus.). (gr. 3-7). 1982. pap. 3.95 (*0-14-031412-1*, Puffin) Puffin Bks.

—Jeremiah in the Dark Woods. (Illus.). 48p. (ps-3). 1990. pap. 4.95 (*0-14-032811-4*, Puffin) Puffin Bks.

—Jolly Christmas Postman. (Illus.). 1991. 17.95 (*0-316-02033-8*) Little.

—The Jolly Postman. Ahlberg, Janet & Ahlberg, Allan, illus. 32p. (gr. k-3). 1986. 16.95 (*0-316-02036-2*) Little.

—Peek-A-Boo! LC 81-1925. (Illus.). 1981. pap. 11.95 (*0-670-54598-8*) Viking Child Bks.

—Peek-A-Boo. (Illus.). 32p. (ps-k). 1984. pap. 4.50 (*0-14-050107-X*, Puffin) Puffin Bks.

Ahler, Stanley A., et al. People of the Willows: The Prehistory & Early History of the Hidatsa Indians. LC 91-50599. (Illus.). 123p. (Orig.). (gr. 9 up). 1991. pap. 19.95 (*0-9608700-8-3*) U NDak Pres.

Ahlers, Julia. Special Topics in Justice & Peace: Nine Articles for Student Handouts. Allaire, Barbara, ed. 48p. (Orig.). (gr. 11-12). 1990. pap. text ed. 8.95 stitched (*0-88489-244-1*) St Marys.

Ahlers, Julia, et al. Growing in Christian Morality. Nagel, Steve, ed. St. George, Carolyn, illus. 304p. (Orig.). (gr. 10-11). 1992. pap. text ed. 13.50 (*0-88489-240-9*); 18.95 (*0-88489-261-1*) St Marys.

Ahlstrom, Mark. The Canada Goose. LC 83-24015. (Illus.). 48p. (gr. 5-6). 1984. RSBE 12.95 (*0-89686-243-7*, Crestwood Hse) Macmillan Child Grp.

—The Foxes. LC 83-5324. (Illus.). 48p. (gr. 5-6). 1983. RSBE 12.95 (*0-89686-220-8*, Crestwood Hse) Macmillan Child Grp.

—The Polar Bear. LC 85-30900. (Illus.). 48p. (gr. 4-5). 1986. RSBE 12.95 (*0-89686-268-2*, Crestwood Hse) Macmillan Child Grp.

—The Pronghorn. LC 85-28054. (Illus.). 48p. (gr. 5-6). 1986. RSBE 12.95 (*0-89686-292-5*, Crestwood Hse) Macmillan Child Grp.

—The Sheep. LC 83-25215. (Illus.). 48p. (gr. 5-6). 1984. RSBE 12.95 (*0-89686-248-8*, Crestwood Hse) Macmillan Child Grp.

—The Snow Goose. LC 85-29933. (Illus.). 48p. (gr. 5-6). 1986. RSBE 12.95 (*0-89686-293-3*, Crestwood Hse) Macmillan Child Grp.

Ahlstrom, Mark & Schroeder, Howard. The Wild Pigs. LC 86-2282. (Illus.). 48p. (gr. 5-6). 1986. RSBE 12.95 (*0-89686-272-0*, Crestwood Hse) Macmillan Child Grp.

Ahlstrom, Mark E. The Black Bear. LC 85-22872. (Illus.). 48p. (gr. 4-5). 1985. RSBE 12.95 (*0-89686-276-3*, Crestwood Hse) Macmillan Child Grp.

—The Coyote. LC 85-24290. (Illus.). 48p. (gr. 4-8). 1985. RSBE 12.95 (*0-89686-277-1*, Crestwood Hse) Macmillan Child Grp.

—The Elk. LC 85-11667. (Illus.). 48p. (gr. 5-6). 1985. RSBE 12.95 (*0-89686-278-X*, Crestwood Hse) Macmillan Child Grp.

—The Moose. LC 85-26931. (Illus.). 48p. (gr. 4-5). 1985. RSBE 12.95 (*0-89686-279-8*, Crestwood Hse) Macmillan Child Grp.

—The Mule Deer. LC 87-614. (Illus.). 48p. (gr. 5-6). 1987. RSBE 12.95 (*0-89686-324-7*, Crestwood Hse) Macmillan Child Grp.

Ahmad, Fazl. Abu Bakr: First Caliph of Islam. 100p. (Orig.). (gr. 7-12). 1984. pap. 3.50 (*1-56744-240-4*) Kazi Pubns.

—Aisha: The Truthful. 140p. (Orig.). (gr. 7-12). 1984. pap. 3.50 (*1-56744-238-2*) Kazi Pubns.

—Ali, the Fourth Caliph of Islam. 103p. (Orig.). (gr. 7-12). 1984. pap. 3.50 (*1-56744-243-9*) Kazi Pubns.

—Husain: The Great Martyr. 150p. (Orig.). (gr. 7-12). 1984. pap. 3.50 (*1-56744-239-0*) Kazi Pubns.

—Khalid bin Walid: The Sword of Allah. 115p. (Orig.). (gr. 7-12). 1984. pap. 3.50 (*1-56744-244-7*) Kazi Pubns.

—Mahmood of Ghazni. 120p. (Orig.). (gr. 7-12). 1984. pap. 3.50 (*1-56744-246-3*) Kazi Pubns.

—Muhammad bin Qasim. 95p. (Orig.). (gr. 7-12). 1984. pap. 3.50 (*1-56744-245-5*) Kazi Pubns.

—Muhammad the Prophet of Islam. 125p. (Orig.). (gr. 7-12). 1984. pap. 3.50 (*1-56744-236-6*) Kazi Pubns.

—Muhy-ud Din Alamgir Aurangzeb. 103p. (Orig.). (gr. 7-12). 1984. pap. 3.50 (*1-56744-247-1*) Kazi Pubns.

—Omar: The Second Caliph of Islam. 100p. (Orig.). (gr. 7-12). 1984. pap. 3.50 (*1-56744-241-2*) Kazi Pubns.

—Othman, the Third Caliph of Islam. 95p. (Orig.). (gr. 7-12). 1984. pap. 3.50 (*1-56744-242-0*) Kazi Pubns.

—Some Companions of the Prophet, Pt. I. 115p. (gr. 4-10). 1985. pap. 3.50 (*1-56744-390-7*) Kazi Pubns.

—Some Companions of the Prophet, Pt. II. 115p. (gr. 4-10). 1985. pap. 3.50 (*1-56744-391-5*) Kazi Pubns.

—Some Companions of the Prophet, Pt. III. 115p. (gr. 4-10). 1985. pap. 3.50 (*1-56744-392-3*) Kazi Pubns.

—Sultan Tipi. 120p. (Orig.). (gr. 7-12). 1984. pap. 3.50 (*1-56744-237-4*) Kazi Pubns.

Ahmad, Khurshid, tr. & intro. by see Al-Maudoodi, Abul A.

Ahmad, P. Color & Learn Salat. pap. 3.50 (*0-935782-58-3*) Kazi Pubns.

Ahmad, Shakil, tr. see Saqr, Abdul B.

Ahnan, Katherine van see Van Ahnan, Katherine & Young Bear, Joan A.

Aho, Jennifer J. & Petras, John W. Learning About Sex: A Guide for Children & Their Parents. Aho, Jennifer J., illus. LC 78-53949. 80p. (gr. 4-6). 1978. pap. 7.95 (*0-8050-1078-5*, Bks Young Read) H Holt & Co.

Ahouse, Jeremy J. Fingerprinting. Bergman, Lincoln & Fairwell, Kay, eds. Klofkorn, Lisa, illus. Hoyt, Richard, photos by. (Illus.). 38p. (Orig.). (gr. 4-8). 1987. pap. 8.50 (*0-912511-21-4*) Lawrence Science.

AHSGR Staff. Kuche Kochen. (Illus.). 238p. (gr. 9-12). 1973. pap. text ed. 10.00 (*0-914222-10-4*) Am Hist Soc Ger.

Aiello. It's Your Turn at Bat. 1991. 0.85 (*0-8050-2014-4*) H Holt & Co.

—Secrets Aren't Always. 1991. 0.85 (*0-8050-2019-5*) H Holt & Co.

Aiello, Barbara & Shulman, Jeffrey. Business Is Looking Up: Featuring Renaldo Rodriguez. Barr, Loel, illus. 48p. (gr. 3-6). 1988. PLB 13.95 (*0-941477-00-2*) TFC Bks NY.

—Friends for Life: Featuring Amy Wilson. Barr, Loel, illus. LC 88-29251. 48p. (gr. 3-6). 1988. PLB 13.95 (*0-941477-03-7*) TFC Bks NY.

—Hometown Hero: Featuring Scott Whittaker. Barr, Loel, illus. 48p. (gr. 3-6). 1989. PLB 13.95 (*0-941477-04-5*) TFC Bks NY.

—It's Your Turn at Bat: Featuring Mark Riley. Barr, Loel, illus. 48p. (gr. 3-6). 1988. PLB 13.95 (*0-8050-3070-0*) TFC Bks NY.

—On with the Show! Featuring Brenda Dubrowski. Barr, Loel, illus. 56p. (gr. 3-6). 1989. PLB 13.95 (*0-941477-06-1*) TFC Bks NY.

—A Portrait of Me: Featuring Christine Kontos. (Illus.). 48p. (gr. 3-6). 1989. PLB 13.95 (*0-941477-05-3*) TFC Bks NY.

—Secrets Aren't (Always) for Keeps: Featuring Jennifer Hauser. Barr, Loel, illus. 48p. (gr. 3-6). 1988. PLB 13.95 (*0-8050-3069-7*) TFC Bks NY.

—Trick or Treat or Trouble: Featuring Brian McDaniel. Barr, Loel, illus. 56p. (gr. 3-6). 1989. PLB 13.95 (*0-941477-07-X*) TFC Bks NY.

Aigner, Jean S. The Eskimo. (Illus.). (gr. 5 up). 1989. 17.95 (*1-55546-705-9*) Chelsea Hse.

Aiken. Haunting Christmas Tales. 1993. pap. 2.95 (*0-590-46025-0*) Scholastic Inc.

Aiken, Conrad. Silent Snow, Secret Snow. LC 83-71788. 48p. (gr. 6 up). 1983. PLB 13.95s.p. (*0-87191-963-X*) Creative Ed.

Aiken, Joan. Black Hearts in Battersea. 224p. (gr. 5 up). 1981. pap. 1.75 (*0-440-90648-2*, LFL) Dell.

—Bridle the Wind. LC 83-5355. 224p. (gr. 7 up). 1983. 14.95 (*0-385-29301-1*) Delacorte.

—Dido & Pa. LC 86-2061. 256p. (gr. 7 up). 1986. 14.95 (*0-385-29480-8*) Delacorte.

—Died on a Rainy Sunday. (gr. k-12). 1988. pap. 2.95 (*0-440-20097-0*, LFL) Dell.

—The Erl King's Daughter. Warren, Paul, illus. 42p. (gr. 2-4). 1989. 3.95 (*0-8120-6137-3*) Barron.

—A Fit of Shivers: Tales for Late at Night. LC 92-6130. 144p. (gr. 6 up). 1992. 15.00 (*0-385-30691-1*) Delacorte.

—A Foot in the Grave. Pienkowski, Jan, illus. 128p. (gr. 5 up). 1992. 15.95 (*0-670-84169-2*) Viking Child Bks.

—Give Yourself a Fright. (gr. 7 up). 1989. 14.95 (*0-440-50120-2*) Delacorte.

—Is Underground. LC 92-27423. 1993. 15.00 (*0-385-30898-1*) Delacorte.

—The Last Slice of Rainbow: And Other Stories. Berenzy, Alix, illus. LC 87-45271. 160p. (gr. 3-7). 1988. PLB 12.89 (*0-06-020043-X*) HarpC Child Bks.

—The Last Slice of Rainbow: And Other Stories. Berenzy, Alix, illus. LC 87-45271. 160p. (gr. 3-7). 1990. pap. 3.50 (*0-06-440334-3*, Trophy) HarpC Child Bks.

—Midnight Is a Place. 1985. pap. 3.50 (*0-440-45634-7*, YB) Dell.

—Midnight Is a Place. (gr. 4-7). 1993. pap. 2.95 (*0-590-45496-X*) Scholastic Inc.

—Night Fall. (gr. 5 up). 1988. pap. 2.95 (*0-440-20054-7*, LFL) Dell.

—Nightbirds on Nantucket. 243p. (gr. k-6). 1981. pap. 1.75 (*0-440-96370-2*, YB) Dell.

—Past Eight O'Clock. Pienkowski, Jan, illus. 128p. (gr. 2-6). 1991. pap. 4.95 (*0-14-032355-4*, Puffin) Puffin Bks.

—Return to Harken House. (gr. 5-9). 1990. 13.95 (*0-385-29975-3*) Delacorte.

—The Shadow Guests. (gr. 5 up). 1986. pap. 2.95 (*0-440-48226-7*, YB) Dell.

—The Shadow Guests. large type ed. (gr. 1-8). 1993. 15.95 (*0-7451-1913-1*, Galaxy Child Lrg Print) Chivers N Amer.

—The Shadow Guests: A Novel. LC 80-65830. 144p. (gr. 7 up). 1980. pap. 11.95 (*0-385-28889-1*) Delacorte.

—The Shoemaker's Boy. Ambrus, Victor, illus. LC 93-6613. (ps-6). 1994. pap. 13.00 (*0-671-86647-8*, S&S BFYR) S&S Trade.

—The Stolen Lake: A Novel. LC 81-5015. 256p. (gr. 7 up). 1981. 10.95 (*0-385-28982-0*) Delacorte.

—A Touch of Chill. LC 79-3331. 124p. (gr. 7 up). 1980. 9.95 (*0-385-29310-0*) Delacorte.

—A Touch of Chill. (gr. k up). 1989. pap. 3.50 (*0-440-20459-3*, LFL) Dell.

—A Whisper in the Night: Tales of Terror & Suspense. (gr. k-12). 1988. pap. 3.25 (*0-440-20185-3*, LE) Dell.

—The Wolves of Willoughby Chase. 176p. (gr. k-6). 1987. pap. 3.50 (*0-440-49603-9*, YB) Dell.

—The Wolves of Willoughby Chase. Marriott, Pat, illus. LC 63-18034. 168p. (gr. 4-6). 1989. pap. 13.95 (*0-385-03594-2*) Doubleday.

Ai-Ling, Louie, retold by. Yeh-Shen: A Cinderella Story from China. Young, Ed, illus. (ps-3). 1988. pap. 5.95 (*0-399-21594-8*, Sandcastle Bks) Putnam Pub Group.

Ain, Diantha. What Do You Know about Succotash? Poems & Drawings. Ain, Diantha, illus. 75p. (Orig.). (gr. 1-6). 1991. pap. 7.95 (*0-925360-01-5*) Geste Pub.

Ainsworth, Catherine H. American Calendar Customs, Vol. I. LC 79-52827. 112p. (Orig.). (ps-12). 1979. pap. 12.00 (*0-933190-06-9*) Clyde Pr.

—American Calendar Customs, Vol. II. LC 79-55784. 110p. (Orig.). (ps-12). 1980. pap. 12.00 (*0-933190-07-7*) Clyde Pr.

—American Folk Foods. LC 84-72828. (Illus.). 224p. (Orig.). (ps-12). 1984. pap. 12.00 (*0-933190-12-3*) Clyde Pr.

—Black & White & Said All over: Riddles. LC 72-5461. 36p. (ps-12). 1976. 5.00 (*0-933190-02-6*) Clyde Pr.

—Family Life of Young Americans. LC 85-72144. 272p. (Orig.). (ps-12). 1986. pap. 12.00 (*0-933190-13-1*) Clyde Pr.

—Folktales of America, Vol. II. LC 80-66300. 212p. (Orig.). (ps-12). 1982. pap. 12.00 (*0-933190-09-3*) Clyde Pr.

—Folktales of America, Vol. I. LC 80-66300. 124p. (ps-12). 1980. pap. 12.00 (*0-933190-08-5*) Clyde Pr.

—Folktales of America, Vol. III. LC 80-66300. 224p. (Orig.). (ps-12). 1988. pap. 12.00 (*0-933190-15-8*) Clyde Pr.

—Games & Lore of Young Americans. LC 83-70191. 251p. (Orig.). (ps-12). 1983. pap. 12.00 (*0-933190-10-7*) Clyde Pr.

—Jump Rope Verses Around the United States. LC 75-4827. 24p. (ps-12). 1976. 5.00 (*0-933190-01-8*) Clyde Pr.

—Legends of New York State. 2nd ed. LC 78-54873. 99p. (ps-12). 1983. 12.00 (*0-933190-11-5*) Clyde Pr.

—Polish-American Folktales. LC 77-80771. 112p. (ps-12). 1977. 12.00 (*0-933190-04-2*) Clyde Pr.

—Superstitions from Seven Towns of the United States. LC 43-7320. 64p. (ps-12). 1973. 5.00 (*0-933190-00-X*) Clyde Pr.

Aird, Hazel B. & Ruddiman, Catherine. Henry Ford: Young Man with Ideas. Wood, Wallace, illus. LC 86-10756. 192p. (gr. 2-6). 1986. pap. 3.95 (*0-02-041910-4*, Aladdin) Macmillan Child Grp.

Aisenberg, Gino & Montes, Elizabeth. Bursting with Joy - Una Celebracion! (Illus., Orig.). (gr. 1-8). 1992. tchr's. ed. 25.00 (*1-55944-025-2*) Franciscan Comns.

AIT Staff. Earth, the Environment, & Beyond from Science Source. Grewar, Mindy, ed. (Orig.). (gr. 7-12). 1992. text ed. write for info. (*0-7842-0605-8*) Agency Instr Tech.

—Our Human Body from Science Source. Grewar, Mindy, ed. (Orig.). (gr. 7-12). 1992. text ed. write for info. (*0-7842-0604-X*) Agency Instr Tech.

Aitken, John & Mills, George. Scientific Problem Solving: An Introduction to Technology. (gr. 4-6). 1989. pap. 10.95 (*0-8224-6324-5*) Fearon Teach Aids.

Aitkens, Maggie. Gun Control. (Illus.). 96p. (gr. 6 up). 1990. PLB 17.50 (*0-8225-2601-8*) Lerner Pubns.

Aixela, Javier F., tr. see Platt, Richard.

Aixela, Javier F., tr. see Puncel, Maria.

Aka, Karen Y. Honolulu, Hawaii: The Travel Guide for Kids. Koch, Susan C., illus. 32p. (gr. k-4). 1992. pap. 4.95 (*0-945600-08-9*) Colormore Inc.

Akass, Susan. Number Nine Duckling. Ayliffe, Alex, illus. 32p. (ps-1). 1993. 13.95 (*1-56397-224-7*) Boyds Mills Pr.

Aker, Suzanne. What Comes in Twos, Threes & Fours? LC 89-35482. 1990. pap. 13.95 (*0-671-67173-1*, S&S BFYR) S&S Trade.

—What Comes in Twos, Threes, & Fours? LC 89-3548. (ps). 1992. pap. 4.95 (*0-671-79247-4*, S&S BFYR) S&S Trade.

Akesson, Samuel K., ed. see True, Adiaha.

Akiko Sueyoshi. Jessica's Friend. Young, Richard G., ed. Kaisei-sha, tr. Akiko Hayashi, illus. LC 89-12050. 32p. (gr. 1-3). 1989. PLB 14.60 (*0-944483-47-X*) Garrett Ed Corp.

Akins, Kelly, illus. My Dinosaur Library, 14 bks. (ps-2). 1992. bds. 17.95 (*1-56293-201-2*, Set, mini-board bks. in a tray) McClanahan Bk.

Akinsheye, Dayo, jt. auth. see Akinsheye, Dexter.

Akinsheye, Dayo, ed. see Akinsheye, Dexter.

Akinsheye, Dexter. African American Inventor Adolphus Samms, Vol. I. Akinsheye, Dayo, ed. Gibbs, C. R., intro. by. (Illus., Orig.). (gr. 1-12). 1992. pap. 3.00 (*1-877835-00-5*); Set of 39 titles. pap. 78.00 (*0-685-26242-1*) TD Pub.

—African American Inventor Adolphus Samms, Vol. III. Akinsheye, Dayo, ed. Gibbs, C. R., intro. by. (Illus., Orig.). (gr. 1-12). 1992. pap. 3.00 (*1-877835-01-3*); Set of 39 titles. pap. 78.00 (*0-685-26244-8*) TD Pub.

—African American Inventor Adolphus Samms, Vol. II. Akinsheye, Dayo, ed. Gibbs, C. R., intro. by. (Illus., Orig.). (gr. 1-12). 1992. pap. 3.00 (*1-877835-02-1*); Set of 39 titles. pap. 78.00 (*0-685-26246-4*) TD Pub.

—African American Inventor Alice H. Parker. Akinsheye, Dayo, ed. Gibbs, C. R., intro. by. (Illus., Orig.). (gr. 1-12). 1992. pap. 3.00 (*1-877835-03-X*); Set of 39 titles. pap. 78.00 (*0-685-26190-5*) TD Pub.

—African American Inventor Andrew J. Beard. Akinsheye, Dayo, ed. Gibbs, C. R., intro. by. (Illus., Orig.). (gr. 1-12). 1992. pap. 3.00 (*1-877835-04-8*); Set of 39 titles. pap. 78.00 (*0-685-26240-5*) TD Pub.

—African American Inventor Benjamin F. Jackson. Akinsheye, Dayo, ed. Gibbs, C. R., intro. by. (Illus., Orig.). (gr. 1-12). 1992. pap. 3.00 (*1-877835-05-6*); Set of 39 titles. pap. 78.00 (*0-685-26206-5*) TD Pub.

—African American Inventor Charles C. Brooks, Vol. II. Akinsheye, Dayo, ed. Gibbs, C. R., intro. by. (Illus., Orig.). (gr. 1-12). 1992. pap. 3.00 (*1-877835-06-4*); Set of 39 titles. pap. 78.00 (*0-685-26208-1*) TD Pub.

—African American Inventor Charles C. Brooks, Vol. I. Akinsheye, Dayo, ed. Gibbs, C. R., intro. by. (Illus., Orig.). (gr. 1-12). 1992. pap. 3.00 (*1-877835-07-2*); Set of 39 titles. pap. 78.00 (*0-685-26210-3*) TD Pub.

—African American Inventor Edward R. Lewis. Akinsheye, Dayo, ed. Gibbs, C. R., intro. by. (Illus., Orig.). (gr. 1-12). 1992. pap. 3.00 (*1-877835-08-0*); Set of 39 titles. pap. 78.00 (*0-685-26226-X*) TD Pub.

—African American Inventor Elijah McCoy. Akinsheye, Dayo, ed. Gibbs, C. R., intro. by. (Illus., Orig.). (gr. 1-12). 1992. pap. 3.00 (*1-877835-09-9*); Set of 39 titles. pap. 78.00 (*0-685-26238-3*) TD Pub.

—African American Inventor Frederick Jones, Vol. I. Akinsheye, Dayo, ed. Gibbs, C. R., intro. by. (Illus., Orig.). (gr. 1-12). 1992. pap. 3.00 (*1-877835-10-2*); Set of 39 titles. pap. 78.00 (*0-685-26174-3*) TD Pub.

—African American Inventor Frederick Jones, Vol. II. Akinsheye, Dayo, ed. Gibbs, C. R., intro. by. (Illus., Orig.). (gr. 1-12). 1992. pap. 3.00 (*1-877835-11-0*); Set of 39 titles. pap. 78.00 (*0-685-26178-6*) TD Pub.

—African American Inventor Garrett T. Morgan, Vol. II. Akinsheye, Dayo, ed. Gibbs, C. R., intro. by. (Illus., Orig.). (gr. 1-12). 1992. pap. 3.00 (*1-877835-12-9*); Set of 39 titles. pap. 78.00 (*0-685-26218-9*) TD Pub.

—African American Inventor Garrett T. Morgan, Vol. I. Akinsheye, Dayo, ed. Gibbs, C. R., intro. by. (Illus., Orig.). (gr. 1-12). 1992. pap. 3.00 (*0-685-26219-7*); Set of 39 titles. pap. 78.00 (*0-685-26220-0*) TD Pub.

—African American Inventor George F. Grant. Akinsheye, Dayo, ed. Gibbs, C. R., intro. by. (Illus., Orig.). (gr. 1-12). 1992. pap. 3.00 (*0-685-26183-2*); Set of 39 titles. pap. 78.00 (*0-685-26184-0*) TD Pub.

—African American Inventor George R. Carruthes. Akinsheye, Dayo, ed. Gibbs, C. R., intro. by. (Illus., Orig.). (gr. 1-12). 1992. pap. 3.00 (*0-685-26191-3*); Set of 39 titles. pap. 78.00 (*0-685-26192-1*) TD Pub.

—African American Inventor George Toliver. Akinsheye, Dayo, ed. Gibbs, C. R., intro. by. (Illus., Orig.). (gr. 1-12). 1992. pap. 3.00 (*1-877835-13-7*); Set of 39 titles. pap. 78.00 (*0-685-26228-6*) TD Pub.

—African American Inventor George W. Murray. Akinsheye, Dayo, ed. Gibbs, C. R., intro. by. (Illus., Orig.). (gr. 1-12). 1992. pap. 3.00 (*1-877835-14-5*); Set of 39 titles. pap. 78.00 (*0-685-26200-6*) TD Pub.

—African American Inventor Gertrude Downing. Akinsheye, Dayo, ed. Gibbs, C. R., intro. by. (Illus., Orig.). (gr. 1-12). 1992. pap. 3.00 (*1-877835-15-3*); Set of 39 titles. pap. 78.00 (*0-685-44653-0*) TD Pub.

—African American Inventor Granville T. Woods, Vol. II. Akinsheye, Dayo, ed. Gibbs, C. R., intro. by. (Illus., Orig.). (gr. 1-12). 1992. pap. 3.00 (*1-877835-16-1*); Set of 39 titles. pap. 78.00 (*0-685-26232-4*) TD Pub.

—African American Inventor Granville T. Woods, Vol. I. Akinsheye, Dayo, ed. Gibbs, C. R., intro. by. (Illus., Orig.). (gr. 1-12). 1992. pap. 3.00 (*1-877835-17-X*); Set of 39 titles. pap. 78.00 (*0-685-26234-0*) TD Pub.

—African American Inventor Harold Linden. Akinsheye, Dayo, ed. Gibbs, C. R., intro. by. (Illus., Orig.). (gr. 1-12). 1992. pap. 3.00 (*1-877835-18-8*); Set of 39 titles. pap. 78.00 (*0-685-26196-4*) TD Pub.

—African American Inventor Henrietta Bradberry. Akinsheye, Dayo, ed. Gibbs, C. R., intro. by. (Illus., Orig.). (gr. 1-12). 1992. pap. 3.00 (*1-877835-19-6*); Set of 39 titles. pap. 78.00 (*0-685-26176-X*) TD Pub.

—African American Inventor Henry Blair. Akinsheye, Dayo, ed. Gibbs, C. R., intro. by. (Illus., Orig.). (gr. 1-12). 1992. pap. 3.00 (*1-877835-20-X*); Set of 39 titles. pap. 78.00 (*0-685-26180-8*) TD Pub.

—African American Inventor Hubert Julian. Akinsheye, Dayo, ed. Gibbs, C. R., intro. by. (Illus., Orig.). (gr. 1-12). 1992. pap. 3.00 (*1-877835-21-8*); Set of 39 titles. pap. 78.00 (*0-685-26182-4*) TD Pub.

—African American Inventor Jack A. Johnson. Akinsheye, Dayo, ed. Gibbs, C. R., intro. by. (Illus., Orig.). (gr. 1-12). 1992. pap. 3.00 (*1-877835-22-6*); Set of 39 titles. pap. 78.00 (*0-685-26170-0*) TD Pub.

—African American Inventor James T. Redding. Akinsheye, Dayo, ed. Gibbs, C. R., intro. by. (Illus., Orig.). (gr. 1-12). 1992. pap. 3.00 (*1-877835-23-4*); Set of 39 titles. pap. 78.00 (*0-685-26212-X*) TD Pub.

—African American Inventor Jan E. Matzeliger. Akinsheye, Dayo, ed. Gibbs, C. R., intro. by. (Illus., Orig.). (gr. 1-12). 1992. pap. 3.00 (*1-877835-24-2*); Set of 39 titles. pap. 78.00 (*0-685-26216-2*) TD Pub.

—African American Inventor John Pickering. Akinsheye, Dayo, ed. Gibbs, C. R., intro. by. (Illus., Orig.). (gr. 1-12). 1992. pap. 3.00 (*1-877835-25-0*); Set of 39 titles. pap. 78.00 (*0-685-26194-8*) TD Pub.

—African American Inventor Joseph H. Smith. Akinsheye, Dayo, ed. Gibbs, C. R., intro. by. (Illus., Orig.). (gr. 1-12). 1992. pap. 3.00 (*1-877835-26-9*); Set of 39 titles. pap. 78.00 (*0-685-26236-7*) TD Pub.

—African American Inventor Lewis H. Latimer, Vol. I. Akinsheye, Dayo, ed. Gibbs, C. R., intro. by. (Illus., Orig.). (gr. 1-12). 1992. pap. 3.00 (*1-877835-27-7*); Set of 39 titles. pap. 78.00 (*0-685-26186-7*) TD Pub.

—African American Inventor Lewis H. Latimer, Vol. II. Akinsheye, Dayo, ed. Gibbs, C. R., intro. by. (Illus., Orig.). (gr. 1-12). 1992. pap. 3.00 (*1-877835-28-5*); Set of 39 titles. pap. 78.00 (*0-685-26204-9*) TD Pub.

—African American Inventor Lewis Latimer. Akinsheye, Dayo, ed. Gibbs, C. R., intro. by. (Illus., Orig.). (gr. 1-12). 1992. pap. 3.00 (*1-877835-29-3*); Set of 39 titles. pap. 78.00 (*0-685-26202-2*) TD Pub.

—African American Inventor Math Pack Workbook. Akinsheye, Dayo, ed. Akinsheye, Addae, illus. 20p. (Orig.). (gr. 2-5). 1992. pap. text ed. 2.50 (*1-877835-53-6*) TD Pub.

—African American Inventor Miriam E. Benjamin. Akinsheye, Dayo, ed. Gibbs, C. R., intro. by. (Illus., Orig.). (gr. 1-12). 1992. pap. 3.00 (*1-877835-30-7*); Set of 39 titles. pap. 78.00 (*0-685-26222-7*) TD Pub.

—African American Inventor Norbert Rillieux. Akinsheye, Dayo, ed. Gibbs, C. R., intro. by. (Illus., Orig.). (gr. 1-12). 1992. pap. 3.00 (*1-877835-31-5*); Set of 39 titles. pap. 78.00 (*0-685-26224-3*) TD Pub.

—African American Inventor Richard Spikes. Akinsheye, Dayo, ed. Gibbs, C. R., intro. by. (Illus., Orig.). (gr. 1-12). 1992. pap. 3.00 (*1-877835-32-3*); Set of 39 titles. pap. 78.00 (*0-685-26172-7*) TD Pub.

—African American Inventor Richard Toomey. Akinsheye, Dayo, ed. Gibbs, C. R., intro. by. (Illus., Orig.). (gr. 1-12). 1992. pap. 3.00 (*1-877835-33-1*); Set of 39 titles. pap. 78.00 (*0-685-26230-8*) TD Pub.

—African American Inventor Sara E. Goode. Akinsheye, Dayo, ed. Gibbs, C. R., intro. by. (Illus., Orig.). (gr. 1-12). 1992. pap. 3.00 (*1-877835-34-X*); Set of 39 titles. pap. 78.00 (*0-685-26204-9*) TD Pub.

—African American Inventor William B. Purvis. Akinsheye, Dayo, ed. Gibbs, C. R., intro. by. (Illus., Orig.). (gr. 1-12). 1992. pap. 3.00 (*1-877835-36-6*); Set of 39 titles. pap. 78.00 (*0-685-26198-0*) TD Pub.

—Discovering American History. Akinsheye, Dayo, ed. Griffin, Charles, illus. 20p. (Orig.). (gr. 2-3). 1992. pap. 4.99 (*1-877835-70-6*) TD Pub.

Akinsheye, Dexter & Akinsheye, Dayo. I Want to Be... Akiwshye, Dexter, illus. 56p. (gr. k-4). 1992. pap. 12.00 (*1-877835-47-1*); pap. text ed. 5.00 (*1-877835-48-X*) TD Pub.

Akio, Terumasa. Me & Alves: A Japanese Journey. Matsui, Susan, tr. Oido, Yukio, illus. 24p. 1993. lib. bdg. 14.95 (*1-55037-223-8*, Pub. by Annick CN); pap. 4.95 (*1-55037-222-X*, Pub. by Annick CN) Firefly Bks Ltd.

Akkerman, Dinie & Van Loon, Paul. To Catch the Moon. (Illus.). 24p. (ps-1). 1993. 12.95 (*0-8120-6341-4*); pap. 5.95 (*0-8120-1559-2*) Barron.

Akmon, Nancy C. Come to My Tea Party: A Cookbook for Children. Akmon, Roni, illus. 84p. (gr. 3-6). 1993. 10.95 (*0-926684-09-4*) Eclectic Oregon.

Aks, Pat. Love Knots. (Orig.). 1992. pap. 3.99 (*0-449-70357-6*, Juniper) Fawcett.

Aks, Patricia. Impossible Love. 144p. (Orig.). (gr. 9-12). 1991. pap. 3.50 (*0-449-70297-9*, Juniper) Fawcett.

Alabado, Ceres S. Kangkong: 1896. (TAG., Illus.). 241p. (Orig.). (gr. 1-6). 1984. pap. 5.50 (*971-10-0106-3*, Pub. by New Day Pub PI) Cellar.

Alaia, Chero, jt. auth. see Rafter, Rusalie.

Albanese, Gayle, jt. auth. see Garrison, Eileen.

Albee, Jo. The Lost Kitten. Goldberg, Grace, illus. 24p. (ps-2). 1992. pap. 0.99 (*1-56293-111-3*) McClanahan Bk.

—The Missing Snowman. Learner, Vicki M., illus. 24p. (Orig.). (gr. k-1). 1990. pap. 0.99 (*1-878624-47-4*) McClanahan Bk.

—There's an Elephant in the Bathtub. Coghlan, Jeanne A., illus. 24p. (Orig.). (gr. k-1). 1990. pap. 0.99 (*1-878624-39-3*) McClanahan Bk.

Alberione, James. Queen of Apostles Prayerbook. rev. ed. Daughters of St. Paul Staff, compiled by. 377p. 1991. blue vinyl bdg. 9.95 (*0-8198-6201-0*); black vinyl bdg. 9.95 (*0-8198-6202-9*); white vinyl bdg. 9.95 (*0-8198-6203-7*); pap. 7.95 (*0-8198-6200-2*) St Paul Bks.

Albers, Maura & Cvikota, Tom, eds. Just Add Color: A Children's Coloring Book with Drawings by Contemporary Artists. Rosenblum, Robert, intros. by. (Illus.). 36p. (Orig.). 1991. pap. text ed. 19.95 (*0-9627744-0-5*) HBP NY.

Albert, Burton. Where Does the Trail Lead? (gr. k-3). 1991. pap. 15.00 jacketed (*0-671-73409-1*, S&S BFYR) S&S Trade.

—Where Does the Trail Lead? Pinkney, Brian, illus. LC 90-21450. 40p. (ps-3). 1993. pap. 5.95 (*0-671-79617-8*, S&S BFYR) S&S Trade.

—Windsongs & Rainbows. Stillman, Susan, illus. LC 92-12012. (ps-2). 1993. pap. 14.00 JRT (*0-671-76004-1*, S&S BFYR) S&S Trade.

Albert, Burton, Jr. Code Busters! Levine, Abby, ed. Warshaw, Jerry, illus. LC 84-2935. 32p. (gr. 3-6). 1985. 11.95 (*0-8075-1235-4*) A Whitman.

—Mine, Yours, Ours. Axeman, Lois, illus. LC 77-9408. (ps-1). 1977. PLB 10.95 (*0-8075-5148-1*) A Whitman.

—Top Secret! Codes to Crack. Levine, Abby, ed. Warshaw, Jerry, illus. LC 87-2146. 32p. (gr. 4-7). 1987. PLB 11.95 (*0-8075-8027-9*) A Whitman.

Albert, Gilbert. Les Champs et Les Forets. Ganim, Barbara, illus. (FRE.). 28p. (gr. 6-8). 1986. pap. text ed. 3.95 (*0-911409-46-7*) Natl Mat Dev.

Albert, Gretchen D. Scribble Art: Kindergarten & Preschool. Albert, Gretchen D., illus. 85p. (ps-3). 1980. pap. text ed. 5.80 (*0-686-28105-5*) GDA Pubns.

Albert, Kristine & Polette, Nancy. Trials. Dillon, Paul, illus. 48p. (Orig.). (gr. 4-8). 1991. pap. 5.95 (*0-913839-99-X*) Bk Lures.

Albert, Richard E. Alejandro's Gift. Long, Sylvia, illus. LC 93-30199. 1994. 13.95 (*0-8118-0436-4*) Chronicle Bks.

Albert, Toni. Ben & Me: A Study Guide. Friedland, Joyce & Kessler, Rikki, eds. (gr. 2-5). 1991. pap. text ed. 14.95 (*0-88122-566-5*) LRN Links.

—The War with Grandpa: A Study Guide. Friedland, Joyce & Kessler, Rikki, eds. (gr. 3-6). 1991. pap. text ed. 14.95 (*0-88122-578-9*) LRN Links.

Alberti, Delbert & Mason, George. Laboratory Laughter. Firmhand, Zelda, illus. (Orig.). (gr. 2-9). 1974. pap. 7.95 (*0-918932-25-4*) Activity Resources.

Alberton, Kathleen. The ABC's of Family Court: A Children's Guide. Clarke, Dorothy J., illus. LC 88-120423. 54p. (gr. 1-12). 1987. pap. 1.50 (*0-9619599-0-8*) NYC Law Dept.

Alberts, Nancy. Teeth Week. (gr. 4-7). 1993. pap. 2.75 (*0-590-45563-X*) Scholastic Inc.

Albertsen, June. Two Are Twins. Anton, Karen, illus. LC 86-70195. 31p. (ps-3). 1987. pap. 5.95 (*0-9615839-0-8*) Double Day.

Albertson, Jon. Falklands Fiasco. Hooper, Anne, ed. Pheris, William E., IV, illus. 284p. (gr. 12). 1989. 16.95 (*0-9621448-1-9*) Aeolus Bks.

—Naked in the Twisted Sky. Hooper, N. John & Hooper, Anne, eds. 300p. (gr. 12). 1989. 16.95 (*0-9621448-2-7*) Aeolus Bks.

—Valley of the Condor. Hooper, Anne, ed. 300p. (gr. 12). 1990. write for info. (*0-9621448-3-5*) Aeolus Bks.

Albertson, Rebecca. The Complete Book of Macra-Tack. 4th, rev. ed. Albertson, Rebecca & Wilhelm, Pamela, illus. 50p. (gr. 3-12). 1983. spiral 9.95 (*0-9611536-0-1*) Macra-Tack Inc.

Alborough, Jez. Beaky. Alborough, Jez, illus. 32p. (ps-3). 1990. 13.45 (*0-395-53348-1*) HM.

—Clothesline. Alborough, Jez, illus. LC 92-54962. 32p. (ps). 1993. pap. 6.99 (*1-56402-243-9*) Candlewick Pr.

—Cuddly Dudley. Alborough, Jez, illus. LC 92-52994. 32p. (ps). 1993. 14.95 (*1-56402-095-9*) Candlewick Pr.

—Where's My Teddy? Alborough, Jez, illus. LC 91-58765. 32p. (ps up). 1992. 14.95 (*1-56402-048-7*) Candlewick Pr.

—Where's My Teddy? LC 91-58765. (Illus.). 32p. (ps up). 1993. 4.95 (1-56402-255-2) Candlewick Pr.
—Where's My Teddy? LC 91-58765. (ps-3). 1994. pap. 4.99 (1-56402-280-3) Candlewick Pr.
Albrecht, Peggy. House Beyond Congo Cross. (gr. 6-8). 1982. pap. 3.95 (0-87508-651-9) Chr Lit.
—Secret of the Old House. (gr. 6-8). 1983. pap. 3.95 (0-87508-653-5) Chr Lit.
Albright, Molly. Best Friends. DeRosa, Dee, illus. LC 87-13874. 96p. (gr. 3-6). 1988. PLB 9.89 (0-8167-1151-8); pap. text ed. 2.95 (0-8167-1152-6) Troll Assocs.
—The Big Showoffs. DeRosa, Dee, illus. LC 87-13872. 96p. (gr. 3-6). 1988. PLB 9.89 (0-8167-1155-0); pap. text ed. 2.95 (0-8167-1156-9) Troll Assocs.
—The Dream Team. DeRosa, Dee, illus. LC 87-13821. 96p. (gr. 3-6). 1988. PLB 9.89 (0-8167-1153-4); pap. text ed. 2.95 (0-8167-1154-2) Troll Assocs.
—Fright Night. Connor, Eulala, illus. LC 88-12388. 96p. (gr. 3-6). 1989. PLB 9.89 (0-8167-1486-X); pap. text ed. 2.95 (0-8167-1487-8) Troll Assocs.
—The Mascot Mess. Connor, Eulala, illus. LC 88-15879. 96p. (gr. 3-6). 1989. PLB 9.89 (0-8167-1484-3); pap. text ed. 2.95 (0-8167-1485-1) Troll Assocs.
—Meet Miss Dracula. DeRosa, Dee, illus. LC 87-13871. 96p. (gr. 3-6). 1988. PLB 9.89 (0-8167-1157-7); pap. text ed. 2.95 (0-8167-1158-5) Troll Assocs.
—The Room of Doom. Connor, Eulala, illus. LC 88-15912. 96p. (gr. 3-6). 1989. PLB 9.89 (0-8167-1482-7); pap. text ed. 2.95 (0-8167-1483-5) Troll Assocs.
—Video Stars. Connor, Eulala, illus. LC 88-15880. 96p. (gr. 3-6). 1989. PLB 9.89 (0-8167-1480-0); pap. text ed. 2.95 (0-8167-1481-9) Troll Assocs.
Albright, Nancy T. Do Tell! Holiday Draw & Tell Stories. rev. & enlg. ed. (ps-4). 1989. pap. 5.00 (0-913545-13-9) Moonlight FL.
Albright, Nancy T., illus. I Know an Old Lady Who Swallowed a Fly. (Orig.). (ps-6). 1985. pap. 3.50 (0-913545-10-4) Moonlight FL.
Albright, Naomi. The Great White Forest-King. 170p. 1992. pap. 12.75 (1-882218-01-9) Blue Star Pubs.
ALC Staff, ed. see Adoff, Arnold.
ALC Staff, ed. see Ahlberg, Allan.
ALC Staff, ed. see Arnold, Caroline.
ALC Staff, ed. see Atkinson, Linda.
ALC Staff, ed. see Avi.
ALC Staff, ed. see Baum, Louis.
ALC Staff, ed. see Child, Lydia M.
ALC Staff, ed. see Clarke, Gus.
ALC Staff, ed. see Clifford, Eth.
ALC Staff, ed. see Cole, Joanna & Calmenson, Stephanie.
ALC Staff, ed. see Gleeson, Libby.
ALC Staff, ed. see Haskins, James.
ALC Staff, ed. see Hayes, Sarah.
ALC Staff, ed. see Haywood, Carolyn.
ALC Staff, ed. see Hodges, Margaret.
ALC Staff, ed. see Hughes, Shirley.
ALC Staff, ed. see Hurwitz, Johanna.
ALC Staff, ed. see Isadora, Rachel.
ALC Staff, ed. see Kellogg, Steven.
ALC Staff, ed. see Monson, A. M.
ALC Staff, ed. see Prelutsky, Jack.
ALC Staff, ed. see Pryor, Bonnie.
ALC Staff, ed. see Rice, Eve.
ALC Staff, ed. see Simon, Seymour.
ALC Staff, ed. see Steptoe, John.
ALC Staff, ed. see Swindells, Robert.
ALC Staff, ed. see Tafuri, Nancy.
ALC Staff, ed. see Van de Wetering, Janwillem.
ALC Staff, ed. see Zolotow, Charlotte.
Alcabes, Sylvan. UPCO's Review of Biology. 2nd ed. (Illus.). 288p. (gr. 9-12). 1988. pap. text ed. 3.00 (0-937323-05-5) United Pub Co.
Alchemy II, Inc. Staff, illus. Goldilocks & the Three Bears. 26p. 1988. incl. cassette 9.95 (1-55578-906-4) Worlds Wonder.
—Jack & the Beanstalk. 26p. (ps). 1988. incl. cassette 9.95 (1-55578-907-2) Worlds Wonder.
—The Little Red Hen. 26p. (ps). 1988. incl. cassette 9.95 (1-55578-905-6) Worlds Wonder.
Alcock, Vivian. The Mysterious Mr. Ross. large type ed. (gr. 1-8). 1990. 13.95 (0-7451-0759-1, Galaxy Child Lrg Print) Chivers N Amer.
Alcock, Vivien. The Cuckoo Sister. LC 85-20648. 158p. (gr. 4-6). 1986. pap. 14.95 (0-385-29467-0) Delacorte.
—The Haunting of Cassie Palmer. LC 81-15230. 160p. (gr. 4-6). 1982. pap. 11.95 (0-385-28402-0) Delacorte.
—Kind of Thief. (gr. 4-7). 1992. 14.00 (0-385-30564-8) Delacorte.
—A Kind of Thief. large type ed. 260p. 1992. 13.95 (0-7451-1608-6, Galaxy Child Lrg Print) Chivers N Amer.
—The Monster Garden. LC 88-6900. 160p. (gr. 5-9). 1988. 13.95 (0-440-50053-2) Delacorte.
—The Monster Garden. (gr. k-6). 1990. pap. 2.95 (0-440-40257-3, YB) Dell.
—The Mysterious Mr. Ross. LC 87-5455. 160p. (gr. 5-9). 1987. pap. 14.95 (0-385-29581-2) Delacorte.
—Singer to the Sea God. LC 92-9832. 1993. 15.00 (0-385-30866-3) Delacorte.
—The Stonewalkers. LC 82-13956. 192p. (gr. 4-6). 1983. pap. 12.95 (0-385-29233-3) Delacorte.
—Travelers by Night. (gr. k-6). 1990. pap. 2.95 (0-440-40292-1, YB) Dell.
—The Trial of Anna Cotman. large type ed. 290p. (gr. 3-7). 1991. 13.95 (0-7451-1322-2, Galaxy Child Lrg Print) Chivers N Amer.
—Trial of Anna Cotman. (gr. 4-7). 1992. pap. 3.25 (0-440-40616-1) Dell.
Alcock, Vivien, jt. auth. see Garfield, Vivien.
Alcorn, Johnny. Rembrandt's Beret. Alcorn, Stephen, illus. LC 90-42330. 32p. (gr. 1 up). 1991. 13.95 (0-688-10206-9, Tambourine Bks); PLB 13.88 (0-688-10207-7, Tambourine Bks) Morrow.
Alcorta, Joe H., Sr. La Historia de un Famoso Equipo: Los Dallas Cowboys. (SPA., Illus.). 410p. (gr. 9-12). 1989. 14.95 (0-685-29025-5) Hermenejildo Pr.
Alcott, Louisa May. Eight Cousins. (gr. 7 up). 1974. 19.95 (0-316-03091-0) Little.
—Eight Cousins. (gr. k-6). 1986. pap. 3.50 (0-440-42231-0, Pub. by Yearling Classics) Dell.
—Eight Cousins or the Aunt Hill. 272p. (gr. 5 up). 1989. pap. 3.50 (0-14-035112-4, Puffin) Puffin Bks.
—Glimpses of Louisa: A Centennial Sampling of the Best Short Stories by Louisa May Alcott. (gr. 7 up). 1968. 19.95 (0-316-03090-2) Little.
—Good Wives. 320p. (gr. 3-7). 1983. pap. 2.95 (0-14-035009-8, Puffin) Puffin Bks.
—Jack & Jill. (gr. 5 up). 1979. 17.95 (0-316-03092-9) Little.
—Jack & Jill. (Illus.). 352p. (gr. 5 up). 1991. pap. 2.95 (0-14-035128-0, Puffin) Puffin Bks.
—Jo's Boys. 352p. (gr. 4-6). 1984. pap. 2.25 (0-14-035015-2, Puffin) Puffin Bks.
—Jo's Boys. Stern, Madelain, afterword by. 304p. (gr. 7-12). 1987. pap. 2.25 (0-451-52089-0, Sig Classics) NAL-Dutton.
—Jo's Boys. 1988. 20.95 (0-8488-0411-2) Amereon Ltd.
—Jo's Boys. 1989. Repr. of 1886 ed. lib. bdg. 79.00 (0-7812-1642-7) Rprt Serv.
—Jo's Boys. 344p. 1992. pap. 3.25 (0-590-45178-2, Apple Classics) Scholastic Inc.
—Jo's Boys & How They Turned Out. (gr. 7 up). 1986. 19.95 (0-316-03093-7) Little.
—Little Men. (Illus.). (gr. 5 up). 1969. pap. 1.95 (0-8049-0194-5, CL-194) Airmont.
—Little Men. (Illus.). (gr. 4-6). 1947. (G&D); 13.95 (0-448-06018-3, G&D) Putnam Pub Group.
—Little Men. (Illus.). 384p. (gr. 4 up). 1982. pap. 6.95 (0-448-11018-0, G&D) Putnam Pub Group.
—Little Men. Brich, Reginald, illus. (gr. 7 up). 1971. 17.95 (0-316-03094-5) Little.
—Little Men. 240p. (gr. 4-6). 1984. pap. 2.99 (0-14-035018-7, Puffin) Puffin Bks.
—Little Men. (Orig.). (gr. 4-6). 1987. pap. 3.25 (0-590-41279-5, Apple Paperbacks) Scholastic Inc.
—Little Men. 1989. Repr. of 1861 ed. lib. bdg. 79.00 (0-7812-1629-X) Rprt Serv.
—Little Men. 1991. 12.99 (0-517-03088-8) Outlet Bk Co.
—Little Women. (Illus.). (gr. 6 up). 1966. pap. 2.95 (0-8049-0106-6, CL-106) Airmont.
—Little Women. Magagna, Anna M. & Jambor, Louis, illus. (gr. 4-6). 1981. (G&D); deluxe ed. 15.95 (0-448-06019-1) Putnam Pub Group.
—Little Women. (gr. 6 up). 1974. 59.95 (0-8490-0547-7) Gordon Pr.
—Little Women. Smith, Jessie W., illus. (gr. 7 up). 1968. 19.95 (0-316-03095-3) Little.
—Little Women. 320p. (gr. 3-7). 1983. pap. 2.25 (0-14-035008-X, Puffin) Puffin Bks.
—Little Women. (gr. 5 up). 1963. 37.50 (0-685-20188-0, 144-7) Saphrograph.
—Little Women. (gr. 6 up). 1983. Repr. lib. bdg. 18.95x (0-89966-408-3) Buccaneer Bks.
—Little Women. Douglas, Ann, intro. by. 480p. (gr. 3 up). 1983. pap. 3.95 (0-451-52341-5, Sig Classic) NAL-Dutton.
—Little Women. Edwards, Gunvor, illus. Gliberry, Lysbeth, retold by. (Illus.). 48p. (gr. 7-12). 1975. pap. text ed. 3.25x (0-19-421804-X) OUP.
—Little Women. LC 62-20197. (gr. 4 up). 1986. pap. 3.95 (0-02-041240-1, Collier Young Ad) Macmillan Child Grp.
—Little Women. Smith, Jessie W. & Merrill, Frank, illus. 400p. (gr. 2 up). 1988. 12.99 (0-517-63489-9) Outlet Bk Co.
—Little Women. (Orig.). (gr. k-6). 1987. pap. 6.95 (0-440-44768-2, Pub. by Yearling Classics) Dell.
—Little Women. Showalter, Elaine, intro. by. 608p. 1989. pap. 5.95 (0-14-039069-3, Penguin Classics) Viking Penguin.
—Little Women. 1989. Repr. of 1867 ed. lib. bdg. 79.00 (0-7812-1627-3) Rprt Serv.
—Little Women. Auerbach, Nina, afterword by. 480p. 1983. pap. 3.95 (0-553-21275-3, Bantam Classics Spectra) Bantam.
—Little Women. large type ed. 336p. 1987. 15.95 (0-7089-8384-7, Charnwood) Ulverscroft.
—Little Women. 1986. pap. 3.25 (0-590-43797-6, Apple Paperbacks) Scholastic Inc.
—Little Women. 1988. 2.98 (0-671-09222-7) S&S Trade.
—Little Women. Kulling, Monica, adapted by. LC 93-38237. 1994. write for info. (0-679-86175-0) Random.
—Little Women, or, Meg, Jo, Beth, & Amy. Hague, Michael, illus. LC 93-18943. 308p. (gr. 4-8). 1993. PLB 15.95 (0-8050-2767-X, Bks Young Read) H Holt & Co.
—Little Women, Vol. 1: Four Funny Sisters. Lindskoog, Kathryn, ed. (Illus.). (gr. 3-7). 1991. pap. 4.99 (0-88070-437-3, Gold & Honey) Questar Pubs.
—Louisa's Wonder Book: An Unknown Alcott Juvenile. Stern, Madeline B., ed. LC 76-358119. (Illus.). 1975. Repr. of 1870 ed. 7.50 (0-916699-08-0) CMU Clarke Hist Lib.
—A Modern Mephistopheles. 1988. 16.95 (0-8488-0412-0) Amereon Ltd.
—Old-Fashioned Girl. Abbot, Elenore, illus. (gr. 7 up). 1969. 19.95 (0-316-03096-1) Little.
—An Old-Fashioned Girl. (Orig.). (gr. k-6). 1987. pap. 4.95 (0-440-46609-1, Pub. by Yearling Classics) Dell.
—Old-Fashioned Girl. (gr. 4-7). 1991. pap. 2.95 (0-14-035137-X, Puffin) Puffin Bks.
—An Old-Fashioned Thanksgiving. McCurdy, Michael, illus. LC 89-1908. 32p. (gr. 3-7). 1989. reinforced 14.95 (0-8234-0772-1) Holiday.
—Quatre Filles du Docteur March. Rozier, J. & Gaudriault, M., illus. (FRE.). (gr. 5-10). 1900. 10.95 (2-07-033413-9) Schoenhof.
—Reader's Digest Best Loved Books for Young Readers: Little Women. Ogburn, Jackie, ed. English, Mark, illus. 176p. (gr. 4-12). 1989. 3.99 (0-945260-25-3) Choice Pub NY.
—Rose in Bloom. Price, Hattie L., illus. (gr. 7 up). 1976. 19.95 (0-316-03098-8) Little.
—Rose in Bloom. (gr. k-6). 1986. pap. 4.95 (0-440-47588-0, YB) Dell.
—Rose in Bloom. 336p. (gr. 5 up). 1989. pap. 3.95 (0-14-035125-6, Puffin) Puffin Bks.
—Under the Lilacs. Davis, Marguerite, illus. (gr. 7 up). 1977. 17.95 (0-316-03099-6) Little.
—Under the Lilacs. 320p. (gr. 2 up). 1991. pap. 2.95 (0-14-035132-9, Puffin) Puffin Bks.
—Work. LC 76-48849. (Illus.). (gr. 10 up). 1977. Schocken.
—Works of Louisa May Alcott. (gr. 5-6). 37.95 (0-88411-173-3, Pub. by Aeonian Pr) Amereon Ltd.
Alcott, Louisa May, adapted by. An Old Fashioned Thanksgiving. adpt. ed. Wheeler, Jody, illus. LC 93-20352. 40p. (ps-3). 1993. PLB 14.00 (0-8249-8630-X, Ideals Child); pap. 13.95 (0-8249-8620-2) Hambleton-Hill.
Alcott, Sarah. Young Amelia Earhart: A Dream to Fly. Hormann, Toni, illus. LC 91-24974. 32p. (gr. k-2). 1992. text ed. 11.59 (0-8167-2528-4); pap. text ed. 2.95 (0-8167-2529-2) Troll Assocs.
Alcoze, Thom. Multiculturalism in Mathematics, Science, & Technology: Reading & Activities. pap. 32.00 (0-201-29595-4) Addison-Wesley.
Alda, Arlene. Arlene Alda's ABC. LC 93-24999. (gr. 3 up). 1993. 13.95 (1-883672-01-5) Tricycle Pr.
—Arlene Alda's ABC. Alda, Arlene, photos by. (Illus.). 32p. (ps-2). 1993. Repr. of 1981 ed. 12.95 (0-89087-348-8) Tricycle Pr.
—Sheep, Sheep, Sheep: Help Me Fall Asleep. Alda, Arlene, photos by. LC 91-43006. (Illus.). 32p. (ps-2). 1992. pap. 13.50 (0-385-30791-8) Doubleday.
Aldag, Kurt. Some Things Never Change. Rush, Ken, illus. LC 91-9907. 32p. (ps-3). 1994. RSBE 13.95 (0-02-700205-5, Macmillan Child Bk) Macmillan Child Grp.
Alden, Joan. A Boy's Best Friend. Hopkins, Catherine, illus. LC 92-8061. 32p. (ps-2). 1992. 12.95 (1-55583-203-2, Alyson Wonderland) Alyson Pubns.
Alden, L. Cat's Adventure in Alphabet Town. McCallum, J., illus. LC 91-3605. 32p. (ps-2). 1992. PLB 14.60 (0-516-05403-1) Childrens.
—Elfin's Adventure in Alphabet Town. Hohag, L., illus. LC 91-20545. 32p. (ps-2). 1992. PLB 14.60 (0-516-05405-8) Childrens.
Alden, Laura. Halloween. McCallum, Jodie, illus. LC 93-7633. (gr. 4 up). 1993. write for info. (0-516-00684-3) Childrens.
—Houdini. Raskin, Betty, illus. LC 88-34126. 100p. (gr. 3-7). 1989. PLB 21.35 (0-89565-456-3); PLB 14.95s.p. (0-685-55993-9) Childs World.
—Learning about Unicorns. Stasiak, Krystyna, illus. LC 85-9926. 48p. (gr. 2-6). 1985. pap. 4.95 (0-516-06539-2) Childrens.
—Megalosaurus. Magnuson, Diana, illus. 32p. (gr. k-4). 1990. PLB 21.35 (0-89565-629-9); PLB 14.95s.p. (0-685-56214-X) Childs World.
—Nightingale's Adventure in Alphabet Town. McCallum, Jodie, illus. LC 92-1069. 32p. (ps-2). 1992. PLB 14.60 (0-516-05414-7) Childrens.
—Ornithomimus. Ching, illus. 32p. (gr. k-4). 1990. PLB 21.35 (0-89565-630-2); PLB 14.95s.p. (0-685-56215-8) Childs World.
—Owl's Adventure in Alphabet Town. McCallum, Jodie, illus. LC 92-4091. 32p. (ps-2). 1992. PLB 14.60 (0-516-05415-5) Childrens.
—Penguin's Adventure in Alphabet Town. Williams, Jenny, illus. LC 92-1068. 32p. (ps-2). 1992. PLB 14.60 (0-516-05416-3) Childrens.
—Saying I'm Sorry. Siculan, Dan, illus. LC 82-19945. 32p. (gr. 1-2). 1983. PLB 21.35 (0-89565-247-1); PLB 14.95s.p. (0-685-55663-8) Childs World.
—Squirrel's Adventure in Alphabet Town. Collins, Judi, illus. LC 92-1314. 32p. (ps-2). 1992. PLB 14.60 (0-516-05419-8) Childrens.
—Umpire's Adventure in Alphabet Town. Hohag, Linda, illus. LC 92-12668. 32p. (ps-2). 1992. PLB 14.60 (0-516-05421-X) Childrens.
—When. Axeman, Lois, illus. LC 83-7305. 32p. (gr. k-2). 1983. pap. 3.95 (0-516-46592-9) Childrens.
Alden, Laura & Lexa-Senning, Susan. Thanksgiving. LC 93-13019. (Illus.). 1993. write for info. (0-516-00688-6) Childrens.

Alden, Laura, compiled by. Dinosaur Jokes. Magnuson, Diana, illus. LC 88-17489. 48p. (gr. 1-5). 1988. lib. bdg. 13.27 (*0-516-01865-5*); pap. 3.95 (*0-516-41865-3*) Childrens.

Alder, David A. The Children of Chelm. Friedman, Arthur, illus. (gr. 1-5). 1979. (Bonim Bks); pap. 4.50 (*0-88482-773-9*, Bonim Bks) Hebrew Pub.

Alder, Elizabeth. The King's Shadow. 1994. 17.00 (*0-374-34182-6*) FS&G.

Alderman, Clifford L. Story of the Thirteen Colonies. Fisher, L. E., illus. (gr. 5-9). 1966. lib. bdg. 9.99 (*0-394-90415-X*) Random Bks Yng Read.

Alderson, Frederick. Outdoor Games. (Illus.). 64p. (gr. 6 up). 1980. 14.95 (*0-7136-2031-5*) Dufour.

Alderson, Sue A. Ida & the Wool Smugglers. Blades, Ann, illus. LC 87-15487. 32p. (gr. k-4). 1988. SBE 13.95 (*0-689-50440-3*, M K McElderry) Macmillan Child Grp.

Alderson, Sueann. Bonnie McSmithers Is at It Again! Garrick, Fiona, illus. 24p. (Orig.). (ps-2). 1990. pap. 0.99 (*1-55037-110-X*, Pub. by Annick CN) Firefly Bks Ltd.

—Bonnie McSmithers You're Driving Me Dithers. Garrick, Fiona, illus. 24p. (Orig.). (ps-2). 1990. pap. 0.99 (*1-55037-108-8*, Pub. by Annick CN) Firefly Bks Ltd.

—Hurry Up, Bonnie! Garrick, Fiona, illus. 24p. (Orig.). (ps-2). 1990. pap. 0.99 (*1-55037-109-6*, Pub. by Annick CN) Firefly Bks Ltd.

Alderton, David. Baby Animals. (Illus.). 64p. 1991. 4.99 (*0-517-05155-9*) Outlet Bk Co.

Aldis, Dorothy. Nothing Is Impossible - The Story of Beatrix Potter. Cuffari, Richard, illus. (gr. 4-6). 1988. 18.75 (*0-8446-6359-X*) Peter Smith.

Aldis, Rodney. Polar Lands. LC 91-34170. (Illus.). 48p. (gr. 5 up). 1992. RSBE 13.95 (*0-87518-494-4*, Dillon) Macmillan Child Grp.

—Rainforests. LC 91-20595. (Illus.). 48p. (gr. 4-6). 1991. RSBE 13.95 (*0-87518-495-2*, Dillon) Macmillan Child Grp.

—Towns & Cities. LC 91-35801. (Illus.). 48p. (gr. 5 up). 1992. RSBE 13.95 (*0-87518-496-0*, Dillon) Macmillan Child Grp.

Aldous, Lynn. Lettering Pack. (Illus.). (gr. 3-6). 1992. pap. 7.95 (*1-56680-505-8*) Mad Hatter Pub.

Aldred, Cyril. Tut-Ankh-Amun-& His Friends. (gr. 8). 1977. pap. 3.95 (*0-88388-043-1*) Bellerophon Bk.

—Tutankhmun. (Illus.). (gr. 5). 1978. pap. 2.95 (*0-88388-059-8*) Bellerophon Bks.

Aldred, Lisa. Thurgood Marshall. King, Coretta Scott, intro. by. (Illus.). 128p. (gr. 5 up). 1990. PLB 17.95 (*1-55546-601-X*); pap. 9.95 (*0-7910-0245-4*) Chelsea Hse.

Aldridge, Josephine H. The Pocket Book. Moreno, Rene K., illus. LC 93-1699. 1994. pap. 14.00 (*0-671-87128-5*, S&S BFYR) S&S Trade.

—A Possible Tree. San Souci, Daniel, illus. LC 92-13704. 32p. (gr. k-3). 1993. RSBE 14.95 (*0-02-700407-4*, Macmillan Child Bk) Macmillan Child Grp.

Aldridge, Ruth. I Remember When. Wilkin, Mike, illus. LC 93-26926. 1994. 4.25 (*0-383-03750-6*) SRA Schl Grp.

Aldrin, Edwin E. see Baird, Anne.

Aleichem, Sholem. Hanukah Money. Shulevitz, Uri & Shub, Elizabeth, trs. Shulevitz, Uri, illus. LC 77-26693. 32p. (ps-3). 1991. pap. 3.95 (*0-688-10993-4*, Mulberry) Morrow.

Aleichem, Sholom. Holiday Tales of Sholom Aleichem. Shevrin, Aliza, tr. DiGrazia, Thomas, illus. LC 79-753. 145p. (gr. 5 up). 1985. pap. 5.95 (*0-689-71034-8*, Aladdin) Macmillan Child Grp.

Alemany, Norah, tr. see Maury, Inez.

Alen, Paule, jt. auth. see Deru, Myriam.

Alessandrini, Jean. Mystery & Chocolate. (Illus.). (gr. 1-8). 1992. PLB 8.95 (*0-89565-898-4*); Resale. 12.75 (*0-685-60996-0*) Childs World.

Alex, Ben, jt. auth. see Thomas, Mack.

Alexander, Alison. Power Magic. 1991. pap. 11.95 (*0-671-74131-4*, S&S BFYR); pap. 6.95 (*0-671-74130-6*, S&S BFYR) S&S Trade.

—Science Magic: Scientific Experiments for Young Children. 1987. (PRHJ); pap. 6.95 (*0-671-66927-3*) S&S Trade.

Alexander, Andrea. Why Do Mice Celebrate Christmas? And Other Fun Questions of the Season. Alexander, Andrea, illus. 64p. (Orig.). (ps-5). 1991. pap. 13.95 (*0-9628006-0-0*) Zenon Pub.

Alexander, Bryan & Alexander, Cherry. An Eskimo Family. (Illus.). 32p. (gr. 2-5). 1985. PLB 13.50 (*0-8225-1656-X*) Lerner Pubns.

—Inuit. LC 92-9894. (Illus.). 48p. (gr. 5-6). 1992. PLB 22.80 (*0-8114-2301-8*) Raintree Steck-V.

Alexander, Cecil. All Things Bright & Beautiful. Heyer, Carol, illus. 32p. (ps-2). 1992. 11.95 (*0-8249-8544-3*, Ideals Child) Hambleton-Hill.

Alexander, Cecil F. All Things Bright & Beautiful. Morgan, Mary, illus. 32p. (Orig.). (ps-2). 1989. pap. 1.95 (*0-448-34304-5*, Platt & Munk Pubs) Putnam Pub Group.

Alexander, Cherry, jt. auth. see Alexander, Bryan.

Alexander, Debra W. All My Dreams. 16p. (gr. 6-12). 1993. 3.95 (*1-56688-067-X*) Bur For At-Risk.

—All My Feelings. 23p. (gr. k-5). 1992. 3.95 (*1-56688-055-6*) Bur For At-Risk.

—Don't Go. 16p. (gr. k-5). 1992. 3.95 (*1-56688-057-2*) Bur For At-Risk.

—I Can't Remember. 16p. (gr. k-5). 1992. 3.95 (*1-56688-059-9*) Bur For At-Risk.

—In This House Called Home. 24p. (gr. 6-12). 1993. 3.95 (*1-56688-065-3*) Bur For At-Risk.

—It Happened in Autumn. 24p. (gr. 6-12). 1993. 3.95 (*1-56688-069-6*) Bur For At-Risk.

—It Happened to Me. 24p. (gr. k-5). 1992. 3.95 (*1-56688-058-0*) Bur For At-Risk.

—It's My Life. 24p. (gr. 6-12). 1993. 3.95 (*1-56688-066-1*) Bur For At-Risk.

—Something Bad Happened. 16p. (gr. k-5). 1992. 3.95 (*1-56688-056-4*) Bur For At-Risk.

—The Way I Feel. 16p. (gr. 6-12). 1993. 3.95 (*1-56688-064-5*) Bur For At-Risk.

—When I Remember. 24p. (gr. 6-12). 1993. 3.95 (*1-56688-068-8*) Bur For At-Risk.

—The World I See. 24p. (gr. k-5). 1992. 3.95 (*1-56688-054-8*) Bur For At-Risk.

Alexander, Ellen. Llama & the Great Flood: A Folktale from Peru. Alexander, Ellen, illus. LC 88-1194. 40p. (gr. k-4). 1989. (Crowell Jr Bks); PLB 13.89 (*0-690-04729-0*) HarpC Child Bks.

Alexander, Frances. Mother Goose on the Rio Grande. (Illus.). 96p. (gr. 4 up). 1983. pap. 6.95 (*0-8442-7641-3*, Passport Bks) NTC Pub Grp.

Alexander, Frank, ed. see Sanford, Doris, Jr.

Alexander, Heather. Look Inside Your Brain. Costa, Nicoletta, illus. LC 90-85544. 16p. (ps-3). 1991. 11.95 (*0-448-40186-X*, G&D) Putnam Pub Group.

Alexander, James E. Depression Kids: Shaping the Character of Our Lives. 260p. (Orig.). 1993. pap. 12.50 (*0-939965-07-0*) Macedon Prod.

Alexander, John L., et al. Handbook for Boys. (Illus.). (gr. 7-12). 1976. pap. 12.75 (*0-8395-3100-1*, 33100) BSA.

Alexander, Kay. Creative Learning Elementary Art Resources, Set 1: Clear. (Illus.). 83p. (gr. k-3). 1989. write for info. tchr's ed. (*0-924509-01-5*) Crystal.

Alexander, Linda. Job Well Done. Petie, Haris, illus. (gr. 1-4). PLB 7.19 (*0-8313-0002-7*) Lantern.

Alexander, Liza. Babysitting with Big Bird. Leigh, Tom, illus. 24p. (ps-4). 1993. 20.00 (*0-307-74029-3*, 64029, Golden Pr) Western Pub.

—I Want to Be a Ballet Dancer. (ps-3). 1993. pap. 2.25 (*0-307-13121-1*, Pub. by Golden Bks) Western Pub.

—I Want to Be a Cowboy. Ewers, Joe, illus. 24p. (ps-k). 1992. write for info. (*0-307-13117-3*) Western Pub.

—Imagine: Big Bird Meets Santa Claus. (ps-3). 1993. pap. 2.25 (*0-307-13119-X*, Golden Pr) Western Pub.

—Nothing to Do. Cooke, Tom, illus. LC 87-81761. 32p. (ps-k). 1988. write for info. (*0-307-12024-4*, Pub. by Golden Bks) Western Pub.

—Scared of the Dark. Cooke, Tom, illus. 32p. (ps-k). 1986. write for info. (*0-307-12020-1*, Pub by Golden Bks) Western Pub.

—Sesame Street: Ernie & Twiddlebug Town Fair. 1990. pap. write for info. (*0-307-10030-8*, Golden Pr) Western Pub.

—Sesame Street Rainforest Adventure. 24p. (ps up). 1992. write for info. (*0-307-74021-8*, 64021) Western Pub.

—Sesame Street: Splish Splashy Day. (Illus.). 24p. (ps-k). 1989. pap. write for info. (*0-307-10064-2*, Pub. by Golden Bks) Western Pub.

—Too Little! Brannon, Tom, illus. 32p. (ps-k). 1992. write for info. (*0-307-12009-0*, 12009) Western Pub.

—A Visit to the Sesame Street Museum. Mathiew, Joe, illus. LC 87-1685. 32p. (gr. k-3). 1987. lib. bdg. 5.99 (*0-394-98715-2*); pap. 2.25 (*0-394-88715-8*) Random Bks Yng Read.

—When Oscar Was a Little Grouch & Other Good-Night Stories. (Illus.). 24p. (ps-1). 1989. write for info. (Pub. by Golden Bks) Western Pub.

Alexander, Liza, et al. The Sesame Street Treasury: Featuring Jim Henson's Sesame Street Muppets. Chartier, Normand, et al, illus. LC 93-8326. Date not set. write for info. (*0-679-84655-7*); PLB write for info. (*0-679-94655-1*) Random.

Alexander, Lloyd. The Beggar Queen. (gr. 6-12). 1985. pap. 3.50 (*0-440-90548-6*, LFL) Dell.

—Black Cauldron. 192p. (gr. k-6). 1980. pap. 3.99 (*0-440-40649-8*, YB) Dell.

—Black Cauldron. LC 65-13868. (gr. 4-6). 1965. 15.95 (*0-8050-0992-2*, Bks Young Read) H Holt & Co.

—The Book of Three. 192p. (gr. 5-9). 1980. pap. 3.50 (*0-440-90702-0*, LFL) Dell.

—Book of Three. LC 64-18250. 224p. (gr. 4-6). 1964. 16.95 (*0-8050-0874-8*, Bks Young Read) H Holt & Co.

—The Book of Three. 192p. (gr. k-6). 1978. pap. 3.50 (*0-440-40702-8*, YB) Dell.

—Book of Three. Date not set. write for info. H Holt & Co.

—The Castle of Llyr. 192p. (gr. 5-9). 1980. pap. 3.50 (*0-440-91125-7*, LFL) Dell.

—Castle of Llyr. 192p. (gr. k-6). 1969. pap. 3.50 (*0-440-41125-4*, YB) Dell.

—Castle of Llyr. LC 66-13461. 204p. (gr. 4-6). 1966. 16.95 (*0-8050-1115-3*, Bks Young Read) H Holt & Co.

—The Cat Who Wished to Be a Man. 120p. (gr. 4-7). 1977. (DCB); (DCB) Dutton Child Bks.

—Cat Who Wished to Be a Man. (gr. 4-7). 1992. pap. 3.50 (*0-440-40580-7*) Dell.

—The Drackenberg Adventure. (gr. k-6). 1990. pap. 3.50 (*0-440-40296-4*, Pub. by Yearling Classics) Dell.

—The Drackenburg Adventure. LC 87-36881. 160p. (gr. 5-9). 1988. 12.95 (*0-525-44389-4*, 01258-370, DCB) Dutton Child Bks.

—The El Dorado Adventure. LC 86-29157. 176p. (gr. 5-9). 1987. 13.95 (*0-525-44313-4*, DCB) Dutton Child Bks.

—The First Two Lives of Lukas-Kasha. LC 77-26699. 224p. (gr. 4-7). 1978. 14.95 (*0-525-29748-0*, DCB) Dutton Child Bks.

—The First Two Lives of Lukas-Kasha. 224p. (gr. 7 up). 1982. pap. 2.25 (*0-440-42784-3*, YB) Dell.

—Fortune Tellers. LC 91-30684. (Illus.). 32p. (gr. k-3). 1992. 15.00 (*0-525-44849-7*, DCB) Dutton Child Bks.

—The Foundling: And Other Tales of Prydain. 128p. (gr. 5 up). 1982. pap. 3.50 (*0-440-42536-0*, YB) Dell.

—The High King. 288p. (gr. 5-9). 1980. pap. 3.50 (*0-440-93574-1*, LFL) Dell.

—The High King. LC 68-11833. 288p. (gr. 4-6). 1968. 16.95 (*0-8050-1114-5*, Bks Young Read) H Holt & Co.

—The High King. 288p. (gr. k-6). 1969. pap. 3.99 (*0-440-43574-9*, YB) Dell.

—The Illyrian Adventure. LC 85-30762. (Illus.). 160p. (gr. 5-9). 1986. 13.95 (*0-525-44250-2*, DCB) Dutton Child Bks.

—The Illyrian Adventure. (gr. k-12). 1987. pap. 3.50 (*0-440-94018-4*, LFL) Dell.

—The Illyrian Adventure. 1990. pap. 3.50 (*0-440-40297-2*) Dell.

—The Jedera Adventure. LC 88-38865. 160p. (gr. 5-9). 1989. 13.95 (*0-525-44481-5*, DCB) Dutton Child Bks.

—The Jedera Adventure. 1990. pap. 3.99 (*0-440-40295-6*, YB) Dell.

—The Kestrel. 256p. (gr. 7 up). 1983. pap. 3.99 (*0-440-94393-0*, LFL) Dell.

—King's Fountain. Keats, Ezra J., illus. LC 72-13310. 32p. (ps-3). 1989. (DCB); pap. 4.95 (*0-525-44537-4*, DCB) Dutton Child Bks.

—Marvelous Misadventures of Sebastian. LC 70-166879. (gr. 4 up). 1973. 14.95 (*0-525-34739-9*, DCB); (DCB) Dutton Child Bks.

—Marvelous Misadventures of Sebastian. (gr. 4-7). 1991. pap. 3.50 (*0-440-40549-1*, YB) Dell.

—The Philadelphia Adventure. LC 89-34990. 160p. (gr. 5-9). 1990. 13.95 (*0-525-44564-1*, DCB) Dutton Child Bks.

—Philadelphia Adventure. (gr. 4-7). 1992. pap. 3.50 (*0-440-40605-6*) Dell.

—Remarkable Journey. 1993. pap. 3.99 (*0-440-40890-3*) Dell.

—The Remarkable Journey of Prince Jen. LC 91-13720. 288p. (gr. 5 up). 1991. 15.00 (*0-525-44826-8*, DCB) Dutton Child Bks.

—Taran Wanderer. 272p. (gr. 5-9). 1980. pap. 3.50 (*0-440-98483-1*, LFL) Dell.

—Taran Wanderer. 272p. (gr. k-6). 1969. pap. 3.50 (*0-440-48483-9*, YB) Dell.

—Taran Wanderer. LC 67-10230. 256p. (gr. 4-6). 1967. 15.95 (*0-8050-1113-7*, Bks Young Read) H Holt & Co.

—Time Cat. Sokol, Bill, illus. (gr. 4-7). 16.25 (*0-8446-6237-2*) Peter Smith.

—Westmark. 192p. (gr. 5-9). 1982. pap. 3.50 (*0-440-99731-3*, LFL) Dell.

—Westmark. LC 80-22242. (gr. 5 up). 1981. 15.95 (*0-525-42335-4*, DCB) Dutton Child Bks.

—The Wizard in the Tree. 144p. (gr. 5 up). 1981. pap. 3.25 (*0-440-49556-3*, Pub. by Yearling Classics) Dell.

—The Wizard in the Tree. Kubinyi, Laszlo, illus. 144p. (gr. 4-7). 1974. 14.95 (*0-525-43128-4*, DCB) Dutton Child Bks.

Alexander, M. Where Does the Sky End, Grandpa? 1992. 12.95 (*0-15-295603-4*, HB Juv Bks) HarBrace.

Alexander, Margaret. Rachel & the Pink & Green Dragon. (Illus.). 44p. (gr. k-3). 1992. 6.95 (*1-55523-518-2*) Winston-Derek.

Alexander, Martha. And My Mean Old Mother Will Be Sorry, Blackboard Bear. Alexander, Martha, illus. LC 72-707. (gr. k-2). 1977. pap. 3.50 (*0-8037-0126-8*) Dial Bks Young.

—Blackboard Bear. Alexander, Martha, illus. (Orig.). (ps-2). 1988. pap. 3.50 (*0-8037-0629-4*) Dial Bks Young.

—Blackboard Bear. (ps-3). 1988. pap. 4.99 (*0-14-054609-X*) Dial Bks Young.

—Even That Moose Won't Listen to Me. Alexander, Martha, illus. 32p. (ps-k). 1988. PLB 11.89 (*0-8037-0188-8*) Dial Bks Young.

—Even That Moose Won't Listen to Me. Alexander, Martha, illus. LC 85-4338. 32p. (ps-2). 1991. pap. 3.95 (*0-8037-0984-6*, Dial Pied Piper) Puffin Bks.

—Four Bears in a Box. (ps-3). 1992. 8.95 (*0-8037-1043-7*, Dial Pied Piper) Puffin Bks.

—Good Night, Lily. Alexander, Martha, illus. LC 92-53005. 14p. (ps). 1993. 4.95 (*1-56402-164-5*) Candlewick Pr.

—How My Library Grew, By Dinah. Alexander, Martha, illus. 32p. (gr. k-5). 1983. 18.00 (*0-8242-0679-7*) Wilson.

—I Sure Am Glad to See You Black. (ps-3). 1992. pap. 3.99 (*0-14-054642-1*) Puffin Bks.

—I Sure Am Glad to See You, Blackboard Bear. LC 76-2280. (Illus.). (ps-3). 1976. Dial Bks Young.

—I Sure Am Glad to See You, Blackboard Bear. (Illus.). (ps-3). 1976. pap. 3.50 (*0-8037-4008-5*, Dial Pied Piper) Puffin Bks.

—I'll Protect You from the Jungle Beasts. Alexander, Martha, illus. LC 73-6015. 32p. (ps-2). 1983. PLB 8.89 (*0-8037-4309-2*) Dial Bks Young.

—Lily & Willy. Alexander, Martha, illus. LC 92-53004. 14p. (ps). 1993. 4.95 (*1-56402-163-7*) Candlewick Pr.

—Maggie's Moon. Alexander, Martha, illus. LC 82-1575. 32p. (ps-2). 1982. Dial Bks Young.

—The Magic Box. (Illus.). 64p. (ps-3). 1994. pap. 1.99 (*0-14-050504-0*, Puffin Pied Piper) Puffin Bks.

—The Magic Hat. (Illus.). 64p. (ps-3). 1994. pap. 1.99 (0-14-050471-0, Puffin Pied Piper) Puffin Bks.
—The Magic Picture. (Illus.). 64p. (ps-3). 1994. pap. 1.99 (0-14-050505-9, Puffin Pied Piper) Puffin Bks.
—Maybe a Monster. Alexander, Martha, illus. LC 68-28732. 32p. (ps-2). 1985. PLB 8.89 (0-8037-5513-9) Dial Bks Young.
—Move over, Twerp. Alexander, Martha, illus. 32p. (ps-2). 1989. pap. 3.95 (0-8037-5814-6) Dial Bks Young.
—Nobody Asked If I Wanted a Babysitter. (ps-3). 1993. pap. 3.99 (0-14-054673-1) Puffin Bks.
—Nobody Asked Me If I Wanted a Baby Sister. Alexander, Martha, illus. LC 78-153731. (ps-2). 1971. 10.95 (0-8037-6401-4); PLB 10.89 (0-8037-6402-2) Dial Bks Young.
—Nobody Asked Me If I Wanted a Baby Sister. Alexander, Martha, illus. (gr. k-2). 1977. pap. 3.95 (0-8037-6410-3) Dial Bks Young.
—Out, Out, Out. Alexander, Martha, illus. LC 68-15251. (gr. k-3). 1968. PLB 6.95 (0-685-01457-6) Dial Bks Young.
—Poems & Prayers for the Very Young. (Illus.). (ps-1). 1973. pap. 2.25 (0-394-82705-8) Random Bks Yng Read.
—Sabrina. Alexander, Martha, illus. LC 72-134855. 32p. (ps-2). 1991. pap. 2.95 (0-8037-0842-4, Dial Pied Piper) Puffin Bks.
—Sabrina. Alexander, Martha, illus. 1991. 8.95 (0-8037-7547-4) Dial Bks Young.
—Three Magic Flip Books. Incl. The Magic Hat; The Magic Picture; The Magic Box. (Illus.). (ps-k). 1984. Three bks. in a shrink-wrapped slipcase. 5.95 (0-8037-0051-2, 0578-170) Dial Bks Young.
—We Never Get to Do Anything. Alexander, Martha, illus. (ps-3). 1985. Dial Bks Young.
—We're in Big Trouble, Blackboard Bear. Alexander, Martha, illus. LC 79-20631. (ps-2). 1980. Dial Bks Young.
—When the New Baby Comes, I'm Moving Out. Alexander, Martha, illus. LC 79-4275. (ps-2). 1979. PLB 9.89 (0-8037-9558-0) Dial Bks Young.
—Where's Willy? Alexander, Martha, illus. LC 92-53006. 14p. (ps). 1993. 4.95 (1-56402-161-0) Candlewick Pr.
—Willy's Boot. Alexander, Martha, illus. LC 92-53007. 14p. (ps). 1993. 4.95 (1-56402-162-9) Candlewick Pr.

Alexander, Matilda. Judges. (Illus.). 57p. (gr. k-6). 1981. pap. text ed. 9.45 (1-55976-016-8) CEF Press.
—Ruth. Butcher, Sam, illus. 48p. (gr. k-6). 1972. pap. text ed. 9.45 (1-55976-017-6) CEF Press.

Alexander, Pat. My Own Book of Bible Stories. (Illus.). 128p. 1983. 9.99 (0-85648-541-1) Lion USA.

Alexander, Pat & Masom, Caroline. Picture Archive of the Bible. (Illus.). 192p. 1987. 29.95 (0-7459-1047-5) Lion USA.

Alexander, Pat, as told by. My Own Book of Bible Stories. 2nd ed. Cox, Carolyn, illus. LC 92-36252. 128p. (gr. k-3). 1993. text ed. 14.95 (0-7459-2635-5) Lion USA.

Alexander, Pat, retold by. Nelson Children's Bible. LC 81-624. 256p. (gr. 2-4). 1991. 9.99 (0-8407-6802-8) Nelson.

Alexander, Paul, jt. auth. see Bridges, Laurie.

Alexander, R. McNeill. Animal Movement. Head, J. J., ed. Botzis, Ka, illus. LC 84-45834. 16p. (Orig). (gr. 10 up). 1985. pap. text ed. 2.75 (0-89278-364-8, 45-9764) Carolina Biological.

Alexander, Rod. BMX Racing: A Step-By-Step Guide. LC 89-27291. (Illus.). 64p. (gr. 4-8). 1990. PLB 9.79 (0-8167-1943-8); pap. text ed. 2.95 (0-8167-1944-6) Troll Assocs.

Alexander, Sally. Mom Can't See Me. Ancona, George, illus. LC 89-13241. 48p. (gr. 1-5). 1990. RSBE 14.95 (0-02-700401-5, Macmillan Child Bk) Macmillan Child Grp.
—Sarah's Surprise. Kastner, Jill, illus. LC 89-36780. 32p. (gr. k-3). 1990. RSBE 13.95 (0-02-700391-4, Macmillan Child Bk) Macmillan Child Grp.

Alexander, Sally H. Maggie's Whopper. Ray, Deborah K., illus. LC 91-7726. 32p. (gr. k-3). 1992. RSBE 14.95 (0-02-700201-2, Macmillan Child Bk) Macmillan Child Grp.
—Mom's Best Friend. Ancona, George, illus. LC 91-43809. 48p. (gr. 1-5). 1992. RSBE 14.95 (0-02-700393-0, Macmillan Child Bk) Macmillan Child Grp.

Alexander, Sandra C. Famous African-Americans in U. S. History. 30p. (gr. 1-8). 1989. tchr's. ed. 2.99 (1-882288-50-5) RonSan Graphics.
—Famous Hispanic-Americans in U. S. History. 34p. (gr. 1-8). 1992. tchr's. ed. 2.99 (1-882288-52-1) RonSan Graphics.
—Famous Native-Americans in U. S. History. 34p. (gr. 1-8). 1992. tchr's. ed. 2.99 (1-882288-51-3) RonSan Graphics.

Alexander, Scott. Rhinoceros Success. 25th ed. Smallwood, Laurie, illus. LC 80-51648. 123p. (Orig). (gr. 1 up). 1985. pap. 5.95 (0-937382-00-0) Rhinos Pr.

Alexander, Sue. America's Own Holidays: Mas de Fiesta de los Estados Unidos. FS Staff, ed. Morrill, Leslie, illus. (ENG & SPA.). 48p. 1988. PLB 11.40 (0-531-01293-9) Watts.
—Ellsworth & Millicent. Meier, David S., illus. LC 92-7705. 28p. (gr. k up). 1993. 14.95 (0-88708-247-5) Picture Bk Studio.
—Finding Your First Job. LC 79-26487. (Illus.). (gr. 9 up). 1980. (DCB); (DCB) Dutton Child Bks.

—More Witch, Goblin & Ghost Stories. Winter, Jeanette, illus. LC 78-3280. (gr. 1-4). 1978. 6.95 (0-394-83933-1) Pantheon.
—Seymour the Prince. Hoban, Lillian, illus. LC 78-31406. (gr. 2-4). 1979. 6.95 (0-685-03943-9) Pantheon.
—Small Plays for Special Days. Huffman, Tom, illus. LC 76-28424. 64p. (ps-1). 1988. pap. 4.95 (0-89919-798-1, Clarion Bks) HM.
—There's More...Much More. Brewster, Patience, illus. LC 86-33632. 32p. (ps-3). 1987. 12.95 (0-15-200605-2, Gulliver Bks) HarBrace.
—Whatever Happened to Uncle Albert? Huffman, Tom, illus. 128p. (gr. 3-6). 1980. 13.45 (0-395-29104-6, Clarion Bks) HM.
—Who Goes Out on Halloween-Bank Street? (ps-3). 1990. PLB 9.99 (0-553-05891-6, Little Rooster); pap. 3.50 (0-553-34922-8) Bantam.
—Witch, Goblin, & Ghost Are Back. Winter, Jeanette, illus. LC 83-22157. 62p. (gr. 1-4). 1985. 6.95 (0-394-86296-1, Pant Bks Young); lib. bdg. 9.99 (0-394-96296-6) Pantheon.
—Witch, Goblin & Ghost in the Haunted Woods. Winter, Jeanette, illus. LC 80-20863. 72p. (gr. 1-4). 1981. 6.95 (0-394-84443-2); lib. bdg. 7.99 (0-394-94443-7) Pantheon.
—Witch, Goblin, & Sometimes Ghost: Six Read-Alone Stories. Winter, Jeanette, illus. LC 76-8657. (ps-3). 1976. 6.95 (0-394-83216-7) Pantheon.
—World Famous Muriel. (gr. k-6). 1988. pap. 2.50 (0-440-49610-1, YB) Dell.
—World Famous Muriel & the Magic Mystery. Frazee, Marla, illus. LC 89-22396. 32p. (gr. k-3). 1990. (Crowell Jr Bks); PLB 12.89 (0-690-04789-4, Crowell Jr Bks) HarpC Child Bks.

Alexander, William. The Case of the Funny Money Man. Ewers, Joe, illus. LC 89-36358. 96p. (gr. 4-7). 1990. PLB 9.89 (0-8167-1692-7); pap. text ed. 2.95 (0-8167-1693-5) Troll Assocs.
—The Case of the Gumball Bandits. Ewers, Joe, illus. LC 89-36558. 96p. (gr. 4-7). 1990. PLB 9.89 (0-8167-1696-X); pap. text ed. 2.95 (0-8167-1697-8) Troll Assocs.
—The Case of the Pizza Pie Spy. Ewers, Joe, illus. LC 89-20156. 96p. (gr. 4-7). 1990. PLB 9.89 (0-8167-1698-6); pap. text ed. 2.95 (0-8167-1699-4) Troll Assocs.
—The Ghost of Shockly Manor. Ewers, Joe, illus. LC 89-36544. 96p. (gr. 4-7). 1990. PLB 9.89 (0-8167-1694-3); pap. text ed. 2.95 (0-8167-1695-1) Troll Assocs.

Alfaya, Javier, tr. see Rodgers, Mary.

Alfredson, Hans. The Night the Moon Came By. Ahlin, Per, illus. Nunnally, Tiina, tr. from SWE. LC 93-663. (Illus.). 1993. Repr. 13.00 (91-29-62246-8, Pub. by R & S Bks) FS&G.

Algarin, Miguel, ed. Aloud! Voices. (gr. 6 up). 1994. pap. write for info. (0-8050-3275-4) H Holt & Co.

Alger, Horatio. The Lost Tales of Horatio Alger: Adventure, Romance & Moral Intrigue, the Best of Alger's Early Tales. Scharnhorst, Gary, ed. LC 89-14919. 240p. (gr. 10 up). 1990. 10.95 (0-934745-11-0) Acadia Pub Co.

Alger, Horatio, Jr. Struggling Upward. 1971. Fasc. 6.95 (0-87874-005-8, Nautilus) Galloway.

Algimantas KEZYS Staff, ed. see Lithuanian Photographers Staff.

Algren, Nelson. He Swung & He Missed. (gr. 5 up). 1992. PLB 13.95 (0-88682-490-7) Creative Ed.

Alhaji Obaba Abdullahi Muhammad. Three Little Africans. McCollin, Russ, illus. 36p. (Orig). (gr. k-4). 1978. pap. 2.50 (0-916157-00-8) African Islam Miss Pubns.

Ali, S. Ameer. Color & Learn the Names of the Family of Prophet Muhammad. 32p. (Orig). (ps). (gr. up). Date not set. pap. 3.50 (0-934905-13-4) Kazi Pubns.

Aliaga, Barbara. Keyboarding for Kids. (Illus.). 99p. (Orig). (gr. 1-6). 1985. pap. 7.95 (0-88908-606-0, 9538) ISC Pr.

Alico, Stella H. Benjamin Franklin-Martin Luther King Jr. Cruz, E. R., illus. (gr. 4-12). 1979. pap. text ed. 2.95 (0-88301-353-3); wkbk 1.25 (0-88301-377-0) Pendulum Pr.
—Elvis Presley - The Beatles. Cruz, E. R. & Guanlao, Ernie, illus. (gr. 4-12). 1979. pap. text ed. 2.95 (0-88301-352-5); wkbk 1.25 (0-88301-376-2) Pendulum Pr.

Ali-El, Yusuf. Once upon a Ryme Tyme for Growing Minds. Pride, Alexis, et al, illus. LC 83-90101. 90p. (gr. k-5). 1983. map. 9.95 (0-912475-09-9) Natl Res Unltd.

Aliki. Aliki's Dinosaur Dig: A Book & Card Game. Aliki, illus. 32p. (gr. k-6). 1992. pap. 9.95 incl. cards (0-694-00286-0) HarpC Child Bks.
—At Mary Bloom's. Aliki, illus. LC 75-45482. 32p. (gr. k-3). 1983. 11.25 (0-688-02480-7); PLB 14.93 (0-688-02481-5) Greenwillow.
—Christmas Tree Memories. Aliki, illus. LC 90-45575. 32p. (ps-3). 1991. 15.00 (0-06-020007-3); PLB 14.89 (0-06-020008-1) HarpC Child Bks.
—Communication. LC 91-48156. (Illus.). 32p. (gr. 5 up). 1993. 14.00 (0-688-10529-7); PLB 13.93 (0-688-11248-X) Greenwillow.
—Corn Is Maize: The Gift of the Indians. Aliki, illus. LC 75-6928. 40p. (gr. k-3). 1976. PLB 14.89 (0-690-00975-5, Crowell Jr Bks) HarpC Child Bks.
—Corn Is Maize: The Gift of the Indians. Aliki, illus. LC 75-6928. 40p. (gr. k-3). 1986. pap. 4.50 (0-06-445026-0, Trophy) HarpC Child Bks.

—Digging up Dinosaurs. rev. ed. Aliki, illus. LC 87-29949. 32p. (ps-3). 1988. 15.00i (0-690-04714-2, Crowell Jr Bks); PLB 14.89 (0-690-04716-9) HarpC Child Bks.
—Digging up Dinosaurs. rev. ed. Aliki, illus. LC 85-42979. 32p. (gr. k-3). 1988. pap. 4.95 (0-06-445078-3, Trophy) HarpC Child Bks.
—Digging up Dinosaurs. 32p. (ps-2). 1991. pap. 7.95 (1-55994-302-5, Caedmon) HarperAudio.
—Dinosaur Bones. Aliki, illus. LC 85-48246. 32p. (ps-3). 1988. 15.00 (0-690-04549-2, Crowell Jr Bks); PLB 14.89 (0-690-04550-6) HarpC Child Bks.
—Dinosaur Bones. Aliki, illus. 32p. (gr. k-4). 1990. 4.50 (0-06-445077-5, Trophy) HarpC Child Bks.
—Dinosaurs Are Different. Aliki, illus. LC 84-45332. 32p. (ps-3). 1985. 14.00 (0-690-04456-9, Crowell Jr Bks); PLB 13.89 (0-690-04458-5) HarpC Child Bks.
—Dinosaurs Are Different. Aliki, illus. LC 84-45332. 32p. (ps-3). 1988. incl. cassette 7.95 (0-694-00236-4, Trophy); pap. 4.50 (0-06-445056-2, Trophy) HarpC Child Bks.
—Feelings. Aliki, illus. LC 84-4098. 32p. (gr. k-3). 1984. 15.00 (0-688-03831-X); PLB 14.93 (0-688-03832-8) Greenwillow.
—Feelings. LC 84-4098. (Illus.). (ps-3). 1986. 3.95 (0-688-06518-X, Mulberry) Morrow.
—Fossils Tell of Long Ago. Aliki, illus. LC 78-170999. 40p. (gr. k-3). 1972. PLB 12.89 (0-690-31379-9, Crowell Jr Bks) HarpC Child Bks.
—Fossils Tell of Long Ago. rev. ed. Aliki, illus. LC 89-17247. 32p. (gr. k-4). 1990. 14.00 (0-690-04844-0, Crowell Jr Bks); PLB 13.89 (0-690-04829-7, Crowell Jr Bks) HarpC Child Bks.
—Fossils Tell of Long Ago. rev. ed. Aliki, illus. LC 89-15468. 32p. (gr. k-4). 1990. pap. 4.95 (0-06-445093-7, JS093, Trophy) HarpC Child Bks.
—Go Tell Aunt Rhody. reissued ed. Aliki, illus. LC 74-681. 32p. (ps-3). 1986. RSBE 14.95 (0-02-700410-4, Macmillan Child Bk) Macmillan Child Grp.
—The Gods & Goddesses of Olympus. LC 93-17834. 1994. 16.00 (0-06-023530-6); PLB 15.89 (0-06-023531-4) HarpC Child Bks.
—La Historia de Johnny Appleseed. Mlawer, Teresa, tr. (Illus.). 32p. (gr. k-2). 1992. 9.95 (0-9625162-6-0) Lectorum Pubns.
—How a Book Is Made. Aliki, illus. LC 85-48156. 32p. (gr. 2 up). 1986. 14.00 (0-690-04496-8, Crowell Jr Bks); PLB 13.89 (0-690-04498-4, Crowell Jr Bks) HarpC Child Bks.
—How a Book Is Made. Aliki, illus. LC 85-48156. 32p. (gr. k-4). 1988. pap. 5.95 (0-06-446085-1, Trophy) HarpC Child Bks.
—Hush Little Baby: A Folk Lullaby. LC 68-12194. (Illus.). 32p. (gr. k-4). 1972. (S&S BFYR); pap. 5.95 (0-671-66742-4, S&S BFYR) S&S Trade.
—I'm Growing! Aliki, illus. LC 91-14087. 32p. (ps-1). 1992. 14.00 (0-06-020244-0); PLB 13.89 (0-06-020245-9) HarpC Child Bks.
—I'm Growing! Aliki, illus. LC 91-14087. 32p. (ps-1). 1993. pap. 4.95 (0-06-445116-X, Trophy) HarpC Child Bks.
—Jack & Jake. Aliki, illus. LC 85-9911. 32p. (ps-1). 1986. 11.75 (0-688-06099-4); PLB 11.88 (0-688-06100-1) Greenwillow.
—Keep Your Mouth Closed, Dear. Aliki, illus. LC 66-19310. (gr. k-3). 1966. PLB 13.89 (0-8037-4418-8) Dial Bks Young.
—King's Day: Louis XIV of France. LC 88-38179. (Illus.). 32p. (gr. 2-6). 1989. 13.95 (0-690-04588-3, Crowell Jr Bks); PLB 13.89 (0-690-04590-5, Crowell Jr Bks) HarpC Child Bks.
—The King's Day: Louis XIV of France. Aliki, illus. LC 88-38179. 32p. (gr. 2-6). 1991. pap. 4.95 (0-06-443268-8, Trophy) HarpC Child Bks.
—Manners. LC 89-34622. (gr. k up). 1990. 14.00 (0-688-09198-9); PLB 13.93 (0-688-09199-7) Greenwillow.
—Manners. LC 92-43788. Date not set. write for info. (0-688-04579-0, Mulberry) Morrow. Postponed.
—The Many Lives of Benjamin Franklin. Aliki, illus. 32p. (ps-3). 1988. pap. 12.95 (0-671-66119-1, S&S BFYR); pap. 5.95 (0-671-66491-3, S&S BFYR) S&S Trade.
—A Medieval Feast. LC 82-45923. (Illus.). 32p. (gr. 2-6). 1983. 14.00 (0-690-04245-0, Crowell Jr Bks); PLB 13.89 (0-690-04246-9, Crowell Jr Bks) HarpC Child Bks.
—A Medieval Feast. LC 82-45923. (Illus.). 32p. (gr. 2-6). 1986. pap. 5.95 (0-06-446050-9, Trophy) HarpC Child Bks.
—Milk from Cow to Carton. rev. ed. LC 91-23807. (Illus.). 32p. (gr. k-4). 1992. 14.00 (0-06-020434-6); PLB 13.89 (0-06-020435-4) HarpC Child Bks.
—Milk from Cow to Carton. rev. ed. LC 91-23807. (Illus.). 32p. (gr. k-4). 1992. pap. 4.50 (0-06-445111-9, Trophy) HarpC Child Bks.
—Mummies Made in Egypt. Aliki, illus. LC 77-26603. 32p. (gr. 2-6). 1979. 14.00 (0-690-03858-5, Crowell Jr Bks); PLB 13.89 (0-690-03859-3, Crowell Jr Bks) HarpC Child Bks.
—Mummies Made in Egypt. Aliki, illus. LC 85-42746. 32p. (gr. 2-6). 1985. pap. 5.95 (0-06-446011-8, Trophy) HarpC Child Bks.
—My Feet. Aliki, illus. LC 89-49357. 32p. (ps-1). 1990. 14.00 (0-690-04813-0, Crowell Jr Bks); PLB 13.89 (0-690-04815-7, Crowell Jr Bks) HarpC Child Bks.
—My Feet. Aliki, illus. LC 89-49357. 32p. (ps-1). 1992. pap. 4.50 (0-06-445106-2, Trophy) HarpC Child Bks.

—My Five Senses. rev. ed. LC 88-35350. (Illus.). 32p. (gr. 1-3). 1989. pap. 4.95 (0-06-445083-X, Trophy) HarpC Child Bks.
—My Five Senses. rev. ed. Aliki, illus. LC 88-35350. 32p. (ps-1). 1991. 19.95 (0-06-020050-2) HarpC Child Bks.
—My Five Senses. rev. ed. Aliki, illus. LC 88-853500. 228p. (ps-3). 1989. 14.00 (0-690-04792-4, Crowell Jr Bks); PLB 13.89 (0-685-58944-7) HarpC Child Bks.
—My Five Senses Library. 1962. PLB 12.89 (0-690-56763-4, Crowell Jr Bks) HarpC Child Bks.
—My Hands. rev. ed. Aliki, illus. LC 89-49158. 32p. (ps-1). 1990. 14.00 (0-690-04878-5, Crowell Jr Bks); PLB 13.89 (0-690-04880-7, Crowell Jr Bks) HarpC Child Bks.
—My Hands. rev. ed. Aliki, illus. LC 89-71728. 32p. (ps-1). 1992. pap. 4.50 (0-06-445096-1, Trophy) HarpC Child Bks.
—My Visit to the Aquarium. Aliki, illus. LC 92-18678. 40p. (ps-3). 1993. 15.00 (0-06-021458-9); PLB 14.89 (0-06-021459-7) HarpC Child Bks.
—My Visit to the Dinosaurs. rev. ed. Aliki, illus. LC 85-47538. 32p. (ps-3). 1985. 14.00 (0-690-04422-4, Crowell Jr Bks); PLB 13.89 (0-690-04423-2) HarpC Child Bks.
—My Visit to the Dinosaurs. 2nd ed. Aliki, illus. LC 85-42748. 32p. (ps-3). 1987. incl. cassette 7.95 (0-694-00201-1, Trophy); pap. 4.95 (0-06-445020-1, Trophy) HarpC Child Bks.
—My Visit to the Dinosaurs Big Book. Aliki, illus. LC 85-47538. 32p. (ps-3). 1994. pap. 19.95 (0-06-443350-1, Trophy) HarpC Child Bks.
—Overnight at Mary Bloom's. Aliki, illus. LC 86-7719. 32p. (ps-3). 1987. 11.75 (0-688-06764-6); lib. bdg. 11.88 (0-688-06765-4) Greenwillow.
—Story of Johnny Appleseed. Aliki, illus. (ps-2). 1987. 11.95 (0-13-850800-3) P-H.
—Story of Johnny Appleseed. LC 88-3145. (ps-3). 1971. pap. 5.95 (0-671-66746-7, S&S BFYR) S&S Trade.
—The Story of William Penn. Aliki, illus. LC 93-26289. (Orig.). Date not set. pap. 12.00 (0-671-88558-8, S&S BFYR) S&S Trade.
—The Two of Them. LC 79-10161. (Illus.). 32p. (gr. k-3). 1979. 14.95 (0-688-80225-7); PLB 14.88 (0-688-84225-9) Greenwillow.
—The Two of Them. LC 79-10161. (ps-3). 1987. pap. 4.95 (0-688-07337-9, Mulberry) Morrow.
—Use Your Head, Dear. Aliki, illus. LC 82-11911. 48p. (gr. k-3). 1983. 13.95 (0-688-01811-4); PLB 13.88 (0-688-01812-2) Greenwillow.
—We Are Best Friends. Aliki, illus. LC 81-6549. 32p. (gr. k-3). 1982. 16.00 (0-688-00822-4); PLB 15.93 (0-688-00823-2) Greenwillow.
—We Are Best Friends. LC 81-6549. (Illus.). 32p. (ps-3). 1987. pap. 3.95 (0-688-07037-X, Mulberry) Morrow.
—A Weed Is a Flower: The Life of George Washington Carver. Aliki, illus. 32p. (ps-3). 1988. pap. 14.00 (0-671-66118-3, S&S BFYR); pap. 5.95 (0-671-66490-5, S&S BFYR) S&S Trade.
—Welcome, Little Baby. LC 86-7648. (Illus.). 24p. (ps up). 1987. 14.00 (0-688-06810-3); PLB 13.93 (0-688-06811-1) Greenwillow.
—Wild & Woolly Mammoths. Aliki, illus. LC 76-18082. 40p. (gr. k-3). 1977. PLB 13.89 (0-690-01276-4, Crowell Jr Bks) HarpC Child Bks.
—Wild & Woolly Mammoths. LC 76-18082. (Illus.). 40p. (ps-3). 1983. pap. 4.50 (0-06-445005-8, Trophy) HarpC Child Bks.
Alimayo, Chikuyo, pseud. Once Around the Track. (Illus.). (gr. 9-12). 1974. 7.95 (0-9606692-2-1); pap. 3.95 (0-9606692-3-X) Eko Pubns.
Aliotta, Jerry. The Puerto Ricans. Moynihan, Daniel P., intro. by. (Illus.). 112p. (gr. 5 up). 1991. lib. bdg. 17.95 (0-87754-897-8) Chelsea Hse.
Al-Kausar, Tawfik, intro. by. Islamic Students Organizations: Role & Challenges, Proceedings of International Conference. 2nd ed. (ARA.). 425p. 1985. pap. write for info. (1-882837-03-7) Wamy Intl.
Alladin, Bilzik. Story of Mohammad the Prophet. Anand, B. M., illus. (gr. 3-10). 1979. 7.25 (0-89744-139-7) Auromere.
Allaire, Barbara, ed. see Ahlers, Julia.
Allaire, Barbara, ed. see Stoutzenberger, Joseph.
Allan, Doug. The Seal on the Rocks. Oxford Scientific Film Staff, illus. LC 87-9950. 32p. (gr. 4-6). 1988. PLB 15.93 (1-55532-271-9) Gareth Stevens Inc.
Allan, Douglas, jt. auth. see Saintsing, David.
Allan, Jay. Blocks. (Illus.). (ps). 1993. pap. 5.95 (0-9631798-1-0) Silver Seahorse.
Allan, Mabel E. The Horns of Danger. 192p. (gr. 7-11). 1981. 8.95 (0-396-07987-3, Putnam) Putnam Pub Group.
Allan, Nicholas. The Hefty Fairy. (Illus.). 32p. (gr. 1-3). 1990. 13.95 (0-09-173751-6, Pub. by Hutchinson UK) Trafalgar.
—Hilltop Hospital. (Illus.). 32p. (ps-1). 1994. 19.95 (Pub. by Hutchinson UK) Trafalgar.
—Jesus' Christmas Party. Allan, Nicholas, illus. LC 91-17092. 32p. 1992. 9.99 (0-679-82688-2) Random Bks Yng Read.
Allan, Ted. Willie the Squowse. Blake, Quentin, illus. (gr. 2 up). 1991. Repr. of 1978 ed. 9.95 (0-8038-9341-8) Hastings.
Allard, Harry. Bumps in the Night. Marshall, James, illus. 48p. (gr. 1-4). 1984. pap. 2.25 (0-553-15284-X, Skylark) Bantam.
—Bumps in the Night. Marshall, James, illus. (gr. k-3). 1984. 2.99 (0-553-15711-6, Skylark) Bantam.

—The Cactus Flower Bakery. Delaney, Ned, illus. LC 90-36565. 32p. (ps-3). 1991. PLB 14.89 (0-06-020047-2) HarpC Child Bks.
—The Cactus Flower Bakery. Delaney, Ned, illus. LC 90-36565. 32p. (ps-3). 1993. pap. 4.95 (0-06-443297-1, Trophy) HarpC Child Bks.
—Miss Nelson Has a Field Day. Marshall, James, illus. LC 84-27791. 32p. (gr. k-3). 1985. 13.45 (0-395-36690-9) HM.
—Miss Nelson Has a Field Day. Marshall, James, illus. 32p. (gr. k-3). 1988. pap. 4.80 (0-395-48654-8, Sandpiper) HM.
—Miss Nelson Has a Field Day. Marshall, James, illus. (ps-3). 1989. pap. 7.70 incl. cassette (0-395-52138-6) HM.
—Miss Nelson Is Back. Marshall, James, illus. 1988. pap. 7.70 incl. cass. (0-395-48872-9) HM.
—Miss Nelson Is Missing. (ps-3). 1993. pap. 7.95 incl. cass. (0-395-45737-8) HM.
—The Stupids Have a Ball. Marshall, James, illus. LC 77-27660. (gr. k-3). 1984. 13.45 (0-395-26497-9); pap. 4.80 (0-395-36169-9) HM.
—The Stupids Step Out. Marshall, James, illus. LC 73-21698. 32p. (gr. k-3). 1974. 14.95 (0-395-18513-0); pap. 4.80 (0-395-25377-2) HM.
—The Stupids Step Out. Marshall, James, illus. (ps-3). 1993. pap. 4.95 incl. cassette (0-395-52139-4) HM.
—The Stupids Take Off. Marshall, James, illus. 32p. (gr. k-3). 1993. pap. 4.95 (0-395-65743-1) HM.
Allard, Harry & Marshall, James. Miss Nelson Is Back. (Illus.). (gr. k-3). 1986. 13.45 (0-395-32956-6); pap. 4.80 (0-395-41668-X) HM.
—Miss Nelson Is Missing! Marshall, James, illus. (gr. k-3). 1985. reinforced bdg. 13.45 (0-395-25296-2); pap. 3.80 (0-395-40146-1) HM.
—The Stupids Die. (Illus.). (gr. k-3). 1985. 13.45 (0-395-30347-8); pap. 4.80 (0-395-38364-1) HM.
—The Stupids Take Off. Allard, Harry & Marshall, James, illus. 32p. (gr. k-3). 1989. 13.45 (0-395-50068-0) HM.
Allasio, John, et al. Sequential Math 1: A Workbook. 148p. (gr. 8-12). 1988. 7.95 (0-937820-54-7); answer key 3.25 (0-937820-55-5) Westsea Pub.
—Sequential Math 2: A Workbook. 141p. (gr. 9-12). 1990. pap. 7.95 (0-937820-65-2); answer key 3.25 (0-937820-66-0) Westsea Pub.
—Sequential Math 3: A Workbook. 156p. (gr. 10-12). 1993. pap. 7.95 (0-937820-67-9); answer key 3.25 (0-937820-68-7) Westsea Pub.
Allee, Marjorie H. Jane's Island. De Gogorza, Maitland, illus. 236p. (gr. 6 up). 1988. Repr. of 1931 ed. 13.95 (0-9611374-2-8) Woods Hole Hist.
Allen. Pharaohs & Pyramids. (gr. 4-9). 1977. (Usborne-Hayes); PLB 13.96 (0-88110-103-6); pap. 6.95 (0-86020-084-1) EDC.
Allen, Adrianne T. Sheila's Show Biz Days. Shelia, illus. 64p. (Orig.). (gr. k-6). 1993. pap. 9.95 (0-685-65119-3) Colonial Pr AL.
Allen, Anne. Sports for the Handicapped. (gr. 6 up). 1981. lib. bdg. 10.85 reinforced (0-8027-6437-1) Walker & Co.
Allen, Bob. Mountain Biking. (Illus.). 48p. (gr. 4-12). 1992. PLB 17.50 (0-8225-2476-7) Lerner Pubns.
Allen, Carol. Earth: All about Earthquakes, Volacnoes, Glaciers, Oceans & More. Pearson, David, illus. 32p. 1993. pap. 5.95 (1-895688-06-X, Pub. by Greey dePencier CN) Firefly Bks Ltd.
—Japan. (Illus.). 64p. (gr. 4-8). 1992. wkbk. 7.95 (0-86653-684-1, 1418) Good Apple.
Allen, Constance. Elmo's Guessing Game. (ps). 1993. 4.95 (0-307-12398-7, Golden Pr) Western Pub.
—Grover's Book of Cute Things to Touch. (ps). 1990. write for info. (0-307-12320-0, Golden Pr) Western Pub.
—Merry Christmas, Everybody! (ps-3). 1993. pap. 2.25 (0-307-10017-0, Golden Pr) Western Pub.
—My Name Is Big Bird. Swanson, Maggie, illus. 24p. (ps-k). 1992. pap. write for info. (0-307-11533-X, 11533, Golden Pr) Western Pub.
—My Name Is Elmo. Swanson, Maggie, illus. 24p. (ps-k). 1993. pap. 1.45 (0-307-11541-0, 11541, Golden Pr) Western Pub.
—Sesame Street: Bert's Beautiful Sights. 1990. pap. write for info. (0-307-12318-9, Golden Pr) Western Pub.
—Sesame Street: Ernie Follows His Nose. (ps). 1990. write for info. (0-307-12321-9) Western Pub.
—Sesame Street: Oscar's Grouchy Sounds. 1990. pap. write for info. (0-307-12319-7, Golden Pr) Western Pub.
—Sesame Street: Sleep Tight! Prebenna, David, illus. (ps-k). 1991. pap. write for info. (0-307-10026-X, Golden Pr) Western Pub.
Allen County Police Officers Assn., compiled by. Kids Talk to Kids. 75p. (gr. 6-12). 1990. pap. write for info. (0-9614659-6-4) Cuchullain Pubns.
Allen County Police Officers Association Staff, compiled by. Kids Talk to Kids. 75p. (Orig.). (gr. 6-12). 1991. pap. write for info. (0-9614659-7-2) Cuchullain Pubns.
Allen, David. Air: All about Cyclones, Rainbows, Clouds, Ozone & More. Bain, Gordon, illus. 32p. 1993. pap. 5.95 (1-895688-08-6, Pub. by Greey dePencier CN) Firefly Bks Ltd.
Allen, Dennis & Allen, Nan. Rip Van Christmas. Date not set. 4.50 (0-685-68513-6, BCMC-74); cassette 9.98 (0-685-68514-4, BCTA-9134C) Lillenas.
Allen, Dennis, jt. auth. see Allen, Nan.

Allen, Derek, retold by. Blood from the Mummy's Tomb. 160p. (gr. 6 up). 1988. pap. 2.95 (0-8120-4074-0) Barron.
Allen, Diane van see Van Allen, Diane.
Allen, Dorothy S. Plaster & Bisque Art: Special Finishes. Cole, Tom, ed. LC 80-70317. (Illus.). 44p. (gr. 4 up). 1981. pap. 2.95 (0-9605204-4-9) Dots Pubns.
—Plaster & Bisque Art: The Soft Touch Technique. Cole, Tom, ed. LC 80-70317. (Illus.). 47p. (gr. 4 up). 1981. pap. 2.95 (0-9605204-6-5) Dots Pubns.
—Plaster & Bisque Art: With Transparent Watercolor. Cole, Tom, ed. LC 80-70317. (Illus.). 57p. (gr. 4 up). 1981. pap. 1.95 (0-9605204-5-7) Dots Pubns.
Allen, Dorothy S. & Cole, Tom. Plaster & Bisque Art: Mist, Museum Bronze, Pastel Chalk, Pearl & Suede Finishes. LC 80-70317. (Illus.). 52p. (gr. 4 up). 1981. pap. 2.95 (0-9605204-3-0) Dots Pubns.
Allen, Douglas. The Penguin in the Snow. Oxford Scientific Film Staff, illus. LC 87-9968. 32p. (gr. 4-6). 1987. PLB 15.93 (1-55532-270-0) Gareth Stevens Inc.
Allen, Edith B. One Hundred Bible Games. (gr. 5 up). 1968. pap. 4.99 (0-8010-0033-5) Baker Bk.
Allen, Eleanor. Home Sweet Home: A History of Housewark. (Illus.). 64p. (gr. 6 up). 1979. 14.95 (0-7136-1927-9) Dufour.
—Wartime Children, Nineteen Thirty-Nine to Nineteen Forty-Five. (Illus.). 64p. (gr. 6 up). 1983. 14.95 (0-7136-1503-6) Dufour.
—Wash & Brush up. (Illus.). 64p. (gr. 7 up). 1984. 14.95 (0-7136-1639-3) Dufour.
Allen, Eugenie. The Best Ever Kids' Book of Lists. 128p. (Orig.). 1991. pap. 2.95 (0-380-76357-5, Camelot) Avon.
Allen, Frances, jt. auth. see Malley, Barbara.
Allen, Gilbert. In Everything: Poems Nineteen Seventy-Two to Nineteen Seventy-Nine. LC 81-82661. 75p. (gr. 9-12). 1982. pap. 4.50x perfect bd. (0-916418-37-5) Lotus.
Allen, Helen S. A Birthday Letter to Lynn: Mandy Learns to Make a Cake. 16p. (ps). 1992. pap. text ed. 5.00 (1-881907-04-X) Two Bytes Pub.
—A Letter to Lynn: Mandy's Day at the Beach. 16p. (ps). 1992. pap. text ed. 5.00 (1-881907-03-1) Two Bytes Pub.
—A Valentine Letter to Lynn: Mandy's Adventure in the Snow. 16p. (ps). 1992. pap. text ed. 5.00 (1-881907-02-3) Two Bytes Pub.
Allen, James. Basketball, Play Like a Pro. LC 89-27351. (Illus.). 64p. (gr. 4-8). 1990. lib. bdg. 9.79 (0-8167-1935-7); pap. text ed. 2.95 (0-8167-1936-5) Troll Assocs.
—Football, Play Like a Pro. LC 89-38633. (Illus.). 64p. (gr. 4-8). 1990. lib. bdg. 9.79 (0-8167-1929-2); pap. text ed. 2.95 (0-8167-1930-6) Troll Assocs.
Allen, Jeffery. Nosey Mrs. Rat. Marshall, James, illus. LC 84-19618. 32p. (ps-3). 1985. pap. 11.95 (0-670-80880-6) Viking Child Bks.
Allen, Jeffrey. Mary Alice Returns. Marshall, James, illus. (ps-3). 1986. lib. bdg. 13.95i (0-316-03429-0) Little.
—Nosey Mrs. Rat. Marshall, James, illus. LC 86-25462. 32p. (ps-3). 1987. pap. 3.95 (0-14-050665-9, Puffin) Puffin Bks.
Allen, Johann. Verse for Grandchildren, Vol. I. 30p. (gr. k-4). 1992. pap. 5.00 (0-9633569-0-9) Home Imag.
Allen, John L. Jedediah Smith & the Mountain Men of the American West. Goetzmann, William H., ed. Collins, Michael, intro. by. (Illus.). 112p. (gr. 5 up). 1991. lib. bdg. 18.95 (0-7910-1319-7) Chelsea Hse.
Allen, Jonathan. Big Owl, Little Towel. Allen, Jonathan, illus. LC 91-39349. 12p. (ps). 1992. 3.95 (0-688-11783-X, Tambourine Bks) Morrow.
—Mucky Moose. Allen, Jonathan, illus. LC 90-6363. 32p. (ps-3). 1991. SBE 12.95 (0-02-700251-9, Macmillan Child Bk) Macmillan Child Grp.
—My Dog. Allen, Jonathan, illus. LC 89-30857. 32p. (gr. 1-2). 1989. PLB 18.60 (0-8368-0095-8) Gareth Stevens Inc.
—One with a Bun. Allen, Jonathan, illus. LC 91-44055. 12p. (ps). 1992. 3.95 (0-688-11781-3, Tambourine Bks) Morrow.
—Purple Sock, Pink Sock. Allen, Jonathan, illus. LC 91-43379. 12p. (ps). 1992. 3.95 (0-688-11782-1, Tambourine Bks) Morrow.
—Up the Steps, Down the Slide. Allen, Jonathan, illus. LC 91-44534. 12p. (ps). 1992. 3.95 (0-688-11784-8, Tambourine Bks) Morrow.
—Who's at the Door? Allen, Jonathan, illus. LC 92-19618. 32p. (ps up). 1993. 11.95 (0-688-12257-4, Tambourine Bks) Morrow.
Allen, Jonathan, jt. auth. see Lear, Edward.
Allen, Joseph. Mikey Goes Whale Watching. Trout, M. D., ed. Woodaman, W., illus. 50p. (Orig.). (gr. 1-5). 1986. PLB 13.50 (0-917071-05-0); pap. 8.95 (0-917071-04-2) Ocean Allen Pub.
Allen, Judy. Eagle. Humphries, Tudor, illus. LC 93-28541. 1994. write for info. reinforced bdg. (1-56402-143-2) Candlewick Pr.
—Elephant. Humphries, Tudor, illus. LC 92-54407. 32p. (ps up). 1993. 14.95 (1-56402-069-X) Candlewick Pr.
—Panda. Humphries, Tudor, illus. LC 92-54411. 32p. (ps up). 1993. 14.95 (1-56402-142-4) Candlewick Pr.
—Seal. Humphries, Tudor, illus. LC 93-3642. 1994. write for info. (1-56402-145-9) Candlewick Pr.
—Tiger. Humphries, Tudor & Humphries, Tudor, illus. LC 91-58760. 32p. (ps up). 1992. 14.95 (1-56402-083-5) Candlewick Pr.

—Tiger. LC 91-58760. (ps-3). 1994. pap. 4.99 (*1-56402-284-6*) Candlewick Pr.

—Whale. Humphries, Tudor, illus. LC 92-53019. 32p. (gr. 1-3). 1993. 14.95 (*1-56402-160-2*) Candlewick Pr.

—What Is a Wall, After All? Baron, Alan, illus. LC 92-54623. 32p. (ps up). 1993. PLB 14.95 (*1-56402-218-8*) Candlewick Pr.

Allen, Julia. My First Animal Ride. Reese, Bob, illus. (gr. k-3). 1987. 7.95 (*0-89868-179-0*); pap. 2.95 (*0-89868-180-4*) ARO Pub.

—My First Camping Trip. Reese, Bob, illus. (gr. k-3). 1987. 7.95 (*0-89868-181-2*); pap. 2.95 (*0-685-50867-6*) ARO Pub.

—My First Camping Trip. Reese, Bob, illus. (gr. k-3). 1987. pap. 20.00 (*0-89868-182-0*) ARO Pub.

—My First Dentist Visit. Reese, Bob, illus. (gr. k-3). 1987. 7.95 (*0-89868-185-5*); pap. 2.95 (*0-89868-186-3*) ARO Pub.

—My First Doctor Visit. Reese, Bob, illus. (gr. k-3). 1987. 7.95 (*0-89868-187-1*); pap. 2.95 (*0-89868-188-X*) ARO Pub.

—My First Job. Reese, Bob, illus. (gr. k-3). 1987. 7.95 (*0-89868-184-7*); pap. 2.95 (*0-89868-183-9*) ARO Pub.

—My First Phone Call. Reese, Bob, illus. (gr. k-3). 1987. 7.95 (*0-89868-189-8*); pap. 2.95 (*0-89868-190-1*) ARO Pub.

—Thirty Word My First Series, 6 bks. Reese, Bob, illus. (gr. k-3). 1987. Set. 47.70 (*0-89868-237-1*); Set. pap. 29.50 (*0-89868-236-3*) ARO Pub.

Allen, Karen K. & Miller, Margery S. Reading the Newspaper: Advanced Level. 190p. (Orig.). (gr. 9-12). 1988. pap. text ed. 9.95 (*0-89061-500-4*) Jamestown Pubs.

Allen, Laura J. Rollo & Tweedy & the Ghost at Dougal Castle. (Illus.). 64p. (gr. k-3). 1992. 13.00 (*0-06-020106-1*); PLB 12.89 (*0-06-020107-X*) HarpC Child Bks.

Allen, Linda. When Grandfather's. 1992. pap. 2.99 (*0-553-15970-4*) Bantam.

—When Granfather's Parrot Inherited Kennington Court. Kew, Katinka, illus. (gr. 3-7). 1990. 12.95 (*0-316-03413-4*, Joy St Bks) Little.

Allen, Linda, retold by. & illus. The Mouse Bride: A Finnish Tale. 32p. (ps-3). 1992. PLB 14.95 (*0-399-22136-0*, Philomel Bks) Putnam Pub Group.

Allen, Linda & Snider, Chrystle L., eds. Washington Songs & Lore. Green, Donald A., illus. 200p. (gr. 1-12). 1988. pap. 15.95 (*0-9616441-3-3*); Abridged ed., 72 pg. comb bdg. 8.95 (*0-9616441-4-1*) Melior Dist.

Allen, Linda B. High Mountain Challenge: A Guide for Young Mountaineers. Trafton, Mary, illus. LC 89-16. 224p. (Orig.). (gr. 6-12). 1989. pap. 9.95 (*0-910146-98-5*) AMC Books.

Allen, Marjorie N. & Rotner, Shelley. Changes. Rotner, Shelley, photos by. LC 90-6601. (Illus.). 32p. (ps-1). 1991. RSBE 13.95 (*0-02-700252-7*, Macmillan Child Bk) Macmillan Child Grp.

Allen, Mayme, et al. One Hundred One Word Puzzlers. Allen, Mayme, illus. LC 92-26302. 128p. (gr. 6 up). 1992. pap. 4.95 (*0-8069-8722-7*) Sterling.

Allen, Missy, jt. auth. see Peissel, Michel.

Allen, Nan & Allen, Dennis. Case of the Missing Christmas. Date not set. 4.50 (*0-685-68521-7*, BCMC-65); cassette 9.98 (*0-685-68522-5*, BCTA-9095C) Lillenas.

Allen, Nan, jt. auth. see Allen, Dennis.

Allen, Pamela. Belinda. Allen, Pamela, illus. 32p. (ps-3). 1993. 13.00 (*0-670-84372-5*) Viking Child Bks.

—How to Raise Butterflies. (gr. 4-7). 1990. 11.99 (*0-399-61286-6*) Putnam Pub Group.

—I Wish I Had a Pirate Suit. (ps). 1990. 12.95 (*0-670-82475-5*) Viking Child Bks.

—I Wish I Had a Pirate Suit. LC 92-12295. (gr. 4 up). 1993. 3.99 (*0-14-050988-7*) Puffin Bks.

—Mr. Archimedes Bath. (Illus.). 26p. (gr. k-3). 1991. 7.95 (*0-7322-7236-X*, Pub. by Angus & Robertson AT) HarpC.

—My Cat Maisie. (Illus.). 32p. (ps-3). 1991. 12.95 (*0-670-83251-0*) Viking Child Bks.

—My Cat Maisie. (Illus.). 32p. (ps-3). 1993. pap. 4.99 (*0-14-054237-X*, Puffin) Puffin Bks.

—Who Sank the Boat? (Illus.). 32p. (ps-1). 1990. pap. 5.95 (*0-698-20679-7*, Sandcastle Bks) Putnam Pub Group.

Allen, Patsy, jt. auth. see Allen, Tom.

Allen, Peter. The Origins of World War II. LC 91-22698. (Illus.). 64p. (gr. 7-12). 1992. PLB 13.40 (*0-531-18410-2*, Pub. by Bookwright Pr) Watts.

Allen, R. E. Ozzy on the Outside. 1991. pap. 3.50 (*0-440-20767-3*) Dell.

Allen, Rebecca. You Can Do It Guide to School Success. 128p. (Orig.). (gr. 5-8). 1989. pap. text ed. 2.25 (*0-87406-414-7*) Willowisp Pr.

Allen, Richard W. Ozzy. 1989. pap. 13.95 (*0-440-50146-6*) Dell.

Allen, Rob, jt. auth. see Gillum, Perry.

Allen, Rob, jt. ed. see Gillum, Perry.

Allen, Robert. Daniel Webster: Defender of the Union. (Illus.). (gr. 3-6). 1989. pap. 6.95 (*0-88062-156-7*) Mott Media.

—William Jennings Bryan. (gr. 3-6). 1992. pap. 6.95 (*0-88062-160-5*) Mott Media.

Allen, Robert A. Billy Sunday: Homerun to Heaven. Rock, Louise, ed. Shaw, Charles, illus. (gr. 3-7). 1985. pap. 6.95 (*0-88062-125-7*) Mott Media.

Allen, Samuel. Every Round & Other Poems. LC 87-80159. 159p. (Orig.). (gr. 9-12). 1987. pap. 9.00 perfect bdg. (*0-916418-65-0*) Lotus.

Allen, Sandra & Dlugokinski, Eric. Ben's Secret. 28p. (gr. k-6). 1992. pap. 9.95 (*1-882801-00-8*) Feelings Factory.

Allen, Sharon, ed. see Mills-Thornton, Serena G.

Allen, Stephen D. Reality: Drugs & Guns--No-Win Solutions. LC 92-64322. 126p. (gr. k-8). 1992. pap. 14.95 (*0-9634084-7-X*) S D A Pub.

Allen, Steve & Meadows, Jayne. Shakin' Loose with Mother Goose. Bullock, Kathleen, illus. 128p. (ps-2). 1987. 4 bks. & 2 forty minute tapes in gift box ed. 19.95 (*0-89411-010-1*) Kids Matter.

Allen, Thomas B. On Grandaddy's Farm. Allen, Thomas B., illus. LC 88-23374. 48p. (ps-3). 1989. 13.95 (*0-394-89613-0*); lib. bdg. 14.99 (*0-394-99613-5*) Knopf Bks Yng Read.

—Where the Children Live. (Illus.). 27p. 1980. 10.95 (*0-13-957126-4*) P-H.

Allen, Tom. Those Buried Texans, No Stone Unturned. LC 80-82288. (Illus.). 172p. (Orig.). (gr. 4 up). 1980. pap. 6.95 (*0-937460-00-1*) Hendrick-Long.

Allen, Tom & Allen, Patsy. Captain Scruffy. (Illus.). 32p. (ps-1). 1993. 15.95 (*0-460-88104-3*, Pub. by J M Dent & Sons) Trafalgar.

—Zizz Cleans Up. (Illus.). 32p. (ps-k). 1993. 15.95 (*0-460-88102-7*, Pub. by J M Dent & Sons) Trafalgar.

Allen, Tom, et al. Dinosaur Days in Texas. Morris, Aaron, illus. LC 88-37237. 64p. (gr. 3 up). 1989. lib. bdg. 14.95 (*0-937460-30-3*) Hendrick-Long.

Allen, Valerie. The Night Thief. Soper, Patrick, illus. LC 89-28459. 32p. (gr. k-3). 1990. 14.95 (*0-88289-774-8*) Pelican.

Allen, Wynell. Nature Stories for Children. 1993. 6.95 (*0-8062-4454-2*) Carlton.

—Tales for Little Children. (Illus.). 32p. 1992. pap. 3.95 (*0-8059-3316-6*) Dorrance.

Allert, Kathy. Kate Greenaway Paper Dolls in Full Color. 1981. pap. 3.50 (*0-486-24153-X*) Dover.

Allert, Kathy, illus. The Golden Nursery Song Book: Favorite Songs & Singing Games for Children. 48p. (ps-k). 1993. 7.95 (*0-307-15863-2*, 15863, Golden Pr) Western Pub.

Alley, David. Sky: All about Planets, Stars, Galaxies, Eclipses & More. Galiman, Ron, illus. 32p. 1993. pap. 5.95 (*1-895688-04-3*, Pub. by Greey dePencier CN) Firefly Bks Ltd.

Alley, R. W. Wee Wheels. (Illus.). 24p. (ps). 1990. bds. 2.50 (*0-448-02260-5*, G&D) Putnam Pub Group.

Alley, R. W., illus. Busy Farm Trucks. 12p. (ps-up). 1986. 6.95 (*0-448-09883-0*, G&D) Putnam Pub Group.

—Old MacDonald Had a Farm. 18p. (ps). 1991. 3.95 (*0-448-40106-1*, G&D) Putnam Pub Group.

Alley, R. W., illus. & photos by see Moche, Dinah.

Alley, Robert. The Ghost in Dobbs Diner. Alley, Robert, illus. LC 81-4864. 48p. (ps-3). 1981. 5.95 (*0-8193-1055-7*); lib. bdg. 5.95 (*0-8193-1056-5*) Parents.

Allgood, Dave & Allgood, Stephanie. Merry Bear Book of Dreams: A Book to Read & Color. 2nd ed. (Illus.). 36p. (ps-3). 1985. pap. 2.95 (*0-933103-00-X*) Merry Bears.

Allgood, Stephanie, jt. auth. see Allgood, Dave.

Alliance Francaise de Londres Staff, compiled by. First Two Hundred Words in French. Sleight, Katy, illus. LC 93-29562. 1994. 3.95 (*1-85697-954-7*) Kingfisher Bks.

Allingham, William. The Fairies. Hague, Michael, illus. LC 88-28474. 32p. (ps-2). 1989. PLB 13.95 (*0-8050-1003-3*, Bks Young Read) H Holt & Co.

Allington, Richard. Communication-Talking. (ps-3). 1990. 14.25 (*0-8172-1320-1*) Raintree Steck-V.

Allington, Richard L. Colors. Spangler, Noel, illus. LC 79-19116. 32p. (gr. k-3). 1985. PLB 15.33 (*0-8172-1280-9*); pap. 3.95 (*0-8114-8240-5*) Raintree Steck-V.

—Numbers. Garcia, Tom, illus. LC 79-19200. 32p. (gr. k-3). 1985. pap. 3.95 (*0-8114-8239-1*) Raintree Steck-V.

—Opposites. Conner, Eulala, illus. LC 79-20525. 32p. (gr. k-3). 1985. pap. 3.95 (*0-8114-8237-5*) Raintree Steck-V.

—Shapes. Ehlert, Lois, illus. LC 79-19852. 32p. (gr. k-3). 1985. pap. 3.95 (*0-8114-8238-3*) Raintree Steck-V.

—Talking. Thrun, Rick, illus. Krull, Kathleen. LC 80-17021. (Illus.). 32p. (ps-2). 1985. pap. 3.95 (*0-8114-8234-0*) Raintree Steck-V.

Allington, Richard L. & Krull, Kathleen. Autumn. Bond, Bruce, illus. LC 80-25190. 32p. (gr. k-3). 1985. PLB 15.96 (*0-8172-1343-0*); pap. text ed. 3.95 (*0-8114-8242-1*) Raintree Steck-V.

—Feelings. Cody, Brian, illus. LC 79-27549. 32p. (ps-2). 1985. pap. text ed. 3.95 (*0-8114-8236-7*) Raintree Steck-V.

—Reading. Naprstek, Joel, illus. LC 80-16547. 32p. (ps-2). 1985. pap. 3.95 (*0-8114-8235-9*) Raintree Steck-V.

—Science. Teason, James, illus. LC 82-101711. 32p. (gr. k-3). 1985. pap. 8.95 (*0-8172-2486-6*) Raintree Steck-V.

—Smelling. Gatzke, Lee, illus. LC 79-27147. 32p. (gr. k-3). 1985. PLB 15.33 (*0-8172-1293-0*); pap. 9.27 (*0-8172-2488-2*) Raintree Steck-V.

—Spring. Rains, Dee, illus. LC 80-25093. 32p. (gr. k-3). 1985. PLB 15.96 (*0-8172-1342-2*); pap. 3.95 (*0-8114-8244-8*) Raintree Steck-V.

—Summer. Hockerman, Dennis, illus. LC 80-25097. 32p. (gr. k-3). 1985. PLB 15.96 (*0-8172-1341-4*); pap. 3.95 (*0-8114-8241-3*) Raintree Steck-V.

—Winter. Wallner, John, illus. LC 80-25115. 32p. (gr. k-3). 1985. PLB 15.95 (*0-8172-1340-6*); pap. 3.95 (*0-8114-8243-X*) Raintree Steck-V.

Allinson, Beverley. Effie. Reid, Barbara, illus. 32p. (ps-1). 1991. 11.95 (*0-590-44045-4*, Scholastic Hardcover) Scholastic Inc.

Allinson, Elaine S. Daniel's Question: A Cesarean Birth Story. DeBiase, Judith, illus. 13p. (ps-5). 1981. staple bdg. 2.95 (*0-9606960-0-8*) Willow Tree NY.

Allison, Alida. The Toddler's Potty Book. 32p. (ps). 1985. softcover 3.95 (*0-8431-0673-5*) Price Stern.

Allison, B., intro. by see Balzar, Howard.

Allison, B., intro. by see Balzer, Howard.

Allison, B., ed. see Balzer, Howard.

Allison, Carol. Ringu of India's Forest. Espe, Marvin, illus. 52p. (gr. k-6). 1987. pap. text ed. 8.99 (*1-55976-050-8*) CEF Press.

Allison, Christine. Teach Your Children Well: A Parent's Guide to the Stories, Poems, Fables, & Tales that Instill Traditional Values. LC 92-42762. 1993. 22.95 (*0-385-30290-8*) Delacorte.

Allison, Diane W. This Is the Key to the Kingdom. Allison, Diane W., illus. 32p. (ps-3). 1992. 15.95 (*0-316-03432-0*) Little.

Allison, John P. & Allison, Lee A. David, the Trash Cop: A Child's Guide to Recycling. McCulloch, Jerry, illus. 21p. (Orig.). (gr. 1-6). 1992. pap. 6.95 (*0-9632789-2-4*) RMC Pub Grp.

Allison, Lee A., jt. auth. see Allison, John P.

Allison, Linda. Blood & Guts. (Illus.). (gr. 5-12). 1976. pap. 9.95 (*0-316-03443-6*) Little.

—The Reasons for Seasons: The Great Cosmic Megagalactic Trip Without Moving from Your Chair. Allison, Linda, illus. 128p. (gr. 4 up). 1975. 14.95 (*0-316-03439-8*); pap. 9.95 (*0-316-03440-1*) Little.

—The Sierra Club Summer Book. Allison, Linda, illus. 160p. (gr. 3-7). 1989. pap. 7.95 (*0-316-03433-9*) Sierra.

—Stethoscope Book & Kit. (gr. 2-7). 1991. pap. 12.95 (*0-201-57096-3*) Addison-Wesley.

—Trash Artists Workshop. LC 80-84184. (gr. 3-8). 1981. pap. 10.95 (*0-8224-9780-8*) Fearon Teach Aids.

—The Wild Inside: Sierra Club's Guide to Great Outdoors. Allison, Linda, illus. 144p. (gr. 3-7). 1988. pap. 7.95 (*0-316-03434-7*) Little.

Allison, Linda & Ferguson, Tom. The Get-Well-Quick Kit. Allison, Linda & Wells, William S., illus. LC 92-42626. 1993. 14.38 (*0-201-63213-6*) Addison-Wesley.

Allison, Linda & Katz, David. Gee Wiz! How to Mix Art & Science or the Art of Thinking Scientifically. Allison, Linda, illus. LC 83-9834. 128p. (gr. 4 up). 1983. 14.95 (*0-316-03444-4*); pap. 8.95 (*0-316-03445-2*) Little.

Allison, Lynda. Lisa Said No. LC 89-32331. 134p. (Orig.). 1989. pap. 6.99 (*0-932581-53-6*) Word Aflame.

Allman, Paul. Exploring Careers in Video. rev. ed. Rosen, Ruth, ed. (gr. 7-12). 1989. PLB 13.95 (*0-8239-1018-0*) Rosen Group.

—The Knot. Rosen, Roger, ed. (gr. 7 up). 1988. PLB 12.95 (*0-8239-0776-7*) Rosen Group.

—No Pain, No Gain. 223p. (gr. 7-12). 1987. 12.95 (*0-8239-0691-4*) Rosen Group.

Allred, David, ed. see Flowers, Sandra H.

Allred, Gordon. Dori the Mallard. Brown, Margery, illus. (gr. 5 up). 1968. 8.95 (*0-8392-3052-4*) Astor-Honor.

—Old Crackfoot. Brown, Margery, illus. (gr. 5 up). 1965. 8.95 (*0-8392-3051-6*) Astor-Honor.

Allred, Michael. Madman: The Oddity Odyssey. (Illus.). 144p. (gr. 4 up). 1993. pap. 12.95 (*0-87816-247-X*) Kitchen Sink.

Allsburg, Chris Van see Van Allsburg, Chris.

Allsburg, Chris van see Van Allsburg, Chris.

Allsburg, Chris Van see Van Allsburg, Chris.

Allsburg, Chris Van see Van Allsburg, Chris.

Allston, Aaron. Mythic Greece: Age of Heroes. Charlton, Coleman, ed. Loubet, Dennis, illus. 160p. (Orig.). (gr. 10-12). 1988. pap. 12.00 (*1-55806-002-2*, 1020) Iron Crown Ent Inc.

Allum, Faith T. Respite. Allum, Lois Saarinen, illus. 48p. (Orig.). (gr. 6 up). 1985. pap. 3.00 (*0-9613349-2-4*) F T Allum.

Allwood, Suzanne E. The Adventures of Sugar-Gum. Allwood, Suzanne E., illus. 1990. 6.95 (*0-533-08801-1*) Vantage.

Almagor. Plum Tree is Taken. Date not set. 15.00 (*0-06-023378-8*, Festival); PLB 14.89 (*0-06-023379-6*, Festival) HarpC Child Bks.

Alman, Mickey. Scene of the Crime. 1990. pap. 3.50 (*0-8041-0600-2*) Ivy Books.

Almaraz, Humberto. Santa Will Love My Tree (Play Format) Almaraz, Humberto, illus. & intro. by. 12p. (Orig.). (ps-3). 1982. pap. 5.00 incl. 45 rpm record (*0-9616528-1-0*) Alpha-Beto Music.

—Santa Will Love My Tree (Story Format) Almaraz, Humberto, illus. & intro. by. 12p. (Orig.). (ps-2). 1982. pap. 5.00 incl. 45 rpm record (*0-9616528-0-2*) Alpha-Beto Music.

Al-Maudoodi, Abul A. Towards Understanding Islam. Ahmad, Khurshid, tr. & intro. by. 116p. 1985. pap. write for info. (*1-882837-25-8*) Wamy Intl.

Almeleh, Fiona, illus. Plants & Flowers of the Desert. 32p. (gr. 3-5). 1985. 7.95x (*0-86685-446-0*) Intl Bk Ctr.

Almon, Russell. Kid Can't Miss. 1992. pap. 3.50 (*0-380-76261-7*, Flare) Avon.

Almonte, Paul. Inside Baseball. 64p. (gr. 4-6). 1994. PLB 12.95 (*1-881889-55-6*) Silver Moon.

Almonte, Paul & Desmond, Theresa. Capital Punishment. (Illus.). 48p. (gr. 5-6). 1991. RSBE 12.95 (0-89686-660-2, Crestwood Hse) Macmillan Child Grp.
—Diabetes. LC 90-45745. (Illus.). 48p. (gr. 5-6). 1991. RSBE 12.95 (0-89686-604-1, Crestwood Hse) Macmillan Child Grp.
—The Immune System. (Illus.). 48p. (gr. 5-6). 1991. RSBE 12.95 (0-89686-661-0, Crestwood Hse) Macmillan Child Grp.
—Interracial Marriage. LC 91-45251. (Illus.). 48p. (gr. 5-6). 1992. RSBE 12.95 (0-89686-749-8, Crestwood Hse) Macmillan Child Grp.
—Learning Disabilities. LC 91-22632. (Illus.). 48p. (gr. 5-6). 1992. RSBE 11.95 (0-89686-721-8, Crestwood Hse) Macmillan Child Grp.
—Medical Ethics. (Illus.). 48p. (gr. 5-6). 1991. RSBE 12.95 (0-89686-662-9, Crestwood Hse) Macmillan Child Grp.
—Police, People & Power. LC 91-46951. (Illus.). 48p. (gr. 5-6). 1992. RSBE 12.95 (0-89686-748-X, Crestwood Hse) Macmillan Child Grp.
—Street Gangs. LC 93-25330. Date not set. write for info. (0-89686-808-7, Crestwood Hse) Macmillan Child Grp.
Aloia, Gregory F. The Legend of the Golden Straw: A Christmas Story. (ps-4). 1989. 14.95 (0-8294-0631-X) Loyola.

Alonso, Fernando. Little Red Hen - La Gallina Paulina. Gimeno, J. M., illus. (SPA & ENG.). 26p. (gr. k-2). 1989. Spanish ed. 5.25 (0-88272-467-3); English ed. 5.25 (0-88272-468-1) Santillana.
The traditional story lovingly retold. A little red hen finds a grain of wheat, but no one to share the work of planting & caring for it. Brightly colored illustrations by J.M. Gimeno brings the story to life. English & Spanish versions are available of this charming story. To order: Santillana, 901 West Walnut, Compton, CA 90220. Telephone 1-310-763-0455.
Publisher Provided Annotation.

Alotaibi, et al. Original People, 4 bks, Set II, Reading Level 5. (Illus.). 288p. (gr. 4-8). 1989. Set. PLB 66.68 (0-86625-269-X); 50.00s.p. (0-685-58809-2) Rourke Corp.
Alper, Ann. Forgotten Voyager: The Story of Amerigo Vespucci. (Illus.). 80p. (gr. 3-6). 1991. PLB 17.50 (0-87614-442-3) Carolrhoda Bks.
Alper, Janis & Grishaver, Joel. Mah la'Asot: What Should I Do? A Book of Ethical Problems & Jewish Responses. Urbanovic, Jackie, illus. 64p. (Orig.). (gr. 4-8). 1992. pap. text ed. 4.95 (0-933873-69-7) Torah Aura.
Alpern, Lynne & Blumenfeld, Esther. In-Laws, Out-Laws & Other Theories of Relativity. Warlick, Cal, illus. 128p. (gr. 7). 1990. pap. 6.95 (0-934601-94-1) Peachtree Pubs.
Alpert, Lou. Dancing with the Shadows in My Room. Alpert, Lou, illus. 32p. (ps-8). 1991. 12.95 (1-879085-06-2) Whsprng Coyote Pr.
—Emma & the Magic Dance. Alpert, Lou, illus. 32p. (ps-8). 1991. smythe sewn reinforced bdg. 12.95 (1-879085-01-1) Whsprng Coyote Pr.
—Emma Giggled. Alpert, Lou, illus. 32p. (ps-8). 1991. smythe sewn reinforced bdg. 12.95 (1-879085-02-X) Whsprng Coyote Pr.
—Emma Lights up the Sky. Alpert, Lou, illus. 32p. (ps-8). 1991. smythe sewn reinforced bdg. 12.95 (1-879085-03-8) Whsprng Coyote Pr.
—Emma Swings. Alpert, Lou, illus. 32p. (ps-8). 1991. smythe sewn reinforced bdg. 12.95 (1-879085-04-6) Whsprng Coyote Pr.
—Emma's Turn to Dance. Alpert, Lou, illus. 32p. (ps-8). 1991. smythe sewn reinforced bdg. 12.95 (1-879085-00-3) Whsprng Coyote Pr.
—The Man in the Moon & His Flying Balloon. Alpert, Lou, illus. 32p. (ps-8). 1991. smythe sewn reinforced bdg. 12.95 (1-879085-05-4) Whsprng Coyote Pr.
—Max & the Great Blueness. Alpert, Lou, illus. LC 92-23313. 32p. (gr-12). 1993. smythe sewn reinforced 13.95 (1-879085-38-0) Whsprng Coyote Pr.
—You & Your Dad. Alpert, Lou, illus. LC 91-44412. 32p. (ps-12). 1992. smythe sewn reinforced 12.95 (1-879085-36-4) Whsprng Coyote Pr.
Alpert, Stanley, jt. auth. see Lindshell, Sheryl.
Alpha Pyramis Publishing Staff. Story Time Stories That Rhyme, Vol. 1: Fish Convention, Rainbow, Miss Divine Sunshine & Others. 106p. (gr. 1-2). 1992. binder 27.95 (0-913597-99-6, Pub. by Alpha Pyramis) Prosperity & Profits.
Alphin, Elaine M. The Ghost Cadet. 192p. (gr. 4-6). 1991. 14.95 (0-8050-1614-7, Bks Young Read) H Holt & Co.
—Ghost Cadet. 192p. 1992. pap. 2.95 (0-590-45244-4, Apple Paperbacks) Scholastic Inc.

—The Proving Ground. LC 92-11356. 192p. (gr. 4-7). 1992. 14.95 (0-8050-2140-X, Bks Young Read) H Holt & Co.
Alpine Partners Staff. See How I Grow. Mitchell, Suzanne, ed. Matthews, Mozelle, illus. 32p. Date not set. 39.95 (0-9637894-0-6) Video Moments.
Al-Sheikh, H. E., intro. by. Issues from the Contemporary Islamic Thoughts: Research Papers & Proceedings of the 2nd International Conference of Wamy. 3rd ed. (ARA.). 433p. 1984. pap. write for info. (1-882837-01-0) Wamy Intl.
Alsop, Peter, et al. In the Hospital. 64p. (Orig.). (gr. k-6). 1989. pap. 12.98g (1-877942-00-6, MS503) Moose Schl Records.
Alstetter, Billy. Speech & Hearing. (Illus.). 112p. (gr. 6-12). 1991. 18.95 (0-7910-0029-X) Chelsea Hse.
Alston, Edith. Let's Visit a Space Camp. Plunkett, Michael, illus. LC 89-34373. 32p. (gr. 2-4). 1990. lib. bdg. 10.79 (0-8167-1743-5); pap. text ed. 2.95 (0-8167-1744-3) Troll Assocs.
Alston, Nelson G. Sonnets in the Names of Love: In the Names of Love. Avent, Barbara P., ed. (Illus.). 96p. (Orig.). 1993. pap. 10.95 (0-9632202-2-5) Alpha Bk Pr.
Alston, Nelson G., ed. see Avent, Barbara P.
Al-Sunaidi, Julie, ed. see Smith, Audrey.
Alt, David, ed. see Frye, Keith.
Altamuro, Vincent J. & Clarkson, Sandra P. Exploring with Pattern Blocks. 64p. (gr. 4-8). 1989. pap. text ed. 8.50 (0-938587-09-9) Cuisenaire.
Alter, Anna. Destination Outer Space. (gr. 6 up). 1988. 4.95 (0-8120-3839-8) Barron.
Alter, Judith. Eli Whitney. LC 90-12222. (Illus.). 64p. (gr. 5-8). 1990. PLB 12.90 (0-531-10875-9) Watts.
—Growing up in the Old West. LC 88-34547. (Illus.). 64p. (gr. 3-5). 1989. PLB 12.90 (0-531-10746-9) Watts.
—Women of the Old West. LC 88-34549. (Illus.). 64p. (gr. 3-5). 1989. PLB 12.90 (0-531-10756-6) Watts.
Alter, Judith M. Luke & the Van Zandt County War. Conoly, Walli, illus. LC 84-101. 132p. (gr. 4 up). 1984. 10.95 (0-912646-88-8) Tex Christian.
Alter, Judy. After Pa Was Shot. Shaw, Charles, illus. LC 89-12176. 192p. (Orig.). (gr. 4-9). 1991. pap. 5.95 (0-936650-12-5) E C Temple.
—Katie & the Recluse. LC 90-23695. 192p. (gr. 4-9). 1991. pap. 5.95 (0-936650-13-3) E C Temple.
—Maggie & a Horse Named Devildust. Shaw, Charles, illus. LC 88-22815. 160p. (gr. 4-9). 1989. pap. 5.95 (0-936650-08-7) E C Temple.
—Maggie & Devildust Ridin' High. Shaw, Charles, illus. LC 89-2683. 176p. (Orig.). (gr. 4-9). 1990. pap. 5.95 (0-936650-10-9) E C Temple.
—Maggie & the Search for Devildust. Shaw, Charles, illus. LC 88-8019. 160p. (gr. 4-9). 1989. pap. 5.95 (0-936650-09-5) E C Temple.
Althea. How Do Things Grow? Douglas, Julie, illus. LC 90-10923. 32p. (gr. k-3). 1991. PLB 11.59 (0-8167-2118-1); pap. text ed. 3.95 (0-8167-2119-X) Troll Assocs.
—Insects & Other Small Creatures. Male, Alan, illus. LC 89-20307. 32p. (gr. 3-6). 1990. PLB 11.59 (0-8167-1961-6); pap. text ed. 3.95 (0-8167-1962-4) Troll Assocs.
—Trees & Leaves. More, David & Allen, Graham, illus. LC 89-20308. 32p. (gr. 3-6). 1990. PLB 11.59 (0-8167-1967-5); pap. text ed. 3.95 (0-8167-1968-3) Troll Assocs.
—Undersea Homes. 24p. (gr. 2 up). 1986. pap. 2.95 (0-685-10901-1) Cambridge U Pr.
—What Makes Things Move? Green, Robina, illus. LC 90-10924. 32p. (gr. k-3). 1991. PLB 11.59 (0-8167-2124-6); pap. text ed. 3.95 (0-8167-2125-4) Troll Assocs.
Althoff, Victoria M. I Won't Leave You. 125p. (Orig.). (gr. 5-8). 1989. pap. text ed. 2.99 (0-87406-426-0) Willowisp Pr.
Altland, Millard, jt. auth. see Cornell, William A.
Altman, Adelaide. Professor Pishposh & the Robots. Altman, Adelaide, illus. 48p. (ps-2). 1988. 12.95 (0-933905-05-X); pap. 9.95 (0-933905-16-5) Claycomb Pr.
Altman, Joyce & Goldberg, Sue. Dear Bronx Zoo. (gr. 4-7). 1992. pap. 3.50 (0-380-71649-6, Camelot) Avon.
Altman, Joyce, jt. auth. see Goldberg, Sue.
Altman, Linda J. Amelia's Road. Sanchez, Enrique O., illus. LC 92-59982. 32p. (gr. k-3). 1993. 14.95 (1-880000-04-0) Lee & Low Bks.
—Migrant Farm Workers: The Temporary People. LC 93-11921. 1994. write for info. (0-531-13033-9) Watts.
—The Pullman Strike of Eighteen Ninety-Four: Turning Point for American Labor. (Illus.). 64p. (gr. 4-6). 1994. 14.90 (1-56294-346-4) Millbrook Pr.
Altman, Susan. Extraordinary Black Americans from Colonial to Contemporary Times. LC 88-11977. (Illus.). 240p. (gr. 4 up). 1989. PLB 30.60 (0-516-00581-2) Childrens.
Altman, Susan & Lechner, Susan. Followers of the North Star: Rhymes about African American Heroes, Heroines, & Historical Times. Wooden, Bryan, illus. LC 93-797. 1993. write for info. (0-516-05151-2) Childrens.
Altman, Tim, jt. auth. see McAllister, Dawson.
Altsheler, Joseph A. After the Battle. rev. ed. (gr. 9-12). 1989. Repr. of 1905 ed. multi-media kit 35.00 (0-685-31125-2) Balance Pub.
—The Forest Runners. 300p. 1990. 13.95 (0-929146-04-2) Voyageur Pub.

—Kentucky Frontiersmen: The Adventures of Henry Ware, Hunter & Border Fighter. rev. ed. Kenton, Nathaniel, ed. Doney, Todd, illus. LC 88-50581. 256p. (gr. 5-10). 1988. 16.95 (0-929146-01-8) Voyageur Pub.
—Riflemen of the Ohio. 1991. 13.95 (0-929146-05-0) Voyageur Pub.
Altshuler, David, ed. see Rossel, Seymour.
Alvarado, Manuel. Spain. (Illus.). 48p. (gr. 5-8). 1990. PLB 13.90 (0-531-18332-7, Pub. by Bookwright Pr) Watts.
Alvarez, Everett, Jr. & Clinton, Susan. Everett Alvarez, Jr. A Hero for Our Times. LC 90-38375. (Illus.). 32p. (gr. 2-4). 1990. PLB 14.60 (0-516-04277-7); pap. 3.95 (0-516-44277-5) Childrens.
Alvarez, Everett, Jr. & Pitch, Anthony S. Chained Eagle. LC 89-45547. (Illus.). 308p. (gr. 8-12). 1989. 18.95 (1-55611-167-3) D I Fine.
Alvarez, Ines, tr. see Berenstain, Stan & Berenstain, Janice.
Alvarez, Ines, tr. see De Cuenca, Pilar.
Alvarez, Ines, tr. see Eastman, P. D.
Alvarez, Ines, tr. see Provensen, Alice & Provensen, Martin.
Alvarez, Juan. Chocolate, Chipmunks, & Canoes: An American Indian Words Coloring Book. Alvarez, Juan, illus. LC 90-60331. 32p. (gr. 1-3). 1991. pap. 3.95 (1-878610-03-1) Red Crane Bks.
—Jose Rabbit's Southwest Adventures: An ABC Coloring Book with Spanish Words. Alvarez, Juan, illus. 32p. (Orig.). (gr. 1-3). 1990. pap. 3.95 (1-878610-00-7) Red Crane Bks.
Alvarez, Julia. How the Garcia Girls Lost Their Accents. 308p. (gr. 10 up). 1991. 16.95 (0-945575-57-2) Algonquin Bks.
Alvarez, Mark. The Official Baseball Hall of Fame Answer Book. (gr. 3 up). 1989. pap. 6.95 (0-671-67377-7, Little Simon) S&S Trade.
—Story of Jackie Robinson. 1990. (S&S BFYR); pap. 2.95 (0-671-69093-0, S&S BFYR) S&S Trade.
Alvarez, Mark, jt. auth. see Cleveland, Will.
Alvarez del Real, Maria E., ed. Cocina Latino Americana. (SPA., Illus.). 304p. (Orig.). 1988. pap. 4.50x (0-944499-44-9) Editorial Amer.
—Como Escribir Cartas De Amor. (SPA., Illus.). 288p. (Orig.). 1988. pap. 4.00x (0-944499-38-4) Editorial Amer.
—Como Reparar 500 Problemas De la Casa. (SPA., Illus.). 352p. (Orig.). 1988. pap. 4.50x (0-944499-33-3) Editorial Amer.
—El Dato Escolar. 3rd ed. LC 81-72099. (SPA., Illus.). 352p. (gr. 2). 1985. pap. 6.00x (0-944499-11-2) Editorial Amer.
—Diccionario EASA Ingles-Espanol Espanol-Ingles. 2nd, rev. ed. (ENG & SPA., Illus.). 808p. (Orig.). 1992. pap. 5.95 (1-56259-017-0) Editorial Amer.
—Diccionario Escolar. 2nd ed. LC 83-80787. (SPA., Illus.). 228p. (gr. 2). 1986. pap. 3.75x (0-944499-13-9) Editorial Amer.
—Diccionario Geografico Universal. 3rd, rev. ed. Rodriguez, Jose L., illus. (SPA.). 876p. (Orig.). 1992. pap. 5.95 (1-56259-020-0) Editorial Amer.
—Fechas Que Han Hecho Historia. (SPA., Illus.). 320p. (Orig.). 1988. pap. 5.00x (0-944499-41-4) Editorial Amer.
—Frases Celebres De Todos los Tiempos. (SPA., Illus.). 336p. (Orig.). 1988. pap. 4.00x (0-944499-40-6) Editorial Amer.
—Guia Practica para la Mujer. (SPA., Illus.). 320p. (Orig.). 1989. pap. 4.00x (0-944499-37-6) Editorial Amer.
Alvaro, Albert M., ed. see Santos, Elsie S.
Alverson, Charles. The Princess & the Mirror. Southgate, Mark, illus. 32p. (gr. k-3). 1989. 13.95 (0-86264-174-8, Pub. by Anderson Pr UK) Trafalgar.
Alvin, Virginia & Silverstein, Robert. Cystic Fibrosis. LC 93-30045. 1994. write for info. (0-531-12552-1) Watts.
Alward, Edgar C. Research Paper, Step-by-Step. rev. ed. (gr. 9 up). 1991. pap. 22.00 (0-9620092-7-X) Pine Isl Pr.
Alward, Edgar C. & Dale, E. Up Your Punctuation! An Almost Non-Grammatical Approach to Punctuation. 112p. (Orig.). (gr. 9-12). 1988. pap. 12.95 (0-9620092-0-2) Pine Isl Pr.
Alwin-Hill, Raymond. Treasure Island. LC 91-52607. (Orig.). 1991. pap. 6.00 (0-88734-412-7) Players Pr.
Alyeshmreni, Mansoor, tr. see Bahar, Mehrdad.
Alyson, Sasha, ed. Young, Gay & Proud! rev. ed. (Illus.). 120p. (Orig.). (gr. 7-12). 1991. pap. 3.95 (1-55583-001-3) Alyson Pubns.
Amado, Jorge. Home Is the Sailor. 1979. pap. 4.50 (0-380-45187-5, Bard) Avon.
Aman, Catherine. The Scottish Americans. (Illus.). 112p. (gr. 5 up). 1991. lib. bdg. 17.95 (1-55546-132-8) Chelsea Hse.
Amari, Suad. Cooking the Lebanese Way. (Illus.). 48p. (gr. 5 up). 1985. PLB 14.95 (0-8225-0913-X) Lerner Pubns.
Amato, Carol. Astronomy. (Illus.). 64p. (gr. 3-7). 1992. 5.98 (0-8317-1012-8) Smithmark.
—The Earth. (Illus.). 64p. (gr. 3-7). 1992. 5.98 (0-8317-1011-X) Smithmark.
Amato, Carol & Ladizinsky, Eric. Fifty Nifty Science Fair Projects. Manwaring, Kerry, illus. 64p. (Orig.). (gr. 3-7). 1993. pap. 3.95 (1-56565-053-0) Lowell Hse.
Amato, Janet D' see D'Amato, Janet & D'Amato, Alex.
Amberg, Jay. The Learning Skills Handbook. 144p. (Orig.). (gr. 6-10). 1993. pap. 7.95 (0-673-36098-9) GdYrBks.

Amberg, Jay & Larson, Mark. The Creative Writing Handbook. (Illus.). 144p. (Orig.). (gr. 6-10). 1991. pap. 7.95 (0-673-36013-X) GdYrBks.

Amberson, Max L., ed. see Stewart, Robert.

Ambrus, Glenys, jt. auth. see Ambrus, Victor.

Ambrus, Victor & Ambrus, Glenys. Santa Claus Takes Off. (Illus.). 28p. (gr. k up). 1991. bds. 13.95 (0-19-279878-2) OUP.

Ambrus, Victor, retold by. & illus. Never Laugh at Bears: A Folk Tale from Transylvania. LC 91-40372. 32p. (gr. k-3). 1992. PLB 14.95 (0-87226-465-3, Bedrick Blackie) P Bedrick Bks.

Ambrus, Victor G. Blackbeard the Pirate. (Illus.). 32p. (gr. 2 up). 1990. pap. 5.95 (0-19-272220-4) OUP.

—Count, Dracula! Ambrus, Victor G., illus. LC 91-40269. 24p. (ps-1). 1992. 3.99 (0-517-58969-9) Crown Bks Yng Read.

—What Time Is It, Dracula? Ambrus, Victor G., illus. LC 91-41260. 24p. (ps-1). 1992. 3.99 (0-517-58970-2) Crown Bks Yng Read.

Ambrus, Victor G., illus. The Canterbury Tales. McCaughrean, Geraldine, retold by. LC 85-60147. (Illus.). 128p. (gr. 4 up). 1985. 14.95 (1-56288-259-7) Checkerboard.

Amdur, Nikki. One of Us. Sanderson, Ruth, illus. LC 81-65847. (gr. 3-6). 1981. Dial Bks Young.

Amdur, Richard. Anne Frank. (Illus.). 112p. (gr. 5 up). 1993. 18.95 (0-7910-1641-2, Am Art Analog) Chelsea Hse.

—Chaim Weizmann. Schlesinger, Arthur M., Jr., intro. by. (Illus.). 112p. (gr. 5 up). 1988. lib. bdg. 17.95 (0-87754-446-8) Chelsea Hse.

—The Fragile Earth. Train, Russell E., intro. by. LC 93-827. 1994. write for info. (0-7910-1572-6); pap. write for info. (0-7910-1597-1) Chelsea Hse.

—Linda Ronstadt: Mexican-American Singer. (Illus.). 112p. (gr. 6-12). 1994. PLB 18.95 (0-7910-1781-8, Am Art Analog); pap. write for info. (0-7910-2025-8, Am Art Analog) Chelsea Hse.

—Menachem Begin. (Illus.). 112p. (gr. 5 up). 1988. 17.95 (0-87754-561-8) Chelsea Hse.

—Moshe Dayan. Schlesinger, Arthur M., intro. by. (Illus.). 112p. (gr. 5 up). 1989. 17.95 (1-55546-829-2) Chelsea Hse.

—Toxic Materials. (Illus.). 112p. (gr. 5 up). 1993. PLB 19.95 (0-7910-1574-2) Chelsea Hse.

Ameiss, Bill & Graver, Jane. Love, Sex & God. 128p. (gr. 9 up). 1988. pap. 7.99 (0-570-08485-7, 14-1625) Concordia.

Amelar, Chris. Stand Alone Rock. 32p. pap. 9.95 (0-88284-544-6, 4430) Alfred Pub.

Amenta, Charles A. Russell Is Extra Special: A Book about Autism for Children. LC 91-41863. 32p. (ps-3). 1992. pap. 8.95 (0-945354-44-4); 16.95 (0-945354-43-6) Magination Pr.

American Academy of Pediatrics Staff. Caring for Your School-Age Child: Ages 5 to 12. 432p. (ps-7). 1994. 21.95 (0-553-08982-X) Am Acad Pediat.

American Association of Diabetes Educators Staff. Healthy Eating for Healthy Growing: A Children's Coloring Book. 26p. (gr. 1-6). 1983. 0.75 (0-686-39262-0) Am Assn Diabetes Ed.

American Automobile Association Staff. Sportsmanlike Driving. 7th ed. 1975. text ed. 25.24 (0-07-001292-X, W) McGraw.

—Sportsmanlike Driving. 9th ed. 352p. (gr. 9-12). 1987. text ed. 22.16 (0-07-001338-1); pap. text ed. 14.48 (0-07-001339-X) McGraw.

American Bible Society Staff, tr. see Hoffman, Elizabeth.

American College Testing Program Staff. Study Power Leader's Guide. 99p. (Orig.). (gr. 7 up). 1987. tchr's. ed. 4.00 (0-937734-63-2) Am Coll Testing.

—Study Power, Managing Time & Environment. 30p. (Orig.). (gr. 7 up). 1987. wkbk. 1.00 (0-937734-65-9) Am Coll Testing.

—Study Power, Preparing for Tests. 14p. (Orig.). (gr. 7 up). 1987. wkbk. 1.00 (0-937734-69-1) Am Coll Testing.

—Study Power, Reading Textbooks. 21p. (Orig.). (gr. 7 up). 1987. wkbk. 1.00 (0-937734-66-7) Am Coll Testing.

—Study Power, Student Workbook Set. (Orig.). (gr. 7 up). 1987. wkbk. 5.00 (0-937734-64-0) Am Coll Testing.

—Study Power, Taking Class Notes. 22p. (Orig.). (gr. 7 up). 1987. wkbk. 1.00 (0-937734-67-5) Am Coll Testing.

—Study Power, Taking Tests. 13p. (Orig.). (gr. 7 up). 1987. wkbk. 1.00 (0-937734-70-5) Am Coll Testing.

—Study Power, Using Resources. 14p. (Orig.). (gr. 7 up). 1987. wkbk. 1.00 (0-937734-68-3) Am Coll Testing.

American Colortype Co., Staff. Cut & Assemble Paper Dollhouse Furniture. 1981. pap. 4.95 (0-486-24150-5) Dover.

American Diabetes Association Staff. Grilled Cheese at Four O'Clock in the Morning. Turner, Jeanne, illus. 90p. (gr. 3-7). 1988. pap. 5.95 (0-945448-02-3, CCHGC) Am Diabetes.

—Teddy Ryder Rides Again! 22p. 1990. pap. 1.50 (0-945448-21-X, CCHTRRA) Am Diabetes.

American Etiquette Institute Staff. Eddycat & Buddy Entertain a Guest, Bk. 5. (Illus.). 32p. (gr. k-3). 1991. 13.95 (1-879322-14-5) Amer Etiquette Inst.

—Eddycat & Gabby Gorilla Babysit, Bk. 9. (Illus.). 32p. (gr. k-3). 1991. 13.95 (1-879322-18-8) Amer Etiquette Inst.

—Eddycat Attends Sunshine's Birthday Party, Bk. 3. (Illus.). 32p. (gr. k-3). 1991. 13.95 (1-879322-12-9) Amer Etiquette Inst.

—Eddycat Brings Soccer to Mannersville, Bk. 8. (Illus.). 32p. (gr. k-3). 1991. 13.95 (1-879322-17-X) Amer Etiquette Inst.

—Eddycat Goes on Vacation with the Ducks, Bk. 11. (Illus.). 32p. (gr. k-3). 1991. 13.95 (1-879322-20-X) Amer Etiquette Inst.

—Eddycat Goes Shopping with Becky Bunny, Bk. 6. (Illus.). 32p. (gr. k-3). 1991. 13.95 (1-879322-15-3) Amer Etiquette Inst.

—Eddycat Helps Sunshine Plan Her Party, Bk. 2. (Illus.). 32p. (gr. k-3). 1991. 13.95 (1-879322-11-0) Amer Etiquette Inst.

—Eddycat Introduces Leonardo Lion, Bk. 12. (Illus.). 32p. (gr. k-3). 1991. 13.95 (1-879322-21-8) Amer Etiquette Inst.

—Eddycat Introduces Mannersville, USA, Bk. 1. (Illus.). 32p. (gr. k-3). 1991. 13.95 (1-879322-10-2) Amer Etiquette Inst.

—Eddycat Serves Grandma's Birthday Brunch, Bk. 10. (Illus.). 32p. (gr. k-3). 1991. 13.95 (1-879322-19-6) Amer Etiquette Inst.

—Eddycat Teaches Telephone Skills, Bk. 4. (Illus.). 32p. (gr. k-3). 1991. 13.95 (1-879322-13-7) Amer Etiquette Inst.

—Eddycat Visits Wright Street School, Bk. 7. (Illus.). 32p. (gr. k-3). 1991. 13.95 (1-879322-16-1) Amer Etiquette Inst.

American Forestry Association Staff. Trees Every Boy & Girl Should Know. (gr. 1-6). 4.50 (0-686-26729-X, 31) Am Forests.

—Trees Every Boy & Girl Should Know. 4th ed. (Illus.). 89p. 1977. pap. text ed. 4.50 (0-685-46347-8) Am Forests.

American Health Foundation Staff. Great Meals, Great Snacks, Great Kids. 1990. pap. 4.95 (0-590-43382-2) Scholastic Inc.

American Heart Association Staff & Moller, James. American Heart Association Kids' Cookbook. Holub, Joan, illus. LC 92-56800. 128p. (gr. 4 up). 1993. pap. 15.00 (0-8129-1930-0, Times Bks) Random.

American Heritage Magazine Editorial Staff. The American Heritage Junior Library, 20 vols. (gr. 5-12). 1989. 14.95 ea. (0-8167-1536-X) Troll Assocs.

American Institute for Character Education Staff. Character Education Curriculum: The Happy Life Series plus Living with Me & Others Including Our Rights & Responsibilities, Levels A-F. (Illus.). (gr. 1-7). 1984. Set. 820.00 (0-685-09646-7); tchr's ed. 95.00 ea. Level A, 124p (0-913413-01-1) Level B, 127p (0-913413-02-X) Level C, 148p (0-913413-03-8) Level D, 152p (0-913413-04-6) Level E, 160p (0-913413-05-4) Level F, 6th gr. 95.00 (0-685-09647-5); Level G, Middle School#Level K, Kindergarten with film strips. 125.00 (0-685-09648-3) Char Ed Inst.

American Institute for Research. Science Success for Students with Disabilities. 1992. pap. 17.95 (0-201-81939-2) Addison-Wesley.

American Map Corp. Staff. Scholastic World Atlas, No. 9552. (gr. 7-9). 1990. pap. 3.25 (0-685-47443-7) Am Map.

American Map Corp. Staff, ed. Atlas Mundial. (Illus.). (gr. 7-12). 1990. pap. 2.75 (0-8416-9555-5); Span. lang. ed. pap. write for info. Am Map.

American Red Cross Staff. American Red Cross Child Story Activity Book. (ps-3). 1992. pap. 39.50 pack of 10 (0-8016-6509-4) Mosby Yr Bk.

—American Red Cross Swimming & Diving. 356p. 1992. pap. 20.00 (0-8016-6506-X) Mosby Yr Bk.

American Red Cross Staff, tr. see Garehime, Ed.

American Society for Engineering Education Staff. Directory of Engineering & Engineering Technology Undergraduate Programs, 1994. (Illus.). (gr. 11 up). 1994. pap. 49.95 (0-87823-147-1) Am Soc Eng Ed.

American Society for the Prevention of Cruelty to Animals Staff. Big Cats, Little Cats. Tompkins, Ptolemy, illus. 48p. (Orig.). (gr. k-4). 1991. stapled bdg. 4.95 (1-879326-09-4) Living Planet Pr.

American Trust Publications, ed. see Simpson, Juwairiah J. L.

Amerikaner, Susan. Gifted & Talented Language Arts. Whitten, Leesa, illus. 96p. (gr. 1-3). 1993. pap. 3.95 (1-56565-064-6) Lowell Hse.

—Gifted & Talented Reading Workbook. Whitten, Leesa, illus. 96p. (ps-3). 1992. pap. 3.95 (0-929923-83-9) Lowell Hse.

—The Gifted & Talented Reading Workbook. Whitten, Leesa, illus. 96p. (gr. 1-3). 1993. pap. 3.95 (1-56565-040-9) Lowell Hse.

—My Silly Book of ABC's. Brook, Bonnie, ed. Ziegler, Judy, illus. 32p. (ps-1). 1989. 5.95 (0-671-68119-2); PLB 8.98 (0-671-68363-2) Silver Pr.

—My Silly Book of Colors. Brook, Bonnie, ed. Ziegler, Judy, illus. 32p. (ps-1). 1989. 5.95 (0-671-68120-6); PLB 8.98 (0-671-68364-0) Silver Pr.

—My Silly Book of Counting. Brook, Bonnie, ed. Ziegler, Judy, illus. 32p. (ps-1). 1989. 5.95 (0-671-68121-4); PLB 8.98 (0-671-68365-9) Silver Pr.

—My Silly Book of Opposites. Brook, Bonnie, ed. Ziegler, Judy, illus. 32p. (ps-1). 1989. 5.90 (0-671-68122-2); PLB 8.98 (0-671-68366-7) Silver Pr.

—One Hundred & One Things to Do to Develop Your Child's Gifts & Talents, Vol. 1. (ps-1). 1989. pap. 5.95 (0-8125-9497-5) Tor Bks.

—One Hundred & One Things to Do to Develop Your Child's Gifts & Talents, Vol. 2. (gr. 1-3). 1989. pap. 5.95 (0-8125-9392-8) Tor Bks.

—Silly Me! Books, 4 bks. Ziegler, Judy, illus. (ps-1). 1990. Set, 24p. ea. 19.80 (0-671-93116-4, J Messner); Set, 24p. ea. lib. bdg. 35.92 (0-671-93137-7) S&S Trade.

Amery. Alphabet Book. (gr. k-2). 1979. (Usborne-Hayes); PLB 11.96 (0-88110-065-X) EDC.

—At the Seaside. Cartwright, illus. 20p. (ps). 1985. 3.95 (0-86020-855-9, Pub. by Usborne) EDC.

—Experiments. (gr. 4-6). 1977. pap. 5.95 (0-86020-135-X, Usborne-Hayes) EDC.

—On the Farm. Cartwright, Stephen, illus. 20p. (ps). 1984. 3.95 (0-86020-853-2, Pub. by Usborne) EDC.

Amery & Adair. Jokes & Tricks. (gr. 4-6). 1977. pap. 5.95 (0-86020-034-5, Usborne-Hayes) EDC.

Amery & Haron. First Thousand Words in Hebrew. Cartwright, Stephen, illus. 62p. (ps-6). 1985. PLB 11.95 (0-86020-863-X, Pub. by Usborne) EDC.

Amery & Mila. First Thousand Words in English. (Illus.). (gr. 1-9). 1979. 11.95 (0-86020-266-6, Usborne-Hayes) English ed. EDC.

Amery & Vanage. Rome & Romans. (gr. 4-9). 1976. (Usborne-Hayes); PLB 13.96 (0-88110-101-X); pap. 6.95 (0-86020-070-1) EDC.

Amery, jt. auth. see Webb.

Amery, H. Action Toys. (Illus.). 32p. (gr. 3-6). 1977. pap. 5.95 (0-86020-021-3) EDC.

—At the Zoo. (Illus.). 16p. (ps-1). 1984. (Usborne); pap. 3.95 (0-7460-1542-9) EDC.

—Barn on Fire. (Illus.). 16p. (ps). 1989. 3.95 (0-7460-0260-2, Usborne); lib. bdg. 7.96 (0-88110-375-6, Usborne) EDC.

—Black Knights Victory. (Illus.). 24p. (ps-2). 1987. 3.95 (0-7460-0157-6) EDC.

—Children's Poems. (Illus.). 96p. (gr. 2-6). 1992. pap. 12.95 (0-7460-0482-6) EDC.

—Cinderella. (gr. 1 up). 1989. 6.96 (0-88110-339-X); 3.95 (0-7460-0250-5) EDC.

—Even More Farmyard Tales. (Illus.). 64p. (ps up). 1993. 9.95 (0-7460-1416-3) EDC.

—The Farm. (Illus.). 12p. (ps up). 1988. bds. 3.50 (0-7460-0128-2) EDC.

—Farmyard Tales. (Illus.). 64p. (ps). 1989. 9.95 (0-7460-0263-7, Usborne) EDC.

—First Stories. Cartwright, Stephen, illus. 48p. 1988. 8.95 (0-7460-0191-6) EDC.

—Going Swimming. (Illus.). 24p. (ps-2). 1987. 3.95 (0-7460-0065-0); PLB 7.96 (0-88110-261-X) EDC.

—Going to the Fair. (Illus.). 24p. (ps-2). 1987. 3.95 (0-7460-0066-9); PLB 7.96 (0-88110-262-8) EDC.

—Goldilocks & the Three Bears. Cartwright, Stephen, illus. 16p. (ps-2). 1988. PLB 6.96 (0-88110-318-7) EDC.

—Grumpy Goat. (Illus.). 64p. (ps up). 1993. pap. 3.95 (0-7460-1413-9) EDC.

—Hungry Donkey. (Illus.). 16p. (ps-3). 1992. pap. 3.95 (0-7460-0586-5) EDC.

—Kitten's Day Out. (Illus.). 16p. (ps-3). 1992. pap. 3.95 (0-7460-1415-5) EDC.

—Little Red Riding Hood. Cartwright, Stephen, illus. 16p. (ps-2). 1987. 2.95 (0-7460-0138-X); PLB 6.96 (0-88110-290-3) EDC.

—The Mammoth Hunt. (Illus.). 24p. 1987. 3.95 (0-7460-0158-4) EDC.

—More Farmyard Tales. (Illus.). 64p. (ps-2). 1992. 9.95 (0-7460-0592-X) EDC.

—The Naughty Sheep. (Illus.). 16p. (ps). 1989. 3.95 (0-7460-0261-0, Usborne); lib. bdg. 7.96 (0-88110-376-4, Usborne) EDC.

—New Pony. (Illus.). 64p. (ps up). 1993. pap. 3.95 (0-7460-1414-7) EDC.

—Pig Gets Lost. (Illus.). 16p. (ps-3). 1992. pap. 3.95 (0-7460-0590-3) EDC.

—Pig Gets Stuck. (Illus.). 16p. (ps). 1989. 3.95 (0-7460-0259-9, Usborne); PLB 7.96 (0-88110-374-8, Usborne) EDC.

—The Runaway Tractor. (Illus.). 16p. (ps). 1989. 3.95 (0-7460-0262-9, Usborne); lib. bdg. 7.96 (0-88110-377-2, Usborne) EDC.

—Scarecrow's Secret. (Illus.). 16p. (ps-3). 1992. pap. 3.95 (0-7460-0584-9) EDC.

—Seaside. (Illus.). 12p. (ps up). 1988. bds. 3.50 (0-7460-0137-1) EDC.

—Silly Sheepdog. (Illus.). 16p. (ps-3). 1992. pap. 3.95 (0-7460-1412-0) EDC.

—Three Little Pigs. Cartwright, Stephen, illus. 16p. (ps-2). 1987. 3.95 (0-7460-0189-4); PLB 6.96 (0-88110-293-8) EDC.

—Tractor in Trouble. (Illus.). 16p. (ps-3). 1992. pap. 3.95 (0-7460-0588-1) EDC.

—The Zoo. (Illus.). 12p. (ps up). 1988. bds. 3.50 (0-7460-0127-4) EDC.

Amery, H. & Cartwright, S. First Hundred Words in German. (GER., Illus.). 32p. (ps-4). 1988. PLB 11.96 (0-88110-324-1, Usborne); pap. 7.95 (0-7460-0365-X, Usborne) EDC.

Amery, H. & Civardi, Anne. Print & Paint: Lots of Ways to Make Pictures & Patterns. (Illus.). 32p. (gr. 3-6). 1977. pap. 5.95 (0-86020-011-6) EDC.

Amery, H. & DiBello, P. The First Thousand Words in Italian. Cartwright, Stephen, illus. 64p. (gr. 1-6). 1983. 11.95 (0-86020-768-4) EDC.

Amery, H. & Littler, A. Batteries & Magnets. (Illus.). 32p. (gr. 3-6). 1977. pap. 5.95 (0-86020-008-6) EDC.

Amery, H., compiled by. Animal Poems. (Illus.). 32p. (gr. 2-6). 1990. (Usborne); pap. 5.95 (*0-7460-0442-7*, Usborne) EDC.
—Christmas Carols. (Illus.). 64p. (ps up) 1990. (Usborne); pap. 7.95 (*0-7460-0432-X*, Usborne) EDC.
—Creepy Poems. (Illus.). 32p. (gr. 2-6). 1990. (Usborne); pap. 5.95 (*0-7460-0440-0*, Usborne) EDC.
—Funny Poems. (Illus.). 32p. (gr. 2-6). 1990. (Usborne); pap. 5.95 (*0-7460-0444-3*, Usborne) EDC.
Amery, Heather. First Thousand Words in French. Cartwright, Stephen, illus. 50p. (ps-7). 1980. 11.95 (*0-86020-267-4*) EDC.
—First Thousand Words in German. Cartwright, Stephen, illus. 50p. (ps-7). 1979. 11.95 (*0-86020-268-2*) EDC.
—First Thousand Words in Spanish. Cartwrigh, Stephen, illus. 50p. (ps-7). 1979. 11.95 (*0-86020-277-1*) EDC.
—Fun with Paper. LC 92-51071. 1994. lib. bdg. 6.99 (*0-679-83493-1*); pap. 9.99 (*0-679-93493-6*) Random.
—Word Detective in French. Cartwright, Stephen, illus 50p. (gr. 3-7). 1983. 8.95 (*0-7460-0399-4*) EDC.
—Word Detective in German. Cartwright, Stephen, illus. 50p. (gr. 3-7). 1983. 11.95 (*0-86020-664-5*) EDC.
Amery, Heather & Cartwright, Stephen. The First Hundred Words. Cartwright, Stephen, illus. 32p. (ps up). 1988. PLB 11.96 (*0-88110-322-5*); pap. 7.95 (*0-7460-0186-X*) EDC.
Amery, Heather & Kirilenko, Katrina. The First Thousand Words in Russian. Cartwright, Stephen, illus. 64p. (gr. k-7). 1983. 11.95 (*0-86020-769-2*) EDC.
Amery, Heather, et al. Looking at... Brachiosaurus: A Dionsaur from the Jurassic Period. Gibbons, Tony, illus. 24p. (gr. 2 up). 1993. PLB 17.27 (*0-8368-1044-9*) Gareth Stevens Inc.
—Looking at... Iguanodon: A Dinosaur from the Cretaceous Period. Gibbons, Tony, illus. 24p. (gr. 2 up). 1993. PLB 17.27 (*0-8368-1045-7*) Gareth Stevens Inc.
—Looking at... Protoceratops: A Dinosaur from the Cretaceous Period. Gibbons, Tony, illus. LC 93-5536. 24p. (gr. 2 up). 1993. PLB 17.27 (*0-8368-1046-5*) Gareth Stevens Inc.
—Looking at... Stegosaurus: A Dinosaur from the Jurassic Period. Gibbons, Tony, illus. LC 93-5535. 24p. (gr. 2 up). 1993. PLB 17.27 (*0-8368-1047-3*) Gareth Stevens Inc.
—Looking at... Triceratops: A Dinosaur from the Cretaceous Period. Gibbons, Tony, illus. 24p. (gr. 2 up). 1993. PLB 17.27 (*0-8368-1048-1*) Gareth Stevens Inc.
—Looking at... Tyrannosaurus Rex: A Dinosaur from the Cretaceous Period. Gibbons, Tony, illus. 24p. (gr. 2 up). 1993. PLB 17.27 (*0-8368-1049-X*) Gareth Stevens Inc.
—The New Dinosaur Collection, 6 titles. Gibbons, Tony, illus. (gr. 2 up). 1993. Set. PLB 103.60 (*0-8368-1043-0*) Gareth Stevens Inc.
Ames, Diane. The Buddy System. 1992. pap. 3.50 (*0-06-106075-5*, Harp PBks) HarpC.
—Campfire Secrets. 1992. pap. 3.50 (*0-06-106076-3*, Harp PBks) HarpC.
—Never Say Good-Bye. 1992. pap. 3.50 (*0-06-106077-1*, Harp PBks) HarpC.
—Summer Fling. 1992. pap. 3.50 (*0-06-106074-7*, Harp PBks) HarpC.
Ames, Evelyn E. & Trucano, Lucille. Becoming Male & Female. LC 88-63796. (Illus.). 116p. (gr. 9-12). 1988. pap. text ed. 12.00 (*0-935529-05-5*) Comprehen Health Educ.
Ames, Felicia. The Bird You Care For. 1970. pap. 1.75 (*0-451-07527-7*, E7527, Sig) NAL-Dutton.
—The Cat You Care For. 1968. pap. 3.50 (*0-451-13041-3*, Sig) NAL-Dutton.
Ames, Gerald & Wyler, Rose. Magic Secrets. Stubis, Talivaldis, illus. LC 67-4229. 64p. (gr. k-3). 1967. PLB 10.89 (*0-06-020069-3*) HarpC Child Bks.
Ames, Gerald, jt. auth. see Wyler, Rose.
Ames, Lee J. Draw Fifty Creepy Crawlies: The Step-by-Step Way to Draw Bugs, Slugs, Spiders, Scorpions. 1992. pap. 8.00 (*0-385-42449-3*) Doubleday.
Ames, Louise B. Why Am I So Noisy? Why Is She So Shy? 48p. (Orig.). (ps-8). 1991. pap. text ed. 7.95 (*0-935493-45-X*) Modern Learn Pr.
Ames, Mary. Memories of the Pasque & Prairie. Wong, Vera M., illus. Thornley, Phyllis, intro. by. (Illus.). 79p. (gr. 9-12). 1987. 13.95 (*0-9619407-0-0*) Country Messenger Inc.
Ames, Mildred. The Dancing Madness: A Novel. LC 80-65831. 144p. (gr. 7 up). 1980. 8.95 (*0-385-28113-7*) Delacorte.
—Grandpa Jake & the Grand Christmas. LC 90-8527. 112p. (gr. 5-7). 1990. SBE 13.95 (*0-684-19241-1*, Scribners Young Read) Macmillan Child Grp.
Amey, Peter. Imperialism. Yapp, Malcolm, et al, eds. (Illus.). (gr. 6-11). 1980. pap. text ed. 3.45 (*0-89908-201-7*) Greenhaven.
—Pax Romana. Yapp, Malcolm, et al, eds. (Illus.). 32p. (gr. 6-11). 1980. pap. text ed. 3.45 (*0-89908-002-2*) Greenhaven.
—The Scientific Revolution. Yapp, Malcolm, et al, eds. (Illus.). (gr. 6-11). 1980. pap. text ed. 3.45 (*0-89908-107-X*) Greenhaven.
Amey, Peter, et al. Leonardo Da Vinci. Yapp, Malcolm, et al, eds. (Illus.). (gr. 6-11). 1980. pap. text ed. 3.45 (*0-89908-016-2*) Greenhaven.
—Luther, Erasmus & Loyola. Yapp, Malcolm, et al, eds. (Illus.). (gr. 6-11). 1980. pap. text ed. 3.45 (*0-89908-018-9*) Greenhaven.
Amicis, Edmondo De see De Amicis, Edmondo.

Amico, Victoria, tr. see Hutchinson, Hanna.
Amigos en Recuperacio. Los Doce Pasos Para los Cristianos: De Familias Adictas y Disfuncionales. LC 93-25095. (SPA.). 144p. (gr. 12 up). 1993. pap. 7.95 (*0-941405-40-0*) Recovery CA.
Amini, Majid. Echo of a Cry. Koliai, Christina, ed. 172p. 1989. pap. text ed. write for info. Afsaneh Pub.
—Paradise Subverted. Kolia, Christina, ed. 350p. 1989. write for info. Afsaneh Pub.
Amir, Tami. The Brave Frog. Kriss, David, tr. from HEB. Elchanan, illus. 24p. (Orig.). (ps) 1992. pap. text ed. 3.00x (*1-56134-158-4*) Dushkin Pub.
—La Rana Valiente. Writer, C. C. & Nielsen, Lisa C., trs. Elchanan, illus. (SPA.). 24p. (Orig.). (ps) 1992. pap. text ed. 3.00x (*1-56134-168-1*) Dushkin Pub.
Amis, Kingsley. We Are All Guilty. 96p. (gr. 7 up). 1992. 14.00 (*0-670-84268-0*) Viking Child Bks.
Amis, Kingsley, ed. The Faber Popular Reciter. 256p. (gr. 10 up). 1979. pap. 9.95 (*0-571-11339-7*) Faber & Faber.
Ammann, Herman. The Little Troll Without a Soul. (Illus.). 27p. (Orig.). (gr. 4-9). 1976. pap. 2.00 (*0-88680-117-6*); royalty on application 20.00 (*0-685-59268-5*) I E Clark.
Ammann, Hermann. Little Match Girl: One-Act Dramatization. (Illus.). 36p. (gr. k up). 1970. pap. 7.50 director's script (*0-88680-112-5*); pap. 2.00 bk. (*0-88680-111-7*); royalty on application 20.00 (*0-685-57900-X*) I E Clark.
—Magic Well. (Illus.). 37p. (gr. k up). 1972. pap. 7.50 director's script (*0-88680-123-0*); pap. 2.00 bk. (*0-88680-122-2*); royalty on application 20.00 (*0-685-57902-6*) I E Clark.
—Steadfast Tin Soldier. (Illus.). 29p. (gr. 1 up). 1969. royalty on application 20.00 (*0-88680-187-7*); pap. 2.00 bk. (*0-88680-186-9*) I E Clark.
Ammon, Richard. Growing up Amish. LC 88-27493. (Illus.). 80p. (gr. 3-7). 1989. SBE 13.95 (*0-689-31387-X*, Atheneum Child Bk) Macmillan Child Grp.
—The Kids' Book of Chocolate. LC 86-26564. (Illus.). 96p. (gr. 3-7). 1987. SBE 12.95 (*0-689-31292-X*, Atheneum Child Bk) Macmillan Child Grp.
—Trains at Work. Ammon, Richard, illus. Peterson, Darrell, photos by. LC 92-33913. (Illus.). 32p. (gr. 1-5). 1993. SBE 14.95 (*0-689-31740-9*, Atheneum Child Bk) Macmillan Child Grp.
Ammons, Nelle P., jt. auth. see Core, Earl L.
Amnesty International, Human Rights for Children Committee Staff. Human Rights for Children. Sinetar, Marsha, illus. LC 92-35575. 80p. (Orig.). (gr. k-6). 1992. spiral bdg. 12.95 (*0-89793-120-3*); pap. 10.95 (*0-89793-121-1*) Hunter Hse.
Amore, JoAnn, jt. auth. see Farr, J. Michael.
Amos, Janine. Afraid. LC 90-46540. (Illus.). 32p. (ps-3). 1991. 15.96 (*0-8172-3775-5*); pap. 3.95 (*0-8114-6908-5*) Raintree Steck-V.
—Angry. LC 90-46540. (Illus.). 32p. (ps-3). 1991. 15.96 (*0-8172-3776-3*); pap. 3.95 (*0-8114-6909-3*) Raintree Steck-V.
—Animals in Danger. McAllister, David, illus. LC 92-16336. 32p. (gr. 2-3). 1992. PLB 18.99 (*0-8114-3404-4*) Raintree Steck-V.
—Feeding the World. LC 92-16337. (Illus.). 32p. (gr. 2-3). 1992. PLB 18.99 (*0-8114-3407-9*) Raintree Steck-V.
—Hurt. LC 90-46540. (Illus.). 32p. (ps-3). 1991. 15.96 (*0-8172-3777-1*); pap. 3.95 (*0-8114-6910-7*) Raintree Steck-V.
—Jealous. LC 90-46540. (Illus.). 32p. (ps-3). 1991. 15.96 (*0-8172-3778-X*); pap. 3.95 (*0-8114-6911-5*) Raintree Steck-V.
—Lonely. LC 90-46540. (Illus.). 32p. (ps-3). 1991. 15.96 (*0-8172-3779-8*); pap. 3.95 (*0-8114-6912-3*) Raintree Steck-V.
—Pollution. LC 92-16338. (Illus.). 32p. (gr. 2-3). 1992. PLB 18.99 (*0-8114-3405-2*) Raintree Steck-V.
—Pollution. (ps-3). 1993. pap. 3.95 (*0-8114-4917-3*) Raintree Steck-V.
—Sad. LC 90-46540. (Illus.). 32p. (ps-3). 1991. 15.96 (*0-8172-3780-1*); pap. 3.95 (*0-8114-6913-1*) Raintree Steck-V.
—Waste & Recycling. LC 92-16339. (Illus.). 32p. (gr. 2-3). 1992. PLB 18.99 (*0-8114-3406-0*) Raintree Steck-V.
Amos, W. J. Mia: Saigon. (ps-12). 1986. pap. 2.50 (*0-87067-274-6*, BH274) Holloway.
Amos, William H. Life in Ponds & Streams. Crump, Donald J., ed. LC 81-47745. 32p. (ps-3). 1981. lib. bdg. 16.95 (*0-87044-404-2*); PLB 13.95 (*0-87044-409-3*) Natl Geog.
Amos, William H. see National Geographic Society Staff.
Amos, Winsom. Youth Poems. Jones, Jean, illus. 24p. (Orig.). (gr. 6-12). 1983. pap. 1.75x (*0-932510-00-0*) Soma Pr.
Amoss, Berthe. Car Seat Games. (Illus.). 10p. (ps-7). 1989. pap. 2.95 (*0-922589-14-3*) More Than Card.
—Cinderella. Amoss, Berthe, illus. 10p. (ps-7). 1989. pap. 2.95 (*0-922589-04-6*) More Than Card.
—David & Goliath. (Illus.). 10p. (ps-7). 1989. pap. 2.95 (*0-922589-12-7*) More Than Card.
—Hansel & Gretel. Amoss, Berthe, illus. 10p. (ps-7). 1989. pap. 2.95 (*0-922589-05-4*) More Than Card.
—Jack & the Beanstalk. Amoss, Berthe, illus. 10p. (ps-7). 1989. pap. 2.95 (*0-922589-00-3*) More Than Card.
—Jonah. (Illus.). 10p. (ps-7). 1989. pap. 2.95 (*0-922589-09-7*) More Than Card.

—Little Red Riding Hood. (Illus.). 10p. (ps-7). 1989. pap. 2.95 (*0-922589-11-9*) More Than Card.
—Lost Magic. 192p. (gr. 5 up). 1993. 14.95 (*1-56282-573-9*) Hyprn Child.
—The Loup Garou. Amoss, Berthe, illus. LC 79-20536. 48p. (ps-4). 1979. 9.95 (*0-88289-189-8*) Pelican.
—Lullaby & Good Night. (Illus.). 10p. (ps-7). 1989. pap. 2.95 (*0-922589-13-5*) More Than Card.
—The Mockingbird Song. LC 87-45272. 128p. (gr. 4-7). 1988. HarpC Child Bks.
—Mother Goose Rhymes. Amoss, Berthe, illus. 10p. (ps-7). 1989. pap. 2.95 (*0-922589-02-X*) More Than Card.
—Noah. (Illus.). 10p. (ps-7). 1989. pap. 2.95 (*0-922589-10-0*) More Than Card.
—Old Hannibal & the Hurricane. Amoss, Berthe, illus. LC 91-71387. 32p. (ps-2). 1991. 14.95 (*1-56282-097-4*); PLB 14.89 (*1-56282-098-2*) Hyprn Child.
—Rumpelstiltskin. Amoss, Berthe, illus. 10p. (ps-7). 1989. pap. 2.95 (*0-922589-03-8*) More Than Card.
—Secret Lives. 192p. (gr. 1-9). 1981. pap. 2.95 (*0-440-47904-5*, YB) Dell.
—Snow White & the Seven Dwarfs. Amoss, Berthe, illus. 10p. (ps-7). 1989. pap. 2.95 (*0-922589-01-1*) More Than Card.
Amsel, Sheri. Cecils Montana Adventure Activity Book. (Illus.). 32p. (Orig.). (gr. 4-7). 1992. pap. 3.95 (*1-56044-138-0*) Falcon Pr MT.
—Deserts. Amsel, Sheri, illus. LC 92-8789. 32p. 1992. lib. bdg. 17.28 (*0-8114-6300-1*) Raintree Steck-V.
—Grasslands. Amsel, Sheri, illus. LC 92-8788. 32p. 1992. lib. bdg. 17.28 (*0-8114-6302-8*) Raintree Steck-V.
—A Wetland Walk. Amsel, Sheri, illus. 32p. (gr. k-3). 1993. PLB 14.90 (*1-56294-213-1*) Millbrook Pr.
—Wetland Walk. LC 92-5105. (ps-3). 1993. pap. 6.95 (*1-56294-719-2*) Millbrook Pr.
Amstutz, Andre, jt. auth. see Ahlberg, Allan.
Amstutz, Beverly. Benjamin & the Bible Donkeys. (Illus.). 36p. (gr. k-7). 1981. pap. 2.50x (*0-937836-03-6*) Precious Res.
—The Fly Has Lots of Eyes. (Illus.). 34p. (gr. k-9). 1981. pap. 2.50x (*0-937836-04-4*) Precious Res.
—I Love My Foster Grandparents. (Illus.). 24p. (gr. k-7). 1981. pap. 2.50x (*0-937836-06-0*) Precious Res.
—Moccasins & Sneakers. (Illus.). 24p. (gr. k-7). 1980. pap. 2.50x (*0-937836-02-8*) Precious Res.
—Sharing Is Fun. Amstutz, Beverly, illus. 24p. (gr. k-7). 1979. pap. 2.50x (*0-937836-00-1*) Precious Res.
—Sprouts: A Diary for the Foster Child. Amstutz, Beverly, illus. 38p. (Orig.). (gr. k-7). 1982. pap. 2.50x (*0-937836-07-9*) Precious Res.
—That Boy, That Girl. LC 80-80372. (Illus.). 24p. (gr. k-7). 1979. pap. 2.50x (*0-937836-01-X*) Precious Res.
—Too Big for the Bag. (Illus.). (gr. k-7). 1981. pap. 2.50x (*0-937836-05-2*) Precious Res.
—Touch Me Not! (Illus.). 20p. (ps-7). 1983. pap. 2.50x (*0-937836-09-5*) Precious Res.
—You Are Number One! (Illus.). 30p. (gr. k-9). 1982. pap. 2.50x (*0-937836-08-7*) Precious Res.
Amthor, Terry, ed. see Lindsay, A. Brook, III.
Amthor, Terry K. Action on Akaisha Outstation. 32p. (gr. 10-12). 1985. 6.00 (*0-915795-46-9*, 9101) Iron Crown Ent Inc.
—Rivendell, the House of Elrond. McBride, Angus, illus. 36p. (Orig.). (gr. 10-12). 1987. pap. 7.00 (*0-915795-87-6*, 8080) Iron Crown Ent Inc.
—Teeth of Mordor. Fenlon, Peter C., Jr., ed. Martin, David & Martin, Elissa, illus. 32p. (gr. 10-12). 1988. pap. 6.00 (*0-915795-96-5*, 8202) Iron Crown Ent Inc.
Amthor, Terry K., ed. see Foley, Tod.
Amthor, Terry K., ed. see Kane, Thomas.
Amthor, Terry K., ed. see LaDell, Leo.
Amuzegar, Hooshang, tr. see Behrangi, Samad.
Anand, Mulk R. Maya of Mohenjo-Daro. 3rd ed. Biswas, Pulak, illus. 24p. (Orig.). (gr. k-3). 1980. pap. 2.50 (*0-89744-214-8*, Pub. by Childrens Bk Trust IA) Auromere.
Anastasia, Dina. Bear Who Couldn't Do Anything. (ps-2). 1989. pap. text ed. 3.95 cased (*0-7214-5227-2*) Ladybird Bks.
Anastasio. Pass the Peas Please, Vol. 1. (gr. 3 up). 1992. pap. 5.95 (*0-316-03833-4*) Little.
Anastasio, Dina. Big Bird Can Share. Leigh, Tom, illus. 32p. (ps-k). 1985. write for info. (*0-307-12016-3*, Pub. by Golden Bks) Western Pub.
—Ghostwriter: Courting Danger & Other Stories. (ps-3). 1992. pap. 2.99 (*0-553-48070-7*) Bantam.
—It's about Time. Smith, Mavis, illus. 24p. (gr. k-3). 1993. 8.95 (*0-448-40551-2*, G&D) Putnam Pub Group.
—Joy to the World! Paterson, Bettina, illus. 32p. (ps-3). 1992. (G&D); pap. 2.25 (*0-448-40479-6*, G&D) Putnam Pub Group.
—My Own Book. (gr. 4-7). 1992. pap. 2.95 (*0-8431-0367-1*) Price Stern.
—My Secret Book. (gr. 4-7). 1992. pap. 2.95 (*0-8431-3373-2*) Price Stern.
—Sesame Street Counting Book. 1985. 1.00 (*0-307-02023-1*) Western Pub.
—The Teddy Bear Who Couldn't Do Anything. Loccisano, Karen, illus. 24p. 1993. 2.95 (*0-7214-3511-4*) Ladybird Bks.
Anatta, Ivan. Flowers. LC 92-35065. 1993. write for info. (*1-56766-005-3*) Childs World.
Anatta, Ivan M. Trees. LC 92-32286. 1993. write for info. (*1-56766-002-9*) Childs World.
Anchondo, Mary, jt. auth. see Rohmer, Harriet.

Ancona, George. The Aquarium Book. (Illus.). 48p. (gr. 3-6). 1991. 14.95 (0-89919-655-1, Clarion Bks) HM.
—Bananas. (gr. 4-7). 1990. pap. 5.70 (0-395-54787-3) HM.
—Bananas: From Manolo to Margie. Ancona, George, illus. 48p. (gr. 3-6). 1982. 15.95 (0-89919-100-2, Clarion Bks) HM.
—Helping Out. (ps-3). 1991. pap. 127.60 (0-395-55774-7, Clarion Bks) HM.
—Man & Mustang. Ancona, George, illus. LC 91-29513. 48p. (gr. 3-7). 1992. RSBE 15.95 (0-02-700802-9, Macmillan Child Bk) Macmillan Child Grp.
—My Camera. LC 91-2288. (Illus.). 48p. (Orig.). (gr. 2-7). 1992. PLB 15.99 (0-517-58280-5); pap. 8.99 (0-517-58279-1) Crown Bks Yng Read.
—Pablo Remembers. LC 92-22819. (gr. 4 up). 1993. write for info. (0-688-11249-8); lib. bdg. write for info. (0-688-11250-1) Lothrop.
—The Pinatamaker: El Pinatero. LC 93-2389. (gr. 5 up). 1994. write for info. (0-15-261875-9) HarBrace.
—Powwow. (gr. 4-7). 1993. pap. 8.95 (0-15-263269-7, HB Juv Bks) HarBrace.
—Riverkeeper. LC 89-36777. (Illus.). 48p. (gr. 3 up). 1990. RSBE 14.95 (0-02-700911-4, Macmillan Child Bk) Macmillan Child Grp.
—Sheep Dog. LC 84-20100. (Illus.). 64p. (gr. 5 up). 1985. 12.95 (0-688-04118-3); PLB 12.88 (0-688-04119-1) Lothrop.
—Turtle Watch. Ancona, George, photos by. LC 87-9316. (Illus.). 48p. (gr. 1-5). 1987. RSBE 14.95 (0-02-700910-6, Macmillan Child Bk) Macmillan Child Grp.

Ancona, George & Miller, Mary B. Handtalk Zoo. Ancona, George, illus. LC 88-36861. 32p. (ps up). 1989. RSBE 14.95 (0-02-700801-0, Four Winds) Macmillan Child Grp.

Ancona, George, jt. auth. see Miller, Mary Beth.

Ancona, George, photos by. Earth Keepers. Anderson, Joan, text by. LC 92-38627. (Illus.). 1993. 17.95 (0-15-242199-8) HarBrace.
—Powwow. LC 92-15912. (Illus.). 1993. write for info. (0-15-263268-9) HarBrace.

Anderheggen, George C. Willie the Weenie Whiner. (Illus.). 20p. (Orig.). (gr. 5 up). 1983. 3.95 (0-910717-01-X) Bookling Pubs.

Anders, Jeanne. Leslie. LC 86-72892. 160p. (gr. 9 up). 1987. pap. 3.99 (0-87123-927-2) Bethany Hse.

Andersdatter, Karla M. Follow the Blue Butterfly. Koff, Deborah, illus. (gr. 4-8). 1980. 6.00 (0-935430-00-8) In Between.
—Marissa the Tooth Fairy. write for info. In Between.
—Witches & Whimsies. write for info. In Between.

Andersen, Hans Christian. Andersen's Fairy Tales. LC 58-6191. (Illus.). 352p. (gr. 3-9). 1981. (G&D); deluxe ed 13.95 (0-448-06005-1) Putnam Pub Group.
—Andersen's Fairy Tales. 1991. lib. bdg. 250.00 (0-8490-4569-X) Gordon Pr.
—Andersen's Fairy Tales. (Illus.). 1992. write for info. (0-89434-122-7) Ferguson.
—Complete Hans Christian Andersen Fairy Tales. 1987. 11.99 (0-517-45375-4) Outlet Bk Co.
—Dulac's the Snow Queen: And Other Stories. Haugaard, Erik C., tr. Dulac, Edmund, illus. LC 76-7308. 144p. (ps up). 1976. 9.95 (0-385-11678-0) Doubleday.
—Emperor & the Nightingale. Watling, James, illus. LC 78-18065. 32p. (gr. k-4). 1979. PLB 9.79 (0-89375-134-0); pap. 1.95 (0-89375-112-X) Troll Assocs.
—The Emperor & the Nightingale. Van Nutt, Robert, illus. Tuber, Joel, adapted by. LC 88-11541. (Illus.). 44p. (gr. up). 1991. pap. 14.95 (0-88708-082-0, Rabbit Ears); bk. & cass. pkg. 19.95 (0-88708-087-1, Rabbit Ears) Picture Bk Studio.
—The Emperor's New Clothes. Burton, Virginia L., illus. LC 83-19610. 48p. (gr. k-3). 1979. pap. 5.70 (0-395-28594-1) HM.
—Emperor's New Clothes. Ford, Pamela B., illus. LC 78-18063. 32p. (gr. k-4). 1979. PLB 9.79 (0-89375-132-4); pap. 1.95 (0-89375-110-3) Troll Assocs.
—The Emperor's New Clothes. Westcott, Nadine B., illus. (ps-3). 1984. pap. 5.95 (0-316-93124-1) Little.
—The Emperor's New Clothes. Duntze, Dorothee, illus. LC 86-2509. 32p. (gr. k-3). 1986. 14.95 (1-55858-036-0) North-South Bks NYC.
—The Emperor's New Clothes. Alchemy II, Inc. Staff, illus. 26p. (ps). 1988. incl. cassette 9.95 (1-55578-901-3) Worlds Wonder.
—The Emperor's New Clothes. Metaxas, Eric, tr. Van Nutt, Robert, illus. LC 90-25376. 32p. (gr. k up). 1991. pap. 14.95 (0-88708-160-6, Rabbit Ears); pap. 19.95 incl. cassette (0-88708-161-4, Rabbit Ears) Picture Bk Studio.
—The Emperor's New Clothes. Levinson, Riki, retold by. Byrd, Robert, illus. LC 89-23820. 40p. (ps-2). 1991. 14.95 (0-525-44611-7, DCB) Dutton Child Bks.
—The Emperor's New Clothes. Easton, Samantha, retold by. Walz, Richard, illus. 1991. 6.95 (0-8362-4928-3) Andrews & McMeel.
—The Emperor's New Clothes. 1991. PLB 13.95s.p. (0-88682-479-6) Creative Ed.
—The Emperor's New Clothes. Layerfeld, Karl, illus. 1992. 40.00 (0-87113-527-2) Grove-Atltic.
—The Emperor's Nightingale. Slater, Teddy, retold by. LC 91-73807. (Illus.). 32p. (gr. k-3). 1992. 13.95 (1-56282-133-4); PLB 13.89 (1-56282-134-2) Disney Pr.

—The Emperor's Nightingale: A Classic Tale. Jose, Eduard, adapted by. Moncure, Jane B., tr. from SPA. Lavarello, Jose M., illus. LC 88-35209. 32p. (gr. 1-4). 1988. PLB 19.95 (0-89565-484-9); PLB 13.95s.p. (0-685-56034-1) Childs World.
—Fairy Tales. Thomas, Charles & Robinson, W. Heath, illus. Spink, Reginald, tr. LC 92-53178. 416p. 1992. 14.95 (0-679-41791-5, Evrymans Lib Childs Class) Knopf.
—Fairy Tales from Hans Christian Andersen. Ash, Russell & Higton, Bernard, eds. (Illus.). 128p. 1992. 16.95 (0-8118-0230-2) Chronicle Bks.
—The Fir Tree. Imsand, Marcel & Marshall, Rita, illus. 40p. (gr. 6 up). 1983. PLB 13.95s.p. (0-87191-949-4) Creative Ed.
—The Fir Tree. Burkert, Nancy E., illus. LC 73-121800. 48p. (ps up). 1986. pap. 5.95 (0-06-443109-6, Trophy) HarpC Child Bks.
—The Fir Tree. Goode, Diane, adapted by. & illus. LC 82-62172. 32p. (ps up). 1988. pap. 1.25 (0-394-81941-1) Random Bks Yng Read.
—Fir Tree. Britt, Stephanie, illus. 24p. (ps-3). 1989. pap. 2.95 (0-8249-8389-0, Ideals Child) Hambleton-Hill.
—Fir Tree. Watts, Bernadette, illus. LC 89-43730. (ps-3). 1990. 14.95 (1-55858-093-X) North-South Bks NYC.
—Four Tales from Hans Andersen: An Anniversary Edition. (Illus.). 96p. (ps up). 1986. 8.50 (0-521-33069-6) Cambridge U Pr.
—Hans Andersen: His Classic Fairy Tales. Haugaard, Erik C., tr. Foreman, Michael, illus. LC 77-74792. 196p. (gr. 1 up). 1978. 15.95 (0-385-13364-2) Doubleday.
—Hans Andersen's Fairy Tales. Kingsland, L. W., tr. Birkett, Rachel, illus. 268p. (ps-6). 1987. 18.95 (0-19-274532-8) OUP.
—Hans Andersen's Fairy Tales: A Selection. Frolich, Lorenz & Pedersen, Vilhelm, illus. Kingsland, L. W., tr. from DAN. Lewis, Naomi, intro. by. LC 84-7120. 1985. pap. 3.95 (0-19-281699-3) OUP.
—Hans Christian Andersen Fairy Tales. Zwerger, Lisbeth, selected by. Bell, Anthea, tr. from DAN. Zwerger, Lisbeth, illus. LC 91-13132. 68p. (ps up). 1992. 19.95 (0-88708-182-7) Picture Bk Studio.
—Hans Christian Andersen's Fairy Tales. Gotlieb, Jules, illus. LC 58-6191. (gr. 3 up). 1958. pap. 1.95 (0-8049-0169-4, CL-169) Airmont.
—It's Perfectly True! LC 87-7567. (Illus.). 32p. (ps-3). 1988. reinforced bdg. 13.95 (0-8234-0672-5) Holiday.
—Little Match Girl. Lent, Blair, illus. LC 68-28050. (gr. k-3). 1975. pap. 1.95 (0-685-02294-3) HM.
—The Little Match Girl. Isadora, Rachel, illus. 32p. (ps-3). 1990. 14.95 (0-399-21336-8, Sandcastle Bks); pap. 5.95 (0-399-22007-0, Sandcastle Bks) Putnam Pub Group.
—Little Match Girl. Augenstine, Erin, illus. 32p. (ps-3). 1992. 6.95 (0-8362-4931-3) Andrews & McMeel.
—The Little Match Girl: A Classic Tale. Jose, Eduard, adapted by. Suire, Diane D., tr. Rovira, Francesc, illus. LC 88-36868. 32p. (gr. 1-4). 1988. PLB 19.95 (0-89565-476-8); PLB 13.95s.p. (0-685-56046-5) Childs World.
—The Little Mermaid. Iwasaki, Chihiro, illus. LC 84-9490. 32p. (gr. 2 up). 1991. pap. 15.95 (0-907234-59-3) Picture Bk Studio.
—The Little Mermaid. Treherne, Katie T., adapted by. & illus. LC 89-31602. 42p. (gr. k-3). 1989. 15.95 (0-15-246320-8) HarBrace.
—The Little Mermaid. Iwasaki, Chihiro, illus. 1991. pap. 3.95 (0-590-44456-5) Scholastic Inc.
—The Little Mermaid. Officer, Robyn, illus. 32p. (ps-3). 1992. 6.95 (0-8362-4918-6) Andrews & McMeel.
—Little Mermaid. pap. 2.95 (0-88388-039-3) Bellerophon Bks.
—The Little Mermaid. Hague, Michael, illus. LC 92-29807. 1993. write for info. (0-8050-1010-6, Bks Young Read) H Holt & Co.
—The Little Mermaid: A Classic Tale. Jose, Eduard, adapted by. Moncure, Jane B., tr. Lavarello, Jose M., illus. LC 88-36869. 32p. (gr. 1-4). 1988. PLB 19.95 (0-89565-477-6); PLB 13.95s.p. (0-685-56045-7) Childs World.
—The Little Mermaid: A Step Three Book. Hautzig, Deborah, adapted by. May, Darcy, illus. LC 91-6632. 48p. (Orig.). (gr. 2-3). 1991. lib. bdg. 7.99 (0-679-92241-5); pap. 3.50 (0-679-82241-0) Random Bks Yng Read.
—The Little Mermaid & Other Fairy Tales. Kliros, Thea, illus. LC 93-14418. 96p. 1993. pap. 1.00 (0-486-27816-6) Dover.
—The Little Mermaid: The Original Story. Santore, Charles, illus. LC 93-20375. 1993. 14.00 (0-517-06495-2) Outlet Bk Co.
—Mary Engelbreit's The Snow Queen. Englebreit, Mary, illus. 48p. (ps-3). 1993. 15.95 (1-56305-438-8, 3438) Workman Pub.
—Michael Hague's Favourite Hans Christian Andersen Fairy Tales. Hague, Michael, illus. LC 81-47455. 168p. (ps-2). 1981. 19.95 (0-8050-0659-1, Bks Young Read) H Holt & Co.
—Die Nachtigall. Palecek, Josef, illus. (GER.). 40p. (gr. k-3). 1992. 13.95 (3-314-00521-0) North-South Bks NYC.
—Nightingale. Le Gallienne, Eva, tr. Burkert, Nancy E., illus. LC 64-18574. 48p. (gr. 3 up). 1965. PLB 14.89 (0-06-023781-3) HarpC Child Bks.
—The Nightingale. Zwerger, Lisbeth, illus. LC 84-9492. (gr. 1 up). 1991. pap. 14.95 (0-907234-57-7) Picture Bk Studio.

—The Nightingale. Le Gallienne, Eva, tr. from DAN. Burkert, Nancy E., illus. LC 64-18574. 48p. (gr. 2-6). 1985. pap. 7.95 (0-06-443070-7, Trophy) HarpC Child Bks.
—The Nightingale. Demi, illus. 32p. (ps-3). 1988. pap. 3.95 (0-15-257428-X, Voyager Bks) HarBrace.
—The Nightingale. Darke, Alison C., illus. 32p. (ps-3). 1989. 13.95 (0-385-26081-4, Zephyr-BFYR); (Zephyr-BFYR) Doubleday.
—The Nightingale. Palecek, Josef, illus. Lewis, Naomi, tr. LC 89-43723. (Illus.). 40p. (gr. k-3). 1990. 13.95 (1-55858-090-5) North-South Bks NYC.
—The Nightingale. Huerta, Catherine, illus. 32p. (ps-3). 1992. 6.95 (0-8362-4927-5) Andrews & McMeel.
—The Nightingale. Bell, Anthea, tr. from DAN. Zwerger, Lisbeth, illus. LC 92-6632. 28p. (gr. 4 up). 1993. Repr. Mini-bk. 4.95 (0-88708-269-6) Picture Bk Studio.
—The Nightingale: European Folk Tales. Wilson, Janet, illus. 24p. (ps-2). 1992. pap. 3.50 (0-88625-284-9) Durkin Hayes Pub.
—The Princess & the Pea. Galdone, Paul, illus. LC 77-12707. (ps-2). 1979. 14.45 (0-395-28807-X, Clarion Bks) HM.
—The Princess & the Pea. Stevens, Janet, adapted by. LC 81-13395. (Illus.). 32p. (ps-3). 1982. reinforced bdg. 14.95 (0-8234-0442-0); pap. 5.95 (0-8234-0753-5) Holiday.
—The Princess & the Pea. Duntze, Dorothee, illus. LC 85-7199. 32p. (gr. k-2). 1985. 14.95 (1-55858-034-4) North-South Bks NYC.
—The Princess & the Pea. Bell, Anthea, tr. Tharlet, Eve, illus. LC 87-13913. (ps up). 1991. pap. 13.95 (0-88708-052-9) Picture Bk Studio.
—The Princess & the Pea. Alchemy II, Inc. Staff, illus. 26p. (ps). 1988. incl. cassette 9.95 (1-55578-909-9) Worlds Wonder.
—The Princess & the Pea. Bell, Anthea, tr. from DAN. Tharlet, Eve, illus. LC 90-25386. 28p. (gr. k up). 1991. pap. 4.95 (0-88708-170-3) Picture Bk Studio.
—The Princess & the Pea. Stevenson, Sucie, retold by. & illus. LC 90-3212. 32p. (gr. k-3). 1992. pap. 15.00 (0-385-41375-0) Doubleday.
—The Princess & the Pea: A Classic Tale. Jose, Eduard, adapted by. Riehecky, Janet, tr. Rovira, Francesc, illus. LC 88-35206. 32p. (gr. 1-4). 1988. PLB 19.95 (0-89565-486-5); PLB 13.95s.p. (0-685-56037-6) Childs World.
—The Red Shoes. Iwasaki, Chihiro, illus. LC 82-61836. 36p. (gr. 3 up). 1991. pap. 15.95 (0-907234-26-7) Picture Bk Studio.
—The Red Shoes. (gr. 7-12). 1983. pap. 3.25x (0-19-421741-8) OUP.
—La Reine Des Neiges. Watts, Bernadette, illus. (FRE.). 32p. (gr. k-3). 1992. 14.95 (3-85539-629-9) North-South Bks NYC.
—Le Rossignol. Palecek, Josef, illus. (FRE.). 40p. (gr. k-3). 1992. 13.95 (3-314-20707-7) North-South Bks NYC.
—Rossignol de l'Empereur de Chine. Lemoine, Georges, illus. (FRE.). 56p. (gr. 3-7). 1990. pap. 8.95 (0-685-60280-X) Schoenhof.
—Die Schneekonigin. Watts, Bernadette, illus. (GER.). 32p. (gr. k-3). 1992. 14.95 (3-85825-292-1) North-South Bks NYC.
—Seven Tales retold by H. C. Andersen. Le Gallienne, Eva, retold by. Sendak, Maurice, illus. LC 59-16151. 144p. (gr. k up). 1991. pap. 7.95 (0-06-443172-X, Trophy) HarpC Child Bks.
—Seven Tales by Hans Christian Andersen. reissued ed. Le Gallienne, Eva, tr. from DAN. Sendak, Maurice, illus. LC 59-16151. 144p. (gr. 3 up). 1959. 13.95 (0-06-023790-2); PLB 13.89 (0-06-023791-0) HarpC Child Bks.
—The Snow Queen. Lewis, Naomi, adapted by. Bogdanovic, Toma, illus. LC 68-17218. 32p. (ps-5). 9.95 (0-87592-048-9) Scroll Pr.
—The Snow Queen. Lewis, Naomi, adapted by. Le Cain, Errol, illus. (ps-3). 1982. pap. 3.95 (0-14-050294-7, Puffin) Puffin Bks.
—The Snow Queen. Jeffers, Susan, illus. LC 82-70199. 40p. (gr. k up). 1982. 15.95 (0-8037-8011-7); PLB 12.89 (0-8037-8029-X); pap. 4.95 (0-8037-0692-8) Dial Bks Young.
—The Snow Queen. Hess, Dick & Edrigewcius, Stasys, illus. LC 83-71172. 48p. (gr. 6 up). 1984. PLB 13.95s.p. (0-87191-950-8) Creative Ed.
—The Snow Queen. Watts, Bernadette, illus. Bell, Anthea, adapted by. LC 87-1518. (Illus.). 32p. (gr. k-3). 1987. 14.95 (1-55858-053-0) North-South Bks NYC.
—The Snow Queen. Philip, Neil, tr. from DAN. Holmes, Sally, illus. LC 89-45289. 64p. 1989. 14.95 (0-688-09047-8); PLB 14.88 (0-688-09048-6) Lothrop.
—The Snow Queen. Lewis, Naomi, retold by. Barrett, Angela, illus. LC 92-54412. 48p. (ps up). 1993. 16.95 (1-56402-215-3) Candlewick Pr.
—The Steadfast Tin Soldier. Di Grazia, Thomas, adapted by. (Illus.). 32p. (gr. 1-4). 1981. 8.95 (0-13-846295-X) P-H.
—The Steadfast Tin Soldier. Lemoine, Georges, illus. 32p. 1983. PLB 13.95s.p. (0-87191-948-6) Creative Ed.
—The Steadfast Tin Soldier. Lewin, Simon, retold by. LC 91-71342. (Illus.). 32p. (gr. 1-4). 1991. 13.95 (1-56282-016-8); PLB 13.89 (1-56282-073-7) Disney Pr.
—The Steadfast Tin Soldier. Easton, Samantha, retold by. Montgomery, Michael, illus. 1991. 6.95 (0-8362-4929-1) Andrews & McMeel.

—The Steadfast Tin Soldier. Lynch, P. J., ed. 1992. write for info. (0-15-200599-4, Gulliver Bks) HarBrace.
—The Steadfast Tin Soldier. Seidler, Tor, retold by. Marcellino, Fred, illus. LC 92-52690. 32p. (ps-3). 1992. 15.00 (0-06-205000-1); PLB 14.89 (0-06-205001-X) HarpC Child Bks.
—The Steadfast Tin Soldier: A Classic Tale. Jose, Eduard, adapted by. Moncure, Jane B., tr. Asensio, Augusti, illus. LC 88-35207. 32p. (gr. 1-4). 1988. PLB 19.95 (0-89565-468-7); PLB 13.95s.p. (0-685-56024-4) Childs World.
—The Swineherd. Lewis, Naomi, tr. Duntze, Dorothee, illus. LC 86-62521. 32p. (gr. k-3). 1987. 14.95 (1-55858-038-7) North-South Bks NYC.
—The Swineherd. Hahn, Deborah, retold by. & illus. LC 90-6248. 32p. (gr. k up). 1991. 14.95 (0-688-10052-X); PLB 14.88 (0-688-10053-8) Lothrop.
—Thumbelina. Jeffers, Susan, illus. LC 79-50146. (ps-3). 1979. PLB 14.89 (0-8037-8814-2) Dial Bks Young.
—Thumbelina. Nigoghossian, Christine W., illus. LC 78-18080. 32p. (gr. k-4). 1979. PLB 9.79 (0-89375-141-3); pap. 1.95 (0-89375-119-7) Troll Assocs.
—Thumbelina. Roberts, Tom, adapted by. Johnson, David, illus. LC 89-8484. 32p. (gr. 1 up). 1991. pap. 14.95 (0-88708-113-4, Rabbit Ears); incl. cassette 19.95 (0-88708-114-2, Rabbit Ears) Picture Bk Studio.
—Thumbelina. abr. ed. Hautzig, Deborah, adapted by. Kaila, Karina, illus. Collins, Judy, contrib. by. (Illus.). 32p. (ps-5). 1990. Incl. 30 min. cassette. slipcased 15.95 (0-679-80810-8) Knopf Bks Yng Read.
—Thumbelina. abr. ed. Hautzig, Deborah, adapted by. Kaila, Karina, illus. LC 89-29700. 32p. (ps-3). 1990. PLB 10.99 (0-679-90667-3) Knopf Bks Yng Read.
—Thumbelina. Jeffers, Susan, illus. LC 79-50146. 32p. (ps-3). 1985. pap. 5.95 (0-8037-0232-9) Dial Bks Young.
—Thumbelina. Officer, Robyn, illus. 32p. (ps-3). 1992. 6.95 (0-8362-4926-7) Andrews & McMeel.
—Thumbelina. McGillis, Kelly, read by. Johnson, David, illus. Isham, Mark, contrib. by. (Illus.). 32p. (ps up). 1992. pap. write for info. slipcase pkg., incl. cassette (0-307-14331-7, 14331, Golden Pr) Western Pub.
—Thumbelina. 1992. pap. 2.99 (0-8125-2318-0) Tor Bks.
—Thumbelina. Johnson, David, illus. 64p. 1992. Repr. of 1989 ed. Mini-bk. incl. cass. 9.95 (0-88708-256-4, Rabbit Ears) Picture Bk Studio.
—Thumbelina: A Classic Tale. Jose, Eduard, adapted by. Riehecky, Janet, tr. Rovira, Francesc, illus. LC 88-35307. 32p. (gr. 1-4). 1988. PLB 19.95 (0-89565-466-0); PLB 13.95s.p. (0-685-56022-8) Childs World.
—Thumbelina & Other Stories. LC 88-43554. 96p. 1989. 4.95 (0-89471-722-7) Running Pr.
—Thumbeline. Zwerger, Lisbeth, illus. LC 85-12062. 28p. (gr. 1 up). 1991. pap. 14.95 (0-88708-006-5) Picture Bk Studio.
—Thumbeline. abr. ed. Bell, Anthea, tr. from DAN. Zwerger, Lisbeth, illus. LC 90-25387. 28p. (gr. k up). 1991. pap. 4.95 (0-88708-171-1) Picture Bk Studio.
—The Tin Soldier. (gr. k-6). 1983. pap. 3.25x (0-19-421742-6) OUP.
—The Tinderbox. Moser, Barry, adapted by. Hutton, Warwick, illus. LC 88-9206. 32p. (gr. 1 up). 1988. SBE 14.95 (0-689-50458-6, M K McElderry) Macmillan Child Grp.
—Tinderbox, Vol. 1. (ps-9). 1990. 14.95 (0-316-03938-1) Little.
—The Top & the Ball. Nyman, Elisabeth, illus. 32p. (gr. k-3). 1992. 14.95 (0-8249-8547-8, Ideals Child); PLB 15.00 (0-8249-8583-4) Hambleton-Hill.
—Twelve Tales. Blegvad, Erik, tr. & illus. LC 93-6927. 1994. write for info. (0-689-50584-1, M K McElderry) Macmillan Child Grp.
—The Ugly Duckling. Bogdanovic, Toma, illus. LC 75-145207. 32p. (ps-3). 9.95 (0-87592-055-1) Scroll Pr.
—Ugly Duckling. Williams, Jennie, illus. LC 78-18059. 32p. (gr. k-2). 1979. PLB 9.79 (0-89375-128-6); pap. 1.95 (0-89375-106-5) Troll Assocs.
—The Ugly Duckling. (gr. k-6). 1983. pap. 3.25x (0-19-421704-3) OUP.
—The Ugly Duckling. Van Nutt, Robert, illus. LC 86-185. 48p. (gr. k up). 1986. 12.95 (0-394-88403-5); incl. cassette 15.95 (0-394-88298-9) Knopf Bks Yng Read.
—The Ugly Duckling. Mayer, Marianna, retold by. Locker, Thomas, illus. LC 85-23869. 40p. (ps up). 1987. RSBE 16.95 (0-02-765130-4, Macmillan Bk) Macmillan Child Grp.
—The Ugly Duckling. Moore, Lilian, retold by. San Souci, Daniel, illus. 48p. (ps-2). 1988. pap. 3.95 (0-590-43794-1); incl. cassette 5.95 (0-590-63231-0) Scholastic Inc.
—The Ugly Duckling. Bell, Anthea, tr. Marks, Alan, illus. LC 89-3975. 42p. (gr. k up). 1991. pap. 14.95 (0-88708-116-9) Picture Bk Studio.
—The Ugly Duckling. Howell, Troy, retold by. & illus. 40p. 1990. 15.95 (0-399-22158-1, Putnam) Putnam Pub Group.
—The Ugly Duckling. (Illus.). 24p. (ps up). 1990. write for info. (0-307-12106-2, Pub. by Golden Bks) Western Pub.
—Ugly Duckling. Ross, Katherine, adapted by. LC 90-61004. (Illus., Orig.). (ps-2). 1991. pap. 2.25 (0-679-81039-0) Random Bks Yng Read.
—Ugly Duckling. Officer, Robyn, illus. 32p. (ps-3). 1992. 6.95 (0-8362-4911-9) Andrews & McMeel.

—The Ugly Duckling. (Illus.). 32p. (gr. k-3). 1993. pap. 2.99 (0-87406-656-5) Willowisp Pr.
—The Ugly Duckling: A Classic Tale. Jose, Eduard, adapted by. McDonnell, Janet, tr. Asensio, Augusti, illus. LC 88-36795. 32p. (gr. 1-4). 1988. PLB 19.95 (0-89565-474-1); PLB 13.95s.p. (0-685-56044-9) Childs World.
—The Ugly Duckling & Other Fairy Tales. (Illus.). 96p. (Orig.). 1992. pap. 1.00t (0-486-27081-5) Dover.
—The Wild Swans. Jeffers, Susan, illus. Ehrlich, Amy, retold by. LC 81-65843. (Illus.). 40p. (gr. k up). 1976. 15.95 (0-8037-9381-2) Dial Bks Young.
—The Wild Swans. Milone, Karen, illus. LC 80-27685. 32p. (gr. k-4). 1981. PLB 9.79 (0-89375-480-3); pap. text ed. 1.95 (0-89375-481-1) Troll Assocs.
—Wild Swans. Jeffers, Susan, illus. LC 81-65843. 40p. (gr. k up). 1987. pap. 5.95 (0-8037-0451-8) Dial Bks Young.
—The Wild Swans. Hautzig, Deborah, adapted by. Kaila, Kaarina, illus. LC 91-47879. 32p. (gr. k-3). 1992. 12.00 (0-679-83446-X); PLB 12.99 (0-679-93446-4) Knopf Bks Yng Read.
Andersen, Hans Christian, jt. auth. see Hawthorne, Nathaniel.
Andersen, Hans Christian, jt. auth. see Tolstoy, Leo.
Andersen, Karen B. An Alphabet in Five Acts. Born, Flint, illus. LC 92-26947. 32p. 1993. 13.99 (0-8037-1440-8); PLB 13.89 (0-8037-1441-6) Dial Bks Young.
Andersen, Maria. Howlin' Marie. Elgaard, Elin, tr. 140p. (gr. 9-12). 1985. 7.95 (0-920806-71-6, Pub. by Penumbra Pr CN) U of Toronto Pr.
Andersen, T. J. Baja Cars. LC 87-29022. (Illus.). 48p. (gr. 5-6). 1988. RSBE 11.95 (0-89686-357-3, Crestwood Hse) Macmillan Child Grp.
—Power Boat Racing. LC 87-30502. (Illus.). 48p. (gr. 5-6). 1988. RSBE 11.95 (0-89686-359-X, Crestwood Hse) Macmillan Child Grp.
Andersen, Torsten. The Christmas Before: Adventures in Babyland & Beyond. 1992. text ed. 7.95 (0-533-10136-0) Vantage.
—Debbie Dare. 1992. 7.95 (0-533-10279-0) Vantage.
Andersen, Yvonne. Make Your Own Animated Movies & Videotapes, Vol. 1. Andersen, Yvonne, illus. (gr. 7 up). 1991. 19.95 (0-316-03941-1) Little.
Anderson, Brad. Marmaduke: Sitting Pretty. 128p. (gr. 9). 1986. pap. 1.95 (0-8125-7350-1) Tor Bks.
Anderson, C. W. Billy & Blaze. (Illus.). 56p. 1992. Repr. PLB 11.95x (0-89966-947-6) Buccaneer Bks.
—Billy & Blaze: A Boy & His Pony. 2nd ed. LC 91-29882. (Illus.). 56p. (gr. k-3). 1992. pap. 3.95 (0-689-71608-7, Aladdin) Macmillan Child Grp.
—Blaze & the Forest Fire: Billy & Blaze Spread the Alarm. 2nd ed. LC 91-26586. (Illus.). 56p. (gr. k-3). 1992. pap. 3.95 (0-689-71605-2, Aladdin) Macmillan Child Grp.
—Blaze & the Lost Quarry: Story & Pictures. Anderson, C. W., illus. LC 93-10721. 48p. (gr. k-3). 1994. pap. 3.95 (0-689-71775-X, Aladdin) Macmillan Child Grp.
—Blaze & the Mountain Lion: Billy & Blaze to the Rescue. Anderson, C. W., illus. LC 92-27148. 48p. (gr. k-3). 1993. pap. 3.95 (0-689-71711-3, Aladdin) Macmillan Child Grp.
—Blaze & Thunderbolt: Billy & Blaze Head West. Anderson, C. W., illus. LC 92-27153. 48p. (gr. k-3). 1993. pap. 3.95 PB (0-689-71712-1, Aladdin) Macmillan Child Grp.
—Blaze Shows the Way: Story & Pictures. Anderson, C. W., illus. LC 93-1454. 48p. (gr. k-3). 1994. pap. 3.95 (0-689-71776-8, Aladdin) Macmillan Child Grp.
Anderson, Carol J. Alphabet Soup. Harding, Trish T., illus. 60p. (gr. k-4). 1989. 12.95 (0-935317-26-0) Blue Heron WA.
Anderson, Carolyn. How to Protect Your Child from Becoming a Missing Person. 46p. (ps-7). 1992. wkbk., incl. audiotape 12.00 (1-883778-00-X); audiotape 5.00 (0-685-68073-8) Starlite Prods.
Anderson, Catherine, ed. see Theo Carus Harter, Kaboblin.
Anderson, Catherine C. John F. Kennedy. (Illus.). 112p. (gr. 5 up). 1991. PLB 21.50 (0-8225-4904-2) Lerner Pubns.
Anderson, Dale. Battles that Changed the Modern World. Gerstle, Gary, contrib. by. LC 93-17028. (Illus.). 48p. (gr. 5-7). 1993. PLB 22.80 (0-8114-4928-9) Raintree Steck-V.
—Explorers Who Found New Worlds. LC 93-19016. (Illus.). 48p. (gr. 5-7). 1993. PLB 22.80 (0-8114-4931-9) Raintree Steck-V.
Anderson, David & Holland, I. I., eds. Forests & Forestry. 4th ed. (gr. 10-12). 1990. 38.60 (0-8134-2854-8); text ed. 28.95 (0-8134-2855-6); tchr's. manual 6.95 (0-685-45077-5) Interstate.
Anderson, David A. The Origin of Life on Earth: An African Creation Myth. Wilson, Kathleen A., illus. 32p. 1991. PLB 18.95 (0-9629978-5-4) Sights Prods.
—What You Can See, You Can Be! Jones, Don, illus. 48p. (Orig.). (gr. 3-8). 1988. 11.95 (0-87516-603-2) DeVorss.

Anderson, David A. & Sankofa. The Rebellion of Humans. Wilson, Kathleen A., illus. 32p. 1993. 18.95 (0-9629978-6-2) Sights Prods. This book, the second in a trilogy of African creation & early mythology, starts where the 1992 African Studies Association African Children's Book Award Winner, THE ORIGIN OF LIFE ON EARTH ends. The narrative tells of humankind's loss of respect for life & its responsibilities, & of the calamities that befall civilization as a result. The story centers on the struggle of one Yoruban individual who attains awareness & ponders how to transmit his knowledge to others. This volume continues the ORIGIN OF LIFE ON EARTH's (ISBN 0-9629978-5-4, $18.95) focus, about which the SCHOOL LIBRARY JOURNAL said, "This story's themes of determination, effort, generosity & the sacredness of life, as well as the attractive art, extend its appeal beyond myth, religion or ethnic collections." Volume discounts available from the publisher. ISBN 0-9629978-6-2, $18.95, SIGHTS PRODUCTIONS, P.O. Box 101, Mt. Airy, MD 21771. Telephone: 410-795-4582; FAX: 301-829-2585. *Publisher Provided Annotation.*

Anderson, Debbie S. Daniel & the Sand Angel: A Florida Christmas Story. Broderick, Michael, illus. 32p. (Orig.). (ps-4). 1988. pap. 9.95 (0-936417-11-0) Axelrod Pub.
Anderson, Debby. All Year Long. (ps-1). 1986. comb bdg. 3.49 (1-55513-043-7, Chariot Bks) Cook.
—Friends. Anderson, Debby, illus. 32p. (ps). 1986. plastic comb bdg. 3.95 (0-89191-932-5, 59329, Chariot Bks) Cook.
—God Is with Me. (ps-1). 1986. comb bdg. 3.95 (0-89191-269-X, Chariot Bks) Cook.
—God Is with Me. Anderson, Debby, illus. 32p. (gr. k-2). 1991. pasted 2.50 (0-87403-821-9, 24-03921) Standard Pub.
—God Loves Even Me. Anderson, Debby, illus. 32p. (gr. k-2). 1991. pasted 2.50 (0-87403-820-0, 24-03920) Standard Pub.
—Here & There, Everywhere! (Illus.). 18p. (ps). 1988. bds. 4.99 (1-55513-643-5, Chariot Bks) Cook.
—Jesus Loves Me. (Illus.). 18p. (ps). 1988. bds. 4.99 (1-55513-647-8, Chariot Bks) Cook.
—Jesus Loves the Little Children. (ps). 1993. 4.99 (0-7814-0687-0) Cook.
—My Friend Noah. (Illus.). 18p. (ps). 1988. bds. 4.99 (1-55513-665-6, Chariot Bks) Cook.
Anderson, Deborah & Finne, Martha. Liza's Story: Neglect & the Police. Swofford, Jeanette, illus. LC 85-25379. 48p. (gr. 1-4). 1986. RSBE 11.95 (0-87518-323-9, Dillon) Macmillan Child Grp.
—Michael's Story: Emotional Abuse & Working with a Counselor. Swofford, Jeanette, illus. LC 85-25400. 48p. (gr. 1-4). 1986. RSBE 11.95 (0-87518-322-0, Dillon) Macmillan Child Grp.
—Robin's Story: Physical Abuse & Seeing the Doctor. Swofford, Jeanette, illus. LC 85-25383. 48p. (gr. 1-4). 1986. RSBE 9.95 (0-87518-321-2, Dillon) Macmillan Child Grp.
Anderson, Deborah, jt. auth. see Evans, Mary J.
Anderson, Ella. Jo-Jo. (gr. 2-7). 1979. pap. 2.95 (0-87508-693-4) Chr Lit.
Anderson, George. American Family Farm. (gr. 3 up). 1989. 18.95 (0-15-203025-5) HarBrace.
Anderson, Gretchen, ed. The Louisa May Alcott Cookbook. Milone, Karen, illus. 96p. (gr. 3 up). 1985. 12.95 (0-316-03951-9) Little.
Anderson, Honey & Reinholdt, Bill. Don't Cut down This Tree. Ruth, Trevor, illus. LC 92-21446. 1993. 3.75 (0-383-03621-6) SRA Schl Grp.
—Getting the Mail. Fleming, Leanne, illus. LC 92-34338. 1993. 3.75 (0-383-03624-0) SRA Schl Grp.
—What Are You Called? Bruere, Justin, illus. LC 92-31953. 1993. 3.75 (0-383-03604-6) SRA Schl Grp.
Anderson, J. I. I Can Read About Dogs & Puppies. LC 72-96455. (Illus.). (gr. 2-4). 1973. pap. 1.95 (0-89375-053-0) Troll Assocs.
—I Can Read About Johnny Appleseed. Krasnoborski, William, illus. LC 76-54445. (gr. 2-5). 1977. pap. 1.95 (0-89375-037-9) Troll Assocs.
—I Can Read About Paul Bunyan. Snyder, Joel, illus. LC 76-54494. (gr. 2-5). 1977. pap. 1.95 (0-89375-041-7) Troll Assocs.
—I Can Read About Pecos Bill. Killgrew, John, illus. LC 76-54575. (gr. 2-5). 1977. pap. 1.95 (0-89375-042-5) Troll Assocs.
—I Can Read About the First Thanksgiving. McKeown, Gloria, illus. LC 76-54400. (gr. 2-5). 1977. pap. 1.95 (0-89375-034-4) Troll Assocs.
—I Can Read About Whales & Dolphins. LC 72-96955. (Illus.). (gr. 2-4). 1973. pap. 1.95 (0-89375-052-2) Troll Assocs.
Anderson, J. K. Birds of California. (gr. 1-9). 1992. pap. 3.95 (0-88388-101-2) Bellerophon Bks.

—Castles. (gr. 1-9). 1992. pap. 3.95 *(0-88388-088-1)* Bellerophon Bks.

—Castles of Scotland. (gr. 1-9). 1992. pap. 3.95 *(0-88388-111-X)* Bellerophon Bks.

—Gorgons. (gr. 1-9). 1992. pap. 3.95 *(0-88388-109-8)* Bellerophon Bks.

—Unicorns-Coloring Book. 1985. pap. 3.95 *(0-88388-086-5)* Bellerophon Bks.

Anderson, James, tr. see Va, Leong.

Anderson, Janet. A Hug for a New Friend. Kong, Emilie, illus. 40p. (ps). 4.00 *(0-910313-88-1)* Parker Bros.

Anderson, Janet S. The Happy Birthday Hug. Ewers, Joe, illus. LC 85-9476. 32p. (ps-3). 1985. pap. 0.99 *(0-87372-006-7)*; 3.50 *(0-910313-90-3)* Parker Bros.

Anderson, Jean, ed. see Bullock, Harold B.

Anderson, Jeff, jt. auth. see Murray, Terry.

Anderson, Jill. Bright Beginnings Storybook: Building Self-Esteem Skills with Pumsy. Soasey, Beverly, illus. 42p. (gr. k-1). 1990. text ed. 3.95 *(0-9608284-7-8)*; leader's guide 80.00 *(0-9608284-6-X)* Timberline Pr.

—The Land of No. Blackwelder, Kathy, ed. Magnuson, Diana, illus. LC 87-51628. 40p. (gr. 1-4). 1990. PLB 14.95 *(0-9608284-5-1)* Timberline Pr.

—Pumsy Storybook. Soasey, Beverly, illus. 40p. (Orig.). (gr. 1-4). 1990. pap. text ed. 3.95 *(0-9608284-2-7)* Timberline Pr.

—Thinking, Changing, Rearranging: Improving Self Esteem in Young People. LC 88-2289. (Illus.). 80p. (gr. 2). 1990. Repr. of 1981 ed. wkbk. 7.50 *(0-943920-30-2)* Metamorphous Pr.

Anderson, Jill & Weinman, Susan. Skill Builders: Course Code 392-2. Schroeder, Bonnie & Doheny, Catherine, eds. Anastasia, Karyn & Black, Jean, illus. 90p. (gr. 4). 1989. pap. text ed. 5.95 *(0-917531-88-4)* CES Compu-Tech.

Anderson, Joan. Christmas on the Prairie. Ancona, George, illus. LC 85-4095. 48p. (gr. 2-6). 1985. 14.95 *(0-89919-307-2,* Clarion Bks) HM.

—Christopher Columbus: From Vision to Voyage. (gr. 4-7). 1991. 14.95 *(0-8037-1041-0)*; PLB 14.89 *(0-8037-1042-9)* Dial Bks Young.

—The First Thanksgiving Feast. Ancona, George, photos by. LC 84-5803. (Illus.). 48p. (gr. 2-6). 1984. 14.95 *(0-89919-287-4,* Clarion Bks) HM.

—The First Thanksgiving Feast. Ancona, George, photos by. LC 84-58040. (Illus.). (gr. 3-6). 1989. pap. 5.70 *(0-395-51886-5,* Clarion Bks) HM.

—From Map to Museum: Uncovering Mysteries of the Past. Ancona, George, photos by. LC 87-31307. (Illus.). 64p. (gr. 3-7). 1988. 12.95 *(0-688-06914-2)*; PLB 12.88 *(0-688-06915-0,* Morrow Jr Bks) Morrow Jr Bks.

—The Glorious Fourth at Prairietown. Ancona, George, photos by. LC 85-28417. (Illus.). 48p. (gr. 2-6). 1986. 11.95 *(0-688-06246-6)*; lib. bdg. 11.88 *(0-688-06247-4,* Morrow Jr Bks) Morrow Jr Bks.

—Harry's Helicopter. Ancona, George, photos by. LC 89-28601. (Illus.). 32p. (gr. k up). 1990. 13.95 *(0-688-09186-5)*; PLB 13.88 *(0-688-09187-3,* Morrow Jr Bks) Morrow Jr Bks.

—Joshua's Westward Journal. Ancona, George, illus. LC 87-5509. 48p. (gr. 2-5). 1987. 13.00 *(0-688-06680-1)*; lib. bdg. 12.88 *(0-688-06681-X,* Morrow Junior Books) Morrow Jr Bks.

—Richie's Rocket. Ancona, George, illus. LC 92-38417. 32p. (gr. k up). 1993. 15.00 *(0-688-11304-4)*; PLB 14.93 *(0-688-11305-2)* Morrow Jr Bks.

—Seventeen Eighty-Seven. (Illus.). 200p. (gr. 3-7). 1987. 14.95 *(0-15-200582-X)* HarBrace.

—Spanish Pioneers of the Southwest. Ancona, George, photos by. LC 88-16121. (Illus.). 64p. (gr. 2-6). 1989. 14.95 *(0-525-67264-8,* Lodestar Bks) Dutton Child Bks.

—Twins on Toes: A Ballet Debut. Ancona, George, photos by. LC 92-35104. (Illus.). 32p. (gr. 3-7). 1993. 14.99 *(0-525-67415-2,* Lodestar Bks) Dutton Child Bks.

Anderson, Joan F., jt. auth. see Pugh, Ann.

Anderson, Joan W. Pioneer Children of Appalachia. (gr. 4-7). 1990. pap. 5.70 *(0-395-54792-X,* Clarion Bks) HM.

—Williamsburg Household. LC 87-33803. (gr. 4-7). 1990. pap. 5.70 *(0-395-54791-1,* Clarion Bks) HM.

Anderson, John A. & Groten, Frank J., Jr. Latin: A Course for Schools & Colleges. rev. ed. LC 71-102077. (Illus.). 357p. (gr. 7-12). 1988. Repr. of 1970 ed. 20.00x *(0-942573-00-5)* Hill School.

Anderson, John K. Horses & Riding. Conkle, Nancy, illus. 48p. (gr. 7-9). 1979. pap. 3.95 *(0-88388-066-0)* Bellerophon Bks.

Anderson, John W. The Tale of the Great Fruit Tree. Stout, John W., illus. 40p. 1992. 15.00 *(0-9633296-0-X)* Koinonia TX.

Anderson, Joy. Juma & the Magic Jinn. Mikolaycak, Charles, illus. LC 85-23815. 40p. (gr. 1-3). 1986. 12.95 *(0-688-05443-9)*; PLB 12.88 *(0-688-05444-7)* Lothrop.

Anderson, Julian G. The New Testament in Everyday American English. rev. ed. RKB Studios Staff, illus. x, 886p. (gr. 10 up). 1989. pap. 4.95 *(0-685-27817-4)* Anderson Bks.

Anderson, Karen. Games Junior Kid's Big Book of Games. LC 89-40727. (Illus.). 176p. (Orig.). (gr. 1-7). 1990. pap. 8.95 *(0-89480-657-2,* 1657) Workman Pub.

—Games Magazine Presents Kids' Giant Book of Games. 1993. pap. 12.00 *(0-8129-2199-2,* Times Bks) Random.

Anderson, Karen C. Disney's Big Book of Puzzlers: Picture Puzzles, Brainteasers, Games, Mazes, & More. LC 91-73805. (Illus.). 176p. (gr. 2-7). 1992. pap. 9.95 *(1-56282-067-2)* Disney Pr.

Anderson, Karen C., jt. auth. see Cumbaa, Stephen.

Anderson, Kathleen. Old Mission San Luis Obispo de Tolosa: A Miniature Cut-Out & Color Model. Fast, Marti, illus. 8p. (Orig.). (gr. 4). 1990. pap. 3.95 *(0-945092-12-1)* EZ Nature.

Anderson, Kathy. Sweet & Sassy: Counted Cross Stitch Designs for Children & Beginners. 32p. (Orig.). 1983. pap. 5.95 *(0-88290-216-4)* Horizon Utah.

Anderson, Kathy P. Illinois: Hello U. S. A. (gr. 4-7). 1993. 17.50 *(0-8225-2723-5)* Lerner Pubns.

Anderson, Kelly. Immigration. (Illus.). 112p. (gr. 5-8). 1993. PLB 14.95 *(1-56006-140-5)* Lucent Bks.

Anderson, L. W. Light & Color. new ed. LC 87-23225. (Illus.). 48p. (gr. 2-6). 1987. PLB 18.64 *(0-8172-3257-5)* Raintree Steck-V.

Anderson, LaVere. Martha Washington: First Lady of the Land. Cary, illus. 80p. (gr. 2-6). 1991. Repr. of 1973 ed. lib. bdg. 12.95 *(0-7910-1452-5)* Chelsea Hse.

—Mary McLeod Bethune: Teacher with a Dream. (Illus.). 80p. (gr. 2-6). 1991. Repr. of 1976 ed. lib. bdg. 12.95 *(0-7910-1405-3)* Chelsea Hse.

—Mary Todd Lincoln: President's Wife. Cary, illus. 80p. (gr. 2-6). 1991. Repr. of 1975 ed. lib. bdg. 12.95 *(0-7910-1415-0)* Chelsea Hse.

Anderson, Lena. Bunny Bath. Anderson, Lena, illus. LC 89-63049. (ps-k). 1991. bds. 3.95 *(91-29-59652-1)* R & S Books.

—Bunny Box. (Illus.). 20p. (ps). 1991. bds. 3.95 *(91-29-59858-3,* Pub. by R&S Bks) FS&G.

—Bunny Fun. (Illus.). 20p. (ps). 1991. bds. 3.95 *(91-29-59860-5,* Pub. by R&S Bks) FS&G.

—Bunny Surprise. Anderson, Lena, illus. LC 89-63050. (ps-k). 1991. bds. 3.95 *(91-29-59654-8)* R & S Books.

—Stina. (Illus.). 40p. (gr. k up). 1989. 11.95 *(0-688-08880-5)*; PLB 11.88 *(0-688-08881-3)* Greenwillow.

—Stina's Visit. LC 89-77716. (Illus.). 32p. (ps up). 1991. 13.95 *(0-688-09665-4)*; PLB 13.88 *(0-688-09666-2)* Greenwillow.

Anderson, Lena, illus. Bunny Party. (ps). 1989. bds. 3.95 *(91-29-59134-1,* Pub. by R & S Bks) FS&G.

—Bunny Story. (ps). 1989. bds. 3.95 *(91-29-59132-5,* Pub. by R & S Bks) FS&G.

Anderson, Leone C. Surprise at Muddy Creek. Endres, Helen, illus. 32p. (gr. 1-3). 1990. PLB 19.95 *(0-89565-698-1)*; PLB 13.95s.p. *(0-685-56164-X)* Childs World.

Anderson, Lisa. Proud to Be Me, Peewee Platypus. Messer, Cathy, illus. 40p. (Orig.). (ps-4). 1990. pap. 12.95 *(0-9628323-0-8)* Ridge Enter.

Anderson, Lydia M., jt. auth. see Ptacek, Greg.

Anderson, Lydia M., jt. auth. see Weidt, Maryann N.

Anderson, Lynn. If I Really Believe, Why Do I Have These Doubts? 224p. (Orig.). 1992. pap. 7.99 *(1-55661-182-X)* Bethany Hse.

Anderson, Lynne, jt. auth. see Terry, Ellen.

Anderson, M. The Unsinkable Molly Malone. (gr. 7 up). 1991. 16.95 *(0-15-213801-3,* HB Juv Bks) HarBrace.

Anderson, Madelyn K. Arthritis. LC 89-5745. (Illus.). 93p. (gr. 5-9). 1989. PLB 12.90 *(0-531-10801-5)* Watts.

—Edgar Allan Poe, a Mystery. (Illus.). 176p. (gr. 9-12). 1993. PLB 14.40 *(0-531-13012-6)* Watts.

—Edgar Allan Poe: A Mystery. (Illus.). 176p. (gr. 7-12). 1993. pap. 6.95 *(0-531-15678-8)* Watts.

—Environmental Diseases. LC 87-8117. (Illus.). 72p. (gr. 4-9). 1987. PLB 10.90 *(0-531-10382-X)* Watts.

—The Nez Perce. LC 93-31422. 1994. write for info. *(0-531-20063-9)*; pap. write for info. *(0-531-15686-9)* Watts.

—Oil Spills. LC 90-32896. (Illus.). 64p. (gr. 5-8). 1990. PLB 12.90 *(0-531-10872-4)* Watts.

—Robert E. Peary & the Fight for the North Pole. Rosoff, Iris, ed. (Illus.). 176p. (gr. 9-12). 1992. 14.45 *(0-531-15246-4)*; PLB 14.40 *(0-531-13004-5)* Watts.

Anderson, Marcie. Exploring Fifty States. 176p. (gr. 3-6). 1983. pap. 2.50 *(0-87406-114-8)* Willowisp Pr.

Anderson, Margaret J. Charles Darwin, Naturalist. LC 93-29839. 1994. write for info. *(0-89490-476-0)* Enslow Pubs.

—The Druid's Gift. LC 88-22028. 192p. 1989. 12.95 *(0-394-81936-5)* Knopf Bks Yng Read.

—Food Chains: The Unending Cycle. LC 90-3282. (Illus.). 64p. (gr. 6 up). 1991. lib. bdg. 15.95 *(0-89490-290-3)* Enslow Pubs.

—In the Circle of Time. LC 78-10156. (gr. 5-9). 1979. lib. bdg. 6.99 *(0-394-94029-6)* Knopf Bks Yng Read.

Anderson, Marilyn. The Haunted Underwear. (Illus.). 128p. (gr. 3-5). 1992. pap. 2.50 *(0-87406-592-5)* Willowisp Pr.

Anderson, Mary. Catch Me, I'm Falling in Love. (gr. k-12). 1987. pap. 2.50 *(0-440-91122-2,* LFL) Dell.

—The Curse of the Demon. (gr. k-6). 1989. pap. 2.95 *(0-440-40203-4,* YB) Dell.

—Do You Call That a Dream Date? LC 86-908. 176p. (gr. 7 up). 1987. pap. 14.95 *(0-385-29488-3)* Delacorte.

—Do You Call That a Dream Date? 176p. (gr. 6 up). 1989. pap. 2.95 *(0-440-20350-3,* LFL) Dell.

—The Hairy Beast in the Woods. (gr. 8-12). 1989. pap. 2.75 *(0-318-42743-5,* Pub. by Yearling Classics) Dell.

—Mostly Monsters, No. 1. (gr. k-6). 1989. pap. 2.95 *(0-440-40178-X,* YB) Dell.

—Mostly Monsters, No. 2. (Orig.). (gr. k-6). 1989. pap. 2.95 *(0-440-40181-X,* YB) Dell.

—Suzy's Secret Snoop Society. (gr. 3-7). 1991. pap. 2.95 *(0-380-75917-9,* Camelot) Avon.

—Terror under the Tent. (gr. k-6). 1987. pap. 2.50 *(0-440-48633-5,* YB) Dell.

—The Three Spirits of Vandermeer Manor. (Orig.). (gr. k-6). 1987. pap. 2.75 *(0-440-48810-9,* YB) Dell.

—Tune in Tomorrow. 192p. (gr. 7 up). 1985. pap. 2.50 *(0-380-69870-6,* Flare) Avon.

—Who Says Nobody's Perfect? LC 87-5336. 160p. (gr. 7 up). 1987. pap. 14.95 *(0-385-29582-0)* Delacorte.

Anderson, Mignon, ed. see Dounuts, Kevin.

Anderson, Myra. Big Enough. Reid, Diana S., illus. 32p. (gr. k-3). 1991. 12.95 *(0-9625620-0-9)* DOT Garnet.

—Kathryn's Mouse. Chapman, Shirley, illus. 48p. (gr. k-6). 1991. 16.95 *(0-9625620-4-1)* DOT Garnet.

—A Tail of a Different Color. Jerome, Debra P., illus. 32p. (gr. k-4). 1992. 13.95 *(0-9625620-3-3)* DOT Garnet.

Anderson, Neil & Park, Dave. Bondage Breaker Youth Edition. 1993. pap. 7.99 *(1-56507-139-5)* Harvest Hse.

Anderson, Neil T. & Park, Dave. Stomping Out the Darkness: Realizing the Incredible Power of Who I Really Are in Christ. Daly, Jean, ed. (Illus.). 180p. (gr. 8-12). 1993. pap. 8.99 *(0-8307-1640-8,* 5422307) Regal.

Anderson, Norma R. An Elfindale Story. Gonzales, Joe, illus. LC 81-5977. 36p. (Orig.). (gr. 1-6). 1981. pap. 5.95 *(0-913504-64-5)* Lowell Pr.

Anderson, Paul L. For Freedom & for Gaul. LC 57-9449. (Illus.). (gr. 7-11). 1931. 16.00 *(0-8196-0102-0)* Biblo.

—Pugnax the Gladiator. LC 61-1111. (Illus.). (gr. 7-11). 1939. 16.00 *(0-8196-0104-7)* Biblo.

—Slave of Catiline. LC 57-9446. 255p. (gr. 7-11). 1930. 18.00 *(0-8196-0101-2)* Biblo.

—Swords in the North. LC 57-9448. 270p. (gr. 7-11). 1935. 20.00 *(0-8196-0103-9)* Biblo.

—With the Eagles. LC 57-9447. (Illus.). (gr. 7-11). 1929. 20.00 *(0-8196-0100-4)* Biblo.

Anderson, Paul S. Storytelling with the Flannel Board, 3 Bks, Bk. 1. Francis, Irene, illus. LC 21-650. 270p. (ps). 1963. 15.95 *(0-513-00105-0)* Denison.

—Storytelling with the Flannel Board, 3 Bks, Bk. 2. Arms, William, illus. LC 21-650. 260p. (ps). 1970. 15.95 *(0-513-00137-9)* Denison.

Anderson, Peggy. First Day Blues. Strecker, Rebekah, illus. LC 91-67808. 64p. (Orig.). (gr. 3-6). 1992. PLB 16.95 *(0-943990-73-4)*; pap. 5.95 *(0-943990-72-6)* Parenting Pr.

Anderson, Peggy K. Coming Home: Children's Stories for Adult Children of Alcoholics. Detterbeck, Nancy, illus. LC 87-73388. 136p. (Orig.). (gr. 5-10). 1988. pap. 7.95 *(0-934125-06-6)* Glen Abbey Bks.

—Safe at Home! LC 90-19133. 128p. (gr. 3-7). 1992. SBE 12.95 *(0-689-31686-0,* Atheneum Child Bk) Macmillan Child Grp.

Anderson, Peggy L. Denver Handwriting Analysis. 80p. (gr. 3-8). 1983. pap. 35.00 manual & wall chart *(0-87879-334-8)*; recording forms 10.00 *(0-87879-335-6)*; remedial checklists 7.00 *(0-685-06661-4)* Acad Therapy.

Anderson, Peggy P. Time for Bed, the Babysitter Said. LC 86-27388. (ps). 1987. 13.45 *(0-395-41851-8)* HM.

—Wendle, What Have You Done? LC 93-11291. 1994. write for info. *(0-395-64346-5)* HM.

Anderson, Penny S. Feeling Frustrated. Siculan, Dan, illus. LC 82-19910. 32p. (gr. 1-2). 1983. PLB 21.35 *(0-89565-245-5)*; PLB 14.95s.p. *(0-685-55660-3)* Childs World.

Anderson, Peter. Charles Eastman: Physician, Reformer, & Native American Leader. LC 91-36654. (Illus.). 152p. (gr. 4 up). 1992. PLB 18.60 *(0-516-03278-X)*; pap. 5.95 *(0-516-43278-8)* Childrens.

—Into the Unknown: Major Powells River Journey. (Illus.). 32p. (Orig.). (gr. 4-7). 1992. pap. 5.95 *(1-56044-133-X)* Falcon Pr MT.

—Maria Martinez: Pueblo Potter. LC 92-4807. (Illus.). 32p. (gr. 2-5). 1992. PLB 14.60 *(0-516-04184-3)* Childrens.

—Maria Martinez: Pueblo Potter. LC 92-4807. (Illus.). 32p. (gr. 2-5). 1993. pap. 3.95 *(0-516-44184-1)* Childrens.

—Will Rogers: American Humorist. LC 91-35057. (Illus.). 32p. (gr. 2-5). 1992. PLB 14.60 *(0-516-04183-5)*; pap. 3.95 *(0-516-44183-3)* Childrens.

Anderson, Rachel. The Bus People. LC 92-1506. 96p. (gr. 5 up). 1992. 13.95 *(0-8050-2297-X,* Bks Young Read) H Holt & Co.

—Paper Faces. large type ed. 216p. 1993. 13.95 *(0-7451-1683-3,* Galaxy Child Lrg Print) Chivers N Amer.

—Paper Faces. 128p. (gr. 4-7). 1993. PLB 14.95 *(0-8050-2527-8,* Bks Young Read) H Holt & Co.

Anderson, Rachel & Bradby, David. Reynard the Fox. (Illus.). 80p. (gr. 5-8). 1987. 18.95 *(0-19-274129-2)* OUP.

Anderson, Robert. Endangered Species: Understanding Words in Context. LC 91-29890. (Illus.). 32p. (gr. 4-7). 1991. PLB 10.95 *(0-89908-608-X)* Greenhaven.

—Forests: Identifying Propaganda Techniques. LC 92-28185. (Illus.). 32p. (gr. 4-7). 1992. PLB 10.95 *(0-89908-099-5)* Greenhaven.

—Garbage: Understanding Words in Context. LC 91-22100. (Illus.). 32p. (gr. 4-7). 1991. PLB 10.95 *(0-89908-609-8)* Greenhaven.

—Pollution: Examining Cause & Effect Relationships. LC 92-25958. (Illus.). 32p. (gr. 4-7). 1992. PLB 10.95 (0-89908-574-1) Greenhaven.
Anderson, Robert, jt. ed. see Rohr, Janelle.
Anderson, Sanna. The Stormy Night. (Illus.). (ps-2). 1991. 12.99 (0-8423-6772-1) Tyndale.
Anderson, Scoular. Land Ahoy! The Story of Christopher Columbus. (Illus.). 96p. (gr. 3-7). 1992. pap. 2.99 (0-14-034617-1) Puffin Bks.
Anderson, Sherwood. The Egg. LC 92-44057. 1994. write for info. (0-88682-573-3) Creative Ed.
Anderson, Sheryl J., jt. auth. see Wolfe, William D.
Anderson, Stephen E. Wee-Sitt Babysitting Guide. Trost, Ed, ed. Anderson, Stephen E., illus. (Orig.). (gr. 6-9). 1989. pap. 4.95 (0-685-29145-6) Chimurenga.
—Wee-Sitt Guide to Babysitting. Trost, Ed, ed. (Illus.). 21p. (Orig.). 1989. pap. text ed. 4.95 (0-9624153-0-8) Chimurenga.
Anderson, Stevens, ed. see Lancaster, Derek.
Anderson, Tammy L., ed. California Redwoods Color Book. 26p. (ps-8). 1988. pap. 1.95 (0-915687-03-8) FVN Corp.
Anderson, Tim, jt. auth. see Hyden, Tom.
Anderson, Tom. Sing Choral Music at Sight. Blakeslee, Michael, ed. (Illus.). 128p. (Orig.). (gr. 1-12). 1992. pap. 36.00 tchr's ed. (1-56545-007-8) Music Ed Natl.
Anderson, Vicki. Fiction Index for Readers Ten to Sixteen: Subject Access to Over 8200 Books (1960-1990) LC 91-50954. 488p. (gr. 7-12). 1992. PLB 35.00x (0-89950-703-4) McFarland & Co.
Anderson, Wayne. Dragon. LC 91-4790. (ps-3). 1992. 15.00 (0-671-78397-1, Green Tiger) S&S Trade.
Anderson, William. Basic Houseplants for Pathfinders: A Youth Enrichment Skill. (Illus.). 20p. (Orig.). 1987. pap. 5.00 tchr's ed (0-936241-21-7) Cheetah Pub.
—Laura Ingalls Wilder: A Biography. LC 91-33805. (Illus.). 240p. (gr. 3-7). 1992. 16.00 (0-06-020113-4); PLB 15.89 (0-06-020114-2) HarpC Child Bks.
Anderson, William & Kelly, Leslie A. Little House Country: A Photo Guide to the Homesites of Laura Ingalls Wilder. (Illus.). 48p. 1989. 9.95 (0-9610088-8-1) Anderson MI.
Anderson, William T. A Wilder in the West: Eliza Jane's Story of a Lady Homesteader. (Illus.). 44p. (gr. 8 up). 1985. pap. 3.95 (0-9610088-4-9) Anderson MI.
Andre, Ken St. see St. Andre, Ken & Perrin, Steve.
Andree, Josephine P., ed. Chips from the Mathematical Log. (gr. 11-12). 1966. pap. 2.00 (0-686-00750-6) Mu Alpha Theta.
Andreev, Tania. Food in Russia. LC 88-32179. (Illus.). 32p. (gr. 3-6). 1989. lib. bdg. 15.94 (0-86625-343-2); 11.95s.p. (0-685-58497-6) Rourke Corp.
Andrejtschitsch, Jan, et al. Action Skateboarding. LC 91-40328. (Illus.). 128p. (gr. 10-12). 1992. 16.95 (0-8069-8500-3) Sterling.
—Action Skateboarding. (Illus.). 128p. (gr. 10-12). 1993. pap. 10.95 (0-8069-8501-1) Sterling.
Andres, Katherine. Fish Story. McGraw, Deloss, illus. LC 92-14677. 1993. pap. 15.00 (0-671-79270-9) S&S Trade.
—Humphrey & Ralph. Day, Brant, illus. LC 93-11478. 1994. write for info. (0-671-88129-9, S&S BFYR) S&S Trade.
Andretti, Michael, et al. Michael Andretti at Indianapolis. LC 91-38815. (Illus.). 64p. (gr. 3-7). 1992. pap. 15.00 jacketed (0-671-75296-0, S&S BFYR) S&S Trade.
—Michael Andretti at Indianapolis. Carver, Douglas, photos by. LC 91-38815. (Illus.). 64p. (gr. 3-7). 1993. pap. 5.95 (0-671-79674-7, S&S BFYR) S&S Trade.
Andrews & McMeel Inc. Staff. Pebbles & Bamm-Bamm's Wedding Album. (ps-3). 1993. 9.95 (1-878685-62-7) Turner Pub GA.
—Tom & Jerry Friends to the End. (ps-3). 1993. 14.95 (1-878685-26-0) Turner Pub GA.
Andrews & McMeel Staff. Beauty & the Beast - Gift Book. (ps-3). 1993. 4.95 (0-8362-3036-1) Andrews & McMeel.
—Cinderella. (ps-3). 1993. 4.95 (0-8362-3034-5) Andrews & McMeel.
—Flintstones Wacky Inventions: How Things Work in the Modern Stone Age. (gr. 4-7). 1993. 15.95 (1-878685-65-1, Bedrock Pr) Turner Pub GA.
—Jack & the Beanstalk. (ps-3). 1993. 4.95 (0-8362-3035-3) Andrews & McMeel.
Andrews, C. L. Story of Sitka. 142p. (gr. 9 up). pap. 9.95 (0-8466-0094-3, S94) Shorey.
Andrews, Clarence A., tr. see Gravel, Fern.
Andrews, Dianne, ed. see Avery, Louisia.
Andrews, Dorothy W. God's World & Johnny. (gr. 5 up). 1983. pap. 4.45 (0-318-01335-5) Rod & Staff.
Andrews, Ed. Caravans of Mars. Hasenauer, Richard, illus. 64p. (Orig.). 1989. pap. 8.00 (1-55878-023-8) Game Designers.
Andrews, Elaine. Indians of the Plains. (Illus.). 96p. (gr. 5-8). 1991. lib. bdg. 18.95x (0-8160-2387-5) Facts on File.
Andrews, Glenn, jt. auth. see Sobol, Donald J.
Andrews, Ian. Pompeii. (Illus.). 48p. (gr. 7 up). 1978. pap. 7.50 (0-521-20973-0) Cambridge U Pr.
Andrews, Jan. The Auction. Reczuch, Karen, illus. LC 90-41378. 32p. (ps-3). 1991. RSBE 13.95 (0-02-705535-3, Macmillan Child Bk) Macmillan Child Grp.
—Pumpkin Time. LaFave, Kim, illus. 32p. (ps-3). 1991. 12.95 (0-88899-112-6, Pub. by Groundwood-Douglas & McIntyre CN) Firefly Bks Ltd.

—Very Last First Time. Wallace, Ian, illus. LC 85-71606. 32p. (gr. k-4). 1986. SBE 14.95 (0-689-50388-1, M K McElderry) Macmillan Child Grp.
Andrews, Janice. Tunes for Tots. (ps). 1987. write for info. incl. tape & tchr's. guide (1-878079-04-2) Arts Pubns.
Andrews, Jean F. The Flying Fingers Club. LC 88-19875. 104p. (gr. 3-5). 1988. pap. 4.95 (0-930323-44-0, Kendall Green Pubns) Gallaudet Univ Pr.
—The Ghost of Tomahawk Creek. Allard, Mike, illus. LC 93-86006. (Orig.). (gr. 2-6). 1993. pap. text ed. 5.95 (1-883120-01-2) Northern St U.
—Hasta Luego, San Diego. LC 90-27125. 104p. (Orig.). (gr. 3-6). 1991. pap. 4.95 (0-930323-83-1, Pub. by K Green Pubns) Gallaudet Univ Pr.
Andrews, Kristi. All That Glitters, No. 2: Take Two. 176p. (Orig.). 1987. pap. 2.50 (0-553-26417-6) Bantam.
—Typecast, No. 5. 176p. (Orig.). 1988. pap. 2.50 (0-553-26569-5) Bantam.
—Upstaged, No. 7. 176p. (Orig.). (gr. 6 up). 1988. pap. 2.50 (0-553-26704-3) Bantam.
Andrews, Linda G., jt. auth. see Leggett, Linda R.
Andrews, Raymond. The Last Radio Baby: A Memoir. Andrews, Benny, illus. LC 90-41751. 224p. 1990. 15.95 (1-56145-004-9) Peachtree Pubs.
Andrews, Sylvia. Rattlebone Rock. Plecas, Jennifer, illus. LC 93-4426. Date not set. 15.00 (0-06-023451-2); PLB 14.89 (0-06-023452-0) HarpC.
Andrews, William G. The Land & People of the Soviet Union. LC 90-5746. (Illus.). 320p. (gr. 6 up). 1991. 17.95 (0-06-020034-0); PLB 17.89 (0-06-020035-9) HarpC Child Bks.
Andrist, Earl W. Monte Superstition Gold. Chavis, Ken, illus. 170p. (Orig.). 1990. pap. 7.95 (1-878431-02-1) Artist Profile Pub.
Andronik, Catherine M. Kindred Spirit: A Biography of L. M. Montgomery, Creator of Anne of Green Gables. LC 92-25869. (Illus.). 160p. (gr. 5-9). 1993. SBE 14.95 (0-689-31671-2, Atheneum Child Bk) Macmillan Child Grp.
—Quest for a King: Searching for the Real King Arthur. LC 88-7381. (Illus.). 160p. (gr. 5 up). 1989. SBE 12.95 (0-689-31411-6, Atheneum Child Bk) Macmillan Child Grp.
Andry, Andrew C. & Schepp, Steven. How Babies Are Made. Hampton, Blake, illus. LC 99-944003. 88p. 1984. pap. 9.95 (0-316-04227-7) Little.
Andryszewski, Tricia. The Dust Bowl: Disaster on the Plains. LC 92-15300. (Illus.). 64p. (gr. 4-6). 1993. PLB 14.40 (1-56294-272-7) Millbrook Pr.
—Marjory Stoneman Douglas, Friend of the Everglades. LC 93-26731. 1994. PLB write for info. (1-56294-384-7) Millbrook Pr.
Andujar, Maria D. & Iglesias, Jose L. Mecanografia Al Dia. rev. ed. (gr. 10 up). 1977. pap. text ed. 3.50 (0-88345-306-1, 18482) Prentice ESL.
Anduze, A. L. Caribbean Crosswords. LC 93-70926. (Illus.). 64p. (gr. 5-12). Date not set. pap. 8.95 (0-932831-10-9) Eastern Caribbean Inst.
Anello, Christine. Farmyard Cat. (ps-3). 1990. pap. 3.95 (0-86896-392-5, Pub. by Ashton Scholastic AT) Heinemann.
Anfenson-Vance, Deborah, et al, eds. see Wert, Debra.
Anfenson-Vance, Deborah, et al, eds. see Wert, Debra L.
Angel, jt. auth. see Fritz.
Angel, Ann. Lech Walesa. LC 91-50539. (Illus.). 68p. (gr. 3-4). 1992. PLB 18.60 (0-8368-0628-X) Gareth Stevens Inc.
—Louis Pasteur. LC 91-19552. (Illus.). 68p. (gr. 3-4). 1992. PLB 18.60 (0-8368-0625-5) Gareth Stevens Inc.
—Real for Sure Sister. LC 87-29217. (Illus.). 72p. (gr. 3-6). 1988. 10.95 (0-9609504-7-8) Perspect Indiana.
Angel, Marie. Marie Angel's Exotic Alphabet: An Alphabet to Unfold in Words & Pictures. LC 92-8850. (Illus.). 1992. 12.95 (0-8037-1247-2) Dial Bks Young.
—Woodland Christmas. 1991. 12.95 (0-8037-1088-7) Dial Bks Young.
Angeli, Marguerite de. The Lion in the Box. 1975. 12.95 (0-385-03317-6) Doubleday.
Angeli, Marguerite De see De Angeli, Marguerite.
Angeli, Marguerite de see De Angeli, Marguerite.
Angell, Judie. The Buffalo Nickel Blues Band. LC 91-3793. 192p. (gr. 3-7). 1991. pap. 3.95 (0-689-71448-3, Aladdin) Macmillan Child Grp.
—Dear Lola: How to Build Your Own Family. 144p. (gr. 5-9). 1986. pap. 1.95 (0-440-91787-5, LFL) Dell.
—Don't Rent My Room. 1991. pap. 3.50 (0-553-29142-4) Bantam.
—A Home Is to Share... & Share... & Share. LC 83-21356. 112p. (gr. 4-6). 1984. SBE 12.95 (0-02-705830-1, Bradbury Pr) Macmillan Child Grp.
—In Summertime, It's Tuffy. 192p. (gr. 5 up). 1979. pap. 2.25 (0-440-94051-6, LFL) Dell.
—Leave the Cooking to Me. (gr. 7 up). 1990. 15.00 (0-553-05849-5); pap. 3.50 (0-553-29055-X) Bantam.
—Ronnie & Rosey. 192p. (gr. 6-9). 1979. pap. 2.25 (0-440-97491-7, LFL) Dell.
—Secret Selves. 192p. (gr. 7 up). 1981. pap. 2.25 (0-440-97716-9, LE) Dell.
—Tina Gogo. 160p. (gr. 5 up). 1980. pap. 1.75 (0-440-98738-5, LFL) Dell.
—What's Best for You? 192p. (gr. 6-9). 1983. pap. 2.25 (0-440-98959-0, LFL) Dell.
—What's Best for You. LC 90-1599. 192p. (gr. 7 up). 1990. pap. 3.95 (0-02-041491-9, Collier Young Ad) Macmillan Child Grp.

—Yours Truly: A Novel. LC 92-29472. 192p. (gr. 7-12). 1993. 14.95 (0-531-05472-1); PLB 14.99 (0-531-08622-4) Orchard Bks Watts.
Angelou, Maya. Life Doesn't Frighten Me. Boyers, Sara J., ed. Basquiat, Jean-Michel, illus. LC 92-40409. (gr. 7 up). 1993. write for info. (Dist. by Workman Pub.) Stewart Tabori & Chang.
Angers, Joann. Meeting the Forgiving Jesus: A Child's First Penance Book. 32p. (gr. 1-3). 1983. pap. 2.95 (0-89243-201-2) Liguori Pubns.
Angers, JoAnn M. My Beginning Mass Book. Read, Maryann, illus. 48p. (Orig.). (gr. 1-4). 1978. pap. 1.95 (0-89622-082-6) Twenty-Third.
Angilillo, Barbara W. Italy. LC 90-10191. (Illus.). 96p. (gr. 6-12). 1990. PLB 19.92 (0-8114-2438-3) Raintree Steck-V.
Anglesky, Zoe, ed. Word Up: Hope for Youth Poetry from El Centro de la Raza. (ENG, SPA & TAG.). 1992. 12.95 (0-9633275-1-8) El Centro de la Raza.
Anglund, Joan W. All about My Family. Anglund, Joan W., illus. 48p. (ps up). 1987. pap. 6.95 (0-590-40828-3) Scholastic Inc.
—Baby's First Book. Anglund, Joan W., illus. 12p. (ps). 1985. 3.99 (0-394-87470-6) Random Bks Yng Read.
—Bedtime Book. (ps-6). 1993. pap. 12.00 (0-671-74176-4, S&S BFYR) S&S Trade.
—Childhood Is a Time of Innocence: Twentieth Anniversary Edition. LC 65-20974. (Illus.). 32p. (gr. k up). 1984. Repr. of 1964 ed. 6.95 (0-15-216952-0, HB Juv Bks) HarBrace.
—A Child's Year. (Illus.). 24p. (ps-k). 1992. write for info. (0-307-00141-5, 312-06, Golden Pr) Western Pub.
—A Christmas Book. (Illus.). 48p. (gr. k-3). 1983. lib. bdg. 7.99 (0-394-95551-X) Random Bks Yng Read.
—Christmas Candy Book. (Illus.). 1983. 5.95 (0-915696-63-0) Determined Prods.
—A Christmas Cookie Book. LC 77-78293. (Illus.). 1982. Repr. of 1977 ed. 3.95 (0-915696-07-X) Determined Prods.
—Christmas Is a Time of Giving. Anglund, Joan W., illus. LC 61-10106. 28p. (ps up). 1961. 9.95 (0-15-217863-5, HB Juv Bks) HarBrace.
—Christmas Is Love. (Illus.). 32p. (ps up). 1988. 7.95 (0-15-200425-4, Gulliver Bks) HarBrace.
—A Friend Is Someone Who Likes You: Silver Anniversary Edition. Anglund, Joan W., illus. LC 58-8624. 32p. (ps up). 1983. 8.95 (0-15-229678-6, HB Juv Bks) HarBrace.
—God Is Love. (Illus.). (gr. 1 up). 5.95 (0-317-13661-5) Determined Prods.
—How Many Days Has Baby To Play? Anglund, Joan W., illus. LC 87-19665. 21p. (ps-k). 1988. 7.95 (0-15-200460-2, Gulliver Bks) HarBrace.
—In a Pumpkin Shell. Anglund, Joan W., illus. LC 60-10243. 32p. (ps-2). 1977. pap. 3.95 (0-15-644425-9, Voyager Bks) HarBrace.
—In a Pumpkin Shell: A Mother Goose ABC. Anglund, Joan W., illus. LC 60-10243. (ps-2). 1960. 10.95 (0-15-238269-0, HB Juv Bks) HarBrace.
—The Joan Walsh Anglund Coloring Book. Anglund, Joan W., illus. 80p. (ps-3). 1984. pap. 2.95 saddle-stitched (0-394-86875-7) Random Bks Yng Read.
—The Joan Walsh Anglund I Love You Book & Doll Set. Anglund, Joan W., illus. LC 88-60060. 24p. (ps-1). 1988. book & doll pkg. 5.95 (0-394-89338-7) Random Bks Yng Read.
—Love Is a Baby. LC 91-1224. 1992. write for info. (0-15-200517-X, HB Juv Bks) HarBrace.
—Morning Is a Little Child. Anglund, Joan W., illus. LC 69-11592. (gr. 4-6). 1969. 7.95 (0-15-255652-4, HB Juv Bks) HarBrace.
—A Mother Goose Book. Van Doren, Liz, ed. Anglund, Joan W., illus. 32p. (ps up). 1991. 7.95 (0-15-200529-3, Gulliver Bks) HarBrace.
—Nibble Nibble Mousekin: A Tale of Hansel & Gretel. Anglund, Joan W., illus. LC 62-14422. 32p. (gr. k-3). 1962. 10.95 (0-15-257400-X, HB Juv Bks) HarBrace.
—Nibble Nibble Mousekin: A Tale of Hansel & Gretel. Anglund, Joan W., illus. LC 62-14422. 32p. (gr. k-3). 1977. pap. 4.95 (0-15-665588-8, Voyager Bks) HarBrace.
—Peace Is a Circle of Love. LC 92-28855. 1993. 8.95 (0-15-259922-3) HarBrace.
—Spring Is a New Beginning. Anglund, Joan W., illus. LC 63-7892. 32p. (ps up). 1991. 8.95 (0-15-278161-7, HB Juv Bks) HarBrace.
Angulo, Jaime De see De Angulo, Jaime.
Angus, Fay, adapted by see Hoffman, E. T.
Anholt, Catherine. Aren't You Lucky! 32p. 1991. 14.95 (0-316-04264-1, Joy St Bks) Little.
—Good Days, Bad Days. (Illus.). 32p. 1991. 14.95 (0-399-22283-9, Putnam) Putnam Pub Group.
—Here Come the Babies. Anholt, Catherine, illus. LC 92-54584. 32p. (gr. 3 up). 1993. 13.95 (1-56402-209-9) Candlewick Pr.
—Kids. LC 91-58739. (ps-3). 1994. pap. 4.99 (1-56402-269-2) Candlewick Pr.
—Snow Fairy & the Spaceman. (ps-3). 1991. 13.95 (0-385-30421-8) Delacorte.
—Tom's Rainbow Walk, Vol. 1. Anholt, Catherine, illus. 32p. (ps-3). 1990. 12.95 (0-316-04261-7, Joy St Bks) Little.
—When I Was a Baby. Anholt, Catherine, illus. 32p. (ps-3). 1989. 11.95 (0-316-04262-5, Joy St Bks) Little.
Anholt, Catherine & Anholt, Laurence. All about You. (Illus.). 32p. (ps). 1992. 14.00 (0-670-84488-8) Viking Child Bks.

—Bear & Baby. Anholt, Laurence & Anholt, Catherine, illus. LC 92-54581. 24p. (ps). 1993. 5.95 (*1-56402-235-8*) Candlewick Pr.
—Come Back, Jack! LC 93-2885. 1994. write for info. (*1-56402-313-3*) Candlewick Pr.
—Kids. Anholt, Catherine & Anholt, Laurence, illus. LC 91-58739. 32p. (ps up). 1992. 13.95 (*1-56402-097-5*) Candlewick Pr.
—Toddlers. Anholt, Catherine & Anholt, Laurence, illus. LC 92-54588. 24p. (ps). 1993. 5.95 (*1-56402-242-0*) Candlewick Pr.
—Twins, Two by Two. Anholt, Catherine & Anholt, Laurence, illus. LC 91-71820. 32p. (ps). 1992. 13.95 (*1-56402-041-X*) Candlewick Pr.
—What I Like. LC 90-27816. (Illus.). 32p. 1991. 14.95 (*0-399-21863-7*, Putnam) Putnam Pub Group.
Anholt, Catherine, jt. auth. see Anholt, Laurence.
Anholt, Laurence. The Forgotten Forest. Anholt, Laurence, illus. 32p. (ps-3). 1992. 14.95 (*0-87156-569-2*) Sierra.
Anholt, Laurence & Anholt, Catherine. Can You Guess? A Lift-the-Flap Birthday Party Book. 16p. (ps-1). 1993. pap. 4.99 (*0-14-054951-X*, Puffin) Puffin Bks.
Anholt, Laurence, jt. auth. see Anholt, Catherine.
Anker, Debby & De Graff, John. David Brower: Friend of the Earth. (Illus.). 80p. (gr. 4-7). 1993. PLB 14.95 (*0-8050-2124-8*) TFC Bks NY.
Ann Arbor Publishers Editorial Staff & Edwards, Susan. Cursive Tracking. large type, reusable ed. 32p. (gr. 2-8). 1973. pap. text ed. 6.50 (*0-87879-738-6*, Ann Arbor Div) Acad Therapy.
Ann Arbor Publishers Editorial Staff. Cursive Writing: Words, Bk. 1: Reusable Edition. 64p. (gr. 2-3). 1977. wkbk. 6.50 (*0-87879-791-2*, Ann Arbor Div) Acad Therapy.
Ann, Fay, ed. see Nixon, Joan L.

Annable, Toni & Kaspar, Maria H. The Four Seasons. Viola, Amy, tr. Lumetta, Lawrence, illus. 80p. (Orig.). (gr. 5 up). 1992. Set. pap. text ed. 8.95 (*1-882828-09-7*) Vol. 1: English-Spanish, Las Cuatro Estaciones. Vol. 2: English-French, Les Quatre Saisons. Kasan Imprints.
What does it mean when the leaves turn red? How does the snow know when to stop falling? What is the dormouse looking for & where do baby birds go to school? Four children discover the joys of seasonal changes. Contains charming poems for each season. Beautifully illustrated. An original dual language book for children grades 5-6. Features our easy line-by-line, side-by-side format. Series contains one each English-Spanish & English-French. 40 pages each. Quantity discounts available. To order: contact: KIP Children's Books, 1239 Nile Dr., Suite 3, Corpus Christi, TX 78412. 1-800-982-5298.
Publisher Provided Annotation.

—*The Four Seasons: Las Cuatro Estaciones.* Viola, Amy, tr. Lumetta, Lawrence, illus. 40p. (Orig.). (gr. 5 up). 1992. pap. 4.95 (*1-882828-02-X*) Kasan Imprints.
—*The Four Seasons: Les Quatre Saisons.* Lumetta, Lawrence, illus. 40p. (Orig.). (gr. 5 up). 1992. pap. 4.95 (*1-882828-03-8*) Kasan Imprints.

—**The Runaway Match. Viola, Amy, tr. 48p. (Orig.). (gr. 3 up). 1992. Set. pap. 8.95 (*1-882828-10-0*) Vol. 1 English-Spanish, La Cerilla Fugitiva. Vol. 2 English-French, L'Alumette Fugitive. Kasan Imprints.**
A tree & a runaway match teach a leaf about fire safety when a careless boy starts a blaze in the park. A charming play in two acts for small or large stage. An hilarious, memorable tool for fire safety. Endorsed by fire-fighter associations. Original dual language play for home, group & school performances as well as community theatres. Written in side-by-side format with line-by-line continuity. Series contains one each English-Spanish & English-French. For children grades 3-4. 24 pages each. Quantity discounts available. To order contact: KIP

Children's Books, 1239 Nile Drive, Suite 3, Corpus Christi, TX 78412. 1-800-982-5298.
Publisher Provided Annotation.

—*The Runaway Match: La Cerilla Fugitiva.* Viola, Amy, tr. 24p. (Orig.). (gr. 3 up). 1992. pap. 4.95 (*1-882828-04-6*) Kasan Imprints.
—*The Runaway Match: L'Alumette Fugitive.* 24p. (Orig.). (gr. 3 up). 1992. pap. 4.95 (*1-882828-05-4*) Kasan Imprints.

—**Sherm the Worm. Viola, Amy, tr. (Illus.). 96p. (Orig.). (gr. k up). 1992. Set. pap. 8.95 (*1-882828-08-9*) Vol. 1 English-Spanish, Lozano el Gusano. Vol. 2 English-French, Valere le Ver. Kasan Imprints.**
The delightful story of a lazy worm looking for an easy life. But, poor Sherm doesn't know what's waiting for him! He just goes from surprise to surprise. What a lesson he learns! Original, dual language, storybook to color in. Beautifully illustrated. Increases the child's interest in the second language. Written in conversational style with line-by-line continuity & in the side-by-side format. Series contains one each English-Spanish & English-French. 48 pages each. Quantity discounts available. To order contact: KIP Children's Books, 1239 Nile Drive, Suite 3, Corpus Christi, TX 78412. 1-800-982-5298.
Publisher Provided Annotation.

—*Sherm the Worm: Lozano El Gusano.* Viola, Amy, tr. Lumetta, Lawrence, illus. 40p. (Orig.). (gr. k up). 1992. pap. 4.95 (*1-882828-00-3*) Kasan Imprints.
—*Sherm the Worm: Valere le ver.* Lumetta, Lawrence, illus. 48p. (Orig.). (gr. k up). 1992. pap. 4.95 (*1-882828-01-1*) Kasan Imprints.

—**The Silver Tree. Viola, Amy, tr. (Illus.). 80p. (Orig.). (gr. 6 up). 1992. Set. pap. 8.95 (*1-882828-11-9*) Vol. 1 English-Spanish, El Arbol de Plata. Vol. 2 English-French, L'Arbre Argente. Kasan Imprints.**
A story about wicked pirates, a village chief with a secret & a magic silver tree. Are true riches found in little silver leaves? Can the chief save his beloved island? A truly classic adventure-folktale that children will treasure for years. Wonderful illustrations. Excellent dual language format. Line-by-line continuity. Series contains one each English-Spanish & English-French. For children grades 6-8. 40 pages each. Quantity discounts available. To order contact: KIP Children's Books, 1239 Nile Drive, Corpus Christi, TX 78412. 1-800-982-5298.
Publisher Provided Annotation.

—*The Silver Tree: El Arbol de Plata.* Viola, Amy, tr. Lumetta, Lawrence, illus. 40p. (Orig.). (gr. 6 up). 1992. pap. 4.95 (*1-882828-06-2*) Kasan Imprints.
Annble, Toni & Kaspar, Maria H. The Silver Tree: L'Arbre Argente. Lumetta, Lawrence, illus. 40p. (Orig.). (gr. 6 up). 1992. pap. 4.95 (*1-882828-07-0*) Kasan Imprints.
Annen, Sharon, tr. see Desnos, Robert.
Annis, Scott, jt. auth. see Canady, Robert.
Annis, Scott E., jt. auth. see Isham, Joy.
Anno, Mitsumasa. Anno's Alphabet: An Adventure in Imagination. Anno, Mitsumasa, illus. LC 73-21652. 64p. (gr. k up). 1975. 16.00 (*0-690-00540-7*, Crowell Jr Bks); PLB 15.89 (*0-690-00541-5*) HarpC Child Bks.
—Anno's Alphabet: An Adventure in Imagination. Anno, Mitsumasa, illus. LC 73-21652. 64p. (ps up). 1988. pap. 7.95 (*0-06-443190-8*, Trophy) HarpC Child Bks.
—Anno's Counting Book. Anno, Mitsumasa, illus. LC 76-28977. 32p. (ps-3). 1977. 16.00 (*0-690-01287-X*, Crowell Jr Bks); PLB 15.89 (*0-690-01288-8*) HarpC Child Bks.

—Anno's Counting Book. LC 76-28977. (Illus.). 32p. (ps-3). 1986. pap. 5.95 (*0-06-443123-1*, Trophy) HarpC Child Bks.
—Anno's Counting Book Big Book. LC 65-28977. (Illus.). 32p. (ps-3). 1992. pap. 19.95 (*0-06-443315-3*, Trophy) HarpC Child Bks.
—Anno's Counting House. (Illus.). 48p. (ps-3). 1982. 16.95 (*0-399-20896-8*, Philomel) Putnam Pub Group.
—Anno's Faces. Anno, Mitsumasa, illus. 32p. (ps). 1989. 11.95 (*0-399-21711-8*, Philomel Bks) Putnam Pub Group.
—Anno's Journey. 48p. (gr. 4 up). 1981. 15.95 (*0-399-20762-7*, Philomel Bks); pap. 7.95 (*0-399-20952-2*, Philomel Bks) Putnam Pub Group.
—Anno's Magic Seed. LC 92-39309. 1994. write for info. (*0-399-22538-2*, Philomel Bks) Putnam Pub Group.
—Anno's Math Games. 104p. (ps-3). 1987. 19.95 (*0-399-21151-9*, Philomel Bks) Putnam Pub Group.
—Anno's Math Games, No. III. (Illus.). 112p. (ps-3). 1991. 19.95 (*0-399-22274-X*, Philomel Bks) Putnam Pub Group.
—Anno's Math Games II. Anno, Mitsumasa, illus. 104p. (gr. 1-4). 1989. 19.95 (*0-399-21615-4*, Philomel Bks) Putnam Pub Group.
—Anno's Medieval World. Anno, Mitsumasa, illus. LC 79-28367. 56p. (gr. 3 up). 1990. 16.95 (*0-399-20742-2*, Philomel Bks) Putnam Pub Group.
—Anno's Mysterious Multiplying Jar. Anno, Mitsumasa, illus. LC 82-22413. 48p. (gr. 3 up). 1983. 16.95 (*0-399-20951-4*, Philomel Bks) Putnam Pub Group.
—Anno's Peekaboo. (Illus.). 32p. (ps-k). 1988. 10.95 (*0-399-21520-4*, Philomel Bks) Putnam Pub Group.
—Anno's U. S. A. 48p. (ps-8). 1992. 16.95 (*0-399-20974-3*, Philomel Bks); pap. 7.95 (*0-399-21595-6*, Philomel Bks) Putnam Pub Group.
—Upside-Downers. (Illus.). (gr. k-4). 1988. 13.95 (*0-399-21522-0*, Philomel Bks) Putnam Pub Group.
Anno, Mitsumasa, jt. auth. see Nozaki, Akihiro.
Anno, Mitsumasa, retold by. & illus. Anno's Aesop: A Book of Fables by Aesop & Mr. Fox. LC 88-60087. 64p. (ps-2). 1989. 18.95 (*0-531-05774-7*); PLB 18.99 (*0-531-08374-8*) Orchard Bks Watts.
Anno, Mitsumasa, retold by. & illu see Grimm, Jacob & Grimm, Wilhelm K.
Annunziata, Jane, jt. auth. see Nemiroff, Marc A.
Anpilogova, B. G., et al. Foundation Dictionary of Russian: Three Thousand High Semantic Frequency Words. (RUS & ENG.). 178p. (gr. 9-12). 1967. pap. 4.95 (*0-486-21860-0*) Dover.
Ansari, Masud. Modern Hypnosis: Theory & Practice. Ansari, Said S., illus. 232p. (gr. 5). 1982. pap. 6.95 (*0-685-05553-1*) MAS-Pr.
Ansary, Mir T. Afghanistan: Fighting for Freedom. LC 91-15648. (Illus.). 128p. (gr. 4-6). 1991. RSBE 14.95 (*0-87518-482-0*, Dillon) Macmillan Child Grp.
Ansell, Rod & Percy, Rachel. To Fight the Wild. LC 85-22023. (Illus.). 156p. (gr. 7 up). 1986. 12.95 (*0-15-289068-8*, HB Juv Bks) HarBrace.
Anson, August. Marine Biology & Ocean Science. (Illus.). 340p. (gr. 9-12). 1990. text ed. 24.95 (*0-9624094-0-5*); pap. text ed. 18.95 (*0-9624094-1-3*) Balaena Bks.
Anson, Mandy. Focus on Love. 1991. pap. 2.99 (*0-553-29290-0*) Bantam.
Anstey, David, jt. auth. see Jennings, Terry.
Anthony, Carl S. America's Most Influential First Ladies. Ford, Betty, frwd. by. LC 92-18444. 160p. (gr. 5-12). 1992. PLB 14.95 (*1-881508-00-5*) Oliver Pr MN.
Anthony, Piers. Balook. Woodroffe, Patrick, illus. 200p. 1990. 24.95 (*0-88733-069-X*); signed ed. 75.00 (*0-685-53972-5*) Underwood-Miller.
Anthony, Susan C. Facts Plus: An Almanac of Essential Information. rev. ed. LC 91-77581. (Illus.). 256p. (gr. 3-9). 1992. pap. 15.95 (*1-879478-03-X*) Instr Res Co.
Anthony, Suzanne. Haiti. (Illus.). 112p. (gr. 5 up). 1989. lib. bdg. 14.95 (*1-55546-796-2*) Chelsea Hse.
Antioch. Away in the Manger. (ps-3). 1991. pap. 2.50 (*0-89954-153-4*) Antioch Pub Co.
Antle, Nancy. The Good Bad Cat. Gregorich, Barbara, ed. (Illus.). 16p. (Orig.). (gr. k-2). 1985. pap. 2.25 (*0-88743-012-0*, 06012) Sch Zone Pub Co.
—The Good Bad Cat. Gregorich, Barbara, ed. (Illus.). 32p. (gr. k-2). 1992. pap. 3.95 (*0-88743-410-X*, 06062) Sch Zone Pub Co.
—Hard Times: A Story of the Great Depression. Watling, James, illus. 64p. (gr. 2-6). 1993. RB 12.99 (*0-670-84665-1*) Viking Child Bks.
—Touch Choices: A Story of the Vietnam War. Laporte, Michele, illus. 64p. (gr. 2-6). 1993. reinforced bdg. 12.99 (*0-670-84879-4*) Viking Child Bks.
Anton, Tina. Sharks, Sharks, Sharks. (Illus.). 32p. (gr. 1-4). 1989. 15.96 (*0-8172-3531-0*); pap. 3.95 (*0-8114-6731-7*) Raintree Steck-V.
Antonson, Joan M. & Hanable, William S. Alaska's Heritage. LC 84-72718. (Illus., Orig.). (gr. 10-12). 1986. Set. text ed. 37.00 (*0-943712-18-1*) Alaska Hist.
Antouopulos, Barbara. The Abominable Snowman. LC 77-21387. (Illus.). 48p. (gr. 4 up). 1983. PLB 18.64 (*0-8172-1053-9*) Raintree Steck-V.
Antwerp, T. Cooper van see Van Antwerp, T. Cooper.
Anyone Can Read Press Staff, ed. see Herr, Selma E.
Anyone Can Read Staff, ed. see Herr, Selma E & Piequet, Miriam.
Anyone Can Read Staff, ed. see Piequet, Miriam.
Anzaldua, Gloria. Friends from the Other Side: Amigos del otro lado. Mendez, Consuelo, illus. LC 92-34384. 32p. (gr. 2-7). 1993. 13.95 (*0-89239-113-8*) Childrens Book Pr.

Aoki, Hisako. Santa's Favorite Story. 2nd ed. Gantschev, Ivan, illus. LC 82-60895. 28p. (gr. k up). 1991. pap. 4.95 (*0-88708-153-3*) Picture Bk Studio.

Aoki, Hisako & Gantschev, Ivan. Santa's Favorite Story. LC 82-60895. (Illus.). 28p. (ps up). 1991. pap. 14.95 (*0-907234-16-X*) Picture Bk Studio.

Apablasa, Bill. Rhymin' Simon & the Mystery of the Fat Cat. Thiesing, Lisa, illus. LC 90-21054. 64p. (gr. 2-5). 1991. 10.95 (*0-525-44702-4*, DCB) Dutton Child Bks.

Apablasa, Bill & Thiesing, Lisa. Rhymin' Simon & the Mystery of the Fake Snake. (Illus.). 64p. (gr. 2-5). 1993. 11.99 (*0-525-44977-9*, DCB) Dutton Child Bks.

Apfel, Necia H. Astronomy Projects for Young Scientists. LC 84-6454. (Illus.). 128p. (gr. 10 up). 1984. pap. 7.95 (*0-668-06006-9*, 6006-9) P-H.

—It's All Elementary: From Atoms to the Quantum World of Quarks, Leptons, & Gluons. LC 84-9718. (Illus.). 160p. (gr. 4 up). 1985. PLB 12.88 (*0-688-04093-4*) Lothrop.

—Nebulae. LC 86-33765. (Illus.). 48p. (gr. 3-6). 1988. 13.95 (*0-688-07228-3*); PLB 13.88 (*0-688-07229-1*) Lothrop.

—Voyager to the Planets. Briley, Dorothy, ed. (Illus.). 48p. (gr. 3 up). 1991. 15.45 (*0-395-55209-5*, Clarion Bks) HM.

Appalachee Center for Human Services Staff. Choosing for Yourself 6-8. (Illus.). 208p. (gr. 6-8). 1988. Repr. of 1984 ed. 3-ring binder 200.00 (*1-8776670-2-1*) Shared Learning.

—Choosing for Yourself 9-12. (Illus.). 222p. 1988. Repr. of 1984 ed. 3-ring binder 200.00 (*1-8776670-3-X*) Shared Learning.

Appalachia Educational Laboratory Staff. Act. For Individualized Career Exploration. (gr. 9-11). 1989. 17.95 (*0-936007-17-6*, 3210) Meridian Educ.

—Work Activities Interest Checklist. (Illus.). 6p. (gr. 9 up). 1990. pap. text ed. 14.00 (*1-877-84-4535*) Meridian Educ.

—Work Situations Temperaments Checklist. (Illus.). 6p. (gr. 9 up). 1990. pap. text ed. 14.00 (*1-877-84-4543*) Meridian Educ.

Appel, Benjamin. Shepherd of the Sun. Bryson, Bernarda, illus. (gr. 5 up). 1961. 10.95 (*0-8392-3033-8*) Astor-Honor.

Appel, Dona J. Charlie Chipmunk's Dilemma. 1993. 7.95 (*0-8062-4711-8*) Carlton.

Appel, Gene. Healing Hidden Hurts: Leaving the Past & Finding New Life. 112p. (Orig.). Date not set. pap. 6.99 (*0-7847-0133-4*) Standard Pub.

Appel, Marty. Joe Dimaggio. (Illus.). 64p. (gr. 3 up). 1990. 14.95 (*0-7910-1164-X*) Chelsea Hse.

—Yogi Berra. (Illus.). 64p. (gr. 3 up). 1992. lib. bdg. 14.95 (*0-7910-1169-0*) Chelsea Hse.

Appel, Sergio, tr. see Rodecker, Stephen B. & Quon-Warner, Maryanna.

Appel, Ted. Jose Marti. (Illus.). (gr. 5 up). 1992. lib. bdg. 17.95 (*0-7910-1246-8*) Chelsea Hse.

Appelbaum, Diana. Giants in the Land. McCurdy, Michael, illus. LC 92-26526. 1993. 14.95 (*0-395-64720-7*) HM.

Appelbaum, Neil. Is There a Hole in Your Head? Appelbaum, Neil, illus. (gr. k-3). 1963. 8.95 (*0-8392-3012-5*) Astor-Honor.

Appelhof, Mary, et al. Worms Eat Our Garbage: Classroom Activities for a Better Environment. Fenton, Mary F. & Kostecke, Nancy, illus. Dindal, Daniel L., pref. by. 232p. (Orig.). (gr. 4 up). 1993. Wkbk. 19.95 (*0-942256-05-0*) Flower Pr. WORMS EAT OUR GARBAGE integrates earthworms with ecology, composting, natural resources, soil science, conservation, the environment, recycling, & biology in a curriculum guide & workbook designed for grades 4-8. Over 150 activities use the world of worms to help students develop science, language, math, problem-solving, & critical-thinking skills. Whether the book is used at home, in a classroom, outdoor education center, nature center or master composting program, users will find themselves drawn in & captivated by the diversity & scope of information presented. Dr. Dan Dindal, Distinguished Professor of Soil Ecology at SUNY in Syracuse, says in the preface, "Even though this book was prepared as a teaching aid for elementary & middle school grades, its potential use extends far beyond. Anyone who is fascinated & wishes to learn more about earthworms, as well as those whose active quest is to be an exciting & creative educator, will be served well by this book." Barbara Hannaford, teacher of 6-8 grade math & science, says, "The format is appealing to both teachers & students & the content is fantastic." Teacher's guide, 400 illustrations, resources, bibliography, 16 appendices, glossary, & index. See also WORMS EAT MY GARBAGE for how to set up & maintain worm composting systems. To order: Flower Press 616-327-0108. *Publisher Provided Annotation.*

Appell, Clara & Appell, Morey. Glenn Learns to Read. 2nd ed. Szasz, Suzanne, photos by. Appell, Clara T., intro. by. LC 87-62285. (Illus.). 64p. (ps-2). 1987. pap. 6.25 (*0-943501-00-8*) M L Appell.

Appell, Morey, jt. auth. see Appell, Clara.

Appelt, Watermelon Day. 1993. 14.95 (*0-8050-2304-6*) H Holt & Co.

Appelt, Kathi. Elephants Aloft. LC 92-4231. (ps-3). 1993. 13.95 (*0-15-225384-X*, HB Juv Bks) HarBrace.

Appelt, Kathi A. The Boy Who Loved to Dance. Morales, Sioux N., illus. 48p. (ps-3). 1986. PLB 11.95 (*0-938169-00-9*); pap. 6.95 (*0-938169-01-7*) Pecan Tree Pr.

Appiah, Peggy. Tales of an Ashanti Father. Dickson, Mona, illus. LC 88-19059. 160p. (gr. 2-6). 1989. lib. bdg. 12.95 (*0-8070-8312-7*); pap. 6.95 (*0-8070-8313-5*, NL4) Beacon Pr.

Appiah, Sonia. Amoko & Efua Bear. Easmon, Carol, illus. LC 88-8343. 32p. (ps-1). 1989. SBE 13.95 (*0-02-705591-4*, Macmillan Child Bk) Macmillan Child Grp.

Apple, Margot. Blanket. Apple, Margot, illus. 32p. (ps-3). 1990. 13.45 (*0-395-51522-X*) HM.

Apple, Victor, II. Tom Swift the Astral Fortress. (gr. 5-6). 17.95 (*0-88411-461-9*, Pub. by Aeonian Pr) Amereon Ltd.

Appleby. The Three Billy-Goats Gruff. 1993. pap. 19.95 (*0-590-71393-0*) Scholastic Inc.

Appleby, Ellen. Ho! Ho! Ho! (Illus.). 5p. 1993. bds. 3.98 (*0-8317-9655-3*) Smithmark.

—In the Gingerbread House. (Illus.). 5p. 1993. bds. 3.98 (*0-8317-9654-5*) Smithmark.

—The Jolly Jack-O-Lantern. (Illus.). 5p. 1993. bds. 3.98 (*0-8317-9656-1*) Smithmark.

—The Three Billy-Goats Gruff. (Illus.). 32p. (gr. k-2). 1985. pap. 2.50 (*0-590-41121-7*) Scholastic Inc.

—Trick or Treat. (Illus.). 5p. 1993. bds. 3.98 (*0-8317-9657-X*) Smithmark.

—Wheels on the Bus. (Illus.). 24p. (ps-k). 1993. 9.00 (*0-307-74815-4*, 64815, Golden Pr) Western Pub.

Appleby, Ellen, jt. auth. see Kroll, Steven.

Appleby, Ellen, illus. A Merry Scary Halloween. 16p. (ps-k). 1990. pap. 3.95 casebound (*0-671-70721-3*, Little Simon) S&S Trade.

—Peek-A-Boo. 16p. (ps-k). 1990. pap. 3.95 casebound (*0-671-70722-1*, Little Simon) S&S Trade.

Applegate, Jill, ed. see Petralia, Joseph F.

Applegate, Katherine. The Haunted Palace. Barnhart, Philo, illus. LC 93-70936. 80p. (gr. 1-4). 1993. pap. 2.95 (*1-56282-503-8*) Disney Pr.

—King Triton, Beware! Barnhart, Philo, illus. LC 93-71030. 80p. (gr. 1-4). 1993. pap. 2.95 (*1-56282-502-X*) Disney Pr.

—Love Shack. 1993. pap. 3.50 (*0-06-106793-8*, Harp PBks) HarpC.

—My Sister's Boyfriend. 1992. pap. 3.50 (*0-06-106717-2*, Harp PBks) HarpC.

—Ocean City. 1993. pap. 3.50 (*0-06-106748-2*, Harp PBks) HarpC.

—Story of Colin Powell & Benjamin Davis. (gr. 4-7). 1992. pap. 3.25 (*0-440-40595-5*) Dell.

—The Unbelievable Truth. (gr. 7 up). 1992. pap. 3.50 (*0-06-106774-1*, Harp PBks) HarpC.

—The World's Best Jinx McGee. 80p. (Orig.). (gr. 2). 1992. pap. 2.99 (*0-380-76728-7*, Camelot Young) Avon.

Appleman, Harlene & Shapiro, Jane. A Seder for Tu B'Shevat. McLean, Chari R., illus. 32p. (ps up). 1984. pap. 2.95 (*0-930494-39-3*) Kar Ben.

Appleman, Marc. Joe Montana. (Illus.). (gr. 3-7). 1991. pap. 4.95 (*0-316-04870-4*, Spts Illus Kids) Little.

Appleton, C. M. Steve Urkel's Super-Cool Guide to Success! (Illus.). 64p. (gr. 3-8). 1992. pap. 2.95 (*0-590-45744-6*) Scholastic Inc.

—Yuk It up with Urkel! (ps-3). 1992. pap. 2.95 (*0-590-45745-4*) Scholastic Inc.

Appleton, Doug, illus. Barbie & the Beat Play Set. 24p. 1991. 6.95 (*0-8431-2920-4*) Price Stern.

Appleton, Victor. The Black Dragon. Greenberg, Anne, ed. 176p. (Orig.). 1991. pap. 2.95 (*0-671-67823-X*, Archway) PB.

—Cyborg Kickboxer. Greenberg, Ann, ed. 160p. (Orig.). 1991. pap. 2.95 (*0-671-67825-6*, Archway) PB.

—Death Quake. Greenberg, Anne, ed. 160p. (Orig.). 1993. pap. 2.99 (*0-671-79529-5*, Archway) PB.

—The DNA Disaster. Greenberg, Anne, ed. 160p. (Orig.). 1991. pap. 2.95 (*0-671-67826-4*, Archway) PB.

—Fire Biker. Greenberg, Anne, ed. 160p. 1992. pap. 2.99 (*0-671-75652-4*, Archway) PB.

—The Invisible Force. Barish, Wendy, ed. 192p. (Orig.). (gr. 3-8). 1983. 8.50 (*0-671-43958-8*) S&S Trade.

—The Microbots. Greenberg, Anne, ed. 160p. (Orig.). 1992. pap. 2.99 (*0-671-75651-6*) PB.

—Mind Games. Greenberg, Anne, ed. 160p. (Orig.). 1992. pap. 2.99 (*0-671-75654-0*, Archway) PB.

—Monster Machine. Greenberg, Anne, ed. 160p. (Orig.). 1991. pap. 2.99 (*0-671-67827-2*, Archway) PB.

—Moonstalker. Greenberg, Ann, ed. 160p. (Orig.). 1992. pap. 2.99 (*0-671-75645-1*) PB.

—Mutant Beach. Greenberg, Anne, ed. 160p. (Orig.). (gr. 7 up). 1992. pap. 2.99 (*0-671-75657-5*, Archway) PB.

—The Negative Zone. Greenberg, Anne, ed. 176p. (Orig.). 1991. pap. 2.95 (*0-671-67824-8*, Archway) PB.

—Tom Swift & His Airship. (ps-3). 1992. 12.95 (*1-55709-177-3*) Applewood.

—Tom Swift & His Motor Boat. (ps-3). 1992. 12.95 (*1-55709-176-5*) Applewood.

—Tom Swift & His Motor Cycle. (ps-3). 1992. 12.95 (*1-55709-175-7*) Applewood.

—The Tom Swift Gift Set, 3 vols. Boxed Set. pap. 7.95 (*0-317-12430-7*) S&S Trade.

—Tom Swift: The Alien Probe. 192p. (Orig.). (gr. 3-7). 1981. 8.95 (*0-671-42538-2*); pap. 2.75 (*0-671-42578-1*) S&S Trade.

—Tom Swift: The City in the Stars. 192p. (Orig.). (gr. 3-7). 1981. 8.95 (*0-671-41120-9*); pap. 3.50 (*0-671-41115-2*) S&S Trade.

—Tom Swift: The War in Outer Space. 192p. (Orig.). (gr. 3-7). 1981. 8.95 (*0-671-42539-0*) S&S Trade.

Appleton, Victor, II. Tom Swift & His Electronic Electroscope. (gr. 5-6). 17.95 (*0-88411-462-7*, Pub. by Aeonian Pr) Amereon Ltd.

—Tom Swift & His Space Solatron. (gr. 5-6). 17.95 (*0-88411-457-0*, Pub. by Aeonian Pr) Amereon Ltd.

—Tom Swift & His Triphibian Atomicar. (gr. 5-6). 16.95 (*0-88411-459-7*, Pub. by Aeonian Pr) Amereon Ltd.

—Tom Swift Terror on the Moons of Jupiter. (gr. 5-6). 17.95 (*0-88411-460-0*, Pub. by Aeonian Pr) Amereon Ltd.

—Tom Swift the Alien Probe. (gr. 5-6). 17.95 (*0-88411-464-3*, Pub. by Aeonian Pr) Amereon Ltd.

—Tom Swift the City in the Stars. (gr. 5-6). 17.95 (*0-88411-463-5*, Pub. by Aeonian Pr) Amereon Ltd.

—Tom Swift the Rescue Mission. (gr. 5-6). 17.95 (*0-88411-458-9*, Pub. by Aeonian Pr) Amereon Ltd.

—Tom Swift the Water in Outer Space. (gr. 5-6). 16.95 (*0-88411-465-1*, Pub. by Aeonian Pr) Amereon Ltd.

Apps, Roy. Trouble Next Door. White, Lorrain, illus. 80p. (ps-2). 1992. 13.95 (*0-09-173975-6*, Pub. by Hutchinson UK) Trafalgar.

Apy, Deborah. Beauty & the Beast. Hague, Michael, illus. LC 83-4395. 80p. (gr. 2-4). 1991. 14.95 (*0-8050-1448-9*, Bks Young Read) H Holt & Co.

Apy, Deborah, retold by. Beauty & the Beast. Hague, Michael, illus. LC 83-5495. 80p. (gr. 2-4). 1988. pap. 6.95 (*0-8050-0948-5*, Bks Young Read) H Holt & Co.

Arabian Nights Staff. The Tale of Aladdin & the Wonderful Lamp. Kimmel, Eric A., retold by. Chen, Ju-Hong, illus. LC 91-814. 32p. (ps-3). 1992. reinforced bdg. 14.95 (*0-8234-0938-4*) Holiday.

Aragon, Hilda, illus. My First Nursery Rhyme Book. 28p. (Orig.). (ps-7). 1981. pap. 3.75 (*0-915347-07-5*) Pueblo Acoma Pr.

—A Pueblo Village. 8p. (Orig.). (ps-7). 1982. pap. 4.00 (*0-915347-17-2*) Pueblo Acoma Pr.

Aragon, Jane C. Salt Hands. Rand, Ted, illus. 24p. (ps-2). 1994. pap. 4.99 (*0-14-050321-8*, Puffin Unicorn) Puffin Bks.

Aragon, Jane Chelsea. Salt Hands. Rand, Ted, illus. LC 88-38470. 24p. (ps-2). 1989. 12.95 (*0-525-44489-0*, DCB) Dutton Child Bks.

Aragon, Ray J. de see De Aragon, Ray J.

Aragones, Sergio & Zone, Ray. Aragones 3-D. Aragones, Sergio, illus. 64p. (Orig.). (gr. 9-12). 1989. pap. 4.95 (*0-317-93126-1*) Three-D Zone.

Araki, Chiyo. Origami in the Classroom, 2 vols. LC 65-13412. (Illus.). (gr. 1 up). 1965-68. bds. 14.95 ea. Vol. 1 (*0-8048-0452-4*) Vol. 2 (*0-8048-0453-2*) C E Tuttle.

Araki, Nancy K. & Horii, Jane. Matsuri: Festival! Japanese American Celebrations & Activities. (Illus., Orig.). 1985. pap. 9.95 (*0-89346-019-2*) Heian Intl.

Araluce, Jose R., tr. see Nicholson, Robert.

Araluce, Jose R., tr. see Nicholson, Robert & Watts, Claire.

Araten, Harry. Two by Two: Favorite Bible Stories. Araten, Harry, illus. LC 90-46841. 32p. (gr. k-3). 1991. pap. 7.95 (*0-929371-54-2*) Kar Ben.

Araujo, Frank P. Nekane, the Lamina & the Bear: A Tale of the Basque Pyrenees. Xiao Jun Li, illus. LC 93-84620. 32p. 1993. 16.95 (*1-877810-01-0*) Rayve Prodns.

Arban, Jean B. Complete Conservatory Method for Trumpet (Cornet) or E-Flat Alto, B-Flat Tenor, Baritone, Euphonium & B-Flat Bass in Treble Clef. Goldman, Edwin F. & Smith, Walter M., eds. 350p. (Orig.). 1936. pap. 24.95 (*0-8258-0010-2*, 021) Fischer Inc NY.

Arbeiter, Jean S., jt. ed. see Katz, Marjorie P.

Arbel, Ilil. Favorite Roses Coloring Book. (Illus.). 32p. (gr. 1-3). 1988. pap. 2.95 (*0-486-25845-9*) Dover.

Arboleda, Alba, et al. Outer Space Adventures. (Illus.). 32p. (gr. 3 up). 1986. incl. hand held Decoder 5.95 (*0-88679-462-5*) Educ Insights.

Arceneaux, Marc. Paper Airplanes. (Illus.). 32p. 1974. pap. 4.50 (*0-8431-1703-6*) Price Stern.

Arch Books Staff. Abraham, Sarah, & the Promised Son: Genesis 17, 18: 1-15, 21: 1-7. 1993. pap. 1.89 (*0-570-06183-0*) Concordia.

—Garden & a Promise: Genesis 1-3. (ps-3). 1992. pap. 1.89 (0-570-06072-9) Concordia.
—Story of Noah's Ark: Genesis 6: 5-9: 17. (ps-3). 1993. pap. 1.89 (0-570-06009-5) Concordia.
Archambault, Alan. Paper Soldiers of Civil War. (Illus.). (gr. 1-9). 1992. pap. 3.95 (0-88388-152-7) Bellerophon Bks.
Archambault, Alan, jt. auth. see Canon, Jill.
Archambault, John. Counting Sheep. Rombola, John, illus. LC 89-11163. 32p. (ps-2). 1989. 14.95 (0-8050-1135-8, Bks Young Read) H Holt & Co.
Archambault, John & Martin, Bill, Jr. A Beautiful Feast for a Big King Cat. Degen, Bruce, illus. LC 92-32331. 32p. (ps-3). 1994. 15.00 (0-06-022903-9); PLB 14.89 (0-06-022904-7) HarpC Child Bks. Postponed.
Archambault, John, jt. auth. see Martin, Bill, Jr.
Archard, Cary, ed. Poetry Wales: Twenty-Five Years. 280p. (Orig.). (gr. 10-12). 1990. pap. 21.00 (1-85411-031-4, Pub. by Seren Bks UK) Dufour.
Archbold, Rick. Deep Sea Explorer: The Story of Robert Ballard, Discoverer of the Titanic. LC 93-1983. 160p. (gr. 3-7). 1994. 13.95 (0-590-47232-1) Scholastic Inc.
Archer, Colleen R. Riding High. 73p. (gr. 9-12). 1986. 7.95 (0-920806-39-2, Pub. by Penumbra Pr CN) U of Toronto Pr.
Archer, James. Breaking Barriers: The Feminist Movement. 1991. 14.95 (0-670-83104-2) Viking Child Bks.
Archer, Jules. Earthquake! LC 90-45370. (Illus.). 48p. (gr. 5-6). 1991. RSBE 12.95 (0-89686-593-2, Crestwood Hse) Macmillan Child Grp.
—Hurricane! LC 90-45369. (Illus.). 48p. (gr. 5-6). 1991. RSBE 12.95 (0-89686-597-5, Crestwood Hse) Macmillan Child Grp.
—The Incredible Sixties: The Stormy Years That Changed America. LC 85-16421. (Illus.). 223p. (gr. 7 up). 1986. 17.95 (0-15-238298-4, HB Juv Bks) HarBrace.
—Rage in the Streets: Mob Violence in America. LC 93-5710. 1994. write for info. (0-15-277691-5, Browndeer Pr) HarBrace.
—Superspies: The Secret Side of Government. LC 77-72640. (gr. 7up). 1977. pap. 7.95 (0-440-08136-X) Delacorte.
—They Had a Dream: The Civil Rights Struggle from Frederick Douglass to Marcus Garvey to Martin Luther King, Jr., & Malcolm X. (Illus.). 288p. (gr. 5 up). 1993. 15.99 (0-670-84494-2) Viking Child Bks.
—Tornado! LC 90-45373. (Illus.). 48p. (gr. 5-6). 1991. RSBE 12.95 (0-89686-594-0, Crestwood Hse) Macmillan Child Grp.
—Winners & Losers: How Elections Work in America. LC 83-18368. (Illus.). 240p. (gr. 7 up). 1984. 14.95 (0-15-297945-X, HB Juv Bks) HarBrace.
Archer, Richard P. Concept Spelling's: Language Awareness Workbook. 56p. (Orig.). (gr. 4-12). 1982. 10.00 (0-935276-06-8) Concept Spelling.
—Concept Spelling's: The Secrets of Spelling-Cassette-Workbook. 30p. (gr. 5-12). 1982. Wkbk. 20.00 (0-935276-07-6) Concept Spelling.
Archibald, Paul. Trumpet & Brass. (Illus.). 32p. (gr. 4-7). 1993. PLB 12.40 (0-531-17423-9, Gloucester Pr) Watts.
Ardai, Charles, jt. ed. see Williams, Sheila.
Arden, William. Alfred Hitchcock & the Three Investigators in the Mystery of the Dancing Devil. LC 80-29350. (Illus.). (gr. 4-7). 1984. pap. 2.95 (0-394-86425-5) Random Bks Yng Read.
—Alfred Hitchcock & the Three Investigators in the Mystery of the Dead Man's Riddle. Hearne, William, illus. LC 74-4934. 160p. (gr. 4-7). 1984. pap. 2.95 (0-394-84422-0) Random Bks Yng Read.
—Alfred Hitchcock & the Three Investigators in the Mystery of the Headless Horse, No. 26. LC 77-74458. (Illus.). (gr. 4-8). 1985. pap. 3.95 (0-394-86426-3) Random Bks Yng Read.
—Alfred Hitchcock & the Three Investigators in the Secret of the Crooked Cat. Hitchcock, Alfred, ed. (Illus.). (gr. 4-9). 1985. pap. 2.95 (0-394-86413-1) Random Bks Yng Read.
—Alfred Hitchcock & the Three Investigators in the Secret of Shark Reef. Hitchcock, Alfred, ed. (Illus.). (gr. 4-7). 1985. pap. 3.95 (0-394-84249-9); pap. 2.95 (0-394-86430-1) Random Bks Yng Read.
—Hot Wheels. LC 88-29695. 144p. (gr. 5 up). 1989. PLB 6.99 (0-394-99959-2) Random Bks Yng Read.
—The Mystery of the Deadly Double. LC 79-29638. 160p. (gr. 4-7). 1985. pap. 2.95 (0-394-86428-X) Random Bks Yng Read.
—The Mystery of the Headless Horse. Hitchcock, Alfred, ed. LC 80-29259. 160p. (gr. 4-7). 1985. pap. 3.95 (0-685-57772-4) Random Bks Yng Read.
—The Mystery of the Purple Pirate. LC 82-372. (Illus.). 192p. (gr. 4-7). 1982. lib. bdg. 6.99 (0-394-94951-X); pap. 2.95 (0-394-84951-5) Random Bks Yng Read.
—The Mystery of the Smashing Glass. LC 83-26984. (Illus.). 192p. (gr. 4-7). 1984. pap. 2.95 (0-394-86550-2) Random Bks Yng Read.
Ardizzone, Edward. The Little Tim & Brave Sea Captain. (Illus.). 48p. (ps-3). 1983. pap. 3.99 (0-14-050175-4, Puffin) Puffin Bks.
—Tim All Alone. (Illus.). 48p. (ps-7). 1990. pap. 6.95 (0-19-272125-9) OUP.
—Tim & Charlotte. (Illus.). 48p. (ps-6). 1987. pap. 6.95 (0-19-272118-6) OUP.
—Tim & Ginger. Ardizzone, Edward, illus. 48p. (ps-3). 1987. pap. 6.95 (0-19-272113-5) OUP.

—Tim in Danger. (Illus.). 48p. (ps-3). 1987. pap. 6.95 (0-19-272106-2) OUP.
—Tim to the Lighthouse. (Illus.). 48p. (gr. 1-4). 1987. pap. 6.95 (0-19-272107-0) OUP.
—Tim's Friend Towser. Ardizzone, Edward, illus. 48p. (ps-3). 1987. pap. 6.95 (0-19-272112-7) OUP.
Ardley, Bridget & Ardley, Neil. The Random House Book of 1001 Questions & Answers. LC 88-23200. (Illus.). 176p. (Orig.). (gr. 3-7). 1989. PLB 12.99 (0-394-99992-4); 13.00 (0-394-89992-X) Random Bks Yng Read.
Ardley, Brigette & Ardley, Neil. Greece. (Illus.). 48p. (gr. 4-8). 1989. lib. bdg. 14.98 (0-382-09822-6) Silver Burdett Pr.
—India. (Illus.). 48p. (gr. 4-8). 1989. lib. bdg. 14.98 (0-382-09795-5) Silver Burdett Pr.
Ardley, N. The Science Book of Gravity. 1992. 9.95 (0-15-200621-4, Gulliver Bks) HarBrace.
—The Science Book of Motion. 1992. 9.95 (0-15-200622-2, Gulliver Bks) HarBrace.
—The Science Book of Weather. 1992. 9.95 (0-15-200624-9, Gulliver Bks) HarBrace.
Ardley, Neil. Bridges. Stefoff, Rebecca, ed. LC 90-40247. (Illus.). 48p. (gr. 4-7). 1990. PLB 17.26 (0-944483-74-7) Garrett Ed Corp.
—Dams. Stefoff, Rebecca, ed. LC 90-40360. (Illus.). 48p. (gr. 4-7). 1990. PLB 17.26 (0-944483-75-5) Garrett Ed Corp.
—Dictionary of Science. LC 93-29811. 1994. write for info. (1-56458-349-X) Dorling Kindersley.
—Electricity. LC 91-4963. (Illus.). 48p. (gr. 8-9). 1992. RSBE 13.95 (0-02-705665-1, New Discovery) Macmillan Child Grp.
—Heat. LC 91-29057. (Illus.). 48p. (gr. 6 up). 1992. RSBE 13.95 (0-02-705666-X, New Discovery) Macmillan Child Grp.
—Language & Communications. (Illus.). 40p. (gr. 5-9). 1989. PLB 12.40 (0-531-17187-6, Gloucester Pr) Watts.
—Light. LC 91-25740. (Illus.). 48p. (gr. 8-9). 1992. RSBE 13.95 (0-02-705667-8, New Discovery) Macmillan Child Grp.
—Muscles to Machines: Projects with Movement. 1990. PLB 12.40 (0-531-17200-7) Watts.
—Music. King, Dave, et al, photos by. LC 88-13394. (Illus.). 64p. (gr. 5 up). 1989. 15.00 (0-394-82259-5); lib. 15.99 (0-394-92259-X) Knopf Bks Yng Read.
—Oil Rigs. Stefoff, Rebecca, ed. LC 90-40246. (Illus.). 48p. (gr. 4-7). 1990. PLB 17.26 (0-944483-76-3) Garrett Ed Corp.
—One Hundred One Great Science Experiments. (Illus.). 120p. (gr. k-3). 1993. 16.95 (1-56458-404-6) Dorling Kindersley.
—Science Book of Air. 29p. (gr. 2-5). 1991. 9.95 (0-15-200578-1) HarBrace.
—Science Book of Color. 29p. (gr. 2-5). 1991. 9.95 (0-15-200576-5) HarBrace.
—Science Book of Electricity. 29p. (gr. 2-5). 1991. 9.95 (0-15-200583-8, HB Juv Bks) HarBrace.
—Science Book of Energy. (gr. 4-7). 1992. 9.95 (0-15-200611-7, HB Juv Bks) HarBrace.
—The Science Book of Hot & Cold. (gr. 4-7). 1992. 9.95 (0-15-200612-5, HB Juv Bks) HarBrace.
—Science Book of Light. 29p. (gr. 2-5). 1991. 9.95 (0-15-200577-3) HarBrace.
—Science Book of Machines. (gr. 4-7). 1992. 9.95 (0-15-200613-3, HB Juv Bks) HarBrace.
—Science Book of Magnets. 29p. (gr. 2-5). 1991. 9.95 (0-15-200581-1, HB Juv Bks) HarBrace.
—Science Book of Sound. 29p. (gr. 2-5). 1991. 9.95 (0-15-200579-X, HB Juv Bks) HarBrace.
—Science Book of the Senses. (gr. 4-7). 1992. 9.95 (0-15-200614-1, HB Juv Bks) HarBrace.
—Science Book of Things That Grow. 29p. (gr. 2-5). 1991. 9.95 (0-15-200586-2, HB Juv Bks) HarBrace.
—Science Book of Water. 29p. (gr. 2-5). 1991. 9.95 (0-15-200575-7) HarBrace.
—Sound Waves to Music: Projects with Sound. (Illus.). 32p. (gr. 5-8). 1990. PLB 12.40 (0-531-17236-8, Gloucester Pr) Watts.
Ardley, Neil, jt. auth. see Ardley, Bridget.
Ardley, Neil, jt. auth. see Ardley, Brigette.
Arehart, Lynda L. & Torrie, Margaret. Understanding HIV-AIDS: A Workbook Suitable for Mainstreamed Students. (Illus.). 48p. (gr. 9-12). 1990. tchrs. ed. 8.95 (0-8138-1619-X); wkbk. 4.95x (0-8138-1618-1) Iowa St U Pr.
Arem, Joel. Rocks & Minerals. Boltin, Lee & Arem, Joel, photos by. LC 91-74106. (Illus.). 160p. (gr. 7-12). 1991. pap. 8.95 (0-945005-06-7) Geoscience Pr.
Arem, Joel E. Descubre Dinosaurios. University of Mexico City Staff, tr. from SPA. O'Neill, Pablo M. & Robare, Lorie, illus. 48p. (gr. 3-8). 1993. PLB 16.95 (1-56674-049-5, HTS Bks) Forest Hse.
—Descubre Rocas y Minerales. University of Mexico City Staff, tr. from SPA. O'Neill, Pablo M. & Robare, Lorie, illus. 48p. (gr. 3-8). 1993. PLB 16.95 (1-56674-051-7, HTS Bks) Forest Hse.
Arem, Tzvi Z. The Story of Reb Baruch Ber: The Kamenitzer Rosh Yeshiba - Rabbi Baruch Ber Leibowitz & His Successor, Rabbi Reuven Grozovsky. (Illus.). 128p. (gr. 6-12). 1987. 11.95 (0-89906-804-9); pap. 8.95 (0-89906-805-7) Mesorah Pubns.
Arenas, Jose F. The Key to Renaissance Art. (Illus.). 80p. (gr. 8 up). 1990. PLB 21.50 (0-8225-2057-5) Lerner Pubns.

Argaman, Shmuel. The Captivity of Mahram. Henlicky, Gregg, illus. LC 90-83947. 120p. (gr. 3-5). 1990. 11.95 (1-56062-045-5); pap. 8.95 (0-685-46904-2) CIS Comm.
Argent, Kerry. Happy Birthday, Wombat! A Lift-the-Flap Book. (ps). 1991. 11.95 (0-316-05097-0, Joy St Bks) Little.
Argent, Kerry & Trinca, Rod. One Woolly Wombat. LC 84-21854. (Illus.). 32p. (ps-1). 1985. 12.95 (0-916291-00-6) Kane Miller Bk.
—One Woolly Wombat. Argent, Kerry, illus. 32p. (ps-1). 1987. pap. 6.95 (0-916291-10-3) Kane-Miller Bk.
Argent, Philip, illus. Sing Nowell! 64p. (gr. 1-6). 1991. pap. 14.95 (0-7136-5695-6, Pub. by A&C Black UK) Talman.
Arginteanu, Judy. The Movies of Alfred Hitchcock. LC 93-23990. 1994. 18.95 (0-8225-1642-X) Lerner Pubns.
Argon, Hilda. Counting Book. (Illus.). 20p. (Orig.). (ps-7). 1981. pap. 3.75 (0-915347-15-6) Pueblo Acoma Pr.
Argueta, Manlio & Ross, Stacey. The Magic Dogs of the Volcanoes (Los perros magicos de los volcanoes) Simmons, Elly, illus. LC 90-2254. (SPA & ENG.). 32p. (gr. k-5). 1990. 13.95 (0-89239-064-6) Childrens Book Pr.
Arico, Diane, ed. A Season of Joy: Favorite Stories & Poems for Christmas. San Souci, Daniel, illus. LC 86-29059. 64p. (gr. k-3). 1987. Doubleday.
Arico, Diane, ed. see Crocker, Chris.
Arico, Diane, ed. see Keene, Carolyn & Dixon, Franklin W.
Arico, Diane, ed. see McGee, Eddie.
Arico, Diane, ed. see Matthews, Gordon.
Arico, Diane, ed. see Rotsler, William.
Arico, Diane, ed. see Sullivan, George.
Aries, Ruby. Dream & Play with Us: Come Share Tim's & Lisa's Adventures & Learn How to Play Their Games. Loft, Randi, ed. Aries, Ruby, illus. 115p. (Orig.). (gr. k-4). 1990. pap. 14.95 (0-9626570-5-0) Perk-Lo Pk Prodns.
Ariev, Lauren. What Can Baby Do? Morgan, Mary, illus. 24p. (ps). 1992. bds. write for info. (0-307-06140-X, 6140) Western Pub.
—Who Are Baby's Friends? Morgan, Mary, illus. 24p. (ps). 1992. bds. write for info. (0-307-06142-6, 6142, Golden Pr) Western Pub.
Aristophanes. Four Major Plays. new ed. Teitel, N. R., intro. by. Incl. The Acharnians; The Birds; The Clouds; Lysistrata. (gr. 11 up). 1968. pap. 2.95 (0-8049-0189-9, CL-189) Airmont.
Aristophanes see Lind, Levi R.
Aristotle. Politics. Barker, Ernest, tr. (gr. 9 up). 1946. pap. 11.95x (0-19-500306-3) OUP.
Arkhurst, Joyce C., retold by. The Adventures of Spider: West African Folk Tales. Pinkney, Jerry, illus. LC 92-444. 1992. 6.95 (0-316-05107-1) Little.
Arkin, Alan. The Lemming Condition. Sandin, Joan, illus. LC 75-6296. 64p. (gr. 4 up). 1976. 13.00 (0-06-020133-9) HarpC Child Bks.
—Some Fine Grampa! Zimmer, Dirk, illus. LC 92-24436. 32p. (gr. k-3). 1994. 14.00 (0-06-021533-X); PLB 13.89 (0-06-021534-8) HarpC Child Bks.
Arkow, Phil. Teacher's Pet Projects: A Pet Education Program. Gress, Jonna, ed. Regan, Dana, illus. 14p. (Orig.). (gr. k-3). 1993. pap. 16.20 incl. tchr's. guide, stickers, board game, bulletin board decos, & 5 reproducibles (0-944943-22-5, 20554-8) Current Inc.
Armbruster, Ann. The American Flag. (Illus.). 64p. (gr. 5-8). 1991. PLB 12.90 (0-531-20045-0) Watts.
Armbruster, Ann & Taylor, Elizabeth A. Astronaut Training. (Illus.). 64p. (gr. 5-8). 1990. PLB 12.90 (0-531-10862-7) Watts.
—Tornadoes. LeMonnier, Joe, illus. LC 89-31827. 64p. (gr. 4-7). 1989. PLB 12.90 (0-531-10755-8) Watts.
—Tornadoes. (Illus.). 64p. (gr. 5-8). 1993. pap. 5.95 (0-531-15666-4) Watts.
Armer, Laura A. Waterless Mountain. Armer, Laura A., illus. LC 8-3. 1931. 11.95 (0-679-20233-1) Random Bks Yng Read.
—Waterless Mountain. LC 92-32066. (Illus.). 240p. (gr. 3-5). 1993. 16.00 (0-679-84502-X) Knopf Bks Yng Read.
Armintrout, W. G. Death Game 2090. Barrett, Kevin, ed. Aulisio, Janet, et al, illus. 48p. (Orig.). (gr. 9-12). 1990. pap. 9.00 (1-55806-132-0, 5106) Iron Crown Ent Inc.
Armitage, Barry. Motorcycles. LC 88-16964. (Illus.). 32p. (gr. 2-8). 1988. 12.95 (0-8069-6892-3) Sterling.
Armitage, David, jt. auth. see Armitage, Ronda.
Armitage, Peter. The Innu. (Illus.). 112p. (gr. 5 up). 1991. lib. bdg. 17.95 (0-685-47584-0) Chelsea Hse.
—The Montagnais-Naskapi. (Illus.). (gr. 5 up). 1989. 17.95 (1-55546-717-2) Chelsea Hse.
Armitage, Ronda & Armitage, David. Harry Hates Shopping! LC 92-27945. (Illus.). 32p. (ps-2). 1993. pap. 2.95 (0-590-45886-8) Scholastic Inc.
Armond, Dale de see De Armond, Dale.
Armour, Peter. Stop That Pickle! Shachat, Andrew, illus. LC 92-903541. 1993. 14.95 (0-395-66375-X) HM.
Armstrong, B. Animal Ecograms. (Illus.). (gr. 1 up). 1991. 20 picture postcards 7.95 (0-88160-202-7, LW296) Learning Wks.
—Birds. 32p. (gr. 1-6). 1988. 3.95 (0-88160-161-6, LW 266) Learning Wks.
—Bodacious Borders. LC 92-81600. 68p. 1992. 9.95 (0-88160-214-0, LW208) Learning Wks.
—Build a Doodle. No. 1. 32p. (gr. k-4). 1985. 2.95 (0-88160-124-1, LW 133) Learning Wks.
—Build a Doodle, No. 2. 32p. (gr. k-4). 1985. 2.95 (0-88160-125-X, LW 134) Learning Wks.

—Dinosaurs. 32p. (gr. 1-7). 1988. 3.95 (*0-88160-160-8*, LW 265) Learning Wks.
—Fishes. 32p. (gr. 1-6). 1988. 3.95 (*0-88160-163-2*, LW 268) Learning Wks.
—Mammals. 32p. (gr. 1-6). 1988. 3.95 (*0-88160-162-4*, LW 267) Learning Wks.
—Primary Awards Galore. (gr. k-3). 1985. 5.95 (*0-88160-121-7*, LW 132) Learning Wks.
—Reptiles. 32p. (gr. 1-6). 1988. 3.95 (*0-88160-164-0*, LW 269) Learning Wks.
Armstrong, Bev. Dinosaur Detective. Armstrong, Bev, illus. 32p. (gr. k-3). 1979. 3.95 (*0-88160-075-X*, LW 808) Learning Wks.
—Have Fun Following Directions. Armstrong, Bev, illus. 32p. (gr. 1-3). 1979. wkbk. 3.95 (*0-88160-077-6*, LW 810) Learning Wks.
—Insects. (Illus.). 48p. (gr. 2-5). 1990. 5.95 (*0-88160-192-6*, LW 151) Learning Wks.
—Who's Following Directions? Armstrong, Bev, illus. 32p. (gr. 4-7). 1979. wkbk. 3.95 (*0-88160-072-5*, LW 805) Learning Wks.
Armstrong, Beverly. Awards Galore. 48p. (gr. 1-6). 1981. 5.95 (*0-88160-040-7*, LW 225) Learning Wks.
—Build a Doodle Circus. (Illus.). 32p. (gr. k-4). 1986. 2.95 (*0-88160-133-0*, LW138) Learning Wks.
—Build a Doodle City. (Illus.). 32p. (gr. k-4). 1986. 2.95 (*0-88160-132-2*, LW136) Learning Wks.
—Build a Doodle Farm. (Illus.). 32p. (gr. k-4). 1986. 2.95 (*0-88160-130-6*, LW135) Learning Wks.
—Build a Doodle Ocean. (Illus.). 32p. (gr. k-4). 1986. 2.95 (*0-88160-131-4*, LW137) Learning Wks.
—Christmas Capers. (Illus.). 24p. (gr. 2-6). 1987. 4.95 (*0-88160-151-9*, LW264) Learning Wks.
—Clip Art Carousel: All Purpose Art. (Illus.). 32p. (gr. 1-6). 1986. 4.95 (*0-88160-137-3*, LW139) Learning Wks.
—Clip Art Carousel: Holidays & Celebrations. (Illus.). 32p. (gr. 1-6). 1986. 4.95 (*0-88160-140-3*, LW140) Learning Wks.
—Clip Art Carousel: People & Places. (Illus.). 32p. (gr. 1-6). 1986. 4.95 (*0-88160-142-X*, LW142) Learning Wks.
—Clip Art Carousel: Science & Math. (Illus.). 32p. (gr. 1-6). 1986. 4.95 (*0-88160-141-1*, LW141) Learning Wks.
—Endangered Animals - Superdoodles. 32p. (gr. 1-6). 1994. 4.95 (*0-88160-228-0*, LW323) Learning Wks.
—The Hanukkah Happening. (Illus.). 24p. (gr. 2-6). 1987. 4.95 (*0-88160-150-0*, LW263) Learning Wks.
—Marine Life - Superdoodles. 32p. (gr. 1-6). 1994. 4.95 (*0-88160-227-2*, LW322) Learning Wks.
—Pirates, Explorers, Tailblazers. 112p. (gr. 4-6). 1987. 9.95 (*0-88160-152-7*, LW 908) Learning Wks.
—Punctuation Passport. 38p. (gr. 4-6). 1979. 6.95 (*0-88160-029-6*, LW 214) Learning Wks.
—Reptiles - Superdoodles. 32p. (gr. 1-6). 1994. 4.95 (*0-88160-229-9*, LW324) Learning Wks.
—Zoo - Superdoodles. 32p. (gr. 1-6). 1994. 4.95 (*0-88160-230-2*, LW325) Learning Wks.
Armstrong, Beverly, jt. auth. see Artell, Mike.
Armstrong, Beverly, jt. auth. see Renfro, Nancy.
Armstrong, Carole & Peppin, Anthea. All My Own Work! Adventures in Art. (Illus.). 48p. (gr. 2-7). 1993. pap. 6.95 (*0-8120-1755-2*) Barron.
Armstrong, Donald see Landau, Elaine.
Armstrong, Jennifer. Ann of the Wild Rose, Seventeen Seventy-Four, No. 2. 1994. pap. 2.94 (*0-553-29867-4*) Bantam.
—Chin Yu Min & the Ginger Cat. GrandPre, Mary, illus. LC 92-8658. 32p. (ps-4). 1993. 15.00 (*0-517-58656-8*); PLB 15.99 (*0-517-58657-6*) Crown Bks Yng Read.
—Hilary to the Rescue. (gr. 3-6). 1990. pap. 2.75 (*0-553-15812-0*) Bantam.
—Hugh Can Do. Root, Kimberly B., illus. LC 90-46275. 40p. (ps-4). 1992. 15.00 (*0-517-58218-X*); PLB 15.99 (*0-517-58219-8*) Crown Bks Yng Read.
—Little Salt Lick & the Sun King. Goodell, Jon, illus. LC 93-18673. 1994. write for info. (*0-517-59620-2*); write for info. (*0-517-59621-0*) Crown Bks Yng Read.
—Steal Away. LC 91-18504. 224p. (gr. 6 up). 1992. 15.95 (*0-531-05983-9*); lib. bdg. 15.99 (*0-531-08583-X*) Orchard Bks Watts.
—Steal Away. 224p. (gr. 3-7). 1993. pap. 3.25 (*0-590-46921-5*, Apple Paperbacks) Scholastic Inc.
—That Champion Chimp. (gr. 4-7). 1990. pap. 2.75 (*0-553-15828-7*) Bantam.
—That Terrible Baby. Meddaugh, Susan, illus. LC 93-14727. 32p. 1994. 14.00 (*0-688-11832-1*, Tambourine Bks); PLB 13.93 (*0-688-11833-X*, Tambourine Bks) Morrow.
—Too Many Pets. (gr. 4-7). 1990. pap. 2.75 (*0-553-15804-X*) Bantam.
—The Whittler's Tale. Vasiliev, Valery, illus. LC 93-14749. 1994. write for info. (*0-688-10751-6*, Tambourine Bks); PLB write for info. (*0-688-10752-4*) Morrow.
—Wild Rose Inn. 1994. pap. 3.99 (*0-553-29866-6*) Bantam.
—Wild Rose Inn, No. 3. (gr. 7 up). 1994. pap. 3.99 (*0-553-29909-3*) Bantam.
Armstrong, John. Track Planning for Realistic Operation. rev. ed. LC 63-5732. (Illus.). 100p. (gr. 6). 1979. pap. 7.95 (*0-89024-504-5*) Kalmbach.
Armstrong, Nancy. Navajo Children. (gr. 2-6). 1975. 1.95 (*0-89992-037-3*) Coun India Ed.
—Navajo Long Walk. (gr. 4-9). 1983. pap. 7.95 (*0-89992-083-7*) Coun India Ed.

Armstrong, Nancy, et al. The Heritage. (gr. 3-6). 1977. 1.95 (*0-89992-065-9*) Coun India Ed.
Armstrong, S., jt. auth. see Hawthorn, P.
Armstrong, Velma. The Banana Horse. Graves, Helen, ed. LC 85-51966. 104p. (gr. 3-6). 1986. pap. 6.95 (*0-938232-98-3*) Winston-Derek.
Armstrong, Vicki. A Dragon Drinks Just One Drop. Armstrong, Bruce, illus. 32p. (gr. 1-6). 1990. wkbk. 5.99 (*0-933367-01-5*) See the Sounds.
—Pigs Pet People. Armstrong, Bruce, illus. (ps-4). 1985. wkbk. 5.99 (*0-933367-00-7*) See the Sounds.
Armstrong, Virgil. The Assassination of General George Armstrong Custer: The True Story Behind the Battle of the Little Big Horn. Whitman, Patricia, ed. 300p. (gr. 9-12). 1990. pap. write for info. (*0-925390-22-4*) Armstrong Assocs.
Armstrong, Wayne. Camping Basics. Schoolcraft, Robert, illus. LC 85-9407. 48p. (gr. 3-7). 1985. 10.95 (*0-13-112657-1*) P-H.
Armstrong, William. Health, Happiness, Humor & Holiness. Graves, Helen, ed. LC 86-51342. (Illus.). 86p. (gr. 3-8). 1987. pap. text ed. 5.95 (*1-55523-065-2*) Winston-Derek.
Armstrong, William H. Sounder. LC 70-85030. (Illus.). 128p. (gr. 6 up). 1969. 14.00 (*0-06-020143-6*); PLB 13.89 (*0-06-020144-4*) HarpC Child Bks.
—Sounder. Barkley, James, illus. LC 70-85030. 128p. (gr. 6 up). 1972. pap. 3.95 (*0-06-440020-4*, Trophy) HarpC Child Bks.
—Sounder. large type ed. Barkley, James, illus. 99p. (gr. 2-6). 1987. Repr. of 1969 ed. lib. bdg. 13.95 (*1-55736-003-0*, Crnrstn Bks) BDD LT Grp.
—Sour Land. LC 70-135783. 128p. (gr. 6 up). 1971. PLB 13.89 (*0-06-020142-8*) HarpC Child Bks.
—Sour Land. LC 70-135783. 128p. (gr. 7 up). 1976. pap. 3.95 (*0-06-440074-3*, Trophy) HarpC Child Bks.
Arnaud, Catherine M. A Gallery of Games. Schwartz, Marc, photos by. Collomb, Etienne. LC 93-25053. (gr. 4 up). 1994. 13.95 (*0-395-68379-3*) Ticknor & Fields.
Arndt, Walter, tr. see Busch, Wilhelm.
Arneach, Lloyd, as told by. The Animals' Ballgame: A Story from the Eastern Band of the Cherokee Nation. LC 92-9416. (Illus.). (ps-3). 1992. PLB 16.93 (*0-516-05139-3*) Childrens.
Arneson, D. J. Bats: A Nature-Fact Book. (Illus.). 32p. 1992. pap. 2.50 (*1-56156-147-9*) Kidsbks.
—The Human Body. (Illus.). 32p. 1991. pap. 2.50 (*1-56156-024-3*) Kidsbks.
—Incredible Insects. (Illus.). 24p. (Orig.). 1990. pap. 2.50 (*0-942025-20-2*) Kidsbks.
—Martin Luther King Poster Book. (Illus.). 6p. 1992. pap. 2.95 (*1-56156-161-4*) Kidsbks.
—Nutrition & Disease: Looking for the Link. LC 92-14473. (Illus.). 128p. (gr. 9-12). 1992. PLB 13.40 (*0-531-12504-1*) Watts.
—Rocks & Minerals. Friedman, Howard, illus. 32p. (Orig.). 1990. pap. 2.50 (*0-942025-90-3*) Kidsbks.
—Toxic Cops. LC 90-13102. (Illus.). 128p. (gr. 7-12). 1991. PLB 13.40 (*0-531-12525-4*) Watts.
Arneson, D. J., retold by see Barrie, J. M.
Arneson, D. J., ed. see London, Jack.
Arneson, D. J., retold by see Pyle, Howard.
Arneson, D. J., retold by see Shelley, Mary Wollstonecraft.
Arneson, D. J., retold by see Swift, Jonathan.
Arno, Roger. The Story of Space & Rockets. (Illus.). (gr. 5). 1978. pap. 3.95 (*0-88388-063-6*) Bellerophon Bks.
Arnold & Posey. Do It Yourself. large type ed. 86p. (gr. 7-12). 1983. Repr. of 1971 ed. 12.16 (*0-317-01883-3*, 4-04720-00) Am Printing Hse.
Arnold, Arnold. Antique Paper Dolls, 1915-1920. 1976. pap. 3.95 (*0-486-23176-3*) Dover.
—Pictures & Stories from Forgotten Children's Books. (Illus.). 170p. (Orig.). (gr. k-6). 1970. pap. 7.50 (*0-486-22041-9*) Dover.
Arnold, Caroline. The Ancient Cliff Dwellers of Mesa Verde. Hewett, Richard, illus. 64p. (gr. 3-6). 1992. 15.45 (*0-395-56241-4*, Clarion Bks) HM.
—Australia Today. LC 87-10660. (Illus.). 96p. (gr. 4-9). 1987. PLB 10.90 (*0-531-10377-3*) Watts.
—Camel. Hewett, Richard, illus. LC 91-26805. 48p. (gr. 2 up). 1992. 15.00 (*0-688-09498-8*); PLB 14.93 (*0-688-09499-6*) Morrow Jr Bks.
—Cats: In from the Wild. Hewett, Richard R., photos by. LC 92-32986. (Illus.). 1993. 19.95 (*0-87614-692-2*) Carolrhoda Bks.
—Cheetah. Hewett, Richard, photos by. LC 88-39940. (Illus.). 48p. (gr. 2 up). 1989. 12.95 (*0-688-08143-6*); PLB 12.88 (*0-688-08144-4*) Morrow Jr Bks.
—Cheetah. ALC Staff, ed. Hewett, Richard, illus. LC 88-39940. (Illus.). 48p. (gr. 3 up). 1992. pap. 5.95 (*0-688-11696-5*, Mulberry) Morrow.
—Coping with Natural Disasters. (gr. 5 up). 1988. 13.95 (*0-8027-6716-8*); PLB 14.85 (*0-8027-6717-6*) Walker & Co.
—Dinosaur Mountain. (gr. 4-7). 1993. pap. 6.95 (*0-395-66503-5*, Clarion Bks) HM.
—Dinosaurs All Around: An Artist's View of the Prehistoric World. Hewett, Richard, photos by. LC 92-5726. (Illus.). 48p. (gr. 3-6). 1993. 14.45 (*0-395-62464-3*, Clarion Bks) HM.
—Dinosaurs Down Under: And Other Fossils from Australia. Hewett, Richard, photos by. (Illus.). 48p. (gr. 3-7). 1990. 15.45 (*0-89919-814-7*) HM.
—Elephant. Hewett, Richard, photos by. LC 92-31095. (Illus.). 48p. (gr. 2 up). 1993. 15.00 (*0-688-11342-7*); PLB 14.93 (*0-688-11343-5*) Morrow Jr Bks.

—Fireflies. Johnson, Pamela, illus. LC 93-30439. 1994. write for info. (*0-590-46944-4*) Scholastic Inc.
—Flamingo. Hewett, Richard, photos by. LC 90-19186. (Illus.). 48p. (gr. 2 up). 1991. 13.95 (*0-688-09411-2*); PLB 13.88 (*0-688-09412-0*) Morrow Jr Bks.
—Giraffe. Hewett, Richard, illus. LC 87-1502. 48p. (gr. 2-5). 1987. 12.95 (*0-688-07069-8*); lib. bdg. 12.88 (*0-688-07070-1*, Morrow Jr Bks) Morrow Jr Bks.
—Giraffe. Hewett, Richard, photos by. LC 92-25550. (Illus.). 48p. (gr. 3 up). 1993. pap. 5.95 (*0-688-12272-8*, Mulberry) Morrow.
—A Guide Dog Puppy Grows Up. Hewett, Richard, photos by. (Illus.). 43p. (gr. 1 up). 1991. 16.95 (*0-15-232657-X*) HarBrace.
—Heart Disease. LC 90-33609. (Illus.). 96p. (gr. 9-12). 1990. PLB 13.90 (*0-531-10884-8*) Watts.
—Hippo. Hewett, Richard, photos by. LC 88-39794. (Illus.). 48p. (gr. 2 up). 1989. 12.95 (*0-688-08145-2*); PLB 12.88 (*0-688-08146-0*, Morrow Jr Bks) Morrow Jr Bks.
—Hippo. ALC Staff, ed. Hewett, Richard, illus. LC 88-39794. 48p. (gr. 3 up). 1992. pap. 5.95 (*0-688-11697-3*, Mulberry) Morrow.
—House Sparrows Everywhere. Hewett, Richard R., photos by. (Illus.). 48p. (gr. 2-5). 1992. 19.95 (*0-87614-696-5*) Carolrhoda Bks.
—Kangaroo. Hewett, Richard, illus. LC 86-18103. 48p. (gr. 2-5). 1987. 12.95 (*0-688-06480-9*); lib. bdg. 12.88 (*0-688-06481-7*, Morrow Jr Bks) Morrow Jr Bks.
—Kangaroo. Hewett, Richard, photos by. LC 86-18103. (Illus.). (gr. 3 up). 1992. pap. 5.95 (*0-688-11502-0*, Mulberry) Morrow.
—Koala. Hewett, Richard, illus. LC 86-18092. 48p. (gr. 2-5). 1987. 13.95 (*0-688-06478-7*); lib. bdg. 13.88 (*0-688-06479-5*, Morrow Jr Bks) Morrow Jr Bks.
—Koala. Hewett, Richard, photos by. LC 86-18092. (Illus.). 48p. (gr. 3 up). 1992. pap. 5.95 (*0-688-11503-9*, Mulberry) Morrow.
—Llama. Hewett, Richard, photos by. LC 87-27130. (Illus.). 48p. (gr. 2-5). 1988. 12.95 (*0-688-07540-1*); PLB 12.88 (*0-688-07541-X*) Morrow Jr Bks.
—Monkey. Hewett, Richard, photos by. LC 92-31094. (Illus.). 48p. (gr. 2 up). 1993. 15.00 (*0-688-11344-3*); PLB 14.93 (*0-688-11345-1*) Morrow Jr Bks.
—The Olympic Summer Games. (Illus.). 64p. (gr. 5-8). 1991. PLB 12.90 (*0-531-20052-3*) Watts.
—The Olympic Winter Games. (Illus.). 64p. (gr. 5-8). 1991. PLB 12.90 (*0-531-20053-1*) Watts.
—On the Brink of Extinction: The California Condor. Wallace, Michael, photos by. LC 92-14914. (Illus.). 1993. write for info. (*0-15-257990-7*) HarBrace.
—On the Brink of Extinction: The California Condor. LC 92-14914. (gr. 4-7). 1993. pap. 8.95 (*0-15-257991-5*) HarBrace.
—Orangutan. Hewett, Richard, photos by. LC 89-38957. (Illus.). 48p. (gr. 2 up). 1990. 13.95 (*0-688-08826-0*); PLB 13.88 (*0-688-08827-9*, Morrow Jr Bks) Morrow Jr Bks.
—Ostriches & Other Flightless Birds. Hewett, Richard R., illus. 48p. (gr. 2-5). 1990. PLB 19.95 (*0-87614-377-X*) Carolrhoda Bks.
—Pain: What Is It? How Do We Deal with It? LC 86-29815. (Illus.). 96p. (gr. 3-7). 1986. 12.95 (*0-688-05710-1*); lib. bdg. 12.88 (*0-688-05711-X*, Morrow Jr Bks) Morrow Jr Bks.
—Panda. Hewett, Richard, illus. LC 91-33251. 48p. (gr. 2 up). 1992. 15.00 (*0-688-09496-1*); PLB 14.93 (*0-688-09497-X*) Morrow Jr Bks.
—Pele: The King of Soccer. Mathews, V., ed. LC 91-33557. (Illus.). 64p. (gr. 3-6). 1992. PLB 12.90 (*0-531-20077-9*) Watts.
—Penguin. Hewett, Richard, photos by. LC 87-31458. (Illus.). 48p. (gr. 2-5). 1988. 12.95 (*0-688-07706-4*); PLB 12.88 (*0-688-07707-2*) Morrow Jr Bks.
—Pets Without Homes. Hewett, Richard, illus. LC 83-2106. 48p. (gr. k-3). 1983. 14.95 (*0-89919-191-6*, Clarion Bks) HM.
—Reindeer. Johnson, Pamela, illus. LC 93-12981. (gr. 4-7). 1993. pap. 3.95 (*0-590-46943-6*) Scholastic Inc.
—Saving the Peregrine Falcon. Hewett, Richard R., photos by. LC 84-15576. (Illus.). 48p. (gr. 2-5). 1985. PLB 19.95 (*0-87614-225-0*); pap. 6.95 (*0-87614-523-3*) Carolrhoda Bks.
—Sea Lion. Hewett, Richard, photos by. LC 93-27007. (Illus.). 1994. write for info. (*0-688-12027-X*); lib. bdg. write for info. (*0-688-12028-8*) Morrow Jr Bks.
—Sea Turtles. Peck, Marshall, illus. LC 93-6353. 1994. 3.95 (*0-590-46945-2*) Scholastic Inc.
—Snake. Hewett, Richard, photos by. LC 90-22591. (Illus.). 48p. (gr. 2 up). 1991. 13.95 (*0-688-09409-0*); PLB 13.88 (*0-688-09410-4*) Morrow Jr Bks.
—Soccer: From Neighborhood Play to the World Cup. LC 91-12830. (Illus.). 64p. (gr. 5-8). 1991. PLB 12.90 (*0-531-20037-X*) Watts.
—The Terrible Hodag. Davis, Lambert, illus. 30p. (ps-3). 1989. 14.95 (*0-15-284750-2*) HarBrace.
—Trapped in Tar: Fossils from the Ice Age. Hewett, Richard. LC 86-17614. (Illus.). 64p. (gr. 3-6). 1987. 13.45 (*0-89919-415-X*, Clarion Bks); pap. 5.95 (*0-395-54783-0*, Clarion Bks) HM.
—Tule Elk. Hewett, Richard R., photos by. (Illus.). 48p. (gr. 2-5). 1989. 19.95 (*0-87614-343-5*) Carolrhoda Bks.
—A Walk by the Seashore. Brook, Bonnie, ed. Tanz, Freya, illus. 32p. (ps-1). 1990. 5.95 (*0-671-68666-6*); lib. bdg. 9.98 (*0-671-68662-3*) Silver Pr.
—A Walk in the Desert. Brook, Bonnie, ed. Tanz, Freya, illus. 32p. (ps-1). 1990. 5.95 (*0-671-68668-2*); lib. bdg. 9.98 (*0-671-68664-X*) Silver Pr.

—A Walk in the Woods. Brook, Bonnie, ed. Tanz, Freya, illus. 32p. (ps-1). 1990. 5.95 (0-671-68665-8); lib. bdg. 9.98 (0-671-68661-5) Silver Pr.
—A Walk on the Great Barrier Reef. (Illus.). 48p. (gr. 2-5). 1988. PLB 19.95 (0-87614-285-4) Carolrhoda Bks.
—A Walk on the Great Barrier Reef. Arnold, Arthur, illus. 48p. (gr. 2-5). 1988. pap. 6.95 (0-87614-501-2, First Ave Edns) Lerner Pubns.
—A Walk up a Mountain. Brook, Bonnie, ed. Tanz, Freya, illus. 32p. (ps-1). 1990. 5.95 (0-671-68667-4); lib. bdg. 9.98 (0-671-68663-1) Silver Pr.
—Watch out for Sharks! Hewett, Richard, photos by. (Illus.). 48p. (gr. 3-6). 1991. 15.45 (0-395-57560-5, Clarion Bks) HM.
—Wild Goat. Hewett, Richard, photos by. LC 89-38958. (Illus.). 48p. (gr. 2 up) 1990. 13.95 (0-688-08824-4); PLB 13.88 (0-688-08825-2, Morrow Jr Bks) Morrow Jr Bks.
—Zebra. Hewett, Richard, illus. LC 87-1503. 48p. (gr. 2-5). 1987. 13.95 (0-688-07067-1); lib. bdg. 13.88 (0-688-07068-X, Morrow Jr Bks) Morrow Jr Bks.
—Zebra. Hewett, Richard, photos by. LC 92-25550. (Illus.). 48p. (gr. 3 up). 1993. pap. 5.95 (0-688-12273-6, Mulberry) Morrow.
Arnold, Eugene. Big Water: Flight to Okeechobee. Siegrist, Wes, illus. LC 92-61845. 201p. (gr. 12). 1993. pap. 12.95 (0-9628828-2-8) Prospector Pr.
Arnold, Frances. Greece. LC 91-24808. (Illus.). 96p. (gr. 6-12). 1992. PLB 19.92 (0-8114-2448-0) Raintree Steck-V.
Arnold, Henri & Lee, Bob. Jumble for Kids. (Illus.). 160p. 1992. pap. 3.95 (0-941263-37-1) Tribune FL.
Arnold, J. Douglas. Awesome Sega Genesis Secrets, No. 1. (Illus.). 256p. (Orig.). 1992. pap. 9.95 (0-9624676-4-2, GV1469.3) Sandwich Islands.
Arnold, J. Douglas, jt. auth. see Meston, Zach.
Arnold, Jeanne G. The Little Cloud That Couldn't: An Environmental Story for Children. Beattie, Linda D., illus. LC 90-62422. 76p. (Orig.). (gr. 3-7). 1990. pap. 4.95 (0-9620887-1-4) Media Serv Unltd.
Arnold, Katya, retold by. & illus. Baba Yaga: A Russian Folktale. LC 92-38199. 32p. (gr. k-3). 1993. 14.95 (1-55858-208-8); PLB 14.88 (1-55858-209-6) North-South Bks NYC.
Arnold, Kevin D. & Bassett, James C. Passing the Ohio Proficiency Test. 288p. (Orig.). (gr. 8-12). 1993. pap. 12.95 (1-884183-01-8) OH Proficiency.
Arnold, Lisa E. You Know You're Really Pregnant When... (Illus.). 64p. 1987. 9.95 (0-8431-1916-0) Price Stern.
Arnold, Marti. Alaska, Uncle Jim & Me. Lesko, Marian, ed. Dessereau, April & Present, David, illus. 146p. (Orig.). (gr. 6 up) 1983. pap. 5.95 (0-912683-00-7) Fireweed.
Arnold, Matthew. Poetry & Criticism of Matthew Arnold. Culler, A. D., ed. LC 61-19991. (gr. 9 up). 1961. pap. 9.16 (0-395-05152-5, RivEd) HM.
Arnold, Nick, jt. auth. see McCarthy, Colin.
Arnold, Sandra M. Alicia Alonso: First Lady of the Ballet. LC 93-18098. 1993. 14.95 (0-8027-8242-6); PLB 15.85 (0-8027-8243-4) Walker & Co.
Arnold, Tedd. Green Wilma. Arnold, Tedd, illus. LC 91-31501. 32p. (ps-3). 1993. 13.99 (0-8037-1313-4); PLB 13.89 (0-8037-1314-2) Dial Bks Young.
—Mother Goose's Words of Wit & Wisdom: A Book of Months. (Illus.). 64p. 1990. 14.95 (0-8037-0825-4); PLB 14.89 (0-8037-0826-2) Dial Bks Young.
—My First Drawing Book. (Illus.). (ps-2). 1986. bds. 5.95 6 bds. (0-89480-350-6, 1350) Workman Pub.
—No Jumping on the Bed! Arnold, Tedd, illus. LC 86-13501. 32p. (ps-2). 1987. 14.00 (0-8037-0038-5); PLB 13.89 (0-8037-0039-3) Dial Bks Young.
—Ollie Forgot. Arnold, Tedd, illus. 32p. (ps-3). 1991. pap. 3.95 (0-8037-0985-4, Dial Pied Piper) Puffin Bks.
—The Signmaker's Assistant. Arnold, Tedd, illus. LC 90-19537. 32p. (ps-3). 1992. 14.00 (0-8037-1010-0); PLB 13.89 (0-8037-1011-9) Dial Bks Young.
—The Simple People. Shachat, Andrew, illus. LC 91-17697. 32p. (ps-3). 1992. 14.00 (0-8037-1012-7); PLB 13.89 (0-8037-1013-5) Dial Bks Young.
Arnold, Tedd, illus. Actions. 16p. (ps). 1992. pap. 3.95 (0-671-77824-2, Little Simon) S&S Trade.
—Colors. 16p. (ps). 1992. pap. 3.95 (0-671-77825-0, Little Simon) S&S Trade.
—Opposites. 16p. (ps). 1992. pap. 3.95 (0-671-77823-4, Little Simon) S&S Trade.
—Sounds. 16p. (ps). 1992. pap. 3.95 (0-671-77826-9, Little Simon) S&S Trade.
Arnold, Terrell E. & Kennedy, Moorhead. Think about Terrorism: The New Warfare. LC 87-21158. (Illus.). 153p. (gr. 9-12). 1988. lib. bdg. 14.85 (0-8027-6757-5); pap. 5.95 (0-8027-6758-3) Walker & Co.
Arnold, Tim. Natural History from A to Z: A Terrestrial Sampler. Arnold, Tim, illus. LC 88-26879. 64p. (gr. 5-9). 1991. SBE 15.95 (0-689-50467-5, M K McElderry) Macmillan Child Grp.
—The Winter Mittens. LC 88-2736. (Illus.). 32p. (gr. 3-6). 1988. RSBE 13.95 (0-689-50449-7, M K McElderry) Macmillan Child Grp.
Arnold, Tim, retold by. & illus. The Three Billy Goats Gruff. LC 92-23992. 32p. (ps-3). 1993. SBE 14.95 (0-689-50575-2, M K McElderry) Macmillan Child Grp.

Arnoldt, Robert P. Insights: A Guide to the American Experience in Vietnam, 1940 to Present. rev. ed. Marx, Jacqueline A. & Carpenter, Robert S., eds. 100p. (Illus.). (gr. 9 up). 1989. pap. text ed. write for info. Visions Unlimited.
Arnoldt, Robert P. & Marx, Jacqueline A. Vietnam Insights: A Guide to the American Experience in Vietnam 1940 to Present. rev. ed. Carpenter, Robert S., ed. Arnoldt, Robert P., intro. by. LC 89-50664. 232p. (Orig.). (gr. 8 up). 1992. pap. 21.95 (0-9622776-0-6) Visions Unlimited.
Arnosky, Jim. All Night Near the Water. LC 93-31078. 1994. write for info. (0-399-22629-X, Putnam) Putnam Pub Group.
—Come out, Muskrats. Arnosky, Jim, illus. LC 88-26611. 40p. (ps-3). 1989. 12.95 (0-688-05457-9); PLB 12.88 (0-688-05458-7) Lothrop.
—Come Out, Muskrats. LC 88-26611. (Illus.). 24p. (ps-3). 1991. pap. 3.95 (0-688-10490-8, Mulberry) Morrow.
—Crinkleroot's Book of Animal Tracking. Arnosky, Jim, illus. LC 88-15353. 48p. (gr. k-5). 1989. RSBE 13.95 (0-02-705851-4, Bradbury Pr) Macmillan Child Grp.
—Crinkleroot's Guide to Knowing the Birds. Arnosky, Jim, illus. LC 91-38234. 32p. (gr. k-5). 1992. RSBE 14.95 (0-02-705857-3, Bradbury Pr) Macmillan Child Grp.
—Crinkleroot's Guide to Knowing the Trees. Arnosky, Jim, illus. LC 91-18651. 40p. (ps-5). 1992. RSBE 13.95 (0-02-705855-7, Bradbury Pr) Macmillan Child Grp.
—Crinkleroot's Guide to Walking in Wild Places. Arnosky, Jim, illus. LC 89-38427. 32p. (gr. k-5). 1990. RSBE 13.95 (0-02-705842-5, Bradbury Pr) Macmillan Child Grp.
—Crinkleroot's Guide to Walking in Wild Places. Arnosky, Jim, illus. LC 92-45775. 32p. (gr. k-5). 1993. pap. 4.95 (0-689-71753-9, Aladdin) Macmillan Child Grp.
—Crinkleroot's Twenty-Five Birds Every Child Should Know. Arnosky, Jim, illus. LC 92-36059. 32p. (gr. k-3). 1993. RSBE 12.95 (0-02-705859-X, Bradbury Pr) Macmillan Child Grp.
—Crinkleroot's Twenty-Five Fish Every Child Should Know. Arnosky, Jim, illus. LC 92-39381. 32p. (gr. k-3). 1993. RSBE 12.95 (0-02-705844-1, Bradbury Pr) Macmillan Child Grp.
—Crinkleroot's Twenty-Five Mammals Every Child Should Know. Arnosky, Jim, illus. LC 93-7585. 32p. (ps-3). 1994. RSBE 12.95 (0-02-705845-X, Bradbury Pr) Macmillan Child Grp.
—Crinkleroot's Twenty-Five More Mammals Every Child Should Know. Arnosky, Jim, illus. LC 93-7584. 32p. (ps-3). 1994. RSBE 12.95 (0-02-705846-8, Bradbury Pr) Macmillan Child Grp.
—Deer at the Brook. LC 84-12239. (Illus.). 32p. (ps-3). 1986. 13.95 (0-688-04099-3); PLB 13.88 (0-688-04100-0) Lothrop.
—Deer at the Brook. LC 84-12239. (Illus.). 32p. (ps-3). 1991. pap. 4.95 (0-688-10488-6, Mulberry) Morrow.
—Drawing from Nature. Arnosky, Jim, illus. LC 82-15327. 64p. (Orig.). 1987. 13.95 (0-688-01295-7) Lothrop.
—Drawing Life in Motion. Arnosky, Jim, illus. LC 83-25129. 48p. (Orig.). 1987. 12.95 (0-688-03803-4) Lothrop.
—Every Autumn Comes the Bear. Arnosky, Jim, illus. LC 92-30515. 32p. (ps-1). 1993. 14.95 (0-399-22508-0, Putnam) Putnam Pub Group.
—Fish in a Flash! A Personal Guide to Spin-Fishing. LC 90-45832. (Illus.). 64p. (gr. 4-9). 1991. SBE 14.95 (0-02-705854-9, Bradbury Pr) Macmillan Child Grp.
—Flies in the Water, Fish in the Air: A Personal Introduction to Fly Fishing. LC 84-29684. (Illus.). 96p. (gr. 5-9). 1986. 12.95 (0-688-05834-5) Lothrop.
—Flies in the Water, Fish in the Air: A Personal Introduction to Fly Fishing. Arnosky, Jim, illus. Randolph, John, frwd. by. (Illus.). 96p. (gr. 6-12). 1992. pap. 10.00 (0-88150-246-4) Countryman.
—Freshwater Fish & Fishing. LC 81-12520. (Illus.). 64p. (gr. 3-7). 1982. SBE 12.95 (0-02-705850-6, Four Winds) Macmillan Child Grp.
—Gray Boy. LC 87-29337. (gr. 4-9). 1988. PLB 13.95 (0-688-07345-X) Lothrop.
—I Was Born in a Tree & Raised by Bees. Arnosky, Jim, illus. LC 88-6121. 48p. (gr. k-5). 1988. Repr. of 1977 ed. RSBE 13.95 (0-02-705841-7, Bradbury Pr) Macmillan Child Grp.
—In the Forest. Arnosky, Jim, illus. LC 89-2341. 32p. (gr. 4 up). 1989. 13.95 (0-688-08162-2); PLB 13.88 (0-688-09138-5) Lothrop.
—A Kettle of Hawks. Arnosky, Jim, illus. LC 89-12459. 32p. (gr. k-4). 1990. 13.95 (0-688-09279-0); lib. bdg. 13.88 (0-688-09280-2) Lothrop.
—Long Spikes. Arnosky, Jim, illus. 96p. (gr. 3-7). 1992. 12.70 (0-395-58830-8, Clarion Bks) HM.
—Near the Sea. 32p. 1990. 13.95 (0-688-08164-9); PLB 13.88 (0-688-09327-2) Lothrop.
—Otters under Water. (Illus.). 32p. (ps-1). 1992. 14.95 (0-399-22339-8, Putnam) Putnam Pub Group.
—Raccoons & Ripe Corn. Arnosky, Jim, illus. LC 87-4243. 32p. (ps-3). 1987. 13.95 (0-688-05455-2); PLB 13.88 (0-688-05456-0) Lothrop.
—Raccoons & Ripe Corn. LC 87-4243. (Illus.). 32p. (ps-3). 1991. pap. 4.95 (0-688-10489-4, Mulberry) Morrow.

—Secrets of a Wildlife Watcher. LC 82-24920. (Illus.). 64p. (gr. 5 up). 1983. 13.95 (0-688-02079-8); lib. bdg. 13.88 (0-688-02081-X) Lothrop.
—Secrets of a Wildlife Watcher. 1991. pap. 7.95 (0-688-10531-9, Pub. by Beech Tree Bks) Morrow.
—Sketching Outdoors in All Seasons. LC 88-2202. (Illus.). 48p. (gr. 5 up). 1988. 12.95 (0-688-06290-3) Lothrop.
—Sketching Outdoors in Autumn. LC 88-1244. (Illus.). 48p. (gr. 5 up). 1988. 12.95 (0-688-06288-1) Lothrop.
—Sketching Outdoors in Spring. Arnosky, Jim, illus. LC 86-21308. 48p. (gr. 4 up). 1987. 12.95 (0-688-06284-9) Lothrop.
—Sketching Outdoors in Summer. LC 87-29728. (gr. 5 up). 1988. PLB 12.95 (0-688-06286-5) Lothrop.
—Watching Foxes. LC 84-20157. (Illus.). 24p. (ps-3). 1984. 12.95 (0-688-04259-7); PLB 12.88 (0-688-04260-0) Lothrop.
Arnothy. I Am Fifteen: And I Don't Want to Die. 1993. pap. 2.95 (0-590-44630-4) Scholastic Inc.
Arnott, Kathleen. African Myths & Legends. Kiddell-Monroe, Joan, illus. 224p. (gr. 4 up). 1990. pap. 10.95 (0-19-274143-8) OUP.
Arnow, Jan. Louisville Slugger: The Making of a Baseball Bat. Arnow, Jan, photos by. LC 84-7049. (Illus.). 48p. (gr. 3-7). 1984. 11.95 (0-394-86297-X, Pant Bks Young); lib. bdg. 12.99 (0-394-96297-4) Pantheon.
Arnsteen, Katy K. Children's Songs: Hide 'n' Seek. 1990. 3.99 (0-517-02569-8) Outlet Bk Co.
—Favorite Fairy Tales. (Illus.). 24p. (ps-1). 1990. 3.99 (0-517-02567-1) Outlet Bk Co.
—Mother Goose Rhymes: Hide 'n' Seek. 1990. 3.99 (0-517-02630-9) Outlet Bk Co.
Arnstein, Helene S. Billy & Our New Baby. Smyth, M. Jane, illus. LC 73-7951. 32p. (ps-3). 1973. 16.95x (0-87705-093-7) Human Sci Pr.
Arntson, Herbert E. Caravan to Oregon. LC 57-13207. (Illus.). (gr. 7-11). 1957. 8.95 (0-8323-0164-7) Binford Mort.
Aron, Jack R. see Hellman, Nina & Brouwer, Norman.
Aroner, Miriam & Haas, Shelly O. The Kingdom of Singing Birds. LC 92-39382. 1993. 13.95 (0-929371-43-7); pap. 5.95 (0-929371-44-5) Kar Ben.
Aronin, Ben. The Secret of the Sabbath Fish. Rieger, Shay, illus. LC 78-63437. (gr. k-4). 1979. 8.95 (0-8276-0110-7) JPS Phila.
Aronoff, Daisy P. ABC Bible & Holiday Stories. Danciger, Leila N., illus. 58p. (ps-7). 1992. pap. 15.95 (1-878612-28-X) Sunflower Co.
Aronow, Sara. Seven Days of Creation. Seligson, Judith, illus. 32p. (ps-2). 1985. 4.95 (0-87203-119-5) Hermon.
Aronson, Billy. They Came from DNA: Mysteries of Science. (gr. 4-7). 1993. 17.95 (0-7167-9006-8) W H Freeman.
Aronson, Joseph. Encyclopedia of Furniture. rev. ed. (Illus.). 496p. (gr. 9 up). 1961. 27.50 (0-517-03735-1, Crown) Crown Pub Group.
Aronson, Rande, jt. auth. see Temple, Nancy M.
Arpi, Erik. A Troll Wedding: The Troll Children's Search for the Magic Wedding Flower. Engen, Kari & Gracey, Kirsten, trs. from SWE. Lidberg, Rolf, illus. LC 92-60297. 30p. (ps-5). 1992. 12.95 (1-881278-00-X) M S Pr.
Arrabito, James. Cameras at the Zoo. Glaser, Mary J., illus. 16p. (Orig.). (gr. 3-10). 1991. pap. 4.95 (0-9622596-0-8) Arraster Pub.
Arrants, Cheryl & Arrants, Dennis. Thimbelina & the Notion Parade. Arrants, Cheryl & Arrants, Dennis, illus. 32p. (Orig.). (gr. k-4). 1983. pap. text ed. 2.50 (0-943704-03-0) Arrants & Assoc.
Arrants, Dennis, jt. auth. see Arrants, Cheryl.
Arrick, Fran. God's Radar. 224p. (gr. 6-12). 1986. pap. 2.95 (0-440-92960-1, LFL) Dell.
—Nice Girl from Good Home. 208p. (gr. 7 up). 1986. pap. 2.75 (0-440-96358-3, LFL) Dell.
—Steffie Can't Come Out to Play. 160p. (gr. 7 up). 1979. pap. 2.50 (0-440-97635-9, LFL) Dell.
—Tunnel Vision. 176p. (gr. 7 up). 1981. pap. 3.50 (0-440-98579-X, LE); tchr's. guide by Lou Stanek 0.50 (0-685-01410-X) Dell.
—What You Don't Know. 1992. 16.00 (0-553-07471-7) Bantam.
—What You Don't Know Can Kill You. LC 91-26617. 160p. (gr. 7-10). 1992. 15.00 (0-685-53824-9) Bantam.
—Where'd You Get the Gun, Billy? (gr. 7 up) 1991. 16.00 (0-553-07135-1, Starfire) Bantam.
—Where'd You Get the Gun, Billy? 1992. pap. 3.50 (0-553-28935-7) Bantam.
Arrigo, Mary & Hargreaves, Connie. When I Visit Yosemite. Nishimura, Chris, illus. 43p. (Orig.). (ps). pap. 2.95 (0-318-21253-6) Arrigo CA.
Arrington, Karen. The Commission on Civil Rights. (Illus.). (gr. 5 up). 1992. 14.95 (1-55546-127-1) Chelsea Hse.
Arroyo, Anita. El Grillo Grunon: Cuentos para Chicos y Grandes. Robain, Armando O., illus. LC 84-13199. (SPA.). 122p. (Orig.). (gr. 1-6). 1984. pap. 5.50 (0-8477-3527-3) U of PR Pr.
Art In-Forms Staff, ed. see Ullom, A. Thomas.
Artell, Mike. The Wackiest Ecology Riddles on Earth. LC 91-45773. (Illus.). 96p. (gr. 3-8). 1992. 12.95 (0-8069-1250-2) Sterling.
—The Wackiest Nature Riddles on Earth. (Illus.). 96p. (gr. 2-8). 1993. pap. 3.95 (0-8069-1251-0) Sterling.
—Who Said Moo? Artell, Mike, illus. 12p. (ps-k). 1994. pap. 7.95 (0-689-71811-X, Aladdin) Macmillan Child Grp.

Artell, Mike & Armstrong, Beverly. Fun with Expressions. LC 91-77126. (Illus.). 40p. (gr. 2-6). 1992. 5.95 (*0-88160-209-4*, LW 299) Learning Wks.

Artell, Mike, illus. T'was the Night Before Christmas. LC 93-37281. 1994. write for info. (*0-689-71801-2*, Aladdin) Macmillan Child Grp.

Arter, Jim. Gruel & Unusual. 1993. pap. 3.50 (*0-440-40891-1*) Dell.

Artes, Dorothy B. Rick & Po, Special Agents, Bk. 1. Weinberger, Jane, ed. LC 87-51328. (Illus.). 66p. (Orig.). (gr. 4-6). 1988. pap. 4.00 (*0-932433-39-1*) Windswept Hse.

—Rick & Po: Village Detectives, Bk. 2. LC 86-50878. (Illus.). 98p. (Orig.). (gr. 4-6). 1987. pap. 4.00 (*0-932433-28-6*) Windswept Hse.

Arthur, Alex. Shell. Einsiedel, Andreas, photos by. LC 88-13449. (Illus.). 64p. (gr. 5 up). 1989. 15.00 (*0-394-82256-0*); lib. bdg. 15.99 (*0-394-92256-5*) Knopf Bks Yng Read.

Arthur, Gayle. Building with BASIC: A Programming Kit for Kids. (Illus., Orig.). (gr. k up). 1992. pap. 19.95 incl. disk (*0-672-30057-5*) Alpha Bks IN.

Arthur, Malcolm, tr. see Perrault, Charles.

Arthur, Robert. Alfred Hitchcock & the Three Investigators in the Mystery of the Green Ghost. Hitchcock, Alfred, ed. (Illus.). (gr. 4-8). 1985. pap. 3.95 (*0-394-86404-2*) Random Bks Yng Read.

—Alfred Hitchcock & the Three Investigators in the Mystery of the Talking Skull. Hitchcock, Alfred, ed. Kane, Harry, illus. LC 69-20274. (gr. 4-7). 1984. 3.95 (*0-394-86411-5*) Random Bks Yng Read.

—Alfred Hitchcock & the Three Investigators in the Mystery of the Vanishing Treasure. Hitchcock, Alfred, ed. Kane, Harry, illus. (gr. 4-8). 1985. lib. bdg. 6.99 (*0-394-91550-X*); pap. 3.95 (*0-394-86405-0*) Random Bks Yng Read.

—Alfred Hitchcock & the Three Investigators in the Mystery of the Whispering Mummy. Hitchcock, Alfred, ed. (Illus.). (gr. 4-8). 1978. pap. 3.95 (*0-394-86403-4*) Random Bks Yng Read.

—Alfred Hitchcock & the Three Investigators in the Mystery of the Fiery Eye. Kane, Harry, illus. LC 77-28860. (gr. 4-8). 1984. pap. 3.95 (*0-394-86407-7*) Random Bks Yng Read.

—Alfred Hitchcock & the Three Investigators in the Mystery of the Silver Spider. Kane, Harry, illus. (gr. 4-8). 1985. pap. 2.95 (*0-394-86408-5*) Random Bks Yng Read.

—Alfred Hitchcock & the Three Investigators in the Secret of Skeleton Island. Hitchcock, Alfred, ed. Kane, Harry, illus. (gr. 4-9). 1985. pap. 3.95 (*0-394-86406-9*) Random Bks Yng Read.

—Mystery of the Screaming Clock. (gr. 4-7). 1991. pap. 3.95 (*0-679-82173-2*) Knopf Bks Yng Read.

Arthur, Robert, ed. Spies & More Spies. Lambert, Saul, illus. (gr. 7-11). 1972. lib. bdg. 5.39 (*0-394-91673-5*) Random Bks Yng Read.

Arthur, Shirley M. Surviving Teen Pregnancy: Your Choices, Dreams & Decisions. LC 91-6931. (Illus.). 192p. (Orig.). (gr. 1-8). 1991. pap. 9.95 (*0-930934-47-4*) Morning Glory.

Artman, John. Ancient Greece. 64p. (gr. 4-8). 1991. 7.95 (*0-86653-583-7*, GA1310) Good Apple.

—Ancient Rome. 64p. (gr. 4-8). 1991. 7.95 (*0-86653-638-8*, GA1343) Good Apple.

—Collectible Correctibles. Filkins, Vanessa, illus. 64p. (gr. 4-8). 1984. wkbk. 7.95 (*0-86653-214-5*, GA 559) Good Apple.

—Cowboys: An Activity Book. 64p. (gr. 4 up). 1982. 7.95 (*0-86653-068-1*, GA 417) Good Apple.

—Explorers. Hyndman, Kathryn, illus. 64p. (gr. 4 up). 1986. 7.95 (*0-86653-340-0*, GA 796) Good Apple.

—Good Apple & Reading Fun. 144p. (gr. 3-7). 1981. 11.95 (*0-86653-046-0*, GA 278) Good Apple.

—Indians: An Activity Book. 64p. (gr. 4 up). 1981. 7.95 (*0-86653-012-6*, GA 240) Good Apple.

—Insights. 112p. (gr. 4-8). 1989. 9.95 (*0-86653-511-X*, GA1096) Good Apple.

—Pioneers. Hyndman, Kathryn, illus. 64p. (gr. 4 up). 1987. pap. 7.95 (*0-86653-401-6*, GA 1027) Good Apple.

—Slanguage. 80p. (gr. 4 up). 1980. 8.95 (*0-916456-60-9*, GA 175) Good Apple.

Artman, John H. The Write Stuff! Filkins, Vanessa, illus. 64p. (gr. 4-8). 1985. wkbk. 7.95 (*0-86653-273-0*, GA 681) Good Apple.

Arturo, Juan G., tr. see Maestro, Betsy & Maestro, Giulio.

Aruego, Ariane, jt. auth. see Aruego, Jose.

Aruego, Jose. Look What I Can Do! Aruego, Jose, illus. LC 87-21743. 32p. (ps-1). 1988. pap. 3.95 (*0-689-71205-7*, Aladdin) Macmillan Child Grp.

Aruego, Jose & Aruego, Ariane. Cuento de un Cocodrilo. Palacios, Argentina, tr. from SPA. (gr. k-3). 1979. pap. 2.95 (*0-590-42695-8*) Scholastic Inc.

Aruego, Jose & Dewey, Ariane. Rockabye Crocodile. LC 87-463. (Illus.). 32p. (ps-3). 1988. 14.00 (*0-688-06738-7*); lib. bdg. 13.93 (*0-688-06739-5*) Greenwillow.

—Rockabye Crocodile. LC 92-24587. 32p. (ps). 1993. pap. 4.95 (*0-688-12333-3*, Mulberry) Morrow.

—We Hide, You Seek. LC 78-13638. (Illus.). 32p. (gr. k-3). 1979. 14.95 (*0-688-80201-X*); PLB 14.88 (*0-688-84201-1*) Greenwillow.

—We Hide, You Seek. LC 78-13638. (Illus.). 32p. (ps-3). 1988. pap. 4.95 (*0-688-07815-X*, Mulberry) Morrow.

Arvetis, Chris & Palmer, Carole. Deserts. LC 93-502. (Illus.). 1993. write for info. (*0-528-83574-2*) Rand McNally.

—Forests. LC 93-500. (Illus.). 1993. write for info. (*0-528-83573-4*) Rand McNally.

—Lakes & Rivers. LC 93-499. (Illus.). 1993. write for info. (*0-528-83572-6*) Rand McNally.

—Mountains. LC 93-501. (Illus.). 1993. write for info. (*0-528-83571-8*) Rand McNally.

—Swamps & Marshes. Buckley, James, illus. LC 93-33675. (gr. 4 up). 1994. write for info. (*0-528-83676-5*) Rand McNally.

Arvey, Michael. The End of the World: Opposing Viewpoints. LC 92-15101. (Illus.). 112p. (gr. 5-8). 1992. PLB 14.95 (*0-89908-096-0*) Greenhaven.

—ESP: Opposing Viewpoints. LC 88-24316. (Illus.). 112p. (gr. 5-8). 1989. PLB 14.95 (*0-89908-057-X*) Greenhaven.

—Miracles: Opposing Viewpoints. LC 90-39156. (Illus.). 112p. (gr. 5-8). 1990. PLB 14.95 (*0-89908-084-7*) Greenhaven.

—Reincarnation: Opposing Viewpoints. LC 89-37443. (Illus.). 112p. (gr. 5-8). 1989. PLB 14.95 (*0-89908-067-7*) Greenhaven.

—UFOs: Opposing Viewpoints. LC 89-11645. (Illus.). 111p. (gr. 5-8). 1989. PLB 14.95 (*0-89908-060-X*) Greenhaven.

Aryai, Sia. Baby Bright Board Books: ABC's. Aryai, Sia, photos by. (Illus.). 1993. 5.95 (*1-56565-049-2*) Lowell Hse.

—Baby Bright Board Books: Colors. Aryai, Sia, photos by. (Illus.). 1993. 5.95 (*1-56565-050-6*) Lowell Hse.

—Baby Bright Board Books: Shapes. Aryai, Sia, photos by. (Illus.). 1993. 5.95 (*1-56565-051-4*) Lowell Hse.

—My Accessories: My Favorite Things. (ps-3). 1992. 3.99 (*0-8431-3402-X*) Price Stern.

—My Hats: My Favorite Things. (ps-3). 1992. 3.99 (*0-8431-3400-3*) Price Stern.

—My Shoes: My Favorite Things. (ps-3). 1992. 3.99 (*0-8431-3401-1*) Price Stern.

—My Toys: My Favorite Things. (ps-3). 1992. 3.99 (*0-8431-3403-8*) Price Stern.

Asala, Joanne. The Green Knight: A Tale of Ancient Britain - Arthurian Romance about Sir Gawain & the Green Knight. Asala, Jason, illus. 64p. (gr. 3). 1992. pap. 6.95 (*1-880954-00-1*) Kalevala Bks.

Asamiya, Kia. Gunhed: Gun Unit - Heavy Elimination Device. Horibuchi, Seiji, ed. Fujii, Satoru, tr. from JPN. (Illus.). 136p. (Orig.). (gr. 10 up). 1991. pap. 14.95 (*0-929279-14-X*) Viz Commns Inc.

Asare, Meshack. Cat in Search of a Friend. LC 86-10583. (Illus.). 32p. (ps-5). 1986. 10.95 (*0-916291-07-3*, Cranky Nell Bk) Kane-Miller Bk.

—Cat in Search of a Friend. LC 88-71622. (Illus.). 32p. (ps-3). 1988. pap. 6.95 (*0-86543-107-8*) Africa World.

Asato, Andrew, jt. auth. see Fuller, Rose.

Asbee, Sue. Woolf. (Illus.). 112p. (gr. 7 up). 1990. lib. bdg. 19.94 (*0-86593-019-8*); lib. bdg. 14.95s.p. (*0-685-46453-9*) Rourke Corp.

Asbjornsen, P. C. & Moe, J. E. The Man Who Kept House. S, Svend O., illus. LC 91-37599. 32p. (gr. k-3). 1992. SBE 13.95 (*0-689-50560-4*, M K McElderry) Macmillan Child Grp.

—The Three Billy Goats Gruff. Brown, Marcia, illus. 28p. (ps-3). 1991. pap. 3.95 (*0-15-690150-1*) HarBrace.

Asch. Bear Shadow. (gr. 6 up). 1993. pap. 19.95 (*0-590-72736-2*) Scholastic Inc.

Asch, Connie. Indians of the Americas Coloring Book. (Illus.). 32p. (Orig.). (gr. k-6). 1987. pap. 2.95 (*0-918080-33-9*) Treasure Chest.

—Tohono O'Odham Indian Coloring Book. rev. ed. (Illus.). 32p. (gr. 2-6). 1990. pap. 2.95 (*0-918080-60-6*) Treasure Chest.

Asch, Frank. Baby in the Box. Gibbons, Gail, illus. LC 88-16452. 32p. (ps-3). 1989. reinforced bdg. 12.95 (*0-8234-0725-X*) Holiday.

—Baby in the Box. LC 88-16452. (Illus.). 32p. (ps-3). 1990. pap. 5.95 (*0-8234-0844-2*) Holiday.

—Bear Shadow. Asch, Frank, illus. LC 82-18250. 32p. (ps-2). 1988. pap. 14.00 jacketed (*0-671-66279-1*, S&S BFYR); pap. 4.95 (*0-671-66686-8*, S&S BFYR) Trade.

—Bear's Bargain. Asch, Frank, illus. LC 85-6355. (ps-2). 1989. pap. 12.95 jacketed (*0-671-66690-8*, S&S BFYR); pap. 4.95 (*0-671-67838-8*, S&S BFYR) S&S Trade.

—Bear's Bargain. (ps-3). 1992. pap. 19.95 (*0-590-72698-6*) Scholastic Inc.

—Bear's Bargain. (gr. 1). 1991. pap. write for info. (*0-663-56211-2*) Silver Burdett Pr.

—Bread & Honey. Asch, Frank, illus. LC 81-16893. 48p. (ps-3). 1982. 5.95 (*0-8193-1077-8*); PLB 5.95 (*0-8193-1078-6*) Parents.

—Bread & Honey. (Illus.). 48p. (ps-2). 1992. pap. 2.95 (*0-448-40319-6*, G&D) Putnam Pub Group.

—The Earth & I. LC 93-237. 1994. write for info. (*0-15-200443-2*, Gulliver Bks) HarBrace.

—The Flower Faerie. Asch, Frank & Vagin, Vladimir. Vagin, Vladimir, illus. LC 91-33763. 32p. (gr. 1-4). 1993. 14.95 (*0-590-45493-5*) Scholastic Inc.

—George's Store. Wiseman, Bernard, illus. LC 82-22298. 48p. (ps-3). 1983. 5.95 (*0-8193-1101-4*); PLB 5.95 (*0-8193-1102-2*) Parents.

—Goodbye House. Asch, Frank, illus. LC 85-19263. (ps-2). 1989. pap. 12.95 jacketed (*0-671-67054-9*, Little Simon); pap. 4.95 (*0-671-67927-9*, Little Simon) S&S Trade.

—Goodnight, Horsey. Asch, Frank, illus. LC 81-7332. 32p. (ps up). 1989. pap. 12.95 jacketed (*0-671-66277-5*, Little Simon); pap. 4.95 (*0-671-66278-3*, Little Simon) S&S Trade.

—Hands Around Lincoln School. LC 92-31246. 144p. 1994. 13.95 (*0-590-44149-3*) Scholastic Inc.

—Happy Birthday Moon. Asch, Frank, illus. 32p. (ps-1). 1988. Bk. & cassette. pap. 7.95 (*0-671-67145-6*, Little Simon) S&S Trade.

—Happy Birthday, Moon. LC 88-6569. (Illus.). 32p. (gr. k-4). 1985. pap. 14.00 jacketed (*0-671-66454-9*, Little Simon); pap. 4.95 (*0-671-66455-7*, Little Simon) S&S Trade.

—Just Like Daddy. (Illus.). 32p. (gr. k-4). 1984. pap. 12.95 jacketed (*0-671-66456-5*, S&S BFYR); pap. 4.95 (*0-671-66457-3*, S&S BFYR) S&S Trade.

—The Last Puppy. Asch, Frank, illus. LC 80-215. 32p. (ps up). 1989. pap. 14.00 (*0-671-66276-7*, S&S BFYR); pap. 4.95 (*0-671-66687-8*, S&S BFYR) S&S Trade.

—Little Fish, Big Fish. (Illus.). (ps). 1992. bds. 8.95 (*0-590-44492-1*, 027, Cartwheel) Scholastic Inc.

—Milk & Cookies. LC 82-7962. (Illus.). 48p. (ps-3). 1982. 5.95 (*0-8193-1087-5*); PLB 5.95 (*0-8193-1088-3*) Parents.

—Milk & Cookies. (Illus.). 48p. (ps-2). 1991. pap. 2.95 (*0-448-40103-7*, G&D) Putnam Pub Group.

—Moonbear. (gr. 4 up). 1993. 3.95 (*0-671-86743-1*, Little Simon) S&S Trade.

—Moonbear's Books. (gr. 3 up). 1993. 3.95 (*0-671-86744-X*, Little Simon) S&S Trade.

—Moonbear's Canoe. (ps-6). 1993. 3.95 (*0-671-86745-8*, Little Simon) S&S Trade.

—Moonbear's Friend. (ps-6). 1993. 3.95 (*0-671-86746-6*, Little Simon) S&S Trade.

—Mooncake. Asch, Frank, illus. 32p. 1986. pap. 4.95 (*0-671-66451-4*) S&S Trade.

—Moondance. Asch, Frank, illus. LC 92-12358. 32p. (gr. k-3). 1993. 12.95 (*0-590-45487-0*) Scholastic Inc.

—Moongame. (Illus.). 32p. (gr. k-4). 1987. pap. 12.95 (*0-671-66452-2*, S&S BFYR); pap. 4.95 (*0-671-66453-0*, S&S BFYR) S&S Trade.

—Moongame. (ps-3). 1992. pap. 19.95 (*0-590-72624-2*) Scholastic Inc.

—Oats & Wild Apples. Asch, Frank, illus. LC 87-17742. 32p. (ps-3). 1988. reinforced bdg. 14.95 (*0-8234-0677-6*) Holiday.

—Pearl's Pirates. Asch, Frank, illus. LC 86-19621. 160p. (gr. k-3). 1987. pap. 13.95 (*0-385-29546-4*) Delacorte.

—Pearl's Pirates. (gr. k-6). 1989. pap. 3.25 (*0-440-40245-X*, YB) Dell.

—Pearl's Promise. Asch, Frank, illus. LC 83-17153. 160p. (gr. 4-6). 1984. PLB 12.95 (*0-385-29321-6*); pap. 12.95 (*0-385-29325-9*) Delacorte.

—Pearl's Promise. 160p. (gr. 1-4). 1984. pap. 2.95 (*0-440-46863-9*, YB) Dell.

—Popcorn. Asch, Frank, illus. LC 79-216. 48p. (ps-3). 1979. 5.95 (*0-8193-1001-8*); lib. bdg. 5.95 (*0-8193-1002-6*) Parents.

—Popcorn. Asch, Frank, illus. 48p. (gr. 3-7). 1990. pap. 2.95 (*0-448-04333-5*, G&D) Putnam Pub Group.

—Sand Cake. Asch, Frank, illus. LC 78-11183. 48p. (ps-3). 1979. 5.95 (*0-8193-0985-0*); lib. bdg. 5.95 (*0-8193-0986-9*) Parents.

—Sand Cake. Asch, Frank, illus. 48p. (ps-2). 1990. pap. 2.95 (*0-448-04341-6*, G&D) Putnam Pub Group.

—Sand Cake. LC 93-15452. 1993. PLB 13.27 (*0-8368-0973-4*) Gareth Stevens Inc.

—Short Train, Long Train. (Illus.). (ps). 1992. bds. 8.95 (*0-590-44493-X*, 028, Cartwheel) Scholastic Inc.

—Skyfire. Asch, Frank, illus. LC 88-3193. 32p. (ps-2). 1988. (Little Simon); pap. 4.95 (*0-671-66861-7*, Little Simon) S&S Trade.

Asch, Frank & Vagin, Vladimir. Dear Brother. 32p. 1992. 13.95 (*0-590-43107-2*, Scholastic Hardcover) Scholastic Inc.

—Here Comes the Cat! Asch, Frank & Vladimir, Vagin, illus. 1991. pap. 3.95 (*0-590-41854-8*) Scholastic Inc.

—Insects from Outer Space. Vagin, Vladimir, illus. LC 93-26876. 1994. 14.95 (*0-590-45489-7*) Scholastic Inc.

Asch, Frank, jt. auth. see Vagin, Vladimir.

Asch, Jan, et al. Flags of the United Nations. 24p. (gr. 2-7). 1991. 4.95 (*0-590-43117-X*) Scholastic Inc.

Aschenbrenner, Gerald. Jack, the Seal, & the Sea. Fink, Joanne, adapted by. Aschenbrenner, Gerald, illus. 30p. (gr. 2-5). 1988. PLB 14.98 (*0-382-09985-0*); PLB 11.24s.p. (*0-685-46995-6*); pap. 6.95 (*0-382-09986-9*); pap. 5.21s.p. (*0-685-46996-4*) Silver Burdett Pr.

AScott, Michael. October Moon. 129p. (gr. 8 up). 1993. pap. 9.95 (*0-86278-300-3*, Pub. by OBrien Pr IE) Dufour.

Asden, Richard. The Professor's Stick Book & Toy. 16p. (gr. 3 up). 1993. pap. text ed. 19.95 (*1-883737-01-X*) Matey Pr.

Aseltine, Lorraine. First Grade Can Wait. Tucker, Kathleen, ed. LC 87-26457. (Illus.). 32p. (ps-2). 1988. PLB 11.95 (*0-8075-2451-4*) A Whitman.

Aseltine, Lorraine, et al. I'm Deaf, & It's Okay. LC 85-26446. (Illus.). 40p. (gr. 1-4). 1986. 11.95 (*0-8075-3472-2*) A Whitman.

Ash, Martha C. Grandmother's Visit with Sam. White, Regina, illus. LC 85-71540. 48p. (Orig.). (ps-2). 1985. pap. 4.25 (*0-933865-00-7*) Doris Pubns.

Ash, Maureen. Alexander the Great: Ancient Empire Builder. LC 91-1386. 128p. (gr. 3 up). 1991. PLB 26.60 (*0-516-03063-9*) Childrens.

—The Story of Harriet Beecher Stowe. LC 89-25364. (Illus.). 32p. (gr. 3-6). 1990. PLB 13.27 (0-516-04746-9); pap. 3.95 (0-516-44746-7) Childrens.
—The Story of the Women's Movement. LC 89-17325. 32p. (gr. 3-6). 1989. PLB 13.27 (0-516-04724-8); pap. 3.95 (0-516-44724-6) Childrens.
—Vasco Nunez de Balboa: Expedition to the Pacific Ocean. LC 90-2230. (Illus.). 128p. (gr. 3 up). 1990. PLB 26.60 (0-516-03057-4) Childrens.
Ash, Russell & Higton, Bernard, eds. Aesop's Fables: A Classic Illustrated Edition. (Illus.). 1990. 15.95 (0-87701-780-8) Chronicle Bks.
Ash, Russell, ed. see Andersen, Hans Christian.
Ashabranner, Brent. Always to Remember: The Story of the Vietnam Veterans Memorial. Ashabranner, Jennifer, photos by. (Illus.). 40p. (gr. 6 up). 1988. 14.95 (0-399-22031-3, Putnam) Putnam Pub Group.
—Always to Remember: The Story of the Vietnam Veterans Memorial. (gr. 4-7). 1992. pap. 2.95 (0-590-44590-1) Scholastic Inc.
—An Ancient Heritage: The Arab-American Minority. Conklin, Paul, illus. LC 90-30641. 160p. (gr. 3-7). 1991. PLB 14.89 (0-06-020049-9) HarpC Child Bks.
—Crazy about German Shepherds. Ashabranner, Jennifer, photos by. LC 90-1303. (Illus.). 96p. (gr. 5 up). 1990. 14.95 (0-525-65032-6, Cobblehill Bks) Dutton Child Bks.
—Dark Harvest: Migrant Farmworkers in America. Conklin, Paul, illus. x, 150p. (gr. 7 up). 1993. Repr. of 1985 ed. PLB 16.50 (0-208-02391-7, Pub. by Linnet) Shoe String.
—A Grateful Nation: The Story of Arlington National Cemetery. (Illus.). 112p. 1990. 15.95 (0-399-22188-3, Putnam) Putnam Pub Group.
—I'm in the Zoo, Too. Stevens, Janet, illus. LC 88-32662. (gr. k-4). 1989. 12.95 (0-525-65002-4, Cobblehill Bks) Dutton Child Bks.
—A Memorial for Mr. Lincoln. Ashabranner, Jennifer, illus. 128p. (gr. 5-9). 1992. 15.95 (0-399-22273-1, Putnam) Putnam Pub Group.
—Morning Star, Black Sun. (Illus.). 160p. (gr. 7-11). 1982. 11.95 (0-396-08045-6, Putnam) Putnam Pub Group.
—A New Frontier: The Peace Corps in Eastern Europe. Conklin, Paul, photos by. LC 93-38535. (gr. 5 up). 1994. write for info (Cobblehill Bks) Dutton Child Bks.
—People Who Make a Difference. LC 89-34593. (Illus.). (gr. 5 up). 1989. 15.95 (0-525-65009-1, Cobblehill Bks) Dutton Child Bks.
—Still a Nation of Immigrants. Ashabranner, Jennifer, photos by. LC 92-44335. (Illus.). 144p. (gr. 5 up). 1993. 15.99 (0-525-65130-6, Cobblehill Bks) Dutton Child Bks.
—The Times of My Life: A Memoir. LC 90-40920. (gr. 4-7). 1990. 14.95 (0-525-65047-4, Cobblehill Bks) Dutton Child Bks.
Ashabranner, Brent & Ashabranner, Melissa. Into a Strange Land. (Illus.). 160p. (gr. 9-12). 1987. 14.95 (0-399-21709-6, Putnam) Putnam Pub Group.
Ashabranner, Brent K., jt. auth. see Davis, Russell B.
Ashabranner, Melissa, jt. auth. see Ashabranner, Brent.
Ashachik, Diane M., retold by see Grahame, Kenneth.
Ashachik, Diane M., ed. see Kipling, Rudyard.
Asham, Roger & Ford, Horace. Toxophilus; Archery – Theory & Practice, 2 vols. in 1. Manley, Dean V., ed. St. Charles, Glenn, frwd. by. (Illus.). (gr. 10 up). 1992. Repr. 39.95 (1-56416-092-0) Derrydale Pr.

Ashbach, Dawn & Veal, Janice. Adventures in Greater Puget Sound: An Educational Guide Exploring the Marine Environment of Greater Puget Sound. Veal, Janice, illus. 56p. (Orig.). (gr. 3-9). 1991. 7.95 (0-9629778-0-2) NW Island.
ADVENTURES IN GREATER PUGET SOUND captures the magic of marine life in this unique region. An educational guide & activity book, it is designed for 8 to 12 year olds, but adults will be tempted to try their hands at a variety of challenges ranging from hidden pictures to crossword puzzles & decoding the "Captain's Secret Message." The rich green waters of Greater Puget Sound are the hub for a multitude of marine activities. Colorful sea anemones & shy octopuses undulate their tentacles on the sea floor, while orca whales breach & yachts & ferry boats wend their watery ways at the surface. ADVENTURES IN GREATER PUGET SOUND includes concise & definitive information on a host of creatures & boats from wrinkled whelks to eagles, to oil freighters. The activities are designed to reinforce text information. The book is illustrated with more than 150 pen & ink drawings. To order: Northwest Island Associates, 444 Guemes Island Road, Anacortes, WA 98221; (206) 293-3721. *Publisher Provided Annotation.*

Ashby, Gwynneth. A Family in South Korea. (Illus.). 32p. (gr. 2-5). 1987. 13.50 (0-8225-1675-6) Lerner Pubns.
Ashby, Ruth. Beetlejuice for President. 96p. (Orig.). 1992. pap. 2.99 (0-671-75552-8) PB.
—Jane Goodall's Animal World: Sea Otters. LC 89-38552. (Illus.). 32p. (gr. 3-7). 1990. SBE 11.95 (0-689-31472-8, Atheneum Child Bk) Macmillan Child Grp.
—Jane Goodall's Animal World: Tigers. LC 89-38549. (Illus.). 32p. (gr. 3-7). 1990. SBE 11.95 (0-689-31474-4, Atheneum Child Bk) Macmillan Child Grp.
—Lydia's Scream Date. 96p. (Orig.). 1992. pap. 2.99 (0-671-75553-6) PB.
—The Orangutan. LC 93-5754. (Illus.). 60p. (gr. 4). 1994. RSBE 13.95 (0-87518-600-9, Dillon) Macmillan Child Grp.
Ashby, Ruth, ed. Monster Mix-Up. 128p. (Orig.). 1991. pap. 3.50 (0-671-74201-9, Archway) PB.
—Nintendo Book, No. 4: Koopa Kapers. 128p. (Orig.). 1991. pap. 3.50 (0-671-74202-7, Archway) PB.
Ashby, Ruth, ed. see Barber, Antonia.
Ashby, Ruth, ed. see Bosco, Clyde.
Ashby, Ruth, ed. see Cohen, Daniel.
Ashby, Ruth, ed. see Gorman, Carol.
Ashby, Ruth, ed. see Harrell, Janice.
Ashby, Ruth, ed. see Hodgeman, Ann.
Ashby, Ruth, ed. see Hodgman, Ann.
Ashby, Ruth, ed. see Kistler, Darci.
Ashby, Ruth, ed. see McEvoy, Seth & Smith, Laure.
Ashby, Ruth, ed. see Specter, B. J.
Ashby, Ruth, ed. see Steiner, Barbara.
Ashby, Ruth, ed. see Wayne, Matt.
Ashby, Sylvia. Don Coyote. (Illus.). 40p. (Orig.). (ps up). 1986. pap. 3.00 (0-88680-260-1); royalty on application 35.00 (0-685-67528-9) I E Clark.
—Once upon a Broomstick: A Halloween Happening in One Act. (Illus.). 28p. (Orig.). (gr. 1-8). 1990. pap. 2.25 (0-88680-329-2); royalty on application 25.00 (0-685-58901-3) I E Clark.
—Professor Zuccini's Traveling Tales. 44p. (gr. k up). 1983. pap. 3.50 (0-88680-208-3); royalty on application 40.00 (0-685-57866-6) I E Clark.
—Santa Claus Is Missing! (Illus.). 22p. (Orig.). (ps up). 1989. Piano Score. 7.50 (0-88680-311-X); pap. 3.00 bk. (0-88680-310-1); royalty on application 35.00 (0-685-58558-1) I E Clark.
—Shining Princess of the Slender Bamboo. (Illus.). 44p. (Orig.). (gr. 6 up). 1987. pap. 3.50 (0-88680-266-0); royalty on application 50.00 (0-685-67658-7) I E Clark.
Ashby, Sylvia, contrib. by. Happily Ever After: Tales Told by the Brothers Grimm. (Illus.). 56p. (Orig.). (gr. k up). 1988. pap. 3.00 (0-88680-290-3); royalty on application 50.00 (0-685-67685-4) I E Clark.
Ashby, Sylvia, adapted by. Once upon a Santa Claus. Halpain, Thomas J., contrib. by. (Illus.). 44p. (Orig.). (ps up). 1988. pap. 3.00 (0-88680-296-2); piano-vocal score 10.00 (0-88680-297-0); royalty on application 35.00 (0-685-58410-0) I E Clark.
Asher. Summer Smith Begins. (gr. 7 up). 1987. pap. 2.50 (0-553-25883-4) Bantam.
Asher, Sandy. Everything Is Not Enough. (gr. k-12). 1988. pap. 2.75 (0-440-20002-4, LFL) Dell.
—Just Like Jenny. LC 82-70315. 160p. (gr. 5-9). 1986. pap. 2.50 (0-440-94289-6) Dell.
—Just Like Jenny. LC 82-70315. (gr. 4-6). 1982. pap. 12.95 (0-385-28496-9) Delacorte.
—Missing Pieces. LC 83-14381. 144p. (gr. 7 up). 1984. 12.95 (0-385-29318-6) Delacorte.
—Missing Pieces. (gr. 6 up). 1986. pap. 2.50 (0-440-95716-8, LFL) Dell.
—Out of Here: A Senior Class Yearbook. LC 92-35188. 160p. (gr. 7 up). 1993. 14.99 (0-525-67418-7, Lodestar Bks) Dutton Child Bks.
—Princess Bee & the Royal Good-Night Story. Mathews, Judith, ed. Smith, Cat B., illus. LC 89-35749. 32p. (ps-1). 1990. 13.95 (0-8075-6624-1) A Whitman.
—Teddy Teaberry's Peanutty Problem. (gr. k-6). 1989. pap. 2.50 (0-440-40229-8, YB) Dell.
—Teddy Teabury's Fabulous Facts. Jones, Bob, illus. 110p. (Orig.). (gr. 4-5). 1985. pap. 2.50 (0-440-48576-2, YB) Dell.
—Things Are Seldom What They Seem. LC 82-72819. 144p. (gr. 7up). 1983. pap. 11.95 (0-385-29250-3) Delacorte.
—Where Do You Get Your Ideas? Hellard, Susan, illus. 96p. (gr. 5 up). 1987. 12.95 (0-8027-6690-0); PLB 13.85 (0-8027-6691-9) Walker & Co.
—Where Do You Get Your Ideas? Helping Young Writers Begin. 124p. (gr. 4-7). 1987. 9.92 (0-685-63804-9, BR7441) W A T Braille.
—Wild Words & How to Tame Them. Kendrick, Dennis, illus. 96p. (gr. 5 up). 1989. 13.95 (0-8027-6887-3); PLB 14.85 (0-8027-6888-1) Walker & Co.

Ashford, Ann. If I Found a Wistful Unicorn: A Gift of Love. Drath, Bill, illus. 40p. 1992. 6.95 (1-56145-047-2) Peachtree Pubs.
Ashford, Moyra. Brazil. LC 90-19250. (Illus.). 96p. (gr. 6-12). 1991. PLB 19.92 (0-8114-2436-7) Raintree Steck-V.
Ashforth, Camilla. Calamity. Ashforth, Camilla, illus. LC 92-54956. 32p. (ps up). 1993. 15.95 (1-56402-252-8) Candlewick Pr.
—Horatio's Bed. Ashforth, Camilla, illus. LC 91-58737. 32p. (ps up). 1992. 15.95 (1-56402-057-6) Candlewick Pr.
—Horatio's Bed. LC 91-58737. (ps-3). 1994. pap. 4.99 (1-56402-277-3) Candlewick Pr.
—Monkey Tricks. Ashforth, Camilla, illus. LC 92-53013. 32p. (ps-3). 1993. 15.95 (1-56402-170-X) Candlewick Pr.
Ashley, Bernard. All My Men. LC 78-12683. (gr. 6 up). 1978. 21.95 (0-87599-228-5) S G Phillips.
—Bad Blood. large type ed. (gr. 1-8). 1990. 13.95 (0-7451-1424-5, Galaxy Child Lrg Print) Chivers N Amer.
—A Break in the Sun. Keeping, Charles, illus. 186p. (gr. 6 up). 1980. 21.95 (0-87599-230-7) S G Phillips.
—Cleversticks. Brazell, Derek, illus. LC 91-34669. 32p. (ps-2). 1992. 10.00 (0-517-58878-1); PLB 10.99 (0-517-58879-X) Crown Bks Yng Read.
—A Kind of Wild Justice. Keeping, Charles, illus. LC 78-10899. (gr. 7 up). 1979. 21.95 (0-87599-229-3) S G Phillips.
—Running Scared. large type ed. 352p. (gr. 1-8). 1990. 13.95 (0-7451-1099-1, Galaxy Child Lrg Print) Chivers N Amer.
—Terry on the Fence. Keeping, Charles, illus. LC 76-39898. (gr. 5-9). 1977. 21.95 (0-87599-222-6) S G Phillips.
Ashley, Ellen. Barri, Take Two. 160p. 1991. pap. 3.50 (0-449-14584-0, Girls Only) Fawcett.
—Encore. 160p. 1991. pap. 3.50 (0-449-14587-5, Girls Only) Fawcett.
Ashley, Jill. Riddles about Christmas. Brook, Bonnie, ed. Gray, Rob, illus. 32p. (ps-3). 1990. 6.95 (0-671-70554-7); PLB 10.98 (0-671-70552-0) Silver Pr.
—Riddles about Easter. Gray, Rob, photos by. (Illus.). 32p. (ps-3). 1991. 6.95 (0-671-72727-3); PLB 10.98 (0-671-72726-5) Silver Pr.
Ashman, I. Make This Egyptian Temple. (Illus.). 32p. 1990. pap. 9.95 (0-7460-0461-3) EDC.
—Make This Lost Temple. 32p. 1992. pap. 9.95 (0-685-59087-9) EDC.
—Make This Model Cathedral. (Illus.). 32p. 1988. pap. 9.95 (0-7460-0182-7) EDC.
—Make This Model: Haunted House. (Illus.). 32p. (gr. 4 up). 1991. pap. 9.95 (0-7460-0647-0, Usborne) EDC.
—Make This Model Village. (Illus.). 32p. 1988. pap. 9.95 (0-86020-579-7) EDC.
—Make This Model: Wizards Castle. (Illus.). 32p. (gr. 4 up). 1991. pap. 9.95 (0-7460-0607-1, Usborne) EDC.
—Make This Roman Fort. (Illus.). 32p. 1989. pap. 9.95 (0-7460-0256-4) EDC.
—Make This Roman Villa. (Illus.). 32p. 1990. pap. 9.95 (0-7460-0462-1) EDC.
—Make This Viking Settlement. (Illus.). 32p. 1989. pap. 9.95 (0-7460-0257-2) EDC.
Ashman, I., jt. auth. see Cartwright, S.
Ashman, Iain. Make This Model Castle. Stitt, Sue & McCaig, Ron, illus. (gr. 4-9). 1983. pap. 5.95 (0-13-545947-8, Pub. by Treehouse) P-H.
—Make This Model Doll's House. (Illus.). 32p. (gr. 4-7). 1993. pap. 9.95 (0-7460-1316-7, Usborne) EDC.
—Make This Model Village. Stitt, Sue & McCaig, Ron, illus. (gr. 4-9). 1983. pap. 5.95 (0-13-545954-0, Pub. by Treehouse) P-H.
Ashman, L. Make This Model Castle. 32p. 1988. pap. 9.95 (0-86020-578-9, Usborne) EDC.
—Make This Model Town. 32p. 1988. pap. 9.95 (0-7460-0181-9, Usborne) EDC.
Ashmore, M. Catherine, et al. Risks & Rewards of Entrepreneurship. LC 87-21787. 128p. (Orig.). 1987. pap. text ed. 7.95 (0-8219-0323-3, 25658); tchr's. resource guide 19.00 (0-8219-0324-1, TRG-25803) EMC.
Ashraf. Lessons in Islam, 5. 8.50 (1-56744-121-1) Kazi Pubns.
Ashrose, Cara. The Very First Americans. Waldman, Bryna, illus. LC 92-38076. 32p. (ps-3). 1993. pap. 2.25 (0-448-40169-X, G&D); (G&D) Putnam Pub Group.
Ashton, Christina. Codes & Ciphers: Hundreds of Unusual & Secret Ways to Send Messages. LC 92-39008. (Illus.). 112p. (Orig.). (gr. 7 up). 1993. pap. 7.95 (1-55870-292-X) Betterway Bks.
—Words Can Tell: A Book about Our Language. LC 87-20333. 128p. (gr. 6-9). 1989. lib. bdg. 12.98 (0-671-65223-0, J Messner) S&S Trade.
Ashton, Elizabeth A. An Old-Fashioned ABC Book. Smith, Jessie W., illus. 32p. (ps-3). 1990. 14.95 (0-670-83048-8) Viking Child Bks.
—An Old-Fashioned ABC Book. Smith, Jessie W., illus. 32p. (ps-3). 1992. pap. 3.99 (0-14-054189-6) Puffin Bks.
—An Old-Fashioned One Two Three Book. Smith, Jesse W., illus. 32p. (ps-3). 1991. 14.95 (0-670-83499-8) Viking Child Bks.
Ashton, Elizabeth Allen. An Old-Fashined One Two Three Book. Smith, Jessie Willcox, illus. LC 92-21109. 32p. (ps-3). 1993. pap. 4.99 (0-14-054310-4) Puffin Bks.

Ashton, Stephen. The British in India. (Illus.). 86p. (gr. 7-9). 1988. 19.95 (0-7134-5475-X, Pub. by Batsford UK) Trafalgar.

Ashwander, Donald, jt. auth. see Martin, Judith.

Ashwill, Beverley. The Blue-Eyed Ninja Warrior. Ashwill, Betty J., illus. LC 90-83313. 43p. (gr. 3-9). 1990. pap. 5.98 (0-941381-05-6) BJO Enterprises.

—Marlina & McGee. Ashwill, Betty J., illus. LC 86-73031. 32p. (ps-3). 1987. pap. 5.95 (0-941381-00-5) BJO Enterprises.

—The Runaways. Ashwill, Betty, illus. LC 87-72441. 48p. (gr. 4-8). 1988. 12.95 (0-941381-02-1); pap. 5.95 (0-941381-01-3) BJO Enterprises.

—Too Little, Too Big, Just Right. Ashwill, Betty J., illus. LC 90-83314. 18p. (ps-3). 1990. pap. 3.98 (0-941381-04-8) BJO Enterprises.

Ashwill, Beverley B. Heather & the New Baby. Ashwill, Betty J., illus. LC 88-63168. 23p. (Orig.). (gr. k-3). 1988. pap. 3.98 (0-941381-03-X) BJO Enterprises.

Ashwill, Beverly. Charley the Fearless Zoo Keeper. Ashwill, Betty J., illus. LC 90-83311. 20p. (ps-3). 1990. pap. 3.98 (0-941381-07-2) BJO Enterprises.

—The Invisible Dawn. Ashwill, Betty J., illus. LC 90-83310. 24p. (ps-5). 1990. pap. 3.98 (0-685-37787-3) BJO Enterprises.

—Jeffrey, the Littlest Pig. Ashwill, Betty J., illus. LC 90-83312. 24p. (ps-3). 1990. pap. 3.98 (0-941381-06-4) BJO Enterprises.

Ashworth, Dennis. Understanding Microcomputers. Hylton, Richard M., ed. Wren, James E. & MacMillan, Marilyn, illus. 32p. (Orig.). (gr. 9-12). 1987. pap. text ed. 6.50 (0-89606-215-5, 801) Am Assn Voc Materials.

Ashworth, L. E. Revelation: Signs of the Times. (Illus.). 240p. (Orig.). (gr. 10). 1990. pap. 5.95 (0-9627415-0-7) Advent Times.

Asian Cultural Center for UNESCO. Folk Tales from Asia for Children Everywhere, Bk. 1. LC 74-82605. (Illus.). 60p. (gr. 1-4). 1975. 6.50 (0-8348-1032-8) Weatherhill.

—Folk Tales from Asia for Children Everywhere, Bk. 2. LC 74-82605. (Illus.). 60p. (gr. 3-6). 1975. 6.50 (0-8348-1033-6) Weatherhill.

—Folk Tales from Asia for Children Everywhere, Bk. 5. LC 74-82605. (Illus.). 60p. (gr. 1-4). 1977. 6.50 (0-8348-1036-0) Weatherhill.

—Folk Tales from Asia for Children Everywhere, Bk. 6. LC 74-82605. (Illus.). 60p. (gr. 3-6). 1978. 6.50 (0-8348-1037-9) Weatherhill.

Asian Cultural Center for UNESCO, ed. Folk Tales from Asia for Children Everywhere, Bk. 3. LC 74-82605. (Illus.). 60p. (gr. 3-6). 1976. 6.50 (0-8348-1034-4) Weatherhill.

—Stories from Asia Today: A Collection for Young Readers, Bk. 2. LC 74-82605. (Illus.). 184p. (gr. 4-7). 1980. pap. 8.95 (0-8348-1040-9) Weatherhill.

Asian Cultural Center for UNESCO Staff. Folk Tales from Asia for Children Everywhere, Bk. 4. 60p. (gr. 3-6). 1986. pap. 6.50 (0-8348-1035-2) Weatherhill.

Asian Cultural Centre for UNESCO, ed. Stories from Asia Today: A Collection for Young Readers, Bk. I. LC 74-82605. (Illus.). 144p. (gr. 4-7). 1980. pap. 7.95 (0-8348-1038-7) Weatherhill.

Asian Women United of California, ed. Making Waves: An Anthology of Writings by & about Asian American Women. LC 88-47661. (Illus.). 480p. (gr. 9-12). 1989. pap. 18.95 (0-8070-5905-6, BP 807) Beacon Pr.

Asifi, Allama M. Children's Guide to Islam. rev. ed. 145p. 1983. pap. 7.00 (0-941724-11-5) Islamic Seminary.

Asimov, Isaac. All the Troubles of World. 40p. (gr. 5). 1989. PLB 13.95s.p. (0-88682-233-5) Creative Ed.

—Ancient Astronomy. LC 88-17564. (Illus.). 32p. (gr. 3-4). 1988. PLB 17.27 (1-55532-368-5) Gareth Stevens Inc.

—Ancient Astronomy. (gr. 4-7). 1991. pap. 4.95 (0-440-40387-1) Dell.

—Ask Isaac Asimov, 41 vols. (Illus.). 24p. 1991. Subscription set. PLB 685.77 (0-8368-0562-3) Gareth Stevens Inc.

—Ask Isaac Asimov, 41 vols. (Illus.). (gr. 1-8). Standing Order. PLB 10.95 ea. (0-8368-0788-X); Subscription Order. PLB 9.95 ea. (0-8368-0789-8) Gareth Stevens Inc.

—The Asteroids. LC 87-42598. (Illus.). (gr. 3-4). 1988. PLB 17.27 (1-55532-353-7) Gareth Stevens Inc.

—Asteroids. (gr. 4-7). 1991. pap. 4.99 (0-440-40443-6) Dell.

—Astronomy Today. LC 89-4631. (Illus.). 32p. (gr. 3-4). 1989. PLB 17.27 (1-55532-402-9) Gareth Stevens Inc.

—The Birth & Death of Stars. LC 88-42892. (Illus.). 32p. (gr. 3-4). 1989. PLB 17.27 (1-55532-367-7) Gareth Stevens Inc.

—Birth & Death of Stars. (gr. 4-7). 1991. pap. 4.99 (0-440-40446-0, YB) Dell.

—Christopher Columbus. LC 90-25836. (Illus.). 64p. (gr. 3-4). 1991. PLB 18.60 (0-8368-0556-9) Gareth Stevens Inc.

—Colonizing Planets & Stars. (gr. 4-7). 1991. pap. 4.99 (0-440-40447-9, YB) Dell.

—Colonizing the Planets & Stars. LC 89-4644. 32p. (gr. 3-4). 1989. PLB 17.27 (1-55532-372-3) Gareth Stevens Inc.

—Comets & Meteors. LC 89-4632. 32p. (gr. 3-4). 1989. PLB 17.27 (1-55532-400-2) Gareth Stevens Inc.

—Comets & Meteors. (gr. 4-7). 1991. pap. 4.99 (0-440-40450-9, YB) Dell.

—Did Comets Kill the Dinosaurs? LC 87-42590. (Illus.). 32p. (gr. 3-4). 1987. PLB 17.27 (1-55532-322-7) Gareth Stevens Inc.

—Did Comets Kill the Dinosaurs? 1990. pap. 4.95 (0-440-40347-2, YB) Dell.

—Earth: Our Home Base. LC 87-42607. (Illus.). 32p. (gr. 3-4). 1988. PLB 17.27 (1-55532-362-6) Gareth Stevens Inc.

—The Earth's Moon. LC 87-42601. (Illus.). 32p. (gr. 3-4). 1988. PLB 17.27 (1-55532-357-X) Gareth Stevens Inc.

—Fantastic Voyage. 192p. (gr. 7 up). 1984. pap. 3.50 (0-553-27151-2, Spectra) Bantam.

—Far As Human Eye Could See. LC 86-16684. 216p. (gr. 7 up). 1987. 15.95 (0-385-23514-3) Doubleday.

—Ferdinand Magellan. LC 91-9207. (Illus.). 64p. (gr. 3-4). 1991. PLB 18.60 (0-8368-0560-7) Gareth Stevens Inc.

—Franchise. 40p. (gr. 5). 1989. PLB 13.95s.p. (0-88682-232-7) Creative Ed.

—Greeks: A Great Adventure. (Illus.). 320p. (gr. 7 up). 1965. 15.45 (0-395-06574-7) HM.

—Henry Hudson. LC 90-23948. (Illus.). 64p. (gr. 3-4). 1991. PLB 18.60 (0-8368-0558-5) Gareth Stevens Inc.

—How Did We Find about Microwaves? Kors, Erika, illus. 64p. (gr. 1-4). 1989. 11.95 (0-8027-6837-7); PLB 12.85 (0-8027-6838-5) Walker & Co.

—How Did We Find Out about Antarctica? Wool, David, illus. (gr. 5-8). 1979. PLB 11.85 (0-8027-6371-5) Walker & Co.

—How Did We Find Out about Atoms. LC 75-3910. 64p. (gr. 5-8). 1976. PLB 12.85 (0-8027-6248-4) Walker & Co.

—How Did We Find Out about Black Holes? Wool, David, illus. LC 73-4320. 64p. (gr. 5 up). 1978. PLB 12.85 reinforced (0-8027-6337-5) Walker & Co.

—How Did We Find Out about Coal. 58p. 1992. text ed. 4.64 (1-56956-114-1) W A T Braille.

—How Did We Find Out about Comets? Wool, David, illus. LC 74-78115. 64p. (gr. 5-8). 1975. lib. bdg. 10.85 (0-8027-6204-2) Walker & Co.

—How Did We Find Out about Computers? Wool, David, illus. LC 83-40401. 64p. (gr. 5 up). 1984. lib. bdg. 11.85 (0-8027-6533-5) Walker & Co.

—How Did We Find Out about Dinosaurs. LC 72-95793. (gr. 5 up). 1981. PLB 11.85 (0-8027-6134-8) Walker & Co.

—How Did We Find Out about DNA? Wool, David, illus. LC 85-15589. 61p. (gr. 9 up). 1985. 9.95 (0-8027-6596-3); PLB 10.85 (0-8027-6604-8) Walker & Co.

—How Did We Find Out about Earthquakes? Wool, David, illus. LC 77-78984. 64p. (gr. 6 up). 1978. PLB 12.85 (0-8027-6306-5) Walker & Co.

—How Did We Find Out About Electricity? Selsam, Millicent E., ed. Kalmenoff, Matthew, illus. LC 72-81380. 64p. (gr. 5-8). 1973. PLB 10.85 (0-8027-6124-0) Walker & Co.

—How Did We Find out about Germs. Wool, David, illus. LC 73-81402. 64p. (gr. 5-8). 1973. PLB 10.85 (0-8027-6166-6) Walker & Co.

—How Did We Find Out about Lasers? Kors, Erika, illus. (gr. 5 up). 1990. 12.95 (0-8027-6935-7); lib. bdg. 13.85 (0-8027-6936-5) Walker & Co.

—How Did We Find Out about Life in the Deep Sea? Wool, David, illus. (gr. 4-7). 1981. lib. bdg. 10.85 (0-8027-6428-2) Walker & Co.

—How Did We Find Out about Neptune? Kors, Erika, illus. 64p. (gr. 5 up). 1990. 12.95 (0-8027-6981-0); lib. bdg. 13.85 (0-8027-6982-9) Walker & Co.

—How Did We Find Out about Nuclear Power? LC 76-12067. (Illus.). (gr. 4 up). 1976. PLB 12.85 (0-8027-6266-2) Walker & Co.

—How Did We Find Out about Oil? Wool, David, illus. 64p. (gr. 5-8). 1980. PLB 10.85 (0-8027-6381-2) Walker & Co.

—How Did We Find Out about Our Genes? Wool, David, illus. LC 83-1211. 64p. (gr. 5-8). 1983. PLB 10.85 (0-8027-6500-9) Walker & Co.

—How Did We Find Out about Our Human Roots? Wool, David, illus. (gr. 4-8). 1979. PLB 10.85 (0-8027-6361-8) Walker & Co.

—How Did We Find Out about Outer Space? 64p. (gr. 5 up). 1977. PLB 11.85 (0-8027-6284-0) Walker & Co.

—How Did We Find out about Photosynthesis. Kors, Erika, illus. 32p. (gr. 1-4). 1989. 11.95 (0-8027-6899-7); PLB 12.85 (0-8027-6886-5) Walker & Co.

—How Did We Find Out about Pluto? Kors, Erika, illus. 64p. (gr. 5 up). 1991. 12.95 (0-8027-6991-8); PLB 13.85 (0-8027-6992-6) Walker & Co.

—How Did We Find Out about Robots? Wool, David, illus. 64p. (gr. 4-7). 1984. PLB 10.85 (0-8027-6563-7) Walker & Co.

—How Did We Find Out about Solar Power? Wool, David, illus. 64p. (gr. 4-7). 1983. PLB 12.85 (0-8027-6423-1) Walker & Co.

—How Did We Find Out about Sunshine. 64p. (gr. 5 up). 1987. 10.95 (0-8027-6697-8); PLB 12.85 (0-8027-6698-6) Walker & Co.

—How Did We Find Out about the Atmosphere? LC 84-27125. 64p. (gr. 5-9). 1985. 9.95 (0-8027-6588-2); PLB 12.85 (0-8027-6580-7) Walker & Co.

—How Did We Find Out about the Beginning of Life? Wool, David, illus. LC 81-71196. 64p. (gr. 4-7). 1982. PLB 10.85 (0-8027-6448-7) Walker & Co.

—How Did We Find Out about the Brain. (gr. 5 up). 1987. 10.95 (0-8027-6736-2); PLB 11.85 (0-8027-6737-0) Walker & Co.

—How Did We Find Out about the Speed of Light? Wool, David, illus. LC 86-4085. 64p. (gr. 5 up). 1986. 10.95 (0-8027-6637-4); PLB 11.85 (0-8027-6613-7) Walker & Co.

—How Did We Find Out about the Universe? Wool, David, illus. LC 82-42531. 64p. (gr. 5-8). 1983. PLB 12.85 (0-8027-6477-0) Walker & Co.

—How Did We Find Out About Vitamins? Wool, David, illus. LC 73-92453. 64p. (gr. 5-8). 1974. PLB 11.85 (0-8027-6184-4) Walker & Co.

—How Did We Find Out about Volcanoes? Wool, David, illus. 64p. (gr. 4-7). 1981. PLB 12.85 (0-8027-6412-6) Walker & Co.

—How did We Find Out about Volcanoes? 64p. (gr. 2-7). 1982. pap. 1.95 (0-380-59626-1, 59626-1, Camelot) Avon.

—How Did We Find Out the Earth Is Round? Selsam, Millicent E., ed. Kalmenoff, Matthew, illus. LC 72-81378. 64p. (gr. 5-8). 1972. PLB 5.85 (0-8027-6122-4) Walker & Co.

—How Do Airplanes Fly? (Illus.). 24p. (gr. 1-8). 1992. PLB 15.93 (0-8368-0800-2); PLB 15.93 s.p. (0-685-61486-7) Gareth Stevens Inc.

—How Do Big Ships Float? (Illus.). 24p. (gr. 1-8). 1992. PLB 15.93 (0-8368-0802-9); PLB 15.93 s.p. (0-685-61488-3) Gareth Stevens Inc.

—How Does a TV Work? (Illus.). 24p. (gr. 1-8). 1992. PLB 15.93 (0-8368-0804-5); PLB 15.93 s.p. (0-685-61490-5) Gareth Stevens Inc.

—How Is Paper Made? (Illus.). 24p. (gr. 1-8). 1992. PLB 15.93 (0-8368-0803-7); PLB 15.93 s.p. (0-685-61489-1) Gareth Stevens Inc.

—How Was the Universe Born. LC 87-42602. (Illus.). 32p. (gr. 3-4). 1988. PLB 17.27 (1-55532-358-8) Gareth Stevens Inc.

—Index. LC 89-43142. (Illus.). 32p. (gr. 3-4). 1990. PLB 17.27 (1-55532-900-4) Gareth Stevens Inc.

—Is Our Planet Warming Up? LC 91-50359. (Illus.). 24p. (gr. 2-3). 1992. PLB 15.93 (0-8368-0744-8) Gareth Stevens Inc.

—Is There Life on Other Planets? LC 87-42603. (Illus.). 32p. (gr. 3-4). 1989. PLB 17.27 (1-55532-359-6) Gareth Stevens Inc.

—Is There Life on Other Planets? 1991. pap. 4.95 (0-440-40348-0, YB) Dell.

—Isaac Asimov's Library of the Universe, 33 vols. Sachner, Mark, ed. (Illus.). 1056p. (gr. 3-4). Set. lib. bdg. 569.91 (1-55532-420-7) Gareth Stevens Inc.

—Isaac Asimov's Pioneers of Science & Exploration, 3 vols. (Illus.). 64p. (gr. 3-4). 1991. Set. PLB 55.80 (0-8368-0754-5) Gareth Stevens Inc.

—It's Such a Beautiful Day. Redpath, Ann, ed. Delessert, Etienne, illus. 64p. (gr. 4 up). 1985. PLB 13.95s.p. (0-88682-008-1) Creative Ed.

—Jupiter: The Spotted Giant. LC 88-42893. (Illus.). 32p. (gr. 3-4). 1989. PLB 17.27 (1-55532-363-4) Gareth Stevens Inc.

—Mars: Our Mysterious Neighbor. LC 87-42599. (Illus.). (gr. 3-4). 1988. PLB 17.27 (1-55532-354-5) Gareth Stevens Inc.

—Mercury: The Quick Planet. LC 87-42605. (Illus.). 32p. (gr. 3-4). 1989. PLB 17.27 (1-55532-360-X) Gareth Stevens Inc.

—Mercury: The Spotted Giant. LC 87-42605. (Illus.). 32p. (gr. 2-5). 1989. PLB 17.27 (0-685-45391-X) Gareth Stevens Inc.

—Mythology & the Universe. LC 89-11360. (Illus.). 32p. (gr. 3-4). 1989. PLB 17.27 (1-55532-403-7) Gareth Stevens Inc.

—Mythology & the Universe. (gr. 4-7). 1991. pap. 4.99 (0-440-40449-5, YB) Dell.

—Neptune: The Farthest Giant. LC 89-43136. (Illus.). 32p. (gr. 3-4). 1990. PLB 17.27 (1-55532-369-3) Gareth Stevens Inc.

—Oceans of Venus & the Big Sun of Mercury. (gr. 4 up). 1993. pap. 4.99 (0-553-56254-1, Spectra) Bantam.

—Our Milky Way & Other Galaxies. LC 87-42597. (Illus.). (gr. 3-4). 1988. PLB 17.27 (1-55532-352-9) Gareth Stevens Inc.

—Our Solar System. LC 87-42606. (Illus.). 32p. (gr. 3-4). 1988. PLB 17.27 (1-55532-361-8) Gareth Stevens Inc.

—Piloted Space Flights. LC 89-11303. (Illus.). (gr. 3-4). 1990. PLB 17.27 (1-55532-371-5) Gareth Stevens Inc.

—Pluto: A Double Planet? LC 89-11290. (Illus.). 32p. (gr. 3-4). 1989. PLB 12.95 (1-55532-373-1) Gareth Stevens Inc.

—Projects in Astronomy. LC 89-43133. (Illus.). 32p. (gr. 3-4). 1990. PLB 17.27 (1-55532-401-0) Gareth Stevens Inc.

—Quasars, Pulsars & Black Holes. LC 87-42596. (Illus.). 32p. (gr. 3-4). 1988. PLB 17.27 (1-55532-351-0) Gareth Stevens Inc.

—Quasars, Pulsars & Black Holes. 1990. pap. 4.95 (0-440-40353-7) Dell.

—Robbie. 40p. (gr. 5). 1989. 13.95 (0-88682-231-9); PLB 10.45s.p. (0-685-21701-9) Creative Ed.

—Rockets, Probes & Satellites. LC 87-42639. (Illus.). 32p. (gr. 3-4). 1988. PLB 17.27 (1-55532-366-9) Gareth Stevens Inc.

—Rockets, Probes & Satellites. 1990. pap. 4.95 (0-440-40351-0, YB) Dell.

—Sally. 40p. (gr. 5). 1989. PLB 13.95s.p. (0-88682-230-0) Creative Ed.

—Saturn: The Ringed Beauty. LC 88-17563. (Illus.). 32p. (gr. 3-4). 1988. PLB 17.27 (1-55532-364-2) Gareth Stevens Inc.

—Science Fiction, Science Fact. LC 87-42591. (Illus.). 32p. (gr. 3-4). 1989. PLB 17.27 (*1-55532-323-5*) Gareth Stevens Inc.
—Science Fiction Science Fact. (gr. 4-7). 1991. pap. 4.95 (*0-440-40352-9*) Dell.
—Space Garbage. LC 88-42894. (Illus.). 32p. (gr. 3-4). 1989. PLB 17.27 (*1-55532-370-7*) Gareth Stevens Inc.
—Space Garbage. (gr. 4-7). 1991. pap. 4.99 (*0-440-40444-4*) Dell.
—Space Spotter's Guide. LC 87-42600. (Illus.). 32p. (gr. 3-4). 1988. PLB 17.27 (*1-55532-356-1*) Gareth Stevens Inc.
—Space Spotters Guide. (gr. 4-7). 1991. pap. 4.95 (*0-440-40388-X*) Dell.
—The Sun. LC 87-42595. (Illus.). 32p. (gr. 3-4). 1988. PLB 17.27 (*1-55532-350-2*) Gareth Stevens Inc.
—Unidentified Flying Objects. LC 87-42604. (Illus.). (gr. 3-4). 1988. PLB 17.27 (*1-55532-355-3*) Gareth Stevens Inc.
—Unidentified Flying Objects. 1990. pap. 4.95 (*0-440-40349-9*, YB) Dell.
—Uranus: The Sideways Planet. LC 87-42594. (Illus.). 32p. (gr. 3-4). 1988. PLB 17.27 (*1-55532-324-3*) Gareth Stevens Inc.
—Venus: A Shrouded Mystery. LC 89-43135. (Illus.). 32p. (gr. 3-4). 1990. PLB 17.27 (*1-55532-365-0*) Gareth Stevens Inc.
—Visions of Fantasy: Tales from the Masters. 1991. pap. 3.50 (*0-553-29356-7*) Bantam.
— What is a Shooting Star? LC 90-25922. (Illus.). 24p. (gr. 2-3). 1991. PLB 15.93 (*0-8368-0436-8*) Gareth Stevens Inc.
—What Is Acid Rain? LC 91-50362. (Illus.). 24p. (gr. 2-3). 1992. PLB 15.93 (*0-8368-0741-3*) Gareth Stevens Inc.
—What Is an Eclipse? LC 90-26062. (Illus.). 24p. (gr. 2-3). 1991. PLB 15.93 (*0-8368-0440-6*) Gareth Stevens Inc.
—What's Happening to the Ozone Layer? LC 92-5347. (Illus.). 24p. (gr. 1-8). 1993. PLB 15.93 (*0-8368-0795-2*); PLB 11.95 s.p. (*0-685-61484-0*) Gareth Stevens Inc.
—Where Does Garbage Go? LC 91-50361. (Illus.). 24p. (gr. 2-3). 1992. PLB 15.93 (*0-8368-0742-1*) Gareth Stevens Inc.
—Why Are Animals Endangered? LC 92-5346. (Illus.). 24p. (gr. 1-8). 1993. PLB 15.93 (*0-8368-0798-7*); PLB 15.93 s.p. (*0-685-61485-9*) Gareth Stevens Inc.
—Why Are Some Beaches Oily? LC 92-5345. 1992. PLB 15.93 (*0-8368-0796-0*) Gareth Stevens Inc.
—Why Are the Rain Forests Vanishing? LC 92-5348. 1992. PLB 15.93 (*0-8368-0797-9*) Gareth Stevens Inc.
—Why Are the Whales Vanishing? (Illus.). 24p. (gr. 2-3). 1992. PLB 15.93 (*0-8368-0745-6*) Gareth Stevens Inc.
—Why Do Stars Twinkle? (Illus.). 24p. (gr. 2-3). 1991. PLB 15.93 (*0-8368-0437-6*) Gareth Stevens Inc.
—Why Do We Have Different Seasons? LC 90-26061. (Illus.). 24p. (gr. 2-3). 1991. PLB 15.93 (*0-8368-0439-2*) Gareth Stevens Inc.
—Why Does Litter Cause Problems? LC 92-5349. 1992. PLB 15.93 (*0-8368-0799-5*) Gareth Stevens Inc.
—Why Does the Moon Change Shape? LC 90-25430. (Illus.). 24p. (gr. 2-3). 1991. PLB 15.93 (*0-8368-0438-4*) Gareth Stevens Inc.
—Why Is the Air Dirty? (Illus.). 24p. (gr. 2-3). 1992. PLB 15.93 (*0-8368-0743-X*) Gareth Stevens Inc.
—Words from the Myths. Barss, William, illus. 224p. (gr. 5-10). 1961. 14.95 (*0-395-06568-2*) HM.
—Words from the Myths. (Illus.). 144p. (gr. 9-12). 1969. pap. 3.95 (*0-451-16252-8*, Sig) NAL-Dutton.
—Words from the Myths. (Illus.). 144p. (gr. 6). 1969. pap. 2.50 (*0-451-14097-4*, Sig) NAL-Dutton.
—The World's Space Program. LC 89-43134. (Illus.). 32p. (gr. 3-4). 1990. PLB 17.27 (*1-55532-374-X*) Gareth Stevens Inc.
Asimov, Isaac & Dierks, Carrie. How Does a Cut Heal? LC 93-18271. 1993. PLB 17.27 (*0-8368-0805-3*) Gareth Stevens Inc.
—Why Do People Come in Different Colors? LC 93-20157. 1993. PLB 17.27 (*0-8368-0808-8*) Gareth Stevens Inc.
—Why Do Some People Need Glasses? LC 93-20156. 1993. PLB 17.27 (*0-8368-0809-6*) Gareth Stevens Inc.
—Why Do We Need Sleep? LC 92-20154. 1993. PLB 17.27 (*0-8368-0806-1*) Gareth Stevens Inc.
—Why Do We Need to Brush Our Teeth. LC 93-20155. 1993. PLB 15.93 (*0-8368-0807-X*) Gareth Stevens Inc.
Asimov, Isaac & Giraud, Robert. The Future in Space. (Illus.). 32p. (gr. 3-8). 1993. PLB 17.27 (*0-8368-0913-0*); PLB 17.27 s.p. (*0-685-61505-7*) Gareth Stevens Inc.
Asimov, Isaac & Sturgeon, Theodore. The Ugly Little Boy & The Widget, the Wadget, & Boff. 1989. 3.50 (*0-8125-5966-5*) Tor Bks.
Asimov, Isaac & White, Frank. Think about Space: Where Have We Been? Where Are We Going? Danziger, Jeff, illus. LC 88-36731. 120p. (gr. 6 up). 1989. PLB 14.85 (*0-8027-6766-4*); pap. 5.95 (*0-8027-6767-2*) Walker & Co.
Asimov, Isaac, jt. auth. see Asimov, Janet.
Asimov, Isaac & Greenberg, Martin H., eds. Visions of Fantasy. Elmore, Larry, illus. 192p. (gr. 5 up). 1989. 14.95 (*0-385-26359-7*, Zephyr-BFYR) Doubleday.
Asimov, Isaac, ed. see Royston, Robert.
Asimov, Isaac, et al, eds. One Hundred Great Science Fiction Short Short Stories. 320p. (gr. 9 up). 1980. pap. 3.95 (*0-380-50733-1*) Avon.

—Young Witches & Warlocks. Asimov, Isaac, intro. by. LC 85-45849. 224p. (gr. 7 up). 1987. HarpC Child Bks.
Asimov, Janet. The Package in Hyperspace. Gampert, John, illus. (gr. 4-7). 1988. 13.95 (*0-8027-6822-9*); PLB 14.85 (*0-8027-6823-7*) Walker & Co.
Asimov, Janet & Asimov, Isaac. Norby & the Court Jester. 128p. (gr. 3-7). 1991. 14.95 (*0-8027-8131-4*); PLB 15.85 (*0-8027-8132-2*) Walker & Co.
—Norby & the Invaders. LC 85-13635. 138p. (gr. 3-5). 1985. 10.95 (*0-8027-6599-8*); PLB 10.85 (*0-8027-6607-2*) Walker & Co.
—Norby & the Oldest Dragon. (gr. 4-9). 1990. 14.95 (*0-8027-6909-8*); PLB 15.85 (*0-8027-6910-1*) Walker & Co.
—Norby & the Queen's Necklace. LC 86-11120. 144p. (gr. 4-9). 1986. 11.95 (*0-8027-6659-5*); PLB 12.85 (*0-8027-6660-9*) Walker & Co.
—Norby & Yobo's Great Adventure. 224p. (gr. 4-9). 1989. 12.95 (*0-8027-6893-8*); PLB 13.85 (*0-8027-6894-6*) Walker & Co.
—Norby Down to Earth. (Illus.). (gr. 4-9). 1989. 12.95 (*0-8027-6866-0*); PLB 13.85 (*0-8027-6867-9*) Walker & Co.
—Norby Finds a Villain. (gr. 4-9). 1987. 12.95 (*0-8027-6710-9*); PLB 13.85 (*0-8027-6711-7*) Walker & Co.
—Norby, the Mixed up Robot. LC 82-25173. 96p. (gr. 5-7). 1983. PLB 10.85 (*0-8027-6496-7*) Walker & Co.
Aska, Warabe. Who Hides in the Park. Aska, Warabe, illus. (ENG, FRE, JPN & CHI.). 36p. (gr. k up). 1990. pap. 7.95 (*0-88776-244-1*) Tundra Bks.
Askinosie, Barbra. A Star for Christmas. (Illus.). 26p. (ps-1). 1988. pap. 2.95 incl. sticker pgs. (*0-671-66870-6*, Little Simon) S&S Trade.
Askounis, Christina. The Dream of the Stone. 272p. (gr. 7 up). 1992. 17.00 (*0-374-31877-8*) FS&G.
Asmann, Lynn & Sprague, Jane. Baby Basics. Asmann, Lynn, illus. (gr. 5 up). 1980. pap. 4.95 (*0-938416-00-6*) BCS Educ Aids.
Asmar, Ramsey. The Birth of a New Tradition. Yerkes, Lane, illus. LC 92-35284. 32p. (gr. 4-6). 1992. PLB 17.96 (*0-8114-3583-0*) Raintree Steck-V.
Asolon, Karel B., ed. The Phantom of Devil's Bridge & the Tale of Buffalo Castle. (Illus.). 41p. (Orig.). (gr. 4). 1985. pap. 12.00 (*0-930329-04-X*) Kabel Pubs.
Aspinall, Anthony. Misadventures of an Aging Mule. 400p. 1990. 34.95 (*0-233-98439-9*, Pub. by A Deutsch UK) Trafalgar.
Aspinwall, Margaret, jt. auth. see Lipman, Jean.
Assaf, Yael. Pete & the Vegetable Soup. Kriss, David, tr. from HEB. Elchanan, illus. 24p. (Orig.). (ps). 1992. pap. text ed. 3.00x (*1-56134-160-6*) Dushkin Pub.
—Pete y la Sopa de Verduras. Writer, C. C. & Nielsen, Lisa C., trs. Elchanan, illus. (SPA.). 24p. (Orig.). (ps). 1992. pap. text ed. 3.00x (*1-56134-170-3*) Dushkin Pub.
Asseng, Nathan. Billy Graham. 112p. (gr. 3-7). 1993. pap. 4.99 (*0-310-39841-X*, Pub. by Youth Spec) Zondervan.
Asseng, Nathan see Carson, Ben.
Assicurato, Thomas see Curato, Guy, pseud.
Astley, Neil, ed. Bossy Parrot. LC 87-73294. (Illus.). 64p. (Orig.). (gr. 1 up). 1988. pap. 10.95 (*1-85224-040-7*, Pub. by Bloodaxe Bks) Dufour.
Astrop, John. John Astrop's Ghastly Games. Astrop, John, illus. 24p. (gr-3). 1983. pop-up bk. 9.95 (*0-385-29307-0*) Delacorte.
Asuka, Ken. Toto Visits Mystic Mountain. Young, Richard Y., ed. Kaisei-sha, tr. Asuka, Ken, illus. LC 89-11754. 32p. (gr. 1-3). 1989. PLB 14.60 (*0-944483-46-1*) Garrett Ed Corp.
Asuka, Ken, jt. auth. see Barnes, Jill.
Ata, Te & Moroney, Lynn, eds. Baby Rattlesnake. LC 89-9892. (Illus.). 32p. (ps-5). 1989. 13.95 (*0-89239-049-2*) Childrens Book Pr.
—Baby Rattlesnake. (Illus.). 32p. (gr. 1-7). 1993. pap. 5.95 (*0-89239-111-1*) Childrens Book Pr.
Atar, Nancy A., jt. auth. see Henningfield, Jack E.
Aten, Jerry. America: From Sea to Shining Sea. 160p. (gr. 4 up). 1988. wkbk. 12.95 (*0-86653-434-2*, GA1044) Good Apple.
—Americans, Too! 80p. (gr. 4 up). 1982. 8.95 (*0-86653-099-1*, GA 444) Good Apple.
—Challenge Across America. 96p. (gr. 4-8). 1990. 12.95 (*0-86653-556-X*, GA1157) Good Apple.
—Challenge Around the World. 96p. (gr. 4-8). 1991. 12.95 (*0-86653-587-X*, GA1308) Good Apple.
—Challenge Through American History. (Illus.). 96p. (gr. 4-8). 1992. 12.95 (*0-86653-659-0*, GA1391) Good Apple.
—Democracy for Young Americans. 112p. (gr. 4-8). 1989. 9.95 (*0-86653-483-0*, GA1083) Good Apple.
—Fifty Nifty States. (Illus.). 320p. (gr. 4 up). 1990. 19.95 (*0-86653-532-2*, GA1138) Good Apple.
—Good Apple & Math Fun. 144p. (gr. 3-7). 1981. 11.95 (*0-86653-023-1*, GA 279) Good Apple.
—Maptime... U. S. A. 69p. (gr. 4 up). 1982. 7.95 (*0-86653-093-2*, GA 422) Good Apple.
—Our Living Constitution - Then & Now. Hyndman, Kathryn, illus. 168p. (gr. 5 up). 1986. wkbk. 12.95 (*0-86653-386-9*, GA 1000) Good Apple.
—Outstanding Women. Hierstein, Judy, illus. 64p. (gr. k-4). 1987. pap. 7.95 (*0-86653-413-X*, GA1008) Good Apple.
—Presidential Leaders. Hierstein, Judy, illus. 64p. (gr. k-4). 1986. wkbk. 7.95 (*0-86653-347-8*, GA 697) Good Apple.

—Presidents. Hyndman, Kathryn, illus. 176p. (gr. 4 up). 1985. wkbk. 12.95 (*0-86653-281-1*, GA 627) Good Apple.
—Prime Time Life Skills. Filkins, Vanessa, illus. 64p. (gr. 2-5). 1983. wkbk. 7.95 (*0-86653-126-2*, GA 487) Good Apple.
—Prime Time Maps. Filkins, Vanessa, illus. 64p. (gr. 2-5). 1983. wkbk. 7.95 (*0-86653-108-4*, GA 470) Good Apple.
—Prime Time Math Skills. Filkins, Vanessa, illus. 64p. (gr. 2-5). 1984. wkbk. 7.95 (*0-86653-155-6*, GA 524) Good Apple.
—Prime Time Reading Skills. Filkins, Vanessa, illus. 64p. (gr. 2-5). 1984. wkbk. 7.95 (*0-86653-185-8*, GA 525) Good Apple.
—Prime Time Thinking Skills. Filkins, Vanessa, illus. 64p. (gr. 2-5). 1985. wkbk. 7.95 (*0-86653-276-5*, GA 628) Good Apple.
—Understanding Our World Through Geography. 208p. (gr. 4-8). 1991. 14.95 (*0-86653-592-6*, GA1309) Good Apple.
—Women in History. Hyndman, Kathryn, illus. 144p. (gr. 4 up). 1986. wkbk. 11.95 (*0-86653-344-3*, GA 692) Good Apple.
Athar, Alia N. Muhammad, the Last Prophet I. 32p. (gr. 2-4). 1992. pap. 3.00 wkbk. (*1-56744-209-9*) Kazi Pubns.
—Muhammad, the Last Prophet II. 32p. (gr. 3-5). 1992. pap. 3.00 (*1-56744-210-2*) Kazi Pubns.
—Prophets: Models for Humanity. 205p. (gr. 10-12). 1993. pap. 14.50 (*1-56744-425-3*) Kazi Pubns.
Atherton, Mary K., et al. Touch with Your Eyes! Frank, Phil, illus. 48p. (Orig.). (gr. k-8). 1982. pap. 4.50 (*0-9613069-0-4*) Orinda Art Coun.
Athey, Virginia. Zonkey, the Donkey. Rutherford, Donna, illus. 20p. (ps-2). 1993. pap. 6.50 saddle stitch (*0-922510-10-5*) Lucky Bks.
Athkins, D. E. Mirror, Mirror. 144p. 1992. pap. 3.25 (*0-590-45246-0*, Point) Scholastic Inc.
—The Ripper. 1992. 3.25 (*0-590-45349-1*, Point) Scholastic Inc.
Atiyeh, Wadeeha. Fourth Wise Man. Vukovich, Charles, illus. (gr. 4 up). 1959. pap. 3.00 (*0-8315-0038-7*) Speller.
Atkin, Abraham. Chelkeinu. 200p. text ed. 6.50 (*0-914131-09-5*, A120) Torah Umesorah.
—Darkeinu Aleph & Bais: In One Volume. pap. text ed. 3.85 (*0-914131-12-5*, A100) Torah Umesorah.
—Darkeinu Daled. text ed. 4.00 (*0-914131-13-3*, A102) Torah Umesorah.
Atkin, K. Le Francais Sans Souci. 304p. (gr. 4-6). 1987. pap. text ed. 42.88 (*0-201-17624-6*) Addison-Wesley.
Atkin, S. Beth. Voices from the Fields: America's Migrant Children. LC 92-32248. 1993. 16.95 (*0-316-05633-2*) Little.
Atkins, Abraham. Darkeinu Gimel. (gr. 4 up). text ed. 3.85 (*0-914131-14-1*, A101) Torah Umesorah.
Atkins, Greg. Through the Storybook. Garabedian, Brian, contrib. by. (Illus.). 24p. (Orig.). (gr-p4). 1988. pap. 2.50 (*0-88680-306-3*); piano-vocal score 7.50 (*0-88680-307-1*); royalty on application 35.00 (*0-685-58414-3*) I E Clark.
Atkins, Kirsten. How Long Is a Piece of String? Posey, Pam, illus. LC 93-18062. 1994. write for info. (*0-383-03672-0*) SRA Schl Grp.
Atkins, Sinclair. From Stone Age to Conquest. LC 85-73167. (Illus.). 96p. (gr. 5-8). 1984. pap. 12.95 (*0-7175-1305-X*) Dufour.
Atkinson, Allen. Old King Cole & Other Favorites. (Illus.). 64p. (Orig.). 1986. pap. 2.50 (*0-553-15355-2*) Bantam.
Atkinson, Allen, illus. The Cat & the Fiddle & Other Favorites. 64p. (Orig.). (gr. k). 1985. pap. 2.50 (*0-553-15321-8*) Bantam.
—Humpty Dumpty & Other Favorites. 64p. (Orig.). (gr. k). 1985. pap. 2.50 (*0-553-15340-4*) Bantam.
—Jack & Jill & Other Favorites. 64p. (Orig.). 1986. pap. 2.50 (*0-553-15354-4*) Bantam.
—Little Bo-Peep & Other Favorites. 64p. (Orig.). 1986. pap. 2.50 (*0-553-15353-6*) Bantam.
—Little Boy Blue & Other Favorites. 64p. (Orig.). (gr. k). 1985. pap. 2.50 (*0-553-15320-X*) Bantam.
—Mary Had a Little Lamb & Other Favorites. (Orig.). (gr. k). 1985. pap. 2.50 (*0-553-15319-6*) Bantam.
—Simple Simon & Other Favorites (Mother Goose) 64p. (Orig.). 1986. pap. 2.50 (*0-553-15322-6*) Bantam.
Atkinson, Elizabeth. Monster Vehicles. (gr. 3-4). 1991. PLB 11.95 (*1-56065-077-X*) Capstone Pr.
Atkinson, Gordon, jt. auth. see Heikkinen, Henry.
Atkinson, I. The Viking Ships. LC 77-17510. (Illus.). 48p. (gr. 7 up). 1979. pap. 8.50 (*0-521-21951-5*) Cambridge U Pr.
Atkinson, John. Bamboo & Friends. Engel, Michael, illus. LC 88-50844. 104p. (gr. 1-12). 1988. 13.95 (*0-929155-05-X*) Windward Bks.
Atkinson, Kathie. The Blue Layer. LC 93-28993. 1994. 4.25 (*0-383-03747-6*) SRA Schl Grp.
—Creepy Crawlies. LC 92-31908. 1993. 3.75 (*0-383-03562-7*) SRA Schl Grp.
—Home & Safe. (ps-3). 1993. pap. 3.95 (*1-86373-373-6*, Pub. by Allen & Unwin Aust Pty AT) IPG Chicago.
—What's For Dinner? (ps-3). 1993. pap. 3.95 (*1-86373-375-2*, Pub. by Allen & Unwin Aust Pty AT) IPG Chicago.
—Worms, Wonderful Worms. LC 93-28968. 1994. 4.25 (*0-383-03788-3*) SRA Schl Grp.

Atkinson, Linda. In Kindling Flame: The Story of Hannah Senesh. ALC Staff, ed. LC 83-24392. (Illus.). 214p. (gr. 8-12). 1992. pap. 4.95 (0-688-11689-2, Pub. by Beech Tree Bks) Morrow.
—In Kindling Flame: The Story of Hannah Senesh 1921-1944. LC 83-24392. 224p. (gr. 9 up). 1985. 14.95 (0-688-02714-8) Lothrop.
Atkinson, Stuart. Journey into Space. Asimov, Isaac, intro. by. 80p. (gr. 5-7). 1988. pap. 14.95 (0-670-82306-6) Viking Child Bks.
Atlan, Liliane. The Passerby. Desimini, Lisa, illus. Owens, Rochelle, tr. (Illus.). 96p. (gr. 7 up). 1993. PLB 13.95 (0-8050-3054-9, Bks Young Read) H Holt & Co.
Atlas, Nick, ed. see Wiseman, Loren K.
Atlas, Susan. Passover Passage. (gr. 4-7). 1991. 5.95 (0-933873-46-8) Torah Aura.
Atlas, Susan, jt. auth. see Crown, Bonnie.
Attalides, Stephanos. Journey into Space: Adventure Box IV. Attalides, Stephanos, illus. 12p. (ps up). 1988. 4.95 (0-694-00266-6) HarpC Child Bks.
Attwood, Teresa K., jt. auth. see North, A. C.
Atungaye, Monifa. Provisions. LC 88-83009. 60p. (gr. 9-12). 1989. pap. 5.00 (0-916418-68-5) Lotus.
Atwater, Florence, jt. auth. see Atwater, Richard.
Atwater, Richard. Mr. Popper's Penguins. (gr. 4-7). 1992. pap. 1.99 (0-440-21370-3) Dell.
—Mr. Popper's Penguins. (gr. 4-7). 1992. pap. 3.50 (0-316-05843-2) Little.
Atwater, Richard & Atwater, Florence. Mr. Popper's Penguins. (Illus.). 144p. (gr. 3-6). 1978. 3.50 (0-440-45934-6, YB) Dell.
—Mr. Popper's Penguins. Lawson, Robert, illus. (gr. 3 up). 1938. 14.95 (0-316-05842-4) Little.
—Mr. Popper's Penguins: A Pop-Up Book. Williams, Karin, illus. LC 92-53195. 1993. 16.95 (0-316-05844-0) Little.
Atwell & Wells. Wide Range Vocabulary Test. large type ed. (gr. 3 up). Repr. of 1945 ed. Form B. 4.28 (0-317-01965-1, 4-27440-00); Form C. 4.28 (0-317-01966-X, 4-27430-00); Form B. directions for bd. with administering 1.95 (0-317-01967-8, 8-54290-00); Form C. directions for bd. with administering 1.70 (0-317-01968-6, 8-54300-00) Am Printing Hse.
Atwell, David L. The Day Hans Got His Way. Atwell, Debby, illus. LC 91-43945. 32p. (ps-3). 1992. 14.45 (0-395-58772-7) HM.
Atwell, Lucy. Lucy Atwell's Goodnight Stories. (Illus.). (ps-1). 1985. 3.98 (0-517-46903-0) Outlet Bk Co.
Atwood, Elizabeth, jt. ed. see Grosseck, Joyce.
Atwood, Margaret. For the Birds. Bianchi, John, illus. 56p. (gr. 8-12). 1991. pap. 9.95 (0-920668-32-1) Firefly Bks Ltd.
Atwood, Marjorie, Jr. Galisteo Legend. Smith, James C., ed. Yamashita, Mina, illus. LC 91-41394. 48p. (Orig.). 1992. pap. 6.95 (0-86534-154-0) Sunstone Pr.
Atyeo, Marilyn, jt. auth. see Uhde, Anna.
Auakian, Monique. The Meiji Restoration & the Rise of Modern Japan. (Illus.). 64p. (gr. 7 up). 1991. PLB 16.98 (0-382-24132-0); pap. 8.95 (0-382-24139-8) Silver Burdett Pr.
Aubin, Michael. A Day at Home. (Illus.). 32p. (gr. 3-5). 1991. 18.50 (0-89565-762-7); 12.95s.p. (0-685-55083-4) Childs World.
Aubinais, Marie. Happy Christmas, God. (Illus.). 48p. (ps-3). 6.99 (0-7459-2238-4) Lion USA.
Aubry, Pam. Youth for Youth Staying Free. 20p. (gr. 1-2). 1990. pap. 1.00 (0-914127-50-0) Univ Class.
Aubyn, Giles St. see St. Aubyn, Giles.
Auch, Mary J. Angel & Me. 1989. 9.95 (0-316-05914-5) Little.
—Angel & Me & the Bayside Bombers. Smith, Cat B., illus. (gr. 2-4). 1991. pap. 2.95 (0-316-05915-3) Little.
—Bird Dogs Can't Fly. Auch, Mary J., illus. LC 93-2746. (ps-3). 1993. reinforced bdg. 15.95 (0-8234-1050-1) Holiday.
—Cry Uncle! LC 87-45330. 224p. (gr. 4-7). 1987. 14.95 (0-8234-0660-1) Holiday.
—Cry Uncle! (gr. 4-7). 1990. pap. 2.95 (0-553-15787-6) Bantam.
—The Easter Egg Farm. Auch, Mary J., illus. LC 91-15681. 32p. (ps-3). 1992. reinforced bdg. 15.95 (0-8234-0917-1) Holiday.
—Glass Slippers Give You Blisters. LC 88-45865. 176p. (gr. 3-7). 1989. 14.95 (0-8234-0752-7) Holiday.
—Kidnapping Kevin Kowalski. LC 89-46065. 128p. (gr. 3-7). 1990. 14.95 (0-8234-0815-9) Holiday.
—Kidnapping Kevin Kowalski. 1992. pap. 2.95 (0-590-44335-6, Apple Paperbacks) Scholastic Inc.
—The Latch-Key Dog. Smith, Cat B., illus. LC 93-18604. 1994. 13.95 (0-316-05916-1) Little.
—Mom Is Dating Weird Wayne. LC 88-45275. 160p. (gr. 4-7). 1988. 14.95 (0-8234-0720-9) Holiday.
—Mom Is Dating Weird Wayne. (gr. 4-7). 1991. pap. 2.99 (0-553-15916-X) Bantam.
—Out of Step. LC 92-4704. 96p. (gr. 4-7). 1992. 13.95 (0-8234-0985-6) Holiday.
—Peeping Beauty. LC 92-16374. (Illus.). 32p. (ps-3). 1993. reinforced bdg. 14.95 (0-8234-1001-3) Holiday.
—Pick of the Litter. LC 87-25205. 160p. (gr. 3-7). 1988. 14.95 (0-8234-0692-X) Holiday.
—Seven Long Years Until College. LC 91-2094. 176p. (gr. 3-7). 1991. 13.95 (0-8234-0901-5) Holiday.
—A Sudden Change of Family. LC 90-55100. 112p. (gr. 3-7). 1990. 13.95 (0-8234-0842-6) Holiday.
—A Sudden Change of Family. MacDonald, Pat, ed. 160p. 1993. pap. 2.99 (0-671-74892-0, Minstrel Bks) PB.

Auch, Mary Jane. Glass Slippers Give You Blisters. 1990. pap. 2.75 (0-590-43501-9) Scholastic Inc.
Audrey de, la Martre see De la Martre, Audrey.
Auer, Jim. Ten Good Reasons to Be a Catholic: A Teenager's Guide to the Church. LC 87-80988. (gr. 7-12). 1987. pap. 2.95 (0-89243-271-3) Liguori Pubns.
—Ten Ways to Get into the New Testament: A Teenager's Guide. LC 90-64270. 80p. (Orig.). (gr. 9-12). 1991. pap. text ed. 2.95 (0-89243-342-6) Liguori Pubns.
—Ten Ways to Meet God: Spirituality for Teens. 64p. (gr. 7-12). 1989. pap. 2.95 (0-89243-299-3) Liguori Pubns.
Auer, Martin. The Blue Boy. Klages, Simone, illus. LC 91-39130. 32p. (gr. 2 up). 1992. POB 11.95 (0-02-707610-5, Macmillan Child Bk) Macmillan Child Grp.
—Now, Now Markus. LC 88-34320. (Illus.). 48p. (ps up). 1989. 12.95 (0-688-08974-7); PLB 12.88 (0-688-08975-5) Greenwillow.
Auer, Varvara, jt. auth. see Linnell, Andrew.
Auerbach, J. H., tr. see Hartling, Peter.
Auerbach, Susan. Queen Elizabeth II. LC 92-46478. 1993. 19.93 (0-86625-481-1); 14.95s.p. (0-685-67777-X) Rourke Pubns.
—Vietnamese Americans. LC 91-15806. 104p. (gr. 5-9). 1991. 13.95s.p. (0-86593-136-4) Rourke Corp.
Auerbacher, Inge. I Am a Star: Child of the Holocaust. Bernbaum, Israel, illus. LC 92-31444. 80p. (gr. 3-7). 1993. pap. 4.99 (0-14-036401-3) Puffin Bks.
Aufderheide, Patricia. Anwar Sadat. (Illus.). 112p. (gr. 5 up). 1985. lib. bdg. 17.95x (0-87754-560-X) Chelsea Hse.
Augelli, John P., ed. American Neighbors. rev. ed. LC 85-81413. (Illus.). (gr. 5 up). 1986. text ed. 12.95 (0-88296-087-3); tchr's. guide 8.95 (0-88296-355-4); unit tests 6.95 (0-934291-49-7); discovery sheets (56 duplicator masters) 9.95 (0-934291-50-0) Gateway Pr MI.
August, Clara see Higgins, Betty.
August, Paul. Brain Function. Mendelson, Jack H. & Mello, Nancyintro. by. (Illus.). 128p. (gr. 5 up). 1988. lib. bdg. 19.95x (1-55546-204-9) Chelsea Hse.
August, Paul N. Drugs & Women. (Illus.). 32p. (gr. 5 up). 1991. pap. 4.49 (0-7910-0002-8) Chelsea Hse.
Augustine, Nicholas & Augustine, Victoria C. Conny the Clown. Augustine, Victoria C., illus. 32p. (Orig.). 1991. pap. write for info. (1-879783-00-2) Staccato Prodns.
—Little Lady Star. Augustine, Victoria C., illus. 32p. 1991. pap. write for info. (1-879783-01-0) Staccato Prodns.
Augustine, Victoria C., jt. auth. see Augustine, Nicholas.
Auh, Yoon-Il. Auh Etudes: Fifth Etude. 35p. (gr. 1-12). 1986. wkbk. 10.00 (1-882858-26-3) Yoon-il Auh.
—Auh Etudes: First Etude. 15p. (gr. 5-12). 1992. wkbk. 10.00 (1-882858-13-1) Yoon-il Auh.
—Auh Etudes: Fourth Etude. 30p. (gr. 1-12). 1985. wkbk. 10.00 (1-882858-16-6) Yoon-il Auh.
—Auh Etudes: Second Etude. 17p. (gr. 5-12). 1992. wkbk. 10.00 (1-882858-14-X) Yoon-il Auh.
—Auh Etudes: The Art of Bowing. 20p. (gr. 1-12). 1993. wkbk. 10.00 (1-882858-07-7) Yoon-il Auh.
—Auh Etudes: The Art of Double Stop, Bk. I. 20p. (gr. 1-12). 1993. wkbk. 10.00 (1-882858-08-5) Yoon-il Auh.
—Auh Etudes: The Art of Double Stop, Bk. II. 20p. (gr. 1-12). 1993. wkbk. 10.00 (1-882858-09-3) Yoon-il Auh.
—Auh Etudes: Third Etude. 19p. (gr. 5-12). 1992. wkbk. 10.00 (1-882858-15-8) Yoon-il Auh.
—Concert Books for the Young: EZ Duet I. 30p. (gr. 1-12). 1993. wkbk. 10.00 (1-882858-22-0) Yoon-il Auh.
—Concert Books for the Young: EZ Duet II. 30p. (gr. 1-12). 1993. wkbk. 10.00 (1-882858-23-9) Yoon-il Auh.
—Concert Books for the Young: Moto Perpetuo III. 9p. (gr. 1-8). 1983. wkbk. 10.00 (1-882858-39-5) Yoon-il Auh.
—Concert Books for the Young: Moto Perpetuo I. 8p. (gr. 1-8). 1990. wkbk. 10.00 (1-882858-37-9) Yoon-il Auh.
—Concert Books for the Young: Moto Perpetuo II. 8p. (gr. 1-8). 1990. wkbk. 10.00 (1-882858-38-7) Yoon-il Auh.
—Concert Books for the Young: My First Concert Book. 35p. (gr. k-5). 1988. wkbk. 10.00 (1-882858-19-0) Yoon-il Auh.
—Concert Books for the Young: My Second Concert Book. 35p. (gr. k-5). 1988. wkbk. 10.00 (1-882858-18-2) Yoon-il Auh.
—Concert Books for the Young: My Third Concert Book. 35p. (gr. k-7). 1988. wkbk. 10.00 (1-882858-21-2) Yoon-il Auh.
—Concert Books for the Young: Pizzicato Wonder Land. 22p. (gr. k-8). 1988. wkbk. 10.00 (1-882858-27-1) Yoon-il Auh.
—Concert Books for the Young: Theme & Variations I. 12p. (gr. 1-6). 1987. wkbk. 10.00 (1-882858-24-7) Yoon-il Auh.
—Concert Books for the Young: Theme & Variations II. 12p. (gr. 1-6). 1987. wkbk. 10.00 (1-882858-25-5) Yoon-il Auh.
—Concert Books for the Young: Twenty-Four Contemporary Easy Duets, Bk. I. 25p. 1987. wkbk. 10.00 (1-882858-41-7) Yoon-il Auh.
—Concert Books for the Young: Twenty-Four Contemporary Easy Duets, Bk. II. 1987. wkbk. 10.00 (1-882858-42-5) Yoon-il Auh.

—Contemporary Rhythm & Dynamics, Bk. I. 20p. (gr. 1-12). 1986. wkbk. 10.00 (1-882858-43-3) Yoon-il Auh.
—Contemporary Rhythm & Dynamics, Bk. II. 20p. (gr. 1-12). 1986. wkbk. 10.00 (1-882858-44-1) Yoon-il Auh.
—Contemporary Rhythm & Dynamics: Ten Contemporary EZ Duets. 20p. (gr. 4-12). 1986. wkbk. 10.00 (1-882858-40-9) Yoon-il Auh.
—Position Studies: Advance Position Study. 35p. (gr. 1-12). 1985. wkbk. 10.00 (1-882858-46-8) Yoon-il Auh.
—Position Studies: Scales & Shifting 1. 30p. (gr. 5-12). 1990. wkbk. 10.00 (1-882858-11-5) Yoon-il Auh.
—Position Studies: Scales & Shifting 2. 30p. (gr. 5-12). 1990. wkbk. 10.00 (1-882858-12-3) Yoon-il Auh.
—Position Studies: Third Position. 35p. (gr. 5-12). 1986. wkbk. 10.00 (1-882858-45-X) Yoon-il Auh.
—Pre-School Virtuoso, Bk. I. 40p. (gr. k-5). 1988. wkbk. 10.00 (1-882858-03-4) Yoon-il Auh.
—Pre-School Virtuoso, Bk. II. 40p. (gr. k-5). 1988. wkbk. 10.00 (1-882858-04-2) Yoon-il Auh.
—Pre-School Virtuoso, Bk. III. 40p. (gr. k-5). 1988. wkbk. 10.00 (1-882858-05-0) Yoon-il Auh.
—Pre-School Virtuoso, Bk. IV. 40p. (gr. k-5). wkbk. 10.00 (1-882858-06-9) Yoon-il Auh.
—Preliminary Advance, Bk. 1. 50p. (gr. 1-8). 1983. wkbk. 14.00 (1-882858-17-4) Yoon-il Auh.
—Preliminary, Bk. 1. 60p. (gr. 1-8). 1983. wkbk. 14.00 (1-882858-00-X) Yoon-il Auh.
—Preliminary, Bk. 2. 60p. (gr. 1-8). 1983. wkbk. 14.00 (1-882858-01-8) Yoon-il Auh.
—Preliminary, Bk. 3. 45p. (gr. 1-8). 1983. wkbk. 14.00 (1-882858-02-6) Yoon-il Auh.
—Scale System for Young: EZ Scales. 45p. (gr. 1-12). 1993. wkbk. 10.00 (1-882858-10-7) Yoon-il Auh.
—Tricks for the Wild Fiddler, Bk. I. 35p. (gr. 1-12). 1985. wkbk. 10.00 (1-882858-28-X) Yoon-il Auh.
—Tricks for the Wild Fiddler, Bk. II. 35p. (gr. 1-12). 1985. wkbk. 10.00 (1-882858-29-8) Yoon-il Auh.
Aukerman, Ruth. Move over, Picasso! A Young Painter's Primer. (Illus.). 44p. (Orig.). (gr. 1-6). 1994. pap. 12.95 (1-884555-01-2) P Depke Bks.
Auld, Janice. Shape-a-Poem. (gr. 1-3). 1986. pap. 6.95 (0-8224-6393-8) Fearon Teach Aids.
—Shape-a-Story. (gr. 1-3). 1986. pap. 6.95 (0-8224-6392-X) Fearon Teach Aids.
Auld, Janice L. Cut & Paste Phonics: Extra Help for Troublesome Letter Combinations. (gr. 1-3). 1985. pap. 8.95 (0-8224-5540-4) Fearon Teach Aids.
Auld-Lonie, Margaret, ed. see Kopelman, Yvonne A.
Aulson, Pam. Crafty Ideas with Placemats. (Illus.). 24p. (gr. 6 up). 1979. pap. 3.00 (0-9601896-3-7) Patch As Patch.
—Placemat Pets 'n Playmates. (Illus.). 24p. (gr. 6 up). 1980. pap. 3.00 (0-9601896-2-9) Patch As Patch.
Ault, Karuna, ed. see Hari Dass, Baba.
Ault, Rosalie S. BASIC Programming for Kids. LC 83-12773. (Illus.). 192p. (gr. 5 up). 1983. 10.95 (0-685-06975-3) HM.
Aunt Eeebs. The Dinosaur Debut. rev. ed. Aunt Eeebs, illus. 24p. (ps-2). 1991. pap. write for info. (1-878908-00-6) Rivercrest Indus.
—The Happy Campers. Aunt Eeebs, illus. 24p. (Orig.). (ps-2). 1991. pap. write for info. (1-878908-02-2) Rivercrest Indus.
Aunt Peggy. Caterpillar. Beeching, Mark, illus. 24p. 1992. pap. 6.95 (0-9636185-0-4); Coloring bk. 8.95 (0-9636185-3-9) Aunt Peggys Pub.

—Caterpillar. 2nd ed. Beeching, Mark, illus. 24p. (ps-k). 1994. 13.95 (0-9636185-2-0) Aunt Peggys Pub. A beautifully illustrated, twenty-four page picture book for children ages 2 to 6 yrs. In this book there are three words that explain the working of nature--COCOON--HIBERNATE--& METAMORPHOSIS. Available in: HARDCOVER--PAPERBACK--COLORING BOOK or "FUN PACK", PAPERBACK/COLOR BOOK. Order from: Aunt Peggy's Publishing, P.O. Box 395, Lowell, IN 46356. 219-696-8707. *Publisher Provided Annotation.*

—Caterpillar: Fun Pack. Beeching, Mark, illus. 24p. (ps-k). 1994. Set, Story bk. & color bk. 8.95 (0-9636185-4-7) Aunt Peggys Pub.
—How Did You Come to School Today. Beeching, Mark, illus. 24p. 1992. pap. 6.95 (0-9636185-1-2) Aunt Peggys Pub.
Auriga. Enciclopedia Juvenil Auriga: Inventos Que Conmovieron el Mundo, Descubrimientos e Inventos, Armas Que Conmovieron el Mundo, Historia Ilustrada de los Barcos, Artistas Que Conmovieron el Mundo. (SPA.). 360p. 1977. leatherette 42.00 (84-201-0202-4, French & Eur) Fr & Eur.
Ausbrook, Michael. Raisa Gorbachev. (Illus.). 112p. (gr. 5 up). 1992. lib. bdg. 17.95 (0-7910-1625-0) Chelsea Hse.

Aushenker, Michael. Get That Goat! Thatch, Nancy R., ed. Aushenker, Michael, illus. Melton, David, intro. by. LC 90-5930. (Illus.). 26p. (gr. k-4). 1990. PLB 14. 95 (0-933849-28-1) Landmark Edns.

Aust, Siegfried. Clocks! How Time Flies. Poppel, Hans, illus. 32p. (gr. 2-5). 1991. PLB 18.95 (0-8225-2154-7) Lerner Pubns.

—Flight! Free As a Bird. Poppel, Hans, illus. 32p. (gr. 2-5). 1991. PLB 18.95 (0-8225-2150-4) Lerner Pubns.

—Lenses! Take a Closer Look. Nyncke, Helge, illus. 32p. (gr. 2-5). 1991. PLB 18.95 (0-8225-2151-2) Lerner Pubns.

—Light! A Bright Idea. Nyncke, Helge, illus. LC 92-9704. 1992. 18.95 (0-8225-2155-5) Lerner Pubns.

—Ships! Come Aboard. Kleinert, Enno, illus. LC 92-12761. 1993. 18.95 (0-8225-2156-3) Lerner Pubns.

Austen, Jane. Emma. Duffy, J. D., intro. by. (gr. 9 up). 1966. pap. 1.95 (0-8049-0102-3, CL-102) Airmont.

—Jane Austen: Her Complete Novels. (gr. 7-10). 1992. 12.99 (0-517-34799-7) Outlet Bk Co.

—Mansfield Park. Threapleton, M. M., intro. by. (gr. 10 up). 1967. pap. 1.95 (0-8049-0131-7, CL-131) Airmont.

—Persuasion. Duffy, J. D., intro. by. (gr. 10 up). 1966. pap. 1.50 (0-8049-0107-4, CL-107) Airmont.

—Pride & Prejudice. (gr. 10 up). 1962. pap. 3.50 (0-8049-0001-9, CL-1) Airmont.

—Pride & Prejudice. Schorer, Mark, ed. LC 56-13877. (gr. 9 up). 1956. pap. 8.36 (0-395-05101-0, RivEd) HM.

—Pride & Prejudice. Cogancherry, Helen, illus. Stewart, Diana, adapted by. LC 81-5215. (Illus.). 48p. (gr. 4 up). 1983. PLB 18.64 (0-8172-1673-1) Raintree Steck-V.

—Pride & Prejudice. LC 92-50183. 368p. 1992. 5.98 (1-56138-171-3) Courage Bks.

—Sense & Sensibility. Spacks, Patricia M., afterword by. 352p. (gr. 9-12). 1983. pap. 3.50 (0-553-21334-2, Bantam Classics) Bantam.

Auster, Benjamin. I Like It When... Winborn, Marsha, illus. 24p. (ps-2). 1990. PLB 14.60 (0-8172-3578-7); PLB 10.95 pkg. of 3 (0-8114-2933-4) Raintree Steck-V.

Austin, Lou. The Little Me & the Great Me, Vol. 1. (ps-5). 1985. 5.95 (0-934538-26-3); pap. 3.95 (0-934538-21-2); parent-tchr's. manual 1.25 (0-934538-06-9) Partnership Foundation.

—My Secret Power, Vol. 2. (gr. 1-6). 1960. 5.95 (0-934538-22-0); pap. 3.95 (0-934538-27-1) Partnership Foundation.

—Why & How Was I Born, Vol. 3. (gr. 1-6). 1963. 5.95 (0-934538-28-X); pap. 3.95 (0-934538-23-9) Partnership Foundation.

Austin, Oliver L., Jr. Families of Birds. Rev. ed. Singer, Arthur, illus. (gr. 9 up). 1985. pap. write for info. (0-307-13669-8); pap. write for info. (0-307-24015-0, Golden Pr) Western Pub.

Austin, Richard H. see Stapler, Harry.

Austin, Trina K. All Aboard the S. S. Nutrient. (Illus.). 26p. (Orig.). (gr. k-4). 1986. pap. 6.50 (0-9615840-0-9) Trinas Pr.

Autenrieth, Georg. A Homeric Dictionary for Schools & Colleges. Flagg, Isaac, ed. Keep, Robert P., tr. (Illus.). 318p. (gr. 9 up). 1976. pap. 15.95x (0-8061-1289-1) U of Okla Pr.

Autry, Peyton. The Eagles of Warrick. LC 90-81703. (Illus.). 200p. (Orig.). 1990. pap. 10.95 (0-9625824-0-9) Avosett Bks.

Autry, Raz. Sam in Flight: Further Adventures of Bad Sam. Myers, Mary B., illus. LC 92-496. 64p. (Orig.). (gr. 1-6). 1992. pap. 5.95 (1-56474-029-3) Fithian Pr.

Avakian, Monique & Smith, Carter, III. A Historical Album of New York. LC 92-41135. (Illus.). 64p. (gr. 4-8). 1993. PLB 15.40 (1-56294-005-8) Millbrook Pr.

Avent, Barbara P. The Leopard Speaks about Changes in Life. Alston, Nelson G., ed. Winchell, Karl, illus. 64p. (Orig.). 1993. pap. 9.95 (0-9632202-1-7) Alpha Bk Pr.

Avent, Barbara P., ed. see Alston, Nelson G.

Aver, Kate. Joey's Way. Himler, Ronald, illus. LC 92-7830. 48p. (gr. 1-4). 1992. SBE 12.95 (0-689-50552-3, M K McElderry) Macmillan Child Grp.

Averill, Esther. Fire Cat. Averill, Esther, illus. LC 60-10234. 64p. (gr. k-3). 1960. PLB 13.89 (0-06-020196-7) HarpC Child Bks.

—The Fire Cat. LC 60-10234. (Illus.). 64p. (gr. k-3). 1983. pap. 3.50 (0-06-444038-9, Trophy) HarpC Child Bks.

—Jenny's Adopted Brothers. (gr. 1-3). 1988. 18.75 (0-8446-6286-0) Peter Smith.

—Jenny's Birthday Book. Averill, Esther, illus. LC 54-6589. 32p. (gr. k-3). 1954. PLB 14.89 (0-06-020251-3) HarpC Child Bks.

—King Philip, the Indian Chief. Belsky, Vera, illus. LC 92-32156. v, 147p. (gr. 6-12). 1993. lib. bdg. 17.50 (0-208-02357-7, Pub. by Linnet); (Pub. by Linnet) Shoe String.

—The School for Cats & Jenny's Moonlight Adventure. Averill, Esther, illus. (gr. k-3). 1990. pap. 2.95 (0-553-15362-5) Bantam.

Averous, Pierre. The Atom. (gr. 6 up). 1988. 4.95 (0-8120-3837-1) Barron.

Avery, Carol. And with a Light Touch: Learning about Reading, Writing, & Teaching with First Graders. LC 92-42680. (gr. 9-12). 1993. pap. text ed. 25.00 (0-435-08787-8, 08787) Heinemann.

Avery, Charles. Everybody Has Feelings - Todos Tenemos Sentimientos: The Moods of Children As Photographed by Charles E. Avery. Marulanda, Sandra, tr. (ENG & SPA., Illus.). 48p. (gr. k-8). 1992. 14.95 (0-940880-33-4) Open Hand.

Avery, Gillian. The Elephant War. (gr. k-6). 1988. pap. 4.95 (0-440-40040-6, Pub by Yearning Classics) Dell.

—A Likely Lad. LC 92-43911. 1994. pap. 15.00 (0-671-79867-7, S&S BFYR) S&S Trade.

—Maria Escapes. Snow, Scott, illus. LC 91-36730. 272p. (gr. 4-8). 1992. pap. 15.00 jacketed, 3-pc. bdg. (0-671-77074-8, S&S BFYR) S&S Trade.

—Maria's Italian Spring. Snow, Scott, illus. LC 92-16955. (gr. 4-8). 1993. pap. 15.00 JR3 (0-671-79582-1, S&S BFYR) S&S Trade.

Avery, Helen P. The Ghost of Canterville Hall. 1977. 4.50 (0-87602-112-7) Anchorage.

—The Secret Garden. (Orig.). (gr. k-3). 1987. pap. 5.00 playscript (0-87602-271-9) Anchorage.

Avery, Lorraine. The Creepy Carousel. Thomas, Linda, illus. LC 89-20279. 96p. (gr. 4-6). 1990. PLB 9.89 (0-8167-1712-5); pap. text ed. 2.95 (0-8167-1713-3) Troll Assocs.

—Movie Madness. Thomas, Linda, illus. LC 89-20333. 96p. (gr. 4-6). 1990. PLB 9.89 (0-8167-1714-1); pap. text ed. 2.95 (0-8167-1715-X) Troll Assocs.

—The Runaway Winner. Thomas, Linda, illus. LC 89-34369. 96p. (gr. 4-6). 1990. PLB 9.89 (0-8167-1708-7); pap. text ed. 2.95 (0-8167-1709-5) Troll Assocs.

—Secret in the Lake. Thomas, Linda, illus. LC 89-5119. 96p. (gr. 4-6). 1990. PLB 9.89 (0-8167-1710-9); pap. text ed. 2.95 (0-8167-1711-7) Troll Assocs.

Avery, Louisia. The Risks of RO - Episode 4: Child's Play. Wimberly, Potice & Andrews, Dianne, eds. Smith, Pauline, illus. 110p. (Orig.). 1988. pap. text ed. 5.95 (0-945779-03-8) Ethnic Role Model.

Avery, Susan. Extraordinary American Indians. LC 92-11358. (Illus.). 260p. (gr. 4 up). 1992. PLB 30.60 (0-516-00583-9) Childrens.

Avi. The Bird, the Frog, & the Light: A Fable. Henry, Matthew, illus. LC 93-4886. 1994. write for info. (0-531-06808-0); PLB write for info. (0-531-08658-5) Orchard Bks Watts.

—Blue Heron. LC 91-4308. 192p. (gr. 5-9). 1992. SBE 14.95 (0-02-707751-9, Bradbury Pr) Macmillan Child Grp.

—Blue Heron. 192p. 1993. pap. 3.99 (0-380-72043-4, Camelot) Avon.

—Bright Shadow. LC 85-5719. 144p. (gr. 5-7). 1985. SBE 13.95 (0-02-707750-0, Bradbury Pr) Macmillan Child Grp.

—Bright Shadow. 2nd ed. LC 88-3339. 176p. (gr. 3-7). 1994. pap. 3.95 (0-689-71783-0, Aladdin) Macmillan Child Grp.

—Captain Grey. LC 92-37643. 160p. 1993. write for info. (0-688-12233-7) Morrow Jr Bks.

—Captain Grey. LC 92-37643. 160p. 1993. pap. 3.95 (0-688-12234-5, Pub. by Beech Tree Bks) Morrow.

—City of Light, City of Dark: A Comic Book Novel. Floca, Brian, illus. LC 93-2887. 192p. (gr. 4 up). 1993. 15.95 (0-531-06800-5); PLB 15.99 (0-531-08650-X) Orchard Bks Watts.

—Devil's Race. LC 84-47636. 160p. (gr. 7 up). 1984. (Lipp Jr Bks); PLB 13.89 (0-397-32095-7, Lipp Jr Bks) HarpC Child Bks.

—Emily Upham's Revenge. ALC Staff, ed. Zelinsky, Paul, illus. 176p. (gr. 5-12). 1992. pap. 3.95 (0-688-11899-2, Pub. by Beech Tree Bks) Morrow.

—Emily Upham's Revenge, or, How Deadwood Dick Saved the Banker's Niece: Massachusetts Adventure. Zelinsky, Paul O., illus. LC 92-390. 192p. 1992. 14.00 (0-688-11898-4) Morrow Jr Bks.

—The Fighting Ground. Thompson, Ellen, illus. LC 82-47719. 160p. (gr. 5 up). 1984. (Lipp Jr Bks) PLB 13. 89 (0-397-32074-4, Lipp Jr Bks) HarpC Child Bks.

—The Fighting Ground. LC 82-47719. 160p. (gr. 4 up). 1987. pap. 3.95 (0-06-440185-5, Trophy) HarpC Child Bks.

—Judy with Punch. LC 92-27157. (Illus.). 176p. (gr. 5-9). 1993. SBE 14.95 (0-02-707755-1, Bradbury Pr) Macmillan Child Grp.

—Man from the Sky. ALC Staff, ed. 96p. (gr. 5-12). 1992. pap. 3.95 (0-688-11897-6, Pub. by Beech Tree Bks) Morrow.

—Man from the Sky. Wiesner, David, illus. LC 92-389. 96p. 1992. 14.00 (0-688-11896-8) Morrow Jr Bks.

—The Man Who Was Poe. LC 89-42537. 224p. (gr. 6-8). 1989. 13.95 (0-531-05833-6); PLB 13.99 (0-531-08433-7) Orchard Bks Watts.

—The Man Who Was Poe. 224p. 1991. pap. 3.99 (0-380-71192-3, Flare) Avon.

—Nothing but the Truth: A Documentary Novel. LC 91-9200. 192p. (gr. 6 up). 1991. 14.95 (0-531-05959-6); RLB 14.99 (0-531-08559-7) Orchard Bks Watts.

—Romeo & Juliet - Together (& Alive!) at Last. LC 87-7680. 128p. (gr. 6-8). 1987. 13.95 (0-531-05721-6); PLB 13.99 (0-531-08321-7) Orchard Bks Watts.

—Romeo & Juliet - Together (& Alive) at Last. 128p. 1988. pap. 3.50 (0-380-70525-7, Camelot) Avon.

—S. O. R. Losers. 96p. (gr. 3-7). 1986. pap. 3.50 (0-380-69993-1, Camelot) Avon.

—Shadrach's Crossing. LC 82-19008. 192p. (gr. 5 up). 1983. 10.95 (0-394-85816-6) Pantheon.

—Something Upstairs: A Tale of Ghosts. LC 88-60094. 128p. (gr. 5-7). 1988. 13.95 (0-531-05782-8); PLB 13. 99 (0-531-08382-9) Orchard Bks Watts.

—Sometimes I Think I Hear My Name. Adams, Jeanette, illus. LC 81-38421. 160p. (gr. 7 up). 1982. 9.95 (0-394-85048-3); lib. bdg. 9.99 (0-394-95048-8) Pantheon.

—S.O.R. Losers. LC 84-11022. 112p. (gr. 5-7). 1984. 12. 95 (0-02-793410-1, Bradbury Pr) Macmillan Child Grp.

—The True Confessions of Charlotte Doyle. Murray, Ruth E., illus. LC 90-30624. 224p. (gr. 6-8). 1990. 15. 95 (0-531-05893-X); PLB 15.99 (0-531-08493-0) Orchard Bks Watts.

—The True Confessions of Charlotte Doyle. 240p. (gr. 6). 1992. pap. 3.99 (0-380-71475-2, Flare) Avon.

—The True Confessions of Charlotte Doyle. large type ed. LC 92-37075. 288p. 1993. Repr. lib. bdg. 15.95 (1-56054-592-5) Thorndike Pr.

—Who Stole the Wizard of Oz? James, Derek, illus. LC 81-15447. 128p. (gr. 3-6). 1990. Repr. of 1981 ed. 3.99 (0-394-84992-2) Random Bks Yng Read.

—Who Was That Masked Man, Anyway? LC 92-7942. 176p. (gr. 4 up). 1992. 14.95 (0-531-05457-8); PLB 14.99 (0-531-08607-0) Orchard Bks Watts.

—Windcatcher. LC 90-40574. 128p. (gr. 3-7). 1991. SBE 13.95 (0-02-707761-6, Bradbury Pr) Macmillan Child Grp.

—Windcatcher. 128p. 1992. pap. 3.50 (0-380-71805-7, Camelot) Avon.

—Wolf Rider: A Tale of Terror. LC 86-13607. 224p. (gr. 7 up). 1986. SBE 14.95 (0-02-707760-8, Bradbury Pr) Macmillan Child Grp.

—Wolf Rider: A Tale of Terror. LC 87-23905. 224p. (gr. 7 up). 1988. pap. 2.95 (0-02-041511-7, Collier Young Ad) Macmillan Child Grp.

—Wolf Rider: A Tale of Terror. 2nd ed. 224p. (gr. 7 up). 1993. pap. 3.95 (0-02-041513-3, Collier Young Ad) Macmillan Child Grp.

Avis, Jen & Ward, Kathy. Just for Kids. Johnson, Colleen C., illus. 166p. 1990. spiral bdg. 12.95 (0-9628683-1-0) Avis & Ward.

Avison, Brigid. I Wonder Why I Blink: And Other Questions about My Body. Green, Ruby & Kenyon, Tony, illus. LC 92-45599. 32p. (gr. k-3). 1993. 8.95 (1-85697-875-3) Kingfisher Bks.

Avi-Yonah, Michael. Dig This! How Archaeologists Uncover Our Past. LC 92-28305. 1993. 22.95 (0-8225-3200-X, Runestone Pr) Lerner Pubns.

Avraham, Regina. The Circulatory System. Koop, C. Everett, intro. by. (Illus.). 112p. (gr. 6-12). 1989. 18.95 (0-7910-0013-3) Chelsea Hse.

—The Digestive System. (Illus.). 104p. (gr. 6-12). 1989. 18.95 (0-7910-0015-X) Chelsea Hse.

—The Downside of Drugs. Mendelson, Jack H. & Mello, Nancyintro. by. (Illus.). 112p. (gr. 5 up). 1988. lib. bdg. 19.95 (1-55546-232-4) Chelsea Hse.

—The Reproductive System. (Illus.). 128p. (gr. 6-12). 1991. 18.95 (0-7910-0025-7) Chelsea Hse.

—Substance Abuse: Prevention & Treatment. Mendelson, Jack H. & Mello, Nancyintro. by. (Illus.). 128p. (gr. 5 up). 1988. lib. bdg. 19.95 (1-55546-219-7) Chelsea Hse.

—Substance Abuse: Prevention & Treatment. 1988. pap. 9.95 (0-7910-0807-X) Chelsea Hse.

Avrett, Robert. Timid Pup. (Illus.). (gr. 1-3). PLB 7.19 (0-8313-0004-3) Lantern.

Awdry, Christopher. Tell the Time with Thomas. Stott, Ken, illus. LC 91-67877. 32p. (ps-3). 1993. 7.99 (0-679-83461-3) Random Bks Yng Read.

—Thomas's Big Book of Words. Stott, Ken, illus. LC 91-62681. 32p. (ps-1). 1992. 7.99 (0-679-82778-1) Random Bks Yng Read.

Awdry, W. Bertie the Bus Wheel Book. Bell, Owain, illus. 14p. (ps-k). 1993. 4.99 (0-679-84469-4) Random Bks Yng Read.

—Breakfast-Time for Thomas: Based on the Railway Series. Bell, Owain, illus. LC 89-62527. 32p. (Orig.). (ps-3). 1990. pap. 1.50 (0-679-80409-9) Random Bks Yng Read.

—Catch Me, Catch Me! A Thomas the Tank Engine Story. Bell, Owain, illus. LC 89-37547. 24p. (Orig.). (ps-2). 1990. pap. 2.25 (0-679-80485-4) Random Bks Yng Read.

—Choo-Choo, Peek-a-Boo. Bell, Owain, illus. LC 91-61250. 14p. (ps). 1992. 3.99 (0-679-82262-3) Random Bks Yng Read.

—A Cow on the Line & Other Thomas the Tank Engine Stories. Mitton, David & Permane, Terry, photos by. LC 91-21706. (Illus.). (Orig.). (ps-3). 1992. PLB 5.99 (0-679-91977-5); pap. 2.25 (0-679-81977-0) Random Bks Yng Read.

—A Cow on the Line & Other Thomas the Tank Engine Stories. reissue ed. Starr, Ringo, narrated by. Mitton, David & Permane, Terry, photos by. (Illus.). 32p. (ps-3). 1992. pap. 5.95 incl. cass. (0-679-83476-1) Random Bks Yng Read.

—Diesel's Devious Deed & Other Thomas the Tank Engine Stories. Mitton, David & Permane, Terry, photos by. LC 91-21133. (Illus.). 32p. (Orig.). (ps-3). 1992. PLB 5.99 (0-679-91976-7); pap. 2.25 (0-679-81976-2) Random Bks Yng Read.

—Diesel's Devious Deed & Other Thomas the Tank Engine Stories. reissue ed. Starr, Ringo, narrated by. Mitton, David & Permane, Terry, photos by. (Illus.). 32p. (ps-3). 1992. pap. 5.95 incl. cass. (0-679-83474-5) Random Bks Yng Read.

—Duck Takes Charge. Mitton, David & Permane, Terry, photos by. LC 92-45564. (Illus.). 32p. (ps-2). 1993. 3.50 (0-679-84763-4) Random Bks Yng Read.

—Good Morning, James. Bell, Owain, illus. 12p. (ps). 1992. 3.99 (0-679-82707-2) Random Bks Yng Read.

—Happy Birthday, Thomas! A Step 1 Book - Preschool-Gr 1. Bell, Owain, illus. LC 89-49649. 32p. (Orig.). (ps-1). 1990. lib. bdg. 7.99 (0-679-90809-9); pap. 3.50 (0-679-80809-4) Random Bks Yng Read.

—Henry & the Elephant: Based on the Railway Series. Bell, Owain, illus. LC 89-62528. 32p. (Orig.). (ps-3). 1990. pap. 1.50 (0-679-80408-0) Random Bks Yng Read.

—Henry the Green Engine & the Tunnel. Spong, Clive, illus. LC 91-67968. 12p. (ps-1). 1992. 3.99 (0-679-83451-6) Random Bks Yng Read.

—James & the Foolish Freight Cars. LC 91-8035. (Illus.). 32p. (ps-2). 1991. 3.50 (0-679-82086-8) Random Bks Yng Read.

—James the Red Engine. Bell, Owain, illus. 7p. (ps-k). 1991. bds. 7.00 with plastic wheels (0-679-81590-2) Random Bks Yng Read.

—Meet Thomas the Tank Engine & His Friends. McArthur, Kenny, et al, illus. LC 89-32299. 32p. (ps-1). 1989. 6.95 (0-679-80102-2) Random Bks Yng Read.

—Percy Runs Away. LC 91-8707. (Illus.). 32p. (ps-2). 1991. 3.50 (0-679-82087-6) Random Bks Yng Read.

—Percy the Small Engine Takes the Plunge. Spong, Clive, illus. LC 91-67970. 12p. (ps-1). 1992. 3.99 (0-679-83453-2) Random Bks Yng Read.

—Percy's Promise. Mitton, David & Permane, Terry, photos by. LC 92-43773. (Illus.). 32p. (ps-2). 1993. 3.50 (0-679-84765-0) Random Bks Yng Read.

—Thomas & the Freight Train. Bell, Owain, illus. LC 90-62371. 22p. (ps). 1991. bds. 2.95 (0-679-81599-6) Random Bks Yng Read.

—Thomas & the Hide-&-Seek Animals: A Thomas the Tank Engine Flap Book. Bell, Owain, illus. LC 90-62114. 24p. (ps-1). 1991. 7.95 (0-679-81316-0) Random Bks Yng Read.

—Thomas & Trevor. Mitton, David & Permane, Terry, photos by. LC 92-43774. (Illus.). 32p. (ps-2). 1993. 3.50 (0-679-84766-9) Random Bks Yng Read.

—Thomas Breaks the Rules. LC 91-2428. (Illus.). 32p. (ps-2). 1991. 3.50 (0-679-82088-4) Random Bks Yng Read.

—Thomas Gets Tricked & Other Stories: Based on the Railway Series. McArthur, Kenny, photos by. LC 89-8502. (Illus.). 32p. (ps-3). 1989. PLB 5.99 (0-679-90100-0); pap. 2.25 (0-679-80100-6) Random Bks Yng Read.

—Thomas Gets Tricked & Other Stories. McArthur, Kenny, et al, photos by. Starr, Ringo, contrib. by. (Illus.). 32p. (Orig.). (ps-2). 1991. pap. 5.95 incl. 20-min. cassette (0-679-80108-1) Random Bks Yng Read.

—Thomas, Percy, & the Post Train. Mitton, David & Permane, Terry, illus. 1994. write for info. (0-679-86046-0) Random Bks Yng Read.

—Thomas the Tank Engine ABC: (Just Right for 2's & 3's) McArthur, Kenny, photos by. LC 89-10605. (Illus.). 24p. (ps). 1990. 5.99 (0-679-80362-9) Random Bks Yng Read.

—Thomas the Tank Engine & the Great Race. Bell, Owain, illus. 7p. (ps-k). 1989. bds. 7.00 with plastic wheels (0-679-80000-X) Random Bks Yng Read.

—Thomas the Tank Engine & the School Trip. Bell, Owain, illus. LC 92-33711. 32p. (ps-1). 1993. PLB 7.99 (0-679-94365-X); pap. 3.50 (0-679-84365-5) Random Bks Yng Read.

—Thomas the Tank Engine & the Tractor. Spong, Clive, illus. LC 91-67969. 12p. (ps-1). 1992. 3.99 (0-679-83452-4) Random Bks Yng Read.

—Thomas the Tank Engine Goes Fishing. Spong, Clive, illus. LC 91-67967. 12p. (ps-1). 1992. 3.99 (0-679-83450-8) Random Bks Yng Read.

—Thomas the Tank Engine Starter Library, 4 bks. Dalby, C. Reginald, illus. (gr. 1-5). 1990. Repr. of 1945 ed. boxed set 19.95 (0-679-80792-6) Random Bks Yng Read.

—Thomas the Tank Engine Take-along Library, 5 bks. McArthur, Kenny, et al, photos by. (Illus.). (ps-3). 1992. Boxed set incls. A Cow on the Line & Other Stories, Thomas Gets Tricked & Other Stories, Diesel's Devious Deed & Other Stories, Trouble for Thomas & Other Stories, & Catch Me! Catch Me!, 32p. ea. 11.50 (0-679-83840-6) Random Bks Yng Read.

—Thomas the Tank Engine Visits a Farm. Bell, Owain, illus. 10p. (ps). 1991. vinyl 3.95 (0-679-81580-5) Random Bks Yng Read.

—Thomas the Tank Engine's Noisy Trip. Bell, Owain, illus. LC 89-60089. 28p. 1989. bds. 2.95 (0-679-80083-2) Random Bks Yng Read.

—Thomas's Big Railway Pop-up Book. Bell, Owain, illus. 14p. (ps up). 1992. 13.00 (0-679-83465-6) Random Bks Yng Read.

—Thomas's Carousel Book. Bell, Owain, illus. 5p. (ps-3). 1993. 8.00 (0-679-84819-3) Random Bks Yng Read.

—Toby the Tram Engine. LC 91-7770. (Illus.). 32p. (ps-2). 1991. 3.50 (0-679-82095-7) Random Bks Yng Read.

—Tracking Thomas the Tank Engine & His Friends: A Book with Finger Tabs. Stott, Ken, illus. LC 91-67876. 16p. (ps-1). 1992. bds. 7.99 (0-679-83458-3) Random Bks Yng Read.

—Trouble for Thomas & Other Stories. reissue ed. McArthur, Kenny, et al, photos by. Starr, Ringo, contrib. by. (Illus.). 32p. (ps-2). 1991. incl. 20-min. cassette 5.95 (0-679-80106-5) Random Bks Yng Read.

—Trouble for Thomas & Other Stories: Based on the Railway Series. McArthur, Kenny, photos by. LC 89-8503. (Illus.). 32p. (ps-3). 1989. pap. 2.25 (0-679-80101-4) Random Bks Yng Read.

Awdry, W., created by. Thomas the Tank Engine Storybook. Mitton, David & Permane, Terry, photos by. LC 92-35915. (Illus.). 1993. 8.00 (0-679-84465-1) Random Bks Yng Read.

Awiakta, Marilou. Rising Fawn & the Fire Mystery. Bringle, Beverly, illus. Easson, Roger R., ed. LC 83-13824. (Illus.). 48p. (Orig.). (gr. 5 up). 1984. pap. 11.95 (0-918518-29-6) Iris Pr.

Axelrod, Alan, commentary by. Songs of the Wild West. Fox, Dan, contrib. by. (Illus.). 128p. 1991. pap. 19.95 jacketed (0-671-74775-4, S&S BFYR) S&S Trade.

Axelrod, Amy. Pigs Will Be Pigs. McGinley-Nally, Sharon, illus. LC 93-7640. 40p. (gr. k-3). 1994. RSBE 14.95 (0-02-765415-X, Four Winds) Macmillan Child Grp.

Axelrod, Herman, jt. auth. see Bachrach, Kalman.

Axelrod, Herman C. In Their Footsteps. 144p. text ed. 6.00 (0-914131-98-2, B015) Torah Umesorah.

Axelsen, Jenny, jt. auth. see Axelsen, Stephen.

Axelsen, Stephen & Axelsen, Jenny. Little Sisters. Axelsen, Stephen & Axelsen, Jenny, illus. LC 92-34261. 1993. 4.25 (0-383-03637-2) SRA Schl Grp.

Axeman, Lois, illus. Holidays. LC 84-9429. 32p. (gr. k-3). 1984. PLB 21.35 (0-89565-266-8); PLB 14.95s.p. (0-685-55700-6) Childs World.

Axiom Information Resources Staff. Celebrity Birthday Guide: Names & Birthdays of Major Movie-TV Stars & Other Famous People. rev. ed. 32p. (Orig.). 1993. pap. 5.95 (0-943213-09-6) Axiom Info Res.

—Star Guide, 1994-1995: Where to Contact over 3200 Movie Stars, TV Stars, Rock Stars, Sports Stars, & Other Famous Celebrities. rev. ed. Robinson, Terry, ed. (Illus.). 208p. 1994. pap. 12.95 (0-943213-12-6) Axiom Info Res.

Axsom, Dora & Pelham, Erra. No Lace for Cricket: Sequel to Mountain Mama. 216p. (Orig.). (gr. 10 up). 1991. pap. 5.50 (0-9621669-2-8) Lil Red Hen OK.

Axtell, Susan, jt. auth. see Bethell, Jean.

Axworthy, Anni. Along Came Toto. Axworthy, Anni, illus. LC 92-52992. 32p. (ps-3). 1993. 12.95 (1-56402-172-6) Candlewick Pr.

—Anni's India Diary. Axworthy, Anni, illus. LC 92-17524. 32p. (ps-12). 1992. smyth sewn reinforced 14.95 (1-879085-59-3) Whsprng Coyote Pr.

Aych, Mary J. Pick of the Litter. (gr. 4-7). 1990. pap. 2.95 (0-553-15808-2) Bantam.

Ayckbourn, Alan. Confusions. (Illus.). 63p. 1988. pap. 9.95 (0-413-53270-4, A0063, Pub. by Methuen UK) Heinemann.

—Mr. A's Amazing Maze Plays. 96p. 1990. pap. 7.95 (0-571-14160-9) Faber & Faber.

Aycock, Theresa. The Banana Pie That Changed the World. (Illus.). 24p. (gr. k-3). 1993. pap. 2.50 (0-87406-611-5) Willowisp Pr.

Aydelott, Jimmie. Art & Math Throughout the Year. (gr. 1-6). 1989. pap. 8.95 (0-8224-0104-5) Fearon Teach Aids.

Ayer, Eleanor. Determination. (gr. 7-12). 1991. PLB 13.95 (0-8239-1226-4) Rosen Group.

—Everything You Need to Know about Teen Fatherhood. Rosen, Ruth, ed. (gr. 7-12). 1993. PLB 13.95 (0-8239-1532-8) Rosen Group.

—Germany. (Illus.). 64p. (gr. 7 up). 1990. lib. bdg. 17.27 (0-86593-093-7); lib. bdg. 12.95s.p. (0-685-36365-1) Rourke Corp.

—Our Flag. LC 91-38892. (Illus.). 48p. (gr. 2-4). 1992. PLB 12.90 (1-56294-107-0) Millbrook Pr.

—Our Great Rivers & Waterways. (Illus.). 48p. (gr. 2-4). 1994. 12.90 (1-56294-441-X) Millbrook Pr.

—Our National Monuments. LC 91-43230. (Illus.). 48p. (gr. 2-4). 1992. PLB 12.90 (1-56294-078-3) Millbrook Pr.

—Teen Suicide: Is It Too Painful to Grow Up? (Illus.). 64p. (gr. 5-8). 1993. PLB 14.95 (0-8050-2573-1) TFC Bks NY.

Ayer, Eleanor H. The Anasazi. LC 92-14701. 112p. 1993. 14.95 (0-8027-8184-5); PLB 15.85 (0-8027-8185-3) Walker & Co.

—Berlin. LC 91-29721. (Illus.). 96p. (gr. 6 up). 1992. RSBE 13.95 (0-02-707800-0, New Discovery) Macmillan Child Grp.

—Boris Yeltsin: Man of the People. LC 92-16607. (Illus.). 144p. (gr. 5 up). 1992. RSBE 13.95 (0-87518-543-6, Dillon) Macmillan Child Grp.

—Hispanic Colorado. Kline, Jane, illus. 48p. (gr. 4-7). 1982. 11.95x (0-939650-11-8); pap. 6.95x (0-939650-10-X) R H Pub.

—Margaret Bourke-White: Photographing the World. LC 91-39800. (Illus.). 112p. (gr. 5 up). 1992. RSBE 13.95 (0-87518-513-4, Dillon) Macmillan Child Grp.

Ayer, Eleanor H., compiled by. Colorado Chronicles Index. Kline, Jane, illus. 48p. (gr. 4-7). 1986. pap. 6.95x (0-939650-26-6) R H Pub.

Ayer, Eleanor H., ed. see Thumhart, Suzanne.

Ayer, Elizabeth. Canada. (Illus.). 64p. (gr. 7 up). 1990. lib. bdg. 17.27 (0-86593-091-0); lib. bdg. 12.95s.p. (0-685-36363-5) Rourke Corp.

Aylesworth, Jim. The Bad Dream. Fay, Ann, ed. LC 85-685. (Illus.). 32p. (ps-2). 1985. 11.95 (0-8075-0506-4) A Whitman.

—The Cat & the Fiddle & More. Hull, Richard, illus. LC 91-30956. 32p. (ps-1). 1992. SBE 13.95 (0-689-31715-8, Atheneum Child Bk) Macmillan Child Grp.

—The Completed Hickory Dickory Dock. Christelow, Eileen, illus. LC 89-38484. 32p. (ps-2). 1990. SBE 13.95 (0-689-31606-2, Atheneum Child Bk) Macmillan Child Grp.

—Country Crossing. Rand, Ted, illus. LC 89-78184. 32p. (ps-2). 1991. SBE 13.95 (0-689-31580-5, Atheneum Child Bk) Macmillan Child Grp.

—The Folks in the Valley: A Pennsylvania Dutch ABC. Vitale, Stefano, illus. LC 91-12451. 32p. (ps-3). 1992. 15.00 (0-06-021672-7); PLB 14.89 (0-06-021929-7) HarpC Child Bks.

—The Good-Night Kiss. Krudop, Walter L., illus. LC 91-40952. 32p. (ps-3). 1993. SBE 14.95 (0-689-31515-5, Atheneum Child Bk) Macmillan Child Grp.

—Hanna's Hog. Rounds, Glen, illus. LC 87-11559. 32p. (gr. k-3). 1988. RSBE 13.95 (0-689-31367-5, Atheneum Child Bk) Macmillan Child Grp.

—McGraw's Emporium. 1994. write for info. (0-8050-3192-8) H Holt & Co.

—Mr. McGill Goes to Town. Graham, Thomas, illus. LC 89-31111. 32p. (ps-2). 1989. 13.95 (0-8050-0772-5, Owlet BYR) H Holt & Co.

—Mr. McGill Goes to Town. Graham, Thomas, illus. LC 89-31111. 32p. (gr. k-2). 1992. pap. 4.95 (0-8050-2096-9, Owlet BYR) H Holt & Co.

—Mother Halverson's New Cat. Goffe, Toni, illus. LC 88-29279. 32p. (gr. k-3). 1989. SBE 13.95 (0-689-31465-5, Atheneum Child Bk) Macmillan Child Grp.

—My Son John. Frampton, David, illus. LC 92-27192. 1993. write for info. (0-8050-1725-9, Bks Young Read) H Holt & Co.

—Old Black Fly. Gammell, Stephen, illus. LC 91-26825. 32p. (ps-2). 1992. 15.95 (0-8050-1401-2, Bks Young Read) H Holt & Co.

—One Crow: A Counting Rhyme. Young, Ruth, illus. LC 85-45856. 32p. (ps-1). 1988. (Lipp Jr Bks); PLB 12.89 (0-397-32175-9) HarpC Child Bks.

—One Crow: A Counting Rhyme. Young, Ruth, illus. LC 85-45856. 32p. (ps-1). 1990. pap. 5.95 (0-06-443242-4, Trophy) HarpC Child Bks.

—Two Terrible Frights. Christelow, Eileen, illus. LC 86-25859. 32p. (ps-2). 1987. SBE 13.95 (0-689-31327-6, Atheneum Child Bk) Macmillan Child Grp.

Aylesworth, Thomas & Aylesworth, Virginia. Chicago. (Illus.). 64p. (gr. 3-7). PLB 14.95 (1-56711-020-7) Blackbirch.

Aylesworth, Thomas G. Government & the Environment: Tracking the Record. LC 92-24515. (Illus.). 104p. (gr. 6 up). 1993. lib. bdg. 17.95 (0-89490-398-5) Enslow Pubs.

—Kids' Almanac of Professional Football. LC 92-16483. (Illus.). 176p. 1992. pap. 8.95 (1-55870-266-0) Shoe Tree Pr.

—The Kids' World Almanac of Baseball. Lane, John, illus. Hershiser, Orel, intro. by. (Illus.). 288p. 1990. text ed. 14.95 (0-88687-463-7, World Almanac); pap. 6.95 (0-88687-563-3, World Almanac) F&W Inc NJ.

—The Kid's World Almanac of Baseball. Ripken, Cal, Jr., intro. by. LC 92-35867. 1993. write for info. (0-88687-721-0, World Almanac) F&W Inc NJ.

—Kids' World Almanac of Baseball. rev. ed. (gr. 4-7). 1993. 14.95 (0-88687-722-9, World Almanac) F&W Inc NJ.

—Kids' World Almanac of the United States. 288p. (gr. 3-7). 1990. 14.95 (0-88687-479-3, World Almanac); pap. 7.95 (0-88687-478-5, World Almanac) F&W Inc NJ.

—Moving Continents: Our Changing Earth. LC 89-33549. (Illus.). 64p. (gr. 6 up). 1990. lib. bdg. 15.95 (0-89490-273-3) Enslow Pubs.

Aylesworth, Thomas G. & Aylesworth, Virginia L. Atlantic: W. Virginia, District of Columbia. (Illus.). 64p. (gr. 3 up). 1991. lib. bdg. 16.95 (0-7910-1041-4) Chelsea Hse.

—The Atlantic (Virginia, West Virginia, District of Columbia). (Illus.). 64p. (Orig.). 1990. lib. bdg. 16.95x (1-55546-555-2); pap. 6.95 (0-7910-0533-X) Chelsea Hse.

—Eastern Great Lakes: Ohio - Indiana - Michigan. (Illus.). 64p. (gr. 3 up). 1991. lib. bdg. 16.95 (0-7910-1045-7) Chelsea Hse.

—Great Plains (Montana, North Dakota, South Dakota, Wyoming, Nebraska) LC 87-18198. (Illus.). 64p. (gr. 3 up). 1988. lib. bdg. 16.95 (1-55546-566-8) Chelsea Hse.

—The Great Plains: Montana, North Dakota, South Dakota, Wyoming, Nebraska. (Illus.). 64p. (gr. 3 up). 1992. lib. bdg. 16.95 (0-7910-1052-X) Chelsea Hse.

—Lower Atlantic (North Carolina, South Carolina). (Illus.). 64p. (gr. 3 up). 1991. lib. bdg. 16.95 (0-7910-1042-2) Chelsea Hse.

—Mid Atlantic: Pennsylvania - Delaware - Maryland. (Illus.). 64p. (gr. 3 up). 1991. lib. bdg. 16.95 (0-7910-1040-6) Chelsea Hse.

—The Mid-Atlantic (Pennsylvania, Delaware, Maryland). (Illus.). 64p. (gr. 3 up). 1988. lib. bdg. 16.95 (1-55546-554-4); pap. 6.95 (0-7910-0537-2) Chelsea Hse.

—Northern New England: Maine - Vermont - New Hampshire. (Illus.). 64p. (gr. 3 up). 1990. lib. bdg. 16.95 (0-7910-1037-6) Chelsea Hse.

—The Northwest (Washington, Oregon, Alaska, Idaho). (Illus.). 64p. (gr. 3 up). 1992. lib. bdg. 16.95 (0-7910-1051-1) Chelsea Hse.

—Pacific: California, Hawaii. (gr. 3 up). 1992. lib. bdg. 16.95 (0-7910-1050-3) Chelsea Hse.

—South Central (Louisiana, Arkansas, Missouri, Kansas, Oklahoma) (Illus.). 64p. (Orig.). (gr. 3 up). 1988. lib. bdg. 16.95 (1-55546-561-7); pap. 6.95 (0-7910-0542-9) Chelsea Hse.
—South Central (Louisiana, Arkansas, Missouri, Kansas, Oklahoma) (Illus.). 64p. (gr. 3 up). 1992. PLB 16.95 (0-7910-1047-3) Chelsea Hse.
—The South (Mississippi, Alabama, Florida) (Illus.). 64p. (gr. 3 up). 1988. 16.95 (1-55546-558-7); pap. 6.95 (0-7910-0541-0) Chelsea Hse.
—The South (Mississippi, Alabama, Florida) (Illus.). 64p. (gr. 3 up). 1991. lib. bdg. 16.95 (0-7910-1044-9) Chelsea Hse.
—The Southeast (Kentucky, Tennessee, Georgia) (Illus.). 64p. (gr. 3 up). 1988. lib. bdg. 16.95 (1-55546-557-9); pap. 6.95 (0-7910-0543-7) Chelsea Hse.
—The Southeast (Kentucky, Tennessee, Georgia) (Illus.). 64p. (gr. 3 up). 1991. lib. bdg. 16.95 (0-7910-1043-0) Chelsea Hse.
—Southern New England: Connecticut - Massachusetts - Rhode Island. (Illus.). 64p. (gr. 3 up). 1990. lib. bdg. 16.95 (0-7910-1038-4) Chelsea Hse.
—Southern New England (Connecticut, Massachusetts, Rhode Island) LC 87-17880. (Illus.). 64p. (Orig.). (gr. 3 up). 1988. lib. bdg. 16.95 (1-55546-552-8); pap. 6.95 (0-7910-0544-5) Chelsea Hse.
—The Southwest (Texas, New Mexico, Colorado) (Illus.). 64p. 1988. lib. bdg. 16.95x (1-55546-562-5); pap. 6.95 (0-7910-0545-3) Chelsea Hse.
—The Southwest (Texas, New Mexico, Colorado) (Illus.). 64p. (gr. 3 up). 1992. lib. bdg. 16.95 (0-7910-1048-1) Chelsea Hse.
—State Reports Series, 17 titles. (Illus.). 1088p. (gr. 3 up). 1990. lib. bdg. 288.15 (0-7910-1036-8) Chelsea Hse.
—Territories & Possessions & Guam, Puerto Rico, U. S. Virgin Islands, American Samoa, North Mariana Islands: Guam, Puerto Rico, U. S. Virgin Islands, American Samoa, North Mariana Islands. (Illus.). 64p. (gr. 3 up). 1992. lib. bdg. 16.95 (0-7910-1053-8) Chelsea Hse.
—Upper Atlantic: New Jersey - New York. (Illus.). 64p. (gr. 3 up). 1987. lib. bdg. 16.95 (1-55546-553-6); pap. 6.95 (0-685-35556-X) Chelsea Hse.
—Upper Atlantic: New Jersey, New York. (Illus.). 64p. (gr. 3 up). 1990. lib. bdg. 16.95x (0-7910-1039-2) Chelsea Hse.
—The West (Arizona, Nevada, Utah) (Illus.). 64p. (Orig.). 1988. lib. bdg. 16.95x (1-55546-563-3); pap. 6.95 (0-7910-0548-8) Chelsea Hse.
—The West (Arizona, Nevada, Utah) (Illus.). 64p. (gr. 3 up). 1992. PLB 16.95 (0-7910-1049-X) Chelsea Hse.
—Western Great Lakes (Illinois, Iowa, Wisconsin, Minnesota) (Illus.). 64p. (Orig.). (gr. 3 up). 1987. lib. bdg. 16.95x (1-55546-560-9); pap. 6.95x (0-7910-0549-6) Chelsea Hse.
—Western Great Lakes (Illinois, Iowa, Wisconsin, Minnesota) (Illus.). 64p. (gr. 3 up). 1992. lib. bdg. 16.95 (0-7910-1046-5) Chelsea Hse.
Aylesworth, Virginia, jt. auth. see Aylesworth, Thomas.
Aylesworth, Virginia L., jt. auth. see Aylesworth, Thomas G.
Ayliffe, Alex. Slither, Swoop, Swing. LC 92-16415. 32p. 1993. 12.99 (0-670-84801-8) Viking Child Bks.
Aylott, Jane. The Soft Secret Word. Andersson, Benny, illus. 32p. 1992. 12.00 (0-9631440-0-6) Winged Peoples.
Ayman, Lily. A Persian Reader Bk. 1: Farsi Biyamuzim: Ketab-E Aval. 2nd, rev. ed. Bolurchian, Flora, illus. LC 93-61060. (PER.). 104p. (Orig.). (gr. 1). 1994. pap. text ed. 9.95x (0-936347-34-1) Iran Bks.
—A Persian Reader: Farsi Biyamuzim: Ravesh-E Tadris. 2nd, rev. ed. LC 93-61059. (PER.). 64p. (Orig.). (gr. 1). 1994. pap. 16.95x tchr's. ed. (0-936347-36-8) Iran Bks.
Aymar, Brant, ed. The Personality of the Cat. (Illus.). 352p. 1989. 8.99 (0-517-00016-4) Outlet Bk Co.
Ayme, Marcel. Boites de Peinture. Sabatier, Roland, illus. (FRE.). 72p. (gr. 1-5). 1990. pap. 9.95 (2-07-031199-6) Schoenhof.
—Canard et la Panthere. Sabatier, C. & Sabatier, R., illus. (FRE.). 63p. (gr. 1-5). 1991. pap. 9.95 (2-07-031128-7) Schoenhof.
—Chien. Sabatier, Roland, illus. (FRE.). 72p. (gr. 1-5). 1990. pap. 9.95 (2-07-031201-1) Schoenhof.
—Cygnes. Sabatier, Roland, illus. (FRE.). 72p. (gr. 1-5). 1990. pap. 9.95 (2-07-031235-6) Schoenhof.
—Mauvais Jars. Sabatier, C. & Sabatier, R., illus. (FRE.). 72p. (gr. 1-5). 1990. pap. 10.95 (2-07-031236-4) Schoenhof.
—Paon. Sabatier, C. & Sabatier, R., illus. (FRE.). 1985. pap. 8.95 (2-07-031087-6) Schoenhof.
—Patte du Chat. Sabatier, Roland, illus. (FRE.). 72p. (gr. 1-5). 1990. pap. 9.95 (2-07-031200-3) Schoenhof.
—Probleme. Sabatier, Roland, illus. (FRE.). 71p. (ps-1). 1989. pap. 9.95 (2-07-031198-8) Schoenhof.
—Vaches. Sabatier, Roland, illus. (FRE.). 72p. (gr. 1-5). 1990. pap. 9.95 (2-07-031215-1) Schoenhof.
Aymerich, Angela F. Los Tres Perritos. Billin-Frye, Paige, illus. (SPA.). 16p. (Orig.). (gr. 1-3). 1991. pap. text ed. 29.95 big bk. (1-56334-021-6); pap. text ed. 6.00 small bk. (1-56334-035-6) Hampton-Brown.
Aymerich, Angela F., jt. auth. see Porter, Mark.
Aymes, Maria de la Cruz see De la Cruz Aymes, Maria, et al.
Ayoub, Abderrahaman, et al. Umm el Madayan: An Islamic City Through the Ages. Corni, Francesco, illus. LC 93-757. (ENG.). (gr. 5 up). 1994. 16.95 (0-395-65967-1) HM.

Ayrai, Sia. Baby Bright Board Books: 123's. Ayrai, Sia, photos by. (Illus.). 1993. 5.95 (1-56565-048-4) Lowell Hse.
Ayres, Becky. Salt Lake City. LC 90-2968. 60p. (gr. 3 up). 1990. RSBE 13.95 (0-87518-436-7, Dillon) Macmillan Child Grp.
—Victoria Flies High. Koontz, Robin M., illus. LC 89-694. 32p. (ps-3). 1990. 12.95 (0-525-65014-8, Cobblehill Bks) Dutton Child Bks.
Ayres, Becky H. Matreshka. Natchev, Alexi, illus. LC 91-36359. 32p. (gr. k-3). 1992. pap. 15.00 (0-385-30657-1) Doubleday.
Ayres, Carter M. Chuck Yeager: Fighter Pilot. (Illus.). 48p. (gr. 4 up). 1988. PLB 13.50 (0-8225-0483-9) Lerner Pubns.
—Pilots & Aviation. (Illus.). 72p. (gr. 5 up). 1990. PLB 21.50 (0-8225-1590-3) Lerner Pubns.
Ayres, Pam. Guess Where? Lacome, Julie, illus. LC 93-24336. 1994. write for info. (1-56402-314-1) Candlewick Pr.
—Guess Why. Lacome, Julie, illus. LC 93-24337. 1994. write for info. (1-56402-315-X) Candlewick Pr.
—Piggo & the Nosebag. Ellis, Andy, illus. 32p. (gr. k-3). 1991. 9.95 (0-563-20922-4, BBC-Parkwest) Parkwest Pubns.
—Piggo Has a Train Ride. Ellis, Andy, illus. 32p. (gr. k-3). 1992. 9.95 (0-563-20921-6, BBC-Parkwest) Parkwest Pubns.
Azaad, Meyer. The Tale of Ringy. Ghanoonparvar, Mohammad R. & Wilcox, Diane L., trs. from PER. Haqiqat, Nahid, illus. 24p. (Orig.). (gr. 3 up). 1983. pap. 4.95 (0-686-43078-6) Mazda Pubs.
Azaad, Meyer, jt. auth. see Farjam, Farideh.
Azaola, Miguel, tr. see Ungerer, Tomi.
Azarian, Mary. A Farmer's Alphabet. LC 80-84938. 56p. (ps-2). 1981. 16.95 (0-87923-394-X); pap. 12.95 (0-87923-397-4) Godine.
—Farmers Alphabet Junior. LC 80-84938. 64p. 1985. pap. 7.95 (0-87923-589-6) Godine.
Aziz, Laurel & Edwards, Frank B. Ottawa: A Kid's Eye View. Kraulis, J. A., illus. 72p. 1993. text ed. 19.95 (0-921285-27-2, Pub. by Bungalo Bks CN); pap. 9.95 (0-921285-26-4, Pub. by Bungalo Bks CN) Firefly Bks Ltd.
Aziz, Laurel, jt. auth. see Forsyth, Adrian.
Aziz, Tariq, tr. see Iqbal, Muhammad.
Azzam, Leila & Gouverneur, Aisha. The Life of the Prophet Muhammad. (Illus.). 135p. 1992. pap. 19.95 (0-946621-02-0, Pub. by Islamic Texts UK) Atrium Pubs.
Azzolino, Agnes. Math Games for Adult & Child: Math Games for 2 Through 7-Year-Olds. rev. ed. LC 93-7994. (Illus.). 84p. (Orig.). (ps-2). 1993. Incl. 3 game boards, a set of cards & plastic game pieces. pap. text ed. 20.00 (0-9623593-4-3) Mathematical.
—Math Games for the Young Child. Vinik, Michael, illus. (Orig.). (ps-2). 1987. pap. text ed. 8.40 (0-9623593-1-9) Mathematical.

B

B. S. S. Music Staff. Christmas Song Favorites (Words Only) large type ed. 60p. (gr. 3). 1963. 4.28 (0-317-01880-9, 4-03590-00) Am Printing Hse.
—Selected Christmas Songs (Words Only) large type ed. 16p. (gr. 3). 1960. 3.31 (0-317-01933-3, 4-23260-00) Am Printing Hse.
Baba, Noboru. Eleven Cats & a Pig. Baba, Noboru, illus. LC 88-9596. 48p. (gr. k-4). 1988. lib. bdg. 18.95 (0-87614-338-9) Carolrhoda Bks.
—Eleven Cats & Albatrosses. Baba, Noboru, illus. LC 88-9598. 48p. (gr. k-4). 1988. lib. bdg. 18.95 (0-87614-335-4) Carolrhoda Bks.
—Eleven Cats in a Bag. Baba, Noboru, illus. LC 88-9597. 48p. (gr. k-4). 1988. lib. bdg. 18.95 (0-87614-336-2) Carolrhoda Bks.
—Eleven Hungry Cats. LC 88-5419. (Illus.). 48p. (gr. k-4). 1988. PLB 18.95 (0-87614-337-0) Carolrhoda Bks.
Baba Hari Dass. Mystic Monkey. Kelley, Elizabeth A., illus. LC 81-51051. 64p. (Orig.). (gr. 4-8). 1984. pap. 9.95 (0-918100-05-4) Sri Rama.
Babbitt, James E., ed. Rainbow Trails: Adventures in Rainbow Bridge Country. Lancaster, John, intro. by. 120p. (Orig.). 1989. pap. 5.95 (0-317-93359-0) Glen Canyon Nat Hist Assn.
Babbitt, Lucy C. Children of the Maker. LC 88-45482. 208p. (gr. 6 up). 1988. 15.00 (0-374-31245-1) FS&G.
—Where the Truth Lies: A Novel. LC 92-34061. 208p. (gr. 7 up). 1993. 15.95 (0-531-05473-X); PLB 15.99 (0-531-08623-2) Orchard Bks Watts.
Babbitt, Natalie. Bub or The Very Best Thing. Babbitt, Natalie, illus. LC 93-78758. 32p. (gr. k up). 1994. 15.00 (0-06-205044-3); PLB 14.89 (0-06-205045-1) HarpC Child Bks.
—The Devil's Other Storybook. LC 86-32760. (Illus.). 112p. (gr. 3 up). 1987. 13.00 (0-374-31767-4) FS&G.
—Devil's Other Storybook. (gr. 4-7). 1989. pap. 3.50 (0-374-41704-0) FS&G.
—The Devil's Storybook. (Illus.). 102p. (gr. 3-7). 1974. 13.00 (0-374-31770-4) FS&G.
—The Devil's Storybook. Babbitt, Natalie, illus. LC 74-5488. 102p. (gr. 3-7). 1984. pap. 3.95 (0-374-41708-3) FS&G.

—The Eyes of the Amaryllis. LC 77-11862. 160p. (gr. 3 up). 1977. 14.00 (0-374-32241-4) FS&G.
—The Eyes of the Amaryllis. 128p. (gr. 3 up). 1986. pap. 3.95 (0-374-42238-9, Sunburst) FS&G.
—Goody Hall. (Illus.). 176p. (gr. 4 up). 1986. pap. 3.50 (0-374-42767-4) FS&G.
—Herbert Rowbarge. LC 82-18274. 216p. (gr. 9 up). 1982. 15.00 (0-374-32959-1); pap. 3.95, 1984 (0-374-51852-1, Sunburst) FS&G.
—Kneeknock Rise. Babbitt, Natalie, illus. LC 79-105622. 96p. (gr. 3 up). 1970. 15.00 (0-374-34257-1); pap. 3. 95, 1984 (0-374-44260-6, Sunburst) FS&G.
—Nellie: A Cat on Her Own. Babbitt, Natalie, illus. (ps up). 1989. 14.00 (0-374-35506-1) FS&G.
—Nellie: A Cat on Her Own. (Illus.). (ps-3). 1992. pap. 4.95 (0-374-45496-5, Sunburst) FS&G.
—Phoebe's Revolt. LC 68-13679. (Illus.). 40p. (ps up). 1988. pap. 3.95 (0-374-45792-1) FS&G.
—The Search for Delicious. Babbitt, Natalie, illus. LC 69-20374. 176p. (gr. 3 up). 1969. 15.00 (0-374-36534-2) FS&G.
—The Something. Babbitt, Natalie, illus. LC 70-125143. 40p. (ps-3). 1987. 11.00 (0-374-37137-7) FS&G.
—The Something. (Illus.). (ps-3). 1987. pap. 2.95 (0-374-46464-2) FS&G.
—Tuck Everlasting. LC 75-33306. 160p. (gr. 3 up). 1975. 15.00 (0-374-37848-7) FS&G.
—Tuck Everlasting. large type ed. 180p. (gr. 3-7). 1987. Repr. of 1975 ed. lib. bdg. 14.95 (1-55736-050-2, Crnrstn Bks); bk. & 3 audio cass. 35.95 (0-685-28641-X) BDD LT Grp.
—Tuck Everlasting. LC 75-33306. 160p. (gr. 3 up). 1985. pap. 3.95 (0-374-48009-5, Sunburst) FS&G.
—Tuck Para Siempre: Tuck Everlasting. Fradera, Narcis, tr. (SPA.). 158p. (gr. 5 up). 1991. 13.95 (0-374-37849-5) FS&G.
—Tuck Para Siempre: Tuck Everlasting. (gr. 4-7). 1993. pap. 3.95 (0-374-48011-7) FS&G.
Babcock, Carl, ed. see Barber, Jacqueline & Willard, Carolyn.
Babcock, Chris. No Moon, No Milk! Teague, Mark, illus. LC 92-40697. 32p. (ps-2). 1993. 12.00 (0-517-58779-3); PLB 12.99 (0-517-58780-7) Crown Bks Yng Read.
Babel, Issac. Benya Krik, the Gangster & Other Stories. Yarmolinsky, Avraham, ed. Guerney, Bernard G., tr. from RUS. LC 70-101637. 128p. (gr. 4 up). 1988. pap. 8.95 (0-8052-0244-7) Wiener Pubs Inc.
Baber, Carolyn S. Pony. Fleischman, Luke T., illus. 22p. 1990. pap. 9.95 (0-9628937-0-6, TX2910777) Richmond Saddlery.
Babin, Veronique. Enciclopedia Mega-Chiquitin. (SPA., Illus.). 116p. (ps-2). 1993. Repr. of 1989 ed. 9.95 (970-607-181-4) CKG Pubs.
Babisch, Donald. Who Is That Peeking in My Windows. Caroland, Mary, ed. LC 90-83590. (Illus.). 44p. 1991. pap. 4.95 (1-55523-374-0) Winston-Derek.
Babor, Thomas. Alcohol: Customs & Rituals. updated ed. (Illus.). (gr. 5 up). 1992. lib. bdg. 19.95 (0-685-52235-0) Chelsea Hse.

Babson, Jane F. Babson's Bestiary. Babson, Jane F., illus. LC 90-71155. 32p. (ps-4). 1991. casebound 10.95 (0-940787-02-4) Winstead Pr. Second in a learning to read series for children & adults. Illustrated with original art, writing designed to stimulate interest, curiosity & intellectual skills. Thought-provoking. Acid-free paper. Special discounts to libraries, literacy programs. "The art book offers a superior presentation... includes some fun animal rhymes within the alphabet form...intriguing, unusual art.--THE MIDWEST BOOK REVIEW. "Attractive alphabet primer with its well-executed illustrations, a fun & funny book about animals."-- THE BLOOMSBURY REVIEW. *Publisher Provided Annotation.*

—The Nest on the Porch. Babson, Jane F., illus. LC 88-51084. 32p. (Orig.). (ps up). 1989. pap. 4.95 (0-940787-01-6) Winstead Pr.
Babyak, Jolene. Reportage uber Alcatraz: Die Geschichte der Gefangnisinsel erzahlt von Fruheren Bewohnern. Chestnut, Renate, tr. from ENG. (GER., Illus.). 30p. (Orig.). 1991. pap. 11.95 (0-9618752-1-6) Ariel Vamp Pr.
Bach, Alice. The Bully of Library Place. (Orig.). 1988. pap. 2.95 (0-440-40030-9, YB) Dell.
—Double Bucky Shanghai. (Orig.). (gr. k-6). 1987. pap. 2.95 (0-440-41996-4, YB) Dell.
—Miriam's Well. 1991. 16.00 (0-385-30435-8) Delacorte.
—Parrot Woman. (Orig.). (gr. k-6). 1987. pap. 2.95 (0-440-46987-2, YB) Dell.
—Ragwars. (Orig.). (gr. k-6). 1987. pap. 2.95 (0-440-47345-4, YB) Dell.

Bach, Alice & Exum, Cheryl. Moses' Ark: Stories from the Bible. Dillon, Leo & Dillon, Diane, illus. (gr. 4-8). 1989. 14.95 (0-685-30899-5) Delacorte.
Bach, Alice & Exum, J. Cheryl. Moses & Noah's Ark: Stories from the Bible. Dillon, Leo & Dillon, Diane, illus. LC 89-1069. 181p. 1989. 14.95 (0-385-29778-5) Delacorte.
Bach, Jennifer & Brost, Amy. The Great Zopper Toothpaste Treasure. 64p. (Orig.). (gr. 5 up). 1988. pap. 2.50 (0-553-15583-0, Skylark) Bantam.
Bach, Julie. Hillary Clinton. LC 93-15325. (Illus.). 1993. 12.94 (1-56239-221-2) Abdo & Dghtrs.
—Princess Diana. Wallner, Rosemary, ed. LC 91-73026. 202p. 1991. 12.94 (1-56239-081-3) Abdo & Dghtrs.
—Tipper Gore. LC 93-15326. (Illus.). 1993. 12.94 (1-56239-220-4) Abdo & Dghtrs.
—Tom Cruise. LC 93-3981. (gr. 4 up). 1993. 12.94 (1-56239-228-X) Abdo & Dghtrs.
Bach, Julie & Modl, Tom, eds. Religion in America: Opposing Viewpoints. LC 88-24359. (Illus.). 250p. (gr. 10 up). 1988. PLB 17.95 (0-89908-437-0); pap. text ed. 9.95 (0-89908-412-5) Greenhaven.
Bach, Julie, ed. see Kincher, Jonni.
Bach, Marcus. I, Monty. 3rd ed. (Illus.). 94p. (gr. 1-6). 1985. Repr. of 1977 ed. deluxe ed. 8.95 (0-89610-000-6) ARE Pr.
—I, Monty. LC 77-82232. 94p. 1992. Repr. 12.95 (0-87516-648-2) DeVorss.
Bach, Richard. Jonathan Livingston Seagull. 128p. (gr. 7 up). 1976. pap. 4.99 (0-380-01286-3) Avon.
Bachelder, Marvin. Snow Treasure: A Study Guide. Friedland, Joyce & Kessler, Rikki, eds. (gr. 5-7). 1991. pap. text ed. 14.95 (0-88122-582-7) LRN Links.
Bachelis, Faren M. El Salvador. LC 89-25419. (Illus.). 128p. (gr. 5-9). 1990. PLB 26.60 (0-516-02718-2) Childrens.
Bacheller, Irving. Lost in the Fog. Krupinski, Loretta, adapted by. & illus. LC 88-25923. (gr. k-3). 1990. 14.95 (0-316-07462-4) Little.
Bachelor, Evelyn, et al, eds. Teen Conflicts. Sullivan, N., pref. by. (Illus.). 240p. (Orig.). (gr. 8 up). 1972. 9.95 (0-87297-006-X); pap. 7.95 (0-87297-007-8) Diablo.
Bacher, June M. Love Follows the Heart. (Orig.). (gr. 9-12). 1990. pap. 6.99 (0-89081-748-0) Harvest Hse.
—Love Is a Gentle Stranger. LC 82-83839. 160p. (gr. 10 up). 1992. pap. 6.99 (0-89081-374-4); pap. 4.99 (0-89081-975-0) Harvest Hse.
—When Hearts Awaken. 192p. 1988. pap. 6.99 (0-89081-610-7) Harvest Hse.
Bachman, Barbara. Frisky Phonics Fun I. Bachman, Barbara, illus. 152p. (gr. 1-3). 1984. wkbk. 11.95 (0-86653-195-5, GA 548) Good Apple.
—Frisky Phonics Fun II. Bachman, Barbara, illus. 152p. (gr. 1-3). 1984. wkbk. 11.95 (0-86653-212-9, GA 549) Good Apple.
Bachmann, Bertha. Memories of Kazakhstan. Duin, Edgar C., tr. from GER. LC 83-73393. 160p. (gr. 7-12). 1984. pap. text ed. 10.50 (0-914222-12-0) Am Hist Soc Ger.
Bachrach, Deborah. Custer's Last Stand: Opposing Viewpoints. LC 90-36967. (Illus.). 112p. (gr. 5-8). 1990. PLB 14.95 (0-89908-077-4) Greenhaven.
—Espionage. LC 92-37438. (Illus.). 112p. (gr. 5-8). 1992. PLB 14.95 (1-56006-134-0) Lucent Bks.
—The Korean War. LC 91-23065. (Illus.). 112p. (gr. 5-8). 1991. PLB 17.95 (1-56006-409-9) Lucent Bks.
—Margaret Sanger. LC 92-46878. (Illus.). 112p. (gr. 5-8). 1993. PLB 14.95 (1-56006-032-8) Lucent Bks.
—Pearl Harbor: Opposing Viewpoints. LC 88-24288. (Illus.). 112p. (gr. 5-8). 1989. PLB 14.95 (0-89908-059-6) Greenhaven.
—The Spanish-American War. LC 91-16730. (Illus.). 112p. (gr. 5-8). 1991. PLB 17.95 (1-56006-405-6) Lucent Bks.
Bachrach, Kalman. Hasefer Alef-Beis Hametzuyar (In Color) Gordon, Ayalah, illus. (HEB.). 67p. (gr. 1). 1960. pap. text ed. 2.50x (1-878530-01-1) K Bachrach Co.
—Hasefer Chelek Rishon, Pt. 1: Alef-Beis. Soyer, Yitzhak, illus. (HEB.). 68p. (gr. 1). 1941. pap. text ed. 2.25x (1-878530-00-3) K Bachrach Co.
—Hasefer Chelek Sheini, Pt. 2. Krukman, Tsvi, illus. (HEB.). 91p. (gr. 2). 1942. pap. text ed. 2.25x (1-878530-09-7) K Bachrach Co.
—Hasefer Chelek Shlishi, Pt. 3. Krukman, Tsvi, illus. (HEB.). 73p. (gr. 3). 1947. pap. text ed. 2.25x (1-878530-10-0) K Bachrach Co.
—Me Ah P'Amim V'Echad - Asid (One Thousand Times & One - Future Tense) Dikduk L'Talmidim (Grammar for Students) (HEB.). 46p. (gr. 1-3). 1937. pap. text ed. 1.00x (1-878530-21-6) K Bachrach Co.
—Meyah P'Amim V'Echad - Haveh (One Thousand Times & One - Present Tense) Dikduk L'Talmidim (Grammar for Students) (HEB.). 32p. (gr. 1-3). 1937. pap. text ed. 1.00x (1-878530-22-4) K Bachrach Co.
—Meyah P'Amim V'Echad - Ovar (One Thousand Times & One - Past Tense) Dikduk L'Talmidim (Grammar for Students) (HEB.). 48p. (gr. 1-3). 1937. pap. text ed. 1.00x (1-878530-20-8) K Bachrach Co.
—Olami Sefer Rishon, Bk. 1. rev. ed. Krukman, Tsvi, illus. (HEB.). 59p. (gr. 2). 1943. pap. text ed. 2.00x (1-878530-14-3) K Bachrach Co.
—Olami Sefer Sheini, Bk. 2. rev. ed. Krukman, Tsvi, illus. (HEB.). 71p. (gr. 3-4). 1950. pap. text ed. 2.00x (1-878530-15-1) K Bachrach Co.
—Olami Sefer Shlishi, Bk. 3. Gutman, Nachum, illus. (HEB.). 92p. (gr. 4-6). 1936. pap. text ed. 2.00x (1-878530-16-X) K Bachrach Co.

—Targilon Hasefer Chelek Rishon, Pt. 1. (HEB.). 42p. (gr. 1). 1950. wkbk. 2.25x (1-878530-11-9) K Bachrach Co.
—Targilon Hasefer Chelek Sheini, Pt. 2. (HEB.). 76p. (gr. 1). 1949. wkbk. 2.25x (1-878530-12-7) K Bachrach Co.
—Targilon Hasefer Chelek Shlishi, Pt. 3. (HEB.). 60p. (gr. 3). 1953. wkbk. 2.25x (1-878530-13-5) K Bachrach Co.
—Targilon Olami Sefer Rishon, Bk. 1. (HEB.). 54p. (gr. 2). 1936. wkbk. 2.00x (1-878530-17-8) K Bachrach Co.
—Targilon Olami Sefer Sheini, Bk. 2. (HEB.). 54p. (gr. 3-4). 1936. wkbk. 2.00x (1-878530-18-6) K Bachrach Co.
—Targilon Olami Sefer Shlishi, Bk. 3. (HEB.). 60p. (gr. 4-6). 1939. wkbk. 2.00x (1-878530-19-4) K Bachrach Co.
Bachrach, Kalman & Axelrod, Herman. Ketivoni Chelek Chamishi, Pt. 5. Vanner, Vera, illus. (HEB.). 64p. (gr. 6). 1972. pap. text ed. 3.50x (1-878530-06-2) K Bachrach Co.
—Ketivoni Chelek Rishon, Pt. 1. Krukman, Tsvi, illus. (HEB.). 72p. (gr. 2). 1957. pap. text ed. 3.50x (1-878530-02-X) K Bachrach Co.
—Ketivoni Chelek R'Viyi, Pt. 4. Vanner, Vera, illus. (HEB.). 55p. (gr. 5). 1972. pap. text ed. 3.50x (1-878530-05-4) K Bachrach Co.
—Ketivoni Chelek Sheni, Pt. 2. Krukman, Tsvi, illus. (HEB.). 62p. (gr. 3). 1958. pap. text ed. 3.50x (1-878530-03-8) K Bachrach Co.
—Ketivoni Chelek Shishi, Pt. 6. Herskowitz, Sarah, illus. (HEB.). 62p. (gr. 7). 1974. pap. text ed. 3.50x (1-878530-07-0) K Bachrach Co.
—Ketivoni Chelek Shlishi, Pt. 3. Hershkowitz, Sarah, illus. (HEB.). 64p. (gr. 4). 1959. pap. text ed. 3.50x (1-878530-04-6) K Bachrach Co.
—Ketivoni Chelek Sh'Viyi, Pt. 7. Hershkowitz, Sarah, illus. (HEB.). 64p. (gr. 8). 1974. pap. text ed. 3.50x (1-878530-08-9) K Bachrach Co.
Back, Christine. Bean & Plant. LC 86-9634. (Illus.). 25p. (gr. 2-5). 1986. PLB 9.98 (0-382-09286-4); pap. 3.95 (0-382-24014-6) Silver Burdett Pr.
—Chicken & Egg. LC 86-10019. (Illus.). 25p. (gr. k-4). 1991. 6.95 (0-382-09292-9); PLB 9.98 (0-382-09284-8); pap. 3.95 (0-382-09959-1) Silver Burdett.
Back, Christine & Watts, Barrie. Spider's Web. LC 86-10017. (Illus.). 25p. (gr. k-4). 1986. pap. 3.95 (0-382-24020-0) Silver Burdett Pr.
—Tadpole & Frog. LC 86-10049. (Illus.). 25p. (gr. k-4). 1986. 6.95 (0-382-09293-7); PLB 9.98 (0-382-09285-6); pap. 3.95 (0-382-24021-9) Silver Burdett Pr.
Backhouse, Halcyon. The Incredible Journey. LC 92-33820. (Illus.). 1993. 9.99 (0-8407-9403-7) Nelson.
—Noah's Story. Press, Jenny, illus. LC 92-952. 1992. 7.99 (0-8407-3417-4) Oliver-Nelson.
Backhouse, Robert. The Big Book of Bible Facts. LC 92-32366. 1993. 9.99 (0-8407-7743-4) Oliver-Nelson.
Backker, Vera De see De Backker, Vera.
Backman, Aidel. One Night, One Hanukkah Night. (Illus.). 32p. (ps-2). 1990. 14.95 (0-8276-0368-1) JPS Phila.
Backman, Margaret E. Coping with Choosing a Therapist: A Young Person's Guide to Counseling & Psychotherapy. LC 93-29661. 1993. write for info. (0-8239-1699-5) Rosen Group.
Backovsky, Jan. Trouble in Paradise. LC 91-47930. (Illus.). 32p. (ps up) 1992. 14.00 (0-688-11857-7, Tambourine Bks); PLB 13.93 (0-688-11858-5, Tambourine Bks) Morrow.
Backstein, Karen. The Blind Men & the Elephant, Level 3. 1992. 2.95 (0-590-45813-2) Scholastic Inc.
—Little Chick's Easter Surprise. (ps-3). 1993. pap. 4.95 (0-590-46263-6) Scholastic Inc.
Backus, Mary L. All the Way Around Green Lake. Newman, Sheila, illus. 24p. (Orig.). (ps). 1984. pap. write for info. (0-9613400-0-2) Grnwillow End.
Bacom, Paul see Tunis, John R.
Bacon. Wind. 1993. pap. 28.67 (0-590-72703-6) Scholastic Inc.
Bacon, Josephine. Cooking the Israeli Way. Wolfe, Bob, et al, illus. LC 85-18059. 48p. (gr. 5 up). 1986. PLB 14.95 (0-8225-0912-1) Lerner Pubns.
Bacon, Joy. Oliver Bean. Weinberger, Jane, ed. DeVito, Pam, illus. LC 90-70907. 68p. (ps-3). 1991. 12.95 (0-932433-71-5); pap. 9.95 (0-932433-73-1) Windswept Hse.
Bacon, Katharine J. Shadow & Light. LC 86-23789. 208p. (gr. 7 up). 1987. SBE 14.95 (0-689-50431-4, M K McElderry) Macmillan Child Grp.
Bacon, M. Songs That Every Child Should Know. (ps-6). 1972. 59.95 (0-8490-1086-1) Gordon Pr.
Bacon, Ron. The Bone Tree. Wilson, Mark, illus. LC 93-20806. 1994. 4.25 (0-383-03738-7) SRA Schl Grp.
—Fish of Our Fathers. 1989. 11.95 (0-85953-301-8) Childs Play.
—Home of the Winds. LC 90-45701. 1989. 11.95 (0-85953-302-6) Childs Play.
—House of the People. LC 90-46408. 1989. 11.95 (0-85953-300-X) Childs Play.
—Wash Day. Greenstein, Susan, illus. LC 92-34270. 1993. 2.50 (0-383-03665-8) SRA Schl Grp.
Baczewski, Paul. Just for Kicks. LC 90-30528. 192p. (gr. 6 up). 1990. 13.95 (0-397-32465-0, Lipp Jr Bks); PLB 13.89 (0-397-32466-9, Lipp Jr Bks) HarpC Child Bks.

Baczewski, Paul C. Just for Kicks. LC 90-30528. 192p. (gr. 7 up). 1992. pap. 3.95 (0-06-447074-1, Trophy) HarpC Child Bks.
Badcock, J., jt. auth. see Tingay, G. I.
Badcock, John & Tingay, Graham. The Romans & Their Empire. (Illus.). 75p. (Orig.). (gr. 6-8). 1992. pap. 14.95x (0-7487-1186-4, Pub. by S Thornes UK) Dufour.
Badcock, John, jt. auth. see Tingay, Graham I.
Baden. The Greatest Gift Is Love. LC 59-1314. 24p. (gr. k-4). 1985. pap. 1.89 (0-570-06196-2) Concordia.
Baden, Robert. Adam & His Family. (Illus.). 24p. (gr. k-4). 1986. pap. 1.89 (0-570-06198-9, 59-1421) Concordia.
—And Sunday Makes Seven. Mathews, Judith, ed. Edwards, Michelle, illus. LC 89-37823. 40p. (ps-3). 1990. 13.95 (0-8075-0356-8) A Whitman.
—Caleb, God's Special Spy. (Illus.). 24p. (Orig.). (ps-4). 1993. pap. 1.89 (0-570-09031-8) Concordia.
—The Coming of the Holy Spirit. (Illus.). 24p. (Orig.). (ps-4). 1992. pap. 1.89 (0-570-09029-6) Concordia.
—Y Domingo, Siete. Mathews, Judith, ed. Ada, Alma F., tr. Edwards, Michelle, illus. LC 89-37823. (SPA.). 40p. (ps-3). 1990. 13.95 (0-8075-9355-9) A Whitman.
Baden-Powell, Robert. My Adventures As a Spy. Baden-Powell, Robert, illus. 132p. (Orig.). Date not set. pap. 16.95 (0-9632054-8-X) Stevens Pub.
—Scouting for Boys: A Handbook for Instruction in Good Citizenship. Baden-Powell, Robert, illus. 273p. (Orig.). 1992. pap. 17.95 (0-9632054-1-2) Stevens Pub.
Bader, Barbara, retold by. Aesop & Company: With Scenes from His Legendary Life. Geisert, Arthur, illus. 64p. 1991. 16.45 (0-395-50597-6, Sandpiper) HM.
Bader, Bonnie. East Side Story. Golub, Sean, illus. 80p. (gr. 4-6). 1993. PLB 12.95 (1-881889-22-X) Silver Moon.
—Golden Quest. LC 93-16461. 64p. (Orig.). (gr. 3-5). 1993. PLB 12.95 (1-881889-30-0) Silver Moon.
—A Philadelphia Story. 80p. (gr. 4-6). 1994. PLB 12.95 (1-881889-51-3) Silver Moon.
Baehr, Patricia. Louisa Eclipsed. LC 88-17709. 160p. (gr. 7 up). 1988. 12.95 (0-688-07682-3) Morrow Jr Bks.
—Mouse in the House. Lydecker, Laura, illus. LC 93-4068. (ps-3). 1994. write for info. (0-8234-1102-8) Holiday.
—School Isn't Fair! Alley, R. W., illus. LC 88-21461. 32p. (ps-k). 1989. RSBE 13.95 (0-02-708130-3, Four Winds) Macmillan Child Grp.
—School Isn't Fair. Alley, R. W., illus. LC 91-38485. 32p. (ps-k). 1992. pap. 4.95 (0-689-71544-7, Aladdin) Macmillan Child Grp.
Baender, Margaret W. Tail Waggings of Maggie. Hinkle, Janet W., illus. 64p. (gr. 8-10). 1982. pap. 6.00x (0-88100-012-4) Philmar Pub.
Baer, Edith. This Is the Way We Go to School. 40p. (ps-2). 1990. 14.95 (0-590-43161-7) Scholastic Inc.
—This Is the Way We Go to School. Bjorkman, Steve, illus. 32p. (ps-1). 1992. pap. 3.95 (0-590-43162-5, Blue Ribbon Bks) Scholastic Inc.
—The Wonder of Hands. rev. & reissued ed. Hoban, Tana, illus. LC 91-31351. 48p. (ps-1). 1992. RSBE 12.95 (0-02-708138-9, Macmillan Child Bk) Macmillan Child Grp.
Baer, Gene. Have You Seen My Finger? Baer, Gene, illus. LC 91-61251. 16p. (ps-k). 1992. 5.99 (0-679-81382-9) Random Bks Yng Read.
—Thump Thump Rat-a-Tat-Tat. LC 88-28469. (Illus.). 32p. (ps-1). 1989. PLB 14.89 (0-06-020362-5) HarpC Child Bks.
—Thump, Thump, Rat-a-Tat-Tat. Ehlert, Lois, illus. LC 88-28469. 32p. (ps-1). 1991. pap. 4.95 (0-06-443265-3, Trophy) HarpC Child Bks.
—Thump, Thump, Rat-a-Tat-Tat Big Book. Ehlert, Lois, illus. LC 88-28469. 32p. (ps-1). 1992. 19.95 (0-694-00386-7) HarpC Child Bks.
Baer, Judy. Adrienne. LC 87-71605. 176p. (Orig.). (gr. 7-12). 1987. pap. 3.99 (0-87123-949-3) Bethany Hse.
—Broken Promises. 128p. (Orig.). (gr. 7 up). 1989. pap. 3.99 (1-55661-087-4) Bethany Hse.
—Cedar River Daydreams, Bks. 1-5. (Orig.). 1991. Giftset. 19.99 (1-55661-763-1) Bethany Hse.
—Cedar River Daydreams, Bks. 6-10. (Orig.). 1991. Giftset. 19.99 (1-55661-764-X) Bethany Hse.
—Cedar River Daydreams, Bks. 11-15. (Orig., Set incls. Something Old, Something New, Vanishing Star, No Turning Back, Second Chance & Lost & Found). (gr. 7-10). 1992. Giftset. pap. 19.99 (1-55661-765-8) Bethany Hse.
—Cedar River Daydreams 16-20 Giftset. 1993. 19.99 (1-55661-772-0) Bethany Hse.
—Dear Judy, Did You Ever Like a Boy Who Didn't Like You? 1993. pap. 7.99 (1-55661-341-5) Bethany Hse.
—Dear Judy, What's It Like at Your House? 160p. (Orig.). (gr. 7-10). 1992. pap. 7.99 (1-55661-291-5) Bethany Hse.
—The Discovery. 144p. (Orig.). 1993. pap. 3.99 (1-55661-330-X) Bethany Hse.
—Fill My Empty Heart. 128p. (Orig.). (gr. 7-10). 1990. pap. 3.99 (1-55661-128-5) Bethany Hse.
—The Intruder. 160p. (Orig.). (gr. 7 up). 1989. pap. 3.99 (1-55661-088-2) Bethany Hse.
—Jennifer's Secret. LC 88-63463. 128p. (Orig.). (gr. 6 up). 1989. pap. 3.99 (1-55661-058-0) Bethany Hse.
—Journey to Nowhere. LC 88-63462. 144p. (Orig.). (gr. 6 up). 1989. pap. 3.99 (1-55661-067-X) Bethany Hse.
—Lonely Girl. 144p. (Orig.). (gr. 7-10). 1992. pap. 3.99 (1-55661-280-X) Bethany Hse.
—Lost & Found. 144p. (Orig.). (gr. 7-10). 1992. pap. 3.99 (1-55661-243-5) Bethany Hse.

—More Than Friends. 144p. (gr. 7-10). 1992. pap. 3.99 (*1-55661-298-2*) Bethany Hse.
—Never Too Late. 144p. (Orig.). 1993. pap. 3.99 (*1-55661-329-6*) Bethany Hse.
—New Girl in Town. LC 88-71504. 176p. (Orig.). (gr. 10-12). 1988. pap. 3.99 (*1-55661-022-X*) Bethany Hse.
—No Turning Back. 144p. (Orig.). 1991. 3.99 (*1-55661-216-8*) Bethany Hse.
—Paige. LC 86-70912. 160p. (Orig.). (gr. 7-9). 1986. pap. 3.99 (*0-87123-894-2*) Bethany Hse.
—Riddles of Love-Sweet Dreams No. 63: Kiss Me Creep. 1991. pap. 2.50 (*0-553-30233-7*) Bantam.
—Second Chance. 144p. (Orig.). (gr. 7-10). 1991. 3.99 (*1-55661-217-6*) Bethany Hse.
—Silent Tears No More. LC 89-82689. 144p. (Orig.). (gr. 7-10). 1990. 3.99 (*1-55661-119-6*) Bethany Hse.
—Something Old, Something New. 144p. (Orig.). (gr. 7-9). 1991. pap. 3.99 (*1-55661-183-8*) Bethany Hse.
—Special Kind of Love. 1993. pap. 3.99 (*1-55661-367-9*) Bethany Hse.
—Tomorrow's Promise. 144p. (Orig.). (gr. 6-9). 1990. pap. 3.99 (*1-55661-143-9*) Bethany Hse.
—Trouble with a Capital T. LC 88-71503. 176p. (Orig.). (gr. 10-12). 1988. pap. 3.99 mass market (*1-55661-021-1*) Bethany Hse.
—Unheard Voices. 144p. (Orig.). (gr. 7-10). 1992. pap. 3.99 (*1-55661-257-5*) Bethany Hse.
—Vanishing Star. 144p. (Orig.). (gr. 7-9). 1991. pap. 3.99 (*1-55661-197-8*) Bethany Hse.
—Yesterday's Dream. 144p. (Orig.). (gr. 8-10). 1990. pap. 3.99 (*1-55661-142-0*) Bethany Hse.
Baer, Ruth. Creation to Canaan, Bk. 1. (gr. 7). 1979. 9.80 (*0-686-30770-4*); tchr's. ed. avail. 6.40 (*0-686-30771-2*) Rod & Staff.
Baez, Josefina. Por Que Mi Nombre Es Marisol? Un Cuento De la Republica Dominicana. Guerrero, Alex, illus. (SPA.). 24p. (Orig.). (gr. k-3). 1993. pap. 12.95 (*1-882161-01-7*) Latinarte.
—Why Is My Name Marisol? A Dominican Children's Story. Guerrero, Alex, illus. 24p. (Orig.). (gr. k-3). 1993. pap. 12.95 (*1-882161-02-5*) Latinarte.
Baez, Kjersti H. Corrie Ten Boom. (Illus.). 224p. (gr. 3 up). 1989. pap. 2.50 perfect bdg. (*1-55748-102-4*) Barbour & Co.
Bagchi, Santosh, tr. see Vishwashrayananda, Swami.
Bagdon, Paul. Scrapper John: Rendezvous at Skull Mountain. 128p. (Orig.). 1992. pap. 3.50 (*0-380-76418-0*, Camelot) Avon.
—Scrapper John: Showdown at Burnt Rock. 128p. (Orig.). (gr. 6). 1992. pap. 3.50 (*0-380-76417-2*, Camelot) Avon.
—Scrapper John: Valley of the Spotted Horse. (gr. 4-7). 1992. pap. 3.50 (*0-380-76416-4*, Camelot) Avon.
Bagert, Brod. Chicken Socks: And Other Contagious Poems. Ellis, Tim, illus. 32p. (gr. 3-7). 1994. 15.95 (*1-56397-292-1*) Boyds Mills Pr.
—Let Me Be the Boss. Smith, Gerald, illus. LC 91-91408. 48p. (gr. 3-7). 1992. 14.95 (*1-56397-099-6*, Wordsong) Boyds Mills Pr.
Baggett, Nancy, jt. auth. see Settel, Joanne.
Baggiani, J. M. & Tewell, V. M. The Chess Set & Other Stories. Birt, Jane L., illus. 21p. (gr. 2-3). 1966. pap. 3.50 (*0-934329-07-9*) Baggiani-Tewell.
—In the Country. Birt, Jane L., illus. 26p. (gr. 2-4). 1966. pap. 3.50 (*0-934329-08-7*) Baggiani-Tewell.
—Phonics; a Tool for Better Reading & Spelling, Bk. I. Birt, Jane L., illus. (gr. 1-2). 1982. pap. 9.50 student's copy (*0-934329-00-1*); tchr's. manual 10.75 (*0-934329-01-X*) Baggiani-Tewell.
—Phonics: A Tool for Better Reading & Spelling, Bk. II. Jacobson, Mary M., illus. (gr. 3-6). 1967. pap. 3.50 (*0-934329-02-8*); wkbk. 2.00 (*0-934329-03-6*) Baggiani-Tewell.
—Phonics: A Tool for Better Reading & Spelling, Bk. III. Jacobson, Mary M. & Davis, Mary I., illus. (gr. 5-12). 1984. pap. 5.75 (*0-934329-04-4*); wkbk. 4.00 (*0-934329-05-2*) Baggiani-Tewell.
—Read & Draw. Birt, Jane L., illus. 12p. (gr. 1-3). 1966. pap. 2.00 (*0-934329-06-0*) Baggiani-Tewell.
Bagley. Suppose the Wolf Were an Octopus: Grades 3-4. 1992. 9.99 (*0-89824-096-4*) Trillium Pr.
—Suppose the Wolf Were an Octopus: Grades 5-6. 1992. 9.99 (*0-89824-097-2*) Trillium Pr.
Bagley & Foley. Suppose the Wolf Were an Octopus: Grades K-2. 1992. 9.99 (*0-89824-087-5*) Trillium Pr.
Bagley, Pat. If You Were a Boy in the Time of the Nephites. Bagley, Pat, illus. 48p. (gr. 3-6). 1989. pap. 4.95 (*0-87579-250-2*) Deseret Bk.
—If You Were a Girl in the Time of the Nephites. Bagley, Pat, illus. 48p. (gr. 3-6). 1989. pap. 4.95 (*0-87579-249-9*) Deseret Bk.
—Norman the Nephite & Rover-Hah Coloring Book. Bagley, Pat, illus. 32p. (Orig.). (gr. 1-6). 1992. pap. 1.95 (*0-87579-673-7*) Deseret Bk.
—Where Have All the Nephites Gone? Bagley, Pat, illus. (gr. 3-12). 1993. 12.95 (*0-87579-757-1*) Deseret Bk.
Baglio, Ben. The First Olympics, No. 77. 176p. (Orig.). (gr. 7 up). 1988. pap. 3.25 (*0-553-27063-X*) Bantam.
Bagnold, Enid. National Velvet. 293p. 1981. Repr. PLB 16.95x (*0-89966-359-1*) Buccaneer Bks.
—National Velvet. 339p. 1981. Repr. PLB 18.95 (*0-89967-033-4*) Harmony Raine.
—National Velvet. Lewin, Ted, illus. LC 85-2982. 207p. (gr. 3 up). 1985. 15.95 (*0-688-05788-8*) Morrow Jr Bks.
—National Velvet. large type ed. 304p. 1990. Repr. lib. bdg. 15.95 (*1-55736-175-4*, Crnrstn Bks) BDD LT Grp.

—National Velvet. 272p. 1991. pap. 3.99 (*0-380-71235-0*, Flare) Avon.
Bagwell, Joyce B. Low Country Quake Tales. 88p. 1986. pap. 7.50 (*0-89308-593-6*, SC 84) Southern Hist Pr.
Bahar, Mehrdad. Bastoor. new & rev. ed. Jabbari, Ahmad, ed. Alyeshmreni, Mansoor, tr. from PER. LC 83-60451. (Illus.). 32p. (Orig.). (gr. 1 up). 1983. pap. 4.95 (*0-939214-17-2*) Mazda Pubs.
Baha'u'llah. Blessed Is the Spot. Stevenson, Anna, illus. LC 58-8815. (gr. k-2). 1958. 14.50 (*0-87743-014-4*, 352-040) Bahai.
Bahlinger, Nanette M. The Jekyll Island Historic District Coloring Book. Bahlinger, Nanette M., illus. 32p. (Orig.). (gr. 5). 1993. wkbk. 4.00 (*0-9638256-1-5*) N M Bahlinger.
Bahous, Sally. Sitti & the Cats. LC 98-80262. 24p. (gr. 3-6). 1993. 13.95x (*1-879373-61-0*) R Rinehart.
Bahr, Amy C., ed. see Durrell, Julie.
Bahr, Amy C., ed. see Tannenbaum, D. Leb.
Bahr, Mary. The Memory Box. Tucker, Kathleen, ed. Cunningham, David, illus. LC 91-21628. 32p. (gr. 1-4). 1992. PLB 13.95 (*0-8075-5052-3*) A Whitman.
Bailer, Darice. Puffin's Homecoming: The Story of an Atlantic Puffin. Thomas, Peter, narrated by. Lee, Katie, illus. LC 92-43762. 32p. (ps-3). 1993. 11.95 (*0-924483-90-3*); incl. audiocassette tape 16.95 (*0-924483-91-1*); incl. audiocassette tape & 7" toy 25. 95 (*0-924483-92-X*); incl. audiocassette tape & 11" toy 39.95 (*0-924483-93-8*); audiocassette tape only avail. (*0-924483-94-6*) Soundprints.
Bailes, Edith G. But Will It Bite Me? A Reference Book of Insects for Children & Their Grownups. 112p. (Orig.). (gr. 1-6). 1985. pap. 9.95 (*0-9611118-1-X*) Cardamom.
Bailey, jt. auth. see Draper.
Bailey, Anne. Burn Up. 144p. (gr. 7 up). 1992. pap. 4.95 (*0-571-16504-4*) Faber & Faber.
—Israel's Babe. 144p. 1991. 16.95 (*0-571-16243-6*) Faber & Faber.
Bailey, Bobbi M. The Christmas Tree That Cried. (Illus.). 36p. (gr. k-6). 1982. 11.95 (*0-9625005-0-X*) Wee Pr.
—Emma's Happy Birthday Piano. DeFazio, Deborah, illus. 36p. (gr. k-4). 1991. pap. 7.95 (*0-9625005-1-8*) Wee Pr.
Bailey, Carolyn S. The Little Rabbit Who Wanted Red Wings. Santoro, Chris, illus. 32p. (ps-1). 1988. pap. 2.25 (*0-448-19089-3*, Platt & Munk); (Platt & Munk) Putnam Pub Group.
—Miss Hickory. Gannett, Ruth, illus. LC 46-7275. (gr. 4-7). 1977. pap. 3.99 (*0-14-030956-X*, Puffin) Puffin Bks.
—Miss Hickory. Gannett, Ruth, illus. (gr. 4-7). 1946. pap. 14.00 (*0-670-47940-3*) Viking Child Bks.
Bailey, Debbie. Brothers. Huszar, Susan, photos by. (Illus.). 14p. 1993. text ed. 4.95 (*1-55037-274-2*, Pub. by Annick CN) Firefly Bks Ltd.
—Hermanas - Sisters. Huszar, Susan, illus. (SPA.). 14p. 1993. 4.95 (*1-55037-307-2*, Pub. by Annick CN) Firefly Bks Ltd.
—Hermanos - Brothers. Huszar, Susan, illus. (SPA.). 14p. 1993. 4.95 (*1-55037-308-0*, Pub. by Annick CN) Firefly Bks Ltd.
—Sisters. Huszar, Susan, illus. 14p. 1993. text ed. 4.95 (*1-55037-275-0*, Pub. by Annick CN) Firefly Bks Ltd.
—The Talk-about-Books Series, 6 vols. Huszar, Susan, photos by. (Illus.). 14p. (ps-k). 1991. bds. 4.95 ea. (Pub. by Annick CN) Toys (*1-55037-165-7*) Hats (*1-55037-159-2*) Shoes (*1-55037-161-4*) Clothes (*1-55037-167-3*) My Mom (*1-55037-163-0*) My Dad. 4.95 (*1-55037-164-9*) Firefly Bks Ltd.
Bailey, Donna. All about Birth & Growth. LC 90-10134. (Illus.). 48p. (gr. 2-6). 1990. PLB 17.28 (*0-8114-2777-3*) Raintree Steck-V.
—All about Digestion. LC 90-41010. (Illus.). 48p. (gr. 2-6). 1990. PLB 17.28 (*0-8114-2781-1*) Raintree Steck-V.
—All about Heart & Blood. LC 90-10052. (Illus.). 48p. (gr. 2-6). 1990. PLB 17.28 (*0-8114-2779-X*) Raintree Steck-V.
—All about Skin, Hair & Teeth. LC 90-10050. (Illus.). 48p. (gr. 2-6). 1990. PLB 17.28 (*0-8114-2783-8*) Raintree Steck-V.
—All about Your Brain. LC 90-41008. (Illus.). 48p. (gr. 2-6). 1990. PLB 17.28 (*0-8114-2778-1*) Raintree Steck-V.
—All about Your Lungs. LC 90-41009. (Illus.). 48p. (gr. 2-6). 1990. PLB 17.28 (*0-8114-2782-X*) Raintree Steck-V.
—All about Your Senses. LC 90-10051. (Illus.). 48p. (gr. 2-6). 1990. PLB 17.28 (*0-8114-2776-5*) Raintree Steck-V.
—All about Your Skeleton. LC 90-10114. (Illus.). 48p. (gr. 2-6). 1990. PLB 17.28 (*0-8114-2780-3*) Raintree Steck-V.
—Australia. LC 89-26124. (Illus.). 32p. (gr. 1-4). 1990. PLB 15.96 (*0-8114-2547-9*); pap. 3.95 (*0-8114-7175-6*) Raintree Steck-V.
—Bears. LC 89-22015. (Illus.). 32p. (gr. 1-4). 1990. PLB 15.96 (*0-8114-2633-5*); pap. 3.95 (*0-8114-4614-X*) Raintree Steck-V.
—Birds. LC 89-21755. (Illus.). 48p. (gr. 2-6). 1990. PLB 17.28 (*0-8114-2509-6*) Raintree Steck-V.
—Butterflies. LC 89-22016. (Illus.). 32p. (gr. 1-4). 1990. PLB 15.96 (*0-8114-2635-1*); pap. 3.95 (*0-8114-4609-3*) Raintree Steck-V.
—Camels. LC 90-22109. (Illus.). 32p. (gr. 1-4). 1992. PLB 15.96 (*0-8114-2644-0*) Raintree Steck-V.

—Canada. LC 91-21292. (Illus.). 32p. (gr. 1-4). 1992. PLB 15.96 (*0-8114-2568-1*); pap. 3.95 (*0-8114-7181-0*) Raintree Steck-V.
—Canoeing. LC 90-23055. (Illus.). 32p. (gr. 1-4). 1991. PLB 15.96 (*0-8114-2903-2*); pap. 3.95 (*0-8114-4706-5*) Raintree Steck-V.
—Cars, Trucks, & Trains. LC 89-21736. (Illus.). 48p. (gr. 2-6). 1990. PLB 17.28 (*0-8114-2505-3*); pap. 4.95 (*0-8114-6625-6*) Raintree Steck-V.
—Cities. LC 89-26153. (Illus.). 48p. (gr. 2-6). 1990. PLB 17.28 (*0-8114-2515-0*) Raintree Steck-V.
—Cycling. LC 90-36488. (Illus.). 32p. (gr. 1-4). 1990. PLB 15.96 (*0-8114-2855-9*); pap. 3.95 (*0-8114-4712-X*) Raintree Steck-V.
—Dancing. LC 90-23057. (Illus.). 32p. (gr. 1-4). 1991. PLB 15.96 (*0-8114-2902-4*); pap. 3.95 (*0-8114-4707-3*) Raintree Steck-V.
—Los Delfines. LC 91-23779. (SPA., Illus.). 32p. (gr. 1-4). 1992. PLB 14.64 (*0-8114-2656-4*) Raintree Steck-V.
—Deserts. LC 89-26120. (Illus.). 48p. (gr. 2-6). 1990. PLB 17.28 (*0-8114-2511-8*) Raintree Steck-V.
—Dolphins. LC 90-22110. (Illus.). 32p. (gr. 1-4). 1992. PLB 15.96 (*0-8114-2647-5*); pap. 3.95 (*0-8114-4616-6*) Raintree Steck-V.
—Energy All Around Us. LC 90-39294. (Illus.). 48p. (gr. 2-6). 1990. PLB 17.28 (*0-8114-2520-7*) Raintree Steck-V.
—Energy for Our Bodies. LC 90-39295. (Illus.). 48p. (gr. 2-6). 1990. PLB 17.28 (*0-8114-2521-5*) Raintree Steck-V.
—Energy from Oil & Gas. LC 90-39300. (Illus.). 48p. (gr. 2-6). 1990. PLB 17.28 (*0-8114-2518-5*) Raintree Steck-V.
—Energy from Wind & Water. LC 90-39388. (Illus.). 48p. (gr. 2-6). 1990. PLB 17.28 (*0-8114-2519-3*) Raintree Steck-V.
—Facts About: Space. (gr. 4-7). 1993. pap. 4.95 (*0-8114-6628-0*) Raintree Steck-V.
—Facts About: The Far Planets. (ps-3). 1993. pap. 4.95 (*0-8114-5200-X*) Raintree Steck-V.
—Facts About: The Near Planets. (ps-3). 1993. pap. 4.95 (*0-8114-5201-8*) Raintree Steck-V.
—Families. LC 89-29232. (Illus.). 48p. (gr. 2-6). 1990. PLB 17.28 (*0-8114-2514-2*) Raintree Steck-V.
—Far Out in Space. LC 90-40083. (Illus.). 48p. (gr. 2-6). 1990. PLB 17.28 (*0-8114-2525-8*) Raintree Steck-V.
—The Far Planets. LC 90-40081. (Illus.). 48p. (gr. 2-6). 1990. PLB 17.28 (*0-8114-2524-X*) Raintree Steck-V.
—Farmers. LC 89-26149. (Illus.). 48p. (gr. 2-6). 1990. PLB 17.28 (*0-8114-2517-7*) Raintree Steck-V.
—Fish. LC 89-21757. (Illus.). 48p. (gr. 2-6). 1990. PLB 17.28 (*0-8114-2508-8*) Raintree Steck-V.
—Fishing. LC 90-9958. (Illus.). 32p. (gr. 1-4). 1990. PLB 15.96 (*0-8114-2851-6*); pap. 3.95 (*0-8114-4713-8*) Raintree Steck-V.
—Forests. LC 89-26106. (Illus.). 48p. (gr. 2-6). 1990. PLB 17.28 (*0-8114-2512-6*) Raintree Steck-V.
—Germany. LC 91-22763. (Illus.). 32p. (gr. 1-4). 1992. PLB 15.96 (*0-8114-2566-5*); pap. 3.95 (*0-8114-7176-4*) Raintree Steck-V.
—Giraffes. LC 90-22108. (Illus.). (gr. 1-4). 1992. PLB 15. 96 (*0-8114-2646-7*) Raintree Steck-V.
—Greece. LC 89-26123. (Illus.). 32p. (gr. 1-4). 1990. PLB 15.96 (*0-8114-2551-7*) Raintree Steck-V.
—Hiking. LC 90-23054. (Illus.). 32p. (gr. 1-4). 1991. PLB 15.96 (*0-8114-2905-9*); pap. 3.95 (*0-8114-4708-1*) Raintree Steck-V.
—Hong Kong. LC 89-28985. (Illus.). 32p. (gr. 1-4). 1990. PLB 15.96 (*0-8114-2552-5*) Raintree Steck-V.
—India. LC 89-26122. (Illus.). 32p. (gr. 2-5). 1990. PLB 15.96 (*0-8114-2548-7*); pap. 3.95 (*0-8114-7182-9*) Raintree Steck-V.
—Insects. LC 89-21738. (Illus.). 48p. (gr. 2-6). 1990. PLB 17.28 (*0-8114-2506-1*); pap. 4.95 (*0-8114-6629-9*) Raintree Steck-V.
—Israel. LC 89-22005. (Illus.). 32p. (gr. 1-4). 1990. PLB 15.96 (*0-8114-2558-4*); pap. 3.95 (*0-8114-7177-2*) Raintree Steck-V.
—Italy. LC 89-22031. (Illus.). 32p. (gr. 1-4). 1990. PLB 15.96 (*0-8114-2553-3*) Raintree Steck-V.
—Japan. LC 89-26093. (Illus.). 32p. (gr. 1-4). 1990. PLB 15.96 (*0-8114-2554-1*); pap. 3.95 (*0-8114-7183-7*) Raintree Steck-V.
—Judo. LC 90-23058. (Illus.). 32p. (gr. 1-4). 1991. PLB 15.96 (*0-8114-2900-8*); pap. 3.95 (*0-8114-4714-6*) Raintree Steck-V.
—Lizards. LC 90-22988. (Illus.). (gr. 1-4). 1992. PLB 15. 96 (*0-8114-2645-9*) Raintree Steck-V.
—Looking at Stars. LC 90-40076. (Illus.). 48p. (gr. 2-6). 1990. PLB 17.28 (*0-8114-2522-3*); pap. 4.95 (*0-8114-6626-4*) Raintree Steck-V.
—Mexico. LC 89-22030. (Illus.). 32p. (gr. 1-4). 1990. PLB 15.96 (*0-8114-2555-X*); pap. 3.95 (*0-8114-7184-5*) Raintree Steck-V.
—Mountains. LC 89-21984. (Illus.). 48p. (gr. 2-5). 1990. PLB 17.28 (*0-8114-2513-4*) Raintree Steck-V.
—The Near Planets. LC 90-40078. (Illus.). 48p. (gr. 2-6). 1990. PLB 17.28 (*0-8114-2523-1*) Raintree Steck-V.
—Netherlands. LC 91-20188. (Illus.). 32p. (gr. 1-4). 1992. PLB 15.96 (*0-8114-2565-7*) Raintree Steck-V.
—Nigeria. LC 89-22033. (Illus.). 32p. (gr. 1-4). 1990. PLB 15.96 (*0-8114-2557-6*); pap. 3.95 (*0-8114-7179-9*) Raintree Steck-V.
—Nomads. LC 89-26136. (Illus.). 48p. (gr. 2-6). 1990. PLB 17.28 (*0-8114-2516-9*) Raintree Steck-V.

—Planes. LC 89-21737. (Illus.). 48p. (gr. 2-6). 1990. PLB 17.28 (*0-8114-2503-7*); pap. 4.95 (*0-8114-6630-2*) Raintree Steck-V.
—Reptiles. LC 89-21756. (Illus.). 48p. (gr. 2-5). 1990. PLB 17.28 (*0-8114-2507-X*); pap. 4.95 (*0-8114-6627-2*) Raintree Steck-V.
—Rivers. LC 89-26132. (Illus.). 48p. (gr. 2-5). 1990. PLB 17.28 (*0-8114-2510-X*) Raintree Steck-V.
—Sailing. LC 90-36489. (Illus.). 32p. (gr. 1-4). 1990. PLB 15.96 (*0-8114-2853-2*); pap. 3.95 (*0-8114-4709-X*) Raintree Steck-V.
—Las Serpientes. LC 91-23778. (SPA., Illus.). 32p. (gr. 1-4). 1992. PLB 14.64 (*0-8114-2657-2*) Raintree Steck-V.
—Sharks. LC 90-22114. (Illus.). 32p. (gr. 1-4). 1992. PLB 15.96 (*0-8114-2649-1*); pap. 3.95 (*0-8114-4618-2*) Raintree Steck-V.
—Ships. LC 89-21727. (Illus.). 48p. (gr. 2-6). 1990. PLB 17.28 (*0-8114-2502-9*); pap. 4.95 (*0-8114-6631-0*) Raintree Steck-V.
—Skating. LC 90-36525. (Illus.). 32p. (gr. 1-4). 1990. PLB 15.96 (*0-8114-2854-0*); pap. 3.95 (*0-8114-4715-4*) Raintree Steck-V.
—Skiing. LC 90-36125. (Illus.). 32p. (gr. 1-4). 1990. PLB 15.96 (*0-8114-2856-7*); pap. 3.95 (*0-8114-4710-3*) Raintree Steck-V.
—Snakes. LC 89-26078. (Illus.). 32p. (gr. 1-4). 1990. PLB 15.96 (*0-8114-2636-X*); pap. 3.95 (*0-8114-4613-1*) Raintree Steck-V.
—Space. LC 89-21762. (Illus.). 48p. (gr. 2-6). 1990. PLB 17.28 (*0-8114-2504-5*) Raintree Steck-V.
—Spain. LC 91-23716. (Illus.). 32p. (gr. 1-4). 1992. PLB 15.96 (*0-8114-2569-X*); pap. 3.95 (*0-8114-7186-1*) Raintree Steck-V.
—Spiders. LC 90-22113. (Illus.). 32p. (gr. 1-4). 1992. PLB 15.96 (*0-8114-2648-3*); pap. 3.95 (*0-8114-4623-9*) Raintree Steck-V.
—Sweden. LC 91-22052. (Illus.). 32p. (gr. 1-4). 1992. PLB 15.96 (*0-8114-2567-3*) Raintree Steck-V.
—Swimming. LC 90-36527. (Illus.). 32p. (gr. 1-4). 1990. PLB 15.96 (*0-8114-2852-4*); pap. 3.95 (*0-8114-4716-2*) Raintree Steck-V.
—Tennis. LC 90-23056. (Illus.). 32p. (gr. 1-4). 1991. PLB 15.96 (*0-8114-2904-0*); pap. 3.95 (*0-8114-4711-1*) Raintree Steck-V.
—Thailand. LC 91-22044. (Illus.). 32p. (gr. 1-4). 1992. PLB 15.96 (*0-8114-2570-3*) Raintree Steck-V.
—Track & Field. LC 90-23053. (Illus.). 32p. (gr. 1-4). 1991. PLB 15.96 (*0-8114-2901-6*); pap. write for info. (*0-8114-4747-2*) Raintree Steck-V.
—Trinidad. LC 89-28567. (Illus.). 32p. (gr. 1-4). 1990. PLB 15.96 (*0-8114-2550-9*) Raintree Steck-V.
—What We Can Do about Conserving Energy. Kline, Marjory, ed. (Illus.). 32p. (gr. 3-5). 1992. PLB 11.40 (*0-531-11079-6*) Watts.
—What We Can Do about Litter. (Illus.). 32p. (gr. k-4). 1991. PLB 11.40 (*0-531-11016-8*) Watts.
—What We Can Do about Noise & Fumes. (Illus.). 32p. (gr. k-4). 1992. PLB 11.40 (*0-531-11018-4*) Watts.
—What We Can Do about Protecting Nature. Kline, Marjory, ed. (Illus.). 32p. (gr. 3-5). 1992. PLB 11.40 (*0-531-11080-X*) Watts.
—What We Can Do about Recycling Garbage. (Illus.). 32p. (gr. k-4). 1991. PLB 11.40 (*0-531-11017-6*) Watts.
—What We Can Do about Wasting Water. (Illus.). 32p. (gr. k-4). 1992. PLB 11.40 (*0-531-11019-2*) Watts.
Bailey, Donna & Sproule, Anna. Bangladesh. LC 90-9652. (Illus.). 32p. (gr. 1-4). 1990. PLB 15.96 (*0-8114-2559-2*) Raintree Steck-V.
—Brazil. LC 90-30534. (Illus.). 32p. (gr. 1-4). 1990. PLB 15.96 (*0-8114-2560-6*) Raintree Steck-V.
—France. LC 90-9647. (Illus.). 32p. (gr. 1-4). 1990. PLB 15.96 (*0-8114-2561-4*) Raintree Steck-V.
—Ireland. LC 90-9645. (Illus.). 32p. (gr. 1-4). 1990. PLB 15.96 (*0-8114-2562-2*) Raintree Steck-V.
—Kenya. LC 90-9644. (Illus.). 32p. (gr. 1-4). 1990. PLB 15.96 (*0-8114-2563-0*); pap. 3.95 (*0-8114-7178-0*) Raintree Steck-V.
—Philippines. LC 90-9547. (Illus.). 32p. (gr. 1-4). 1990. PLB 15.96 (*0-8114-2564-9*); pap. 3.95 (*0-8114-7185-3*) Raintree Steck-V.
—Poland. LC 89-13358. (Illus.). 32p. (gr. 1-4). 1990. PLB 15.96 (*0-8114-2556-8*) Raintree Steck-V.
Bailey, Donna, jt. auth. see Butterworth, Christine.
Bailey, Eva. Amy Johnson. (Illus.). 64p. (gr. 5-9). 1991. 11.95 (*0-237-60032-3*, Pub. by Evans Bros Ltd) Trafalgar.
Bailey, Harold P. The Quadruple of the Merry Folbolly: or The Golden Adventure. 1993. 11.95 (*0-533-10590-0*) Vantage.
Bailey, Jill. Discovering Deer. Caulkins, Janet, ed. (Illus.). 48p. (gr. 1-6). 1988. PLB 12.40 (*0-531-18196-0*, Pub. by Bookwright Pr) Watts.
—Discovering Shrews, Moles, & Voles. (Illus.). 48p. (gr. k-6). 1989. PLB 12.40 (*0-531-18291-6*) Watts.
—Facts of Records. LC 92-19026. 1993. 13.00 (*0-671-79149-4*, S&S BFYR); pap. 8.00 (*0-671-79151-6*, S&S BFYR) S&S Trade.
—Frogs in Three Dimensions. Bruandet, Jerome, illus. 12p. (ps). 1992. 16.00 (*0-670-84336-9*) Viking Child Bks.
—Gorilla Rescue. LC 90-9678. (Illus.). 48p. (gr. 3-7). 1990. PLB 18.60 (*0-8114-2705-6*); pap. 4.95 (*0-8114-6553-5*) Raintree Steck-V.
—Life Cycle of a Bee. (ps-3). 1990. PLB 11.90 (*0-531-18316-5*, Pub. by Bookwright Pr) Watts.

—Life Cycle of a Crab. (ps-3). 1990. PLB 11.90 (*0-531-18317-3*, Pub. by Bookwright Pr) Watts.
—Life Cycle of a Grasshopper. (ps-3). 1990. PLB 11.90 (*0-531-18314-9*, Pub. by Bookwright Pr) Watts.
—The Life Cycle of a Ladybug. (Illus.). 32p. (gr. k-4). 1989. PLB 11.90 (*0-531-18292-4*, Pub. by Bookwright Pr) Watts.
—The Life Cycle of a Spider. (Illus.). 32p. (gr. k-4). 1989. PLB 11.90 (*0-531-18288-6*, Pub. by Bookwright Pr) Watts.
—Life Cycle of an Owl. (ps-3). 1990. PLB 11.90 (*0-531-18315-7*, Pub. by Bookwright Pr) Watts.
—Mission Rhino. LC 90-32529. (Illus.). 48p. (gr. 3-7). 1990. PLB 18.60 (*0-8114-2702-1*); pap. 4.95 (*0-8114-6550-0*) Raintree Steck-V.
—Operation Elephant. Green, John, illus. LC 90-46056. 48p. (gr. 3-7). 1991. PLB 18.60 (*0-8114-2706-4*); pap. 4.96 (*0-8114-6554-3*) Raintree Steck-V.
—Operation Turtle. Green, John, illus. LC 91-19874. 48p. (gr. 3-7). 1992. PLB 18.60 (*0-8114-2713-7*); pap. 4.95 (*0-8114-6546-2*) Raintree Steck-V.
—Otter Rescue. Baum, Ann, illus. LC 91-19277. 48p. (gr. 3-7). 1992. PLB 18.60 (*0-8114-2710-2*); pap. 4.95 (*0-8114-6548-9*) Raintree Steck-V.
—Polar Bear Rescue. Green, John, illus. LC 90-4490. 48p. (gr. 3-7). 1991. PLB 18.60 (*0-8114-2708-0*); pap. 4.95 (*0-8114-6556-X*) Raintree Steck-V.
—Project Dolphin. Green, John, illus. LC 91-16007. 48p. (gr. 3-7). 1992. PLB 18.60 (*0-8114-2711-0*); pap. 4.95 (*0-8114-6547-0*) Raintree Steck-V.
—Project Panda. LC 90-9802. (Illus.). 48p. (gr. 3-7). 1990. PLB 18.60 (*0-8114-2704-8*); pap. 4.95 (*0-8114-6552-7*) Raintree Steck-V.
—Project Whale. Green, John, illus. LC 90-45159. 48p. (gr. 3-7). 1991. PLB 18.60 (*0-8114-2707-2*); pap. 4.95 (*0-8114-6555-1*) Raintree Steck-V.
—Save the Macaw. Baum, Ann, illus. LC 91-19871. 48p. (gr. 3-7). 1992. PLB 18.60 (*0-8114-2712-9*); pap. 4.95 (*0-8114-6549-7*) Raintree Steck-V.
—Save the Snow Leopard. Green, John, illus. LC 90-45917. 48p. (gr. 3-7). 1991. PLB 18.60 (*0-8114-2709-9*); pap. 4.95 (*0-8114-6557-8*) Raintree Steck-V.
—Save the Tiger. LC 89-48770. (Illus.). 48p. (gr. 3-7). 1990. PLB 18.60 (*0-8114-2703-X*); pap. 4.95 (*0-8114-6551-9*) Raintree Steck-V.
Bailey, Jill & Felts, Shirley. Naturescapes. LC 88-50187. (ps up). 1988. pap. 15.95 (*0-670-82038-5*) Viking Child Bks.
Bailey, Jill & Seddon, Tony. Animal Movement. (Illus.). 64p. 1988. 15.95x (*0-8160-1656-9*) Facts on File.
—Animal Parenting. (Illus.). 64p. 1989. 15.95x (*0-8160-1654-2*) Facts on File.
—Animal Vision. (Illus.). 64p. 1988. 15.95x (*0-8160-1652-6*) Facts on File.
—Anticipating the Seasons. (Illus.). 64p. 1988. 15.95x (*0-8160-1653-4*) Facts on File.
—Birds of Prey. (Illus.). 64p. (gr. 5 up). 1988. 15.95x (*0-8160-1655-0*) Facts On File.
—Mimicry & Camouflage. 64p. (gr. 5 up). 1988. 15.95x (*0-8160-1657-7*) Facts on File.
Bailey, Jill, jt. auth. see Seddon, Tony.
Bailey, Joe, jt. auth. see Stone, Jon.
Bailey, John, et al, eds. Gods & Men: Myths & Legends from the World's Religions. (Illus.). 144p. 1993. pap. 10.95 (*0-19-274145-4*) OUP.
Bailey, John B. The Legend of the Cherokee Rose. Griffin, James D., Jr., ed. Smith, Rick, illus. 10p. (Orig.). (gr. k-8). 1991. pap. 3.00 (*0-9628023-1-X*) J Laina Pub.
Bailey, Katharine R. & Bourne, Gloria. U. S. Virgin Islands: Jewels of the Caribbean--St. Croix, St. Thomas, St. John. Henle, Fritz, photos by. LC 86-82891. (Illus.). 48p. (Orig.). (gr. 7-12). 1987. pap. 6.95 (*0-88714-012-2*) KC Pubns.
Bailey, Kenneth. Enciclopedia Infantil Molino. (SPA.). 234p. 1973. 95.00 (*0-8288-6277-X*, S22860) Fr & Eur.
—Enciclopedia Juvenil Molino en Color, 5 vols. (SPA.). 510p. 1972. Set. 150.00 (*0-8288-6301-0*, S22861) Fr & Eur.
Bailey, Marilyn. Evolution: Opposing Viewpoints. LC 90-3837. (Illus.). 112p. (gr. 5-8). 1990. PLB 14.95 (*0-89908-078-2*) Greenhaven.
—Single-Parent Families. LC 89-1415. (Illus.). 48p. (gr. 4 up). 1989. RSBE 12.95 (*0-89686-437-5*, Crestwood Hse) Macmillan Child Grp.
—Stepfamilies. LC 89-25325. (Illus.). 48p. (gr. 5-6). 1990. RSBE 12.95 (*0-89686-495-2*, Crestwood Hse) Macmillan Child Grp.
Bailey, Mark W. Electricity. rev. ed. LC 87-20796. (Illus.). 48p. (gr. 2-6). 1988. PLB 18.64 (*0-8172-3253-2*); pap. 4.49 (*0-8114-8218-9*) Raintree Steck-V.
Bailey, Vanessa. Animal Colors. Stillwell, Stella, illus. 16p. (ps). 1991. 5.95 (*0-8120-6245-0*) Barron.
—Animal Opposites. (ps). 1991. 5.95 (*0-8120-6244-2*) Barron.
—Animal Sounds. Stillwell, Stella, illus. 16p. (ps). 1991. 5.95 (*0-8120-6243-4*) Barron.
—Card Tricks: Games & Projects for Children. LC 90-32666. (Illus.). 32p. (gr. k-4). 1990. PLB 11.90 (*0-531-17255-4*, Gloucester Pr) Watts.
—Magic Tricks: Games & Projects for Children. LC 90-32664. (Illus.). 32p. (gr. k-4). 1990. PLB 11.90 (*0-531-17256-2*, Gloucester Pr) Watts.
—Puppets: Games & Projects. LC 90-44841. (Illus.). 32p. (gr. 2-4). 1991. PLB 11.90 (*0-531-17269-4*, Gloucester Pr) Watts.

—Shadow Theater: Games & Projects. (Illus.). 32p. (gr. 2-4). 1991. PLB 11.90 (*0-531-17270-8*, Gloucester Pr) Watts.
Baillie, Allan. Adrift. 128p. (gr. 3-7). 1992. 14.00 (*0-670-84474-8*) Viking Child Bks.
—Drac & the Gremlin. Tanner, Jane, illus. LC 88-20275. 32p. (ps-3). 1989. 11.95 (*0-8037-0628-6*) Dial Bks Young.
—Drac & the Gremlin. Tanner, Jane, illus. LC 88-20275. 32p. (ps-3). 1992. pap. 4.99 (*0-14-054542-5*, Puffin Pied Piper) Puffin Bks.
—Little Brother. 144p. (gr. 3-7). 1992. 14.00 (*0-670-84381-4*) Viking Child Bks.
—Little Brother. 144p. (gr. 5 up). 1994. pap. 3.99 (*0-14-036862-0*) Puffin Bks.
Baily, Jane B. Dottie, the Unfoolish Mule. Parker, Carolyn, illus. LC 90-93258. 32p. (Orig.). (gr. k-3). 1990. pap. 6.95 (*0-9626642-1-9*) J B Baily.
Baines, Chris. The Nest. Ives, Penny, illus. LC 89-77653. 24p. (ps-3). 1990. 7.95 (*0-940793-55-5*, Crocodile Bks) Interlink Pub.
—The Picnic. Ives, Penny, illus. LC 89-77746. 24p. (ps-3). 1990. 7.95 (*0-940793-54-7*, Crocodile Bks) Interlink Pub.
Baines, Gwendolyn L. People in the Web of Life. 2nd ed. (gr. 7 up). 1992. pap. 9.95 (*0-9614505-1-7*) Nevada Pub.
Baines, John. Environmental Disasters. LC 93-8526. (Illus.). 48p. (gr. 4-6). 1993. 15.95 (*1-56847-086-X*) Thomson Lrning.
—Exploring Humans & the Environment. Hughes, Jenny, illus. LC 92-24734. 48p. (gr. 4-8). 1992. PLB 19.92 (*0-8114-2604-1*) Raintree Steck-V.
—Japan. LC 93-23948. (gr. 5 up). 1994. write for info. (*0-8114-1847-2*) Raintree Steck-V.
—Water. LC 92-45668. 32p. (gr. 3-6). 1993. 13.95 (*1-56847-041-X*) Thomson Lrning.
Baines, John D. Acid Rain. LC 89-21656. (Illus.). 48p. (gr. 4-9). 1990. PLB 19.92 (*0-8114-2385-9*); pap. 5.95 (*0-685-58659-6*) Raintree Steck-V.
—Atmosphere. LC 89-22042. (Illus.). 48p. (gr. 4-9). 1990. PLB 19.92 (*0-8114-2388-3*); pap. 5.95 (*0-8114-3450-8*) Raintree Steck-V.
—Protecting the Oceans. LC 90-10208. (Illus.). 48p. (gr. 4-9). 1990. PLB 19.92 (*0-8114-2391-3*); pap. 5.95 (*0-8114-3454-0*) Raintree Steck-V.
—The U. S. A. LC 93-26533. 1993. write for info. (*0-8114-1857-X*) Raintree Steck-V.
Bains, Rae. Abraham Lincoln. Smolinski, Dick, illus. LC 84-2581. 32p. (gr. 3-6). 1985. PLB 9.49 (*0-8167-0146-6*); pap. text ed. 2.95 (*0-8167-0147-4*) Troll Assocs.
—Ancient Greece. Frenck, Hal, illus. LC 84-2685. 32p. (gr. 3-6). 1985. PLB 9.49 (*0-8167-0244-6*); pap. text ed. 2.95 (*0-8167-0245-4*) Troll Assocs.
—Babe Ruth. Smolinski, Dick, illus. LC 84-2595. 32p. (gr. 3-6). 1985. PLB 9.49 (*0-8167-0144-X*); pap. text ed. 2.95 (*0-8167-0145-8*) Troll Assocs.
—Benito Juarez, Hero of Modern Mexico. Davis, Allen, illus. LC 92-2291. 48p. (gr. 4-6). 1992. lib. bdg. 10.79 (*0-8167-2825-9*); pap. 3.50 (*0-8167-2826-7*) Troll Assocs.
—Case of the Great Train Robbery. Harvey, Paul, illus. LC 81-7525. 48p. (gr. 2-4). 1982. PLB 10.89 (*0-89375-588-5*); pap. text ed. 3.50 (*0-89375-589-3*) Troll Assocs.
—Christopher Columbus. Smolinski, Dick, illus. LC 84-2585. 32p. (gr. 3-6). 1985. lib. bdg. 9.49 (*0-8167-0150-4*); pap. text ed. 2.95 (*0-8167-0151-2*) Troll Assocs.
—Clara Barton: Angel of the Battlefield. LC 81-23123. (Illus.). 48p. (gr. 4-6). 1982. PLB 10.79 (*0-89375-752-7*); pap. text ed. 3.50 (*0-89375-753-5*) Troll Assocs.
—Discovering Electricity. Snyder, Joel, illus. LC 81-3339. 32p. (gr. 2-4). 1982. PLB 11.59 (*0-89375-564-8*); pap. 2.95 (*0-89375-565-6*) Troll Assocs.
—Europe. Eitzen, Allan, illus. LC 84-8598. 32p. (gr. 3-6). 1985. PLB 9.49 (*0-8167-0304-3*); pap. text ed. 2.95 (*0-8167-0305-1*) Troll Assocs.
—Forests & Jungles. Snyder, Joel, illus. LC 84-8641. 32p. (gr. 3-6). 1985. PLB 9.49 (*0-8167-0312-4*); pap. text ed. 2.95 (*0-8167-0313-2*) Troll Assocs.
—Gandhi, Peaceful Warrior. Snow, Scott, illus. LC 89-5101. 48p. (gr. 4-6). 1990. lib. bdg. 10.79 (*0-8167-1767-2*); pap. 3.50 (*0-8167-1768-0*) Troll Assocs.
—Harriet Tubman: The Road to Freedom. LC 81-23145. (Illus.). 48p. (gr. 4-6). 1982. PLB 10.79 (*0-89375-760-8*); pap. text ed. 3.50 (*0-89375-761-6*) Troll Assocs.
—Health & Hygiene. Zink-White, Nancy, illus. LC 84-2627. 32p. (gr. 3-6). 1985. PLB 9.49 (*0-8167-0180-6*); pap. text ed. 2.95 (*0-8167-0181-4*) Troll Assocs.
—Hiccups, Hiccups. Coontz, Otto, illus. LC 81-4638. 32p. (gr. k-2). 1981. PLB 11.59 (*0-89375-537-0*); pap. text ed. 2.95 (*0-89375-538-9*) Troll Assocs.
—Indians of the Eastern Woodlands. Hannon, Mark, illus. LC 84-2664. 32p. (gr. 3-6). 1985. PLB 9.49 (*0-8167-0118-0*); pap. text ed. 2.95 (*0-8167-0119-9*) Troll Assocs.
—Indians of the Plains. Baxter, Robert, illus. LC 84-2645. 32p. (gr. 3-6). 1985. PLB 9.49 (*0-8167-0188-1*); pap. text ed. 2.95 (*0-8167-0189-X*) Troll Assocs.
—Indians of the West. Guzzi, George, illus. LC 84-2600. 32p. (gr. 3-6). 1985. PLB 9.49 (*0-8167-0134-2*); pap. text ed. 2.95 (*0-8167-0135-0*) Troll Assocs.

—Jack London: A Life of Adventure. Geehan, Wayne, illus. LC 91-3927. 48p. (gr. 4-6). 1992. PLB 10.79 (*0-8167-2513-6*); pap. text ed. 3.50 (*0-8167-2514-4*) Troll Assocs.

—James Monroe, Young Patriot. Frenck, Hal, illus. LC 85-1071. 48p. (gr. 4-6). 1986. lib. bdg. 10.79 (*0-8167-0557-7*); pap. text ed. 3.50 (*0-8167-0558-5*) Troll Assocs.

—Light. Harriton, Chuck, illus. LC 84-2719. 32p. (gr. 3-6). 1985. PLB 9.49 (*0-8167-0202-0*); pap. text ed. 2.95 (*0-8167-0203-9*) Troll Assocs.

—Louis Pasteur. Smolinski, Dick, illus. LC 84-2748. 32p. (gr. 3-6). 1985. PLB 9.49 (*0-8167-0148-2*); pap. text ed. 2.95 (*0-8167-0149-0*) Troll Assocs.

—Martin Luther King. Frenck, Hal, illus. LC 84-2666. 32p. (gr. 3-6). 1985. PLB 9.49 (*0-8167-0160-1*); pap. text ed. 2.95 (*0-8167-0161-X*) Troll Assocs.

—Molecules & Atoms. Harriton, Chuck, illus. LC 84-2712. 32p. (gr. 3-6). 1985. PLB 9.49 (*0-8167-0284-5*); pap. text ed. 2.95 (*0-8167-0285-3*) Troll Assocs.

—Pilgrims & Thanksgiving. Wenzel, David, illus. LC 84-2686. 32p. (gr. 3-6). 1985. PLB 9.49 (*0-8167-0222-5*); pap. text ed. 2.95 (*0-8167-0223-3*) Troll Assocs.

—Prehistoric Animals. Acosta, Andres, illus. LC 84-2735. 32p. (gr. 3-6). 1985. PLB 9.49 (*0-8167-0296-9*); pap. text ed. 2.95 (*0-8167-0297-7*) Troll Assocs.

—Robert E. Lee: Brave Leader. Smolinski, Dick, illus. LC 85-1092. 48p. (gr. 4-6). 1986. lib. bdg. 10.79 (*0-8167-0545-3*); pap. text ed. 3.50 (*0-8167-0546-1*) Troll Assocs.

—Rocks & Minerals. Maccabe, Richard, illus. LC 84-8644. 32p. (gr. 3-6). 1985. PLB 9.49 (*0-8167-0186-5*); pap. text ed. 2.95 (*0-8167-0187-3*) Troll Assocs.

—Simples Machines. Veno, Joseph, illus. LC 84-2607. 32p. (gr. 3-6). 1985. PLB 9.49 (*0-8167-0166-0*); pap. text ed. 2.95 (*0-8167-0167-9*) Troll Assocs.

—Supreme Court. Dole, Bob, illus. LC 84-2736. 32p. (gr. 3-6). 1985. PLB 9.49 (*0-8167-0272-1*); pap. text ed. 2.95 (*0-8167-0273-X*) Troll Assocs.

—Thurgood Marshall: Fight for Justice. Griffith, Gershom, illus. LC 92-37302. 48p. (gr. 4-6). 1993. 10.79 (*0-8167-2827-5*); tchr's. ed. 3.50 (*0-8167-2828-3*) Troll Assocs.

—Water. Garcia, T. R., illus. LC 84-2718. 32p. (gr. 3-6). 1985. PLB 9.49 (*0-8167-0194-6*); pap. text ed. 2.95 (*0-8167-0195-4*) Troll Assocs.

—Wonders of Rivers. Miyake, Yoshi, illus. LC 81-7423. 32p. (gr. 2-4). 1982. PLB 11.59 (*0-89375-570-2*); pap. text ed. 2.95 (*0-89375-571-0*) Troll Assocs.

Bair, Elmer O. Elmer Bair's Story: 1899-1987, Vol. 1. Mangan, Velda B., ed. Chaffin, Maureen A., illus. LC 87-80294. 484p. (gr. 9 up). 1987. 20.00 (*0-9618269-0-8*) Elmer Bair.

Bair, Lowell, tr. see Dumas, Alexandre.

Baird, Anne. The Christmas Lamb. Baird, Anne, illus. LC 88-5137. 32p. (ps-2). 1989. 12.95 (*0-688-07774-9*); PLB 12.88 (*0-688-07775-7*, Morrow Jr Bks) Morrow Jr Bks.

—Guppies of Hilly Dale House. LC 89-11562. (Illus.). 40p. (ps). 1991. pap. 13.95 incl. jacket (*0-671-69201-1*, Little Simon) S&S Trade.

—Space Camp: The Great Adventures for NASA Hopefuls. Koropp, Robert, photos by. Shepard, Alan B. & Buckbee, Edward O.frwd. by. LC 91-21587. (Illus.). 48p. (gr. 3 up). 1992. 14.00 (*0-688-10227-1*); PLB 13.93 (*0-688-10228-X*) Morrow Jr Bks.

—The U. S. Space Camp Book of Rockets. Graham, David, photos by. Aldrin, Edwin E. & Buckbee, Edward O.frwd. by. LC 93-26148. 1993. write for info. (*0-688-12228-0*); PLB write for info. (*0-688-12229-9*) Morrow Jr Bks.

Baird, Bil. Art of the Puppet. (Illus.). (gr. 9 up). 1966. 35.00 (*0-8238-0067-9*) Plays.

Baird, Daniel, jt. auth. see Oram, Hiawyn.

Baird, Kristin, jt. auth. see Kile, Marilyn.

Baird, Mary & Larrivee-Cohen, Donna, eds. Painting Our Way to a Better Future: An Art-Coloring Book of Contemporary Career Options for Women. Grigsby, Diane, illus. 56p. (Orig.). (gr. 1-9). 1990. pap. 6.95 (*0-9627833-0-7*) Hard Hatted Women.

Baird, Tate, ed. see Morgan, Judith.

Baird, Tate, ed. see Oana, Katherine.

Baird, Tate, ed. see Spataro, Lucian.

Baird, Thomas. Where Time Ends. LC 87-45864. 288p. (gr. 7 up). 1988. HarpC Child Bks.

Baird, W. David. The Quapaws. Porter, Frank. (Illus.). 112p. (gr. 5 up). 1989. lib. bdg. 17.95 (*1-55546-728-8*) Chelsea Hse.

Baird, W. David, ed. see Zane, Alex.

Baisden, E. Bertram, et al. Anthology of Caribbean Short Stories. 125p. (Orig.). (gr. 7-12). 1989. pap. text ed. write for info. Caribbean Rsch Ctr.

Baize, Timothy. Broc: The Littlest Champion. LC 89-92510. (Illus.). 185p. (Orig.). (gr. 6-12). 1989. pap. 9.95 (*0-9625193-0-8*) T Baize.

Bak, Linda, jt. auth. see Fanning, Margaret.

Baker. Soviet Air Force. LC 88-12121. (Illus.). 48p. (gr. 3-8). 1987. PLB 18.60 (*0-86625-331-9*); PLB 13.95s.p. (*0-685-58301-5*) Rourke Corp.

—Soviet Forces in Space. LC 88-14050. (Illus.). 48p. (gr. 3-8). 1987. PLB 18.60 (*0-86625-335-1*); PLB 13.95s.p. (*0-685-58299-X*) Rourke Corp.

—The Time Machine & The Chef. Abell, ed. & illus. (Orig.). (gr. 9 up). 1992. 24.00 (*1-56611-014-9*); pap. 7.00 (*0-685-66202-0*) Jones.

—Where the Forest Meets the Sea. 1993. pap. 28.67 (*0-590-72453-3*) Scholastic Inc.

—You & HIV: A Day at a Time. (Illus.). 272p. 1991. pap. text ed. 18.95 (*0-7216-3606-3*) Saunders.

Baker & Boyington. Down East Puzzles & Word Games. Hassett, John, illus. 80p. (Orig.). 1989. pap. 3.95 (*0-89272-272-X*) Down East.

Baker, Alan. Benjamin's Balloon. 32p. 1990. 12.95 (*0-688-09744-8*) Lothrop.

—Benjamin's Portrait. Baker, Alan, illus. LC 86-10396. 32p. (ps-2). 1987. PLB 11.88 (*0-688-06878-2*) Lothrop.

—Black & White Rabbit's ABC. LC 93-29760. 1994. 7.95 (*1-85697-951-2*) Kingfisher Bks.

—Brown Rabbit's Shape Book. LC 93-29758. 1994. 7.95 (*1-85697-950-4*) Kingfisher Bks.

—Gray Rabbit's 1, 2, 3. 1994. 7.95 (*1-85697-952-0*) Kingfisher Bks.

—Two Tiny Mice. Baker, Alan, illus. LC 90-13939. 32p. (ps-1). 1991. 12.95 (*0-8037-0973-0*) Dial Bks Young.

—Where's Mouse? Baker, Alan, illus. LC 92-53117. 16p. (ps-k). 1992. 12.95 (*1-85697-821-4*) Kingfisher Bks.

—White Rabbit's Color Book. LC 93-32316. 1994. 7.95 (*1-85697-953-9*) Kingfisher Bks.

Baker, Arthur. Cut & Assemble Paper Airplanes That Fly. 1982. pap. 3.95 (*0-486-24302-8*) Dover.

Baker, Barbara. Digby & Kate. Winborn, Marsha, illus. LC 87-24455. 48p. (ps-2). 1988. 9.95 (*0-525-44370-3*, 0966-290, DCB) Dutton Child Bks.

—Digby & Kate. Windborn, Marsha, illus. LC 93-6555. (gr. k-3). 1993. pap. 3.25 (*0-14-036547-8*, Puffin) Puffin Bks.

—Digby & Kate Again. Winborn, Marsha, illus. LC 88-25677. 48p. (ps-2). 1989. 9.95 (*0-525-44477-7*, DCB) Dutton Child Bks.

—N-O Spells No. LC 90-19714. (Illus.). 64p. (gr. 2-5). 1991. 10.95 (*0-525-44639-7*, DCB) Dutton Child Bks.

—Oh, Emma. Stock, Catharine, illus. LC 91-2578. 96p. (gr. 2-5). 1991. 12.95 (*0-525-44771-7*, DCB) Dutton Child Bks.

—Oh, Emma. Stock, Catherine, illus. LC 93-7767. 144p. (gr. 2-5). 1993. pap. 3.99 (*0-14-036357-2*, Puffin) Puffin Bks.

—Staying with Grandmother. Schachner, Judith B., illus. LC 93-13749. 48p. (gr. 1-4). 1994. 12.99 (*0-525-44603-6*, DCB) Dutton Child Bks.

—Third Grade Is Terrible. Shepherd, Roni, illus. LC 88-3631. 80p. (gr. 2-5). 1989. 11.95 (*0-525-44425-4*, DCB) Dutton Child Bks.

—Third Grade Is Terrible. MacDonald, Patricia, ed. Shepard, Roni, illus. 112p. 1991. pap. 2.99 (*0-671-70379-X*, Minstrel Bks) PB.

Baker, Barbara & Winborn, Martha. Digby & Kate Again. (Illus.). (gr. k-3). 1994. pap. 3.25 (*0-14-036665-2*) Puffin Bks.

Baker, Betty. Little Runner of the Longhouse. Lobel, Arnold, illus. LC 62-8040. 64p. (gr. k-3). 1962. PLB 13.89 (*0-06-020341-2*) HarpC Child Bks.

—Little Runner of the Longhouse. Lobel, Arnold, illus. LC 62-8040. 64p. (gr. k-3). 1989. pap. 3.50 (*0-06-444122-9*, Trophy) HarpC Child Bks.

—Walk the World's Rim. LC 65-11458. 192p. (gr. 5 up). 1965. PLB 14.89 (*0-06-020381-1*) HarpC Child Bks.

Baker, Bonnie J. A Pear by Itself. LC 82-4430. 32p. (ps-2). 1982. 11.93 (*0-516-02032-3*); pap. 2.95 (*0-516-42032-1*) Childrens.

Baker, C. David. The Fencerow Tails. Harman, Julie, illus. 48p. (gr. k-5). 1991. 12.95x (*0-9630669-0-0*) Liberty Lines.

Baker, C. G. Taking Charge. LC 93-15038. 144p. (gr. 3-7). 1993. pap. 3.50 (*0-14-036568-0*, Puffin) Puffin Bks.

Baker, Carin G. Fight for Honor. 128p. (gr. 3-7). 1992. pap. 3.50 (*0-14-036024-7*) Puffin Bks.

—Girl Trouble. 144p. (gr. 3-7). 1992. pap. 3.50 (*0-14-036074-3*, Puffin) Puffin Bks.

—High Pressure. 128p. (gr. 3-7). 1992. pap. 3.50 (*0-14-036025-5*) Puffin Bks.

—Karate Club, No. 5: Out of Control. LC 92-19941. 144p. (gr. 3-7). 1992. pap. 3.50 (*0-14-036264-9*) Puffin Bks.

—Road Warriors. 144p. (gr. 3-7). 1992. pap. 3.50 (*0-14-036076-X*, Puffin) Puffin Bks.

Baker, Carin Greenberg. To Catch a Thief! LC 92-39517. 144p. (gr. 3-7). 1993. pap. 3.50 (*0-14-036291-6*) Puffin Bks.

Baker, Charles F., III. The Struggle for Freedom: Plays on the American Revolution, 1762-1788. Yoder, Carolyn P., ed. Zarins, Joyce A. & Porter, Coni, illus. 144p. (Illus.). (gr. 4-9). 1990. pap. 15.95 (*0-942389-05-0*) Cobblestone Pub.

Baker, Charlotte. Trails North - Stories of Texas Yesterdays. Roberts, Melissa, ed. Gholson, Virginia, illus. 128p. (gr. 4-7). 1991. 10.95 Eakin-Sunbelt.

Baker, D. Danger on Apollo Thirteen. (Illus.). 32p. (gr. 4 up). 1988. PLB 17.27 (*0-86592-871-1*); 12.95 (*0-685-58289-2*) Rourke Corp.

—Today's World in Space, 6 bks, Set I, Reading Level 5. (Illus.). 288p. (gr. 3-8). 1988. Set. PLB 111.60 (*0-86592-403-1*); PLB 83.70s.p. (*0-685-58830-0*) Rourke Corp.

Baker, Darrell. Disney Babies Nursery Rhymes. (ps). 1988. 1.95 (*0-307-01137-2*, Golden Pr) Western Pub.

Baker, Darrell, illus. Baby Donald's Busy Play Group. LC 87-81947. 14p. (ps-1). 1988. write for info. (*0-307-12316-2*) Western Pub.

—Disney Babies Nursery Rhymes. LC 87-83006. 12p. (ps). 1988. write for info. (*0-307-06082-9*) Western Pub.

—Disney Babies on the Go. LC 87-83008. 12p. (ps). 1988. write for info. (*0-307-06099-3*) Western Pub.

—Disney Babies Rock-a-Bye. LC 87-83007. 12p. (ps). 1988. write for info. (*0-307-06084-5*) Western Pub.

—Disney Babies What's up High? LC 87-83009. 12p. (ps). 1988. write for info. (*0-307-06100-0*) Western Pub.

Baker, Dave, et al. How Big is the Moon: Whole Maths in Action. LC 90-5187. (Illus.). 110p. (Orig.). (gr. k-6). 1990. pap. 15.95 (*0-435-08312-0*, 08312) Heinemann.

Baker, David. Airborne Early Warning. (Illus.). 48p. (gr. 3-8). 1989. lib. bdg. 18.60 (*0-86592-533-X*) Rourke Corp.

—Airlift. (Illus.). 48p. (gr. 3-8). 1989. lib. bdg. 18.60 (*0-86592-531-3*) Rourke Corp.

—Anti-Submarine Warfare. 48p. (gr. 3-8). 1989. lib. bdg. 18.60 (*0-86592-532-1*) Rourke Corp.

—Believe It Or Not Space Facts, Reading Level 5. (Illus.). 48p. (gr. 3-8). 1988. 18.60 (*0-86592-407-4*) Rourke Corp.

—Bombers. (Illus.). 48p. (gr. 3-8). 1987. PLB 18.60 (*0-86592-355-8*) Rourke Corp.

—Earth Watch. (Illus.). 48p. (gr. 3-8). 1989. lib. bdg. 18.60 (*0-86592-372-8*); 13.95s.p. (*0-685-58641-3*) Rourke Corp.

—Exploring Mars. (Illus.). 48p. (gr. 3-8). 1987. PLB 18.60 (*0-86592-404-X*); lib. bdg. 13.95s.p. (*0-685-67598-X*) Rourke Corp.

—Exploring Venus & Mercury. LC 88-33707. (Illus.). 48p. (gr. 4-6). 1989. PLB 18.60 (*0-86592-371-X*); lib. bdg. 13.95s.p. (*0-685-58638-3*) Rourke Corp.

—Factories in Space. LC 87-16689. (Illus.). 48p. (gr. 3-8). 1987. PLB 18.60 (*0-86592-409-0*); lib. bdg. 13.95s.p. (*0-685-67602-1*) Rourke Corp.

—Flight to the Stars. (Illus.). 48p. (gr. 3-8). 1989. lib. bdg. 18.60 (*0-86592-373-6*); 13.95s.p. (*0-685-58640-5*) Rourke Corp.

—Future Fighters. (Illus.). 48p. (gr. 3-8). 1989. lib. bdg. 18.60 (*0-86592-535-6*); 13.95s.p. (*0-685-58601-4*) Rourke Corp.

—Ground Attack Planes. 48p. (gr. 3-8). 1989. lib. bdg. 18.60 (*0-86592-536-4*); 13.95s.p. (*0-685-58603-0*) Rourke Corp.

—Helicopters. (Illus.). 48p. (gr. 3-8). 1987. PLB 18.60 (*0-86592-356-6*); 13.95s.p. (*0-685-67593-9*) Rourke Corp.

—I Want to Fly the Shuttle. LC 87-20467. (Illus.). 48p. (gr. 3-8). 1987. PLB 18.60 (*0-86592-406-6*); 13.95s.p. (*0-685-67600-5*) Rourke Corp.

—Journey to the Outer Planets. LC 87-19888. (Illus.). 48p. 1987. PLB 18.60 (*0-86592-405-8*); 13.95 (*0-685-67599-8*) Rourke Corp.

—Land-Based Fighters. (Illus.). 48p. (gr. 3-8). 1987. PLB 18.60 (*0-86592-351-5*); 13.95s.p. (*0-685-67591-2*) Rourke Corp.

—Living in Space. (Illus.). 48p. (gr. 3-8). 1989. lib. bdg. 18.60 (*0-86592-401-5*); 13.95s.p. (*0-685-58639-1*) Rourke Corp.

—Living on the Moon. (Illus.). 48p. (gr. 3-8). 1989. lib. bdg. 18.60 (*0-86592-374-4*); 13.95s.p. (*0-685-58642-1*) Rourke Corp.

—Military Aircraft Library, 6 bks, Set II, Reading Level 5. (Illus.). 288p. (gr. 3-8). 1989. Set. PLB 111.60 (*0-86592-530-5*); 83.70s.p. (*0-685-58763-0*) Rourke Corp.

—Navy Fighters. (Illus.). 48p. (gr. 3-8). 1987. PLB 18.60 (*0-86592-352-3*); 13.95s.p. (*0-685-67594-7*) Rourke Corp.

—Navy Strike Planes. (Illus.). 48p. (gr. 3-8). 1989. lib. bdg. 18.60 (*0-86592-534-8*); 13.95s.p. (*0-685-58602-2*) Rourke Corp.

—Peace in Space. LC 87-19885. (Illus.). 48p. (gr. 3-8). 1987. PLB 18.60 (*0-86592-408-2*); 13.95s.p. (*0-685-67601-3*) Rourke Corp.

—Research Planes. (Illus.). 48p. (gr. 3-8). 1987. PLB 18.60 (*0-86592-354-X*); 13.95s.p. (*0-685-67595-5*) Rourke Corp.

—Spy Planes. (Illus.). 48p. (gr. 3-8). 1987. PLB 18.60 (*0-86592-353-1*); PLB 13.95s.p. (*0-685-67592-0*) Rourke Corp.

—Starwatch. (Illus.). 48p. (gr. 3-8). 1989. lib. bdg. 18.60 (*0-86592-400-7*); lib. bdg. 13.95s.p. (*0-685-58637-5*) Rourke Corp.

—Today's World in Space, 6 bks, Set II, Reading Level 5. (Illus.). 288p. (gr. 3-8). 1989. Set. PLB 111.60 (*0-86592-370-1*); PLB 83.70s.p. (*0-685-58762-2*) Rourke Corp.

Baker, Dianne. Ted Bear's Magic Swing. Krum, Ronda, illus. LC 91-65819. 32p. (gr. 1-3). 1992. 12.95 (*0-87159-162-6*) Unity Bks.

Baker, Elizabeth. The Gourmet Uncook Book. (gr. 11 up). 1994. pap. 12.95 (*0-937766-15-1*) Drelwood Comns.

Baker, Eugene. At the Scene of the Crime. Axeman, Lois, illus. LC 80-14091. 32p. (gr. 2-5). 1980. PLB 18.50 (*0-89565-151-3*); PLB 12.95s.p. (*0-685-55474-0*) Childs World.

—In the Detective's Lab. Axeman, Linda, illus. LC 80-17787. 32p. (gr. 2-5). 1980. PLB 18.50 (*0-89565-154-8*); PLB 12.95s.p. (*0-685-55489-9*) Childs World.

—Master of Disguise. Axeman, Lois, illus. LC 80-11297. 32p. (gr. 2-5). 1980. PLB 18.50 (*0-89565-149-1*); PLB 12.95s.p. (*0-685-55504-6*) Childs World.

—Shadowing the Suspect. Axeman, Lois, illus. LC 80-13982. 32p. (gr. 2-5). 1980. PLB 18.50 (*0-89565-152-1*); PLB 12.95s.p. (*0-685-55542-9*) Childs World.

—Spotting the Fakes-Forgeries & Counterfeits. Axeman, Lois, illus. LC 80-15998. 32p. (gr. 2-5). 1980. PLB 18. 50 *(0-89565-153-X)*; PLB 12.95s.p. *(0-685-55551-8)* Childs World.
—What's Right? A Handbook about Values. 112p. (gr. 2-6). 1980. PLB 21.35 *(0-89565-208-0)*; PLB 14.95s.p. *(0-685-66237-3)* Childs World.
Baker, Harri T. & Browning, Jane. An Arkansas History for Young People. (gr. 8). 1991. student wkbk. 28.00 *(1-55728-083-5)*; write for info. tchr's. manual *(1-55728-201-3)* U of Ark Pr.
Baker, Houston. A Many Colored Coat: Countee Cullen. (gr. 12 up). 1974. pap. 3.00 *(0-910296-36-7)* Broadside Pr.
Baker, Houston A. Blues Journeys Home. LC 85-80142. (Illus.). 59p. (Orig.). (gr. 7-12). 1985. pap. 5.00 perfect bdg. *(0-916418-61-8)* Lotus.
—Spirit Run. LC 81-82664. 38p. (gr. 9-12). 1982. pap. 3. 00x *(0-916418-38-3)* Lotus.
Baker, Howard, text by. & photos by Big South Fork Country. (Illus.). 120p. (gr. 9 up). 1993. 29.95 *(1-55853-258-7)* Rutledge Hill Pr.
Baker, James W. April Fools' Day Magic. Overlie, George, illus. 48p. (gr. 2-5). 1989. 11.95 *(0-8225-2230-6)* Lerner Pubns.
—Birthday Magic. Overlie, George, illus. LC 88-2717. 48p. (gr. 2-5). 1988. lib. bdg. 11.95 *(0-8225-2226-8,* First Ave Edns); pap. 3.95 *(0-8225-9536-2,* First Ave Edns) Lerner Pubns.
—Christmas Magic. Overlie, George, illus. 48p. (gr. 2-5). 1988. lib. bdg. 11.95 *(0-8225-2227-6)*; pap. 3.95 *(0-8225-9537-0)* Lerner Pubns.
—Halloween Magic. Overlie, George, illus. 48p. (gr. 2-5). 1988. lib. bdg. 11.95 *(0-8225-2228-4,* First Ave Edns); pap. 3.95 *(0-8225-9551-6,* First Ave Edns) Lerner Pubns.
—Illusions Illustrated: A Professional Magic Show for Young Performers. Ayres, Carter M., photos by. Swofford, Jeanette, illus. LC 83-19549. 120p. (gr. 6 up). 1984. PLB 22.95 *(0-8225-0768-4,* First Ave Edns); pap. 6.95 *(0-8225-9512-5,* First Ave Edns) Lerner Pubns.
—Independence Day Magic. Overlie, George, illus. 48p. (gr. 2-5). 1989. 11.95 *(0-8225-2236-5)* Lerner Pubns.
—New Year's Magic. Overlie, Goerge, illus. 48p. (gr. 2-5). 1989. 11.95 *(0-8225-2231-4)* Lerner Pubns.
—Presidents' Day Magic. Overlie, George, illus. 48p. (gr. 2-5). 1989. 11.95 *(0-8225-2232-2)* Lerner Pubns.
—St. Patrick's Day Magic. Overlie, George, illus. 48p. (gr. 2-5). 1989. 11.95 *(0-8225-2234-9)* Lerner Pubns.
—Thanksgiving Magic. Overlie, George, illus. 48p. (gr. 2-5). 1989. 11.95 *(0-8225-2233-0)* Lerner Pubns.
—Valentine Magic. Overlie, George, illus. LC 88-2710. 48p. (gr. 2-5). 1988. lib. bdg. 11.95 *(0-8225-2229-2,* First Ave Edns); pap. 3.95 *(0-8225-9550-8,* First Ave Edns) Lerner Pubns.
Baker, Jeannie. Home in the Sky. Baker, Jeannie, illus. LC 83-25379. 32p. (gr. k-3). 1984. 13.00 *(0-688-03841-7)*; PLB 11.96 *(0-688-03842-5)* Greenwillow.
—Home in the Sky. Baker, Jeannie, illus. 32p. (ps-3). 1993. pap. 4.95 *(0-590-44704-1)* Scholastic Inc.
—Where the Forest Meets The Sea. LC 87-7551. (Illus.). 32p. (ps-3). 1988. 15.00 *(0-688-06363-2)*; lib. bdg. 14. 93 *(0-688-06364-0)* Greenwillow.
—Window. LC 90-3922. (Illus.). 32p. (ps up). 1991. 14.00 *(0-688-08917-8)*; PLB 13.93 *(0-688-08918-6)* Greenwillow.
—Window. (Illus.). 32p. (ps-3). 1993. pap. 4.99 *(0-14-054830-0)* Puffin Bks.
Baker, Keith. Big Fat Hen. LC 93-19160. 1994. write for info. *(0-15-292869-3)* HarBrace.
—The Dove's Letter. Baker, Keith, illus. LC 87-8530. 32p. (ps-3). 1988. 14.95 *(0-15-224133-7,* HB Juv Bks) HarBrace.
—The Dove's Letter. LC 87-8530. (ps-3). 1993. pap. 5.95 *(0-15-224134-5,* Voyager Bks) HarBrace.
—Hide & Snake. (ps-3). 1991. 12.95 *(0-15-233986-8,* HB Juv Bks) HarBrace.
—The Magic Fan. 16p. (gr. k-3). 1989. 14.95 *(0-15-250750-7)* HarBrace.
—Who Is the Beast? Baker, Keith, illus. 28p. (ps-3). 1991. pap. 19.95 *(0-15-296059-7)* HarBrace.
—Who Is the Beast? Baker, Keith, illus. LC 89-29365. 28p. (ps-2). 1990. 12.95 *(0-15-296057-0)* HarBrace.
Baker, Leslie. The Antique Store Cat. Baker, Leslie, illus. 32p. (ps-3). 1992. 14.95 *(0-316-07837-9)* Little.
—Morning Beach. (ps-3). 1990. 14.95 *(0-316-07835-2)* Little.
—Third Story Cat. (ps-3). 1990. pap. 4.95 *(0-316-07836-0)* Little.
Baker, Lucy. Eagles. (Illus.). 32p. (gr. 2-6). 1990. pap. 4.95 *(0-14-034437-3,* Puffin) Puffin Bks.
—Life in the Deserts. (Illus.). 32p. (gr. 5-8). 1990. PLB 12.40 *(0-531-10980-1)* Watts.
—Life in the Deserts. (gr. 4-7). 1993. pap. 4.95 *(0-590-46129-X)* Scholastic Inc.
—Life in the Oceans. (Illus.). 32p. (gr. 5-8). 1990. PLB 12.40 *(0-531-10981-X)* Watts.
—Life in the Oceans. (gr. 4-7). 1993. pap. 4.95 *(0-590-46132-X)* Scholastic Inc.
—Life in the Rainforests. (Illus.). 32p. (gr. 5-8). 1990. PLB 12.40 *(0-531-10983-6)* Watts.
—Polar Bears. (Illus.). 32p. (gr. 2-6). 1990. pap. 4.95 *(0-14-034435-7,* Puffin) Puffin Bks.
—Seals. (Illus.). 32p. (gr. 2-6). 1990. pap. 4.95 *(0-14-034436-5,* Puffin) Puffin Bks.

—Snakes. (Illus.). 32p. (gr. 2-6). 1990. pap. 4.95 *(0-14-034434-9,* Puffin) Puffin Bks.
Baker, Margaret. Food & Cooking. (Illus.). 64p. (gr. 6 up). 1979. 14.95 *(0-7136-1465-X)* Dufour.
Baker, Michael K. The Sword. LC 84-90678. 303p. (gr. 5up). 1985. text ed. 8.00 *(0-932543-01-4)*; pap. 8.00 *(0-932543-00-6)* M B Pub.
Baker, Nancy & Hoffman, Richard L., eds. Virginia Insects: An Activity Book. 32p. (gr. 4-6). 1993. pap. 2.95 *(0-9625801-8-X)* VA Mus Natl Hist.
Baker, Olaf. Where the Buffaloes Begin. Gammell, Stephen, illus. LC 85-5682. 48p. (ps-4). 1989. 14.95 *(0-670-82760-6)*; pap. 5.99 *(0-14-050560-1)* Viking Child Bks.
Baker, Pamela J. My First Book of Sign. Gillen, Patricia B, illus. LC 86-14937. iv, 76p. (ps-3). 1986. 14.95 *(0-930323-20-3,* Kendall Green Pubns) Gallaudet Univ Pr.
Baker, Pat. Dear Diary. (gr. 3-8). 1990. pap. 4.99 *(0-8423-0536-X)* Tyndale.
Baker, Patricia. The Nineteen Fifties. Cumming, Valerie & Feldman, Elane, eds. (Illus.). 64p. (gr. 7-12). 1991. 16.95x *(0-8160-2468-5)* Facts on File.
—The Nineteen Forties. (Illus.). 64p. (gr. 6-10). 1992. lib. bdg. 16.95x *(0-8160-2467-7)* Facts on File.
Baker, R. Ray. Red Brother. 1927. 5.00x *(0-911586-03-2)* Wahr.
Baker, R. Robin, jt. auth. see Oram, Liz.
Baker, Rachel. The First Woman Doctor. Copelman, Evelyn, illus. 192p. (gr. 4-6). 1987. pap. 2.95 *(0-590-44767-X)* Scholastic Inc.
Baker, Richard, jt. ed. see Keller, Charles.
Baker, Robert H., jt. auth. see Zim, Herbert S.
Baker, Sanna A. Who's a Friend of the Water-Spurting Whale? De Paola, Tomie, illus. LC 86-23423. (ps-1). 1987. 9.99 *(0-89191-587-7,* Chariot Bks) Cook.
Baker, Sue. The Birds & the Bees. LC 91-39758. (gr. 3 up). 1991. 9.95 *(0-85953-404-0)* Childs Play.
—Child's Play Weather. (ps-3). 1993. 12.95 *(0-85953-929-6)* Childs Play.
Baker, Susan. Explorers of North America. LC 89-26364. (Illus.). 48p. (gr. 4-8). 1990. PLB 19.92 *(0-8114-2752-8)* Raintree Steck-V.
—First Look at Mountains. LC 91-9420. (Illus.). 32p. (gr. 1-2). 1991. PLB 15.93 *(0-8368-0703-0)* Gareth Stevens Inc.
—First Look at Rivers. LC 91-9419. (Illus.). 32p. (gr. 1-2). 1991. PLB 15.93 *(0-8368-0679-4)* Gareth Stevens Inc.
—First Look at Using Energy. LC 91-2372. (Illus.). 32p. (gr. 1-2). 1991. PLB 15.93 *(0-8368-0680-8)* Gareth Stevens Inc.
—First Look under the Sea. (Illus.). 32p. (gr. 1-2). 1991. PLB 15.93 *(0-8368-0702-2)* Gareth Stevens Inc.
Baker, Tanya & Holm, Carlton. Harvey the Hiccupping Hippopotamus. Wilkinson, Sue, illus. 32p. (ps-k). 1992. lib. bdg. 10.95 with dust jacket *(0-8120-6248-5)*; pap. 5.95 *(0-8120-4927-6)* Barron.
Baker, Thomas A. Second Chance in Centerville. 96p. (gr. 3-9). 1991. pap. 11.00 *(0-87879-908-7)* High Noon Bks.
Baker, Tom. High School Highways, 5 novels in ea. set, 48p.ea, Sets 1 & 2. (Illus.). 32p. (gr. 2-7). 1988. pap. 15.00 ea. set Set 1 *(0-87879-536-7)* Set 2 *(0-87879-582-0)* High Noon Bks.
Baker, Wendy & Haslam, Andrew. Earth: A Creative Hands-on Approach to Science. LC 92-27573. (Illus.). 48p. (gr. 2-5). 1993. POB 12.95 *(0-689-71662-1,* Aladdin) Macmillan Child Grp.
—Electricity: A Creative Hands-on Approach to Science. LC 92-24566. (Illus.). 48p. (gr. 2-5). 1993. POB 12.95 *(0-689-71663-X,* Aladdin) Macmillan Child Grp.
—Plants: A Creative Hands-on Approach to Science. LC 92-24559. (Illus.). 48p. (gr. 2-5). 1993. POB 12.95 *(0-689-71664-8,* Aladdin) Macmillan Child Grp.
—Sound: A Creative Hands-on Approach to Science. LC 92-30104. (Illus.). 48p. (gr. 2-5). 1993. POB 12.95 *(0-689-71665-6,* Aladdin) Macmillan Child Grp.
Bakhtiar, Laleh. History of Islam, Pt. I. 205p. (gr. 10-12). 1993. pap. 19.95 *(1-56744-427-X)* Kazi Pubns.
—History of Islam, Pt. II. 205p. (gr. 10-12). 1993. pap. 19.95 *(1-56744-428-8)* Kazi Pubns.
—Muhammad's Companions: Essays on Those Who Bore Witness, Pt. I. 205p. (gr. 10-12). 1993. pap. 14.95 *(1-56744-426-1)* Kazi Pubns.
—Muhammad's Companions: Essays on Those Who Bore Witness, Pt. II. 205p. (gr. 10-12). 1993. pap. 12.95 *(1-56744-318-4)* Kazi Pubns.
Bakke, Jean, ed. see League of Women Voters Staff.
Bakken, Edna. Alberta. LC 91-951144. (Illus.). 144p. (gr. 5-8). 1992. PLB 26.60 *(0-516-06611-0)* Childrens.
Bakken, Harald. The Fields & the Hills: The Journey, Once Begun, Book I. 240p. (gr. 5 up). 1992. 15.45 *(0-395-59397-2,* Clarion Bks) HM.
Bakoske, Sharon & Davidson, Margaret. Dolphins. Courtney, illus. 48p. (Orig.). (gr. 1-3). 1993. PLB 7.99 *(0-679-94437-0)*; pap. 3.50 *(0-679-84437-6)* Random Bks Yng Read.
Balaban, John. The Hawk's Tale. Delamare, David, illus. LC 87-14938. 148p. (gr. 3-7). 1988. 14.95 *(0-15-200462-9,* Gulliver Bks) HarBrace.
Balamore, Usha, tr. see Muhaiyaddeen, M. R.
Balan, Bruce. The Cherry Migration. Lane, Dan, illus. 32p. 1991. 12.95 *(0-88138-098-9,* Green Tiger Bks) S&S Trade.
—Jeremy Quacks. Meier, David S., illus. LC 89-31372. 32p. (ps up). 1991. pap. 14.95 *(0-88708-104-5)* Picture Bk Studio.

—The Moose in the Dress. Teasdale, Denise, illus. LC 90-86345. 32p. (ps-1). 1991. 14.00 *(0-517-58564-2,* Clarkson Potter) Crown Bks Yng Read.
—Pie in the Sky. Skilbeck, Clare, illus. 32p. (ps-3). 1993. 13.99 *(0-670-85150-7)* Viking Child Bks.
Balazs, Eva. Alessandra. LC 93-60233. (Illus.). 34p. (gr. k-3). 1994. 12.00 *(1-55523-604-9)* Winston-Derek.
Balcells, Jacqueline. The Enchanted Raisin. Miller, Elizabeth G., tr. from SPA. Miller, L. Dennis, illus. LC 88-28587. 104p. (gr. 3-7). 1989. pap. 11.00 *(0-935480-38-2)* Lat Am Lit Rev Pr.
Balcer, Bernadette & O'Byrne-Pelham, Fran. Philadelphia. LC 88-20198. (Illus.). 60p. (gr. 3 up). 1988. RSBE 13.95 *(0-87518-388-3,* Dillon) Macmillan Child Grp.
Balcer, Bernadette, jt. auth. see O'Byrne-Pelham, Fran.
Balch, Glenn. Christmas Horse. Crowell, Pers, illus. Woodward, Tim, intro. by. (Illus.). 1990. pap. 9.95 *(0-931659-10-8)* Limberlost Pr.
Balcomb, Kenneth C., III & Minasian, Stanley M. The Whales of Hawaii: Including All Species of Marine Mammals in Hawaiian & Adjacent Waters. Foster, Larry A., illus. Gilmartin, William, intro. by. (Illus.). 114p. (Orig.). (gr. 9 up). 1987. pap. 9.95 *(0-9617803-0-4)* Marine Mammal Fund.
Balcomb, Philip E. The Clock Repair First Reader: Second Steps for the Beginner. Balcomb, Philip E., illus. 160p. (Orig.). (gr. 9 up). 1989. pap. 14.95 *(0-9620456-1-6)* Tempus Pr.
Balcziak, B. Movies. (Illus.). 48p. (gr. 4-8). 1989. lib. bdg. 17.27 *(0-86592-058-3)*; 12.95 *(0-685-58623-5)* Rourke Corp.
—Music. (Illus.). 48p. (gr. 4-8). 1989. lib. bdg. 17.27 *(0-86592-056-7)*; 12.95s.p. *(0-685-58627-8)* Rourke Corp.
—Newspapers. (Illus.). 48p. (gr. 4-8). 1989. lib. bdg. 17. 27 *(0-86592-069-9)*; 12.95s.p. *(0-685-58624-3)* Rourke Corp.
—Radio. (Illus.). 48p. (gr. 4-8). 1989. lib. bdg. 17.27 *(0-86592-057-5)*; 12.95s.p. *(0-685-58625-1)* Rourke Corp.
—Television. (Illus.). 48p. (gr. 4-8). 1989. lib. bdg. 17.27 *(0-86592-059-1)*; lib. bdg. 12.95s.p. *(0-685-58628-6)* Rourke Corp.
Balcziak, Bill, jt. auth. see Frisch, Carlienne.
Balczon, Mary-Lynne J., jt. auth. see Johnson, Kathryn T.
Bald, Robert C., ed. Six Elizabethan Plays. Incl. Tamburlaine, Pt. 1. Marlowe, Christopher; Shoemaker's Holiday. Dekker, Thomas; Knight of the Burning Pestle. Beaumont, Francis & Fletcher, John.; Epicoene. Jonson, Ben; Duchess of Malfi. Webster, John; Broken Heart. Ford, John. LC 63-4440. (gr. 9up). 1959. pap. 9.16 *(0-395-05135-5,* RivEd) HM.
Baldauski, Karen. Cat-Coloring Book. 1950. pap. 2.95 *(0-486-24011-8)* Dover.
Balderas, Eduardo, tr. see Dean, Bessie.
Balderose, Nancy W. Once upon a Pony: A Mountain Christmas. LC 92-13814. 32p. 1992. 12.95 *(0-8192-7000-8)* Morehouse Pub.
Baldner, Jean V. Pebbles in the Wind. Webster, Carroll, illus. 52p. (Orig.). (gr. 7 up). pap. 5.95 *(0-9615317-0-3)* Baldner J V.
Baldry, Cherith. A Rush of Golden Wings. Bishop, Lila, ed. 160p. (gr. 8-12). pap. 5.95 *(0-89107-634-4)* Good News.
Balducci, Rita. Disney's Beauty & the Beast. Cardona, Jose, illus. 24p. (ps-k). 1992. write for info. *(0-307-10021-9,* 10021) Western Pub.
—Disney's the Little Mermaid. (ps). 1993. 3.95 *(0-307-12537-8,* Golden Pr) Western Pub.
—Walt Disney's Alice in Wonderland: Book of Colors. DiCicco, Sue, illus. 12p. (ps). 1993. bds. 1.95 *(0-307-06079-9,* 6079, Golden Pr) Western Pub.
—Walt Disney's Bambi: Thumper's Book of Opposites. Pacheco, David & Wakeman, Diana, illus. 12p. (ps). 1993. bds. 1.95 *(0-307-06124-8,* 6124, Golden Pr) Western Pub.
Balducci, Rita, retold by. Little Red Riding Hood. Eubank, Mary G., illus. (ps-k). 1991. pap. 1.25 *(0-307-11511-9,* Golden Pr) Western Pub.
Balducci, Rita, adapted by. Walt Disney's Cinderella. Mones, illus. 28p. (ps). 1992. bds. write for info. *(0-307-12530-0,* 12530, Golden Pr) Western Pub.
—Walt Disney's Dumbo. Ortiz, Phil & Wakeman, Diana, illus. 28p. (ps). 1992. bds. write for info. *(0-307-12533-5,* 12533, Golden Pr) Western Pub.
—Walt Disney's Snow White & The Seven Dwarfs. Williams, Don, illus. 24p. (ps-k). 1992. write for info. laminated covers *(0-307-10037-5,* 10037, Golden Pr) Western Pub.
Baldwin, Cathy, ed. see Youngs, Bettie B. & Tracy, Brian S.
Baldwin, Dorothy. Health & Drugs. (Illus.). 32p. 1987. PLB 17.27 *(0-86592-292-6)*; 12.95s.p. *(0-685-67609-9)* Rourke Corp.
—Health & Exercise. (Illus.). 32p. (gr. 3-8). 1987. PLB 17.27 *(0-86592-293-4)*; 12.95s.p. *(0-685-67611-0)* Rourke Corp.
—Health & Feelings. (Illus.). 32p. (gr. 3-8). 1987. PLB 17.27 *(0-86592-290-X)*; 12.95s.p. *(0-685-58167-5)* Rourke Corp.
—Health & Food. (Illus.). 32p. (gr. 3-8). 1987. PLB 17.27 *(0-86592-294-2)*; 12.95s.p. *(0-685-67608-0)* Rourke Corp.
—Health & Friends. (Illus.). 32p. (gr. 3-8). 1987. PLB 17. 27 *(0-86592-289-6)*; 12.95s.p. *(0-685-67612-9)* Rourke Corp.

—Health & Hygiene. (Illus.). 32p. (gr. 3-8). 1987. PLB 17.27 (0-86592-291-8); 12.95s.p. (0-685-67610-2) Rourke Corp.

Baldwin, James & Mead, Margaret. A Rap on Race. (gr. 9 up). 1992. pap. 5.99 (0-440-21176-X) Dell.

Baldwin, Joyce. To Heal the Heart of a Child: Helen Taussig, M.D. 128p. 1992. 14.95 (0-8027-8166-7); lib. bdg. 15.85 (0-8027-8167-5) Walker & Co.

Balent, Matthew, jt. auth. see Wujcik, Erick.

Bales, Carol A. Tales of the Elders: A Memory Book of Men & Women Who Came to America as Immigrants, 1900-1930. Bales, Carol A., photos by. LC 92-46729. (Illus.). 160p. (gr. 5 up). 1993. Repr. of 1977 ed. 10.98 (0-382-24373-0); PLB 12.98 (0-382-24364-1) Silver Burdett Pr.

Balestrino, Philip. The Skeleton Inside You. Bolognese, Don, illus. LC 85-42982. 40p. (ps-3). 1986. pap. 4.95 (0-06-445039-2, Trophy) HarpC Child Bks.

—The Skeleton Inside You. rev. ed. Kelley, True, illus. LC 88-23672. 32p. (gr. k-3). 1989. 14.00 (0-690-04731-2, Crowell Jr Bks); PLB 13.89 (0-690-04733-9) HarpC Child Bks.

—The Skeleton Inside You. rev. ed. Kelley, True, illus. LC 88-24600. 32p. (gr. k-3). 1989. pap. 4.50 (0-06-445087-2, Trophy) HarpC Child Bks.

Balian, Lorna. Amelia's Nine Lives. Balian, Lorna, illus. 32p. (ps-3). 1987. Repr. of 1986 ed. 7.50 (0-687-37096-5) Humbug Bks.

—Amelia's Nine Lives. Balian, Lorna, illus. 32p. (ps-3). 1986. PLB 13.95 (0-687-01250-3) Humbug Bks.

—The Aminal. Balian, Lorna, illus. 32p. (ps-3). 1987. Repr. of 1972 ed. 7.50 (0-687-37101-5) Humbug Bks.

—Bah! Humbug? Balian, Lorna, illus. 32p. (ps-3). 1988. Repr. of 1978 ed. 7.50 (0-687-37107-4) Humbug Bks.

—A Garden for a Groundhog. Balian, Lorna, illus. 32p. (gr. k up). 1985. PLB 13.95 (0-687-14009-9) Humbug Bks.

—Humbug Potion: An A-B-Cipher. Balian, Lorna, illus. 32p. (ps-3). 1988. Repr. of 1985 ed. 7.50 (0-687-37102-3) Humbug Bks.

—Humbug Potion: An A-B-Cipher. Balian, Lorna, illus. 32p. (ps-3). 1985. PLB 12.95 (0-687-18021-X) Humbug Bks.

—Humbug Rabbit. Balian, Lorna, illus. 32p. (ps-3). 1987. Repr. of 1975 ed. 7.50 (0-687-37098-1) Humbug Bks.

—Humbug Witch. Balian, Lorna, illus. 32p. (gr. k up). 1992. Repr. of 1987 ed. PLB 13.95 (1-881772-24-1) Humbug Bks.

—I Love You, Mary Jane. Balian, Lorna, illus. 48p. (ps-3). 1988. Repr. of 1966 ed. 7.50 (0-687-37100-7) Humbug Bks.

—Leprechauns Never Lie. Balian, Lorna, illus. 32p. (ps-3). 1988. Repr. of 1981 ed. 7.50 (0-687-37110-4) Humbug Bks.

—Mother's, Mother's Day. Balian, Lorna, illus. 32p. (ps-3). 1987. Repr. of 1982 ed. 7.50 (0-687-37097-3) Humbug Bks.

—The Socksnatchers. Balian, Lorna, illus. 32p. (ps-3). 1988. PLB 12.95 (0-687-39047-8) Humbug Bks.

—Sometimes It's Turkey, Sometimes It's Feathers. Balian, Lorna, illus. 32p. (ps-3). 1987. Repr. of 1973 ed. 7.50 (0-687-37106-6) Humbug Bks.

—A Sweetheart for Valentine. Balian, Lorna, illus. 32p. (ps-3). 1988. Repr. of 1980 ed. 7.50 (0-687-37109-0) Humbug Bks.

—Wilbur's Space Machine. Balian, Lorna, illus. LC 90-55095. 32p. (ps-3). 1990. reinforced 14.95 (0-8234-0836-1) Holiday.

Balibar, Francoise & Maury, Jean-Pierre. How Things Fly. 80p. (gr. 8 up). 1989. pap. 4.95 (0-8120-4215-8) Barron.

Balick, Don. Animal Survival. Marson, Ron, ed. Marson, Peg, illus. 80p. (gr. 5-10). 1986. 13.95 (0-941008-37-1) Tops Learning.

Balis, Andrea & Reiser, Robert. P. J. (gr. k-6). 1987. pap. 2.95 (0-440-46880-9, YB) Dell.

Baljo, Wallace, Jr. Grand Coulee: A Story of the Columbia River from Molten Lavas & Ice to Grand Coulee Dam. rev. ed. Hemsley, Roberta G., illus. 80p. (gr. 4-6). pap. write for info. (0-9606084-0-0) Clipboard.

Balkin, Rick, ed. see Gregory, Ross.

Balkin, Rick, ed. see Shifflett, Crandall A.

Balkwill, Fran. Amazing Schemes within Your Genes. Rolph, Mic, illus. LC 92-42942. (gr. 3 up). 1993. 17.50 (0-87614-804-6) Carolrhoda Bks.

—Cell Wars. Rolph, Mic, illus. LC 92-6377. 1992. 17.50 (0-87614-761-9) Carolrhoda Bks.

—Cells Are Us. Rolph, Mic, illus. 32p. (gr. 3-6). 1993. 17.50 (0-87614-762-7) Carolrhoda Bks.

—DNA Is Here to Stay. Rolph, Mic, illus. 32p. (gr. 3-6). 1993. 17.50 (0-87614-763-5) Carolrhoda Bks.

Balkwill, Richard. Trafalgar. LC 93-2650. (Illus.). 32p. (gr. 6 up). 1993. RSBE 13.95 (0-02-726326-6, New Discovery Bks) Macmillan Child Grp.

Ball, Ann. Holy Names of Jesus: Devotions, Litanies, Meditations. LC 90-60646. 192p. (Orig.). 1990. pap. 7.95 (0-87973-428-0, 428) Our Sunday Visitor.

Ball, Brian. Quest for Queenie. (ps-5). 1991. 10.95 (0-316-07961-8) Little.

Ball, Douglas H., et al. Stories Worth Reading. Bruns, Stan & Capron, Michael W., illus. 192p. (Orig.). (gr. 8-11). 1989. pap. text ed. write for info. (0-9621844-0-3) Printemps Bks.

Ball, Duncan. Emily Eyefinger. Ulrich, George, illus. LC 91-20751. 96p. (gr. 2-5). 1992. pap. 13.00 jacketed (0-671-74618-9, S&S BFYR) S&S Trade.

—Emily Eyefinger & the Lost Treasure. Ulrich, George, illus. LC 93-39648. Date not set. write for info. (0-671-86535-8, S&S BFYR) S&S Trade.

—Emily Eyefinger, Secret Agent. Ulrich, George, illus. LC 92-30518. 96p. (gr. 2-5). 1993. pap. 13.00 JRT (0-671-79827-8, S&S BFYR) S&S Trade.

—Grandfather's Wheeliething. Smith, Cat B., illus. LC 93-12524. 1994. pap. 14.00 (0-671-79817-0, S&S BFYR) S&S Trade.

—Jeremy's Tail. Rawlins, Donna, illus. LC 90-28952. 32p. (ps-1). 1991. 14.95 (0-531-05951-0); RLB 14.99 (0-531-08551-1) Orchard Bks Watts.

—Spy Code Handbook. (gr. 4-7). 1992. pap. 3.95 (0-207-16018-X, Pub. by Angus & Robertson AT) HarpC.

—Spy Code Handbook. (gr. 4-7). 1992. pap. 3.95 (0-207-17718-X, Pub. by Angus & Robertson AT) HarpC.

Ball, Jacqueline. Everything You Need to Know about Drug Abuse. rev. ed. (gr. 4-7). 1992. 13.95 (0-8239-1402-X) Rosen Group.

—Let's Party. (Illus.). 32p. (gr. 5 up). 1990. lib. bdg. 15.94 (0-86625-418-8); lib. bdg. 11.95s.p. (0-685-36382-1) Rourke Corp.

—Looking Good, 8 bks, Set 11. (Illus.). 64p. (gr. 5 up). 1990. Set. lib. bdg. 127.52 (0-86625-287-8); 95.60 (0-685-58754-1) Rourke Corp.

—Riddles about Baby Animals. Brook, Bonnie, ed. (Illus.). 32p. (ps-3). 1989. 6.95 (0-671-68577-5); PLB 10.98 (0-671-68576-7) Silver Pr.

—Riddles about Our Bodies. Brook, Bonnie, ed. (Illus.). 32p. (ps-3). 1989. 6.95 (0-671-68579-1); PLB 10.98 (0-671-68578-3) Silver Pr.

—Riddles about the Seasons. Brook, Bonnie, ed. (Illus.). 32p. (ps-3). 1989. 6.95 (0-671-68583-X); PLB 10.98 (0-671-68582-1) Silver Pr.

—Riddles about the Senses. Brook, Bonnie, ed. (Illus.). 32p. (ps-3). 1989. 6.95 (0-671-68581-3); PLB 10.98 (0-671-68580-5) Silver Pr.

Ball, Jacqueline A. Battle of the Class Clowns. 1990. pap. 2.95 (0-06-106007-0, PL) HarpC.

—Halloween Double Dare. (gr. 4-7). 1990. pap. 2.95 (0-06-106006-2, PL) HarpC.

—A Kitten Named Cuddles. (gr. 4-7). 1991. pap. 2.95 (0-06-106038-0, PL) HarpC.

—A Puzzle for Apatosaurus. (gr. 4-7). 1990. pap. 2.95 (0-06-106002-X, PL) HarpC.

—Revenge of the Terror Dactyls. (gr. 4-7). 1991. pap. 2.95 (0-06-106081-X, PL) HarpC.

—Sara's Biggest Valentine. (gr. 4-7). 1991. pap. 2.95 (0-06-106043-7, PL) HarpC.

—Sneeze-O-Saurus. (gr. 4-7). 1990. pap. 2.95 (0-06-106008-9, PL) HarpC.

—T. Rex's Missing Tooth. (gr. 4-7). 1991. pap. 2.95 (0-06-106055-0, Harp PBks) HarpC.

—What Can It Be, 8 bks. (Illus.). (gr. k-3). 1990. Set, 32p. ea. 47.60 (0-671-94104-6); Set, 32p. ea. lib. bdg. 109.80 (0-671-94103-8) Silver Pr.

Ball, Jacqueline A. & Conant, Catherine. Georgia O'Keeffe: Painter of the Desert. (Illus.). 64p. (gr. 3-7). PLB 14.95 (1-56711-033-9) Blackbirch.

Ball, Jane A., jt. auth. see Littlefield, Robert S.

Ball, John & Fairclough, Chris. Fiji. (Illus.). 96p. (gr. 5 up). 1988. 14.95 (0-222-00984-5) Chelsea Hse.

Ball, Karen. Choice Adventures: Hazardous Homestead. 160p. (gr. 4-8). 1992. pap. text ed. 4.99 (0-8423-5032-2) Tyndale.

Ball, Nancy. Boots: The Story of a Saint. Decker, Tim, illus. LC 88-72340. 44p. (Orig.). (gr. 2-5). 1989. pap. 5.00 (0-916383-72-5) Aegina Pr.

—Shy Ann. Christie, Robert D., illus. LC 88-51305. 55p. (Orig.). (gr. k-4). 1989. pap. 3.95 (0-931563-03-8) Wishing Rm.

Ball, Sara. The Animal Show Mix & Match Book. (Illus.). (ps-1). 1992. 4.20 (1-56021-141-5) W J Fantasy.

—The Teddy Bear Book of Days. (Illus.). (gr. 4-12). 1992. 15.00 (1-56021-185-7) W J Fantasy.

Ball, W. W. Fun with String Figures. LC 76-173664. (Illus.). 89p. (gr. k-3). 1971. pap. 2.95 (0-486-22809-6) Dover.

Ball, Zachary. Bristle Face. LC 62-2219. 206p. (gr. 4-7). 1991. 14.95 (0-8234-0915-5) Holiday.

—Bristle Face. LC 93-10394. 208p. (gr. 5 up). 1993. pap. 3.99 (0-14-036444-7, Puffin) Puffin Bks.

Ballantyne, Kay, et al. Hands-On Science: Ten Themes for the Whole Year. (Illus.). 96p. (gr. 1-3). 1993. pap. 12.95 (1-55799-250-9) Evan-Moor Corp.

Ballard, Bob. Explorer. Seymour, Peter, ed. (Illus.). 12p. (gr. 4-8). 1992. 19.95 (1-878685-08-2) Turner Pub GA.

Ballard, John. Monsoon. school ed. LC 84-62121. (Illus.). 240p. (gr. 9 up). 1986. pap. text ed. 9.95 (0-932279-02-3) World Citizens.

—Monsoon: Christian Edition. LC 84-62121. (Illus.). 240p. (gr. 8-12). 1986. pap. 9.95 (0-932279-03-1) World Citizens.

Ballard, Kimberly M. Light at Summer's End. 160p. (Orig.). (gr. 9-12). 1991. pap. 6.99 (0-87788-503-6) Shaw Pubs.

Ballard, Lois. Reptiles. LC 81-38525. (Illus.). 48p. (gr. k-4). 1982. PLB 15.27 (0-516-01644-X); pap. 4.95 (0-516-41644-8) Childrens.

Ballard, Robert D. Exploring the Bismarck: The Real-Life Quest to Find Hitler's Greatest Battleship. (gr. 4-7). 1993. pap. 6.95 (0-590-44269-4) Scholastic Inc.

—Exploring the Titanic. (gr. 4-7). 1991. 14.95 (0-590-41953-6); pap. 6.95 (0-590-41952-8) Scholastic Inc.

Ballard, Robin. Good-bye, House. LC 93-252. (Illus.). 24p. (ps up). 1994. write for info. (0-688-12525-5); PLB write for info. (0-688-12526-3) Greenwillow.

—Gracie. LC 92-14245. (Illus.). 24p. (ps up). 1993. 14.00 (0-688-11806-2); PLB 13.93 (0-688-11807-0) Greenwillow.

—Granny & Me. LC 90-24170. (Illus.). 24p. (ps up). 1992. 14.00 (0-688-10548-3); PLB 13.93 (0-688-10549-1) Greenwillow.

—My Father Is Far Away. LC 91-29580. (Illus.). 32p. (ps-6). 1992. 14.00 (0-688-10953-5); PLB 13.93 (0-688-10954-3) Greenwillow.

Ballenbera, Birdie. Looking at Ballet. LC 89-7176. (Illus.). 48p. (gr. 4-8). 1990. 13.95 (1-85435-105-2) Marshall Cavendish.

Ballenger, Sharon. Adventures of the Ballenger Bears. Colley, Molly, illus. 62p. (Orig.). (ps-6). 1992. Spiral bdg. pap. 11.95 (1-880734-00-1) SharLew Ent.

How many of us have treasured a Teddy Bear friend? Lots of people have them as children but more & more adults have become engrossed in the wonderful world of Teddy Bears & live "real life adventures" with them. This book is composed of 12 stories, each of which recounts a new adventure had by members of a very large collection of Teddy Bears. "...you will enjoy this book for the entertaining stories about Teddy Bears entering the world & looking for adventure. This is just the sort of whimsy loved by all our readers!" (The Teddy Tribune, May, 1993). These stories are illustrated by over 30 charming, gentle drawings that make these characters look so real you could just reach out & give them a hug. While stories aren't preachy, they do encourage the reader to share, to set goals & meet them, to care for family & friends, & to try new things as the Bears do. You will find yourself smiling when you read about the Bears calling on Grandma Bear to help finish up the apricot pie adventure, or trying to learn the polite way to eat cupcakes & drink tea at Bear School. This is definitely a "feel good" book, one which makes you feel you've spent an afternoon with good friends. Order from: SharLew Enterprises, P.O. Box 971, Ridgecrest, CA 93556. (619) 375-8540.

Publisher Provided Annotation.

Ballinger, Erich. Monster Manual: A Complete Guide to Your Favorite Creatures. LC 93-34219. 1994. 18.95 (0-8225-0722-6) Lerner Pubns.

Ballman, Wanda. Jack the Jack Rabbit. (Illus.). 16p. (gr. k-4). 1991. 1.95 (0-8059-3178-3) Dorrance.

Ballonga, Jordi, jt. auth. see Hernandez, Xavier.

Balmer, Helen. Jungle Adventure. (gr. 6). 1993. pap. 14.00 (0-671-86768-7, S&S BFYR) S&S Trade.

Balow, Tom, jt. auth. see Carpenter, Allan.

Balsamo, Kathy. Exploring the Lives of Gifted People-The Sciences. Johnson, Phyllis, illus. 80p. (gr. 4 up). 1987. pap. 8.95 (0-86653-417-2, GA 1038) Good Apple.

—Exploring the Lives of Gifted People-The Arts. Johnson, Phyllis, illus. 80p. (gr. 4 up). 1987. pap. 8.95 (0-86653-406-7, GA1037) Good Apple.

Balsamo, Kathy L. It's about Writing: A Writing Resource for Science, Social Studies, Math & Language. (Illus.). 112p. (Orig.). 1990. pap. 9.95 (0-9623835-2-X) Pieces of Lrning.

Balseiro, Jose A., ed. see Casona, Alejandro.

Balsley, Irol W. Where on Earth? 144p. (gr. 4-8). 1986. wkbk. 11.95 (0-86653-336-2, GA 691) Good Apple.

Balter, Lawrence. A. J.'s Mom Gets a New Job. Schanzer, Roz, illus. 40p. (gr. 3-7). 1990. 5.95 (0-8120-6151-9) Barron.

—Alfred Goes to the Hospital. Schanzer, Roz, illus. 40p. (gr. 3-7). 1990. 5.95 (0-8120-6150-0) Barron.

—A Funeral for Whiskers: Understanding Death. Schanzer, Roz, illus. 40p. (ps-3). 1991. 5.95 (0-8120-6153-5) Barron.

—Linda Saves the Day: Understanding Fear. Schanzer, Roz, illus. 40p. (ps-2). 1989. 5.95 (0-8120-6117-9) Barron.
—Sue Lee Starts School: Adjusting to School. Schanzer, Roz, illus. 40p. (ps-3). 1991. 5.95 (0-8120-6152-7) Barron.
—Sue Lee's New Neighborhood: Adjusting to a New Move. Schanzer, Roz, illus. 40p. (ps-2). 1989. 5.95 (0-8120-6116-0) Barron.
—The Wedding: Adjusting to a Parent's Remarriage. Schanzer, Roz, illus. 40p. (ps-2). 1989. 5.95 (0-8120-6118-7) Barron.
—What's the Matter with A. J? Understanding Jealousy. Schanzer, Roz, illus. 40p. (ps-2). 1989. 5.95 (0-8120-6119-5) Barron.
Balterman, Lee. Girders & Cranes: A Skyscraper Is Built. Levine, Abby, ed. Balterman, Lee, illus. LC 90-37028. 32p. (gr. k-4). 1991. PLB 14.95 (0-8075-2923-0) A Whitman.
Balthis, Frank, ed. see Beach-Balthis, Judy.
Balthis, Frank S., ed. see Beach-Balthis, Judy.
Baltuck, Naomi. Crazy Gibberish & Other Story Hour Stretches from a Storyteller's Bag of Tricks. (Illus.). 1993. PLB 25.00 (0-208-02336-4, Pub. by Linnet); pap. text ed. 15.00 (0-208-02337-2, Pub. by Linnet) Shoe String.
Balzac, Honore De see De Balzac, Honore.
Balzac, Honore de see De Balzac, Honore.
Balzar, Howard. Baseball Super Stars. Allison, B., intro. by. (Illus.). 23p. (Orig.). (gr. 1-8). 1990. pap. 2.50 (0-943409-14-4) Marketcom.
—Baseball Superstars. Allison, B., intro. by. 29p. (Orig.). 1991. pap. 4.95 (0-943409-18-7) Marketcom.
—Basketball Super Stars. Allison, B., intro. by. (Illus.). 23p. (Orig.). (gr. 1-8). 1990. pap. 2.50 (0-943409-15-2) Marketcom.
—Basketball Superstars. Allison, B., intro. by. (Illus.). 29p. (Orig.). 1991. pap. 4.95 (0-943409-17-9) Marketcom.
—Football Super Stars. Allison, B., intro. by. (Illus.). 23p. (Orig.). (gr. 1-8). 1990. pap. 2.50 (0-943409-13-6) Marketcom.
—NFL Superstars. Allison, B., intro. by. (Illus.). 29p. (Orig.). 1991. pap. 4.95 (0-943409-16-0) Marketcom.
—Quarterbacks of the NFL. Allison, B., intro. by. (Illus.). 23p. (Orig.). (gr. 1-8). 1990. pap. 2.50 (0-943409-12-8) Marketcom.
Balzer, Howard. Football All Pro Defense. Allison, B., intro. by. Focus on Sports-New York Staff, illus. 28p. (Orig.). 1989. pap. 2.50 (0-943409-10-1) Marketcom.
—Football All Pro Offense. Allison, B., intro. by. Focus On Sports-New York Staff, illus. (Orig.). 1989. pap. 2.50 (0-943409-09-8) Marketcom.
—Football All Pro Super Stars. Allison, B., ed. Focus On Sports-New York Staff, illus. 28p. (Orig.). 1989. pap. 2.50 (0-943409-11-X) Marketcom.
Balzola, Asun. Munia & the Day Things Went Wrong. (Illus.). 24p. (gr. k-2). 1988. 11.95 (0-521-35643-1) Cambridge U Pr.
—Munia & the Moon. (Illus.). 1989. 11.95 (0-521-37143-0) Cambridge U Pr.
—Munia & the Orange Crocodile. (Illus.). 24p. (gr. k-2). 1988. 11.95 (0-521-35642-3) Cambridge U Pr.
—Munia & the Red Shoes. (Illus.). 1989. 11.95 (0-521-37142-2) Cambridge U Pr.
Bambara, Toni C. Raymond's Run. (gr. 4-9). Date not set. 13.95 (0-88682-351-X, 97222-098) Creative Ed.
Bamberger, David. Judaism & the World's Religions. (gr. 7-8). 7.95 (0-317-70158-4); tchr's guide 14.95 (0-685-43978-X) Behrman.
—A Young Person's History of Israel. Mandelkern, Nicholas, ed. (Illus.). 150p. (Orig.). (gr. 5-7). 1985. pap. 6.95 (0-87441-393-1); By Sara M. Schacheer & Priscilla Fishman. tchr's guide 12.50x (0-87441-419-9); student's activity bk. 4.25 (0-87441-429-6) Behrman.
Banchek, Linda. Snake In, Snake Out. Arnold, Elaine, illus. 32p. (ps-1). 1992. pap. 2.99 (0-440-40738-9, YB) Dell.
Bancroft, Catherine & Gruenberg, Hannah C. Felix's Hat. Greunberg, Hannah, illus. LC 92-10868. 32p. (ps-2). 1993. RSBE 14.95 (0-02-708325-X, Four Winds) Macmillan Child Grp.
Bancroft, Henrietta & Van Gelder, Richard G. Animals in Winter. Di Palma, Gaetano, illus. 40p. (gr. k-3). pap. 1.95 (0-590-01321-1) Scholastic Inc.
Bandele, Ramla. Nzinga. 1992. pap. 6.95 (0-88378-023-2) Third World.
Bandes, Hanna. Sleepy River. Winter, Jeanette, illus. LC 92-26198. 32p. (ps). 1993. 14.95 (0-399-22349-5, Philomel Bks) Putnam Pub Group.
Bandon, Alexandra. Chinese Americans. (Illus.). 112p. (gr. 6 up). 1994. PLB 13.95 RSBE (0-02-768149-1, New Discovery Bks) Macmillan Child Grp.
—Date Rape. LC 93-24063. (gr. 10 up). Date not set. write for info. (0-89686-806-0, Crestwood Hse) Macmillan Child Grp.
—Filipino Americans. LC 92-42205. (Illus.). 112p. (gr. 6 up). 1993. RSBE 13.95 (0-02-768143-2, New Discovery Bks) Macmillan Child Grp.
—Mexican Americans. LC 92-41001. (Illus.). 112p. (gr. 6 up). 1993. RSBE 13.95 (0-02-768142-4, New Discovery Bks) Macmillan Child Grp.
—West Indian Americans. LC 93-27201. (Illus.). 112p. (gr. 6 up). 1994. RSBE 13.95 (0-02-768148-3, New Discovery Bks) Macmillan Child Grp.
Bane, Rosemary, jt. auth. see Poffenberg, Nancy.
Banfield, Beryle, jt. ed. see Myers, Ruth S.

Banfield, Susan. Charlemagne. Schlesinger, Arthur M., Jr., intro. by. (Illus.). 112p. (gr. 5 up). 1986. lib. bdg. 17.95 (0-87754-592-8) Chelsea Hse.
—Charles de Gaulle. Schlesinger, Arthur M., Jr., intro. by. (Illus.). 112p. (gr. 5 up). 1985. lib. bdg. 17.95 (0-87754-551-0) Chelsea Hse.
—Joan of Arc. (Illus.). 112p. (gr. 5 up). 1985. lib. bdg. 17.95 (0-87754-556-1) Chelsea Hse.
—The Rights of Man, the Reign of Terror: The Story of the French Revolution. LC 89-2742. 224p. (gr. 7 up). 1990. 15.00 (0-397-32353-0, Lipp Jr Bks); PLB 14.89 (0-397-32354-9, Lipp Jr Bks) HarpC Child Bks.
Bang. Ten, Nine, Eight. 1993. pap. 28.67 (0-590-73313-3) Scholastic Inc.
Bang, Molly. Dawn. LC 83-886. (Illus.). 32p. (ps up). 1983. 11.95 (0-688-02400-9); PLB 13.88 (0-688-02404-1) Morrow Jr Bks.
—Dawn. LC 83-886. (Illus.). 32p. (ps-3). 1991. pap. 3.95 (0-688-10989-6, Mulberry) Morrow.
—Delphine. Bang, Molly, illus. LC 87-34958. 32p. (gr. 2 up). 1988. 12.95 (0-688-05636-9); PLB 12.88 (0-688-05637-7, Morrow Jr Bks) Morrow Jr Bks.
—The Grey Lady & the Strawberry Snatcher. LC 85-29224. (Illus.). 48p. (ps-3). 1984. RSBE 14.95 (0-02-708140-0, Four Winds) Macmillan Child Grp.
—The Paper Crane. Bang, Molly, illus LC 84-13546. 32p. (gr. k-3). 1985. 13.95 (0-688-04108-6); lib. bdg. 13.93 (0-688-04109-4) Greenwillow.
—The Paper Crane. LC 84-13546. (gr. k-3). 1987. pap. 4.95 (0-688-07333-6, Mulberry) Morrow.
—Ten, Nine, Eight. Bang, Molly, illus. LC 81-20106. 24p. (ps-1). 1983. 14.00 (0-688-00906-9); PLB 13.93 (0-688-00907-7) Greenwillow.
—Ten, Nine, Eight. LC 81-20106. (Illus.). 24p. (ps-3). 1991. pap. 3.95 (0-688-10480-0, Mulberry) Morrow.
—Wiley & the Hairy Man: Adapted from an American Folk Tale. Bang, Molly G., illus. LC 75-38581. 64p. (gr. 1-4). 1976. RSBE 11.95 (0-02-708370-5, Macmillan Child Bk) Macmillan Child Grp.
—Yellow Ball. Bang, Molly, illus. LC 90-46077. 24p. (ps up). 1991. 55.99 (0-688-06314-4); PLB 12.88 (0-688-06315-2, Morrow Jr Bks) Morrow Jr Bks.
—Yellow Ball. LC 92-40722. (Illus.). 32p. (ps-1). 1993. pap. 4.50 (0-14-054828-9, Puffin) Puffin Bks.
Bang, Molly, ed. & illus. The Goblins Giggle & Other Stories. (gr. 3-5). 1988. 17.25 (0-8446-6360-3) Peter Smith.
Bang, Molly G. Tye May & the Magic Brush. LC 80-16488. (Illus.). 56p. (gr. 1 up). 1992. pap. 4.95 (0-688-11504-7, Mulberry) Morrow.
—Wiley & the Hairy Man: Adapted from an American Folk Tale. Bang, Molly G., illus. LC 87-2540. 64p. (gr. 1-4). 1987. pap. 3.95 (0-689-71162-X, Aladdin) Macmillan Child Grp.
Bangs, Edward. Yankee Doodle. Kellogg, Steven, illus. LC 80-17024. 40p. (ps-3). 1989. SBE 13.95 (0-02-749800-X, Four Winds) Macmillan Child Grp.
Banim, Lisa. American Dreams. Golub, Nan, illus. LC 93-22573. 80p. (gr. 4-6). 1993. PLB 12.95 (1-881889-34-3) Silver Moon.
—Drums at Saratoga. LC 93-16460. 64p. (Orig.). (gr. 4-6). 1993. PLB 12.95 (1-881889-20-3) Silver Moon.
—A Spy in Boston. (Illus.). 80p. (gr. 4-6). 1994. PLB 12.95 (1-881889-54-8) Silver Moon.
Banish, Roslyn. A Forever Family: A Book About Adoption. Banish, Roslyn, illus. LC 90-28725. 48p. (gr. k-3). 1992. 14.00 (0-06-021673-5); PLB 13.89 (0-06-021674-3) HarpC Child Bks.
—A Forever Family: A Book About Adoption. Banish, Roslyn, illus. LC 90-28726. 48p. (gr. k-3). 1992. pap. 5.95 (0-06-446116-5, Trophy) HarpC Child Bks.
Banister, Manly. Making Picture Frames in Wood. LC 81-50985. (Illus.). 128p. (gr. 10-12). 1981. pap. 9.95 (0-8069-7542-3) Sterling.
Bank Street College Media Group, ed. see Hooks, William A., et al.
Bank Street College of Education Editors. ABC Come Play with Me. (Illus.). 64p. (ps-k). 1985. 3.95 (0-8120-3617-4) Barron.
—All Around the House. (Illus.). 64p. (ps-k). 1985. 2.95 (0-8120-3613-1) Barron.
—All Around the Neighborhood. (Illus.). 64p. (ps-k). 1985. 2.95 (0-8120-3612-3) Barron.
—Animals, Animals, Animals: At Home - In the Circus - At the Zoo. (Illus.). 64p. (ps-k). 1985. pap. 2.95 (0-8120-3610-7) Barron.
—Get Ready to Read. (Illus.). 64p. (ps-k). 1985. 3.95 (0-8120-3616-6) Barron.
—It's about Time: Play Time - Work Time - Learning Time. (Illus.). 64p. (ps-k). 1985. 2.95 (0-8120-3611-5) Barron.
—Let's Do Math. (gr. 1-2). 1986. pap. 3.95 (0-8120-3627-1) Barron.
—Let's Explore Land, Water, Air. (gr. 1-2). 1986. pap. 2.95 (0-8120-3624-7) Barron.
—Let's Explore the Seasons. (gr. 1-2). 1986. pap. 2.95 (0-8120-3625-5) Barron.
—Let's Learn about Money. (gr. 1-2). 1986. pap. 3.95 (0-8120-3626-3) Barron.
—Let's Play Word Games. (gr. 1-2). 1986. pap. 3.95 (0-8120-3628-X) Barron.
—Let's Take a Ride. (gr. 1-2). 1986. pap. 2.95 (0-8120-3623-9) Barron.
—One to Ten More Counting Fun. (Illus.). 64p. (ps-k). 1985. 3.95 (0-8120-3614-X) Barron.
—One, Two, Three Come Count with Me. (Illus.). 64p. (ps-k). 1985. 3.95 (0-8120-3615-8) Barron.

Bank Street College of Education Staff. Barron's Book of Fun & Learning. 384p. (gr. k). 1987. pap. 19.95 (0-8120-3822-3) Barron.
—Let's Make Word Games. (gr. 1-2). 1986. pap. 3.95 (0-8120-3629-8) Barron.
—Let's Stay Safe & Sound. (gr. 1-2). 1986. pap. 2.95 (0-8120-3622-0) Barron.
Banks, Ann. It's My Money: A Kid's Guide to the Green Stuff. Natti, Susanna, illus. LC 92-12618. 32p. (gr. 2-6). 1993. pap. 3.99 (0-14-036086-7, Puffin) Puffin Bks.
—It's My Money: A Kid's Guide to the Green Stuff. Natti, Susanna, illus. LC 93-12618. 32p. (gr. 3-7). 1993. 3.99 (0-670-36086-4) Puffin Bks.
—When Your Parents Get a Divorce. Bobak, Cathy, illus. 64p. (gr. 3 up). 1990. pap. 7.95 (0-14-034340-7, Puffin) Puffin Bks.
Banks, Ann & Evans, Nancy. Goodbye, House. Russo, Marisabina, illus. 64p. (gr. 2-6). 1988. pap. 7.95 (0-517-53907-1, Harmony) Crown Pub Group.
Banks, David. Sarah Ferguson: The Royal Redhead. LC 87-15567. (Illus.). 64p. (gr. 3 up). 1988. RSBE 13.95 (0-87518-369-7, Dillon) Macmillan Child Grp.
Banks, Doris, ed. see Hollenbeck, Joan W.
Banks, Jacqueline T. Project Wheels. LC 92-10843. 112p. (gr. 3-6). 1993. 13.95 (0-395-64378-3) HM.
Banks, Joann. Brandon's First Baseball Game. Robinson, Famous, illus. LC 90-63290. 37p. (Orig.). (gr. ps-6). 1990. pap. text ed. 5.00 (0-9627951-0-0) JRBB Pubs.
Banks, Kate. Alphabet Soup. Sis, Peter, illus. LC 87-3191. 32p. (ps-2). 1988. 12.95 (0-394-89151-1) Knopf Bks Yng Read.
—Big, Bigger, Biggest Adventure. Yalowitz, Paul, illus. LC 89-34919. 40p. (ps-3). 1990. 12.95 (0-394-89857-5); lib. bdg. 13.99 (0-394-99857-X) Knopf Bks Yng Read.
—The Bunnysitters. Sims, Blanche, illus. LC 90-27441. 80p. (Orig.). (gr. 2-4). 1991. lib. bdg. 6.99 (0-679-91232-0); pap. 2.50 (0-679-81232-6) Random Bks Yng Read.
Banks, Katherine A. Peter & the Talking Shoes. Date not set. write for info. (0-394-82723-6) Knopf Bks Yng Read.
Banks, Lynne R. The Adventures of King Midas. Smith, Jos A., illus. LC 92-3795. 160p. (gr. 3 up). 1992. 14.00 (0-688-10894-6) Morrow Jr Bks.
—The Adventures of King Midas. 160p. (gr. 4). 1993. pap. 3.99 (0-380-71564-3, Camelot) Avon.
—The Fairy Rebel. Geldart, William, illus. LC 87-28740. 128p. (gr. 5 up). 1988. 12.95 (0-385-24483-5) Doubleday.
—The Fairy Rebel. 128p. (gr. 4). 1989. pap. 3.50 (0-380-70650-4, Camelot) Avon.
—The Fairy Rebel. large type ed. (Illus.). 227p. 1989. lib. bdg. 15.95 (1-55736-124-X, Crnrstn Bks) BDD LT Grp.
—Farthest-Away Mountain. (gr. 4-7). 1991. pap. 14.95 (0-385-41534-6) Doubleday.
—The Farthest-Away Mountain. 144p. 1992. pap. 3.50 (0-380-71303-9, Camelot) Avon.
—I, Houdini. (Orig.). (gr. 4-7). 1989. pap. 3.50 (0-380-70649-0, Camelot) Avon.
—I, Houdini: The Autobiography of a Self-Educated Hamster. Riley, Terry, illus. LC 87-22284. 128p. (gr. 5 up). 1988. pap. 12.95 (0-385-24482-7) Doubleday.
—The Indian in the Cupboard. Cole, Brock, illus. 192p. (gr. 4-7). 1982. pap. 3.99 (0-380-60012-9, Camelot) Avon.
—The Indian in the Cupboard. (gr. 4). 1985. 15.00 (0-385-17051-3) Doubleday.
—Indian in the Cupboard. large type ed. (gr. 5 up). 1988. Repr. of 1980 ed. lib. bdg. 15.95 (1-55736-034-0, Crnrstn Bks) BDD LT Grp.
—Lynne Reid Banks, 3 vols. (gr. 4-7). 1991. See. pap. 10. 50 boxed (0-380-71680-1) Avon.
—The Magic Hare. Moser, Barry, illus. LC 92-10585. 64p. 1993. 15.00 (0-688-10895-4); PLB 14.93 (0-688-10896-2) Morrow Jr Bks.
—Melusine: A Mystery. LC 88-32798. 256p. (gr. 7 up). 1989. HarpC Child Bks.
—Melusine: A Mystery. LC 88-32798. 224p. (gr. 7 up). 1991. pap. 3.95 (0-06-447054-7, Trophy) HarpC Child Bks.
—The Mystery of the Cupboard. Newsom, Tom, illus. LC 92-39295. 256p. (gr. 5 up). 1993. 13.95 (0-688-12138-1); PLB 13.88 (0-688-12635-9) Morrow Jr Bks.
—One More River. rev. ed. 256p. (gr. 5 up). 1992. 14.00 (0-688-10893-8) Morrow Jr Bks.
—One More River. 256p. 1993. pap. 3.99 (0-380-71563-5, Camelot) Avon.
—Return of the Indian. Geldart, William, illus. LC 85-31119. 192p. (gr. 4-6). 1986. pap. 13.95 (0-385-23497-X) Doubleday.
—The Return of the Indian. (gr. 3-7). 1987. pap. 3.99 (0-380-70284-3, Camelot) Avon.
—The Return of the Indian. large type ed. (Illus.). 227p. 1989. PLB 15.95 (1-55736-104-5, Crnrstn Bks) BDD LT Grp.
—The Secret of the Indian. (gr. 5 up). 1989. pap. 14.95 (0-385-26292-2) Doubleday.
—The Secret of the Indian. 160p. 1990. pap. 3.99 (0-380-71040-4, Camelot) Avon.
Banks, M. Endangered Wildlife. (Illus.). 48p. (gr. 5 up). 1988. PLB 18.60 (0-86592-284-5); 13.95 (0-685-58319-8) Rourke Corp.
Banks, Marcus. The Soup Kitchen. 32p. (gr. 9 up). 1993. pap. 5.95 (0-8059-3322-0) Dorrance.

Banks, Martin. Conserving Rain Forests. LC 89-21658. (Illus.). 48p. (gr. 4-9). 1990. PLB 19.92 (0-8114-2387-5); pap. 5.95 (0-8114-3452-4) Raintree Steck-V.
—Discovering Badgers. Caulkins, Janet, ed. (Illus.). 48p. (gr. 1-6). 1988. PLB 12.40 (0-531-18225-8, Pub. by Bookwright Pr) Watts.
—Discovering Otters. Caulkins, Janet, ed. (Illus.). 48p. (gr. 1-6). 1988. PLB 12.40 (0-531-18227-4, Pub. by Bookwright Pr) Watts.
—The Polar Bear on the Ice. Oxford Scientific Films Staff, photos by. LC 89-4472. (Illus.). 32p. (gr. 4-6). 1989. PLB 15.93 (0-8368-0114-8) Gareth Stevens Inc.
Banks, Martin, jt. auth. see Harrison, Virginia.
Banks, Merry. Animals of the Night. Himler, Ronald, illus. LC 89-6194. 32p. (ps-k). 1990. SBE 13.95 (0-684-19093-1, Scribners Young Read) Macmillan Child Grp.
Banks, Sara H. Remember My Name. Saflund, Birgitta, illus. LC 92-61905. 120p. (Orig.). (gr. 4-8). 1993. pap. 8.95 (1-879373-31-6) R Rinehart.
—Tomo-Chi Chi: Gentle Warrior. 2nd ed. LC 93-85477. 80p. (gr. 5 up). 1993. pap. 7.95 (1-879373-59-9) R Rinehart.
Banks, Valerie J. Flags of the African People: Benderas of the African Diaspora, 2 vols. Tony Productions Staff & Tyler, Brian, illus. (Orig.). (gr. k-8). 1990. pap. 9.95 (0-9622340-9-5) Sala Enterp.
—Kwanzaa: An African Celebration. (Illus.). 16p. 1991. pap. 3.00 (0-685-59710-5) Sala Enterp.
—Kwanzaa Coloring Book. 6th ed. (ENG & SWA., Illus.). 46p. (gr. k-8). 1992. pap. 5.95 (0-9622340-6-0) Sala Enterp.
Bannan, Jan G. Sand Dunes. (Illus.). 48p. (gr. 3-6). 1989. lib. bdg. 19.95 (0-87614-321-4); pap. 6.95 (0-87614-513-6) Carolrhoda Bks.
Bannatyne-Cugnet, Jo. A Prairie Alphabet. Moore, Yvette, illus. LC 92-80414. 32p. (gr. k up). 1992. 19. 95 (0-88776-292-1) Tundra Bks.
Banner, Angela. Ant & Bee: Alphabetical Story for Tiny Tots. Ward, Bryan, illus. 96p. (ps-1). 1991. 6.95 (0-434-92966-2, Pub. by W Heinemann Ltd) Trafalgar.
—Ant & Bee & Kind Dog. Ward, Bryan, illus. 96p. (ps-1). 1992. 6.95 (0-434-92960-3, Pub. by W Heinemann Ltd) Trafalgar.
—Ant & Bee & the ABC. (Illus.). 96p. (ps-1). 1989. 6.95 (0-434-92967-0, Pub. by W Heinemann Ltd) Trafalgar.
—Ant & Bee & the Doctor. Ward, Bryan, illus. 96p. (ps-1). 1992. 6.95 (0-434-92968-9, Pub. by W. Heinemann Ltd) Trafalgar.
—Ant & Bee & the Rainbow. Ward, Bryan, illus. 96p. (ps-1). 1992. 6.95 (0-434-92972-7, Pub. by W. Heinemann Ltd) Trafalgar.
—Ant & Bee & the Secret. (Illus.). 96p. (ps-1). 1989. 6.95 (0-434-92959-X, Pub. by W Heinemann Ltd) Trafalgar.
—Ant & Bee Go Shopping. Ward, Bryan, illus. 96p. (ps-1). 1992. 6.95 (0-434-92970-0, Pub. by W Heinemann Ltd) Trafalgar.
—Ant & Bee Time. (Illus.). 94p. (ps-3). 1988. 6.95 (0-434-92961-1, Pub. by W Heinemann Ltd) Trafalgar.
—Around the World with Ant & Bee. (Illus.). 96p. (ps-1). 1989. 6.95 (0-434-92958-1, Pub. by W Heinemann Ltd) Trafalgar.
—Happy Birthday with Ant & Bee. (Illus.). 96p. (ps-1). 1989. 6.95 (0-434-92963-8, Pub. by W Heinemann Ltd) Trafalgar.
—More & More Ant & Bee. (Illus.). 96p. (ps-1). 1989. 6.95 (0-434-92962-X, Pub. by W Heinemann Ltd) Trafalgar.
—More Ant & Bee. (Illus.). 96p. (ps-1). 1989. 6.95 (0-434-92965-4, Pub. by W Heinemann Ltd) Trafalgar.
—One, Two, Three with Ant & Bee. (Illus.). 96p. (ps-1). 1989. 6.95 (0-434-92964-6, Pub. by W Heinemann Ltd) Trafalgar.
Bannerman, Helen. The Story of Little Black Mingo. (Illus.). 72p. (ps-4). 1990. Repr. of 1901 ed. 12.95 (0-9616844-5-3) Greenhouse Pub.
—The Story of Little Black Quasha. (Illus.). 56p. (ps-4). 1990. Repr. of 1908 ed. 10.95 (0-9616844-3-7) Greenhouse Pub.
—The Story of Little Black Quibba. (Illus.). 68p. (ps-4). 1990. Repr. of 1902 ed. 10.95 (0-9616844-4-5) Greenhouse Pub.
—Story of Little Black Sambo. (Illus.). (gr. k-3). 1923. 12. 00 (0-397-30006-9, HarpT) HarpC.
Bannister, Barbara F. Reading Round-Ups: One Hundred Ten Ready-to-Use Literature Enrichment Activities. 288p. (gr. 5-8). 1988. pap. 24.95x (0-87628-750-X) Ctr Appl Res.
Bannister, Ned. Cadets: Code Name: Snowball, No. 1. (gr. 3 up). 1988. pap. 2.95 (0-345-35115-0) Ballantine.
—Code Name: North Star. (gr. 4 up). 1989. pap. 2.95 (0-345-35921-6) Ballantine.
Bannister, Roberta. Math: Grade 1. Hoffman, Joan, ed. Cook, Chris, illus. 32p. (gr. 1). 1979. wkbk. 1.99 (0-938256-28-9) Sch Zone Pub Co.
—Math: Grade 2. Hoffman, Joan, ed. Cook, Chris, illus. 32p. (gr. 2). 1979. wkbk. 1.99 (0-938256-30-0) Sch Zone Pub Co.
—Math: Grade 3. Hoffman, Joan, ed. Cook, Chris, illus. 32p. (gr. 3). 1979. wkbk. 1.99 (0-938256-31-9) Sch Zone Pub Co.
—Math: Grade 4. Hoffman, Joan, ed. Cook, Chris, illus. 32p. (gr. 4). 1979. wkbk. 1.99 (0-938256-33-5) Sch Zone Pub Co.

—Math: Grades 5-6. Hoffman, Joan, ed. Cook, Chris, illus. 32p. (gr. 5-6). 1980. wkbk. 1.99 (0-938256-35-1) Sch Zone Pub Co
Bannon, Troy. Aggro Moves. (gr. 4-7). 1991. pap. 2.99 (0-440-40506-8) Dell.
—Air Walk. (gr. 4-7). 1991. pap. 2.99 (0-440-40532-7, YB) Dell.
—Mean Street. 1992. pap. 2.99 (0-440-40588-2, YB) Dell.
—Power Grind. (gr. 4-7). 1992. pap. 2.99 (0-440-40559-9) Dell.
Bansemer, Roger, jt. auth. see May, Daryl.
Banta, Melissa. Frederick Douglass. (Illus.). 80p. (gr. 3-5). 1993. PLB 12.95 (0-7910-1765-6) Chelsea Hse.
—Frederick Douglass. (gr. 4-7). 1993. pap. 4.95 (0-7910-1973-X) Chelsea Hse.
Banta, Robert. Grandpa Says: You Can Make It a Wonderful Life. LC 89-52115. 148p. (gr. 2-6). 1990. 7.95 (1-55523-312-0) Winston-Derek.
Banta, Susan, illus. Animals. 10p. (ps-1). 1993. bds. 2.95 (1-56293-311-6) McClanahan Bk.
—Colors. 10p. (ps-1). 1993. bds. 2.95 (1-56293-309-4) McClanahan Bk.
—Opposites. 10p. (ps-1). 1993. bds. 2.95 (1-56293-312-4) McClanahan Bk.
—Shapes. 10p. (ps-1). 1993. bds. 2.95 (1-56293-310-8) McClanahan Bk.
Bantam. Cop & a Half. (gr. 4-6). 1993. pap. 3.50 (0-553-48138-X) Bantam.
Bantam Staff. Things to Cuddle. (ps). 1994. 2.99 Bantam.
—Things to Eat. (ps). 1994. 2.99 Bantam.
—Things to Wear. (ps). 1994. 2.99 Bantam.
—Things with Wheels. (ps). 1994. 2.99 Bantam.
Bantock, Nick. Kubla Khan: A Pop-up Version of Coleridge's Classic. (Illus.). 19p. 1994. 12.95 (0-670-85242-2, Viking) Viking Penguin.
—Nick Bantock Boxed Set: Jabberwocky; The Walrus & the Carpenter. (Illus.). 1993. 18.90 (0-670-77265-8, Viking) Viking Penguin.
—Nick Bantock Boxed Set: Robin Hood; Solomon Grundy; There Was an Old Lady. (Illus.). 1993. 27.85 (0-670-77264-X, Viking) Viking Penguin.
—Runners, Sliders, Bouncers, Climbers: A Pop-up Look at Animals in Motion. Bantock, Nick, illus. 15p. (gr. 1-5). 1992. 14.95 (1-56282-219-5) Hyprn Child.
—The Walrus & the Carpenter. (Illus.). 12p. 1992. 9.95 (0-670-84503-5, Viking) Viking Penguin.
—Wings: A Pop-up Book of Things That Fly. Bantock, Nick, illus. LC 90-60979. 12p. (ps-5). 1991. 14.95 (0-679-81041-2) Random Bks Yng Read.
Bantock, Nick, retold by. & illus. Solomon Grundy: A Pop-up Rhyme. 12p. 1992. 8.95 (0-670-84319-9) Viking Child Bks.
—There Was an Old Lady. (gr. 4 up). 1990. pap. 8.95 (0-670-83194-8) Viking Child Bks.
Baquedano, Elizabeth. Aztec, Inca, & Maya. Zabe, Michel & Rudkin, David, illus. 64p. (gr. 5 up). 1993. 15.00 (0-679-83883-X); PLB 15.99 (0-679-93883-4) Knopf Bks Yng Read.
Bar, Amos. Gary el Jardinero. Writer, C. C. & Nielsen, Lisa C., trs. Elchanan, illus. (SPA.). 24p. (Orig.). (ps). 1992. pap. text ed. 3.00x (1-56134-172-X) Dushkin Pub.
—Gary the Gardener. Kriss, David, tr. from HEB. Elchanan, illus. 24p. (Orig.). (ps). 1992. pap. text ed. 3.00x (1-56134-162-2) Dushkin Pub.
Baraldi, Giani, jt. auth. see Brewster, Scott.
Baraldi, Severino, jt. auth. see Montgomery, Mary.
Baram, Bella. The Cat Who Looked for a House. Kriss, David, tr. from HEB. Elchanan, illus. 24p. (Orig.). (ps). 1992. pap. text ed. 3.00x (1-56134-140-1) Dushkin Pub.
—La Gata Que Buscaba un Hogar. Writer, C. C. & Nielsen, Lisa C., trs. Elchanan, illus. (SPA.). 24p. (Orig.). (ps). 1992. pap. text ed. 3.00x (1-56134-150-9) Dushkin Pub.
Baranoff, Timy. Kindergarten Minute by Minute. LC 78-72076. (gr. k). 1991. pap. 10.95 (0-8224-4100-4) Fearon Teach Aids.
Baranzini, Marlene S., jt. auth. see Bovert, Howard E.
Barasch, Lynne. Rodney's Inside Story. LC 91-24405. (Illus.). 32p. (ps-1). 1992. 13.95 (0-531-05993-6); PLB 13.99 (0-531-08593-7) Orchard Bks Watts.
—A Winter Walk. LC 92-39804. 1993. 13.45 (0-395-65937-X) Ticknor & Fields.
Barasch, Marc I. No Plain Pets! Drescher, Henrik, illus. LC 90-22518. 40p. (ps-3). 1991. 14.95 (0-06-022472-X); PLB 14.89 (0-06-022473-8) HarpC Child Bks.
Barba, Harry & Barba, Marian, eds. What's Cooking in Congress? LC 79-83777. (Illus.). 144p. (gr. 5 up). 1979. pap. 9.95 (0-911906-15-0) Harian Creative Bks.
Barba, Marian, jt. ed. see Barba, Harry.
Barba, Roberta A. Kids Know. (gr. 3 up). 1992. 7.95 (0-8062-4260-4) Carlton.
Barbadillo, Pedro, tr. see Cole, Brock.
Barbadillo, Pedro, tr. see L'Engle, Madeleine.
Barbalet, Margaret. The Wolf. Tanner, Jane, illus. LC 91-25202. 32p. (gr. 1-4). 1992. 14.95 (0-02-711840-1, Macmillan Child Bk) Macmillan Child Grp.
Barbaresi, Nina. Snow White & the Seven Dwarfs - Coloring Book. 1989. pap. 1.00 (0-486-25911-0) Dover.
Barbato, Juli. From Bed to Bus. Schatell, Brian, illus. LC 84-20159. 32p. (ps-2). 1985. RSBE 13.95 (0-02-708380-2, Macmillan Child Bk) Macmillan Child Grp.

Barber. Buzzard Is My Best Friend. 1981. 12.95 (0-02-507260-9) Macmillan.
Barber, Antonia. Gemma & the Baby Chick. Littlewood, Karin, illus. 32p. (ps-3). 1993. 14.95 (0-590-45479-X) Scholastic Inc.
—The Ghosts. Ashby, Ruth, ed. 224p. (gr. 6-9). 1989. pap. 2.99 (0-671-70714-0, Archway) PB.
—The Mousehole Cat. Bayley, Nicola, illus. LC 90-31533. 40p. (gr. k-3). 1990. SBE 14.95 (0-02-708331-4, Macmillan Child Bk) Macmillan Child Grp.
Barber, Barbara E. Saturday at The New You. Rich, Anna, illus. LC 93-5165. 1994. 14.95 (1-880000-06-7) Lee & Low Bks.
Barber, Ezekiel. Instant Encyclopedia of Indian History. Narang, Rajanini, ed. Zimmerman, L., intro. by. (Illus.). 413p. (gr. 8-9). 1981. write for info. (0-911799-01-X) Simplex Ent.
Barber, Jacqueline. Bubble-ology. Bergman, Lincoln & Fairwell, Kay, eds. Baker, Lisa H., et al, illus. Barber, Jacqueline & Sneider, Cary I., photos by. 53p. (gr. 5-9). 1987. pap. 8.50 (0-912511-11-7) Lawrence Science.
—Chemical Reactions. Bergman, Lincoln & Fairwell, Kay, eds. Baker, Lisa H. & Craig, Rose, illus. Barber, Jacqueline, et al, photos by. 24p. (Orig.). (gr. 7-10). 1986. pap. 7.50 (0-912511-13-3) Lawrence Science.
—Crime Lab Chemistry. rev. ed. Bergman, Lincoln & Fairwell, Kay, eds. (Illus.). 10p. (gr. 4-8). 1989. pap. 7.50 (0-912511-16-8) Lawrence Science.
—Solids, Liquids, & Gases. Bergman, Lincoln & Fairwell, Kay, eds. Baker, Lisa H. & Peterson, Adria, illus. Barber, Jacqueline, et al, photos by. 56p. (Orig.). (gr. 3-6). 1986. pap. 10.00 (0-912511-69-9) Lawrence Science.
—Vitamin C Testing. Bergman, Lincoln & Fairwell, Kay, eds. Bevilacqua, Carol, illus. Barber, Jacqueline & Hoyt, Richard, photos by. (Illus.). 48p. (Orig.). (gr. 4-8). 1988. pap. 8.50 (0-912511-70-2) Lawrence Science.
Barber, Jacqueline & Willard, Carolyn. Bubble Festival. Bergman, Lincoln & Babcock, Carl, eds. (Illus.). 184p. (gr. k-6). 1992. pap. 12.00 (0-912511-80-X) Lawrence Science.
Barber, Jacqueline, jt. auth. see Sneider, Cary I.
Barber, Joel. Wild Fowl Decoys. 2nd ed. Barber, Joel, illus. 151p. (gr. 10 up). 1989. Repr. of 1934 ed. 39.95 (1-56416-002-5) Derrydale Pr.
Barber, Lilian S. The New Complete Italian Greyhound. Cooper, Joan M. & Cooper, William J., eds. Barber, Lilian S. (Illus.). 1993. 21.95 (0-9611986-2-1) Ital Greyhnd.
Barber, Linda & Gabriel, Nancy. I Can Write! I Can Read! My Writing Book for Names & Telephone Numbers. (Illus.). 128p. (gr. ps-2). 1994. wkbk. 9.95 (0-9632868-0-3) Going Places.
Barber, Nicola. Building for Tomorrow. LC 92-24925. (Illus.). 48p. (gr. 5). 1992. PLB 22.80 (0-8114-2805-2) Raintree Steck-V.
Barber, Phyllis. Legs: The Story of a Giraffe. Baumann, Ann, illus. LC 90-47679. 80p. (gr. 4-7). 1991. SBE 13. 95 (0-689-50526-4, M K McElderry) Macmillan Child Grp.
Barberis, France. Would You Like a Parrot? Barberis, Franco, illus. LC 67-28671. 32p. (ps-k). 8.95 (0-87592-060-8) Scroll Pr.
Barbey, Dorine. Giant Works: Underground, over Water, in the Air. Bogard, Vicki, tr. from FRE. Favreau, Luc, illus. LC 91-48167. 38p. (gr. k-5). 1992. 4.95 (0-944589-44-8) Young Discovery Lib.
—Giant Works: Underground, over Water, in the Air. Favreau, Luc, illus. 40p. (gr. k-5). 1993. PLB 12.95 (1-56674-059-2, HTS Bks) Forest Hse.
—What Are the Five Senses? (ps-3). 1994. 4.95 (0-944589-48-0) Young Discovery Lib.
Barbic, Ivo. Playing Tennis with Bouncy & Fuzzy. Blanc, Henry, illus. 96p. 1987. pap. 9.95 (0-88289-654-7) Pelican.
Barbieri, Roberto, jt. auth. see Dambrosio, Monica.
Barbieri-McGrath, Barbara. The M & M's Counting Book. Glass, Roger R., illus. 1994. write for info. (0-88106-854-3); PLB write for info. (0-88106-855-1); pap. write for info. (0-88106-853-5) Charlesbridge Pub.
Barbosa, Rogerio A. African Animal Tales. Guthrie, Feliz, tr. from POR. Fittipaldi, Cica, illus. LC 92-42378. 60p. (gr. 1-3). 1993. 17.95 (0-912078-96-0) Volcano Pr.
Barbosa-Lima, Carlos, jt. auth. see Griggs, John.
Barbot, Daniel. A Bicycle for Rosaura. Fuenmayor, Morella, illus. 24p. (ps-3). 1991. 9.95 (0-916291-34-0) Kane-Miller Bk.
Barbour, Harriot B. & Freeman, Warren S. Story of Music. rev. ed. (Illus.). 312p. (gr. 7-9). 1958. text ed. 13.95 (0-87487-033-X) Summy-Birchard.
Barbour, Karen. Little Nino's Pizzeria. 32p. (ps-3). 1990. pap. 4.95 (0-15-246321-6, Voyager Bks) HarBrace.
—Little Nino's Pizzeria. (ps). 1991. pap. 19.95 (0-15-246322-4, HB Juv Bks) HarBrace.
—Mr. Bow Tie. (ps-3). 1991. 13.95 (0-15-256165-X, HB Juv Bks) HarBrace.
—Nancy. (Illus.). 30p. (ps-3). 1989. 13.95 (0-15-256675-9) HarBrace.
Barboza, Ronald, ed. A Salute to Cape Verdean Musicians & Their Music. (Illus.). 48p. (gr. 9-12). 1989. pap. 10.00 (0-9627637-0-5) D&C Cape Verdeans.

Barboza, Steven. Door of No Return: The Legend of Goree Island. LC 93-21163. 1994. write for info. (*0-525-65188-8*, Cobblehill Bks) Dutton Child Bks.
—I Feel Like Dancing: A Year with Jacques D'Amboise & the National Dance Institute. D'Amboise, Carolyn G., photos by. LC 91-28439. (Illus.). 48p. (gr. 2-6). 1992. 13.00 (*0-517-58454-9*); PLB 13.99 (*0-517-58455-7*) Crown Bks Yng Read.
Barchas. I Was Walking down the Road. 1993. pap. 28. 67 (*0-590-71883-5*) Scholastic Inc.
Barchas, Sarah. Pinata: Bilingual Songs for Children. 24p. (gr. k-6). 1991. pap. 12.95 incl. audiocassette (*0-9632621-0-6*) High Haven Mus.
Barclay, John, ed. see Maitland, William J.
Barclay, Shinan N. Who Am I? What Am I? Where Do I Belong? The Storytale about the Search for Meaning, Identity & Purpose. (Illus.). 40p. (ps-4). 1990. 5.95 (*0-317-89505-2*); pap. write for info. (*0-945086-08-3*) Sunlight Prodns.
Barclay, William. Prayers for Young People. LC 92-38164. 96p. (Orig.). 1993. pap. 4.95 (*0-687-33328-8*) Abingdon.
Barclay-Smith, Phyllis, jt. auth. see Pollard, H. B.
Bard, Roberta. Francis Drake: First Englishman to Circle the Globe. LC 91-34522. (Illus.). 128p. (gr. 3 up). 1992. PLB 26.60 (*0-516-03067-1*) Childrens.
Bard, Tate, ed. see Buch, Jane.
Bard, Tate, ed. see McClure, Patricia.
Barden. Base Stealers. 1991. 12.50s.p. (*0-86593-126-7*) Rourke Corp.
—MVPs. 1991. 16.67 (*0-86593-127-5*); 12.50s.p. (*0-685-66095-8*) Rourke Corp.
—Prisons. 1991. 12.95s.p. (*0-86593-110-0*); 17.27 (*0-685-59207-3*) Rourke Corp.
Barden, Helen. Busy Little Gardener. 1990. 5.99 (*0-517-03603-7*) Outlet Bk Co.
Barden, Renardo. The Discovery of America: Opposing Viewpoints. LC 89-11709. (Illus.). 112p. (gr. 5-8). 1989. PLB 14.95 (*0-89908-071-5*) Greenhaven.
—Fears & Phobias. LC 89-1340. (Illus.). 48p. (gr. 4 up). 1989. RSBE 12.95 (*0-89686-441-3*, Crestwood Hse) Macmillan Child Grp.
—Gangs. LC 89-1413. (Illus.). 48p. (gr. 4 up). 1989. RSBE 12.95 (*0-89686-440-5*, Crestwood Hse) Macmillan Child Grp.
—Gangs. (Illus.). 64p. (gr. 7 up). 1990. lib. bdg. 17.27 (*0-86593-073-2*); 12.95s.p. (*0-685-36324-4*) Rourke Corp.
—Gun Control. (Illus.). 64p. (gr. 7 up). 1990. lib. bdg. 17. 27 (*0-86593-072-4*); lib. bdg. 12.95s.p. (*0-685-36325-2*) Rourke Corp.
—Playoff Pressure. LC 92-9143. 1992. 17.26 (*0-86593-162-3*); 12.95s.p. (*0-685-59400-9*) Rourke Pubns.
Barden, Robert, jt. auth. see Hacker, Michael.
Barden, Rosalind. TV Monster. (Illus.). 32p. (ps-2). 1988. 12.95 (*0-517-56934-5*) Crown Bks Yng Read.
Bardill, Donald R., jt. auth. see Mueller, Charles S.
Bardon, Keith. Exploring Forces & Structures. Clay, Marilyn, illus. LC 91-38318. 48p. (gr. 4-8). 1992. PLB 19.92 (*0-8114-2602-5*) Raintree Steck-V.
Bare, Colleen S. Busy, Busy Squirrels. Bare, Colleen S., photos by. LC 90-44219. (Illus.). 32p. (gr. 1-4). 1991. 12.95 (*0-525-65063-6*, Cobblehill Bks) Dutton Child Bks.
—Critter: The Class Cat. (Illus.). 32p. (ps-2). 1993. pap. 3.99 (*0-14-055266-9*, Puffin Unicorn) Puffin Bks.
—Elephants on the Beach. Bare, Colleen S., photos by. LC 89-32267. (Illus.). 32p. (ps-3). 1990. 12.95 (*0-525-65018-0*, Cobblehill Bks) Dutton Child Bks.
—Guinea Pigs Don't Read Books. (Illus.). 32p. (ps-2). 1993. pap. 3.99 (*0-14-054995-1*, Puffin Unicorn) Puffin Bks.
—Love a Llama. LC 92-39928. (Illus.). 32p. (gr. 1-4). 1994. 13.99 (*0-525-65146-2*, Cobblehill Bks) Dutton Child Bks.
—Never Grab a Deer by the Ear. Bare, Colleen S., photos by. LC 92-7702. (Illus.). 32p. (gr. 1-4). 1993. 13.00 (*0-525-65112-8*, Cobblehill Bks) Dutton Child Bks.
—Never Kiss an Alligator. LC 88-32659. (Illus.). (ps-3). 1989. 12.95 (*0-525-65003-2*, Cobblehill Bks) Dutton Child Bks.
—This Is a House. Bare, Colleen S., photos by. (Illus.). 32p. (gr. 1-5). 1992. 14.00 (*0-525-65090-3*, Cobblehill Bks) Dutton Child Bks.
—Who Comes to the Water Hole? Bare, Colleen S., photos by. LC 91-7915. (Illus.). 32p. (ps-3). 1991. 13. 95 (*0-525-65073-3*, Cobblehill Bks) Dutton Child Bks.
Barenbaum, Ruth, ed. see Barrows, Clifford, et al.
Bargar & Johnson. Anacondas. (Illus.). 24p. (gr. 1-4). 1987. PLB 11.94 (*0-86592-249-7*) Rourke Corp.
—Coral Snakes. (Illus.). 24p. (gr. 1-4). 1987. PLB 11.94 (*0-86592-246-2*) Rourke Corp.
—King Snakes. (Illus.). 24p. (gr. 1-4). 1987. PLB 11.94 (*0-86592-248-9*); 8.95s.p. (*0-685-67603-X*) Rourke Corp.
—Pythons. (Illus.). 24p. (gr. 1-4). 1987. PLB 11.94 (*0-86592-244-6*) Rourke Corp.
—Rat Snakes. (Illus.). 24p. (gr. 1-4). 1987. PLB 11.94 (*0-86592-247-0*) Rourke Corp.
—Tree Vipers. (Illus.). 24p. (gr. 1-4). 1987. PLB 11.94 (*0-86592-245-4*); PLB 8.95s.p. (*0-685-67604-8*) Rourke Corp.
Bargar, Sherie & Johnson, Linda. Boas Constrictoras. Palacios, Argentina, tr. from ENG. Van Horn, George, photos by. LC 93-8391. (SPA., Illus.). 1993. write for info. (*0-86593-333-2*) Rourke Corp.

Barger & Johnson. Boa Constrictors, Reading Level 2. (Illus.). 24p. (gr. k-5). 1986. PLB 11.94 (*0-86592-959-9*) Rourke Corp.
—Cobras, Reading Level 2. (Illus.). 24p. (gr. k-5). 1986. PLB 11.94 (*0-86592-955-6*) Rourke Corp.
—Copperheads, Reading Level 2. (Illus.). 24p. (gr. k-5). 1986. PLB 11.94 (*0-86592-957-2*) Rourke Corp.
—Cottonmouths, Reading Level 2. (Illus.). 24p. (gr. k-5). 1986. PLB 11.94 (*0-86592-958-0*) Rourke Corp.
—Mambas, Reading Level 2. (Illus.). 24p. (gr. k-5). 1986. PLB 11.94 (*0-86592-960-2*); 8.95s.p. (*0-685-58805-X*) Rourke Corp.
—Rattlesnake, Reading Level 2. (Illus.). 24p. (gr. k-5). 1986. PLB 11.94 (*0-86592-956-4*) Rourke Corp.
—Snake Discovery Library, 6 bks, Set I, Reading Level 2. (Illus.). 144p. (gr. k-5). 1986. Set. PLB 71.60 (*0-86592-954-8*); PLB 53.70s.p. (*0-685-58804-1*) Rourke Corp.
Barger, Amy & Barger, Andrew. MacFroggy Teaches BASIC. (gr. 5-10). 1993. pap. text ed. 12.00 (*0-944838-39-1*) Med Physics Pub.
Barger, Andrew, jt. auth. see Barger, Amy.
Barger, Eric. From Rock to Rock. LC 87-70776. (Illus.). 190p. 1990. pap. 8.99 (*0-910311-61-7*) Huntington Hse.
Barger, James. James Joyce: Modern Irish Writer. Rahmas, D. Steve, ed. LC 74-14701. 32p. (gr. 7-12). 1974. lib. bdg. 4.95 incl. catalog cards (*0-87157-577-9*) SamHar Pr.
—William Faulkner: Modern American Novelist & Nobel Prize Winner. Rahmas, D. Steve, ed. 32p. (Orig.). (gr. 7-12). 1973. lib. bdg. 4.95 incl. catalog cards (*0-87157-563-9*) SamHar Pr.
Barham, Scott, illus. Of the Jigsaw. 248p. (Orig.). (gr. 5-8). 1986. pap. 12.95 (*0-920541-07-0*); tchr's. guide, 51p. 5.95 (*0-920541-48-8*) Peguis Pubs Ltd.
—Pieces. 120p. (Orig.). (gr. k-4). 1986. pap. 12.95 (*0-920541-05-4*); tchr's. guide, 24p. 5.95 (*0-920541-46-1*) Peguis Pubs Ltd.
—Puzzle. 178p. (Orig.). (gr. 9-12). 1986. pap. 12.95 (*0-920541-09-7*); tchr's. guide, 44p. 5.95 (*0-920541-50-X*) Peguis Pubs Ltd.
Baring-Gould, S. A Book of Nursery Songs & Rhymes. (ps-4). 1972. 59.95 (*0-87968-768-1*) Gordon Pr.
Barish, Wendy, jt. auth. see Lawson, Don.
Barish, Wendy, jt. auth. see Riedman, Sarah R.
Barish, Wendy, ed. I Can Draw Horses. Speirs, Gill, illus. 64p. (gr. 3-7). 1983. pap. 3.95 (*0-671-46447-7*, Little Simon) S&S Trade.
Barish, Wendy, ed. see Appleton, Victor.
Barish, Wendy, ed. see Beal, George.
Barish, Wendy, ed. see Benton, Michael J.
Barish, Wendy, ed. see Dixon, Franklin W.
Barish, Wendy, ed. see Heck, Joseph.
Barish, Wendy, ed. see Hope, Laura L.
Barish, Wendy, ed. see Hyman, Jane & Millen-Posner, Barbara.
Barish, Wendy, ed. see Keene, Carolyn.
Barish, Wendy, ed. see Keene, Carolyn & Dixon, Franklin W.
Barish, Wendy, ed. see Packard, Mary.
Barish, Wendy, ed. see Rotsler, William.
Barish, Wendy, ed. see Sheldon, Ann.
Barish, Wendy, ed. see Wright, Jill & Wright, David.
Barkan, Joanne. Abraham Lincoln. Brook, Bonnie, ed. Miller, Lyle, illus. 32p. (gr. k-2). 1990. 5.95 (*0-671-69113-9*); PLB 10.98 (*0-671-69107-4*) Silver Pr.
—Air, Air All Around. Brook, Bonnie, ed. Petach, Heidi, illus. 32p. (ps-1). 1990. 5.95 (*0-671-68659-3*); PLB 9.98 (*0-671-68655-0*) Silver Pr.
—Animal Car. Ong, Christina, illus. 12p. (ps). 1993. bds. 3.50 (*0-689-71676-1*, Aladdin) Macmillan Child Grp.
—Anna Marie's Blanket. Maze, Deborah, illus. 32p. 1990. 12.95 (*0-8120-6124-1*) Barron.
—Boxcar. Walz, Richard, illus. 12p. (ps-k). 1992. POB 3.50 (*0-689-71573-0*, Aladdin) Macmillan Child Grp.
—Caboose. Walz, Richard, illus. 12p. (ps-k). 1992. POB 3.50 (*0-689-71574-9*, Aladdin) Macmillan Child Grp.
—Circus Locomotive. Ong, Christina, illus. 12p. (ps). 1993. bds. 3.50 (*0-689-71674-5*, Aladdin) Macmillan Child Grp.
—Clown Caboose. Ong, Christina, illus. 12p. (ps). 1993. bds. 3.50 (*0-689-71675-3*, Aladdin) Macmillan Child Grp.
—Creatures That Glow. (gr. 9-12). 1991. PLB 13.99 (*0-385-41979-1*) Doubleday.
—Fire, Fire Burning Bright. Brook, Bonnie, ed. Petach, Heidi, illus. 32p. (ps-1). 1990. 5.95 (*0-671-68658-5*); PLB 9.98 (*0-671-68654-2*) Silver Pr.
—Glow in the Dark Spooky House. (ps-3). 1990. write for info. (*0-307-06252-X*) Western Pub.
—Kermit's Mixed-up Message. Attinello, Lauren, illus. 32p. (Orig.). (gr. 1-4). 1987. pap. 2.75 (*0-590-44011-X*) Scholastic Inc.
—Locomotive. Walz, Richard, illus. 12p. (ps-k). 1992. bds. 3.50 (*0-689-71576-5*, Aladdin) Macmillan Child Grp.
—Passenger Car. Walz, Richard, illus. 12p. (ps-k). 1992. bds. 3.50 (*0-689-71575-7*, Aladdin) Macmillan Child Grp.
—Performers' Car. Ong, Christina, illus. 12p. (ps). 1993. bds. 3.50 (*0-689-71673-7*, Aladdin) Macmillan Child Grp.
—Rocks, Rocks Big & Small. Brook, Bonnie, ed. Petach, Heidi, illus. 32p. (ps-1). 1990. 5.95 (*0-671-68660-7*); PLB 9.98 (*0-671-68656-9*) Silver Pr.

—That Fat Hat. Swanson, Maggie, illus. LC 92-7414. 1992. 2.95 (*0-590-45643-1*) Scholastic Inc.
—A Very Merry Santa Story. 1992. 3.95 (*0-590-46020-X*, Cartwheel) Scholastic Inc.
—A Very Merry Snowman Story. 1992. 3.95 (*0-590-46021-8*, Cartwheel) Scholastic Inc.
—A Very Scary Haunted House. Wheeler, Jodie, illus. 24p. 1991. pap. 3.95 (*0-590-44497-2*) Scholastic Inc.
—The Very Scary Jack'O Lantern. Wheeler, Jodie, illus. 24p. 1991. pap. 3.95 (*0-590-44496-4*) Scholastic Inc.
—Very Scary Witch Story. (ps-3). 1992. pap. 5.50 (*0-590-45936-8*) Scholastic Inc.
—Water, Water Everywhere. Brook, Bonnie, ed. Petach, Heidi, illus. 32p. (ps-1). 1990. 5.95 (*0-671-68657-7*); PLB 9.98 (*0-671-68653-4*) Silver Pr.
—Whiskerville Bake Shop. Schmidt, Karen L., illus. 12p. (ps-k). 1990. bds. 3.50 (*0-448-19467-8*, G&D) Putnam Pub Group.
—Whiskerville Firehouse. Schmidt, Karen L., illus. 12p. (ps-k). 1990. bds. 3.50 (*0-448-19468-6*, G&D) Putnam Pub Group.
—Whiskerville Grocery. (Illus.). 12p. (ps-k). 1991. bds. 3.95 (*0-448-40091-X*, G&D) Putnam Pub Group.
—Whiskerville Post Office. Schmidt, Karen L., illus. 12p. (ps-k). 1990. bds. 3.50 (*0-448-19466-X*) Putnam Pub Group.
—Whiskerville School. Schmidt, Karen L., illus. 12p. (ps-k). 1990. bds. 3.50 (*0-448-19465-1*, G&D) Putnam Pub Group.
—Whiskerville Theater. (Illus.). 12p. (ps-k). 1991. bds. 3.95 (*0-448-40084-7*, G&D) Putnam Pub Group.
—Whiskerville Toy Shop. (Illus.). 12p. (ps-k). 1991. bds. 3.95 (*0-448-40089-8*, G&D) Putnam Pub Group.
—Whiskerville Train Station. (Illus.). 12p. (ps-k). 1991. bds. 3.95 (*0-448-40088-X*, G&D) Putnam Pub Group.
Barkan, Joanne, et al. The Muppet Babies in Let's Imagine....A Trip to the Stars. Chauhan, Man har, illus. 26p. (ps up). 1987. pap. 14.95 (*1-55578-806-8*) Worlds Wonder.
—The Muppet Babies in Let's Imagine...The Missing Toy's Adventure. Wilson, Ann, illus. 26p. (ps up). 1987. pap. 14.95 (*1-55578-805-X*) Worlds Wonder.
—The Muppet Babies in Let's Imagine...What Happened in the Nursery. Venning, Sue, illus. (ps up). 1987. pap. 14.95 (*1-55578-808-4*) Worlds Wonder.
Barken, Joanne, et al. The Muppet Babies in Let's Imagine...Music Everywhere. Brannon, Tom, illus. 26p. (ps up). 1987. pap. 14.95 (*1-55578-807-6*) Worlds Wonder.
Barker, Carol. A Family in Nigeria. LC 85-6932. (Illus.). 32p. (gr. 2-5). 1985. PLB 13.50 (*0-8225-1659-4*) Lerner Pubns.
Barker, Cicely M. Fairy Magic: Pop-up Book. (Illus.). 5p. (ps-3). 1993. 7.95 (*0-7232-4038-8*) Warne.
—The Fairy Necklaces. (Illus.). 64p. 1992. 6.95 (*0-7232-4000-0*) Warne.
—Fairy Places: Pop-up Book. (Illus.). 5p. (ps-3). 1993. 7.95 (*0-7232-4039-6*) Warne.
—The Flower Fairies Activity Book. (Illus.). 24p. (gr. 3 up). 1992. pap. 5.95 (*0-7232-3994-0*) Warne.
—Flower Fairies Baby Book. 1992. pap. 8.95 (*0-7232-3787-5*) Warne.
—Flower Fairies Birthday Book. 1992. 6.95 (*0-7232-3785-9*) Warne.
—The Flower Fairies Changing Seasons: A Sliding Picture Book. (Illus.). 140p. 1992. 9.95 (*0-7232-4001-9*) Warne.
—Flower Fairies of the Autumn. (Illus.). 1991. 5.95 (*0-7232-3755-7*) Warne.
—Flower Fairies of the Garden. Barker, Cicely M., illus. (ps up). 1991. 5.95 (*0-7232-3758-1*) Warne.
—Flower Fairies of the Spring. Barker, Cicely M., illus. (ps up). 1991. 5.95 (*0-7232-3753-0*) Warne.
—Flower Fairies of the Summer. Barker, Cicely M., illus. (ps up). 1991. 5.95 (*0-7232-3754-9*) Warne.
—Flower Fairies of the Trees. Barker, Cicely M., illus. (ps up). 1991. 5.95 (*0-7232-3760-3*) Warne.
—Flower Fairies of the Wayside. (Illus.). 1991. 5.95 (*0-7232-3757-3*) Warne.
—Flower Fairies of the Winter. (Illus.). 1991. 5.95 (*0-7232-3756-5*) Warne.
—The Flower Fairies Poster Activity Book. (Illus.). 24p. 1993. 6.95 (*0-7232-4037-X*) Warne.
—Flower Fairies Year: A Frieze. 1992. 6.00 (*0-7232-3761-1*) Warne.
—A Flower Fairy Alphabet. (Illus.). 1991. 5.95 (*0-7232-3759-X*) Warne.
—Four Seasons of the Flower Fairies: A Flower Fairies Gift Set, 4 bks. (Illus.). 1992. Boxed Set. 24.00 (*0-7232-5181-9*) Warne.
—The Lord of the Rushie River & Simon the Swan. (Illus.). 98p. (ps-3). 1992. 14.00 (*0-7232-3980-0*) Warne.
—A Treasury of Flower Fairies. (Illus.). 128p. 1992. deluxe ed. 19.95 (*0-7232-3796-4*, Warne) Viking Child Bks.
—A World of Flower Fairies. (Illus.). 128p. 1993. 20.00 (*0-7232-4002-7*) Warne.
Barker, Cicely M., illus. A Flower Fairies Postcard Book. 30p. (ps up). 1991. pap. 7.95 (*0-7232-3710-7*) Warne.
—Old Rhymes for All Times. 112p. (gr. 4-7). 1994. 12.99 (*0-7232-3751-4*) Warne.
Barker, Cicley M. Flower Fairies Address Book. 1992. 6.95 (*0-7232-3762-X*) Warne.
Barker, Clive. The Thief of Always: A Fable. LC 92-53428. 1992. 20.00 (*0-06-017724-1*, HarpT) HarpC.

Barker, Clive & Niles, Steve. London, Vol. 1: Bloodline. Skulan, Tom, ed. Kastro, Carlos, illus. 48p. (Orig.). 1993. pap. 5.95 (*0-938782-25-8*) Fantaco.
—London, Vol. 2: End of the Line. Skulan, Tom, ed. Kastro, Carlos, illus. 48p. 1993. pap. 5.95 (*0-938782-26-6*) Fantaco.
Barker, Clive, et al. Demons & Deviants. Brown, Mike, ed. Lang, Charles, et al, illus. 62p. (Orig.). 1993. pap. 4.95 (*0-938782-24-X*) Fantaco.
Barker, Dan. Just Pretend: A Freethought Book for Children. Cuebas, Alma, illus. 72p. (Orig.). (ps-6). 1988. pap. 10.00 (*0-318-42495-9*) Freedom Rel Found.
—Maybe Right, Maybe Wrong: A Guide for Young Thinkers. Strassburg, Brian, illus. 72p. 1992. pap. 12. 95 (*0-87975-731-0*) Prometheus Bks.
—Maybe Yes, Maybe No: A Guide for Young Skeptics. Stassburg, Brain, illus. 80p. (Orig.). (gr. 2-6). 1991. pap. 12.95 (*0-87975-607-1*) Prometheus Bks.
Barker, Ernest, tr. see Aristotle.
Barker, Jane, jt. auth. see Downing, Sybil.
Barker, Jane V. Trappers & Traders. Downing, Sybil, ed. (Illus.). 36p. (gr. k-6). pap. 3.95 (*1-878611-03-8*) Silver Rim Pr.
Barker, Jane V. & Downing, Sybil. Colorado Heritage Series, 10 vols. (Illus.). (ps-8). Set. pap. 39.50 (*1-878611-00-3*) Silver Rim Pr.
—Mountain Treasures. (Illus.). 44p. (gr. k-6). pap. 3.95 (*1-878611-01-1*) Silver Rim Pr.
Barker, Jane V., jt. auth. see Downing, Sybil.
Barker, Larry L. Communication Skills: Objectives & Criterion Referenced Exercises for Grades 7-12. (Illus.). 321p. (Orig.). 1988. pap. text ed. 84.95 incl. Listening Skills (*0-685-27248-6*) SPECTRA Inc.
Barker, Marjorie. Magical Hands. Yoshi, illus. LC 89-31373. 32p. (ps up). 1991. pap. 14.95 (*0-88708-103-7*) Picture Bk Studio.
Barker, Shane. Surviving As a Teenager in a Grown-up's World. 1993. pap. 6.95 (*0-88494-881-1*) Bookcraft Inc.
Barker, Shane R. Finding a Friend in the Mirror. LC 88-21743. viii, 113p. (gr. 7-12). 1988. 8.95 (*0-87579-178-6*) Deseret Bk.
Barker, Wayne G. Cryptograms. 119p. (gr. 9 up). 1980. lib. bdg. 14.45 (*0-89412-090-5*); pap. text ed. 4.95 (*0-89412-043-3*) Aegean Park Pr.
Barkey, Tom. Forbid Not Prophecy. Mills, Dick, frwd. by. 125p. (Orig.). (gr. 8). 1991. pap. 5.95 (*0-9626910-1-1*) Power Comm Ch.
—God Is... My Strength. Mackall, Phyllis, ed. 86p. (Orig.). (gr. 8). 1990. pap. 6.95 (*0-9626910-0-3*) Power Comm Ch.
Barkhausen, Annette. Penguins. LC 93-13050. (gr. 3 up). 1993. write for info. (*0-8368-1002-3*) Gareth Stevens Inc.
Barkhausen, Annette & Geiser, Franz. Elephants. LC 93-13049. (gr. 3 up). 1993. write for info. (*0-8368-1001-5*) Gareth Stevens Inc.
—Rabbits & Hares. Daniel, Jamie, tr. from GER. LC 93-15932. 1993. write for info. (*0-8368-1004-X*) Gareth Stevens Inc.
Barkin, Carol & James, Elizabeth. Happy Thanksgiving! Carmi, Giora, illus. LC 86-33734. 96p. (gr. 4-7). 1987. 12.95 (*0-688-06800-6*); PLB 12.88 (*0-688-06801-4*) Lothrop.
—Happy Valentines Day. LC 87-35812. (Illus.). 96p. (gr. 4-7). 1988. 12.95 (*0-688-06796-4*); PLB 12.88 (*0-688-06797-2*) Lothrop.
—The Holiday Handbook. LC 92-29846. 1993. 15.45 (*0-395-65011-9*, Clarion Bks) HM.
—Jobs for Kids. Doty, Roy, illus. LC 89-45900. 128p. (gr. 5-9). 1989. lib. bdg. 11.88 (*0-688-09324-8*) Lothrop.
—Jobs for Kids. Doty, Roy, illus. LC 89-45900. 128p. (gr. 5-9). 1991. pap. 6.95 (*0-688-09323-X*, Pub. by Beech Tree Bks) Morrow.
—The Scary Halloween Costume Book. Coville, Katherine, illus. LC 81-14249. (gr. 3-6). 1983. 12.95 (*0-688-00956-5*); PLB 12.88 (*0-688-00957-3*) Lothrop.
Barkin, Carol, jt. auth. see James, Elizabeth.
Barklem, Jill. Autumn Story. (ps-3). 1989. 10.95 (*0-399-21754-1*, Philomel Bks) Putnam Pub Group.
—The Four Seasons of Brambly Hedge. (Illus.). 144p. (gr. 3 up). 1990. 25.95 (*0-399-21869-6*, Philomel Bks) Putnam Pub Group.
—High Hills: Mini Edition. (Illus.). (ps-3). 1991. 9.95 (*0-399-22271-5*, Philomel Bks) Putnam Pub Group.
—The Secret Staircase. Barklem, Jill, illus. 32p. (ps-3). 1989. pap. 5.95 (*0-399-21726-6*, Sandcastle Bks) Putnam Pub Group.
—The Secret Staircase. 32p. (ps-3). 1992. 10.95 (*0-399-21865-3*, Philomel Bks) Putnam Pub Group.
—Spring Story. Barklem, Jill, illus. LC 80-15300. 32p. (gr. 1 up). 1986. 10.95 (*0-399-20746-5*, Philomel) Putnam Pub Group.
—Summer Story. Barklem, Jill, illus. LC 80-15423. 32p. (gr. 1 up). 1986. 10.95 (*0-399-20747-3*, Philomel) Putnam Pub Group.
—Winter Story. Barklem, Jill, illus. LC 80-15422. 32p. (gr. 1 up). 1986. 10.95 (*0-399-20748-1*, Philomel) Putnam Pub Group.
—World of Brambly Hedge. LC 92-25306. (Illus.). 24p. (ps up). 1993. 17.95 (*0-399-22012-7*, Philomel Bks) Putnam Pub Group.
Barklow, Irene. From Trails to Rails: The Post Offices, Stage Stops, & Wagon Roads of Union County, Oregon. Evans, Jack, ed. (Illus.). 306p. (Orig.). (gr. 8up). 1987. 24.95 (*0-9618185-2-1*); pap. 18.95 (*0-9618185-0-6*) Enchant Pub Oregon.

—The Old & the New: History of the Post Offices of Wallowa County. (Illus.). 184p. (Orig.). (gr. 8 up). 1987. pap. 11.95 (*0-9618185-1-4*) Enchant Pub Oregon.
Barkman, Betty & Barkman, Paul. A Well Trained Llama: A Trainers Guide. rev. ed. LC 88-93027. (Illus.). 95p. (Orig.). (gr. 9 up). 1989. pap. text ed. 25. 00 (*0-945860-01-3*) Birch Bark Pr.
Barkman, Paul, jt. auth. see Barkman, Betty.
Barks, Carl. Walt Disney's Donald & Daisy Comic Album. Barks, Carl, illus. Blum, Geoffrey, intro. by. (Illus.). 48p. (Orig.). (ps up). 1988. pap. 5.95 (*0-944599-11-7*) Gladstone Pub.
—Walt Disney's Donald & Gladstone Album. (Illus.). 48p. (Orig.). (ps up). 1988. pap. 5.95 (*0-944599-12-5*) Gladstone Pub.
—Walt Disney's Donald Duck Adventures Album. Barks, Carl, illus. Blum, Geoffrey, intro. by. (Illus.). 48p. (Orig.). (ps up). 1988. pap. 5.95 (*0-944599-08-7*) Gladstone Pub.
—Walt Disney's Donald Duck Adventures Album. Barks, Carl, illus. Blum, Geoffrey, intro. by. (Illus.). 48p. (Orig.). (ps up). 1988. pap. 5.95 (*0-944599-13-3*) Gladstone Pub.
—Walt Disney's Donald Duck Adventures Album. Barks, Carl, illus. Blum, Geoffrey, intro. by. (Illus.). 48p. (Orig.). (ps up). 1989. pap. 5.95 (*0-944599-15-X*) Gladstone Pub.
—Walt Disney's Donald Duck Adventures Comic Album. Barks, Carl, illus. Blum, Geoffrey, intro. by. (Illus.). 48p. (Orig.). (ps up). 1988. pap. 5.95 (*0-944599-04-4*) Gladstone Pub.
—Walt Disney's Donald Duck Album. Barks, Carl, illus. Blum, Geoffrey, intro. by. (Illus.). 48p. (Orig.). (ps up). 1988. pap. 5.95 (*0-944599-06-0*) Gladstone Pub.
—Walt Disney's Donald Duck Album. Blum, Geoffrey, intro. by. (Illus.). 48p. (Orig.). 1989. pap. 5.95 (*0-944599-26-5*) Gladstone Pub.
—Walt Disney's Donald Duck Album. Blum, Geoffrey, intro. by. (Illus.). 48p. (Orig.). 1989. pap. 5.95 (*0-944599-23-0*) Gladstone Pub.
—Walt Disney's Donald Duck Comic Album. Barks, Carl, illus. Blum, Geoffrey, intro. by. (Illus.). 48p. (ps up). 1987. pap. 5.95 (*0-944599-01-X*) Gladstone Pub.
—Walt Disney's Donald Duck Family Album. Blum, Geoffrey, intro. by. (Illus.). 48p. (Orig.). 1989. pap. 5.95 (*0-944599-22-2*) Gladstone Pub.
—Walt Disney's Uncle Scrooge Album. Barks, Carl, illus. Blum, Geoffrey, intro. by. (Illus.). 48p. (Orig.). (ps up). 1988. pap. 5.95 (*0-944599-14-1*) Gladstone Pub.
—Walt Disney's Uncle Scrooge Album. Blum, Geoffrey, intro. by. (Illus.). 48p. (Orig.). 1989. pap. 5.95 (*0-944599-24-9*) Gladstone Pub.
—Walt Disney's Uncle Scrooge & Donald Duck Giant Album. Blum, Geoffrey, intro. by. (Illus.). 72p. (Orig.). 1989. pap. 8.95 (*0-944599-27-3*) Gladstone Pub.
—Walt Disney's Uncle Scrooge Comic Album. Barks, Carl, illus. Blum, Geoffrey, intro. by. (Illus.). 48p. (ps up). 1987. pap. 5.95 (*0-944599-02-8*) Gladstone Pub.
—Walt Disney's Uncle Scrooge Comic Album. Barks, Carl, illus. Blum, Geoffrey, intro. by. (Illus.). 48p. (ps up). 1988. pap. 5.95 (*0-944599-05-2*) Gladstone Pub.
—Walt Disney's Uncle Scrooge Comic Album. Barks, Carl, illus. Blum, Geoffrey, intro. by. (Illus.). 48p. (Orig.). (ps up). 1987. pap. 5.95 (*0-944599-00-1*) Gladstone Pub.
—Walt Disney's Uncle Scrooge Comic Album. Barks, Carl, illus. Blum, Geoffrey, intro. by. (Illus.). 48p. (Orig.). (ps up). 1988. pap. 5.95 (*0-944599-10-9*) Gladstone Pub.
—Walt Disney's Uncle Scrooge Comic Album. Barks, Carl, illus. Blum, Geoff, intro. by. (Illus.). 48p. (Orig.). 1989. pap. 5.95 (*0-944599-16-8*) Gladstone Pub.
—Walt Disney's Uncle Scrooge Comic Album. Barks, Carl, illus. Blum, Geoff, intro. by. (Illus.). 48p. (Orig.). 1989. pap. 5.95 (*0-944599-19-2*) Gladstone Pub.
Barks, Carl & Hannah, Jack. Walt Disney's Donald Duck Giant Comic Album. Barks, Carl & Hannah, Jack, illus. Blum, Geoff, intro. by. 72p. (gr. k up). 1989. pap. 8.95 (*0-944599-20-6*) Gladstone Pub.
Barks, Carl & Rosa, Don. Walt Disney's Uncle Scrooge Giant Album. Blum, Geoffrey, intro. by. (Illus.). 96p. (Orig.). 1989. pap. 11.95 (*0-944599-28-1*) Gladstone Pub.
Barks, Carl, intro. by. Donald Duck. (Illus.). 195p. 1991. 17.99 (*0-517-69714-9*) Outlet Bk Co.
Barks, Carl, illus. Uncle Scrooge McDuck: His Life & Times. Summer, Edward, ed. Lucas, George, intro. by. LC 81-66953. (Illus.). 376p. (ps-3). 1987. pap. 34.95 (*0-89087-510-3*); text ed. 59.95 (*0-89087-511-1*) Celestial Arts.
—Walt Disney's Comics in Color, Vol. 4. rev. ed. 192p. 1990. pap. 19.95 (*0-944599-42-7*) Gladstone Pub.
Barks, Carl & Gollub, Mo, illus. Walt Disney's Comics in Color, Vol. 1. rev. ed. 192p. 1990. pap. 19.95 (*0-944599-39-7*) Gladstone Pub.
Barks, Carl & Gottfredson, Floyd, illus. Walt Disney's Comics in Color. rev. ed. 192p. (ps up). 1990. pap. 19. 95 (*0-944599-35-4*) Gladstone Pub.
—Walt Disney's Comics in Color, Vol. 2. rev. ed. 192p. 1990. pap. 19.95 (*0-944599-40-0*) Gladstone Pub.
—Walt Disney's Comics in Color, Vol. 3. rev. ed. 192p. 1990. pap. 19.95 (*0-944599-41-9*) Gladstone Pub.
—Walt Disney's Comics in Color, Vol. 5. rev. ed. 200p. 1990. pap. 19.95 (*0-944599-38-9*) Gladstone Pub.

—Walt Disney's Comics in Color, Vol. 6. rev. ed. 184p. (ps up). 1990. pap. 19.95 (*0-944599-37-0*) Gladstone Pub.
Barks, Carl & Rosa, Don, illus. Walt Disney's Comics in Color, Vol. 7. rev. ed. 206p. (ps up). 1990. pap. 19.95 (*0-944599-36-2*) Gladstone Pub.
Barlass, Gail. Dinosquares: A Modern Dinosaur Book for Imaginative Children. Hansen, Ron, ed. & illus. LC 87-62124. 24p. (ps-3). 1988. pap. 3.95 (*0-943925-07-X*) Purple Turtle Bks.
Bar-Lev, Geoffrey & Sakkal, Joyce. Jewish Amerian Struggle for Equality. LC 92-7473. 1992. 22.60 (*0-86593-182-8*); 16.95s.p. (*0-685-59291-X*) Rourke Corp.
Barlow, Jeffrey. Sun Yat-sen. Schlesinger, Arthur M., Jr., intro. by. (Illus.). 112p. (gr. 5 up). 1987. lib. bdg. 17.95 (*0-87754-441-7*) Chelsea Hse.
Barlowe, Dorothea & Barlowe, Sy, illus. Dinosaurs. LC 77-70862. (ps-3). 1977. 8.99 (*0-394-83538-7*) Random Bks Yng Read.
Barlowe, Dot & Barlowe, Sy. Who Lives Here? Barlowe, Dot & Barlowe, Sy, illus. LC 79-27494. 32p. (ps-3). 1980. pap. 2.25 (*0-394-83740-1*) Random Bks Yng Read.
Barlowe, Sy, jt. auth. see Barlowe, Dot.
Barmat, Jeanne. Foster Families. LC 90-46834. (Illus.). 48p. (gr. 5-6). 1991. RSBE 12.95 (*0-89686-605-X*, Crestwood Hse) Macmillan Child Grp.
Barnard, Alan. Kalahari Bushmen. LC 93-32423. (Illus.). 48p. (gr. 6-10). 1994. 16.95 (*1-56847-160-2*) Thomson Lrning.
Barnard, Stephen. The Illustrated History of Rock. (Illus.). 256p. (gr. 7 up). 1987. text ed. 70.00 (*0-02-870251-4*) Schirmer Bks.
Barnes, Caroline. It's No Fun to Be Sick! (Illus.). 32p. (ps-k). 1989. write for info. (*0-307-12031-7*, Pub. by Golden Bks) Western Pub.
Barnes, F. A. & Kuehne, Tom. Canyon Country: Mountain Biking. LC 87-73014. (Illus.). 144p. (Orig.). (gr. 7 up). 1988. pap. 8.00 (*0-9614586-5-8*) Canyon Country Pubns.
Barnes, Frances. Figaro. Fairbridge, John, illus. LC 93-132. 1994. write for info. (*0-383-03686-0*) SRA Schl Grp.
Barnes, Jeremy. Samuel Goldwyn. Furstinger, Nancy, ed. (Illus.). 128p. (gr. 7-10). 1989. PLB 13.98 (*0-382-09586-3*) Silver Burdett Pr.
Barnes, Jill & Asuka, Ken. Smile for Toto. Rubin, Caroline, ed. Japan Foreign Rights Centre Staff, tr. from JPN. Asuka, Ken, illus. LC 90-37747. 32p. (gr. k-4). 1990. PLB 14.60 (*0-944483-87-9*) Garrett Ed Corp.
—Toto in Trouble. Rubin, Caroline, ed. Japan Foreign Rights Centre Staff, tr. from JPN. Asuka, Ken, illus. LC 90-37749. 32p. (gr. k-4). 1990. PLB 14.60 (*0-944483-86-0*) Garrett Ed Corp.
Barnes, Jill & Ishinabe, Fusako. Spring Snowman. Rubin, Caroline, ed. Japan Foreign Rights Centre Staff, tr. from JPN. Ishinabe, Fusako, illus. LC 90-37748. 32p. (gr. k-3). 1990. PLB 14.60 (*0-944483-83-6*) Garrett Ed Corp.
Barnes, Jill & Kanabe, Junkichi. Road Roller Saves the Day. Rubin, Caroline, ed. Japan Foreign Rights Centre Staff, tr. from JPN. Emu, Namae, illus. LC 90-3841. 40p. (gr. k-3). 1990. PLB 15.93 (*0-944483-81-X*) Garrett Ed Corp.
Barnes, Jill & Sato, Wakiko. Granny, Let Me In. Rubin, Caroline, ed. Japan Foreign Rights Centre Staff, tr. from JPN. Sato, Wakiko, illus. LC 90-37752. 40p. (gr. k-3). 1990. PLB 15.93 (*0-944483-82-8*) Garrett Ed Corp.
Barnes, Jill & Sueyoshi, Akiko. Great Day for Bears. Rubin, Caroline, ed. Japan Foreign Rights Centre Staff, tr. from JPN. Fujita, Miho, illus. LC 90-37753. 32p. (gr. k-3). 1990. PLB 14.60 (*0-944483-84-4*) Garrett Ed Corp.
Barnes, Jill & Teramura, Terua. Elephant Rescue. Rubin, Caroline, ed. Japan Foreign Rights Centre Staff, tr. from JPN. Murakami, Tsutomu, illus. LC 90-37750. 40p. (gr. k-3). 1990. PLB 15.93 (*0-944483-85-2*) Garrett Ed Corp.
Barnes, Jill & Tsurmi, Masao. Giant Tree & the Boy. Rubin, Caroline, ed. Japan Foreign Rights Centre Staff, tr. from JPN. Suzuki, Mamoru, illus. LC 90-37751. 40p. (gr. k-4). 1990. PLB 15.93 (*0-944483-80-1*) Garrett Ed Corp.
Barnes, Joe, jt. auth. see Puckett, Christine S.
Barnes, Joyce A. The Baby Grand, the Moon in July, & Me. LC 93-17984. Date not set. write for info. (*0-8037-1586-2*); PLB write for info. (*0-8037-1600-1*) Dial Bks Young.
Barnes, Joyce B. Patches, the Blessed Beast of Burden. Ramirez-Walker, Linda J., illus. 36p. 1990. 15.00 (*0-9628493-0-8*) J B Barnes.
Barnes, Lilly. Lace Them Up. Fernandes, Eugenie, illus. 36p. (ps-2). 1992. 8.95 (*1-56282-282-9*) Hyprn Child.
Barnes, Maryke. Setting Wonder Free. Marton, Jirina, illus. 24p. 1993. lib. bdg. 14.95 (*1-55037-241-6*, Pub. by Annick CN); pap. 4.95 (*1-55037-238-6*, Pub. by Annick CN) Firefly Bks Ltd.
Barnes, Michael, jt. auth. see Ely, Vivian K.
Barnes, Peter W. Nat, Nat, the Nantucket Cat. Arciero, Susan, illus. 30p. 1993. 15.95 (*0-9637688-0-8*) Vacation Spot.
Barnes, Richard, jt. auth. see Williams, George A.
Barnes, Susan, ed. see Demuth, Patricia B.
Barnes-Murphy, Rowan. Colors. 16p. (ps). 1992. bds. 3.95 (*0-8249-8530-3*, Ideals Child) Hambleton-Hill.

—Numbers. 16p. (ps). 1992. bds. 3.95 (*0-8249-8531-1*, Ideals Child) Hambleton-Hill.
—Opposites. Barnes-Murphy, Rowan, illus. 16p. (ps). 1993. bds. 3.95 (*0-8249-8611-3*, Ideals Child) Hambleton-Hill.
—Shapes. Barnes-Murphy, Rowan, illus. 16p. (ps). 1993. bds. 3.95 (*0-8249-8606-7*, Ideals Child) Hambleton-Hill.
Barnes-Svarney, Patricia. The National Science Foundation. Schlesinger, Arthur M., Jr., intro. by. (Illus.). 112p. (gr. 5 up). 1989. lib. bdg. 14.95 (*1-55546-117-4*) Chelsea Hse.
—Traveler's Guide to the Solar System. LC 93-17313. (Illus.). 80p. (gr. 4-10). 1993. 14.95 (*0-8069-8672-7*) Sterling.
—Zimbabwe. (Illus.). 128p. (gr. 5 up). 1989. 14.95 (*1-55546-799-7*) Chelsea Hse.
Barnes-Svarney, Patricia L. Born of Heat & Pressure: Mountains & Metamorphic Rocks. LC 89-25856. (Illus.). 64p. (gr. 6 up). 1991. lib. bdg. 15.95 (*0-89490-276-8*) Enslow Pubs.
—Clocks in the Rocks: Learning about Earth's Past. LC 89-7698. (Illus.). 64p. (gr. 6 up). 1990. lib. bdg. 15.95 (*0-89490-275-X*) Enslow Pubs.
—Fossils: Stories from Bones & Stones. LC 90-19408. (Illus.). 64p. (gr. 6 up). 1991. lib. bdg. 15.95 (*0-89490-294-6*) Enslow Pubs.
Barnett, Ada & Wurfer, Nicole. Eddycat Brings Soccer to Mannersville. Hoffmann, Mark, illus. LC 92-56879. 1993. PLB 17.27 (*0-8368-0941-6*) Gareth Stevens Inc.
Barnett, Ada, et al. Eddycat & Buddy Entertain a Guest. Hoffmann, Mark, illus. LC 92-56883. 32p. (gr. 1 up). 1993. Repr. of 1991 ed. PLB 17.27 incl. tchr's. guide (*0-8368-0946-7*) Gareth Stevens Inc.
—Eddycat Attends Sunshine's Birthday Party. Hoffmann, Mark, illus. LC 92-56881. 1993. PLB 17.27 (*0-8368-0943-2*) Gareth Stevens Inc.
—Eddycat Goes Shopping with Becky Bunny. Hoffmann, Mark, illus. LC 93-56884. 32p. (gr. 1 up). 1993. Repr. of 1991 ed. PLB 17.27 incl. tchr's. guide (*0-8368-0947-5*) Gareth Stevens Inc.
—Eddycat Helps Sunshine Plan Her Party. Hoffmann, Mark, illus. LC 92-56880. 1993. PLB 17.27 (*0-8368-0942-4*) Gareth Stevens Inc.
—Eddycat Introduces Mannersville. Hoffmann, Mark, illus. LC 92-56877. 1993. PLB 17.27 (*0-8368-0939-4*) Gareth Stevens Inc.
—Eddycat Teaches Telephone Skills. Hoffmann, Mark, illus. LC 92-56882. 1993. PLB 17.27 (*0-8368-0944-0*) Gareth Stevens Inc.
—Eddycat Visits Wright Street School. Hoffmann, Mark, illus. LC 92-56878. 1993. PLB 17.27 (*0-8368-0940-8*) Gareth Stevens Inc.
Barnett, Carol. Boy & the Donkey. (ps-3). 1990. 7.95 (*0-8442-9417-9*, Natl Textbk) NTC Pub Grp.
—Boy Who Cried Wolf. (ps-3). 1990. 7.95 (*0-8442-9419-5*, Natl Textbk) NTC Pub Grp.
—Goldilocks & the Three Bears. (ps-3). 1990. 7.95 (*0-8442-9416-0*, Natl Textbk) NTC Pub Grp.
—Lion & the Mouse. (ps-3). 1990. 7.95 (*0-8442-9420-9*, Natl Textbk) NTC Pub Grp.
—Little Red Hen. (ps-3). 1990. 7.95 (*0-8442-9418-7*, Natl Textbk) NTC Pub Grp.
—Milkmaid & Her Pail. (ps-3). 1990. 7.95 (*0-8442-9421-7*, Natl Textbk) NTC Pub Grp.
Barnett, Jeanie M. Ghana. (Illus.). 104p. (gr. 5 up). 1989. lib. bdg. 14.95 (*1-55546-789-X*) Chelsea Hse.
Barnett, Robert J. Baptism: Who Needs It? 16p. (Orig.). (gr. 6 up). 1991. pap. text ed. 1.25 (*0-87227-171-4*) Reg Baptist.
Barnhart, jt. auth. see Thorndike.
Barnhart, Clarence L. & Barnhart, Robert K., eds. The World Book Dictionary - 1993. LC 92-61263. (Illus.). 2554p. 1993. lib. bdg. write for info. (*0-7166-0293-8*) World Bk.
Barnhart, Diana & Leon, Vicki. Tidepools: The Bright World of the Rocky Shoreline. rev. ed. Balthis, Frank, et al, photos by. LC 93-21338. (Illus.). 48p. (gr. 5 up). 1993. pap. 9.95 (*0-918303-37-0*) Blake Pub.
Barnhart, Robert K., jt. ed. see Barnhart, Clarence L.
Barns, Rebecca B., ed. see Blizzard, Gladys S.
Baro, Ana B., tr. see Marshall, James.
Barofsky, Semour, tr. see Sendak, Philip.
Baroja. Las Inquietudes de Shanti Andia. (gr. 7-12). 1973. pap. 5.95 (*0-88436-062-8*, 70267) EMC.
Baron, Connie. The Physically Disabled. LC 88-21554. (Illus.). 48p. (gr. 5-6). 1988. RSBE 12.95 (*0-89686-417-0*, Crestwood Hse) Macmillan Child Grp.
Baron, Jane & Jones, Barbara. The Word Book. 106p. (gr. 10-12). 1981. pap. text ed. 16.50 (*1-881678-05-9*) CRIS.
Baron, Lindamichelle. The Sun Is On. rev. ed. Elam, Keith, illus. Dee, Ruby, intro. by. (Illus.). 48p. (gr. 1-6). 1982. pap. 5.95 (*0-940938-02-2*) Harlin Jacque.
Baron, Michelle. Hey Diddle Diddle. Alchemy II, Inc. Staff, illus. 26p. (ps). 1988. incl. cassette 9.95 (*1-55578-919-6*) Worlds Wonder.
—Hickory Dickory Dock. Alchemy II, Inc. Staff, illus. 26p. (ps). 1988. incl. cassette 9.95 (*1-55578-923-4*) Worlds Wonder.
—Little Bo Peep. Alchemy II, Inc. Staff, illus. 26p. (ps). 1988. incl. cassette 9.95 (*1-55578-921-8*) Worlds Wonder.
—Little Boy Blue. Alchemy II, Inc. Staff, illus. 26p. (ps). 1988. incl. cassette 9.95 (*1-55578-918-8*) Worlds Wonder.

—Nanny Piggy. Alchemy II, Inc, illus. 26p. (ps up). 1987. 12.95 (*1-55578-602-2*) Worlds Wonder.
—Safe at Home with Teddy Ruxpin. Armstrong, Julie, et al, illus. 34p. (ps). 1988. write for info. incl. audio tape (*0-934323-70-4*) Alchemy Comms.
—Water Safety with Teddy Ruxpin. Armstrong, Julie, et al, illus. 34p. (ps). 1988. incl. audio tape 9.95 (*0-934323-74-7*) Alchemy Comms.
Baron, Nancy. Getting Started in Calligraphy. Baron, Nancy, illus. LC 78-66311. (gr. 7 up) 1979. spiral bdg. 9.95 (*0-8069-8840-1*) Sterling.
Baron, Nick. Glory's End. (gr. 9-12). 1990. pap. 3.50 (*0-06-106013-5*, PL) HarpC.
Baron, Phil. The Do-Along Songbook. Forse, Ken, ed. High, David, et al, illus. 26p. (ps). 1986. 9.95 (*0-934323-34-8*); pre-programmed audio cass. tape incl. Alchemy Comms.
—Fire Safety with Teddy Ruxpin. Armstrong, Julie, et al, illus. 22p. (ps). 1988. write for info. incl. pre-programmed audiotape (*0-934323-75-5*) Alchemy Comms.
—Gizmos & Gadgets. (Illus.). 34p. (ps). 1987. packaged with pre-programmed audio cass. tape 9.95 (*0-934323-45-3*) Alchemy Comms.
—The Mushroom Forest. Forsse, Ken & Becker, Mary, eds. Conley-Gorniak, Allyn & Armstrong, Julie A., illus. 26p. (ps). 1986. 9.95 (*0-934323-36-4*); pre-programmed audio cass. tape incl. Alchemy Comms.
—Quiet Please. Hicks, Russell, et al, illus. 34p. (ps). 1987. incl. pre-programmed audio cass. 9.95 (*0-934323-40-2*) Alchemy Comms.
—Wooly & the Giant Snowzos. Hicks, Russell, et al, illus. 34p. (ps). 1987. incl. pre-programmed audio cass. 9.95 (*0-934323-42-9*) Alchemy Comms.
Baron, Stanley, jt. auth. see Mitchell, Janis.
Barone, Shirley A. Bugs - Bugs - Bugs, Vol. 10. Coleman, Debbie, illus. 44p. (Orig.). (ps-2). 1989. pap. write for info. Toad Hse Bks.
—Easter Parade, Vol. 6. Coleman, Debbie, illus. 44p. (Orig.). (ps-2). 1990. pap. write for info. Toad Hse Bks.
—Funny Dinosaurs, Vol. 4. Coleman, Debbie, illus. 44p. (Orig.). (ps-2). 1989. pap. write for info. Toad Hse Bks.
—Halloween Fun for Everyone, Vol. 1. Coleman, Debbie, illus. 44p. (Orig.). (ps-2). 1989. pap. 1.69 (*0-685-30447-7*) Toad Hse Bks.
—Happy Valentines, Vol. 5. Coleman, Debbie, illus. 44p. (Orig.). (ps-2). 1990. pap. text ed. write for info. Toad Hse Bks.
—I Know My ABC's, Vol. 13. Coleman, Debbie, illus. 44p. (Orig.). (ps-2). 1989. pap. write for info. Toad Hse Bks.
—I Know My Numbers, Vol. 14. Coleman, Debbie, illus. 44p. (Orig.). (ps-2). 1989. pap. write for info. Toad Hse Bks.
—I Like Monsters, Vol. 9. Coleman, Debbie, illus. 44p. (Orig.). (ps-2). 1989. pap. write for info. Toad Hse Bks.
—In My Toy Box, Vol. 8. Coleman, Debbie, illus. 44p. (Orig.). (ps-2). 1989. pap. write for info. Toad Hse Bks.
—Kittens & Puppies, Vol. 11. Coleman, Debbie, illus. 44p. (Orig.). (ps-2). 1989. pap. write for info. Toad Hse Bks.
—Let's Give Thanks, Vol. 2. Coleman, Debbie, illus. 44p. (Orig.). (ps-2). 1989. pap. 1.75 (*0-685-30448-5*) Toad Hse Bks.
—Meet My Friends: Children of the World, Vol. 15. Coleman, Debbie, illus. 44p. (Orig.). (ps-2). 1989. pap. write for info. Toad Hse Bks.
—My Teddy Bears, Vol. 12. Coleman, Debbie, illus. 44p. (Orig.). (ps-2). 1989. pap. write for info. Toad Hse Bks.
—A Shoe for You, Vol. 7. Coleman, Debbie, illus. 44p. (Orig.). (ps-2). 1989. pap. write for info. Toad Hse Bks.
—A Time for Joy (Christmas, Vol. 3. Coleman, Debbie, illus. 44p. (Orig.). (ps-2). 1989. pap. write for info. Toad Hse Bks.
Baroness Orczy. The Scarlet Pimpernel. (gr. k-6). 1989. pap. 3.50 (*0-440-40220-4*, YB) Dell.
Barquist, Larry E. The Little Bird That Couldn't Fly. 1993. 7.95 (*0-533-10456-4*) Vantage.
Barr, George. Fascinating Science Experiments for Young People. LC 93-8111. (Illus.). 160p. (gr. 7-8). 1993. pap. text ed. 3.95t (*0-486-27670-8*) Dover.
—Outdoor Science Projects for Young People. (Illus.). 160p. pap. 3.95 (*0-486-26855-1*) Dover.
—Science Projects for Young People. 153p. (gr. 5 up). 1986. pap. 3.50 (*0-486-25235-3*) Dover.
—Science Tricks & Magic for Young People. (Illus.). 126p. (gr. 3-11). 1987. pap. 3.50 (*0-486-25453-4*) Dover.
—Sports Science for Young People. 1990. pap. 3.95 (*0-486-26527-7*) Dover.
Barr, Linda & Monserrat, Catherine. Student Study Guide for Teenage Pregnancy: A New Beginning. rev. ed. 60p. (gr. 6-12). 1992. wkbk. 4.95 (*0-945886-11-X*) New Futures.
—Teenage Pregnancy: A New Beginning. rev. ed. Behm, Kim, et al, illus. Jones, Lyn, et al, photos by. 112p. (gr. 6-12). 1992. pap. 14.95 (*0-945886-07-1*) New Futures.
Barr, Linda, ed. see Cosby, Bill, et al.
Barr, Linda, ed. see Resnik, Hank.

Barr, Marilyn. Fearon's Animal Theme Activity Sheets. (ps-1). 1989. pap. 6.95 (*0-8224-0501-6*) Fearon Teach Aids.
Barr, Marilyn G. Paper Bags: Patterns for Cut-&-Play Fun. (Illus.). 64p. (ps-k). 1989. 6.95 (*0-685-31233-X*, MM1915) Monday Morning Bks.
Barr, Marilynn G. Bear Days. (Illus.). 48p. (ps-1). 1993. pap. 5.95 (*1-878279-55-6*) Monday Morning Bks.
—Build-a-Board. (Illus.). 128p. (gr. 1-6). 1991. pap. 10.95 (*1-878279-32-7*) Monday Morning Bks.
—Bunny Days. (Illus.). 48p. (ps-1). 1993. pap. 5.95 (*1-878279-54-8*) Monday Morning Bks.
—Dinosaur Days. (Illus.). 48p. (ps-1). 1993. pap. 5.95 (*1-878279-56-4*) Monday Morning Bks.
—Duck Days. (Illus.). 48p. (ps-1). 1993. pap. 5.95 (*1-878279-53-X*) Monday Morning Bks.
—Gameboard Round-up. (Illus.). 128p. (gr. 1-6). 1991. pap. 10.95 (*1-878279-33-5*) Monday Morning Bks.
—Mother Goose Caboose. 256p. (gr. 2). 1991. 16.95 (*0-86653-618-3*, GA1337) Good Apple.
—Paper Plates. (Illus.). 64p. (ps-k). 1989. 6.95 (*0-912107-98-7*, MM1916) Monday Morning Bks.
—Paper Rolls. (Illus.). 64p. (ps-k). 1989. 6.95 (*1-878279-00-9*, MM1917) Monday Morning Bks.
—Pop-up Theater. (gr. 4-6). 1991. pap. 14.95 (*0-8224-5586-2*) Fearon Teach Aids.
—Shortcuts for Fall. (Illus.). 80p. (ps-4). 1992. pap. 8.95 (*1-878279-43-2*) Monday Morning Bks.
—Shortcuts for Spring. (Illus.). 80p. (gr. k-4). 1992. pap. 8.95 (*1-878279-45-9*) Monday Morning Bks.
—Shortcuts for Winter. (Illus.). 80p. (gr. k-4). 1992. pap. 8.95 (*1-878279-44-0*) Monday Morning Bks.
Barr, Mike. Batman: Full Circle. O'Neil, Dennis, ed. 64p. (gr. 3 up). 1991. pap. 5.95 (*0-930289-98-6*) DC Comics.
Barr, Mike, et al. The Best of Star Trek. Greenberger, Bob & Hill, Michael, eds. Purcell, Gordon & Villagran, Ricardo, illus. 240p. (Orig.). 1991. pap. 19.95 (*1-56389-009-7*) DC Comics.
Barr, Roger. Radios: Wireless Sound. LC 93-12988. 1994. 15.95 (*1-56006-225-8*) Lucent Bks.
—Richard Nixon. LC 92-25566. (Illus.). 112p. (gr. 5-8). 1992. PLB 14.95 (*1-56006-035-2*) Lucent Bks.
—The Vietnam War. LC 91-23067. (Illus.). 112p. (gr. 5-8). 1991. PLB 17.95 (*1-56006-410-2*) Lucent Bks.
Barr, Stephen. Mathematical Brain Benders: Second Miscellany of Puzzles. (Illus.). 224p. (gr. 6 up). 1982. pap. 4.95 (*0-486-24260-9*) Dover.
Barr, Vilma, ed. see Bernstein, Louis & Garibaldi, Louis E.
Barracca, Debra & Barracca, Sal. Maxi, the Hero. Buehner, Mark, illus. (ps-3). 1991. 12.95 (*0-8037-0939-0*); PLB 12.89 (*0-8037-0940-4*) Dial Bks Young.
Barracca, Debra, jt. auth. see Barracca, Sal.
Barracca, Sal & Barracca, Debra. The Adventures of Taxi Dog. Fogelman, Phyllis J., ed. Buehner, Mark, illus. LC 89-1056. 32p. (ps-3). 1990. 13.00 (*0-8037-0671-5*); PLB 12.89 (*0-8037-0672-3*) Dial Bks Young.
—Maxi, the Star. Ayers, Alan, illus. LC 91-44962. 32p. (ps-3). 1993. 13.99 (*0-8037-1348-7*); PLB 13.89 (*0-8037-1349-5*) Dial Bks Young.
Barracca, Sal, jt. auth. see Barracca, Debra.
Barraclough, Geoffrey. Introduction to Contemporary History. (gr. 9 up). 1968. pap. 5.95 (*0-14-020827-5*, Penguin Bks) Viking Penguin.
Barratt, C. Mother Goose Songbook. (gr. k up). 1986. 4.98 (*0-685-16882-4*, 615754) Outlet Bk Co.
Barratt, Dorothy, et al. Becoming Friends, What Friends Believe. Eichorn, Chris & Nelson, Lois, illus. 78p. (gr. 5-6). 1990. tchr's. ed. 7.50 (*0-943701-16-3*) George Fox Pr.
Barre, Shelley A. Chive. LC 93-16202. (gr. 4). 1993. pap. 14.00 (*0-671-75641-9*, S&S BFYR) S&S Trade.
Barrett, Anna P. Juneteenth. rev. ed. Goodman, Frances B., ed. Costner, Howard, illus. 64p. (gr. k-8). 1993. pap. 9.95 (*0-89896-111-4*) Larksdale.
—The Middlebatchers: Throw a Party for the Marriage of Hetty Wish & Lester Leg, Vol. 1. Darst, Shelia S., ed. Russell, Dave, illus. 118p. (Orig.). (gr. 3-7). 1984. pap. 7.95 (*0-89896-105-X*) Larksdale.
Barrett, Bonnie. Cantus Cunarum: English Nursery Rhymes in Latin. Farrar, Rick, illus. (LAT). 30p. (Orig.). (gr. 6-12). 1991. spiral bdg. 2.10 (*0-939507-00-5*, B707) Amer Classical.
Barrett, Ethel. Abraham: God's Faithful Pilgrim. LC 82-12330. 128p. (Orig.). (gr. 3 up). 1982. pap. 3.99 (*0-8307-0769-7*, 5810906) Regal.
Barrett, Jennifer. Kiki's New Sister. 1992. 13.50 (*0-553-07567-5*, Little Rooster) Bantam.
Barrett, Joanne, jt. auth. see Long, Ron E.
Barrett, Joanne, et al. Zeroes into Heroes. (gr. 3-6). Date not set. 4.50 (*0-685-68191-2*, BCMB-628); cassette 9.98 (*0-685-68192-0*, BCTA-9130C) Lillenas.
Barrett, John. Daniel Discovers Daniel. Servello, Joe, illus. LC 79-17897. 32p. (gr. k-1). 1980. 16.95 (*0-87705-423-1*) Human Sci Pr.
—The Day the Toys Came to Silver Dollar City. Ruth, Rod, illus. (gr. k-10). 1978. 1.99 (*0-686-22891-X*) Silver Dollar.
—The Littlest Mule. Silver Dollar City, Inc. Staff, ed. Baer, Jane & Baer, Dale, illus. (ps-5). 1977. 2.99g (*0-686-19125-0*) Silver Dollar.
—Oscar, the Selfish Octopus. Servello, Joseph, illus. LC 78-18760. 32p. (ps-3). 1978. 16.95 (*0-87705-335-9*) Human Sci Pr.

—Zeke Hatfield & a Ghost Named Rocky. Ruth, Red, illus. (gr. k-10). 1978. 1.99 (*0-686-22892-8*) Silver Dollar.

Barrett, John, et al. Stories of God's Love: Creation, Noah's Ark, Christmas, Joshua & the Wall of Jericho. Haines, Bill, illus. (ps-2). 1990. 9.99 (*1-55513-399-1*, 63990, Chariot Bks) Cook.

—Stories of People Who Loved God: Jonah, Daniel, David, Esther. Haines, Bill, illus. (ps-2). 1991. 9.99 (*1-55513-539-0*, 65391, Chariot Bks) Cook.

Barrett, John E., photos by. Big Bird Is Yellow: A Sesame Street Book of Colors. LC 89-63996. (Illus.). 14p. (ps-3). bds. 3.95 (*0-679-80752-7*) Random Bks Yng Read.

Barrett, John E. & View-Master International, photos by. Big Bird's Mother Goose. LC 83-63404. (Illus.). 28p. (ps). 1984. bds. 2.95 (*0-394-86745-9*) Random Bks Yng Read.

Barrett, John M. It's Hard Not to Worry: Stories for Children about Poverty. (Illus., Orig.). (gr. 1-6). 1988. pap. 4.75 (*0-377-00178-3*) Friendship Pr.

—No Time for Me: Learning to Live with Busy Parents. Servello, Joe, illus. LC 78-21257. 32p. (ps-3). 1985. 16.95 (*0-87705-385-5*) Human Sci Pr.

Barrett, Joyce D. Willie's Not the Hugging Kind. Cummings, Pat, illus. LC 89-1868. 32p. (gr. k-3). 1989. 14.00 (*0-06-020416-8*); PLB 13.89 (*0-06-020417-6*) HarpC Child Bks.

—Willie's Not the Hugging Kind. Cummings, Pat, illus. LC 89-1868. 32p. (gr. k-3). 1991. pap. 3.95 (*0-06-443264-5*, Trophy) HarpC Child Bks.

Barrett, Judi. Animals Should Definitely Not Act Like People. Barrett, Ron, illus. LC 80-13364. 32p. (ps-2). 1980. SBE 13.95 (*0-689-30768-3*, Atheneum Child Bk) Macmillan Child Grp.

—Animals Should Definitely Not Act Like People. Barrett, Ron, illus. 32p. (ps-1). 1988. pap. 3.95 (*0-689-71287-1*, Aladdin) Macmillan Child Grp.

—Animals Should Definitely Not Wear Clothing. Barrett, Ron, illus. LC 70-115078. 32p. (ps-2). 1970. SBE 13. 95 (*0-689-20592-9*, Atheneum Child Bk) Macmillan Child Grp.

—Animals Should Definitely Not Wear Clothing. Barrett, Ron, illus. 32p. (ps-1). 1988. pap. 3.95 (*0-689-70807-6*, Aladdin) Macmillan Child Grp.

—Animals Should Definitely Not Wear Clothing. Barrett, Ron, illus. 32p. (gr. k-3). 1990. incl. cass. 19.95 (*0-87499-147-1*); pap. 12.95 incl. cass. (*0-87488-146-3*); Set; incl. 4 bks., cass., & guide. pap. 27.95 (*0-87499-148-X*) Live Oak Media.

—Benjamin's Three Hundred Sixty-Five Birthdays. reissue ed. Barrett, Ron, illus. LC 92-2497. 40p. (ps-1). 1992. RSBE 13.95 (*0-689-31791-3*, Atheneum Child Bk) Macmillan Child Grp.

—Benjamin's 365 Birthdays. 2nd ed. Barrett, Ron, illus. LC 92-2497. 40p. (ps-1). 1992. pap. 4.95 (*0-689-71635-4*, Aladdin) Macmillan Child Grp.

—Cloudy with a Chance of Meatballs. Barrett, Ron, illus. LC 78-2945. 32p. (ps-3). 1978. RSBE 14.95 (*0-689-30647-4*, Atheneum Child Bk) Macmillan Child Grp.

—Cloudy with a Chance of Meatballs. Barrett, Ron, illus. (gr. 2-5). 1985. pap. 12.95 incl. cassette (*0-941078-91-4*); PLB incl. cassette 19.95 (*0-941078-93-0*); incl. cassette, 4 paperbacks guide 27. 95 (*0-941078-92-2*) Live Oak Media.

—Pickles Have Pimples: And Other Silly Statements. Johnson, Lonnie S., illus. LC 85-20073. 32p. (ps-2). 1986. SBE 13.95 (*0-689-31187-7*, Atheneum Child Bk) Macmillan Child Grp.

—A Snake Is Totally Tail. Johnson, Lonni S., illus. LC 83-2657. 32p. (ps-1). 1983. SBE 13.95 (*0-689-30979-1*, Atheneum Child Bk) Macmillan Child Grp.

Barrett, Judith. Cloudy with a Chance of Meatballs. LC 87-29643. (Illus.). (ps-3). 1982. pap. 3.95 (*0-689-70749-5*, Aladdin) Macmillan Child Grp.

—A Snake Is Totally Tail. Johnson, Lonni S., illus. LC 87-1123. 32p. (ps-1). 1987. pap. 3.95 (*0-689-71148-4*, Aladdin) Macmillan Child Grp.

Barrett, Katharine. Animals in Action. Bergman, Lincoln & Fairwell, Kay, eds. Baker, Lisa H., illus. Barrett, Reginald & Craig, Rose, photos by. (Illus.). 44p. (Orig.). (gr. 6-9). 1986. pap. 8.50 (*0-912511-10-9*) Lawrence Science.

—Mapping Animal Movements. Bergman, Lincoln & Fairwell, Kay, eds. Baker, Lisa H. & Bevilacqua, Carol, illus. Barrett, Reginald, et al, photos by. 41p. (Orig.). (gr. 5-9). 1987. pap. 8.50 (*0-912511-60-5*) Lawrence Science.

Barrett, Katharine, et al. Investigating Artifacts. Bergman, Lincoln & Fairwell, Kay, eds. (Illus.). 120p. (gr. k-6). 1992. pap. 12.00 (*0-912511-83-4*) Lawrence Science.

Barrett, Katherine & Greene, Richard. The Man Behind the Magic: The Story of Walt Disney. (Illus.). 208p. (gr. 5 up). 1991. 18.00 (*0-670-82259-0*) Viking Child Bks.

Barrett, Kevin. Black Guard. Charlton, S. Coleman, ed. Jones, J. Wallace, et al, illus. 40p. (Orig.). (gr. 12). 1990. pap. 8.00 (*1-55806-115-0*, 7012) Iron Crown Ent Inc.

—Imperial Crisis: House Devon in Turmoil. (Illus.). 56p. (gr. 10-12). 1985. pap. 12.00 (*0-915795-37-X*, 9300) Iron Crown Ent Inc.

Barrett, Kevin, jt. auth. see Brinkley, Chad.

Barrett, Kevin, ed. see Armintrout, W. G.

Barrett, Kevin, ed. see Bouton, Steve.

Barrett, Kirt K. The Flight of Fancy. Barrett, Brett K., illus. LC 89-60346. 38p. (gr. 3-9). 1989. PLB 12.95 (*0-9622496-0-2*) Roanoke Park.

Barrett, Linda & Guengerich, Galen. Health Care. Culleton, P., ed. LC 90-13020. (Illus.). 96p. (gr. 6-12). 1991. PLB 13.90 (*0-531-11102-4*) Watts.

—Personal Services. LC 90-13010. (Illus.). 96p. (gr. 6-12). 1991. PLB 14.40 (*0-531-11103-2*) Watts.

—Sales & Distribution. LC 90-12991. (Illus.). 96p. (gr. 6-12). 1991. PLB 14.40 (*0-531-11105-9*) Watts.

—Telecommunications. LC 90-13024. (Illus.). 96p. (gr. 6-12). 1991. PLB 14.40 (*0-531-11104-0*) Watts.

Barrett, Mark, et al. The Word Test--Adolescent - Complete Kit: A Test of Expressive Vocabulary & Semantics. (gr. 7-12). 1989. complete kit 49.95 (*1-55999-096-1*) LinguiSystems.

—The Word Test--Adolescent - Examiner's Manual: A Test of Expressive Vocabulary & Semantics. (gr. 7-12). 1989. examiner's manual 33.00 (*1-55999-097-X*) LinguiSystems.

Barrett, Marsha. Early Christians: Workers for Jesus. Hester, Ron, illus. (gr. 1-6). 1979. 5.99 (*0-8054-4247-2*, 4242-47) Broadman.

—Servant with a Smile. Swain, John & Stevens, Bill, photos by. (Illus.). 40p. (Orig.). (gr. 1-3). 1985. pap. 2.00 (*0-317-18029-0*) Home Mission.

—Vena Aguillard: Woman of Faith. LC 82-73664. (gr. 4-6). 1983. 5.95 (*0-8054-4281-2*, 4242-81) Broadman.

Barrett, Marvin. Meet Thomas Jefferson. Fogarty, Pat, illus. LC 88-19069. 72p. (gr. 2-4). 1989. pap. 2.99 (*0-394-81964-0*) Random Bks Yng Read.

Barrett, Mary B. Sing to the Stars. Speidel, Sandra, illus. LC 92-41773. 1994. 14.95 (*0-316-08224-4*) Little.

Barrett, N. S. Bears. FS Staff, ed. LC 87-50846. 32p. (Orig.). (gr. 1-6). 1988. PLB 11.90 (*0-531-10526-1*) Watts.

—Monkeys & Apes. FS Staff, ed. (Illus.). 32p. (gr. 1-6). 1988. PLB 11.90 (*0-531-10529-6*); pap. 4.95 (*0-531-15205-7*) Watts.

—Pandas. FS Staff, ed. (Illus.). 32p. (gr. 4-9). 1988. PLB 11.90 (*0-531-10530-X*) Watts.

—Polar Animals. FS Staff, ed. (Illus.). 32p. (gr. 1-6). 1988. PLB 11.90 (*0-531-10531-8*) Watts.

Barrett, Norman. Animales Polares. LC 90-70882. (SPA., Illus.). 32p. (gr. k-4). 1990. PLB 11.90 (*0-531-07900-7*) Watts.

—Aranas. LC 88-51514. (SPA., Illus.). 32p. (gr. k-4). 1990. PLB 11.90 (*0-531-07901-5*) Watts.

—Artes Marciales. LC 90-70884. (SPA., Illus.). 32p. (gr. k-4). 1990. PLB 11.90 (*0-531-07902-3*) Watts.

—Ballenas. LC 90-70885. (SPA., Illus.). 32p. (gr. k-4). 1990. PLB 11.90 (*0-531-07903-1*) Watts.

—Bicicross. LC 90-70885. (SPA., Illus.). 32p. (gr. k-4). 1990. PLB 11.90 (*0-531-07904-X*) Watts.

—Birds of Prey. (Illus.). 32p. (gr. k-4). 1991. PLB 11.90 (*0-531-14151-9*) Watts.

—Canoeing. Franklin Watts Ltd., ed. (Illus.). 32p. (ps-3). 1988. PLB 11.90 (*0-531-10349-8*) Watts.

—Canoeing. (Illus.). 32p. (gr. 2 up). 1990. pap. 4.95 (*0-531-15178-6*) Watts.

—Carros de Carrera. LC 90-70887. (SPA., Illus.). 32p. (gr. k-4). 1990. PLB 11.90 (*0-531-07905-8*) Watts.

—Cats. (Illus.). 32p. (gr. k-4). 1990. PLB 11.90 (*0-531-14045-8*) Watts.

—Cocodrilos y Caimanes. LC 90-71415. (SPA., Illus.). 32p. (gr. k-4). 1991. PLB 11.40 (*0-531-07919-8*) Watts.

—Coral Reef. LC 90-42931. (Illus.). 32p. (gr. k-4). 1991. PLB 11.90 (*0-531-14110-1*) Watts.

—Coral Reef. (Illus.). 32p. (gr. k-4). 1991. pap. 4.95 (*0-531-15608-7*) Watts.

—Crocodiles & Alligators. LC 88-51517. (Illus.). 32p. (gr. k-6). 1990. 11.90 (*0-531-10705-1*) Watts.

—Custom Cars. LC 86-50639. (Illus.). 32p. (gr. k-3). 1990. PLB 11.90 (*0-531-10273-4*) Watts.

—Delfines. LC 90-71418. (SPA., Illus.). 32p. (gr. k-4). 1991. PLB 11.90 (*0-531-07920-1*) Watts.

—Deserts. (Illus.). (ps-3). 1990. PLB 11.90 (*0-531-10832-5*) Watts.

—Deserts. (Illus.). 32p. (gr. 2 up). 1991. pap. 4.95 (*0-531-24619-1*) Watts.

—Desiertos. (SPA., Illus.). 32p. (gr. k-4). 1990. PLB 11. 90 (*0-531-07924-4*) Watts.

—Dogs. (Illus.). 32p. (gr. k-4). 1990. PLB 11.90 (*0-531-14040-7*) Watts.

—Dragons & Lizards. LC 90-43335. (Illus.). 32p. (gr. k-4). 1991. PLB 11.90 (*0-531-14111-X*) Watts.

—Dragons & Lizards. (Illus.). 32p. (gr. k-4). 1991. pap. 4.95 (*0-531-15609-5*) Watts.

—Flightless Birds. LC 90-42382. (Illus.). 32p. (gr. k-4). 1991. PLB 11.90 (*0-531-14112-8*) Watts.

—Flightless Birds. (Illus.). 32p. (gr. k-4). 1991. pap. 4.95 (*0-531-15611-7*) Watts.

—Flying Machines. LC 93-33238. 1994. write for info. (*0-531-14301-5*) Watts.

—Gerbils. LC 89-21529. (Illus.). 32p. (gr. k-4). 1990. PLB 11.90 (*0-531-14030-X*) Watts.

—Gimnasia. LC 90-70888. (SPA., Illus.). 32p. (gr. k-4). 1990. PLB 11.90 (*0-531-07906-6*) Watts.

—Guinea Pigs. (Illus.). 32p. (gr. k-4). 1990. PLB 11.90 (*0-531-14031-8*) Watts.

—Gymnastics. (Illus.). 32p. (gr. 2 up). 1991. pap. 4.95 (*0-531-24614-0*) Watts.

—Hamsters. (Illus.). 32p. (gr. k-4). 1990. PLB 11.40 (*0-531-14032-6*) Watts.

—Hang Gliding. Franklin Watts Ltd., ed. (Illus.). 32p. (ps-9). 1988. 11.90 (*0-531-10350-1*) Watts.

—Huracanes y Tornados. LC 90-70889. (SPA., Illus.). 32p. (gr. k-4). 1990. PLB 11.90 (*0-531-07907-4*) Watts.

—Hurricanes & Tornadoes. (Illus.). 32p. (gr. 2 up). 1991. pap. 4.95 (*0-531-24615-9*) Watts.

—Kangaroos & Other Marsupials. LC 90-42383. (Illus.). 32p. (gr. k-4). 1991. PLB 11.90 (*0-531-14113-6*) Watts.

—Kangaroos & Other Marsupials. (Illus.). 32p. (gr. k-4). 1991. pap. 4.95 (*0-531-15612-5*) Watts.

—Martial Arts. (Illus.). 32p. (gr. 2 up). 1991. pap. 4.95 (*0-531-24617-5*) Watts.

—Monos y Simios. LC 90-71420. (SPA., Illus.). 32p. (gr. k-4). 1991. PLB 11.90 (*0-531-07918-X*) Watts.

—Monsters of the Deep. (Illus.). 32p. (gr. k-4). 1991. PLB 11.90 (*0-531-14150-0*) Watts.

—Montanas. LC 90-71419. (SPA., Illus.). 32p. (gr. k-4). 1991. PLB 11.90 (*0-531-07923-6*) Watts.

—Mountains. (Illus.). 32p. (gr. 2 up). 1991. pap. 4.95 (*0-531-24616-7*) Watts.

—Osos. LC 90-71417. (SPA., Illus.). 32p. (gr. k-4). 1991. PLB 11.90 (*0-531-07917-1*) Watts.

—Pandas. (SPA., Illus.). 32p. (gr. k-4). 1990. PLB 11.90 (*0-531-07908-2*); pap. 4.95 (*0-531-15206-5*) Watts.

—Penguins. LC 90-32151. (Illus.). 32p. (gr. k-4). 1991. PLB 11.90 (*0-531-14114-4*) Watts.

—Penguins. (Illus.). 32p. (gr. k-4). 1991. pap. 4.95 (*0-531-15613-3*) Watts.

—Picture World of Air Rescue. LC 90-31222. (Illus.). 32p. (gr. k-4). 1991. PLB 12.40 (*0-531-14089-X*) Watts.

—Picture World of Airport Rescue. LC 90-31221. (Illus.). 32p. (gr. k-4). 1991. PLB 12.40 (*0-531-14088-1*) Watts.

—Picture World of Ambulances. LC 90-31223. (Illus.). 32p. (gr. k-4). 1991. PLB 12.40 (*0-531-14090-3*) Watts.

—The Picture World of Astronauts. (Illus.). 32p. (gr. k-4). 1990. PLB 12.40 (*0-531-14053-9*) Watts.

—Picture World of Fire Engines. LC 90-31035. (Illus.). 32p. (gr. k-4). 1991. PLB 12.40 (*0-531-14091-1*) Watts.

—The Picture World of Planets. (Illus.). 32p. (gr. k-4). 1990. PLB 12.40 (*0-531-14054-7*) Watts.

—Picture World of Police Vehicles. LC 90-31020. (Illus.). 32p. (gr. k-4). 1991. PLB 12.40 (*0-531-14092-X*) Watts.

—The Picture World of Rockets & Satellites. (Illus.). 32p. (gr. k-4). 1990. PLB 12.40 (*0-531-14055-5*) Watts.

—Picture World of Sea Rescue. LC 90-31019. (Illus.). 32p. (gr. k-4). 1991. PLB 12.40 (*0-531-14093-8*) Watts.

—The Picture World of Space Shuttles. (Illus.). 32p. (gr. k-4). 1990. PLB 12.40 (*0-531-14056-3*) Watts.

—The Picture World of Space Voyages. (Illus.). 32p. (gr. k-4). 1990. PLB 12.40 (*0-531-14057-1*) Watts.

—The Picture World of Sun & Stars. (Illus.). 32p. (gr. k-4). 1990. PLB 12.40 (*0-531-14058-X*) Watts.

—Poisonous Insects. (Illus.). 32p. (gr. k-4). 1991. PLB 11. 90 (*0-531-14152-7*) Watts.

—Poisonous Snakes. (Illus.). 32p. (gr. k-4). 1991. PLB 11. 90 (*0-531-14153-5*) Watts.

—Rabbits. (Illus.). 32p. (gr. k-4). 1990. PLB 11.90 (*0-531-14033-4*) Watts.

—Racing Cars. (Illus.). 32p. (gr. 2 up). 1990. pap. 4.95 (*0-531-15143-3*) Watts.

—Sailing. Franklin Watts Ltd., ed. (Illus.). 32p. (ps-6). 1988. 11.90 (*0-531-10351-X*) Watts.

—Scuba Diving. (Illus.). 32p. (gr. k-6). 1990. 11.90 (*0-531-10631-4*) Watts.

—Seals & Walruses. LC 90-32150. (Illus.). 32p. (gr. k-4). 1991. PLB 11.90 (*0-531-14115-2*) Watts.

—Seals & Walruses. (Illus.). 32p. (gr. k-4). 1991. pap. 4.95 (*0-531-15614-1*) Watts.

—Serpientes. LC 90-70891. (SPA., Illus.). 32p. (gr. k-4). 1990. PLB 11.90 (*0-531-07909-0*) Watts.

—Space Machines. LC 93-33237. 1994. write for info. (*0-531-14300-7*) Watts.

—Sport: Players, Games & Spectacle. (Illus.). 48p. (gr. 5-8). 1993. 13.95 (*0-531-15262-6*) Watts.

—Sports Machines. LC 93-33236. 1994. write for info. (*0-531-14299-X*) Watts.

—Stunt Riding. (Illus.). 32p. (gr. k-3). 1987. PLB 11.90 (*0-531-10276-9*) Watts.

—Tanques. (SPA., Illus.). 32p. (gr. k-4). 1991. PLB 11.90 (*0-531-07922-8*) Watts.

—Tiburones. (SPA., Illus.). 32p. (gr. k-4). 1990. PLB 11. 90 (*0-531-07910-4*) Watts.

—Transport Machines. LC 93-33235. 1994. write for info. (*0-531-14298-1*) Watts.

—Trucks. (Illus.). 32p. (gr. 2 up). 1990. pap. 4.95 (*0-531-15146-8*) Watts.

—Volcanes. (SPA., Illus.). 32p. (gr. k-4). 1990. PLB 11.90 (*0-531-07911-2*) Watts.

—Volcanoes. (Illus.). 32p. (gr. 2 up). 1991. pap. 4.95 (*0-531-24618-3*) Watts.

—Wild Cats. (Illus.). 32p. (gr. k-4). 1991. PLB 11.90 (*0-531-14155-1*) Watts.

—Windsurfing. Franklin Watts Ltd., ed. (Illus.). 32p. (ps-9). 1988. 10.90 (*0-531-10354-4*) Watts.

—Wolves & Wild Dogs. (Illus.). 32p. (gr. k-4). 1991. PLB 11.90 (*0-531-14154-3*) Watts.

Barrett, Norman & Mulherin, Jenny. Rivers & Lakes. LC 84-5713. (Illus.). 32p. (gr. 1-4). 1990. PLB 11.90 (*0-531-10840-6*) Watts.

Barrett, Norman S. Airliners. LC 84-50697. (Illus.). 32p. (gr. 3-6). 1989. pap. 4.95 (*0-531-15137-9*) Watts.

—BMX Bikes. LC 86-50638. (Illus.). 32p. (gr. k-3). 1987. PLB 11.90 (*0-531-10272-6*) Watts.
—BMX Bikes. (Illus.). (gr. 3-6). 1989. pap. 4.95 (*0-531-15138-7*) Watts.
—Dolphins. (Illus.). 32p. (gr. k-6). 1989. PLB 11.90 (*0-531-10706-X*) Watts.
—Elephants. FS Staff, ed. (Illus.). 32p. (gr. 1-6). 1988. PLB 11.90 (*0-531-10528-8*); pap. 4.95 (*0-531-15204-9*) Watts.
—Spiders. (Illus.). 32p. (gr. k-6). 1989. PLB 11.90 (*0-531-10702-7*) Watts.
—Sport: Players, Games, & Spectacle. LC 93-7936. 1993. write for info. (*0-531-14280-9*) Watts.
—Whales. (Illus.). 32p. (gr. k-6). 1989. PLB 11.90 (*0-531-10703-5*) Watts.
Barrett, Pamela. Becky's Braces. 1993. 7.75 (*0-8042-4689-8*) Carlton.
Barrett, Peter & Barrett, Susan. The Circle Sarah Drew. Barrett, Peter & Barrett, Susan, illus. Incl. The Line Sophie Drew (*0-87592-029-2*); The Square Ben Drew (*0-87592-049-7*). LC 72-89449. (Illus.). 32p. (ps-2). 1973. 8.95 ea. (*0-87592-012-8*) Scroll Pr.
Barrett, Sally. The Sound of the Week. 144p. (gr. k-4). 1980. 11.95 (*0-916456-63-3*, GA 184) Good Apple.
Barrett, Susan, jt. auth. see Barrett, Peter.
Barrett, Susan L. It's All in Your Head: A Guide to Understanding Your Brain & Boosting Your Brain Power. rev. ed. Espeland, Pamela, ed. Urbanovic, Jackie, illus. LC 92-18090. 160p. (gr. 3-7). 1992. pap. 9.95 (*0-915793-45-8*) Free Spirit Pub.
Barrett, Tracy. Harper's Ferry: The Story of John Brown's Raid. LC 92-39810. (Illus.). 64p. (gr. 4-6). 1993. PLB 14.90 (*1-56294-380-4*) Millbrook Pr.
—Nat Turner & the Slave Revolt. LC 92-12086. (Illus.). 32p. (gr. 2-4). 1993. PLB 12.40 (*1-56294-275-1*) Millbrook Pr.
Barrett, William E. Lilies of the Field. Silverman, Burt, illus. LC 62-8085. (gr. 7 up). 1967. 3.95 (*0-685-01491-6*, Im); pap. 3.95 (*0-385-07246-5*, Im) Doubleday.
Barrett-Dragan, Patricia & Dalton, Rosemary. The Kid's Cookbook. rev. ed. Nelson, Mike, illus. 192p. (gr. 2-8). 1992. pap. 8.95 (*1-55867-043-2*, Nitty Gritty Ckbks) Bristol Pub Ent CA.
Barrie, Anmarie. A Step-by-Step Book about Our First Aquarium. (Illus.). 64p. 1987. 3.95 (*0-86622-454-8*, SK003) TFH Pubns.
Barrie, Barbara. Adam Zigzag. LC 93-8735. 1994. 14.95 (*0-385-31172-9*) Delacorte.
—Lone Star. 192p. (gr. 4-7). 1992. pap. 3.50 (*0-440-40718-4*, YB) Dell.
Barrie, J. M. The Little Minister. 232p. 1981. Repr. PLB 18.95 (*0-89966-329-X*) Buccaneer Bks.
—The Little Minister. 300p. 1980. Repr. PLB 18.95x (*0-89967-007-5*) Harmony Raine.
—Peter Pan. (Illus.). (ps). 1985. bds. 1.00 (*0-517-48144-8*) Outlet Bk Co.
—Peter Pan. Shebar, Susan, ed. Lewis, T., illus. LC 87-15480. 48p. (gr. 2-6). 1988. PLB 12.89 (*0-8167-1199-2*); pap. text ed. 3.95 (*0-8167-1200-X*) Troll Assocs.
—Peter Pan. 15.95 (*0-8488-0427-9*) Amereon Ltd.
—Peter Pan. Gustafson, Scott, illus. 192p. 1991. 20.00 (*0-670-84180-3*) Viking Child Bks.
—Peter Pan. Dubowski, Cathy, adapted by. Zallinger, Jean, illus. LC 90-23077. 96p. (Orig.). (gr. 2-7). 1991. lib. bdg. 5.99 (*0-679-91044-1*); pap. 2.95 (*0-679-81044-7*) Random Bks Yng Read.
—Peter Pan. 1985. pap. 2.95 (*0-553-21178-1*, Bantam Classics) Bantam.
—Peter Pan. Arneson, D. J., retold by. Clift, Eva, illus. 128p. 1991. pap. 2.95 (*1-56156-029-4*) Kidsbks.
—Peter Pan. Hildebrandt, Greg, illus. 160p. 1987. 14.95 (*0-88101-270-X*) Unicorn Pub.
—Peter Pan. Bedford, F. D., illus. LC 92-53172. 224p. 1992. 12.95 (*0-679-41792-3*, Evrymans Lib Childs Class) Knopf.
—Peter Pan. Ormerod, Jan, illus. 208p. (gr. 5 up). 1993. pap. 3.99 (*0-14-032007-5*) Puffin Bks.
—Peter Pan. (gr. 4-7). 1993. pap. 3.25 (*0-590-46735-2*) Scholastic Inc.
—Peter Pan: A Changing Picture & Lift-the-Flap Book. abr. ed. Caswell, Edmund, illus. 32p. (ps-3). 1992. 15.95 (*0-670-83608-7*) Viking Child Bks.
—Peter Pan & Wendy. Foreman, Michael, illus. 160p. (gr. k-6). 1992. (Pub. by Pavilion UK); pap. 17.95 (*1-85145-449-7*, Pub. by Pavilion UK) Trafalgar.
—Peter Pan in Kensington Gardens. 175p. 1981. Repr. PLB 16.95x (*0-89966-328-1*) Buccaneer Bks.
—Peter Pan in Kensington Gardens. 150p. 1980. Repr. PLB 16.95x (*0-89967-006-7*) Harmony Raine.
—Peter Pan in Kensington Gardens & Peter & Wendy. Hollindale, Peter, intro. by. (Illus.). 288p. 1991. pap. 5.95 (*0-19-282593-3*) OUP.
—Peter Pan: Return to Never-Never Land. Forten, Ron, adapted by. (Illus.). 56p. 1991. pap. 5.95 (*1-56398-016-9*) Malibu Graphics.
Barrie, James. Little Minister. (gr. 10 up). 1968. pap. 0.75 (*0-8049-0187-2*, CL-187) Airmont.
—Peter Pan. White, Flora & Bedford, F. D., illus. 304p. (gr. k-5). 1988. Repr. of 1911 ed. 12.99 (*0-517-63222-5*) Outlet Bk Co.
Barrie, James M. Peter Pan. 176p. (gr. 3 up). 1985. 39. 50x (*0-685-00703-0*, Bantam Classics); pap. 12.95 (*0-685-00704-9*) Bantam.

—Peter Pan. LC 80-14510. (Illus.). 192p. (gr. k up). 1980. SBE 19.95 (*0-684-16611-9*, Scribners Young Read) Macmillan Child Grp.
—Peter Pan. Frank, Josette, adapted by. Goode, Diane, illus. LC 82-13288. 72p. (ps-4). 1983. lib. bdg. 8.99 (*0-394-95717-2*); pap. 8.95 (*0-394-85717-8*) Random Bks Yng Read.
—Peter Pan. 1986. pap. 2.95 (*0-14-035066-7*, Puffin) Puffin Bks.
—Peter Pan. Lurie, Alison, afterword by. 208p. 1987. pap. 3.50 (*0-451-52088-2*, Sig Classics) NAL-Dutton.
—Peter Pan. Frank, Josette, adapted by. Goode, Diane, illus. Redgrave, Lynn, contrib. by. (Illus.). 72p. (ps-5). 1987. incl. cass. 15.95 (*0-394-89226-7*) Random Bks Yng Read.
—Peter Pan. Hague, Michael, illus. LC 87-403. 144p. (gr. 4-6). 1987. 19.95 (*0-8050-0276-6*, Bks Young Read) H Holt & Co.
—Peter Pan. 176p. 1992. 9.49 (*0-8167-2554-3*); pap. 2.95 (*0-8167-2555-1*) Troll Assocs.
—Peter Pan. Oremerod, Jan, illus. (FRE.). 239p. (gr. 5-10). 1988. pap. 9.95 (*2-07-033411-2*) Schoenhof.
—The Study of Peter Pan. unabr., slightly altered ed. O'Connor, Daniel, adapted by. Woodward, Alice B., illus. Kliros, Thea, contrib. by. LC 29-18641. (Illus.). 96p. 1992. Repr. 1.00 (*0-486-27294-X*) Dover.
Barrie, James Matthew. Peter Pan & Wendy. 1988. 7.99 (*0-517-66189-6*) Outlet Bk Co.
Barrier, Jean & Kennedy, Alice. English Is Fun. McCombs, Toni, illus. Barrier, Jean & Kennedy, Aliceintro. by. (Illus.). 96p. (gr. k-5). 1981. pap. 6.00 (*0-911743-01-4*) Barrier & Kennedy.
—English Is Fun Books. McCombs, Toni, illus. 192p. (gr. k-8). 1991. pap. text ed. 12.00 (*0-911743-07-3*) Barrier & Kennedy.
—English Is Fun II. Catoe, Kaye, et al, eds. McCombs, Toni, illus. 96p. (gr. 2-8). 1985. pap. text ed. 6.00 (*0-911743-04-9*); tchr's ed. 8.00 (*0-911743-06-5*) Barrier & Kennedy.
Barrier, Jean see Barrier, Jean & Kennedy, Alice.
Barrington, Margaret. My Cousin Justin. 288p. (Orig.). (gr. 10-12). 1990. pap. 11.95 (*0-85640-456-X*, Pub. by Blackstaff Pr Belfast) Dufour.
Barris, Sara L. & Seltzer, Doryle P. Together Forever: An Adoption Story Coloring Book. Mazer, Susan, illus. 32p. 1992. pap. 3.95 (*0-9632023-0-8*) Shoot Star Pr.
Barron, T. A. The Merlin Effect. LC 93-36234. 1994. write for info. (*0-399-22689-3*, Philomel Bks) Putnam Pub Group.
Barron, Thomas A. Heartlight. 272p. (gr. 5-9). 1990. 15. 95 (*0-399-22180-8*, Philomel Bks) Putnam Pub Group.
Barron, Tom. The Ancient One. (Illus.). 368p. (gr. 6 up). 1992. 17.95 (*0-399-21899-8*, Philomel Bks) Putnam Pub Group.
Barrow, Lloyd H. Adventures with Rocks & Minerals: Geology Experiments for Young People. LC 90-30444. (Illus.). 96p. (gr. 4-9). 1991. lib. bdg. 16.95 (*0-89490-263-6*) Enslow Pubs.
Barrow, Madeline H., ed. see Dickson, Sandy L.
Barrow, Reginald H. The Romans. (Orig.). (gr. 9 up). 1975. pap. 5.95 (*0-14-020196-3*, Penguin Bks) Viking Penguin.
Barrowman, Tom, et al. MS-DOS Technic Control One Technology Pack. Helgoe, Cathy & Lough, Tom, eds. Graf, Heidi & Sturms, Aina, illus. 416p. (gr. 6-12). 1991. 595.00 (*0-914831-78-X*, 968) Lego Dacta.
—Technic Control One Resource Guide. Helgoe, Cathy & Lough, Tom, eds. Graf, Heidi & Sturms, Aina, illus. 416p. (gr. 6-12). 1991. text ed. 75.00 (*0-914831-74-7*, 959) Lego Dacta.
—Apple Technic Control One Technology Pack. Helgoe, Cathy & Lough, Tom, eds. Graf, Heidi & Sturms, Aina, illus. 416p. (gr. 6-12). 1991. 575.00 (*0-914831-75-5*, 958) Lego Dacta.
Barrows, Clifford, et al. The Opening Doors Series, 6 bks, Series 1. Barenbaum, Ruth, ed. Lane, Barry, ed. Beckwith, Joel. Seals, Elayne, illus. (Orig.). (gr. 6 up). 1989. Set. pap. 22.95 (*1-877829-00-5*) Opening Doors.
Barry, Jan. Draw, Design & Paint. (Illus.). 144p. (gr. 2-6). 1990. 12.95 (*0-86653-536-5*, GA1142) Good Apple.
Barry, Jimi, ed. see Cahill, Robert B. & Hrebic, Herbert J.
Barry, Mark. Car Books & Puzzle. Barry, Mark, illus. (ps). 1993. Gift box set of 4 bks, 12p. ea. bds. 14.95 (*1-56828-039-4*) Red Jacket Pr.
—The City Car Book. 12p. (ps). 1992. 4.95 (*1-56828-004-1*) Red Jacket Pr.
—A Drive in the Country. 12p. (ps). 1992. 4.95 (*1-56828-006-8*) Red Jacket Pr.
—The Highway Car Book. 12p. (ps). 1992. 4.95 (*1-56828-005-X*) Red Jacket Pr.
—Sirens & Lights. 12p. (ps). 1992. 4.95 (*1-56828-007-6*) Red Jacket Pr.
Barry, Mary J. Seward, Alaska: A History of the Gateway City, Vol. II: 1914-1923. Barry, Richard E., illus. 225p. (gr. 8 up). 1993. pap. 25.00 (*0-9617009-2-0*) M J P Barry.
Barry, Robert. Mr. Willowby's Christmas Tree. (Illus.). 32p. 1992. Repr. PLB 11.95x (*0-89966-935-2*) Buccaneer Bks.
—Mr. Willowby's Christmas Tree. Barry, Robert, illus. 32p. (ps-2). 1992. pap. 3.99 (*0-440-40726-5*, YB) Dell.
Barry, S. L., et al. Amazing Animals of Australia. Crump, Donald J., ed. LC 84-29558. (Illus.). 104p. (gr. 3-8). 1985. 8.95 (*0-87044-515-4*); PLB 12.50 (*0-87044-520-0*) Natl Geog.

Barry, Sebastian. Elsewhere. (gr. 1-12). 1985. 15.95 (*0-85105-903-1*, Pub. by Colin Smythe Ltd Britain) Dufour.
Barry, Sheila A. Super-Colossal Book of Puzzles, Tricks & Games. (Illus.). 640p. 1992. Repr. of 1978 ed. 9.99 (*0-517-07769-8*, Pub. by Wings Bks) Outlet Bk Co.
—The World's Best Party Games. Anderson, Doug, illus. LC 86-30038. 128p. (gr. 6-10). 1987. pap. 4.95 (*0-8069-6484-7*) Sterling.
—World's Best Travel Games. LC 87-7065. (Illus.). 128p. (gr. 5 up). 1988. pap. 4.95 (*0-8069-6776-5*) Sterling.
—The World's Most Spine-Tingling True Ghost Stories. Sharpe, Jim, illus. LC 92-19862. 96p. (gr. 3 up). 1992. 12.95 (*0-8069-8686-7*); pap. 3.95 (*0-8069-8687-5*) Sterling.
Barry, Sheila A., ed. Kids' Funniest Jokes. Sinclair, Jeff, illus. LC 93-23045. 96p. (gr. 2-10). 1993. 12.95 (*0-8069-0449-6*); pap. write for info. (*0-8069-0448-8*) Sterling.
Barss, Karen J. Clean Water. (Illus.). (gr. 5 up). 1992. lib. bdg. 19.95 (*0-7910-1583-1*) Chelsea Hse.
Barstow, Robbins. Grandiosas Criaturas del Mar: Una Introduccion al Mundo de las Ballenas y Otros Cetaceos. Accent, Inc. Staff, tr. from ENG. Sineti, Donald, illus. (SPA.). 46p. (Orig.). (gr. 7-12). 1988. pap. 5.00 (*0-9618858-2-3*) Cetacean Society.
—Meet the Great Ones: An Introduction to Whales & Other Cetaceans. Sineti, Donald, illus. LC 87-70553. 46p. (Orig.). (gr. 7-12). 1987. pap. 5.95 (*0-9618858-1-5*) Cetacean Society.
—Meet the Great Whales: An Illustrated Introduction to the Marvels of Cetaceans. 2nd ed. Sineti, Donald, illus. LC 87-70553. 56p. 1993. pap. 8.95 (*0-685-67826-1*) Parnassus Imprints.
Barsuhn, Rochelle N. Feeling Afraid. Connelly, Gwen, illus. LC 82-19946. (gr. 1-2). 1983. PLB 21.35 (*0-89565-246-3*); PLB 14.95s.p. (*0-685-55658-1*) Childs World.
—Feeling Angry. Hutton, Kathryn, illus. LC 82-19911. 32p. (gr. 1-2). 1983. PLB 21.35 (*0-89565-244-7*); PLB 14.95s.p. (*0-685-55659-X*) Childs World.
Barsy, Kalman. Del Nacimiento de la Isla de Boriken. Quintero, Nora, illus. LC 82-83288. (SPA.). 76p. (gr. 6). 1982. pap. 7.50 (*0-940238-01-2*) Ediciones Huracan.
Barta, Beverly, ed. see Gilbert, Jeanette.
Bartch, Marian, jt. auth. see Mallett, Jerry.
Bartel, Marvin. My Own Picture Book about Getting Older. Bartel, Marvin, illus. LC 89-80248. 43p. (gr-7). 1989. wkbk. 4.95 (*0-87303-135-0*) Faith & Life.
Bartel, Nettie R., et al. SIDA: Lo Que Todos Debemos Saber: Cuaderno del Estudiante. Rojas, Miriam M., tr. from ENG. (SPA., Illus.). (gr. 7-12). 1989. Level I, 96 p. wkbk. 8.00 (*0-929853-00-8*); Level II, 112 p. wkbk. 9.00 (*0-929853-01-6*); parents hdbk. 3.00 (*0-929853-02-4*) Condor Pubns Inc.
Bartels, Alice. The Beast. Tibo, Gilles, illus. 32p. (ps-2). 1990. 14.95 (*1-55037-101-0*, Pub. by Annick CN); pap. 6.95 (*1-55037-102-9*, Pub. by Annick CN) Firefly Bks Ltd.
Bartelt, Jeanine, et al. A Fence Too High. French, Marty, et al, illus. 26p. (ps up). 1986. 7.95 (*1-55578-103-9*); cass. incl. Worlds Wonder.
Barth, Edna. Hearts, Cupids, & Red Roses: The Story of the Valentine Symbols. Arndt, Ursula, illus. LC 73-7128. 64p. (gr. 3-6). 1982. pap. 5.95 (*0-89919-036-7*, Clarion Bks) HM.
—Holly, Reindeer, & Colored Lights: The Story of the Christmas Symbols. Arndt, Ursula, illus. LC 71-157731. 96p. (gr. 3-6). 1981. pap. 5.95 (*0-89919-037-5*, Clarion Bks) HM.
—Holly, Reindeer, & Colored Lights: The Story of the Christmas Symbols. Arndt, Ursula, illus. LC 71-157731. 96p. (gr. 3-6). 1979. 15.45 (*0-395-28842-8*, Calrion Bks) HM.
—I'm Nobody, Who Are You: The Story of Emily Dickinson. Cuffari, Richard, illus. LC 72-129211. 128p. (gr. 3-6). 1979. 15.45 (*0-395-28843-6*, Clarion Bks) HM.
—Lilies, Rabbits, & Painted Eggs: The Story of the Easter Symbols. Arndt, Ursula, illus. LC 74-79033. (gr. 3-6). 1979. (Clarion Bks); pap. 5.95 (*0-395-30550-0*, Clarion Bks) HM.
—Shamrocks, Harps, & Shillelaghs: The Story of the St. Patrick's Day Symbols. Arndt, Ursula, illus. LC 77-369. 96p. (gr. 3-6). 1982. 15.45 (*0-395-28845-2*, Clarion Bks); pap. 5.95 (*0-89919-038-3*, Clarion) HM.
—Turkeys, Pilgrims, & Indian Corn: The Story of the Thanksgiving Symbols. Arndt, Ursula, illus. LC 75-4703. 96p. (gr. 3-6). 1981. pap. 4.95 (*0-89919-039-1*, Clarion Bks) HM.
—Turkeys, Pilgrims, & Indian Corn: The Story of the Thanksgiving Symbols. Arndt, Ursula, illus. LC 75-4703. 96p. (gr. 3-6). 1979. 13.95 (*0-395-28846-0*, Clarion Bks) HM.
—Witches, Pumpkins & Grinning Ghosts: The Story of the Halloween Symbols. Arndt, Ursula, illus. LC 72-75705. 96p. (gr. 3-6). 1981. 4.95 (*0-89919-040-5*, Clarion Bks); pap. 4.95 (*0-317-03145-7*, Clarion Bks) HM.
—Witches, Pumpkins & Grinning Ghosts: The Story of the Halloween Symbols. Arndt, Ursula, illus. LC 72-75705. 96p. (gr. 3-6). 1979. 13.45 (*0-395-28847-9*, Clarion Bks) HM.
Barth, Jeff. A Thanksgiving Story in Vermont - 1852. Mitchinson, Shelia, illus. 60p. (Orig.). (gr. 3-8). 1989. pap. write for info. (*0-9624067-0-8*) Parable Pub.

Barth, Nancy & Wittenborn, Sally. But Will You Be My Valentine? (Illus., Orig.). (ps-k). 1987. pap. 4.95 (0-942565-01-0) Country Schl Pubns.
—On Halloween Night. Wittenborn, Sally, illus. 12p. (Orig.). (ps-1). 1987. pap. 4.95 (0-942565-00-2) Country Schl Pubns.

Barth, Shannon. Show! Don't Tell! How to Personalize College Applications. Berescik, Susan, ed. Dirgo, Ray, illus. 175p. (Orig.). (gr. 11-12). 1993. plastic comb 19.95 (0-9638297-0-X) Intl Editing.

Barthelme, Donald. Snow White. LC 67-14324. 1972. pap. 7.95 (0-689-70331-7, 191, Atheneum Child Bk) Macmillan Child Grp.

Bartholomew. Jimmy & the White Lie. (Illus.). 32p. (gr. k-9). 1976. 4.99 (0-570-03460-4, 56-1341) Concordia.
—My Friend Horace. McKissack, Patricia & McKissack, Fredrick, eds. LC 87-61650. (Illus.). 32p. (Orig.). (gr. 1-3). 1987. text ed. 8.95 (0-88335-721-6); pap. text ed. 4.95 (0-88335-741-0) Milliken Pub Co.

Bartimole, John, ed. see Lena, Daniel S. & Howard, Marie.

Bartle, Brian. Here Comes Tow Truck. Bartle, Brian, illus. 12p. (ps-1). 1992. 4.95 (0-448-40593-8, G&D) Putnam Pub Group.

Bartlett, J. A., jt. auth. see Helmrath, M. O.

Bartlett, Jaye. Caterpillar Had a Dream: A Poetic Story about Dreams Coming True. (Illus.). 1991. 8.95 (1-878064-02-9) TLC Bks.
—Caterpillar Had a Dream: A Story about Dreams Coming True. Dubina, Alan, illus. 38p. (Orig.). (ps up). 1990. PLB 11.95 incl. cassette (1-878064-00-2) New Age CT.
—Freddy the Elephant: The Story of a Sensitive Leader. Dubina, Alan, illus. 45p. (Orig.). (ps up). 1991. pap. 11.95 incl. cassette (1-878064-01-0) New Age CT.

Barto, Renzo. How to Draw Cartoon Characters. LC 92-23057. (Illus.). 32p. (gr. k-6). 1993. PLB 10.65 (0-8167-3265-5); pap. text ed. 1.95 (0-8167-3218-3) Troll Assocs.
—How to Draw Monster, Weirdoes, & Aliens. LC 92-23056. (Illus.). 32p. (gr. k-6). 1993. PLB 10.65 (0-8167-3245-0); pap. text ed. 1.95 (0-8167-3217-5) Troll Assocs.

Bartok, Mira & Ronan, Christine. Ancient Celts: Stencils. 32p. (Orig.). (gr. 3 up). 1993. pap. 9.95 (0-673-36101-2) GdYrBks.
—Ancient Japan: Stencils. (Illus.). 32p. (Orig.). (gr. 3 up). 1992. pap. 9.95 (0-673-36054-7) GdYrBks.
—Ancient Mexico: Stencils. 32p. (Orig.). (gr. 3 up). 1992. pap. 9.95 (0-673-36055-5) GdYrBks.
—Indians of the Great Plains: Stencils. 32p. (Orig.). 1993. pap. 9.95 (0-673-36138-1) GdYrBks.
—Northwest Coast Indians: Stencils. (Illus.). 32p. (Orig.). (gr. 3 up). 1992. pap. 9.95 (0-673-36056-3) GdYrBks.
—Pueblo Indians of the Southwest: Stencils. (Illus.). 32p. (Orig.). (gr. 3 up). 1993. pap. 9.95 (0-673-36102-0) GdYrBks.
—West Africa: Ghana: Stencils. (Illus.). 32p. (Orig.). (gr. 3 up). 1992. pap. 9.95 (0-673-36053-9) GdYrBks.
—West Africa: Nigeria: Stencils. (Illus.). 32p. (Orig.). 1993. pap. 9.95 (0-673-36137-3) GdYrBks.

Bartold, Thomas, jt. auth. see Siembieda, Kevin.

Bartold, Thomas, ed. see Siembieda, Kevin.

Bartold, Thomas, ed. see Siembieda, Kevin & Long, Kevin.

Bartold, Thomas, ed. see Wallis, James & Siembieda, Kevin.

Bartold, Thomas, ed. see Siembieda, Kevin & Long, Kevin.

Bartoletti, Susan & Lisandrelli, Elaine. Easy Writer: Student Worksheets, Level G. Gompper, Gail, illus. 38p. (Orig.). (gr. 7-9). 1986. pap. text ed. 14.95 (0-913935-37-9) ERA-CCR.
—Easy Writer: Student Worksheets, Level H. (Illus.). 38p. (Orig.). (gr. 8-10). 1986. pap. text ed. 14.95 (0-913935-38-7) ERA-CCR.

Bartoletti, Susan C. Silver at Night. Ray, David, illus. (gr. 4 up). 1994. 15.00 (0-517-59426-9); PLB 15.99 (0-517-59427-7) Crown Bks Yng Read.

Barton. Wee Little Woman. Date not set. 13.00 (0-06-023387-7, Festival); PLB 12.89 (0-06-023388-5, Festival) HarpC Child Bks.

Barton, Byron. Airplanes. LC 85-47899. (Illus.). 32p. (ps-k). 1986. 4.95 (0-694-00060-4, Crowell Jr Bks); PLB 12.89 (0-690-04532-8) HarpC Child Bks.
—Airport. Barton, Byron, illus. LC 79-7816. 32p. (ps-k). 1982. 15.00 (0-690-04168-3, Crowell Jr Bks); PLB 14.89 (0-690-04169-1) HarpC Child Bks.
—Airport. Barton, Byron, illus. LC 79-7816. 32p. (ps-1). 1987. pap. 4.95 (0-06-443145-2, Trophy) HarpC Child Bks.
—Boats. Barton, Byron, illus. LC 85-47900. 32p. (ps-k). 1986. 4.95 (0-694-00059-0, Crowell Jr Bks); PLB 12.89 (0-690-04536-0) HarpC Child Bks.
—Bones, Bones, Dinosaur Bones. Barton, Byron, illus. LC 89-71306. 32p. (ps-1). 1990. 11.00 (0-690-04825-4, Crowell Jr Bks); PLB 12.89 (0-690-04827-0, Crowell Jr Bks) HarpC Child Bks.
—Building a House. LC 80-22674. (Illus.). 32p. (ps-1). 1981. PLB 14.88 (0-688-84291-7) Greenwillow.
—Building a House. LC 80-22674. (Illus.). (ps-3). 1990. pap. 4.95 (0-688-09356-6, Mulberry) Morrow.
—Dinosaurs, Dinosaurs. Barton, Byron, illus. LC 88-22938. 40p. (ps-1). 1989. 10.95 (0-694-00269-0, Crowell Jr Bks); PLB 13.89 (0-690-04768-1) HarpC Child Bks.
—Dinosaurs, Dinosaurs. Barton, Byron, illus. LC 88-22938. 40p. (ps-1). 1991. 19.95 (0-06-020410-9) HarpC Child Bks.
—Dinosaurs, Dinosaurs. Barton, Byron, illus. LC 88-22938. 40p. (ps-1). 1993. pap. 4.95 (0-06-443298-X, Trophy) HarpC Child Bks.
—Hester. LC 75-9668. (Illus.). 32p. (ps-3). pap. 3.95 (0-688-09240-3, Mulberry) Morrow.
—I Want to Be an Astronaut. Barton, Byron, illus. LC 87-24311. 32p. (ps-1). 1988. 7.95 (0-694-00261-5, Crowell Jr Bks); PLB 12.89 (0-690-04744-4) HarpC Child Bks.
—I Want to Be an Astronaut. Barton, Byron, illus. LC 87-24311. 32p. (ps-1). 1992. pap. 4.95 (0-06-443280-7, Trophy) HarpC Child Bks.
—Little Red Hen. Barton, Byron, illus. LC 91-4051. 32p. (ps-1). 1993. 12.95 (0-06-021675-1); PLB 12.89 (0-06-021676-X) HarpC Child Bks.
—Machines at Work. Barton, Byron, illus. LC 86-24221. 32p. (ps-1). 1987. 14.00 (0-694-00190-2, Crowell Jr Bks); PLB 13.89 (0-690-04573-5) HarpC Child Bks.
—Trains. Barton, Byron, illus. LC 85-47898. 32p. (ps-k). 1986. 4.95 (0-694-00061-2, Crowell Jr Bks); PLB 12.89 (0-690-04534-4) HarpC Child Bks.
—Trucks. Barton, Byron, illus. LC 85-47901. 32p. (ps-k). 1986. 4.95 (0-694-00062-0, Crowell Jr Bks); PLB 12.89 (0-690-04530-1) HarpC Child Bks.
—Where's Al? LC 78-171866. (Illus.). 32p. (ps). 1989. pap. 5.70 (0-395-51582-3, Clarion Bks) HM.

Barton, Byron, retold by. & illus. The Three Bears. LC 90-43151. 32p. (ps-1). 1991. 15.00 (0-06-020423-0); PLB 14.89 (0-06-020424-9) HarpC Child Bks.

Barton, Charles D. Changes in Youth Morality: What Caused Them, No. 1. rev. ed. Barton, David, illus. 40p. 1988. pap. 3.00 (0-317-93057-5) Wallbuilders.
—The Myth of Separation. 296p. (Orig.). (gr. 7 up). 1989. pap. 7.95 (0-925279-04-8) Wallbuilders.
—What Happened to SAT Scores, No. 1. rev. ed. Barton, David, illus. 52p. 1988. pap. 3.00 (0-317-93056-7) Wallbuilders.

Barton, Chris & Shulman, Dee. Cream Cake. (Illus.). 32p. (ps-2). 1993. 16.95 (0-370-31766-1, Pub. by Bodley Head UK) Trafalgar.

Barton, Clara. Story of the Red Cross. Gemme, Francis R., illus. (gr. 4 up). 1968. pap. 1.50 (0-8049-0170-8, CL-170) Airmont.

Barton, Julia, jt. auth. see Campbell, Alison.

Barton, Miles. Vanishing Species. LC 91-8379. (Illus.). 40p. (gr. 5-8). 1991. PLB 12.90 (0-531-17306-2, Gloucester Pr) Watts.

Bartone, Elisa. The Angel Who Forgot. Cline, Paul, illus. LC 91-34233. 48p. (Orig.). (ps up). 1992. 10.00 (0-671-76037-8, Green Tiger) S&S Trade.
—Peppe the Lamplighter. LC 92-1397. (ps-3). 1993. 14.00 (0-688-10268-9); PLB 13.93 (0-688-10269-7) Lothrop.

Bartos-Hoppner, Barbara. The Pied Piper of Hamelin. Fuchshuber, Annegert, illus. LC 87-45150. 32p. (gr. k-3). 1987. (Lipp Jr Bks) HarpC Child Bks.

Bartusch, Nancy. Sign Numbers. (Illus.). 54p. (Orig.). (ps-3). 1988. pap. 5.00 (0-916708-17-9) Modern Signs.

Barty-King, Hugh. Worst Poverty: A History of Debt & Debtors. (Illus.). 224p. (gr. 9-12). 1991. 30.00 (0-86299-868-9) A Sutton Pub.

Bartz, Carl. The Department of State. Schlesinger, Arthur M., Jr., intro. by. (Illus.). 120p. (gr. 5 up). 1989. lib. bdg. 14.95 (0-87754-846-3) Chelsea Hse.

Bartz, Paul A. Letting God Create Your Day, Vol. 1, No. 1: Scripts from the International Broadcast Creation Moments. 84p. (Orig.). 1989. pap. write for info. Colorsong Prodns.

Baruch, Andrea, ed. see Cardinal, Michael S.

Baruch, Jacques-Olivier. Incredibly Fast. LC 93-462. (Illus.). 48p. (gr. 6 up). 1993. lib. bdg. 14.95 RSBE (0-02-708435-3, New Discovery Bks) Macmillan Child Grp.

Barufaldi, J., et al. Heath Science. large type ed. Incl. Gr. II. 264p; Gr. III, 2 vols. 342p; Gr. V, 3 vols. 604p. Set. 121.00 (0-317-02448-5, J-10180). (gr. 2-6). 1985. Am Printing Hse.

Barwick, Mary. The Alabama Angels. 3rd ed. Barwick, Mary, illus. 28p. (gr. 1-6). 1989. pap. 8.95 (0-9622815-1-4) Black Belt Pr.
—The Alabama Angels in Anywhere, L. A. (Lower Alabama) Barwick, Mary, illus. 32p. (Orig.). 1991. pap. 8.95 (0-9622815-6-5) Black Belt Pr.

Barysh, Ann, et al. The Suitcase Scholar Goes to Kenya. Lerner Geography Department Staff, ed. (gr. 4-6). Set incls. teaching guide, Kenya in Pictures, A Family in Kenya, Count Your Way Through Africa, Safari, Cooking the African Way & wall map. saddle-stitch bdg. 49.95 (0-685-55161-X); teaching guide 15.95 (0-685-55162-8) Lerner Pubns.
—The Suitcase Scholar Goes to Mexico. Lerner Geography Department Staff, ed. (Illus.). (gr. 4-6). 1992. Set incls. teaching guide, Mexico in Pictures, A Family in Mexico, Count Your Way Through Mexico, Cooking the Mexican Way, Focus on Mexico: Modern Life in an Ancient Land & wall map. saddle-stitch bdg. 49.95 (0-8225-4003-7); teaching guide 15.95 (0-685-55160-1) Lerner Pubns.

Barz, Brigitte. Festivals with Children. 1988. pap. 10.50 (0-86315-055-1, 20241) Gryphon Hse.

Barzun, Jacques & Taylor, Wendell H. A Catalogue of Crime: A Reader's Guide to the Literature of Mystery, Detection, & Related Genres. LC 88-45884. 864p. (gr. 7 up). 1989. 50.00 (0-06-010263-2, HarpT) HarpC.

Base, Graeme. Animalia. Base, Graeme, illus. 32p. (ps up). 1987. 17.95 (0-8109-1868-4) Abrams.
—Animalia. (Illus.). 32p. 1993. 11.95 (0-8109-1939-7) Abrams.
—The Eleventh Hour: A Curious Mystery. (Illus.). 32p. 1989. 17.95 (0-8109-0851-4) Abrams.
—The Eleventh Hour: A Curious Mystery. (Illus.). 32p. 1993. 11.95 (0-8109-3265-2) Abrams.

Base, Graeme, illus. Jabberwocky: From Lewis Carroll's Through the Looking Glass. 32p. 1989. 16.95 (0-8109-1150-7) Abrams.

Basford, Teri M. Ten Steps to Becoming a Model. (Illus.). 50p. (Orig.). (gr. 9). 1989. pap. write for info.; pap. text ed. write for info. T Mack Glamour.

Bash, Barbara. Desert Giant, Vol. 1. (gr. 4-7). 1990. pap. 5.95 (0-316-08307-0) Little.
—Desert Giant: The World of the Saguaro Cactus. Bash, Barbara, illus. 32p. (gr. 1-5). 1989. 15.95 (0-316-08301-1) Little.
—Shadows of Night: The Hidden World of the Little Brown Bat. LC 92-22713. (Illus.). 32p. (gr. 1-5). 1993. 16.95 (0-87156-562-5) Sierra.
—Tree of Life: The World of the African Baobab. (gr. 1-5). 1989. 14.95 (0-316-08305-4, Sierra Club) Little.
—Urban Roosts: Where Birds Nest in the City. Bash, Barbara, illus. (gr. 1-5). 1990. 15.95 (0-316-08306-2) Little.
—Urban Roosts: Where Birds Nest in the City. Bash, Barbara, illus. 32p. (gr. 4-7). 1992. pap. 5.95 (0-316-08312-7) Little.

Bashe, Philip, jt. auth. see Snider, Dee.

Basinger, Missy, jt. auth. see Basinger, Sherry.

Basinger, Sherry & Basinger, Missy. Wizzer Rabbit Wants You to Be Drug Free. (Illus.). 17p. (Orig.). 1988. pap. write for info. (0-9620945-0-1) S & M Basinger.

Baskerville, Judith. Bread. Stefoff, Rebecca, ed. Barber, Ed, photos by. LC 91-18189. (Illus.). 32p. (gr. 3-5). 1991. PLB 15.93 (1-56074-001-9) Garrett Ed Corp.

Baskin, Leonard. Leonard Baskin's Miniature Natural History. Baskin, Leonard, illus. 28p. (gr. k up). 1993. Repr. 14.95 (0-88708-265-3) Picture Bk Studio.

Baskin-Salzberg, Anita & Salzberg, Allen. Flightless Birds. LC 93-9553. (Illus.). 64p. (gr. 4-6). 1993. PLB 12.90 (0-531-20117-1) Watts.
—Predators! LC 90-47672. (Illus.). 64p. (gr. 3-5). 1991. PLB 12.90 (0-531-20009-4) Watts.

Basow, Lynn. The Room Parent's Party Planner: How to Host Great Parties in Your Child's Classroom. Marsh, Chuck, ed. Wallace, Dan, illus. 56p. (Orig.). 1993. pap. 9.95 (0-9638975-0-0) Inverness Pr.
Busy parents of grade-schoolers will love this warm, wonderful guidebook that shows them how to be heroes to their kids - & their kid's teachers & classmates - by helping with classroom parties. Full of practical advice, specific examples & encouragement, THE ROOM PARENT'S PARTY PLANNER is perfect for busy parents who want hands-on participation in their children's education. Lynn Basow, a working mother of two, shares a decade of classroom party planning with tips on organizing a parents' team to spread the word & the work; involving kids in party planning; pacing & controlling the party to keep everyone involved; planning snacks, crafts & games; keeping plans flexible & ready for the unexpected, & building on successes as kids progress through school. With help from THE ROOM PARENT'S PARTY PLANNER, parents don't have to spend a lot of time or money to have a lot of fun - & show their commitment to their children's education. Single copy price: $9.95 plus $3.00 shipping & handling. Quantity discounts available. Order directly from Inverness Press, P.O. Box 1174, Lawrence, KS 66044 or FAX 913-843-2640.
Publisher Provided Annotation.

Basquez, Juan J., jt. ed. see Puncel, Maria.

Bass, Althea. Grandfather Grey Owl Told Me. (gr. 4 up). 1973. 1.75 (0-89992-051-9) Coun India Ed.
—Nightwalker & the Buffalo. (gr. 4-9). 1972. 4.95 (0-89992-032-2) Coun India Ed.

Bass, Sophie F. Pig-Tail Days in Old Seattle. Clark, Florenz, illus. LC 72-77591. 190p. (gr. 4-6). 1973. 12. 50 (*0-8323-0206-6*) Binford Mort.

Bassano, Sharron, jt. auth. see Christison, MaryAnn.

Bassett, Harmon. Behavior, Teaching & Understanding of Motivational Learning in Enhancing Child Performance with Models & Morals in Poetry. rev. ed. LC 86-47708. (Illus.). 289p. (gr. 2-6). 1991. 29.50 (*1-55914-500-5*); pap. 22.50 (*1-55914-501-3*) ABBE Pubs Assn.

—Children's Daily Verses for Growing up the Easy Way with Fun & Play. LC 88-47545. (Illus.). 150p. (gr. 2-7). 1988. 19.95 (*0-88164-712-8*); pap. 15.95 (*0-88164-713-6*) ABBE Pubs Assn.

—F. U. N-D. A. T. E. S. with a Likeable You for Adolescents & Juveniles. rev. ed. LC 88-47848. 175p. (gr. 7-12). 1991. 19.50 (*1-55914-490-4*); pap. 14.50 (*1-55914-491-2*) ABBE Pubs Assn.

Bassett, James C., jt. auth. see Arnold, Kevin D.

Bassett, Jeni. Little Treasury of the Little People's Mother Goose, 6 vols. (Illus.). 1990. Boxed set. 5.99 (*0-517-01478-5*) Outlet Bk Co.

Bassett, Jeni, photos by & text by. The Chicks' Trick. LC 93-18471. 1994. write for info. (*0-525-65152-7*, Cobblehill Bks) Dutton Child Bks.

Bassett, Kerry. My Very Own Special Body Book. 4th ed. McDaniel, Diane, illus. Wooley, Marilyn J., intro. by. (Illus.). 18p. (ps-2). 1987. pap. 3.25 (*0-9620154-0-7*) Hawthorne Pr.

Bassett, Lisa. The Bunny's Alphabet Eggs. Bassett, Jeni, illus. LC 92-37987. (gr. 2 up). 1993. 3.99 (*0-517-08153-9*) Outlet Bk Co.

—Koala Christmas. Bassett, Jeni, illus. LC 90-47628. 32p. (ps-2). 1991. 12.95 (*0-525-65065-2*, Cobblehill Bks) Dutton Child Bks.

—Ten Little Bunnies. Bassett, Jeni, illus. LC 92-37986. (gr. 2 up). 1993. 3.99 (*0-517-08154-7*) Outlet Bk Co.

—Very Truly Yours, Charles L. Dodgson, Alias Lewis Carroll. LC 85-10972. (Illus.). 118p. (gr. 5 up). 1987. 15.95 (*0-688-06091-9*) Lothrop.

Bassett, Patrick F. & Moore, Malcolm. The English Companion. (Illus.). 144p. (gr. 9-12). 1989. pap. text ed. 10.00 (*1-877653-04-7*) Wayside Pub.

Bassett, Scott & Bassett, Tammy. Artemus & the Alphabet. Bassett, Scott, illus. 32p. (ps-k). 1980. 6.95x (*0-9605548-0-7*); PLB 6.95x (*0-9605548-1-5*) Bassett & Brush.

Bassett, Tammy, jt. auth. see Bassett, Scott.

Basta, Margo M., jt. auth. see Siegel, Alice.

Bastardo, Peter J., jt. auth. see Iozzi, Louis A.

Bastin, Marjoleine. A Little Dog for Vera. LC 90-49938. (Illus.). 48p. 1991. 10.95 (*1-55670-208-6*) Stewart Tabori & Chang.

—My Name Is Vera. (Illus.). 28p. (ps-2). 1985. 2.95 (*0-8120-5690-6*) Barron.

—Vera & Her Friends. (Illus.). 28p. (ps-2). 1985. 2.95 (*0-8120-5689-2*) Barron.

—Vera the Mouse. (ps-k). 1986. Four-bk. boxed set. 11. 95 (*0-8120-7391-6*); 2.95 ea Barron.

—Vera's Dresses Up. 28p. (ps-2). 1985. 2.95 (*0-8120-5691-4*) Barron.

—Vera's Special Hobbies. (Illus.). 28p. (ps-2). 1985. 2.95 (*0-8120-5692-2*) Barron.

Bastyra, Judy. Busy Little Cook. 1990. 5.99 (*0-517-03602-9*) Outlet Bk Co.

Basu, Romen. The Street Corner Boys. Hauge, Veronica, tr. 154p. (gr. 9-10). 1992. 14.95 (*0-932377-40-8*) Facet Bks.

Bat-Ami, Miriam. Sea, Salt, & Air. Young, Mary O., illus. LC 91-34140. 32p. (gr. 1-5). 1993. RSBE 14.95 (*0-02-708495-7*, Macmillan Child Bk) Macmillan Child Grp.

—When the Frost Is Gone. Ramsey, Marcy D., illus. LC 92-26181. 64p. (gr. 4 up). 1994. SBE 14.95 (*0-02-708497-3*, Macmillan Child Bk) Macmillan Child Grp.

Batchelor, C. Fun, Magic & Jokes. (Illus.). 32p. (gr. 2-6). 1985. pap. 5.95 (*0-88625-072-2*) Durkin Hayes Pub.

Batchelor, Mary. Children's Bible in Three Hundred Sixty-Five Stories. Haysom, John, illus. 416p. (ps up). 1987. 15.95 (*0-7459-1333-4*) Lion USA.

—The Children's Bible in Three Hundred Sixty-Five Stories: Red Gift Edition. (Illus.). 416p. (gr. k up). 1988. 26.95 (*0-7459-1019-X*) Lion USA.

—Children's Bible in Three Hundred Sixty-Five Stories: White Gift Edition. (Illus.). 416p. (gr. k up). 1988. 26. 95 (*0-7459-1375-X*) Lion USA.

—The Lion Book of Bible Stories & Prayers. (Illus.). 96p. (gr. 1-5). 1989. 11.95 (*0-85648-239-0*) Lion USA.

—Lion Book of Children's Prayers. (Illus.). 96p. 1984. 11. 95 (*0-85648-070-3*) Lion USA.

—Lion Christmas Book. (Illus.). 96p. (Orig.). 1988. pap. 7.99 (*0-7459-1511-6*) Lion USA.

—The Story of Jesus. Haysom, John, illus. 192p. (gr. 1-6). 1992. 14.95 (*0-7459-1884-0*) Lion USA.

Batchelor, Phil. Love Is a Verb. 1991. pap. 3.99 (*0-312-92427-5*) St Martin.

Batdorf, Carol. Gifts of the Season: Life among the Northwest Indians. Graves, Katheryn, illus. 24p. (Orig.). (gr. 1-6). 1990. pap. 5.95 (*0-88839-246-X*) Hancock House.

—Seawolf: Building a Canoe. Clark, Patricia, illus. 24p. (Orig.). (gr. 1-6). 1990. pap. 4.95 (*0-88839-247-8*) Hancock House.

—Tinka: A Day in a Little Girl's Life. Batdorf, Carol, illus. 32p. (Orig.). (gr. 1-6). 1990. pap. 5.95 (*0-88839-249-4*) Hancock House.

—Totem Poles: An Ancient Art. Cheney, Tracy, illus. 24p. (Orig.). (gr. 1-6). 1990. pap. 4.95 (*0-88839-248-6*) Hancock House.

Bate, Lucy. How Georgina Drove the Car Very Carefully from Boston to New York. Taylor, Tamar, illus. LC 88-22861. 32p. (ps-k). 1992. pap. 4.99 (*0-517-59324-6*) Crown Bks Yng Read.

—Little Rabbit's Loose Tooth. De Groat, Diane, illus. LC 75-6833. 32p. (gr. k-3). 1988. PLB 15.00 (*0-517-52240-3*); pap. 4.99 (*0-517-55122-5*) Crown Bks Yng Read.

Bateman, Penny, et al. The Arabs. (Illus.). (gr. 2-6). pap. 3.95 (*0-7141-1583-5*, Pub. by Brit Mus UK) Parkwest Pubns.

Bates, A. Dead Game. 1993. pap. 3.25 (*0-590-45829-9*) Scholastic Inc.

—Final Exam. 1990. pap. 3.25 (*0-590-43291-5*, Point) Scholastic Inc.

—Mother's Helper. 144p. 1991. 3.25 (*0-590-44582-0*, Point) Scholastic Inc.

—Party Line. (gr. 6 up). 1989. pap. 3.25 (*0-590-44238-4*) Scholastic Inc.

—What's the Opposite of a Best Friend? (gr. 4-7). 1993. pap. 2.95 (*0-590-44415-8*) Scholastic Inc.

Bates, Betty. Call Me Friday the Thirteenth. Edwards, Linda S., illus. 112p. (gr. 3-7). 1985. pap. 2.50 (*0-440-40984-5*, LFL) Dell.

—Everybody Say Cheese. (gr. 3-6). 1986. pap. 2.50 (*0-440-42446-1*, YB) Dell.

—The Great Male Conspiracy. (gr. k-6). 1990. pap. 2.95 (*0-440-40247-6*, YB) Dell.

—Thatcher Payne-in-the-Neck. (gr. k-6). 1987. pap. 3.25 (*0-440-48598-3*, YB) Dell.

—Tough Beans. Morrill, Leslie, illus. 96p. (gr. 3-7). 1992. pap. 3.50 (*0-440-40689-7*, YB) Dell.

Bates, Gale. Tales of Tutu Nene & Nele. McCarthy, Carole H., illus. 36p. (ps-4). 1991. 7.95 (*0-89610-193-2*) Island Heritage.

Bates, Katherine L. America the Beautiful. Waldman, Neil, illus. LC 92-46199. 32p. 1993. SBE 14.95 (*0-689-31861-8*, Atheneum Child Bk) Macmillan Child Grp.

Bates, Robert L. The Challenge of Mineral Resources. (Illus.). 32p. (gr. 5-9). 1991. PLB 12.40 (*0-531-17292-9*, Gloucester Pr) Watts.

—Industrial Minerals: How They Are Found & Used. LC 87-36537. (Illus.). 64p. (gr. 6 up). 1988. lib. bdg. 15.95 (*0-89490-174-5*) Enslow Pubs.

—Mineral Resources A-Z. LC 90-34301. 128p. (gr. 6 up). 1991. lib. bdg. 17.95 (*0-89490-244-X*) Enslow Pubs.

Bateson, Margaret, jt. auth. see Lellie, Herman.

Bateson, Margaret, jt. auth. see Leslie, Herman.

Batherman, Muriel. Before Columbus. Batherman, Muriel, illus. 32p. (gr. k-3). 1990. pap. 4.80 (*0-395-54954-X*) HM.

Bathersfield, Arnold, et al. Gurus & Griots. Gibbs, C. Jeanean, ed. Mark, Joan G., et al, illus. LC 87-90523. 108p. (gr. 7 up). 1987. pap. 6.00 (*0-9618755-0-X*) Palm Tree Ent.

Batin, Adela. Best Recipes of Alaska's Fishing Lodges. Batin, Christopher, ed. 320p. (Orig.). Date not set. pap. 24.95 (*0-685-65892-9*) Alaska Angler.

Batin, Christopher, ed. see Batin, Adela.

Batmanglij, M. & Batmanglij, N. The Wonderful Story of Zaal. Franta, illus. LC 86-12665. 48p. (gr. 4 up). 1986. 18.50 (*0-934211-01-9*) Mage Pubs Inc.

Batmanglij, M., ed. see Yushij, Nima.

Batmanglij, M., tr. see Hedayat, Sadegh & Batmanglij, N.

Batmanglij, N, jt. auth. see Batmanglij, M.

Batmanglij, N., jt. auth. see Hedayat, Sadegh.

Batmanglij, N., tr. see Hedayat, Sadegh & Batmanglij, N.

Batmanglij, N. Khalili, tr. see Wilde, Oscar.

Battaglia, Aurelius, ed. Mother Goose. (ps-1). 1973. 2.25 (*0-394-82661-2*) Random Bks Yng Read.

Battaglia, Aurelius, illus. Animal Sounds. 22p. (ps). 1981. write for info. (*0-307-12122-4*, Golden Bks) Western Pub.

—Seasons. LC 76-43128. (ps-1). 1978. 3.95 (*0-448-46514-0*, G&D) Putnam Pub Group.

—Three Little Pigs. LC 76-24170. 32p. (ps-2). 1982. lib. bdg. 5.99 (*0-394-93459-8*) Random Bks Yng Read.

Battanyi-Petose, Laura. Downtown Boy. 1993. pap. 3.50 (*0-06-106154-9*, Harp PBks) HarpC.

Batten, Mary. Nature's Tricksters: Animals & Plants That Aren't What They Seem. Lovejoy, Lois, illus. (gr. 3-6). 1992. 14.95 (*0-316-08371-2*) Little.

Battestin, Martin C., ed. see Fielding, Henry.

Battistella, B. The Gospel for Young Children. (Illus.). (ps-4). 1988. 39.00x (*0-85439-193-2*, Pub. by St Paul Pubns UK) St Mut.

—The Legend of Little White Hood. (gr. 1 up). 1988. pap. 1.75 (*0-8198-4405-5*) St Paul Bks.

Battles, Edith. The Witch in Room Six. LC 86-45785. 144p. (gr. 3-7). 1987. HarpC Child Bks.

—The Witch in Room Six. LC 86-45785. 160p. (gr. 3-7). 1989. pap. 3.50 (*0-06-440204-5*, Trophy) HarpC Child Bks.

Bauer, jt. auth. see Hirschi.

Bauer, Caroline F. Halloween: Stories & Poems. Sis, Peter, illus. LC 88-2675. 96p. (gr. 2-5). 1992. pap. 4.95 (*0-06-446111-4*, Trophy) HarpC Child Bks.

—Midnight Snowman. Stock, Catherine, illus. LC 86-26540. 32p. (ps-2). 1987. SBE 13.95 (*0-689-31294-6*, Atheneum Child Bk) Macmillan Child Grp.

—My Mom Travels a Lot. 48p. (ps-3). 1985. pap. 3.95 (*0-14-050545-8*, Puffin) Puffin Bks.

Bauer, Caroline F., ed. Halloween: Stories & Poems. LC 88-2675. (Illus.). 96p. (gr. 2-5). 1989. 13.00 (*0-397-32300-X*, Lipp Jr Bks); PLB 12.89 (*0-397-32301-8*, Lipp Jr Bks) HarpC Child Bks.

—Rainy Day: Stories & Poems. Chessare, Michele, illus. LC 85-45170. 96p. (gr. 2-5). 1986. (Lipp Jr Bks); PLB 13.89 (*0-397-32105-8*, Lipp Jr Bks) HarpC Child Bks.

—Snowy Day: Stories & Poems. Tomes, Margot, illus. LC 85-45858. 80p. (gr. 2-5). 1986. (Lipp Jr Bks); PLB 13. 89 (*0-397-32177-5*) HarpC Child Bks.

—Snowy Day: Stories & Poems. Tomes, Margot, illus. LC 85-45858. 80p. (gr. 2-5). 1992. pap. 3.95 (*0-06-446123-8*, Trophy) HarpC Child Bks.

—Thanksgiving: Stories & Poems. Westcott, Nadine b., illus. LC 93-18631. (gr. 4 up). 1994. 14.00 (*0-06-023326-5*); PLB 13.89 (*0-06-023327-3*) HarpC Child Bks.

—Valentine's Day: Stories & Poems. Sims, Blanche L., illus. LC 91-37641. 96p. (gr. 2-5). 1993. 14.00 (*0-06-020823-6*); PLB 13.89 (*0-06-020824-4*) HarpC Child Bks.

—Windy Day: Stories & Poems. Zimmer, Dirk, illus. LC 86-42994. 96p. (gr. 2-5). 1988. (Lipp Jr Bks); PLB 13. 89 (*0-397-32208-9*) HarpC Child Bks.

Bauer, Caroline Feller. My Mom Travels a Lot. Parker, Nancy W., illus. (gr. k-3). 1982. incl. cassette 19.95 (*0-941078-23-X*); pap. 12.95 incl. cassette (*0-941078-21-3*); pap. 27.95 4 bks., cassette & guide (*0-941078-22-1*); sound filmstrip 22.95 (*0-941078-24-8*) Live Oak Media.

Bauer, Fred & Reufenacht, Peter. Chilp. LC 72-89351. (Illus.). 24p. (gr. k-4). 1973. 7.95 (*0-87592-011-X*) Scroll Pr.

Bauer, Gerhard. Soccer Techniques, Tactics & Teamwork. Beckenbauer, Franz, intro. by. (Illus.). 160p. (gr. 10-12). 1993. pap. 14.95 (*0-8069-8730-8*) Sterling.

Bauer, Helen. Hawaii: The Aloha State. rev. ed. Rayson, Ann, rev. by. McCurdy, Bruce S., illus. LC 82-72319. 192p. (gr. 4-7). 1982. 25.95 (*0-935848-13-4*); pap. 16. 95 (*0-935848-15-0*); wkbk. 5.95 (*0-935848-34-7*); tchr's. manual 5.00 (*1-880188-46-5*) Bess Pr.

Bauer, Joan. Squashed. LC 91-44905. 192p. (gr. 7 up). 1992. 15.00 (*0-385-30793-4*) Delacorte.

Bauer, Judith. What's It Like to Be a Doctor. Burns, Raymond, illus. LC 89-34398. 32p. (gr. k-3). 1990. lib. bdg. 10.89 (*0-8167-1801-6*); pap. text ed. 2.95 (*0-8167-1802-4*) Troll Assocs.

—What's It Like to Be a Nurse. Pellaton, Karen E., illus. LC 89-34387. 32p. (gr. k-3). 1990. lib. bdg. 10.89 (*0-8167-1809-1*); pap. text ed. 2.95 (*0-8167-1810-5*) Troll Assocs.

—What's It Like to Be an Airline Pilot. Iosa, Ann W., illus. LC 89-34397. 32p. (gr. k-3). 1990. PLB 10.89 (*0-8167-1791-5*); pap. text ed. 2.95 (*0-8167-1792-3*) Troll Assocs.

Bauer, Lois M. & Reed, Barbara A. Dance & Play Activities for the Elementary Grades, 2 Vols. (Illus.). (gr. 1-6). 1967. Vol. 1. 4.50 (*0-910354-02-2*); Vol. 2. 4.98 (*0-910354-07-3*) Chartwell.

Bauer, Marion D. Am I Blue: Coming Out from the Silence. LC 93-29574. 1994. 15.00 (*0-06-024253-1*, Festival); PLB 14.89 (*0-06-024254-X*, Festival) HarpC Child Bks.

—A Dream of Queens & Castles. (gr. 3-7). 1990. 13.95 (*0-395-51330-8*) HM.

—Dream of Queens & Castles. (gr. 4-7). 1992. pap. 3.25 (*0-440-40554-8*) Dell.

—Face to Face. 192p. (gr. 5-9). 1991. 13.45 (*0-395-55440-3*, Clarion Bks) HM.

—Face to Face. 1993. pap. 3.50 (*0-440-40791-5*) Dell.

—Ghost Eye. 1992. 12.95 (*0-590-45298-3*, Scholastic Hardcover) Scholastic Inc.

—On My Honor. LC 86-2679. 96p. (gr. 4-7). 1987. 12.95 (*0-89919-439-7*, Clarion Bks) HM.

—On My Honor. (gr. k-6). 1987. pap. 3.50 (*0-440-46633-4*, YB) Dell.

—A Question of Trust. 128p. (gr. 4-7). 1994. 13.95 (*0-590-47915-6*, Scholastic Hardcover) Scholastic Inc.

—Rain of Fire. LC 83-2065. 160p. (gr. 4-8). 1983. 14.45 (*0-89919-190-8*, Clarion Bks) HM.

—Shelter from the Wind. LC 75-28184. 112p. (gr. 6 up). 1979. 13.95 (*0-395-28890-8*, Clarion Bks) HM.

—A Taste of Smoke. LC 92-32585. (gr. 5 up). 1993. 13. 95 (*0-395-64341-4*, Clarion Bks) HM.

—Touch the Moon. (gr. k-6). 1990. pap. 2.95 (*0-440-40256-5*, YB) Dell.

—What's Your Story? A Young Person's Guide to Writing Fiction. 144p. (gr. 5 up). 1992. 13.45 (*0-395-57781-0*, Clarion Bks); pap. 6.70 (*0-395-57780-2*, Clarion Bks) HM.

Bauer, Marion Dane. Touch the Moon. Berenzy, Alix, illus. LC 87-663. 96p. (gr. 4-7). 1987. 12.95 (*0-89919-526-1*, Clarion Bks) HM.

Bauer, Martha J. Hey, This Is Fun! Dresselhaus, Richard, frwd. by. LC 90-80992. (Illus.). 128p. (gr. 6-12). 1990. pap. 6.95 (*0-9624398-1-9*) Abel II Pub.

Bauer, P., jt. auth. see Hirschi, E.

Bauldock, Gerald. Reaching for the Moon. LC 88-92848. 303p. (Orig.). (gr. 7-12). 1989. pap. text ed. 14.95 (*0-9621728-0-4*) B-Dock Pr.

Bauleke, Ann. Kirby Puckett: Fan Favorite. LC 92-15271. 1993. 13.50 (*0-8225-0490-1*) Lerner Pubns.

—Kirby Puckett: Fan Favorite. (gr. 4-7). 1993. pap. 4.95 (*0-8225-9633-4*) Lerner Pubns.
—Rickey Henderson: Record Stealer. (Illus.). 48p. (gr. 4-9). 1991. PLB 13.50 (*0-8225-0541-X*) Lerner Pubns.
—Rickey Henderson: Record Stealer. (Illus.). 64p. (gr. 4-9). 1992. pap. 4.95 (*0-8225-9597-4*) Lerner Pubns.
Baum, Arline & Baum, Joseph. Opt: An Illusionary Tale. LC 86-28130. (ps-3). 1987. pap. 11.95 (*0-670-80870-9*) Viking Child Bks.
—Opt: An Illusionary Tale. (Illus.). 32p. (ps-3). 1989. pap. 3.99 (*0-14-050573-3*, Puffin) Puffin Bks.
Baum, Joseph, jt. auth. see Baum, Arline.
Baum, L. Frank. Adventures in Oz: Ozma of Oz & Marvelous Land of Oz, The Original Editions Complete & Unabridged. 575p. (gr. 2 up). 1985. pap. 11.90 (*0-486-24880-1*) Dover.
—Adventures in Oz: Wonderful Wizard of Oz Pop-Ups. 1991. 2.99 (*0-517-05267-9*) Outlet Bk Co.
—Animal Fairy Tales. Bull, Charles L., illus. 48p. (ps-3). 1989. pap. 7.95 (*0-929605-04-7*) Books Wonder.
—Cyclone. 6p. 1991. 2.99 (*0-517-05269-5*) Outlet Bk Co.
—Dorothy & the Wizard in Oz. Neill, John R., illus. 256p. (gr. 5-10). 1984. pap. 5.95 (*0-486-24714-7*) Dover.
—Dorothy & the Wizard in Oz. (gr. 4 up). 18.25 (*0-8446-6141-4*) Peter Smith.
—Dorothy & the Wizard in Oz. facsimile ed. Neill, John R., illus. Glassman, Peter, afterword by. LC 90-592. (Illus.). 272p. (ps up) 1990. Repr. 19.95g (*0-688-09826-6*) Morrow Jr Bks.
—Emerald City. (Illus.). 6p. 1991. 2.99 (*0-517-05266-0*) Outlet Bk Co.
—The Emerald City of Oz. LC 52-2380. 1985. pap. 4.99 (*0-345-33464-7*, Del Rey) Ballantine.
—The Emerald City of Oz. (gr. 4 up). 18.75 (*0-8446-6399-9*) Peter Smith.
—The Emerald City of Oz. Neill, John R., illus. Glassman, Peter, afterword by. LC 92-61765. (Illus.). 304p. 1993. 20.00 (*0-688-11558-6*) Morrow Jr Bks.
—Glinda of Oz. 224p. 1985. pap. 3.95 (*0-345-33394-2*, Del Rey) Ballantine.
—Land of Oz. (Illus.). (gr. 4 up). 1968. pap. 1.25 (*0-8049-0181-3*, CL-181) Airmont.
—The Land of Oz. LC 79-52645. 1985. pap. 4.99 (*0-345-33568-6*) Ballantine.
—The Life & Adventures of Santa Claus. Clark, Mary, illus. Gardner, Martin, intro. by. (Illus.). (gr. 3-8). 18.25 (*0-8446-5450-7*) Peter Smith.
—The Life & Adventures of Santa Claus. (gr. 2-6). 1985. 4.98 (*0-517-42062-7*) Outlet Bk Co.
—Life & Adventures of Santa Claus. 160p. 1986. pap. 2.95 (*0-451-52064-5*, Sig Classics) NAL-Dutton.
—The Life & Adventures of Santa Claus. 15.95 (*0-8488-0428-7*) Amereon Ltd.
—The Life & Adventures of Santa Claus. Ploog, Mike, illus. 96p. 1992. text ed. 24.95 (*1-879450-76-3*) Tundra MA.
—The Life & Adventures of Santa Claus. (Illus.). 1993. Repr. PLB 18.95x (*1-56849-175-1*) Buccaneer Bks.
—Little Wizard Stories of Oz. (Illus.). 96p. 1988. pap. 2.95 (*0-553-15617-9*, Skylark) Bantam.
—The Magical Monarch of Mo. (Illus.). (gr. 4-8). 19.50 (*0-8446-1609-5*) Peter Smith.
—Marvelous Land of Oz. Neill, John R., illus. Gardner, M., intro. by. (Illus.). xvii, 287p. (gr. 4-6). 1969. pap. 5.95 (*0-486-20692-0*) Dover.
—Marvelous Land of Oz. McKee, David, illus. 192p. (gr. 4-6). 1985. pap. 2.25 (*0-14-035041-1*, Puffin) Puffin Bks.
—The Marvelous Land of Oz. Neill, John R., illus. LC 85-4856. 288p. (gr. 4-6). 1985. 15.00 (*0-688-05439-0*) Morrow Jr Bks.
—Mother Goose in Prose. (gr. k up). 1986. 4.98 (*0-685-16878-6*, 519046) Outlet Bk Co.
—Ozma of Oz. LC 77-89301. (Orig.). 1986. pap. 3.95 (*0-345-33589-9*, Del Rey) Ballantine.
—Ozma of Oz. 272p. (gr. 2 up). 1985. pap. 5.95 (*0-486-24779-1*) Dover.
—Ozma of Oz. (gr. 5 up). 18.25 (*0-8446-6180-5*) Peter Smith.
—Ozma of Oz. Neill, John R., illus. LC 88-63291. 288p. 1989. 19.95 (*0-688-06632-1*) Morrow Jr Bks.
—Ozma of Oz. 160p. (gr. 5 up). 1992. pap. 2.95 (*0-14-035119-1*) Puffin Bks.
—The Patchwork Girl of Oz. LC 79-88483. 1985. pap. 4.99 (*0-345-33290-3*) Ballantine.
—Patchwork Girl of Oz. 1990. pap. 6.95 (*0-486-26514-5*) Dover.
—Policeman Bluejay. LC 81-9044. (gr. 1-6). 1981. Repr. of 1907 ed. 50.00x (*0-8201-1367-0*) Schol Facsimiles.
—Queen Zixi of Ix: Or, the Story of the Magic Cloak. Richardson, Frederick, illus. Gardner, M., intro. by. (Illus.). 231p. (gr. 1-3). 1971. pap. 4.95 (*0-486-22691-3*) Dover.
—Queen Zixi of Ix: The Story of the Magic Cloak. (Illus.). (gr. 2-6). 17.75 (*0-8446-0026-1*) Peter Smith.
—The Road to Oz. LC 79-88480. 1986. pap. 4.95 (*0-345-33467-1*, Del Rey) Ballantine.
—The Road to Oz. Neill, John R., illus. Glassman, Peter, afterword by. LC 90-48349. (Illus.). 272p. 1991. Repr. of 1909 ed. 16.95 (*0-688-09997-1*) Morrow Jr Bks.
—The Road to Oz. 160p. (gr. 5 up). 1993. pap. 2.99 (*0-14-035121-3*, Puffin) Puffin Bks.
—The Sea Fairies. Neill, John R., illus. 240p. 1987. 19.95 (*0-929605-03-9*); pap. 11.95 (*0-929605-00-4*) Books Wonder.

—Sky Island. Neill, John R., illus. 288p. (gr. 3 up). 1988. 19.95 (*0-929605-02-0*); pap. 11.95 (*0-929605-01-2*) Books Wonder.
—Surprising Adventures of the Magical Monarch of Mo & His People. Ver Beck, Frank, illus. (ps-4). 1968. pap. 6.95 (*0-486-21892-9*) Dover.
—The Surprising Adventures of the Magical Monarch of Mo & His People. (gr. 5-6). 19.95 (*0-88411-771-5*, Pub. by Aeonian Pr) Amereon Ltd.
—Tik Tok of Oz. (Illus.). 192p. (gr. 5 up). 1991. pap. 2.25 (*0-14-035124-8*, Puffin) Puffin Bks.
—The Wizard of Oz. LC 79-52644. 1979. pap. 4.99 (*0-345-33590-2*, Del Rey) Ballantine.
—Wizard of Oz. Copelman, Evelyn, et al, illus. (gr. 4-6). 1956. il. jr. lib. o.p. 5.95 (*0-448-05826-X*, G&D); deluxe ed. 12.95 (*0-448-06026-4*) Putnam Pub Group.
—The Wizard of Oz. Hague, Michael, illus. LC 82-1109. 232p. (gr. 4-6). 1982. 19.95 (*0-8050-0221-9*, Bks Young Read) H Holt & Co.
—The Wizard of Oz. (gr. 3-7). 1983. pap. 2.99 (*0-14-035001-2*, Puffin) Puffin Bks.
—The Wizard of Oz. Smith, Jos A., illus. Hautzig, Deborah, adapted by. LC 83-13792. (Illus.). 64p. (ps-3). 1984. lib. bdg. 8.99 (*0-394-95331-2*) Random Bks Yng Read.
—The Wizard of Oz. Santore, Charles, illus. Hearn, Michael P., intro. by. (Illus.). 96p. 1991. 15.00 (*0-517-69506-5*, Pub. by Jellybean Pr); lib. bdg. 20.00 (*0-517-06655-6*, Pub. by Jellybean Pr) Outlet Bk Co.
—Wizard of Oz. Hildebrandt, Greg, illus. 160p. 1985. 14.95 (*0-88101-273-4*) Unicorn Pub.
—Wizard of Oz. 1993. pap. 2.95 (*0-590-44089-6*) Scholastic Inc.
—Wizard of Oz-Color Book. 1978. pap. 2.95 (*0-486-20452-9*) Dover.
—The Wizard of Oz: (El Mago de Oz) (SPA.). 9.95 (*84-204-3509-0*) Santillana.
—The Wizard of Oz Waddle Book. Denslow, W. W., illus. LC 93-10069. 1993. 24.95 (*1-55709-205-2*); ltd. collector's ed. 85.00 (*1-55709-203-6*) Applewood.
—The Woggle-Bug Book. LC 78-6887. (gr. 1-6). 1978. Repr. of 1905 ed. 50.00x (*0-8201-1308-5*) Schol Facsimiles.
—The Wonderful Wizard of Oz. Krenkel, Roy, illus. (gr. 4 up). 1965. pap. 1.75 (*0-8049-0069-8*, CL-69) Airmont.
—The Wonderful Wizard of Oz. 139p. 1981. Repr. PLB 15.95x (*0-89966-347-8*) Buccaneer Bks.
—Wonderful Wizard of Oz. Denslow, W. W., illus. Gardner, Martin, intro. by. (Illus.). vii, 268p. (gr. k-6). 1960. pap. 7.95 (*0-486-20691-2*) Dover.
—The Wonderful Wizard of Oz. 193p. 1981. Repr. PLB 11.95x (*0-89967-021-0*) Harmony Raine.
—Wonderful Wizard of Oz. Denslow, W. W., illus. (gr. 4 up). 19.25 (*0-8446-1610-9*) Peter Smith.
—The Wonderful Wizard of Oz. (gr. 5-6). 19.95 (*0-88411-772-3*, Pub. by Aeonian Pr) Amereon Ltd.
—The Wonderful Wizard of Oz. Denslow, W. W., illus. Glassman, Peter, afterword by. LC 86-62556. (Illus.). 316p. (ps up) 1987. 19.95 (*0-688-06944-4*) Morrow Jr Bks.
—The Wonderful Wizard of Oz. Moser, Barry, illus. 1986. 29.95 (*0-520-05822-4*) U CA Pr.
—The Wonderful Wizard of Oz. large type ed. Denslow, W. W., illus. 188p. (gr. 2-6). 1987. lib. bdg. 13.95 (*1-55736-013-8*, Crnrstn Bks) BDD LT Grp.
—The Wonderful Wizard of Oz. Leach, William R., ed. 188p. 1991. pap. 16.95 (*0-534-14736-4*) Wadsworth Pub.
—Wonderful Wizard of Oz. 176p. 1992. 9.49 (*0-8167-2564-0*); pap. 2.95 (*0-8167-2565-9*) Troll Assocs.
—The Wonderful Wizard of Oz. Mabie, Grace, ed. Newsom, Tom, illus. LC 92-12704. 48p. (gr. 3-6). 1992. PLB 12.89 (*0-8167-2864-X*); pap. text ed. 3.95 (*0-8167-2865-8*) Troll Assocs.
—The Wonderful Wizard of Oz. Denslow, W. W., illus. LC 92-53173. 192p. 1992. 12.95 (*0-679-41794-X*, Evrymans Lib Childs Class) Knopf.
—Wonderful Wizard of Oz Pop Ups. 1991. slipcased 12.99 (*0-517-06094-9*) Outlet Bk Co.
—Yellow Brick Road. (Illus.). 6p. 1991. 2.99 (*0-517-05268-7*) Outlet Bk Co.
Baum, Louis. After Dark. Varley, Susan, illus. LC 89-16123. 32p. (ps-3). 1990. 11.95 (*0-87951-382-9*) Overlook Pr.
—I Want to See the Moon. Daly, Niki, illus. LC 88-33061. 32p. (ps-3). 1989. cloth 11.95 (*0-87951-367-5*) Overlook Pr.
—One More Time. Bouma, Paddy, illus. LC 85-31050. 32p. (ps-k). 1986. lib. bdg. 11.88 (*0-688-06587-2*, Morrow Jr Bks) Morrow Jr Bks.
—One More Time. ALC Staff, ed. Bouma, Paddy, illus. LC 85-31050. 32p. (ps up). 1992. pap. 3.95 (*0-688-11698-1*, Mulberry) Morrow.
Baum, Roger. The Rewolf of Oz. LC 91-24058. (Illus.). 1991. 13.95 (*0-671-74982-X*, Green Tiger) S&S Trade.
Baum, Roger S. Dorothy of Oz. Miles, Elizabeth, illus. LC 89-6918. 176p. 1989. 14.95 (*0-688-07848-6*) Morrow Jr Bks.
—The SillyOZbul of OZ & the Magic Merry-Go-Round. 32p. 1992. 15.95 (*0-9630101-2-3*) Yellow Brick Rd.
—The SillyOZbul of OZ & Toto. Mertins, Lisa, illus. 1992. 15.95 (*0-9630101-1-5*) Yellow Brick Rd.
—The SillyOZbuls of OZ. Mertins, Lisa, illus. LC 91-66003. 1991. 15.95 (*0-9630101-0-7*) Yellow Brick Rd.
Baum, Susan. Beach. Baum, Susan, illus. 16p. (ps-1). 1991. pap. 4.95 (*0-06-107416-0*) HarpC Child Bks.

Bauman, A. F. Guess Where You're Going, Guess What You'll Do. Kelley, True, illus. 32p. (ps-k). 1989. 13.45 (*0-395-50211-X*) HM.
Bauman, Chris & Fishman, Sylvia E. Childhood Inventory of Language & Development Chart (CHILD) (ps-1). 1991. 7.50 (*0-937857-27-0*, 1592) Speech Bin.
Bauman, Elizabeth H. Coals of Fire. LC 53-12197. (Illus.). (gr. 5-9). 1954. 4.95 (*0-8361-1957-6*) Herald Pr.
Bauman, Kenneth. Invitation to Life: Student Work Sheets. Raney, Ken, illus. LC 86-81531. 27p. (gr. 9-12). 1986. P. 27. student wkbk. 7.95 (*0-87303-102-4*); P. 45. Leader's Guide 5.95 (*0-87303-121-0*) Faith & Life.
Bauman, Toni & Zinkgraf, June. Celebrations. Wunderlin, Linda W., illus. 240p. (gr. k-6). 1985. wkbk. 14.95 (*0-86653-330-3*, GA 666) Good Apple.
—Spring Surprises. 240p. (gr. k-6). 1979. 15.95 (*0-916456-54-4*, GA109) Good Apple.
—Winter Wonders. 240p. (gr. k-6). 1978. 15.95 (*0-916456-29-3*, GA89) Good Apple.
Bauman, Toni, jt. auth. see Zinkgraf, June.
Baumann, Hans. What Time Is It Around the World? LC 75-24710. (Illus.). (gr. k-5). 1979. 6.95 (*0-87592-061-6*) Scroll Pr.
Baumann, K., ed. see Hopkins, L. B.
Baumann, Kurt. The Hungry One. Eidrigevicius, Stasys, illus. Lewis, Naomi, tr. from GER. LC 92-31030. (Illus.). 32p. (gr. k-3). 1993. 14.95 (*1-55858-121-9*); PLB 14.88 (*1-55858-196-0*) North-South Bks NYC.
—Three Kings. Gantschev, Ivan, illus. Lewis, Naomi, tr. LC 89-43729. (Illus.). 32p. (gr. 1-3). 1990. 13.95 (*1-55858-094-8*) North-South Bks NYC.
Baumann, Kurt, retold by. The Story of Jonah. Reed, Allison, illus. LC 86-62522. 32p. (gr. k-3). 1987. 13.95 (*1-55858-050-6*) North-South Bks NYC.
Baumann, Susan K. & Mandell, Steven L. QBASIC. Perlee, ed. 450p. 1992. text ed. 37.75 (*0-314-78351-2*) West Pub.
Baumgardner, Mary A. Alexandra, Keeper of Dreams. Wheeler, Penny & Wilson, Miriam W., eds. Baumgardner, Mary A., illus. 37p. (gr. k-4). 1993. 12.95 (*0-944576-08-7*) Rocky River Pubs.
Baumgart, Klaus. Anna & the Little Green Dragon. Baumgart, Klaus, illus. LC 91-26639. 32p. (ps-3). 1992. 12.95 (*1-56282-166-0*); PLB 12.89 (*1-56282-167-9*) Hyprn Child.
—The Little Green Dragon Steps Out. Baumgart, Klaus, illus. LC 92-5120. 32p. (ps-3). 1992. Repr. of 1989 ed. PLB 12.89 (*1-56282-255-1*); text ed. 12.95 (*1-56282-254-3*) Hyprn Child.
—Where Are You, Little Green Dragon? Baumgart, Klaus, illus. LC 92-72026. 32p. (ps-3). 1993. 12.95 (*1-56282-344-2*); PLB 12.89 (*1-56282-345-0*) Hyprn Child.
Baumgartner, Barbara, retold by. Crocodile! Crocodile! And Other Folktales. Moffatt, Judith, illus. LC 93-28027. 1994. write for info. (*1-56458-463-1*) Dorling Kindersley.
Bausch, William J. Becoming a Man: Basic Information, Guidance, & Attitudes on Sex for Boys. LC 87-51569. 324p. (Orig.). (gr. 5-12). 1988. pap. 9.95 (*0-89622-357-4*) Twenty Third.
Bautista, Bezalie P. The Boy Who Looked Different. Saprid, Pearle R., illus. 24p. (Orig.). (gr. k-2). 1990. pap. 3.50x (*971-10-0406-2*, Pub. by New Day Pub PI) Cellar.
Bauzen, Peter & Bauzen, Susanne. Flower Pressing. Kuttner, Paul, tr. from GER. LC 77-167661. (gr. 7 up). 1982. pap. 4.95 (*0-8069-7674-8*) Sterling.
Bauzen, Susanne, jt. auth. see Bauzen, Peter.
Baw, Cindy & Brownlow, Paul C. Children of the Bible: Exciting Stories about Children in the Bible. (Illus.). (ps-3). 1984. 8.99 (*0-915720-19-1*) Brownlow Pub Co.
Bawa, Ujagar S. Aasaa Di Vaar: (A Part of Sikh Scriptures) 184p. (gr. 8-12). 1993. 12.50x (*0-942245-08-3*) Wash Sikh Ctr.
—Bichitra Naatik: A Part of Sikh Scriptures. 172p. (gr. 8-12). 1991. pap. 10.00x (*0-942245-06-7*) Wash Sikh Ctr.
—Sikhism: A Short Expose. 30p. (gr. 8-12). 1988. pap. 2.00x (*0-942245-02-4*) Wash Sikh Ctr.
—Sri Sukhmani Sahib: A Part of Sikh Scriptures. 304p. (gr. 8-12). 1990. pap. 10.00x (*0-942245-05-9*) Wash Sikh Ctr.
Bawa, Ujagar S., jt. auth. see Singh, Vir.
Bawa, Ujagar S., jt. auth. see Singh, Vir S.
Bawden, Juliet. Fun with Fabric. Venus, Joanna, illus. Johnson, David, photos by. LC 92-51070. (Illus.). 48p. (gr. 1-5). 1993. 6.99 (*0-679-83494-X*); PLB 9.99 (*0-679-93494-4*) Random Bks Yng Read.
—Making Presents. Kerr, Elizabeth, illus. LC 92-18649. 48p. (gr. 1-5). 1994. 6.99 (*0-679-83495-8*); PLB 9.99 (*0-679-93495-2*) Random Bks Yng Read.
—One Hundred One Things to Make: Fun Craft Projects with Everyday Materials. Pang, Alex, illus. LC 93-29633. 1994. write for info. (*0-8069-0596-4*) Sterling.
Bawden, Nina. Carrie's War. LC 72-13253. (gr. 4-7). 1973. PLB 14.89 (*0-397-31450-7*, Lipp Jr Bks) HarpC Child Bks.
—Carrie's War. 160p. 1989. pap. 4.95 (*0-440-40142-9*, Pub. by Yearling Classics) Dell.
—The Finding. LC 84-25069. 160p. (gr. 3 up). 1985. 11.95 (*0-688-04979-6*) Lothrop.
—The Finding. (gr. k-6). 1988. pap. 2.95 (*0-440-40004-X*) Dell.

—A Handful of Thieves. 192p. (gr. 3-7). 1991. 13.45 (*0-395-58634-8*, Clarion Bks) HM.
—Henry. Powzyk, Joyce, illus. LC 87-29339. (gr. 3 up). 1988. PLB 13.95 (*0-688-07894-X*) Lothrop.
—The House of Secrets. 192p. (gr. 3-7). 1992. 13.45 (*0-395-58670-4*, Clarion Bks) HM.
—Humbug. 144p. (gr. 4-7). 1992. 13.45 (*0-395-62149-6*, Clarion Bks) HM.
—Humbug. large type ed. 208p. 1993. 13.95 (*0-7451-1670-1*, Galaxy Child Lrg Print) Chivers N Amer.
—Humbug. 144p. (gr. 5 up). 1994. pap. 3.99 (*0-14-036586-9*) Puffin Bks.
—The Outside Child. LC 88-27349. (Illus.). 160p. (gr. 4-9). 1989. 12.95 (*0-688-08965-8*) Lothrop.
—The Outside Child. large type ed. (gr. 1-8). 1991. 13.95 (*0-7451-1425-3*, Galaxy Child Lrg Print) Chivers N Amer.
—The Outside Child. 240p. (gr. 5 up). 1994. pap. 3.99 (*0-14-036858-2*) Puffin Bks.
—The Peppermint Pig. LC 74-26922. 192p. (gr. 3-6). 1975. PLB 13.89 (*0-397-31618-6*, Lipp Jr Bks) HarpC Child Bks.
—The Peppermint Pig. 160p. (gr. 5 up). 1988. pap. 4.95 (*0-440-40122-4*, Pub. by Yearling Classics) Dell.
—The Real Plato Jones. LC 92-43873. 1993. 13.95 (*0-395-66972-3*, Clarion Bks) HM.
—The Robbers. LC 79-4152. (Illus.). 160p. (gr. 4-7). 1989. Repr. of 1979 ed. 12.95 (*0-688-41902-X*) Lothrop.
—The Robbers. 1990. pap. 3.25 (*0-440-40316-2*, YB) Dell.
—Squib. LC 82-75. (Illus.). 160p. (gr. 4-6). 1982. 12.95 (*0-688-01299-X*) Lothrop.
—Squib. (gr. k-6). 1990. pap. 3.50 (*0-440-40326-X*, YB) Dell.
—White Horse Gang. Bawden, Nina, illus. 176p. (gr. 4-7). 1992. 13.95 (*0-395-58709-3*, Clarion Bks) HM.
—The Witch's Daughter. 192p. (gr. 3-7). 1991. 13.45 (*0-395-58635-6*, Clarion Bks) HM.
Bax, Martin. Edmond Went Far Away. Foreman, Michael, illus. 32p. (ps-3). 1989. 12.95 (*0-15-225105-7*, HB Juv Bks) HarBrace.
Baxter, Kathleen M. Come & Get It: A Natural Foods Cookbook for Children. rev. ed. LC 81-70782. (Illus.). 128p. (ps-6). 1989. PLB 13.95 (*0-9603696-4-3*); pap. 8.95 spiral bdg. (*0-9603696-3-5*) Children First.
Baxter, Leon. The Drawing Book. Baxter, Leon, illus. 64p. (ps-4). 1990. 13.95 (*0-8249-8475-7*, Ideals Child) Hambleton-Hill.
—The Drawing Book. rev. ed. (Illus.). 62p. 1991. Repr. of 1990 ed. PLB 15.95 (*1-878363-38-7*) Forest Hse.
—The Drawing Book. Baxter, Leon, illus. 64p. (ps-4). 1993. pap. 5.95 (*0-8249-8633-4*, Ideals Child) Hambleton-Hill.
—Famous Automobiles. 48p. (gr. 2-5). 1992. pap. 7.95 (*0-8249-8559-1*, Ideals Child) Hambleton-Hill.
—Famous Flying Machines. (Illus.). 48p. (gr. 1-5). 1992. pap. 7.95 (*0-8249-8532-X*, Ideals Child) Hambleton-Hill.
—Famous Ships. Baxter, Leon, illus. 48p. (gr. 2-5). 1993. pap. 7.95 (*0-685-65409-5*, Ideals Child) Hambleton-Hill.
—Famous Ships. (gr. 4-7). 1993. pap. 7.95 (*0-8249-8612-1*, Ideals Child) Hambleton-Hill.
Baxter, Nancy N. Gallant Fourteenth: The Story of an Indiana Civil War Regiment. Niblack, John L., pref. by. 205p. 1986. 16.95 (*0-9617367-8-X*); pap. 12.00 (*0-9617367-0-4*) Guild Pr IN.
—The Miamis! 100p. (gr. 4-6). 1987. 13.95 (*0-9617367-3-9*) Guild Pr IN.
Baxter, Nancy N., ed. Hoosier Farmboy in Lincoln's Army: The Civil War Letters of Pvt. John R. McClure. 2nd ed. (Illus.). 67p. (gr. 6-10). 1971. 14.95 (*0-9617367-2-0*) Guild Pr IN.
Baxter, Nancy N., ed. see Hale, Janet.
Baxter, Nicola. Romans. (Illus.). 32p. (gr. 5-8). 1992. PLB 11.90 (*0-531-14143-8*) Watts.
Baxter, Roberta. Number Fun. Sagasti, Miriam, illus. 32p. (ps-2). Date not set. 11.95 (*1-56065-147-4*) Capstone Pr. Postponed.
—The Shape of Your World. Sagasti, Miriam, illus. 32p. (ps-2). Date not set. 11.95 (*1-56065-144-X*) Capstone Pr. Postponed.
—Turn of the Seasons. Sagati, Miriam, illus. 32p. (ps-2). Date not set. 11.95 (*1-56065-146-6*) Capstone Pr. Postponed.
Bay, Timothy. First to the Moon. LC 92-75989. 1993. 9.95 (*0-383-03818-9*) SRA Schl Grp.
Bay, William. Children's Guitar Method, Vol. 1. (Illus.). 1993. 4.95 (*0-685-63840-5*, 93833); cass. 9.98 (*0-685-63841-3*, 93833) Mel Bay.
—Children's Guitar Method, Vol. 2. (Illus.). 1993. 4.95 (*0-685-63842-1*, 93834) Mel Bay.
—Children's Guitar Method, Vol. 3. 1993. 4.95 (*0-685-63843-X*, 93835) Mel Bay.
—Kids' Rock Guitar Method. 1993. 5.95 (*0-685-63861-8*, 94360); cass. 9.98 (*0-685-63862-6*, 94360); CD 14.95 (*0-685-63863-4*, 94360) Mel Bay.
Bayer, Jane. A, My Name Is Alice. Kellogg, Steven, illus. LC 84-7059. (gr. k-3). 1984. 15.00 (*0-8037-0123-3*); PLB 14.89 (*0-8037-0124-1*) Dial Bks Young.
—A, My Name Is Alice. Kellogg, Steven, illus. LC 84-7059. 32p. (ps-2). 1987. pap. 4.95 (*0-8037-0130-6*) Dial Bks Young.

Bayles, Miriam. Si Bantay, Si Puti, at Si Ngaw. Bayles, Arthur, illus. (TAG., Orig.). (gr. k-2). 1988. pap. 3.75x (*971-10-0359-7*, Pub. by New Day Pub PI) Cellar.
—Si Wayt at Ang Kanyang Mga Kaibigan. Tiano, Bethoven, illus. (TAG.). 35p. (Orig.). (gr. k-2). 1990. pap. 4.00x (*971-10-0416-X*, Pub. by New Day Pub PI) Cellar.
Bayley, Monica & Schulz, Charles M. Snoopy Omnibus. LC 82-71285. (Illus.). 1983. 6.95 (*0-915696-54-1*); pap. 4.95 (*0-915696-81-9*) Determined Prods.
Bayley, Nicola. Copycats. Bayley, Nicola, illus. LC 91-58722. 96p. (ps up). 1992. 14.95 (*1-56402-114-9*) Candlewick Pr.
Baylis-White, Mary. Sheltering Rebecca. 112p. (gr. 3-7). 1991. 14.95 (*0-525-67349-0*, Lodestar Bks) Dutton Child Bks.
—Sheltering Rebecca. 112p. (gr. 5-9). 1993. pap. 3.99 (*0-14-036448-X*, Puffin) Puffin Bks.
Baylor, Byrd. Amigo. Williams, Garth, illus. 48p. (gr. 1-3). 1989. pap. 4.95 (*0-689-71299-5*, Aladdin) Macmillan Child Grp.
—The Best Town in the World. Himler, Ronald, illus. LC 83-9033. 32p. (gr. 1-3). 1983. SBE 14.95 (*0-684-18035-9*, Scribners Young Read) Macmillan Child Grp.
—The Best Town in the World. Himler, Ronald, illus. LC 86-3381. 32p. (gr. 1-3). 1986. pap. 3.95 (*0-689-71086-0*, Aladdin) Macmillan Child Grp.
—The Desert Is Theirs. Parnall, Peter, illus. LC 74-24417. 32p. (ps-3). 1975. SBE 14.95 (*0-684-14266-X*, Scribners Young Read) Macmillan Child Grp.
—The Desert Is Theirs. Parnall, Peter, illus. LC 86-17323. 32p. (gr. 1-5). 1987. pap. 4.95 (*0-689-71105-0*, Aladdin) Macmillan Child Grp.
—Desert Voices. Parnall, Peter, illus. LC 80-17061. 32p. (ps-3). 1981. SBE 14.95 (*0-684-16712-3*, Scribners Young Read) Macmillan Child Grp.
—Desert Voices. Parnall, Peter, illus. LC 92-24475. 32p. (gr. 1-5). 1993. pap. 3.95 (*0-689-71691-5*, Aladdin) Macmillan Child Grp.
—Everybody Needs a Rock. Parnall, Peter, illus. LC 74-9163. 32p. (ps-3). 1974. RSBE 14.95 (*0-684-13899-9*, Scribners Young Read) Macmillan Child Grp.
—Everybody Needs a Rock. Parnall, Peter, illus. LC 74-9163. 32p. (gr. k-3). 1985. pap. 4.95 (*0-689-71051-8*, Aladdin) Macmillan Child Grp.
—Guess Who My Favorite Person Is. Parker, Robert A., illus. LC 77-7151. 32p. (gr. 1-5). 1985. pap. 4.95 (*0-689-71052-6*, Aladdin) Macmillan Child Grp.
—Guess Who My Favorite Person Is. reissued ed. Parker, Robert A., illus. LC 77-7151. 32p. (gr. 1-4). 1992. RSBE 14.95 (*0-684-19514-3*, Scribners Young Read) Macmillan Child Grp.
—Hawk, I'm Your Brother. Parnall, Peter, illus. LC 75-39296. 48p. (ps-3). 1976. SBE 14.95 (*0-684-14571-5*, Scribners Young Read) Macmillan Child Grp.
—Hawk, I'm Your Brother. reissued ed. Parnall, Peter, illus. LC 86-10742. 48p. (gr. 1-5). 1986. pap. 3.95 (*0-689-71102-6*, Aladdin) Macmillan Child Grp.
—If You Are a Hunter of Fossils. Parnall, Peter, illus. LC 79-17926. 32p. (ps-3). 1980. SBE 14.95 (*0-684-16419-1*, Scribners Young Read) Macmillan Child Grp.
—If You Are a Hunter of Fossils. Parnall, Peter, illus. LC 79-17926. 32p. (gr. 3-6). 1984. pap. 4.95 (*0-689-70773-8*, Aladdin) Macmillan Child Grp.
—I'm in Charge of Celebrations. Parnall, Peter, illus. LC 85-19633. 32p. (gr. 1-4). 1986. SBE 14.95 (*0-684-18579-2*, Scribners Young Read) Macmillan Child Grp.
—And It Is Still That Way. Jelinek, Lucy, illus. 96p. (gr. k-8). 1987. pap. 6.95 (*0-939729-06-7*) Trails West Pub.
—Moon Song. Himler, Ronald, illus. LC 81-18427. 24p. (gr. 3-6). 1982. SBE 12.95 (*0-684-17463-4*, Scribners Young Read) Macmillan Child Grp.
—One Small Blue Bead. 2nd ed. Himler, Ronald, illus. LC 90-28160. 32p. (gr. 2-5). 1992. SBE 13.95 (*0-684-19334-5*, Scribners Young Read) Macmillan Child Grp.
—The Other Way to Listen. Parnall, Peter, illus. LC 78-23430. 32p. (ps-3). 1978. SBE 14.95 (*0-684-16017-X*, Scribners Young Read) Macmillan Child Grp.
—The Table Where Rich People Sit. Parnall, Peter, illus. LC 93-1251. 1994. text ed. 14.95 (*0-684-19653-0*, Scribner) Macmillan.
—The Way to Start a Day. Parnall, Peter, illus. LC 78-113. 32p. (ps-3). 1978. SBE 14.95 (*0-684-15651-2*, Scribners Young Read) Macmillan Child Grp.
—The Way to Start a Day. Parnall, Peter, illus. LC 85-28802. 32p. (gr. 1-4). 1986. pap. 3.95 (*0-689-71054-2*, Aladdin) Macmillan Child Grp.
—When Clay Sings. Bahti, Tom, illus. LC 70-180758. 32p. (ps-3). 1987. Repr. of 1977 ed. SBE 13.95 (*0-684-18829-5*, Scribners Young Read) Macmillan Child Grp.
—When Clay Sings. Bahti, Tom, illus. LC 86-20587. 32p. (gr. 1-4). 1987. pap. 3.95 (*0-689-71106-9*, Aladdin) Macmillan Child Grp.
—Your Own Best Secret Place. LC 78-21243. (Illus.). 32p. (gr. 1-3). 1991. SBE 14.95 (*0-684-16111-7*, Scribners Young Read) Macmillan Child Grp.
Baynes, John. How Maps Are Made. (Illus.). 32p. (gr. 5-12). 1987. 12.95x (*0-8160-1691-7*) Facts on File.
Baynes, Pauline. Let There Be Light. Baynes, Pauline, illus. LC 90-44572. 32p. (gr. 1 up). 1991. SBE 13.95 (*0-02-708542-2*, Macmillan Child Bk) Macmillan Child Grp.
Baynes, Pauline, jt. auth. see Lewis, C. S.

Baynes, Pauline, compiled by. & illus. Thanks Be to God: Prayers from Around the World. 32p. (ps up). 1990. 12.95 (*0-02-708541-4*, Macmillan Child Bk) Macmillan Child Grp.
Baynes, Pauline, illus. Prince Caspian. LC 93-11514. (gr. 5 up). 1994. 15.00 (*0-06-023483-0*); PLB 14.89 (*0-06-023484-9*) HarpC Child Bks.
Baynton, Martin. Why Do You Love Me? LC 89-1861. (Illus.). 32p. (ps up). 1990. 15.00 (*0-688-09156-3*); PLB 14.93 (*0-688-09157-1*) Greenwillow.
Bazaldua, Barbara. Disney's Aladdin: Monkey Business. (ps-3). 1993. pap. 2.25 (*0-307-12788-5*, Golden Pr) Western Pub.
—Disney's Beauty & the Beast Word Book. Baker, Darrell, illus. 14p. (ps-k). 1992. write for info. (*0-307-12391-X*, 12391) Western Pub.
—Disney's Darkwing Duck in Clean Money. DiCicco, Sue, illus. 24p. (ps-3). 1992. write for info. (*0-307-12668-4*, 12668) Western Pub.
—Walt Disney's Goofy Joke Book. Baker, Darrell, illus. 24p. (ps-3). 1993. pap. 1.95 (*0-307-12683-8*, 12683, Golden Pr) Western Pub.
Bazar, Ronald, jt. auth. see Dehr, Roma.
Beach, James C. Theodore Roosevelt: Man of Action. (Illus.). 80p. (gr. 2-6). 1991. Repr. of 1960 ed. lib. bdg. 12.95 (*0-7910-1450-9*) Chelsea Hse.
Beach, Judy & Spencer, Kathleen. Big Fearon Book of Teachers' Holiday Helpers. (gr. 1-3). 1987. pap. 19.95 (*0-8224-6776-3*) Fearon Teach Aids.
—Christmas. (gr. 1-3). 1987. pap. 5.95 (*0-8224-6773-9*) Fearon Teach Aids.
—Halloween. (gr. 1-3). 1987. pap. 5.95 (*0-8224-6771-2*) Fearon Teach Aids.
—Minds-on Fun for Fall. (gr. k-4). 1991. pap. 9.95 (*0-86653-948-4*) Fearon Teach Aids.
—Minds-on Fun for Spring. (gr. k-4). 1991. pap. 9.95 (*0-86653-946-8*) Fearon Teach Aids.
—Minds-on Fun for Summer. (gr. k-4). 1991. pap. 9.95 (*0-86653-945-X*) Fearon Teach Aids.
—Minds-on Fun for Winter. (gr. k-4). 1991. pap. 9.95 (*0-86653-947-6*) Fearon Teach Aids.
—Springtime. (gr. 1-3). 1987. pap. 5.95 (*0-8224-6775-5*) Fearon Teach Aids.
—Thanksgiving. (gr. 1-3). 1987. pap. 5.95 (*0-8224-6772-0*) Fearon Teach Aids.
—Valentine's Day. (gr. 1-3). 1987. pap. 5.95 (*0-8224-6774-7*) Fearon Teach Aids.
Beach, Lynn. The Dark. MacDonald, Patricia, ed. 128p. (Orig.). 1991. pap. 2.99 (*0-671-74089-X*, Minstrel Bks) PB.
—Dead Man's Secret. MacDonald, Pat, ed. 128p. (Orig.). 1992. pap. 2.99 (*0-671-75924-8*, Minstrel Bks) PB.
—The Evil One. 128p. (Orig.). 1991. pap. 2.99 (*0-671-74088-1*, Minstrel Bks) PB.
—Invisibility Island. (gr. 8 up). 1988. pap. 2.95 (*0-345-35097-9*) Ballantine.
—Phantom Valley: In the Mummy's Tomb. MacDonald, Pat, ed. 128p. (Orig.). 1992. pap. 2.99 (*0-671-75925-6*, Minstrel Bks) PB.
—Phantom Valley: The Headless Ghost. McDonald, Pat, ed. 128p. (Orig.). (gr. 3-6). 1992. pap. 2.99 (*0-671-75926-4*, Minstrel Bks) PB.
—Scream of the Cat. MacDonald, Patricia, ed. 128p. (Orig.). 1992. pap. 2.99 (*0-671-74090-3*) PB.
—The Spell. MacDonald, Pat, ed. 128p. (Orig.). 1992. pap. 2.99 (*0-671-75923-X*, Minstrel Bks) PB.
Beach, Stewart. Good Morning-Sun's Up. Sugita, Yataka, illus. LC 79-108178. 32p. (ps-3). 8.95 (*0-87592-021-7*) Scroll Pr.
Beach-Balthis, Judy. Ano Nuevo: A Children's Guide. Balthis, Frank S., ed. Beach-Balthis, Judy, illus. 24p. (Orig.). (gr. k-8). 1985. pap. 2.95 (*0-918355-02-8*) Firehole Pr.
—Point Reyes: A Children's Guide. Balthis, Frank S., ed. Beach-Balthis, Judy, illus. 24p. (Orig.). (gr. k-8). 1983. pap. 2.95 (*0-685-53258-5*) Firehole Pr.
—Yellowstone: A Children's Guide. Balthis, Frank, ed. Beach-Balthis, Judy, illus. 36p. (Orig.). (gr. k-8). 1981. pap. 2.95 (*0-918355-01-X*) Firehole Pr.
Beachy, J. Wayne. A Bird of Peace Is Born in Petersburg. Hawkins, Beverly, illus. (Orig.). (gr. 5). 1981. pap. 2.50 (*0-9608084-0-X*) B Hawkins Studio.
—The Extraordinary Ordinary Christmas Matoaca, 1870. Hawkins, Beverly, illus. 20p. (Orig.). (gr. 5). 1984. pap. 2.50 (*0-9608084-2-6*) B Hawkins Studio.
—The Ghost of Rat Castle: A Story of Old Petersburg. Hawkins, Beverly, illus. 24p. (Orig.). (gr. 5). 1983. pap. 2.50 (*0-9608084-1-8*) B Hawkins Studio.
—Richmond Theater Fire, 1862. Hawkins, Beverly, illus. 24p. (Orig.). (gr. 5 up). 1987. pap. 3.00 (*0-9608084-3-4*) B Hawkins Studio.
Beachy, Mary D. & Wolferman, Kristie. When Peanut Butter Is Not Enough. Flick, Deborah M., illus. 100p. (gr. 2-7). 1986. pap. 7.95 (*0-9616883-0-0*) Petit Appetit.
Beak, Barbara. Octavia Warms Up. LC 91-31644. 1992. 2.95 (*0-85953-786-2*) Childs Play.
—Walter Worm's Good Turn. LC 91-33548. 1992. 2.95 (*0-85953-785-4*) Childs Play.
Beake, Lesley. The Song of Be. 110p. (gr. 7 up). 1993. PLB 14.95 (*0-8050-2905-2*, Bks Young Read) H Holt & Co.
Beal, George. The Julian Messner Young Reader's Thesaurus. 1984. pap. 6.95 (*0-685-09676-9*) S&S Trade.

—The Kingfisher Book of Words: A-Z Guide to Quotations, Proverbs, Origins, Usage, & Idioms. Stevenson, Peter, illus. LC 92-53105. 192p. (gr. 4 up). 1992. 10.95 (1-85697-805-2) Kingfisher Bks.

—The Simon & Schuster Young Readers' Thesaurus. Barish, Wendy, ed. (Illus.). 192p. (gr. 3-7). 1984. pap. 6.95 (0-685-09127-9, Little Simon) S&S Trade.

—Simon & Schuster Young Readers' Thesaurus. (Illus.). 192p. 1984. pap. 7.95 (0-671-50816-4, S&S BFYR) S&S Trade.

Beal, George & Chatterton, Martin. The Kingfisher First Thesaurus. LC 92-45572. (Illus.). 144p. (gr. 2-6). 1993. 14.95 (1-85697-914-8) Kingfisher Bks.

Beal, K. Big Book Package, 4 vols. (Illus.). 16p. (gr. 1-3). 1990. Set. pap. text ed. 80.25 (0-201-52205-5) Addison-Wesley.

—Here It's Winter Big Book. (Illus.). 16p. (gr. 1-3). 1990. pap. text ed. 22.95 (0-201-52203-9) Addison-Wesley.

—I Like You Big Book. (Illus.). 16p. (gr. 1-3). 1990. pap. text ed. 22.95 (0-201-52204-7) Addison-Wesley.

—I Like You Little Book. (Illus.). 16p. (gr. 1-3). 1990. pap. text ed. 4.50 (0-201-52209-8) Addison-Wesley.

—I Like You Little Books Four-Pack. (Illus.). 16p. (gr. 1-3). 1990. Set. pap. text ed. 12.95 (0-201-52213-6) Addison-Wesley.

—I Love My Family Big Book. (Illus.). 16p. (gr. 1-3). 1990. pap. text ed. 22.95 (0-201-52202-0) Addison-Wesley.

—I Love My Family Little Book. (Illus.). 16p. (gr. 1-3). 1990. pap. text ed. 4.50 (0-201-52207-1) Addison-Wesley.

—I Love My Family Little Books Four-Pack. (Illus.). 16p. (gr. 1-3). 1990. Set. pap. text ed. 12.95 (0-201-52211-X) Addison-Wesley.

—It's Pink I Think Big Book. (Illus.). 16p. (gr. 1-3). 1990. pap. text ed. 22.95 (0-201-52201-2) Addison-Wesley.

—It's Pink I Think Little Book. (Illus.). 16p. (gr. 1-3). 1990. pap. text ed. 4.50 (0-201-52206-3) Addison-Wesley.

—It's Pink I Think Little Books Four-Pack. (Illus.). 16p. (gr. 1-3). 1990. Set. pap. text ed. 12.95 (0-201-52210-1) Addison-Wesley.

—It's Winter Little Book. (Illus.). 16p. (gr. 1-3). 1990. pap. text ed. 4.50 (0-201-52208-X) Addison-Wesley.

—It's Winter Little Books Four-Pack. (Illus.). 16p. (gr. 1-3). 1990. Set. pap. text ed. 12.95 (0-201-52212-8) Addison-Wesley.

Beale, Jane G. Keyboard Arithmetic. 29p. (Orig.). (gr. 1-8). 1986. pap. 3.50 (0-937781-09-6) G Beale Pr.

Bealer, Alex. Only the Names Remain: The Cherokees & the Trail of Tears. Bock, William S., illus. (gr. 4-6). 1972. lib. bdg. 15.95 (0-316-08520-0) Little.

Beales, Valerie. Emma & Freckles. Rogers, Jacqueline, illus. LC 91-20751. 208p. (gr. 5-9). 1992. pap. 13.00 jacketed, 3-pc. bdg. (0-671-74686-3, S&S BFYR) S&S Trade.

Beall, Alan. Braves on the Warpath: The Fifty Greatest Games in the History of the Washington Redskins. Baugh, Sammy, frwd. by. LC 88-81470. (Illus.). 400p. (gr. 6-12). 1988. 24.95 (0-929639-00-6) Kinloch Bks.

Beall, Pamela C. & Nipp, Susan. Wee Sing. (ps-2). 1982. pap. 2.95 (0-8431-0676-X); pap. 9.95 incl. cassette (0-8431-0522-4) Price Stern.

—Wee Sing & Play. (Illus.). 64p. (Orig.). (ps-6). 1983. pap. 2.95 (0-8431-0391-4); pap. 9.95 incl. cassette (0-8431-0743-X) Price Stern.

—Wee Sing for Christmas. (Illus.). 64p. (Orig.). (ps-2). 1984. incl. cass. 9.95 (0-8431-1071-6); pap. 2.95 (0-8431-1197-6) Price Stern.

—Wee Sing Sing-Alongs. (Illus.). 64p. (ps-6). 1983. pap. 2.95 (0-8431-0311-6); pap. 9.95 incl. cassette (0-8431-0742-1) Price Stern.

Beall, Pamela C. & Nipp, Susan H. King Cole's Party. Klein, Nancy, illus. (ps-2). 1987. 19.95 (0-8431-4714-8); incl. audiocassette soundtrack 24.95 (0-8431-4715-6) Price Stern.

—Wee Sing America. Klein, Nancy, illus. 64p. (ps-2). 1987. pap. 2.95 (0-8431-4702-4); incl. cass. 9.95 (0-8431-1983-7) Price Stern.

—Wee Sing Bible Songs. Klein, Nancy, illus. 64p. (ps-2). 1986. pap. 2.95 (0-8431-1566-1); bk. & cass. 9.95 (0-8431-1780-X) Price Stern.

—Wee Sing Dinosaurs. (Illus.). 64p. 1991. pap. 2.95 (0-8431-2921-2); pap. 9.95 incl. cassette (0-8431-2946-8) Price Stern.

—Wee Sing Fun 'n Folk Songs. (Illus.). 64p. (Orig.). (ps-2). pap. 2.95 (0-8431-2760-0); bk. & cassette 9.95 (0-8431-2759-7) Price Stern.

—Wee Sing Nursery Rhymes & Lullabies. (Illus.). 64p. (Orig.). (ps-2). 1985. pap. 9.95 incl. cass. (0-8431-1422-3); pap. 2.95 (0-8431-1438-X) Price Stern.

—Wee Sing Pop-up Nursery Rhymes. Bracken, Carolyn, illus. 7p. 1993. 13.95 (0-8431-3599-9) Price Stern.

—Wee Sing Silly Songs. (Illus.). 64p. (ps-6). 1983. pap. 2.95 (0-8431-0310-8); pap. 9.95 incl. cass. (0-8431-0741-3) Price Stern.

Beall, Pamela C., et al. Wee Sing over in the Meadow. Reasoner, Charles A., illus. 64p. (ps). 10.95 (0-8431-1949-7); incl. cass. 14.95 (0-8431-1978-0) Price Stern.

Beame, Rona. Backyard Explorer Kit. LC 88-51582. (Illus.). 64p. (gr. k-5). 1989. pap. 9.95 (0-89480-343-3, 1343) Workman Pub.

Beamer, Nona. Helu Papa-Counting in Hawaiian: Pi'a Pa-Hawaiian Alphabet. Ching, Patrick, illus. 40p. 1991. text ed. write for info. (0-9627294-0-X) Hawaiian Resources.

Beamer, Winona D. Talking Story with Nona Beamer: Stories of a Hawaiian Family. Kahalewai, Marilyn, illus. Hannahs, Neil J., afterword by. LC 83-70357. (Illus.). 80p. (gr. 2-6). 1984. 9.95 (0-935848-20-7) Bess Pr.

Beames, Margaret. The Lunch That Mom Made. Curtis, Neil, illus. LC 92-21454. 1993. 4.25 (0-383-03639-9) SRA Schl Grp.

Bean, Barbara & Bennett, Shari. The Me Nobody Knows: A Guide for Teen Survivors. LC 93-12624. 200p. 1993. pap. 9.95 (0-02-902015-8) Free Pr.

Bean, James H., ed. see Lynch, Don & Thompson, David.

Bean, Lowell J. & Bourgeault, Lisa. The Cahuilla. Porter, Frank W., III, intro. by. (Illus.). 112p. (gr. 5 up). 1989. 17.95 (1-55546-693-1) Chelsea Hse.

Bean, Suzanne M., jt. auth. see Karnes, Frances A.

Bean, Vaughan. The ABC's of Meditation & More, (A Guide for Children) (Illus.). 88p. (Orig.). (gr. 2-5). 1994. pap. 11.95 (0-9631740-1-0) Millinnium-Holographic.
This book is recommended for children ages seven to eleven & introduces young readers to the subjects of elementary meditation & relaxation, lucid dreaming, creative visualization & other positive concepts which, according to the author, are easily learned when children are allowed to exercise their individual creativity & "innate intelligence."
Publisher Provided Annotation.

Beane, Kelly D. My Life in the City. Iscaro, Nancy L., frwd. by. West Side High School Students, illus. 48p. (Orig.). (gr. 10-12). 1989. pap. text ed. write for info. West Side Pubns.

Bear, Magdalen, jt. auth. see Jenkins, Gerald.

Beard, Adelia, jt. auth. see Beard, Lina.

Beard, Charles A. & Vagts, Detlev. Presidents in American History. 2nd, rev. ed. Steltenpohl, Jane, ed. (Illus.). 240p. (gr. 6-10). 1989. lib. bdg. 14.98 (0-671-68574-0, J Messner); pap. 6.95 (0-671-68575-9) S&S Trade.

Beard, Daniel C. American Boys Handy Book: What to Do & How to Do It. facs. ed. LC 66-15858. (Illus.). 392p. (gr. 4 up). 1966. 14.95 (0-8048-0006-5) C E Tuttle.

—The American Boy's Handy Book: What to Do & How to Do It. Perrin, Noel, frwd. by. LC 82-3155. (Illus.). 320p. (gr. 4 up). 1983. pap. 10.95 (0-87923-449-0) Godine.

Beard, Lina & Beard, Adelia. American Girls Handybook: How to Amuse Yourself & Others. LC 86-46262. 480p. 1987. 11.95 (0-87923-666-3) Godine.

Beard, Ray, jt. auth. see Matthews, Velda.

Bearden, Donna & Muller, Jim. One-Two-Three, My Computer & Me: A LOGO Fun Book for Kids. (gr. 3 up). 1983. pap. 16.50 (0-8359-5228-2, Reston) P-H.

Beardsley, John. Pablo Picasso. (Illus.). 92p. 1991. 19.95 (0-8109-3713-1) Abrams.

Bearman, Jane. David. Bearman, Jane, illus. LC 65-21753. (gr. 3 up). 1975. 3.95 (0-8246-0085-1) Jonathan David.

—The Eight Nights: A Chanukah Counting Book. Bearman, Jane, illus. LC 78-60781. (gr. k-3). 1979. pap. 5.00 (0-8074-0237-0, 102562) UAHC.

—Jonathan. Bearman, Jane, illus. LC 65-21754. (gr. 3 up). 1975. 3.95 (0-8246-0089-4) Jonathan David.

Beasant. Medicine. (Illus.). 32p. (gr. 4-8). 1986. PLB 13.96 (0-88110-221-0); pap. 6.95 (0-86020-948-2) EDC.

Beasant, Pam. Space. LC 92-53103. (Illus.). 48p. (Orig.). (gr. 3-8). 1992. pap. 5.95 (1-85697-811-7) Kingfisher Bks.

Beasant, Pam & Findly, Ian. Electronics. Newton, Martin & Andrews, Jane, illus. 48p. (gr. 5-8). 1985. (Pub. by Usborne); pap. 6.95 (0-86020-809-5) EDC.

Beasant, Pam & Smith, Alastair. How to Draw Maps & Charts. (Illus.). 32p. (gr. 3 up). 1993. lib. bdg. 12.96 (0-88110-650-X, Usborne); pap. 4.95 (0-7460-1002-8, Usborne) EDC.

Beasley, Barbara & Wolkoff, Judie. Ace Hits Rock Bottom. (gr. k-12). 1987. pap. 2.75 (0-440-90048-4, LFL) Dell.

Beasley, Mrs. Jim. Missions Studies: Brazil. (Illus.). 32p. (Orig.). (ps). 1985. pap. 2.25 (0-89114-155-3) Baptist Pub Hse.

Beasley, Roberta, illus. Baby's Cradle Songs. 12p. (ps). 1986. 3.99 (0-394-88242-3) Random Bks Yng Read.

Beasley, Sterling. Captain Miraculous & the Bound for Glory Kid. (Illus.). 32p. (Orig.). 1993. pap. 4.95 (8059-3421-9) Dorrance.

Beaton, Clare. Cards. Beaton, Clare, illus. 24p. (gr. k-4). 1990. PLB 10.90 (0-531-19096-X); pap. 2.95 (0-531-15159-X) Watts.

—Costumes. Beaton, Clare, illus. LC 89-21520. 24p. (gr. k-4). 1990. PLB 10.90 (0-531-19094-3); pap. 2.95 (0-531-15160-3) Watts.

—Face Painting. Beaton, Clare, illus. LC 90-11956. 24p. (gr. k-4). 1990. PLB 10.90 (0-531-19095-1); pap. 2.95 (0-531-15161-1) Watts.

—Hats. Beaton, Clare, illus. 24p. (gr. k-4). 1990. PLB 10.90 (0-531-19097-8); pap. 2.95 (0-531-15162-X) Watts.

—Masks. Beaton, Clare, illus. 24p. (gr. k-4). 1990. PLB 10.90 (0-531-19098-6); pap. 2.95 (0-531-15163-8) Watts.

—Monster Party Kit. (Illus.). (gr. 1 up). 1993. pap. 19.95 (1-56138-338-4) Running Pr.

—T-Shirt Painting. Beaton, Clare, illus. 24p. (gr. k-4). 1990. PLB 10.90 (0-531-19099-4); pap. 2.95 (0-531-15164-6) Watts.

Beaton, Jane, et al. Family Celebrations: Advent & Christmas. 64p. 1984. pap. 2.50 (0-8146-1389-6) Liturgical Pr.

Beaton, Margaret. Oprah Winfrey: TV Talk Show Host. LC 90-2150. (Illus.). (gr. 4 up). 1990. PLB 18.60 (0-516-03270-4) Childrens.

—Syria. LC 88-18697. (Illus.). 128p. (gr. 5-9). 1988. PLB 26.60 (0-516-02708-5) Childrens.

Beattie, Kurt, jt. auth. see Falls, Gregory A.

Beattie, Laura. Discover Rocks & Minerals at the Carnegie. (Illus.). 24p. (gr. 1-8). 1991. wkbk. 2.95 (0-911239-37-5) Carnegie Mus.

Beattie, Laura C. Discover African Wildlife: Activity Book. Creative Company Staff, illus. 24p. (Orig.). (gr. 3-7). 1993. wkbk. 2.95 (0-911239-38-3) Carnegie Mus.

—Discover African Wildlife at the Carnegie. (Illus.). 24p. (gr. 3-7). 1993. wkbk. 2.95 (0-911239-39-1) Carnegie Mus.

—Discover Rocks & Minerals: Activity Book. Creative Company Staff, illus. 24p. (gr. 3-8). 1991. wkbk. 2.95 (0-911239-36-7) Carnegie Mus.

Beattie, Owen & Geiger, John. Buried in Ice. 64p. 1992. 15.95 (0-590-43848-4, Scholastic Hardcover) Scholastic Inc.

Beattie, Owen, jt. auth. see Geiger, John.

Beatty, Jerome. Arctic Rovings: Or the Adventures of a New Bedford Boy on Sea & Land by Daniel Weston Hall. Hogarth, William, illus. LC 91-40359. xiv, 144p. (gr. 7-10). 1992. Repr. of 1968 ed. lib. bdg. 17.50 (0-208-02324-0, Pub. by Linnet) Shoe String.

Beatty, Judith, jt. auth. see Kraul, Edward G.

Beatty, Noelle B. Suriname. (Illus.). 96p. (gr. 5 up). 1988. lib. bdg. 14.95 (1-55546-196-4) Chelsea Hse.

Beatty, Patricia. Be Ever Hopeful, Hannalee. LC 88-21581. 208p. (gr. 5-9). 1988. 13.00 (0-688-07502-9) Morrow Jr Bks.

—Be Ever Hopeful Hannalee. 216p. (gr. 5-9). 1990. pap. 2.95 (0-8167-2259-5) Troll Assocs.

—Behave Yourself, Bethany Brant. LC 86-12517. 160p. (gr. 5-9). 1986. 12.95 (0-688-05923-6) Morrow Jr Bks.

—Bonanza Girl. LC 92-23317. 224p. (gr. 5 up). 1993. 14.00 (0-688-12361-9) Morrow Jr Bks.

—Bonanza Girl. LC 92-27682. 224p. 1993. 4.95 (0-688-12280-9) Morrow Jr Bks.

—Charley Skedaddle. LC 87-12270. 192p. (gr. 5-9). 1987. 12.95 (0-688-06687-9) Morrow Jr Bks.

—Charley Skedaddle. 192p. 1988. pap. 2.95 (0-8167-1317-0) Troll Assocs.

—The Coach That Never Came. LC 85-15213. 176p. (gr. 5-9). 1985. 11.95 (0-688-05477-3) Morrow Jr Bks.

—Eight Mules from Monterey. LC 81-22284. 224p. (gr. 4-6). 1982. 13.95 (0-688-01047-4) Morrow Jr Bks.

—Eight Mules from Monterey. LC 81-22284. 272p. (gr. 5 up). 1993. pap. 4.95 (0-688-12279-5, Pub. by Beech Tree Bks) Morrow.

—Jayhawker. LC 91-17890. 224p. (gr. 5 up). 1991. 13.95 (0-688-09850-9) Morrow Jr Bks.

—Lupita Manana. LC 81-505. (gr. 7-9). 1981. PLB 12.93 (0-688-00359-1) Morrow Jr Bks.

—Lupita Manana. LC 81-505. 192p. (gr. 6 up). 1992. pap. 4.95 (0-688-11497-0, Pub. by Beech Tree Bks) Morrow.

—The Nickel-Plated Beauty. LC 92-23318. 272p. (gr. 5 up). 1993. 14.00 (0-688-12360-0); pap. 3.95 (0-685-61089-6) Morrow Jr Bks.

—The Nickel Plated Beauty. LC 92-27683. 240p. (gr. 5 up). 1993. pap. 4.95 (0-688-12281-7, Pub. by Beech Tree Bks) Morrow.

—Sarah & Me & Lady from the Sea. LC 89-33624. 224p. (gr. 5 up). 1989. 11.95 (0-688-08045-6) Morrow Jr Bks.

—Turn Homeward, Hannalee. LC 84-8960. 208p. (gr. 5-9). 1984. 12.95 (0-688-03871-9) Morrow Jr Bks.

—Turn Homeward, Hannalee. 193p. (gr. 5-9). 1990. pap. 2.95 (0-8167-2260-9) Troll Assocs.

—Wait for Me, Watch for Me, Eula Bee. LC 78-12782. (gr. 5 up). 1990. Repr. of 1978 ed. 3.95 (0-688-10077-5, Pub. by Beech Tree Bks) Morrow.

—Who Comes with Cannons? LC 92-6317. 192p. (gr. 5 up). 1992. 14.00 (0-688-11028-2) Morrow Jr Bks.

Beatty, Patricia & Robbins, Phillip. Eben Tyne, Powdermonkey. LC 90-35330. 240p. (gr. 5 up). 1990. 12.95 (0-688-08884-8) Morrow Jr Bks.

Beatty, Willard W., ed. see Clark, Ann N.

Beaty, Dave. Moths & Butterflies. LC 92-29741. 1993. write for info. (1-56766-001-0) Childs World.

—Primates. (gr. 1-8). 1992. PLB 15.95 (0-89565-851-8); Resale. 22.75 (0-685-61002-0) Childs World.

—Waterfowl. LC 92-32319. 1993. write for info. (1-56766-006-1) Childs World.

Beaubeau, Anne, jt. auth. see Keckeis, M. B.

Beauchamp, Andre. Teenage Mothers: Their Experience, Strength, & Hope. Fisher, Rosemarie, tr. from FRE. LC 90-38476. (Illus.). 96p. (Orig.). (gr. 7-12). 1990. pap. 8.95 (0-89390-180-6) Resource Pubns.

Beaude, Pierre-Marie. The Book of Creation. Clements, Andrew, tr. Lemoine, Georges, illus. LC 90-35418. 56p. (gr. 5 up). 1991. pap. 16.95 (0-88708-141-X) Picture Bk Studio.

Beaudin, Margery. Winning Is Responsibility. LC 80-85339. (gr. 7-10). PLB write for info. (0-938762-27-3) Eagle Mktg Corp.

Beaudry, Jo & Ketchum, Lynne. Carla Goes to Court. Hamilton, Jack, illus. LC 82-2854. 32p. (gr. 1-5). 1982. 14.95 (0-89885-088-6); pap. 9.95 (0-89885-354-0) Human Sci Pr.

Beaufay, Gabriel. Dinosaurs & Other Extinct Animals. (Illus.). 80p. (gr. 7 up). 1987. pap. 4.95 (0-8120-3836-3) Barron.

Beaumont, de Leprince De see De Leprince de Beaumont.

Beaumont, Francis see Bald, Robert C.

Beaumont, Madame de see De Beaumont, Madame.

Beauregard, Diane C. de see De Beauregard, Diane C.

Beauregard, Diane Costa De see Costa de Beauregard, Diane.

Beautier, Francois. Descubrir la Tierra (Discover the Earth) Calzada, Francisco-Javier, tr. Davot, Francois, illus. (SPA.). 96p. (gr. 4 up). 1992. PLB 15.90 (1-56294-175-5) Millbrook Pr.

Beauvoir, Simone de see De Beauvoir, Simone.

Beauzile, Anthony L. & Beauzile, Gerard, Jr. Kartik Trivedi, Contemporary Impressionist. Fairhall, Winnifred, ed. Trivedi, Kartik, illus. (Orig.). (gr. 10-12). 1992. 95.95g (0-9633124-1-3); pap. 34.95g (0-685-62455-2) T&T Dyno-Srvs.

Beauzile, Gerard, Jr., jt. auth. see Beauzile, Anthony L.

Beaver, Edmund. Travel Games. (gr. 4 up). 1974. pap. 1.00 (0-910208-01-8) Beavers.

Beazley, Frank, jt. auth. see Norman, Jane.

Becerra de Jenkins, Lyll. Celebrating the Hero. (Illus.). 160p. (gr. 7 up). 1993. 15.99 (0-525-67399-7, Lodestar Bks) Dutton Child Bks.

Bech, Bente, illus. Hot on the Scent. Lind, Peter, contrib. by. LC 92-8782. (Illus.). 32p. (ps-3). 1993. PLB 17.27 (0-8368-0510-0); PLB 17.27 s.p. (0-685-61501-4) Gareth Stevens Inc.

Bechard, Margaret. My Sister, My Science Report. 96p. (gr. 3-7). 1990. pap. 11.95 (0-670-83290-1) Viking Child Bks.

—My Sister, My Science Report. 96p. (gr. 3-7). 1992. pap. 4.99 (0-14-034408-X, Puffin) Puffin Bks.

—Tory & Me & the Spirit of True Love. LC 92-5821. 156p. (gr. 3-7). 1992. 14.00 (0-670-84688-0) Viking Child Bks.

Bechtel, Beverly. Lancelot the Ocelot. Horvat, Laurel M., illus. 32p. (gr. k-3). 1991. PLB 18.95 (0-87614-687-6) Carolrhoda Bks.

Bechtel, Faythelma. God's Marvelous Gifts. (gr. 5). 1982. 13.75x (0-87813-920-6) Christian Light.

Beck, Amanda. The Pegasus Club & Me. Yoshi Miyake, illus. LC 91-38330. 32p. (gr. 2-6). 1992. PLB 17.96 (0-8114-3577-6) Raintree Steck-V.

Beck, Ian. Emily & the Golden Acorn. LC 91-4510. (ps-3). 1992. pap. 14.00 (0-671-75979-5, S&S BFYR) S&S Trade.

—Five Little Ducks. LC 92-27193. (Illus.). 32p. (ps-2). 1993. PLB 14.95 (0-8050-2525-1, Bks Young Read) H Holt & Co.

—The Teddy Robber. (Illus.). 32p. (ps-3). 1993. 12.95 (0-8120-6401-1); pap. text ed. 5.95 (0-8120-1711-0) Barron.

Beck, Ian, jt. ed. see Williams, Sarah.

Beck, Jerry. I Tawt I Taw a Puddy Tat: Tweety & Sylvester's Golden Jubilee. 192p. 1991. 35.00 (0-8050-1644-9) H Holt & Co.

Beck, Margaret. Madugu. Whitney, Dick, illus. 26p. (gr. k-6). 1987. pap. text ed. 5.50 (1-55976-052-4) CEF Press.

Beck, Martine. Rescue of Brown Bear & White Bear. (ps-3). 1991. 14.95 (0-316-08654-1) Little.

—Wedding of Brown Bear & White Bear, Vol. 1. (ps-3). 1990. 12.95 (0-316-08652-5) Little.

Beck, Mary L. Heroes & Heroines in Tlingit-Haida Legend. DeWitt, Nancy, illus. LC 89-14931. 126p. (Orig.). (gr. 8 up). 1989. pap. 12.95 (0-88240-334-6) Alaska Northwest.

Beck, Michael & Scott, Judy. Geography: United States: Geography - History - Maps - Flags (Through Research Activities) Beck, Michael, illus. 240p. (Orig.). (gr. 4-6). 1990. pap. text ed. 20.00 (0-927867-00-1) Skippingstone Pr.

Beck, Ray & Gabriel, Suellen. Project RIDE Program Manual: Responding to Individual Differences in Education. (gr. k-6). 1988. tchr's. ed. 13.00 (0-944584-09-8) Sopris.

Beck, Sara. Fanshen the Magic Bear. (Illus.). (gr. 1-5). 1973. 4.95 (0-938678-01-9) New Seed.

Beck, Susan E. God Loves Me Bible. (ps) 1993. 7.99 (0-310-91652-6) Zondervan.

Beck, Trudy, jt. auth. see Green, Laurel.

Beckelman, Laurie. Alzheimer's Disease. LC 89-25251. (Illus.). 48p. (gr. 4 up). 1990. RSBE 12.95 (0-89686-489-8, Crestwood Hse) Macmillan Child Grp.

—Body Blues. LC 93-31778. 1994. write for info. (0-89686-842-7, Crestwood Hse) Macmillan Child Grp.

—The Homeless. LC 89-1432. (Illus.). 48p. (gr. 4 up). 1989. RSBE 12.95 (0-89686-439-1, Crestwood Hse) Macmillan Child Grp.

—Loneliness. LC 93-5625. 1994. write for info. (0-89686-843-5, Crestwood Hse) Macmillan Child Grp.

—Transplants. LC 90-33665. (Illus.). 48p. (gr. 5-6). 1990. RSBE 12.95 (0-89686-572-X, Crestwood Hse) Macmillan Child Grp.

Becker, Antoinette & Reuter, Eisabeth. Best Friends. (gr. 1-4). 1993. 12.95 (0-943706-18-1) Yllw Brick Rd.

Becker, Elizabeth. America's Vietnam War: A Narrative History. 160p. (gr. 7 up). 1992. 15.45 (0-395-59094-9, Clarion Bks) HM.

Becker, Eve. The Love Potion. (gr. 4-7). 1989. pap. 2.75 (0-553-15731-0, Skylark) Bantam.

—The Magic Mix-Up. (gr. 4-7). 1989. pap. 2.75 (0-553-15770-1, Skylark) Bantam.

—The Sneezing Spell. (gr. 4-7). 1990. pap. 2.75 (0-553-15774-4, Skylark) Bantam.

—Thirteen Means Magic. (gr. 4-7). 1989. pap. 2.75 (0-553-15730-2, Skylark) Bantam.

—Too Much Magic. (gr. 4-7). 1990. pap. 2.75 (0-553-15785-X) Bantam.

Becker, Jan, et al. Enhance Chance. (Illus., Orig.). (gr. k-9). 1973. pap. 7.95 (0-918932-10-6) Activity Resources.

Becker, Jane R., tr. see Billiet, Daniel.

Becker, Jim. You Can Name 100 Trucks! Chewning, Randy, illus. 14p. (ps). 1994. bds. 8.95 (0-590-46302-0, Cartwheel) Scholastic Inc.

Becker, Jim & Mayer, Andy. Build Your Own Radio. (Illus.). 64p. (Orig.). (gr. 3 up). 1992. incls. radio kit 19.95 (1-56138-071-7) Running Pr.

—Build Your Own Telephone. LC 93-83372. (Illus.). 64p. (Orig.). (gr. 5 up). 1993. pap. 25.00 (0-679-83444-3) Random Bks Yng Read.

—Where Does Little Car Go? 1992. 4.95 (0-590-44911-7, Cartwheel) Scholastic Inc.

—Where Does Little Puppy Go? 1992. 4.95 (0-590-44912-5, Cartwheel) Scholastic Inc.

Becker, John. Seven Little Rabbits. Cooney, Barbara, illus. 32p. 1991. pap. 3.95 (0-590-44849-8, Blue Ribbon Bks) Scholastic Inc.

Becker, Kayla M. & Heckert, Connie K. To Keera with Love: Abortion, Adoption, or Keeping the Baby, The Story of One Teen's Choice. LC 87-62400. (Illus.). 190p. (Orig.). 1987. pap. 8.95 (1-55612-072-9) Sheed & Ward MO.

Becker, Lois & Stratton, Mark. Little Miss Muffet. Alchemy II, Inc. Staff, illus. 26p. (ps). 1988. incl. cassette 9.95 (1-55578-922-6) Worlds Wonder.

—Mistress Mary. Alchemy II, Inc. Staff, illus. 26p. (ps). 1988. incl. cassette 9.95 (1-55578-920-X) Worlds Wonder.

—Muppet Babies on Twinkledink. Alchemy II, Inc., illus. 26p. (ps up). 1987. 12.95 (1-55578-606-5) Worlds Wonder.

Becker, Lois, ed. see Grimm, Jacob & Grimm, Wilhelm K.

Becker, Mary, ed. see Baron, Phil.

Becker, Mary, ed. see Forsse, Ken & Hughes, Margaret.

Becker, Mary, ed. see Hughes, Margaret A.

Becker, Mary, ed. see Ryan, Will.

Becker, Maurice. Biology Flipper. (Illus.). 49p. (gr. 5 up). 1988. Repr. of 1977 ed. 15.95 (1-878383-05-1) C Lee Pubns.

Becker, Melissa. My Family Helps: A Missions Activity Book for Preschoolers. Gross, Karen, ed. 24p. (Orig.). (ps). 1993. pap. text ed. 3.95 (1-56309-080-5, New Hope) Womans Mission Union.

Becker, R. Margot. Ann M. Martin: The Story of the Author of the Baby-Sitters Club. (gr. 4-7). 1993. pap. 3.50 (0-590-45877-9) Scholastic Inc.

Becker, Sandi, jt. auth. see Kaplan, Carol.

Becker, Sheila. VerbMaster: French. Collins, Stephen, ed. (FRE.). 28p. (Orig.). (gr. 9 up). 1990. pap. 4.95 (0-9626328-2-1) F One Servs.

Becker, Shirley. Buddy's Shadow. Fargo, Todd, illus. 32p. (ps-2). 1992. Repr. of 1991 ed. 13.95 (0-944727-19-0) Jason & Nordic Pubs.

—Buddy's Shadow. (Illus.). 32p. (ps-2). 1991. pap. 6.95 (0-944727-08-5) Jason & Nordic Pubs.

Becker, Suzy, et al. The All Better Book. LC 92-50282. (Illus.). 1992. pap. 5.95 (1-56305-314-4, 3314) Workman Pub.

Becker, Verne. Campus Life Guide to Surviving High School. 1990. pap. 7.99 (0-310-71001-4) Zondervan.

Beckett, Jim. Incan Gold. 176p. (Orig.). 1988. pap. 2.50 (0-553-27415-5) Bantam.

Beckett, John. World's Weirdest "True" Ghost Stories. Hayhurst, Steve, illus. LC 91-15408. 96p. (gr. 4 up). 1992. 12.95 (0-8069-8410-4); pap. 3.95 (0-8069-8411-2) Sterling.

Becklahn, John. Population Explosion. 1990. PLB 12.90 (0-531-17198-1, Gloucester Pr) Watts.

Becklake, John & Becklake, Sue. Food & Farming. (Illus.). 40p. (gr. 6-9). 1991. PLB 12.90 (0-531-17288-0, Gloucester Pr) Watts.

Becklake, Sue. Space, Stars, Planets & Spacecraft. LC 91-60144. (Illus.). 64p. (gr. 3 up). 1991. 11.95 (1-879431-14-9); PLB 12.99 (1-879431-29-7) Dorling Kindersley.

—Traveling in Space. LC 90-11017. (Illus.). 32p. (gr. 4-6). 1991. PLB 11.89 (0-8167-2136-X); pap. text ed. 3.95 (0-8167-2137-8) Troll Assocs.

—Waste Disposal & Recycling. LC 91-9702. (Illus.). 40p. (gr. 5-8). 1991. PLB 12.90 (0-531-17305-4, Gloucester Pr) Watts.

Becklake, Sue, jt. auth. see Becklake, John.

Beckman, Beatrice. I Can Be a Teacher. LC 84-23236. (Illus.). 32p. (gr. k-3). 1985. PLB 14.60 (0-516-01843-4); pap. 3.95 (0-516-41843-2) Childrens.

—I Can Be President. LC 84-12653. (Illus.). 32p. (gr. k-3). 1984. PLB 14.60 (0-516-01841-8); pap. 3.95 (0-516-41841-6) Childrens.

—Puedo Ser Maestra: (I Can Be a Teacher) LC 84-23236. (SPA.). 32p. (gr. k-3). 1989. PLB 13.93 (0-516-31843-8); pap. 3.95 (0-516-51843-7) Childrens.

Beckman, Beverly. Senses in God's World. 24p. (ps). 1986. 6.99 (0-570-04150-3, 56-1604) Concordia.

—Shapes in God's World. LC 56-1462. (ps-k). 1984. 6.99 (0-570-04094-9) Concordia.

—Sizes in God's World. (ps-k). 1984. 6.99 (0-570-04095-7, 56-1463) Concordia.

Beckman, Gunnel. Mia Alone. Tate, Joan, tr. 112p. (gr. 7 up). 1978. pap. 1.25 (0-440-95586-6, LFL) Dell.

Beckman, Jean, ed. see Lindstrom, Marilyn.

Beckman, Jean E. Why? There Is More to You Than Meets the Eye. (Illus.). 50p. (Orig.). (gr. 9-12). 1981. pap. 4.25 (0-941992-00-4) Los Arboles Pub.

Beckman, Kaj. Lisa Can't Sleep. Beckman, Per, illus. 28p. (ps). 1990. 7.95 (91-29-59768-4, Pub. by R & S Bks) FS&G.

Beckman, Beverly. Emotions in God's World. 24p. (ps-1). 1986. 6.99 (0-570-04149-X, 56-1610) Concordia.

—Numbers in God's World. (ps). 1983. 6.99 (0-570-04083-3, 56-1438) Concordia.

—Seasons in God's World. Bowser, Carolyn E., illus. 24p. (gr. 2-5). 1985. 6.99 (0-570-04127-9, 56-1538) Concordia.

—Time in God's World. Edler, Jules, illus. 24p. (gr. 2-5). 1985. 6.99 (0-570-04128-7, 56-1539) Concordia.

Bedard, Michael. A Darker Magic. LC 86-28829. 208p. (gr. 5-9). 1987. SBE 14.95 (0-689-31342-X, Atheneum Child Bk) Macmillan Child Grp.

—A Darker Magic. 192p. 1989. pap. 2.95 (0-380-70611-3, Flare) Avon.

—Emily. Cooney, Barbara, illus. LC 91-41806. 40p. (gr. k-3). 1992. 16.00 (0-385-30697-0) Doubleday.

—The Nightingale. Ricci, Regolo, illus. (gr. k-4). 1992. 14.95 (0-395-60735-3, Clarion Bks) HM.

—Painted Devil. LC 92-35637. 224p. (gr. 5-9). 1994. SBE 16.95 (0-689-31827-8, Atheneum Child Bk) Macmillan Child Grp.

—Redwork. LC 89-27983. 240p. (gr. 7 up). 1990. SBE 15.95 (0-689-31622-4, Atheneum Child Bk) Macmillan Child Grp.

—Redwork. 224p. 1992. pap. 3.50 (0-380-71612-7, Flare) Avon.

Beddow, Bruce R. Draw a Dragon Book: An Artbook for Children Who Draw Their Own Thing. (ps-5). 1991. pap. 6.95 (0-533-09240-X) Vantage.

Bedford, Nancy, tr. see Caldwell, Louise.

Bedford, Viola & Richtel, Anne. It's Okay to Paint a Purple Turtle. Pocick, Margo, illus. 24p. (Orig.). (gr. k-8). 1991. 8.95 (0-938911-07-4) Indiv Educ Syst.

Bedik. Our President: Bill Clinton. 1993. pap. 2.50 (0-590-47126-0) Scholastic Inc.

Bedley, Janet. Promises Broken, Promises Kept. 224p. 1991. pap. 5.99 (1-55513-609-5, 36095) Cook.

Bedoukian, Kerop. Some of Us Survived: The Story of an Armenian Boy. LC 79-10601. 186p. (gr. 6 up). 1979. 15.00 (0-374-37132-6) FS&G.

Bedoyere, C. de la see Johnson, Peter D.

Bee, Cindy. A Big House, a Little Girl & a Few Things That Made Them Laugh. Jesionowski, Mary & Schnickel, Jacob, illus. 20p. (Orig.). (ps-5). 1990. pap. 2.75 (0-9616308-1-7) Hearthstn Inn.

Bee, Clair. Dugout Jinx. (Illus.). 208p. 1990. Repr. lib. bdg. 21.95x (0-89966-741-4) Buccaneer Bks.

Bee, Robert L. The Yuma. (Illus.). 112p. (gr. 5 up). 1989. 17.95 (1-55546-737-7) Chelsea Hse.

Bee, Ronald J., jt. auth. see Feldbaum, Carl B.

Beebe, Brooke M. & Rosenblatt, Ruth Y. The Dictionary. Maas, Mieke, illus. LC 77-730283. (gr. 3-5). 1977. pap. text ed. 165.00 4 filmstrips, 4 cass., 24 skill sheets, Guide (0-89290-121-7, A151-SATC) Soc for Visual.

Beebe, Catherine. Saint John Bosco & the Children's Saint Dominic Savio. 2nd ed. LC 92-71930. 157p. 1992. pap. 9.95 (0-89870-416-2) Ignatius Pr.

Beebe, Hank. The Other Person's Shoes. (Illus.). 20p. (Orig.). (gr. 6-12). 1992. pap. 3.00 (0-88680-366-7); piano-vocal score 10.00 (0-88680-367-5); royalty on application 35.00 (0-685-62711-X) I E Clark.

Beecham, Jahnna. Dance With Me. 192p. 1987. pap. 2.50 (0-317-65473-X, Sweet Dreams) Bantam.

—The Right Combination, No. 139. 192p. (Orig.). (gr. 5 up). 1988. pap. 2.50 (0-553-27005-2, Sweet Dreams) Bantam.

Beechick, Ruth. An Easy Start in Arithmetic: Grades K-3. 32p. (Orig.). (gr. k-3). 1986. pap. text ed. 4.00 (0-940319-01-2) Arrow Press.

—A Home Start in Reading: Grades K-3. 1985. pap. 4.00 (0-940319-00-4) Arrow Press.

—A Strong Start in Language: Grades K-3. 32p. (Orig.). (gr. k-3). 1986. pap. 4.00 (0-940319-02-0) Arrow Press.

Beechman, Dolly, jt. auth. see Sternberg, Pat.

Beeck, Johannes, et al. Telefon. Baker, Syd, illus. Winitz, Harris, intro. by. (GER., Illus.). 50p. (gr. 7 up). 1990. Incls. cass. tape. pap. text ed. 22.00 (0-939990-70-9) Intl Linguistics.

Beegle, Shirley. Bible Double Trouble Puzzles. Dilley, Romilda, illus. 64p. (gr. 5 up). 1992. wkbk. 6.99 (0-87403-671-2, 28-02791) Standard Pub.

Beek, Deborah van der see Van der Beek, Deborah.
Beek, Tom Van see Van Beek, Tom.
Beer, Hans de see Bos, Burny.
Beer, Hans de see De Beer, Hans.
Beer, Hans de see De Beer, Hans & De Beer, Hans.
Beers, Dorothy S. The Gecko. (Illus.). 60p. (gr. 3 up). 1990. RSBE 13.95 (0-87518-441-3, Dillon) Macmillan Child Grp.
—The Prairie Dog. LC 90-3327. (Illus.). 60p. (gr. 3 up). 1990. RSBE 13.95 (0-87518-444-8, Dillon) Macmillan Child Grp.

Beers, Gil & Hagler, Elizabeth. The Early Reader's Bible. 528p. (gr. 3-8). 1991. 15.99 (0-945564-43-0, Gold & Honey) Questar Pubs.
Fun to Learn...Easy to Read! Here's the Bible young children can fully enjoy on their own--& one that's specially designed to strengthen their beginning reader skills! This is a once-in-a-lifetime book for kids, a special companion during a special time in childhood when the discovery of reading unfolds. And this book will help develop not only their love for reading, but also their love for the Bible. THE EARLY READER'S BIBLE is vocabulary-controlled. The text in each story is taken from a 250-word basic vocabulary list developed from public school reading materials. (In each story, an average of three new words are also taught.) The text is written in short, simple sentences, & set in a clear typeface particularly recommended for children. And on every page of each story is a big, bright, colorful picture to enhance the text! 64 short, easy-to-read Bible stories; Activity pages & fun, life-centered questions following each story; Complete listing of all basic words & all new words used in the text; Bright, colorful pictures on every page; Includes list of moral & spiritual values taught in each story; Complete index to stories & Scriptural references. Order from Questar Publishers, P.O. Box 1720, Sisters, OR 97759, 503-549-1144.
Publisher Provided Annotation.

Beers, Ronald A., jt. auth. see Beers, V. Gilbert.
Beers, V. Gilbert. Friends Are Helpers. Eubank, Mary G., illus. 12p. (ps-2). 1991. bds. 3.99 (0-8010-0997-9) Baker Bk.
—Friends Give Good Gifts. Eubank, Mary G., illus. 12p. (ps-2). 1991. bds. 3.99 (0-8010-0998-7) Baker Bk.
—Friends Play Together. Eubank, Mary G., illus. 12p. (ps-2). 1991. bds. 3.99 (0-8010-0999-5) Baker Bk.
—Friends Share. Eubank, Mary G., illus. 12p. (ps-2). 1991. bds. 3.99 (0-8010-0996-0) Baker Bk.
—Growing up with God's Friends. Endres, Helen, illus. LC 87-81046. 94p. (Orig.). (ps-7). 1987. 12.99 (0-89081-528-3) Harvest Hse.
—Growing up with Jesus. Endres, Helen, illus. LC 87-81043. 94p. (Orig.). (ps-7). 1987. 12.99 (0-89081-525-9) Harvest Hse.
—Little Talks about God & You. 224p. (Orig.). (ps-2). 1986. pap. 9.99 (0-89081-519-4) Harvest Hse.
—More Little Talks about God & You. LC 87-81042. 224p. (Orig.). (ps-3). 1987. pap. 9.99 (0-89081-586-0) Harvest Hse.
—My Bedtime Anytime Storybook. O'Connor, Tim, illus. LC 92-8376. 1992. 12.99 (0-8407-9166-6) Oliver-Nelson.
—My Picture Bible to See & to Share. 189p. (ps-4). 1982. text ed. 14.99 (0-88207-818-6, Sonflower Bks) SP Pubns.
—My Sunny Day, & Day Nursery Rhyme Book. O'Connor, Tim, illus. LC 93-17261. 1993. 12.99 (0-8407-9253-0) Nelson.
—Precious Moments Read-Aloud Stories, Bk. 1. Wiersma, Debbie B., ed. Butcher, Samuel J., tr. (Illus.). 256p. (gr. 4 up). 1991. 11.95 (0-8010-1015-2) Baker Bk.
—Precious Moments Through-the-Day Stories. Butcher, Samuel J., illus. LC 90-1265. 256p. 1991. 14.99 (0-8010-0992-8) Baker Bk.
—Toddlers Bedtime Storybook. Boerke, Carol, illus. 352p. (ps). 1993. 14.99 (1-56476-181-9, Victor Books) SP Pubns.

—The Toddler's Bible. (ps). 1992. 14.99 (0-89693-077-7, Victor Books) SP Pubns.
—Toddlers Bible Library. (ps). 1993. 10.99 (1-56476-150-9, Victor Books) SP Pubns.
Beers, V. Gilbert & Beers, Ronald A. Bible Stories to Live by, Old Testament. De Jonge, Reint, illus. 96p. (gr. k-3). 1991. 12.99 (0-8407-3506-5) Nelson.
—The Big Book of All-Time Favorite Bible Stories. Hochstatter, Daniel J., illus. LC 92-8306. 1992. 12.99 (0-8407-9165-8) Oliver-Nelson.
—Growing God's Way to See & Share. 192p. (gr. 7 up). 1987. pap. 14.99 (0-89693-801-8, Victor Books) SP Pubns.
—Little People in Tough Spots: Bible Answers for Young Children. (Illus.). 144p. 1992. 7.99 (0-8407-9157-7) Oliver-Nelson.
Beers, V. Gilbert & Morris, C. Spencer. Beginners ABC Bible Memory Book. 288p. (Orig.). (ps-8). 12.99 (0-945564-41-4, Gold & Honey) Questar Pubs.
Beers, V. Gilbert, text by. Precious Moments Through-the-Year Stories. Butcher, Samuel J., illus. LC 89-17848. 288p. (gr. 2-6). 1989. 14.99 (0-8010-0973-1) Baker Bk.
Beeson, Bob. Ten Little Circus Mice. Beeson, Bob, illus. 32p. (ps-1). 1993. 11.95 (0-8249-8616-4, Ideals Child) Hambleton-Hill.
Begarnie, Luke. Fighters, Choppers & Bombers. (Illus.). 32p. 1987. pap. 3.95 (0-590-40738-4) Scholastic Inc.
Begay, Shonto. Ma'ii & Cousin Horned Toad. (Illus.). 1992. 14.95 (0-590-45391-2, Scholastic Hardcover) Scholastic Inc.
Begaye, Lisa S. Building a Bridge. Tracy, Libba, illus. LC 92-82138. 32p. (gr. k). 1993. 14.95 (0-87358-557-7) Northland AZ.
Begin, S., et al. Suspicious Minds: A Radio Play Developing Listening Strategies & Lifeskills. 1990. pap. text ed. 13.50 (0-8013-0287-0, 75937); cass. 37.95 (0-8013-0288-9, 75938) Longman.
Beglar, David & Murray, Neil. Contemporary Topics: Advanced Listening Comprehension. LC 92-39791. 1993. pap. text ed. 19.95 (0-8013-0928-X); 4 cassettes 66.00 (0-8013-0929-8) Longman.
Beguinot, Brigitte. The Mouse Party: An Open-the-Door Book. Beguinot, Brigitte, illus. 12p. (ps-3). 1992. bds. 10.95 (1-878093-50-9) Boyds Mills Pr.
Behal, J. K. India Today. 200p. (Orig.). (gr. 12). 1993. pap. text ed. 14.95 (0-9628328-1-2) Starlite Inc.
Behm, Barbara. The Story of Medicine. LC 91-11739. (Illus.). 64p. (gr. 2-3). 1991. PLB 19.93 (0-8368-0049-4) Gareth Stevens Inc.
Behm, Barbara, ed. The Index. (Illus.). 96p. (gr. 3-8). 1987. PLB 233.33 set (0-317-62824-0); pap. 13.25 (0-8172-3062-9) Raintree Steck-V.
Behm, Barbara J., ed. Ask about the Earth & the Sky. (Illus.). 64p. (gr. 4-5). 1987. PLB 19.92 (0-8172-2876-4) Raintree Steck-V.
Behm, Barbara J., adapted by. Investigating the Color Blue. LC 93-23815. 1993. write for info. (0-8368-1028-7) Gareth Stevens Inc.
Behm, Barbara J., ed. Investigating the Color Green. LC 93-23816. 1993. write for info. (0-8368-1029-5) Gareth Stevens Inc.
Behm, Barbara J., adapted by. Investigating the Color Red. LC 93-23817. 1993. write for info. (0-8368-1027-9) Gareth Stevens Inc.
—Investigating the Color Yellow. LC 93-23814. 1993. write for info. (0-8368-1030-9) Gareth Stevens Inc.
Behm, Tom. How Things Happen in Three: A Participation Musical. (Orig.). (gr. k-3). 1992. pap. 4.50 playscript (0-87602-317-0) Anchorage.
Behm, Tom, adapted by. Tarheel Tales. 35p. (Orig.). 1990. Playscript. pap. 4.50 (0-87602-292-1) Anchorage.
Behme, Robert L. Incredible Plants: Oddities, Curiosities & Eccentricities. LC 91-38788. (Illus.). 132p. (gr. 6-12). 1992. 14.95 (0-8069-8244-6) Sterling.
—Incredible Plants: Oddities, Curiosities & Eccentricities. (Illus.). 128p. (gr. 5-10). 1993. pap. 7.95 (0-8069-8245-4) Sterling.
Behn, Harry. Trees. Endicott, James, illus. LC 91-25179. 32p. (ps-2). 1992. 14.95 (0-8050-1926-X, B Martin BYR) H Holt & Co.
Behn, Robin. Paper Bird. LC 87-51682. 88p. 1988. 15.95 (0-89672-164-7); pap. 9.95 (0-89672-163-9) Tex Tech Univ Pr.
Behr, Sheila, jt. auth. see Brainard, Beth.
Behrangi, Samad. The Tale of the Little Black Fish: Mahi Siah Kuchulu. Amuzegar, Hooshang, tr. Javan, Yousef J., illus. LC 91-73480. (PER & ENG). 72p. (Orig.). 1992. pap. 6.95 (0-936347-20-1) Iran Bks.
Behrendt, Bill L. Pocket Magic: Graphic Games for the Pocket Computer. LC 82-80271. (Illus.). 96p. (Orig.). 1982. 17.95 (0-685-05521-3); pap. 9.95 (0-942412-01-X); pre-recorded cassette 8.95 (0-686-87025-5) Micro Text Pubns.
Behrendt, Fred, et al. Perils of the Young Kingdoms. Brooks, Les, ed. Bjorksten, Gus, et al, illus. 128p. (Orig.). (gr. 7 up). 1991. pap. text ed. 18.95 (0-933635-82-6, 2113) Chaosium.
—Tales of the Miskatonic Valley. Brooks, Les, ed. Bjorksten, Gus, et al, illus. 128p. (Orig.). (gr. 7 up). 1992. pap. text ed. 18.95 (0-933635-83-4, 2334) Chaosium.
Behrens, Debra J., ed. see Thompson-Peters, Flossie E.
Behrens, June. Barbara Bush: First Lady of Literacy. LC 90-2201. (Illus.). 32p. (gr. 2-5). 1990. PLB 14.60 (0-516-04275-0); pap. 3.95 (0-516-44275-9) Childrens.

—Dolphins! LC 89-33846. 48p. (gr. 1-4). 1989. PLB 15.00 (0-516-00517-0); pap. 5.95 (0-516-40517-9) Childrens.
—Fiesta! Taylor, Scott, illus. LC 78-8468. 32p. (gr. k-4). 1978. PLB 15.00 (0-516-08815-7, Golden Gate); pap. 3.95 (0-516-48815-5) Childrens.
—Fiesta! Kratky, Lada, tr. LC 85-23271. (SPA, Illus.). 32p. (ps-3). 1986. PLB 15.00 (0-516-38815-0); pap. 3.95 (0-516-58815-X) Childrens.
—George Bush: Forty-First President of the United States. LC 89-693. (Illus.). 32p. (gr. 2-4). 1989. PLB 14.60 (0-516-04172-X); pap. 3.95 (0-516-44172-8) Childrens.
—Gung Hay Fat Choy. LC 81-17077. (gr. 1-4). 1982. 15.00 (0-516-08842-4); pap. 3.95 (0-516-48842-2) Childrens.
—Hanukkah. Behrens, Terry, illus. LC 82-17890. 32p. (gr. k-4). 1983. PLB 15.00 (0-516-02386-1); pap. 3.95 (0-516-42386-X) Childrens.
—I Can Be a Nurse. LC 85-29086. (Illus.). 32p. (gr. k-3). 1986. PLB 14.60 (0-516-01893-0) Childrens.
—I Can Be a Pilot. LC 85-10961. 32p. (gr. k-3). 1985. PLB 14.60 (0-516-01888-4); pap. 3.95 (0-516-41888-2) Childrens.
—I Can Be a Truck Driver. LC 84-23246. (Illus.). 32p. (gr. k-3). 1985. PLB 14.60 (0-516-01848-5) Childrens.
—I Can Be an Astronaut. LC 84-7601. (Illus.). 32p. (gr. k-3). 1984. PLB 14.60 (0-516-01837-X); pap. 3.95 (0-516-41837-8) Childrens.
—Juliette Low: Founder of the Girl Scouts of America. LC 88-11976. (Illus.). 32p. (gr. 2-4). 1988. PLB 14.60 (0-516-04171-1); pap. 3.95 (0-516-44171-X) Childrens.
—El Libro de los Modales (The Manners Book) LC 79-22377. (SPA., Illus.). 32p. (gr. k-3). 1987. PLB 15.00 (0-516-38750-2); pap. 3.95 (0-516-58750-1) Childrens.
—Martin Luther King, Jr. The Story of a Dream. Siberell, Anne, illus. LC 78-23873. 32p. (gr. k-4). 1979. PLB 15.93 (0-516-08879-3, Golden Gate) Childrens.
—Passover. Behrens, Terry, illus. LC 87-5161. 32p. (gr. k-4). 1987. pap. 3.95 (0-516-42389-4) Childrens.
—Puedo Ser Conductor de Camion (I Can Be a Truck Driver) Kratky, Lada, tr. LC 85-31402. (SPA, Illus.). 32p. (gr. k-3). 1986. PLB 13.93 (0-516-31848-9); pap. 3.95 (0-516-51848-8) Childrens.
—Puedo Ser Enfermera (I Can Be a Nurse) LC 85-29086. (SPA., Illus.). 32p. (ps-2). 1988. PLB 13.93 (0-516-31893-4); pap. 3.95 (0-516-51893-3) Childrens.
—Puedo Ser un Astronauta (I Can Be an Astronaut) Kratky, Lada, tr. from ENG. LC 84-7601. (SPA., Illus.). 32p. (gr. k-3). 1984. PLB 13.93 (0-516-31837-3); pap. 3.95 (0-516-51837-2) Childrens.
—Ronald Reagan: An All-American. LC 81-9993. (Illus.). 32p. (gr. 2 up). 1981. PLB 14.60 (0-516-03565-7) Childrens.
—Sally Ride, Astronaut: An American First. LC 83-23173. (Illus.). 32p. (gr. 2-5). 1984. PLB 14.60 (0-516-03606-8); pap. 3.95 (0-516-43606-6) Childrens.
—Sharks! LC 89-25375. (Illus.). 48p. (gr. 1-4). 1990. PLB 15.00 (0-516-00571-5); pap. 5.95 (0-516-40571-3) Childrens.
—Whales of the World. LC 87-8046. (Illus.). 48p. (gr. 1-4). 1987. PLB 15.00 (0-516-08877-7); pap. 4.95 (0-516-48877-5) Childrens.
—Whalewatch! Olguin, John, illus. LC 78-7338. 32p. (gr. k-4). 1978. PLB 13.67 (0-516-08873-4, Golden Gate); pap. 3.95 (0-516-48873-2) Childrens.
Behrens, June & Brower, Pauline. California Missions. LC 93-13190. 1993. write for info. (0-516-05371-X) Childrens.
Behrens, Michael. At the Edge. 208p. (gr. 7 up). 1988. pap. 2.95 (0-380-75610-2, Flare) Avon.
Behrens, Terry. Powwow. LC 83-7274. (Illus.). 32p. (gr. k-4). 1983. pap. 3.95 (0-516-42387-8) Childrens.
Behrman, Carol H. The Lancaster Witch. 160p. (gr. 5-8). 1993. pap. 2.99 (0-87406-645-X) Willowisp Pr.
Beil, Karen M. Grandma According to Me. Rand, Ted, illus. LC 91-10624. 32p. (ps-3). 1992. pap. 15.00 (0-385-41484-6) Doubleday.
Beilenson, John. Sukarno. Schlsinger, Arthur M., intro. by. (Illus.). 112p. (gr. 5 up). 1990. 17.95 (1-55546-853-5) Chelsea Hse.
Beiler, Edna. Mattie Mae. Graber, E. R., illus. LC 67-24800. 128p. (gr. 3-7). 1967. pap. 5.95 (0-8361-1789-1) Herald Pr.
Beiner, Stan J. Sedra Scenes: Skits for Every Torah Portion. LC 82-71282. 225p. (Orig.). (gr. 6-12). 1982. pap. text ed. 9.75 (0-86705-007-1) A R E Pub.
Beirne, Barbara. A Pianist's Debut: Preparing for the Concert Stage. Beirne, Barbara, photos by. (Illus.). 56p. (gr. 2-5). 1990. PLB 21.50 (0-87614-432-6) Carolrhoda Bks.
—Riders Up: Preparing for a Pony Race. (ps-3). 1992. 21.50 (0-87614-714-7) Carolrhoda Bks.
—Siothan's Journey: A Belfast Girl Visits the United States. (ps-3). 1993. 19.95 (0-87614-728-7) Carolrhoda Bks.
—Under the Lights: A Child Model at Work. (Illus.). 56p. (gr. 2-5). 1988. PLB 21.50 (0-87614-316-8) Carolrhoda Bks.
Beisel, Marvin. Hopalong Purrsnickity. Hill, Sarah, illus. 192p. (ps). 1990. pap. 15.95 (0-9626309-0-X) HoppyTalk Prodns.
Beisert, Heide H. My Magic Cloth: A Story for a Whole Week. Beisert, Heide H., illus. Lewis, Naomi, tr. LC 86-60490. (Illus.). 32p. (gr. k-3). 1986. 14.95 (1-55858-069-7) North-South Bks NYC.

Beisner, Monika. Catch That Cat! A Picture Book of Rhymes & Puzzles. (Illus.). 32p. 1990. 15.00 (0-374-31226-5) FS&G.
—Monika Beisner's Book of Riddles. LC 83-81529. (Illus.). 32p. (ps up). 1983. 15.00 (0-374-30866-7) FS&G.
—Secret Spells & Curious Charms. Beisner, Monika, illus. LC 85-45323. 32p. (ps up). 1986. 15.00 (0-374-36692-6) FS&G.
—Topsy Turvy. LC 87-45751. (Illus.). 32p. (ps up). 1988. 15.00 (0-374-37679-4) FS&G.
Beit-Hallahmi, Benjamin. The Illustrated Encyclopedia of Active New Religions, Sects, & Cults. Rosen, Roger, ed. 1992. 49.95 (0-8239-1505-0) Rosen Group.
Beitler, Stanley, ed. see Green, Belva.
Beittel, Joan N., jt. auth. see Beittel, Kenneth R.
Beittel, Kenneth R. & Beittel, Joan N. Ralph & Deno in Vermont. Beittel, Kenneth R., illus. LC 90-86028. 32p. (Orig.). (gr. 5 up). 1990. pap. 6.00 (0-9628511-0-8) HVHA.
Bekker, Cajus. Hitler's Naval War. (gr. 7 up). 1981. pap. 2.75 (0-89083-759-7) Zebra.
Belanger, Mark. Old Slippery. (gr. 4-7). 1993. pap. 3.95 (0-8114-4305-1) Raintree Steck-V.
—Old Slippery. (Illus.). (gr. 2-6). 1992. PLB 17.96 (0-8114-3576-8) Raintree Steck-V.
Belcastro, Jani. The Old House on the Hill. Belcastro, Jani, illus. LC 92-59951. 44p. (gr. k-3). 1993. 6.95 (1-55523-575-1) Winston-Derek.
Belcher, J. A., ed. Sign Language Dot-to-Dot. new ed. 32p. (ps-3). 1979. 2.95 (0-917002-40-7) Joyce Media.
Belchez, Chito & Moguet, Pamela J. Bikol Newspaper Reader. LC 91-70529. 1992. 44.00 (0-931745-76-4); cassettes 20.00 (0-931745-88-8) Dunwoody Pr.
Belden, Wilanne S. Frankie! LC 86-33507. (Illus.). 163p. (gr. 3-7). 1987. 14.95 (0-15-229380-9) HarBrace.
—Mind-Find. LC 87-11979. 191p. (gr. 7 up). 1988. 14.95 (0-15-254270-1) HarBrace.
Belfiglio, Val. Pride of the Southwest: Outstanding Athletes of the Southwest Conference. Carter, Bo, intro. by. (Illus.). 144p. (gr. 4-7). 1992. 14.95 (0-89015-822-3) Eakin-Sunbelt.
Belfiore, Sammantha. Little, Little Fairy Tales. 1993. 7.95 (0-533-10203-0) Vantage.
Belgrano, Giovanni. Let's Make a Movie. LC 72-90235. (Illus.). 48p. (gr. 4-9). 1973. 9.95 (0-87592-028-4) Scroll Pr.
Belgum, Erik. Artificial Intelligence: Opposing Viewpoints. LC 90-3519. (Illus.). 112p. (gr. 5-8). 1990. PLB 14.95 (0-89908-085-5) Greenhaven.
Belgum, Erik, jt. auth. see Nardo, Don.
Belk, Bradford, jt. auth. see Gangelhoff, Jeanne M.
Belk, C. Joy. Conscious Directional Recipes for the 90s. (Illus.). 50p. (Orig.). 1990. pap. text ed. write for info. (0-9620258-3-6) Babe Co.
Belk, Gordon G., ed. see Schmid-Belk, Donna D.
Bell, Alison. Fifty Frightening Things to Do & Make. Suckow, Will, illus. 64p. 1993. pap. 4.95 (1-56565-067-0) Lowell Hse.
Bell, Alison & Rooney, Lisa. My Body, Myself: An Assuring, Candid Guide for Girls. (Illus.). 144p. 1993. pap. 4.95 (1-56565-045-X) Lowell Hse.
Bell, Anthea. Animal Antics. Janosch, illus. 128p. (gr. k-2). 1987. 17.95 (0-86264-033-4, Pub. by Anderson Pr UK) Trafalgar.
—Swan Lake. Iwasaki, Chihiro, illus. LC 86-9509. 28p. (gr. 1 up). 1991. pap. 15.95 (0-88708-028-6) Picture Bk Studio.
Bell, Anthea, adapted by see Hoffmann, E. T.
Bell, Anthea, tr. see Andersen, Hans Christian.
Bell, Anthea, tr. see Chapouton, Anne-Marie.
Bell, Anthea, tr. see Ende, Michael.
Bell, Anthea, tr. see Fontane, Theodor.
Bell, Anthea, tr. see Grimm, Jacob & Grimm, Wilhelm K.
Bell, Anthea, tr. see Hoffmann, E. T.
Bell, Anthea, tr. see Janisch, Heinz.
Bell, Anthea, tr. see Janosch.
Bell, Anthea, tr. see Nostlinger, Christine.
Bell, Anthea, tr. see Pacovska, Kveta.
Bell, Anthea, tr. see Pfister, Marcus.
Bell, Anthea, tr. see Preussler, Otfried.
Bell, Anthea, tr. see Sonnleitner, A. T.
Bell, Anthea, tr. see Velthuijs, Max.
Bell, Anthea, tr. see Velthuis, Max.
Bell, Bill, illus. Let's Pretend: Poems Collected by Natalie Bober. 72p. (ps-3). 1990. pap. 4.95 (0-14-032132-2, Puffin) Puffin Bks.
Bell, Christina. The Boy with a Toucan in His Heart. 160p. 1990. 39.00x (0-85439-397-8, Pub. by St Paul Pubns UK) St Mut.
Bell, Clare. Clan Ground. (gr. k-12). 1987. pap. 2.95 (0-440-91287-3, LFL) Dell.
—Ratha & Thistle-Chaser. LC 89-36807. 240p. (gr. 7 up). 1990. SBE 14.95 (0-689-50462-4, M K McElderry) Macmillan Child Grp.
—Ratha's Creature. (gr. k-12). 1987. pap. 2.95 (0-440-97298-1, LFL) Dell.
—Tomorrow's Sphinx. (gr. k-12). 1988. pap. 3.25 (0-440-20124-1, LFL) Dell.
Bell, Clarisa. Animals del Circo de Sonora. Sanchez, Jose R., illus. (SPA.). 24p. (Orig.). (gr. k-5). 1993. pap. 9. 95x (1-56492-081-X) Laredo.
—At the Olympics. Kohen, Gabriela, tr. from SPA. Sanchez, Jose R., illus 24p. (Orig.). (gr. 2-6). 1992. pap. 9.95x (1-56492-007-0) Laredo.

—El Circo. Sanchez, Jose R., illus. (SPA.). 24p. (Orig.). (gr. 2-6). 1992.

PLB 9.95x (1-56492-078-X) Laredo. A great artist & a fabulous author have combined efforts to provide an unusual view of circus people. Sparkling color & humor further enhance this book. In Spanish.
Publisher Provided Annotation.

—**En Las Olimpidas. Sanchez, Jose R., illus. (SPA.). 24p. (Orig.). (gr. 2-6). 1992. PLB 9.95x (1-56492-051-8) Laredo. Whoever expected to read about the Olympic games in rhyme...In this simple yet imaginative book, this topic is beautifully brought to life. In Spanish.**
Publisher Provided Annotation.

—Games People Play. Kohen, Gabriela, tr. from SPA. Sanchez, Jose R., illus. 24p. (gr. 2-6). 1992. pap. 9.95x (1-56492-004-6) Laredo.
—Games People Play: Big Book. Kohen, Gabriela, tr. from SPA. Sanchez, Jose R., illus. 24p. (Orig.). (gr. 2-6). 1992. pap. 19.95x (1-56492-005-4) Laredo.
—El Teatro. Sanchez, Jose R., illus. (SPA.). 24p. (gr. 2-6). 1992. pap. 9.95x (1-56492-056-9) Laredo.
—El Teatro: Big Book. Sanchez, Jose R., illus. (SPA.). 24p. (Orig.). (gr. 2-6). 1992. pap. 19.95x (1-56492-057-7) Laredo.
—Vamos a Jugar. Sanchez, Jose R., illus. (SPA.). 24p. (Orig.). (gr. 2-6). 1992. pap. 9.95x (1-56492-048-8) Laredo.
—Vamos a Jugar: Big Book. Sanchez, Jose R., illus. (SPA.). 24p. (Orig.). (gr. 2-6). 1992. pap. 19.95x (1-56492-049-6) Laredo.
Bell, D. Morgans. The Adventures of Ecomunk: Mr. Beaver Builds a Dam. 1992. 8.95 (0-533-10212-X) Vantage.
Bell, Irene W. Literature Cross-A-Word Book I: Crossword Learning Experiences with Animal Stories, Modern Fantasy, & Space & Time. Kirby, Keith, illus. 96p. 1982. pap. 14.75 (0-89774-062-9) Oryx Pr.
Bell, J. L. Soap Science: A Science Book Bubbling with 36 Experiments. (gr. 4-7). 1993. pap. write for info. (0-201-62451-6) Addison-Wesley.
Bell, Jo G. The Day Small Circle Changed His Shape. Conahan, Carolyn, illus. 32p. (ps-2). Date not set. 11. 95 (1-56065-160-1) Capstone Pr. Postponed.
—Hide & Seek with Colors. Conahan, Carolyn, illus. 32p. (ps-2). Date not set. 11.95 (1-56065-158-X) Capstone Pr. Postponed.
—Sometimes I Wish I Were Big. Conahan, Carolyn, illus. 32p. (ps-2). Date not set. 11.95 (1-56065-159-8) Capstone Pr. Postponed.
Bell, Joseph. Sandy of Laguna. Garrison, Ben, illus. 72p. (Orig.). (gr. k-8). 1992. pap. 9.95 (1-880812-01-0) S Ink WA.
Bell, Louise P. Kitchen Fun. 1988. 3.99 (0-517-66927-7) Outlet Bk Co.
Bell, Lucille H. Glow in the Dark Trip to the Planets. (ps-3). 1990. write for info. (0-307-06250-3) Western Pub.
Bell, Marty. The Legend of Dr. J. The Story of Julius Erving. (RL 8). 1976. pap. 2.95 (0-451-12179-1, AE2179, Sig) NAL-Dutton.
—The Legend of Dr. J. The Story of Julius Erving. updated & expanded ed. (Illus.). 192p. (gr. 9-12). 1976. pap. 4.95 (0-451-15464-9, Sig) NAL-Dutton.
Bell, Mary S. Sonata for Mind & Heart. LC 91-20588. 224p. (gr. 7 up). 1992. SBE 14.95 (0-689-31734-4, Atheneum Child Bk) Macmillan Child Grp.
Bell, Nanci & Lindamood, Phyllis. Vanilla Vocabulary: Visualized-Verbalized Vocabulary Book. Lindamood, Phyllis, illus. 200p. (gr. 4-7). Date not set. pap. 19.00 (0-945856-03-2) Acad Reading.
Bell, Neill. The Book of Where: Or How to Be Naturally Geographic. 140p. (gr. 7 up). 1982. pap. 9.95 (0-316-08831-5) Little.
—Only Human: Why We Are the Way We Are. Clifford, Sandy, illus. LC 83-9826. 128p. (gr. 4 up). 1983. 14.95 (0-316-08816-1); pap. 9.95 (0-316-08818-8) Little.
Bell, Owain, illus. The Midnight Ride of Thomas the Tank Engine. LC 93-26587. 1994. 4.99 (0-679-85643-9) Random Bks Yng Read.
—Thomas the Tank Engine Says Goodnight. 12p. (ps-k). 1990. sponge filled 3.99 (0-679-80791-8) Random Bks Yng Read.
—Wave Hello to Thomas! A Thomas the Tank Engine Lift-&-Peek-a-Board Book. Awdry, W., contrib. by. LC 92-80747. (Illus.). 14p. (ps-k). 1993. bds. 3.99 (0-679-83877-5) Random Bks Yng Read.
Bell, Peg, intro. by. Batchin' It Specialties: Cooking for "1 or 2" Can Be Fun. rev. ed. LC 88-92429. 198p. (gr. 8). 1988. plastic comb bdg. 12.95 (0-9621056-0-0) P A Bell Enterps.
Bell, Richard. Deep in the Wood. (Illus.). 28p. (ps-2). 1988. pap. 6.95 (0-434-92849-6, Pub. by W Heinemann Ltd) Trafalgar.
Bell, Rivian, jt. auth. see Koenig, Teresa.
Bell, Rob, ed. see Bennie, Scott.
Bell, Rob, ed. see Brown, Charles.

Bell, Rob, ed. see Dershem, Kurt.
Bell, Robert. My First Book of Space Coloring & Activity Book. Epstein, Len, et al, illus. 160p. (gr. 1 up). 1986. pap. 6.95 (0-671-62407-5, Little Simon) S&S Trade.
Bell, Robert, jt. auth. see Hansen, Rosanna.
Bell, Robert, ed. see Matalon, David.
Bell, Robert A. Crystals. Lopez, Paul, illus. 24p. (gr. k-5). 1992. pap. write for info. blister pk., incl. 3 crystal specimens & magnifying glass (0-307-12856-3, 12856, Golden Pr) Western Pub.
—Fossils. Spence, James, illus. 24p. (gr. k-5). 1992. pap. write for info. blister pk., incl. 4 fossil specimens (0-307-12855-5, 12855, Golden Pr) Western Pub.
Bell, Rosemary. Yurok Tales. Webb, Kathy, illus. 90p. (Orig.). (gr. 4-8). 1992. pap. 9.95 (1-880922-01-0) Bell Bks CA.
Bell, Sally. The Young Indiana Jones Chronicles: Safari in Africa. Vicente, Gonzalez, illus. 48p. (gr. 2-4). 1992. pap. write for info. (0-307-11470-8, 11470, Golden Pr) Western Pub.
Bell, Sam H. The Hollow Ball. 256p. (Orig.). (gr. 10-12). 1990. pap. 11.95 (0-85640-452-7, Pub. by Blackstaff Pr Belfast) Dufour.
Bell, William. Forbidden City. (gr. 7 up). 1990. 14.95 (0-553-07131-9, Starfire); pap. 3.99 (0-553-28864-4, Starfire) Bantam.
Bellairs, John. Chessman of Doom. 1989. 13.95 (0-8037-0729-0) Dial Bks Young.
—Chessman of Doom. (gr. 4-7). 1991. pap. 3.50 (0-553-15884-8) Bantam.
—The Chessmen of Doom. (gr. 4-8). 1992. 16.50 (0-8446-6579-7) Peter Smith.
—The Curse of the Blue Figurine. 208p. (gr. 4-6). 1984. pap. 3.50 (0-553-15540-7, RL6IL4, Skylark) Bantam.
—Dark Secret - Weather. 1986. pap. 3.50 (0-553-15621-7) Bantam.
—The Dark Secret of Weatherend. Gorey, Edward, illus. 208p. (gr. 5 up). 1984. 13.95 (0-8037-0072-5) Dial Bks Young.
—The Dark Secret of Weatherend. 192p. 1986. pap. 2.50 (0-553-15375-7, Skylark) Bantam.
—The Eyes of the Killer Robot. LC 86-2148. 176p. (gr. 5 up). 1986. 11.95 (0-8037-0324-4) Dial Bks Young.
—The Figure in the Shadows. 192p. (gr. 4-7). 1977. pap. 3.50 (0-440-42551-4, YB) Dell.
—The Figure in the Shadows. Mayer, Mercer, illus. LC 74-2885. 168p. (gr. 4-7). 1975. Dial Bks Young.
—The Figure in the Shadows. Mayer, Mercer, illus. LC 92-31362. 160p. (gr. 3 up). 1993. pap. 3.50 (0-14-036337-8, Puffin) Puffin Bks.
—The Ghost in the Mirror. Strickland, Brad, contrib. by. LC 92-18369. 1993. 14.99 (0-8037-1370-3); PLB 14. 89 (0-8037-1371-1) Dial Bks Young.
—The House with a Clock in Its Walls. 192p. (gr. 3 up). 1974. pap. 3.50 (0-440-43742-3, YB) Dell.
—The House with a Clock in Its Walls. Gorey, Edward, illus. LC 92-26794. 192p. (gr. 3 up). 1993. pap. 3.50 (0-14-036336-X, Puffin) Puffin Bks.
—The Lamp from the Warlock's Tomb. LC 87-21404. 176p. (gr. 5 up). 1988. 12.95 (0-8037-0512-3) Dial Bks Young.
—The Lamp from the Warlock's Tomb. (gr. 4-8). 1989. pap. 3.50 (0-553-15697-7, Skylark) Bantam.
—The Letter, the Witch & the Ring. 192p. (gr. 3-6). 1977. pap. 3.25 (0-440-44722-4, YB) Dell.
—The Letter, the Witch, & the Ring. Egielski, Richard, illus. LC 75-28968. (gr. 4-7). 1976. Dial Bks Young.
—The Letter, the Witch, & the Ring. Egielski, Richard, illus. LC 92-31361. 208p. (gr. 3 up). 1993. pap. 3.50 (0-14-036338-6, Puffin) Puffin Bks.
—The Mansion in the Mist. LC 91-29639. 176p. (gr. 5 up). 1992. 15.00 (0-8037-0845-9); PLB 14.89 (0-8037-0846-7) Dial Bks Young.
—The Mansion in the Mist. 176p. (gr. 5 up). 1993. pap. 3.99 (0-14-034933-2, Puffin) Puffin Bks.
—The Mummy, the Will & the Crypt. 176p. (gr. 6). 1985. pap. 2.75 (0-553-15498-2) Bantam.
—Mummy, Will & Crypt. 1985. pap. 3.50 (0-553-15701-9) Bantam.
—The Revenge of the Wizard's Ghost. Gorey, Edward, illus. LC 85-4550. 160p. (gr. 5 up). 1985. 13.95 (0-8037-0170-5) Dial Bks Young.
—The Revenge of the Wizard's Ghost. 160p. 1986. pap. 3.50 (0-553-15451-6) Bantam.
—Secret of the Underground Room. (Illus.). 160p. (ps-3). 1990. 14.00 (0-8037-0863-7); PLB 13.89 (0-8037-0864-5) Dial Bks Young.
—The Secret of the Underground Room. LC 92-17304. 128p. (gr. 5 up). 1992. pap. 3.99 (0-14-034932-4, Puffin) Puffin Bks.
—The Spell of the Sorcerer's Skull. 176p. 1985. pap. 2.75 (0-553-15357-9, Skylark) Bantam.
—The Treasure of Alpheus Winterborn. 192p. (gr. 3-8). 1985. pap. 2.75 (0-553-15527-X, Skylark) Bantam.
—The Trolley to Yesterday. LC 88-7113. (Illus.). 192p. (gr. 5 up). 1989. 13.95 (0-8037-0581-6); PLB 13.89 (0-8037-0582-4) Dial Bks Young.
—Trolley to Yesterday. (gr. 4-7). 1990. pap. 3.99 (0-553-15795-7) Bantam.
—The Vengeance of the Witch-Finder. Gorey, Edward, illus. Strickland, Brad, contrib. by. LC 93-10081. (Illus.). 176p. (gr. 5 up). 1993. 14.99 (0-8037-1450-5); lib. bdg. 14.89 (0-8037-1451-3) Dial Bks Young.

Bellamy, David. How Green Are You? Dann, Penny, illus. LC 90-19453. 32p. (gr. 1-4). 1991. 14.95 (*0-517-58429-8*, Clarkson Potter); PLB 15.99 (*0-517-58447-6*, C N Potter Bks) Crown Bks Yng Read.
—Our Changing World: The Forest. Dow, Jill, illus. 24p. (gr. 1-4). 1988. bds. 12.00 (*0-517-56800-4*, Clarkson Potter) Crown Bks Yng Read.
—Our Changing World: The River. Dow, Jill, illus. 24p. (gr. 1-4). 1988. bds. 12.00 (*0-517-56801-2*, Clarkson Potter) Crown Bks Yng Read.
—Our Changing World: The Rock Pool. Dow, Jill, illus. 32p. (gr. 1-5). 1988. 9.95 (*0-517-56977-9*, Clarkson Potter) Crown Bks Yng Read.
—Tomorrow's Earth: A Squeaky-Green Guide. Jacques, Benoit, illus. LC 91-58652. 68p. (gr. 3 up). 1992. Repr. of 1991 ed. 9.98 (*1-56138-124-1*) Courage Bks.
Bellamy, Edward. Looking Backward: Two Thousand to Eighteen Eighty-Seven. Elliott, Robert C., ed. LC 67-2787. (gr. 9 up). 1966. pap. 7.96 (*0-395-05194-0*, RivEd) HM.
Bellamy, H. A. & Shaw, Joan. My First Birthday Book. Lippincott, Laurene, illus. 32p. 1991. write for info. (*0-9629039-0-6*) Happy Rainbow.
Bellamy, John. Doubleday Children's Thesaurus. Stevenson, Peter, illus. LC 86-16217. 192p. (gr. k-6). 1987. 15.00 (*0-385-23833-9*) Doubleday.
Belle, Barbara. Pixel Helps Pooper out of a Pickle. (Illus.). 24p. (Orig.). (gr. 1-5). pap. 3.25 (*0-935163-02-6*) Pixel Prods Pubns.
Belle, Susan La see Jacobsen, Mark & Kozlovski, Jane.
Bellegarde. Black Heroes & Heroines, Bk 5: Benjamin Banneker's Great Achievements. 64p. (gr. 5 up). 1985. 8.95 (*0-918340-14-4*) Bell Ent.
Bellegarde, Ida R. Black Heroes & Heroines, Bk. 3. LC 79-51798. 61p. (gr. 5 up). 1983. 8.95 (*0-918340-11-X*) Bell Ent.
—Black Heroes & Heroines, Bk. 4. LC 79-51798. 64p. (gr. 5 up). 1984. 8.95 (*0-918340-13-6*) Bell Ent.
—Lisping Leaves. (gr. 9 up) 1976. 8.95 (*0-918340-03-9*) Bell Ent.
Bellem, Robert L. Dan Turner, Hollywood Detective: Lights! Camera! Murder! Mason, Tom, ed. Wilber, Ron, illus. 62p. 1990. pap. 7.95 (*0-944735-65-7*) Malibu Graphics.
Beller, Joel. So You Want to Do a Science Project! LC 81-7943. (Illus.). 160p. (gr. 5 up). 1984. pap. 13.20 (*0-668-04987-1*, 4987) P-H.
Beller, Susan P. Cadets at War: The True Story of Teenage Heroism at the Battle of New Market. LC 90-21952. (Illus.). 96p. (gr. 3-7). 1991. 9.95 (*1-55870-196-6*) Shoe Tree Pr.
—Medical Practices in the Civil War. LC 92-14960. (Illus.). 96p. (Orig.). (gr. 3-7). 1992. pap. 6.95 (*1-55870-264-4*) Shoe Tree Pr.
—Mosby & His Rangers: Adventures of the Gray Ghost. LC 92-17475. (Illus.). 96p. (Orig.). (gr. 3-7). 1992. pap. 6.95 (*1-55870-265-2*) Shoe Tree Pr.
—Roots for Kids: Genealogy Anyone Can Understand. LC 88-35134. 128p. (Orig.). (gr. 6 up). 1989. pap. 8.95 (*1-55870-112-5*) Betterway Bks.
Bellerophon Books Staff. Ancient Buildings. (gr. 4-7). 1992. pap. 3.95 (*0-88388-121-7*) Bellerophon Bks.
—Billy Yank. (gr. 4-7). 1992. pap. 3.95 (*0-88388-155-1*) Bellerophon Bks.
—California Indian Tribes, Vol. 1: Northern. (gr. 1-9). 1993. pap. 3.95 (*0-88388-153-5*) Bellerophon Bks.
—California Indian Tribes, Vol. 2: Southern. (gr. 4-7). 1992. pap. 3.95 (*0-88388-184-5*) Bellerophon Bks.
—Don Quixote. (gr. 4-7). 1992. pap. 3.95 (*0-88388-182-9*) Bellerophon Bks.
—Johnny Reb. (gr. 1-9). 1993. pap. 3.95 (*0-88388-180-2*) Bellerophon Bks.
—Old Testament. (gr. 1-9). 1992. pap. 3.95 (*0-88388-003-2*) Bellerophon Bks.
—Story of California: 1849 to Present, Vol. 2. (gr. 4-7). 1992. pap. 3.95 (*0-88388-171-3*) Bellerophon Bks.
—Tournament. (gr. 4-7). 1992. pap. 3.95 (*0-88388-181-0*) Bellerophon Bks.
Bellerophon Staff. Aces & Airplanes of WW One. (gr. 1-9). 1992. pap. 3.95 (*0-88388-037-7*) Bellerophon Bks.
—Ancient Africa, Vol. 1. (gr. 1-9). 1992. pap. 2.50 (*0-88388-090-3*) Bellerophon Bks.
—Ancient China. (gr. 1-9). 1992. pap. 3.95 (*0-88388-077-6*) Bellerophon Bks.
—Ancient Greece. (gr. 1-9). 1992. pap. 3.95 (*0-88388-008-8*) Bellerophon Bks.
—Ancient Hawaii. (gr. 1-9). 1992. pap. 2.95 (*0-88388-091-1*) Bellerophon Bks.
—Ancient Near East. (gr. 1-9). 1992. pap. 3.95 (*0-88388-002-4*) Bellerophon Bks.
—Ancient Rome. (gr. 1-9). 1992. pap. 3.95 (*0-88388-061-X*) Bellerophon Bks.
—Caps & Helmets American Revolution, Set I. (gr. 1-9). 1992. pap. 5.95 (*0-88388-029-6*) Bellerophon Bks.
—Caps & Helmets American Revolution, Set II. (gr. 1-9). 1992. pap. 5.95 (*0-88388-040-7*) Bellerophon Bks.
—Caps & Helmets American Revolution, Set III. (gr. 1-9). 1992. pap. 5.95 (*0-88388-041-5*) Bellerophon Bks.
—French Revolution Paper Dolls. (gr. 1-9). 1993. pap. 5.95 (*0-88388-141-1*) Bellerophon Bks.
—George Caleb Bingham. (gr. 1-9). 1992. pap. 1.95 (*0-88388-151-9*) Bellerophon Bks.
—Great American Airplanes. (gr. 1-9). 1992. pap. 3.95 (*0-88388-113-6*) Bellerophon Bks.
—Great Composers Post Cards. (gr. 1-9). 1992. pap. 3.95 (*0-88388-163-2*) Bellerophon Bks.
—Great Indian Chiefs. (gr. 1-9). 1992. pap. 3.95 (*0-88388-033-4*) Bellerophon Bks.
—Helmets of the Renaissance. (gr. 1-9). 1992. pap. 5.95 (*0-88388-105-5*) Bellerophon Bks.
—Henry the Eighth & His Wives. (gr. 1-9). 1992. pap. 3.95 (*0-88388-009-1*) Bellerophon Bks.
—Incas, Aztecs, & Mayas. (gr. 1-9). 1992. pap. 3.95 (*0-88388-010-5*) Bellerophon Bks.
—Infamous Women. (gr. 1-9). 1992. pap. 3.95 (*0-88388-035-0*) Bellerophon Bks.
—A Medieval Alphabet. (gr. 1-9). 1992. pap. 3.95 (*0-88388-001-6*) Bellerophon Bks.
—Middle Ages. (gr. 1-9). 1992. pap. 3.95 (*0-88388-007-5*) Bellerophon Bks.
—A Musical Alphabet. (gr. 1-9). 1992. pap. 3.95 (*0-88388-137-3*) Bellerophon Bks.
—New Testament. (gr. 1-9). 1992. pap. 3.95 (*0-88388-004-0*) Bellerophon Bks.
—Queen Elizabeth the First. (gr. 1-9). 1992. pap. 3.95 (*0-88388-013-X*) Bellerophon Bks.
—Queen Nefertiti. (gr. 1-9). 1992. pap. 2.50 (*0-88388-154-3*) Bellerophon Bks.
—Ramses the Great. (gr. 1-9). 1992. pap. 2.50 (*0-88388-148-9*) Bellerophon Bks.
—Renaissance. (gr. 1-9). 1992. pap. 3.95 (*0-88388-011-3*) Bellerophon Bks.
—Royal Family Paper Dolls. (gr. 1-9). 1992. pap. 3.95 (*0-88388-097-0*) Bellerophon Bks.
—Shakespeare. (gr. 1-9). 1992. pap. 3.95 (*0-88388-008-3*) Bellerophon Bks.
—Ships. (gr. 1-9). 1992. pap. 3.95 (*0-88388-016-4*) Bellerophon Bks.
—Totem Poles. (gr. 1-9). 1992. pap. 4.95 (*0-88388-081-4*) Bellerophon Bks.
Bellerose, Albert J. Princess Kaiulani: Color Me Hawaii. (Illus.). 128p. (gr. k-6). 1990. pap. 3.95 (*0-935848-84-3*) Bess Pr.
Bellew, Bob. Gymnastics. Kline, Marjory, ed. (Illus.). 32p. (gr. 2-5). 1992. PLB 11.90 (*0-531-18463-3*, Pub. by Bookwright Pr) Watts.
Bellina, Joan, jt. auth. see Cronin, Gaynell B.
Belling, Andrew. Let's Sing about America. O'Malley, Kevin, illus. LC 92-763081. 32p. (gr. k-2). 1992. PLB 11.89 (*0-8167-2982-4*); pap. text ed. 3.95 (*0-8167-2983-2*) Troll Assocs.
Bellison, Simeon, ed. see Klose, Hyacinthe.
Bello, Rosario De see De Bello, Rosario.
Belloc, Hilaire. The Bad Child's Book of Beasts. rev. ed. Tripp, Wallace, illus. 48p. (Orig.). (gr. 7 up). 1982. pap. 4.95 (*0-9605776-3-7*) Sparhawk.
—Jim, Who Ran Away from His Nurse, & Was Eaten by a Lion. Chess, Victoria, illus. (gr. 2 up). 1987. pap. 4.95 (*0-316-13816-9*) Little.
—Matilda Who Told Lies. Kellogg, Steven, illus. LC 78-121812. 32p. (gr. k up). 1992. 13.00 (*0-8037-1101-8*) Dial Bks Young.
—Matilda Who Told Lies. Kellogg, Steven, illus. LC 78-121812. 32p. (ps up). 1992. pap. 3.99 (*0-14-054547-6*, Puffin Pied Piper) Puffin Bks.
—Matilda: Who Told Such Dreadful Lies. Simmonds, Posy, illus. LC 91-15852. 32p. 1992. 15.00 (*0-679-82658-0*); PLB 15.99 (*0-679-92658-5*) Knopf Bks Yng Read.
Bellows, Cathy. The Grizzly Sisters. LC 90-38787. (Illus.). 32p. (ps-3). 1991. RSBE 14.95 (*0-02-709032-9*, Macmillan Child Bk) Macmillan Child Grp.
—Toad School. Bellows, Cathy, illus. LC 89-212562. 32p. (ps-3). 1990. RSBE 13.95 (*0-02-708835-9*, Macmillan Child Bk) Macmillan Child Grp.
Bellows, Dena, jt. auth. see Lamb, Sandra.
Bellville, Cheryl W. The Airplane Book. Bellville, Cheryl W., illus. 48p. (gr. k-4). 1991. PLB 19.95 (*0-87614-686-8*) Carolrhoda Bks.
—Airplane Book. (ps-3). 1993. pap. 5.95 (*0-87614-618-3*) Carolrhoda Bks.
—Farming Today Yesterday's Way. LC 84-3215. (Illus.). 32p. (gr. k-4). 1984. PLB 13.50 (*0-87614-220-X*) Carolrhoda Bks.
—Flying in a Hot Air Balloon. LC 92-37390. 1993. 19.95 (*0-87614-750-3*) Carolrhoda Bks.
—Rodeo. LC 84-14981. (Illus.). 32p. (gr. k-4). 1985. PLB 19.95 (*0-87614-272-2*) Carolrhoda Bks.
—Rodeo. (Illus.). 32p. (gr. k-4). 1985. pap. 5.95 (*0-87614-492-X*, First Ave Edns) Lerner Pubns.
—Theater Magic: Behind the Scenes at a Children's Theater. Bellville, Cheryl W., illus. LC 86-9757. 48p. (gr. k-4). 1986. PLB 19.95 (*0-87614-278-1*) Carolrhoda Bks.
Bellville, Cheryl W., jt. auth. see Bellville, Rod.
Bellville, Rod & Bellville, Cheryl W. Large Animal Veterinarians. LC 82-19750. (Illus.). 32p. (gr. k-4). 1983. PLB 13.50 (*0-87614-211-0*) Carolrhoda Bks.
Belpre, Pura. Perez & Martina. Sanchez, Carlos, illus. 64p. 1991. 15.95 (*0-670-84166-8*) Viking Child Bks.
—Perez y Martina. (ps-3). 1991. 15.95 (*0-670-84167-6*) Viking Child Bks.
Belpre, Pura, tr. see Leaf, Munro.
Belsey, William, jt. auth. see Kalman, Bobbie.
Belting, Natalia M. Moon Was Tired of Walking on Air. Hillenbrand, Will, illus. LC 91-20946. 48p. (gr. 4-7). 1992. 15.95 (*0-395-53806-8*) HM.
Belton, Sandra. From Miss Ida's Porch. Cooper, Floyd, illus. LC 92-31239. 40p. (gr. 2-5). 1993. RSBE 14.95 (*0-02-708915-0*, Four Winds) Macmillan Child Grp.

Bemelmans, Ludwig. Mad about Madeline. Quindlen, Anna, intro. by. (Illus.). 352p. 1993. 35.00 (*0-670-85187-6*) Viking Child Bks.
—Madeline. Bemelmans, Ludwig, illus. LC 39-21791. (gr. k-3). 1977. pap. 4.50 incl. cassette (*0-14-050198-3*, Puffin) Puffin Bks.
—Madeline. (Illus.). 32p. (ps-3). 1993. pap. 17.99 (*0-14-054845-9*, Puffin) Puffin Bks.
—Madeline. (Illus.). 1993. pap. 6.99 incl. cassette (*0-14-095120-2*, Puffin) Puffin Bks.
—Madeline. Grosman, Ernesto L., tr. (SPA., Illus.). 64p. (ps-3). 1993. 14.99 (*0-670-85154-X*) Viking Child Bks.
—Madeline & the Bad Hat. Bemelmans, Ludwig, illus. LC 57-62. (gr. k-3). 1977. pap. 4.99 (*0-14-050206-8*, Puffin) Puffin Bks.
—Madeline & the Gypsies. Bemelmans, Ludwig, illus. 56p. (ps-3). 1977. pap. 4.50 (*0-14-050261-0*, Puffin) Puffin Bks.
—Madeline & the Gypsies. Bemelmans, Ludwig, illus. (gr. k-3). 1959. pap. 14.99 (*0-670-44682-3*) Viking Child Bks.
—Madeline Book & Toy Box. (ps-3). 1991. pap. 19.95 (*0-14-034880-8*, Puffin) Puffin Bks.
—Madeline in London. Bemelmans, Ludwig, illus. 56p. (ps-3). 1977. pap. 4.50 (*0-14-050199-1*, Puffin) Puffin Bks.
—Madeline Pop Up. LC 86-51634. (Illus.). (ps-3). 1987. Pop-Up ed. pap. 15.00 (*0-670-81667-1*) Viking Child Bks.
—Madeline's Christmas. LC 85-40092. (Illus.). 32p. (ps-3). 1985. pap. 14.00 (*0-670-80666-8*) Viking Child Bks.
—Madeline's Christmas. (ps-3). 1988. pap. 3.99 (*0-14-050666-7*, Puffin) Puffin Bks.
—Madeline's Christmas. (Illus.). (ps-3). 1993. pap. 6.99 incl. cassette (*0-14-095108-3*, Puffin) Puffin Bks.
—Madeline's House: Includes: Madeline; Madeline's Rescue; Madeline & the Bad Hat. Bemelmans, Ludwig, illus. (ps-3). 1989. pap. 12.50 (*0-14-095028-1*, Puffin) Puffin Bks.
—Madeline's Rescue. Bemelmans, Ludwig, illus. 64p. (gr. k-3). 1977. pap. 4.50 (*0-14-050207-6*, Puffin) Puffin Bks.
—Madeline's Rescue. Bemelmans, Ludwig, illus. LC 53-8709. 56p. (gr. k-3). 1953. pap. 14.00 (*0-670-44716-1*) Viking Child Bks.
—Madeline's Rescue. (ps-3). 1989. incl. cassette 6.95 (*0-14-095034-6*, Puffin) Puffin Bks.
—Madeline's Rescue. (Illus.). 1993. pap. 6.99 incl. cassette (*0-14-095122-9*, Puffin) Puffin Bks.
—Rosebud. Bemelmans, Ludwig, illus. LC 92-47046. 40p. (ps-2). 1993. 8.99 (*0-679-84913-0*); PLB 9.99 (*0-679-94913-5*) Knopf Bks Yng Read.
Bemister, Margaret. Thirty Indian Legends of Canada. Tait, Douglas, illus. 158p. (gr. 3-7). 1991. pap. 9.95 (*0-88894-025-4*, Pub. by Groundwood-Douglas & McIntyre CN) Firefly Bks Ltd.
Bemmelmans, Ludwig. Madeline. Bemelmans, Ludwig, illus. LC 68-666. (gr. k-3). 1958. pap. 15.00 (*0-670-44580-0*) Viking Child Bks.
—Madeline & the Bad Hat. Bemelmans, Ludwig, illus. (gr. k-3). 1957. pap. 14.00 (*0-670-44614-9*) Viking Child Bks.
—Madeline in London. Bemelmans, Ludwig, illus. (gr. k-3). 1961. pap. 15.00 (*0-670-44648-3*) Viking Child Bks.
Benagh, Jim. Sports Great Herschel Walker. LC 89-28385. (Illus.). 64p. (gr. 4-10). 1990. lib. bdg. 15.95 (*0-89490-207-5*) Enslow Pubs.
Benamy, Arnon, tr. see Chimenti, Elisa.
Benander, Carl D. Little Elk's Miracle. Teasley, Jamie, ed. Beyer, Paul, illus. LC 89-51758. 45p. (gr. k-3). 1991. 7.95 (*0-685-31291-7*) Winston-Derek.
Benanti, Carol. Real Fossils. Frank, Michael, ed. Dickens, Earl, illus. 32p. (Orig.). (gr. 3-8). Date not set. pap. 6.95 (*1-880592-06-1*) Pace Prods.
Benanti, Carol, ed. see Frank, Mike.
Benard, Robert. A Catholic Education. (gr. k-12). 1987. pap. 3.50 (*0-440-91124-9*, LFL) Dell.
Benard, Robert, ed. All Problems Are Simple. (Orig.). (gr. k-12). 1988. pap. 3.95 (*0-440-20164-0*, LFL) Dell.
Benarde, Anita. Games from Many Lands. Benarde, Anita, illus. Winskill, Mary, frwd. by. LC 71-86975. (Illus.). 64p. (gr. 3-7). 1971. PLB 13.95 (*0-87460-147-9*) Lion Bks.
Ben-Asher, Naomi & Leaf, Hayim. The Junior Jewish Encyclopedia. 12th, rev. ed. LC 84-51583. (Illus.). 352p. (gr. 9-12). 1993. 22.95 (*0-88400-162-8*) Shengold.
Benavidez, Barbara. My School Years: Kindergarten Through Graduation. (Illus.). (gr. 5-12). 24.95 (*0-9619463-0-X*) Barmarle Pubns.
Benchley, Nathaniel. George the Drummer Boy. Bolognese, Don, illus. LC 76-18398. 64p. (gr. k-3). 1977. PLB 13.89 (*0-06-020501-6*) HarpC Child Bks.
—George the Drummer Boy. Bolognese, Don, illus. LC 76-18398. 64p. (gr. k-3). 1987. pap. 3.50 (*0-06-444106-7*, Trophy) HarpC Child Bks.
—Ghost Named Fred. Shecter, Ben, illus. LC 68-24322. 64p. (gr. k-3). 1968. PLB 13.89 (*0-06-020474-5*) HarpC Child Bks.
—A Ghost Named Fred. Shecter, Ben, illus. LC 68-24322. 64p. (gr. k-3). 1979. 3.50 (*0-06-444022-2*, Trophy) HarpC Child Bks.
—Kilroy & the Gull. Schoenherr, John, illus. LC 76-24309. (gr. 4-6). 1978. pap. 3.95 (*0-06-440090-5*, Trophy) HarpC Child Bks.

—Only Earth & Sky Last Forever. LC 72-82891. 204p.
(gr. 7 up). 1974. pap. 4.95 (0-06-440049-2, Trophy)
HarpC Child Bks.
—Only Earth & Sky Last Forever. (gr. 7 up). 1992. 17.25
(0-8446-6583-5) Peter Smith.
—Oscar Otter. Lobel, Arnold, illus. LC 66-11499. 64p.
(gr. k-3). 1966. PLB 13.89 (0-06-020472-9) HarpC
Child Bks.
—Oscar Otter. Lobel, Arnold, illus. LC 66-11499. 64p.
(gr. k-3). 1980. pap. 3.50 (0-06-444025-7, Trophy)
HarpC Child Bks.
—Red Fox & His Canoe. Lobel, Arnold, illus. LC 64-
16650. 64p. (gr. k-3). 1964. PLB 13.89
(0-06-020476-1) HarpC Child Bks.
—Red Fox & His Canoe. Lobel, Arnold, illus. LC 64-
16650. 64p. (gr. k-3). 1985. pap. 3.50 (0-06-444075-3,
Trophy) HarpC Child Bks.
—Sam the Minuteman. Lobel, Arnold, illus. LC 68-
10211. 64p. (gr. k-3). 1969. PLB 13.89
(0-06-020480-X) HarpC Child Bks.
—Sam the Minuteman. Lobel, Arnold, illus. LC 68-
10211. 64p. (gr. k-3). 1987. pap. 3.50 (0-06-444107-5,
Trophy) HarpC Child Bks.
—Several Tricks of Edgar Dolphin. Funai, Mamoru, illus.
LC 79-85038. 64p. (gr. k-3). 1970. PLB 13.89
(0-06-020468-0) HarpC Child Bks.
—Small Wolf. Sandin, Joan, illus. LC 70-183170. 64p.
(gr. k-3). 1972. PLB 13.89 (0-06-020492-3) HarpC
Child Bks.
—Small Wolf. Sandin, Joan, illus. 1994. pap. write for
info. (0-06-444180-6) HarpC Child Bks.
—Strange Disappearance of Arthur Cluck. Lobel, Arnold,
illus. LC 67-4151. 64p. (gr. k-3). 1967. PLB 13.89
(0-06-020478-8) HarpC Child Bks.
Benda, Andreas. The Good Samaritan. Jacobsen, Walter,
illus. 10p. (gr. k-2). 1993. puzzle bk. 6.99
(0-8028-5083-9) Eerdmans.
—The Good Shepherd. Jacobsen, Walter, illus. 10p. (gr.
k-2). 1993. puzzle bk. 6.99 (0-8028-5084-7) Eerdmans.
Bendall-Brunello, John. Seven-&-One-Half Labors of
Hercules. Bendall-Brunello, John, illus. LC 91-36176.
64p. (gr. 2-5). 1991. 10.95 (0-525-44780-6, DCB)
Dutton Child Bks.
Bender, David L., ed. American Government: Opposing
Viewpoints. LC 87-19791. (Illus.). (gr. 10 up). 1988.
lib. bdg. 17.95 (0-89908-398-6); pap. 9.95
(0-89908-373-0) Greenhaven.
—American Values: Opposing Viewpoints. LC 89-36526.
(Illus.). 312p. (gr. 10 up). 1989. lib. bdg. 17.95
(0-89908-436-2); pap. text ed. 9.95 (0-89908-411-7)
Greenhaven.
—Constructing a Life Philosophy: Opposing Viewpoints.
(Illus.). 264p. (gr. 10 up). 1993. PLB 17.95
(0-89908-198-3); pap. text ed. 9.95 (0-89908-173-8)
Greenhaven.
Bender, Evelyn. Brazil. (Illus.). 112p. (gr. 5 up). 1990. 14.
95 (0-7910-1108-9) Chelsea Hse.
Bender, Lionel. Animals of the Night. 1990. pap. 4.95
(0-531-17257-0) Watts.
—Around the Home. (Illus.). 32p. (gr. 5-8). 1991. PLB
12.40 (0-531-17348-8, Gloucester Pr) Watts.
—Atoms & Cells. (ps-3). 1990. PLB 12.40
(0-531-17219-8, Gloucester Pr) Watts.
—Birds & Mammals. Franklin Watts Ltd., ed. Khan,
Aziz, illus. 40p. (gr. 7-9). 1988. PLB 12.40
(0-531-17091-8, Gloucester Pr) Watts.
—The Body. (Illus.). 32p. (gr. 5-6). 1989. PLB 12.40
(0-531-17183-3) Watts.
—Canada. (Illus.). 48p. (gr. 4-8). 1987. PLB 14.98
(0-382-09508-1) Silver Burdett Pr.
—Cave. LC 89-5531. (Illus.). 32p. (gr. k-6). 1989. PLB
11.90 (0-531-10819-8) Watts.
—Crocodiles & Alligators. 1990. pap. 4.95
(0-531-17258-9) Watts.
—Desert. LC 88-51612. (Illus.). 32p. (gr. 3-6). 1989. PLB
11.90 (0-531-10707-8) Watts.
—Fish to Reptiles. Franklin Watts Ltd., ed. Khan, Aziz,
illus. 40p. (gr. 7-9). 1988. PLB 12.40 (0-531-17093-4,
Gloucester Pr) Watts.
—Forensic Detection. LC 90-3242. (Illus.). 32p. (gr. 5-8).
1990. PLB 12.40 (0-531-17250-3) Watts.
—France. (Illus.). 48p. (gr. 4-8). 1987. PLB 14.98
(0-382-09505-7) Silver Burdett Pr.
—Frontiers of Medicine. (Illus.). 32p. (gr. 5-8). 1991.
PLB 12.40 (0-531-17298-8, Gloucester Pr) Watts.
—Geography. LC 91-29406. (Illus.). 96p. (gr. 1-5). 1992.
pap. 13.00 (0-671-75996-5, S&S BFYR); pap. 8.00
(0-671-75997-3, S&S BFYR) S&S Trade.
—Glacier. LC 88-50369. (Illus.). 32p. (gr. 3-5). 1989.
PLB 11.90 (0-531-10647-0) Watts.
—Invention. King, Dave, photos by. LC 90-4888. (Illus.).
64p. (gr. 5 up). 1991. 15.00 (0-679-80782-9); PLB 15.
99 (0-679-90782-3) Knopf Bks Yng Read.
—Invertebrates. Khan, Aziz, illus. 40p. (gr. 1). 1988. 12.
40 (0-531-17092-6) Watts.
—Island. (Illus.). 32p. (gr. k-6). 1989. PLB 11.90
(0-531-10820-1) Watts.
—Lake. LC 88-51613. (Illus.). 32p. (gr. 3-5). 1989. PLB
11.90 (0-531-10708-6) Watts.
—Lizards & Dragons. 1990. pap. 4.95
(0-531-17259-7) Watts.
—Mountain. LC 88-50370. (Illus.). 32p. (gr. 3-5). 1989.
PLB 11.90 (0-531-10646-2) Watts.
—Our Planet. LC 91-30843. (Illus.). 96p. (gr. 1-5). 1992.
pap. 13.00 (0-671-75995-7, S&S BFYR); pap. 8.00
(0-671-75994-9, S&S BFYR) S&S Trade.
—Polar Animals. (Illus.). 32p. (gr. k-6). 1989. PLB 12.40
(0-531-17164-7, Gloucester Pr) Watts.

—Pythons & Boas. (Illus.). 32p. (gr. 4 up). 1990. pap.
3.95 (0-531-17261-9, Gloucester Pr) Watts.
—River. FS-Watts Staff, ed. (Illus.). 32p. (gr. 1-6). 1988.
PLB 11.90 (0-531-10554-7) Watts.
—Telescopes. LC 91-7802. (Illus.). 32p. (gr. 5-8). 1991.
PLB 12.40 (0-531-17265-1, Gloucester Pr) Watts.
—Volcano. FS-Watts Staff, ed. (Illus.). 32p. (gr. 1-6).
1988. PLB 11.90 (0-531-10553-9) Watts.
Bender, Robert. A Little Witch Magic. LC 92-4054.
(Illus.). 32p. (ps-3). 1992. 14.95 (0-8050-2126-4, Bks
Young Read) H Holt & Co.
—A Most Unusual Lunch. LC 93-34068. (gr. 3 up). 1994.
pap. write for info. (0-8037-1710-5); PLB write for
info. (0-8037-1711-3) Dial Bks Young.
—The Preposterous Rhinoceros: or Alvin's Beastly
Birthday. LC 93-14200. 1994. write for info.
(0-8050-2806-4) H Holt & Co.
—The Three Billy Goats Gruff. Bender, Robert, illus. LC
92-41077. 32p. (ps-2). 1993. PLB 14.90
(0-8050-2529-4, Bks Young Read) H Holt & Co.
Bendick. Explore an Ocean. 1994. pap. write for info.
(0-8050-3273-8) H Holt & Co.
Bendick, Jeanne. Artificial Satellites: Helpers in Space.
(Illus.). 32p. (gr. k-2). 1991. PLB 12.40
(1-56294-002-3) Millbrook Pr.
—Caves. 1994. write for info. (0-8050-2764-5) H Holt &
Co.
—Comets & Meteors: Visitors from Space. (Illus.). 32p.
(gr. k-2). 1991. PLB 12.40 (1-56294-001-5) Millbrook
Pr.
—Egyptians Tombs. (Illus.). 64p. (gr. 3-5). 1989. PLB 12.
90 (0-531-10462-1) Watts.
—Eureka! It's a Telephone! Murdocca, Sal, illus. LC 92-
5085. 48p. (gr. 2-6). 1993. PLB 14.90 (1-56294-215-8)
Millbrook Pr.
—Eureka! It's an Airplane! Murdocca, Sal, illus. LC 91-
34791. 48p. (gr. 2-6). 1992. PLB 14.90
(1-56294-058-9) Millbrook Pr.
—Eureka! It's an Automobile! Murdocca, Sal, illus. LC
91-34790. 48p. (gr. 2-6). 1992. PLB 14.90
(1-56294-057-0) Millbrook Pr.
—Eureka! It's Television. (ps-3). 1993. pap. 6.95
(1-56294-718-4) Millbrook Pr.
—Exploring an Ocean Tide Pool. Telander, Todd, illus.
LC 91-34572. 64p. (gr. 2-4). 1992. 14.95
(0-8050-2043-8, Bks Young Read) H Holt & Co.
—Mathematics Illustrated Dictionary: Facts, Figures, &
People. rev. ed. LC 89-8977. (Illus.). 247p. (gr. 5-9).
1989. PLB 14.90 (0-531-10664-0) Watts.
—Moons & Rings: Companions to the Planets. (Illus.).
32p. (gr. k-2). 1991. PLB 12.40 (1-56294-000-7)
Millbrook Pr.
—The Planets: Neighbors in Space. Brodie, Caroline,
illus. 32p. (gr. k-2). 1991. PLB 12.40 (1-878841-03-3)
Millbrook Pr.
—The Stars: Lights in the Night Sky. Brodie, Caroline,
illus. 32p. (gr. k-2). 1991. PLB 12.40 (1-878841-00-9)
Millbrook Pr.
—The Sun: Our Very Own Star. Brodie, Caroline, illus.
32p. (gr. k-2). 1991. PLB 12.40 (1-878841-02-5)
Millbrook Pr.
—Tombs of the Ancient Americas. LC 92-24546. (Illus.).
64p. (gr. 5-8). 1993. PLB 12.40 (0-531-20148-1)
Watts.
—The Universe: Think Big! Brodie, Caroline, illus. 32p.
(gr. k-2). 1991. PLB 12.40 (1-878841-01-7) Millbrook
Pr.
Bendick, Jeanne & Bendick, Robert. Eureka! It's
Television! Murdocca, Sal, illus. & designed by. LC
92-15652. 48p. (gr. 2-6). 1993. PLB 14.90
(1-56294-214-X) Millbrook Pr.
Bendick, Robert, jt. auth. see Bendick, Jeanne.
Bendix, Jane. Mi'Ca: Buffalo Hunter. Bendix, Jane, illus.
189p. (Orig.). (gr. 5-10). 1992. 14.95 (0-89992-431-X);
pap. 9.95 (0-89992-131-0) Coun India Ed.
Ben-Dov, Meir, jt. auth. see Rappel, Yoel.
Benedek, Elissa P., jt. auth. see Cain, Barbara.
Benedict, Helen. Safe, Strong & Streetwise: The
Teenager's Guide to Preventing Sexual Assualt.
(Illus.). 192p. (gr. 7 up). 1987. 14.95 (0-316-08899-4);
pap. 6.95 (0-87113-100-5) Little.
Benedict, Kitty. Air. (gr. 5 up). 1992. PLB 10.95
(0-88682-547-4) Creative Ed.
—Air: My First Nature Books. Felix, Monique, illus. 32p.
(gr. k-2). 1993. pap. 2.95 (1-56189-167-3) Amer Educ
Pub.
—The Ant. Soutter-Perrot, Andrienne, contrib. by. LC
92-15122. (gr. 5 up). 1992. PLB 10.95
(0-88682-564-4) Creative Ed.
—The Ant: My First Nature Books. Felix, Monique, illus.
32p. (gr. k-2). 1993. pap. 2.95 (1-56189-174-6) Amer
Educ Pub.
—The Cow. Wuest, Gerard, illus. Soutter-Perrot,
Andrienne, contrib. by. LC 92-14456. (Illus.). (gr. 5
up). 1992. PLB 10.95 (0-88682-567-9) Creative Ed.
—The Cow: My First Nature Books. Felix, Monique,
illus. 32p. (gr. k-2). 1993. pap. 2.95 (1-56189-177-0)
Amer Educ Pub.
—The Earth. (gr. 5 up). 1992. PLB 10.95
(0-88682-548-2) Creative Ed.
—Earth: My First Nature Books. Felix, Monique, illus.
32p. (gr. k-2). 1993. pap. 2.95 (1-56189-168-1) Amer
Educ Pub.
—The Earthworm. Delessert, Etienne, illus. Soutter-
Perrot, Andrienne, concept by. LC 92-15024. (Illus.).
(gr. 5 up). 1992. PLB 10.95 (0-88682-566-0) Creative
Ed.

—The Earthworm: My First Nature Books. Felix,
Monique, illus. 32p. (gr. k-2). 1993. pap. 2.95
(1-56189-176-2) Amer Educ Pub.
—The Egg. Pache, Jocelyne, illus. Soutter-Perrot,
Andrienne, concept by. LC 92-15014. (Illus.). (gr. 5
up). 1992. PLB 10.95 (0-88682-565-2) Creative Ed.
—The Egg: My First Nature Books. Felix, Monique, illus.
32p. (gr. k-2). 1993. pap. 2.95 (1-56189-175-4) Amer
Educ Pub.
—The Fall of the Bastille. (Illus.). 64p. (gr. 7 up). 1991.
PLB 16.98 (0-382-24129-0); pap. 8.95 (0-382-24135-5)
Silver Burdett Pr.
—Fire. (gr. 5 up). 1992. PLB 10.95 (0-88682-553-9)
Creative Ed.
—Fire: My First Nature Books. Felix, Monique, illus.
32p. (gr. k-2). 1993. pap. 2.95 (1-56189-173-8) Amer
Educ Pub.
—The Gnat. (gr. 5 up). 1992. PLB 10.95 (0-88682-551-2)
Creative Ed.
—The Gnat: My First Nature Books. Felix, Monique,
illus. 32p. (gr. k-2). 1993. pap. 2.95 (1-56189-171-1)
Amer Educ Pub.

—**My First Nature Book Series, 12 bks.
Delessert, Etienne, illus. 32p. (Orig.).
(gr. 1-4). 1993. Set. pap. 35.40
(1-56189-149-5) Amer Educ Pub.
What is soil made of? What happens
when an earthworm is cut in half?
What do toads eat? Children will find
the answers to these questions & more
in twelve Nature Books--& they'll have
a lot of fun along the way! MY FIRST
NATURE BOOKS are designed to
arouse & encourage a child's curiosity
about the world around us. Each book
introduces a fascinating topic--from
essentials of life such as air & earth, to
the beneficial cow & the mighty oak
tree. The text is engagingly simple &
there's a charming illustration on each
page. Children will quickly take to
heart the most important fact of all:
that learning about nature is a natural
thing to do! Titles include: Air, ISBN
1-56189-167-3, $2.95; Earth, ISBN 1-
56189-168-1, $2.95; Water, ISBN 1-
56189-169-X, $2.95; The Oak, ISBN 1-
56189-170-3, $2.95; The Gnat, ISBN 1-
56189-171-1, $2.95; The Wolf, ISBN 1-
56189-172-X, $2.95; Fire, ISBN 1-
56189-173-8, $2.95; The Ant, ISBN 1-
56189-174-6, $2.95; The Egg, ISBN 1-
56189-175-4, $2.95; The Earthworm,
ISBN 1-56189-176-2, $2.95; The Cow,
ISBN 1-56189-177-0, $2.95; The Toad,
ISBN 1-56189-178-9, $2.95.**
Publisher Provided Annotation.

—The Oak. (gr. 5 up). 1992. PLB 10.95 (0-88682-550-4)
Creative Ed.
—The Oak: My First Nature Books. Felix, Monique,
illus. 32p. (gr. k-2). 1993. pap. 2.95 (1-56189-170-3)
Amer Educ Pub.
—The Toad. Felix, Monique, illus. Soutler-Perrot,
Andrienne, contrib. by. LC 92-14165. (gr. 5 up). 1992.
PLB 10.95 (0-88682-568-7) Creative Ed.
—The Toad: My First Nature Books. Felix, Monique,
illus. 32p. (gr. k-2). 1993. pap. 2.95 (1-56189-178-9)
Amer Educ Pub.
—Water. (gr. 5 up). 1992. PLB 10.95 (0-88682-549-0)
Creative Ed.
—Water: My First Nature Books. Felix, Monique, illus.
32p. (gr. k-2). 1993. pap. 2.95 (1-56189-169-X) Amer
Educ Pub.
—The Wolf. (gr. 5 up). 1992. PLB 10.95 (0-88682-552-0)
Creative Ed.
—The Wolf: My First Nature Books. Felix, Monique,
illus. 32p. (gr. k-2). 1993. pap. 2.95 (1-56189-172-X)
Amer Educ Pub.
Benedict, Rex. Oh, Brother Juniper. Berg, Joan, illus. (gr.
5-6). 1963. lib. bdg. 4.99 (0-394-91457-0) Pantheon.
—Run for Your Sweet Life. Christiana, David, illus. LC
86-45507. 128p. (gr. 5 up). 1986. 14.00
(0-374-36359-5) FS&G.
Beneduce, Ann K. A Weekend with Winslow Homer. LC
93-12189. (Illus.). 64p. 1993. 19.95 (0-8478-1622-2)
Rizzoli Intl.
Beneduce, Ann K., retold by see Swift, Jonathan.
Beneduce, Ann K., tr. A Weekend with Velazquez.
Rodari, Florian, text by. LC 92-33350. (Illus.). 64p.
1993. 19.95 (0-8478-1647-8) Rizzoli Intl.
Benet, Rosemary, jt. auth. see Benet, Stephen Vincent.
Benet, Stephen Vincent. By the Waters of Babylon. 32p.
(gr. 6). 1990. PLB 13.95s.p. (0-88682-294-7) Creative
Ed.

—The Devil & Daniel Webster. 48p. (gr. 6). 1990. PLB 13.95s.p. (0-88682-295-5) Creative Ed.

Benet, Stephen Vincent & Benet, Rosemary. A Book of Americans. Child, Charles, illus. LC 33-27433. 128p. (gr. 4-6). 1944. 12.95 (0-8050-0284-7, Bks Young Read); pap. 5.95 (0-8050-0297-9) H Holt & Co.

Benforado, Sally. Bring Me a Story. rev. ed. (gr. 6-10). 14.95 (0-915745-08-9) Floricanto Pr.

Bengston, Gary. Kelly, Adam's Secret Dream. 40p. 1991. smythe-sewn, casebound 19.95 (0-9631057-0-1) Five Corn Danforth.

Beni, Ruth. The Family Next Door. (Illus.). 48p. (gr. 2-4). 1990. pap. 6.95 (0-233-98383-X, Pub. by A Deutsch UK) Trafalgar.

Benitez, Miena. George Washington Carver, Plant Doctor. 32p. 1989. PLB 15.96 (0-8172-3522-1); pap. 3.95 (0-8114-6719-8) Raintree Steck-V.

Benitez, Mirna. How Spider Tricked Snake. (Illus.). 32p. (gr. 1-4). 1989. PLB 15.96 (0-8172-3524-8); pap. 3.95 (0-8114-6725-2) Raintree Steck-V.

—Super Parrot. (Illus.). 32p. (gr. 1-4). 1989. PLB 15.96 (0-8172-3503-5); pap. 3.95 (0-8114-6704-X) Raintree Steck-V.

Benjamin, A. What's up the Coconut Tree? Biro, Val, illus. 32p. (ps up) 1992. laminated boards 11.95 (0-19-279896-0) OUP.

Benjamin, Alan. Buck. Morley, Carol, illus. LC 93-17090. 1994. write for info. (0-06-023454-7); PLB write for info. (0-06-023459-8) HarpC Child Bks.

—Buck. Morley, Carol, illus. LC 93-31161. 1994. write for info. (0-671-88718-1, S&S BFYR) S&S Trade.

—Busy Bunnies. Santoro, Christopher, illus. 16p. (ps) 1988. pap. 3.95 (0-671-64807-1, Little Simon) S&S Trade.

—Christmas Wishes. 16p. 1989. pap. 3.95 (0-671-68268-7, Little Simon) S&S Trade.

—Dear Santa Chubby Board Book. (ps-6). 1993. pap. 3.95 (0-671-87068-8, Little Simon) S&S Trade.

—Ducky's Easter Surprise. Santoro, Christopher, illus. 16p. 1988. pap. 3.95 (0-671-64808-X, Little Simon) S&S Trade.

—Halloween Riddles Chubby Board Book. (ps-6). 1993. pap. 3.95 (0-671-87067-X, Little Simon) S&S Trade.

—Hallowhat? A Chubby Board Book. (ps). 1992. pap. 3.95 (0-671-77009-8, Little Simon) S&S Trade.

—Hanukkah Chubby Board Book. (ps-6). 1993. 3.95 (0-671-87069-6, Little Simon) S&S Trade.

—Howl-O-Ween Chubby Board Book. (ps-6). 1993. pap. 3.95 (0-671-87066-1, Little Simon) S&S Trade.

—Let's Count, Dracula: A Chubby Board Book. (ps). 1992. pap. 3.95 (0-671-77008-X, Little Simon) S&S Trade.

—Let's Eat: Vamos a Comer. (SPA & ENG). (ps) 1992. pap. 2.95 (0-671-76927-8, Little Simon) S&S Trade.

—Let's Play: Vamos a Jugar. (ENG & SPA). (ps) 1992. pap. 2.95 (0-671-76928-6, Little Simon) S&S Trade.

—Let's Take a Walk: Vamos a Caminar. (ENG & SPA). (ps). 1992. pap. 2.95 (0-671-76929-4, Little Simon) S&S Trade.

—A Nickel Buys a Rhyme. Schmidt, Karen L., illus. LC 92-6475. 40p. (ps up) 1993. 15.00 (0-688-06698-4); PLB 14.93 (0-688-06699-2) Morrow Jr Bks.

—Rat-a-Tat, Pitter Pat. Miller, Margaret, illus. LC 87-568. 40p. (ps-k). 1987. (Crowell Jr Bks); PLB 11.89 (0-690-04611-1) HarpC Child Bks.

—What Color? Que Color? (ENG & SPA.). (ps). 1992. pap. 2.95 (0-671-76930-8, Little Simon) S&S Trade.

Benjamin, Alan, adapted by see Maugham, W. Somerset.

Benjamin, Anne. Young Harriet Tubman: Freedom Fighter. Beier, Ellen, illus. LC 91-26404. 32p. (gr. k-2). 1992. PLB 11.59 (0-8167-2538-1); pap. text ed. 2.95 (0-8167-2539-X) Troll Assocs.

—Young Helen Keller: Woman of Courage. Durrell, Julie, illus. LC 91-26406. 32p. (gr. k-2). 1992. PLB 11.59 (0-8167-2530-6); pap. text ed. 2.95 (0-8167-2531-4) Troll Assocs.

—Young Pocahontas: Indian Princess. Powers, Christine, illus. LC 91-32654. 32p. (gr. k-2). 1992. PLB 11.59 (0-8167-2534-9); pap. text ed. 2.95 (0-8167-2535-7) Troll Assocs.

Benjamin, Carol L. Cartooning for Kids. Benjamin, Carol L., illus. LC 81-43876. 80p. (gr. 3-7). 1982. PLB 12.89 (0-690-04208-6, Crowell Jr Bks) HarpC Child Bks.

—The Wicked Stepdog. 128p. (gr. 5 up). 1986. pap. 2.50 (0-380-70089-1, Flare) Avon.

—Writing for Kids. Benjamin, Carol L., illus. LC 85-47542. 80p. (gr. 3-7). 1985. PLB 12.89 (0-690-04490-9, Crowell Jr Bks) HarpC Child Bks.

Benjamin, Christopher. The Sport Americana Price Guide to the Non-Sports Cards, No. 4. (Illus.). 720p. 1992. pap. 14.95 (0-937424-57-9) Edgewater.

Benjamin, Cynthia. I Am a Doctor. Sagasti, Miriam, illus. 24p. (ps). 1994. 8.95 (0-8120-6380-5) Barron.

—Yo Soy un Medico. Sagasti, Miriam, illus. 24p. (ps). 1994. 8.95 (0-8120-6414-3) Barron.

Benjamin, Don-Paul & Miner, Ron. Come Sit with Me Again: Sermons for Children. LC 86-30588. (Illus.). 128p. (Orig.). 1987. pap. 8.95 (0-8298-0748-9) Pilgrim OH.

Benjamin, Saragail K. My Dog Ate It. LC 93-25218. 128p. (gr. 8-12). 1994. 14.95 (0-8234-1047-1) Holiday.

Benjamin, Starrn J., jt. auth. see Jenison, Norma J.

Ben-Jochannan, Yosef. Black Man of the Nile & His Family. LC 89-61274. 460p. 1990. pap. 24.95 (0-933121-26-1) Black Classic.

Ben-Ner, Yitzhak, et al. Teenage Soldiers-Adult Wars: From the Barracks to the Battlefield. (gr. 7-12). 1991. PLB 16.95 (0-8239-1304-X); pap. 8.95 (0-8239-1305-8) Rosen Group.

Bennet, Marian. My First Valentine's Day Book. LC 84-21511. (Illus.). 32p. (ps-2). 1985. PLB 15.00 (0-516-02906-1); pap. 3.95 (0-516-42906-X) Childrens.

Bennet, Olivia. A Family in Egypt. LC 84-19468. (Illus.). 32p. (gr. 2-5). 1985. PLB 13.50 (0-8225-1652-7) Lerner Pubns.

Bennett, Alan D., ed. Journey Through Judaism: The Best of Keeping Posted. LC 90-19938. (gr. 10 up). 1991. pap. 12.00 (0-8074-0311-3, 160500) UAHC.

Bennett, Andrew. Paper Hats: Six Incredible Hats to Assemble & Wear. (Illus.). 64p. (Orig.). (gr. 3 up). 1993. pap. 19.95 (1-56138-256-6) Running Pr.

Bennett, Anna E. Little Witch. Stone, Helen, illus. LC 52-13721. 128p. (gr. 3-5). 1981. pap. 3.95 (0-06-440119-7, Trophy) HarpC Child Bks.

Bennett, Barbara J. Stonewall Jackson: Lee's Greatest Lieutenant. (Illus.). 160p. (gr. 5 up). 1990. lib. bdg. 18.98 (0-382-09939-7); pap. 8.95 (0-382-24048-0) Silver Burdett Pr.

Bennett, Benjamin K. Burgers on the Moon. (Illus.). 10p. (Orig.). 1990. pap. 2.00 (0-935350-21-7) Luna Bisonte.

Bennett, Bill & Tatchell, Judy. Understanding the Micro. (Illus.). 48p. (gr. 7-9). 1982. (Usborne-Hayes); pap. 3.95 (0-86020-637-8) EDC.

Bennett, Cherie. The Fall of the Perfect Girl. 224p. (gr. 7 up). 1993. pap. 3.50 (0-14-036319-X, Puffin) Puffin Bks.

—Good-Bye, Best Friend. 1992. pap. 3.50 (0-440-21247-2) Dell.

—Good-Bye, Best Friend. 1993. pap. 3.50 (0-06-106739-3, Harp PBks) HarpC.

—Only Love Can Break Your Heart, No. 3. 224p. (gr. 7 up). 1993. pap. 3.50 (0-14-036320-3) Puffin Bks.

—Sunset Heat. 1992. pap. 3.99 (0-425-13383-4) Berkley Pub.

—Sunset, No. 01: Sunset Island. 1991. pap. 3.50 (0-425-12969-1, Splash) Berkley Pub.

—Sunset, No. 04: Sunset Farewell. 1991. pap. 3.50 (0-425-12772-9, Splash) Berkley Pub.

—Sunset, No. 05: Sunset Reunion. 1991. pap. 3.50 (0-425-13318-4, Splash) Berkley Pub.

—Sunset Scandal. 224p. (Orig.). (gr. 4-7). 1992. pap. 3.50 (0-425-13385-0) Berkley Pub.

—Sunset Touch. 1993. pap. 3.99 (0-425-13708-2) Berkley Pub.

—Sunset Whispers. 224p. (Orig.). 1992. pap. 3.50 (0-425-13386-9) Berkley Pub.

—Surviving Sixteen, No. 3: Did You Hear about Amber? 224p. (gr. 7 up). 1993. pap. 3.50 (0-14-036318-1, Puffin) Puffin Bks.

—Wild Hearts on Fire. 1994. pap. 3.50 (0-671-86514-5, Archway) PB.

Bennett, David. Bear Facts: Sounds. Kightley, Rosalinda, illus. (ps-k). 1989. 3.95 (0-553-05494-5, Little Rooster) Bantam.

—Bear Facts: Water. Kightley, Rosalinda, illus. 1989. pap. 3.95 (0-553-05811-8) Bantam.

—Day & Night. Kightley, Rosalinda, illus. 32p. (ps up). 1988. pap. 3.95 (0-553-05479-1) Bantam.

—Earth. Kightley, Rosalinda, illus. 32p. (ps-12). 1988. pap. 3.95 (0-553-05481-3) Bantam.

—Fire. Kightley, Rosalinda, illus. 1989. 3.95 (0-553-05813-4) Bantam.

—One Cow Moo Moo. Cooke, Andy, illus. LC 90-32065. 32p. (ps-2). 1990. 11.95 (0-8050-1416-0, Bks Young Read) H Holt & Co.

—Rain, No. 1. Knight, Rosalinda, illus. 32p. (Orig.). 1988. pap. 3.95 (0-553-05474-0) Bantam.

—Seasons. Kightley, Rosalinda, illus. 32p. (ps up). 1988. pap. 3.95 (0-553-05480-5) Bantam.

—What Am I Made Of? Trotter, Stuart, illus. LC 91-278. 32p. (gr. k-3). 1991. POB 5.95 (0-689-71490-4, Aladdin) Macmillan Child Grp.

Bennett, Denise. The Color Tree. 32p. (gr. 4-5). 1993. 12.95 (1-880851-07-5) Greene Bark Pr.

Bennett, Gay. A Family in Sri Lanka. LC 85-6891. (Illus.). 32p. (gr. 2-5). 1985. PLB 13.50 (0-8225-1661-6) Lerner Pubns.

Bennett, George, ed. Great Tales of Action & Adventure. 256p. (gr. 7 up). 1978. pap. 2.75 (0-440-93202-5, LFL) Dell.

Bennett, Gerald M. Rebecca Tells of a Miracle of Life: A Special Belief in the Healing Power of Love. Rider, Tracy & Sheil, Audrey, eds. Varno, John, illus. LC 92-83744. 42p. (Orig.). (gr. 3-8). 1993. pap. 7.98 (0-9630718-4-X) New Dawn NY.

Bennett, Geraldine M. Katrina & Elishia Teach about the Aura. Rider, Tracy & Sheil, Audrey, eds. Varno, John, illus. LC 92-83709. 32p. (gr. 3-8). 1993. pap. 7.98 (0-9630718-9-0) New Dawn NY.

—Katrina Tells Jamie about John's Invisible Lesson. Rider, Tracy & Sheil, Audrey, eds. Varno, John, illus. 42p. (gr. 3-8). 1993. pap. 7.98 (0-9630718-8-2) New Dawn NY.

—**The Katrina Tells Series. (gr. k up). 1994. pap. write for info. (1-882786-99-8) New Dawn NY. KATRINA TELLS JAMIE ABOUT JOHN'S INVISIBLE LESSON, ISBN 0-9630718-8-2, This delightful tale, told through a child's eyes,** explains in simple terms how we can influence the disposition of others with our minds. An ability we all possess & can learn to use is told in language even a child can understand. All ages will benefit from this story. KATRINA & ELISHA TEACH ABOUT THE AURA, ISBN 0-9630718-9-0, A charming tale about two baby-sitters who devise an ingenious way to entertain their young charges. They teach useful techniques for calming, how to recognize & cleanse one's aura, & how to harness & direct one's own natural energy. This captivating story brings the aura into focus & enables anyone to understand what it is & how to begin working with it. Highly recommended! REBECA TELLS OF THE MIRACLE OF LIFE, ISBN 0-9630718-4-X, A story about young Conrad & his mother & how they miraculously overcome, against all medical odds, some major health problems. The story will touch the hearts of anyone who has grown doubtful of the healing power of love. *Publisher Provided Annotation.*

—**Opening the Door to Your Inner Self: My Lessons.** Bennett, Geraldine M., illus. 122p. (Orig.). (gr. 2 up). 1993. pap. 12.98 (0-9630718-5-8, 1-87122) New Dawn NY. **OPENING THE DOOR TO YOUR INNER SELF, MY LESSONS,** emphasizes the positive, teaching love using Happy faces versus Ugly bugs. Carefully formatted steps teach both young & old how to be the best person they possibly can be by taking the reader on a journey of self-discovery which builds self-confidence & self-respect. Emphasis is placed on the free will to choose which path to take. Charts, fun filled exercises, & clear illustrated demonstrations make this choice very clear, & it is the hope of the author that the majority prefer to travel the path of the Happy faces or Love. The beginning to understanding one's own inner nature & how to apply it to daily living. Order from The New Dawn Publishing Company, RD 1, Box 133, Dexter, NY 13634. Phone: 315-639-6764. *Publisher Provided Annotation.*

Bennett, Helen S. Jack's Amazing Magic Bed. Hone, Michael J., illus. 32p. (gr. 2). 1993. pap. 9.95 (0-9638747-0-5) Tomac Pubng.

Bennett, J. A Cup of Starshine: Poems & Pictures for Children. 57p. (ps-1). 1991. 16.95 (0-15-220982-4, HB Juv Bks) HarBrace.

Bennett, Jack. The Voyage of the Lucky Dragon. 156p. (gr. 7 up). 1982. 9.95 (0-13-944165-4) P-H.

—The Voyage of the Lucky Dragons. 156p. (gr. 5 up). 1985. pap. 5.95 (0-13-944158-1) P-H.

Bennett, James. Dakota Dream. LC 93-17854. 144p. (gr. 7 up). 1994. 14.95 (0-590-46680-1) Scholastic Inc.

—I Can Hear the Mourning Dove. 224p. (gr. 7 up). 1990. 14.45 (0-395-53623-5) HM.

—I Can Hear the Mourning Dove. 1993. pap. 3.25 (0-590-45691-1) Scholastic Inc.

Bennett, Jay. Coverup. LC 87-13716. 144p. (gr. 9-12). 1991. 14.45 (0-531-15224-3); PLB 14.40 (0-531-11091-5) Watts.

—Coverup. 1992. pap. 3.99 (0-449-70409-2, Juniper) Fawcett.

—The Dark Corridor. (gr. 6 up). 1990. pap. 3.50 (0-449-70337-1, Juniper) Fawcett.

—The Dark Corridor: A Novel of Suspense for Young Adults. 176p. (gr. 7 up). 1988. 13.95 (0-531-15090-9) Watts.

—The Haunted One. (gr. 7 up). 1989. pap. 3.99 (0-449-70314-2, Juniper) Fawcett.

—Say Hello to the Hit Man. 144p. (gr. 7 up). 1981. pap. 1.95 (0-440-97618-9, LFL) Dell.

—Sing Me a Death Song. LC 89-24812. 160p. (gr. 7-12).
1990. PLB 14.40 (*0-531-10853-8*) Watts.
—Sing Me a Death Song. 144p. (gr. 7 up). 1990. pap.
3.99 (*0-449-70369-X*, Juniper) Fawcett.
—Skinhead. 128p. (gr. 7-12). 1991. 14.45
(*0-531-15218-9*); PLB 14.40 (*0-531-11001-X*) Watts.
Bennett, Jill. Animal Fair. (ps-3). 1990. 12.95
(*0-670-82691-X*) Viking Child Bks.
—Machine Poems. Sharratt, Nick, illus. 32p. (ps up).
1991. bds. 9.95 (*0-19-276094-7*) OUP.
—Noisy Poems. Sharratt, Nick, illus. 32p. (gr. k-3). 1990.
10.95 (*0-19-276063-7*); pap. 4.95 (*0-19-278219-3*)
OUP.
—Teeny Tiny. De Paola, Tomie, illus. LC 85-12347. 32p.
(ps-1). 1986. 10.95 (*0-399-21293-0*, Putnam) Putnam
Pub Group.
Bennett, Jill, ed. Machine Poems. Sharratt, Nick, illus.
32p. 1993. pap. 5.95 (*0-19-276114-5*) OUP.
—People Poems. Sharratt, Nick, illus. 28p. (gr. k up).
1990. bds. 11.00 laminated (*0-19-276086-6*) OUP.
—Tasty Poems. Sharratt, Nick, illus. 28p. 1992. bds. 9.95
(*0-19-276109-9*) OUP.
Bennett, Jill, compiled by see Cummings, e. e., et al.
Bennett, Jim, jt. auth. see Oxenbury, Helen.
Bennett, John. Master Skylark. Hogan, Alice H., intro.
by. (gr. 5 up). 1965. 1.95 (*0-8049-0092-2*, CL-92)
Airmont.
Bennett, Lori J. Plug in the Sun. (gr. 1-8). 1992. pap.
9.95 (*1-878347-20-9*) NL Assocs.
—Think Plus Science. (gr. 4-8). 1993. pap. 9.95
(*1-878347-23-3*) NL Assocs.
Bennett, Marian. God Made Kittens. (Illus.). 24p. (ps).
1980. 2.50 (*0-87239-404-2*, 3636) Standard Pub.
—God Made Puppies. (Illus.). 24p. (ps). 1980. 2.50
(*0-87239-403-4*, 3635) Standard Pub.
Bennett, Marian & Stortz, Diane. Jesus Grew. Munger,
Nancy, illus. 12p. (ps). 1992. deluxe ed. 4.99
(*0-87403-995-9*, 24-03115) Standard Pub.
—My Family & Friends. Oliviera, Gerry, illus. 12p. (ps).
1992. deluxe ed. 4.99 (*0-87403-994-0*, 24-03114)
Standard Pub.
Bennett, Marian, ed. Baby Jesus. Karch, Paul, illus. 10p.
(ps). 1985. 4.99 (*0-87239-907-9*, 2747) Standard Pub.
Bennett, Nancy & Bennett, Pearl. My ABC Book.
Bennett, Pearl, illus. 54p. (ps-1). 1988. wkbk. 12.00
(*0-9622242-0-0*) Red Baron Pub Co.
Bennett, Olivia. Annie Besant. (Illus.). 64p. (gr. 6-10).
1991. 13.95 (*0-237-60038-2*, Pub. by Evans Bros Ltd)
Trafalgar.
—Colin's Baptism. (Illus.). 25p. (gr. 2-4). 1991. 12.95
(*0-237-60134-6*, Pub. by Evans Bros Ltd) Trafalgar.
—A Family in Brazil. (Illus.). 32p. (gr. 2-5). 1986. lib.
bdg. 13.50 (*0-8225-1665-9*) Lerner Pubns.
—A Farm in the City. (Illus.). 29p. (gr. 2-4). 1991. 12.95
(*0-237-60121-4*, Pub. by Evans Bros Ltd) Trafalgar.
—Holi: Hindi Festival of Spring. (Illus.). 25p. (gr. 2-4).
1991. 11.95 (*0-237-60135-4*, Pub. by Evans Bros Ltd)
Trafalgar.
—Kikar's Drum. (Illus.). 25p. (gr. 2-4). 1991. 12.95
(*0-237-60122-2*, Pub. by Evans Bros Ltd) Trafalgar.
—Our New Home. (Illus.). 26p. (gr. 2-4). 1991. 16.95
(*0-237-60149-4*, Pub. by Evans Bros Ltd) Trafalgar.
—Sikh Wedding. (Illus.). 27p. (gr. 2-4). 1991. 12.95
(*0-237-60128-1*, Pub. by Evans Bros Ltd) Trafalgar.
—Turkish Afternoon. (Illus.). 25p. (gr. 2-4). 1991. 12.95
(*0-237-60119-2*, Pub. by Evans Bros Ltd) Trafalgar.
Bennett, Pearl. My One-Two-Three Book. (Illus.). 12p.
(Orig.). (ps-1). 1990. wkbk. 4.00 (*0-9622242-1-9*) Red
Baron Pub Co.
Bennett, Pearl, jt. auth. see Bennett, Nancy.
Bennett, Rainey, jt. auth. see Preston, Edna M.
Bennett, Rowena. Creative Plays & Programs for
Holidays. (gr. 2-6). 1989. pap. 15.00 (*0-8238-0005-9*)
Plays.
Bennett, S. Christopher. Pterosaurs: The Flying Reptiles.
Franczak, Brian, illus. LC 93-29845. 1994. write for
info. (*0-531-11181-4*) Watts.
Bennett, Shari, jt. auth. see Bean, Barbara.
Bennie, Scott. Day of the Destroyer. Bell, Rob, ed.
Phillips, Joe & Dunn, Ben, illus. 32p. (Orig.). (gr. 12).
1990. pap. 7.00 (*1-55806-101-0*, 408) Iron Crown Ent
Inc.
Benning, Elizabeth. Dying of the Light. 1993. pap. 3.50
(*0-06-106796-2*, Harp PBks) HarpC.
—Life without Alice. (gr. 4-7). 1993. pap. 3.50
(*0-06-106156-5*, Harp PBks) HarpC.
—Losing David. 1994. pap. 3.50 (*0-06-106147-6*, Harp
PBks) HarpC.
—Please Don't Go. (gr. 9-12). 1993. pap. 3.50
(*0-06-106148-4*, Harp PBks) HarpC.
Benny, Mike. The World's Punniest Joke Book. Hoffman,
Sanford, illus. LC 94-42578. 96p. 1993. 12.95
(*0-8069-8544-5*) Sterling.
—World's Punniest Joke Book. Hoffman, Sanford, illus.
96p. (gr. 2-8). 1993. pap. 3.95 (*0-8069-8545-3*)
Sterling.
Benoit, David & Graff, Charles G. Theft by Deception.
(Illus.). 12p. (Orig.). (gr. 7 up). 1987. pap. text ed.
1.50 (*0-923105-08-5*) Glory Ministries.
Benoit, Marie. Mauritius. (Illus.). 96p. (gr. 5 up). 1989.
14.95 (*0-7910-0126-1*) Chelsea Hse.
Benson, B. J. Tandy. LC 88-50930. 179p. 1989. pap. 9.95
(*1-55523-169-1*) Winston-Derek.
Benson, Elizabeth. My Sister, My Sorrow. (gr. 9-12).
1993. pap. 3.50 (*0-06-106760-1*, Harp PBks) HarpC.
Benson, Kathleen, jt. auth. see Haskins, James.

Benson, Laura. This Is Our Earth. (Illus.). 32p. (ps-4).
1994. 14.95 (*0-88106-445-9*); PLB 15.00
(*0-88106-446-7*) Charlesbridge Pub.
Benson, Mary C., ed. see Root, Loretta P.
Benson, Michael. Coping with Birth Control. rev. ed.
Benson, Roger, ed. (gr. 4-7). 1992. PLB 13.95
(*0-8239-1489-5*) Rosen Group.
—Dream Teams: The Best Teams of All Time. (gr. 4-7).
1991. 17.95 (*0-316-08993-1*, Spts Illus Kids) Little.
Benson, Patrick. Little Penguin. (Illus.). 32p. (ps-2).
1991. 14.95 (*0-399-21757-6*, Philomel Bks) Putnam
Pub Group.
Benson, Rita. Looking after the Babysitter. Forss, Ian,
illus. LC 93-26221. 1994. 4.25 (*0-383-03760-3*) SRA
Schl Grp.
—Rosa's Diary. Campbell, Caroline, illus. LC 93-28972.
1994. 4.25 (*0-383-03772-7*) SRA Schl Grp.
—What Angela Needs. McClelland, Linda, illus. LC 92-
34266. 1993. 14.00 (*0-383-03666-6*) SRA Schl Grp.
Benson, Robert B. The Wizard of Bergen. 125p. (Orig.).
(gr. 7-12). 1987. pap. 7.50 (*0-9616327-1-2*) Brandt
Bks.
Benson, Roger, ed. see Benson, Michael.
Bentheim, Rozelle. King Kid. LC 91-2058. (Illus.). 128p.
(gr. 4-7). 1991. 13.95 (*0-8050-1633-3*, Bks Young
Read) H Holt & Co.
Bentley, Bill. Ulysses S. Grant. LC 93-416. (Illus.). 64p.
(gr. 4-6). 1993. PLB 12.90 (*0-531-20162-7*) Watts.
Bentley, Eric, ed. see Brecht, Bertolt.
Bentley, Gerald E., ed. see Shakespeare, William.
Bentley, James. Albert Schweitzer: The Doctor Who
Devoted His Life to Africa's Sick. Lantier, Patricia,
adapted by. LC 90-9974. (Illus.). 64p. (gr. 3-4). 1991.
PLB 18.60 (*0-8368-0457-0*) Gareth Stevens Inc.
—Albert Schweitzer: The Doctor Who Gave up a
Brilliant Career to Serve the People of Africa. LC 88-
17731. (Illus.). 68p. (gr. 5-6). 1989. PLB 18.60
(*1-55532-823-7*) Gareth Stevens Inc.
Bentley, John & Charlton, Bill. Finding Out about
Streams. (Illus.). 64p. (gr. 7-12). 1985. 19.95
(*0-7134-4425-8*, Pub. by Batsford UK) Trafalgar.
—Finding Out about Villages. (Illus.). 48p. (gr. 5-8).
1983. 19.95 (*0-7134-4291-3*, Pub. by Batsford UK)
Trafalgar.
Bentley, Judith. Archbishop Tutu of South Africa. LC
88-410. (Illus.). 96p. (gr. 6 up). 1988. lib. bdg. 16.95
(*0-89490-180-X*) Enslow Pubs.
—Fidel Castro. 128p. (gr. 4-7). 1991. lib. bdg. 13.98
(*0-671-70198-3*, J Messner); pap. 7.95
(*0-671-70199-1*) S&S Trade.
—Harriet Tubman. (Illus.). 144p. (gr. 9-12). 1990. PLB
14.40 (*0-531-10948-8*) Watts.
Bentley, Nancy. I've Got Your Nose. (ps-3). 1991. pap.
12.00 (*0-385-41297-5*) Doubleday.
Bentley, Ray. Shopping with Darby. (Illus.). 24p. (ps-k).
1989. pap. 2.50 (*0-685-51901-5*) Durkin Hayes Pub.
Bentley, Ray R. Darby the Dinosaur in Shopping with
Darby. Hamby, Michael B., illus. LC 89-51111. 24p.
(ps-1). 1989. pap. 2.50 (*0-9623481-0-4*) Darby
Dinosaur.
Bentley, Victor. Possessing Truth in Balance & Anatomy
of a Backslider. LC 89-8945. 128p. (Orig.). 1989. pap.
5.99 (*0-932581-48-X*) Word Aflame.
Bentley, W. A. & Humphreys, W. J. Snow Crystals.
(Illus.). (gr. 5 up). 23.75 (*0-8446-1660-5*) Peter Smith.
Bentley, William G. Indoor & Outdoor Games. (gr. k-6).
1966. pap. 7.95 (*0-8224-3910-7*) Fearon Teach Aids.
Bently, Judith. Brides, Midwives, & Wives. 1994. PLB
write for info. (*0-8050-2994-X*) H Holt & Co.
—Explorer's Guide. 1994. PLB write for info.
(*0-8050-2995-8*) H Holt & Co.
Benton, Allen H. & Bunting, Richard L. Young People's
Nature Guide. De Santo, Rita, et al, illus. 177p. (gr.
2-4). 1978. pap. text ed. 3.00 (*0-942788-05-2*)
Marginal Med.
Benton, Michael. Dinosaur & Other Prehistoric Animal
Factfinder. Channell, Jim & Maddison, Kevin, illus.
LC 92-53119. 256p. (Orig.). (gr. 4-8). 1992. pap. 12.95
(*1-85697-802-8*) Kingfisher Bks.
—Dinosaurs. LC 90-30837. (Illus.). 96p. (gr. 1-5). 1992.
pap. 13.00 (*0-671-75998-1*, S&S BFYR); pap. 8.00
(*0-671-75999-X*, S&S BFYR) S&S Trade.
—Dinosaurs. (Illus.). 32p. (gr. 5-7). 1993. PLB 12.40
(*0-531-17370-4*, Gloucester Pr) Watts.
—Prehistoric Animals: An A-Z Guide. (Illus.). 176p.
1989. 7.99 (*0-517-69190-6*) Outlet Bk Co.
Benton, Michael J. The Dinosaur Encyclopedia. Barish,
Wendy, ed. Channell, Jim, et al, illus. 192p. (gr. 3-7).
1984. (S&S BFYR); pap. 7.95 (*0-671-51046-0*, S&S
BFYR) S&S Trade.
—Dinosaurs. LC 93-19072. (Illus.). 1993. 12.95
(*1-56458-382-1*) Dorling Kindersley.
Ben-Uri, Galila. Dark Island. LC 93-72271. 172p. (gr.
5-8). 1993. write for info. (*1-56062-206-7*); pap. write
for info. (*1-56062-207-5*) CIS Comm.
—The Missing Crown. Hinlicky, Gregg, illus. 223p. (gr.
5-7). 1988. 13.95 (*0-935063-41-2*); pap. 8.95
(*0-935063-42-0*) CIS Comm.
—The Mysterious Cargo. Hinlicky, Gregg, illus. 285p.
(gr. 5-7). 1989. 13.95 (*1-56062-006-4*); pap. 10.95
(*1-56062-007-2*) CIS Comm.
Ben-Vri, Galilia. Hijacked. 190p. 1993. 12.95
(*0-685-66698-0*) CIS Comm.
Benzel, David. Psyching for Slalom: An Illustrated Guide
to the Mind & Muscle of the Complete Skier.
Robertson, Jo, ed. (Illus.). 127p. (Orig.). 1989. pap. 15.
95 (*0-944406-05-X*) World Pub FL.

Benziger, John. The Corpuscles: Adventurers in Inner
Space. Benziger, John & Benziger, Mary, illus. LC 88-
92390. 64p. (gr. k-6). 1989. 11.95 (*0-9620961-0-5*)
Corpuscles Intergalactica.
—The Corpuscles Meet the Virus Invaders. Benziger,
John & Benziger, Mary, illus. LC 90-80327. 30p. (gr.
3-6). 1990. 14.95 (*0-9620961-1-3*) Corpuscles
Intergalactica.
Benzwie, Teresa. A Moving Experience: Dance for
Lovers of Children & the Child Within. Bender,
Robert, illus. 216p. (ps-6). 1988. pap. text ed. 21.95
(*0-913705-25-X*) Zephyr Pr AZ.
Berck, Judith. No Place to Be: Voices of Homeless
Children. Coles, Robert, frwd. by. (Illus.). 144p. (gr. 5
up). 1992. 14.45 (*0-395-53350-3*) HM.
Berdan, Frances F. The Aztecs. Porter, Frank W., III,
intro. by. (Illus.). 112p. (gr. 5 up). 1989. 17.95
(*1-55546-692-3*); pap. 9.95 (*0-7910-0354-X*) Chelsea
Hse.
Berdugo, A., et al. Ositos Nada Mas. (SPA & ENG.).
159p. (gr. k-6). 1992. pap. text ed. 16.95
(*1-881431-30-4*) AIMS Educ Fnd.
Berends, Polly B. The Case of the Elevator Duck.
Allison, Diane, illus. LC 88-23971. 64p. (gr. 2-4).
1989. PLB 6.99 (*0-394-92646-3*); pap. 2.50
(*0-394-82646-9*) Random Bks Yng Read.
Berenstain, Jan, jt. auth. see Berenstain, Stan.
Berenstain, Janice & Berenstain, Stan. The Berenstain
Bears Get in a Fight. Berenstain, Janice & Berenstain,
Stan, illus. LC 81-15866. 32p. (ps-1). 1982. lib. bdg.
5.99 (*0-394-95132-8*); pap. 2.25 (*0-394-85132-3*)
Random Bks Yng Read.
—The Berenstain Bears Go to Camp. Berenstain, Janice
& Berenstain, Stan, illus. LC 81-15864. 32p. (ps-1).
1982. pap. 2.25 (*0-394-85131-5*) Random Bks Yng
Read.
Berenstain, Janice, jt. auth. see Berenstain, Stan.
Berenstain, Michael. The Biggest Dinosaurs. (Illus.). 24p.
(ps-k). 1989. pap. write for info. (*0-307-11977-7*, Pub.
by Golden Bks) Western Pub.
—The Dwarks at the Mall. 48p. (Orig.). (gr. 2 up). 1985.
pap. 2.25 (*0-553-15341-2*) Bantam.
—Flying Dinosaurs - Pterodactyls. Berenstain, Michael,
illus. (ps-3). 1991. pap. 1.75 (*0-307-12620-X*, Golden
Pr) Western Pub.
—Hop, Waddle, Swim! (Illus.). 40p. (ps-1). 1992. write
for info. (*0-307-11578-X*, 11578) Western Pub.
—The Horned Dinosaur: Triceratops. (Illus.). 24p. (ps-k).
1989. pap. write for info. (*0-307-11979-3*, Pub. by
Golden Bks) Western Pub.
—King of the Dinosaurs: Tyrannosaurus Rex. (Illus.).
24p. (ps-k). 1989. pap. write for info. (*0-307-11976-9*,
Pub. by Golden Bks) Western Pub.
—Michael Berenstain's Butterfly Book. Berenstain,
Michael, illus. 24p. (ps-k). 1992. pap. write for info.
laminated covers (*0-307-10023-5*, 10023, Golden Pr)
Western Pub.
—Peat Moss & Ivy's Backyard Adventure. Berenstain,
Michael, illus. LC 85-43097. 32p. (ps-3). 1986. lib.
bdg. 5.99 (*0-394-97604-5*); pap. 1.95 (*0-394-87604-0*)
Random Bks Yng Read.
—Ready For School. (ps). 1990. pap. write for info.
(*0-307-11642-5*) Western Pub.
—The Ship Book. (Illus.). (gr. k-3). 1978. 6.95
(*0-679-20449-0*) McKay.
—Who Am I? A First Book of Famous People.
Berenstain, Michael, illus. 40p. (gr. 2-4). 1992. write
for info. (*0-307-11551-8*, 11551, Golden Pr) Western
Pub.
Berenstain, S. Los Osos Berenstain dia de Mudanza. LC
93-37312. (SPA., Illus.). 1994. 2.25 (*0-679-85430-4*)
Random.
Berenstain, Stan. Berenstain Bear's Around the Clock-
Coloring Book. 1987. pap. 0.49 (*0-394-88263-6*)
Random Bks Yng Read.
—Berenstain Bear's Bear Scout-Coloring Book. 1987. pap.
0.49 (*0-394-88260-1*) Random Bks Yng Read.
—Berenstain Bear's Count on Numbers Coloring Book.
1987. pap. 0.49 (*0-394-88264-4*) Random Bks Yng
Read.
—Berenstain Bear's On the Farm Coloring Book. 1987.
pap. 0.49 (*0-394-88262-8*) Random Bks Yng Read.
—Berenstain Bear's Safety First-Coloring Book. 1987.
pap. 0.49 (*0-394-88259-8*) Random Bks Yng Read.
—Berenstain Bears Storytime Color Book. 1989. pap.
0.66 (*0-394-82368-0*) Random Bks Yng Read.
Berenstain, Stan & Berenstain, Jan. The Berenstain
Bears Accept No Substitutes. Berenstain, Stan &
Berenstain, Jan, illus. 112p. (Orig.). (gr. 2-6). 1993.
PLB 7.99 (*0-679-94035-9*); pap. 2.99 (*0-679-84035-4*)
Random Bks Yng Read.
—The Berenstain Bears & the Bad Dream. (Illus.). 32p.
(ps-1). 1992. incl. cassette 5.95 (*0-679-82761-7*)
Random Bks Yng Read.
—The Berenstain Bears & the Bully. Berenstain, Stan &
Berenstain, Jan, illus. 32p. (ps-3). 1993. PLB 5.99
(*0-679-94805-8*); pap. 2.25 (*0-679-84805-3*) Random
Bks Yng Read.
—The Berenstain Bears & the Drug Free Zone.
Berenstain, Stan & Berenstain, Jan, illus. LC 92-
31604. 112p. (Orig.). (gr. 2-6). 1993. PLB 7.99
(*0-679-93612-2*); pap. 2.99 (*0-679-83612-8*) Random
Bks Yng Read.
—The Berenstain Bears & the Female Fullback.
Berenstain, Stan & Berenstain, Jan, illus. 112p. (Orig.).
(gr. 2-6). 1993. PLB 7.99 (*0-679-93611-4*); pap. 2.99
(*0-679-83611-X*) Random Bks Yng Read.

—The Berenstain Bears & the Nerdy Nephew. Berenstain, Stan & Berenstain, Jan, illus. LC 92-32564. 112p. (Orig.). (gr. 2-6). 1993. PLB 7.99 (0-679-93610-6); pap. 2.99 (0-679-83610-1) Random Bks Yng Read.

—The Berenstain Bears & the New Girl in Town. Berenstain, Jan & Berenstain, Stan, illus. LC 92-32570. 112p. (Orig.). (gr. 2-6). 1993. PLB 7.99 (0-679-93613-0); pap. 2.99 (0-679-83613-6) Random Bks Yng Read.

—The Berenstain Bears & the Red-Handed Thief. Berenstain, Stan & Berenstain, Jan, illus. 112p. (Orig.). (gr. 2-6). 1993. PLB 7.99 (0-679-94033-2); pap. 2.99 (0-679-84033-8) Random Bks Yng Read.

—The Berenstain Bears & the School Scandal Sheet. Berenstain, Stan & Berenstain, Jan, illus. 112p. (Orig.). (gr. 2-6). 1993. PLB 7.99 (0-679-95812-6); pap. 2.99 (0-679-85812-1) Random Bks Yng Read.

—The Berenstain Bears & the Trouble with Grownups. Berenstain, Stan & Berenstain, Jan, illus. LC 91-27430. 32p. (Orig.). (ps-1). 1992. PLB 5.99 (0-679-93000-0); pap. 2.25 (0-679-83000-6) Random Bks Yng Read.

—The Berenstain Bears & the Wheelchair Commando. Berenstain, Stan & Berenstain, Jan, illus. 112p. (Orig.). (gr. 2-6). 1993. PLB 7.99 (0-679-94034-0); pap. 2.99 (0-679-84034-6) Random Bks Yng Read.

—The Berenstain Bears & Too Much Pressure. Berenstain, Stan & Berenstain, Jan, illus. LC 92-6544. 32p. (Orig.). (ps-1). 1992. PLB 5.99 (0-679-93671-8); pap. 2.25 (0-679-83671-3) Random Bks Yng Read.

—Berenstain Bears' Big Rummage Sale. 24p. (ps up). 1992. write for info. (0-307-74020-X, 64020) Western Pub.

—The Berenstain Bears Don't Pollute (Anymore) (Illus.). 1992. pap. write for info. (0-679-83230-0) Random Bks Yng Read.

—The Berenstain Bears Don't Pollute (Anymore) Berenstain, Stan & Berenstain, Jan, illus. 32p. (ps-1). 1993. incl. cass. 5.95 (0-679-83889-9) Random Bks Yng Read.

—The Berenstain Bears: Family Tree House. 2p. (ps-2). 1993. write for info. (1-883366-06-2) Yes Ent.

—The Berenstain Bears Gotta Dance. Berenstain, Stan & Berenstain, Jan, illus. LC 92-32565. 112p. (Orig.). (gr. 2-6). 1993. PLB 7.99 (0-679-94032-4); pap. 2.99 (0-679-84032-X) Random Bks Yng Read.

—The Berenstain Bears on Wheels. Berenstain, Stan & Berenstain, Jan, illus. 14p. (ps-k). 1992. bds. 3.99 (0-679-83245-9) Random Bks Yng Read.

—Eager Beavers: The Berenstain Bears. 16p. (ps-2). 1993. write for info. (1-883366-02-X) Yes Ent.

—Life with Pa Pa: The Berenstain Bears. 16p. (ps-2). 1993. write for info. (1-883366-01-1) Yes Ent.

—Mysterious Numbers: The Berenstain Bears. 16p. (ps-2). 1993. write for info. (1-883366-00-3) Yes Ent.

—Los Osos Berenstain en la Oscuridad. Guibert, Rita, tr. from ENG. Berenstain, Stan & Berenstain, Jan, illus. LC 91-51092. (SPA). 32p. (ps-3). 1992. pap. 2.25 (0-679-83471-0) Random Bks Yng Read.

—Los Osos Berenstain, No Se Permiten Ninas. LC 93-29904. (SPA). 1994. 2.25 (0-679-85431-2) Random Bks Yng Read.

—Los Osos Berenstain y Demasiada Fiesta. Guibert, Rita, tr. Berenstain, Stan & Berenstain, Jan, illus. LC 92-45874. (SPA). 32p. (ps-3). 1993. pap. 2.25 (0-679-84745-6) Random Bks Yng Read.

—Los Osos Berenstain y Demasiada Television. Guibert, Rita, tr. Berenstain, Stan & Berenstain, Jan, illus. LC 92-16251. (SPA). 32p. (ps-3). 1993. pap. 2.25 (0-679-84007-9) Random Bks Yng Read.

—Los Osos Berenstain y el Cuarto Desordenado. Guibert, Rita, tr. from ENG. Berenstain, Stan & Berenstain, Jan, illus. LC 91-50191. (SPA). 32p. (ps-3). 1992. pap. 2.25 (0-679-83470-2) Random Bks Yng Read.

—Los Osos Berenstain y la Ninera. Guibert, Rita, tr. Berenstain, Stan & Berenstain, Jan, illus. LC 92-46719. (SPA). 32p. (ps-3). 1993. pap. 2.25 (0-679-84746-4) Random Bks Yng Read.

—Los Osos Berenstain y las Peleas Entre Amigos. Guibert, Rita, tr. Berenstain, Stan & Berenstain, Jan, illus. LC 92-14807. (SPA). 32p. (ps-3). 1993. pap. 2.25 (0-679-84006-0) Random Bks Yng Read.

Berenstain, Stan & Berenstain, Janice. After the Dinosaurs. Berenstain, Stan & Berenstain, Janice, illus. LC 88-42588. 32p. (Orig.). (gr. k-3). 1988. lib. bdg. 5.99 (0-394-90518-0); (Random Juv) Random Bks Yng Read.

—The B Book. (Illus.). (ps-1). 1971. lib. bdg. 7.99 (0-394-92324-3) Random Bks Yng Read.

—The Bear Detectives. Berenstain, Stan & Berenstain, Janice, illus. LC 75-1603. 48p. (gr. k-3). 1975. 6.95 (0-394-83127-6); lib. bdg. 7.99 (0-394-93127-0) Beginner.

—The Bear Detectives. Berenstain, Stan & Berenstain, Janice, illus. (ps-1). 1988. pap. 5.95 bk. & cassette pkg. (0-394-80499-6) Random Bks Yng Read.

—Bear Scouts. Berenstain, Stan & Berenstain, Janice, illus. LC 67-21919. 72p. (gr. k-3). 1967. 6.95 (0-394-80046-X) Beginner.

—Bears' Christmas. LC 79-117542. (Illus.). 72p. (gr. k-3). 1987. 6.95 (0-394-80090-7); lib. bdg. 6.99 (0-394-90090-1) Beginner.

—The Bears' Christmas. Berenstain, Stan & Berenstain, Janice, illus. 64p. (ps-1). 1988. pap. 6.95 bk. & cassette pkg. (0-394-89835-4) Random Bks Yng Read.

—Bears in the Night. (Illus.). (ps-1). 1971. 6.95 (0-394-82286-2); lib. bdg. 7.99 (0-394-92286-7) Random Bks Yng Read.

—Bears on Wheels. LC 72-77840. (Illus.). (ps-1). 1969. 6.95 (0-394-80967-X); lib. bdg. 7.99 (0-394-90967-4) Random Bks Yng Read.

—Bears' Picnic. LC 66-10156. (Illus.). 72p. (gr. k-3). 1966. 6.95 (0-394-80041-9); lib. bdg. 7.99 (0-394-90041-3) Beginner.

—Bears' Vacation. Berenstain, Stan & Berenstain, Janice, illus. LC 68-28460. 72p. (gr. k-3). 1968. 6.95 (0-394-80052-4) Beginner.

—The Bears' Vacation. Berenstain, Stan & Berenstain, Janice, illus. 64p. (ps-1). 1987. 6.95 (0-394-88848-0) Random Bks Yng Read.

—El Bebe de los Osos Berenstain: (The Berenstain Bears' New Baby) De Cuenca, Pilar & Alvarez, Ines, trs. from ENG. Berenstain, Stan & Berenstain, Janice, illus. LC 81-12193. (SPA). 32p. (Orig.). (ps-3). 1982. lib. bdg. 5.99 (0-394-95144-1); pap. 2.25 (0-394-85144-7) Random Bks Yng Read.

—The Berenstain Bears' Almanac. Berenstain, Stan, illus. LC 73-2298. 72p. (ps-4). 1984. pap. 6.99 (0-394-86601-0) Random Bks Yng Read.

—The Berenstain Bears & Mama's New Job. Berenstain, Stan & Berenstain, Jan, illus. LC 84-4787. 32p. (ps-1). 1984. lib. bdg. 5.99 (0-394-96881-6); pap. 2.25 (0-394-86881-1) Random Bks Yng Read.

—The Berenstain Bears & the Bad Dream. Berenstain, Stan & Berenstain, Janice, illus. LC 87-27295. 32p. (ps-1). 1988. lib. bdg. 5.99 (0-394-97341-0); pap. 2.25 (0-394-87341-6) Random Bks Yng Read.

—The Berenstain Bears & the Bad Habit. Berenstain, Stan & Berenstain, Janice, illus. LC 86-3205. 32p. (ps-1). 1987. lib. bdg. 5.99 (0-394-97340-2); pap. 2.25 (0-394-87340-8) Random Bks Yng Read.

—The Berenstain Bears & the Big Election. Berenstain, Stan & Berenstain, Janice, illus. LC 83-62399. 32p. (ps-3). 1984. pap. 1.50 (0-394-86542-1) Random Bks Yng Read.

—The Berenstain Bears & the Big Road Race. Berenstain, Stan & Berenstain, Janice, illus. LC 87-4581. 32p. (gr. k-3). 1987. lib. bdg. 5.99 (0-394-99134-6); pap. 2.25 (0-394-89134-1) Random Bks Yng Read.

—The Berenstain Bears & the Dinosaurs. Berenstain, Stan & Berenstain, Janice, illus. LC 84-60384. 32p. (ps-3). 1984. pap. 1.50 (0-394-86883-8) Random Bks Yng Read.

—The Berenstain Bears & the Double Dare. Berenstain, Stan & Berenstain, Janice, illus. LC 87-27296. 32p. (ps-1). 1988. lib. bdg. 5.99 (0-394-99748-4); pap. 2.25 (0-394-89748-X) Random Bks Yng Read.

—The Berenstain Bears & the Ghost of the Forest. Berenstain, Stan & Berenstain, Janice, illus. LC 88-42586. 32p. (Orig.). (gr. k-3). 1988. lib. bdg. 5.99 (0-394-90565-2); 2.25 (0-394-80565-8, Random Juv) Random Bks Yng Read.

—The Berenstain Bears & the In-Crowd. LC 88-32095. (Illus.). 32p. (Orig.). (ps-1). 1989. lib. bdg. 5.99 (0-394-93013-4); pap. 2.25 (0-394-83013-X) Random Bks Yng Read.

—The Berenstain Bears & the Messy Room. Berenstain, Janice & Berenstain, Stan, illus. Lerner, Sharon, ed. 32p. (ps-2). 1983. lib. bdg. 5.99 (0-394-95639-7); pap. 2.25 (0-394-85639-2) Random Bks Yng Read.

—The Berenstain Bears & the Missing Dinosaur Bone. Berenstain, Stan & Berenstain, Janice, illus. LC 79-3458. 48p. (ps-3). 1980. lib. bdg. 7.99 (0-394-94447-X) Beginner.

—The Berenstain Bears & the Missing Honey. Berenstain, Stan & Berenstain, Janice, illus. LC 87-4549. 32p. (ps-3). 1987. lib. bdg. 5.99 (0-394-99133-8); pap. 2.25 (0-394-89133-3) Random Bks Yng Read.

—The Berenstain Bears & the Prize Pumpkin. Berenstain, Stan & Berenstain, Janice, illus. LC 90-32865. 32p. (Orig.). (ps-1). 1990. lib. bdg. 5.99 (0-679-90847-1); pap. 2.25 (0-679-80847-7) Random Bks Yng Read.

—The Berenstain Bears & the Sitter. Berenstain, Stan & Berenstain, Janice, illus. LC 81-50046. 32p. (ps-1). 1981. lib. bdg. 5.99 (0-394-94837-8); pap. 2.25 (0-394-84837-3) Random Bks Yng Read.

—The Berenstain Bears & the Sitter. Berenstain, Stan & Berenstain, Janice, illus. 32p. (ps-1). 1987. 2.95 (0-394-88890-1) Random Bks Yng Read.

—The Berenstain Bears & the Slumber Party. Berenstain, Stan & Berenstain, Janice, illus. LC 89-35223. 32p. (Orig.). 1990. PLB 5.99 (0-679-90419-0); pap. 2.25 (0-679-80419-6) Random Bks Yng Read.

—The Berenstain Bears & the Spooky Old Tree. LC 77-93771. (Illus.). (ps-2). 1978. 6.95 (0-394-83910-2); lib. bdg. 7.99 (0-394-93910-7) Random Bks Yng Read.

—The Berenstain Bears & the Trouble with Friends. Berenstain, Stan & Berenstain, Janice, illus. LC 85-30165. 32p. (ps-1). 1987. lib. bdg. 5.99 (0-394-97339-9); pap. 2.25 (0-394-87339-4) Random Bks Yng Read.

—The Berenstain Bears & the Truth. LC 83-3304. (Illus.). 32p. (ps-k). 1983. lib. bdg. 5.99 (0-394-95640-0); pap. 2.25 (0-394-85640-6) Random Bks Yng Read.

—The Berenstain Bears & the Truth. Berenstain, Stan & Berenstain, Janice, illus. LC 83-3304. 32p. (ps-1). 1988. bk. & cassette pkg. 5.95 (0-394-89771-4) Random Bks Yng Read.

—The Berenstain Bears & the Week at Grandma's. Berenstain, Stan & Berenstain, Janice, illus. LC 85-25743. (ps-1). 1986. lib. bdg. 5.99 (0-394-97335-6); pap. 2.25 (0-394-87335-1) Random Bks Yng Read.

—The Berenstain Bears & the Week at Grandma's. Berenstain, Stan & Berenstain, Janice, illus. LC 85-25743. 32p. (ps-1). 1990. pap. 3.50 incl. puppet (0-394-82714-7) Random Bks Yng Read.

—The Berenstain Bears & the Wild, Wild Honey. LC 83-60057. (Illus.). 32p. (ps). 1983. pap. 1.50 (0-394-85924-3) Random Bks Yng Read.

—The Berenstain Bears & Too Much Birthday. Berenstain, Stan & Berenstain, Janice, illus. LC 85-14529. 32p. (ps-1). 1986. lib. bdg. 5.99 (0-394-97332-1); pap. 2.25 (0-394-87332-7) Random Bks Yng Read.

—The Berenstain Bears & Too Much Junk Food. Berenstain, Stan & Berenstain, Janice. Lerner, Sharon, ed. LC 84-40393. 32p. (ps-2). 1985. lib. bdg. 5.99 (0-394-97217-1); pap. 2.25 (0-394-87217-7) Random Bks Yng Read.

—The Berenstain Bears & Too Much TV. Berenstain, Stan & Berenstain, Jan, illus. LC 83-22887. (gr. 3-6). 1984. lib. bdg. 5.99 (0-394-96570-1); pap. 2.25 (0-394-86570-7) Random Bks Yng Read.

—The Berenstain Bears & Too Much TV. Berenstain, Stan & Berenstain, Janice, illus. (ps-1). 1989. bk. & cassette 5.95 (0-394-82894-1) Random Bks Yng Read.

—The Berenstain Bears & Too Much Vacation. LC 88-32094. (Illus.). 32p. (Orig.). (ps-1). 1989. PLB 5.99 (0-679-93014-2); pap. 2.25 (0-679-83014-8) Random Bks Yng Read.

—The Berenstain Bears & Too Much Vacation. Berenstain, Stan & Berenstain, Janice, illus. LC 88-32094. 32p. (ps-1). 1990. pap. 5.95 (0-679-80311-4); cass. incl. Random Bks Yng Read.

—The Berenstain Bears Are a Family. Berenstain, Stan & Berenstain, Janice, illus. LC 90-63082. 24p. (Orig.). (ps). 1991. 2.95 (0-679-80746-2) Random Bks Yng Read.

—The Berenstain Bears at the Super-Duper Market. Berenstain, Stan & Berenstain, Janice, illus. LC 90-63080. 24p. (Orig.). (ps). 1991. 2.95 (0-679-80748-9) Random Bks Yng Read.

—The Berenstain Bears' Bath Book. Berenstain, Stan & Berenstain, Janice, illus. 10p. (ps). 1985. vinyl 3.95 (0-394-87116-2) Random Bks Yng Read.

—The Berenstain Bears Blaze a Trail. Berenstain, Stan & Berenstain, Janice, illus. LC 87-4552. 32p. (ps-1). 1987. lib. bdg. 5.99 (0-394-99132-X); pap. 2.25 (0-394-89132-5) Random Bks Yng Read.

—The Berenstain Bears' Christmas Tree. LC 80-5087. (Illus.). 72p. (ps-3). 1980. 10.95 (0-394-84566-8); lib. bdg. 9.99 (0-394-94566-2) Random Bks Yng Read.

—The Berenstain Bears' Christmas Tree. reissue ed. Berenstain, Stan & Berenstain, Janice, illus. 64p. (ps-2). 1991. incl. 20-min. cassette 8.95 (0-679-81974-6) Random Bks Yng Read.

—The Berenstain Bears Don't Pollute (Anymore) Berenstain, Stan & Berenstain, Janice, illus. LC 91-9147. 32p. (Orig.). (ps-1). 1991. lib. bdg. 5.99 (0-679-92351-9); pap. 2.25 (0-679-82351-4) Random Bks Yng Read.

—Berenstain Bears Forget Their Manners. Berenstain, Stan & Berenstain, Janice, illus. LC 84-43156. 32p. (gr. k-3). 1985. lib. bdg. 5.99 (0-394-97333-X); pap. 2.25 (0-394-87333-5) Random Bks Yng Read.

—The Berenstain Bears Forget Their Manners. Berenstain, Stan & Berenstain, Janice, illus. 32p. (ps-1). 1986. pap. 5.95 with cassette (0-394-88343-8) Random Bks Yng Read.

—The Berenstain Bears' Four Seasons. Berenstain, Stan & Berenstain, Janice, illus. LC 90-63079. 24p. (Orig.). (ps). 1991. 2.95 (0-679-80749-7) Random Bks Yng Read.

—The Berenstain Bears Get in a Fight. Berenstain, Stan & Berenstain, Janice, illus. 32p. (ps-1). 1987. pap. 3.50 (0-394-88893-6) Random Bks Yng Read.

—The Berenstain Bears Get in a Fight. Berenstain, Stan & Berenstain, Janice, illus. 32p. (ps-1). 1988. pap. 4.95 bk. & cassette pkg. (0-394-89778-1) Random Bks Yng Read.

—The Berenstain Bears Get Stage Fright. Berenstain, Stan & Berenstain, Janice, illus. LC 85-25716. 32p. (gr. 3-6). 1986. lib. bdg. 5.99 (0-394-97337-2); pap. 2.25 (0-394-87337-8) Random Bks Yng Read.

—The Berenstain Bears Get the Gimmies. Berenstain, Stan & Berenstain, Janice, illus. LC 88-42587. 32p. (Orig.). (ps-1). 1988. lib. bdg. 5.99 (0-394-90566-0); pap. 2.25 (0-394-80566-6) Random Bks Yng Read.

—The Berenstain Bears Get the Gimmies. Berenstain, Stan & Berenstain, Janice, illus. LC 88-42587. 32p. (ps-1). 1990. pap. 5.95 (0-679-80313-0); cass. incl. Random Bks Yng Read.

—The Berenstain Bears Go Fly a Kite. LC 83-60056. (Illus.). 32p. (ps-2). 1983. pap. 1.50 (0-394-85921-9) Random Bks Yng Read.

—The Berenstain Bears Go Out for the Team. LC 85-30164. (Illus.). 32p. (ps-1). 1987. 2.25 (0-394-87338-6) Random Bks Yng Read.

—The Berenstain Bears Go Out for the Team. reissued ed. Berenstain, Stan & Berenstain, Janice, illus. LC 85-30164. 32p. (ps-1). 1991. pap. 5.95 incls. cassette (0-679-81495-7) Random Bks Yng Read.

—The Berenstain Bears Go to Camp. Berenstain, Stan & Berenstain, Janice, illus. (ps-1). 1989. 5.95 (0-394-82896-8) Random Bks Yng Read.

—The Berenstain Bears Go to School. LC 77-79853. (Illus.). (ps-2). 1978. lib. bdg. 5.99 (0-394-93736-8); pap. 2.25 (0-394-83736-3) Random Bks Yng Read.

—The Berenstain Bears Go to the Doctor. Berenstain, Stan & Berenstain, Janice, illus. LC 81-50043. 32p. (ps-1). 1981. lib. bdg. 5.99 (0-394-94835-1); pap. 2.25 (0-394-84835-7) Random Bks Yng Read.
—The Berenstain Bears in the Dark. LC 82-5395. 32p. (ps-1). 1982. pap. 2.25 saddle-stitched (0-394-85443-8) Random Bks Yng Read.
—Berenstain Bears Learn about Strangers. Berenstain, Stan & Berenstain, Jan, illus. LC 84-43157. 32p. (ps-1). 1985. lib. bdg. 5.99 (0-394-97338-8); 2.25 (0-394-87334-3) Random Bks Yng Read.
—The Berenstain Bears Learn about Strangers. (Illus.). 32p. (ps-1). 1986. pap. 5.95 (0-394-88346-2) Random Bks Yng Read.
—The Berenstain Bears' Make & Do Book. Berenstain, Stan & Berenstain, Janice, illus. 64p. (ps-3). 1984. pap. 3.95 (0-394-86895-1) Random Bks Yng Read.
—The Berenstain Bears Meet Santa Bear. Berenstain, Stan & Berenstain, Jan, illus. LC 84-4829. 32p. (ps-1). 1984. lib. bdg. 5.99 (0-394-96880-8); pap. 2.25 (0-394-86880-3) Random Bks Yng Read.
—The Berenstain Bears Meet Santa Bear. Berenstain, Stan & Berenstain, Janice, illus. LC 84-4829. 32p. (ps-1). 1989. pap. 5.95 incl. cassette (0-394-85228-1) Random Bks Yng Read.
—The Berenstain Bears' Moving Day. Berenstain, Stan & Berenstain, Janice, illus. LC 81-50044. 32p. (ps-1). 1981. lib. bdg. 5.99 (0-394-94838-6); pap. 2.25 (0-394-84838-1) Random Bks Yng Read.
—The Berenstain Bears' Nature Guide. Berenstain, Stan & Berenstain, Jan, illus. LC 75-8070. 72p. (ps-4). 1984. pap. 7.95 (0-394-86602-9) Random Bks Yng Read.
—The Berenstain Bears' New Baby. Berenstain, Stan & Berenstain, Janice, illus. LC 74-2535. 32p. (Orig.). (ps-1). 1974. pap. 2.25 (0-394-82908-5) Random Bks Yng Read.
—The Berenstain Bears' New Baby. Berenstain, Stan & Berenstain, Janice, illus. 32p. (gr. 1-3). 1985. pap. 5.95 incl. cass. (0-394-87661-X) Random Bks Yng Read.
—The Berenstain Bears: No Girls Allowed. Berenstain, Stan & Berenstain, Janice, illus. LC 85-18246. 32p. (ps-1). 1986. pap. 2.25 (0-394-87331-9) Random Bks Yng Read.
—The Berenstain Bears' Nursery Tales. (Illus.). (ps-1). 1973. pap. 2.25 (0-394-82665-5) Random Bks Yng Read.
—The Berenstain Bears on the Job. Berenstain, Stan & Berenstain, Janice, illus. LC 87-9739. 32p. (gr. k-3). 1987. lib. bdg. 5.99 (0-394-99131-1); pap. 2.25 (0-394-89131-7) Random Bks Yng Read.
—The Berenstain Bears on the Moon. Berenstain, Stan & Berenstain, Janice, illus. LC 84-20428. 48p. (ps-3). 1985. 6.95 (0-394-87180-4); lib. bdg. 7.99 (0-394-97180-9) Random Bks Yng Read.
—The Berenstain Bears Ready, Set, Go! Berenstain, Stan & Berenstain, Janice, illus. LC 88-42589. 32p. (Orig.). (gr. k-3). 1988. lib. bdg. 5.99 (0-394-90564-4); 2.25 (0-394-80564-X) Random Bks Yng Read.
—The Berenstain Bears Say Good Night. Berenstain, Stan & Berenstain, Janice, illus. LC 90-63081. 24p. (Orig.). (ps). 1991. 2.95 (0-679-80747-0) Random Bks Yng Read.
—The Berenstain Bears' Science Fair. Berenstain, Stan & Berenstain, Janice, illus. LC 76-8121. (gr. 1-4). 1977. PLB 11.99 (0-394-93294-3) Random Bks Yng Read.
—The Berenstain Bears' Science Fair. Berenstain, Stan & Berenstain, Janice, illus. LC 76-8121. 72p. (ps-4). 1984. pap. 6.95 (0-394-86603-7) Random Bks Yng Read.
—The Berenstain Bears Shoot the Rapids. Berenstain, Stan & Berenstain, Janice, illus. LC 83-60055. 32p. (ps-3). 1984. pap. 1.50 (0-394-86543-X) Random Bks Yng Read.
—The Berenstain Bears' Soccer Star. LC 83-60055. (Illus.). 32p. (ps-2). 1983. pap. 1.50 (0-394-85922-7) Random Bks Yng Read.
—The Berenstain Bears' Take-Along Library. Berenstain, Stan & Berenstain, Janice, illus. Incl. The Berenstain Bears Visit the Dentist. 32p; The Berenstain Bears & Too Much TV. 32p; The Berenstain Bears & the Sitter. 32p; The Berenstain Bears in the Dark. 32p; The Berenstain Bears & the Messy Room. 32p. (Illus.). (ps-3). 1985. 11.50 (0-394-87615-6) Random Bks Yng Read.
—The Berenstain Bears to the Rescue. LC 83-60058. (Illus.). 32p. (ps-2). 1983. pap. 1.50 (0-394-85923-5) Random Bks Yng Read.
—The Berenstain Bears' Toy Time. (Illus.). 12p. (ps). 1985. 2.95 (0-394-87449-8) Random Bks Yng Read.
—The Berenstain Bears Trick or Treat. Berenstain, Stan & Berenstain, Janice, illus. LC 89-30884. 32p. (Orig.). (ps-1). 1989. PLB 5.99 (0-679-90091-8); pap. 2.25 (0-679-80091-3) Random Bks Yng Read.
—The Berenstain Bears Trick or Treat. reissue ed. Berenstain, Stan & Berenstain, Janice, illus. 32p. (ps-1). 1991. incl. 20-min. cassette 6.00 (0-679-81497-3) Random Bks Yng Read.
—The Berenstain Bears' Trouble at School. Berenstain, Stan & Berenstain, Janice, illus. LC 86-4999. 32p. (ps-1). 1987. lib. bdg. 5.99 (0-394-97336-4); pap. 2.25 (0-394-87336-X) Random Bks Yng Read.
—The Berenstain Bears' Trouble at School. Berenstain, Stan & Berenstain, Janice, illus. LC 86-4999. 32p. (ps-1). 1990. pap. 3.50 incl. puppet (0-394-82715-5) Random Bks Yng Read.

—The Berenstain Bears' Trouble with Money. LC 83-3305. (Illus.). 32p. (ps-k). 1983. pap. 1.95 (0-394-85917-0) Random Bks Yng Read.
—The Berenstain Bears' Trouble with Pets. Berenstain, Stan & Berenstain, Janice, illus. LC 90-32956. 32p. (Orig.). (ps-1). 1990. lib. bdg. 5.99 (0-679-90848-X); pap. 2.25 (0-679-80848-5) Random Bks Yng Read.
—The Berenstain Bears Visit the Dentist. Berenstain, Stan & Berenstain, Janice, illus. LC 81-50045. 32p. (ps-1). 1981. lib. bdg. 5.99 (0-394-94836-X); pap. 2.25 (0-394-84836-5) Random Bks Yng Read.
—Big Honey Hunt. LC 62-15115. (Illus.). 64p. (gr. 1-2). 1962. 6.95 (0-394-80028-1) Beginner.
—Bike Lesson. LC 64-11460. (Illus.). 64p. (ps-1). 1966. 6.95 (0-394-80036-2); lib. bdg. 7.99 (0-394-90036-7) Random Bks Yng Read.
—C Is for Clown. (Illus.). (ps-1). 1972. lib. bdg. 7.99 (0-394-92492-4) Random Bks Yng Read.
—The Day of the Dinosaur. Berenstain, Michael, illus. LC 87-9828. 32p. (gr. k-3). 1987. lib. bdg. 5.99 (0-394-99130-3); pap. 2.25 (0-394-89130-9) Random Bks Yng Read.
—He Bear, She Bear. Berenstain, Stan & Berenstain, Janice, illus. LC 74-5518. 48p. (ps-1). 1974. 6.95 (0-394-82997-2); lib. bdg. 7.99 (0-394-92997-7) Random Bks Yng Read.
—He Bear She Bear & Bears on Wheels. Berenstain, Stan & Berenstain, Janice, illus. (ps-1). 1989. bk. & cassette 7.95 (0-394-82952-2) Random Bks Yng Read.
—Inside, Outside, Upside Down. LC 68-28465. (Illus.). (ps-1). 1968. 6.95 (0-394-81142-9); lib. bdg. 7.99 (0-394-91142-3) Random Bks Yng Read.
—Old Hat, New Hat. (Illus.). (ps-1). 1970. 6.95 (0-394-80669-7); lib. bdg. 7.99 (0-394-90669-1) Random Bks Yng Read.
Berenstain, Stan, jt. auth. see Berenstain, Janice.
Berenstain, Stan & Berenstain, Janice, illus. The Berenstain Kids: I Love Colors. LC 87-9722. (ps-3). 1987. PLB 5.99 (0-394-99129-X); pap. 2.25 (0-394-89129-5) Random Bks Yng Read.
Berenzy, A. Puss in Boots. 1994. 14.95 (0-8050-1284-2) H Holt & Co.
—Rapunzel. 1992. 14.95 (0-8050-1283-4) H Holt & Co.
Berenzy, Alix. A Frog Prince. Berenzy, Alix, illus. 32p. (ps up). 1989. 14.95 (0-8050-0426-2, Bks Young Read) H Holt & Co.
Berenzy, Alix, retold by. & illus. A Frog Prince. LC 88-29628. 32p. (ps up). 1991. pap. 4.95 (0-8050-1848-4, Owlet BYR) H Holt & Co.
Berescik, Susan, ed. see Barth, Shannon.
Berg, Adriane G. & Bochner, Arthur B. Totally Awesome Money Book for Kids (& Their Parents) (Illus.). 176p. (gr. 4-12). 1993. 18.95 (1-55704-183-0); pap. 9.95 (1-55704-176-8) Newmarket.
Berg, Cami. D Is for Dolphin. Bionoi, Janet, illus. 64p. 1991. 18.95 (1-879244-01-2) Windom Bks.
—Sky Bear. (Illus.). 40p. (ps up) 1994. 15.95 (1-879244-87-X) Windom Bks.
Berg, Daniel & Berg, Denise. Tropical Shipwrecks: A Vacationing Divers Guide to the Bahamas & Caribbean. (Illus.). 160p. (Orig.). 1989. pap. text ed. 12.95 (0-9616167-2-5) Aqua Explorers.
Berg, Denise, jt. auth. see Berg, Daniel.
Berg, Eric. Bernie's Safe Ideas. LC 93-8905. 1993. write for info. (1-56071-324-0) ETR Assocs.
—Five Special Senses. LC 93-8906. 1993. write for info. (1-56071-328-3) ETR Assocs.
—The Pink Medicine Lesson. LC 93-8908. (gr. 4 up). 1993. write for info. (1-56071-326-7) ETR Assocs.
—Try It, You'll Like It! LC 93-8907. 1993. write for info. (1-56071-325-9) ETR Assocs.
Berg, Francie M. How to Be Slimmer, Trimmer & Happier: An Action Plan for Young People with a Step-by Step Guide to Losing Weight Through Positive Living. rev. ed. Cook, Tim, illus. LC 82-90690. 200p. (Orig.). (gr. 9 up). 1983. 11.95 (0-918532-10-8); pap. 6.95 (0-918532-11-6); Leader's Guide 64p. 4.95 (0-918532-12-4) Healthy Liv Inst.
Berg, Hans, jt. auth. see Berg, Karin.
Berg, Jean H. Daniel in the Lions' Den. Darwin, Beatrice, illus. Jareaux, Robin, contrib. by. (Illus.). 32p. (Orig.). (gr. k-3). 1973. pap. 9.95 incl. audiocassette (0-87510-178-X) Christian Sci.
—Joseph & His Brothers. Krush, Beth & Krush, Joe, illus. 32p. (Orig.). (gr. k-3). 1976. pap. 9.95 incl. audiocassette (0-87510-104-6) Christian Sci.
—Mr. Koonan's Bargain. LC 70-158559. (gr. 1-4). 1971. 7.95 (0-87874-002-3, Nautilus) Galloway.
—Nehemiah Builds the Wall. Madden, Don, illus. 32p. (Orig.). (gr. k-3). 1978. pap. 9.95 incl. audiocassette (0-87510-114-3) Christian Sci.
—Noah & the Ark. Madden, Don, illus. 32p. (Orig.). (gr. k-3). 1974. pap. 9.95 incl. audiocassette (0-87510-180-1) Christian Sci.
—The Story of Jesus. Krush, Beth & Krush, Joe, illus. 40p. (Orig.). (gr. k-3). 1977. pap. 9.95 incl. audiocassette (0-87510-185-2) Christian Sci.
Berg, Jean H., jt. auth. see Stauffer, Russell G.
Berg, Jean H., retold by. The Story of Peter. Palm, Felix, illus. 40p. (Orig.). (gr. k-3). 1990. pap. 9.95 incl. audiocassette (0-87510-216-6) Christian Sci.
Berg, Jean H., adapted by. The Story of Ruth. Palm, Felix & Crouch, Ellen, illus. 32p. pap. 9.95 (0-87510-213-5, G&I244) Christian Sci.
Berg, Julie. The Berenstains. LC 93-12959. 1993. 13.99 (1-56239-224-7) Abdo & Dghtrs.
—Beverly Cleary. Berg, Julie, illus. LC 93-12958. (gr. 6 up). 1993. 13.99 (1-56239-222-0) Abdo & Dghtrs.

—Maurice Sendak. LC 93-15738. 1993. 13.99 (1-56239-225-5) Abdo & Dghtrs.
—Tomie de Paola. Berg, Julie, illus. LC 93-12960. 1993. 13.95 (1-56239-223-9) Abdo & Dghtrs.
Berg, Julie, jt. auth. see Kallen, Stuart A.
Berg, Julie, jt. auth. see Nielsen, Shelly.
Berg, Julie, ed. see Kallen, Stuart A.
Berg, Julie, ed. see Neilsen, Shelly.
Berg, Julie, ed. see Nielsen, Shelly.
Berg, Julie, ed. see Wheeler, Jill C.
Berg, Karin & Berg, Hans. Greenland Through the Year. LC 72-90689. (Illus.). 24p. (gr. k-4). 1973. 7.95 (0-87592-023-3) Scroll Pr.
Berg, Kevin A. Jibberish & Rhyme. Hansen, Trisha, illus. 104p. (gr. 2-4). 1993. PLB 12.95 (0-9636795-0-3) Child Tech Bks.
Bergen, Lara R. Farm Babies. Ogden, Betina, illus. LC 93-26192. 1994. pap. write for info. (0-448-40212-2, G&D) Putnam Pub Group.
Berger. The Outer Space Tracing Fun Book. 1992. pap. 1.95 (0-590-45133-2) Scholastic Inc.
Berger, Barbara. When the Sun Rose. (Illus.). 32p. (ps-3). 1990. pap. 5.95 (0-399-22175-1, Sandcastle Bks) Putnam Pub Group.
Berger, Barbara H. The Donkey's Dream. Berger, Barbara H., illus. LC 84-18905. 32p. (ps-5). 1986. 14.95 (0-399-21233-7, Philomel) Putnam Pub Group.
—Donkey's Dream. LC 84-18905. (Illus.). 32p. (ps-5). 1986. pap. 5.95 (0-399-22014-3, Sandcastle Bks) Putnam Pub Group.
—Grandfather Twilight. Berger, Barbara H., illus. 32p. (ps-3). 1986. 14.95 (0-399-20996-4, Philomel) Putnam Pub Group.
—Grandfather Twilight. (ps-3). 1990. pap. 5.95 (0-399-21596-4, Sandcastle Bks) Putnam Pub Group.
—Grandfather Twilight: Mini Edition. (Illus.). 32p. (ps-3). 1992. 5.95 (0-399-21999-4, Philomel Bks) Putnam Pub Group.
—Gwinna. (Illus.). 128p. 1990. 18.95 (0-399-21738-X, Philomel Bks) Putnam Pub Group.
—When the Sun Rose. Berger, Barbara H., illus. LC 86-2484. 32p. (ps-2). 1986. 14.95 (0-399-21360-0, Philomel) Putnam Pub Group.
Berger, Bruce. A Dazzle of Hummingbirds. Leon, Vicki, ed. (Illus.). 40p. (Orig.). (gr. 5 up). 1989. pap. 7.95 (0-918303-19-2) Blake Pub.
Berger, Fredericka. The Green Bottle & the Silver Kite. LC 92-10073. 144p. (gr. 5 up). 1993. 14.00 (0-688-11785-6) Greenwillow.
—Robots - What They Are, What They Do. Huffman, Tom, illus. LC 91-14128. 48p. (gr. k up). 1992. 14.00 (0-688-09863-0); PLB 13.93 (0-688-09864-9) Greenwillow.
Berger, Gilda. Addiction. rev. ed. LC 92-17093. 176p. (gr. 9-12). 1992. PLB 13.90 (0-531-11144-X) Watts.
—Alcoholism & the Family. LC 93-10898. (Illus.). 128p. (gr. 7-12). 1993. PLB 13.40 (0-531-12548-3) Watts.
—Crack-The New Drug Epidemic. (Illus.). 128p. (gr. 7-12). 1987. PLB 13.40 (0-531-10410-9) Watts.
—Drug Abuse: The Impact on Society. Rakos, Jennie, ed. LC 88-10620. (Illus.). 160p. (gr. 6-12). 1988. PLB 13.90 (0-531-10579-2) Watts.
—Joey's Story: Straight Talk about Drugs. Kirk, Barbara, photos by. (Illus.). 64p. (gr. 7 up). 1991. PLB 12.90 (1-56294-003-1) Millbrook Pr.
—Joey's Story: Straight Talk about Drugs. 1992. pap. 4.95 (0-395-63559-4) HM.
—Magic Slippers: Stories from the Ballet. 1990. 17.00 (0-385-24935-7) Doubleday.
—Making up Your Mind about Drugs. Enik, Ted, illus. LC 88-3609. 80p. (gr. 4-6). 1988. (Lodestar Bks); pap. 4.95 (0-525-67256-7, Lodestar Bks) Dutton Child Bks.
—Meg's Story: Straight Talk about Drugs. LC 91-21515. (Illus.). 64p. (gr. 7 up). 1992. PLB 12.90 (1-56294-102-X) Millbrook Pr.
—Meg's Story: Straight Talk about Drugs. 1992. pap. 4.95 (0-395-63557-8) HM.
—Patty's Story: Straight Talk about Drugs. Kirk, Barbara, photos by. (Illus.). 64p. (gr. 7 up). 1991. PLB 12.90 (1-878841-04-1) Millbrook Pr.
—Patty's Story: Straight Talk about Drugs. 1992. pap. 4.95 (0-395-63558-6) HM.
—Premenstrual Syndrome: A Guide for Young Women. 3rd, rev. ed. LC 91-34647. (Illus.). 96p. (gr. 7-12). 1991. pap. 7.95 (0-89793-088-6) Hunter Hse.
—Psychology Words. LC 85-8889. (Illus.). 96p. (gr. 7 up). 1986. lib. bdg. 9.59 (0-671-54291-5, J Messner) S&S Trade.
—Sharks. Santoro, Christopher, illus. LC 85-29327. 48p. (gr. k-4). 1987. pap. 10.95 (0-385-23418-X) Doubleday.
—Violence & Drugs. LC 89-34154. 112p. (gr. 7 up). 1989. PLB 13.40 (0-531-10818-X) Watts.
—Violence & Sports. LC 89-28069. 1990. PLB 13.90 (0-531-10907-0) Watts.
—Violence & the Family. 1990. PLB 13.90 (0-531-10906-2) Watts.
—Violence & the Media. LC 89-31502. (Illus.). 176p. (gr. 7-12). 1989. PLB 14.40 (0-531-10808-2) Watts.
—Whales. Bonaforte, Lisa, illus. LC 86-16500. 48p. (gr. k-3). 1987. 11.99 (0-685-18308-4); PLB 10.95 (0-685-18309-2) Doubleday.
Berger, Gilda & Berger, Melvin. Drug Abuse A-Z. LC 89-1512. 144p. (gr. 6 up). 1990. lib. bdg. 18.95 (0-89490-193-1) Enslow Pubs.
Berger, Gilda, jt. auth. see Berger, Melvin.
Berger, Helen, jt. auth. see Sefkow, Paula.

Berger, Larry B. & Lithwick, Dahlia, eds. I Will Sing Life: Voices from the Hole in the Wall Gang Camp. Benson, Robert, photos by. Newman, Paul, intro. by. (Illus.). 288p. 1992. 22.95 *(0-316-09273-8)* Little.

Berger, Melvin. All about Magnifying Glasses. (ps-3). 1993. pap. 4.95 *(0-590-45510-9)* Scholastic Inc.

—All about Seeds: A Hands-On Science Book. 32p. 1992. pap. 2.95 *(0-590-44909-5)* Scholastic Inc.

—Animals & Their Babies. 16p. (ps-2). 1992. pap. 14.95 *(1-56784-005-1)* Newbridge Comms.

—Animals in Danger. 16p. (gr. 2-4). 1993. pap. 14.95 *(1-56784-202-X)* Newbridge Comms.

—Animals in Hiding. 16p. (ps-2). 1993. pap. 14.95 *(1-56784-010-8)* Newbridge Comms.

—An Apple a Day. 16p. (ps-2). 1993. pap. 14.95 *(1-56784-201-1)* Newbridge Comms.

—As Big As a Whale. 16p. (gr. 2-4). 1993. pap. 14.95 *(1-56784-201-1)* Newbridge Comms.

—As Old as the Hills. Schindler, Stephen D., illus. LC 88-37403. 32p. (gr. k-4). 1989. PLB 12.90 *(0-531-10699-3)* Watts.

—A Butterfly Is Born. 16p. (ps-2). 1993. pap. 14.95 *(1-56784-012-4)* Newbridge Comms.

—Can Kids Save the Earth? 16p. (gr. 2-4). 1994. pap. 14.95 *(1-56784-209-7)* Newbridge Comms.

—Dinosaurs. 128p. 1990. pap. 2.95 *(0-380-76052-5,* Camelot) Avon.

—Discovering Mars: The Amazing Story of the Red Planet. (gr. 4-7). 1992. pap. 3.95 *(0-590-45221-5)* Scholastic Inc.

—From Peanuts to Peanut Butter. 16p. (ps-2). 1992. pap. 14.95 *(1-56784-001-9)* Newbridge Comms.

—Germs Make Me Sick! Hafner, Marilyn, illus. LC 84-45334. 32p. (ps-3). 1985. (Crowell Jr Bks); PLB 14.89 *(0-690-04429-1)* HarpC Child Bks.

—Germs Make Me Sick! Hafner, Marylin, illus. LC 84-45334. 32p. (ps-3). 1987. (Trophy); pap. 4.50 *(0-06-445053-8,* Trophy) HarpC Child Bks.

—Germs Make Me Sick! Hafner, Marylin, illus. LC 93-27059. 1995. write for info. *(0-06-024249-3);* lib. bdg. write for info. *(0-06-024250-7)* HarpC Child Bks.

—Hazardous Substances: A Reference. LC 86-8806. 128p. (gr. 6 up). 1986. lib. bdg. 17.95 *(0-89490-116-8)* Enslow Pubs.

—If You Lived on Mars. LC 88-9105. (Illus.). 80p. (gr. 4-6). 1989. 13.95 *(0-525-67260-5,* Lodestar Bks) Dutton Child Bks.

—Life in a Coral Reef. 16p. (gr. 2-4). 1994. pap. 14.95 *(1-56784-204-6)* Newbridge Comms.

—Life in the Polar Regions. 16p. (gr. 2-4). 1994. pap. 14.95 *(1-56784-210-0)* Newbridge Comms.

—Life in the Rainforest. 16p. (gr. 2-4). 1993. pap. 14.95 *(1-56784-200-3)* Newbridge Comms.

—Look Out for Turtles! Lloyd, Megan, illus. LC 90-36894. 32p. (gr. k-4). 1992. 15.00 *(0-06-022539-4);* PLB 14.89 *(0-06-022540-8)* HarpC Child Bks.

—Make Mine Ice Cream. 16p. (ps-2). 1993. pap. 14.95 *(1-56784-007-8)* Newbridge Comms.

—Monsters. 128p. 1991. pap. 2.95 *(0-380-76053-3,* Camelot) Avon.

—The Native Americans Told Us So. 16p. (gr. 2-4). 1994. pap. 14.95 *(1-56784-211-9)* Newbridge Comms.

—Oil Spill! Mirocha, Paul, illus. LC 92-34779. 1994. 14.00 *(0-06-022909-8);* PLB 13.89 *(0-06-022912-8)* HarpC Child Bks.

—One Hundred & One Spooky Halloween Jokes. (gr. 4-7). 1993. pap. 1.95 *(0-590-47143-0)* Scholastic Inc.

—One Hundred & One Wacky Science Jokes. 1989. pap. 1.95 *(0-590-42388-6)* Scholastic Inc.

—One Hundred & One Wacky State Jokes. 1991. pap. 1.95 *(0-590-44487-5)* Scholastic Inc.

—One Hundred One President Jokes. 1990. pap. 1.95 *(0-590-43166-8)* Scholastic Inc.

—Ouch! A Book about Cuts, Scratches, & Scrapes. Stewart, Pat, illus. 32p. (gr. k-3). 1991. 12.95 *(0-525-67323-7,* Lodestar Bks) Dutton Child Bks.

—The Science of Music. Buchanan, Yvonne, illus. LC 87-24921. 16p. (gr. 5-9). 1989. (Crowell Jr Bks); PLB 13.89 *(0-690-04647-2,* Crowell Jr Bks) HarpC Child Bks.

—See, Hear, Touch, Taste, Smell. 16p. (ps-2). 1993. pap. 14.95 *(1-56784-009-4)* Newbridge Comms.

—Seeds Get Around. 16p. (ps-2). 1992. pap. 14.95 *(1-56784-006-X)* Newbridge Comms.

—Sports Medicine. LC 81-43891. (Illus.). 128p. (gr. 5 up). 1982. (Crowell Jr Bks); (Crowell Jr Bks) HarpC Child Bks.

—Squirrels All Year Long. 16p. (ps-2). 1992. pap. 14.95 *(1-56784-003-5)* Newbridge Comms.

—The Story of Folk Music. LC 76-18159. (Illus.). (gr. 6 up). 1976. PLB 24.95 *(0-87599-215-3)* S G Phillips.

—Stranger Than Fiction: Killer Bugs. 128p. (Orig.). 1990. pap. 3.50 *(0-380-76036-3,* Camelot) Avon.

—Stranger Than Fiction: Sea Monsters. 96p. 1991. pap. 2.95 *(0-380-76054-1,* Camelot) Avon.

—Switch On, Switch Off. Croll, Carolyn, illus. LC 88-17638. 32p. (gr. k-3). 1989. (Crowell Jr Bks); PLB 13.89 *(0-690-04786-X,* Crowell Jr Bks) HarpC Child Bks.

—Switch on, Switch Off. Croll, Carolyn, illus. LC 88-17638. 32p. (gr. k-3). 1990. pap. 4.50 *(0-06-445097-X,* Trophy) HarpC Child Bks.

—Those Fabulous Frogs. 16p. (gr. 2-4). 1994. pap. 14.95 *(1-56784-208-9)* Newbridge Comms.

—A Tour of the Planets. 16p. (gr. 2-4). 1994. pap. 14.95 *(1-56784-207-0)* Newbridge Comms.

—UFO's, ET's, & Visitors from Space. 100p. (gr. 6-9). 1989. 8.00 *(0-685-63803-0,* BR8091) W A T Braille.

—The Web of Life. 16p. (gr. 2-4). 1994. pap. 14.95 *(1-56784-206-2)* Newbridge Comms.

—Where Does All the Garbage Go? 16p. (ps-2). 1992. pap. 14.95 *(1-56784-002-7)* Newbridge Comms.

—Who Cares about the Weather? 16p. (ps-2). 1992. pap. 14.95 *(1-56784-004-3)* Newbridge Comms.

—Why I Cough, Sneeze, Shiver, Hiccup, & Yawn. Keller, Holly, illus. LC 82-45587. 40p. (gr. k-3). 1983. PLB 13.89 *(0-690-04254-X,* Crowell Jr Bks) HarpC Child Bks.

—Wild Weather. 16p. (gr. 2-4). 1993. pap. 14.95 *(1-56784-203-8)* Newbridge Comms.

—The World of Ants. 16p. (ps-2). 1993. pap. 14.95 *(1-56784-008-6)* Newbridge Comms.

—The World of Dance. LC 78-14498. (Illus.). (gr. 7 up). 1978. 24.95 *(0-87599-221-8)* S G Phillips.

Berger, Melvin & Berger, Gilda. How's the Weather? Cymerman, John, illus. 48p. (gr. 1-5). 1993. PLB 12.00 *(0-8249-8599-0,* Ideals Child); pap. 13.95 *(0-8249-8641-5)* Hambleton-Hill.

—Round & Round the Money Goes. Cymerman, John, illus. 48p. (gr. 1-5). 1993. PLB 12.00 *(0-8249-8640-7,* Ideals Child); pap. 3.95 *(0-8249-8598-2)* Hambleton-Hill.

—Telephones, Televisions, & Toilets: How They Work & What Can Go Wrong. Madden, Don, illus. LC 92-18198. (gr. k-3). 1993. 12.00 *(0-8249-8645-8,* Ideals Child); pap. 3.95 *(0-8249-8608-3)* Hambleton-Hill.

—Where Are the Stars During the Day? A Book about Stars. Sims, Blanche, illus. LC 92-18200. (gr. k-3). 1993. 12.00 *(0-8249-8644-X,* Ideals Child); pap. 3.95 *(0-8249-8607-5)* Hambleton-Hill.

—Where Did Your Family Come From? A Book about Immigrants. Quackenbush, Robert, illus. LC 92-28626. (gr. k-3). 1993. 12.00 *(0-8249-8647-4,* Ideals Child); pap. 3.95 *(0-8249-8610-5)* Hambleton-Hill.

—The Whole World in Your Hands: Looking at Maps. Quackenbush, Robert, illus. LC 92-18199. (gr. k-3). 1993. 12.00 *(0-8249-8646-6,* Ideals Child); pap. 3.95 *(0-8249-8609-1)* Hambleton-Hill.

Berger, Melvin, jt. auth. see Berger, Gilda.

Berger, Neal J. The Only Purple Dinosaur. 1991. 6.95 *(0-533-09141-1)* Vantage.

Berger, Sidney. Bird Boy. (Illus.). 36p. (Orig.). (gr. 2 up). 1988. pap. 3.00 *(0-88680-295-4);* royalty on application 50.00 *(0-685-58403-8)* I E Clark.

—Rapunzel. (Illus.). 32p. (Orig.). (ps up). 1991. pap. 3.00 *(0-88680-359-4);* royalty on application 40.00 *(0-685-59134-4)* I E Clark.

Berger, Sidney L. & Fanidi, Theo. The Little Match Girl: The Musical. (Illus.). 32p. (Orig.). (gr. 4 up). 1985. pap. 3.00 *(0-88680-230-X);* piano & vocal score 10.00 *(0-88680-231-8);* royalty on application 60.00 *(0-685-58018-0)* I E Clark.

Berger, Terry. Ben's ABC Day. Kandell, Alice, illus. LC 81-13754. 32p. (gr. k-3). 1982. PLB 14.88 *(0-688-00882-8)* Lothrop.

—I Have Feelings. Spivak, I. Howard, photos by. LC 70-147123. (Illus.). 32p. (ps-3). 1971. 14.95 *(0-87705-021-X);* pap. 9.95 *(0-89885-342-7)* Human Sci Pr.

—I Have Feelings Too. LC 79-15863. 32p. (ps-3). 1979. 16.95 *(0-87705-441-X)* Human Sci Pr.

—Lucky. LC 73-16817. 48p. (ps-3). 1976. 6.95 *(0-87955-110-0)* *(0-87955-710-9)* O'Hara.

Berger, Terry, ed. Black Fairy Tales. White, David O., illus. LC 70-75517. (gr. 3-7). 1974. (Atheneum Childrens Bk); pap. 3.95 *(0-689-70402-X)* Macmillan Child Grp.

Berger, Thomas. The Christmas Craft Book. Lawson, Polly, tr. (Illus.). 86p. 1990. pap. 12.95 *(0-86315-110-8,* Pub. by Floris Bks UK) Gryphon Hse.

—The Little Troll. Lawson, Polly, tr. Heuninck, Ronald, illus. (GER.). 32p. (gr-3). 1992. 14.95 *(0-86315-112-4,* Pub. by Floris Bks UK) Gryphon Hse.

—The Mouse & the Potato. Lawson, Polly, tr. Grillis, Carla, illus. (DUT.). 32p. (ps-2). 1990. Repr. 14.95 *(0-86315-103-5,* Pub. by Floris Bks UK) Gryphon Hse.

Bergey, Alyce. David & Jonathan. (Illus.). 24p. (gr. k-4). 1987. pap. 1.89 *(0-570-09006-7,* 59-1434) Concordia.

—World God Made: Genesis 1-2. (ps-3). 1965. pap. 1.89 *(0-570-06011-7)* Concordia.

—Young Jesus in the Temple. (Illus.). (gr. k-4). 1986. pap. 1.89 saddlestitched *(0-570-06203-9,* 59-1426) Concordia.

Bergez, John, ed. see Reinstedt, Randall A.

Bergh, Jerald E., ed. see Kipling, Rudyard.

Berghammer, Gretta, jt. ed. see Jennings, Coleman A.

Bergin, Feryl J. You...& Being a Teenager. rev. ed. Bergin, James E., illus. 112p. 1991. 6.95 *(0-936955-00-7)* Eminent Pubns.

Bergin, Mark, jt. auth. see MacDonald, Fiona.

Bergman, Carol. Mae West. Horner, Matina. (Illus.). 112p. (gr. 5 up). 1988. lib. bdg. 17.95 *(1-55546-681-8)* Chelsea Hse.

—Sidney Poitier. King, Coretta Scott, intro. by. (Illus.). 112p. (Orig.). (gr. 5 up). 1988. 17.95 *(1-55546-605-2);* pap. 9.95 *(0-7910-0209-8)* Chelsea Hse.

Bergman, David, jt. auth. see Plante, Patricia.

Bergman, Donna. City Fox. Hanson, Peter E., illus. LC 90-27019. 32p. (gr. k-3). 1992. SBE 13.95 *(0-689-31687-9,* Atheneum Child Bk) Macmillan Child Grp.

—Timmy Green's Blue Lake. Ohlsson, Ib, illus. LC 91-30232. 32p. (ps up). 1992. 14.00 *(0-688-10747-8,* Tambourine Bks); PLB 13.93 *(0-688-10748-6,* Tambourine Bks) Morrow.

Bergman, Irwin. Jackie Robinson: Baseball Pioneer. (Illus.). 1993. 13.95 *(0-7910-1771-0,* Am Art Analog); pap. 4.95 *(0-7910-2113-0,* Am Art Analog) Chelsea Hse.

Bergman, Lincoln, ed. see Agler, Leigh.

Bergman, Lincoln, ed. see Ahouse, Jeremy J.

Bergman, Lincoln, ed. see Barber, Jacqueline.

Bergman, Lincoln, ed. see Barber, Jacqueline & Willard, Carolyn.

Bergman, Lincoln, ed. see Barrett, Katharine.

Bergman, Lincoln, ed. see Barrett, Katharine, et al.

Bergman, Lincoln, ed. see Buegler, Marion E.

Bergman, Lincoln, ed. see Cossey, Ruth, et al.

Bergman, Lincoln, ed. see Echols, Jean C.

Bergman, Lincoln, ed. see Goodman, Jan M.

Bergman, Lincoln, ed. see Gould, Alan.

Bergman, Lincoln, ed. see Hocking, Colin, et al.

Bergman, Lincoln, ed. see Kopp, Jaine.

Bergman, Lincoln, ed. see Sneider, Cary & Gould, Alan.

Bergman, Lincoln, ed. see Sneider, Cary I.

Bergman, Lincoln, ed. see Sneider, Cary I., et al.

Bergman, Lincoln, ed. see Sneider, Cary I.

Bergman, Lincoln, ed. see Sneider, Cary I. & Barber, Jacqueline.

Bergman, Lincoln, ed. see Sneider, Cary I. & Gould, Alan.

Bergman, Tamar. Along the Tracks. Swirsky, Michael, tr. 256p. (gr. 6-9). 1991. 14.45 *(0-395-55328-8,* Sandpiper) HM.

—The Boy from over There. Halkin, Hillel, tr. from HEB. LC 87-36634. 192p. (gr. 3-7). 1988. 13.45 *(0-395-43077-1)* HM.

—Boy from over There. (gr. 4-7). 1992. pap. 3.95 *(0-395-64370-8)* HM.

Bergman, Thomas. Don't Turn Away, 8 vols. Bergman, Thomas, illus. 56p. (gr. 4-5). 1989. Set. PLB 138.16 *(0-8368-0759-6)* Gareth Stevens Inc.

—Finding a Common Language: Children Living with Deafness. LC 88-42969. (Illus.). 48p. (gr. 4-5). 1989. PLB 17.27 *(1-55532-916-0)* Gareth Stevens Inc.

—Going Places: Children Living with Cerebral Palsy. Bergman, Thomas, illus. LC 90-48266. 48p. (gr. 4-5). 1991. PLB 17.27 *(0-8368-0199-7)* Gareth Stevens Inc.

—Meeting the Challenge: Children Living with Diabetes. LC 91-50334. (Illus.). 56p. (gr. 3-8). 1992. PLB 17.27 *(0-8368-0738-3);* PLB 17.27 s.p. *(0-685-61496-4)* Gareth Stevens Inc.

—Moments That Disappear: Children Living with Epilepsy. LC 91-50335. (Illus.). 56p. (gr. 3-8). 1992. PLB 17.27 *(0-8368-0739-1);* PLB 17.27 s.p. *(0-685-61495-6)* Gareth Stevens Inc.

—On Our Own Terms: Children Living with Physical Handicaps. LC 88-42973. (Illus.). 48p. (gr. 4-5). 1989. PLB 17.27 *(1-55532-942-X)* Gareth Stevens Inc.

—One Day at a Time: Children Living with Leukemia. LC 88-42972. (Illus.). 48p. (gr. 4-5). 1989. PLB 17.27 *(1-55532-913-6)* Gareth Stevens Inc.

—Seeing in Special Ways: Children Living with Blindness. LC 88-42970. (Illus.). 56p. (gr. 4-5). 1989. PLB 17.27 *(1-55532-915-2)* Gareth Stevens Inc.

—We Laugh, We Love, We Cry: Children Living with Mental Retardation. LC 88-42971. (Illus.). 48p. (gr. 4-5). 1989. PLB 17.27 *(1-55532-914-4)* Gareth Stevens Inc.

Bergreen, Gary. Coping with Difficult Teachers. Rosen, Roger, ed. LC 88-20107. (gr. 7 up). 1988. PLB 13.95 *(0-8239-0788-0)* Rosen Group.

—Coping with Study Strategies. rev. ed. (gr. 7-12). 1990. 13.95 *(0-8239-1140-3)* Rosen Group.

Bergsmo, Morten, ed. Studying the Writings of Shoghi Effendi. 216p. (Orig.). (gr. 12). 1991. pap. 14.95 *(0-85398-336-4)* G Ronald Pub.

Bergstralh, Jay T., et al, eds. Uranus. LC 90-21185. 1076p. 1991. 75.00x *(0-8165-1208-6)* U of Ariz Pr.

Bergstrom, Corinne. Losing Your Best Friend. Rosamilia, Patricia, illus. LC 79-20622. 32p. (ps-3). 1980. 16.95 *(0-87705-471-1)* Human Sci Pr.

Bergstrom, Craig, jt. auth. see Bergstrom, Joan M.

Bergstrom, Evelyn J., ed. see Perle, Ruth L.

Bergstrom, Gunilla. Is That a Monster, Alfie Atkins? Swindells, Robert, tr. (Illus.). 28p. (ps up). 1989. 6.95 *(91-29-59136-8,* Pub. by R & S Bks) FS&G.

—Who's Scaring Alfie Atkins? Sandin, Joan, tr. from SWE. Bergstrom, Gunilla, illus. 32p. (ps up). 1987. 6.95 *(91-29-58318-7,* Pub. by R & S Bks) FS&G.

Bergstrom, Joan M. & Bergstrom, Craig. All the Best Contests for Kids, 1992-1993. 3rd ed. 288p. (gr. k-9). 1992. pap. 9.95 *(0-89815-451-0)* Ten Speed Pr.

Berhard, Emery, retold by. The Tree That Rains: The Flood Myth of the Huichol Indians of Mexico. Bernhard, Durga, illus. LC 93-8294. (gr. 4-8). 1994. 15.95 *(0-8234-1108-7)* Holiday.

Beringer, Joan E. God's Gifts. Leder, Dora, illus. LC 81-82908. 32p. (gr. k-3). 1984. 8.95 *(0-87510-160-7)* Christian Sci.

Berk, Fred. Chasidic Dance. (gr. 9 up). 1975. pap. 5.00 *(0-8074-0083-1,* 582050) UAHC.

Berk, Meridith & Vavrus, Toni. Go Ahead - Make Me Laugh. LC 92-48261. (Illus.). 96p. (gr. 4-8). 1992. 12.95 *(0-8069-8442-2)* Sterling.

—Go Ahead - Make Me Laugh. Sinclair, Jeff, illus. 96p. (gr. 3-8). 1993. pap. 3.95 *(0-8069-8443-0)* Sterling.

Berke, Art. Babe Ruth: The Best There Ever Was. Rakos, Jennie, ed. LC 87-27366. (Illus.). 128p. (gr. 7-9). 1988. PLB 14.40 (0-531-10472-9) Watts.
—Gymnastics. Solomon, Maury, ed. LC 87-23745. (Illus.). 96p. (gr. 4 up). 1988. PLB 10.90 (0-531-10478-8) Watts.
Berke, Sally. Monster at Loch Ness. LC 77-24715. (Illus.). 48p. (gr. 4 up). 1983. PLB 18.64 (0-8172-1054-7) Raintree Steck-V.
Berke, Tina, ed. see Murphy, Linda.
Berkemeyer, Kathy, ed. see Heartland, Amanda.
Berkemeyer, Kathy, ed. see Reidelbach, Maria.
Berkow, Ira. Hank Greenberg: Hall-of-Fame Slugger. Ellison, Mick, illus. LC 90-43005. 108p. (gr. 3-7). 1991. 12.95t (0-8276-0376-2) JPS Phila.
Berkowitz, Henry. Amphibians & Reptiles. Berkowitz, Henry, illus. 32p. (Orig.). (gr. 1-9). 1985. pap. 2.50 (0-317-66182-5) Banyan Bks.
—The Dinosaurs: An Educational Coloring Book. Berkowitz, Henry, illus. 32p. (Orig.). (gr. 1-9). 1986. pap. 2.50 (0-938059-00-9) Henart Bks.
—Sharks: An Educational Coloring Book. (Illus.). 32p. (Orig.). (gr. 1-9). 1988. pap. 2.50 (0-938059-01-7) Henart Bks.
Berksen, Barbara. Island of the Blue Dolphins: A Study Guide. (gr. 4-7). 1984. tchr's. ed. & wkbk. 14.95 (0-88122-088-4) LRN Links.
Berkus, Clara W. Charlsie's Chuckle. Dodd, Margaret, illus. LC 91-46655. 32p. (gr. k-6). 1992. 14.95 (0-933149-50-6) Woodbine House.
Berlan, Kathryn H. Andrew's Amazing Monsters. Chambliss, Maxie, illus. LC 91-39131. 32p. (ps-2). 1993. SBE 13.95 (0-689-31739-5, Atheneum Child Bk) Macmillan Child Grp.
Berle, Arnie. New Guitar Techniques for Sightreading. Stang, Aaron, ed. 104p. (Orig.). 1991. pap. text ed. 9.95 (0-89898-583-8) CPP Belwin.
Berleth, Richard. Samuel's Choice. Mathews, Judith, ed. Watling, James, illus. LC 89-77186. 40p. (gr. 3-6). 1990. PLB 14.95 (0-8075-7218-7) A Whitman.
Berlfein, Judy. Teen Pregnancy. LC 92-9673. (Illus.). 112p. (gr. 5-8). 1992. PLB 14.95 (1-56006-130-8) Lucent Bks.
Berlin, Evelyn, jt. auth. see Hubbard, Kate.
Berliner, Don. Before the Wright Brothers. (Illus.). 72p. (gr. 5 up). 1990. 19.95 (0-8225-1588-1) Lerner Pubns.
—Distance Flights. (Illus.). 72p. (gr. 5 up). 1990. 21.50 (0-8225-1589-X) Lerner Pubns.
—Living in Space. LC 92-24847. (Illus.). 72p. (gr. 5 up). 1993. 14.95 (0-8225-1599-7) Lerner Pubns.
—Our Future in Space. (Illus.). 72p. (gr. 5 up). 1991. PLB 19.95 (0-8225-1592-X) Lerner Pubns.
—Research Airplanes: Testing the Boundaries of Flight. (Illus.). 64p. (gr. 5 up). 1988. PLB 21.50 (0-8225-1582-2) Lerner Pubns.
—Unusual Airplanes. (Illus.). 48p. (gr. 4-9). 1985. lib. bdg. 14.95 (0-8225-0431-6) Lerner Pubns.
—The World Aerobatics Championships. (Illus.). 64p. (gr. 5 up). 1989. 17.50 (0-8225-0531-2) Lerner Pubns.
Berliner, Franz. Miserable Marabou. Hedlund, Irene, illus. LC 89-30852. 23p. (gr. k-3). 1989. PLB 18.60 (0-8368-0094-X) Gareth Stevens Inc.
—Wildebeest. Gyldendal, tr. Brogger, Lilian, illus. LC 90-82449. 32p. (ps-2). 1991. 13.95 (0-8249-8488-9, Ideals Child) Hambleton-Hill.
Berliner, Larry & Berliner, Susan. ReWriter, Bk. I. Gompper, Gail, illus. 38p. (Orig.). (gr. 5 up). 1985. pap. text ed. 17.95 ea. Bk. I, gr. 5-8 & high school sp. needs (0-913935-28-X) Bk. II, gr. 6-9 & high school sp. needs (0-913935-29-8) ERA-CCR.
Berliner, Susan, jt. auth. see Berliner, Larry.
Berlitz. Berlitz Jr. French. (FRE., Illus.). 64p. (Orig.). (ps-2). 1989. bds. 19.95 incl. cassette (0-689-71314-2, Aladdin) Macmillan Child Grp.
—Berlitz Jr. French Dictionary. LC 91-40123. (Illus.). 144p. (ps-2). 1992. POB 11.95 (0-689-71539-0, Aladdin) Macmillan Child Grp.
—Berlitz Jr. German: Ich Spreche Deutsch. (Illus.). 64p. (ps-2). 1992. POB 19.95 (0-689-71598-6, Aladdin) Macmillan Child Grp.
—Berlitz Jr. Italian: Parlo Italiano. LC 91-21143. (Illus.). 64p. (ps-2). 1992. POB 19.95 (0-689-71595-1, Aladdin) Macmillan Child Grp.
—Berlitz Jr. Spanish. (ps-2). 1989. bds. 19.95 incl. cassette (0-689-71317-7, Aladdin) Macmillan Child Grp.
—Berlitz Jr. Spanish Dictionary. LC 91-43927. (Illus.). 144p. (ps-2). 1992. POB 11.95 (0-689-71538-2, Aladdin) Macmillan Child Grp.
Berlitz, Charles. Bermuda Triangle. 272p. 1978. pap. 5.99 (0-380-00465-8) Avon.
Berman, Aaron, ed. see Olshtain, Elite, et al.
Berman, Avis. James McNeill Whistler. LC 93-9453. 1993. 19.95 (0-8109-3968-1) Abrams.
Berman, Claire. What Am I Doing in a Stepfamily? Wilson, Dick, illus. (gr. k-7). 1992. pap. 8.95 (0-8184-0563-5, L Stuart) Carol Pub Group.
Berman, Claire G. What Am I Doing in a Step-Family? Wilson, Dick, illus. 48p. (gr. 2 up). 1982. 12.00 (0-8184-0325-X) Carol Pub Group.
Berman, Julie S., jt. auth. see Clapp, Steve.
Berman, Linda. The Goodbye Painting. Hannon, Mark, illus. LC 81-20217. 32p. (ps-3). 1982. 16.95 (0-89885-074-6) Human Sci Pr.
Berman, Melanie. Building Jewish Life Prayers & Blessings. Bleicher, David, illus. 32p. (Orig.). (gr. k-2). 1991. pap. text ed. 1.85 (0-933873-66-2) Torah Aura.

Berman, Russell. Paul von Hindenburg. Schlesinger, Arthur M., Jr., intro. by. (Illus.). 112p. (gr. 5 up). 1987. lib. bdg. 17.95 (0-87754-532-4) Chelsea Hse.
Berman, Ruth. American Bison. (ps-3). 1992. 19.95 (0-87614-697-3) Carolrhoda Bks.
Berman, Sally. Catch Them Thinking in Science: A Handbook of Classroom Strategies. LC 93-78421. (Illus.). 112p. (gr. 6-12). 1993. pap. 15.95 (0-932935-55-9) IRI-Skylght.
Berman, William. How to Dissect. 4th ed. LC 83-27510. (Illus.). 224p. (gr. 8 up). 1985. pap. 8.95 (0-668-05941-9) P-H.
Bermejo, Ana, tr. see Platt, Richard.
Bernadot, Dan. Four Steps to Less Fat & Better Nutrition: A Rational Approach to Weight Loss. (Illus.). 127p. (Orig.). (gr. 9-12). 1983. pap. 6.95 (0-936007-19-2, 2550) Meridian Educ.
Bernal, Diaz Del Castillo see Bernal-Diaz, Del Castillo.
Bernal-Diaz, Del Castillo. Conquest of New Spain. Cohen, John M., tr. (Illus.). (gr. 9 up). 1963. pap. 7.95 (0-14-044123-9) Viking Child Bks.
Bernard, Elizabeth. Center Stage. 1987. pap. 2.95 (0-449-13300-1, Girls Only) Fawcett.
—Changing Partners. (gr. 6 up). 1988. pap. 2.95 (0-449-13303-6, Girls Only) Fawcett.
Bernard, Eunice C. Honey Bee Milly: Honey Bee - Apis Mellifera. Tausch, Cheryl C., illus. 72p. (Orig.). (gr. 4 up). 1994. pap. write for info. (0-9629950-5-3) Ashbook Pr.
Bernard, Felix, jt. auth. see Smith, Dick.
Bernard, Lodge, retold by. Prince Ivan & the Firebird: A Russian Folk Tale. Lodge, Bernard, illus. LC 93-12343. (ps-12). 1993. smythe sewn reinforced 14.95 (1-879085-86-0) Whsprng Coyote Pr.
Bernard, Patricia. Kangaroo Kids. 1992. pap. 3.50 (0-553-15959-3) Bantam.
Bernard, Robert, ed. All Problems Are Simple & Other Stories: Nineteen Views of the College Years. (gr. 12 up). 1988. 3.50 (0-318-37398-X, LF) Dell.
Bernardini, Robert. Southern Love for Christmas. Rice, James, illus. 32p. (gr. k-3). 1993. 14.95 (0-88289-974-0) Pelican.
—A Southern Time Christmas. Rice, James, illus. LC 91-12467. 32p. 1991. 14.95 (0-88289-828-0) Pelican.
Bernards, Neal. Advertising: Distinguishing Between Fact & Opinion. LC 91-28266. (Illus.). 32p. (gr. 4-7). 1991. PLB 10.95 (0-89908-614-4) Greenhaven.
—Elections: Locating the Author's Main Idea. LC 92-21793. (Illus.). 32p. (gr. 4-7). 1992. PLB 10.95 (1-56510-022-0) Greenhaven.
—Gun Control. LC 91-15561. (Illus.). 112p. (gr. 5-8). 1991. PLB 14.95 (1-56006-127-8) Lucent Bks.
—Living in Space: Opposing Viewpoints. LC 90-3727. (Illus.). 112p. (gr. 5-8). 1990. PLB 14.95 (0-89908-075-8) Greenhaven.
—Nuclear Power: Examining Cause & Effect Relationships. LC 90-40412. (Illus.). 32p. (gr. 3-6). 1990. PLB 10.95 (0-89908-607-1) Greenhaven.
—The Palestinian Conflict: Identifying Propaganda Techniques. LC 90-37741. (Illus.). 32p. (gr. 3-6). 1990. PLB 10.95 (0-89908-602-0) Greenhaven.
—Population: Detecting Bias. Buggey, JoAnne, contrib. by. LC 92-17419. (Illus.). 32p. (gr. 4-7). 1992. PLB 10.95 (0-89908-622-5) Greenhaven.
—The War on Drugs: Examining Cause & Effect Relationships. LC 91-22021. (Illus.). 32p. (gr. 4-7). 1991. PLB 10.95 (0-89908-612-8) Greenhaven.
Bernards, Neal & Szumski, Bonnie. Prisons: Detecting Bias. LC 90-45284. (Illus.). 32p. (gr. 3-6). 1990. PLB 10.95 (0-89908-604-7) Greenhaven.
Bernards, Neal, ed. The Environmental Crisis: Opposing Viewpoints. (Illus.). 264p. (gr. 10 up). 1991. PLB 17.95 (0-89908-175-4); pap. 9.95 (0-89908-150-9) Greenhaven.
—Euthanasia: Opposing Viewpoints. LC 89-2181. (Illus.). 235p. (gr. 10 up). 1989. PLB 17.95 (0-89908-442-7); pap. 9.95 (0-89908-417-6) Greenhaven.
—The Mass Media: Opposing Viewpoints. LC 87-14848. (Illus.). 32p. (gr. 10 up). 1987. lib. bdg. 17.95 (0-89908-425-7); pap. 9.95 (0-89908-400-1) Greenhaven.
—The War on Drugs: Opposing Viewpoints. LC 90-39795. (Illus.). 240p. (gr. 10 up). 1990. PLB 17.95 (0-89908-483-4); pap. text ed. 9.95 (0-89908-458-3) Greenhaven.
Bernards, Neal, jt. ed. see O'Neill, Terry.
Bernards, Neal, et al, eds. Teenage Sexuality: Opposing Viewpoints. LC 87-37268. (Illus.). (gr. 10 up). 1988. lib. bdg. 17.95 (0-89908-430-3); pap. 9.95 (0-89908-405-2) Greenhaven.
Bernardson, Derek. Emma's Rat-Tastic Adventure. Wilcox, Cathy, illus. 96p. (Orig.). (gr. k-4). 1993. pap. 6.95 (0-04-442345-4, Pub. by Allen & Unwin Aust Pty AT) IPG Chicago.
—The Sparrows & the Circus. Kelly, Geoff, illus. 96p. (Orig.). (gr. 1-3). 1993. pap. 6.95 (1-86373-061-3, Pub. by Allen & Unwin Aust Pty AT) IPG Chicago.
—The Sparrows & the Spies. Kelly, Geoff, illus. 96p. (Orig.). (gr. 1-3). 1993. pap. 6.95 (1-86373-042-7, Pub. by Allen & Unwin Aust Pty AT) IPG Chicago.
Bernatas, Bob. Sitting Bull. (gr. 4-7). 1993. pap. 7.95 (0-7910-1968-3) Chelsea Hse.
Bernath, Stefen. Garden Flowers-Coloring Book. 1978. pap. 2.95 (0-486-23142-9) Dover.
—Tropical Fish-Coloring Book. pap. 2.95 (0-486-23620-X) Dover.

Bernet, Elizabeth C. Wings of Love. Whiting, William T., illus. 40p. (ps). 1991. 11.95 (0-88138-109-8, Green Tiger) S&S Trade.
Bernhard, Brendan. The Iranian Americans. Moynihan, Daniel P., intro. by. (Illus.). 112p. (gr. 7-12). 1991. lib. bdg. 17.95 (0-87754-885-4) Chelsea Hse.
—Pizarro, Orellana, & the Exploration of the Amazon. Goetzmann, William H., ed. Collins, Michael, intro. by. (Illus.). 112p. (gr. 5 up). 1991. lib. bdg. 18.95 (0-7910-1305-7) Chelsea Hse.
Bernhard, Durga. Alphabeasts. LC 92-24980. (Illus.). 32p. (ps-3). 1993. reinforced bdg. 14.95 (0-8234-0993-7) Holiday.
—What's Maggie up To? Bernhard, Durga, illus. LC 91-42915. 32p. (ps-3). 1992. reinforced bdg. 14.95 (0-8234-0969-4) Holiday.
Bernhard, Emery. Dragonfly. Bernhard, Durga, illus. LC 92-39930. 32p. (ps-3). 1993. reinforced bdg. 15.95 (0-8234-1033-1) Holiday.
—Eagles: Lions of the Sky. Bernhard, Durga, illus. LC 93-1833. 32p. (gr. 4-8). 1994. 15.95 (0-8234-1105-2) Holiday.
—Ladybug. Bernhard, Durga, illus. LC 92-52714. 32p. (ps-3). 1992. reinforced bdg. 14.95 (0-8234-0986-4) Holiday.
Bernhard, Emery, retold by. How Snowshoe Hare Rescued the Sun: A Yuit Folktale. Bernhard, Durga, illus. LC 92-47124. (ps-3). 1993. reinforced bdg. 15.95 (0-8234-1043-9) Holiday.
—Spotted Eagle & Black Crow: A Lakota Legend. Bernhard, Durga, illus. LC 92-23950. 32p. (ps-3). 1993. reinforced bdg. 15.95 (0-8234-1007-2) Holiday.
Bernhard, Gwyn K. Gwyn Karon Bernhard's Kids' Talk: Kids' Talk in the Classroom Workbook, No. 1. 125p. (gr. 5-9). 1989. 85.00 (1-87-781904-2) Kids Talk CT.
Bernhardt, Barbara A., et al. The Marfan Syndrome: A Booklet for Teenagers. LeHew, Ronald, illus. 20p. 1988. pap. 1.00 (0-918335-03-5) Natl Marfan Foun.
Bernhardt, Edythe. ABC's of Thinking with Caldecott Books. Polette, Nancy. (Illus.). 112p. (gr. 1-4). 1988. pap. 12.95 (0-913839-70-1) Bk Lures.
Bernholz, Jean F. & Sumner, Patricia H. Success in Reading & Writing. 2nd ed. (Illus.). 288p. (gr. 3 up). 1991. 27.95 (0-673-36005-9) GdYrBks.
Bernie, Shirley A., jt. auth. see Sansom-Flood, Renee.
Bernier, Evariste. Baxter Bear & Moses Moose. Peterson, Dawn, illus. LC 90-61408. 48p. (gr. 1-4). 1990. 12.95 (0-89272-287-8) Down East.
Bernier-Grand, Carmen. Juan Bobo: Four Silly Tales from Puerto Rico. Nieves, Ernesto R., illus. LC 93-12936. Date not set. 14.00 (0-06-023389-3); PLB 13.89 (0-06-023390-7) HarpC.
Bernos de Gasztold, Carmen. Prayers from the Ark: Selected Poems. Godden, Rumer, tr. Moser, Barry, illus. 32p. 1992. 16.00 (0-670-84496-9) Viking Child Bks.
Bernotas, Bob. Amiri Baraka (Le Roi Jones) King, Coretta Scott, intro. by. (Illus.). 112p. (gr. 5 up). 1991. lib. bdg. 17.95 (0-7910-1117-8) Chelsea Hse.
—Brigham Young. (Illus.). 112p. (gr. 5 up). 1993. PLB 17.95 (0-7910-1642-0) Chelsea Hse.
—Department of Housing & Urban Development. Schlesinger, Arthur M., Jr., intro. by. (Illus.). 104p. (gr. 5 up). 1991. lib. bdg. 14.95 (0-87754-841-2) Chelsea Hse.
—Jim Thorpe. (Illus.). (gr. 5 up). 1993. PLB 17.95 (0-7910-1722-2) Chelsea Hse.
—Jim Thorpe. (gr. 4-7). 1992. pap. 7.95 (0-7910-1695-1) Chelsea Hse.
—Sitting Bull. (Illus.). 112p. (gr. 5 up). 1992. lib. bdg. 17.95 (0-7910-1703-6) Chelsea Hse.
—Spike Lee: Filmmaker. LC 92-41234. (Illus.). 112p. (gr. 6 up). 1993. lib. bdg. 17.95 (0-89490-416-7) Enslow Pubs.
Bernotas, Bob, Jr. The Federal Government: How it Works. (Illus.). 144p. (gr. 5 up). 1990. 14.95 (0-87754-859-5) Chelsea Hse.
Bernstein, Bob. Friday Afternoon Fun. Schmidt, Ross, illus. 64p. (gr. 2-6). 1984. wkbk. 7.95 (0-86653-206-4, GA 558) Good Apple.
—Math Thinking Motivators. 96p. (gr. 2-7). 1988. wkbk. 9.95 (0-86653-431-8, GA1049) Good Apple.
—Mathemactivities. 112p. (gr. 2-7). 1991. 9.95 (0-86653-617-5, GA1336) Good Apple.
—Monday Morning Magic. 64p. (gr. k-6). 1982. 7.95 (0-86653-080-0, GA 425) Good Apple.
—Numbers Count. 96p. (gr. 2-7). 1990. 9.95 (0-86653-542-X, GA1151) Good Apple.
—Thinking Numbers. 96p. (gr. 2-7). 1989. 9.95 (0-86653-506-3, GA1094) Good Apple.
Bernstein, Bonnie. Day By Day. 2nd ed. (gr. k-6). 1989. pap. 16.95 (0-8224-4253-1) Fearon Teach Aids.
—Writing Crafts Workshop. LC 81-85351. (gr. 3-8). 1982. pap. 10.95 (0-8224-9785-9) Fearon Teach Aids.
Bernstein, Bonnie & Blair, Leigh. Native American Crafts Workshop. LC 81-82041. (gr. 3-8). 1982. pap. 10.95 (0-8224-9784-0) Fearon Teach Aids.
Bernstein, Daryl. Better Than a Lemonade Stand: Business Ideas for Kids. (Illus.). (gr. 2-10). 1992. pap. 7.95 (0-941831-75-2) Beyond Words Pub.
—Kids Can Succeed! Fifty-One Tips for Real Life from One Kid to Another. (Illus.). 216p. (Orig.). (gr. 3-7). 1993. pap. 5.95 (1-55850-285-8) Adams Inc MA.
Bernstein, David. Parshas Beshalach. Shapiro, Sara, illus. (ENG & HEB.). 192p. (gr. 5-8). 1991. pap. text ed. 6.00 (0-914131-96-6, A148) Torah Umesorah.

Bernstein, Joanne & Cohen, Paul. Creepy, Crawly, Critter Riddles. Tucker, Kathleen, ed. Hoffman, Rosekrans, illus. LC 86-15911. 32p. (gr. 1-5). 1986. PLB 8.95 (0-8075-1345-8) A Whitman.
—Unidentified Flying Riddles. Fay, Ann, ed. Seltzer, Meyer, illus. LC 83-17097. 32p. (gr. 1-5). 1983. PLB 8.95 (0-8075-8329-4) A Whitman.
Bernstein, Joanne E. & Blue, Rose. Judith Resnik: Challenger Astronaut. Gerber, Alan J., contrib. by. (Illus.). 144p. (gr. 5-9). 1990. 14.95 (0-525-67305-9, Lodestar Bks) Dutton Child Bks.
Bernstein, Joanne E. & Cohen, Paul. Dizzy Doctor Riddles. Tucker, Kathy, ed. Whiting, Carl, illus. LC 89-35392. 32p. (gr. 1-5). 1989. 8.95 (0-8075-1648-1) A Whitman.
—Happy Holiday Riddles to You. Fay, Ann, ed. Seltzer, Meyer, illus. LC 85-717. 32p. (gr. 1-5). 1985. PLB 8.95 (0-8075-3154-5) A Whitman.
—Out to Pasture! Jokes about Cows. Hanson, Joan, illus. 32p. (gr. 1-4). 1988. PLB 11.95 (0-8225-0998-9) Lerner Pubns.
—Riddles to Take on Vacation. Fay, Ann, ed. LC 87-2071. (Illus.). (gr. 1-5). 1987. PLB 8.95 (0-8075-6999-2) A Whitman.
—Sporty Riddles. Mathews, Judith, ed. Harvey, Paul, illus. LC 89-5294. 32p. (gr. 1-5). 1989. PLB 8.95 (0-8075-7590-9) A Whitman.
—Touchdown Riddles. Levine, Abby, ed. Signorino, Slug, illus. LC 88-21761. 32p. (gr. 1-5). 1989. 8.95g (0-8075-8036-8) A Whitman.
—What Was the Wicked Witch's Real Name? & Other Character Riddles. Iosa, Ann, illus. LC 86-1648. 32p. (gr. 1-5). 1986. 8.95 (0-8075-8854-7) A Whitman.
—Why Didn't the Dinosaur Cross the Road? And Other Prehistoric Riddles. Tucker, Kathy, ed. Whiting, Carl, illus. LC 90-12726. 32p. (gr. 2-5). 1990. 8.95 (0-8075-9077-0) A Whitman.
Bernstein, Joanne E. & Fireside, Bryna. Special Parents, Special Children. Mathews, Judith, ed. Bernstein, Michael, photos by. LC 90-42442. (Illus.). 64p. (gr. 3-7). 1991. 11.95 (0-8075-7559-3) A Whitman.
Bernstein, Joanne E., jt. auth. see Blue, Rose.
Bernstein, Leonard. Leonard Bernstein's Young People's Concerts. 1992. pap. 15.00 (0-385-42435-3, Anchor Pr) Doubleday.
Bernstein, Louis & Garibaldi, Louis E. Reflections on an Aquarium. Barr, Vilma, ed. Capa, Cornell, intro. by. LC 92-70602. (Illus.). 96p. (Orig.). 1992. text ed. 26.95 smyth stitch bdg. (0-9632150-0-0); pap. text ed. 16.95 (0-9632150-1-9) Drum Comns.
Bernstein, Richard & Agel, Jerome. The Congress. LC 88-21025. (gr. 7 up). 1989. 12.95 (0-8027-6832-6); PLB 13.85 (0-8027-6833-4) Walker & Co.
—The Presidency. LC 88-21026. (gr. 7 up). 1989. 12.95 (0-8027-6829-6); PLB 13.85 (0-8027-6831-8) Walker & Co.
—The Supreme Court. LC 88-21027. (gr. 7 up). 1989. 12.95 (0-8027-6834-2); PLB 13.85 (0-8027-6835-0) Walker & Co.
Bernstein, Sharon C. A Family That Fights. Levine, Abby, ed. Ritz, Karen, illus. LC 90-29889. 32p. (gr. k-4). 1991. 11.95 (0-8075-2248-1) A Whitman.
Bernstein, V. America's Story: Worktext, 2 bks. large type ed. (gr. 8-12). 1983. Repr. of 1978 ed. 24.15 ea.; Bk. 1, 19 pt. 24.15 (0-317-03355-7, 4-00830-00) Bk. 2, 20 pt (4-00840-00) Am Printing Hse.
Berridge, Celia. Hannah's New Boots. LC 92-14124. (Illus.). (ps-1). 1993. 10.95 (0-590-45888-4) Scholastic Inc.
—Hannah's Temper. LC 92-10874. (Illus.). 24p. (ps-1). 1993. 10.95 (0-590-45887-6) Scholastic Inc.
Berrill, Margaret. Chanticleer. Bottomley, Jane, illus. LC 86-6746. 32p. (gr. 2-5). PLB 17.96 (0-8172-2626-5) Raintree Steck-V.
—Mummies, Masks, & Mourners. Molan, Chris, illus. LC 89-31822. 48p. (gr. 4-7). 1990. 14.95 (0-525-67282-6, Lodestar Bks) Dutton Child Bks.
Berry. Don't Leave an Elephant. Date not set. 15.00 (0-06-023509-8, Festival); PLB 14.89 (0-06-023510-1, Festival) HarpC Child Bks.
—First Palm Trees. Date not set. 15.00 (0-06-023504-7, Festival); PLB 14.89 (0-06-023508-X, Festival) HarpC Child Bks.
Berry, Christine. Mama Went Walking. Brusca, Maria C., illus. LC 89-39789. 32p. (ps-2). 1990. 14.95 (0-8050-1261-3, Bks Young Read) H Holt & Co.
Berry, Gail. Little Fox & the Golden Hawk. Arnold, Elaine, illus. Kremer, John, intro. by. (Illus.). 32p. (gr. 1-9). 1991. 9.50 (0-912411-36-8) Open Horizons.
Berry, Gaynor, illus. First Five Hundred Words. 28p. 1993. 3.50 (0-7214-1520-2) Ladybird Bks.
—First Picture Dictionary. 26p. 1993. 3.50 (0-7214-1519-9) Ladybird Bks.
—First Words for Me. 26p. 1993. 3.50 (0-7214-1522-9) Ladybird Bks.
Berry, Jake, ed. see MisKowski, Mike & Foley, Jack.
Berry, James. Ajeemah & His Son. LC 92-6615. 96p. (gr. 7 up). 1992. 13.00 (0-06-021043-5); PLB 12.89 (0-06-021044-3) HarpC Child Bks.
—Ajeemah & His Son. LC 92-6615. 96p. (gr. 7 up). 1994. pap. 3.95 (0-06-440523-0, Trophy) HarpC Child Bks.
—The Future-Telling Lady: and Other Stories. LC 92-13759. 144p. (gr. 5 up). 1993. 14.00 (0-06-021434-1); PLB 13.89 (0-06-021435-X) HarpC Child Bks.
—Spiderman Anancy. Olubo, Joseph, illus. LC 89-33418. 148p. (gr. 4-6). 1989. 13.95 (0-8050-1207-9, Bks Young Read) H Holt & Co.

—A Thief in the Village & Other Stories. LC 87-24695. 160p. (gr. 6 up). 1988. PLB 12.95 (0-531-05745-3); PLB 12.99 (0-531-08345-4) Orchard Bks Watts.
—A Thief in the Village: And Other Stories of Jamaica. 156p. (gr. 4 up). 1990. pap. 4.99 (0-14-034357-1, Puffin Bks) Puffin Bks.
—When I Dance. Ingber, Bonnie V., ed. Barbour, Karen, illus. 120p. (gr. 7 up). 1991. 15.95 (0-15-295568-2) HarBrace.
Berry, John R. Good Words for New Christians. (Orig.). (gr. 6-12). 1987. pap. 2.95 (0-9616900-0-3) J R Berry.
Berry, Joy. About Change & Moving. Bartholomew, illus. 48p. (gr. 3 up). 1990. PLB 15.00 (0-516-02951-7) Childrens.
—About Death. Bartholomew, illus. 48p. (gr. 3 up). 1990. PLB 15.00 (0-516-02952-5) Childrens.
—About Dependence & Separation. (Illus.). 48p. (gr. 3 up). 1990. 15.00 (0-516-02957-6); pap. 4.95 (0-516-42957-4) Childrens.
—About Disasters. (Illus.). 48p. (gr. 3 up). 1990. 15.00 (0-516-02959-2); pap. 4.95 (0-516-42959-0) Childrens.
—About Divorce. Bartholomew, illus. 48p. (gr. 3 up). 1990. PLB 15.00 (0-516-02953-3) Childrens.
—About Handling Traumatic Experiences. (Illus.). 48p. (gr. 3 up). 1990. 15.00 (0-516-02958-4); pap. 4.95 (0-516-42958-2) Childrens.
—About Physical Disabilities. Bartholomew, illus. 48p. (gr. 3 up). 1990. PLB 15.00 (0-516-02954-1) Childrens.
—About Step Families. Bartholomew, illus. 48p. (gr. 3 up). 1990. 15.00 (0-516-02955-X) Childrens.
—About Substance Abuse. Bartholomew, illus. 48p. (gr. 3 up). 1990. PLB 15.00 (0-516-02956-8) Childrens.
—About Weight Problems & Eating Disorders. (Illus.). 48p. (gr. 3 up). 1990. 15.00 (0-516-02960-6); pap. 4.95 (0-516-42960-4) Childrens.
—Every Kid's Guide to Being a Communicator. (Illus.). 48p. (gr. 3-7). 1987. 5.95 (0-516-21418-7) Childrens.
—Every Kid's Guide to Being Special. Bartholemew, illus. 48p. (gr. 3-7). 1987. 5.95 (0-516-21401-2) Childrens.
—Every Kid's Guide to Coping with Childhood Traumas. Bartholomew, illus. 48p. (gr. 3-7). 1988. 5.95 (0-516-21426-8) Childrens.
—Every Kid's Guide to Decision Making & Problem Solving. Bartholomew, illus. 48p. (gr. 3-7). 1987. 4.95 (0-516-21410-1) Childrens.
—Every Kid's Guide to Good Manners. (Illus.). 48p. (gr. 3-7). 1987. 4.95 (0-516-21420-9) Childrens.
—Every Kid's Guide to Handling Disagreements. (Illus.). 48p. (gr. 3-7). 1987. 4.95 (0-516-21421-7) Childrens.
—Every Kid's Guide to Handling Family Arguments. Bartholomew, illus. 48p. (gr. 3-7). 1987. 4.95 (0-516-21402-0) Childrens.
—Every Kid's Guide to Handling Feelings. Bartholemew, illus. 48p. (gr. 3-7). 1987. 4.95 (0-516-21403-9) Childrens.
—Every Kid's Guide to Handling Fights with Brothers & Sisters. Bartholemew, illus. 48p. (gr. 3-7). 1987. 5.95 (0-516-21404-7) Childrens.
—Every Kid's Guide to Laws That Relate to Kids in the Community. (Illus.). 48p. (gr. 3-7). 1987. 5.95 (0-516-21423-3) Childrens.
—Every Kid's Guide to Laws That Relate to Parents & Children. Bartholomew, illus. 48p. (gr. 3-7). 1987. 4.95 (0-516-21411-X) Childrens.
—Every Kid's Guide to Laws That Relate to School & Work. Bartholomew, illus. 48p. (gr. 3-7). 1987. 4.95 (0-516-21412-8) Childrens.
—Every Kid's Guide to Making & Managing Money. Bartholomew, illus. 48p. (gr. 3-7). 1986. 4.95 (0-516-21405-5) Childrens.
—Every Kid's Guide to Making Friends. Bartholemew, illus. 48p. (gr. 3-7). 1987. 5.95 (0-516-21406-3) Childrens.
—Every Kid's Guide to Saving the Earth. (Illus.). 64p. (gr. 1-6). 1992. PLB 16.95 (1-878363-72-7) Forest Hse.
—Every Kid's Guide to the Juvenile Justice System. (Illus.). 48p. (gr. 3-7). 1987. 5.95 (0-516-21422-5) Childrens.
—Every Kid's Guide to Thinking & Learning. (Illus.). 48p. (gr. 3-7). 1987. 4.95 (0-516-21424-1) Childrens.
—Every Kid's Guide to Watching TV Intelligently. Bartholomew, illus. 48p. (gr. 3-7). 1987. 4.95 (0-516-21417-9) Childrens.
Berry, Joy W. Teach Me about Brothers & Sisters. Dickey, Kate, ed. LC 85-45079. (Illus.). 36p. (ps). 1986. 4.98 (0-685-10718-3) Grolier Inc.
—Teach Me about Friends. Dickey, Kate, ed. LC 85-45083. (Illus.). 36p. (ps). 1986. 4.98 (0-685-10721-3) Grolier Inc.
—Teach Me about Listening. Dickey, Kate, ed. LC 85-45087. (Illus.). 36p. (ps). 1986. 4.98 (0-685-10726-4) Grolier Inc.
—Teach Me about Looking. Dickey, Kate, ed. LC 85-45086. (Illus.). 36p. (ps). 1986. 4.98 (0-685-10725-6) Grolier Inc.
—Teach Me About Mommies & Daddies. Dickey, Kate, ed. LC 85-45078. (Illus.). 36p. (ps). 1986. 4.98 (0-685-10717-5) Grolier Inc.
—Teach Me about My Body. Dickey, Kate, ed. LC 85-45092. (Illus.). 36p. (ps). 1986. 4.98 (0-685-10730-2) Grolier Inc.
—Teach Me about Pets. Dickey, Kate, ed. LC 85-45081. (Illus.). 36p. (ps). 1986. 4.98 (0-685-10720-5) Grolier Inc.

—Teach Me about Pretending. Dickey, Kate, ed. LC 85-45091. (Illus.). 36p. (ps). 1986. 4.98 (0-685-10731-0) Grolier Inc.
—Teach Me about Relatives. Dickey, Kate, ed. LC 85-45080. (Illus.). 36p. (ps). 1986. 4.98 (0-685-10719-1) Grolier Inc.
—Teach Me about School. Dickey, Kate, ed. LC 85-45093. (Illus.). 36p. (ps). 1986. 4.98 (0-685-10732-9) Grolier Inc.
—Teach Me about Tasting. Dickey, Kate, ed. LC 85-45088. (Illus.). 36p. (ps). 1986. 4.98 (0-685-10727-2) Grolier Inc.
—Teach Me about the Baby Sitter. Dickey, Kate, ed. LC 85-45077. (Illus.). 36p. (ps). 1986. 4.98 (0-685-10722-1) Grolier Inc.
—Teach Me about the Dentist. Dickey, Kate, ed. LC 85-45084. (Illus.). 36p. (ps). 1986. 4.98 (0-685-10724-8) Grolier Inc.
—Teach Me about the Doctor. Dickey, Kate, ed. (Illus.). 36p. (ps). 1986. 4.98 (0-685-10723-X) Grolier Inc.
—Teach Me about Touching. Dickey, Kate, ed. LC 85-45089. (Illus.). 36p. (ps). 1986. 4.98 (0-685-10728-0) Grolier Inc.
Berry, Linda. Christmas Plays for Older Children. (gr. 5-7). 1981. saddle wire 2.95 (0-8054-9733-1) Broadman.
Berry, Liz. Mel. 224p. (gr. 7 up). 1991. 13.95 (0-670-83925-6) Viking Child Bks.
—Mel. LC 93-7484. 224p. (gr. 7 up). 1993. pap. 3.99 (0-14-036534-6, Puffin) Puffin Bks.
Berry, Lori S. How to Bead Earrings: An Artistic Approach. Knight, Denise E., ed. (Illus.). 96p. (Orig.). 1993. perfect bdg. 9.95 (0-943604-34-6) Eagles View.
Berry, Louise A., jt. auth. see Miller, Christina G.
Berry, Lynn. Wojciech Jaruzelski. (Illus.). 112p. (gr. 5 up). 1990. 17.95 (1-55546-838-1) Chelsea Hse.
Berry, Marilyn. Help Is on the Way for Listening Skills. (Illus.). 48p. (gr. 4-6). 1987. pap. 4.95 (0-516-43285-0) Childrens.
—Help Is on the Way for Reading Skills. (Illus.). 48p. (gr. 4-6). 1987. pap. 4.95 (0-516-43286-9) Childrens.
Berry, Michael. Georgia O'Keeffe. Horner, Matina, intro. by. (Illus.). 112p. (Orig.). (gr. 5 up). 1988. 17.95 (1-55546-673-7); pap. 9.95 (0-7910-0420-1) Chelsea Hse.
Berry, Michael & Berry, Nora. Seek & Ye Shall Find New Testament. (ps-3). 1992. 12.99 (0-929216-74-1) HSH Edu Media Co.
—Seek & Ye Shall Find Old Testament. (ps-3). 1992. 12.99 (0-929216-78-4) HSH Edu Media Co.
Berry, Nora, jt. auth. see Berry, Michael.
Berry, Roger L. Into All the World. (gr. 4). 1991. 17.50 (0-87813-925-7) Christian Light.
Berry, Ron, et al. Crassy the Crude Beastie: A Beastie Book about Good Manners. Bartholomew, illus. 48p. (ps-1). 1993. write for info. (1-883761-03-4) Fmly Life Prods.
—Fritter the Wasteful Beastie: A Beastie Book about Conserving Resources. Bartholomew, illus. 48p. (ps-1). 1993. write for info. (1-883761-02-6) Fmly Life Prods.
—Glumby the Grumbler: A Beastie Book about Being Grateful. Bartholomew, illus. 48p. (ps-1). 1993. write for info. (1-883761-00-X) Fmly Life Prods.
—Hogger the Hoarding Beastie: A Beastie Book about Sharing. Bartholomew, illus. 48p. (ps-1). 1993. write for info. (1-883761-01-8) Fmly Life Prods.
—Moogie the Messy Beastie: A Beastie Book about Being Neat. Bartholomew, illus. 48p. (ps-1). 1993. write for info. (1-883761-05-0) Fmly Life Prods.
—Scrappy the Squabbler: A Beastie Book about Getting along with Others. Bartholomew, illus. 48p. (ps-1). 1993. write for info. (1-883761-04-2) Fmly Life Prods.
Berry, S. L. Gwendolyn Brooks. LC 93-742. 1993. PLB 18.95 (0-88682-612-8) Creative Ed.
—Indianapolis. (Illus.). 60p. (gr. 3 up). 1990. RSBE 13.95 (0-87518-426-X, Dillon) (0-685-33006-0) Macmillan Child Grp.
—Langston Hughes. LC 93-741. 1993. PLB 18.95s.p. (0-88682-616-0) Creative Ed.
—Truman Capote. LC 93-10625. (gr. 5 up). 1994. write for info. (0-88682-619-5) Creative Ed.
Berry, S. L., jt. auth. see Loewen, Nancy.
Berry, Skip. Gordon Parks. King, Coretta Scott, intro. by. (Illus.). 112p. (gr. 5 up). 1991. lib. bdg. 17.95 (1-55546-604-4) Chelsea Hse.
—Little League World Series. (gr. 5 up). 1992. PLB 14.95 (0-88682-538-5) Creative Ed.
—The Tour de France. (gr. 5 up). 1992. PLB 14.95 (0-88682-539-3) Creative Ed.
Berry, Skip L. E. E. Cummings. LC 93-743. 1993. PLB 18.95s.p. (0-88682-611-X) Creative Ed.
Berry, Steve. The Boy Who Wouldn't Speak. Betteridge, Deirdre, illus. 32p. 1992. PLB 14.95 (1-55037-231-9, Pub. by Annick CN); pap. 4.95 (1-55037-230-0, Pub. by Annick CN) Firefly Bks Ltd.
Berry, T. The Day God Came. 44p. (gr. 6 up). 1992. pap. 5.95 (1-55523-515-8) Winston-Derek.
Berry, William D. Buffalo Land. Berry, William D., illus. 48p. (gr. 5-8). 1985. pap. 9.95 (0-938271-01-6) Press N Amer.
—Deneki, An Alaskan Moose. (Illus.). 48p. (gr. 5-8). 1983. pap. 8.95 (0-938271-00-8) Press N Amer.
Berst, Barbara. We Are Farmers. Berst, Barbara, illus. 24p. (Orig.). (ps-2). 1990. acid-free cotton paper 25.00, (0-9614126-3-1); pap. 9.95 (0-9614126-2-3) Natl Lilac Pub.

Berst, Barbara J. I Love Softball. LC 84-62470. (Illus.). 72p. (Orig.). (gr. 3-6). 1985. pap. 4.25 (*0-9614126-0-7*) Natl Lilac Pub.

Berthier, Rene. Jesus, Friend of Children. (Illus.). 80p. (gr. 2-8). 1990. 9.99 (*0-85648-053-3*); pap. 6.99 (*0-85648-316-8*) Lion USA.

Berthon, Prue, illus. Answering the Call. 40p. 1991. 17. 95 (*0-9629140-0-2*) White Dove NM.

Bertolini, Dewey. Secret Wounds & Silent Cries. rev. ed. LC 93-18867. 156p. 1993. pap. 7.99 (*1-56476-116-9*, Victor Books) SP Pubns.
—Sometimes I Really Hate You. 132p. 1991. pap. 4.99 (*0-89693-041-6*) SP Pubns.

Berton, Pierre. Canada under Siege. (Illus.). 88p. (gr. 5-8). 1992. pap. 5.99 (*0-7710-1431-7*, Pub. by McClelland & Stewart CN) Firefly Bks Ltd.
—The Capture of Detroit. (Illus.). 84p. (gr. 5 up). 1992. pap. 5.95 (*0-7710-1425-2*, Pub. by McClelland & Stewart CN) Firefly Bks Ltd.
—The Death of Isaac Brock. (Illus.). 84p. (gr. 5 up). 1992. pap. 5.95 (*0-7710-1426-0*, Pub. by McClelland & Stewart CN) Firefly Bks Ltd.
—Revenge of the Tribes. (Illus.). 88p. 1992. pap. 5.99 (*0-7710-1429-5*, Pub. by McClelland & Stewart CN) Firefly Bks Ltd.

Bertram, John, jt. auth. see Gravelle, Karen.

Bertrand, Armand L., Jr. How to Start Understanding the Computer. LC 83-90306. (Illus.). 208p. (Orig.). (gr. 7 up). 1986. pap. 12.95 (*0-912447-02-8*) Eclectical.

Bertrand, Cecile. Let's Pretend. LC 92-54431. (ps-3). 1993. 13.00 (*0-688-12377-5*) Lothrop.
—Mr. & Mrs. Smith Have Only One Child, but What a Child. LC 91-2757. (ps-3). 1992. PLB 12.93 (*0-688-11331-1*) Lothrop.
—Mr. & Mrs. Smith Have Only One Child, but What a Child! LC 91-2757. (ps-3). 1992. 13.00 (*0-688-11330-3*) Lothrop.
—Noni Hears. (ps). 1993. 4.95 (*0-307-15686-9*, Artsts Writrs) Western Pub.
—Noni Sees. (ps). 1993. 4.95 (*0-307-15685-0*, Artsts Writrs) Western Pub.
—Noni Tastes. (ps). 1993. 4.95 (*0-307-15687-7*, Artsts Writrs) Western Pub.
—Noni Touches. (ps). 1993. 4.95 (*0-307-15688-5*, Artsts Writrs) Western Pub.

Bertrand, Lynne. Good Night, Teddy Bear: A Book for Helping Get Ready for Bed, with Special Things to Touch, Smell, See & Do. Street, Janet, illus. 24p. (ps). 1992. comb-bound 9.95 (*0-9631591-1-9*) Chapters Pub.
—Let's Go! Teddy Bear. Street, Janet, illus. LC 93-71172. 24p. (ps). 1993. combbound 9.95 (*1-881527-15-8*) Chapters Pub.
—One Day, Two Dragons. Street, Janet, illus. LC 91-32743. 32p. (ps-3). 1992. 14.00 (*0-517-58411-5*); PLB 14.99 (*0-517-58413-1*) Crown Bks Yng Read.

Bertsch, Aida C. & Bertsch, Werner J. Florida: Educational & Historical Coloring Book. (Illus.). 24p. (Orig.). (gr. 1-6). 1989. pap. 2.99 (*1-877833-01-0*) Pro Pub Inc.

Bertsch, Werner J., jt. auth. see Bertsch, Aida C.

Bertschmann, Harry, jt. auth. see Sampson, Mary Y.

Bertschmann, Mary, ed. see Sampson, Mary Y.

Bertschmann, Mary, ed. see Sampson, Mary Y. & Bertschmann, Harry.

Beshara, Raymond, et al. What You Should Know about AIDS. (Illus.). 72p. (gr. 6-10). 1989. pap. text ed. 9.85 (*0-9623161-2-1*); tchr's. ed. 3.00 (*0-9623161-3-X*) ERN Inc.

Beshore, George. Science in Ancient China. LC 87-23748. (Illus.). 96p. (gr. 5-8). 1988. PLB 10.90 (*0-531-10485-0*) Watts.
—Science in Early Islamic Culture. Rasof, Henry, ed. LC 88-2660. (Illus.). 72p. (gr. 5-8). 1988. PLB 10.90 (*0-531-10596-2*) Watts.

Beskow, Elsa. Around the Year. (Illus.). (ps-2). 1988. 14. 95 (*0-86315-075-6*, 20245) Gryphon Hse.
—The Flowers' Festival. Beskow, Elsa, illus. 32p. (gr. k-4). 1991. Repr. of 1914 ed. 14.95g (*0-86315-120-5*, Pub. by Floris Bks UK) Gryphon Hse.
—Ollie's Ski Trip. Ernest Benn Ltd. Staff, tr. from SWE. Beskow, Elsa, illus. (ps-2). Repr. of 1960 ed. 14.95 (*0-86315-091-8*, Pub. by Floris Bks UK) Gryphon Hse.
—Pelle's New Suit. Beskow, Elsa, illus. 16p. (ps-1). 1929. PLB 13.89 (*0-06-020496-6*) HarpC Child Bks.
—Pelle's New Suit. Woodburn, Marion L., tr. from SWE. Beskow, Elsa, illus. 32p. (ps-2). Repr. of 1979 ed. 14. 95 (*0-86315-092-6*, Pub. by Floris Bks UK) Gryphon Hse.
—Peter in Blueberry Land. (ps-2). 1988. 14.95 (*0-86315-050-0*, 20237) Gryphon Hse.
—Peter's Old House. 28p. (ps-k). 1990. 14.95 (*0-86315-102-7*, 1479, Pub. by Floris Bks UK) Anthroposophic.
—The Tale of the Little, Little Old Woman. Beskow, Elsa, illus. (ps). 1989. 10.95 (*0-86315-079-9*, 20246) Gryphon Hse.

Bess, Clayton. The Mayday Rampage. DiCicco, Dan, illus. LC 92-74268. 208p. (gr. 9-12). 1993. 14.95 (*1-882405-00-5*); pap. 7.95 (*1-882405-01-3*); 3 audiocassettes, incl. AIDS curriculum w/ tchr's. guide 21.95 (*1-882405-02-1*) Lookout Pr.
—Story for a Black Night. LC 81-13396. (gr. 7 up). 1982. 13.45 (*0-395-31857-2*) HM.
—The Truth about the Moon. Hoffman, Rosekrans, illus. 48p. (gr. k-3). 1983. 13.45 (*0-395-34551-0*) HM.

—Truth about the Moon. (ps-3). 1992. pap. 4.95 (*0-395-64371-6*) HM.

Bessant, P. & Smith, L. Dance. (Illus.). 48p. (gr. 5 up). 1987. PLB 14.96 (*0-88110-245-8*); pap. 7.95 (*0-7460-0087-1*) EDC.

Besson, Jean-Louis. Livre de l'Histoire de France. (FRE.). 124p. (gr. 4-9). 1986. 17.95 (*2-07-039525-1*) Schoenhof.

Best, Anthony. That Makes Me Angry. Cooke, Tom, illus. (ps-3). 1990. pap. write for info. (*0-307-12026-0*, Pub. by Golden Bks) Western Pub.

Best, Cari. Taxi! Taxi! Gottlieb, Dale, illus. LC 92-32249. 1993. 14.95 (*0-316-09259-2*) Little.

Best, Elizabeth. Mr. McGillicuddy's Clocks. Culic, Ned, illus. LC 93-26928. 1994. 4.25 (*0-383-03765-4*) SRA Schl Grp.
—What Happened to Aunt Cordelia? Webb, Phillip, illus. LC 93-167. 1994. write for info. (*0-383-03725-5*) SRA Schl Grp.

Betancourt, Jeanne. Crazy Christmas. 128p. (gr. 4 up). 1988. pap. 2.95 (*0-553-15643-8*, Skylark) Bantam.
—Home Sweet Home. (gr. 7 up). 1989. pap. 2.95 (*0-553-27857-6*, Starfire) Bantam.
—Home Sweet Home. 1988. 13.95 (*0-553-05469-4*) Bantam.
—Kate's Turn. 192p. 1992. 13.95 (*0-590-43103-X*, Scholastic Hardcover) Scholastic Inc.
—Kate's Turn. (gr. 4-7). 1993. pap. 2.95 (*0-590-43104-8*) Scholastic Inc.
—More Than Meets the Eye. 1990. 14.95 (*0-553-05871-1*) Bantam.
—More Than Meets the Eye. 1991. pap. 3.50 (*0-553-29351-6*) Bantam.
—My Name Is Brain Brian. LC 92-16513. 176p. (gr. 3-7). 1993. 13.95 (*0-590-44921-4*) Scholastic Inc.
—Not Just Party Girls. 176p. (gr. 7 up). 1989. 13.95 (*0-553-05497-X*, Starfire) Bantam.
—Puppy Love. 96p. (gr. 4-8). 1986. pap. 2.50 (*0-380-89958-2*, Camelot) Avon.
—The Rainbow Kid. 112p. (Orig.). (gr. 3-7). 1983. pap. 2.50 (*0-380-84665-9*, Camelot) Avon.
—Sweet Sixteen & Never... 144p. (Orig.). (gr. 7-12). 1991. pap. 3.50 (*0-553-25534-7*, Starfire) Bantam.

Bethancourt, T. Ernesto. The Me Inside of Me. LC 85-10292. 156p. (gr. 5 up). 1985. 15.95 (*0-8225-0728-5*) Lerner Pubns.

Bethell, Jean & Axtell, Susan. A Colonial Williamsburg Activities Book: Fun Things to Do for Children 4 & Up. Wallner, Susan, illus. 40p. (Orig.). 1984. pap. 3.95 (*0-87935-068-7*) Williamsburg.

Bettencourt, Michael. Guy de Maupassant. LC 93-10633. (gr. 6 up). 1994. write for info. (*0-88682-624-1*) Creative Ed.
—Stephen Crane. LC 93-17132. 1994. write for info. (*0-88682-621-7*) Creative Ed.

Better Homes & Gardens Editors. Better Homes & Gardens Step-by-Step Kids' CookBook. 1984. pap. 8.95 (*0-696-01325-8*) Meredith Bks.
—Bugs, Bugs, Bugs. (Illus.). 32p. 1989. 8.95 (*0-696-01884-5*) Meredith Bks.
—New Junior Cookbook. rev. ed. (Illus.). 96p. (gr. 3-5). 1989. Repr. of 1979 ed. 8.95 (*0-696-01147-6*) Meredith Bks.

Better Homes & Gardens Staff. Holiday Crafts Kids Can Make: Includes Fifty Fun & Easy Holiday Projects for Kids with How To. 1992. pap. 14.95 (*0-696-01606-0*) Meredith Bks.

Bettison, Joan. Baba Nangko. Fleming, Leanne, illus. LC 93-26225. 1994. 4.25 (*0-383-03733-6*) SRA Schl Grp.

Betts, Keith & McCollam, Dan. Junior High Game Nights: Wild & Crazy Outreach Events for Junior High Ministry. 96p. 1991. pap. 9.99 (*0-310-53811-4*, Pub. by Youth Spec) Zondervan.

Betts, Louise, adapted by see Burnett, Frances H.

Betts, Louise, adapted by see Dodge, Mary M.

Betty Crocker Staff, ed. Betty Crocker's Boys & Girls Microwave Cookbook. 160p. 1992. pap. 15.00 (*0-13-085549-9*, B Crocker Cbkbs) P-H Gen Ref & Trav.

Betz, Dieter. The Bear Family. LC 91-42698. (Illus.). 60p. (gr. 2-6). 1992. 15.00 (*0-688-11647-7*, Tambourine Bks); PLB 14.93 (*0-688-11648-5*, Tambourine Bks) Morrow.

Beuth, Eugene. We Love Our New Home. Beuth, Eugene, illus. LC 93-77946. 34p. (ps). 1993. pap. 12.95 (*0-9636417-2-7*) Make-Hawk Pub.

Beutler, Bryce D., jt. auth. see Beutler, Eve R.

Beutler, Cora. Baptism Journal, Boy. (Illus.). 28p. (Orig.). 1992. pap. 2.95 (*1-56684-005-8*, Sigma Pub) Pubs Wholesale.

Beutler, Cora R. Baptism Journal, Girl. (Illus.). 28p. (Orig.). 1992. pap. 2.95 (*1-56684-002-3*, Sigma Pub) Pubs Wholesale.

Beutler, Eve R. & Beutler, Bryce D. Whinosaurus Rex. (Illus.). 36p. (ps-3). 1993. pap. 9.00 (*0-9637262-0-X*) Evening Pearl.

Beven, Annette. The Spade Sage. Hall, Diane, illus. 24p. (gr. 1-3). 1976. pap. 7.95 (*0-913546-71-2*) Dharma Pub.

Beveridge, Barbara. Honey, My Rabbit. Love, Judith D., illus. LC 92-34272. 1993. 2.50 (*0-383-03630-5*) SRA Schl Grp.
—Hooray for Snow. Greenhatch, Betty, illus. LC 92-27098. 1993. 3.75 (*0-383-03573-2*) SRA Schl Grp.
—Over the Marble Mountain. Mancini, Rob, illus. LC 92-27097. (gr. 4 up). 1993. 2.50 (*0-383-03589-9*) SRA Schl Grp.

—The Stream. Crossett, Warren, illus. LC 92-33738. 1993. 3.75 (*0-383-03657-7*) SRA Schl Grp.
—Waves. Costeloe, Brenda, illus. LC 92-31948. 1993. 3.75 (*0-383-03603-8*) SRA Schl Grp.

Bevis, Phillip, ed. see Moore, Clement C.

Beyer, Don E. Castro! LC 92-34534. (Illus.). 176p. (gr. 9-12). 1993. PLB 14.40 (*0-531-13027-4*) Watts.
—The Manhattan Project: America Makes the First Atomic Bomb. LC 90-13049. (Illus.). 128p. (gr. 7-12). 1991. PLB 13.90 (*0-531-11008-7*) Watts.
—The Totem Pole Indians of the Northwest. LC 89-31170. (Illus.). 64p. (gr. 4-7). 1989. PLB 12.90 (*0-531-10750-7*) Watts.
—The Totem Pole Indians of the Northwest. (Illus.). 64p. (gr. 3 up). 1991. pap. 5.95 (*0-531-15607-9*) Watts.

Beyer, Fred. North Carolina, the Years Before Man: A Geologic History. LC 91-70197. (Illus.). 240p. (gr. 10). 1991. text ed. 34.95 (*0-89089-400-0*) Carolina Acad Pr.

Beyer, Kay. Coping with Teen Parenting. rev. ed. Rosen, Ruth, ed. (gr. 7-12). 1992. PLB 13.95 (*0-8239-1525-5*) Rosen Group.
—The Value of Good Manners. (gr. 7-12). 1992. PLB 15. 95 (*0-685-58964-1*) Rosen Group.

Beyer, W. F. & Keydel, D. F., eds. Deeds of Valor: How America's Civil War Heroes Won the Congressional Medal of Honor. (Illus.). 544p. (gr. 3-7). 1992. 9.98 (*0-681-41567-3*) Longmeadow Pr.

Beyl, Judith. Sunshine, Rainbows & Friends. Sydlik, Danilea & Campbell, Elisa L., illus. LC 80-50828. 83p. (Orig.). 1980. pap. 5.95 (*0-933308-01-9*) Harper SF.

Beylon, Cathy. Hush Little Baby. (ps). 1992. 4.95 (*1-56288-284-8*) Checkerboard.
—The Mulberry Bush. (ps). 1992. 4.95 (*1-56288-282-1*) Checkerboard.
—Old Macdonald. (ps). 1992. 4.95 (*1-56288-281-3*) Checkerboard.
—There Was a Tree. (ps). 1992. 4.95 (*1-56288-283-X*) Checkerboard.

Beylon, Cathy, jt. auth. see Kahn, Peggy.

Beylon, Cathy, illus. Over in the Meadow. 28p. (ps). 1990. 2.95 (*0-02-689484-X*) Checkerboard.
—Wynken, Blynken, & Nod. 24p. (ps). 1992. bds. write for info. (*0-307-06141-8*, 6141, Golden Pr) Western Pub.

Bhajan, Yogi. Seventy-Two Stories of God, Good, & Goods. Khalsa, Tej K., ed. Khalsa, Mahan K., illus. 241p. (Orig.). (gr. 10). 1989. pap. 9.95 (*0-685-29452-8*) Harimander Pub.

Bhaktipada, Swami. Lila in the Land of Illusion: A Re-Telling of Lewis Carroll's Alice in Wonderland. New Vrindaban Community Artists, illus. LC 87-18626. 127p. (gr. 3-8). 1987. 12.95 (*0-932215-22-X*); pap. text ed. 7.95 (*0-932215-19-X*) Palace Pub.

Bhaktivedanta, Swami A. C. Prahlad, Picture & Story Book. LC 72-2032. (Illus.). (gr. 2-6). 1973. pap. 4.00 (*0-685-47513-1*) Bhaktivedanta.

Bhaktivedanta Swami Prabhupado, A. C., tr. see Yogesvara dosa-Jyotirmayi.

Bhanji, Lindley. Cocoon. Winkler, Chris, ed. Bhanji, Lindley, illus. 28p. (Orig.). (gr. 10 up). 1988. pap. 2.00 saddle stapled (*0-929611-00-4*) Plutonium Pr.

Bhatt, H. D. Kalidas. (Illus.). (gr. 3-8). 1979. pap. 3.95 (*0-89744-144-3*) Auromere.

Bhi, Karen. The Lumbee: Southeast. (Illus.). (gr. 5 up). 1993. 18.95 (*1-55546-713-X*, Am Art Analog); pap. write for info. (*0-7910-0386-8*, Am Art Analog) Chelsea Hse.

Bial, Morrison D., jt. auth. see Simon, Solomon.

Bial, Morrison D., ed. see Stadtler, Bea.

Bial, Raymond. Amish Home. Bial, Raymond, illus. 40p. (gr. 4-7). 1993. 14.45 (*0-395-59504-5*) HM.
—Corn Belt Harvest. (Illus.). 48p. (gr. 3-6). 1991. 14.45 (*0-395-56234-1*, Sandpiper) HM.
—County Fair. Bial, Raymond, illus. 40p. (gr. 3-6). 1992. 14.45 (*0-395-57644-X*) HM.
—Prairie Home. LC 92-36449. 1993. 15.95 (*0-395-64046-6*) HM.
—Shaker Home. LC 93-17917. 1994. write for info. (*0-395-64047-4*) HM.

Bianchi, Anne. C. Everett Koop: The Health of a Nation. LC 92-1230. (Illus.). 104p. (gr. 7 up). 1992. PLB 14.90 (*1-56294-103-8*) Millbrook Pr.

Bianchi, J. Bushmen Brouhaha. (Illus.). 24p. (ps-8). 1987. 12.95 (*0-921285-10-8*, Pub. by Bungalo Bks CN); pap. 4.95 (*0-921285-08-6*, Pub. by Bungalo Bks CN) Firefly Bks Ltd.
—Champions of Hockey. (Illus.). 24p. (ps-8). 1989. 12.95 (*0-921285-18-3*, Pub. by Bungalo Bks CN); pap. 4.95 (*0-921285-16-7*, Pub. by Bungalo Bks CN) Firefly Bks Ltd.
—The Last of the Tree Ranchers. (Illus.). 24p. (ps-8). 1986. 12.95 (*0-921285-02-7*, Pub. by Bungalo Bks CN); pap. 4.95 (*0-921285-00-0*, Pub. by Bungalo Bks CN) Firefly Bks Ltd.
—Princess Frownsalot. (Illus.). 24p. (ps-8). 1987. 12.95 (*0-921285-06-X*, Pub. by Bungalo Bks CN); pap. 4.95 (*0-921285-04-3*, Pub. by Bungalo Bks CN) Firefly Bks Ltd.
—The Swine Snafu. (Illus.). 24p. (ps-8). 1988. 12.95 (*0-921285-14-0*, Pub. by Bungalo Bks CN); pap. 4.95 (*0-921285-12-4*, Pub. by Bungalo Bks CN) Firefly Bks Ltd.

Bianchi, John. Flight of the Space Quester. Bianchi, John, illus. 24p. 1993. lib. bdg. 14.95 (*0-921285-31-0*, Pub. by Bungalo Bks CN); pap. 4.95 (*0-921285-30-2*, Pub. by Bungalo Bks CN) Firefly Bks Ltd.

—Penelope Penguin: The Incredibly Good Baby. Bianchi, John, illus. 24p. (ps-3). 1992. PLB 14.95 (0-921285-13-2, Pub. by Bungalo Bks CN); pap. 4.95 (0-921285-11-6, Pub. by Bungalo Bks CN) Firefly Bks Ltd.
—Snowed in at Pokeweed Public School. Bianchi, John, illus. 24p. (gr. 6-9). 1991. 14.95 (0-921285-07-8, Pub. by Bungalo Bks CN); pap. 4.95 (0-921285-05-1, Pub. by Bungalo Bks CN) Firefly Bks Ltd.
Bianchi, John & Edwards, Frank B. Grandma Mooner Lost Her Voice. Bianchi, John, illus. 24p. (ps-2). 1992. PLB 14.95 (0-921285-19-1, Pub. by Bungalo Bks CN); pap. 4.95 (0-921285-17-5, Pub. by Bungalo Bks CN) Firefly Bks Ltd.

—Snow: Learning for the Fun of It. Binachi, John, illus. 48p. (gr. 5 up). 1992. PLB 17.95 (0-921285-15-9, Pub. by Bungalo Bks CN); pap. 7.95 (0-921285-09-4, Pub. by Bungalo Bks CN) Firefly Bks Ltd. By combining a wealth of factual information about snow with the cartoon illustrations of John Bianchi, this book serves up science in a painless way that both kids & adults will love. Bianchi & author Frank B. Edwards examine snow from dozens of perspectives, keeping their approach light & the facts interesting. Their explanation of snowflake formation is accompanied by a sidebar about the meteorological pioneer who devoted his lifetime to photographing snowflakes (yes, he died of pneumonia). The movement of glaciers is introduced with an illustration of an advancing icesheet creeping along the main street of a city, eroding office towers instead of mountains. After explaining how animals adapt to snow, the book offers a blueprint of the ultimate winter beast--the long-eared snow scooter. Advice on tracking species in the snow includes abominable snowmen as well as rabbits & birds. After thoroughly tracing how snow has affected the planet & how people have learned to cope with its inevitable presence (through such inventions as the snow shovel, skis & the igloo), the book presents a romp through the snow hall of fame, a useful collection of snow trivia that is guaranteed to delight readers. Publisher Provided Annotation.

Bianchi, John, jt. auth. see Edwards, Frank.
Bianchi, John, jt. auth. see Edwards, Frank B.
Bianchi, Robert S. The Nubians: People of the Ancient Nile. LC 93-13273. (Illus.). 72p. (gr. 4-6). 1994. PLB 14.90 (1-56294-356-1) Millbrook Pr.
Bibb, Eric, tr. see Lindgren, Astrid.
Bibb, Eric, tr. see Rehnman, Mats.
Bibb, Eric, tr. see Sundvall, Viveca.
Bibeau, Simone. Developing the Early Learner: Level 1. rev. ed. Kruck, Gerry, illus. 64p. (ps-2). 1983. pap. text ed. 4.95 (0-940406-01-2) Perception Pubns.
—Developing the Early Learner: Level 2. rev. ed. Kruck, Gerry, illus. 64p. (ps-2). 1983. pap. text ed. 4.95 (0-940406-02-0) Perception Pubns.
—Developing the Early Learner: Level 3. rev. ed. Kruck, Gerry, illus. 64p. (ps-2). 1983. pap. text ed. 4.95 (0-940406-03-9) Perception Pubns.
—IQ Booster Kit: Developing the Early Learner Levels 1-4. Kruck, Gerry, illus. 256p. (ps-2). 1983. pap. text ed. 85.00 (bks. & cassettes) (0-940406-05-5) Perception Pubns.
—Writing the Advanced Short Story. Kruck, Gerry, illus. 32p. (gr. 1-12). 1983. pap. text ed. 1.95 (0-940406-07-1) Perception Pubns.
—Writing the Beginning Short Story. Kruck, Gerry, illus. 32p. (Orig.). (gr. 1-9). 1983. pap. text ed. 1.95 (0-940406-06-3) Perception Pubns.
—Writing the Fantasy Story. Kruck, Gerry, illus. 32p. (Orig.). (gr. 1-9). 1983. pap. text ed. 1.95 (0-940406-08-X) Perception Pubns.
Bibee, John. Bicycle Hills: How One Halloween Almost Got out of Hand. LC 89-15316. (Illus.). 204p. (Orig.). (gr. 7-8). 1989. pap. 6.99 (0-8308-1203-2, 1203) InterVarsity.
—The Journey of Wishes. Turnbaugh, Paul, illus. LC 93-8173. 192p. (Orig.). (gr. 4-8). 1993. pap. 6.99 (0-8308-1207-5, 1207) InterVarsity.

—The Last Christmas. LC 90-4870. (Illus.). 204p. (Orig.). (gr. 3-8). 1990. pap. 6.99 (0-8308-1204-0, 1204) InterVarsity.
—The Magic Bicycle. LC 83-240. (Illus.). 215p. (Orig.). (gr. 4-9). 1983. pap. 6.99 (0-87784-348-1, 348) InterVarsity.
—The Only Game in Town. Turnbaugh, Paul, illus. LC 88-9369. 209p. (ps-6). 1988. pap. 6.99 (0-8308-1202-4, 1202) InterVarsity.
—The Perfect Star. LC 92-5686. (Illus.). 192p. (Orig.). (gr. 5-12). 1992. pap. 6.99 (0-8308-1206-7, 1206) InterVarsity.
—The Runaway Parents: A Parable of Problem Parents. Turnbaugh, Paul, illus. LC 91-22762. 204p. (gr. 3-8). 1991. pap. 6.99 (0-8308-1205-9, 1205) InterVarsity.
—The Spirit Flyers Series, 4 bks, Set A. Turnbaugh, Paul, illus. (Orig.). 1992. Boxed Set. pap. 24.99 (0-8308-1208-3, 1208) InterVarsity.
—The Spirit Flyers Series, 4 bks, Set B. Turnbaugh, Paul, illus. (Orig.). 1993. Set. pap. 24.99 boxed (0-8308-1289-X, 1289) InterVarsity.
—The Toy Campaign. Turnbaugh, Paul, illus. LC 87-3261. 225p. (Orig.). (gr. 4 up). 1987. pap. 6.99 (0-8308-1201-6, 1201) InterVarsity.
Bible Adventures Staff. Noah's Adventure in the Ark. (Illus.). (ps). 1991. bds. 8.99 (0-8007-7122-2) Revell.
Bible, Ken, compiled by. A Pocketful of Praise. (gr. 3-7). Date not set. songbk. 3.25 (0-685-68220-X, BCMB-574); double-length cassette, split-channel 11.98 (0-685-68221-8, BCTA-9085C) Lillenas.
—Primary Praise. Date not set. songbk. 5.95 (0-685-68214-5, BCMB-620); double-length split-channel cassette 11.98 (0-685-68215-3, BCTA-9122C) Lillenas.
—Sing a Song of Scripture. (gr. 3-7). Date not set. 5.95 (0-685-68216-1, BCMB-558); Vols. 1 & 2. double-cassette pack 18.98 (0-685-68217-X, BCTA-9075B); Vol. 1. cassette 11.98 (0-685-68218-8, BCTA-9074C); Vol. 2. cassette 11.98 (0-685-68219-6, BCTA-9075C) Lillenas.
Bibliotheca Press Staff. Black English, Chocolate Slang: or English Too??? 15p. (gr. 9-12). 1989. pap. text ed. 4.00 (0-318-42724-9, Pub. by Biblio Pr Ga) Prosperity & Profits.
—Posie the Positive Train: Story Edition. (gr. 4-9). 1990. 12.95 (0-939476-27-4, Pub. by Biblio Pr GA); pap. 9.95 (0-939476-28-2, Pub. by Biblio Pr GA) Prosperity & Profits.
Bickel, Kurt. Getting along with Parents. 48p. (Orig.). (gr. 9-12). 1990. pap. 7.99 (1-55945-202-1) Group Pub.
Bicknell, Arthur. Scavenger's Hunt. (Orig.). (gr. k-12). 1987. pap. 2.95 (0-440-97672-3, LFL) Dell.
Bicknell, Treld, compiled by. Seven Is Heaven. LC 86-45415. (Illus.). 64p. (gr. 2). 1986. 8.95 (0-15-200580-3, Gulliver Bks) HarBrace.
Biddle, Steve. Amazing Origami for Children. 1993. 8.95 (1-55521-944-6) Bk Sales Inc.
Bider, Djemma. A Drop of Honey. Kojoyian, Armen, illus. (ps-4). 1989. pap. 14.95 jacketed (0-671-66265-1, S&S BFYR) S&S Trade.
Bidwell, John, et al. First Three Wagon Trains. Remington, Frederic, illus. 118p. (gr. 7-9). 1993. pap. 11.95 (0-8323-0504-9) Binford Mort.
Bie, Catherine F. De see De Bie, Catherine F.
Biel, Timothy. The Civil War. LC 91-29500. (Illus.). 112p. (gr. 5-8). 1991. PLB 17.95 (1-56006-404-8) Lucent Bks.
Biel, Timothy L. Atoms: Building Blocks of Matter. LC 90-13214. (Illus.). 96p. (gr. 5-8). 1990. PLB 15.95 (1-56006-207-X) Lucent Bks.
—The Black Death. LC 89-112269. (Illus.). 64p. (gr. 5-8). 1989. PLB 11.95 (1-56006-001-8) Lucent Bks.
—The Challenger. McGovern, Brian, illus. LC 90-6255. 64p. (gr. 5-8). 1990. PLB 11.95 (1-56006-013-1) Lucent Bks.
—Pompeii. LC 89-9395. (Illus.). 64p. (gr. 5-8). 1989. PLB 11.95 (1-56006-000-X) Lucent Bks.
Biel, Timothy L., jt. auth. see Glaser, Elizabeth.
Biel, Timothy L., jt. auth. see Migneco, Ronald.
Biemer, Linda. New York City: Our Community. (Illus.). 100p. (gr. 4). 1986. 9.30 (0-685-24532-2, Peregrine Smith) Gibbs Smith Pub.
—New York: Our Communities. (Illus.). 328p. (gr. 4). 1983. text ed. 18.60x (0-87905-111-6, Peregrine Smith) Gibbs Smith Pub.
Biene, Susanna & Moneli, illus. Sing Through the Seasons: Ninety-Nine Songs for Children. Society of Brothers Staff, ed. LC 70-164916. 144p. (gr. k-6). 1972. 17.00 (0-87486-006-7); cassette 7.00 (0-87486-048-2) Plough.
Biener, Laurence, et al. How to Study Study Aid. 1978. pap. 2.50 (0-317-64276-6) Youth Ed.
Bierce, Ambrose. An Occurrence at Owl Creek Bridge. Neumeier, Marty, illus. 40p. (gr. 6 up). 1980. PLB 13.95s.p. (0-87191-770-X) Creative Ed.
Bierce, Rose, ed. see Center for Environmental Education Staff.
Bierhorst, John. A Cry from the Earth: Music of the North American Indians. LC 91-59002. (Illus.). 113p. 1992. pap. 14.95 (0-941270-53-X) Ancient City Pr.
—Doctor Coyote: A Native American Aesop's Fables. Watson, Wendy, illus. LC 86-8669. 48p. (gr. 2-5). 1987. SBE 15.95 (0-02-709780-3, Macmillan Child Bk) Macmillan Child Grp.

—The Girl Who Married a Ghost & Other Tales from the North American Indians. reissued ed. LC 77-21515. (Illus.). (gr. 7 up). 1984. SBE 12.95 (0-02-709740-4, Four Winds) Macmillan Child Grp.
—Is My Friend at Home? Pueblo Fireside Tales. Watson, Wendy, illus. LC 93-14249. 1994. text ed. 14.95 (0-02-709733-1) Macmillan.
—The Mythology of Mexico & Central America. LC 90-5879. (Illus.). 256p. (gr. 7 up). 1990. 14.95g (0-688-06721-2) Morrow Jr Bks.
—The Mythology of North America: Introduction to Classic American Crods, Heroes & Tricksters. LC 85-281. (Illus.). 272p. (gr. 7 up). 1986. 13.00 (0-688-04145-0); pap. 6.95 (0-688-06666-6, Morrow Jr Bks) Morrow Jr Bks.
—The Mythology of South America. LC 87-26237. (Illus.). 256p. (gr. 7 up). 1988. 15.95 (0-688-06722-0) Morrow Jr Bks.
—The Sacred Path. LC 82-14118. 192p. (gr. 7 up). 1983. 15.95 (0-688-01699-5); pap. 7.95 (0-688-02647-8, Morrow Jr Bks) Morrow Jr Bks.
—The Way of the Earth: Native America & the Environment. LC 93-28971. (gr. 5 up). 1994. write for info. (0-688-11560-8) Morrow.
Bierhorst, John, ed. The Hungry Woman: Myths & Legends of the Aztecs. LC 92-22217. 1993. 9.00 (0-688-12301-5, Quill) Morrow.
—In the Trail of the Wind: American Indian Poems & Ritual Orations. Bierhorst, Jane B., illus. (gr. 8 up). 1987. pap. 4.95 (0-374-43576-6) FS&G.
Bierhorst, John, ed. & tr. Lightning Inside You: And Other Native American Riddles. Brierley, Louise, illus. LC 91-21744. 112p. (gr. 2 up). 1992. 14.00 (0-688-09582-8) Morrow Jr Bks.
Bierhorst, John, ed. The Monkey's Haircut: And Other Stories Told by the Maya. Parker, Robert A., illus. LC 85-28471. 160p. (gr. 5 up). 1986. 13.00 (0-688-04269-4) Morrow Jr Bks.
—The Naked Bear: Folktales of the Iroquois. Zimmer, Dirk, illus. LC 86-21836. 144p. (gr. 3 up). 1987. 14.95 (0-688-06422-1) Morrow Jr Bks.
Bierhorst, John, selected by. On the Road of Stars: Native American Night Poems & Sleep Charms. Pedersen, Judy, illus. LC 92-20001. 32p. (gr. 1). 1994. RSBE 14.95 (0-02-709735-8, Macmillan Child Bk) Macmillan Child Grp.
Bierhorst, John, retold by. The Woman Who Fell from the Sky: The Iroquois Story of Creation. Parker, Robert A., illus. LC 92-5591. 32p. (gr. k up). 1993. 15.00 (0-688-10680-3); PLB 14.93 (0-688-10681-1) Morrow Jr Bks.
Bierhorst, John, tr. Spirit Child: A Story of the Nativity. Cooney, Barbara, illus. LC 84-720. 32p. (ps-2). 1990. pap. 4.95 (0-688-09926-2, Mulberry) Morrow.
Biernot, Michele M. Mystery at Loon Lake. LC 91-67496. 44p. (gr. 4-7). 1992. 6.95 (1-55523-495-X) Winston-Derek.
Biesty, Stephen & Platt, Richard. Man-of-War. Biesty, Steven, illus. LC 92-21227. 32p. (gr. 3 up). 1993. 16.95 (1-56458-321-X) Dorling Kindersley.
Biffi, Inos. The First Sacraments. Walsh, Kevin, tr. from ITA. Vignazia, Franco, illus. Martini, Carlo, intro. by. LC 88-80658. (Illus.). 94p. (gr. 4-9). 1989. 15.95 (0-89870-206-2) Ignatius Pr.
—Prayer. Vignazia, Franco, illus. LC 93-41090. 1994. write for info. (0-8028-3759-X) Eerdmans.
—The Story of the Eucharist. Drury, John, tr. from ITA. Vignazia, Franco, illus. LC 85-82173. 125p. (gr. 5 up). 1986. 16.95 (0-89870-089-2) Ignatius Pr.
Bigelow, Horatio. Gunnerman. 2nd ed. Sheldon, Harold, intro. by. (Illus.). 246p. (gr. 10 up). 1990. Repr. of 1939 ed. 35.00 (1-56416-007-6) Derrydale Pr.
Bigelow, William. Strangers in Their Own Country: A Curriculum Guide on South Africa. Brutus, Dennis, frwd. by. LC 85-71369. (Illus.). 104p. (Orig.). (gr. 8 up). 1987. pap. 12.95 (0-86543-010-1) Africa World.
Biggar, Joan R. Danger at Half-Moon Lake. (Illus.). 128p. (gr. 5-8). 1991. pap. 3.99 (0-570-04194-5) Concordia.
—High Desert Secrets. 160p. (Orig.). (gr. 5-8). 1992. pap. 3.99 (0-570-04711-0) Concordia.
—Shipwreck on the Lights. 160p. (Orig.). (gr. 5-8). 1992. pap. 3.99 (0-570-04710-2) Concordia.
—Treasure at Morning Gulch. (Illus.). 152p. (Orig.). (gr. 5-8). 1991. pap. 3.99 (0-570-04193-7) Concordia.
Bigge, Tanya. Gardening Projects for Children. 1992. pap. 10.95 (1-878767-31-3) Murdoch Bks.
Biggs, Betsey. Kidding Around Spain: A Young Person's Guide. D'Agostino, Anthony, illus. 108p. (Orig.). (gr. 3 up). 1991. pap. 12.95 (0-945465-97-1) John Muir.
Bigler, Karen R. Big Bulletin Boards: A Cooperative Approach. (Illus.). 96p. (Orig.). (gr. k-5). 1990. pap. 9.95 (0-673-46240-4) GdYrBks.
Bilderback, Allen H. Revelation & Apocalyptic Symbols: Bible Stories of the Planets & Stars. Anderson, Cindy & Flippin, Terry, illus. 180p. (gr. 8 up). 1992. 24.95 (0-9630710-1-7); pap. 19.95 (0-9630710-0-9) ABCO Pub.
Bilezikian, Gary. While I Slept. Bilezikian, Gary, illus. LC 90-52514. 32p. (ps-1). 1990. 12.95 (0-531-05875-1); PLB 12.99 (0-531-08475-2) Orchard Bks Watts.
Bilger, Burkhard. Global Warming. (Illus.). 120p. (gr. 5 up). 1992. PLB 19.95 (0-7910-1575-0) Chelsea Hse.
Bill, J. Brent. The Secret Survival Manual: A Guidebook for Teens. (Illus.). 160p. (gr. 6-9). 1993. pap. 7.99 (0-8007-5473-5) Revell.

Bill, J. Brent & Brent, Bill J. Cruisin' & Choosin' (Orig.). 1989. pap. 6.99 (*0-8007-5298-8*) Revell.

Billac, Pete. The Annihilator: All Must Die. Davis, Sharon K., ed. LC 80-85318. 176p. (Orig.). (gr. 12 up). 1987. pap. 1.95 (*0-317-67266-5*) Swan Pub.

—The Last Medal of Honor: A True Story of Unbelievable Valor. Davis, Sharon, et al, eds. Alder, Andy, illus. LC 90-70069. 224p. (Orig.). (gr. 9 up). 1990. pap. 11.95 (*0-685-32912-7*) Swan Pub.

Billam, Rosemary. Fuzzy Rabbit. Julian-Ottie, Vanessa, illus. LC 83-17637. 32p. (ps-3). 1984. pap. 2.25 (*0-394-86346-1*) Random Bks Yng Read.

—Fuzzy Rabbit Saves Christmas. Julian-Ottie, Vanessa, illus. LC 89-77934. 32p. (Orig.). (ps-3). 1991. pap. 2.25 (*0-679-80460-9*) Random Bks Yng Read.

Billiet, Daniel. The Great Invasion of the Stone Moles. Becker, Jane R., tr. from FRE. Rutten, Nicole, illus. LC 89-26371. 32p. 1990. 13.95 (*1-55670-153-5*) Stewart Tabori & Chang.

Billin-Frye, Paige, illus. The Sleepy Little Puppy. 12p. (ps). 1993. bds. 4.95 (*0-448-40541-5*, G&D) Putnam Pub Group.

Billings, Charlene W. Christa McAuliffe: Pioneer Space Teacher. LC 86-13453. (Illus.). 64p. (gr. 6 up). 1986. lib. bdg. 15.95 (*0-89490-148-6*) Enslow Pubs.

—Grace Hopper: Navy Admiral & Computer Pioneer. LC 89-1523. (Illus.). 128p. (gr. 6 up). 1989. lib. bdg. 17.95 (*0-89490-194-X*) Enslow Pubs.

—Lasers: The New Technology of Light. LC 92-7324. (Illus.). 128p. 1992. PLB 17.95 (*0-8160-2630-0*) Facts on File.

—Pesticides: Necessary Risk. LC 92-30394. (Illus.). 112p. (gr. 6 up). 1993. lib. bdg. 17.95 (*0-89490-299-7*) Enslow Pubs.

—Superconductivity: From Discovery to Breakthrough. LC 90-20782. (Illus.). 64p. (gr. 3-7). 1991. 15.95 (*0-525-65048-2*, Cobblehill Bks) Dutton Child Bks.

Billings, Henry & Billings, Melissa. Eccentrics. (Illus.). 160p. (gr. 6 up). 1987. pap. text ed. 7.75x (*0-89061-464-4*) Jamestown Pubs.

—Heroes. (Illus.). 160p. (gr. 6 up). 1985. pap. text ed. 7.75x (*0-89061-450-4*) Jamestown Pubs.

Billings, Henry F. Introduction to Economics. (Illus.). 448p. (gr. 11-12). 1990. text ed. 25.95 (*0-8219-0495-7*, 75450); tchr's. ed. 29.00 (*0-8219-0499-X*, 75801); tchr's. resource binder 59.00 (*0-8219-0498-1*, 75801); wkbk. 6.95 (*0-8219-0496-5*, 75650); software program IBM 280.00 (*0-8219-0650-X*, 955006); test generator IBM 198.00 (*0-8219-0840-5*, 75903) EMC.

Billings, John. My Pet Crocodile: And Other Slightly Outrageous Verse. Todd, Janette, illus. LC 93-72718. 128p. (gr. k-12). 1993. 16.95 (*1-884035-55-8*) Chokecherry.

Billings, Melissa, jt. auth. see Billings, Henry.

Billingsley, Derrell, jt. auth. see Billingsley, Veteria.

Billingsley, Veteria & Billingsley, Derrell. The First Christmas Gift. Date not set. 3.95 (*0-685-68603-5*, BCMC-33) Lillenas.

Billington, Rachel. The First Christmas. Brown, Barbara, illus. LC 87-20383. 32p. (gr. k-5). 1987. pap. 6.95 (*0-8192-1410-8*) Morehouse Pub.

Billout, Guy. By Camel or by Car: A Look at Transportation. Billout, Guy, illus. 32p. 1983. 8.95 (*0-13-109603-6*, Pub. by Treehouse); pap. 5.95 (*0-13-109595-1*) P-H.

—The Journey. Billout, Guy, illus. LC 93-17094. 1993. PLB 16.95 (*0-88682-626-8*) Creative Ed.

—Journey. (Illus.). 32p. 1993. 16.95 (*1-56846-081-3*) Creat Editions.

—Squid & Spider: A Look at the Animal Kingdom. Billout, Guy, illus. 32p. (Orig.). (gr. 6 up). 1982. 10.95 (*0-13-839958-X*) P-H.

—Thunderbolt & Rainbow: A Look at Greek Mythology. (Illus.). 1981. 9.95 (*0-13-920637-X*) P-H.

Bilyeu, Linda M. Celebrate Spring. Grossmann, Dan, illus. 144p. (gr. k-3). 1984. wkbk. 11.95 (*0-86653-209-9*, SS 836, Shining Star Pubns) Good Apple.

Bimes, James D., jt. auth. see Stacy, Darryl.

Bimler, Rich, illus. Sex & the New You. 64p. (gr. 6-9). 1988. pap. 7.99 (*0-570-08484-9*, 14-1624) Concordia.

Binato, Leonardo. What Grows in a Flower Pot? 12p. (ps-3). 1992. 4.95 (*1-56566-010-2*) Thomasson-Grant.

—What Hatches from an Egg? Turn & Learn. 12p. (ps-3). 1992. 4.95 (*1-56566-007-2*) Thomasson-Grant.

—What Lives in the Grass? 12p. (ps-3). 1993. 4.95 (*1-56566-028-5*) Thomasson-Grant.

—What Swims in the Sea? 12p. (ps-3). 1993. 4.95 (*1-56566-027-7*) Thomasson-Grant.

—What's Behind the Clouds? 12p. (ps-3). 1993. 4.95 (*1-56566-029-3*) Thomasson-Grant.

—What's Hidden in the Pirate's Chest? 12p. (ps-3). 1992. 4.95 (*1-56566-009-9*) Thomasson-Grant.

—What's in the Magician's Hat? 12p. (ps-3). 1992. 4.95 (*1-56566-008-0*) Thomasson-Grant.

—What's in the Tree? 12p. (ps-3). 1993. 4.95 (*1-56566-030-7*) Thomasson-Grant.

Binch, Caroline. Gregory Cool. LC 93-11845. 1994. write for info. (*0-8037-1577-3*) Dial Bks Young.

Binder, Otto, ed. see Shelley, Mary Wollstonecraft.

Binder, Otto, ed. see Verne, Jules.

Binder, Otto, ed. see Wells, H. G.

Binford, Dale. Rabbits Can't Dance! Binford, Dale, illus. LC 89-42640. 24p. (gr. 1-2). 1989. PLB 18.60 (*0-8368-0106-7*) Gareth Stevens Inc.

Binford, Shari, et al, eds. AIDS: What Is It All About? 44p. 1991. pap. text ed. 11.95 (*1-878623-19-2*) Info Plus TX.

—Child Abuse: Fear in the Home. 44p. 1991. pap. text ed. 11.95 (*1-878623-24-9*) Info Plus TX.

—Crime: Is It Out of Control? 52p. 1991. pap. text ed. 11.95 (*1-878623-21-4*) Info Plus TX.

—Education: Is It Improving or Declining. 48p. 1991. pap. text ed. 11.95 (*1-878623-20-6*) Info Plus TX.

—Growing Up: New Challenges for a New Generation. 48p. 1991. pap. text ed. 11.95 (*1-878623-22-2*) Info Plus TX.

—Homeless: Struggling to Survive. 40p. 1991. pap. text ed. 11.95 (*1-878623-23-0*) Info Plus TX.

Bingham, jt. auth. see Stryker.

Bingham, Caroline & Foster, Karen, eds. Crafts for Celebration. 48p. (gr. 2-6). 1993. PLB 13.90 (*1-56294-099-6*) Millbrook Pr.

—Crafts for Decoration. (Illus.). 48p. (gr. 2-6). 1993. PLB 13.90 (*1-56294-098-8*) Millbrook Pr.

—Crafts for Everyday Life. (Illus.). 48p. (gr. 2-6). 1993. PLB 13.90 (*1-56294-097-X*) Millbrook Pr.

—Crafts for Play. (Illus.). 48p. (gr. 2-6). 1993. PLB 13.90 (*1-56294-096-1*) Millbrook Pr.

Bingham, Clifton, jt. auth. see Nister, Ernest.

Bingham, Edwin. Oregon! LC 79-2296. (Illus.). 300p. (gr. 4). 1985. text ed. 17.25x (*0-87905-103-5*, Peregrine Smith) Gibbs Smith Pub.

Bingham, J. Science Experiments. (Illus.). 64p. (gr. 5 up). 1992. PLB 13.96 (*0-88110-515-5*, Usborne); pap. 7.95 (*0-7460-0806-6*, Usborne) EDC.

Bingham, Mindy. Berta Benz & the Motorwagen. Maeno, Itoko, illus. 48p. (gr. 1-6). 1992. with dust jacket 14.95 (*0-911655-38-7*) Advocacy Pr.

—Minou. Maeno, Itoko, illus. LC 86-26539. 64p. (gr. k-6). 1987. 14.95 (*0-911655-36-0*) Advocacy Pr.

Bingham, Mindy & Stryker, Sandy. Career Choices: A Guide for Teens & Young Adults: Who Am I? What Do I Want? How Do I Get It? Shafer, Robert, ed. Maeno, Itoko, et al, illus. LC 90-81785. 288p. (Orig.). (gr. 9 up). 1990. pap. 19.95 (*1-878787-02-0*) Able Pub.

Bingham, Mindy, jt. auth. see Paine, Penelope C.

Bingham, Mindy, et al. Choices: A Teen Woman's Journal for Self-Awareness & Personal Planning. updated ed. Green, Barbara & Peters, Kathleen, eds. (Illus.). 240p. (gr. 8 up). 1993. 18.95 (*0-911655-21-2*); pap. 18.95 (*0-911655-22-0*); wkbk. 5.95 Advocacy Pr.

—Challenges: A Young Man's Journal for Self-Awareness & Personal Planning. updated ed. Greene, Barbara & Peters, Kathleen, eds. LC 84-70108. (Illus.). 240p. (gr. 8 up). 1993. 18.95 (*0-911655-26-3*, Dist. by Ingram Book Co Bookpeople); pap. 18.95 (*0-911655-24-7*, Dist. by Ingram Book Co Bookpeople); wkbk. 5.95 (*0-911655-25-5*, Dist. by Ingram Book Co Bookpeople) Advocacy Pr.

Bingham, Thomas R. Program for Affective Learning (PAL) A Cognitive Supplementary Curriculum Teaching Positive Mental Health Rules. rev. ed. Ellis, Albert, intro. by. (Illus.). (gr. 3-6). Set. pap. text ed. 84.00 (*0-939707-05-5*) Starter Kit (*0-939707-01-2*) SK Seat Work (*0-939707-03-9*) Feeling Good Concept Kit (*0-939707-02-0*) Seat Work (*0-939707-04-7*) Set. tchr's guide 5.95 (*0-939707-00-4*) Thinking Kids Pr.

Binkley, Benny. Ben & His Friends. (gr. 4 up). 1993. 7.75 (*0-8062-4511-5*) Carlton.

Binnamin, Vivian. The Case of the Anteater's Missing Lunch. Brook, Bonnie, ed. Nelsen, Jeffrey S., illus. 32p. (gr. k-3). 1990. PLB 6.98 (*0-671-68816-2*); pap. 2.95 (*0-671-68820-0*) Silver Pr.

—The Case of the Mysterious Mermaid. Brook, Bonnie, ed. Nelsen, Jeffrey S., illus. 32p. (gr. k-3). 1990. PLB 6.98 (*0-671-68817-0*); pap. 2.95 (*0-671-68821-9*) Silver Pr.

—The Case of the Planetarium Puzzle. Brook, Bonnie, ed. Nelsen, Jeffrey S., illus. 32p. (gr. k-3). 1990. PLB 6.98 (*0-671-68819-7*); pap. 2.95 (*0-671-68823-5*) Silver Pr.

—The Case of the Snoring Stegosaurus. Brook, Bonnie, ed. Nelsen, Jeffrey S., illus. 32p. (gr. k-3). 1990. PLB 6.98 (*0-671-68818-9*); pap. 2.95 (*0-671-68822-7*) Silver Pr.

—Field Trip Mysteries Series, 4 vols. Nelsen, Jeffrey S., illus. 128p. (gr. k-3). 1990. Set. PLB 27.92 (*0-671-94436-3*) Set. pap. 11.80 (*0-671-94437-1*) Silver Pr.

Binney, Don. Inside Great Britain. FS Staff, ed. (Illus.). 32p. (gr. 1-6). 1988. PLB 11.90 (*0-531-10612-8*) Watts.

—Inside Italy. FS Staff, ed. (Illus.). 32p. (gr. 1-6). 1988. PLB 11.90 (*0-531-10613-6*) Watts.

Bin-Nun, Judy & Cooper, Nancy. Pesach: A Holiday Funtext. Steinberger, Heidi, illus. 32p. (Orig.). (gr. 1-3). 1983. pap. text ed. 5.00 (*0-8074-0161-7*, 101310) UAHC.

Bin-Nun, Judy & Einhorn, Franne. Rosh Hashanah: A Holiday Funtext. Steinberger, Heidi, illus. (gr. 1-3). 1978. pap. 5.00 (*0-8074-0230-3*, 101300) UAHC.

Biracree, Tom. Althea Gibson. Horner, Matina, intro. by. (Illus.). 112p. (gr. 5 up). 1990. lib. bdg. 17.95 (*1-55546-654-0*) Chelsea Hse.

—Wilma Rudolph. Horner, Matina, intro. by. (Illus.). 112p. (Orig.). (gr. 5 up). 1988. 17.95 (*1-55546-675-3*); pap. 9.95 (*0-7910-0217-9*) Chelsea Hse.

Birch, Beverley. Louis Braille: Bringer of Hope to the Blind. Lantier, Patricia, adapted by. LC 90-9969. (Illus.). 64p. (gr. 3-4). 1991. PLB 18.60 (*0-8368-0454-6*) Gareth Stevens Inc.

—Marie Curie: Pioneer in the Study of Radiation. LC 89-77762. (Illus.). 64p. (gr. 3-4). 1990. PLB 18.60 (*0-8368-0388-4*) Gareth Stevens Inc.

—Marie Curie: The Polish Scientist Who Discovered Radium & Its Life-Saving Properties. Sherwood, Rhoda, ed. LC 88-2091. (Illus.). 68p. (gr. 5-6). 1988. PLB 18.60 (*1-55532-818-0*) Gareth Stevens Inc.

—Our Hidden Garden. (Illus.). 26p. (gr. 2-4). 1991. 12.95 (*0-237-60147-8*, Pub. by Evans Bros Ltd) Trafalgar.

—Our Victorian Stall. (Illus.). 25p. (gr. 2-4). 1991. 16.95 (*0-237-60154-0*, Pub. by Evans Bros Ltd) Trafalgar.

—Shakespeare's Stories: Histories. Green, Robina, illus. LC 88-15693. 126p. (gr. 7-12). 1990. pap. 6.95 (*0-87226-226-X*) P Bedrick Bks.

—Shakespeare's Stories: Tragedies. Kerins, Tony, illus. LC 88-18112. 126p. (gr. 7-12). 1990. pap. 6.95 (*0-87226-227-8*) P Bedrick Bks.

Birch, Beverley, retold by. Shakespeare's Stories: Comedies. Tarrant, Carol, illus. LC 88-16947. 126p. 1990. pap. 6.95 (*0-87226-225-1*) P Bedrick Bks.

—Shakespeare's Stories: Comedies. Tarrant, Carol, illus. LC 93-13366. 1993. 6.99 (*0-517-09358-8*) Outlet Bk Co.

—Shakespeare's Stories: Histories. Green, Robina, illus. LC 93-13203. 1993. 6.99 (*0-517-09359-6*, Pub. by Wings Bks) Outlet Bk Co.

—Shakespeare's Stories: Tragedies. Kerins, Tony, illus. LC 93-13199. 1993. 6.99 (*0-517-09360-X*, Pub. by Wings Bks) Outlet Bk Co.

Birch, Beverley, adapted by see Brown, Pam.

Birch, Beverley, adapted by see Nicholson, Michael.

Birch, Beverley, adapted by see Schloredt, Valerie.

Birch, Beverly. Marie Curie. LC 88-2091. (Illus.). 68p. (Orig.). (gr. 5-6). 1990. pap. 7.95 (*0-8192-1522-8*) Morehouse Pub.

Birch, Beverly, retold by. Shakespeare's Stories: Comedies. Tarrant, Carol, illus. LC 88-16947. 126p. (gr. 7-12). 1988. 12.95 (*0-87226-191-3*) P Bedrick Bks.

—Shakespeare's Stories: Histories. Green, Robina, illus. LC 88-15693. 126p. (gr. 7-12). 1988. 12.95 (*0-87226-192-1*) P Bedrick Bks.

—Shakespeare's Stories: Tragedies. Kerins, Tony, illus. LC 88-18112. 126p. (gr. 7-12). 1988. 12.95 (*0-87226-193-X*) P Bedrick Bks.

Birch, Claire. Collision Course. (gr. 4-7). 1991. pap. 2.99 (*0-440-40512-2*, YB) Dell.

—Double Danger. (gr. 4-7). 1991. pap. 2.99 (*0-440-40525-4*, YB) Dell.

—False Lead. (gr. 4-7). 1991. pap. 2.99 (*0-440-40550-5*, YB) Dell.

—High Stakes. (gr. 4-7). 1992. pap. 2.99 (*0-440-40583-1*) Dell.

—Tight Spot. (gr. 4-7). 1991. pap. 2.99 (*0-440-40502-5*) Dell.

—Triple Threat. (gr. 4-7). 1991. pap. 2.99 (*0-440-40501-7*) Dell.

Birch, Cyril, ed. Chinese Myths & Fantasies. Kiddell-Monroe, Joan, illus. 144p. 1993. pap. 10.95 (*0-19-274152-7*) OUP.

Birch, David. The King's Chessboard. Grebu, Devis, illus. LC 87-20164. 32p. (gr. k up). 1988. PLB 10.89 (*0-8037-0367-8*) Dial Bks Young.

—The King's Chessboard. Grebu, Devis, illus. 32p. (gr. k up). 1993. pap. 4.99 (*0-14-054880-7*, Puffin Pied Piper) Puffin Bks.

—Wrestle the Angel. LC 93-60917. (Illus.). 44p. (gr. k-3). 1994. 7.95 (*1-55523-652-9*) Winston-Derek.

Birch Lane Press Staff. Cinderella. (ps-3). 1990. 12.95 (*1-55972-054-9*, Birch Ln Pr) Carol Pub Group.

—Jack & the Beanstalk. (ps). 1990. 12.95 (*1-55972-048-4*, Birch Ln Pr) Carol Pub Group.

Birchman, David. A Tale of Tulips, a Tale of Onions. Hunt, Jonathan, illus. LC 92-31240. 40p. (gr. 1-4). 1994. RSBE 15.95 (*0-02-710112-6*, Four Winds) Macmillan Child Grp.

Birchman, David F. Brother Billy Bronto's Bygone Blues Band. O'Brien, John, illus. LC 90-2611. (ps-3). 1992. 14.00 (*0-688-10423-1*); PLB 13.93 (*0-688-10424-X*) Lothrop.

—The Raggly, Scraggly, No-Soap, No-Scrub Girl. Porfirio, Guy, illus. LC 92-40339. (gr. 3 up). 1995. write for info. (*0-688-11060-6*); PLB write for info. (*0-688-11061-4*) Lothrop.

—Victorious Paints the Great Balloon. LC 90-1746. (Illus.). 64p. (gr. 2-6). 1991. RSBE 13.95 (*0-02-710111-8*, Bradbury Pr) Macmillan Child Grp.

Bird, E. J. The Blizzard of Eighteen Ninety-Six. Bird, E. J., illus. 72p. (gr. 2-6). 1990. PLB 14.95 (*0-87614-651-5*) Carolrhoda Bks.

—Chuck Wagon Stew. (Illus.). 72p. (gr. 2-6). 1988. 14.95 (*0-87614-313-3*); pap. 4.95 (*0-87614-498-9*) Carolrhoda Bks.

—How Do Bears Sleep? (Illus.). 32p. (ps-3). 1989. PLB 18.95 (*0-87614-384-2*) Carolrhoda Bks.

—How Do Bears Sleep? Bird, E. J., illus. 32p. (ps-3). pap. 5.95 (*0-87614-522-5*) Carolrhoda Bks.

—The Rainmakers. LC 92-29739. 1993. 19.95 (*0-87614-748-1*) Carolrhoda Bks.

—Ten Tall Tales. LC 84-12086. (Illus.). 56p. (gr. 2-6). 1984. PLB 14.95 (*0-87614-267-6*) Carolrhoda Bks.

Bird, Malcolm. The School in Murky Wood. (Illus.). 40p. (ps-3). 1993. 10.95 (*0-8118-0544-1*) Chronicle Bks.

—The Witch's Handbook. Bird, Malcolm, illus. LC 88-911. 96p. (ps up). 1988. POB 7.95 (*0-689-71237-5*, Aladdin) Macmillan Child Grp.

Bird, Malcolm & Dart, Alan. The Magic Handbook. (Illus.). 96p. (gr. 1-5). 1992. pap. 12.95 (*0-8118-0284-1*) Chronicle Bks.

Bird, Tate, ed. see McClure, Patricia.

Birdseye, Debbie, jt. auth. see Birdseye, Tom.

Birdseye, Tom. Airmail to the Moon. Gammell, Stephen, illus. LC 87-21199. 32p. (ps-3). 1988. reinforced bdg. 14.95 *(0-8234-0683-0)*; pap. 5.95 *(0-8234-0754-3)* Holiday.
—I'm Going to Be Famous. LC 86-45401. 144p. (gr. 3-7). 1986. 14.95 *(0-8234-0630-X)* Holiday.
—Just Call Me Stupid. (gr. 4-7). 1993. 14.95 *(0-8234-1045-5)* Holiday.
—A Kids' Guide to Building Forts. Klein, Bill, illus. LC 92-45908. 64p. (Orig.). (gr. 3-9). 1993. pap. 8.95 *(0-943173-69-8)* Harbinger AZ.
—A Regular Flood of Mishap. Loyd, Megan, illus. LC 93-9888. 32p. (gr. 4-8). 1994. 15.95 *(0-8234-1070-6)* Holiday.
—A Song of Stars. Ju-Hong Chen, illus. LC 89-20066. 32p. (gr. 4-8). 1990. reinforced bdg. 14.95 *(0-8234-0790-X)* Holiday.
—Tucker. LC 89-46243. 120p. (gr. 3-7). 1990. 13.95 *(0-8234-0813-2)* Holiday.
—Waiting for Baby. Leedy, Loreen, illus. LC 90-29076. 32p. (ps-3). 1991. reinforced 14.95 *(0-8234-0892-2)* Holiday.
Birdseye, Tom & Birdseye, Debbie. She'll Be Comin' Round the Mountain. Glass, Andrew, illus. LC 92-37641. 1994. write for info. *(0-8234-1032-3)* Holiday.
Birenbaum, Barbara. Candle Talk. Birenbaum, Barbara, illus. LC 90-33299. 54p. (gr. 2-5). 1991. 10.95 *(0-935343-10-5)*; pap. 5.95g *(0-935343-15-6)* Peartree.
—The Cupdeer. Birenbaum, Barbara, illus. LC 92-33093. 1993. PLB write for info. *(0-935343-04-0)*; pap. write for info. *(0-935343-02-4)* Peartree.
—The Gooblins Night. Birenbaum, Barbara, illus. LC 85-62585. 44p. (gr. 2-5). 1985. 10.95 *(0-935343-32-6)*; pap. 5.95 *(0-935343-31-8)* Peartree.
—The Hidden Shadow. Birenbaum, Barbara, illus. LC 86-12187. 54p. (gr. 1-4). 1986. 10.95 *(0-935343-42-3)*; pap. 5.95 *(0-935343-43-1)* Peartree.
—Lady Liberty's Light. Birenbaum, Barbara, illus. LC 85-32061. 50p. (gr. 3-5). 1986. 10.95 *(0-935343-12-1)*; pap. 5.95 *(0-935343-11-3)* Peartree.
—The Lighthouse Christmas. Birenbaum, Barbara & Sapp, Patt, illus. LC 90-7284. 48p. (Orig.). (gr. k-5). 1991. 10.95 *(0-935343-26-1)*; pap. 5.95 *(0-935343-25-3)* Peartree.
—The Lost Side of the Dreydl. Birenbaum, Barbara, illus. 50p. (gr. 3-5). 1987. 10.95 *(0-935343-17-2)*; pap. 5.95 *(0-935343-16-4)* Peartree.
—The Olympic Glow. (Illus.). 48p. (gr. 3-5). 1990. 10.95 *(0-935343-40-7)*; pap. 5.95 *(0-935343-41-5)* Peartree.
—The Olympic Glow. (Illus.). (gr. 3-5). 10.95 *(0-935343-45-8)*; pap. 5.95 *(0-935343-46-6)* Peartree.
Birger, Trudy & Green, Jeffrey M. A Daughter's Gift of Love: A Holocaust Memoir. LC 92-15503. 224p. 1992. 22.95 *(0-8276-0420-3)* JPS Phila.
Birkby, Robert C. Boy Scout Handbook. 10th ed. (Illus.). 672p. (gr. 6-12). 1992. 5.00 *(0-685-48068-2, 33229)* BSA.
—Conservation Handbook. Boy Scouts of America Staff, ed. LC 91-58676. (Illus.). 136p. 1991. pap. 6.00 *(0-8395-3570-8, 33570)* BSA.
Birkenhead. Biggest Horse You Ever Did See. Date not set. 15.00 *(0-06-023467-9, Festival)*; PLB 14.89 *(0-06-023468-7, Festival)* HarpC Child Bks.
—Melanie Jane. Date not set. 15.00 *(0-06-023391-5, Festival)*; PLB 14.89 *(0-685-68963-8, Festival)* HarpC Child Bks.
Birker, Stefan. Drawing & Painting with Colored Pencils. LC 92-41349. (Illus.). 128p. (gr. 9-12). 1993. pap. 16.95 *(0-8069-0312-0)* Sterling.
Birkett, Alaric. Vikings. (gr. 5-8). 1985. pap. 10.95 *(0-7175-1321-1)* Dufour.
Birkhead, Mike. The Falcon over the Town. Oxford Scientific Films, photos by. LC 87-42615. (Illus.). 32p. (gr. 4-6). 1988. PLB 15.93 *(1-55532-304-9)* Gareth Stevens Inc.
Birkner, Karen, jt. auth. see Birkner, Malthias.
Birkner, Malthias & Birkner, Karen. Denizens of the Dark Wood. Ney, Jessica, ed. McBride, Angus & Danforth, Liz, illus. 32p. (Orig.). (gr. 12). 1989. pap. 6.00 *(1-55806-081-2, 8111)* Iron Crown Ent Inc.
Birky, Lela. Truth for Life Bible Studies. (gr. 7-9). 1965. pap. write for info. *(0-686-15481-9)* Rod & Staff.
Birmingham, Duncan. Look Twice: Mirror Reflections, Logical Thinking. (gr. 3 up). 1991. pap. 6.95 *(0-906212-86-3, Pub. by Tarquin UK)* Parkwest Pubns.
—The Maya, Aztecs & Incas Pop-up. (Illus.). 32p. (gr. 3 up). 1985. pap. 7.95 *(0-906212-37-5, Pub. by Tarquin UK)* Parkwest Pubns.
Birminham, Duncan. M Is for Mirror. (Illus.). 33p. (gr. 2-5). 1989. pap. 6.95 *(0-906212-66-9, Pub. by Tarquin UK)* Parkwest Pubns.
Birnbaum, Alfred, tr. see Murakami, Haruki.
Birnbaum, Bette. Jane Goodall & the Wild Chimpanzees. (Illus.). 32p. (gr. 1-4). 1989. PLB 15.96 *(0-8172-3509-4)*; pap. 3.95 *(0-8114-6709-0)* Raintree Steck-V.
—My School, Your School. (Illus.). 24p. 1990. PLB 14.60 *(0-8172-3583-3)*; pap. 10.95 pkg. of 3 *(0-8114-2931-8)* Raintree Steck-V.
Birnbaum, Steve & Lefkon, Wendy, eds. Birnbaum's Walt Disney World for Kids by Kids, 1994. (Illus.). 128p. 1993. pap. 9.95 *(1-56282-750-2)* Hyperion.
Birnes, William J., jt. auth. see Shadow Lawn Press Staff.
Birney, Betty. Bambi's Snowy Day. Pacheco, David & Wakeman, Diana, illus. 32p. (ps-k). 1992. write for info. *(0-307-15704-0, 15704, Golden Pr)* Western Pub.

—Disney's Beauty & the Beast. (ps). 1993. 3.95 *(0-307-12536-X, Golden Pr)* Western Pub.
—Disney's Winnie the Pooh Helping Hands: Oh, Bother! Somebody's Grumpy! Baker, Darrell, illus. 24p. (ps-3). 1992. write for info. *(0-307-12667-6, 12667)* Western Pub.
—Disney's Winnie the Pooh Helping Hands: Oh, Bother! Someone's Messy! Stevenson, Nancy, illus. 24p. (ps-3). 1992. write for info. *(0-307-12690-0, 12690, Golden Pr)* Western Pub.
—Piglet Bakes Half a Haycorn Pie. Baker, Darrell, illus. 24p. (ps-2). 1992. write for info. *(0-307-12338-3, 12338)* Western Pub.
—Walt Disney's Sleeping Beauty. (ps). 1993. 3.95 *(0-307-12528-9, Golden Pr)* Western Pub.
—Walt Disney's Winnie the Pooh Helping Hands: Oh, Bother! Someone Won't Share. Stevenson, Nancy, illus. 24p. (ps-3). 1993. pap. 1.95 *(0-307-12766-4, 12766, Golden Pr)* Western Pub.
—Wee Sing in Sillyville. Beall, Pamela C., created by. (Illus.). 24p. 1993. pap. 3.95 *(0-8431-3649-9)* Price Stern.
—Wee Sing Together. Beall, Pamela C., created by. (Illus.). 24p. 1993. pap. 3.95 *(0-8431-3648-0)* Price Stern.
—Who Am I? Berret, Lisa, illus. 16p. (ps). 1992. pap. 5.95 pop-up bk. *(0-671-76914-6, Little Simon)* S&S Trade.
—Winnie the Pooh & the Little Lost Bird: A Big Golden Book. (ps-3). 1993. 3.95 *(0-307-12369-3, Golden Pr)* Western Pub.
—Winnie the Pooh & the Missing Pots. Hicks, Russell, illus. 24p. (ps-2). 1992. write for info. *(0-307-12337-5, 12337)* Western Pub.
—Winnie the Pooh: The Merry Christmas Mystery. (ps-3). 1993. pap. 2.25 *(0-307-12774-5, Golden Pr)* Western Pub.
Birney, Betty, adapted by. Disney's The Little Mermaid. Martin, Kerry & Marvin, Fred, illus. 28p. (ps). 1992. bds. write for info. *(0-307-12534-3, 12534, Golden Pr)* Western Pub.
Birnhack, Sara. Promise Me Tomorrow. LC 90-82061. (gr. 6 up). 1990. 12.95 *(1-56062-025-0)*; pap. 9.95 *(1-56062-026-9)* CIS Comm.
Biro, Val. Jack & the Beanstalk. (Illus.). 32p. (ps up). 1990. bds. 9.95 *(0-19-278218-5)* OUP.
—Rub-a-Dub-Dub: Val Biro's Seventy-Seven Favorite Nursery Rhymes. Biro, Val, illus. LC 90-14402. 62p. (ps). 1991. PLB 16.95 *(0-87226-449-1, Bedrick Blackie)* P Bedrick Bks.
—Tobias & the Dragon: A Hungarian Folk Tale. Biro, Val, illus. LC 89-18492. 32p. (gr. k-3). 1990. PLB 12.95 *(0-87226-427-0, Bedrick Blackie)* P Bedrick Bks.
Biro, Val, jt. auth. see Todd, H. E.
Biro, Val, retold by. & illus. Hungarian Folk-Tales. 192p. (gr. 4 up). 1992. pap. 10.95 *(0-19-274148-9)* OUP.
Biro, Val, retold by. The Three Little Pigs. (Illus.). 28p. (ps-1). 1991. bds. 7.95 *(0-19-279880-4, 12353)* OUP.
Biros, Florence K. Dog Jack. Libb, Melva, ed. (Illus.). 192p. (Orig.). 1988. pap. 6.95 *(0-936369-22-1)* Son-Rise Pubns.
Biros, Florence W. Dog Jack. 2nd ed. (Illus.). (gr. 5 up). 1990. 7.95 *(0-936369-47-7)* Son Rise Pubns.
Birrer, Cynthia & Birrer, William. The Lady & the Unicorn. Birrer, Cynthia & Birrer, William, illus. LC 86-20872. 32p. (ps-3). 1987. 12.95 *(0-688-04037-3)* Lothrop.
Birrer, William, jt. auth. see Birrer, Cynthia.
Biscardi, Cyrus H. The Storybook of Opera, Vol. II. Blythe, Anne, frwd. by. LC 86-81155. (Illus.). 224p. (gr. 7 up). 1987. lib. bdg. 23.95 *(0-918452-99-6)*; pap. 23.95 *(1-55691-006-1)* Learning Pubns.
Bischof, Larry & Lowry, William B. Amazon Adventure. LC 92-12844. (gr. 2). 1992. 13.99 *(1-56239-150-X)* Abdo & Dghtrs.
Bischoff, David. Some Kind of Wonderful: Movie Tie-In. (gr. 9 up). 1987. pap. 2.50 *(0-440-98042-9)* Dell.
Bischoff, David, jt. auth. see Preiss, Byron.
Bisel, Sara. Secrets of Vesuvius: Exploring the Mysteries of an Ancient Buried City. (gr. 4-7). 1993. pap. 6.95 *(0-590-43851-4)* Scholastic Inc.
Bisel, Sara C. Secrets of Vesuvius: Exploring the Mysteries of an Ancient Buried City. (gr. 4-7). 1991. 15.95 *(0-590-43850-6, Scholastic Hardcover)* Scholastic Inc.
Biser, Len. Meet Mrs. Wiggywaggle: Mrs. Wiggywaggle Goes to Town. Beach, Katharina, illus. 32p. (ps-1). 1991. write for info. *(1-880015-29-3)* Petra Pub Co.
Biser, Len, jt. auth. see Sprock, Inge.
Bishop, Adela. The Christmas Polar Bear. Czapla, Carole, illus. 32p. (gr. k-3). 1991. 12.95 *(0-9625620-2-5)* DOT Garnet.
—The Easter Wolf. Czapla, Carole, illus. 28p. (ps-3). 1991. 12.95 *(0-9625620-1-7)* DOT Garnet.
Bishop & Leechman. The Adventures of Jozedek. Nudd, Stacy, illus. LC 86-72946. 62p. (Orig.). (gr. 4-5). 1987. pap. 6.00 *(0-916383-23-7)* Aegina Pr.
Bishop, Ann. Hello, God! Rubin, Caroline, ed. Warshaw, Jerry, illus. LC 77-12828. (gr. 1-4). 1977. PLB 8.95 *(0-8075-6965-8)* A Whitman.
Bishop, Claire H. All Alone. Rojanovsky, Feodor, illus. 96p. (gr. 2-5). 1953. 15.00 *(0-670-11336-0)* Viking Child Bks.
—The Five Chinese Brothers. (Illus.). (gr. k-3). 1938. 11.95 *(0-698-20044-6, Coward)* Putnam Pub Group.
—The Five Chinese Brothers. Wiese, Kurt, illus. 64p. (ps-3). 1989. pap. 4.95 *(0-698-20642-8, Sandcastle Bks)* Putnam Pub Group.

—Twenty & Ten. Pene du Bois, William, illus. (gr. 3-7). 1978. pap. 3.99 *(0-14-031076-2, Puffin)* Puffin Bks.
—Twenty & Ten. Pene du Bois, William, illus. (gr. 5-9). 1984. 16.75 *(0-8446-6168-6)* Peter Smith.
Bishop, Conrad & Fuller, Elizabeth. Get Happy. 36p. (Orig.). (gr. 9-12). 1991. pap. 4.00 acting ed. *(0-9624511-0-X)* WordWorkers.
Bishop, Dorothy S. The City Mouse & the Country Mouse. (FRE & ENG., Illus.). 72p. 1989. pap. 4.95 *(0-8442-1086-2, Passport Bks)* NTC Pub Grp.
—Habia Una Vez. (SPA., Illus.). 96p. 1991. pap. 9.95 incl. 60-min. cassette *(0-8442-7349-X, Passport Bks)* NTC Pub Grp.
—The Lion & the Mouse. (FRE & ENG., Illus.). 72p. 1989. pap. 4.95 *(0-8442-1084-6, Passport Bks)* NTC Pub Grp.
—The Tortoise & the Hare. (ENG & FRE.). 72p. (gr. 4 up). pap. 4.95 *(0-8442-1085-4, Passport Bks)* NTC Pub Grp.
Bishop, Dorothy S., et al. Bilingual Fables & Folk Tales. Incl. Perez y Martina *(0-8442-7167-5)*; El Pajaro Cu: The Cu Bird *(7163-5)*; Las Manchos del Sapo: How the Toad Lost its Spots *(7171-5)*; Chiquita y Pepita: The City Mouse & the Country Mouse *(0-8442-7446-1)*; Tina la Tortuga y Carlos el Conejo: The Tortoise & the Hare *(0-8442-7444-5)*; Leonardo el Leon y Ramon el Raton: The Lion & The Mouse *(0-8442-7445-3)*; Poniendo el Cascabel el Gato: Belling the Cat *(0-8442-7282-5)*; El Muchacho Que Grito EL Lobo!: The Boy Who Cried Wolf *(7295-5)*; La Lechera y Su Cubeta: The Milkmaid & Her Pail. 1991 *(0-8442-7250-7)*. (SPA & ENG., Illus.). 72p. (gr. 4 up). 1983. pap. 4.95 ea. (Passport Bks) NTC Pub Grp.
—Las Manchos Del Sapo. (SPA & ENG., Illus.). 72p. 1991. pap. 3.95 *(0-8442-7171-3, Passport Bks)* NTC Pub Grp.
—El Muchacho Que Grito el Lobo! (ENG & SPA., Illus.). 72p. 1991. pap. 4.95 *(0-8442-7295-7, Passport Bks)* NTC Pub Grp.
—El Pajaro Cu. (SPA & ENG., Illus.). 72p. 1991. pap. 4.95 *(0-8442-7163-2, Passport Bks)* NTC Pub Grp.
Bishop, Eleanor. Prints in the Sand: The U. S. Coast Guard Beach Patrol During WWII. LC 89-62184. (Illus.). 92p. (Orig.). (gr. 8-12). 1989. pap. 9.95 *(0-929521-22-6)* Pictorial Hist.
Bishop, Jack. Ralph Ellison. King, Coretta Scott, intro. by. (Illus.). 112p. (Orig.). (gr. 5 up). 1988. 17.95 *(1-55546-585-4)*; pap. 9.95 *(0-7910-0202-0)* Chelsea Hse.
Bishop, James, Jr., et al. Experience Jerome & the Verde Valley Legends & Legacies, No. II. Henry, Ron, illus. LC 90-71606. 356p. (Orig.). (gr. 8-12). 1990. pap. 12.95 *(0-9628329-1-X)* Thorne Enterprises.
Bishop, Kathleen. A White Face Painted Brown: A Young Girl's Journey into the Bosom of a Black & Mexican Los Angeles Ghetto Called Aliso Village. Shwed, Joanne, ed. 180p. (Orig.). (gr. 8-12). 1993. pap. text ed. 12.95 *(0-9636217-1-8)* Pallas Athena.
Bishop, Kathryn, ed. see Heisch, Glan & Heisch, Elisabeth.
Bishop, Lila, ed. see Baldry, Cherith.
Bishop, Lila, ed. see Bly, Stephen.
Bishop, Lila, ed. see Minar, Barbra.
Bishop, Lila, ed. see Stahl, Hilda.
Bishop, M., et al. Merrill Science Program. large type ed. Incl. Focus on Physical Science. 800p. 1981. 210.50 *(0-317-02420-5, J-06620-00)*. (gr. 7-9). 1982. Repr. of 1981 ed (J-06620-00) Am Printing Hse.
Bishop, Pamela R. Exploring Your Skeleton: Funny Bones & Not-So-Funny Bones. Callen, Liz, illus. LC 90-31026. 32p. (gr. 1-4). 1991. PLB 12.90 *(0-531-10970-4)* Watts.
Bishop, Roma. Animals. (Illus.). 14p. (ps-k). 1991. pap. 2.95 casebound pop-up *(0-671-74833-5, Little Simon)* S&S Trade.
—At the Zoo: Match It Up. 1989. 3.99 *(0-517-68251-6)* Outlet Bk Co.
—Colors. (ps). 1992. pap. 2.95 *(0-671-79120-6, Little Simon)* S&S Trade.
—Mommy & Baby. (ps). 1992. pap. 2.95 *(0-671-79119-2, Little Simon)* S&S Trade.
—Numbers. (Illus.). 14p. (ps-k). 1991. pap. 2.95 *(0-671-74832-7, Little Simon)* S&S Trade.
—Opposites. (ps). 1992. pap. 2.95 *(0-671-79128-1, Little Simon)* S&S Trade.
—Perfect Pom-Pom: Where Does It Belong? (ps-3). 1993. 9.95 *(0-307-17602-9, Golden Pr)* Western Pub.
—Shapes. (Illus.). 14p. (ps-k). 1991. pap. 2.95 *(0-671-74830-0, Little Simon)* S&S Trade.
—Things That Go. 1992. pap. 2.95 *(0-671-79129-X, Little Simon)* S&S Trade.
—Toys. (Illus.). 14p. (ps-k). 1991. pap. 2.95 *(0-671-74831-9, Little Simon)* S&S Trade.
Bishop, Roma, illus. Christmas Songs & Prayers for Children. 32p. (ps). 1993. 9.98 *(0-8317-5168-1)* Smithmark.
Bishops' Committee for Pastoral Research Staff & National Conference of Catholic Bishops Staff. The Sexual Challenge: Growing up Christian. 16p. (Orig.). (gr. 9-12). 1990. pap. 0.95 *(1-555-86364-7)* US Catholic.
Bisignano, Alphonse. Cooking the Italian Way. LC 82-12641. (Illus.). 48p. (gr. 5 up). 1982. PLB 14.95 *(0-8225-0906-7)* Lerner Pubns.
Bisignano, Judith. Trivial Pursuit - Science (Junior High) (Illus.). 64p. (gr. 7-9). 1992. 12.95 *(0-86653-651-5, GA1387)* Good Apple.

Bisignano, Judith & Sanders, Corine. Saints Alive! Mirocha, Kay, illus. LC 86-63988. 64p. (gr. 5-7). 1987. wkbk. 7.95 (1-55612-038-9) Sheed & Ward MO.

Bisignano, Judy. Relating. Tom, Darcy, illus. 64p. (gr. 3-8). 1985. wkbk. 7.95 (0-86653-331-1, GA 678) Good Apple.

Bisignano, Judy, jt. auth. see Carswell, Evelyn.

Biskup, Michael & Wekesser, Carol, eds. Suicide: Opposing Viewpoints. LC 92-6093. (Illus.). 240p. (gr. 10 up). 1992. PLB 17.95 (0-89908-193-2); pap. text ed. 9.95 (0-89908-168-1) Greenhaven.

Biskup, Michael D., ed. Criminal Justice: Opposing Viewpoints. (Illus.). 264p. (gr. 10 up). 1993. PLB 17.95 (0-89908-624-1); pap. text ed. 9.95 (0-89908-623-3) Greenhaven.

Biskup, Michael D. & Cozic, Charles P., eds. Youth Violence. LC 92-23592. 200p. (gr. 10 up). 1992. PLB 16.95 (1-56510-017-4); pap. text ed. 9.95 (1-56510-016-6) Greenhaven.

Biskup, Michael D. & Swisher, Karin L., eds. AIDS: Opposing Viewpoints. LC 92-19874. (Illus.). 240p. (gr. 10 up). 1992. PLB 17.95 (0-89908-190-8); pap. text ed. 9.95 (0-89908-165-7) Greenhaven.

Biskup, Michael D., jt. ed. see Wekesser, Carol.

Bisnignano, Judith. Living with Death - Middle School. 64p. (gr. 5-9). 1991. 7.95 (0-86653-584-5, GA1317) Good Apple.

Bispham, W. Bispham: Memoranda Concerning the Family of Bispham in Great Britain & the U. S. 348p. 1992. lib. bdg. 67.00 (0-8328-2635-9); pap. 57.00 (0-8328-2636-7) Higginson Bk Co.

Bissell, LeClair & Watherwax, Richard. The Cat Who Drank Too Much. (ENG & SPA., Illus.). 48p. (gr. 4 up). 1982. pap. 5.00 (0-911153-00-4) Spanish ed., 03/1984 (0-911153-01-2) Bibulophile Pr.

Bissett, Isabel. Here Comes Annette! Vane, Mitch, illus. LC 92-27267. 1993. 3.75 (0-383-03628-3) SRA Schl Grp.

—How to Make Cheese Muffins. Costeloe, Brenda, illus. LC 93-21247. 1994. 4.25 (0-383-03748-4) SRA Schl Grp.

—Molly's Bracelet. Strahan, Heather, illus. LC 92-34337. 1993. 3.75 (0-383-03641-0) SRA Schl Grp.

—That's Dangerous. Tulloch, Coral, illus. LC 92-31947. 1993. 3.75 (0-383-03596-1) SRA Schl Grp.

—Wheels. Wood, Bill, illus. LC 92-21399. 1993. 3.75 (0-383-03605-4) SRA Schl Grp.

Bisson, Terry. Harriet Tubman. King, Coretta Scott, intro. by. (Illus.). 112p. (Orig.). (gr. 5 up). 1991. pap. 9.95 (0-7910-0249-7) Chelsea Hse.

—Nat Turner. King, Coretta Scott, intro. by. (Illus.). 112p. (Orig.). (gr. 5 up). 1988. 17.95 (1-55546-613-3); pap. 9.95 (0-7910-0214-4) Chelsea Hse.

Bissonnette-Lamendella, Denise. Pathways: A Job Search Curriculum. 275p. (Orig.). 1987. student wkbk. 7.95 (0-942071-05-0) M Wright & Assocs.

—Pathways: A Job Search Curriculum. rev. ed. 265p. 1987. Repr. of 1986 ed. tchr's. ed. 87.95 (0-942071-02-6) M Wright & Assocs.

Bitker, Marian. Thanks for Giving & Other Poems. LC 90-93454. 63p. (Orig.). 1991. 15.00x (0-9628150-0-4); pap. 10.00x (0-9628150-1-2) M Bitker.

Bitmead, Michele, jt. auth. see Pryor, Nick.

Bitney, James. First Communion: A Parish Celebration Family Book. 48p. 1993. pap. text ed. 6.30 (1-55944-038-4) Franciscan Comns.

Bitney, James & Nelson, Yvette. Welcome to the Family. 112p. (gr. 4-6). 1988. student ed. 6.95 (0-89505-658-5, T18X1) Tabor Pub.

—Welcome to the Way, Jr. High Student Edition. (Illus.). 80p. (Orig.). (gr. 6-8). 1989. pap. text ed. 7.50 (0-89505-585-6, T2512) Tabor Pub.

—Welcome to the Way, Sr. High Student Edition. (Illus.). 80p. (gr. 9-12). 1989. pap. text ed. 7.50 (0-89505-580-5, T2513) Tabor Pub.

Bitter, Gary G. & Camuse, Ruth A. Using a Microcomputer in the Classroom. (gr. k-12). 1983. pap. text ed. 25.00 (0-8359-8144-4, Reston) P-H.

Bittinger, Gayle. Exploring Sand & the Desert: And the Desert. Harrison, Brenda M., ed. Mohrann, Gary, illus. LC 92-62463. 96p. (Orig.). (ps-1). 1993. pap. 8.95 (0-911019-58-8) Warren Pub Hse.

—Exploring Water & the Ocean: And the Ocean. Harrison, Brenda M., ed. Mohrann, Gary, illus. LC 92-62462. 96p. (Orig.). (ps-1). 1993. pap. 8.95 (0-911019-59-6) Warren Pub Hse.

—Exploring Wood & the Forest: And the Forest. Harrison, Brenda M., ed. Mohrann, Gary, illus. LC 92-62464. 96p. (Orig.). (ps-1). 1993. pap. 8.95 (0-911019-60-X) Warren Pub Hse.

—Our Selves. Kotomaimoce, Kathy, illus. LC 91-67076. 80p. 1992. 8.95 (0-911019-51-0, WPH 1202) Warren Pub Hse.

—Our World. McKinnon, Elizabeth, ed. Jones, Kathy, illus. LC 89-52145. 80p. (Orig.). (ps-1). 1990. pap. 8.95 (0-911019-30-8) Warren Pub Hse.

—Play & Learn with Magnets. Warren, Jean, ed. Mohrmann, Gary, illus. LC 93-61084. 64p. (Orig.). 1994. pap. text ed. 7.95 (0-911019-92-8) Warren Pub Hse.

Bittinger, Gayle, ed. Holiday Piggyback Songs. Warren, Jean, compiled by. Ekberg, Marion H., illus. LC 88-50593. 96p. (Orig.). (ps-1). 1988. pap. 8.95 (0-911019-18-9) Warren Pub Hse.

Bittinger, Gayle, ed. see McKinnon, Elizabeth.

Bittinger, Gayle, ed. see Warren, Jean.

Bittinger, Gayle, jt. ed. see Warren, Jean.

Bittinger, Gayle, ed. see Warren, Jean & McKinnon, Elizabeth S.

Bittner, Bob, ed. see Wallace, Jeffery S.

Bivens, Christopher, illus. The Perfect Tree & Favorite Christmas Carols. Ingram, John W., ed. Bivins, Christopher, illus. LC 90-34514. 48p. (ps-2). 1990. 4.95 (0-88101-104-5) Unicorn Pub.

Bivens, Ruth. Aunt Ruth's Puppet Scripts, Bk. I. (Orig.). (gr. 1-8). 1986. Incl. cassette narration. pap. 19.95 (0-89265-096-6) Randall Hse.

—Aunt Ruth's Puppet Scripts, Bk. III. 55p. (gr. 1-6). 1987. 19.95 (0-89265-119-9); cassette incl. Randall Hse.

Bivens, Tom. The Perfect Tree. Bivens, Chris, illus. 48p. (ps-2). 1991. 6.95 (0-88101-179-7) Unicorn Pub.

Bix, Cynthia O., jt. auth. see Rauzon, Mark.

Bixenman, Judy. Dinosaur Jokes. (Illus.). 32p. 1991. 19.95 (0-89565-728-7); 13.95s.p. (0-685-55123-7) Childs World.

Bizer, Linda, jt. auth. see Nathan, Beverly.

Bizette, Genevieve. The Cardinal. 12p. (ps) 1992. 4.95 (1-56828-011-4) Red Jacket Pr.

—The Dove. 12p. (ps). 1992. 4.95 (1-56828-009-2) Red Jacket Pr.

—The Mallard. 12p. (ps). 1992. 4.95 (1-56828-012-2) Red Jacket Pr.

—Nell's Aviary. (ps). 1992. 11.95 (1-56828-013-0) Red Jacket Pr.

—The Seagull. 12p. (ps). 1992. 4.95 (1-56828-010-6) Red Jacket Pr.

Bizette, Genevieve, illus. Nell's Aviary. (ps). 1993. Gift box set of 4 bks., 12p. ea. incl 4 hanging birds. bds. 14.95 (1-56828-038-6) Red Jacket Pr.

Bjarkman, Peter. Duke Snider. (Illus.). 64p. (gr. 3 up). 1994. PLB 14.95 (0-7910-1190-9, Am Art Analog) Chelsea Hse.

—Ernie Banks. (Illus.). 64p. (gr. 3 up). 1994. PLB 14.95 (0-7910-1167-4, Am Art Analog) Chelsea Hse.

—Warren Spahn. (Illus.). 1994. 14.95 (0-7910-1191-7, Am Art Analog) Chelsea Hse.

Bjarkman, Peter C. Roberto Clemente. Murray, Jim, intro. by. (Illus.). 64p. (gr. 3 up). 1991. lib. bdg. 14.95 (0-7910-1171-2) Chelsea Hse.

Bjener, Tamiko. Children of the World: Finland. LC 87-42580. (Illus.). 64p. (gr. 5-6). 1987. PLB 19.93 (1-55532-218-2) Gareth Stevens Inc.

—Children of the World: Philippines. LC 86-42805. (Illus.). 64p. (gr. 5-6). 1987. PLB 19.93 (1-55532-167-4) Gareth Stevens Inc.

—Children of the World: Sweden. LC 86-42803. (Illus.). 64p. (gr. 5-6). 1987. PLB 19.93 (1-55532-164-X) Gareth Stevens Inc.

Bjork, Christina. Elliot's Extraordinary Cookbook. Sandin, Joan, tr. Anderson, Lena, illus. 60p. 1991. 11.95 (91-29-59658-0, Pub. by R & S Bks) FS&G.

—Linnea in Monet's Garden. Sandin, Joan, tr. from SWE. Anderson, Lena, illus. 56p. (gr. 3-6). 1987. 11.95 (91-29-58314-4, Pub. by R & S Bks) FS&G.

—Linnea's Alamanac. Anderson, Lena, illus. Sandin, Joan, tr. (gr. k-3). 1989. 11.95 (91-29-59176-7, Pub. by R & S Bks) FS&G.

—Linnea's Windowsill Garden. Anderson, Lena, illus. 60p. 1988. 11.95 (91-29-59064-7, Pub. by R & S Bks) FS&G.

—The Other Alice: The Story of Alice Liddell & Alice in Wonderland. Eriksson, Inga-Karin, illus. Sandlin, Joan, tr. from SWE. LC 93-662. (Illus.). 1993. 18.00 (91-29-62242-5, Pub. by R & S Bks) FS&G.

Bjorke, Drew. Arne & Loki. Bjorke, Drew, illus. 12p. (ps). 1993. 4.95 (1-56828-033-5) Red Jacket Pr.

—Arne the Viking. Bjorke, Drew, illus. (ps). 1993. Gift box set of 4 bks., 12p. ea. incl. viking ship. bds. 14.95 (1-56828-037-8) Red Jacket Pr.

—The Artic Trip. Bjorke, Drew, illus. 12p. (ps). 1993. 4.95 (1-56828-035-1) Red Jacket Pr.

—The Magic Sail. Bjorke, Drew, illus. 12p. (ps). 1993. 4.95 (1-56828-036-X) Red Jacket Pr.

—The Viking Counting Book. Bjorke, Drew, illus. 12p. (ps). 1993. 4.95 (1-56828-034-3) Red Jacket Pr.

Bjorkman, jt. auth. see Marzollo.

Black, Albert, ed. see Friendly, Alfred.

Black, Albert, ed. see Stewart, Celeste.

Black, Albert, ed. see White, Sylvia.

Black, Ann N. & Smith, Jo R. Ten Tools of Language-Written. 2nd ed. (Illus.). 166p. (gr. 11-12). 1982. pap. text ed. 12.60x (0-910513-00-7) Mayfield Printing.

Black, Auguste R. Miracles at the Inn. Sherentz, Michael K., illus. 24p. (Orig.). (gr. 1-12). 1990. pap. 4.95 (0-9628010-1-1) A R Black.

—The Shelby Avenue Gang. Black, Candice N., illus. 66p. (Orig.). (gr. 2-5). 1990. pap. 3.95 (0-9628010-0-3) A R Black.

—The Year That Santa Goofed & Other Short Stories. Sherentz, Michael & Horton, Terri, illus. 22p. (Orig.). (gr. 1-5). 1990. pap. 2.95 (0-9628010-2-X) A R Black.

Black, Beryl. Coping with Sexual Harassment. rev. ed. Rosen, Ruth, ed. 149p. (gr. 7 up). 1992. PLB 13.95 (0-8239-1174-8); pap. 8.95 (0-8239-0764-3) Rosen Group.

Black, Brian. America at War: Battles That Turned the Tide. (gr. 4-7). 1992. pap. 3.50 (0-590-45505-2) Scholastic Inc.

Black, Christopher. The Android Invasion. (Orig.). (gr. 4-8). 1984. pap. 2.50 (0-440-40081-3, YB) Dell.

Black, Claudia. My Dad Loves Me, My Dad Has a Disease. LC 59-776. (Illus.).

88p. (Orig.). (gr. k-9). 1982. pap. 9.95 (0-9607940-2-6) MAC Pub.

MY DAD LOVES ME, MY DAD HAS A DISEASE is an 88 page illustrated workbook for children whose mothers or fathers are affected by alcoholism & other forms of chemical dependencies. It is designed to help children better understand alcoholism & to better understand their own feelings. The basic premise of this book is that alcoholism is a disease, affecting not only the alcoholic but those who love them as well. Professionals & non-professionals can use this book as a tool when addressing these children. Although this workbook was designed for & illustrated by children through age fourteen, it may also hold insights for the now adult child, raised in an alcoholic home. Every child should have their own copy to express their feelings & perceptions. Remember, this is a workbook; you will need colored pens or crayons as you read. Written by Claudia Black, Ph.D., MSW. MAC Publishing, 5005 East 39th Avenue, Denver, CO 80207-1106. 303-331-0148. $9.95 plus $1.50 shipping.
Publisher Provided Annotation.

Black, Cynthia, ed. see Joyer, Mike & Roberts, Zack.

Black, Donald O. Lama's SuperAmerican Coloring Book. (Illus.). 7p. (gr. 3). 1991. map. write for info. (0-9625753-1-3) SuperAmerican Bks.

Black, Fiona. Aesop's Fables. (ps-3). 1991. 6.95 (0-8362-4914-3) Andrews & McMeel.

Black, Fiona, retold by see Grimm, Jacob & Grimm, Wilhelm K.

Black, Fiona, retold by see Hoffman, E. T.

Black, Fiona, retold by see Hoffmann, E. T.

Black, Irma S. Little Old Man Who Could Not Read. Fleishman, Seymour, illus. LC 68-9115. (gr. k-2). 1968. PLB 11.95 (0-8075-4621-6) A Whitman.

Black, J. R. The Ghost of Chicken Liver Hill. 120p. (Orig.). (gr. 3-7). 1993. pap. 3.50 (0-679-85007-4) Random Bks Yng Read.

—Guess Who's Dating a Werewolf? 120p. (Orig.). (gr. 3-7). 1993. pap. 3.50 (0-679-85008-2) Random Bks Yng Read.

—Revenge of the Computer Phantoms. 132p. (gr. 3-5). 1993. pap. 3.50 (0-679-85407-X) Random Bks Yng Read.

—The Undead Express. 132p. (Orig.). (gr. 3-7). 1994. pap. 3.50 (0-679-85408-8) Random Bks Yng Read.

—The Witches Next Door. 120p. (Orig.). (gr. 3-7). 1993. pap. 3.50 (0-679-85108-9) Random Bks Yng Read.

Black, John & Evans, Patrick. John Black Presents Power Build. (Illus.). 92p. 1990. pap. 9.95 (0-929994-05-1) Crains Muscle.

Black, Judy. Fashion. LC 93-4639. (gr. 9 up). 1994. write for info. (0-89686-791-9, Crestwood Hse) Macmillan Child Grp.

Black, Kaye. Kidvid: Fun-Damentals of Video Instruction. Murray, Joe, illus. 112p. (Orig.). (gr. 4-8). 1989. pap. 15.95 (0-913705-44-6) Zephyr Pr AZ.

Black, Matthew W., ed. see Shakespeare, William.

Black, Patti & Morrison, Ann, eds. Walter Anderson for Children: An Activity Book from the Mississippi State Historical Museum. Anderson, Walter, illus. 64p. (Orig.). (ps-8). 1984. pap. 12.95 (0-685-09182-1) Mississippi Archives.

Black, S. Fabulous Facts about Fifty States. (gr. 4-7). 1991. pap. 2.75 (0-590-44886-2) Scholastic Inc.

Black, Sheila. Sitting Bull. Furstinger, Nancy, ed. (Illus.). 144p. (gr. 7-9). 1989. PLB 12.98 (0-382-09572-3); pap. 7.95 (0-382-09761-0) Silver Burdett Pr.

—The Story of the Easter Bunny. Officer, Robyn, illus. LC 87-81934. 32p. (gr. 1-5). 1988. write for info. (0-307-10415-X, Pub. by Golden Bks) Western Pub.

Black, Sheila, ed. Andersen's Fairy Tales. LC 90-55649. (Illus.). 56p. (gr. 1-4). 1991. 9.98 (0-89471-981-5) Courage Bks.

Black, Shelia. Hansel & Gretel & the Witch's Story. (ps-3). 1991. 13.95 (1-55972-080-8, Birch Ln Pr) Carol Pub Group.

—Story of the Tooth Fairy. (ps-3). 1990. write for info. incl. tooth pillow (0-307-14004-0) Western Pub.

Black, Sonia. All about Baby Animals Activity Book. (ps-3). 1993. pap. 1.95 (0-590-46286-5) Scholastic Inc.

—Full House Trivia & Puzzle Fun Book. (gr. 4-7). 1993. pap. 2.95 (0-590-47145-7) Scholastic Inc.

—Laugh-A-Minute Joke Book. (gr. 4up). 1989. pap. 1.95 (0-590-42154-9) Scholastic Inc.

—One Hundred One Outer Space Jokes. 1990. pap. 1.95 (0-590-42972-8) Scholastic Inc.

Black, Sonia & Brigandi, Pat. Baby-Sitters Club Notebook. (Illus.). (gr. 5 up). 1991. pap. 2.50 (0-590-45074-3) Scholastic Inc.
Black, Wallace, jt. auth. see Blashfield, Jean.
Black, Wallace B. & Blashfield, Jean F. America Prepares for War. LC 90-46581. (Illus.). 48p. (gr. 5-6). 1991. RSBE 12.95 (0-89686-554-1, Crestwood Hse) Macmillan Child Grp.
—Bataan & Corregidor. (Illus.). 48p. (gr. 5-6). 1991. RSBE 12.95 (0-89686-557-6, Crestwood Hse) Macmillan Child Grp.
—Battle of Britain. LC 90-46579. (Illus.). 48p. (gr. 5-6). 1991. RSBE 12.95 (0-89686-553-3, Crestwood Hse) Macmillan Child Grp.
—Battle of the Atlantic. LC 91-7989. (Illus.). 48p. (gr. 5-6). 1991. RSBE 12.95 (0-89686-558-4, Crestwood Hse) Macmillan Child Grp.
—Battle of the Bulge. LC 92-1722. (Illus.). 48p. (gr. 5-6). 1993. RSBE 12.95 (0-89686-568-1, Crestwood Hse) Macmillan Child Grp.
—Blitzkrieg. LC 90-46580. (Illus.). 48p. (gr. 5-6). 1991. RSBE 12.95 (0-89686-552-5, Crestwood Hse) Macmillan Child Grp.
—Bombing Fortress Europe. LC 91-31452. (Illus.). 48p. (gr. 6 up). 1992. RSBE 12.95 (0-89686-562-2, Crestwood Hse) Macmillan Child Grp.
—D-Day. LC 91-45951. (Illus.). 48p. (gr. 5-6). 1992. RSBE 12.95 (0-89686-566-5, Crestwood Hse) Macmillan Child Grp.
—Desert Warfare. LC 91-27186. (Illus.). 48p. (gr. 6 up). 1992. RSBE 12.95 (0-89686-561-4, Crestwood Hse) Macmillan Child Grp.
—Flattops at War. LC 91-7916. (Illus.). 48p. (gr. 5-6). 1991. RSBE 12.95 (0-89686-559-2, Crestwood Hse) Macmillan Child Grp.
—Guadalcanal. LC 91-19902. (Illus.). 48p. (gr. 6 up). 1992. RSBE 12.95 (0-89686-560-6, Crestwood Hse) Macmillan Child Grp.
—Hiroshima & the Atomic Bomb. LC 92-33974. (Illus.). 48p. (gr. 5-6). 1993. RSBE 12.95 (0-89686-571-1, Crestwood Hse) Macmillan Child Grp.
—Invasion of Italy. LC 91-41484. (Illus.). 48p. (gr. 5-6). 1992. RSBE 12.95 (0-89686-565-7, Crestwood Hse) Macmillan Child Grp.
—Island Hopping in the Pacific. LC 92-2505. (Illus.). 48p. (gr. 7 up). 1992. RSBE 12.95 (0-89686-567-3, Crestwood Hse) Macmillan Child Grp.
—Iwo Jima & Okinawa. LC 92-25868. (Illus.). 48p. (gr. 5-6). 1993. RSBE 12.95 (0-89686-569-X, Crestwood Hse) Macmillan Child Grp.
—Jungle Warfare. LC 91-31533. (Illus.). 48p. (gr. 6 up). 1992. RSBE 12.95 (0-89686-563-0, Crestwood Hse) Macmillan Child Grp.
—Pearl Harbor. LC 90-45621. (Illus.). 48p. (gr. 5-6). 1991. RSBE 12.95 (0-89686-555-X, Crestwood Hse) Macmillan Child Grp.
—Russia at War. (Illus.). 48p. (gr. 5-6). 1991. RSBE 12.95 (0-89686-556-8, Crestwood Hse) Macmillan Child Grp.
—Victory in Europe. LC 92-23234. (Illus.). 48p. (gr. 5-6). 1993. RSBE 12.95 (0-89686-570-3, Crestwood Hse) Macmillan Child Grp.
—War Behind the Lines. LC 91-40866. (Illus.). 48p. (gr. 5-6). 1992. RSBE 12.95 (0-89686-564-9, Crestwood Hse) Macmillan Child Grp.
Black, Wallace B. & Willis, Terri. Cars: An Environmental Challenge. LC 92-9797. (Illus.). 128p. (gr. 4-8). 1992. PLB 26.60 (0-516-05504-6) Childrens.
Black, Wallace B., jt. auth. see Blashfield, Jean F.
Blackburn. Waiting for Sunday. 1993. pap. 28.67 (0-590-50158-5) Scholastic Inc.
Blackburn, Francis, et al, eds. see White, Terence.
Blackburn, Joyce. The Bloody Summer of Seventeen Forty-Two: A Colonial Boy's Journal. Graham, Critt, illus. 64p. (gr. 5-8). 1985. pap. 4.25 (0-930803-00-0) Fort Frederica.
—Martha Berry: A Woman of Courageous Spirit & Bold Dreams. 1992. pap. 8.95 (1-56145-071-5) Peachtree Pubs.
Blackburn, Lorraine A., jt. ed. see Brewton, John E.
Blackburn, Lynn B. The Class in Room Forty-Four: When a Classmate Dies. Johnson, Joy, ed. Borum, Shari, illus. 24p. (Orig.). (gr. 1-6). 1990. pap. 3.50 (1-56123-025-1) Centering Corp.
—I Know I Made It Happen: A Book about Children & Guilt. Johnson, Joy, ed. Borum, Shari, illus. 24p. (Orig.). (ps-6). 1990. pap. 3.50 (1-56123-016-2) Centering Corp.
—Timothy Duck: The Story of the Death of a Friend. Johnson, Joy, ed. Borum, Shari, illus. 24p. (Orig.). (gr. 1-6). 1989. pap. 3.25 (1-56123-013-8) Centering Corp.
Blackburn, Roderic H. Okiek. (Illus.). 42p. (gr. 6-9). 1991. pap. 4.95 (0-237-50631-9, Pub. by Evans Bros Ltd) Trafalgar.
Blacke, Terry L. & Hill, Donald. Pabulum Pig: The Yule Swine. Blacke, Terry L., illus. 30p. (gr. 4). 1992. pap. 7.98 (0-9630718-2-3) New Dawn NY.
Blacker, Terence. Herbie Hamster, Where Are You? Unwin, Myra, illus. LC 90-8053. 32p. (ps-3). 1990. 10. 95 (0-679-80838-8) Random Bks Yng Read.
—Homebird. LC 92-23536. 144p. (gr. 7 up). 1993. SBE 13.95 (0-02-710685-3, Bradbury Pr) Macmillan Child Grp.
—In Control, Ms. Wiz? Goffe, Toni, illus. 64p. (gr. 2-5). 1990. pap. 2.95 (0-8120-4500-9) Barron.
—Ms Wiz Spells Trouble. Goffe, Toni, illus. 64p. (gr. 3-6). 1990. pap. 2.95 (0-8120-4420-7) Barron.

—You're Under Arrest, Ms. Wiz. Goffe, Toni, illus. 64p. (gr. 2-5). 1990. pap. 2.95 (0-8120-4499-1) Barron.
Blackistone, Mick. Broken Wings Will Fly. Wharton, Jennifer H., illus. 32p. (gr. 2-6). 1992. 10.95 (0-87033-439-5) Tidewater.
—The Day They Left the Bay. 2nd ed. Boynton, Lee, illus. (gr. 1-6). 1991. Repr. of 1988 ed. PLB 14.95 (0-9627726-3-1) Blue Crab MD.
Blackman, Malorie. Girl Wonder & the Terrific Twins. Toft, Lis, illus. LC 92-27667. (gr. 2-5). 1993. 12.99 (0-525-45065-3, DCB) Dutton Child Bks.
—A New Dress for Maya. James, Rhian N., illus. LC 91-50337. 32p. (ps-3). 1993. PLB 17.27 (0-8368-0713-8); PLB 17.27 s.p. (0-685-61500-6) Gareth Stevens Inc.
Blackman, Steve. Land Transportation. LC 93-1473. (Illus.). 32p. (gr. 5-7). 1993. PLB 11.90 (0-531-14276-0) Watts.
—Ships & Shipwrecks. (Illus.). 32p. (gr. 5-7). 1993. PLB 11.90 (0-531-14278-7) Watts.
—Space Travel. LC 93-13310. 1993. 11.90 (0-531-14275-2) Watts.
—Space Travel. (Illus.). 32p. (gr. 5-7). 1993. PLB 11.90 (0-685-65605-5) Watts.
Blackman, Steven. Planes & Flight. LC 93-17392. (Illus.). 32p. (gr. 5-7). 1993. PLB 11.90 (0-531-14277-9) Watts.
Blackmore, Michael. Your Book of Watching Wildlife. (gr. 7 up). 1972. 7.95 (0-571-08347-1) Transatl Arts.
Blackmore, R. D. Lorna Doone. 272p. (gr. 4-6). 1984. pap. 2.95 (0-14-035021-7, Puffin) Puffin Bks.
Blackmore, Richard. Lorna Doone. 345p. 1981. Repr. PLB 24.95 (0-89966-350-8) Buccaneer Bks.
Blackmore, Richard D. Lorna Doone. Threapleton, M. M., intro. by. (gr. 8 up). 1967. pap. 2.50 (0-8049-0149-X, CL-149) Airmont.
—Lorna Doone. 378p. 1981. Repr. PLB 24.95 (0-89967-024-5) Harmony Raine.
Blacknall, Carolyn. Sally Ride: America's First Woman in Space. LC 84-12671. (Illus.). 80p. (gr. 3 up). 1985. RSBE 13.95 (0-87518-260-7, Dillon) Macmillan Child Grp.
Blackshear, Helen F. The Creek Captives: And Other Alabama Stories. Raymond, Thomas, illus. 112p. (Orig.). (gr. 4-9). 1990. pap. 9.95 (0-9622815-2-2) Black Belt Pr.
Blackstone, Harry, Jr., et al. The Blackstone Book of Magic & Illusion. Bradbury, Ray, frwd. by. Mason, Eric, illus. LC 84-29486. 248p. (gr. 7 up). 1985. 22.95 (0-937858-45-5) Newmarket.
Blackstone, Margaret. This Is Baseball. O'Brien, John, photos by. LC 92-22921. (Illus.). 32p. (ps-k). 1993. 14. 95 (0-8050-2390-9, Bks Young Read) H Holt & Co.
—This is Mini Golf. 1994. write for info. (0-8050-2800-5) H Holt & Co.
Blackwelder, Kathy, ed. see Anderson, Jill.
Blackwell, B. Believe It or Not Stories. 15p. (gr. 7-10). 1986. 23.00x (0-7223-2003-5, Pub. by A H Stockwell England) St Mut.
Blackwell, Muriel. Peter: The Prince of Apostles. Karch, Paul, illus. (gr. 1-6). 1978. 5.95 (0-8054-4227-8, 4242-27) Broadman.
Blackwell, Muriel F. How Do I Become a Christian? LC 89-34347. (gr. 4-6). 1991. 7.95 (0-8054-4341-X) Broadman.
Blackwood, Alan. The Age of Exploration. (Illus.). 24p. (gr. k-4). 1990. PLB 10.90 (0-531-18342-4, Pub. by Bookwright Pr) Watts.
—Hungarian Uprising, Reading Level 8. LC 86-20341. (Illus.). 80p. (gr. 7 up). 1988. 13.95s.p. (0-86592-032-X); PLB 18.60 (0-685-58793-2) Rourke Corp.
—Music. LC 89-11479. (Illus.). 48p. (gr. 6-11). 1990. PLB 19.92 (0-8114-2358-1) Raintree Steck-V.
—New Year. (Illus.). 48p. (gr. 3-8). 1987. PLB 15.94 (0-86592-981-5); 11.95s.p. (0-685-67597-1) Rourke Corp.
—The Orchestra: An Introduction to the World of Classical Music. LC 92-18412. (Illus.). 96p. (gr. 3 up). 1993. PLB 16.90 (1-56294-202-6); pap. 9.95 (1-56294-708-7) Millbrook Pr.
—Piano & Keyboards. (Illus.). 32p. (gr. 4-7). 1993. PLB 12.40 (0-531-17422-0, Gloucester Pr) Watts.
—Twenty Tyrants. LC 89-23853. (Illus.). 48p. (gr. 3-8). 1990. PLB 12.95 (1-85435-255-5) Marshall Cavendish.
Blackwood, Gary L. Beyond the Door. LC 90-23414. 176p. (gr. 5-8). 1991. SBE 13.95 (0-689-31645-3, Atheneum Child Bk) Macmillan Child Grp.
—The Dying Sun. LC 88-27517. 224p. (gr. 6-9). 1989. SBE 14.95 (0-689-31482-5, Atheneum Child Bk) Macmillan Child Grp.
—Wild Timothy. LC 87-937. 160p. (gr. 4-8). 1987. SBE 13.95 (0-689-31352-7, Atheneum Child Bk) Macmillan Child Grp.
Blackwood, Mary. Derek the Knitting Dinosaur. Argent, Kerry, illus. 32p. (ps-3). 1990. PLB 18.95 (0-87614-400-8) Carolrhoda Bks.
—Derek the Knitting Dinosaur: Picture Book. (ps-3). 1991. pap. 5.95 (0-87614-540-3) Carolrhoda Bks.
Blades, Ann. Fall. Blades, Ann, illus. (ps-k). 1990. bds. 4.95 (0-688-09232-2) Lothrop.
—Mary of Mile 18. LC 74-179430. (Illus.). (gr. 1-4). 1971. pap. 6.95 (0-88776-059-7) Tundra Bks.
—Spring. Blades, Ann, illus. LC 89-2424. 10p. (ps). 1990. board 4.95 (0-688-09230-6) Lothrop.
—Summer. (Illus.). (ps-k). 1990. bds. 4.95 (0-688-09231-4) Lothrop.
—Winter. Blades, Ann, illus. (ps-k). 1990. bds. 4.95 (0-688-09233-0) Lothrop.

Bladon, Rachel. French for Beginners Workbook. (gr. 4-7). 1993. pap. 6.95 (0-8442-1415-9, Passport Bks) NTC Pub Grp.
—German for Beginners Workbook. (gr. 4-7). 1993. pap. 6.95 (0-8442-2181-3, Passport Bks) NTC Pub Grp.
Blady, Ken. The Jewish Boxers' Hall of Fame. LC 88-29367. (Illus.). (gr. 7 up). 1989. 14.95 (0-933503-87-3) Shapolsky Pubs.
Blaebst, Werner. Maxi's Bed Magicians. Blaebst, Werner, illus. 28p. (ps-k). 1991. smythe sewn reinforced bdg. 9.95 (1-56182-020-2) Atomium Bks.
Blagowidow, George. In Search of the Lady Lion Tamer. 249p. 1987. 15.95 (0-15-144500-1) HarBrace.
Blain, Diane. The Boxcar Children Cookbook. Tucker, Kathy, ed. Deal, L. Kate & Neill, Eileen M., illus. LC 91-15080. 96p. (gr. 2-8). 1991. 13.95g (0-8075-0859-4); pap. 9.95g (0-8075-0856-X) A Whitman.
Blaine, John. The Magic Talisman. Frolich, Dany, illus. Goodwin, Hal, afterword by. (Illus.). 213p. (gr. 8-12). 1989. 25.00 (0-936414-06-5) Manuscript Pr.
Blaine, Marge. The Terrible Thing That Happened at Our House. Wallner, John, illus. LC 86-4827. 40p. (ps-3). 1984. Repr. of 1975 ed. RSBE 13.95 (0-02-710720-5, Four Winds) Macmillan Child Grp.
—The Terrible Thing That Happened at Our House. Wallner, John C., illus. 32p. (gr. 1-4). 1991. pap. 3.95 (0-590-42371-1) Scholastic Inc.
Blair, Al. Mooshwhopper: A Juicy, Moosey Min-Min-Minnesota Burger Tale. 3rd ed. McMurray, Chuck, illus. LC 83-61092. 32p. (gr. 3). 1983. pap. 3.95 (0-930366-04-2) Northcountry Pub.
Blair, Alison. Back to School. (gr. 10 up). 1989. pap. 2.95 (0-8041-0329-1) Ivy Books.
—Class Act. 192p. (gr. 10 up). 1988. pap. 2.95 (0-8041-0076-4) Ivy Books.
—Higher Education. (gr. 10 up). 1988. pap. 2.95 (0-8041-0070-5) Ivy Books.
—Love by the Book. (gr. 10 up). 1989. pap. 2.95 (0-8041-0331-3) Ivy Books.
—Making the Grade. 192p. (gr. 10 up). 1988. pap. 2.95 (0-8041-0082-9) Ivy Books.
—School's Out! 192p. (gr. 10 up). 1987. pap. 2.50 (0-8041-0059-4) Ivy Books.
—Social Studies. (gr. 10 up). 1989. pap. 2.95 (0-8041-0330-5) Ivy Books.
—Study Break. (gr. 10 up). 1988. pap. 2.95 (0-8041-0327-5) Ivy Books.
Blair, Carvel. Exploring the Sea: Oceanography Today. Rimson, Ole & Luke, Melinda, eds. McNaught, Harry, illus. LC 85-43336. 96p. (gr. 5 up). 1986. pap. 8.95 (0-394-85927-8) Random Bks Yng Read.
Blair, Cynthia. Apple Pie Adventure. (gr. 4 up). 1989. pap. 3.99 (0-449-70308-8, Juniper) Fawcett.
—Chocolate Is My Middle Name. (gr. 7 up). 1992. pap. 3.99 (0-449-70400-9, Juniper) Fawcett.
—The Curse. 1993. pap. 3.99 (0-06-106158-1, Harp PBks) HarpC.
—The Hot Fudge Sunday Affair. 1985. pap. 3.99 (0-449-70158-1, Juniper) Fawcett.
—The Lollipop Plot. 144p. (Orig.). (gr. 4 up). 1990. pap. 3.95 (0-449-70377-0, Juniper) Fawcett.
—The Pink Lemonade Charade. 128p. (gr. 4 up). 1988. pap. 3.50 (0-449-70258-8, Juniper) Fawcett.
—The Popcorn Project. (gr. 5 up). 1989. pap. 3.99 (0-449-70309-6, Juniper) Fawcett.
—The Rebellion. 1993. pap. 3.99 (0-06-106160-3, Harp PBks) HarpC.
—Warning: Baby-sitting May Be Hazardous to Your Health. 1993. pap. 3.99 (0-449-70412-2, Juniper) Fawcett.
Blair, David, retold by see Carroll, Lewis.
Blair, David N. Fear the Condor. 160p. (gr. 7 up). 1992. 15.00 (0-525-67381-4, Lodestar Bks) Dutton Child Bks.
—The Land & People of Bolivia. LC 89-39721. (Illus.). 224p. (gr. 6 up). 1990. (Lipp Jr Bks); PLB 15.89 (0-397-32383-2, Lipp Jr Bks) HarpC Child Bks.
Blair, Grandpa. The Gospel Rag: Adam & Eve Straight Up. 2nd ed. 16p. (gr. 11 up). 1992. 5.95 (0-930366-71-9) Northcountry Pub.
—The Gospel Rag: Jesus Straight Up. 2nd ed. 16p. (gr. 11 up). 1992. 5.95 (0-930366-85-9) Northcountry Pub.
—The Gospel Rag: Noah Straight Up. 16p. (gr. 11 up). 1992. 5.95 (0-930366-69-7) Northcountry Pub.
—Vexillophily: A Capsule History of the Stars & Stripes. 2nd, rev. ed. (Illus.). 46p. (gr. 11 up). 1992. 9.95 (0-930366-74-3) Northcountry Pub.
—Willie the Groundhog. 6p. (gr. 10 up). 1991. 4.75 (0-930366-63-8) Northcountry Pub.
—Ziggy the Zombie from Zumbrota. 14p. (gr. 10 up). 1991. 5.75 (0-930366-62-X) Northcountry Pub.
Blair, Gwenda. Laura Ingalls Wilder. Allen, Thomas B., illus. 64p. (gr. 1-4). 1981. (Putnam); pap. 6.95 (0-399-20953-0) Putnam Pub Group.
Blair, L. E. Baby Talk. 128p. (gr. 4-7). 1992. 2.95 (0-307-22021-4, 22021) Western Pub.
—Beauty Queens. 128p. (gr. 3-7). 1992. pap. 2.95 (0-307-22026-5, 22026, Golden Pr) Western Pub.
—Blue Ribbon. 128p. (gr. 3-7). 1992. pap. 2.95 (0-307-22025-7, 22025, Golden Pr) Western Pub.
—Center Stage. 128p. (gr. 3-7). 1992. pap. 2.95 (0-307-22028-1, 22028, Golden Pr) Western Pub.
—Expectations. 128p. (gr. 4-7). 1992. 2.95 (0-307-22024-9, 22024) Western Pub.
—Face Off! 128p. (gr. 2 up). 1990. pap. write for info. (0-307-22002-8, Pub. by Golden Bks) Western Pub.

—Falling in Like. (gr. 4-8). 1990. pap. 2.95
(*0-307-22010-9*) Western Pub.
—Family Affair. 128p. (gr. 4-7). 1992. 2.95
(*0-307-22019-2*, 22019) Western Pub.
—Family Rules. (gr. 3-7). 1992. pap. 2.95
(*0-307-22029-X*, 22029, Golden Pr) Western Pub.
—The Ghost of Eagle Mountain. 128p. (gr. 2 up). 1990.
pap. write for info. (*0-307-22006-0*, Pub. by Golden
Bks) Western Pub.
—It's All in the Stars. 128p. (gr. 2 up). 1990. pap. write
for info. (*0-307-22005-2*, Pub. by Golden Bks)
Western Pub.
—The New You. 128p. (gr. 2 up). 1990. pap. write for
info. (*0-307-22003-6*, Pub. by Golden Bks) Western
Pub.
—Odd Couple. (gr. 4-7). 1990. pap. 2.95 (*0-307-22008-7*)
Western Pub.
—Party Central. 128p. (gr. 4-7). 1992. 2.95
(*0-307-22023-0*, 22023) Western Pub.
—Peer Pressure Girl Talk, No. 9. 1991. pap. 2.95
(*0-307-22009-5*) Western Pub.
—Perfect Match. 128p. (gr. 3-7). 1992. pap. 2.95
(*0-307-22027-3*, 22027, Golden Pr) Western Pub.
—Problem Dad. (gr. 4-7). 1992. pap. 2.95
(*0-307-22022-2*, 22022) Western Pub.
—Rebel, Rebel. 128p. (gr. 2 up). 1990. pap. write for info.
(*0-307-22004-4*, Pub. by Golden Bks) Western Pub.
—Rockin' Class Trip. 128p. (gr. 4-7). 1992. 2.95
(*0-307-22020-6*, 22020) Western Pub.
—Thin Ice. (gr. 4-7). 1990. pap. write for info.
(*0-307-22007-9*) Western Pub.
—Welcome to Junior High. 128p. (gr. 2 up). 1990. pap.
write for info. (*0-307-22001-X*, Pub. by Golden Bks)
Western Pub.
Blair, Leigh, jt. auth. see Bernstein, Bonnie.
Blair, Shannon. Kiss & Tell. 176p. (Orig.). (gr. 5 up).
1985. pap. 2.50 (*0-553-26843-0*) Bantam.
Blair, Susan M. Unexpected Company. Blair, Susan M.,
illus. 56p. (ps-7). 1992. 19.95 (*0-9631956-0-3*) Pendant
Pr.
Blair, Walter, ed. see Twain, Mark.
Blair, Yogi. Minnesota Fortune Cookies. 5th ed. 26p. (gr.
11 up). 1993. 8.95 (*0-930366-73-5*) Northcountry Pub.
Blaisdell, Frank. More of Magic. Dawson, Steve, ed.
Walker, Barbara, illus. iv, 97p. (gr. 8). 1980. 10.00
(*0-915926-48-2*) Magic Ltd.
Blake, Doron W. The Adventure of George the
Dinosaur. Lucas, Winafred B., ed. Gremard, David,
illus. (ps-2). Date not set. English ed. write for info.
(*1-882530-04-7*); Spanish ed. write for info.
(*1-882530-09-8*) Deep Forest Pr.
Blake, James L. Common Sense in a Complex World:
What Every Young Person Should Know. LC 88-
72165. 192p. (Orig.). (gr. 8-11). 1989. pap. 8.95
(*0-9621230-0-5*) CSI Pub.
Blake, Jon. Daley B. Scheffler, Axel & Scheffler, Axel,
illus. LC 91-58725. 32p. (ps up). 1992. 13.95
(*1-56402-078-9*) Candlewick Pr.
—Wriggly Pig. Jenkin-Pearce, Susie, illus. LC 91-24171.
32p. (ps-3). 1992. 14.00 (*0-688-11295-1*, Tambourine
Bks); PLB 13.93 (*0-688-11296-X*, Tambourine Bks)
Morrow.
Blake, Olive. The Grape Jelly Mystery. Goodman, Joan
E., illus. LC 78-18040. 48p. (gr. 2-4). 1979. PLB 10.89
(*0-89375-096-4*); pap. 3.50 (*0-89375-084-0*) Troll
Assocs.
—Mystery of the Lost Letter. Kossin, Sanford, illus. LC
78-18037. 48p. (gr. 2-4). 1979. PLB 10.89
(*0-89375-093-X*); pap. 3.50 (*0-89375-081-6*) Troll
Assocs.
—Mystery of the Lost Pearl. Parker, Ed, illus. LC 78-
60121. 48p. (gr. 2-4). 1979. PLB 10.89
(*0-89375-086-7*); pap. 3.50 (*0-89375-074-3*) Troll
Assocs.
Blake, Quentin. All Join In. (ps-3). 1991. 14.95
(*0-316-09934-1*) Little.
—Cockatoos. (ps-3). 1992. 14.95 (*0-316-09951-1*) Little.
—Simpkin. Blake, Quentin, illus. 32p. (ps-1). 1994. 14.99
(*0-670-85371-2*) Viking Child Bks.
Blake, Richard see Zimelman, Nathan.
Blake, Robert J. Dog. LC 92-39313. 1994. write for info.
(*0-399-22019-4*, Philomel Bks) Putnam Pub Group.
—The Perfect Spot. Blake, Robert J., illus. 32p. (ps-8).
1992. PLB 14.95 (*0-399-22132-8*, Philomel Bks)
Putnam Pub Group.
Blake, Susan. A Change of Heart. 224p. (Orig.). (gr. 7-
12). 1986. pap. 2.95 (*0-553-26168-1*) Bantam.
—Head over Heels. 192p. (gr. 7 up). 1988. pap. 2.95
(*0-8041-0234-1*) Ivy Books.
—Stealing Josh. 128p. (Orig.). 1990. pap. 3.50
(*0-449-14606-5*) Fawcett.
Blake, William. The Tyger. Waldman, Neil, illus. LC 92-
23378. 1993. 15.95 (*0-15-292375-6*) HarBrace.
Blakeley, Given. What the Bible Says about the Kingdom
of God. LC 88-71154. 466p. 1988. text ed. 13.95
(*0-89900-260-9*) College Pr Pub.
Blakely, Henry. A Windy Place. (gr. 12 up). 1974. 6.00
(*0-685-00875-4*); pap. 2.50 (*0-910296-15-4*) Broadside
Pr.
Blakely, Nora B. Shani on the Hill. Gilchrist, Jan S.,
illus. (gr. 1). 1988. pap. 3.95 (*0-88378-123-9*) Third
World.
Blakely, Roger K. Wolfgang Amadeus Mozart. (Illus.).
111p. (gr. 5-8). 1993. PLB 14.95 (*1-56006-028-X*)
Lucent Bks.

Blakeman, Sarah. Elephant. Field, James, illus. LC 91-
44728. 32p. (gr. 4-6). 1993. PLB 11.59
(*0-8167-2769-4*); tchr's. ed. 3.95 (*0-8167-2770-8*) Troll
Assocs. Postponed.
Blakemore, Sally, jt. auth. see Breslow, Susan.
Blaker, Charles W. The College Matchmaker. New,
Dwight, illus. LC 80-67604. 56p. (Orig.). (gr. 11-12).
1980. pap. text ed. 3.50 (*0-9604614-0-X*) Rekalb Pr.
Blakeslee, Ann. After the Fortune Cookies. 128p. (gr.
3-7). 1989. 13.95 (*0-399-21562-X*, Putnam) Putnam
Pub Group.
Blakeslee, Michael, ed. see Anderson, Tom.
Blakey, Nancy. The Mudpies Activity Book: Recipes for
Invention. Watts, Melissah, illus. 144p. (ps-6). pap.
7.95 (*0-89815-576-2*) Ten Speed Pr.
Blanc, Esther S. Berchick, My Mother's Horse. Dixon,
Tennessee, illus. LC 87-37172. 36p. (gr. k-5). 1989.
14.95 (*0-912078-81-2*) Volcano Pr.
Blanc, Iris. Learning WordPerfect 5.0 & 5.1: Through
Step-by-Step Exercises & Applications. (gr. 9-12).
1991. pap. 20.00 comb bdg. (*1-56243-046-7*, W-9);
tchr's. ed. 10.00 (*1-56243-047-5*, W-106);
transparencies of exercises 250.00 (*1-56243-049-1*,
PW-1); cancelled (*1-56243-050-5*, PW-2); answer key
on diskette 65.00 (*1-56243-048-3*, SW-25) DDC Pub.
—Lotus 1-2-3 (Ver. 2.2) Quick Reference Guide. (gr. 9-
12). 1990. spiral bdg. 8.95 (*1-56243-000-9*, L2-17);
transparencies 225.00 (*1-56243-026-2*, TT19) DDC
Pub.
—Step-by-Step Skill Building Exercises for the Word
Processor Solutions Booklet. 100p. (gr. 9-12). 1989.
pap. text ed. avail. (*1-56243-004-1*, RWP-SOL) DDC
Pub.
Blanc, L. Le see Le Blanc, L.
Blanchard, Anne. Navigation: A Three-Dimensional
Exploration. Peacock, Irvine, illus. LC 92-80434. 12p.
(gr. 2-6). 1992. 15.95 (*0-531-05455-1*) Orchard Bks
Watts.
Blanchard, Arlene. The Naughty Lamb. Wells, Tony,
illus. LC 88-4098. 32p. (ps-1). 1989. 9.95
(*0-8037-0577-8*) Dial Bks Young.
Blanchard, G. L., jt. auth. see Turner, Herschell.
Blanchard, Gerald. The Black West. (gr. 4-6). 1992. print
set 75.00 (*1-882205-04-9*) All Media Prods.
Blanchard, James J. see Stapler, Harry.
Blanchard, Robert. Graphiti, Bk. 1. rev. ed. 24p. (gr.
2-9). 1986. pap. 5.50 (*0-918932-89-0*) Activity
Resources.
—Graphiti, Bk. 2. rev. ed. 24p. (gr. 2-9). 1986. 5.50
(*0-918932-90-4*) Activity Resources.
Blanchette, Rick. Choice Adventure: Class Project
Showdown. LC 92-30501. 1993. 4.99 (*0-8423-5047-0*)
Tyndale.
Blanco, Alberto. Desert Mermaid (La sirena del desierto)
LC 92-1105. (Illus.). 32p. (gr. k-5). 1992. 13.95
(*0-89239-106-5*) Childrens Book Pr.
Blanco, Richard L. Rommel the Desert Warrior: The
Afrika Korps in World War II. LC 82-2293. 192p. (gr.
7 up). 1982. (J Messner); lib. bdg. write for info.
(*0-671-49582-8*) S&S Trade.
Bland, Celia. Harriet Beecher Stowe: Antislavery Author.
(Illus.). 80p. (gr. 3-5). 1993. PLB 13.95
(*0-7910-1773-7*, Am Art Analog) Chelsea Hse.
Bland, Geneva F. Herman & the Mini-Bus with Soul.
28p. 1993. 14.95 (*0-9638969-0-3*) GBL Pubng.
Bland, Joellen. Stage Plays from the Classics. LC 87-
14669. (Orig.). (gr. 7-12). 1987. pap. 14.95
(*0-8238-0281-7*) Plays.
Blaney, Christine. My Dog's Day: A Moving Picture
Book. Blaney, Christine, illus. 8p. (ps). 1993. 11.99
(*0-670-85202-3*) Viking Child Bks.
Blank, Florence W. & Guertin, Carolyn W. Sound Skill
Builder: Use with Sure Steps to Reading & Spelling, 3
bks. Incl. Bk. 1. price not set (*0-916720-04-7*); Bk. 2.
price not set (*0-916720-05-5*); Bk. 3. price not set
(*0-916720-06-3*). (gr. 1-7). Date not set. Weiss Pub.
Blank, Grace W. Grace Delight & Tricksey. Witte,
Suzanne, illus. LC 91-75093. 111p. (gr. k-3). 1992.
8.95 (*1-55523-459-3*) Winston-Derek.
—Jennie & Sue Visit a Kentucky Farm. Witte-Barrett,
Suzanne, illus. 70p. (gr. 3-6). Date not set. write for
info. (*0-9634122-5-6*) Feather Fables.
Blank, Joani. The Kids' First Book about Sex.
Quackenbush, Marcia, illus. LC 89-14800. 48p.
(Orig.). (ps-3). 1983. pap. 5.50 (*0-940208-07-5*, Yes
Pr) Down There Pr.
—Playbook for Kids About Sex. Costanzo, Lana, illus.
56p. (gr. 2-6). 1980. pap. 5.00 (*0-9602324-6-X*, Yes
Pr) Down There Pr.
Blank, Peter. The First Spell of Winnefred Broomstock.
Sperling, Thomas, illus. 32p. 1992. 7.95
(*1-56288-273-2*) Checkerboard.
Blankenbaker, Frances. What the Bible Is All about for
Young Explorers. LC 86-22488. (Illus.). 364p. (gr.
6-8). 1988. 12.99 (*0-8307-1179-1*, 5111647); pap. 8.99
(*0-8307-1162-7*, 5418877) Regal.
Blankenship, Judy, illus. Teddy Beddy Bear's Bedtime
Songs & Poems. LC 84-4837. 32p. (ps). 1984. pap.
2.25 saddle-stitched (*0-394-86826-9*) Random Bks
Yng Read.
Blankholm, Robert F. Twenty-Six Friends: The Shape of
the Alphabet Letters. 2nd ed. LC 90-71355. (Illus.).
64p. 1990. pap. 7.95 (*0-933499-02-7*) Stagecoach Rd
Pr.
Blansett, Mary L. & Schimminger, Lorraine. Put a Frog
in Your Pocket. (Illus.). 112p. (gr. 3-6). 1985. guide
8.95 (*0-86530-085-2*, IP 85-2) Incentive Pubns.
Blaricom, Colleen Van see Van Blaricom, Colleen.

Blaricom, Colleen Von see Van Blaricom, Colleen.
Blashfield, Jean & Black, Wallace. Oil Spills. LC 91-
25861. 128p. (gr. 4-8). 1991. PLB 26.60
(*0-516-05508-9*) Childrens.
Blashfield, Jean F. & Black, Wallace B. Endangered
Species. LC 92-9083. (Illus.). 128p. (gr. 4-8). 1992.
PLB 26.60 (*0-516-05514-3*) Childrens.
—Global Warming. LC 90-7119. (Illus.). 128p. (gr. 4-8).
1991. PLB 26.60 (*0-516-05501-1*) Childrens.
—Recycling. LC 90-400. (Illus.). 128p. (gr. 4-8). 1991.
PLB 26.60 (*0-516-05502-X*) Childrens.
—Too Many People? LC 91-34603. 128p. (gr. 4-8). 1992.
PLB 26.60 (*0-516-05513-5*) Childrens.
Blashfield, Jean F., jt. auth. see Black, Wallace B.
Blasky, A. & Chafconloff, E. Faces: Exchanging Views in
English. 96p. 1985. pap. 13.95
(*0-8013-0526-8*, 78372); tchr's. ed. 13.50
(*0-8013-0527-6*, 78373); cassette 22.95
(*0-8013-0528-4*, 78374) Longman.
Blass, Jacqueline. My Playhouse. Blass, Jacqueline, illus.
8p. (ps-4). 1989. bds. 6.99 (*1-55037-033-2*, Pub. by
Annick CN) Firefly Bks Ltd.
Blassingame, Wyatt. Jim Beckwourth: Black Trapper &
Indian Chief. (Illus.). 80p. (gr. 2-6). 1991. Repr. of
1973 ed. lib. bdg. 12.95 (*0-7910-1404-5*) Chelsea Hse.
—The Look-It-Up Book of Presidents. rev. & updated ed.
LC 89-10519. (Illus.). (gr. 5-9). 1990. 10.95
(*0-679-80353-X*); PLB 11.99 (*0-679-90353-4*); pap.
5.95 (*0-679-80358-0*) Random Bks Yng Read.
—Ponce de Leon. (Illus.). 96p. (gr. 3-5). 1991. Repr. of
1965 ed. lib. bdg. 12.95 (*0-7910-1493-2*) Chelsea Hse.
—Stephen Decatur: Fighting Sailor. (Illus.). 80p. (gr. 2-6).
1993. Repr. of 1964 ed. lib. bdg. 12.95
(*0-7910-1435-5*) Chelsea Hse.
Blatchford, Claire. El Cielo Azul de Shawna. Writer, C.
C. & Nielsen, Lisa C., trs. Eagle, Mike, illus. (SPA.).
24p. (Orig.). (ps). 1992. pap. text ed. 3.00x
(*1-56134-174-6*) Dushkin Pub.
—Down the Path. Eagle, Mike, illus. 24p. (Orig.). (ps).
1992. pap. text ed. 3.00x (*1-56134-142-8*) Dushkin
Pub.
—Por el Camino. Writer, C. C. & Nielsen, Lisa C., trs.
Eagle, Mike, illus. (SPA.). 24p. (Orig.). (ps). 1992.
pap. text ed. 3.00x (*1-56134-152-5*) Dushkin Pub.
—Shawna's Bit of Blue Sky. Eagle, Mike, illus. 24p.
(Orig.). (ps). 1992. pap. text ed. 3.00x (*1-56134-164-9*)
Dushkin Pub.
—Una Sorpresa para Reggie. Writer, C. C. & Nielsen,
Lisa C., trs. Eagle, Mike, illus. (SPA.). 24p. (Orig.).
(ps). 1992. pap. text ed. 3.00x (*1-56134-151-7*)
Dushkin Pub.
—A Surprise for Reggie. Eagle, Mike, illus. 24p. (Orig.).
(ps). 1992. pap. text ed. 3.00x (*1-56134-141-X*)
Dushkin Pub.
Blathwayt, Benedict. Stories from Firefly Island. LC 92-
40786. 128p. (ps up). 1993. 16.00 (*0-688-12487-9*)
Greenwillow.
Blau, Judith. Bunny Mitten's Book. Blau, Judith, illus. 7p.
(ps). 1991. incl. puppet 5.95 (*0-679-81315-2*) Random
Bks Yng Read.
—Ducky Mitten's Book. Blau, Judith, illus. 7p. (ps). 1991.
incl. puppet 5.95 (*0-679-81314-4*) Random Bks Yng
Read.
—Kitten Mitten's Stocking. Blau, Judith, illus. 7p. (ps).
1992. incl. puppet 5.99 (*0-679-83046-4*) Random Bks
Yng Read.
—Puppy Mitten's Present. Blau, Judith, illus. 7p. (ps).
1992. incl. puppet 5.99 (*0-679-83045-6*) Random Bks
Yng Read.
—Stop & Go Potty. Blau, Judith, illus. LC 92-61706. 6p.
(ps). 1993. 6.99 (*0-679-84021-4*) Random Bks Yng
Read.
Blau, Justine. Betty Friedan. Horner, Matina, intro. by.
(Illus.). 112p. (gr. 5 up). 1990. lib. bdg. 17.95
(*1-55546-653-2*) Chelsea Hse.
Blau, Melinda. Whatever Happened to Amelia Earhart?
LC 77-22173. (Illus.). 48p. (gr. 4 up). 1983. PLB 18.64
(*0-8172-1057-1*) Raintree Steck-V.
Blau, Melinda E. Killer Bees. LC 77-10010. (Illus.). 48p.
(gr. 4 up). 1983. PLB 18.64 (*0-8172-1055-5*) Raintree
Steck-V.
Blauer, Ettagale & Laure, Jason. Tanzania. LC 93-35495.
1994. write for info. (*0-516-02622-4*) Childrens.
Blaustein, Muriel. Jim Chimp's Story. LC 91-18001.
(Illus.). 40p. (ps-2). 1992. pap. 14.00 jacketed
(*0-671-74779-7*, S&S BFYR) S&S Trade.
—Play Ball, Zachary! Blaustein, Muriel, illus. LC 87-
45274. 32p. (ps-2). 1988. HarpC Child Bks.
**Blazquez, Maria Del Carmen see Gomez-Navarro, Maria
J., et al.**
Blazquez, Maria Del Carmen see Puncel, Maria.
Bleaney, C. H., jt. auth. see Lawless, Richard.
Blecher, George, tr. see Nilsson, Ulf.
Blecher, Lone T., tr. see Nilsson, Ulf.
Bledsoe, Sara. Colorado. LC 92-31054. 1993. 17.50
(*0-8225-2750-2*) Lerner Pubns.
Bledsoe, Shirley, jt. auth. see MacKenzie, Joy.
Bleeker, Sonia. The Sioux Indians: Hunters & Warriors
of the Plains. Sasaki, Kisa N., illus. LC 62-7713. 160p.
(gr. 3-6). 1962. PLB 11.88 (*0-688-31457-0*) Morrow Jr
Bks.
Blegvad, Erik, tr. & illus. see Andersen, Hans Christian.
Blegvad, Lenore. Anna Banana & Me. Blegvad, Erik,
illus. LC 84-547. 32p. (gr. k-3). 1985. SBE 13.95
(*0-689-50274-5*, M K McElderry) Macmillan Child
Grp.

—Anna Banana & Me. Blegvad, Erik, illus. LC 86-22220. 32p. (ps-3). 1987. pap. 3.95 (0-689-71114-X, Aladdin) Macmillan Child Grp.
—Anna Banana & Me. Blegvad, Erik, illus. (gr. 1-3). 1988. bk. & cassette 19.95 (0-87499-104-8); bk. & cassette 12.95 (0-87499-103-X); 4 cassettes & guide 27.95 (0-87499-105-6) Live Oak Media.
—Once upon a Time & Grandma. Blegvad, Lenore, illus. LC 92-7407. 32p. (ps-3). 1993. SBE 14.95 (0-689-50548-5, M K McElderry) Macmillan Child Grp.
—Rainy Day Kate. LC 87-16805. (Illus.). 32p. (gr. k-4). 1988. SBE 13.95 (0-689-50442-X, M K McElderry) Macmillan Child Grp.
Bleich, Alan R. Coping with Health Risks & Risky Behavior. Rosen, Roger, ed. (gr. 7-12). 1990. PLB 13. 95 (0-8239-1072-5) Rosen Group.
Bleifeld, Maurice. Botany Projects for Young Scientists. LC 91-43704. 144p. (gr. 9-12). 1992. PLB 13.90 (0-531-11046-X) Watts.
—Botany Projects for Young Scientists. (gr. 4-7). 1992. pap. 6.95 (0-531-15650-8) Watts.
—Experimenting with a Microscope. Rasof, Henry, ed. LC 88-14043. (Illus.). 112p. (gr. 7-12). 1988. PLB 13. 40 (0-531-10580-6) Watts.
—How to Prepare for the SAT II, Biology: Including Modern Biology in Review. 11th, rev. ed. LC 93-28545. 1994. pap. 11.95 (0-8120-1701-3) Barron.
Bleifeld, Maurice, jt. auth. see Johnson, Gaylord.
Bleiler, E. F. Mother Goose Melodies. 128p. (ps up). 1985. pap. 2.95 (0-486-22577-1) Dover.
Bleiler, E. F., ed. see Hoffmann, E. T.
Blevins, George, jt. auth. see Gilford, Henry.
Blevins, Wade. And Then the Feather Fell. Blevins, Wade, illus. Sargent, Dave, intro. by. (Illus.). 48p. (Orig.). (gr. k-8). 1993. text ed. 11.95 (1-56763-060-X); pap. text ed. 5.95 (0-685-67465-7) Ozark Pub.
—Ganseti & the Legend of the Little People. Blevins, Wade, illus. Sargent, Dave, intro. by. (Illus.). 48p. (Orig.). (gr. k-8). 1993. text ed. 11.95 (1-56763-065-0); pap. text ed. 5.95 (1-56763-066-9) Ozark Pub.
—Legend of Little Deer. Blevins, Wade, illus. Sargent, Dave, intro. by. (Illus.). 48p. (Orig.). (gr. k-8). 1993. text ed. 11.95 (1-56763-073-1); pap. text ed. 5.95 (1-56763-074-X) Ozark Pub.
—Path of Destiny. Blevins, Wade, illus. Sargent, Dave, intro. by. (Illus.). 48p. (Orig.). (gr. k-8). 1993. text ed. 11.95 (1-56763-071-5); pap. text ed. 5.95 (1-56763-072-3) Ozark Pub.
—The Wisdom Circle. Blevins, Wade, illus. Sargent, Dave, intro. by. (Illus.). 48p. (Orig.). (gr. k-8). 1993. text ed. 11.95 (1-56763-075-1); pap. text ed. 5.95 (1-56763-076-6) Ozark Pub.
Blickenstaff, James P. Flight of Fantasy. 1991. 15.95 (0-533-09169-1) Vantage.
Bligh, William. Mutiny on Board HMS Bounty. Teitel, N. R., intro. by. (gr. 8 up). 1965. pap. 1.95 (0-8049-0088-4, CL-88) Airmont.
Blight, Cathy. Primary Crafts for Kids. 1991. pap. 8.95 (0-88494-789-0) Bookcraft Inc.
Blinks, William, et al. Memories of Early Michigan City. Lewis, Patricia, ed. (Orig.). (gr. 6 up). 1990. pap. 2.00 (0-935549-14-5) MI City Hist.
Blinn, William. Brian's Song. (Illus.). 128p. (Orig.). (gr. 6 up). 1983. pap. 3.99 (0-553-26618-7) Bantam.
Blishen, Edward, ed. Children's Classics to Read Aloud. LC 92-53097. (Illus.). 256p. (gr. 2 up). 1992. 16.95 (1-85697-825-7) Kingfisher Bks.
—Oxford Book of Poetry for Children. Wildsmith, Brian, illus. 168p. (gr. k-5). 1987. 16.95 (0-19-276031-9) OUP.
Blishen, Edward, selected by. Science Fiction Stories. Littlewood, Karin, illus. LC 92-26453. 256p. (gr. 4-9). 1993. 6.95 (1-85697-889-3) Kingfisher Bks.
Blishen, Edward & Blishen, Nancy, eds. A Treasury of Stories for Five Year Olds. Noakes, Polly, illus. LC 92-53107. 160p. (Orig.). (gr. k-5). 1992. pap. 5.95 (1-85697-827-3) Kingfisher Bks.
—A Treasury of Stories for Seven Year Olds. Ludlow, Patricia, illus. LC 92-53109. 160p. (Orig.). (gr. k-5). 1992. pap. 5.95 (1-85697-829-X) Kingfisher Bks.
—A Treasury of Stories for Six Year Olds. Knowles, Tizzie, illus. LC 92-53108. 160p. (Orig.). (gr. k-5). 1992. pap. 5.95 (1-85697-828-1) Kingfisher Bks.
Blishen, Nancy, jt. ed. see Blishen, Edward.
Bliss. Aging. 1991. 12.95s.p. (0-86593-114-3) Rourke Corp.
—Batting Champs. 1991. 12.50s.p. (0-86593-129-1) Rourke Corp.
—Home Run Leaders. 1991. 12.50s.p. (0-86593-128-3); PLB 16.67 (0-685-66094-X) Rourke Corp.
Bliss, Jonathan. Child Abuse. (Illus.). 64p. (gr. 7 up). 1990. lib. bdg. 17.27 (0-86593-081-3); lib. bdg. 12. 95s.p. (0-685-46438-5) Rourke Corp.
—China. (Illus.). 64p. (gr. 7 up). 1990. lib. bdg. 17.27 (0-86593-090-2); lib. bdg. 12.95s.p. (0-685-36364-3) Rourke Corp.
—Dynasties. LC 92-412. 1992. 17.26 (0-86593-156-9); 12.95s.p. (0-685-66121-0) Rourke Corp.
Bliss, Richard, et al. Fossils: Key to the Present. (gr. 6-12). 1990. pap. 4.95 (0-89051-058-X) Master Bks.
Bliss, Richard B., ed. Dinosaur ABC's Activity Book. rev. ed. Schmitt, Doug, illus. 32p. (gr. k-3). 1986. pap. 3.95 (0-89051-113-6) Master Bks.
Bliss, Ronald G. Eagle Trap. LC 82-71045. (Illus.). 108p. (gr. 3-5). 1990. pap. 3.50x (0-943864-05-4) Davenport.

Bliss, Sands & Co. Staff. The Magic Moving Picture Book. 32p. (gr. 4 up). 1975. pap. 3.95 (0-486-23224-7) Dover.
Bliven, Bruce, Jr. American Revolution. (Illus.). (gr. 4-6). 1963. lib. bdg. 8.99 (0-394-90383-8) Random Bks Yng Read.
—The Story of D-Day. LC 81-483. (Illus.). 160p. (gr. 5-9). 1981. pap. 4.99 (0-394-84886-1) Random Bks Yng Read.
—Story of D-Day: June 6, 1944. (Illus.). (gr. 6-8). 1963. lib. bdg. 8.99 (0-394-90362-5) Random Bks Yng Read.
—The Story of D-Day: June 6, 1944. LC 93-24776. 15.00 (0-679-84503-8) Random.
Blizzard, Gladys. Come Look with Me: Exploring Landscape Art with Children. LC 91-34320. (Illus.). 32p. (gr. 1-8). 1992. 13.95 (0-934738-95-5) Thomasson-Grant.
Blizzard, Gladys S. Come Look with Me: Animals in Art. LC 92-5357. 32p. (gr. 1-8). 1992. 13.95 (1-56566-013-7) Thomasson-Grant.
—Come Look with Me: Enjoying Art with Children. LC 90-19627. (Illus.). 32p. (gr. 1-8). 1991. 13.95 (0-934738-76-9) Thomasson-Grant.
—Come Look with Me: World of Play. Barns, Rebecca B., ed. LC 92-36263. (Illus.). 32p. (gr. 1 up). 1993. 13. 95 (1-56566-031-5) Thomasson-Grant.
Bloch. Beth Doxy. 1993. PLB 13.95 (0-8050-2233-3) H Holt & Co.
Bloch, Carol Z. Sticker Atlas of the United States. Nichols, K., illus. (Orig.). 1990. pap. 3.95 (1-879424-10-X) Nickel Pr.
Bloch, Lawrence W., ed. see Farr, Naunerle.
Bloch, Lolla, tr. see Taubes, Hella.
Block, Arlene. Phonics Consonants. Nayer, Judith E., ed. Schanzer, Roz, illus. 32p. (gr. k-1). 1991. wkbk. 1.95 (1-878624-64-4) McClanahan Bk.
Block, Arlene, jt. auth. see Wise, Beth A.
Block, Francesca L. Cherokee Bat & the Goat Guys. LC 91-30706. 112p. (gr. 7 up). 1992. 14.00 (0-06-020269-6); PLB 13.89 (0-06-020270-X) HarpC Child Bks.
—Cherokee Bat & the Goat Guys. LC 91-20706. 128p. (gr. 7 up). 1993. pap. 3.95 (0-06-447095-4, Trophy) HarpC Child Bks.
—Missing Angel Juan. Braun, Wendy, illus. LC 92-38299. 144p. (gr. 7 up). 1993. 14.00 (0-06-023004-5); PLB 13.89 (0-06-023007-X) HarpC Child Bks.
—Weetzie Bat. LC 88-6214. 96p. (gr. 7 up). 1989. 12.95 (0-06-020534-2); PLB 12.89 (0-06-020536-9) HarpC Child Bks.
—Weetzie Bat. LC 88-6214. 96p. (gr. 6 up). 1991. pap. 3.95 (0-06-447068-7, Trophy) HarpC Child Bks.
—Witch Baby. LC 90-28916. 112p. (gr. 7 up). 1991. 14. 00 (0-06-020547-4); PLB 13.89 (0-06-020548-2) HarpC Child Bks.
—Witch Baby. LC 90-28916. 128p. (gr. 7 up). 1992. 3.95 (0-06-447065-2, Trophy) HarpC Child Bks.
Block, Linda F. & Dubin, Debbie I. Chanukah on Noah's Ark. 72p. (Orig.). (gr. 1-7). 1987. pap. 6.95 (0-9619082-0-3) Noahs Ark.
Block, Richard. Discover Rain Forests. (Illus.). 48p. (gr. 3-6). 1992. PLB 14.95 (1-56674-030-4, HTS Bks) Forest Hse.
Blocksma, Dewey & Blocksma, Mary. Easy-to-Make Spaceships That Really Fly. Russo, Marisabina, illus. LC 83-10986. 64p. (gr. 2-6). 1985. pap. 11.95 jacketed (0-671-66301-1, S&S BFYR); pap. 5.95 (0-671-66302-X, S&S BFYR) S&S Trade.
—Easy-to-Make Water Toys That Really Work. Seiden, Art, illus. LC 84-24913. 64p. (gr. 2-6). 1988. pap. 5.95 (0-671-66259-7, S&S BFYR) S&S Trade.
Blocksma, Mary. All My Toys Are on the Floor. Kalthoff, Sandra C., illus. LC 85-27000. 24p. (ps-2). 1986. PLB 12.33 (0-516-01579-6); pap. 3.95 (0-516-41579-4) Childrens.
—Amazing Mouths & Menus. Ames, Lee J., illus. 64p. (gr. 2-6). 1986. 12.95 (0-13-023854-6) P-H.
—Apple Tree! Apple Tree! Kalthoff, Sandra C., illus. LC 82-19852. 24p. (ps-2). 1983. PLB 12.33 (0-516-01584-2); pap. 3.95 (0-516-41584-0) Childrens.
—Apple Tree! Apple Tree! Big Book. 24p. (ps-2). 1990. PLB 30.60 (0-516-49514-3) Childrens.
—The Best-Dressed Bear. Kalthoff, Sandra C., illus. LC 84-9565. 24p. (ps-2). 1984. lib. bdg. 12.33 (0-516-01585-0); pap. text ed. 3.95 (0-516-41585-9) Childrens.
—The Best Dressed Bear Big Book. (Illus.). 24p. (ps-2). 1989. PLB 30.60 (0-516-49510-0) Childrens.
—Chirrinchinchina - Que Hay en la Tina? (Rub-a-Dub-Dub - What's in the Tub?) Martin, Sandra K., illus. LC 84-12139. (SPA.). 24p. (ps-2). 1988. PLB 12.33 (0-516-31586-2); pap. 3.95 (0-516-51586-1) Childrens.
—Donde Esta el Pato? - Where's That Duck? Martin, Sandra K., illus. LC 85-15001. (SPA.). 24p. (ps-2). 1990. PLB 12.33 (0-516-31587-0); pap. 3.95 (0-516-51587-X) Childrens.
—Grandma Dragon's Birthday. Kalthoff, Sandra C., illus. LC 82-19851. 24p. (ps-2). 1983. pap. 3.95 (0-516-41582-4) Childrens.
—Manzano, Manzano! - Libro Grande: Apple Tree! Apple Tree! - Big Book. (Illus.). 24p. (ps-2). 1990. PLB 30.60 (0-516-59514-8) Childrens.
—Manzano, Manzano! Apple Tree! Apple Tree! LC 86-19270. (Illus.). 24p. (ps-2). 1986. PLB 12.33 (0-516-31584-6); pap. 3.95 (0-516-51584-5) Childrens.
—The Marvelous Music Machine: A Story of the Piano. Richter, Mischa, illus. LC 84-4892. 64p. (gr. 3-7). 1984. 10.95 (0-13-559410-3) P-H.

—El Oso Mas Elegante (The Best Dressed Bear) LC 86-19272. (Illus.). 24p. (ps-2). 1986. PLB 12.33 (0-516-31585-4); pap. 3.95 (0-516-51585-3) Childrens.
—The Pup Went Up. Kalthoff, Sandra C., illus. LC 82-19862. 24p. (ps-2). 1983. PLB 12.33 (0-516-01583-4) Childrens.
—Rub-a-Dub-Dub - What's in the Tub? Kalthoff, Sandra C., illus. LC 84-12139. 24p. (ps-2). 1984. lib. bdg. 12. 33 (0-516-01586-9); pap. 3.95 (0-516-41586-7) Childrens.
—Rub-a-dub-dub-What's in the Tub? Big Book. 24p. (ps-2). 1987. PLB 30.60 (0-516-49505-4) Childrens.
—Ticket to the Twenties: A Time Traveler's Guide. Dennen, Susan, illus. LC 92-24303. 1993. 15.95 (0-316-09974-0) Little.
—Todos Mis Juquetes (All My Toys Are on the Floor) Kalthoff, Sandra C., illus. LC 85-27000. (SPA.). 24p. (ps-2). 1989. pap. 3.95 (0-516-51579-9) Childrens.
—Where's That Duck? LC 85-15001. (Illus.). 32p. (ps-2). 1985. PLB 12.33 (0-516-01587-7); pap. 3.95 (0-516-41587-5) Childrens.
—Yoo Hoo, Moon! 1991. pap. 9.99 (0-553-07094-0) Bantam.
—Yoo Hoo, Moon! 1992. pap. 3.50 (0-553-35212-1) Bantam.
Blocksma, Mary, jt. auth. see Blocksma, Dewey.
Blodgett, Elizabeth G., jt. auth. see Miller, Viola P.
Blohm, Hans, jt. auth. see Haas, Rudi.
Blomquist, Geraldine M. Coping As a Foster Child. (gr. 7-12). 1992. PLB 13.95 (0-8239-1346-5) Rosen Group.
Blomquist, Geraldine M. & Blomquist, Paul B. Zachary's New Home: A Story for Foster & Adopted Children. Lemieux, Margo, illus. LC 90-41914. 32p. (ps-2). 1990. 16.95 (0-945354-28-2); pap. 6.95 (0-945354-27-4) Magination Pr.
—Zachary's New Home: A Story for Foster & Adopted Children. Lemieux, Margo, illus. LC 92-56876. 1993. PLB 17.26 (0-8368-0937-8) Gareth Stevens Inc.
Blomquist, Paul B., jt. auth. see Blomquist, Geraldine M.
Blonder. Wee Wonders of Nature. (gr. 2 up). 1988. 2.50 (0-448-09254-9, G&D) Putnam Pub Group.
Blonder, Ellen, illus. My Very First Things. (ps). 1988. bds. 2.50 (0-448-09253-0, G&D) Putnam Pub Group.
Blonigen, Julie A. Biking for a Better Voice. (Illus.). 48p. (gr. k-8). 1992. wkbk. 39.95 (0-937857-26-2, 1597) Speech Bin.
Blood, Charles L. & Link, Martin. The Goat in the Rug. Parker, Nancy W., illus. LC 80-17315. 40p. (ps-3). 1984. Repr. of 1976 ed. RSBE 14.95 (0-02-710920-8, Four Winds) Macmillan Child Grp.
—The Goat in the Rug. Parker, Nancy W., illus. LC 89-77701. 40p. (ps-3). 1990. pap. 4.95 (0-689-71418-1, Aladdin) Macmillan Child Grp.
Bloom, Daniel H. The Magic of Johnny Readingseed. Julien, Claudia, illus. 48p. (gr. 5-9). 1990. 9.95 (0-944007-60-0) Shapolsky Pubs.
Bloom, Edgar B. It All Starts with Counting: A Short Guide to Old-Fashioned Arithmetic & Other Mathematical Concepts. Holliman, Mary C., ed. viii, 122p. (Orig.). (gr. 6-12). 1993. pap. 10.00 (0-936015-26-8); wkbk. 10.00 (0-685-58700-2) Pocahontas Pr.
Bloom, Hanya. Friendly Fangs. (gr. 4-7). 1991. pap. 2.95 (0-06-106032-1, Harp PBks) HarpC.
—Science Spook. (gr. 4-7). 1990. pap. 2.95 (0-06-106020-8, PL) HarpC.
—Vampire Cousins. (gr. 4-7). 1990. pap. 2.95 (0-06-106025-9, PL) HarpC.
—Vic the Vampire, No. 1: School Ghoul. (gr. 4-7). 1990. pap. 2.95 (0-06-106004-6, Harp PBks) HarpC.
Bloom, Marc. Know Your Game: Football. (gr. 4-7). 1990. pap. 2.95 (0-590-43312-1) Scholastic Inc.
Bloom, Marjorie. Estimate! Calculate! Evaluate! Calculator Activities for the Middle Grades. (gr. 4-7). 1990. pap. 9.50 (0-201-48032-8) Addison-Wesley.
Bloom, Marjorie W. & Galton, Grace C. Estimate! Calculate! Evaluate! Calculator Activities for the Middle Grades. Berger, Joshua, illus. 88p. (gr. 5-8). 1990. pap. text ed. 9.50 (0-938587-12-9) Cuisenaire.
Bloom, Suzanne. A Family for Jamie: An Adoption Story. Bloom, Suzanne, illus. LC 90-42589. 24p. (ps-1). 1991. 13.00 (0-517-57492-6, Clarkson Potter); PLB 13.99 (0-517-57493-4, C N Potter Bks) Crown Bks Yng Read.
—We Keep a Pig in the Parlor. Bloom, Suzanne, illus. 32p. (ps-1). 1988. 13.95 (0-517-56829-2, Clarkson Potter) Crown Bks Yng Read.
Bloomfield, William. Career Action Plan: Implementation Guide. (gr. 9 up). 1989. 12.95 (0-936007-16-8, 3301) Meridian Educ.
Blos, Joan. Brothers of the Heart. LC 85-40293. 176p. (gr. 6 up). 1985. SBE 13.95 (0-684-18452-4, Scribners Young Read) Macmillan Child Grp.
—Brothers of the Heart. LC 87-1089. 176p. (gr. 7 up). 1987. pap. 3.95 (0-689-71166-2, Aladdin) Macmillan Child Grp.
Blos, Joan W. Brooklyn Doesn't Rhyme. Birling, Paul, illus. 96p. (gr. 3-6). 1994. SBE 12.95 (0-684-19694-8, Scribners Young Read) Macmillan Child Grp.
—Brothers of the Heart: A Story of the Old Northwest, 1837-1838. 2nd ed. LC 92-39668. 176p. (gr. 3-7). 1993. pap. 3.95 (0-689-71724-5, Aladdin) Macmillan Child Grp.
—A Gathering of Days: A New England Girl's Journal, 1830-1832. LC 90-32. 160p. (gr. 3-7). 1990. pap. 3.95 (0-689-71419-X, Aladdin) Macmillan Child Grp.

—A Gathering of Days: A New England Girl's Journal, 1830-32. LC 79-16898. 144p. (gr. 4-7). 1979. SBE 13.95 (0-684-16340-3, Scribners Young Read) Macmillan Child Grp.
—The Grandpa Days. McCully, Emily A., illus. LC 88-19801. 32p. (ps). 1989. pap. 8.95 jacketed (0-671-64640-0, Little Simon) S&S Trade.
—Grandpa Days. LC 88-19801. (ps-3). 1994. pap. 3.95 (0-671-88244-9, Halfmoon) S&S Trade.
—The Heroine of the Titanic: A Tale Both True & Otherwise of the Life of Molly Brown. Dixon, Tennessee, illus. LC 90-35369. 40p. (gr. 1 up). 1991. 14.95 (0-688-07546-0); PLB 14.88 (0-688-07547-9) Morrow Jr Bks.
—Lottie's Circus. Trivas, Irene, illus. LC 88-39035. 32p. (ps up). 1989. 13.95 (0-688-06746-8); PLB 13.88 (0-688-06747-6, Morrow Jr Bks) Morrow Jr Bks.
—Martin's Hats. Simont, Marc, illus. LC 83-13389. 32p. (ps-3). 1984. 11.95 (0-688-02027-5); PLB 11.88 (0-688-02033-X, Morrow Jr Bks) Morrow Jr Bks.
—Martin's Hats. LC 83-13389. (Illus.). 32p. (ps-3). 1984. pap. 4.95 (0-688-07039-6, Mulberry) Morrow.
—Old Henry. Gammell, Stephen, illus. LC 86-21745. 32p. (ps-4). 1987. lib. bdg. 13.95 (0-688-06399-3); 13.88 (0-688-06400-0) Morrow Jr Bks.
—Old Henry. Gammell, Stephen, illus. LC 86-21745. 32p. (ps-2). 1990. pap. 4.95 (0-688-09935-1, Mulberry) Morrow.
—One Very Best Valentine's Day. 1990. pap. 8.95 (0-671-64639-7) S&S Trade.
—One Very Best Valentine's Day. McCully, Emily A., illus. 32p. (ps-2). 1992. pap. 2.25 (0-671-75297-9, Little Simon) S&S Trade.
—A Seed, a Flower, a Minute, an Hour. Poppel, Hans, illus. LC 91-4992. 40p. (ps-2). 1992. pap. 14.00 jacketed, 3-pc. bdg. (0-671-73214-5, S&S BFYR) S&S Trade.
—A Seed, Flower a Minute, an Hour. LC 91-4992. (ps-3). 1994. pap. 4.95 (0-671-88632-0, Half Moon Bks) S&S Trade.
Blos, Joan W., ed. see Brown, Margaret Wise.
Blos, Sarah I. & Davis, Julie N. Katsu & the Kite. (Illus.). 14p. 1988. pap. 0.96 (0-912303-43-3) Michigan Mus.

Blount, Lucy D. The Story of Lucy What's-Her-Name! And Your Name Too! Long, Woodie, illus. 48p. 1992. Spiral bdg. pap. 12.00 (0-9630017-2-8) Light-Bearer.

Author Lucy Blount has created an uplifting children's story peppered with special hints & clues to help little ones uncover the secret name God has chosen for each of His children. Through THE STORY OF LUCY WHAT'S-HER-NAME (AND YOUR NAME TOO!), Mrs. Blount has woven a comforting tapestry of love, self-confidence, reassurance & joy. The book is designed to lift the spirits of children, build their self-esteem, & help them discover their individuality. "...because each one of us has received God's loving light differently, so each one of us gives His Light off differently. We are all to shine, like our God's created stars in the night, but each of us twinkles differently." Illustrated with honesty & simplicity by Alabama folk artist Woodie Long, whose work is featured in art galleries across the nation. Spiral-bound, with blank pages for little artists to create their own special illustrations.
Publisher Provided Annotation.

Blount, Trevor, ed. see Dickens, Charles.
Bloyd, Sunni. Animal Rights. LC 90-6197. (Illus.). 96p. (gr. 5-8). 1990. PLB 14.95 (1-56006-114-6) Lucent Bks.
—Endangered Species. LC 89-12895. (Illus.). 96p. (gr. 5 up). 1989. PLB 14.95 (1-56006-106-5) Lucent Bks.
Blue Lantern Studio Staff. Baby's Own Book: A Treasury for Special Moments. 1993. 13.95 (0-8118-0003-2) Chronicle Bks.
Blue, Rose. Me & Einstein: Breaking Through the Reading Barrier. Luks, Peggy, illus. (gr. 3 up). 1984. 14.95 (0-87705-388-X); pap. 9.95 (0-89885-185-8) Human Sci Pr.
—Wishful Lying. Hartman, Laura, illus. LC 79-21806. 32p. (ps-3). 1980. 16.95 (0-87705-473-8) Human Sci Pr.
Blue, Rose & Bernstein, Joanne E. Diane Sawyer: Super Newswoman. LC 89-16817. (Illus.). 128p. (gr. 6 up). 1990. lib. bdg. 17.95 (0-89490-288-1) Enslow Pubs.

Blue, Rose & Naden, Corinne J. Barbara Bush: First Lady. LC 90-48318. (Illus.). 104p. (gr. 6 up). 1991. lib. bdg. 17.95 (0-89490-350-0) Enslow Pubs.
—Barbara Jordan. (Illus.). 112p. (gr. 5 up). 1992. lib. bdg. 17.95 (0-7910-1131-3) Chelsea Hse.
—Colin Powell: Straight to the Top. LC 91-19121. (Illus.). 48p. (gr. 2-4). 1991. PLB 12.40 (1-56294-052-X) Millbrook Pr.
—People of Peace. LC 93-30547. 1994. PLB write for info. (1-56294-409-6) Millbrook Pr.
—The U. S. Air Force. LC 92-13431. (Illus.). 64p. (gr. 3-6). 1993. PLB 14.90 (1-56294-217-4) Millbrook Pr.
Blue, Rose, jt. auth. see Bernstein, Joanne E.
Blue, Rose, jt. auth. see Naden, Corinne J.
Blueford, J. R., et al. Life Cycle - A Diversity in a Balance. (gr. k-6). 1992. 24.95 (1-56638-157-6) Math Sci Nucleus.
—Universe Cycle - Search for Our Beginning. (gr. k-6). 1992. 20.95 (1-56638-055-3) Math Sci Nucleus.
—Water Cycle - The Earth's Gift. (gr. k-6). 1992. 19.95 (1-56638-146-0) Math Sci Nucleus.
Bluestein, Janet. Being a Successful Teacher. (gr. k-6). 1988. pap. 25.95 (0-8224-6791-7) Fearon Teach Aids.
Bluestone, Carol & Irwin, Susan. Washington, D. C. Guidebook for Kids. rev. ed. LC 87-50322. (Illus.). 64p. (gr. 3-9). 1987. pap. 5.95 (0-9601022-2-1) Noodle Pr.
Blum, Laurie. Free Money for Foreign Study: A Guide to More Than 1,000 Grants & Scholarships for Study Abroad. 256p. (gr. 8 up). 1991. lib. bdg. 24.95x (0-8160-2450-2) Facts on File.
Blum, Raymond. Mathemagic. Sinclair, Jeff, illus. LC 91-22523. 128p. (gr. 4-11). 1991. 12.95 (0-8069-8354-X) Sterling.
—Mathemagic. Sinclair, Jeff, illus. LC 91-22523. 128p. (gr. 8 up). 1992. pap. 4.95 (0-8069-8355-8) Sterling.
Blumberg, Leda. Breezy. 96p. (gr. 3-7). 1988. pap. 2.50 (0-380-89942-6, Camelot) Avon.
Blumberg, Rhoda. Bloomers! Morgan, Mary, illus. LC 92-27154. 40p. (gr. k-5). 1993. RSBE 14.95 (0-02-711684-0, Bradbury Pr) Macmillan Child Grp.
—Commodore Perry in the Land of the Shogun. LC 84-21800. (Illus.). 128p. (gr. 4 up). 1985. 14.95 (0-688-03723-2) Lothrop.
—The First Travel Guide to the Moon: What to Pack, How to Go, & What to See When You Get There. Doty, Roy, illus. LC 84-28757. 96p. (gr. 3-7). 1984. Repr. of 1980 ed. 13.95 (0-02-711680-8, Four Winds) Macmillan Child Grp.
—The Great American Gold Rush. LC 89-736. (Illus.). 144p. (gr. 5 up). 1989. SBE 17.95 (0-02-711681-6, Bradbury Pr) Macmillan Child Grp.
—The Incredible Journey of Lewis & Clark. LC 87-4235. (Illus.). 144p. (gr. 4 up). 1987. 17.95 (0-688-06512-0) Lothrop.
—Jumbo. Hunt, Jonathan, illus. LC 91-34789. 48p. (gr. k-5). 1992. RSBE 15.95 (0-02-711683-2, Bradbury Pr) Macmillan Child Grp.
—The Remarkable Voyages of Captain Cook. LC 91-11219. (Illus.). 160p. (gr. 5 up). 1991. SBE 18.95 (0-02-711682-4, Bradbury Pr) Macmillan Child Grp.
Blume, Judy. Are You There, God? It's Me, Margaret. 156p. (gr. 5-8). 1972. pap. 3.99 (0-440-40419-3, YB) Dell.
—Are You There God? It's Me, Margaret. reissued ed. LC 90-44484. 156p. (gr. 4-7). 1990. Repr. of 1970 ed. SBE 13.95 (0-02-710991-7, Bradbury Pr) Macmillan Child Grp.
—Are You There, God? It's Me, Margaret. (gr. 4-7). 1991. pap. 3.99 (0-440-90419-6, YB) Dell.
—La Ballena "Blubber" Ada, Alma F., tr. LC 83-2731. (SPA). 160p. (gr. 4-6). 1983. SBE 12.95 (0-02-710940-2, Bradbury Pr) Macmillan Child Grp.
—Blubber. LC 73-94116. 160p. (gr. 4-6). 1982. SBE 13.95 (0-02-711010-9, Bradbury Pr) Macmillan Child Grp.
—Blubber. 160p. (gr. 3-6). 1976. pap. 3.50 (0-440-40707-9, YB) Dell.
—Blubber. large type ed. 190p. (gr. 4-9). 1988. Repr. of 1974 ed. lib. bdg. 15.95 (1-55736-025-1, Crnrstn Bks) BDD LT Grp.
—Deenie. LC 73-80197. 192p. (gr. 6-8). 1982. SBE 13.95 (0-02-711020-6, Bradbury Pr) Macmillan Child Grp.
—Deenie. 144p. (gr. 7 up). 1991. pap. 3.50 (0-440-93259-9, LFL) Dell.
—Deenie. large type ed. 215p. (gr. 5 up). 1988. Repr. of 1973 ed. lib. bdg. 15.95 (1-55736-026-X, Crnrstn Bks) BDD LT Grp.
—Estas Ahi Dios? Soy Yo, Margaret. Ada, Alma F., tr. LC 83-2730. (SPA). 160p. (gr. 4-6). 1983. 13.95 (0-02-710950-X, Bradbury Pr) Macmillan Child Grp.
—Forever. LC 74-28850. 216p. (gr. 7 up). 1975. SBE 14.95 (0-02-711030-3, Bradbury Pr) Macmillan Child Grp.
—Freckle Juice. Lisker, Sonia O., illus. LC 85-280. 48p. (gr. 1-3). 1978. pap. 3.50 (0-440-42813-0, YB) Dell.
—Freckle Juice. Lisker, Sonia O., illus. LC 85-280. 40p. (gr. 1-3). 1984. Repr. of 1971 ed. 12.95 (0-02-711690-5, Four Winds) Macmillan Child Grp.
—Fudge, 3 vols. (gr. 4-7). 1992. Set. pap. 14.00 boxed (0-440-36051-X) Dell.
—Fudge-A-Mania. LC 90-39627. 128p. (gr. 3-7). 1990. 12.95 (0-525-44672-9, DCB) Dutton Child Bks.
—Fudge-a-Mania. (gr. 4-7). 1991. pap. 3.50 (0-440-40490-8, YB) Dell.
—Fudge-a-Mania. 1991. pap. 3.50 (0-440-70695-5) Dell.
—Fudge-a-Mania. (gr. 4-7). 1992. pap. 1.99 (0-440-21369-X) Dell.

—Fudge-a-Mania. 169p. (gr. 3-6). 1990. 13.52 (0-685-66377-9, BR8443) W A T Braille.
—Fudge-a-Mania. 169p. 1991. text ed. 13.52 (1-56956-235-0) W A T Braille.
—Here's to You, Rachel Robinson. LC 93-9631. 208p. (gr. 5 up). 1993. 14.95 (0-531-06801-3); PLB 14.99 (0-531-08651-8) Orchard Bks Watts.
—Iggie's House. LC 70-104340. 128p. (gr. 4-6). 1970. SBE 12.85 (0-02-711040-0, Bradbury Pr) Macmillan Child Grp.
—Iggie's House. 128p. (gr. 3-6). 1986. pap. 3.99 (0-440-44062-9, YB) Dell.
—Iggie's House. large type, unabr. ed. 158p. (gr. 3-6). 1989. lib. bdg. 13.95 (0-8161-4449-4) G K Hall.
—It's Not the End of the World. LC 70-181739. 176p. (gr. 5-7). 1982. SBE 14.95 (0-02-711050-8, Bradbury Pr) Macmillan Child Grp.
—It's Not the End of the World. (gr. k-6). 1986. pap. 3.25 (0-440-44158-7, YB) Dell.
—It's Not the End of the World. (gr. k-6). 1982. pap. 3.99 (0-440-94140-7) Dell.
—It's Not the End of the World. 1979. pap. 1.95 (0-553-13628-3) Bantam.
—Judy Blume, 4 vols. (gr. 4-7). 1992. Set. pap. 14.00 boxed (0-440-36053-6) Dell.
—Judy Blume Collection, 5 bks. Incl. Are You There God, It's Me, Margaret; Otherwise Known As Sheila the Great; Starring Sally J. Freedman As Herself; Superfudge; Tales of a Fourth Grade Nothing. (gr. 3-8). 1986. Boxed Set. pap. 16.25 (0-440-44356-3) Dell.
—Judy Blume: Judy Blume & You, Friends for Life, 4 vols. (gr. 4-7). 1991. pap. 13.50 boxed set (0-440-36013-7) Dell.
—Just as Long as We're Together. LC 87-7980. 304p. (gr. 5-8). 1987. 12.95 (0-531-05729-1); PLB 12.99 (0-531-08329-2) Orchard Bks Watts.
—Just As Long As We're Together. 304p. (gr. k-6). 1988. pap. 3.99 (0-440-40075-9, YB) Dell.
—Just As Long As We're Together. large type ed. 210p. (gr. 5 up). 1988. Repr. of 1987 ed. lib. bdg. 15.95 (1-55736-046-4, Crnrstn Bks) BDD LT Grp.
—Just As Long As We're Together. (gr. 4-7). 1991. pap. 3.99 (0-440-21094-1, YB) Dell.
—Just As Long As We're Together. 1988. pap. 3.50 (0-440-70013-2) Dell.
—Just As Long As We're Together. large type ed. (gr. 1-8). 1990. 13.95 (0-7451-0826-1, Galaxy Child Lrg Print) Chivers N Amer.
—The One in the Middle Is the Green Kangaroo. Aitken, Amy, illus. 48p. (gr. k-2). 1982. pap. 3.99 (0-440-46731-4, YB) Dell.
—The One in the Middle Is the Green Kangaroo. 2nd ed. Trivas, Irene, illus. LC 80-29664. 32p. (gr. k-2). 1991. Repr. of 1981 ed. 13.95 (0-02-711055-9, Bradbury Pr) Macmillan Child Grp.
—The One in the Middle is the Green Kangaroo. Trivas, Irene, illus. (ps-3). 1992. pap. 3.99 (0-440-40668-4, YB) Dell.
—Otherwise Known As Sheila the Great. 128p. (gr. 3-6). 1976. pap. 3.99 (0-440-46701-2, YB) Dell.
—Otherwise Known As Sheila the Great. (gr. 3-6). 1972. 13.99 (0-525-36455-2, DCB) Dutton Child Bks.
—The Pain & the Great One. Trivas, Irene, illus. LC 84-11009. 32p. (gr. k-3). 1984. RSBE 13.95 (0-02-711100-8, Bradbury Pr) Macmillan Child Grp.
—The Pain & the Great One. (gr. k-12). 1985. pap. 4.99 (0-440-46819-1, YB) Dell.
—Sheila la Magnifica - Sheila the Great. Salazar-Alonso, Olvido, tr. (SPA.). 151p. (gr. 5-8). 1991. pap. 8.50 (84-204-4577-0) Santillana.
—Starring Sally J. Freedman As Herself. LC 76-57805. 296p. (gr. 4-7). 1982. SBE 15.95 (0-02-711070-2, Bradbury Pr) Macmillan Child Grp.
—Superfudge. 176p. (gr. 2-6). 1981. pap. 3.99 (0-440-48433-2, YB) Dell.
—Superfudge. LC 80-10439. 176p. (gr. 3-6). 1980. 13.00 (0-525-40522-4, DCB) Dutton Child Bks.
—Superfudge. large type ed. 239p. (gr. 2-6). 1987. Repr. of 1980 ed. lib. bdg. 14.95 (1-55736-014-6, Crnrstn Bks) BDD LT Grp.
—Superfudge. (gr. 4-7). 1993. pap. 1.99 (0-440-21619-2) Dell.
—Tales of a Fourth Grade Nothing. (gr. k-6). 1976. pap. 3.99 (0-440-48474-X, YB) Dell.
—Tales of a Fourth Grade Nothing. Doty, Roy, illus. LC 70-179050. 128p. (gr. 2-5). 1972. 11.95 (0-525-40720-0, DCB) Dutton Child Bks.
—Tales of a Fourth Grade Nothing. large type ed. Doty, Roy, illus. 174p. (gr. 2-6). 1987. Repr. of 1972 ed. lib. bdg. 14.95 (1-55736-015-4, Crnrstn Bks) BDD LT Grp.
—Tales of a Fourth Grade Nothing. large type ed. (gr. 1-8). 1991. 13.95 (0-7451-0722-2, Galaxy Child Lrg Print) Chivers N Amer.
—Then Again, Maybe I Won't. LC 77-156548. 176p. (gr. 5-7). 1971. SBE 13.95 (0-02-711090-7, Bradbury Pr) Macmillan Child Grp.
—Then Again, Maybe I Won't. 164p. (gr. 5-8). 1986. pap. 3.99 (0-440-48659-9, YB) Dell.
—Tiger Eyes. LC 81-6152. 256p. (gr. 7 up). 1981. SBE 14.95 (0-02-711080-X, Bradbury Pr) Macmillan Child Grp.
—Tiger Eyes. 224p. (gr. 7 up). 1982. 3.99 (0-440-98469-6, LFL) Dell.
Blumenfeld, Esther, jt. auth. see Alpern, Lynne.
Blumenthal, Howard J. Careers in Television. (Illus.). (gr. 7 up). 1992. 16.95 (0-316-10076-5) Little.

—You Can Do It! Careers in Baseball. LC 92-9542. 1993. 16.95 (*0-316-10095-1*) Little.
Blumenthal, Nancy. Count-a-Saurus. Kaufman, Robert, illus. LC 88-21320. 24p. (ps-3). 1989. RSBE 12.95 (*0-02-749391-1*, Four Winds) Macmillan Child Grp.
—Count-A-Saurus. Kaufman, Robert J., illus. LC 91-41250. 24p. (gr. k-3). 1992. pap. 3.95 (*0-689-71633-8*, Aladdin) Macmillan Child Grp.
Blumenthal, Richard, jt. auth. see Despres, Joseph.
Blundell, Kim & Tyler, Jenny. Animal Mazes. (Illus.). 24p. (gr. k-2). 1993. pap. 3.95 (*0-7460-1323-X*, Usborne) EDC.
Blundell, Tony. Beware of Boys. LC 90-24299. (Illus.). 32p. (ps up). 1992. 14.00 (*0-688-10924-1*); PLB 13.93 (*0-688-10925-X*) Greenwillow.
Blustein, Lotte & Geary, Rosemary J. Writing the Research Paper. 70p. (gr. 9 up). 1992. pap. text ed. 7.50 (*0-9605248-3-5*) Blustein-Geary.
Bly, Leon. An Analysis of Leadership & How to Be a Better Leader. 117p. (Orig.). (gr. 9). 1988. text & wkbk. 24.95 (*0-9621505-0-9*) Cnsltnts Unlimited.
Bly, Stephen. Coyote True. LC 92-8224. 128p. 1992. pap. 4.99 (*0-89107-680-8*, Crossway Bks) Good News.
—The Dog Who Would Not Smile. Bishop, Lila, ed. 128p. (gr. 4-7). 1992. pap. 4.99 (*0-89107-656-5*) Good News.
—Final Justice at Adobe Wells. LC 93-14185. 192p. (Orig.). (gr. 9 up). 1993. pap. 7.99 (*0-89107-744-8*, Crossway Bks) Good News.
—The Last Stubborn Buffalo in Nevada. 128p. (Orig.). (gr. 6-9). 1993. pap. 4.99 (*0-89107-746-4*, Crossway Bks) Good News.
—You Can Always Trust a Spotted Horse. LC 92-46667. 128p. (Orig.). (gr. 4-7). 1993. pap. 4.99 (*0-89107-716-2*, Crossway Bks) Good News.
Bly, Stephen A. Rivers in Arizona. 140p. (Orig.). (gr. 7-12). 1991. pap. 4.95 (*0-8474-6624-8*) Back to Bible.
Blyler, Allison. Finding Foxes. (Illus.). 32p. (ps-3). 1991. 14.95 (*0-399-22264-2*, Philomel Bks) Putnam Pub Group.
Blymire, Lynn, et al. A. C. T. I. (gr. k-4). 1981. pap. 3.00 (*0-931992-40-0*) Penns Valley.
Blystone, Peter L., tr. see Volkov, Alexander.
Blystone, Peter L., tr. from RUS. & a see Volkov, Alexander M.
Blythe, William B. The Human Kidney. Head, J. J., ed. Imrick, Ann T., illus. LC 86-72196. 16p. (Orig.). (gr. 10 up). 1991. pap. text ed. 2.75 (*0-89278-167-X*, 45-9767) Carolina Biological.
Blyton, Enid. Christmas Tales. 1993. 9.98 (*0-8317-1272-4*) Smithmark.
—Five Get Into Trouble. large type ed. (gr. 1-8). 1993. 15.95 (*0-7451-1910-7*, Galaxy Child Lrg Print) Chivers N Amer.
—Five Go off in a Caravan. large type ed. 272p. 1992. 13.95 (*0-7451-1466-0*, Galaxy Child Lrg Print) Chivers N Amer.
—Five Go off to Camp. large type ed. (gr. 1-8). 1991. 13.95 (*0-7451-1701-5*, Galaxy Child Lrg Print) Chivers N Amer.
—Five Go to Smuggler's Top. 264p. 1991. text ed. 15.95x (*0-7451-1368-0*, Pub. by Chivers Pr UK) Hall.
—Five on Kirrin Island Again. large type ed. 233p. 1992. 13.95 (*0-7451-1620-5*, Galaxy Child Lrg Print) Chivers N Amer.
BMA Staff. The Baby ABCs: A Memory Book for Boys & Girls ages 3-5. Lautermilch, John, illus. 54p. (ps). 1980. pap. text ed. 4.95 (*0-89323-051-0*) Bible Memory.
Boardman, Bob. Red Hot Peppers. Boardman, Diane, illus. 64p. (Orig.). (gr. 3 up). 1993. pap. 12.95 incl. speed rope (*0-912365-78-1*) Sasquatch Bks.
—Red Hot Peppers. (Illus.). 64p. (Orig.). (gr. 3 up). 1993. pap. 12.95 incl. beaded-rope kit (*0-912365-94-3*) Sasquatch Bks.
—Red Hot Peppers: The Skookum Book of Jump Rope Games, Rhymes, & Fancy Footwork. Boardman, Diane, illus. 64p. (Orig.). (gr. 3 up). 1993. pap. 8.95 (*0-912365-74-9*) Sasquatch Bks.
Boart, Jeff, ed. see Richards, R. W.
Boatness, Marie E. Travel Games for the Family. Westheimer, Mary, ed. Woodruff, Mark, illus. LC 93-90005. 144p. (Orig.). (gr. 1-8). 1993. pap. 9.95 (*0-9635619-0-1*) Canyon Creek.
Bobbi. Grandma's Teapot. Simbrom, Janine C., illus. 37p. 1992. pap. 3.95 (*0-9626608-3-3*) Magik NY.
—Matthew's Dream. Simbrom, Janine C., illus. 51p. 1993. pap. 5.95 (*0-9626608-6-8*) Magik NY.
—T-Neck. 63p. 1992. pap. 5.95 (*0-9626608-4-1*) Magik NY.
Bober, Natalie. Thomas Jefferson: Man on a Mountain. LC 87-37462. (Illus.). 288p. (gr. 7 up). 1988. SBE 15.95 (*0-689-31154-0*, Atheneum Child Bk) Macmillan Child Grp.
Bober, Natalie S. Marc Chagall: Painter of Dreams. Rosenberry, Vera, illus. LC 91-25463. 124p. (gr. 4-8). 1991. 14.95 (*0-8276-0379-7*) JPS Phila.
—A Restless Spirit: The Story of Robert Frost. (Illus.). 192p. (gr. 5 up). 1991. 19.95 (*0-8050-1672-4*, Bks Young Read) H Holt & Co.
—Thomas Jefferson: Man on a Mountain. LC 92-35604. (Illus.). 288p. (gr. 7 up). 1993. pap. 6.95 (*0-02-041797-7*, Collier Young Ad) Macmillan Child Grp.
Bobo, Betty, jt. auth. see Embry, Lynn.
Bobo, Carmen P. Sarah's Growing-up Summer. LC 88-62111. 52p. 1989. 6.95 (*1-55523-187-X*) Winston-Derek.

Bobrow, Jerry. Cliffs Elm Review: For the California State University Entry Level Mathematics Test. 330p. (Orig.). (gr. 12). 1987. pap. text ed. 8.95 (*0-8220-2071-8*) Cliffs.
Boccaccio. Andreuccio de Perugia. (gr. 7-12). pap. 4.95 (*0-88436-049-0*, 55250) EMC.
Boccaccio, Giovanni. Chichibo & the Crane. Luzatti, Lele, illus. (gr. 1-6). 1961. 8.95 (*0-8392-3004-4*) Astor-Honor.
Bochinski, Julianne B. Complete Handbook of Science Fair Projects. 1991. pap. text ed. 12.95 (*0-471-52728-9*) Wiley.
—The Complete Handbook of Science Fair Projects. 1991. text ed. 29.95 (*0-471-52729-7*) Wiley.
Bochner, Arthur B., jt. auth. see Berg, Adriane G.
Bock, Fred. Charlie Brown's Favorite Sunday School Songs. Schulz, Charles, illus. 24p. (Orig.). (gr. 1-6). 1992. pap. 7.95 (*1-56516-012-6*) Houston IN.
Bock, Glenn H., ed. see Haensel, Phyllis C.
Bock, Glenn N & Hoff, Marshall G., eds. Someone Special. Belding, Pam & Lasley, Susan K., illus. 32p. (gr. k-6). 1981. write for info. (*0-940210-00-2*) Minn Med Found.
Bock, Shelly V. Lonely Lyla. 1992. 7.95 (*0-533-09389-9*) Vantage.
Bockris, Victor. Life & Death of Andy Warhol. (ps-3). 1990. pap. 14.95 (*0-553-34929-5*) Bantam.
Bodart, Joni R. One Hundred World Class Thin Books: or What to Read When Your Book Report Is Due Tomorrow. 300p. (Orig.). (gr. 7-12). 1993. PLB 27.50 (*0-87287-986-0*) Libs Unl.
Bodden, Ilona, jt. auth. see Poppel, Hans.
Boddy, Joe, illus. A Christmas Carol. 48p. (ps-2). 1992. 5.95 (*0-88101-263-7*) Unicorn Pub.
—Countdown to Christmas. 48p. (ps-3). 1992. 6.95 (*0-88101-230-0*) Unicorn Pub.
Boddy, Marlys. ABC Book of Feelings. (Illus.). 32p. (ps-3). 1991. 8.99 (*0-570-04190-2*, 56-1649) Concordia.
Bode, Janet. Beating the Odds: Stories of Unexpected Achievers. LC 91-14215. 160p. (gr. 9-12). 1991. 14.45 (*0-531-15230-8*); PLB 14.40 (*0-531-10985-2*) Watts.
—Death Is Hard to Live With. 1993. 15.00 (*0-553-08410-0*) Bantam.
—Kids Still Having Kids: People Talk about Teen Pregnancy. LC 92-14175. (Illus.). 192p. (gr. 9-12). 1992. 15.45 (*0-531-15254-5*); PLB 14.90 (*0-531-11132-6*) Watts.
—New Kids in Town: Oral Histories of Immigrant Teens. 128p. 1991. pap. 2.95 (*0-590-44144-2*) Scholastic Inc.
—Truce: Ending the Sibling War. 144p. (gr. 8-12). 1991. 13.95 (*0-531-15221-9*); PLB 13.90 (*0-531-10996-8*) Watts.
—Truce: Ending the Sibling War. (gr. 12 up). 1993. pap. 3.99 (*0-440-21891-8*) Dell.
—The Voices of Rape. 144p. (gr. 9-12). 1990. 13.95 (*0-531-15184-0*); PLB 13.90 (*0-531-10959-3*) Watts.
—The Voices of Rape: Healing the Hurt. 144p. (gr. 7 up). 1992. pap. 3.99 (*0-440-21301-0*, LFL) Dell.
Bodecker, N. M. Carrot Holes & Frisbee Trees. Winters, Nina, illus. LC 83-2799. 48p. (gr. 3-5). 1983. SBE 12.95 (*0-689-50097-1*, M K McElderry) Macmillan Child Grp.
—Hurry, Hurry, Mary Dear! LC 76-14811. (Illus.). 128p. 1976. SBE 12.95 (*0-689-50066-1*, Pub. by M K McElderry) Macmillan Child Grp.
—Water Pennies & Other Poems. Blegvad, Erik, illus. LC 90-6477. 64p. 1991. SBE 12.95 (*0-689-50517-5*, M K McElderry) Macmillan Child Grp.
Boden, Arthur & Woodside, John. Boden's Beasts. Boden, Art, illus. (gr. 1-5). 1964. 8.95 (*0-8392-3045-1*) Astor-Honor.
Boden, Robert. Teen Talks with God. (gr. 7-12). 1980. pap. 3.99 (*0-570-03812-X*, 12-2921) Concordia.
Bodett, Tom. Irish Rebellion. 1993. pap. 3.25 (*0-553-56349-1*) Bantam.
Bodger, Lorraine. Great American Cakes. 1990. 7.99 (*0-517-02740-2*) Outlet Bk Co.
Bodha, Daji, ed. see John, Da Free.
Bodie, Idella. Ghost in the Capitol. Kovach, Gay H., illus. 116p. (gr. 5-9). 1986. pap. 6.95 (*0-87844-072-0*) Sandlapper Pub Co.
—A Hunt for Life's Extras: The Story of Archibald Rutledge. (Illus.). 176p. (gr. 5-12). 1986. pap. 6.95 (*0-87844-073-9*) Sandlapper Pub Co.
—The Mystery of the Pirate's Treasure. Yancey, Louise, illus. LC 72-94930. 136p. (gr. 5-9). 1984. pap. 6.95 (*0-87844-059-3*) Sandlapper Pub Co.
—The Secret of Telfair Inn. Yancy, Louise, illus. LC 79-177909. 98p. (gr. 5-9). 1983. pap. 6.95 (*0-87844-050-X*) Sandlapper Pub Co.
—Stranded! Sookikian, Charles J., illus. LC 84-14098. 132p. (Orig.). (gr. 5-9). 1984. pap. 6.95 (*0-87844-060-7*) Sandlapper Pub Co.
Bodily, Jolene & Kreiswirth, Kinny. The Lunch Book & Bag: A Fit Kid's Guide to Making Delicious (& Nutritious) Lunches. Kreiswirth, Kinny, illus. LC 92-2815. 56p. (gr. 2-6). 1992. pap. 12.95 (*0-688-11624-8*, Tambourine Bks) Morrow.
Bodker, Cecil. Mary of Nazareth. 1989. 14.95 (*91-29-59178-3*, Pub. by R & S Bks) FS&G.
Bodkin, Odds. The Banshee Train. Rose, Ted, illus. LC 93-39635. Date not set. write for info. (*0-395-69426-4*, Clarion Bks) HM.
Bodman, D., jt. auth. see Fairbanks, Ellen.

Bodnar, Judit Z., adapted by. The Fox, the Bear, & the Fish. Sandford, John, illus. Bodnar, Judit Z., tr. LC 93-19046. (Illus.). 1995. write for info. (*0-688-12174-8*); lib. bdg. write for info. (*0-688-12175-6*) Lothrop.
Bodnar, Judit Z., ed. see Maestro, Betsy.
Bodnar, Judit Z., ed. see Reddix, Valerie.
Bodourian, Marilyn, jt. auth. see Hendee, Stephanie.
Bodow, Steven. Sitting Bull. LC 92-16518. (Illus.). 128p. (gr. 7-10). 1992. PLB 22.80 (*0-8114-2328-X*) Raintree Steck-V.
Bodsworth, Nan. A Nice Walk in the Jungle. (Illus.). 32p. (ps-2). 1990. pap. 12.95 (*0-670-82476-3*) Viking Child Bks.
—A Nice Walk in the Jungle. (Illus.). 32p. (ps-3). 1992. pap. 4.99 (*0-14-054573-5*, Puffin) Puffin Bks.
Boe, David C. De see De Boe, David C.
Boegehold, Betty. Here's Pippa! Szekeres, Cyndy, illus. LC 88-27256. 128p. (gr. k-3). 1989. pap. 2.95 (*0-394-82702-3*) Knopf Bks Yng Read.
—Three to Get Ready. Chalmers, Mary, illus. LC 62-8042. (gr. k-3). 1965. PLB 13.89 (*0-06-020551-2*) HarpC Child Bks.
Boegehold, Betty, jt. auth. see Hooks, William H.
Boegehold, Betty D. Fight. (ps-3). 1991. 9.99 (*0-553-07086-X*) Bantam.
—Fight. (ps-3). 1991. pap. 3.50 (*0-553-35206-7*) Bantam.
—Horse Called Starfire. 1990. 9.99 (*0-553-05861-4*) Bantam.
—Pippa Pops Out! Szekeres, Cyndy, illus. 64p. (ps-3). 1980. pap. 0.95 (*0-440-46865-5*, YB) Dell.
—You Are Much Too Small-Bank Street. (ps-3). 1990. PLB 9.99 (*0-553-05895-9*, Little Rooster); pap. 3.50 (*0-553-34925-2*) Bantam.
Boehm, Ann E. & Slater, Barbara R. Cognitive Skills Assessment Battery. 2nd ed. (ps-k). 1981. complete kit 51.95 (*0-8077-5975-9*); refill 8.95x (*0-8077-5976-7*); assessor's manual 3.50x (*0-8077-5977-5*); sampler 3. 95x (*0-8077-5978-3*) Tchrs Coll.
Boehr, Karren. Ants in the Sugar Bowl. 165p. (gr. 4 up). 1986. 3.99 (*0-570-03638-0*, 39-1122) Concordia.
Boelts, Darwin, jt. auth. see Boelts, Maribeth.
Boelts, Maribeth. Dry Days, Wet Nights. Parkinson, Kathy, illus. LC 93-28674. 1994. write for info. (*0-8075-1723-2*) A Whitman.
—Tornado. Hansen-Cole, Robin, illus. LC 92-27988. 32p. 1993. pap. 3.95 (*0-8091-6607-0*) Paulist Pr.
Boelts, Maribeth & Boelts, Darwin. Kids to the Rescue! First-Aid Techniques for Kids. Megale, Marina, illus. LC 91-50666. 80p. (Orig.). (ps-6). 1992. PLB 17.95 (*0-943990-83-1*); pap. 7.95 (*0-943990-82-3*) Parenting Pr.
Boelts, Meribeth. With My Mom - with My Dad. 32p. 1992. pap. 5.95 (*0-8163-1060-2*) Pacific Pr Pub Assn.
Boericke, Arthur, et al. The Complete Adventures of Olga da Polga. Helweg, Hans, illus. LC 82-72753. 512p. (gr. 4-6). 1983. 16.95 (*0-440-00981-2*) Delacorte.
Boerner, Lee A. Job Seeker's Workbook. Botterbusch, Karl F., ed. (Illus.). 169p. (Orig.). 1988. pap. 10.00 (*0-916671-83-6*) Material Dev.
Boesky, Amy. Planet Was, Vol. 1. (ps-3). 1990. 14.95 (*0-316-10084-6*, Joy St Bks) Little.
Boettcher, Sue. Sue Boettcher's Black Cat ABC. 32p. 1993. 5.95 (*0-285-63062-8*, Pub. by Souvenir UK) Atrium Pubs.

Boga, Steve. On Their Own: Adventure Athletes in Solo Sports, 3 bks. Kratoville, B. L., ed. (Illus.). (gr. 3-9). 1992. Set, 64p. ea. bk. pap. text ed. 11. 00 (*0-87879-928-1*); wkbk. 12.50 (*0-87879-929-X*) High Noon Bks. ON THEIR OWN: ADVENTURE ATHLETES IN SOLO SPORTS - Examples of personal courage & achievement in solo sports endeavors are highlighted in three titles written for a 3rd grade reading level. All 15 stories (5 in each book) are true stories of the action-packed adventures of real people. Children will receive encouraging insights from the stories of others who have had to overcome obstacles to winning. BOOK ONE details the achievements of rock climber John Bachar, who once climbed Yosemite's El Capitan & Half Dome in the same day, swimmer Lynne Cox, first to swim the Bering Strait. BOOK TWO tells of Jericho Poppler, U.S. Women's Surfing Champ, Steve McKinney, World Record Speed Skier, John Lubill, World Champion White Water Canoe Racer, among others. BOOK THREE describes Eric Heiden, winner of five gold medals for speed

skating, Jan Case, hang glider pilot, & more. ON THEIR OWN was awarded as one of the Public Library Association's "1991 Top Titles for New Adult Readers." *Publisher Provided Annotation.*

Bogad, Carolyn. Fraction Fantasy. (gr. 5-7). 1979. pap. 3.95 (*0-88160-067-9*, LW 707) Learning Wks.
Bogaerts, Gert, jt. auth. see Bogaerts, Rascal.
Bogaerts, Rascal & Bogaerts, Gert. Socrates. LC 92-24120. 1993. 14.95 (*0-8118-0314-7*) Chronicle Bks.
Bogan, Rachel, ed. see Hughes, Barb.
Bogard, Vicki, tr. from FRE. Monkeys, Apes & Other Primates. Wallis, Diz, illus. LC 89-5378. 38p. (gr. k-5). 1989. 4.95 (*0-944589-26-X*, 026) Young Discovery Lib.
Bogard, Vicki, tr. see Barbey, Dorine.
Bogard, Vicki, tr. see Brice, Raphaelle.
Bogard, Vicki, tr. see Busuttil, Joelle.
Bogard, Vicki, tr. see Costa de Beauregard, Diane.
Bogard, Vicki, tr. see Courtault, Martine.
Bogard, Vicki, tr. see De Beauregard, Diane C.
Bogard, Vicki, tr. see Dievart, Roger.
Bogard, Vicki, tr. see Fontanel, Beatrice.
Bogard, Vicki, tr. see Gandiol-Coppin, Brigitte.
Bogard, Vicki, tr. see Henry-Biabaud, Chantal.
Bogard, Vicki, tr. see Krafft, Maurice.
Bogard, Vicki, tr. see Laurencin, Genevieve.
Bogard, Vicki, tr. see Lazier, Christine.
Bogard, Vicki, tr. see Limousin, Odile & Neumann, Daniele.
Bogard, Vicki, tr. see Morel, Gaud.
Bogard, Vicki, tr. see Pfeffer, Pierre.
Bogard, Vicki, tr. see Prot, Viviane A.
Bogard, Vicki, tr. see Riquier, Aline.
Bogard, Vicki, tr. see Tordjman, Nathalie.
Bogard, Vicki, tr. see Verdat, Jean-Pierre.
Bogart. Ten for Dinner. 1993. pap. 28.67 (*0-590-73173-4*) Scholastic Inc.
Bogart, Ann, photos by. Thinking Green: My Home. (Illus.). 24p. (ps-k). 1993. 3.98 (*0-8317-2530-3*) Smithmark.
—Thinking Green: My Neighborhood. (Illus.). 24p. (ps-k). 1993. 3.98 (*0-8317-2529-X*) Smithmark.
Bogart, Jeffrey, ed. see Richards, R. W.
Bogart, Jo-Ellen. Daniel's Dog. Wilson, Janet, illus. 1992. pap. 3.95 (*0-590-43401-2*, Blue Ribbon Bks) Scholastic Inc.
Bogart, Max see Stuart, Jesse.
Boggs, Juanita, jt. auth. see Strand, Julie.
Bogot, Howard. Yoni. (ps). 1982. pap. 4.00 (*0-8074-0166-8*, 101980) UAHC.
Bogot, Howard & Orkand, Robert. Hagadah Shel Pesah: A Passover Haggadah. LC 93-21340. 1993. 9.95 (*0-88123-059-6*); write for info. (*0-88123-060-X*) Central Conf.
Bogot, Howard & Syme, Daniel. My Body Is Something Special. (Illus.). (ps). 1982. pap. 4.00 (*0-8074-0152-8*, 101715) UAHC.
—Prayer Is Reaching. Ruthen, Marlene L., illus. 32p. (ps). 1982. text ed. 4.00 (*0-8074-0172-2*, 101230) UAHC.
Bogot, Howard & Syme, Daniel B. I Learn about God. Ruthen, Marlene L., illus. 32p. (ps). 1982. pap. 4.00 (*0-8074-0159-5*, 101970) UAHC.
Bogot, Howard, jt. auth. see Kipper, Lenore.
Bogot, Howard, jt. auth. see Syme, Daniel.
Bogot, Howard I. My First One Hundred Hebrew Words: A Young Person's Dictionary of Judaism. Carmi, Giora, illus. (gr. k-3). 1993. 11.95 (*0-8074-0509-4*, 101716) UAHC.
Bograd, Larry. The Fourth-Grade Dinosaur Club. Lauter, Richard, illus. LC 88-22876. (gr. 3 up). 1989. 13.95 (*0-440-50128-8*) Delacorte.
—Poor Gertie. Zimmer, Dirk, illus. LC 86-3091. 96p. (gr. 3-6). 1986. pap. 12.95 (*0-385-29487-5*) Delacorte.
Bogus, SDiane A., ed. The Poetry Workbook: A Poet's Workbook. 3rd, rev. ed. 25p. (gr. 11-12). 1991. pap. 10.00 (*0-934172-20-X*) WIM Pubns.
Bohatta, Ida. Day with Heinzel. (Illus.). (ps-3). 1992. 4.00 (*0-86724-008-3*) W J Fantasy.
—Flipp & Flir. (Illus.). (ps-3). 1992. 4.00 (*0-86724-017-2*) W J Fantasy.
—Heinzel the Innkeeper. (Illus.). (ps-3). 1992. 4.00 (*0-86724-003-2*) W J Fantasy.
—Ice Men. (Illus.). (ps-3). 1992. 4.00 (*0-86724-021-0*) W J Fantasy.
—The Little Advent Book. (Illus.). (ps-3). 1992. 4.00 (*1-56021-139-3*) W J Fantasy.
—Little Men Underground. (Illus.). (ps-3). 1992. 4.00 (*0-86724-019-9*) W J Fantasy.
—Saint Nicholas. (Illus.). (ps-3). 1992. 4.00 (*0-86724-024-5*) W J Fantasy.
—Winter House. (Illus.). (ps-3). 1992. 4.00 (*0-86724-023-7*) W J Fantasy.
Bohl, Al. Zaanan: Fatal Limit. Bohl, Al, illus. 224p. (gr. 4-8). 1989. pap. text ed. 2.50 (*1-55748-101-6*) Barbour & Co.
—Zaanan: The Dream of Delasor. (Illus.). 224p. (gr. 3 up). 1990. pap. 2.50 (*1-55748-124-5*) Barbour & Co.
—Zaanan: The Ransom of Renaissance. (Illus.). 224p. (gr. 9-12). 1990. pap. text ed. 2.50 (*1-55748-136-9*) Barbour & Co.

Bohlke, Dorothee. Cokolina & the Wild Island. Max, Jill & Bradford, Elizabeth, eds. Verlag, Mangold, tr. Bohlke, Dorothee, illus. LC 91-24337. 24p. (gr. k-3). 1991. PLB 14.60 (*1-56074-032-9*) Garrett Ed Corp.
—Mr. Chang & the Yellow Robe. Bradford, Elizabeth, ed. Verlag, Mangold, tr. from GER. Bohlke, Dorothee, illus. LC 91-21303. 32p. (gr. k-3). 1991. PLB 14.60 (*1-56074-029-9*) Garrett Ed Corp.
Bohn, Raymond J., jt. auth. see Wool, John D.
Bohner, Charles. Bold Journey: West with Lewis & Clark. LC 84-19328. (Illus.). 171p. (gr. 5 up). 1985. 13.45 (*0-395-36691-7*); pap. 4.80 (*0-395-54978-7*) HM.
Boholm-Olsson, Eva. Tuan. Van Don, Pham, illus. Jonasson, Dianne, tr. (Illus.). 32p. (ps up). 1988. 11.95 (*91-29-58766-2*, R & S Bks) FS&G.
Bohonek, Jan B. & Bohonek, Stan B. How Peter Molar Looked for a Smile. Bohonek, Jan & Bohonek, Stan B., illus. Johnsen, David C. LC 83-73507. 32p. (gr. 1-3). 1984. PLB 9.95 (*0-914827-00-6*) Adonis Studio.
Bohonek, Stan B., jt. auth. see Bohonek, Jan B.
Boice, Tara. If You Find a Baby Bird: How to Protect & Care for Wild Baby Birds. 36p. (gr. 4-9). 1992. pap. 7.95 (*0-9631916-0-8*) Seawind Pub.
Boies, Janice. Heart & Soul. 192p. (gr. 7 up). 1988. pap. 2.50 (*0-553-26949-6*) Bantam.
—Just the Way You Are. 176p. (Orig.). (gr. 7-12). 1986. pap. 2.50 (*0-553-25815-X*) Bantam.
—Love on Strike. (gr. 9-12). 1990. pap. 2.75 (*0-553-28633-1*) Bantam.
—Wright Boy, Wrong Girl. LC 88-91249. 186p. (gr. 6 up). 1989. pap. 2.95 (*0-8041-0239-2*) Ivy Books.
Boiko, Claire. Children's Plays for Creative Actors. 384p. (gr. 3-7). 1985. pap. 15.00 (*0-8238-0267-1*) Plays.
Boileau, Michele, tr. see Taylor, C. J.
Boileau, Michele, tr. see Zeman, Ludmila.
Bois, William P. du see Du Bois, William P.
Bois, William Pene Du see Pene Du Bois, William.
Bois, William Pene Du see Pene du Bois, William.
Boivin, Kelly. What's in a Box? Skivington, Janice, illus. LC 91-4062. 32p. (ps-2). 1991. PLB 11.93 (*0-516-02010-2*); pap. 2.95 (*0-516-42010-0*) Childrens.
—Where Is Mittens? Martin, Clovis, illus. LC 90-2220. 32p. (ps-2). 1990. PLB 11.93 (*0-516-02060-9*); pap. 2.95 (*0-516-42060-7*) Childrens.
Bokich, Obren. Christmas Card for Mr. McFizz. (Illus.). 40p. (gr. k-6). 1991. 11.95 (*0-88138-097-0*, Green Tiger) S&S Trade.
Bolam, Emily, illus. House That Jack Built. LC 91-40927. 32p. (gr. k up). 1993. 14.00 (*0-525-44972-8*, DCB) Dutton Child Bks.
Boland, Charles M. Ring in the Jubilee: The Story of America's Liberty Bell. LC 72-80407. (Illus.). 96p. (gr. 6 up). 1973. pap. 5.95 (*0-85699-055-8*) Chatham Pr.
Boland, Janice. Annabel. Halsey, Megan, illus. LC 91-46490. 32p. (ps-2). 1993. 12.99 (*0-8037-1254-5*); PLB 12.89 (*0-8037-1255-3*) Dial Bks Young.
Bolch, Judy, ed. see Goldstein, Helen H.
Bold, Ethan. The Flip Chart of Good Grammar. Bold, Mary, ed. (Illus.). 20p. (Orig.). (gr. 4-7). 1993. pap. 10.00 (*0-938267-08-6*) Bold Prodns.
—The Flip Chart of Math Tips. Bold, Mary, ed. 20p. (Orig.). (gr. 6-7). 1992. pap. 10.00 (*0-938267-09-4*) Bold Prodns.
Bold, Mary. How to Improve Your Mind over Summer Vacation. Small, Carol B., illus. 65p. (gr. 4-6). 1987. wkbk. 6.95 (*0-938267-05-1*) Bold Prodns.
—Publish Your Own Book: A Resource Book for Young Authors. Small, Carol B., illus. LC 86-91615. 36p. (Orig.). (gr. 5 up). 1986. pap. 6.95 (*0-938267-02-7*) Bold Prodns.
Bold, Mary, jt. auth. see Brown, Ann.
Bold, Mary, ed. see Bold, Ethan.
Bold, Mary, ed. see Pugh, Ann, et al.
Bolden, Tonya, jt. auth. see Higginsen, Vy.
Bolden, Tonya, ed. Rites of Passage: Stories about Growing up by Black Writers from Around the World. Johnson, Charles, frwd. by. LC 93-31304. 1993. 16.95 (*1-56282-688-3*) Hyprn Child.
Boldorini, Maria G., illus. My First Bible. 12p. (ps-1). 1994. 6.99 (*0-679-85621-8*) Random Bks Yng Read.
Boldt, Jeanine, jt. ed. see Jones, Michael P.
Boldt, Jeanine see Jones, Michael P.
Boles, Lisa P., et al. Just the Facts: A Guide to Teenage Health Issues. Moriarty, Nancy, ed. (Illus.). 54p. (Orig.). (gr. 9-12). 1990. pap. 5.00 (*0-9627714-0-6*) MMI Pubns.
Bolger, William F., intro. by. All about Letters. Rev. ed. LC 82-600601. (Illus.). 64p. (gr. 9-12). 1982. pap. 2.50x (*0-685-06202-3*, 01135) USPS.
—P. S. Write Soon! All about Letters. LC 82-600641. (Illus.). 64p. (Orig.). (gr. 4-8). 1982. pap. 2.50x (*0-8141-3796-2*, 37962) USPS.
Bolick, Nancy, jt. auth. see Randolph, Sallie.
Bolick, Nancy O. & Randolph, Sallie G. Shaker Villages. LoTurco, Laura, illus. LC 92-34587. 96p. (gr. 5 up). 1993. 12.95 (*0-8027-8209-4*); PLB 13.85 (*0-8027-8210-8*) Walker & Co.
Bolinske, Janet L., ed. Big Bug Big Book Package, 6 bks. (Illus.). (gr. k-1). 1987. Set of 6 bks., 24 pgs. ea. bk. spiral bdg. 80.00 (*0-88335-760-7*) Milliken Pub Co.
—Big Bug Softcover Package. (Illus., Orig.). (gr. k-1). 1989. Set of 6 bks., 24 pgs. ea. bk. pap. 27.00 (*0-88335-539-6*) Milliken Pub Co.
—Children's Classics Big Book Package, 6 bks. (Illus.). (gr. 1-3). 1987. Set of 6 bks., 32 pgs. ea. bk. spiral bdg. 80.00 (*0-88335-540-X*) Milliken Pub Co.

—Children's Classics Hardcover Package, 18 bks. (Illus., Orig.). (gr. 1-3). 1987. Set, 32p. ea. 145.00 (*0-88335-550-7*) Milliken Pub Co.
—Children's Classics Softcover Package, 18 bks. (Illus., Orig.). (gr. 1-3). 1987. Set, 32p. ea. pap. 80.00 (*0-88335-570-1*) Milliken Pub Co.
Bolinske, Janet L., ed. see Christian, Mary B.
Bolinske, Janet L., jt. ed. see Dolan, Ellen M.
Bolinske, Janet L., ed. see Kaplan, Carol B.
Bolkosky, Sidney, jt. auth. see Lipson, Greta.
Boll. Die Erzahlungen. (Illus.). pap. 5.95 (*0-88436-108-X*, 45275) EMC.
Bollen, Roger, jt. auth. see Sadler, Marilyn.
Bollendorf, Robert. Sober Spring. LC 91-17474. 176p. 1991. pap. 5.99 (*0-8066-2539-2*, 9-2539) Augsburg Fortress.
Bolliger, Max. Three Little Bears. Wilkon, Jozef, illus. (ps-3). 1987. 12.95 (*1-55774-006-2*) Modan-Adama Bks.
Bolognese, Don. Drawing Horses & Foals. (ps-3). 1990. pap. 3.95 (*0-531-15200-6*) Watts.
—Drawing Spaceships & Other Spacecraft. (ps-3). 1990. pap. 3.95 (*0-531-15201-4*) Watts.
Bolognese, Don & Raphael, Elaine. Drawing America: The Story of the First Thanksgiving. 32p. 1991. 10.95 (*0-590-44373-9*, Scholastic Hardcover) Scholastic Inc.
—The Way to Draw & Color Dinosaurs. Bolognese, Don & Raphael, Elaine, illus. LC 90-8636. 48p. (Orig.). (gr. 1-7). 1991. lib. bdg. 10.99 (*0-679-90477-8*); pap. 6.00 (*0-679-80477-3*) Random Bks Yng Read.
—The Way to Draw & Color Monsters. Bolognese, Don & Raphael, Elaine, illus. LC 90-8637. 48p. (Orig.). (gr. 1-7). 1991. lib. bdg. 10.99 (*0-679-90478-6*); pap. 5.99 (*0-679-80478-1*) Random Bks Yng Read.
Bolognese, Don, jt. auth. see Raphael, Elaine.
Bolt, Bruce A. Discover Volcanoes & Earthquakes. (Illus.). 48p. (gr. 3-6). 1992. PLB 14.95 (*1-56674-031-2*, HTS Bks) Forest Hse.
Bolt, Stephen, jt. auth. see Jensen, Antony.
Bolte, Carl E., Jr. Elvin: The Little Black Elf. Turner, Vernon K., ed. LC 87-28960. 150p. (Orig.). 1988. pap. 8.95 (*0-89865-554-4*) Donning Co.
Bolton, Clyde. Ivy. (ps-12). 1986. pap. 3.95 (*0-87067-832-9*, BH832) Holloway.
Bolton, Elizabeth. Case of the Wacky Cat. Harvey, Paul, illus. LC 84-8725. 48p. (gr. 2-4). 1985. PLB 10.89 (*0-8167-0400-7*); pap. text ed. 3.50 (*0-8167-0401-5*) Troll Assocs.
—Ghost in the House. Burns, Ray, illus. LC 84-20530. 48p. (gr. 2-4). 1985. PLB 10.89 (*0-8167-0418-X*); pap. 3.50 (*0-8167-0419-8*) Troll Assocs.
—Secret of the Ghost Piano. Fiammenghi, Gioia, illus. LC 84-8745. 48p. (gr. 2-4). 1985. PLB 10.89 (*0-8167-0410-4*); pap. text ed. 3.50 (*0-8167-0411-2*) Troll Assocs.
—Secret of the Magic Potion. Sims, Blanche, illus. LC 84-8881. 48p. (gr. 2-4). 1985. PLB 10.89 (*0-8167-0420-1*); pap. text ed. 3.50 (*0-8167-0421-X*) Troll Assocs.
—The Tree House Detective Club. Schindler, S. D., illus. LC 84-8762. 48p. (gr. 2-4). 1985. PLB 10.89 (*0-8167-0404-X*); pap. text ed. 3.50 (*0-8167-0405-8*) Troll Assocs.
Bolton, Jane. My Grandmother's Patchwork Quilt: A Book & Portfolio of Patchwork Pieces. LC 93-17279. 1994. 17.95 (*0-385-31155-9*) Doubleday.
Bolton, Jonathan, jt. auth. see Wilson, Claire.
Bolton, Jonathan W. & Wilson, Claire M. Scholars, Writers, & Professionals. LC 93-31683. 1994. write for info. (*0-8160-2896-6*) Facts on File.
Bolton, Linda. Hidden Pictures. LC 92-10528. 1993. 14.99 (*0-8037-1378-9*) Dial Bks Young.
Bolton, Martha. Humorous Monologues. LC 88-25977. (Illus.). 128p. 1990. pap. 4.95 (*0-8069-6751-X*) Sterling.
—T. V. Jokes & Riddles. LC 91-25297. (Illus.). 96p. (gr. 3-10). 1991. 12.95 (*0-8069-7244-0*) Sterling.
—TV Jokes & Riddles. Sinclair, Jeff, illus. LC 91-25297. 96p. 1992. pap. 3.95 (*0-8069-7246-7*) Sterling.
—What's Growing under Your Bed? Date not set. 7.95 (*0-685-68720-1*, BCMP-634) Lillenas.
Bolton, Mimi D. Merry-Go-Round Family. 2nd ed. (Illus.). 225p. (gr. 3-7). 1990. Repr. of 1954 ed. 14.95x (*0-9614274-2-6*) Wisla Pubs.
Boltz, C. W. How Electricity Is Made. (Illus.). 32p. (gr. 7 up). 12.95x (*0-8160-0039-5*) Facts on File.
Boluch, Kathleen A. Julia's World, Pt. 1: Better Times. Christiansen, Lee & Selwyn, Paul, illus. 58p. 1990. 14.95 (*0-9626365-0-9*) Swarovski Amer Ltd.
Bomans, Godfried. Eric in the Land of the Insects. Kornblith, Regina L., tr. from DUT. LC 93-24071. 1994. write for info. (*0-395-65231-6*) HM.
Bombarde, Odile. The Barbarians. Grant, Donald, illus. LC 87-34092. 38p. (gr. k-5). 1988. 4.95 (*0-944589-10-3*, 103) Young Discovery Lib.
Bombarde, Odile & Moatti, Claude. Living in Ancient Rome. Matthews, Sarah, tr. from FRE. Place, Francois, illus. LC 87-37113. 38p. (gr. k-5). 1988. 4.95 (*0-944589-08-1*, 081) Young Discovery Lib.
—Living in Ancient Rome. Place, Francois, illus. 40p. (gr. k-5). 1993. PLB 9.95 (*1-56074-060-6*, HTS Bks) Forest Hse.
Bombardem, Odile. Glory That Was Greece. (ps-3). 1994. 4.95 (*0-944589-46-4*) Young Discovery Lib.
Bombaugh, Ruth. Science Fair Success. LC 89-7798. (Illus.). 96p. (gr. 6 up). 1990. lib. bdg. 16.95 (*0-89490-197-4*) Enslow Pubs.

Bomer, John M., tr. from FRE. A Child's Life of Jesus. Napoli, Lizzi, illus. LC 89-81355. 40p. (Orig.). (ps-2). 1990. 8.95 (*0-87793-415-0*) Ave Maria.

Bonafoux, Pascal. A Weekend with Rembrandt. LC 91-40507. (Illus.). 64p. (gr. 1-6). 1992. 19.95 (*0-8478-1441-6*) Rizzoli Intl.

Bonagurio, Susan. Animal Count. Tunmore, Gary, ed. Bonagurio, Susan, illus. 22p. (ps). 1991. 12.95 (*0-924649-09-7*); PLB 15.95 (*0-924649-08-9*); pap. text ed. 9.95 (*0-685-48844-6*) Scribblers Pub.

Bonar, Veronica & Daniel, Jamie, eds. Coping with--Food Trash. Kenyon, Tony, illus. LC 93-32478. 1994. write for info. (*0-8368-1056-2*) Gareth Stevens Inc.

Bond, jt. auth. see Castillo.

Bond, Alan & Bond, Jill, eds. Our Planet, His Creation. (Illus.). 112p. (Orig.). (gr. k-12). 1992. pap. 5.00 (*0-9631992-2-6*) Bonding Place.

Bond, Felicia. The Chicks' Christmas. LC 82-45918. (Illus.). 32p. (ps-3). 1988. 4.95 (*0-694-00156-2*, Crowell Jr Bks) HarpC Child Bks.

—Four Valentines in a Rainstorm. Bond, Felicia, illus. LC 82-45586. 32p. (gr. k-3). 1990. pap. 3.95 (*0-06-443216-5*, Trophy) HarpC Child Bks.

—The Halloween Performance. Bond, Felicia, illus. LC 82-45920. 32p. (ps-3). 1987. pap. 4.95 (*0-06-443155-X*, Trophy) HarpC Child Bks.

—Poinsettia & Her Family. Bond, Felicia, illus. LC 81-43035. 32p. (ps-3). 1981. PLB 13.89 (*0-690-04145-4*, Crowell Jr Bks) HarpC Child Bks.

—Poinsettia & Her Family. Bond, Felicia, illus. LC 81-43035. 32p. (ps-3). 1985. pap. 4.95i (*0-06-443076-6*, Trophy) HarpC Child Bks.

—Poinsettia & the Firefighters. LC 83-46169. (Illus.). 32p. (ps-3). 1984. PLB 15.89 (*0-690-04401-1*, Crowell Jr Bks) HarpC Child Bks.

—Poinsettia & the Firefighters. Bond, Felicia, illus. LC 83-46169. 32p. (ps-3). 1988. pap. 4.95 (*0-06-443160-6*, Trophy) HarpC Child Bks.

Bond, Jill, jt. ed. see Bond, Alan.

Bond, Larry. Data Annex Upgrade. Venters, Steve, illus. 136p. (Orig.). 1990. pap. 10.00 (*1-55878-053-X*) Game Designers.

Bond, Michael. Bear Called Paddington. Fortnum, Peggy, illus. LC 60-9096. 128p. (gr. 3-7). 1968. pap. 3.50 (*0-440-40483-5*, YB) Dell.

—Bear Called Paddington. Fortnum, Peggy, illus. 128p. (gr. 1-5). 1960. 13.45 (*0-395-06390-8*) HM.

—The Caravan Puppets. Julian-Ottie, Vanessa, illus. LC 85-109047. 130p. (gr. 3 up). 1983. write for info. (*0-00-184135-1*) Harper SF.

—The Hilarious Adventures of Paddington, 5 bks. Incl. A Bear Called Paddington; More about Paddington; Paddington at Large; Paddington at Work; Paddington Helps Out. (Illus.). 1986. Boxed set. pap. 14.75 (*0-440-43668-0*) Dell.

—More about Paddington. Fortnum, Peggy, illus. (gr. 4-6). 1962. 13.45 (*0-395-06640-9*) HM.

—More about Paddington. large type ed. Fortnum, Peggy, illus. 176p. (gr. 8-12). 1991. 13.95 (*0-7451-1297-8*, Galaxy Child Lrg Print) Chivers N Amer.

—Paddington Abroad. Fortnum, Peggy, illus. 128p. (gr. 2-6). 1992. pap. 3.25 (*0-440-47352-7*, YB) Dell.

—Paddington Abroad. Fortnum, Peggy, illus. LC 72-2753. 128p. (gr. 1-5). 1973. 14.45 (*0-395-14331-4*) HM.

—Paddington Abroad. large type ed. Fortnum, Peggy, illus. 168p. 1992. 13.95 (*0-7451-1547-0*, Galaxy Lrg Print) Chivers N Amer.

—Paddington at Large. Fortnum, Peggy, illus. 128p. (gr. 3-7). 1970. pap. 2.95 (*0-440-46801-9*, YB) Dell.

—Paddington at Large. (Illus.). (gr. 1-5). 1963. 13.95 (*0-395-06641-7*) HM.

—Paddington at Large. large type ed. Fortnum, Peggy, illus. 168p. 1993. 13.95 (*0-7451-1657-4*, Galaxy Lrg Print) Chivers N Amer.

—Paddington at the Circus. Lobban, John, illus. LC 91-44210. 32p. (ps-2). 1992. 8.95 (*0-694-00415-4*, Festival) HarpC Child Bks.

—Paddington at the Seashore. Lobban, John, illus. 28p. (ps). 1992. 2.95 (*0-694-00397-2*) HarpC Child Bks.

—Paddington at Work. 128p. (gr. k-8). 1971. pap. 2.95 (*0-440-40797-4*, YB) Dell.

—Paddington at Work. Fortnum, Peggy, illus. LC 67-20372. (gr. 1-5). 1967. 13.95 (*0-395-06637-9*) HM.

—Paddington Bear. Lobban, John, illus. LC 91-29781. 32p. (ps-3). 1992. 8.95 (*0-694-00394-8*) HarpC Child Bks.

—Paddington Book & Bear Box. (Illus.). 32p. (ps-1). 1993. incl. plush toy 16.95 (*0-670-84683-X*) Viking Child Bks.

—Paddington Goes Shopping. Lobban, John, illus. 28p. (ps). 1992. 2.95 (*0-694-00395-6*) HarpC Child Bks.

—Paddington Goes to Town. 128p. (gr. 2-5). 1992. pap. 3.25 (*0-440-46793-4*, YB) Dell.

—Paddington Goes to Town. Fortnum, Peggy, illus. LC 68-28043. (gr. 1-5). 1977. 14.95 (*0-395-06635-2*) HM.

—Paddington Helps Out. Fortnum, Peggy, illus. 128p. (gr. 3-7). 1982. pap. 2.95 (*0-440-46802-7*, YB) Dell.

—Paddington Helps Out. Fortnum, Peggy, illus. (gr. 4-6). 1973. 13.45 (*0-395-06639-5*) HM.

—Paddington Helps Out. large type ed. (gr. 1-8). 1991. 13.95 (*0-7451-1426-1*, Galaxy Child Lrg Print) Chivers N Amer.

—Paddington in the Kitchen. Lobban, John, illus. 28p. (ps). 1992. 2.95 (*0-694-00396-4*) HarpC Child Bks.

—Paddington Marches On. (Illus.). (gr. 4-6). 1965. 13.45 (*0-395-06642-5*) HM.

—Paddington Marches On. (gr. 4-7). 1991. pap. 3.25 (*0-440-46799-3*) Dell.

—Paddington Marches On. large type ed. Fortnum, Peggy, illus. 1993. 15.95 (*0-7451-1806-2*, Galaxy Child Lrg Print) Chivers N Amer.

—Paddington Meets the Queen. Lobban, John, illus. LC 92-24938. 32p. (ps-3). 1993. 3.95 (*0-694-00460-X*, Festival) HarpC Child Bks.

—Paddington on Screen. Macey, Barry, illus. (gr. 2-5). 1982. 14.45 (*0-395-32950-7*) HM.

—Paddington on Screen. (gr. k-6). 1992. pap. 3.25 (*0-440-40029-5*, YB) Dell.

—Paddington on Stage. (gr. 4-7). 1992. pap. 3.25 (*0-440-46846-9*, YB) Dell.

—Paddington on Top. Fortnum, Peggy, illus. 128p. (gr. 1-5). 1975. 13.95 (*0-395-21897-7*) HM.

—Paddington on Top. 1991. pap. 3.25 (*0-440-46818-3*) Dell.

—Paddington Rides On! Lobban, John, illus. LC 92-24937. 32p. (ps-3). 1993. 3.95 (*0-694-00461-8*, Festival) HarpC Child Bks.

—Paddington Takes a Bath. Lobban, John, illus. 28p. (ps). 1992. 2.95 (*0-694-00398-0*) HarpC Child Bks.

—Paddington Takes the Air. 128p. (gr. 2-6). 1991. pap. 3.25 (*0-440-47321-7*, YB) Dell.

—Paddington Takes the Air. Fortnum, Peggy, illus. LC 78-147902. (gr. 3-7). 1971. 14.45 (*0-395-10909-4*) HM.

—Paddington Takes the Test. (Illus.). (gr. 3-6). 1980. 13.45 (*0-395-29519-X*) HM.

—Paddington Takes the Test. 128p. (gr. k-6). 1982. 1.95 (*0-440-47021-8*, YB) Dell.

—Paddington Takes to TV. Wood, Ivor, illus. 128p. (gr. 1-5). 1974. 14.45 (*0-395-19881-X*) HM.

—Paddington Takes to TV. (gr. 4-7). 1991. pap. 3.25 (*0-440-45930-3*) Dell.

—Paddington's ABC. (ps-3). 1991. 10.99 (*0-670-84104-8*) Viking Child Bks.

—Paddington's Colors. Lobban, John, illus. 32p. (ps-1). 1991. 10.99 (*0-670-84102-1*) Viking Child Bks.

—Paddington's Garden. Lobban, John, illus. LC 92-24527. 32p. (ps-3). 1993. 8.95 (*0-694-00462-6*, Festival) HarpC Child Bks.

—Paddington's Magical Christmas. Lobban, John, illus. 32p. (ps-3). 1993. 8.95 (*0-694-00503-7*, Festival) HarpC Child Bks.

—Paddington's Opposites. (ps-3). 1991. 10.95 (*0-670-84105-6*) Viking Child Bks.

—Paddington's-Pop Up. 1989. 9.95 (*0-8167-0900-9*) Troll Assocs.

—Paddington's Storybook. Fortnum, Peggy, illus. 160p. (gr. 1-5). 1984. 16.45 (*0-395-36667-4*) HM.

—Paddington's 1 2 3. (ps-3). 1991. 10.99 (*0-670-84103-X*) Viking Child Bks.

—The Tales of Olga da Polga. Helweg, Hans, illus. LC 88-31444. 128p. (gr. 3-7). 1989. Repr. of 1973 ed. SBE 13.95 (*0-02-711731-6*, Macmillan Child Bk) Macmillan Child Grp.

Bond, Michael, jt. auth. see Bradley, Alfred.

Bond, Michael, compiled by. Michael Bond's Book of Bears. LC 92-14120. (Illus.). 144p. (ps-12). 1992. SBE 16.95 (*0-689-71649-4*, Aladdin) Macmillan Child Grp.

Bond, Nancy. Another Shore. LC 87-3907. 320p. (gr 7 up). 1988. SBE 16.95 (*0-689-50463-2*, M K McElderry) Macmillan Child Grp.

—A Place to Come Back To. LC 83-48745. 204p. (gr 7 up). 1984. SBE 15.95 (*0-689-50302-4*, M K McElderry) Macmillan Child Grp.

—A String in the Harp. LC 75-28181. 384p. (gr. 4-8). 1976. SBE 15.95 (*0-689-50036-X*, M K McElderry) Macmillan Child Grp.

—A String on the Harp. (gr. 5-9). 1987. pap. 5.99 (*0-14-032376-7*, Puffin) Puffin Bks.

—Truth to Tell. LC 93-11248. 336p. (gr. 5 up). 1994. SBE 17.95 (*0-689-50601-5*, M K McElderry) Macmillan.

—The Voyage Begun. LC 81-3481. 336p. (gr. 7 up). 1981. SBE 16.95 (*0-689-50204-4*, M K McElderry) Macmillan Child Grp.

Bond, Reed. Betsy's Butter. Bond, Reed, illus. 16p. (Orig.). (gr. 1-3). 1992. pap. 4.50 (*0-9631992-1-8*) Bonding Place.

Bond, Ruskin. Cherry Tree. Eitzen, Allan, illus. LC 90-85731. 32p. (ps-3). 1991. 14.95 (*1-878093-21-5*) Boyds Mills Pr.

—Grandfather's Private Zoo. (Illus.). 95p. (gr. 3-5). 1.00 (*0-88253-345-2*) Ind-US Inc.

—The Hidden Pool. Das, Arup, illus. 64p. (Orig.). (gr. k-3). 1980. pap. 2.75 (*0-89744-211-3*, Pub. by Childrens Bk Trust IA) Auromere.

—Tales Told at Twilight. 166p. (gr. 4-6). 1970. 1.25 (*0-88253-394-0*) Ind-US Inc.

Bond, Victor. Ride with Me Through ABC. Lemke, Horst, illus. LC 67-19376. 32p. (ps-k). 6.95 (*0-87592-043-8*) Scroll Pr.

Bondar, Barbara & Bondar, Roberta. On the Shuttle: Eight Days in Space. 64p. Date not set. PLB 16.95 (*1-895688-12-4*, Pub. by Greey dePencier CN); pap. 8.95 (*1-895688-10-8*, Pub. by Greey dePencier CN) Firefly Bks Ltd.

Bondar, Roberta, jt. auth. see Bondar, Barbara.

Bone, Jan. Opportunities in Plastics Careers. LC 90-50732. 160p. (Orig.). (gr. 7-12). 1991. 13.95 (*0-8442-8673-7*, VGM Career Bks); pap. 10.95 (*0-8442-8674-5*, VGM Career Bks) NTC Pub Grp.

Boney, Lesley, illus. Cities. 48p. (gr. k-5). 1988. pap. 2.95 (*0-8431-2248-X*) Price Stern.

—Dinosaurs. 48p. (gr. k-5). 1988. pap. 2.95 (*0-8431-2245-5*) Price Stern.

—Space. 48p. (gr. k-5). 1988. pap. 2.95 (*0-8431-2247-1*) Price Stern.

—Wild Animals. 48p. (gr. k-5). 1988. pap. 2.95 (*0-8431-2246-3*) Price Stern.

Bonforte, Lisa. Fifty Favorite Birds-Coloring Book. 1983. pap. 2.95 (*0-486-24261-7*) Dover.

—I Can Draw Dinosaurs. (Illus.). 64p. (Orig.). (gr. 2-7). 1984. pap. 3.95 (*0-671-52756-8*, Little Simon) S&S Trade.

Bonham, Frank. Mystery of the Fat Cat. Smith, Alvin, illus. 160p. (gr. 5-9). 1971. pap. 1.25 (*0-440-46226-6*, YB) Dell.

Bonham, Tal D. The Treasury of Clean Jokes for Children. (Orig.). (gr. 1-6). 1987. pap. 3.95 (*0-8054-5721-6*) Broadman.

—The Treasury of Clean Teenage Jokes. LC 85-4134. (gr. 7 up). 1985. pap. 3.95 (*0-8054-5713-5*, 4257-13) Broadman.

Bonica, Diane. Biblical Easter & Spring Performances. (Illus.). 96p. (ps-2). 1989. 10.95 (*0-86653-478-4*, SS1869, Shining Star Pubns) Good Apple.

—Hand-Shaped Art. Renard, Jan, illus. 112p. (ps-2). 1989. wkbk. 9.95 (*0-86653-474-1*, GA1079) Good Apple.

—Hand-Shaped Gifts. 144p. (ps-4). 1991. 11.95 (*0-86653-612-4*, GA1331) Good Apple.

—Writing & Art Go Hand in Hand. 80p. (gr. 2-6). 1988. pap. text ed. 7.95 (*0-86530-068-2*, IP 13-2) Incentive Pubns.

Bonifer, Michael. The Making of Tron. Ellenshaw, Harrison, illus. 96p. (Orig.). (gr. 1-4). 1982. pap. 7.95 (*0-671-45575-3*) S&S Trade.

Bonilla, Jayne. If Hurricanes Were Candy Canes. Moss, Barbara, illus. 16p. (Orig.). (gr. k-6). 1992. pap. 4.95 (*0-9635105-0-9*) J R Bonilla.

Boning, R. D & W Supportive Reading Skills Series: Rhyme Time, 5 pts. large type ed. Incl. Bk. A1. (gr. 1); Bk. A2. 52p. (gr. 1). 6.18 (*0-317-02134-6*, 4-22490-00); Bk. A3. 56p. (gr. 1). 6.18 (*0-317-02135-4*, 4-22500-00). 1976. Am Printing Hse.

—Multiple Skills Series. large type ed. Incl. Set B, Nos. 1-4. 60p. (gr. 2). 9.87 ea. Bklet. 1 (4-32720-00) Bklet. 2 (4-32730-00) Bklet. 3 (4-32740-00) Bklet. 4 (4-32750-00); Set C, Nos. 1-4. 60p. (gr. 3). 9.87 ea. Bklet. 1 (4-32760-00) Bklet. 2 (4-32770-00) Bklet. 3 (4-32780-00) Bklet. 4 (4-32790-00); Set D, Nos. 1-4. 60p. (1977). (gr. 4). Booklet 1. 8.97 (*0-317-04461-3*, 4-32800-00); Booklet 2. 17.50 (*0-317-04462-1*, J-32810-00); Booklet 3. 16.50 (*0-317-04463-X*, J-32820-00); Booklet 4. 9.87 (*0-317-04464-8*, 4-32830-00); Set E, Nos. 1-4. 60p. (1976). (gr. 4). 9.87 ea. Bklet. 1 (4-32840-00) Bklet. 2 (4-32850-00) Bklet. 3 (4-32860-00) Bklet. 4 (4-32870-00); Set F, Nos. 1-4. 60p. (gr. 6). Bklet. 1. 16.00 (*0-317-03528-2*, J-32880-00). (gr. 2-9). 1980. Repr. Am Printing Hse.

—Specific Skill Series: Drawing Conclusions, 12 pts. 2nd, large type ed. Incl. Booklet A. 60p. (gr. 1). 1976. 16.50 (*0-317-04548-2*, J-32120-00); Booklet B. 60p. (gr. 2). 1979. 15.00 (*0-317-04549-0*, J-32130-00); Booklet C. 60p. (gr. 3). 1979. 15.00 (*0-317-04550-4*, J-32140-00); Booklet D. 60p. (gr. 4). 1976. 15.00 (*0-317-04551-2*, J-32150-00); Booklet E. 112p. (gr. 5). 1979. 28.00 (*0-317-04736-1*, J-32160-00); Booklet F. 112p. (gr. 6). 1979. 16.86 (*0-317-04553-9*, 4-32170-00); Booklet G. 112p. (gr. 7). 1979. 16.86 (*0-317-04554-7*, 4-32180-00); Booklet H. 112p. (gr. 8). 1979. 16.86 (*0-317-04555-5*, 4-32190-00); Booklet I. 112p. (gr. 9). 1979. 28.00 (*0-317-04556-3*, J-32200-00); Booklet J. 112p. (gr. 10). 1979. 16.86 (*0-317-04557-1*, 4-32210-00); Booklet K. 112p. (gr. 11). 1979. 16.86 (*0-317-04737-X*, 4-32220-00); Booklet L. 112p. (gr. 12). 1979. 16.86 (*0-317-04559-8*, 4-32230-00). (gr. 1-12) Am Printing Hse.

—Specific Skill Series: Following Directions, 12 pts. 2nd, large type ed. Incl. Booklet A. 112p. (gr. 1). 1979. 31.50 (*0-317-04560-1*, J-32240-00); Booklet B. 112p. (gr. 2). 1979. 28.00 (*0-317-04561-X*, J-32250-00); Booklet C. 112p. (gr. 3). 1980. 28.00 (*0-317-04562-8*, J-32260-00); Booklet D. 112p. (gr. 4). 1979. 28.00 (*0-317-04563-6*, J-32270-00); Booklet E. 112p. (gr. 5). 1979. 28.00 (*0-317-03631-9*, J-32280-00); Booklet F. 112p. (gr. 6). 1979. 16.86 (*0-317-03632-7*, 4-32290-00); Booklet G. 112p. (gr. 7). 1980. 16.86 (*0-317-03633-5*, 4-32300-00); Booklet H. 112p. (gr. 8). 1979. 16.86 (*0-317-03634-3*, 4-32310-00); Booklet I. 112p. (gr. 9). 1980. 16.86 (*0-317-03635-1*, 4-32320-00); Booklet J. 112p. (gr. 10). 1979. 16.86 (*0-317-03636-X*, 4-32330-00); Booklet K. 112p. (gr. 11). 1980. 16.86 (*0-317-03637-8*, 4-32340-00); Booklet L. 112p. (gr. 12). 1980. 16.86 (*0-317-03638-6*, 4-32350-00). (gr. 1-12) Am Printing Hse.

—Specific Skill Series: Getting the Facts, 12 pts. 2nd, large type ed. Incl. Booklet A. 60p. (gr. 1). 1976. 15.00 (0-317-03639-4, J-32360-00); Booklet B. 60p. (gr. 2). 1980. 15.00 (0-317-03640-8, J-32370-00); Booklet C. 60p. (gr. 3). 1980. 15.00 (0-317-03641-6, J-32380-00); Booklet D. 116p. (gr. 4). 1980. 28.50 (0-317-03642-4, J-32390-00); Booklet E. 116p. (gr. 5). 1980. 16.86 (0-317-03643-2, 4-32400-00); Booklet F. 116p. (gr. 6). 1980. 16.86 (0-317-03644-0, 4-32410-00); Booklet G. 116p. (gr. 7). 16.86 (0-317-03645-9, 4-32420-00); Booklet H. 116p. (gr. 8). 16.86 (0-317-03646-7, 4-32430-00); Booklet I. 116p. (gr. 9). 1980. 16.86 (0-317-03647-5, 4-32440-00); Booklet J. 116p. (gr. 10). 16.86 (0-317-03648-3, 4-32450-00); Booklet K. 116p. (gr. 11). 1980. 16.86 (0-317-03649-1, 4-32460-00); Booklet L. 116p. (gr. 12). 1980. 16.86 (0-317-02558-9, 4-32470-00). (gr. 1-12) Am Printing Hse.

—Specific Skill Series: Getting the Main Idea, 12 pts. 2nd, large type ed. Incl. Booklet A. 112p. (gr. 1). 1976. 31.50 (0-317-04564-4, J-32480-00); Booklet B. 60p. (gr. 2). 1979. 15.50 (0-317-04565-2, J-32490-00); Booklet C. 60p. (gr. 3). 1979. 15.00 (0-317-04738-8, J-32500-00); Booklet D. 60p. (gr. 4). 1979. 15.00 (0-317-04567-9, J-32510-00); Booklet E. 112p. (gr. 5). 1979. 16.86 (0-317-04568-7, 4-32520-00); Booklet F. 112p. (gr. 6). 1979. 16.86 (0-317-04569-5, 4-32530-00); Booklet G. 112p. (gr. 7). 1979. 16.86 (0-317-04570-9, 4-32540-00); Booklet H. 112p. (gr. 8). 1979. 16.86 (0-317-04739-6, 4-32550-00); Booklet I. 112p. (gr. 9). 1980. 16.86 (0-317-04572-5, 4-32560-00); Booklet J. 112p. (gr. 10). 1979. 16.86 (0-317-04573-3, 4-32570-00); Booklet K. 112p. (gr. 11). 1979. 16.86 (0-317-02570-8, 4-32590-00). (gr. 1-12) Am Printing Hse.

—Specific Skill Series: Locating the Answer, 12 pts. 2nd, large type ed. Incl. Booklet A. 60p. (gr. 1). 1980. 15.00 (0-317-03660-2, J-32600-00); Booklet B. 116p. (gr. 2). 1979. 29.00 (0-317-03661-0, J-32610-00); Booklet C. 116p. (gr. 3). 1980. 29.00 (0-317-03662-9, J-32620); Booklet D. 116p. (gr. 4). 1980. 16.86 (0-317-03663-7, 4-32630-00); Booklet E. 116p. (gr. 5). 1980. 16.86 (0-317-03664-5, 4-32640-00); Booklet F. 116p. (gr. 6). 1980; Booklet G. 116p. (gr. 7); Booklet H. 116p. (gr. 8); Booklet I. 116p. (gr. 9). 1980. 16.86 (0-317-03668-8, 4-32680-00); Booklet J. 116p. (gr. 10); Booklet K. 116p. (gr. 11); Booklet L. 116p. (gr. 12). (gr. 1-12) Am Printing Hse.

Bonner. Two-Way Pitcher. (gr. 7 up). PLB 7.19 (0-8313-0008-6) Lantern.

Bonner, Ann & Bonner, Roger. Earlybirds...Earlywords. LC 72-89449. (Illus.). 32p. (ps-2). 1973. 7.95 (0-87592-013-6) Scroll Pr.

Bonner, Darlene, ed. see Walsh, Jeff.

Bonner, Roger, jt. auth. see Bonner, Ann.

Bonner, Staci. Sports. LC 93-9887. (Illus.). 48p. (gr. 5-6). 1994. RSBE 14.95 (0-89686-789-7, Crestwood Hse) Macmillan Child Grp.

Bonners, Susan. Fragile Predator: The Lynx. LC 93-24975. (gr. 4 up). 1994. 14.95 (0-316-10201-6) Little.

—Just in Passing. Bonners, Susan, illus. LC 88-22021. 32p. (ps-2). 1989. 11.95 (0-688-07711-0); PLB 11.88 (0-688-07712-9) Lothrop.

—Panda. LC 78-50404. (Illus.). 32p. (ps-3). 1978. pap. 6.95 (0-385-28772-0); pap. 6.46 (0-385-28775-5) Delacorte.

—A Penguin Year. Bonners, Susan, illus. LC 79-53595. 48p. (ps-3). 1981. 11.95 (0-685-01398-7); PLB 12.95 (0-385-28022-X) Delacorte.

—Wooden Doll. (ps-3). 1991. 13.95 (0-688-08280-7) Lothrop.

—Wooden Doll. (ps-3). 1991. PLB 13.88 (0-688-08282-3) Lothrop.

Bonnet, Robert L. Computers: Forty-Nine Science Fair Projects. (Illus.). 160p. (gr. 4-7). 1990. 16.95 (0-8306-7524-8, 3524); pap. 9.95 (0-8306-3524-6) TAB Bks.

—Environmental Science: Forty-Nine Science Fair Projects. (Illus.). 160p. 1990. 17.95 (0-8306-7369-5); pap. 9.95 (0-8306-3369-3) TAB Bks.

Bonnet, Robert L. & Keen, G. Daniel. Botany: Forty-Nine More Science Fair Projects. (Illus.). 170p. (gr. 4-7). 1990. 16.95 (0-8306-7416-0, 3416); pap. 9.95 (0-8306-3416-9) TAB Bks.

—Space & Astronomy: Forty-Nine Science Fair Projects. 144p. 1991. 16.95 (0-8306-3939-X); pap. 9.95 (0-8306-3938-1) TAB Bks.

Bonnette, Charlotte A., ed. see Dennie, Joseph & Weathers, Joseph.

Bonnette, Jeanne. Three Friends. (ps-2). 1982. pap. 1.95 (0-89992-066-7) Coun India Ed.

Bonnici, Peter. Lost in Town. Kopper, Lisa, illus. 32p. (gr. k-2). 1990. 11.95 (0-340-48612-0, Pub. by Hodder & Stoughton UK) Trafalgar.

—The Special Event. Kopper, Lisa, illus. 32p. (gr. k-2). 1990. 11.95 (0-340-48609-0, Pub. by Hodder & Stoughton UK) Trafalgar.

—The Village Show. Kopper, Lisa, illus. 32p. (gr. k-2). 1990. 11.95 (0-340-48610-4, Pub. by Hodder & Stoughton UK) Trafalgar.

Bonnici, Roberta L. I'm Scared to Witness! Clore, Chuck, illus. 48p. (Orig.). (gr. 9-12). 1979. pap. 1.50 (0-88243-931-6, 02-0931); leader's guide 3.95 (0-88243-330-X, 02-0330) Gospel Pub.

—Your Right to Be Different. Clore, Chuck, illus. 48p. (gr. 9-12). 1982. pap. 1.50 (0-88243-842-5, 02-0842); leader's guide 3.95 (0-88243-333-4, 02-0333) Gospel Pub.

Bonniwell, William R. The Life of Blessed Margaret of Castello. LC 83-70524. 113p. (gr. 8). 1983. pap. 6.00 (0-89555-213-2) TAN Bks Pubs.

Bonno, Chris, jt. auth. see Deschaine, Scott.

Bonomi, Kathryn. Italy. (Illus.). 128p. (gr. 5 up). 1991. 14.95 (1-55546-752-0) Chelsea Hse.

Bonsall, Crosby. Amazing the Incredible Super Dog. LC 85-45811. (Illus.). 32p. (gr. k-3). 1986. PLB 14.89 (0-06-020591-1) HarpC Child Bks.

—And I Mean It, Stanley. LC 73-14324. (Illus.). 32p. (ps-1). 1984. pap. 3.50 (0-06-444046-X, Trophy) HarpC Child Bks.

—And I Mean It, Stanley. 32p. (ps-2). 1990. pap. 6.95 (1-55994-265-7, Caedmon) HarperAudio.

—The Case of the Cat's Meow. Bonsall, Crosby, illus. LC 65-11451. 64p. (gr. k-3). 1978. pap. 3.50 (0-06-444017-6, Trophy) HarpC Child Bks.

—The Case of the Double Cross. LC 80-7768. (Illus.). 64p. (gr. k-3). 1982. pap. 3.50 (0-06-444029-X, Trophy) HarpC Child Bks.

—The Case of the Dumb Bells. LC 66-8267. (Illus.). 64p. (gr. k-3). 1982. pap. 3.50 (0-06-444030-3, Trophy) HarpC Child Bks.

—The Case of the Hungry Stranger. newly illustrated ed. Bonsall, Crosby, illus. LC 91-14365. 64p. (gr. k-3). 1980. pap. 3.50 (0-06-444026-5, Trophy) HarpC Child Bks.

—The Case of the Scaredy Cats. LC 75-159039. (Illus.). 64p. (ps-3). 1984. pap. 3.50 (0-06-444047-8, Trophy) HarpC Child Bks.

—The Day I Had to Play with My Sister. Bonsall, Crosby, illus. LC 72-76507. 32p. (ps-2). pap. 3.50 (0-06-444117-2, Trophy) HarpC Child Bks.

—Mine's the Best. LC 72-9863. (Illus.). 32p. (gr. k-3). 1984. pap. 3.50 (0-06-444054-0, Trophy) HarpC Child Bks.

—Who's a Pest? Bonsall, Crosby, illus. LC 62-13310. 64p. (gr. k-3). 1986. pap. 3.50 (0-06-444099-0, Trophy) HarpC Child Bks.

—Who's Afraid of the Dark? Bonsall, Crosby, illus. LC 79-2700. 32p. (ps-2). 1985. pap. 3.50 (0-06-444071-0, Trophy) HarpC Child Bks.

Bonsall, Crosby N. And I Mean It, Stanley. LC 73-14324. (Illus.). 32p. (gr. k-3). 1974. PLB 13.89 (0-06-020568-7) HarpC Child Bks.

—Case of the Cat's Meow. Bonsall, Crosby N., illus. LC 65-11451. 64p. (gr. k-3). 1965. PLB 13.89 (0-06-020561-X) HarpC Child Bks.

—The Case of the Double Cross. (Illus.). 64p. (gr. k-3). 1980. PLB 13.89 (0-06-020603-9) HarpC Child Bks.

—Case of the Dumb Bells. Bonsall, Crosby N., illus. LC 66-8267. 64p. (gr. k-3). 1966. PLB 13.89 (0-06-020624-1) HarpC Child Bks.

—Case of the Hungry Stranger. newly illus. ed. Bonsall, Crosby N., illus. LC 91-13345. 64p. (gr. k-3). 1963. 13.00 (0-06-020570-9); PLB 12.89 (0-06-020571-7) HarpC Child Bks.

—Case of the Scaredy Cats. LC 75-159039. (Illus.). 64p. (gr. k-3). 1971. PLB 13.89 (0-06-020566-0) HarpC Child Bks.

—The Day I Had to Play with My Sister. Bonsall, Crosby N., illus. LC 72-76507. 32p. (ps-2). 1972. PLB 13.89 (0-06-020576-8) HarpC Child Bks.

—It's Mine: A Greedy Book. Bonsall, Crosby N., illus. LC 64-11839. 32p. (gr. k-3). 1964. PLB 13.89 (0-06-020586-5) HarpC Child Bks.

—Mine's the Best. Bonsall, Crosby, illus. LC 72-9863. 32p. (ps-2). 1973. PLB 13.89 (0-06-020578-4) HarpC Child Bks.

—Piggle. Bonsall, Crosby, illus. LC 73-5478. 64p. (gr. k-3). 1973. PLB 13.89 (0-06-020580-6) HarpC Child Bks.

—Tell Me Some More. Siebel, Fritz, illus. LC 61-5773. 64p. (gr. k-3). 1961. PLB 13.89 (0-06-020601-2) HarpC Child Bks.

—What Spot? Bonsall, Crosby N., illus. LC 63-8005. 64p. (gr. k-3). 1963. PLB 13.89 (0-06-020611-X) HarpC Child Bks.

—Who's a Pest? Bonsall, Crosby N., illus. LC 62-13310. 64p. (gr. k-3). 1962. PLB 13.89 (0-06-020621-7) HarpC Child Bks.

—Who's Afraid of the Dark? LC 79-2700. (Illus.). 32p. (ps-3). 1980. PLB 13.89 (0-06-020599-7) HarpC Child Bks.

Bonsignori, Martina. Baby Birds. Torriani, Graziella, illus. 18p. (ps-k). 1992. Set of 3 bks. bds. 11.95 (1-56397-158-5); bds. 3.95 (1-56397-153-4) Boyds Mills Pr.

Bontemps, Arna. Lonesome Boy. Topolski, Feliks, illus. LC 88-3434. 32p. (gr. k-3). 1988. pap. 4.95 (0-8070-8307-0, NL 2) Beacon Pr.

Bontemps, Arna & Hughes, Langston. Popo & Fifina. Campbell, E. Simms, illus. Rampersad, Arnold & Rampersad, Arnoldintro. by. (Illus.). 120p. 1993. jacketed 14.95 (0-19-508765-8) OUP.

Bonvicini, Joan. Women's Basketball Drills: General Drills. (Orig.). (gr. 7 up). 1988. pap. 6.95 (0-932741-59-2) Championship Bks & Vid Prodns.

Bonvillain, Nancy. The Haidas: People of the Northwest Coast. LC 93-34902. 1994. PLB write for info. (1-56294-491-6) Millbrook Pr.

—Hiawatha. (Illus.). 112p. (gr. 5 up). 1992. lib. bdg. 17.95 (0-7910-1707-9) Chelsea Hse.

—The Huron. (Illus.). 112p. (gr. 5 up). 1989. 17.95 (1-55546-708-3) Chelsea Hse.

—Mohawk. (Illus.). 112p. (gr. 5 up). 1992. lib. bdg. 17.95 (0-7910-1636-6) Chelsea Hse.

Booher, Dianna. They're Playing Our Secret. (Orig.). Date not set. pap. 5.99 (0-8010-5273-4) Revell.

Booher, Dianna D. Coping: When Your Family Falls Apart. LC 79-17342. 192p. (gr. 7 up). 1979. lib. bdg. 11.98 (0-671-33083-7, J Messner) S&S Trade.

—Love: First Aid for the Young. LC 84-27245. 160p. (gr. 7 up). 1985. lib. bdg. 11.98 (0-671-54401-2, J Messner) S&S Trade.

—Rape: What Would You Do If...? LC 81-914. 128p. (gr. 7 up). 1983. lib. bdg. 12.98 (0-671-42201-4, J Messner); lib. bdg. 4.95 (0-671-49485-6) S&S Trade.

Booher, Dianne D. Rape: What Would You Do If? rev. ed. 160p. (gr. 7 up). 1991. lib. bdg. 13.98 (0-671-74538-7, J Messner); pap. 6.95 (0-671-74546-8) S&S Trade.

Booht, David. Til All the Stars Have Fallen. (gr. 4-7). 1990. 14.95 (0-670-83272-3) Viking Child Bks.

Book, David L. Problems for Puzzlebusters. LC 92-90284. (Illus.). 358p. (gr. 7-12). 1992. 24.95 (0-9633217-0-6) Enigmatics.

Book, Linda. A Frog's Tale. Armstrong, Robert, illus. 32p. (Orig.). (gr. k-6). 1990. PLB 5.00 (0-9626294-0-5) Words & Muse Prodns.

Bookless, George, ed. see Sanford, Monard G.

Bookmaker & Raquin, Michele. My First French Vocabulary. (Illus.). 48p. 1991. spiral bdg. 9.95 (0-13-377607-7, Harraps) P-H Gen Ref & Trav.

—My First German Vocabulary. (Illus.). 48p. 1991. pap. 9.95 spiral bdg. (0-13-377599-2, Harraps) P-H Gen Ref & Trav.

—My First Spanish Vocabulary. (Illus.). 48p. 1991. spiral bdg. 11.95 (0-13-377581-X, Harraps) P-H Gen Ref & Trav.

Books, Cyrus, tr. see Kastner, Erich.

Books, Emma K. Frere Jacques. Bushell, Isobel, illus. 14p. (ps). 1994. 5.95 (0-694-00574-6, Festival) HarpC Child Bks.

—Twinkle, Twinkle, Little Star. Bushell, Isobel, illus. 12p. (ps). 1994. 5.95 (0-694-00575-4, Festival) HarpC Child Bks.

Boon, Emilie. It's Spring, Peterkin. Boon, Emilie, illus. LC 85-62015. 14p. (ps). 1986. bds. 3.95 (0-394-87997-X) Random Bks Yng Read.

Boone, Debby. Bedtime Hugs for Little Ones. Ferrer, Gabriel, illus. LC 87-81035. 64p. (ps-1). 1988. 11.99 (0-89081-616-6) Harvest Hse.

—The Snow Angel. Ferrer, Gabri, illus. 32p. (ps-1). 1991. text ed. 12.99 (0-89081-871-1) Harvest Hse.

Boone, Debby & Ferrer, Gabriel. Tomorrow Is a Brand New Day. (Illus.). 32p. (Orig.). (ps-3). 1989. 11.99 (0-89081-770-7) Harvest Hse.

Boone, E., jt. auth. see Motai, L.

Boone, E., et al. Basics in Reading: An Introduction to American Magazines. 115p. 1988. pap. text ed. 13.95 (0-8013-0514-4, 78360); tchr's. ed. 14.50 (0-8013-0513-6, 78359) Longman.

Boone, J. Allen & Leonard, Paul H. Adventures in Kinship with All Life. Leonardo, Bianca, ed. 128p. (gr. 9-12). 1990. pap. 9.95 (0-930852-08-7) Tree Life Pubns. This inspirational title, with warm humor, is one high school youth -- especially those who are fond of animals -- can enjoy. Author J. Allen Boone devoted his life to human-animal relationships. He developed a consciousness of the oneness of all living beings & the soul of the universe. This book contains heartwarming, inspiring, true stories of the amazing power of extra-sensory perception in animals. It is also about the bond of love & trust that can exist between people & animals of all kinds, & a new & wonderful world of silent communication. ADVENTURES... salutes the divinity within all living creatures. In his encounter with "Just Joe," his monkey companion, Boone struggles to become the pupil, with the small simian the teacher - a teacher whose wisdom is not measured in words, but in his ability to vibrate with life's pulsations. When Boone & "Just Joe" sat rocking & embracing, they felt their "echoing heartbeats." Other characters in this epic drama of life with love between people & animals are horses, gophers, seagulls & dogs. The stories of two faithful dogs, Sally &

Bomber Dog, are remarkable. A chapter entitled "The Love Compass" tells of a mysterious power animals possess. Boone teaches the reader how to become a master at interspecies relationships; the silent language can be learned. ADVENTURES... was the last book by Boone, published posthumously. (Original title, THE LANGUAGE OF SILENCE.) His three earlier books (still in print) are: KINSHIP WITH ALL LIFE (Harper & Row), LETTERS TO STRONGHEART, & YOU ARE THE ADVENTURE. Order from Atrium Publishers Group (800) 275-2606. *Publisher Provided Annotation.*

Boone-Thomas, Del. For Kids Who Are Coming of Age: Talking to Teenagers in Language They Understand. LC 84-91735. (Illus.). 57p. (Orig.). (gr. 7-12). 1983. pap. 7.95x (0-9611780-0-0) Boone-Thomas.

Boore, Sara. Bedtime Book. (ps). 1992. pap. 12.95 (1-878257-20-X) Klutz Pr.

Boorer, Wendy. Dogs. Coombs, Roy, illus. LC 88-17653. 24p. (Orig.). (gr. 2-5). 1989. lib. bdg. 5.99 (0-394-99988-6) Random Bks Yng Read.

Boorstin, Daniel J. The Americans, Vol. 1: The Colonial Experience. (gr. 7-12). 1964. pap. text ed. 8.95 (0-07-553700-1) McGraw.

—The Americans, Vol. 2: The National Experience. (gr. 7-12). 1967. pap. text ed. 8.95 (0-07-553701-X) McGraw.

Booss, Claire, ed. Scandinavian Folk & Fairy Tales. (Illus.). 704p. (gr. 7-10). 1984. 12.99 (0-517-43620-5) Outlet Bk Co.

Booth, Barbara D. Mandy. LaMarche, Jim, illus. LC 90-19989. 32p. (gr. 1 up). 1991. 14.95 (0-688-10338-3); PLB 14.88 (0-688-10339-1) Lothrop.

Booth, Basil. Earthquakes & Volcanoes. LC 91-44878. (Illus.). 48p. (gr. 4-6). 1992. RSBE 13.95 (0-02-711735-9, New Discovery) Macmillan Child Grp.

—Temperate Forests. Furstinger, Nancy, ed. (Illus.). 48p. (gr. 5-8). 1989. PLB 16.98 (0-382-09791-2) Silver Burdett Pr.

—Volcanoes & Earthquakes. (Illus.). 48p. (gr. 5-8). 1991. PLB 16.98 (0-382-24227-0) Silver Burdett Pr.

Booth, Coleen E. Going Live. LC 91-21607. 192p. (gr. 5-7). 1992. SBE 14.95 (0-684-19392-2, Scribners Young Read) Macmillan Child Grp.

Booth, David, compiled by. Doctor Knickerbocker & Other Rhymes. Kovalski, Maryann, illus. LC 92-46266. (ps). 1993. 16.45 (0-395-67168-X) Ticknor & Fields.

Booth, David, selected by. Til All the Stars Have Fallen: A Collection of Poems for Children. Denton, Kady M., illus. 96p. (ps-3). 1994. pap. 6.99 (0-14-034438-1) Puffin Bks.

Booth, David, ed. Voices on the Wind: Poems for All Seasons. Lemieux, Michele, illus. LC 90-5566. 48p. (ps up). 1990. 13.95 (0-688-09554-2); PLB 13.88 (0-688-09555-0, Morrow Jr Bks) Morrow Jr Bks.

Booth, Ernest S. Field Record for Birds. (gr. 7 up). 1960. pap. 2.00 (0-911080-03-1) Outdoor Pict.

—Life List for Birds. (gr. 7 up). 1969. pap. 2.00 (0-911080-04-X) Outdoor Pict.

Booth, Eugene. At the Beach. LC 77-7659. (Illus.). (gr. k-3). 1985. PLB 13.32 (0-8393-0111-1); pap. text ed. 9.27 (0-8393-0161-8) Raintree Steck-V.

—At the Circus. Collard, Derek, illus. LC 77-7946. 24p. (gr. k-3). 1985. PLB 13.32 (0-8393-0112-X); pap. text ed. 9.27 (0-8393-0162-6) Raintree Steck-V.

—At the Fair. Collard, Derek, illus. LC 77-7961. 24p. (gr. k-3). 1985. PLB 13.32 (0-8393-0114-6); pap. text ed. 9.27 (0-8393-0163-4) Raintree Steck-V.

—At the Zoo. LC 77-7627. (Illus.). (gr. k-3). 1977. PLB 13.32 (0-8393-0107-3) Raintree Steck-V.

—In the Air. LC 77-7984. (Illus.). 24p. (gr. k-3). 1977. PLB 13.32 (0-8393-0105-7) Raintree Steck-V.

—In the City. LC 77-7949. (Illus.). 24p. (gr. k-3). 1985. PLB 13.32 (0-8393-0109-X); pap. 9.27 (0-8393-0166-9) Raintree Steck-V.

—In the Garden. LC 77-7628. (Illus.). 24p. (gr. k-3). 1977. PLB 13.32 (0-8393-0115-4) Raintree Steck-V.

—In the Jungle. LC 77-7947. (Illus.). 24p. (gr. k-3). 1977. PLB 13.32 (0-8393-0104-9) Raintree Steck-V.

—In the Park. LC 77-7622. (Illus.). 24p. (gr. k-3). 1977. PLB 13.32 (0-8393-0106-5) Raintree Steck-V.

Booth, Jerry. The Big Beast Book: Dinosaurs & How They Got That Way. Weston, Martha, illus. LC 87-36206. (gr. 3-7). 1988. 14.95 (0-316-10263-6); pap. 9.95 (0-316-10266-0) Little.

Booth, Julianne. Books of the New Testament. (gr. k-4). 1981. pap. 1.89 (0-570-06150-4, 59-1305) Concordia.

—Books of the Old Testament. (ps-3). 1988. pap. 1.89 (0-570-06151-2) Concordia.

—Parables of Jesus. (gr. k-4). 1982. pap. 1.89 (0-570-06163-6, 59-1309) Concordia.

Booth, Martin, et al. Bismarck. Yapp, Martin & Killingray, Margaret, eds. (Illus.). 32p. (gr. 6-11). 1980. pap. text ed. 3.45 (0-89908-023-5) Greenhaven.

Booth, Mary L., tr. see Mace, Jean.

Booth, Zilpha M. Finding a Friend. Breeden, Teisha, illus. LC 86-50987. 54p. (gr. 1-5). 1987. pap. 3.95 (0-932433-22-7) Windswept Hse.

Boraks, Lucius. Religions of the West. LC 87-63499. 116p. (Orig.). 1988. pap. 7.95 (1-55612-141-5) Sheed & Ward MO.

Borba, Craig & Borba, Michele. The Good Apple Guide to Learning Centers. Volpe, Nancee, illus. 208p. (gr. k-6). 1978. 14.95 (0-916456-33-1, GA86) Good Apple.

Borba, Michele. Esteem Builders: A Self-Esteem Curriculum for Improving Student Achievement, Behavior & School-Home Climate. Taylor-McMillan, Birah, ed. Highpoint Type & Graphics Staff, illus. LC 88-80769. 444p. (Orig.). (gr. k-8). 1989. pap. 49.95 spiral bdg. (0-915190-53-2, JP9053-2) Jalmar Pr.

Borba, Michele & Ungaro, Dan. Bookends. 128p. (gr. 1-4). 1982. 11.95 (0-86653-065-7, GA 432) Good Apple.

—The Complete Letter Book. 112p. (ps-3). 1980. 11.95 (0-916456-80-3, GA 182) Good Apple.

Borba, Michele, jt. auth. see Borba, Craig.

Borchardt, Lois M. Learning about God's Love: Word-Picture Activities for Children in Grades 1 & 2. 48p. (gr. 1-2). 1986. pap. 2.99 (0-570-04354-9, 61-2017) Concordia.

Borchers, Deena. Changing the World. (Illus.). 48p. (gr. 9-12). 1993. pap. 7.99 (1-55945-236-6) Group Pub.

—Communicating with Friends. (Illus.). 48p. (gr. 9-12). 1992. pap. 7.99 (1-55945-228-5) Group Pub.

—What is the Church? (Illus.). 48p. (gr. 9-12). 1992. pap. 7.99 (1-55945-222-6) Group Pub.

Borchers, E., jt. auth. see Charpentreau, J.

Bordeaux, Michelle, compiled by. Poetry: Friends for a Lifetime. (Illus.). 40p. (gr. 5 up). 1992. pap. 2.99 (0-87406-633-6) Willowisp Pr.

Bordeaux, Norma N., jt. auth. see Szekely, Edmond B.

Borden, Beatrice B. Wild Animals of Africa. (Illus.). 48p. (ps-2). 1982. lib. bdg. 6.99 (0-394-95306-1) Random Bks Yng Read.

Borden, Louise. Albie the Lifeguard. Sayles, Elizabeth, illus. LC 91-11327. 32p. (ps-3). 1993. 14.95 (0-590-44585-5) Scholastic Inc.

—Caps, Hats, Socks, & Mittens: A Book about the Four Seasons. Lillian, Lillian, illus. 1992. pap. 3.95 (0-590-44872-2, Blue Ribbon Bks) Scholastic Inc.

—Neighborhood Trucker. 1990. pap. 12.95 (0-590-42584-6) Scholastic Inc.

Borden, Margie. Mincemeat Pie. Graves, Helen, ed. 54p. (gr. 4-8). 1987. 5.95 (1-55523-048-2) Winston-Derek.

Borden, Merritt W. Coping with Life the Principle Way: A Plain-English Common-Sense Approach to Solving the Problems of Everyday Living. rev. ed. Glines, Shane, illus. 119p. (gr. 7-12). 1993. spiral bdg. 12.95 (0-929393-11-2) Diogenes Pub Co.

Border, Rosy. Beginners Guide to Magic. Everett, Mimi, illus. 48p. (gr. 3-6). 1992. pap. 2.95 (1-56680-008-0) Mad Hatter Pub.

—A "Spot-It" Guide to Nature. Banazi, Pauline, illus. 48p. (gr. 3-6). 1992. pap. 2.95 (1-56680-012-9) Mad Hatter Pub.

Border, Rosy, ed. Jokes, Jokes & More Jokes. Green, Barry, illus. 48p. (gr. 3-6). 1992. pap. 2.95 (1-56680-002-1) Mad Hatter Pub.

Bordewich, Fergus M. Peach Blossom Spring. Yang Ming-Yi, illus. LC 92-19676. 1994. 15.00 (0-671-78710-1, Green Tiger) S&S Trade.

Bordman, Marcia B., et al. Practical English Structure, Vol. 2. Butler, Paul, illus. LC 80-85299. 224p. (gr. 9-12). 1981. text ed. 15.95 (0-913580-67-8, Clerc Bks) Gallaudet Univ Pr.

—Practical English Structure, Vol. 3. Butler, Paul, illus. LC 80-85299. 220p. (gr. 9-12). 1981. text ed. 15.95 (0-913580-68-6, Clerc Bks) Gallaudet Univ Pr.

—Practical English Structure, Vol. 4. Butler, Paul, illus. LC 80-85299. 218p. (gr. 9-12). 1981. text ed. 15.95 (0-913580-69-4, Clerc Bks) Gallaudet Univ Pr.

—Practical English Structure, Vol. 5. Butler, Paul, illus. LC 80-85299. 340p. (gr. 9-12). 1982. text ed. 15.95 (0-913580-70-8, Clerc Bks) Gallaudet Univ Pr.

Bordman, Marcia Beth, et al. Practical English Structure, Vol. 1. Butler, Paul, illus. LC 80-85299. 200p. (gr. 9-12). 1981. text ed. 15.95 (0-913580-66-X, Clerc Bks) Gallaudet Univ Pr.

Bordon, Louise. Caps, Hats, Socks, & Mittens. (ps-3). 1992. pap. 19.95 (0-590-72429-0) Scholastic Inc.

Borenson, Henry. The Hands-on Equations Learning System. 2nd ed. (Illus.). 66p. (gr. 3-8). 1988. Repr. of 1986 ed. Incl. worksheets, pawns & cubes. 34.95 (0-9618105-0-5) Borenson & Assocs.

Borenstein. Five-Minute Bible Games & Fun. (Illus.). 96p. (ps-3). 1992. 10.95 (0-86653-698-1, SS2828, Shining Star Pubns) Good Apple.

Borg, Mary. Writing Your Life: Autobiographical Writing Activities for Young People. Blackstone, Ann, illus. 46p. (gr. 5-12). 1989. pap. text ed. 14.95 (1-877673-09-9) Cottonwood Pr.

Borg, Veronique. The Next Balcony Down. (Illus.). 32p. (gr. 3-5). 1991. 18.50 (0-89565-757-0); 12.95s.p. (0-685-55088-5) Childs World.

Borgardt, Marianne. Deadly Storms in Action: An Early Reader Pop-up Book. Harris, Greg, illus. 16p. (Orig.). (ps-3). 1993. bds. 8.95 (0-689-71719-9, Aladdin) Macmillan Child Grp.

—Volcanoes & Earthquakes in Action: An Early Reader Pop-up Book. Harris, Greg, illus. 16p. (Orig.). 1993. bds. 8.95 (0-689-71720-2, Aladdin) Macmillan Child Grp.

Borgenicht, David. Start Exploring Folktales of Native Americans: A Story-Filled Coloring Book. Driggs, Helen, illus. 128p. (Orig.). (gr. 3 up). 1993. pap. 8.95 (1-56138-303-1) Running Pr.

Borgese, Paul. If Fish Went Peopling. (gr. k up). 1989. pap. 11.95 (1-878347-05-5) NL Assocs.

—On the Other Side. (gr. k up). 1986. pap. 6.95 (1-878347-06-3) NL Assocs.

Borgia, Rubi, jt. auth. see Wilkes, Angela.

Borgo, Deborah C., illus. Thomas the Tank Engine - Shapes & Sizes. Awdry, W., contrib. by. (Illus.). 14p. (ps). 1993. bds. 2.29 (0-679-81643-7) Random Bks Yng Read.

—Thomas the Tank Engine Counts to Ten. Awdry, W., contrib. by. (Illus.). 14p. (ps). 1993. bds. 2.29 (0-679-81644-5) Random Bks Yng Read.

Borie, Marcia & Wilkerson, Tichi. Hollywood Legends: The Golden Years of the Hollywood Reporter. 2nd ed. (Illus.). 350p. (gr. 7 up). 1988. pap. 14.95 (0-942139-03-8) Tale Weaver.

Boring, Mel. Incredible Constructions & the People Who Built Them. LC 84-19522. 96p. (gr. 4 up). 1985. PLB 13.85 (0-8027-6560-2) Walker & Co.

Borisoff, Norman. Bewitched & Bewildered: A Spooky Love Story. 112p. (Orig.). (gr. 7-11). 1982. pap. 1.75 (0-440-90905-8, LFL) Dell.

Boritzer, Etan. What Is God? Marantz, Robbie, illus. 32p. (Orig.). (gr. 1-7). 1990. 14.95 (0-920668-89-5); pap. 5.95 (0-920668-88-7) Firefly Bks Ltd.

—What Is Love? Marantz, Robbie, illus. LC 93-94066. 32p. (gr. k-5). 1994. 14.95 (0-9637597-2-8); pap. 5.95 (0-9637597-3-6) V Lane Bks.

Borja, Corinne & Borja, Robert. Making Chinese Paper Cuts. Tucker, Kathleen, ed. Borja, Corinne & Borja, Robert, illus. LC 79-18358. (gr. 3-8). 1980. PLB 13.95 (0-8075-4948-7) A Whitman.

Borja, Robert, jt. auth. see Borja, Corinne.

Borland, Hal. Plants of Christmas. Dowden, Anne O., illus. LC 87-552. 32p. (gr. 3 up). 1987. Repr. of 1969 ed. 14.95 (0-690-04649-9, Crowell Jr Bks); (Crowell Jr Bks) HarpC Child Bks.

—When the Legends Die. 224p. (gr. 6-12). 1984. pap. 3.99 (0-553-25738-2) Bantam.

Borland, Kathryn K. & Speicher, Helen R. Harry Houdini: Young Magician. LC 90-23321. (Illus.). 192p. (gr. 3-7). 1991. pap. 3.95 (0-689-71476-9, Aladdin) Macmillan Child Grp.

Borlenghi, Patricia. From Albatross to Zoo. (Illus.). (ps up). 1992. 14.95 (0-590-45483-8, 018, Scholastic Hardcover) Scholastic Inc.

Borlenghi, Patricia & Wright, Rachel. Italy. LC 93-14702. (Illus.). 32p. (gr. 5-7). 1993. PLB 11.90 (0-531-14264-7) Watts.

Bormuth, Robert, jt. auth. see Usher, Michael A.

Born, Anne, tr. see Holmas, Stig.

Bornet, Vaughn D. It's a Dog's Life & I Like It! LC 91-78055. 40p. (gr. 3-8). 1991. pap. 8.95 (0-9632366-0-1) Bornet Bks.

Bornstein. Gorilita. (SPA.). 1993. pap. 3.95 (0-590-12086-7) Scholastic Inc.

Bornstein, Harry. All by Myself. (Illus.). 16p. (ps). 1975. pap. 3.50 (0-913580-43-0, Pub. by K Green Pubns) Gallaudet Univ Pr.

—Be Careful. (Illus.). 32p. (ps-3). 1976. pap. 5.50 (0-913580-55-4, Pub. by K Green Pubns) Gallaudet Univ Pr.

—A Book about Me. (Illus.). 16p. (ps). 1973. pap. 3.50 (0-913580-19-8, Pub. by K Green Pubns) Gallaudet Univ Pr.

—Circus Time. (Illus.). 16p. (ps). 1976. pap. 3.50 (0-913580-51-1, Pub. by K Green Pubns) Gallaudet Univ Pr.

—The Clock Book. (Illus.). 36p. (ps-2). 1975. pap. 5.95 (0-913580-48-1, Pub. by K Green Pubns) Gallaudet Univ Pr.

—Count & Color. (Illus.). 16p. (ps). 1973. pap. 3.50 (0-913580-20-1, Pub. by K Green Pubns) Gallaudet Univ Pr.

—Fire Fighter Brown. Tom, Linda C., illus. 16p. (ps). 1976. pap. 3.50 (0-913580-50-3, Pub. by K Green Pubns) Gallaudet Univ Pr.

—The Gingerbread Man. (Illus.). 48p. (ps-2). 1976. pap. 5.95 (0-913580-52-X, Pub. by K Green Pubns) Gallaudet Univ Pr.

—The Holiday Book. (Illus.). 48p. (ps-2). 1974. pap. 6.50 (0-913580-30-9) Gallaudet Univ Pr.

—I Want to Be a Farmer. LC 72-84675. (Illus.). 48p. (ps-2). 1972. pap. 5.95 (0-913580-14-7) Gallaudet Univ Pr.

—Jack & the Beanstalk. (Illus.). 64p. (ps-3). 1975. pap. 6.50 (0-913580-47-3, Pub. by K Green Pubns) Gallaudet Univ Pr.

—Little Poems for Little People. (Illus.). 56p. (ps-3). 1974. pap. 6.50 (0-913580-31-7, Pub. by K Green Pubns) Gallaudet Univ Pr.

—Mealtime at the Zoo. Hrivnak, Suzette & Hrivnak, James R., illus. 48p. (ps-2). 1973. pap. 5.95 (0-913580-11-2) Gallaudet Univ Pr.

—Mouse's Christmas Eve. (Illus.). 44p. (ps-3). 1974. pap. 5.95 (0-913580-28-7, Pub. by K Green Pubns) Gallaudet Univ Pr.

—My Animal Book. (Illus.). 16p. (ps). 1973. pap. 3.50 (0-913580-21-X) Gallaudet Univ Pr.

—My Toy Book. (Illus.). 16p. (ps). 1973. pap. 3.50 (*0-913580-22-8*, Pub. by K Green Pubns) Gallaudet Univ Pr.

—The Night Before Christmas. (Illus.). 56p. (ps-3). 1973. pap. 6.50 (*0-913580-15-5*, Pub. by K Green Pubns) Gallaudet Univ Pr.

—Night-Day - Work-Play. (Illus.). 48p. (ps-2). 1974. pap. 5.95 (*0-913580-23-6*) Gallaudet Univ Pr.

—Oliver in the City. (Illus.). 56p. (ps-3). 1975. pap. 6.50 (*0-913580-49-X*) Gallaudet Univ Pr.

—The Pet Shop. (Illus.). 16p. (ps). 1976. pap. 3.50 (*0-913580-54-6*, Pub. by K Green Pubns) Gallaudet Univ Pr.

—Police Officer Jones. (Illus.). 16p. (ps) 1976. pap. 3.50 (*0-913580-53-8*, Pub. by K Green Pubns) Gallaudet Univ Pr.

—Questions & More Questions. (Illus.). 52p. (ps-3) 1973. pap. 6.50 (*0-913580-24-4*) Gallaudet Univ Pr.

—Songs in Signed English. (Illus.). 44p. (ps-2) 1973. pap. 9.00 incl. record (*0-913580-12-0*, Pub. by K Green Pubns) Gallaudet Univ Pr.

—Spring Is Green. (Illus.). 52p. (ps-2) 1973. pap. 6.50 (*0-913580-17-1*) Gallaudet Univ Pr.

—Three Little Kittens. (Illus.). 32p. (ps-2) 1973. pap. 5.50 (*0-913580-16-3*) Gallaudet Univ Pr.

—Three Little Pigs. (Illus.). 44p. (ps-3) 1972. pap. 6.50 (*0-913580-09-0*, Pub. by K Green Pubns) Gallaudet Univ Pr.

—The Ugly Duckling. (Illus.). 48p. (ps-2) 1974. pap. 6.50 (*0-913580-29-5*, Pub. by K Green Pubns) Gallaudet Univ Pr.

—We're Going to the Doctor. (Illus.). 28p. (ps-3). 1985. pap. 5.50 (*0-913580-26-0*, Pub. by K Green Pubns) Gallaudet Univ Pr.

—With My Legs. (Illus.). 16p. (ps). 1975. pap. 3.50 (*0-913580-42-2*, Pub. by K Green Pubns) Gallaudet Univ Pr.

Bornstein, Harry & Saulnier, Karen. Little Red Riding Hood. Pomeroy, Bradley O., illus. 48p. (gr. 1-6). 1990. PLB 15.95 (*1-878363-26-3*) Forest Hse.

Bornstein, Harry & Saulnier, Karen L. Little Red Riding Hood: Told in Signed English. Pomeroy, Bradley O., illus. LC 90-3477. 48p. (ps-2). 1990. 14.95 (*0-930323-63-7*, Pub. by K Green Pubns) Gallaudet Univ Pr.

—Mother Goose: Nursery Rhymes. Peters, Patricia & Tom, Linda C., illus. 48p. (gr. k-3). 1992. PLB 15.95 (*1-56674-034-7*) Forest Hse.

—Nursery Rhymes from Mother Goose: Told in Signed English. Peters, Patricia & Tom, Linda, illus. 48p. (ps-2). 1992. 14.95 (*0-930323-99-8*, Pub. by K Green Pubns) Gallaudet Univ Pr.

—The Signed English Starter. Miller, Ralph R., Sr., illus. LC 84-4042. 232p. (gr-6). 1984. pap. text ed. 13.95 (*0-913580-82-1*, Clerc Bks) Gallaudet Univ Pr.

Bornstein, Harry, et al. Don't Be a Grumpy Bear: A Coloring Book about Manners in Signed English. Miller, Ralph R., illus. 32p. (ps-2). 1986. pap. 3.95 (*0-930323-26-2*, Pub. by K Green Pubns) Gallaudet Univ Pr.

Bornstein, Harry, et al, eds. The Comprehensive Signed English Dictionary. LC 82-82830. (Illus.). x, 464p. 1983. 29.95 (*0-913580-81-3*, Clerc Bks) Gallaudet Univ Pr.

Bornstein, Jerry. The Neo-Nazis. LC 85-5363. (Illus.). 192p. (gr. 7 up). 1986. lib. bdg. 11.98 (*0-671-50238-7*, J Messner) S&S Trade.

—Police Brutality: A National Debate. LC 92-42146. (Illus.). 112p. (gr. 6 up). 1993. lib. bdg. 17.95 (*0-89490-430-2*) Enslow Pubs.

Bornstein, Ruth. Little Gorilla. Bornstein, Ruth, illus. LC 75-25508. 32p. (ps-3). 1986. 15.45 (*0-395-28773-1*, Clarion Bks); pap. 4.95 (*0-89919-421-4*, Clarion Bks) HM.

Bornstein, Ruth L. The Seedling Child. LC 86-19581. (Illus.). 28p. (ps-3). 1987. 12.95 (*0-15-272459-1*) HarBrace.

Bornstein, Sandy. What Makes You What You Are? A First Look at Genetics. Steltenpohl, Jane, ed. (Illus.). 128p. (gr. 7 up). 1989. (J Messner); lib. bdg. 6.95 (*0-671-68650-X*) S&S Trade.

Bornstein, Scott. Vocabulary Mastery. Vincent, Ben, illus. 272p. (gr. 9-12). 1982. 22.50 (*0-9602610-1-X*); pap. 14.95 (*0-9602610-2-8*) Bornstein Memory.

Bornthal, Mark. Baby Bop's ABC's. Hartley, Linda, ed. 24p. (ps-k). Date not set. pap. 2.25 (*0-7829-0377-0*) Barney Pub.

Borntrager, Mary C. Daniel. large type ed. 160p. (gr. 4 up). 1993. pap. 8.95 (*0-8361-3639-X*) Herald Pr.

—Ellie. LC 88-2779. 168p. (gr. 7-12). 1988. pap. 6.95 (*0-8361-3468-0*) Herald Pr.

—Rebecca. 176p. (Orig.). (gr. 8-12). 1989. pap. 6.95 (*0-8361-3500-8*) Herald Pr.

Borovetz, Fran. Ha Motzi Bracha Kit. (Illus.). 32p. (Orig.). (gr. 3-4). 1985. pap. text ed. 4.95 (*0-933873-03-4*) Torah Aura.

Borovsky, Paul. A Fish for Paulina. (Illus.). 32p. (ps-2). 1994. 14.95 (*1-56282-581-X*); PLB 14.89 (*1-56282-582-8*) Hyprn Child.

—George. Borovsky, Paul, illus. LC 89-2022. (ps up). 1990. 12.95 (*0-688-09150-4*); PLB 12.88 (*0-688-09151-2*) Greenwillow.

—Nico. Borovsky, Paul, illus. LC 92-13924. 32p. (ps-2). 1993. 14.00 (*0-517-58854-4*); PLB 14.99 (*0-517-58855-2*) Crown Bks Yng Read.

—The Strange Blue Creature. Borovsky, Paul, illus. LC 92-54864. 32p. (ps-2). 1993. 13.95 (*1-56282-434-1*); PLB 13.89 (*1-56282-435-X*) Hyprn Child.

Borowitz, Eugene & Patz, Naomi. Explaining Reform Judaism. 183p. (gr. 6-8). 1985. pap. text ed. 7.95 (*0-87441-394-X*); By Kerry Olitzky. tchr's. ed., 96pps. 14.95x (*0-87441-436-9*); wkbk., 90pps. 4.25 (*0-317-60043-5*) Behrman.

Borowsky, Irvin J. Artists Confronting the Inconceivable. (Illus.). 136p. 1992. 100.00 (*1-881060-00-4*) Am Interfaith.

Borrelli, Susan. Freedom in the Sun. LC 91-67500. (Illus.). 44p. (gr. k-3). 1992. pap. 6.95 (*1-55523-494-1*) Winston-Derek.

Borten. Halloween. Date not set. 15.00 (*0-06-023582-9*, Festival); PLB 14.89 (*0-06-023583-7*, Festival) HarpC Child Bks.

Borton, Enrique R. Trevino, tr. see De Trevino, Elizabeth Borton.

Borton, Lady. Fat Chance! Ray, Deborah K., illus. 32p. (ps-3). 1993. 14.95 (*0-399-21963-3*, Philomel) Putnam Pub Group.

Bortz, Alfred B. Superstuff! Materials That Have Changed Our Lives. LC 90-12565. (Illus.). 128p. (gr. 9-12). 1990. PLB 13.40 (*0-531-10887-2*) Watts.

Bortz, Fred. Mind Tools: The Science of Artificial Intelligence. LC 92-16653. (Illus.). 128p. (gr. 9-12). 1992. PLB 13.40 (*0-531-12515-7*) Watts.

Borzendowski, Janice. John Russwurm. (Illus.). 112p. (gr. 5 up). 1989. 17.95 (*1-55546-610-9*) Chelsea Hse.

Bos, Burny. Olli, der Kleine Elefant. De Beer, Hans, illus. (GER.). 32p. (gr. k-3). 1992. 13.95 (*3-85825-328-6*) North-South Bks NYC.

—Olli, le Petit Elephant. De Beer, Hans, illus. (FRE.). 32p. (gr. k-3). 1992. 13.95 (*3-85539-659-0*) North-South Bks NYC.

—Ollie the Elephant. De Beer, Hans, illus. LC 89-42608. 32p. (gr. k-3). 1989. 13.95 (*1-55858-012-3*) North-South Bks NYC.

—Ollie the Elephant. De Beer, Hans, illus. 32p. (gr. k-3). 1991. pap. 2.95 (*1-55858-110-3*) North-South Bks NYC.

—Le Prince Ferdinand. De Beer, Hans, illus. (FRE.). 32p. (gr. k-3). 1992. 13.95 (*3-85539-703-1*) North-South Bks NYC.

—Prince Valentino. De Beer, Hans, illus. LC 89-43247. 32p. (gr. k-3). 1990. 13.95 (*1-55858-089-1*) North-South Bks NYC.

—Valentino Frosch und das Himbeerrote Cabrio. De Beer, Hans, illus. (GER.). 32p. (gr. k-3). 1992. 13.95 (*3-85825-346-4*) North-South Bks NYC.

Bosca, Francesca. Caspar & the Star. Ferri, Giuliano, illus. 40p. (gr. 1-8). 1991. 12.95 (*0-7459-2120-5*) Lion USA.

—Caspar & the Star. (ps-3). 1993. pap. 4.99 (*0-7459-2770-X*) Lion USA.

Bosch, Carl. Bully on the Bus. Strecker, Rebekah, illus. LC 88-42650. 64p. (Orig.). (gr. 2-5). 1988. PLB 16.95 (*0-943990-43-2*); pap. 5.95 (*0-943990-42-4*) Parenting Pr.

Bosch, Carl W. Making the Grade. Strecker, Rebekah, illus. LC 90-62674. 64p. (Orig.). (gr. 3). 1991. lib. bdg. 16.95 (*0-943990-49-1*); pap. 5.95 (*0-943990-48-3*) Parenting Pr.

Boschini, Henny & Boschini, Luciano. Chasing Whales off Norway. LC 72-90690. (Illus.). 32p. (gr. k-4). 1973. 7.95 (*0-87592-010-1*) Scroll Pr.

Boschini, Luciano, jt. auth. see Boschini, Henny.

Bosco, Clyde. Pipe Down. Ashby, Ruth, ed. 128p. (Orig.). 1991. pap. 3.50 (*0-671-74203-5*, Archway) PB.

Bosco, James. The Misadventures of Wags & Freckles Kid-Pak: A Lesson in the Dangers of Alcohol. rev. ed. Lupo, Ann, ed. Bosco, James & Carter, Fred, illus. 28p. (ps-3). 1991. map. text ed. 3.95 (*1-56230-136-5*); pap. text ed. 4.95 incl. audiotape (*1-56230-126-8*) Syndistar.

Bosco, Peter. World War I. (Illus.). 144p. (gr. 9-12). 1991. 17.95x (*0-8160-2460-X*) Facts on File.

Bosco, Peter I. Roanoke: The Story of the Lost Colony. LC 91-19887. (Illus.). 64p. (gr. 4-6). 1992. PLB 14.40 (*1-56294-111-9*) Millbrook Pr.

—War of 1812. (Illus.). 128p. (gr. 7 up). 1991. PLB 16.90 (*1-56294-004-X*) Millbrook Pr.

Bosnia, Nella, jt. auth. see Turin, Adela.

Bosschere, Jean de & Morris, M. C. Christmas Tales of Flanders. (Illus.). (gr. 4-8). 7.75 (*0-8446-4516-8*) Peter Smith.

Bosse, Malcolm. Captives of Time. LC 86-32943. 256p. (gr. 7 up). 1987. pap. 14.95 (*0-385-29583-9*) Delacorte.

—Captives of Time. (gr. k-12). 1989. pap. 3.50 (*0-440-20311-2*, LFL) Dell.

—Deep Dream of the Rain Forest. LC 92-55095. 1993. 15.00 (*0-374-31757-7*) FS&G.

—Ganesh. LC 93-7956. 1993. 3.95 (*0-374-42517-5*) FS&G.

Bosson, Jo-Ellen. Platypus. Bosson, Jo-Ellen, illus. 10p. (ps-1). 1992. bds. 2.95 (*1-56293-218-7*) McClanahan Bk.

—Robin. Bosson, Jo-Ellen, illus. 10p. (ps-1). 1992. bds. 2.95 (*1-56293-217-9*) McClanahan Bk.

—Swan. Bosson, Jo-Ellen, illus. 10p. (ps-1). 1992. bds. 2.95 (*1-56293-216-0*) McClanahan Bk.

—Turtle. Bosson, Jo-Ellen, illus. 10p. (ps-1). 1992. bds. 2.95 (*1-56293-219-5*) McClanahan Bk.

—Wild & Free: The Story of a Black-Footed Ferret. Bosson, Jo-Ellen, illus. Thomas, Peter, narrated by. (Illus.). 32p. (ps-3). 1992. 11.95 (*0-924483-68-7*); incl. audiocassette 16.95 (*0-924483-67-9*); incl. audiocassette tape & 16 inch stuffed animal toy 39.95 (*0-924483-66-0*); write for info. audiocass. tape (*0-924483-75-X*) Soundprints.

Boss-Ribs, Mary C. & Running-Crane, Jenny. Stories of Our Blackfeet Grandmothers. (Orig.). (gr. 1-6). 1984. pap. 4.95 (*0-89992-096-9*) Coun India Ed.

Bostick, William A. Calligraphy for Kids. (Illus.). 32p. (Orig.). (gr. 3-12). 1991. wkbk. 9.95 (*0-9606630-1-0*) La Stampa Calligrafica.

A fun way for youngsters to learn calligraphy as well as beautiful & legible handwriting. Unfortunately, these skills aren't usually acquired in schools today. Before printing, sample pages were tested on sixth & seventh graders. The students' enthusiastic participation & delightful testimonials such as, "I think your book is great!" &, "If I saw it in a bookstore I would buy it," encouraged us to proceed. The budding calligrapher goes over the author's large Chancery quotation for each letter & then repeats the calligraphy on his own, both large & at normal handwriting size. Cartoon 'live letters' liven each page & students are encouraged to draw their own. The cover reproduces Chancery & six other alphabets for kids to explore. It opens up the whole wonderful world of calligraphy to a youngster. But, of course, adults can also learn from it: the age range is 6 to 96! Book dealers & stores selling educational material for children tell us that there is nothing like "Calligraphy for Kids" on the market today. It's unique!
Publisher Provided Annotation.

Boston, Gypsy D. The Rainbow Fairies. Adair, Laura, illus. 1991. 12.95 (*0-9631503-0-8*); pap. 4.95 (*0-9631503-1-6*) Gypsy Damaris.

Pre-school & primary-grade children will delight in the folklore of this wonderfully written & beautifully illustrated book...& its size is perfect for small hands. "Who washes the flower's face?" "Who teaches baby owls to fly?" "Who colors the rainbow?" Why, the fairies -- of course!! Order directly from Gypsy Damaris Books, P.O. Box 8417, Shreveport, LA 71148-8417.
Publisher Provided Annotation.

Boston, Linda M. Huff & Puff & Me. 2nd ed. 1988. 15.00 (*0-941549-09-7*) Creative Hlth.

Boston, Lucy. The Children of Green Knowe. Deeter, Catherine & Boston, Peter, illus. 183p. (gr. 3-7). 1989. pap. 3.95 (*0-15-217151-7*, Odyssey) HarBrace.

—An Enemy at Green Knowe. Deeter, Catherine & Boston, Peter, illus. 176p. (gr. 4-7). 1989. pap. 3.95 (*0-15-225973-2*, Odyssey) HarBrace.

—A Stranger at Green Knowe. Deeter, Catherine & Boston, Peter, illus. 199p. (gr. 3-7). 1989. pap. 3.95 (*0-15-281755-7*, Odyssey) HarBrace.

—Treasure of Green Knowe. Deeter, Catherine & Boston, Peter, illus. 214p. (gr. 3-7). 1989. pap. 3.95 (*0-15-289982-0*, Odyssey) HarBrace.

Boston, Lucy M. The Chimneys of Green Knowe. large type ed. Boston, Peter, illus. 272p. (gr. 3 up). 1990. 18.95 (*0-7451-1175-0*) G K Hall.

—River at Green Knowe. 161p. (gr. 3-7). 1989. pap. 3.95 (*0-15-267450-0*, Odyssey) HarBrace.

—The River at Greene Knowe. large type ed. Boston, Peter, illus. 208p. 1992. 13.95 (*0-7451-1467-9*, Galaxy Child Lrg Print) Chivers N Amer.

—Sea Egg. Boston, Peter, illus. LC 67-10200. (gr. 2-6). 1967. 8.95 (*0-15-271050-7*, HB Juv Bks) HarBrace.

—Stranger at Green Knowe. Boston, Peter, illus. LC 61-10108. (gr. 5-9). 1961. 9.95 (*0-15-281752-2*, HB Juv Bks) HarBrace.

Bostrom, Alice. David Livingstone, Missionary to Africa. Lautermilch, John, illus. 32p. (Orig.). 1982. pap. 1.30 (0-89323-027-8) Bible Memory.

Boswell, James, jt. auth. see Johnson, Samuel.

Boswell, Kathryn, jt. auth. see O'Connor, Francine.

Boswell, Kathryn, jt. auth. see O'Connor, Francine M.

Bosworth, et al. AIDS. (gr. 7-12). Date not set. incl. software 120.00 (0-912899-53-0) Lrning Multi-Systs.

—Alcohol & Other Drugs. (gr. 7-12). Date not set. incl. software 120.00 (0-912899-59-X) Lrning Multi-Systs.

—Body Management. (gr. 7-12). Date not set. incl. software 120.00 (0-912899-58-1) Lrning Multi-Systs.

—Human Sexuality. (gr. 7-12). Date not set. incl. software 120.00 (0-912899-55-7) Lrning Multi-Systs.

—Implementing BARN. (gr. 7-12). Date not set. write for info. incl. software (0-912899-54-9) Lrning Multi-Systs.

—Smoking. (gr. 7-12). Date not set. incl. software 120.00 (0-912899-56-5) Lrning Multi-Systs.

—Stress Management. (gr. 7-12). Date not set. incl. software 120.00 (0-912899-57-3) Lrning Multi-Systs.

Bosworth, Michael. My Own Place. Wilkin, Mike, illus. LC 93-27058. 1994. 4.25 (0-383-03766-2) SRA Schl Grp.

Boteler, Alison. Disney Party Handbook. LC 91-58610. (Illus.). 196p. 1992. PLB 13.89 (1-56282-200-4); pap. 9.95 (1-56282-173-3) Disney Pr.

Bothell, Diane J., et al. Nashramh: The Gold Threads. 2nd, rev. ed. 392p. 1991. 12.95 (0-933673-18-3) Three-Stones Pubns.

—Nashramh: The White Threads. 2nd, rev. ed. 392p. 1991. 12.95 (0-933673-19-1) Three-Stones Pubns.

Bothell, Lisa J. Nashramh: The Blue Thread. 3rd, rev. ed. 392p. 1991. 12.95 (0-933673-17-5) Three-Stones Pubns.

—Nashramh: The Red Thread. 3rd, rev. ed. 382p. 1991. pap. 12.95 (0-933673-16-7) Three-Stones Pubns.

Bothmer, Gerry, tr. see Lindgren, Astrid.

Botner, Barbara. The World's Greatest Expert on Everything...Is Crying. (gr. 3-7). 1986. pap. 2.95 (0-440-49739-6, YB) Dell.

Botterbusch, Karl F., ed. see Boerner, Lee A.

Bottner, Barbara. Bootsie Barker Bites. Rathman, Peggy, illus. 32p. 1992. 14.95 (0-399-22125-5, Putnam) Putnam Pub Group.

—Hurricane Music. Yalowitz, Paul, illus. LC 92-43697. 1994. write for info. (0-399-22544-7, Putnam) Putnam Pub Group.

—Let Me Tell You Everything: Memoirs of a Lovesick Intellectual. LC 88-22066. 160p. (gr. 7 up). 1989. HarpC Child Bks.

—Messy. Bottner, Barbara, illus. LC 78-50420. (gr. k-2). 1979. 6.95 (0-440-05492-3); pap. 6.46 (0-440-05493-1) Delacorte.

—Nothing in Common. (gr. 5 up). 1988. pap. 2.95 (0-553-27060-5, Starfire) Bantam.

Bottomley, Jim. Paper Projects for Creative Kids of All Ages. 160p. (gr. 5 up). 1983. pap. 12.95 (0-316-10349-7) Little.

Bouchard, Elizabeth. Benazir Bhutto: Prime Minister. (Illus.). 64p. (gr. 3-7). PLB 14.95 (1-56711-027-4) Blackbirch.

—Everything You Need to Know about Sexual Harassment. rev. ed. (gr. 4-7). 1992. 13.95 (0-8239-1490-9) Rosen Group.

Bouchard, Robert. Let's Play the Recorder. (gr. 6 up). 9.95 (0-8283-1471-3) Branden Pub Co.

Boucher, Helene & Major, Henriette. Make up Magic. (Illus.). 32p. (gr. 3-7). 1993. 7.95 (2-7625-5270-2, Pub. by Les Edits Herit CN) Adams Inc MA.

Boucher, Jerry. Fire Truck Nuts & Bolts. LC 92-37476. 1993. 9.95 (0-87614-783-X) Carolrhoda Bks.

—Fire Truck Nuts & Bolts. (ps-3). 1993. pap. 5.95 (0-87614-619-1) Carolrhoda Bks.

Boudreau, Cathy. Speech Takes Off. (Illus.). 176p. (gr. k-6). 1991. 24.95 (0-937857-30-0, 1595) Speech Bin.

Boughton, Richard. Rent-A-Puppy, Inc. LC 91-22842. 112p. (gr. 3-7). 1992. SBE 12.95 (0-689-31730-1, Atheneum Child Bk) Macmillan Child Grp.

Boulais, Sue. Learning How: BMX Riding. James, Jody, ed. Concept of Design Staff, illus. 48p. (gr. 4-7). 1992. lib. bdg. 14.95 (0-944280-36-6); pap. 5.95 (0-944280-41-2) Bancroft-Sage.

—Learning How: Football. James, Jody, ed. Concept of Design Staff, illus. 48p. (gr. 4-7). 1992. lib. bdg. 14.95 (0-944280-37-4); pap. 5.95 (0-944280-43-9) Bancroft-Sage.

Boulden, Jim. All Together. (Illus.). 32p. (Orig.). (gr. 1-7). 1991. pap. 4.95 (1-878076-10-8) Boulden Pub.

—Alone Together. Eberly, Keith, illus. 32p. (Orig.). (gr. 1-7). 1991. pap. 4.95 (1-878076-09-4) Boulden Pub.

—Feeling Good. (Illus.). 32p. (Orig.). (gr. 1-7). 1991. pap. 4.95 (1-878076-11-6) Boulden Pub.

—Feelings & Faces: Feelings Activity Book. Winter, Peter, illus. 32p. (Orig.). (gr. 1-7). 1993. pap. 4.95 (1-878076-20-5) Boulden Pub.

—Glad to Be Me. Fountain, Phil, illus. 32p. (Orig.). (gr. 1-6). 1993. pap. 4.95 (1-878076-26-4) Boulden Pub.

—How I Feel: Feelings Activity Book. Vecchio, Tony, illus. 32p. (Orig.). (gr. 1-7). Date not set. pap. 4.95 (1-878076-21-3) Boulden Pub.

—My Secret. Vachio, Tony, illus. 32p. (Orig.). (gr. 1-7). 1991. pap. 4.95 (1-878076-13-2) Boulden Pub.

—Saying Goodbye. 2nd ed. (SPA., Illus., Orig.). (gr. 1-7). 1991. pap. 3.95 (1-878076-02-7) Boulden Pub.

—Saying Goodbye. rev. ed. Eberly, Keith, illus. 32p. (Orig.). (gr. 1-7). 1991. pap. 3.95 (1-878076-12-4) Boulden Pub.

—Uncle Jerry Has AIDS. Winter, Peter, illus. 32p. (Orig.). (gr. 3-7). 1992. pap. 3.95 (1-878076-18-3) Boulden Pub.

Boulden, Jim & Boulden, Joan. Let's Talk. (Illus., Orig.). (gr. 1-7). 1991. pap. 4.95 wkbk. (1-878076-05-1) Boulden Pub.

—Mom & Me. Winter, Peter, illus. 32p. (Orig.). (gr. 1-6). 1993. pap. 4.95 (1-878076-25-6) Boulden Pub.

—My Story. (Orig.). (gr. 1-7). 1991. pap. 4.95 wkbk. (1-878076-06-X) Boulden Pub.

—Secrets That Hurt. Winter, Peter, illus. 32p. (Orig.). (gr. 1-6). 1993. pap. 4.95 (1-878076-28-0) Boulden Pub.

—Tough Times. Fountain, Phil, illus. 32p. (Orig.). (gr. 1-6). 1993. pap. 4.95 (1-878076-29-9) Boulden Pub.

Boulden, Joan, jt. auth. see Boulden, Jim.

Boulding, J. Russell. Thora's Saga: A Tale of Old Iceland. LC 85-73124. (Illus.). 184p. (Orig.). (gr. 6-12). 1986. pap. 4.95 (0-936001-00-3) Peaceable Pr.

Boule, Mary N. The California Native American Tribes. Liddell, Dan, illus. (gr. 1-8). 1991. pap. 85.00 boxed ed. (1-877599-23-9) Merryant Pubs.

—California's Native American Tribes, No. 1: Achumawi Tride. Liddell, Daniel, illus. 40p. (Orig.). (gr. 2-3). 1992. pap. 4.50 (1-877599-25-5) Merryant Pubs.

—California's Native American Tribes, No. 11: Coast Miwok. Liddell, Daniel, illus. 40p. (Orig.). (gr. 2-4). 1992. pap. 4.50 (1-877599-35-2) Merryant Pubs.

—California's Native American Tribes, No. 17: East & S. E. Pomo Tribe. Liddell, Daniel, illus. 40p. (Orig.). (gr. 3-4). 1992. pap. 4.50 (1-877599-40-9) Merryant Pubs.

—California's Native American Tribes, No. 12: Eastern Miwok Tribe. Liddell, Daniel, illus. 40p. (Orig.). (gr. 3-5). 1992. pap. 4.50 (1-877599-36-0) Merryant Pubs.

—California's Native American Tribes, No. 13: Lake Miwok Tribe. Liddell, Daniel, illus. 40p. (Orig.). (gr. 3-5). 1992. pap. 4.50 (1-877599-37-9) Merryant Pubs.

—California's Native American Tribes, No. 10: Maidu-KonKow Tribe. Liddell, Daniel, illus. 40p. (Orig.). (gr. 4-5). 1992. pap. 4.50 (1-877599-34-4) Merryant Pubs.

—California's Native American Tribes, No. 14: Ohlone Tribe. Liddell, Daniel, illus. 40p. (Orig.). (gr. 4-5). 1992. pap. 4.50 (1-877599-38-7) Merryant Pubs.

—California's Native American Tribes, No. 15: Patwin Tribe. Liddell, Daniel, illus. 60p. (Orig.). (gr. 3-5). 1992. pap. text ed. 4.50 (1-877599-49-2) Merryant Pubs.

—California's Native American Tribes, No. 18: Salinan Tribe. Liddell, Daniel, illus. 40p. (Orig.). (gr. 4-5). 1992. pap. 4.50 (1-877599-41-7) Merryant Pubs.

—California's Native American Tribes, No. 19: Shasta Tribe. Liddell, Daniel, illus. 40p. (Orig.). (gr. 2-4). 1992. pap. 4.50 (1-877599-42-5) Merryant Pubs.

—California's Native American Tribes, No. 16: Western & N. E. Pomo Tribe. Liddell, Daniel, illus. 40p. (Orig.). (gr. 2-3). 1992. pap. 4.50 (1-877599-39-5) Merryant Pubs.

—California's Native American Tribes, No. 2: Atsugewi Tribe. Liddell, Daniel, illus. 40p. (Orig.). (gr. 2-3). 1992. pap. 4.50 (1-877599-26-3) Merryant Pubs.

—California's Native American Tribes, No. 24: Foothill Yokuts Tribe. Liddell, Daniel, illus. 40p. (Orig.). (gr. 3-5). 1992. pap. 4.50 (1-877599-46-8) Merryant Pubs.

—California's Native American Tribes, No. 20: Tolowa Tribe. Liddell, Daniel, illus. 40p. (Orig.). (gr. 2-3). 1992. pap. 4.50 (1-877599-43-3) Merryant Pubs.

—California's Native American Tribes, No. 21: Tubatulabal Tribe. Liddell, Daniel, illus. 60p. (gr. 2-4). 1992. pap. 4.50 (1-877599-24-7) Merryant Pubs.

—California's Native American Tribes, No. 23: Valley Yokuts Tribe. Liddell, Daniel, illus. 40p. (Orig.). (gr. 4-5). 1992. pap. 4.50 (1-877599-45-X) Merryant Pubs.

—California's Native American Tribes, No. 22: Wintu Tribe. Liddell, Daniel, illus. 40p. (Orig.). (gr. 4-5). 1992. pap. 4.50 (1-877599-44-1) Merryant Pubs.

—California's Native American Tribes, No. 25: Yuki Tribe. Liddell, Daniel, illus. 40p. (Orig.). (gr. 2-3). 1992. pap. 4.50 (1-877599-47-6) Merryant Pubs.

—California's Native American Tribes, No. 26: Yurok Tribe. Liddell, Daniel, illus. 40p. (Orig.). (gr. 2-4). 1992. pap. 4.50 (1-877599-48-4) Merryant Pubs.

—California's Native American Tribes, No. 3: Cahuilla Tribe. Liddell, Daniel, illus. 40p. (Orig.). (gr. 2-4). 1992. pap. 4.50 (1-877599-27-1) Merryant Pubs.

—California's Native American Tribes, No. 4: Chumash Tribe. Liddell, Daniel, illus. 40p. (Orig.). (gr. 3-5). 1992. pap. 4.50 (1-877599-28-X) Merryant Pubs.

—California's Native American Tribes, No. 5: Diegueno (Ipai-Tipai) Liddell, Daniel, illus. 40p. (Orig.). (gr. 2-4). 1992. pap. 4.50 (1-877599-29-8) Merryant Pubs.

—California's Native American Tribes, No. 6: Gabrielino Tribe. Liddell, Daniel, illus. 40p. (Orig.). (gr. 4-5). 1992. pap. 4.50 (1-877599-30-1) Merryant Pubs.

—California's Native American Tribes, No. 7: Hupa Tribe. Liddell, Daniel, illus. 40p. (Orig.). (gr. 2-4). 1992. pap. 4.50 (1-877599-31-X) Merryant Pubs.

—California's Native American Tribes, No. 8: Karok Tribe. Liddell, Daniel, illus. 40p. (Orig.). (gr. 2-3). 1992. pap. 4.50 (1-877599-32-8) Merryant Pubs.

—California's Native American Tribes, No. 9: Luiseno Tribe. Liddell, Daniel, illus. 40p. (Orig.). (gr. 4-5). 1992. pap. 4.50 (1-877599-33-6) Merryant Pubs.

—The Missions: California's Heritage, No. 1: Mission San Diego de Alcala. Grim, Ellen & De Batuc, Alfredo, illus. 24p. (Orig.). (gr. 4-6). 1988. pap. 3.50 (1-877599-00-X) Merryant Pubs.

—The Missions: California's Heritage, No. 10: Mission Santa Barbara. Grim, Ellen & De Batuc, Alfredo, illus. 24p. (Orig.). (gr. 4-6). 1988. pap. 3.50 (1-877599-09-3) Merryant Pubs.

—The Missions: California's Heritage, No. 11: Mission la Purisima Concepcion. Grim, Ellen & De Batuc, Alfredo, illus. 24p. (Orig.). (gr. 4-6). 1988. pap. 3.50 (1-877599-10-7) Merryant Pubs.

—The Missions: California's Heritage, No. 12: Mission Santa Cruz. Grim, Ellen & De Batuc, Alfredo, illus. 24p. (Orig.). (gr. 4-6). 1988. pap. 3.50 (1-877599-11-5) Merryant Pubs.

—The Missions: California's Heritage, No. 13: Mission Nuestra Senora de la Soledad. Grim, Ellen & De Batuc, Alfredo, illus. 20p. (Orig.). (gr. 4-6). 1988. pap. 3.50 (1-877599-12-3) Merryant Pubs.

—The Missions: California's Heritage, No. 14: Mission San Jose. Grim, Ellen & De Batuc, Alfredo, illus. 28p. (Orig.). (gr. 4-6). 1988. pap. 3.50 (1-877599-13-1) Merryant Pubs.

—The Missions: California's Heritage, No. 15: Mission San Juan Bautista. Grim, Ellen & De Batuc, Alfredo, illus. 24p. (Orig.). (gr. 4-6). 1988. pap. 3.50 (1-877599-14-X) Merryant Pubs.

—The Missions: California's Heritage, No. 16: Mission San Miguel Arcangel. Grim, Ellen & De Batuc, Alfredo, illus. 24p. (Orig.). (gr. 4-6). 1988. pap. 3.50 (1-877599-15-8) Merryant Pubs.

—The Missions: California's Heritage, No. 17: Mission San Fernando Rey de Espana. Grim, Ellen & De Batuc, Alfredo, illus. 24p. (Orig.). (gr. 4-6). 1988. pap. 3.50 (1-877599-16-6) Merryant Pubs.

—The Missions: California's Heritage, No. 18: Mission San Luis Rey de Francia, 21 Bks. De Batuc, Alfredo & Grim, Ellen, illus. 24p. (Orig.). (gr. 4). 1988. pap. 3.50 (1-877599-17-4) Merryant Pubs.

—The Missions: California's Heritage, No. 19: Mission Santa Ines. Grim, Ellen & De Batuc, Alfredo, illus. 24p. (Orig.). (gr. 4-6). 1988. pap. 3.50 (1-877599-18-2) Merryant Pubs.

—The Missions: California's Heritage, No. 2: Mission San Carlos Borromeo de Carmelo. Grim, Ellen & De Batuc, Alfredo, illus. 24p. (Orig.). (gr. 4-6). 1988. pap. 3.50 (1-877599-01-8) Merryant Pubs.

—The Missions: California's Heritage, No. 20: Mission San Rafael Arcangel. Grim, Ellen & De Batuc, Alfredo, illus. 24p. (Orig.). (gr. 4-6). 1988. pap. 3.50 (1-877599-19-0) Merryant Pubs.

—The Missions: California's Heritage, No. 21: Mission San Francisco Solano. Grim, Ellen & De Batuc, Alfredo, illus. 24p. (Orig.). (gr. 4-6). 1988. pap. 3.50 (1-877599-20-4) Merryant Pubs.

—The Missions: California's Heritage, No. 3: Mission San Antonio de Padua. Grim, Ellen & De Batuc, Alfredo, illus. 24p. (Orig.). (gr. 4-6). 1988. pap. 3.50 (1-877599-02-6) Merryant Pubs.

—The Missions: California's Heritage, No. 4: Mission San Gabriel Arcangel. Grim, Ellen & De Batuc, Alfredo, illus. 24p. (Orig.). (gr. 4-6). 1988. pap. 3.50 (1-877599-03-4) Merryant Pubs.

—The Missions: California's Heritage, No. 5: Mission San Luis Obispo de Tolosa. Grim, Ellen & De Batuc, Alfredo, illus. 24p. (Orig.). (gr. 4-6). 1988. pap. 3.50 (1-877599-04-2) Merryant Pubs.

—The Missions: California's Heritage, No. 6: Mission San Francisco de Asis. Grim, Ellen & De Batuc, Alfredo, illus. 24p. (Orig.). (gr. 4-6). 1988. pap. 3.50 (1-877599-05-0) Merryant Pubs.

—The Missions: California's Heritage, No. 7: Mission San Juan Capistrano. Grim, Ellen & De Batuc, Alfredo, illus. 24p. (Orig.). (gr. 4-6). 1988. pap. 3.50 (1-877599-06-9) Merryant Pubs.

—The Missions: California's Heritage, No. 8: Mission Santa Clara de Asis. Grim, Ellen & De Batuc, Alfredo, illus. 24p. (Orig.). (gr. 4-6). 1988. pap. 3.50 (1-877599-07-7) Merryant Pubs.

—The Missions: California's Heritage, No. 9: Mission San Buenaventura. Grim, Ellen & De Batuc, Alfredo, illus. 24p. (Orig.). (gr. 4-6). 1988. pap. 3.50 (1-877599-08-5) Merryant Pubs.

Boulle, Pierre. Bridge over the River Kwai. (gr. 8 up). 1990. pap. 4.50 (0-553-24850-2) Bantam.

—Planet of the Apes. 128p. (RL 7). 1964. pap. 2.50 (0-451-14324-8, AJ2318, Sig) NAL-Dutton.

Boulton, Alexander O. Frank Lloyd Wright, Architect: A Picture Biography. Pfeiffer, Bruce B., intro. by. LC 93-12188. 1993. write for info. (0-8478-1683-4) Rizzoli Intl.

Boulton, Harold. All Through the Night. Fasen, Steve & Fasen, Gary, illus. (gr. 2 up). 1988. 13.95 (0-687-01015-2) Abingdon.

Boulton, Jane, adapted by see Whiteley, Opal.

Boundy, Donna, jt. auth. see Washton, Arnold M.

Bouquet, Jeff S. Young Man's Guide to Autos: Basics, Operation, Safety & Maintenance. Kimmel, Nita, illus. 80p. 1991. 55.00x (1-56216-017-6); pap. 25.00x (1-56216-018-4) Systems Co.

Bour, Daniele. The House from Morning to Night. LC 84-21873. (Illus.). 16p. (ps-3). 1985. 9.95 (0-916291-01-4) Kane Miller Bk.

Bour, Laura. Bears. (Illus.). (ps). 1992. bds. 10.95 (0-590-45270-3, 038, Cartwheel) Scholastic Inc.

—Whales. Bour, Laura, illus. LC 92-41413. 24p. (ps-3). 1993. 11.95 (0-590-47130-9, Cartwheel) Scholastic Inc.

Bour, Laura, jt. ed. see Jeunesse, Gallimard.

Bourgeault, Lisa, jt. auth. see Bean, Lowell J.

Bourgeois, Jean-Francois. Los Ninos de la Biblia. Maecha, Alberto, ed. Landgraff, Michael, illus. (SPA.). 40p. (gr. 3-5). 1984. pap. write for info. (0-942504-11-9) Overcomer Pr.
Bourgeois, Paulette. Amazing Dirt Book. 1990. pap. 6.68 (0-201-55096-2) Addison-Wesley.
—Amazing Paper Book. (gr. 4-8). 1990. pap. 6.68 (0-201-52377-9) Addison-Wesley.
—Amazing Potato Book. LC 91-23847. 1991. pap. 6.68 (0-201-56761-X) Addison-Wesley.
—Big Sarah's Little Boots. Clark, Brenda, illus. LC 89-4224. (ps-k). 1989. pap. 11.95 (0-590-42622-2) Scholastic Inc.
—Big Sarah's Little Boots. Clark, Brenda, illus. 1992. pap. 3.95 (0-590-42623-0, Blue Ribbon Bks) Scholastic Inc.
—Franklin Fibs. (Illus.). 1992. pap. 3.95 (0-590-44647-9) Scholastic Inc.
—Franklin in the Dark. Clark, Brenda, illus. 32p. (ps-2). 1987. pap. 3.95 (0-590-44506-5) Scholastic Inc.
—Franklin in the Dark. (ps-3). 1992. pap. 19.95 (0-590-72701-X) Scholastic Inc.
—Franklin Is Lost. (ps-3). 1993. pap. 3.95 (0-590-46255-5) Scholastic Inc.
—Too Many Chickens! (ps-3). 1991. 12.95 (0-316-10358-6) Little.
Bourgoing, Pascale de see De Bourgoing, Pascale.
Bourke, Linda. Eye Spy: A Mysterious Alphabet. Bourke, Linda, illus. 64p. (ps up). 1991. 15.95 (0-87701-805-7) Chronicle Bks.
Bourke, Linda, jt. auth. see Sullivan, Mary B.
Bourne, Cheryl. Sam the Big Blue Bear. LC 93-60235. (Illus.). 44p. (ps-3). 1994. 6.95 (1-55523-599-9) Winston-Derek.
Bourne, Gloria, jt. auth. see Bailey, Katharine R.
Bourne, Miriam A. A Day in the Life of a Chef. Jann, Gayle, illus. LC 87-13762. 32p. (gr. 4-8). 1988. PLB 11.79 (0-8167-1115-1); pap. text ed. 2.95 (0-8167-1116-X) Troll Assocs.
—A Day in the Life of a Cross-Country Trucker. Jann, Gayle, illus. LC 87-13582. 32p. (gr. 4-8). 1988. PLB 11.79 (0-8167-1117-8); pap. text ed. 2.95 (0-8167-1118-6) Troll Assocs.
—Let's Visit a Toy Factory. Plunkett, Micheal, illus. LC 87-3489. 32p. (gr. 2-4). 1988. PLB 10.79 (0-8167-1159-3); pap. text ed. 2.95 (0-8167-1160-7) Troll Assocs.
Bourne, Phyllis, tr. see Wright, Bob.
Bourque, Nina. The Best Trade of All. Urbanovic, Jackie, illus. LC 83-7352. 32p. (gr. 3-6). 1983. PLB 14.65 (0-940742-33-0) Raintree Steck-V.
—The Best Trade of All. Urbanovic, Jackie, illus. LC 83-7352. 32p. (gr. 3-6). 1984. PLB 27.99 incl. cassette (0-8172-2280-4); cassette only 14.00 (0-317-19659-6) Raintree Steck-V.
Bousquet, Catherine. Incredibly Hidden. LC 93-9459. (Illus.). 48p. (gr. 6 up). 1993. lib. bdg. 14.95 RSBE (0-02-711737-5, New Discovery Bks) Macmillan Child Grp.
Boutan, Mila. Collages. (Illus.). (ps-1). 1992. 4.50 (1-56021-196-2) W J Fantasy.
—Decoupage. (Illus.). (ps-1). 1992. 4.50 (1-56021-194-6) W J Fantasy.
—Mosaiques. (Illus.). (ps-1). 1992. 4.50 (1-56021-195-4) W J Fantasy.
Boutiaul, Claudine. The Hen with the Wooden Leg. (Illus.). 32p. (gr. 3-5). 1991. 18.50 (0-89565-751-1); 12.95s.p. (0-685-55084-2) Childs World.
Bouton, Bud. B Is for Buffalo. (Illus.). 64p. (gr. 1 up). 1994. 15.95 (1-879244-03-9) Windom Bks.
Bouton, Steve. Cyber Rogues. Barrett, Kevin, ed. Aulisio, Janet, illus. 32p. (Orig.). (gr. 12). 1990. pap. 10.00 (1-55806-125-8, 5103) Iron Crown Ent Inc.
Bouvier, Leon F. Immigration. 160p. (gr. 7 up). 1992. PLB 14.85 (0-8027-6755-9); pap. 5.95 (0-8027-6756-7) Walker & Co.
Bouwman, Constance, et al. Beginning Spanish: A Teacher's Manual: Comprehension Based Activities for the Learnables, Book One. Baker, Syd, illus. 163p. (gr. 7 up). 1989. pap. text ed. 28.00 (0-939990-78-4) Intl Linguistics.
Bovaird, A. Goodbye U. S. A. - Bonjour France: A Language Learning Adventure. (Illus.). 48p. (gr. 3-7). 1993. 12.95 (0-8120-6406-2); pap. 5.95 (0-8120-4960-8) Barron.
Bovaird, Anne. Goodbye U. S. A. - Ola Mexico! Ballouhey, Pierre, illus. (gr. 3-7). 1994. 12.95 (0-8120-6374-0); pap. 5.95 (0-8120-1388-3) Barron.
Bove, Eugene. Uncle Gene's Breadbook for Kids! Bove, Eugene, illus. 64p. (gr. 5-12). 1986. pap. 11.95 (0-937395-00-5) Happibook Pr.
Bove, Linda. Sesame Street Sign Language ABC with Linda Bove. Cooke, Tom, illus. Shevett, Anita & Shevett, Anita, photos by. LC 85-1845. (Illus.). 32p. (gr. 3-8). 1985. lib. bdg. 5.99 (0-394-97516-2); 2.25 (0-394-87516-8) Random Bks Yng Read.
Bovert, Howard E. & Baranzini, Marlene S. Book of the American Indians. Sanchez, Bill, illus. LC 93-3068. (gr. 1-8). 1993. 19.95 (0-316-96921-4); pap. 10.95 (0-316-22208-9) Little.
Bovet, Howard E., et al. Book of the American Revolution. Sanchez, Bill, illus. LC 93-21769. (gr. 9-12). 1994. 19.95 (0-316-96922-2) Little.
Bowden, Joan. The Amazing Rhino. Cremins, Bob, illus. Moseley, Keith, contrib. by. LC 92-18891. (Illus.). (ps-3). 1993. 7.99 (0-8037-1383-5) Dial Bks Young.
—Planes of the Aces: A Three-Dimensional Collection of the Most Famous Aircraft in the World. 1993. pap. 14.95 (0-385-30910-4) Doubleday.

—A Pop-up Book of Monster Machines. Paris, Pat, designed by. (Illus.). 14p. (gr. k-5). 1991. 14.95 (0-8120-6205-1) Barron.
—Pop up Just Ben. 1989. 4.95 (0-671-67555-9) S&S Trade.
—Where Does Our Garbage Go? Paris, Pat, illus. (gr. 1-5). 1992. pap. 10.00 (0-385-30652-0) Doubleday.
—Why the Tides Ebb & Flow. (gr. k-3). 1979. 14.45 (0-395-28378-7) HM.
—Why the Tides Ebb & Flow. Brown, Marc, illus. 48p. (gr. k-3). 1990. pap. 5.95 (0-395-54952-3) HM.
—A World Without Elephants. Cremins, Bob, illus. Moseley, Keith, contrib. by. LC 92-18889. (Illus.). (ps-3). 1993. 7.99 (0-8037-1382-7) Dial Bks Young.
—A World Without Tigers. Cremins, Bob, illus. Moseley, Keith, contrib. by. LC 92-18890. (Illus.). (ps-3). 1993. 7.99 (0-8037-1381-9) Dial Bks Young.
Bowden, Julie see Mansmann, Patricia A. & Neuhausel, Patricia A.
Bowden, Miriam. The Adventures of Paz in the Land of Numbers. Crum, Anna M., illus. LC 89-71741. 32p. (ps-3). 1992. 12.95 (0-89334-150-9, 150-9) Humanics Ltd.
Bowe, Frank. Equal Rights for Americans with Disabilities. LC 92-25484. (Illus.). 144p. (gr. 9-12). 1992. 13.40 (0-531-13030-4) Watts.
Bowe-Gutman, Sonia. Teen Pregnancy. 72p. (gr. 6 up). 1987. PLB 15.95 (0-8225-0039-6) Lerner Pubns.
Bowen & Bowen Type Setters Staff, ed. see Potter, Jerold C.
Bowen, Annette P. Get a Life, Jennifer Parker. (Orig.). (gr. 8-12). 1993. pap. write for info. (0-87579-756-3) Deseret Bk.
Bowen, Betsy. Antler, Bear, Canoe: A Northwoods Alphabet Year. Bowen, Betsy, illus. 32p. (ps-3). 1991. 15.95 (0-316-10376-4, Joy St Bks) Little.
—Tracks in the Wild. LC 92-28691. 1993. 15.95 (0-316-10377-2) Little.
Bowen, Elizabeth. Friends & Relations. 192p. (gr. 7 up). 1980. pap. 2.25 (0-380-49601-1, 49601-1) Avon.
Bowen, Judith C., et al. The College Admissions Game... How to Play & Win. (Illus.). 112p. (gr. 9-12). 1992. pap. 19.95 (1-882707-02-8) Coll Info Srv.
Bowen, Marjorie. Viper of Milan. LC 65-25494. (gr. 4-8). 1965. 12.95 (0-8023-1014-1) Dufour.
Bowen, Richard. The First Helping. Bowen, Richard, illus. (gr. k-6). Date not set. pap. 9.95 (1-56883-009-2) Colonial Pr AL.
Bowen, Robert S. Infield Flash. LC 69-14320. (gr. 7-12). 1969. PLB 11.88 (0-688-51007-8) Lothrop.
Bowen, Sally. Down by the Christmas Stream. Wasmer, Kristina, illus. 38p. 1992. pap. 10.95 (0-9633546-0-4, Dist. by BookWorld Services, Inc.) Bowen & Assocs.
—Down by the Enchanted Stream. Wasmer, Kristina, illus. 38p. 1992. pap. 10.95 (0-9633546-1-2, Dist. by BookWorld Services, Inc.) Bowen & Assocs.
Bowen-Woodward, Kathy. Coping with a Negative Body Image. Rosen, Ruth, ed. (gr. 7-12). 1989. PLB 13.95 (0-8239-0978-6) Rosen Group.
Bower, B. M. Cabin Fever. 290p. 1981. Repr. of 1918 ed. PLB 16.35x (0-89966-017-7) Buccaneer Bks.
—Flying U Ranch. 280p. 1981. Repr. PLB 16.95x (0-89966-018-5) Buccaneer Bks.
Bower, Miranda. Experiment with Weather. LC 92-41126. 1993. 17.50 (0-8225-2458-9) Lerner Pubns.
Bower, Paula R. Apartheid Is Wrong: A Curriculum for Young People. (Illus.). 280p. (gr. 1-12). 1989. 3-ring hard cover notebook 15.00 (1-878537-00-8) Educ Racism & Apart.
Bower, Tom. Albert Blows a Fuse. Bower, Tom, illus. 32p. (gr. 5-8). 1991. 11.95 (0-7459-1906-5) Lion USA.
Bowers, Grace A., jt. auth. see Campbell, Louise A.
Bowers, R. G., et al. Talking about Grammar. (gr. 9-12). 1987. pap. text ed. 13.95 (0-582-55899-9, 78323) Longman.
Bowers, Ruth B. Little Thumb. LC 88-51387. (Illus.). 110p. (gr. k-3). 1989. pap. 5.95 (1-55523-196-9) Winston-Derek.
Bowes, Clare. The Hippo Bus. Bowes, Clare, illus. LC 92-34264. 1993. 14.00 (0-383-03629-1) SRA Schl Grp.
Bowkett, Gerald E. Reaching for a Star: The Final Campaign for Alaska Statehood. Matson, Sue, ed. Stevens, Ted, intro. by. LC 87-83742. (Illus.). 162p. (Orig.). (gr. 9-12). 1989. 22.95 (0-945397-04-6); pap. 14.95 (0-945397-05-4) Epicenter Pr.
Bowkett, Stephen. Dualists. (gr. 5-8). 1990. pap. 17.95 (0-575-04106-4, Pub. by Gollancz UK) Trafalgar.
Bowlby, Linda A. & Thomas, Mary L. Side Saddle Riding: Four-H Manual. Frank, Gayle, illus. 23p. (Orig.). (gr. 9-12). 1984. pap. 5.00 (1-884011-01-2) Wrld Sidesaddle.
—Side Saddle Riding: Four-H Manual. 2nd, rev. ed. John-Petrie, Sandi, illus. 24p. (gr. 9-12). 1993. pap. 5.00 (1-884011-06-3) Wrld Sidesaddle.
Bowles, Brad. Grandma's Band. Chan, Anthony, illus. 48p. (gr. k-4). 1989. PLB 14.95 (0-88045-112-2) Stemmer Hse.
Bowles, Charles. The Sometimes Invisible Spaceship. LC 87-71712. 113p. (Orig.). 1987. pap. 6.00 (0-916383-25-3) Aegina Pr.
Bowling, David L. Clean up Your Act, Dirty Dinjy Daryl. Bowling, Patricia H., illus. 32p. (Orig.). (gr. 1-4). 1993. 9.95 (0-939700-06-9); pap. 5.95 (0-939700-05-0); pap. 5.95 (0-939700-04-2) I D I C P.
Bowling, David L. & Bowling, Patricia H. Dirty Dingy Daryl. Martz, John, ed. Bowling, Patricia H., illus. LC 81-83120. 24p. (ps-4). 1981. 6.00 (0-939700-00-X); pap. 3.00 (0-939700-01-8) I D I C P.

—Dirty Dingy Daryl for President. Martz, John, ed. Bowling, Patricia H., illus. LC 83-82273. 40p. (gr. 1-4). 1983. 6.00 (0-939700-02-6); pap. 3.00 (0-939700-03-4) I D I C P.
Bowling, Patricia H., jt. auth. see Bowling, David L.

Bowman, Crystal. Cracks in the Sidewalk: Children's Daily Adventures. Hartman, Alan G., ed. Williams, Aaron, illus. 128p. (gr. k-8). 1993. 12.00 (0-9636050-1-1); pap. 6.00 (0-9636050-0-3) Cygnet Pub. Crystal Bowman is a homemaker, lyricist, & freelance writer. She especially enjoys writing for children & draws from her experience as a mother & former school teacher. When Crystal began sharing her poems with students in the local schools, the response was so positive that she wanted to make her poems available to the students. CRACKS IN THE SIDEWALK is a wonderful collection of these poems that children of all ages & backgrounds will enjoy. These poems address everyday issues such as the hiccups, mosquito bites, vegetables, & bubble gum. The reader will have an opportunity to meet such characters as Charles with snarles, messy Bess, Walter who hates his name, & a unique set of twins named Marilyn May & Mike. CRACKS IN THE SIDEWALK allows the reader to observe life through the eyes of an innocent child. It is warm, sensitive, humorous, & thought provoking. The poems are cleverly written in precise rhythm & rhyme, often with delightful endings. The poems are richly enhanced by outstanding illustrations. The illustrator, a fourteen year old boy, beautifully captures the warmth, humor, & emotions in unique & refreshing drawings. This book will appeal to all children, regardless of age, race or creed. To order: Cygnet Publishing Co., 2153 Wealthy Street, SE #238. East Grand Rapids, MI 49506.
Publisher Provided Annotation.

Bowman, John. Andrew Carnegie. Furstinger, Nancy, ed. (Illus.). 128p. (gr. 7-10). 1989. PLB 13.98 (0-382-09582-0) Silver Burdett Pr.
Bowman, John, ed. see Golay, Michael.
Bowman, John, ed. see Isserman, Maurice.
Bowman, John, ed. see Mills, Bronwyn.
Bowman, John S. Sportmanship. (Illus.). 64p. (gr. 7-12, RL 4-6). 1990. PLB 13.95 (0-8239-1110-1) Rosen Group.
Bowman, Margret & Millhouse, Nicholas. Blue-Footed Booby: Bird of the Galapagos. Bowman, Margret, illus. LC 85-27617. 32p. (gr. 1-7). 1986. 11.95 (0-8027-6628-5); lib. bdg. 11.85 (0-8027-6629-3) Walker & Co.
Bowman, Pete. A Surprise for Easter: A Revolving Picture Book. (Illus.). 12p. (Orig.). (ps-2). 1992. POB 11.95 (0-689-71552-8, Aladdin) Macmillan Child Grp.
Bowman-Kruhm, Mary, jt. auth. see Wirths, Claudine.
Bowman-Kruhm, Mary, jt. auth. see Wirths, Claudine G.
Bown, Deni. Orchids. LC 91-14937. (Illus.). 48p. (gr. 5-9). 1992. PLB 19.92 (0-8114-2736-6) Raintree Steck-V.
Bowser, Milton. Tobias, Vol. I, Bk. I: Follow Me to Yesterday. MacLean, Alistair, ed. Bowser, M., illus. 72p. 1993. PLB 20.00 (0-685-65016-2) (0-940178-30-3) Sitare.
Bowser, Milton & Haramilio, Alyce, eds. Saucer Sam. Cantrell, Ray, illus. 72p. 1992. 10.00 (0-940178-38-9) Sitare.
Bowyer. Houses & Homes. (gr. 4-9). 1978. (Usborne-Hayes); PLB 13.96 (0-88110-117-6); pap. 6.95 (0-86020-191-0) EDC.
Boy Scouts of America. Agribusiness. (Illus.). 72p. (Orig.). (gr. 6-12). 1987. pap. 1.85 (0-8395-3272-5, 3272) BSA.
—American Labor. (Illus.). 48p. (Orig.). (gr. 6-12). 1987. pap. 1.85 (0-8395-3326-8, 33326) BSA.
—Archery. (Illus.). 56p. (gr. 6-12). 1986. pap. 1.85 (0-8395-3381-0, 33259) BSA.

—Architecture. (Illus.). 46p. (gr. 6-12). 1966. pap. 1.85 (0-8395-3321-7, 33321) BSA.
—Art. (Illus.). 48p. (gr. 6-12). 1968. pap. 1.85 (0-8395-3320-9, 33320) BSA.
—Astronomy. (Illus.). 80p. (gr. 6-12). 1983. pap. 1.85 (0-8395-3303-9, 33303) BSA.
—Atomic Energy. (Illus.). 80p. (gr. 6-12). 1983. pap. 1.85 (0-8395-3275-X, 33275) BSA.
—Basketry. (Illus.). 32p. (gr. 6-12). 1986. pap. 1.85 (0-8395-3313-6, 33313) BSA.
—Beekeeping. (Illus.). 56p. (gr. 6-12). 1983. pap. 1.85 (0-8395-3362-4, 33362) BSA.
—Bird Study. (Illus.). 64p. (gr. 6-12). 1984. pap. 1.85 (0-8395-3282-2, 33282) BSA.
—Botany. (Illus.). 64p. (gr. 6-12). 1983. pap. 1.85 (0-8395-3379-9, 33379) BSA.
—Boy Scout Songbook. 128p. (gr. 6-12). 1970. pap. 1.55 (0-8395-3224-5, 33224) BSA.
—Camping. (Illus.). 96p. (gr. 6-12). 1984. pap. 1.85 (0-8395-3256-3, 33256) BSA.
—Consumer Buying. (Illus.). 64p. (gr. 6-12). 1975. pap. 1.85 (0-8395-3387-X, 33387) BSA.
—Cooking. LC 19-600. (Illus.). 80p. (gr. 6-12). 1986. pap. 1.85 (0-8395-3257-1, 33257) BSA.
—Cub Scout Leader Book. (Illus.). 192p. (gr. 9). 1982. pap. 4.75x (0-8395-3220-2, 33220) BSA.
—Cub Scout Magic. (Illus.). 146p. (gr. 3-5). 1960. pap. 7.00x (0-8395-3219-9, 33219) BSA.
—Cub Scout Songbook. (Illus.). 80p. (gr. 3-5). 1969. pap. 2.40x (0-8395-3222-9, 33222) BSA.
—Cub Scout Sports: Badminton. (Illus.). 32p. (Orig.). (gr. 2-5). 1986. pap. 1.35x (0-8395-4081-7, 2106) BSA.
—Cub Scout Sports: Bicycling. (Illus.). 64p. (Orig.). (gr. 2-5). 1986. pap. 1.35 (0-8395-4082-5, 34082) BSA.
—Cub Scout Sports: Gymnastics. (Illus.). 40p. (gr. 2-5). 1987. pap. 1.35 (0-8395-4085-X, 2110) BSA.
—Cub Scout Sports: Skating. (Illus.). 64p. (Orig.). (gr. 2-5). 1986. pap. 1.35 (0-8395-4083-3, 34083) BSA.
—Cub Scout Sports: Ultimate. (Illus.). 32p. (Orig.). (gr. 2-5). 1986. pap. 1.35x (0-8395-4084-1, 34084) BSA.
—Cycling. (Illus.). 40p. (gr. 6-12). 1984. pap. 1.85 (0-8395-3277-6, 33277) BSA.
—Dentistry. (Illus.). 32p. (gr. 6-12). 1975. pap. 1.85 (0-8395-3394-2, 33394) BSA.
—Dog Care. (Illus.). 48p. (gr. 6-12). 1984. pap. 1.85 (0-8395-3289-X, 33289) BSA.
—Drafting. (Illus.). 32p. (gr. 6-12). 1965. pap. 1.85 (0-8395-3273-3, 33273) BSA.
—Electronics. (Illus.). 72p. (gr. 6-12). 1977. pap. 1.85 (0-8395-3279-2, 33279) BSA.
—Emergency Preparedness. (Illus.). 64p. (gr. 6-12). 1972. pap. 1.85 (0-8395-3366-7, 33366) BSA.
—Energy. (Illus.). 64p. (gr. 6-12). 1978. pap. 1.85 (0-8395-3335-7, 33335) BSA.
—Engineering. (Illus.). 48p. (gr. 6-12). 1978. pap. 1.85 (0-8395-3376-4, 33376) BSA.
—Environmental Science. (Illus.). 72p. (gr. 6-12). 1983. pap. 1.85 (0-8395-3363-2, 33363) BSA.
—Farm Mechanics. (Illus.). 64p. (gr. 6-12). 1984. pap. 1.85 (0-8395-3346-2, 33346) BSA.
—First Aid. (Illus.). 96p. (gr. 6-12). 1988. pap. 1.85 (0-8395-3276-8, 33276) BSA.
—Geology. (Illus.). 96p. (gr. 6-12). 1985. pap. 1.85 (0-8395-3284-9, 33284) BSA.
—Handicap Awareness. (Illus.). 48p. (gr. 6-12). 1981. pap. 1.85 (0-8395-3370-5, 3370) BSA.
—Hiking. (Illus.). 36p. (gr. 6-12). 1991. pap. 1.85 (0-8395-3380-2, 33380) BSA.
—Home Repairs. (Illus.). 42p. (gr. 6-12). 1961. pap. 1.85 (0-8395-3329-2, 33329) BSA.
—Horsemanship. (Illus.). 64p. (gr. 6-12). 1986. pap. 1.85 (0-8395-3298-9, 33298) BSA.
—Insect Study. (Illus.). 64p. (gr. 6-12). 1985. pap. 1.85 (0-8395-3353-5, 33353) BSA.
—Machinery. (Illus.). 58p. (gr. 6-12). 1983. pap. 1.85 (0-8395-3337-3, 33337) BSA.
—Masonry. (Illus.). 64p. (gr. 6-12). 1980. pap. 1.85 (0-8395-3339-X, 33339) BSA.
—Metals Engineering. (Illus.). 64p. (gr. 6-12). 1984. pap. 1.85 (0-8395-3269-5, 33269) BSA.
—Metalwork. (Illus.). 36p. (gr. 6-12). 1969. pap. 1.85 (0-8395-3312-8, 33312) BSA.
—Model Design & Building. (Illus.). 44p. (gr. 6-12). 1964. pap. 1.85 (0-8395-3280-6, 3280) BSA.
—Nature. (Illus.). 48p. (gr. 6-12). 1973. pap. 1.85 (0-8395-3285-7, 33285) BSA.
—Pulp & Paper. (Illus.). 40p. (gr. 6-12). 1974. pap. 1.85 (0-8395-3343-8, 33343) BSA.
—Salesmanship. LC 19-600. (Illus.). 40p. (gr. 6-12). 1987. pap. 1.85 (0-8395-3351-9, 33351) BSA.
—Sea Exploring Manual. 272p. (gr. 6-12). 1987. pap. 12.85 (0-8395-3229-6, 33239) BSA.
—Stamp Collecting. (Illus.). 48p. (gr. 6-12). 1974. pap. 1.85 (0-8395-3359-4, 33296) BSA.
—Textile. 64p. (gr. 6-12). 1972. pap. 1.85 (0-8395-3344-6, 33344) BSA.
—Theater. 64p. (gr. 6-12). 1968. pap. 1.85 (0-8395-3328-4, 33328) BSA.
—Woodwork. (Illus.). 48p. (gr. 6-12). 1970. pap. 1.85 (0-8395-3316-0, 33316) BSA.
Boy Scouts of America Staff. Canoeing. (Illus.). 88p. (gr. 6-12). 1989. pap. 1.85 (0-8395-3308-X, 33308) BSA.
—Collections. (Illus.). 48p. (gr. 6-12). 1991. pap. 1.85 (0-8395-3242-5, 33242) BSA.
—Cub Scout Academics: Art. (Illus.). 44p. 1991. pap. 1.35 (0-8395-3031-5, 33031) BSA.
—Cub Scout Academics: Communicating. (Illus.). 112p. 1992. pap. 1.35 (0-8395-3033-1, 33033) BSA.
—Cub Scout Academics: Music. (Illus.). 40p. 1991. pap. 1.35 (0-8395-3034-X, 33034) BSA.
—Cub Scout Academics: Science. (Illus.). 44p. 1991. pap. 1.35 (0-8395-3030-7, 33030) BSA.
—Cub Scout Sports: Fishing. 40p. (Orig.). (gr. 2-5). 1988. pap. 1.35 (0-8395-4086-8, 34086) BSA.
—Electricity. (Illus.). 56p. (gr. 6-12). 1991. pap. 1.85 (0-8395-3236-9, 33236) BSA.
—Explorer Leader Handbook. (Illus.). 186p. (gr. 4-9). 1991. pap. 8.25 (0-8395-4637-8, 34637) BSA.
—Family Life. (Illus.). 40p. (gr. 6-12). 1991. pap. 1.85 (0-8395-3243-1, 33243) BSA.
—Junior Leader Handbook. (Illus.). 168p. 1990. pap. 2.25 (0-8395-3500-7, 33500) BSA.
—Learning for Life: Fifth Grade. (Illus.). 168p. (gr. 5). 1991. pap. 5.00 (0-8395-2130-8, 32130) BSA.
—Learning for Life: First Grade. (Illus.). 139p. (gr. 1). 1991. pap. 5.00 (0-8395-2126-X, 32126) BSA.
—Learning for Life: Fourth Grade. (Illus.). 154p. (gr. 4). 1991. pap. 5.00 (0-8395-2129-4, 32129) BSA.
—Learning for Life: High School. (Illus.). 160p. (gr. 9-12). 1991. pap. 5.00 (0-8395-2133-2, 32133) BSA.
—Learning for Life: Junior High. (Illus.). 62p. (gr. 7-8). 1991. pap. 5.00 (0-8395-2132-4, 32132) BSA.
—Learning for Life: Kindergarten. (Illus.). 134p. (gr. k). 1991. pap. 5.00 (0-8395-2125-1, 32125) BSA.
—Learning for Life: Second Grade. (Illus.). 156p. (gr. 2). 1991. pap. 5.00 (0-8395-2127-8, 32127) BSA.
—Learning for Life: Sixth Grade. (Illus.). 162p. (gr. 6). 1991. pap. 5.00 (0-8395-2131-6, 32131) BSA.
—Learning for Life: Special Education. (Illus.). 130p. 1991. pap. 5.00 (0-8395-2134-0, 32134) BSA.
—Learning for Life: Third Grade. (Illus.). 136p. (gr. 3). 1991. pap. 5.00 (0-8395-2128-6, 32128) BSA.
—Medicine. (Illus.). 70p. (gr. 6-12). 1991. pap. 1.85 (0-8395-3244-X, 33244) BSA.
—My Scout Advancement Trail. (Illus.). 16p. (Orig.). (gr. 5). 1990. pap. 0.95 (0-8395-3424-8, 33424) BSA.
—Order of the Arrow Handbook. rev. ed. (Illus.). 96p. (gr. 6 up). 1990. pap. 1.85 (0-8395-4996-2, 34996) BSA.
—Scoutmaster Handbook. (Illus.). 272p. 1992. pap. 6.50 (0-8395-3002-1, 33002) BSA.
—Varsity Shooting Sports. (Illus.). 87p. 1990. pap. 3.15 (0-8395-3457-4, 3457) BSA.
—Varsity Tennis. (Illus.). 42p. 1990. pap. 3.15 (0-8395-3455-8, 3455) BSA.
—Varsity Triathlon. (Illus.). 41p. 1990. pap. 3.15 (0-8395-3456-6, 3456) BSA.
—Venture Backpacking. (Illus.). 82p. 1990. pap. 3.15 (0-8395-3442-6, 33442) BSA.
—Venture Discovering Adventure. (Illus.). 20p. 1990. pap. 3.15 (0-8395-3472-8, 33472) BSA.
—Venture Freestyle Biking. (Illus.). 52p. 1990. pap. 3.15 (0-8395-3447-7, 3447) BSA.
—Venture Whitewater. (Illus.). 70p. 1990. pap. 3.15 (0-8395-3465-5, 33465) BSA.
—Webelos Scout Book. rev. ed. (Illus.). 416p. (gr. 4-6). 1987. pap. 4.95 (0-8395-3235-0, 33235) BSA.
Boy Scouts of America Staff, ed. see Birkby, Robert C.
Boyce, Kim & Abraham, Ken. In Focus: Devotions to Help You Make Sense Out of a Senseless World. LC 92-31299. (Illus.). 1993. write for info. (0-7814-0814-8, Chariot Bks) Cook.
Boyce-Ballweber, Hettie. The First People of Maryland. LC 87-61066. 110p. (gr. 1-6). 1987. casebound 15.00 (0-917882-24-5) MD Hist Pr.
Boyd, Aaron. First Lady: The Story of Hillary Rodham Clinton. (Illus.). 128p. (gr. 6 up). 1994. PLB 18.95 (1-883846-02-1) M Reynolds.
Boyd, Aaron & Causey, Michael. Ross Perot: Businessman Politician. 128p. (gr. 8 up). 1994. PLB 18.95 (1-883846-04-8) M Reynolds.
Boyd, Aaron, jt. auth. see Martin, Gene L.
Boyd, Anne. Life in a Medieval Monastery. 2nd ed. (Illus.). 48p. (gr. 7 up). 1988. pap. 7.50 (0-521-33724-0) Cambridge U Pr.
Boyd, Brendan, text by. Hoops: Behind the Scenes with the Boston Celtics. Horenstein, Henry, photos by. (Illus.). 32p. (gr. 3-7). 1989. (Spts Illus Kids); pap. 8.95 (0-316-37309-5) Little.
Boyd, Candy D. Charlie Pippin. LC 86-23780. 192p. (gr. 3-7). 1987. SBE 14.95 (0-02-726350-9, Macmillan Child Bk) Macmillan Child Grp.
—Charlie Pippin. 192p. (gr. 3-7). 1988. pap. 3.99 (0-14-032587-5, Puffin) Puffin Bks.
—Chevrolet Saturdays. LC 92-32119. 176p. (gr. 3-7). 1993. SBE 14.95 (0-02-711760-0, Macmillan Child Bk) Macmillan Child Grp.
—Circle of Gold. 128p. (Orig.). (gr. 4-6). 1984. pap. 2.95 (0-590-43266-4, Apple Paperbacks) Scholastic Inc.
—Circle of Gold. LC 93-19020. 128p. (gr. 3-7). 1994. 13.95 (0-590-49426-0) Scholastic Inc.
—Forever Friends. 192p. (gr. 5-9). 1986. pap. 4.99 (0-14-032077-6, Puffin) Puffin Bks.
—Forever Friends. (gr. 4-8). 1992. 17.00 (0-8446-6571-1) Peter Smith.
Boyd, Frances & Quinn, David. Stories from Lake Wobegon: Advanced Listening & Conversation Skills. 1990. map. text ed. 18.95 (0-8013-0312-5, 78017); cass. 37.95 (0-8013-0492-X, 78344) Longman.
Boyd, George A. Drugs & Sex. LC 93-5873. 1993. 14.95 (0-8239-1538-7) Rosen Group.
Boyd, John R. & Boyd, Mary A. Input - Output. (Illus.). 272p. (Orig.). (gr. 7-12). 1989. pap. 8.95 (0-933759-14-2); 4.95 (0-933759-15-0); cassette tape set 29.95 (0-933759-16-9) Abaca Bks.

Boyd, Kevin W. The Complete Aquarium Problem Solver. (Illus.). 32p. (gr. 10). 1989. pap. write for info. Boylen.
Boyd, L. M. Clancy's Treasure Book for Children. Boyd, L. M., illus. 166p. (Orig.). (gr. k-5). 1981. pap. 7.95 (0-941620-34-4) Carson Ent.
Boyd, Liz. Baby Wiggles - Bunny Hops. LC 92-50279. (ps). 1992. 8.95 (1-56305-308-X) Workman Pub.
Boyd, Lizi. Baby Wiggles - Baby Plays. LC 92-50278. (ps). 1992. 8.95 (1-56305-310-1) Workman Pub.
—Bailey the Big Bully. 32p. (ps-3). 1991. 3.95 (0-14-054051-2, Puffin) Puffin Bks.
—Black Dog Red House. Boyd, Lizi, illus. (ps-2). 1993. 12.95 (0-316-10443-4) Little.
—Half Wild & Half Child. (Illus.). 32p. (ps-3). 1991. pap. 3.95 (0-14-050825-2, Puffin) Puffin Bks.
—Mouse in a House: A Toy, Book, & Crafts Kit. (ps-3). 1993. 12.95 (0-316-10444-2) Little.
—The Not-So-Wicked Stepmother. (Illus.). 32p. (ps-3). 1989. pap. 3.95 (0-14-050720-5, Puffin) Puffin Bks.
—Sam Is My Half Brother. (Illus.). 32p. (ps-2). 1990. pap. 11.95 (0-670-83046-1) Viking Child Bks.
—Sam Is My Half Brother. (Illus.). 32p. (ps-3). 1992. pap. 3.99 (0-14-054190-X, Puffin) Puffin Bks.
—Sweet Dreams, Willy. Boyd, Lizi, illus. 32p. (ps-1). 1992. PLB 12.50 (0-670-84382-2) Viking Child Bks.
—Willy & the Cardboard Boxes. (Illus.). 32p. (ps-1). 1991. 11.95 (0-670-83636-2) Viking Child Bks.
Boyd, Mary A., jt. auth. see Boyd, John R.
Boyd, Patricia R. The Furry Wind. Spring, Grace J., illus. 28p. (gr. 2-3). 1982. pap. 2.25 (0-9603840-4-9) Andrew Mtn Pr.
Boyd, Patti, illus. Oh So Noisy! 12p. (ps). 1993. bds. 4.95 (0-448-40538-5, G&D) Putnam Pub Group.
Boyd, Pauline, jt. auth. see Boyd, Selma.
Boyd, Selma & Boyd, Pauline. The How: Making the Best of a Mistake. Luks, Peggy, illus. LC 80-13513. 32p. (ps-3). 1981. 16.95 (0-87705-176-3) Human Sci Pr.
Boyd, Susan, et al. Global Warming & Energy Choices: A Community Action Guide. (Illus.). 38p. (Orig.). (gr. 5-12). 1991. 4.00 (0-937345-07-5) Concern.
Boyde, Florence C. Slightly Dotty. 160p. 1993. 15.95 (0-8059-3406-5) Dorrance.
Boyd-Smith, Wendy. The No Barking at the Table Cookbook: Canine Recipes Most Begged For. Saltzberg, Barney, illus. 106p. (Orig.). 1991. pap. text ed. write for info. (0-9629459-0-0) Lip Smackers.
Boyer. Accident Kids. LC 73-93019. (Illus.). 32p. (gr. 2-5). 1974. PLB 9.95 (0-87783-119-X); pap. 3.94 deluxe ed. (0-87783-120-3) cassettes o.s.i. 7.94x (0-87783-175-0) Oddo.
—Let's Walk Safely. LC 80-82953. (Illus.). 32p. (gr. 1-6). 1981. PLB 9.95 (0-87783-159-9) Oddo.
—Lucky Bus. LC 73-87801. (Illus.). 32p. (gr. k-2). 1974. PLB 12.35 prebound (0-87783-131-9); cassette o.s.i. 7.94x (0-87783-193-9) Oddo.
—Oddo Safety Series. (Illus.). (ps-6). Set of 4 vols. PLB 44.60 (0-87783-170-X); three cassettes o.s.i. 23.82x (0-87783-235-8) Oddo.
—Safety on Wheels. LC 73-87802. (Illus.). 32p. (gr. k-5). 1974. PLB 12.35 prebound (0-87783-134-3); pap. 3.94 deluxe ed. (0-87783-134-3); cassette 7.94x (0-87783-199-8) Oddo.
Boyer, Jill, et al. Blacksongs, Series I: Four Poetry Broadsides by Black Women. (gr. 7-12). 1977. pap. 5.00 (0-916418-15-4) Lotus.
Boyer, Jill W. Breaking Camp. LC 83-82772. (Illus.). 61p. (gr. 9-12). 1984. pap. 6.00 perf. bnd. (0-916418-52-9) Lotus.
Boyer, Robert E. Oceanography. 2nd ed. LC 74-1649. (Illus.). 48p. (gr. 7-12). 1987. pap. 7.50 (0-8331-6611-5, 6611) Hubbard Sci.
Boyer, Robert E. & Snyder, P. B. Geology Fact Book. 2nd ed. LC 75-138627. (Illus.). 48p. (gr. 4-7). 1986. pap. text ed. 7.50 (0-8331-0572-8) Hubbard Sci.
Boyers, Sara J., ed. see Angelou, Maya.
Boyette, William. Soviet Georgia. (Illus.). 104p. (gr. 5 up). 1988. lib. bdg. 14.95 (1-55546-779-2) Chelsea Hse.
Boyice, Lester L., jt. auth. see Simmons, Herbert R.
Boyington, jt. auth. see Baker.
Boykin, Phyllis. I Like to Go to Church. (ps). 1987. 5.95 (0-8054-4174-3) Broadman.

Boylan, Kristi M. Spenser's Important Work: Introducing Your Child To Day Care. Featherman, John, illus. 32p. (Orig.). 1993. pap. 7.99 (1-883497-00-0) Parent Track.
SPENSER'S IMPORTANT WORK is the first in a series of 32-page, four-color illustrated children's books for children who attend child care centers. Each of the five books in the series is designed to help young children become acquainted with the day to day events of child care facilities. At the back of each book is a section called Parent's Guide which presents parents with effective ways to make their child's experience at day care a positive one.

SPENSER'S IMPORTANT WORK introduces children to the day care experience & helps lessen separation anxiety. Book II/SPENSER'S NEW FRIEND, teaches children how to make friends at day care. Book III/ SPENSER GETS THE POX teaches children & parents about communicable diseases at day care. Book IV/LATE TO SCHOOL AGAIN teaches children the importance of being on time. Book V/SPENSER'S NEW ROOM helps children make the adjustment in changing teachers or rooms at day care. Each book retails at $7.99. Cost for ordering 5 or more books in the series is $4.00 per book. Order by sending check or money order to The Parent Track Publications, 3210 Commander Rd., Carrollton, TX 75006. Or call 214-269-2160.
Publisher Provided Annotation.

Boyle, Alison. Playdays Colours & Shapes. Johnson, Paul, illus. 32p. (ps-2). 1992. pap. 2.95 (0-563-20887-2, BBC-Parkwest) Parkwest Pubns.
—Playdays Letters & Words. Johnson, Paul, illus. 32p. (ps-2). 1992. pap. 2.95 (0-563-20890-2, BBC-Parkwest) Parkwest Pubns.
—Playdays Numbers. Johnson, Paul, illus. 32p. (ps-2). 1992. pap. 2.95 (0-563-20889-9, BBC-Parkwest) Parkwest Pubns.
—Playdays Out & About. Johnson, Paul, illus. 32p. (ps-2). 1992. pap. 2.95 (0-563-20888-0, BBC-Parkwest) Parkwest Pubns.
Boyle, Doe. Gray Wolf Pup. Thomas, Peter, narrated by. Domm, Jeff, illus. 32p. (gr. k-3). 1993. 11.95 (1-56899-010-3); incl. audiocassette 16.95 (1-56899-009-X); incl. audiocassette, 14 in. plush toy 39.95 (1-56899-007-3); incl. audiocassette, 8 in. plush toy 25.95 (1-56899-008-1) Soundprints.
—Summer Coat, Winter Coat: The Story of a Snowshoe Hare. Komisar, Alexi, narrated by. Davis, Alton, illus. 32p. (gr. k-3). 1993. 11.95 (1-56899-015-4); incl. audiocassette 8 in. brown plush toy 25.95 (1-56899-018-9); incl. audiocassette 16.95 (1-56899-014-6); incl. audiocassette, 11 in. white plush toy 39.95 (1-56899-012-X); incl. audiocassette, 11 in. brown plush toy 39.95 (1-56899-017-0); incl. audiocassette, 8 in. white plush toy 25.95 (1-56899-013-8) Soundprints.
Boyle, Doe & Thomas, Peter, eds. Big Town Trees: From an Original Article which Appeared in Ranger Rick Magazine, Copyright National Wildlife Federation. Beylon, Cathy, illus. 20p. (gr. k-3). 1993. 6.95 (0-924483-83-0); incl. audio tape 9.95 (0-924483-84-9); incl. audio tape & 13 inch plush toy 35.95 (0-924483-87-3); incl. 9 inch plush toy 21.95 (0-924483-89-X) Soundprints.
—Caribou Country: From an Original Article Which Appeared in Ranger Rick Magazine, Copyright National Wildlife Federation. Langford, Alton, illus. Luther, Sallie, contrib. by. (Illus.). 20p. (gr. k-3). 1992. 6.95 (0-924483-53-9); incl. audiocass. tape & 13" toy 35.95 (0-924483-50-4); incl. 9" toy 21.95 (0-924483-51-2); incl. audiocass. tape 9.95 (0-924483-52-0); write for info. audiocass. tape (0-924483-80-6) Soundprints.
—Deputy Scarlett: From an Original Article Which Appeared in Ranger Rick Magazine, copyright National Wildlife Federation. Langford, Alton, illus. Luther, Sallie, contrib. by. (Illus.). 20p. (gr. k-3). 1992. 6.95 (0-924483-49-0); incl. audiocass. tape & 11" toy 35.95 (0-924483-46-0); incl. 8" toy 21.95 (0-924483-47-4); incl. audiocass. tape 9.95 (0-924483-48-2); write for info. audiocass. tape (0-924483-79-2) Soundprints.
—Earth Day Every Day: From an Original Article which Appeared in Ranger Rick Magazine, Copyright National Wildlife Federation. Beylon, Cathy, illus. 20p. (gr. k-3). 1993. 6.95 (0-924483-82-2); incl. audio tape 9.95 (0-924483-85-7); incl. audio tape & 13 inch plush toy 35.95 (0-924483-86-5); incl. 9 inch plush toy 21.95 (0-924483-88-1) Soundprints.
—Gift from the Trees from an Original Article Which Appeared in Ranger Rick Magazine, Copyright National Wildlife Federation. Beylon, Cathy, illus. 20p. (gr. k-3). 1993. 6.95 (1-56899-022-7); incl. audiocassette 9.95 (1-56899-021-9); incl. audiocassette, 13 in. plush toy 35.95 (1-56899-019-7); incl. 13 in. plush toy 21.95 (1-56899-020-0) Soundprints.

—Operation Beaver: From an Original Article Which Appeared in Ranger Rick Magazine, Copyright National Wildlife Federation. Beylon, Cathy, illus. Luther, Sallie, contrib. by. (Illus.). 20p. (gr. k-3). 1992. 6.95 (0-924483-57-1); incl. audiocass. tape & 13" toy 35.95 (0-924483-54-7); incl. 9" toy 21.95 (0-924483-55-5); incl. audiocass. tape 9.95 (0-924483-56-3); write for info. audiocass. tape (0-924483-81-4) Soundprints.
—Rick's First Adventure: From an Original Article Which Appeared in Ranger Rick Magazine, Copyright National Wildlife Federation. Langford, Alton, illus. Luter, Sallie, contrib. by. (Illus.). 20p. (gr. k-3). 1992. 6.95 (0-924483-45-8); incl. audiocass. tape & 13" toy 35.95 (0-924483-42-3); incl. 9" toy 21.95 (0-924483-43-1); incl. audiocass. tape 9.95 (0-924483-44-X); write for info. audiocass. tape (0-924483-78-4) Soundprints.
Boyle, Kay. Winter Night. LC 92-44043. 1994. write for info. (0-88682-576-8) Creative Ed.
Boylston, Helen D. Clara Barton, Founder of American Red Cross. (Illus.). (gr. 4-6). 1963. lib. bdg. 11.99 (0-394-90358-7) Random Bks Yng Read.
Boyne, Walter J. The Smithsonian Book of Flight for Young People. LC 88-985. (Illus.). (gr. 3-7). 1988. pap. 10.95 (0-689-71212-X, Aladdin) Macmillan Child Grp.
—Smithsonian Book of Flight for Young People. LC 87-35912. 128p. (gr. 3-7). 1988. SBE 16.95 (0-689-31422-1, Atheneum Child Bk) Macmillan Child Grp.
Boynton, Alice. Halloween KidDoodles, No. 3. Silver, Pattie, illus. 64p. (ps-2). 1992. pap. 0.99 (1-56293-261-6) McClanahan Bk.
Boynton, Alice B. Priscilla Alden & the Story of the First Thanksgiving. Brook, Bonnie, ed. Kiefer, Christa, illus. 32p. (gr. k-2). 1990. 6.95 (0-671-69111-2); PLB 10.98 (0-671-69105-8) Silver Pr.
Boynton, LaVerne L. The Enchantment of Beaver Creek. Richards, Linda, illus. 248p. 1988. 12.95 (0-685-44325-6) Starlite Pub.
Boynton, Robert W., ed. see Shakespeare, William.
Boynton, Sandra. A Is for Angry: An Animal & Adjective Alphabet. LC 83-40038. 48p. (ps-k). 1987. pap. 5.95 (0-89480-507-X, 1507) Workman Pub.
—A to Z. Boynton, Sandra, illus. 14p. (ps). 1984. 3.95 (0-671-49317-5, Little Simon) S&S Trade.
—Blue Hat Green Hat. 14p. 1984. 3.95 (0-671-49320-5, Little Simon) S&S Trade.
—Boynton on Board: Barnyard Dance! Boynton, Sandra, illus. 24p. (ps). 1993. bds. 6.95 (1-56305-442-6, 3442) Workman Pub.
—Boynton on Board: Birthday Monsters! Boynton, Sandra, illus. 24p. (ps). 1993. bds. 6.95 (1-56305-443-4) Workman Pub.
—Boynton on Board: Oh My Oh My Oh Dinosaurs! Boynton, Sandra, illus. 24p. (ps). 1993. bds. 6.95 (1-56305-441-8, 3441) Workman Pub.
—Boynton on Board: One, Two, Three! Boynton, Sandra, illus. 24p. (ps). 1993. bds. 6.95 (1-56305-444-2, 3444) Workman Pub.
—But Not the Hippopotamus. Klimo, Kate, ed. Boynton, Sandra, illus. 14p. (ps-k). 1982. 3.95 (0-671-44904-4, Little Simon) S&S Trade.
—Doggies. 1984. 3.95 (0-671-49318-3, Little Simon) S&S Trade.
—The Going to Bed Book. Klimo, Kate, ed. Boynton, Sandra, illus. 14p. (ps-k). 1982. 3.95 (0-671-44902-8, Little Simon) S&S Trade.
—Good Night, Good Night. Boynton, Sandra, illus. LC 85-2098. 40p. (ps-1). 1985. 6.95 (0-394-87285-1) Random Bks Yng Read.
—Horns to Toes. 12p. 1984. 3.95 (0-671-49319-1, Little Simon) S&S Trade.
—Moo Baa La La La. Klimo, Kate, ed. Boynton, Sandra, illus. 14p. 1982. 3.95 (0-671-44901-X, Little Simon) S&S Trade.
—Opposites. Klimo, Kate, ed. Boynton, Sandra, illus. (ps-k). 1982. 3.95 (0-671-44903-6, Little Simon) S&S Trade.
Bozanich, Tony L. Captain Flounder, His Sole Brothers & Friends. Isaksen, Lisa A., ed. Isaksen, Patricia, illus. 16p. (ps-4). 1984. pap. 4.95 (0-930655-00-1) Antarctic Pr.
Bozylinsky, Hannah H. Lala Salama. LC 92-23928. (Illus.). 40p. (ps-2). 1993. PLB 14.95 (0-399-22022-4, Philomel Bks) Putnam Pub Group.
Bracale, Carla. Fair-Weather Love. (gr. 5 up). 1989. pap. 2.95 (0-8041-0240-6) Ivy Books.
—Fair-Weather Love. 1992. pap. 2.99 (0-553-29449-0) Bantam.
—Puppy Love. (gr. 9-12). 1991. pap. 2.95 (0-553-28830-X) Bantam.
Brace, Ian. Play the Game: Ice Hockey. (Illus.). 80p. (gr. 10-12). 1991. pap. 6.95 (0-7063-6853-3, Pub. by Ward Lock UK) Sterling.
Bracken, Carolyn. Peter Rabbit's Pockets. Bracken, Carolyn, illus. 8p. (ps). 1982. pap. 3.95 (0-671-44528-6, Little Simon) S&S Trade.
Bracken, Carolyn, illus. The Busy School Bus. 12p. (ps up). 1986. 6.95 (0-448-09880-6, G&D) Putnam Pub Group.
—Fast Rolling Fire Trucks. 1984. 6.95 (0-448-09876-8, G&D) Putnam Pub Group.
—Santa's Pockets. (ps). 1983. pap. 3.95 (0-671-47660-2, Little Simon) S&S Trade.
—Teddy Bear's Pockets. 8p. (ps). 1983. pap. 3.95 washable (0-671-46448-5, Little Simon) S&S Trade.

Bracken, Carolyn & Barbaresi, Nina, illus. Baby Seal. (ps). 1984. pap. 2.95 vinyl (0-671-50031-7, Little Simon) S&S Trade.
—Duckling. (ps). 1984. pap. 2.95 vinyl (0-671-50030-9, Little Simon) S&S Trade.
Bracken, Charles. Tennis: Play Like a Pro. LC 89-27341. (Illus.). 64p. (gr. 4-8). 1990. PLB 9.79 (0-8167-1931-4); pap. text ed. 2.95 (0-8167-1932-2) Troll Assocs.
—Volleyball, A Step-by-Step Guide. LC 89-27352. (Illus.). 64p. (gr. 4-8). 1990. lib. bdg. 9.79 (0-8167-1951-9); pap. text ed. 2.95 (0-8167-1952-7) Troll Assocs.
Bracken, Sarah, jt. auth. see Pulleyn, Micah.
Brackenbury, Gill. My Picture Number Book. 1990. 3.99 (0-517-03206-6) Outlet Bk Co.
Brackenbury, John. Insects in Flight. (Illus.). 192p. (gr. 10-12). 1992. 35.00 (0-7137-2301-7, Pub. by Blandford Pr UK) Sterling.
Brackett, Karen & Manley, Rosie. Beautiful Junk. (gr. 1-6). 1990. pap. 10.95 (0-8224-0626-8) Fearon Teach Aids.
Brackett, Rona N. Harry's Grandpa Takes a Mysterious Journey. Johnson, Mackenzie, illus. LC 86-1233. 55p. (Orig.). (gr. 3-6). 1986. text ed. 12.50 (0-916955-04-4); pap. 6.75 (0-916955-05-2) Arcus Pub.
Brackin, A. J. Clocks: Chronicling Time. LC 91-16713. (Illus.). 96p. (gr. 5-8). 1991. PLB 15.95 (1-56006-208-8) Lucent Bks.
Brackman, Barbara, jt. auth. see Waldvogel, Merikay.
Bracons, Jose. The Key to Gothic Art. (Illus.). 80p. (gr. 8 up). 1990. PLB 21.50 (0-8225-2051-6) Lerner Pubns.
Bracy, Norma M. Light Bulbs. Bracy, Norma M., illus. 22p. (gr. k up). 1984. pap. text ed. 2.00 (0-915783-01-0) Book Binder.
—Poe & Pog. (Illus.). 22p. (gr. k-12). 1986. pap. text ed. 2.00 (0-915783-02-9) Book Binder.
—Rule of Gold. Bracy, Norma M., illus. 20p. (gr. k-12). 1983. pap. text ed. 2.00g (0-915783-00-2) Book Binder.
—Salt. (Illus.). 32p. (gr. k-12). 1986. pap. text ed. 2.00 (0-915783-03-7) Book Binder.
Bracy, Norma N. The Tool Box. (Illus.). 35p. (gr. k-12). 1987. pap. text ed. 2.00 (0-915783-04-5) Book Binder.
Bradbury, Frances M. American Hooked Rug Patterns. Bradbury, Frances, illus. 48p. (Orig.). 1986. pap. 5.95 (0-88045-084-3) Stemmer Hse.
Bradbury, Lynne. The First Christmas: Bible Stories. Williams, Jenny, illus. 28p. (ps-2). 1989. 3.95 (0-7214-5197-7, S846-1 SER.) Ladybird Bks.
—Shapes & Colors. Grundy, Lynn N., illus. 28p. (ps). 1992. Series 921. 3.50 (0-7214-1510-5) Ladybird Bks.
—What Is the Time? Grundy, Lynn N., illus. 28p. (ps). 1992. Series 921. 3.50 (0-7214-1511-3) Ladybird Bks.
Bradbury, Pamela, jt. auth. see Smith, Kathie B.
Bradbury, Pamela Z., jt. auth. see Smith, Kathie B.
Bradbury, Ray. Dandelion Wine. (gr. 6 up). 1985. pap. 4.99 (0-553-27753-7) Bantam.
—The Foghorn. Kelley, Gary, illus. 32p. 1987. PLB 13.95s.p. (0-88682-107-X) Creative Ed.
—The Halloween Tree. 192p. (gr. 7 up). 1984. pap. 4.99 (0-553-25823-0) Bantam.
—The Halloween Tree. Mugnaini, Joseph, illus. LC 72-2433. 160p. (gr. 6 up). 1988. Repr. of 1972 ed. 15.00 (0-394-82409-1); PLB 13.99 (0-394-92409-6) Knopf Bks Yng Read.
—Illustrated Man. (gr. 6-12). 1969. pap. 3.50 (0-553-25483-9) Bantam.
—The Smile. 1991. PLB 13.95s.p. (0-88682-466-4) Creative Ed.
—Something Wicked This Way Comes. (gr. 6-12). 1983. pap. 3.50 (0-553-25774-9) Bantam.
—Switch on the Night. Dillon, Leo & Dillon, Diane, illus. LC 92-25321. 40p. (ps-2). 1993. 8.99 (0-394-80486-4); PLB 9.99 (0-394-90486-9) Knopf Bks Yng Read.
—The Toynbee Convector. Kunz, Anita, illus. 32p. (gr. 7-9). 1992. 10.95 (1-878685-15-5) Turner Pub GA.
Bradbury, Thomas E. Scraggly's New Home. Goyette, Ron & Funk, Nancy C., trs. (Illus.). 32p. (Orig.). (gr. k-5). 1987. pap. text ed. write for info. (0-9618945-0-4) Tern Pubns.
Bradby, David, jt. auth. see Anderson, Rachel.
Braden, Vic & Phillips, Louis. Sportsathon Puzzles, Jokes, Facts & Games. Eberbach, Andrea, illus. (ps-k). 1986. pap. 4.95 (0-14-032028-8, Puffin) Puffin Bks.
Bradfield, Carl. Getting in Shape with Wendell & Myrtle: The Wendells Family, at It Again. (Illus.). 216p. (Orig.). (gr. 8-12). Date not set. pap. write for info. (0-9632319-4-4) ASDA Pub.
—Hawaii Calls Wendell & Myrtle: The Wendells Family Make It to the Big Island. (Illus.). 196p. (Orig.). (gr. 8-12). Date not set. pap. write for info. (0-9632319-5-2) ASDA Pub.
—The Sullivans of Little Horsepen Creek: A Tale of Colonial North Carolina's Regulator Era, Circa: 1760s. (Illus.). 350p. (gr. 8-12). Date not set. write for info. (0-9632319-2-8) ASDA Pub.
—Tecumseh's Trail: The Appalachian Trail, Then & Now. (Illus.). 137p. (Orig.). (gr. 8-12). Date not set. pap. write for info. (0-9632319-3-6) ASDA Pub.
Bradford, Ann & Gezi, Kal. The Mystery at the Tree House. McLean, Mina G., illus. LC 80-15654. 32p. (gr. k-4). 1980. PLB 18.50 (0-89565-148-3); PLB 12.95s.p. (0-685-55526-7) Childs World.

—The Mystery of the Midget Clown. McLean, Mina G., illus. LC 80-72513. 32p. (gr. k-4). 1980. PLB 18.50 (0-89565-146-7); PLB 12.95s.p. (0-685-55530-5) Childs World.
—The Mystery of the Missing Dogs. McLean, Mina G., illus. LC 80-10436. 32p. (gr. k-4). 1980. PLB 18.50 (0-89565-143-2); PLB 12.95s.p. (0-685-55531-3) Childs World.
Bradford, Ann, jt. auth. see Gezi, Kal.
Bradford, Betsy A. Princess Patty in Peace on Earth. 56p. (gr. k-6). 1993. write for info. (0-9633846-3-5) Scope Pub.
Bradford, Elizabeth, ed. see Bohlke, Dorothee.
Bradford, Elizabeth, ed. see Mann, Marek.
Bradford, Elizabeth, ed. see Wolf, Andrea.
Bradford, Gigi & Moos, Michael, eds. Sixteen Toes: Anthology. (Illus.). (gr. 2-7). 1978. pap. 2.50 (0-930970-00-4) O'Neill Pr.
Bradford, Jan. Caroline Zucker & the Birthday Disaster. Ramsey, Marcy, illus. LC 90-11159. 96p. (gr. 2-5). 1991. lib. bdg. 9.89 (0-8167-2021-5); pap. text ed. 2.95 (0-8167-2022-3) Troll Assocs.
—Caroline Zucker Gets Even. Ramsey, Marcy D., illus. LC 89-20630. 96p. (gr. 2-5). 1991. lib. bdg. 9.89 (0-8167-2015-0); pap. text ed. 2.95 (0-8167-2016-9) Troll Assocs.
—Caroline Zucker Gets Her Wish. Ramsey, Marcy D., illus. LC 90-31549. 96p. (gr. 2-5). 1991. PLB 9.89 (0-8167-2019-3); pap. text ed. 2.95 (0-8167-2020-7) Troll Assocs.
—Caroline Zucker Helps Out. Ramsey, Marcy, illus. LC 90-11156. 96p. (gr. 2-5). 1991. PLB 9.89 (0-8167-2025-8); pap. text ed. 2.95 (0-8167-2026-6) Troll Assocs.
—Caroline Zucker Makes a Big Mistake. Ramsey, Marcy, illus. LC 90-11160. 96p. (gr. 2-5). 1991. PLB 9.89 (0-8167-2023-1); pap. text ed. 2.95 (0-8167-2024-X) Troll Assocs.
—Caroline Zucker Meets Her Match. Ramsey, Marcy D., illus. LC 90-10813. 96p. (gr. 2-5). 1991. lib. bdg. 9.89 (0-8167-2017-7); pap. text ed. 2.95 (0-8167-2018-5) Troll Assocs.
Bradford, John. Everything's Coming up Fractions: With Cuisenaire Rods. 64p. (gr. 3-6). 1981. pap. text ed. 8.50 (0-914040-91-X) Cuisenaire.
Bradford, Leigh, jt. auth. see Fryer, Lee.
Bradford, Sarah. Harriet Tubman, the Moses of Her People. LC 93-34223. 160p. (gr. 4-6). 1993. pap. 8.95 (1-55709-217-6) Applewood.
Bradlee, Dick. Instant Tennis. (Illus.). 124p. (gr. 7 up). 1962. 9.95 (0-8159-5811-0) Devin.
Bradley, Alfred & Bond, Michael. Paddington on Stage. Fortnum, Peggy, illus. LC 76-62497. (gr. 2-5). 1977. 14.45 (0-395-25155-9) HM.
Bradley, Ann. Cows Are Vegetarians! A Book for Vegetarian Kids. Kramer, Stephen & Huffman, Elise, illus. 24p. (gr. 2-8). 1992. pap. 7.95 (0-9630893-0-7) Healthways.
Bradley, Catherine. Kazakhstan. Channon, John, contrib. by. LC 92-2243. (Illus.). 32p. (gr. 4-6). 1992. PLB 13.90 (1-56294-308-1) Millbrook Pr.
—Life in the Mountains. (gr. 4-7). 1993. pap. 4.95 (0-590-47608-4) Scholastic Inc.
Bradley, Catherine, jt. auth. see Bradley, John.
Bradley, John. Eastern Europe: The Road to Democracy. rev. ed. LC 93-11186. (Illus.). 40p. (gr. 6-8). 1993. PLB 12.90 (0-531-17430-1, Gloucester Pr) Watts.
Bradley, John & Bradley, Catherine. Germany: The Reunification of a Nation - Update. rev. ed. (Illus.). 40p. (gr. 6-8). 1993. PLB 12.90 (0-531-17431-X, Gloucester Pr) Watts.
Bradley, John, jt. auth. see Marshall, Ray.
Bradley, Melvin. Mules: Missouri's Long Eared Miners. Gwin, Paul, ed. (Illus.). 116p. (Orig.). 1987. pap. 7.50 (0-933842-06-6) Extension Div.
Bradley, Michael R. On the Job: Safeguarding Workers' Rights. LC 92-9015. 1992. 22.60 (0-86593-175-5); 16.95s.p. (0-685-59322-3) Rourke Corp.
Bradley, Mignon L. Cinco de Mayo: An Historical Play. Huber, Carrie, illus. LC 81-8341. (ENG & SPA.). 60p. (Orig.). (gr. 4 up). 1981. pap. 6.95 (0-939584-00-X) LUISA Prods.
Bradley, Patricia, jt. auth. see Minor, Nancy.
Bradley, R. C. Teaching for "Self-Directed" Living & Learning in Students - How to Help Students Get in Charge of Their Lives: "Self-Directed" Living & Learning. LC 90-85800. 224p. 1991. text ed. 19.95 (0-9628624-0-1) Bassi Bk.
Bradley, Richard, ed. see Clary, Linda & Harms, Larry.
Bradley, Susannah. Busy Bee Pack. Banazi, Pauline, illus. (gr. 3-6). 1992. pap. 7.95 (1-56680-503-1) Mad Hatter Pub.
—Cuddly Teddies' Activity Book. Banazi, Pauline, illus. (gr. 3-6). 1992. pap. 5.95 (1-56680-507-4) Mad Hatter Pub.
—Freaky Frank's Cut Out Fun Book. Mostyn, David, illus. (gr. 3-6). 1992. pap. 3.95 (1-56680-506-6) Mad Hatter Pub.
—How to Draw Cartoons. Archer, Rebecca, illus. 48p. (gr. 3-6). 1992. pap. 2.95 (1-56680-003-X) Mad Hatter Pub.
—Paper Fun Pack. (Illus.). (gr. 3-6). 1992. pap. 7.95 (1-56680-504-X) Mad Hatter Pub.
—The Turbulent Triangle. Neary, Bryan, illus. 48p. (gr. 3-6). 1992. pap. 2.95 (1-56680-001-3) Mad Hatter Pub.

Bradley, Susannah, ed. Beginner's Guide to French. Archer, Rebecca, illus. 48p. (gr. 3-6). 1992. pap. 2.95 (1-56680-004-8) Mad Hatter Pub.
—Ghosts, Monsters & Legends. Appleby, Barrie, illus. 48p. (gr. 3-6). 1992. pap. 2.95 (1-56680-005-6) Mad Hatter Pub.
Bradley, Virginia. Wait & See. 1994. write for info. (0-525-65158-6, Cobblehill Bks) Dutton Child Bks.
Bradley-Johnson, Sharon & Johnson, C. Merle. Baby Power: A New Addition. (Illus.). 32p. (Orig.). 1981. pap. 3.00 (1-878526-05-7) Pineapple MI.
Bradman, Tony. The Bad Babies' Book of Colors. Schulman, Janet, ed. Van der Beek, Debbie, illus. Greenstein, Mina, designed by. LC 86-27860. (Illus.). 32p. (ps-2). 1987. 5.95 (0-394-89046-9) Knopf Bks Yng Read.
—The Bad Babies' Counting Book. Van der Beek, Debbie, illus. LC 86-71. 32p. (ps-2). 1986. Set. 4.95 (0-394-88352-7) Knopf Bks Yng Read.
—A Bad Week for the Three Bears. Williams, Jenny, illus. LC 91-41871. 32p. (Orig.). 1993. pap. 2.25 (0-679-83379-X) Random Bks Yng Read.
—Billy & the Baby. (ps-3). 1992. 11.95 (0-8120-6328-7); pap. 5.95 (0-8120-1387-5) Barron.
—The Bluebeards: Adventure on Skull Island. Murphy, Rowan B., illus. 64p. (gr. 3-6). 1990. pap. 2.95 (0-8120-4421-5) Barron.
—The Bluebeards: Mystery at Musket Bay. Murphy, Rowan B., illus. 64p. (gr. 3-6). 1990. pap. 2.95 (0-8120-4422-3) Barron.
—The Bluebeards: Peril at the Pirate School. Murphy, Rowan B., illus. 64p. (gr. 2-5). 1990. pap. 2.95 (0-8120-4502-5) Barron.
—The Bluebeards: Revenge at Ryan's Reef. Murphy, Rowan B., illus. 52p. (ps-3). 1992. pap. 3.50 (0-8120-4903-9) Barron.
—Dilly & the Horror Movie. Hellard, Susan, illus. 64p. (gr. 2-5). 1991. pap. 3.95 (0-14-032799-1, Puffin) Puffin Bks.
—Dilly Speaks Up. Hellard, Susan, illus. 32p. (ps-3). 1991. 11.95 (0-670-83680-X) Viking Child Bks.
—Dilly the Dinosaur. Hellard, Susan, illus. 64p. (Orig.). (gr. 2-5). 1988. pap. 3.95 (0-14-032337-6, Puffin) Puffin Bks.
—It Came from Outer Space. LC 91-17882. (Illus.). 32p. (ps-3). 1992. 12.00 (0-8037-1098-4) Dial Bks Young.
—John Lennon. (Illus.). 64p. (gr. 5-9). 1991. 11.95 (0-237-60021-8, Pub. by Evans Bros Ltd) Trafalgar.
—Michael. Ross, Tony, illus. LC 90-40523. 32p. (ps-2). 1991. SBE 13.95 (0-02-711850-9, Macmillan Child Bk) Macmillan Child Grp.
—The Story Tree. Ravilious, Robin, illus. 32p. (gr. 1-3). 1993. 17.95 (0-460-88093-4, Pub. by J M Dent & Sons) Trafalgar.
—That's Not a Fish. Pearce, Susie J., illus. (ps-k). 1993. 15.95 (0-460-88039-X, Pub. by J M Dent & Sons) Trafalgar.
—This Little Baby. Williams, Jenny, illus. 32p. (ps-k). 1990. 13.95 (0-399-22202-2, Putnam) Putnam Pub Group.
Bradshaw, Georgene & Wrighton, Charlene A. Zoo-Phonics Level B Reader: (a-b-c) (Illus.). 48p. (gr. 1). 1987. pap. text ed. 4.50 (0-9617342-2-1) Zoo-phonics.
Bradshaw, Georgene E. & Wrighton, Charlene A. Zoo-Phonics. Clark, Irene, illus. 32p. (gr. k-4). 1986. pap. text ed. 10.00 (0-9617342-0-5); tchr's manual (incl. basic kit) 50.00 (0-685-17464-6) Zoo-Phonics.
—A Zoo-Phonics Reader: Level A. Clark, Irene, illus. 32p. (ps-1). 1986. pap. text ed. 3.50 (0-9617342-1-3) Zoo-Phonics.
—Zoo-Phonics Reader: Level B (d-e-f) (Illus.). 48p. (gr. 1). 1987. pap. text ed. 4.50 (0-9617342-3-X) Zoo-phonics.
—Zoo-Phonics Reader: Level C (g-h-i) (Illus.). 48p. (gr. 1). 1988. pap. text ed. 5.50 (0-9617342-4-8) Zoo-phonics.
Bradshaw, Gillian. Beyond the North Wind. LC 92-9671. 192p. (gr. 5 up). 1993. 14.00 (0-688-11357-5) Greenwillow.
—The Dragon & the Thief. LC 90-48259. (Illus.). (gr. 5 up). 1991. 13.95 (0-688-10575-0) Greenwillow.
—The Land of Gold. LC 91-31810. 160p. (gr. 5 up). 1992. 14.00 (0-688-10576-9) Greenwillow.
Bradshaw, Jeremy. The Wolf: The World's Wild Dogs. Stefoff, Rebecca, ed. LC 92-10244. (Illus.). 31p. (gr. 3-6). 1992. PLB 17.26 (1-56074-055-8) Garrett Ed Corp.
Brady, Esther W. Toliver's Secret. Cuffari, Richard, illus. 176p. (gr. 3-7). 1988. pap. 4.99 (0-517-56910-8) Crown Bks Yng Read.
Brady, Irene. America's Horses & Ponies. Brady, Irene, illus. 202p. (gr. 4 up). 1976. pap. 15.45 (0-395-24050-6, Sandpiper) HM.
Brady, Janeen. I Have a Song for You, Vol. 1: About People & Nature. rev. ed. (Illus.). (ps-4). Illus. by Linda Howard, 1986, 50pgs. pap. text ed. 6.95 activity bk. (0-944803-02-4); Ed. by Ted Brady, Illus. by Phyllis & Warren Luch, 1979, 39pgs. songbook 6.95 (0-944803-00-8); cassette 7.95 (0-944803-01-6) Brite Intl.
—I Have a Song for You, Vol. 2: About Seasons & Holidays. (Illus., Orig.). (ps-4). Illus. by Linda Howard, 1987, 50pgs. pap. text ed. 6.95 activity bk. (0-944803-05-9); Ed. by Ted Brady, Illus. by Phyllis & Warren Luch, 1979, 45 pgs. songbook 6.95 (0-944803-03-2); cassette 7.95 (0-944803-04-0) Brite Intl.

—I Have a Song for You, Vol. 3: About Animals. Howard, Linda, illus. 50p. (ps-4). 1988. pap. text ed. 6.95 activity bk. (0-944803-08-3); Ed. by Ted Brady, Illus. by Phyllis & Warren Luch, 1979, 42pgs. songbook 6.95 (0-944803-06-7); cassette 7.95 (0-944803-07-5) Brite Intl.
—The Metrics Are Coming! (gr. k-4). 1980. cassette 7.95 (0-944803-14-8) Brite Intl.
—My Body Machine. Twede, Evan, illus. (ps-6). 1989. songbk. 45p. 7.95 (0-944803-65-2); cassette & activity bk. 9.95 (0-944803-66-0) Brite Intl.
—My Body Machine. 29p. (ps-6). 1990. Dialogue Bk. 1.25 (0-944803-73-3) Brite Intl.
—Safety Kids Personal Safety, Vol. 1. Underwood, Oscar, tr. (SPA., Orig.). (gr. k-6). 1984. dialogue bk. 1.25 (0-944803-18-0); Trans. by Oscar Underwood, in Spanish, 1984, 6pgs. pap. text ed. 1.25 dialogue bk. (0-944803-19-9); songbk. 5.95 (0-944803-15-6); act. bk. 2.25 (0-944803-16-4); cassette & bk. 9.95 (0-944803-17-2) Brite Intl.
—Safety Kids Personal Safety, Vol. 1. Twede, Evan, illus. 14p. (gr. k-6). 1983. Set of 20. wkbk. 12.00 (0-944803-20-2) Brite Intl.
—Safety Kids Play it Smart: Stay Safe from Drugs, Vol. 2. Twede, Evan, illus. 14p. (gr. k-6). 1985. Set of 20. wkbk. 12.00 (0-944803-25-3) Brite Intl.
—Safety Kids Play It Smart, Vol. 2: Stay Safe from Drugs. Twede, Evan, illus. (Orig.). (gr. k-6). 1985. pap. text ed. 5.95 songbook (0-944803-21-0); pap. text ed. 1.25 dialogue bk., 1985, 16pgs. (0-944803-24-5); act. bk. 2.25 (0-944803-22-9); cassette & bk. 9.95 (0-944803-23-7); video avail. (0-944803-72-5) Brite Intl.
—Show a Little Love. Grover, Nina, illus. 48p. (gr. k-6). 1981. songbk. 6.95 (0-944803-26-1); cassette 7.95 (0-944803-28-8) Brite Intl.
—Someone Special - You! Clarkson & Twede, illus. 26p. (gr. k-9). 1991. activity bk. 2.25 (0-944803-76-8); cassette & bklt. 9.95 (0-944803-74-1) Brite Intl.
—Standin' Tall Cleanliness. Galloway, Neil, illus. 22p. (Orig.). 1984. pap. text ed. 1.50 activity bk. (0-944803-54-7); cassette & bk. 8.95 (0-944803-55-5) Brite Intl.
—Standin' Tall Courage. Wilson, Grant, illus. 22p. (Orig.). (ps-6). 1982. pap. text ed. 1.50 activity bk. (0-944803-43-1); cassette & bk. 8.95 (0-944803-45-8) Brite Intl.
—Standin' Tall Forgiveness. Wilson, Grant & Galloway, Neil, illus. 22p. (Orig.). (ps-6). 1981. pap. text ed. 1.50 activity bk. (0-944803-39-3); cassette & bk. 8.95 (0-944803-40-7) Brite Intl.
—Standin' Tall Honesty. Wilson, Grant & Galloway, Neil, illus. 22p. (Orig.). (ps-6). 1981. pap. text ed. 1.50 activity bk. (0-944803-37-7); cassette & bk. 8.95 (0-944803-38-5) Brite Intl.
—Standin' Tall Obedience. Wilson, Grant & Galloway, Neil, illus. 22p. (Orig.). (ps-6). 1981. pap. text ed. 1.50 activity bk. (0-944803-35-0); cassette & bk. 8.95 (0-944803-36-9) Brite Intl.
—Standin' Tall Songbook, Vol. 1. 52p. (ps-6). 1987. pap. text ed. 6.95 (0-944803-62-8) Brite Intl.
—Standin' Tall Songbook, Vol. 2. 71p. (ps-6). 1988. pap. text ed. 6.95 (0-944803-63-6) Brite Intl.
—Standin' Tall Songbook, Vol. 3. 72p. (ps-6). 1989. pap. text ed. 6.95 (0-944803-64-4) Brite Intl.
—Standin' Tall Work. Wilson, Grant & Galloway, Neil, illus. 22p. (Orig.). (ps-6). 1981. pap. text ed. 1.50 activity bk. (0-944803-41-5); cassette & bk. 8.95 (0-944803-42-3) Brite Intl.
—Take Your Hat Off When the Flag Goes By. Perry, Scott & Hulet, Grant, illus. 22p. (gr. k-6). 1987. activity bk. 2.25 (0-944803-31-8); Set of 20. wkbk. 12.00 (0-944803-34-2); cassette & bk. 9.95 (0-944803-32-6); dialogue bk. 1.25 (0-944803-33-4); songbk. 7.95 (0-944803-29-6) Brite Intl.
—Watch Me Sing, Vol. 1. Noyce, Robert, illus. 31p. (ps-2). 1977. pap. text ed. 5.95 songbk (0-944803-09-1); cassette 7.95 (0-944803-10-5) Brite Intl.
—Watch Me Sing, Vol. 2. Twede, Evan & Nelson, Eloise, illus. 30p. (ps-2). 1986. pap. text ed. 5.95 songbk. (0-944803-11-3); cassette 7.95 (0-944803-12-1) Brite Intl.
Brady, Janeen & Woolley, Diane. Brite Dreams. Twede, Evan, illus. 32p. (Orig.). (ps). 1988. pap. 2.25 (0-944803-79-2); pap. 9.95 incl. cassette (0-944803-80-6) Brite Intl.
—Standin' Tall Dependability. Galloway, Neil, illus. 22p. (Orig.). (ps-6). 1984. pap. text ed. 1.50 activity bk. (0-944803-59-8); cassette & bk. 8.95 (0-944803-60-1) Brite Intl.
—Standin' Tall Gratitude. Wilson, Grant, illus. 22p. (Orig.). (ps-6). 1982. pap. text ed. 1.50 activity bk. (0-944803-48-2); cassette & bk. 8.95 (0-944803-49-0) Brite Intl.
—Standin' Tall Happiness. Wilson, Grant, illus. 22p. (Orig.). (ps-6). 1982. pap. text ed. 1.50 activity bk. (0-944803-46-6); cassette & bk. 8.95 (0-944803-47-4) Brite Intl.
—Standin Tall Love. Wilson, Grant, illus. 22p. (Orig.). (ps-6). 1982. pap. text ed. 1.50 activity bk. (0-944803-50-4); cassette & bk. 8.95 (0-944803-51-2) Brite Intl.
—Standin' Tall Self-Esteem. Wilson, Grant, illus. 22p. (Orig.). (ps-6). 1984. pap. text ed. 1.50 activity bk. (0-944803-56-3); cassette & bk. 8.95 (0-944803-57-1) Brite Intl.

—Standin' Tall Service. Wilson, Grant, illus. 22p. (Orig.). (ps-6). 1984. pap. text ed. 1.50 activity bk. (0-944803-52-0); cassette & bk. 8.95 (0-944803-53-9) Brite Intl.

Brady, Janeen J. Safety Kids, Vol. 3: Protect Their Minds. Twede, Evan, illus. 32p. (Orig.). (gr. k-6). 1992. pap. 2.25 (0-944803-78-4); pap. 9.95 incl. cassette (0-944803-77-6) Brite Intl.

Brady, Jennifer. Jambi & the Lions. Thatch, Nancy R., ed. Brady, Jennifer, illus. Melton, David, intro. by. LC 92-17593. (Illus.). 26p. (gr. 3-5). 1992. PLB 14.95 (0-933849-41-9) Landmark Edns.

Brady, Kathleen, illus. Oh, A-Hunting We Will Go Big Book. (ps-2). 1988. pap. text ed. 14.00 (0-922053-14-6) N Edge Res.

Brady, Maxine. The Monopoly Book. (Illus.). (gr. 7 up). 1976. pap. 4.95 (0-679-14401-3) McKay.

Brady, Philip. Reluctant Hero: A Snowy Road to Salem in 1802. 144p. (gr. 7 up). 1990. 16.95 (0-8027-6972-1); lib. bdg. 17.85 (0-8027-6974-8) Walker & Co.

Brady, Susan. Find My Blanket. Brady, Susan, illus. LC 87-45310. 32p. (ps-1). 1988. (Lipp Jr Bks) HarpC Child Bks.

Braff Brodzinsky, Anne. The Mulberry Bird: Story of an Adoption. LC 86-2460. (Illus.). 48p. (gr. k-5). 1986. 10.95 (0-9609504-5-1) Perspect Indiana.

Braga, Meg. Cosas Que Hacer para Navidad. (gr. 4-6). 1989. Repr. of 1981 ed. 2.75 (0-311-26607-X) Casa Bautista.

Bragg, Bea. The Very First Thanksgiving: Pioneers on the Rio Grande. LC 89-15562. (Illus.). 64p. (Orig.). (gr. 3-5). 1989. pap. 7.95 (0-943173-22-1) Harbinger AZ.

Bragg, Michael, illus. Monday's Child. 32p. (ps-1). 1989. 15.95 (0-575-04097-1, Pub. by Gollancz England) Trafalgar.

Bragg, Ruth. Mrs. Muggle's Sparkle. Bragg, Ruth, illus. LC 89-31371. 28p. (ps up). 1991. pap. 15.95 (0-88708-106-1) Picture Bk Studio.

Bragg, Ruth G. Alphabet Out Loud. LC 91-14546. (Illus.). 32p. (gr. k up). 1991. pap. 14.95 (0-88708-172-X) Picture Bk Studio.

—The Birthday Bears. Bragg, Ruth G., illus. LC 90-7385. 28p. (gr. k up). 1991. pap. 14.95 (0-88708-139-8) Picture Bk Studio.

—Colors of the Day. Bragg, Ruth G., illus. LC 92-7790. 40p. 1992. pap. 14.95 (0-88708-245-9) Picture Bk Studio.

Bragger & Rice. On y Va, Level 2. (gr. 7-12). 1989. text ed. 35.95 (0-8384-1682-9); 38.95 (0-8384-1684-5); 10.95 (0-8384-1683-7); 275.00 (0-8384-1697-7) Heinle & Heinle.

—On y Va, Level 3. (gr. 7-12). 1990. text ed. 37.95 (0-8384-1925-9); 39.95 (0-8384-1926-7); 11.95 (0-8384-1927-5); 275.00 (0-8384-1928-3) Heinle & Heinle.

Braille International, Inc. Staff & Henry, James, illus. No More Nightmares: Keeper of the Dreams. 17p. (Orig.). (gr. 1). 1992. pap. 10.95 (1-56956-002-1) W A T Braille.

Brainard, Beth & Behr, Sheila. Soup Should Be Seen, Not Heard! The Kids' Etiquette Book. (Illus.). 107p. (Orig.). (ps-7). 1988. pap. 10.00 (0-9621908-0-2) Good Idea Kids.

Braithwaite, E. R. To Sir, with Love. (gr. 9-12). 1992. pap. 3.50 (0-515-10519-8) Jove Pubns.

Braithwaite, Pamela A. Byron's Double Discovery. Bauer, Eleanor L., illus. 120p. (Orig.). (gr. 4-10). 1991. pap. 4.00 (1-880960-00-1) Script Memory FI.

Braly, David. Cattle Barons of Early Oregon. LC 78-105220. (Illus.). 44p. (gr. 7-12). 1982. pap. 4.50 (0-942206-00-2) Mediaor Co.

Bramhall, Elizabeth. Ty Loves Flowers: A Toddlers' Environmental Awareness Book. (Illus.). 16p. (ps-1). 1993. pap. write for info. (0-9636038-0-9) E Bramhall.

Bramley, Peter, illus. Florida's Vanishing Wildlife. 32p. (Orig.). (gr. k-4). 1992. pap. 2.95 (0-8200-1101-0) Great Outdoors.

Bramos, Ann S., jt. auth. see Bramos, Helen.

Bramos, Ann S., tr. & illus. see Bramos, Helen.

Bramos, Ann S., tr. from GRE see Bramos, Helen.

Bramos, Helen. My Favorite Bed Time Stories. Bramos, Ann S., tr. & illus. LC 91-76687. 63p. (Orig.). 1992. pap. 7.00 (1-56002-152-7) Aegina Pr.

—My Red Storybook. Bramos, Ann S., tr. from GRE & FRE. & illus. 77p. (Orig.). (ps-7). 1993. pap. 8.00 (0-9635333-1-2) A S Bramos.

Bramos, Helen & Bramos, Ann S. My Little Storybook. Bramos, Ann S., illus. (gr. 1-6). 1992. pap. 7.00 (0-9635333-0-4) A S Bramos.

Bramwell, M, jt. auth. see Cork, B.

Bramwell, Martyn. How Things Work. Mostyn, David, illus. 38p. (ps-3). 1985. PLB 10.95 (0-86020-847-8, Pub. by Usborne) EDC.

—The Simon & Schuster Young Readers' Book of Planet Earth. LC 91-38216. (Illus.). 192p. (gr. 4 up). 1992. pap. 13.00 (0-671-77830-7, S&S BFYR); pap. 8.00 (0-671-77831-5, S&S BFYR) Trade.

Bramwell, Martyn, ed. Mammals. LC 93-4336. 48p. (gr. k-3). 1993. 12.95 (1-56458-386-4) Dorling Kindersley.

Branca, Nicholas. Rectiles: A Geometric Introduction to Algebra. 48p. (gr. 5-9). 1991. pap. text ed. 24.95 (0-938587-19-6) Cuisenaire.

Brancato, Robin F. Come Alive at 505. LC 79-19144. 224p. (gr. 7 up). 1980. 8.95 (0-394-84294-4); lib. bdg. 8.99 (0-394-94294-9) Knopf Bks Yng Read.

—Uneasy Money. Hendrix, Bryan, designed by. LC 86-45296. (Illus.). 256p. (gr. 7-10). 1989. PLB 11.99 (0-394-96954-5) Knopf Bks Yng Read.

—Winning. LC 77-5632. 224p. (gr. 7 up). 1988. Repr. of 1977 ed. 3.95 (0-394-80751-0) Knopf Bks Yng Read.

Branch, Hazel F. Just for Me. LC 92-62879. (Illus.). 57p. (Orig.). (gr. 4-9). 1992. pap. 3.95 (0-931563-04-6) Wishing Rm.

Branch, James H., III. Multicultural Stories. Ward, Dick, ed. Douglass, S., illus. LC 92-93449. 29p. 1992. 12.50 (0-9635840-0-6) Guttenburg Pub.

Branch, Mary. Tell Me a Story 2. 31p. (ps-4). 1982. pap. 0.25 (0-8163-0477-7) Pacific Pr Pub Assn.

Brand, Jill, ed. The Green Umbrella. (Illus.). 96p. (gr. 2-6). 1991. pap. 18.95 spiral bdg. (0-7136-3390-5, Pub. by A&C Black UK) Talman.

Brand, Oscar. Songs of Seventy Six: A Folksinger's History of the Revolution. LC 72-83733. (Illus.). 176p. 1972. 16.95 (0-87131-092-9); pap. 8.95 (0-87131-170-4) M Evans.

Brandel, Marc. An Ear for Danger. LC 88-45880. 144p. (Orig.). (gr. 5 up). 1989. pap. 2.95 (0-394-89943-1) Knopf Bks Yng Read.

Brandenberg, Aliki. Welcome Little Baby: Miniature Edition. Brandenberg, Aliki, illus. 32p. (ps up). 1993. Repr. text ed. 4.95 (0-688-12665-0, Tupelo Bks) Morrow.

Brandenberg, Franz. Aunt Nina & Her Nephews & Nieces. Aliki, illus. LC 82-12004. 32p. (gr. k-3). 1983. PLB 14.93 (0-688-01870-X); 15.00 (0-688-01869-6) Greenwillow.

—Aunt Nina, Good Night. Aliki, illus. LC 88-18777. 32p. (ps up). 1989. 12.95 (0-688-07463-4); PLB 12.88 (0-688-07464-2) Greenwillow.

—Aunt Nina's Visit. Aliki, illus. LC 83-16531. 32p. (gr. k-3). 1984. 15.00 (0-688-01764-9); PLB 14.93 (0-688-01766-5) Greenwillow.

—I Wish I Was Sick, Too! Aliki, illus. LC 75-46610. 32p. (gr. k-3). 1976. PLB 15.88 (0-688-84047-7) Greenwillow.

—I Wish I Was Sick, Too! Aliki, illus. LC 75-46610. 32p. (ps-3). 1990. pap. 3.95 (0-688-09354-X, Mulberry) Morrow.

—It's Not My Fault. Aliki, illus. LC 79-24157. 64p. (gr. 1-3). 1980. 14.00 (0-688-80235-4) Greenwillow.

—Leo & Emily. Aliki, illus. LC 80-19657. 56p. (gr. 1-3). 1981. 15.00 (0-688-80292-3) Greenwillow.

—Leo & Emily. (gr. k-6). 1990. pap. 2.95 (0-440-40294-8, YB) Dell.

—Leo & Emily & the Dragon. Aliki, illus. LC 83-14091. 56p. (gr. 1-3). 1984. 12.95 (0-688-02531-5); PLB 12.88 (0-688-02532-3) Greenwillow.

—Leo & Emily's Big Idea. (gr. k-6). 1990. pap. 2.95 (0-440-40302-2, Pub. by Yearling Classics) Dell.

—Leo & Emily's Big Ideas. Aliki, illus. LC 81-6424. 56p. (gr. 1-3). 1982. 13.88 (0-688-00754-6); PLB 13.95 (0-688-00755-4) Greenwillow.

—Leo & Emily's Zoo. Abolafia, Yossi, illus. LC 87-17907. 32p. (ps-1). 1988. 11.95 (0-688-07457-X); lib. bdg. 11.88 (0-688-07458-8) Greenwillow.

—Leo & Emily's Zoo. 1990. pap. 2.95 (0-440-40319-7) Dell.

—Nice New Neighbors. Aliki, illus. LC 77-1651. 56p. (gr. 1-4). 1977. PLB 13.88 (0-688-84105-8) Greenwillow.

—Nice New Neighbors. Aliki, illus. 32p. (ps-2). 1990. pap. 2.75 (0-590-44117-5) Scholastic Inc.

—Nice New Neighbors. Aliki, illus. LC 77-1651. 56p. (ps-3). 1991. pap. 4.95 (0-688-10997-7, Mulberry) Morrow.

—Otto Is Different. Stevenson, James, illus. LC 84-13654. 24p. (gr. k-3). 1985. 11.75 (0-688-04253-8); PLB 11.88 (0-688-04254-6) Greenwillow.

Brandenburg, Franz. A Fun Weekend. Brandenburg, Alexa, illus. LC 89-77502. 24p. (ps up). 1991. 13.95 (0-688-09720-0); PLB 13.88 (0-688-09721-9) Greenwillow.

Brandenburg, Jim. Sand & Fog: Adventures in Southern Africa. Guernsey, JoAnn B., ed. LC 93-30425. 1994. write for info. (0-8027-8232-9); PLB write for info. (0-8027-8233-7) Walker & Co.

—To the Top of the World: Adventures with Arctic Wolves. Guernsey, JoAnn B., ed. LC 93-12105. (gr. 4-7). 1993. 16.95 (0-8027-8219-1); PLB 17.85 (0-8027-8220-5) Walker & Co.

Brandes, Louis G. Can You Believe What You See? Illusions. Laycock, Mary, ed. Brandes, Louis G., illus. 96p. (Orig.). (gr. 4-10). 1988. pap. 12.50 (0-918932-92-0) Activity Resources.

Brandes, Mary J., ed. see Vincent, Richard J.

Brandeth, Gyles. The Do-It-Yourself Genius Kit, 4 bks. Brown, Judy, illus. (ps-3). 1989. Gift Set. pap. 3.95 (0-14-095331-0, Puffin) Puffin Bks.

—The Emergency Excuses Kit, 4 bks. Brown, Judy, illus. (gr. 2-5). 1992. Boxed Set. pap. 4.50 (0-14-034832-8) Puffin Bks.

—The Emergency Joke Kit. Brown, Judy, illus. (Orig.). (ps-3). 1988. pap. 3.95 (0-14-095322-1, Puffin) Puffin Bks.

—The Emergency Joke Kite. Brown, Judy, illus. (ps-3). 1988. pap. 3.50 (0-317-69598-3, Puffin) Puffin Bks.

Brandon, Fran. The Day the Woods Went Crazy. LC 89-51294. 44p. (gr. 4-7). 1990. 5.95 (1-55523-256-6) Winston-Derek.

Brandreth, Gyles. Amazing Facts about Your Body. Craig, Bobby, illus. LC 80-1088. 32p. (gr. 5-8). 1981. pap. 2.95 (0-385-17018-1, Zephyr-BFYR) Doubleday.

—The Biggest Tongue Twister Book in the World. (Illus.). 128p. 1992. Repr. of 1986 ed. 3.99 (0-517-07768-X, Pub. by Wings Bks) Outlet Bk Co.

—Famous Last Words & Tombstone Humor. LC 88-24966. 128p. (Illus.). (gr. 4 up). 1989. pap. 5.95 (0-8069-6950-4) Sterling.

—The Great Book of Optical Illusions. Murphy, Rowan B. & Murphy, Albert, illus. LC 85-9898. 96p. (Illus.). (gr. 2 up). 1985. pap. 4.95 (0-8069-6258-5) Sterling.

—A Joke-a-Day Book. McGee, Shelagh, illus. 96p. 1992. Repr. of 1979 ed. 3.99 (0-517-07766-3, Pub. by Wings Bks) Outlet Bk Co.

—Quick & Easy Magic Tricks. (Illus.). 96p. (Orig.). 1988. pap. 1.95 (0-942025-33-4) Kidsbks.

—The Super Joke Book. Barrenger, Nick, illus. LC 83-397. 128p. (gr. 3 up). 1985. 12.95 (0-8069-4672-5); pap. 3.95 (0-8069-6200-3) Sterling.

—Super Silly Riddles. 1991. 3.99 (0-517-07352-8) Outlet Bk Co.

Brandt, Betty. The Adventures of Nicolet. Brandt, Laura, ed. Craig, Jennifer, illus. 160p. (Orig.). (gr. 8-12). 1991. 12.95 (0-9622014-2-1) Beaver Valley.

—Special Delivery. Haubrich, Kathy, illus. 48p. (gr. k-4). 1988. lib. bdg. 14.95 (0-87614-312-5) Carolrhoda Bks.

—The Story of Nicolet. Nestingen, Jan, ed. Smith, Dan, illus. 64p. (Orig.). (gr. 3-5). 1991. pap. 6.95 (0-9622014-3-X) Beaver Valley.

Brandt, Catharine. We Light the Candles: Devotions Related to Family Use of the Advent Wreath. 40p. pap. 4.99 (0-8066-1544-3, 10-15443, Augsburg) Augsburg Fortress.

Brandt, Keith. Abe Lincoln: The Young Years. LC 81-23172. (Illus.). 48p. (gr. 4-6). 1982. PLB 10.79 (0-89375-750-0); pap. text ed. 3.50 (0-89375-751-9) Troll Assocs.

—Air. Burns, Raymond, illus. LC 84-2608. 32p. (gr. 3-6). 1985. PLB 9.49 (0-8167-0130-X); pap. text ed. 2.95 (0-8167-0131-8) Troll Assocs.

—Ancient Rome. Frenck, Hal, illus. LC 84-2684. 32p. (gr. 3-6). 1985. PLB 9.49 (0-8167-0298-5); pap. text ed. 2.95 (0-8167-0299-3) Troll Assocs.

—Babe Ruth, Home Run Hero. Frenck, Hal, illus. LC 85-1091. 48p. (gr. 4-6). 1986. lib. bdg. 10.79 (0-8167-0553-4); pap. text ed. 3.50 (0-8167-0554-2) Troll Assocs.

—Cabeza de Vaca: New World Explorer. Martinez, Sergio, illus. LC 92-36960. 48p. (gr. 4-6). 1993. lib. bdg. 10.79 (0-8167-2829-1); 3.50 (0-8167-2830-5) Troll Assocs.

—Case of the Missing Dinosaur. Wallner, John, illus. LC 81-7620. 48p. (gr. 2-4). 1982. PLB 10.89 (0-89375-586-9); pap. text ed. 3.50 (0-89375-587-7) Troll Assocs.

—Caves. Schneider, Rex, illus. LC 84-2573. 32p. (gr. 3-6). 1985. PLB 9.49 (0-8167-0142-3); pap. text ed. 2.95 (0-8167-0143-1) Troll Assocs.

—Daniel Boone: Frontier Adventures. Lawn, John, illus. LC 82-15915. 48p. (gr. 4-6). 1983. PLB 10.79 (0-89375-843-4); pap. text ed. 3.50 (0-89375-844-2) Troll Assocs.

—Deserts. Watling, James, illus. LC 84-8623. 32p. (gr. 3-6). 1985. PLB 9.49 (0-8167-0262-4); pap. text ed. 2.95 (0-8167-0263-2) Troll Assocs.

—Discovering Trees. Nigoghossian, Christine W., illus. LC 81-7522. 32p. (gr. 2-4). 1982. PLB 11.59 (0-89375-566-4); pap. text ed. 2.95 (0-89375-567-2) Troll Assocs.

—Earth. Jones, John, illus. LC 84-8444. 32p. (gr. 3-6). 1985. PLB 9.49 (0-8167-0250-0); pap. text ed. 2.95 (0-8167-0251-9) Troll Assocs.

—Electricity. Harriton, Chuck, illus. LC 84-2705. 32p. (gr. 3-6). 1985. PLB 9.49 (0-8167-0198-9); pap. text ed. 2.95 (0-8167-0199-7) Troll Assocs.

—Five Senses. Green, Gloria, illus. LC 84-2633. 32p. (gr. 3-6). 1985. PLB 9.49 (0-8167-0168-7); pap. text ed. 2.95 (0-8167-0169-5) Troll Assocs.

—George Washington. Frenck, Hal, illus. LC 84-8624. 32p. (gr. 3-6). 1985. PLB 9.49 (0-8167-0256-X); pap. text ed. 2.95 (0-8167-0257-8) Troll Assocs.

—Indian Crafts. Guzzi, George, illus. LC 84-2588. 32p. (gr. 3-6). 1985. lib. bdg. 9.49 (0-8167-0132-6); pap. text ed. 2.95 (0-8167-0133-4) Troll Assocs.

—Indian Festivals. Guzzi, George, illus. LC 84-2644. 32p. (gr. 3-6). 1985. PLB 9.49 (0-8167-0182-2); pap. text ed. 2.95 (0-8167-0183-0) Troll Assocs.

—Indian Homes. Guzzi, George, illus. LC 84-2650. 32p. (gr. 3-6). 1985. PLB 9.49 (0-8167-0126-1); pap. text ed. 2.95 (0-8167-0127-X) Troll Assocs.

—Insects. Brickman, Robin, illus. LC 84-2659. 32p. (gr. 3-6). 1985. PLB 9.49 (0-8167-0184-9); pap. text ed. 2.95 (0-8167-0185-7) Troll Assocs.

—Jackie Robinson: A Life of Courage. Ramsey, Marcy, illus. LC 91-17852. 48p. (gr. 4-6). 1992. PLB 10.79 (0-8167-2505-5); pap. text ed. 3.50 (0-8167-2506-3) Troll Assocs.

—John Paul Jones: Hero of the Seas. Swan, Susan, illus. LC 82-16045. 48p. (gr. 4-6). 1983. PLB 10.79 (0-89375-849-3); pap. text ed. 3.50 (0-89375-850-7) Troll Assocs.

—Lafayette, Hero of Two Nations. Snow, Scott, illus. LC 89-33981. 48p. (gr. 4-6). 1990. PLB 10.79 (0-8167-1771-0); pap. text ed. 3.50 (0-8167-1772-9) Troll Assocs.

—Lou Gehrig, Pride of the Yankees. Lawn, John, illus. LC 85-1075. 48p. (gr. 4-6). 1986. lib. bdg. 10.79 (0-8167-0549-6); pap. text ed. 3.50 (0-8167-0550-X) Troll Assocs.

—Marie Curie: Brave Scientist. Milone, Karen, illus. LC 82-16092. 48p. (gr. 4-6). 1983. PLB 10.79 *(0-89375-855-8)*; pap. text ed. 3.50 *(0-89375-856-6)* Troll Assocs.

—Mexico & Central America. Eitzen, Allan, illus. LC 84-2668. 32p. (gr. 3-6). 1985. PLB 9.49 *(0-8167-0264-0)*; pap. text ed. 2.95 *(0-8167-0265-9)* Troll Assocs.

—Mountains. Cumings, Art, illus. LC 84-2577. 32p. (gr. 3-6). 1985. PLB 9.49 *(0-8167-0154-7)*; pap. text ed. 2.95 *(0-8167-0155-5)* Troll Assocs.

—Paul Revere: Son of Liberty. LC 81-23147. (Illus.). 48p. (gr. 4-6). 1982. PLB 10.79 *(0-89375-766-7)*; pap. text ed. 3.50 *(0-89375-767-5)* Troll Assocs.

—Pearl Bailey: With a Song in Her Heart. Griffith, Gershom, illus. LC 92-20190. 48p. (gr. 4-6). 1992. PLB 10.79 *(0-8167-2921-2)*; pap. text ed. 3.50 *(0-8167-2922-0)* Troll Assocs.

—Planets & the Solar System. Veno, Joseph, illus. LC 84-2714. 32p. (gr. 3-6). 1985. PLB 9.49 *(0-8167-0300-0)*; pap. text ed. 2.95 *(0-8167-0301-9)* Troll Assocs.

—President. Dole, Bob, illus. LC 84-2652. 32p. (gr. 3-6). 1985. PLB 9.49 *(0-8167-0268-3)*; pap. text ed. 2.95 *(0-8167-0269-1)* Troll Assocs.

—Robert E. Lee. Lawn, John, illus. LC 84-2687. 32p. (gr. 3-6). 1985. PLB 9.49 *(0-8167-0278-0)*; pap. text ed. 2.95 *(0-8167-0279-9)* Troll Assocs.

—Rosa Parks: Fight for Freedom. Griffith, Gershom, illus. LC 91-34939. 48p. (gr. 4-6). 1993. lib. bdg. 10.79 *(0-8167-2831-3)*; pap. text ed. 3.50 *(0-8167-2832-1)* Troll Assocs.

—Sound. Sweat, Lynn, illus. LC 84-2632. 32p. (gr. 3-6). 1985. PLB 9.49 *(0-8167-0128-8)*; pap. text ed. 2.95 *(0-8167-0129-6)* Troll Assocs.

—Sun. Sweat, Lynn, illus. LC 84-2715. 32p. (gr. 3-6). 1985. PLB 9.49 *(0-8167-0190-3)*; pap. text ed. 2.95 *(0-8167-0191-1)* Troll Assocs.

—Transportation. Schneider, Rex, illus. LC 84-2584. 32p. (gr. 3-6). 1985. PLB 9.49 *(0-8167-0172-5)*; pap. text ed. 2.95 *(0-8167-0173-3)* Troll Assocs.

—What Makes It Rain? Miyake, Yoshi, illus. LC 81-7495. 32p. (gr. 2-4). 1982. PLB 11.59 *(0-89375-582-6)*; pap. text ed. 2.95 *(0-89375-583-4)* Troll Assocs.

—Wonders of the Seasons. Watling, James, illus. LC 81-7411. 32p. (gr. 2-4). 1982. PLB 11.59 *(0-89375-580-X)*; pap. text ed. 2.95 *(0-89375-581-8)* Troll Assocs.

Brandt, Laura, ed. see **Brandt, Betty.**

Brandt, Sue R. Facts about the Fifty States. 2nd, rev. ed. Greenberg, Lorna, ed. LC 87-25437. (Illus.). 72p. (gr. 4-9). 1988. PLB 12.90 *(0-531-10476-1)* Watts.

—State Flags: Including the Commonwealth of Puerto Rico. LC 92-8948. 1992. 13.90 *(0-531-20001-9)* Watts.

—State Flags: Including the Commonwealth of Puerto Rico. (gr. 4-7). 1992. pap. 6.95 *(0-531-15630-3)* Watts.

—State Trees: Including the Commonwealth of Puerto Rico. LC 92-8946. 1992. 13.90 *(0-531-20000-0)* Watts.

—State Trees: Including the Commonwealth of Puerto Rico. (gr. 4-7). 1992. pap. 6.95 *(0-531-15632-X)* Watts.

Branfield, John. The Day I Shot My Dad: And Other Stories. 160p. (gr. 6-9). 1990. 18.95 *(0-575-04486-1,* Pub. by Gollancz England) Trafalgar.

—Lanhydrock Days. 96p. (gr. 7-10). 1992. 18.95 *(0-575-04880-8,* Pub. by Gollancz UK); pap. 8.95 *(0-575-05081-0,* Pub. by Gollancz UK) Trafalgar.

Branley, Franklyn. It's Raining Cats & Dogs: All Kinds of Weather & Why We Have It. 128p. 1993. pap. 3.50 *(0-380-71849-9,* Camelot) Avon.

—Keeping Time. Van Rynbach, Iris, illus. LC 92-6783. 1993. 13.95 *(0-395-47777-8)* HM.

Branley, Franklyn M. Air Is All Around You. Rev. ed. Keller, Holly, illus. LC 85-47884. 32p. (gr. k-3). 1986. (Crowell Jr Bks); PLB 13.89 *(0-690-04503-4)* HarpC Child Bks.

—Air Is All Around You. Keller, Holly, illus. LC 85-45405. 32p. (gr. k-3). 1987. incl. cassette 7.95 *(0-694-00202-X,* Trophy); pap. 4.50 *(0-06-445048-1,* Trophy) HarpC Child Bks.

—The Beginning of the Earth. rev. ed. Maestro, Giulio, illus. LC 84-47765. 32p. (ps-3). 1988. (Crowell Jr Bks); PLB 13.89 *(0-690-04654-5,* Crowell Jr Bks) HarpC Child Bks.

—The Beginning of the Earth. rev. ed. Maestro, Giulio, illus. LC 87-45677. 32p. (ps-3). 1988. pap. 4.50 *(0-06-445074-0,* Trophy) HarpC Child Bks.

—The Big Dipper. rev. ed. Coxe, Molly, illus. LC 90-33198. 32p. (ps-1). 1991. pap. 4.95 *(0-06-445100-3,* Trophy) HarpC Child Bks.

—The Big Dipper. rev. ed. Coxe, Molly, illus. LC 90-31199. 32p. (ps-1). 1991. 13.95 *(0-06-020511-3)*; PLB 13.89 *(0-06-020512-1)* HarpC Child Bks.

—The Christmas Sky. rev. ed. Fieser, Stephen, illus. LC 89-71210. 48p. (gr. 3-7). 1990. 14.95 *(0-690-04770-3,* Crowell Jr Bks) PLB 14.89 *(0-690-04772-X,* Crowell Jr Bks) HarpC Child Bks.

—The Christmas Sky. Fieser, Stephen, illus. LC 89-71210. 48p. (gr. 3-7). 1992. pap. 5.95 *(0-06-446133-5,* Trophy) HarpC Child Bks.

—Comets. rev. ed. Maestro, Giulio, illus. LC 83-46161. 32p. (gr. k-3). 1984. (Crowell Jr Bks); PLB 13.89 *(0-690-04415-1)* HarpC Child Bks.

—Comets. Maestro, Giulio, illus. LC 83-46161. 32p. (ps-3). 1989. 7.95 *(0-694-00199-6,* Trophy); pap. 4.50 *(0-06-445088-0,* Trophy) HarpC Child Bks.

—Earthquakes. Rosenblum, Richard, illus. LC 89-35424. 32p. (gr. k-4). 1990. 14.00 *(0-690-04661-8,* Crowell Jr Bks); PLB 13.89 *(0-690-04663-4,* Crowell Jr Bks) HarpC Child Bks.

—Eclipse: Darkness in Daytime. rev. ed. Crews, Donald, illus. LC 87-47692. 32p. (ps-3). 1988. (Crowell Jr Bks); PLB 14.89 *(0-690-04619-7,* Crowell Jr Bks) HarpC Child Bks.

—Eclipse: Darkness in Daytime. rev. ed. Crews, Donald, illus. LC 87-45276. 32p. (ps-3). 1988. pap. 4.50 *(0-06-445081-3,* Trophy) HarpC Child Bks.

—Flash, Crash, Rumble, & Roll. rev. ed. Emberley, Ed E. & Emberley, Barbara, illus. LC 84-45333. 32p. (ps-3). 1985. PLB 13.89 *(0-690-04425-9,* Crowell Jr Bks) HarpC Child Bks.

—Flash, Crash, Rumble & Roll. Emberley, Barbara & Emberley, Ed E., illus. LC 84-48532. 32p. (ps-3). 1987. (Trophy); pap. 4.50 *(0-06-445012-0,* Trophy) HarpC Child Bks.

—From Sputnik to Space Shuttle: Into the New Space Age. LC 85-43186. (Illus.). 80p. (gr. 3-6). 1986. (Crowell Jr Bks); (Crowell Jr Bks) HarpC Child Bks.

—Gravity Is a Mystery. rev. ed. Madden, Don, illus. LC 85-48247. 32p. (ps-3). 1986. (Crowell Jr Bks); PLB 14.89 *(0-690-04527-1)* HarpC Child Bks.

—Hurricane Watch. Maestro, Giulio, illus. LC 85-47534. 32p. (ps-3). 1985. PLB 13.89 *(0-690-04471-2,* Crowell Jr Bks) HarpC Child Bks.

—Hurricane Watch. Maestro, Giulio, illus. LC 85-47534. 32p. (gr. k-3). 1987. pap. 4.50 *(0-06-445062-7,* Trophy) HarpC Child Bks.

—Is There Life in Outer Space? Madden, Don, illus. LC 83-45057. 32p. (ps-3). 1984. (Crowell Jr Bks); PLB 14.89 *(0-690-04375-9)* HarpC Child Bks.

—Is There Life in Outer Space? Madden, Don, illus. LC 85-45057. 32p. (gr. k-3). 1986. pap. 4.50 *(0-06-445049-X,* Trophy) HarpC Child Bks.

—It's Raining Cats & Dogs: All Kinds of Weather & Why We Have It. Kelley, True, illus. LC 86-27546. 128p. (gr. 3-8). 1987. 14.45 *(0-395-33070-X)* HM.

—Journey into a Black Hole. Simont, Marc, illus. LC 85-48249. 32p. (ps-3). 1986. PLB 13.89 *(0-690-04544-1,* Crowell Jr Bks) HarpC Child Bks.

—Journey into a Black Hole. Simont, Marc, illus. LC 85-48249. 32p. (gr. k-3). 1988. pap. 4.50 *(0-06-445075-9,* Trophy) HarpC Child Bks.

—The Moon Seems to Change. rev. ed. Emberley, Barbara & Emberley, Ed E., illus. LC 86-47747. 32p. (ps-3). 1987. (Crowell Jr Bks); PLB 13.89 *(0-690-04585-9)* HarpC Child Bks.

—The Moon Seems to Change. rev. ed. Emberley, Barbara & Emberley, Ed E., illus. LC 86-27097. 32p. (ps-3). 1987. pap. 4.50 *(0-06-445065-1,* Trophy) HarpC Child Bks.

—Neptune: Voyager's Final Target. LC 91-2469. (Illus.). 64p. (gr. 3-6). 1992. 15.00 *(0-06-022519-X)*; PLB 14.89 *(0-06-022520-3)* HarpC Child Bks.

—The Planets in Our Solar System. rev. ed. Madden, Don, illus. LC 86-47530. 32p. (ps-3). 1987. 15.00 *(0-690-04579-4,* Crowell Jr Bks); PLB 14.89 *(0-690-04581-6)* HarpC Child Bks.

—The Planets in Our Solar System. rev. ed. Madden, Don, illus. LC 86-45171. 32p. (ps-3). 1987. pap. 4.50 *(0-06-445064-3,* Trophy) HarpC Child Bks.

—Rain & Hail. Barton, Harriett, illus. LC 83-45058. 40p. (gr. k-3). 1983. PLB 13.89 *(0-690-04353-8,* Crowell Jr Bks) HarpC Child Bks.

—Rockets & Satellites. rev. ed. Maestro, Giulio, illus. LC 86-27047. 32p. (ps-3). 1987. pap. 4.50 *(0-06-445061-9,* Trophy) HarpC Child Bks.

—Shooting Stars. Keller, Holly, illus. LC 88-14190. 32p. (ps-1). 1989. 13.95 *(0-690-04701-0,* Crowell Jr Bks); PLB 13.89 *(0-690-04703-7,* Crowell Jr Bks) HarpC Child Bks.

—Shooting Stars. Keller, Holly, illus. LC 88-14190. 32p. (ps-1). 1991. pap. 4.50 *(0-06-445103-8,* Trophy) HarpC Child Bks.

—The Sky Is Full of Stars. Bond, Felicia, illus. LC 81-43037. 40p. (gr. k-3). 1981. PLB 13.89 *(0-690-04123-3,* Crowell Jr Bks) HarpC Child Bks.

—The Sky Is Full of Stars. Bond, Felicia, illus. LC 81-43037. 40p. (gr. k-3). 1983. pap. 4.50 *(0-06-445002-3,* Trophy) HarpC Child Bks.

—Snow Is Falling. rev. ed. Keller, Holly, illus. LC 85-48256. 32p. (ps-3). 1986. pap. 4.50 *(0-06-445058-9,* Trophy) HarpC Child Bks.

—Snow Is Falling. rev. ed. Keller, Holly, illus. LC 85-48256. 32p. (ps-3). 1986. (Crowell Jr Bks); PLB 14.89 *(0-690-04548-4,* Crowell Jr Bks) HarpC Child Bks.

—Star Guide. Eagle, Ellen, illus. LC 84-45928. 64p. (gr. 3-6). 1987. (Crowell Jr Bks); PLB 12.89 *(0-690-04351-1,* Crowell Jr Bks) HarpC Child Bks.

—Sun Dogs & Shooting Stars: A Skywatcher's Calendar. (Illus.). (gr. 5 up). 1980. 14.45 *(0-395-29520-3)* HM.

—Sun Dogs & Shooting Stars: A Skywatcher's Guide. 128p. 1992. pap. 3.50 *(0-380-71848-0,* Camelot) Avon.

—The Sun: Our Nearest Star. rev. ed. Madden, Don, illus. LC 87-47764. 32p. (ps-3). 1988. (Crowell Jr Bks); PLB 13.89 *(0-690-04678-2)* HarpC Child Bks.

—Sunshine Makes the Seasons. rev. ed. Maestro, Giulio, illus. LC 85-47540. 32p. (ps-3). 1985. PLB 14.89 *(0-690-04442-8,* Crowell Jr Bks) HarpC Child Bks.

—Sunshine Makes the Seasons. rev. ed. Maestro, Giulio, illus. LC 85-42750. 32p. (ps-3). 1988. incl. cassette 7.95 *(0-694-00203-8,* Trophy); pap. 4.50 *(0-06-445019-8,* Trophy) HarpC Child Bks.

—Tornado Alert. Maestro, Giulio, illus. LC 87-29379. 32p. (ps-3). 1988. (Crowell Jr Bks); PLB 13.89 *(0-690-04688-X)* HarpC Child Bks.

—Tornado Alert. Maestro, Giulio, illus. LC 87-29379. 32p. (gr. k-4). 1990. pap. 4.95 *(0-06-445094-5,* Trophy) HarpC Child Bks.

—Uranus: The Seventh Planet. Buchanan, Yvonne, illus. LC 87-35046. 64p. (gr. 3-6). 1988. (Crowell Jr Bks); PLB 12.89 *(0-690-04687-1,* Crowell Jr Bks) HarpC Child Bks.

—Venus: Magellan Explores Our Twin Planet. LC 92-32990. (Illus.). 64p. (gr. 3-6). 1994. 14.95 *(0-06-020298-X)*; PLB 14.89 *(0-06-020384-6)* HarpC Child Bks.

—Volcanoes. Simont, Marc, illus. LC 84-45344. 32p. (ps-3). 1985. (Crowell Jr Bks); PLB 13.89 *(0-690-04431-3)* HarpC Child Bks.

—Volcanoes. Simont, Marc, illus. LC 84-45344. 32p. (ps-3). 1986. pap. 4.50 *(0-06-445059-7,* Trophy) HarpC Child Bks.

—What Happened to the Dinosaurs? Simont, Marc, illus. LC 88-37626. 32p. (gr. k-3). 1989. (Crowell Jr Bks); PLB 13.89 *(0-690-04749-5,* Crowell Jr Bks) HarpC Child Bks.

—What Happened to the Dinosaurs? Simont, Marc, illus. LC 88-37626. 32p. (gr. k-4). 1991. pap. 4.50 *(0-06-445105-4,* Trophy) HarpC Child Bks.

—What Makes Day & Night? rev. ed. Dorros, Arthur, illus. LC 85-40657. 32p. (gr. k-3). 1986. pap. 4.95 *(0-06-445050-3,* Trophy) HarpC Child Bks.

—What Makes Day & Night? rev. ed. Dorros, Arthur, illus. LC 85-47903. 32p. (ps-3). 1986. PLB 14.89 *(0-690-04524-7,* Crowell Jr Bks) HarpC Child Bks.

—What the Moon Is Like. rev. ed. Kelley, True, illus. LC 85-47904. 32p. (ps-3). 1986. PLB 14.89 *(0-690-04512-3,* Crowell Jr Bks) HarpC Child Bks.

—What the Moon Is Like. Kelley, True, illus. LC 85-45400. 32p. (gr. k-3). 1987. Book & Cassette Set. 7.95 *(0-694-00205-4,* Trophy); pap. 4.50 *(0-06-445052-X,* Trophy) HarpC Child Bks.

Brannan, Linda, jt. auth. see **McCombs, Barbara L.**

Brannon, Brian, jt. auth. see **Thatcher, Kevin.**

Brannon, Tom. Baby Natasha's Busy Day. (ps). 1993. pap. 2.25 *(0-307-06035-7,* Golden Pr) Western Pub.

—Flash Cards Get Ready Numbers. (ps). 1986. pap. 3.25 *(0-307-04981-7,* Golden Pr) Western Pub.

Brannon, Tom, illus. Jim Henson's Muppet Babies' Christmas Book. 48p. (ps-2). 1992. 6.95 *(0-307-15955-8,* 15955, Golden Pr) Western Pub.

—Sesame Street: Little Elmo's Toy Box. (ps). 1990. pap. write for info. *(0-307-06038-1,* Golden Pr) Western Pub.

—Sesame Street: Little Ernie Loves Rubber Duckie. 12p. (ps). 1992. write for info. nontoxic, washable *(0-307-06064-0,* 6064, Golden Pr) Western Pub.

—Sesame Street: Little Grover Takes a Walk. (ps-k). 1991. pap. write for info. *(0-307-06062-4,* Golden Pr) Western Pub.

—What Does Baby Kermit Say? 12p. (ps). 1993. pap. 1.95 *(0-307-06036-5,* 6036, Golden Pr) Western Pub.

Brannon, Tom & Cooke, Tom, illus. Open Sesame Multilevel Book. Baigelman, Simon, photos by. pap. 7.95 *(0-19-434261-1)* OUP.

Branscum, Robbie. Johnny May Grows Up. Marstall, Bob, illus. LC 86-45780. 128p. (gr. 4-8). 1987. HarpC Child Bks.

—Old Blue Tilley. LC 90-6348. 96p. (gr. 5-9). 1991. SBE 12.95 *(0-02-711931-9,* Macmillan Child Bk) Macmillan Child Grp.

Branson, Margaret & Coombs, Fred. Civics for Today. (Illus.). (gr. 7-9). 1980. text ed. 36.72 *(0-395-26201-1)*; wkbk. 11.28 *(0-395-26203-8)* HM.

Branson, Mary. Adventures in Prayer: A Prayer Guide for Children. (Illus.). 127p. (Orig.). (gr. k-6). 1988. pap. 4.95 *(0-936625-14-7,* New Hope AL) Womans Mission Union.

—Fun Around the World: Games, Crafts, Food & Dress Ideas You Can Use! Gross, Karen, ed. 64p. (Orig.). (gr. 1-6). 1992. pap. text ed. 4.95 *(1-56309-052-X,* New Hope) Womans Mission Union.

Branson, Mary K. A Carousel of Countries: Games, Songs, Recipes & Customs from Around the World. (Illus.). 96p. (gr. 1-6). 1986. pap. 5.95 *(0-936625-53-8,* New Hope AL) Womans Mission Union.

Branson, O. T. Apache Indian Coloring Book. 32p. (gr. 1-6). 1983. pap. 2.95 *(0-918080-13-4)* Treasure Chest.

—Indian Dancer Coloring Book. 32p. (gr. 1-6). 1982. pap. 2.95 *(0-918080-03-7)* Treasure Chest.

Branston, Brian. Gods & Heroes from Viking Mythology. Caselli, Giovanni, illus. LC 92-29705. 1993. write for info. *(0-87226-905-1)* P Bedrick Bks.

Branton, Leslie B. Colorful Kansas City. Hsu, Serena, illus. LC 90-50125. 64p. (Orig.). (gr. 2 up). 1990. pap. 4.95 *(0-933701-47-0)* Westport Pubs.

Brashear, William. A Northwood Lad. Costa, Gwen, ed. LC 90-1137. (gr. 6 up). 1992. pap. 14.95 *(0-87949-333-X)* Ashley Bks.

Brashler, William. The Story of Negro League Baseball. LC 93-36547. (gr. 5 up). 1994. 15.95 *(0-395-67169-8)*; pap. 9.95 *(0-395-69721-2)* Ticknor & Fields.

Bratman, Fred. Becoming a Citizen: Adopting a New Home. LC 92-24061. (Illus.). 48p. (gr. 5-6). 1992. PLB 21.34 *(0-8114-7354-6)* Raintree Steck-V.

—Everything You Need to Know When a Parent Dies. (gr. 7-12). 1992. PLB 13.95 *(0-8239-1324-4)* Rosen Group.

—War in the Persian Gulf. (Illus.). 64p. (gr. 7 up). 1991. PLB 15.90 (*1-56294-051-1*) Millbrook Pr.
Bratvold, Gretchen. Oregon. (Illus.). 72p. (gr. 3-6). 1991. PLB 17.50 (*0-8225-2704-9*) Lerner Pubns.
—Wisconsin. (Illus.). 72p. (gr. 3-6). 1991. PLB 17.50 (*0-8225-2700-6*) Lerner Pubns.
Braumiller, Tanya. Visiting Gig Harbor. Hamer, Bonnie, illus. (Orig.). (gr. 1-4). 1983. pap. 2.75 (*0-933992-28-9*) Coffee Break.
Braun, Elisabeth. Profiles in Conservation: Africa. (Illus.). 250p. (gr. 9 up). 1994. text ed. 26.50x (*1-55591-914-9*) Fulcrum Pub.
Braun, Lilian J. The Cat Who Sniffed Glue. 1989. pap. 4.99 (*0-515-09954-6*) Jove Pubns.
Braun, Lutz. Faster Than the Bull. Moore, Stephen, illus. LC 92-37947. 32p. (gr. 4-6). 1992. PLB 17.96 (*0-8114-3580-6*) Raintree Steck-V.
Brautigan, Richard. In Watermelon Sugar. 176p. (gr. 9 up). 1973. pap. 1.75 (*0-440-34026-8*) Dell.
Bravo, Olga. Olga's Cup & Saucer. 1994. write for info. (*0-8050-3301-7*) H Holt & Co.
Bray, Marian. World's Biggest Chicken. 1992. pap. 4.99 (*1-55513-929-9*) Cook.
Bray, Marian F. Ever So Slightly. LC 91-12469. 144p. 1991. pap. 4.99 (*0-8066-2536-8, 9-2536*) Augsburg Fortress.
—Springtime of Khan. LC 88-19917. (gr. 7-9). 1988. pap. 3.99 (*1-55513-123-9, Chariot Bks*) Cook.
—Stars over East L. A. (Orig.). (gr. 8-12). 1993. pap. 6.99 (*0-87788-798-5*) Shaw Pubs.
Bray, Vivieene, illus. Little Bear's Bedtime. 10p. (ps-2). 1993. bds. 16.95 (*1-56293-317-5*) McClanahan Bk.
—Little Bear's Breakfast. 10p. (ps-2). 1993. bds. 16.95 (*1-56293-318-3*) McClanahan Bk.
Braybrooks, Ann. Disney's Aladdin. Ortiz, Phil & Michaels, Serge, illus. 24p. (ps-3). 1992. pap. write for info. (*0-307-12692-7, 12692, Golden Pr*) Western Pub.
—Disney's Aladdin: The Cave of Wonders. (ps-3). 1993. 4.95 (*0-307-11565-8, Golden Pr*) Western Pub.
—Disney's Aladdin: The Cave of Wonders. (ps-3). 1993. pap. 3.50 (*0-307-15974-4, Golden Pr*) Western Pub.
—Disney's Mickey Mouse Reading Kit. (Illus.). 24p. 1993. kit 19.95 (*1-56138-145-4*) Running Pr.
Braybrooks, Ann & Rifkin, Mark. The Disney Treasury of Princesses: Stories from the Films. Thompkins, Kenny, illus. LC 92-56163. 80p. 1993. 14.95 (*1-56282-497-X*); PLB 14.89 (*1-56282-498-8*) Disney Pr.
Braybrooks, Ann, adapted by. Walt Disney's One Hundred One Dalmatians. LC 90-85424. (Illus.). 96p. 1991. 14.95 (*1-56282-010-9*); PLB 14.89 (*1-56282-011-7*) Disney Pr.
—Walt Disney's One Hundred One Dalmatians. Dicicco, Gil, illus. LC 90-85425. 72p. (Orig.). (gr. 2-6). 1991. pap. 2.95 (*1-56282-013-3*) Disney Pr.
Braynard, Frank O. U. S. Steamships: A Picture Postcard History. Cronkite, Walter, intro. by. (Illus.). 144p. (Orig.). 1991. pap. 14.95 (*0-930256-20-4*) Almar.
Brazile, Lionel J., Jr. Arithmetic Summary Booklet. (Illus.). 16p. (Orig.). (gr. 1-9). 1990. pap. 12.95 (*0-9624016-0-9*) Scholar Pub Co.
Brazouski, Antoinette & Klatt, Mary J., eds. Children's Books on Ancient Greek & Roman Mythology: An Annotated Bibliography. 1993. 49.95 (*0-313-28973-5, Greenwood Pr*) Greenwood.
Brazz, Marlene L., jt. auth. see Terkel, Susan N.
Breakstone, Steve. Washington Walkabout. Marsh, Jerry & Hurt, Rory, eds. (Illus.). 256p. (Orig.). 1992. pap. 13.95 (*0-9632724-4-6*) Balance Pubns.
Brearley, Sue. Adventure Holiday. Mathews, Jenny, photos by. (Illus.). 28p. (gr. 1-4). 1991. 12.95 (*0-7136-3382-4, Pub. by A&C Black UK*) Talman.
—Talk to Me. (Illus.). 26p. (gr. 1-4). 10.95 (*0-7136-3192-9, Pub. by A&C Black UK*) Talman.
Breathed, Berkeley. Goodnight Opus. (Illus.). 1993. 15. 95 (*0-316-10853-7*) Little.
—The Last Basselope: One Ferocious Story. LC 92-14467. (Illus.). 1992. 14.95 (*0-316-10761-1*) Little.
—A Wish for Wings That Work: An Opus Christmas Story. Breathed, Berkeley, illus. 32p. 1991. 14.95 (*0-316-10758-1*) Little.
Brebeuf, Jean de see De Brebeuf, Jean.
Brebner, Daphne B., ed. see Wallower, Lucille.
Brecht, Bertolt. Galileo. Bentley, Eric, ed. Laughton, Charles, tr. from GER. Bentley, Eric, intro. by. 160p. (Orig.). (gr. 9 up). 1966. pap. 6.95 (*0-8021-3059-3*) Grove-Atltic.
Breckenridge, Judy. Simple Physics Experiments with Everyday Materials. Zweifel, Frances, illus. LC 92-25312. 128p. (gr. 4 up). 1993. 12.95 (*0-8069-8606-9*) Sterling.
—Simple Physics Experiments with Everyday Materials. Zweifel, Frances, illus. 128p. (gr. 4-10). 1993. pap. 4.95 (*0-8069-8607-7*) Sterling.
Breckler, Rosemary K. Hoang Breaks the Lucky Teapot. Frankel, Adrian, illus. 32p. (gr. k-3). 1992. 13.45 (*0-395-57031-X*) HM.
Bredeson, Carmen. Jonas Salk: Discoverer of the Polio Vaccine. (Illus.). 104p. (gr. 6 up). 1993. lib. bdg. 17.95 (*0-89490-415-9*) Enslow Pubs.
Bredin, Henrietta. Christmas Eve. LC 92-1235. 1992. 5.95 (*0-85953-145-7*) Childs Play.
—The Prince & the Goosegirl. LC 92-260. 1992. 5.95 (*0-85953-146-5*) Childs Play.
Bree, Loris T. & Bree, Marlin. Kid's Squish Book: Slimy, Pasty, Sticky Things to Do That Should Only Be Done When Wearing Your Oldest Clothes. (Illus.). 96p. 1993. pap. 8.95 (*0-943400-76-7*) Marlor Pr.

Bree, Marlin, jt. auth. see Bree, Loris T.
Breebaart, Joeri & Breebaart, Piet. When I Die, Will I Get Better? Kushner, Harold, intro. by. LC 93-2713. (Illus.). 32p. (gr. k-4). 1993. 11.95 (*0-87226-375-4*) P Bedrick Bks.
Breebaart, Piet, jt. auth. see Breebaart, Joeri.
Breeding, Robert L. From London to Appalachia. Moore, Erin C., illus. 200p. (gr. 4-7). 1991. pap. 9.95 (*1-880258-03-X*) Thriftecon.
Breen, Michael, jt. auth. see McEntee, Sean.
Breese, Gillian & Langham, Tony. The Amazing Adventures of Teddy Tum Tum. Lowry, Patrick, illus. 32p. (ps-3). 1992. 11.95 (*1-55970-185-4*) Arcade Pub Inc.
Breeze, Lynn. Baby's Clothes. (Illus.). 14p. (ps). 1994. bds. 4.50 fold-outs (*0-8120-6410-0*) Barron.
—Baby's Food. (Illus.). 14p. (ps). 1994. bds. 4.50 fold-outs (*0-8120-6413-5*) Barron.
—Baby's Pets. (Illus.). 14p. (ps). 1994. bds. 4.50 fold-outs (*0-8120-6411-9*) Barron.
—Baby's Toys. (Illus.). 14p. (ps). 1994. bds. 4.50 fold-outs (*0-8120-6412-7*) Barron.
Breeze, Lynn, illus. This Little Baby Goes Out. Morris, Ann, text by. LC 92-30880. (Illus.). (ps). 1993. 5.95 (*0-316-10854-5*) Little.
—This Little Baby's Bedtime. Morris, Ann, text by. LC 92-30879. (Illus.). (ps). 1993. 5.95 (*0-316-58419-3*) Little.
—This Little Baby's Morning. Morris, Ann, text by. LC 92-30881. (Illus.). (ps). 1993. 5.95 (*0-316-58420-7*) Little.
—This Little Baby's Playtime. Morris, Ann, text by. LC 92-30878. (Illus.). (ps). 1993. 5.95 (*0-316-10855-3*) Little.
Breinburg, Petronella. Shawn Goes to School. Lloyd, Errol, illus. LC 73-8003. 32p. (ps-2). 1974. PLB 14.89 (*0-690-00277-7, Crowell Jr Bks*) HarpC Child Bks.
Breiter, Herta S. Pollution. LC 87-23233. (Illus.). 48p. (Orig.). (gr. 2-6). 1987. PLB 18.64 (*0-8172-3259-1*); pap. 4.49 (*0-8114-8216-2*) Raintree Steck-V.
—Time & Clocks. rev. ed. LC 87-23229. (Illus.). 48p. (gr. 2-6). 1987. PLB 18.64 (*0-8172-3262-1*) Raintree Steck-V.
—Weather. rev. ed. LC 87-23226. (Illus.). 48p. (gr. 2-6). 1987. PLB 18.64 (*0-8172-3265-6*) Raintree Steck-V.
Breitmeyer, Lois & Leithauser, Gladys. Who Should I Be? (gr. 4 up). 1991. pap. 2.95 (*0-8091-6599-6*) Paulist Pr.
Breitter, Herta S. Fuel & Energy. rev. ed. LC 87-20804. (Illus.). 48p. (gr. 2-6). 1987. PLB 18.64 (*0-8172-3255-9*); pap. 4.49 (*0-8114-8223-5*) Raintree Steck-V.
Bremmer. How Birds Live. (gr. 4-6). 1981. (Usborne-Hayes), PLB 13.96 (*0-88110-082-X*); pap. 6.95 (*0-86020-157-0*) EDC.
Bremmer, T., et al. Book of Knowledge. (Illus.). 243p. (gr. 3 up). 21.95 (*0-7460-0360-9*) EDC.
Bremyer, Jayne. Not Like Other Girls. 162p. (ps up). 1982. pap. 9.95 (*0-944996-09-4*) Carlsons.
Brenan, Kathleen M. & Mandell, Steven L. Introduction to Computers & Basic Programming. 2nd ed. 564p. (gr. 9-12). 1987. text ed. 32.75 (*0-314-32166-7*); Tchr's. manual. 15.95 (*0-314-43635-9*); wkbk. 9.50 (*0-314-36064-6*) West Pub.
Brendon, Stuart, illus. Children's Giant World Atlas. Lye, Keith, contrib. by. (Illus.). 14p. (gr. k-4). 1987. 19.95 (*0-681-40268-7*) Longmeadow Pr.
Breneman, Steven B. Fly Away Home. LC 84-6252. 74p. (Orig.). (gr. 2-6). 1984. pap. 8.50 (*0-87743-183-3, Pub. by Bellwood Pr*) Bahai.
Bren Guernsey, JoAnn. Missing Children. LC 89-25210. (Illus.). 48p. (gr. 4 up). 1990. RSBE 13.95 (*0-89686-494-4, Crestwood Hse*) Macmillan Child Grp.
Brennan, Frank. Reptiles. Livingstone, Malcolm, illus. LC 91-26684. 32p. (Orig.). (ps-2). 1992. pap. 5.95 (*0-689-71587-0, Aladdin*) Macmillan Child Grp.
Brennan, Gale. Earl the Squirrel. Flint, Russ, illus. 16p. (Orig.). (gr. k-6). 1981. pap. 1.25 (*0-685-02455-5*) Brennan Bks.
—Toulouse the Mouse. Flint, Russ, illus. 16p. (Orig.). (gr. k-6). 1981. pap. 1.25 (*0-685-02458-X*) Brennan Bks.
Brennan, Gale, jt. auth. see LaFleur, Tom.
Brennan, Herbie. Emily & the Werewolf. Pace, David, illus. 96p. (ps-3). 1993. SBE 16.95g (*0-689-50593-0, M K McElderry*) Macmillan Child Grp.
Brennan, J. H. The Castle of Darkness. 192p. (Orig.). (gr. 6 up). 1986. pap. 2.50 (*0-440-91120-6, LFL*) Dell.
—The Den of Dragons. 192p. (gr. 6 up). 1986. pap. 2.50 (*0-440-91873-1, LFL*) Dell.
—The Gateway of Doom. (Orig.). (gr. k-12). 1987. pap. 2.50 (*0-440-92800-1, LFL*) Dell.
—Kingdom of Horror. (gr. 6-12). 1987. pap. 2.50 (*0-440-94540-2*) Dell.
—Realm of Chaos. (Orig.). (gr. k-12). 1987. pap. 2.50 (*0-440-97325-2, LFL*) Dell.
—Shiva Accused: An Adventure of the Ice Age. LC 90-25888. 288p. (gr. 5 up). 1991. 16.95 (*0-06-020741-8*); PLB 16.89 (*0-06-020742-6*) HarpC Child Bks.
—Shiva Accused: An Adventure of the Ice Age. LC 90-25888. 288p. (gr. 5 up). 1991. pap. 4.95 (*0-06-440431-5, Trophy*) HarpC Child Bks.
—Shiva: An Adventure of the Ice Age. LC 89-77654. 208p. (gr. 5 up). 1992. pap. 3.95 (*0-06-440392-0, Trophy*) HarpC Child Bks.

—Shiva's Challenge: An Adventure of the Ice Age. LC 91-40676. 224p. (gr. 5 up). 1992. 17.00 (*0-06-020825-2*); PLB 16.89 (*0-06-020826-0*) HarpC Child Bks.
—Shiva's Challenge: An Adventure of the Ice Age. LC 91-40676. 224p. (gr. 5 up). 1993. pap. 4.95 (*0-06-440460-9, Trophy*) HarpC Child Bks.
—Voyage of Terror. (Orig.). (gr. k-12). 1987. pap. 2.50 (*0-440-99324-5, LFL*) Dell.
Brennan, Jan. Born Two-Gether. (Illus.). 40p. (Orig.). (ps-2). Date not set. pap. 5.95 (*0-9613536-1-9*) J & L Bks.
Brennan, John & Keaney, Leonie. Zoo Day. (Illus.). 32p. (ps-2). 1989. PLB 13.50 (*0-87614-358-3*) Carolrhoda Bks.
Brennan, Melissa. Careless Kisses. 1991. pap. 3.50 (*0-06-106052-6, Harp PBks*) HarpC.
—Could This Be Love? 1991. pap. 3.50 (*0-06-106067-4, Harp PBks*) HarpC.
—Paradise Lost? 1991. pap. 3.50 (*0-06-106068-2, Harp PBks*) HarpC.
—The Real Thing. (gr. 7 up). 1992. pap. 3.50 (*0-06-106070-4, Harp PBks*) HarpC.
—Sneaking Around. 1992. pap. 3.50 (*0-06-106069-0, Harp PBks*) HarpC.
—Whispers & Rumors. 1991. pap. 3.50 (*0-06-106049-6, Harp PBks*) HarpC.
Brennan, Steve. Sharing Susan. LC 90-27097. 128p. (gr. 4-7). 1994. pap. 3.95 (*0-06-440430-7, Trophy*) HarpC Child Bks.
Brennan-Nichols, Patricia. Getting to Know Jesus. Haberson, Lydia, illus. 68p. (Orig.). (gr. k-3). 1984. pap. 4.95 (*0-89505-130-3, R0610*) Tabor Pub.
—Getting to Know Jesus: Teacher's Guide. (Illus.). 80p. (gr. k-3). 1984. 11.95 (*0-89505-131-1, R0620*) Tabor Pub.
—Learning to Love Jesus. (Illus.). 80p. (Orig.). (gr. 4-6). 1985. tchr's. guide 15.95 (*0-89505-329-2, R0520*); pap. 4.95 72p. (*0-89505-328-4, R0510*) Tabor Pub.
Brenner, Anita. The Boy Who Could Do Anything: And Other Mexican Folktales. Charlot, Jean, illus. LC 92-3903. 128p. (gr. 3-7). 1992. Repr. of 1942 ed. lib. bdg. 17.50 (*0-208-02353-4, Pub. by Linnet*) Shoe String.
Brenner, Barbara. Beef Stew. Siracusa, Catherine, illus. LC 89-36769. 32p. (Orig.). (ps-1). 1990. lib. bdg. 7.99 (*0-394-95046-1*); pap. 3.50 (*0-394-85046-7*) Random Bks Yng Read.
—Bodies. Ancona, George, illus. (ps-3). 1973. 13.95 (*0-525-26770-0, DCB*) Dutton Child Bks.
—The Color Wizard: Level 1. Dillon, Leo & Dillon, Diane, illus. (ps-3). 1989. pap. 3.50 (*0-553-34690-3*) Bantam.
—Dinosaurium. LC 91-6335. (ps-3). 1993. pap. 9.50 (*0-553-35427-2*) Bantam.
—Faces. Ancona, George, illus. LC 70-102737. 48p. (ps-2). 1970. 14.95 (*0-525-29518-6, DCB*) Dutton Child Bks.
—Good News. 1991. 9.99 (*0-553-07091-6*); pap. 3.50 (*0-553-35209-1*) Bantam.
—Group Soup. Munsinger, Lynn, illus. 32p. (ps-3). 1992. PLB 12.50 (*0-670-82867-X*) Viking Child Bks.
—If You Were There in Seventeen Seventy-Six. (Illus.). 128p. (gr. 3-7). 1994. SBE 14.95 (*0-02-712322-7, Bradbury Pr*) Macmillan Child Grp.
—If You Were There in 1492. LC 90-24099. (Illus.). 112p. (gr. 3-7). 1991. SBE 13.95 (*0-02-712321-9, Bradbury Pr*) Macmillan Child Grp.
—Lion & Lamb Step Out. 1990. 9.99 (*0-553-05860-6*) Bantam.
—The Magic Box, Level 3. Boix, Manuel, illus. 1990. PLB 9.99 (*0-553-05896-7, Little Rooster*); pap. 3.50 (*0-553-34926-0, Little Rooster*) Bantam.
—Mr. Tall & Mr. Small. Shenon, Mike, illus. LC 93-8256. 1994. write for info. (*0-8050-2757-2*) H Holt & Co.
—Moon Boy. 1990. 9.99 (*0-553-05858-4*) Bantam.
—Mystery of the Disappearing Dogs. Sims, Blanche, illus. LC 82-186. 128p. (gr. 3-6). 1982. pap. 1.95 (*0-394-85162-5*) Knopf Bks Yng Read.
—The Mystery of the Plumed Serpent. Sims, Blanche, illus. LC 80-17316. 128p. (gr. 3-6). 1981. lib. bdg. 4.99 (*0-394-94531-X*) Knopf Bks Yng Read.
—Planetarium. LC 91-6629. (ps-3). 1993. pap. 9.50 (*0-553-35428-0*) Bantam.
—Rosa & Marco & the Three Wishes. Halsey, Megan, illus. LC 90-26855. 32p. (gr. 1-3). 1992. RSBE 11.95 (*0-02-712315-4, Bradbury Pr*) Macmillan Child Grp.
—A Snake-Lover's Diary. Brenner, Barbara, illus. LC 84-43136. 96p. (gr. 4-6). 1990. PLB 15.89 (*0-06-020697-7*) HarpC Child Bks.
—Ups & Downs with Lion & Lamb. (ps-3). 1991. 9.99 (*0-553-07088-6*); pap. 3.50 (*0-553-35207-5*) Bantam.
—Wagon Wheels. newly illus. ed. Bolognese, Don, illus. LC 92-18780. 64p. (gr. k-3). 1978. 14.00 (*0-06-020668-3*); PLB 13.89 (*0-06-020669-1*) HarpC Child Bks.
—Wagon Wheels. newly illustrated ed. Bologneze, Don, illus. LC 92-18780. 64p. (gr. k-3). 1984. pap. 3.50 (*0-06-444052-4, Trophy*) HarpC Child Bks.
Brenner, Barbara & Chardiet, Bernice. Hide & Seek Science: Where's That Reptile? Schwartz, Carol, illus. LC 92-20905. 1993. 10.95 (*0-590-45212-6*) Scholastic Inc.
—Where's That Fish? Schwartz, Carol, illus. LC 93-2929. 32p. (ps-3). 1994. 10.95 (*0-590-45214-2, Cartwheel*) Scholastic Inc.

—Where's That Insect? Hide & Seek Science. Schwartz, Carol, illus. LC 92-20906. 32p. 1993. 10.95 (*0-590-45210-X*) Scholastic Inc.
Brenner, Barbara & Garelick, May. The Tremendous Tree Book. Brenner, Fred, illus. LC 91-73753. 40p. (ps-3). 1992. 14.95 (*1-878093-56-8*) Boyds Mills Pr.
—Two Orphan Cubs. Kors, Erika, illus. (ps-1). 1989. 12. 95 (*0-8027-6868-7*); PLB 13.85 (*0-8027-6869-5*) Walker & Co.
Brenner, Barbara, jt. auth. see Hooks, William H.
Brenner, Barbara, ed. The Earth Is Painted Green: A Garden of Poems about Our Planet. Schindler, S. D., illus. LC 93-21466. 96p. 1993. 16.95 (*0-590-45134-0*) Scholastic Inc.
Brenner, Barbara A. Annie's Pet: Level 2. Ziegler, Jack, illus. (ps-3). 1989. 9.99 (*0-553-05833-9*); pap. 3.50 (*0-553-34693-8*) Bantam.
—The Color Wizard: Level 1. Dillon, Leo & Dillon, Diane, illus. (ps-3). 1989. 9.99 (*0-553-05825-8*) Bantam.
Brenner, Barbara A., jt. auth. see Hooks, William H.
Brenner, Peter. King for One Day. Wyss, Manspeter, illus. LC 74-151271. 36p. (ps-3). 7.95 (*0-87592-027-6*) Scroll Pr.
Brenner, Richard J. The Complete Super Bowl Story: Games I-XXIII. (Illus.). 112p. (gr. 5 up). 1989. PLB 15.95 (*0-8225-1503-2*) Lerner Pubns.
—The World Series: The Great Contests. (Illus.). 88p. (gr. 5 up). 1989. PLB 15.95 (*0-8225-1502-4*) Lerner Pubns.
Brenner, Robert C. Modems Made Easy. Brenner, Veronica L., ed. Technical Support Services Staff, illus. 270p. (Orig.). (gr. 9-12). 1991. pap. 19.95 (*0-929535-09-X*) Brenner Info Group.
Brenner, Summer. Dancers & the Dance. LC 90-30312. 144p. (Orig.). 1990. pap. 9.95 (*0-918273-75-7*) Coffee Hse.
Brenner, Veronica L., ed. see Brenner, Robert C.
Brent, Bill J., jt. auth. see Bill, J. Brent.
Brent, Isabelle. The Christmas Story. (Illus.). 1989. 13.95 (*0-8037-0730-4*) Dial Bks Young.
—Noah's Ark. 1992. 12.95 (*0-316-10837-5*) Little.
Brent, Isabelle, illus. An Alphabet of Animals. LC 92-54652. 1993. 12.95 (*0-316-10852-9*) Little.
Brentano, Clemens. The Legend of Rosepetal. Zwerger, Lisbeth, illus. LC 84-27386. 32p. (gr. 2-6). 1991. pap. 16.95 (*0-907234-71-2*) Picture Bk Studio.
Breskin, jt. auth. see Zalben, Jane.
Bresler, L. Earth Facts. (Illus.). 48p. (gr. 3-7). 1987. PLB 12.96 (*0-88110-239-3*); pap. 5.95 (*0-7460-0022-7*) EDC.
Breslow, Ronald. Enzymes: The Machines of Life. Head, J. J., ed. Steffen, Ann T., illus. LC 84-45828. 16p. (Orig.). (gr. 10 up). 1986. pap. text ed. 2.75 (*0-89278-155-6*, 45-9755) Carolina Biological.
Breslow, Susan. I Really Want a Dog. LC 89-38567. (Illus.). 40p. (ps-3). 1990. 12.95 (*0-525-44589-7*, DCB) Dutton Child Bks.
Breslow, Susan & Blakemore, Sally. I Really Want a Dog. Kelley, True, illus. 40p. (ps-3). 1993. pap. 4.99 (*0-14-054941-2*, Puffin Unicorn) Puffin Bks.
Bresnick-Perry, Roslyn. Leaving for America. Reisberg, Mira, illus. LC 92-8450. 32p. (ps-7). 1992. PLB 13.95 (*0-89239-105-7*) Childrens Book Pr.
Bretecher, Claire. Agrippina. 50p. 1992. pap. 9.95 (*0-7493-0812-5*, Pub. by Mandarin UK) Heinemann.
Brett, Bernard. The Fighting Ship. Batchelor, John & Lapper, Ivan, illus. 96p. (gr. 7 up). 1988. 17.95 (*0-19-273155-6*) OUP.
—Monsters. LC 82-13452. (Illus.). 128p. (gr. 4-8). 1983. (J Messner); pap. 3.95 (*0-671-46160-5*) S&S Trade.
Brett, Caroline. The Whale: The Sovereigns of the Sea. Stefoff, Rebecca, ed. LC 92-10242. (Illus.). 31p. (gr. 3-6). 1992. PLB 17.26 (*1-56074-054-X*) Garrett Ed Corp.
Brett, Jan. Annie & the Wild Animals. Brett, Jan, illus. LC 84-19818. 32p. (gr. k-3). 1985. 14.95 (*0-395-37800-1*); pap. 7.95 (*0-395-53962-5*) HM.
—Annie & the Wild Animals. Brett, Jan, illus. (ps-3). 1989. pap. 4.80 (*0-395-51006-6*, Sandpiper) HM.
—Beauty & the Beast. Brett, Jan, illus. LC 88-16965. 48p. (gr. 1-7). 1989. 14.95 (*0-89919-497-4*, Clarion Bks) HM.
—Beauty & the Beast. (ps-3). 1990. pap. 5.70 (*0-395-55702-X*, Clarion Bks) HM.
—Berlioz the Bear. LC 90-37634. (Illus.). 32p. 1991. 14. 95 (*0-399-22248-0*, Putnam) Putnam Pub Group.
—Christmas Trolls. Brett, Jan, illus. LC 93-10106. 32p. (ps-3). 1993. PLB 15.95 (*0-399-22507-2*, Putnam) Putnam Pub Group.
—The First Dog. (Illus.). 28p. (ps-3). 1988. 13.95 (*0-15-227650-5*) HarBrace.
—First Dog. LC 88-222. (ps-3). 1992. pap. 5.95 (*0-15-227651-3*, Voyager Bks) HarBrace.
—Fritz & the Beautiful Horses. Brett, Jan, illus. 32p. (gr. k-3). 1987. 13.45 (*0-395-30850-X*); pap. 4.80 (*0-395-45356-9*) HM.
—Goldilocks & the Three Bears. (Illus.). 32p. (ps-3). 1990. pap. 6.95 (*0-399-22004-6*, Sandcastle Bks) Putnam Pub Group.
—The Mitten: A Ukrainian Folktale. Brett, Jan, illus. 32p. (ps-3). 1990. 15.95 (*0-399-21920-X*, Putnam) Putnam Pub Group.
—The Trouble with Trolls. (Illus.). 32p. (ps-3). 1992. 14. 95 (*0-399-22336-3*, Putnam) Putnam Pub Group.
—The Twelve Days of Christmas. (Illus.). 32p. 1990. 14. 95 (*0-399-22197-2*, Putnam) Putnam Pub Group.

—Twelve Days of Christmas. (Illus.). 32p. 1990. 14.95 (*0-399-22037-2*, Putnam) Putnam Pub Group.
—The Wild Christmas Reindeer. Brett, Jan, illus. 32p. (ps-3). 1990. 14.95 (*0-399-22192-1*, Putnam) Putnam Pub Group.
Brett, Jan & Lear, Edward. Owl & the Pussycat. (Illus.). 32p (ps-3). 1991. 14.95 (*0-399-21925-0*, Putnam) Putnam Pub Group.
Breverton, David. Here Comes Bulldozer. Bartle, Brian, illus. 12p. (ps-1). 1992. 4.95 (*0-448-40590-3*, G&D) Putnam Pub Group.
—Here Comes Dump Truck. Bartle, Brian, illus. 12p. (ps-1). 1992. 4.95 (*0-448-40591-1*, G&D) Putnam Pub Group.
—Here Comes Fire Truck. Bartle, Brian, illus. 12p. (ps-1). 1992. 4.95 (*0-448-40592-X*, G&D) Putnam Pub Group.
Brew, Annie S., jt. auth. see Brew, Lydia E.
Brew, Lydia E. & Brew, Annie S. Dr. Edith Irby Jones: A Story of Triumph. 58p. (gr. k-2). 1992. pap. text ed. 3.50 (*0-9635351-0-2*) Lydias Educ.
Brew, Virginia & McCabe, Michael. Arizona: Studies. rev. ed. (Illus.). 160p. (gr. 4-6). 1994. text ed. 19.45 (*0-911981-58-6*) Cloud Pub.
Brew, Virginia, jt. auth. see McCabe, Michael.
Brewer, Annie M. & Brewer, Donald E. Chemicals du Jour: A Traveler's Guide to Tanker Contents. 250p. (Orig.). (gr. 8). 1993. pap. 19.95 (*0-9632341-3-7*) Whiteford.
Brewer, Donald E., jt. auth. see Brewer, Annie M.
Brewer, Duncan. Comets, Asteroids & Meteorites. LC 90-40813. (Illus.). 64p. (gr. 5-9). 1992. PLB 15.95 (*1-85435-376-4*) Marshall Cavendish.
—Jupiter. LC 90-40812. (Illus.). 64p. (gr. 5-9). 1992. PLB 13.95 (*1-85435-373-X*) Marshall Cavendish.
—Mars. LC 90-40806. (Illus.). 64p. (gr. 5-9). 1992. PLB 13.95 (*1-85435-372-1*) Marshall Cavendish.
—Mercury. LC 90-40807. (Illus.). 64p. (gr. 5-9). 1992. PLB 13.95 (*0-685-57609-4*) Marshall Cavendish.
—The Outer Planets: Uranus, Neptune, Pluto. LC 90-40810. (Illus.). 64p. (gr. 5-9). 1992. PLB 15.95 (*1-85435-375-6*) Marshall Cavendish.
—Planet Earth. LC 90-40809. (Illus.). 64p. (gr. 5-9). 1992. PLB 15.95 (*1-85435-371-3*) Marshall Cavendish.
—Planet Guides, 8 vols. (Illus.). 512p. (gr. 5-9). 1992. Set. PLB 127.60 (*1-85435-368-3*) Marshall Cavendish.
—Saturn. LC 90-40811. (Illus.). 64p. (gr. 5-9). 1992. PLB 15.95 (*1-85435-374-8*) Marshall Cavendish.
—Venus. LC 90-40808. (Illus.). 64p. (gr. 5-9). 1992. PLB 13.95 (*1-85435-370-5*) Marshall Cavendish.
Brewer, Lewis, jt. auth. see United States Tennis Association Staff.
Brewer, Linda S., jt. auth. see Turner, Peggy.
Brewster, Dorothy P. Discovering Torrance: A Guide & Coloring Book. Haggott, Mikko, tr. Brewster, Karen, et al, illus. 52p. (Orig.). (gr. 3). 1987. pap. 4.50 (*0-9619944-0-1*); tchr's manual 8.00 (*0-9619944-1-X*); write for info. Japanese suppl. (*0-9619944-2-8*) Rodor & Co.
Brewster, Patience. Rabbit Inn, Vol. 1. (ps-3). 1991. 14. 95 (*0-316-10747-6*) Little.
—Two Bushy Badgers. LC 92-40696. 1994. 14.95 (*0-316-10862-6*) Little.
Brewster, Scott & Baraldi, Giani. Ferdinand Magellan. (Illus.). 104p. (gr. 5-8). 1990. lib. bdg. 16.98 (*0-382-09979-6*); pap. 8.95 (*0-382-24005-7*) Silver Burdett Pr.
Brewton, Barney. California Studies. (gr. 4). 1987. text incl. activity program 229.00 (*0-318-41079-6*) Southwinds Pr.
Brewton, John E. & Blackburn, Lorraine A., eds. They've Discovered a Head in the Box for the Bread & Other Laughable Limericks. Krahn, Fernando, illus. LC 77-26598. 144p (gr. 3-7). 1978. PLB 13.89 (*0-690-03883-6*, Crowell Jr Bks) HarpC Child Bks.
Brewton, John E., et al. In the Witch's Kitchen: Poems for Halloween. Barton, Harriett, illus. LC 79-7822. 96p. (gr. 2-5). 1980. PLB 13.89 (*0-690-04062-8*, Crowell Jr Bks) HarpC Child Bks.
Brewton, Sara, et al, eds. My Tang's Tungled & Other Ridiculous Situations. Booth, Graham, illus. LC 73-254. 128p. (gr. 5 up). 1989. PLB 13.89 (*0-690-04778-9*, Crowell Jr Bks) HarpC Child Bks.
—Of Quarks, Quasars, & Other Quirks: Quizzical Poems for the Supersonic Age. Blake, Quentin, illus. LC 76-54747. 128p. (gr. 5 up). 1990. PLB 13.89 (*0-690-04885-8*, Crowell Jr Bks) HarpC Child Bks.
Briais, Bernard. Celts. LC 91-15842. (Illus.). 48p. (gr. 4-8). 1991. PLB 13.95 (*1-85435-266-0*) Marshall Cavendish.
Brian, J. & Freeman, Jodi L. The Old Ones: A Children's Book about the Anasazi Indians. Flanagan, Terry, illus. LC 86-50383. 64p. (Illus.). (gr. k-4). 1986. pap. 2.95 (*0-937871-27-3*) Think Shop.
Brice, Donald. Robin Hood. Lanawn-Shee Studios Staff, illus. 28p. (Orig.). (gr. k up). 1991. pap. 3.95 (*1-878452-04-5*) Tory Corner Editions.
Brice, Donald & Dandola, John. Explorers Before Columbus. (Illus., Orig.). (gr. k up). 1991. write for info. (*1-878452-07-X*) Tory Corner Editions.
Brice, Raphaelle. From Oil to Plastic. Matthews, Sarah, tr. from FRE. Kniffke, Sophie, illus. LC 87-31753. 38p. (gr. k-5). 1988. 4.95 (*0-944589-17-0*, 170) Young Discovery Lib.
—Rice: The Little Grain That Feeds the World. Bogard, Vicki, tr. from FRE. Riquier, Aline, illus. LC 90-50775. 38p. (gr. k-5). 1991. 4.95 (*0-944589-30-8*, 308) Young Discovery Lib.

Bricker, Sandra D. Freeze Frame. Parker, Liz, ed. Taylor, Marjorie, illus. 45p. (Orig.). (gr. 6-12). 1992. pap. text ed. 2.95 (*1-56254-050-5*) Saddleback Pubns.
Brickey, Louise. Pouche: The Assistant to the Easter Bunny. rev. ed. (Illus.). 36p. (gr. k-3). 1989. Repr. of 1987 ed. write for info. Cottontail Creations.
Brickhill, Joan. South Africa: The End of Apartheid? (Illus.). 40p. (gr. 5-9). 1991. PLB 12.90 (*0-531-17283-X*, Gloucester Pr) Watts.
Bridge, Michael. Moses Goodleaf Learns to Walk: A Short Tale of Discovery. Brennan, Christine, illus. 32p. 1992. PLB 22.95 (*0-944963-19-6*); pap. 16.95 (*0-944963-19-6*); audio tape 7.95 (*0-944963-33-1*) Glastonbury Pr.
—Starseed: An Introduction (for children) to the World. Haughey, Karen, illus. 32p. 1992. 22.95 (*0-944963-34-X*); PLB 20.95 (*0-944963-15-3*); pap. 16. 95 (*0-685-60191-9*) Glastonbury Pr.
Bridgers, Sue E. All Together Now. 192p. (gr. 7 up). 1980. pap. 2.75 (*0-553-26845-7*) Bantam.
—All Together Now. (gr. 7 up). 1990. pap. 3.99 (*0-553-24530-9*, Starfire) Bantam.
—Home Before Dark. (gr. 6 up). 1985. pap. 2.50 (*0-553-26432-X*) Bantam.
—Keeping Christina. LC 92-22061. 288p. (gr. 7 up). 1993. 15.00 (*0-06-021504-6*); PLB 14.89 (*0-06-021505-4*) HarpC Child Bks.
—Notes for Another Life. 208p. (gr. 7 up). 1989. pap. 2.95 (*0-553-27185-7*) Bantam.
—Notes for Another Life. LC 81-1673. 256p. (gr. 7 up). 1981. Repr. of 1981 ed. lib. bdg. 13.99 (*0-394-94889-0*) Knopf Bks Yng Read.
—Permanent Connections. LC 86-45491. 283p. (gr. 7 up). 1987. 14.00 (*0-06-020711-6*); PLB 13.89 (*0-06-020712-4*) HarpC Child Bks.
—Permanent Connections. LC 86-45491. 288p. (gr. 7 up). 1988. pap. 3.95 (*0-06-447020-2*, Trophy) HarpC Child Bks.
Bridges, Christina. The Hero. Batten, Linda, illus. 29p. (gr. k-6). 1981. pap. text ed. 8.95 (*0-917002-39-3*) Joyce Media.
Bridges, L. T. Flags of Louisiana. (ps-8). 1971. 3.95 (*0-87511-010-X*) Claitors.
Bridges, Laurie. The Ashton Horror. 160p. (gr. 7 up). 1984. pap. 2.50 (*0-553-26609-8*) Bantam.
—Magic Show. (ps-7). 1987. pap. 2.25 (*0-553-25096-5*) Bantam.
Bridges, Laurie & Alexander, Paul. Swamp Witch, No. 6. 160p. (Orig.). (gr. 7-12). 1987. pap. 2.50 (*0-553-26792-2*) Bantam.
Bridges, Steve. Today's Media. (Illus.). 48p. (gr. 6-8). 1993. pap. 7.99 (*1-55945-144-0*) Group Pub.
Bridgewater, Alan. I Made It Myself: Kids Craft Projects. (Illus.). 192p. 1990. 19.95 (*0-8306-8339-9*, 3339); pap. 11.95 (*0-8306-3339-1*) TAB Bks.
Bridgewater, Alan & Bridgewater, Gill. Holiday Crafts: More Year-Round Crafts Kids Can Make. (Illus.). 256p. 1990. 25.95 (*0-8306-7409-8*, 3409); pap. 16.95 (*0-8306-3409-6*) TAB Bks.
—Making Noah's Ark Toys in Wood. LC 88-21040. (Illus.). 164p (Orig.). (gr. 10-12). 1988. pap. 10.95 (*0-8069-6726-9*) Sterling.
Bridgewater, Alan, ed. see Hayward, Charles H.
Bridgewater, Gill, jt. auth. see Bridgewater, Alan.
Bridgewater, Gill, ed. see Hayward, Charles H.
Bridgman, Roger. Electronics. (Illus.). 64p. (gr. 3-6). 1993. 15.95 (*1-56458-324-4*) Dorling Kindersley.
Bridner, E. L., Jr., jt. auth. see Wilson, Richard.
Bridwell. Clifford Grow Chart. 1993. pap. 2.95 (*0-590-53637-5*) Scholastic Inc.
—Clifford's Birthday Party. 1993. pap. 19.95 (*0-590-73102-5*) Scholastic Inc.
—La Familia de Clifford. (SPA). 1993. pap. 28.67 (*0-590-73228-5*) Scholastic Inc.
Bridwell, Norman. Clifford & the Grouchy Neighbors. Bridwell, Norman, illus. 32p. (gr. k-3). 1989. pap. 2.25 (*0-590-44261-9*); pap. 5.95 incl. cass. (*0-590-63437-2*) Scholastic Inc.
—Clifford at the Circus. (Illus.). 32p. (ps-2). 1989. 2.25 (*0-590-44293-7*); incl. cassette 5.95 (*0-590-63340-6*) Scholastic Inc.
—Clifford Gets a Job. Bridwell, Norman, illus. 32p. (gr. k-3). 1985. pap. 2.25 (*0-590-44296-1*) Scholastic Inc.
—Clifford Goes to Hollywood. Bridwell, Norman, illus. 32p. (gr. k-3). 1990. pap. 2.25 (*0-590-44289-9*); pap. 5.95 incl. cass. (*0-590-63435-6*) Scholastic Inc.
—Clifford Takes a Trip. (ps-3). 1985. pap. 2.25 (*0-590-44260-0*) Scholastic Inc.
—Clifford Takes a Trip. 1991. pap. 5.95 incl. cassette (*0-590-63823-8*) Scholastic Inc.
—Clifford the Big Red Dog. Bridwell, Norman, illus. (ps-3). 1988. 2.25 (*0-590-44297-X*); pap. 5.95 incl. cassette (*0-590-63212-4*) Scholastic Inc.
—Clifford the Big Red Dog. Bridwell, Norman, illus. 32p. (ps-3). 1988. 10.95 (*0-590-40743-0*, Pub. by Scholastic Hardcover) Scholastic Inc.
—Clifford the Small Red Puppy. (ps-2). 1988. 2.25 (*0-590-44294-5*); incl. cassette 5.95 (*0-590-63211-6*) Scholastic Inc.
—Clifford the Small Red Puppy. (ps-3). 1990. 10.95 (*0-590-43496-9*) Scholastic Inc.
—Clifford the Small Red Puppy Follows His Nose. 32p. 1992. bds. 5.95 (*0-590-44345-3*, Scholastic Hardcover) Scholastic Inc.
—Clifford Treasury, No. I: Small Puppy - Big Red - Pals - Grouchy - Neighbors. 1991. pap. 9.00 (*0-590-63953-6*) Scholastic Inc.

—Clifford Treasury, No. II: Birthday - Puppy - Days - Family - Kitten. 1991. pap. 9.00 (*0-590-63952-8*) Scholastic Inc.
—Clifford Va de Viaje. rev. ed. Palacios, Argentina, tr. (SPA., Illus.). 32p. (Orig.). (gr. k-3). 1987. pap. 2.95 (*0-590-40844-5*) Scholastic Inc.
—Clifford Wants a Cookie. (Illus.). 16p. (ps-3). 1988. Book & Cookie Cutter Package. pap. 3.95 (*0-590-63282-5*) Scholastic Inc.
—Clifford, We Love You. (ps-3). 1991. pap. 2.25 (*0-590-43843-3*); pap. 5.95 incls. cass. (*0-590-63604-9*) Scholastic Inc.
—Clifford's ABC. (ps-3). 1986. pap. 2.25 (*0-590-44286-4*) Scholastic Inc.
—Clifford's Animal Sounds. (ps). 1991. 3.95 (*0-590-44734-3*) Scholastic Inc.
—Clifford's Bathtime. (ps). 1991. 3.95 (*0-590-44735-1*) Scholastic Inc.
—Clifford's Bedtime. (ps). 1991. 3.95 (*0-590-44736-X*) Scholastic Inc.
—Clifford's Big Book of Stories. LC 93-31367. (Illus.). 64p. (ps-3). 1994. 9.95 (*0-590-47925-3*, Cartwheel) Scholastic Inc.
—Clifford's Birthday Party. Bridwell, Norman, illus. 32p. (Orig.). (gr. k-3). 1991. 8.95 (*0-590-44232-5*); pap. 5.95 incl. cassette (*0-590-63237-X*) Scholastic Inc.
—Clifford's Christmas. Bridwell, Norman, illus. 32p. (Orig.). (gr. k-3). 1987. 2.25 (*0-590-44288-0*); incl. cassette 5.95 (*0-590-63210-8*) Scholastic Inc.
—Clifford's Family. Bridwell, Norman, illus. 32p. (gr. k-3). 1984. pap. 2.25 (*0-590-44290-2*) Scholastic Inc.
—Clifford's Good Deeds. Bridwell, Norman, illus. 32p. (gr. k-3). 1985. pap. 2.25 (*0-590-44292-9*) Scholastic Inc.
—Clifford's Good Deeds. 1991. pap. 5.95 incl. cassette (*0-590-63824-6*) Scholastic Inc.
—Clifford's Halloween. Bridwell, Norman, illus. 32p. (gr. k-3). 1989. pap. 2.25 (*0-590-44287-2*); pap. 5.95 (*0-590-63436-4*) Scholastic Inc.
—Clifford's Happy Day: A Pop-up Book. Bridwell, Norman, illus. 16p. (Orig.). (gr. k-3). 1990. pap. 12.95 (*0-590-42926-4*) Scholastic Inc.
—Clifford's Happy Easter. (Illus.). 32p. (ps-3). 1994. pap. 2.25 (*0-590-47782-X*, Cartwheel) Scholastic Inc.
—Clifford's Kitten. Bridwell, Norman, illus. 32p. (gr. k-3). 1984. pap. 2.25 (*0-590-44280-5*) Scholastic Inc.
—Clifford's Manners. Bridwell, Norman, illus. 32p. (gr. k-3). 1987. pap. 2.25 (*0-590-44285-6*) Scholastic Inc.
—Clifford's Noisy Day. (Illus.). 1992. bds. 3.95 (*0-590-45737-3*, 036, Cartwheel) Scholastic Inc.
—Clifford's Pals. Bridwell, Norman, illus. 32p. (gr. k-3). 1985. pap. 2.25 (*0-590-44295-3*) Scholastic Inc.
—Clifford's Peekaboo. (ps). 1991. 3.95 (*0-590-44737-8*) Scholastic Inc.
—Clifford's Puppy Days. 1989. pap. 1.95 (*0-590-42189-1*) Scholastic Inc.
—Clifford's Puppy Days. (ps-3). 1988. pap. 2.25 (*0-590-44262-7*) Scholastic Inc.
—Clifford's Puppy Days. (ps-3). 1992. pap. 19.95 (*0-590-72612-9*) Scholastic Inc.
—Clifford's Puppy Days. LC 93-1802. (Illus.). 32p. (ps-6). 1994. 12.95 (*0-590-43339-3*, Cartwheel) Scholastic Inc.
—Clifford's Riddles. Bridwell, Norman, illus. 32p. (gr. k-3). 1984. pap. 2.25 (*0-590-44282-1*) Scholastic Inc.
—Clifford's Sticker Book. Bridwell, Norman, illus. 24p. (ps-3). 1984. pap. 3.95 (*0-590-33657-6*) Scholastic Inc.
—Clifford's Tricks. Bridwell, Norman, illus. 32p. (gr. k-3). 1986. pap. 2.25 (*0-590-44291-0*) Scholastic Inc.
—Clifford's Word Book. Bridwell, Norman, illus. 32p. (Orig.). (gr.-p1). 1990. pap. 2.25 (*0-590-43095-5*) Scholastic Inc.
—Count on Clifford. (Illus.). 32p. (gr. k-3). 1987. 5.95 (*0-590-33614-2*); pap. 2.25 (*0-590-44284-8*) Scholastic Inc.
—Count on Clifford. (Illus.). 32p. (ps-k). 1987. pap. 2.25 (*0-685-67546-7*) Scholastic Inc.
—Hello, Clifford: A Puppet Book. (ps-3). 1991. 7.95 (*0-590-44673-8*) Scholastic Inc.
—The Witch Goes to School. LC 92-12091. (ps-3). 1992. pap. 2.95 (*0-590-45831-0*) Scholastic Inc.
—The Witch Grows Up. 32p. (Orig.). (gr. k-3). 1987. pap. 2.50 (*0-590-40559-4*) Scholastic Inc.
—The Witch Next Door. Bridwell, Norman, illus. 32p. (gr. k-3). 1986. pap. 2.50 (*0-590-40433-4*) Scholastic Inc.
—The Witch's Christmas. Bridwell, Norman, illus. (gr. k-3). 1972. pap. 1.50 (*0-590-09216-2*) Scholastic Inc.
—The Witch's Christmas. Bridwell, Norman, illus. 32p. (gr. k-3). 1986. pap. 1.95 (*0-590-40434-2*) Scholastic Inc.
—The Witch's Vacation. Bridwell, Norman, illus. 32p. (Orig.). (gr. k-3). 1987. pap. 2.50 (*0-590-40558-6*) Scholastic Inc.
Bridwell, Norman & Bridwell, Norman. Clifford's Thanksgiving Visit. (Illus.). 32p. (ps-3). 1993. pap. 2.25 (*0-590-46987-8*, Cartwheel) Scholastic Inc.
Briere, Euphemia. The Nativity of Our Lord: The Birth of the Messiah. Briere, Euphemia, illus. (Orig.). (gr. 1-3). 1993. pap. 6.00 (*0-913026-38-7*) St Nectarios.
Brigance, Albert. Victory! Times, Bk. 2: Grade Six. (Illus.). 110p. (gr. 6). 1991. pap. 6.95 (*1-55999-201-8*) LinguiSystems.
Brigandi & Lovitt. Super Word Find Fun. 1993. pap. 1.95 (*0-590-40044-4*) Scholastic Inc.
Brigandi, Pat. String Magic: String Designs & How to Make Them. (gr. 4-7). 1993. pap. 2.95 (*0-590-46974-6*) Scholastic Inc.

Brigandi, Pat, jt. auth. see Black, Sonia.
Briggs, Carole S. At the Controls: Women in Aviation. (Illus.). 72p. (gr. 5 up). 1991. PLB 21.50 (*0-8225-1593-8*) Lerner Pubns.
—Diving Is for Me. Sutter, Greg, illus. LC 82-17242. 48p. (gr. 2-5). 1983. PLB 13.50 (*0-8225-1135-5*) Lerner Pubns.
—Research Balloons: Exploring Hidden Worlds. (Illus.). 64p. (gr. 5 up). 1988. PLB 21.50 (*0-8225-1585-7*) Lerner Pubns.
—Waterskiing Is for Me. (Illus.). 48p. (gr. 2-5). 1986. lib. bdg. 13.50 (*0-8225-1140-1*) Lerner Pubns.
—Women in Space: Reaching the Last Frontier. (Illus.). 80p. (gr. 5 up). 1988. PLB 21.50 (*0-8225-1581-4*, First Ave Edns); pap. 5.95 (*0-8225-9547-8*, First Ave Edns) Lerner Pubns.
Briggs, Jean P. Birds Have a Barbecue. 1994. 7.95 (*0-8062-4847-5*) Carlton.
Briggs, K. M. Kate Crackernuts. LC 79-9229. (Illus.). 224p. (gr. 7 up). 1980. 13.50 (*0-688-80240-0*) Greenwillow.
Briggs, Katharine M. An Encyclopedia of Fairies: Hobgoblins, Brownies, Bogies, & Other Supernatural Creatures. LC 76-12939. (Illus.). (gr. 4 up). 1977. 12.95 (*0-394-40918-3*); pap. 19.00 (*0-394-73467-X*) Pantheon.
Briggs, Michael. Stamps. LC 92-17278. (Illus.). 80p. (gr. 5 up). 1993. 13.00 (*0-679-82664-5*); PLB 13.99 (*0-679-92664-X*) Random Bks Yng Read.
Briggs, Noreen V. Bugaboo Words. (Illus.). 160p. (gr. 3 up). 1989. 25.00 (*0-937857-13-0*, 1570) Speech Bin.
Briggs, Raymond. The Fairy Tale Treasury. Haviland, Virginia, ed. (gr. k up). 1986. pap. 8.95 (*0-440-42556-5*, YB) Dell.
—Father Christmas. (Illus.). 32p. (gr. k-3). 1981. pap. 3.95 (*0-14-050125-8*, Puffin) Puffin Bks.
—Father Christmas Goes on Holiday. LC 77-1980. (Illus.). 32p. (gr. k-3). 1977. pap. 3.95 (*0-14-050187-8*, Puffin) Puffin Bks.
—Jim & the Beanstalk. Briggs, Raymond, illus. 40p. (ps-2). 1989. pap. 5.95 (*0-698-20641-X*, Sandcastle Bks) Putnam Pub Group.
—The Mother Goose Treasury. Briggs, Raymond, illus. 1986. pap. 8.95 (*0-440-46408-0*, YB) Dell.
—The Snowman. Briggs, Raymond, illus. LC 78-55904. 32p. (Orig.). (ps-2). 1986. pap. 4.95 book & doll pkg. (*0-394-88466-3*) Random Bks Yng Read.
—The Snowman. Briggs, Raymond, illus. LC 78-55904. 32p. (ps-3). 1978. 13.95 (*0-394-83973-0*) Random Bks Yng Read.
—The Snowman. miniature ed. LC 90-60078. (Illus.). 32p. (ps-8). 1990. 4.95 (*0-679-80906-6*) Random Bks Yng Read.
—The Snowman, No. 8612-4. (Illus.). (ps-4). 1990. 3.50 (*0-7214-1109-6*) Ladybird Bks.
—The Snowman Board Books. Briggs, Raymond, illus. Incl. Building the Snowman (*0-316-10813-8*); Dressing up. 1985. pap. 3.95 (*0-316-10814-6*); Walking in the Air. 1985. pap. 3.95 (*0-316-10815-4*); The Party. (Illus.). (ps-k). 1985. pap. 3.95 ea. Little.
—The Snowman Clock Book. Briggs, Raymond, illus. LC 91-67874. 16p. (ps-3). 1992. pap. 7.99 (*0-679-83261-0*) Random Bks Yng Read.
—The Snowman Cuddle Cloth Book. Briggs, Raymond, illus. 12p. (ps). 3.99 (*0-679-82696-3*) Random Bks Yng Read.
—The Snowman Flap Book. Sliwinska, Sara, illus. 16p. 1991. 7.00 (*0-679-81572-4*) Random Bks Yng Read.
—Snowman: Songbook. 1993. pap. 10.95 (*0-7935-1831-8*, 50489170) H Leonard Pub Corp.
—The Snowman Storybook. Briggs, Raymond, illus. LC 90-8029. 24p. (ps). 1990. 6.00 (*0-679-80840-X*) Random Bks Yng Read.
Bright, Leonard D. The Gifted Kids Guide to Puzzles & Mind Games. (Illus.). 143p. 1985. pap. 7.95 (*0-936750-15-4*) Paradon Pub Co.
Bright, Michael. Acid Rain. (Illus.). 32p. (gr. 2-4). 1991. PLB 11.90 (*0-531-17303-8*, Gloucester Pr) Watts.
—Alligators & Crocodiles. (Illus.). 32p. (gr. 5-8). 1990. PLB 12.40 (*0-531-17245-7*) Watts.
—The Dying Sea. (Illus.). 32p. (gr. 5-8). 1992. PLB 12.40 (*0-531-17385-2*, Gloucester Pr) Watts.
—Eagles. Kline, M., ed. (Illus.). 32p. (gr. 4-8). 1991. PLB 12.40 (*0-531-17262-7*) Watts.
—Elephants. (ps-3). 1990. PLB 12.40 (*0-531-17215-5*) Watts.
—Giant Panda. (Illus.). 32p. (gr. 5-6). 1989. PLB 12.40 (*0-531-17140-X*, Gloucester Pr) Watts.
—The Greenhouse Effect. (Illus.). 32p. (gr. 2-4). 1991. PLB 11.90 (*0-531-17304-6*, Gloucester Pr) Watts.
—Killing for Luxury. (Illus.). 32p. (gr. 5-8). 1992. PLB 12.40 (*0-531-17386-0*, Gloucester Pr) Watts.
—Koalas. (Illus.). 32p. (gr. 5-8). 1990. PLB 12.40 (*0-531-17246-5*, Gloucester Pr) Watts.
—The Ozone Layer. 32p. (gr. 2-4). 1991. PLB 11.90 (*0-531-17302-X*, Gloucester Pr) Watts.
—Polar Bear. LC 89-50446. (Illus.). 32p. (gr. 5-7). 1989. PLB 12.40 (*0-531-17180-9*, Gloucester Pr) Watts.
—Polluting the Oceans. (Illus.). 32p. (gr. k-4). 1991. PLB 11.90 (*0-531-17353-4*, Gloucester Pr) Watts.
—Pollution & Wildlife. (Illus.). 32p. (gr. 5-8). 1992. PLB 12.40 (*0-531-17384-4*, Gloucester Pr) Watts.
—Seals. Kline, M., ed. (Illus.). 32p. (gr. 4-8). 1991. PLB 12.40 (*0-531-17263-5*) Watts.
—Tiger. (Illus.). 32p. (gr. 5-6). 1989. PLB 12.40 (*0-531-17141-8*, Gloucester Pr) Watts.
—Traffic Pollution. (Illus.). 32p. (gr. k-4). 1991. PLB 11.90 (*0-531-17349-6*, Gloucester Pr) Watts.

—Tropical Rainforest. (Illus.). 32p. (gr. 2-4). 1991. PLB 11.90 (*0-531-17301-1*, Gloucester Pr) Watts.
Bright, Robert. Georgie. Bright, Robert, illus. 44p. (gr. k-1). 1944. pap. 7.95 (*0-385-07307-0*) Doubleday.
—Georgie. 48p. (gr. k-3). pap. 1.50 (*0-590-01617-2*) Scholastic Inc.
—Georgie & the Robbers. Bright, Robert, illus. LC 63-11384. 28p. (ps-1). 1963. pap. 5.95 (*0-385-04483-6*); pap. 2.50 (*0-385-13341-3*) Doubleday.
—My Red Umbrella. LC 59-7928. (Illus.). 32p. (ps-1). 1985. 8.95 (*0-688-05249-5*); pap. 3.95 (*0-688-05250-9*) Morrow Jr Bks.
Bright, Velma. The Story of the Little Round Barn. Schultz, Patty, illus. LC 81-65540. 48p. (Illus.). (gr. 2-3). 1981. 10.00x (*0-9605968-2-8*); pap. 5.00 (*0-9605968-3-6*) Bright Bks.
—What Would You Like to Be? Schultz, Patty, illus. 32p. (gr. 1). 1976. PLB 10.00 (*0-9605968-0-1*) Bright Bks.
Bright, Wesley. Play the Game: Weight Training. (Illus.). 80p. (gr. 10-12). 1991. pap. 6.95 (*0-7063-6858-4*, Pub. by Ward Lock UK) Sterling.
Brightfield, Richard. African Safari. (gr. 4-7). 1993. pap. 3.25 (*0-553-29953-0*) Bantam.
—Behind the Great Wall. (gr. 4-7). 1993. pap. 3.25 (*0-553-56103-0*) Bantam.
—Curse of Batterslea. 1984. pap. 1.95 (*0-553-23937-6*) Bantam.
—The Curse of Batterslea Hall, No. 30. 128p. (gr. 4 up). 1984. pap. 2.25 (*0-553-26374-9*) Bantam.
—The Deadly Shadow. 128p. (gr. 4 up). 1985. pap. 2.25 (*0-553-25498-7*) Bantam.
—The Dragon's Den. (Illus.). 128p. (gr. 5-9). 1984. pap. 2.25 (*0-553-25918-0*) Bantam.
—Escape. (ps-7). 1987. pap. 1.95 (*0-553-23294-0*) Bantam.
—Escape from the Kingdom of Frome, No. 3: The Caverns of Mornas. 144p. (Orig.). (gr. 7-12). 1987. pap. 2.50 (*0-553-26200-9*) Bantam.
—Escape from the Kingdom of Frome, No. 4: The Battle of Astar. 128p. (Orig.). (gr. 7-12). 1987. pap. 2.50 (*0-553-26290-4*, Starfire) Bantam.
—The Forest of the King. 128p. (Orig.). (gr. 7-12). 1986. pap. 2.50 (*0-553-26155-X*) Bantam.
—The Gruesome Guests. LC 89-36334. 96p. (gr. 7 up). 1990. PLB 9.89 (*0-8167-1690-0*); pap. text ed. 2.95 (*0-8167-1691-9*) Troll Assocs.
—Hijacked. (gr. 9-12). 1990. pap. 3.25 (*0-553-28635-8*) Bantam.
—Hurricane! 176p. (Orig.). (gr. 4 up). 1988. pap. 2.50 (*0-553-27356-6*) Bantam.
—Hyperspace. (ps-7). 1987. pap. 2.25 (*0-553-26371-4*) Bantam.
—Invaders of the Planet Earth. 128p. (Orig.). (gr. 4 up). 1987. pap. 2.50 (*0-553-26669-1*) Bantam.
—Master of Karate. (gr. 9-12). 1990. pap. 3.25 (*0-553-28202-6*) Bantam.
—Master of Kung Fu. 128p. 1989. pap. 2.99 (*0-553-27718-9*) Bantam.
—Master of Martial Arts. 1992. pap. 3.25 (*0-553-29296-X*) Bantam.
—Master of Tae Kwon Do. 1990. pap. 2.99 (*0-553-28516-5*) Bantam.
—Masters of the Louvre. (gr. 4-7). 1993. pap. 3.25 (*0-553-29969-7*) Bantam.
—Murder Comes to Life. LC 89-36329. 96p. (gr. 7 up). 1990. PLB 9.89 (*0-8167-1686-2*); pap. text ed. 2.95 (*0-8167-1687-0*) Troll Assocs.
—Planet of the Dragons. (gr. 5 up). 1988. pap. 2.50 (*0-553-26887-2*) Bantam.
—Revolution in Russia. 1992. pap. 3.25 (*0-553-29784-8*) Bantam.
—The Roaring Twenties. (gr. 4-7). 1993. pap. 3.25 (*0-553-56348-3*) Bantam.
—Secret of the Pyramids. (ps-7). 1987. pap. 2.25 (*0-553-25761-7*) Bantam.
—The Secret Treasure of Tibet. 128p. (Orig.). (gr. 4). 1984. pap. 2.25 (*0-553-25501-0*) Bantam.
—South of the Border. (gr. 4-7). 1992. pap. 3.25 (*0-553-29757-0*, Starfire) Bantam.
—Star System Tenopia, No. 4. 144p. (Orig.). 1986. pap. 2.50 (*0-553-25637-8*) Bantam.
—Terror on Kabran. 144p. (Orig.). 1986. pap. 2.50 (*0-553-25636-X*) Bantam.
—Trapped in the Sea Kingdom. 128p. 1986. pap. 2.50 (*0-553-25473-1*) Bantam.
—The Valley of the Kings. (gr. 4-7). 1992. pap. 3.25 (*0-553-29756-2*, Starfire) Bantam.
Brighton, Catherine. Hope's Gift. 1988. 12.95 (*0-385-24598-X*) Doubleday.
—Mozart: Scenes from the Childhood of the Great Composer. (ps-3). 1990. PLB 15.99 (*0-385-41538-9*) Doubleday.
—Nijinsky: Scenes from the Childhood of the Great Dancer. (Illus.). 32p. (ps-3). 1989. 13.95 (*0-385-24663-3*, Zephyr-BFYR); PLB 14.99 (*0-385-24926-8*, Zephyr-BFYR) Doubleday.
Briley, Cathryn, ed. see Falwell, Cathryn.
Briley, D., ed. see Hamley, Dennis.
Briley, D., ed. see McKee, David.
Briley, D., ed. see McMillan, Bruce.
Briley, D., ed. see Ormerod, Jan.
Briley, D., ed. see Waddell, Martin.
Briley, Dorothy, ed. see Apfel, Necia H.
Briley, Dorothy, ed. see Watson, Wendy.
Briley, Dorothy, ed. see Wiesner, David.
Briley, Dorthy, ed. see Falwell, Cathryn.

Brill, Ethel C. Copper Country Adventure. LC 87-31485. 213p. (gr. 4 up). 1988. 8.50 (0-933249-05-5) Mid-Peninsula Lib.

Brill, M. I Can Be a Lawyer. LC 87-13227. (Illus.). 32p. (gr. k-3). 1987. PLB 14.60 (0-516-01911-2); pap. 3.95 (0-516-41911-0) Childrens.

Brill, Marlene T. Algeria. LC 89-25436. (Illus.). 128p. (gr. 5-9). 1990. PLB 26.60 (0-516-02717-4) Childrens.

—Allen Jay & the Underground Railroad. Porter, Janice L., illus. LC 92-25279. 1993. 14.95 (0-87614-776-7); pap. write for info. (0-87614-605-1) Carolrhoda Bks.

—James Buchanan. LC 88-10884. (Illus.). 100p. (gr. 3 up). 1988. PLB 17.27 (0-516-01358-0) Childrens.

—John Adams. (Illus.). 100p. (gr. 3 up). 1986. PLB 17.27 (0-516-01384-X); pap. 6.95 (0-516-41384-8) Childrens.

—Libya. LC 87-13192. (Illus.). 128p. (gr. 5-9). 1987. PLB 26.60 (0-516-02776-X) Childrens.

—Mongolia. LC 91-34172. 128p. (gr. 5-9). 1992. PLB 26.60 (0-516-02605-4) Childrens.

Brill, Marlene T. & Targ, Harry R. Guatemala. LC 92-39099. (Illus.). 128p. (gr. 5-9). 1993. PLB 26.60 (0-516-02614-3) Childrens.

Brill, Michael E. Bamboozled. (Orig.). (gr. 6 up). 1985. pap. 4.50 (0-87602-240-9) Anchorage.

—The Masque of Beauty & the Beast. 1979. 4.50 (0-87602-156-9) Anchorage.

Brillhart, Julie. Anna's Goodbye Apron. Mathews, Judith, ed. Brillhart, Julie, illus. LC 89-49362. 32p. (ps-1). 1990. PLB 13.95 (0-8075-0375-4) A Whitman.

—The Dino Expert. LC 92-43474. 1993. write for info. (0-8075-1597-3) A Whitman.

—Story Hour - Starring Megan! Levine, Abby, ed. Brillhart, Julie, illus. LC 91-19523. 32p. (ps-2). 1992. PLB 13.95 (0-8075-7628-X) A Whitman.

Brim, C. Arthur: Tales of the Young King. (Illus.). 32p. (gr. 2-6). 1989. 10.95 (0-88625-236-9) Durkin Hayes Pub.

Brimhall, John. Children's Piano Method. (Illus.). 64p. (Orig.). (gr. 1-6). 1984. pap. text ed. 5.95 (0-8494-2887-4, T430) Hansen Ed Mus.

—Children's Songs for Piano. 96p. (Orig.). (gr. 1-6). 1985. pap. text ed. 7.95 (0-8494-2264-7, 0496) Hansen Ed Mus.

—My Favorite Classics Level One. 120p. (Orig.). (gr. 3-6). pap. text ed. 10.95 (0-8494-2180-2, 0114) Hansen Ed Mus.

—My Favorite Easy Classics, Bk. 5. 128p. (Orig.). (gr. 1-3). 1984. pap. text ed. 10.95 (0-8494-2182-9, 0116) Hansen Ed Mus.

Brimmer, Andrew F. Economic Development: International & African Perspectives. 1990. 15.95 (0-87498-093-3) Assoc Pubs DC.

Brimmner, Larry D. Max & Felix. 32p. (ps-3). 1993. 12.95 (1-56397-010-4) Boyds Mills Pr.

Brimner, Larry D. Animals That Hibernate. LC 90-13116. (Illus.). 64p. (gr. 3-6). 1991. PLB 12.90 (0-531-20018-3) Watts.

—Cory Coleman, Grade Two. Ritz, Karen, illus. 80p. (gr. 2-4). 1990. 12.95 (0-8050-1312-1, Bks Young Read) H Holt & Co.

—Cory Coleman, Grade 2. Ritz, Karen, illus. LC 89-24694. 80p. (gr. 2-4). 1991. pap. 4.95 (0-8050-1844-1, Bks Young Read) H Holt & Co.

—Country Bear's Good Neighbor. Councell, Ruth T., illus. LC 87-5704. 32p. (ps-2). 1988. 12.95 (0-531-05708-9); PLB 12.99 (0-531-08308-X) Orchard Bks Watts.

—Country Bear's Surprise. Councell, Ruth T., illus. LC 90-7717. 32p. (ps-2). 1991. 12.95 (0-531-05811-5); PLB 12.99 (0-531-08411-6) Orchard Bks Watts.

—Elliot Fry's Goodbye. Fernandes, Eugenie, illus. 32p. (ps-3). 1994. 14.95 (1-56397-113-5) Boyds Mills Pr.

—Karate. Rakos, Jennie, ed. LC 87-25341. (Illus.). 72p. (gr. 7-9). 1988. PLB 10.90 (0-531-10480-X) Watts.

—A Migrant Family. (Illus.). 40p. (gr. 4-8). 1992. PLB 17.50 (0-8225-2554-2) Lerner Pubns.

—Snowboarding. Brimner, Larry D., photos by. LC 89-9088. (Illus.). 64p. (gr. 4-6). 1989. PLB 12.90 (0-531-10748-5) Watts.

—Unusual Friendships: Symbiosis in the Animal World. LC 92-24953. (Illus.). 64p. (gr. 5-8). 1993. PLB 12.40 (0-531-20106-6) Watts.

—Unusual Friendships: Symbiosis in the Animal World. (Illus.). 64p. (gr. 5-8). 1993. pap. 5.95 (0-531-15675-3) Watts.

—Voices from the Camps: Internment of Japanese Americans in World War II. LC 93-30201. 1994. write for info. (0-531-11179-2) Watts.

Brims, Bernagh, ed. Five Potato, Six Potato. (Illus.). 80p. (Orig.). (gr. 1-6). 1992. pap. 5.95 (0-86281-344-1, Pub. by Appletree Pr ER) Irish Bks Media.

Brin, Susannah. The Seal Killers. Parker, Liz, ed. Taylor, Marjorie, illus. 45p. (Orig.). (gr. 6-12). 1992. pap. text ed. 2.95 (1-56254-051-3) Saddleback Pubns.

Brin, Susannah, jt. auth. see Sundquist, Nancy.

Brincat, Matthew De. Salt & Light. 56p. (gr. 6up). 1983. pap. 3.00 (0-911423-00-1) Bible-Speak.

Brinckloe, Julie. Fireflies! Brinckloe, Julie, illus. LC 84-20158. 32p. (gr. k-2). 1985. RSBE 13.95 (0-02-713310-9, Macmillan Child Bk) Macmillan Child Grp.

—Fireflies. LC 85-26767. (Illus.). 32p. (gr. k-2). 1986. pap. 3.95 (0-689-71055-0, Aladdin) Macmillan Child Grp.

—Playing Marbles. Brinckloe, Julie, illus. LC 88-1608. 32p. (gr. k-3). 1988. 12.95 (0-688-07143-0); PLB 12.88 (0-688-07144-9, Morrow Jr Bks) Morrow Jr Bks.

—Stitch in Time for the Brothers Rhyme. (ps-3). 1993. pap. 4.95 (0-8114-8400-9) Raintree Steck-V.

Brinckmann, Caren, et al. Beforderung. Baker, Syd, illus. Winitz, Harris, intro. by. (GER., Illus.). 40p. (gr. 7 up). 1990. Incls. cass. tape. pap. text ed. 22.00 (0-939990-71-7) Intl Linguistics.

Brindle, Susan A., jt. auth. see Hooker, Irene H.

Brink, Carol R. Baby Island. Sewell, Helen, illus. LC 92-45577. 160p. (gr. 3-7). 1993. pap. 3.95 (0-689-71751-2, Aladdin) Macmillan Child Grp.

—The Bad Times of Irma Baumlein. 2nd ed. Hyman, Trina S., illus. LC 91-13976. 144p. (gr. 3-7). 1991. pap. 3.95 (0-689-71513-7, Aladdin) Macmillan Child Grp.

—Caddie Woodlawn. Hyman, Trina S., illus. LC 73-588. 288p. (gr. 4-6). 1973. SBE 14.95 (0-02-713670-1, Macmillan Child Bk) Macmillan Child Grp.

—Caddie Woodlawn. LC 89-18357. (Illus.). 288p. (gr. 4-6). 1990. 3.95 (0-689-71370-3, Aladdin) Macmillan Child Grp.

—Caddie Woodlawn. large type ed. (gr. 5 up). 1988. Repr. of 1973 ed. lib. bdg. 15.95 (1-55736-043-X, Crnrstn Bks) BDD LT Grp.

—Caddie Woodlawn. 1970. pap. 3.95 (0-02-041880-9, Collier Young Ad) Macmillan Child Grp.

—Magical Melons. Davis, Marguerite, illus. LC 90-144. 208p. (gr. 3-7). 1990. pap. 3.95 (0-689-71416-5, Aladdin) Macmillan Child Grp.

—The Pink Motel. Greenwald, Sheila, illus. LC 92-17953. 224p. (gr. 3-7). 1993. pap. 3.95 (0-689-71677-X, Aladdin) Macmillan Child Grp.

Brinkley, Chad & Barrett, Kevin. The Body Bank. Aulisio, Janet, illus. 32p. (Orig.). (gr. 12). 1990. pap. 10.00 (1-55806-128-2, 5104) Iron Crown Ent Inc.

Brinkley, Ginny & Sampson, Sherry. Joven y Embarazada: Un Libro Para Usted. Salmon, Otilia & Rodriquez, Judy, trs. from ENG. Cooper, Gail S., illus. Mahan, Charles S., pref. by. (SPA., Illus.). 80p. (gr. 7-12). 1992. pap. text ed. 4.95 (0-9622585-3-9) Pink Inc.

—Promises: A Teen's Guide to Pregnancy. Cooper, Gail, illus. Mahan, Charles, pref. by. (Illus.). 48p. (gr. 7-12). 1993. pap. text ed. write for info. (0-9622585-4-7) Pink Inc.

—Usted y Su Nuevo Bebe: Un Libro Para Madres Jovenes. Salmon, Otilia & Rodriquez, Judy, trs. from ENG. Cooper, Gail S., illus. LC 92-80146. (SPA.). 80p. (gr. 7-12). 1992. pap. text ed. 4.95 (0-9622585-2-0) Pink Inc.

—You & Your New Baby: A Book for Young Mothers. Cooper, Gail S., illus. 70p. (Orig.). (gr. 7 up). 1991. pap. text ed. 3.95 (0-9622585-1-2) Pink Inc.

—Young & Pregnant: A Book for You. Cooper, Gail S., illus. Mahan, Charles, intro. by. (Illus.). 80p. (Orig.). (gr. 7-12). 1989. pap. text ed. 4.95x (0-317-93681-6) Pink Inc.

Brinmer. Cory Coleman Grade 2. 1991. 12.95 (0-8050-1425-X) H Holt & Co.

Brinn, Ross. To the Woods & Waters Wild: A Collection of Irish Writings. O'Mahony, Kieran, ed. LC 90-80516. 150p. (Orig.). 1990. pap. 9.95 (0-944638-02-3) Educare Pr.

Brinn, Ruth Esrig. Jewish Holiday Crafts for Little Hands. Kahn, Katherine Janus, illus. LC 92-39638. (gr. k up). 1993. pap. 10.95 (0-929371-47-X) Kar Ben.

Brinsmead, Hesba. Bianca & Roja. Brooks, Ron, illus. 112p. (Orig.). (gr. 2-6). 1993. pap. 7.95 (1-86373-082-6, Pub. by Allen & Unwin Aust Pty AT) IPG Chicago.

Briscoe, Jill. Harrow Sparrow. Cummings, Ann L., illus. 143p. (gr. 6). 1989. pap. write for info. Jilcoe.

—Jonah & the Worm. Armstrong, Tom & Davis, Florence, illus. 143p. (gr. 6). 1989. pap. write for info. Jilcoe.

—The Man Who Would Not Hate: Festo Kivengere. 1991. pap. 4.99 (0-8499-3309-9) Word Inc.

—Paint the Prisons Bright: Corrie Ten Boom. (gr. 5 up). 1991. pap. 4.99 (0-8499-3308-0) Word Inc.

Briscoe, Jill, jt. auth. see Briscoe, Stuart.

Briscoe, Stuart & Briscoe, Jill. Danny D Books, 4 vols. Marinin, Sally, illus. 12p. (gr. 2-5). 1993. Set. pap. 9.99 (0-8010-1061-6) Baker Bk.

—How Much Does God Know? Marinin, Sally, illus. 12p. 1993. pap. 2.99 (0-8010-1040-3) Baker Bk.

—How Strong Is God? Marinin, Sally, illus. 12p. (Orig.). (gr. 4 up). 1993. pap. 2.99 (0-8010-1037-3) Baker Bk.

—Is God Ever Naughty? Marinin, Sally, illus. 12p. 1993. pap. 2.99 (0-8010-1041-1) Baker Bk.

—Where Is God? Marinin, Sally, illus. 12p. 1993. pap. 2.99 (0-8010-1038-1) Baker Bk.

Brissac, Elvire de see De Brissac, Elvire.

Brisson, Lynn. Three-D Art Projects That Teach. (Illus.). 80p. (gr. k-6). 1989. pap. text ed. 7.95 (0-86530-084-4, IP 166-1) Incentive Pubns.

—Three-D Teaching Aids. (Illus.). 64p. (gr. k-6). 1989. pap. text ed. 6.95 (0-86530-072-0, IP 166-2) Incentive Pubns.

Brisson, Pat. Benny's Pennies. (gr. 4 up). 1993. pap. 14.95 (0-385-41602-4) Doubleday.

—Kate Heads West. Brown, Rick, illus. LC 89-27590. 40p. (gr. k-3). 1990. RSBE 13.95 (0-02-714345-7, Bradbury Pr) Macmillan Child Grp.

—Kate on the Coast. Brown, Rick, illus. LC 91-17046. 40p. (gr. 2-5). 1992. RSBE 13.95 (0-02-714341-4, Bradbury Pr) Macmillan Child Grp.

—Magic Carpet. Schwartz, Amy, illus. LC 89-35993. 32p. (ps-3). 1991. RSBE 14.95 (0-02-714340-6, Bradbury Pr) Macmillan Child Grp.

—Your Best Friend, Kate. Brown, Rick, illus. LC 88-6037. 40p. (gr. k-3). 1989. RSBE 13.95 (0-02-714350-3, Bradbury Pr) Macmillan Child Grp.

—Your Best Friend, Kate. Brown, Rick, illus. LC 91-15245. 40p. (gr. 1-7). 1992. pap. 4.50 (0-689-71545-5, Aladdin) Macmillan Child Grp.

British Hedgehog Society Staff. Prickly Poems. (Illus.). 64p. (gr. 3-5). 1993. 18.95 (0-09-176379-7, Pub. by Hutchinson UK) Trafalgar.

British Museum, Geological Department Staff. Earthquakes. (Illus.). 36p. (Orig.). (gr. 7 up). 1986. pap. 5.95 (0-521-32411-4) Cambridge U Pr.

—Moon, Mars & Meteorites. (Illus.). 36p. (gr. 7 up). 1986. pap. 5.95 (0-521-32414-9) Cambridge U Pr.

British Museum Staff. Nature at Work. LC 78-66795. (Illus.). (gr. 7 up). 1978. pap. 12.95 (0-521-29469-X) Cambridge U Pr.

Britt, Dorothy. The Water Bug Story. Shearer, Renee, illus. 10p. (Orig.). 1992. pap. 4.95 (1-881809-32-3) Gabriel TX.

Britt, Helen. Ye Gods. 1987. pap. text ed. 11.16 (0-88334-196-4, 76161) Longman.

Britt, Stephanie M., illus. My Little Prayers. Ward, Brenda C., compiled by. LC 93-578. (Illus.). (gr. 3 up). 1993. pap. 5.99 (0-8499-1064-1) Word Pub.

Brittain, Bill. All the Money in the World. LC 77-25635. (Illus.). 160p. (gr. 3-7). 1979. PLB 14.89 (0-06-020676-4) HarpC Child Bks.

—All the Money in the World. Robinson, Charles, illus. LC 77-25635. 160p. (gr. 4-7). 1982. pap. 3.95 (0-06-440128-6, Trophy) HarpC Child Bks.

—Devil's Donkey. Glass, Andrew, illus. LC 80-7907. 128p. (gr. 3-7). 1981. PLB 13.89 (0-06-020683-7) HarpC Child Bks.

—Devil's Donkey. Glass, Andrew, illus. LC 80-7907. 128p. (gr. 3-7). 1982. pap. 3.95 (0-06-440129-4, Trophy) HarpC Child Bks.

—Dr. Dredd's Wagon of Wonders. Glass, Andrew, illus. LC 86-45775. 208p. (gr. 3-7). 1987. PLB 13.89 (0-06-020714-0) HarpC Child Bks.

—Dr. Dredd's Wagon of Wonders. Glass, Andrew, illus. LC 86-45775. 192p. (gr. 3-7). 1989. pap. 3.50 (0-06-440294-9, Trophy) HarpC Child Bks.

—The Fantastic Freshman. LC 87-35051. 160p. (gr. 5-9). 1988. PLB 12.89 (0-06-020719-1) HarpC Child Bks.

—The Fantastic Freshman. LC 87-35051. 160p. (gr. 7 up). 1990. pap. 3.25 (0-06-447016-4, Trophy) HarpC Child Bks.

—The Ghost from Beneath the Sea. Chessare, Michele, illus. LC 92-1091. 148p. (gr. 4-7). 1992. 14.00 (0-06-020827-9); PLB 13.89 (0-06-020828-7) HarpC Child Bks.

—My Buddy, the King. LC 88-35704. 144p. (gr. 5-8). 1989. 13.00 (0-06-020724-8); PLB 12.89 (0-06-020725-6) HarpC Child Bks.

—My Buddy, the King. LC 88-35704. 144p. (gr. 5-8). 1992. pap. 3.95 (0-06-440339-4, Trophy) HarpC Child Bks.

—Professor Popkin's Prodigious Polish. Glass, Andrew, illus. LC 89-78221. 160p. (gr. 3-7). 1991. pap. 3.95 (0-06-440386-6, Trophy) HarpC Child Bks.

—Professor Popkin's Prodigious Polish: A Tale of Coven Tree. Glass, Andrew, illus. LC 89-78221. 160p. (gr. 3-7). 1991. PLB 13.89 (0-06-020727-2) HarpC Child Bks.

—Shape-Shifter. LC 93-27268. Date not set. 13.00 (0-06-024238-8); PLB 12.89 (0-06-024239-6) HarpC Child Bks.

—Who Knew There'd Be Ghosts? Chessare, Michele, illus. LC 84-48496. 128p. (gr. 4-7). 1985. PLB 13.89 (0-06-020700-0) HarpC Child Bks.

—Who Knew There'd Be Ghosts? Chessare, Michele, illus. LC 84-48496. 128p. (gr. 4-7). 1988. pap. 3.95 (0-06-440224-X, Trophy) HarpC Child Bks.

—Wings. LC 90-19785. 128p. (gr. 4-7). 1991. 13.95 (0-06-020686-9) HarpC Child Bks.

—The Wish Giver: Three Tales of Coven Tree. Glass, Andrew, illus. LC 82-48264. 192p. (gr. 3-7). 1983. 14.00i (0-06-020686-1); PLB 13.89 (0-06-020687-X) HarpC Child Bks.

—The Wish Giver: Three Tales of Coven Tree. Glass, Andrew, illus. LC 82-48264. 192p. (gr. 3-7). 1986. pap. 3.95 (0-06-440168-5, Trophy) HarpC Child Bks.

Brittain, Grady B. Platy: The Child in Us. McBoon, Linda, illus. LC 81-6503. 53p. (Orig.). (ps-8). 1981. pap. 2.00 (0-86663-761-3) Ide Hse.

Brittain, Mary Ann. A Whale Called Trouble. (Illus.). 24p. (gr. 1-12). 1985. pap. 1.50 (0-917134-08-7) NC Natl Sci.

Britto, Betty, adapted by. The Bat Poet. Stahl, Jule, contrib. by. (Illus.). 40p. (Orig.). (gr. 3 up). 1988. pap. 3.00 (0-88680-300-4); piano-vocal score 10.00 (0-88680-301-2); royalty on application 50.00 (0-685-58402-X) I E Clark.

Britton, Colleen. Celebrate Communion. 79p. (gr. 1-6). 1984. pap. 9.95 (0-940754-26-6) Ed Ministries.

—Palestine Thirty A. D. You Are There. Britton, Colleen, illus. 79p. (ps-6). 1987. pap. 12.95 (0-940754-38-X) Ed Ministries.

Britton, Dorothy, tr. see Higa, Tomiko.

Britton, Dorothy, tr. see Higa, Tomiko & Yorimitsu.

Britton, James N. Literature in Its Place. LC 92-24089. 136p. (gr. 7 up). 1993. pap. 15.00 (0-86709-315-3, 0315) Boynton Cook Pubs.

Broadhurst, Alan. The Great Cross-Country Race. 1965. 5.50 (0-87602-133-X) Anchorage.

—Young Dick Whittington. (gr. 1-7). 1964. 4.50 (0-87602-224-7) Anchorage.

Broadman, Muriel, jt. auth. see Suib, Leonard.
Broberg, Merle. Barbados. (Illus.). 96p. (gr. 5 up). 1989. lib. bdg. 14.95 (*1-55546-792-X*) Chelsea Hse.
—Department of Health & Human Services. (Illus.). 128p. (gr. 5 up). 1989. lib. bdg. 14.95 (*0-87754-840-4*) Chelsea Hse.
Brock, Betty. No Flying in the House. Tripp, Wallace, illus. LC 79-104755. 144p. (gr. 2-5). 1982. pap. 3.95 (*0-06-440130-8*, Trophy) HarpC Child Bks.
Brock, John M. An Illustrated History of Kern County. Ambriz, Don & Reed, Libby, illus. 83p. (gr. 3-8). 1976. pap. 5.00 (*0-943500-05-2*) Kern Historical.
Brock, Ray. Go Fly a Kite. (Illus.). (gr. 4 up). 1976. pap. 8.00 (*0-912846-17-8*) Bookstore Pr.
Brock, Raymond T. Dating & Waiting for Marriage. LC 81-84763. 128p. (gr. 9-12). 1982. pap. 2.95 (*0-88243-881-6*, 02-0881) tchr's. guide 4.50 (*0-88243-192-7*, 32-0192) Gospel Pub.
Brock, William E. Rating Contenders. (Illus.). 27p. 1986. pap. 9.00 plastic spiral bound (*0-9616551-0-0*) Trifecta Charley.
Brockel, Ray, jt. auth. see White, Lawrence B.
Brockman, Alfred. Bears. (ps-3). 1989. pap. 1.95 (*0-8167-1541-6*) Troll Assocs.
Brockman, C. Frank. Trees of North America. Zim, Herbert S. & Fichter, George S., eds. Merrilees, Rebecca, illus. (gr. 9 up). 1968. pap. write for info (*0-307-13658-2*, Golden Pr) Western Pub.
Brockman, Chris. What about Gods? (Illus.). (gr. 1-5). 1978. pap. 7.95 (*0-87975-106-1*) Prometheus Bks.
Brockmeyer, Lloyd & Collison, Kathleen. New Beginnings: A Confirmation Resource. 58p. (Orig.). (gr. 7-8). pap. text ed. 4.50 (*0-941988-00-7*); tchr's ed. 3.50 (*0-941988-01-5*) K Q Assocs.
Brockway, Warren H. Gnomes I Have Known. 1992. pap. 10.00 (*0-533-10223-5*) Vantage.
Brod, Alexandra. Who Stole Travada? Lucke, Peggy, ed. Stotz, Gunther, illus. 128p. (gr. 3-6). 1987. pap. 4.95 (*0-940589-00-1*) Adventure Pr.
Brode, Douglas. Lost Films of the Fifties. (Illus.). 288p. (Orig.). 1988. pap. 15.95 (*0-8065-1092-7*, Citadel Pr) Carol Pub Group.
Broderick, Patricia. Megan Mole Meets a Monster. 1993. 7.95 (*0-8062-4571-9*) Carlton.
Brodeur, Ruth W. Stories from the Big Chair. De Groat, Diane, illus. LC 88-35230. 48p. (gr. 1-4). 1989. SBE 12.95 (*0-689-50481-0*, M K McElderry) Macmillan Child Grp.
Brodien-Jones, Chris. The Dreamkeepers. LC 92-10884. 144p. (gr. 5-9). 1992. SBE 13.95 (*0-02-747862-9*, Bradbury Pr) Macmillan Child Grp.
Brodley, Sue, jt. auth. see Nash, Margaret.
Brodmann, Aliana. Gift. (gr. 5 up). 1993. pap. 14.00 (*0-671-75110-7*, S&S BFYR) S&S Trade.
—Que Ruido! What Noise! Krohn, Hildegard M., tr. from GER. Poppel, Hans, illus. (SPA). 26p. (gr. 3 up). 1990. 13.95 (*968-6465-08-1*) Hispanic Bk Dist.
—Such a Noise! Fillingham, David, tr. from GER. Poppel, Hans, illus. 32p. (gr. k-3). 1989. 11.95 (*0-916291-25-1*) Kane-Miller Bk.
Brodsky, Anna, tr. see Dolson, Gina.
Brody, Ed, et al, eds. Spinning Tales, Weaving Hope: Stories, Storytelling & Activities for Peace, Justice, & the Environment. Bond, Lahki, illus. 288p. (Orig.). 1992. lib. bdg. 49.95 (*0-86571-228-X*); pap. 22.95 (*0-86571-229-8*) New Soc Pubs.
Brody, Jean. Elephants. Leon, Vicki, ed. LC 93-12668. (Illus.). 48p. (Orig.). (gr. 5 up). 1993. pap. 9.95 perfect bdg. (*0-918303-32-X*) Blake Pub.
Brody, Norma. Thoughts on Thinking. (SPA., Orig.). (gr. 11 up). 1991. pap. 7.95 (*0-925360-09-0*) Geste Pub.
Brodzinsky, Anne Braff see Braff Brodzinsky, Anne.
Broeck, Fabricio Banden see Dupre, Judith.
Broekel, Ray. Animal Observations. LC 89-25363. (Illus.). 48p. (gr. k-4). 1990. PLB 15.27 (*0-516-01182-0*); pap. 4.95 (*0-516-41182-9*) Childrens.
—Aquariums & Terrariums. LC 82-4428. (gr. k-4). 1982. 15.27 (*0-516-01660-1*) Childrens.
—Baseball. LC 81-38480. (Illus.). 48p. (gr. k-4). 1982. PLB 15.27 (*0-516-01616-4*); pap. 4.95 (*0-516-41616-2*) Childrens.
—Dangerous Fish. LC 82-4464. (gr. k-4). 1982. 15.27 (*0-516-01635-0*); pap. 4.95 (*0-516-41635-9*) Childrens.
—Experiments with Air. LC 87-34146. (Illus.). 48p. (gr. k-4). 1988. PLB 15.27 (*0-516-01213-4*); pap. 4.95 (*0-516-41213-2*) Childrens.
—Experiments with Light. LC 85-30888. (Illus.). 48p. (gr. k-4). 1986. PLB 15.27 (*0-516-01278-9*); pap. 4.95 (*0-516-41278-7*) Childrens.
—Experiments with Straws & Paper. LC 90-2173. (Illus.). 48p. (gr. k-4). 1990. PLB 15.27 (*0-516-01104-9*); pap. 4.95 (*0-516-41104-7*) Childrens.
—Experiments with Water. LC 87-34147. (Illus.). 48p. (gr. k-4). 1988. PLB 15.27 (*0-516-01215-0*); pap. 4.95 (*0-516-41215-9*) Childrens.
—Fire Fighters. LC 81-7655. (Illus.). 48p. (gr. k-4). 1981. PLB 15.27 (*0-516-01620-2*); pap. 4.95 (*0-516-41620-0*) Childrens.
—Football. LC 81-15484. (Illus.). 48p. (gr. k-4). 1982. PLB 15.27 (*0-516-01629-6*); pap. 4.95 (*0-516-41629-4*) Childrens.
—Gerbil Pets & Other Small Rodents. LC 82-23501. (Illus.). 48p. (gr. k-4). 1983. PLB 15.27 (*0-516-01679-2*) Childrens.
—I Can Be an Author. LC 85-28050. (Illus.). 32p. (gr. k-3). 1986. PLB 14.60 (*0-516-01891-4*); pap. 3.95 (*0-516-41891-2*) Childrens.
—I Can Be an Auto Mechanic. LC 85-11303. 32p. (gr. k-3). 1985. PLB 14.60 (*0-516-01885-X*); pap. 3.95 (*0-516-41885-8*) Childrens.
—Jet Planes. LC 86-32675. (Illus.). 48p. (gr. k-4). 1987. PLB 15.27 (*0-516-01235-5*) Childrens.
—Maps & Globes. LC 83-7509. (Illus.). 48p. (gr. k-4). 1983. PLB 15.27 (*0-516-01695-4*); pap. 4.95 (*0-516-41695-2*) Childrens.
—Police. LC 81-7693. (Illus.). 48p. (gr. k-4). 1981. PLB 15.27 (*0-516-01643-1*) Childrens.
—La Policia (Police) Kratky, Lada, tr. from ENG. LC 81-7693. (SPA., Illus.). 48p. (gr. k-4). 1984. PLB 15. 27 (*0-516-31643-5*); pap. 4.95 (*0-516-51643-4*) Childrens.
—Snakes. LC 81-38487. (Illus.). 48p. (gr. k-4). 1982. PLB 15.27 (*0-516-01649-0*); pap. 4.95 (*0-516-41649-9*) Childrens.
—Sound Experiments. LC 82-17869. (Illus.). 48p. (gr. k-4). 1983. PLB 15.27 (*0-516-01686-5*); pap. 4.95 (*0-516-41686-3*) Childrens.
—Storms. LC 81-15455. (Illus.). 48p. (gr. k-4). 1982. PLB 15.27 (*0-516-01654-7*) Childrens.
—Trains. (Illus.). 48p. (gr. k-4). 1981. PLB 15.27 (*0-516-01652-0*); pap. 4.95 (*0-516-41652-9*) Childrens.
—Tropical Fish. LC 82-19738. (Illus.). 48p. (gr. k-4). 1983. PLB 15.27 (*0-516-01687-3*) Childrens.
—Trucks. LC 82-17907. (Illus.). 48p. (gr. k-4). 1983. PLB 15.27 (*0-516-01688-1*) Childrens.
—Tus Cinco Sentidos (Your Five Senses) LC 84-7603. (SPA.). 48p. (gr. k-4). 1987. PLB 15.27 (*0-516-31932-9*); pap. 4.95 (*0-516-51932-8*) Childrens.
—Your Five Senses. LC 84-7603. (Illus.). 48p. (gr. k-4). 1984. PLB 15.27 (*0-516-01932-5*); pap. 4.95 (*0-516-41932-3*) Childrens.
—Your Skeleton & Skin. LC 84-7746. (Illus.). 48p. (gr. k-4). 1984. PLB 15.27 (*0-516-01934-1*) Childrens.
Broekel, Ray & White, Laurence. Now You See It: Easy Magic for Beginners. Morrison, William, illus. (gr. 1-3). 1979. 13.95 (*0-316-93595-6*) Little.
Broekel, Ray & White, Laurence B., Jr. Abra-Ca-Dazzle: Easy Magic Tricks. Fay, Ann, ed. Thelan, Mary, illus. LC 81-11578. 48p. (gr. 3 up). 1982. PLB 11.95 (*0-8075-0121-2*) A Whitman.
—Hocus Pocus: Magic You Can Do. Fay, Anne, ed. Thelen, Mary, illus. LC 83-26096. 48p. (gr. 3 up). 1984. PLB 11.95 (*0-8075-3350-5*) A Whitman.
Broekel, Ray, jt. auth. see White, Larry.
Broekel, Ray, jt. auth. see White, Laurence B., Jr.
Broger, Achim. The Red Armchair. Schluter, Manfred, illus. 28p. (ps-2). 1991. smythe sewn reinforced bdg. 9.95 (*1-56182-034-2*) Atomium Bks.
—The Wonderful Bedmobile. Kalow, Gisela, illus. 28p. (ps-2). 1991. smythe sewn reinforced bdg. 9.95 (*1-56182-033-4*) Atomium Bks.
Broger, Achim, retold by. The Santa Clauses. Krause, Ute, illus. LC 86-2147. 28p. (ps-3). 1986. 11.95 (*0-8037-0266-3*) Dial Bks Young.
—The Santa Clauses. Krause, Ute, illus. LC 86-2147. 28p. (ps-3). 1988. pap. 3.95 (*0-8037-0557-3*) Dial Bks Young.
Brokaw, Meredith & Gilbar, Annie. The Penny Whistle Christmas Party Book: Including Hanukkah, New Year's, & Twelfth Night Family Parties. Weber, Jill, illus. 128p. (Orig.). 1991. (Fireside); pap. 12.00 (*0-671-73794-5*, Fireside) S&S Trade.
Broker, Loretta. Ellie the Elephant. Meyer, Jacque S., illus. 28p. (Orig.). (ps-k). 1990. pap. 2.95 (*0-916109-09-7*) Summers Pub.
Brokering, Herbert. I Opener. LC 74-4912. (gr. 7 up). 1974. pap. 2.99 (*0-570-06472-4*, 12-2584) Concordia.
—The Night Before Jesus. (ps-4). 1983. 7.99 (*0-570-04084-1*, 56-1439) Concordia.
Bromberg, Murray & Liebb, Julius. The English You Need to Know: Reading, Writing, Grammar. 192p. (gr. 9-12). 1987. pap. 8.95 (*0-8120-2407-9*) Barron.
—Hot Words for the SAT: The Three Hundred Fifty Words You Need to Know. 2nd ed. LC 93-6742. 180p. (gr. 9 up). 1993. pap. 8.95 (*0-8120-1731-5*) Barron.
Brommer, Gerald F. Relief Printmaking. LC 77-113860. (Illus.). (gr. 7-12). 1970. 14.95 (*0-87192-034-4*) Davis Mass.
—Wire Sculpture & Other Three Dimensional Construction. LC 68-19999. (Illus.). (gr. 5-12). 1968. 14.95 (*0-87192-025-5*) Davis Mass.
Brommer, Gerald F. & Horn, George F. Art in Your World. 2nd ed. LC 84-73493. (Illus.). 256p. (gr. 7-8). 1985. text ed. 27.95 (*0-87192-168-5*, 168-5); tchr's. guide 10.95 (*0-685-01368-5*, 168-5G) Davis Mass.
Bronner, Stephen E. Leon Blum. Schlesinger, Arthur M., Jr., intro. by. (Illus.). 112p. (gr. 5 up). 1987. 17.95x (*0-87754-511-1*) Chelsea Hse.
Bronson, Marsha. Amnesty International. LC 93-26367. 1994. write for info. (*0-02-714550-6*, New Discovery Bks) Macmillan Child Grp.
Bronstein, Leona B. & McGrain, Eleanore. Chemistry Flipper. 49p. (gr 7 up) 1989. Repr. of 1978 ed. trade edition 5.95 (*1-878383-06-X*) C Lee Pubns.
Bronstein, Ruth L. Rabbit's Good News. LC 93-30719. (gr. 4 up). Date not set. write for info. (*0-395-68700-4*, Clarion Bks) HM.
Bronte, Charlotte. Jane Eyre. (gr. 9 up). 1964. pap. 3.95 (*0-8049-0017-5*, CL-17) Airmont.
—Jane Eyre. 461p. (RL 7). 1960. pap. 2.50 (*0-451-52332-6*, Sig Classics) NAL-Dutton.
—Jane Eyre. Farr, Naunerle, ed. (Illus.). (gr. 4-12). 1977. pap. text ed. 2.95 (*0-88301-266-9*); wkbk. 1.25 (*0-88301-290-1*) Pendulum Pr.
—Jane Eyre. Shaw, Charlie, illus. Stewart, Diana, adapted by. LC 80-14426. (Illus.). 48p. (gr. 4 up). 1983. PLB 18.64 (*0-8172-1661-8*) Raintree Steck-V.
—Jane Eyre. Mitchell, Kathy, illus. (gr. 4 up). 1983. deluxe ed. 15.95 (*0-448-06031-0*, G&D) Putnam Pub Group.
—Jane Eyre. 448p. (gr. 5 up). 1992. pap. 2.95 (*0-14-035131-0*, Puffin) Puffin Bks.
Bronte, Emily. Wuthering Heights. (gr. 9 up). 1964. pap. 2.95 (*0-8049-0011-6*, CL-11) Airmont.
—Wuthering Heights. Pritchett, V. S., ed. LC 56-14017. (gr. 9 up). 1956. pap. 9.16 (*0-395-05102-9*, RivEd) HM.
—Wuthering Heights. new & abr. ed. Farr, Naunerle, ed. Amongo, Jo, illus. (gr. 4-12). 1977. pap. text ed. 2.95 (*0-88301-272-3*) Pendulum Pr.
—Wuthering Heights. Wright, Betty R., adapted by. Cogancherry, Helen, illus. LC 81-15786. 48p. (gr. 4 up). 1982. PLB 18.64 (*0-8172-1682-0*) Raintree Steck-V.
—Wuthering Heights. 3rd, rev. ed. Sale, William M., Jr. & Dunn, Richard, eds. (gr. 9-12). 1990. pap. text ed. 7.95 (*0-393-95760-8*) Norton.
—Wuthering Heights. 224p. 1989. pap. 2.50 (*0-8125-0516-6*) Tor Bks.
—Wuthering Heights. 1992. 3.50 (*0-590-46030-7*, Apple Classics) Scholastic Inc.
Bronze, Lewis, et al. The Blue Peter Green Book. (Illus.). 64p. (gr. 7-9). 1992. 9.95 (*0-563-20886-4*, BBC-Parkwest) Parkwest Pubns.
Brook, Bonnie. Let's Celebrate Easter: A Book of Drawing Fun. Klein, Susan, illus. LC 87-50428. 32p. (gr. 2-6). 1988. PLB 10.65 (*0-8167-1051-1*); pap. text ed. 1.95 (*0-8167-1052-X*) Troll Assocs.
Brook, Bonnie, jt. auth. see Kraus, Robert.
Brook, Bonnie, ed. see Amerikaner, Susan.
Brook, Bonnie, ed. see Arnold, Caroline.
Brook, Bonnie, ed. see Ashley, Jill.
Brook, Bonnie, ed. see Ball, Jacqueline.
Brook, Bonnie, ed. see Barkan, Joanne.
Brook, Bonnie, ed. see Binnamin, Vivian.
Brook, Bonnie, ed. see Boynton, Alice B.
Brook, Bonnie, ed. see Calder, S. J.
Brook, Bonnie, ed. see Carter, Polly.
Brook, Bonnie, ed. see Himmelman, John.
Brook, Bonnie, ed. see Hoobler, Dorothy & Hoobler, Thomas.
Brook, Bonnie, ed. see Kraus, Robert.
Brook, Bonnie, ed. see Kuhn, Dwight.
Brook, Bonnie, ed. see Leonard, Marcia.
Brook, Bonnie, ed. see Pearce, Q. L. & Pearce, W. J.
Brook, Bonnie, ed. see Pearce, Q. L. & Pearce, W. L.
Brook, Bonnie, ed. see Please Touch Museum Staff.
Brook, Bonnie, ed. see Poskanzer, Susan.
Brook, Bonnie, ed. see Woodson, Jacqueline.
Brook, Bonnie, ed. see Young, Robert.
Brook, Leeanne. The Great Big, Enormous, Gigantic Cardboard Box. Vanzet, Gaston, illus. LC 92-29957. (gr. 3 up). 1993. 14.00 (*0-383-03571-6*) SRA Schl Grp.
Brook, Ruth. Bitty's Halloween Surprise. Kondo, Vala, illus. LC 86-30730. 32p. (gr. k-3). 1988. PLB 11.89 (*0-8167-0916-5*); pap. text ed. 2.95 (*0-8167-0917-3*) Troll Assocs.
—Good for You, Lolly. Kondo, Vala, illus. LC 86-30733. 32p. (gr. k-3). 1988. PLB 11.89 (*0-8167-0914-9*); pap. text ed. 2.95 (*0-8167-0915-7*) Troll Assocs.
—Happy Birthday, Baby. Kondo, Vala, illus. LC 86-30750. 32p. (gr. k-3). 1988. PLB 11.89 (*0-8167-0912-2*); pap. text ed. 2.95 (*0-8167-0913-0*) Troll Assocs.
—Jingle's Big Race. Kondo, Vala, illus. LC 86-30729. 32p. (gr. k-3). 1988. PLB 11.89 (*0-8167-0902-5*); pap. text ed. 2.95 (*0-8167-0903-3*) Troll Assocs.
—Jump for Joy, Betty. Kondo, Vala, illus. LC 86-30731. 32p. (gr. k-3). 1988. PLB 11.89 (*0-8167-0908-4*); pap. text ed. 2.95 (*0-8167-0909-2*) Troll Assocs.
—Play It Again, Rosie! Kondo, Vala, illus. LC 86-30749. 32p. (gr. k-3). 1988. PLB 11.89 (*0-8167-0904-1*); pap. text ed. 2.95 (*0-8167-0905-X*) Troll Assocs.
—Sweet Hearts for Dolly. Kondo, Vala, illus. LC 86-30732. 32p. (gr. k-3). 1988. PLB 11.89 (*0-8167-0906-8*); pap. text ed. 2.95 (*0-8167-0907-6*) Troll Assocs.
—Toony & the Midnight Monster. Kondo, Vala, illus. LC 86-30739. 32p. (gr. k-3). 1988. lib. bdg. 11.89 (*0-8167-0910-6*); pap. text ed. 2.95 (*0-8167-0911-4*) Troll Assocs.
Brooke, Bob. Solar Energy. (Illus.). (gr. 5 up). 1992. lib. bdg. 19.95 (*0-7910-1590-4*) Chelsea Hse.
Brooke, Janet, jt. auth. see Landaw, Jonathan.
Brooke, L. Leslie. Golden Goose Book. Brooke, L. Leslie, illus. 96p. (ps-3). 1992. 16.45 (*0-395-61303-5*, Clarion Bks) HM.
—Ring O'Roses. Brooke, L. Leslie, illus. 96p. (ps-3). 1992. 16.95 (*0-395-61304-3*, Clarion Bks) HM.
Brooke, Roger. Santa's Christmas Journey. LC 84-9796. (Illus.). 32p. (gr. k-5). 1984. PLB 17.96 (*0-8172-2116-6*); PLB 29.28 incl. cassette (*0-8172-2244-8*) Raintree Steck-V.
—Santa's Christmas Journey. (gr. k-5). 1993. pap. 3.95 (*0-8114-8356-8*) Raintree Steck-V.
Brooke, William J. A Brush with Magic. LC 92-41744. 160p. (gr. 3 up). 1993. 15.00 (*0-06-022973-X*); PLB 14.89 (*0-06-022974-8*) HarpC Child Bks.

—A Telling of the Tales: Five Stories. Egielski, Richard, illus. LC 89-36588. 144p. (gr. 3-7). 1990. 13.00 (*0-06-020688-8*); PLB 12.89 (*0-06-020689-6*) HarpC Child Bks.
—A Telling of the Tales: Five Stories. Egielski, Richard, illus. LC 89-36588. 144p. (gr. 3-7). 1993. pap. 5.95 (*0-06-440467-6*, Trophy) HarpC Child Bks.
—Untold Tales. LC 91-4179. 160p. (gr. 5 up). 1992. 15. 00 (*0-06-020271-8*); PLB 14.89 (*0-06-020272-6*) HarpC Child Bks.
—Untold Tales. LC 91-4179. 176p. (gr. 5 up). 1993. pap. 5.95 (*0-06-440483-8*, Trophy) HarpC Child Bks.
Brooke-Ball, Peter. Swimming. 1990. 7.95x (*0-86685-478-9*) Intl Bk Ctr.
Brookes, Diane. Passing the Peace: A Counting Book for Kids. (FRE & ENG., Illus.). 24p. 1990. pap. 8.95 (*0-921254-20-2*, Pub. by Penumbra Pr CN) U of Toronto Pr.
Brookes, Florence W. The Adventures of Elmer the Pet Worm. 1992. 8.75 (*0-8062-4289-2*) Carlton.
Brookfield, Karen. Book. Fordes, Laurence, illus. 64p. (gr. 5 up). 1993. 15.00 (*0-679-84012-5*); PLB 15.99 (*0-679-94012-X*) Knopf Bks Yng Read.
Brooks. Each a Piece. Date not set. 16.00 (*0-06-023594-2*, Festival); PLB 14.89 (*0-06-023595-0*, Festival) HarpC Child Bks.
—Heracles. Date not set. 16.00 (*0-06-023592-6*, Festival); PLB 15.89 (*0-06-023593-4*, Festival) HarpC Child Bks.
Brooks, B. The Seminole. (Illus.). 32p. (gr. 5-8). 1989. lib. bdg. 15.94 (*0-86625-377-7*); 11.95 (*0-685-58584-0*) Rourke Corp.
—The Sioux. (Illus.). 32p. (gr. 5-8). 1989. lib. bdg. 15.94 (*0-86625-382-3*); 11.95 (*0-685-58585-9*) Rourke Corp.
Brooks, B. David & Paull, Robert C. How to Be Successful in Less Than Ten Minutes a Day. 180p. (gr. 7 up). 1991. tchr's. ed. 65.00 (*0-938308-11-4*); wkbk. 65.00 (*0-685-20975-X*) T Jefferson Ctr.
Brooks, Bearl. Basic Skills Reading Comprehension Workbook, 4 bks. 128p. 1983. 1.98 ea. Grades 1-2 (*0-8209-0554-2*, RCW-1) Grades 3-4 (*0-8209-0555-0*, RCW-2) Grades 5-6 (*0-8209-0556-9*, RCW-3) Grades 7-8 (*0-8209-0557-7*, RCW-4) ESP.
—Jumbo Reading Yearbook: Kindergarten. 96p. (gr. k). 1980. 18.00 (*0-8209-0011-7*, JRY R) ESP.
Brooks, Ben. Lemonade Parade. Tucker, Kathleen, ed. Slavin, Bill, illus. LC 91-34870. 32p. (gr. k-3). 1992. PLB 13.95 (*0-8075-4432-9*) A Whitman.
Brooks, Bruce. Boys Will Be. 128p. (gr. 6 up). 1993. PLB 14.95 (*0-8050-2420-4*, Bks Young Read) H Holt & Co.
—Everywhere. LC 90-4073. 80p. (gr. 4 up). 1990. 13.00 (*0-06-020728-0*); PLB 12.89 (*0-06-020729-9*) HarpC Child Bks.
—Everywhere. LC 90-4073. 80p. (gr. 4 up). 1992. pap. 3.95 (*0-06-440433-1*, Trophy) HarpC Child Bks.
—Making Sense: Animal Perception & Communication. LC 93-10474. 1993. write for info. (*0-374-34742-5*) FS&G.
—Midnight Hour Encores. LC 86-45035. 288p. (gr. 7 up). 1986. 14.00 (*0-06-020709-4*); PLB 13.89 (*0-06-020710-8*) HarpC Child Bks.
—Midnight Hour Encores. LC 86-45035. 288p. (gr. 7 up). 1988. pap. 3.95 (*0-06-447021-0*, Trophy) HarpC Child Bks.
—The Moves Make the Man. LC 83-49476. 320p. (gr. 7 up). 1984. 15.00 (*0-06-020679-9*); PLB 14.89 (*0-06-020698-5*) HarpC Child Bks.
—The Moves Make the Man. LC 83-49476. 288p. (gr. 7 up). 1987. pap. 3.95 (*0-06-447022-9*, Trophy) HarpC Child Bks.
—Moves Make the Man. large type ed. 189p. (gr. 5 up). 1988. Repr. of 1984 ed. lib. bdg. 15.95 (*1-55736-048-0*, Crnrstn Bks) BDD LT Grp.
—Nature by Design. (Illus.). 80p. (gr. 5 up). 1991. bds. 13.95 bds. (*0-374-30334-7*) FS&G.
—No Kidding. LC 88-22057. 224p. (gr. 7 up). 1989. 14. 00 (*0-06-020722-1*); PLB 13.89 (*0-06-020723-X*) HarpC Child Bks.
—No Kidding. LC 88-22057. 224p. (gr. 7 up). 1991. pap. 3.95 (*0-06-447051-2*, Trophy) HarpC Child Bks.
—Predator! 80p. (gr. 5 up). 1991. bds. 13.95 bds. (*0-374-36111-8*) FS&G.
—What Hearts? LC 92-5305. 208p. (gr. 5 up). 1992. 14. 00 (*0-06-021131-8*); PLB 13.89 (*0-06-021132-6*) HarpC Child Bks.
Brooks, Bruce see Tunis, John R.
Brooks, Caryl. The Empty Summer. LC 92-12818. 1993. 13.95 (*0-590-45863-9*) Scholastic Inc.
Brooks, Cathleen. The Secret Everyone Knows. 40p. (gr. 5-10). 1989. pap. 3.00 (*0-89486-483-1*, 5165B) Hazelden.
Brooks, Chalsea. Who Can You Trust? 160p. (Orig.). (gr. 5 up). 1993. pap. 2.95 (*0-02-041973-2*, Collier Young Ad) Macmillan Child Grp.
Brooks, Charles, ed. Best Editorial Cartoons of the Year: 1976 Edition. (Illus.). 160p. 1976. 16.95 (*0-88289-122-7*) Pelican.
—Best Editorial Cartoons of the Year: 1977 Edition. Hill, Draper, frwd. by. LC 74-29707. (Illus.). 1977. 16.95 (*0-88289-170-7*); pap. 10.95 (*0-88289-171-5*) Pelican.
Brooks, Chelsea. Beauty & the Blues. 144p. (gr. 5 up). 1994. pap. 2.95 (*0-02-041974-0*, Collier Young Ad) Macmillan Child Grp.
—Behind the Scenes. (Illus.). 64p. (gr. 5 up). 1993. pap. 7.95 (*0-02-041650-4*, Collier Young Ad) Macmillan Child Grp.

—Don't Tell a Soul. 144p. (Orig.). (gr. 5 up). 1994. pap. 2.95 (*0-02-042783-2*, Collier Young Ad) Macmillan Child Grp.
—The Dream Team. 144p. (Orig.). (gr. 5 up). 1994. pap. 2.95 (*0-02-041976-7*, Collier Young Ad) Macmillan Child Grp.
—Perfect Harmony. LC 93-12876. 160p. (Orig.). (gr. 5 up). 1993. pap. 2.95 (*0-02-041972-4*, Aladdin) Macmillan Child Grp.
—Playing for Keeps. 160p. (Orig.). (gr. 5 up). 1993. pap. 2.95 (*0-02-041971-6*, Collier Young Ad) Macmillan Child Grp.
—Power of Love. 144p. (Orig.). (gr. 5 up). 1994. pap. 2.95 (*0-02-041975-9*, Collier Young Ad) Macmillan Child Grp.
Brooks, Cleanth. The Well Wrought Urn: Studies in the Structure of Poetry. LC 47-3143. 300p. (Orig.). (gr. 7 up). 1956. pap. 9.95 (*0-15-695705-1*, Harvest Bks) HarBrace.
Brooks, Clifford, et al. Music! Words! Opera, 4 vols, Level 2. Vogelsang, Johanna, illus. Fowler, Charles, frwd. by. LC 91-45210. (Illus.). (gr. 3-5). 1991. One vol., 460p. tchr's. manual 82.50 (*0-918812-66-6*); Three vols., 48p. ea. wkbk. 4.95 (*0-918812-68-2*) MMB Music.
Brooks, Courtaney. The Case of the Stolen Dinosaur: A Play in Two Versions: Stage & Radio. Way, Merrilee, illus. 26p. (Orig.). (gr. 4 up). 1983. pap. text ed. 4.00x (*0-941274-02-0*) Belnice Bks.
—Eight Steps to Choral Reading. Way, Marrilee, illus. (Orig.). (gr. 1 up). 1983. pap. text ed. 3.00x (*0-941274-01-2*) Belnice Bks.
—Little Red & the Wolf: A Puppet Play. Way, Merrilee, illus. (gr. k up). 1983. pap. text ed. 2.50x (*0-941274-04-7*) Belnice Bks.
—Pardner & Freddie: A Puppet Play. Way, Merrilee, illus. (gr. k up). 1983. pap. text ed. 2.50x (*0-941274-03-9*) Belnice Bks.

— Plays & Puppets &cetera. 7th ed. Runyan, Merrilee, illus. LC 81-68933. 100p. (Orig.). (gr. k up). 1981. pap. text ed. 14.95 (*0-941274-00-4*) Belnice Bks. "Drama celebrates our differences & uses them. Plays draw out our individuality (which) is never wrong; it is ours--unique. We can all learn, for we're not like little cups waiting to be filled, but like lamps ready to be turned on." These excerpts sum up the philosophy that makes PLAYS & PUPPETS &CETERA much more powerful than the average how-to text. Brooks mixes a complete outlining of puppet & drama basics with a wonderfully positive attitude of respect & joy for life & its possibilities. Her explanations offer sufficient know-how to allow any teacher to carry a group through a show from start to curtain. "As a first time student teacher, I used the book to coordinate a play-project with six fourth-graders. One parent wrote a thank-you note telling us it was the first time she had heard her daughter speak above a whisper in public. I used the book again to help an adult troupe of Spanish-speaking novice players stage a Christmas story."-- BREAKTHROUGH Winter/Summer 1990. (Illustrated puppet directions; 7 sample plays for puppets or people actors with casts of 4 to 6, simple costuming such as ears for a dog or cat & props).
Publisher Provided Annotation.

Brooks, F. Clothes & Fashion. (Illus.). 24p. (gr. 2-4). 1990. PLB 3.95 (*0-7460-0448-6*, Usborne) EDC.
—Clothes & Fashion. (Illus.). 24p. (gr. 2-4). 1990. lib. bdg. 11.96 (*0-88110-400-0*, Usborne) EDC.
—Food & Eating. (Illus.). 24p. (gr. 2-4). 1989. lib. bdg. 11.96 (*0-88110-399-3*, Usborne) EDC.
—Protecting Endangered Species. (Illus.). 24p. (gr. 2-5). 1991. lib. bdg. 11.96 (*0-88110-500-7*, Usborne); pap. 4.50 (*0-7460-0608-X*, Usborne) EDC.
—Protecting Our World. (Illus.). 72p. (gr. 2-5). 1992. 10.95 (*0-7460-1082-6*, Usborne) EDC.
—Protecting Rivers & Seas. (Illus.). 24p. (gr. 2-5). 1992. PLB 11.96 (*0-88110-529-5*, Usborne); pap. 4.50 (*0-7460-0687-X*, Usborne) EDC.
—Protecting Trees & Forests. (Illus.). 24p. (gr. 2-5). 1991. PLB 11.96 (*0-88110-528-7*, Usborne); pap. 4.50 (*0-7460-0656-X*, Usborne) EDC.

Brooks, F., jt. auth. see Edom, H.
Brooks, Garth. The Best of Garth Brooks. Cuellar, Carol & Stang, Aaron, eds. 116p. (Orig.). 1992. pap. text ed. 16.95 (*0-89898-633-8*) CPP Belwin.
Brooks, Gwendolyn. Aloneness. LC 74-147270. (gr. 1-4). 1971. map. 5.00 (*0-910296-55-3*) Broadside Pr.
—Beckonings. (gr. 12). 1975. pap. 5.00 (*0-910296-37-5*) Broadside Pr.
—Bronzeville Boys & Girls. Solbert, Ronni, illus. LC 56-8152. 48p. (gr. 3-6). 1967. PLB 13.89 (*0-06-020651-9*) HarpC Child Bks.
—Family Pictures. LC 70-139494. (gr. 12). 1970. 5.00 (*0-685-00861-4*) tape o.p. 5.00 (*0-685-24799-6*) Broadside Pr.
—Report from Part One: An Autobiography. 1st ed. LC 72-77308. 192p. (gr. 12). 1972. 17.95 (*0-910296-82-0*); 22.95 (*0-685-42016-7*) Broadside Pr.
—The Tiger Who Wore White Gloves: Or What You Are You Are. LC 74-75589. 1974. pap. 6.95 (*0-88378-031-3*) Third World.
Brooks, Gwendolyn, et al. A Capsule Course in Black Poetry Writing. 64p. (gr. 12). 1975. pap. 6.00 (*0-910296-32-4*) Broadside Pr.
Brooks, Hindi. Captain Noah. (Illus.). 36p. (Orig.). (gr. 1 up). 1989. pap. 4.00 bk. (*0-88680-317-9*); Piano-Vocal Score 15.00 (*0-88680-318-7*); royalty on application 60.00 (*0-685-58559-X*) I E Clark.
—Wising Up. (Illus.). (gr. 7-12). 1986. pap. 3.50 (*0-88680-255-5*); royalty on application 50.00 (*0-685-67538-6*) I E Clark.

Brooks, Jennifer. Princess Jessica Rescues a Prince. Flores, Lennie, illus. Ridley, Chas, ed. LC 93-92628. (Illus.). 40p. (ps-2). 1994. 15.95 (*0-9636335-0-3*) Nadja Pub.
In 1991, the American Association of University Women appointed a study on the emotional development of girls. The study revealed that girls have a much lower self-image & less self-confidence than boys. Strong female characters featured in quality books can provide positive role models to help improve girls' self-esteem. Little girls have always loved the popular princess stories. They adore the glamorous young women & dream of growing up to be just like them. The early impressions made by the classic fairy tales stay with us a lifetime. Considering this, a princess should be worthy of such a high regard. Rather than passively wasting her life away waiting for a Prince Charming, an admirable young princess would independently create adventures of her own. When finding herself in a dangerous situation, instead of crying helplessly, a deserving princess would exhibit courage & determination. Lastly, a princess should be beloved not merely for her physical characteristics but for all the inner qualities that constitute real beauty. Princess Jessica doesn't really care if she's considered beautiful or not. She has lots of interesting things to do. One day, three handicapped gnomes arrive at Princess Jessica's castle. They tell her of a prince far away whose singing is so beautiful that he was carried off by a lonesome sea serpent. Princess Jessica & her vain sister, Edith, set out to rescue Prince Ryan. Through her trials Princess Jessica learns about strength & love.
Publisher Provided Annotation.

Brooks, Jerome. Knee Holes. LC 91-25398. 144p. (gr. 7 up). 1992. 14.95 (*0-531-05994-4*); lib. bdg. 14.99 (*0-531-08594-5*) Orchard Bks Watts.
—Naked in Winter. LC 89-35651. 224p. (gr. 7 up). 1990. 14.95 (*0-531-05866-2*); PLB 14.99 (*0-531-08466-3*) Orchard Bks Watts.
Brooks, L., et al. Business Mathematics. 10th ed. 576p. (gr. 9-12). 1987. text ed. 24.96 (*0-07-008166-2*) McGraw.
Brooks, Laura. Disney's Beauty & the Beast: The Beast's Story, Level 2. Gutierrez, Ed & Michaels, Serge, illus. 40p. (gr. k-2). 1992. write for info. (*0-307-11552-6*, 11552, Golden Pr) Western Pub.

Brooks, Laura, adapted by. Disney's Beauty & the Beast: The Beast's Story. Gutierrez, Ed & Michaels, Serge, illus. 32p. (gr. k-2). 1993. pap. 3.25 (*0-307-15976-0*, 15976, Golden Pr) Western Pub.

Brooks, Les, ed. see Behrendt, Fred, et al.

Brooks, Martha. Paradise Cafe & Other Stories. (gr. 7 up). 1990. 14.95 (*0-316-10978-9*, Joy St Bks) Little.
—Paradise Cafe: And Other Stories. 1993. pap. 2.95 (*0-590-45562-1*) Scholastic Inc.
—Two Moons in August. (gr. 7 up). 1992. 15.95 (*0-316-10979-7*) Little.
—Two Moons in August. 208p. (gr. 7 up). 1993. pap. 3.25 (*0-590-45923-6*, Point) Scholastic Inc.

Brooks, Polly S. Beyond the Myth: The Story of Joan of Arc. LC 89-37327. (Illus.). 192p. (gr. 7 up). 1990. 16. 00 (*0-397-32422-7*, Lipp Jr Bks); PLB 15.89 (*0-397-32423-5*, Lipp Jr Bks) HarpC Child Bks.
—Queen Eleanor: Independent Spirit of the Medieval World: a Biography of Eleanor of Aquitaine. LC 82-48776. 160p. (gr. 6 up). 1983. PLB 13.89 (*0-397-31995-9*, Lipp Jr Bks) HarpC Child Bks.

Brooks, Rebecca. Inside Art: Culture History Expression, Bk. 1. Crawford, A. F., ed. (Illus.). 224p. (gr. 7). 1992. text ed. 44.40 (*0-87443-101-8*); tchr's. ed. 40.00 (*0-87443-103-4*) Benson.

Brooks, Robert. So That's How I Was Born. Perl, Susan, illus. LC 81-20859. 48p. (ps-2). 1993. pap. 4.95 (*0-671-78344-0*, S&S BYR) S&S Trade.

Brooks, Robert F. Children's Stories for Teenage Adults. rev. ed. (Illus.). 32p. (Orig.). (gr. 5-9). pap. 3.00 (*0-936868-05-8*) Freeland Pubns.
—Nwandu's Child of Life Reader. (Illus.). 20p. (Orig.). (gr. k-4). pap. 2.00 (*0-936868-00-7*) Freeland Pubns.

Brooks, Robin R. Latin for Elementary School Students. 16p. (Orig.). (gr. 2-3). 1991. pap. text ed. 2.80 (*0-939507-23-4*, B8) Amer Classical.

Brooks, Sandra. The Goose with Three Wings. 32p. (Orig.). (gr. k-2). 1987. pap. 1.99 (*0-8163-0683-4*) Pacific Pr Pub Assn.

Brooks, Walter R. Freddy & the Men from Mars. Morrill, Leslie & Wiese, Kurt, illus. LC 86-40421. 256p. (gr. 3-7). 1987. pap. 3.95 (*0-394-88887-1*) Knopf Bks Yng Read.
—Freddy & the Perilous Adventure. Morrill, Leslie & Wiese, Kurt, illus. LC 85-14653. 256p. (gr. 3-7). 1986. lib. bdg. 9.99 (*0-394-97601-0*) Knopf Bks Yng Read.
—Freddy Goes Camping. Morrill, Leslie & Wiese, Kurt, illus. LC 48-8629. 264p. (gr. 3-7). 1986. lib. bdg. 9.99 (*0-394-97602-9*); pap. 4.95 (*0-394-87602-4*) Knopf Bks Yng Read.
—Freddy Plays Football. 1992. Repr. lib. bdg. 18.95x (*0-89968-302-9*) Lightyear.
—Freddy Rides Again. 1992. Repr. lib. bdg. 18.95x (*0-89968-300-2*) Lightyear.
—Freddy the Cowboy. 1992. Repr. lib. bdg. 18.95x (*0-89968-301-0*) Lightyear.
—Freddy the Politician. Morrill, Leslie, illus. LC 85-14713. 264p. (gr. 3-7). 1986. pap. 3.95 (*0-394-87600-8*) Knopf Bks Yng Read.

Brooman, Josh. The World Since Nineteen Hundred. 1989. pap. text ed. 16.00 (*0-582-00989-8*, 78443) Longman.

Brooman, Josh, ed. The End of Old Europe: Causes of the First World War 1914-18. (Illus.). 32p. (Orig.). (gr. 4-12). 1985. pap. text ed. 10.92 (*0-582-22368-7*, 70921) Longman.
—The Great War: The First World War, 1914-18. (Illus.). 40p. (Orig.). (gr. 4-12). 1985. pap. text ed. 10.92 (*0-582-22369-5*, 70922) Longman.
—The World Re-Made: The Results of the First World War. (Illus.). 32p. (Orig.). (gr. 4-12). 1985. pap. text ed. 10.92 (*0-582-22370-9*, 70923) Longman.

Broome, Errol. Dear Mr. Sprouts. LC 92-13490. 128p. (gr. 5-9). 1993. 15.00 (*0-679-83714-0*) Knopf Bks Yng Read.
—The Smallest Koala. Mason, Gwen, illus. (ps-1). 1988. 11.95 (*0-949447-65-X*) Terra Nova.
—Tangles. James, Ann, illus. LC 93-30637. 1994. 13.00 (*0-679-85713-3*) Knopf Bks Yng Read.

Brophy, Ann. John Ericson & the Inventions of War. Gallin, Richard, ed. Steele, Henry, intro. by. (Illus.). 160p. (gr. 5 up). 1990. PLB 18.98 (*0-382-09943-5*); pap. 8.95 (*0-382-24052-9*) Silver Burdett Pr.

Brophy, Hope F. A Letter to Sarah about God. LC 91-67504. (Illus.). 44p. (gr. 1-5). 1992. 7.95 (*1-55523-497-6*) Winston-Derek.

Brophy, Michael. Michael Faraday. LC 90-33893. (Illus.). 48p. (gr. 4-8). 1991. PLB 12.40 (*0-531-18376-9*, Pub. by Bookwright Pr) Watts.

Brophy, Nannette. The Color of My Fur. LC 91-65704. (Illus.). 44p. (gr. k-3). 1992. lib. bdg. 12.95 (*1-55523-456-9*); pap. 8.95 (*1-55523-443-7*) Winston-Derek.

Brophy, Susan. The Fighting Ground: A Study Guide. (gr. 4-7). 1988. tchr's. ed. & wkbk. 14.95 (*0-88122-082-5*) LRN Links.

Brose, David S. Yesterday's River: The Archaeology of Ten Thousand Years along the Tennessee-Tombigbee Waterway. Schornak, Mark, et al, illus. 160p. (gr. 10). 1990. pap. 9.75 (*1-878600-00-1*) Cleve Mus Nat Hist.

Bros. Grimm. King of the Golden Mountain. Cutts, David, ed. Watling, James, illus. LC 87-11262. 32p. (gr. 2-4). 1988. PLB 9.79 (*0-8167-1055-4*); pap. text ed. 1.95 (*0-8167-1056-2*) Troll Assocs.

Brost, Amy, jt. auth. see Bach, Jennifer.

Brothers, Don. West Indies. (Illus.). 128p. (gr. 5 up). 1989. lib. bdg. 14.95 (*1-55546-793-8*) Chelsea Hse.

Brott, Ardyth. Jeremy's Decision. Martchenko, Michael, illus. 32p. (ps-3). 1990. 12.95 (*0-916291-31-6*) Kane-Miller Bk.

Broughton, Bruno. Fishing. (Illus.). 32p. (gr. k-4). 1991. 11.90 (*0-531-18432-3*, Pub. by Bookwright Pr) Watts.

Broughton, Jacqueline P. Garden Flowers to Color. (Illus.). 32p. (ps-2). 1972. pap. 1.25 (*0-913456-51-9*) Interbk Inc.

Brouillard, Anne. Three Cats. LC 91-34180. (Illus.). 32p. 1992. 13.95 (*0-934738-97-1*) Thomasson-Grant.

Broukal, Milada & Murphy, Peter. Introducing the U. S. A. A Cultural Reader. LC 92-35468. (Illus.). (gr. 5 up). 1993. pap. text ed. 11.95 (*0-8013-0984-0*) Longman.

Broun, Heywood. The Fifty-First Dragon. Redpath, Ann, ed. Delessert, Etienne, illus. 32p. (gr. 4 up). 1985. PLB 13.95s.p. (*0-88682-005-7*) Creative Ed.

Broussard, Lucretia-del J., jt. auth. see Johnson, Zenobia M.

Broutin, Christian, illus. Arbre. (FRE.). (ps-1). 1989. 14. 95 (*2-07-035712-0*) Schoenhof.

Brouwer, Norman, jt. auth. see Hellman, Nina.

Brouwer, Sigmund. Barbarians from the Isle. 132p. (gr. 5-8). 1992. pap. 4.99 (*0-89693-116-1*) SP Pubns.
—A City of Dreams. 132p. (Orig.). (gr. 4-8). 1993. pap. 4.99 (*1-56476-048-0*, Victor Books) SP Pubns.
—Doctor Drabbles Remarkable Underwater Breathing Pills. (gr. 4-7). 1991. pap. 5.99 (*0-89693-903-0*, Victor Books) SP Pubns.
—The Downtown Desperadoes. 132p. 1991. pap. 4.99 (*0-89693-860-3*) SP Pubns.
—The Forsaken Crusade. (Orig.). 1992. pap. 46.00 (*0-89693-118-8*, Victor Books) SP Pubns.
—The Legend of Burning Water. (Orig.). 1992. pap. 4.99 (*0-89693-117-X*, Victor Books) SP Pubns.
—Madness at Moonshiner's Bay. 132p. (gr. 5-8). 1992. pap. 4.99 (*0-89693-056-4*) SP Pubns.
—Merlin's Destiny. 132p. (Orig.). (gr. 4-8). 1993. pap. 4.99 (*1-56476-049-9*, Victor Books) SP Pubns.
—Race for the Part Street Treasure. 132p. 1991. pap. 4.99 (*0-89693-859-X*) SP Pubns.
—Short Cuts. LC 93-26411. 132p. (Orig.). (gr. 3-7). 1993. pap. 4.99 (*1-56476-158-4*, Victor Books) SP Pubns.
—Sunrise at the Mayan Temple. (gr. 3-6). 1992. pap. 4.99 (*0-89693-057-2*, Victor Books) SP Pubns.
—Wings of an Angel. 132p. (gr. 5-8). 1992. pap. 4.99 (*0-89693-115-3*) SP Pubns.

Brouwer, Sigmund & Davidson, Wayne. Dr. Drabble's Amazing Invisibility Mirror. 24p. 1992. 5.99 (*0-89693-970-7*) SP Pubns.
—Dr. Drabble's Astounding Musical Mesmerizer. Bell, Bill, illus. 24p. (ps-2). 1991. 5.99 (*0-89693-904-9*) SP Pubns.
—Dr. Drabble's Incredible Identical Robot Innovation. Bell, Bill, illus. 24p. (ps-2). 1991. 5.99 (*0-89693-902-2*) SP Pubns.
—Dr. Drabble's Phenomenal Anti-Gravity Dust Machine. Bell, Bill, illus. 24p. (ps-2). 1991. 5.99 (*0-89693-901-4*) SP Pubns.
—Dr. Drabble's Spectacular Shrinker-Enlarger. 24p. 1992. 5.99 (*0-89693-969-3*) SP Pubns.

Brow, Marc. Arthur's Baby. (ps-3). 1990. 4.95 (*0-316-11007-8*, Joy St Bks) Little.

Browder, Anne, ed. see Browder, Atlantis T. & Browder, Anthony T.

Browder, Anthony T., jt. auth. see Browder, Atlantis T.

Browder, Atlantis T. & Browder, Anthony T. My First Trip to Africa. Browder, Anne, ed. Aaron, Malcolm, illus. LC 91-70328. 38p. (Orig.). 1991. 16.95 (*0-924944-02-1*); pap. 8.95 (*0-924944-01-3*) Inst Karmic.

Brower, Bob, illus. Latter-Day Saints Temple Coloring Book. 80p. (Orig.). (gr. 2-6). 1993. pap. 5.95 (*0-910523-22-3*) Grandin Bk Co.
—Presidents of the LDS Church Coloring Book. 50p. (Orig.). (gr. 2-6). 1993. pap. 5.95 (*0-910523-21-5*) Grandin Bk Co.

Brower, Jamil L. Do Unto Others. (gr. 4 up). 1992. 6.95 (*0-533-09665-0*) Vantage.

Brower, Nancy, ed. see Martin, Michael.

Brower, Pauline. Baden-Powell: Founder of the Boy Scouts. LC 89-33750. 32p. (gr. 2-4). 1989. PLB 14.60 (*0-516-04173-8*) Childrens.

Brower, Pauline, jt. auth. see Behrens, June.

Brown. On Christmas Eve. Date not set. 15.00 (*0-06-023648-5*, Festival); PLB 14.89 (*0-06-023649-3*, Festival) HarpC Child Bks.
—Sleepy ABC. Date not set. 14.00 (*0-06-024284-1*, Festival); PLB 13.89 (*0-06-024285-X*, Festival) HarpC Child Bks.
—Where Have You Been? 1993. pap. 28.67 (*0-590-71408-2*) Scholastic Inc.

Brown, Adam. Nuclear Weapons. (Illus.). 48p. (gr. 5 up). 1987. PLB 18.60 (*0-86592-278-0*); 13.95 (*0-685-67572-6*) Rourke Corp.

Brown, Alan & Perkins, Judy. Christianity. (Illus.). 68p. (gr. 7-9). 1989. 19.95 (*0-7134-5319-2*, Pub. by Batsford UK) Trafalgar.

Brown, Alan, tr. see Hemon, Louis.

Brown, Alice, jt. auth. see Kirk, Pat.

Brown, Alice H. Tom Dooley, Jungle Doctor. (Illus.). (gr. 1-3). 1979. pap. 1.95 (*0-03-049441-9*) Harper SF.

Brown, Angela. Prayers That Avail Much for Children. (Illus.). 32p. (Orig.). (gr. 1-3). 1983. pap. 3.98 (*0-89274-296-8*) Harrison Hse.

Brown, Ann. Handmade Christmas Gifts That Are Actually Usable. Small, Carol B., illus. LC 87-31993. 75p. (Orig.). (gr. k-6). 1987. pap. 6.95 (*0-938267-03-5*) Bold Prodns.
—TV or Not TV. Leigh, Tom, illus. 24p. (ps-3). 1992. 1.95 (*0-307-12652-8*, 12652, Golden Pr) Western Pub.

Brown, Ann & Bold, Mary. Travel-Ogs: The Do-It-Yourself Survival Kit for Traveling with Parents, Siblings, & Dirty Socks. Small, Carol B., illus. 80p. (Orig.). (gr. 1-6). 1988. wkbk. 6.95 (*0-938267-06-X*) Bold Prodns.

Brown, Anthony. Gorilla. Brown, Anthony, illus. LC 85-13. 32p. (ps-2). 1989. pap. 6.00 (*0-394-82225-0*) Knopf Bks Yng Read.

Brown, Arlene. Booklinks: Writing Connections to Children's Literature. 96p. (gr. 3-8). 1993. pap. text ed. 13.95 (*0-944459-61-7*) ECS Lrn Systs.

Brown, B. Holborrk, ed. see Lassik, Grace E.

Brown, Bernice. The Magic Caterpillar. Eberspacher, Jeff, ed. Brown, Bernice, illus. 48p. (gr. k-3). 1992. PLB 9.95 casebound (*1-877740-19-5*); pap. 5.50 (*1-877740-20-9*) Nel-Mar Pub.

Brown, Beth, compiled by. Fairy Tales of Birds & Beasts, Vol. 1. (Illus.). 128p. (gr. 3-7). 1991. PLB 13.95 (*0-87460-375-7*) Lion Bks.

Brown, Betty A. & Raven, Arlene. Exposures, Women & Their Art. Love, Kenna, photos by. Comini, Alessandra, intro. by. (Illus.). 128p. (gr. 9 up). 1989. 39.95 (*0-939165-10-4*); ltd. ed. 60.00 (*0-939165-13-9*); pap. 24.95 (*0-939165-11-2*) NewSage Press.

Brown, Bill & Glass, Malcolm. Important Words: A Book for Poets & Writers. Stafford, William, frwd. by. 198p. (Orig.). (gr. 9-12). 1991. pap. text ed. 16.00x (*0-86709-271-8*, 0271) Boynton Cook Pubs.

Brown, Bill, ed. see Dichmann, Kurt.

Brown, Bob. More Science for You: One Hundred Twelve Illustrated Experiments. (Illus.). 128p. (ps-8). 1988. 12.95 (*0-8306-9125-1*, 3125); pap. 7.95 (*0-8306-3125-9*, 3125) TAB Bks.
—The Turtle's Darshan for All the Animals. (Illus.). 32p. (gr. 2 up). 1973. pap. 5.00 (*0-913078-17-4*) Sheriar Pr.

Brown, Carol S., jt. auth. see Glazer, Susan M.

Brown, Cathy J. & Paterson, Debi. Bouncy Bunny's Birthday: A Family Story about Bravery. Adams, Kathy R., illus. LC 86-61065. 32p. (Orig.). (gr. 1-3). 1985. pap. 8.75 (*0-9614796-0-4*) C J Brown.
—Bouncy Bunny's Birthday: A Family Story about Bravery. Adams, Kathy R., illus. 32p. (Orig.). (gr. 1-3). 1985. pap. 8.75 (*0-318-19386-8*) Offset Hse.

Brown, Charlene. Consumer Guide to Public Auctions: Everything You Need to Know to Profit from Public Auctions. (ps-3). 1993. pap. 7.95 (*0-929230-18-3*) United Res Bks.

Brown, Charlene & Davis, Carolyn. Clay Fun. (Illus.). 64p. (Orig.). (gr. k up). 1989. pap. 5.95 (*0-929261-28-3*, BA03) W Foster Pub.
—Color Fun. Davis, Carolyn, illus. 64p. (Orig.). (gr. k up). 1990. pap. 5.95 (*0-929261-27-5*, BA02) W Foster Pub.
—Colored Pencil Fun: How to Use Color Pencils. Davis, Carolyn, illus. 64p. (Orig.). (gr. k up). 1990. pap. 5.95 (*1-56010-058-3*, BA10) W Foster Pub.
—Comic Strip Fun. (Illus.). 64p. (Orig.). (gr. k up). 1989. pap. 5.95 (*0-929261-29-1*, BA04) W Foster Pub.
—Craft Painting Fun: How to Paint on Objects. Sprague, Sydney, ed. Davis, Carolyn, illus. 64p. (Orig.). 1991. pap. 5.95 (*1-56010-071-0*, BA12) W Foster Pub.
—Drawing Fun. Davis, Carolyn, illus. 64p. (Orig.). (gr. k up). 1988. pap. 5.95 (*0-929261-26-7*, BA01) W Foster Pub.
—Felt Tip Fun: How to Use Felt Tip Pens. Davis, Carolyn, illus. 64p. (Orig.). (gr. k up). 1990. pap. 5.95 (*1-56010-057-5*, BA09) W Foster Pub.
—Paper Art Fun. Davis, Carolyn, illus. 64p. (Orig.). (gr. k up). 1988. pap. 5.95 (*0-929261-31-3*, BA06) W Foster Pub.
—Poster Fun. (Illus.). 64p. (Orig.). (gr. k up). 1988. pap. 5.95 (*0-929261-30-5*, BA05) W Foster Pub.

Brown, Charlene, jt. auth. see Davis, Carolyn.

Brown, Charles. Demons Rule. Bell, Rob, ed. Boonthanakit, Ted & Chacon, Joe, illus. 32p. (Orig.). (gr. 12). 1990. pap. 7.00 (*1-55806-110-X*, 412) Iron Crown Ent Inc.

Brown, Charlotte, adapted by. The Taming of the Shrew. (Illus.). 32p. (gr. 5 up). 1987. pap. 2.00 (*0-88680-276-8*); royalty on application 20.00 (*0-685-67569-5*) I E Clark.

Brown, Christopher, as told by. Favorite Bible Stories, Vol. 1. pap. 2.50 (*0-89954-378-2*) Antioch Pub Co.
—Favorite Bible Stories, Vol. 2. (Illus.). 24p. (gr. 3-7). 1985. pap. 2.50 (*0-89954-416-9*) Antioch Pub Co.
—Favorite Bible Stories, Vol. 3. 1989. pap. 2.50 (*0-89954-597-1*) Antioch Pub Co.

Brown, Christopher, ed. Noah's Ark. Rudegeair, Jean, illus. 24p. (gr. 2-6). 1984. pap. 2.50 (*0-89954-287-5*) Antioch Pub Co.

Brown, Claude. Manchild in the Promised Land. 432p. (RL 7). 1966. pap. 4.95 (*0-451-15741-9*, Sig) NAL-Dutton.

Brown, Craig. City Sounds. LC 90-25632. (Illus.). 24p. (ps-4). 1992. 14.00 (*0-688-10028-7*); PLB 13.93 (*0-688-10029-5*) Greenwillow.
—In the Spring. LC 92-17465. (Illus.). 24p. (ps up). 1994. write for info. (*0-688-10983-7*); PLB write for info. (*0-688-10984-5*) Greenwillow.
—My Barn. LC 90-41758. (Illus.). 24p. (ps up). 1991. 13. 95 (*0-688-08785-X*); PLB 13.88 (*0-688-08786-8*) Greenwillow.

—Patchwork Farmer. LC 88-29229. 24p. (ps up). 1989. 12.95 (*0-688-07735-8*); PLB 12.88 (*0-688-07736-6*) Greenwillow.

Brown, David. The Random House Book of How Things Were Built. LC 91-27638. (Illus.). 144p. (Orig.). (gr. 3-7). 1992. PLB 19.99 (*0-679-92044-7*); pap. 15.00 (*0-679-82044-2*) Random Bks Yng Read.

Brown, Dean R. Simply Science: Discovering the Fascinations of Our World. Goede, Don, illus. 206p. (gr. 7-12). 1993. pap. text ed. 24.95 (*1-880293-02-1*) Alaken.

Brown, Dee. Cavalry Scout. (gr. 7 up). 1989. pap. 2.95 (*0-440-20227-2*) Dell.

—Wounded Knee: An Indian History of the American West. Ehrlick, Emy, adapted by. 192p. (gr. 7 up). 1975. pap. 1.50 (*0-440-95768-0*, LFL) Dell.

—Wounded Knee: An Indian History of the American West. Ehrlich, Amy, adapted by. (Illus.). 224p. (gr. 7 up). 1993. pap. 9.95 (*0-8050-2700-9*, Bks Young Read) H Holt & Co.

—Yellow Horse. 1989. pap. 2.95 (*0-440-20246-9*) Dell.

Brown, Diane B., jt. auth. see Hawthorne, Terri B.

Brown, Don. Ruth Law Thrills a Nation. LC 92-45701. (gr. 9-12). 1993. 13.45 (*0-395-66404-7*) Ticknor & Fields.

Brown, Dottie. Alabama. LC 93-37796. 1994. PLB write for info. (*0-8225-2741-3*) Lerner Pubns.

—Delaware. LC 92-44845. 1993. PLB 17.50 (*0-8225-2733-2*) Lerner Pubns.

—Kentucky. Lerner Geography Department Staff, ed. (Illus.). 72p. (gr. 4-7). 1992. 17.50 (*0-8225-2715-4*) Lerner Pubns.

—New Hampshire. LC 92-28662. (Illus.). 1993. 17.50 (*0-8225-2730-8*) Lerner Pubns.

—Ohio. Lerner Geography Department Staff, ed. (Illus.). 72p. (gr. 3-6). 1992. PLB 17.50 (*0-8225-2725-1*) Lerner Pubns.

Brown, Drollene. Belva Lockwood Wins Her Case. Levine, Abby, ed. LC 87-2114. (Illus.). 48p. (gr. 3-7). 1987. PLB 11.95 (*0-8075-0630-3*) A Whitman.

—Sybil Rides for Independence. Levine, Abby, ed. Apple, Margot, illus. LC 84-17219. 48p. (gr. 2-5). 1985. 11.95 (*0-8075-7684-0*) A Whitman.

Brown, Edward. Just Around the Corner in New Jersey. (Illus.). 112p. (gr. 6 up). 1987. pap. 7.95 (*0-912608-17-X*) Mid Atlantic.

Brown, Eric. Different Shades of Courage: A Coloring & Activities Book of African American Achievement, Vol. 1. Sheen, Jen, ed. (Illus.). 53p. (Orig.). (gr. 4 up). 1993. pap. 9.95 (*0-9636468-0-X*) Little Tike. Introducing from Little Tike Publishing Company, DIFFERENT SHADES OF COURAGE, a coloring & activities book. This book is set with sixteen historical African American influentials starting from early eighteenth century to the late nineteenth century. Volume one in a series of new books from the author & illustrator Eric Brown, shows children a different way of learning about very different heroes. It has over fifty pages, with games & mazes to enhance a child's learning of their new heroes. All the artwork is hand done on a computer by the author & writer, & has been painstakingly drawn to ensure full features of the contemporaries. The purpose of this work is to celebrate the achievements & goals gained by people of African Descent earlier in the history of America, & in other countries as well. It is also a book that hopefully will not only educate African Americans, but also educate other cultures on the struggle & achievements of early 18th & 19th century Black contemporaries. To order: Little Tike Publishing Co., P.O. Box 191743, Roxbury, MA 02119. *Publisher Provided Annotation.*

Brown, Evelyn M. Kateri Tekakwitha: Mohawk Maid. LC 91-72271. (Illus.). 178p. 1991. pap. 9.95 (*0-89870-380-8*) Ignatius Pr.

Brown, F. K. Last Hurdle. Spier, Peter, illus. LC 87-29761. 202p. (gr. 3-9). 1988. Repr. of 1953 ed. 17.50 (*0-208-02212-0*, Linnet) Shoe String.

Brown, Faye. Chinch Bugs, Chinky Pins, & Chinie-Berry Beads. Brown, Trillie, illus. 191p. (Orig.). 1990. pap. 9.95 (*0-943487-24-2*) Sevgo Pr.

Brown, Fern. Baby-Sitter on Horseback. (gr. 5 up). 1988. pap. 2.95 (*0-449-70283-9*, Juniper) Fawcett.

Brown, Fern G. Franklin Pierce: Fourteenth President of the United States. Young, Richard G., ed. LC 88-30050. (Illus.). (gr. 5-9). 1989. PLB 17.26 (*0-944483-25-9*) Garrett Ed Corp.

—Hereditary Disease. LC 87-8139. (Illus.). 96p. (gr. 4-9). 1987. PLB 10.90 (*0-531-10386-2*) Watts.

—Indians of North America. 1995. PLB write for info. (*0-8050-3251-7*); pap. write for info. (*0-8050-3250-9*) H Holt & Co.

—James A. Garfield: Twentieth President of the United States. Young, Richard G., ed. LC 89-39953. (Illus.). 128p. (gr. 5-9). 1990. PLB 17.26 (*0-944483-63-1*) Garrett Ed Corp.

—Owls. Perrotta, Mary, ed. LC 90-13093. (Illus.). 64p. (gr. 3-5). 1991. PLB 12.90 (*0-531-20008-6*) Watts.

—Special Olympics. Rich, Mary P., ed. LC 91-31661. (Illus.). 64p. (gr. 3-5). 1992. PLB 12.90 (*0-531-20062-0*) Watts.

—Teen Guide to Caring for Your Unborn Baby. LC 88-51487. (Illus.). 62p. (gr. 7-12). 1989. PLB 13.40 (*0-531-10668-3*) Watts.

—Teen Guide to Childbirth. (Illus.). 64p. (gr. 7 up). 1990. pap. 4.95 (*0-531-15208-1*) Watts.

Brown, Forman. The Generous Jefferson Bartleby Jones. (Illus.). 32p. (Orig.). (gr. 1-5). 1991. pap. 7.95 (*1-55583-198-2*) Alyson Pubns.

Brown, Frances. My First Book of Words. LC 78-58344. 144p. (gr. k-6). 1979. Walker Educ.

Brown, Gene. Anne Frank: Child of the Holocaust. (Illus.). 64p. (gr. 3-7). PLB 14.95 (*1-56711-030-4*) Blackbirch.

—Anne Frank: Child of the Holocaust. (Illus.). 64p. (gr. 3-7). 1993. pap. 7.95 (*1-56711-049-5*) Blackbirch.

—Bette Davis: Film Star. (Illus.). 64p. (gr. 3-7). PLB 14.95 (*1-56711-028-2*) Blackbirch.

—Conflict in Europe & the Great Depression: World War I (1914-1940) LC 93-24998. (Illus.). 64p. (gr. 5-8). 1993. PLB 14.95 (*0-8050-2585-5*) TFC Bks Ny.

—Discovery & Settlement: Europe Meets the "New World", 1490-1700. LC 93-8537. (gr. 5-8). 1993. PLB 14.95 (*0-8050-2574-X*) TFC Bks NY.

—Duke Ellington. Easton, Emily, ed. (Illus.). 128p. (gr. 7-9). 1990. lib. bdg. 17.98 (*0-382-09906-0*); pap. 14.95 (*0-382-24034-0*) Silver Burdett Pr.

—H. Ross Perot. LC 93-11998. (gr. 1-8). 1993. 15.93 (*0-86592-060-5*); 11.95s.p. (*0-685-66543-7*) Rourke Enter.

—The Nation in Turmoil: Civil Rights & the Vietnam War, 1960-1973. LC 93-24995. (Illus.). 64p. (gr. 5-8). 1993. PLB 14.95 (*0-8050-2588-X*) TFC Bks Ny.

—The Nineteen Ninety-Two Election. LC 92-19963. (Illus.). 64p. (gr. 5-8). 1992. PLB 15.90 (*1-56294-080-5*) Millbrook Pr.

—The Struggle to Grow: Expansionism & Industrialization, 1880-1913. LC 93-24992. (Illus.). 64p. (gr. 5-8). 1993. PLB 14.95 (*0-8050-2584-7*) TFC Bks NY.

—Violence on America's Streets. LC 91-28929. (Illus.). 64p. (gr. 5-8). 1992. PLB 15.90 (*1-56294-155-0*) Millbrook Pr.

—Violence on America's Streets. 1992. pap. 4.95 (*0-395-62469-X*) HM.

Brown, George H., ed. see Donaldson, Judith E.

Brown, H. Jackson, Jr., ed. A Father's Book of Wisdom. 160p. 1988. pap. 5.95 (*0-9606550-1-8*) Porch Swing.

Brown, Harriet, jt. auth. see Friedhoffer.

Brown, Hayden & Dickins, Roberts. The Sombrero. Dickins, Robert, illus. LC 93-6633. 1994. write for info. (*0-383-03714-X*) SRA Schl Grp.

Brown, Irene B. Before the Lark. Milam, Larry, illus. 180p. (gr. 4 up). 1992. pap. 7.95 (*0-936085-22-3*) Blue Heron OR.

—Morning Glory Afternoon. Milam, Larry, illus. 224p. (gr. 7 up). 1991. pap. 8.95 (*0-936085-20-7*) Blue Heron OR.

—Skitterbrain. Milam, Larry, illus. LC 78-18349. 128p. (gr. 4 up). 1992. pap. 6.95 (*0-936085-21-5*) Blue Heron OR.

—Willow Whip. 208p. (Orig.). (gr. 5 up). pap. 8.95 (*0-936085-23-1*) Blue Heron OR.

Brown, J. Aaron, ed. A Child's Gift of Lullabyes. Vienneau, Jim, illus. 14p. (ps). 1987. Book packaged with cassette. 12.95 (*0-927945-01-0*) Someday Baby.

—Un Regalo de Arrullos Para Ninos. Vienneau, Jim, illus. Pineda, Sysy, tr. (SPA., Illus.). 14p. (ps). 1988. Book with cassette. 12.95 (*0-927945-02-9*) Someday Baby.

—The Rock-a-Bye Collection. Vienneau, Jim, illus. 12p. (Orig.). (ps). 1989. lyric bk. of lullabies & cassette 9.95 (*0-927945-00-2*) Someday Baby.

—The Rock-a-Bye Collection, Vols. 1 & 2. rev. ed. Vienneau, Jim, illus. 14p. (ps). 1990. incl. cassette 12.95 ea. Vol. 1 (*0-927945-03-7*) Vol. 2 (*0-927945-04-5*) Someday Baby.

—Snuggle Up: A Gift of Songs for Sweet Dreams. Vienneau, Jim, illus. 14p. (ps). 1992. incl. cass. tape 12.95 (*0-927945-05-3*) Someday Baby.

Brown, J. Aaron, ed. see Burnsed, Linda & Chaffin, Garry.

Brown, James E. Old Freight Train Coloring Book. (SPA & ENG.). 24p. (Orig.). 1992. pap. 0.50 (*0-9632358-0-X*) J E Brown.

Brown, Jane C. Whonk & Whonk Again. (ps-3). 1989. 13.45 (*0-395-49211-4*) HM.

Brown, Janice. Missing! 192p. 1990. pap. 4.99 (*0-7459-1876-X*) Lion USA.

—Sweet 'n' Sour Summer. 128p. (gr. 9-12). 1989. pap. text ed. 4.99 (*0-7459-1803-4*) Lion USA.

Brown, Jeff. Clement Aplati. Ross, Tony, illus. (FRE.). 79p. 1989. pap. 10.95 (*2-07-031196-1*) Schoenhof.

—Flat Stanley. Ungerer, Tomi, illus. LC 63-17525. 64p. (gr. 1-5). 1964. PLB 13.89 (*0-06-020681-0*) HarpC Child Bks.

—Flat Stanley. Ungerer, Tomi, illus. LC 63-17525. 48p. (gr. 2-5). 1989. pap. 4.95 (*0-06-440293-2*, Trophy) HarpC Child Bks.

—We Like Kids! Letters & Numbers Songbook. (Illus.). 88p. (ps-3). 1994. pap. 13.95 (*0-673-36126-8*) GdYrBks.

Brown, Jeff, et al. We Like Kids! Songbook. (Illus.). 88p. (Orig.). (ps-3). 1992. pap. 13.95 (*0-673-36038-5*) GdYrBks.

—We Like Kids! Songs for the Earth. (Illus.). 80p. (Orig.). (ps-3). 1992. pap. 13.95 (*0-673-36052-0*) GdYrBks.

Brown, Jerome C. Classics Papercrafts. (gr. k-5). 1991. 8.95 (*0-8224-1352-3*) Fearon Teach Aids.

—Dinosaur Color & Pattern Book. (gr. k-3). 1989. pap. 9.95 (*0-8224-2322-7*) Fearon Teach Aids.

—Fables & Tales PaperCrafts. (gr. k-5). 1989. pap. 8.95 (*0-8224-3155-6*) Fearon Teach Aids.

—Folk Tale PaperCrafts. (gr. k-5). 1989. pap. 8.95 (*0-8224-3156-4*) Fearon Teach Aids.

—Great Gifts for All Accasions That Kids Can Make for Practically Nothing. (gr. 1-6). 1986. pap. 10.95 (*0-8224-3596-9*) Fearon Teach Aids.

—Holiday Art Projects. (gr. 3-12). 1984. pap. 5.95 (*0-8224-5190-5*) Fearon Teach Aids.

—Holiday Crafts & Greeting Cards. (gr. 3-6). 1982. pap. 6.95 (*0-8224-5194-8*) Fearon Teach Aids.

—Holiday Gifts & Decorations Kids Can Make for Practically Nothing. (gr. 1-6). 1986. pap. 10.95 (*0-8224-3595-0*) Fearon Teach Aids.

—Legends & Fables Papercrafts. (gr. k-5). 1991. 8.95 (*0-8224-4234-5*) Fearon Teach Aids.

—Mother Goose PaperCrafts. (gr. k-5). 1989. pap. 8.95 (*0-8224-3154-8*) Fearon Teach Aids.

—Paper Designs. (gr. 1-6). 1982. pap. 6.95 (*0-8224-5193-X*) Fearon Teach Aids.

—Tales from Many Lands Papercrafts. (gr. k-5). 1991. 8.95 (*0-8224-3157-2*) Fearon Teach Aids.

Brown, John J. American Angler's Guide: or Complete Fisher's Manual for the U. S. (Illus.). 332p. (gr. 10 up). 1993. Repr. of 1858 ed. 42.90 (*1-56416-117-X*) Derrydale Pr.

Brown, John R. Living Legends. LC 89-50186. 124p. (Orig.). 1990. pap. 5.95 (*0-916383-89-X*) Aegina Pr.

—Shakespeare & His Theatre. Gentleman, David, illus. LC 81-8441. 64p. (gr. 6 up). 1982. 14.95 (*0-688-00850-X*) Lothrop.

Brown, Jordan. Elizabeth Blackwell. Horner, Matina S., intro. by. (Illus.). 112p. (gr. 5 up). 1989. 17.95 (*1-55546-642-7*) Chelsea Hse.

Brown, Judy, jt. auth. see Cresswell, Helen.

Brown, Julie. How People Worship. LC 90-23939. (Illus.). 64p. (gr. 2-3). 1991. PLB 19.93 (*0-8368-0047-8*) Gareth Stevens Inc.

Brown, Julie & Brown, Robert. Earth's Energy & Fuel. LC 91-2803. (Illus.). 64p. (gr. 2-3). 1991. PLB 19.93 (*0-8368-0077-X*) Gareth Stevens Inc.

Brown, Julie & Hott, Michael. Inventing Things. LC 89-11506. (Illus.). 64p. (gr. 2-3). 1990. PLB 19.93 (*0-8368-0035-4*) Gareth Stevens Inc.

Brown, Julie, ed. see Taylor-Boyd, Susan.

Brown, Kathryn. Muledred. (Illus.). 32p. (ps-3). 1990. 12.95 (*0-15-256265-6*) HarBrace.

Brown, Kay. Willy's Summer Dream. 132p. (gr. 7 up). 1989. 13.95 (*0-15-200064-1*, Gulliver Bks) HarBrace.

Brown, Ken. Nellie's Knot. LC 92-27910. (Illus.). 32p. (ps-1). 1993. SBE 13.95 (*0-02-714930-7*, Four Winds) Macmillan Child Grp.

Brown, Kenneth. Barn House Book: Rhymes, Riddles, & Jokes. Brown, Kenneth, illus. Date not set. 12.95 (*1-56743-046-5*) Amistad Pr.

Brown, Kenneth, illus. Dollhouse Book: Color & Counting Concepts. 1994. 12.95 (*1-56743-044-9*) Amistad Pr.

Brown, Kent. Why Can't I Fly? 1990. 13.95 (*0-385-41208-8*) Doubleday.

Brown, Keven, ed. see Cuevas, Lou.

Brown, Kevin. Romare Bearden. King, Coretta Scott, intro. by. (Illus.). 112p. (gr. 5 up). 1993. PLB 17.95 (*0-7910-1119-4*) Chelsea Hse.

Brown, Kevin & Mitsch, Ray. The Quest. LC 92-26406. 1993. 9.99 (*0-8407-4560-5*) Nelson.

—Step by Step. LC 93-18823. Date not set. 7.99 (*0-8407-3426-3*) Nelson.

Brown, Laurene K. & Brown, Marc. Dinosaurs Divorce: A Guide for Changing Families. Brown, Marc, illus. 32p. (ps-3). 1988. 14.95 (*0-316-11248-8*); pap. 5.95 (*0-316-10996-7*) Little.

—Dinosaurs Travel: A Guide for Families on the Go. Brown, Marc, illus. 32p. (ps-3). 1988. 13.95 (*0-316-11076-0*) Little.

—Visiting the Art Museum. LC 85-32552. (Illus.). 32p. (ps-1). 1986. 14.99 (*0-525-44233-2*, DCB); (DCB) Dutton Child Bks.

Brown, Laurie K. Dinosaurs Alive & Well! A Guide to Good Health. (ps-3). 1992. pap. 5.95 (*0-316-11009-4*, Joy St Bks) Little.

—Dinosaurs Travel, Vol. 1. (ps-3). 1991. pap. 5.95 (*0-316-11253-4*) Little.

—Rex & Lilly at Play. Brown, Marc, illus. LC 93-25877. 1994. 12.95 (*0-316-11386-7*) Little.

—Toddler Time: A Book to Share with Your Toddler. Brown, Marc, illus. 48p. 1990. 14.95 (*0-316-11263-1*, Joy St Bks) Little.

Brown, Laurie K. & Brown, Marc. Dinosaurs Alive & Well! A Guide to Good Health. (ps-3). 1990. 14.95 (*0-316-10998-3*, Joy St Bks) Little.

—Dinosaurs to the Rescue: A Guide to Protecting Our Planet. Brown, Marc, illus. (ps-3). 1992. 14.95 (*0-316-11087-6*, Joy St Bks) Little.

Brown, Lawrence. Thinking about the World: Building Geography Foundations. 1993. pap. 16.00 (*0-201-45546-3*) Addison-Wesley.

Brown, Lewis S., ed. see Ellenberger, W., et al.

Brown, Lynn. Fire & Firecrackers. 3rd ed. Walker, Granville, Jr., ed. Jackson, Gregory A., illus. 14p. (Orig.). (ps-6). 1982. pap. 2.97x (*0-9608466-1-1*) Fun Reading.

—Ms. Worm. 3rd ed. Walker, Granville, Jr., ed. Jackson, Gregory A., illus. (Orig.). (ps-6). 1982. pap. 2.95x (*0-9608466-0-3*) Fun Reading.

Brown, M. K. Let's Go Swimming with Mr. Sillypants. Brown, M. K., illus. LC 85-29900. 32p. (ps-2). 1992. pap. 4.99 (*0-517-59030-1*) Crown Bks Yng Read.

—Sally's Room. 32p. 1992. 13.95 (*0-590-44709-2*, Scholastic Hardcover) Scholastic Inc.

—Sally's Room. (gr. 5-8). 1993. pap. 3.95 (*0-590-44710-6*) Scholastic Inc.

Brown, Maggie W. Making Decisions. Proof Positive-Farrowlyne Associates, Inc. Staff, illus. 61p. (Orig.). 1990. text ed. 2.80 stitched (*0-88489-200-X*); tchr's ed. 6.00 (*0-88489-201-8*) St Marys.

Brown, Marc. Arthur Babysits. (Illus.). 32p. (ps-3). 1992. 14.95 (*0-316-11293-3*, Joy St Bks) Little.

—Arthur Goes to Camp. Brown, Marc, illus. LC 81-15588. 32p. (ps-3). 1984. 14.95 (*0-316-11218-6*, Joy St Bks); pap. 4.95 (*0-316-11058-2*, Joy St Bks) Little.

—Arthur Meets the President. (ps-3). 1991. 14.95 (*0-316-11265-8*) Little.

—Arthur Meets the President: An Arthur Adventure. (ps-3). 1992. pap. 4.95 (*0-316-11291-7*, Joy St Bks) Little.

—Arthur's April Fool. LC 82-20368. (Illus.). 32p. (ps-3). 1985. 14.95 (*0-316-11196-1*, Joy St Bks); pap. 4.95 (*0-316-11234-8*, Joy St Bks) Little.

—Arthur's Baby, Vol. 1. 32p. 1987. 14.95 (*0-316-11123-6*, Joy St Bks) Little.

—Arthur's Birthday. Brown, Marc, illus. 32p. (ps-3). 1989. 14.95 (*0-316-11073-6*, Joy St Bks) Little.

—Arthur's Birthday. (ps-3). 1991. pap. 4.95 (*0-316-11074-4*) Little.

—Arthur's Chicken Pox. LC 93-22996. 1994. 14.95 (*0-316-11384-0*) Little.

—Arthur's Christmas. Brown, Marc, illus. LC 84-4373. (ps-3). 1985. 14.95 (*0-316-11180-5*, Joy St Bks); pap. 4.95 (*0-316-10993-2*) Little.

—Arthur's Eyes. Brown, Marc, illus. LC 79-11734. (ps-3). 1979. lib. bdg. 14.95 (*0-316-11063-9*, Joy St Bks) Little.

—Arthur's Eyes. Brown, Marc, illus. 32p. (ps-3). 1986. pap. 4.95 (*0-316-11069-8*, Joy St Bks) Little.

—Arthur's Family Vacation. LC 92-26650. 1993. 14.95 (*0-316-11312-3*) Little.

—Arthur's Halloween. Brown, Marc, illus. LC 82-14286. 32p. (ps-3). 1983. 14.95 (*0-316-11116-3*, Joy St Bks); pap. 4.95 (*0-316-11059-0*, Joy St Bks) Little.

—Arthur's Nose. Brown, Marc, illus. 32p. (ps-3). 1986. lib. bdg. 14.95 (*0-316-11193-7*, Joy St Bks); pap. 4.95 (*0-316-11070-1*, Joy St Bks) Little.

—Arthur's Pet Business. (ps-3). 1990. 14.95 (*0-316-11262-3*, Joy St Bks) Little.

—Arthur's Pet Business. (ps-3). 1993. pap. 4.95 (*0-316-11316-6*) Little.

—Arthur's Puppy. LC 92-46342. (gr. 1-8). 1993. 14.95 (*0-316-11355-7*, Joy St Bks) Little.

—Arthur's Teacher Trouble. Brown, Marc, illus. 32p. (ps-3). 1989. 13.95 (*0-316-11244-5*, Joy St Bks); pap. 4.95 (*0-316-11186-4*, Joy St Bks) Little.

—Arthur's Thanksgiving. Brown, Marc, illus. LC 83-798. 32p. (gr. 1-3). 1984. 14.95 (*0-316-11060-4*, Joy St Bks); pap. 4.95 (*0-316-11232-1*) Little.

—Arthur's Tooth. Brown, Marc, illus. 32p. (ps-3). 1985. 14.95 (*0-316-11245-3*, Joy St Bks) Little.

—Arthur's Tooth, Vol. 1. (ps-3). 1986. pap. 4.95 (*0-316-11246-1*) Little.

—Arthur's Valentine. Brown, Marc, illus. (ps-3). 1980. 14.95 (*0-316-11062-0*, Joy St Bks) Little.

—Arthur's Valentine. Brown, Marc, illus. 32p. (ps-3). 1988. pap. 4.95 (*0-316-11187-2*, Joy St Bks) Little.

—The Bionic Bunny Show. Brown, Laurene K., illus. 32p. (ps-3). 1985. 14.95 (*0-316-11120-1*, Joy St Bks); pap. 5.95 (*0-316-10992-4*, Joy St Bks) Little.

—D. W. All Wet. Brown, Marc, illus. (ps-3). 1988. 10.95 (*0-316-11077-9*, Joy St Bks) Little.

—D. W. All Wet. (ps-3). 1991. pap. 4.95 (*0-316-11268-2*) Little.

—D. W. Flips. Brown, Marc, illus. (ps-2). 1987. 12.95 (*0-316-11239-9*, Joy St Bks) Little.

—D. W. Flips. (ps-3). 1991. write for info.; pap. 4.95 (*0-316-11269-0*) Little.

—D. W. Just Big Enough. LC 92-19947. 1993. 11.95 (*0-316-11305-0*, Joy St Bks) Little.

—D. W. Rides Again! LC 93-7192. 1993. 12.95 (*0-316-11356-5*) Little.

—Finger Rhymes. LC 80-10173. (Illus.). 32p. (ps-2). 1980. 12.95 (*0-525-29732-4*, DCB) Dutton Child Bks.

—Hand Rhymes. Brown, Marc, illus. 32p. (ps-1). 1993. pap. 4.99 (*0-14-054939-0*, Puffin Unicorn) Puffin Bks.

—Party Rhymes. (Illus.). 48p. (ps-3). 1994. pap. 4.99 (*0-14-050318-8*, Puffin Unicorn) Puffin Bks.

—Pickle Things. Brown, Marc, illus. LC 80-10540. 48p. (ps-3). 1980. 5.95 (*0-8193-1027-1*) Parents.

—The Silly Tail Book. Brown, Marc, illus. LC 83-2250. 48p. (ps-3). 1983. 5.95 (*0-8193-1109-X*); pap. 2.95 (*0-8193-1158-8*) Parents.

—Spooky Riddles. LC 83-6051. (Illus.). 48p. (gr. k-3). 1983. 6.95 (*0-394-86093-4*) Beginner.

—There's No Place Like Home. Brown, Marc, illus. LC 84-4229. 48p. (ps-3). 1984. 5.95 (*0-8193-1125-1*) Parents.

—There's No Place Like Home. LC 93-13040. write for info. (*0-8368-0978-5*) Gareth Stevens Inc.

—The True Francine. Brown, Marc, illus. 32p. (ps-3). 1981. 15.95 (*0-316-11212-7*, Joy St Bks) Little.

—The True Francine. Brown, Marc, illus. (ps-3). 1987. pap. 5.95 (*0-316-11243-7*, Joy St Bks) Little.

—What Do You Call a Dumb Bunny? & Other Rabbit Riddles, Games, Jokes & Cartoons. Brown, Marc, illus. LC 82-21650. 32p. (ps-3). 1983. (Joy St Bks); pap. 4.95 (*0-316-11119-8*, Joy St Bks) Little.

—Witches Four. Brown, Marc, illus. LC 79-5263. 48p. (ps-3). 1980. 5.95 (*0-8193-1013-1*); PLB 5.95 (*0-8193-1014-X*) Parents.

—Witches Four. Brown, Marc, illus. 48p. (ps-2). 1991. pap. 2.95 (*0-448-41079-6*, G&D) Putnam Pub Group.

—Your First Garden Book. Brown, Marc, illus. (gr. 1 up). 1981. 12.45i (*0-316-11217-8*, Pub. by Atlantic Pr); pap. 6.95 (*0-316-11215-1*) Little.

Brown, Marc & Krensky, Stephen. Dinosaurs, Beware! A Safety Guide. Brown, Marc & Krensky, Stephen, illus. LC 82-15207. 32p. (ps-3). 1984. 14.95 (*0-316-11228-3*, Joy St Bks); pap. 6.95 (*0-316-11219-4*, Joy St Bks) Little.

—Perfect Pigs: An Introduction to Manners. LC 83-746. (Illus.). (ps-3). 1983. 15.95 (*0-316-11079-5*, Joy St Bks); pap. 6.95 (*0-316-11080-9*, Joy St Bks) Little.

Brown, Marc, jt. auth. see Brown, Laurene K.

Brown, Marc, jt. auth. see Brown, Laurie K.

Brown, Marc, ed. Hand Rhymes. Brown, Marc, illus. LC 84-25918. 32p. (ps-1). 1985. 13.95 (*0-525-44201-4*, DCB) Dutton Child Bks.

Brown, Marc, compiled by. & illus. Party Rhymes. LC 88-17680. 48p. (ps-3). 1988. 13.95 (*0-525-44402-5*, DCB) Dutton Child Bks.

—Play Rhymes. LC 87-13537. 32p. (ps-1). 1987. 12.95 (*0-525-44336-3*, DCB) Dutton Child Bks.

—Play Rhymes. 32p. (ps-1). 1993. pap. 4.99 (*0-14-054936-6*, Puffin Unicorn) Puffin Bks.

Brown, Marc, illus. Can You Jump Like a Frog? 8p. (ps-k). 1989. 5.95 (*0-525-44463-7*, DCB) Dutton Child Bks.

—One, Two Buckle My Shoe. 8p. (ps-k). 1989. 5.95 (*0-525-44462-9*, DCB) Dutton Child Bks.

—Teddy Bear, Teddy Bear. 8p. (ps-k). 1989. 5.95 (*0-525-44531-5*, DCB) Dutton Child Bks.

—Two Little Monkeys. 8p. (ps-k). 1989. 5.95 (*0-525-44533-1*, DCB) Dutton Child Bks.

Brown, Marcia. Award Puzzles: Shadow. 1990. 5.95 (*0-938971-63-8*) JTG Nashville.

—Backbone of the King. (Illus.). 180p. (gr. 4-8). 1984. Repr. of 1966 ed. 12.95 (*0-8248-0963-7*) UH Pr.

—Dick Whittington & His Cat. Brown, Marcia, illus. LC 50-9157. 32p. (gr. k-3). 1988. Repr. of 1950 ed. RSBE 14.95 (*0-684-18998-4*, Scribners Young Read) Macmillan Child Grp.

—Lotus Seeds: Children. LC 85-40288. 192p. (gr. 7 up). 1986. SBE 13.95 (*0-684-18490-7*, Scribners Young Read) Macmillan Child Grp.

—Once a Mouse. Brown, Marcia, illus. LC 61-14769. 32p. (ps-3). 1972. SBE 13.95 (*0-684-12662-1*, Scribners Young Read) Macmillan Child Grp.

—Once a Mouse. Brown, Marcia, illus. LC 89-32057. 32p. (gr. k-4). 1989. pap. 3.95 (*0-689-71343-6*, Aladdin) Macmillan Child Grp.

—Shadow. Brown, Marcia, illus. LC 86-3432. 38p. (ps up). 1986. pap. 3.95 (*0-689-71084-4*, Aladdin) Macmillan Child Grp.

—Sopa de Piedras. Mlawer, Teresa, tr. from ENG. Brown, Marcia, illus. (gr. 5-7). 1991. PLB 12.95 (*0-9625162-1-X*) Lectorum Pubns.

—Stone Soup. Brown, Marcia, illus. LC 47-11630. 48p. (ps-4). 1979. RSBE 13.95 (*0-684-92296-7*, Scribners Young Read); (Scribner) Macmillan Child Grp.

—Stone Soup. reissued ed. Brown, Marcia, illus. LC 86-10964. 48p. (ps-2). 1986. pap. 3.95 (*0-689-71103-4*, Aladdin) Macmillan Child Grp.

—Stone Soup. Brown, Marcia, illus. (gr. 1-4). 1987. incl. cassette 19.95 (*0-87499-053-X*); pap. 12.95 incl. cassette (*0-87499-052-1*); 4 paperbacks, cassette & guide 27.95 (*0-87499-054-8*) Live Oak Media.

Brown, Marcia & Perrault, Charles. Cinderella. (Illus.). (ps-5). 1971. RSBE 13.95 (*0-684-12676-1*, Scribners Young Read) Macmillan Child Grp.

Brown, Marcia, tr. from FRE see Cendrars, Blaise.

Brown, Marcia, tr. from FRE see Perrault, Charles.

Brown, Margaret. Xmas in the Barn. 1952. 14.00 (*0-690-19271-1*, Crowell Jr Bks) HarpC Child Bks.

Brown, Margaret F. Careers in Occupational Therapy. Rosen, Ruth, ed. (gr. 7-12). 1989. PLB 13.95 (*0-8239-0981-6*) Rosen Group.

Brown, Margaret W. Baby Animals. LC 88-18481. (Illus.). 32p. (ps-1). 1989. Repr. of 1941 ed. 10.95 (*0-394-82040-1*); lib. bdg. 11.99 (*0-394-92040-6*) Random Bks Yng Read.

—Big Red Barn. rev. ed. Bond, Felicia, illus. LC 85-45814. 32p. (ps-1). 1989. 14.00 (*0-06-020748-5*); PLB 13.89 (*0-06-020749-3*) HarpC Child Bks.

—Big Red Barn. Bond, Felicia, illus. LC 85-45814. 32p. (ps-1). 1991. 19.95 (*0-06-020750-7*) HarpC Child Bks.

—Big Red Barn. Bond, Felicia, illus. 32p. (ps-1). 1993. pap. 5.95 (*0-06-443349-8*, Trophy) HarpC Child Bks.

—A Child's Good Night Book. Charlot, Jean, illus. LC 84-43123. 32p. (ps-2). 1986. pap. 4.95 (*0-06-443114-2*, Trophy) HarpC Child Bks.

—A Child's Good Night Book. Charlot, Jean, illus. LC 91-45340. 32p. (ps-3). 1992. 10.00 (*0-06-021028-1*); PLB 9.89 (*0-06-020752-3*) HarpC Child Bks.

—Christmas in the Barn. Cooney, Barbara, illus. LC 52-7858. 32p. (gr. k-3). 1961. PLB 13.89 (*0-690-19272-X*, Crowell Jr Bks) HarpC Child Bks.

—Christmas in the Barn. Cooney, Barbara, illus. LC 85-42738. 32p. (ps-3). 1985. pap. 4.95 (*0-06-443082-0*, Trophy) HarpC Child Bks.

—David's Little Indian. Charlip, Remy, illus. 48p. (gr. 2-5). 1989. Repr. of 1954 ed. 10.95 (*0-929077-02-4*, Hopscotch Bks); PLB 10.95 (*0-317-92547-4*, Hopscotch Bks) Watermark Inc.

—David's Little Indian. (ps-3). 1992. pap. 3.25 (*0-440-40587-4*) Dell.

—The Dead Bird. (gr. 3 up). 1979. pap. 2.50 (*0-440-41775-9*) Dell.

—The Dead Bird. Charlip, Remy, illus. LC 84-43124. 48p. (gr. k-3). 1989. Repr. of 1958 ed. PLB 11.89 (*0-06-020758-2*) HarpC Child Bks.

—Don't Frighten the Lion! Rey, H. A., illus. 32p. (ps-2). 1993. pap. 4.95 (*0-06-443262-9*, Trophy) HarpC Child Bks.

—Dream Book. (ps-3). 1991. pap. 3.99 (*0-440-40567-X*, YB) Dell.

—Dream Book. (ps). 1990. 9.95 (*0-929077-12-1*) WaterMark Inc.

—The Fish with a Deep Sea Smile. (gr. 5 up). 1993. pap. 8.95 (*0-385-31112-5*) Dell.

—The Fish with the Deep Sea Smile: Stories & Poems for Reading to Young Children. LC 87-26227. (Illus.). 128p. (ps-3). 1988. Repr. of 1938 ed. PLB 18.00 (*0-208-02193-0*, Linnet) Shoe String.

—Four Fur Feet. Charlip, Remy, illus. 48p. (gr. 1-3). 1989. Repr. of 1961 ed. 13.95 (*0-929077-03-2*, Hopscotch Bks); PLB 12.95 (*0-317-92548-2*, Hopscotch Bks) Watermark Inc.

—Four Fur Feet. (ps-3). 1993. pap. 3.99 (*0-440-40684-6*) Dell.

—Four Fur Feet. Hubbard, Woodleigh, illus. LC 93-31523. 1994. write for info. (*0-7868-0002-X*); PLB write for info. (*0-7868-2000-4*) Hyprn Child.

—The Golden Egg Book. Wisegard, Leonard, illus. 32p. (ps-1). 1976. write for info. (*0-307-12045-7*, Golden Pr); PLB 9.15 (*0-685-05367-9*) Western Pub.

—Goodnight Moon. Hurd, Clement, illus. LC 47-30762. 36p. (ps-1). 1947. 13.00 (*0-06-020705-1*); PLB 12.89 (*0-06-020706-X*) HarpC Child Bks.

—Goodnight Moon. Hurd, Clement, illus. LC 47-30762. (ps-2). 1977. pap. 3.95 (*0-06-443017-0*, Trophy) HarpC Child Bks.

—Goodnight Moon. (gr. k-3). 1984. incl. cassette 19.95 (*0-941078-30-2*); pap. 12.95 incl. cassette (*0-941078-28-0*); incl. 4 bks., cassette, & guide 27.95 (*0-317-07120-3*) Live Oak Media.

—Goodnight Moon. 1993. pap. 19.95 (*0-590-73302-8*) Scholastic Inc.

—Goodnight Moon Bedtime Box. Hurd, Clement, illus. 32p. (ps-3). 1992. incl. bunny 19.95 (*0-694-00373-5*) HarpC Child Bks.

—Goodnight Moon Board Book. Hurd, Clement, illus. LC 47-30762. 34p. (ps). 1991. 6.95 (*0-694-00361-1*) HarpC Child Bks.

—The Goodnight Moon Room: A Pop-Up Book. Hurd, Clement, illus. LC 83-48169. 10p. (ps-1). 1985. 10.95 (*0-694-00003-5*) HarpC Child Bks.

—The Grasshopper & the Ants. Moore, Larry, illus. LC 93-70938. 32p. 1993. 12.95 (*1-56282-534-8*); PLB 12.89 (*1-56282-535-6*) Disney Pr.

—Important Book. Weisgard, Leonard, illus. LC 49-9133. 22p. (ps-1). 1949. 13.00 (*0-06-020720-5*); PLB 12.89 (*0-06-020721-3*) HarpC Child Bks.

—The Important Book. Weisgard, Leonard, illus. LC 49-9133. 24p. (gr. k-3). 1990. pap. 4.95 (*0-06-443227-0*, Trophy) HarpC Child Bks.

—Indoor Noisy Book. new ed. Weisgard, Leonard, illus. LC 92-46879. 48p. (ps-3). 1976. pap. 4.95 (*0-06-443003-0*, Trophy) HarpC Child Bks.

—Little Chicken. Weisgard, Leonard, illus. LC 43-16942. 32p. (ps-3). 1943. 13.00 (*0-06-020739-6*); PLB 12.89 (*0-06-020740-X*) HarpC Child Bks.

—The Little Fir Tree. Cooney, Barbara, illus. LC 85-42743. 40p. (ps-3). 1985. pap. 4.95 (*0-06-443083-9*, Trophy) HarpC Child Bks.

—The Little Fir Tree. Cooney, Barbara, illus. LC 54-5534. 24p. (gr. k-3). 1979. PLB 13.89 (*0-690-04016-4*, Crowell Jr Bks) HarpC Child Bks.

—The Little Fireman. Slobodkina, Esphyr, illus. LC 84-43127. 40p. 1952. 11.95 (*0-201-09261-1*) HarpC Child Bks.

—The Little Fireman. new ed. Slobodkina, Esphyr, illus. LC 92-17571. 40p. (ps-3). 1993. 12.00 (*0-06-021476-7*); PLB 11.89 (*0-06-021477-5*) HarpC Child Bks.

—Little Fur Family. 16p. (ps-1). 1985. boxed ed. 7.95 (*0-694-00004-3*) HarpC Child Bks.

—Little Fur Family. special rel. ed. Williams, Garth, illus. LC 51-11657. 32p. (ps-3). 1951. 14.00 (0-06-020745-0); PLB 13.89 (0-06-020746-9) HarpC Child Bks.
—Nibble Nibble: Poems for Children. Weisgard, Leonard, illus. LC 84-43128. 64p. (ps-3). 1959. PLB 13.89 (0-201-09291-3) HarpC Child Bks.
—The Noisy Book. new ed. Weisgard, Leonard, illus. LC 92-8322. 48p. (ps-1). 1939. 15.00 (0-06-020830-9); PLB 14.89 (0-06-020831-7) HarpC Child Bks.
—The Noisy Book. new ed. Weisgard, Leonard, illus. LC 92-8322. 48p. (ps-1). 1939. pap. 4.95 (0-06-443001-4, Trophy) HarpC Child Bks.
—A Pussycat's Christmas. LC 93-4424. (Illus.). (gr. 3 up). 1994. 15.00 (0-06-023532-2); PLB 14.89 (0-06-023533-0) HarpC Child Bks.
—The Quiet Noisy Book. new ed. Weisgard, Leonard, illus. LC 92-8320. 40p. (ps-1). 1993. 15.00 (0-06-020845-7); PLB 14.89 (0-06-021220-9) HarpC Child Bks.
—The Quiet Noisy Book. new ed. Weisgard, Leonard, illus. LC 92-8320. 40p. (ps-1). 1993. pap. 4.95 (0-06-443215-7, Trophy) HarpC Child Bks.
—Red Light, Green Light. Weisgard, Leonard, illus. 40p. 1992. 14.95 (0-590-44558-8, Scholastic Hardcover) Scholastic Inc.
—The Runaway Bunny. Hurd, Clement, illus. LC 71-183168. 40p. (ps-2). 1942. 13.00 (0-06-020765-5); PLB 12.89 (0-06-020766-3) HarpC Child Bks.
—The Runaway Bunny. Hurd, Clement, illus. LC 71-183168. 40p. (ps-2). 1977. pap. 3.95 (0-06-443018-9, Trophy) HarpC Child Bks.
—The Runaway Bunny. Hurd, Clement, illus. (gr. k-3). 1985. incl. cassette 19.95 (0-941078-78-7); pap. 12.95 incl. cassette (0-941078-76-0); cassette, 4 paperbacks & guide 27.95 (0-941078-77-9) Live Oak Media.
—The Runaway Bunny Board Book. Hurd, Clement, illus. LC 71-183168. 32p. (ps). 1991. pap. 6.95 (0-06-107429-2) HarpC Child Bks.
—The Sailor Dog. reissued ed. Williams, Garth, illus. 24p. (ps-k). 1992. write for info. (0-307-00143-1, 312-08, Golden Pr) Western Pub.
—The Seashore Noisy Book. new ed. Weisgard, Leonard, illus. LC 92-31433. 48p. (ps-1). 1993. 15.00 (0-06-020840-6); PLB 15.89 (0-06-020841-4) HarpC Child Bks.
—Sleepy Little Lion. Ylla, photos by. LC 47-11482. (Illus.). 24p. (gr. k-3). 1947. PLB 12.89 (0-06-020771-X) HarpC Child Bks.
—Sneakers: Seven Stories About a Cat. Charlot, Jean, illus. (ps-3). 1985. PLB 14.89 (0-06-020767-1) HarpC Child Bks.
—The Summer Noisy Book. new ed. Weisgard, Leonard, illus. LC 92-31435. 40p. (ps-1). 1993. 15.00 (0-06-020855-4); PLB 15.89 (0-06-020856-2) HarpC Child Bks.
—Summer Noisy Book. new ed. Weisgard, Leonard, illus. LC 92-31435. 40p. (ps-1). 1993. pap. 4.95 (0-06-443228-5, Trophy) HarpC Child Bks.
—Two Little Trains. LC 84-43138. 40p. 1986. PLB 12.89 (0-06-020768-X) HarpC Child Bks.
—Under the Sun & Moon: And Other Poems. Leonard, Tom, illus. 40p. (ps-3). 1993. 14.95 (1-56282-354-X); PLB 14.89 (1-56282-355-8) Hyprn Child.
—Wait Till the Moon Is Full. Williams, Garth, illus. LC 48-9278. 32p. (ps-1). 1948. 15.00 (0-06-020800-7); PLB 14.89 (0-06-020801-5) HarpC Child Bks.
—Wait Till the Moon Is Full. Williams, Garth, illus. LC 48-9278. (Illus.). 32p. (ps-3). 1989. pap. 4.95 (0-06-443222-X, Trophy) HarpC Child Bks.
—Wheel on the Chimney. Gergely, Tibor, illus. LC 84-48379. 32p. (ps-3). 1954. 14.00 (0-397-30288-6, Lipp Jr Bks); PLB 13.89 (0-397-30296-7) HarpC Child Bks.
—Wheel on the Chimney New. Gergely, Tibor, illus. LC 93-29423. 1994. 15.00 (0-06-024247-7, Festival); PLB 14.89 (0-06-024248-5, Festival) HarpC Child Bks.
—Where Have You Been? (Illus.). 32p. (ps). 1990. Repr. of 1952 ed. 8.95 (0-8038-8018-9) Hastings.
—The Whispering Rabbit. Szekeres, Cyndy, illus. 24p. (ps-k). 1992. write for info. (0-307-00138-5, 312-03, Golden Pr) Western Pub.
—Willie's Adventures. LC 84-43141. 72p. (ps-3). 1988. PLB 11.89 (0-06-020769-8) HarpC Child Bks.
—The Winter Noisy Book. new ed. Shaw, Charles G., illus. LC 92-46880. 48p. (ps-1). 1986. 15.00 (0-06-020865-1); PLB 15.89 (0-06-020866-X) HarpC Child Bks.
—The Winter Noisy Book. new ed. Weisgard, Leonard, illus. LC 92-46880. 48p. (ps-1). 1976. pap. 4.95 (0-06-443004-9, Trophy) HarpC Child Bks.
—Young Kangaroo. Shimin, Simeon, illus. 48p. (ps). 1992. pap. 3.99 (0-440-40670-6, YB) Dell.
—Young Kangaroo. Dewey, Jennifer, illus. 48p. (ps-3). 1993. 13.95 (1-56282-409-0); PLB 13.89 (1-56282-410-4) Hyprn Child.
Brown, Margaret W., ed. Homes in the Wilderness: A Pilgrim's Journal of Plymouth Plantation in 1620, by William Bradford & Others of the Mayflower Company. LC 87-27321. (Illus.). 76p. (gr. 5-12). 1988. PLB 16.00 (0-208-02197-3, Linnet); pap. 8.95 (0-208-02269-4, Linnet) Shoe String.
Brown, Margaret W., illus. Three Best-Loved Tales: Mister Dog; The Color Kittens; Seven Little Postmen. 80p. (ps-2). 1992. write for info. (0-307-15634-6, 15634, Golden Pr) Western Pub.

Brown, Margaret Wise. The Country Noisy Book. Weisgard, Leonard, photos by. LC 93-4755. 1988. 15.00 (0-06-020810-4, Festival); PLB 14.89 (0-06-020811-2) HarpC Child Bks.
—David's Little Indian. LC 89-40295. (Illus.). 48p. (gr. k-4). 1992. Repr. 11.95 (1-56282-209-8) Hyprn Child.
—The Day Before Now. Blos, Joan W., ed. Allen, Thomas B., illus. LC 93-12814. 1994. pap. 15.00 (0-671-79628-3, S&S BFYR) S&S Trade.
—The Dream Book. LC 90-81630. (Illus.). 32p. (ps-k). 1992. Repr. 9.95 (1-56282-211-X) Hyprn Child.
—The Dream Book: First Comes the Dream. Floethe, Richard, illus. 32p. (gr. 1-3). 1990. Repr. of 1950 ed. 9.95 (0-685-45149-6) WaterMark Inc.
—Four Fur Feet. LC 89-40210. (Illus.). 32p. (ps-3). 1992. Repr. 9.95 (1-56282-213-6) Hyprn Child.
—The Indoor Noisy Book. new ed. Weisgard, Leonard, illus. LC 92-46879. (ps-1). 1986. 15.00 (0-06-020820-1); PLB 15.89 (0-06-020821-X) HarpC Child Bks.
Brown, Margery W. Afro-Bets: Book of Colors. Blair, Culverson, illus. LC 91-76333. 24p. (Orig.). (ps-1). 1991. pap. 3.95 (0-940975-29-7) Just Us Bks.
—Afro-Bets: Book of Shapes. Blair, Culverson, illus. LC 91-76334. 24p. (Orig.). (ps-1). 1991. pap. 3.95 (0-940975-28-9) Just Us Bks.
Brown, Marion M. Sacagawea: Indian Interpreter to Lewis & Clark. LC 87-33810. (Illus.). 119p. (gr. 4 up). 1988. PLB 18.60 (0-516-03262-3); pap. 5.95 (0-516-43262-1) Childrens.
—Singapore. LC 89-34280. 128p. (gr. 5-9). 1989. PLB 26.60 (0-516-02715-8) Childrens.
—Susette La Flesche: Advocate for Native American Rights. LC 91-35296. (Illus.). 152p. (gr. 4 up). 1992. PLB 18.60 (0-516-03277-1); pap. 5.95 (0-516-43277-X) Childrens.
Brown, Mary B. Wings along the Waterway. LC 91-18559. (Illus.). 80p. (gr. 3-6). 1992. 17.95 (0-531-05981-2); lib. bdg. 17.99 (0-531-08581-3) Orchard Bks Watts.
Brown, Marzella. Activities for Cooperative Learning. Rivera, Doreen, et al, illus. 48p. (gr. 2-5). 1990. wkbk. 5.95 (1-55734-109-5) Tchr Create Mat.
—All about Cooperative Learning. Wright, Theresa, illus. 48p. (gr. 2-5). 1990. wkbk. 5.95 (1-55734-107-9) Tchr Create Mat.
—Great Games for Cooperative Learning. Rivera, Doreen, et al, illus. 48p. (gr. 2-5). 1990. wkbk. 5.95 (1-55734-108-7) Tchr Create Mat.
—Newspaper Reporters. Coan, Sharon, ed. Apodaca, Blanqui, illus. 48p. (gr. 3-6). 1990. wkbk. 5.95 (1-55734-137-0) Tchr Create Mat.
—Writing & Cooperative Learning: Writing & Cooperative Learning. Rivera, Doreen, et al, illus. 48p. (gr. 2-5). 1990. wkbk. 5.95 (1-55734-110-9) Tchr Create Mat.
Brown, Michael. Soccer Techniques in Pictures. (Illus.). 80p. (Orig.). 1991. pap. 7.95 (0-399-51701-4, Perigee Bks) Putnam Pub Group.
Brown, Mike, ed. see Barker, Clive, et al.
Brown, Mirella. In the Land of la Fustera. 32p. 1993. pap. 9.95 (0-8059-3348-4) Dorrance.
Brown, Pam. Charlie Chaplin: Comic Genius Who Brought Laughter & Hope to Millions. LC 88-27568. (Illus.). 64p. (gr. 5-6). 1991. PLB 18.60 (1-55532-838-5) Gareth Stevens Inc.
—Father Damien: Missionary to a Forgotten People. Birch, Beverley, adapted by. LC 89-49751. (Illus.). 64p. (gr. 3-4). 1990. PLB 18.60 (0-8368-0389-2) Gareth Stevens Inc.
—Father Damien: The Man Who Lived & Died for the Victims of Leprosy. Sherwood, Rhoda, ed. LC 88-2106. (Illus.). 68p. (gr. 5-6). 1988. PLB 18.60 (1-55532-815-6) Gareth Stevens Inc.
—Florence Nightingale: The Founder of Modern Nursing. Tolan, Mary, adapted by. LC 90-9972. (Illus.). 64p. (gr. 3-4). 1991. PLB 18.60 (0-8368-0456-2) Gareth Stevens Inc.
—It Was Always Africa. LC 86-2240. (gr. 7-10). 1986. pap. 4.95 (0-8054-4335-5) Broadman.
—Lean on Me: How to Help a Friend with a Problem. Nelson, Becky, ed. (Orig.). (gr. 7-12). 1993. pap. text ed. 1.95 (1-56309-068-6) Womans Mission Union.
Brown, Paula. Moon Jump. LC 92-22216. 32p. 1993. 13.50 (0-670-84237-0) Viking Child Bks.
Brown, Peter L. Astronomy. LC 84-1654. (Illus.). 64p. (gr. 7 up). 15.95x (0-87196-985-8) Facts on File.
Brown, Regina. Little Brother. Bornschlegel, Ruth, illus. (gr. 3-7). 1962. 8.95 (0-8392-3019-2) Astor-Honor.
—Play at Your House. Brown, Regina, illus. (gr. 3-7). 1962. 8.95 (0-8392-3027-3) Astor-Honor.
Brown, Richard. Cookie Monster's Good Time to Eat! (Illus.). 14p. (ps-k). 1989. write for info. (0-307-12259-X, Pub. by Golden Bks) Western Pub.
—One Hundred Words about Animals. Brown, Richard, illus. LC 86-22774. 27p. (ps-k). 1987. 5.95 (0-15-200550-1, Gulliver Bks) HarBrace.
—One Hundred Words about Animals. Brown, Richard, illus. (gr. k-2). 1990. incl. cass. 19.95 (0-87488-183-8); pap. 12.95 incl. cass. (0-87499-182-X); Set; incl. 4 bks., cass., & guide. pap. 27.95 (0-87499-184-6) Live Oak Media.
—One Hundred Words about My House. LC 87-7574. (Illus.). 28p. (ps-k). 1988. 6.95 (0-15-200552-8, Gulliver Bks) HarBrace.
—One Hundred Words about Transportation. Brown, Richard, illus. LC 86-22781. 27p. (ps-k). 1987. 5.95 (0-15-200551-X, Gulliver Bks) HarBrace.

—One Hundred Words about Working. LC 87-8368. (Illus.). 27p. (ps-k). 1988. 6.95 (0-15-200553-6, Gulliver Bks) HarBrace.
Brown, Richard, jt. auth. see Ziefert, Harriet.
Brown, Richard, illus. Gulliver's Travels: A Kid's Guide to Southern California. 135p. (gr. 1 up). 1988. 6.95 (0-318-33430-5, Gulliver Bks) HarBrace.
—A Kid's Guide to National Parks. 160p. (gr. 1 up). 1989. pap. 6.95 (0-318-37140-5, Gulliver Bks) HarBrace.
—A Kid's Guide to New York City. 138p. (gr. 1 up). 1988. pap. 6.95 (0-15-200458-0, Gulliver Bks) HarBrace.
—A Kid's Guide to Southern California. 135p. (gr. 1 up). 1988. pap. 6.95 (0-15-200457-2, Gulliver Bks) HarBrace.
—Muchas Palabras Sobre Animals. (SPA). 32p. (ps-1). 1989. pap. 3.95 (0-15-200531-5) HarBrace.
—Muchas Palabras Sobre Mi Casa. (SPA). 28p. (ps-1). 1989. pap. 3.95 (0-15-200532-3, Gulliver Bks) HarBrace.
—One Hundred Words about Animals. (ps-1). 1989. pap. 4.95 (0-15-200554-4, Voy B) HarBrace.
—One Hundred Words about My House. (ps-1). 1989. pap. 3.95 (0-15-200556-0, Voy B) HarBrace.
—One Hundred Words about Transportation. (ps-1). 1989. pap. 3.95 (0-15-200555-2, Voy B) HarBrace.
—One Hundred Words about Working. (ps-1). 1989. pap. 3.95 (0-15-200557-9, Voy B) HarBrace.
—Sesame Street, Cookie Monster's Book of Cookie Shapes. 24p. (ps-k). 1979. pap. write for info (0-307-10074-X, Pub. by Golden Bks) Western Pub.
Brown, Richard C., jt. auth. see Nishiyama, Hidetaka.
Brown, Rick. What Rhymes with Snake? A Word & Picture Flap Book. Brown, Rick, illus. LC 92-37870. 24p. 1994. 11.95 (0-688-12328-7, Tambourine Bks) Morrow.
Brown, Rick, illus. Old MacDonald Had a Farm. (ps-k). 1993. 9.99 (0-670-85157-4) Viking Child Bks.
—Who Built the Ark? (ps-3). 1994. fold-outs 9.99 (0-670-85160-4) Viking Child Bks.
Brown, Robert. How Weather Works. LC 91-2021. (Illus.). 64p. (gr. 2-3). 1991. PLB 19.93 (0-8368-0087-7) Gareth Stevens Inc.
—Luke: Doctor-Writer. Hester, Ron, illus. (gr. 1-6). 1977. bds. 5.95 (0-8054-4233-2, 4242-33) Broadman.
—Stand Alone Blues. 32p. pap. 9.95 (0-88284-543-8, 4428) Alfred Pub.
Brown, Robert & Jones, Brian. Exploring Space. LC 89-11278. (Illus.). 64p. (gr. 2-3). 1989. PLB 19.93 (0-8368-0029-X) Gareth stevens Inc.
Brown, Robert, jt. auth. see Brown, Julie.
Brown, Robert M. Spirit of Protestantism. (gr. 9 up). 1961. pap. 10.95 (0-19-500724-7) OUP.
Brown, Roberta. The Walking Tree & Other Scary Stories. (gr. 4 up). 1991. 8.95 (0-87483-143-1) August Hse.
Brown, Roberta S. Queen of the Cold-Blooded Tales. 176p. (gr. 7 up). 1993. 19.00 (0-685-67270-0) August Hse.
Brown, Rodney. Noah's Great Adventure. (Illus.). 20p. 1993. 15.95 (1-883909-00-7) Wisdom Tree.
Brown, Roger S., ed. see DeGraf, Anna.
Brown, Ron. The Hag of Halloween. Shand, Jim & Brown, Ron, illus. LC 88-92081. 12p. (Orig.). (gr. 6). 1988. pap. 2.95 (0-685-24339-7) Deer Creek Pub.
Brown, Rose M. The PMS Zone. Skeeter, illus. 80p. (Orig.). 1988. pap. 7.95 (0-9622109-0-0) Skeetoonies.
Brown, Ruth. Alphabet Times Four: An International ABC. LC 91-3162. (Illus.). 32p. (ps-k). 1991. 13.95 (0-525-44831-4, DCB) Dutton Child Bks.
—The Big Sneeze. LC 84-23385. (Illus.). 32p. (ps-1). 1985. 13.95 (0-688-04665-7); lib. bdg. 12.88 (0-688-04666-5) Lothrop.
—A Dark Dark Tale. Brown, Ruth, illus. LC 81-66798. 32p. (ps-3). 1981. 12.95 (0-8037-1672-9); PLB 12.89 (0-8037-1673-7) Dial Bks Young.
—A Dark Dark Tale. Brown, Ruth, illus. LC 81-66798. 32p. (ps-3). 1984. pap. 3.95 (0-8037-0093-8) Dial Bks Young.
—Dark Dark Tale. giant ed. (ps-3). 1991. pap. 17.95 (0-8037-1074-7, Dial Pied Piper) Puffin Bks.
—The Grizzly Revenge. Brown, Ruth, illus. 32p. (gr. 3-6). 1987. 15.95 (0-86264-024-5, Pub. by Anderson Pr UK) Trafalgar.
—If at First You Do Not See. Brown, Ruth, illus. LC 82-15527. 48p. (ps-2). 1983. 14.95 (0-8050-1053-X, Bks Young Read) H Holt & Co.
—If at First You Do Not See. LC 82-15527. (Illus.). 48p. (ps-2). 1989. pap. 5.95 (0-8050-1031-9, Bks Young Read) H Holt & Co.
—Ladybug, Ladybug. Brown, Ruth, illus. LC 88-14852. 32p. (ps-1). 1988. 12.95 (0-525-44423-8, DCB) Dutton Child Bks.
—Ladybug, Ladybug. LC 88-14852. (Illus.). 32p. (ps-1). 1992. pap. 3.99 (0-14-054543-3, Puffin Unicorn) Puffin Bks.
—One Stormy Night. Brown, Ruth, illus. LC 92-27004. 32p. (ps-1). 1993. 13.99 (0-525-45091-2, DCB) Dutton Child Bks.
—Our Cat Flossie. Brown, Ruth, illus. LC 86-19895. 32p. (ps-1). 1986. 10.95 (0-525-44256-1, DCB) Dutton Child Bks.
—Our Cat Flossie. Brown, Ruth, illus. LC 86-19895. 32p. (ps-1). 1990. pap. 3.95 (0-525-44608-7, DCB) Dutton Child Bks.
—Our Puppy's Vacation. LC 87-5433. (Illus.). 32p. (ps-1). 1987. 10.95 (0-525-44326-6, DCB) Dutton Child Bks.

—Our Puppy's Vacation. LC 87-5433. (Illus.). 32p. (ps-1). 1991. pap. 3.95 (*0-525-44701-6*, Puffin) Puffin Bks.
—The Picnic. LC 92-5718. (ps-2). 1993. 14.00 (*0-525-45012-2*, DCB) Dutton Child Bks.
—The World That Jack Built. Brown, Ruth, illus. LC 90-25034. 32p. (ps-1). 1991. 13.95 (*0-525-44635-4*, DCB) Dutton Child Bks.
Brown, Ruthanne, jt. auth. see Clark, Raymond C.
Brown, Ryan & Clarrian, Dean. The Collected Teenage Mutant Ninja Turtles Adventures, Vol. 1. Gaydos, Michael, et al, illus. 96p. 1991. pap. 5.95 (*1-879450-03-8*) Tundra MA.
—The Collected Teenage Mutant Ninja Turtles Adventures, Vol. 2. Mitchroney, Ken, et al, illus. 88p. 1991. pap. 5.95 (*1-879450-04-6*) Tundra MA.
Brown, Ryan, jt. auth. see Clarrain, Dean.
Brown, Ryan, et al. Teenage Mutant Ninja Turtles, Vol. 1. Berger, Dan, et al, illus. 150p. 1990. pap. 9.95 (*1-879450-00-3*) Tundra MA.
Brown, Sam E. Bubbles, Rainbows & Worms: Science Experiments for Pre-School Children. Stamper, Silas, illus. LC 80-84598. 105p. (ps-1). 1981. pap. 8.95 (*0-87659-100-4*) Gryphon Hse.
—Gentle Rain & Loving Sun: Activities for Developing a Healthy Self-Concept in Young Children. LC 91-72221. 380p. (Orig.). 1992. pap. text ed. 29.95 (*1-55959-031-9*) Accel Devel.
Brown, Sandford. Louis Armstrong: Singing, Swinging Satchmo. (Illus.). 144p. (gr. 9-12). 1993. PLB 14.40 (*0-531-13028-2*) Watts.
—Louis Armstrong: Swinging, Singing Satchmo. (Illus.). (gr. 7-12). 1993. pap. 6.95 (*0-531-15680-X*) Watts.
Brown, Stephen. Tlingit Totem Poles. (gr. 1-9). 1992. pap. 4.95 (*0-88388-150-0*) Bellerophon Bks.
Brown, Stephen F. Taoism. (Illus.). 128p. (gr. 7-12). 1992. bds. 17.95x (*0-8160-2448-0*) Facts on File.
Brown, Sterling A. The Last Ride of Wild Bill & Eleven Narrative Poems. 53p. (gr. 12 up). 1975. pap. 5.00 (*0-910296-02-2*) Broadside Pr.
Brown, Steven J., ed. see Spainhower, Steven D.
Brown, Stoney. Encino High: Stoney's Notebook. (Illus.). 96p. 1992. pap. 7.95 (*1-56282-896-7*) Hyprn Child.
Brown, Susan. Pakistan & Bangladesh. (Illus.). 48p. (gr. 4-8). 1989. lib. bdg. 14.98 (*0-382-09825-0*) Silver Burdett Pr.
Brown, Sylvia, jt. auth. see Parrett, Sherii.
Brown, Tom, Jr. Tom Brown's Field Guide to Nature & Survival for Children. 1989. pap. 8.95 (*0-425-11106-7*, Berkley Trade) Berkley Pub.
Brown, Towana J. Leave, Retard, Leave! Brown, Becky, illus. 127p. (Orig.). (gr. 8-12). 1988. pap. 3.50 (*0-9622060-0-8*) T J Brown.
—Raglagger. Brown, Becky, illus. LC 89-90647. 168p. (Orig.). (gr. 5-7). 1989. pap. 3.50 (*0-9622060-2-4*) T J Brown.
—Scottie. Brown, Becky E., illus. LC 88-93029. 150p. (Orig.). (gr. 5-6). 1989. pap. 3.50 (*0-9622060-1-6*) T J Brown.
Brown, Tricia. Chinese New Year. Ortiz, Fran, photos by. LC 87-8532. (Illus.). 48p. (ps-2). 1987. 14.95 (*0-8050-0497-1*, Bks Young Read) H Holt & Co.
—Hello, Amigos! Ortiz, Fran, photos by. LC 86-9882. (Illus.). 48p. (ps-2). 1992. 15.95 (*0-8050-1891-3*, Owlet BYR); pap. 5.95 (*0-8050-0090-9*) H Holt & Co.
—Japanese American. 1994. write for info. (*0-8050-2353-4*) H Holt & Co.
—Lee-Ann: The Story of a Vietnamese-American Girl. (Illus.). 48p. 1991. 14.95 (*0-399-21842-4*, Putnam) Putnam Pub Group.
—Russian Emigre. 1994. write for info. (*0-8050-2354-2*) H Holt & Co.
Brown, Tricia, jt. auth. see Junior League of San Francisco Staff.
Brown, Vinson. Exploring Pacific Coast Tide Pools. rev. & enl. ed. Rovetta, Ane, illus. 80p. (gr. 4 up). 1966. 16.95 (*0-87961-216-9*); pap. 8.95 (*0-87961-217-7*) Naturegraph.
—Pomo Indians of California & Their Neighbors. Elsasser, Albert B., ed. Andrews, Douglas, illus. LC 78-13946. 64p. (Orig.). (gr. 4 up). 1969. 15.95 (*0-911010-31-9*); pap. 7.95 (*0-911010-30-0*) Naturegraph.
—Return of the Indian Spirit. Johnson, W. Cameron, illus. LC 81-65887. 64p. (gr. 5 up). 1982. pap. 7.95 (*0-89087-401-8*) Celestial Arts.
Brown, Vinson & Lawrence, George. Californian Wildlife Region. 3rd, rev. ed. (Illus.). 224p. (gr. 4 up). Date not set. 16.95 (*0-87961-200-2*); pap. 8.95 (*0-87961-201-0*) Naturegraph.
Brown, Vinson & Livezey, Robert. The Sierra Nevadan Wildlife Region. 3rd, rev. ed. (Illus.). 192p. (gr. 4 up). 1962. 16.95 (*0-911010-03-3*); pap. 8.95 (*0-911010-02-5*) Naturegraph.
Brown, Vinson, jt. auth. see Willoya, William.
Brown, Vinson, et al. Rocks & Minerals of California. 3rd. rev. ed. LC 72-13423. (Illus.). 200p. (gr. 4 up). 1972. 16.95 (*0-911010-59-9*); pap. 8.95 (*0-911010-58-0*) Naturegraph.
—Wildlife of the Intermountain West. (Illus.). 144p. (gr. 4 up). 1968. 15.95 (*0-911010-15-7*); pap. 7.95 (*0-911010-14-9*) Naturegraph.
Brown, Virginia P. & Owens, Laurella. World of the Southern Indians. Gokie, Nathan, illus. LC 83-6376. 176p. (gr. 6-9). 1983. 15.95 (*0-912221-00-3*) Beechwood.

Brown, Warren. Alternative Sources of Energy. LC 93-7470. (Illus.). 112p. (gr. 5 up). 1993. PLB 19.95 (*0-7910-1588-2*); pap. write for info. (*0-7910-1613-7*) Chelsea Hse.
—Colin Powell. (Illus.). 112p. (gr. 5 up). 1992. lib. bdg. 17.95 (*0-7910-1647-1*); pap. 9.95 (*0-7910-1648-X*) Chelsea Hse.
—Fidel Castro: Cuban Revolutionary. LC 93-25211. (Illus.). 128p. (gr. 7 up). 1994. 15.90 (*1-56294-385-5*) Millbrook Pr.
—John C. Calhoun. (Illus.). 112p. (gr. 5 up). 1993. 18.95 (*0-7910-1727-3*, Am Art Analog); pap. write for info. (*0-7910-1728-1*, Am Art Analog) Chelsea Hse.
—Robert E. Lee. facsimile ed. (gr. 4-7). 1982. pap. 7.95 (*0-7910-0698-0*) Chelsea Hse.
—The Search for the Northwest Passage. Goetzmann, William H., ed. Collins, Michael, intro. by. (Illus.). 112p. (gr. 5 up). 1991. lib. bdg. 18.95 (*0-7910-1297-2*) Chelsea Hse.
Brown, William F. True Texas Tales. Mazzu, Kenneth, illus. LC 92-93887. 64p. (Orig.). (gr. 7 up). 1992. pap. 8.75 perfect bdg. (*1-881936-14-7*) WFB Ent.
—Wood Works: Experiments with Common Wood & Tools. LC 83-15905. (Illus.). 128p. (gr. 3 up). 1984. SBE 13.95 (*0-689-31033-1*, Atheneum Child Bk) Macmillan Child Grp.
Brown, William F. & Gadzella, Bernadette. Study Skills Test. 28p. (Orig.). 1987. pap. text ed. 3.50 (*1-881936-01-5*) WFB Ent.
Browne, A., jt. auth. see McAfee, A.
Browne, Anthony. The Big Baby: A Little Joke. LC 93-20210. (gr. 1-3). 1994. 13.00 (*0-679-84737-5*) Knopf Bks Yng Read.
—Changes. Browne, Anthony, illus. LC 90-4283. 32p. (ps-3). 1991. Repr. of 1990 ed. 14.95 (*0-679-81029-3*); PLB 15.99 (*0-679-91029-8*) Knopf Bks Yng Read.
—Gorilla. Browne, Anthony, illus. LC 85-13. 32p. (ps-3). 1985. PLB 13.99 (*0-394-97525-1*) Knopf Bks Yng Read.
—Gorilla: Miniature Edition. Browne, Anthony, illus. 32p. (ps-3). 1991. 4.95 (*0-679-81453-1*) Knopf Bks Yng Read.
—Piggybook. Browne, Anthony, illus. LC 86-3008. 32p. (ps-3). 1986. 14.95 (*0-394-88416-7*); lib. bdg. 14.99 (*0-394-98416-1*) Knopf Bks Yng Read.
—Through the Magic Mirror. LC 90-23166. 32p. (ps up). 1992. 14.00 (*0-688-10725-7*) Greenwillow.
—The Tunnel. Browne, Anthony, illus. (gr. 4-8). 1990. 14.00 (*0-394-84582-X*); lib. bdg. 12.99 (*0-394-94582-4*) Random Bks Yng Read.
—Willy & Hugh. Browne, Anthony, illus. LC 90-4938. 32p. (ps-3). 1991. 13.00 (*0-679-81446-9*); lib. bdg. 13.99 (*0-679-91446-3*) Knopf Bks Yng Read.
—Willy the Wimp. Browne, Anthony, illus. LC 84-14320. 32p. (ps-3). 1985. PLB 13.99 (*0-394-97061-6*) Knopf Bks Yng Read.
—Willy the Wimp. Browne, Anthony, illus. LC 84-14320. 32p. (ps-2). 1989. Repr. of 1985 ed. 5.99 (*0-394-82610-8*) Knopf Bks Yng Read.
—Zoo. Browne, Anthony, illus. LC 92-11708. 32p. 1993. lib. bdg. 15.99 (*0-679-93946-6*) Knopf Bks Yng Read.
—Zoo. LC 92-11708. (Illus.). 32p. 1993. 15.00 (*0-679-83946-1*) Knopf Bks Yng Read.
Browne, Dik. Hagar the Horrible: Pillage Idiot. 128p. (Orig.). 1986. pap. 1.95 (*0-8125-6788-9*, Dist. by Warner Pub Services & Saint Martin's Press) Tor Bks.
—Hi & Lois: Dawg Day Afternoon. 128p. 1986. pap. 1.95 (*0-8125-6908-3*) Tor Bks.
Browne, Dik, jt. auth. see Walker, Mort.
Browne, Eileen. No Problem. Parkins, David, illus. LC 92-53134. 40p. (gr. k-3). 1993. bk. ed. 14.95 (*1-56402-176-9*); bk. & kit ed. 14.99 (*1-56402-200-5*) Candlewick Pr.
—Tick-Tock. Parkins, David, illus. LC 93-927. 1994. write for info. (*1-56402-300-1*) Candlewick Pr.
—Where's That Bus? Browne, Eileen, illus. LC 90-20885. 32p. (ps-1). 1991. pap. 13.95 jacketed (*0-671-73810-0*, S&S BFYR) S&S Trade.
—Where's That Bus? LC 90-20885. (Illus.). 32p. (ps-1). 1993. pap. 7.95 (*0-671-79854-5*, S&S BYR) S&S Trade.
Browne, Gerard, illus. The Aircraft Lift-the-Flap Book. 18p. (gr. 2-5). 1992. 13.00 (*0-525-67351-2*, Lodestar Bks) Dutton Child Bks.
Browne, Gerard & Browne, Gerard, illus. The Car & Truck Lift-the-Flap Book. LC 88-29994. 18p. (gr. 2-5). 1989. 12.95 (*0-525-67273-7*, Lodestar Bks) Dutton Child Bks.
Browne, Jane. The Little One. (Illus.). 24p. 1993. 14.95 (*1-85681-102-6*, Pub. by J MacRae UK) Trafalgar.
Browne, Juanita K. Thomasina & the Tommyknocker. Bridgman, Allison, illus. LC 93-13732. viii, 85p. (Orig.). (gr. 4-7). 1993. pap. 8.75 (*0-9636621-0-4*) Browne Bks.
Browne, Roger, jt. auth. see Stephenson, Robert.
Browne, Rollo. An Aboriginal Family. LC 84-19447. (Illus.). 32p. (gr. 2-5). 1985. PLB 13.50 (*0-8225-1655-1*) Lerner Pubns.
—A Family in Australia. (Illus.). 32p. (gr. 2-5). 1987. PLB 13.50 (*0-8225-1671-3*) Lerner Pubns.
Browne, Vee. Monster Birds: A Navajo Folktale. Whitethorne, Baje, illus. LC 92-82139. 32p. (gr. 2 up). 1993. 14.95 (*0-87358-558-5*) Northland AZ.
—Monster Slayer: A Navajo Folktale. Whitethorne, Baje, illus. LC 91-52603. 32p. (gr. k-6). 1991. 14.95 (*0-87358-525-9*) Northland AZ.
Browne-Gutnik, Natalie, jt. auth. see Gutnik, Martin J.

Brownell, David. Great Composers, Bk. 1. Conkle, Nancy, illus. (gr. 7 up). 1978. pap. 3.95 (*0-88388-058-X*) Bellerophon Bks.
—Great Composers, Bk. 2. (gr. 1-9). 1992. pap. 3.95 (*0-88388-046-6*) Bellerophon Bks.
—Great Composers, Bk. 3. (gr. 1-9). 1992. pap. 3.95 (*0-88388-134-9*) Bellerophon Bks.
—Great Lawyers. Conkle, Nancy, illus. 48p. (Orig.). (gr. 8). 1988. pap. 3.95 (*0-88388-133-0*) Bellerophon Bks.
—Heroes of the American Revolution. (gr. 1-9). 1992. pap. 3.95 (*0-88388-050-4*) Bellerophon Bks.
—Nutcracker. (gr. 1-9). 1992. pap. 3.95 (*0-88388-052-0*) Bellerophon Bks.
—Peter & the Wolf. (gr. 1-9). 1992. pap. 3.95 (*0-88388-093-8*) Bellerophon Bks.
Brownell, M. Barbara. Mammals. LC 93-19467. (gr. 1-3). 1993. write for info. (*0-87044-890-0*) Natl Geog.
Browning, James. Read the Label Carefully: Separating New Age & Christianity. Nelson, Becky, ed. 22p. (Orig.). (gr. 7-12). 1992. pap. text ed. 1.95 (*1-56309-062-7*, Wrld Changers Res) Womans Mission Union.
Browning, Jane, jt. auth. see Baker, Harri T.
Browning, Robert. The Pied Piper of Hamelin. rev. ed. Small, Terry, illus. 47p. (gr. 1 up). 1988. 10.95 (*0-15-200566-8*, Gulliver Bks) HarBrace.
—The Pied Piper of Hamelin. Greenaway, Kate, illus. LC 93-767. 1993. 5.99 (*0-517-09347-2*, Pub. by Derrydale Bks) Outlet Bk Co.
—The Pied Piper of Hamelin. 1993. 12.95 (*0-679-42812-7*, Everymans Lib) Knopf.
—The Pied Piper of Hamelin: A Classic Tale. Jose, Eduard, adapted by. Suire, Diane D., tr. Rovira, Francesc, illus. LC 88-35313. 32p. (gr. 1-4). 1988. PLB 19.95 (*0-89565-471-7*); PLB 13.95s.p. (*0-685-56031-7*) Childs World.
—Poems of Robert Browning. Smalley, Donald, ed. LC 56-3004. (gr. 9 up). 1956. pap. 9.16 (*0-395-05103-7*, RivEd) HM.
Brownlee, Juanita. Tangram Geometry in Metric. Merrick, Paul, illus. (Orig.). (gr. 5-10). 1976. pap. 7.95 (*0-918932-43-2*, 0140701407) Activity Resources.
Brownlee, Walter. The First Ships Round the World. LC 73-91815. (Illus.). 48p. (gr. 7 up). 1974. pap. 7.50 (*0-521-20438-0*) Cambridge U Pr.
—The Navy That Beat Napoleon. LC 78-18091. (Illus.). 48p. 1981. pap. 7.50 (*0-521-22145-5*) Cambridge U Pr.
—Warrior: The First Modern Battleship. (Illus.). 48p. (gr. 7 up). 1985. pap. 7.50 (*0-521-27579-2*) Cambridge U Pr.
Brownley, Margaret. A Youths' Guide to Job Hunting. 28p. (Orig.). (gr. 8-12). 1988. pap. 3.95 (*0-945485-02-6*) Comm Intervention.

Brownlow, Bette H. Tyler's Descent. (Illus.). 32p. (Orig.). 1993. pap. 5.25 (*1-883516-00-5*) Peregrine & Hayes. TYLER'S DESCENT is the story about the conflicts & joys of a Light Being's descent from the spirit into three-dimensional reality. TYLER'S DESCENT is the first of three stories written for the purpose of teaching basic metaphysical lessons, facilitating children's connection with spirit, & for stimulating memory of their origins. The three stories will be known collectively as TYLER'S TRILOGY. Unhampered by time & space, Tyler is free to explore the universe & multidimensional realities at will as a spark of Light. Although reluctant to give up his freedom, he anticipates his descent into three-dimensional reality through the birth process. He knows that life experience on Earth will contribute to his soul's growth & eventual complete reunion with the Creator. Even as a newborn infant, Tyler still maintains his connection with spirit. But he worries that as he gets older his connection with spirit will be more difficult to maintain. Dr. Brownlow, a clinical psychologist, has discovered that TYLER'S DESCENT, adapted as a guided imagery technique is a "powerful" tool in assisting clients to resolve abortion issues. To order, write P.O. Box 64101, Tuscon, AZ 85728 or call/fax (602) 887-7194 or call (602) 299-1504. If no answer, leave message.
Publisher Provided Annotation.

Brownlow, Paul C., jt. auth. see Baw, Cindy.
Brownmiller, Arlan J. Nixie's Wild Zoo. 1992. pap. 11.95 (*0-533-10308-8*) Vantage.
Brownrigg, Sheri. All Tutus Should Be Pink. Johnson, Meredith, illus. 32p. 1992. pap. 2.95 (*0-590-43904-9*, Cartwheel) Scholastic Inc.
—Best Friends Wear Pink Tutus. Johnson, Meredith, illus. 1993. write for info. (*0-590-46437-X*) Scholastic Inc.
Brownstein, Robin & Guttmacher, Peter. The Scotch-Irish Americans. (Illus.). 112p. (gr. 5 up). 1988. lib. bdg. 17.95 (*0-87754-875-7*) Chelsea Hse.
Brownstein, Samuel C., et al. How to Prepare for SAT I. 18th ed. 800p. 1994. pap. 12.95 (*0-8120-1856-7*) Barron.
—How to Prepare for the SAT. 17th ed. 780p. (gr. 9 up). 1993. pap. 11.95 (*0-8120-1633-5*) Barron.
—PSAT - NMSQT: How to Prepare for the Preliminary Scholastic Aptitude Test - National Merit Scholarship Qualifying Test. 8th ed. LC 93-21849. 380p. (gr. 9 up). 1993. pap. 10.95 (*0-8120-1414-6*) Barron.
Brownstone & Franck, eds. The Scandinavian-American Heritage. LC 88-45086. 128p. (gr. 5-9). 1988. 16.95x (*0-8160-1626-7*) Facts On File.
Brownstone, David & Franck, Irene. Historic Places of Early America. LC 88-27521. (Illus.). 64p. (gr. 3-7). 1989. pap. 7.95 (*0-689-71234-0*, Aladdin) Macmillan Child Grp.
Brownstone, David M. The Chinese-American Heritage. (Illus.). 144p. 1988. 16.95x (*0-8160-1627-5*) Facts on File.
—The Jewish-American Heritage. LC 87-19905. (Illus.). 128p. (gr. 7 up). 1988. 16.95x (*0-8160-1628-3*) Facts on File.
Brownstone, David M. & Franck, Irene M. Healers. (Illus.). 240p. (gr. 6-10). 1989. 17.95x (*0-8160-1446-9*) Facts on File.
—Historic Places of Early America. LC 88-27521. (Illus.). 64p. (gr. 3-7). 1989. SBE 14.95 (*0-689-31439-6*, Atheneum Child Bk) Macmillan Child Grp.
—Manufacturers & Miners. (Illus.). 176p. 1988. 17.95x (*0-8160-1447-7*) Facts on File.
—Natural Wonders of America. LC 88-32707. (Illus.). 64p. (gr. 3-7). 1989. pap. 7.95 (*0-689-71229-4*, Aladdin) Macmillan Child Grp.
—Natural Wonders of America. LC 88-27487. (Illus.). 64p. (gr. 3-7). 1989. SBE 14.95 (*0-689-31430-2*, Atheneum Child Bk) Macmillan Child Grp.
Brownstone, David M., jt. auth. see Franck, Irene M.
Bruccoli, M. J., ed. see James, Henry.
Bruce, C., ed. see Maher, Robert.
Bruce, C., ed. see Reum, Earl.
Bruce, Harry. Maud: The Life of L. M. Montgomery. 1992. 17.00 (*0-553-08770-3*) Bantam.
Bruce, Linda. Al Phillip Bettle. Bruce, Linda, illus. (gr. k-3). 1965. 8.95 (*0-8392-3050-8*) Astor-Honor.
Bruce, Lisa. Oliver's Alphabets. Gliori, Debi, illus. LC 92-39471. 24p. (ps-1). 1993. SBE 13.95 (*0-02-735996-4*, Bradbury Pr) Macmillan Child Grp.
Bruce, Preston & Johnson, Katharine. From the Door of the White House. LC 81-23672. (Illus.). 160p. (gr. 6 up). 1984. 12.95 (*0-688-00883-6*) Lothrop.
Bruch, Marilyn. Phonics Art Projects. (gr. 1-3). 1985. pap. 8.95 (*0-8224-5541-2*) Fearon Teach Aids.
Bruchac, Joseph. A Boy Called Slow. Baviera, Rocco, illus. LC 93-21233. 1994. write for info. (*0-399-22692-3*, Philomel Bks) Putnam Pub Group.
—Fox Song. Morin, Paul, illus. LC 92-24815. 32p. (ps). 1993. 14.95 (*0-399-22346-0*, Philomel Bks) Putnam Pub Group.
—The Great Ball Game: A Muskogee Story. Roth, Susan L., illus. LC 93-6269. 1994. write for info. (*0-8037-1539-0*); PLB write for info. (*0-8037-1540-4*) Dial Bks Young.
—Iroquois Stories: Heroes & Heroines, Monsters & Magic. Burgevin, Daniel, illus. LC 85-5705. 198p. (gr. 3-7). 1985. pap. 8.95 (*0-89594-234-8*) Crossing Pr.
Bruchac, Joseph, jt. auth. see Caduto, Michael.
Bruchac, Joseph, jt. auth. see Caduto, Michael J.
Bruchac, Joseph, retold by. The First Strawberries: A Cherokee Story. Vojtech, Anna, illus. LC 91-31058. 32p. (ps-3). 1993. 13.99 (*0-8037-1331-2*); lib. bdg. 13.89 (*0-8037-1332-0*) Dial Bks Young.
Bruchac, Joseph, as told by. Flying with Eagle, Racing the Great Bear: Stories from Native North America. LC 93-21966. (Illus.). 128p. (gr. 5-8). 1993. PLB 13.95 (*0-8167-3026-1*); pap. write for info. (*0-8167-3027-X*) BrdgeWater.
Bruchac, Joseph, retold by. Gluskabe & the Four Wishes. Shrader, Christine, illus. LC 93-26924. 1995. write for info. (*0-525-65164-0*, Cobblehill Bks) Dutton Child Bks.
Bruchac, Joseph & London, Jonathan, eds. Thirteen Moons on Turtle's Back: A Native American Year of Moons. Locker, Thomas, illus. 32p. (ps-8). 1992. PLB 15.95 (*0-399-22141-7*, Philomel Bks) Putnam Pub Group.
Bruck, Michael von see Schneider, D. Douglas.
Bruestle, Beaumont. The Wonderful Tang. (gr. 1-7). 1952. 4.50 (*0-87602-222-0*) Anchorage.
Brugge, David. Hubbell Trading Post National Historic Site. Foreman, Ronald J. & Priehs, T. J., eds. 16p. (Orig.). 1992. pap. 2.95 (*1-877856-18-5*) SW Pks Mnmts.
Bruggen, Bill & Wade, Tom. Carve Your Own Carousel Horse. LC 89-85082. (Illus.). 96p. (Orig.). 1989. pap. 14.95 (*0-929758-04-8*) Beeman Jorgensen.
Bruggen, Bill, jt. auth. see Machan, Wayne.

Bruguier, Leonard R., ed. see Sansom-Flood, Renee & Bernie, Shirley A.
Brumagin, Wayne, ed. see Young, Philip G.
Brumbeau, Jeff. The Man in the Moon in Love. Couch, Greg, illus. LC 91-37804. 32p. 1992. 14.95 (*1-55670-229-9*) Stewart Tabori & Chang.
Brumley, Karen. Saving Our Planet. Altop, Tammy, illus. 40p. (gr. 6). 1991. wkbk. 3.95 (*1-561894-06-0*) Amer Educ Pub.
—Saving Our Planet. Altop, Tammy, illus. 40p. (gr. 5). 1991. wkbk. 3.95 (*1-561894-05-2*) Amer Educ Pub.
—Saving Our Planet. Altop, Tammy, illus. 40p. (gr. 4). 1991. wkbk. 3.95 (*1-561894-04-4*) Amer Educ Pub.
Brummett, Nancy V., ed. see Hefley, Lynn C.
Brumpton, Karen B. Freeman Earns a Bike. Feldman, Roper, illus. LC 84-60947. 32p. (ps-4). 1984. 10.95 (*0-917487-00-1*) McVie Pub.
Bruna, Dick. Dick Bruna's Picture Wordbook. (Illus.). 64p. 1991. 5.99 (*0-517-05662-3*) Outlet Bk Co.
Bruneau, Thomas C. The Political Transformation of the Brazilian Catholic Church. LC 73-79318. (gr. 4-7). pap. 71.00 (*0-317-28009-0*, 2025579) Bks Demand.
Brunelli, Jean, jt. auth. see Lindsay, Jeanne W.
Brunhoff, Jean de. A. B. C. de Babar. new ed. (FRE.). 46p. 1978. 15.95 (*0-8288-4858-0*, M11808) Fr & Eur.
—Babar au Cirque. (Illus.). 16p. 1974. 4.95 (*0-686-54121-9*, FC241) Fr & Eur.
—Babar en Famille. 26p. 1975. 15.95 (*0-7859-0672-X*, FC589) Fr & Eur.
—Babar et le Crocodile. 16p. 1975. 4.95 (*0-7859-0673-8*, FC242) Fr & Eur.
—Babar et le Pere Noel. 29p. 1975. 15.95 (*0-7859-0674-6*, FC582) Fr & Eur.
—Le Couronnement de Babar. 16p. 1975. 4.95 (*0-686-54126-X*, FC251) Fr & Eur.
—L' Enfance de Babar. 16p. 1975. 4.95 (*0-686-54127-8*) Fr & Eur.
—Histoire de Babar, le Petite Elephant. (Illus.). 32p. 18.95 (*0-686-54129-4*, FC593) Fr & Eur.
—Vive le Roi Babar. 20p. 1976. 4.95 (*0-7859-0675-4*, FC253) Fr & Eur.
—Le Voyage de Babar. 27p. 1975. 15.95 (*0-7859-0676-2*, FC581) Fr & Eur.
Brunhoff, Jean De see De Brunhoff, Jean.
Brunhoff, Jean de see De Brunhoff, Jean.
Brunhoff, Jean De see De Brunhoff, Jean & De Brunhoff, Laurent.
Brunhoff, L. De see De Brunhoff, L.
Brunhoff, Laurent de. L' Anniversaire de Babar. 28p. 1975. 15.95 (*0-7859-0677-0*, M11806) Fr & Eur.
—Les Aventures de Babar. 18p. 1977. 15.95 (*0-686-54134-0*) Fr & Eur.
—Babar a Celesteville. 16p. 1974. 4.95 (*0-7859-0678-9*, F12062*) Fr & Eur.
—Babar aux Sports d'Hiver. (Illus.). 20p. 1976. 4.95 (*0-7859-0679-7*, FC250) Fr & Eur.
—Babar Aviateur. 16p. 1974. 4.95 (*0-7859-0680-0*, M5989) Fr & Eur.
—Babar Campeur. 16p. 1974. 4.95 (*0-686-54138-3*) Fr & Eur.
—Babar dans l'Ile aux Oiseaux. 29p. 15.95 (*0-7859-0681-9*, F2002) Fr & Eur.
—Babar en Amerique. 23p. 1975. 15.95 (*0-686-54140-5*) Fr & Eur.
—Babar et le Docteur. 16p. 1975. 4.95 (*0-686-54141-3*) Fr & Eur.
—Babar et le Wouly-Wouly. 26p. 15.95 (*0-7859-0682-7*, M11805) Fr & Eur.
—Babar et Sa Famille. 26p. 1976. 4.95 (*0-686-54143-X*) Fr & Eur.
—Babar Patissier. 16p. 1975. 4.95 (*0-686-54144-8*) Fr & Eur.
Brunhoff, Laurent De see De Brunhoff, Jean & De Brunhoff, Laurent.
Brunhoff, Laurent De see De Brunhoff, Laurent.
Brunhoff, Laurent de see De Brunhoff, Laurent.
Brunhoff, Laurent de see De Brunhoff, Laurent.
Brunhoff, Laurent de see De Brunhoff, Laurent.
Brunhoff, Laurent de see De Brunhoff, Laurent.
Brunhoff, Laurent De see De Brunhoff, Laurent.
Brunhoff, Laurent de see De Brunhoff, Laurent.
Brunhoff, Laurent De see De Brunhoff, Laurent.
Bruni, Mary A. Rosita's Christmas Wish. Ricks, Thom, illus. LC 85-52040. 48p. (gr. k-8). 1985. 13.95 (*0-935857-00-1*); ltd. ed. 125.00 (*0-935857-03-6*); write for info. (*0-935857-09-5*); pap. write for info. (*0-935857-01-X*); pap. write for info. (*0-935857-10-9*) Texart.
Bruni, Mary-Ann S. Elif: Child of Turkey. (Illus.). 48p. (gr. k-8). 1988. 12.95 (*0-935857-13-3*); pap. text ed. write for info. (*0-935857-14-1*) Texart.
—El Sueno de Rosita. De Castro, Rogelio, tr. from ENG. Ricks, Thom, illus. (SPA.). 48p. (gr. k-8). 1987. 13.95 (*0-935857-02-8*); pap. write for info. (*0-935857-04-4*) (*0-935857-11-7*) (*0-935857-12-5*) Texart.
Bruni, Mary-Ann S., ed. see Cormier, Larry.
Bruning, Nancy. Cities Against Nature. LC 91-34604. 128p. (gr. 4-8). 1992. PLB 26.60 (*0-516-05510-0*) Childrens.
Brunke, Dawn B. Who Lives Here, Bk. 1. Linder, Greg, ed. Shafer, Mary A., illus. (Orig.). (gr. k-6). 1993. pap. 6.95 (*1-55971-152-3*) NorthWord.
—Who Lives Here, Bk. 2. Linder, Greg, ed. Shafer, Mary A., illus. (Orig.). (gr. k-6). 1993. pap. 6.95 (*1-55971-153-1*) NorthWord.

—Who Lives Here, Bk. 3. Linder, Greg, ed. Shafer, Mary A., illus. (Orig.). (gr. k-6). 1993. pap. 6.95 (*1-55971-154-X*) NorthWord.
—Who Lives Here, Bk. 4. Linder, Greg, ed. Shafer, Mary A., illus. (Orig.). (gr. k-6). 1993. pap. 6.95 (*1-55971-155-8*) NorthWord.
Brunn, Robert. The Initiation. 160p. (gr. 5 up). 1992. pap. 3.50 (*0-440-94047-8*, LFL) Dell.
Brunner, Rick, et al. Soviet Training & Recovery Methods: For Competitive Athletes. LC 90-62005. (Illus.). 200p. (Orig.). (gr. 10 up). 1990. pap. 18.95 (*0-9622039-2-0*) Sports Focus Pub.
Brunner, Robert F., et al. Listen to Your Mother. Johnson, Saundra L., illus. 70p. (Orig.). (ps-3). 1991. PLB write for info. (*1-879209-00-4*); pap. text ed. write for info.; tchr's. ed. avail. Saundras Story Bks.
—When You Feel Like Your Out of Luck. Johnson, Saundra L., illus. LC 90-92036. 58p. (Orig.). (ps-3). 1991. PLB 24.95 (*1-879209-01-2*); pap. text ed. write for info.; tchr's. ed. avail. Saundras Story Bks.
Bruno, Bonnie. Kwitcherbellyakin: Devotions for Young Families. 144p. 1992. pap. 5.99 (*0-310-54811-X*, Youth Bks) Zondervan.
Bruno, Clara E. see Charley, Aunt, pseud.
Bruno, Janet & Dakan, Peggy. Cooking in the Classroom. (ps-3). 1974. pap. 7.95 (*0-8224-1610-7*) Fearon Teach Aids.
Brunoff, Laurent De see De Brunoff, Laurent.
Bruns, Roger. Abraham Lincoln. Schlesinger, Arthur M., Jr., intro. by. (Illus.). 112p. (gr. 5 up). 1986. lib. bdg. 17.95 (*0-87754-597-9*); pap. 9.95 (*0-7910-0649-2*) Chelsea Hse.
—George Washington. Schlesinger, Arthur M., Jr., intro. by. (Illus.). 112p. (gr. 5 up). 1987. lib. bdg. 17.95 (*0-87754-584-7*); pap. 9.95 (*0-7910-0668-9*) Chelsea Hse.
—Julius Caesar. Schlesinger, Arthur M., Jr., intro. by. (Illus.). 112p. (gr. 5 up). 1988. lib. bdg. 17.95 (*0-87754-514-6*) Chelsea Hse.
—Thomas Jefferson. (Illus.). 112p. (gr. 5 up). 1986. lib. bdg. 17.95 (*0-87754-583-9*); pap. 9.95 (*0-7910-0644-1*) Chelsea Hse.
Brunswick, G., illus. The Haunted House Three-D Coloring Book. 32p. (Orig.). (gr. 4-7). 1988. pap. 3.95 (*0-942025-57-1*) Kidsbks.
—Wild Wheels Three-D Coloring Book. 32p. (Orig.). (gr. 4-7). 1988. pap. 3.95 (*0-942025-60-1*) Kidsbks.
Brunton, Paul. Inspiration & the Overself: The Notebooks of Paul Brunton, Vol. 14. Cash, Paul & Smith, Timothy, eds. (Illus.). 256p. (gr. 7 up). 1988. 25.00 (*0-943914-40-X*, Dist. by NBN); pap. 14.95 (*0-943914-41-8*, Dist. by NBN) Larson Pubns.
Brusca, Maria C. My Mama's Little Ranch on the Pampas. LC 93-28113. 1994. write for info. (*0-8050-2782-3*) H Holt & Co.
—On the Pampas. Brusca, Maria C., illus. LC 90-40938. 40p. (ps-2). 1991. 14.95 (*0-8050-1548-5*, Bks Young Read) H Holt & Co.
—On the Pampas. Brusca, Maria C., illus. LC 90-40938. 40p. (ps-2). 1993. pap. 5.95 (*0-8050-2919-2*, Bks Young Read) H Holt & Co.
—When Jaguar's Moon. 1994. write for info. (*0-8050-2797-1*) H Holt & Co.
Brusca, Maria C. & Wilson, Tona. The Blacksmith & the Devils. Brusca, Maria C., illus. LC 92-176. 40p. (gr. 1-4). 1992. 15.95 (*0-8050-1954-5*, Bks Young Read) H Holt & Co.
—The Cook & the King. Brusca, Maria C., illus. LC 92-25812. 40p. (gr. 1-4). 1993. 14.95 (*0-8050-2355-0*, Bks Young Read) H Holt & Co.
Brusic, Sharon A. Launching Science & Technology Across the Curriculum Design. (ps-3). 1992. pap. 4.75 (*0-8273-4950-5*) Delmar.
—Launching Science & Technology Across the Curriculum Explore. (ps-3). 1992. pap. 4.75 (*0-8273-4951-3*) Delmar.
—Launching Science & Technology Across the Curriculum Space. (ps-3). 1992. pap. 4.75 (*0-8273-4948-3*) Delmar.
—Launching Science & Technology Across the Curriculum Transportation. (ps-3). 1992. pap. 4.75 (*0-8273-4949-1*) Delmar.
Brusic, Sharon A. & Wells, John G. Kids & Technology: Mission Twenty-One, 4 bks, Level 1. 1993. Set. pap. text ed. 19.00 (*0-8273-5997-7*); tchr's. resource bk., binder 95.00 (*0-8273-4952-1*) Delmar.
Brusselmans, Christiane, et al. Sunday: Book of Readings Adapted for Children Year A. 176p. (ps-7). 1989. text ed. 49.95 (*0-929496-38-8*) Treehaus Comns.
—Sunday: Book of Readings Adapted for Children, Year B. 176p. (ps-8). 1990. text ed. 49.95 (*0-929496-57-4*) Treehaus Comns.
—Sunday: Book of Readings Adapted for Children Year C. 176p. text ed. 49.95 (*0-929496-91-4*) Treehaus Comns.
—Sunday: Leaders Weekly Guidebook, Year B. 160p. (ps-8). 1990. text ed. 49.95 (*0-929496-58-2*) Treehaus Comns.
—Sunday: Leaders Weekly Guidebook Year C. 160p. text ed. 49.95 (*0-929496-92-2*) Treehaus Comns.
Brust, Beth W. The Amazing Paper Cuttings of Hans Christian Andersen. LC 93-24532. 1994. 14.95 (*0-395-66787-9*) Ticknor & Fields.
Brutschy, Jennifer. Celeste & Crabapple Sam. Christelow, Eileen, illus. LC 92-1587. (gr. k-3). 1994. 14.99 (*0-525-67416-0*, Lodestar Bks) Dutton Child Bks.

—The Winter Fox. Garns, Allen, illus. LC 92-33467. 40p.
(ps-3). 1993. 15.00 (*0-679-81524-4*); PLB 15.99
(*0-679-91524-9*) Knopf Bks Yng Read.
Bruun, Bertel, jt. auth. see Bruun, Ruth D.
Bruun, Ruth D. & Bruun, Bertel. Brain: What It Is, What
It Does. Brunn, Peter, illus. LC 88-21182. 64p. 1989.
12.95 (*0-688-08453-2*); PLB 12.88 (*0-688-08454-0*)
Greenwillow.
—The Human Body. Wynne, Patricia, illus. LC 82-5210.
96p. (gr. 5 up). 1982. lib. bdg. 12.99 (*0-394-94424-0*);
pap. 11.95 smythe-sewn (*0-394-84424-6*) Random Bks
Yng Read.
Bruvelaitis, Lisa. Nearly Noodles. Bruvelaitis, Lisa, illus.
24p. (Orig.). (ps-2). 1990. pap. 0.99 (*1-55037-128-2*,
Pub. by Annick CN) Firefly Bks Ltd.
Bruzonik, Erika. El Color De la Memoria. (SPA., Illus.).
106p. (Orig.). (gr. 9-12). 1992. pap. 4.95
(*1-881791-00-9*) In One EAR.
Bruzzone, Catherine. Christmas Activity Book. Beaton,
Clare, illus. 24p. (gr. k-5). 1993. pap. 3.95
(*0-8120-1745-5*) Barron.
—French for Children. (FRE.). 80p. 1993. pap. 11.95
(*0-685-62822-1*, F9175-7, Natl Textbk); pap. 29.95
pkg. incl. 2 60-min. children's audiocassettes, 1 60-
min. tchr's. audiocassette (*0-685-62823-X*, F9179-X,
Natl Textbk) NTC Pub Grp.
—German for Children. (GER.). 80p. 1993. pap. 11.95
(*0-685-62832-9*, F9281-8, Natl Textbk); pap. 29.95
pkg. incl. 2 60-min. children's audiocassettes, 1 60-
min. tchr's. audiocassette (*0-685-62833-7*, F9281-8,
Natl Textbk) NTC Pub Grp.
—Italian for Children. (ITA.). 80p. 1993. pap. 11.95
(*0-685-62835-3*, F9285-0, Natl Textbk); pap. 29.95
pkg. incl. 2 60-min. children's audiocassettes, 1 60-
min. tchr's. audiocassette (*0-685-62836-1*, F9313-X,
Natl Textbk) NTC Pub Grp.
—My First Family Tree Book. Church, Caroline, illus.
24p. (gr. k-2). 1992. pap. 3.95 (*0-8249-8546-X*, Ideals
Child) Hambleton-Hill.
—Passport's French for Children. 80p. (gr. 1-6). 1992.
pap. 29.95 incl. audiocassettes (*0-8442-9179-X*,
Passport Bks) NTC Pub Grp.
—Passport's German for Children. 80p. (gr. 1-6). 1992.
pap. 29.95 incl. audiocassettes (*0-8442-9280-X*,
Passport Bks) NTC Pub Grp.
—Passport's Italian for Children. 80p. (gr. 1-6). 1992.
pap. 29.95 incl. audiocassettes (*0-8442-9313-X*,
Passport Bks) NTC Pub Grp.
—Passport's Spanish for Children. 80p. (gr. 1-6). 1992.
pap. 29.95 incl. audiocassettes (*0-8442-9165-X*,
Passport Bks) NTC Pub Grp.
—Spanish for Children: For Young Learners. (SPA.). 80p.
1993. pap. 11.95 (*0-685-62809-4*, F9166-8, Natl
Textbk); pap. 29.95 pkg. incl. 2 60-min children's
audiocassettes, 1 60-min. tchr's, audiocassette
(*0-685-62810-8*, F9165-X, Natl Textbk) NTC Pub
Grp.
Bruzzone, Catherine & Morton, Lone. All about Me.
Church, Caroline J., illus. 24p. (Orig.). (gr. k-3). 1993.
pap. 3.95 (*0-8249-8605-9*, Ideals Child) Hambleton-
Hill.
Bryan see Sohn, David A.
Bryan, Antonia D., jt. auth. see O'Neill, Richard.
Bryan, Ashley. All Night, All Day: A Child's First Book
of African-American Spirituals. Bryan, Ashley, illus.
LC 90-753145. 48p. (ps-4). 1991. SBE 14.95
(*0-689-31662-3*, Atheneum Child Bk) Macmillan
Child Grp.
—Beat the Story-Drum, Pum-Pum. LC 80-12045. (Illus.).
80p. (gr. 3-6). 1987. SBE 13.95 (*0-689-31356-X*,
Atheneum Child Bk) Macmillan Child Grp.
—Beat the Story-Drum, Pum-Pum. Bryan, Ashley, illus.
LC 86-20598. 80p. (gr. 4-6). 1987. pap. 7.95
(*0-689-71107-7*, Aladdin) Macmillan Child Grp.
—The Cat's Purr. LC 84-21534. (Illus.). 48p. (ps-3). 1985.
SBE 11.95 (*0-689-31086-2*, Atheneum Child Bk)
Macmillan Child Grp.
—The Dancing Granny. Bryan, Ashley, illus. LC 87-
1140. 64p. (gr. k-4). 1987. pap. 6.95 (*0-689-71149-2*,
Aladdin) Macmillan Child Grp.
—Lion & the Ostrich Chicks & Other African Folk Tales.
Ashley, Bryan, illus. LC 86-3349. 96p. (gr. 2-6). 1986.
SBE 13.95 (*0-689-31311-X*, Atheneum Child Bk)
Macmillan Child Grp.
—The Ox of the Wonderful Horns: And Other African
Folktales. reissue ed. Bryan, Ashley, illus. LC 75-
154749. 48p. (ps-4). 1993. RSBE 14.95
(*0-689-31799-9*, Atheneum Child Bk) Macmillan
Child Grp.
—Sh-Ko & His Eight Wicked Brothers. Yoshimura,
Fumio, illus. LC 88-892. 32p. (ps-3). 1988. SBE 13.95
(*0-689-31446-9*, Atheneum Child Bk) Macmillan
Child Grp.
—Sing to the Sun. LC 91-38359. (Illus.). 32p. (gr. 2 up).
1992. 15.00 (*0-06-020829-5*); PLB 14.89
(*0-06-020833-3*) HarpC Child Bks.
—The Story of Lightning & Thunder. Bryan, Ashley,
illus. LC 92-40509. 32p. (ps-3). 1993. SBE 14.95
(*0-689-31836-7*, Atheneum Child Bk) Macmillan
Child Grp.
—Turtle Knows Your Name. Bryan, Ashley, illus. LC
89-2. 32p. (ps-3). 1989. SBE 13.95 (*0-689-31578-3*,
Atheneum Child Bk) Macmillan Child Grp.
Bryan, Ashley, jt. auth. see Langstaff, John.
Bryan, Ashley, retold by. & illus. Turtle Knows Your
Name. LC 92-33553. 32p. (ps-3). 1993. pap. 4.95
(*0-689-71728-8*, Aladdin) Macmillan Child Grp.

Bryan, Betsy & Cohen, Judith. Tu Puedes Ser una
Egiptologa. Yanez, Juan, tr. from ENG. Katz, David,
illus. (SPA.). 40p. (gr. 4-7). 1993. pap. 6.00
(*1-880599-11-2*) Cascade Pass.
—You Can Be a Woman Egyptologist. Katz, David, illus.
LC 93-1267. 40p. (Orig.). (gr. 3-6). 1993. pap. 6.00
(*1-880599-10-4*) Cascade Pass.
Bryan, Jenny. Breathing: The Respiratory System. LC
92-36353. (Illus.). 48p. (gr. 5 up). 1993. RSBE 13.95
(*0-87518-563-0*, Dillon) Macmillan Child Grp.
—Digestion: The Digestive System. LC 92-35052. (Illus.).
48p. (gr. 5 up). 1993. RSBE 13.95 (*0-87518-564-9*,
Dillon) Macmillan Child Grp.
—Medical Technology. LC 90-25027. (Illus.). 48p. (gr.
5-8). 1991. 12.90 (*0-531-18398-X*, Pub. by Bookwright
Pr) Watts.
—Mind & Matter. (Illus.). 48p. (gr. 5 up). 1993. lib. bdg.
13.95 RSBE (*0-87518-588-6*, Dillon) Macmillan Child
Grp.
—Movement: The Muscular & Skeletal System. LC 92-
35092. (Illus.). 48p. (gr. 5 up). 1993. RSBE 13.95
(*0-87518-565-7*, Dillon) Macmillan Child Grp.
—The Pulse of Life: The Circulatory System. LC 92-
36410. (Illus.). 48p. (gr. 5 up). 1993. RSBE 13.95
(*0-87518-566-5*, Dillon) Macmillan Child Grp.
—Reproduction. (Illus.). 48p. (gr. 5 up). 1993. lib. bdg.
13.95 RSBE (*0-87518-589-4*, Dillon) Macmillan Child
Grp.
—Smell, Taste & Touch. (Illus.). 48p. (gr. 5). 1994. PLB
13.95 RSBE (*0-87518-590-8*, Dillon) Macmillan Child
Grp.
—Sound & Vision. (Illus.). 48p. (gr. 5). 1994. PLB 13.95
RSBE (*0-87518-591-6*, Dillon) Macmillan Child Grp.
Bryan, T. Scott. Geysers: What They Are & How They
Work. (Illus.). 48p. (Orig.). 1990. pap. 5.95
(*0-911797-74-2*) R Rinehart.
Bryansky, Faina. The Key to Music Making, Pt. I: Piano
Method for Beginners. Squillace, Albert & Kuznetsov,
Eugene, illus. LC 88-50726. 48p. (gr. 1-5). 1988. pap.
8.00 (*0-929571-00-2*) White Lilac Pr.
Bryant. Anne Abrams. 1991. 0.85 (*0-8050-2037-3*) H
Holt & Co.
—Carol Thomas-Weaver. 1991. 0.85 (*0-8050-2012-8*) H
Holt & Co.
—Sharon Oehler. 1991. 0.85 (*0-8050-2022-5*) H Holt &
Co.
—Zoe McCully: Park Ranger. 1991. 0.85 (*0-8050-2016-0*)
H Holt & Co.
Bryant, Ashley. Starstruck. 160p. (Orig.). 1990. pap. 3.50
(*0-449-14583-2*, Girls Only) Fawcett.
Bryant, Bonnie. Autumn Trail, No. 30. 1993. pap. 3.25
(*0-553-48077-4*) Bantam.
—Beach Ride. (gr. 4-7). 1993. pap. 3.25 (*0-553-48073-1*)
Bantam.
—Bridle Path. (gr. 4-7). 1993. pap. 3.25 (*0-553-48074-X*)
Bantam.
—Chocolate Horse. (gr. 4-7). 1994. pap. 3.50
(*0-553-48146-0*) Bantam.
—Fox Hunt. (gr. 4-7). 1992. pap. 3.25 (*0-553-15990-9*)
Bantam.
—Ghost Rider. (gr. 4-7). 1992. pap. 3.25 (*0-553-48067-7*)
Bantam.
—Hayride. (gr. 4-7). 1993. pap. 3.25 (*0-553-48145-2*)
Bantam.
—Horse Games. (gr. 4-7). 1991. pap. 3.25
(*0-553-15882-1*) Bantam.
—Horse Shy, Bk. No. 2. (gr. 3-7). 1988. pap. 2.75
(*0-317-69287-9*) Bantam.
—Horse Trouble. 1992. pap. 3.25 (*0-553-48025-1*)
Bantam.
—Horse Wise. (gr. 4 up). 1990. pap. 3.25 (*0-553-15805-8*)
Bantam.
—Pack Trip. (gr. 4-7). 1991. pap. 3.25 (*0-553-15928-3*)
Bantam.
—Ranch Hands. (gr. 4-6). 1993. pap. 3.25
(*0-553-48076-6*) Bantam.
—Rodeo Rider. (gr. 4 up). 1990. pap. 3.25
(*0-553-15821-X*) Bantam.
—Saddle Club. 1992. pap. 3.25 (*0-553-15983-6*) Bantam.
—Saddle Club, No. 17: Horsenapped! 144p. 1991. pap.
3.25 (*0-553-15937-2*) Bantam.
—Sea Horse. (gr. 4-7). 1991. pap. 3.25 (*0-553-15847-3*)
Bantam.
—Show Horse. (gr. 4-7). 1992. pap. 3.25 (*0-553-48072-3*)
Bantam.
—Snow Ride. 1992. pap. 3.25 (*0-553-15907-0*) Bantam.
—Stable Manners. (gr. 4-6). 1993. pap. 3.25
(*0-553-48075-8*) Bantam.
—Star Rider. (gr. 4-7). 1991. pap. 3.25 (*0-553-15938-0*)
Bantam.
—Starlight Christmas. (gr. 4-7). 1990. pap. 3.25
(*0-553-15832-5*) Bantam.
—Team Play. (gr. 4-7). 1991. pap. 3.25 (*0-553-15862-7*)
Bantam.
Bryant, Donna. My Cat Buster. Wood, Jakki, illus. 20p.
(ps-3). 1991. 8.95 (*0-8120-6211-6*) Barron.
—My Dog Jessie. Wood, Jakki, illus. 20p. (ps-3). 1991.
8.95 (*0-8120-6212-4*) Barron.
—My Guinea Pigs Pip & Gus. Wood, Jakki, illus. 20p.
(ps-3). 1991. 8.95 (*0-8120-6213-2*) Barron.
—My Rabbit Roberta. Wood, Jakki, illus. 20p. (ps-3).
1991. 8.95 (*0-8120-6210-8*) Barron.
Bryant, Gary. The First Ride: The Real Story of Santa
Claus. 40p. 1992. pap. 4.95 (*1-881442-00-4*) New
Legends Pub.
—The True-Life Adventures of Nicky Ridge. 78p. (gr.
4-8). 1992. pap. 6.95 (*1-881442-02-0*) New Legends
Pub.

Bryant, Jennifer. Anne Abrams: Engineering Drafter.
Brown, Pamela & Adkins, Bill, photos by. (Illus.). 40p.
(gr. 2-4). 1991. PLB 15.95 (*0-941477-51-7*) TFC Bks
NY.
—Carol Thomas-Weaver: Music Teacher. Brown, Pamela
& Adkins, Bill, photos by. (Illus.). 40p. (gr. 2-4). 1991.
PLB 15.95 (*0-941477-56-8*) TFC Bks NY.
—Jane Sayler: Veterinarian. Brown, Pamela & Adkins,
Bill, photos by. (Illus.). 40p. (gr. 2-4). 1991. PLB 15.
95 (*0-941477-55-X*) TFC Bks NY.
—Margaret Murie: A Wilderness Life. Castro, Antonio,
illus. 80p. (gr. 4-7). 1993. PLB 14.95 (*0-8050-2220-1*)
TFC Bks NY.
—Marjory Stoneman Douglas: Voice of the Everglades.
Raymond, Larry, illus. 72p. (gr. 4-7). 1992. PLB 14.95
(*0-8050-2113-2*) TFC Bks NY.
—Sharon Oehler: Pediatrician. Brown, Pamela & Adkins,
Bill, photos by. (Illus.). 40p. (gr. 2-4). 1991. PLB 15.
95 (*0-941477-53-3*) TFC Bks NY.
—Ubel Velez: Lawyer. Brown, Pamela & Adkins, Bill,
photos by. (Illus.). 40p. (gr. 2-4). 1991. PLB 15.95
(*0-941477-52-5*) TFC Bks NY.
—Zoe McCully: Park Ranger. Brown, Pamela & Adkins,
Bill, photos by. (Illus.). 40p. (gr. 2-4). 1991. PLB 15.
95 (*0-941477-54-1*) TFC Bks NY.
Bryant, Linda, et al, eds. see Pondsmith, Michael.
Bryant, Martha F. Sacajawea: A Native American
Heroine. Gilliland, Hap, ed. Sargent, Heather &
Gilliland, Hap, illus. 256p. (Orig.). 1989. 21.95
(*0-89992-420-4*); pap. 15.95 (*0-89992-120-5*) Coun
India Ed.
Bryant, Thomas A. Rodeo, America's Number One Sport.
2nd ed. Wagner, E. Vernel, illus. 64p. (gr. 3-5). 1986.
pap. 3.00 (*0-941875-00-8*) Wolverine Gallery.
Bryant-Mole, K. Colors. (Illus.). 24p. (ps up). 1990. pap.
3.50 (*0-7460-0594-6*, Usborne) EDC.
—Dot to Dot Nature. (Illus.). 24p. (ps-4). 1993. pap. 3.50
(*0-7460-1375-2*, Usborne) EDC.
—Numbers. (Illus.). 24p. (ps up). 1992. pap. 3.50
(*0-7460-1042-7*) EDC.
—Second Big Dot to Dot. (Illus.). 96p. (gr. k-4). 1993.
pap. 9.95 (*0-7460-1377-9*, Usborne) EDC.
—Shapes. (Illus.). 24p. (ps up). 1991. pap. 3.50
(*0-7460-0593-8*, Usborne) EDC.
Bryant-Mole, K. & Tyler, J. Dot to Dot (B - U). (Illus.).
72p. (ps-2). 1992. 6.95 (*0-7460-1448-1*) EDC.
Bryant-Mole, K., jt. auth. see Gee, R.
Bryant-Mole, K., jt. auth. see Tyler, J.
Bryant-Mole, Karen. Dot-to-Dot at the Seaside. (Illus.).
24p. (gr. k-1). 1993. pap. 3.50 (*0-7460-1376-0*,
Usborne) EDC.
—Dot-to-Dot Dinosaurs. (Illus.). 24p. (gr. k-1). 1993.
pap. 3.50 (*0-7460-1374-4*, Usborne) EDC.
—Dot-to-Dot Space. (Illus.). 24p. (gr. k-1). 1993. pap.
3.50 (*0-7460-1373-6*, Usborne) EDC.
Bryant-Mole, Karen & Gee, Robyn. Multiplying &
Dividing Puzzles. (Illus.). 32p. (gr. 2-6). 1993. pap.
4.95 (*0-7460-1073-7*, Usborne) EDC.
Bryce, James & Polick, Bill. The Power Basics of
Football. LC 84-22838. 112p. 1986. 5.95
(*0-13-688318-4*, Busn) P-H.
Bryce, James, et al. Power Basics of Soccer. LC 84-
22839. 112p. 1984. 5.95 (*0-13-688326-5*, Busn) P-H.
Brychta, Alex. The Arrow. (ps-k). 1987. 2.95
(*0-19-272166-6*) OUP.
Bryer, James. Reading Skills Songbook, Vol. 1: Read,
Rapp, & Rock to the Skills of Reading. Evangelist,
Gary, illus. 48p. (Orig.). (gr. 2-6). 1989. pap. 14.95
incl. audiocassette (*0-9622499-0-4*) Soundbox Pubns.
Bryson, Jamie S. The War Canoe. LC 89-17580. 198p.
(Orig.). 1990. pap. 9.95 (*0-88240-368-0*) Alaska
Northwest.
BSA Staff. Junior Leader Training Conference Staff
Guide. (Illus.). 336p. (gr. 6-12). 1992. pap. 11.00
(*0-8395-4535-5*, 34535) BSA.
BSCS Staff. Science for Life & Living: Integrating
Science, Technology & Health. 368p. (gr. 5). 1991.
case-sewn 22.90 (*0-8403-5998-5*) Kendall-Hunt.
—Science for Life & Living: Integrating Science,
Technology, & Health, Grade 2. 464p. (gr. 2). 1992.
tchr's. ed., 3-hole binder 43.90 (*0-8403-5993-4*)
Kendall-Hunt.
—Science for Life & Living: Integrating Science,
Technology, & Health, Grade 3. 368p. (gr. 3). 1992.
case-sewn 19.90 (*0-8403-5994-2*); tchr's. ed., 3-ring
binder, 480 p. 39.90 (*0-8403-5995-0*) Kendall-Hunt.
—Science for Life & Living: Integrating Science,
Technology, & Health, Grade 4. 320p. (gr. 4). 1992.
case-sewn 20.90 (*0-8403-5996-9*); tchr's. ed., 3-ring
binder, 432p. 43.90 (*0-8403-5997-7*) Kendall-Hunt.
Buak, Karen. Grandma's Cookies. Kita, Helen M., illus.
40p. (Orig.). (ps-4). 1992. pap. text ed. 6.95 chapbk.
(*1-56315-055-7*) Guyasuta Pubs.
Buban, Peter & Schmitt, Marshall L. Understanding
Electricity & Electronics. 3rd ed. 1974. text ed. 28.32
(*0-07-008675-3*, W) McGraw.
Bubniuk, Irena. Preliminary Piano Work for the Student
of Music, Vol. 1. (Illus.). (gr. k up). 1992. Set; Incl.
music wkbk. & text bk. 75.00 (*1-882596-00-5*); Text
bk., 159p. write for info. (*1-882596-01-3*); Music
wkbk., spiral bdg., 200p. write for info.
(*1-882596-02-1*) BML.

Buch, Jane. Fitness & Nutrition: The Winning Combination. 2nd ed. Bard, Tate, ed. LC 84-51951. (Illus.). 160p. (gr. 7-12). 1990. text ed. 19.93 (0-685-58645-6); pap. text ed. 12.60 (0-914127-55-1); tchr's. planning guide 17.27 (0-914127-49-7); wkbk., 160p. 5.27 (0-914127-19-5); testing program 7.67 (0-914127-48-9) Univ Class.

Buchan, Elizabeth. Beatrix Potter. 64p. 1991. 10.95 (0-7232-3780-8) Warne.

Buchan, John, pref. by. The Poetry of Neil Munro. 88p. (gr. 9 up). 1989. 12.95 (0-907590-24-1, Pub. by SPA Bks Ltd UK) Seven Hills Bk Dists.

Buchan, Stuart. Guys Like Us. (gr. 7 up). 1986. 14.95 (0-385-29448-4) Delacorte.
—Guys Like Us. (gr. k-12). 1989. pap. 2.95 (0-440-20244-2, LFL) Dell.
—Love & Lucy Bloom. (gr. 7 up). 1988. pap. 2.25 (0-373-98022-1) S&S Trade.
—When We Lived with Pete. (Orig.). (gr. 4-7). 1986. pap. 2.95 (0-440-49483-4, YB) Dell.

Buchanan, Carol, ed. see Ruskin, Thelma.

Buchanan, D. H. The Gob-Gob-Goblin's Feast. Balkovek, James, illus. 64p. (ps-4). 1993. pap. 9.95 (0-8449-4275-8); FRE Translation Tool, "Trans-it" 4.95 (0-8449-4289-8); CHI Translation Tool, "Trans-it" 4.95 (0-8449-4291-X); GER Translation Tool, "Trans-it" 4.95 (0-8449-4290-1); SPA Translation Tool, "Trans-it" 4.95 (0-8449-4288-X) Good Morn Tchr.

Buchanan, David. Greek Athletics. McLeish, Kenneth & McLeish, Valerie, eds. (Illus.). 48p. (gr. 7-12). 1976. pap. text ed. 9.00 (0-582-20059-8, 70659) Longman.

Buchanan, Dawna. The Falcon's Wing. 128p. (gr. 4). 1993. pap. 3.50 (0-380-72102-3, Camelot) Avon.

Buchanan, Dawna L. The Falcon's Wing. LC 91-22545. 144p. (gr. 5 up). 1992. 13.95 (0-531-05986-3); lib. bdg. 13.99 (0-531-08586-4) Orchard Bks Watts.

Buchanan, Debby, jt. auth. see Buchanan, Ken.

Buchanan, Doris A. Mr. Grumpuss. 1991. 7.95 (0-533-09546-8) Vantage.

Buchanan, Elizabeth. Mole Moves House. 1991. 9.95 (0-385-26538-7); PLB 10.99 (0-385-26539-5) Doubleday.

Buchanan, George. The Children's Book of Woodwork. (Illus.). 64p. (gr. 3-6). 1990. 24.95 (0-7134-6122-5, Pub. by Batsford UK) Trafalgar.

Buchanan, George, jt. auth. see Robins, Deri.

Buchanan, Heather S. George & Matilda Mouse & the Floating School. LC 89-22036. (Illus.). 40p. (ps-3). 1990. map. 3.95 (0-671-70613-6) S&S Trade.
—George & Matilda Mouse & the Moon Rocket. LC 91-24318. (Illus.). 40p. (ps-3). 1992. pap. 14.00 jacketed (0-671-75864-0, S&S BFYR) S&S Trade.
—Little Pig Goes to Market. LC 92-11895. 1993. pap. 14.00 (0-671-79351-9, S&S BYR) S&S Trade.

Buchanan, J. Nothing Else but Yams for Supper. (Illus.). 24p. (ps-8). 1988. pap. 4.95 (0-88753-182-2, Pub. by Black Moss Pr CN) Firefly Bks Ltd.
—Taking Care of My Cold. (Illus.). 24p. (ps-8). 1990. pap. 4.95 (0-88753-197-0, Pub. by Black Moss Pr CN) Firefly Bks Ltd.

Buchanan, Jami L. Letters to My Little Sisters. LC 84-27612. (Orig.). (gr. 7-8). 1985. pap. 5.99 (0-8307-0999-1, S185100) Regal.

Buchanan, John G. Thomas Paine: American Revolutionary Writer. Rahmas, D. Steve, ed. (gr. 7-12). 1976. lib. bdg. 4.95 incl. catalog cards (0-87157-585-X) SamHar Pr.

Buchanan, John G., ed. see Pangburn, Thelma I.

Buchanan, Ken. This House Is Made of Mud. Tracy, Libba, illus. LC 90-53589. 32p. (ps-k). 1991. 14.95 (0-87358-518-6) Northland AZ.

Buchanan, Ken & Buchanan, Debby. It Rained on the Desert Today. Tracy, Libba, illus. 32p. (ps up). 1994. 14.95 (0-87358-575-5) Northland AZ.
—Lizards on the Wall. Schweitzer-Johnson, Betty, illus. LC 92-13664. (gr. 1-4). 1992. 12.95 (0-943173-77-9) Harbinger AZ.

Buchanan, Patricia. Robert E Lee: A Hero for Young Americans. LC 90-70314. 142p. (gr. 5-8). 1990. pap. 6.95 (1-55523-334-1) Winston-Derek.

Buchanan, Paul. The Return of the Eagle. Parker, Liz, ed. Taylor, Marjorie, illus. 45p. (Orig.). (gr. 6-12). 1992. pap. text ed. 2.95 (1-56254-052-1) Saddleback Pubns.

Buchanan, William J. One Last Time. 128p. (Orig.). 1992. pap. 2.99 (0-380-76152-1, Flare) Avon.

Buchanan-Hedman, Pat. Patrick & Patty Go to Time Out. Koop, Christie, illus. 24p. (Orig.). (ps-5). 1991. 8.95 (1-880121-50-6) Three Cs Ent.
—Stepmothers & Moonkisses. Koop, Christie, illus. 23p. (Orig.). (ps-5). 1991. 8.95 (1-880121-00-X) Three Cs Ent.
—Tracy & the Lavender Piece of Paper: A Realistic Story to Help Children Cope with Painful & Bitter Divorces. Koop, Christie, illus. (Orig.). (gr. 1-6). 1991. write for info. (1-880121-75-1) Three Cs Ent.

Buchanan-Hedman, Pat & Kingsbury, Kenneth. A Stepfather Named Buddy. Koop, Christie, illus. (Orig.). (ps-5). 1991. write for info. (1-880121-25-5) Three Cs Ent.

Buchart & Associates, Inc. Staff. Indianapolis Guide Book for Kids. 36p. (ps-5). 1993. pap. 2.75 (1-883900-01-8) Buchart & Assocs.
—Knoxville Guide Book for Kids. 28p. (ps-5). 1993. pap. 1.50 (1-883900-03-4) Buchart & Assocs.
—Louisville Guide Book for Kids. 36p. (ps-5). 1993. pap. 2.75 (1-883900-02-6) Buchart & Assocs.

Bucheit, Kelly S., ed. see Mooney, Chuck, III.

Buchheit, Paul. The Gospel of Mark in Verse. Jones, M. L., ed. 73p. (Orig.). 1993. pap. text ed. 5.95 (1-882270-06-1) Old Rugged Cross.

Buchignani, Walter. Tell No One Who You Are: The Secret Childhood of Regine Miller. LC 92-80412. 160p. (gr. 5-8). 1994. 17.95 (0-88776-286-7); pap. 9.95 (0-88776-303-0) Tundra Bks.

Buchman, Dian D. Medical Mysteries: Six Deadly Cases. (gr. 4-7). 1993. pap. 2.75 (0-590-43468-3) Scholastic Inc.
—Our Forty-Second President. (gr. 4-7). 1993. pap. 2.95 (0-590-46572-4) Scholastic Inc.

Buchter, Carol & Quigley, Elaine. Developing Basic Writing Skills, Bk. 1. (gr. 3-4). 1983. wkbk. 4.95 (0-89525-391-7) Ed Activities.
—Developing Basic Writing Skills, Bk. 2. (gr. 5-6). 1983. wkbk. 4.95 (0-89525-392-5) Ed Activities.

Buchwald, Ann, jt. auth. see Stewart, Marjabelle Y.

Buchwald, Ann, jt. auth. see Young, Marjabelle Y.

Buchwald, Claire. The Puppet Book: How to Make & Operate Puppets & Stage a Puppet-Play. Jakubiszyn, Audrey, illus. LC 90-38080. 134p. (Orig.). 1990. pap. 13.95 (0-8238-0293-0) Plays.

Buchwald, Emilie. Gildaen: The Heroic Adventures of a Most Unusual Rabbit. Flynn, Barbara, illus. LC 93-16255. 1993. 12.95 (0-915943-38-7) Milkweed Ed.

Buck, Nola. Not-Too-Sweet Trick or Treat. Karas, G. Brian, illus. 16p. (ps-3). 1993. 4.95 (0-694-00489-8, Festival) HarpC Child Bks.

Buck, Pearl S. The Big Wave. LC 85-45402. (Illus.). 80p. (gr. 3-6). 1986. pap. 3.95 (0-06-440171-5, Trophy) HarpC Child Bks.
—The Big Wave. LC 48-244. (Illus.). 80p. (gr. 2-6). 1973. PLB 13.89 (0-381-99923-8, Crowell Jr Bks) HarpC Child Bks.
—The Enemy. LC 85-30005. 64p. (gr. 6 up). 1986. PLB 13.95s.p. (0-88682-059-6) Creative Ed.
—The Old Demon. Higashi, Sandra, illus. 40p. (gr. 4 up). 1982. PLB 13.95s.p. (0-87191-828-5) Creative Ed.

Buck, Peggy J. Tommy Learns about Time & Eternity. Lautermilch, John, illus. 68p. (Orig.). (gr. 1-3). 1980. pap. 1.25 (0-89323-006-5, 023) Bible Memory.

Buck, Ray. Cal Ripken, Jr. All Star Shortstop. LC 85-485. (Illus.). 48p. (gr. 2-8). 1985. lib. bdg. 13.27 (0-516-04343-9) Childrens.

Buckalew, M. W., Jr. Learning to Control Stress. rev. ed. Gahan, Nancy L., illus. (gr. 7-12). 1982. PLB 13.95 (0-8239-0496-2) Rosen Group.

Buckalew, M. Walker. Drugs & Stress. Rosen, Ruth, ed. (gr. 7-12). 1993. 14.95 (0-8239-1418-6) Rosen Group.

Buckalew, Marshall, ed. see Coffey, William E., et al.

Buckalew, Marshall, ed. see Coffey, William E. & Riddel, Frank S.

Buckalew, Marshall, ed. see Doherty, William T.

Buckalew, Marshall, ed. see Williams, Tony L.

Buckalew, Walker. Coping with Choosing a College. Rosen, Roger, ed. 64p. (gr. 7-12). 1990. PLB 13.95 (0-8239-1079-2) Rosen Group.

Buckbee, Edward O. see Baird, Anne.

Buckel, Marian C. & Buckel, Tiffany. Mom, I Have a Staring Problem: A True Story of Petit Mal Seizures & the Hidden Problem It Can Cause: Learning Disability. LC 92-90113. (Illus.). 1992. pap. 3.95 saddle stitch (0-317-04291-2) M C Buckel.

Buckel, Tiffany, jt. auth. see Buckel, Marian C.

Bucki, Lisa, et al. Mathemagic. (Illus., Orig.). 1992. pap. 19.95 (0-672-30267-5) Alpha Bks IN.

Buckingham, Betty Jo, ed. Women at the Well: Expressions of Faith, Life & Worship Drawn from Our Own Wisdom. Carachei, Maria E., tr. LC 87-6224. (Orig.). (gr. 12). 1987. pap. 7.95 (0-9618243-0-1) Ch Brethren Womens Caucus.

Buckingham, Jack. The Accompaniment Guitar: A Beginner's Guide to Song Accompaniment for Individual or Classroom Use. (Illus.). 80p. 1979. pap. 7.00 (0-8258-0003-X, 05065) Fischer Inc NY.

Buckingham, Jamie. Let's Talk about Life. rev. ed. LC 86-61987. (Illus.). 112p. (gr. k up). 1987. pap. 6.99 (0-930525-07-8, Creation Hse) Strang Comms Co.

Buckingham, Nash. Blood Lines. 2nd ed. Burke, Edgar, illus. Davis, Henry P., intro. by. (Illus.). 227p. (gr. 10 up). 1991. Repr. of 1938 ed. 35.00 (1-56416-004-1) Derrydale Pr.
—Mark Right. 2nd ed. Buckingham, Nash, photos by. (Illus.). 250p. (gr. 10 up). 1989. Repr. 35.00 (1-56416-005-X) Derrydale Pr.

Buckingham, Sandra. Stencil It! (Illus.). 64p. Date not set. PLB 17.95 (0-921820-75-5, Pub. by Camden Hse CN); pap. 9.95 (0-921820-73-9, Pub. by Camden Hse CN) Firefly Bks Ltd. In STENCIL IT!, kids will learn how to decorate almost everything they own, from sneakers to school notebooks & denim jackets. With step-by-step instructions & colorful how-to photographs, this beginner's guide is perfect not only for kids who insist they can't draw but also for kids who do nothing but. Sandra Buckingham describes how to set up, how to select materials & how to master the basic techniques involved in creating both original & classic designs, including birds, leaves, flowers, lizards, turtles, cave figures & much more. STENCIL IT! features sample stencil designs that can be copied & adapted for use in more than a dozen projects. The author's message is simple: with these easy-to-learn methods & a few affordable supplies, ANYONE can learn to stencil. Chapters include: Getting Started, Stencilling Silhouettes, Using Color, Painting on Fabric, Wearable Art, Lettering, Art Prints, Personalizing Your Room, Creating Your Own Stencil Designs. The author is especially careful to offer both safety & cleanup tips. Sandra Buckingham is the author of Stencilling: A Harrowsmith Guide with more than 50,000 copies in print. *Publisher Provided Annotation.*

Buckingham, Simon. Alec & His Flying Bed. LC 90-52939. (Illus.). 32p. (gr. k up). 1991. 14.95 (0-688-10555-6); PLB 14.88 (0-688-10556-4) Lothrop.

Buckle, Mariette. All Dressed Up. Strahan, Heather, illus. LC 92-21447. 1993. 3.75 (0-383-03613-5) SRA Schl Grp.

Buckler, William E., ed. Prose of the Victorian Period. (gr. 9 up). 1958. pap. 9.16 (0-395-05128-2, RivEd) HM.

Buckler, William E., ed. see Hardy, Thomas.

Buckley, Helen. Take Care of Things, Edward Said. Coville, Katherine, illus. LC 88-1578. 32p. (ps up). 1991. 13.95 (0-688-07731-5); PLB 13.88 (0-688-07732-3) Lothrop.

Buckley, Helen E. Grandfather & I. Ormerod, Jan, illus. LC 93-22936. 1994. write for info. (0-688-12533-6); PLB write for info. (0-688-12534-4) Lothrop.
—Grandmother & I. Ormerod, Jan, illus. LC 93-22937. (gr. 3 up). 1994. write for info. (0-688-12531-X); PLB write for info. (0-688-12532-8) Lothrop.

Buckley, Joe. Donny in London. 160p. (gr. 7-11). 1993. pap. 9.95 (0-86327-360-2, Pub. by Wolfhound Pr EIRE) Dufour.
—Run Donny Run. 140p. (gr. 6-10). 1991. pap. 7.95 (0-86327-297-5, Pub. by Wolfhound Pr EIRE) Dufour.

Buckley, John. The Magical Round Wall. (gr. 3-7). 1991. 6.95 (0-533-08849-6) Vantage.

Buckley, Ramon, tr. see Dahl, Roald.

Buckley, Richard. The Follish Tortoise. Carle, Eric, illus. LC 93-20123. (gr. 1-8). 1993. pap. 4.95 (0-88708-323-4) Picture Bk Studio.
—The Foolish Tortoise & the Greedy Python. Carle, Eric, illus. LC 86-25468. 48p. (ps). 1991. pap. 12.95 (0-88708-039-1) Picture Bk Studio.
—The Greedy Python. Carle, Eric, illus. LC 92-6633. 28p. (ps). 1993. Repr. Mini-bk. 4.95 (0-88708-268-8) Picture Bk Studio.

Buckley, Richard & Williams, Alex. The Bird Who Couldn't Fly. (Illus.). 32p. (ps-1). 1989. 15.95 (0-340-41990-3, Pub. by Hodder & Stoughton UK) Trafalgar.

Buckman, Mary. The Alphabet Cookbook. (Illus.). (gr. k-2). 1988. pap. text ed. 9.95 (1-879414-03-1) Mary Bee Creat.
—The Alphagator. (Illus.). 32p. (ps). 1992. pap. 8.95 (1-879414-10-4) Mary Bee Creat.
—The Animal Cookbook. (Illus.). (gr. k-2). 1982. text ed. 9.95 (1-879414-01-5) Mary Bee Creat.
—Ben. Morgan, Connie, illus. 32p. (gr. k-5). 1992. pap. 8.95 (1-879414-09-0) Mary Bee Creat.
—The Count & Cook Book. (Illus.). (gr. k-2). 1982. pap. text ed. 9.95 (1-879414-00-7) Mary Bee Creat.
—Leap Frog. LC 89-63379. (Illus., Orig.). (gr. k-2). 1989. pap. text ed. 12.95 (1-879414-05-8) Mary Bee Creat.
—Magical Muriel. LC 90-60453. (Illus., Orig.). (gr. k-2). 1991. pap. text ed. 12.95 (1-879414-07-4) Mary Bee Creat.
—The Shape & Cook Book. (Illus.). (gr. k-2). 1982. pap. text ed. 9.95 (1-879414-02-3) Mary Bee Creat.
—Wiggle Worm. LC 89-63502. (Illus., Orig.). (gr. k-2). 1989. pap. text ed. 12.95 (1-879414-06-6) Mary Bee Creat.

Bucknall, Caroline. One Bear All Alone. Bucknall, Caroline, illus. LC 85-6968. 32p. (ps-2). 1989. 4.95 (0-8037-0645-6) Dial Bks Young.
—One Bear in the Hospital. Bucknall, Caroline, illus. LC 90-2994. 32p. (ps-2). 1991. 11.95 (0-8037-0847-5) Dial Bks Young.
—One Bear in the Picture. (Illus.). 32p. (ps-2). 1993. pap. 3.99 (0-14-054591-3) Puffin Bks.
—The Three Little Pigs. Bucknall, Caroline, illus. LC 86-16716. 32p. (ps-2). 1987. 10.95 (0-8037-0100-4) Dial Bks Young.

Buckwalter, Leoda. Conquest & Glory: True Tales from the Land of the Taj. Johns, Helen, ed. LC 92-74955. (Illus.). 171p. (Orig.). 1992. pap. 7.95 (0-916035-56-5) Evangel Indiana.

Bucur, Mike, jt. auth. see Molyneux, Lynn.

Budbill, David. Bones on Black Spruce Mountain. 128p. (gr. 5 up). 1994. pap. 3.99 (0-14-036854-X) Puffin Bks.
—Snowshoe Trek to Otter River. (Illus.). 96p. (gr. 4-6). 1984. pap. 2.75 (0-553-15469-9, Skylark) Bantam.

Buddhist Text Translation Society Staff. Cherishing Life, Vol. I. (Illus.). 150p. (Orig.). (gr. 3 up). 1983. pap. 7.00 (0-88139-004-6) Buddhist Text.
—Cherishing Life, Vol. II. (Illus.). 160p. (gr. 3 up). 1983. pap. 7.00 (0-88139-015-1) Buddhist Text.
—Filiality, the Human Source, Vol. 1. 132p. (gr. 3 up). 1983. pap. 7.00 (0-88139-006-2) Buddhist Text.
—Filiality, the Human Source, Vol. 2. 120p. (Orig.). (gr. 3 up). 1983. pap. 7.00 (0-88139-020-8) Buddhist Text.

Buddinger, Peyton B., jt. auth. see Chamberlain, Valerie M.

Buddle, Jackie. Fun with Words. Davis, Annelies, illus. 32p. (gr. 2). 1988. PLB 14.97 (0-88625-164-8); pap. 2.97 (0-88625-161-3) Durkin Hayes Pub.

Buddle, Jacqueline. Fun with Sizes & Shapes. Davis, Annelies, illus. 32p. (gr. k). 1988. PLB 14.97 (0-88625-162-1); pap. 2.95 (0-88625-143-5) Durkin Hayes Pub.

Budworth, Geoffrey. The Knot Book. LC 84-26843. (Illus.). 160p. (gr. 7 up). 1985. pap. 8.95 (0-8069-7944-5) Sterling.

Bue, Henri, tr. see Carroll, Lewis.

Buegler, Marion E. Discovering Density. Bergman, Lincoln & Fairwell, Kay, eds. Klofkorn, Lisa, illus. Hoyt, Richard, photos by. (Illus.). 49p. (Orig.). (gr. 6-10). 1988. pap. 8.50 (0-912511-17-6) Lawrence Science.

Buehler, Paula. Who's on Second Beach? 8p. (gr. k-2). 1993. pap. write for info. (1-882563-07-7) Lamont Bks.

Buehler, Stephanie J. There's No Surf in Cleveland. LC 92-11981. 144p. (gr. 3-7). 1993. 13.95 (0-395-62162-3, Clarion Bks) HM.

Buehner, Caralyn. A Job for Wittilda. Buehner, Mark, illus. LC 91-15630. 32p. (ps-3). 1993. 13.99 (0-8037-1149-2); lib. bdg. 13.89 (0-8037-1150-6) Dial Bks Young.

Buehner, Caralyn & Buehner, Mark. The Courtesy Quiz Book. LC 93-36293. (gr. 5 up). 1994. write for info. (0-8037-1494-7); PLB write for info. (0-8037-1495-5) Dial Bks Young.
—The Escape of Marvin the Ape. LC 91-10795. (Illus.). 32p. (ps-3). 1992. 14.00 (0-8037-1123-9); PLB 13.89 (0-8037-1124-7) Dial Bks Young.

Buehner, Mark, jt. auth. see Buehner, Caralyn.

Buehrens, Adam. Hi, I'm Adam: A Child's Book of Tourette Syndrome. LC 90-47552. (Illus.). 35p. (Orig.). (gr. k-8). 1991. pap. 4.95 (1-878267-29-9) Hope Pr CA.

Buehrens, Adam & Buehrens, Carol. Adam & the Magic Marble: A Magical Adventure. LC 90-23906. (Illus.). 108p. (Orig.). (gr. k-10). 1991. pap. 6.95 (1-878267-30-2) Hope Pr CA.

Buehrens, Carol, jt. auth. see Buehrens, Adam.

Buell, Ellen L., ed. Treasury of Little Golden Books. 120p. (ps-2). 1989. write for info. (0-307-86540-1, Golden Bks) Western Pub.

Buerger, Jane. Obedience. rev. ed. Endres, Helen, illus. LC 80-39520. 32p. (gr. k-3). 1981. PLB 21.35 (0-89565-206-4); PLB 14.95s.p. (0-685-55536-4) Childs World.

Buerger, Jane & Davis, Jenine. Helping. 32p. (gr. k-3). 1985. PLB 21.35 (0-89565-302-8); PLB 14.95s.p. (0-685-62604-0) Childs World.

Buffalo, Audreen. Meet Oprah Winfrey. (Illus.). 112p. (gr. 3-5). 1993. pap. 2.99 (0-679-85425-8) Random Bks Yng Read.

Buffet, Jimmy. Jimmy Buffet. 76p. (Orig.). pap. text ed. 13.95 (0-89898-473-4) CPP Belwin.

Buffet, Savannah J., jt. ed. see Buffett, Jimmy.

Buffett, Jimmy. Jolly Man. LC 87-8573. (gr. 4 up). 1993. pap. 4.95 (0-15-240538-0, HB Juv Bks) HarBrace.

Buffett, Jimmy & Buffett, Savannah J. The Jolly Man. Davis, Lambert, illus. (ps-3). 1990. Incl. cassette. 19.95 (0-15-240531-3) HarBrace.
—Trouble Dolls. Ingber, Bonnie V., intro. by. Davis, Lambert, illus. 32p. (gr. 1 up). 1991. 14.95 (0-15-290790-4) HarBrace.

Buffett, Jimmy & Buffett, Savannah J., eds. The Jolly Mon. Davis, Lambert, illus. 32p. (gr. 4-8). 1988. 14.95 (0-15-240530-5) HarBrace.

Buffett, Savannah J., jt. auth. see Buffett, Jimmy.

Buffie, Margaret. The Haunting of Frances Rain. 1989. pap. 12.95 (0-590-42834-9) Scholastic Inc.
—Warnings. 1991. 13.95 (0-590-43665-1, Scholastic Hardcover) Scholastic Inc.

Buhay, Debra. Black & White of Finance. 30p. (gr. 12). 1990. pap. 2.00 (1-878056-02-6) D Hockenberry.
—Black & White of Marriage. 30p. (gr. 12). 1990. pap. 2.00 (1-878056-04-2) D Hockenberry.
—Black & White of Politics. 30p. (gr. 12). 1990. pap. 2.00 (1-878056-03-4) D Hockenberry.
—Black & White of Success. 30p. (gr. 12). 1990. pap. 2.00 (1-878056-01-8) D Hockenberry.
—Black & White of Writing. 30p. (gr. 12). 1990. pap. 2.00 (0-685-37411-4) D Hockenberry.

Buhler, Cheyl, et al. Thematic Bibliography. Buhler, Cheryl, et al, illus. 176p. (gr. k-8). 1993. wkbk. 14.95 (1-55734-373-X) Tchr Create Mat.

Buhler, June H., et al. Let's Celebrate Texas: Past, Present & Future. LC 86-11961. (Illus.). 171p. (gr. 4-7). 1986. 15.95x (0-937460-23-0) Hendrick-Long.

Buholzer, Theres. Life of the Snail. Simon, Noel, tr. from GER. (Illus.). 48p. (gr. 2-5). 1987. PLB 19.95 (0-87614-246-3) Carolrhoda Bks.

Bulfinch, Thomas. Age of Chivalry. (gr. 8 up). 1965. pap. 1.95 (0-8049-0061-2, CL-61) Airmont.
—Bulfinch's Mythology, 3 vols. Bovie, Palmer, intro. by. Incl. Vol. 1. The Age of Fable. 408p. 1962. pap. 3.95 (0-451-62444-0, ME2230); Vols 2 & 3. The Age of Chivalry & Legends of Charlemagne. 608p. pap. 4.95 (0-451-62252-9). (RL 7). 1962. pap. 4.95 (0-451-62659-1, Ment) NAL-Dutton.

Bulfinch, Thomas & Sewell, H. A Book of Myths. Sewell, Helen, illus. LC 42-25450. 128p. (gr. 5-9). 1969. SBE 14.95 (0-02-782280-X, Macmillan Child Bk) Macmillan Child Grp.

Bull, Angela. Anne Frank. (Illus.). 64p. (gr. 5-9). 1991. 11.95 (0-237-60015-3, Pub. by Evans Bros Ltd) Trafalgar.
—Elizabeth Fry. (Illus.). 64p. (gr. 5-9). 1991. 11.95 (0-237-60028-5, Pub. by Evans Bros Ltd) Trafalgar.
—Florence Nightingale. (Illus.). 64p. (gr. 5-9). 1991. 11.95 (0-237-60018-8, Pub. by Evans Bros Ltd) Trafalgar.
—Marie Curie. (Illus.). 64p. (gr. 5-9). 1991. 11.95 (0-237-60024-2, Pub. by Evans Bros Ltd) Trafalgar.

Bull, Emma. The Princess & the Lord of Night. Gaber, Susan, illus. LC 93-19151. 1994. write for info. (0-15-263543-2, J Yolen Bks) HarBrace.

Bull, George, tr. see Machiavelli, Niccolo.

Bull, Norman. Church of Jesus Grows. (gr. 2-7). 1979. 10.95 (0-7175-0454-9) Dufour.
—Church of the Jews. (gr. 2-7). 1975. 10.95 (0-7175-0450-6) Dufour.
—Founders of the Jews. (gr. 2-7). 1985. pap. 10.95 (0-7175-0977-X) Dufour.
—Jesus the Nazarene. (gr. 2-7). 1984. pap. 10.95 (0-7175-0981-8) Dufour.
—Prophets of the Jews. (gr. 2-7). 1984. pap. 10.95 (0-7175-0979-6) Dufour.

Bull, Rene. The Arabian Knights. (gr. 2-6). 1986. 8.98 (0-685-16864-6, 619342) Outlet Bk Co.

Bulla, Clyde R. The Chalk Box Kid. Allen, Thomas B., illus. LC 87-4683. 64p. (gr. 2-4). 1987. lib. bdg. 6.99 (0-394-99102-8); pap. 1.50 (0-394-89102-3) Random Bks Yng Read.
—Charlie's House. Flavin, Teresa, illus. LC 92-23998. 96p. (gr. 3-6). 1993. 14.00 (0-679-83841-4) Knopf Bks Yng Read.
—The Christmas Coat. Wickstrom, Sylvie, illus. LC 89-2380. 48p. (gr. k-2). 1990. 13.95 (0-394-89385-9); PLB 14.99 (0-394-99385-3) Knopf Bks Yng Read.
—Daniel's Duck. Sandin, Joan, illus. LC 77-25647. 64p. (gr. k-3). 1979. PLB 13.89 (0-06-020909-7) HarpC Child Bks.
—Daniel's Duck. Sandin, Joan, illus. LC 78-22156. 64p. (gr. k-3). 1982. pap. 3.50 (0-06-444031-1, Trophy) HarpC Child Bks.
—Ghost of Windy Hill. Bolognese, Don, illus. LC 68-11059. (gr. 3-7). 1968. PLB 13.89 (0-690-32764-1, Crowell Jr Bks) HarpC Child Bks.
—The Ghost of Windy Hill. 96p. (Orig.). (gr. 2-5). 1990. pap. 2.75 (0-590-43286-9) Scholastic Inc.
—Keep Running, Allen! Ichikawa, Satomi, illus. LC 77-23311. (gr. k-2). 1978. PLB 14.89 (0-690-01375-2, Crowell Jr Bks) HarpC Child Bks.
—A Lion to Guard Us. Chessare, Michele, illus. LC 80-2455. (gr. 2-5). 1981. (Crowell Jr Bks); PLB 13.89 (0-690-04097-0, Crowell Jr Bks) HarpC Child Bks.
—Lion to Guard Us. LC 80-2455. (Illus.). 128p. (gr. 3-5). 1989. pap. 3.95 (0-06-440333-5, Trophy) HarpC Child Bks.
—A Lion to Guard Us. 105p. (gr. 4-7). 1981. 8.40 (0-685-66374-4, BR8236) W A T Braille.
—Pocahontas & the Strangers. (Illus.). 176p. (gr. 2-6). 1987. pap. 2.95 (0-590-43481-0) Scholastic Inc.
—Secret Valley. Paull, Grace, illus. LC 49-10917. 112p. (gr. 2-5). 1993. pap. 3.95 (0-06-440456-0, Trophy) HarpC Child Bks.
—Shoeshine Girl. Grant, Leigh, illus. LC 75-8516. 64p. (gr. 2-5). 1989. pap. 3.95 (0-06-440228-2, Trophy) HarpC Child Bks.
—Shoeshine Girl. LC 75-8516. (Illus.). 80p. (gr. 3-5). 1989. PLB 13.89 (0-690-04830-0, Crowell Jr Bks) HarpC Child Bks.
—Singing Sam. Magurn, Susan, illus. LC 88-19758. 48p. (Orig.). (gr. 1-3). 1989. PLB 7.99 (0-394-91977-7); pap. 3.50 (0-394-81977-2) Random Bks Yng Read.
—Squanto, Friend of the Pilgrims. 112p. 1990. pap. 2.95 (0-590-44055-1) Scholastic Inc.
—The Sword in the Tree. Galdone, Paul, illus. LC 56-5699. 128p. (gr. 2-5). 1962. PLB 13.89 (0-690-79909-8, Crowell Jr Bks) HarpC Child Bks.
—What Makes a Shadow? rev. ed. Otani, June, illus. LC 92-36350. 32p. (ps-1). 1994. 15.00 (0-06-022915-2); PLB 14.89 (0-06-022916-0) HarpC Child Bks.
—What Makes a Shadow? Otani, June, illus. LC 92-36350. 32p. (ps-1). 1994. pap. 4.95 (0-06-445118-6, Trophy) HarpC Child Bks.
—White Bird. Cook, Donald, illus. LC 89-70231. 64p. (Orig.). (gr. 2-4). 1990. lib. bdg. 6.99 (0-679-90662-2); pap. 2.50 (0-679-80662-8) Random Bks Yng Read.

Bulla, Dale. The Magic Box. Arkenberg, Rebecca N., illus. 24p. (gr. 2-6). 1993.

12.95 (1-884197-00-0) N Horizon Educ. As a poor couple work in their garden, they discover a box that reproduces anything that is placed into it. The choices they make are reminiscent of a modern day rags to riches story. The mixture of old to new, past & present, rich & poor, provide a playful adaptation of an ancient tale. When youngsters read or listen to this story, they may be encouraged to talk about the mistakes made & issues raised as they think about the consequences of their choices. Children may be asked, "What would you do if you found such a box?" Storyteller Dale Bulla shares this comical retelling of an old folktale which is the most often requested story in his repertoire.
Publisher Provided Annotation.

Bullard, Sara. Free At Last: A History of the Civil Rights Movement & Those Who Died in the Struggle. Bond, Julian, intro. by. LC 92-38174. (Illus.). 112p. 1993. PLB 18.00 (0-19-508381-4) OUP.

Bullen, Susan. The Alps & Their People. (Illus.). 48p. (gr. 5-8). 1994. 15.95 (1-56847-165-3) Thomson Lrning.
—The Arctic & Its People. LC 93-27125. (Illus.). 48p. (gr. 5-8). 1994. 15.95 (1-56847-153-X) Thomson Lrning.

Buller, Jon. I Love You Good Night. 1990. pap. 2.25 (0-671-70297-1, Little Simon) S&S Trade.

Buller, Jon & Schade, Susan. I Love You, Good Night. 1988. pap. 5.95 (0-671-66561-8, S&S BFYR) S&S Trade.
—Mike & the Magic Cookies. (Illus.). 48p. (gr. 2-4). 1992. (G&D); pap. 3.50 (0-448-40386-2, G&D) Putnam Pub Group.
—No Tooth, No Quarter! A Step 3 Book. Buller, Jon, illus. LC 89-30250. 48p. (Orig.). (gr. 2-3). 1989. lib. bdg. 7.99 (0-394-94956-0); pap. 3.50 (0-394-84956-6, Random Juv) Random Bks Yng Read.
—Toad on the Road. Buller, Jon, illus. LC 91-4246. 32p. (Orig.). (ps-1). 1992. PLB 7.99 (0-679-92689-5); pap. 3.50 (0-679-82689-0) Random Bks Yng Read.
—Twenty-Thousand Baseball Cards under the Sea: A Step Three Book. Buller, Jon, illus. LC 90-40704. 48p. (Orig.). (gr. 2-3). 1991. lib. bdg. 7.99 (0-679-91569-9); pap. 3.50 (0-679-81569-4) Random Bks Yng Read.
—The Video Kids. LC 93-26923. 1994. PLB write for info. (0-448-40181-9, G&D); pap. write for info. (0-448-40180-0, G&D) Putnam Pub Group.
—Yo! It's Captain Yo-Yo. Buller, Jon & Schade, Susan, illus. LC 92-44306. 48p. (gr. 2-3). 1993. PLB 3.50 (0-448-40192-4, G&D); (G&D) Putnam Pub Group.

Buller, Jon, jt. auth. see Schade, Susan.

Bullock, Gloria S. & Crocitto, Jane B. Shopping at the Ani-Mall. Weinberger, Jane, ed. DeVito, Pam, illus. LC 90-70475. 44p. (ps-3). 1991. pap. 9.95 (0-932433-72-3) Windswept Hse.

Bullock, Harold B. The Battle for the Worlds. Anderson, Jean, ed. Menefee, Paige & Smith, Patti, illus. 1990. 14.95 (0-9626219-4-3) Summit TX.

Bullock, Judy. Uncle Wiley Whiskers: Tells How the Catfish Got Its name. Barber, Liz A., illus. 16p. (gr. k-6). 1992. pap. 4.95 (0-937552-49-6) Quail Ridge.

Bullock, Kathleen. A Friend for Mitzi Mouse. LC 90-31559. (Illus.). 40p. (ps-1). 1990. pap. 13.95 jacketed (0-671-68867-7, Little Simon) S&S Trade.
—It Chanced to Rain. Bullock, Kathleen, illus. LC 87-32070. (ps-1). 1992. pap. 13.95 jacketed (0-671-66005-5, S&S BFYR); pap. 3.95 (0-671-77820-X, S&S BFYR) S&S Trade.
—Rabbits Are Coming. (ps). 1991. pap. 13.95 jacketed (0-671-72963-2, S&S BFYR) S&S Trade.
—The Rabbits Are Coming! LC 90-49830. (Illus.). 40p. (ps-1). 1993. pap. 4.95 (0-671-79609-7, Little Simon) S&S Trade.
—She'll Be Comin' Round the Mountain. LC 92-17340. 1993. pap. 14.00 (0-671-79153-2, S&S BFYR) S&S Trade.

Bullock, Robert. Wilderness Habitat: The Great Plains - A Young Reader's Journal. Bullock, Robert, illus. LC 86-81461. 64p. (Orig.). (gr. k-8). 1987. pap. 5.95 (0-943972-10-8) Homestead WY.
—Wilderness Habitat: The Rocky Mountains: A Young Reader's Journal. Bullock, Robert, illus. LC 93-77117. 64p. (Orig.). (gr. k-5). 1993. pap. 7.95 (0-943972-18-3) Homestead WY.

Bullock, Waneta B. & Loveless, Ganelle. ABC Mazes. (Illus.). 56p. (gr. k-1). 1979. pap. 7.00 (0-87879-713-0, Ann Arbor Div) Acad Therapy.

Bullshows, Harry & Gilliland, Hap. Legends of Chief Bald Eagle. (gr. 2-10). 1977. 1.95 (0-89992-034-9) Coun India Ed.

Bulman, George. Play the Game: Volleyball. (Illus.). 80p. (Orig.). (gr. 10-12). 1990. pap. 6.95 (0-7063-6774-X, Pub. by Ward Lock UK) Sterling.

Bulmer-Thomas, Barbara. Journey Through Mexico. Camm, Martin, et al, illus. LC 90-10950. 32p. (gr. 3-5). 1991. PLB 11.89 (*0-8167-2116-5*); pap. text ed. 3.95 (*0-8167-2117-3*) Troll Assocs.

Bulow, Von Hans see Cramer, J. B.

Bulpin, Tom V. The Hunter Is Death. Astley-Maberly, C. T., illus. 348p. (gr. 10 up). 1987. Repr. of 1962 ed. 30.00 (*0-940143-08-9*) Safari Pr.

Bumann, Joan & Patterson, John. All-New Edition of Our American Presidents. 176p. (gr. 5 up). 1993. pap. 2.99 (*0-87406-644-1*) Willowisp Pr.

Bumpus, Jerry. Dawn of the Flying Pigs. (Illus.). 144p. (Orig.). 1992. pap. 12.50x (*0-914140-16-7*) Carpenter Pr.

Bunce, Vincent J. Japan. LC 93-20426. 1994. write for info. (*0-531-14270-1*) Watts.

Bunch, Lewis, ed. see Woodard, Lynette & Cook, Kevin.

Bundschuh, Rick. The Church. LC 88-9692. (Illus.). 154p. (Orig.). (gr. 9-12). 1988. pap. 5.99 (*0-8307-1182-1*, S184102) Regal.

—How to Survive Middle School: A Humorous Guide to the Wonder Years. 160p. 1991. pap. 5.99 (*0-310-53521-2*, Pub. by Youth Spec) Zondervan.

—A Shadow of a Man. LC 86-22048. 120p. (Orig.). (gr. 6-9). 1986. pap. 5.99 (*0-8307-1143-0*, S185116) Regal.

Bungum, Jane. Money & Financial Institutions. (Illus.). 88p. (gr. 5 up). 1991. PLB 21.50 (*0-8225-1781-7*) Lerner Pubns.

Bunin, Catherine & Bunin, Sherry. Is That Your Sister? A True Story of Adoption. Welch, Sheila K., illus. 32p. (gr. 2-6). 1992. Repr. of 1976 ed. 14.95 (*0-9611872-6-3*) Our Child Pr.

Bunin, Sherry, jt. auth. see Bunin, Catherine.

Bunn, Scott. Just Hold On. LC 82-70316. 160p. (gr. 7 up). 1982. pap. 9.95 (*0-385-28490-X*) Delacorte.

Bunn, T. Davis. Florian's Gate. 400p. 1992. pap. 8.99 (*1-55661-244-3*) Bethany Hse.

—Winter Palace. 400p. (Orig.). 1993. pap. 8.99 (*1-55661-324-5*) Bethany Hse.

Bunnell, Jean. Children at Shaker Village: Rural Life in the 19th Century, Using Primary Sources to Learn about History. (Illus.). 54p. (Orig.). (gr. 5-9). 1991. pap. text ed. 25.00x (*0-915836-16-5*) United Soc Shakers.

Bunnett, Chris, jt. auth. see McSweeney, Sean.

Bunnett, Rochelle. Friends in the Park. Sahlhoff, Carl, illus. 32p. 1993. 7.95 (*1-56288-347-X*) Checkerboard.

—Friends Together: More Alike Than Different. Brown, Matt & Sahloff, Carl, photos by. (Illus.). 12p. (gr. k-4). 1993. tchr's. ed. 24.95 (*1-56288-429-8*) Checkerboard.

Bunny. Tigger: Story of a Mayan Ocelot. LC 66-12746. (Illus.). (gr. k-2). 1974. 6.95 (*0-87208-009-9*) Island Pr Pubs.

Bunsen, Rick, ed. Golden Christmas Treasury. rev. & enl. ed. LC 84-72934. (Illus.). 96p. (gr. k-12). 1989. write for info. (*0-307-95585-0*, Pub. by Golden Bks) Western Pub.

Bunson, Margaret & Bunson, Matthew. Kateri Tekakwitha. Bunson, Margaret, illus. LC 92-61548. 56p. (Orig.). 1993. 9.95 (*0-87973-786-7*, 786); pap. 6.95 (*0-87973-560-0*, 560) Our Sunday Visitor.

—St. Patrick. Bunson, Margaret, illus. LC 92-61547. 56p. (Orig.). 1993. 9.95 (*0-87973-785-9*, 785); pap. 6.95 (*0-87973-559-7*, 559) Our Sunday Visitor.

Bunson, Matthew, jt. auth. see Bunson, Margaret.

Bunt, Sandra K. The Other Side of the Desk. DeVito, Pam, illus. LC 90-71374. 135p. (Orig.). (gr. 3-6). 1992. pap. 9.95 (*0-932433-80-4*) Windswept Hse.

Bunte, Pamela A. & Franklin, Robert J. The Paiute. (Illus.). 112p. (gr. 5 up). 1990. 17.95 (*1-55546-723-7*) Chelsea Hse.

Bunting. Days. Date not set. 15.00 (*0-06-023609-4*, Festival); PLB 14.89 (*0-06-023612-4*, Festival) HarpC Child Bks.

Bunting, E. Jumping the Nail. 148p. (gr. 7 up). 1991. 15.95 (*0-15-241357-X*, HB Juv Bks) HarBrace.

—Summer Wheels. 1992. 14.95 (*0-15-207000-1*, HB Juv Bks) HarBrace.

Bunting, E. & Rand, T. Night Tree. (ps-3). 1991. 13.95 (*0-15-257425-5*, HB Juv Bks) HarBrace.

Bunting, E., et al. Sprint Library Three-A. large type ed. Incl. Summer at Ravenswood. 102p. (3 up). 1982. Repr. of 1976 ed. 18.98 (*0-317-03698-X*, 4-23080-00) Am Printing Hse.

Bunting, Eve. The Big Red Barn. Knotts, Howard, illus. LC 78-12186. 32p. (gr. k-3). 1979. pap. 6.95 (*0-15-611938-2*, Voyager Bks) HarBrace.

—Coffin on a Case. LC 92-855. 112p. (gr. 4-7). 1992. 13.00 (*0-06-020273-4*); PLB 12.89 (*0-06-020274-2*) HarpC Child Bks.

—Coffin on a Case. LC 92-855. (Illus.). 112p. (gr. 4-7). 1993. pap. 3.95 (*0-06-440461-7*, Trophy) HarpC Child Bks.

—Day Before Christmas. Peck, Beth, illus. 32p. (ps-3). 1992. 14.95 (*0-89919-866-X*, Clarion Bks) HM.

—A Day's Work. Himler, Ronald, illus. 1995. write for info. (*0-395-67321-6*, Clarion Bks) HM.

—Demetrius & the Golden Goblet. Hague, Michael, illus. LC 79-14865. 48p. (gr. 1-5). 1980. 8.95 (*0-15-223186-2*, HB Juv Bks) HarBrace.

—Dream Dancer. (Illus.). 64p. 1992. 12.75 (*0-89565-779-1*); 8.95s.p. (*0-685-55119-9*) Childs World.

—Face at the Edge of the World. LC 85-2684. 192p. (gr. 7 up). 1988. 13.95 (*0-89919-399-4*, Clarion Bks); pap. 4.95 (*0-89919-800-7*) HM.

—Fifteen. (Illus.). (gr. 3-8). 1992. PLB 12.75 (*0-685-62602-4*); PLB 8.95s.p. (*0-685-62603-2*) Childs World.

—Flower Garden. Hewitt, Kathryn, illus. LC 92-25766. 1994. write for info. (*0-15-228776-0*) HarBrace.

—Fly Away Home. Giblin, James, ed. Himler, Ronald, illus. 32p. (ps-2). 1991. 14.45 (*0-395-55962-6*, Clarion Bks) HM.

—Fly Away Home. Himler, Ronald, illus. 32p. (gr. k-3). 1993. pap. 5.70 (*0-395-66415-2*, Clarion Bks) HM.

—The Followers. (Illus.). 64p. 1992. 12.75 (*0-89565-764-3*); 8.95s.p. (*0-685-55108-3*) Childs World.

—For Always. LC 92-11478. (Illus.). (gr. 1-8). 1992. PLB 8.95 (*0-89565-969-7*); Resale. 12.75 (*0-685-59403-3*) Childs World.

—Ghost Behind Me. (gr. 7-9). 1986. pap. 2.50 (*0-671-62211-0*, Archway) PB.

—Ghost Children. (gr. 4-7). 1991. pap. 3.50 (*0-553-15879-1*) Bantam.

—Ghost's Hour, Spook's Hour. Carrick, Donald, illus. LC 86-31674. 32p. (ps-1). 1987. 14.45 (*0-89919-484-2*, Clarion Bks) HM.

—Ghost's Hour, Spook's Hour. Carrick, Donald, illus. LC 86-31674. 32p. (ps). 1989. pap. 4.95 (*0-395-51583-1*, Clarion Bks) HM.

—Ghost's Hour, Spook's Hour. Carrick, Donald, illus. 1990. pap. 7.70 incl.cassette (*0-395-56244-9*, Clarion Bks) HM.

—The Ghosts of Departure Point. LC 81-48602. 113p. (gr. 6 up). 1982. (Lipp Jr Bks); (Lipp Jr Bks) HarpC Child Bks.

—The Girl in the Painting. (Illus.). 64p. 1992. 12.75 (*0-89565-770-8*); 8.95s.p. (*0-685-55115-6*) Childs World.

—Happy Birthday, Dear Duck. Brett, Jan, illus. LC 87-15694. 32p. (ps-1). 1988. 13.95 (*0-89919-541-5*, Clarion Bks) HM.

—Happy Birthday, Dear Duck. Brett, Jan, illus. LC 87-15694. 32p. (ps). 1990. pap. 4.80 (*0-395-52594-2*, Clarion Bks) HM.

—The Hideout. D'Andrade, Diane, ed. 133p. (gr. 3-7). 1991. 14.95 (*0-15-233990-6*) HarBrace.

—Hideout. (gr. 4-7). 1993. pap. 4.95 (*0-15-233991-4*) HarBrace.

—How Many Days to America? A Thanksgiving Story. Peck, Beth, illus. LC 88-2590. 32p. (gr. k-4). 1988. 15.45 (*0-89919-521-0*, Clarion Bks) HM.

—How Many Days to America: A Thanksgiving Story. Bunting, Eve, illus. 32p. (ps-3). 1990. pap. 5.70 (*0-395-54777-6*, Clarion Bks) HM.

—If I Asked You, Would You Stay? LC 82-49052. 160p. (gr. 7 up). 1987. PLB 12.89x (*0-397-32066-3*, Trophy); pap. 3.95 (*0-06-447023-7*, Trophy) HarpC Child Bks.

—In the Haunted House. Meddaugh, Susan, illus. LC 89-77663. 32p. (ps-3). 1990. 13.45 (*0-395-51589-0*, Clarion Bks) HM.

—Is Anybody There? LC 87-45881. 176p. (gr. 4-7). 1990. (Trophy); PLB 12.89x (*0-397-32303-4*, Trophy); pap. 3.95 (*0-06-440347-5*, Trophy) HarpC Child Bks.

—The Island of One. (Illus.). 64p. 1992. 12.75 (*0-89565-768-6*); 8.95s.p. (*0-685-55109-1*) Childs World.

—Jane Martin, Dog Detective. Schwartz, Amy, illus. 44p. (ps-3). 1988. pap. 3.95 (*0-15-239587-3*, Voyager Bks) HarBrace.

—Janet Hamm Needs a Date for the Dance. 112p. 1987. pap. 2.95 (*0-553-15537-7*, Skylark) Bantam.

—Jumping the Nail. LC 94-11090. (gr. 9-12). 1993. pap. 4.95 (*0-15-241358-8*) HarBrace.

—Just Like Everyone Else. LC 92-11455. (Illus.). (gr. 1-8). 1992. PLB 8.95 (*0-89565-972-7*); Resale. 12.75 (*0-685-59327-4*) Childs World.

—Karen Kepplewhite Is the World's Best Kisser. LC 83-2066. 96p. (gr. 3-6). 1983. 13.45 (*0-89919-182-7*, Clarion Bks) HM.

—Lady's Girl. (Illus.). 64p. 1992. 12.75 (*0-89565-777-5*); 8.95s.p. (*0-685-55120-2*) Childs World.

—Maggie the Freak. (Illus.). 64p. 1992. 12.75 (*0-89565-775-9*); 8.95s.p. (*0-685-55144-X*) Childs World.

—The Man Who Could Call Down Owls. Mikolaycak, Charles, illus. LC 83-17568. 32p. (gr. k-3). 1984. RSBE 13.95 (*0-02-715380-0*, Macmillan Child Bk) Macmillan Child Grp.

—The Mask. (Illus.). 64p. 1992. 12.75 (*0-89565-769-4*); 8.95s.p. (*0-685-55110-5*) Childs World.

—The Mirror Planet. (Illus.). 64p. 1992. 12.75 (*0-89565-767-8*); 8.95s.p. (*0-685-55111-3*) Childs World.

—The Mother's Day Mice. Brett, Jan, illus. LC 85-13991. (ps-3). 1986. 13.95 (*0-89919-387-0*, Clarion Bks) HM.

—The Mother's Day Mice. Brett, Jan, illus. (gr. 4 up). 1988. pap. 4.95 (*0-89919-702-7*, Clarion Bks) HM.

—Nasty Stinky Sneakers. LC 93-34641. 1994. 13.00 (*0-06-024236-1*, Festival); PLB 12.89 (*0-06-024237-X*, Festival) HarpC Child Bks.

—Night of the Gargoyles. Wiesner, David, illus. LC 93-8160. 1994. write for info. (*0-395-66553-1*, Clarion Bks) HM.

—No Nap. Meddaugh, Susan, illus. LC 88-35256. 32p. (ps-k). 1989. 15.45 (*0-89919-813-9*, Clarion Bks) HM.

—Nobody Knows but Me. LC 92-8537. (Illus.). (gr. 1-8). 1992. PLB 8.95 (*0-89565-971-9*); Resale. 12.75 (*0-685-59394-0*) Childs World.

—Oh, Rick. (Illus.). 64p. 1992. 12.75 (*0-89565-774-0*); 8.95s.p. (*0-685-55116-4*) Childs World.

—Our Sixth-Grade Sugar Babies. LC 90-5487. 160p. (gr. 4-6). 1990. 13.00 (*0-397-32451-0*, Lipp Jr Bks); PLB 12.89 (*0-397-32452-9*, Lipp Jr Bks) HarpC Child Bks.

—Our Sixth-Grade Sugar Babies. LC 90-5487. 160p. (gr. 4-6). 1992. pap. 3.95 (*0-06-440390-4*, Trophy) HarpC Child Bks.

—Our Teacher's Having a Baby. De Groat, Diane, illus. 32p. (ps-3). 1992. 13.45 (*0-395-60470-2*, Clarion Bks) HM.

—A Part of the Dream. (Illus.). 64p. 1992. 12.75 (*0-89565-771-6*); 8.95s.p. (*0-685-55117-2*) Childs World.

—A Perfect Father's Day. Giblin, James, ed. Meddaugh, Susan, illus. 32p. (ps-1). 1991. 13.95 (*0-395-52590-X*, Clarion Bks) HM.

—A Perfect Father's Day. Meddaugh, Susan, illus. 32p. (gr. k-3). 1993. pap. 5.70 (*0-395-66416-0*, Clarion Bks) HM.

—Red Fox Running. (ps-3). 1993. 15.95 (*0-395-58919-3*, Clarion Bks) HM.

—Ride When You're Ready. (Illus.). 64p. 1992. 12.75 (*0-89565-776-7*); 8.95s.p. (*0-685-55121-0*) Childs World.

—St. Patrick's Day in the Morning. Brett, Jan, illus. LC 79-15934. 32p. (ps-3). 1983. 13.95 (*0-395-29098-8*, Clarion Bks); pap. 5.95 (*0-89919-162-2*, Clarion Bks) HM.

—Scary, Scary Halloween. Brett, Jan, illus. LC 86-2642. 32p. (ps-3). 1988. 12.95 (*0-89919-414-1*, Clarion Bks); pap. 5.95 (*0-89919-799-X*, Clarion Bks) HM.

—The Sea World Book of Sharks. LC 79-63920. (Illus.). 80p. (gr. 4-7). 1984. pap. 9.95 (*0-15-271952-0*, HB Juv Bks) HarBrace.

—The Sea World Book of Whales. LC 85-16409. (Illus.). 96p. (gr. 4-7). 1988. 14.95 (*0-15-271948-2*, HB Juv Bks); pap. 9.95 (*0-15-271953-9*) HarBrace.

—Sharing Susan. LC 90-27097. 128p. (gr. 4-7). 1991. 14.00 (*0-06-021693-X*); PLB 13.89 (*0-06-021694-8*) HarpC Child Bks.

—Sixth-Grade Sleepover. LC 86-4679. 96p. (gr. 4-7). 1986. 13.95 (*0-15-275350-8*, HB Juv Bks) HarBrace.

—Sixth Grade Sleepover. 112p. (gr. 3-7). 1987. pap. 2.95 (*0-590-42882-9*, Apple Paperbacks) Scholastic Inc.

—The Skate Patrol. Tucker, Kathleen, ed. LC 80-18640. (Illus.). 40p. (gr. 2-5). 1980. PLB 8.95 (*0-8075-7393-0*) A Whitman.

—Smoky Night. Diaz, David, illus. LC 93-14885. (gr. 4 up). 1994. write for info (*0-15-269954-6*) Harbrace.

—Someday a Tree. Himler, Ronald, illus. LC 92-24074. 32p. (gr. k-3). 1993. 14.45 (*0-395-61309-4*, Clarion Bks) HM.

—Someone Is Hiding on Alcatraz Island. LC 84-5019. 144p. (gr. 5-8). 1984. 13.45 (*0-89919-219-X*, Clarion Bks) HM.

—Someone Is Hiding on Alcatraz Island. 144p. 1986. pap. 3.50 (*0-425-10294-7*, Berkley-Pacer) Berkley Pub.

—The Space People. (Illus.). 64p. 1992. 12.75 (*0-89565-765-1*); 8.95s.p. (*0-685-55112-1*) Childs World.

—Such Nice Kids. 160p. (gr. 4-9). 1990. 13.45 (*0-395-54998-1*, Clarion Bks) HM.

—A Sudden Silence. 107p. (gr. 7 up). 1988. 14.95 (*0-15-282058-2*) HarBrace.

—Sunshine Home. De Groat, Diane, illus. LC 93-570. Date not set. write for info. (*0-395-63309-5*, Clarion Bks) HM.

—Survival Camp. LC 92-11689. (Illus.). (gr. 1-8). 1992. PLB 8.95 (*0-89565-970-0*); Resale. 12.75 (*0-685-59404-1*) Childs World.

—Terrible Things: An Allegory of the Holocaust. rev. ed. Gammell, Stephen, illus. 24p. (gr. 1-4). 1989. 11.95 (*0-8276-0325-8*); pap. 7.95 (*0-8276-0507-2*) JPS Phila.

—A Turkey for Thanksgiving. De Groat, Diane, illus. 32p. (ps-1). 1991. 13.95 (*0-89919-793-0*, Clarion Bks) HM.

—Two Different Girls. (Illus.). 64p. 1992. 12.75 (*0-89565-772-4*); 8.95s.p. (*0-89565-773-2*) Childs World.

—The Undersea People. (Illus.). 64p. 1992. 12.75 (*0-89565-766-X*); 8.95s.p. (*0-685-55113-X*) Childs World.

—The Valentine Bears. Brett, Jan, illus. 32p. (gr. 3). 1985. 14.95 (*0-89919-138-X*, Clarion Bks); pap. 4.95 (*0-89919-313-7*, Clarion) HM.

—The Wall. Himler, Ronald, illus. 32p. (ps-3). 1990. 14.45 (*0-395-51588-2*, Clarion Bks) HM.

—Wall. (ps-3). 1992. pap. 5.70 (*0-395-62977-2*, Clarion Bks) HM.

—The Wednesday Surprise. Garrick, Donald, illus. 32p. (gr. k-3). 1989. 14.45 (*0-89919-721-3*, Clarion Bks) HM.

—The Wednesday Surprise. Carrick, Donald, illus. 32p. (ps-3). 1990. pap. 4.80 (*0-395-54776-8*, Clarion Bks) HM.

—The Wild Horses. (Illus.). 64p. 1992. 12.75 (*0-89565-778-3*); 8.95s.p. (*0-685-55122-9*) Childs World.

—Will You Be My POSSLQ. LC 87-322. 181p. (gr. 7 up). 1987. 12.95 (*0-15-297399-0*, HB Juv Bks) HarBrace.

—Winter's Coming. Knotts, Howard, illus. LC 76-28321. 32p. (ps-3). 1990. pap. 3.95 (*0-15-298037-7*) HarBrace.

Bunting, Jane. My First ABC. (Illus.). 32p. (gr. k-4). 1993. 12.95 (*1-56458-403-8*) Dorling Kindersley.

Bunting, Janet. My First Recorder Book. (Illus.). 32p. (gr. 2-6). 1989. Incl. recorder. pap. 14.95 (*0-8120-7618-4*) Barron.

Bunting, Philippa, jt. auth. see Hunka, Alison.
Bunting, Richard L., jt. auth. see Benton, Allen H.
Buntline, Ned. Buffalo Bill: His Adventures in the West. LC 74-15731. (Illus.). 320p. (gr. 7 up). 1974. Repr. of 1886 ed. 23.00x (0-405-06366-0) Ayer.
Bunuel. Las Tres de la Madrugada. 1972. pap. 4.95 (0-88436-061-X, 70265) EMC.
Bunyan, John. Pilgrim's Progress. (gr. 9 up). 1968. pap. 1.95 (0-8049-0183-X, CL-183) Airmont.
—The Pilgrim's Progress. (Illus.). 232p. (gr. 4 up). 1981. pap. text ed. 2.00 (0-89323-016-2, 119) Bible Memory.
—Pilgrim's Progress. Leavis, Frank R., frwd. by. (RL 10). 1964. pap. 4.95 (0-451-52399-7, CE1813, Sig Classics) NAL-Dutton.
—The Pilgrim's Progress. Larsen, Dan, ed. Bohl, Al, illus. 224p. (gr. 4-8). 1989. pap. text ed. 2.50 (1-55748-099-0) Barbour & Co.
—The Pilgrim's Progress. Larsen, Dan, adapted by. (gr. 3 up). 1992. 9.95 (1-55748-276-4) Barbour & Co.
Burack, Jonathan. A Trip to the Planets. (Illus.). 12p. (ps-3). incl. filmstrip, cass. 25.00 (0-915291-90-8, 5154) Know Unltd.
Buranelli, Vincent. Thomas Alva Edison. (Illus.). 144p. (gr. 5-9). 1989. PLB 13.98 (0-382-09522-7) Silver Burdett Pr.
Burbank, Jonathan. Nepal. LC 91-15866. (Illus.). 128p. (gr. 5-9). 1991. PLB 21.95 (1-85435-401-9) Marshall Cavendish.
Burbank, Linda. Sylvan: The Magic Tree. Van Treese, James B., ed. Upman, Michael, illus. 30p. 1993. pap. 7.95 (1-56901-201-6) NW Pub.
Burch, Gladys. Famous Violinists for Young People. LC 75-38316. (gr. 7 up). Repr. of 1946 ed. 18.75 (0-8369-8118-9) Ayer.
Burch, Joann. Chico Mendes: Defender of the Rain Forest. (Illus.). 48p. (gr. 2-4). 1994. 12.40 (1-56294-413-4) Millbrook Pr.
Burch, Joann J. Fine Print: A Story about Johann Gutenberg. Aldrich, Kent A., illus. 64p. (gr. 3-6). 1991. lib. bdg. 14.95 (0-87614-682-5) Carolrhoda Bks.
—Fine Print: A Story about Johann Gutenberg. (ps-3). 1992. pap. 5.95 (0-87614-565-9) Carolrhoda Bks.
—Isabella of Castile: Queen on Horseback. LC 91-3173. (Illus.). 64p. (gr. 5-8). 1991. PLB 12.90 (0-531-20033-7) Watts.
—Kenya: Africa's Tamed Wilderness. LC 91-43104. (Illus.). 128p. (gr. 4 up). 1992. RSBE 14.95 (0-87518-512-6, Dillon) Macmillan Child Grp.
Burch, Jonathan. Astronauts. Stefoff, Rebecca, ed. LC 91-45925. (Illus.). 32p. (gr. 5-9). 1992. PLB 17.26 (1-56074-041-8) Garrett Ed Corp.
Burch, Marilyn. Phonics Seatwork. (gr. 1-3). 1985. pap. 8.95 (0-8224-5543-9) Fearon Teach Aids.
—Shape-a-Sound. (gr. 1-3). 1986. pap. 6.95 (0-8224-6394-6) Fearon Teach Aids.
Burch, Robert. Christmas with Ida Early. LC 83-5792. 144p. (gr. 3-7). 1983. pap. 12.95 (0-670-22131-7) Viking Child Bks.
—Christmas with Ida Early. LC 85-5680. 158p. (gr. 3-7). 1985. pap. 4.99 (0-14-031971-9, Puffin) Puffin Bks.
—D. J.'s Worst Enemy: A Novel by Robert Burch. Weiss, Emil, illus. LC 92-44783. 144p. (gr. 4-6). 1993. Repr. of 1965 ed. 19.95 (0-8203-1554-0) U of Ga Pr.
—Home-Front Heroes. 144p. (gr. 3-7). 1992. pap. 3.99 (0-14-036030-1) Puffin Bks.
—Ida Early Comes over the Mountain. 152p. (gr. 3-7). 1982. pap. 2.50 (0-380-57091-2, Camelot) Avon.
—Ida Early Comes Over the Mountain. LC 79-20532. (gr. 3-7). 1980. pap. 14.99 (0-670-39169-7) Viking Child Bks.
—Ida Early Comes over the Mountain. (gr. 4 up). 1990. pap. 3.99 (0-14-034534-5, Puffin) Puffin Bks.
—King Kong & Other Poets. LC 86-5512. 160p. (gr. 3-7). 1986. pap. 11.95 (0-670-80927-6) Viking Child Bks.
—Queenie Peavy. 160p. (gr. 3-7). 1987. pap. 3.99 (0-14-032305-8, Puffin) Puffin Bks.
—Renfroe's Christmas: A Novel by Robert Burch. Negri, Rocco, illus. LC 92-44773. 56p. (gr. 4-6). 1993. Repr. of 1971 ed. 14.95 (0-8203-1553-2) U of Ga Pr.
—Skinny. LC 89-28225. 128p. (gr. 4-6). 1990. Repr. of 1964 ed. 19.95 (0-8203-1223-1) U of Ga Pr.
—Traveling Bird. (gr. 1-4). 1959. 9.95 (0-8392-3038-9) Astor-Honor.
—Tyler, Wilkin & Skee. LC 89-28245. 160p. (gr. 4-6). 1990. Repr. of 1963 ed. 19.95 (0-8203-1194-4) U of Ga Pr.
Burchard, Peter. Venturing: An Introduction to Sailing. (Illus.). 160p. (gr. 5 up). 1986. 17.95 (0-316-11613-0) Little.
Burchard, S. H. Sports Star: Fernando Valenzuela. LC 82-47932. (Illus.). 64p. (ps-3). 1982. 8.95 (0-15-278044-0, HB Juv Bks) HarBrace.
—The Statue of Liberty: Birth to Rebirth. LC 85-5525. (Illus.). 192p. (gr. 4-7). 1985. 13.95 (0-15-279969-9, Pub. by HJ) HarBrace.
Burchfield, Ellen, jt. auth. see Hall, Betty L.
Burchill, James V., et al. Ghosts & Haunts from the Appalachian Foothills. 192p. (Orig.). (gr. 10 up). 1993. pap. 9.95 (1-55853-253-6) Rutledge Hill Pr.
Burckhardt, Ann, jt. auth. see Germaine, Elizabeth.
Burda, Margaret. Amazing States. Sodac, David, illus. 160p. (gr. 4-8). 1984. wkbk. 12.95 (0-86653-205-6, GA 546) Good Apple.
Burden-Patmon, Denise. Imani's Gift at Kwanzaa. Cooper, Floyd, illus. 32p. (gr. 2-5). 1993. pap. 4.95 (0-671-79841-3, S&S BYR) S&S Trade.

Burden-Patmon, Denise & Jones, Kathryn D. Carnival. Ruffins, Reynold, illus. 32p. (gr. 2-5). 1993. pap. 4.95 (0-671-79840-5, S&S BYR) S&S Trade.
Burdett, Alice. Nature's Savage Cats. LC 92-33536. 1993. 14.99 (0-8037-1608-7) Dial Bks Young.
Burdick, Gerry & Schuett, Julie. Puzzling about South Dakota. Gleich, Shannon & Long, Lori, illus. 61p. (Orig.). (gr. 8 up). 1992. pap. 4.95 (0-9632844-0-1, 050111557) Dakota Desktop.
Burdick, Margaret. Sara Raccoon & the Secret Place: A Maple Forest Story. (gr. 3). 1992. 14.95 (0-316-11617-3) Little.
Burditt, Faraday & Holley, Cynthia. Every Day in Every Way. (ps). 1989. pap. 12.95 (0-8224-2507-6) Fearon Teach Aids.
Burell, Roy. Moctezuma & the Aztecs. McBride, Angus, illus. LC 92-5823. 63p. (gr. 6-7). 1992. PLB 24.26 (0-8114-3351-X) Raintree Steck-V.
Bureloff, Morris. Algebra Acrobatic Puzzles. (Illus.). (gr. 7-12). 1988. pap. 7.95 (0-918932-93-9) Activity Resources.
—Brain-Busting Decode Puzzles. Laycock, Mary, ed. Bureloff, Morris, illus. 64p. (gr. 7-10). 1985. pap. 7.95 (0-918932-86-6) Activity Resources.
Bureloff, Morris & Johnson, Connie. Calculators, Number Patterns, & Magic. Roes, Ruth, illus. (gr. 4-12). 1977. pap. text ed. 7.95 (0-918932-49-1) Activity Resources.
Bureloff, Morris, et al. Number Triangles. Laycock, Mary & Merrick, Paul, eds. Merrick, Paul, illus. (Orig.). (gr. 5-12). 1977. pap. 7.95 (0-918932-36-X) Activity Resources.
Bures, Ruth A. Here Comes Christmas. 40p. (gr. k-8). 1982. pap. 14.95 (0-86704-008-4) Clarus Music.
Burge, Michael C. Vaccines: Preventing Disease. LC 92-27851. (Illus.). 96p. (gr. 5-8). 1992. PLB 15.95 (1-56006-223-1) Lucent Bks.
Burgel, Paul H. Gorillas. (ps-3). 1992. 19.95 (0-87614-758-9) Carolrhoda Bks.
—Gorillas. (gr. 4-7). 1993. pap. 6.95 (0-87614-612-4) Carolrhoda Bks.
Burger, Warren E. see Kennon, Donald R. & Strincer, Richard.
Burgeson, Nancy. The Baby-Sitter's Guide. LC 91-14959. (Illus.). 32p. (gr. 5-9). 1991. pap. text ed. 1.95 (0-8167-2467-9) Troll Assocs.
—The Money Book for Kids. LC 91-15108. (Illus.). 32p. (gr. 5-9). 1991. pap. text ed. 1.95 (0-8167-2465-2) Troll Assocs.
—My Family History. Janums, Aija, illus. LC 92-3086. 32p. (gr. 3-6). 1992. pap. text ed. 1.95 (0-8167-2794-5) Troll Assocs.
Burgess. Angel for May. Date not set. 15.00 (0-06-023513-6, Festival); PLB 14.89 (0-06-023514-4, Festival) HarpC Child Bks.
—Burning Issy. Date not set. 15.00 (0-06-023511-X, Festival); PLB 14.89 (0-06-023512-8, Festival) HarpC Child Bks.
Burgess & Molgard. A Child's Book of Mormon Activity Book, 2 bks. Bk. 1. pap. 3.95 ea. (0-88494-625-8) Bk. 2 (0-88494-661-4) Bookcraft Inc.
—A Child's Church Presidents Activity Book. pap. 3.95 (0-88494-686-X) Bookcraft Inc.
—A Child's New Testament Activity Book. pap. 3.95 (0-88494-771-8) Bookcraft Inc.
—A Child's Old Testament Activity Book. pap. 3.95 (0-88494-720-3) Bookcraft Inc.
Burgess, jt. auth. see Hague.
Burgess, Allan. From Twisted Ear to Reverent Tear. Heston, Claudia, illus. 96p. (gr. 7-12). 1983. 5.98 (0-941518-25-6) Perry Enterprises.
Burgess, Allan & Molgard, Max. A Child's Introduction to the Scriptures Activity Book. 1991. pap. 3.95 (0-88494-793-9) Bookcraft Inc.
Burgess, Anna. The Do-It-Yourself Lettering Book. (Illus.). 64p. (gr. 4-7). 1993. pap. 5.95 (0-8167-3036-9) Troll Assocs.
Burgess, Barbara H. The Fred Field. LC 93-14260. 1994. write for info. (0-385-31070-6) Delacorte.
—Oren Bell. 1991. 15.00 (0-385-30325-4) Delacorte.
—Oren Bell. (ps-3). 1992. pap. 3.50 (0-440-40747-8) Dell.
Burgess, Beverly C. Chicken Little. (Orig.). (gr. 1-3). 1987. 3.98 (0-89274-414-6) Harrison Hse.
—God Are You Really Real? Titolo, Nancy, illus. 30p. (Orig.). (gr. 1-3). 1985. pap. 1.98 (0-89274-309-3) Harrison Hse.
—God Is My Best Friend. Linder, Elizabeth, illus. 32p. (Orig.). (gr. 1-3). 1986. pap. 1.98 (0-89274-293-3) Harrison Hse.
—God Is Never to Busy to Listen. Linder, Elizabeth, illus. (Orig.). (gr. 1-3). 1987. pap. 1.98 (0-89274-457-X) Harrison Hse.
—How Can I Please You, God? Mckee, Vici, illus. 32p. (ps-5). 1991. Repr. of 1989 ed. 3.98 (1-879470-00-4) Burgess Pub.
—Is Easter Just for Bunnies? Titolo, Nancy, illus. 30p. (Orig.). (gr. 1-3). 1985. pap. 1.98 (0-89274-310-7) Harrison Hse.
—Jack & the Beanstalk. (gr. k-6). 1985. pap. 3.98 (0-89274-384-0) Harrison Hse.
—The Little Red Hen. (Illus.). 32p. (gr. 1-3). 1984. pap. 3.98 (0-89274-312-3) Harrison Hse.
—Little Red Riding Hood. (Illus.). 32p. (Orig.). (gr. 1-3). 1983. pap. 3.98 (0-89274-289-5) Harrison Hse.
—Prayers for Pre-Schoolers. (Illus., Orig.). (ps-2). 1991. pap. 4.98 (1-879470-02-0) Burgess Pub.

—Seedtime Stories: Bedtime Stories with Poems & Devotionals. Mckee, Vici, illus. (Orig.). (gr. 2-6). 1991. pap. 4.95 (1-879470-01-2) Burgess Pub.
—Three Bears in the Ministry. 32p. (Orig.). (ps). 1982. pap. 3.98 (0-89274-252-6) Harrison Hse.
Burgess, Beverly Capps. How Can I Please You God? McKee, Vicki, illus. 29p. (Orig.). 1989. pap. text ed. 4.00 (0-9618975-1-1) Annette Capps.
Burgess, Gelett. Goop Tales. LC 72-93766. (Illus.). 128p. (gr. 1-6). 1973. pap. 3.95 (0-486-22914-9) Dover.
—Goop Tales. (Illus.). (gr. 4-8). 17.00 (0-8446-4717-9) Peter Smith.
—Goops & How to Be Them: A Manual of Manners for Polite Infants. Burgess, Gelett, illus. LC 68-55630. 96p. (gr. 1-6). 1968. pap. 3.95 (0-486-22233-0) Dover.
—The Little Father. Egielski, Richard, illus. LC 84-46171. 32p. (ps up). 1985. 14.00 (0-374-34596-1) FS&G.
—More Goops & How Not to Be Them: A Manual of Manners for Impolite Infants. Burgess, Gelett, illus. LC 68-55531. 96p. (ps-4). 1968. pap. 3.95 (0-486-22234-9) Dover.
Burgess, Joe. Basic Air Conditioning. Gorham, Kelly, ed. Bergwall, Jim, contrib. by. (Illus.). 24p. (gr. 10 up). Date not set. wkbk. 7.00 (0-8064-0005-6) Bergwall.
Burgess, Mark. One Little Teddy Bear. (ps-3). 1991. 10.95 (0-670-84079-3) Viking Child Bks.
Burgess, Melvin. The Cry of the Wolf. LC 91-47690. 128p. (gr. 5 up). 1992. 13.00 (0-688-11744-9, Tambourine Bks) Morrow.
Burgess, Mike. Magic & Magicians. 48p. (gr. 3-4). 1991. PLB 11.95 (1-56065-044-3) Capstone Pr.
Burgess, Thonrton W. The Adventures of Johnny Chuck. (gr. 5-6). 17.95 (0-88411-787-1, Pub. by Aeonian Pr) Amereon Ltd.
Burgess, Thornton. The Adventures of Bob White. 1992. Repr. lib. bdg. 17.95x (0-89966-994-8) Buccaneer Bks.
—The Adventures of Bobby Coon. 1992. Repr. lib. bdg. 17.95x (0-89966-992-1) Buccaneer Bks.
—The Adventures of Buster Bear. 1986. Repr. lib. bdg. 17.95 (0-89966-525-X) Buccaneer Bks.
—The Adventures of Jimmy Skunk. 1992. Repr. lib. bdg. 17.95x (0-89966-993-X) Buccaneer Bks.
—The Adventures of Johnny Chuck. 1992. Repr. lib. bdg. 17.95x (0-89966-991-3) Buccaneer Bks.
—The Adventures of Ol'Mistah Buzzard. 1992. Repr. lib. bdg. 17.95x (0-89966-995-6) Buccaneer Bks.
—The Adventures of Peter Cottontail. (Illus.). (ps-8). 1990. Repr. lib. bdg. 18.95x (0-89966-664-7) Buccaneer Bks.
—The Adventures of Reddy Fox. 1992. Repr. lib. bdg. 17.95x (0-89966-990-5) Buccaneer Bks.
—Billy Mink. 91p. 1981. Repr. PLB 17.95x (0-89966-352-4) Buccaneer Bks.
—Billy Mink. 178p. 1981. Repr. PLB 17.95 (0-89967-026-1) Harmony Raine.
—Blacky the Crow. 93p. 1981. Repr. PLB 17.95 (0-89966-351-6) Buccaneer Bks.
—Blacky the Crow. 198p. 1981. Repr. PLB 17.95 (0-89967-025-3) Harmony Raine.
—Buster Bear's Twins. 1992. Repr. lib. bdg. 17.95x (0-89966-981-6) Buccaneer Bks.
—Jerry Muskrat at Home. 1986. Repr. lib. bdg. 17.95 (0-89966-527-6) Buccaneer Bks.
—Little Joe Otter. 103p. 1981. Repr. PLB 17.95x (0-89966-353-2) Buccaneer Bks.
—Little Joe Otter. 169p. 1981. Repr. PLB 17.95 (0-89967-027-X) Harmony Raine.
—Longlegs the Heron. 1992. Repr. lib. bdg. 17.95x (0-89966-979-4) Buccaneer Bks.
—Mother West Wind's Neighbors. (Illus.). 160p. 1992. Repr. PLB 14.95x (0-89966-901-8) Buccaneer Bks.
—Old Mother West Wind. Hague, Michael, illus. LC 89-20088. 90p. (gr. 2-4). 1990. 18.95 (0-8050-1005-X, Bks Young Read) H Holt & Co.
—Old Mother West Wind. 1992. Repr. PLB 14.95x (0-89966-900-X) Buccaneer Bks.
—Paddy the Beaver. 1986. Repr. lib. bdg. 17.95 (0-89966-528-4) Buccaneer Bks.
—Whitefoot the Wood Mouse. 1992. Repr. lib. bdg. 17.95x (0-89966-980-8) Buccaneer Bks.
Burgess, Thornton W. The Adventures of Buster Bear. Kliros, Thea, adapted by. Cady, Harrison, illus. LC 92-36949. 96p. 1993. pap. 1.00 (0-486-27564-7) Dover.
—The Adventures of Chatterer the Red Squirrel. unabr. ed. Kliros, Thea, adapted by. Cady, Harrison, illus. LC 92-14627. 96p. 1992. pap. 1.00 (0-486-27399-7) Dover.
—The Adventures of Danny Meadow Mouse. Cady, Harrison & Kliros, Thea, illus. LC 92-36950. 96p. 1993. pap. 1.00 (0-486-27565-5) Dover.
—The Adventures of Grandfather Frog. (gr. 5-6). 17.95 (0-88411-777-4, Pub. by Aeonian Pr) Amereon Ltd.
—The Adventures of Grandfather Frog. unabr. ed. Kliros, Thea, adapted by. Cady, Harrison, illus. LC 92-13146. 96p. 1992. pap. text ed. 1.00 (0-486-27400-4) Dover.
—The Adventures of Jerry Muskrat. (gr. 5-6). 17.95 (0-88411-782-0, Pub. by Aeonian Pr) Amereon Ltd.
—The Adventures of Jerry Muskrat. (Illus.). 96p. 1993. pap. text ed. 1.00t (0-486-27817-4) Dover.
—The Adventures of Jimmy Skunk. Cady, Harrison, illus. 128p. (ps-3). 1987. pap. 3.98 (0-316-11662-9) Little.
—The Adventures of Ol' Mistah Buzzard. (gr. 5-6). 17.95 (0-88411-784-7, Pub. by Aeonian Pr) Amereon Ltd.
—The Adventures of Old Man Coyote. (gr. 5-6). 17.95 (0-88411-781-2, Pub. by Aeonian Pr) Amereon Ltd.
—The Adventures of Old Mr. Toad. (gr. 5-6). 17.95 (0-88411-785-5, Pub. by Aeonian Pr) Amereon Ltd.

—The Adventures of Peter Cottontail. large type ed. 96p. 1992. pap. 1.00 (*0-486-26929-9*) Dover.
—The Adventures of Poor Mrs. Quack. (gr. 5-6). 17.95 (*0-88411-775-8*, Pub. by Aeonian Pr) Amereon Ltd.
—The Adventures of Poor Mrs. Quack. (Illus.). 96p. 1993. pap. text ed. 1.00t (*0-486-27818-2*) Dover.
—The Adventures of Prickly Porky. (gr. 5-6). 17.95 (*0-88411-783-9*, Pub. by Aeonian Pr) Amereon Ltd.
—The Adventures of Reddy Fox. large type ed. 96p. 1992. pap. 1.00 (*0-486-26930-2*) Dover.
—The Dear Old Briar-Patch. Cady, Harrison, illus. 192p. (ps-3). 1983. pap. 8.95 (*0-316-11654-8*) Little.
—Mother West Wind's Children. rev. ed. (Illus.). (gr. 1-3). 1962. 16.95 (*0-316-11645-9*) Little.
—Mother West Wind's Children. Cady, Harrison, illus. 156p. (ps-3). 1985. pap. 8.95 (*0-316-11657-2*) Little.
—Mother West Wind's Neighbors. Cady, Harrison, illus. LC 68-21862. (gr. 1 up). 1985. pap. 8.95 (*0-316-11656-4*) Little.
—Old Mother West Wind. golden anniversary ed. Cady, Harrison, illus. (gr. 1 up). 1985. 16.95 (*0-316-11648-3*); pap. 8.95 (*0-316-11655-6*) Little.
—Old Mother West Wind's Neighbors. (gr. 5-6). 18.95 (*0-88411-786-3*, Pub. by Aeonian Pr) Amereon Ltd.
Burgest, David R. Proverbs for the Young...& the Not So Young. Burgest, David R., II, illus. 75p. (Orig.). (gr. 7-12). 1989. pap. write for info. Self-Taught Pubs.
Burgie, Irving. Caribbean Carnival: Songs of the West Indies. Lessac, Frane, illus. Guy, Rosa, intro. by. LC 91-760838. (Illus.). 32p. (gr. 1 up). 1992. 15.00 (*0-688-10779-6*, Tambourine Bks); PLB 14.93 (*0-688-10780-X*, Tambourine Bks) Morrow.
Buria, Maria E. Billy the Bean. Siu, Emma, illus. 36p. (Orig.). (ps-k). 1989. pap. 5.95 (*1-878926-04-7*) Colorful Lrngs.
Burke. Red Acre Farm. 1993. 14.95 (*0-8050-2047-0*) H Holt & Co.
Burke & Kranhold. Big Fearon Bulletin Board Book. (gr. k-8). 1978. pap. 20.95 (*0-8224-0702-7*) Fearon Teach Aids.
Burke see Sohn, David A.
Burke, Amy M. Not Just Schoolwork, Vol. 2. (gr. 4-12). 1993. pap. 19.95 (*1-878347-24-1*) NL Assocs.
—Not Just Schoolwork, Vol. 3. (gr. 4-12). 1993. pap. 19.95 (*1-878347-25-X*) NL Assocs.
Burke, Amy M. & Wallace, Roger. Not Just Schoolwork. LC 76-9524. 201p. (Orig.). (gr. 3-12). 1990. pap. 29.95 (*0-8290-0354-1*) NL Assocs.
Burke, Amy M., jt. auth. see Levy, Nathan.
Burke, Bronwen. Christian Slater. (Illus.). 48p. 1992. 1.49 (*0-440-21425-4*) Dell.
—Garth Brooks. (Illus.). 48p. 1992. 1.49 (*0-440-21433-5*) Dell.
—Jason Priestley: Who's Hot! 48p. (gr. 4-7). 1992. pap. 1.49 (*0-440-21378-9*) Dell.
—Who's Hot! Grant Show. (gr. 4-7). 1993. pap. 1.49 (*0-440-21477-7*) Dell.
Burke, Deidre. Food & Fasting. LC 93-537. 32p. (gr. 4-8). 1993. 13.95 (*1-56847-034-7*) Thomson Lrning.
Burke, James L. & Davison, Kenneth E. Ohio's Heritage. LC 83-20091. (Illus.). 340p. (gr. 7). 1984. text ed. 19.50x (*0-87905-109-4*, Peregrine Smith) Gibbs Smith Pub.
Burke, Kathleen. Louisa May Alcott. Horner, Matina, intro. by. (Illus.). 112p. (gr. 5 up). 1988. lib. bdg. 17.95 (*1-55546-637-0*) Chelsea Hse.
Burke, Patricia A., et al. Adventures from God's Word. rev. ed. Miller, Marge, ed. (Illus.). 128p. (gr. 3). 1983. text ed. 9.99 (*0-87239-663-0*, 2953) Standard Pub.
Burke, Roma N. Whiskers, a Kitten's Story. LC 87-62417. 120p. (gr. 3-8). 1988. pap. 8.95 (*0-88100-058-2*) Natl Writ Pr.
Burke, Terrill M. Dolphin Magic: The Ancient Knowledge. 310p. (Orig.). (gr. 6 up). 1993. pap. 12.25 (*1-880485-51-6*) Alpha-Dolphin.
—Dolphin Magic: The First Encounter. 305p. (gr. 6 up). 1993. pap. 12.25 (*1-880485-69-9*) Alpha-Dolphin.
Burke, Timothy. Cocoa Puppy. Burke, Ann & Burke, Ann, illus. LC 89-50890. 32p. (Orig.). (ps-3). 1989. 5.00 (*0-9623227-0-9*) Thunder & Ink.
—Tugboats in Action. LC 93-9131. 1993. write for info. (*0-8075-8112-7*) A Whitman.
Burkert, Nancy E. Valentine & Orson. Burkert, Nancy E., illus. 56p. (gr. 5 up). 1989. 16.95 (*0-374-38078-3*) FS&G.
Burkett, Larry. Get a Grip on Your Money - Student Text. Slonim, David, illus. 136p. (Orig.). (gr. 9-12). 1990. pap. text ed. 7.95 (*0-929608-75-5*) Focus Family.
—Get a Grip on Your Money - Teacher's Guide. Slonim, David, illus. 116p. (Orig.). (gr. 9-12). 1990. pap. text ed. 10.95 (*0-929608-74-7*) Focus Family.
—Surviving the Money Jungle. Day, Bruce, illus. 72p. (Orig.). (gr. 7-9). 1990. pap. text ed. 7.95 (*0-929608-77-1*) Focus Family.
Burkett, Lucille F. Barbadian Fairy Tales. Roberts, Anne F., ed. (Illus.). 38p. (Orig.). (gr. 1 up). 1987. pap. 5.00 (*0-317-62575-6*) Libr Commns Servs.
Burke-Weiner, Kimberly. The Maybe Garden. Roehm, Michelle, ed. Spillman, Fredrika, illus. 36p. (gr. 1-4). 1992. 14.95 (*0-941831-56-6*); pap. 7.95 (*0-941831-57-4*) Beyond Words Pub.
Burkhardt, Robert. The Federal Aviation Administration. Schlesinger, Arthur M., Jr., intro. by. (Illus.). 112p. (gr. 5 up). 1989. lib. bdg. 14.95 (*1-55546-107-7*) Chelsea Hse.

Burkhart, Joyce L. & Mercer, Deborah B. Scripture Concepts for Children Activity-Story Book: Building Godly Character, Vol. 2. Burkhart, Joyce L., illus. 43p. (ps-2). 1992. pap. 7.95 (*0-9633166-1-3*) Penta Ent.
—Scripture Concepts for Children Activity-Story Book, Vol. 1: Building Godly Self-Esteem. Burkhart, Joyce L., illus. 43p. (ps-2). 1991. pap. 7.95 (*0-9633166-0-5*) Penta Ent.
Burkholder, Ruth C. Mi Jun's Difficult Decision. O'Dwyer, Chung S. & Fwhang, Duk S., illus. LC 83-20494. 14p. (Orig.). (gr. 4-6). 1984. pap. 4.95 (*0-377-00139-2*) Friendship Pr.
—Won Gil's Secret Diary. O'Dwyer, Chung S. & Fwhang, Duk S., illus. LC 83-16529. 14p. (Orig.). (gr. 1-3). 1984. pap. 4.95 (*0-377-00138-4*) Friendship Pr.
Burkle, Diane, et al. Big Fearon Book of Dinosaurs. (gr. 1-3). 1989. pap. 12.95 (*0-8224-0698-5*) Fearon Teach Aids.
Burks, James F., jt. ed. see Therio, Adrien.
Burla, Oded. El Nombre Secreto. Writer, C. C. & Nielsen, Lisa C., trs. Elchanan, illus. (SPA.). 24p. (Orig.). (ps). 1992. pap. text ed. 3.00x (*1-56134-156-8*) Dushkin Pub.
—The Secret Name. Kriss, David, tr. from HEB. Elchanan, illus. 24p. (Orig.). (ps). 1992. pap. text ed. 3.00x (*1-56134-146-0*) Dushkin Pub.
Burland, C. A. Way of the Buddha. (gr. 3-7). 1988. pap. 10.95 (*0-7175-0590-1*) Dufour.
Burland, Cottie A. Ancient China. Puulton, Yvonne, illus. (gr. 4-8). 1974. Repr. of 1960 ed. 10.95 (*0-7175-0018-7*) Dufour.
—Ancient Egypt. (Illus.). (gr. 4-8). 1974. Repr. of 1957 ed. 10.95 (*0-7175-0014-4*) Dufour.
—Ancient Rome. (Illus.). (gr. 4-8). 1974. Repr. of 1958 ed. 10.95 (*0-7175-0015-2*) Dufour.
Burleigh, Bob. Flight: The Journey of Charles Lindbergh. Wimmer, Mike, illus. 32p. (ps-3). 1991. 14.95 (*0-399-22272-3*, Philomel) Putnam Pub Group.
Burleigh, Robert. A Man Named Thoreau. Bloom, Lloyd, illus. LC 85-7947. 48p. (gr. 3 up). 1985. SBE 13.95 (*0-689-31122-2*, Atheneum Child Bk) Macmillan Child Grp.
Burman, Margaret, jt. auth. see Saal, Jocelyn.
Burma-Washington, Marcay & Schroeder, Mary A. Math in Bloom (Addition & Subtraction) (gr. 1-4). 1989. spiral wkbk. 39.95 (*1-55999-058-9*) LinguiSystems.
—Math in Bloom (Multiplication & Division) (gr. 2-6). 1989. spiral wkbk. 39.95 (*1-55999-059-7*) LinguiSystems.
Burnes, Diane & Burns, Andy. Home on the Range: Ranch-Style Riddles. Burke, Susan S., photos by. LC 93-19158. (gr. 4 up). 1994. 11.95 (*0-8225-2341-8*) Lerner Pubns.
Burness, Tad. Joshua. Burness, Tad, illus. 90p. (Orig.). (gr. 3 up). 1987. pap. 4.95 (*1-55523-082-2*) Winston-Derek.
Burnett, Frances. The Secret Garden. (gr. 5 up). 1989. pap. 2.50 (*0-451-52080-7*) NAL-Dutton.
Burnett, Frances H. Little Lord Fauntleroy. (Illus.). 252p. 1981. Repr. PLB 21.95x (*0-89966-288-9*) Buccaneer Bks.
—Little Lord Fauntleroy. 190p. (gr. 1 up). 1985. pap. 2.95 (*0-14-035025-X*, Puffin) Puffin Bks.
—Little Lord Fauntleroy. (gr. k-6). 1986. pap. 4.95 (*0-440-44764-X*, Pub. by Yearling Classics) Dell.
—Little Lord Fauntleroy. Butts, Dennis, intro. by. LC 92-13794. 208p. (gr. 4 up). 1993. pap. 7.95 (*0-19-282961-0*) OUP.
—Little Lord Fauntleroy. (Illus.). 160p. (gr. 5 up). 1993. 18.95 (*0-87923-958-1*) Godine.
—A Little Princess. 232p. 1981. Repr. PLB 15.95 (*0-89966-327-3*) Buccaneer Bks.
—A Little Princess. 240p. (gr. 5-9). 1975. pap. 3.50 (*0-440-44767-4*, YB) Dell.
—Little Princess. Tudor, Tasha, illus. LC 63-15435. (gr. 4-6). 1963. 15.00 (*0-397-30693-8*, Lipp Jr Bks); PLB 14.89 (*0-397-31339-X*, Lipp Jr Bks) HarpC Child Bks.
—A Little Princess. 300p. 1977. PLB 15.95x (*0-89967-005-9*) Harmony Raine.
—A Little Princess. 224p. (gr. 4-6). 1984. pap. 2.99 (*0-14-035028-4*, Puffin) Puffin Bks.
—A Little Princess. Tudor, Tasha, illus. LC 63-15435. 240p. (gr. 4-8). 1987. pap. 3.95 (*0-06-440187-1*, Trophy) HarpC Child Bks.
—A Little Princess. 256p. (Orig.). (gr. 4-6). 1987. pap. 3.25 (*0-590-40719-8*, Apple Classics) Scholastic Inc.
—A Little Princess. Adorjan, Carol M., adapted by. Marvin, Frederic, illus. LC 87-15485. 48p. (gr. 3-6). 1988. PLB 12.89 (*0-8167-1201-8*); pap. text ed. 3.95 (*0-8167-1202-6*) Troll Assocs.
—A Little Princess. LC 88-46102. (Illus.). 192p. (gr. 5 up). 1989. 17.95 (*0-87923-784-8*) Godine.
—A Little Princess. Henterly, Jamichael, illus. 288p. (gr. 4 up). 1989. 13.95 (*0-448-09299-9*, G&D) Putnam Pub Group.
—A Little Princess. Schwartz, Lynne S., intro. by. 240p. 1990. pap. 2.95 (*0-451-52509-4*, Sig Classics) NAL-Dutton.
—A Little Princess. 1990. pap. 3.50 (*0-440-40386-3*, Pub. by Yearling Classics) Dell.
—Little Princess. (gr. 3 up). 1993. pap. 4.99 (*0-88070-527-2*, Gold & Honey) Questar Pubs.
—A Little Princess. Dubowski, Cathy E., ed. LC 93-14000. Date not set. write for info. (*0-679-85090-2*) Random.
—The Lost Prince. (gr. 4-6). 1986. pap. 2.95 (*0-14-035071-2*, Puffin) Puffin Bks.

—Racketty-Packetty House: As Told by Queen Crosspatch. Cady, Harrison, illus. 72p. (gr. 3-6). 1992. 4.99 (*0-517-07249-1*, Pub. by Derrydale Bks) Outlet Bk Co.
—Sara Crewe. 96p. (gr. 3-7). 1986. pap. 2.75 (*0-590-42323-1*) Scholastic Inc.
—The Secret Garden. 302p. 1981. Repr. PLB 21.95x (*0-89966-326-5*) Buccaneer Bks.
—Secret Garden. (gr. k-6). 1989. pap. 3.50 (*0-440-47709-3*, Pub. by Yearling Classics); pap. 3.50 (*0-440-97709-6*, Dell Trade Pbks) Dell.
—The Secret Garden. (gr. 4-6). 1987. pap. 2.95 (*0-14-035004-7*, Puffin) Puffin Bks.
—The Secret Garden. Mitchell, Kathy, illus. 320p. (gr. 4 up). 1987. 13.95 (*0-448-06029-9*, G&D) Putnam Pub Group.
—The Secret Garden. Tudor, Tasha, illus. LC 62-17457. 256p. (gr. 4-8). 1987. pap. 3.50 (*0-06-440188-X*, Trophy) HarpC Child Bks.
—The Secret Garden. McNulty, Faith, afterword by. 1987. pap. 2.95 (*0-451-52417-9*, Sig Classics) NAL-Dutton.
—The Secret Garden. Allen, Thomas B., illus. Howe, James, adapted by. LC 86-17788. (Illus.). 72p. (gr. k-5). 1993. 13.95 (*0-394-86467-0*) Random Bks Yng Read.
—The Secret Garden. Howell, Troy, illus. 288p. (gr. k-6). 12.99 (*0-517-63225-X*) Outlet Bk Co.
—The Secret Garden. Hague, Michael, illus. LC 86-22780. 240p. (gr. 4-6). 1987. 19.95 (*0-8050-0277-4*, Bks Young Read) H Holt & Co.
—The Secret Garden. Lowry, Lois, intro. by. 256p. 1987. pap. 3.50 (*0-553-21201-X*, Bantam Classics) Bantam.
—The Secret Garden. Betts, Louise, adapted by. LC 87-15490. (Illus.). (gr. 3-6). 1988. PLB 12.89 (*0-8167-1203-4*); pap. 3.95 (*0-8167-1204-2*) Troll Assocs.
—The Secret Garden. 360p. 1987. pap. 4.95 (*0-19-281772-8*) OUP.
—The Secret Garden. Sanderson, Ruth, illus. LC 86-46002. 240p. 1988. 18.95 (*0-394-55431-0*) Knopf Bks Yng Read.
—The Secret Garden. Hughes, Shirley, illus. 240p. (gr. 5 up). 1989. pap. 18.95 (*0-670-82571-9*) Viking Child Bks.
—The Secret Garden. 304p. (gr. 4-7). 1987. pap. 2.95 (*0-590-43346-6*) Scholastic Inc.
—The Secret Garden. 1987. pap. 3.50 (*0-440-40055-4*) Dell.
—The Secret Garden. (Illus.). (gr. 3-5). 3.50 (*0-7214-0632-7*) Ladybird Bks.
—Secret Garden. 288p. 1990. pap. 2.50 (*0-8125-0501-8*) Tor Bks.
—The Secret Garden. 1991. pap. 3.99 (*0-8125-1910-8*) Tor Bks.
—The Secret Garden. 288p. 1992. 9.49 (*0-8167-2558-6*); pap. 2.95 (*0-8167-2559-4*) Troll Assocs.
—The Secret Garden. 1979. pap. 3.25 (*0-440-77706-2*) Dell.
—The Secret Garden. 288p. (gr. 5-8). 1991. pap. 2.99 (*0-87406-575-5*) Willowisp Pr.
—The Secret Garden. 1993. 14.95 (*0-679-42309-5*, Everymans Lib) Knopf.
—The Secret Garden. Howe, James, adapted by. Allen, Thomas A., illus. LC 93-18509. 128p. (Orig.). (gr. 2-6). 1993. pap. 2.99 (*0-679-84751-0*) Random Bks Yng Read.
—The Secret Garden. Bishop, Michael, illus. 200p. 1993. 25.00 (*0-88363-202-0*) H L Levin.
—The Spring Cleaning: As Told by Queen Crosspatch. Cady, Harrison, illus. 56p. (gr. 3-6). 1992. 4.99 (*0-517-07248-3*, Pub. by Derrydale Bks) Outlet Bk Co.
—The Troubles of Queen Silver-Bell: As Told by Queen Crosspatch. Cady, Harrison, illus. 56p. (gr. 3-6). 1992. 4.99 (*0-517-07247-5*, Pub. by Derrydale Bks) Outlet Bk Co.
Burnett, Francis H. The Secret Garden: A Young Reader's Edition of the Classic Story. Abr. ed. Crawford, Dale, illus. LC 90-80198. 56p. (gr. 1 up). 1990. 9.98 (*0-89471-860-6*) Courage Bks.
Burnett, Yumiko M., tr. see Rodieck, Jorma.
Burnford, Sheila. The Incredible Journey. (gr. 6-8). 1977. pap. 2.95 (*0-553-26218-1*) Bantam.
—The Incredible Journey. (gr. 6-8). 15.95 (*0-88411-099-0*, Pub. by Aeonian Pr) Amereon Ltd.
—The Incredible Journey. Burger, Carl, illus. (gr. 4-8). 1990. 16.00 (*0-553-05874-6*, Skylark) Bantam.
—The Incredible Journey. 1985. pap. 3.99 (*0-553-15616-0*) Bantam.
—The Incredible Journey. 1984. pap. 3.50 (*0-553-27442-2*) Bantam.
Burnie, David. Bird. Chadwick, Peter, photos by. LC 87-26441. (Illus.). 64p. (gr. 5 up). 1988. 15.00 (*0-394-89619-X*); lib. bdg. 15.99 (*0-394-99619-4*) Knopf Bks Yng Read.
—Communication. LC 91-31946. (Illus.). 32p. (gr. 4-7). 1992. PLB 12.40 (*0-531-17312-7*, Gloucester Pr) Watts.
—Dictionary of Nature. LC 93-30696. 1994. write for info. (*1-56458-473-9*) Dorling Kindersley.
—How Nature Works: One Hundred Ways Parents & Kids Can Share the Secrets of Nature. LC 91-12432. (Illus.). 192p. (gr. 3 up). 1991. 24.00 (*0-89577-391-0*, Dist. by Random) RD Assn.
—Machines & How They Work. LC 91-60147. (Illus.). 64p. (gr. 3 up). 1991. 11.95 (*1-879431-15-7*); PLB 12.99 (*1-879431-30-0*) Dorling Kindersley.

—Mammals. LC 92-54312. (Illus.). 64p. (gr. 3 up). 1993. 9.95 (*1-56458-228-0*) Dorling Kindersley.
—Plant & Flower. King, Dave, et al, illus. LC 88-27172. 64p. (gr. 5 up). 1989. 15.00 (*0-394-82252-8*); PLB 15.99 (*0-394-92252-2*) Knopf Bks Yng Read.
—Seashore. LC 93-31075. 1994. write for info. (*1-56458-323-6*) Dorling Kindersley.
—Tree. Chadwick, Peter, photos by. LC 88-1572. (Illus.). 64p. (gr. 5 up). 1988. 15.00 (*0-394-89617-3*); lib. bdg. 15.99 (*0-394-99617-8*) Knopf Bks Yng Read.
Burnie, David A. Animals. LC 92-15434. 1993. pap. 13. 00 (*0-671-79130-3*, S&S BFYR); pap. 8.00 (*0-671-79135-4*, S&S BFYR) S&S Trade.
Burningham, John. Aldo. Burningham, John, illus. LC 91-19589. 32p. (ps-2). 1992. 15.00 (*0-517-58701-7*); PLB 15.99 (*0-517-58699-1*) Crown Bks Yng Read.
—Avocado Baby. Burningham, John, illus. LC 81-43844. 24p. (ps-3). 1982. 16.00 (*0-690-04243-4*, Crowell Jr Bks); PLB 15.89 (*0-690-04244-2*) HarpC Child Bks.
—Come Away from the Water, Shirley. Burningham, John, illus. LC 77-483. 32p. (gr. 1-2). 1977. (Crowell Jr Bks); PLB 14.89 (*0-690-01361-2*) HarpC Child Bks.
—Come Away from the Water, Shirley. LC 77-483. (Illus.). 32p. (ps-3). 1983. pap. 5.95 (*0-06-443039-1*, Trophy) HarpC Child Bks.
—The Dog. 2nd ed. LC 93-10344. 1994. write for info. (*1-56402-326-5*) Candlewick Pr.
—Granpa. Burningham, John, illus. LC 84-17464. 32p. (ps-1). 1985. 14.00 (*0-517-55643-X*) Crown Bks Yng Read.
—Granpa. (ps-2). 1992. pap. 4.99 (*0-517-58797-1*) Crown Bks Yng Read.
—Harvey Slumfenberger's Christmas Present. Burningham, John, illus. LC 92-54957. 32p. (ps up). 1993. 15.95 (*1-56402-246-3*) Candlewick Pr.
—Hey! Get off Our Train. Burningham, John, illus. LC 89-15802. 48p. (ps-4). 1990. 15.00 (*0-517-57638-4*); PLB 15.99 (*0-517-57643-0*) Crown Bks Yng Read.
—John Burningham's ABC. Burningham, John, illus. LC 92-42765. 64p. (ps-2). 1993. 13.00 (*0-517-59503-6*); PLB 13.99 (*0-517-59504-4*) Crown Bks Yng Read.
—John Burningham's Book of First Concepts: Letters, Numbers, Colors, Opposites. LC 93-18844. 1994. lib. bdg. write for info. (*1-56402-205-6*) Candlewick Pr.
—John Patrick Norman McHennessey: The Boy Who Was Always Late. (Illus.). 32p. (ps-3). 1987. 14.95 (*0-517-56805-5*) Crown Bks Yng Read.
—Mr. Gumpy's Motor Car. Burningham, John, illus. LC 75-4582. 48p. (ps-3). 1976. PLB 14.89 (*0-690-00799-X*, Crowell Jr Bks) HarpC Child Bks.
—Mr. Gumpy's Outing. LC 77-159507. (Illus.). 32p. (ps-2). 1971. 14.95 (*0-8050-0708-3*, Bks Young Read) H Holt & Co.
—Mr. Gumpy's Outing. LC 77-159507. (Illus.). 32p. (ps-2). 1990. pap. 5.95 (*0-8050-1315-6*, Bks Young Read) H Holt & Co.
—Time to Get out of the Bath, Shirley. Burningham, John, illus. LC 76-58503. 32p. (gr. k-2). 1978. 13.95 (*0-690-01378-7*, Crowell Jr Bks); PLB 13.89 (*0-690-01379-5*) HarpC Child Bks.
—Would You Rather... Burningham, John, illus. LC 78-7088. 32p. (ps-3). 1978. 17.00 (*0-690-03917-4*, Crowell Jr Bks); PLB 16.89 (*0-690-03918-2*, Crowell Jr Bks) HarpC Child Bks.
Burnnett, Carroll. Kikko's Tracks. Burnnett, Carroll, illus. 28p. (Orig.). (ps up). 1988. pap. 6.95 (*0-9619414-1-3*) Foto Fantasi Pr.
Burns, Andy, jt. auth. see Burnes, Diane.
Burns, Bree. Harriet Tubman: And the Fight Against Slavery. (Illus.). 80p. 1993. 13.95 (*0-7910-1751-6*, Am Art Analog); pap. 4.95 (*0-7910-1995-0*, Am Art Analog) Chelsea Hse.
Burns, Charles. Charles Burns Sketchbook. Vance, Jim, ed. (Illus.). 64p. (gr. 4 up). 1993. pap. 6.95 (*0-87816-250-X*) Kitchen Sink.
Burns, Clint, jt. auth. see Burns, Diane.
Burns, Deborah, ed. see Tilgner, Linda.
Burns, Diane. Cranberries: Fruit of the Bogs. Bellville, Cheryl W., photos by. LC 93-29620. 1994. write for info. (*0-87614-822-4*) Carolrhoda Bks.
—Rocky Mountain Seasons: From Valley to Mountaintop. Dannen, Kent & Dannen, Donna, photos by. LC 92-22833. (Illus.). 32p. (gr. 1-5). 1993. RSBE 14.95 (*0-02-716142-0*, Macmillan Child Grp) Macmillan Child Grp.
—Sugaring Season: Making Maple Syrup. Nygren, Tord, illus. 32p. (gr. k-4). 1990. PLB 19.95 (*0-87614-420-2*) Carolrhoda Bks.
—Sugaring Season: Making Maple Syrup. (ps-3). 1992. pap. 5.95 (*0-87614-554-3*) Carolrhoda Bks.
Burns, Diane & Burns, Clint. Hail to the Chief! Jokes about the Presidents. Hanson, Joan, illus. 32p. (gr. 1-4). 1989. 11.95 (*0-8225-0971-7*, First Ave Edns); pap. 2.95 (*0-8225-9561-3*, First Ave Edns) Lerner Pubns.
Burns, Diane L. Arbor Day. Rogers, Kathy, illus. 48p. (gr. k-4). 1989. 14.95 (*0-87614-346-X*) Carolrhoda Bks.
—Elephants Never Forget! A Book of Elephant Jokes. (Illus.). 32p. (gr. 1-4). 1987. pap. 2.95 (*0-8225-9518-4*, First Ave Edns) Lerner Pubns.
—Snakes Alive! Jokes about Snakes. Hanson, Joan, illus. (gr. 1-4). 1988. PLB 11.95 (*0-8225-0096-2*, First Ave Edns); pap. 2.95 (*0-8225-9543-5*, First Ave Edns) Lerner Pubns.
Burns, Diane L. & Scholten, Dan. Here's to Ewe: Riddles about Sheep. Burke, Susan S., illus. 32p. (gr. 1-4). 1989. PLB 11.95 (*0-8225-2326-4*) Lerner Pubns.

Burns, Elizabeth. Hanky Panky: Traditional Handkerchief Toys. Burns, Elizabeth, illus 24p. (ps-6). 1989. pap. 4.50 (*0-9624152-0-0*) E Burns.
—Hanky Panky: Traditional Handkerchief Toys, Benefit Edition. (Illus.). 24p. (ps-6). 1991. pap. 4.50 (*0-9624152-2-7*) E Burns.
Burns, Jim. Spirit Wings: Taking Off in Your Relationship with God & Learning to Soar a Spirit-Filled Devotional for Youth. LC 92-15247. 290p. (Orig.). 1992. pap. 8.99 (*0-89283-783-7*, Vine Bks) Servant.
Burns, Julie & Swan, Dorothy. Reading Without Books. LC 78-72078. (gr. 4-6). 1979. pap. 8.95 (*0-8224-5830-6*) Fearon Teach Aids.
Burns, Marilyn. The Book of Think: Or How to Solve Problems Twice Your Size. Weston, Martha, illus. (gr. 5 up). 1976. 15.95 (*0-316-11742-0*); pap. 9.95 (*0-316-11743-9*) Little.
—Collection of Math Lessons: Grades Six to Eight. (gr. 6-8). 1990. pap. 14.95 (*0-201-48042-5*) Addison-Wesley.
—Collection of Math Lessons: Grades Three to Six. (gr. 3-6). 1987. pap. 14.95 (*0-201-48040-9*) Addison-Wesley.
—Good for Me! All about Food in 32 Bites. Clifford, Sandy, illus. LC 78-6727. (gr. 5 up). 1978. pap. 9.95 (*0-316-11747-1*) Little.
—The Hanukkah Book. Weston, Martha, illus. LC 80-27935. 128p. (gr. 3-7). 1981. SBE 13.95 (*0-02-716140-4*, Four Winds) Macmillan Child Grp.
—The Hanukkah Book. 128p. 1991. pap. 3.50 (*0-380-71520-1*, Camelot) Avon.
—I Am Not a Short Adult: Getting Good at Being a Kid. (Illus.). (gr. 5 up). 1977. 14.95 (*0-316-11745-5*); pap. 8.95 (*0-316-11746-3*) Little.
—The I Hate Mathematics! Book. Hairston, Martha, illus. 128p. (gr. 5 up). 1975. 15.95 (*0-316-11740-4*); pap. 9.95 (*0-316-11741-2*) Little.
—Math by All Means: Multiplication. Friedman, Aileen, ed. (Illus.). 160p. (Orig.). (gr. 3). 1991. pap. text ed. 16.50 (*0-941355-04-7*) M Burns Educ Assocs.
—Math for Smarty Pants: Or Who Says Mathematicians Have Little Pig Eyes. Weston, Martha, illus. 140p. (gr. 7 up). 1982. 15.95 (*0-316-11738-2*); pap. 9.95 (*0-316-11739-0*) Little.
—The One Dollar Word Riddle Book. Weston, Martha, illus. 48p. (Orig.). (gr. 3-8). 1990. pap. 6.95 (*0-938587-29-3*) Cuisenaire.
—One Dollar Word Riddle Book. (gr. 4-7). 1990. pap. 6.95 (*0-201-48025-5*) Addison-Wesley.
—This Book Is about Time. Weston, Martha, illus. LC 78-6614. (gr. 5 up). 1978. pap. 9.95 (*0-316-11750-1*) Little.
Burns, Peggy. Nothing Ever Stays the Same. 128p. (gr. 9-12). 1989. pap. text ed. 4.99 (*0-7459-1805-0*) Lion USA.
—The Splitting Image of Rosie Brown. 128p. (Orig.). (gr. 7-10). 1990. pap. 4.99 (*0-7459-1831-X*) Lion USA.
Burns, Phillis B. Iron Lady at Sea: From Shipyard to Voyage: A Story of the Great Iron-Hulled Sailing Ship, Star of India. (Illus.). 108p. (Orig.). 1988. pap. 6.95 (*0-685-20061-2*) Cove Pr CA.
Burns, Virginia L. Gentle Hunter: Biography of Alice Evans, Bacteriologist. (Illus.). 224p. (gr. 5-12). 1993. PLB 22.00 (*0-9604726-5-7*) Enterprise Pr.
Burnsed, Linda & Chaffin, Garry. A Child's Gift of Bedtime Stories, Vol. 1. Brown, J. Aaron, ed. Ragland, Teresa, illus. 28p. (gr. 1-4). 1993. incl. cass. 12.95 (*0-927945-07-X*) Someday Baby.
Burnsed, Linda, jt. auth. see Chaffin, Gary.
Burnside, Julian. Matilda & the Dragon. Guthridge, Bettina, illus. 32p. (Orig.). (gr. k-2). 1993. 14.95 (*1-86373-127-X*, Pub. by Allen & Unwin Aust Pty AT); pap. 7.95 (*1-86373-144-X*, Pub. by Allen & Unwin Aust Pty AT) IPG Chicago.
—Matilda & the Dragon. (ps-3). 1993. pap. 7.95 (*1-86373-179-2*, Pub. by Allen & Unwin Aust Pty AT) IPG Chicago.
Burow, Daniel, jt. auth. see Frank, Penny.
Burr, Daniella. Don't Just Sit There! Fifty Ways to Have a Nickelodeon Day. Henry, Steve, illus. LC 90-86411. 96p. (Orig.). (gr. 2-6). 1992. pap. 2.95 (*0-448-40202-5*, G&D) Putnam Pub Group.
Burrage, Barbara. The Bible Quiz Book. 30p. (gr. 5 up). 1979. pap. 2.95 (*0-8192-1256-3*) Morehouse Pub.
Burrell, jt. auth. see Hirschi.
Burrell, Roy. The Greeks. Connolly, Peter, illus. 112p. (gr. 7 up). 1990. 17.95 (*0-19-917161-0*) OUP.
—Oxford First Ancient History. Connolly, Peter, illus. 320p. 1993. bds. 35.00 (*0-19-521058-1*) OUP.
—The Romans. Connolly, Peter, illus. 112p. (gr. 5-9). 1991. bds. 17.95 (*0-19-917162-9*, 5084) OUP.
Burrill, Gail, et al. Data Analysis & Statistics Across the Curriculum. Schoen, Harold L., contrib. by. LC 92-16923. (Illus.). 88p. (Orig.). (gr. 9-12). 1992. pap. 15. 00 (*0-87353-329-1*) NCTM.
Burrill, Richard. The Human Almanac: People Through Time. 432p. (gr. 9-12). 1983. pap. 12.95 (*0-943238-00-5*) Anthro Co.

— **Protectors of the Land: An Environmental Journey to Understanding the Conservation Ethic. Macias, Regina, ed. Waters, Robyn & Ipina, David, illus. 300p. (gr. 3-12). 1993. pap. text ed. 22.95**

(*1-878464-02-7*); write for info. (*1-878464-03-5*) Anthro Co. An environmental survival guide about "belongingness" for students, teachers & parents. For thousands of years, the native Californians lived in harmony with the Earth. Their wise elders understand a 'conservation ethic' that all things are connected in one giant web & that our rightful place as human beings is to preserve it. The California Indians respect that elders are the link to the past & the children are the hope for the future. PROTECTORS OF THE LAND calls young people --& all of us-- to environmental action. Grizzly Bear Heart, a fictional Maidu medicine man, prepares us to become protectors of the land. In the first section of the book, he takes us on an environmental journey to understanding the conservation ethic. We fly above the Sacramento Valley to observe the dying Sacramento River & the brown smog from automobiles. We witness the devastating impacts of clear cut logging & overgrazing in the Sierra Nevada rangeland & mountains. We visit Auburn RANCHERIA to learn about energy & fire making from a Maidu-Nisenan elder. The Sierra Mewuk from Yosemite Valley share with us their story of TOO-TAUK-A NOOLAH, the inchworm -- a story that reminds us we make a difference in the world no matter how small we are. In the Cooperative Games & Songs section, we learn more about the Indian cultural ways through activities that instill the values of cooperation & sharing. Maps & charts, Indian storytelling & wisdom words, 'stepping outdoor' environmental activities, & discussion questions also are included. Volume discount available from the publisher, The Anthro Company. Post Office Box 661765, Sacramento, CA 95866-1765. Telephone: 916-971-1675. Resource book for parents & teachers of 4th & 5th grade. Students will want to read & use the book themselves. *Publisher Provided Annotation.*

—Somewhere Behind the Eyes: A New Way of Being & Seeing. (Orig.). (gr. 9-12). 1990. 15.95 (*1-878464-04-3*); pap. 8.95 (*1-878464-05-1*) Anthro Co.
Burrill, Richard, ed. Closest to God: The Life-Stories of Muhammad & the Five God-Men of History. (gr. 9-12). 1990. 17.95 (*1-878464-06-X*); pap. 10.95 (*1-878464-07-8*) Anthro Co.
Burrill, Richard L. Ishi: America's Last Stone Age Indian. Ipina, David, illus. 50p. 1990. pap. 8.95 (*1-878464-01-9*) Anthro CO.
Burroughs, Edgar Rice. Monster Men. LC 62-8707. (Illus.). 25.00 (*0-940724-06-5*) P Hunt.
Burroughs, Margaret G., jt. ed. see Randall, Dudley.
Burroughs, Nigel. Nature's Chicken: A Book for Animal Lovers. LC 92-13799. (Illus.). 32p. 1992. 5.95 (*0-913990-92-2*) Book Pub Co.
Burrow, Barbara. Christmas Time at Santa's Workshop. 1989. 8.95 (*0-8167-1442-8*) Troll Assocs.
Burroway, Jane, jt. auth. see Lord, John V.
Burroway, Janet, jt. auth. see Lord, John V.
Burrows, Arthur A. Grammar Exercises Part One: Elementary-Intermediate ESL. 2nd, rev. ed. Clark, Raymond C., ed. MacLean, Robert & Sempe, Jean J., illus. 256p. (Orig.). (gr. 8 up). 1992. pap. text ed. 10. 95x (*0-86647-011-5*) Pro Lingua.
Burrows, Arthur A., ed. see Fuchs, Marjorie S., et al.
Burrows, Roger. The Little Tugboat That Sneezed. Hawley, Kevin, illus. 24p. (Orig.). (gr. k-1). 1990. pap. 0.99 (*1-878624-40-7*) McClanahan Bk.
Burrows, William E. Mission to Deep Space: Voyager's Interplanetary Odyssey. LC 92-29746. 1993. write for info. (*0-7167-6500-4*) W H Freeman.
Bursell, Susan. Haunted Houses. LC 93-4296. (gr. 5 up). 1994. 14.75 (*1-56510-153-7*) Lucent Bks.

Bursik, Rose. Amelia's Fantastic Flight. Bursik, Rose, illus. LC 91-28809. 32p. (ps-2). 1992. 14.95 *(0-8050-1872-7,* Bks Young Read) H Holt & Co.
—Zoe's Sheep. 1994. write for info. *(0-8050-2530-8)* H Holt & Co.
Bursill, Henry. Hand Shadows to Be Thrown upon a Wall. 42p. (gr. 1-6). pap. 1.95 *(0-486-21779-5)* Dover.
—More Hand Shadows to Be Thrown Upon a Wall. (Illus.). 39p. (gr. 1-6). 1971. pap. 1.95 *(0-486-21384-6)* Dover.
Burstein, Chaya. Benjy's Bible Trails. LC 90-25421. (Illus.). 32p. (gr. 1-5). 1992. pap. 3.95 *(0-929371-27-5)* Kar Ben.
Burstein, Chaya M. A First Jewish Holiday Cookbook. Burstein, Chaya M., illus. (gr. 3-8). 1979. (Bonim Bks); pap. 8.95 *(0-88482-775-5,* Bonim Bks) Hebrew Pub.
—The Jewish Kids Catalog. Burstein, Chaya M., illus. 224p. (gr. 3-7). 1983. pap. 14.95 *(0-8276-0215-4)* JPS Phila.
—Jewish Kids Hebrew-English Wordbook. Burstein, Chaya M., illus. 40p. (gr. 1 up). 1993. 16.95 *(0-8276-0319-9)* JPS Phila.
—A Kid's Catalog of Israel. Burstein, Chaya, illus. 288p. (gr. 3 up). 1988. 14.95 *(0-8276-0263-4)* JPS Phila.
—The Mystery of the Coins. Burstein, Chaya M., illus. 160p. (Orig.). (gr. 4-6). 1988. pap. text ed. 9.95 *(0-8074-0350-4,* 123000) UAHC.
—The UAHC Kids Catalog of Jewish Living. Burstein, Chaya M., illus. LC 91-42815. (gr. 4-6). 1992. pap. 8.95 *(0-8074-0464-0,* 123934) UAHC.
Burstein, Fred. The Dancer. Auclair, Joan, illus. LC 91-41429. 40p. (ps-3). 1993. RSBE 14.95 *(0-02-715625-7,* Bradbury Pr) Macmillan Child Grp.
—Whispering in the Park. Cogancherry, Helen, illus. LC 91-239. 32p. (ps-2). 1992. SBE 13.95 *(0-02-715621-4,* Bradbury Pr) Macmillan Child Grp.
Burt, Denise. Birth of a Koala. LC 88-14578. (Illus.). 40p. (gr. 3-7). 1988. Repr. of 1986 ed. 12.95 *(0-944176-02-X)* Terra Nova.
—I'm Not a Bear. Ryan, Ron, photos by. (Illus.). 32p. (gr. k-5). 1987. pap. 5.95 *(0-944176-00-3)* Terra Nova.
Burt, Erica. Natural Materials. (Illus.). 32p. (gr. 2-6). 1990. lib. bdg. 15.94 *(0-86592-486-4);* lib. bdg. 11.95s.p. *(0-685-46442-3)* Rourke Corp.
—Paper. (Illus.). 32p. (gr. 2-6). 1990. lib. bdg. 15.94 *(0-86592-488-0);* lib. bdg. 11.95s.p. *(0-685-46443-1)* Rourke Corp.
Burt, Katherine. The Scariest Stories You've Ever Heard, Pt. II. 96p. (gr. 4-8). 1988. 2.99 *(0-87406-419-8,* 39-19157-7)* Willowisp Pr.
Burt, Stephen. RVs & Vans. (Illus.). 48p. (gr. 3-6). 1992. PLB 12.95 *(1-56065-071-0)* Capstone Pr.
Burt, William F. The Adventures of Herby. 1993. 7.95 *(0-8062-4782-7)* Carlton.
Burton, Grace, et al. Fifth-Grade Book. Leiva, Miriam A., ed. LC 91-45680. (Illus.). 32p. (Orig.). (gr. k-6). 1992. pap. 11.00 *(0-87353-315-1)* NCTM.
—Fourth-Grade Book. Leiva, Miriam A., ed. LC 91-47648. (Illus.). 32p. (gr. k-6). 1992. pap. text ed. 11.00 *(0-87353-314-3)* NCTM.
—Second-Grade Book. Leiva, Miriam A., ed. LC 92-16408. (Illus.). 32p. (Orig.). (gr. k-6). 1992. pap. 9.50 *(0-87353-312-7)* NCTM.
—Sixth-Grade Book. Leiva, Miriam A., ed. LC 92-16924. (Illus.). 32p. (Orig.). (gr. k-6). 1992. pap. 11.50 *(0-87353-316-X)* NCTM.
—Third-Grade Book. Leiva, Miriam A., ed. LC 91-34131. (Illus.). 32p. (Orig.). (gr. k-6). 1992. pap. 11.00 *(0-87353-313-5)* NCTM.
Burton, Jane. Animal Activities, 4 vols. Burton, Jane & Taylor, Kim, illus. 128p. (gr. 2-3). 1989. Set. PLB 63.72 *(0-8368-0184-9)* Gareth Stevens Inc.
—Animals at Home. (Illus.). 24p. (gr. k-4). 1991. PLB 9.90 *(1-878137-12-3)* Newington.
—Animals at Night. (Illus.). 24p. (gr. k-4). 1991. PLB 9.90 *(1-878137-13-1)* Newington.
—Animals at Rest. (Illus.). 24p. (gr. k-4). 1991. PLB 9.90 *(1-878137-14-X)* Newington.
—Animals at Work. (Illus.). 24p. (gr. k-4). 1991. PLB 9.90 *(1-878137-15-8)* Newington.
—Animals Eating. (Illus.). 24p. (gr. k-4). 1991. PLB 9.90 *(1-878137-00-X)* Newington.
—Animals Fighting. (Illus.). 24p. (gr. k-4). 1991. PLB 9.90 *(1-878137-03-4)* Newington.
—Animals Keeping Clean. LC 88-43144. (Illus.). 24p. (Orig.). (ps-3). 1989. lib. bdg. 5.99 *(0-394-92261-1)* Random Bks Yng Read.
—Animals Keeping Cool. LC 88-43143. (Illus.). 24p. (Orig.). (ps-3). 1989. lib. bdg. 5.99 *(0-394-92260-3)* Random Bks Yng Read.
—Animals Learning. (Illus.). 24p. (gr. k-4). 1991. PLB 9.90 *(1-878137-01-8)* Newington.
—Animals Talking. (Illus.). 24p. (gr. k-4). 1991. PLB 9.90 *(1-878137-02-6)* Newington.
—Baby Animals Growing Up, 12 vols. Burton, Jane, illus. 384p. (gr. 2-3). 1989. Set. PLB 191.16 *(0-8368-0201-2)* Gareth Stevens Inc.
—Buffy the Barn Owl. LC 89-11410. (Illus.). 32p. (gr. 2-3). 1989. PLB 15.93 *(0-8368-0202-0)* Gareth Stevens Inc.
—Caper the Kid. Burton, Jane, photos by. LC 89-11566. (Illus.). 32p. (gr. 2-3). 1989. PLB 15.93 *(0-8368-0203-9)* Gareth Stevens Inc.
—Chester the Chick. LC 89-11421. (Illus.). 32p. (gr. 2-3). 1989. PLB 15.93 *(0-8368-0204-7)* Gareth Stevens Inc.

—Dabble the Duckling. Burton, Jane, photos by. LC 89-11398. (Illus.). 32p. (gr. 2-3). 1989. PLB 15.93 *(0-8368-0205-5)* Gareth Stevens Inc.
—Dazy the Guinea Pig. LC 89-11397. (Illus.). 32p. (gr. 2-3). 1989. PLB 15.93 *(0-8368-0206-3)* Gareth Stevens Inc.
—Dizzie the Pony. LC 89-11395. (Illus.). 32p. (gr. 2-3). 1989. PLB 15.93 *(0-8368-0207-1)* Gareth Stevens Inc.
—Freckles the Rabbit. Taylor, Kim, illus. LC 89-11396. 32p. (gr. k-3). 1989. PLB 15.93 *(0-8368-0208-X)* Gareth Stevens Inc.
—Ginger the Kitten. Burton, Jane, photos by. LC 87-16660. (Illus.). 32p. (ps-3). 1988. pap. 2.25 *(0-394-89638-6)* Random Bks Yng Read.
—Ginger the Kitten. LC 89-11417. (Illus.). 32p. (gr. 2-3). 1989. PLB 15.93 *(0-8368-0213-6)* Gareth Stevens Inc.
—Jack the Puppy. LC 89-11422. (Illus.). 32p. (gr. 2-3). 1989. PLB 15.93 *(0-8368-0209-8)* Gareth Stevens Inc.
—Keeping Clean. Burton, Jane & Taylor, Kim, photos by. LC 89-11557. (Illus.). 32p. (gr. 2-3). 1989. PLB 15.93 *(0-8368-0187-3)* Gareth Stevens Inc.
—Keeping Cool. Burton, Jane & Taylor, Kim, photos by. LC 89-11412. (Illus.). 32p. (gr. 2-3). 1989. PLB 15.93 *(0-8368-0188-1)* Gareth Stevens Inc.
—Keeping Safe. Burton, Jane & Taylor, Kim, photos by. LC 89-11416. (Illus.). 32p. (gr. 2-3). 1989. PLB 15.93 *(0-8368-0186-5)* Gareth Stevens INc.
—Surfer the Seal. LC 89-11368. (Illus.). 32p. (gr. 2-3). 1989. PLB 15.93 *(0-8368-0210-1)* Gareth Stevens Inc.
—Taddy the Toad. LC 89-11409. (Illus.). 32p. (gr. 2-3). 1989. PLB 15.93 *(0-8368-0211-X)* Gareth Stevens Inc.
—Trill the Fox Cub. LC 89-11370. (Illus.). 32p. (gr. 2-3). 1989. PLB 18.60 *(0-8368-0212-8)* Gareth Stevens Inc.
Burton, Jane, ed. & photos by Keeping Warm. LC 89-11411. (Illus.). 32p. (gr. 2-3). 1989. PLB 15.93 *(0-8368-0185-7)* Gareth Stevens Inc.
Burton, Jane, photos by. Chick. (Illus.). 24p. (gr. k-3). 1992. 6.95 *(0-525-67355-5,* Lodestar Bks) Dutton Child Bks.
—See How They Grow: Kitten. (Illus.). 24p. (gr. k-3). 1991. 6.95 *(0-525-67343-1,* Lodestar Bks) Dutton Child Bks.
—See How They Grow: Puppy. (Illus.). 24p. (gr. k-3). 1991. 6.95 *(0-525-67342-3,* Lodestar Bks) Dutton Child Bks.
Burton, John. Mammals. (gr. 5 up). 1992. 9.98 *(0-8317-6973-4)* Smithmark.
Burton, John A. Close to Extinction. (Illus.). 32p. (gr. 5-8). 1992. PLB 12.40 *(0-531-17383-6,* Gloucester Pr) Watts.
Burton, Marilee R. My Best Shoes. Ransome, James E., illus. LC 92-33863. 32p. 1994. 15.00 *(0-688-11756-2,* Tambourine Bks); PLB 14.93 *(0-688-11757-0,* Tambourine Bks) Morrow.
—One Little Chickadee. Street, Janet, illus. LC 93-27271. (gr. 2 up). write for info. *(0-688-12651-0,* Tamborine Bks); PLB write for info. *(0-688-12652-9)* Morrow.
—Tail Toes Eyes Ears Nose. Burton, Marilee R., illus. LC 87-33276. 32p. (ps-1). 1988. PLB 11.89 *(0-06-020874-0)* HarpC Child Bks.
—Tail Toes Eyes Ears Nose. Burton, Marilee R., illus. LC 87-32276. 32p. (ps-1). 1992. pap. 4.95 *(0-06-443260-2,* Trophy) HarpC Child Bks.
Burton, Maurice. Birds. (Illus.). 64p. (gr. 4-7). 1985. 15.95x *(0-8160-1063-3)* Facts on File.
—Insects & Their Relatives. (Illus.). 64p. 1984. 15.95x *(0-87196-986-6)* Facts on File.
—Warm-Blooded Animals. (Illus.). 64p. (gr. 4-7). 1985. 15.95x *(0-8160-1059-5)* Facts on File.
Burton, Michael H. In the Light of a Child: Fifty-Two Verses for Children & the Child in Every Human Being. McHenry, Kitsy & Geard, David, illus. 62p. (Orig.). (gr. 4). 1989. pap. text ed. 12.95 *(0-932776-17-5)* Adonis Pr.
Burton, Miyo, ed. see Japanese American Curriculum Project, Inc. Staff.
Burton, Richard, ed. see Gibbons, Dave.
Burton, Richard F., tr. see Lubin, Leonard.
Burton, Richard T., tr. see Lubin, Leonard.
Burton, Robert. Arctic. (Illus.). 24p. (gr. k-4). 1991. PLB 9.90 *(1-878137-16-6)* Newington.
—Desert. (Illus.). 24p. (gr. k-4). 1991. PLB 9.90 *(1-878137-17-4)* Newington.
—Discovering Owls. (Illus.). 48p. (gr. 5-8). 1990. PLB 12.40 *(0-531-18318-1,* Pub. by Bookwright Pr) Watts.
—The Egg Book. Burton, Jane & Taylor, Kim, photos by. LC 93-28365. 1994. 14.95 *(1-56458-460-7)* Dorling Kindersley.
—The Mouse in the Barn. Oxford Scientific Films, photos by. LC 87-42614. (Illus.). 32p. (gr. 4-6). 1988. PLB 15.93 *(1-55532-305-7)* Gareth Stevens Inc.
—Seashore. (Illus.). 24p. (gr. k-4). 1991. PLB 9.90 *(1-878137-19-0)* Newington.
—Towns. (Illus.). 24p. (gr. k-4). 1991. PLB 9.90 *(1-878137-18-2)* Newington.
Burton, Teresa, jt. auth. see Cajacob, Thomas.
Burton, Tim. The Nightmare Before Christmas. Burton, Tim, illus. LC 92-54867. 40p. 1993. 15.95 *(1-56282-411-2);* PLB 15.89 *(1-56282-412-0)* Hyprn Child.
—Tim Burton's Nightmare Before Christmas Pop-Up. (ps-3). 1993. 14.98 *(0-453-03132-3)* Mouse Works.
Burton, Virginia L. Choo Choo. (Illus.). 48p. (gr. k-3). 1973. 14.45 *(0-395-17684-0)* HM.
—Choo Choo: The Story of a Little Engine Who Ran Away. Burton, Virginia L., illus. LC 37-19461. 56p. (Orig.). (gr. k-8). 1988. pap. 4.80 *(0-395-47942-8)* HM.

—Katy & the Big Snow. (Illus.). (gr. k-3). 1973. reinforced bdg. 13.45 *(0-395-18155-0)* HM.
—Katy & the Big Snow. Burton, Virginia L., illus. 40p. (gr. k-3). 1974. pap. 4.80 *(0-395-18562-9,* Sandpiper) HM.
—Life Story. (Illus.). (gr. k-3). 1989. 15.45 *(0-395-16030-8);* pap. 6.70 *(0-395-52017-7)* HM.
—Mike Mulligan & His Steam Shovel. (Illus.). (gr. k-3). 1939. PLB 11.95 *(0-395-06681-6)* HM.
—Mike Mulligan & His Steam Shovel. (gr. 3 up). 1993. pap. 7.95 incl. cass. *(0-395-45738-6)* HM.
—Mike Mulligan & His Steam Shovel. (gr. k-3). 1977. 13.45 *(0-395-16961-5);* pap. 4.80 *(0-395-25939-8)* HM.
Burton, Virginia Lee. The Little House. (Illus.). (gr. k-3). 1978. 13.95 *(0-395-18156-9);* pap. 4.95 *(0-395-25938-X)* HM.
Buscaglia, Leo F. A Memory for Tino. Newsom, Carol, illus. 50p. (ps up). 1988. 12.95 *(0-688-07482-0)* SLACK Inc.
—Seven Stories of Christmas Love. Newsom, Tom, illus. 110p. 1987. 12.95 *(0-688-07521-5)* SLACK Inc.
Busch, Laura C. Ant Books. 180p. (ps-1). 1990. 13.95 *(1-880642-01-8)* Little Read.
—Bunny Books. (ps-2). 1990. 13.95 *(1-880642-06-9)* Little Read.
—Butterfly Books. (ps-2). 1989. 13.95 *(1-880642-03-4)* Little Read.
—Canary Books. (ps-2). 1990. 13.95 *(1-880642-04-2)* Little Read.
—Caterpillar Books. 180p. (ps-1). 1990. 13.95 *(1-880642-02-6)* Little Read.
—Kitty Books. (ps-2). 1991. 13.95 *(1-880642-07-7)* Little Read.
—Letter Sound Books. (ps-2). 1991. pap. 13.95 *(1-880642-00-X)* Little Read.
—Turtle Books, 12 bks. (ps-2). 1990. Set. 13.95 *(1-880642-05-0)* Little Read.
Busch, Wilhelm. Max & Moritz. Klein, H. Arthur, ed. 216p. (Orig., Bilingual Eng & Ger). (gr. 3-6). 1962. pap. 4.95 *(0-486-20181-3)* Dover.
—Max & Moritz. Arndt, Walter, tr. LC 85-1241. (Illus.). (gr. 4 up). 1985. 9.95 *(0-915361-19-1)* Modan-Adama Bks.
Buschemeyer, Robin Q. Alphabet Pal. Launching Pad Studio, Inc. Staff, illus. 64p. (Orig.). (ps-3). 1986. pap. 2.99 *(0-935609-01-6)* Eduplay.
—Number Pal. Launching Pad Studios, Inc. Staff, illus. 40p. (Orig.). (ps-3). 1986. pap. 2.99 *(0-935609-02-4)* Eduplay.
—Word Pal. Launching Pad Studio, Inc. Staff, illus. 40p. (Orig.). (ps-3). 1986. pap. 2.99 *(0-935609-00-8)* Eduplay.
Buschini, Henny & Buschini, Luciano. The Ship in the Field. Buschini, Henny & Buschini, Luciano, illus. LC 77-174719. 32p. (gr. k-3). 1973. 6.95 *(0-87592-045-4)* Scroll Pr.
Buschini, Luciano, jt. auth. see Buschini, Henny.
Buschman, Janis & Hunley, Debbie. Strangers Don't Look Like the Big Bad Wolf! Lyons, Carole & Meyer, Linda D., eds. Megale, Marina, illus. McMorris, Sharon, intro. by. LC 85-80513. (Illus.). 38p. (Orig.). (gr. 2-4). 1985. lib. bdg. 9.00 *(0-932091-04-0);* pap. 3.95 *(0-932091-05-9)* Franklin Pr WA.
Busenberg, Bonnie. Vanilla, Chocolate, & Strawberry: The Story of Your Favorite Flavors. LC 93-15101. 1993. 23.95 *(0-8225-1573-3)* Lerner Pubns.
Bush, Catherine. Elizabeth I. (Illus.). 112p. (gr. 5 up). 1985. lib. bdg. 17.95x *(0-87754-579-0)* Chelsea Hse.
—Mohandas K. Gandhi. (Illus.). 112p. (gr. 5 up). 1985. lib. bdg. 17.95 *(0-87754-555-3)* Chelsea Hse.
Bush, Don. Jack Snake. Carbonneau, Lana, illus. 48p. (gr. k up). 1985. 5.50x *(0-943978-01-7)* Rolling Hills Pr.
—Little Brook Series, 3 bks. (Illus.). (gr. 3). lib. bdg. 16.50 *(0-943978-03-3)* Rolling Hills Pr.
—Magic Smith the Chameleon. 62p. (gr. 3). text ed. 6.50 *(0-943978-02-5)* Rolling Hills Pr.
Bush, Douglas, ed. see Keats, John.
Bush, Douglas, ed. see Shakespeare, William.
Bush, Florence C. Dorie: Woman of the Mountains. LC 91-12875. (Illus.). 254p. (gr. 6 up). 1992. text ed. 24.95x *(0-87049-725-1);* pap. 10.95 *(0-87049-726-X)* U of Tenn Pr.
—If Life Gives You Scraps, Make a Quilt: Short Stories of the Smoky Mountains. Bush, Florence C. & Bush, Margaret C., illus. 180p. (Orig.). 1993. pap. 9.95 *(0-9634680-0-6)* Misty Cove Pr.
Bush, John. The Fish Who Could Wish. Paul, Korky, illus. 32p. (ps-3). 1991. 9.95 *(0-916291-35-9)* Kane-Miller Bk.
—The Fish Who Could Wish. Paul, Korky, illus. 32p. 1994. pap. 6.95 *(0-916291-48-0)* Kane-Miller Bk.
Bush, John & Geraghty, Paul. The Bungle in the Jungle. (Illus.). (ps-2). 1992. 13.95 *(0-09-174056-8,* Pub. by Hutchinson UK) Trafalgar.
Bush, Lawrence. Emma Ansky-Levine & Her Mitzvah Machine. Iskowitz, Joel, illus. (gr. 4-6). 1991. pap. 7.95 *(0-8074-0458-6,* 123933) UAHC.
—Rooftop Secrets & Other Stories of Anti-Semitism. Vorspan, Albert, commentary by. LC 86-1362. (Illus.). 144p. (Orig.). (gr. 7 up). 1986. pap. text ed. 7.95 *(0-8074-0314-8,* 121702) UAHC.
Bush, Max. Thirteen Bells of Boglewood. (Orig.). (gr. k-3). 1987. pap. 4.50 *(0-87602-272-7)* Anchorage.
—The Troll & the Elephant Prince. (gr. 4 up). 1985. pap. 4.50 *(0-87602-254-9)* Anchorage.
—The Voyage of the Dragonfly. 1989. Playscript. 4.50 *(0-87602-287-5)* Anchorage.

Bush, Timothy. James in the House of Aunt Prudence. Bush, Timothy, illus. LC 92-40127. 32p. (ps-2). 1993. 13.00 (*0-517-58881-1*); PLB 13.99 (*0-517-58882-X*) Crown Bks Yng Read.
—Three at Sea. LC 93-3677. 1994. 13.00 (*0-517-59299-1*, Crown); lib. bdg. 13.99 (*0-517-59300-9*, Crown) Crown Bks Yng Read.
Bushell, Isobel & Bushell, John. Alexander & the Cardboard Box. (Illus.). (ps). 1994. Set (4) slipcased. bds. 9.95 (*0-8120-6393-7*) Barron.
—Alexander & the Little Fish. (Illus.). (ps). 1994. Set (4) slipcased. bds. 9.95 (*0-8120-6396-1*) Barron.
—Alexander & the New Bicycle. (Illus.). (ps). 1994. bds. 9.95 (*0-8120-6394-5*) Barron.
—Alexander & the Special Cake. (Illus.). (ps). 1994. Set (4) slipcased. bds. 9.95 (*0-8120-6395-3*) Barron.
Bushell, Isobel, illus. Santa Claus Is Coming to Town: Musical Board Book. 12p. (ps). 1993. 5.95 (*0-694-00563-0*) HarpC Child Bks.
Bushell, John, jt. auth. see Bushell, Isobel.
Bushey, Jeanne. A Sled Dog for Moshi. (Illus.). 1994. write for info. (*1-56282-631-X*); PLB write for info. (*1-56282-632-8*) Hyprn Child.
Bushey, Jerry. Farming the Land: Modern Farmers & Their Machines. Bushey, Jerry, photos by. (Illus.). 40p. (gr. k-4). 1987. PLB 13.50 (*0-87614-314-1*) Carolrhoda Bks.
—Farming the Land: Modern Farmers & Their Machines. (Illus.). (gr. k-4). 1987. pap. 4.95 (*0-87614-493-8*, First Ave Edns) Lerner Pubns.
—Monster Trucks & Other Giant Machines on Wheels. LC 84-23160. (Illus.). 32p. (gr. k-4). 1985. PLB 19.95 (*0-87614-271-4*); pap. 4.95 (*0-87614-491-1*) Carolrhoda Bks.
Bushnell, Jack. Circus of the Wolves. Parker, Robert A., illus. LC 93-8092. 1994. write for info. (*0-688-12554-9*); lib. bdg. write for info. (*0-688-12555-7*) Lothrop.
Bushong, George L. Where's Doopey? 1991. 7.95 (*0-533-09435-6*) Vantage.
Bushwick, Nathan. Understanding the Jewish Calendar. 114p. (gr. 9-12). 1989. 9.95 (*0-940118-17-3*) Moznaim.
Busiek, Kurt. The Wizard's Tale, Bk. 1. Yronwode, Catherine & Adair, Lynn, eds. Wenzel, David, illus. 42p. (Orig.). (gr. 1-4). 1993. pap. 4.95t (*1-56060-206-6*) Eclipse Bks.
—The Wizard's Tale, Bk. 2. Yronwode, Catherine & Adair, Lynn, eds. Wenzel, David, illus. 42p. (Orig.). (gr. 1-4). 1993. pap. 4.95t (*1-56060-207-4*) Eclipse Bks.
—The Wizard's Tale, Bk. 3. Yronwode, Catherine & Adair, Lynn, eds. Wenzel, David, illus. 42p. (Orig.). (gr. 1-4). 1994. pap. 4.95t (*1-56060-208-2*) Eclipse Bks.
—The Wizard's Tale, Collection, 3 bks. Yronwode, Catherine & Adair, Lynn, eds. Wenzel, David, illus. 42p. (Orig.). (gr. 1-4). Date not set. write for info. (*1-56060-210-4*); pap. write for info. (*1-56060-209-0*) Eclipse Bks.
Business Kids Staff. The Business Kit. Ashemimry, Nasir M., intro. by. (Illus.). 129p. (gr. 8-12). 1989. tchr's. ed. 14.95 (*0-9625075-1-2*); kit of 5 booklets 49.95 (*0-9625075-0-4*) Lemonade Kids.
Buskin, David. Outdoor Games. Kline, Dick, illus. Thompson, Morton, intro. by. (Illus.). (gr. k-4). 1966. PLB 12.95 (*0-87460-000-1*) Lion Bks.
Buskohl, Esther E. Honey: Story of a Little Brown Mule. Buskohl, Esther E., illus. LC 85-80216. 80p. (Orig.). (gr. 3-5). 1985. 9.95 (*0-9614991-0-9*); pap. 4.95 (*0-9614991-1-7*) EEBART.
Busnar, Gene. It's Rock 'n' Roll. LC 79-10927. (Illus.). 256p. (gr. 7 up). 1979. (J Messner); pap. 4.95 (*0-685-03343-0*) S&S Trade.
Busoni, Rafaello. The Man Who Was Don Quixote. (Illus.). (gr. 5 up). 1982. 9.95 (*0-13-548107-4*, Pub. by Treehouse) P-H.
Buss, Fran L. Journey of the Sparrows. 160p. (gr. 5-9). 1991. 15.00 (*0-525-67362-8*, Lodestar Bks) Dutton Child Bks.
Buss, Nancy. The Lobster & Ivy Higgins. Mulkey, Kim, illus. LC 91-72868. 64p. (gr. 3-7). 1992. 13.95 (*1-56397-011-2*) Boyds Mills Pr.
—Rose-Petal & the Evil Weeds. Paris, Pat, illus. 1984. incl. cassette 7.95 (*0-685-08159-1*) Parker Bros.
Busselle, Rebecca. Bathing Ugly. LC 88-17929. 192p. (gr. 7 up). 1989. 12.95 (*0-531-05801-8*); PLB 12.99 (*0-531-08401-9*) Orchard Bks Watts.
—A Frog's-Eye View. LC 90-30645. 208p. (gr. 7 up). 1990. 14.95 (*0-531-05907-3*); PLB 14.99 (*0-531-08507-4*) Orchard Bks Watts.
Bussey, M. T., ed. see Otto, Simon.
Bussolati, Emanuela. The Horse. Michelini, Carlo A., illus. LC 92-72118. 10p. (ps). 1993. 6.95 (*1-56397-201-8*) Boyds Mills Pr.
Bustard, Anne. T Is for Texas. (Illus.). 32p. (ps-2). 1989. 12.95 (*0-89658-113-6*) Voyageur Pr.
Busuttil, Joelle. Behind the Wall of China. Bogard, Vicki, tr. from FRE. Quentin, Laurence, illus. LC 92-969. (gr. k-5). 1992. 4.95 (*0-944589-42-1*) Young Discovery Lib.
—Behind the Wall of China. Quentin, Laurence, illus. 40p. (gr. k-5). 1993. PLB 9.95 (*1-56674-057-6*, HTS Bks) Forest Hse.
Butcher, Jon, jt. auth. see Butcher, Samuel J.
Butcher, Sam. Bible Promises. (Illus.). 1992. 4.99 (*0-8407-4263-0*) Oliver-Nelson.

—Christmas. (Illus.). 1992. 4.99 (*0-8407-4264-9*) Oliver-Nelson.
—Gift of Love. (Illus.). 1992. 4.99 (*0-8407-4265-7*) Oliver-Nelson.
—Itty Bitty Books: Precious Moments, 4 bks. (Illus.). 1992. Set. 19.99 (*0-8407-6882-6*) Oliver-Nelson.
—Prayers for Boys & Girls. (Illus.). 1992. 4.99 (*0-8407-4266-5*) Oliver-Nelson.
—Precious Moments Prayers for Boys & Girls. 1989. 10.99 (*0-8407-7230-0*) Nelson.
Butcher, Samuel. Precious Moments Christmas Story. (ps-3). 1991. 7.25 (*0-307-15506-4*) Western Pub.
Butcher, Samuel J. Precious Moments Bedtime Stories. Butcher, Sam, illus. LC 88-24047. 248p. 1989. 14.99 (*0-8010-0959-6*) Baker Bk.
Butcher, Samuel J. & Butcher, Jon. Precious Moments Learning Can Be Fun. (Illus.). 176p. (ps). 1993. 14.99 (*0-8010-1059-4*) Baker Bk.
Butcher, Samuel J., tr. see Beers, V. Gilbert.
Butenhoff, Lisa K. Nina's Magic. Thatch, Nancy R., ed. Butenhoff, Lisa K., illus. Melton, David, intro. by. LC 92-18293. (Illus.). 26p. (gr. 3-4). 1992. PLB 14.95 (*0-933849-40-0*) Landmark Edns.
Butler, Beverly. Ghost Cat. 1988. pap. 2.75 (*0-590-43443-8*, Scholastic) Scholastic Inc.
—Witch's Fire. LC 93-44. 144p. (gr. 5 up). 1993. 14.99 (*0-525-65132-2*, Cobblehill Bks) Dutton Child Bks.
Butler, Cathy, ed. see Cummings, Margaret A.
Butler, Cathy, ed. see Solomon, Marti.
Butler, Dale. Blossom. Caffin, Liz, illus. LC 92-34265. 1993. 14.00 (*0-383-03620-8*) SRA Schl Grp.
Butler, Daphne. First Look - Complete Set, 16 vols. (Illus.). (gr. 1-2). 1991. Set. PLB 2254.88 (*0-8368-0706-5*) Gareth Stevens Inc.
—First Look at Boats. LC 90-10256. (Illus.). 32p. (gr. 1-2). 1991. PLB 15.93 (*0-8368-0502-X*) Gareth Stevens Inc.
—First Look at Cars. LC 90-10265. (Illus.). 32p. (gr. 1-2). 1991. PLB 15.93 (*0-8368-0503-8*) Gareth Stevens Inc.
—First Look at Day & Night. LC 90-10246. (Illus.). 32p. (gr. 1-2). 1991. PLB 15.93 (*0-8368-0505-4*) Gareth Stevens Inc.
—First Look at the Airports. LC 90-10266. (Illus.). 32p. (gr. 1-2). 1991. PLB 15.93 (*0-8368-0501-1*) Gareth Stevens Inc.
—First Look at the Changing Seasons. LC 90-10246. (Illus.). 32p. (gr. 1-2). 1991. PLB 15.93 (*0-8368-0504-6*) Gareth Stevens Inc.
—First Look in the Forest. LC 90-10240. (Illus.). 32p. (gr. 1-2). 1991. PLB 15.93 (*0-8368-0506-2*) Gareth Stevens Inc.
—First Look in the Hospital. LC 90-10245. (Illus.). 32p. (gr. 1-2). 1991. PLB 15.93 (*0-8368-0563-1*) Gareth Stevens Inc.
—First Look under the Ground. LC 90-10250. (Illus.). 32p. (gr. 1-2). 1991. PLB 15.93 (*0-8368-0507-0*) Gareth Stevens Inc.
—France. LC 92-16648. (Illus.). 32p. (gr. 3-4). 1992. PLB 19.24 (*0-8114-3675-6*) Raintree Steck-V.
—Italy. LC 92-16649. (Illus.). 32p. (gr. 3-4). 1992. PLB 19.24 (*0-8114-3677-2*) Raintree Steck-V.
—Spain. LC 92-17032. (Illus.). 32p. (gr. 3-4). 1992. PLB 19.24 (*0-8114-3678-0*) Raintree Steck-V.
—U. S. A. LC 92-13647. (Illus.). 32p. (gr. 3-4). 1992. PLB 19.24 (*0-8114-3676-4*) Raintree Steck-V.
Butler, Dorothy. Another Happy Tale. Hurford, John, illus. LC 91-23133. 32p. (ps-3). 1991. 12.95 (*0-940793-88-1*, Crocodile Bks) Interlink Pub.
—A Happy Tale. Hurford, John, illus. LC 90-34500. 32p. (ps-5). 1990. 11.95 (*0-940793-61-X*, Crocodile Bks) Interlink Pub.
—Higgledy Piggledy Hobbledy Hoy. LC 89-77503. (Illus.). 30p. (ps up). 1991. 13.95 (*0-688-08660-8*); PLB 13.88 (*0-688-08661-6*) Greenwillow.
—My Brown Bear Barney. Fuller, Elizabeth, illus. LC 88-21199. 24p. (ps up). 1989. 14.00 (*0-688-08567-9*); PLB 13.93 (*0-688-08568-7*) Greenwillow.
—My Brown Bear Barney in Trouble. Fuller, Elizabeth, illus. LC 90-24776. 24p. (ps-6). 1993. 14.00 (*0-688-10521-1*); PLB 13.93 (*0-688-10522-X*) Greenwillow.
Butler, Elvie. Celebrate Thanksgiving with Stickers. 1989. pap. 3.95 (*0-590-42505-6*) Scholastic Inc.
—Celebrate Valentine's Day. Van Horn, William, illus. 48p. (gr. 1-4). 1989. pap. 2.95 (*0-590-42052-6*) Scholastic Inc.
Butler, Francelia. Indira Gandhi. Schlesinger, Arthur M., Jr., intro. by. (Illus.). 112p. (gr. 5 up). 1987. lib. bdg. 17.95 (*0-87754-596-0*) Chelsea Hse.
Butler, Joan & Walker, Katherine S. Ballet for Boys & Girls. (Illus.). (gr. 3-7). 1980. 9.95x (*0-13-055574-6*) P-H.
Butler, John, jt. auth. see Strong, Stacie.
Butler, Linda P. Maxine & the Ghost Dog. Goldberg, Grace, illus. 24p. (ps-2). 1992. pap. 0.99 (*1-56293-114-8*) McClanahan Bk.
Butler, M. Christina. Picnic Pandemonium. Rutherford, Meg, illus. LC 90-10148. 28p. (gr. 1-2). 1991. PLB 15.93 (*0-8368-0433-3*) Gareth Stevens Inc.
—Stanley in the Dark. Rutherford, Meg, illus. 32p. (ps-1). 1990. with dust jacket 12.95 (*0-8120-6158-6*) Barron.
—Too Many Eggs. LC 83-49007. (Illus.). (gr. k-12). 1988. 12.95 (*0-87923-741-4*) Godine.
Butler, M. Christine. The Dinosaur Egg Mystery. (ps-3). 1992. 11.95 (*0-8120-6297-3*); pap. 5.95 (*0-8120-1379-4*) Barron.
Butler, Mary K. Papa's Old Trunk. LC 81-68812. (Illus.). (gr. 6-12). 1981. 10.00 (*0-934530-03-3*) Buck Pub.

Butler, Mike. Colorado - Mile by Mile. 36p. (gr. 3-8). 1991. pap. 6.95 (*1-880372-12-6*) Mile By Mile.
Butler, Samuel. Erewhon. Threapleton, M. M., intro. by. (gr. 11 up). 1967. pap. 1.25 (*0-8049-0130-9*, CL-130) Airmont.
—Way of All Flesh. Rudzik, O. H., intro. by. (gr. 11 up). 1965. pap. 2.50 (*0-8049-0090-6*, CL-90) Airmont.
Butler, Sandra L., ed. see Ziegler, J. F.
Butler, Stephen. Henny Penny. Butler, Stephen, illus. LC 90-35115. 32p. (ps-1). 1991. 12.95 (*0-688-09921-1*, Tambourine Bks); PLB 12.88 (*0-688-09922-X*, Tambourine Bks) Morrow.
—The Mouse & the Apple. Butler, Stephen, illus. LC 93-15951. 32p. (ps up). 1994. 15.00 (*0-688-12810-6*, Tambourine Bks); PLB 14.93 (*0-688-12811-4*, Tambourine Bks) Morrow.
Butler, Susan. A Trip to the Jungle. (Illus.). 40p. (Orig.). (ps-2). 1978. pap. 3.95 (*0-931416-00-0*) Open Books.
Butler, William V. The Young Detective's Handbook. Landon, Lucinda, illus. (gr. 3-7). 1986. (Pub. by Atlantic Monthly Pr); pap. 6.95 (*0-316-11889-3*) Little.
Butrick, Lyn M. If This... & That.. Then What. Cooper, William R., ed. Butrick, Lyn M., illus. LC 83-50783. 27p. (gr. 1-3). 1983. Set. pap. 15.80 (*0-914127-13-6*); Vol. 1. 3.93 (*0-914127-04-7*) Univ Class.
—Logic for Space Age Kids. Cooper, William H., ed. Butrick, Lyn M., illus. LC 84-50892. 32p. (gr. 3-6). 1984. pap. 5.27 (*0-914127-16-0*) Univ Class.
—Thinking Makes a Difference. Tate, Baird, ed. LC 86-50146. (Illus.). (gr. 4-8). 1986. pap. 6.60 (*0-914127-20-9*); Avail. tchrs. ed. Univ Class.
Butson, Thomas. Ivan the Terrible. Schlesinger, Arthur M., Jr., intro. by. (Illus.). 112p. (gr. 5 up). 1988. lib. bdg. 17.95 (*0-87754-534-0*) Chelsea Hse.
—Mikhail Gorbachev. Schlesinger, Arthur M., Jr., intro. by. (Illus.). 112p. (Orig.). (gr. 5 up). 1989. 17.95 (*1-55546-200-6*); pap. 9.95 (*0-7910-0571-2*) Chelsea Hse.
—Pierre Elliott Trudeau. Schlesinger, Arthur M., Jr., intro. by. (Illus.). 112p. (gr. 5 up). 1986. lib. bdg. 17.95 (*0-87754-445-X*) Chelsea Hse.
Buttenwieser, Paul. Their Pride & Joy. (gr. 6 up). 1988. pap. 8.95 (*0-440-50073-7*, LE) Dell.
Butterfield, M. Air Travel Games. (Illus.). 32p. (gr. 2 up). 1986. pap. 4.95 (*0-86020-997-0*) EDC.
—How to Draw Machines. 32p. (gr. 2 up). 1988. PLB 12.96 (*0-88110-316-0*); pap. 4.95 (*0-7460-0175-4*) EDC.
Butterfield, M., jt. auth. see Peach, S.
Butterfield, M., jt. auth. see Potter, T.
Butterfield, Maira, jt. auth. see Ganeri, Anita.
Butterfield, Maira, jt. auth. see Langley, Andrew.
Butterfield, Moira. Amazon Rainforest. Johnson, Paul, illus. 16p. (gr. k-5). 1992. pap. 6.95 (*0-8249-8566-4*, Ideals Child) Hambleton-Hill.
—Bird. Johnson, Paul, illus. 24p. (ps-1). 1992. pap. 3.95 (*0-671-75892-6*, Little Simon) S&S Trade.
—Butterfly. Johnson, Paul, illus. 24p. (ps-1). 1992. pap. 3.95 (*0-671-75894-2*, Little Simon) S&S Trade.
—The Earth. LC 92-53101. (Illus.). 48p. (Orig.). (gr. 3-8). 1992. pap. 5.95 (*1-85697-808-7*) Kingfisher Bks.
—Flower. Johnson, Paul, illus. 24p. (ps-1). 1992. pap. 3.95 (*0-671-75891-8*, Little Simon) S&S Trade.
—Frog. Johnson, Paul, illus. 24p. (ps-1). 1992. pap. 3.95 (*0-671-75893-4*, Little Simon) S&S Trade.
—Fun with Paint. Venus, Joanna & Kerr, Elizabeth, illus. 48p. (gr. 1-5). 1993. 6.99 (*0-679-83492-3*); PLB 9.99 (*0-679-93492-8*) Random Bks Yng Read.
—People & Places. Forsey, Chris, illus. LC 91-214. 40p. (Orig.). (gr. 2-5). 1991. pap. 3.99 (*0-679-80868-X*) Random Bks Yng Read.
—Undersea World. Johnson, Paul, illus. 16p. (gr. 1-5). 1992. pap. 6.95 (*0-8249-8589-3*, Ideals Child) Hambleton-Hill.
—Wild Animals. LC 92-53114. (Illus.). 48p. (Orig.). (gr. 3-8). 1992. pap. 5.95 (*1-85697-809-5*) Kingfisher Bks.
Butterfield, Moira & Wright, Nicola. Getting to Know Britain: People, Places. Wooley, Kim, illus. LC 93-29716. (gr. 3-7). 1994. 12.95 (*0-8120-6392-9*); pap. 5.95 (*0-8120-1854-0*) Barron.
Butterfield, Ron. Woodcarving: A Complete Course. (Illus.). 128p. (gr. 10-12). 1992. pap. 14.95 (*0-946819-04-1*, Pub. by Guild Mstr Craftsman) Sterling.
Butterfield, S. Borders & Beyond. (gr. 1-6). 1985. 5.95 (*0-88160-118-7*, LW250) Learning Wks.
—Gold Medal Games. rev. ed. (gr. 1-3). 1992. Repr. of 1983 ed. 3.95 (*0-88160-106-3*, LW 125) Learning Wks.
Butterfield, Sherri. Seasons. (Illus.). 48p. (gr. 2-5). 1990. 5.95 (*0-88160-190-X*, LW 149) Learning Wks.
Butters, Dorothy G. The Bells of Freedom. Wilde, Carol, illus. (gr. 4-8). 1984. 15.50 (*0-8446-6162-7*) Peter Smith.
Butterworth, Christine. Alligators. LC 90-9927. (Illus.). 32p. (gr. 1-4). 1990. PLB 15.96 (*0-8114-2639-4*); pap. 3.95 (*0-8114-4608-5*) Raintree Steck-V.
—Eagles. LC 89-26076. (Illus.). 32p. (gr. 1-4). 1990. PLB 15.96 (*0-8114-2632-7*) Raintree Steck-V.
—Frogs. LC 89-22014. (Illus.). 32p. (gr. 1-4). 1990. PLB 15.96 (*0-8114-2637-8*); pap. 3.95 (*0-8114-4611-5*) Raintree Steck-V.
—Kangaroos. LC 89-26077. (Illus.). 32p. (gr. 1-4). 1990. PLB 15.96 (*0-8114-2634-3*); pap. 3.95 (*0-8114-4612-3*) Raintree Steck-V.
Butterworth, Christine & Bailey, Donna. Las Aguilas. LC 91-22808. (SPA., Illus.). 32p. (gr. 1-4). 1992. PLB 14.64 (*0-8114-2660-2*) Raintree Steck-V.

—Chimpanzees. LC 90-9928. (Illus.). 32p. (gr. 1-4). 1990. PLB 15.96 (0-8114-2642-4); pap. 3.95 (0-8114-4615-8) Raintree Steck-V.
—Crabs. LC 90-36168. (Illus.). 32p. (gr. 1-4). 1990. PLB 15.96 (0-8114-2640-8) Raintree Steck-V.
—Deer. LC 90-9960. (Illus.). 32p. (gr. 1-4). 1990. PLB 15.96 (0-8114-2638-6) Raintree Steck-V.
—Foxes. LC 90-36169. (Illus.). 32p. (gr. 1-4). 1990. PLB 15.96 (0-8114-2641-6) Raintree Steck-V.
—Owls. LC 90-37529. (Illus.). 32p. (gr. 1-4). 1990. PLB 15.96 (0-8114-2643-2) Raintree Steck-V.
Butterworth, Emma M. As the Waltz Was Ending. LC 82-70402. 192p. (gr. 7 up). 1984. SBE 14.95 (0-02-716190-0, Four Winds) Macmillan Child Grp.
—As the Waltz Was Ending. 262p. (gr. 7 up). 1991. pap. 3.25 (0-590-44440-9, Point); tchr's. guide 1.25 (0-590-40665-5) Scholastic Inc.
Butterworth, Jim, jt. auth. see Jones, Tim.
Butterworth, Nick. Busy People. Butterworth, Nick, illus. LC 91-58719. 32p. (ps). 1992. 9.95 (1-56402-056-8) Candlewick Pr.
—Field Day. (ps-3). 1991. 14.00 (0-385-30328-9) Delacorte.
—Field Day. (gr. 1-3). 1993. pap. 2.99 (0-553-37250-5) Bantam.
—Making Faces. Butterworth, Nick, illus. LC 92-54578. 32p. (ps). 1993. 12.95 (1-56402-212-9) Candlewick Pr.
—My Dad Is Awesome. Butterworth, Nick, illus. LC 91-71832. 32p. (ps up). 1992. pap. 4.99 (1-56402-033-9) Candlewick Pr.
—My Grandma Is Wonderful. Butterworth, Nick, illus. LC 91-58747. 32p. (ps up). 1992. pap. 4.99 (1-56402-100-9) Candlewick Pr.
—My Grandpa Is Amazing. Butterworth, Nick, illus. LC 91-58746. 32p. (ps up). 1992. pap. 4.99 (1-56402-099-1) Candlewick Pr.
—Nativity Play. (ps-3). 1991. pap. 3.99 (0-440-40541-6, YB) Dell.
—Nick Butterworth's Book of Nursery Rhymes. (ps-3). 1991. 14.95 (0-670-83551-X) Viking Child Bks.
—One Blowy Night. (ps-3). 1992. 14.95 (0-316-11919-9) Little.
—One Snowy Night. (ps-3). 1990. 13.95 (0-316-11918-0) Little.
—Rescue Party, Vol. 1. (ps-3). 1993. 14.95 (0-316-11923-7) Little.
—School Trip. 1990. 13.95 (0-385-30242-8) Delacorte.
—School Trip. (gr. 1-3). 1993. pap. 2.99 (0-553-37249-1) Bantam.
Butterworth, Nick & Inkpen, Mich. Jasper's Beanstalk. Inkpen, Mick, illus. LC 92-14886. 32p. (ps-3). 1993. SBE 13.95 (0-02-716231-1, Bradbury Pr) Macmillan Child Grp.
Butterworth, Nick & Inkpen, Mick. The Good Stranger. Butterworth, Nick & Inkpen, Mick, illus. 32p. (ps-3). 1992. 3.99 (0-551-02507-7) HarpC.
—The Little Gate. Butterworth, Nick & Inkpen, Mick, illus. 32p. (ps-3). 1992. pap. 3.99 (0-551-02506-9) HarpC.
—The Rich Farmer. Butterworth, Nick & Inkpen, Mick, illus. 32p. (ps-3). 1992. pap. 3.99 (0-551-02508-5) HarpC.
—The Ten Silver Coins. Butterworth, Nick & Inkpen, Mick, illus. 32p. (ps-3). 1992. 3.99 (0-551-02505-0) HarpC.
Butterworth, Nick & Inkpen, Mick, illus. Who Made Me? Doney, Malcolm, text by. LC 92-20748. 1992. write for info. (0-551-01476-8) Zondervan.
Butterworth, Oliver. The Enormous Egg. (gr. k-6). 1987. pap. 3.50 (0-440-42337-6, YB) Dell.
—The Enormous Egg. Darling, Louis, illus. (gr. 4-6). 1956. 14.95 (0-316-11904-0, Pub. by Atlantic Monthly Pr) Little.
—Enormous Egg; You Won't Believe Your Eyes! (gr. 4-7). 1993. pap. 3.95 (0-316-11920-2) Little.
—Trouble with Jenny's Ear. (gr. 4-7). 1993. 4.95 (0-316-11922-9) Little.
—A Visit to the Big House. Avishai, Susan, illus. LC 92-9787. 48p. (gr. 2-5). 1993. 13.95 (0-395-52805-4) HM.
Butterworth, Rod R. & Flodin, Mickey. The Pocket Dictionary of Signing. rev. ed. 224p. (Orig.). 1992. pap. 5.95 (0-399-51743-X, Perigee Bks) Putnam Pub Group.
Butterworth, W., et al. Double Action Library Four Program. large type ed. Incl. The Air Freight Mystery. 132p. 24.15 (0-317-02180-X, 4-04140-00); Apprentice to a Rip-Off. 132p. 24.15 (0-317-02181-8, 4-04150-00); The Drop-In. 132p. 24.15 (0-317-02182-6, 4-04160-00); Flying Wheels. 132p; The Promise Ring. 132p. 24.15 (0-317-02184-2, 4-04180-00); Teacher's Guide. 16p. 5.24 (0-317-02185-0, 4-04190-00). (gr. 7-12). 1981. Repr. of 1979 ed. Am Printing Hse.
Butterworth, W. E. Leroy & the Old Man. 168p. (gr. 7 up). 1989. pap. 3.25 (0-590-42711-3) Scholastic Inc.
Butts, Dennis, intro. by see Burnett, Frances H.
Butts, Dennis, intro. by see Nesbit, Edith.
Butts, Donna R. & Corder, S. Scott. UFO Contact, the Four. Stevens, Wendelle C., ed. Butts, Donna R., illus. Caulfield, William, intro. by. (Illus.). 240p. (gr. 9-12). 1989. PLB 17.95 (0-934269-18-1) UFO Photo.
Butts, W. E. The Inheritance. Seiger, Jamie, illus. 32p. (gr. 7-9). 1981. pap. 5.00 (0-939622-27-0) Four Zoas Night.
Butwin, Frances. The Jews in America. rev. ed. 87p. (gr. 5 up). 1991. PLB 15.95 (0-8225-0217-8) Lerner Pubns.
—Jews in America. 1991. pap. 5.95 (0-8225-1044-8) Lerner Pubns.

Buxton, Jane H; see Crump, Donald J.
Buxton, Jane H., ed. Dinosaur Babies, Bk. 1 of 2. (Illus.). (ps-3). 1991. Set. 24.50 (0-87044-841-2) Natl Geog.
—Playful Pandas, Bk. 1 of 2. (Illus.). (ps-3). 1991. Set. 24.50 (0-87044-840-4) Natl Geog.
Buxton, John, illus. Secret Treasures. LC 93-9767. (Illus.). 1993. write for info. (0-87044-956-7) Natl Geog.
Buxton, Marilyn. Advanced Projects for Children. Harrison, Gaye, illus. 59p. (gr. 5-7). 1984. pap. text ed. 11.95 (0-88193-105-5) Create Learn.
—Beginning Projects for Children. Harrison, Gaye, illus. 47p. (gr. 4-7). 1983. pap. text ed. 11.95 (0-88193-101-2) Create Learn.
—Intermediate Projects for Children. Harrison, Gaye, illus. 60p. (gr. 5-7). 1983. pap. text ed. 11.95 (0-88193-103-9) Create Learn.
Buxton, Marilyn & Buxton, Robin. PET, Vol. 3. 58p. (gr. 5-12). 1983. pap. text ed. 11.95 (0-88193-023-7) Create Learn.
—PET, Vol. 4. 54p. (gr. 5-12). 1983. pap. text ed. 11.95 (0-88193-024-5) Create Learn.
—VIC-20, Vol. 4. 63p. (gr. 5-12). 1983. pap. text ed. 11.95 (0-88193-064-4) Create Learn.
Buxton, Marilyn & Buxton, Tammy. TI 99-4A, Vol. 3. 65p. (gr. 5-12). 1983. pap. text ed. 11.95 (0-88193-053-9) Create Learn.
—TI 99-4A, Vol. 4. 45p. (gr. 5-12). 1983. pap. text ed. 11.95 (0-88193-054-7) Create Learn.
Buxton, Marilyn, jt. auth. see Buxton, Robin.
Buxton, Robin. Commodore 64, Vol. 1. 50p. (gr. 4-12). 1983. pap. text ed. 11.95 (0-88193-041-5) Create Learn.
—Commodore 64, Vol. 2. 58p. (gr. 4-12). 1983. pap. text ed. 11.95 (0-88193-042-3) Create Learn.
—Commodore 64, Vol. 5. 66p. (gr. 6-12). 1984. pap. text ed. 11.95 (0-88193-045-8) Create Learn.
—Commodore 64, Vol. 6. 76p. (gr. 6-12). 1984. pap. text ed. 11.95 (0-88193-046-6) Create Learn.
—PET, Vol. 1. 51p. (gr. 4-12). 1983. pap. text ed. 11.95 (0-88193-021-0) Create Learn.
—PET, Vol. 2. 51p. (gr. 5-12). 1983. pap. text ed. 11.95 (0-88193-022-9) Create Learn.
—PET, Vol. 5. 72p. (gr. 6-12). 1984. pap. text ed. 11.95 (0-88193-025-3) Create Learn.
—PET, Vol. 6. 56p. (gr. 6-10). 1984. pap. text ed. 11.95 (0-88193-026-1) Create Learn.
—VIC-20, Vol. 1. 51p. (gr. 4-12). 1983. pap. text ed. 11.95 (0-88193-061-X) Create Learn.
—VIC-20, Vol. 2. 59p. (gr. 4-12). 1983. pap. text ed. 11.95 (0-88193-062-8) Create Learn.
—VIC-20, Vol. 3. 59p. (gr. 5-12). 1983. pap. text ed. 11.95 (0-88193-063-6) Create Learn.
Buxton, Robin & Buxton, Marilyn. Commodore 64, Vol. 3. 59p. (gr. 5-12). 1983. pap. text ed. 11.95 (0-88193-043-1) Create Learn.
—Commodore 64, Vol. 4. 59p. (gr. 5-12). 1983. pap. text ed. 11.95 (0-88193-044-X) Create Learn.
Buxton, Robin, jt. auth. see Buxton, Marilyn.
Buxton, Tammy. TI 99-4A, Vol. 1. 54p. (gr. 4-12). 1983. pap. text ed. 11.95 (0-88193-051-2) Create Learn.
—TI 99-4A, Vol. 2. 53p. (gr. 4-12). 1983. pap. text ed. 11.95 (0-88193-052-0) Create Learn.
Buxton, Tammy, jt. auth. see Buxton, Marilyn.
Buzhardt, Gail & Hawthorne, Margaret. Recontres sur le Mississippi, 1682-1763. (Illus.). 280p. (gr. 10-12). Date not set. set. 28.00x (0-87805-665-3) U Pr of Miss.
Byam, Michele. Arms & Armor. King, Dave, photos by. LC 87-26449. (Illus.). 64p. (gr. 5 up). 1988. 15.00 (0-394-89622-X); lib. bdg. 15.99 (0-394-99622-4) Knopf Bks Yng Read.
Byard, C., ed. see Williams, S.
Byars, Betsy. The Animal, the Vegetable, & John D. Jones. Sanderson, Ruth, illus. 160p. (gr. 5 up). 1983. pap. 3.25 (0-440-40356-1, YB) Dell.
—The Animal, the Vegetable, & John D. Jones. large type ed. 166p. (gr. 3-6). 1984. Repr. of 1982 ed. 44.03 (0-317-01868-X, 4-00950-00) Am Printing Hse.
—The Animal, the Vegetable & John D. Jones. large type ed. 156p. 1992. 13.95 (0-7451-1609-4, Galaxy Child Lrg Print) Chivers N Amer.
—Beans on the Roof. Rosales, Melodye, illus. 80p. (gr. k-3). 1988. pap. 13.95 (0-440-50055-9) Delacorte.
—Beans on the Roof. 1990. pap. 3.25 (0-440-40314-6, YB) Dell.
—Bingo Brown & the Language of Love. large type ed. 152p. 1989. lib. bdg. 15.95 (1-55736-146-0, Crnrstn Bks) BDD LT Grp.
—Bingo Brown & the Language of Love. (Illus.). 144p. (gr. 3-7). 1991. pap. 3.99 (0-14-034141-2, Puffin) Puffin Bks.
—Bingo Brown, Gypsy Lover. 160p. (gr. 3 up). 1990. 12.95 (0-670-83322-3) Viking Child Bks.
—Bingo Brown, Gypsy Lover. 128p. (gr. 3-7). 1992. pap. 3.99 (0-14-034518-3) Puffin Bks.
—Bingo Brown, Gypsy Lover. large type ed. 152p. (gr. 1-8). 1992. 13.95 (0-7451-1499-7, Galaxy Child Lrg Print) Chivers N Amer.
—Bingo Brown's Guide to Romance. 160p. (gr. 3-7). 1992. 14.00 (0-670-84491-8) Viking Child Bks.
—A Blossom Promise. Rogers, Jacqueline, illus. 160p. (gr. k-6). 1989. pap. 2.95 (0-440-40137-2, YB) Dell.
—The Blossoms & the Green Phantom. Rogers, Jacqueline, illus. 160p. (gr. 4-6). 1987. pap. 14.95 (0-385-29533-2) Delacorte.
—The Blossoms & the Green Phantom. Rogers, Jacqueline, illus. 160p. (gr. k-6). 1988. pap. 2.95 (0-440-40069-4) Dell.

—The Blossoms Meet the Vulture Lady. (gr. k-6). 1987. pap. 2.75 (0-440-40677-3, YB) Dell.
—The Blossoms Meet the Vulture Lady. large type ed. (gr. 1-8). 1990. 13.95 (0-7451-0824-5, Galaxy Child Lrg Print) Chivers N Amer.
—The Burning Questions of Bingo Brown. large type ed. 232p. (gr. 3-7). 1989. lib. bdg. 14.95 (0-8161-4770-1, Large Print Bks) Hall.
—The Burning Questions of Bingo Brown. 176p. (gr. 3 up). 1990. pap. 3.99 (0-14-032479-8, Puffin) Puffin Bks.
—The Cartoonist. 128p. (gr. k-6). 1981. pap. 1.95 (0-440-41046-0, YB) Dell.
—The Cartoonist. large type ed. 152p. (gr. 1-8). 1991. 13.95 (0-7451-1317-6, Galaxy Child Lrg Print) Chivers N Amer.
—Coast to Coast. LC 91-46451. (Illus.). 176p. (gr. 5-9). 1992. 14.00 (0-385-30787-X) Delacorte.
—The Computer Nut. large type ed. Byars, Betsy, illus. 200p. 1993. 13.95 (0-7451-1680-9, Galaxy Child Lrg Print) Chivers N Amer.
—The Cybil War. large type ed. 136p. 1991. 13.95 (0-7451-1403-2, Galaxy Child Lrg Print) Chivers N Amer.
—The Golly Sisters Go West. Truesdell, Sue, illus. LC 84-48474. 64p. (gr. k-3). 1986. PLB 13.89 (0-06-020884-8) HarpC Child Bks.
—Golly Sisters Go West. LC 84-48474. (Illus.). 64p. (gr. k-3). 1989. pap. 3.50 (0-06-444132-6, Trophy) HarpC Child Bks.
—The Golly Sisters Ride Again. Truesdell, Sue, photos by. LC 92-23394. (Illus.). 1994. 13.00 (0-06-021563-1); PLB 12.89 (0-06-021564-X) HarpC Child Bks.
—Good-Bye, Chicken Little. LC 78-19829. 112p. (gr. 5 up). 1979. PLB 13.89 (0-06-020911-9) HarpC Child Bks.
—Good-Bye, Chicken Little. LC 78-19829. 112p. (gr. 5 up). 1990. pap. 3.95 (0-06-440291-6, Trophy) HarpC Child Bks.
—Hooray for the Golly Sisters! Truesdell, Sue, illus. LC 89-48147. 64p. (gr. k-3). 1990. 14.00 (0-06-020898-8); PLB 13.89 (0-06-020899-6) HarpC Child Bks.
—Hooray for the Golly Sisters! Truesdell, Sue, contrib. by. LC 89-48147. (Illus.). 64p. (gr. k-3). 1992. pap. 3.50 (0-06-444156-3, Trophy) HarpC Child Bks.
—The Moon & I. (Illus.). 96p. (gr. 5 up). 1992. 12.95 (0-671-74166-7, J Messner); lib. bdg. 14.98 (0-671-74165-9, J Messner) S&S Trade.
—The Night Swimmers. Howell, Troy, illus. LC 79-53597. 160p. (gr. 4-6). 1980. 9.95 (0-685-01397-9); pap. 11.95 (0-385-28709-7) Delacorte.
—The Night Swimmers. Howell, Troy, illus. 144p. (gr. 5-9). 1983. pap. 3.50 (0-440-45857-9, YB) Dell.
—Night Swimmers. large type ed. 1990. Repr. PLB 15.95 (1-55736-177-0, Crnrstn Bks) BDD LT Grp.
—The Not-Just-Anybody Family. (gr. k-6). 1987. pap. 3.50 (0-440-45951-6, YB) Dell.
—The Pinballs. LC 76-41518. 144p. (gr. 5 up). 1977. 15.00 (0-06-020917-8); PLB 14.89 (0-06-020918-6) HarpC Child Bks.
—The Pinballs. LC 76-41518. 144p. (gr. 5 up). 1987. pap. 3.95 (0-06-440198-7, Trophy) HarpC Child Bks.
—Pinballs. large type ed. 185p. (gr. 5-8). 1988. Repr. of 1977 ed. lib. bdg. 15.95 (1-55736-028-6, Crnrstn Bks); bk. & 2 audio cass. 29.95 (1-55736-090-1) BDD LT Grp.
—Seven Treasure Hunts. Barrett, Jennifer, illus. LC 90-32043. 80p. (gr. 2-6). 1991. 14.00 (0-06-020885-6); PLB 13.89 (0-06-020886-4) HarpC Child Bks.
—The Seven Treasure Hunts. Barrett, Jennifer, illus. LC 90-32043. 80p. (gr. 2-6). 1992. pap. 3.95 (0-06-440435-8, Trophy) HarpC Child Bks.
—Summer of the Swans. large type ed. 185p. (gr. 5 up). 1988. Repr. of 1970 ed. lib. bdg. 15.95 (1-55736-030-8, Crnrstn Bks) BDD LT Grp.
—The T. V. Kid. large type ed. 312p. (gr. 4-7). 1990. 15.95 (0-7451-1179-3) G K Hall.
—The Two-Thousand-Pound Goldfish. LC 81-48652. 160p. (gr. 5 up). 1982. PLB 14.89 (0-06-020890-2) HarpC Child Bks.
—The Two-Thousand Pound Goldfish. large type ed. 160p. 1989. Repr. of 1982 ed. lib. bdg. 15.95 (1-55736-131-2, Crnrstn Bks) BDD LT Grp.
—The Two-Thousand-Pound Goldfish. 160p. (gr. 3-7). 1991. pap. 2.95 (0-590-42368-1) Scholastic Inc.
—Wanted...Mud Blossom. (gr. 4-7). 1991. 14.00 (0-385-30428-5) Delacorte.
—Wanted...Mud Blossom. (gr. 4-7). 1993. pap. 3.50 (0-440-40761-3) Dell.
—The Winged Colt of Casa Mia. Cuffari, Richard, illus. 132p. (gr. 3-7). 1981. pap. 2.95 (0-380-00201-9, Camelot) Avon.
Byars, Betsy C. After the Goat Man. Himler, Ronald, illus. (gr. 3-7). 1982. pap. 3.95 (0-14-031533-0, Puffin) Puffin Bks.
—Bingo Brown & the Language of Love. 160p. (gr. 3-7). 1989. 12.95 (0-670-82791-6) Viking Child Bks.
—The Burning Questions of Bingo Brown. LC 87-21022. 160p. (gr. 3-7). 1988. pap. 14.00 (0-670-81932-8) Viking Child Bks.
—The Cartoonist. Cuffari, Richard, illus. LC 77-12782. 128p. (gr. 3-7). 1978. 13.95 (0-670-20556-7) Viking Child Bks.
—The Cartoonist. Cuffari, Richard, illus. (gr. 3-7). 1987. pap. 3.99 (0-14-032309-0, Puffin) Puffin Bks.
—The Computer Nut. LC 84-7239. 144p. (gr. 3-7). 1984. pap. 12.95 (0-670-23548-2) Viking Child Bks.

—The Computer Nut. Byars, Guy, illus. 144p. (gr. 3-7). 1986. pap. 3.99 (0-14-032086-5, Puffin) Puffin Bks.
—Cracker Jackson. LC 84-24684. 168p. (gr. 5-7). 1985. pap. 12.95 (0-670-80546-7) Viking Child Bks.
—Cracker Jackson. 160p. (gr. 5-9). 1986. pap. 3.95 (0-14-031881-X, Puffin) Puffin Bks.
—The Cybil War. Owens, Gail, illus. LC 80-26912. 144p. (gr. 8-12). 1981. pap. 12.95 (0-670-25248-4) Viking Child Bks.
—The Cybil War. Owens, Gail, illus. 144p. (gr. 3 up). 1990. pap. 3.99 (0-14-030356-3, Puffin) Puffin Bks.
—The Eighteenth Emergency. Grossman, Robert, illus. (gr. 4-6). 1981. pap. 3.99 (0-14-031451-2, Puffin) Puffin Bks.
—The Eighteenth Emergency. Grossman, Robert, illus. LC 72-91399. 128p. (gr. 4-6). 1973. pap. 12.95 (0-670-29055-6) Viking Child Bks.
—The Glory Girl. LC 83-5927. 144p. (gr. 5-9). 1983. pap. 12.95 (0-670-34261-0) Viking Child Bks.
—The Glory Girl. (ps-3). 1985. pap. 3.95 (0-14-031785-6, Puffin) Puffin Bks.
—Go & Hush the Baby. McCully, Emily A., illus. (ps-3). 1982. pap. 4.99 (0-14-050396-X, Puffin) Puffin Bks.
—The House of Wings. Schwartz, Daniel, illus. 136p. (gr. 3-7). 1982. pap. 3.99 (0-14-031523-3, Puffin) Puffin Bks.
—The House of Wings. Schwartz, Daniel, illus. 160p. (gr. 4-6). 1972. pap. 14.95 (0-670-38025-3) Viking Child Bks.
—McMummy. LC 93-16717. 160p. (gr. 5-9). 1993. 13.99 (0-670-84995-2) Viking Child Bks.
—The Midnight Fox. Grifalconi, Ann, illus. (gr. 3-7). 1981. pap. 3.99 (0-14-031450-4, Puffin) Puffin Bks.
—The Midnight Fox. Grifalconi, Ann, illus. LC 68-27566. (gr. 3-7). 1968. pap. 13.95 (0-670-47473-8) Viking Child Bks.
—The Summer of the Swans. CoConis, Ted, illus. 144p. 1981. pap. 3.99 (0-14-031420-2, Puffin) Puffin Bks.
—Summer of the Swans. CoConis, Ted, illus. (gr. 7 up). 1970. pap. 14.00 (0-670-68190-3) Viking Child Bks.
—Trouble River. Negri, Rocco, illus. (gr. 3-7). 1969. pap. 13.95 (0-670-73257-5) Viking Child Bks.
—Trouble River. Negri, Rocco, illus. 160p. (gr. 3-7). 1989. pap. 3.99 (0-14-034243-5, Puffin) Puffin Bks.
—The TV Kid. Cuffari, Richard, illus. 128p. (gr. 4-6). 1976. pap. 12.95 (0-670-73331-8) Viking Child Bks.
—The TV Kid. Cuffari, Richard, illus. (gr. 2-7). 1987. pap. 3.99 (0-14-032308-2, Puffin) Puffin Bks.
Byck, Robert. Treating Mental Illness. updated ed. (Illus.). (gr. 5 up). 1992. lib. bdg. 19.95 (0-685-52256-3) Chelsea Hse.
Byczynski, Lynn. Genetics: Nature's Blueprints. LC 91-15568. (Illus.). 96p. (gr. 5-8). 1991. PLB 15.95 (1-56006-213-4) Lucent Bks.
Bye, Holly, jt. auth. see Stone, Sylvia.
Byer, Carol, illus. Henny Penny. LC 80-28146. 32p. (gr. k-3). 1981. PLB 9.79 (0-89375-490-0); pap. text ed. 1.95 (0-89375-491-9) Troll Assocs.
Byers, Helen. Kidding Around Boston: A Young Person's Guide. 2nd ed. Blakemore, Sally, illus. 64p. (gr. 3 up). 1993. pap. 9.95 (1-56261-092-9) John Muir.
Byers, Ken. The Father & Son Survival Kit: A Journey into the Wilderness of Relationships. (gr. 9 up). 1988. 19.95 (0-9619040-1-1); pap. 12.95 (0-9619040-0-3); wkbk. 12.95 (0-9619040-2-X) Journeys Together.
Byers, Patricia & Preston, Julia. The Kids' Money Book. LC 82-184275. (Illus.). 144p. (gr. 2-6). 1983. pap. 4.95 (0-89709-041-1) Liberty Pub.
Byers, Reggie. The Esteem Team in "The Best I Can Be" Byers, Reggie, illus. 48p. (gr. k-4). 1993. 9.95 (1-882732-05-7) Ctr Applied Psy.
Byers, Rinda M. Mycca's Baby. Tamura, David, illus. LC 88-27320. 32p. (ps-2). 1990. 13.95 (0-531-05828-X); PLB 13.99 (0-531-08428-0) Orchard Bks Watts.
Byles, Monica. Experiment with Senses. LC 92-41110. 1993. 17.50 (0-8225-2455-4) Lerner Pubns.
—Experiments with Plants. Anderson, Nancy, illus. LC 92-43117. 1993. 17.50 (0-8225-2456-2) Lerner Pubns.
—Life in the Polar Lands. (Illus.). 32p. (gr. 5-8). 1990. PLB 12.40 (0-531-10982-8) Watts.
—Life in the Polar Lands. (Illus.). (gr. 4-7). 1993. pap. 4.95 (0-590-46130-3) Scholastic Inc.
Bynum, Margaret M., ed. Power English & Word Command, Bk. 1. 64p. (Orig.). (gr. 10-12). 1986. wkbk. 15.00 (0-912686-97-4) Learn Inc.
Byrd, Elizabeth L. A Fonalfubet Pronunciation Dictionary of American English Words. (Orig.). (gr. k up). 1986. pap. text ed. 20.00 (0-9615393-2-1) U Assocs.
Byrd, Robert, retold by. & illu see Grimm, Jacob & Grimm, Wilhelm K.
Byres, Terence. Adam Smith, Malthus & Marx. Yapp, Malcolm, et al, eds. (Illus.). 32p. (gr. 6-11). 1980. pap. text ed. 3.45 (0-89908-021-9) Greenhaven.
Byrne, Art & McMahon, Sean. Lives: One Hundred Thirteen Great Irishwomen & Irishmen. Short, John, illus. 230p. (Orig.). (gr. 9-12). 1990. pap. 16.95 (1-85371-094-6, Pub. by Poolbeg Pr ER) Dufour.
Byrne, David. Stay up Late. Kalman, Maira, illus. LC 87-10399. (ps up). 1987. pap. 14.95 (0-670-81895-X) Viking Child Bks.
—Stay Up Late. (gr. 3 up). 1989. pap. 5.99 (0-14-050791-4, Puffin) Puffin Bks.
Byrnes, Lynne, illus. The Three Little Pigs. 24p. (ps-1). 1991. pap. 1.25 (0-7214-5305-8, S9016-6 SER.) Ladybird Bks.
—The Ugly Duckling. 24p. (ps-1). 1991. pap. 1.25 (0-7214-5304-X, S9016-5) Ladybird Bks.

Byrnes, Patricia & Krenz, Nancy. Southwestern Arts & Crafts Projects. Rev. ed. LC 77-18988. (Illus.). (gr. 1-8). 1979. pap. 9.95 (0-913270-62-8) Sunstone Pr.
Byrnes, Ron. Exploring the Developing World: Life in Africa & Latin America. (Illus.). (gr. 7-12). 1993. pap. 26.95 (0-943804-78-7) U of Denver Teach.
Byron, George Gordon. Don Juan. Marchand, Leslie A., ed. LC 81-3011. (gr. 9 up). 1972. pap. 9.16 (0-395-05138-X, RivEd) HM.
Byrum, Isabel. How John Became a Man. 64p. (gr. 7 up). pap. 0.75 (0-686-29118-2) Faith Pub Hse.

C

Caballero, Jane & Christman-Rothlein, Liz. Back to Basics in Early Reading Skills. rev. ed. LC 80-83232. (Illus.). 113p. (Orig.). (ps-1). 1987. pap. 14.95 (0-89334-098-7) Humanics Ltd.
Caballero, Jane A. & Whordley, Derek. Children Around the World. rev. ed. LC 82-81892. 176p. (Orig.). (ps-4). 1991. pap. 16.95 (0-89334-112-6) Humanics Ltd.
Caban, Janice, ed. & illus. see Lipton, Alfred.
Cabat, Erni, illus. Erni Cabat's Magical ABC: Animals Around the Farm. Rule, Michael, notes by. LC 90-5242. (Illus.). 64p. (ps-2). 1992. 15.95 (0-943173-73-6) Harbinger AZ.
—Erni Cabat's Magical World of Monsters. Cohen, Daniel, text by. (Illus.). 32p. (gr. 4 up). 1992. 14.00 (0-525-65087-3, Cobblehill Bks) Dutton Child Bks.
Cabellero, Jane A. Aerospace Projects for Young Children. rev. ed. LC 79-90481. (Illus.). 112p. (Orig.). (ps-3). 1987. pap. 14.95 (0-89334-100-2) Humanics Ltd.
Cabral, Brian & Parolini, Stephen. Second String Champion. 108p. (Orig.). (gr. 7-12). 1990. pap. 7.99 (1-55945-008-8) Group Pub.
Cabral, Olga. So Proudly She Sailed. (Illus.). (gr. 5-9). 1981. 13.45 (0-395-31670-7) HM.
Caddy, John, ed. A Box of Night Mirrors. Schanilec, Gaylord, illus. 120p. (Orig.). 1980. pap. 5.00 (0-927663-11-2) COMPAS.
Cadnum, Michael. Breaking the Fall. LC 92-5829. 160p. (gr. 7 up). 1992. 15.00 (0-670-84687-2) Viking Child Bks.
—Calling Home. 192p. (gr. 7 up). 1991. 14.95 (0-670-83566-8) Viking Child Bks.
—Calling Home. 144p. (gr. 7 up). 1993. pap. 3.99 (0-14-034569-8, Puffin) Puffin Bks.
Caduto, Michael & Bruchac, Joseph. Keepers of the Animals: Native American Stories & Wildlife Activities for Children. Fadden, John K., illus. Deloria, Vine, Jr., intro. by. LC 91-71364. (Illus.). 288p. (gr. k-7). 1991. 19.95 (1-55591-088-2); tchr's. guide, 48p. 9.95 (1-55591-107-2) Fulcrum Pub.
Caduto, Michael J. & Bruchac, Joseph. Keepers of the Earth: Native American Stories, & Environmental Activities for Children. Fadden, John K. & Wood, Carol, illus. Momaday, N. Scott, intro. by. LC 88-3620. 209p. (gr. 1-6). 1988. indexed 19.95 (1-55591-027-0) Fulcrum Pub.
Cadwallader, Sharon. Cookie McCorkle & the Case of the Crooked Key. 112p. (Orig.). 1993. pap. 3.50 (0-380-76896-8, Camelot Young) Avon.
—Cookie McCorkle & the Case of the King's Ghost. 112p. (Orig.). 1991. pap. 2.99 (0-380-76350-8, Camelot) Avon.
—Cookie McCorkle & the Case of the Mystery Map. 128p. (Orig.). 1993. pap. 3.50 (0-380-76895-X, Camelot Young) Avon.
—Cookie McCorkle & the Case of the Emerald Earrings. 128p. (Orig.). (gr. 3-4). 1991. pap. 2.95 (0-380-76098-3, Camelot Young) Avon.
—Cookie McCorkle & the Case of the Missing Castle. 128p. 1991. pap. 2.99 (0-380-76348-6, Camelot) Avon.
—Cookie McCorkle & the Case of the Polka-Dot Safecracker. 128p. (Orig.). (gr. 3-4). 1991. pap. 2.95 (0-380-76099-1, Camelot Young) Avon.
—Star-Crossed Love. 176p. (Orig.). (gr. 7-12). 1987. pap. 2.50 (0-553-26339-0) Bantam.
Cady, Edwin H., ed. see Howells, William Dean.
Caen, Herb. The Cable Car & the Dragon. Byfield, Barbara N., illus. LC 85-32004. 40p. 1986. 9.95 (0-87701-390-X) Chronicle Bks.
Caffrey, Stephanie & Kenslea, Timothy. The Family That Wanted a Home. 16p. (Orig.). (gr. 3-5). 1978. pap. 1.95 (0-8192-1235-0) Morehouse Pub.
—How the World Began. 16p. (Orig.). (gr. 3-5). 1978. pap. 1.95 (0-8192-1233-4) Morehouse Pub.
—The Shepherds Find a King. 16p. (Orig.). (ps-1). 1978. pap. 1.95 (0-8192-1232-6) Morehouse Pub.
Caffrey, Stephanie & Kenslea, Timothy, eds. The Boy in the Striped Coat. 16p. (gr. 3-5). 1978. pap. 1.95 (0-8192-1234-2) Morehouse Pub.
Cafiero, Renee V., tr. see Sommer-Bodenburg, Angela.
Caggiano, Rosemary & Martinez, Larry. The Circus. 48p. (gr. k-6). 1978. pap. 14.95 (0-86704-000-9) Clarus Music.
Caggiano, Rosemary, jt. auth. see Fass, Bernie.
Caggiano, Rosemary, jt. auth. see Young, Roger.
Cahill, Chris. Bear Magic. Young, Ruth & Rose, Mitchell, illus. LC 89-61636. 12p. (ps-1). 1990. bds. 5.95 incl. finger puppet (1-877779-00-8) Schneider Educational.

—Bunny Magic. Young, Ruth & Rose, Mitchell, illus. LC 89-61633. 12p. (ps-1). 1990. bds. 5.95 incl. finger puppet (1-877779-02-4) Schneider Educational.
—Un Conejito Encantador - Bunny Magic. LC 90-62627. (Illus.). 12p. 1991. bds. 5.95 incl. finger puppet (1-877779-20-2) Schneider Educational.
—Un Osito Encantador - Bear Magic. LC 90-62628. (Illus.). 12p. 1991. bds. 5.95 incl. finger puppet (1-877779-19-9) Schneider Educational.
Cahill, Keri M., ed. see Cahill, Robert E.
Cahill, Mary J. Israel. (Illus.). 112p. (gr. 5 up). 1988. lib. bdg. 14.95 (1-55546-791-1) Chelsea Hse.
Cahill, Robert B. & Hrebic, Herbert J. Cut the Deck. rev. ed. Barry, Jimi, ed. (gr. 8-9). 1985. text ed. 9.10 (0-933282-16-8); pap. text ed. 6.00 (0-933282-15-X) Stack the Deck.
Cahill, Robert E. Olde New England's Sugar & Spice & Everything... America's First Cookbook & Food History. Cahill, Keri M., ed. (Illus.). 63p. (Orig.). 1991. pap. 3.95 (0-9626162-2-2) Old Saltbox Pub Hse.
Cahill, Susan, ed. Women & Fiction: Short Stories by & About Women. (gr. 7 up). 1975. pap. 4.50 (0-451-62411-4, ME2263, Ment) NAL-Dutton.
Cahn, Julie. The Dating Book. Schneider, Meg, ed. 160p. 1983. 9.29 (0-685-06228-7) S&S Trade.
—Spotlight on Love. (gr. 2-7). 1984. pap. 2.95 (0-671-52625-1) S&S Trade.
Cailloux, Michel. Learning Magic with Michel the Magician. (Illus.). 32p. (gr. 3-7). 1993. 7.95 (2-7625-6854-4, Pub. by Les Edits Herit CN) Adams Inc MA.
Cain, Barbara & Benedek, Elissa P. What Would You Do? A Child's Book about Divorce. Cummins, James, illus. 50p. 1976. text ed. 9.00 (0-88048-300-8) Am Psychiatric.
Cain, Barbara S. Double-Dip Feelings: A Book to Help Children Understand Emotions. O'Brien, Ann S., illus. LC 89-49382. 32p. 1990. 16.95 (0-945354-23-1); pap. 8.95 (0-945354-20-7) Magination Pr.
—Double-Dip Feelings: Stories to Help Children Understand Emotions. Patterson, Anne, illus. LC 92-56870. 1993. Repr. of 1990 ed. PLB 17.26 (0-8368-0931-9) Gareth Stevens Inc.
Cain, Clifford. Five-Minute Bible Object Lessons. (Illus.). 96p. (ps-5). 1992. 10.95 (0-86653-694-9, SS2824, Shining Star Pubns) Good Apple.
Cain, E. Le see Price, M. & Le Cain, E.
Cain, Joy D. The Team on & off the Set. (gr. 1-3). 1993. pap. 3.50 (0-553-48090-1) Bantam.
Cain, Michael. The Legend of Sir Miguel. Thatch, Nancy R., ed. Melton, David, intro. by. LC 90-5927. (Illus.). 26p. (gr. 3-6). 1990. PLB 14.95 (0-933849-26-5) Landmark Edns.
—Louise Nevelson. Horner, Matina S., intro. by. (Illus.). 112p. (gr. 5 up). 1989. 17.95 (1-55546-671-0) Chelsea Hse.
—Mary Cassatt. Horner, Matina, intro. by. (Illus.). 112p. (gr. 5 up). 1989. lib. bdg. 17.95 (1-55546-647-8) Chelsea Hse.
Cain, V. M. Steps of Love: Single Adoptive Parenting. 133p. (Orig.). 1988. text ed. write for info.; pap. write for info. V M H Cain.
Cain, Wilma W., ed. Story of Transportation. rev. ed. LC 87-81355. (Illus.). 128p. (gr. 4 up). 1988. 1-4 copies 14.95 ea. (0-934291-24-1); 5 or more copies 11.95 (0-317-91142-2) Gateway Pr MI.
Caines, Jeannette. Abby. Kellogg, Steven, illus. LC 73-5480. 32p. (ps-3). 1973. PLB 12.89 (0-06-020922-4) HarpC Child Bks.
—Abby. Kellogg, Steven, illus. LC 73-5480. 32p. (ps-3). 1984. pap. 4.95 (0-06-443049-9, Trophy) HarpC Child Bks.
—Chilly Stomach. Cummings, Pat, illus. LC 85-45250. 32p. (ps-2). 1986. HarpC Child Bks.
—I Need a Lunch Box. Cummings, Pat, illus. LC 85-45829. 32p. (ps-1). 1993. 14.00i (0-06-020984-4); PLB 13.89 (0-06-020985-2) HarpC Child Bks.
—I Need a Lunch Box. Cummings, Pat, illus. LC 85-45829. 32p. (ps-1). 1993. pap. 4.95 (0-06-443341-2, Trophy) HarpC Child Bks.
—Just Us Women. Cummings, Pat, illus. LC 81-48655. (gr. k-3). 1982. PLB 14.89 (0-06-020942-9) HarpC Child Bks.
—Just Us Women. Cummings, Pat, illus. LC 81-48655. 32p. (gr. k-3). 1984. pap. 4.95 (0-06-443056-1, Trophy) HarpC Child Bks.
—Window Wishing. LC 79-2698. (Illus.). 32p. (gr. k-3). 1980. PLB 13.89 (0-06-020934-8) HarpC Child Bks.
Cairis, Nicholas T. Era of the Passenger Liner. Mathers, Pamela, ed. (Illus.). 288p. 1992. 49.95 (0-929624-03-3); PLB 39.00 (0-685-59281-2) Pegasus Bks.
—Island of the Titans. Mather, Pamela, ed. (Illus.). 90p. (Orig.). 1989. pap. 4.95 (0-929624-02-5) Pegasus Bks.
Cairns, Trevor. Europe Rules the World. LC 79-41598. (Illus.). 96p. (Orig.). (gr. 7 up). 1981. pap. 12.95 (0-521-22710-0) Cambridge U Pr.
—Medieval Knights. (Illus.). 64p. 1992. pap. 9.95 (0-521-38953-4) Cambridge U Pr.
—Middle Ages. (Illus.). 96p. (gr. 7 up). 1973. pap. 12.95 (0-521-07726-5) Cambridge U Pr.
—Power for the People. LC 76-30607. (Illus.). 96p. (gr. 7 up). 1978. pap. 12.95 (0-521-20902-1) Cambridge U Pr.
—Romans & Their Empire. LC 69-11026. (Illus.). 96p. (gr. 7 up). 1970. pap. 13.95 (0-521-07227-1) Cambridge U Pr.

—The Twentieth Century. LC 82-4251. (Illus.). 144p. (gr. 7 up). 1984. pap. 12.95 (*0-521-28270-5*) Cambridge U Pr.

Cairns, Trevor, ed. The Coming of Civilization. 2nd ed. (Illus.). 96p. (gr. 7 up). 1986. pap. 11.95 (*0-521-33711-9*) Cambridge U Pr.

Cairo, Jane, et al. I Can't, God Can, I Think I'll Let Him: Daily Devotions for Teenaged Girls' Recovery. LC 92-19115. 1992. 7.99 (*0-8407-3458-1*) Nelson.

Caisley, Raewyn. Hannah & Her Dad. Thomas, Meredith, illus. LC 93-28997. 1994. 4.25 (*0-383-03787-5*) SRA Schl Grp.

—The Leaf Raker. Power, Margaret, illus. LC 93-26218. 1994. 4.25 (*0-383-03756-5*) SRA Schl Grp.

—Raewyn's Got the Writing Bug Again. LC 93-24529. 1994. 4.25 (*0-383-03734-4*) SRA Schl Grp.

Caistor, Nicholas. Argentina. LC 91-7215. 96p. (gr. 6-11). 1991. PLB 19.92 (*0-8114-2443-X*) Raintree Steck-V.

Caitlin, Stephen. Amazing World of Birds. Snyder, Joel, illus. LC 89-4968. 32p. (gr. 2-4). 1990. PLB 11.59 (*0-8167-1747-8*); pap. text ed. 2.95 (*0-8167-1748-6*) Troll Assocs.

—Busy Bunnies. Mahan, Ben, illus. LC 87-10912. 32p. (gr. k-2). 1988. PLB 11.59 (*0-8167-1083-X*); pap. text ed. 2.95 (*0-8167-1084-8*) Troll Assocs.

—Discovering Reptiles & Amphibians. Johnson, Pamela, illus. LC 89-4972. 32p. (gr. 2-4). 1990. PLB 11.59 (*0-8167-1753-2*); pap. text ed. 2.95 (*0-8167-1754-0*) Troll Assocs.

—Skateboard Fun. LC 87-19179. (ps-1). 1988. PLB 7.06 (*0-8167-1233-6*); pap. 1.95 (*0-8167-1234-4*) Troll Assocs.

—Wonders of Swamps & Marshes. Watling, James, illus. LC 89-4967. 32p. (gr. 2-4). 1990. PLB 11.59 (*0-8167-1765-6*); pap. text ed. 2.95 (*0-8167-1766-4*) Troll Assocs.

—You Dirty Dog. LC 87-19182. (Illus.). (gr. k-2). 1988. PLB 11.59 (*0-8167-1103-8*); pap. 2.95 (*0-8167-1104-6*) Troll Assocs.

Cajacob, Thomas & Burton, Teresa. Close to the Wild: Siberian Tigers in a Zoo. Cajacob, Thomas, photos by. (Illus.). 48p. (gr. 2-5). 1986. PLB 19.95 (*0-87614-227-7*); pap. 6.95 (*0-87614-451-2*) Carolrhoda Bks.

Cake, J. C. Good Knight Stories. Stickler, Ruth, ed. 190p. (gr. 1 up). 1967. pap. 5.95 (*0-932785-49-2*) Philos Pub.

Calabro, Marian. Operation Grizzly Bear. Craighead, John, et al, illus. LC 88-37497. 112p. (gr. 5 up). 1989. SBE 12.95 (*0-02-716241-9*, Four Winds) Macmillan Child Grp.

—Zap! A Brief History of Television. LC 91-744. (Illus.). 224p. (gr. 5 up). 1992. SBE 15.95 (*0-02-716242-7*, Four Winds) Macmillan Child Grp.

Calamaro, Emanuel. Les Trois Ours: The Three Bears. rev. ed. Nofziger, Edward, illus. (FRE.). 22p. (gr. k-2). 1990. pap. 2.95 (*0-922852-07-3*) AIMS Intl.

Calamaro, Emanuel, adapted by see De la Fontaine, Jean.

Calaprice, Alice, adapted by see Heinrich, Bernd.

Caldecott, Barrie. Jewelry Crafts. Kline, Marjory, ed. (Illus.). 48p. (gr. 5-8). 1992. PLB 12.40 (*0-531-14203-5*) Watts.

—Papier Mache. LC 92-6259. (Illus.). 48p. (gr. 4-6). 1993. PLB 12.40 (*0-531-14217-5*) Watts.

Caldecott, Barry. Kites. (Illus.). 48p. (gr. 5-8). 1990. PLB 12.40 (*0-531-14075-X*) Watts.

Caldeira, Ernesto. Jefferson Davis Coloring Book. Rice, James, illus. 32p. (Orig.). (gr. 1-6). 1982. pap. 2.95 (*0-88289-256-8*) Pelican.

Calder, Alexander. Fables of Aesop According to Sir Roger L'Estrange. (Illus.). 124p. (gr. k-6). pap. 3.95 (*0-486-21780-9*) Dover.

Calder, Angus, ed. see Dickens, Charles.

Calder, Lyn. Blue-Ribbon Friends. LC 90-85433. (Illus.). 32p. (gr. k-3). 1991. 5.95 (*1-56282-034-6*) Disney Pr.

—Gold-Star Homework. LC 90-85434. (Illus.). 32p. (gr. k-3). 1991. 5.95 (*1-56282-035-4*) Disney Pr.

—Minnie 'n Me: Lemonade for Sale. Vaccaro Associates, Inc. Staff, illus. 24p. (ps-k). 1992. pap. write for info. (*0-307-11649-2*, 11649, Golden Pr) Western Pub.

—Minnie 'n Me: That's What Friends Are For. Vaccaro Associates, Inc. Staff, illus. 24p. (ps-k). 1992. pap. write for info. (*0-307-11629-8*, 11629, Golden Pr) Western Pub.

—Minnie 'n Me: The Perfect Bow. Shakespeare, Sue, illus. (ps-k). 1991. pap. write for info. (*0-307-10025-1*, Golden Pr) Western Pub.

—Minnie 'n Me: What Will I Wear? Mateu, Franc, illus. 32p. (ps-1). 1992. pap. write for info. (*0-307-15967-1*, 15967) Western Pub.

—Walt Disney's Alice's Tea Party. LC 99-73810. (Illus.). 48p. (gr. k-4). 1992. 12.95 (*1-56282-145-8*); PLB 12. 89 (*1-56282-199-7*) Disney Pr.

—Walt Disney's The Little Mermaid: Ariel above the Sea. Mateu, Franc, illus. 32p. (ps-2). 1992. pap. write for info. (*0-307-15965-5*, 15965) Western Pub.

Calder, Nigel & Newell, John. On the Frontiers of Science: How Scientists See Our Future. (Illus.). 256p. 1989. 35.00x (*0-8160-2205-4*) Facts on File.

Calder, S. J. First Facts 6 bks. Van Wright, Cornelius, illus. (ps-1). 1989. Set, 32p. ea. write for info. (*0-671-94108-9*, J Messner); Set, 32p. ea. lib. bdg. write for info. (*0-671-94107-0*) S&S Trade.

—If You Were a Bird. Brook, Bonnie. ed. Van Wright, Cornelius, illus. 32p. (ps-1). 1989. 5.95 (*0-671-68599-6*); PLB 9.98 (*0-671-68595-3*) Silver Pr.

—If You Were a Cat. Brook, Bonnie, ed. Van Wright, Cornelius, illus. 32p. (ps-1). 1989. 5.95 (*0-671-68604-6*); PLB 9.98 (*0-671-68598-8*) Silver Pr.

—If You Were a Fish. Brook, Bonnie, ed. (Illus.). 32p. (ps-1). 1989. 5.95 (*0-671-68672-0*); PLB 9.98 (*0-671-68596-1*) Silver Pr.

—If You Were an Ant. Brook, Bonnie, ed. Van Wright, Cornelius, illus. 32p. (ps-1). 1989. 5.95 (*0-671-68603-8*); PLB 9.98 (*0-671-68798-0*) Silver Pr.

Calderazzo, John. One Hundred One Questions: Volcanoes. Foreman, Ronald J., et al, eds. LC 93-84875. (Illus.). 48p. (Orig.). Date not set. pap. write for info. (*1-877856-33-9*) SW Pks Mnmts.

Calderon, Frank, ed. Ingles Facil. (ENG & SPA., Illus.). 416p. (Orig.). 1992. pap. 5.00x (*1-56291-022-7*) Editorial Amer.

—Pequeneces (Little Things), Retos y Necesidades. (SPA., Illus.). 80p. 1991. pap. 3.95 (*1-56259-005-7*) Editorial Amer.

—Washington Irving's Pilgrim of Love: From the Tales of the Alhambra. 2nd ed. Pontet, Daniel G., illus. 64p. (gr. 4 up). 1990. text ed. 19.95 (*0-939193-20-5*) Edit Concepts.

Calders, Pere. Brush. Feitlowitz, Marguerite, tr. from SPA. Vendrell, Carme S., illus. LC 85-23873. 32p. (ps-3). 1986. 10.95 (*0-916291-05-7*) Kane-Miller Bk.

—Brush. Feitlowitz, Marguerite, tr. from SPA. Vendrell, Carme S., illus. 32p. (ps-3). 1988. pap. 6.95 (*0-916291-16-2*) Kane-Miller Bk.

Calderwood, Simone. Clothes. Cullo, Ned, illus. LC 92-27086. 1993. 2.50 (*0-383-03560-0*) SRA Schl Grp.

Caldwell, E. S. She's Gone. Quigley, Ed, illus. LC 75-43158. 128p. (Orig.). (gr. 8-11). 1976. pap. 2.95 (*0-88243-893-X*, 02-0893); tchr's. guide 4.50 (*0-88243-167-6*, 32-0167) Gospel Pub.

Caldwell, Louise. Como Guiar a Los Escolares: How to Guide Children. Bedford, Nancy, tr. from ENG. (SPA.). 160p. (Orig.). (gr. 1-3). 1990. pap. text ed. 4.95 (*0-311-11821-6*) Casa Bautista.

—Timothy: Young Pastor. Karch, Paul, illus. (gr. 1-6). 1978. 5.95 (*0-8054-4239-1*, 4242-39) Broadman.

Caldwell, S. Playing Chess. (Illus.). 64p. (gr. 5 up). 1987. PLB 12.96 (*0-88110-288-1*); pap. 6.95 (*0-7460-0135-5*) EDC.

Caldwell, Willie W. Stonewall Jim: A Biography of General James A. Walker, C. S. A. Savage, Lon, ed. Butler, M. Caldwell, intro. by. (Illus.). 280p. (gr. 10-12). 1990. 24.95 (*0-9617256-4-8*); pap. 12.95 (*0-9617256-5-6*) Northcross Hse.

Calenberg, Laura K., jt. auth. see Hunt, Angela E.

Calhoun, D'Ann, ed. see Farr, Naunerle.

Calhoun, D'Ann, ed. see Verne, Jules.

Calhoun, Mary. Henry the Sailor Cat. Ingraham, Erick, illus. LC 92-29794. 1994. write for info. (*0-688-10840-7*); lib. bdg. write for info. (*0-688-10841-5*) Morrow Jr Bks.

—High-Wire Henry. Ingraham, Erick, illus. LC 89-35642. 40p. (gr. k up). 1991. 13.95 (*0-688-08983-6*); PLB 13. 88 (*0-688-08984-4*, Morrow Jr Bks) Morrow Jr Bks.

—Hungry Leprechaun. Duvoisin, Roger, illus. LC 62-7214. 32p. (gr. k-3). 1962. PLB 12.88 (*0-688-31713-8*) Morrow Jr Bks.

—Jack & the Whoopee Wind. Gackenbach, Dick, illus. LC 86-1630. 32p. (ps-3). 1987. 13.95 (*0-688-06137-0*); lib. bdg. 13.88 (*0-688-06138-9*, Morrow Jr Bks) Morrow Jr Bks.

—Katie Join. Frame, Paul, illus. LC 60-5775. (gr. 3-6). 1960. PLB 12.89 (*0-06-020951-8*) HarpC Child Bks.

—While I Sleep. Young, Ed, illus. LC 90-25488. 32p. (ps up). 1992. 14.00 (*0-688-08200-9*); PLB 13.93 (*0-688-08201-7*) Morrow Jr Bks.

—The Witch of Hissing Hill. McCaffery, Janet, illus. LC 64-15475. (gr. k-3). 1964. PLB 13.88 (*0-688-31762-6*) Morrow Jr Bks.

—Wobble the Witch Cat. Duvoisin, Roger, illus. LC 58-5018. 32p. (gr. k-3). 1958. PLB 13.88 (*0-688-31621-2*) Morrow Jr Bks.

Calhoun, Sharon C. & English, Billy J. The Wisconsin Story. 202p. (gr. 4). 1987. 12.95 (*0-9619484-0-X*, TXU-299476); 49.95 (*0-318-23764-4*) Apple Corps Pubs.

Calif, Ruth. The Over-the-Hill Ghost. Holub, Joan, illus. LC 87-30523. 160p. (gr. 3-8). 1988. 10.95 (*0-88289-667-9*) Pelican.

—The Over-the-Hill Witch. Holub, Joan, illus. LC 89-35371. 144p. (gr. 5). 1990. 10.95 (*0-88289-754-3*) Pelican.

California Afro-American Museum Foundation, Los Angeles Staff, jt. auth. see Turenne des Pres, Francois.

Call, Betty & Souther, Shelia. Children Can Worship: Book Two. (gr. 1-4). 1982. pap. 5.99 (*0-87148-176-6*) Pathway Pr.

Callaghan, Steven. Brainercise Mental Exercise Program: Arithmetic, 2 bks, Vol. 1. (gr. k-12). 1991. comb. bdg. 5.00 ea. Bk. 3, 25p (*0-925395-18-8*) Bk. 4, 25p (*0-925395-21-8*) SGC Biomedical.

—Brainercise Mental Exercise Program: Arithmetic, Vol. 1, Bk. 8. large type ed. 25p. (gr. k up). 1991. comb binding 5.00 (*0-925395-23-4*) SGC Biomedical.

—Brainercise Mental Exercise Program: Arithmetic, Vol. 1, Bk. 7. large type ed. 25p. (gr. k up). 1991. comb binding 5.00 (*0-925395-22-6*) SGC Biomedical.

—Brainercise Mental Exercise Program: Arithmetic, Vol. 1, Bk. 9. large type ed. 25p. (gr. k up). 1991. comb binding 5.00 (*0-925395-29-3*) SGC Biomedical.

—Brainercise Mental Exercise Program: Arithmetic, Vol. 1, Bk. 10. large type ed. 25p. (gr. k up). 1991. comb binding 5.00 (*0-925395-30-7*) SGC Biomedical.

—Brainercise Mental Exercise Program: Arithmetic, Vol. 2, Bk. 1. large type ed. 25p. (gr. k up). 1991. comb binding 5.00 (*0-925395-27-7*) SGC Biomedical.

—Brainercise Mental Exercise Program: Arithmetic, Vol. 2, Bk. 3. large type ed. 25p. (gr. k up). 1991. comb binding 5.00 (*0-925395-32-3*) SGC Biomedical.

—Brainercise Mental Exercise Program: Arithmetic, Vol. 2, Bk. 2. large type ed. 25p. (gr. k up). 1991. comb binding 5.00 (*0-925395-31-5*) SGC Biomedical.

—Brainercise Mental Exercise Program: Arithmetic, Vol. 3, Bk. 1. large type ed. 25p. (gr. k up). 1991. comb binding 5.00 (*0-925395-28-5*) SGC Biomedical.

—Brainercise Mental Exercise Program, Vol. 1, Bk. 2: Arithmetic. 25p. (gr. k-12). 1991. comb. bdg. 5.00 (*0-925395-15-3*) SGC Biomedical.

—Brainercise Mental Exercise Program, Vol. 1, Bk. 3: Arithmetic. large type ed. 25p. (gr. k-12). 1991. comb bdg. 5.00 (*0-925395-16-1*) SGC Biomedical.

—Brainercise Mental Exercise Program, Vol. 1, Bk. 4: Arithmetic. large type ed. 25p. (gr. k-12). 1991. comb bdg. 5.00 (*0-925395-17-X*) SGC Biomedical.

Callahan, Dorothy M. Julie Krone: A Winning Jockey. LC 89-26061. (Illus.). 64p. (gr. 3 up). 1990. RSBE 13. 95 (*0-87518-425-1*, Dillon) (*0-685-31386-7*) Macmillan Child Grp.

Callahan, Rosemary. This Is Thumb Book. LC 92-56931. (Illus.). 35p. (gr. k-3). 1993. pap. 5.95 (*1-55523-571-9*) Winston-Derek.

Callan, Jamie. Over the Hill at Fourteen. 176p. (gr. 7 up). pap. 1.95 (*0-451-13090-1*, Sig Vista) NAL-Dutton.

Callaway, Colin G. Indians of the Northeast. (Illus.). 96p. (gr. 5-12). 1991. lib. bdg. 18.95x (*0-8160-2389-1*) Facts on File.

Callejas, Juan, et al, eds. see Cosby, Bill, et al.

Callejas, Juan, et al, eds. see Resnik, Hank, et al.

Callen, Larry. Contrary Imaginations. LC 90-33181. (Illus.). 128p. (gr. 6 up). 1991. 12.95 (*0-688-09961-0*) Greenwillow.

—The Just-Right Family. McQueen, Lucinda, illus. 40p. 1984. 5.95 (*0-910313-26-1*) Parker Bros.

—Pinch. Friedman, Marvin, illus. (gr. 5 up). 1976. 14.95 (*0-316-12495-8*, Joy St Bks) Little.

—Who Kidnapped the Sheriff? Gammill, Stephen L., illus. 176p. (gr. 4 up). 1985. 14.95 (*0-316-12499-0*, Joy St Bks) Little.

Callenbach, Ernest & Leefeldt, Christine. Humphrey the Wayward Whale. Buell, Carl, illus. 24p. (Orig.). (gr. k-6). 1986. pap. 3.95 (*0-930588-23-1*) Heyday Bks.

Callihan, D. Jeanne & Nesmith, Samuel P. Our Mexican Ancestors, Vol. I. (Illus.). 124p. (gr. 5-8). 8.95 (*0-933164-39-4*); pap. 5.95 (*0-933164-38-6*) U of Tex Inst Tex Culture.

Callinan, Karen. Autumn. Marden, Carol K., illus. 32p. (ps-2). Date not set. 11.95 (*1-56065-153-9*) Capstone Pr. Postponed.

—Circles. Marden, Carol K., illus. 32p. (ps-2). Date not set. 11.95 (*1-56065-151-2*) Capstone Pr. Postponed.

—Green. Marden, Carol K., illus. 32p. (ps-2). 1992. 11.95 (*1-56065-152-0*) Capstone Pr.

—O'Clock. Marden, Carol K., illus. 32p. (ps-2). Date not set. 11.95 (*1-56065-149-0*) Capstone Pr. Postponed.

—Rectangles. Marden, Carol K., illus. 32p. (ps-2). Date not set. 11.95 (*1-56065-150-4*) Capstone Pr. Postponed.

Callister, Joann I. Teenagers in Crisis: Not Alone. LC 90-23970. 128p. (Orig.). 1991. pap. 8.95 (*0-931832-80-2*) Fithian Pr.

Callou, Nadia, ed. see Walley, Deborah.

Calloway, Colin G. The Abenaki. Porter, Frank, intro. by. (Illus.). 112p. (gr. 5 up). 1989. lib. bdg. 17.95x (*1-55546-687-7*) Chelsea Hse.

Calmenson, Stephanie. Babies. Wilburn, Kathy, illus. LC 86-81490. 22p. (ps). 1987. write for info. (*0-307-12118-6*, Golden Bks) Western Pub.

—Dinner at the Panda Palace. Westcott, Nadine B., illus. LC 90-33720. 32p. (ps-3). 1991. 15.00 (*0-06-021010-9*); PLB 14.89 (*0-06-021011-7*) HarpC Child Bks.

—The Giggle Book. Chambliss, Maxie, illus. LC 87-9085. 48p. (ps-3). 1987. 5.95 (*0-8193-1140-5*) Parents.

—Hotter Than a Hot Dog! Savadier, Elivia, illus. LC 93-313. (gr. 1-8). 1994. 14.95 (*0-316-12479-6*) Little.

—It Begins with an A. Russo, Marisabina, illus. LC 92-72016. 32p. (ps-2). 1993. 12.95 (*1-56282-122-9*); PLB 12.89 (*1-56282-123-7*) Hyprn Child.

—Little Bunny. (ps-1). 1985. pap. 3.50 (*0-671-53110-7*, Little Simon) S&S Trade.

—The Little Bunny. Chambliss, Maxie, illus. (gr. 2-6). 1986. 4.95 (*0-671-62079-7*, Little Simon) S&S Trade.

—Little Chick. (ps-1). 1985. 3.50 (*0-671-53111-5*, Little Simon) S&S Trade.

—The Little Witch Sisters. Alley, R. W., illus. LC 89-3320. 48p. (ps-3). 1989. 5.95 (*0-8193-1191-X*) Parents.

—The Little Witch Sisters. Alley, R. W., illus. LC 93-15454. 1993. write for info. (*0-8368-0970-X*) Gareth Stevens Inc.

—Marigold & Grandma on the Town. Chalmers, Mary, illus. LC 89-31147. 64p. (gr. k-3). 1994. 14.00 (*0-06-020812-0*); PLB 13.89 (*0-06-020813-9*) HarpC Child Bks.

—One Hundred & One Funny Bunny Jokes. (gr. 5-7). 1990. pap. 1.95 (*0-590-43165-X*) Scholastic Inc.

—One Hundred One Silly Summertime Jokes. 1989. pap. 1.95 (*0-590-42556-0*) Scholastic Inc.

—One Little Monkey. Appleby, Ellen, illus. LC 82-7958. 48p. (ps-3). 1982. pap. 5.95 (*0-8193-1091-3*); PLB 5.95 (*0-8193-1092-1*) Parents.
—The Principal's New Clothes. Brunkus, Denise, illus. (ps-3). 1989. pap. 12.95 (*0-590-41822-X*) Scholastic Inc.
—The Principal's New Clothes. Brunkus, Denise, illus. 40p. (ps-2). 1991. pap. 3.95 (*0-590-44778-5*, Blue Ribbon Bks) Scholastic Inc.
—Roller Skates! 1992. 2.95 (*0-590-45716-0*, Cartwheel) Scholastic Inc.
—Rosie, a Visiting Dog's Story. Sutcliffe, Justin, photos by. LC 93-21243. (Illus.). 1994. write for info. (*0-395-65477-7*, Clarion Bks) HM.
—Ten Furry Monsters. Chambliss, Maxie, illus. LC 84-4998. 48p. (ps-3). 1984. 5.95 (*0-8193-1128-6*) Parents.
—Tom & Jerry: The Movie--Digest Novelization. (gr. 4-7). 1993. pap. 3.25 (*0-590-47115-5*) Scholastic Inc.
—Wanted: Warm, Furry Friend. Schwartz, Amy, illus. LC 88-13405. 32p. (gr. k-3). 1990. RSBE 13.95 (*0-02-716390-3*, Macmillan Child Bk) Macmillan Child Grp.
—What Am I? Very First Riddles. Gundersheimer, Karen, illus. LC 87-22959. 32p. (ps-2). 1989. 11.95 (*0-06-020997-6*); PLB 11.89 (*0-06-020998-4*) HarpC Child Bks.
—What Am I? Very First Riddles. Gundersheimer, Karen, illus. LC 87-22959. 32p. (ps-2). 1992. pap. 4.95 (*0-06-443291-2*, Trophy) HarpC Child Bks.
—Where Will the Animals Stay? Appleby, Ellen, illus. LC 83-13479. 48p. (ps-3). 1984. 5.95 (*0-8193-1119-7*) Parents.
—Where's Rufus? Chambliss, Maxie, illus. LC 88-4092. 48p. (ps-3). 1988. 5.95 (*0-8193-1177-4*) Parents.
—Zip, Whiz, Zoom! Stott, Dorothy, illus. (ps-1). 1992. 13.95 (*0-316-12478-8*, Joy St Bks) Little.
Calmenson, Stephanie, jt. auth. see Cole, Joanna.
Calmenson, Stephanie, retold by. The Children's Aesop: Selected Fables. Byrd, Robert, illus. LC 91-73884. 64p. (ps-3). 1992. 11.95 (*1-56397-041-4*) Boyds Mills Pr.
Calmenson, Stephanie, adapted by. Race to Danger. LC 92-56396. 136p. (Orig.). (gr. 4-8). 1993. pap. 3.50 (*0-679-84388-4*) Random Bks Yng Read.
—Walt Disney Pictures Presents the Little Mermaid. Maten, Frenc, illus. (ps-k). 1991. pap. write for info. (*0-307-10027-8*, Golden Pr) Western Pub.
Calmenson, Stephanie, jt. ed. see Cole, Joanna.
Calmera, Brenda. Dallas Cowboys. (gr. 4 up). 1991. PLB 14.95s.p. (*0-88682-364-1*) Creative Ed.
Calrenson, Stephanie. Tiger's Bedtime. Cooke, Tom, illus. (ps-k). 1991. pap. write for info. (*0-307-11510-0*, Golden Pr) Western Pub.
Calvera, Elizabeth C., ed. see Fugate, Clara T.
Calverley, Dianne. Claire. rev. ed. (Illus.). 1992. 6.95 (*0-8062-4590-5*) Carlton.
Calvert, Jacquelyn, jt. auth. see Noonan, Janet.
Calvert, Patricia. Bigger. LC 93-14415. 144p. (gr. 4-6). 1994. SBE 13.95 (*0-684-19685-9*, Scribners Young Read) Macmillan Child Grp.
—Hadder MacColl. 144p. (gr. 5-9). 1986. pap. 3.95 (*0-14-032158-6*, Puffin) Puffin Bks.
—Picking up the Pieces. LC 92-27909. 192p. (gr. 7 up). 1993. SBE 14.95 (*0-684-19558-5*, Scribner's Young Read) Macmillan Child Grp.
—The Snowbird. 192p. (gr. 7 up). 1982. pap. 1.95 (*0-451-13353-6*, AE1354, Sig Vista) NAL-Dutton.
—The Snowbird. LC 80-19139. 160p. (gr. 7 up). 1989. SBE 13.95 (*0-684-19120-2*, Scribners Young Read) Macmillan Child Grp.
—The Stone Pony. 160p. (gr. 7-9). 1983. pap. 2.99 (*0-451-13729-9*, Sig) NAL-Dutton.
—Stranger, You & I. 160p. (gr. 7 up). 1988. pap. 2.50 (*0-380-70600-8*, Flare) Avon.
—When Morning Comes. LC 89-5854. 160p. (gr. 7 up). 1989. SBE 13.95 (*0-684-19105-9*, Scribners Young Read) Macmillan Child Grp.
—Yesterday's Daughter. LC 86-13753. 144p. (gr. 7 up). 1986. SBE 13.95 (*0-684-18746-9*, Scribners Young Read) Macmillan Child Grp.
—Yesterday's Daughter. 1988. pap. 2.75 (*0-380-70470-6*, Flare) Avon.
Calvin, Margaret. An Alaskan A B C Coloring Book. Griffith, Sandy, illus. 32p. (Orig.). (ps-4). 1986. pap. 3.95 (*0-9615529-3-X*) Old Harbor Pr.
Calzada, Francisco-Javier, tr. see Beautier, Francois.
Cambell, Janet, ed. see Canright, David.
Cambridge, Barbara S. And This I Know. 2nd ed. Anderson, Lin, illus. Blackburn, Jim, contrib. by. (Illus.). 24p. 1987. pap. write for info. (*0-9621018-1-8*) CBridge Pubns.
—And This I Know: Affirmations for Children. rev. ed. Anderson, Lin, illus. 28p. 1987. pap. 6.95 (*0-317-91380-8*) CBridge Pubns.
Camburn, Herbert, jt. auth. see Gaughenbaugh, Michael.
Cameron, Ann. Julian, Dream Doctor. Strugnell, Ann, illus. LC 89-37562. 64p. (Orig.). (gr. 2-4). 1993. PLB 6.99 (*0-679-90524-3*); pap. 2.50 (*0-679-80524-9*) Random Bks Yng Read.
—Julian, Dream Doctor. 46p. 1992. text ed. 3.68 (*1-56956-116-8*) W A T Braille.
—Julian, Secret Agent. Allison, Diane W., illus. LC 88-4428. 64p. (Orig.). (gr. 2-4). 1988. lib. bdg. 6.99 (*0-394-91949-1*); pap. 2.50 (*0-394-81949-7*) Random Bks Yng Read.

—Julian's Glorious Summer. Leder, Dora, illus. LC 86-33828. 64p. (gr. 2-4). 1987. lib. bdg. 6.99 (*0-394-99117-6*); 2.50 (*0-394-89117-1*) Random Bks Yng Read.
—More Stories Julian Tells. Strugnell, Ann, illus. LC 84-10095. 96p. (gr. k-4). 1986. PLB 13.99 (*0-394-96969-3*) Knopf Bks Yng Read.
—More Stories Julian Tells. Strugnell, Ann, illus. LC 84-10095. 96p. (gr. k-3). 1989. pap. 2.99 (*0-394-82454-7*) Knopf Bks Yng Read.
—The Most Beautiful Place in the World. Allen, Thomas B., illus. LC 88-4228. 64p. (ps-3). 1988. 11.95 (*0-394-89463-4*); lib. bdg. 12.99 (*0-394-99463-9*) Knopf Bks Yng Read.
—The Stories Julian Tells. Strugness, Ann, illus. LC 80-18023. 96p. (gr. k-5). 1981. 8.95 (*0-394-84301-0*); lib. bdg. 10.99 (*0-394-94301-5*) Pantheon.
—The Stories Julian Tells. Strugnell, Ann, illus. LC 80-18023. 88p. (gr. k-3). 1989. Repr. of 1981 ed. 3.25 (*0-394-82892-5*) Knopf Bks Yng Read.
Cameron, Ann, adapted by. The Kidnapped Prince: The Life of Olaudah Equiano. Gates, Henry L., Jr., intro. by. LC 93-29914. Date not set. write for info. (*0-679-85619-6*); pap. write for info. (*0-679-95619-0*) Knopf.
Cameron, Dana, ed. see Ricketts, Marijane G.
Cameron, Eleanor. Beyond Silence. LC 80-10350. 208p. (gr. 5-9). 1980. 9.95 (*0-525-26463-9*, DCB) Dutton Child Bks.
—The Court of the Stone Children. 192p. (gr. 4 up). 1990. pap. 4.99 (*0-14-034289-3*, Puffin) Puffin Bks.
—Julia & the Hand of God. Owens, Gail, illus. LC 77-4507. (gr. 4-7). 1977. 12.95 (*0-525-32910-2*, DCB) Dutton Child Bks.
—Julia & the Hand of God. Owens, Gail, illus. 176p. (gr. 3-7). 1989. pap. 3.95 (*0-14-034042-4*, Puffin) Puffin Bks.
—Julia's Magic. Owens, Gail, illus. LC 84-8118. 144p. (gr. 2-5). 1984. 13.95 (*0-525-44114-X*, DCB) Dutton Child Bks.
—Julia's Magic. Owens, Gail, illus. 160p. (gr. 3-7). 1989. pap. 3.95 (*0-14-034040-8*, Puffin) Puffin Bks.
—Mr. Bass's Planetoid. Darling, Louis, illus. (gr. 3-7). 1958. 14.95 (*0-316-12525-3*, Joy St Bks) Little.
—The Private World of Julia Redfern. 224p. (gr. 5 up). 1990. pap. 4.95 (*0-14-034043-2*, Puffin) Puffin Bks.
—The Private Worlds of Julia Redfern. LC 87-30695. 224p. (gr. 6 up). 1988. 14.95 (*0-525-44394-0*, 01354-410, DCB) Dutton Child Bks.
—A Room Made of Windows. (gr. 7 up). 1971. 15.95 (*0-316-12523-7*, Joy St Bks) Little.
—A Room Made of Windows. Hyman, Trina S., illus. 288p. (gr. 4 up). 1990. pap. 4.95 (*0-14-034156-0*, Puffin) Puffin Bks.
—The Seed & the Vision: On the Writing & Appreciation of Children's Books. 400p. (gr. 10 up). 1993. 22.99 (*0-525-44949-3*, DCB) Dutton Child Bks.
—Stowaway to the Mushroom Planet. Henneberger, Robert, illus. (gr. 3-7). 1956. 14.95 (*0-316-12534-2*, Joy St Bks) Little.
—Stowaway to the Mushroom Planet. (gr. 3-7). 1988. pap. 5.95 (*0-316-12541-5*); pap. text ed. write for info. Little.
—That Julia Redfern. Owens, Gail, illus. LC 82-2405. 144p. (gr. 2-5). 1982. 12.95 (*0-525-44015-1*, DCB) Dutton Child Bks.
—That Julia Redfern. Owens, Gail, illus. 144p. (gr. 3-7). 1989. pap. 3.95 (*0-14-034041-6*, Puffin) Puffin Bks.
—The Wonderful Flight to the Mushroom Planet. Henneberger, Robert, illus. (gr. 4-6). 1988. 14.95 (*0-316-12537-7*, Joy St Bks); pap. 5.95 (*0-316-12540-7*, Joy St Bks) Little.
Cameron, Euan, tr. see Green, Julian.
Cameron, J., ed. see Coccola, Raymond de & King, Paul.
Camille, Pamela, intro. by. Children of the Mountains: Short Stories by the Elementary School Children of Pagosa Springs, Colorado. LC 88-81602. (Illus.). 150p. (Orig.). (gr. 4-8). 1988. pap. 7.95 (*0-945985-01-0*) Freedom Lights Pr.
Camilli, Thomas. Make It Metric. (Illus.). 32p. (gr. 4-6). 1993. pap. text ed. 4.95 (*1-55799-251-7*) Evan-Moor Corp.
Cammarata, Joe. Student Survival Guide. Tunmore, Gary, ed. Cammarata, Sharon, illus. 108p. (gr. 6-12). 1991. wkbk. 9.95 (*0-924649-03-8*) Scribblers Pub.
Camp, L. Sprague de see De Camp, L. Sprague.
Camp, Lindsay. Dinosaurs at the Supermarket. Skilbeck, Clare, illus. LC 92-16936. 32p. (gr. 3-8). 1993. 13.99 (*0-670-84802-6*) Viking Child Bks.
—Keeping Up with Cheetah. Newton, Jill, illus. LC 92-44162. (gr. k-4). 1993. write for info. (*0-688-12655-3*) Lothrop.
Camp, Norma C. George Washington: Man of Courage & Prayer. Manderfield, Diane, illus. LC 76-3084. (gr. 3-6). 1977. pap. 6.95 (*0-915134-25-X*) Mott Media.
Campbell, Aileen, illus. The Wee Scot Book: Scottish Poems & Stories. Greenberg, Linda, ed. LC 93-28728. (Illus.). 1994. write for info. (*1-56554-018-2*) Pelican.
Campbell, Alexander & Haff, Gerry. Live with Jesus. 90p. (Orig.). (gr. 1-6). 1984. pap. 12.95 (*0-940754-20-7*) Ed Ministries.
—Live with Moses. 90p. (Orig.). (gr. 1-6). 1982. pap. 12.95 (*0-940754-13-4*) Ed Ministries.
Campbell, Alison & Barton, Julia. Are You Asleep, Rabbit? Scriven, Gill, illus. LC 89-12974. 32p. (ps-1). 1990. 12.95 (*0-688-09490-2*); lib. bdg. 12.88 (*0-688-09491-0*) Lothrop.

—Are You Asleep, Rabbit? Scriven, Gill, illus. 32p. (ps-3). 1992. pap. 3.99 (*0-14-054495-X*) Puffin Bks.
Campbell, Andrea. Great Games for Great Parties: How to Throw a Perfect Party. LC 91-22983. (Illus.). 160p. (gr. 1-9). 1991. 14.95 (*0-8069-8318-3*) Sterling.
—Great Games for Great Parties: How to Throw a Perfect Party. Hoffman, Sanford, illus. 160p. (gr. 3-10). 1992. pap. 7.95 (*0-8069-8319-1*) Sterling.
Campbell, Ann. Once upon a Princess & a Pea. Young, Kathy O., illus. LC 92-30526. 32p. 1993. 13.95 (*1-55670-289-2*) Stewart Tabori & Chang.
Campbell, Barbara. Bob II. 224p. (gr. 6-9). 1994. write for info. (*1-56282-346-9*); PLB write for info. (*1-56282-347-7*) Hyprn Child.
—Taking Care of Yoki. LC 85-46040. 160p. (gr. 3-7). 1986. pap. 3.95 (*0-06-440173-1*, Trophy) HarpC Child Bks.
Campbell, Carol A. Wildflower Field Guide & Press for Kids. 1993. pap. 13.95 (*1-56305-242-3*, 3242) Workman Pub.
Campbell, Chris. No Guarantees: A Young Woman's Fight to Overcome Drug & Alcohol Addiction. LC 92-25183. (Illus.). 192p. (gr. 6 up). 1993. RSBE 14.95 (*0-02-716445-4*, New Discovery) Macmillan Child Grp.
Campbell, Civardi. Viking Raiders. (gr. 4-9). 1977. (Usborne-Hayes); PLB 13.96 (*0-88110-102-8*); pap. 6.95 (*0-86020-085-X*) EDC.
Campbell, Dennis. International Immigration & Nationality Law. LC 93-16497. (gr. 7 up). 1993. write for info. (*0-7923-2203-7*, Pub. by M Nihoff); write for info. (*0-7923-2204-5*) Kluwer Ac.
Campbell, E. Year of the Leopard Song. 1992. write for info. (*0-15-299806-3*, HB Juv Bks) HarBrace.
Campbell, Elisabeth, ed. see McKinzie, Harry & Tindimwebwa, Issy.
Campbell, Elizabeth. Castle Hopping in the U. K. with Elizabeth. (Illus.). 60p. (Orig.). (gr. 9-12). 1988. pap. 12.95 (*0-9618324-0-1*) EFC Pub.
Campbell, Elizabeth A. Jamestown: The Beginning. Bock, William S., illus. 96p. (gr. 4-6). 1974. lib. bdg. 15.95 (*0-316-12599-7*) Little.
Campbell, Eric. Place of Lions. 185p. (gr. 3 up). 1991. 15.95 (*0-15-262408-2*, HB Juv Bks) HarBrace.
Campbell, Fergus W., jt. auth. see Legge, Gordon E.
Campbell, George V. North Shore Line Memories. LC 80-51353. (Illus.). 288p. (gr. 11). 1990. Repr. of 1980 ed. 45.95 (*0-916374-96-3*) Interurban.
Campbell, James A. The Secret Places: The Story of a Child's Adventure with Grief. McConnell, Mary, illus. 45p. (Orig.). (gr. 4-9). 1992. pap. 5.25 (*1-56123-051-0*) Centering Corp.
Campbell, Janet, adapted by. Walt Disney's Three Little Pigs. DiCicco, Gil, illus. LC 92-53443. 32p. 1993. 12.95 (*1-56282-381-7*); PLB 12.89 (*1-56282-382-5*) Disney Pr.
—Walt Disney's Winnie the Pooh & the Honey Tree. Kurtz, John, illus. LC 92-53442. 48p. (ps-4). 1993. 12.95 (*1-56282-379-5*) Disney Pr.
Campbell, Jeff, jt. auth. see Clean Team Staff.
Campbell, Joanna. Ashleigh's Dream. (gr. 4-7). 1993. pap. 3.50 (*0-06-106737-7*, Harp PBks) HarpC.
—Battlecry Forever. (gr. 7 up). 1992. pap. 3.50 (*0-06-106771-7*, Harp PBks) HarpC.
—A Horse Called Wonder. (gr. 4-7). 1991. pap. 3.50 (*0-06-106120-4*, Harp PBks) HarpC.
—Sierra's Steeplechase. (gr. 4-7). 1993. pap. 3.50 (*0-06-106164-6*, Harp PBks) HarpC.
—Star of Shadowbrook Farm. 1992. pap. 3.50 (*0-06-106783-0*, Harp PBks) HarpC.
—Thoroughbred: A Horse Called Wonder. 1992. pap. 3.50 (*0-06-106724-5*, Harp PBks) HarpC.
—The Wild Mustang. (gr. 3-5). 1989. pap. 2.99 (*0-553-15698-5*, Skylark) Bantam.
—Wonder's First Race. (gr. 6-9). 1991. pap. 3.50 (*0-06-106082-8*, Harp PBks) HarpC.
—Wonder's First Race. 1993. pap. 3.50 (*0-06-106704-0*, Harp PBks) HarpC.
—Wonder's Promise. 1991. pap. 3.50 (*0-06-106085-2*, Harp PBks) HarpC.
—Wonder's Promise. 1992. pap. 3.50 (*0-06-106705-9*, Harp PBks) HarpC.
—Wonder's Victory. (gr. 7-9). 1991. pap. 3.50 (*0-06-106083-6*, Harp PBks) HarpC.
—Wonder's Victory. (gr. 4-7). 1993. pap. 3.50 (*0-06-106703-2*, Harp PBks) HarpC.
—Wonder's Yearling. (gr. 4-7). 1993. pap. 3.50 (*0-06-106747-4*, Harp PBks) HarpC.
Campbell, John C. Two Dogs Plus. Cunningham, Imogen & Richardson, David, illus. 95p. (gr. 8 up). 1984. pap. text ed. 9.95 (*0-9613596-0-9*); pap. 7.95 (*0-685-09160-0*) Deer Creek Pr.
Campbell, John N. Gator: The Cowpony Goes to School. (Illus.). 72p. (gr. 4-7). 1990. 9.95 (*0-89015-699-9*, Pub. by Panda Bks) Eakin-Sunbelt.
Campbell, John P. Campbell's High School-College Quiz Book: The Quiz Contestant's Vade Mecum. rev. ed. LC 84-19012. 524p. (gr. 9 up). 1984. pap. 16.95x (*0-9609412-3-1*) Patricks Pr.
—Campbell's Middle School Quiz Book, No. 2. 332p. (Orig.). (gr. 5-8). 1986. pap. 14.95x (*0-9609412-6-6*) Patricks Pr.
—Campbell's Middle School Quiz Book No. 1. 326p. (Orig.). (gr. 5-8). 1985. pap. 14.95x (*0-9609412-4-X*) Patricks Pr.
—Campbell's Potpourri I of Quiz Bowl Questions. LC 83-83076. 318p. (Orig.). (gr. 9 up). 1984. pap. 14.95x (*0-9609412-1-5*) Patricks Pr.

—Campbell's Potpourri III of Quiz Bowl Questions. 288p. (Orig.). (gr. 7-12). 1985. pap. 14.95x (*0-9609412-5-8*) Patricks Pr.

—Campbell's Potpourri Two of Quiz Bowl Questions. rev. ed. LC 84-61238. 354p. (gr. 9 up). 1991. pap. 14.95x (*0-9609412-2-3*) Patricks Pr.

Campbell, Ken. Skungpoomery. 47p. 1988. pap. text ed. 5.95x (*0-413-33910-6*, A0263, Pub. by Methuen UK) Heinemann.

Campbell, Ken, jt. auth. see Waechter, F. K.

Campbell, Louisa. Ernie Gets Lost. Cooke, Tom, illus. 32p. (gr. k-3). write for info. (*0-307-12015-5*, Pub. by Golden Bks) Western Pub.

—A World of Holidays. LC 93-22591. 64p. (gr. 1-3). 1993. PLB 11.95 (*1-881889-08-4*) Silver Moon.

Campbell, Louise A. & Bowers, Grace A. Muffin, The Maine Puffin. Mason, MacAdam L., illus. 40p. (Orig.). (gr. k-3). 1988. pap. 9.95 (*0-9621949-0-5*) Muffin Enter.

Campbell, Margaret F., jt. auth. see Mostoller, Dwight E.

Campbell, Maria. People of the Buffalo: How the Plains Indians Lived. Tait, Douglas & Twofeathers, Shannon, illus. 48p. (gr. 3-7). 1992. pap. 7.95 (*0-88894-329-6*, Pub. by Groundwood-Douglas & McIntyre CN) Firefly Bks Ltd.

Campbell, Martha S. Patrick Packrat & His Very Old House. Light-Waller, Sara, illus. 32p. (Orig.). (gr. 1-5). 1993. pap. 6.95 (*0-9630468-1*) Treasure Chest.

Campbell, Mary. Quattro Pro for Windows 2.0. 1993. pap. write for info. (*0-679-79199-X*) Random.

Campbell, Patricia J. Presenting Robert Cormier. 1990. pap. 4.95 (*0-440-20544-1*, LFL) Dell.

Campbell, Richard & Thompson, Mary. Working: Today & Tomorrow. rev. ed. (Illus.). 416p. (gr. 9-12). 1991. text ed. 25.95 (*0-8219-0739-5*, 25661); tchr's. ed. 29. 00 (*0-8219-0743-3*, 25811); tchr's. resource guide 59. 00 (*0-8219-0740-9*, 50828); wkbk. 6.95 (*0-8219-0192-3*, 25662); test bklt. 4.95 (*0-8219-0193-1*, 25901); software Apple 158.00 (*0-8219-0194-X*, 95428F) EMC.

Campbell, Robert M. First Twenty-One: Life, History & Thoughts. 247p. (Orig.). (gr. 10-12). 1984. pap. 6.95 (*0-9613542-0-8*) R M Campbell.

Campbell, Rod. Book of Board Games. (Illus.). 12p. 1984. 5.95 (*0-13-079872-X*) P-H.

—Buster Gets Dressed. (gr. 1-3). 1988. 4.95 (*0-8120-5922-0*) Barron.

—Buster Keeps Warm. (gr. 1-3). 1988. 4.95 (*0-8120-5923-9*) Barron.

—Dear Zoo. Campbell, Rod, illus. LC 82-83224. 22p. (ps-1). 1983. bds. 10.95 (*0-02-716440-3*, Four Winds) Macmillan Child Grp.

—Dear Zoo. (ps-k). 1987. pap. 4.95 (*0-317-62180-7*, Puffin) Puffin Bks.

—Dear Zoo. Campbell, Rod, illus. 24p. (ps-1). 1988. bds. 3.95 (*0-689-71230-8*, Aladdin) Macmillan Child Grp.

—I'm a Mechanic. 12p. (ps-2). 1986. bds. 6.95 (*0-8120-5768-6*) Barron.

—I'm a Nurse. 12p. (ps-2). 1986. bds. 6.95 (*0-8120-5769-4*) Barron.

—It's Mine. (Illus.). 24p. (ps). 1988. 8.95 (*0-8120-5921-2*) Barron.

—It's Mine: (Miniature Version) (Illus.). 22p. (ps). 1991. 3.95 (*0-8120-6229-9*) Barron.

—My Pop-up Garden Friends. LC 92-4382. (Illus.). 14p. (ps). 1993. POB 4.95 (*0-689-71643-5*, Aladdin) Macmillan Child Grp.

—My Presents. Campbell, Rod, illus. 24p. (ps-1). 1989. Repr. of 1989 ed. POB 3.95 (*0-689-71286-3*, Aladdin) Macmillan Child Grp.

—Oh Dear! Campbell, Rod, illus. LC 84-3993. 20p. (ps-1). 1986. bds. 8.95 (*0-02-716430-6*, Four Winds) Macmillan Child Grp.

—Oh Dear! Campbell, Rod, illus. 20p. (ps-k). 1994. Repr. of 1986 ed. bds. 4.95 (*0-689-71774-1*, Aladdin) Macmillan Child Grp.

—Pop-up Pet Shop. 18p. (ps-1). 1990. bds. 4.95 (*0-689-71385-1*, Aladdin) Macmillan Child Grp.

Campbell, Sid. Mastering Bruce Lee's Devastating 1 & 3 Inch Punch...with the BRUTUS Power Punch System. Evans, Ed & Campbell, Sid, illus. Campbell, Sid, intro. by. 16p. 1986. pap. 1.00 (*0-318-20215-8*) Gong Prods.

Campbell, Stan. Fighters & Writers. 144p. (gr. 8 up). 1988. pap. text ed. 5.99 (*0-89693-863-8*, Victor Books) SP Pubns.

—Growing Pains: The Church Hits the Road. 144p. (gr. 9-12). 1989. pap. 5.99 (*0-89693-384-9*, Victor Books) SP Pubns.

—Higher Love. 96p. 1991. pap. 2.99 student bk. (*0-89693-790-9*) SP Pubns.

—Nobody Like Me. 96p. (gr. 7-9). 1986. pap. 2.99 student bk. (*0-89693-515-9*, Victor Books); tchr's. ed. 12.99 (*0-89693-188-9*) SP Pubns.

—The Saga Begins. 156p. (gr. 8 up). 1988. pap. 5.99 (*0-89693-656-2*, Victor Books) SP Pubns.

—That's the Way the Kingdom Crumbles. 144p. (gr. 8 up). 1988. pap. text ed. 5.99 (*0-89693-658-9*, Victor Books) SP Pubns.

—What's This World Coming To? 144p. (gr. 8 up). 1988. pap. text ed. 5.99 (*0-89693-865-4*, Victor Books) SP Pubns.

Campbell, Tammie L. Honey Brown in Search of Her Identity, Vol. 1. Jammer, Cornelius C., Jr., illus. Moon, Felicia, intro. by. 24p. (Orig.). (gr. k-5). 1990. pap. 4.95 (*0-9623947-0-X*) T L Campbell.

Campbell, William A. Casting Your Vote in North Carolina. 2nd ed. 25p. (gr. 10-12). 1990. pap. text ed. 5.00 (*1-56011-171-2*) Institute Government.

Camphouse, Marylyn J., frwd. by see Rankin, William.

Campion, Nardi R. Kit Carson: Pathfinder of the West. (Illus.). 80p. (gr. 2-6). 1993. Repr. of 1963 ed. lib. bdg. 12.95 (*0-7910-1433-9*) Chelsea Hse.

—Mother Ann Lee, Morning Star of the Shakers. Sprigg, June, frwd. by. LC 90-50305. (Illus.). 205p. (gr. 9-10). 1990. pap. 12.95 (*0-87451-527-0*) U Pr of New Eng.

Campling, Elizabeth. Portrait of a Decade: Nineteen Eighties. (Illus.). 72p. (gr. 7-11). 1990. 19.95 (*0-7134-6209-4*, Pub. by Batsford UK) Trafalgar.

—Portrait of a Decade: The 1970s. (Illus.). 72p. (gr. 7-10). 1989. 19.95 (*0-7134-5998-3*, Pub. by Batsford UK) Trafalgar.

—Portrait of a Decade: 1900-1909. (Illus.). 72p. (gr. 7-11). 1990. 19.95 (*0-7134-5989-1*, Pub. by Batsford UK) Trafalgar.

—The Postwar World: The USA since 1945. (Illus.). 64p. (gr. 7-9). 1988. 19.95 (*0-7134-5756-2*, Pub. by Batsford UK) Trafalgar.

—Timeline: The Police. (Illus.). 64p. (gr. 7-10). 1989. 19. 95 (*0-85219-789-6*, Pub. by Batsford UK) Trafalgar.

—U. S. S. R. Since Nineteen Forty-Five. (Illus.). 64p. (gr. 7-11). 1990. 19.95 (*0-7134-6063-6*, Pub. by Batsford UK) Trafalgar.

Campolo, Anthony. Ideas for Social Action. 160p. (gr. 9-12). 1985. pap. 9.99 (*0-310-45251-1*, 11375P, Pub. by Youth Specialities) Zondervan.

Campton, David, retold by. Frankenstein. 160p. (gr. 6 up). 1988. pap. 2.95 (*0-8120-4076-7*) Barron.

—The Vampyre. 160p. (gr. 6 up). 1988. pap. 2.95 (*0-8120-4070-8*) Barron.

Campus Crusade for Christ Staff. Good News Comic Booklet. (Illus.). 25p. (gr. 1-6). 1970. 8.99 (*0-86605-069-8*) Nelson.

Camsey, Terry, jt. auth. see Smart, Janette.

Camus, Albert. The Guest. (gr. 4-9). Date not set. 13.95 (*0-88682-356-0*, 97217-098) Creative Ed.

Camuse, Ruth A., jt. auth. see Bitter, Gary G.

Canadeo, Anne. The Fact or Fiction Files: Ghosts. (Illus.). (gr. 7 up). 1990. 14.95 (*0-8027-6929-2*); lib. bdg. 15.85 (*0-8027-6930-6*) Walker & Co.

—The Fact or Fiction Files: UFOs. (Illus.). (gr. 7 up). 1990. 14.95 (*0-8027-6927-6*); lib. bdg. 15.85 (*0-8027-6928-4*) Walker & Co.

—Ralph Lauren: Master of Fashion. Young, Richard G., ed. LC 91-32777. (Illus.). 64p. (gr. 4-8). 1992. PLB 17. 26 (*1-56074-021-3*) Garrett Ed Corp.

—Sam Walton: The Giant of Wal-Mart. Young, Richard G., ed. LC 91-32776. (Illus.). 64p. (gr. 4-8). 1992. PLB 17.26 (*1-56074-025-6*) Garrett Ed Corp.

—Warren G. Harding: Twenty-Ninth President of the United States. Young, Richard G., ed. LC 89-39952. (Illus.). 128p. (gr. 5-9). 1990. PLB 17.26 (*0-944483-64-X*) Garrett Ed Corp.

Canady, Robert & Annis, Scott. Color in Iowa Coloring Album. (Illus.). 32p. (Orig.). (gr. 1-5). 1984. pap. 3.95 (*0-9615584-0-7*) Little Gnome.

Canault, Nina. Incredibly Small. (Illus.). 48p. (gr. 6 up). 1993. RSBE 14.95 (*0-02-716455-1*, New Discovery Bks) Macmillan Child Grp.

Canesso, Claudia. Cambodia. (Illus.). 96p. (gr. 6 up). 1989. lib. bdg. 14.95 (*1-55546-798-9*) Chelsea Hse.

Caney, Steven. Make Your Own Time Capsule. LC 89-40725. (Illus.). 64p. (Orig.). (gr. 2-6). 1991. pap. 12.95 (*0-89480-418-9*, 1418) Workman Pub.

—Start Your Own Lemonade Stand. LC 89-40724. (Illus.). 64p. (Orig.). (gr. 2-6). 1991. pap. 12.95 (*0-89480-398-0*, 1398) Workman Pub.

—Steve Caney's Toybook. LC 75-8814. (Illus.). 176p. (ps-5). 1972. pap. 7.95 (*0-911104-17-8*, 023) Workman Pub.

—Steven Caney's Invention Book. LC 84-40679. (Illus.). 208p. (gr. 3-8). 1985. pap. 8.95 (*0-89480-076-0*, 406) Workman Pub.

—Steven Caney's Kids' America. LC 77-27465. (Illus.). 416p. (ps-9). 1978. pap. 13.95 (*0-911104-80-1*, 114) Workman Pub.

—Steven Caney's Play Book. LC 75-9816. (Illus.). 240p. (ps-5). 1975. pap. 9.95 (*0-911104-38-0*, 050) Workman Pub.

—Teach Yourself Tap Dancing. LC 89-40726. (Illus.). 64p. (Orig.). (gr. 2-5). 1991. pap. 12.95 (*0-89480-428-6*, 1428) Workman Pub.

Canfield, Anita. The Young Woman & Her Self-Esteem. 93p. (gr. 7-12). 1990. pap. 4.95 (*0-87579-365-7*) Deseret Bk.

Canfield, Dorothy. The Bent Twig. 334p. 1981. Repr. PLB 17.95x (*0-89966-343-5*) Buccaneer Bks.

—The Bent Twig. 340p. 1981. Repr. PLB 13.95x (*0-89967-018-0*) Harmony Raine.

—Understood Betsy. 219p. 1981. Repr. PLB 21.95 (*0-89966-342-7*) Buccaneer Bks.

—Understood Betsy. 213p. 1980. Repr. PLB 21.95 (*0-89967-019-9*) Harmony Raine.

Caniff, Milton. The Complete Color Terry & the Pirates, Vol. 1. Marschall, Richard, intros. by. Feiffer, Jules. (Illus.). 96p. (gr. 6 up). 1990. 34.95 (*0-924359-19-6*) Remco Wrldserv Bks.

Cannastra, Lyn & Raynor, Tom, eds. Career Sourcebook I: A Guide to Career Planning & Job Hunting. 2nd, rev. ed. (Illus.). 184p. (gr. 9-12). 1988. pap. text ed. 10.00 (*0-931032-25-3*) Edison Electric.

Cannon, A. E. Amazing Gracie. LC 91-6781. 214p. (gr. 6-9). 1991. 15.00 (*0-385-30487-0*) Delacorte.

—Cal Cameron by Day, Spider-Man by Night. LC 87-24655. 160p. (gr. 7 up). 1988. pap. 13.95 (*0-385-29635-5*) Delacorte.

—Cal Cameron by Day, Spiderman by Night. (gr. k-12). 1989. pap. 3.25 (*0-440-20313-9*, LFL) Dell.

—Shadow Brothers. 1992. pap. 3.50 (*0-440-21167-0*) Dell.

—Will the Real Cal Cameron Please Stand Up? (gr. 7 up). 1988. write for info. Delacorte.

Cannon, Bettie. Begin the World Again. LC 90-46596. 192p. (gr. 7 up). 1991. SBE 14.95 (*0-684-19292-6*, Scribners Young Read) Macmillan Child Grp.

—A Bellsong for Sarah Raines. LC 87-4299. 192p. (gr. 7 up). 1987. 14.95 (*0-684-18839-2*, Scribners Young Read) Macmillan Child Grp.

Cannon, Devereaux D., Jr. Flags of Tennessee. Tullier, Debra L., illus. LC 90-7679. 112p. (gr. 6-8). 1990. 14. 95 (*0-88289-794-2*) Pelican.

Cannon, Elaine. Baptized & Confirmed Your Lifeline to Heaven. 9.95 (*0-88494-617-7*) Bookcraft Inc.

—Eight Is Great. pap. 5.95 (*0-88494-612-6*) Bookcraft Inc.

—Turning Twelve or More: Living by the Articles of Faith. 9.95 (*0-88494-732-7*) Bookcraft Inc.

Cannon, Frances A. A Picture Book. Petz, Rita K., ed. Carr, Linda, illus. (gr. 4-6). write for info. Rapcom Enter.

Cannon, Janell. Stellaluna. LC 92-16439. 1993. write for info. (*0-15-280217-7*) HarBrace.

Cannon, Jim, et al. The Contemporary World: Conflict or Co-Operation? 2nd ed. (Illus.). 128p. (Orig.). (gr. 9-12). 1979. pap. text ed. 23.76 (*0-05-003734-X*, 70092) Longman.

Cannon, Kelly, et al. Becoming Kingdom Kids. (Illus., Orig.). (gr. 2-5). 1989. pap. 6.99 (*0-89081-727-8*) Harvest Hse.

Cannon, LeGrand. Look to the Mountain. Daniell, Jere, frwd. by. 416p. 1991. pap. 5.95 (*0-88150-215-4*) Countryman.

Cannon, Marian G. Dwight David Eisenhower: War Hero & President. LC 89-24791. (gr. 4-7). 1990. PLB 14.40 (*0-531-10915-1*) Watts.

—Robert E. Lee: Defender of the South. LC 93-415. (Illus.). 64p. (gr. 4-6). 1993. PLB 12.90 (*0-531-20120-1*) Watts.

Canon & Howe, G. E. Stories from The Catechist: Nine Hundred Seven Traditional Catholic Stories Illustrating the Truths of the Catholic Catechism. LC 82-50589. 387p. 1989. pap. 15.00 (*0-89555-184-5*) Tan Bks Pubs.

Canon, Jill. Civil War Heroines. Archambault, Alan, illus. (Orig.). (gr. 7 up). 1989. pap. 3.95 (*0-88388-147-0*) Bellerophon Bks.

Canon, Jill & Archambault, Alan. Civil War Heroes. Archambault, Alan, illus. 48p. (Orig.). (gr. 7). 1988. pap. 3.95 (*0-88388-130-6*) Bellerophon Bks.

Canon, Joel. Heroines of the American Revolution. (gr. 1-9). 1993. pap. 3.95 (*0-88388-173-X*) Bellerophon Bks.

Canright, David. Ships & the River. Cambell, Janet, ed. Canright, David, intro. by. (Illus.). 32p. (gr. 2-6). 1975. pap. 2.00 (*0-913344-22-2*) South St Sea Mus.

Canterbury, Joyce C. Time We Talk: The Pre-Teen Years. Canterbury, Joyce C., illus. LC 92-73621. 24p. (Orig.). (gr. 4-7). 1993. pap. 4.25 (*0-9634737-0-0*) Hoffman Spec.

Cantoni, Louise B. Leaving Matters to God. Gomez-Milan, Francis, illus. LC 92-9984. 164p. (gr. 3-8). 1984. 3.00 (*0-8198-4424-1*) St Paul Bks.

Cantor, Clarence. Good Times in Rhyme. 1993. 7.95 (*0-533-10420-3*) Vantage.

Cantor, David. The Baltic Americans. Moynihan, Daniel P., intro. by. (Illus.). 112p. (gr. 5 up). 1991. 17.95 (*0-87754-890-0*) Chelsea Hse.

Cantwell, Lee G. Cross Currents. LC 93-12389. x, 244p. (Orig.). (gr. 8-12). 1993. pap. 9.95 (*0-87579-672-9*) Deseret Bk.

Capdevila, Roser, illus. Let's Count. Ballar, Elisabet, text by. LC 92-2813. 44p. (ps-3). 1992. 13.95 (*1-56566-011-0*) Thomasson-Grant.

Capek, Jindra. A Child Is Born. Capek, Jindra, illus. (gr. 5 up). 1987. 12.95 (*1-55774-007-0*) Modan-Adama Bks.

Capes, Richard. Richard Capes' Drawings Capture Siesta Key: An Artistic Tour of the Island. Peelen, Julie & Whitley, Marvin, eds. (Illus.). 184p. (Orig.). (gr. 12 up). 1992. 49.95 (*0-9635417-1-4*); pap. 24.95 (*0-9635417-0-6*) Capes Studio FL.

Caple, Kathy. The Biggest Nose. Caple, Kathy, illus. LC 84-17545. 32p. (gr. k-3). 1985. 14.45 (*0-395-36894-4*); pap. 5.70 (*0-395-47943-6*) HM.

—The Coolest Place in Town. Caple, Kathy, illus. 32p. (gr. k-3). 1990. 13.45 (*0-395-51523-8*) HM.

—Fox & Bear. Caple, Kathy, illus. 40p. (gr. k-3). 1992. 13.45 (*0-395-55634-1*) HM.

—Harry's Smile. Caple, Kathy, illus. LC 87-5094. 32p. (gr. k-3). 1987. 13.95 (*0-395-43417-3*) HM.

—The Purse. Caple, Kathy, illus. LC 86-2889. 32p. (gr. k-3). 1986. 13.95 (*0-395-41852-6*) HM.

—The Purse. 32p. (gr. k-3). 1992. pap. 4.80 (*0-395-62981-0*, Sandpiper) HM.

Capocy, Edward J. The Magic of Christmas. rev. ed. Capocy, Edward J., illus. 48p. 1991. 14.00 (*1-880210-00-2*); PLB 18.00 (*1-880210-01-0*); pap. 4.50 (*1-880210-02-9*); coloring bk. 2.29 (*1-880210-03-7*) Am Classic Ent.

Capote, Truman. A Christmas Memory. Delessert, Etienne, illus. 40p. (gr. 4 up). 1984. PLB 13.95s.p. (0-87191-956-7) Creative Ed.
—A Christmas Memory. Peck, Beth, illus. LC 88-36452. 48p. (gr. 2 up). 1989. 16.00 (0-679-80040-9) Knopf Bks Yng Read.
—Jug of Silver. Hoys, James, illus. LC 86-4230. 48p. (gr. 4 up). 1986. PLB 13.95s.p. (0-88682-076-6) Creative Ed.
—Miriam: A Classic Story of Loneliness. (Illus.). (gr. 4 up). 1982. PLB 13.95s.p. (0-87191-829-3) Creative Ed.
Cappelloni, Nancy. Ethnic Cooking the Microwave Way. Wolfe, Robert L. & Wolfe, Diane, photos by. LC 93-29543. (gr. 6 up). 1994. 14.95 (0-8225-0929-6) Lerner Pubns.
Capps, Benjamin. The Great Chiefs. LC 75-744. (Illus.). (gr. 7 up). 1975. 19.93 (0-8094-1494-5) Time-Life.
Captain Comal's Staff. Cartridge Graphics & Sound. Hejndorf, Frank, illus. 64p. (Orig.). (gr. 6 up). 1984. pap. 6.95 (0-928411-02-8) Comal Users.
Capucilli, Alyssa S. Good Morning, Pond. (Illus.). 32p. (ps-2). 1994. write for info. (1-56282-674-3); PLB write for info. (1-56282-675-1) Hyprn Child.
—Peekaboo Bunny. Melcher, Mary, illus. 24p. (ps). 1994. 6.95 (0-590-46754-9, Cartwheel) Scholastic Inc.
Carabillo, Toni & Meuli, Judith. The Feminization of Power. Smeal, Eleanor, intro. by. (Illus.). 166p. (Orig.). (gr. 8-12). 1988. pap. 8.95 (0-929037-02-2) Fund Feminist Majority.
Carabis, Anne. The Magic Rocking Chair. Carabis, Anne, illus. 28p. (Orig.). (ps-3). 1980. pap. 3.50 (0-9605802-0-4) Carabis.
Caraccilo, Dominic J. The Ready Brigade of the Eighty-Second Airborne in Desert Storm: A Combat Memoir by a Headquarters Company Commander. LC 92-50945. 223p. (gr. 8-12). 1993. pap. 16.95x (0-89950-829-4) McFarland & Co.
Carachei, Maria E., tr. see Buckingham, Betty Jo.
Caraher, Kim. There's a Bat on the Balcony. Sofilas, Mark, illus. LC 92-34260. 1993. 4.25 (0-383-03660-7) SRA Schl Grp.
Caraker, Mary. The Faces of Ceti. LC 90-38065. 208p. (gr. 7 up). 1991. 14.45 (0-395-54698-2) HM.
—Snows of Jaspre. 1990. pap. 4.95 (0-395-56149-3) HM.
Caraway, Jane. One Windy Day. Smath, Jerry, illus. 24p. (ps-2). 1990. PLB 14.60 (0-8172-3579-5); PLB 10.95 3 bk. set (0-685-67712-5) Raintree Steck-V.
Carbone, Elisa L. My Dad's Definitely Not a Drunk! Weber, Susan B., ed. Neuhaus, Roy, illus. LC 92-53883. 116p. (Orig.). (gr. 4-9). 1992. text ed. 11.95 (0-914525-21-2); pap. text ed. 7.95 (0-914525-22-0) Waterfront Bks.
Carbone, Terry. Happy As a Tapir. DuQuette, Keith, illus. 32p. 1992. 13.00 (0-670-84227-3) Viking Child Bks.
Carbotti, Richard. Newport Houses. 8p. (gr. k-2). 1993. pap. write for info. (1-882563-01-8) Lamont Bks.
—Summer Festivals. 8p. (gr. k-2). 1993. pap. write for info. (1-882563-09-3) Lamont Bks.
Carden, Gary, jt. auth. see Davenport, Tom.
Cardiel, Patrice H., jt. auth. see Trisler, Alana.

Cardinal, Catherine S. The Button Box. (Illus.). 40p. (Orig.). (gr. 3 up). 1992. write for info. (0-9630655-1-3); pap. write for info. Garden Gate.

Introducing, THE BUTTON BOX, the second in a collection of childrens' stories offered by the author, Catherine S. Cardinal. Her first collection, "Mud Grape Pie", was published in 1990. THE BUTTON BOX, a tin, a cardboard box, or sewing cabinet drawer often serve as a place to store buttons, old or new. It is also a gathering place for all sorts of odds & ends, such as safety pins, rubber bands, & perhaps an occasional hair curler. On a rainy day the button box is a grand form of entertainment. This book, not unlike the button box, holds a collection of stories. Liza, Mary, Gladys, Sampson, Katie & Grandpa Arthur are characters that are kept in this volume, as is the assortment of buttons in the button box. The story, Mud Grape Pie, is a compilation of tales. These stories deal with a fanciful herb garden & its fairy-like caretaker, Princess Jill. In this garden, along with the Princess, lives her companion Ashes the cat, & the humanistic bugs & insects. The Princess & her friend have many adventures, each one imparting a lesson about the herbs & imposing a moral applicable to life.

Both, THE BUTTON BOX & MUD GRAPE PIE, are stories to be read to children of all ages. Sug. retail price for both MUD GRAPE PIE & THE BUTTON BOX is $6.00. Please look forward to LITTLE ALBY. For more information or to order write: Garden Gate Publishing, Cathy Cardinal, 1655 Washington Avenue, Vincennes, IN 47591. Telephone reverse charges to: 1-812-882-2626.
Publisher Provided Annotation.

—Mud Grape Pie. 29p. (gr. k-6). 1991. pap. 6.00 (0-9630655-0-5) Garden Gate.
Cardinal, Michael S. The Dynamo's Guide to the Lowlife. Baruch, Andrea, ed. Cardinal, Michael S., illus. 64p. (Orig.). 1989. pap. 8.95 (0-9623902-0-8) Dreamworld.
Cardona, Jose, illus. Pop-Up Book of Actions. LC 92-70935. 12p. (ps-k). 1993. 7.95 (1-56282-506-2) Disney Pr.
—A Pop-up Book of Things That Go. LC 92-56160. 12p. (ps-k). 1993. 7.95 (1-56282-509-7) Disney Pr.
Cardoso, Ersillo, jt. auth. see Rouse.
Carey, Belva. Poetry of Love: Baby Boomers. New South Press Staff, illus. 72p. (Orig.). (gr. 6 up). 1987. pap. 5.95 (0-9617859-0-X) Careys Pub Co.
Carey, Ernestine G., jt. auth. see Gilbreth, Frank B.
Carey, Ernestine G., jt. auth. see Gilbreth, Frank B., Jr.
Carey, Helen, jt. auth. see Greenberg, Judith.
Carey, Helen H., jt. auth. see Greenberg, Judith E.
Carey, Karla. Julie & Jackie & the Calendar: The Music Book (with Song Lyrics, Complete Narration & Cassette) Nolan, Dennis, illus. LC 88-12894. 61p. 1990. pap. 9.95 complete pkg. (1-55768-200-3); pap. 9.95 book only (1-55768-175-9); cass. 9.95 (0-317-67817-5) LC Pub.
—Julie & Jackie & the Calendar: The Play & Musical Play (with Music Book, Story-&-Song Cassette & Piano Cassette) Nolan, Dennis, illus. LC 88-12894. 61p. 1990. pap. 35.00 complete pkg. (1-55768-150-3); pap. 25.00 book only (0-317-89494-3); story-&-song or piano cass. 8.00 (0-317-89495-1) LC Pub.
—Julie & Jackie at Christmas-Time: The Narration & Music Book. Nolan, Dennis, illus. 69p. 1990. pap. 18.95 complete pkg. (0-685-35761-9); pap. 9.95 (1-55768-201-1); cassette 9.95 (0-685-35762-7) LC Pub.
—Julie & Jackie at Christmas-Time: The Play & Musical Play (with Music Book, Story-&-Song Cassette & Piano Cassette) Nolan, Dennis, illus. LC 88-12909. 39p. 1990. pap. 35.00 complete pkg. (1-55768-151-1); pap. 25.00 book only (1-55768-026-4); story-&-song or piano cass. 8.00 (0-685-19710-7) LC Pub.
—Julie & Jackie at the Circus: The Narration & Music Book. Nolan, Dennis, illus. 57p. 1990. pap. 18.95 complete pkg. (0-685-35759-7); pap. 9.95 (1-55768-202-X); cassette 9.95 (0-685-35760-0) LC Pub.
—Julie & Jackie at the Circus: The Play & Musical Play (with Music Book, Story-&-Song Cassette & Piano Cassette) Nolan, Dennis, illus. LC 88-12910. 44p. 1990. pap. 35.00 complete pkg. (1-55768-152-X); pap. 25.00 book only (1-55768-177-5); story-&-song or piano cass. 8.00 (1-55768-027-2) LC Pub.
—Julie & Jackie Go a'Journeying: The Narration & Music Book. Nolan, Dennis, illus. 76p. 1990. pap. 18.95 complete pkg. (0-685-35755-4); pap. 9.95 (1-55768-203-8); cassette 9.95 (0-685-35756-2) LC Pub.
—Julie & Jackie Go a'Journeying: The Play & Musical Play (with Music Book, Story-&-Song Cassette & Piano Cassette) Nolan, Dennis, illus. LC 88-9171. 73p. 1990. pap. 35.00 complete pkg. (1-55768-153-8); pap. 25.00 book only (1-55768-028-0); story-&-song or piano cass. 8.00 (0-685-19711-5) LC Pub.
—Julie & Jackie on the Ranch: The Narration & Music Book. Nolan, Dennis, illus. 91p. 1990. pap. 18.95 complete pkg. (0-685-35757-0); pap. 9.95 (1-55768-204-6); cassette 9.95 (0-685-35758-9) LC Pub.
—Julie & Jackie on the Ranch: The Play & Musical Play (with Music Book, Story-&-Song Cassette & Piano Cassette) Nolan, Dennis, illus. LC 88-12911. 46p. 1990. pap. 35.00 complete pkg. (1-55768-154-6); pap. 25.00 book only (1-55768-029-9); story-&-song or piano cass. 8.00 (0-685-19712-3) LC Pub.
Carey, Mary. Donald Duck, TV Star! LC 87-83491. (Illus.). 40p. (gr. k-2). 1988. write for info. (0-307-11695-6) Western Pub.
—Texas Brat in Alaska: The Cat Train Kid. (Illus.). 96p. (gr. 5-7). 1991. 10.95 (0-89015-831-2) Eakin-Sunbelt.
Carey, Mary V. Alfred Hitchcock & the Three Investigators in the Mystery of the Magic Circle. Hearne, Jack, illus. LC 78-55915. (gr. 4-7). 1978. lib. bdg. 6.99 (0-394-93607-8) Random Bks Yng Read.
—Alfred Hitchcock & the Three Investigators in the Mystery of Death Trap Mine. Hearne, Jack, illus. LC 76-8135. (gr. 4-7). 1985. pap. 3.95 (0-394-84449-1); pap. 2.95 (0-394-86424-7) Random Bks Yng Read.

—Alfred Hitchcock & the Three Investigators in the Mystery of Monster Mountain. Hitchcock, Alfred, ed. (Illus.). (gr. 4-7). 1985. pap. 3.95 (0-394-86420-4) Random Bks Yng Read.
—The Mystery of the Blazing Cliffs. Hitchcock, Alfred, ed. LC 80-10954. 192p. (gr. 4-7). 1981. lib. bdg. 6.99 (0-394-94504-2); pap. 2.95 (0-394-84504-8) Random Bks Yng Read.
—The Mystery of the Missing Mermaid. LC 83-3030. (Illus.). 192p. (gr. 4-7). 1983. lib. bdg. 6.99 (0-394-95875-6); pap. 3.95 (0-394-85875-1) Random Bks Yng Read.
—The Mystery of the Wandering Cave Man. LC 82-3667. (Illus.). 192p. (gr. 4-7). 1982. PLB 7.99 (0-394-95278-2) Random Bks Yng Read.
—Walt Disney's Peter Pan & Captain Hook. (Illus.). (ps-3). 1973. 6.95 (0-394-82517-9); lib. bdg. 4.99 (0-394-92517-3) Random Bks Yng Read.
Carey, Valerie S. The Devil & Mother Crump. Lobel, Arnold, illus. LC 87-64. 40p. (gr. k-3). 1987. HarpC Child Bks.
—The Devil & Mother Crump. Lobel, Arnold, illus. LC 87-64. 40p. (gr. 2-5). 1992. pap. 4.95 (0-06-443278-5, Trophy) HarpC Child Bks.
—Harriet & William & the Terrible Creature. LC 90-13721. (Illus.). 32p. (ps-1). 1990. bap. 3.95 (0-525-44652-4, DCB) Dutton Child Bks.
—Maggie Mab & the Bogey Beast. Westerman, Johanna, illus. 32p. (ps-3). 1992. 14.95 (1-55970-155-2) Arcade Pub Inc.
—Tsugele's Broom. Zimmer, Dirk, illus. LC 92-9873. 48p. (gr. k-3). 1993. 15.00 (0-06-020986-0); PLB 14.89 (0-06-020987-9) HarpC Child Bks.
Carfi, John & Carle, Cliff. No Hang-Ups III: Funny Answering Machine Messages. Tenorio, Greg, illus. 96p. (Orig.). 1988. pap. 3.95 (0-918259-12-6) CCC Pubns.
Carick, Valery. Picture Folk-Tales. (Illus.). 96p. 1992. pap. 1.00t (0-486-27083-1) Dover.
Carini, E. Take Another Look. (ps-3). 1969. pap. 1.50 (0-685-03910-2) P-H.
Carkeet, David. Quiver River. LC 90-24095. 224p. (gr. 7 up). 1991. 14.95 (0-06-022453-3); PLB 14.89 (0-06-022454-1) HarpC Child Bks.
—The Silent Treatment. LC 87-45567. 288p. (gr. 7 up). 1988. PLB 13.89 (0-06-020979-8) HarpC Child Bks.
Carl, Angela R. A Matter of Choice. Speirs, John, illus. 32p. (gr. 1-3). 1990. PLB 19.95 (0-89565-699-X); PLB 13.95s.p. (0-685-56165-8) Childs World.
Carl, Angela R. & Holmes, Alice C. Growing with Bible Heroes: Grade 4. rev. ed. Miller, Marge, ed. (Illus.). 128p. (gr. 4). 1983. text ed. 9.99 (0-87239-664-9, 2954) Standard Pub.
Carl, Kathy, jt. auth. see Cook, Shirley.
Carle, Cliff, jt. auth. see Carfi, John.
Carle, Eric. All Around Us. Carle, Eric, illus. LC 86-9354. (ps up). 1991. bds. 11.95 3 friezes, incl. carry case (0-88708-016-2) Picture Bk Studio.
—The Art of Eric Carle. Carle, Eric, illus. LC 91-646. 124p. (gr. k up). 1993. pap. 29.95 (0-88708-176-2) Picture Bk Studio.
—La Chenille Affamee. (FRE., Illus.). 32p. (ps up). 1992. PLB 16.95 (0-399-21870-X, Philomel Bks) Putnam Pub Group.
—Do You Want to Be My Friend? Carle, Eric, illus. LC 70-140643. 32p. (ps-2). 1971. 15.00 (0-690-24276-X, Crowell Jr Bks); PLB 14.89 (0-690-01137-7, Crowell Jr Bks) HarpC Child Bks.
—Do You Want to Be My Friend? Carle, Eric, illus. LC 70-140643. 32p. (ps-2). 1987. pap. 5.95 (0-06-443127-4, Trophy) HarpC Child Bks.
—Dragons Dragons & Other Creatures That Never Were. Carle, Eric, illus. 72p. (ps up). 1991. 18.95 (0-399-22105-0, Philomel) Putnam Pub Group.
—Draw Me a Star. (Illus.). 40p. (ps up) 1992. PLB 15.95 (0-399-21877-7, Philomel Bks) Putnam Pub Group.
—The Eric Carle Slipcase Collection: The Very Hungry Caterpillar; the Very Bust Spider; the Very Quiet Cricket. Carle, Eric, illus. 32p. (ps-3). Date not set. 52.85 (0-399-22623-0, Philomel) Putnam Pub Group. Postponed.
—The Grouchy Ladybug. Carle, Eric, illus. LC 77-3170. 48p. (gr-1). 1977. 15.00i (0-690-01391-4, Crowell Jr Bks); PLB 14.89 (0-690-01392-2) HarpC Child Bks.
—The Grouchy Ladybug. LC 77-3170. (Illus.). 48p. (ps-2). 1986. pap. 5.95 (0-06-443116-9, Trophy) HarpC Child Bks.
—Have You Seen My Cat? LC 87-15262. (Illus.). (ps up). 1991. pap. 14.95 (0-88708-054-5) Picture Bk Studio.
—Have You Seen My Cat? Carle, Eric, illus. 1991. pap. 3.95 (0-590-44461-1, Blue Ribbon Bks) Scholastic Inc.
—A House for Hermit Crab. LC 87-29261. (Illus.). 32p. (ps up). 1991. pap. 15.95 (0-88708-056-1) Picture Bk Studio.
—A House for Hermit Crab. Carle, Eric, illus. LC 90-25388. 32p. (gr. k up). 1991. pap. 4.95 (0-88708-168-1) Picture Bk Studio.
—La Mariquita Malhumorada. Carle, Eric, illus. LC 91-28582. 48p. (ps-3). 1992. 15.00 (0-06-020549-0); PLB 14.89 (0-06-020569-5) HarpC Child Bks.
—La Mariquita Malhumorada. Carle, Eric, illus. LC 91-28582. 48p. (gr. k-3). 1992. pap. 5.95 (0-06-443301-3, Trophy) HarpC Child Bks.
—The Mixed-Up Chameleon. 2nd ed. Carle, Eric, illus. LC 83-45950. 32p. (ps-3). 1984. 15.00 (0-690-04396-1, Crowell Jr Bks); PLB 14.89 (0-690-04397-X) HarpC Child Bks.

—The Mixed-Up Chameleon. rev. ed. LC 83-45950. (Illus.). 32p. (ps-3). 1988. pap. 5.95 (*0-06-443162-2*, Trophy) HarpC Child Bks.
—Mixed-up Chameleon: Miniature Edition. Carle, Eric, illus. LC 91-2497. 32p. (ps-3). 1991. 4.95 (*0-06-020103-7*) HarpC Child Bks.
—The Mixed-up Chameleon Sticker Book. Carle, Eric, illus. LC 75-5505. 32p. (ps-2). 1993. 7.95 (*0-694-00448-0*, Festival) HarpC Child Bks.
—My Very First Book of Colors. reissued ed. Carle, Eric, illus. LC 72-83776. 10p. (ps-1). 1985. 4.95 (*0-694-00011-6*, Crowell Jr Bks) HarpC Child Bks.
—My Very First Book of Food. Carle, Eric, illus. LC 85-45259. 10p. (ps-k). 1986. 2.95 (*0-694-00130-9*, Crowell Jr Bks) HarpC Child Bks.
—My Very First Book of Heads & Tails. Carle, Eric, illus. LC 85-45260. 10p. (ps-k). 1986. 2.95 (*0-694-00128-7*, Crowell Jr Bks) HarpC Child Bks.
—My Very First Book of Numbers. reissued ed. Carle, Eric, illus. LC 72-83777. 10p. (ps-1). 1985. 4.95 (*0-694-00012-4*, Crowell Jr Bks) HarpC Child Bks.
—My Very First Book of Shapes. reissued ed. Carle, Eric, illus. LC 72-83778. 10p. (ps-1). 1985. 4.95 (*0-694-00013-2*, Crowell Jr Bks) HarpC Child Bks.
—My Very First Book of Tools. Carle, Eric, illus. LC 85-45258. 10p. (ps-k). 1986. 2.95 (*0-694-00129-5*, Crowell Jr Bks) HarpC Child Bks.
—My Very First Book of Touch. Carle, Eric, illus. LC 84-47894. 10p. (ps-k). 1986. 2.95 (*0-694-00095-7*, Crowell Jr Bks) HarpC Child Bks.
—My Very First Book of Words. Carle, Eric, illus. LC 72-83779. 10p. (ps-1). 1985. 4.95 (*0-694-00014-0*, Crowell Jr Bks) HarpC Child Bks.
—One, Two, Three to the Zoo. LC 68-26967. (Illus.). (ps-2). 1989. 15.95 (*0-399-61172-X*, Philomel); pap. 5.95 (*0-399-20847-X*, Sandcastle Bks) Putnam Pub Group.
—One, Two, Three to the Zoo. (Illus.). 34p. (ps-2). 1990. pap. 5.95 (*0-399-21970-6*, Sandcastle Bks) Putnam Pub Group.
—La Oruga Muy Hambrienta. (SPA.). 32p. 1989. 16.95 (*0-685-32965-8*, Philomel Bks) Putnam Pub Group.
—Pancakes, Pancakes! Carle, Eric, illus. LC 88-32438. 36p. (gr. k up). 1991. pap. 15.95 (*0-88708-120-7*) Picture Bk Studio.
—Pancakes, Pancakes! Carle, Eric, illus. LC 92-6633. 28p. 1992. pap. 4.95 minibk. (*0-88708-275-0*) Picture Bk Studio.
—Pancakes, Pancakes. 1992. 5.95 (*0-590-44453-0*, Blue Ribbon Bks) Scholastic Inc.
—Papa, Please Get the Moon for Me. LC 85-29785. (Illus.). 32p. (ps up). 1991. pap. 17.95 (*0-88708-026-X*) Picture Bk Studio.
—Papa, Please Get the Moon for Me. LC 91-14561. (Illus.). 24p. (gr. k up). 1991. pap. 5.95 (*0-88708-177-0*) Picture Bk Studio.
—Rooster's Off to See the World. LC 86-25509. (Illus.). 28p. (ps up). 1991. pap. 15.95 (*0-88708-042-1*) Picture Bk Studio.
—Rooster's Off to See the World. Carle, Eric, illus. LC 91-15246. 28p. (gr. k up). 1992. pap. 4.95 (*0-88708-178-9*) Picture Bk Studio.
—Secret Birthday Message. Carle, Eric, illus. LC 75-168726. 26p. (ps-3). 1972. 15.00 (*0-690-72347-4*, Crowell Jr Bks); PLB 14.89 (*0-690-72348-2*) HarpC Child Bks.
—Secret Birthday Message. Carle, Eric, illus. LC 85-45403. 26p. (ps-3). 1986. pap. 5.95 (*0-06-443099-5*, Trophy) HarpC Child Bks.
—The Secret Birthday Message: Miniature Edition. Carle, Eric, illus. LC 91-8306. 26p. (ps-3). 1991. 4.95 (*0-06-020102-9*) HarpC Child Bks.
—The Tiny Seed. Carle, Eric, illus. LC 86-2534. 32p. (gr. k up). 1991. pap. 15.95 (*0-88708-015-4*) Picture Bk Studio.
—The Tiny Seed. 2nd ed. Carle, Eric, illus. LC 86-2534. 36p. (gr. k up). 1991. pap. 4.95 (*0-88708-155-X*) Picture Bk Studio.
—Today Is Monday. Carle, Eric, illus. 32p. (ps-3). 1993. 14.95 (*0-399-21966-8*, Philomel Bks) Putnam Pub Group.
—The Very Busy Spider. Carle, Eric, illus. 32p. (ps-2). 1989. 16.95 (*0-399-21166-7*, Philomel Bks); mini ed. 5.95 (*0-399-21592-1*) Putnam Pub Group.
—The Very Hungry Caterpillar. Carle, Eric, illus. LC 70-82764. (ps-2). 1981. 15.95 (*0-399-20853-4*, Philomel) Putnam Pub Group.
—The Very Hungry Caterpillar. Carle, Eric, illus. 32p. (ps up). 1986. miniature ed. 4.95 (*0-399-21301-5*, Putnam) Putnam Pub Group.
—The Very Hungry Caterpillar: Mini & Plush Package. Carle, Eric, illus. 32p. (ps-3). 1991. 13.95 (*0-399-22049-6*, Philomel) Putnam Pub Group.
—The Very Quiet Cricket: A Multi-Sensory Book. LC 89-78317. (Illus.). 32p. (ps-1). 1990. 18.95x (*0-399-21885-8*, Philomel Bks) Putnam Pub Group.
—Walter the Baker. LC 93-20124. (gr. 1-8). 1993. 15.95 (*0-88708-331-5*) Picture Bk Studio.
Carle, Eric, illus. & retold by see Aesop, et al.
Carless, Jennifer. Renewable Energy: A Concise Guide to Green Alternatives. LC 92-35137. 224p. 1993. 19.95 (*0-8027-8214-0*) Walker & Co.
Carleton, Nancy, ed. see Loomans, Diane.
Carlile, Candy. Book Report Big Top. 48p. (gr. 1-4). 1980. 5.95 (*0-88160-009-1*, LW 111) Learning Wks.
Carlin, Matthew, jt. auth. see Tissot, John.

Carlin, Mike, ed. Superman: Panic in the Sky. (Illus.). 192p. (Orig.). 1993. pap. text ed. 9.95 (*1-56389-094-1*) DC Comics.
Carlin, Richard. European Classical Music, 1600-1855. (Illus.). 144p. 1988. 17.95x (*0-8160-1382-9*) Facts on File.
—Jazz. (Illus.). 128p. (gr. 7-12). 1991. 17.95x (*0-8160-2229-1*) Facts on File.
Carlisle, Jody, jt. auth. see Cook, Carole.
Carlisle, Madelyn. Let's Investigate Beautiful, Bouncy Balloons. (gr. 4-7). 1992. pap. 4.95 (*0-8120-4734-6*) Barron.
—Let's Investigate Magical, Mysterious Meteorites. Banek, Yvette, illus. LC 92-12776. (gr. 4-7). 1992. pap. 4.95 (*0-8120-4733-8*) Barron.
—Let's Investigate Mesmerizing, Masterful Maps. (gr. 4-7). 1992. pap. 4.95 (*0-8120-4735-4*) Barron.
—Let's Investigate Sparkling, Silent Snow. (gr. 4-7). 1992. pap. 4.95 (*0-8120-4736-2*) Barron.
Carlisle, Madelyn, jt. auth. see Carlisle, Norman.
Carlisle, Madelyn W. Let's Investigate Soft, Shimmering Sand. Banek, Yvette S., illus. 32p. (gr. 3-7). 1993. pap. 4.95 (*0-8120-4972-1*) Barron.
—Let's Investigate Weird & Wonderful Sea Creatures. Banek, Yvette S., illus. LC 92-45206. 32p. (gr. 3-7). 1993. pap. 4.95 (*0-8120-4974-8*) Barron.
Carlisle, Norman & Carlisle, Madelyn. Bridges. LC 82-17874. (Illus.). 48p. (gr. k-4). 1983. PLB 15.27 (*0-516-01677-6*) Childrens.
—Rivers. LC 81-38448. (Illus.). 48p. (gr. k-4). 1982. PLB 15.27 (*0-516-01645-8*) Childrens.
Carlisle, Robert L. Tower, This Is Andy & Other Flying Stories from Northeast Nebraska. Plimpton, George, frwd. by. LC 91-18416. (Illus.). 178p. (Orig.). 1991. pap. 8.95 (*0-934988-24-2*, CIP) Foun Bks.
Carlson. A Christmas Lullaby. 24p. (gr. k-4). 1985. pap. 1.69 (*0-570-06195-4*, 59-1296) Concordia.
Carlson, Anna L. The Candy Cruncher. 2nd. ed. LC 80-83738. (Illus.). 24p. (gr. k-4). 1983. pap. 1.95 (*0-939938-03-0*) Karwyn Ent.
—The Cookie Looker. 2nd. ed. LC 80-82182. (Illus.). (gr. k-4). 1983. pap. 1.95 (*0-939938-01-4*) Karwyn Ent.
—Homer Bear's Secret. 1st. ed. Wynne, Dianna, illus. 24p. (Orig.). (gr. k-4). 1983. pap. 1.95 (*0-939938-05-7*) Karwyn Ent.
—The Mouse Family's Christmas. 1st. ed. (Illus.). 24p. (Orig.). (gr. k-4). 1983. pap. 1.95 (*0-939938-04-9*) Karwyn Ent.
—Stories to Treasure. Wynne, Diana, illus. 24p. (Orig.). (ps-5). 1984. pap. 62.40 (*0-939938-06-5*) Karwyn Ent.
—Toady Tales. 2nd. ed. LC 80-83018. 24p. (gr. k-4). 1983. pap. 1.95 (*0-939938-02-2*) Karwyn Ent.
Carlson, Anna L. & Wynne, Diana. My Brother & I Like Cookies. 2nd. ed. Wynne, Diana, illus. LC 80-81624. 96p. (Orig.). (gr. 1-7). 1983. pap. 4.95 (*0-939938-00-6*) Karwyn Ent.
Carlson, Barbara. Our Nation's Capital City. (Illus.). 8p. (ps-3). 1988. incl. filmstrip 19.00 (*1-55933-003-1*, 3187) Know Unltd.
Carlson, Bruce, ed. see Thomas, Robert.
Carlson, Chris. Troubled Waters. 80p. (Orig.). 1992. pap. 10.00 (*1-55878-098-X*) Game Designers.
Carlson, Dale. The Plant People. 96p. (gr. 5 up). 1979. pap. 1.25 (*0-440-96959-X*, LFL) Dell.
Carlson, Donna, ed. see Melville, Herman.
Carlson, Donna E., ed. Let the Games Begin! Trilingual Coloring Book. (Illus.). 32p. (Orig.). (ps up) 1988. pap. 0.99 (*0-9619653-1-2*) DEC Special Stuff.
Carlson, Eric. The Holiday Wreath Book: Eighty Wreaths to Celebrate Birthdays, Anniversaries & Holidays Throughout the Year. LC 92-47698. (Illus.). 112p. (gr. 10-12). 1992. 21.95 (*0-8069-8696-4*, Pub. by Lark Bks) Sterling.
Carlson, Faith. A Cookie Christmas. Carlson, Faith, illus. 28p. (Orig.). (ps-2). 1986. pap. 5.00 (*0-932591-05-1*) Baggeboda Pr.
Carlson, George. I Can Draw, 8 vols. in 1. 1988. 5.99 (*0-517-62540-7*) Outlet Bk Co.
Carlson, Jeanne, et al, illus. A King, a Hunter & a Golden Goose. Tulku, Tarthang, intro. by. LC 86-24154. 32p. (gr. 1-4). 1987. PLB 14.95 (*0-89800-155-2*) Dharma Pub.
Carlson, Jeffrey D. A Historical Album of Minnesota. LC 92-41136. (Illus.). 64p. (gr. 4-8). 1993. PLB 15.40 (*1-56294-006-6*) Millbrook Pr.
Carlson, Judy. Here Comes Kate! (Illus.). 32p. (gr. 1-4). 1989. PLB 15.96 (*0-8172-3515-9*); pap. 3.95 (*0-8114-6713-9*) Raintree Steck-V.
—Life with Max. 1989. PLB 15.96 (*0-8172-3525-6*); pap. 3.95 (*0-8114-6727-9*) Raintree Steck-V.
—Nothing Is Impossible, Said Nelly Bly. (Illus.). 32p. (gr. 1-4). 1989. PLB 15.96 (*0-8172-3521-3*); pap. 3.95 (*0-8114-6721-X*) Raintree Steck-V.
Carlson, Karyl & Gjovaag, Eric. Queen Ann in Oz. (Illus.). 117p. (gr. 2 up). 1993. 29.95 (*0-929605-26-8*); pap. 9.95 (*0-929605-25-X*) Books Wonder.
Carlson, Larry G. Molecular Ramjet: And Other Bedtime Stories... Valenzuela, Walter V., illus. 32p. (gr. 7-9). 1989. pap. 4.95 (*0-929301-01-3*) TadAlex Bks.
Carlson, Laurie. EcoArt! Earth-Friendly Art & Craft Experiences for 3- to 9-Year-Olds. Braren, Loretta, illus. LC 92-21347. 160p. (Orig.). (ps-5). 1993. pap. 12.95 (*0-913589-68-3*) Williamson Pub Co.
—If I Were an Indian: A Kid's Activity Guide to Traditional North American Indian Life. LC 93-39922. 1994. pap. 12.95 (*1-55652-213-4*) Chicago Review.

—Kids Create! Art & Craft Experiences for 3- to 9-Year-Olds. Williamson, Susan, ed. Braren, Loretta T., illus. LC 90-33677. 160p. (Orig.). (gr. k-3). 1990. pap. 12.95 (*0-913589-51-9*) Williamson Pub Co.
Carlson, Linda. Everything You Need to Know about Your Parents' Divorce. rev. ed. Rosen, Ruth, ed. (gr. 7-12). 1992. PLB 13.95 (*0-8239-1510-7*) Rosen Group.
Carlson, Lisa. Your Uvula Is Showing: Names to Call Your Sister or Brother. Nedobeck, Don, illus. (Orig.). (gr. 3 up). Date not set. pap. write for info. (*0-942679-11-3*) Upper Access.
Carlson, Lori. English con Salsa. 1994. write for info. (*0-8050-3135-9*) H Holt & Co.
Carlson, Lori M. & Ventura, Cynthia L. Where Angels Glide at Dawn. LC 90-6697. 128p. (gr. 5 up). 1993. pap. 3.95 (*0-06-440464-1*, Trophy) HarpC Child Bks.
Carlson, Lori M. & Ventura, Cynthia L., eds. Where Angels Glide at Dawn: New Stories from Latin America. Ortega, Jose, illus. LC 90-6697. 128p. (gr. 5 up). 1990. 14.00 (*0-397-32424-3*, Lipp Jr Bks); PLB 13.89 (*0-397-32425-1*, Lipp Jr Bks) HarpC Child Bks.
Carlson, Maria, tr. see Prokofiev, Sergei.
Carlson, Mary, jt. auth. see Riley, Jane.
Carlson, Nancy. Arnie & the New Kid. (Illus.). 32p. (ps-2). 1990. pap. 12.00 (*0-670-82449-2*) Viking Child Bks.
—Arnie & the New Kid. (Illus.). 32p. (ps-3). 1992. pap. 3.99 (*0-14-050945-3*, Puffin) Puffin Bks.
—Arnie & the Stolen Markers. (Illus.). 32p. (ps-3). 1987. pap. 11.95 (*0-670-81548-9*) Viking Child Bks.
—Arnie & the Stolen Markers. (Illus.). 32p. (ps-3). 1989. pap. 3.95 (*0-14-050707-8*, Puffin) Puffin Bks.
—Arnie Goes to Camp. 1988. pap. 11.95 (*0-670-81549-7*) Viking Child Bks.
—Bunnies & Their Hobbies. Carlson, Nancy, illus. LC 83-23161. 32p. (ps-3). 1984. PLB 13.50 (*0-87614-257-9*) Carolrhoda Bks.
—Bunnies & Their Hobbies. LC 84-26458. (Illus.). 32p. (ps-3). 1985. pap. 3.99 (*0-14-050538-5*, Puffin) Puffin Bks.
—Bunnies & Their Sports. (Illus.). 32p. (ps-3). 1989. pap. 3.95 (*0-14-050617-9*, Puffin) Puffin Bks.
—Harriet & the Garden. LC 81-18136. (Illus.). 32p. (ps-3). 1982. lib. bdg. 13.50 (*0-87614-184-X*) Carolrhoda Bks.
—Harriet & the Garden. Carlson, Nancy, illus. 32p. (ps-3). 1985. pap. 3.95 (*0-14-050466-4*, Puffin) Puffin Bks.
—Harriet & the Garden. Carlson, Nancy, illus. (gr. k-3). 1985. bk. & cassette 19.95 (*0-941078-66-3*); pap. 12.95 bk. & cassette (*0-317-14686-6*); cassette, 4 paperbacks & guide 27.95 (*0-317-14687-4*) Live Oak Media.
—Harriet & the Roller Coaster. LC 81-18138. (Illus.). 32p. (ps-3). 1982. lib. bdg. 13.50 (*0-87614-183-1*) Carolrhoda Bks.
—Harriet & the Roller Coaster. (Illus.). 32p. (gr. k-3). 1984. pap. 3.95 (*0-14-050467-2*, Puffin) Puffin Bks.
—Harriet & the Roller Coaster. Carlson, Nancy, illus. (gr. k-3). 1985. bk. & cassette 19.95 (*0-941078-56-6*); pap. 12.95 bk. & cassette (*0-941078-54-X*); cassette, 4 paperbacks & guide 27.95 (*0-941078-55-8*) Live Oak Media.
—Harriet & Walt. LC 81-18137. (Illus.). 32p. (ps-3). 1982. lib. bdg. 13.50 (*0-87614-185-8*) Carolrhoda Bks.
—Harriet & Walt. Carlson, Nancy, illus. (gr. k-3). 1984. bk. & cassette 19.95 (*0-941078-59-0*); pap. 12.95 bk. & cassette (*0-317-14688-2*); cassette, 4 paperbacks & guide 27.95 (*0-317-14689-0*) Live Oak Media.
—Harriet's Halloween Candy. LC 81-18140. (Illus.). 32p. (ps-3). 1982. lib. bdg. 13.50 (*0-87614-182-3*) Carolrhoda Bks.
—Harriet's Halloween Candy. 32p. (gr. k-3). 1984. pap. 3.99 (*0-14-050465-6*, Puffin) Puffin Bks.
—Harriet's Halloween Candy. Carlson, Nancy, illus. (gr. k-3). 1985. bk. & cassette 19.95 (*0-941078-53-1*); pap. 12.95 bk. & cassette (*0-941078-51-5*); cassette, 4 paperbacks & guide 27.95 (*0-941078-52-3*) Live Oak Media.
—Harriet's Recital. LC 81-18135. (Illus.). 32p. (ps-3). 1982. lib. bdg. 13.50 (*0-87614-181-5*) Carolrhoda Bks.
—Harriet's Recital. (Illus.). 32p. (ps-3). 1985. pap. 3.95 (*0-14-050464-8*, Puffin) Puffin Bks.
—Harriet's Recital. Carlson, Nancy, illus. (gr. k-3). 1985. bk. & cassette 19.95 (*0-941078-69-8*); pap. 12.95 bk. & cassette (*0-941078-67-1*); cassette, 4 paperbacks & guide 27.95 (*0-941078-68-X*) Live Oak Media.
—How to Lose All of Your Friends. LC 92-28368. 1994. write for info. (*0-670-84906-5*) Viking Child Bks.
—I Like Me. (Illus.). (ps-1). 1988. pap. 14.00 (*0-670-82062-8*) Viking Child Bks.
—I Like Me! (Illus.). 32p. (ps-1). 1990. pap. 3.99 (*0-14-050819-8*, Puffin) Puffin Bks.
—I Like Me! Read-Aloud Set. (Illus.). (ps-3). 1993. Set incls. 1 Giant copy, 6 paperbacks, giant-sized bookmark & tchr's. guide in a free- standing easel. pap. 41.93 (*0-14-778977-X*) Puffin Bks.
—Life Is Fun! Carlson, Nancy, illus. 32p. (ps-3). 1993. reinforced bdg. 13.99 (*0-670-84206-0*) Viking Child Bks.
—Louanne Pig in Making the Team. Carlson, Nancy, illus. (ps-3). 1986. pap. 3.99 (*0-14-050601-2*, Puffin) Puffin Bks.
—Louanne Pig in Making the Team. Carlson, Nancy, illus. (gr. k-3). 1987. 19.95 (*0-685-18332-7*); pap. 12.95 (*0-87499-038-6*); 4 paperbacks, cassette & guide 27.95 (*0-87499-036-X*) Live Oak Media.

—Louanne Pig in the Mysterious Valentine. (ps-3). 1987. pap. 3.95 (0-14-050604-7, Puffin) Puffin Bks.
—Louanne Pig in the Mysterious Valentine. Carlson, Nancy, illus. (gr. 1-3). 1988. bk. & cassette 19.95 (0-87499-087-4); bk. & cassette 12.95 (0-87499-086-6); 4 cassettes & guide 27.95 (0-87499-088-2) Live Oak Media.
—Louanne Pig in the Perfect Family. (Illus.). 32p. (ps-3). 1986. pap. 3.95 (0-14-050600-4, Puffin) Puffin Bks.
—Louanne Pig in The Perfect Family. Carlson, Nancy, illus. (gr. k-3). 1987. incl. cassette 19.95 (0-87499-037-8); pap. 12.95 incl. cassette (0-87499-035-1); 4 paperbacks, cassette & guide 27.95 (0-685-18333-5) Live Oak Media.
—Louanne Pig in the Talent Show. Carlson, Nancy, illus. 32p. (ps-3). 1986. pap. 3.95 (0-14-050603-9, Puffin) Puffin Bks.
—Louanne Pig in The Talent Show. Carlson, Nancy, illus. (gr. k-3). 1987. incl. cassette 19.95 (0-87499-065-3); pap. 12.95 incl. cassette (0-87499-064-5); 4 paperbacks, cassette & guide 27.95 (0-87499-066-1) Live Oak Media.
—Louanne Pig in the Witch Lady. Carlson, Nancy, illus. 32p. (ps-3). 1986. pap. 3.95 (0-14-050602-0, Puffin) Puffin Bks.
—Louanne Pig in Witch Lady. Carlson, Nancy, illus. (gr. k-3). 1987. incl. cassette 19.95 (0-87499-068-8); pap. 12.95 incl. cassette (0-87499-067-X); 4 paperbacks, guide & cassette 27.95 (0-87499-069-6) Live Oak Media.
—Loudmouth George & the Big Race. LC 83-5191. (Illus.). 32p. (ps-3). 1983. PLB 13.50 (0-87614-215-3) Carolrhoda Bks.
—Loudmouth George & the Big Race. Carlson, Nancy, illus. 32p. (ps-3). 1986. pap. 3.95 (0-14-050516-4, Puffin) Puffin Bks.
—Loudmouth George & The Big Race. Carlson, Nancy, illus. (gr. k-3). 1986. incl. cassette 19.95 (0-317-59227-0); pap. 12.95 incl. cassette (0-87499-029-7); 4 paperbacks, cassette & guide 27.95 (0-87499-031-9) Live Oak Media.
—Loudmouth George & the Cornet. LC 82-22171. (Illus.). 32p. (ps-3). 1983. PLB 13.50 (0-87614-214-5) Carolrhoda Bks.
—Loudmouth George & the Cornet. Carlson, Nancy, illus. (gr. k-3). 1986. pap. 12.95 incl. cassette (0-87499-011-4); PLB incl. cassette 19.95 (0-87499-013-0); incl. cassette 4 paperbacks guide 27.95 (0-87499-012-2) Live Oak Media.
—Loudmouth George & the Fishing Trip. LC 82-22159. (Illus.). 32p. (ps-3). 1983. PLB 13.50 (0-87614-213-7) Carolrhoda Bks.
—Loudmouth George & the Fishing Trip. LC 84-18119. (Illus.). 32p. (ps-3). 1985. pap. 3.95 (0-14-050508-3, Puffin) Puffin Bks.
—Loudmouth George & the Fishing Trip. Carlson, Nancy, illus. (gr. k-3). 1986. pap. 12.95 incl. cassette (0-87499-017-3); PLB incl. cassette 19.95 (0-87499-019-X); write for info. incl. cassette, 4 paperbacks guide (0-87499-018-1) Live Oak Media.
—Loudmouth George & the New Neighbors. LC 83-7298. (Illus.). 32p. (ps-3). 1983. PLB 13.50 (0-87614-216-1) Carolrhoda Bks.
—Loudmouth George & the New Neighbors. Carlson, Nancy, illus. (ps-3). 1986. pap. 3.99 (0-14-050515-6, Puffin) Puffin Bks.
—Loudmouth George & The New Neighbors. Carlson, Nancy, illus. (gr. k-3). 1987. incl. cassette 19.95 (0-87499-034-3); pap. 12.95 incl. cassette (0-87499-032-7); 4 paperbacks, cassette & guide 27.95 (0-87499-033-5) Live Oak Media.
—Loudmouth George & the Sixth-Grade Bully. LC 83-7178. (Illus.). 32p. (ps-3). 1983. PLB 13.50 (0-87614-217-X) Carolrhoda Bks.
—Loudmouth George & the Sixth Grade Bully. LC 84-18120. (Illus.). 32p. (ps-3). 1985. pap. 3.95 (0-14-050510-5, Puffin) Puffin Bks.
—Loudmouth George & the Sixth Grade Bully. Carlson, Nancy, illus. (gr. k-3). 1986. pap. 12.95 incl. cassette 19.95 (0-87499-016-5); incl. cassette, 4 paperbacks guide 27.95 (0-317-40166-1) Live Oak Media.
—Making the Team. Carlson, Nancy, illus. LC 85-3775. 32p. (ps-3). 1985. PLB 13.50 (0-87614-281-1) Carolrhoda Bks.
—The Perfect Family. Carlson, Nancy, illus. LC 85-4123. 32p. (ps-3). 1985. PLB 13.50 (0-87614-280-3) Carolrhoda Bks.
—Poor Carl. (Illus.). 32p. (ps-3). 1991. pap. 3.95 (0-14-050773-6, Puffin) Puffin Bks.
—Take Time to Relax. (ps-3). 1991. 14.00 (0-670-83287-1) Viking Child Bks.
—Take Time to Relax! LC 92-26584. 1993. pap. 4.99 (0-14-054242-6, Puffin) Puffin Bks.
—The Talent Show. Carlson, Nancy, illus. LC 85-4122. 32p. (ps-3). 1985. PLB 13.50 (0-87614-284-6) Carolrhoda Bks.
—Visit to Grandma's. (ps-3). 1991. 13.95 (0-670-83288-X) Viking Child Bks.
—A Visit to Grandma's. LC 93-18607. (Illus.). 32p. (ps-3). 1993. pap. 4.99 (0-14-054243-4, Puffin) Puffin Bks.
—What If It Never Stops Raining? Carlson, Nancy, illus. 32p. (ps-3). 1992. 14.00 (0-670-81775-9) Viking Child Bks.
—Witch Lady. Carlson, Nancy, illus. LC 85-3756. 32p. (ps-3). 1985. PLB 13.50 (0-87614-283-8) Carolrhoda Bks.

Carlson, Natalie S. A Brother for the Orphelines. (gr. k-6). 1969. pap. 2.75 (0-440-40827-X, YB) Dell.
—Family under the Bridge. Williams, Garth, illus. LC 58-5292. 112p. (gr. 3-7). 1958. PLB 14.89 (0-06-020991-7) HarpC Child Bks.
—The Family under the Bridge. Williams, Garth, illus. LC 58-5292. 112p. (gr. 2-5). 1989. pap. 3.95 (0-06-440250-9, Trophy) HarpC Child Bks.
—The Happy Orpheline. (gr. k-6). 1987. pap. 2.75 (0-440-43455-6, YB) Dell.
—The Orphelines in the Enchanted Castle. (gr. k-6). 1988. pap. 2.75 (0-440-40015-5, YB) Dell.
—A Pet for the Orphelines. (gr. k-6). 1988. pap. 2.75 (0-440-46838-8, YB) Dell.
—A Pet for the Orphelines. (gr. 1-4). 1988. 2.75 (0-440-40014-7, Pub. by Yearling Classics) Dell.
—Spooky & the Bad Luck Raven. Glass, Andrew, illus. LC 87-15471. (ps-1). 1988. 12.95 (0-688-07650-5); lib. bdg. 12.88 (0-688-07651-3) Lothrop.
—Spooky & the Ghost Cat. Glass, Andrew, illus. LC 84-17146. 32p. (ps-1). 1985. 13.00 (0-688-04316-X); lib. bdg. 12.88 (0-688-04317-8) Lothrop.
—Spooky & the Witch's Goat. Stevenson, Dinah, ed. Glass, Andrew, illus. LC 88-21628. 32p. (gr. k-4). 1989. 12.95 (0-688-08540-7); PLB 12.88 (0-685-22781-2) Lothrop.
—Spooky & the Wizard's Bats. Glass, Andrew, illus. LC 85-18020. 32p. (ps-1). 1986. 12.95 (0-688-06280-6); PLB 12.88 (0-688-06281-4) Lothrop.
—Spooky Night. Glass, Andrew, illus. LC 82-54. 32p. (ps-3). 1982. 13.95 (0-688-00934-4); PLB 13.88 (0-688-00935-2) Lothrop.

Carlson, Nolan. Summer & Shiner. Carlson, John, illus. LC 92-71256. 158p. 1992. pap. text ed. 8.95 (0-9627947-4-0) Hearth KS.

Carlson, Rick. Bubba's Berry Picking Expedition Value: Obedience. 32p. 1992. pap. 1.95 saddle stitched (0-310-58181-8, Youth Bks) Zondervan.
—Danny Buys a Blobit Value: Truthfulness. 32p. 1992. pap. 1.95 saddle stitched (0-310-58142-7, Youth Bks) Zondervan.
—Spike's Big Blue Babble Balloon Machine Value: Sharing. 32p. 1992. pap. 1.95 saddle stitched (0-310-58171-0, Youth Bks) Zondervan.

Carlson-Savage, Natalie. A Grandmother for the Orphelines. (gr. k-6). 1988. pap. 2.75 (0-440-40016-3, YB) Dell.

Carlsruh, Dan K. The Cannibals of Sunset Drive. LC 92-40568. 160p. (gr. 3-7). 1993. SBE 13.95 (0-02-717110-8, Macmillan Child Bk) Macmillan Child Grp.

Carlston, Eloise, jt. auth. see Wolfersperger, Shirley K.

Carlstorm, Nancy W. How Does the Wind Walk? Ray, Deborah K., illus. LC 90-25958. 32p. (ps-3). 1993. RSBE 14.95 (0-02-717275-9, Macmillan Child Bk) Macmillan Child Grp.

Carlstrom, Nancy. Goodbye Geese. Young, Ed, illus. 32p. (ps-3). 1991. 14.95 (0-399-21832-7, Philomel) Putnam Pub Group.
—Northern Lullaby. Dillon, Leo & Dillon, Diane, illus. 32p. (ps-3). 1992. PLB 15.95 (0-399-21806-8, Philomel Bks) Putnam Pub Group.

Carlstrom, Nancy W. Baby-O. Stevenson, Sucie, illus. 32p. (ps-3). 1992. 14.95 (0-316-12851-1) Little.
—Barney Is Best. Hale, James G., illus. LC 92-30376. 32p. (gr. k-3). 1994. 15.00 (0-06-022875-X); PLB 14.89 (0-06-022876-8) HarpC Child Bks.
—Better Not Get Wet, Jesse Bear. Degen, Bruce, illus. LC 87-10810. 32p. (ps-1). 1988. RSBE 13.95 (0-02-717280-5, Macmillan Child Bk) Macmillan Child Grp.
—Blow Me a Kiss, Miss Lilly. Schwartz, Amy, illus. LC 89-34505. 32p. (ps-3). 1990. 13.00 (0-06-021012-5); PLB 12.89 (0-06-021013-3) HarpC Child Bks.
—Does God Know How to Tie Shoes? McElrath-Eslick, Lori, illus. 40p. (ps-3). 1993. 14.99 (0-8028-5074-X) Eerdmans.
—Fish & Flamingo. Desimini, Lisa, illus. (ps-3). 1993. 14.95 (0-316-12859-7) Little.
—Grandpappy. Molk, Laurel, illus. (ps-3). 1990. 14.95 (0-316-12855-4) Little.
—Happy Birthday, Jesse Bear! Degen, Bruce, illus. LC 93-25180. 1994. write for info. (0-02-717277-5, Macmillan Child Bk) Macmillan Child Grp.
—How Do You Say It Today, Jesse Bear? Degen, Bruce, illus. LC 91-21939. 32p. (ps-1). 1992. RSBE 13.95 (0-02-717276-7, Macmillan Child Bk) Macmillan Child Grp.
—I'm Not Moving, Mama! Wickstrom, Thor, illus. LC 89-38151. 32p. (ps-1). 1990. RSBE 13.95 (0-02-717286-4, Macmillan Child Bk) Macmillan Child Grp.
—It's About Time, Jesse Bear: And Other Rhymes. Degen, Bruce, illus. LC 88-8511. 32p. (ps-1). 1990. RSBE 13.95 (0-02-717351-8, Macmillan Child Bk) Macmillan Child Grp.
—Jesse Bear, What Will You Wear? Degen, Bruce, illus. LC 85-10610. 32p. (ps-k). 1986. RSBE 13.95 (0-02-717350-X, Macmillan Child Bk) Macmillan Child Grp.
—Kiss Your Sister, Rose Marie! Wickstrom, Thor, illus. LC 90-48671. 32p. (ps-1). 1992. RSBE 13.95 (0-02-717271-6, Macmillan Child Bk) Macmillan Child Grp.

—The Moon Came Too. Ormai, Stella, illus. LC 86-18046. 32p. (ps-1). 1987. SBE 13.95 (0-02-717380-1, Macmillan Child Bk) Macmillan Child Grp.
—No Nap for Benjamin Badger. Nolan, Dennis, illus. LC 90-42564. 32p. (ps-1). 1991. RSBE 13.95 (0-02-717285-6, Macmillan Child Bk) Macmillan Child Grp.
—Rise & Shine. Catalano, Dominic, illus. LC 92-21696. 32p. (ps-2). 1993. 15.00 (0-06-021451-1); PLB 14.89 (0-06-021452-X) HarpC Child Bks.
—The Snow Speaks. Dyer, Jane, illus. (ps-3). 1992. 14.95 (0-316-12861-9) Little.
—Swim the Silver Sea, Joshie Otter. (Illus.). 40p. (ps-3). 1993. PLB 14.95 (0-399-21872-6, Philomel Bks) Putnam Pub Group.
—What Does the Rain Play? Sorensen, Henry, illus. LC 91-47712. 32p. (ps-2). 1993. RSBE 14.95 (0-02-717273-2, Macmillan Child Bk) Macmillan Child Grp.
—What Would You Do If You Lived at the Zoo? Boyd, Lizi, illus. LC 93-7036. 1993. 13.95 (0-316-12867-8) Little.
—Where Does the Night Hide? Allen, Thomas B. & Allen, Laura H., illus. LC 89-32910. 32p. (ps-1). 1990. RSBE 13.95 (0-02-717390-9, Macmillan Child Bk) Macmillan Child Grp.
—Who Gets the Sun Out of Bed? (ps-3). 1992. 14.95 (0-316-12862-7) Little.
—Wild Wild Sunflower Child Anna. Pinkney, Jerry, illus. LC 86-18226. 32p. (ps-1). 1987. RSBE 14.95 (0-02-717360-7, Macmillan Child Bk) Macmillan Child Grp.
—Wild Wild Sunflower Child Anna. Pinkney, Jerry, illus. LC 90-40679. 32p. (ps-1). 1991. pap. 4.95 (0-689-71445-9, Aladdin) Macmillan Child Grp.
—Wishing at Dawn in Summer. Allison, Diane W., illus. (ps-2). 1993. 14.95 (0-316-12854-6) Little.

Carlyle, Carolyn. Mercy Hospital: Crisis! 128p. (Orig.). (gr. 5). 1993. pap. 3.50 (0-380-76846-1, Camelot) Avon.
—Mercy Hospital: Dr. Cute. 128p. (Orig.). 1993. pap. 3.50 (0-380-76849-6, Camelot) Avon.
—Mercy Hospital: Don't Tell Mrs. Harris. 128p. (Orig.). 1993. pap. 3.50 (0-380-76848-8, Camelot) Avon.
—Mercy Hospital: The Best Medicine. 128p. (Orig.). 1993. pap. 3.50 (0-380-76847-X, Camelot) Avon.

Carlyle, Linda P. God & Joseph & Me. 25p. 1992. 6.95 (0-8163-1092-0) Pacific Pr Pub Assn.
—Grandma Stepped on Fire. 25p. 1992. 6.95 (0-8163-1094-7) Pacific Pr Pub Assn.
—I Can Choose. 32p. 1992. pap. 5.95 (0-8163-1082-3) Pacific Pr Pub Assn.
—Max Moves In. 26p. 1992. 6.95 (0-8163-1095-5) Pacific Pr Pub Assn.
—Rescued from the River. 25p. 1992. 6.95 (0-8163-1093-9) Pacific Pr Pub Assn.

Carmel, Paula, jt. auth. see Toomey, Marilyn M.

Carmelich, Christina M. Friends. 1993. 7.95 (0-8062-4700-2) Carlton.

Carmen Blazquez, Maria Del see Gomez-Navarro, Maria J., et al.

Carmen Blazquez, Maria Del see Puncel, Maria.

Carmichael, Carrie. Bigfoot: Man, Monster, or Myth? LC 77-21317. (Illus.). 48p. (gr. 4 up). 1977. PLB 18.64 (0-8172-1052-0) Raintree Steck-V.
—Bigfoot: Man, Monster, or Myth? LC 77-13297. (Illus.). 48p. (gr. 4up). 1983. Raintree Steck-V.

Carmichael, Jack B. Black Knight. 89p. (Orig.). (gr. 12). 1991. pap. 9.95 (0-9626948-1-9) Dynamics MI.

Carmichael, Stanrod, intros. by see Knight, Tanis & Lewin, Larry.

Carmine, Mary. Daniel's Dinosaurs. (gr. 4-7). 1991. 12.95 (0-590-44638-X, Scholastic Hardcover) Scholastic Inc.

Carn, John B. Vietnam Blues. (Orig.). (ps-12). 1988. pap. 3.25 (0-87067-730-6) Holloway.

Carnegie Museum of Natural History, Division of Education Staff. Dippy Diplodocus: Story & Gameboard. Kelley, Patte, illus. 16p. (Orig.). (ps-2). 1988. pap. 5.95 (0-911239-23-5) Carnegie Mus.
—Dippy Diplodocus: Story Only. (Illus.). 16p. (Orig.). (ps-2). 1988. pap. 1.50 (0-911239-40-5) Carnegie Mus.

Carnegie, Vicky. The Nineteen Eighties. Cumming, Valerie & Feldman, Elane, eds. (Illus.). 64p. 1990. 16.95x (0-8160-2471-5) Facts on File.

Carnes, Pauline. A Squirrel's Tale. 1993. 7.75 (0-8062-4664-2) Carlton.

Carnes, Ruth J. David G. Burnet: From New Jersey to Texas. 64p. (gr. 4-7). 1986. 10.95 (0-89015-583-6, Pub. by Panda Bks) Eakin-Sunbelt.

Carney, Charles. Twenty Thousand Leaks under the Sea. Kong, Emilie, illus. 24p. (ps-4). 1993. 20.00 (0-307-04030-7, 64030, Golden Pr) Western Pub.

Carney, Mary L. Angel in My Backpack. 128p. (gr. 7-9). 1987. pap. 6.99 (0-310-28501-1, 11342P, Pub. by Youth Spec.) Zondervan.
—Bible Knock-Knocks & Other Fun Stuff. LC 88-939. (ps-6). 1988. pap. 4.95 (0-687-03180-X) Abingdon.
—How Do You Hug an Angel? A Devotional Novel for Junior Highers. 144p. (gr. 6-9). 1993. pap. 6.99 (0-310-59411-1, Pub. by Youth Spec) Zondervan.
—Stepping Out. (Illus.). 128p. (gr. 3-7). 1992. pap. write for info. (0-8007-5425-5) Revell.
—There's an Angel in My Locker. 112p. (Orig.). (gr. 7-9). 1986. pap. 6.99 (0-310-28471-6, 11341P, Pub. by Youth Spec.) Zondervan.
—Too Tough to Hurt. 128p. 1991. pap. 6.99 (0-310-28621-2, Youth Bks) Zondervan.

—Wrestling with an Angel: A Devotional Novel for Junior Highers. rev. ed. 160p. (gr. 6-9). 1993. pap. 6.99 (0-685-63320-9, Pub. by Youth Spec) Zondervan.
Carola, Robert. How Do I Grow? rev. ed. Crawford, Mel, illus. 32p. (gr. 2-4). 1990. Repr. of 1988 ed. PLB 9.95 (1-878363-14-X) Forest Hse.
—How Do I Know? Crawford, Mel, illus. 32p. (gr. 2-4). 1990. Repr. of 1988 ed. PLB 9.95 (1-878363-12-3) Forest Hse.
Caroland, Mary, ed. see Babisch, Donald.
Caroland, Mary, ed. see Drake, Ann.
Caroland, Mary, ed. see Elliott, Lisa E.
Caroland, Mary, ed. see Korte, Gene J.
Caroland, Mary, ed. see Osborne, Thelma.
Caroland, Mary, ed. see Petroske, Mimi.
Caroland, Mary, ed. see Reasonover, Ila.
Caroland, Mary, ed. see Schultz, Janice.
Caroland, Mary, ed. see Williams, Monique M.
Caroli, Betty L. Immigrants Who Returned Home. (Illus.). (gr. 5 up). 1990. 17.95 (0-87754-864-1) Chelsea Hse.
Carolock, G. M., ed. see Lassik, Grace E.
Carpenter. The Captain Hook Affair. write for info. HM.
—Elephants Don't Bounce. write for info. HM.
—The Joshers: Or London to Birmingham with Albert & Victoria. write for info. HM.
—The Solitary Volcano. write for info. HM.
—The Wind in the Willows. write for info. HM.
Carpenter & Prichard, Mari. The Oxford Companion to Children's Literature. write for info. HM.
Carpenter, Allan. Alabama. LC 77-13920. (Illus.). 96p. (gr. 4 up). 1978. PLB 19.93 (0-516-04101-0) Childrens.
—Alaska. LC 78-12419. (Illus.). 96p. (gr. 4 up). 1979. PLB 19.93 (0-516-04102-9) Childrens.
—Arizona. LC 79-11802. (Illus.). 96p. (gr. 4 up). 1979. PLB 19.93 (0-516-04103-7) Childrens.
—Arkansas. LC 78-3786. (Illus.). 96p. (gr. 4 up). 1978. PLB 19.93 (0-516-04104-5) Childrens.
—Benin (Dahomey) Owen, Wilfred, Jr., ed. LC 77-20877. (gr. 6-12). pap. 26.00 (0-8357-3475-7, 2039762) Bks Demand.
—California. LC 77-21101. (Illus.). 96p. (gr. 4 up). 1978. PLB 19.93 (0-516-04105-3) Childrens.
—Colorado. LC 77-13921. (Illus.). 96p. (gr. 4 up). 1978. PLB 19.93 (0-516-04106-1) Childrens.
—Connecticut. LC 79-4173. (Illus.). 96p. (gr. 4 up). 1979. PLB 19.93 (0-516-04107-X) Childrens.
—Delaware. LC 78-15915. (Illus.). 96p. (gr. 4 up). 1979. PLB 19.93 (0-516-04108-8) Childrens.
—District of Columbia. new ed. LC 78-31683. (Illus.). 96p. (gr. 4 up). 1979. PLB 19.93 (0-516-04151-7) Childrens.
—Far-Flung America. new ed. LC 79-12505. (Illus.). 96p. (gr. 4 up). 1979. PLB 19.93 (0-516-04152-5) Childrens.
—Florida. LC 78-8108. (Illus.). 96p. (gr. 4 up). 1979. PLB 19.93 (0-516-04109-6) Childrens.
—Georgia. LC 79-12095. (Illus.). 96p. (gr. 4 up). 1979. PLB 19.93 (0-516-04110-X) Childrens.
—Hawaii. LC 79-9991. (Illus.). 96p. (gr. 4 up). 1979. PLB 19.93 (0-516-04111-8) Childrens.
—Idaho. new ed. LC 79-9804. (Illus.). 96p. (gr. 4 up). 1979. PLB 19.93 (0-516-04112-6) Childrens.
—Illinois. new ed. LC 78-32064. (Illus.). 96p. (gr. 4 up). 1979. PLB 19.93 (0-516-04113-4) Childrens.
—Indiana. new ed. LC 78-12459. (Illus.). 96p. (gr. 4 up). 1979. PLB 19.93 (0-516-04114-2) Childrens.
—Iowa. LC 79-11802. (Illus.). 96p. (gr. 4 up). 1979. PLB 19.93 (0-516-04115-0) Childrens.
—Kansas. new ed. LC 79-12433. (Illus.). 96p. (gr. 4 up). 1979. PLB 19.93 (0-516-04116-9) Childrens.
—Kentucky. new ed. LC 79-12696. (Illus.). 96p. (gr. 4 up). 1979. PLB 19.93 (0-516-04117-7) Childrens.
—Louisiana. LC 78-3390. (Illus.). 96p. (gr. 4 up). 1978. PLB 19.93 (0-516-04118-5) Childrens.
—Maine. new ed. LC 79-10804. (Illus.). 96p. (gr. 4 up). 1979. PLB 19.93 (0-516-04119-3) Childrens.
—Maryland. new ed. LC 78-14892. (Illus.). 96p. (gr. 4 up). 1979. PLB 19.93 (0-516-04120-7) Childrens.
—Massachusetts. new ed. LC 78-3785. (Illus.). 96p. (gr. 4 up). 1978. PLB 19.93 (0-516-04121-5) Childrens.
—Michigan. LC 78-8001. (Illus.). 96p. (gr. 4 up). 1978. PLB 19.93 (0-516-04122-3) Childrens.
—Minnesota. new ed. LC 78-8000. (Illus.). 96p. (gr. 4 up). 1978. PLB 19.93 (0-516-04123-1) Childrens.
—Mississippi. LC 78-3400. (Illus.). 96p. (gr. 4 up). 1978. PLB 19.93 (0-516-04124-X) Childrens.
—Missouri. LC 78-3551. (Illus.). 96p. (gr. 4 up). 1978. PLB 19.93 (0-516-04125-8) Childrens.
—Montana. new ed. LC 79-683. (Illus.). 96p. (gr. 4 up). 1979. PLB 19.93 (0-516-04126-6) Childrens.
—Nebraska. LC 78-10480. (Illus.). 96p. (gr. 4 up). 1979. PLB 19.93 (0-516-04127-4) Childrens.
—Nevada. LC 79-4355. (Illus.). 96p. (gr. 4 up). 1979. PLB 19.93 (0-516-04128-2) Childrens.
—New Hampshire. LC 79-11454. (Illus.). 96p. (gr. 4 up). 1979. PLB 19.93 (0-516-04129-0) Childrens.
—New Jersey. LC 78-14891. (Illus.). 96p. (gr. 4 up). 1979. PLB 19.93 (0-516-04130-4) Childrens.
—New Mexico. LC 78-2695. (Illus.). 96p. (gr. 4 up). 1978. PLB 19.93 (0-516-04131-2) Childrens.
—New York. new ed. LC 78-3395. (Illus.). 96p. (gr. 4 up). 1978. PLB 19.93 (0-516-04132-0) Childrens.
—North Carolina. new ed. LC 79-682. (Illus.). 96p. (gr. 4 up). 1979. PLB 19.93 (0-516-04133-9) Childrens.
—North Dakota. new ed. LC 79-11470. (Illus.). 96p. (gr. 4 up). 1979. PLB 19.93 (0-516-04134-7) Childrens.

—Ohio. new ed. LC 78-16162. (Illus.). 96p. (gr. 4 up). 1979. PLB 19.93 (0-516-04135-5) Childrens.
—Oklahoma. new ed. LC 79-10592. (Illus.). 96p. (gr. 4 up). 1979. PLB 19.93 (0-516-04136-3) Childrens.
—Oregon. new ed. LC 78-13955. (Illus.). 96p. (gr. 4 up). 1979. PLB 19.93 (0-516-04137-1) Childrens.
—Pennsylvania. new ed. LC 78-5089. (Illus.). 96p. (gr. 4 up). 1978. PLB 19.93 (0-516-04138-X) Childrens.
—Rhode Island. LC 78-16446. (Illus.). 96p. (gr. 4 up). 1979. PLB 19.93 (0-516-04139-8) Childrens.
—South Carolina. LC 79-11453. (Illus.). 96p. (gr. 4 up). 1979. PLB 19.93 (0-516-04140-1) Childrens.
—South Dakota. new ed. LC 78-3385. (Illus.). 96p. (gr. 4 up). 1978. PLB 19.93 (0-516-04141-X) Childrens.
—Tennessee. LC 78-11522. (Illus.). 96p. (gr. 4 up). 1979. PLB 19.93 (0-516-04142-8) Childrens.
—Texas. LC 78-18430. (Illus.). 96p. (gr. 4 up). 1979. PLB 19.93 (0-516-04143-6) Childrens.
—Utah. new ed. LC 79-12433. (Illus.). 96p. (gr. 4 up). 1979. PLB 19.93 (0-516-04144-4) Childrens.
—Vermont. new ed. LC 79-829. (Illus.). 96p. (gr. 4 up). 1979. PLB 19.93 (0-516-04145-2) Childrens.
—Virginia. LC 78-8002. (Illus.). 96p. (gr. 4 up). 1978. PLB 19.93 (0-516-04146-0) Childrens.
—Washington. new ed. LC 79-13390. (Illus.). 96p. (gr. 4 up). 1979. PLB 19.93 (0-516-04147-9) Childrens.
—West Virginia. new ed. LC 79-12900. (Illus.). 96p. (gr. 4 up). 1979. PLB 19.93 (0-516-04148-7) Childrens.
—Wisconsin. new ed. LC 77-13666. (Illus.). 96p. (gr. 4 up). 1978. PLB 19.93 (0-516-04149-5) Childrens.
—Wyoming. new ed. LC 78-32135. (Illus.). 96p. (gr. 4 up). 1979. PLB 19.93 (0-516-04150-9) Childrens.
Carpenter, Allan & Balow, Tom. Algeria. LC 72-20876. (gr. 6-12). pap. 26.00 (0-8357-3474-9, 2039761) Bks Demand.
—Botswana. Cohen, Ronald, ed. LC 72-10379. (gr. 6-12). pap. 25.40 (0-8357-3476-5, 2039763) Bks Demand.
Carpenter, Allan & Maginnis, Matthew. Burundi. Rowe, John, ed. LC 73-4971. (gr. 6-12). pap. 25.20 (0-8357-2700-9, 2039764) Bks Demand.
Carpenter, Angelica S. Frances Hodgson Burnett: Beyond the Secret Garden. (gr. 4-7). 1992. pap. 6.95 (0-8225-9610-5) Lerner Pubns.
—L. Frank Baum: Royal Historian of Oz. (gr. 4-7). 1993. pap. 7.95 (0-8225-9617-2) Lerner Pubns.
Carpenter, Angelica S. & Shirley, Jean. Frances Hodgson Burnett: Beyond the Secret Garden. (Illus.). 128p. (gr. 5 up). 1990. PLB 21.50 (0-8225-4905-0) Lerner Pubns.
—L. Frank Baum: Royal Historian of Oz. (gr. 5 up). 1991. PLB 21.50 (0-8225-4910-7) Lerner Pubns.
Carpenter, Eric. Young Christopher Columbus: Discoverer of the New Worlds. Himmelman, John, illus. LC 91-24975. 32p. (gr. k-2). 1992. PLB 11.59 (0-8167-2526-8); pap. text ed. 2.95 (0-8167-2527-6) Troll Assocs.
Carpenter, Frances. Tales of a Chinese Grandmother. Hasselriie, Malthe, illus. LC 72-77514. 302p. (gr. 3-8). 1972. pap. 8.95 (0-8048-1042-7) C E Tuttle.
—Tales of a Korean Grandmother. LC 72-77515. (Illus.). 320p. (gr. 3-8). 1972. pap. 8.95 (0-8048-1043-5) C E Tuttle.
Carpenter, Francis. Tales of a Chinese Grandmother. 293p. (gr. 5-6). Repr. of 1937 ed. lib. bdg. 22.95x (0-89190-481-6, Pub. by River City Pr) Amereon Ltd.
Carpenter, Humphrey. Mr. Majeika. large type ed. Rodgers, Frank, illus. 96p. (gr. 1-8). 1992. 13.95 (0-7451-1582-9, Galaxy Child Lrg Print) Chivers N Amer.
—Secret Gardens: The Golden Age of Children's Literature. (Illus.). 272p. 1991. pap. 9.70 (0-395-57374-2) HM.
Carpenter, Karen & Howard, Susie. Something Happened in My House: A Journey of Children's Grief. (Illus.). 36p. (Orig.). (gr. 3-8). 1993. pap. 9.95 (1-883613-01-9) Byte Size.
Carpenter, Mark. Brazil: An Awakening Giant. LC 87-13417. (Illus.). 128p. (gr. 5 up). 1988. RSBE 14.95 (0-87518-366-2, Dillon) Macmillan Child Grp.
Carpenter, Mimi G. Mermaid in a Tidal Pool. Carpenter, Mimi G., illus. 32p. (Orig.). (gr. p-6). 1985. pap. 8.95 (0-9614628-0-9) Beachcomber Pr.
—What the Sea Left Behind. Carpenter, Mimi G., illus. LC 81-66251. 32p. (gr. 1-4). 1981. pap. 7.95 (0-89272-123-5) Down East.
Carpenter, Robert S., ed. see Arnoldt, Robert P.
Carpenter, Robert S., ed. see Arnoldt, Robert P. & Marx, Jacqueline A.
Carpentier, Marcel. Your First Puppy. (Illus.). 34p. (Orig.). (gr. 1-6). 1991. pap. 1.95 (0-86622-064-X, YF-119) TFH Pubns.
Carper, Helen, ed. see West Virginia Writers, Inc., Staff & McClure, Patricia.
Carr & Paquet. God, I've Got to Talk to You Again! LC 59-1315. 24p. (Orig.). (gr. k-4). 1985. pap. 1.89 (0-570-06197-0, 59-1315) Concordia.
Carr, Barbara. The Planet of the Dinosaurs. Bear, Alice, illus. LC 92-9287. 32p. (gr. k-3). 1992. 12.95 (0-89334-161-4, 161-4) Humanics Ltd.
Carr, Dan. Cheating. (Illus.). (gr. k-4). 1984. pap. 0.99 (0-570-08725-2, 56-1469) Concordia.
—Hurting Others. (Illus.). (gr. k-4). 1984. pap. 0.99 (0-570-08727-9, 56-1471) Concordia.
—Lying. (Illus.). (gr. k-4). 1984. pap. 0.99 (0-570-08732-5, 56-1476) Concordia.
—My Bad Temper. (Illus.). (gr. 1-3). 1984. pap. 0.99 (0-570-08730-9, 56-1474) Concordia.

—Our Savior Is Born. (gr. 1 up). 1984. 7.99 (0-570-04092-2, 56-1460) Concordia.
—Paying Attention. (Illus.). (gr. k-4). 1984. pap. 0.99 (0-570-08729-5, 56-1473) Concordia.
—Sharing. (Illus.). (gr. k-4). 1984. pap. 0.99 (0-570-08728-7, 56-1472) Concordia.
—Stealing. (Illus.). (gr. k-4). 1984. pap. 0.99 (0-570-08731-7, 56-1475) Concordia.
—Vandalism. (Illus.). (gr. k-4). 1984. pap. 0.99 (0-570-08726-0, 56-1470) Concordia.
Carr, J., jt. auth. see Steffens, J.
Carr, Jan. Beauty & the Beast. Bratun, Katy, illus. 32p. (ps-3). 1993. pap. 2.50 (0-590-46451-5, Cartwheel) Scholastic Inc.
—I Am Curious about Me. Campana, Manny, illus. 48p. (ps-2). 1990. pap. 1.95 (0-590-44032-2) Scholastic Inc.
—Secret Garden. (Illus.). (ps-3). 1993. pap. 3.25 (0-590-47172-4) Scholastic Inc.
—Wizard of Oz. (ps-3). 1993. pap. 3.25 (0-590-46993-2) Scholastic Inc.
Carr, Jo. Trouble with Tikki. Petie, Haris, illus. LC 71-115459. (gr. k-2). 1970. 7.19 (0-8313-0013-2) Lantern.
Carr, M. J. Ariel the Spy. LC 92-54512. (Illus.). 80p. (gr. 1-4). 1993. pap. 2.95 (1-56282-372-8) Disney Pr.
—Arista's New Boyfriend. LC 92-54511. (Illus.). 80p. (gr. 1-4). 1993. pap. 2.95 (1-56282-371-X) Disney Pr.
—Be My Valentine. (ps-3). 1992. pap. 2.50 (0-590-45131-6) Scholastic Inc.
—Cabbage Patch Kids Visit the Doctor. (ps-3). 1993. pap. 2.50 (0-685-64929-6) Scholastic Inc.
—The Cabbage Patch Kids Visit the Doctor. (ps-3). 1993. pap. 2.50 (0-590-46631-3) Scholastic Inc.
Carr, Richard, tr. see Guillen, Nicholas.
Carr, Roberta, ed. Art & Music Scholarships. 75p. (Orig.). (gr. 9-12). 1992. pap. text ed. 12.50x (1-880468-06-9) Col Connect.
—Directory of Pre-College Programs. 75p. (Orig.). (gr. 9-12). 1992. pap. text ed. 25.00x (1-880468-05-0) Col Connect.
—Scholarships for Catholic Colleges & Universities. 75p. (Orig.). (gr. 9-12). 1992. pap. text ed. 12.50x (1-880468-07-7) Col Connect.
Carr, Roger. The Clinker. 144p. (gr. 5-9). 1989. 14.45 (0-395-51737-0) HM.
Carr, Terry. Spill! The Story of the Exxon Valdez. (Illus.). 64p. (gr. 5-8). 1991. 18.95 (0-531-15217-0); PLB 18.90 (0-531-10998-4) Watts.
Carran, Betty B. Romania. LC 87-35423. (Illus.). 124p. (gr. 5-9). 1988. PLB 26.60 (0-516-02703-4) Childrens.
Carrara, Larry, jt. auth. see Wakefield, Pat.
Carrara, Larry, jt. auth. see Wakefield, Pat A.
Carraro, J. M., ed. see Rudner, Barry.
Carratello, John & Carratello, Patty. All about Science Fairs. Chellton, Anna, illus. 96p. (gr. 1-8). 1989. wkbk. 9.95 (1-55734-228-8) Tchr Create Mat.
—Connecting Math & Literature. Apodaca, Blanca, et al, illus. Vasconcelles, Keith, intro. by. 144p. (gr. k-3). 1991. wkbk. 12.95 (1-55734-342-X) Tchr Create Mat.
—Great Americans. Fullam, Sue, illus. 112p. (Orig.). (gr. 2-5). 1991. 10.95 (1-55734-112-5) Tchr Create Mat.
—Hands on Science: Animals. Wright, Terry, illus. 32p. (gr. 2-5). 1988. wkbk. 4.95 (1-55734-225-3) Tchr Create Mat.
—Hands on Science: Our Changing Earth. Wright, Terry, illus. 32p. (gr. 2-5). 1988. wkbk. 4.95 (1-55734-226-1) Tchr Create Mat.
—Hands on Science: Plants. Wright, Terry, illus. 32p. (gr. 2-5). 1988. wkbk. 4.95 (1-55734-224-5) Tchr Create Mat.
—Hands on Science: Simple Machines. Wright, Terry & Spence, Paula, illus. 32p. (gr. 2-5). 1988. wkbk. 4.95 (1-55734-227-X) Tchr Create Mat.
—Hooray for the USA! Fullam, Sue & Wright, Theresa, illus. 112p. (Orig.). (gr. 2-5). 1991. 10.95 (1-55734-113-3) Tchr Create Mat.
—Literature Activities for Reluctant Readers: Intermediate. Buhler, Cheryl, et al, illus. 112p. (gr. 3-5). 1991. wkbk. 10.95 (1-55734-354-3) Tchr Create Mat.
—Literature Activities for Reluctant Readers: Primary. Fullam, Sue & Vasconcelles, Keith, illus. 112p. (gr. k-3). 1991. wkbk. 10.95 (1-55734-353-5) Tchr Create Mat.
—Literature & Critical Thinking. Spence, Paula & Wright, Terry, illus. 96p. (gr. 5-8). 1989. wkbk. 9.95 (1-55734-310-1) Tchr Create Mat.
—Literature & Critical Thinking. Spivak, Darlene, ed. Wright, Theresa & Spence, Paula, illus. 96p. (gr. k-3). 1989. wkbk. 9.95 (1-55734-311-X) Tchr Create Mat.
—Literature & Critical Thinking. Wright, Theresa & et al, illus. 96p. (gr. 3-5). 1989. wkbk. 9.95 (1-55734-313-6) Tchr Create Mat.
—Literature & Critical Thinking. Apodaca, Blanqui, et al, illus. 96p. (gr. 5-8). 1990. wkbk. 9.95 (1-55734-314-4) Tchr Create Mat.
—Literature & Critical Thinking. Apodaca, Blanqui, et al, illus. 96p. (gr. 3-5). 1990. wkbk. 9.95 (1-55734-315-2) Tchr Create Mat.
—Literature & Critical Thinking. Wright, Theresa, illus. 96p. (gr. 3-5). 1987. wkbk. 9.95 (1-55734-355-1) Tchr Create Mat.
—Literature & Critical Thinking, CB. Wright, Theresa, illus. 96p. (gr. k-3). 1987. wkbk. 9.95 (1-55734-356-X) Tchr Create Mat.
—Literature & Critical Thinking. Wright, Theresa & Smythe, Linda, illus. 96p. (gr. k-3). 1988. wkbk. 9.95 (1-55734-357-8) Tchr Create Mat.

—Literature & Critical Thinking. Chellton, Anna, et al, illus. 96p. (gr. k-3). 1989. wkbk. 9.95 (*1-55734-361-6*) Tchr Create Mat.
—Literature & Critical Thinking. Chellton, Anna, et al, illus. 96p. (gr. 3-5). 1989. wkbk. 9.95 (*1-55734-362-4*) Tchr Create Mat.
—Literature & Critical Thinking. Spence, Paula, et al, illus. 96p. (gr. 5-8). 1989. wkbk. 9.95 (*1-55734-364-0*) Tchr Create Mat.
—Problem Solving Science Investigations. Chellton, Anna, illus. 96p. (gr. 1-8). 1989. wkbk. 9.95 (*1-55734-229-6*) Tchr Create Mat.
—United States Geography. Chellton, Anna, et al, illus. 48p. (gr. 3-6). 1989. wkbk. 5.95 (*1-55734-160-5*) Tchr Create Mat.
—World Geography. Chellton, Anna, illus. 48p. (gr. 3-6). 1989. wkbk. 5.95 (*1-55734-161-3*) Tchr Create Mat.
—Writing a Country Report. Chellton, Anna, illus. 48p. (gr. 3-6). 1989. wkbk. 5.95 (*1-55734-163-X*) Tchr Create Mat.
—Writing a State Report. Chellton, Anna, illus. 48p. (gr. 3-6). 1989. wkbk. 5.95 (*1-55734-162-1*) Tchr Create Mat.
Carratello, John, jt. auth. see Carratello, Patricia.
Carratello, John, jt. auth. see Carratello, Patty.
Carratello, Patricia. Food & Nutrition. Carratello, Patricia, illus. 40p. (gr. 1-4). 1980. wkbk. 5.95 (*1-55734-212-1*) Tchr Create Mat.
—I Can Capitalize. Chacon, Rick, illus. 32p. (gr. 3-6). 1983. wkbk. 4.95 (*1-55734-331-4*) Tchr Create Mat.
—I Can Give a Speech. Chacon, Rick, illus. 32p. (gr. 3-6). 1981. 4.95 (*1-55734-327-6*) Tchr Create Mat.
—I Can Punctuate. Chacon, Rick, illus. 32p. (gr. 3-6). 1983. wkbk. 4.95 (*1-55734-332-2*) Tchr Create Mat.
—I Can Write a Book Report. Chacon, Rick, illus. 32p. (gr. 3-6). 1985. wkbk. 4.95 (*1-55734-336-5*) Tchr Create Mat.
—I Can Write a Letter. Chacon, Rick, illus. 32p. (gr. 3-6). 1983. wkbk. 4.95 (*1-55734-333-0*) Tchr Create Mat.
—I Can Write a Paragraph. Chacon, Rick, illus. 32p. (gr. 3-6). 1981. wkbk. 4.95 (*1-55734-330-6*) Tchr Create Mat.
—I Can Write a Poem. Chacon, Rick, illus. 32p. (gr. 3-6). 1981. wkbk. 4.95 (*1-55734-326-8*) Tchr Create Mat.
—I Can Write a Research Paper. Chacon, Rick, illus. 32p. (gr. 3-6). 1985. wkbk. 4.95 (*1-55734-334-9*) Tchr Create Mat.
—I Can Write a Short Story. Chacon, Rick, illus. 32p. (gr. 3-6). 1985. wkbk. 4.95 (*1-55734-335-7*) Tchr Create Mat.
—Let's Investigate Health & Safety. (Illus.). 48p. (gr. 1-4). 1984. wkbk. 5.95 (*1-55734-214-8*) Tchr Create Mat.
—My Body. Carratello, Patricia, illus. 38p. (gr. 1-4). 1980. wkbk. 5.95 (*1-55734-211-3*) Tchr Create Mat.
Carratello, Patricia & Carratello, John. Let's Investigate Space. Carratello, Patricia & Carratello, John, illus. 48p. (gr. 1-4). 1984. wkbk. 5.95 (*1-55734-216-4*) Tchr Create Mat.
—Let's Investigate the Senses. Chacon, Rick, illus. 48p. (gr. 1-4). 1984. wkbk. 5.95 (*1-55734-213-X*) Tchr Create Mat.
Carratello, Patty. The Bee & the Seed. Spivak, Darlene, ed. Smythe, Linda, illus. 16p. (gr. k-2). 1987. wkbk. 1.95 (*1-55734-381-0*) Tchr Create Mat.
—Body Basics. Wright, Theresa, illus. 48p. (gr. 1-5). 1987. wkbk. 5.95 (*1-55734-220-2*) Tchr Create Mat.
—Brett, My Pet. Spivak, Darlene, ed. Spence, Paula, illus. 16p. (gr. k-2). 1988. wkbk. 1.95 (*1-55734-387-X*) Tchr Create Mat.
—Dot's Pot. Spivak, Darlene, ed. Brostrom, Eileen, illus. 16p. (gr. k-2). 1988. wkbk. 1.95 (*1-55734-389-6*) Tchr Create Mat.
—Duke the Blue Mule. Spivak, Darlene, ed. Smythe, Linda, illus. 16p. (gr. k-2). 1988. wkbk. 1.95 (*1-55734-384-5*) Tchr Create Mat.
—Gail's Paint Pail. Spivak, Darlene, ed. Olsen, Shirley, illus. 16p. (gr. k-2). 1988. wkbk. 1.95 (*1-55734-385-3*) Tchr Create Mat.
—It's Easy to Capitalize. Wright, Theresa, illus. 32p. (gr. 1-4). 1988. 4.95 (*1-55734-322-5*) Tchr Create Mat.
—It's Easy to Punctuate. Spence, Paula & Wright, Theresa, illus. 32p. (gr. 1-4). 1988. wkbk. 4.95 (*1-55734-321-7*) Tchr Create Mat.
—It's Easy to Write a Paragraph. Wright, Theresa, illus. 32p. (gr. 1-4). 1988. wkbk. 4.95 (*1-55734-324-1*) Tchr Create Mat.
—Literature & Critical Thinking. Wright, Theresa, et al, illus. 96p. (gr. 3-5). 1988. wkbk. 9.95 (*1-55734-358-6*) Tchr Create Mat.
—Literature & Critical Thinking. Wright, Theresa, et al, illus. 96p. (gr. 3-5). 1988. wkbk. 9.95 (*1-55734-359-4*) Tchr Create Mat.
—Literature & Critical Thinking. Wright, Theresa, et al, illus. 96p. (gr. 5-8). 1988. wkbk. 9.95 (*1-55734-360-8*) Tchr Create Mat.
—Literature & Critical Thinking. Apodaca, Blanqui & Vasconcelles, Keith, illus. 96p. (gr. 5-8). 1990. wkbk. 9.95 (*1-55734-316-0*) Tchr Create Mat.
—Mice on Ice. Spivak, Darlene, ed. Smythe, Linda, illus. 16p. (gr. k-2). 1988. wkbk. 1.95 (*1-55734-382-9*) Tchr Create Mat.
—My Cap. Spivak, Darlene, ed. Smythe, Linda, illus. 16p. (gr. k-2). 1988. wkbk. 1.95 (*1-55734-386-1*) Tchr Create Mat.
—My Old Gold Boat. Spivak, Darlene, ed. Smythe, Linda, illus. 16p. (gr. k-2). 1988. wkbk. 1.95 (*1-55734-383-7*) Tchr Create Mat.

—My Truck & My Pup. Spivak, Darlene, ed. Brostrom, Eileen, illus. 16p. (gr. k-2). 1988. wkbk. 1.95 (*1-55734-390-X*) Tchr Create Mat.
—Nutrition & Me. Wright, Theresa, illus. 48p. (gr. 1-5). 1987. wkbk. 5.95 (*1-55734-222-9*) Tchr Create Mat.
—Skate, Kate, Skate. Spivak, Darlene, ed. Smythe, Linda, illus. 16p. (gr. k-2). 1988. wkbk. 1.95 (*1-55734-380-2*) Tchr Create Mat.
—This Is Fred. Spivak, Darlene, ed. Brostrom, Eileen, illus. 16p. (gr. k-2). 1988. wkbk. 1.95 (*1-55734-391-8*) Tchr Create Mat.
—Will Bill? Spivak, Darlene, ed. Olsen, Shirley, illus. 16p. (gr. k-2). 1988. wkbk. 1.95 (*1-55734-388-8*) Tchr Create Mat.
Carratello, Patty & Carratello, John. Literature & Critical Thinking. Apodaca, Blanqui & Wright, Theresa, illus. 96p. (gr. 3-5). 1989. wkbk. 9.95 (*1-55734-312-8*) Tchr Create Mat.
—Literature & Critical Thinking. (Illus.). 96p. (gr. 5-8). 1989. wkbk. 9.95 (*1-55734-363-2*) Tchr Create Mat.
Carratello, Patty, jt. auth. see Carratello, John.
Carraway, Mary. Jill. LC 85-71473. 144p. (Orig.). (gr. 6-9). 1985. pap. 3.99 (*0-87123-847-0*) Bethany Hse.
—Wendy. LC 87-72793. 160p. (Orig.). (gr. 9-12). 1988. pap. 3.99 (*0-87123-942-6*) Bethany Hse.
Carre, John le see Le Carre, John.
Carrell, M. Understanding English. large type ed. 78p. (gr. 7-12). 1983. Repr. of 1972 ed. 13.84 (*0-317-01953-8*, 4-26600-00) Am Printing Hse.
Carrick. Aladdin & the Wonderful Lamp. 1993. pap. 4.95 (*0-590-41680-4*) Scholastic Inc.
Carrick, Carol. The Accident. Carrick, Donald, illus. LC 76-3532. 32p. (ps-3). 1981. (Clarion Bks); pap. 5.95 (*0-89919-041-3*) HM.
—Ben & the Porcupine. Carrick, Donald, illus. LC 80-214020. 32p. (ps-3). 1985. pap. 5.70 (*0-89919-348-X*, Clarion Bks) HM.
—Big Old Bones: A Dinosaur Tale. Carrick, Donald, illus. 32p. (gr. k-2). 1989. 13.95 (*0-89919-734-5*, Clarion Bks) HM.
—Big Old Bones: A Dinosaur Tale. (ps-3). 1992. pap. 5.70 (*0-395-61582-8*, Clarion Bks) HM.
—The Crocodiles Still Wait. Carrick, Donald, illus. LC 79-23519. 32p. (gr. 1-4). 1980. 14.45 (*0-395-29102-X*, Clarion Bks) HM.
—The Elephant. Carrick, Donald, illus. write for info. (Clarion Bks) HM.
—The Elephant in the Dark. Carrick, Donald, photos by. write for info. (Clarion Bks) HM.
—The Elephant in the Dark. Carrick, Donald, illus. LC 88-2591. 144p. (gr. 3-7). 1988. 13.95 (*0-89919-757-4*, Clarion Bks) HM.
—Elephant in the Dark. (gr. 4-7). 1990. pap. 2.95 (*0-590-42995-7*) Scholastic Inc.
—The Foundling. Carrick, Donald, illus. LC 77-1587. 32p. (ps-4). 1979. 14.45 (*0-395-28775-8*, Clarion Bks) HM.
—The Foundling. Carrick, Donald, illus. LC 77-1587. (ps-3). 1986. pap. 4.95 (*0-89919-466-4*, Clarion Bks) HM.
—In the Moonlight, Waiting. Carrick, Donald, illus. 32p. (ps-1). 1990. 13.95 (*0-89919-867-8*) Clarion Pr.
—Left Behind. Carrick, Donald, illus. LC 88-1040. 32p. (gr. k-3). 1988. 13.95 (*0-89919-535-0*, Clarion Bks) HM.
—Left Behind. Carrick, Donald, illus. 32p. (ps-3). 1991. pap. 4.80 (*0-395-54380-0*, Clarion Bks) HM.
—Lost in the Storm. Carrick, Donald, illus. LC 74-1051. 32p. (ps-3). 1979. 14.45 (*0-395-28776-6*, Clarion Bks) HM.
—Lost in the Storm. Carrick, Donald, illus. (ps-3). 1987. pap. 5.95 (*0-89919-493-1*, Clarion Bks) HM.
—Norman Fools the Tooth Fairy. McCue, Lisa, illus. 32p. 1992. 13.95 (*0-590-42240-5*, Scholastic Hardcover) Scholastic Inc.
—Octopus. Carrick, Donald, illus. 32p. (ps-3). 1991. pap. 5.70 (*0-395-59759-5*, Clarion Bks) HM.
—Old Mother Witch. Carrick, Donald, illus. LC 75-4609. 32p. (ps-4). 1979. 14.45 (*0-395-28778-2*, Clarion Bks) HM.
—Old Mother Witch. Carrick, Donald, illus. LC 75-4609. 32p. (ps). 1989. pap. 4.80 (*0-395-51584-X*, Clarion Bks) HM.
—Patrick's Dinosaurs. Carrick, Donald, illus. LC 83-2049. 32p. (gr. k-3). 1983. 13.95 (*0-89919-189-4*, Clarion Bks) HM.
—Patrick's Dinosaurs. Carrick, Donald, illus. LC 83-2049. (gr. k-3). 1985. pap. 7.95 (*0-89919-402-8*, Clarion Bks) HM.
—Paul's Christmas Birthday. Carrick, Donald, illus. LC 77-28408. 32p. (gr. k-3). 1978. PLB 13.88 (*0-688-84159-7*) Greenwillow.
—Sand Tiger Shark. Carrick, Donald, illus. 32p. (ps-3). 1991. pap. 5.70 (*0-395-59701-3*, Clarion Bks) HM.
—Sleep Out. Carrick, Donald, illus. LC 72-88539. 32p. (gr. 1-3). 1979. (Clarion Bks); pap. 4.95 (*0-89919-083-9*, Clarion) HM.
—Some Friend. Carrick, Donald, illus. LC 79-11490. 112p. (gr. 3-6). 1987. pap. 5.70 (*0-89919-525-3*, Clarion Bks) HM.
—Stay Away from Simon. Carrick, Donald, illus. LC 84-14289. 64p. (gr. 2-5). 1985. 12.95 (*0-89919-343-9*, Clarion Bks) HM.
—Stay Away from Simon! Carrick, Donald, illus. (gr. 3-6). 1989. pap. 5.70 (*0-89919-849-X*, Clarion Bks) HM.
—Two Very Little Sisters. (ps-3). 1993. 14.95 (*0-395-60927-5*, Clarion Bks) HM.

—Whaling Days. Frampton, David, illus. 40p. (gr. 4-7). 1993. 15.45 (*0-395-50948-3*, Clarion Bks) HM.
—What a Wimp! Carrick, Donald, illus. LC 82-9597. (gr. 3-6). 1988. pap. 3.95 (*0-89919-703-5*, Clarion Bks) HM.
—What Happened to Patrick's Dinosaurs? Carrick, Donald, illus. LC 85-13989. (gr. k-3). 1988. 14.95 (*0-89919-406-0*, Clarion Bks); pap. 5.95 (*0-89919-797-3*, Clarion Bks) HM.
—What Happened to Patrick's Dinosaurs? Carrick, Doral, illus. 1988. pap. 7.70 incl. cass. (*0-89919-838-4*, Clarion Bks) HM.
Carrick, Donald. Harald & the Giant Knight. 32p. (gr. 1-3). 1982. 15.95 (*0-89919-060-X*, Clarion Bks) HM.
—Harald & the Great Stag. Carrick, Donald, illus. LC 87-17875. 32p. (gr. k-4). 1988. 14.95 (*0-89919-514-8*, Clarion Bks) HM.
—Harald & the Great Stag. Carrick, Donald, illus. 32p. (ps-3). 1990. pap. 4.80 (*0-395-52596-9*, Clarion Bks) HM.
—Milk. Carrick, Donald, illus. LC 84-25879. 24p. (ps-1). 1985. lib. bdg. 13.88 (*0-688-04823-4*) Greenwillow.
—Morgan & the Artist. LC 84-14267. (Illus.). 32p. (ps-4). 1985. 14.45 (*0-89919-300-5*, Clarion Bks) HM.
—Patrick's Dinosaurs. (ps-3). 1987. incl. cass. 6.95 (*0-317-64570-6*) HM.
Carrick, Graham. Wood. (Illus.). 32p. (gr. 2-6). 1990. lib. bdg. 15.94 (*0-86592-484-8*); lib. bdg. 11.95s.p. (*0-685-36306-6*) Rourke Corp.
Carrick, Noel. Luxembourg. (Illus.). 96p. (gr. 5 up). 1988. 14.95 (*0-222-01144-0*) Chelsea Hse.
—New Guinea. (Illus.). 96p. (gr. 5 up). 1989. 14.95 (*0-222-00916-0*) Chelsea Hse.
Carricle, Noel. San Marino. (Illus.). 96p. (gr. 5 up). 1988. 14.95 (*0-7910-0101-6*) Chelsea Hse.
Carrie, Christopher. Adventure in the Arctic Circle. (Illus.). 40p. (gr. k up). 1990. 1.59 (*0-86696-249-2*) Binney & Smith.
—Alphabet. (Illus.). 12p. (Orig.). (gr. 3-6). 1987. pap. 4.70 (*0-86696-204-2*) Binney & Smith.
—Amazing Animals. (Illus.). 40p. (gr. k up). 1991. 1.49 (*0-86696-305-7*) Binney & Smith.
—Amazing Discoveries. (Illus.). 40p. (gr. k up). 1991. 1.49 (*0-86696-308-1*) Binney & Smith.
—Amazing People. (Illus.). 40p. (gr. k up). 1991. 1.49 (*0-86696-307-3*) Binney & Smith.
—Amazing Places. (Illus.). 40p. (gr. k up). 1991. 1.49 (*0-86696-306-5*) Binney & Smith.
—Animals. (Illus.). 12p. (Orig.). (gr. 3-6). 1987. pap. 4.70 (*0-86696-201-8*) Binney & Smith.
—Astronauts to Diving Ducks. (Illus.). 40p. (Orig.). (gr. k up). 1989. pap. 1.49 (*0-86696-219-0*) Binney & Smith.
—Chase Through the Desert Wilds. (Illus.). 40p. (gr. k up). 1990. 1.59 (*0-86696-244-1*) Binney & Smith.
—Colorful Days Calendar. (Illus.). 32p. (Orig.). (gr. 5 up). 1989. pap. 1.99 (*0-86696-240-9*) Binney & Smith.
—Crazy Monster Mix-Ups. (Illus.). 32p. (gr. k up). 1991. 1.49 (*0-86696-301-4*) Binney & Smith.
—Elephants to Haunted Houses. (Illus.). 40p. (Orig.). (gr. k up). 1989. pap. 1.49 (*0-86696-225-5*) Binney & Smith.
—Enchanted Toyland. (Illus.). 32p. (ps-k). 1991. 1.99 (*0-86696-314-6*) Binney & Smith.
—Everything Has a Shape. (Illus.). 40p. (Orig.). (ps up). 1989. pap. 1.99 (*0-86696-222-0*) Binney & Smith.
—Fun with Colors. (Illus.). 28p. (ps-k). 1991. 2.59 (*0-86696-312-X*) Binney & Smith.
—Fun with Letters. (Illus.). 28p. (ps-k). 1991. 2.59 (*0-86696-310-3*) Binney & Smith.
—Fun with Numbers. (Illus.). 28p. (ps-k). 1991. 2.59 (*0-86696-309-X*) Binney & Smith.
—Fun with Opposites. (Illus.). 28p. (ps-k). 1991. 2.59 (*0-86696-311-1*) Binney & Smith.
—Funny Animal Mix-Ups. (Illus.). 32p. (gr. k up). 1991. 1.49 (*0-86696-302-2*) Binney & Smith.
—Going Places. (Illus.). 40p. (Orig.). (ps up) 1989. pap. 1.99 (*0-86696-221-2*) Binney & Smith.
—Growing Up. (Illus.). 40p. (Orig.). (ps up) 1989. pap. 1.99 (*0-86696-220-4*) Binney & Smith.
—Holiday Fun. (Illus.). 32p. (Orig.). (ps up) 1989. 1.99 (*0-685-27062-9*) Binney & Smith.
—Icebergs to Lazy Lizards. (Illus.). 40p. (Orig.). (gr. k up). 1989. pap. 1.49 (*0-86696-226-3*) Binney & Smith.
—Little Holiday Shop. (Illus.). 32p. (Orig.). (gr. 2-5). 1989. pap. 1.99 (*0-86696-241-7*) Binney & Smith.
—The Magic Garden. (Illus.). 32p. (ps-k). 1991. 1.99 (*0-86696-313-8*) Binney & Smith.
—Measurement. (Illus.). 12p. (Orig.). (gr. 3-6). 1987. pap. 4.70 (*0-86696-206-9*) Binney & Smith.
—Mission to the Space Station. (Illus.). 40p. (gr. k up). 1990. 1.59 (*0-86696-247-6*) Binney & Smith.
—Mixed up Farm. (Illus.). 32p. (ps-k). 1990. 1.99 (*0-86696-236-0*) Binney & Smith.
—Monsters to Playful Penguins. (Illus.). 40p. (Orig.). (gr. k up). 1989. pap. 1.49 (*0-86696-227-1*) Binney & Smith.
—My Perfect Pet. (Illus.). 40p. (Orig.). (ps up). 1989. pap. 1.99 (*0-86696-218-2*) Binney & Smith.
—Mystery of the Forest Phantom. (Illus.). 40p. (gr. k up). 1990. 1.59 (*0-86696-243-3*) Binney & Smith.
—Numbers. (Illus.). 12p. (Orig.). (ps). 1987. pap. 4.70 (*0-86696-203-4*) Binney & Smith.
—Over the Rainbow. (Illus.). 32p. (Orig.). (ps-k). 1990. 1.99 (*0-86696-239-5*) Binney & Smith.
—Playful Jungle Friends. (Illus.). 32p. (Orig.). (ps-k). 1990. 1.99 (*0-86696-238-7*) Binney & Smith.
—Quest for the Jungle City. (Illus.). 40p. (gr. k up). 1990. 1.59 (*0-86696-245-X*) Binney & Smith.

—Quilts to Unusual Unicorns. (Illus.). 40p. (Orig.). (gr. k up). 1989. pap. 1.49 (0-86696-229-8) Binney & Smith.
—Search for the Sea Treasure. (Illus.). 40p. (gr. k up). 1990. 1.59 (0-86696-246-8) Binney & Smith.
—Shapes. (Illus.). 12p. (Orig.). (gr. 3-6). 1987. pap. 4.70 (0-86696-202-6) Binney & Smith.
—Silly People Mix-Ups. (Illus.). 32p. (gr. k up). 1991. 1.49 (0-86696-304-9) Binney & Smith.
—Smiles, Giggles & Frowns. (Illus.). 40p. (Orig.). (ps up). 1989. pap. 1.99 (0-86696-223-9) Binney & Smith.
—So Big. (Illus.). 32p. 1988. 2.70 (0-86696-205-0) Binney & Smith.
—Time. (Illus.). 12p. (Orig.). (gr. 3-6). 1987. pap. 4.70 (0-86696-207-7) Binney & Smith.
—Tiny Town Tale. (Illus.). 32p. (Orig.). (ps-k). 1990. 1.99 (0-86696-237-9) Binney & Smith.
—Volcanoes to Zany Zebras. (Illus.). 40p. (Orig.). (gr. k up). 1989. pap. 1.49 (0-86696-230-1) Binney & Smith.
—Wacky Vehicle Mix-Ups. (Illus.). 32p. (gr. k up). 1991. 1.49 (0-86696-303-0) Binney & Smith.
—Wild about Color. (Illus.). 40p. (gr. k up). 1990. 1.99 (0-86696-234-4) Binney & Smith.

Carrier, Lark. A Christmas Promise. LC 86-12356. (Illus.). 36p. (ps up). 1991. pap. 15.95 (0-88708-032-4) Picture Bk Studio.
—A Christmas Promise. LC 91-14556. (Illus.). 28p. (gr. k up). 1991. pap. 4.95 (0-88708-180-0) Picture Bk Studio.
—Do Not Touch. LC 87-32730. (Illus.). (ps-12). 1991. pap. 15.95 (0-88708-061-8) Picture Bk Studio.
—A Perfect Spring. Carrier, Lark, illus. LC 89-49262. 32p. (ps up). 1991. pap. 14.95 (0-88708-131-2) Picture Bk Studio.
—Scout & Cody. Carrier, Lark, illus. LC 86-883. 28p. (ps up). 1991. pap. 14.95 (0-88708-013-8) Picture Bk Studio.
—Snowy Path: A Christmas Journey. Carrier, Lark, illus. LC 89-8449. 28p. (ps up). 1991. pap. 15.95 (0-88708-121-5) Picture Bk Studio.
—There Was a Hill... Carrier, Lark, illus. LC 84-25536. 40p. (ps up). 1991. pap. 15.95 (0-907234-70-4) Picture Bk Studio.

Carrier, Roch. Un Bonne et Heureuse Annee. Pelletier, Gilles, illus. LC 91-65366. (FRE.). 24p. (gr. 3 up). 1991. 14.95 (0-88776-268-9) Tundra Bks.
—The Boxing Champion. Cohen, Sheldon, illus. LC 90-70133. 24p. (gr. 3 up). 1991. 14.95 (0-88776-249-2) Tundra Bks.
—The Boxing Champion. Cohen, Sheldon, illus. 24p. (gr. 3 up). 1993. pap. 6.95 (0-88776-308-1) Tundra Bks.
—Canada Je T'Aime - I Love You. Tanobe, Miyuki, illus. LC 90-70137. 72p. 1991. 29.95 (0-88776-253-0) Tundra Bks.
—Un Champion. Cohen, Sheldon, illus. LC 90-70134. (FRE.). 24p. (gr. 3 up). 1991. 14.95 (0-88776-250-6) Tundra Bks.
—Le Chandail de Hockey. Cohen, Sheldon, illus. (FRE.). 24p. (Orig.). (gr. 1 up). 1985. pap. 6.95 (0-88776-176-3, Dist. by U of Toronto Pr); 14.95 (0-88776-171-2) Tundra Bks.
—A Happy New Year's Day. Gilles, Pelletier, illus. LC 91-65367. 24p. (gr. 3 up). 1991. 14.95 (0-88776-267-0) Tundra Bks.
—The Hockey Sweater. Fischman, Sheila, tr. from FRE. Cohen, Sheldon, illus. 24p. (gr. 1 up). 1984. text ed. 14.95 (0-88776-169-0, Dist. by U of Toronto Pr); pap. 6.95 (0-88776-174-7) Tundra Bks.
—El Jonron Mas Largo. Zeller, Beatriz, tr. Cohen, Sheldon, illus. (SPA.). 24p. (gr. 3 up). 1993. 14.95 (0-88776-304-9) Tundra Bks.
—The Longest Home Run. Fischman, Sheila, tr. from FRE. Cohen, Sheldon, illus. LC 92-62364. 24p. (gr. 3 up). 1993. 14.95 (0-88776-300-6) Tundra Bks.
—Le Plus Long Circuit (The Longest Home Run) Cohen, Sheldon, illus. LC 92-62362. (FRE.). 24p. (gr. 2 up). 1993. 14.95 (0-88776-301-4) Tundra Bks.

Carriker, S. David. North Carolina Railroads: The Common Carrier Railroads of North Carolina. 66p. 1989. pap. 15.00 (0-936013-08-7) Herit Pub NC.

Carris, Joan. Aunt Morbelia & the Screaming Skulls. Cushman, Doug, illus. (gr. 3-7). 1990. 14.95 (0-316-12945-3) Little.
—Aunt Morbelia & the Screaming Skulls. MacDonald, Pat, ed. Cushman, Doug, illus. 144p. (gr. 3-6). 1992. pap. 2.99 (0-671-74784-3, Minstrel Bks) PB.
—A Ghost of a Chance. Henry, Paul, illus. 160p. (gr. 3-7). 1992. 14.95 (0-316-13016-8) Little.
—The Greatest Idea Ever. Newsom, Carol, illus. LC 89-34516. 176p. (gr. 3-7). 1990. (Lipp Jr Bks); PLB 13.89 (0-397-32379-4, Lipp Jr Bks) HarpC Child Bks.
—Howling for Home. (ps). 1992. 12.95 (0-316-13017-6) Little.
—Just a Little Ham, Vol. 1. 1989. 13.95 (0-316-12990-9) Little.
—Stolen Bones: A Novel. LC 92-36479. 1993. 14.95 (0-316-13018-4) Little.

Carris, Joan D. Pets, Vets, & Marty Howard. (gr. k-6). 1987. pap. 2.95 (0-440-46855-8, Yearling) Dell.
—Witch Cat. (gr. 5 up). 1986. pap. 2.95 (0-440-49477-X, YB) Dell.

Carris, Joan D., et al. SAT Success. 3rd ed. LC 91-19039. 600p. (gr. 10-12). 1991. pap. 11.95 (1-56079-049-0) Petersons Guides.

Carrogio. Enciclopedia Infantil, 10 vols. (SPA.). 2400p. 1974. Set. leather 495.00 (0-8288-6033-5, S50480) Fr & Eur.

Carroll, Bill. Ford V8 Performance Guide. LC 76-16836. (Illus., Orig.). (gr. 7 up). 1972. 15.00 (0-910390-17-7) Auto Bk.

Carroll, Bob. The Major League Way to Play Baseball. (Illus.). 96p. (gr. 3 up). 1991. pap. 12.95 (0-671-73316-8, S&S BFYR); pap. 5.95 (0-671-70441-9, S&S BFYR) S&S Trade.
—Official Baseball Hall of Fame Sticker Book of Records. 1990. pap. 7.95 (0-671-69091-4, Little Simon) S&S Trade.

Carroll, David. Make Your Own Chess Set. Carroll, David, photos by. (Illus.). (gr. 5 up). 1975. (Pub. by Treehouse); pap. 2.95 (0-13-547768-7) P-H.

Carroll, Jeri. The Complete Color Book. (Illus.). 112p. (ps-3). 1991. 9.95 (0-86653-585-3, GP1300) Good Apple.
—Learning Centers for Little Kids. Foster, Tom, illus. 64p. (ps-2). 1983. wkbk. 7.95 (0-86653-103-3, GA 458) Good Apple.
—Let's Learn about Magnificent Me. Foster, Tom, illus. 64p. (ps-2). 1987. pap. 7.95 (0-86653-384-2, GA1010) Good Apple.

Carroll, Jeri & Dunlavy, Kathy. My Very First Books to Make & Read. 144p. (ps-2). 1990. 11.95 (0-86653-557-8, GA1163) Good Apple.

Carroll, Jeri & Kear, Dennis. Writing Fun with Phonics. (Illus.). 160p. (ps-2). 1992. wkbk. 12.95 (0-86653-686-8, 1420) Good Apple.

Carroll, Jeri & Wells, Candace. Founders. Foster, Tom, illus. 64p. (ps-3). 1986. wkbk. 7.95 (0-86653-345-1, GA 695) Good Apple.
—Inventors. Foster, Tom, illus. 64p. (gr. k-4). 1987. pap. 7.95 (0-86653-381-8, GA1006) Good Apple.

Carroll, Jeri & Wells, Candance. Pathfinders. Foster, Tom, illus. 64p. (gr. k-4). 1986. wkbk. 7.95 (0-86653-357-5, GA 696) Good Apple.

Carroll, Jeri, jt. auth. see Wells, Candace.

Carroll, Jeri, et al. Back to School in January. Smith, Bron, illus. 144p. (gr. k-5). 1989. wkbk. 11.95 (0-86653-470-9, GA1067) Good Apple.

Carroll, Jeri A. Let's Learn about Getting Along with Others. 64p. (ps-2). 1988. wkbk 7.95 (0-86653-439-3, GA1042) Good Apple.

Carroll, Jeri A. & Wells, Candace B. Learning about Fall & Winter Holidays. 112p. (ps-2). 1988. wkbk. 9.95 (0-86653-441-5, GA1048) Good Apple.

Carroll, Jeri A., jt. auth. see Wells, Candace B.

Carroll, Joan. The Black College Career Guide. 140p. (gr. 9-12). 1992. pap. 6.95 (1-881223-00-0) Zulema Ent.

Carroll, Kathleen S. One Red Rooster. Barbier, Suzette, illus. 32p. (ps). 1992. 13.45 (0-395-60195-9) HM.

Carroll, Lewis. Alice au Pays de Merveilles. (FRE.). (gr. 3-8). 7.95 (0-8288-6095-5, M5497) Fr & Eur.
—Alice au Pays des Merveilles. Tenniel, John, illus. (FRE.). 223p. (gr. 5-10). 1987. pap. 9.95 (2-07-033437-6) Schoenhof.
—Alice in Wonderland. 215p. 1981. Repr. PLB 15.95x (0-89966-345-1) Buccaneer Bks.
—Alice in Wonderland. 299p. 1981. Repr. PLB 12.95x (0-89967-019-9) Harmony Raine.
—Alice in Wonderland. Tenniel, John, illus. 160p. (gr. 3-6). 1988. pap. 2.95 (0-590-42035-6, Apple Classics) Scholastic Inc.
—Alice in Wonderland. 1930. 7.99 (0-517-05191-5) Outlet Bk Co.
—Alice in Wonderland. (Illus.). 192p. 1993. 4.95 (1-56138-246-9) Running Pr.
—Alice in Wonderland: A Classic Tale. Jose, Eduard, adapted by. Riehecky, Janet, tr. from SPA. Rovira, Francesc, illus. LC 88-35309. 32p. (gr. 1-4). 1988. PLB 19.95 (0-89565-467-9); PLB 13.95s.p. (0-685-56033-3) Childs World.
—Alice in Wonderland & Through the Looking Glass. Tenniel, John, illus. (gr. 4-6). 1963. 13.95 (0-448-06004-3, G&D) Putnam Pub Group.
—The Alice in Wonderland Pop-up. Thorne, Jenny, illus. LC 80-7615. 12p. (gr. k-4). 1980. pap. 6.95 (0-385-28038-6) Delacorte.
—Alice in Wonderland Pop-up Book. (ps-3). 1991. 14.00 (0-440-40540-8, YB) Dell.
—Alice's Adventures in Wonderland. Tenniel, John, illus. Bd. with Through the Looking Glass. LC 82-242973. (gr. 5 up). 1965. pap. 1.95 (0-8049-0079-5, CL-79) Airmont.
—Alice's Adventures in Wonderland. Todd, Justin, illus. LC 82-242973. 160p. (gr. 3 up). 1984. 3.99 (0-517-55591-3) Outlet Bk Co.
—Alice's Adventures in Wonderland. Tenniel, John, illus. LC 82-242973. (gr. 7 up). 1985. pap. 2.25 (0-14-035038-1, Puffin) Puffin Bks.
—Alice's Adventures in Wonderland. Hague, Michael, illus. LC 85-856. 128p. (gr. 4-6). 1985. 19.95 (0-8050-0212-X, Bks Young Read) H Holt & Co.
—Alice's Adventures in Wonderland. Hitchner, Earle, adapted by. Billin-Frye, Paige, illus. LC 89-33889. 48p. (gr. 3-6). 1990. PLB 12.89 (0-8167-1861-X); pap. text ed. 3.95 (0-8167-1862-8) Troll Assocs.
—Alice's Adventures in Wonderland. abr. ed. Blair, David, retold by. Bradley, John, illus. LC 91-58124. 56p. 1992. 9.98 (1-56138-100-4) Courage Bks.
—Alice's Adventures in Wonderland. Tenniel, John, illus. Glassman, Peter, intro. by. LC 91-31482. (Illus.). 208p. 1992. 15.00 (0-688-11087-8) Morrow Jr Bks.
—Alice's Adventures in Wonderland. Tenniel, John, illus. LC 93-571. 240p. 1993. Repr. of 1866 ed. 6.00 (1-56957-900-8) Shambhala Pubns.

—Alice's Adventures in Wonderland. Ross, Tony, illus. LC 93-72323. 128p. (gr. 2 up). 1994. SBE 16.95 (0-689-31864-2, Atheneum Child Bk) Macmillan Child Grp.
—Alice's Adventures in Wonderland & Through the Looking Glass. (RL 4). 1960. pap. 2.75 (0-451-52320-2, Sig Classics) NAL-Dutton.
—Alice's Adventures in Wonderland & Through the Looking Glass. Tenniel, John, illus. Cohen, Morton N., intro. by. (Illus.). 256p. 1984. pap. 2.75 (0-553-21345-8, Bantam Classics Spectra) Bantam.
—Alice's Adventures in Wonderland & Through the Looking Glass: And What Alice Found There. Tenniel, John, illus. 416p. 1992. pap. 3.99 (0-440-40743-5, Pub. by Yearling Classics) Dell.
—Alice's Adventures in Wonderland & Through the Looking Glass. Tenniel, John, illus. LC 92-53181. 336p. 1992. 12.95 (0-679-41795-8, Evrymans Lib Childs Class) Knopf.
—Alice's Adventures in Wonderland & Through the Looking-Glass, 2 bks. Tenniel, John, illus. 1993. Boxed Set. 29.95 (0-688-12050-4) Morrow Jr Bks.
—Alice's Adventures in Wonderland: The Ultimate Illustrated Edition. Edens, Cooper, compiled by. (ps up). 1989. 22.50 (0-553-05385-X) Bantam.
—Alice's Adventures under Ground: The Story That Became Alice in Wonderland. (Illus.). 112p. 1992. 17.95 (1-85145-471-3, Pub. by Pavilion UK) Trafalgar.
—Alice's Adventures Underground. Carroll, Lewis, illus. Gardner, Martin. (Illus.). 128p. (gr. 4-9). 1965. pap. 2.95 (0-486-21482-6) Dover.
—Aventures D'Alice au Pays des Merveilles. Bue, Henri, tr. from ENG. Tenniel, John, illus. Cohen, Morton N., intro. by. (FRE., Illus.). 196p. (gr. 4-8). 1972. pap. 4.95 (0-486-22836-3) Dover.
—Best of Lewis Carroll. 1992. 7.98 (0-89009-700-3) Bk Sales Inc.
—Humorous Verse of Lewis Carroll. (Illus.). 446p. (gr. 1 up). 1933. pap. 9.95 (0-486-20654-8) Dover.
—The Hunting of the Snark: A Musical Comedy. Jackson, R. Eugene & Ellis, David, eds. 36p. (Orig.). (gr. 2 up). 1987. pap. 3.00 (0-88680-273-3); piano & vocal score 10.00 (0-88680-274-1); royalty on application 60.00 (0-685-58254-X) I E Clark.
—Jabberwocky. LC 91-58968. (Illus.). 1992. 13.95 (1-56282-245-4); PLB 13.89 (1-56282-246-2) Disney Pr.
—Jabberwocky Pop Up Book. 1991. 8.95 (0-670-84085-8) Viking Child Bks.
—Lewis Carroll's Jabberwocky. reissue ed. Zalben, Jane B., illus. Humpty Dumpty, annotations by. (Illus.). 32p. 1992. PLB 14.95 (1-56397-080-5) Boyds Mills Pr.
—The Little Alice Editions: Alice's Adventures in Wonderland; Through the Looking-Glass. Tenniel, John, illus. 416p. (ps up). 1988. slipcased set 12.95 (0-8037-0589-1) Dial Bks Young.
—Reader's Digest Best Loved Books for Young Readers: Alice's Adventures in Wonderland & Through the Looking Glass. Ogburn, Jackie, ed. Tenniel, John, illus. 192p. (gr. 4-12). 1989. 3.99 (0-945260-21-0) Choice Pub NY.
—A Tangled Tale. Frost, Arthur B., illus. LC 87-50437. 208p. (gr. 5-12). 1987. pap. 7.95 (0-940561-06-9) White Rose Pr.
—Through the Looking Glass. 176p. (gr. 7 up). 1985. pap. 2.99 (0-14-035039-X, Puffin) Puffin Bks.
—Through the Looking Glass. Tenniel, John, illus. 224p. 1977. Repr. 14.95 (0-312-80374-5) St Martin.
—Through the Looking-Glass. abr. ed. Ross, Tony, illus. 128p. (gr. 4-7). 1993. Repr. of 1993 ed. SBE 16.95 (0-689-31863-4, Atheneum Child Bk) Macmillan Child Grp.
—Through the Looking Glass, & What Alice Found There. Tenniel, John, illus. LC 84-60960. 184p. (gr. 2 up). 1984. Repr. of 1941 ed. 6.95 (0-88088-991-8, 889918) Peter Pauper.
—Through the Looking Glass & What Alice Found There. 1990. 12.99 (0-517-03346-1) Outlet Bk Co.
—Through the Looking Glass & What Alice Found There. (Illus.). 127p. 1991. 7.99 (0-517-00233-7) Outlet Bk Co.
—Through the Looking Glass & What Alice Found There. Tenniel, John, illus. LC 92-20642. 240p. (gr. 1 up). 1993. 15.00 (0-688-12049-0) Morrow Jr Bks.
—Through the Looking-Glass & What Alice Found There (California-Pennyroyal Edition) Goodacres, Selwyn H. & Kincaid, James R.intro. by. Incl. Deluxe Edition. 198p. LC 83-47520. 198p. (gr. 8 up). 1983. 35.00 (0-520-05039-8) U CA Pr.
—The Walrus & the Carpenter. Zalben, Jane B., illus. LC 85-7591. 32p. (gr. 2-4). 1986. 13.95 (0-8050-0071-2, Bks Young Read) H Holt & Co.
—The Walrus & the Carpenter. Zalben, Jane B., illus. LC 85-7591. 32p. (gr. 2-4). 1990. pap. 4.95 (0-8050-1482-9, Owlet BYR) H Holt & Co.

Carroll, Lewis & Tenniel, Sir John. Alice's Adventures in Wonderland. LC 82-242973. (Illus.). (gr. 5 up). 1977. 14.95 (0-312-01821-5) St Martin.

Carroll, Lewis see Dodgson, Charles, pseud.

Carroll, Lewis, jt. auth. see Lear, Edward.

Carroll, Louann. Journeys: The Adventures of Leaf. LC 92-13485. (Illus.). (gr. 4). 1992. pap. 9.95 (1-880090-03-1) Galde Pr.

Carroll, Merle T. This Is Alabama. 3rd, rev. & updated ed. (Illus.). 336p. (gr. 4). 1993. Repr. of 1975 ed. text ed. 14.50 (0-9632262-0-7) J Y Carroll.

Carroll, Susan. How Big Is a Brachiosaurus? Marvin, Frederic, illus. 32p. (ps-2). 1986. pap. 1.95 (*0-448-19077-X*, G&D) Putnam Pub Group.

Carroll, Teresa P. Mommy Breastfeeds Our Baby. Gray, Linda, illus. (Orig.). (ps) 1990. pap. 4.95 (*0-9626614-0-6*) NuBaby AL.

Carrozzi, Craig J. Wedding of the Waters. LC 88-60526. (Illus.). 396p. (Orig.). 1988. pap. 10.95 (*0-9620286-0-6*) Suthrn Trails Pub.

Carruth, Gordon, ed. The Young Reader's Companion. LC 93-6662. 681p. (gr. 4 up). 1993. 39.95 (*0-8352-2765-0*) Bowker.

Carruth, Jane. Little Treasury of Alice in Wonderland. 1992. 5.99 (*0-517-06720-X*) Outlet Bk Co.
—Little Treasury of Peter Pan. 1992. 5.99 (*0-517-06718-8*) Outlet Bk Co.
—My Giant Treasury of Fairy Tales. 1988. 9.98 (*0-671-09118-2*) S&S Trade.

Carryl, Charles. The Walloping Window Blind. Rand, Ted, illus. 32p. (ps-3). 1992. 14.95 (*1-55970-154-4*) Arcade Pub Inc.

Carryl, Charles E. The Walloping Window-Blind. LaMarche, Jim, illus. LC 92-40338. (gr. k-5). 1993. write for info. (*0-688-12517-4*); lib. bdg. write for info. (*0-688-12518-2*) Lothrop.

Carser, S. X. Motocross Cycles. (Illus.). 48p. (gr. 3-6). 1992. PLB 12.95 (*1-56065-069-9*) Capstone Pr.

Carson. Make the Team: Swimming & Diving. 1991. 13. 95 (*0-316-13027-3*) Little.

Carson, Ben. Ben Carson. Murphy, Cecil & Asseng, Nathancontrib. by. 112p. (gr. 3-9). 1992. pap. 4.99 (*0-310-58641-0*, Pub. by Youth Spec) Zondervan.

Carson, Carol D., jt. auth. see Marzollo, Jean.

Carson, Charles. Make the Team: Swimming & Diving. (gr. 4-7). 1991. pap. 5.95 (*0-316-13028-1*, Spts Illus Kids) Little.

Carson, Gordon, et al, eds. see White, Gregory.

Carson, Jane. Rex & Rita Saurus' Big Surprise. (ps-3). 1990. pap. 2.50 (*0-590-43292-3*) Scholastic Inc.

Carson, Jo. Pulling My Leg. Downing, Julie, illus. LC 89-70978. 32p. (ps-2). 1990. 14.95 (*0-531-05817-4*); PLB 14.99 (*0-531-08417-5*) Orchard Bks Watts.
—Pulling My Leg. Downing, Julie, illus. LC 89-70978. 32p. (ps-2). 1994. pap. 5.95 (*0-531-07046-8*) Orchard Bks Watts.
—Stories I Ain't Told Nobody Yet: Selections from the People Pieces. LC 88-19821. 96p. (gr. 7 up). 1989. 13. 95 (*0-531-05808-5*); PLB 13.99 (*0-531-08408-6*) Orchard Bks Watts.
—You Hold Me & I'll Hold You. Cannon, Annie, illus. LC 91-16370. 32p. (ps-2). 1992. 14.95 (*0-531-05895-6*); lib. bdg. 14.99 (*0-531-08495-7*) Orchard Bks Watts.

Carson, Mary S. The Scientific Kid: Projects, Experiments, Adventures. LC 88-45551. 80p. (Orig.). 1989. pap. 14.00 (*0-06-096316-6*, PL 6316, PL) HarpC.

Carson, Rob. The Living Mountain: Mount St. Helens. Hoffmann, Duane, illus. 84p. (Orig.). (gr. k-8). 1992. pap. 10.95 (*0-9623072-9-7*) S Ink WA.

Carson, Robert. Hernando de Soto: Expedition to the Mississippi River. LC 91-12665. 128p. (gr. 3 up). 1991. PLB 26.60 (*0-516-03065-5*) Childrens.
—Mississippi. LC 88-11747. (Illus.). 144p. (gr. 4 up). 1988. PLB 26.60 (*0-516-00470-0*) Childrens.
—Mississippi. 193p. 1993. text ed. 15.40 (*1-56956-167-2*) W A T Braille.

Carson, S. L. Maximilien Robespierre. Schlesinger, Arthur M., Jr., intro. by. (Illus.). 112p. (gr. 5 up). 1988. lib. bdg. 17.95 (*0-87754-549-9*) Chelsea Hse.

Carson-Finnerty, LaVonne. Environmental Health. Garell, Dale C. & Snyder, Solomon H., eds. (Illus.). (gr. 6-12). 1990. PLB 19.95 (*0-7910-0082-6*, Am Art Analog) Chelsea Hse.

Carstensen, Karol. BMX Bikes. 48p. (gr. 3-4). 1991. PLB 11.95 (*1-56065-076-1*) Capstone Pr.

Carswell, Evelyn & Bisignano, Judy. Living. Tom, Darcy, illus. 64p. (gr. 3-8). 1985. wkbk. 7.95 (*0-86653-332-X*, GA 679) Good Apple.

Carter, Adam. A Day in the Life of a Medical Detective. Duncan, Bob, illus. LC 84-8851. 32p. (gr. 4-8). 1985. PLB 11.79 (*0-8167-0097-4*); pap. text ed. 2.95 (*0-8167-0098-2*) Troll Assocs.

Carter, Alden R. The American Revolution: At the Forge of Liberty. LC 88-5624. (Illus.). 96p. (gr. 6 up). 1988. PLB 10.90 (*0-531-10569-5*) Watts.
—The American Revolution: Colonies in Revolt. Kline, M., ed. LC 88-5624. (Illus.). 96p. (gr. 6 up). 1988. PLB 10.90 (*0-531-10576-8*) Watts.
—The American Revolution: The Darkest Hours. Kline, M., ed. LC 88-5626. (Illus.). 96p. (gr. 6 up). 1988. PLB 10.90 (*0-531-10578-4*) Watts.
—The American Revolution: War for Independence. LC 92-5586. (Illus.). 64p. (gr. 5-8). 1992. PLB 12.90 (*0-531-20082-5*) Watts.
—The American Revolution: War for Independence. (Illus.). 64p. (gr. 5-8). 1993. pap. 5.95 (*0-531-15652-4*) Watts.
—Battle of the Ironclads: The Monitor & the Merrimack. LC 93-417. (Illus.). 64p. (gr. 4-6). 1993. PLB 12.90 (*0-531-20091-4*) Watts.
—China Past - China Future. LC 93-13537. 1994. write for info. (*0-531-11161-X*) Watts.
—The Civil War: American Tragedy. (Illus.). 64p. (gr. 5-8). 1992. PLB 12.90 (*0-531-20039-6*) Watts.
—The Civil War: American Tragedy. (Illus.). 64p. (gr. 5-8). 1993. pap. 5.95 (*0-531-15653-2*) Watts.

—The Colonial Wars: Clashes in the Wilderness. Clipson, Bill, illus. LC 92-9906. 64p. (gr. 5-8). 1992. PLB 12.90 (*0-531-20079-5*) Watts.
—The Colonial Wars: Clashes in the Wilderness. (Illus.). 64p. (gr. 5-8). 1993. pap. 5.95 (*0-531-15654-0*) Watts.
—Last Stand at the Alamo. LC 89-22688. (ps-3). 1990. PLB 12.90 (*0-531-10888-0*) Watts.
—The Mexican War: Manifest Destiny. LC 92-10334. (Illus.). 64p. (gr. 5-8). 1992. PLB 12.90 (*0-531-20081-7*) Watts.
—The Mexican War: Manifest Destiny. (Illus.). 64p. (gr. 5-8). 1993. pap. 5.95 (*0-531-15656-7*) Watts.
—Radio: From Marconi to the Space Age. LC 86-23335. (Illus.). 96p. (gr. 4-9). 1987. PLB 10.90 (*0-531-10310-2*) Watts.
—Robodad. 144p. 1990. 14.95 (*0-399-22191-3*, Putnam) Putnam Pub Group.
—The Shoshoni. LC 89-31102. (Illus.). 64p. (gr. 3-5). 1989. PLB 12.90 (*0-531-10753-1*) Watts.
—The Shoshoni. (Illus.). 64p. (gr. 3 up). 1991. pap. 5.95 (*0-531-15605-2*) Watts.
—The Spanish-American War: Imperial Ambitions. (Illus.). 64p. (gr. 5-8). 1992. PLB 12.90 (*0-531-20078-7*) Watts.
—The Spanish-American War: Imperial Ambitions. (Illus.). 64p. (gr. 5-8). 1993. pap. 5.95 (*0-531-15657-5*) Watts.
—Up Country. 224p. (gr. 7 up). 1989. 15.95 (*0-399-21583-2*, Putnam) Putnam Pub Group.
—Up Country. 256p. 1991. pap. 2.95 (*0-590-43638-4*, Point) Scholastic Inc.
—The War of Eighteen Twelve: Second Fight for Independence. LC 92-11438. (Illus.). 64p. (gr. 5-8). 1992. PLB 12.90 (*0-531-20080-9*) Watts.
—The War of 1812: Second Fight for Independence. (Illus.). 64p. (gr. 5-8). 1993. pap. 5.95 (*0-531-15659-1*) Watts.
—Wart, Son of Toad. 1986. pap. 2.50 (*0-425-08885-5*) Berkley Pub.

Carter, Angela. Sleeping Beauty: And Other Favourite Fairy Tales. 1991. pap. 10.70 (*0-395-60727-2*) HM.

Carter, Ann, compiled by. Birds, Beasts, & Fishes: A Selection of Animal Poems. Cartwright, Reg, illus. Carter, Ann, intros. by. LC 90-21493. (Illus.). 64p. (ps up). 1993. SBE 16.95 (*0-02-717776-9*, Macmillan Child Bk) Macmillan Child Grp.

Carter, Anne. The Fisherwoman. Brierley, Louise, illus. 32p. (gr. 1-4). 1991. 14.95 (*0-688-09872-X*); PLB 14. 88 (*0-688-09873-8*) Lothrop.

Carter, Anne, retold by see Grimm, Jacob & Grimm, Wilhelm K.

Carter, Brian. State Government in Iowa. 5th ed. Institute of Public Affairs Staff, ed. (Illus.). (gr. 10). 1990. pap. text ed. 7.00 (*0-317-02886-3*) U Iowa IPA.

Carter, Darleen. Uh-Oh Not Me. LC 90-71360. (Illus.). 44p. (gr. k-3). 1991. 5.95 (*1-55523-398-8*) Winston-Derek.

Carter, David. Baby Bug Colors. (gr. 3 up). 1993. pap. 4.95 (*0-671-86875-6*, Little Simon) S&S Trade.
—Baby Bug Counting. (Illus.). (ps-6). 1993. pap. 4.95 (*0-671-86876-4*, Little Simon) S&S Trade.
—Baby Bug In & Out. (gr. 3 up). 1993. pap. 4.95 (*0-671-86630-3*, Little Simon) S&S Trade.
—Baby Bug Opposites. (Illus.). (ps-6). 1993. pap. 4.95 (*0-671-86877-2*, Little Simon) S&S Trade.
—George Santayana. (Illus.). (gr. 5 up). 1992. lib. bdg. 17.95 (*0-7910-1254-9*) Chelsea Hse.
—Over in the Meadow. (Illus.). 32p. 1992. 13.95 (*0-590-44498-0*, Scholastic Hardcover) Scholastic Inc.

Carter, David, jt. auth. see Carter, Noelle.

Carter, David A. How Many Bugs in a Box? (ps-1). 1988. pap. 12.95 (*0-671-64965-5*, S&S BFYR) S&S Trade.
—In a Dark, Dark Wood: An Old Tale with a New Twist. (Illus.). 28p. (ps-3). 1991. pap. 10.95 casebound, pop-up (*0-671-74134-9*, S&S BFYR) S&S Trade.
—Jingle Bugs. (ps). 1992. pap. 16.00 (*0-671-72924-1*, S&S BFYR) S&S Trade.
—What's in My Pocket? A Pop-up & Peek-in Book. Carter, David A., illus. 10p. (ps-k). 1989. 8.95 (*0-399-21685-5*, Putnam) Putnam Pub Group.

Carter, Debby L., illus. Help Save Us Stickerbooks of Wild Animals, Bks. 1 & 2. 16p. (ps-2). 1989. Bk. 1. 4.95 (*0-525-44460-2*, DCB); Bk. 2. pap. 4.95 (*0-525-44461-0*, DCB) Dutton Child Bks.

Carter, Dorothy S. His Majesty, Queen Hatshepsut. Chessare, Michele, illus. LC 85-45855. 256p. (gr. 5 up). 1987. (Lipp Jr Bks) PLB 13.89 (*0-397-32179-1*, Lipp Jr Bks) HarpC Child Bks.

Carter, Eneida & Mikalac, Miriam. Break Dance: The Free & Easy Way! Forman, Jan A., illus. 32p. (gr. 7 up). 1984. pap. 9.95 (*0-916391-00-0*) Free & Easy Pubns.

Carter, Hodding. The Commandos of World War II. LC 80-21142. (Illus.). 160p. (gr. 5-9). 1981. 4.95 (*0-394-84735-0*) Random Bks Yng Read.

Carter, Jimmy. Talking Peace. (Illus.). 160p. (gr. 7 up). 1993. 16.99 (*0-525-44959-0*, DCB) Dutton Child Bks.

Carter, Katharine J. Oceans. LC 81-17093. (Illus.). 48p. (gr. k-4). 1982. PLB 15.27 (*0-516-01639-3*); pap. 4.95 (*0-516-41639-1*) Childrens.

Carter, Katherine. Ships & Seaports. LC 82-4463. (Illus.). (gr. k-4). 1982. pap. 4.95 (*0-516-41656-1*) Childrens.

Carter, Kathryn T. At the Battle of San Jacinto: With Rip Cavitt. (Illus.). 96p. (gr. 4-7). 1987. 9.95 (*0-89015-374-4*, Pub. by Panda Bks) Eakin-Sunbelt.

Carter, Kit, jt. auth. see Clark, I. E.

Carter, Laurel S., jt. auth. see D'Amato, Janet P.

Carter, Lin, ed. Weird Tales, No. 3. (gr. 7 up). 1981. pap. 2.50 (*0-89083-803-8*) Zebra.

Carter, Margaret. The Young Child's Busy Book: Of Playing, Learning, Stories & Rhymes. Maclean, Colin & Maclean, Moira, illus. LC 92-53094. 96p. (ps-k). 1992. 14.95 (*1-85697-822-2*) Kingfisher Bks.

Carter, Margaret, retold by. Beauty & the Beast & Other Stories. Offen, Hilda, illus. LC 93-5772. 1994. 3.95 (*1-85697-967-9*) Kingfisher Bks.
—Cinderella & Other Stories. Offen, Hilda, illus. LC 93-5770. 1994. 3.95 (*1-85697-968-7*) Kingfisher Bks.
—Goldilocks & Other Stories. Offen, HIlda, illus. LC 93-5771. 1994. 3.95 (*1-85697-969-5*) Kingfisher Bks.
—Little Red Riding Hood & Other Stories. Offen, Hilda, illus. LC 93-5768. 1994. 3.95 (*1-85697-970-9*) Kingfisher Bks.
—Sleeping Beauty & Other Stories. Offen, Hilda, illus. LC 93-5769. 1994. 3.95 (*1-85697-971-7*) Kingfisher Bks.
—Snow White & Other Stories. Offen, HIlda, illus. LC 93-5767. 1994. 3.95 (*1-85697-972-5*) Kingfisher Bks.
—The Three Little Pigs & Other Stories. Offen, Hilda, illus. LC 93-11741. 1994. 3.95 (*1-85697-973-3*) Kingfisher Bks.
—The Ugly Duckling & Other Stories. Offen, Hilda, illus. LC 93-5766. 1994. 3.95 (*1-85697-974-1*) Kingfisher Bks.

Carter, Marilyn. Peluk, an Eskimo Boy. (Illus.). 44p. (gr. 3 up). pap. text ed. 5.95 (*0-944677-04-5*) Aladdin Pub.

Carter, Mary. Reading for Comprehension Skills. (Illus.). (gr. 2-7). 1982. wkbk. 4.50 (*0-89525-177-9*) Ed Activities.

Carter, Mary C., ed. see Sandling, R. Harris.

Carter, Michael C., jt. auth. see Jackson, Bobby L.

Carter, Michelle W. The Bookworm That Went to College. (gr. k-6). 1992. 7.95 (*0-8062-4419-4*) Carlton.

Carter, Noelle. I'm a Little Mouse. Carter, David, illus. LC 90-80318. 12p. (ps-2). 1991. 10.95 (*0-8050-1420-9*, Bks Young Read) H Holt & Co.
—My House. (Illus.). 6p. (ps-1). 1991. 7.95 (*0-670-83922-1*) Viking Child Bks.
—My Pet. (Illus.). (ps-1). 1991. 7.95 (*0-670-83923-X*) Viking Child Bks.
—Peek-a-Boo, Little Mouse. Carter, David, illus. LC 91-78193. 12p. 1992. 10.95 (*0-8050-2253-8*, Bks Young Read) H Holt & Co.
—Where's My Fuzzy Blanket? 14p. 1991. pap. 6.95 (*0-590-44466-2*) Scholastic Inc.
—Where's My Squishy Ball? A Lift & Touch Book. Carter, Noelle, illus. 14p. (ps). 1993. 6.95 (*0-590-47385-9*, Cartwheel) Scholastic Inc.

Carter, Noelle & Carter, David. Merry Christmas, Little Mouse: A Lift-the-Flap, Scratch-the-Scent Book. Carter, David, illus. 12p. (ps). 1993. PLB 11.95 (*0-8050-2712-2*, Bks Young Read) H Holt & Co.

Carter, Patricia. Illuminated Calligraphy: Borders & Letters. (Illus.). 64p. (Orig.). 1992. pap. 15.95 (*0-85532-642-5*, Pub. by Search Pr UK) A Schwartz & Co.

Carter, Penny. A New House for the Morrisons. Carter, Penny, illus. LC 93-12463. 32p. (ps-1). 1993. 12.99 (*0-670-84567-1*) Viking Child Bks.

Carter, Peter. Borderlands. 1993. pap. 4.95 (*0-374-40883-1*) FS&G.
—Bury the Dead. LC 85-45995. 374p. (gr. 6 up). 1987. 17.00 (*0-374-31011-4*) FS&G.
—The Hunted. 1994. 17.00 (*0-374-33520-6*) FS&G.

Carter, Peter, jt. auth. see Paul, Korky.

Carter, Peter, ed. & tr. see Grimm, Jacob & Grimm, Wilhelm K.

Carter, Peter, tr. see Harranth, Wolf.

Carter, Philip & Russell, Ken, eds. Power Puzzles. LC 92-43427. (Illus.). 128p. (gr. 10-12). 1993. pap. 5.95 (*0-8069-0381-3*) Sterling.

Carter, Philip J. & Russell, Ken. Children's Challenging Brain Teasers. (Illus.). 96p. (gr. 6-12). 1991. pap. 4.95 (*0-7063-6944-0*, Pub. by Ward Lock UK) Sterling.

Carter, Philip J. & Russell, Ken A. Baffling Brain Teasers. (Illus.). 128p. (gr. 10-12). 1992. pap. 4.95 (*0-7063-7090-2*, Pub. by Ward Lock UK) Sterling.
—Beat the IQ Challenge. (Illus.). 128p. (gr. 10-12). 1993. pap. 4.95 (*0-7063-7128-3*, Pub. by Ward Lock UK) Sterling.
—Brain Busters. (Illus.). 368p. (gr. 10-12). 1992. pap. 8.95 (*0-7063-7097-X*, Pub. by Ward Lock UK) Sterling.

Carter, Polly. Bridge Book. LC 91-4464. (ps-3). 1992. pap. 9.95 (*0-671-77741-6*, S&S BFYR) S&S Trade.
—Harriet Tubman. Brook, Bonnie, ed. Pinkney, Brian, illus. 32p. (gr. k-2). 1990. 6.95 (*0-671-69115-5*); PLB 10.98 (*0-671-69109-0*) Silver Pr.

Carter, Rosalyn see Sawyer, Kem K.

Carter, Rosalynn see Sawyer, Kem K.

Carter, Russell G. A Patriot Lad of Old Cape Cod. Pitz, Henry & Sousa, Joseph, illus. LC 75-5092. 224p. (gr. 6-8). 1975. 4.95 (*0-88492-007-0*); pap. 1.95 (*0-88492-008-9*) W S Sullwold.

Carter, Sharon. Careers in Aviation. Rosen, Ruth, ed. (gr. 7-12). 1989. PLB 13.95 (*0-8239-0965-4*) Rosen Group.
—Coping Through Friendship. Rosen, Roger, ed. (gr. 7 up). 1988. PLB 13.95 (*0-8239-0789-9*) Rosen Group.

Carter, Sharon & Monnig, Judith. Coping with a Hospital Stay. Rosen, Ruth, ed. 128p. (gr. 7 up). 1987. PLB 13.95 (*0-8239-0682-5*) Rosen Group.

Carter, Sharon, jt. auth. see Clayton, Lawrence.

Carter, Sharon, jt. auth. see Wheeler, Joan.

Carter, Sharon, et al. Coping with Medical Emergencies. rev. ed. 121p. (gr. 7-12). 1988. PLB 13.95 (*0-8239-0782-1*) Rosen Group.

Carter, Tonya R., jt. auth. see Thompson, Paul B.

Cartier, Randi, ed. see Reed, Gary.

Cartier, Randi, ed. see Wujcik, Erick.

Cartlidge, Michelle. Baby Mice at Home. Cartlidge, Michelle, illus. 24p. (ps). 1992. bds. 2.95 (*0-525-44840-3*, DCB) Dutton Child Bks.

—Bear in the Forest. Cartlidge, Michelle, illus. 12p. (ps). 1991. bds. 3.50 (*0-525-44674-5*, DCB) Dutton Child Bks.

—Bears on the Go. Cartlidge, Michelle, illus. 24p. (ps). 1992. bds. 2.95 (*0-525-44841-1*, DCB) Dutton Child Bks.

—Bunny's Birthday. Cartlidge, Michelle, illus. 24p. (ps). 1992. bds. 2.95 (*0-525-44843-8*, DCB) Dutton Child Bks.

—Doggy Days. Cartlidge, Michelle, illus. 24p. (ps). 1992. bds. 2.95 (*0-525-44844-6*, DCB) Dutton Child Bks.

—Duck in the Pond. Cartlidge, Michelle, illus. 12p. (ps). 1991. bds. 3.50 (*0-525-44675-3*, DCB) Dutton Child Bks.

—Elephant in the Jungle. Cartlidge, Michelle, illus. 12p. (ps). 1991. bds. 3.50 (*0-525-44676-1*, DCB) Dutton Child Bks.

—Good Night, Teddy. Cartlidge, Michelle, illus. LC 91-58732. 24p. (ps). 1992. 5.95 (*1-56402-076-2*) Candlewick Pr.

—A House for Lily Mouse. (gr. 1-5). 1987. 10.95 (*0-13-395849-3*) P-H.

—Mouse House. (Illus.). 24p. (ps). 1990. 4.95 (*0-525-44638-9*, DCB) Dutton Child Bks.

—Mouse in the House. Cartlidge, Michelle, illus. 12p. (ps). 1991. bds. 3.50 (*0-525-44678-8*, DCB) Dutton Child Bks.

—Mouse Letters. Cartlidge, Michelle, illus. 24p. (ps). 1993. 4.99 (*0-525-45089-0*, DCB) Dutton Child Bks.

—Mouse Theater. (Illus.). 22p. (ps). 1992. 4.95 (*0-525-44980-9*, DCB) Dutton Child Bks.

—Mouse Time. Cartlidge, Michelle, illus. 24p. (ps). 1991. 3.95 (*0-525-44766-0*, DCB) Dutton Child Bks.

—The Mouse Wedding: A Pres-out Model Book. (Illus.). 32p. 1993. pap. 8.95 (*0-8362-4504-0*) Andrews & McMeel.

—Mouse's Christmas House: A Press-out Model House. (Illus.). 32p. (Orig.). 1992. pap. 9.95 (*0-8362-4500-8*) Andrews & McMeel.

—Teddy's Friends. Cartlidge, Michelle, illus. LC 91-58758. 24p. (ps). 1992. 5.95 (*1-56402-077-0*) Candlewick Pr.

Cartlidge, Michelle & Cartlidge, Michelle. A Mouse's Diary. (Illus.). 32p. (ps-2). 1994. 4.50 (*0-525-45195-1*, DCB) Dutton Child Bks.

Cartwright & Rawson. Gnomes, Goblins & Fairies. (gr. k-4). 1980. (Usborne-Hayes); pap. 4.50 (*0-86020-384-0*) EDC.

—Princes & Princesses. (gr. k-4). 1980. (Usborne-Hayes); pap. 3.95 (*0-86020-382-4*) EDC.

—Princes, Wizards & Gnomes. (gr. k-4). 1980. 10.95 (*0-86020-508-8*, Usborne-Hayes) EDC.

—Wizards. (gr. k-4). 1980. (Usborne-Hayes); pap. 4.50 (*0-86020-380-8*) EDC.

Cartwright, Ann. The Winter Hedgehog. Cartwright, Reg, illus. LC 90-5593. 32p. (ps-3). 1990. SBE 12.95 (*0-02-717775-0*, Macmillan Child Bk) Macmillan Child Grp.

Cartwright, Ann & Cartwright, Reg. Proud & Fearless Lion. 32p. (ps-1). 1987. 8.95 (*0-8120-5800-3*) Barron.

Cartwright, Hal V. Granny Boy & the Puny Warbler. Matheson, Hedda, illus. LC 92-71096. 48p. (Orig.). (gr. 4). 1992. pap. 8.50 (*0-923687-16-5*) Celo Valley Bks.

Cartwright, John. Inside Harry's Brain Maze Book. 1989. pap. 1.50 (*0-8167-1222-0*) Troll Assocs.

—More Amazing Dinosaurs Maze Book. 32p. 1989. pap. 1.50 (*0-8167-1221-2*) Troll Assocs.

—Those Amazing Dinosaur Mazes. 1989. pap. 1.50 (*0-8167-1220-4*) Troll Assocs.

Cartwright, Pauline. All Creatures. LC 90-10021. (Illus.). 16p. (gr. 1-4). 1990. PLB 14.64 (*0-8114-2695-5*) Raintree Steck-V.

—Arthur & the Dragon. LC 90-10091. (Illus.). 32p. (gr. 1-4). 1990. PLB 17.28 (*0-8114-2689-0*) Raintree Steck-V.

—Escape from Zarcay. Campbell, Caroline, illus. LC 90-10075. 32p. (gr. 2-5). 1990. PLB 17.28 (*0-8114-2694-7*) Raintree Steck-V.

—Taking Our Photo. Strahan, Heather, illus. LC 92-31950. 1993. 3.75 (*0-383-03595-3*) SRA Schl Grp.

Cartwright, Reg, jt. auth. see Cartwright, Ann.

Cartwright, S. One, Two, Three. (Illus.). 32p. 1992. (Usborne); pap. 8.95 (*0-7460-0726-4*, Usborne) EDC.

Cartwright, S. & Ashman, I. Apple Tree Farm: Press Out Model. Cartwright, S., illus. 32p. 1991. pap. 8.95 (*0-7460-0664-0*, Usborne) EDC.

Cartwright, S., jt. auth. see Amery, H.

Cartwright, S., jt. auth. see Tyler, J.

Cartwright, Stephen. Find the Bird. Cartwright, Stephen, illus. Zeff, C. (Illus.). 12p. (ps). 1984. bds. 3.50 (*0-86020-719-6*, Pub. by Usborne) EDC.

—Find the Duck. Cartwright, Stephen, illus. Zeff, C. (Illus.). 12p. (ps). 1984. bds. 3.50 (*0-86020-714-5*, Pub. by Usborne) EDC.

—Find the Kitten. Cartwright, Stephen, illus. Zeff, C. (Illus.). 12p. (ps). 1984. bds. 3.50 (*0-86020-718-8*, Pub. by Usborne) EDC.

—Find the Piglet. Cartwright, Stephen, illus. Zeff, C. (Illus.). 12p. (ps). 1984. bds. 3.50 (*0-86020-716-1*, Pub. by Usborne) EDC.

—Find the Puppy. Cartwright, Stephen, illus. Zeff, C. (Illus.). 12p. (ps). 1984. bds. 3.50 (*0-86020-717-X*, Pub. by Usborne) EDC.

—Find the Teddy. Cartwright, Stephen, illus. Zeff, C. (Illus.). 12p. (ps). 1984. bds. 3.50 (*0-86020-715-3*, Pub. by Usborne) EDC.

Cartwright, Stephen, jt. auth. see Amery, Heather.

Cartwright, Stephen, jt. auth. see Civardi, Anne.

Cartwright, Stephen, illus. Going to School. 16p. (ps up). 1986. pap. 3.95 (*0-7460-1269-1*) EDC.

—Moving House. 16p. (ps up). 1986. PLB write for info.; pap. 3.95 (*0-685-58332-5*) EDC.

—The New Baby. 16p. (ps up). 1986. 3.95 (*0-86020-966-0*) EDC.

Carty, Margaret F. Christmas in Vermont: Three Stories. Langley, Marilynn, illus. LC 83-62750. 48p. (Orig.). (gr. 5 up). 1983. pap. 2.95 (*0-933050-21-6*) New Eng Pr VT.

Caruana, Claudia M. The Abortion Debate. LC 92-22417. (Illus.). 64p. (gr. 5-8). 1992. PLB 15.90 (*1-56294-311-1*) Millbrook Pr.

Caruso, Joseph G. Adam's Diary. (Illus.). 26p. (Orig.). (gr. k up). 1989. pap. 3.00 (*0-88680-313-6*); Piano-Vocal Score 15.00 (*0-88680-314-4*); royalty on application 60.00 (*0-685-58566-2*) I E Clark.

—The Phantom of the Old Opera House. 48p. (gr. 4 up). 1982. pap. 3.50 (*0-88680-153-2*); royalty on application 35.00 (*0-317-03574-6*) I E Clark.

—Tom Sawyer, Detective. 34p. (Orig.). (gr. 2 up). 1991. pap. 3.00 (*0-88680-358-6*); royalty on application 35. 00 (*0-685-59132-8*) I E Clark.

Caruso, Lenore, ed. see Pilurs, David B.

Caruso, Lenore R., ed. see Pilurs, David B.

Caruso, Sara, ed. see Pilurs, David B.

Caruso, Sara L., ed. see Pilurs, David B.

Carvin, Ruth. Color It Christmas: With Three Christmas Posters. Carvin, Ruth, illus. 8p. (gr. 3 up). 1987. write for info. Carvin Pub.

—A Visit to New Orleans Coloring Book. Dolobowsky, Mena, illus. 28p. (gr. k-4). 1986. 3.50 (*0-9616390-0-8*) Carvin Pub.

—A Visit to New Orleans: With Pictures to Color & Verses to Read. rev. ed. Dolobowsky, Mena, illus. 32p. (gr. k-4). 1988. coloring bk. 3.50 (*0-9616390-2-4*) Carvin Pub.

Carwardine, Mark. Animals in the Cold. Young, Richard G., ed. Channell, Jim, illus. LC 89-32827. 45p. (gr. 3-5). 1989. PLB 14.60 (*0-944483-26-7*) Garrett Ed Corp.

—Animals on the Move. Young, Richard G., ed. Francis, John, illus. LC 89-32809. 45p. (gr. 3-5). 1989. PLB 14. 60 (*0-944483-27-5*) Garrett Ed Corp.

—Monkeys & Apes. Young, Richard G., ed. Camm, Martin, illus. LC 89-32808. 45p. (gr. 3-5). 1989. PLB 14.60 (*0-944483-28-3*) Garrett Ed Corp.

—Nibblers & Gnawers. Young, Richard G., ed. Twinney, Dick, illus. LC 89-32807. 45p. (gr. 3-5). 1989. PLB 14.60 (*0-944483-29-1*) Garrett Ed Corp.

—Night Animals. Young, Richard G., ed. Camm, Martin, illus. LC 89-7880. 45p. (gr. 3-5). 1989. PLB 14.60 (*0-944483-30-5*) Garrett Ed Corp.

—Water Animals. Young, Richard G., ed. Camm, Martin, illus. LC 89-7879. 45p. (gr. 3-5). 1989. PLB 14.60 (*0-944483-31-3*) Garrett Ed Corp.

—Whales, Dolphins, & Porpoises. LC 92-7624. (Illus.). 64p. (gr. 3 up). 1992. 11.95 (*1-56458-144-6*) Dorling Kindersley.

Carwell, Hattie. Blacks in Science: Astrophysicist to Zoologist. Earls, Julian, intro. by. (Illus.). 96p. (gr. 8 up). 1988. pap. 7.00 (*0-682-48911-5*); 10.00 (*0-685-22950-5*) H Carwell.

Cary, Barbara. Meet Abraham Lincoln. Marchesi, Stephen, illus. LC 88-19066. 72p. (gr. 2-4). 1989. PLB 6.99 (*0-394-91966-1*); pap. 2.99 (*0-394-81966-7*) Random Bks Yng Read.

Cary, Mara. Basic Baskets. LC 75-14222. 127p. 1975. HM.

Casad, Mary B. Bluebonnet at Dinosaur Valley State Park. Vinvent, Benjamin, illus. LC 90-7338. 32p. (gr. k-3). 1990. 13.95 (*0-88289-776-4*) Pelican.

—Bluebonnet at the Alamo. (Illus.). 40p. (gr. 4-7). 1984. 11.95 (*0-89015-445-7*, Pub. by Panda Bks) Eakin-Sunbelt.

—Bluebonnet at the State Fair. Binder, Pat, illus. 40p. (gr. 2-4). 1985. 11.95 (*0-89015-530-5*) Eakin-Sunbelt.

—Bluebonnet of the Hill Country. Binder, Pat, illus. (gr. k-4). 1983. 11.95 (*0-89015-395-7*, Pub. by Panda Bks) Eakin-Sunbelt.

Casagrande, Louis B. & Johnson, Sylvia A. Focus on Mexico: Modern Life in an Ancient Land. (Illus.). 96p. (gr. 5up). 1986. lib. bdg. 21.50 (*0-8225-0645-9*) Lerner Pubns.

Casanova, Mary. The Golden Retriever. LC 90-34141. (Illus.). 48p. (gr. 5-6). 1990. RSBE 12.95 (*0-89686-525-8*, Crestwood Hse) Macmillan Child Grp.

Casas, Bartholomew Las see Las Casas, Bartholomew.

Casas, Rosa, jt. auth. see Vazquez, Ana.

Case, Adam. Who Tells the Truth? A Collection of Logical Puzzles to Make You Think. 39p. 1991. 4.95 (*0-906212-77-4*, Pub. by Tarquin UK) Parkwest Pubns.

Case, Dianne. Love, David. Andreasen, Dan, illus. 144p. (gr. 3-7). 1991. 14.95 (*0-525-67350-4*, Lodestar Bks) Dutton Child Bks.

Case, Elinor. Humphrey, Wimsey & Doo. Taylor, Marie, illus. 48p. (Orig.). (ps-6). 1984. pap. 5.95 (*0-910781-02-8*) G Whittell Mem.

Case, Evelyn C., jt. auth. see Volz, Jim.

Case, Mary. The Green Jellybean. Shaffer, Dianna, illus. 32p. (ps-8). 1989. pap. text ed. 4.95 (*1-877995-01-0*) Koala Pub Co.

—Katie Koala Bear, Vol. 1: What Will Katie Wear to School? Shaffer, Dianna, illus. LC 89-83279. 28p. (gr. 2-4). 1989. pap. text ed. 4.95 (*0-685-28857-9*) Koala Pub Co.

—Katie Koala Bear, Vol. 2: Katie's Tree of Designs. Shaffer, Dianna, illus. 28p. (gr. 2-4). 1989. pap. text ed. 4.95 (*1-877995-00-2*) Koala Pub Co.

—Katie Koala Bear, Vol. 3: Katie & Karla Make Pizza. Shaffer, Dianna, illus. 28p. (gr. 2-4). 1989. pap. text ed. 4.95 (*1-877995-05-3*) Koala Pub Co.

—Katie Koala Bear, Vol. 4: Katie Loves Math. Shaffer, Dianna, illus. 28p. (gr. 2-4). 1989. pap. text ed. 4.95 (*1-877995-13-4*) Koala Pub Co.

—Katie Koala Bear, Vol. 5: Katie Learns to Read. Shaffer, Dianna, illus. 28p. (gr. 2-4). 1989. pap. text ed. 4.95 (*1-877995-04-5*) Koala Pub Co.

Case, Mary & Shaffer, Dianna. Katie Koala Bear in What Will Katie Wear to School? (Illus.). 20p. (Orig.). 1989. pap. 4.95 (*1-877995-06-1*) Koala Pub Co.
Katie Koala in What Will Katie Wear To School? is the first of a series of story books for primary students. It is designed for whole language strategies in the classroom. Katie is a charming Koala bear. In this book, she gets ready for school & dresses for cold weather. What Katie wears to school each day is carefully recorded on the Koala's family calendar. A paper reproducible cutout is available with each book, so the add-on story can be told using the feltboard. A blank calendar & graphing strategies are included also.
Publisher Provided Annotation.

Case, Riley B. & Keysor, Charles W. We Believe: Jr. High. rev. ed. Heidinger, James V., II, et al, eds. Myers, Glenn, illus. 60p. (gr. 6-9). 1988. wkbk. 4.35 (*0-917851-20-X*) Bristol Hse.

Case, Riley B., et al. We Believe--Sr. High. rev. ed. 64p. 1988. wkbk. 4.35 (*0-917851-26-9*) Bristol Hse.

Caseley, Judith. Ada Potato. LC 87-19738. (Illus.). 24p. (ps up). 1989. 11.95 (*0-688-07742-0*); PLB 11.88 (*0-688-07743-9*) Greenwillow.

—Annie's Potty. LC 89-34717. (Illus.). 24p. (ps up). 1990. 12.95 (*0-688-09065-6*); lib. bdg. 12.88 (*0-688-09066-4*) Greenwillow.

—Apple Pie & Onions. Caseley, Judith, illus. LC 86-9804. 32p. (gr. 1-4). 1987. 11.75 (*0-688-06762-X*); PLB 11.88 (*0-688-06763-8*) Greenwillow.

—Chloe in the Know. LC 92-14757. (Illus.). 144p. (gr. 1 up). 1993. 14.00 (*0-688-11055-X*) Greenwillow.

—Cousins. LC 88-34903. (Illus.). 24p. (ps up). 1990. 12. 95 (*0-688-08433-8*); lib. bdg. 12.88 (*0-688-08434-6*) Greenwillow.

—Dear Annie. LC 90-39793. (Illus.). 32p. (ps up). 1991. 13.95 (*0-688-10010-4*); PLB 13.88 (*0-688-10011-2*) Greenwillow.

—Grandpa's Garden Lunch. LC 89-23325. (Illus.). 32p. (ps up). 1990. 12.95 (*0-688-08816-3*); PLB 12.88 (*0-688-08817-1*) Greenwillow.

—Harry & Arney. LC 93-20787. 1994. write for info. (*0-688-12140-3*) Greenwillow.

—Harry & Willy & Carrothead. LC 90-30291. (Illus.). 24p. (ps up). 1991. 13.95 (*0-688-09492-9*); PLB 13.88 (*0-688-09493-7*) Greenwillow.

—Hurricane Harry. LC 90-13809. (Illus.). 128p. (gr. 1 up). 1991. 13.95 (*0-688-10027-9*) Greenwillow.

—Hurricane Harry. Caseley, Judith, illus. LC 93-6991. 112p. (gr. 2 up). 1994. pap. 3.95 (*0-688-12549-2*, Pub. by Beech Tree Bks) Morrow.

—Kisses. LC 89-15221. 192p. (gr. 7 up). 1990. 12.95 (*0-679-80166-9*); PLB 13.99 (*0-679-90166-3*) Random Bks Yng Read.

—Mama, Coming & Going. LC 92-29402. (Illus.). 32p. (ps up). 1994. write for info. (*0-688-11441-5*); PLB write for info. (*0-688-11442-3*) Greenwillow.

—Mr. Green Peas. LC 93-24183. 1994. write for info. (*0-688-12859-9*); PLB write for info. (*0-688-12860-2*) Greenwillow.

—My Father, the Nutcase. LC 91-46750. 196p. (gr. 7 up). 1992. 15.00 (*0-679-83394-3*); PLB 15.99 (*0-679-93394-8*) Knopf Bks Yng Read.

—The Noisemakers. LC 90-2806. (Illus.). 24p. (ps-6). 1992. 14.00 (*0-688-09394-9*); PLB 13.93 (*0-688-09395-7*) Greenwillow.

—Silly Baby. LC 87-4097. (Illus.). 24p. (ps-3). 1988. 11. 95 (*0-688-07355-7*); lib. bdg. 11.88 (*0-688-07356-5*) Greenwillow.

—Sophie & Sammy's Library Sleepover. LC 91-48160. (Illus.). 32p. (ps-6). 1993. 14.00 (0-688-10615-3); PLB 13.93 (0-688-10616-1) Greenwillow.
—Starring Dorothy Kane. LC 90-24172. (gr. 1 up). 1992. 13.00 (0-688-10182-8) Greenwillow.
—Starring Dorothy Kane. Caseley, Judith, illus. LC 93-6992. 160p. (gr. 2 up). 1994. pap. 3.95 (0-688-12548-4, Pub. by Beech Tree Bks) Morrow.
—Three Happy Birthdays. LC 88-18788. (Illus.). 32p. (ps up). 1989. 12.95 (0-688-08179-7); PLB 12.88 (0-688-08180-0) Greenwillow.
—Three Happy Birthdays. LC 92-24583. 40p. (gr. 1 up). 1993. pap. 4.95 (0-688-11699-X, Mulberry) Morrow.
—When Grandpa Came to Stay. Caseley, Judith, illus. LC 85-12616. 32p. (gr. k-2). 1986. 11.75 (0-688-06128-1); PLB 11.88 (0-688-06129-X) Greenwillow.
Caselli, Giovanni. An Egyptian Craftsman. Caselli, Giovanni, illus. LC 85-30685. 32p. (gr. 3-6). 1991. lib. bdg. 12.95 (0-87226-100-X) P Bedrick Bks.
—The Everyday Life of a Cathedral Builder. Caselli, Giovanni, illus. LC 87-29787. 32p. (gr. 3-6). 1992. PLB 12.95 (0-87226-115-8) P Bedrick Bks.
—The Everyday Life of a Florentine Merchant. Caselli, Giovanni, illus. LC 86-4365. 32p. (gr. 3-6). 1991. PLB 12.95 (0-87226-107-7) P Bedrick Bks.
—The First Civilizations. LC 84-6179. (Illus.). 48p. (gr. 5 up). 1985. 16.95 (0-911745-59-9) P Bedrick Bks.
—A Greek Potter. Caselli, Giovanni, illus. LC 85-30637. 32p. (gr. 3-6). 1991. lib. bdg. 12.95 (0-87226-101-8) P Bedrick Bks.
—An Ice Age Hunter. Caselli, Giovanni, illus. LC 91-33261. 32p. (gr. 3-6). 1992. lib. bdg. 12.95 (0-87226-103-4) P Bedrick Bks.
—Life Through the Ages. LC 92-52838. (Illus.). 64p. (gr. 3 up). 1992. 11.95 (1-56458-143-8) Dorling Kindersley.
—The Middle Ages. LC 87-27105. 48p. (gr. 5 up). 1988. 16.95 (0-87226-176-X) P Bedrick Bks.
—The Middle Ages. Caselli, Giovanni, illus. 48p. (gr. 5 up). 1993. pap. 8.95 sewn (0-685-66005-2) P Bedrick Bks.
—Middle Ages. (gr. 4-7). 1993. pap. 8.95 (0-87226-263-4) P Bedrick Bks.
—The Renaissance & the New World. Caselli, Giovanni, illus. LC 85-22900. 48p. (gr. 5 up). 1986. 16.95 (0-87226-050-X) P Bedrick Bks.
—The Roman Empire & the Dark Ages. LC 84-6480. (Illus.). 48p. (gr. 5 up). 1985. 16.95 (0-911745-58-0) P Bedrick Bks.
—A Roman Soldier. Sergio, illus. LC 86-4366. 32p. (gr. 3-6). 1991. PLB 12.95 (0-87226-106-9) P Bedrick Bks.
—A Viking Settler. Caselli, Giovanni, illus. LC 86-3302. 32p. (gr. 3-6). 1991. lib. bdg. 12.95 (0-87226-104-2) P Bedrick Bks.
—Wonders of the World. LC 92-52798. (Illus.). 64p. (gr. 3 up). 1992. 11.95 (1-56458-145-4) Dorling Kindersley.
Casey, Barbara W. Grandma Jock & Christabelle. LC 93-60737. 61p. (gr. 7-12). 1993. pap. 6.95 (1-55523-406-2) Winston-Derek.
—Leilani Zan. LC 90-71707. 113p. (gr. 9-12). 1992. 7.95 (1-55523-405-4) Winston-Derek.
Casey, Denise. Big Birds. Gilmore, Jackie, photos by. LC 92-17275. (Illus.). 48p. (gr. 1-5). 1993. 14.99 (0-525-65121-7, Cobblehill Bks) Dutton Child Bks.
—Weather Everywhere. Gilmore, Jackie, photos by. LC 92-23239. (Illus.). 40p. (gr. k-4). 1993. RSBE 13.95 (0-02-717777-7, Bradbury Pr) Macmillan Child Grp.
Casey, Jane C. Millard Fillmore. LC 87-35183. (Illus.). 100p. (gr. 3 up). 1988. PLB 17.27 (0-516-01353-X) Childrens.
—William Howard Taft. LC 88-8675. (Illus.). 100p. (gr. 3 up). 1988. PLB 17.27 (0-516-01366-1) Childrens.
Casey, Maude. Over the Water. 1994. write for info. (0-8050-3276-2) H Holt & Co.
Casey, Patricia. Cluck, Cluck. LC 87-30435. (Illus.). 32p. (ps-1). 1988. 12.95 (0-688-07767-6) Lothrop.
—Quack Quack. LC 87-17301. (Illus.). (ps-1). 1988. 12. 95 (0-688-07765-X) Lothrop.
Cash, Angela. Dreamskate. 1993. pap. 3.50 (0-553-56475-7) Bantam.
Cash, Judy. Kidding Around Los Angeles: A Young Person's Guide to the City. (Illus.). 64p. (gr. 3 up). 1989. pap. 9.95 (0-945465-34-3) John Muir.
Cash, Paul, ed. see Brunton, Paul.
Cash, Terry. Bricks. Stefoff, Rebecca, ed. Barber, Ed, photos by. LC 90-40249. (Illus.). 32p. (gr. 3-5). 1990. PLB 15.93 (0-944483-68-2) Garrett Ed Corp.
—One Hundred One Physics Tricks: Fun Experiments with Everyday Materials. LC 92-21859. (Illus.). 104p. (gr. 3-9). 1992. 14.95 (0-685-60095-5) Sterling.
—One Hundred One Physics Tricks: Fun Experiments with Everyday Materials. (Illus.). 104p. (gr. 3 up). 1993. pap. 9.95 (0-8069-8785-5) Sterling.
—Plastics. Stefoff, Rebecca, ed. Barber, Ed, photos by. LC 90-40368. (Illus.). 32p. (gr. 3-5). 1990. PLB 15.93 (0-944483-70-4) Garrett Ed Corp.
—Sound. Chen, Kuo K. & Bull, Peter, illus. 40p. (gr. 5-6). 1989. PLB 12.90 (0-531-19064-1, Warwick) Watts.
Cashman, Greer F. & Frankel, Alona. Jewish Days & Holidays. LC 86-70789. (Illus.). 64p. (gr up). 1986. 11.95 (0-915361-58-2) Modan-Adama Bks.
Cashman, Mary M. Toby the Friendly Turtle. (Illus.). 16p. (gr. 3 up). 1994. saddle-stitched 4.95 (0-8059-3461-8) Dorrance.
Cashman, S., jt. ed. see Quinn, Bridie.

Casler, Leigh. The Boy Who Dreamed of an Acorn. LC 92-44902. 1994. write for info. (0-399-22547-1, Philomel) Putnam Pub Group.
Casn, Terry & Taylor, Barbara. One Hundred Seventy-Five More Science Experiments to Amuse & Amaze Your Friends. Kuo Kang Chen & Bull, Peter, illus. LC 90-39250. 176p. (Orig.). (gr. 4-7). 1991. pap. 12.00 (0-679-80390-4) Random Bks Yng Read.
Casolaro, Nancy. The Gifted & Talented Math Workbook. Whitten, Leesa, illus. 96p. (gr. 1-3). 1993. pap. 3.95 (1-56565-039-5) Lowell Hse.
Casolaro, Nancy, jt. auth. see Furlong, Kaye.
Casona, Alejandro. Barca Sin Pescador. Balseiro, Jose A. & Owre, J. Riis, eds. (gr. 9 up). 1975. pap. 11.95x (0-19-501984-9) OUP.
Caspi, Mishael M., jt. auth. see Gold, Sharlya.
Cassabois, Jacques. Port Englouti. Boucher, Michel, illus. (FRE.). 79p. (gr. 3-7). 1989. pap. 8.95 (2-07-031204-6) Schoenhof.
Cassady, David. Dating Decisions. (Illus.). 48p. (gr. 9-12). 1991. pap. 7.99 (1-55945-215-3) Group Pub.
—Faith for Tough Times. (Illus.). 48p. (gr. 9-12). 1991. pap. 7.99 (1-55945-216-1) Group Pub.
Cassady, Marsh, jt. auth. see Sturkie, Joan.
Cassat, Julie. What I Like Best about Christmas. Rigo, Christina, illus. 14p. (gr. 4-7). 1989. pap. text ed. 5.95 (0-927106-02-7) Prod Concept.
Cassatt, Mary, illus. Lullabies & Good Night. 32p. 1989. 13.95 (0-8249-8441-2, Ideals Child); incl. 60-min. cassette 17.95 (0-8249-7351-8) Hambleton-Hill.
Cassedy, Sylvia. Behind the Attic Wall. LC 82-45922. 320p. (gr. 4-7). 1983. (Crowell Jr Bks); PLB 14.89 (0-690-04337-6, Crowell Jr Bks) HarpC Child Bks.
—Behind the Attic Wall. 320p. (gr. 4 up). 1985. pap. 3.99 (0-380-69843-9, Camelot) Avon.
—Best Cat Suit of All. LC 87-24659. (ps-3). 1991. 10.95 (0-8037-0516-6); PLB 10.89 (0-8037-0517-4) Dial Bks Young.
—In Your Own Words: A Beginner's Guide to Writing. rev. ed. LC 89-78079. 240p. (gr. 5 up). 1990. (Crowell Jr Bks); PLB 13.89 (0-690-04823-8, Crowell Jr Bks) HarpC Child Bks.
—In Your Own Words: A Beginner's Guide to Writing. rev. ed. LC 89-78079. 240p. (gr. 5 up). 1990. pap. 7.95 (0-06-446102-5, Trophy) HarpC Child Bks.
—Lucie Babbidge's House. LC 89-1296. 256p. (gr. 4-7). 1989. (Crowell Jr Bks); PLB 13.89 (0-690-04798-3, Crowell Jr Bks) HarpC Child Bks.
—Lucie Babbidge's House. 256p. 1993. pap. 3.99 (0-380-71812-X, Camelot) Avon.
—M. E. & Morton. LC 85-48251. 320p. (gr. 4-7). 1989. pap. 3.95 (0-06-440306-8, Trophy) HarpC Child Bks.
—Roomrimes. Chessare, Michele, illus. LC 86-4583. 80p. (gr. k-3). 1987. (Crowell Jr Bks); PLB 12.89 (0-690-04467-4, Crowell Jr Bks) HarpC Child Bks.
—Zoomrimes: Poems About Things That Go. Chessare, Michele, illus. LC 90-1463. 64p. (gr. 3-7). 1993. 14.00 (0-06-022632-3); PLB 13.89 (0-06-022633-1) HarpC Child Bks.
Cassedy, Sylvia & Suetake, Kunihiro. Red Dragonfly on My Shoulder: Haiku. Bang, Molly, illus. LC 91-18443. 32p. (gr. k-5). 1992. 15.00 (0-06-022624-2); PLB 14. 89 (0-06-022625-0) HarpC Child Bks.
Casserly, Constance D. A Fine Line. LC 93-70368. 218p. (gr. 8-12). 1993. pap. 7.95x (0-943864-71-2) Davenport.
Cassidy, John. The Time Book. (ps-8). 1991. wire-o bdg. incl. watch 10.95 (1-878257-08-0) Klutz Pr.
Cassidy, John & Cassidy, Nancy. Kids Songs Two: Another Holler-along Handbook. M'Guinness, Jim, illus. 70p. (Orig.). 1989. pap. 10.95 incl. 48-min. stereo cassette (0-932592-20-1) Klutz Pr.
Cassidy, John & Stillinger, Scott. The New Official Koosh Book. Taber, Ed, illus. 88p. 1992. perfect bdg., incl. 3 mini-Koosh balls 9.95 (1-878257-30-7) Klutz Pr.
Cassidy, John, jt. auth. see Cassidy, Nancy.
Cassidy, Nancy. Kids Songs: Sleepyheads. 50p. 1991. Incl. cassette tape. wiro-bound 10.95 (1-878257-11-0) Klutz Pr.
Cassidy, Nancy & Cassidy, John. Kid's Songs: A Holler along Handbook. M'Guinness, Jim, illus. 86p. (Orig.). 1986. pap. 10.95 incl. 48 min. stereo cassette (0-932592-13-9) Klutz Pr.
Cassidy, Nancy, jt. auth. see Cassidy, John.
Cassidy, Pat & Close, Jim. Kids, BASIC & the Coleco Adam. (Illus.). 200p. 1984. 17.95 (0-13-515446-4) P-H.
Cassidy, Vincent & Simpson, Amos. Traveling Man: The Life Story of Henry Watkins Allen. 1967. 4.50 (0-87511-017-7) Claitors.
Cassin, Sue. Fascinating Facts about Animals. 1990. 9.95 (1-55782-329-4, Pub. by Warner Juvenile Bks) Little.
—Fascinating Facts about Your Body. 1990. 9.95 (1-55782-328-6, Pub. by Warner Juvenile Bks) Little.
Cassin-Scott, Jack. Amateur Dramatics. (Illus.). 144p. (gr. 10-12). 1992. 24.95 (0-304-34146-0, Pub. by Cassell UK) Sterling.
Casson, Lee. My Uncle Max. Desputeaux, Helene, illus. 24p. (ps-2). 1990. pap. 0.99 (1-55037-130-4, Pub. by Annick CN) Firefly Bks Ltd.
Cassorla, Albert. The Ultimate Skateboard Book. LC 88-42604. (Illus.). 128p. (Orig.). (gr. 6 up). 1988. pap. 9.95 (0-89471-564-X) Running Pr.
Cassway, Esta. Five Books of Moses for Young People. LC 92-8013. 248p. 1992. 40.00 (0-87668-451-7) Aronson.

Cast, C. Vance. Where Did the Dinosaurs Go? Wilkinson, Sue, illus. 40p. (ps-2). 1994. pap. 4.95 (0-8120-1573-8) Barron.
—Where Does Electricity Come From? Wilkinson, Sue, illus. 40p. (ps-2). 1992. pap. 5.95 (0-8120-4835-0) Barron.
—Where Does Oil Come From? Wilkinson, Sue, illus. 40p. (ps-2). 1993. pap. 4.95 (0-8120-1467-7) Barron.
—Where Does Paper Come From? Wilkinson, Sue, illus. 40p. (ps-2). 1993. pap. 4.95 (0-8120-1468-5) Barron.
—Where Does Pollution Come From? Wilkinson, Sue, illus. 40p. (ps-2). 1994. pap. 4.95 (0-8120-1571-1) Barron.
—Where Does Water Come From? Wilkinson, Sue, illus. 40p. (ps-2). 1992. pap. 5.95 (0-8120-4642-0) Barron.
Castagnola, Larry. More Parables for Little People. Muren, Nancy L., illus. LC 87-62532. 88p. (Orig.). (gr. 4-5). 1987. pap. 8.95 (0-89390-095-8) Resource Pubns.
Castagnola, Lawrence. Parables for Little People. Muren, Nancy LaBerge, illus. Quinn, Francis A. LC 86-60029. (Illus.). 104p. (Orig.). (gr. 4 up). 1982. pap. 7.95 (0-89390-034-6) Resource Pubns.
Castalanas, Guadalupe, tr. see Mozeleski, Peter A.
Castaneda, Omar. Among the Volcanoes. 192p. (gr. 7 up). 1991. 14.95 (0-525-67332-6, Lodestar Bks) Dutton Child Bks.
Castaneda, Omar S. Abuela's Weave. Sanchez, Enrique O., illus. LC 92-71927. 32p. (gr. k-3). 1993. 14.95 (1-880000-00-8) Lee & Low Bks.
—Among the Volcanoes. (ps-3). 1993. pap. 3.50 (0-440-40746-X) Dell.
—Imagining Isabel. 192p. (gr. 7 up). 1994. 15.99 (0-525-67431-4, Lodestar Bks) Dutton Child Bks.
Casterline, Charlotte L. The Asthma Attack by Bo B. Bear. Brunza-Horn, Nanette, illus. (Orig.). (ps-6). 1988. pap. 5.95 (0-9617218-2-0) Info All Bk.
—My Friend Has Asthma. Zabroski, Patricia, illus. 24p. (Orig.). (ps-6). 1985. pap. 4.95 (0-9617218-0-4) Info All Bk.
—Sam the Allergen. (Illus.). 26p. (Orig.). (ps-6). 1985. pap. 4.95 (0-9617218-1-2) Info All Bk.
Castiglia, Julie. Margaret Mead. (Illus.). 144p. (gr. 5-9). 1989. PLB 13.98 (0-382-09525-1) Silver Burdett Pr.
Castillo & Bond. University of Chicago Spanish Dictionary: A New Concise Spanish-English & English-Spanish Dictionary of Words & Phrases Basic to the Written & Spoken Language of Today, 8 vols. large type ed. 1740p. (gr. 9 up). 1967. Repr. of 1948 ed. Set. 435.00 (0-317-01954-6, J-23870-00) Am Printing Hse.
Castillo, Bernal D. de. Cortez & the Conquest of Mexico by the Spaniards in 1521. Herzog, B. G., abridged by. LC 88-581. xii, 165p. (gr. 5 up). 1988. Repr. of 1942 ed. 19.50 (0-208-02221-X, Linnet) Shoe String.
Castillo, Bernal Diaz Del see Castillo, Bernal D. de.
Castillo, Steve. Maximum Happiness: Jack & Jill Discover True Love. Castillo, Steve, illus. 58p. (Orig.). (gr. 9). 1989. 5.95 (0-317-93187-3) Paisley Bks.
Castillo Bernal, Diaz Del see Bernal-Diaz, Del Castillo.
Castine, Joseph, et al. The Foreign Language Teacher's Handbook: Aiming for Proficiency in German. (GER., Illus.). 200p. (Orig.). (gr. 8-9). 1991. tchr's ed. 28.95 (1-879279-06-1) Proficiency Pr.
Castle, Barbara G. The Adventures of Captain Rhema. rev. ed. LC 91-6082. (gr. 5-9). 1991. pap. 4.00 (0-915541-61-0) Star Bks Inc.
Castle, Caroline. Grandpa Baxter & the Photographs. Bowman, Peter, illus. LC 92-44192. 32p. (ps-1). 1993. 14.95 (0-531-05487-X); PLB 14.99 (0-531-08637-2) Orchard Bks Watts.
—The Hare & the Tortoise. Weevers, Peter, illus. LC 84-9569. 32p. (ps-3). 1985. 10.95 (0-8037-0138-1) Dial Bks Young.
—Herbert Binns & the Flying Tricycle. 1990. pap. 3.95 (0-8037-0739-8, Dial Pied Piper) Puffin Bks.
Castle, Caroline, retold by. Hare & the Tortoise. Weevers, Peter, illus. LC 84-9569. 32p. (ps-3). 1987. pap. 4.95 (0-8037-0147-0) Dial Bks Young.
Castoldi, Maggiorina. Chirpy the Chick. 30p. (ps-1). 1987. 3.95 (0-8120-5819-4) Barron.
Castor, Harriet. Trucks. (Illus.). 12p. (ps). 1993. bds. 4.50 (0-7460-1098-2, Usborne) EDC.
Castor, Harriet, jt. auth. see Young, Caroline.
Castro, Rogelio de see Bruni, Mary-Ann S.
Caswell, Helen. Daniel & His Friends. LC 93-25305. 24p. 1993. 11.95 (0-687-10085-2) Abingdon.
—God Makes Us Different. LC 87-33466. (ps-3). 1988. pap. 5.95 (0-687-15336-0) Abingdon.
—God Must Like to Laugh. Caswell, Helen, illus. LC 87-1362. (ps-3). 1987. pap. 5.95 (0-687-15188-0) Abingdon.
—God's Love Is for Sharing. Caswell, Helen, illus. LC 87-11580. (gr. k-3). 1987. pap. 5.95 (0-687-15335-2) Abingdon.
—Loaves & Fishes. LC 93-25308. 24p. 1993. 11.95 (0-687-22526-4) Abingdon.
—My Big Family at Church. LC 88-30630. 1990. pap. 5.95 (0-687-27533-4) Abingdon.
—Parable of the Bridesmaids. Caswell, Helen, illus. 24p. (ps-3). 1992. 11.95 (0-687-30022-3) Abingdon.
—Parable of the Good Samaritan. Caswell, Helen, illus. 24p. (ps-3). 1992. 11.95 (0-687-30023-1) Abingdon.
—Parable of the Leaven. Caswell, Helen, illus. LC 92-15161. 24p. (ps-3). 1992. pap. 5.95 (0-687-30024-X) Abingdon.

—Parable of the Mustard Seed. Caswell, Helen, illus. LC 92-15160. 24p. (ps-3). 1992. pap. 5.95 (0-687-30025-8) Abingdon.
—Parable of the Sower. LC 90-23200. (ps-3). 1991. 11.95 (0-687-30020-7) Abingdon.
—Parable of the Vineyard. LC 90-23228. (ps-3). 1991. 11.95 (0-687-30021-5) Abingdon.
Caswell, Helen R. God's World Makes Me Feel So Little. Caswell, Helen R., illus. LC 84-14545. 32p. (gr. k-3). 1988. 5.95 (0-687-15510-X) Abingdon.
Cat, Countee & Cullen, Countee. My Lives & How I Lost Them. Owens, Nubia, illus. Strickland, Dorothy, frwd by. LC 92-46738. (Illus.). 174p. (gr. 3-5). 1993. PLB 14.98 (0-382-24360-9); 12.95 (0-382-24369-2) Silver Burdett Pr.
Cat, Christopher & Cullen, Countee. Lost Zoo. Pinkney, Brian, illus. 96p. (gr. 3-5). 1991. PLB 14.98 (0-382-24255-6); 12.95 (0-382-24256-4) Silver Burdett Pr.
Catalano, Dominic. Wolf Plays Alone. (Illus.). 32p. (ps up). 1992. PLB 14.95 (0-399-21868-8, Philomel Bks) Putnam Pub Group.
Catalano, Grace. Alyssa Milano: She's the Boss. (gr. 7 up). 1989. pap. 2.95 (0-318-41642-5, Starfire) Bantam.
—Alyssa Milano: She's the Boss. (gr. 6-9). 1989. pap. 2.75 (0-553-28158-5) Bantam.
—Kirk Cameron: Dream Guy. 112p. (Orig.). (gr. 7-9). 1987. pap. 2.75 (0-553-27135-0, Starfire) Bantam.
—River Phoenix: Hero & Heartthrob. (gr. 7 up). 1988. pap. 2.75 (0-553-27728-6, Starfire) Bantam.
Catalano, Julie. Animal Welfare. Train, Russell E., intro. by. LC 93-26841. 1994. write for info. (0-7910-1591-2); pap. write for info. (0-7910-1616-1) Chelsea Hse.
—Mexican Americans. Moynihan, Daniel P., intro. by. 112p. (gr. 5 up). 1988. 17.95 (0-87754-857-9); pap. 9.95 (0-7910-0272-1) Chelsea Hse.
Catalanotto, Peter. Christmas Always. LC 90-28712. (Illus.). 32p. (ps-1). 1991. 14.95 (0-531-05946-4); RLB 14.99 (0-531-08546-5) Orchard Bks Watts.
—Dylan's Day Out. LC 88-36440. (Illus.). 32p. (ps-1). 1989. 14.95 (0-531-05829-8); PLB 14.99 (0-531-08429-9) Orchard Bks Watts.
—Dylan's Day Out. Catalanotto, Peter, illus. LC 88-36440. 32p. (ps-1). 1993. pap. 5.95 (0-531-07034-4) Orchard Bks Watts.
—Mr. Mumble. Catalanotto, Peter, illus. LC 89-48940. 32p. (ps-2). 1990. 14.95 (0-531-05880-8); PLB 14.99 (0-531-08480-9) Orchard Bks Watts.
Catchpole, Brian. A Map History of the British People Since 1700. 2nd ed. (gr. 7-12). 1975. pap. text ed. 15.00x (0-435-31160-3) Heinemann.
—A Map History of the United States. (gr. 7-12). 1972. pap. text ed. 15.00x (0-435-31158-1) Heinemann.
Catchpole, Clive. Deserts. McIntyre, Brian, illus. LC 83-7757. 32p. (ps-4). 1985. pap. 4.95 (0-8037-0037-7, 0481-140) Dial Bks Young.
—Grasslands. Snowball, Peter, illus. LC 83-27123. 32p. (gr. k-4). 1985. pap. 4.95 (0-8037-0083-0, 0481-140) Dial Bks Young.
—Jungles. Finney, Denise, illus. LC 83-7796. 32p. (ps-4). 1985. pap. 4.95 (0-8037-0036-9, 0481-140) Dial Bks Young.
—Mountains. McIntyre, Brian, illus. LC 83-25273. 32p. (gr. k-4). 1985. pap. 4.95 (0-8037-0087-3, 0481-140) Dial Bks Young.
Cate, Dick. Twisters. Binch, Caroline, illus. 160p. (gr. 5-8). 1989. 17.95 (0-575-04099-8, Pub. by Gollancz England) Trafalgar.
Cate, Jean M. & Raskin, Selma. It's Easy to Say Crepidula! A Phonetic Guide to Pronunciation of the Scientific Names of Sea Shells. Vasquez, Gina, illus. 158p. (Orig.). (gr. 5-7). 1986. pap. 19.95 (0-938509-00-4) Pretty Penny Pr.
Cateland, Grace. Joey Forever. 1993. pap. 3.99 (0-553-56611-3) Bantam.
Cates, Emily. The Ghost Ferry. (gr. 4-7). 1991. pap. 2.95 (0-553-15863-5) Bantam.
—The Ghost in the Attic. Cates, Emily, illus. (gr. 3-7). 1990. pap. 2.95 (0-553-15826-0, Skylark) Bantam.
—The Mystery of Misty Island Inn. 1990. pap. 2.95 (0-553-15858-9) Bantam.
Cates, Joe W. Buzbee. Cates, Joe W., illus. 96p. (gr. 3-8). 1987. PLB write for info. (0-942403-04-5) J Barnaby Dist.
—Carl the Cactus. Cates, Joe W., illus. 64p. (Orig.). (gr. k-6). 1986. PLB 9.95 (0-942403-03-7); pap. 7.00 (0-942403-01-0) J Barnaby Dist.
—The Crooked Tree. Cates, Joe W., illus. 48p. (Orig.). (gr. k-6). 1986. PLB 9.95 (0-942403-02-9); pap. 6.00 (0-942403-00-2) J Barnaby Dist.
Cather, Willa. My Antonia, 2 vols. large type ed. (gr. 10 up). Repr. of 1949 ed. Set. write for info. NAVH.
—Neighbor Rosicky. LC 85-46058. 88p. (gr. 6 up). 1986. PLB 13.95s.p. (0-88682-065-0) Creative Ed.
Catherall, Ed. Exploring Electricity. LC 89-26117. (Illus.). 48p. (gr. 4-8). 1990. PLB 19.92 (0-8114-2594-0) Raintree Steck-V.
—Exploring Energy Sources. LC 90-21764. (Illus.). 48p. (gr. 4-8). 1991. PLB 19.92 (0-8114-2597-5) Raintree Steck-V.
—Exploring Light. LC 89-28063. (Illus.). 48p. (gr. 4-8). 1990. PLB 19.92 (0-8114-2591-6) Raintree Steck-V.
—Exploring Magnets. LC 89-26116. (Illus.). 48p. (gr. 4-8). 1990. PLB 19.92 (0-8114-2593-2) Raintree Steck-V.
—Exploring Plants. LC 91-40544. (Illus.). 48p. (gr. 4-8). 1992. PLB 19.92 (0-8114-2601-7) Raintree Steck-V.

—Exploring Soil & Rocks. LC 90-10024. (Illus.). 48p. (gr. 4-8). 1990. PLB 19.92 (0-8114-2595-9) Raintree Steck-V.
—Exploring Sound. LC 89-38614. (Illus.). 48p. (gr. 4-8). 1990. PLB 19.92 (0-8114-2592-4) Raintree Steck-V.
—Exploring the Human Body. (Illus.). 48p. (gr. 4-8). 1992. PLB 19.92 (0-8114-2599-1) Raintree Steck-V.
—Exploring Uses of Energy. LC 90-46703. (Illus.). 48p. (gr. 4-8). 1990. PLB 19.92 (0-8114-2598-3) Raintree Steck-V.
—Exploring Weather. LC 90-10025. (Illus.). 48p. (gr. 4-8). 1990. PLB 19.92 (0-8114-2596-7) Raintree Steck-V.
Catley, Alison. The Party in the Sky. (Illus.). 32p. (ps-2). 1992. 17.95 (0-09-174036-3, Pub. by Hutchinson UK) Trafalgar.
—Rabbit. (Illus.). 32p. (ps-1). 1993. 15.95 (0-09-174408-3, Pub. by Hutchinson UK) Trafalgar.
Catley, Alison, jt. auth. see Wilson, Gina.
Catling, Patrick S. The Chocolate Touch. Apple, Morgot, illus. 96p. 1981. pap. 2.75 (0-553-15479-6) Bantam.
—The Chocolate Touch. Apple, Margot, illus. LC 78-31100. 96p. (gr. 4-6). 1979. Repr. of 1952 ed. PLB 11.88 (0-688-32187-9) Morrow Jr Bks.
—The Chocolate Touch. 1984. pap. 3.50 (0-553-15639-X) Bantam.
—John Midas in Dreamtime. 96p. (gr. 3-7). 1987. pap. 2.75 (0-553-15567-9, Skylark) Bantam.
Catoe, Kaye, et al, eds. see Barrier, Jean & Kennedy, Alice.
Catron, Carol & Parks, Barbara. Super Story Telling. 239p. (ps). 1986. 15.95 (0-513-01793-3) Denison.
Catt, Louis. Little Ghost. Prater, John, illus. LC 93-29804. 1994. write for info. (1-56402-394-X) Candlewick Pr.
Cattaneo, F. Shop Made Easy Worktext, 2 vols. large type ed. 290p. (gr. 7-12). 1983. Set. 51.81 (0-317-01935-X, 4-23230-00) AM Printing Hse.
Cattaneo, Pietro, jt. auth. see Morgan, Lee.
Catterwell, Thelma. Sebastian Lives in a Hat. Argent, Kerry, illus. 32p. (ps-1). 1990. 13.95 (0-916291-30-8) Kane-Miller Bk.
Catucci, Thomas F. Time with Jesus: Twenty Guided Meditations for Youth. LC 93-71891. 160p. (Orig.). (gr. 9-12). 1993. pap. 13.95 spiral bdg. (0-87793-499-1) Ave Maria.
Caudell, Marian. Listen to Your Heart. 176p. (Orig.). (gr. 7-12). 1986. pap. 2.50 (0-553-25727-7) Bantam.
Caudill, Happy. Happy Little Family. (gr. k-6). 1989. pap. 2.75 (0-440-40164-X, YB) Dell.
Caudill, Rebecca. The Best-Loved Doll. Gilbert, Elliot, illus. LC 92-898. 64p. (ps-2). 1992. 12.95 (0-8050-2103-5, Bks Young Read) H Holt & Co.
—A Certain Small Shepherd. (gr. k-6). 1987. pap. 2.99 (0-440-41194-7, YB) Dell.
—Did You Carry the Flag Today, Charley? Grossman, Nancy, illus. LC 66-11422. 96p. (gr. 2-4). 1966. reinforced bdg. 15.95 (0-8050-1201-X, Bks Young Read) H Holt & Co.
—Did You Carry the Flag Today, Charley? (gr. k-6). 1988. pap. 3.25 (0-440-40092-9) Dell.
—A Pocketful of Cricket. Ness, Evaline, illus. LC 64-12617. 48p. (gr. k-2). 1964. reinforced bdg. 7.95 (0-03-089752-1, Bks Young Read); pap. 5.95 (0-8050-1275-3) H Holt & Co.
—Saturday Cousins. (gr. k-6). 1989. pap. 2.75 (0-440-40208-5, YB) Dell.
—Schoolhouse in the Woods. (gr. k-6). 1989. pap. 2.75 (0-440-40170-4, YB) Dell.
—Schoolroom in the Parlor. (gr. k-6). 1989. pap. 2.75 (0-440-40200-X, YB) Dell.
—Tree of Freedom. 284p. (gr. 5-9). 1988. pap. 5.99 (0-14-032908-0, Puffin) Puffin Bks.
—Tree of Freedom. (gr. 5-9). 17.50 (0-8446-6401-4) Peter Smith.
Caudron, C. & Childs, C. Face Painting Kit. (Illus.). 32p. (gr. 2-6). 1993. pap. 12.95 incl. facepaints & brush (0-88110-656-9, Usborne) EDC.
Caujolle, Claude, jt. auth. see Price, Betty G.
Cauley, Lorinda B. Clap Your Hands. Cauley, Lorinda B., illus. 32p. (ps-1). 1992. PLB 14.95 (0-399-22118-2, Putnam) Putnam Pub Group.
—Puss in Boots. LC 86-7629. (Illus.). 32p. (ps-3). 1988. 13.95 (0-15-264227-7, HB Juv Bks); pap. 3.95 (0-15-264228-5) HarBrace.
—Three Blind Mice. (Illus.). 32p. (ps-3). 1991. 14.95 (0-399-21775-4, Putnam) Putnam Pub Group.
—The Three Little Kittens. (Illus.). 32p. (ps-1). 1982. 3.95 (0-448-10216-1, G&D); (G&D) Putnam Pub Group.
—Treasure Hunt. LC 93-14043. 1994. write for info. (0-399-22447-5, Putnam) Putnam Pub Group.
—The Trouble with Tyrannosaurus Rex. Cauley, Lorinda B., illus. 32p. (ps-3). 1988. 14.95 (0-15-290880-3) HarBrace.
—The Trouble with Tyrannosaurus Rex. 32p. (ps-3). 1990. pap. 4.95 (0-15-290881-1, Voyager Bks) HarBrace.
—The Ugly Duckling. Canley, Lorinda B., illus. LC 79-12340. 40p. (gr. k-3). 1979. pap. 4.95 (0-15-692528-1, Voyager Bks) HarBrace.
Cauley, Lorinda B., retold by. & illus. Goldilocks & the Three Bears. 32p. (ps-2). 1981. 14.95 (0-399-20794-5, Putnam) Putnam Pub Group.
—Goldilocks & the Three Bears. (ps-3). 1992. pap. 5.95 (0-399-22326-6, Sandcastle Bks) Putnam Pub Group.

Cauley, Lorinda B., retold by. The Town Mouse & the Country Mouse. (Illus.). 32p. (ps-3). 1990. pap. 5.95 (0-399-22009-7, Sandcastle Bks) Putnam Pub Group.
Cauley, Lorinda B., illus. Old MacDonald Had a Farm. 32p. (ps-3). 1989. 14.95 (0-399-21628-6, Putnam) Putnam Pub Group.
Caulkins, Janet. Joseph Stalin. (Illus.). 160p. (gr. 9-12). 1990. PLB 14.40 (0-531-10945-3) Watts.
—Pets of the Presidents. LC 91-33179. (Illus.). 72p. (gr. 3-6). 1992. PLB 14.90 (1-56294-060-0) Millbrook Pr.
Caulkins, Janet, ed. see Bailey, Jill.
Caulkins, Janet, ed. see Banks, Martin.
Caulkins, Janet, ed. see Losito, Linda.
Caulkins, Janet, ed. see MacQuitty, Miranda.
Caulkins, Janet, ed. see Milburn, Constance.
Caulkins, Janet, ed. see Williams, John.
Cauper, Eunice. Martin Luther King, Jr. & Our January 15th Holiday for Children. Tonra, Ian, illus. 32p. (Orig.). (gr. k-3). 1991. pap. text ed. 6.00 (0-9617551-3-X) E Cauper.
—The Story of Christopher Columbus & Our October 12th Holiday for Kindergarten Children. Cauper, David, illus. 16p. (Orig.). (gr. k-3). 1985. pap. 3.95 (0-9617551-0-5) E Cauper.
—The Story of the Pilgrims & Their Indian Friends: A Thanksgiving Story for Children. 5th ed. Cauper, David, illus. 15p. (gr. k). 1990. pap. 4.95 (0-9617551-1-3) E Cauper.
Causey, Michael, jt. auth. see Boyd, Aaron.
Cavalier, Richard. Practical Word Power: Dictionary-Based Skills in Pronunciation & Vocabulary Development. reissued ed. Haskell, John F., ed. (Illus.). 265p. (Orig.). (gr. 6 up). 1993. pap. text ed. 23.95 (0-9601096-0-9) Program Counsel.
Cavan, Seamus. Daniel Boone & the Opening of the Ohio Country. Goetzmann, William H., ed. Collins, Michael, intro. by. (Illus.). 112p. (gr. 5 up). 1991. lib. bdg. 18.95 (0-7910-1309-X) Chelsea Hse.
—The Irish-American Experience. Shenton, James, contrib. by. LC 92-7512. (Illus.). 64p. (gr. 4-6). 1993. PLB 14.90 (1-56294-218-2) Millbrook Pr.
—Lewis & Clark & the Route to the Pacific. (gr. 4-7). 1992. pap. 7.95 (0-7910-1538-6) Chelsea Hse.
—Thurgood Marshall & Equal Rights. LC 92-12995. (Illus.). 32p. (gr. 2-4). 1993. PLB 12.40 (1-56294-277-8) Millbrook Pr.
—W. E. B. Du Bois & Racial Relations. LC 92-33015. (Illus.). 32p. (gr. 2-4). 1993. PLB 12.40 (1-56294-288-3) Millbrook Pr.
Cavanagh, Helen. Panther Glade. LC 92-23406. 160p. (gr. 5-9). 1993. pap. 15.00 JR3 (0-671-75617-6, S&S BFYR) S&S Trade.
Cavanagh, Mary. Favorite Menus. Kubo, Chad & Filarca, Josie, illus. 13p. (gr. 3-5). 1980. pap. 3.95 (0-8431-2573-X) Enrich.
—Telephone Power. Quinn, Kaye, illus. 13p. (gr. 3-5). 1980. pap. 3.95 (0-8431-2572-1) Enrich.
Cavanaugh, Arthur, jt. auth. see Horn, Geoffrey.
Cavanaugh, Kate. I Can't Sleep with Those Elves Watching Me. Kiner, K. C., illus. 24p. (ps-8). 1990. pap. text ed. 4.95 (0-9622353-1-8) KAC.
—Pete & His Elves Series. Kiner, K. C., illus. 28p. 1992. Set. pap. write for info. (0-9622353-4-2) KAC.
—Pete Goes to Grand Island. Kiner, K. C., illus. 24p. 1992. pap. 5.95 (0-9622353-3-4) KAC.
—Pete's Lost. Kiner, K. C., illus. 24p. (Orig.). 1991. pap. 4.95 (0-9622353-2-6) KAC.
Cavanna, Betty. Angel on Skis. (gr. 4-7). 1992. pap. 2.50 (0-8167-1268-9) Troll Assocs.
—Banner Year. LC 87-23692. 224p. (gr. 7 up). 1987. 12.95 (0-688-05779-9) Morrow Jr Bks.
—Banner Year. 217p. (gr. 4-7). 1992. pap. 2.50 (0-8167-1265-4) Troll Assocs.
—Boy Next Door. (gr. 4-7). 1992. pap. 2.50 (0-8167-1270-0) Troll Assocs.
—Going on Sixteen. LC 85-4877. 224p. (gr. 5-9). 1985. Repr. of 1946 ed. 11.95 (0-688-05892-2) Morrow Jr Bks.
—Going on Sixteen. 188p. (gr. 6-9). 1992. pap. 2.50 (0-8167-1266-2) Troll Assocs.
—Paintbox Summer. 212p. 1981. Repr. PLB 19.95 (0-89966-357-5) Buccaneer Bks.
—Paintbox Summer. 239p. 1981. Repr. PLB 16.95x (0-89967-031-8) Harmony Raine.
—Ruffles & Drums. (gr. 4-7). 1992. pap. 2.50 (0-8167-1267-0) Troll Assocs.
—Two's Company. Smith, Edward J., illus. 190p. (gr. 5-9). 1951. 7.00 (0-664-32080-5, Westminster) Westminster John Knox.
—Wanted: A Girl for the Horses. 224p. (gr. 7 up). 1984. 12.95 (0-688-02757-1) Morrow Jr Bks.
Cave, Edward. The Boy Scout's Hike Book. 243p. (gr. 10). 1992. pap. 12.95 (0-9632054-0-4) Stevens Pub.
Cave, Kathryn. Out for the Count. Riddell, Chris, illus. LC 91-22096. 32p. (ps-3). 1992. pap. 14.00 jacketed (0-671-75591-9, S&S BFYR) S&S Trade.
Cavendish, Marshall. Wildlife of the World. LC 93-3581. (gr. 5 up). 1993. Set. 249.95 (1-85435-592-9); Vol. 1. write for info. (1-85435-593-7) Marshall Cavendish.
Cavendish, Maxwell P. The True Story of Christmas. LeBaudour, RoseMarie, illus. 56p. (Orig.). (gr. 4 up). 1991. pap. 15.00 (0-9628016-2-3) Gentian Servs.
Caveney, Sylvia & Giesen, Rosemary. Where Am I? Stern, Simon, illus. LC 76-22476. 24p. (gr. k-3). 1977. PLB 7.95 (0-8225-1365-X) Lerner Pubns.

Cavin, Diantha S. Scripture by Picture: Make Memorizing the Bible Fun & Easy. Cavin, Diantha S., illus. 78p. (Orig.). (ps-6). 1992. pap. 10.95 (0-9628012-3-2) Dexter KS.

Cawley, Sherry. Braves Fun Book I. 80p. (Orig.). 1986. pap. 3.95 (0-937511-00-5) Fun Bk Enter.

Cayford, John E. Maine Firsts. 3rd, rev. & enl. ed. LC 79-56551. 68p. (Orig.). pap. text ed. 18.50 (pack of 10) (0-941216-11-X); tchr's. ed. incl. pack of 10 20.00 (0-941216-12-8) Cay-Bel.

Cayne, Bernard S., ed. see Williams, Bill.

Cazet, Denys. Are There Any Questions? LC 91-42977. (Illus.). 32p. (ps-2). 1992. 14.95 (0-531-05451-9); PLB 14.99 (0-531-08601-1) Orchard Bks Watts.

—Born in the Gravy. Cazet, Denys, illus. LC 92-44523. 32p. (ps-1). 1993. 14.95 (0-531-05488-8); PLB 14.99 (0-531-08638-0) Orchard Bks Watts.

—Christmas Moon. Cazet, Denys, illus. LC 84-10969. 32p. (ps-2). 1984. RSBE 13.95 (0-02-717810-2, Bradbury Pr) Macmillan Child Grp.

—Christmas Moon. Cazet, Denys, illus. LC 87-37434. 32p. (ps-2). 1988. pap. 4.95 (0-689-71259-6, Aladdin) Macmillan Child Grp.

—Daydreams. Cazet, Denys, illus. LC 89-48939. 32p. (ps-2). 1990. 14.95 (0-531-05881-6); PLB 14.99 (0-531-08481-7) Orchard Bks Watts.

—December Twenty-Fourth. Cazet, Denys, illus. LC 86-8247. 32p. (ps-2). 1986. RSBE 13.95 (0-02-717950-8, Bradbury Pr) Macmillan Child Grp.

—A Fish in His Pocket. Cazet, Denys, illus. LC 87-5462. 32p. (ps-2). 1987. 13.95 (0-531-05713-5); PLB 13.99 (0-531-08313-6) Orchard Bks Watts.

—A Fish in His Pocket. LC 87-5462. (Illus.). 32p. (ps-2). 1991. pap. 4.95 (0-531-07021-2) Orchard Bks Watts.

—Frosted Glass. Cazet, Denys, illus. LC 86-26822. 32p. (ps-2). 1987. RSBE 13.95 (0-02-717960-5, Bradbury Pr) Macmillan Child Grp.

—Good Morning, Maxine! Cazet, Denys, illus. LC 88-2889. 32p. (ps-1). 1989. RSBE 13.95 (0-02-717940-0, Bradbury Pr) Macmillan Child Grp.

—Great-uncle Felix. Cazet, Denys, illus. LC 87-24682. 32p. (ps-1). 1988. 12.95 (0-531-05750-X); PLB 12.99 (0-531-08350-0) Orchard Bks Watts.

—I'm Not Sleepy. Cazet, Denys, illus. LC 91-15958. 32p. (ps-1). 1992. 14.95 (0-531-05898-0); lib. bdg. 14.99 (0-531-08498-1) Orchard Bks Watts.

—Mother Night. LC 88-36439. (Illus.). 32p. (ps-1). 1989. 14.95 (0-531-05830-1); PLB 14.99 (0-531-08430-2) Orchard Bks Watts.

—Never Spit on Your Shoes. LC 89-35164. (Illus.). 32p. (ps-1). 1990. 14.95 (0-531-05847-6); PLB 14.99 (0-531-08447-7) Orchard Bks Watts.

—Never Spit on Your Shoes. Cazet, Denys, illus. LC 89-35164. 32p. (ps-1). 1993. pap. 5.95 (0-531-07039-5) Orchard Bks Watts.

—Nothing at All. LC 93-25204. (Illus.). 32p. (ps-1). 1994. 14.95 (0-531-06822-6); lib. bdg. 14.99 RLB (0-531-08672-0) Orchard Bks Watts.

—Saturday. Cazet, Denys, illus. LC 87-2388. 64p. (gr. 1-4). 1988. pap. 3.95 (0-689-71065-8, Aladdin) Macmillan Child Grp.

Cazin, Lorraine. Karts. (Illus.). 48p. (gr. 3-6). 1992. PLB 12.95 (1-56065-072-9) Capstone Pr.

Cazin, Lorraine J. Yosemite. LC 88-20236. (Illus.). 48p. (gr. 4-5). 1988. RSBE 13.95 (0-89686-407-3, Crestwood Hse) Macmillan Child Grp.

Cazzola, Gus. The Bells of Santa Lucia. Morgan, Pierr, illus. 32p. (ps-3). 1991. 14.95 (0-399-21804-1, Philomel) Putnam Pub Group.

CCC of America Staff. Nicholas: The Boy Who Became Santa. CCC of America Staff, illus. 35p. (Orig.). (ps-4). 1989. incl. video 21.95 (1-56814-003-7); pap. text ed. 2.95 book (0-685-62400-5) CCC of America.

Ceasar, Lisbeth D. Big Fearon Book of Comprehension Capers. (gr. 1-6). 1986. pap. 23.95 (0-8224-1479-1) Fearon Teach Aids.

Ceasor, Ebraska, et al. Blacks in Ohio: Seven Portraits. McCluskey, John, ed. (Orig.). (gr. 7-12). 1976. pap. 5.00 (0-913678-13-9) New Day Pr.

Ceasor, Ebraska D. Mae C. Jemison: First Black Female Astronaut. Durant, Charlotte & Pye, Ethel, eds. Johnson, Leonard J., illus. 40p. (Orig.). (ps-1). 1992. pap. 4.00 (0-913678-22-8) New Day Pr.

Ceasor, Frank, Sr. & Gaines, Edith. Can You Count?; Carpetbaggers in Action; Mr. Impossible. 2nd ed. McCluskey, John A., ed. Pryor, Ernest, et al, illus. (gr. 4-7). 1993. pap. 3.00 (0-913678-27-9) New Day Pr.

Cebulash, Mel. Baseball Players Do Amazing Things. (Illus.). (gr. 2-5). 1973. 8.95 (0-394-82611-6) Random Bks Yng Read.

—Batboy. Krych, Duane, illus. (gr. 1-8). 1992. PLB 8.95 (0-89565-882-8); Resale. 12.75 (0-685-60975-8) Childs World.

—Catnapper. (gr. 1-8). 1992. PLB 8.95 (0-89565-878-X); Resale. 12.75 (0-685-60971-5) Childs World.

—Flippers Boy. Krych, Duane, illus. (gr. 1-8). 1992. PLB 8.95 (0-89565-881-X); Resale. 12.75 (0-685-60974-X) Childs World.

—Muscle-Bound. Krych, Duane, illus. (gr. 1-8). 1992. PLB 8.95 (0-89565-883-6); Resale. 12.75 (0-685-60976-6) Childs World.

—Rattler. (gr. 1-8). 1992. PLB 8.95 (0-89565-880-1); Resale. 12.75 (0-685-60973-1) Childs World.

—Snooperman. (gr. 1-8). 1992. PLB 12.75 (0-89565-879-8); Resale. 12.95 (0-685-60972-3) Childs World.

—Willie's Wonderful Pet. Ford, George, illus. 32p. (ps-2). 1993. pap. 2.95 (0-590-45787-X) Scholastic Inc.

Cecerallo, Julius & Dent, Anne. Independence: A Life Skills Guide for Teens. 96p. 1988. pap. 14.95 (0-87868-350-X, 3500) Child Welfare.

Cech, John. First Snow, Magic Snow. McGinley-Nally, Sharon, illus. LC 91-42988. 40p. (gr. k-2). 1992. RSBE 14.95 (0-02-717971-0, Four Winds) Macmillan Child Grp.

—My Grandmother's Journey. McGinley-Nally, Sharon, illus. LC 90-35731. 40p. (ps-4). 1991. RSBE 14.95 (0-02-718135-9, Bradbury Pr) Macmillan Child Grp.

Cecil, Barbara, jt. auth. see Cecil, Terry.

Cecil, Laura. Listen to This. Clark, Emma C., illus. LC 87-8556. 96p. (ps-3). 1988. 15.00 (0-688-07617-3) Greenwillow.

—Stuff & Nonsense. Clark, Emma C., illus. LC 89-1647. 96p. (ps up). 1989. 15.95 (0-688-08898-8) Greenwillow.

Cecil, Laura, compiled by. Boo! Young Scary Stories. Clark, Emma C., illus. LC 90-2824. (ps up). 1990. 20.00 (0-688-09842-8) Greenwillow.

—A Thousand Yards of Sea. Clark, Emma C., illus. LC 91-35687. 80p. (ps up). 1993. 18.00 (0-688-11437-7) Greenwillow.

Cecil, Mirabel. Lottie's Cats. Martin, Francesca, illus. LC 89-29038. 32p. (ps-3). 1990. 12.95 (0-517-57707-0) Crown Bks Yng Read.

Cecil, Terry & Cecil, Barbara. Chrisgopher Columbus in Stowaway on the Santa Maria. Smallwood, Steve, illus. 32p. (Orig.). (gr. k-6). 1992. PLB 4.00 (0-9633016-0-8) Infiniti.

Cecire, Kenneth. Multiple Choice Questions in Preparation for the AP Physics ("B" & "C") Examination. 72p. (gr. 11-12). 1991. wkbk. 15.95 (1-878621-10-6); tchr's. manual, 80p. avail. (1-878621-11-4) D & S Mktg Syst.

Ceckowski, Karen. The Joy of Serving. (Illus.). 48p. (gr. 9-12). 1991. pap. 7.99 (1-55945-210-2) Group Pub.

Cecotti, Loralie. Seattle Center. Hamer, Bonnie, illus. 24p. (Orig.). (gr. 1-4). 1983. pap. 2.75 (0-933992-30-0) Coffee Break.

—Washington Wildlife. Hamer, Bonnie, illus. 24p. (Orig.). (gr. k-5). 1984. pap. text ed. 2.75 (0-318-04105-7) Coffee Break.

Cedarbaum, Sophia. A First Book of Jewish Holidays. Ruthen, Marlene L., illus. LC 85-105348. 80p. (gr. 1-3). 1984. pap. text ed. 6.95 (0-8074-0274-5, 301500) UAHC.

Cedeno, Maria E. Cesar Chavez: Labor Leader. LC 92-22620. (Illus.). 32p. (gr. 2-4). 1993. PLB 12.40 (1-56294-280-8) Millbrook Pr.

CEF Staff, ed. Growing Songs for Children. 60p. (gr. k-6). 1978. pap. text ed. 2.99 (1-55976-205-5) CEF Press.

Celestri, John. The Christian Crusader: The Quest Begins. 72p. (gr. 3-6). 1992. pap. 3.49 (0-9634183-0-0) CC Comics.

—The Christian Crusader: The Quest Begins. rev. ed. Celestri, John, illus. 80p. 1992. pap. 3.99 (0-9634183-1-9) CC Comics.

—The Christian Crusader: Web of Lies...Chains of Sin. (Illus.). 80p. (Orig.). 1993. pap. 3.99 (0-9634183-2-7) CC Comics.

Cellino, Maria E., ed. see Williams, Thelma.

Celsi, Teresa. The Fourth Little Pig. Cushman, Doug, illus. 24p. (ps-3). 1990. PLB 14.60 (0-8172-3577-9); pap. 10.95 pkg. of 3 (0-685-67711-7) Raintree Steck-V.

—Jesse Jackson & Political Power. (Illus.). 32p. (gr. 2-4). 1991. PLB 12.40 (1-56294-040-6) Millbrook Pr.

—Ralph Nader: The Consumer Revolution. (Illus.). 104p. (gr. 7 up). 1991. PLB 14.90 (1-56294-044-9) Millbrook Pr.

—Rosa Parks & the Montgomery Bus Boycott. (Illus.). 32p. (gr. 2-4). 1991. PLB 12.40 (1-878841-14-9) Millbrook Pr.

Celsi, Teresa N. Squanto & the First Thanksgiving. (Illus.). 32p. (gr. 1-4). 1989. PLB 15.96 (0-8172-3511-6); pap. 3.95 (0-8114-6710-4) Raintree Steck-V.

Cendejas, Deena L., jt. auth. see Smith, M. Sherry.

Cendrars, Blaise. Shadow. Brown, Marcia, tr. from FRE. & illus. LC 81-9424. 40p. (gr. 2 up). 1982. SBE 16.95 (0-684-17226-7, Scribners Young Read) Macmillan Child Grp.

Center for Attitudinal Healing Staff. Advice to Doctors & Other Big People...from Kids. Jampolsky, Gerald, intro. by. (Illus.). 164p. (Orig.). (gr. 8-12). 1990. pap. 7.95 (0-89087-618-5) Celestial Arts.

—Another Look at the Rainbow. LC 82-12951. (gr. 1-5). 1983. pap. 8.95 (0-89087-341-0) Celestial Arts.

Center for Environmental Education Staff. The Ocean: Consider the Connections. Maraniss, Linda & Bierce, Rose, eds. Perry, Jill, illus. Asimov, Isaac, frwd. by. (Illus.). 104p. (Orig.). (gr. 2-6). 1985. pap. 8.95 wkbk. (0-9615294-0-7) Ctr Env Educ.

Center for Learning Network. Abortion: Beyond Personal Choice: Looking at Life. 12p. (gr. 9-12). 1992. pap. text ed. 0.80 (1-56077-222-0) Ctr Learning.

—Chastity: the Only Choice: Looking at Life. 12p. (gr. 7-12). 1992. pap. text ed. 0.80 (1-56077-221-2) Ctr Learning.

—Connections: A Summer Bible Program for Children. 78p. (gr. k-3). 1990. pap. text ed. 12.95 (1-56077-053-8) Ctr Learning.

—Divorce: Adjusting to Change: Looking at Life. 12p. (gr. 7-12). 1992. pap. text ed. 0.80 (1-56077-223-9) Ctr Learning.

—Fundamentalism: A Catholic Response. 98p. (gr. 9-12). 1992. pap. text ed. 12.95 (1-56077-062-7) Ctr Learning.

—My Journey, My Prayer. 96p. (gr. 9-12). 1991. pap. text ed. 5.95 (1-56077-128-3) Ctr Learning.

—Praying with Children, Bk. 1. 119p. (gr. 1-3). 1991. pap. text ed. 12.95 (1-56077-028-7) Ctr Learning.

—Praying with Children, Bk. 2. 107p. (gr. 4-6). 1991. pap. text ed. 12.95 (1-56077-029-5) Ctr Learning.

—Stepfamilies: Personal Adjustment: Looking at Life. 12p. (gr. 7-12). 1992. pap. text ed. 0.80 (1-56077-224-7) Ctr Learning.

Center for Learning Network Staff. Animal Farm by George Orwell & The Book of the Dun Cow by Walter Wangerin: Curriculum Unit. 107p. (gr. 9-12). 1992. 17.95 (1-56077-150-X) Ctr Learning.

—Babbitt by Sinclair Lewis: Curriculum Unit. 61p. (gr. 9-12). 1992. tchr's. ed. 17.95 (1-56077-210-7) Ctr Learning.

—Brave New World by Aldous Huxley: Curriculum Unit. 85p. (gr. 9-12). 1993. tchr's. ed. 18.95 (1-56077-281-6) Ctr Learning.

—Christian Service: Workshop Models. 101p. (gr. 7-8). 1992. tchr's. ed. 15.95 (1-56077-182-8) Ctr Learning.

—Coming to Terms with Divorce: A Guided Support Program for Primary Grades Workbook. 98p. (gr. 1-3). 1992. wkbk. 6.95 (1-56077-146-1) Ctr Learning.

—Coming to Terms with Divorce: A Guided Support Program for Primary Grades Leader's Manual. 75p. (gr. 1-3). 1992. tchr's. ed. 8.95 (1-56077-147-X) Ctr Learning.

—Crime & Punishment by Fyodor Dostoevsky: Curriculum Unit. 79p. (gr. 9-12). 1991. Repr. of 1987 ed. 17.95 (1-56077-176-3) Ctr Learning.

—Cyrano de Bergerac by Edmond Rostand: Curriculum Unit. 78p. (gr. 9-12). 1992. Repr. of 1989 ed. tchr's. ed. 17.95 (1-56077-209-3) Ctr Learning.

—A Doll's House & Hedda Gabler by Henrik Ibsen: Curriculum Unit. 71p. (gr. 9-12). 1991. Repr. of 1989 ed. 17.95 (1-56077-174-7) Ctr Learning.

—Faith & Belief: Workshop Models. 95p. (gr. 7-8). 1992. tchr's. ed. 15.95 (1-56077-181-X) Ctr Learning.

—A Farewell to Arms by Ernest Hemingway: Curriculum Unit. 64p. (gr. 9-12). 1993. tchr's. ed. 18.95 (1-56077-274-3) Ctr Learning.

—Hiroshima by John Hersey - On the Beach by Nevil Shute: Curriculum Unit. 82p. (gr. 6-12). 1992. 17.95 (1-56077-153-4) Ctr Learning.

—Justice & Peace: Workshop Models. 79p. (gr. 7-8). 1992. tchr's. ed. 15.95 (1-56077-183-6) Ctr Learning.

—Let's Talk to Teens about Chastity. (SPA.). 64p. (gr. 7-12). 1992. tchr's. ed. 5.95 (1-56077-155-0) Ctr Learning.

—Macbeth by William Shakespeare: Curriculum Unit. 92p. (gr. 9-12). 1991. 17.95 (1-56077-175-5) Ctr Learning.

—Oedipus the King by Sophocles: Curriculum Unit. 116p. (gr. 9-12). 1991. 17.95 (1-56077-167-4) Ctr Learning.

—The Old Man & the Sea by Ernest Hemingway - Ethan Frome by Edith Wharton: Curriculum Unit. 83p. (gr. 9-12). 1993. tchr's. ed. 18.95 (1-56077-279-4) Ctr Learning.

—Our Town by Thornton Wilder: Curriculum Unit. 84p. (gr. 9-12). Repr. of 1989 ed. 17.95 (1-56077-172-0) Ctr Learning.

—Personal Growth. 46p. (gr. 7-8). 1992. tchr's. ed. 7.95 (1-56077-184-4); student book, 72p. 5.95 (1-56077-233-6) Ctr Learning.

—Prayer & Worship: Workshop Models. 112p. (gr. 7-8). 1992. tchr's. ed. 15.95 (1-56077-185-2) Ctr Learning.

—A Raisin in the Sun by Lorraine Hansberry: Curriculum Unit. 90p. (gr. 9-12). 1992. Repr. of 1988 ed. tchr's. ed. 17.95 (1-56077-214-X) Ctr Learning.

—Relationships. 48p. (gr. 7-8). 1992. tchr's. ed. 7.95 (1-56077-186-0); student ed., 88p. 5.95 (1-56077-232-8) Ctr Learning.

—Searching for Yourself: A Journey to Discover Values. rev. ed. 212p. (gr. 7-9). 1992. tchr's. ed. 34.95 (1-56077-152-6) Ctr Learning.

—The Slave Dancer by Paula Fox & I, Juan De Pareja by Elizabeth Borton de Trevino: Curriculum Unit. 89p. (gr. 6-9). 1992. 17.95 (1-56077-180-1) Ctr Learning.

—A Streetcar Named Desire by Tennessee Williams: Curriculum Unit. 87p. (gr. 9-12). 1992. 17.95 (1-56077-169-0) Ctr Learning.

—Tale of Two Cities by Charles Dickens: Curriculum Unit. 73p. (gr. 9-12). 1991. 17.95 (1-56077-173-9) Ctr Learning.

—The Taming of the Shrew by William Shakespeare: Curriculum Unit. 2nd, rev. ed. 115p. (gr. 9-12). 1992. 17.95 (1-56077-170-4) Ctr Learning.

—To the Lighthouse by Virginia Woolf: Curriculum Unit. 99p. (gr. 9-12). 1992. 17.95 (1-56077-177-1) Ctr Learning.

—Today Is: An Ecumenical Prayer Journal for Young Teens. rev. ed. 80p. (gr. 6-9). 1992. pap. text ed. 3.95 (1-56077-217-4) Ctr Learning.

—A Tree Grows in Brooklyn by Betty Smith: Curriculum Unit. 88p. (gr. 9-12). 1993. tchr's. ed. 18.95 (1-56077-277-8) Ctr Learning.

—Twelfth Night by William Shakespeare: Curriculum Unit. 2nd, rev. ed. 111p. (gr. 9-12). 1992. 17.95 (1-56077-171-2) Ctr Learning.

—Uncle Tom's Cabin by Harriet Beecher Stowe: Curriculum Unit. 102p. (gr. 9-12). 1992. 17.95 (1-56077-151-8) Ctr Learning.

—U. S. Biographies, Bk. 1: Beginning to 1800. (gr. 4-8). 1992. student text, 48p. 4.95 (*1-56077-200-X*); tchr's. ed., 141p. 19.95 (*1-56077-160-7*) Ctr Learning.

—U. S. Biographies, Bk. 2: 1800-1830. (gr. 4-8). 1992. student text, 56p. 4.95 (*1-56077-201-8*); tchr's. ed., 148p. 19.95 (*1-56077-161-5*) Ctr Learning.

—U. S. Biographies, Bk. 3: 1830-1850. (gr. 4-8). 1992. student text, 56p. 4.95 (*1-56077-202-6*); tchr's. ed., 154p. 19.95 (*1-56077-162-3*) Ctr Learning.

—U. S. Biographies, Bk. 4: 1850-1890. (gr. 4-8). 1992. student text, 56p. 4.95 (*1-56077-203-4*); tchr's. ed., 146p. 19.95 (*1-56077-163-1*) Ctr Learning.

—U. S. Biographies, Bk. 5: 1890-1930. (gr. 4-8). 1992. student text, 54p. 4.95 (*1-56077-204-2*); tchr's. ed., 145p. 19.95 (*1-56077-164-X*) Ctr Learning.

—U. S. Biographies, Bk. 6: 1930-1960. (gr. 4-8). 1992. student text, 54p. 4.95 (*1-56077-205-0*); tchr's. ed., 140p. 19.95 (*1-56077-165-8*) Ctr Learning.

—U. S. Biographies, Bk. 7: 1960-1990. (gr. 4-8). 1992. student text, 56p. 4.95 (*1-56077-206-9*); tchr's. ed., 140p. 19.95 (*1-56077-166-6*) Ctr Learning.

—U. S. History & Geography, Bk. 1: Beginnings to 1877. 192p. (gr. 4-8). 1992. curriculum unit 24.95 (*1-56077-119-4*) Ctr Learning.

—U. S. History & Geography, Bk. 2: 1878 to the Present. 194p. (gr. 4-8). 1992. curriculum unit 24.95 (*1-56077-120-8*) Ctr Learning.

—Valuing Others: A Journey to Discover Values. rev. ed. 199p. (gr. 9-12). 1992. tchr's. ed. 34.95 (*1-56077-141-0*) Ctr Learning.

Center for Marine Conservation Staff. The Ocean Book: Aquarium & Seaside Activities & Ideas for All Ages. (gr. k-6). 1989. pap. text ed. 12.95 (*0-471-62078-5*) Wiley.

Center for Self Sufficiency, Research Division Staff. Finding Bargains by Using the Newspapers & or Telephone Directory: A Workbook. 21p. (gr. 11-12). pap. 14.95 (*0-91081187-3*) Ctr Self Suff.

Center, Y., jt. auth. see Yin-lien C. Chin.

Century, Douglas. Toni Morrison: Author. LC 93-31166. (Illus.). 1994. 18.95 (*0-7910-1877-6*, Am Art Analog); pap. write for info. (*0-7910-1906-3*, Am Art Analog) Chelsea Hse.

Cera, Mary J. Living with Death - Primary. 64p. (gr. 1-4). 1991. 7.95 (*0-86653-588-8*, GA1316) Good Apple.

Cera, Mary J. & Else, JoAnn. Trivial Pursuit - Language Arts (Intermediate) (Illus.). 64p. (gr. 4-6). 1992. 12.95 (*0-86653-648-5*, GA1383) Good Apple.

—Trivial Pursuit - Language Arts (Primary) (Illus.). 64p. (gr. 1-3). 1992. 12.95 (*0-86653-646-9*, GA1382) Good Apple.

Cerbus, Deborah P. & Rice, Cheryl F. Connecting Science & Literature. Apodaca, Blanca, et al, illus. 144p. (gr. k-3). 1991. wkbk. 12.95 (*1-55734-341-1*) Tchr Create Mat.

Cerf, Bennett. Riddle-De-Dee. 144p. (ps-8). 1990. pap. 3.95 (*0-345-36872-X*) Ballantine.

—Stories to Make You Feel Better. 1972. 12.95 (*0-394-47553-4*) Random Bks Yng Read.

Cerf, Bennett, ed. Riddle-De-Dee. 1962. 10.95 (*0-394-44304-7*) Random Bks Yng Read.

Cerf, Bennett A. Bennett Cerf's Book of Animal Riddles. LC 64-11246. (gr. 2-3). 1964. lib. bdg. 7.99 (*0-394-90034-0*) Beginner.

—Bennett Cerf's Book of Laughs. LC 59-13387. (Illus.). 72p. (gr. 1-2). 1959. lib. bdg. 7.99 (*0-394-90011-1*) Beginner.

—Bennett Cerf's Book of Riddles. LC 60-13492. (Illus.). 72p. (gr. 1-2). 1989. 6.95 (*0-394-80015-X*); lib. bdg. 7.99 (*0-394-90015-4*) Beginner.

—More Riddles. LC 61-11727. (Illus.). 72p. (gr. k-3). 1961. 6.95 (*0-394-80024-9*); lib. bdg. 7.99 (*0-394-90024-3*) Beginner.

Cernobous, Wayne J. Millie Milkweed Seed Meets the Genny Geranium Gang. Wyman, Helen B., illus. 46p. (Orig.). (gr. k-5). 1984. pap. 5.95 (*0-9615065-0-4*) Kinnickinnic Pr.

Cerro, Ana M., tr. see Ada, Alma F.

Cerullo, Mary M. Lobsters: Gangsters of the Sea. Rotman, Jeffrey L., photos by. LC 93-1288. (Illus.). 64p. (gr. 4 up). 1993. 15.95 (*0-525-65153-5*, Cobblehill Bks) Dutton Child Bks.

—Sharks: Challengers of the Deep. Rotman, Jeffrey L., photos by. LC 92-14206. 64p. (gr. 4 up). 1993. 15.00 (*0-525-65100-4*, Cobblehill Bks) Dutton Child Bks.

Cervantes. Don Quijote de la Mancha: Primer Parte. (gr. 7-12). pap. 5.95 (*0-88436-056-3*, 70275) EMC.

Cervantes, Miguel De see De Cervantes, Miguel.

Cervantes, Miguel de see De Cervantes, Miguel.

Cervantes, Miguel Saavedra De see De Cervantes, Miguel Saavedra.

CES Industries, Inc. Staff. Ed-Lab Eight Hundred Experiment Manual: EPROM Programming. (Illus., Orig.). (gr. 9-12). 1984. pap. write for info. (*0-86711-084-8*) CES Industries.

—Ed-Lab Eight Hundred Experiment Manual: Thermal Probe Sensor. (Illus., Orig.). (gr. 9-12). 1983. pap. write for info. (*0-86711-073-2*) CES Industries.

—Ed-Lab Experiment Manual: CES 380-85 Microprocessors. (Illus., Orig.). (gr. 9-12). 1984. pap. write for info. (*0-86711-076-7*) CES Industries.

—Ed-Lab Experiment Manual: CES 6010 Microwave Training System. (Illus., Orig.). (gr. 9-12). 1984. pap. write for info. (*0-86711-083-X*) CES Industries.

—Ed-Lab Experiment Manual: CES 6016 Telephone Modem. (Illus., Orig.). (gr. 9-12). 1984. pap. write for info. (*0-86711-085-6*) CES Industries.

Cesal, Barbara P. Heart to Heart for Primary Grades: Family Involvement in Primary Reading. (ps-3). 1993. pap. 14.95 (*0-201-49004-8*) Addison-Wesley.

Chacon, Rick. Big & Easy Art. Chacon, Rick, illus. 32p. (ps-1). 1986. wkbk. 4.95 (*1-55734-074-9*) Tchr Create Mat.

—Grocery Bag Art: Farm. Chacon, Rick, illus. 48p. (ps-3). 1986. wkbk. 5.95 (*1-55734-071-4*) Tchr Create Mat.

—Grocery Bag Art: Holidays. Chacon, Rick, illus. 48p. (ps-3). 1986. wkbk. 5.95 (*1-55734-073-0*) Tchr Create Mat.

Chadefaud, Catherine & Coblence, Jean-Michel. The First Empires. Ridett, Anthea, tr. from FRE. Tarride, Michel, illus. 77p. (gr. 7 up). 1988. 17.98 (*0-39481-6*); 10.37s.p. (*0-685-18824-8*) Silver Burdett Pr.

Chadwick, Charley G., et al. Wall Framing. Harrington, Lois G., ed. Smith, George W., Jr. & Edwards, Jason, illus. 72p. (Orig.). (gr. 10-12). 1989. pap. text ed. 8.00 (*0-89606-266-X*, 701); tchr's. key 3.00 (*0-685-27030-0*, 701TK) Am Assn Voc Materials.

Chadwick, Frank. Cloud Captains of Mars. Aulisio, Janet, illus. 64p. (Orig.). 1989. pap. 8.00 (*1-55878-043-2*) Game Designers.

—Ironclads & Ether Flyers. Deitrick, David, illus. 112p. (Orig.). 1990. pap. 12.00 (*0-943580-96-X*) Game Designers.

Chadwick, Frank A. Conklin's Atlas. Ryan, Shea, illus. 80p. (Orig.). 1989. pap. 10.00 (*1-55878-024-6*) Game Designers.

—Twilight: Two Thousand. Harris, Dell, illus. 280p. (Orig.). 1990. pap. 20.00 (*1-55878-070-X*) Game Designers.

Chadwick, Frank S. Cadillacs & Dinosaurs. Schultz, Mark, illus. 144p. (Orig.). (gr. 9-12). 1990. pap. 18.00 (*1-55878-073-4*) Game Designers.

Chadwick, Kenneth E. A Hear Do'n Sing Book: Little Bitty You Little Bitty Me. Boss, Jackie, illus. (ps). 1979. 4.25 (*0-9603698-0-5*) Bet-Ken Prods.

Chadwick, Roxane. Amelia Earhart: Aviation Pioneer. (Illus.). 56p. (gr. 4 up). 1987. PLB 13.50 (*0-8225-0484-7*); pap. 4.95 (*0-8225-9515-X*) Lerner Pubns.

—Anne Morrow Lindbergh: Pilot & Poet. (Illus.). 56p. (gr. 4 up). 1987. PLB 13.50 (*0-8225-0488-X*); pap. 4.95 (*0-8225-9516-8*) Lerner Pubns.

—Once upon a Felt Board. Skiles, Janet, illus. 128p. (gr. k-4). 1986. wkbk. 10.95 (*0-86653-338-9*, GA 798) Good Apple.

Chadwick, Tim. Cabbage Moon. Harper, Piers, illus. LC 93-28952. 1994. 14.95 (*0-531-06827-7*); lib. bdg. write for info. (*0-531-08677-1*) Orchard Bks Watts.

Chadwick, Valerie A., illus. Book of Mormon Story & Coloring Book. (Orig.). (gr. 3-6). Date not set. pap. 4.95 (*0-87579-702-4*) Deseret Bk.

Chafconloff, E., jt. auth. see Blasky, A.

Chafe, William. The Road to Equality: American Women Since 1962. (Illus.). 144p. 1994. lib. bdg. 20.00 (*0-19-508325-3*) OUP.

Chaffin, Charles, jt. auth. see Neufeld, Herm.

Chaffin, Garry, jt. auth. see Burnsed, Linda.

Chaffin, Gary & Burnsed, Linda. A Child's Gift of Bedtime Stories. Ragland, Teresa, illus. LC 93-17766. 44p. (ps-6). 1993. 13.95 (*1-56566-044-7*) Thomasson-Grant.

Chaffin, Ken. Computers. Nolte, Larry, illus. 48p. (gr. 3-6). Date not set. PLB 12.95 (*1-56065-115-6*) Capstone Pr. Postponed.

Chaffin, Lillie D. Tommy's Big Problem. Petie, Haris, illus. (ps-2). PLB 7.19 (*0-8313-0016-7*) Lantern.

Chaikin, Linda. Silk. 400p. (Orig.). 1993. pap. 8.99 (*1-55661-248-6*) Bethany Hse.

Chaikin, Miriam. Ask Another Question: The Story & Meaning of Passover. Friedman, Marvin, illus. LC 84-12744. 96p. (gr. 3-6). 1985. (Clarion Bks); pap. 4.95 (*0-89919-423-0*, Clarion Bks) HM.

—Esther. Rosenberry, Vera, illus. LC 86-20183. 32p. (gr. 2-6). 1987. 9.95 (*0-8276-0272-3*); pap. 7.95 (*0-8276-0508-0*) JPS Phila.

—Exodus. Mikolaycak, Charles, illus. LC 85-27361. 32p. (gr. 1-4). 1987. reinforced bdg. 15.95 (*0-8234-0607-5*) Holiday.

—Feathers in the Wind. Saldutti, Denise, illus. LC 88-10978. 64p. (gr. 3-5). 1989. HarpC Child Bks.

—Hanukkah. Weiss, Ellen, illus. LC 89-77512. 32p. (ps-3). 1990. reinforced bdg. 15.95 (*0-8234-0816-7*) Holiday.

—Hanukkah. Weiss, Ellen, illus. LC 89-77512. 32p. (ps-3). 1990. pap. 5.95 (*0-8234-0905-8*) Holiday.

—Hinkl & Other Schlemiel Stories. (Illus.). 96p. (Orig.). (gr. 3-12). 1987. 10.95 (*0-933503-15-6*) Shapolsky Pubs.

—Hinkl & Other Shlemiel Stories. Posner, Marcia, illus. LC 86-29755. 96p. (Orig.). (gr. 7 up). 1987. pap. 6.95 (*0-933503-37-7*) Shapolsky Pubs.

—Joshua in the Promised Land. Frampton, David, illus. (gr. 3-6). 1990. pap. 6.70 (*0-395-54797-0*, Clarion Bks) HM.

—Light Another Candle: The Story & Meaning of Hanukkah. 1987 ed. Demi, illus. (gr. 7 up). 1981. pap. 6.95 (*0-89919-057-X*, Clarion Bks) HM.

—Make Noise, Make Merry. (gr. 4-7). 1983. 11.95 (*0-89919-140-1*, Clarion Bks) HM.

—Make Noise, Make Merry: The Story & Meaning of Purim. Demi, illus. LC 82-12926. 96p. (gr. 3-6). 1986. pap. 4.95 (*0-89919-424-9*, Clarion Bks) HM.

—Menorahs, Mezuzas, & Other Jewish Symbols. Weihs, Erika, illus. (gr. 5 up). 1990. 14.95 (*0-89919-856-2*, Clarion Bks) HM.

—Shake a Palm Branch: The Story & Meaning of Sukkot. Friedman, Marvin, illus. LC 84-5022. 96p. (gr. 3-6). 1984. 12.95 (*0-89919-254-8*, Clarion Bks); pap. 4.95 (*0-89919-428-1*, Clarion Bks) HM.

—Sound the Shofar: The Story & Meaning of Rosh HaShanah & Yom Kippur. Weihs, Erika, illus. LC 86-2651. 96p. (gr. 3-7). 1986. (Clarion Bks); pap. 4.95 (*0-89919-427-3*, Clarion Bks) HM.

—Three Aesop Fox Fables. (gr. 4-7). 1992. pap. 7.70 (*0-395-61580-1*, Clarion Bks) HM.

Chaikin, Miriam, retold by. Children's Bible Stories: From Genesis to Daniel. Gilbert, Yvonne, illus. LC 90-42588. 96p. (gr. 1-5). 1993. 17.99 (*0-8037-0956-0*); PLB 17.89 (*0-8037-0990-0*) Dial Bks Young.

Chalabian, Antranig. Revolutionary Figures (in Armenian) Mihran Damadian, Hambartzum Boyajian, Serob Aghbiur, Hrair-Dzhoghk, Gevorg Chavush, Sebastasti Murad, Nigol Tuman. (Illus.). 464p. 1991. 25.00 (*0-9622741-2-7*) A Chalabian.

Chalk, Gary. Yankee Doodle. Chalk, Gary, illus. LC 92-53482. 48p. (gr. k-3). 1993. 14.95 (*1-56458-202-7*) Dorling Kindersley.

Chalk, Gary, jt. auth. see Dever, Joe.

Chall, Marsha W. Mattie. LC 91-3042. (ps-3). 1992. 11.00 (*0-688-09730-8*) Lothrop.

—Mattie. 48p. 1994. pap. 3.50 (*0-380-72116-3*, Camelot Young) Avon.

—Up North at the Cabin. LC 91-3035. (ps-3). 1992. PLB 14.93 (*0-688-09733-2*) Lothrop.

—Up North at the Cabin. (ps-3). 1992. 15.00 (*0-688-09732-4*) Lothrop.

Challand, Helen. Activities in the Earth Sciences. LC 82-9444. (Illus.). (gr. 5 up). 1982. PLB 17.27 (*0-516-00506-5*) Childrens.

—Activities in the Life Sciences. LC 82-9442. (Illus.). (gr. 5 up). 1982. PLB 17.27 (*0-516-00507-3*) Childrens.

—Earthquakes. LC 82-9699. (Illus.). (gr. k-4). 1982. PLB 15.27 (*0-516-01636-9*); pap. 4.95 (*0-516-41636-7*) Childrens.

—Experiments with Electricity. LC 85-30887. (Illus.). 48p. (gr. k-4). 1986. PLB 15.27 (*0-516-01276-2*); pap. 4.95 (*0-516-41276-0*) Childrens.

—Experiments with Magnets. LC 85-30851. (Illus.). 48p. (gr. k-4). 1986. PLB 15.27 (*0-516-01279-7*); pap. 4.95 (*0-516-41279-5*) Childrens.

—Plants Without Seeds. LC 85-30935. (Illus.). 48p. (gr. k-4). 1986. PLB 15.27 (*0-516-01280-0*) Childrens.

Challand, Helen J. Activities in the Physical Sciences. LC 83-26224. (Illus.). 96p. (gr. 5 up). 1984. PLB 17.27 (*0-516-00504-9*) Childrens.

—Disappearing Wetlands. LC 91-38243. 128p. (gr. 4-8). 1992. PLB 26.60 (*0-516-05511-9*) Childrens.

—Experiments with Chemistry. LC 88-11862. (Illus.). 48p. (gr. k-4). 1988. PLB 15.27 (*0-516-01151-0*) Childrens.

—Science Projects & Activities. Kimball, Linda H., illus. LC 84-23252. 93p. (gr. 5-8). 1985. PLB 17.27 (*0-516-00569-3*) Childrens.

—Vanishing Forests. LC 91-25863. 128p. (gr. 4-8). 1991. PLB 26.60 (*0-516-05505-4*) Childrens.

—Volcanoes. LC 82-17888. (Illus.). 48p. (gr. k-4). 1983. PLB 15.27 (*0-516-01690-3*); pap. 4.95 (*0-516-41690-1*) Childrens.

Challoner, J. The Science Book of Numbers. 1992. 9.95 (*0-15-200623-0*, Gulliver Bks) HarBrace.

Challoner, Jack. Energy. LC 92-54479. (Illus.). 64p. (gr. 7 up). 1993. 15.95 (*1-56458-232-9*) Dorling Kindersley.

—My First Batteries & Magnets. LC 92-52825. (Illus.). 48p. (gr. k-4). 1992. 12.95 (*1-56458-133-0*) Dorling Kindersley.

Chalmers, Mary. A Christmas Story. Chalmers, Mary, illus. LC 56-8143. 24p. (ps-1). 1962. Repr. of 1956 ed. PLB 12.89 (*0-06-021191-1*) HarpC Child Bks.

—Easter Parade. Chalmers, Mary, illus. LC 87-45277. 32p. (ps-1). 1988. PLB 11.89 (*0-06-021233-0*) HarpC Child Bks.

—Easter Parade. Chalmers, Mary, illus. LC 87-45277. 32p. (ps-1). 1990. pap. 4.95 (*0-06-443219-X*, Trophy) HarpC Child Bks.

—Merry Christmas, Harry. new ed. LC 90-27516. (Illus.). 32p. (ps-2). 1992. 13.00 (*0-06-022739-7*); PLB 12.89 (*0-06-022742-7*) HarpC Child Bks.

—Take a Nap, Harry. Chalmers, Mary, illus. LC 89-77655. 32p. (ps-2). 1991. PLB 13.89 (*0-06-021244-6*) HarpC Child Bks.

—Throw a Kiss, Harry. Chalmers, Mary, illus. LC 89-49064. 32p. (ps-2). 1990. 12.95 (*0-06-021246-2*) HarpC Child Bks.

Chamberlain, E. R. Florence in the Time of the Medici. Reeves, Marjorie, illus. LC 83-6929. (gr. 7-12). 1982. pap. 8.76 (*0-582-20489-5*, 70771) Longman.

Chamberlain, Eugene. Carol Beth Learns about Following Jesus. LC 89-38428. (gr. 1-3). 1991. 6.95 (*0-8054-4340-1*) Broadman.

—Jesus: God's Son, Saviour, Lord. Padgett, James, illus. (gr. 1-6). 1976. pap. 5.95 (*0-8054-4226-X*, 4242-26) Broadman.

—Loyd Corder: Traveler for God. LC 82-73663. (gr. 4-6). 1983. 5.95 (*0-8054-4284-7*, 4242-84) Broadman.

Chamberlain, Margaret, jt. auth. see Mahy, Margaret.

Chamberlain, Margaret, jt. auth. see Umansky, Kaye.

Chamberlain, Margaret, illus. The Little Christmas Fold-Out Book. 28p. (ps-4). 1991. accordian bk. 4.99 (*0-7459-2121-3*) Lion USA.

Chamberlain, Martha E. Surviving Junior High. LC 88-2937. 296p. (Orig.). (gr. 7-9). 1988. pap. 9.95 (0-8361-3462-1) Herald Pr.
Chamberlain, Sarah, illus. Friendly Beasts: A Traditional Christmas Carol. LC 91-2115. 24p. (ps-2). 1991. 13.95 (0-525-44743-3, DCB) Dutton Child Bks.
Chamberlain, Shannin. My ABC Book of Cancer. (Illus.). 40p. (Orig.). (ps-8). 1991. pap. 6.95 (0-912184-07-8) Synergistic Pr.
Chamberlain, Valerie M. & Buddinger, Peyton B. Teen Guide. 6th ed. O'Neill, Martha, ed. Evelyne Johnson Associates Staff, illus. 528p. 1985. text ed. 30.00 (0-07-007842-4); pap. text ed. 11.68 (0-07-007831-9) McGraw.
Chambers. Tollbridge. Date not set. 15.00 (0-06-023598-5, Festival); PLB 14.89 (0-06-023599-3, Festival) HarpC Child Bks.
Chambers, Aidan, ed. A Haunt of Ghosts. LC 86-45486. 192p. (gr. 7 up). 1987. HarpC Child Bks.
Chambers, Barry. Willy the Hit Man. 94p. (gr. 4-8). 1992. pap. 5.25 (1-880384-01-9) Coldwater Pr.
Chambers, Cally, jt. auth. see Peacock, Graham.
Chambers, Catherine & Wright, Rachel. Spain. LC 92-27137. 1993. 11.90 (0-531-14257-4) Watts.
Chambers, Catherine E. California Gold Rush: Search for Treasure. Eitzen, Alan, illus. LC 83-18280. 32p. (gr. 5-9). 1984. PLB 11.59 (0-8167-0051-6); pap. text ed. 2.95 (0-8167-0052-4) Troll Assocs.
—Daniel Boone & the Wilderness Road. Guzzi, George, illus. LC 83-18291. 32p. (gr. 5-9). 1984. PLB 11.59 (0-8167-0037-0); pap. text ed. 2.95 (0-8167-0038-3) Troll Assocs.
—Flatboats on the Ohio: Westward Bound. Lawn, John, illus. LC 83-18278. 32p. (gr. 5-9). 1984. PLB 11.59 (0-8167-0049-4); pap. text ed. 2.95 (0-8167-0050-8) Troll Assocs.
—Frontier Dream: Life on the Great Plains. Smolinski, Dick, illus. LC 83-18282. 32p. (gr. 5-9). 1984. PLB 11.59 (0-8167-0039-7); pap. text ed. 2.95 (0-8167-0040-0) Troll Assocs.
—Frontier Farmer: Kansas Adventures. Epstein, Len, illus. LC 83-18279. 32p. (gr. 5-9). 1984. PLB 11.59 (0-8167-0053-2); pap. text ed. 2.95 (0-8167-0054-0) Troll Assocs.
—Frontier Village: A Town Is Born. Smolinski, Dick, illus. LC 83-18271. 32p. (gr. 5-9). 1984. PLB 11.59 (0-8167-0045-1); pap. text ed. 2.95 (0-8167-0046-X) Troll Assocs.
—Indiana Days: Life in a Frontier Town. Lawn, John, illus. LC 83-18283. 32p. (gr. 5-9). 1984. PLB 11.59 (0-8167-0055-9); pap. text ed. 2.95 (0-8167-0056-7) Troll Assocs.
—Log Cabin Home: Pioneers in the Wilderness. Eitzen, Alan, illus. LC 83-18277. 32p. (gr. 5-9). 1984. PLB 11.59 (0-8167-0041-9); pap. text ed. 2.95 (0-8167-0042-7) Troll Assocs.
—Texas Roundup: Life on the Range. Lawn, John, illus. LC 83-18281. 32p. (gr. 5-9). 1984. PLB 11.59 (0-8167-0047-X); pap. text ed. 2.95 (0-8167-0048-6) Troll Assocs.
—Wagons West: Off to Oregon. Smolinski, Dick, illus. LC 83-18276. 32p. (gr. 5-9). 1984. PLB 11.59 (0-8167-0043-5); pap. text ed. 2.95 (0-8167-0044-3) Troll Assocs.
Chambers, John. One Hundred One Irish Lives. (Illus.). 348p. (Orig.). (gr. 4-8). 1992. pap. 21.95 (0-7171-1725-1, Pub. by Gill & Macmillan EIRE) Irish Bks Media.
Chambers, Vickie. In the Silence of the Hills. Taylor, LaVonne, ed. (Illus.). (gr. 9-12). Date not set. write for info. (0-9627735-1-4) Excllnc Entrps.
Chambless, Jane. Tucker & the Bear. LC 89-30244. (ps-2). 1989. pap. 13.95 (0-671-67357-2, S&S BFYR) S&S Trade.
Chambliss, Maxie, illus. I Know an Old Lady. 1987. pap. 6.99 incl. audiocassette (0-553-45901-5) Bantam.
Champanier, jt. auth. see Stewart.
Champion, Joyce. Emily & Alice. Stevenson, Sucie, illus. LC 92-13575. 1993. 13.95 (0-15-200588-9) HarBrace.
—Emily & Alice Again. Stevenson, Sucie, illus. LC 93-5004. 1994. write for info. (0-15-200439-4, Gulliver Bks) HarBrace.
Champlin, Allen R., Sr., jt. auth. see Ross, Elena.
Champlin, Connie & DeVasure, John. Storytelling with the Computer. (Illus.). 64p. (gr. k-6). 1986. pap. 29.95 (0-938594-09-5); diskette incl. Spec Lit Pr.
Champlin, Connie, jt. auth. see Champlin, John.
Champlin, Dale, illus. Down by the Bay Big Book. (ps-2). 1988. pap. text ed. 14.00 (0-922053-02-2) N Edge Res.
—The Wheels on the Bus Big Book. (ps-2). 1988. pap. text ed. 14.00 (0-922053-15-4) N Edge Res.
Champlin, John & Champlin, Connie. Books, Puppets & the Mentally Retarded Student. Anderson, Carol A., illus. 162p. (Orig.). 1981. pap. 15.95 (0-938594-00-1) Spec Lit Pr.
Champlin, John, ed. see Connelly, Tony & Holley, Cindy.
Champlin, John, ed. see Keefe, Betty.
Chan, Barbara J. Kid Pix Around the World: A Computer & Activities Book. Chan, Barbara J., illus. LC 92-46141. 1993. pap. 12.95 (0-201-62226-2) Addison-Wesley.
Chan, Janis F. Getting Help. (Illus.). 64p. (gr. 7 up). 1982. pap. text ed. 3.95 (0-915510-61-8) Fearon-Janus.
Chan, Jeffery, ed. The Big AIIIEEEEE! (gr. 9-12). 14.95 (0-685-61040-3) JACP Inc.

Chan, Jennifer L. One Small Girl. Lee, Wendy K., illus. LC 92-35423. 32p. (gr. k-2). 1993. 12.95 (1-879965-05-4) Polychrome Pub.
Chan, Margie. The Eye 'N' Hand, Book One for Violin. (gr. 2). 1988. write for info. GIM-Ho.
—Music Concepts & Vocabulary for Violin, Bk. 1. 41p. (gr. 2 up). 1984. wkbk. 4.95 (0-9615006-0-3) Gim-Ho.
—Music Concepts & Vocabulary for Violin, Bk. 2. 48p. (gr. 2 up). 1985. wkbk. 4.95 (0-9615006-1-1) Gim Ho.
Chana Faiga Brander. A Blick of Tzurik. Bayer, Breindy, illus. 126p. (Orig.). (gr. 4). 1990. pap. text ed. 9.50 (0-9629684-0-4) K K Aharon.
Chance, Suzanne. Dig Me Up. 176p. (Orig.). 1992. pap. 3.50 (0-380-76917-4, Flare) Avon.
Chancellor, Betty. A Child's Christmas Cookbook. Obering, Kay & Nast, Thomas, illus. 40p. (Orig.). (gr. 1-8). 1969. pap. 4.00 (0-914510-00-2) Evergreen.
Chandler, Ann. Black Women: A Salute to Black Inventors. rev. ed. Ivery, Evelyn L., ed. Chandler, Alton, et al, illus. Chandler, Alton, intro. by. 24p. (gr. 3-7). 1992. pap. text ed. 1.50 (1-877804-06-1) Chandler White.
Chandler, David. Exploring the Night Sky with Binoculars. Davis, Don, illus. 48p. (Orig.). 1983. pap. 4.95 (0-9613207-0-2) D Chandler.
Chandler, David P. The Land & People of Cambodia. LC 90-5907. (Illus.). 224p. (gr. 6 up). 1991. 17.95 (0-06-021129-6); PLB 17.89 (0-06-021130-X) HarpC Child Bks.
Chandler, Jane. Glass. Stefoff, Rebecca, ed. Barber, Ed, photos by. LC 91-18191. (Illus.). 32p. (gr. 3-5). 1991. PLB 15.93 (1-56074-004-3) Garrett Ed Corp.
Chandler, Linda S. When I Talk to God. LC 84-4967. (Illus.). 1984. 6.95 (0-8054-4291-X, 4242-91) Broadman.
Chandonnet, Ann. Chief Stephen's Parky: One Year in the Life of an Athapascan Girl. Gilliland, Hap, ed. (Illus.). 72p. (Orig.). (gr. 4-12). 1989. pap. 7.95 (0-89992-119-1) Coun India Ed.
—Chief Stephen's Parky: One Year in the Life of An Athapascan Girl. 2nd ed. Kasl, Janette, illus. LC 92-61910. 80p. (gr. 4-6). 1993. pap. 7.95 (1-879373-39-4) R Rinehart.
Chandra, Deborah. Balloons: And Other Poems. (gr. 4-7). 1993. pap. 3.95 (0-374-40492-5) FS&G.
—Miss Mabel's Table. Grover, Max, illus. LC 93-9137. (ps-2). 1993. write for info. (0-15-276712-6, Browndeer Pr) HarBrace.
—Rich Lizard: And Other Poems. (gr. 4-7). 1993. 14.00 (0-374-36274-2) FS&G.
Chandrasekhar, Aruna. Oliver & the Oil Spill. Thatch, Nancy R., ed. Chandrasekhar, Aruna, illus. Melton, David, intro. by. LC 91-3340. (Illus.). 26p. (gr. k-4). 1991. PLB 14.95 (0-933849-33-8) Landmark Edns.
Chaney, Casey. Ready, Willing & Terrified: A Coward's Guide to Risk-Taking. Moffett, Berdell & Rhiannon, Thea, eds. Craghead, Gary, illus. 144p. (Orig.). 1991. pap. 10.95 (0-9626403-1-X) Mocha Pub.
Chaney, J. R. Aleksandr Pushkin: Poet for the People. 112p. (gr. 5 up). 1991. PLB 21.50 (0-8225-4911-5) Lerner Pubns.
Chaney, Lisa. Breakfast. (Illus.). 32p. (gr. 3-6). 1992. 12.95 (0-7136-3186-4, Pub. by A&C Black UK) Talman.
Chaney, Sky & Fisher, Pam, eds. The Discovery Book: A Helpful Guide for the World Written by Children with Disabilities. rev. ed. (Illus.). 100p. (gr. 3-10). 1989. pap. 7.95 (0-9616891-1-0) UCPANB.
Chaney, Steve. The Puppet in the Big Black Box. Katz, Richard, illus. 32p. (gr. k-3). 1989. write for info. Stiff Lip.
Chang, Florence C. Believe It or Not: An Anthology of Ancient Tales Retold. Chang, Shou-Jen, illus. LC 80-68258. 80p. (gr. 10-12). 1980. pap. 6.25x (wkbk. incl.) (0-936620-02-1) Ginkgo Hut.
—China Is Farther Than the Sun? A Beginning Chinese-English Reader. LC 80-68256. (Illus.). 51p. (gr. 3-4). 1980. pap. 5.50x incl. wkbk. (0-936620-00-5) Ginkgo Hut.
—Maomao & Mimi. Chang, Tao-Yuan, illus. LC 81-80784. 80p. (Orig.). (gr. 5-9). 1981. pap. 4.15x incl. exercises (0-936620-05-6) Ginkgo Hut.
—Puppy's Tail. Chang, Tao-Yuan, illus. LC 81-82176. 72p. (Orig.). (gr. 1-2). 1981. pap. 4.15x incl. exercises (0-936620-06-4) Ginkgo Hut.
—With Sound & Color: An Intermediate Chinese-English Reader. Chai, Florence, illus. LC 80-68257. 71p. (Orig.). (gr. 7-9). 1980. pap. 6.00x (wkbk. incl.) (0-936620-01-3) Ginkgo Hut.
Chang, Heidi. Elaine & the Flying Frog. Chang, Heidi, illus. LC 90-33721. 64p. (Orig.). (gr. 2-4). 1991. PLB 6.99 (0-679-90870-6); pap. 2.50 (0-679-80870-1) Random Bks Yng Read.
—Elaine, Mary Lewis, & the Frogs. (Illus.). 64p. (gr. 2-5). 1988. PLB 9.95 (0-517-56752-0) Crown Bks Yng Read.
Chang, Ina. A Separate Battle: Women & the Civil War. (Illus.). 112p. (gr. 5-9). 1991. 16.00 (0-525-67365-2, Lodestar Bks) Dutton Child Bks.
Chang, Margaret & Chang, Raymond. The Cricket Warrior. Hutton, Warwick, illus. LC 93-35395. (gr. 3 up). 1994. write for info. (0-689-50605-8, Atheneum Child Bk) MacMillan.
—In the Eye of War. LC 89-38027. 208p. (gr. 4-7). 1990. SBE 14.95 (0-689-50503-5, M K McElderry) Macmillan Child Grp.
Chang, Monica. The Mouse Bride: A Chinese Folktale. Lin, Lesley, illus. LC 91-44296. 32p. (gr. k-4). 1992. 14.95 (0-87358-533-X) Northland AZ.

Chang, Raymond, jt. auth. see Chang, Margaret.
Chanin, Michael. Grandfather Four Winds & Rising Moon. Smith, Sally, illus. LC 93-2689. 1994. 14.95 (0-915811-47-2) H J Kramer Inc.
Channen, Don. Tallis Ends & Other Tales. 184p. 1992. pap. 14.95 (965-229-053-X, Pub. by Gefen Pub Hse IS) Gefen Bks.
—UH! OH! Hanukkah. (gr. 3-7). 1993. 12.95 (0-943706-15-7) Yllw Brick Rd.
Chanover, Alice, jt. auth. see Chanover, Hyman.
Chanover, Hyman & Chanover, Alice. Pesah Is Coming. Kessler, Leonard, illus. (gr. k-2). 1956. 5.95 (0-8381-0713-3, 10-713) United Syn Bk.
—Pesah Is Here. Kessler, Leonard, illus. (gr. k-2). 1956. 5.95 (0-8381-0714-1) United Syn Bk.
Chanover, Hyman & Zusman, Evelyn. A Book of Prayer for Junior Congregations: Sabbath & Festivals. (ENG & HEB.). 256p. (gr. 4-7). 4.50x (0-8381-0174-7, 10-174) United Syn Bk.
Chanover, Hyman, adapted by. Service for the High Holy Days Adapted for Youth. LC 72-2058. 192p. (gr. 8 up). 1972. pap. 4.95x (0-87441-123-8) Behrman.
Chant, Barry. Spindles & the Giant Eagle Rescue. 1991. PLB 3.99 (0-8423-6214-2) Tyndale.
—Spindles & the Mystery of the Missing Numbat. 1991. PLB 3.99 (0-8423-6213-4) Tyndale.
Chant, Chris. Airliners. Batchelor, John, illus. LC 88-28762. 63p. (gr. 3 up). 1990. PLB 16.95 (1-85435-088-9) Marshall Cavendish.
—Sailing Ships. Batchelor, John, illus. LC 88-28706. 63p. (gr. 3 up). 1990. PLB 16.95 (1-85435-091-9) Marshall Cavendish.
—Steam Locomotives. Batchelor, John, illus. LC 88-28763. 63p. (gr. 3-9). 1989. PLB 16.95 (1-85435-087-0) Marshall Cavendish.
—Steamships. Batchelor, John, illus. LC 88-28764. 63p. (gr. 3-9). 1989. PLB 16.95 (1-85435-086-2) Marshall Cavendish.
Chant, Christopher. Military History of the United States, 16 vols. (Illus.). 2000p. 1992. PLB 459.95 (1-85435-351-9) Marshall Cavendish.
Chapian, Marie. Am I the Only One Here with Faded Genes? LC 87-11611. (Illus.). 192p. 1987. pap. 7.99 (0-87123-945-0) Bethany Hse.
—Feeling Small... Walking Tall. 176p. (Orig.). (gr. 8 up). 1989. pap. 7.99 (1-55661-029-7) Bethany Hse.
—Mothers & Daughters. LC 88-4199. 176p. (Orig.). (gr. 8 up). 1988. pap. 7.99 (1-55661-007-6) Bethany Hse.
—The Secret Place of Strength. 208p. (Orig.). 1991. 10.99 (1-55661-219-2) Bethany Hse.
Chapian, Marie, jt. auth. see Coyle, Neva.
Chapin, Laurie & Flagenheimer-Riggle, Ellen. Looking into Literature & Seeing Myself. (Illus.). 128p. (gr. k-3). 1992. wkbk. 10.95 (0-86653-706-6, 1427) Good Apple.
Chapin, Laurie & Flegenheimer-Riggle, Ellen. Leaping into Literature. 144p. (gr. k-3). 1990. 11.95 (0-86653-561-6, GA1164) Good Apple.
Chapin, Tom & Forster, John. Sing a Whale Song. Smath, Jerry, illus. 32p. 1993. incl. cass. 14.00 (0-679-83478-8) Random Bks Yng Read.
Chapin, Tom, narrated by see Elliott, Joey.
Chapin, Tom, narrated by see Harms, Valerie.
Chapin, Tom, narrated by see Thompson-Hoffman, Susan.
Chaplan, Roberta. Tell Me a Story, Paint Me the Sun: When a Girl Feels Ignored by Her Father. LC 91-7233. (Illus.). 48p. (gr. 3-6). 1991. pap. 7.95 (0-945354-24-X) Magination Pr.
Chaplik, Dorothy. Jesse Jackson: Up with Hope: A Biography of Jesse Jackson. rev. ed. LC 86-11634. (Illus.). 128p. (gr. 6 up). 1987. RSBE 13.95 (0-87518-347-6, Dillon) Macmillan Child Grp.
Chaplin, Susan. I Can Sign My ABC's. McCaul, Laura, illus. LC 86-22890. 56p. (ps-1). 1986. 9.95 (0-930323-19-X, Kendall Green Pubns) Gallaudet Univ Pr.
Chapman. Superbikes. rev. ed. (gr. 4-6). 1984. (Usborne-Hayes); pap. 5.95 (0-86020-182-1) EDC.
Chapman, Al. Coloring Book of New Mexico Santos. Ortega, Pedro R., tr. Chapman, Al, illus. (SPA & ENG.). 32p. (gr. 1-8). 1982. pap. 3.00 (0-913270-19-9) Sunstone Pr.
Chapman, Carl. Who Am I among So Many? An Autobiography Plus Special Articles: The Biggest Exception in the Bible, Paul's Thorn in the Flesh, & Not Discerning the Lord's Body. LC 88-92635. 132p. (Orig.). (gr. 9-12). 1989. pap. 4.99 (0-9621529-0-0) C Chapman.
Chapman, Carol. Barney Bipple's Magic Dandelions. Kellogg, Steven, illus. LC 77-5747. 32p. (gr. k-3). 1988. 13.95 (0-525-44449-1, DCB) Dutton Child Bks.
—Barney Bipple's Magic Dandelions. Kellogg, Steven, illus. LC 77-14852. 32p. (gr-3). 1992. pap. 3.99 (0-14-054540-9, Puffin Unicorn) Puffin Bks.
—The Tale of Meshka the Kvetch. Lobel, Arnold, illus. LC 80-11225. 32p. (gr. k-3). 1980. 13.95 (0-525-40745-6, DCB) Dutton Child Bks.
—The Tale of Meshka the Kvetch. Lobel, Arnold, illus. LC 80-11225. 32p. (gr. k-3). 1989. pap. 3.95 (0-525-44494-7, DCB) Dutton Child Bks.
—Tale of Meshka the Kvetch. (ps-3). 1993. pap. 4.99 (0-14-054787-8) Puffin Bks.
Chapman, Charles, ed. see Claire, Elizabeth.
Chapman, Charles, ed. see Olshtain, Elite, et al.
Chapman, Cheryl. Pass the Fritters, Critters. Roth, Susan L., illus. LC 91-45055. 40p. (ps-k). 1993. RSBE 14.95 (0-02-717975-3, Four Winds) Macmillan Child Grp.

—Snow on Snow on Snow. St. James, Synthia, illus. 1994. write for info. (*0-8037-1456-4*); PLB write for info. (*0-8037-1457-2*) Dial Bks Young.

Chapman, Christina. Treasure in the Attic. Hoggan, Pat, illus. LC 92-35814. 32p. (gr. 4-6). 1992. PLB 17.96 (*0-8114-3582-2*) Raintree Steck-V.

Chapman, Dorothy. My Body Is Where I Live. (gr. k-4). 1989. text ed. 17.95 (*0-88671-297-1*, 5102) Am Guidance.

Chapman, Geoffrey. Book of Gospels. (Illus.). 672p. 1985. 95.00 (*0-225-66351-1*) Harper SF.

Chapman, Gillian. Maps & Mazes: A First Guide to Map Making. (gr. 3). 1993. pap. 6.95 (*1-56294-715-X*) Millbrook Pr.

Chapman, Gillian & Robson, Pam. Making Books: A Step by Step Guide to Your Own Publishing. (Illus.). 32p. (gr. 3-6). 1992. 12.95 (*1-56294-169-0*); PLB 12. 90 (*1-56294-154-2*) Millbrook Pr.

—Maps & Mazes: A First Guide to Mapmaking. LC 93-1234. (Illus.). 32p. (gr. 2-4). 1993. PLB 12.90 (*1-56294-405-3*) Millbrook Pr.

Chapman, John. Welcome to English: Let's Begin. (Illus.). 48p. (gr. 1 up). 1980. pap. 3.25 (*0-88345-422-X*, 18480); tchr's manual 4.50 (*0-88345-423-8*, 18493); tchr's. manual 4-5 7.50 (*0-88345-368-1*, 18499) Prentice ESL.

Chapman, Kathryn. God & I Can Talk: A Prayer Guide for Children. (Illus.). 104p. (Orig.). (gr. 1-3). 1988. pap. 4.95 (*0-936625-15-5*, New Hope AL) Womans Mission Union.

Chapman, Kim W. The Magic Hat. 2nd ed. LC 76-20842. (Illus.). 46p. (gr. k up). 1976. 5.00 (*0-914996-10-X*) Lollipop Power.

Chapman, Laura. Adventures in Art. (Illus.). (gr. 1-6). 1994. Bk. 1. text ed. 19.95 (*0-87192-251-7*); Bk. 2. text ed. 19.95 (*0-87192-252-5*); Bk. 3. text ed. 23.95 (*0-87192-253-3*); Bk. 1. tchr's ed. 27.95 (*0-87192-257-6*); Bk. 2. tchr's. ed. 27.95 (*0-87192-258-4*); Bk. 3. tchr's ed. 27.95 (*0-87192-259-2*) Davis Mass.

—Adventures in Art. (Illus.). (gr. 1-6). 1994. Bk. 4. text ed. 23.95 (*0-87192-254-1*); Bk. 5. text ed. 23.95 (*0-87192-255-X*); Bk. 6. text ed. 23.95 (*0-87192-256-8*); Bk. 4. tchr's. ed. 27.95 (*0-87192-260-6*); Bk. 5. tchr's. ed. 27.95 (*0-87192-261-4*); Bk. 6. tchr's. ed. 27.95 (*0-87192-262-2*) Davis Mass.

—Art: Images & Ideas. (Illus.). (gr. 8). 1992. 39.95 (*0-87192-231-2*); tchr's. guide 25.00 (*0-87192-233-9*) Davis Mass.

—A World of Images. (Illus.). (gr. 7). 1992. 39.95 (*0-87192-230-4*); tchr's. guide 25.00 (*0-87192-232-0*) Davis Mass.

Chapman, Lynne F. Leo Tolstoy. LC 93-10629. (gr. 5 up). 1994. write for info. (*0-88682-620-9*) Creative Ed.

—Sylvia Plath. LC 93-3354. 1993. PLB 18.95 (*0-88682-614-4*) Creative Ed.

Chapman, Mary W. Why? McKissack, Patricia & McKissack, Fredrick, eds. LC 88-60387. (Illus.). 32p. (Orig.). (gr. 1-3). 1988. text ed. 8.95 (*0-88335-781-X*); pap. text ed. 4.95 (*0-88335-793-3*) Milliken Pub Co.

Chapman, Phil. Electricity. (gr. 5-9). 1976. (Usborne-Hayes); PLB 13.96 (*0-88110-006-4*); pap. 6.95 (*0-86020-078-7*) EDC.

Chapman, William G. Green-Timber Trails: Wild Animal Stories of the North Country. Berle, Peter A., frwd. by. (Illus.). 304p. (gr. 5 up). 1992. pap. 13.00 (*0-88150-240-5*) Countryman.

Chapouton, A. M. King Clawley Dragon, the First. (Illus.). (gr. 1-8). 1992. PLB 8.95 (*0-89565-885-2*); Resale. 12.75 (*0-685-60988-X*) Childs World.

Chapouton, Anne-Marie. Billy the Brave. Bell, Anthea, tr. from FRE. Claverie, Jean, illus. LC 85-63307. 32p. (gr. k-2). 1986. 8.95 (*1-55858-070-0*) North-South Bks NYC.

—Downy, Pistachio & Fanny. (Illus.). 48p. (gr. k-4). 1990. 12.75 (*0-89565-808-9*); 8.95s.p. (*0-685-55098-2*) Childs World.

—If Sophie... (Illus.). 32p. (gr. 3-5). 1991. 18.50 (*0-89565-760-0*); 12.95s.p. (*0-685-55085-0*) Childs World.

—Krustnkrum. (Illus.). 32p. (gr. k-2). 1991. 18.50 (*0-89565-744-9*); 12.95s.p. (*0-685-55073-7*) Childs World.

—Tim Tidies Up. (Illus.). 32p. (gr. 3-5). 1991. 18.50 (*0-89565-750-3*); 12.95s.p. (*0-685-55094-X*) Childs World.

Chappell, David, illus. Five Things God Cannot Do. 16p. (gr. k-6). 1989. pap. text ed. 4.25 (*1-55976-129-6*) CEF Press.

Chappell, James A. Little Johnny Raindrop. Shaw, Charles, illus. LC 88-2173. 32p. (ps-3). 1988. 12.95 (*0-938349-28-7*) State House Pr.

Chappell, Stephen. Dragons & Demons, Angels & Eagles: Morality Tales for Teens. LC 89-63202. 128p. (Orig.). 1990. pap. 6.95 (*0-89243-314-0*) Liguori Pubns.

Chappell, Warren, jt. auth. see Prokofiev, Sergei.

Chapple, Judy. Your Horse: A Step-by-Step Guide to Horse Ownership. LC 84-22280. (Illus.). 144p. (gr. 8 up). 1984. (Garden Way Pub); pap. 12.95 (*0-88266-353-4*, Graden Way Pub) Storey Comm Inc.

Charaleone. All I See Is Part of Me. Aldrich, Cynthia, illus. 56p. (gr. 2-8). 1989. 14.95 (*0-935699-03-1*) Illum Arts.

Charbonneau, Claudette & Lander, Patricia. The Land & People of Norway. LC 91-35029. (Illus.). 256p. (gr. 6 up). 1993. 18.00 (*0-06-020573-3*); PLB 17.89 (*0-06-020583-0*) HarpC Child Bks.

Charbonneau, Claudette, jt. auth. see Lander, Patricia S.

Charbonneau, Manon. Hidden Rods - Hidden Numbers. 78p. (gr. 1-8). 1975. pap. text ed. 5.95 (*0-914040-13-8*) Cuisenaire.

Charbonnet, Gabrielle. Snakes Are Nothing to Sneeze At. Carter, Abby, illus. 80p. (gr. 2-4). 1990. 13.95 (*0-8050-1373-3*, Bks Young Read) H Holt & Co.

—Snakes Are Nothing to Sneeze At. Carter, Abby, illus. LC 89-26919. 80p. (gr. 2-4). 1991. pap. 4.95 (*0-8050-1842-5*, Bks Young Read) H Holt & Co.

Charbonnet, Gabrielle, retold by see Lindenbaum, Pija.

Charbonnet, Varela G. Ballet for Charlotte. 1994. write for info. (*0-8050-3063-8*) H Holt & Co.

Chardiet, Bernice. Come Out, Mouse. Dinardo, Jeffrey, illus. 20p. (ps-1). 1994. pap. 4.99 (*0-14-054997-8*) Puffin Bks.

—The Great Carrot Top Mystery. Hartelius, Margaret A., illus. 24p. (ps-1). 1994. pap. 3.50 (*0-590-33426-3*, Cartwheel) Scholastic Inc.

—Rapunzel. 1990. pap. 2.50 (*0-590-42281-2*) Scholastic Inc.

—Somethins Is Coming. Cote, Pamela, illus. (ps-1). 1994. pap. 4.99 (*0-14-054996-X*) Puffin Bks.

Chardiet, Bernice & Maccarone, Grace. The Best Teacher in the World. Karas, G. Brian, illus. 32p. (ps-2). 1991. Repr. 2.50 (*0-590-43307-5*) Scholastic Inc.

—Bunny Runs Away. 1992. pap. 2.50 (*0-590-44932-X*) Scholastic Inc.

—Martin & the Teacher's Pet. Karas, Brian, illus. 48p. 1992. pap. 2.50 (*0-590-44931-1*) Scholastic Inc.

—Merry Christmas, What's Your Name School Friends. Karas, G. Brian, illus. 32p. (ps-2). 1991. 2.50 (*0-590-43306-7*) Scholastic Inc.

—The Snowball War. 1992. 2.50 (*0-590-44933-8*) Scholastic Inc.

—We Scream for Ice Cream. Karas, G. Brain, illus. 48p. (ps-3). 1992. pap. 2.50 (*0-590-44934-6*) Scholastic Inc.

Chardiet, Bernice, jt. auth. see Brenner, Barbara.

Chardiet, Bernice, jt. auth. see Maccarone, Grace.

Chardiet, Jon. The Magic Fish Rap. 1993. incl. cassette 5.95 (*0-590-66152-3*) Scholastic Inc.

—The Magic Fish Rap. 1993. pap. 3.95 (*0-590-45859-0*) Scholastic Inc.

—The Rough Gruff Goat Brothers. Suares, J. C., illus. (gr. k-3). 1993. pap. 5.95 incl. cass. (*0-590-69004-3*) Scholastic Inc.

Chariot Books Staff. Please. (ps). 1993. 3.29 (*0-7814-0107-0*) Cook.

—Sorry. (ps). 1993. 3.29 (*0-7814-0105-4*) Cook.

—Thank You. (ps). 1993. 3.29 (*0-7814-0106-2*) Cook.

Chariot Family Staff. Noah's Ark. Tallarico, Tony, illus. 1987. plastic 6.47 (*1-55513-653-2*, 56531, Chariot Bks) Cook.

Chariot Staff. Christmas Counting Book. (ps). 1993. 9.99 (*0-7814-0127-5*) Cook.

—My Jesus Pocketbook Christmas Is Coming. (ps-3). 1993. pap. 0.69 (*0-7814-0143-7*) Cook.

Charles, Arthur H., Jr. How to Learn a Foreign Language. LC 93-29573. 1994. write for info. (*0-531-11098-2*) Watts.

Charles, Carole. The Boston Tea Party. Seible, Bob, illus. LC 75-33156. (gr. 2-6). 1992. PLB 21.95 (*0-913778-18-4*); pap. 14.95 (*0-685-57677-9*) Childs World.

—General George at Yorktown. Seible, Bob, illus. LC 75-33158. 32p. (gr. 2-6). 1975. PLB 21.35 (*0-913778-23-0*); pap. 14.95 (*0-685-57679-5*) Childs World.

—John Paul Jones, Victory at Sea. Seible, Bob, illus. LC 75-33157. 32p. (gr. 2-6). 1975. PLB 21.35 (*0-913778-21-4*); pap. 14.95 (*0-685-57680-9*) Childs World.

—Martha Helps the Rebel. Seible, Bob, illus. LC 75-33126. (gr. 2-6). 1975. PLB 5.95 (*0-913778-22-2*) Childs World.

Charles, Chuck D., ed. see Stuart, Jesse.

Charles, Donald. El Ano de Gato Galano (Calico Cat's Year) Kratky, Lada, tr. from GER. Charles, Donald, illus. (SPA.). 32p. (ps-3). 1984. PLB 15.00 (*0-516-33461-1*); pap. 3.95 (*0-516-53461-0*) Childrens.

—Calico Cat at School. LC 81-6096. (Illus.). 32p. (ps-3). 1981. 15.00 (*0-516-03445-6*); pap. 3.95 (*0-516-43445-4*) Childrens.

—Calico Cat at the Zoo. Charles, Donald, illus. LC 80-25380. 32p. (gr. 3). 1981. PLB 15.00 (*0-516-03443-X*) Childrens.

—Calico Cat Looks at Shapes. Charles, Donald, illus. LC 75-12947. 32p. (ps-3). 1975. PLB 15.00 (*0-516-03436-7*) Childrens.

—Calico Cat Meets Bookworm. LC 78-6557. (Illus.). 32p. (gr. 3). 1978. PLB 15.00 (*0-516-03441-3*) Childrens.

—Calico Cat's Exercise Book. LC 82-9640. (Illus.). (ps-3). 1982. PLB 15.00 (*0-516-03457-X*) Childrens.

—Calico Cat's Sunny Smile. Charles, Donald, illus. LC 90-37981. 32p. (ps-3). 1990. PLB 15.00 (*0-516-03482-0*) Childrens.

—Calico Cat's Year. LC 83-23160. (Illus.). 32p. (ps-3). 1984. PLB 15.00 (*0-516-03461-8*) Childrens.

—Chancay & the Secret of Fire. (Illus.). 32p. (ps-3). 1992. 14.95 (*0-399-22129-8*, Putnam) Putnam Pub Group.

—Count on Calico Cat. Charles, Donald, illus. LC 74-8007. 32p. (ps-3). 1974. PLB 15.00 (*0-516-03435-9*) Childrens.

—Cuenta con Gato Galano (Count on Calico Cat) Kratky, Lada, tr. from ENG. Charles, Donald, illus. LC 74-8007. (SPA.). 32p. (ps-3). 1984. PLB 15.00 (*0-516-33479-4*); pap. 3.95 (*0-516-53479-3*) Childrens.

—Fat, Fat Calico Cat. LC 77-7154. (Illus.). 32p. (gr. 3). 1977. PLB 15.00 (*0-516-03456-1*) Childrens.

—Gata Galano Mira los Colores: Calico Cat Looks at Colors. LC 75-12948. (SPA., Illus.). 32p. (ps-3). 1992. PLB 15.00 (*0-516-33437-9*); pap. 3.95 (*0-516-53437-8*) Childrens.

—Gordito, Gordon Gato Galano: (Fat, Fat Calico Cat) Charles, Donald, illus. LC 77-7154. (SPA.). 32p. (ps-2). 1988. PLB 15.00 (*0-516-33456-5*); pap. 3.95 (*0-516-53456-4*) Childrens.

—El Libro de Ejercicios de Gato Galano (Calico Cat's Exercise Book) Kratky, Lada, tr. from ENG. Charles, Doanld, illus. LC 82-9640. (SPA.). 32p. (ps-3). 1984. pap. 3.95 (*0-516-53457-2*) Childrens.

—Mira las Formas con Gato Galano (Calico Cat Looks at Shapes) LC 75-12947. (SPA., Illus.). 32p. (ps-3). 1987. PLB 15.00 (*0-516-33436-0*); pap. 3.95 (*0-516-53436-X*) Childrens.

—Paddy Pigs Poems. 1989. pap. 13.95 (*0-671-67081-6*) S&S Trade.

—Paddy Pig's Poems. (gr. 2). 1991. pap. write for info. (*0-663-56223-6*) Silver Burdett Pr.

—Shaggy Dog's Birthday. Charles, Donald, illus. LC 86-9566. 32p. (ps-3). 1986. PLB 15.00 (*0-516-03576-2*) Childrens.

—Shaggy Dog's Christmas. LC 85-14972. (Illus.). 32p. (ps-3). 1985. PLB 15.00 (*0-516-03675-0*) Childrens.

—Shaggy Dog's Tall Tale. Charles, Donald, illus. LC 79-26493. 32p. (ps-3). 1980. PLB 15.00 (*0-516-03616-5*) Childrens.

—Ugly Bug. LC 92-835. (ps-3). 1994. 13.99 (*0-8037-1204-9*); 13.89 (*0-8037-1205-7*) Dial Bks Young.

Charles, Kirk. Amazing Card Tricks. LC 92-5482. (Illus.). (gr. 1-8). 1992. PLB 14.95 (*0-89565-965-4*); Resale. 21.35 (*0-685-59285-5*) Childs World.

—Amazing Coin Tricks. Woodworth, Viki, illus. LC 93-29259. 1994. write for info. (*1-56766-084-3*) Childs World.

—Amazing String Tricks. Woodworth, Viki, illus. LC 93-35866. 1994. write for info. (*1-56766-085-1*, Pub. by Childs World) Standard Pub.

—Magic Tricks. LC 92-9012. (Illus.). (gr. 1-8). 1992. PLB 14.95 (*0-89565-964-6*); Resale. 21.35 (*0-685-59293-6*) Childs World.

Charles, Oz. How Does Soda Get Into a Bottle? LC 87-11534. (Illus.). 32p. (gr. 1-5). 1988. pap. 9.95 (*0-671-63755-X*, S&S BFYR) S&S Trade.

—How Does Soda Get Into the Bottle? 32p. (ps-3). 1990. pap. 3.95 (*0-671-69436-7*, S&S BFYR) S&S Trade.

—How Is a Crayon Made? LC 87-11436. (Illus.). 32p. (gr. 1-5). 1990. (S&S BFYR); pap. 3.95 (*0-671-69437-5*, S&S BFYR) S&S Trade.

Charles, Ray. Ray Charles: A Man & His Soul. Olsen, David C., ed. 84p. (Orig.). 1986. pap. 13.95 (*0-89898-500-5*) CPP Belwin.

Charles, Veronika M. The Crane Girl. LC 92-50843. (Illus.). 32p. (ps-1). 1993. 14.95 (*0-531-05485-3*) Orchard Bks Watts.

Charleston, Gordon. Armstrong Lands on the Moon. (Illus.). 32p. (gr. 5). 1994. PLB 13.95 RSBE (*0-87518-530-4*, Dillon) Macmillan Child Grp.

—Peary Reaches the North Pole. LC 92-44500. (Illus.). 32p. (gr. 5 up). 1993. RSBE 13.95 (*0-87518-535-5*, Dillon) Macmillan Child Grp.

Charlet, James D., et al. North Carolina: Our People, Places, & Past Student Workbook. Charlet, James D., illus. 300p. 1988. wkbk. 49.95 (*0-935911-13-8*) Cornucop Pub.

—North Carolina: Our People, Places & Past. Long, C. Mayapriya, et al, illus. 320p. (gr. 4 up). 1987. lib. bdg. 22.95 (*0-89089-319-5*) Carolina Acad Pr.

Charley, Aunt, pseud. The Raindrop Children, Vol. 1. Bruno, Clara E., illus. 24p. (gr. 1-2). 1991. pap. 5.95 (*1-880945-00-2*) Animated Elements.

Charlier, J. M. The Blue Coats. Starwatcher Graphics Staff, tr. from FRE. Giraud, Jean M., illus. 56p. (gr. 12 up). 1990. pap. 7.95 (*0-87416-093-6*, Comcat Comics) Catalan Communs.

—A Yankee Named Blueberry. Starwatcher Graphics Staff, tr. from FRE. Giraud, Jean m., illus. 56p. (Orig.). (gr. 12 up). 1990. pap. 7.95 (*0-87416-087-1*, Comcat Comics) Catalan Communs.

Charlip, Remy. Fortunately. Charlip, Remy, illus. LC 80-36956. 48p. (ps-3). 1980. Repr. of 1964 ed. RSBE 14. 95 (*0-02-718100-6*, Four Winds) Macmillan Child Grp.

—Fortunately. Charlip, Remy, illus. LC 92-22794. 48p. (ps-3). 1993. pap. 4.95 (*0-689-71660-5*, Aladdin) Macmillan Child Grp.

Charlip, Remy & Joyner, Jerry. Thirteen. LC 75-8875. (Illus.). 40p. (gr. 1-3). 1984. Repr. of 1975 ed. RSBE 13.95 (*0-02-718120-0*, Four Winds) Macmillan Child Grp.

Charlip, Remy & Miller, Mary B. Handtalk: An ABC of Finger Spelling & Sign Language. Ancona, George, illus. LC 85-3667. 48p. (ps-up). 1984. Repr. of 1974 ed. SBE 15.95 (*0-02-718130-8*, Four Winds) Macmillan Child Grp.

—Handtalk: An ABC of Finger Spelling & Sign Language. Ancona, George, illus. LC 86-20585. 48p. (ps-12). 1987. pap. 4.95 (*0-689-71108-5*, Aladdin) Macmillan Child Grp.

—Handtalk Birthday: A Number & Story Book in Sign Language. Ancona, George, illus. LC 86-22755. 48p. (ps up). 1987. SBE 15.95 (0-02-718080-8, Four Winds) Macmillan Child Grp.

Charlip, Remy & Supree, Burton. Mother Mother I Feel Sick Send for the Doctor Quick Quick Quick. (Illus.). 1993. pap. 14.95x (1-56849-172-7) Buccaneer Bks.

Charlip, Remy, jt. auth. see Martin, Judith.

Charlip, Remy, jt. auth. see Miller, Mary B.

Charlton, Bill, jt. auth. see Bentley, John.

Charlton, Coleman, ed. see Allston, Aaron.

Charlton, Coleman, ed. see Crutchfield, Charles.

Charlton, Coleman, ed. see McKeage, Jeff.

Charlton, S. C., ed. see Colborn, Mark.

Charlton, S. Coleman. Creatures & Treasures. (Illus.). 96p. (gr. 10-12). 1985. 12.00 (0-915795-30-2, 1400) Iron Crown Ent Inc.

Charlton, S. Coleman & Ruemmler, John D. Middle-Earth Role Playing (MERP). (Illus.). 128p. (gr. 10-12). 1986. pap. 10.00 (0-915795-31-0, 8000) Iron Crown Ent Inc.

Charlton, S. Coleman, ed. see Barrett, Kevin.

Charlton, S. Coleman, ed. see Robinson, Andrew.

Charlton, S. Coleman, ed. see Staplehurst, Graham.

Charman, Andrew. Air. LC 93-31748. 1994. write for info. (0-8114-5509-2) Raintree Steck-V.

—Earth. LC 93-31791. 1994. write for info. (0-8114-5510-6) Raintree Steck-V.

—Energy. LC 92-6079. (Illus.). 32p. (gr. 5-8). 1993. PLB 12.40 (0-531-14233-7) Watts.

—Fire. LC 93-20873. 1994. write for info. (0-8114-5511-4) Raintree Steck-V.

—Lonely Christmas Tree. (gr. ps-3). 1992. pap. 5.95 (0-671-78452-8, Little Simon) S&S Trade.

—Materials. LC 92-6078. (Illus.). 32p. (gr. 5-8). 1993. PLB 12.40 (0-531-14232-9) Watts.

—Water. LC 93-20880. 1994. write for info. (0-8114-5508-4) Raintree Steck-V.

Charnas, Suzy M. The Bronze King. 208p. 1987. pap. 2.95 (0-553-15493-1, Skylark) Bantam.

—The Bronze King. 208p. 1988. pap. 2.95 (0-553-27104-0, Starfire) Bantam.

—The Golden Thread. 1989. 13.95 (0-553-05821-5, Starfire) Bantam.

—The Kingdom of Kevin Malone. LC 92-40720. 1993. 16.95 (0-15-200756-3, J Yolen Bks) HarBrace.

—The Silver Glove. (gr. 7 up). 1989. pap. 2.95 (0-318-41646-8, Starfire) Bantam.

—The Silver Glove. 1988. 13.95 (0-553-05470-8) Bantam.

Charney, Steve. Let's Sing about Silly People. Barnes-Murphy, Rowan, illus. LC 92-24713. 32p. (gr. k-2). 1992. PLB 11.89 (0-8167-2978-6); pap. text ed. 3.95 (0-8167-2979-4) Troll Assocs.

Charpentier, Aristide-Christian. The Violin of Passing Time. (gr. 1-7). 1972. 4.50 (0-87602-217-4) Anchorage.

Charpentreau, J. & Borchers, E. Livre de Tous les Jours. (FRE). (gr. 4-9). 1980. 15.95 (2-07-039514-6) Schoenhof.

Charpentreau, J. & Jean, G. Dictionnaire des Poetes et de la Poesie. (FRE). 427p. (gr. 5-10). 1983. 27.95 (2-07-051019-0) Schoenhof.

Charren, Peggy & Hulsizer, Carol. The TV-Smart Book for Kids: Puzzles, Games, & Other Good Stuff. Hafner, Marylin, illus. 48p. (gr. 2-7). 1986. Parent's Guide, 16 p. 6.95 (0-525-44249-9, DCB) Dutton Child Bks.

Charry, Elias & Segal, Abraham. The Eternal People. (Illus.). 448p. (gr. 9-11). 7.50x (0-8381-0206-9, 10-206) United Syn Bk.

Chartier, Genevieve. La Fille des Michettes. (FRE). 242p. (gr. 7). 1992. pap. 15.95 (0-9634891-0-0) La Presse des Mich.

Chartier, Jack W. The Art of Whistling. (Illus.). 40p. (gr. 1 up). 1993. PLB 4.95 (0-9636343-1-3) Chartier.

Chartier, Normand. Jingle Bells. 16p. 1989. pap. 3.95 (0-671-68269-5, Little Simon) S&S Trade.

—Over the River & Thro' the Woods. (Illus.). 24p. (ps-3). 1990. 5.95 (0-671-64150-6, Little Simon); pap. 2.25 (0-671-72337-5) S&S Trade.

—Sesame Street: Who Am I? 22p. (ps-1). 1978. write for info. (0-307-12124-0, 12124, Pub. by Golden Bks) Western Pub.

Chartier, Normand, illus. Jingle Bells. 1986. pap. 2.25 (0-671-63202-9, Little Simon) S&S Trade.

Chartrand, Mark R. Planets. 1990. pap. write for info. (0-307-24077-0) Western Pub.

Chartrand, Micheline. Lollypop at Nursery School. (Illus.). 12p. (ps). 1993. bds. 3.95 (2-921198-11-8, Pub. by Les Edits Herit CN) Adams Inc MA.

—Lollypop Is Angry. (Illus.). 12p. (ps). 1993. bds. 3.95 (2-921198-09-6, Pub. by Les Edits Herit CN) Adams Inc MA.

—Lollypop Knows How. (Illus.). 12p. (ps). 1993. bds. 3.95 (2-921198-08-8, Pub. by Les Edits Herit CN) Adams Inc MA.

—Visit for Lollypop. (Illus.). 12p. (ps). 1993. bds. 3.95 (2-921198-10-X, Pub. by Les Edits Herit CN) Adams Inc MA.

Charvat, William, et al, eds. see Hawthorne, Nathaniel.

Charyn, Jerome. Back to Bataan. (gr. 4-7). 1993. 15.00 (0-374-30476-9) FS&G.

Chase, Alyssa. Jomo & Mata. Chase, Andra, illus. LC 93-25206. 32p. (gr. 1-4). 1993. 16.95 (1-55942-051-0, 7656); video, tchr's. guide & storybook 79.95 (1-55942-054-5, 9375) Marshfilm.

Chase, Edith N. New Baby Calf. (Illus.). 32p. (gr. k-3). 1991. pap. 2.95 (0-590-44776-9) Scholastic Inc.

Chase, Jan B. The Golden Song. Chase, Jan B., illus. 32p. (gr. k-3). 1993. 16.95 (1-880158-01-9) J N Townsend.

Chase, John. Louisiana Purchase: An American Story. Chase, John, illus. 96p. 1991. 4.95 (0-911116-24-9); pap. 8.95 (0-911116-68-0) Pelican.

Chase, Mary. Loretta Mason Potts. (gr. 4-8). 19.00 (0-8446-6428-6) Peter Smith.

Chase, Richard. Grandfather Tales. (Illus.). 240p. (gr. 4-6). 1973. 17.45 (0-395-06692-1) HM.

—Grandfather Tales. (gr. 4-7). 1990. pap. 5.95 (0-395-56150-7) HM.

—Jack Tales. (Illus.). 202p. (gr. 4-6). 1943. 13.45 (0-395-06694-8) HM.

—Jack Tales. (gr. 4-7). 1993. pap. 4.95 (0-395-66951-0) HM.

—Singing Games & Playparty Games. Tolford, Joshua, illus. 63p. (gr. 1-4). 1949. pap. 2.50 (0-486-21785-X) Dover.

—Singing Games & Playparty Games. Tolford, Joshua, illus. Rufty, Hilton, contrib. by. (Illus.). (gr. 4-8). 16.50 (0-8446-4721-7) Peter Smith.

Chase, Richard, ed. see Crane, Stephen.

Chase, Richard, ed. see Harris, Joel C.

Chastain, Frances. Animals of Ancient China. (Illus.). 34p. (ps-2). 1986. text ed. 5.95 (0-8351-1790-1) China Bks.

Chastain, Gerald, Jr., jt. auth. see Kamm, Karlyn.

Chatt, Andy. Cocaine the Silent Killer: Self Help Manual. (Orig.). (gr. 7 up). 1991. pap. text ed. 8.95 (0-9626964-0-4) Nocaine.

Chatterjee, Debjani. The Elephant-Headed God & Other Hindu Tales. LC 92-20454. 1992. 13.00 (0-19-508112-9) OUP.

Chatterton, Martin, jt. auth. see Beal, George.

Chattington, Jenny & Firman, Mary. The Ancient Greeks. (Illus.). (gr. 2-6). pap. 3.95 (0-7141-1283-6, Pub. by Brit Mus UK) Parkwest Pubns.

Chatton, Ray, jt. auth. see Mulqueen, Jack.

Chaucer, Geoffrey. Canterbury Tales. Coghill, Nevill, tr. (Orig.). (gr. 9 up). 1951. pap. 3.95 (0-14-044022-4) Viking Child Bks.

—The Canterbury Tales. Stewart, Diana, adapted by. Hubrich, Dan, illus. LC 80-22141. 48p. (gr. 4 up). 1983. PLB 18.64 (0-8172-1666-9) Raintree Steck-V.

—Canterbury Tales. Cohen, Barbara, adapted by. Hyman, Trina S., illus. LC 86-21045. 96p. (gr. 5 up). 1988. 17.95 (0-688-06201-6) Lothrop.

—The Canterbury Tales. 496p. (ps-8). 1990. Repr. lib. bdg. 29.95x (0-89966-671-X) Buccaneer Bks.

—Chanticleer & the Fox. Cooney, Barbara, illus. LC 58-10449. 40p. (ps-3). 1982. 14.00 (0-690-18561-8, Crowell Jr Bks); PLB 13.89 (0-690-18562-6); pap. 3.95 (0-690-04318-X) HarpC Child Bks.

—Chanticleer & the Fox. Cooney, Barbara, illus. LC 58-10449. 32p. (gr. k-3). 1982. pap. 5.95 (0-06-443087-1, Trophy) HarpC Child Bks.

—Chanticleer & the Fox. Roberts, Fulton, retold by. Davis, Marc, illus. LC 91-71341. 32p. 1991. 13.95 (1-56282-022-2); PLB 13.89 (1-56282-072-9) Disney Pr.

—Chaucer. (gr. 1-9). 1992. pap. 3.95 (0-88388-017-2) Bellerophon Bks.

Chaudhry, Saida. Call to Prophethood. (Illus.). (gr. 2-5). pap. 4.00 (0-89259-046-7) Am Trust Pubns.

—We Are Muslim Children. (gr. 4). 1984. pap. 4.00 (0-89259-126-9) Am Trust Pubns.

Chaudron, Chris & Childs, Caro. Face Painting. (Illus.). 32p. (gr. 2-6). 1993. PLB 12.95 (0-88110-649-6, Usborne); pap. 5.95 (0-7460-1445-7) EDC.

Chauhan, Manhar, illus. Muppet Babies Take a Bath. 10p. (ps). 1992. vinyl 3.95 (0-394-86362-3) Random Bks Yng Read.

Chavez, Joseph, ed. see Mendelsohn, A.

Chavez, Juana. Mother Deer & Her Spotted Fawns. Aragon, Hilda, illus. 14p. (Orig.). (ps-7). 1981. pap. 3.75 (0-915347-10-5) Pueblo Acoma Pr.

Chavez, Vivian, tr. see Lehman, Yvette K.

Chbosky, Stacy. Who Owns the Sun? Chbosky, Stacy, illus. LC 88-12694. 26p. (gr. 3-12). 1988. PLB 14.95 (0-933849-14-1) Landmark Edns.

Cheadle, J. A. A Donkey's Life: A Story for Children. Thomas, Toni, illus. LC 80-123421. iii, 88p. (Orig.). (gr. 2-6). 1979. pap. 3.50 (0-9604244-0-7) Heahstan Pr.

Cheasebro, Margaret. The Prodigal Son & Other Parables As Plays. LC 92-7232. (gr. 5 up). 1993. 6.99 (0-8054-6065-9) Broadman.

Cheatham, Ann. The Beggar's Curse. (Orig.). (gr. k-12). 1987. pap. 2.50 (0-440-91024-2, LFL) Dell.

—Black Harvest. (Orig.). (gr. k-12). 1987. pap. 2.50 (0-440-91039-0, LFL) Dell.

—The Witch of Lagg. (Orig.). (gr. k-12). 1987. pap. 2.50 (0-440-99412-8, LFL) Dell.

Check, William A. AIDS. (Illus.). 128p. (gr. 6-12). 1988. lib. bdg. 18.95 (0-7910-0054-0); pap. 9.95 (0-7910-0481-3) Chelsea Hse.

—Alzheimer's Disease. Koop, C. Everett, intro. by. (Illus.). 112p. (gr. 6-12). 1989. 18.95 (0-7910-0056-7); pap. 9.95 (0-7910-0483-X) Chelsea Hse.

—Child Abuse. (Illus.). 104p. (gr. 6-12). 1990. lib. bdg. 18.95 (0-7910-0043-5); pap. 9.95 (0-7910-0509-7) Chelsea Hse.

—Drugs & Perception. Mendelson, Jack H. & Mello, Nancyintro. by. (Illus.). 112p. (gr. 5 up). 1988. lib. bdg. 19.95 (1-55546-214-6) Chelsea Hse.

—The Mind-Body Connection. (Illus.). 112p. (gr. 6-12). 1990. 18.95 (0-7910-0068-0) Chelsea Hse.

Checkerboard Staff. Classic Junior Elf. 1989. 46.98 (0-02-898104-9) Macmillan.

Cheetham, Ann. The Pit. LC 89-26868. 160p. (gr. 4-6). 1990. 14.95 (0-8050-1142-0, Bks Young Read) H Holt & Co.

—The Pit. 192p. (gr. 3-7). 1993. pap. 3.95 (0-06-440448-X, Trophy) HarpC Child Bks.

Cheever, John. The Enormous Radio. 32p. (gr. 6 up). 1983. PLB 13.95s.p. (0-87191-959-1) Creative Ed.

Chekhov, Anton. A Day in the Country. Redpath, Ann, ed. (Illus.). 32p. (gr. 4 up). 1986. PLB 19.95 (0-88682-004-9); PLB 13.95s.p. Creative Ed.

—Kashtanka. Pevear, Richard, tr. from RUS. Moser, Barry, illus. LC 89-10866. 1991. 16.95 (0-399-21905-6, Putnam) Putnam Pub Group.

Chelepi, Chris. Growing up in Ancient Greece. Molan, Chris, illus. LC 91-14852. 32p. (gr. 3-5). 1993. PLB 11.89 (0-8167-2719-8); pap. text ed. 3.95 (0-8167-2720-1) Troll Assocs. Postponed.

Chemielewski, Gary. Riddles. Clark, Ron G., illus. LC 86-17720. (gr. 2-3). 1986. PLB 13.27 (0-86592-686-7); 9.95 (0-685-58363-5) Rourke Corp.

Chen, Gerald H., jt. auth. see Rockefeller, R. D.

Chenel, Pascale. Life & Death of Dinosaurs. (Illus.). 80p. (gr. 7 up). 1987. pap. 4.95 (0-8120-3840-1) Barron.

Chenery, Janet. Toad Hunt. (ps-3). 1992. pap. 2.99 (0-440-40561-0) Dell.

—Wolfie. (ps-3). 1991. pap. 2.75 (0-440-40496-7) Dell.

Cheney, Cora. Vermont, the State with the Storybook Past. rev. ed. MacLean, Robert, illus. Muller, H. N., III, intro. by. LC 86-60341. (Illus.). 272p. (gr. 5-9). 1986. pap. 14.95 (0-933050-36-4) New Eng Pr VT.

Cheney, David M. Son of Minos. LC 64-25838. (gr. 7). 18.00 (0-8196-0142-X) Biblo.

Cheney, Glenn A. Chernobyl: The Ongoing Story of the World's Deadliest Nuclear Disaster. LC 93-17508. (gr. 5 up). 1994. write for info. (0-02-718305-X, New Discovery) Macmillan Child Grp.

—Drugs, Teens, & Recovery: Real-Life Stories of Trying to Stay Clean. LC 92-39722. (Illus.). 104p. (gr. 6 up). 1993. lib. bdg. 17.95 (0-89490-431-0) Enslow Pubs.

—El Salvador: Country in Crisis. LC 89-38708. (gr. 4-7). 1990. PLB 13.40 (0-531-10916-X) Watts.

Cheney, Patricia. The Land & People of Zimbabwe. LC 89-36244. (Illus.). 256p. (gr. 6 up). 1990. (Lipp Jr Bks); PLB 15.89 (0-397-32393-X, Lipp Jr Bks) HarpC Child Bks.

Cheney, Roland J., jt. auth. see Hedge-Cheney, Jacquelyn.

Cheney-Coker, Syl. The Last Harmattan of Alusine Dunbar. 398p. (Orig.). (gr. 9-12). 1990. pap. 9.95 (0-435-90572-4, 90572) Heinemann.

Cheng, Andrea. Let's Make a Present. (Illus.). 128p. PLB 16.95 (1-878363-64-6) Forest Hse.

—Let's Make a Present! Easy to Make Gifts for Friends & Relatives of Any Age. Macdonald, Roland B. & Gray, Dan, illus. 128p. (gr. k-5). 1991. pap. 9.95 (1-878767-16-X) Murdoch Bks.

Cheng An Jiang, jt. auth. see Wei Jiang.

Chenier, Norman J. Chenier Math Method: A Practical Math Dictionary & Workbook-Textbook. (Illus.). 268p. (gr. 9 up). 1989. text ed. 24.95 (0-9626061-0-3) Chenier Educ Enter.

Chenoweth, Margaret. Scaredy Cat Finds a Home. (ps-3). 1991. pap. 2.50 (0-89954-515-7) Antioch Pub Co.

Chenoweth, Russ. Shadow Walkers. LC 92-18798. 176p. (gr. 5 up). 1993. SBE 13.95 (0-684-19447-3, Scribner Young Read) Macmillan Child Grp.

Cherfas, Jeremy. Animal Builders. (Illus.). 32p. (gr. 4-6). 1991. PLB 15.95 (0-8225-2255-1) Lerner Pubns.

—Animal Communicators. (Illus.). 32p. (gr. 4-6). 1991. PLB 15.95 (0-8225-2252-7) Lerner Pubns.

—Animal Defenses. (Illus.). 32p. (gr. 4-6). 1991. PLB 15.95 (0-8225-2253-5) Lerner Pubns.

—Animal Navigators. (Illus.). 32p. (gr. 4-6). 1991. PLB 15.95 (0-8225-2250-0) Lerner Pubns.

—Animal Parents. (Illus.). 32p. (gr. 4-6). 1991. PLB 15.95 (0-8225-2251-9) Lerner Pubns.

—Animal Societies. (Illus.). 32p. (gr. 4-6). 1991. PLB 15.95 (0-8225-2254-3) Lerner Pubns.

Cheripko, Jan. Voices of the River: Adventures on the Delaware. (Illus.). 48p. (gr. 7 up). 1994. 15.95 (1-56397-325-1) Boyds Mills Pr.

Cherkerzian, Diane. Easter Fun. (ps-3). 1993. pap. 3.95 (1-56397-164-X); Set of 3 bks. pap. 11.85 (1-56397-166-6) Boyds Mills Pr.

—Indoor Sunshine: Great Things to Make & Do on Rainy Days. LeHew, Ron, illus. LC 92-73628. 32p. (gr. 2-7). 1993. Set of 3 bks. 11.85 (1-56397-169-0); pap. 3.95 (1-56397-163-1) Boyds Mills Pr.

—Outdoor Fun: Great Things to Make & Do on Sunny Days. LeHew, Ron, illus. LC 92-74583. 32p. (gr. 2-7). 1993. Set of 3 bks. 11.85 (1-56397-168-2); pap. 3.95 (1-56397-162-3) Boyds Mills Pr.

Chermayeff, Ivan. Fishy Facts. LC 93-31091. 1994. 9.95 (0-15-228175-4, Gulliver Bks) HarBrace.

—Furry Facts. LC 93-30147. 1994. 9.95 (0-15-230425-8, Gulliver Bks) HarBrace.

—Tomato & Other Colors. (ps-3). 1981. 13.55 (0-13-924753-X) P-H.

Chermayeff, Ivan & Chermayeff, Jane C. First Shapes. (Illus.). 32p. 1991. 16.95 (0-8109-3819-7) Abrams.

Chermayeff, Jane C., jt. auth. see Chermayeff, Ivan.

Cherness, Claudia. Leroy, the Lizard Coloring Book. (ENG, SPA & FRE.). 24p. (ps-2). 1993. 3.95 (0-943864-66-6) Davenport.

Cherney, Ila. My Haggadah. Paiss, Jana, illus. 66p. (gr. 4-7). 1985. pap. text ed. 4.25 (0-317-60058-3) Behrman.

Chernoff, Goldie T. Easy Costumes You Don't Have to Sew. LC 76-46428. (Illus.). 48p. (gr. 1-3). 1984. RSBE 13.95 (0-02-718230-4, Four Winds) Macmillan Child Grp.

Chernow, Carol, jt. auth. see Chernow, Fred B.

Chernow, Fred B. & Chernow, Carol. Not for Me. (Illus.). 36p. (gr. 1-7). 1986. pap. 3.95 (0-9610742-1-3); tchr's. guide 2.00 (0-685-17181-7) Purcell Prods.

Chernow, Ron, jt. auth. see Johnson, Charles.

Chernus-Mansfield, Nancy & Horn, Marilyn. My Fake Eye: The Story of My Prosthesis. LC 91-73190. 24p. (ps-9). 1991. pap. write for info. (0-9630118-0-4) Inst Fam Blind Child.

Cherrell, Gwen. How Movies Are Made. (Illus.). 32p. 1989. 12.95x (0-8160-2039-6) Facts on File.

Cherrington, Mark. Degradation of the Land. (Illus.). (gr. 5 up). 1992. lib. bdg. 19.95 (0-7910-1589-0) Chelsea Hse.

Cherry, Charles W., II. Excellence Without Excuse: The Black Student's Guide to Academic Excellence. LC 91-35248. (gr. 7 up). 1993. 26.95 (1-56385-497-X); pap. 19.95 (1-56385-498-8) Intl School Pr.

Cherry, Clare. Creative Art for the Developing Child. 2nd ed. (ps-1). 1990. pap. 15.95 (0-8224-1633-6) Fearon Teach Aids.

—Creative Movement for the Developing Child: A Nursery School Handbook for Non-Musicians. rev. ed. LC 79-125140. (ps-1). 1971. pap. 9.95 (0-8224-1660-3) Fearon Teach Aids.

—Creative Play for the Developing Child. LC 75-16950. (ps-1). 1976. pap. 14.95 (0-8224-1632-8) Fearon Teach Aids.

—Please Don't Sit on the Kids: Alternatives to Punitive Discipline. LC 82-81981. (ps-3). 1982. pap. 12.95 (0-8224-5474-2) Fearon Teach Aids.

—Think of Something Quiet. LC 80-82981. (ps-4). 1981. pap. 10.95 (0-8224-6949-9) Fearon Teach Aids.

Cherry, Denise. Step by Step Children's Guide to Dog Training. (Illus.). 64p. 1993. pap. 3.95 (0-86622-518-8, SK044) TFH Pubns.

Cherry, Frances. Legs & Bizou. Tounsi, Corinne, illus. 36p. (ps-8). 1986. 7.95 (0-920806-60-0, Pub. by Penumbra Pr CN) U of Toronto Pr.

Cherry, L. A River Ran Wild. 1992. 14.95 (0-15-200542-0, HB Juv Bks) HarBrace.

Cherry, Leon P. First Call. 8p. 1992. pap. 2.95 (0-685-61428-X) Crnrstone Pub.

—Heart & Soul. 164p. (Orig.). 1993. pap. 10.95 (1-882185-13-7) Crnrstone Pub.

Cherry, Lynne. Archie, Follow Me. LC 89-77160. (Illus.). 32p. (ps-1). 1990. 12.95 (0-525-44647-8, DCB) Dutton Child Bks.

—The Armadillo from Amarillo. LC 93-11185. 1994. write for info. (0-15-200359-2, Gulliver Bks) HarBrace.

—The Dragon & the Unicorn. LC 92-30321. 1994. write for info. (0-15-224193-0) HarBrace.

—Great Kapok Tree: A Tale of the Amazon Rain Forest. 33p. (ps-3). 1990. 14.95 (0-15-200520-X) HarBrace.

—Who's Sick Today? Cherry, Lynne, illus. LC 87-22185. 24p. (ps-1). 1988. 11.95 (0-525-44380-0, 01160-350, DCB) Dutton Child Bks.

—Who's Sick Today? (Illus.). 24p. (ps-1). 1993. pap. 3.99 (0-14-054839-4) Puffin Bks.

Cherry, Lynne, illus. Snow Leopard. LC 86-24033. 12p. (ps). 1987. (DCB) book & toy package 13.95 (0-685-14571-9, DCB) Dutton Child Bks.

Cherry, Winky. My First Embroidery Book. Cherry, Winky, illus. 40p. (ps-6). 1990. pap. 12.00 (0-317-93838-X) ITS Pub.

—My First Machine Sewing Book. Cherry, Winky, illus. 40p. (Orig.). (gr. 2 up). 1989. pap. 12.00 (0-317-93839-8) ITS Pub.

—My First Sewing Book. Cherry, Winky, illus. 40p. (Orig.). (ps-6). 1984. pap. 10.00 (0-317-93840-1) ITS Pub.

Cherryholmes, C. & Manson, G. Investigating Societies. (Illus.). (gr. 6). 1979. text ed. 28.04 (0-07-011986-4) McGraw.

—Studying Cultures. (Illus.). (gr. 4). 1979. text ed. 24.64 (0-07-011984-8) McGraw.

Chesely, Mary. Miss Purdy's Problem. Weinberger, Jane, ed. (Illus.). 48p. (gr. 1-5). 1994. pap. 9.95 (0-932433-15-4) Windswept Hse.

Chesney, Sandy. The Zapped Tadpole & More. 93p. (gr. 4 up). 1991. pap. 6.95 (0-8163-1029-7) Pacific Pr Pub Assn.

Chestney, P. L. When the Animals Left. Chestney, P. L., illus. 52p. (gr. 1-6). 1994. pap. 12.95 (1-883533-00-7) PL&R Chestney.

Chestnut, Renate, tr. see Babyak, Jolene.

Chestnutt, David, illus. Beauty & the Beast. LC 78-54959. 32p. (Orig.). (gr. k-4). 1991. pap. 2.25 (0-394-83954-4) Random Bks Yng Read.

Chesto, Elizabeth, jt. auth. see Chesto, Kathleen O.

Chesto, Kathleen O. & Chesto, Elizabeth. Children's Scripture Puzzles: Reproducible Activities & Family Discussion for Sundays Through the Church Year (Cycle B) (Illus.). 64p. (Orig.). (gr. k-8). 1993. pap. 39.95 (1-55612-619-0) Sheed & Ward MO.

Chesworth, Michael. Party at the Ghost House. (gr. 4 up). 1993. 9.95 (0-89577-507-7, Readers Digest Kids) RD Assn.

—Rainy Day Dream. (ps-3). 1992. 14.00 (0-374-36177-0) FS&G.

—This Is the Story of Archibald Frisby: Who Was As Crazy for Science as Any Kid Could Be. 1994. 15.00 (0-374-30392-4) FS&G.

Chetin, Helen. Angel Island Prisoner. Harvey, Catherine, tr. Lee, Jan, illus. LC 82-51170. (CHI & ENG.). (gr. 3 up). 1982. 7.95 (0-938678-09-4) New Seed.

—My Father Raped Me: Frances Ann Speaks Out. 2nd ed. Olsen, Karen, illus. 20p. (gr. 5 up). 1977. pap. 4.95 (0-938678-05-1) New Seed.

—Perihan's Promise. LC 91-67696. (Illus.). 140p. (gr. 4-9). 1992. pap. 10.95 (0-938678-13-2) New Seed.

Chetwin, Grace. Box & Cox. Small, David, illus. LC 88-35337. 32p. (gr. k-3). 1990. SBE 13.95 (0-02-718314-9, Bradbury Pr) Macmillan Child Grp.

—Child of the Air. LC 90-47565. 256p. (gr. 5 up). 1991. SBE 14.95 (0-02-718317-3, Bradbury Pr) Macmillan Child Grp.

—The Chimes of Alyafaleyn. LC 92-44156. 192p. (gr. 5-9). 1993. RSBE 14.95 (0-02-718222-3, Bradbury Pr) Macmillan Child Grp.

—Collidescope. LC 89-38255. 240p. (gr. 5-9). 1990. SBE 15.95 (0-02-718316-5, Bradbury Pr) Macmillan Child Grp.

—The Crystal Stair. (gr. k up). 1990. pap. 3.25 (0-440-20585-9, LFL) Dell.

—The Crystal Stair: From Tales of Gom in the Legends of Ulm. LC 87-27395. 240p. (gr. 5 up). 1988. SBE 14.95 (0-02-718311-4, Bradbury Pr) Macmillan Child Grp.

—Friends in Time. LC 91-33178. 144p. (gr. 3-7). 1992. SBE 13.95 (0-02-718318-1, Bradbury Pr) Macmillan Child Grp.

—Gom on Windy Mountain. LC 85-18166. (Illus.). 224p. (gr. 6 up). 1986. 12.95 (0-688-05767-5) Lothrop.

—Gom on Windy Mountain. 1990. pap. 3.50 (0-440-20543-7, LFL) Dell.

—Jason's Seven Magical Night Rides. Chetwin, Grace, illus. 128p. (gr. 2-5). 1994. SBE 14.95 (0-02-718221-5, Bradbury Pr) Macmillan Child Grp.

—On All Hallows' Eve. LC 91-46440. 160p. (gr. 3-7). 1992. pap. 3.95 (0-689-71617-6, Aladdin) Macmillan Child Grp.

—Out of the Dark World. 160p. (gr. 6 up). 1985. 11.95 (0-688-04272-4) Lothrop.

—The Riddle & the Rune: From Tales of Gom in the Legends of Ulm. LC 87-10284. 256p. (gr. 5 up). 1987. SBE 15.95 (0-02-718312-2, Bradbury Pr) Macmillan Child Grp.

—The Starstone. (gr. k up). 1990. pap. 3.25 (0-440-20634-0, LFL) Dell.

—The Starstone: From Tales of Gom in the Legends of Ulm. LC 88-30249. 256p. (gr. 5 up). 1989. SBE 15.95 (0-02-718315-7, Bradbury Pr) Macmillan Child Grp.

Chevalier, Christa. Spence & the Mean Old Bear. Levine, Abby, ed. LC 86-1570. (Illus.). 32p. (ps-1). 1986. 11.95 (0-8075-7572-0) A Whitman.

—Spence & the Sleepytime Monster. Tucker, Kathleen, ed. Chevalier, Christa, illus. LC 83-25988. 32p. (ps-1). 1984. PLB 11.95 (0-8075-7574-7) A Whitman.

—Spence Is Small. Levine, Abby, ed. Chevalier, Christa, illus. LC 87-2054. (ps-1). 1987. PLB 11.95 (0-8075-7567-4) A Whitman.

—Spence Isn't Spence Anymore. Levine, Abby, ed. Chevalier, Christa, illus. LC 84-29195. 32p. (ps-1). 1985. 11.95 (0-8075-7565-8) A Whitman.

Chevance, Audrey. Tutu. Chevance, Audrey, illus. LC 91-3506. 32p. (ps-4). 1991. 13.95 (0-525-44769-5, DCB) Dutton Child Bks.

Chevat, Richard. Ready, Set, Recycle! (ps-3). 1993. pap. 1.95 (0-307-10554-7, Golden Pr) Western Pub.

Chevat, Richie. Amazement Park Adventure. (gr. 1-3). 1994. pap. 0.99 (0-553-48091-X) Bantam.

Chew, Ruth. Magic of the Black Mirror. (gr. 4-7). 1990. pap. 2.50 (0-590-43186-2) Scholastic Inc.

—No Such Thing As a Witch. Chew, Ruth, illus. LC 79-18153. (gr. 2 up). 1980. 8.95 (0-8038-5073-5) Hastings.

—Royal Magic. 128p. 1991. pap. 2.75 (0-590-44742-4) Scholastic Inc.

—What the Witch Left. (gr. 4-7). 1993. pap. 2.75 (0-590-45531-1) Scholastic Inc.

—Witch in the House. (gr. 4-7). 1993. pap. 2.75 (0-590-46281-4) Scholastic Inc.

—Wrong Way Around Magic. (gr. 4-7). 1993. pap. 2.75 (0-590-46023-4) Scholastic Inc.

Cheyney, Arnold, jt. auth. see Cheyney, Jeanne.

Cheyney, Jeanne & Cheyney, Arnold. Bulletin Boards for Every Month. (Illus.). 112p. (Orig.). (gr. k-3). 1990. pap. 9.95 (0-673-38828-X) GdYrBks.

—The Continents: Puzzles for Learning World Geography. (Illus.). 184p. (gr. 4-6). 1994. pap. 11.95 (0-673-36072-5) GdYrBks.

—States of Wonder: Puzzles for Learning State Facts. (Illus.). 128p. (Orig.). (gr. 4-6). 1991. pap. 9.95 (0-673-46352-4) GdYrBks.

Chial, Debra. M Is for Minnesota. LC 93-34643. 1994. write for info. (0-89658-234-5) Voyageur Pr.

Chiasson, John. African Journey. Chiasson, John, photos by. LC 86-8233. (Illus.). 64p. (gr. 3-6). 1987. SBE 17.95 (0-02-718530-3, Bradbury Pr) Macmillan Child Grp.

Chicadee Editors, jt. auth. see Owl Editors.

Chicago Zoological Society Staff, ed. Animal Families. (Orig.). (gr. k-2). 1986. pap. text ed. 30.00 (0-913934-04-6) Chicago Zoo.

—Brookfield Zoo Connections: A Program to Enhance Classroom Studies. (Orig.). (gr. k-8). 1986. pap. text ed. 30.00 (0-913934-03-8) Chicago Zoo.

—Creature Features. (Orig.). (gr. 2-3). 1986. pap. text ed. 30.00 (0-913934-05-4) Chicago Zoo.

—Desert Communities. (Orig.). (gr. 4-6). 1986. pap. text ed. 30.00 (0-913934-06-2) Chicago Zoo.

Chichester, A. Lee, jt. auth. see Matthews, Billie P.

Chick, Jack T. Rey de Reyes: La Biblia en Cuadros. (SPA., Illus.). 64p. (Orig.). 1989. pap. 2.25 (0-937958-37-9) Chick Pubns.

Chick, Sandra. I Never Told Her I Loved Her. 128p. (Orig.). (gr. 8-12). 1991. pap. 5.95 (0-7043-4912-4, Pub. by Women's Pr UK) InBook.

Chickadee Magazine Editors. The Chickadee Book of Puzzles & Fun. Perna, Debi, ed. & illus. 32p. (ps up). 1992. pap. 4.95 (0-920075-82-9, Pub. by Greey de Pencier CN) Firefly Bks Ltd.

Chickadee Magazine Editors, jt. auth. see Owl Magazine Editors.

Chickadee Magazine Staff, jt. auth. see OWL Magazine Staff.

Chief Little Summer & Warm Night Rain. The Misfit. 356p. (gr. 8-12). 1991. pap. write for info. (1-880440-03-2) Piqua Pr.

—Reflections on a Rainy April Day. 43p. (gr. 1-5). 1991. pap. write for info. (1-880440-02-4) Piqua Pr.

Chiel, Kinneret. Complete Book of Hanukah. (Illus.). (gr. 6-8). pap. 6.95x (0-87069-367-5) Ktav.

Chiemroum, Sothea. Dara's Cambodian New Year. (ps-3). 1994. pap. 4.95 (0-671-88607-X, Half Moon Bks) S&S Trade.

Chiesa, Carol D., tr. see Collodi, C.

Chiesa, Pierre. Volcanes y Terremotos (Volcanos & Earthquakes) Cobielles, Antonio, tr. Henroit, Jean-Louis, illus. (SPA.). 96p. (gr. 4 up). 1992. PLB 15.90 (1-56294-176-3) Millbrook Pr.

Chijioke, F. A. Ancient Africa. LC 75-80850. (Illus.). 48p. (gr. 5-8). 1969. pap. 5.50 (0-8419-0013-2, Africana) Holmes & Meier.

Child, A. The Cloud Song. 15p. (gr. 1). 1992. pap. text ed. 23.00 big bk. (1-56843-023-X); pap. text ed. 4.50 (1-56843-073-6) BGR Pub.

—My Best Friend & Me. 19p. (gr. 1). 1992. pap. text ed. 23.00 big bk. (1-56843-022-1); pap. text ed. 4.50 (1-56843-072-8) BGR Pub.

—Show Me a Face. 14p. (ps-k). 1992. pap. text ed. 23.00 big bk. (1-56843-006-X); pap. text ed. 4.50 (1-56843-056-6) BGR Pub.

—What Would It Be? 13p. (gr. k). 1992. pap. text ed. 23.00 big bk. (1-56843-011-6); pap. text ed. 4.50 (1-56843-061-2) BGR Pub.

—Yabba Dabba Dinosaur. 23p. (gr. k). 1992. pap. text ed. 23.00 big bk. (1-56843-009-4); pap. text ed. 4.50 (1-56843-059-0) BGR Pub.

Child, Lydia M. Over the River & Through the Wood. ALC Staff, ed. Van Rynbach, Iris, illus. LC 88-4712. 32p. (ps up). 1992. pap. 3.95 (0-688-11839-9, Mulberry) Morrow.

—Over the River & Through the Wood. Westcott, Nadine B., illus. LC 92-14979. 32p. (gr. 1-5). 1993. 14.00 (0-06-021303-5); PLB 13.89 (0-06-021304-3) HarpC Child Bks.

—Over the River & Through the Wood. Manson, Christopher, illus. 32p. (gr. k-3). 1993. 14.95 (1-55858-210-X); lib. bdg. 14.88 (1-55858-211-8) North-South Bks NYC.

Child, Lydia Maria. Girls Own Book. LC 92-10815. (ps-3). 1991. 12.95 (1-55709-134-X) Applewood.

—Over the River & Through the Wood. Turkle, Brinton, illus. 32p. (gr. k-3). 1987. pap. 3.95 (0-590-41190-X, Blue Ribbons Bks) Scholastic Inc.

—Over the River & Through the Wood, Vol. 1. Van Rynbach, Iris, illus. 1989. 15.95 (0-316-13873-8) Little.

Child Study Association of America Staff. Read-to-Me Storybook. Lenski, Lois L., illus. LC 47-31488. (ps-1). 1947. 16.95i (0-690-68832-6, Crowell Jr Bks) HarpC Child Bks.

Child, Vivian M. Puffy & Buttons. 1991. 7.95 (0-533-09365-1) Vantage.

Childers, Norman H. The Great Monkey Debate. Childers, Norman H., illus. 44p. (gr. k-5). 1988. 14.95g (0-940561-12-3) White Rose Pr.

Childre, Doc L. The How-to Book of Teen Self Discovery: Helping Teens Find Balance, Security & Esteem. 2nd ed. Cryer, Bruce & Rozman, Deborah, eds. Putman, Brian, illus. (SPA.). 128p. 1992. pap. 8.95 (1-879052-18-0) Planetary Pubns.

Children at Sunrise Ranch, illus. Songs for the Joy of Living. 50p. (gr. 1-10). 1985. ring-bound 11.95 (0-932869-01-7) Emissaries Divine.

Children's Etiquette Institute Staff, et al. Social Skill Builders for Children: Eddycat, 6 titles. Hoffmann, Mark, illus. 32p. (gr. 1 up). 1993. Set incl. parent-tchr. guide. PLB 103.60 (0-8368-0938-6); PLB 17.27 ea. Gareth Stevens Inc.

Children's Museum of Oak Ridge, Tennessee Staff & Overholt, Jim, eds. Ridges & Valleys: A Mini-Encyclopedia of Anderson County, TN. 3rd ed. (Illus.). 126p. (Orig.). (gr. 5-12). 1990. pap. 5.50 (0-9606832-5-9) Chldrns Mus.

Children's Museum Staff. Original Shirley Temple Dolls in Full Color. (Illus.). 32p. (gr. 2 up). 1988. pap. 3.95 (0-486-25461-5) Dover.

Children's Television Workshop Staff. Who's Hiding? Cooke, Tom, illus. LC 84-81602. 14p. (ps-k). 1986. write for info. (0-307-12157-7, Pub. by Golden Bks) Western Pub.

Children's Writers' Workshop Staff. Shivers in Your Nightshirt: Eerie Stories to Read in Bed. Kaulbach, Kathy, illus. 106p. 1991. pap. 6.95 (0-920852-94-7, Pub. by Nimbus Publishing Ltd CN) Chelsea Green Pub.

Childress, Alice. A Hero Ain't Nothin' but a Sandwich. 100p. (gr. 5-9). 1973. 14.95 (0-698-20278-3, Coward) Putnam Pub Group.

—A Hero Ain't Nothin but a Sandwich. 128p. (gr. 7 up). 1977. pap. 3.50 (0-380-00132-2, Flare) Avon.

—A Hero Ain't Nothin' but a Sandwich. large type ed. 144p. 1989. lib. bdg. 15.95 (1-55736-112-6, Crnrstn Bks) BDD LT Grp.

—Those Other People. 144p. (gr. 8 up). 1989. 14.95 (0-399-21510-7, Putnam) Putnam Pub Group.

Childress, Casey & McKenzie, Linda. A Beginner's Guide to Baseball Card Collecting: A Step-by-Step Guide for the Young Collector. LC 88-90757. (Illus.). 46p. (Orig.). (gr. 4-8). 1990. Repr. of 1988 ed. vinyl covers 7.95 (0-9620167-0-5) C Mack Pub.

—A Kid's Guide to Collecting Baseball Cards. rev. ed. (Illus.). 80p. (gr. 3-9). 1994. pap. 9.95 (0-943173-93-0) Harbinger AZ.

Childress, Mark. Joshua & Bigtooth. Meyerowitz, Rick, illus. 32p. (ps-3). 1992. 14.95 (0-316-14011-2) Little.

—Joshua & the Big Bad Blue Crabs. Brown, Mary B., illus. LC 93-30351. 1995. reinforced bdg. 15.95 (0-316-14118-6) Little.

Childress, Valerie & Nelson, Jane. Drill Team Is for Me. LC 85-19737. (Illus.). 48p. (gr. 2-5). 1986. lib. bdg. 13. 50 (0-8225-1148-7) Lerner Pubns.

Childs, C., jt. auth. see Caudron, C.

Childs, Caro, jt. auth. see Chaudron, Chris.

Childs, N. Flashpoints, 6 bks, Set II, Reading Level 8. (Illus.). 560p. (gr. 7 up). 1988. Set. PLB 111.60 (0-685-58794-0); 83.70s.p. (0-685-58795-9) Rourke Corp.

Childs, Phyllis. Color Me. 35p. (ps-k). 1985. wkbk. 2.95 (0-931749-03-4) PJC Lrng Mtrls.

—The Language Ladder, Bk. I. Sterling, Suzanne, illus. 76p. (ps-k). 1985. wkbk. 6.50 (0-931749-01-8) PJC Lrng Mtrls.

—Language Ladder, Bk. 2. 54p. (ps-k). 1987. pap. 5.95 wkbk. (0-317-60748-0) PJC Lrng Mtrls.

—Speak Up. 78p. (ps-k). 1985. wkbk. 6.50 (0-931749-00-X) PJC Lrng Mtrls.

Childs, Phyllis, et al. First Book of Numbers. 55p. (ps-k). 1985. wkbk. 4.95 (0-931749-02-6) PJC Lrng Mtrls.

—I've Got Something for You to Do...& It's Fun! (ps-k). 1986. wkbk. 2.25 (0-931749-04-2) PJC Lrng Mtrls.

Childs, Valerie. Walt Disney World & Epcot Center. 1990. 7.99 (0-517-48085-9) Outlet Bk Co.

Chiles, John. Teenage Depression & Drugs. (Illus.). 32p. (gr. 5 up). 1991. pap. 4.49 (0-7910-0005-2) Chelsea Hse.

—Teenage Depression & Drugs. updated ed. (Illus.). (gr. 5 up). 1992. lib. bdg. 19.95 (0-685-52254-7); pap. 9.95 (0-685-52255-5) Chelsea Hse.

Chiltosky, Mary U., jt. auth. see Galloway, Mary R.

Chimenti, Elisa. Tales & Legends of Morocco. Benamy, Arnon, tr. (Illus.). (gr. 5 up). 1965. 10.95 (0-8392-3049-4) Astor-Honor.

Chimeric Inc. Staff. Illustory. 12p. (gr. k-4). Date not set. write for info. (0-9636796-0-0) Chimeric.

Chin, Charlie. China's Bravest Girl: The Legend of Hua Mu Lan. LC 93-15255. (Illus.). 32p. (gr. 6-12). 1993. 13.95 (0-89239-120-0) Childrens Book Pr.

Chin, Frank. Donald Duk. LC 90-29994. 173p. (Orig.). 1991. pap. 10.95 (0-918273-83-8) Coffee Hse.

Chin, Steven A. Dragon Parade: A Chinese New Year Story. Tseng, Mou-Sien, illus. LC 92-18079. 32p. (gr. 2-5). 1992. PLB 21.34 (0-8114-7215-9) Raintree Steck-V.

—When Justice Failed: The Fred Korematsu Story. Tamura, David, illus. LC 92-18086. 105p. (gr. 2-5). 1992. PLB 21.34 (0-8114-7236-1) Raintree Steck-V.

Chin, Yin-lien C., intros. by. Traditional Chinese Folktales. Center, Y. LC 88-31129. (Illus.). 192p. (gr. 8-12). 1989. 24.95 (0-87332-507-9) M E Sharpe.

Chinery, Michael. All Kinds of Animals. LC 92-21677. (Illus.). 128p. (ps-3). 1993. 10.00 (0-679-83697-7); PLB 11.99 (0-679-93697-1) Random Bks Yng Read.

—Ant. Armstrong, Nicholas, illus. Watts, Barrie, photos by. LC 90-10947. (Illus.). 32p. (gr. 4-6). 1991. PLB 11.59 (0-8167-2098-3); pap. text ed. 3.95 (0-8167-2099-1) Troll Assocs.

—Butterfly. Senior, Helen, illus. Watts, Barrie, photos by. LC 90-10942. (Illus.). 32p. (gr. 4-6). 1991. lib. bdg. 11. 59 (0-8167-2100-9); pap. text ed. 3.95 (0-8167-2101-7) Troll Assocs.

—Desert Animals. Wright, David, illus. LC 91-53146. 40p. (Orig.). (gr. 2-5). 1992. PLB 8.99 (0-679-92048-X); pap. 4.99 (0-679-82048-5) Random Bks Yng Read.

—Frog. Watts, Barrie, photos by. Camm, Martin, illus. LC 90-10962. 32p. (gr. 4-6). 1991. lib. bdg. 11.59 (0-8167-2102-5); pap. text ed. 3.95 (0-8167-2103-3) Troll Assocs.

—Grassland Animals. Butler, John & McIntyre, Brian, illus. LC 91-53145. 40p. (Orig.). (gr. 2-5). 1992. PLB 8.99 (0-679-92045-5); pap. 4.99 (0-679-82045-0) Random Bks Yng Read.

—Lake & River Animals. Ford, Wayne & Robson, Eric, illus. LC 92-20471. 1993. write for info. (0-679-93704-8); pap. write for info. (0-679-83704-3) Knopf Bks Yng Read.

—Ocean Animals. Robson, Eric, illus. LC 91-53144. 40p. (Orig.). (gr. 2-5). 1992. PLB 8.99 (0-679-92046-3); pap. 4.99 (0-679-82046-9) Random Bks Yng Read.

—Questions & Answers about Forest Animals. Long, Bernard & Robson, Eric, illus. LC 93-29427. 1994. 5.95 (1-85697-963-6) Kingfisher Bks.

—Questions & Answers about Freshwater Animals. Ford, Wayne & Robson, Eric, illus. LC 93-29415. 1994. 5.95 (1-85697-962-8) Kingfisher Bks.

—Questions & Answers about Polar Animals. Butler, John & McIntyre, Brian, illus. LC 93-29426. 1994. 5.95 (1-85697-964-4) Kingfisher Bks.

—Questions & Answers about Seashore Animals. Ford, Wayne, et al, illus. LC 93-29428. 1994. 5.95 Kingfisher Bks.

—Rainforest Animals. Holmes, David & Robinson, Bernard, illus. LC 91-53143. 40p. (Orig.). (gr. 2-5). 1992. PLB 8.99 (0-679-92047-1); pap. 4.99 (0-679-82047-7) Random Bks Yng Read.

—Shark. Doubilet, David, et al, illus. LC 90-33361. 32p. (gr. 4-6). 1991. lib. bdg. 11.59 (0-8167-2104-1); pap. text ed. 3.95 (0-8167-2105-X) Troll Assocs.

—Snake. Ovenden, Denys, illus. Watts, Barrie, photos by. LC 90-10951. (Illus.). 32p. (gr. 4-6). 1991. PLB 11.59 (0-8167-2106-8); pap. text ed. 3.95 (0-8167-2107-6) Troll Assocs.

—Spider. Male, Alan, illus. Watts, Barrie, photos by. LC 90-10941. (Illus.). 32p. (gr. 4-6). 1991. lib. bdg. 11.59 (0-8167-2108-4); pap. text ed. 3.95 (0-8167-2109-2) Troll Assocs.

Chinery, Michael, ed. The Kingfisher Illustrated Encyclopedia of Animals. LC 92-53113. (Illus.). 380p. (gr. 4 up). 1992. 19.95 (1-85697-801-X) Kingfisher Bks.

Ching. The Baboon's Umbrella. LC 91-7952. (Illus.). 24p. (ps-3). 1991. PLB 15.53 (0-516-05131-8); pap. 4.95 (0-516-45131-6) Childrens.

Ching, Emily, ed. see Wonder Kids Publications Group Staff (USA) & Hwa-I Publishing Co., Staff.

Ching, Emily, et al, eds. see Hwa-I Publishing Co., Staff.

Ching, Emily, et al, eds. see Wonder Kids Publications Group Staff.

Ching, Emily, et al, eds. see Wonder Kids Publications Group Staff & Hwa-I Publishing Co., Staff.

Ching, Emily, et al, eds. see Wonder Kids Publications Group Staff (USA) & Hwa-I Publishing Co., Staff.

Ching, Ko-Shee, ed. see Wonder Kids Publications Group Staff (USA) & Hwa-I Publishing Co., Staff.

Ching, Patrick. Exotic Animals in Hawaii. Ching, Patrick, illus. 32p. (Orig.). (ps-6). 1988. pap. 3.95 (0-935848-56-8) Bess Pr.

—Native Animals of Hawaii. Ching, Patrick, illus. 32p. (Orig.). (ps-6). 1988. pap. 3.95 (0-935848-55-X) Bess Pr.

Ching, Patrick & Ching, Patrick. Beautiful Birds of Hawaii Coloring Book. (Illus.). 32p. (ps-2). 1992. pap. 3.95 (1-880188-43-0) Bess Pr.

Ching Yee, Janice. God's Busiest Angels. (Illus.). (gr. k-6). 1975. pap. 3.00 (0-931420-09-1) Pi Pr.

—God's Meekest Angels. (Illus.). (gr. k-6). 1981. pap. 3.00 (0-931420-10-5) Pi Pr.

—God's Naughtiest Angels. (Illus.). (gr. k-6). 1974. pap. 3.00 (0-931420-08-3) Pi Pr.

Chin-Lee, Cynthia. Almond Cookies & Dragon Well Tea. Tang, You S., illus. LC 92-21518. 36p. (gr. k-3). 1993. 12.95 (1-879965-03-8) Polychrome Pub.

Chipangu, Florita. Bird Meets Fish. Donovan, Bob, illus. 36p. 1993. pap. 2.50 (1-878181-07-6) Discovery Comics.

Chippindale, Jenny & Thorp, Kate. Christmas Stitchery. (Illus.). 144p. (gr. 10-12). 1992. pap. 16.95 (0-7153-9965-9, Pub. by David & Charles Pub UK) Sterling.

Chirian, Helene. Crossword Mysteries: Who Dunnit Challenge. (gr. 4-7). 1991. pap. 2.95 (0-8431-2788-0) Price Stern.

Chirinian, Alain. Motorcycles. (Illus.). 64p. (gr. 5-9). 1989. lib. bdg. 10.98 (0-671-68029-3, J Messner); PLB 8.24s.p. (0-685-47093-8); pap. 3.71s.p. (0-685-47094-6) S&S Trade.

—Muscle Cars. Steltenpohl, Jane, ed. (Illus.). 64p. (gr. 5-9). 1989. (J Messner); PLB 8.24s.p. (0-685-47091-1); pap. 3.71s.p. (0-685-47092-X) S&S Trade.

—Race Cars. (Illus.). 64p. (gr. 5-9). 1989. (J Messner); PLB 8.24s.p. (0-685-54167-3); pap. 3.71s.p. (0-685-47098-9) S&S Trade.

—Tough Wheels Series, 4 vols. (Illus.). 256p. (gr. 5-9). 1989. Set. PLB 43.92 (0-671-94096-1, J Messner); Set. PLB 32.94s.p. (0-685-54166-5); Set. pap. 19.80 (0-671-93115-6); Set. pap. 14.85s.p. (0-685-47090-3) S&S Trade.

—Weird Wheels. Steltenpohl, Jane, ed. (Illus.). 64p. (gr. 5-9). 1989. (J Messner); lib. bdg. 4.95 (0-671-68036-6); PLB 8.24s.p. (0-685-47095-4); pap. 3.71s.p. (0-685-47096-2) S&S Trade.

Chirinian, Helene. Camping Out. (Illus.). 48p. (Orig.). (gr. k-3). 1989. pap. 2.95 (0-8431-2415-6) Price Stern.

—Crossword Mysteries: Daring Detectives. 48p. 1990. pap. 2.95 (0-8431-2791-0) Price Stern.

—Crossword Mysteries: Super Sleuth Challenge. 48p. 1990. pap. 2.95 (0-8431-2789-0) Price Stern.

—Future Park. (Illus.). 48p. (Orig.). (gr. k-3). 1989. pap. 2.95 (0-8431-2416-4) Price Stern.

—Scavenger Hunt. (Illus.). 48p. (Orig.). (gr. k-3). 1989. pap. 2.95 (0-8431-2414-8) Price Stern.

Chisa, jt. auth. see Obaba, Al-Imam.

Chisholm. Our Earth. (gr. 2-5). 1982. (Usborne-Hayes); pap. 3.95 (0-86020-582-7) EDC.

—Prehistoric Times. (gr. 2-5). 1983. pap. 4.50 (0-86020-623-8); lib. bdg. 11.96 (0-685-57845-3) EDC.

Chisholm, Gloria. Andrea. LC 83-71614. 160p. (Orig.). (gr. 9 up). 1983. pap. 3.99 (0-87123-297-9) Bethany Hse.

—Jocelyn. LC 87-72794. 176p. (Orig.). (gr. 9-12). 1988. pap. 3.99 (0-87123-846-2) Bethany Hse.

Chisholm, J. Biology. Beeson, D., illus. 48p. (gr. 3-6). 1984. PLB 13.96 (0-88110-166-4); pap. 6.95 (0-86020-707-2) EDC.

—Book of Science. Beeson, D., illus. 48p. (gr. 3-6). 1984. 14.95 (0-86020-721-8) EDC.

—World History Dates. (Illus.). 128p. (gr. 6 up). 1987. PLB 17.96 (0-88110-232-6); pap. 12.95 (0-86020-954-7) EDC.

Chisholm, J. & Gee, R. First Book of History: Prehistoric Times, Castle Times, Roman Times. (Illus.). (gr. 4-7). 1993. pap. 9.95 (0-7460-1304-3, Usborne) EDC.

Chisholm, J., jt. auth. see Milard, A.

Chisholm, Jan. Roman Times. McCaig, Rob, illus. 24p. (gr. 3-6). 1982. PLB 11.96 (0-88110-105-2); pap. 4.50 (0-86020-619-X); lib. bdg. 11.96 (0-685-57844-5) EDC.

Chisholm, Louey, ed. The Golden Staircase: Poems & Verses for Children. LC 79-51973. (Illus.). (gr. 3-8). 1980. Repr. of 1906 ed. 23.50x (0-89609-182-1) Roth Pub Inc.

Chisholm, Sarah. My Christmas Angel. (ps). 1993. pap. 5.99 (0-8066-2601-1) Augsburg Fortress.

—My Christmas Star: A Hide & Seek Story. (ps). 1993. pap. 5.99 (0-8066-2600-3) Augsburg Fortress.

Chishom, J. & Lynnington, M. Chemistry. Ashman, Iain, illus. 48p. (gr. 6 up). 1983. lib. bdg. 13.96 (0-88110-151-6); pap. 6.95 (0-86020-709-9) EDC.

Chislett, G. Whump. (Illus.). 24p. (ps-8). 1989. 12.95 (1-55037-041-3, Pub. by Annick CN); pap. 4.95 (1-55037-040-5, Pub. by Annick CN) Firefly Bks Ltd.

Chislett, Gail. Melinda's No's Gold. Desputeaux, Helene, illus. 32p. (ps-2). 1991. PLB 14.95 (1-55037-196-7, Pub. by Annick CN); pap. 4.95 (1-55037-198-3, Pub. by Annick CN) Firefly Bks Ltd.

—Whump. Krykorka, Vladyana, illus. (ps-1). 1992. 0.99 (1-55037-253-X, Pub. by Annick Pr) Firefly Bks Ltd.

Chisum, Elizabeth. Lizard Tales. (Illus.). 64p. (Orig.). 1993. pap. 8.95 (0-86534-201-6) Sunstone Pr.

Chittum, Ida. The Cat's Pajamas. Cumings, Art, illus. 48p. (ps-3). 1980. 5.95 (0-8193-1029-8) Parents.

—The Ghost Boy of el Toro. LC 78-1079. (gr. 4 up). 1978. 8.00 (0-8309-0201-5) Ind Pr MO.

Chitwood, Deb. The Magic Ring. Fraydas, Stan, illus. LC 82-62432. 32p. (ps-3). 1983. 9.95 (0-942044-01-0) Polestar.

Chlad, Dorothy. Animals Can be Special Friends. Halverson, Lydia, illus. LC 84-23300. 32p. (ps-2). 1985. pap. 3.95 (0-516-41978-1) Childrens.

—Bicycles Are Fun. Martin, Clovis, illus. LC 92-12193. 32p. (ps-2). 1992. PLB 15.00 (0-516-01971-6) Childrens.

—Bicycles Are Fun to Ride. Halverson, Lydia, illus. LC 83-23234. 32p. (ps-2). 1984. pap. 3.95 (0-516-41975-7) Childrens.

—Los Cerillos, los Encendedores y los Triquitraques No Son Juguetes (Matches, Lighters & Firecrackers Are Not Toys) Halverson, Lydia, illus. LC 81-18125. (SPA.). 32p. (ps-2). 1987. PLB 15.00 (0-516-31982-5); pap. 3.95 (0-516-51982-4) Childrens.

—Cuando Cruzo la Calle (When I Cross the Street) Kratky, Lada, tr. Halverson, Lydia, illus. LC 85-31397. (SPA.). 32p. (ps-2). 1986. PLB 15.00 (0-516-31985-X); pap. 3.95 (0-516-51985-9) Childrens.

—Cuando Hay un Incendio Sal Para Afuera (When There Is a Fire...Go Outside) Kratky, Lada, tr. from ENG. Halverson, Lydia, illus. LC 85-9636. (SPA.). 32p. (ps-2). 1986. PLB 15.00 (0-516-31986-8); pap. 3.95 (0-516-51986-7) Childrens.

—Cuando viajo en auto (When I Ride in a Car) Halverson, Lydia, illus. LC 83-7382. (ENG & SPA.). 32p. (ps-2). 1989. PLB 15.00 (0-516-31987-6); pap. 3.95 (0-516-51987-5) Childrens.

—Los Desconocidos (Strangers) Kratky, Lada, tr. from ENG. Halverson, Lydia, illus. LC 81-18109. (SPA.). 32p. (ps-2). 1984. PLB 15.00 (0-516-31984-1); pap. 3.95 (0-516-51984-0) Childrens.

—Es Divertido Andar en Bicicleta (Bicycles Are Fun to Ride) Kratky, Lada, tr. Halverson, Lydia, illus. LC 85-23263. (SPA.). 32p. (ps-2). 1986. pap. 3.95 (0-516-51975-1) Childrens.

—In the Water...On the Water. Halverson, Lydia, illus. LC 88-12065. 32p. (ps-2). 1988. pap. 3.95 (0-516-41974-9) Childrens.

—Jugando en el Patio de Recreo (Playing on the Playground) Halverson, Lydia, illus. LC 87-5197. (SPA.). 32p. (ps-2). 1988. pap. 3.95 (0-516-51989-1) Childrens.

—Matches, Lighters, & Firecrackers are not Toys. LC 81-18125. (Illus.). (gr. k-3). 1982. pap. 3.95 (0-516-41982-X) Childrens.

—Playing on the Playground. Halverson, Lydia, illus. LC 87-5197. 32p. (ps-2). 1987. pap. 3.95 (0-516-41989-7) Childrens.

—Playing Outdoors in the Winter. Halverson, Lydia, illus. LC 90-22258. 32p. (ps-2). 1991. pap. 3.95 (*0-516-41972-2*) Childrens.
—Poisons Make You Sick. Halverson, Lydia, illus. LC 83-24029. 32p. (ps-2). 1984. PLB 15.00 (*0-516-01976-7*); pap. 3.95 (*0-516-41976-5*) Childrens.
—Riding on a Bus. LC 85-12750. (Illus.). 32p. (ps-2). 1985. pap. 3.95 (*0-516-41979-X*) Childrens.
—Stop, Look, & Listen for Trains. LC 83-7213. (Illus.). 32p. (ps-2). 1983. pap. 3.95 (*0-516-41988-9*) Childrens.
—Strangers. LC 81-18109. (Illus.). (gr. k-3). 1982. pap. 3.95 (*0-516-41984-6*) Childrens.
—Los Venenos Te Hacen Dano (Poisons Make You Sick) Kratky, Lada, tr. Halverson, Lydia, illus. LC 85-30738. (SPA.). 32p. (ps-2). 1986. PLB 15.00 (*0-516-31976-0*); pap. 3.95 (*0-516-51976-X*) Childrens.
—Viajando en Autobus (Riding on a Bus) Halverson, Lydia, illus. LC 85-12570. (SPA.). 32p. (ps-2). 1988. PLB 15.00 (*0-516-31979-5*); pap. 3.95 (*0-516-51979-4*) Childrens.
—When I Cross the Street. LC 81-18108. (Illus.). (gr. k-3). 1982. pap. 3.95 (*0-516-41985-4*) Childrens.
—When I Ride in a Car. LC 83-7382. (Illus.). 32p. (ps-2). 1983. pap. 3.95 (*0-516-41987-0*) Childrens.
—When There Is a Fire Go Outside. LC 81-18018. (Illus.). (gr. k-3). 1982. pap. 3.95 (*0-516-41986-2*) Childrens.

Chmielarz, Sharon. Down at Angel's. Kastner, Jill, illus. LC 93-11020. 1994. for info. 14.95 (*0-395-65993-0*) Ticknor & Fields.
—End of Winter. Cable, Annette, illus. LC 91-30304. 32p. (ps-3). 1992. 14.00 (*0-517-58745-9*); PLB 14.99 (*0-517-58746-7*) Crown Bks Yng Read.

Chmielarz, Sharon, adapted by. The Pied Piper of Hamelin. DeWitt, Pat & DeWitt, Robin, illus. 40p. (gr. k-6). 1990. 14.95 (*0-88045-115-7*) Stemmer Hse.

Chmielewski, Gary. Animal Jokes. Clark, Ron G., illus. LC 86-17684. (gr. 2-3). 1986. 13.27 (*0-86592-687-5*); 9.95s.p. (*0-685-58362-7*) Rourke Corp.
—Sports Jokes. Clark, Ron G., illus. (gr. 2-3). 1986. 13.27 (*0-86592-683-2*); lib. bdg. 9.95 (*0-685-58364-3*) Rourke Corp.
—Teacher Jokes. Clark, Ron G., illus. LC 86-17773. (gr. 2-3). 1986. 13.27 (*0-86592-688-3*); 9.95s.p. (*0-685-58365-1*) Rourke Corp.
—Tongue Twisters. Clark, Ron G., illus. LC 86-17701. (gr. 2-3). 1986. 13.27 (*0-86592-685-9*); 9.95s.p. (*0-685-58366-X*) Rourke Corp.
—Why Do Bees Hum: And 265 Other Great Jokes for Kids. 1990. 6.99 (*0-517-02536-1*) Outlet Bk Co.

Cho, Byung K. Korean Culture Tourism & Language: For Everything You Need to Know about Korea. 357p. (gr. 7 up). 1988. 29.00 (*0-685-30452-3*) B K Cho.

Chochola, Frantisek. The Forest. (Illus.). (ps). 1988. bds. 5.50 (*0-86315-073-X*, 20234) Gryphon Hse.
—On the Farm. (ps). 1988. bds. 5.50 (*0-86315-051-9*, 20235) Gryphon Hse.

Chock, Eric, ed. Small Kid Time. 204p. (gr. k-12). 1989. 5.00 (*0-910043-03-5*) Bamboo Ridge Pr.

Chock, Eric & Lum, Darrell, eds. The Best of Bamboo Ridge. LC 83-73232. 325p. (gr. 9-12). 1986. pap. 9.00 (*0-910043-07-8*) Bamboo Ridge Pr.

Chocolate, Debbi. Elizabeth's Wish. 1993. pap. 3.95 (*0-940975-45-9*) Just Us Bks.

Chocolate, Debbi & Hudson, Wade. NEATE: To the Rescue. LC 92-72004. 112p. (Orig.). (gr. 5 up). 1992. pap. 3.95 (*0-940975-42-4*) Just Us Bks.

Chocolate, Deborah M. Kwanzaa. Rosales, Melodye, illus. LC 89-25418. 32p. (ps-3). 1990. PLB 15.00 (*0-516-03991-1*); pap. 3.95 (*0-516-43991-X*) Childrens.
—My First Kwanzaa Book. 1992. bds. 10.95 (*0-590-45762-4*, Cartwheel) Scholastic Inc.
—Spider & the Sky God: An Akan Legend. Albers, Dave, illus. LC 92-13277. 32p. (gr. 2-5). 1992. PLB 11.89 (*0-8167-2811-9*); pap. text ed. 3.95 (*0-8167-2812-7*) Troll Assocs.
—Talk, Talk: An Ashanti Legend. Albers, Dave, illus. LC 92-13279. 32p. (gr. 2-5). 1992. PLB 11.89 (*0-8167-2817-8*); pap. text ed. 3.95 (*0-8167-2818-6*) Troll Assocs.

Chodak, Yurek, ed. see Perrin, Steve.

Chodkowski, Dick. Camp Catastrophe. (Illus.). 48p. 1990. pap. 6.95 (*0-8431-2435-0*) Price Stern.
—Snakes Alive! It's Reptile Clive! McKissack, Patricia & McKissack, Fredrick, eds. Chodkowski, Dick, illus. LC 88-60391. 32p. (Orig.). (gr. 1-3). 1990. text ed. 8.95 (*0-88335-787-9*); pap. text ed. 4.95 (*0-88335-799-2*) Milliken Pub Co.

Choi, Sook N. Echoes of the White Giraffe. LC 92-17476. 144p. (gr. 5 up). 1993. 13.45 (*0-395-64721-5*) HM.
—Year of Impossible Goodbyes. (gr. 4-7). 1993. pap. 3.50 (*0-440-40759-1*) Dell.

Choi Sook Nyul. Halmoni & the Picnic. (ps-3). 1993. 14.95 (*0-395-61626-3*) HM.

Chokai, M. Sherlock Holmes & the Jewel & Other Short Plays. Biswas, Dolly, illus. 169p. (gr. 6). 1983. pap. 3.95x (*0-86131-330-5*) Apt Bks.

Chorao, Kay. Annie & Cousin Precious. LC 93-32611. 1994. write for info. (*0-525-45238-9*, DCB) Dutton Child Bks.
—The Baby's Bedtime Book. Chorao, Kay, illus. LC 84-6067. 64p. (ps). 1989. 13.95 (*0-525-44149-2*, DCB); bk & cassette 18.95 (*0-525-44506-4*) Dutton Child Bks.
—The Baby's Lap Book. (Illus.). (ps-k). 1977. 12.95 (*0-525-26100-1*, DCB) Dutton Child Bks.
—Baby's Lap Book. Rashad, Phylicia, read by. LC 89-23273. (Illus.). 64p. (ps). 1991. 13.95 (*0-525-44604-4*, DCB); incl. audiocassette 18.95 (*0-525-44628-1*) Dutton Child Bks.
—The Baby's Story Book. Chorao, Kay, illus. LC 84-26005. 64p. (ps-1). 1989. 13.95 (*0-525-44200-6*, DCB); bk. & cassette 17.95 (*0-525-44507-2*) Dutton Child Bks.
—Carousel Round & Round. LC 93-35520. 1995. write for info. (*0-395-63632-9*, Clarion Bks) HM.
—Cathedral Mouse. Chorao, Kay, illus. LC 87-33398. 32p. (ps-2). 1988. 12.95 (*0-525-44400-9*, DCB) Dutton Child Bks.
—Cathedral Mouse. LC 87-33398. (Illus.). 32p. (ps-2). 1991. pap. 4.95 (*0-525-44823-3*, Puffin) Puffin Bks.
—The Cherry Pie Baby. Chorao, Kay, illus. LC 88-2630. 32p. (ps-3). 1989. 12.95 (*0-525-44435-1*, DCB) Dutton Child Bks.
—Child's Fairy Tale Book. LC 89-49480. (Illus.). 64p. (ps-3). 1990. 14.95 (*0-525-44630-3*, DCB) Dutton Child Bks.
—The Child's Story Book. Chorao, Kay, illus. LC 87-8899. 64p. (ps-3). 1987. 12.95 (*0-525-44328-2*, 01258-370, DCB) Dutton Child Bks.
—Ida & Betty & the Secret Eggs. Giblin, James, ed. Chorao, Kay, illus. 32p. (ps-2). 1991. 13.45 (*0-395-52591-8*, Clarion Bks) HM.
—Rock, Rock, My Baby. Chorao, Kay, illus. LC 92-61268. 22p. (ps). 1993. 3.25 (*0-679-84333-7*) Random Bks Yng Read.

Chorao, Kay, compiled by. & illus. Baby's Christmas Treasury. LC 90-45872. 48p. (μs). 1991. 10.00 (*0-679-80198-7*); lib. bdg. 10.99 (*0-679-90198-1*) Random Bks Yng Read.

Chorao, Kay, illus. Baby's Good Morning Book. Collins, Judy, contrib. by. LC 86-6415. (Illus.). 64p. (ps). 1990. 13.95 (*0-525-44257-X*, DCB); incl. audio cass. 17.95 (*0-525-44627-3*, DCB) Dutton Child Bks.
—Mother Goose Magic. LC 92-37160. 64p. (ps-k). 1994. 15.99 (*0-525-45064-5*, DCB) Dutton Child Bks.

Chorlian, Ruth W. Long Trail of the Texas Longhorns. 80p. (gr. 4-7). 1986. 9.95 (*0-89015-540-2*, Pub. by Panda Bks) Eakin-Sunbelt.

Chorlton, David. The Human Flower. 8p. (Orig.). (gr. 10 up). 1993. pap. 1.50 (*0-916155-22-6*) Trout Creek.

Chorpenning, Charlotte B. Cinderella. (gr. 1-7). 1940. 4.50 (*0-87602-116-X*) Anchorage.
—Jack & the Beanstalk. 1935. 4.50 (*0-87602-143-7*) Anchorage.
—Little Red Riding Hood. 47p. (Orig.). 1946. 4.50 (*0-87602-149-6*) Anchorage.
—Robinson Crusoe. (gr. 1-9). 1952. 4.50 (*0-87602-192-5*) Anchorage.
—Rumpelstiltskin. (gr. 1-7). 1944. 4.50 (*0-87602-195-X*) Anchorage.
—The Sleeping Beauty. (gr. 1-7). 1947. 4.50 (*0-87602-203-4*) Anchorage.
—The Three Bears. 50p. (Orig.). 1949. 4.50 (*0-87602-208-5*) Anchorage.

Chorpenning, Charlotte B., jt. auth. see McAlvay, Nora.

Chorzempa, Rosemary A. My Family Tree Workbook: Genealogy for Beginners. 64p. (gr. 5 up). 1982. pap. 2.50 (*0-486-24229-3*) Dover.

Chotianovsky, Olga, ed. see Kogan, Mark.

Chottin, Ariane. Beaver Gets Lost. Geneste, Marcelle, illus. LC 91-40651. 22p. (ps). 1992. 6.99 (*0-89577-419-4*, Readers Digest Kids) RD Assn.
—The Curious Little Dolphin. Raquois, Olivier, illus. LC 91-46500. 22p. (ps). 1992. 6.99 (*0-89577-425-9*, Readers Digest Kids) RD Assn.
—A Home for Little Turtle. Wirth, Pascale, illus. LC 91-40650. 22p. (ps). 1992. 6.99 (*0-89577-420-8*, Readers Digest Kids) RD Assn.
—Little Goat's New Horns. Jensen, Patricia, adapted by. Wirth, Pascale, illus. LC 93-4241. 1993. write for info. (*0-89577-544-1*, Readers Digest Kids) RD Assn.
—Little Kangaroo Finds His Way. Jensen, Patricia, adapted by. Fichaux, Catherine, illus. LC 93-4242. 1993. write for info. (*0-89577-543-3*, Readers Digest Kids) RD Assn.
—Little Mouse's Rescue: Little Animal Adventures Ser. Dzierzawska, Malgorzata, illus. Jensen, Patricia, adapted by. LC 93-2949. (Illus.). (ps-3). 1993. write for info. (*0-89577-505-0*) RD Assn.

Choudhary, Bani. Story of Mahabharata. (ps up). 1988. 7.50 (*0-318-37379-3*) Auromere.

Choudhary, Bani R. Stories from Panchatantra. Bhushan, Reboti, illus. (gr. 3-10). 1979. 7.25 (*0-89744-136-2*) Auromere.
—The Story of Krishna. (Illus.). (gr. 3-10). 1979. 7.25 (*0-89744-134-6*) Auromere.
—The Story of Ramayan. (Illus.). (gr. 3-10). 1979. 7.50 (*0-89744-133-8*) Auromere.

Chouinard, Marika. Brave Little Toaster Goes to Mars. 1988. pap. 11.95 (*0-385-24162-3*) Doubleday.

Choy, Carol E., jt. auth. see Yarber, Yvonne.

Christenson, Shawna, et al. The Biggest Little Girl. French, Marty & Warter, Fred, illus. 26p. (ps up). Book & Cassette. 7.95 (*1-55578-108-X*) Worlds Wonder.
—The Biggest Little Girl. French, Marty & Warter, Fred, illus. 26p. (ps up). 1988. incl. cassette 7.95 (*1-55578-916-1*) Worlds Wonder.

Chrisfield, Debbie. Radio. LC 93-26393. Date not set. write for info. (*0-89686-794-3*, Crestwood Hse) Macmillan Child Grp.

Chrisman, Arthur B. Shen of the Sea. Hasselriis, Else, illus. (gr. 4-7). 1968. 15.00 (*0-525-39244-0*, DCB) Dutton Child Bks.

Chrisp, Peter. Blitzkrieg. (Illus.). 64p. (gr. 7-10). 1991. PLB 13.40 (*0-531-18373-4*, Pub. by Bookwright Pr) Watts.
—The Farmer Through History. Smith, Tony, illus. LC 92-38485. 48p. (gr. 5-8). 1993. 15.95 (*1-56847-011-8*) Thomson Lrning.
—The Rise of Fascism. LC 90-46774. (Illus.). 64p. (gr. 9-12). 1991. 13.40 (*0-531-18438-2*, Pub. by Bookwright Pr) Watts.
—The Romans. LC 93-29441. 1994. write for info. (*0-7910-2707-4*); write for info. (*0-7910-2731-7*) Chelsea Hse.
—Search for a Northern Route. LC 93-30920. (Illus.). 48p. (gr. 4-6). 1993. 14.95 (*1-56847-122-X*) Thomson Lrning.
—The Search for the East. LC 93-12826. (Illus.). 48p. (gr. 4-6). 1993. 14.95 (*1-56847-120-3*) Thomson Lrning.
—The Soldier Through History. Smith, Tony, illus. LC 92-40639. 48p. (gr. 5-8). 1993. 15.95 (*1-56847-010-X*) Thomson Lrning.
—The Spanish Conquests in the New World. LC 93-24396. (Illus.). 48p. (gr. 4-6). 1993. 14.95 (*1-56847-123-8*) Thomson Lrning.
—Voyages to the New World. LC 93-9473. 48p. (gr. 4-6). 1993. 14.95 (*1-56847-121-1*) Thomson Lrning.

Christ, Dean, jt. auth. see Sumichrast, Michael J.

Christain, Mary B. Hats Are for Watering Horses: Why the Cowboy Dressed That Way. Miller, Lyle, illus. 64p. (gr. 2 up). 1994. write for info. (*0-937460-89-3*); pap. write for info. (*0-937460-95-8*) Hendrick-Long.

Christelow, Eileen. Don't Wake up Mama! Another Five Little Monkeys Story. Christelow, Eileen, illus. 32p. (ps-3). 1992. 13.45 (*0-395-60176-2*, Clarion Bks) HM.
—The Five-Dog Night. LC 92-36958. 1993. 14.45 (*0-395-62399-5*, Clarion Bks) HM.
—Five Little Monkeys Jumping on the Bed. Christelow, Eileen, illus. (ps-3). 1993. pap. 5.70 (*0-395-55701-1*, Clarion Bks); pap. 7.95 incl. cassette 4.95 (*0-395-60115-0*, Clarion Bks) HM.
—Five Little Monkeys Sitting in a Tree. Giblin, James, ed. Christelow, Eileen, illus. 32p. (ps-1). 1991. 13.45 (*0-395-54434-3*, Clarion Bks) HM.
—Five Little Monkeys Sitting in a Tree. Christelow, Eileen, illus. 32p. (gr. k-3). 1993. pap. 5.70 (*0-395-66413-6*, Clarion Bks) HM.
—Gertrude, the Bulldog Detective. Christelow, Eileen, illus. 32p. (gr. k-3). 1992. 13.45 (*0-395-58701-8*, Clarion Bks) HM.
—Henry & the Dragon. Christelow, Eileen, illus. LC 83-14405. 32p. (ps-2). 1984. 13.45 (*0-89919-220-3*, Clarion Bks) HM.
—Henry & the Dragon. (Illus.). (ps-3). 1990. pap. 4.80 (*0-395-55697-X*, Clarion Bks) HM.
—Henry & the Red Stripes. Christelow, Eileen, illus. 32p. (ps-3). 1982. 14.45 (*0-89919-118-5*, Clarion Bks) HM.
—Jerome & the Witchcraft Kids. Christelow, Eileen, illus. LC 88-2597. 32p. (gr. k-3). 1988. 13.95 (*0-89919-742-6*, Clarion Bks) HM.
—Jerome & the Withcraft Kids. Christelow, Eileen, illus. 32p. (ps-3). 1990. pap. 4.80 (*0-395-54428-9*, Clarion Bks) HM.
—Jerome the Babysitter. Christelow, Eileen, illus. LC 84-12738. 32p. (ps-3). 1987. pap. 4.95 (*0-89919-520-2*, Clarion Bks) HM.
—Olive & the Magic Hat. Christelow, Eileen, illus. LC 87-672. 32p. (gr. k-3). 1987. 12.95 (*0-89919-513-X*, Clarion Bks) HM.
—The Robbery at the Diamond Dog Diner. LC 86-2682. (Illus.). 32p. (ps-3). 1988. 13.95 (*0-89919-425-7*, Clarion Bks); pap. 4.95 (*0-89919-722-1*, Clarion Bks) HM.

Christen, William & Murphy, Thomas. Smart Learning: A Study Skills Guide for Teens. Strother, Deborah B. & Strother, William C., eds. Coverly, Dave, illus. LC 91-48274. 120p. (Orig.). (gr. 6 up). 1992. pap. 10.95 (*0-9628556-5-0*) Grayson Bernard Pubs.

Christensen, Bonnie. An Edible Alphabet. LC 93-7799. 1994. write for info. (*0-8037-1404-1*); lib. bdg. write for info. (*0-8037-1406-8*) Dial Bks Young.

Christensen, J. A. Young Writer. LC 74-88375. (Illus.). xii, 364p. (gr. 8-12). 1970. text ed. 16.95x (*0-87015-180-0*) Pacific Bks.

Christensen, Kathryn. Good Math Beginnings. Jones, Allan & Gorney, Janifer, eds. Gorney, Janifer & Jones, Allan, illus. (Orig.). (ps). 1987. pap. 9.95 (*0-9607458-5-8*) Arts Pubns.

Christensen, Loren. Missing Children. (Illus.). 64p. (gr. 7 up). 1990. lib. bdg. 17.27 (*0-86593-076-7*); lib. bdg. 12.95s.p. (*0-685-46440-7*) Rourke Corp.

Christensen, N. Good Night, Little Kitten. (Illus.). 28p. (ps-2). 1990. 12.33 (*0-516-05354-X*); pap. 3.95 (*0-516-45354-8*) Childrens.

Christenson, Larry. Trinity Teacher Training Workshop Booklet. 80p. (gr. 4-6). 1975. pap. 2.99 (*0-87123-552-8*) Bethany Hse.
—The Wonderful Way That Babies Are Made. LC 82-12813. 48p. (Orig.). (ps up). 1982. 10.99 (*0-87123-627-3*) Bethany Hse.

Christian, Cheryl, ed. What Happens Next? Dwight, Laura, illus. 12p. (ps). 1991. 4.95 (*1-56288-131-0*) Checkerboard.
—Where's the Baby? Dwight, Laura, illus. 12p. (ps). 1992. 4.95 (*1-56288-128-0*) Checkerboard.
—Where's the Kitten? Dwight, Laura, illus. 12p. (ps). 1992. 4.95 (*1-56288-130-2*) Checkerboard.

—Where's the Puppy? Dwight, Laura, illus. 12p. (ps). 1992. 4.95 (1-56288-129-9) Checkerboard.

Christian, Mary B. Bigfoot. LC 87-9024. (Illus.). 48p. (gr. 5-6). 1987. RSBE 12.95 (0-89686-341-7, Crestwood Hse) Macmillan Child Grp.

—But Everybody Does It: Peer Pressure. Brubaker, Lee W., illus. LC 85-17112. 72p. (Orig.). (gr. 4-7). 1986. pap. 3.99 (0-570-03636-4, 39-1098) Concordia.

—Determined Detectives. (gr. 2-4). 1988. pap. 2.50 ea. Maltese Feline, 64p (0-8167-1369-3) Merger on the Orient Expressway, 48p (0-8167-1313-8) Mysterious Case Case, 64p (0-8167-1311-1) Phantom of the Operetta, 64p (0-8167-1312-X) Troll Assocs.

—The Doggone Mystery. Fay, Ann, ed. LC 80-10448. (Illus.). (gr. 1-3). 1980. PLB 8.95 (0-8075-1656-2) A Whitman.

—Go West, Swamp Monsters. Brown, Marc, illus. LC 84-12686. 48p. (ps-3). 1985. 8.95 (0-8037-0091-1) Dial Bks Young.

—Go West, Swamp Monsters. LC 84-12686. (Illus.). 48p. (ps-3). 1987. pap. 4.95 (0-8037-0438-0) Dial Bks Young.

—Goody Sherman's Pig. Zimmer, Dirk, illus. LC 90-35181. 48p. (gr. 2-6). 1991. RSBE 12.95 (0-02-718251-7, Macmillan Child Bk) Macmillan Child Grp.

—Growin' Pains. LC 86-30246. 188p. (gr. 5-12). 1987. pap. 3.95 (0-317-63785-1, Puffin Bks.

—Hats off to John Stetson. Ohlsson, Ib, illus. LC 91-34272. 64p. (gr. 2-6). 1992. SBE 13.95 (0-02-718465-X, Macmillan Child Bk) Macmillan Child Grp.

—Linc. LC 91-3596. 128p. (gr. 7 up). 1991. SBE 13.95 (0-02-718580-X, Macmillan Child Bk) Macmillan Child Grp.

—The Mystery of the Fallen Tree. Boddy, Joe, illus. (ps-8). 1991. 8.95 (0-88335-274-5, AH56); pap. 4.95 (0-88335-288-5, AS56) Milliken Pub Co.

—The Mystery of the Message from the Sky. Boddy, Joe, illus. (ps-8). 1991. 8.95 (0-88335-298-2, AH57); pap. 4.95 (0-88335-289-3, AS57) Milliken Pub Co.

—The Mystery of the Message from the Sky. Boddy, Joe, illus. 32p. 1991. pap. 4.95 (0-685-50187-6) Milliken Pub Co.

—The Mystery of the Midnight Raider. Boddy, Joe, illus. (ps-8). 1991. 8.95 (0-88335-271-0, AH53); pap. 4.95 (0-88335-285-0, AS53) Milliken Pub Co.

—The Mystery of the Missing Red Wagon. Boddy, Joe, illus. (ps-8). 1991. 8.95 (0-88335-286-9, AH54); pap. 4.95 (0-88335-272-9, AS54) Milliken Pub Co.

—The Mystery of the Missing Scarf. Bolinske, Janet L., ed. Boddy, Joe, illus. LC 88-60630. 32p. (Orig.). (gr. 1-3). 1989. text ed. 8.95 (0-88335-596-5); pap. text ed. 4.95 (0-88335-549-3) Milliken Pub Co.

—The Mystery of the Polluted Stream. Boddy, Joe, illus. (ps-8). 1991. 8.95 (0-88335-299-0, AH58); pap. 4.95 (0-88335-290-7, AS58) Milliken Pub Co.

—The Mystery of the Unsigned Valentine. Boddy, Joe, illus. (ps-8). 1991. 8.95 (0-88335-273-7, AH55); pap. 4.95 (0-88335-287-7, AS55) Milliken Pub Co.

—The North Pole Mystery. Bolinske, Janet L., ed. Boddy, Joe, illus. LC 88-60633. 32p. (Orig.). (gr. 1-3). 1989. text ed. 8.95 (0-88335-593-0); pap. text ed. 4.95 (0-88335-597-3) Milliken Pub Co.

—Penrod Again. Dyer, Jane, illus. LC 86-21846. 56p. (gr. 1-4). 1987. RSBE 11.95 (0-02-718550-8, Macmillan Child Bk) Macmillan Child Grp.

—Penrod Again. Dyer, Jane, illus. LC 90-29. 56p. (gr. 1-4). 1990. pap. 3.95 (0-689-71432-7, Aladdin) Macmillan Child Grp.

—Penrod's Pants. Dyer, Jane, illus. LC 85-11545. 56p. (gr. 1-4). 1986. RSBE 11.95 (0-02-718520-6, Macmillan Child Bk) Macmillan Child Grp.

—Penrod's Pants. LC 89-32228. (Illus.). 56p. (gr. 1-4). 1989. pap. 3.95 (0-689-71340-1, Aladdin) Macmillan Child Grp.

—Penrod's Party. Schindler, S. D., illus. LC 89-37203. 48p. (gr. 1-4). 1990. RSBE 11.95 (0-02-718525-7, Macmillan Child Bk) Macmillan Child Grp.

—Penrod's Picture. Schindler, S. D., illus. LC 90-39808. 48p. (gr. 1-4). 1991. RSBE 11.95 (0-02-718523-0, Macmillan Child Bk) Macmillan Child Grp.

—The Pet Day Mystery. Bolinske, Janet L., ed. Boddy, Joe, illus. LC 88-60631. 32p. (Orig.). (gr. 1-3). 1989. text ed. 8.95 (0-88335-595-7); pap. text ed. 4.95 (0-88335-595-X) Milliken Pub Co.

—Sebastian & the Bone to Pick Mystery. 64p. 1986. pap. 2.25 (0-553-15385-4, Skylark) Bantam.

—Sebastian (Super Sleuth) & the Baffling Bigfoot. McCue, Lisa, illus. LC 89-13049. 64p. (gr. 2-6). 1990. SBE 10.95 (0-02-718215-0, Macmillan Child Bk) Macmillan Child Grp.

—Sebastian (Super Sleuth) & the Bone to Pick Mystery. McCue, Lisa, illus. LC 83-5406. 64p. (gr. 2-5). 1983. RSBE 11.95 (0-02-718440-4, Macmillan Child Bk) Macmillan Child Grp.

—Sebastian (Super Sleuth) & the Clumsy Cowboy. McCue, Lisa, illus. LC 84-21758. 64p. (gr. 2-5). 1985. RSBE 11.95 (0-02-718480-3, Macmillan Child Bk) Macmillan Child Grp.

—Sebastian (Super Sleuth) & the Copycat Crime. McCue, Lisa, illus. 64p. (gr. 4-7). 1993. SBE 11.95 (0-02-718211-8, Macmillan Child Bk) Macmillan Child Grp.

—Sebastian (Super Sleuth) & the Crummy Yummies Caper. McCue, Lisa, illus. LC 82-20861. 64p. (gr. 2-5). 1983. RSBE 10.95 (0-02-718430-7, Macmillan Child Bk) Macmillan Child Grp.

—Sebastian (Super Sleuth) & the Egyptian Connection. McCue, Lisa, illus. 64p. (gr. 2-5). 1988. RSBE 10.95 (0-02-718560-5, Macmillan Child Bk) Macmillan Child Grp.

—Sebastian (Super Sleuth) & the Egyptian Connection. McCue, Lisa, illus. 64p. (gr. 3-7). 1991. pap. 3.95 (0-689-71514-5, Aladdin) Macmillan Child Grp.

—Sebastian (Super Sleuth) & the Hair of the Dog Mystery. McCue, Lisa, illus. LC 82-10066. 64p. (gr. 2-5). 1982. RSBE 10.95 (0-02-718260-6, Macmillan Child Bk) Macmillan Child Grp.

—Sebastian (Super Sleuth) & the Impossible Crime. McCue, Lisa, illus. LC 91-28633. 64p. (gr. 2-6). 1992. SBE 11.95 (0-02-718435-8, Macmillan Child Bk) Macmillan Child Grp.

—Sebastian (Super Sleuth) & the Mystery Patient. McCue, Lisa, illus. LC 90-45092. 64p. (gr. 2-6). 1991. SBE 10.95 (0-02-718571-0, Macmillan Child Bk) Macmillan Child Grp.

—Sebastian (Super Sleuth) & the Purloined Sirloin. McCue, Lisa, illus. LC 85-15238. 64p. (gr. 2-5). 1986. RSBE 10.95 (0-02-718210-X, Macmillan Child Bk) Macmillan Child Grp.

—Sebastian (Super Sleuth) & the Secret of the Skewered Skier. McCue, Lisa, illus. LC 83-19569. 64p. (gr. 2-5). 1984. RSBE 10.95 (0-02-718450-1, Macmillan Child Bk) Macmillan Child Grp.

—Sebastian (Super Sleuth) & the Stars-In-His-Eyes Mystery. McCue, Lisa, illus. LC 86-21771. 64p. (gr. 2-5). 1987. RSBE 10.95 (0-02-718540-0, Macmillan Child Bk) Macmillan Child Grp.

—Sebastian (Super Sleuth) & the Time Capsule Caper. McCue, Lisa, illus. LC 88-29295. 64p. (gr. 2-6). 1989. SBE 10.95 (0-02-718570-2, Macmillan Child Bk) Macmillan Child Grp.

—Sebastian (SuperSleuth) & the Crummy Yummies Caper. 64p. (gr. up). 1985. pap. 2.25 (0-553-15293-9) Bantam.

—The Sherlock Street Detectives Package. Bolinske, Janet L., ed. Boddy, Joe, illus. (Orig.). (gr. 1-3). 1989. text ed. 32.00 (0-88335-591-4); pap. text ed. 18.00 (0-88335-592-2) Set of 4 books, 32 pp. each. Milliken Pub Co.

—Singin' Somebody Else's Song. LC 88-12000. 192p. (gr. 7 up). 1988. SBE 14.95 (0-02-718500-1, Macmillan Child Bk) Macmillan Child Grp.

—Swamp Monsters. Brown, Marc, illus. LC 82-1574. 56p. (ps-3). 1983. pap. 4.95 (0-8037-7614-4) Dial Bks Young.

—Swamp Monsters. Brown, Marc, illus. LC 93-25616. (gr. 1-4). 1994. pap. 3.25 (0-14-036841-8, Puffin) Puffin Bks.

—The UFO Mystery. Bolinske, Janet L., ed. Boddy, Joe, illus. LC 88-60632. 32p. (Orig.). (gr. 1-3). 1989. text ed. 8.95 (0-88335-594-9); pap. text ed. 4.95 (0-88335-598-1) Milliken Pub Co.

—Who'd Believe John Colter? Kubinyi, Laszlo, illus. LC 92-33822. 64p. (gr. 2-6). 1993. SBE 13.95 (0-02-718477-3, Macmillan Child Bk) Macmillan Child Grp.

Christian, Peggy. The Old Coot. LC 90-1115. (Illus.). 64p. (gr. 3-5). 1991. SBE 11.95 (0-689-31627-5, Atheneum Child Bk) Macmillan Child Grp.

Christian, Rebecca. Cooking the Spanish Way. LC 82-4709. (Illus.). 48p. (gr. 5 up). 1982. PLB 14.95 (0-8225-0908-3) Lerner Pubns.

Christian, S. Rickly. Alive: Daily Devotions for Young People. (Illus.). 1990. pap. 8.99 (0-310-71031-6, Campus Life) Zondervan.

—Alive Two. (Illus.). 1990. pap. 8.99 (0-310-71041-3, Campus Life) Zondervan.

Christiana, David. Drawer in a Drawer. 32p. (ps-3). 1990. 13.95 (0-374-31874-3) FS&G.

—Drawer in a Drawer. 32p. (ps-3). 1992. pap. 4.95 (0-374-41881-0, Sunburst) FS&G.

—White Nineteens. (Illus.). 32p. (ps-3). 1992. 15.00 (0-374-38390-1) FS&G.

Christiansen, C. B. Mara in the Morning. Stock, Catherine, illus. LC 90-25049. 32p. (gr. k-3). 1991. RSBE 13.95 (0-689-31616-X, Atheneum Child Bk) Macmillan Child Grp.

—My Mother's House, My Father's House. Trivas, Irene, illus. LC 88-16802. 32p. (gr. k-3). 1989. SBE 13.95 (0-689-31394-2, Atheneum Child Bk) Macmillan Child Grp.

—My Mother's House, My Father's House. (ps-3). 1990. pap. 3.95 (0-14-054210-8, Puffin) Puffin Bks.

—A Small Pleasure. LC 87-19313. 144p. (gr. 7 up). 1988. SBE 13.95 (0-689-31369-1, Atheneum Child Bk) Macmillan Child Grp.

—A Small Pleasure. 128p. (gr. 7 up). 1989. pap. 2.95 (0-380-70699-7, Flare) Avon.

—Sycamore Street. Sweet, Melissa, illus. LC 92-33685. 48p. (gr. 1-3). 1993. SBE 13.95 (0-689-31784-0, Atheneum Child Bk) Macmillan Child Grp.

Christiansen, Candace. Calico & Tin Horns. Locker, Thomas, illus. LC 91-3706. 32p. 1992. 16.00 (0-8037-1179-4); PLB 15.89 (0-8037-1180-8) Dial Bks Young.

—The Ice Horse. Locker, Thomas, illus. LC 92-28964. 1993. PLB write for info. Dial Bks Young.

—The Ice Horse. LC 92-28964. (Illus.). 32p. (gr. 1-5). 1993. 15.99 (0-8037-1400-9); lib. bdg. 15.89 (0-8037-1401-7) Dial Bks Young.

Christiansen, Helen E. Trinkets & Treasures: A Collection of Favorite Bits of Wisdom. 130p. (Orig.). (gr. 7 up). 1988. pap. 8.50 (0-9621419-0-9) H Christiansen.

Christie, Agatha. Best Detective Stories of Agatha Christie. 136p. (Orig.). 1986. pap. text ed. 5.95 (0-582-54087-9) Longman.

—The Clocks. 1988. 9.95 (0-553-35071-4) Bantam.

Christie, Sally & Kavanaugh, Peter. Mean & Mighty Me. LC 90-21200. (Illus.). 64p. (gr. 2-5). 1991. 10.95 (0-525-44700-8, DCB) Dutton Child Bks.

Christie, Tom. Global Alert! (Illus.). 112p. (gr. 5-8). 1992. wkbk. 12.95 (0-86653-692-2, 1426) Good Apple.

Christison, Mary Ann. English Through Poetry. Peterson, Kathleen, illus. 130p. (gr. 3-6). 1982. pap. text ed. 8.95 (0-88084-002-1) Alemany Pr.

Christison, MaryAnn & Bassano, Sharron. Purple Cows & Potato Chips. (Illus.). 120p. (gr. 5-12). 1987. pap. text ed. 19.95 (0-13-739178-1) Alemany Pr.

Christman, Catherine, jt. auth. see Christman, Ernest H.

Christman, Catherine A., jt. auth. see Christman, Ernest H.

Christman, E. Daniel. Danny's Travel Journals: Eight Stories, Level Four, Progressive Phonics. LC 90-71309. (Illus.). 56p. 1990. pap. text ed. 10.95 perfect bdg. (0-912329-13-0) Tutorial Press.

Christman, Ernest. Dr. Christman's Learn to Read Book. Christman, Catherine, illus. 256p. (Orig.). 1990. pap. 15.95 (0-933025-17-3) Blue Bird Pub.

Christman, Ernest H. Cat, Kite, Bike, Cave: Four Stories, Level One, Progressive Phonics. LC 90-71307. (Illus.). 52p. 1990. pap. text ed. 10.95 perfect bdg. (0-912329-07-6) Tutorial Press.

—Progressive Phonics, Level 1. Christman, Catherine A., illus. LC 90-71304. 84p. 1990. pap. text ed. 15.95 perfect bdg. (0-912329-06-8) Tutorial Press.

—Progressive Phonics, Level 2. LC 90-71304. (Illus.). 48p. 1990. pap. text ed. 12.95 perfect bdg. (0-912329-03-3) Tutorial Press.

—Progressive Phonics, Level 3. LC 90-71304. (Illus.). 44p. 1990. pap. text ed. 10.95 perfect bdg. (0-912329-09-2) Tutorial Press.

—Progressive Phonics, Level 4. LC 90-71304. (Illus.). 48p. 1990. pap. text ed. 10.95 perfect bdg. (0-912329-12-2) Tutorial Press.

—Progressive Phonics, Level 5. LC 90-71304. (Illus.). 40p. 1990. pap. text ed. 10.95 perfect bdg. (0-912329-15-7) Tutorial Press.

Christman, Ernest H. & Christman, Catherine A. Darby's Friends: Fourteen Stories, Level Three, Progressive Phonics. LC 90-71308. (Illus.). 60p. 1990. pap. text ed. 10.95 perfect bdg. (0-912329-10-6) Tutorial Press.

Christman, Ernest H. & Christman, Catherine. Darby's Stable: Cartoons & Stories, Level Two, Progressive Phonics. LC 84-50859. (Illus.). 88p. (Orig.). (gr. k-12). 1984. pap. text ed. 7.50 (0-912329-04-1) Tutorial Press.

Christman-Rothlein, Liz, jt. auth. see Caballero, Jane.

Christopher, Debbonnaire. The Day the Ohio Canal Turned Eerie. Christopher, Debbonnaire, illus. LC 93-6614. 1993. 3.00 (1-880443-10-4) Roscoe Village.

Christopher, Garrett. Annie & the Old One: A Study Guide. Friedland, Joyce & Kessler, Rikki, eds. (gr. 1-4). 1991. pap. text ed. 14.95 (0-88122-564-9) LRN Links.

—Caps for Sale: A Study Guide. Friedland, Joyce & Kessler, Rikki, eds. (gr. k-3). 1991. pap. text ed. 14.95 (0-88122-587-8) LRN Links.

—Corduroy: A Study Guide. Friedland, Joyce & Kessler, Rikki, eds. (gr. k-3). 1991. pap. text ed. 14.95 (0-88122-588-6) LRN Links.

—A Gathering of Days: A Study Guide. Friedland, J. & Kessler, R., eds. 24p. (gr. 4-7). 1992. pap. text ed. 14.95 (0-88122-698-X) Lrn Links.

—Gregory the Terrible Eater: A Study Guide. Friedland, Joyce & Kessler, Rikki, eds. (gr. k-3). 1991. pap. text ed. 14.95 (0-88122-589-4) LRN Links.

—Ira Sleeps Over: A Study Guide. Friedland, Joyce & Kessler, Rikki, eds. (gr. k-3). 1991. pap. text ed. 14.95 (0-88122-590-8) LRN Links.

—Leo the Late Bloomer: A Study Guide. Friedland, Joyce & Kessler, Rikki, eds. (gr. k-3). 1991. pap. text ed. 14.95 (0-88122-591-6) LRN Links.

—The Little Island: A Study Guide. Friedland, Joyce & Kessler, Rikki, eds. (gr. k-3). 1991. pap. text ed. 14.95 (0-88122-592-4) LRN Links.

—Make Way for Ducklings: A Study Guide. Friedland, Joyce & Kessler, Rikki, eds. (gr. k-3). 1991. pap. text ed. 14.95 (0-88122-593-2) LRN Links.

—The Story of Ferdinand: A Study Guide. Friedland, Joyce & Kessler, Rikki, eds. (gr. k-3). 1991. pap. text ed. 14.95 (0-88122-594-0) LRN Links.

—Sylvester & the Magic Pebble: A Study Guide. Friedland, Joyce & Kessler, Rikki, eds. (gr. k-3). 1991. pap. text ed. 14.95 (0-88122-595-9) LRN Links.

—Tales of a Fourth-Grade Nothing: A Study Guide. Friedland, Joyce & Kessler, Rikki, eds. (gr. 2-5). 1991. pap. text ed. 14.95 (0-88122-575-4) LRN Links.

—Whistle for Willie: A Study Guide. Friedland, Joyce & Kessler, Rikki, eds. (gr. k-3). 1991. pap. text ed. 14.95 (0-88122-596-7) LRN Links.

Christopher, John. Beyond the Burning Lands. (gr. 5-9). 1991. 16.50 (0-8446-6447-2) Peter Smith.

—Beyond the Burning Lands: The Sword of the Spirits Trilogy. LC 78-152288. 180p. (gr. 5-9). 1989. pap. 3.95 (0-02-042572-4, Collier Young Ad) Macmillan Child Grp.

—City of Gold & Lead. LC 67-21245. 224p. (gr. 5-9). 1970. SBE 14.95 (0-02-718380-7, Macmillan Child Bk); (Collier Young Ad) Macmillan Child Grp.

—The City of Gold & Lead. 2nd ed. LC 88-16118. (Illus.). 224p. (gr. 7 up). 1988. pap. 3.95 (*0-02-042701-8*, Collier Young Ad) Macmillan Child Grp.
—The City of Gold & Lead. large type ed. 280p. (gr. 1-8). 1990. 13.95 (*0-7451-1100-9*, Galaxy Child Lrg Print) Chivers N Amer.
—Dragon Dance. LC 85-31149. 160p. (gr. 5-9). 1986. 12.95 (*0-525-44227-8*, DCB) Dutton Child Bks.
—A Dusk of Demons. LC 92-31730. 176p. (gr. 5-9). 1994. SBE 14.95 (*0-02-718425-0*, Macmillan Child Bk) Macmillan Child Grp.
—The Guardians. 2nd ed. LC 91-44197. 224p. (gr. 7 up). 1992. pap. 4.95 (*0-02-042681-X*, Collier Young Ad) Macmillan Child Grp.
—The Lotus Caves. LC 74-78074. 160p. (gr. 5-9). 1971. pap. 4.95 (*0-02-042690-9*, Collier Young Ad) Macmillan Child Grp.
—The Lotus Caves. 2nd ed. LC 91-27715. 224p. (gr. 7 up). 1992. pap. 4.95 (*0-02-042691-7*, Collier Young Ad) Macmillan Child Grp.
—Pool of Fire. LC 68-23062. 192p. (gr. 5-9). 1968. SBE 13.95 (*0-02-718350-5*, Macmillan Child Bk); pap. 3.95 (*0-02-042720-4*, Collier Young Ad) Macmillan Child Grp.
—The Pool of Fire. 2nd ed. LC 88-16117. 224p. (gr. 7 up). 1988. pap. 3.95 (*0-02-042721-2*, Collier Young Ad) Macmillan Child Grp.
—The Pool of Fire. large type ed. 280p. (gr. 3 up). 1990. 18.95 (*0-7451-1176-9*) G K Hall.
—The Prince in Waiting. (gr. 5-9). 1984. 16.75 (*0-8446-6157-0*) Peter Smith.
—The Prince in Waiting. (Illus.). 224p. (gr. 7 up). 1989. pap. 3.95 (*0-02-042573-2*, Collier Young Ad) Macmillan Child Grp.
—The Sword of the Spirit. (gr. 6-12). 1984. 16.50 (*0-8446-6158-9*) Peter Smith.
—The Sword of the Spirits. 224p. (gr. 7 up). 1989. pap. 3.95 (*0-02-042574-0*, Collier Young Ad) Macmillan Child Grp.
—The Tripods Trilogy. 2nd ed. 224p. (gr. 7 up). 1988. Boxed Set. pap. 11.95 (*0-02-042571-6*, Collier Young Ad) Macmillan Child Grp.
—When the Tripods Came. LC 90-1436. 160p. (gr. 7 up). 1990. pap. 3.95 (*0-02-042575-9*, Collier Young Ad) Macmillan Child Grp.
—The White Mountains. LC 67-10362. 192p. (gr. 5-9). 1967. SBE 14.95 (*0-02-718360-2*, Macmillan Child Bk); pap. 3.95 (*0-02-042710-7*, Collier Young Ad) Macmillan Child Grp.
—The White Mountains. 2nd ed. LC 88-16119. 224p. (gr. 7 up). 1988. pap. 3.95 (*0-02-042711-5*, Collier Young Ad) Macmillan Child Grp.
—The White Mountains. large type ed. 256p. (gr. 3 up). 1990. 16.95 (*0-7451-1043-6*) G K Hall.
—Wild Jack. 2nd ed. 160p. (gr. 7 up). 1991. pap. 3.95 (*0-02-042576-7*, Collier Young Ad) Macmillan Child Grp.

Christopher, Marlowe de see De Christopher, Marlowe.
Christopher, Matt. Baseball Pals. Henneberger, Robert, illus. (gr. 4-6). 1990. pap. 3.95 (*0-316-14005-8*) Little.
—The Basket Counts. Swearingen, Karen M., illus. (gr. 3-6). 1991. pap. 3.95 (*0-316-14076-7*) Little.
—Beloved St. Anne. LC 92-56932. (Illus.). 69p. (gr. 6-11). 1993. pap. 6.95 (*1-55523-569-7*) Winston-Derek.
—Catch That Pass, Vol. 1. Kidder, Harvey, illus. LC 77-77442. (gr. 4-6). 1989. lib. bdg. 14.95 (*0-316-13932-7*); pap. 3.95 (*0-316-13924-6*) Little.
—Catcher with a Glass Arm. Caddell, Foster, illus. (gr. 4-6). 1985. pap. 3.95 (*0-316-13985-8*) Little.
—Centerfield Ballhawk. Beier, Ellen, illus. 64p. (gr. 2-4). 1992. 11.95 (*0-316-14079-1*) Little.
—Challenge at Second Base. Ramsey, Marcy, illus. 144p. (gr. 3-6). 1992. pap. 3.95 (*0-316-14249-2*) Little.
—The Counterfeit Tackle. (gr. 4-7). 1990. pap. 3.95 (*0-316-14243-3*) Little.
—Diamond Champs. (gr. 4-7). 1990. pap. 3.95 (*0-316-14006-6*) Little.
—Dirt Bike Racer. Bomzer, Barry, illus. LC 79-745. (gr. 4-6). 1986. 14.95 (*0-316-13977-7*); pap. 3.95 (*0-316-14053-8*) Little.
—Dirt Bike Runaway. Stewart, Edgar, illus. LC 83-13538. 160p. (gr. 4-6). 1986. pap. 3.95 (*0-316-14002-3*) Little.
—The Dog That Called the Signals. Ogden, Bill, illus. LC 82-15234. 48p. (gr. 3-5). 1982. 12.95 (*0-316-13980-7*) Little.
—The Dog That Pitched a No-Hitter. Vasconcellos, Daniel, illus. (gr. 1-3). 1988. 11.95 (*0-316-14057-0*) Little.
—Dog That Pitched a No-Hitter. (ps-3). 1993. pap. 3.95 (*0-316-14103-8*) Little.
—The Dog That Stole Football Plays. Ogden, Bill, illus. 48p. (gr. 3-5). 1980. 13.95 (*0-316-13978-5*) Little.
—The Dog That Stole Home. Vasconcellos, Daniel, illus. LC 92-15613. 1993. 12.95 (*0-316-14082-1*) Little.
—Face Off, Vol. 1. 144p. 1989. pap. 3.95 (*0-316-13994-7*) Little.
—Fielder's Dream. (Illus.). 13p. (gr. 3-6). 1991. incls. puzzle 12.50 (*0-922242-19-4*) Lombard Mktg.
—Football Fugitive. Johnson, Larry, illus. 128p. (gr. 4-6). 1988. 14.95 (*0-316-13971-8*); pap. 3.95 (*0-316-14064-3*) Little.
—The Fox Steals Home. Johnson, Lary, illus. LC 78-17526. (gr. 4-6). 1985. 14.95 (*0-316-13976-9*); pap. 3.95 (*0-316-13986-6*) Little.
—The Great Quarterback Switch. Jones, Eric, illus. LC 83-25628. (gr. 4-6). 1984. 14.95 (*0-316-13903-3*) Little.

—The Great Quarterback Switch. Nones, Eric J., illus. (gr. 3-6). 1991. pap. 3.95 (*0-316-14077-5*) Little.
—Hard Drive to Short. (gr. 4-7). 1991. pap. 3.95 (*0-316-14071-6*) Little.
—The Hit-Away Kid. (gr. 2-4). 1988. 12.95 (*0-316-13995-5*) Little.
—The Hit-Away Kid. (gr. 2-4). 1990. pap. 3.95 (*0-316-14007-4*) Little.
—The Hockey Machine. Schroeppel, Richard, illus. (gr. 4 up). 1986. 14.95 (*0-316-14055-4*) Little.
—Hockey Machine. (gr. 4-7). 1992. pap. 3.95 (*0-316-14087-2*) Little.
—Ice Magic. Goto, Byron, illus. (gr. 4-6). 1987. PLB 14.95 (*0-316-13958-0*); pap. 3.95 (*0-316-13991-2*) Little.
—Johnny Long Legs. Kidder, Harvey, illus. 144p. (gr. 3-6). 1988. pap. 3.95 (*0-316-14065-1*) Little.
—The Kid Who Only Hit Homers. Kidder, Harvey, illus. (gr. 4-6). 1972. lib. bdg. 14.95 (*0-316-13918-1*) Little.
—The Kid Who Only Hit Homers. Kidder, Harvey, illus. 160p. (gr. 4 up). 1986. pap. 3.95 (*0-316-13987-4*) Little.
—Lefty's Lost Pitch. (Illus.). 13p. (gr. 3-6). 1991. incls. puzzle 12.95 (*0-922242-18-6*) Lombard Mktg.
—Legend under the Boards: Back Court Mysteries. (Illus.). (gr. 2-7). 1992. incl. puzzle 12.95 (*0-922242-39-9*) Lombard Mktg.
—Little Lefty. Ramsey, Marcy, illus. (gr. 4-7). 1993. pap. 3.95 (*0-316-14100-3*) Little.
—Long Shot For Paul. (gr. 3-7). 1990. pap. 3.95 (*0-316-14244-1*) Little.
—Long Stretch at First Base. (gr. 4-7). 1993. pap. 3.95 (*0-316-14101-1*) Little.
—Look Who's Playing First Base. Kidder, Harvey, illus. (gr. 4-6). 1987. pap. 3.95 (*0-316-13989-0*) Little.
—Lucky Baseball Bat. (ps-3). 1991. pap. 11.95 (*0-316-14073-2*) Little.
—Lucky Baseball Bat. (ps-3). 1993. pap. 3.95 (*0-316-14260-3*) Little.
—Man Out At First. LC 92-31130. 1993. 12.95 (*0-316-14084-8*) Little.
—Matt Christopher Baseball. (gr. 4-7). 1991. Boxed set 2. pap. 11.85 (*0-316-14075-9*) Little.
—Matt Christopher Hockey Boxed Set: Face-Off, Ice Magic, & the Hockey Machine. (gr. 4-7). 1993. 11.85 (*0-316-14271-9*) Little.
—Miracle at the Plate. Caddell, Foster, illus. 144p. (gr. 3-6). 1989. pap. 3.95 (*0-316-13926-2*) Little.
—No Arm in Left Field. Goto, Byron, illus. (gr. 4-6). 1987. lib. bdg. 14.95 (*0-316-13964-5*); pap. 3.95 (*0-316-13990-4*) Little.
—Pressure Play. LC 92-37276. 1993. 14.95 (*0-316-14098-8*) Little.
—Red-Hot Hightops. Mock, Paul D., illus. 128p. (gr. 4-6). 1987. 14.95 (*0-316-14056-2*) Little.
—Red-Hot Hightops. (gr. 4-7). 1992. pap. 3.95 (*0-316-14089-9*) Little.
—Return of the Home Run Kid. Casale, Paul, illus. 168p. (gr. 3-7). 1992. 14.95 (*0-316-14080-5*) Little.
—Run, Billy, Run. (gr. 3-6). 1988. pap. 3.95 (*0-316-13993-9*) Little.
—Shortstop from Tokyo. Kidder, Harvey, illus. (gr. 3-6). 1988. pap. 3.95 (*0-316-13992-0*) Little.
—Skateboard Tough. (gr. 4-7). 1991. 14.95 (*0-316-14247-6*) Little.
—Soccer Halfback. Johnson, Karla, illus. (gr. 4-6). 1985. 14.95 (*0-316-13946-7*); pap. 3.95 (*0-316-13981-5*) Little.
—The Spy on Third Base. Ulrich, George, illus. LC 88-8914. (gr. 2-4). 1988. 12.95 (*0-316-13996-3*) Little.
—Spy on Third Base, Vol. 1. (ps-3). 1990. pap. 3.95 (*0-316-14008-2*) Little.
—The Submarine Pitch. Ramsey, Marcy, illus. 144p. (gr. 3-6). 1992. pap. 3.95 (*0-316-14250-6*) Little.
—Tackle Without a Team. Sanfilippo, Margaret, illus. LC 88-22644. 128p. (gr. 3-7). 1989. 14.95 (*0-316-14067-8*) Little.
—Tackle Without a Team. (gr. 4-7). 1993. pap. 3.95 (*0-316-14268-9*) Little.
—Takedown. Sanfilippo, Margaret, illus. (gr. 3-7). 1990. 14.95 (*0-316-13930-0*) Little.
—Tight End. 128p. (gr. 3 up) 1981. 14.95 (*0-316-14017-1*) Little.
—Tight End. (gr. 4-6). 1986. write for info.; pap. 3.95 (*0-316-14074-0*) Little.
—Too Hot to Handle. (gr. 4-7). 1991. pap. 3.95 (*0-316-14099-6*) Little.
—Top Wing. (Illus.). (gr. 8-12). 1994. 14.95 (*0-316-14099-6*) Little.
—Touchdown for Tommy. Caddell, Foster, illus. 145p. (gr. 4-6). 1985. pap. 3.95 (*0-316-13982-3*) Little.
—Tough to Tackle. Kidder, Harvey, illus. 152p. (gr. 4-6). 1987. pap. 3.95 (*0-316-14058-9*) Little.
—Undercover Tailback. LC 92-19770. (Illus.). 1992. 14.95 (*0-316-14251-4*) Little.
—Wingman on Ice. (gr. 4-7). 1993. pap. 3.95 (*0-316-14269-7*) Little.
—The Year Mom Won the Pennant. Caddell, Foster, illus. 160p. (gr. 4 up). 1986. pap. 3.95 (*0-316-13988-2*) Little.

Christopher, Tracy. Joan of Arc: Soldier Saint. (Illus.). 80p. (gr. 3-5). 1993. PLB 13.95 (*0-7910-1767-2*, Am Art Analog) Chelsea Hse.
Christophersen, Susan & Farr, J. Michael. Career Preparation: Getting the Most from Training & Education. Croy, Greg, ed. Kreffel, Mike, illus. 64p. (gr. 9-12). 1990. pap. 6.95 (*0-942784-59-6*, CP) JIST Works.

—Knowing Yourself: Learning about Your Skills, Values & Planning Your Life. Croy, Greg, ed. Kreffel, Mike, illus. 64p. (gr. 9-12). 1990. pap. 6.95 (*0-942784-58-8*, KM) JIST Works.
—Your Career: Thinking about Jobs & Careers. Croy, Greg, ed. Kreffel, Mike, illus. 64p. (gr. 9-12). 1990. pap. 6.95 (*0-942784-60-X*, MC) JIST Works.
Christophersen, Susan, jt. auth. see Farr, J. Michael.
Chromey, Rick. Christians in a Non-Christian World. (Illus.). 48p. (gr. 9-12). 1992. pap. 7.99 (*1-55945-224-2*) Group Pub.
—Money: A Christian Perspective. (Illus.). 48p. (gr. 9-12). 1991. pap. 7.99 (*1-55945-212-9*) Group Pub.
—Revelation. (Illus.). 48p. (gr. 9-12). 1992. pap. 7.99 (*1-55945-229-3*) Group Pub.
—Turning Depression Upside Down. (Illus.). 48p. (gr. 9-12). 1992. pap. 7.99 (*1-55945-135-1*) Group Pub.
Chronicle Books, tr. see Gomi, Taro.
Chu, Daniel & Skinner, Eliott. A Glorious Age in Africa: The Story of Three Great African Empires. Barnett, Moneta, illus. LC 90-80150. 124p. (gr. 6-12). 1990. 19.95 (*0-86543-166-3*); pap. 7.95 (*0-86543-167-1*) Africa World.
Chua-Eoan, Howard. Corazon Aquino. (Illus.). 112p. (gr. 5 up). 1988. 17.95x (*1-55546-825-X*) Chelsea Hse.
Chuchill, E. Richard. Sneaky Tricks to Fool Your Friends. Behr, Joyce, illus. LC 86-14448. 128p. (gr. 6-12). 1987. pap. 3.95 (*0-8069-4808-6*) Sterling.
Chudnovsky, Elynne, illus. Bare, Beautiful Feet & Other Missionary Stories. (gr. 1-5). 1992. 3.99 (*0-87509-485-6*) Chr Pubns.
—The Potato Story & Other Missionary Stories. (gr. 1-5). 1992. 3.99 (*0-87509-484-8*) Chr Pubns.
Chukovsky, Kornei. From Two to Five. Morton, Miriam, ed. & tr. LC 63-19028. (gr. 7 up). 1963. pap. 12.00x (*0-520-00238-5*) U CA Pr.
Chung, Okwha & Monroe, Judy. Cooking the Korean Way. (Illus.). 48p. (gr. 5 up). 1988. PLB 14.95 (*0-8225-0921-0*) Lerner Pubns.
Chupick, Carol O. Celebrate Autumn. Grossman, Dan, illus. 144p. (gr. k-3). 1985. wkbk. 11.95 (*0-86653-264-1*, SS 838, Shining Star Pubns) Good Apple.
Church, Alfred J. Lucius, Adventures of a Roman Boy. LC 60-16706. (gr. 7-11). 1969. 20.00 (*0-8196-0108-X*) Biblo.
—Roman Life in the Days of Cicero. LC 61-24994. (gr. 7-11). 1968. 22.00 (*0-8196-0105-5*) Biblo.
Church, Ellen C. Learning Things: Games That Make Learning Fun for Children 3-8 Years Old. LC 81-82033. (ps-3). 1982. pap. 14.95 (*0-8224-4268-X*) Fearon Teach Aids.
Church, Elmer T. Walk with Me in White. LC 86-81184. 154p. 1986. perfect bdg. 5.98 (*0-318-21723-6*) E T Church.
Church, Francis P. Yes, Virginia, There Is a Santa Claus. Allison, Christine, intro. by. LC 92-12268. 1992. 10.00 (*0-385-30854-X*) Delacorte.
Church, J. R. Guardians of the Grail: And the Men Who Plan to Rule the World. Griffin, Ralph G. & Stearman, G. G., eds. LC 89-91688. (Illus.). 318p. (Orig.). (gr. 12). 1989. pap. 9.95 (*0-941241-02-5*) Prophecy Pubns.
Church, Jeff. Dick Whittington & His Cat: A Musical Play Based on an English Folk Tale. (Illus.). 56p. (Orig.). (ps-7). 1990. pap. 3.75 (*0-88680-340-3*); piano/vocal score 10.00 (*0-88680-341-1*); royalty on application 50.00 (*0-685-58895-5*) I E Clark.
—The Pied Piper of New Orleans. (Orig.). 1993. pap. 4.50 playscript (*0-87602-324-3*) Anchorage.
Church, Jok. You Can with Beakman: Science Stuff You Can Do. LC 92-24979. (Illus.). 156p. (Orig.). 1992. pap. 8.95 (*0-8362-7004-5*) Andrews & McMeel.
Church, Jok, created by. Beakman's World: Behind the Scenes of the Hit TV Show. (Illus.). 96p. 1993. pap. 8.95 (*0-8362-7005-3*) Andrews & McMeel.
Church, Kristine. My Brother John. Niland, Kilmeny, illus. LC 90-25868. 32p. (ps-3). 1991. 12.95 (*0-688-10800-8*, Tambourine Bks); PLB 12.88 (*0-688-10801-6*, Tambourine Bks) Morrow.
Church, Vivian. Colors Around Me. LC 75-154209. (Illus.). 28p. (gr. k-3). 1971. 4.95 (*0-910030-15-4*) Afro Am.
Churchill, E. Richard. Amazing Science Experiments with Everyday Materials. Zweifel, Frances, illus. LC 90-20641. 128p. (gr. 4-12). 1992. 12.95 (*0-8069-7372-2*); pap. 4.95 (*0-8069-7371-4*) Sterling.
—Building with Paper. LC 89-26220. (Illus.). 128p. 1990. 14.95 (*0-8069-5772-7*) Sterling.
—Fabulous Paper Airplanes. Michaels, James, illus. LC 91-10490. 128p. (gr. 5 up). 1992. pap. 7.95 (*0-8069-8343-4*) Sterling.
—Fantastic Flying Paper Toys. LC 90-39007. (Illus.). 96p. (Orig.). (gr. 4-10). 1990. pap. 3.95 (*0-8069-7460-5*) Sterling.
—Fast & Funny Paper Toys You Can Make. LC 89-32411. (Illus.). 128p. (gr. 7-12). 1989. 14.95 (*0-8069-5770-0*) Sterling.
—Fast & Funny Paper Toys You Can Make. Michaels, James, illus. LC 89-32411. 128p. (gr. 4-10). 1991. pap. 7.95 (*0-8069-5771-9*) Sterling.
—Geography Flipper. 49p. (gr. 5 up). 1989. Repr. of 1987 ed. trade edition 5.95 (*1-878383-07-8*) C Lee Pubns.
—Holiday Paper Projects. Michaels, James, illus. LC 92-12100. 128p. (gr. 3-9). 1992. 14.95 (*0-8069-8512-7*) Sterling.
—Holiday Paper Projects. Michaels, James, illus. 128p. (gr. 6 up). 1993. pap. 7.95 (*0-8069-8513-5*) Sterling.

—How to Make Optical Illusion Tricks & Toys. LC 89-26169. (Illus.). 128p. (Orig.). 1990. pap. 4.95 (*0-8069-6869-9*) Sterling.
—Instant Paper Airplanes. Michaels, James, illus. LC 88-12325. 128p. (gr. 3 up). 1988. 14.95 (*0-8069-6796-X*) Sterling.
—Instant Paper Airplanes. LC 88-12325. (Illus.). 128p. 1990. pap. 7.95 (*0-8069-6797-8*) Sterling.
—Instant Paper Toys to Pop, Spin, Whirl & Fly. Kendrick, Dennis, illus. LC 85-26229. 112p. (gr. 1-8). 1987. pap. 7.95 (*0-8069-6278-X*) Sterling.
—Paper Action Toys. Michaels, James, illus. LC 93-23860. 128p. (gr. 6 up). 1993. 14.95 (*0-8069-0368-6*) Sterling.
—Paper Science Toys. LC 90-9891. (Illus.). 128p. (gr. 3-10). 1990. 14.95 (*0-8069-5834-0*) Sterling.
—Paper Science Toys. Michaels, James, illus. LC 90-9891. 128p. (gr. 4-11). 1991. pap. 7.95 (*0-8069-5835-9*) Sterling.
—Paper Toys That Fly, Soar, Zoom & Whistle. Michaels, James, illus. LC 88-30311. 192p. (gr. 10-12). 1989. 14.95 (*0-8069-6840-0*) Sterling.
—Paper Tricks & Toys. LC 91-38789. 128p. 1992. 14.95 (*0-8069-8416-3*) Sterling.
—Paper Tricks & Toys. Michaels, James, illus. 128p. (gr. 2-8). 1993. pap. 7.95 (*0-8069-8417-1*) Sterling.
—Terrific Paper Toys. LC 90-24115. (Illus.). 128p. (gr. 3-9). 1991. 14.95 (*0-8069-7496-6*) Sterling.
—Terrific Paper Toys. LC 90-24115. (Illus.). 128p. (gr. 7-12). 1992. pap. 7.95 (*0-8069-7497-4*) Sterling.
Churchill, Eric R. Algebra Flipper. 49p. (gr. 5 up). 1989. Repr. of 1987 ed. trade edition 5.95 (*1-878383-03-5*) C Lee Pubns.
—BASIC Programming Flipper. 49p. (gr. 5 up). 1989. trade edition 5.95 (*1-878383-10-8*) C Lee Pubns.
—Geometry Flipper. 49p. (gr. 5 up). 1989. Repr. of 1988 ed. trade edition 5.95 (*1-878383-04-3*) C Lee Pubns.
Churchman, C. West. The Systems Approach. rev. & updated ed. (gr. 7-12). 1983. pap. 3.95 (*0-440-38407-9*, LE) Dell.
Churchwell, Kay. Baby Jesus. LC 85-24335. (Illus.). (ps). 1986. 4.99 (*0-8054-4170-0*) Broadman.
Chusid, Nancy. Favorite Folk Songs. Chusid, Nancy, illus. 32p. (Orig.). (gr. 2-6). 1990. pap. 6.95 incl. cassette (*1-878624-07-5*) McClanahan Bk.
—Favorite Lullabies. Chusid, Nancy, illus. 32p. (Orig.). (gr. 2-6). 1990. pap. 6.95 incl. cassette (*1-878624-06-7*) McClanahan Bk.
—Favorite Nursery Songs. Chusid, Nancy, illus. 32p. (Orig.). (gr. 2-6). 1990. pap. 6.95 incl. cassette (*1-878624-05-9*) McClanahan Bk.
Chuska, Kenneth R. Teaching the Process of Thinking, k-12. LC 86-61753. 50p. (gr. k-12). 1986. pap. 1.25 (*0-87367-244-5*) Phi Delta Kappa.
Chutkow, Paul. Gerard Depardieu: A Biography. LC 93-26514. 1994. 24.00 (*0-679-40943-2*) Knopf Bks Yng Read.
Chwast, E., ed. see Drucker, M.
Chwast, Seymour. Alphabet Parade. 30p. (ps-2). 1991. 13.95 (*0-15-200351-7*, HB Juv Bks) HarBrace.
—Paper Pets: Make Your Own Three Dogs, 2 Cats, 1 Parrot, 1 Rabbit, 1 Monkey. LC 92-23609. (Illus.). 24p. 1993. pap. 19.95 (*0-8109-2531-1*) Abrams.
—The Twelve Circus Rings. LC 92-13576. 1993. write for info. (*0-15-200627-3*) HarBrace.
Chwast, Seymour, illus. Bushy Bride: Norwegian Fairy Tale. LC 83-71174. 32p. (gr. 6 up). 1983. PLB 13.95p. (*0-87191-952-4*) Creative Ed.
Ciaravino, John. A Christmas Dream. LC 88-51890. (Illus.). 44p. (gr. k-3). 1989. 5.95 (*1-55523-215-9*) Winston-Derek.
Ciardi, John. Doodle Soup. Nacht, Merle, illus. LC 85-814. 64p. (gr. 2-5). 1985. 13.45 (*0-395-38395-1*) HM.
—Doodle Soup. (gr. 4-7). 1992. pap. 3.80 (*0-395-61617-4*) HM.
—Fast & Slow: Poems for Advanced Children of Beginning Parents. Gaver, Becky, intro. by. LC 74-22405. (Illus.). 68p. (gr. k-3). 1975. 14.95 (*0-395-20282-5*) HM.
—The Hopeful Trout & Other Limericks. LC 87-23587. 1989. 13.45 (*0-395-43606-0*) HM.
—Hopeful Trout & Other Limericks. (gr. 4-7). 1992. pap. 3.80 (*0-395-61616-6*) HM.
—I Met a Man. Osborne, Robert. (Illus.). 80p. (gr. k-3). 1973. pap. 6.95 (*0-395-17447-3*, Sandpiper) HM.
—The Monster Den: or Look What Happened at My House - & to It. Gorey, Edward, illus. LC 90-85904. 64p. (gr. k up). 1991. Repr. 13.95 (*1-878093-35-5*, Wordsong) Boyds Mills Pr.
—Someone Could Win a Polar Bear. 64p. (ps-3). 1993. 13.95 (*1-56397-205-0*) Boyds Mills Pr.
—You Know Who. Gorey, Edward, illus. LC 90-85903. 48p. (gr. k up). 1991. Repr. 13.95 (*1-878093-34-7*, Wordsong) Boyds Mills Pr.
—You Read to Me, I'll Read to You. Gorey, Edward, illus. LC 62-16296. 64p. (gr. k-6). 1961. (Lipp Jr Bks) PLB 12.89 (*0-397-30646-6*) HarpC Child Bks.
—You Read to Me, I'll Read to You. Gorey, Edward, illus. LC 62-16296. 64p. (gr. k-4). 1987. pap. 5.95 (*0-06-446060-6*, Trophy) HarpC Child Bks.
Ciconte, Marie, ed. see Shles, Larry.
Ciliotta, Claire & Livingston, Carole. Why Am I Going to the Hospital? Wilson, Dick, illus. (gr. k-7). 1992. pap. 8.95 (*0-8184-0568-6*, L Stuart) Carol Pub Group.
Ciliotta, Claire, jt. auth. see Livingston, Carole.
Cincerelli, Carol J. Opening Five: Art for Grade Five. LC 79-3013. 192p. (gr. 5). 1980. pap. text ed. 10.25 (*0-934902-10-0*) Learn Concepts OH.
—Opening One: Art for Grade One. LC 79-3013. 174p. (gr. 1). 1979. pap. text ed. 9.75 (*0-934902-07-0*) Learn Concepts OH.
—Opening Six: Art for Grade Six. LC 79-3013. 192p. (gr. 6). 1980. pap. text ed. 10.25 (*0-934902-11-9*) Learn Concepts OH.
—Opening Three: Art for Grade Three. LC 79-3013. 195p. (gr. 3). 1980. pap. text ed. 9.75 (*0-934902-09-7*) Learn Concepts OH.
—Opening-Two: Art for Grade Two. LC 79-3013. (gr. 2). 1979. pap. text ed. 9.75 (*0-934902-06-2*) Learn Concepts OH.
—Opening VII: Art for Grade Seven. LC 79-3013. (gr. 7). 1980. pap. text ed. 10.25 (*0-934902-12-7*) Learn Concepts OH.
—Opening VIII: Art for Grade Eight. LC 79-3013. (gr. 8). 1979. pap. text ed. 10.25 (*0-934902-13-5*) Learn Concepts OH.
—A Russian Folktale - My Mother Is the Most Beautiful Woman in the World. 96p. (gr. 1-6). 1990. 10.95 (*0-86653-539-X*, GA1162) Good Apple.
—The Selfish Giant by Oscar Wilde. 96p. (gr. 1-6). 1990. 10.95 (*0-86653-537-3*, GA1158) Good Apple.
—The Tales of Hans Christian Andersen. 144p. (gr. 1-6). 1990. 11.95 (*0-86653-544-6*, GA1159) Good Apple.
—The Tales of the Brothers Grimm. 144p. (gr. 1-6). 1990. 11.95 (*0-86653-562-4*, GA1160) Good Apple.
Cipkowski, Peter. Understanding the Crisis in the Persian Gulf. 192p. 1992. text ed. 24.95 (*0-471-54815-4*); pap. text ed. 12.95 (*0-471-54816-2*) Wiley.
Cirker, Hayward & Steadman, Barbara. French Picture Word Book: Learn over Five Hundred Commonly Used French Words Through Pictures. (FRE & ENG., Illus.). 32p. (Orig.). 1993. pap. text ed. 2.95t (*0-486-27777-1*) Dover.
—German Picture Word Book: Learn over Five Hundred Commonly Used German Words Through Pictures. (GER & ENG., Illus.). 32p. (Orig.). 1993. pap. text ed. 2.95t (*0-486-27778-X*) Dover.
—Spanish Picture Word Book: Learn over Five Hundred Commonly Used Spanish Words Through Pictures. (SPA & ENG., Illus.). 32p. (Orig.). 1993. pap. text ed. 2.95t (*0-486-27779-8*) Dover.
Cirou, Alain. Incredibly Far. (Illus.). 48p. (gr. 6 up). 1993. RSBE 14.95 (*0-02-718650-4*, New Discovery) Macmillan Child Grp.
—Incredibly Far. LC 93-20078. (Illus.). 48p. (gr. 6 up). 1993. RSBE 14.95 (*0-02-781650-8*, New Discovery Bks) Macmillan Child Grp.
Cissom, Joan. The Enchanted Unicorn. Transue, David, illus. 20p. (Orig.). 1989. pap. 3.95 (*0-929560-01-9*) Southern Rose Prodns.
Citrin, Paul J. Joseph's Wardrobe. (Illus.). (gr. 4-6). 1987. pap. 6.95 (*0-8074-0319-9*, 123924) UAHC.
Citron, Howard. Families Make a Difference. 12p. (gr. 3-6). 1993. pap. text ed. 1.30 (*0-9639216-0-6*) Educ Research.
Ciuffreda, Lillian, ed. see Erben, Karel J.
Ciupik, Larry. The Universe. rev. ed. LC 87-20805. (Illus.). 48p. (gr. 2-6). 1987. PLB 18.64 (*0-8172-3264-8*); pap. 4.49 (*0-8114-8221-9*) Raintree Steck-V.
Civardi. Clues & Suspects. (gr. 2-5). 1979. (Usborne-Hayes); PLB (*0-88110-039-0*); pap. 4.50 (*0-86020-227-5*) EDC.
Civardi & Kilpatrick. How Animals Live. (gr. k-6). 1981. (Usborne-Hayes); PLB 13.96 (*0-88110-081-1*); pap. 6.95 (*0-86020-196-1*) EDC.
Civardi, A., et al. Detective's Handbook (B - U) (Illus.). 192p. (gr. 2-6). 1992. pap. 8.95 (*0-86020-278-X*) EDC.
Civardi, Anne. Around the World with the Word Friends. (ps-6). 1989. 4.99 (*0-517-69407-7*) Outlet Bk Co.
—The Big Match. (Illus.). 24p. (ps-2). 1987. 3.95 (*0-7460-0160-6*) EDC.
—The Builder. (Illus.). 24p. (ps-2). 1987. 3.95 (*0-7460-0053-7*) EDC.
—The Farmer. (Illus.). 24p. (gr. 1-3). 1987. 3.95 (*0-7460-0052-9*) EDC.
—The Great Race. (Illus.). 24p. 1988. 3.95 (*0-7460-0163-0*) EDC.
—Moving House. (ps-3). 1993. pap. 3.95 (*0-7460-1281-0*, Usborne) EDC.
—Potty Time. Langley, Jonathan, illus. 24p. (ps). 1988. 6.95 (*0-671-65896-4*, Little Simon) S&S Trade.
—Potty Time. Langley, Jonathan, illus. LC 87-21910. 24p. (ps). 1993. pap. 3.95 (*0-671-79618-6*, S&S BYR) S&S Trade.
—Things People Do. Cartwright, Stephen, illus. 38p. (ps-4). 1986. 10.95 (*0-86020-864-8*, Pub. by Usborne); PLB 12.96 (*0-88110-236-9*) EDC.
—Wacky Book of Witches. (ps-3). 1992. 14.95 (*0-590-45094-8*) Scholastic Inc.
—Word Finder in German. Cartwright, Stephen, illus. 48p. (gr. k-3). 1984. 11.95 (*0-86020-771-4*) EDC.
—Word Finders in English. 48p. (gr. k-3). 1984. 11.95 (*0-86020-767-6*) EDC.
Civardi, Anne & Cartwright, Stephen. Going to a Party. 16p. (ps up). 1987. pap. 3.95 (*0-7460-0072-3*) EDC.
—Going to the Dentist. 16p. (ps up). 1987. pap. 3.95 (*0-7460-1515-1*) EDC.
—Going to the Hospital. 16p. (ps up). 1987. pap. 3.95 (*0-7460-1511-9*) EDC.
Civardi, Anne & Rashbrook, F. Fishing. (Illus.). 32p. (gr. 3-6). 1977. pap. 5.95 (*0-86020-032-9*) EDC.
Civardi, Anne, jt. auth. see Amery, H.
Civardi, Annie. The Secrets of Santa. Scruton, Clive, illus. LC 91-130. 32p. (ps-1). 1991. 13.95 jacketed (*0-671-74270-1*, S&S BFYR) S&S Trade.
Claesson, Stig. Sophie the Circus Princess. Henstra, Friso, illus. Stevens, Susanna, tr. from SWE. LC 93-16780. (Illus.). 1994. 14.00 (*0-671-87008-4*, Green Tiger) S&S Trade.
Claflin, Edward B. Sojourner Truth & the Struggle for Freedom. LC 87-19325. (Illus.). 144p. (gr. 3-6). 1987. pap. 5.95 (*0-8120-3919-X*) Barron.
Clair, Barry St. see St. Clair, Barry & Jones, Bill.
Clair, Barry St. see St. Clair, Barry & Naylor, Keith.
Clair, Bevan. Run Roadrunner. LC 80-82912. (ps-6). 1980. pap. 1.50 (*0-686-30719-4*) B A Scott.
Clair, Nancy. The Grammar Handbook Part One: Elementary-Intermediate ESL. 2nd, rev. ed. Clark, Raymond C., ed. Moran, Patrick & Sempe, Jean J., illus. LC 84-11548. 176p. (gr. 6 up). 1991. pap. text ed. 9.95x (*0-86647-042-5*) Pro Lingua.
Claire, Elizabeth. ESL Wonder Workbook, No. 1: This Is Me. Flamm, Jackie, ed. Frazier, J. D., illus. 104p. (Orig.). (gr. 1-6). 1990. pap. 7.65 (*1-878598-00-7*) Alta Bk Co Pubs.
—ESL Wonder Workbook, No. 2: All Around Me. Chapman, Charles, ed. Frazier, J. D., illus. 104p. (Orig.). (gr. 1-6). 1991. pap. write for info. (*1-878598-01-5*) Alta Bk Co Pubs.
Clancey, Eleanor, ed. see Diggs, Richard N.
Clancey, Lisa, ed. see Reisfeld, Randi.
Clancy, Lisa, ed. Stephanie: The Boy-Oh-Boy Next Door. (Orig.). 1993. pap. 3.50 (*0-671-88121-3*, Minstrel Bks) PB.
Clancy, Lisa, ed. see Gorman, S. S.
Clancy, Lisa, ed. see Gutman, Bill.
Clancy, Lisa, ed. see Nash, Bruce & Zullo, Allan.
Clante, Iben, tr. see Hertz, Grete J.
Clapp, Patricia. Constance. LC 85-43127. 256p. (gr. 4-6). 1991. pap. 3.95 (*0-688-10976-4*, Pub. by Beech Tree Bks) Morrow.
—Jane-Emily. 160p. (gr. 5 up). 1971. pap. 1.75 (*0-440-94185-7*, LFL) Dell.
—Jane-Emily. LC 92-46598. 160p. (gr. 7 up). 1993. 3.95 (*0-688-04592-8*, Pub. by Beech Tree Bks) Morrow.
—The Tamarack Tree. LC 86-108. 224p. (gr. 7 up). 1986. 11.95 (*0-688-02852-7*) Morrow.
—Witches' Children. (gr. 4-8). 1992. 17.00 (*0-8446-6572-X*) Peter Smith.
Clapp, Patricia C. Constance. 256p. (gr. 5 up). 1986. pap. 4.95 (*0-14-032030-X*, Puffin) Puffin Bks.
—The Tamarack Tree. 256p. (Orig.). (gr. 5-9). 1988. pap. 3.95 (*0-14-032406-2*, Puffin) Puffin Bks.
—Witches' Children. (gr. 5-9). 1987. pap. 4.99 (*0-14-032407-0*, Puffin) Puffin Bks.
Clapp, Steve & Berman, Julie S. Repairing Christian Lifestyles. 2nd, rev. ed. (Illus.). 80p. (gr. 6-12). 1992. wkbk. 24.95 (*0-87178-737-7*) Brethren.
Clapp, Steve & Mauck, Sue I. Repairing Christian Lifestyles. 2nd ed. Buck, Eunice & Clapp, E. J., illus. 174p. (gr. 7-12). 1983. pap. 6.00 (*0-914527-21-4*); pap. 5.00 leader's guide (*0-914527-27-4*) C-Four Res.
Clara Barton Elementary School First-Graders. I Need a Hug! (Illus.). 32p. (gr. k-3). 1992. pap. 3.50 (*0-87406-605-0*) Willowisp Pr.
Clardy, Andrea F. Dusty Was My Friend. Alexander, Eleanor, illus. 32p. (gr. 5 up). 1984. 16.95 (*0-89885-141-6*) Human Sci Pr.
Clare, J., ed. Knights in Armor. (gr. 4-7). 1992. 16.95 (*0-15-200508-0*, Gulliver Bks) HarBrace.
—Pyramids of Ancient Egypt. (gr. 4-7). 1992. 16.95 (*0-15-200509-9*, Gulliver Bks) HarBrace.
—Vikings. (gr. 4-7). 1992. 16.95 (*0-15-200512-9*, Gulliver Bks) HarBrace.
—Voyages of Christopher Columbus. (gr. 4-7). 1992. 16.95 (*0-15-200507-2*, Gulliver Bks) HarBrace.
Clare, John D., ed. Ancient Greece. LC 93-6267. 1994. 16.95 (*0-15-200516-1*, Gulliver Bks) HarBrace.
—Classical Rome. LC 92-30502. 1993. write for info. (*0-15-200513-7*, Gullivar Bks) HarBrace.
—Industrial Revolution. LC 93-2554. 1994. write for info. (*0-15-200514-5*) HarBrace.
Claret, Maria. The Chocolate Rabbit. LC 84-24610. 28p. (ps-3). 1985. 7.95 (*0-8120-5624-8*); pap. 5.95 (*0-8120-4926-8*) Barron.
Claridge, M. Geography Quizbook. (Illus.). 32p. (gr. 4 up). 1993. PLB 13.96 (*0-88110-535-X*, Usborne); pap. 6.95 (*0-7460-0710-8*, Usborne) EDC.
—History Quizbook. (Illus.). 32p. (gr. 4 up). 1992. PLB 13.96 (*0-88110-534-1*, Usborne); pap. 6.95 (*0-7460-0641-1*, Usborne) EDC.
—How to Draw Buildings. (Illus.). 32p. (gr. 4 up). 1992. PLB 12.96 (*0-88110-539-2*, Usborne); pap. 4.95 (*0-7460-0747-7*, Usborne) EDC.
—How to Draw Dinosaurs. (Illus.). 32p. (gr. 4 up). 1991. lib. bdg. 12.96 (*0-88110-502-3*, Usborne); pap. 4.95 (*0-7460-0673-X*, Usborne) EDC.
—Skiing. (Illus.). 64p. (gr. 6 up). 1987. pap. 7.95 (*0-7460-0096-0*) EDC.
Claridge, M. & Downswell, P. Animal Quizbook. (Illus.). 32p. (gr. 4 up). 1993. PLB 13.96 (*0-88110-536-8*, Usborne); pap. 6.95 (*0-7460-0720-5*, Usborne) EDC.
Claridge, Marit & Shackell, John. Living Things. (Illus.). 40p. (gr. 3-6). 1986. 10.95 (*0-86020-986-5*) EDC.
Clark, Ann N. In My Mother's House. Herrara, Velino, illus. 64p. (ps up). 1991. 15.95 (*0-670-83917-5*) Viking Child Bks.
—In My Mother's House. Herrara, Velino, illus. 64p. 1992. pap. 4.99 (*0-14-054496-8*) Puffin Bks.

—Little Boy with Three Names: Stories of Taos Pueblo. reformatted ed. Lujan, Tonita, illus. LC 89-81747. 50p. (gr. 1-5). 1990. pap. 8.95 (0-941270-59-9) Ancient City Pr.
—Little Herder in Autumn. Harrington, John P., ed. Young, Robert W., tr. Denetsosie, Hoke, illus. LC 88-70848. (ENG & NAV.). 96p. (gr. 1-5). 1988. pap. 9.95 (0-941270-46-7) Ancient City Pr.
—Secret of the Andes. Charlot, Jean, illus. (gr. 3-7). 1976. pap. 4.99 (0-14-030926-8, Puffin) Puffin Bks.
—Secret of the Andes. Charlot, Jean, illus. (gr. 4-8). 1952. pap. 14.99 (0-670-62975-8) Viking Child Bks.
—Sun Journey: A Story of Zuni Pueblo. reissued ed. Sandy, Percy T., illus. LC 88-70955. 96p. (gr. 3 up). 1988. 19.95 (0-941270-49-1); pap. 9.95 (0-941270-48-3) Ancient City Pr.
—There Still Are Buffalo. Beatty, Willard W., ed. Tongier, Steve, illus. LC 90-85645. 40p. (gr. 1-4). 1992. pap. 8.95 (0-941270-67-X) Ancient City Pr.
Clark, Barbara, intro. by. Conversations & Constructions. 64p. (gr. k-12). 1978. pap. 4.95 (0-945349-01-7) Journeys Into Language.
Clark, Barbara R. Reflections. Davis, Ruby & Gerstung, Estella, eds. Clark, Carl R. & Williams, Cecil J. 72p. (Orig.). (gr. 4-12). 1982. pap. 4.95 (0-686-37922-5) Williams SC.
Clark, Billy C. A Long Row to Hoe. rev. ed. Gifford, James M., ed. Norma, Gurney, intro. by. LC 91-40399. (Illus.). 285p. (gr. 6 up). 1992. Repr. of 1960 ed. 20.00 (0-945084-27-7); ltd. ed. 30.00 (0-945084-28-5) J Stuart Found.
—Song of the River. rev. ed. Gifford, James M., et al, eds. LC 92-31483. (Illus.). 176p. (gr. 7 up). 1993. Repr. of 1957 ed. 15.00 (0-945084-35-8) J Stuart Found.
Clark, Carl R. see Clark, Barbara R.
Clark, Catherine. What's So Funny about Ninth Grade? LC 91-2494. 128p. (gr. 6-9). 1992. lib. bdg. 9.89 (0-8167-2396-6); pap. text ed. 2.95 (0-8167-2397-4) Troll Assocs.
Clark, Cathy. Girl of the Year. (gr. 9-12). 1993. pap. 3.50 (0-06-106744-X, Harp PBks) HarpC.
Clark, Christopher. Oxford Activity Books for Children. Brychta, Alex, illus. (gr. k-4). 1985. Bk. 4. pap. 3.95x (0-19-421833-3); Bk. 5. pap. 3.95x (0-19-421834-1); Bk. 6. pap. 3.95x (0-19-421835-X); Bk. 3. pap. 3.95x (0-19-421832-5); Bk. 1. pap. 3.95x (0-19-421830-9); Bk. 2. pap. 3.95x (0-19-421831-7) OUP.
Clark, Clara E. A Tangram Diary. (Illus.). 64p. (Orig.). (gr. 3-6). 1980. pap. 6.95 (0-934734-05-4) Construct Educ.
Clark, Clara E. & Sternberg, Betty J. Math in Stride, Bk. 1. (Illus.). 166p. (Orig.). (gr. k-2). 1980. pap. 5.95 (0-934734-06-2); tchr's. manual 19.95 (0-934734-12-7) Construct Educ.
—Math in Stride, Bk. 2. (Illus.). 203p. (Orig.). (gr. 1-3). 1980. pap. 6.50 (0-934734-07-0); tchr's. manual 19.95 (0-934734-13-5) Construct Educ.
—Math in Stride, Bk. 3. (Illus.). 219p. (Orig.). (gr. 2-4). 1980. pap. 6.95 (0-934734-08-9) Construct Educ.
Clark, Clara G. Annie's Choice. (Illus.). 196p. (gr. 5 up). 1993. 14.95 (1-56397-053-8) Boyds Mills Pr.
Clark, Colin. Journey Through Italy. Burns, Robert, illus. LC 91-46174. 32p. (gr. 3-5). 1993. PLB 11.89 (0-8167-2763-5); pap. text ed. 3.95 (0-8167-2764-3) Troll Assocs. Postponed.
Clark, Della R. Quiet One. Mignard, Phyllis D., illus. 64p. (ps-5). 1992. 15.00 (0-9631252-0-6) Desert Rose.
Clark, E., ed. see Frankel, B.
Clark, Eleanor B. Kitty's Cousins. 1993. 7.95 (0-533-10569-2) Vantage.
Clark, Elizabeth. Fish. (Illus.). 32p. (gr. 1-4). 1990. PLB 14.95 (0-87614-376-1) Carolrhoda Bks.
—Meat. (Illus.). 32p. (gr. 1-4). 1990. PLB 14.95 (0-87614-375-3) Carolrhoda Bks.
Clark, Ella. Guardian Spirit Quest. (gr. 5-12). 1974. pap. 4.95 (0-89992-045-4) Coun India Ed.
Clark, Ella, ed. In the Beginning. (gr. 5 up). 1977. 1.95 (0-89992-055-1) Coun India Ed.
Clark, Ella E. Indian Legends of the Pacific Northwest. (Illus.). (gr. 9-12). 1953. pap. 13.00x (0-520-00243-1) U CA Pr.
Clark, Emma C. Across the Blue Mountains. LC 93-12118. 1993. 14.95 (0-15-201220-6) HarBrace.
—The Bouncing Dinosaur. (Illus.). 32p. (ps-3). 1990. 13.95 (0-374-30912-4) FS&G.
—Catch That Hat! LC 89-34881. (Illus.). (ps-2). 1990. 12.95 (0-316-14496-7) Little.
—Lunch with Aunt Augusta. LC 91-11969. (Illus.). 32p. (ps-3). 1992. 14.00 (0-8037-1104-2) Dial Bks Young.
Clark, Emma C., illus. I Never Saw a Purple Cow. 96p. (ps-3). 1991. 18.95 (0-316-14500-9) Little.
Clark, Frances. Look & Listen, Pt. A. Goss, Louise & Kraehenbuehl, Davidcontrib. by. 48p. (Orig.). (gr. k-6). 1962. pap. text ed. 6.95 (0-87487-176-X) Summy-Birchard.
—Look & Listen, Pt. B. Goss, Louise & Kraehenbuehl, Davidcontrib. by. 48p. (Orig.). (gr. k-12). 1962. pap. text ed. 6.95 (0-87487-177-8) Summy-Birchard.
—Look & Listen, Pt. C. Goss, Louise & Kraehenbuehl, Davidcontrib. by. 48p. (Orig.). (gr. k-12). 1962. pap. text ed. 6.95 (0-87487-178-6) Summy-Birchard.
—Look & Listen, Pt. D. Goss, Louise & Kraehenbuehl, Davidcontrib. by. 48p. (Orig.). (gr. k-12). 1962. pap. text ed. 6.95 (0-87487-179-4) Summy-Birchard.
Clark, Frances & Goss, Louise. Music Maker, Pt. A. (Illus.). 56p. (gr. 2 up). 1986. pap. text ed. 6.95 wkbk. (0-913277-20-7) New Schl Mus Study.

—Write & Play Time, Pt. A. 64p. (Orig.). (gr. k-6). 1974. pap. text ed. 9.95 (0-87487-196-4) Summy-Birchard.
Clark, Frances, ed. see Kraehenbuehl, David, et al.
Clark, Frances, ed. see Pearce, Elvina T.
Clark, Francis, ed. see George, Jon & Kraehenbuehl, David.
Clark, Gary B., ed. see Clark, Sue A.
Clark, I. E. Hansel & Gretel. (Illus.). 38p. (ps up). 1970. pap. 3.00 (0-88680-075-7); Director's Production Script. pap. 15.00 (0-88680-076-5); royalty on application 35.00 (0-317-03602-5) I E Clark.
—The Happy Scarecrow. (Illus.). 17p. (Orig.). (gr. 5-12). 1966. pap. 2.00 (0-88680-077-3); director's script 7.50 (0-88680-078-1); royalty on application 20.00 (0-685-59264-2) I E Clark.
—Pandora & the Magic Box. (Illus.). 20p. (gr. 2 up). 1968. pap. 6.50 director's script (0-88680-148-6); pap. 1.75 bk. (0-88680-147-8); royalty on application 15.00 (0-685-57905-0) I E Clark.
—Twelve Dancing Princesses. 40p. (ps up). 1969. pap. 3.00 (0-88680-197-4); Director's Production Script. pap. 15.00 (0-88680-198-2); royalty on application 35.00 (0-317-03614-9) I E Clark.
Clark, I. E. & Carter, Kit. It's a Dungaree World. (Illus.). 40p. (ps up). 1974. pap. 3.00 (0-88680-097-8) Piano-Vocal Score, Music & Lyrics. pap. 15.00 (0-88680-098-6); Director's Production Script. pap. 15.00 (0-88680-099-4); royalty on application 60.00 (0-685-08243-1) I E Clark.
Clark, James & Drum, William. Structured BASIC: Apple Version. 3rd ed. LC 93-4720. 1993. write for info. (0-538-61801-9) S-W Pub.
Clark, James I., jt. auth. see Turner Educational Services, Inc. Staff.
Clark, James I., jt. auth. see Turner Educational Services Inc. Staff.
Clark, James I., jt. auth. see Turner Educational Services, Inc. Staff.
Clark, James I., jt. auth. see Turner Program Services, Inc. Staff.
Clark, James I., jt. auth. see Turner Programs Services, Inc. Staff.
Clark, John. Earthquakes to Volcanoes: Projects with Geography. LC 91-35076. (Illus.). 32p. (gr. 5-9). 1992. PLB 12.40 (0-531-17316-X, Gloucester Pr) Watts.
—Mining to Minerals: Projects with Geography. LC 91-34411. (Illus.). 32p. (gr. 5-9). 1992. PLB 12.40 (0-531-17272-4, Gloucester Pr) Watts.
Clark, John G. Science Project Puzzlers: Starter Ideas for the Curious. Schwarz, Frank, illus. Stone, Harris. (Illus.). 61p. (gr. 7 up). 1981. pap. 4.95 (0-13-795450-6, Pub. by Treehouse) P-H.
Clark, John O. The Atmosphere: Projects with Geography. LC 92-1514. (Illus.). 32p. (gr. 5-8). 1992. PLB 12.40 (0-531-17367-4, Gloucester Pr) Watts.
—Seas & Oceans: Projects with Geography. LC 92-1515. (Illus.). 32p. (gr. 5-8). 1992. PLB 12.40 (0-531-17368-2, Gloucester Pr) Watts.
Clark, Judith F. Awesome Facts to Blow Your Mind. Morrow, Skip, illus. 48p. (gr. 2 up). 1993. pap. 4.99 (0-8431-3577-8) Price Stern.
—Gross Facts to Blow Your Mind. Morrow, Skip, illus. LC 93-12250. 48p. 1993. pap. 4.99 (0-8431-3578-6) Price Stern.
—Scary Facts to Blow Your Mind. Morrow, Skip, illus. 48p. (gr. 2 up). 1993. pap. 4.99 (0-8431-3580-8) Price Stern.
—Weird Facts to Blow Your Mind. Morrow, Skip, illus. 48p. (gr. 2 up). 1993. pap. 4.99 (0-8431-3579-4) Price Stern.
Clark, Kay, ed. see Stronck, David.
Clark, Kenneth B., ed. Traditional Black Music Series, 15 vols. (Illus.). (gr. 5 up). 1993. Set. PLB 224.25 (0-7910-1826-1, Am Art Analog) Chelsea Hse.
Clark, Leon E. Through African Eyes, Vol. 2: The Present: Tradition & Change. (Illus.). 292p. (Orig.). (gr. 9-12). 1994. pap. text ed. 19.95x (0-938960-28-8) CITE.
Clark, Leon E., ed. see Seybolt, Peter J.
Clark, Margaret G. Best of Aesop's Fables. (ps-4). 1990. 16.95 (0-316-14499-1, Joy St Bks) Little.
—The Endangered Florida Panther. LC 92-14816. (Illus.). (gr. 4 up). 1993. 14.99 (0-525-65114-4, Cobblehill Bks) Dutton Child Bks.
—Freedom Crossing. 160p. (gr. 3-7). 1991. 2.95 (0-590-44569-3) Scholastic Inc.
—The Vanishing Manatee. LC 89-38676. (Illus.). 64p. (gr. 4 up). 1990. 14.00 (0-525-65024-5, Cobblehill Bks) Dutton Child Bks.

Clark, Marnie, et al, eds. Lighting Candles in the Dark. Thomas, Sylvia, illus. 215p. (Orig.). 1992. pap. 9.50 (0-9620912-3-5) Friends Genl Conf. LIGHTING CANDLES IN THE DARK is an illustrated anthology of 45 exciting stories about the courage of everyday people in the face of danger who use the power of love to save themselves & others. Divided into five sections "Courage & Nonviolence," "The Power of Love," "Acts of Loving Service," "Fairness & Equality," &

"Belonging & Care of the Earth," the stories tell of characters dating from the 17th century to the present all over the world. The stories emphasize Quaker values of using love to heal ourselves, others, & our earth. Many stories have multicultural settings. From a recent review in FRIENDS JOURNAL: "How do we help our children choose love, courage, forgiveness, honesty, & fairness in a world saturated with violence, fear, selfishness, injustice & oppression? LIGHTING CANDLES IN THE DARK is a valuable resource in facing this awesome challenge....There's a good range of situations here, always something to catch a young reader's interest. The book looks bright & fresh, with appealing line drawings & open-looking typeface...this reader finds this book a welcome resource for kids, parents & teachers."--Margaret Springer. Friends General Conference, 1216 Arch Street 2B, Philadelphia, PA 19107. 800-966-4556, Libraries: 10% Bookstores: 40% actual postage. *Publisher Provided Annotation.*

Clark, Marvin, ed. see Redding, Robert.
Clark, Marvin, ed. see Warbelow, Willy L.
Clark, Marvin, ed. see Wilson, Jack.
Clark, Mary. Dinosaurios: Dinosaurs. Kratky, Lada, tr. from ENG. (SPA., Illus.). 48p. (gr. k-4). 1984. PLB 15.27 (0-516-31612-5); pap. 4.95 (0-516-51612-4) Childrens.
Clark, Mary J. The Commonwealth of Independent States. LC 92-20745. (Illus.). 64p. (gr. 5-8). 1992. PLB 15.90 (1-56294-081-3) Millbrook Pr.
Clark, Mary L. Dinosaurs. LC 81-7750. (Illus.). 48p. (gr. k-4). 1981. PLB 15.27 (0-516-01612-1); pap. 4.95 (0-516-41612-X) Childrens.
Clark, Nicholas L., intro. by. Woodland Peoples: An Educational Unit. 32p. (Orig.). 1993. pap. write for info. (0-9623291-6-9) Minnetrista.
Clark, Penny, illus. A Coloring Book of Bible Proverbs. 32p. (ps-5). 1988. 2.50 (0-9618608-2-0) Lynn's Bookshelf.
Clark, Philip. American Civil War. (Illus.). 32p. (gr. 3-9). 1988. PLB 10.95 (0-86307-933-4) Marshall Cavendish.
—American Revolution. (Illus.). 32p. (gr. 3-9). 1988. PLB 10.95 (0-86307-930-X) Marshall Cavendish.
—Russian Revolution. (Illus.). 32p. (gr. 3-9). 1988. PLB 10.95 (0-86307-935-0) Marshall Cavendish.
Clark, Raymond C. Money: Exploring the Ways We Use It. (Illus.). 96p. (gr. 7 up). 1989. 9.50x (0-86647-029-8) Pro Lingua.
—Potluck: Exploring American Foods & Meals. MacLean, Robert, illus. 128p. (Orig.). (gr. 5 up). 1985. text ed. 9.50x (0-86647-012-3) Pro Lingua.
—Story Cards: The Tales of Nasreddin Hodja - Pairwork Conversation Activities. (Illus.). 44p. (gr. 6 up). 1991. 13.95x (0-86647-044-1) Pro Lingua.
Clark, Raymond C. & Brown, Ruthanne. Index Card Games for ESL. 2nd, rev. ed. Moran, Patrick R., illus. LC 82-9786. 80p. (Orig.). (gr. 3 up). 1992. pap. 9.50x (0-86647-002-6) Pro Lingua.
Clark, Raymond C. & Duncan, Janie L. Getting a Fix on Vocabulary, Using Words in the News: The System of Affixation & Compounding in English. (Illus.). 96p. (gr. 7 up). 1991. 9.95x (0-86647-038-7) Pro Lingua.
Clark, Raymond C. & Jerald, Michael. Summer Olympic Games: Exploring International Athletic Competition. (Illus.). 96p. (gr. 5 up). 1987. 9.50x (0-86647-021-2) Pro Lingua.
Clark, Raymond C., ed. Max in America, Pt. 1: Communcating in the Culture. (Illus.). 128p. (gr. 8 up). 1987. 5.00x (0-86647-024-7) Pro Lingua.
—Max in America, Pt. 2: Communcating in the Culture. (Illus.). 128p. (gr. 8 up). 1987. 5.00x (0-86647-025-5) Pro Lingua.
Clark, Raymond C., ed. see Burrows, Arthur A.
Clark, Raymond C., ed. see Clair, Nancy.
Clark, Roberta. Why? Axeman, Lois, illus. LC 83-7306. 32p. (gr. k-2). 1983. pap. 3.95 (0-516-46594-5) Childrens.
Clark, Roland. Gunner's Dawn. 2nd ed. Clark, Roland, illus. 125p. (gr. 10 up). 1991. Repr. of 1937 ed. 40.00 (1-56416-017-3) Derrydale Pr.
—Roland Clark's Etchings. 2nd ed. (Illus.). 187p. (gr. 10 up). 1990. Repr. of 1938 ed. 45.00 (1-56416-016-5) Derrydale Pr.
Clark, Roland & Derrydale Press Staff. Stray Shots & a Decade of American Sporting Books & Prints. (Illus.). 195p. (gr. 10 up). 1993. Repr. of 1937 ed. 40.00 (1-56416-048-3) Derrydale Pr.

Clark, Steve. Illustrated Basketball Dictionary for Young People. Baginski, Frank, illus. (gr. 4 up). 1978. pap. 2.50 (*0-13-450940-4*, Pub. by Treehouse) P-H.
—Wade Boggs: Baseball's Star Hitter. LC 87-33292. (Illus.). 64p. (gr. 3 up). 1988. RSBE 13.95 (*0-87518-377-8*, Dillon) Macmillan Child Grp.
Clark, Sue A. The Rainbow Tree. Clark, Gary B., ed. (Illus.). 18p. (gr. 4-7). 1990. write for info. Point View Pr.
Clark, Suzanne. Blackboard Blackmail. La Haye, Beverly. 220p. (Orig.). 1989. pap. 8.95 (*1-877818-02-X*) Footstool Pubns.
Clark, Thomas D. Simon Kenton, Kentucky Scout. 2nd ed. Hay, Melba P., intro. by. Shenton, Edward, illus. 256p. (gr. 6-12). 17.95 (*0-945084-38-2*); pap. 8.95 (*0-945084-39-0*) J Stuart Found.
Clark, Walter V. The Ox-Bow Incident. 224p. (gr. 9-12). 1943. pap. 4.50 (*0-451-52386-5*, CE1497, Sig Classics) NAL-Dutton.
Clark, Zane. My Royal Service. (Illus.). 165p. (gr. 9 up). 1989. pap. 9.00 (*0-89114-164-2*) Baptist Pub Hse.
Clarke. Torment of Mr. Gully. 1991. 11.95 (*0-8050-1554-X*) H Holt & Co.
Clarke, Arthur C. The Other Side of the Sky: Stories of the Future. 160p. (gr. 7 up). 1985. pap. 2.95 (*0-451-14018-4*, Sig) NAL-Dutton.
—The Sands of Mars. (RL 7). pap. 2.50 (*0-451-12312-3*, AE2312, Sig) NAL-Dutton.
—The Wind from the Sun: Stories of the Space Age. 176p. (RL 7). 1973. pap. 1.95 (*0-451-11475-2*, AJ1475, Sig) NAL-Dutton.
Clarke, Barry. Amazing Frogs & Toads. Young, Jerry, photos by. LC 90-31882. (Illus.). 32p. (Orig.). (gr. 1-5). 1990. lib. bdg. 9.99 (*0-679-90688-6*); pap. 7.99 (*0-679-80688-1*) Knopf Bks Yng Read.
Clarke, Barry, et al. Amphibian. 64p. (gr. 5 up). 1993. 15.00 (*0-679-83879-1*); PLB 16.99 (*0-679-93879-6*) Knopf Bks Yng Read.
Clarke, Brenda. Caring for Others. LC 89-26296. (Illus.). 48p. (gr. 4-8). 1990. PLB 19.92 (*0-8114-2751-X*) Raintree Steck-V.
—Charles Darwin. (Illus.). 32p. (gr. 3-8). 1988. PLB 10.95 (*0-86307-923-7*) Marshall Cavendish.
—Fighting for Their Faith. LC 89-71372. (Illus.). 48p. (gr. 4-8). 1990. PLB 19.92 (*0-8114-2753-6*) Raintree Steck-V.
—Gandhi. (Illus.). 32p. (gr. 3-8). 1988. PLB 10.95 (*0-86307-926-1*) Marshall Cavendish.
Clarke, Donald & Dartford, Mark, eds. The New Illustrated Science & Invention Encyclopedia: How It Works. LC 93-3331. (Illus.). 1994. Set. 349.95 (*0-86307-491-X*) Marshall Cavendish.
Clarke, Elizabeth L. We Ain't Arrived Yet. 61p. (Orig.). 1991. pap. 10.00 (*0-9630882-0-3*) Clarke Prods.
Clarke, Gillian, tr. see Jones, T. Llew.
Clarke, Gus. Along Came Eric. LC 90-6561. (Illus.). 32p. (ps up). 1991. 13.95 (*0-688-10300-6*); PLB 13.88 (*0-688-10301-4*) Lothrop.
—Eddie & Teddy. (ps-3). 1991. 13.88 (*0-688-10039-2*) Lothrop.
—Eddie & Teddy. (ps-3). 1991. 13.95 (*0-688-10038-4*); PLB 13.88 (*0-685-47818-1*) Lothrop.
—Eddie & Teddy. ALC Staff, ed. LC 90-5795. (Illus.). 32p. (ps up). 1992. pap. 3.95 (*0-688-11700-7*, Mulberry) Morrow.
—How Many Days to My Birthday? Pearson, Susan, ed. LC 91-53022. (Illus.). 32p. (ps up). 1992. 14.00 (*0-688-11236-6*); PLB 13.93 (*0-688-11237-4*) Lothrop.
Clarke, Gus, illus. E I E I O: The Story of Old MacDonald, Who Had a Farm. LC 92-53462. (gr. 3 up). 1993. write for info. (*0-688-12215-9*) Lothrop.
Clarke, J. Al Capsella & the Watchdogs. LC 90-26090. 160p. (gr. 6 up). 1991. 14.95 (*0-8050-1598-1*, Bks Young Read) H Holt & Co.
—Al Capsella Takes a Vacation. 160p. (gr. 7 up). 1993. PLB 14.95 (*0-8050-2685-1*, Bks Young Read) H Holt & Co.
—The Heroic Life of Al Capsella. LC 89-24629. 160p. (gr. 6 up). 1990. 14.95 (*0-8050-1310-5*, Bks Young Read) H Holt & Co.
—Riffraff. LC 92-9928. 96p. (gr. 9-12). 1992. 14.95 (*0-8050-1774-7*, Bks Young Read) H Holt & Co.
—Teddy B. Zoot. Hewitt, Margaret, illus. LC 90-34120. 64p. (gr. 2-4). 1992. pap. 4.95 (*0-8050-2210-4*, Redfeather BYR) H Holt & Co.
Clarke, Joy A. Multicultural Social Studies Unit: Who Am I? Blocker, Kearn, illus. 150p. (gr. 3-8). 1991. 3-ring binder 79.95 (*0-9626984-1-5*); pap. 69.95 (*0-685-62443-9*) Clarke Enterprise.
Clarke, Leah. Ghandymeir & Silvermane. rev. ed. 32p. 1991. 6.95 (*0-8062-4022-9*) Carlton.
Clarke, Mary & Ashton, Frederick, illus. Antoinette Sibley. Ashton, Frederick, intro. by. 128p. (gr. 8-12). 1981. 29.95 (*0-903102-64-1*, Pub. by Dance Bks UK) Princeton Bk Co.
Clarke, Nita. Timothy & the Blanket Fairy. (gr. k-6). 1981. 6.95 (*0-933184-06-9*); pap. 4.95 (*0-933184-16-6*) Flame Intl.
Clarke, Nora, compiled by. A Treasury of Bedtime Stories. Spenceley, Annabel, illus. LC 92-43152. 160p. (gr. k-4). 1993. pap. 5.95 (*1-85697-931-8*) Kingfisher Bks.
Clarke, Norman. Patrick in Person. Julian-Otte, Vanessa, illus. 130p. (gr. 3 up). 1992. bds. 16.95 laminated (*0-571-16225-8*) Faber & Faber.
Clarke, Pauline. Return of the Twelve. (Orig.). (gr. 3-7). 1986. pap. 4.95 (*0-440-47536-8*) Dell.

Clarke, Sue. The Tombs of the Paraohs. (Illus.). 10p. 1994. 16.95 (*1-56282-485-6*) Hyprn Child.
Clarkson, G. Fairy Tales: Musical Dramas for Children. 48p. (gr. k-6). 1986. pap. 9.00 (*0-918812-49-6*) MMB Music.
Clarkson, Ginger. Stop, Look & Listen: Songs of Awareness for Young Children. (ps). 1986. pap. text ed. 4.95 (*0-8497-5924-2*, WE8) KJOS.
Clarkson, Margaret. Susie's Babies: A Clear & Simple Explanation of the Everyday Miracle of Birth. 72p. 1992. pap. 8.99 (*0-8028-4053-1*) Eerdmans.
Clarkson, Sandra P., jt. auth. see Altamuro, Vincent J.
Clarkson, Virginia C. The Alphabet of Civility. Vehslage, Cynthia, illus. LC 93-16585. 1993. write for info. (*0-913515-86-8*) Starrhill Pr.
Claro, Nicole. The Apache Indians. (Illus.). 80p (gr. 2-5). 1993. PLB 12.95 (*0-7910-1656-0*) Chelsea Hse.
—The Cherokee Indians. (Illus.). 80p. (gr. 2-5). 1991. lib. bdg. 12.95 (*0-7910-1652-8*) Chelsea Hse.
—Madonna. LC 93-30227. (Illus.). 1994. 18.95 (*0-7910-2330-3*, Am Art Analog); pap. write for info. (*0-7910-2355-9*) Chelsea Hse.
Clarrain, Dean & Brown, Ryan. Collected Teenage Mutant Ninja Turtles Adventures, Vol. 3. Mutchroney, Ken, et al, illus. 88p. 1991. pap. 5.95 (*1-879450-05-4*) Tundra MA.
—The Collected Teenage Mutant Ninja Turtles Adventures, Vol. 4. Mitchroney, Ken, et al, illus. 88p. 1991. pap. 5.95 (*1-879450-06-2*) Tundra MA.
Clarrain, Dean & Lawson, Jim. Teenage Mutant Ninja Turtles: The Secret of the Ooze - Movie Adaptation. Lawson, Jim, illus. 64p. (Orig.). 1991. pap. 5.95 (*1-879450-08-9*) Tundra MA.
Clarrian, Dean, jt. auth. see Brown, Ryan.
Clary, Linda & Harms, Larry. Christmas Music for Little People. Bradley, Richard, ed. (Illus.). 32p. (ps). 1985. bk & cassette 9.95 (*0-89748-160-7*) Bradley Pubns.
Clary, Linda, jt. auth. see Collins, Ann.
Clasing, Elisabeth. Sesame Street: Come to the Playground. Cooke, Tom, illus. 12p. (ps). 1992. write for info. (*0-307-12003-1*, 12003, Golden Pr) Western Pub.
Claudius, Christel, jt. auth. see Huber, Joanna.
Claudius, Christel, jt. auth. see Huber, Johanna.
Clausen, Josie, jt. auth. see Ramos, Teresita V.
Clauser, Suzanne. A Girl Named Sooner. (gr. 7 up). 1974. pap. 2.95 (*0-380-00216-7*) Avon.
Clauss, J., ed. Timeless Children's Tales from Around the World. (Illus.). (gr. 5-6). 1976. lib. bdg. 20.95x (*0-88411-992-0*, Pub. by Aeonian Pr) Amereon Ltd.
Clauss, J., intro. by see Aesop.
Clavell, James. Shogun. 1976. pap. 6.99 (*0-440-17800-2*) Dell.
Claverie, Jean. Die Drei Kleinen Schweinchen. Claverie, Jean, illus. (GER). 32p. (gr. k-3). 1992. 13.95 (*3-85825-330-8*) North-South Bks NYC.
—Little Lou. Claverie, Jean, illus. LC 90-1531. 48p. 1990. 16.95 (*1-55670-162-4*) Stewart Tabori & Chang.
—Little Lou. Claverie, Jean, illus. 48p. (gr. 3 up). 1990. PLB 17.95s.p. (*0-88682-329-3*) Creative Ed.
—The Three Little Pigs. Claverie, Jean, illus. Crawford, Elizabeth, tr. from GER. LC 88-25327. (Illus.). 32p. (gr. k-3). 1989. 13.95 (*1-55858-004-2*) North-South Bks NYC.
—Les Trois Petits Cochons. Claverie, Jean, illus. (FRE). 32p. (gr. k-3). 1992. 13.95 (*3-314-20655-0*) North-South Bks NYC.
Clawson, Elmer. Activities & Investigations in Economics. 1993. pap. 9.95 (*0-201-49005-6*) Addison-Wesley.
—Activities & Investigations in Economics. 1993. pap. 12.95 tchr's ed. (*0-201-49006-4*) Addison-Wesley.
Clawson, Jan. Baptism My Promise to Jesus. Fletcher, Amy, illus. 24p. (Orig.). (gr. 1-3). 1988. pap. 3.95 (*0-88290-298-9*) Horizon Utah.
—Let's Learn about Tithing. Pardew, Les, illus. 24p. (gr. k-6). 1988. pap. 3.95 (*0-88290-339-X*) Horizon Utah.
Clay, Gwen, jt. auth. see Komarc, Marilyn.
Clay, Marie. Stones: Concepts About Print Test. (Orig.). (ps-2). 1980. pap. text ed. 3.00x (*0-435-00556-1*, 00556) Heinemann.
Clay, Rebecca. Kidding Around Paris: A Young Person's Guide to the City. Lambert, Mary, illus. 64p. (Orig.). (gr. 3 up). 1991. pap. 9.95 (*0-945465-82-3*) John Muir.
—Kidding Around Philadelphia: A Young Person's Guide to the City. (Illus.). 64p. (gr. 3 up). 1990. pap. 9.95 (*0-945465-71-8*) John Muir.
Clay, Stanley B. Diva. (Orig.). (ps-12). 1988. pap. 3.50 (*0-87067-839-6*) Holloway.
Claydon, Dina. The Cabin Faced West: A Study Guide. Friedland, Joyce & Kessler, Rikki, eds. 21p. (gr. 9-12). 1990. pap. text ed. 14.95 (*0-88122-409-X*) Lrn Links.
—Maurice's Room: A Study Guide. Friedland, Joyce & Kessler, Rikki, eds. (gr. 2-4). 1991. pap. text ed. 14.95 (*0-88122-569-X*) LRN Links.
—Shoeshine Girl: A Study Guide. Friedland, Joyce & Kessler, Rikki, eds. 20p. (gr. 9-12). 1990. pap. text ed. 14.95 (*0-88122-396-4*) Lrn Links.
—Stone Fox: A Study Guide. Friedland, Joyce & Kessler, Rikki, eds. 21p. (gr. 9-12). 1990. pap. text ed. 14.95 (*0-88122-407-3*) Lrn Links.
Claypool, Jane. Alcohol & You. rev. ed. Greenberg, Lorna, ed. LC 88-10258. (Illus.). 112p. 1988. PLB 13.40 (*0-531-10566-0*) Watts.
—Saddam Hussein. LC 92-46994. 1993. 19.93 (*0-86625-477-3*); 14.95s.p. (*0-685-67775-3*) Rourke Pubns.

Clayton, C. Sing a Song of Gladness. (Illus.). 32p. (gr. k-4). 1974. pap. 1.89 (*0-570-06087-7*, 59-1302) Concordia.
Clayton, Constance, jt. auth. see Potter, Joan.
Clayton, Ed. Martin Luther King: Peaceful Warrior. (gr. 5). 1991. pap. write for info. (*0-663-56247-3*) Silver Burdett Pr.
Clayton, Elaine. Pup in School. Clayton, Elaine, illus. LC 92-18457. 24p. (ps-1). 1993. 12.00 (*0-517-59085-9*); PLB 12.99 (*0-517-59086-7*) Crown Bks Yng Read.
Clayton, Gordon, photos by. Lamb. (Illus.). 24p. (gr. k-3). 1992. 6.95 (*0-525-67359-8*, Lodestar Bks) Dutton Child Bks.
Clayton, Lawrence. Amphetamines & Other Stimulants. Rosen, Ruth, ed. (gr. 7-12). 1993. 14.95 (*0-8239-1534-4*) Rosen Group.
—Barbiturates & Other Depressants. Rosen, Ruth, ed. (gr. 7-12). 1993. 14.95 (*0-8239-1535-2*) Rosen Group.
—Careers in Psychology. Rosen, Ruth, ed. (gr. 7-12). 1992. PLB 13.95 (*0-8239-1457-7*) Rosen Group.
—Coping with a Drug Abusing Parent. 176p. (gr. 7-12). 1991. PLB 13.95 (*0-8239-1300-7*) Rosen Group.
—Coping with Sports Injuries. 1992. 13.95 (*0-8239-1453-4*) Rosen Group.
—Designer Drugs. Rosen, Ruth, ed. (gr. 7-12). 1993. 14.95 (*0-8239-1519-0*) Rosen Group.
Clayton, Lawrence & Carter, Sharon. Coping with Being Gifted. Rosen, Ruth, ed. (gr. 7-12). 1992. PLB 13.95 (*0-8239-1430-5*) Rosen Group.
—Coping with Depression. rev. ed. Rosen, Ruth, ed. (gr. 7-12). 1992. 13.95 (*0-8239-1488-7*) Rosen Group.
Clayton, Lawrence & Morrison, Jaydene. Coping with a Learning Disability. Rosen, Ruth, ed. (gr. 7-12). 1992. PLB 13.95 (*0-8239-1436-4*) Rosen Group.
Clayton, Michael & Howard, Tom. The Love of Horses. (Illus.). 96p. 1993. Repr. 12.98 (*0-8317-4597-5*) Smithmark.
Clayton, Sandra. The Giant. Hunnam, Lucinda, illus. LC 93-28992. 1994. 4.25 (*0-383-03745-X*) SRA Schl Grp.
Clayton, Sheryl H., ed. Black Women Role Models of Greater St. Louis. LC 81-71873. 381p. (Orig.). (gr. 6 up). 1982. 14.95 (*0-9607958-0-4*) Essai Seay Pubns.
Clean Team Staff & Campbell, Jeff. Spring Cleaning. (Orig.). (gr. 7 up). 1989. pap. 5.95 (*0-440-50162-8*, Dell Trade Pbks) Dell.
Cleary, Beverly. Beezus & Ramona. Darling, Louis, illus. LC 55-7623. 192p. (gr. 3-7). 1955. 12.95 (*0-688-21076-7*); PLB 12.88 (*0-688-31076-1*, Morrow Jr Bks) Morrow Jr Bks.
—Beezus & Ramona. 160p. (gr. 5-6). 1990. pap. 3.99 (*0-380-70918-X*, Camelot) Avon.
—Beezus & Ramona. 130p. 1992. text ed. 10.40 (*1-56956-108-7*) W A T Braille.
—The Beezus & Ramona Diary. Tiegreen, Alan, illus. 224p. (gr. 5-7). 1986. pap. 9.95 (*0-688-06353-5*, Pub. by Beech Tree Bks) Morrow.
—Beverly Cleary, 4 vols. (gr. 4-7). 1991. Set. pap. 14.00 boxed (*0-380-71719-0*, Camelot) Avon.
—Dear Mr. Henshaw. Zelinsky, Paul O., illus. LC 83-5372. 144p. (gr. 3-7). 1983. 12.95 (*0-688-02405-X*); PLB 12.88 (*0-688-02406-8*, Morrow Jr Bks) Morrow Jr Bks.
—Dear Mr. Henshaw. Zelinsky, Paul O., illus. 144p. (gr. k-6). 1984. pap. 3.99 (*0-440-41794-5*, YB) Dell.
—Dear Mr. Henshaw. large type ed. Zelinsky, Paul O., illus. 141p. (gr. 2-6). 1987. Repr. of 1983 ed. lib. bdg. 14.95 (*1-55736-001-4*, Crnrstn Bks) BDD LT Grp.
—Dear Mr. Henshaw. (gr. 4-7). 1992. pap. 1.99 (*0-440-21366-5*) Dell.
—Ellen Tebbits. Darling, Louis, illus. LC 51-11430. 160p. (gr. 3-7). 1951. 12.95 (*0-688-21264-6*); PLB 12.88 (*0-688-31264-0*, Morrow Jr Bks) Morrow Jr Bks.
—Ellen Tebbits. 160p. 1990. pap. 3.99 (*0-380-70913-9*, Camelot) Avon.
—Emily's Runaway Imagination. Krush, Joe & Krush, Beth, illus. LC 61-10939. 224p. (gr. 3-7). 1961. 12.95 (*0-688-21267-0*); PLB 12.88 (*0-688-31267-5*, Morrow Jr Bks) Morrow Jr Bks.
—Emily's Runaway Imagination. 224p. 1990. pap. 3.99 (*0-380-70923-6*, Camelot) Avon.
—Fifteen. Krush, Joe & Krush, Beth, illus. LC 56-7509. 256p. (gr. 6-9). 1956. 12.95 (*0-688-21285-9*); PLB 12.88 (*0-688-31285-3*, Morrow Jr Bks) Morrow Jr Bks.
—Fifteen. 192p. 1991. pap. 3.99 (*0-380-70920-1*, Flare) Avon.
—A Girl from Yamhill. (gr. k-6). 1989. pap. 4.50 (*0-440-40185-2*, YB) Dell.
—A Girl from Yamhill: A Memoir. LC 87-31554. (Illus.). 320p. (gr. 7 up). 1988. 15.95 (*0-688-07800-1*) Morrow Jr Bks.
—The Growing-Up Feet. DiSalvo-Ryan, DyAnne, illus. LC 86-12585. 32p. (ps-1). 1987. 11.95 (*0-688-06619-4*); lib. bdg. 11.88 (*0-688-06620-8*) Morrow Jr Bks.
—The Growing up Feet. DiSalvo-Ryan, DyAnne, illus. (gr. k-6). 1988. pap. 3.95 (*0-440-40109-7*, YB) Dell.
—Henry & Beezus. Darling, Louis, illus. LC 52-5930. 192p. (gr. 3-7). 1952. 13.95 (*0-688-21383-9*); PLB 13.88 (*0-688-31383-3*, Morrow Jr Bks) Morrow Jr Bks.
—Henry & Beezus. 1923. pap. 1.75 (*0-440-73295-6*) Dell.
—Henry & Ribsy. Darling, Louis, illus. LC 54-6402. 192p. (gr. 3-7). 1954. 12.95 (*0-688-21382-0*); PLB 12.88 (*0-688-31382-5*, Morrow Jr Bks) Morrow Jr Bks.
—Henry & Ribsy. 1923. pap. 1.75 (*0-440-73296-4*) Dell.
—Henry & the Clubhouse. Darling, Louis, illus. LC 62-7161. (gr. 3-7). 1962. 12.95 (*0-688-21381-2*); PLB 12.88 (*0-688-31381-7*, Morrow Jr Bks) Morrow Jr Bks.

—Henry & the Paper Route. Darling, Louis, illus. LC 57-8562. (gr. 3-7). 1957. 15.95 (0-688-21380-4); PLB 15.80 (0-688-31380-9) Morrow Jr Bks.

—Henry & the Paper Route. 192p. 1990. pap. 3.99 (0-380-70921-X, Camelot) Avon.

—Henry & the Paper Route. 1923. pap. 1.75 (0-440-73298-0) Dell.

—Henry Huggins. Darling, Louis, illus. LC 50-8615. (gr. 3-7). 1950. 13.95 (0-688-21385-5); PLB 13.88 (0-688-31385-X, Morrow Jr Bks) Morrow Jr Bks.

—Henry Huggins, 4 vols. (gr. 4-7). 1990. Boxed set. pap. 14.00 (0-380-71206-7, Camelot) Avon.

—Henry Huggins. 1923. pap. 1.75 (0-440-73551-3) Dell.

—Henry Huggins Clubhouse, 6 vols. (gr. 4-7). 1990. pap. 19.50 boxed set (0-440-36015-3) Dell.

—Janet's Thingamajigs. DiSalvo-Ryan, DyAnne, illus. (gr. k-6). 1988. pap. 4.95 (0-440-40108-9, YB) Dell.

—Jean & Johnny. 224p. (gr. 6-9). 1981. pap. 2.95 (0-440-94358-2, LE) Dell.

—Jean & Johnny. Krush, Beth & Krush, Joe, illus. LC 59-7806. 288p. (gr. 6-9). 1959. 12.95 (0-688-21740-0); PLB 12.88 (0-688-31740-5, Morrow Jr Bks) Morrow Jr Bks.

—Jean & Johnny. 240p. 1991. pap. 3.99 (0-380-70927-9, Flare) Avon.

—The Luckiest Girl. LC 58-6667. 228p. (gr. 7 up). 1958. PLB 12.88 (0-688-31741-3) Morrow Jr Bks.

—The Luckiest Girl. 224p. (gr. 5-6). 1991. pap. 3.99 (0-380-70922-8, Flare) Avon.

—Lucky Chuck. Higginbottom, J. Winslow, illus. LC 83-13386. 40p. (gr. k-3). 1984. 13.95 (0-688-02736-9); PLB 13.88 (0-688-02738-5, Morrow Jr Bks) Morrow Jr Bks.

—Meet Ramona Quimby, 5 bks. Incl. Ramona & Her Family; Ramona & Her Mother; Ramona Forever; Ramona Quimby Age Eight; Ramona the Pest. (gr. k-7). Boxed Set. pap. 15.50 (0-685-19114-1) Dell.

—Mitch & Amy. Porter, George, illus. LC 67-10041. 224p. (gr. 3-7). 1967. 15.95 (0-688-21688-9); PLB 15.88 (0-688-31688-3, Morrow Jr Bks) Morrow Jr Bks.

—Mitch & Amy. 224p. 1991. 3.50 (0-380-70925-2, Camelot) Avon.

—Mitch & Amy. reissued ed. Marstall, Bob, illus. LC 67-10041. 224p. (gr. 2 up). 1991. 13.95 (0-688-10806-7); PLB 13.88 (0-688-10807-5) Morrow Jr Bks.

—The Mouse & the Motorcycle. Darling, Louis, illus. LC 65-20956. (gr. 2-6). 1965. 13.95 (0-688-21698-6); PLB 13.88 (0-688-31698-0) Morrow Jr Bks.

—The Mouse & the Motorcycle. large type ed. 1989. Repr. of 1965 ed. lib. bdg. 15.95 (1-55736-137-1, Crnrstn Bks) BDD LT Grp.

—The Mouse & the Motorcycle. 160p. 1990. pap. 3.99 (0-380-70924-4, Camelot) Avon.

—Mouse House Trio, 3 vols. (gr. 4-7). 1990. pap. 9.75 (0-440-36016-1) Dell.

—Muggie Maggie. Life, Kay, illus. LC 89-38959. 80p. (gr. 7 up). 1990. 11.95 (0-688-08553-9); PLB 11.88 (0-688-08554-7) Morrow Jr Bks.

—Muggie Maggie. 80p. (3-4). 1991. pap. 3.99 (0-380-71087-0, Camelot) Avon.

—Otis Spofford. Darling, Louis, illus. LC 53-6660. 192p. (gr. 3-7). 1953. 12.95 (0-688-21720-6); PLB 12.88 (0-688-31720-0) Morrow Jr Bks.

—Otis Spofford. 192p. 1990. pap. 3.99 (0-380-70919-8, Camelot) Avon.

—Pen Pals, 6 vols. (gr. 4-7). 1990. pap. 17.70 boxed set (0-440-36028-5) Dell.

—Petey's Bedtime Story. Small, David, illus. LC 92-6184. 32p. (gr. k up). 1993. 15.00 (0-688-10660-9); PLB 14.93 (0-688-10661-7) Morrow Jr Bks.

—Ralph S. Mouse. Zelinsky, Paul O., illus. LC 82-3516. 160p. (gr. 4-6). 1982. 14.95 (0-688-01452-6); lib. bdg. 14.88 (0-688-01455-0) Morrow Jr Bks.

—Ralph S. Mouse. Zelinsky, Paul O., illus. 144p. (gr. 2-6). 1983. pap. 3.25 (0-440-47582-1, YB) Dell.

—Ralph S. Mouse. large type ed. 160p. 1989. Repr. of 1982 ed. lib. bdg. 15.95 (1-55736-136-3, Crnrstn Bks) BDD LT Grp.

—Ralph S. Mouse. 160p. (gr. 5). 1993. pap. 3.99 (0-380-70957-0, Camelot) Avon.

—Ramona & Her Father. Tiegreen, Alan, illus. LC 77-1614. 192p. (gr. 3-7). 1977. 13.95 (0-688-22114-9); PLB 13.88 (0-688-32114-3) Morrow Jr Bks.

—Ramona & Her Father. large type ed. 155p. (gr. 3-8). 1988. Repr. of 1977 ed. lib. bdg. 15.95 (1-55736-076-6, Crnrstn Bks) BDD LT Grp.

—Ramona & Her Father. 192p. (gr. 5-6). 1990. pap. 3.99 (0-380-70916-3, Camelot) Avon.

—Ramona & Her Father. 1923. pap. 2.95 (0-440-77241-9) Dell.

—Ramona & Her Friends. pap. 9.00 (0-440-47222-9) Dell.

—Ramona & Her Mother. LC 79-10323. (Illus.). 208p. (gr. 4-6). 1979. 13.95 (0-688-22195-5); PLB 13.88 (0-688-32195-X) Morrow Jr Bks.

—Ramona & Her Mother. 208p. 1990. pap. 3.99 (0-380-70952-X, Camelot) Avon.

—Ramona & Her Mother. 1923. pap. 2.95 (0-440-77243-5) Dell.

—Ramona, Forever. Tiegreen, Alan, illus. LC 84-704. 192p. (gr. 3-7). 1984. 13.95 (0-688-03785-2); PLB 13.88 (0-688-03786-0, Morrow Jr Bks) Morrow Jr Bks.

—Ramona, Forever. 192p. (gr. k-6). 1985. pap. 3.50 (0-440-47210-5, YB) Dell.

—Ramona Forever. large type ed. 192p. 1989. Repr. of 1984 ed. lib. bdg. 15.95 (1-55736-139-8, Crnrstn Bks) BDD LT Grp.

—Ramona Forever. 1985. pap. 2.95 (0-440-77210-9) Dell.

—Ramona Forever. (gr. 4-7). 1993. pap. 1.99 (0-440-21616-8) Dell.

—Ramona, Mouse, 4 vols. (gr. 4-7). 1990. Boxed Set. pap. 14.00 (0-380-71483-3, Camelot) Avon.

—Ramona Quimby, Age Eight. Tiegreen, Alan, illus. LC 80-28425. 192p. (gr. 4-6). 1981. 13.95 (0-688-00477-6); PLB 13.88 (0-688-00478-4) Morrow Jr Bks.

—Ramona Quimby, Age Eight. Tiegreen, Alan, illus. 192p. (gr. 3-7). 1982. pap. 3.25 (0-440-47350-0, YB) Dell.

—Ramona Quimby, Age Eight. 192p. 1992. pap. 3.99 (0-380-70956-2, Camelot) Avon.

—Ramona Quimby, Age 8. large type ed. Tiegreen, Alan, illus. 142p. (gr. 2-6). 1987. Repr. of 1981 ed. lib. bdg. 14.95 (1-55736-000-6, Crnrstn Bks) BDD LT Grp.

—The Ramona Quimby Diary. Tiegreen, Alan, illus. 160p. (gr. 3-7). 1984. pap. 10.95 spiral bdg. (0-688-03883-2, Pub. by Beech Tree Bks) Morrow.

—Ramona the Brave. Tiegreen, Alan, illus. LC 74-16494. 192p. (gr. 3-7). 1975. 13.95 (0-688-22015-0); PLB 13.88 (0-688-32015-5) Morrow Jr Bks.

—Ramona the Brave. Tiegreen, Alan, illus. 192p. (gr. k-6). 1984. pap. 3.25 (0-440-47351-9, YB) Dell.

—Ramona the Brave. large type ed. (Illus.). 143p. (gr. k-6). 1989. Repr. lib. bdg. 15.95 (1-55736-159-2, Crnrstn Bks) BDD LT Grp.

—Ramona the Brave. 1984. pap. 2.95 (0-440-77351-2) Dell.

—Ramona the Pest. 192p. (gr. 4-7). 1982. pap. 3.25 (0-440-47209-1, YB) Dell.

—Ramona the Pest. Darling, Louis, illus. LC 68-12981. (gr. 3-7). 1968. 13.95 (0-688-21721-4); PLB 13.88 (0-688-31721-9) Morrow Jr Bks.

—Ramona the Pest. large type ed. (Illus.). 175p. (gr. k-6). 1990. Repr. PLB 15.95 (1-55736-158-4, Crnrstn Bks) BDD LT Grp.

—Ramona the Pest. 192p. 1992. pap. 3.99 (0-380-70954-6, Camelot) Avon.

—Ramona the Pest. 1923. pap. 2.95 (0-440-77209-5) Dell.

—The Real Hole. rev. ed. Stevens, Mary, illus. LC 85-18815. 32p. (ps-1). 1986. 11.95 (0-688-05850-7); PLB 11.88 (0-688-05851-5) Morrow Jr Bks.

—The Real Hole. large type ed. (gr. k-6). 1987. pap. 3.95 (0-440-47521-X, YB) Dell.

—Ribsy. Darling, Louis, illus. 192p. (gr. 3-7). 1982. pap. 3.50 (0-440-47456-6, YB) Dell.

—Ribsy. Darling, Louis, illus. LC 64-13263. (gr. 3-7). 1964. 15.95 (0-688-21662-5); PLB 15.88 (0-688-31662-X) Morrow Jr Bks.

—Ribsy. 1923. pap. 2.50 (0-440-77456-X) Dell.

—Ribsy. 144p. 1992. pap. 3.99 (0-380-70955-4, Camelot) Avon.

—Runaway Ralph. 176p. (gr. k-6). 1981. pap. 3.25 (0-440-47519-8, YB) Dell.

—Runaway Ralph. LC 77-95786. (Illus.). (gr. 3-7). 1970. 14.95 (0-688-21701-X); PLB 14.88 (0-688-31701-4, Morrow Jr Bks) Morrow Jr Bks.

—Runaway Ralph. 176p. 1991. pap. 3.99 (0-380-70953-8, Camelot) Avon.

—Sister of the Bride. 128p. (gr. 6-9). 1981. pap. 2.75 (0-440-97596-4, LE) Dell.

—Sister of the Bride. Krush, Beth & Krush, Joe, illus. LC 63-8802. 256p. (gr. 7 up). 1963. PLB 13.88 (0-688-31742-1) Morrow Jr Bks.

—Sister of the Bride. 240p. (Orig.). (gr. 6). 1992. pap. 3.99 (0-380-70928-7, Flare) Avon.

—Socks. Darwin, Beatrice, illus. LC 72-10298. 160p. (gr. 3-7). 1973. 11.95 (0-688-20067-2); PLB 11.88 (0-688-30067-7, Morrow Jr Bks) Morrow Jr Bks.

—Socks. 160p. 1990. pap. 3.99 (0-380-70926-0, Camelot) Avon.

—Strider. Zelinsky, Paul O., illus. LC 90-6608. 192p. (gr. 3 up). 1991. 13.95 (0-688-09900-9); PLB 13.88 (0-688-09901-7) Morrow Jr Bks.

—Strider. 160p. 1992. pap. 3.99 (0-380-71236-9, Camelot) Avon.

—Two Dog Biscuits. rev. ed. DeSalvo-Ryan, Dyanne, illus. LC 85-18816. 32p. (ps-1). 1986. 11.95 (0-688-05847-7); lib. bdg. 11.88 (0-688-05848-5, Morrow Jr Bks) Morrow Jr Bks.

Cleary, Florence D. Discovering Books & Libraries: A Handbook for Students in the Middle & Upper Grades. 2nd ed. LC 76-55368. 196p. (gr. 7-12). 1977. pap. 10.00 (0-8242-0594-4) Wilson.

Cleave, Andrew, jt. auth. see Starry, Paul.

Cleaver. Moonlake Angel. (gr. k-6). 1989. pap. 2.95 (0-440-40165-8, YB) Dell.

Cleaver, Bill. Where the Lillies Bloom. LC 75-82402. 224p. (gr. 7 up). 1989. pap. 3.95 (0-06-447005-9, Trophy) HarpC Child Bks.

Cleaver, Bill, jt. auth. see Cleaver, Vera.

Cleaver, Elizabeth. The Loon's Necklace. Toye, William, retold by. Cleaver, Elizabeth, photos by. (Illus.). 24p. (ps up). 1990. pap. 7.50 (0-19-540675-3) OUP.

Cleaver, Vera. Belle Pruitt. LC 87-45879. 176p. (gr. k-7). 1988. (Lipp Jr Bks); PLB 13.89 (0-397-32305-0, Lipp Jr Bks) HarpC Child Bks.

—Ellen Grae. Raskin, Ellen, illus. LC 67-10623. 96p. 1967. PLB 12.89 (0-397-30938-4, Lipp Jr Bks) HarpC Child Bks.

—Hazel Rye. LC 85-42741. 192p. (gr. 5-8). 1985. pap. 3.95 (0-06-440156-1, Trophy) HarpC Child Bks.

—Moon Lake Angel. LC 86-15242. 160p. (gr. 7 up). 1987. 12.95 (0-688-04952-4) Lothrop.

—Sugar Blue. Nomes, Eric J., illus. LC 83-19910. 160p. (gr. 5 up). 1984. 13.00 (0-688-02720-2) Lothrop.

—Sugar Blue. (gr. 3-6). 1986. pap. 2.95 (0-440-48422-7, YB) Dell.

—Sweetly Sings the Donkey. LC 85-40098. 160p. (gr. 5-9). 1985. (Lipp Jr Bks); PLB 12.89 (0-397-32157-0, Lipp Jr Bks) HarpC Child Bks.

Cleaver, Vera & Cleaver, Bill. Delpha Green & Company. LC 79-172141. 144p. (gr. 6 up). 1972. (Junior Bks); pap. 2.95 (0-397-31344-6, LSC-8) HarpC.

—Grover. Marvin, Frederic, illus. LC 69-12001. 128p. (gr. 4-7). 1970. 13.00 (0-397-31118-4, Lipp Jr Bks) HarpC Child Bks.

—Hazel Rye. LC 81-48603. 160p. (gr. 5-8). 1983. (Lipp Jr Bks); PLB 13.89 (0-397-31952-5, Lipp Jr Bks) HarpC Child Bks.

—The Kissimmee Kid. LC 80-29262. 160p. (gr. 5 up). 1981. PLB 12.88 (0-688-51992-X) Lothrop.

—The Kissimmee Kid. LC 80-29262. 160p. (gr. 4-6). 1991. pap. 3.95 (0-688-10975-6, Pub. by Beech Tree Bks) Morrow.

—Queen of Hearts. LC 77-18252. 160p. (gr. 6 up). 1978. 14.00 (0-397-31771-9, Lipp Jr Bks) HarpC Child Bks.

—Queen of Hearts. LC 77-18252. 160p. (gr. 5 up). 1987. pap. 3.50 (0-06-440196-0, Trophy) HarpC Child Bks.

—Where the Lilies Bloom. LC 75-82402. (Illus.). 176p. (gr. 7 up). 1991. PLB 14.89 (0-397-32500-2, Lipp Jr Bks) HarpC Child Bks.

Cleeve, Roger. The Earth. Steltenpohl, Jane, ed. (Illus.). 32p. (gr. 3-5). 1990. lib. bdg. 10.98 (0-671-68626-7, J Messner); lib. bdg. 4.95 (0-671-68629-1) S&S Trade.

—The Living World. Steltenpohl, Jane, ed. (Illus.). 32p. (gr. 3-5). 1990. lib. bdg. 10.98 (0-671-68627-5, J Messner); pap. 4.95 (0-671-68630-5) S&S Trade.

—Outer Space. Steltenpohl, Jane, ed. (Illus.). 32p. (gr. 3-5). 1990. lib. bdg. 10.98 (0-671-68628-3, J Messner) S&S Trade.

—Science up Close Series, 3 vols. (Illus.). 96p. (gr. 3-5). 1990. Set. PLB 32.94 (0-671-94434-7, J Messner); Set. PLB 24.71s.p. (0-685-47007-5); Set. pap. 14.85 (0-671-94435-5); Set. pap. 11.14s.p. (0-685-47008-3) S&S Trade.

Clem, Stephen D. Study Guide: Advanced Placement French Literature, Prose & Theater for the 1992 Exam. (FRE.). 304p. (Orig.). (gr. 11-12). 1991. pap. text ed. 17.27 (1-877653-15-2) Wayside Pub.

Clemence, John. Electricity. Young, Richard, ed. LC 91-20534. (Illus.). 32p. (gr. 3-5). 1991. PLB 15.93 (1-56074-008-6) Garrett Ed Corp.

Clemens, Peter & Delgado, Jose. Super Wings: The Step-by-Step Paper Airplane Book. 64p. (ps-3). 1992. pap. 4.95 (0-929923-87-1) Lowell Hse.

Clemens, Samuel. Huckleberry Finn. Farr, Naunerle, ed. Redondo, Francisco, illus. LC 73-75468. 64p. (Orig.). (gr. 5-10). 1973. pap. 2.95 (0-88301-098-4) Pendulum Pr.

—Tom Sawyer. new ed. Shapiro, Irwin, ed. Cruz, E. R., illus. LC 73-75465. 64p. (Orig.). (gr. 5-10). 1973. pap. 2.95 (0-88301-103-4); student activity bk. 1.25 (0-88301-179-4) Pendulum Pr.

Clemens, Samuel see Twain, Mark, pseud.

Clemens, Samuel L. see Twain, Mark, pseud.

Clemens, Virginia P. Horse in Your Backyard: A First-Time Owner's Primer of Horse-Keeping. 1991. 19.95 (0-13-395088-3) P-H.

Clement, Claude. Be Careful, Little Antelope. Jensen, Patricia, adapted by. Pio, illus. LC 93-2950. 1993. write for info. (0-89577-504-2, Readers Digest Kids) RD Assn.

—Be Patient, Little Chick. Jensen, Patricia, adapted by. Erost, illus. LC 93-2951. 1993. write for info. (0-89577-503-4, Readers Digest Kids) RD Assn.

—Gentle Little Lion. Jensen, Patricia, adapted by. Geneste, Marcelle, illus. LC 93-27047. 1994. write for info. (0-89577-562-X, Readers Digest Kids) RD Assn.

—Go to Sleep, Little Groundhog. Nouvelle, Catherine, illus. LC 91-46234. 22p. (ps). 1992. 6.99 (0-89577-424-0, Readers Digest Kids) RD Assn.

—The Hungry Duckling. Geneste, Marcelle, illus. LC 91-40648. 22p. (ps). 1992. 6.99 (0-89577-418-6, Readers Digest Kids) RD Assn.

—Kitty's Special Job. Raquois, Olivier, illus. LC 91-46233. 22p. (ps). 1992. 6.99 (0-89577-427-5, Readers Digest Kids) RD Assn.

—Little Donkey Learns to Help. Jensen, Patricia, adapted by. Pascal, Robin, illus. LC 93-2952. 1993. write for info. (0-89577-502-6, Readers Digest Kids) RD Assn.

—Little Squirrel's Special Nest. Pons, Bernadette, illus. LC 93-4243. (gr. 4 up). 1993. write for info. (0-89577-542-5, Reader's Digest Kids) RD Assn.

—The Man Who Lit the Stars. Howe, John, illus. (ps-3). 1992. 15.95 (0-316-14741-9) Little.

—The Painter & the Wild Swans. Clement, Frederic, illus. LC 86-2154. 32p. (gr. k up). 1986. 13.95 (0-8037-0268-X) Dial Bks Young.

—The Voice of the Wood. Clement, Frederic, photos by. LC 88-22892. (Illus.). 32p. (gr. k up). 1989. 14.95 (0-8037-0635-9) Dial Bks Young.

—The Voice of the Wood. Clement, Frederic, illus. 32p. (gr. k-8). 1993. pap. 5.99 (0-14-054594-8) Puffin Bks.

Clement, Fred. Department of the Interior. Schlesinger, Arthur M., Jr., intro. by. (Illus.). 112p. (gr. 5 up). 1989. lib. bdg. 14.95 (0-87754-842-0) Chelsea Hse.

—The Nuclear Regulatory Commission. (Illus.). 104p. (gr. 5 up). 1988. 14.95 (1-55546-129-8) Chelsea Hse.

Clement, Jane T. The Sparrow. 4th ed. Hutterian Brethren Staff, ed. Mow, Kathy, illus. Moody, Ruby, intro. by. LC 68-21133. (Illus.). 212p. (gr. 4 up). 1992. pap. 10.00 (0-87486-009-1) Plough.

Clement, Rod. Counting on Frank. LC 90-27558. (Illus.). 32p. (gr. 1-3). 1991. PLB 18.60 (0-8368-0358-2) Gareth Stevens Inc.

Clements, Andrew. Big Al. Yoshi, illus. LC 88-15129. 28p. (ps up). 1991. pap. 14.95 (0-88708-075-8) Picture Bk Studio.

—Big Al. 2nd ed. Yoshi, illus. LC 88-15129. 32p. (gr. k up). 1991. pap. 4.95 (0-88708-154-1) Picture Bk Studio.

—Big Al. Yoshi, illus. 1991. pap. 3.95 (0-590-44455-7, Blue Ribbon Bks) Scholastic Inc.

—Billy & the Bad Teacher. Savadier, Elivia, illus. LC 92-6619. 28p. 1992. pap. 14.95 (0-88708-244-0) Picture Bk Studio.

—Mother Earth's Counting Book. Johnson, Lonni S., illus. LC 90-7343. 44p. (gr. k up). 1992. pap. 15.95 (0-88708-138-X) Picture Bk Studio.

—Noah & the Ark & the Animals. Gantschev, Ivan, illus. LC 84-9438. 28p. (gr. 1 up). 1991. pap. 14.95 (0-907234-58-5) Picture Bk Studio.

—Noah & the Ark & the Animals. Gantschev, Ivan, illus. 1992. pap. 4.95 (0-590-44457-3, Blue Ribbon Bks) Scholastic Inc.

—Noah & the Ark & the Animals. Gantschev, Ivan, illus. LC 90-24898. 28p. (gr. k up). 1991. pap. 4.95 (0-88708-169-X) Picture Bk Studio.

—Santa's Secret Helper. Santini, Debrah, illus. LC 90-8601. 32p. (gr. k up). 1991. pap. 14.95 (0-88708-136-3) Picture Bk Studio.

—Santa's Secret Helper. Santini, Debrah, illus. LC 93-20119. (gr. 1-8). 1993. 4.95 (0-88708-325-0) Picture Bk Studio.

Clements, Andrew, adapted by see Gantschev, Ivan.
Clements, Andrew, adapted by see Hirokazu Miyazaki.
Clements, Andrew, adapted by see Pacovska, Kveta.
Clements, Andrew, adapted by see Tharlet, Eve.
Clements, Andrew, tr. see Beaude, Pierre-Marie.
Clements, Andrew, tr. see Gantschev, Ivan.
Clements, Andrew, tr. see Lobato, Arcadio.
Clements, Andrew, tr. see Tharlet, Eve.

Clements, Bruce. Coming About. LC 83-47841. 180p. (gr. 5 up). 1984. 14.00 (0-374-31457-8) FS&G.

—Coming About. 1993. pap. 3.95 (0-374-41339-8) FS&G.

—I Tell a Lie Every So Often. LC 73-22356. 160p. (gr. 5 up). 1984. pap. 3.50 (0-374-43539-1) FS&G.

—Tom Loves Anna Loves Tom. (gr. 7 up). 1992. pap. 3.95 (0-374-47939-9) FS&G.

—The Treasure of Plunderell Manor. 192p. (gr. 7 up). 1991. pap. 3.95 (0-374-47962-3) FS&G.

—Two Against the Tide. 224p. (gr. 4 up). 1987. pap. 3.50 (0-374-48016-8) FS&G.

Clements, Gillian. Illustrated History of the World: How We Got to Where We Are. (Illus.). (gr. 4-7). 1992. 16.00 (0-374-33258-4) FS&G.

—The Picture History of Great Inventors. LC 93-21705. 1994. 13.00 (0-679-84787-1); 17.00 (0-679-84788-X) Knopf Bks Yng Read.

—The Truth about Castles. Clements, Gillian, illus. 40p. (gr. 2-6). 1990. PLB 18.95 (0-87614-401-6) Carolrhoda Bks.

—Truth about Castles. (gr. 4-7). 1991. pap. 6.95 (0-87614-552-7) Carolrhoda Bks.

Clements, Jan, jt. auth. see Windle, Jeanette.

Clements, Jehan. Alfred the Ant: The First Storytelling "Flip Over" Picture Book. Clements, Jehan, illus. LC 89-61138. 48p. (gr. k-3). 1991. 20.00 (0-9622500-0-7) Strytllr Co.

Clements, Samuel see Twain, Mark, pseud.

Clemesha, David, jt. auth. see Zimmerman, Andrea.

Clemmer Steiner, Susan. God Has No Favorites. Shelley, Maynard, ed. LC 89-84827. 97p. (Orig.). (gr. 8-12). 1989. pap. 4.95 (0-87303-134-2) Faith & Life.

Clemmons, Bradley & Witwer, Julia, illus. The Fish King's Power of Truth. Tulku, Tarthang, intro. by. LC 86-24159. 32p. (gr. k-4). 1987. PLB 14.95 (0-89800-158-7); pap. 7.95 (0-89800-144-7) Dharma Pub.

Clemons, Jack. Gruesome John Frederick: A Tale of Christmas. Hamel, Tom, illus. LC 87-71713. 73p. (Orig.). (gr. 4-5). 1988. pap. 6.00 (0-916383-30-X) Aegina Pr.

Clempner, Jane. Here, There & Everywhere: A Find & Name Picture Word Book. Moss, David, illus. 32p. (ps). 1993. 6.95 (0-8249-8590-7, Ideals Child) Hambleton-Hill.

Clemson, David & Clemson, Wendy. My Second Number Book. LC 93-25425. 1994. write for info. (1-56458-457-7) Dorling Kindersley.

Clemson, Wendy, jt. auth. see Clemson, David.

Clendenin, Mary J. Gonzalo, Coronado's Shepherd Boy. Roberts, Melissa, ed. (Illus.). 128p. (gr. 4-7). 1990. 10.95 (0-89015-700-6, Pub. by Panda Bks) Eakin-Sunbelt.

Cleveland, David. The April Rabbits. Karlin, Nurit, illus. 32p. (gr. k-3). 1986. pap. 2.95 (0-590-42369-X) Scholastic Inc.

—That's Life, 13 vols. Pascarella, Sam, illus. (gr. k-8). 1986. Each individual grade level: k-12. tchrs ed. 65.00 (1-56117-028-3); Eng. wkbk. 3.50 (0-685-29914-7); Span. wkbk. 3.95 (0-685-58484-4); preschool 35.00 (0-685-58485-2); complete k-12 curriculum set 795.00 (0-685-58486-0) Telesis CA.

Cleveland, Will & Alvarez, Mark. Yo! Millard Fillmore: And All Those Other Presidents You Never Heard Of. Nation, Tate, illus. 112p. (gr. 5). 1992. pap. 7.95 (0-9632778-0-4) Goodwood Pr.

—Yo, Millard Fillmore! And All Those Other Presidents You Never Heard Of. 2nd, rev. ed. Nation, Tate, illus. 112p. (Orig.). (gr. 5). 1993. pap. write for info. (0-9632778-1-2) Goodwood Pr.

Cleveland-Peck, Patricia. City Cat, Country Cat. Marklew, Gilly, illus. LC 91-42402. 32p. (ps). 1992. 14.00 (0-688-11644-2); PLB 13.93 (0-688-11645-0) Morrow Jr Bks.

Clevenger, Ernest A., Jr. Bible Characters. (gr. 3 up). 1990. pap. 4.75 (0-88428-018-7) Parchment Pr.

—The Church. 104p. (gr. 3 up). 1990. pap. 4.75 (0-88428-016-0) Parchment Pr.

Clevenger, Ernest, Jr. General Bible Knowledge Bible Drill: Flash Cards Flipbook. 104p. (gr. 3 up). 1990. pap. 4.75 (0-88428-017-9) Parchment Pr.

Clezio, J. M. Le see Le Clezio, J. M.

Cliff, Donna, ed. Simply Funtastic! Creative Play Ideas from Current (R) Kennedy-Smith, Kristin, illus. 32p. (gr. 1 up). 1993. pap. 6.10 (0-944943-31-4, CODE 21165-7) Current Inc.

Cliff, Donna, ed. see McConnell, Nancy P.

Clifford, Alan. The Middle Ages. Yapp, Malcolm, et al, eds. (Illus.). 1980. pap. text ed. 3.45 (0-89908-003-0) Greenhaven.

Clifford, E. Harvey's Horrible Snake Disaster. 1990. pap. 2.95 (0-671-72957-8, Minstrel Bks) PB.

Clifford, Eth. The Dastardly Murder of Dirty Pete. Hughes, George, illus. 128p. (gr. 2-5). 1981. 13.45 (0-395-31671-5) HM.

—Flatfoot Fox & the Case of the Missing Eye. Lies, Brian, illus. 48p. (gr. 2-5). 1990. 12.70 (0-395-51945-4) HM.

—Flatfoot Fox & the Case of the Missing Whoooo. Lies, Brian, illus. LC 92-21903. 1993. 13.95 (0-395-65364-9) HM.

—Flatfoot Fox & the Case of the Missing Eye. (gr. 4-7). 1992. pap. 2.95 (0-590-45812-4) Scholastic Inc.

—Flatfoot Fox & the Case of the Nosy Otter. Lies, Brian, illus. LC 91-26930. 48p. (gr. 2-5). 1992. 13.45 (0-395-60289-0) HM.

—Harvey's Horrible Snake Disaster. LC 83-27299. 128p. (gr. 3-6). 1984. 13.45 (0-395-35378-5, S-83913) HM.

—Harvey's Marvelous Monkey Mystery. LC 86-20837. (gr. 3-6). 1987. 13.45 (0-395-42622-7) HM.

—Harvey's Marvelous Monkey Mystery. (gr. 3-7). 1990. pap. 2.95 (0-671-70927-5) PB.

—Harvey's Wacky Parrot Adventure. 112p. (gr. 3-7). 1990. 13.45 (0-395-53352-X) HM.

—Harvey's Wacky Parrot Adventure. MacDonald, Patricia, ed. 128p. 1991. pap. 2.95 (0-671-72908-X, Minstrel Bks) PB.

—Help! I'm a Prisoner in the Library. (Illus.). 112p. (gr. 2-5). 1979. 13.45 (0-395-28478-3) HM.

—Help! I'm a Prisoner in the Library. 96p. (gr. 4-6). 1991. pap. 2.95 (0-590-44351-8, Apple Paperbacks) Scholastic Inc.

—I Hate Your Guts, Ben Brooster. 112p. (gr. 3-7). 1989. 13.45 (0-395-51079-1) HM.

—I Hate Your Guts, Ben Brooster. 144p. 1990. pap. 2.75 (0-590-43534-5) Scholastic Inc.

—Just Tell Me When We're Dead! Hughes, George, illus. LC 83-10865. 144p. (gr. 2-5). 1983. 13.45 (0-395-33071-8) HM.

—Just Tell Me When We're Dead! (gr. 5-7). 1985. pap. 2.75 (0-590-44010-1, Apple Paperbacks) Scholastic Inc.

—The Man Who Sang in the Dark. Owen, Mary B., illus. 96p. (gr. 2-5). 1987. 13.95 (0-395-43664-8) HM.

—Never Hit a Ghost with a Baseball Bat. Hughes, George, illus. LC 92-8347. 128p. (gr. 3-5). 1993. 13.95 (0-395-61587-9) HM.

—The Remembering Box. Diamond, Donna, illus. 64p. (gr. 2-5). 1985. 13.45 (0-395-38476-1) HM.

—The Remembering Box. ALC Staff, ed. LC 85-10851. 96p. (gr. 5-12). 1992. pap. 3.95 (0-688-11777-5, Pub. by Beech Tree Bks) Morrow.

—Scared Silly. Hughes, George, illus. LC 87-30694. 128p. (gr. 3-7). 1988. 13.45 (0-395-46845-0) HM.

—Scared Silly. 1989. pap. 2.75 (0-590-42382-7) Scholastic Inc.

—The Summer of the Dancing Horse. Owens, Mary B., illus. LC 90-4939. 112p. (gr. 3-7). 1991. 13.45 (0-395-50066-4) HM.

—The Summer of the Dancing Horse. 1992. pap. 2.95 (0-590-45400-5, Apple Paperbacks) Scholastic Inc.

—Will Somebody Please Marry My Sister? Eagle, Ellen, illus. 128p. (gr. 3-6). 1992. 13.45 (0-395-58037-4) HM.

—Will Somebody Please Marry My Sister? (gr. 4-7). 1993. pap. 2.95 (0-590-46624-0) Scholastic Inc.

Clifford, Mary L. The Land & People of Afghanistan. LC 88-21419. (Illus.). 240p. (gr. 6 up). 1989. 18.00 (0-397-32338-7, Lipp Jr Bks); PLB 14.89 (0-397-32339-5, Lipp Jr Bks) HarpC Child Bks.

—When the Great Canoes Came. Haynes, Joyce, illus. LC 92-27913. 1993. 12.95 (0-88289-926-0) Pelican.

Clifton. Everett Anderson's Nine Month Long. LC 78-2402. (ps-2). 1988. pap. 4.95 (0-8050-0295-2, Bks Young Read) H Holt & Co.

Clifton, Fred. Darl. (Illus.). 104p. (gr. 2-6). 1973. 12.00 (0-89388-098-1) Okpaku Communications.

Clifton, James A. The Potawatomi. Porter, Frank, intro. by. (Illus.). 99p. (gr. 5 up). 1987. lib. bdg. 17.95x (1-55546-725-3) Chelsea Hse.

Clifton, Lucille. The Boy Who Didn't Believe in Spring. Turkle, Brinton, illus. (gr. 3-4). 1973. 13.95 (0-525-27145-7, DCB); pap. 1.95 (0-525-45038-6, DCB) Dutton Child Bks.

—The Boy Who Didn't Believe in Spring. Turkle, Brinton, illus. LC 87-27145. 32p. (ps-3). 1988. pap. 4.95 (0-525-44365-7, 0383-120, DCB) Dutton Child Bks.

—The Boy Who Didn't Believe in Spring. 06/1992 ed. (ps-3). 1992. pap. 4.99 (0-14-054739-8) Viking Child Bks.

—Everett Anderson's Christmas Coming. Gilchrist, Jan S., illus. LC 91-2041. 32p. (ps-4). 1991. 14.95 (0-8050-1549-3, Bks Young Read) H Holt & Co.

—Everett Anderson's Christmas Coming. Gilchrist, Jan S., illus. LC 91-2041. 32p. (ps-4). 1993. pap. 4.95 (0-8050-2949-4, Bks Young Read) H Holt & Co.

—Everett Anderson's Friend. Grifalconi, Ann, illus. LC 92-8030. 32p. (ps-3). 1992. 14.95 (0-8050-2246-5, Bks Young Read) H Holt & Co.

—Everett Anderson's Goodbye. Grifalconi, Ann, illus. LC 82-23426. 32p. (Orig.). (ps-2). 1988. pap. 5.95 (0-8050-0800-4, Bks Young Read) H Holt & Co.

—Everett Anderson's Nine Month Long. Grifalconi, Ann, illus. LC 78-2402. 32p. (ps-2). 1978. 13.95 (0-8050-0287-1, Bks Young Read) H Holt & Co.

—Everett Anderson's Year. rev. ed. Grifalconi, Ann, illus. LC 92-4683. 32p. (ps-2). 1992. 14.95 (0-8050-2247-3, Bks Young Read) H Holt & Co.

—Everett Anderson's 1-2-3. Grifalconi, Ann, illus. LC 92-8031. 32p. (ps-2). 1992. 14.95 (0-8050-2310-0, Bks Young Read) H Holt & Co.

—The Lucky Stone. Payson, Dale, illus. LC 78-72862. 64p. (gr. 4-6). 1979. pap. 6.46 (0-385-28600-7) Delacorte.

—Lucky Stone. Payson, Dale, illus. (gr. 2-5). 1986. pap. 2.99 (0-440-45110-8, YB) Dell.

—The Lucky Stone. (gr. 1-4). 1992. 16.25 (0-8446-6592-4) Peter Smith.

—Some of the Days of Everett Anderson. Ness, Evaline, illus. LC 78-98922. 32p. (ps-2). 1988. 13.95 (0-8050-0290-1, Bks Young Read) H Holt & Co.

—Some of the Days of Everett Anderson. 32p. (ps-2). 1987. pap. 5.95 (0-8050-0289-8, Bks. Young Read) H Holt & Co.

—Three Wishes. (ps-3). 1992. 15.00 (0-385-30497-8) Doubleday.

—Three Wishes. (ps-3). 1994. pap. 4.99 (0-440-40921-7) Dell.

Clifton, Lucille, et al. Everett Anderson's Goodbye. Grifalconi, Ann, illus. LC 82-23426. 32p. (ps-2). 1983. 14.95 (0-8050-0235-9, Bks Young Read) H Holt & Co.

Climo. If You Meet a Mermaid. Date not set. 15.00 (0-06-023876-3, Festival); PLB 14.89 (0-06-023877-1, Festival) HarpC Child Bks.

Climo, Lindee. Chester's Barn. Climo, Lindee, illus. LC 82-50243. (gr. 1-5). 1982. pap. 6.95 (0-88776-155-0) Tundra Bks.

Climo, Shirley. City! New York. Ancona, George, illus. LC 89-13482. 64p. (gr. 3-7). 1990. RSBE 16.95 (0-02-719020-X, Macmillan Child Bk) Macmillan Child Grp.

—City! San Francisco. LC 89-32912. (Illus.). 64p. (gr. 3-7). 1990. RSBE 16.95 (0-02-719030-7, Macmillan Child Bk) Macmillan Child Grp.

—City! Washington, D. C. Ancona, George, illus. LC 90-1785. 64p. (gr. 3-7). 1991. SBE 16.95 (0-02-719036-6, Macmillan Child Bk) Macmillan Child Grp.

—Cobweb Christmas. Lasker, Joe, illus. LC 81-43879. 32p. (ps-3). 1982. 15.00 (0-690-04215-9, Crowell Jr Bks); PLB 14.89 (0-690-04216-7) HarpC Child Bks.

—The Cobweb Christmas. Lasker, Joe, illus. LC 81-43879. 32p. (ps-3). 1986. pap. 4.50 (0-06-443110-X, Trophy) HarpC Child Bks.

—The Egyptian Cinderella. Heller, Ruth, illus. LC 88-37547. 32p. (gr. k-3). 1989. 15.00 (0-690-04822-X, Crowell Jr Bks); PLB 14.89 (0-690-04824-6, Crowell Jr Bks) HarpC Child Bks.

—The Egyptian Cinderella. Heller, Ruth, illus. LC 88-37547. 32p. (gr. k-3). 1992. pap. 4.95 (0-06-443279-3, Trophy) HarpC Child Bks.

—King of the Birds. Heller, Ruth, illus. LC 87-47693. 32p. (gr. k-3). 1988. 15.00 (0-690-04621-9, Crowell Jr Bks); PLB 14.89 (0-690-04623-5) HarpC Child Bks.

—King of the Birds. Heller, Ruth, illus. LC 87-47693. 32p. (gr. k-3). 1991. pap. 4.95 (0-06-443273-4, Trophy) HarpC Child Bks.

—Korean Cinderella. Heller, Ruth, illus. LC 93-23268. 48p. (gr. k-3). 1993. 15.00 (0-06-020432-X); PLB 14.89 (0-06-020433-8) HarpC Child Bks.

—The Match Between the Winds. Shepherd, Roni, illus. LC 90-1785. 32p. (ps-3). 1991. RSBE 13.95 (0-02-719035-8, Macmillan Child Bk) Macmillan Child Grp.

—A Month of Seven Days. LC 87-5259. 192p. (gr. 5 up). 1987. (Crowell Jr Bks); PLB 12.89 (0-690-04656-1, Crowell Jr Bks) HarpC Child Bks.

—Month of Seven Days. 192p. (gr. 2-9). 1989. pap. 2.95 (0-8167-1476-2) Troll Assocs.

—Someone Saw a Spider: Spider Facts & Folktales. LC 85-45340. (Illus.). 128p. (gr. 4-7). 1985. 14.00 (0-690-04435-6, Crowell Jr Bks); PLB 13.89 (0-690-04436-4, Crowell Jr Bks) HarpC Child Bks.

—Stolen Thunder: A Norse Myth. Koshkin, Alexander, illus. LC 93-24627. 1994. write for info. (0-395-64368-6, Clarion Bks) HM.

Cline, Don. Antrim & Billy. Metz, Leon, intro. by. LC 90-1598. (Illus.). 170p. 1990. 21.95 (0-932702-48-1) Creative Texas.

Cline, Paul. Booboo's Dream. Cline, Paul & Sieck, Judyth, illus. 32p. (ps-8). 1990. 12.95 (*0-9625261-1-8*) Medlicott Pr.
—Ginger's Moon. Sieck, Judythe, illus. (ps-8). 1990. 11.95 (*0-9625261-0-X*); PLB write for info. Medlicott Pr.
—Grummit's Day. 1991. 12.95 (*0-9625261-3-4*) Medlicott Pr.
—My Mother's Hands. 1991. pap. 5.95 (*0-9625261-2-6*) Medlicott Pr.
Cline, Paul, jt. auth. see McGraw, Sheila.
Cline, Ruth K. J. Focus on Families: A Reference Handbook. 230p. (gr. 9-12). 1989. lib. bdg. 39.00 (*0-87436-508-2*) ABC Clio.
Cline, Starr. Teaching for Talent. Taylor, Christina, illus. Tannenbaum, A. J., intro. by. (Illus.). 56p. (Orig.). (gr. k-6). 1984. 6.50 (*0-88047-040-2*, 8406) DOK Pubs.
Clinton, Bill see Williams, C. Fred.
Clinton, Patrick. I Can Be a Father. LC 88-11749. (Illus.). 32p. (gr. k-3). 1988. pap. 3.95 (*0-516-41904-8*) Childrens.
—The Story of the Empire State Building. LC 87-25687. (Illus.). 32p. (gr. 3-6). 1987. pap. 3.95 (*0-516-44730-0*) Childrens.
Clinton, Susan. Benjamin Harrison. LC 89-33751. 100p. (ps up). 1989. PLB 17.27 (*0-516-01370-X*) Childrens.
—Henry Stanley & David Livingstone: Explorers of Africa. LC 90-2172. (Illus.). 128p. (gr. 3 up). 1990. PLB 26.60 (*0-516-03055-8*) Childrens.
—Herbert Hoover. LC 87-35711. (Illus.). 100p. (gr. 3 up). 1988. PLB 17.27 (*0-516-01355-6*); pap. 6.95 (*0-516-41355-4*) Childrens.
—I Can Be an Architect. LC 85-28004. (Illus.). 32p. (gr. k-3). 1986. PLB 14.60 (*0-516-01890-6*); pap. 3.95 (*0-516-41890-4*) Childrens.
—James Madison. LC 86-13630. (Illus.). 100p. (gr. 3 up). 1986. PLB 17.27 (*0-516-01382-3*); pap. 6.95 (*0-516-41382-1*) Childrens.
—Live Aid. LC 92-33423. (Illus.). 32p. (gr. 3-6). 1993. PLB 15.27 (*0-516-06665-X*); pap. 3.95 (*0-516-46665-8*) Childrens.
—The Story of Susan B. Anthony. Canaday, Ralph, illus. LC 86-9613. 32p. (gr. 3-6). 1986. PLB 13.27 (*0-516-04705-1*) Childrens.
Clinton, Susan, jt. auth. see Alvarez, Everett, Jr.
Clinton, Susan M. The Cuban Missile Crisis. LC 93-12689. (Illus.). 32p. (gr. 3-6). 1993. PLB 15.93 (*0-516-06667-6*) Childrens.
Clise, Michele D. No Bad Bears: Ophelia's Book of Manners. (Illus.). 32p. 1992. 14.00 (*0-670-83883-7*) Viking Child Bks.
Clohe, Rene. Fairyland Favorites: Town Mouse & Country Mouse. 1989. 2.98 (*0-671-06188-7*) S&S Trade.
Cloke, Rene. Br'er Rabbit Stories. 1988. 2.98 (*0-671-06187-9*) S&S Trade.
Cloonan, Paula, illus. The Twelve Days of Christmas. 24p. (gr. k-3). 1990. PLB 14.95 (*0-87226-438-6*, Bedrick Blackie) P Bedrick Bks.
Clooney, Francis X. Confucianism. (Illus.). 128p. (gr. 7-12). 1992. bds. 17.95x (*0-8160-2445-6*) Facts on File.
Close, Arthur C. National Directory of Corporate Public Affairs, 1994. 13th ed. 1994. pap. 90.00 (*1-880873-05-2*) Columbia Bks.
Close, Glenn, read by see Irving, Washington.
Close, Jim, jt. auth. see Cassidy, Pat.
Close Up Foundation Staff. The American Economy: Government's Role, Citizen's Choice. (Illus.). 61p. (gr. 9-12). 1991. pap. text ed. 9.95 (*0-932765-37-8*); tchr's. guide 9.95 (*0-685-62333-5*) Close Up.
—International Relations: Understanding the Behavior of Nations. (Illus.). 80p. (gr. 9-12). 1991. pap. text ed. 9.95 (*0-932765-35-1*); tchr's. guide 9.95 (*0-685-62333-7*) Close Up.
—U. S.-Soviet Relations. rev. ed. (Illus.). 43p. (gr. 11-12). 1986. pap. text ed. 9.95 (*0-932765-07-6*); video & tchr's. guide avail. Close Up.
Closser, Lynne, ed. see John, Da Free.
Clough, Brenda W. An Impossumble Summer. 160p. (gr. 3-6). 1992. 14.95 (*0-8027-8150-0*) Walker & Co.
Clough, Fred. Sal T. Dog. Kirehoff, Dan, illus. 48p. (gr. 1-3). 1990. 12.95 (*0-89272-281-9*) Down East.
Clouse, Nancy, jt. auth. see Aardema, Verna.
Clouse, Nancy L. Puzzle Maps U. S. A. Clouse, Nancy L., illus. LC 89-24604. 32p. (ps-2). 1990. 15.95 (*0-8050-1143-9*, Bks Young Read) H Holt & Co.
Cloutier, James. This Day in Oregon. Cloutier, James, illus. LC 80-83719. 128p. 1981. pap. 6.95 (*0-918966-06-X*) Image West.
Cloverdale Press Editors. Out of Bounds. 160p. (gr. 6 up). 1987. pap. 2.50 (*0-553-26338-2*, Starfire) Bantam.
Cloverdale Press, Inc. Editors, ed. Varsity Takedown Coach, No. 2. 128p. 1987. pap. 2.50 (*0-553-26209-2*) Bantam.
Cloverdale Press Staff. Cheating Heart. 1992. pap. 2.99 (*0-553-29451-2*) Bantam.
—Down with Love! 144p. 1991. pap. 2.99 (*0-553-29144-0*) Bantam.
—Love on the Upbeat. 1992. pap. 2.99 (*0-553-29453-9*) Bantam.
—Lucky in Love. 1992. pap. 2.99 (*0-553-29456-3*) Bantam.
—Play Me a Love Song. 1992. pap. 2.99 (*0-553-29450-4*) Bantam.
—Sweet Dreams. 1992. pap. 2.99 (*0-553-29452-0*) Bantam.
—Trust in Love. 176p. (Orig.). 1988. pap. 2.50 (*0-553-27229-2*, Sweet Dreams) Bantam.

Cloverdale Staff. Finders, Keepers. 1994. pap. 3.50 (*0-553-56478-1*) Bantam.
—Highland Hearts. 1994. 3.50 (*0-553-56477-3*) Bantam.
Clowney, Earle D., tr. see Middlebrooks-Hutcherson, Gracie.
Clucas, Joan. Mother Teresa. Schlesinger, Arthur M., Jr., intro. by. (Illus.). 112p. (Orig.). (gr. 5 up). 1988. 17.95 (*1-55546-855-1*); pap. 9.95 (*0-7910-0602-6*) Chelsea Hse.
Clute, jt. auth. see Fritz.
Clutterbuck, Mary, illus. Animals & Birds of the Desert. 32p. (gr. 3-5). 1985. 7.95x (*0-86685-445-2*) Intl Bk Ctr.
Clutton-Brock, Juliet. Cat. King, Dave, photos by. LC 91-9399. (Illus.). 64p. (gr. 5 up). 1991. 15.00 (*0-679-81458-2*); lib. bdg. 15.99 (*0-679-91458-7*) Knopf Bks Yng Read.
—Dog. Young, Jerry, photos by. LC 91-10135. (Illus.). 64p. (gr. 5 up). 1991. 15.00 (*0-679-81459-0*); lib. bdg. 15.99 (*0-679-91459-5*) Knopf Bks Yng Read.
—Horse. Young, Jerry, photos by. LC 91-53132. (Illus.). 64p. (gr. 5 up). 1992. 15.00 (*0-679-81681-X*); PLB 15.99 (*0-679-91681-4*) Knopf Bks Yng Read.
Clyde, Ahmad. Cheng Ho's Voyage. Durkee, Noura, illus. LC 81-66951. 32p. (Orig.). (gr. 3-7). 1981. pap. 2.00 (*0-89259-021-1*) Am Trust Pubns.
Clymer, E. The Spider, the Cave, & the Pottery Bowl. 80p. (gr. k-6). 1989. pap. 2.99 (*0-440-40166-6*, YB) Dell.
Clymer, Eleanor. The Horse in the Attic. Lewin, Ted, illus. LC 83-6377. 96p. (gr. 3-6). 1983. SBE 12.95 (*0-02-719040-4*, Bradbury Pr) Macmillan Child Grp.
—The Horse in the Attic. 96p. (gr. 4-6). 1985. pap. 2.50 (*0-440-43798-9*, YB) Dell.
—Luke Was There. (gr. 4-6). 1992. 16.00 (*0-8446-6599-1*) Peter Smith.
—My Mother Is the Smartest Woman in the World. Kincade, Nancy, illus. LC 82-1685. 96p. (gr. 4-6). 1982. SBE 12.95 (*0-689-30916-3*, Atheneum Child Bk) Macmillan Child Grp.
—Santiago's Silver Mine. 80p. (Orig.). (gr. k-6). 1989. pap. 2.75 (*0-440-40157-7*, YB) Dell.
—A Search for Two Bad Mice. Gill, Margery, illus. LC 91-2453. 80p. (gr. 1-4). 1991. pap. 3.50 (*0-689-71537-4*, Aladdin) Macmillan Child Grp.
—The Spider, the Cave & the Pottery Bowl. (gr. k-6). 1992. 16.50 (*0-8446-6578-9*) Peter Smith.
—We Lived in the Almont. 112p. (Orig.). (gr. k-6). 1989. pap. 2.75 (*0-440-40144-5*, YB) Dell.
Clymer, Susan. Halloween Echo. (gr. 4-7). 1993. pap. 2.75 (*0-590-46164-8*) Scholastic Inc.
—Scrawny, the Classroom Duck. Ormai, Stella, illus. 96p. (gr. 2-5). 1991. pap. 2.50 (*0-590-43729-1*) Scholastic Inc.
Clyne, Densey. Catch Me If You Can! 1993. pap. 6.95 (*0-685-63824-3*) Routledge Chapman & Hall.
—Catch Me If You Can! (gr. 4-7). 1993. pap. 6.95 (*1-86373-205-5*, Pub. by Allen & Unwin Aust Pty AT) IPG Chicago.
—Plants of Prey. (Illus.). 32p. (Orig.). (gr. 1-5). 1993. pap. 6.95 (*1-86373-132-6*, Pub. by Allen & Unwin Aust Pty AT) IPG Chicago.
Clyne, Patricia E. The Corduroy Road. Cary, illus. (gr. 5-9). 1984. 15.25 (*0-8446-6163-5*) Peter Smith.
CMSP Projects. Applied Math Concepts: Lines & Perimeters Area & Volume. rev. ed. (Illus.). 91p. pap. text ed. write for info. (*0-942851-01-3*) CMSP Projects.
—Prealgebra. rev. ed. (Illus.). 101p. pap. text ed. write for info. (*0-942851-00-5*) CMSP Projects.
Co-Op Kids, jt. auth. see Higgins, Susan O.
Coad, Penelope. Goodnight. Falla, Dominique, illus. LC 92-31960. 1993. 4.25 (*0-383-03569-4*) SRA Schl Grp.
Coady, Christopher, retold by. & illus. Red Riding Hood. LC 91-25567. 32p. (ps-6). 1992. 15.00 (*0-525-44896-9*, DCB) Dutton Child Bks.
Coalition for Child Advocacy Staff. Touching. Bergsma, Jody, illus. 32p. (Orig.). (ps). 1985. pap. 5.95 (*0-934671-00-1*) Whatcom Cty Corp.
Coan, Sharon, ed. see Brown, Marzella.
Coates, Anna. Dog Magic. (gr. 4-7). 1991. pap. 2.99 (*0-553-15910-0*, Skylark) Bantam.
Coates, Bryan E. Japan. (Illus.). 32p. (gr. k-4). 1991. 12.40 (*0-531-18392-0*, Pub. by Bookwright Pr) Watts.
Coates, Earl J. & Thomas, Dean S. An Introduction to Civil War Small Arms. (Illus.). 96p. 1990. pap. text ed. 7.95 (*0-939631-25-3*) Thomas Publications.
Coats, Carolyn & Smith, Pamela. Come Cook with Me! A Cookbook for Kids. Coats, Carolyn, illus. 133p. 1989. pap. 10.00 spiral bound (*1-878722-06-9*) C Coats Bestsellers.
Coats, Laura J. The Almond Orchard. LC 90-38009. (Illus.). 32p. (gr. 1-4). 1991. RSBE 14.95 (*0-02-719041-2*, Macmillan Child Bk) Macmillan Child Grp.
—Alphabet Garden. Coats, Laura J., illus. LC 92-6235. 32p. (ps-1). 1993. RSBE 13.95 (*0-02-719042-0*, Macmillan Child Bk) Macmillan Child Grp.
—Mr. Jordan in the Park. Coats, Laura J., illus. LC 88-13295. 32p. (gr. k-3). 1989. RSBE 14.95 (*0-02-719053-6*, Macmillan Child Bk) Macmillan Child Grp.
—Ten Little Animals. Coats, Laura J., illus. LC 89-36778. 32p. (ps-1). 1990. RSBE 12.95 (*0-02-719054-4*, Macmillan Child Bk) Macmillan Child Grp.

Coatsworth, Elizabeth. The Cat Who Went to Heaven. reissued ed. Ward, Lynd, illus. LC 58-10917. 72p. (gr. 4-6). 1967. RSBE 13.95 (*0-02-719710-7*, Macmillan Child Bk) Macmillan Child Grp.
—The Cat Who Went to Heaven. (gr. 4-6). 1972. pap. 4.95 (*0-02-042580-5*, Aladdin) Macmillan Child Grp.
—The Cat Who Went to Heaven. rev. ed. Ward, Lynd & Jael, illus. LC 90-175. 80p. (gr. 3-7). 1990. pap. 3.95 (*0-689-71433-5*, Aladdin) Macmillan Child Grp.
—Under the Green Willow. Domanska, Janina, illus. LC 84-1471. 24p. (gr. k-3). 1984. 9.25 (*0-688-03845-X*); PLB 8.59 (*0-688-03846-8*) Greenwillow.
Cobb, Alice, jt. auth. see Fahs, Sophia L.
Cobb, Annie. Bear's New House. Wilburn, Kathy, illus. 32p. (gr. k-3). 1991. 6.95 (*0-671-70397-8*); PLB 10.98 (*0-671-70393-5*) Silver Pr.
—Detective Duckworth to the Rescue. Wilburn, Kathy, illus. 32p. (gr. k-3). 1991. 6.95 (*0-671-70398-6*); PLB 10.98 (*0-671-70394-3*) Silver Pr.
—Going Places Series, 4 vols. Wilburn, Kathy, illus. (gr. k-3). 1991. Set, 32p. ea. 27.80 (*0-671-31248-0*); Set, 32p. ea. lib. bdg. 43.92 (*0-671-31247-2*) Silver Pr.
—Mouse's Birthday Party. Wilburn, Kathy, illus. 32p. (gr. k-3). 1991. 6.95 (*0-671-70396-X*); PLB 10.98 (*0-671-70392-7*) Silver Pr.
—Squirrel's Treasure Hunt. Wilburn, Kathy, illus. 32p. (gr. k-3). 1991. PLB 10.98 (*0-671-70391-9*); 6.95 (*0-671-70395-1*) Silver Pr.
Cobb, Joshua, jt. auth. see Cobb, Vicki.
Cobb, Vicki. Bet You Can: Science Possibilities to Fool You. 112p. 1990. 12.95 (*0-688-09865-7*) Lothrop.
—Brush, Comb, Scrub: Inventions to Keep You Clean. Hafner, Marylin, illus. LC 88-2930. 32p. (gr. 1-4). 1993. pap. 3.95 (*0-06-446107-6*, Trophy) HarpC Child Bks.
—Chemically Active! Experiments You Can Do at Home. Cobb, Theo, illus. LC 83-49490. 160p. (gr. 5-8). 1985. (Lipp Jr Bks); PLB 14.89 (*0-397-32080-9*, Lipp Jr Bks) HarpC Child Bks.
—Chemically Active: Experiments You Can Do at Home. reissue ed. Cobb, Theo, illus. LC 83-49490. 160p. (gr. 6-8). 1990. pap. 4.95 (*0-06-446101-7*, Trophy) HarpC Child Bks.
—Feeding Yourself. Hafner, Marylin, illus. LC 88-14192. 32p. (gr. k-3). 1989. (Lipp Jr Bks); PLB 11.89 (*0-397-32325-5*, Lipp Jr Bks) HarpC Child Bks.
—For Your Own Protection: Stories Science Photos Tell. LC 89-2342. (Illus.). 32p. (gr. 3-6). 1989. 14.95 (*0-688-08787-6*); PLB 14.88 (*0-688-08788-4*) Lothrop.
—Fun & Games: Stories Science Photos Tell. LC 90-22792. (Illus.). 32p. (gr. 3 up). 1991. 15.95 (*0-688-09315-9*); PLB 15.88 (*0-688-09316-7*) Lothrop.
—Getting Dressed. Hafner, Marylin, illus. LC 87-26097. 32p. (gr. k-3). 1989. (Lipp Jr Bks); PLB 11.89 (*0-397-32143-0*) HarpC Child Bks.
—Gobs of Goo. Schatell, Brain, illus. LC 82-48457. 40p. (gr. 1-3). 1983. (Lipp Jr Bks); PLB 13.89 (*0-397-32022-1*) HarpC Child Bks.
—How to Really Fool Yourself: Illusions for All Your Senses. LC 79-9620. (Illus.). 160p. (gr. 5 up). 1981. (Lipp Jr Bks); PLB 13.89 (*0-397-31907-X*, Lipp Jr Bks) HarpC Child Bks.
—Keeping Clean. Hafner, Marylin, illus. LC 88-2930. 32p. (gr. k-3). 1989. 11.95 (*0-397-32312-3*, Lipp Jr Bks); PLB 11.89 (*0-397-32313-1*) HarpC Child Bks.
—Lots of Rot. Schatell, Brian, illus. LC 80-8726. 40p. (gr. 1-3). 1981. (Lipp Jr Bks); PLB 15.89 (*0-397-31939-8*) HarpC Child Bks.
—Magic...Naturally: Science Entertainments & Amusements. new ed. Kalish, Lionel, illus. LC 90-21829. 160p. (gr. 4 up). 1993. pap. 4.95 (*0-06-446031-2*, Trophy) HarpC Child Bks.
—Magic...Naturally! Science Entertainments & Amusements. Kalish, Lionel, illus. LC 90-21829. 160p. (gr. 4 up). 1993. 15.00 (*0-06-022474-6*); PLB 14.89 (*0-06-022475-4*) HarpC Child Bks.
—The Monsters Who Died: A Mystery about Dinosaurs. Wenzel, Greg, illus. 64p. (gr. 3-6). 1983. 13.95 (*0-698-20571-5*, Coward) Putnam Pub Group.
—More Power to You! Ogden, Bill, illus. 64p. (gr. 3-5). 1986. lib. bdg. 11.95 (*0-316-14899-7*) Little.
—More Science Experiments You Can Eat. Maestro, Giulio, illus. LC 78-12732. (gr. 5 up). 1979. 13.00 (*0-397-31828-6*, Lipp Jr Bks); PLB 14.89 (*0-397-31878-2*, Lipp Jr Bks) HarpC Child Bks.
—More Science Experiments You Can Eat. LC 78-12732. (Illus.). 128p. (gr. 5-8). 1984. pap. 4.95 (*0-06-446000-3*, Trophy) HarpC Child Bks.
—Natural Wonders: Stories Science Photos Tell. 32p. 1990. 14.95 (*0-688-09317-5*); PLB 14.88 (*0-688-09318-3*) Lothrop.
—Science Experiments You Can Eat. Lippman, Peter, illus. LC 71-151474. 127p. (gr. 5-8). 1972. PLB 14.89 (*0-397-31487-6*, Lipp Jr Bks) HarpC Child Bks.
—Science Experiments You Can Eat. LC 71-151474. (Illus.). 128p. (gr. 5-8). 1972. pap. 4.95 (*0-685-31398-0*, Trophy) HarpC Child Bks.
—Science Experiments You Can Eat. (ps-3). 1984. pap. 4.95 (*0-06-446002-9*, PL) HarpC.
—Science Experiments You Can Eat. rev. ed. Cain, David, illus. LC 93-13679. 1994. Repr. of 1972 ed. 15.00 (*0-06-023534-9*); PLB 14.89 (*0-06-023551-9*) HarpC Child Bks.
—The Scoop on Ice Cream. Karas, Brian, illus. 48p. (gr. 4 up). 1985. Little.

—The Secret Life of Cosmetics: A Science Experiment Book. Cobb, Theo, illus. LC 85-40097. 128p. (gr. 5-9). 1985. 14.00 (*0-397-32121-X*, Lipp Jr Bks); PLB 13.89 (*0-397-32122-8*, Lipp Jr Bks) HarpC Child Bks.
—The Secret Life of Hardware: A Science Experiment Book. Morrison, Bill, illus. LC 81-48607. 96p. (gr. 5 up). 1982. (Lipp Jr Bks); (Lipp Jr Bks) HarpC Child Bks.
—The Secret Life of School Supplies. Morrison, Bill, illus. LC 81-47108. 96p. (gr. 5 up). 1981. PLB 13.89 (*0-397-31925-8*, Lipp Jr Bks) HarpC Child Bks.
—Snap, Button, Zip: Inventions to Keep Your Clothes On. Hafner, Marylin, illus. LC 87-26097. 32p. (gr. 1-4). 1993. pap. 3.95 (*0-06-446106-8*, Trophy) HarpC Child Bks.
—Sneakers Meet Your Feet. Cobb, Theo, illus. 48p. (gr. 4-6). 1985. 11.95 (*0-316-14896-2*) Little.
—This Place Is Cold. Lavallee, Barbara, illus. (gr. 2-4). 1989. 14.95 (*0-8027-6852-0*); PLB 13.85 (*0-8027-6853-9*) Walker & Co.
—This Place Is Cold. Lavallee, Barbara, illus. 32p. (gr. 2-5). 1990. pap. 7.95 (*0-8027-7340-0*) Walker & Co.
—This Place Is Crowded. (gr. 4-7). 1993. pap. 6.95 (*0-8027-7407-5*) Walker & Co.
—This Place Is Crowded: Japan. 32p. (gr. 2-4). 1992. 14.95 (*0-8027-8145-4*); lib. bdg. 15.85 (*0-8027-8146-2*) Walker & Co.
—This Place Is Dry. Lavallee, Barbara, illus. (gr. 2-4). 1989. 12.95 (*0-8027-6854-7*); PLB 13.85 (*0-8027-6855-5*) Walker & Co.
—This Place Is Dry. Lavallee, Barbara, illus. 32p. (Orig.). (gr. 2-5). 1993. pap. 6.95 (*0-8027-7400-8*) Walker & Co.
—This Place Is High. Lavallee, Barbara, illus. 32p. (gr. 2-4). 1989. 12.95 (*0-8027-6882-2*); PLB 13.85 (*0-8027-6883-0*) Walker & Co.
—This Place Is High. (gr. 4-7). 1993. pap. 6.95 (*0-8027-7406-7*) Walker & Co.
—This Place Is Lonely. Lavallee, Barbara, illus. 32p. (gr. 7-8). 1991. 13.95 (*0-8027-6959-4*); lib. bdg. 14.85 (*0-8027-6960-8*) Walker & Co.
—This Place Is Wet. Lavallee, Barbara, illus. 32p. (gr. 2-4). 1989. 12.95 (*0-8027-6880-6*); PLB 13.85 (*0-8027-6881-4*) Walker & Co.
—This Place Is Wet. Lavallee, Barbara, illus. 32p. (Orig.). (gr. 2-5). 1993. pap. 6.95 (*0-8027-7399-0*) Walker & Co.
—Vicki Cobb's Papermaking Book & Kit. Bloom, Tom, illus. 32p. (gr. 2-6). 1993. 16.95 (*0-694-00467-7*, Festival) HarpC Child Bks.
—Why Can't You Unscramble an Egg? Enik, Ted, illus. LC 89-33465. 40p. (gr. 2-5). 1990. 12.95 (*0-525-67293-1*, Lodestar Bks) Dutton Child Bks.
—Why Doesn't the Earth Fall Up? And Other Not Such Dumb Questions about Motion. Enik, Ted, illus. LC 88-11108. 40p. (gr. 2-5). 1989. 13.00 (*0-525-67253-2*, Lodestar Bks) Dutton Child Bks.
—Why Doesn't the Sun Burn Out? Enik, Ted, illus. 40p. (gr. 2-5). 1990. 13.95 (*0-525-67301-6*, Lodestar Bks) Dutton Child Bks.
—Writing It Down. Hafner, Marylin, illus. LC 88-14191. 32p. (gr. k-3). 1989. (Lipp Jr Bks); PLB 11.89 (*0-397-32327-1*, Lipp Jr Bks) HarpC Child Bks.
Cobb, Vicki & Cobb, Joshua. Light Action! Amazing Experiments with Optics. Cobb, Theo, illus. LC 92-25528. 208p. (gr. 6 up). 1993. 15.00 (*0-06-021436-8*); PLB 14.89 (*0-06-021437-6*) HarpC Child Bks.
Cobb, Vicki & Darling, Kathy. Bet You Can! Science Possibilities to Fool You. Ormai, Stella, illus. 112p. (gr. 3-7). 1983. pap. 3.50 (*0-380-82180-X*, Camelot) Avon.
—Bet You Can't! Science Impossibilities to Fool You. Weston, Martha, illus. LC 79-9254. 128p. (gr. 5 up). 1980. 12.95 (*0-688-41905-4*); PLB 12.88 (*0-688-51905-9*) Lothrop.
—Bet You Can't: Science Impossibilities to Fool You. Weston, Martha, illus. 128p. (gr. 3-7). 1983. pap. 3.50 (*0-380-54502-0*, Camelot) Avon.
—Wanna Bet! Science Challenges Bound to Fool You. LC 92-8962. 1992. write for info. (*0-688-11213-7*) Lothrop.
Cobban, Alfred. History of Modern France: 3 vols. rev. ed. (Orig.). (gr. 9 up). 1961. pap. 6.95 (*0-14-020403-2*); pap. 9.95 (*0-14-020525-X*); pap. 6.95 (*0-14-020711-2*) Viking Child Bks.
Cobblestone Publishing, Inc Staff. Recipes from Around the World: For Young People 8-14. (Illus.). 36p. (gr. 4-8). 1987. pap. text ed. 4.95 (*0-942389-03-4*) Cobblestone Pub.
Cobblestone Publishing, Inc. Staff. U. S. History Cartoons: For Young People 8-14. (Illus.). 36p. (gr. 4-8). 1987. pap. text ed. 4.95 (*0-942389-02-6*) Cobblestone Pub.
Cobblestone Publishing Inc. Staff. U. S. History Crosswords: For Young People 8-14. (Illus.). 36p. (gr. 4-8). 1987. pap. text ed. 4.95 (*0-942389-01-8*) Cobblestone Pub.
Cobblestone Publishing, Inc. Staff. U. S. History Word Finds: For Young People 8-14. (Illus.). 36p. (gr. 4-8). 1987. pap. 4.95 (*0-9607638-9-9*) Cobblestone Pub.
Cobielles, Antonio, tr. see Chiesa, Pierre.
Coblence, Jean-Michel. Asian Civilizations. Lamb, Jane C., tr. from FRE. Ageorges, Veronique, illus. 77p. (gr. 7 up). 1988. 17.98 (*0-382-09483-2*); 13.49s.p. (*0-685-18822-1*) Silver Burdett Pr.
Coblence, Jean-Michel, jt. auth. see Chadefaud, Catherine.

Coblentz, Catherine C. The Blue Cat of Castle Town. Holland, Janice, illus. LC 74-14930. 124p. (gr. 3-7). 1983. pap. 8.00 (*0-914378-05-8*) Countryman.
Coburn, John B. Anne & the Sand Dobbies. LC 86-12650. 121p. (gr. 7-12). 1986. pap. 8.95 (*0-8192-1354-3*) Morehouse Pub.
Coburn, Mark, jt. auth. see Petersen, David.
Cocca-Leffler, Maryann. Count the Days Till Christmas. Cocca-Leffler, Maryann, illus. LC 92-82915. 16p. (ps-3). 1993. pap. 3.95 (*0-590-46929-0*, Cartwheel) Scholastic Inc.
—Grandma & Me. Cocca-Leffler, Maryann, illus. LC 90-61044. 28p. (ps). 1991. bds. 2.95 (*0-679-80758-6*) Random Bks Yng Read.
—Ice-Cold Birthday. (Illus.). 32p. (ps-1). 1992. (G&D); pap. 3.50 (*0-448-40380-3*, G&D) Putnam Pub Group.
—Me Too! (Illus.). 1994. 3.50 (*0-448-40399-4*, G&D); pap. write for info. (*0-448-40393-5*, G&D) Putnam Pub Group.
—Wednesday Is Spaghetti Day. (ps-3). 1992. pap. 2.50 (*0-590-42895-0*) Scholastic Inc.
Cocca-Leffler, Maryann, illus. The Elves & the Shoemaker. 18p. (ps). 1993. bds. 3.95 (*0-448-40177-0*, G&D) Putnam Pub Group.
—Hey Diddle Diddle: My First Book of Nursery Rhymes. 18p. (ps). 1991. 3.95 (*0-448-40107-X*, G&D) Putnam Pub Group.
Coccola, Raymond de & King, Paul. The Incredible Eskimo. Cameron, J., ed. Houston, James, illus. 435p. (Orig.). (gr. 9). 1986. pap. 16.95 (*0-88839-189-7*) Hancock House.
Cocetti, Robert A. & Snyder, Lee. Talk That Matters: An Introduction to Public Speaking. rev. ed. 338p. (gr. 10 up). 1992. 18.00 (*1-878276-44-1*) Educ Systs Assocs Inc.
Cochran, Belinda & Reid, Carol. Wings for Independent Thinking. Taylor, Christina, illus. 56p. (Orig.). (gr. 3-8). 1984. 6.50 (*0-88047-038-0*, 8403) DOK Pubs.
Cochran, Sallie B. Brave Star & the Necklace. (Illus.). 23p. (Orig.). (gr. 4-7). 1991. pap. 10.95 (*0-9629612-0-5*) Isabels.
Cochran, Vicki. My Daddy Is a Stranger. Aitken, J. Susan, illus. 24p. (Orig.). (gr. k up). 1992. pap. 3.75 (*1-56123-049-9*) Centering Corp.
Cochrane, Jennifer. Food Plants. LC 90-37226. (Illus.). 48p. (gr. 5-9). 1990. PLB 19.92 (*0-8114-2733-1*) Raintree Steck-V.
—Nature. LC 91-9194. (Illus.). 48p. (gr. 5-8). 1991. PLB 13.90 (*0-531-19143-5*, Warwick) Watts.
—Nature. LC 92-53091. (Illus.). 48p. (Orig.). (gr. 3-8). 1992. pap. 5.95 (*1-85697-813-3*) Kingfisher Bks.
—Trees of the Tropics. LC 90-10023. (Illus.). 48p. (gr. 5-9). 1990. PLB 19.92 (*0-8114-2731-5*) Raintree Steck-V.
Cochrane, Orin, ed. Reading Experiences in Science: Apes; Bats; Bees; Beavers; Dinosaurs; Frogs; Spiders; Whales, 8 bks. Gillespie, Robert, illus. 128p. (Orig.). (gr. 2-4). 1980. Set. pap. 28.95 (*1-895411-12-2*) Peguis Pubs Ltd.
Cochrane, Shirley G. & Townsend, Betsy B. The Jones Family. Robey, Adele, illus. 50p. (Orig.). 1992. pap. 10.00 (*0-9609062-2-3*) WA Expatriates Pr.
Cockcroft, James D. Diego Rivera. (Illus.). 112p. (gr. 5 up). 1991. lib. bdg. 17.95 (*0-7910-1252-2*) Chelsea Hse.
—Mohammed Reza Pahlevi. Schlesinger, Arthur M., intro. by. (Illus.). 112p. (gr. 5 up). 1989. 17.95x (*1-55546-847-0*) Chelsea Hse.
Cockley, Dave. Kids' Country: A Musical Play in Two Acts. Gulick, Lissy, contrib. by. (Illus.). 68p. (Orig.). (gr. 4 up). 1990. pap. 4.25 (*0-88680-331-4*); piano-vocal score 15.00 (*0-88680-332-2*); royalty on application 75.00 (*0-685-58898-X*) I E Clark.
Cockley, David H. Over the Falls: A Child's Guide to Chagrin Falls. Ascherman, Herbert, Jr., photos by. (Illus.). 24p. (Orig.). (gr. 1-6). 1981. pap. 2.25 (*0-940900-00-9*) Aschley Pr.
Cockrell, Marcille, jt. auth. see Vestavia Elementary School Fourth Grade Class.
Coco, Eugene. The Boy Who Wouldn't Eat Breakfast. Iosa, Ann, illus. 24p. (ps-2). 1993. pap. text ed. 0.99 (*1-56293-349-3*) McClanahan Bk.
—Jokes & Riddles. Jarka, Jeff, illus. 24p. (ps-2). 1993. pap. text ed. 0.99 (*1-56293-350-7*) McClanahan Bk.
—The Magic Clown. Pavia, Cathy, illus. 24p. (ps-2). 1993. pap. text ed. 0.99 (*1-56293-348-5*) McClanahan Bk.
—Sammy the Steamroller. Samuels, Mark, illus. 24p. (ps-2). 1993. pap. text ed. 0.99 (*1-56293-347-7*) McClanahan Bk.
Coco, Eugene B. The Fiddler's Son. Sabuda, Robert, illus. 32p. 1991. pap. 5.95 (*0-88138-111-X*, Green Tiger) S&S Trade.
—Glow in Dark Stars, Moon & Clouds. (ps-3). 1990. write for info. (*0-307-06253-8*) Western Pub.
—The Wishing Well. Sabuda, Robert, illus. 36p. 1991. pap. 7.95 (*0-88138-112-8*, Green Tiger) S&S Trade.
Coco, Gregory A., ed. see Powell, Robert M.
Cocquyt, Kathryn. Little Freddie at the Kentucky Derby. Corbett, Sylvia, illus. LC 91-23540. 128p. (gr. 4-7). 1992. 13.95 (*0-88289-856-6*) Pelican.
—Little Freddie's Legacy. Corbett, Sylvia, illus. LC 93-5558. 1994. write for info. (*1-56554-000-X*) Pelican.
Codor, Dick & Teitelbaum, Michael. Follow that Sleigh: The Reindeer Who Saved Christmas. Oren, Rony, contrib. by. (Illus.). (gr. k-5). 1990. 9.95 (*0-944007-51-1*) Shapolsky Pubs.

Cody, Iron Eyes. Indian Talk: Hand Signals of the North American Indians. Cody, Iron Eyes, illus. LC 73-16246. 112p. (gr. 1 up). 1970. 14.95 (*0-911010-83-1*); pap. 6.95 (*0-911010-82-3*) Naturegraph.
Codye, Corinn. Luis W. Alvarez. De Varona, Frank, intro. by. Masheris, Bob, illus. (SPA & ENG.). 32p. (gr. 3-6). 1990. PLB 15.96 (*0-8172-3376-8*); pap. 4.95 (*0-8114-6750-3*) Raintree Steck-V.
—Queen Isabella the First. De Varona, Frank, intro. by. Whipple, Rick, illus. (SPA & ENG.). 32p. (gr. 3-6). 1990. PLB 15.96 (*0-8172-3380-6*); pap. 4.95 (*0-8114-6758-9*) Raintree Steck-V.
—Vilma Martinez. De Varona, Frank, intro. by. Kilgore, Susie, illus. (ENG & SPA.). 32p. (gr. 3-6). 1990. PLB 15.96 (*0-8172-3382-2*); pap. 4.95 (*0-8114-6762-7*) Raintree Steck-V.
Coe, Joyce. Jesus Rides into Jerusalem. (Illus.). 24p. (gr. k-4). 1987. pap. 1.89 (*0-570-09007-5*, 59-1435) Concordia.
Coe, Rachel. I Have a Family. LC 86-17629. (ps). 1987. 5.95 (*0-8054-4172-7*) Broadman.
Coerr, Eleanor. Big Balloon Race. newly illus. ed. Croll, Carolyn, illus. LC 91-13607. 64p. (gr. k-3). 1984. pap. 3.50 (*0-06-444053-2*, Trophy) HarpC Child Bks.
—The Big Balloon Race. newly illus. ed. Croll, Carolyn, illus. LC 91-13606. 64p. (gr. k-3). 1981. 13.00 (*0-06-021352-3*); PLB 12.89 (*0-06-021353-1*) HarpC Child Bks.
—Buffalo Bill & the Pony Express. Bolognese, Don, illus. LC 93-24261. 1995. write for info. (*0-06-023372-9*); PLB write for info. (*0-06-023373-7*) HarpC Child Bks.
—Chang's Paper Pony. Ray, Deborah K., illus. LC 87-45679. 64p. (gr. k-3). 1988. 14.00 (*0-06-021328-0*); PLB 13.89 (*0-06-021329-9*) HarpC Child Bks.
—Chang's Paper Pony. Croll, Carolyn & Ray, Deborah K., illus. LC 87-45679. 64p. (gr. k-3). 1993. pap. 3.50 (*0-06-444163-6*, Trophy) HarpC Child Bks.
—The Josefina Story Quilt. Degen, Bruce, illus. LC 85-45260. 64p. (gr. k-3). 1986. 14.00 (*0-06-021348-5*); PLB 13.89 (*0-06-021349-3*) HarpC Child Bks.
—The Josefina Story Quilt. Degen, Bruce, illus. LC 85-45260. 64p. (gr. k-3). 1989. pap. 3.50 (*0-06-444129-6*, Trophy) HarpC Child Bks.
—Mieko & the Fifth Treasure. LC 92-14660. 64p. 1993. 14.95 (*0-399-22434-3*, Putnam) Putnam Pub Group.
—Sadako. Young, Ed, illus. LC 92-41483. 48p. (gr. 1-4). 1993. TLB 16.95 (*0-399-21771-1*, Putnam) Putnam Pub Group.
—Sadako & the Thousand Paper Cranes. Himler, Ronald, illus. 64p. (gr. 2-5). 1979. pap. 3.50 (*0-440-47465-5*, YB) Dell.
Coerr, Eleanor B. Sadako & the Thousand Paper Cranes. Himler, Ronald, illus. LC 76-9872. (gr. 3-5). 1977. 14.95 (*0-399-20520-9*, Putnam) Putnam Pub Group.
Coffelt, N. Good Night, Sigmund! 1992. 13.95 (*0-15-200464-5*, HB Juv Bks) HarBrace.
Coffelt, Nancy. Dogs in Space. (Illus.). 32p. (ps-3). 1993. 14.95 (*0-15-200440-8*) HarBrace.
—Tom's Fish. LC 92-44114. 1994. write for info. (*0-15-200587-0*, Gulliver Bks) HarBrace.
Coffen, Richard, ed. see Mills, Charles.
Coffen, Richard W., ed. see Taggart, George.
Coffen, Richard W., ed. see Van Pelt, Nancy L.
Coffen, Ron. K-Zoo News. 72p. 1992. pap. 8.95 (*0-8163-1086-6*) Pacific Pr Pub Assn.
Coffey, Vincent J. The Battle of Gettysburg. LC 84-40834. (Illus.). 64p. (gr. 5 up). 1985. PLB 8.95 (*0-382-06830-0*); pap. 8.95 (*0-382-09911-7*) Silver Burdett Pr.
Coffey, Wayne. Carl Lewis. (Illus.). 64p. (gr. 3-7). 1993. PLB 14.95 (*1-56711-006-1*) Blackbirch.
—Carl Lewis. Taylor, Dave, illus. 64p. (gr. 3-7). 1993. pap. 7.95 (*1-56711-052-5*) Blackbirch.
—Jesse Owens. (Illus.). 64p. (gr. 3-7). 1992. PLB 14.95 (*1-56711-000-2*) Blackbirch.
—Jim Thorpe. (Illus.). 64p. (gr. 3-7). 1993. PLB 14.95 (*1-56711-005-3*) Blackbirch.
—Katarina Witt. (Illus.). 64p. (gr. 3-7). 1992. PLB 14.95 (*1-56711-001-0*) Blackbirch.
—Kip Keino. (Illus.). 64p. (gr. 3-7). 1993. PLB 14.95 (*1-56711-003-7*) Blackbirch.
—Olga Korbut. (Illus.). 64p. (gr. 3-7). 1992. PLB 14.95 (*1-56711-002-0*) Blackbirch.
—Olympic Gold, 8 vols. (Illus.). 512p. (gr. 3-7). 1992. Set. PLB 119.60 (*1-56711-008-8*) Blackbirch.
—Straight Talk about Drinking: Teenagers Speak Out about Alcohol. LC 87-32446. 256p. (gr. 7 up). 1988. pap. 9.00 (*0-452-26061-2*, Plume) NAL-Dutton.
—The U. S. Hockey Team, 1980. (Illus.). 64p. (gr. 3-7). 1993. PLB 14.95 (*1-56711-007-X*) Blackbirch.
—Wilma Rudolph. (Illus.). 64p. (gr. 3-7). 1993. PLB 14.95 (*1-56711-004-5*) Blackbirch.
Coffey, William E. & Riddel, Frank S. American Government: The U. S. A. & West Virginia. Buckalew, Marshall, ed. Harvey, Eve S. & Harvey, Cliff, illus. 304p. (gr. 8). 1990. 25.00 (*0-914498-08-8*) WV Hist Ed Found.
Coffey, William E., et al. West Virginia Government. Buckalew, Marshall & Thoenen, Eugenia G., eds. (Illus.). 112p. (Orig.). (gr. 8). 1984. pap. 10.00 (*0-914498-05-3*) WV Hist Ed Found.
Coffin, Carlyn. Noel & His Friends. (Illus.). 130p (ps up). 1987. pap. 10.95 over boards (*0-931474-30-2*) TBW Bks.
Coffland, Jack A. & Cuevas, Gilbert J. Primary Problem Solving in Math. (Illus.). 200p. (Orig.). (gr. k-3). 1992. pap. 13.95 (*0-673-38745-3*) GdYrBks.
Cogger, Virginia, ed. see Saloom, Barbara B.

COHEN, MIRIAM

Coghill, Nevill, tr. see Chaucer, Geoffrey.
Coghlan see Sohn, David A.
Cohan, Leo M. The Hebrew Alphabet: From Generation to Generation. (Illus.). 21p. (Orig.). (gr. 4). 1989. pap. 5.95 (*0-9636415-0-6*) Kol Yisrael Pub.
Cohen. Second Grade Friends. 1993. pap. 2.75 (*0-590-47463-4*) Scholastic Inc.
Cohen, Andrew, jt. auth. see Heinsohn, Beth.
Cohen, Barbara. The Carp in the Bathtub. Halpern, Joan, illus. 48p. (gr. 1-5). 1972. PLB 13.88 (*0-688-51627-0*) Lothrop.
—The Carp in the Bathtub. Halpern, Joan, photos by. LC 87-80446. 32p. (gr. k-5). 1987. pap. 4.95 (*0-930494-67-9*) Kar-Ben.
—The Christmas Revolution. De Groat, Diane, illus. LC 86-21340. 96p. (gr. 3-6). 1987. 12.95 (*0-688-06806-5*) Lothrop.
—The Christmas Revolution. Degroat, Diane, illus. 176p. (gr. 4 up). 1988. pap. 2.95 (*0-553-15642-X*, Skylark) Bantam.
—Christmas Revolution. 1993. pap. 3.50 (*0-440-40871-7*) Dell.
—First Fast. (Illus.). 32p. (gr. 4-6). 1987. 7.95 (*0-8074-0354-7*, 101066) UAHC.
—Headless Roommate. (gr. 7-12). 1987. pap. 2.25 (*0-553-26679-9*) Bantam.
—The Innkeeper's Daughter. LC 79-2421. 159p. (gr. 4-6). 1990. pap. 3.95 (*0-688-10076-7*, Pub. by Beech Tree Bks) Morrow.
—King of the Seventh Grade. LC 82-15247. (gr. 4 up). 1982. 13.95 (*0-688-01302-3*) Lothrop.
—The Long Way Home. 176p. 1990. 12.95 (*0-688-09674-3*) Lothrop.
—The Long Way Home. Cohen, Barbara, illus. 1992. pap. 3.50 (*0-553-15984-4*) Bantam.
—Make a Wish, Molly. Jones, Jan N., illus. LC 93-17901. 1994. 14.95 (*0-385-31079-X*) Delacorte.
—Molly's Pilgrim. Deraney, Michael J., illus. LC 83-797. 32p. (gr. 2-5). 1983. 12.95 (*0-688-02103-4*); PLB 12.88 (*0-688-02104-2*) Lothrop.
—Molly's Pilgrim. Deraney, Michael J., illus. LC 83-797. 1990. pap. 3.25 (*0-553-15833-3*) Bantam.
—The Orphan Game. DeGroat, Diane, illus. LC 87-29340. (gr. 3-6). 1988. PLB 12.95 (*0-688-07615-7*) Lothrop.
—The Orphan Game. (gr. 3-7). 1989. pap. 2.75 (*0-553-15706-X*, Skylark) Bantam.
—People Like Us. 1987. 13.95 (*0-553-05441-4*) Bantam.
—Secret Grove. (Illus.). 32p. (gr. 4-6). 1985. 7.95 (*0-8074-0301-6*, 101065) UAHC.
—Tell Us Your Secret. 1989. 13.95 (*0-553-05810-X*, Starfire) Bantam.
—Thank You, Jackie Robinson. Cuffari, Richard, illus. LC 87-29341. (gr. 3-6). 1988. PLB 13.95 (*0-688-07909-1*) Lothrop.
—Thank You, Jackie Robinson. 1989. pap. 2.95 (*0-590-42378-9*) Scholastic Inc.
—Two Hundred Thirteen Valentines. Clay, Wil, illus. LC 91-7151. 64p. (gr. 2-4). 1991. 13.95 (*0-8050-1536-1*, Redfeather BYR) H Holt & Co.
—Two Hundred Thirteen Valentines. Clay, Wil, illus. LC 91-7151. 64p. (gr. 2-4). 1993. pap. 4.95 (*0-8050-2627-4*, Redfeather BYR) H Holt & Co.
—Unicorns in the Rain. LC 87-23843. 176p. (gr. 7 up). 1988. pap. 2.95 (*0-02-042210-5*, Collier Young Ad) Macmillan Child Grp.
—Yussel's Prayer. Deraney, Michael J., illus. LC 80-25377. 32p. (gr. k-4). 1981. PLB 12.88 (*0-688-00461-X*) Lothrop.
Cohen, Barbara, adapted by. The Donkey's Story. Cohen, Susan J., illus. LC 85-27. 32p. (gr. k-5). 1988. 12.95 (*0-688-04104-3*); PLB 12.88 (*0-688-04105-1*) Lothrop.
Cohen, Barbara, retold by. Yussel's Prayer: A Yom Kippur Story. Deraney, Michael J., illus. LC 92-44551. 32p. 1993. pap. 4.95 (*0-688-04581-2*, Mulberry) Morrow.
Cohen, Barbara, adapted by see Chaucer, Geoffrey.
Cohen, Caron L. Bronco Dogs. Shepherd, Roni, illus. LC 90-47952. 32p. (ps-3). 1991. 12.95 (*0-525-44721-0*, DCB) Dutton Child Bks.
—Mud Pony. 1989. pap. 3.95 (*0-590-41526-3*) Scholastic Inc.
—Pigeon, Pigeon. LC 91-36177. (Illus.). 32p. (ps-1). 1992. 12.00 (*0-525-44866-7*, DCB) Dutton Child Bks.
Cohen, Caron L., retold by. Sally Ann Thunder Ann Whirlwind Crockett. Dewey, Ariane, illus. LC 92-24585. 40p. 1993. pap. 4.95 (*0-688-12331-7*, Mulberry) Morrow.
Cohen, Caron Lee. Sally Ann Thunder Ann Whirlwind Crockett. Dewey, Ariane, illus. LC 84-7978. 40p. (gr. 1-3). 1985. 11.75 (*0-688-04006-3*); PLB 11.88 (*0-688-04007-1*) Greenwillow.
Cohen, Caron Lee, adapted by. The Mud Pony: A Traditional Skidi Pawnee Tale. Begay, Shonto, illus. LC 87-23451. 32p. (gr. k-4). 1988. pap. 14.95 (*0-590-41525-5*) Scholastic Inc.
Cohen, Charles. See You Tomorrow, Charles. 32p. (gr. k-6). 1989. pap. 2.95 (*0-440-40162-3*, YB) Dell.
Cohen, Charles Z. Your Future As a Lawyer. (gr. 7-12). 1977. PLB 7.97 (*0-8239-0382-6*) Rosen Group.
Cohen, Dan, jt. auth. see Cohen, Susan.
Cohen, Daniel. Ancient Egypt. Lippincott, Gary A., illus. 48p. (gr. 2-6). 1990. 10.95 (*0-385-24586-6*, Zephyr-BFYR*); (Zephyr-BFYR) Doubleday.
—Ancient Greece. (gr. 4-7). 1990. 11.95 (*0-385-26064-4*) Doubleday.
—Ancient Rome. Bond, Higgins, illus. LC 90-1410. 48p. (gr. 2-6). 1992. 13.00 (*0-385-26066-0*) Doubleday.

—Animal Rights: A Handbook for Young Adults. LC 92-40875. (Illus.). 128p. (gr. 7 up). 1993. PLB 15.90 (*1-56294-219-0*) Millbrook Pr.
—Beverly Hills 90210. 1991. pap. 3.99 (*0-671-77052-7*) S&S Trade.
—Carl Sagan: Superstar Scientist. (Illus.). 160p. (gr. 7-11). 1987. 14.95 (*0-399-21702-9*, Putnam) Putnam Pub Group.
—Dinosaurs. (ps-3). 1993. pap. 4.99 (*0-440-40784-2*) Dell.
—Ghost in the House. Caponigro, John P., illus. LC 92-37858. (gr. 3-5). 1993. 13.99 (*0-525-65131-4*, Cobblehill Bks) Dutton Child Bks.
—Ghostly Tales of Love & Revenge. 96p. (gr. 5-9). 1992. 14.95 (*0-399-22117-4*, Putnam) Putnam Pub Group.
—Ghostly Terrors. 128p. 1990. pap. 2.99 (*0-671-70507-5*, Minstrel Bks) PB.
—Ghosts of the Deep. LC 92-34669. 112p. (gr. 5-9). 1993. 14.95 (*0-399-22435-1*, Putnam) Putnam Pub Group.
—The Ghosts of War. 96p. (gr. 5-8). 1990. 13.95 (*0-399-22200-6*, Putnam) Putnam Pub Group.
—Gold: The Fascinating Study of the Noble Metal Through the Ages. LC 76-18067. (Illus.). 192p. (gr. 7 up). 1976. 10.95 (*0-87131-218-2*) M Evans.
—Great Ghosts. LC 90-34333. (Illus.). (gr. 4-7). 1990. 13.00 (*0-525-65039-3*, Cobblehill Bks) Dutton Child Bks.
—Great Ghosts. 48p. (gr. 4-7). 1992. pap. 1.95 (*0-590-45734-9*, Apple Paperbacks) Scholastic Inc.
—The Last Hundred Years: Medicine. LC 81-14357. (Illus.). 192p. (gr. 5 up). 1981. 8.95 (*0-87131-356-1*) M Evans.
—Phantom Animals. 96p. 1991. 14.95 (*0-399-22230-8*, Putnam) Putnam Pub Group.
—Phantom Animals. Ashby, Ruth, ed. 112p. 1993. pap. 2.99 (*0-671-75930-2*, Minstrel Bks) PB.
—Phone Call from a Ghost: Strange Tales from Modern America. MacDonald, Patricia, ed. Lynn, David, illus. 112p. (gr. 5-7). 1990. pap. 3.50 (*0-671-68242-3*, Minstrel) PB.
—Prehistoric Animals. Johnson, Pamela F., illus. LC 86-19666. 48p. (gr. k-3). 1988. 9.95 (*0-385-23416-3*) Doubleday.
—Prehistoric Animals. (ps-3). 1993. pap. 4.99 (*0-440-40787-7*) Dell.
—Prophets of Doom. LC 91-34509. (Illus.). 144p. (gr. 7 up). 1992. PLB 15.90 (*1-56294-068-6*) Millbrook Pr.
—Railway Ghosts & Highway Horrors. Marchesi, Stephen, illus. LC 91-11161. 112p. (gr. 4 up). 1991. 13.95 (*0-525-65071-7*, Cobblehill Bks) Dutton Child Bks.
—Railway Ghosts & Railway Horrors. 112p. (gr. 3-7). 1993. pap. 2.95 (*0-590-45423-4*, Apple Paperbacks) Scholastic Inc.
—Real Ghosts. MacDonald, Pat, ed. 128p. (gr. 4-7). 1992. pap. 2.99 (*0-671-78622-9*, Minstrel Bks) PB.
—Southern Fried Rat & Other Gruesome Tales. Brier, Peggy, illus. LC 82-25120. 128p. (gr. 7 up). 1982. 9.95 (*0-87131-400-2*) M Evans.
—Southern Fried Rat & Other Gruesome Tales. 128p. (gr. 5). 1989. pap. 3.50 (*0-380-70655-5*, Flare) Avon.
—The UFOS Third Wave. LC 88-16558. 172p. (gr. 7 up). 1988. 9.95 (*0-87131-541-6*) M Evans.
—The World's Most Famous Ghosts. (Illus.). 112p. (gr. 3-6). 1989. pap. 2.99 (*0-671-69145-7*, Minstrel Bks) PB.
Cohen, Daniel & Cohen, Susan. A Six-Pack & a Fake I.D. Teens Look at the Drinking Question. LC 85-25337. 156p. (gr. 7 up). 1985. 13.95 (*0-87131-459-2*) M Evans.
—Teenage Stress. 176p. (gr. 7 up). 1992. pap. 3.99 (*0-440-21391-6*, LFL) Dell.
—Teenage Stress: Understanding the Tensions You Feel at Home, at School & among Your Friends. LC 83-16477. 160p. (gr. 5 up). 1984. 13.95 (*0-87131-423-1*) M Evans.
—What Kind of Dog Is That? Rare & Unusual Breeds of Dogs. LC 89-34462. (Illus.). 144p. (gr. 5 up). 1989. 12.95 (*0-525-65011-3*, Cobblehill Bks) Dutton Child Bks.
—When Someone You Know Is Gay. LC 89-1260. (gr. 12 up). 1989. 13.95 (*0-87131-567-X*) M Evans.
—Where to Find Dinosaurs Today. LC 91-32084. (Illus.). 224p. 1992. 15.00 (*0-525-65098-9*, Cobblehill Bks) Dutton Child Bks.
—Where to Find Dinosaurs Today. (Illus.). 224p. (ps up). 1992. pap. 6.99 (*0-14-036154-5*, Puffin Unicorn) Puffin Bks.
Cohen, Daniel, jt. auth. see Cohen, Susan.
Cohen, Della. Jeff Rides a Spaceship. Van Wright, Cornelius, illus. 24p. (ps-2). 1992. pap. 0.99 (*1-56293-107-5*) McClanahan Bk.
Cohen, Diana, jt. auth. see Steinbaum, Michael.
Cohen, Donald. Analysis mit und fur Kinder (7, tatsachlich 7 Jahre alt und alter) Reimerth, Gudrun, tr. (GER., Illus.). 179p. (gr. 1-12). 1991. pap. write for info. spiral bdg. (*0-9621674-6-0*) D Cohen Mathman.
—Calculus by & for Young People: (Ages 7, Yes 7 & Up) Cohen, Donald, illus. 177p. (Orig.). (gr. 2 up). 1988. pap. 12.00 spiral bdg. (*0-9621674-0-1*) D Cohen Mathman.

—Calculus by & for Young People: (Ages 7, Yes 7 & Up) rev. ed. Honda, Noriko, tr. (Illus.). 177p. (gr. 1 up). 1989. English ed. spiral bdg. 13.95 (*0-9621674-1-X*); Japanese ed. pap. write for info. (*0-9621674-7-9*); package, incl. bk., worksheets, & 2 videotapes 110.00 (*0-9621674-9-5*) Worksheets (*0-9621674-5-2*) Videotape 1: Infinite Series by & for 6 Year Olds & Up (*0-9621674-2-8*) Videotape 2: Iteration with 6 to 11 Year Olds (*0-9621674-4-4*) D Cohen Mathman.
Cohen, Eliot. My Greatest Day in Baseball. (Illus.). 160p. (gr. 3 up). 1991. pap. 11.95 (*0-671-73319-2*, S&S BFYR); (S&S BFYR) S&S Trade.
Cohen, F. Fred's First Book of Poetry. (Orig.). (gr. 9-12). 1990. pap. 15.00 (*1-878109-10-3*) ASP PA.
Cohen, Frumi. Try a Little Shakespeare. LC 93-32493. 1993. write for info. (*0-88734-519-0*) Players Pr.
Cohen, John M., tr. see Bernal-Diaz, Del Castillo.
Cohen, John M., tr. see De Cervantes, Miguel Saavedra.
Cohen, Joy & Pranis, Eve. GrowLab, Activities for Growing Minds. 307p. (ps-8). 1990. 19.95 (*0-685-48838-1*) Natl Gardening Assn.
Cohen, Judith, jt. auth. see Bryan, Betsy.
Cohen, Judith, jt. auth. see Gabriel, Diane.
Cohen, Judith, jt. auth. see Gordon, Sol.
Cohen, Judith L. Tu Puedes Ser una Ingeniera. Yanez, Juan, tr. from ENG. Katz, David A., illus. (SPA.). 40p. (Orig.). (gr. 4-7). 1992. pap. 6.00 (*1-880599-03-1*) Cascade Pass.
—You Can Be a Woman Engineer. 40p. (Orig.). (gr. 3-7). 1991. pap. 6.00 (*1-880599-01-5*); cassette 4.00 (*1-880599-02-3*) Cascade Pass.
Cohen, Judith L. & Siegel, Margot. Tu Puedes Ser una Arquitecta. Yanez, Juan, tr. from ENG. Katz, David A., illus. (SPA.). 40p. (Orig.). (gr. 4-7). 1992. pap. 6.00 (*1-880599-05-8*) Cascade Pass.
—You Can Be a Woman Architect. Katz, David A., illus. 40p. (Orig.). 1992. pap. 6.00 (*1-880599-04-X*) Cascade Pass.
Cohen, Judith L. & Thompson, Valerie. Tu Puedes Ser una Zoologa. Yanez, Juan, tr. Katz, David, illus. (SPA.). 40p. (gr. 4-7). 1993. pap. 6.00 (*1-880599-09-0*) Cascade Pass.
—You Can Be a Woman Zoologist. Katz, David, illus. LC 93-1092. 40p. (Orig.). (gr. 3-7). 1992. pap. 6.00 (*1-880599-08-2*) Cascade Pass.
Cohen, Judith L., jt. auth. see McAlary, Florence.
Cohen, Judith L., jt. auth. see McAlary, Florence.
Cohen, Keri, ed. see Mazzola, Toni & Guten, Mimi.
Cohen, Lois, ed. see MacHovec, et al.
Cohen, Lorraine. Scenes for Young Actors. 384p. (gr. 6 up). 1982. pap. 5.99 (*0-380-00997-8*) Avon.
Cohen, Lynn. Air & Space. 64p. (ps-2). 1988. 6.95 (*0-912107-80-4*, MM984) Monday Morning Bks.
—Energy & Machines. 64p. (ps-2). 1988. 6.95 (*0-912107-78-2*, MM982) Monday Morning Bks.
—Exploring My World. 64p. (ps-k). 1986. 6.95 (*0-912107-47-2*) Monday Morning Bks.
—Fairy Tale World. 64p. (ps-k). 1986. 6.95 (*0-912107-48-0*) Monday Morning Bks.
—Me & My World. Pinkerton, Susan, illus. 64p. 1986. 6.95x (*0-912107-46-4*, Dist. by Good Apple) Monday Morning Bks.
—Weather & Seasons. 64p. (ps-2). 1988. 6.95 (*0-912107-79-0*, MM983) Monday Morning Bks.
Cohen, Marc J., ed. Hunger, 1993: Third Annual Report on the State of World Hunger - Uprooted People. Anchor-Hoch, Timothy, illus. (Illus.). 175p. (Orig.). (gr. 12 up). 1992. pap. text ed. 12.95 (*0-9628058-6-6*) Bread for the World.
Cohen, Marc J. & Hoehn, Richard A., eds. Hunger 1992: Second Annual Report on the State of World Hunger - Ideas That Work. (Illus.). (gr. 11 up). 1991. pap. 12.95 (*0-9628058-3-1*); study aid 3.00 (*0-9628058-4-X*) Bread for the World.
Cohen, Marsha, illus. Baby's Favorite Things. 12p. (ps). 1986. 3.95 (*0-394-88243-1*) Random Bks Yng Read.
Cohen, Mel, ed. see Garay, Julio.
Cohen, Milton. Ilana & the Monsters. Elfring, Harriet, illus. 40p. (Orig.). Date not set. pap. 3.00 (*0-9616076-0-2*) Jomilt Pubns.
Cohen, Miriam. Bee My Valentine. Hoban, Lillian, illus. LC 77-21950. 32p. (gr. k-3). 1978. PLB 11.88 (*0-688-84129-5*) Greenwillow.
—Bee My Valentine! Hoban, Lillian, illus. (gr. k-3). 1983. pap. 2.95 (*0-440-40507-6*, YB) Dell.
—Best Friends. Hoban, Lillian, illus. LC 70-146620. 32p. (ps-1). 1971. RSBE 13.95 (*0-02-722800-2*, Macmillan Child Bk) Macmillan Child Grp.
—Best Friends. Hoban, Lillian, illus. 32p. (ps-1). 1989. pap. 3.95 (*0-689-71334-7*, Aladdin) Macmillan Child Grp.
—Don't Eat Too Much Turkey! Hoban, Lillian, illus. LC 86-25660. 32p. (gr. k-3). 1987. 15.00 (*0-688-07141-4*); lib. bdg. 14.93 (*0-688-07142-2*) Greenwillow.
—Don't Eat Too Much Turkey. (gr. k-6). 1988. pap. 2.95 (*0-440-40106-2*, YB) Dell.
—First Grade Takes a Test. Hoban, Lillian, illus. (gr. k-3). 1983. pap. 2.95 (*0-440-42500-X*, YB) Dell.
—It's George! Hoban, Lillian, illus. LC 86-19384. 24p. (ps-2). 1988. 11.95 (*0-688-06812-X*); lib. bdg. 11.88 (*0-688-06813-8*) Greenwillow.
—It's George. (gr. k-6). 1989. pap. 2.95 (*0-440-40198-4*) Dell.
—Jim Meets the Thing. 49p. (gr. k-6). 1989. pap. 2.95 (*0-440-40149-6*, YB) Dell.
—Jim's Dog Muffins. Hoban, Lillian, illus. LC 83-14090. 32p. (gr. k-3). 1984. 13.95 (*0-688-02564-1*); PLB 13.88 (*0-688-02565-X*) Greenwillow.

—Jim's Dog Muffins. (gr. k-6). 1986. pap. 2.95 (0-440-44224-9, YB) Dell.
—Liar, Liar, Pants on Fire! (gr. k-6). 1987. pap. 3.25 (0-440-44755-0, YB) Dell.
—Lost in the Museum. Hoban, Lillian, illus. (gr. k-3). 1983. pap. 2.95 (0-440-44780-1, YB) Dell.
—Marijuana: Its Effects on Mind & Body. (Illus.). 32p. (gr. 5 up). 1991. pap. 4.49 (0-7910-0000-1) Chelsea Hse.
—The New Teacher. Hoban, Lillian, illus. LC 78-163239. 32p. (ps-1). 1989. pap. 3.95 (0-689-71332-0, Aladdin) Macmillan Child Grp.
—No Good in Art. Hoban, Lillian, illus. LC 79-16566. 32p. (gr. k-3). 1980. PLB 14.93 (0-688-84234-8) Greenwillow.
—No Good in Art. (gr. k-6). 1986. pap. 3.25 (0-440-46389-0, YB) Dell.
—The Real-Skin Rubber Monster Mask. Hoban, Lillian, illus. LC 89-34620. 32p. (gr. k up). 1990. 12.95 (0-688-09122-9); PLB 12.88 (0-688-09123-7) Greenwillow.
—See You in Second Grade! Hoban, Lillian, illus. LC 87-14869. 32p. (ps up). 1989. 13.95 (0-688-07138-4); PLB 13.88 (0-688-07139-2) Greenwillow.
—See You in Second Grade. (gr. k-6). 1990. pap. 2.95 (0-440-40303-0, Pub. by Yearling Classics) Dell.
—So What? Hoban, Lillian, illus. LC 81-20101. 32p. (gr. k-3). 1982. PLB 15.93 (0-688-01203-5) Greenwillow.
—So What? (gr. k-6). 1988. pap. 3.25 (0-440-40048-1, YB) Dell.
—Starring First Grade. Hoban, Lillian, illus. LC 84-5929. 32p. (gr. k-3). 1985. PLB 15.93 (0-688-04030-6) Greenwillow.
—Starring First Grade. (gr. k-6). 1987. pap. 3.25 (0-440-48250-X, YB) Dell.
—When Will I Read? Hoban, Lillian, illus. LC 76-28320. 32p. (ps-3). 1977. 13.95 (0-688-80073-4); PLB 13.88 (0-688-84073-6) Greenwillow.
—When Will I Read? Hoban, Lillian, illus. (gr. k-3). 1987. pap. 3.25 (0-440-49333-1, YB) Dell.
—Will I Have a Friend? Hoban, Lillian, illus. LC 67-10127. 32p. (ps-1). 1967. RSBE 13.95 (0-02-722790-1, Macmillan Child Bk) Macmillan Child Grp.
—Will I Have a Friend? Hoban, Lillian, illus. LC 89-31340. 32p. (ps-1). 1989. pap. 3.95 (0-689-71333-9, Aladdin) Macmillan Child Grp.
Cohen, Neil. Jackie Joyner-Kersee. (Illus.). 144p. (gr. 3-7). 1992. pap. 4.95 (0-316-15047-9, Spts Illus Kids) Little.
—Shaquille O'Neal. McGarry, Steve, illus. (gr. 8 up). 1993. pap. 3.99 (0-553-48158-4) Bantam.
Cohen, Nora. From Apple to Zipper. Kern, Donna, illus. LC 92-43691. 32p. (ps-1). 1993. POB 8.95 (0-689-71708-3, Aladdin) Macmillan Child Grp.
Cohen, Paul & Cohen, Shari. Careers in Law Enforcement & Security. Rosen, Ruth, ed. (gr. 7-12). 1990. PLB 13.95 (0-8239-1026-1) Rosen Group.
Cohen, Paul, jt. auth. see Bernstein, Joanne.
Cohen, Paul, jt. auth. see Bernstein, Joanne E.
Cohen, Peter. Olson's Meat Pies. Landstrom, Olof, illus. Fisher, Richard E., tr. (Illus.). (gr. k-4). 1989. 12.95 (91-29-59180-5, Pub. by R & S Bks) FS&G.
Cohen, Peter Z. Deadly Game at Stony Creek. Deas, Michael J., illus. LC 93-9364. 96p. (gr. 5 up). 1993. pap. 3.99 (0-14-036476-5, Puffin) Puffin Bks.
Cohen, Philip. Tobacco. LC 91-32583. (Illus.). 64p. (gr. 6-12). 1991. PLB 19.92 (0-8114-3202-5) Raintree Steck-V.
Cohen, Richard, et al. Snail Trails & Tadpole Tails: Nature Education for Young Children. Seaberg, Kurt, illus. Peterson, Roger T., intro. by. LC 93-5850. (Illus.). 96p. (Orig.). (ps-1). 1993. pap. text ed. 12.95 (0-934140-78-2) Redleaf Pr.

**Cohen, Richard A. Alfie's Home. Sherman, Elizabeth, illus. 30p. 1993. 14.95 (0-9637058-0-6) Intl Healing. ALFIE'S HOME is the story of a young boy who thinks he's gay but finds out he's not. Written in simple language, it gives hope to children & adults of all ages who are struggling with their sexual orientation & choose not to be gay. ALFIE'S HOME is the first resource of its kind for teachers, students, parents, counselors, pastors-- anyone helping children heal their sexual identity. Alfie grows up in a dysfunctional family & experiences both abuse & neglect from a distant father, a dominating mother, & an abusive uncle. In his teen years he experiences feelings & attraction for other boys. A counselor explains to Alfie the meaning of his homosexual feelings & helps guide him to deeper healing. "Richard Cohen has hit upon the essential causal & curative themes of the homosexual condition. Many of my adult clients would not have needed psychotherapy today if their parents had read ALFIE'S HOME."--Joseph Nicolosi, Ph.D., Psychologist, Author, REPARATIVE THERAPY OF MALE HOMOSEXUALITY. "ALFIE'S HOME is most definitely a vitally needed book for our children & for our school systems throughout America."--Dr. Thomas L. Brown, Indianapolis School Commissioner. To order contact: International Healing Foundation, P.O. Box 901, Bowie, MD 20718; phone: 301-773-5573. *Publisher Provided Annotation.*

Cohen, Ronald, ed. see Carpenter, Allan & Balow, Tom.
Cohen, Seth. Baby Safari. Cohen, Helena, illus. 28p. (ps). 1993. 3.25 (0-679-83608-X) Random Bks Yng Read.
Cohen, Shari. Coping with Being Adopted. Rosen, Ruth, ed. 132p. (gr. 7 up). 1988. PLB 13.95 (0-8239-0770-8) Rosen Group.
—Coping with Sibling Rivalry. Rosen, Ruth, ed. (gr. 7-12). 1989. PLB 13.95 (0-8239-0977-8) Rosen Group.
—Prime Time Rhyme. (gr. k-6). 1990. 10.95 (0-9620467-4-4) Forward March.
Cohen, Shari, jt. auth. see Cohen, Paul.
Cohen, Sharron. Mysteries of Research. 144p. (Orig.). (gr. 4-8). 1992. pap. text ed. 15.95 (0-913853-21-6, 115-120) Alleyside Pr.
Cohen, Sholem. Yitzy & the G.O.L.E.M. 128p. (gr. 4-8). 1992. pap. text ed. 6.95 (0-922613-50-8) Hachai Pubns.
Cohen, Stan B., jt. auth. see Guth, A. Richard.
Cohen, Stu, et al. Schools Face the Challenge of AIDS. 150p. (Orig.). (gr. 7-12). 1991. pap. text ed. 25.00 (0-89292-094-7) Educ Dev Ctr.
Cohen, Susan & Cohen, Dan. What You Can Believe. 1993. pap. 3.99 (0-440-21890-X) Dell.
Cohen, Susan & Cohen, Daniel. A Six Pack & a Fake I. D. Teens Look at the Drinking Question. 176p. (gr. 7 up). 1992. pap. 3.99 (0-440-21297-9, LFL) Dell.
—Teenage Competition: A Survival Guide. LC 86-24307. 156p. (gr. 7 up). 1986. 13.95 (0-87131-487-8) M Evans.
—When Someone You Know Is Gay. 196p. (gr. 7 up). 1992. pap. 3.99 (0-440-21298-7, LFL) Dell.
Cohen, Susan, jt. auth. see Cohen, Daniel.
Cohen, Ted, ed. International Directory of Pageants. rev. ed. 400p. (gr. 6 up). 1988. PLB 50.00 (0-9620855-0-2) World Pageants.
Cohen, William E., jt. auth. see Inaba, Darryl S.
Cohlene, Terri. Clamshell Boy. (Illus.). 48p. (gr. 4-8). 1990. lib. bdg. 19.93 (0-86593-001-5); lib. bdg. 14.95s.p. (0-685-46446-6) Rourke Corp.
—Clamshell Boy: A Makah Legend. 48p. (gr. 4-7). 1990. pap. 3.95 (0-8167-2361-3) Troll Assocs.
—Dancing Drum. (Illus.). 48p. (gr. 4-8). 1990. lib. bdg. 19.93 (0-86593-007-4); lib. bdg. 14.95s.p. (0-685-46447-4) Rourke Corp.
—Dancing Drum: A Cherokee Legend. 48p. (gr. 4-7). 1990. pap. 3.95 (0-8167-2362-1) Troll Assocs.
—Ka-Ha-Si & the Loon. (Illus.). 48p. (gr. 4-8). 1990. lib. bdg. 19.93 (0-86593-002-3); lib. bdg. 14.95s.p. (0-685-46448-2) Rourke Corp.
—Ka-Ha-Si & the Loon: An Eskimo Legend. 48p. (gr. 4-7). 1990. pap. 3.95 (0-8167-2359-1) Troll Assocs.
—Little Firefly. (Illus.). 48p. (gr. 4-8). 1990. lib. bdg. 19.93 (0-86593-005-8); lib. bdg. 14.95s.p. (0-685-36333-3) Rourke Corp.
—Little Firefly: An Algonquian Legend. 48p. (gr. 4-7). 1990. pap. 3.95 (0-8167-2363-X) Troll Assocs.
—Native American Legends, 6 bks. (Illus.). 288p. (gr. 4-8). 1990. Set. lib. bdg. 119.58 (0-86593-000-7); Set. lib. bdg. 89.70s.p. (0-685-46445-8) Rourke Corp.
—Quillworker. (Illus.). 48p. (gr. 4-8). 1990. lib. bdg. 19.93 (0-86593-004-X); lib. bdg. 14.95s.p. (0-685-36334-1) Rourke Corp.
—Quillworker: A Cheyenne Legend. 48p. (gr. 4-7). 1990. pap. 3.95 (0-8167-2358-3) Troll Assocs.
—Turquoise Boy. (Illus.). 48p. (gr. 4-8). 1990. lib. bdg. 19.93 (0-86593-003-1); lib. bdg. 14.95s.p. (0-685-36335-X) Rourke Corp.
—Turquoise Boy: A Navajo Legend. 48p. (gr. 4-7). 1990. pap. 3.95 (0-8167-2360-5) Troll Assocs.
Cohn, Amy, selected by. From Sea to Shining Sea. Bang, Molly, et al, illus. LC 92-30598. 1993. 29.95 (0-590-42868-3) Scholastic Inc.
Cohn, Janice. I Had a Friend Named Peter: Talking to Children about the Death of a Friend. Owens, Gail, illus. LC 86-31150. 32p. (ps-2). 1987. 13.00 (0-688-06685-2); lib. bdg. 13.88 (0-688-06686-0, Morrow Jr Bks) Morrow Jr Bks.
Cohn, Janice I. Why Did It Happen? Helping Young Children Cope with the Existence of Violence. Owens, Gail, illus. LC 93-1573. 1994. write for info. (0-688-12312-0); PLB write for info. (0-688-12313-9) Morrow Jr Bks.
Cohn, Leigh, jt. auth. see Hall, Lindsey.
Cohn, Tom, ed. see Feldman, Robert S.
Cohn, Tom, ed. see Katz, Phyllis & Frekko, Janet.
Cohn, Tom, ed. see Lampton, Christopher.

Cohn, Tom, ed. see Newman, Gerald & Layfield, Eleanor N.
Cohn, Tom, ed. see Nielsen, Nancy J.
Cohn, Tom, ed. see Sandak, Cass R.
Cohn, Tom, ed. see Yoslow, Mark.
Cohn-Gilletly, Joanne. Ten Minutes with Me. 3rd ed. (Illus., Orig.). (gr. k-3). 1980. pap. 2.00 (0-916634-05-1) Double M Pr.
Coil, Suzanne. Battle for Women's Suffrage. 1995. PLB write for info. (0-8050-2985-0) H Holt & Co.
—Robert Hutchings Goddard. (Illus.). 128p. (gr. 7-12). 1992. lib. bdg. 16.95x (0-8160-2591-6) Facts on File.
—Struggle of Child Labor. 1995. PLB write for info. (0-8050-2986-9) H Holt & Co.
Coil, Suzanne M. Campaign Financing: Politics & the Power of Money. (Illus.). 128p. (gr. 7 up). 1994. 15.90 (1-56294-220-4) Millbrook Pr.
—Civil Rights Movement. 1995. PLB write for info. (0-8050-2987-7) H Holt & Co.
—George Washington Carver. (Illus.). 64p. (gr. 5-8). 1990. PLB 12.90 (0-531-10864-3) Watts.
—Harriet Beecher Stowe. LC 93-13710. (Illus.). 192p. (gr. 7-12). 1993. PLB 14.40 (0-531-13006-1) Watts.
—Mardi Gras! Osborne, Mitchel, illus. LC 92-21166. 48p. (gr. 2 up). 1994. RSBE 15.95 (0-02-722805-3, Macmillan Child Bk) Macmillan Child Grp.
—Poisonous Plants. (Illus.). 64p. (gr. 3-5). 1991. PLB 12.90 (0-531-20017-5) Watts.
—Poisonous Plants. (Illus.). 64p. (gr. 5-8). 1992. pap. 5.95 (0-531-15647-8) Watts.
—The Poor in America. Steltenpohl, Jane, ed. (Illus.). 136p. (gr. 7-10). 1989. lib. bdg. 13.98 (0-671-69052-3, J Messner) S&S Trade.
—Slavery & Abolition. 1995. PLB write for info. (0-8050-2984-2) H Holt & Co.
Coiley, John. Train. Dunning, Mike, photos by. LC 92-4711. (Illus.). 64p. (gr. 5 up). 1992. 15.00 (0-679-81684-4); PLB 16.99 (0-579-91684-9) Knopf Bks Yng Read.
Coit, Margaret L. Andrew Jackson. LC 90-48986. (Illus.). 176p. (gr. 6-10). 1991. PLB 13.95 (1-55905-082-9) Marshall Cavendish.
Coker, William S. John Forbes & Company & the War of 1812 in the Spanish Borderlands. Coling, Jerome F., illus. 37p. (gr. 7 up). 1979. pap. 2.50 (0-933776-08-X) Perdido Bay.
Colbert, Cynthia & Taunton, Martha. Discover Art - Kindergarten. (gr. k). 1989. kit 184.50 (0-87192-219-3, 219-3) Davis Mass.
Colbert, Roz. Zora Neale Hurston. (Illus.). 80p. (gr. 3-5). 1993. PLB 12.95 (0-7910-1766-4) Chelsea Hse.
Colbery, Katie. Find the Mistakes Science: Incredible Insects. (gr. 4-7). 1991. pap. 2.95 (0-8431-2814-3) Price Stern.
Colborn, Mark. Rolemaster Companion. Charlton, S. C., ed. McBride, Angus, illus. 96p. (gr. 10-12). 1986. pap. 12.00 (0-915795-12-4, 1500) Iron Crown Ent Inc.
Colborn, Mark, jt. auth. see Fenlon, Peter C.
Colburn, Rhonda. The Story of Elijah. Pickett, Stacy, illus. 24p. (ps-3). 1990. pap. 3.95 (0-8249-8419-6, Ideals Child) Hambleton-Hill.
—The Story of Shadrach, Meshach & Abednego. Connelly, Gwen, illus. 24p. (ps-3). 1990. pap. 3.95 (0-8249-8421-8, Ideals Child) Hambleton-Hill.
Colby, C. B. World's Best Lost Treasure Stories. LC 91-14377. (Illus.). 96p. (gr. 3-10). 1991. 12.95 (0-8069-8420-1) Sterling.
—World's Best Lost Treasure Stories. LC 91-14377. (Illus.). 96p. (gr. 3-10). 1992. pap. 3.95 (0-8069-8421-X) Sterling.
—World's Best "True" Ghost Stories. LC 88-11703. (Illus.). 128p. (Orig.). (gr. 4 up). 1989. pap. 3.95 (0-8069-6898-2) Sterling.
Colby, J. Disney's the Little Mermaid: Sebastian's Story. Kurtz, John, illus. 24p. (ps-k). 1992. write for info. (0-307-10020-0, 10020) Western Pub.
Colby, Sas & Shirkus, Lorraine. The Pocket Book: A Child's Activity Book. Shirkus, Lorraine, illus. 10p. (ps-k). 1988. 39.95 (0-922656-00-2) Design Matters Inc.
Colby-Newton, Katie. Jack the Ripper: Opposing Viewpoints. LC 90-3835. (Illus.). 112p. (gr. 5-8). 1990. PLB 14.95 (0-89908-081-2) Greenhaven.
Coldrey, Jennifer. Chicken on the Farm. LC 86-5716. (Illus.). 32p. (gr. 4-6). 1986. PLB 15.93 (1-55532-067-8) Gareth Stevens Inc.
—The Crab on the Seashore. LC 85-30293. (Illus.). 32p. (gr. 4-6). 1987. PLB 15.93 (1-55532-060-0) Gareth Stevens Inc.
—Frog in the Pond. LC 85-30300. (Illus.). 32p. (gr. 4-6). 1987. 15.93 (1-55532-059-7) Gareth Stevens Inc.
—Life in the Sea. LC 90-38113. (Illus.). 32p. (gr. 4-7). 1991. PLB 12.40 (0-531-18360-2) Watts.
—The Owl in the Tree. Oxford Scientific Film Staff, illus. LC 87-9915. 32p. (gr. 4-6). 1987. PLB 15.93 (1-55532-272-7) Gareth Stevens Inc.
—The Rabbit in the Fields. LC 85-30293. (Illus.). 32p. (gr. 4-6). 1987. 15.93 (1-55532-061-5) Gareth Stevens Inc.
—Shells. LC 92-54310. (Illus.). 64p. (gr. 3 up). 1993. 9.95 (1-56458-229-9) Dorling Kindersley.
—The Squirrel in the Trees. LC 85-30292. (Illus.). 32p. (gr. 4-6). 1986. 15.93 (1-55532-062-7) Gareth Stevens Inc.
—Strawberry. (Illus.). 25p. (gr. k-4). 1990. 6.95 (0-382-09802-1); PLB 9.98 (0-382-09801-3); pap. 3.95 (0-382-24340-4) Silver Burdett Pr.

—The Swan on the Lake. LC 86-5719. (Illus.). 32p. (gr. 4-6). 1987. 15.93 (*1-55532-066-X*) Gareth Stevens Inc.
—The World of Chickens. LC 86-5718. (Illus.). 32p. (gr. 2-3). 1986. 15.93 (*1-55532-071-6*) Gareth Stevens Inc.
—The World of Crabs. LC 85-30294. (Illus.). 32p. (gr. 2-3). 1986. 15.93 (*1-55532-063-5*) Gareth Stevens Inc.
—The World of Frogs. LC 85-30297. (Illus.). 32p. (gr. 2-3). 1987. 15.93 (*1-55532-024-4*) Gareth Stevens Inc.
—The World of Rabbits. LC 85-28988. (Illus.). 32p. (gr. 2-3). 1986. 15.93 (*1-55532-064-3*) Gareth Stevens Inc.
—The World of Squirrels. LC 85-30296. (Illus.). 32p. (gr. 2-3). 1987. PLB 15.93 (*1-55532-065-1*) Gareth Stevens Inc.
—The World of Swans. LC 86-5721. (Illus.). 32p. (gr. 2-3). 1987. PLB 15.93 (*1-55532-070-8*) Gareth Stevens Inc.
Coldrey, Jennifer, jt. auth. see Shale, David.
Cole. Big Goof & Little Goof. 1992. pap. 3.95 (*0-590-41592-1*) Scholastic Inc.
Cole, Ann & Haas, Carolyn. Purple Cow to the Rescue. LC 82-47913. (Illus.). 160p. (gr. 1-5). 1982. 14.95 (*0-316-15104-1*) Little.
Cole, Ann, et al. Children Are Children Are Children: An Activity Approach to Exploring Brazil, France, Iran, Japan, Nigeria, & the U. S. S. R. (Illus.). (gr. 3-7). 1978. Little.
—I Saw a Purple Cow & 100 Other Recipes for Learning. Kelley, True, illus. 96p. (gr. 4 up). 1972. pap. 8.95 (*0-316-15175-0*) Little.
—A Pumpkin in a Pear Tree: Creative Ideas for Twelve Months of Holiday Fun. (Illus.). 112p. (gr. 1 up). 1976. pap. 8.95 (*0-316-15111-4*) Little.
Cole, Babette. Hurray for Ethelyn. (Illus.). (ps-3). 1991. 14.95 (*0-316-15189-0*) Little.
—Mommy Laid an Egg. (ps-3). 1992. 13.95 (*0-8118-0350-3*) Chronicle Bks.
—Prince Cinders. Cole, Babette, illus. 32p. (gr. 1-3). 1988. 14.95 (*0-399-21502-6*, Putnam) Putnam Pub Group.
—Prince Cinders. Cole, Babette, illus. 32p. (gr. 1-3). 1992. pap. 5.95 (*0-399-21882-3*, Sandcastle Bks) Putnam Pub Group.
—Princess Smartypants. Cole, Babette, illus. LC 86-12381. (ps-3). 1987. 13.95 (*0-399-21409-7*, Putnam) Putnam Pub Group.
—Princess Smartypants. (Illus.). 32p. (ps-3). 1991. pap. 5.95 (*0-399-21779-7*, Sandcastle Bks) Putnam Pub Group.
—Supermoo! LC 92-8967. (Illus.). 32p. (ps-3). 1993. 14.95 (*0-399-22422-X*, Putnam) Putnam Pub Group.
—Tarzanna. Cole, Babette, illus. 32p. (ps-3). 1992. 14.95 (*0-399-21837-8*, Putnam) Putnam Pub Group.
—The Trouble with Dad. 32p. (ps-3). 1986. 13.95 (*0-399-21206-X*, Putnam); pap. 5.95 (*0-399-21467-4*) Putnam Pub Group.
—Trouble with Dad. (ps-3). 1993. pap. 5.95 (*0-399-22534-X*, Sandcastle Bks) Putnam Pub Group.
—The Trouble with Gran. 32p. 1991. pap. 5.95 (*0-399-21791-6*, Sandcastle Bks) Putnam Pub Group.
—The Trouble with Mom. Cole, Babette, illus. 32p. (gr. 5-8). 1984. 13.95 (*0-698-20597-9*, Putnam); pap. 5.95 (*0-698-20681-9*, Sandcastle Bks) Putnam Pub Group.
—Trouble with Mom. LC 83-7750. (ps-3). 1986. pap. 5.95 (*0-698-20624-X*) Putnam Pub Group.
—The Trouble with Uncle. (Illus.). (ps-3). 1992. 14.95 (*0-316-15190-4*) Little.
—Winni Allfours. Cole, Babette, illus. LC 93-28447. (gr. k-4). 1993. PLB 13.95 (*0-8167-3307-4*); pap. 3.95t (*0-8167-3308-2*) Troll Assocs.
Cole, Babette & Van Der Meer, Ron. The Bible Beasties. (Illus.). 12p. 1993. 15.00 (*0-551-02595-6*, Pub. by HarperCollins UK) Harper SF.
Cole, Barbara H. Texas Star. Minton, Barbara, illus. LC 88-25205. 32p-205. 1990. 14.95 (*0-531-05820-4*); PLB 14.99 (*0-531-08420-5*) Orchard Bks Watts.
Cole, Barbara S. Don't Tell a Soul. Rosen, R., ed. 175p. (gr. 7-12). 1987. PLB 12.95 (*0-8239-0701-5*) Rosen Group.
Cole, Betsy. Green Creatures Ten to One. Happe, Cary, illus. LC 88-71429. 32p. (Orig.). (gr. k-3). 1988. pap. 4.95 (*0-9620606-0-7*) Adventure VA.
—Is Aetosaur a Dinosaur? Spear, Scott, illus. Hager, Michael, contrib. by. (Illus.). 64p. (Orig.). (gr. k-3). 1992. pap. 11.95 (*0-9625801-4-7*) VA Mus Natl Hist.
Cole, Brock. Alfa y el Bebe Sucio: Alpha & the Dirty Baby. Gottlieb, T., tr. (SPA., Illus.). 32p. (ps-3). 1991. 14.95 (*0-374-30242-1*) FS&G.
—Celine. (gr. 7 up). 1989. 15.00 (*0-374-31234-6*) FS&G.
—Celine. 224p. (gr. 7 up). 1991. pap. 3.95 (*0-374-41082-8*, Sunburst) FS&G.
—Celine. 1993. pap. 3.95 (*0-374-41083-6*) FS&G.
—Celine. Barbadillo, Pedro, tr. (SPA.). 172p. (gr. 9-12). 1992. pap. write for info. (*84-204-4711-0*) Santillana.
—The Giant's Toe. LC 85-20569. 32p. (ps up). 1986. 15.00 (*0-374-32559-6*) FS&G.
—The Giant's Toe. (Illus.). 32p. (ps up) 1988. pap. 3.95 (*0-374-42557-4*) FS&G.
—The Goats. large type ed. (Illus.). 208p. 1989. lib. bdg. 15.95 (*1-55736-113-4*, Crnrstn Bks) BDD LT Grp.
—The Goats. (gr. 5 up). 1990. pap. 3.95 (*0-374-42575-2*, Sunburst) FS&G.
—The Goats. (gr. 7 up). 1992. pap. 3.95 (*0-374-42576-0*) FS&G.
—King at the Door. (ps-3). 1992. pap. 4.95 (*0-374-44041-7*) FS&G.
—No More Baths. 40p. (ps up) 1989. pap. 3.95 (*0-374-45514-7*, Sunburst) FS&G.

—The Winter Wren. LC 84-1583. (Illus.). 32p. (gr. 2 up). 1984. 15.00 (*0-374-38454-1*, Sunburst) FS&G.
—The Winter Wren. LC 84-1583. (Illus.). 32p. (gr. 2 up). 1988. pap. 4.95 (*0-374-48408-2*) FS&G.
Cole, Bruce. The Pumpkinville Mystery. Warhola, James, illus. (gr. 1-4). 1987. 10.95 (*0-13-741620-2*) P-H.
—The Pumpkinville Mystery. Gwynne, Fred, narrated by. (Illus.). 32p. (gr. 1-4). 1988. Incl. cassettes. pap. 6.95 (*0-671-67147-2*) S&S Trade.
—The Pumpkinville Mystery. Warhola, James, illus. LC 87-2533. 32p. (gr. 1-4). 1991. pap. 3.95 (*0-671-74199-3*, Little Simon) S&S Trade.
Cole, Carole O., jt. auth. see Kramer, Lyneve W.
Cole, Deena. A Child's Guide to Historical Places. Cole, Jeff, illus. 64p. (ps-6). 1993. pap. 3.95 (*1-878893-32-7*); tchr's. guide 6.95 (*1-878893-31-9*) Telcraft Bks.
—A Child's Guide to Natural Wonders. Cole, Jeff, illus. 64p. (ps-6). 1993. pap. 3.95 (*1-878893-34-3*); tchr's. guide 6.95 (*1-878893-33-5*) Telcraft Bks.
Cole, Jacci. Animal Communication: Opposing Viewpoints. LC 88-24401. (Illus.). 112p. (gr. 5-8). 1989. PLB 14.95 (*0-89908-062-6*) Greenhaven.
Cole, Jan, jt. auth. see Dixon, Michael B.
Cole, Joann. Norma Jean, Jumping Bean. Munsinger, Lynn, illus. LC 86-15588. 48p. (gr. 1-3). 1987. lib. bdg. 7.99 (*0-394-98668-7*); 3.50 (*0-394-88668-2*) Random Bks Yng Read.
Cole, Joanna. Aren't You Forgetting Something, Fiona? Delaney, Ned, illus. LC 83-13457. 48p. (ps-3). 1984. 5.95 (*0-8193-1121-9*) Parents.
—A Bird's Body. Wexler, Jerome, illus. LC 82-6446. 48p. (gr. k-3). 1982. 12.95 (*0-688-01470-4*); lib. bdg. 12.88 (*0-688-01471-2*, Morrow Jr Bks) Morrow Jr Bks.
—Bony-Legs. Zimmer, Dirk, illus. LC 85-5070. 48p. (ps-3). 1984. RSBE 13.95 (*0-02-722970-X*, Four Winds) Macmillan Child Grp.
—Bony-Legs. Zimmer, Dirk, illus. 48p. (ps-2). 1986. pap. 2.95 (*0-590-40516-0*) Scholastic Inc.
—Bully Trouble: A Step Two Book. Hafner, Marilyn, illus. LC 89-3757. 48p. (Orig.). (gr. 1-3). 1989. lib. bdg. 7.99 (*0-394-94949-8*); pap. 3.50 (*0-394-84949-3*) Random Bks Yng Read.
—Cars & How They Go. Gibbons, Gail, illus. LC 82-45575. 32p. (gr. 2-6). 1983. (Crowell Jr Bks); PLB 13.89 (*0-690-04262-0*, Crowell Jr Bks) HarpC Child Bks.
—Cars & How They Go. Gibbons, Gail, illus. LC 82-45575. 32p. (gr. 2-6). 1986. pap. 4.95 (*0-06-446052-5*, Trophy) HarpC Child Bks.
—A Cat's Body. Wexler, Jerome, illus. LC 81-22386. 48p. (gr. k-3). 1982. lib. bdg. 12.88 (*0-688-01054-7*, Morrow Jr Bks) Morrow Jr Bks.
—A Chick Hatches. LC 76-29017. (Illus.). 48p. (gr. k-3). 1976. PLB 13.88 (*0-688-32087-2*) Morrow Jr Bks.
—The Clown-Arounds. Smath, Jerry, illus. LC 81-4662. 48p. (ps-3). 1981. 5.95 (*0-8193-1059-X*); PLB 5.95 (*0-8193-1060-3*) Parents.
—The Clown-Arounds. Smath, Jerry, illus. 48p. (ps-2). 1992. pap. 2.95 (*0-448-40321-8*, G&D) Putnam Pub Group.
—The Clown-Arounds Go on Vacation. Smath, Jerry, illus. LC 83-13480. 48p. (ps-3). 1984. 5.95 (*0-8193-1120-0*) Parents.
—The Clown-Arounds Go on Vacation. Smath, Jerry, illus. LC 93-15471. 1993. write for info. (*0-8368-0966-1*) Gareth Stevens Inc.
—The Clown-Arounds Have a Party. Smath, Jerry, illus. LC 82-2128. 48p. (ps-3). 1982. 5.95 (*0-8193-1085-9*); PLB 5.95 (*0-8193-1086-7*) Parents.
—Cuts, Breaks, Bruises, & Burns: How Your Body Heals. Kelley, True, illus. LC 84-45335. 48p. (gr. 2-6). 1985. (Crowell Jr Bks); PLB 13.89 (*0-690-04438-0*) HarpC Child Bks.
—Daytime Animals. Lilly, Kenneth, illus. LC 85-4301. 32p. (ps-2). 1985. PLB 12.99 (*0-394-97188-4*) Knopf Bks Yng Read.
—Dinosaur Story. Kunstler, Mort, illus. LC 74-5931. 32p. (gr. k-3). 1974. PLB 13.88 (*0-688-31826-6*) Morrow Jr Bks.
—Doctor Change. Carrick, Donald, illus. LC 86-881. 32p. (ps-3). 1986. 12.95 (*0-688-06135-4*); lib. bdg. 12.88 (*0-688-06136-2*, Morrow Jr Bks) Morrow Jr Bks.
—A Dog's Body. Wexler, Jerome, illus. LC 85-25885. 48p. (gr. k-3). 1986. 12.95 (*0-688-04153-1*); lib. bdg. 12.88 (*0-688-04154-X*, Morrow Jr Bks) Morrow Jr Bks.
—Don't Call Me Names! (Just Right for 4's & 5's) Munsinger, Lynn, illus. LC 89-35412. 32p. (ps). 1990. 4.95 (*0-679-80258-4*); PLB 5.99 (*0-679-90258-9*) Random Bks Yng Read.
—Don't Tell the Whole World! Duke, Kate, illus. LC 89-29283. 32p. (gr. k-3). 1992. pap. 4.95 (*0-06-443292-0*, Trophy) HarpC Child Bks.
—Evolution. Aliki, illus. LC 87-638. 32p. (gr. k-3). 1987. (Crowell Jr Bks); PLB 13.89 (*0-690-04598-0*, Crowell Jr Bks) HarpC Child Bks.
—Evolution. Aliki, illus. LC 87-638. 32p. (ps-3). 1989. pap. 4.50 (*0-06-445086-4*, Trophy) HarpC Child Bks.
—A Fish Hatches. LC 78-13445. (Illus.). 40p. (gr. k-3). 1978. PLB 12.88 (*0-688-32153-4*, Morrow Jr Bks) Morrow Jr Bks.
—A Frog's Body. Wexler, Jerome, illus. LC 80-10705. 48p. (gr. k-3). 1980. PLB 12.88 (*0-688-32228-X*, Morrow Jr Bks) Morrow Jr Bks.
—Get Well, Clown-Arounds! Smath, Jerry, illus. LC 82-8148. 48p. (ps-3). 1983. 5.95 (*0-8193-1095-6*); PLB 5.95 (*0-8193-1096-4*) Parents.

—Get Well, Clown-Arounds. (Illus.). 42p. (ps-3). 1993. PLB 13.26 (*0-8368-0895-9*); PLB 13.26 s.p. (*0-685-61526-X*) Gareth Stevens Inc.
—A Gift from Saint Francis: The First Creche. Lemieux, Michele, illus. LC 88-22048. 40p. 1989. 13.95 (*0-688-06502-3*); PLB 13.88 (*0-688-06503-1*, Morrow Jr Bks) Morrow Jr Bks.
—Golly Gump Swallowed a Fly. Weissman, Bari, illus. LC 81-11072. 48p. (ps-3). 1982. 5.95 (*0-8193-1069-7*); lib. bdg. 5.95 (*0-8193-1070-0*) Parents.
—A Horse's Body. Wexler, Jerome, photos by. LC 80-28147. (Illus.). 48p. (gr. k-3). 1981. 13.95 (*0-688-00362-1*); PLB 13.88 (*0-688-00363-X*, Morrow Jr Bks) Morrow Jr Bks.
—How You Were Born. LC 83-17314. (Illus.). 48p. (ps-3). 1984. 12.95 (*0-688-01710-X*); lib. bdg. 12.88 (*0-688-01709-6*, Morrow Jr Bks); pap. 4.95 (*0-685-08263-6*, Mulberry Bks) Morrow Jr Bks.
—How You Were Born. LC 83-17314. (ps-3). 1985. pap. 4.95 (*0-688-05801-9*, Mulberry) Morrow.
—How You Were Born. rev. ed. Miller, Margaret, photos by. (Illus.). 48p. (ps up). 1994. pap. 4.95 (*0-688-12061-X*, Mulberry) Morrow.
—How You Were Born: Illustrated with Photographs. rev. ed. Miller, Margaret, photos by. LC 92-23970. (Illus.). 48p. (ps up). 1993. 15.00 (*0-688-12059-8*); PLB 14.93 (*0-688-12060-1*) Morrow Jr Bks.
—The Human Body: How We Evolved. Gaffney-Kessell, Walter, illus. LC 86-23679. 64p. (ps-3). 1987. 12.95 (*0-688-06719-0*); lib. bdg. 12.88 (*0-688-06720-4*, Morrow Jr Bks) Morrow Jr Bks.
—Hungry, Hungry Sharks: A Step Two Book. Wynne, Patricia, illus. LC 85-2218. 48p. (gr. 1-3). 1986. lib. bdg. 7.99 (*0-394-97471-9*); pap. 3.50 (*0-394-87471-4*) Random Bks Yng Read.
—An Insect's Body. Wexler, Jerome & Mendez, Raymond A., photos by. LC 83-22027. (Illus.). 48p. (ps-3). 1984. 13.95 (*0-688-02771-7*); PLB 13.88 (*0-688-02772-5*, Morrow Jr Bks) Morrow Jr Bks.
—It's Too Noisy. Duke, Kate, illus. LC 88-3865. 32p. (ps-3). 1989. (Crowell Jr Bks); PLB 12.89 (*0-690-04737-1*, Crowell Jr Bks) HarpC Child Bks.
—Large As Life Animals in Beautiful Life-Size Paintings. Lilly, Kenneth, illus. LC 89-15391. 56p. (ps-5). 1990. 14.95 (*0-679-80459-5*) Knopf Bks Yng Read.
—The Magic School Bus at the Waterworks. Degen, Bruce, illus. 40p. (gr. 1-4). 1988. pap. 3.95 (*0-590-40360-5*, Scholastic Hardcover) Scholastic Inc.
—The Magic School Bus at the Waterworks. 1993. pap. 3.95 (*0-590-72488-6*) Scholastic Inc.
—The Magic School Bus: In the Time of the Dinosaurs. Degen, Bruce, illus. LC 93-5753. 1994. 14.95 (*0-590-44688-6*) Scholastic Inc.
—The Magic School Bus Inside the Earth. Degen, Bruce, illus. LC 87-4563. 48p. (gr. k-3). 1987. 14.95 (*0-590-40759-7*, Scholastic Hardcover) Scholastic Inc.
—The Magic School Bus Inside the Earth. Degen, Bruce, illus. 1989. pap. 3.95 (*0-590-40760-0*, Scholastic Hardcover) Scholastic Inc.
—The Magic School Bus Inside the Human Body. Degen, Bruce, illus. (ps-3). 1990. pap. 3.95 (*0-590-41427-5*, Scholastic Hardcover) Scholastic Inc.
—The Magic School Bus Inside the Human Body. Degen, Bruce, illus. 1992. pap. 3.95 (*0-685-53602-5*) Scholastic Inc.
—The Magic School Bus Lost in the Solar System. Degen, Bruce, illus. (ps-3). 1990. 14.95 (*0-590-41428-3*, Scholastic Hardcover) Scholastic Inc.
—The Magic School Bus Lost in the Solar System. Degen, Bruce, illus. 40p. 1992. pap. 3.95 (*0-590-41429-1*, Scholastic Hardcover) Scholastic Inc.
—The Magic School Bus on the Ocean Floor. (Illus.). (ps up). 1992. 14.95 (*0-590-41430-5*, 003, Scholastic Hardcover) Scholastic Inc.
—The Missing Tooth. Hafner, Marilyn, illus. LC 88-1903. 48p. (Orig.). (gr. 1-3). 1988. lib. bdg. 7.99 (*0-394-99279-2*); pap. 3.50 (*0-394-89279-8*) Random Bks Yng Read.
—Mixed-Up Magic. Donnelly, Judy, ed. Kelley, True, illus. LC 87-14965. 32p. (gr. k-3). 1987. 8.95 (*0-8038-9298-5*) Hastings.
—Monster Valentines. 1990. pap. 2.50 (*0-590-42216-2*) Scholastic Inc.
—My Puppy Is Born. rev. ed. Miller, Margaret, photos by. LC 90-42011. (Illus.). 48p. (ps up). 1991. pap. 4.95 (*0-688-10198-4*, Mulberry) Morrow.
—My Puppy Is Born. rev. ed. Miller, Margaret, photos by. LC 90-42011. (Illus.). 48p. (ps up). 1991. 13.95 (*0-688-09770-7*); PLB 13.88 (*0-688-09771-5*, Morrow Jr Bks) Morrow Jr Bks.
—New Treasury of Children's Poetry. Brown, Judith G., illus. LC 83-20821. 224p. (ps-8). 1984. pap. 18.50 (*0-385-18539-1*) Doubleday.
—Ready Set Read. 1990. pap. 17.95 (*0-385-41416-1*) Doubleday.
—Riding the Magic School Bus with Joanna Cole & Bruce Degen. 1993. pap. 39.95 (*0-590-45904-X*) Scholastic Inc.
—Six Sick Sheep. LC 92-5715. 1993. pap. 6.95 (*0-688-11068-1*, Pub. by Beech Tree Bks) Morrow.
—A Snake's Body. Wexler, Jerome, photos by. LC 81-9443. (Illus.). 48p. (gr. k-3). 1981. 12.95 (*0-688-00702-3*); 12.88 (*0-688-00703-1*, Morrow Jr Bks) Morrow Jr Bks.
—Sweet Dreams, Clown-Arounds. Smath, Jerry, illus. LC 85-6348. 48p. (ps-3). 1985. 5.95 (*0-8193-1138-3*) Parents.

—Sweet Dreams, Clown-Arounds. Smath, Jerry, illus. LC 93-13038. 1994. PLB 13.27 (*0-8368-0976-9*) Gareth Stevens Inc.
—This Is the Place for Me. Van Horn, William, illus. 32p. (Orig.). (gr. k-3). 1986. pap. 2.50 (*0-590-33996-6*) Scholastic Inc.
—Who Put the Pepper in the Pot? Alley, R. W., illus. LC 88-36625. 48p. (ps-3). 1989. 5.95 (*0-8193-1189-8*) Parents.
—Who Put the Pepper in the Pot? Alley, R. W., illus. 48p. (ps-2). 1991. pap. 2.95 (*0-448-41077-X*, G&D) Putnam Pub Group.
—Who Put the Pepper in the Pot? Alley, Robert W., illus. 42p. (ps-3). 1992. PLB 13.26 (*0-8368-0883-5*); PLB 13.26 s.p. (*0-685-61515-4*) Gareth Stevens Inc.
—You Can't Smell a Flower with Your Ear. Smith, Mavis, illus. LC 93-27264. 1994. write for info. (*0-448-40469-9*, G&D); pap. write for info. (*0-448-40470-2*, G&D) Putnam Pub Group.
—Your Insides. Meisel, Paul, illus. 40p. (ps-1). 1992. 14.95 (*0-399-22123-9*, Putnam) Putnam Pub Group.
Cole, Joanna & Calmenson, Stephanie. Crazy Eights & Other Card Games. Tiegreen, Alan, illus. LC 93-5427. 1994. write for info. (*0-688-12199-3*); PLB write for info. (*0-688-12200-0*); pap. write for info. (*0-688-12201-9*) Morrow Jr Bks.
—The Laugh Book. Hafner, Marilyn, illus. LC 85-13113. 320p. (gr. 2-6). 1986. 17.00 (*0-385-18559-6*) Doubleday.
—Pat a Cake: And Other Play Phymes. Tiegreen, Alan, illus. LC 91-32264. 48p. (ps). 1992. 14.00 (*0-688-11038-X*); PLB 13.93 (*0-688-11039-8*) Morrow Jr Bks.
—Pat-a-Cake & Other Play Rhymes. ALC Staff, ed. Tiegreen, illus. LC 91-32264. 48p. (ps up). 1992. pap. 6.95 (*0-688-11533-0*, Mulberry) Morrow.
—Pin the Tail on the Donkey & Other Party Games. Tiegreen, Alan, illus. LC 92-29786. 48p. (ps up). 1993. 15.00 (*0-688-11891-7*); PLB 14.93 (*0-688-11892-5*); pap. 6.95 (*0-688-12521-2*) Morrow Jr Bks.
—Six Sick Sheep: One Hundred One Tongue Twisters. Tiegreen, Alan, illus. LC 92-5715. 64p. (gr. 3 up). 1993. 15.00 (*0-688-11139-4*); PLB 14.93 (*0-688-11140-8*) Morrow Jr Bks.
Cole, Joanna & Degen, Bruce. The Magic School Bus Inside the Human Body. 1989. 14.95 (*0-590-41426-7*, Scholastic Hardcover) Scholastic Inc.
Cole, Joanna & Calmenson, Stephanie, eds. Give a Dog a Bone: Stories, Poems, Jokes, & Riddles about Dogs. Speirs, John, illus. LC 93-2536. 1994. write for info. (*0-590-46374-8*) Scholastic Inc.
—The Read-Aloud Treasury: Favorite Nursery Rhymes, Poems, Stories & More for the Very Young. Schweninger, Ann, illus. 256p. 1988. pap. 18.95 (*0-385-18560-X*) Doubleday.
—The Scary Book. Demarest, Chris, et al, illus. LC 90-26330. 128p. (gr. 2 up). 1991. 12.95 (*0-688-10654-4*) Morrow Jr Bks.
Cole, Joannna. The Magic School Bus at the Waterworks. (gr. 1-4). 1986. 13.95 (*0-590-43739-9*, Scholastic Hardcover) Scholastic Inc.
Cole, Judith. Another Tortoise & a Different Hare. Van Dun, Anke, illus. 32p. (gr. k-6). 1993. 12.95 (*0-918080-31-2*) Treasure Chest.
—The Moon, the Sun & the Coyote. (gr. k-3). 1991. pap. 13.95 jacketed (*0-671-69628-9*, S&S BFYR) S&S Trade.
—The Moon, the Sun, & the Coyote. (gr. 3). 1992. pap. write for info. (*0-663-56232-5*) Silver Burdett Pr.
Cole, Michael. Head in the Sand. Clifford, Rowan, illus. LC 90-30086. 24p. (ps-3). 1990. PLB 13.50 (*0-87614-435-0*) Carolrhoda Bks.
Cole, Michael D. Bill Clinton: United States President. LC 93-37411. 1994. write for info. (*0-89490-437-X*) Enslow Pubs.
—John Glenn: Astronaut & Senator. LC 92-20285. (Illus.). 104p. (gr. 6 up). 1993. lib. bdg. 17.95 (*0-89490-413-2*) Enslow Pubs.
Cole, Norma. Blast Off! A Space Counting Book. Peck, Marshall, III, illus. LC 93-28794. 32p. (ps-4). 1994. 14.95 (*0-88106-499-8*); PLB 15.00 (*0-88106-493-9*); pap. 6.95 (*0-88106-498-X*) Charlesbridge Pub.
—The Final Tide. LC 90-6072. 160p. (gr. 5 up). 1990. SBE 14.95 (*0-689-50510-8*, M K McElderry) Macmillan Child Grp.
Cole, Robin H. Pablo & the Miracle of Saint Anton. Cole, Robin H., illus. LC 89-37973. 48p. 1990. pap. 3.95 (*0-8091-6590-2*) Paulist Pr.
Cole, Ronald P. Sawdust "Fair Dinkum" LC 92-91125. 88p. 1993. pap. 8.00 (*1-56002-256-6*, Univ Edtns) Aegina Pr.
Cole, Ronny M. Zany Knock Knocks. Garramone, Rich, illus. LC 92-43068. 96p. (gr. 2-7). 1993. pap. 3.95 (*0-8069-8889-5*) Sterling.
Cole, Sharon A. The Emperor's New Clothes. (Illus.). 30p. (ps up). 1976. pap. 3.50 (*0-88680-045-5*); royalty on application 40.00 (*0-317-03604-1*) I E Clark.
Cole, Sheila. The Hen That Crowed. LC 92-4907. (ps-3). 1993. 14.00 (*0-688-10112-7*); PLB 13.93 (*0-688-10113-5*) Lothrop.
—When the Rain Stops. Sorensen, Henri, illus. LC 90-19124. 32p. (ps up). 1991. 13.95 (*0-688-07654-8*); PLB 13.88 (*0-688-07655-6*) Lothrop.
—When the Tide Is Low. Wright-Frierson, Virginia, illus. LC 84-10023. 32p. (ps-1). 1985. 12.95 (*0-688-04066-7*); PLB 12.88 (*0-688-04067-5*) Lothrop.

Cole, Shelia. The Dragon in the Cliff: A Novel Based on the Life of Mary Anning. Farrow, T. C., illus. LC 90-40455. (gr. 4-7). 1991. 12.95 (*0-688-10196-8*) Lothrop.
Cole, Tom, jt. auth. see Allen, Dorothy S.
Cole, Tom, ed. see Allen, Dorothy S.
Cole, W. Owen, ed. see Connolly, Holly & Connolly, Peter.
Cole, Wendy M. Vietnam. (Illus.). 112p. (gr. 5 up). 1989. lib. bdg. 14.95 (*1-55546-800-4*) Chelsea Hse.
Cole, William. Arkful of Animals. (gr. 4-7). 1992. pap. 3.80 (*0-395-61618-2*) HM.
—Beastly Boys & Ghastly Girls. (gr. 4 up). 1977. pap. 1.25 (*0-440-40467-3*, YB) Dell.
—Have I Got Dogs! Apple, Margot, illus. 32p. (ps-3). 1993. reinforced bdg. 13.99 (*0-670-83070-4*) Viking Child Bks.
—Oh, How Silly! Ungerer, Tomi, illus. 80p. (gr. 2 up). 1990. pap. 3.95 (*0-14-034441-1*, Puffin) Puffin Bks.
—Oh, What Nonsense. Ungerer, Tomi, illus. 80p. (gr. 2 up). 1990. pap. 3.95 (*0-14-034442-X*, Puffin) Puffin Bks.
Cole, William, selected by. Oh, Such Foolishness! Poems Selected by William Cole. De Paola, Tomie, illus. LC 78-1622. 96p. (gr. 4-6). 1991. PLB 13.89 (*0-397-32502-9*, Lipp Jr Bks) HarpC Child Bks.
—Oh, That's Ridiculous! Ungerer, Tomi, illus. 80p. (gr. 1-4). 1988. pap. 3.95 (*0-14-032857-2*, Puffin) Puffin Bks.
Cole, William, ed. Poem Stew. Weinhaus, Karen, illus. LC 81-47106. 96p. (gr. 3-6). 1981. (Lipp Jr Bks); PLB 12.89 (*0-397-31964-9*) HarpC Child Bks.
—Poem Stew. Weinhaus, Karen, illus. LC 81-47106. 96p. (gr. 2-6). 1983. pap. 4.95 (*0-06-440136-7*, Trophy) HarpC Child Bks.
Cole, William, selected by. A Zooful of Animals. Munsinger, Lynn, illus. 96p. (ps-8). 1992. 17.45 (*0-395-52278-1*) HM.
Cole, William E., ed. An Arkful of Animals: Poems for the Very Young. Munsinger, Lynn, illus. 128p. (gr. 3-7). 1978. 13.45 (*0-395-27205-X*) HM.
Coleman. Straight Answers for Kids. (gr. 7 up). 1992. write for info. (*1-55513-336-3*, Chariot Bks) Cook.
Coleman, Anne. Fabrics & Yarns. (Illus.). 32p. (gr. 2-6). 1990. lib. bdg. 15.94 (*0-86592-483-X*); lib. bdg. 11.95s.p. (*0-685-46441-5*) Rourke Corp.
Coleman, Bill & Coleman, Patty. My Confirmation Journal. rev. ed. 112p. (gr. 6-9). 1991. pap. 4.95 (*0-89622-483-X*, B67) Twenty-Third.
Coleman, Clay. Attack. (gr. 9-12). 1990. pap. 2.95 (*0-06-106022-4*, PL) HarpC.
—Discovered! (gr. 9-12). 1991. pap. 2.95 (*0-06-106044-5*, PL) HarpC.
—Mutiny. (gr. 4-7). 1991. pap. 2.95 (*0-06-106039-9*, PL) HarpC.
—Resolved: Your Dead. 1990. pap. 3.50 (*0-06-106019-4*, PL) HarpC.
—Stranded. 1990. pap. 2.95 (*0-06-106021-6*, PL) HarpC.
Coleman, Evelyn. Cymbals. Brown, Sterling, illus. LC 93-8690. 1995. write for info. (*0-02-722817-7*) Macmillan.
—The Footwarmer & the Black Crow. Minter, Daniel, illus. LC 92-38352. (gr. 3 up). 1994. text ed. 14.95 (*0-02-722816-9*) MacMillan.
Coleman, Hila. Weekend Sisters. (gr. 6 up). 1988. pap. 2.95 (*0-449-70206-5*, Juniper) Fawcett.
Coleman, Janet W. Fast Eddie. Gillman, Alec, illus. LC 92-31243. 144p. (gr. 3-5). 1993. SBE 13.95 (*0-02-722815-0*, Four Winds) Macmillan Child Grp.
Coleman, John. Your Book of Veteran & Edwardian Cars. (gr. 7 up). 1972. 7.95 (*0-571-09375-2*) Transatl Arts.
—Your Book of Vintage Cars. Tucker, Harry, illus. (gr. 7 up). 1969. 7.95 (*0-571-08276-9*) Transatl Arts.
Coleman, Kate. Who's Hot -- Blossom. (gr. 4-7). 1993. pap. 1.49 (*0-440-21602-8*) Dell.
Coleman, Larry G. Up from the Eagles' Nest. (Illus.). 44p. 1993. 12.95 (*0-9629978-8-9*) Sights Prods.
Coleman, Mary A. The Dreams of Hummingbirds: Poems from Nature. Mathews, Judith, ed. Masheris, Robert, illus. LC 92-36169. 32p. (gr. 3-7). 1993. PLB 14.95 (*0-8075-1720-8*) A Whitman.
—Secret Passageway. Nix, Harriet, illus. 48p. (Orig.). (gr. 1-6). 1989. pap. 8.50 (*0-685-28398-4*) Agee Pub.
Coleman, Nancy, et al. Hopes, Dreams & Wishes, 3 bks. Duris, Ellen, illus. 24p. (Orig.). (ps-k). 1991. Set. pap. 8.95 (*0-8249-7419-0*, Ideals Child) Hambleton-Hill.
Coleman, Patty, jt. auth. see Coleman, Bill.
Coleman, Sheila S. The Best Story about Jesus. Ham, John, illus. 32p. (gr. k-2). 1989. pamphlet pasted 2.50 (*0-87403-602-X*, 3862) Standard Pub.
Coleman, Willaim L. What You Should Know about Accepting People Who Aren't Like You. 1994. 5.99 (*0-8066-2637-2*, Augsburg) Augsburg Fortress.
Coleman, William. Animals That Show & Tell. LC 85-15122. 144p. (gr. 2-7). 1985. pap. 6.99 (*0-87123-807-1*) Bethany Hse.
—Before You Tuck Me In. LC 85-26703. 128p. (Orig.). (ps-k). 1986. pap. 6.99 (*0-87123-830-6*) Bethany Hse.
—Brave & Bashful. (gr. 3-7). 1989. pap. 3.69 (*0-89191-988-0*, Chariot Bks) Cook.
—Chesapeake Charlie & Blackbeard's Treasure. LC 80-70573. 128p. (Orig.). (gr. 5-9). 1981. pap. 3.99 (*0-87123-116-6*) Bethany Hse.
—Chesapeake Charlie & the Bay Bank Robbers. LC 80-66638. 112p. (Orig.). (gr. 2-6). 1980. pap. 3.99 (*0-87123-113-1*) Bethany Hse.
—Earning Your Wings. LC 84-6299. 140p. (gr. 7 up). 1984. pap. 6.99 (*0-87123-311-8*) Bethany Hse.

—Far Out Facts of the Bible. (gr. 3-7). 1989. pap. 3.69 (*1-55513-865-9*, Chariot Bks) Cook.
—Friends Forever. LC 87-700. 160p. (Orig.). 1987. pap. 6.99 (*0-87123-959-0*) Bethany Hse.
—Getting Ready for Our New Baby. LC 84-432. 112p. (ps-2). 1984. pap. 5.99 (*0-87123-295-2*) Bethany Hse.
—Just 'Cuz You Married My Mom Doesn't Mean You're My Dad: A Survival Guide for Teenagers with Step Parents. 132p. (gr. 7 up). 1993. 9.95 (*0-89638-285-0*) CompCare.
—Kings & Critters. (gr. 3-7). 1989. pap. 3.69 (*0-89191-989-9*, Chariot Bks) Cook.
—The Warm Hug Book. LC 85-6175. 128p. (Orig.). (ps). 1985. pap. 6.99 (*0-87123-794-6*) Bethany Hse.
Coleman, William L. Chesapeake Charlie & the Haunted Ship. LC 82-73912. 112p. (Orig.). (gr. 2-6). 1983. pap. 3.99 (*0-87123-282-0*) Bethany Hse.
—Chesapeake Charlie & the Stolen Diamonds. LC 81-68077. 112p. (Orig.). (gr. 5-8). 1981. pap. 3.99 (*0-87123-170-0*) Bethany Hse.
—Cupid is Stupid! How to Fall in Love Without Falling on Your Face. LC 91-21852. 164p. (Orig.). (gr. 9 up). 1991. pap. 7.99 (*0-8308-1335-7*, 1335) InterVarsity.
—Entering the Teen Zone: Devotions to Guide You. LC 90-43092. 112p. (Orig.). (gr. 7-10). 1991. pap. 5.99 (*0-8066-2499-X*, 9-2499, Augsburg) Augsburg Fortress.
—God Doesn't Play Favorites: Gutsy Devotions for Teens. 176p. (Orig.). (gr. 7-12). 1992. pap. 7.99 (*0-8007-5430-1*) Revell.
—If Animals Could Talk. LC 87-7141. (Illus.). 144p. (Orig.). (gr. 2-6). 1987. pap. 6.99 (*0-87123-961-2*) Bethany Hse.
—Listen to the Animals. LC 79-11312. 128p. (ps-6). 1979. pap. 6.99 (*0-87123-341-X*) Bethany Hse.
—My Hospital Book. Walles, Dwight, illus. LC 81-10094. 96p. (Orig.). (gr. 2-7). 1981. pap. 5.99 (*0-87123-354-1*) Bethany Hse.
—Singing Penguins & Puffed-up Toads. LC 81-1079. 125p. (ps-4). 1981. pap. 6.99 (*0-87123-554-4*) Bethany Hse.
—Today I Feel Like a Warm Fuzzy. Koechel & Peterson, illus. LC 80-19708. 126p. (Orig.). (ps-2). 1980. pap. 6.99 (*0-87123-565-X*) Bethany Hse.
—Today I Feel Shy. LC 83-9216. 128p. (Orig.). (gr. 3-4). 1983. pap. 6.99 (*0-87123-588-9*) Bethany Hse.
—What Children Need to Know When Parents Get Divorced. LC 83-6006. 91p. (gr. k-5). 1983. pap. 5.99 (*0-87123-612-5*) Bethany Hse.
—What You Should Know about a Parent Who Drinks Too Much. LC 92-18314. 96p. (Orig.). (gr. 3-8). 1992. pap. 5.99 (*0-8066-2610-0*, 9-2610, Augsburg) Augsburg Fortress.
—What You Should Know about Getting along with a New Parent. LC 92-18335. 96p. (Orig.). (gr. 3-8). 1992. pap. 5.99 (*0-8066-2611-9*, 9-2611, Augsburg) Augsburg Fortress.
—What You Should Know about Living with One Parent. LC 93-31851. 1993. 5.99 (*0-8066-2636-4*) Augsburg Fortress.
Coleridge, Ann. Stranded. 1989. pap. 13.95 (*0-385-29825-0*) Delacorte.
Coleridge, Samuel Taylor. Portable Coleridge. Richards, Ivor A., ed. (gr. 10 up). 1977. pap. 11.00 (*0-14-015048-X*, P48, Penguin Bks) Viking Penguin.
—The Rime of the Ancient Mariner. Young, Ed, illus. LC 90-20403. 64p. (ps up). 1992. SBE 16.95 (*0-689-31613-5*, Atheneum Child Bk) Macmillan Child Grp.
Coleridge, Sara. January Brings the Snow. Chartier, Normand, illus. (ps-3). 1990. (Little Simon); pap. 2.25 (*0-671-72338-3*) S&S Trade.
—January Brings the Snow. 1989. pap. 4.95 (*0-8037-0704-5*, Dial) Doubleday.
Coles, Allison. Mandy & the Hospital. Charlton, Michael, illus. 28p. (ps). 1985. 3.95 (*0-88110-269-5*) EDC.
—Michael & the Sea. Charlton, Michael, illus. 28p. (ps up). 1985. 3.95 (*0-88110-268-7*) EDC.
—Michael in the Dark. Charlton, Michael, illus. 28p. (ps up). 1985. 3.95 (*0-88110-267-9*) EDC.
Coles, William E., Jr. & Schwandt, Stephen. Funnybone. LC 91-13174. 208p. (gr. 7 up). 1992. SBE 14.95 (*0-689-31666-6*, Atheneum Child Bk) Macmillan Child Grp.
Colin, Patrick L. Marine Invertebrates & Plants of the Living Reef. (Illus.). 512p. (gr. 7 up). 1988. lib. bdg. 29.95 (*0-86622-875-6*, H-971) TFH Pubns.
Collaci, Dorothy. The Contender: A Study Guide. 1989. tchr's. ed. & wkbk. 14.95 (*0-88122-059-0*) LRN Links.
Colladi, Carlo. The Adventures of Pinocchio: The Ultimate Illustrated Edition. (Illus.). 160p. (ps up). write for info. Bantam.
Collard, Sneed. Green Giants. Linder, Greg, ed. (gr. 1-5). Date not set. 11.95 (*0-685-65011-1*) NorthWord.
—Smart Survivors. Linder, Greg, ed. (gr. 1-5). Date not set. 14.95 (*1-55971-219-8*) NorthWord.
—Tough Terminators. Linder, Greg, ed. (gr. 1-5). Date not set. 14.95 (*1-55971-218-X*) NorthWord.
Collard, Sneed B. Sea Snakes. (gr. 4-7). 1993. write for info. (*1-56397-004-X*) Boyds Mills Pr.
Collard, Sneed, III. Do They Scare You? Creepy Creatures. (Illus.). 32p. (ps-4). 1993. 14.95 (*0-88106-491-2*); PLB 15.00 (*0-88106-492-0*); pap. 6.95 (*0-88106-490-4*) Charlesbridge Pub.
College Research Group of Concord, MA Staff, compiled by. The Right College 1988. 1545p. (gr. 10-11). 1987. (Arco Test); pap. 14.95 (*0-13-044850-4*) P-H Gen Ref & Trav.

Collen, Arne. Friends & Fiends. (Illus.). 72p. (Orig.). (gr. 7 up). pap. write for info. Eagleye Bks Intl.
Collette, Paul & Wright, Robert. Huddles. LC 91-51081. (Orig.). (gr. 3-12). 1985. pap. 6.00 play script (0-88734-512-3) Players Pr.
Colli, Monica. Twins. LC 91-36606. 1992. 5.95 (0-85953-394-8) Childs Play.
—Twins' Party. (ps-3). 1993. 5.95 (0-85953-404-9) Childs Play.
Collier, Christopher. My Brother Sam Is Dead. large type ed. (gr. 5 up). 1988. Repr. of 1974 ed. 15.95 (1-55736-038-3, Crnrstn Bks) BDD LT Grp.
Collier, Christopher, jt. auth. see Collier, James.
Collier, Christopher, jt. auth. see Collier, James L.
Collier, Christopher, jt. auth. see James L.
Collier, Cynthia. ed. see Wang, Wally & Millard, Scott.
Collier, James & Collier, Christopher. War Comes to Willy Freeman. (gr. 4-6). 1992. 16.50 (0-8446-6596-7) Peter Smith.
Collier, James L. Duke Ellington. LC 90-26303. 144p. (gr. 5-9). 1991. SBE 12.95 (0-02-722985-8, Macmillan Child Bk) Macmillan Child Grp.
—Duke Ellington. LC 92-39793. 144p. (gr. 7 up). 1994. pap. 5.95 (0-02-042675-5, Aladdin) Macmillan Child Grp.
—The Jazz Kid. 1994. write for info. (0-8050-2821-8) H Holt & Co.
—Louis Armstrong: An American Success Story. LC 84-42982. (Illus.). 176p. (gr. 5-9). 1985. SBE 14.95 (0-02-722830-4, Macmillan Child Bk) Macmillan Child Grp.
—Louis Armstrong: An American Success Story. LC 92-45767. (Illus.). 176p. (gr. 7 up). 1994. pap. 5.95 (0-02-042555-4, Aladdin) Macmillan Child Grp.
—My Crooked Family. LC 90-27747. 288p. (gr. 5-9). 1991. pap. 15.00 jacketed, 3-pc. bdg. (0-671-74224-8, S&S BFYR) S&S Trade.
—My Crooked Family. LC 90-27747. 288p. (gr. 5-9). 1993. pap. 3.95 (0-671-86693-1, Half Moon Bks) S&S Trade.
—Outside Looking In. LC 86-21845. 192p. (gr. 5-9). 1987. SBE 13.95 (0-02-723100-3, Macmillan Child Bk) Macmillan Child Grp.
—The Teddy Bear Habit. (gr. 5-9). 15.50 (0-8446-6191-0) Peter Smith.
—The Winchesters. 176p. (gr. 4). 1989. pap. 2.95 (0-380-70808-6, Flare) Avon.
Collier, James L. & Collier, Christopher. The Bloody Country. 180p. (gr. 9 up). 1985. pap. 3.25 (0-590-43126-9) Scholastic Inc.
—Jump Ship to Freedom. LC 81-65492. 192p. (gr. 4-6). 1981. pap. 13.95 (0-385-28484-5) Delacorte.
—Jump Ship to Freedom. (gr. k-6). 1987. pap. 3.50 (0-440-44323-7, Yearling) Dell.
—My Brother Sam Is Dead. LC 84-28787. 224p. (gr. 7 up). 1984. SBE 14.95 (0-02-722980-7, Four Winds) Macmillan Child Grp.
—My Brother Sam Is Dead. 192p. (gr. 9 up). 1985. pap. 2.95 (0-590-42792-X) Scholastic Inc.
—War Comes to Willy Freeman. LC 82-70317. 192p. (gr. 4-6). 1983. pap. 13.95 (0-385-29235-X) Delacorte.
—Who Is Carrie? LC 83-23947. 192p. (gr. 4-6). 1984. 14.95 (0-385-29295-3) Delacorte.
—Who Is Carrie? (gr. k-6). 1987. pap. 3.50 (0-440-49536-9, YB) Dell.
—The Winter Hero. 132p. (gr. 9 up). 1985. pap. 2.75 (0-590-42604-4) Scholastic Inc.
Collier, Jaunell & Hill, Marie. I Love You. Collier, Jaunell, illus. 27p. (Orig.). 1983. write for info. (0-918464-58-7) Irresistible.
Collier, John. In My Backyard. Collier, John, illus. 32p. (ps-3). 1993. reinforced bdg. 14.99 (0-670-83609-5) Viking Child Bks.
Collier, Roberta, illus. Sing with Me Lullabies. (ps-1). 1987. Incl cassette. 5.95 (0-394-88811-1) Random Bks Yng Read.
Colligan-Taylor, Karen, tr. see Michio Hoshino.
Collington, Peter. The Angel & the Soldier Boy. miniature ed. Collington, Peter, illus. 32p. (ps-3). 1991. 4.95 (0-679-81441-8) Knopf Bks Yng Read.
—The Coming of the Surfman. Collington, Peter, illus. LC 92-41844. 32p. (gr. 3 up). 1994. 16.00 (0-679-84721-9) Knopf Bks Yng Read.
—The Midnight Circus. Collington, Peter, illus. 32p. (ps-2). 1993. 15.00 (0-679-83262-9); PLB 15.99 (0-679-93262-3) Knopf Bks Yng Read.
—On Christmas Eve. Collington, Peter, illus. LC 90-4202. 32p. 1990. 14.95 (0-679-80830-2); PLB 15.99 (0-679-90830-7) Knopf Bks Yng Read.
Collini, Emanuela, jt. auth. see Padoan, Gianni.
Collins, A. Frederick. Rapid Math Without a Calculator. 120p. 1987. pap. 5.95 (0-8065-1058-7, Pub. by Citadel Pr) Carol Pub Group.
Collins, Ace, jt. auth. see Mandrell, Louise.
Collins, Ann & Clary, Linda. Sing & Play--Preschool Piano Book One. (Illus.). 60p. (ps). 1987. spiral bdg. 5.00 (0-87563-307-2) Stipes.
Collins, Betty, jt. auth. see Collins, Kevin.
Collins, Bonnie, jt. auth. see Harshman, Marc.
Collins, Crystal. Teddy Bear Paper Dolls. 1983. pap. 3.50 (0-486-24550-0) Dover.
Collins, David. Florence Nightingale. (gr. 3-6). 1985. pap. 6.95 (0-88062-126-5) Mott Media.
—Francis Scott Key. Van Seversen, Joe, illus. 113p. (gr. 3-6). 1982. pap. 6.95 (0-915134-91-8) Mott Media.
—George Washington Carver. Van Seversen, Joe, illus. 131p. (gr. 3-6). 1981. pap. 6.95 (0-915134-90-X) Mott Media.

—Johnny Appleseed. LC 84-60315. (gr. 3-6). 1985. pap. 6.95 (0-88062-134-6) Mott Media.
—Noah Webster: Master of Words. (Illus.). (gr. 3-6). 1989. pap. 6.95 (0-88062-158-3) Mott Media.
Collins, David R. Abraham Lincoln. Quinton, Myron, illus LC 76-2456. (gr. 3-6). 1976. pap. 6.95 (0-915134-93-4) Mott Media.
—Ara's Amazing Spinning Wheel. (Illus.). (ps-2). 1991. PLB 6.95 (0-8136-5181-6, TK7275); pap. 3.50 (0-8136-5681-8, TK7276) Modern Curr.
—Ceb's Amazing Tail. (Illus.). (ps-2). 1987. PLB 6.95 (0-8136-5185-9, TK7273); pap. 3.50 (0-8136-5685-0, TK7274) Modern Curr.
—Charles Lindbergh: Hero Pilot. Mays, Victor, illus. 80p. (gr. 2-6). 1991. Repr. of 1978 ed. lib. bdg. 12.95 (0-7910-1417-7) Chelsea Hse.
—The Country Artist: A Story about Beatrix Potter. Wilken, Mark, illus. 56p. (gr. 3-6). 1989. 14.95 (0-87614-344-3); pap. 5.95 (0-87614-509-8) Carolrhoda Bks.
—Eng & Chang: The Original Siamese Twins. LC 93-26295. Date not set. write for info. (0-87518-602-5, Dillon Pr) Macmillan Child Grp.
—Gerald R. Ford: Thirty-Eighth President of the United States. Young, Richard G., ed. LC 89-39945. (Illus.). 128p. (gr. 5-9). 1990. PLB 17.26 (0-944483-65-8) Garrett Ed Corp.
—Grandfather Woo Goes to School. McKissack, Patricia & McKissack, Fredrick, eds. Wilson, Deborah, illus. LC 88-60389. 32p. (Orig.). (gr. 1-3). 1990. text ed. 8.95 (0-88335-784-4); pap. text ed. 4.95 (0-88335-796-8) Milliken Pub Co.
—Grover Cleveland: 22nd & 24th President of the United States. Young, Richard G., ed. LC 87-35794. (Illus.). (gr. 5-9). 1988. PLB 17.26 (0-944483-01-1) Garrett Ed Corp.
—Hali's Amazing Wings. (Illus.). (ps-2). 1987. PLB 6.95 (0-8136-5183-2, TK7271); pap. 3.50 (0-8136-5683-4, TK7272) Modern Curr.
—Harry S. Truman: People's President. Frame, Paul, illus. 80p. (gr. 2-6). 1991. Repr. of 1985 ed. lib. bdg. 12.95 (0-7910-1421-5) Chelsea Hse.
—Harry S. Truman: 33rd President of the United States. Young, Richard G., ed. LC 87-32750. (Illus.). (gr. 5-9). 1988. PLB 17.26 (0-944483-00-3) Garrett Ed Corp.
—J. R. R. Tolkien: Master of Fantasy. Heagy, William, illus. 144p. (gr. 4-7). 1992. 21.50 (0-8225-4906-9) Lerner Pubns.
—J. R. R. Tolkien: Master of Fantasy. (gr. 4-7). 1993. pap. 7.95 (0-8225-9618-0) Lerner Pubns.
—James Buchanan: Fifteenth President of the United States. Young, Richard G., ed. LC 89-39948. (Illus.). 128p. (gr. 5-9). 1990. PLB 17.26 (0-944483-62-3) Garrett Ed Corp.
—Lee Iacocca: Chrysler's Good Fortune. Young, Richard G., ed. LC 91-31989. (Illus.). 64p. (gr. 4-8). 1992. PLB 17.26 (1-56074-017-5) Garrett Ed Corp.
—Leo's Amazing Paws & Jaws. (Illus.). (ps-2). 1987. PLB 6.95 (0-8136-5182-4, TK7269); pap. 3.50 (0-8136-5682-6, TK7270) Modern Curr.
—Malcolm X: Center of the Storm. LC 91-39951. (Illus.). 104p. (gr. 5 up). 1992. RSBE 13.95 (0-87518-498-7, Dillon) Macmillan Child Grp.
—Mark T-W-A-I-N! A Story about Samuel Clemens. Carey, Vicky, illus. LC 93-15164. 1993. write for info. (0-87614-801-1) Carolrhoda Bks.
—Phillip H. Knight: Running with Nike. Young, Richard G., ed. LC 91-32316. (Illus.). 64p. (gr. 4-8). 1992. PLB 17.26 (1-56074-020-5) Garrett Ed Corp.
—Pioneer Plowmaker: A Story about John Deere. Michaels, Steve, illus. 64p. (gr. 3-6). 1990. PLB 14.95 (0-87614-424-5) Carolrhoda Bks.
—Probo's Amazing Trunk. (Illus.). (ps-2). 1987. PLB 6.95 (0-8136-5184-0, TK7267); pap. 3.50 (0-8136-5684-2, TK7268) Modern Curr.
—Ride a Red Dinosaur. McKissack, Patricia & McKissack, Fredrick, eds. Nolte, Larry, illus. LC 87-61645. 32p. (Orig.). (gr. 1-3). 1987. text ed. 8.95 (0-88335-726-7); pap. text ed. 4.95 (0-88335-746-1) Milliken Pub Co.
—Tales for Hard Times: A Story about Charles Dickens. Mataya, David, illus. 64p. (gr. 3-6). 1990. PLB 14.95 (0-87614-433-4) Carolrhoda Bks.
—To the Point: A Story about E. B. White. Johnson, Amy, illus. 56p. (gr. 3-6). 1989. 14.95 (0-87614-345-1); pap. 5.95 (0-87614-508-X) Carolrhoda Bks.
—Ursi's Amazing Fur Coat. (Illus.). (ps-2). 1987. PLB 6.95 (0-8136-5186-7, TK7265); pap. 3.50 (0-8136-5686-9, TK7266) Modern Curr.
—William McKinley: Twenty-Fifth President of the United States. Young, Richard G., ed. LC 89-39954. (Illus.). 128p. (gr. 5-9). 1990. PLB 17.26 (0-944483-55-0) Garrett Ed Corp.
—The Wisest Answer. McKissack, Patricia & McKissack, Fredrick, eds. Wilson, Deborah, illus. LC 87-61640. 32p. (Orig.). (gr. 1-3). text ed. 8.95 (0-88335-731-3); pap. text ed. 4.95 (0-88335-751-8) Milliken Pub Co.
—Woodrow Wilson: Twenty-Eighth President of the United States. Young, Richard G., ed. LC 88-24563. (gr. 5-9). 1989. PLB 17.26 (0-944483-18-6) Garrett Ed Corp.
—Zachary Taylor: Twelfth President of the United States. Young, Richard G., ed. LC 88-24539. (Illus.). (gr. 5-9). 1989. PLB 17.26 (0-944483-17-8) Garrett Ed Corp.

Collins, David R. & Witter, Evelyn. The Golden Circle. 2nd ed. Nolte, Larry, illus. LC 91-67503. 105p. (gr. 4-8). 1992. pap. 6.95 (1-55523-492-5) Winston-Derek.
Collins, Doris. Fun Times Growing Up. Walsh, Janice, illus. 24p. (Orig.). (gr. k-3). 1988. pap. 7.95 (0-9621650-0-X) Periwinkle MA.
Collins, Grace. Willy, Zilly & the Little Bantams. LC 88-51662. (Illus.). 32p. (gr. 1-3). 1988. 10.25x (0-943864-54-2) Davenport.
Collins, Gretchen. English Grammar Flipper: A Guide to Correct English Usage. 49p. (gr. 5 up). 1989. Repr. of 1977 ed. trade edition 5.95 (1-878383-01-9) C Lee Pubns.
Collins, H. When You Were Little & I Was Big. (Illus.). 32p. (ps-8). 1984. 12.95 (0-920236-84-7, Pub. by Annick CN); pap. 4.95 (0-920236-71-5, Pub. by Annick CN) Firefly Bks Ltd.
Collins, James L. John Brown & the Fight Against Slavery. (Illus.). 32p. (gr. 2-4). 1991. PLB 12.40 (1-56294-043-0) Millbrook Pr.
—Lawmen of the Old West. LC 89-22555. (ps-3). 1990. PLB 12.90 (0-531-10893-7) Watts.
Collins, Jim. The Bermuda Triangle. LC 77-21808. (Illus.). 48p. (gr. 4 up). 1983. PLB 18.64 (0-8172-1050-4) Raintree Steck-V.
—Settling the American West. LC 92-28301. 1993. PLB 12.90 (0-531-20070-1) Watts.
—Unidentified Flying Objects. LC 77-13040. (Illus.). 48p. (gr. 4 up). 1983. PLB 18.64 (0-8172-1065-2) Raintree Steck-V.
Collins, Joseph T., jt. auth. see Cross, Frank B.
Collins, Julie, jt. auth. see Collins, Miki.
Collins, Kevin & Collins, Betty. Experimenting with Science Photography. LC 93-31074. 1994. write for info. (0-531-11166-0) Watts.
Collins, Linda B. & Spangler, Carol S. The Communication Program Planning Book: A Plan Book for Speech-Language Pathologists. 200p. (gr. k-12). 1989. 21.95 (0-937857-10-6, 1567) Speech Bin.
Collins, Miki & Collins, Julie. Trapline Twins. LC 88-34231. (Illus.). 224p. (Orig.). (gr. 7). 1989. pap. 12.95 (0-88240-332-X) Alaska Northwest.
Collins, Nancy. Places to Sleep. Neaville, Michelle, illus. LC 92-14392. 32p. (ps-2). Date not set. 11.95 (1-56065-165-2) Capstone Pr. Postponed.
Collins, Pat L. Don't Feed the Guppies. Hafner, Marylin, illus. LC 92-25336. 1994. write for info. (0-399-22530-7) Putnam Pub Group.
—I Am an Artist. Brickman, Robin, illus. LC 91-42071. 32p. (gr. k-3). 1992. 14.95 (1-56294-702-8); PLB 14.90 (1-56294-082-1) Millbrook Pr.
—Tomorrow, up & Away. Munsinger, Lynn, illus. 32p. (gr. k-3). 1990. 13.45 (0-395-51524-6) HM.
—Waiting for Baby Joe. Tucker, Kathy, ed. Dunn, Joan W., illus. LC 89-21457. 48p. (ps-2). 1990. PLB 11.95 (0-8075-8625-0) A Whitman.
Collins, Patrick, jt. ed. see Temple, Charles.
Collins, Robert F. America at Its Best: Opportunities in the National Guard. Rosen, Ruth, ed. (gr. 7-12). 1989. PLB 14.95 (0-8239-1024-5) Rosen Group.
—Qualifying for Admission to the Service Academies: A Student's Guide. rev. ed. Rosen, Ruth, ed. (Illus.). 154p. (gr. 7 up). 1990. lib. bdg. 14.95 (0-8239-1187-X) Rosen Group.
—Reserve Officer Training Corps: Campus Paths to Service Commissions. (Illus.). 148p. (gr. 7-12). 1986. PLB 14.95 (0-8239-0695-7) Rosen Group.

Collins, S. Harold. Caring for Young Children: Signing for Day Care Providers & Sitters. Kifer, Kathy, illus. 32p. (Orig.). (gr. 1-8). 1993. pap. text ed. 2.95 (0-931993-58-X, GP-058) Garlic Pr OR.
CARING FOR YOUNG CHILDREN is one of four books in the Beginning Sign Language Series. This book is geared to those who work with or care for young hearing impaired children. CAN I HELP? (ISBN 0-931993-57-1, 32p., $2.95) presents signs, sentences & information to help a beginning signer of any age communicate with a hearing impaired person who may need help. The FINGER ALPHABET BOOK (ISBN 0-931993-46-6, 32p., $2.95) teaches alphabet signs & starts you on your way to TALKING with your hands. Its companion book, SIGNING AT SCHOOL, (ISBN 0-931993-47-4, 32p., $2.95) presents signs, sentences & vocabulary to enable a beginning signer to ask questions, get information, give greetings, & give directions. These wonderful books with glossy durable covers provide easy-to-follow illustrations & activities to make sign language fascinating & fun for both

children & adults.
Publisher Provided Annotation.

Collins, Stephen. VerbMaster: Spanish. (SPA.). 29p. (Orig.). (gr. 9 up). 1990. pap. 4.95 (0-9626328-1-3) F One Servs.
Collins, Stephen, ed. see Becker, Sheila.
Collins, Sterling C. Doll-Victorian Mouse Paper Dolls in Full Color. 1986. pap. 3.95 (0-486-25045-8) Dover.
Collins, Thomas & Czarra, Fred. Global Primer - Skills for a Changing World. rev. ed. Webb, Allice, illus. 293p. (gr. k-8). 1991. pap. 26.95 (0-943804-60-4) U of Denver Teach.
Collins, Tom. Steven Spielberg: Creator of E. T. LC 83-21068. (Illus.). 64p. (gr. 3 up). 1983. RSBE 13.95 (0-87518-249-6, Dillon) Macmillan Child Grp.
Collins, William & Levene, Bruce. Black Bart: The True Story of California's Most Famous Stagecoach Robber. LC 91-67893. (Illus.). 224p. (Orig.). (gr. 4-7). 1992. pap. 15.95 (0-933391-10-2) Pac Transcript.
Collins, William W. Moonstone. Lane, L., Jr., intro. by. (gr. 10 up). 1965. pap. 2.95 (0-8049-0076-0, CL-76) Airmont.
Collinson, Alan. Choosing Health. LC 90-25849. (Illus.). 48p. (gr. 5-8). 1991. PLB 19.92 (0-8114-2801-X) Raintree Steck-V.
—Grasslands. LC 92-4021. (Illus.). 48p. (gr. 5 up). 1992. RSBE 13.95 (0-87518-492-8, Dillon) Macmillan Child Grp.
—Pollution. LC 91-24081. (Illus.). 48p. (gr. 4-6). 1992. RSBE 13.95 (0-02-722995-5, New Discovery) Macmillan Child Grp.
—Renewable Energy. LC 90-19791. (Illus.). 48p. (gr. 5-8). 1991. PLB 19.92 (0-8114-2802-8) Raintree Steck-V.
Collinson, Allan. Mountains. LC 91-34171. (Illus.). 48p. (gr. 5 up). 1992. RSBE 13.95 (0-87518-493-6, Dillon) Macmillan Child Grp.
Collins-Sterling, Crystal. Panda-Paper Dolls. 1989. pap. 2.95 (0-486-25929-3) Dover.
Collis, Annabel. You Can't Catch Me! LC 92-54486. 1993. 13.95 (0-316-15237-4) Little.
Collis, Len. Card Games for Children. Carter, Terry & George, Bob, illus. 96p. (ps up) 1989. pap. 5.95 (0-8120-4290-5) Barron.
—Magic Tricks for Children. Carter, Terry & George, Bob, illus. 96p. (gr. 3 up). 1989. pap. 4.95 (0-8120-4289-1) Barron.
Collison, David, jt. auth. see Pryor, Francis.
Collison, Joanne, ed. see Timothy, Kevin.
Collison, Kathleen, jt. auth. see Brockmeyer, Lloyd.
Collman, Barbera J. Kid's Book to Welcome a New Baby: A Fun Activity Book of Things to Do & to Learn for a "Big Brother" or "Big Sister" (Illus.). 96p. (Orig.). 1992. pap. 8.95 (0-943400-65-1) Marlor Pr.
Collman, Marthamarie C. Ballads & Other Island Things. Collman, Martha R., illus. 104p. (Orig.). (gr. 9 up). 1992. pap. 8.95 (0-9631903-0-X) M R Collman.
Collodi. Le Avventure di Pinocchio. (gr. 7-12). pap. 5.95 (0-88436-050-4, 55254) EMC.
Collodi, C. The Adventures of Pinocchio. reissued ed. Chiesa, Carol D., tr. from ITA. Mussino, Attilio, illus. LC 88-26684. 320p. (gr. 3 up). 1989. SBE 24.95 (0-02-722821-5, Macmillan Child Bk) Macmillan Child Grp.
Collodi, Carlo. Adventures of Pinocchio. (Illus.). (gr. 4 up). 1966. pap. 1.75 (0-8049-0101-5, CL-101) Airmont.
—Adventures of Pinocchio. Kredel, Fritz, illus. (gr. 4-6). 1982. 12.95 (0-448-06001-9, G&D) Putnam Pub Group.
—The Adventures of Pinocchio. Harden, E., tr. from ITA. Innocenti, Roberto, illus. LC 88-8918. 144p. (ps up). 1988. 18.95 (0-394-82110-6) Knopf Bks Yng Read.
—The Adventures of Pinocchio. Kassirer, Sue, adapted by. Haverfield, Mary, illus. LC 92-2503. 32p. (Orig.). (ps-2). 1992. pap. 2.25 (0-679-83466-4) Random Bks Yng Read.
—The Adventures of Pinocchio. Innocenti, Roberto, illus. 144p. (gr. 1-12). Date not set. lib. bdg. 19.95 RLB smythe-sewn (0-8211-0394-6, 97080-098) Creative Ed.
—Pinocchio. (FRE., Illus.). (gr. 3-8). 5.95 (0-685-11495-3, S16273) Fr & Eur.
—Pinocchio. (gr. 4-6). 1985. pap. 2.99 (0-14-035037-3, Puffin) Puffin Bks.
—Pinocchio. LC 87-15789. 1988. 10.99 (0-517-61815-X) Outlet Bk Co.
—Pinocchio. Hildebrandt, Greg, illus. 160p. 1986. 14.95 (0-88101-271-8) Unicorn Pub.
—Pinocchio. Chiostri, Carlo, illus. (FRE.). 235p. (gr. 5-10). 1985. pap. 9.95 (2-07-033283-7) Schoenhof.
—Pinocchio. Mattotti, Lorenzo, illus. LC 92-44161. (ENG.). (gr. 2 up). 1993. write for info. (0-688-12450-X); lib. bdg. write for info. (0-688-12451-8) Lothrop.
—Pinocchio: A Classic Tale. Jose, Eduard, adapted by. Moncure, Jane B., tr. from SPA. Asensio, Augusti, illus. LC 88-35308. 32p. 1988. PLB 19.95 (0-89565-458-X); PLB 13.95s.p. (0-685-56023-6) Childs World.
—Walt Disney's Pinocchio. Walt Disney Studios Staff, illus. 80p. 1989. 19.95 (0-8109-1467-0) Abrams.
Collyer, J., jt. auth. see Fraser, K.
Colman, Hila. Claudia, Where Are You? (gr. 7-9). 1985. (Archway); pap. 2.25 (0-671-42450-5) PB.

—Diary of a Frantic Kid Sister. (gr. 4-6). 1985. pap. 2.95 (0-671-61926-8, Archway) PB.
—The Double Life of Angela Jones. LC 87-33246. 160p. (gr. 7 up). 1988. 12.95 (0-688-06781-6) Morrow Jr Bks.
—Forgotten Girl. LC 89-38482. 160p. (gr. 5-9). 1990. PLB 13.99 (0-517-57592-2) Crown Bks Yng Read.
—Nobody Told Me What I Need to Know. LC 84-8673. 176p. (gr. 7 up). 1984. 11.95 (0-688-03869-7) Morrow Jr Bks.
—Rich & Famous Like My Mom. LC 87-27448. 144p. (gr. 4-7). 1988. 10.95 (0-517-56836-5) Crown Bks Yng Read.
—Suddenly. LC 86-28460. 160p. (gr. 7 up). 1987. 12.95 (0-688-05865-5) Morrow Jr Bks.
—Weekend Sisters. LC 85-5665. 176p. (gr. 7 up). 1985. 11.95 (0-688-05785-3) Morrow Jr Bks.
Colman, Penny. Breaking the Chains: The Crusade of Dorothea Lynde Dix. LC 91-17986. (Illus.). 144p. (gr. 6 up). 1992. pap. 5.95 (1-55870-219-9) Shoe Tree Pr.
—Dark Closets & Noises in the Night. 1991. pap. 3.95 (0-8091-6600-3) Paulist Pr.
—Fannie Lou Hamer & the Fight for the Vote. LC 92-21380. (Illus.). 32p. (gr. 2-4). 1993. PLB 12.40 (1-56294-323-5) Millbrook Pr.
—Madame C. J. Walker: Building a Business Empire. (Illus.). 48p. (gr. 2-4). 1994. 12.40 (1-56294-338-3) Millbrook Pr.
—Mother Jones & the March of the Mill Children. (Illus.). 48p. (gr. 3-6). 1994. 14.90 (1-56294-402-9) Millbrook Pr.
—One Hundred One Ways to Do Better in School. Bogan, Paulette, illus. LC 93-30872. 1993. pap. write for info. (0-8167-3285-X) Troll Assocs.
—Spies! Women in the Civil War. LC 92-18097. (Illus.). 96p. (Orig.). (gr. 3-7). 1992. pap. 6.95 (1-55870-267-9) Shoe Tree Pr.
—A Woman Unafraid: The Achievements of Frances Perkins. LC 92-46524. (Illus.). 128p. (gr. 5-9). 1993. SBE 14.95 (0-689-31853-7, Atheneum Child Bk) Macmillan Child Grp.
Colman, Warren. The Bill of Rights. LC 86-33437. (Illus.). 48p. (gr. k-4). 1987. PLB 15.27 (0-516-01232-0); pap. 4.95 (0-516-41232-9) Childrens.
—La Carta de Derechos: (The Bill of Rights) LC 86-33437. (SPA.). 48p. (gr. k-4). 1989. PLB 15.27 (0-516-31232-4); pap. 4.95 (0-516-51232-3) Childrens.
—La Constitucion: (The Constitution) LC 86-30968. (SPA.). 48p. (gr. k-4). 1989. PLB 15.27 (0-516-31231-6); pap. 4.95 (0-516-51231-5) Childrens.
—The Constitution. LC 86-30968. (Illus.). 48p. (gr. k-4). 1987. PLB 15.27 (0-516-01231-2); pap. 4.95 (0-516-41231-0) Childrens.
—Understanding & Preventing Teen Suicide. LC 90-1400. (Illus.). 48p. (gr. k-4). 1990. PLB 17.27 (0-516-00594-4); pap. 4.95 (0-516-40594-2) Childrens.
Colmenson, Stephanie. Walt Disney Pictures Presents the Little Mermaid: Ariel above the Sea. Mateu, Franc, illus. (gr. k-2). 1991. 4.25 (0-307-11697-2, Golden Pr) Western Pub.
Colmenson, Stephenie. Hopscotch, the Tiny Bunny. Lanza, Barbara, illus. (ps-3). 1991. pap. 1.75 (0-307-12617-X, Golden Pr) Western Pub.
Colombo, Monica. The Islamic World. LC 93-31449. 1994. write for info. (0-8114-3328-5) Raintree Steck-V.
Colonial Williamsburg Foundation Staff. Animals at Colonial Williamsburg. (Illus.). 8p. (ps). 1993. bds. 3.95 (0-87935-092-X) Williamsburg.
—The Apprentice. (Illus.). 38p. (Orig.). (gr. 5-7). 1984. pap. 2.95 (0-87935-103-9) Williamsburg.
—Colonial Colors. (Illus.). 8p. (ps). 1993. bds. 3.95 (0-87935-094-6) Williamsburg.
—Count with the Cooper. (Illus.). 8p. (ps). 1993. bds. 3.95 (0-87935-093-8) Williamsburg.
Colonna, Phyllia & Phillips, Ana M. The Power of Caring. LC 81-50388. (gr. k-7). lib. bdg. write for info. (0-911712-87-9) Eagle Mktg Corp.
Colonna, Phyllis & Ramussen, Della M. The Power of Courage. LC 80-85338. (gr. k-7). write for info. Eagle Mktg Corp.
Colonna, Phyllis & Rasmussen, Della M. The Power of Cheerfulness. LC 80-85337. (gr. k-7). lib. bdg. write for info. Eagle Mktg Corp.
—The Power of Determination. LC 80-85339. (gr. k-7). lib. bdg. write for info. Eagle Mktg Corp.
—The Power of Enthusiasm. LC 81-50864. (gr. k-7). lib. bdg. write for info. Eagle Mktg Corp.
—The Power of Integrity. LC 81-50390. (gr. k-7). lib. bdg. write for info. (0-911712-85-2) Eagle Mktg Corp.
—The Power of Sportsmanship. LC 81-50868. (gr. k-7). lib. bdg. write for info. (0-911712-94-1) Eagle Mktg Corp.
—The Power of Trying Again. LC 81-50389. (gr. k-7). lib. bdg. write for info. (0-911712-86-0) Eagle Mktg Corp.
Colonna, Phyllis & Rassmussen, Della M. Power of Dreaming. LC 81-50866. (gr. k-7). PLB write for info. (0-911712-92-5) Eagle Mktg Corp.
Coltharp, Barbara. Colonel Neverfail's Christmas. Sandifer, Shannon & Woolfolk, Doug, eds. Turner, James, illus. (Orig.). (gr. 1-3). 1981. 7.95 (0-86518-019-9) Moran Pub Corp.
Coltharpe, Barbara A. Mr. Rumples Recycles. Gullic, Bob, ed. Coltharpe, Barbara A., illus. 30p. (Orig.). (gr. 3-7). 1989. pap. 4.25x (0-9622702-0-4) Hyacinth Hse.
Coltman, Paul. Tinker Jim. (ps-3). 1992. 15.00 (0-374-37611-5) FS&G.

—Tog the Ribber: Or Granny's Tales. McClure, Gillian, illus. LC 84-82555. 32p. (ps-5). 1985. 15.00 (0-374-37630-1) FS&G.
Colton, Ann R. Precepts for the Young. 66p. (gr. 1-8). 1959. pap. 2.50 (0-917187-15-6) A R Colton Fnd.
Colton, Kitty, jt. ed. see Fetterolf, Michele.
Colton, Kitty, ed. see Miller, Robert F.
Colton, Kitty, ed. see Richardson, Allen F.
Colum, Padraic. The Boy Apprenticed to an Enchanter. Leight, Edward, illus. (gr. 3-7). 1991. 20.00 (0-8446-6482-0) Peter Smith.
—The Children of Odin: The Book of Northern Myths. reissued ed. Pogany, Willy, illus. LC 83-20368. 280p. (gr. 5up). 1984. SBE 15.95 (0-02-722890-8, Collier Young Ad); pap. 8.95 (0-02-042100-1, Collier Young Ad) Macmillan Child Grp.
—The Children's Homer: The Adventures of Odysseus & the Tale of Troy. Pogany, Willy, illus. LC 82-12643. 256p. (gr. 5 up). 1982. pap. 7.95 (0-02-042520-1, Collier Young Ad) Macmillan Child Grp.
—The Golden Fleece: And the Heroes Who Lived Before Achilles. reissued ed. Pogany, Willy, illus. LC 82-21667. 320p. (gr. 5 up). 1983. SBE 15.95 (0-02-723620-X, Macmillan Child Bk); pap. 7.95 (0-02-042260-1, Collier Young Ad) Macmillan Child Grp.
—Legends of Hawaii. (Illus.). (gr. 8 up). 1937. text ed. 32.00x (0-300-00376-5) Yale U Pr.
Columbu, Franco & Tyler, Dick. Weight Training & Body Building for Young Athletes. (Illus.). (gr. 4-8). 1979. pap. 6.95 (0-671-33006-3) S&S Trade.
Columbus, Christopher. Christopher Columbus. (gr. 1-9). 1992. pap. 2.50 (0-88388-156-X) Bellerophon Bks.
—I, Columbus. 49p. 1992. text ed. 3.92 (1-56956-115-X) W A T Braille.
—I, Columbus: My Journal 1492-3. Roop, Peter & Roop, Connie, eds. 64p. (gr. 5). 1991. pap. 5.99 (0-380-71545-7, Camelot) Avon.
—The Log of Christopher Columbus: The First Voyage: Spring, Summer & Fall, 1492. Lowe, Steve, ed. Sabuda, Robert, illus. 32p. (ps-3). 1992. 14.95 (0-399-22139-5, Philomel Bks) Putnam Pub Group.
Columbus Metropolitan Library Staff. Science Fair Projects Index. (gr. 6-9). 1993. text ed. 40.00 (0-917846-31-1, 95577) Highsmith Pr.
Colver, Anne. Abraham Lincoln: For the People. (Illus.). 80p. (gr. 2-6). 1992. Repr. of 1960 ed. lib. bdg. 12.95 (0-7910-1414-2) Chelsea Hse.
—Florence Nightingale: War Nurse. (Illus.). 80p. (gr. 2-6). 1992. Repr. of 1961 ed. PLB 12.95 (0-7910-1466-5) Chelsea Hse.
—Thomas Jefferson: Author of Independence. (Illus.). 80p. (gr. 2-6). 1993. Repr. of 1963 ed. lib. bdg. 12.95 (0-7910-1443-6) Chelsea Hse.
Colvin, L. & Irving, N. Essential French. (Illus.). 64p. 1990. lib. bdg. 12.96 (0-88110-420-5); pap. 5.95 (0-7460-0316-1) EDC.
—Essential German. (Illus.). 64p. 1990. lib. bdg. 12.96 (0-88110-419-1); pap. 5.95 (0-7460-0318-8) EDC.
—Essential Spanish. (Illus.). 64p. 1990. lib. bdg. 12.96 (0-88110-421-3); pap. 5.95 (0-7460-0320-X) EDC.
Colvin, L., jt. auth. see Stockley, C.
Colwell, Lynn H. Erma Bombeck: Writer & Humorist. LC 91-40924. (Illus.). 112p. (gr. 6 up). 1992. lib. bdg. 17.95 (0-89490-384-5) Enslow Pubs.
Coman, Carolyn. Losing Things at Mr. Mudd's. Hidy, Lance, illus. 32p. (ps-3). 1992. 14.00 (0-374-34657-7) FS&G.
—Tell Me Everything. 1993. 15.00 (0-374-37390-6) FS&G.
Comber, Geoffrey & Zeiderman, Howard. Worksheets for Touchstones for Middle Schools, Vol. A. 31p. (Orig.). (gr. 6-7). 1992. wkbk. 1.95 (1-878461-17-6) CZM Pr.
—Worksheets for Touchstones for Middle Schools, Vol. B. 32p. (Orig.). (gr. 7-8). 1993. wkbk. 1.95 (1-878461-18-4) CZM Pr.
Comber, Geoffrey, et al. Courage to Care, Strength to Serve: Reflections on Community Service. 161p. (Orig.). (gr. 7-10). 1989. pap. 9.00 (0-685-68116-5) CZM Pr.
—Guide & Worksheets for Touchstones, Vol. II, Pt. 2. 66p. (Orig.). (gr. 9-12). 1992. pap. 4.50 wkbk. (1-878461-13-3) CZM Pr.
—Investigating Mathematics: The Touchstones Approach. 150p. (Orig.). (gr. 9-12). 1993. pap. 22.00 (1-878461-20-6) CZM Pr.
—Touchstones for Middle Schools en Espanol, Vol. A. Hannum, Thomasina, tr. from ENG. (SPA.). 92p. (Orig.). (gr. 6-8). 1993. pap. 8.50 (1-878461-21-4) CZM Pr.
—Worksheets for Touchpebbles. 32p. (Orig.). (gr. 4-5). 1993. pap. 1.95 wkbk. (1-878461-16-8) CZM Pr.
Comber, Geoffrey, et al, eds. Touchstones, Vol. II, Pt. 1: Texts for Discussion. 157p. (Orig.). (gr. 9-12). 1988. pap. text ed. 11.00 (1-878461-02-8) CZM Pr.
—Touchstones, Vol. II, Pt. 2: Texts for Discussion. 182p. (Orig.). (gr. 9-12). 1986. pap. text ed. 12.00 (1-878461-03-6) CZM Pr.
—Touchstones, Vol. III: Texts for Discussion. 178p. (Orig.). (gr. 9-12). 1987. pap. text ed. 13.00 (1-878461-04-4) CZM Pr.
—Touchstones, Vol. 1: Texts for Discussion. 201p. (Orig.). (gr. 9-12). 1985. pap. text ed. 11.00 (1-878461-01-X) CZM Pr.
Combs, Ann. How Old Is Old? Smith-Moore, J. J., illus. 32p. (gr. k-2). 1988. 8.95 (0-8431-2219-6) Price Stern.
Combs, Eunice A., ed. see Davis, James.
Combs, Eunice A., ed. see Davis, James E.

Comeaux, Maureen N., jt. auth. see Ristow, Kate S.

Comer, Fred R. Coming of Age: Teachers in Iowa 1954 to 1993. LC 93-78742. (Illus.). 240p. 1993. 20.00 (*0-9637413-0-6*) Iowa St Educ. From tea & cookies, conflict & confrontation, & ultimately to collaboration & cooperation, COMING OF AGE chronicles the emergence of teaching as a profession in Iowa. Written by the Iowa State Education Association Executive Director, COMING OF AGE is also the story of teachers everywhere--the "new breed" of college-educated, licensed, socially conscious professionals--who were determined to take charge of their professional destinies. It is about tenacity, courage, & upon occasion, reckless abandon. From the winning of collective bargaining rights, job security, political muscle, & professional autonomy, to their wresting the Association from administrator dominance & making it their own, Fred Comer captures the metamorphosis with a clever wit, remarkable candor, & keen insight. COMING OF AGE offers a fresh behind-the-scenes perspective on the origins of the school reform movement & the Association's role in it. Anyone who cares about public education will delight in the stories, the anecdotes, & the personal reflections about a profession COMING OF AGE. Also included is a chronology of significant education events of the past 40 years. To order, write COMING OF AGE, Iowa State Education Association, 4025 Tonawanda Drive, Des Moines, IA 50312; or FAX 515-279-2659. Also through Baker & Taylor. *Publisher Provided Annotation.*

Comes, Pilar & Hernandez, Xavier. Barmi: A Mediterranean City Through the Ages. Ballonga, Jordi, illus. 64p. (gr. 5 up). 1990. 14.45 (*0-395-54227-8*) HM.

Commager, Henry S. America's Robert E. Lee. LC 90-48983. (Illus.). 128p. (gr. 6-10). 1991. PLB 13.95 (*1-55905-088-8*) Marshall Cavendish.

Commire, Anne, ed. Something about the Author: Facts & Pictures about Contemporary Authors & Illustrators of Books for Young People. Incl. Vol. 1. 1971. 83.00 (*0-8103-0050-8*); Vol. 2. 1972. 83.00 (*0-8103-0052-4*); Vol. 3. 1972. 83.00 (*0-8103-0054-0*); Vol. 4. 1973. 83. 00 (*0-8103-0056-7*); Vol. 5. 1974. 83.00 (*0-8103-0058-3*); Vol. 6. 1974. 83.00 (*0-8103-0060-5*); Vol. 7. 1975. 83.00 (*0-8103-0062-1*); Vol. 8. 1976. 83. 00 (*0-8103-0064-8*); Vol. 9. 1976. 83.00 (*0-8103-0066-4*); Vol. 10. 1976. 83.00 (*0-8103-0068-0*); Vol. 11. 1977. 83.00 (*0-8103-0070-2*); Vol. 12. 1977. 83.00 (*0-8103-0072-9*); Vol. 13. 1978. 83.00 (*0-8103-0094-X*); Vol. 14. 1978. 83.00 (*0-8103-0095-8*); Vol. 15. 1979. 83.00 (*0-8103-0096-6*); Vol. 16. 1979. 83.00 (*0-8103-0097-4*); Vol. 17. 1979. 83.00 (*0-8103-0098-2*); Vol. 18. 1980. 83.00 (*0-8103-0099-0*); Vol. 19. 1980. 83.00 (*0-8103-0051-6*); Vol. 20. 1980. 83.00 (*0-8103-0053-2*); Vol. 21. 1981. 83.00 (*0-8103-0093-1*); Vol. 22. 1981. 83.00 (*0-8103-0085-0*); Vol. 23. 1981. 83.00 (*0-8103-0086-9*); Vol. 24. 1981. 83.00 (*0-8103-0087-7*); Vol. 25. 1981. 83.00 (*0-8103-0084-2*); Vol. 26. 1982. 83.00 (*0-8103-0089-3*); Vol. 27. 1982. 83.00 (*0-8103-0083-4*); Vol. 28. 296p. 1982. 83.00 (*0-8103-0082-6*); Vol. 29. 328p. 1982. 83.00 (*0-8103-0081-8*). LC 72-27107. (gr. 7-12). 74.00x ea. Gale.
—Something about the Author: Facts & Pictures about Contemporary Authors & Illustrators of Books for Young People, Vol. 30. (Illus.). 304p. (gr. 9-12). 1983. 83.00 (*0-8103-0055-9*) Gale.
—Something about the Author: Facts & Pictures about Contemporary Authors & Illustrators of Books for Young People, Vol. 34. (Illus.). 224p. (gr. 9-12). 1984. 83.00 (*0-8103-0063-X*) Gale.
—Something about the Author: Facts & Pictures about Contemporary Authors & Illutrators of Books for Young People, Vol. 44. 300p. (gr. 9-12). 1986. 83.00 (*0-8103-2254-4*) Gale.
—Yesterday's Authors of Books for Children: Facts & Pictures about Authors & Illustrators of Books for Young People, 2 vols. (Illus.). (gr. 7-12). 1977. Vol. 1, 1977. 93.00 (*0-8103-0073-7*); Vol. 2, 1978. 93.00 (*0-8103-0090-7*) Gale.

Communication & Learning Center Staff. One Hundred Twenty-Five Ways to Be a Better Student: A Program for Study Skills Success. 1987. spiral reproducible wkbk. 27.95 (*1-55999-063-5*) LinguiSystems.

Community Intervention, Inc. Staff. Participant Guidebook: My Life... Right Now. (Illus.). 52p. (gr. 7-12). 1988. wkbk. 3.50 (*0-9613416-9-6*) Comm Intervention.
—Saying Yes, Saying No: You & Drugs--A Positive Approach to Staying Drug Free. 24p. (Orig.). (gr. 8-12). 1986. pap. 3.95 (*0-9613416-4-5*) Comm Intervention.

Como, Jay. Career Choice & Job Search. 96p. (Orig.). (gr. 9-12). 1986. wkbk. 5.95 (*0-936007-01-X*, 3070); instr's. guide 3.95 (*0-936007-02-8*, 3070) Meridian Educ.

Company, Merce. Don Gil y el Paraguas Magico: Sir Gil & the Magic Umbrella. Serra, Aurora M., tr. from GER. Asensio, Agusti, illus. (SPA.). 26p. (gr. 1-4). 1990. 13.95 (*968-6465-03-0*) Hispanic Bk Dist.

Compass Productions. Grasslands & Deserts. (Illus.). 10p. (gr. k-4). 1993. 5.95 (*0-694-00444-8*, Festival) HarpC Child Bks.
—Jungles & Islands. (Illus.). 10p. (gr. k-4). 1993. 5.95 (*0-694-00443-X*, Festival) HarpC Child Bks.
—Mountains & Forests. (Illus.). 10p. (gr. k-4). 1993. 5.95 (*0-694-00442-1*, Festival) HarpC Child Bks.
—Oceans & Arctic. (Illus.). 10p. (gr. k-4). 1993. 5.95 (*0-694-00441-3*, Festival) HarpC Child Bks.

Compass Productions Staff. Awesome Animal Actions. Mirocha, Paul, illus. 10p. (gr. k-4). 1992. 5.95 (*0-694-00409-X*, Festival) HarpC Child Bks.
—Baffling Bird Behavior. Mirocha, Paul, illus. 10p. (gr. k-4). 1992. 5.95 (*0-694-00410-3*, Festival) HarpC Child Bks.
—Freaky Fish Facts. Mirocha, Paul, illus. 10p. (gr. k-4). 1992. 5.95 (*0-694-00411-1*, Festival) HarpC Child Bks.
—Incredible Insect Instincts. Mirocha, Paul, illus. 10p. (gr. k-4). 1992. 5.95 (*0-694-00412-X*, Festival) HarpC Child Bks.

Compher, Catherine. Shoes on, Shoes Off. Gross, Karen, ed. 24p. (Orig.). (ps). 1993. pap. text ed. 6.95 (*1-56309-076-7*, New Hope) Womans Mission Union.

Compton, Anita. Marriage Customs. LC 93-16317. (Illus.). 32p. (gr. 4-8). 1993. 13.95 (*1-56847-033-9*) Thomson Lrning.

Compton, Joanne. Ashpet: An Appalachian Tale. Compton, Kenn, illus. LC 93-16034. 40p. (gr. 4-8). 1994. 15.95 (*0-8234-1106-0*) Holiday.

Compton, Joanne, jt. auth. see Compton, Kenn.

Compton, Kenn. Happy Christmas to All! Compton, Kenn, illus. LC 90-29078. 32p. (ps-3). 1991. reinforced 14.95 (*0-8234-0890-6*) Holiday.
—Jack the Giant Chaser: An Appalachian Tale. LC 92-15911. (Illus.). 32p. (ps-3). 1993. reinforced bdg. 14.95 (*0-8234-0998-8*) Holiday.
—Little Rabbit's Easter Surprise. Compton, Kenn & Compton, Joanne, illus. (ps-3). 1992. reinforced bdg. 14.95 (*0-8234-0920-1*) Holiday.

Compton, Kenn & Compton, Joanne. Granny Greenteeth & the Noise in the Night. LC 93-18232. (Illus.). (ps-3). 1993. reinforced bdg. 14.95 (*0-8234-1051-X*) Holiday.

Compton, Patricia. Terrible Eek. (ps-6). 1993. pap. 5.95 (*0-671-87169-2*, S&S BFYR) S&S Trade.

Compton, Patricia A. Terrible Eek. LC 91-6421. (Illus.). 40p. (gr. 4-8). 1991. pap. 14.95 jacketed (*0-671-73737-6*, S&S BFYR) S&S Trade.

Compton, Sara. Daredevil Park. 1991. pap. 3.25 (*0-553-28795-8*) Bantam.
—Stranded. 1989. pap. 2.99 (*0-553-15762-0*) Bantam.

Comstock, Esther J. Feliciana's California Miracle. Comstock, David A., illus. LC 85-9707. xiv, 178p. (Orig.). (gr. 6). 1985. 14.50 (*0-933994-03-6*); pap. 8.75 (*0-933994-04-4*) Comstock Bon.
—Vallejo & the Four Flags. Comstock, Floyd B., illus. LC 79-21636. xvi, 142p. (gr. 4). 1988. 12.50 (*0-933994-01-X*); pap. 8.75 (*0-933994-07-9*) Comstock Bon.

Conant, Catherine, jt. auth. see Ball, Jacqueline A.

Conant, Richard. The Race to Save Christmas. LC 91-65291. (Illus.). 44p. (gr. k-3). 1991. pap. 5.95 (*1-55523-432-1*) Winston-Derek.

Conant, Roger, et al. Peterson First Guide to Reptiles & Amphibians. Conant, Roger, et al, illus. 128p. (gr. 5 up). 1992. pap. 4.80 (*0-395-62232-8*) HM.

Conari Press Editors. Kids' Random Acts of Kindness. (Illus.). 168p. (Orig.). 1994. pap. 8.95 (*0-943233-62-3*) Conari Press.

Conaway, Judith. Detective Tricks You Can Do. Barto, Renzo, illus. LC 85-28881. 48p. (gr. 1-5). 1986. PLB 11.89 (*0-8167-0672-7*); pap. text ed. 3.50 (*0-8167-0673-5*) Troll Assocs.
—Dollhouse Fun! Furniture You Can Make. Barto, Renzo, illus. LC 86-16133. 48p. (gr. 1-5). 1987. PLB 11.89 (*0-8167-0862-2*); pap. text ed. 3.50 (*0-8167-0863-0*) Troll Assocs.
—Easy-to-Make Christmas Crafts. Barto, Renzo, illus. LC 85-16475. 48p. (gr. 1-5). 1986. PLB 11.89 (*0-8167-0674-3*); pap. text ed. 3.50 (*0-8167-0675-1*) Troll Assocs.
—Fun-to-Make Nature Crafts. Barto, Renzo, illus. LC 80-23999. 48p. (gr. 1-5). 1981. PLB 11.89 (*0-89375-440-4*); pap. 3.50 (*0-89375-441-2*) Troll Assocs.
—Great Gifts to Make. Barto, Renzo, illus. LC 85-16498. 48p. (gr. 1-5). 1986. PLB 11.89 (*0-8167-0676-X*); pap. text ed. 3.50 (*0-8167-0677-8*) Troll Assocs.
—Happy Day! Things to Make & Do. Barto, Renzo, illus. LC 86-7131. 48p. (gr. 1-5). 1987. PLB 11.89 (*0-8167-0842-8*); pap. text ed. 3.50 (*0-8167-0843-6*) Troll Assocs.
—Happy Haunting: Halloween Costumes You Can Make. Barto, Renzo, illus. LC 85-28840. 48p. (gr. 1-5). 1986. PLB 11.89 (*0-8167-0666-2*); pap. text ed. 3.50 (*0-8167-0667-0*) Troll Assocs.
—Happy Thanksgiving: Things to Make & Do. Barto, Renzo, illus. LC 85-16463. 48p. (gr. 1-5). 1986. PLB 11.89 (*0-8167-0668-9*); pap. text ed. 3.50 (*0-8167-0669-7*) Troll Assocs.
—Make Your Own Costumes & Disguises. Barto, Renzo, illus. LC 86-11212. 48p. (gr. 1-5). 1987. PLB 11.89 (*0-8167-0840-1*); pap. text ed. 3.50 (*0-8167-0841-X*) Troll Assocs.
—More Magic Tricks You Can Do. LC 86-11351. (Illus.). 48p. (gr. 1-5). 1987. PLB 11.89 (*0-8167-0864-9*); pap. text ed. 3.50 (*0-8167-0865-7*) Troll Assocs.
—More Science Secrets. LC 86-16084. (Illus.). 48p. (gr. 1-5). 1987. PLB 11.89 (*0-8167-0866-5*); pap. text ed. 3.50 (*0-8167-0867-3*) Troll Assocs.
—Springtime Surprises: Things to Make & Do. Barto, Renzo, illus. LC 85-16497. 48p. (gr. 1-5). 1986. PLB 11.89 (*0-8167-0670-0*); pap. text ed. 3.50 (*0-8167-0671-9*) Troll Assocs.
—Things That Go! How to Make Toy Boats, Cars, & Planes. Barto, Renzo, illus. LC 86-7130. 48p. (gr. 1-5). 1987. PLB 11.89 (*0-8167-0838-X*); pap. text ed. 3.50 (*0-8167-0839-8*) Troll Assocs.

Conaway, Judith, adapted by. Twenty-Thousand Leagues under the Sea. D'Achille, Gino, illus. 96p. (gr. 2-5). 1983. 2.95 (*0-394-85333-4*); lib. bdg. 4.99 (*0-394-95333-9*) Random Bks Yng Read.

Conaway, Judith, ed. see Doyle, Arthur Conan.

Conaway, Judith, ed. see Lovelace, Delos W.

Concordia Staff. Boy Who Gave His Lunch Away: John 6: 1-15. 1993. pap. 1.89 (*0-570-06027-3*) Concordia.
—Night the Angels Sang: Luke 2: 8-20. (ps-3). 1993. pap. 1.89 (*0-570-06095-8*) Concordia.

Conder, Edyce. Nite-Nite Stories for Little Sleepy Eyes. 1993. 7.95 (*0-8062-4740-1*) Carlton.

Condit, A. Lloyd. Piffin. 1992. pap. 7.95 (*0-533-10143-3*) Vantage.

Condit, Erin. Francois & Jean-Claude Duvalier. Schlesinger, Arthur M., Jr., intro. by. (Illus.). 112p. (gr. 5 up). 1989. 17.95 (*1-55546-832-2*) Chelsea Hse.

Condon, Judith. Energy. LC 92-32911. 1994. write for info. (*0-531-14252-3*) Watts.
—Farming. LC 92-32910. 1994. write for info. (*0-531-14251-5*) Watts.
—Patterns of Work. LC 92-7838. (Illus.). 32p. (gr. 5-8). 1993. PLB 11.90 (*0-531-14228-0*) Watts.
—Pressure to Take Drugs. 1990. PLB 12.40 (*0-531-10934-8*) Watts.
—Recycling Glass. LC 89-70710. 32p. (gr. 5-8). 1991. PLB 12.40 (*0-531-14077-6*) Watts.
—Recycling Paper. LC 89-70742. 1991. PLB 12.40 (*0-531-14078-4*) Watts.

Condon, Robert J. Great Women Athletes of the Twentieth Century. LC 91-52633. 190p. (gr. 9-12). 1991. lib. bdg. 25.95x (*0-89950-555-4*) McFarland & Co.

Cone, Molly. About Belonging. Perl, Susan, illus. 64p. (Orig.). (gr. 1-2). 1972. pap. 6.00 (*0-8074-0234-6*, 101083) UAHC.
—About Learning. Schweitzer, Iris, illus. (Orig.). (gr. 1). 1972. pap. 6.00 (*0-8074-0233-8*, 101082) UAHC.
—Come Back, Salmon: How a Group of Dedicated Kids Adopted a Stream & Brought It Back to Life. Wheelwright, Sidnee, photos by. (Illus.). 48p. (gr. 2-6). 1992. 16.95 (*0-87156-572-2*) Sierra.
—Dance Around the Fire. Friedman, Marvin, illus. LC 74-9378. 160p. (gr. 7 up). 1974. 5.95 (*0-395-19490-3*) HM.
—Mishmash. MacDonald, Patricia, ed. Shortall, Leonard, illus. 128p. 1991. pap. 2.95 (*0-671-70937-2*, Minstrel Bks) PB.
—Mishmash. (gr. 4-7). 1962. 13.95 (*0-395-06711-1*) HM.
—Mishmash & The Big Fat Problem. Shortall, Leonard, illus. (gr. 2-5). 1982. 13.45 (*0-395-32078-X*) HM.
—Mishmash & The Sauerkraut Mystery. Shortall, Leonard, illus. (gr. 4-6). 1974. pap. 0.95 (*0-395-18556-4*) HM.
—Mystery of Being Jewish. 176p. (gr. 7-9). 1989. pap. 7.95 (*0-8074-0401-2*, 123929) UAHC.

Cone, Patrick. Grand Canyon. Cone, Patrick, photos by. LC 93-31066. (Illus.). 1994. write for info. (*0-87614-820-8*) Carolrhoda Bks.

Conford. Seven Days to a Brand New Life. 1993. pap. 2.95 (*0-685-66035-4*) Scholastic Inc.

Conford, Ellen. The Alfred G. Graebner Memorial High School Handbook of Rules & Regulations. (gr. 7-12). 1976. 14.95 (*0-316-15293-5*) Little.
—And This Is Laura. (Illus.). 192p. (gr. 3-7). 1992. pap. 4.95 (*0-316-15354-0*) Little.

—Anything for a Friend. LC 78-27843. (gr. 3-7). 1979. 14.95 (*0-316-15308-7*) Little.
—Anything for a Friend. 192p. 1987. pap. 2.95 (*0-553-26786-8*, Starfire) Bantam.
—Anything for a Friend. (gr. 4-7). 1992. pap. 3.50 (*0-553-48081-2*) Bantam.
—Can Do, Jenny Archer. Palmisciano, Diane, illus. (gr. 2-4). 1991. 11.95 (*0-316-15356-7*) Little.
—Can Do, Jenny Archer. (gr. 4-7). 1993. pap. 3.95 (*0-316-15372-9*) Little.
—A Case for Jenny Archer. Palmisciano, Diane, illus. LC 88-14169. (gr. 2-4). 1988. 10.95 (*0-316-15266-8*) Little.
—A Case for Jenny Archer. (ps-3). 1990. pap. 2.95 (*0-316-15352-4*) Little.
—Dear Lovey Hart: I Am Desperate. 224p. (gr. 4-6). 1975. 14.95 (*0-316-15306-0*) Little.
—Dear Mom, Get Me Out of Here! LC 92-438. 1992. 14.95 (*0-316-15370-2*) Little.
—Dreams of Victory. Rockwell, Gail, illus. 144p. (gr. 4-6). 1973. 14.95 (*0-316-15294-3*) Little.
—Felicia, the Critic. Stewart, Arvis, illus. (gr. 4-6). 1973. 14.95 (*0-316-15295-1*) Little.
—Felicia the Critic. (Illus.). 160p. (gr. 3-7). 1992. pap. 4.95 (*0-316-15358-3*) Little.
—Hail, Hail Camp Timberwood. Owens, Gail, illus. LC 78-18715. (gr. 3-7). 1978. 14.95 (*0-316-15291-9*) Little.
—I Love You, I Hate You, Get Lost. LC 93-8588. 176p. 1994. 13.95 (*0-590-45558-3*) Scholastic Inc.
—If This Is Love, I'll Take Spaghetti. LC 82-84251. 176p. (gr. 7 up). 1983. SBE 13.95 (*0-02-724250-1*, Four Winds) Macmillan Child Grp.
—If This Is Love, I'll Take Spaghetti. 1990. pap. 2.95 (*0-590-43819-0*) Scholastic Inc.
—Jenny Archer. (ps-3). 1991. pap. 2.95 (*0-316-15353-2*) Little.
—Jenny Archer, Author. Palmisciano, Diane, illus. 64p. (gr. 2-4). 1989. 10.95 (*0-316-15255-2*) Little.
—A Job for Jenny Archer. (gr. 2-4). 1990. pap. 2.95 (*0-316-15349-4*) Little.
—Loving Someone Else. 160p. 1991. 15.00 (*0-553-07353-2*) Bantam.
—Loving Someone Else. 1992. pap. 3.50 (*0-553-29787-2*) Bantam.
—The Luck of Pokey Bloom. Lowenstein, Bernice, illus. 144p. (gr. 4-6). 1975. 14.95 (*0-316-15305-2*) Little.
—Luck of Pokey Bloom. (gr. 4-7). 1991. pap. 4.95 (*0-316-15565-9*) Little.
—Me & the Terrible Two. (gr. 4-7). 1991. pap. 4.95 (*0-316-15366-4*) Little.
—Nibble, Nibble, Jenny Archer. Palmisciano, Diane, illus. LC 92-34306. 1993. 12.95 (*0-316-15371-0*) Little.
—The Revenge of the Incredible Dr. Rancid & His Youthful Assistant, Jeffrey. 132p. (gr. 1-8). 1980. 14.95 (*0-316-15288-9*) Little.
—Royal Pain. (gr. 4-7). 1990. pap. 2.95 (*0-590-43821-2*) Scholastic Inc.
—The Things I Did for Love. 144p. 1988. pap. 2.95 (*0-553-27374-4*, Starfire) Bantam.
—Things I Did Love. 1987. 13.95 (*0-553-05431-7*) Bantam.
—We Interrupt This Semester for an Important Bulletin. 1990. pap. 2.95 (*0-590-43822-0*) Scholastic Inc.
—What's Cooking, Jenny Archer? Palmisciano, Diane, illus. (gr. 2-4). 1989. 12.95 (*0-316-15254-4*) Little.
—What's Cooking, Jenny Archer? (ps-3). 1991. pap. 2.95 (*0-316-15357-5*) Little.
—Why Me? 156p. (gr. 5 up). 1985. 14.95 (*0-316-15326-5*) Little.
—Why Me? (gr. 4-7). 1990. pap. 3.50 (*0-671-74152-7*) PB.
—You Never Can Tell. (Illus.). 156p. (gr. 7 up). 1984. 14.95 (*0-316-15267-6*) Little.
Conforth, Kellie. A Picture Book of Arctic Animals. Conforth, Kellie, illus. LC 90-44896. 24p. (gr. 1-4). 1991. lib. bdg. 9.59 (*0-8167-2144-0*); pap. text ed. 2.50 (*0-8167-2145-9*) Troll Assocs.
—A Picture Book of Australian Animals. Conforth, Kellie, illus. LC 91-18706. 24p. (gr. 1-4). 1992. PLB 9.59 (*0-8167-2470-9*); pap. 2.50 (*0-8167-2471-7*) Troll Assocs.
Conger, David, retold by. Many Lands, Many Stories: Asian Folk Tales for Children. Ra, Ruth, illus. LC 87-50167. 94p. 1987. 12.95 (*0-8048-1527-5*) C E Tuttle.
Congreve, William see Wilson, John H.
Conkie, Heather. Dreamer of Dreams. (gr. 4-6). 1993. pap. 3.99 (*0-553-48044-8*) Bantam.
—Malcolm & the Baby. (gr. 4-7). 1992. pap. 3.99 (*0-553-48034-0*) Bantam.
—The Materializing of Duncan McTavish, No. 4. (gr. 3-7). 1992. pap. 3.99 (*0-553-48030-8*, Skylark) Bantam.
—Old Quarrels, Old Love. (gr. 4-6). 1993. pap. 3.99 (*0-553-48041-3*) Bantam.
—Sara's Homecoming. (gr. 4-7). 1993. pap. 3.99 (*0-553-48038-3*) Bantam.

Conkle, Nancy E. Terrific Bee on Terrific Me. Blackard, Sandy, illus. 32p. (Orig.). (ps-1). 1993. pap. 9.50 (*0-9639061-0-0*) N Conkle.
A brightly colored picture book that uses repetitive language to describe the adventures of Terrific Bee. The flight

line can be traced as the bee flys from one body part to another. Fun & understanding can be enhanced through the use of a bee hand puppet or bee stickers that the children enjoy placing on each body part as the story is read. The characters are from various ethnic backgrounds & some children have a handicap. All children are in play situations & aside from a fun way to learn body parts the book also gives adults an opportunity to satisfy a child's natural curiosity by talking about apparatus that some children need for more efficient function. As understanding develops differences become less significant.
Publisher Provided Annotation.

Conklin. Ten Great Mysteries of Edgar Allan Poe. 1993. pap. 2.95 (*0-590-43344-X*) Scholastic Inc.
Conklin, Barbara P. P. S. I Love You, No. 1. 1984. pap. 2.99 (*0-553-26976-3*) Bantam.
Conklin, Paul, et al, photos by. Land of Yesterday, Land of Tomorrow: Discovering Chinese Central Asia. Ashabranner, Brent, text by. (Illus.). 96p. (gr. 5 up). 1992. 16.00 (*0-525-65086-5*, Cobblehill Bks) Dutton Child Bks.
Conklin, Thomas. Meet Steven Spielberg. LC 93-4315. (gr. 4 up). 1994. 2.99 (*0-679-85445-2*) Knopf Bks Yng Read.
—Muhammad Ali: The Fight for Respect. 1992. pap. 5.95 (*0-395-63556-X*) HM.
Conklin, Tom. Muhammad Ali: The Fight for Respect. LC 91-25950. (Illus.). 104p. (gr. 7 up). 1992. PLB 14.90 (*1-56294-112-7*) Millbrook Pr.
Conley, Andrea. Window on the Deep: The Adventures of Underwater Explorer Sylvia Earle. (Illus.). 40p. (gr. 5-8). 1991. 14.95 (*0-531-15232-4*); PLB 14.90 (*0-531-11119-9*) Watts.
Conley, Andrea, jt. auth. see Mallory, Kenneth.

Conley, Bruce H. Butterflies, Grandpa & Me. (Illus.). 25p. (gr. 4 up). 1976. pap. 2.00 (*0-685-65885-6*) Thum Print. BUTTERFLIES, GRANDPA & ME is a simple story about the unexpected death of a grandfather. Written from a child's point of view, twenty-five pages of text & coloring book pictures follow the main character, Richie, from the first time he learns of grandpa's fatal heart attack through the funeral & into the first week afterward. Shock & numbness, fear, anger, loss of appetite & loneliness are among the many feelings Richie expresses. In search of answers he runs to the creek where the realities of life & death were gently taught by his loving grandfather. Richie's experience includes going to the funeral home, seeing his grandfather's body & asking questions such as, "Where are his feet?", "What are the flowers for...?", & "...is he dead or is he just sleeping?" He spends some time with one of grandpa's older friends, attends the funeral & burial & is surprised to find how hungry he is by the end of the day. In the week that follows, as Richie experiences some of the emptiness of his grandfather's absence he also discovers that doing some of the old things in new ways can bring unexpected pleasure & hope.
Publisher Provided Annotation.

Conley, Kevin. Benjamin Banneker. King, Coretta Scott, intro. by. (Illus.). (gr. 5 up). 1989. 17.95 (*1-55546-573-0*) Chelsea Hse.
Conley, Lucy A. Tattletale Sparkie. (gr. 3 up). 1983. 7.70 (*0-318-01337-1*) Rod & Staff.
Conley, Pauline C. The Code Breaker. (Orig.). (gr. 4 up). 1983. pap. 4.50 (*0-87602-241-7*) Anchorage.
Conley, Phil, jt. auth. see Doherty, William T.
Conlin, Susan & Friedman, Susan L. Ellie's Day. Smith, M. Kathryn, illus. Illsley-Clarke, Jean, intro. by. LC 89-60334. (Illus.). 32p. (Orig.). (ps-2). 1989. PLB 16.95 (*0-943990-45-9*); pap. 5.95 (*0-943990-44-0*) Parenting Pr.

—Nathan's Day. Smith, M. Kathryn, illus. LC 90-62679. 32p. (Orig.). (ps-k). 1991. lib. bdg. 16.95 (*0-943990-61-0*); pap. 5.95 (*0-943990-60-2*) Parenting Pr.
Conlon, Laura. Earthquakes. LC 92-43124. 1993. 12.67 (*0-86593-247-6*); 9.50s.p. (*0-685-66353-1*) Rourke Corp.
—Fire. LC 92-43123. 1993. 12.67 (*0-86593-246-8*); 9.50s.p. (*0-685-66352-3*) Rourke Corp.
—Floods. LC 92-43122. 1993. 12.67 (*0-86593-245-X*); 9.50s.p. (*0-685-66355-8*) Rourke Corp.
Conlon-McKenna, Marita. Little Star. Coady, Christopher, illus. LC 92-22132. 1993. 13.95 (*0-316-15375-3*) Little.
—Under the Hawthorn Tree. Teskey, Donald, illus. LC 90-55097. 160p. (gr. 3-7). 1990. 13.95 (*0-8234-0838-8*) Holiday.
—Under the Hawthorn Tree: Children of the Famine. LC 92-18955. 160p. (gr. 5 up). 1992. pap. 3.99 (*0-14-036031-X*) Puffin Bks.
—Wildflower Girl. Teskey, Donald, illus. LC 92-52711. 176p. (gr. 5-9). 1992. 14.95 (*0-8234-0988-0*) Holiday.
—Wildflower Girl. 176p. (gr. 5 up). 1994. pap. 3.99 (*0-14-036292-4*) Puffin Bks.
Conly, Jane L. Crazy Lady! LC 92-18348. 192p. (gr. 5 up). 1993. 13.00 (*0-06-021357-4*); PLB 12.89 (*0-06-021360-4*) HarpC Child Bks.
—R-T, Margaret, & the Rats of NIMH. Lubin, Leonard, illus. LC 89-19968. 288p. (gr. 4-7). 1990. 14.00 (*0-06-021363-9*); PLB 13.89 (*0-06-021364-7*) HarpC Child Bks.
—R-T, Margaret, & the Rats of NIMH. 1990. PLB 15.89 (*0-06-023647-7*) HarpC Child Bks.
—R-T, Margaret, & the Rats of NIMH. Lubin, Leonard, illus. LC 89-19968. 272p. (gr. 4-7). 1991. pap. 3.95 (*0-06-440387-4*, Trophy) HarpC Child Bks.
—Racso & the Rats of NIMH. Lubin, Leonard, illus. LC 85-42634. 288p. (gr. 4-7). 1988. pap. 3.95 (*0-06-440245-2*, Trophy) HarpC Child Bks.
—Rasco & the Rats of NIMH. Lubin, Leonard, illus. LC 85-42634. 288p. (gr. 4-7). 1986. 13.00 (*0-06-021361-2*); PLB 12.89 (*0-06-021362-0*) HarpC Child Bks.
Connell, David D. Case of the Unnatural. (gr. 4-7). 1993. pap. 4.50 (*0-7167-6504-7*) W H Freeman.
Connell, David D. & Thurman, Jim. The Case of the Willing Parrot: Mathnet, the Book. 1994. write for info. (*0-7167-6528-4*); pap. write for info. (*0-7167-6522-5*) W H Freeman.
—Despair in Monterey Bay: A Mathnet Casebook. LC 93-183351. (gr. 4-7). 1993. 9.95 (*0-7167-6505-5*, Sci Am Yng Rdrs); pap. 3.95 (*0-7167-6502-0*) W H Freeman.
—The Unnatural: A Mathnet Casebook. LC 93-18352. (gr. 4-7). 1993. 9.95 (*0-7167-6506-3*, Sci Am Yng Rdrs) W H Freeman.
Connell, Donna. Writing is Child's Play: A Guide for Teaching Young Children to Write. 2nd ed. (ps-3). 1993. pap. 12.95 (*0-201-81884-1*) Addison-Wesley.
Connell, Kate. Tales from the Underground Railroad. Heller, Debbe, illus. LC 92-14415. 68p. (gr. 2-5). 1992. PLB 21.34 (*0-8114-7223-X*) Raintree Steck-V.
—These Lands Are Ours: Tecumseh's Fight for the Old Northwest. Jones, Jan N., illus. LC 92-14417. 96p. (gr. 2-5). 1992. PLB 21.34 (*0-8114-7227-2*) Raintree Steck-V.
—They Shall Be Heard: The Story of Susan B. Anthony & Elizabeth Cady Stanton. Kiwak, Barbara, illus. LC 92-18088. 85p. (gr. 2-5). 1992. PLB 21.34 (*0-8114-7228-0*) Raintree Steck-V.
Connelly, Bernardine. Follow the Drinking Gourd. Buchanan, Yvonne, illus. LC 93-19247. 1993. 14.95 (*0-88708-336-6*, Rabbit Ears); incl. cass. 19.95 (*0-88708-335-8*, Rabbit Ears) Picture Bk Studio.
Connelly, Gwen, illus. Adventures. LC 83-25212. 32p. (gr. k-3). 1984. PLB 21.35 (*0-89565-265-X*); PLB 14.95s.p. (*0-685-55698-0*) Childs World.
—El Alfabeto: A Child's Introduction to the Letters & Sounds of Spanish. 32p. 1990. 7.95 (*0-8442-7564-6*, Natl Textbk) NTC Pub Grp.
Connelly, H. W. Forty-Seven Object Lessons for Youth Programs. (gr. 5-8). 1964. pap. 5.99 (*0-8010-2314-9*) Baker Bk.
Connelly, John P. You're Too Sweet. (gr. 4-9). 1968. 9.95 (*0-8392-1173-2*) Astor-Honor.
Connelly, Tony & Holley, Cindy. Holiday Stories. Champlin, John, ed. (Illus.). 38p. (gr. 3-6). 1982. pap. 8.95 (*0-938594-02-8*) Spec Lit Pr.
Connett, Eugene V. Fishing a Trout Stream. 2nd ed. Smith, Lawrence, photos by. (Illus.). (gr. 10 up). 1989. Repr. of 1934 ed. 35.00 (*1-56416-006-8*) Derrydale Pr.
Connett, Eugene V., intro. by. American Big Game Fishing. Hunt, Lynn B., illus. 251p. (gr. 10 up). 1993. Repr. of 1935 ed. 50.00 (*1-56416-070-X*) Derrydale Pr.
Connikie, Yvonne. The Nineteen Sixties. Cumming, Valerie & Feldman, Elane, eds. (Illus.). 1990. 16.95x (*0-8160-2469-3*) Facts on File.
Connolly, Austin J. KeyMath Teach & Practice. (gr. k-6). 1985. 574.95 (*0-88671-385-4*, 6880) Am Guidance.
Connolly, Brian A. Bradley's Christmas Adventure. Diamanti, Gina, illus. 38p. (Orig.). (gr. 1-6). 1989. pap. 7.95 (*0-96424282-0-5*) Steele Hollow.
Connolly, Francis X. St. Philip of the Joyous Heart. Rethi, Lili, illus. LC 92-74761. 189p. (gr. 5-8). 1993. pap. 9.95 (*0-89870-431-6*) Ignatius Pr.

Connolly, Holly & Connolly, Peter. Buddhism. Cole, W. Owen, ed. (Illus.). 140p. (Orig.). (gr. 9 up). 1992. pap. 14.95x (*1-871402-07-7*, Pub. by S Thornes UK) Dufour.

Connolly, James E., ed. Why the Possum's Tail Is Bare: And Other North American Indian Nature Tales. Adams, Andrea, illus. LC 84-26871. 64p. (gr. 4-8). 1992. 15.95 (*0-88045-069-X*); pap. 7.95 (*0-88045-107-6*) Stemmer Hse.

Connolly, Maureen. Dragsters. (Illus.). 48p. (gr. 3-6). 1992. PLB 12.95 (*1-56065-074-5*) Capstone Pr.

Connolly, Pat. Coaching Evelyn: Fast, Faster, Fastest Woman in the World. LC 90-4835. (Illus.). 224p. (gr. 7 up). 1991. PLB 15.89 (*0-06-021283-7*) HarpC Child Bks.

Connolly, Peter. The Legend of Odysseus. (Illus.). 80p. (gr. 7-12). 1988. 17.95 (*0-19-917065-7*) OUP.
—The Legend of Odysseus. (Illus.). 80p. (gr. 8 up). 1991. pap. 9.95 (*0-19-917143-2*) OUP.
—Pompeii. (Illus.). 80p. (gr. 6 up). 1990. bds. 17.95 laminated (*0-19-917159-9*) OUP.
—The Roman Fort. (Illus.). 32p. (gr. 6-9). 1991. bds. 16.95 (*0-19-917108-4*) OUP.
—Tiberius Claudius Maximus: The Cavalryman. (Illus.). 32p. (gr. 5-7). 1989. bds. 16.95 laminated (*0-19-917106-8*) OUP.
—Tiberius Claudius Maximus: The Legionary. (Illus.). 32p. (gr. 5-7). 1989. bds. 16.95 laminated (*0-19-917105-X*) OUP.

Connolly, Peter, jt. auth. see Connolly, Holly.

Connolly, Thomas E. A Coeur D'Alene Indian Story. 85p. pap. 4.50 (*0-685-38689-9*) Ye Galleon.

Connor, Brooke, jt. auth. see Kittelson, Pat.

Connors, Patricia & Perucci, Dorianne. Runaways: Coping at Home & on the Street. Rosen, Ruth, ed. (gr. 7-12). 1989. PLB 13.95 (*0-8239-1019-9*) Rosen Group.

Conord, Bruce W. Bill Cosby. (Illus.). 80p. (gr. 3-5). 1993. PLB 12.95 (*0-7910-1761-3*) Chelsea Hse.
—Cesar Chavez: Union Leader. (Illus.). 80p. (gr. 3-5). 1993. 13.95 (*0-7910-1757-5*, Am Art Analog); pap. 4.95 (*0-7910-1999-3*, Am Art Analog) Chelsea Hse.
—John Lennon. LC 92-39113. (Illus.). 1994. 18.95 (*0-7910-1739-7*, Am Art Analog); pap. 7.95 (*0-7910-1740-0*, Am Art Analog) Chelsea Hse.

Conover, Chris. Froggie Went A-Courting. LC 86-45289. (Illus.). 32p. (ps up). 1986. 15.00 (*0-374-32466-2*) FS&G.
—Mother Goose & the Sly Fox. (Illus.). (ps-3). 1989. 15.00 (*0-374-35072-8*) FS&G.
—Mother Goose & the Sly Fox. (Illus.). (ps-3). 1991. pap. 4.95 (*0-374-45397-7*) FS&G.
—Sam Panda & Thunder Dragon. (ps-3). 1992. 16.00 (*0-374-36393-5*) FS&G.

Conoway, Judith, jt. auth. see Tilkin, Sheldon L.

Conoway, Judith, jt. auth. see Tlkin, Sheldon L.

Conrad. Call Me Ahnighito. Date not set. 15.00 (*0-06-023322-2*, Festival); PLB 14.89 (*0-06-023323-0*) HarpC Child Bks.

Conrad, Barnaby. Time Is All We Have. 1989. pap. 4.95 (*0-440-20245-0*) Dell.

Conrad, Earl. Harriet Tubman. 1990. 21.95 (*0-87498-036-4*); pap. 15.95 (*0-685-55179-2*) Assoc Pubs DC.

Conrad, Joseph. The Lagoon. 32p. (gr. 6). 1990. PLB 13.95s.p. (*0-88682-309-9*) Creative Ed.
—Lord Jim. Gemme, F. R., intro. by. (gr. 10 up). 1965. pap. 1.95 (*0-8049-0054-X*, CL-54) Airmont.
—Outcast of the Islands. Teitel, N. R., intro. by. (gr. 9 up). 1966. pap. 1.50 (*0-8049-0113-9*, CL-113) Airmont.

Conrad, Joseph, jt. auth. see London, Jack.

Conrad, Lynn. All Aboard Trucks. Courtney, Richard, illus. 32p. (Orig.). (ps-2). 1989. pap. 2.25 (*0-448-19094-X*, Platt & Munk Pubs) Putnam Pub Group.

Conrad, Pam. Animal Lingo. Falk, Barbara, illus. LC 93-22163. Date not set. 15.00 (*0-06-023401-6*); PLB 14.89 (*0-06-023402-4*) HarpC Child Bks.
—Dollface Has a Party. Selznick, Brian, illus. LC 93-33207. 1994. 15.00 (*0-06-024262-0*, Festival); PLB 14.89 (*0-06-024263-9*, Festival) HarpC Child Bks.
—Holding Me Here. LC 85-45254. 192p. (gr. 7 up). 1986. PLB 11.89 (*0-06-021339-6*) HarpC Child Bks.
—Holding Me Here. 160p. (gr. 7 up). 1987. pap. 2.95 (*0-553-26525-3*, Starfire) Bantam.
—The Lost Sailor. Egielski, Richard, illus. LC 91-39640. 32p. (gr. k-4). 1992. 15.00 (*0-06-021695-6*); PLB 14.89 (*0-06-021696-4*) HarpC Child Bks.
—My Daniel. LC 88-19850. 144p. (gr. 5 up). 1989. 13.00 (*0-06-021313-2*); PLB 12.89 (*0-06-021314-0*) HarpC Child Bks.
—My Daniel. LC 88-19850. 144p. (gr. 5 up). 1991. pap. 3.95 (*0-06-440309-2*, Trophy) HarpC Child Bks.
—Pedro's Journal. 1992. pap. 2.95 (*0-590-46206-7*, 058, Apple Paperbacks) Scholastic Inc.
—Pedro's Journal: A Voyage with Christopher Columbus. Koeppen, Peter, illus. LC 90-85723. 96p. (gr. 3-7). 1991. 13.95 (*1-878093-17-7*) Boyds Mills Pr.
—Prairie Songs. reissue ed. Zudeck, Darryl S., illus. LC 85-42635. 176p. (gr. 5 up). 1987. pap. 3.95 (*0-06-440206-1*, Trophy) HarpC Child Bks.
—Prairie Visions: The Life & Times of Solomon Butcher. Zudeck, Darryl, illus. LC 90-38658. 96p. (gr. 5 up). 1991. 17.00 (*0-06-021373-6*); PLB 16.89 (*0-06-021375-2*) HarpC Child Bks.
—Prairie Visions: The Life & Times of Solomon Butcher. Butcher, Solomon, illus. LC 90-38658. 96p. (gr. 5 up). 1994. pap. 8.95 (*0-06-446135-1*, Trophy) HarpC Child Bks.
—Seven Silly Circles. Wimmer, Mike, illus. LC 85-45835. 64p. (gr. 2-5). 1987. HarpC Child Bks.
—Staying Nine. Wimmer, Mike, illus. LC 87-45862. 80p. (gr. 2-5). 1988. 13.00 (*0-06-021319-1*); PLB 12.89 (*0-06-021320-5*) HarpC Child Bks.
—Staying Nine. LC 87-45862. (Illus.). 80p. (gr. 2-5). 1990. pap. 3.95 (*0-06-440377-7*, Trophy) HarpC Child Bks.
—Stonewords: A Ghost Story. LC 89-36382. 144p. (gr. 5 up). 1990. 14.00 (*0-06-021315-9*); PLB 13.89 (*0-06-021316-7*) HarpC Child Bks.
—Stonewords: A Ghost Story. LC 89-36382. 144p. (gr. 5 up). 1991. pap. 3.95 (*0-06-440354-8*, Trophy) HarpC Child Bks.
—Taking the Ferry Home. LC 87-45856. 224p. (gr. 7 up). 1988. PLB 11.89 (*0-06-021318-3*) HarpC Child Bks.
—Taking the Ferry Home. LC 87-45856. 224p. (gr. 7 up). 1990. pap. 3.95 (*0-06-447011-3*, Trophy) HarpC Child Bks.
—The Rooster's Gift. Beddows, Eric, illus. LC 93-14490. 1995. write for info. (*0-06-023603-5*); PLB write for info. (*0-06-023604-3*) HarpC Child Bks.
—The Tub Grandfather. Egielski, Richard, illus. LC 92-31770. 32p. (gr. k-3). 1993. 15.00 (*0-06-022895-4*); PLB 14.89 (*0-06-022896-2*) HarpC Child Bks.
—The Tub People. Egielski, Richard, illus. LC 88-32804. 32p. (ps-3). 1989. 15.00 (*0-06-021340-X*); PLB 14.89 (*0-06-021341-8*) HarpC Child Bks.
—The Tub People. Egielski, Richard, illus. LC 88-32804. 32p. (gr. k-3). 1995. pap. 4.95 (*0-06-443306-4*, Trophy) HarpC Child Bks.
—What I Did for Roman. LC 86-45497. 224p. (gr. 7 up). 1987. PLB 14.89 (*0-06-021332-9*) HarpC Child Bks.

Conrad, Steven R. & Flegler, Daniel. Math Contests - Grades Seven & Eight, Vol. 2: School Years: 1982-83 Through 1990-91. 166p. (Orig.). (gr. 5-8). 1992. pap. 12.95 (*0-940805-05-7*) Math Leagues.
—Math Contests - Grades 4, 5, & 6, Vol. 2: School Years: 1986-87 Through 1990-91. 102p. (Orig.). (gr. 3-8). 1991. pap. 12.95 (*0-940805-03-0*) Math Leagues.
—Math Contests - High School, Vol. 2: School Years: 1982-83 Through 1990-91. 118p. (Orig.). (gr. 9-12). 1992. pap. 12.95 (*0-940805-04-9*) Math Leagues.

Conradson, Shari. Just Junior High. new ed. 32p. (Orig.). (gr. 6-9). 1992. pap. 5.00 (*0-9620445-1-2*) KSJ Publishing.

Conran, Sebastian. My First ABC Book. Conran, Sebastian, illus. LC 87-14562. 64p. (ps-1). 1988. POB 6.95 (*0-689-71198-0*, Aladdin) Macmillan Child Grp.
—My First 1-2-3 Book. Conran, Sebastian, illus. LC 88-6275. 64p. (ps-1). 1988. POB 7.95 (*0-689-71267-7*, Aladdin) Macmillan Child Grp.

Conroy, Joseph F. Danger sur la Cote d'azur: Reader 4. Bakke, Eric, illus. LC 81-7820. (FRE.). 40p. (Orig.). (gr. 7-12). 1982. pap. 2.95 (*0-88436-857-2*, 40262) EMC.
—Destination: France! Reader 1. Bakke, Eric, illus. LC 81-7816. (FRE.). 40p. (Orig.). (gr. 7-12). 1982. pap. 2.95 (*0-88436-854-8*, 40259) EMC.
—Sur la Route de la Contrebande. Bakke, Eric, illus. LC 81-7817. (FRE.). 40p. (Orig.). (gr. 7-12). pap. 2.95 (*0-88436-856-4*, 40261) EMC.

Conry, Kieran. The Vatican. (Illus.). 96p. (gr. 5 up). 1988. 14.95 (*0-222-01009-6*) Chelsea Hse.

Consentino, Phyllis. Teddy Bear Junction: Stop Here for Fine Collector Bears. (Illus.). 104p. (Orig.). 1985. pap. 10.95 (*0-935855-00-9*) T B J Pubns.

Conservation Treaty Support Group Staff. Cites Endangered Species Coloring Book. rev. ed. Dollinger, Peter, ed. Silk, Linda, illus. 72p. 1993. pap. 4.95 (*1-56002-281-7*) Aegina Pr.

Considine, June. When the Luvenders Came to Merrick Town. LC 89-82487. 240p. (Orig.). (gr. 8-12). 1990. pap. 6.95 (*0-685-46916-6*, Pub. by Poolbeg Pr ER) Dufour.

Constable, David. Candlemaking. (Illus.). 80p. (Orig.). 1993. pap. 16.95 (*0-85532-683-2*, Pub. by Search Pr UK) A Schwartz & Co.

Constantine, R., ed. see Woe, Jonathan.

Constantopoulos, E. Aesop's Fables. (GRE., Illus.). 160p. (gr. 2-3). 4.00 (*0-686-79630-6*); wkbk. 2.50 (*0-686-79631-4*) Divry.

Constanzo, Christie. Hot Air Ballooning. 48p. (gr. 3-4). 1991. PLB 11.95 (*1-56065-049-4*) Capstone Pr.

Consumer Guide Staff, ed. Strategies for Nintendo Games. (Illus.). 128p. 1991. spiralbd. 5.99 (*0-517-03208-2*) Outlet Bk Co.

Consumer Guides Staff. Super Strategies for Nintendo. 1991. 1.99 (*0-517-07330-7*) Outlet Bk Co.

Consumer Reports Books Editors, et al. AIDS: Trading Fears for Facts: A Guide for Young People. rev. ed. (Illus.). 176p. (gr. 8 up). 1992. pap. 4.95 (*0-89043-481-6*) Consumer Reports.

Conteh-Morgan, Jane, illus. Colors. 9p. (ps-1). 1993. bds. 4.95 (*0-448-40522-9*, G&D) Putnam Pub Group.
—Noah's Ark. 18p. (ps). 1994. bds. 3.95 (*0-448-40185-1*, G&D) Putnam Pub Group.

Contreras, Gloria, ed. Latin American Culture Studies: Information & Materials for Teaching about Latin America. rev. ed. Adams, Richard N., intro. by. 310p. (gr. k-12). 1987. pap. text ed. 19.95 (*0-86728-020-4*) U Tx Inst Lat Am Stud.

Contreras, Moyra, tr. see Rodieck, Jorma.

Conway, Celeste. Where Is Papa Now? (Illus.). 32p. (ps-1). 1994. 14.95 (*1-56397-130-5*) Boyds Mills Pr.

Conway, L. M. Goal Getters. 48p. (gr. 3-7). 1984. 5.95 (*0-88160-105-5*, LW 245) Learning Wks.

Conway, Lisa. I Like Ketchup Sandwiches. Conway, Lisa, illus. LC 90-64218. 24p. (Orig.). (ps-2). 1991. pap. 2.25 (*0-679-81719-0*) Random Bks Yng Read.

Conway, Lorraine. Ancient Egypt. Akins, Linda, illus. 64p. (gr. 4-8). 1987. pap. 7.95 (*0-86653-399-0*, GA 1021) Good Apple.
—Animals. 64p. (gr. 5 up). 1980. 7.95 (*0-916456-68-4*, GA 177) Good Apple.
—Body Systems. Atkins, Linda, illus. 64p. (gr. 5 up). 1984. wkbk. 7.95 (*0-86653-153-X*, GA 552) Good Apple.
—Chemistry Concepts. Akins, Linda, illus. 64p. (gr. 5 up). 1983. wkbk. 7.95 (*0-86653-100-9*, GA 460) Good Apple.
—Earth Science: Tables & Tabulations. Akins, Linda, illus. 64p. (gr. 5 up). 1984. wkbk. 7.95 (*0-86653-154-8*, GA 553) Good Apple.
—Energy. Akins, Linda, illus. 64p. (gr. 5 up). 1985. wkbk. 7.95 (*0-86653-267-6*, GA 639) Good Apple.
—Heredity & Embryology. (gr. 5 up). 1980. 6.95 (*0-916456-90-0*, GA 179) Good Apple.
—The Human Body. 64p. (gr. 5 up). 1980. 7.95 (*0-916456-67-6*, GA 178) Good Apple.
—Marine Biology. 64p. (gr. 5 up). 1982. 7.95 (*0-86653-056-8*, GA 400) Good Apple.
—The Middle Ages. Akins, Linda, illus. 64p. (gr. 4-8). 1987. pap. 7.95 (*0-86653-400-8*, GA 1022) Good Apple.
—Oceanography. 64p. (gr. 5 up). 1982. 7.95 (*0-86653-066-5*, GA401) Good Apple.
—Plants. 64p. (gr. 5 up). 1980. 7.95 (*0-916456-69-2*, GA 176) Good Apple.
—Plants & Animals in Nature. Akins, Linda, illus. 64p. (gr. 5 up). 1986. wkbk. 7.95 (*0-86653-356-7*, GA 797) Good Apple.
—Science Graphs & Word Games. 48p. (gr. 5 up). 1981. 7.95 (*0-86653-029-0*, GA 257) Good Apple.

Conwell, Russell H. Acres of Diamonds: All Good Things Are Possible, Right Where You Are, & Now! Leonardo, Bianca, ed. 160p. (gr. 8-12). 1993. pap. text ed. 10.95 (*0-930852-25-7*) Tree Life Pubns.
Here is an excellent & much-needed title for high-school youth. ACRES OF DIAMONDS is a spiritual book. It is not similar to the "get-rich-quick" books that abound. The author saw that success is a spiritual idea, & that when we succeed in a noble effort, we can bless mankind more than if we are poor. Russell H. Conwell was a minister & the founder of Temple University. His lecture ACRES OF DIAMONDS, was delivered personally over 6,000 times & earned over \$4,000,000. (About \$145,000,000 in current dollars.) With this he financed the college education of many poor & worthy high school graduates, never forgetting what a hard time he had in putting himself through college. Conwell lived a SELFLESS life, & died "in harness" at age 82. He lived many lives in one, because he literally worked sixteen hours a day, seven days a week. HE BELIEVED THAT EACH OF US IS PLACED HERE ON EARTH FOR ONE MAIN PURPOSE--TO HELP OTHERS. He inspired thousands of people, & two generations of Americans, many of whom became successes & helped America grow great -- all through the simple but profound concept found in ACRES OF DIAMONDS -- "all good things are possible -- right where you are -- & now!" This new (Fall '93) edition is the only complete text edition. Up to now, only a booklet containing the lecture was available. It has a new cover, new biographical material, new foreword, etc. It appears 68 years after Conwell's passing, to inspire a new generation. The truths & principles in this book are as valid

today as when the great humanitarian lived. There are many opportunities for success today as in Conwell's age, if not more so, because THEY ARE FOUND FIRST & FOREMOST, IN ONE'S OWN CONSCIOUSNESS. Teachers & parents should use this book for young people in their care. ACRES OF DIAMONDS...is published by Tree of Life Publications -- "Books That Heal & Inspire." Bianca Leonardo, N.D. & former teacher, is Editor. *Publisher Provided Annotation.*

Cony, Sue, illus. Colors. 8p. (ps-k). 1991. bds. 4.95 (*1-56293-148-2*) McClanahan Bk.
—Opposites. 8p. (ps-k). 1991. bds. 4.95 (*1-56293-150-4*) McClanahan Bk.
—Shapes. 8p. (ps-k). 1991. bds. 4.95 (*1-56293-149-0*) McClanahan Bk.
—Where Do We Live? 8p. (ps-k). 1991. bds. 4.95 (*1-56293-151-2*) McClanahan Bk.
Coogan, John W. A Workbook of Words. 1987. pap. text ed. 16.20 (*0-8013-0116-5*, 75780) Longman.
Cook. German Americans. 1991. 13.95s.p. (*0-86593-140-2*); PLB 18.60 (*0-685-59184-0*) Rourke Corp.
—The Little Fish That Got Away. 1993. pap. 2.50 (*0-590-41989-7*) Scholastic Inc.
Cook, Amber. Nature Crafts for All the Seasons. LC 93-16749. (Illus.). 128p. (gr. 7 up). 1993. 24.95 (*0-8069-8602-6*) Sterling.
Cook, Bernadine. Looking for Susie. Scull, Marie-Louise, illus. LC 90-41001. 32p. (gr. 1-3). 1991. lib. bdg. 14.50 (*0-208-02241-4*, Pub. by Linnet) Shoe String.
Cook, Bob. Speaking in Tongues: Is That All There Is? Van Someron, Terry, illus. 48p. (gr. 9-12). 1982. pap. text ed. 1.50 (*0-88243-932-4*, 02-0932); leader's guide 3.95 (*0-88243-935-9*, 02-0935) Gospel Pub.
Cook, Carole & Carlisle, Jody. Practical Activities for Practically Everything. (gr. k-3). 1990. 13.95 (*0-8224-5576-5*) Fearon Teach Aids.
Cook, D. Dinosaur's Adventure in Alphabet Town. Rigo, R., illus. LC 91-20544. 32p. (ps-2). 1992. PLB 14.60 (*0-516-05404-X*) Childrens.
Cook, David. Land Animals. Cook, David, illus. LC 84-12072. 32p. (gr. 3-7). 1985. bds. 5.95 (*0-517-55430-5*) Crown Bks Yng Read.
Cook, Donald, tr. see Standiford, Natalie.
Cook, Elizabeth, adapted by. Rabbit Who Overcame Fear: A Jataka Tale. Meller, Eric, illus. Tulku, Tarthang, intro. by. (Illus.). 32p. (Orig.). (gr. k-4). 1991. 14.95 (*0-89800-212-5*); pap. 7.95 (*0-89800-211-7*) Dharma Pub.
Cook, Elizabeth, jt. ed. see Wallace, Zara.
Cook, Fred J. Ku Klux Klan: America's Recurring Nightmare. LC 80-19325. (Illus.). 224p. (gr. 7 up). 1980. lib. bdg. 9.79 (*0-671-34055-7*, J Messner) S&S Trade.
—The Ku Klux Klan: America's Recurring Nightmare. rev. ed. Steltenpohl, Jane, ed. (Illus.). 176p. (gr. 7 up). 1989. lib. bdg. 13.98 (*0-671-68421-3*, J Messner) S&S Trade.
Cook, Hugh, ed. Cracked Wheat & Other Stories. LC 84-18878. 127p. (Orig.). (gr. 7 up). 1984. 12.95 (*0-931940-09-5*); pap. 6.95 (*0-931940-08-7*) Middleburg Pr.
Cook, J. Business. 48p. (gr. 6 up). 1987. pap. 6.95 (*0-86020-934-2*) EDC.
—How to Draw Robots. (Illus.). 32p. (gr. 4 up). 1993. PLB 12.96 (*0-88110-538-4*, Usborne) pap. 4.95 (*0-7460-0745-0*, Usborne) EDC.
—Mountain Bikes. (Illus.). 48p. (gr. 6-10). 1990. lib. bdg. 12.96 (*0-88110-426-4*, Usborne) pap. 5.95 (*0-7460-0520-2*, Usborne) EDC.
—Politics & Governments. 48p. (gr. 6 up). 1981. pap. 6.95 (*0-7460-0047-2*) EDC.
—Understanding Modern Art. (Illus.). 64p. (gr. 5 up). 1992. PLB 13.96 (*0-88110-512-0*, Usborne) pap. 7.95 (*0-7460-0475-3*, Usborne) EDC.
Cook, J. & Way, P. Windsurfing. (Illus.). (gr. 6 up). 1988. pap. 7.95 (*0-7460-0195-9*) EDC.
Cook, Jan L. The Mysterious Undersea World. LC 79-1791. (Illus.). 104p. (gr. 3-8). 1980. 8.95 (*0-87044-317-8*); PLB 12.50 (*0-87044-322-4*) Natl Geog.
Cook, Jean T. Hugs for Our New Baby. (Illus.). (ps-2). 1987. 5.99 (*0-570-04165-1*, 56-1622) Concordia.
Cook, Joel. Rat's Daughter: From an Old Tale. 32p. (ps-3). 1993. 14.95 (*1-56397-140-2*) Boyds Mills Pr.
Cook, John M. Inside Four Ninety-Five. Haye, Caroline, ed. (Illus.). 128p. 1989. write for info. J M Cook Pub.
Cook, Kevin. Disappearing Grasslands. LC 93-1193. 1993. write for info. (*0-8368-0483-X*) Gareth Stevens Inc.
Cook, Kevin, jt. auth. see Woodard, Lynette.
Cook, Lyn. The Secret of Willow Castle. Goodwin, Judith, illus. 236p. (Orig.). (gr. 3-10). 1984. pap. 7.95 (*0-920656-30-7*, Pub. by Camden Hse CN) Firefly Bks Ltd.

Cook, Lynn. A Canadian ABC: An Alphabet Book for Kids. MacDonald, Thoreau, illus. 60p. 1990. pap. 8.95 (*0-921254-24-5*, Pub. by Penumbra Pr CN) U of Toronto Pr.
Cook, Marcy. Daily Math Adventures. Formaro, Rita, illus. 64p. (gr. 3-8). 1987. pap. text ed. 8.50 (*0-914040-51-0*) Cuisenaire.
—Numbers & Words: A Problem Per Day. (gr. 4-7). 1987. pap. 8.50 (*0-201-48002-6*) Addison-Wesley.
—Numbers & Words: A Problem Per Day. Formaro, Rita, illus. 64p. (gr. 3-8). 1987. pap. text ed. 8.50 (*0-914040-52-9*) Cuisenaire.
Cook, Olive R. Trails to Poosey. Sammel, Chelsea, illus. Cook, George R., intro. by. LC 86-8602. (Illus.). 200p. (Orig.). (gr. 3-6). 1986. pap. 5.95 (*0-930079-01-9*) Misty Hill Pr.
Cook, Roy J., ed. One Hundred & One Famous Poems. (Illus.). 186p. (gr. 9-12). 1990. Repr. lib. bdg. 21.95x (*0-89966-667-1*) Buccaneer Bks.
Cook, Sam. CampSights. Cary, Bob, illus. LC 91-62787. 192p. (gr. 10-12). 1991. 16.95 (*0-938586-49-1*) Pfeifer-Hamilton.
Cook, Scott, selected by. & illus. Mother Goose. LC 92-18296. 1993. write for info. (*0-679-80949-X*); PLB write for info. (*0-679-90949-4*) Knopf.
Cook, Shirley & Carl, Kathy. Linking Literature & Writing. (Illus.). 48p. (gr. k-3). 1989. pap. text ed. 14.95 (*0-86530-064-X*, IP 166-5) Incentive Pubns.
Cook, Sue C. The Numbers Book: Student Syllabus, 2 vols. (gr. k-2). 1974. Vol. 1. pap. text ed. 11.85 ea. packs of 10 (*0-89420-081-X*, 193050); Vol. 2. pap. text ed. 11.85 ea. packs of 10 (*0-89420-082-8*, 193051); cass. recordings 17.38 (*0-89420-208-1*, 193000) Natl Book.
Cook, Sybilla. Library Flipper: A Dewey Decimal System Guide. 49p. (gr. 1 up). 1988. trade edition 5.95 (*1-878383-08-6*) C Lee Pubns.
—Reference Flipper: A Guide to Reference Material. 49p. (gr. 1 up). 1988. Repr. of 1983 ed. trade edition 5.95 (*1-878383-09-4*) C Lee Pubns.
Cook, T. S., jt. auth. see Lee, Joanna.
Cook, Veronica L. Editorials of My Mind: Inpirational Messages. 100p. (Orig.). (gr. 9-12). 1989. pap. 7.00 (*0-685-29992-9*) Ronnie Two Pub.
—Mike the Copycat: Adventures & Stories of Cat Tails. Cook, Veronica L., illus. 50p. (Orig.). (gr. 9 up). 1989. pap. text ed. write for info. Ronnie Two Pub.
Cook, Wanda D., jt. auth. see Edwards, Ronald R.
Cooke, Frank E. Kids Can Write Songs, Too! Cooke, Jeff, illus. Franck, Eddie. (Illus.). 120p. (gr. 6-12). 1993. pap. 10.95 (*0-940076-02-0*) Fiesta City.
Cooke, Jean, jt. auth. see Rowland-Entwistle, Theodore.
Cooke, Tim. Calenhad: A Beacon of Gondor. Ney, Jessica, ed. Martin, David, et al, illus. 48p. (Orig.). (gr. 12). 1990. pap. 9.00 (*1-55806-097-9*, 8203) Iron Crown Ent Inc.
Cooke, Tom. Flash Cards Get Ready Colors. (ps). 1986. pap. 2.60 (*0-307-04982-5*, Golden Pr) Western Pub.
—Flash Cards Get Ready Words. (ps). 1986. pap. 5.25 (*0-307-04983-3*, Golden Pr) Western Pub.
Cooke, Tom, illus. Bert & Ernie on the Go. LC 80-54574. 16p. (ps-2). 1981. 8.99 (*0-394-84869-1*) Random Bks Yng Read.
—Bert's Little Garden: A Sesame Street Book. LC 90-61311. 22p. (ps). 1991. bds. 2.95 (*0-679-81061-7*) Random Bks Yng Read.
—Big Bird's Animal Game. 14p. (ps). 1993. bds. 3.95 (*0-307-12395-2*, 12395, Golden Pr) Western Pub.
—Grover's Adventure under the Sea. LC 88-61629. 14p. (ps). 1989. bds. 3.99 (*0-394-81951-9*) Random Bks Yng Read.
—Hide & Seek Camping Trip: A Sesame Street Book. LC 89-61021. 14p. (ps). 1990. bds. 3.99 (*0-679-80138-3*) Random Bks Yng Read.
—Hide-&-Seek with Big Bird: A Sesame Street Book. LC 89-64284. 14p. (ps). 1991. bds. 3.99 (*0-679-80785-3*) Random Bks Yng Read.
—Open Sesame Picture Dictionary. Malecki, Ed, designed by. (ENG & JPN.). 1987. pap. 7.75 (*0-19-434170-4*) OUP.
—Sesame Street Hide-&-Seek Safari. LC 87-61638. 14p. (ps). 1988. bds. 3.99 (*0-394-89474-X*) Random Bks Yng Read.
Cookson, Catherine. Go Tell It to Mrs. Golightly. large type ed. 288p. 1993. LC 7451-1658-2, Galaxy Child Lrg Print) Chivers N Amer.
Cool, Joyce. The Kidnapping of Courtney Van Allen & What's-Her-Name. 176p. 1988. pap. 2.75 (*0-553-15597-0*, Starfire) Bantam.
Cooley, Regina F. The Magic Christmas Pony. Hansen, Han H., illus. LC 91-76342. 36p. (gr. 1-5). 1991. 19.95 (*1-880450-04-6*) Capstone Pub.
Coolidge. Golden Days of Greece. (gr. 5 up). 1968. 14.95 (*0-690-33473-7*, Crowell Jr Bks) HarpC Child Bks.
Coolidge, Archibald C., ed. see Harris, Joel C.
Coolidge, Olivia. Greek Myths. Sandoz, E., illus. 256p. (gr. 7 up). 1949. 13.45 (*0-395-06721-9*) HM.
—Lives of Famous Romans. Johnson, Milton, illus. LC 91-40360. 248p. (gr. 8-12). 1992. Repr. of 1965 ed. lib. bdg. 19.50 (*0-208-02333-X*, Pub. by Linnet) Shoe String.
Coolidge, Olivia E. Trojan War. Sandoz, E., illus. (gr. 7-12). 1952. 16.95 (*0-395-06731-6*) HM.
—Trojan War. 1990. pap. 4.80 (*0-395-56151-5*) HM.
Coolidge, Susan. What Katy Did. (gr. 3-7). 15.75 (*0-8446-6184-8*) Peter Smith.
—What Katy Did. 190p. 1988. Repr. lib. bdg. 19.95x (*0-89966-585-3*) Buccaneer Bks.

—What Katy Did Next. (gr. k-6). 1989. pap. 3.50 (*0-440-40244-1*, Pub. by Yearling Classics) Dell.
Coomaraswamy, Ananda K. & Nivedita, Sr. Myths of the Hindus & Buddhists. (Illus.). 400p. (gr. 4-8). pap. 7.95 (*0-486-21759-0*) Dover.
Coombs, Charles. All-Terrain Bicycling. LC 86-14980. (Illus.). 144p. (gr. 5-9). 1987. 14.95 (*0-8050-0204-9*) H Holt & Co.
—Young Atom Detective. (Illus.). (gr. 4-7). PLB 7.19 (*0-8313-0021-3*) Lantern.
Coombs, Charles I. Ultralights: The Flying Featherweights. LC 83-17411. (Illus.). 160p. (gr. 5 up). 1984. 12.95 (*0-688-02775-X*) Morrow Jr Bks.
Coombs, Fred, jt. auth. see Branson, Margaret.
Coombs, H. Samm. Teenage Survival Manual: How to Reach '20' in One Piece & Enjoy Every Step of the Journey) 4th, rev. ed. Lipney, Stephanie & Moore, Dick, illus. 235p. (gr. 9-12). 1993. pap. 9.95 (*0-925258-08-3*) DB Inc CA.
Coombs, Karen M. Beating Bully O'Brien. (gr. 3-7). 1991. pap. 2.95 (*0-380-75935-7*, Camelot) Avon.
—Samantha Gill, Belly Dancer. 128p. 1989. pap. 2.75 (*0-380-75737-0*, Camelot) Avon.
—Saving Casey. 192p. (Orig.). 1992. pap. 3.50 (*0-380-76634-5*, Camelot) Avon.
Coombs, Patricia. Dorrie & the Blue Witch. Coombs, Patricia, illus. 48p. (gr. k-6). 1980. pap. 1.50 (*0-440-42210-8*, YB) Dell.
—Dorrie & the Dreamyard Monsters. Coombs, Patricia, illus. 48p. (gr. k-6). 1982. pap. 2.25 (*0-440-40896-2*, YB) Dell.
—Dorrie & the Halloween Plot. LC 76-3643. (Illus.). 48p. (gr. 1-5). 1976. PLB 12.88 (*0-688-51764-1*) Lothrop.
—Dorrie & the Haunted House. 48p. (gr. k-6). 1980. pap. 1.50 (*0-440-42212-4*, YB) Dell.
—Dorrie & the Haunted Schoolhouse. Coombs, Patricia, illus. 32p. (ps-3). 1992. 13.45 (*0-395-60116-9*, Clarion Bks) HM.
—Dorrie & the Museum Case. LC 84-27812. (Illus.). 48p. (gr. 1-5). 1986. 11.95 (*0-688-04278-3*); PLB 11.88 (*0-688-04279-1*) Lothrop.
—Dorrie & the Pin Witch. Coombs, Patricia, illus. LC 88-12697. 32p. (gr. 1-4). 1989. 12.95 (*0-688-08055-3*); PLB 12.88 (*0-688-08056-1*) Lothrop.
—Dorrie & the Screebit Ghost. Coombs, Patricia, illus. LC 79-4443. (gr. 1-4). 1979. 9.95 (*0-688-41883-X*) Lothrop.
—Dorrie & the Witches' Camp. Coombs, Patricia, illus. LC 82-9986. 48p. (gr. 1-5). 1983. PLB 12.88 (*0-688-01508-5*) Lothrop.
—Dorrie & the Wizard's Spell. Coombs, Patricia, illus. LC 68-27601. 48p. (gr. 1-5). 1968. PLB 12.88 (*0-688-51083-3*) Lothrop.
—The Magician & McTree. Coombs, Patricia, illus. LC 83-11984. (gr. 1-4). 1984. 11.95 (*0-688-02109-3*) Lothrop.
Coombs, Samm. Teenage Survival Manual: Taking Charge of Your Life. 235p. (Orig.). 1991. pap. 9.95 (*0-685-54351-X*) Halo Bks.
Coon, Alma S. Amy, Ben, & Catalpa the Cat: A Fanciful Story of This & That. Owens, Gail, illus. 40p. (ps-2). 1990. 7.95 (*0-87935-079-2*) Williamsburg.
—The Mouse & the Mill & the Bottle Babies. Shoemaker, Kathryn, illus. 44p. (ps-1). 1992. 5.95 (*0-87935-061-X*) Williamsburg.
Coon, Pam. The Vowel Vow. 72p. (gr. k-3). 1980. 7.95 (*0-88160-010-5*, LW 112) Learning Wks.
Cooney. Christmas. Date not set. 15.00 (*0-06-023433-4*, Festival); PLB 14.89 (*0-06-023434-2*, Festival) HarpC Child Bks.
—The Fog. 1993. pap. 3.25 (*0-590-43806-9*) Scholastic Inc.
—Last Dance. 1992. pap. 3.25 (*0-590-45785-3*, Point) Scholastic Inc.
—Saturday Night. 1992. pap. 3.25 (*0-590-45784-5*, Point) Scholastic Inc.
—Summer Nights. 1992. pap. 3.25 (*0-590-45786-1*, Point) Scholastic Inc.
Cooney, Barbara. Hattie & the Wild Waves. Cooney, Barbara, illus. (ps-3). 1990. 14.95 (*0-670-83056-9*) Viking Child Bks.
—Hattie & the Wild Waves: A Story from Brooklyn. Cooney, Barbara, illus. LC 92-40723. 40p. 1993. pap. 4.99 (*0-14-054193-4*, Puffin) Puffin Bks.
—Island Boy. LC 88-175. (ps-3). 1988. 15.00 (*0-670-81749-X*) Viking Child Bks.
—Island Boy. 40p. (ps-3). 1991. pap. 4.95 (*0-14-050756-6*, Puffin) Puffin Bks.
—Miss Rumphius. Cooney, Barbara, illus. LC 82-2837. 32p. (gr. k-3). 1982. pap. 14.95 (*0-670-47958-6*) Viking Child Bks.
—Miss Rumphius. LC 85-40447. (Illus.). 32p. (ps-3). 1985. pap. 4.99 (*0-14-050539-3*, Puffin) Puffin Bks.
—Miss Rumphius. Cooney, Barbara, illus. (ps-3). 1994. pap. 6.99 incl. cassette (*0-14-095026-5*, Puffin) Puffin Bks.
—Snow White & Rose Red. (ps-3). 1991. pap. 13.95 (*0-685-54227-0*) Delacorte.
—Snow White & Rose Red. LC 89-78013. (ps-3). 1991. 13.95 (*0-385-30175-8*) Delacorte.
Cooney, Barbara, tr. see Hall, Donald.
Cooney, Caroline. The Return of the Vampire. 176p. 1992. pap. 2.95 (*0-590-44884-6*, Point) Scholastic Inc.
—Twenty Pageants Later. (gr. 4-7). 1993. pap. 3.99 (*0-553-29672-8*) Bantam.
Cooney, Caroline B. Among Friends. 176p. (gr. 6 up). 1987. 13.95 (*0-553-05446-5*, Starfire) Bantam.

—Cheerleader. 1991. pap. 3.25 (*0-590-44316-X*, Point) Scholastic Inc.
—Don't Blame the Music. LC 85-21727. 172p. (gr. 8 up). 1986. 14.95 (*0-448-47778-5*, G&D) Putnam Pub Group.
—The Face on the Milk Carton. (gr. 7 up). 1990. 16.00 (*0-553-05853-3*) Bantam.
—Face on the Milk Carton. 1991. pap. 3.99 (*0-553-28958-6*) Bantam.
—Family Reunion. (gr. 7 up). 1989. 14.95 (*0-553-05836-3*, Starfire) Bantam.
—Family Reunion. 1990. pap. 2.95 (*0-553-28573-4*) Bantam.
—The Fire. 1990. pap. 3.25 (*0-590-41641-3*) Scholastic Inc.
—Flight Number 116 Is Down. 176p. 1992. 13.95 (*0-590-44465-4*, Scholastic Hardcover) Scholastic Inc.
—Flight Number 116 is Down. 1993. pap. 3.25 (*0-590-44479-4*) Scholastic Inc.
—Forbidden. (gr. 9-12). 1993. pap. 3.50 (*0-590-46574-0*) Scholastic Inc.
—Freeze Tag. 1992. 3.25 (*0-590-45681-4*, Point) Scholastic Inc.
—New Year's Eve. 224p. (Orig.). (gr. 9 up). 1988. pap. 2.95 (*0-590-44627-4*) Scholastic Inc.
—Operation: Homefront. 1992. pap. 3.99 (*0-553-29685-X*) Bantam.
—Party's Over. 1991. 13.95 (*0-590-42552-8*, Scholastic Hardcover) Scholastic Inc.
—The Party's Over. 192p. (gr. 7 up). 1992. pap. 3.25 (*0-590-42553-6*, Point) Scholastic Inc.
—The Perfume. 1992. pap. 3.25 (*0-590-45402-1*, Point) Scholastic Inc.
—The Snow. 176p. (Orig.). (gr. 7 up). 1990. pap. 3.25 (*0-590-41640-5*) Scholastic Inc.
—Stranger. 1993. pap. 3.50 (*0-590-45680-6*) Scholastic Inc.
—Twenty Pageants Late. 1991. 15.00 (*0-553-07254-4*) Bantam.
—Vampires Promise. 1993. pap. 3.50 (*0-590-45682-2*) Scholastic Inc.
—Whatever Happened to Janie? LC 92-32334. 1993. 15.95 (*0-385-31035-8*) Delacorte.
Cooney, James A. Foreign Policy. rev. ed. 160p. (gr 7 up). 1992. PLB 15.85 (*0-8027-8116-0*); pap. 9.95 (*0-8027-7368-0*) Walker & Co.
Cooney, Judith. Coping with Sexual Abuse. rev. ed. Rosen, R., ed. 118p. (gr. 7-12). 1991. PLB 13.95 (*0-8239-1336-8*); leader's guide 5.95 (*0-8239-0846-1*) Rosen Group.
Cooney, Kevin, jt. auth. see Cooney, Linda A.
Cooney, Linda A. Breaking Away. 224p. 1991. pap. 2.95 (*0-590-44561-8*) Scholastic Inc.
—Freshman Affair. 1992. pap. 3.50 (*0-06-106711-3*, Harp PBks) HarpC.
—Freshman Breakup. 1993. pap. 3.99 (*0-06-106165-4*, Harp PBks) HarpC.
—Freshman Celebrity. 1993. pap. 3.99 (*0-06-106767-9*, Harp PBks) HarpC.
—Freshman Changes. 1991. pap. 3.50 (*0-06-106078-X*, Harp PBks) HarpC.
—Freshman Choices. 1991. pap. 3.50 (*0-06-106128-X*, Harp PBks) HarpC.
—Freshman Christmas. 1992. pap. 4.50 (*0-06-106723-7*, Harp PBks) HarpC.
—Freshman Dorm. 1990. pap. 3.99 (*0-06-106000-3*, Harp PBks) HarpC.
—Freshman Dreams. (gr. 9-12). 1991. pap. 3.50 (*0-06-106040-2*, PL) HarpC.
—Freshman Feud. 1992. pap. 3.50 (*0-06-106141-7*, Harp PBks) HarpC.
—Freshman Flames. 1991. pap. 3.50 (*0-06-106127-1*, Harp PBks) HarpC.
—Freshman Fling. 1991. pap. 3.50 (*0-06-106121-2*, Harp PBks) HarpC.
—Freshman Follies. 1992. pap. 3.50 (*0-06-106142-5*, Harp PBks) HarpC.
—Freshman Games. (gr. 9-12). 1991. pap. 3.50 (*0-06-106035-6*, Harp PBks) HarpC.
—Freshman Guys. (gr. 9-12). 1990. pap. 3.50 (*0-06-106011-9*, PL) HarpC.
—Freshman Heartbreak. (gr. 7 up). 1992. pap. 3.50 (*0-06-106140-9*, Harp PBks) HarpC.
—Freshman Heat. (gr. 9-12). 1993. pap. 3.99 (*0-06-106738-5*, Harp PBks) HarpC.
—Freshman Holiday. 1993. pap. 4.50 (*0-06-106170-0*, Harp PBks) HarpC.
—Freshman Lies. 1990. pap. 3.50 (*0-06-106005-4*, Harp PBks) HarpC.
—Freshman Nights. (gr. 9-12). 1990. pap. 3.50 (*0-06-106012-7*, PL) HarpC.
—Freshman Obsession. 1993. pap. 3.99 (*0-06-106734-2*, Harp PBks) HarpC.
—Freshman Passion. (gr. 9-12). 1993. pap. 3.99 (*0-06-106745-8*, Harp PBks) HarpC.
—Freshman Promises. 1992. pap. 3.50 (*0-06-106134-4*, Harp PBks) HarpC.
—Freshman Rivals. 1991. pap. 3.50 (*0-06-106122-0*, Harp PBks) HarpC.
—Freshman Roommate. 1993. pap. 3.99 (*0-06-106730-X*, Harp PBks) HarpC.
—Freshman Scandal. 1992. pap. 3.50 (*0-06-106718-0*, Harp PBks) HarpC.
—Freshman Summer. 1992. pap. 3.99 (*0-06-106780-6*, Harp PBks) HarpC.
—Freshman Suspect. 1994. pap. 3.99 (*0-06-106168-9*, Harp PBks) HarpC.
—Freshman Taboo. (gr..9-12). 1993. pap. 3.99 (*0-06-106741-5*, Harp PBks) HarpC.
—Freshman Temptation. (gr. 4-7). 1993. pap. 3.99 (*0-06-106166-2*, Harp PBks) HarpC.
—Freshman Truths. 1992. pap. 3.50 (*0-06-106713-X*, Harp PBks) HarpC.
—Freshman Wedding. 1992. pap. 3.50 (*0-06-106135-2*, Harp PBks) HarpC.
—Losing Control. 176p. 1991. 2.95 (*0-590-44560-X*) Scholastic Inc.
—Playing Games. 1992. pap. 2.95 (*0-590-44565-0*, Point) Scholastic Inc.
Cooney, Linda A. & Cooney, Kevin. Making Changes. 176p. 1992. pap. 2.95 (*0-590-44563-4*) Scholastic Inc.
—Standing Alone. 176p. 1991. pap. 2.95 (*0-590-44562-6*) Scholastic Inc.
Cooney, Nancy E. Chatterbox Jamie. Hafner, Marylin, illus. LC 92-11001. 32p. (ps-1). 1993. PLB 14.95 (*0-399-22208-1*, Putnam) Putnam Pub Group.
—Go Away Monsters, Lickety Split! Chambliss, Maxie, illus. 32p. (ps-1). 1990. 13.95 (*0-399-21935-8*, Putnam) Putnam Pub Group.
Cooper, Alan. Rail Travel. LC 93-16804. 32p. (gr. 5-9). 1993. 14.95 (*1-56847-039-8*) Thomson Lrning.
Cooper, Amy J. Aunt Abigail's Beau. (gr. 4-7). 1992. pap. 3.99 (*0-553-48033-2*) Bantam.
Cooper, Ann. Bats: Swift Shadows of the Twilight. Denver Museum of Art Staff, illus. 64p. (gr. 3-6). 1993. pap. text ed. 7.95x (*1-879373-52-1*) R Rinehart.
—Eagles: Hunters of the Sky. (Illus., illus). (gr. 4-6). 1992. pap. 7.95 (*1-879373-11-4*) R Rinehart.
Cooper, Ann K. Gallery of Pioneers. 68p. (gr. 9-12). 1986. pap. text ed. write for info. (*0-910463-05-0*) Edit Heliodor.
Cooper, Carolyn, ed. see Watkins, Dawn L.
Cooper, Charlotte. Fifty Object Stories for Children. (ps-4). 1988. pap. 5.99 (*0-8010-2523-0*) Baker Bk.
Cooper, Chris & Insley, Jane. How Does It Work? 64p. (gr. 4-7). 15.95x (*0-8160-1066-8*) Facts on File.
Cooper, Chris & Osmond, Tony. How Everyday Things Work. 64p. (gr. 7 up). 15.95x (*0-87196-988-2*) Facts on File.
Cooper, Clare. Ashar of Qarius. 163p. (gr. 3-7). 1990. 14.95 (*0-15-200409-2*, Gulliver Bks) HarBrace.
Cooper, Don. Boogie-Woogie Bugs. Forrest, Sandra, illus. (ps-3). 1989. bk. & cassette 5.95 (*0-394-82950-6*) Random Bks Yng Read.
—Dino-Songs. Boyd, Patti, illus. 32p. (ps-3). 1988. bk. & cassette pkg. 6.95 (*0-394-89810-9*) Random Bks Yng Read.
—Hanukkah Songs & Games. Cook, Donald, illus. 32p. (ps-3). 1989. pap. 6.95 incl. cassette (*0-679-80041-7*) Random Bks Yng Read.
—Happy Birthday Songs & Games. Freeze, Marla, illus. Elkins, Stephen, contrib. by. (Illus.). 32p. (Orig.). (ps-3). 1988. pap. 5.95 bk. & cassette pkg. (*0-394-80826-6*) Random Bks Yng Read.
—Merry Christmas Songs & Games. Fritz, Ronald, illus. 32p. (ps-3). 1989. pap. 5.95 incl. cassette (*0-394-82230-7*) Random Bks Yng Read.
—Recycled Songs. Alley, R. W., illus. 32p. (ps-3). 1992. incl. cassette 7.99 (*0-679-82643-2*) Random Bks Yng Read.
—Spooky Tunes. Daniel, Frank, illus. 32p. (Orig.). (ps-3). 1990. pap. 6.95 incl. cassette (*0-679-80303-3*) Random Bks Yng Read.
Cooper, Don, read by. Songs of America. Fritz, Ron, illus. 32p. (ps-3). 1990. 6.95 (*0-394-85225-7*); cass. incl. Random Bks Yng Read.
—Star Tunes. Fritz, Ronald, illus. 32p. (Orig.). (ps-3). 1991. pap. 6.95 incls. cassette (*0-679-81243-1*) Random Bks Yng Read.
Cooper, F. T., tr. see Donauer, Friedrich.
Cooper, Floyd. Langston Hughes. Cooper, Floyd, illus. LC 93-36332. 1994. write for info. (*0-399-22682-6*, Philomel Bks) Putnam Pub Group.
Cooper, Harold. Believing Truth about the Church. (Illus.). 80p. (gr. 8-9). 1975. pap. 3.50 (*0-89114-070-0*); P. 64. tchr's. ed. 1.50 (*0-89114-071-9*) Baptist Pub Hse.
Cooper, Helen. The Bear under the Stairs. Cooper, Helen, illus. LC 92-23840. (ps-2). 1993. 12.99 (*0-8037-1279-0*) Dial Bks Young.
—Ella & the Rabbit. Cooper, Helen, illus. LC 90-34499. 32p. (ps-3). 1990. 12.95 (*0-940793-62-8*, Crocodile Bks) Interlink Pub.
—The House Cat. LC 93-34217. 1994. 15.95 (*0-590-48172-X*) Scholastic Inc.
Cooper, Ilene. Choosing Sides. (Illus.). 218p. (gr. 3-7). 1992. pap. 3.99 (*0-14-036097-2*, Puffin) Puffin Bks.
—Choosing Sides. LC 89-13669. 224p. (gr. 4-7). 1990. 12.95 (*0-688-07934-2*) Morrow Jr Bks.
—Hollywood Wars, No. 4: Trouble in Paradise. 144p. (gr. 3-7). 1993. pap. 3.25 (*0-14-036158-8*, Puffin) Puffin Bks.
—Lights, Camera, Attitude. 144p. (gr. 3-7). 1993. pap. 3.25 (*0-14-036155-3*) Puffin Bks.
—Mean Streak. LC 90-23103. 208p. (gr. 4 up). 1991. 13.95 (*0-688-08431-1*) Morrow Jr Bks.
—Mean Streak. 192p. (gr. 3-7). 1992. pap. 3.99 (*0-14-034978-2*, Puffin) Puffin Bks.
—My Co-Star, My Enemy. 144p. (gr. 3-7). 1993. pap. 3.25 (*0-14-036156-1*) Puffin Bks.
—The New, Improved Gretchen Hubbard. LC 92-6197. 208p. (gr. 4 up). 1992. 14.00 (*0-688-08432-X*) Morrow Jr Bks.
—Queen of the Sixth Grade. LC 88-18859. 128p. (gr. 4-7). 1988. 12.95 (*0-688-07933-4*) Morrow Jr Bks.
—Queen of the Sixth Grade. 160p. (gr. 3 up). 1992. pap. 3.99 (*0-14-036098-0*, Puffin) Puffin Bks.
—Queen of the Sixth Grade. LC 89-36938. (gr. 3 up). 1990. pap. 3.95 (*0-14-034028-9*, Puffin) Puffin Bks.
—Seeing Red. LC 92-42426. 144p. (gr. 3-7). 1993. pap. 3.25 (*0-14-036157-X*, Puffin) Puffin Bks.
—The Winning of Miss Lynn Ryan. Magurn, Susan, illus. LC 87-15233. 128p. (gr. 3-6). 1987. 11.95 (*0-688-07231-3*) Morrow Jr Bks.
Cooper, J. Airplanes. 1991. 8.95s.p. (*0-86592-493-7*) Rourke Enter.
—Arboles (Trees) 1991. 8.95s.p. (*0-86592-498-8*) Rourke Enter.
—Automobiles. 1991. 8.95s.p. (*0-86592-495-3*) Rourke Enter.
—Automoviles (Automobiles) 1991. 8.95s.p. (*0-86592-510-0*) Rourke Enter.
—Aviones (Airplanes) 1991. 8.95s.p. (*0-86592-507-0*) Rourke Enter.
—Boats & Ships. 1991. 8.95s.p. (*0-86592-492-9*) Rourke Enter.
—Botes y Barcos (Boats & Ships) 1991. 8.95s.p. (*0-86592-474-0*) Rourke Enter.
—Bridges. 1991. 8.95s.p. (*0-86592-628-X*) Rourke Enter.
—Cactos (Cactus) 1991. 8.95s.p. (*0-86592-546-1*) Rourke Enter.
—Cactus. 1991. 8.95s.p. (*0-86592-622-0*) Rourke Enter.
—Camiones (Trucks) 1991. 8.95s.p. (*0-86592-509-7*) Rourke Enter.
—Canales (Canals) (SPA.). 1991. 8.95s.p. (*0-86592-923-8*) Rourke Enter.
—Canals. 1991. 8.95s.p. (*0-86592-638-7*) Rourke Enter.
—Castillos (Castles) (SPA.). 1991. 8.95s.p. (*0-86592-937-8*) Rourke Enter.
—Castles. 1991. 8.95s.p. (*0-86592-629-8*) Rourke Enter.
—Dams. 1991. 8.95s.p. (*0-86592-627-1*) Rourke Enter.
—The Earth's Garden Series, 6 bks. 1991. Set. 53.70s.p. (*0-86592-619-0*) Rourke Enter.
—Faros (Lighthouses) (SPA.). 1991. 8.95s.p. (*0-86592-936-X*) Rourke Enter.
—Flores (Flowers) 1991. 8.95s.p. (*0-86592-497-X*) Rourke Enter.
—Flowers. 1991. 8.95s.p. (*0-86592-620-4*) Rourke Enter.
—Insect-Eating Plants. 1991. 8.95s.p. (*0-86592-624-7*) Rourke Enter.
—Lighthouses. 1991. 8.95s.p. (*0-86592-630-1*) Rourke Enter.
—Man-Made Wonders Series, 6 bks. 1991. Set. 53.70s.p. (*0-86592-626-3*) Rourke Enter.
—Maravillas de la Humanidad (Man-Made Wonders) Series, 6 bks, Set VI. (SPA.). 1991. 53.70s.p. (*0-685-53670-X*) Rourke Enter.
—Motocicletas (Motorcycles) 1991. 8.95s.p. (*0-86592-508-9*) Rourke Enter.
—Motorcycles. 1991. 8.95s.p. (*0-86592-494-5*) Rourke Enter.
—Mushrooms. 1991. 8.95s.p. (*0-86592-623-9*) Rourke Enter.
—Plantas Insectivoras (Insect-Eating Plants) 1991. 8.95s.p. (*0-86592-548-8*) Rourke Enter.
—Plantas Singulares (Strange Plants) 1991. 8.95s.p. (*0-86592-547-X*) Rourke Enter.
—Puentes (Bridges) (SPA.). 1991. 8.95s.p. (*0-86592-934-3*) Rourke Enter.
—Rascacielos (Skyscrapers) (SPA.). 1991. 8.95s.p. (*0-86592-935-1*) Rourke Enter.
—Represas (Dams) (SPA.). 1991. 8.95s.p. (*0-86592-924-6*) Rourke Enter.
—Setas y Hongos (Mushrooms) 1991. 8.95s.p. (*0-86592-499-6*) Rourke Enter.
—Skyscrapers. 1991. 8.95s.p. (*0-86592-637-9*) Rourke Enter.
—Spanish Language Books, Set 3: Los Jardines de la Tierra (The Earth's Garden, 6 bks. 1991. 53.70s.p. (*0-86592-496-1*) Rourke Enter.
—Spanish Language Books, Set 5: Maquinas de Viaje (Traveling Machines, 6 bks. 1991. 53.70s.p. (*0-86592-473-2*) Rourke Enter.
—Strange Plants. 1991. 8.95s.p. (*0-86592-625-5*) Rourke Enter.
—Trains. 1991. 8.95s.p. (*0-86592-490-2*) Rourke Enter.
—Traveling Machines Series, 6 bks. 1991. Set. 53.70s.p. (*0-86592-489-9*) Rourke Enter.
—Trees. 1991. 8.95s.p. (*0-86592-621-2*) Rourke Enter.
—Trenes (Trains) 1991. 8.95s.p. (*0-86592-515-1*) Rourke Enter.
—Trucks. 1991. 8.95s.p. (*0-86592-491-0*) Rourke Enter.
Cooper, J. B. Picture Perfect Romance. 1993. pap. 2.99 (*0-553-29983-2*) Bantam.
Cooper, James Fenimore. Deerslayer. (gr. 6 up). 1964. pap. 1.25 (*0-8049-0031-0*, CL31) Airmont.
—Deerslayer. 544p. (gr. RL 7). 1963. pap. 3.95 (*0-451-52484-5*, CE1645, Sig Classics) NAL-Dutton.
—The Deerslayer. 528p. (gr. 9-12). 1991. pap. 3.50 (*0-553-21085-8*, Bantam Classics) Bantam.
—The Deerslayer: or The First War-Path. Wyeth, N. C., illus. LC 90-34326. 480p. 1994. SBE 24.95 (*0-684-19224-1*, Scribners Young Read); (Scribner) Macmillan Child Grp.
—Last of the Mohicans. (gr. 6 up). 1964. pap. 2.95 (*0-8049-0005-1*, CL-5) Airmont.
—Last of the Mohicans. 432p. (Orig.). (RL 7). 1962. pap. 4.95 (*0-451-52503-5*, Sig Classics) NAL-Dutton.
—The Last of the Mohicans. new & abr. ed. Farr, Naunerle, ed. Carrillo, Fred, illus. (gr. 4-12). 1977. pap. text ed. 2.95 (*0-88301-267-7*) Pendulum Pr.

—The Last of the Mohicans. reissue ed. Wyeth, N. C., illus. LC 86-17694. 376p. 1986. SBE 24.95 (0-684-18711-6, Scribners Young Read); deluxe ed. 75.00 (0-684-18716-7, Scribner) Macmillan Child Grp.
—The Last of the Mohicans. 1989. 26.95 (0-89968-254-5) Buccaneer Bks.
—The Last of the Mohicans. Martin, Les, adapted by. Stirnweis, Shannon, illus. 96p. (Orig.). (gr. 2-7). 1993. PLB 5.99 (0-679-94706-X); pap. 2.95 (0-679-84706-5) Random Bks Yng Read.
—The Leatherstocking Saga. (gr. 5-6). 42.95 (0-8488-0059-1, Pub. by Amereon Hse) Amereon Ltd.
—Pathfinder. (gr. 6 up). 1964. pap. 2.95 (0-8049-0035-3, CL-35) Airmont.
—Pathfinder. 488p. (RL 10). 1982. pap. 5.95 (0-451-52257-5, Sig Classics) NAL-Dutton.
—Pioneers. (gr. 8 up). 1964. pap. 1.95 (0-8049-0049-3, CL-49) Airmont.
—Pioneers. 448p. (RL 10). 1964. pap. 4.95 (0-451-52521-3, Sig Classics); pap. 4.50 (0-451-52339-3) NAL-Dutton.
—Prairie. (gr. 8 up). 1964. pap. 1.95 (0-8049-0041-8, CL-41) Airmont.
—Prairie. 416p. (Orig.). (RL 10). 1964. pap. 4.95 (0-451-52516-7, CE1780, Sig Classics) NAL-Dutton.
—The Two Admirals: A Tale. LC 88-12190. 511p. (Orig.). (gr. 9-12). 1990. 49.50x (0-88706-905-3); pap. 18.95x (0-88706-907-X) State U NY Pr.
Cooper, Jason. Airports. LC 92-8677. 1992. 12.67 (0-86593-208-5); lib. bdg. 9.50s.p. (0-685-59384-3) Rourke Corp.
—Coral Reefs. LC 92-16077. 1992. 12.67 (0-86593-229-8); lib. bdg. 9.50s.p. (0-685-59719-9) Rourke Corp.
—Fire Stations. LC 92-8676. 1992. 12.67 (0-86593-210-7); 9.50s.p. (0-685-59383-5) Rourke Corp.
—Large Sea Creatures. LC 92-16072. 1992. 12.67 (0-86593-231-X); 9.50s.p. (0-685-59714-8) Rourke Corp.
—Light. LC 92-8808. 1992. 12.67 (0-86593-166-6); 9.50s.p. (0-685-59295-2) Rourke Corp.
—Magnetism. LC 92-8807. 1992. 11.94 (0-86593-165-8); 8.95s.p. (0-685-59294-4) Rourke Corp.
—Museums. LC 92-12556. 1992. 12.67 (0-86593-209-3); 9.50s.p. (0-685-59389-4) Rourke Corp.
—Sea Plants. LC 92-16076. 1992. 12.67 (0-86593-232-8); 9.50s.p. (0-685-66141-5) Rourke Corp.
—Sea Shells. LC 92-16075. 1992. 12.67 (0-86593-233-6); 9.50s.p. (0-685-66140-7) Rourke Corp.
—Small Sea Creatures. LC 92-16073. 1992. 12.67 (0-86593-230-1); 9.50s.p. (0-685-59715-6) Rourke Corp.
—Sound. LC 92-8809. 1992. 12.67 (0-86593-167-4); 9.50s.p. (0-685-59296-0) Rourke Corp.
—Tide Pools. LC 92-16074. 1992. 12.67 (0-86593-234-4); lib. bdg. 9.50s.p. (0-685-59716-4) Rourke Corp.
—Wind. LC 92-8811. 1992. 12.67 (0-86593-171-2); 9.50s.p. (0-685-59297-9) Rourke Corp.
—Zoos. LC 92-12555. 1992. 12.67 (0-86593-212-3); 9.50s.p. (0-685-59348-6) Rourke Corp.
Cooper, Joan M., ed. see Barber, Lilian S.
Cooper, John & Morris, Susan. Cromwell Family. 52p. (gr. 6 up). 1987. pap. 7.95 (0-85950-546-4, Pub. by S Thornes UK) Dufour.
Cooper, Kay. Discover It Yourself: Where Did You Get Those Eyes? 80p. 1993. pap. 3.50 (0-380-71304-7, Camelot) Avon.
—Discover It Yourself: Where in the World Are You? Novak, Justin, illus. 96p. 1993. pap. 3.50 (0-380-71299-7, Camelot) Avon.
—Discover It Yourself: Who Put the Canon in the Courthouse Square? 96p. 1993. pap. 3.50 (0-380-71298-9, Camelot) Avon.
—Where Did You Get Those Eyes: A Guide to Discovering Your Family History. Accardo, Anthony, illus. (gr. 5 up). 1988. 13.95 (0-8027-6802-4); PLB 14.85 (0-8027-6803-2) Walker & Co.
—Where in the World Are You? Novak, Justin, illus. 80p. (gr. 3-7). 1990. 13.95 (0-8027-6912-8); lib. bdg. 14.85 (0-8027-6913-6) Walker & Co.
—Who Put the Cannon in the Courthouse Square: A Guide to Uncovering the Past. Accardo, Anthony, illus. LC 84-17251. (gr. 4 up). 1984. PLB 12.85 (0-8027-6561-0) Walker & Co.
Cooper, Lee. Fun with German. Githens, Elizabeth, illus. (gr. 3 up). 1972. lib. bdg. 15.95 (0-316-15588-8) Little.
Cooper, Louise. The Sleep of Stone. LC 91-4268. (Illus.). 144p. (gr. 7 up). 1991. SBE 14.95 (0-689-31572-4, Atheneum Child Bk) Macmillan Child Grp.
Cooper, Margaret C. The Riddle of Changewater Pond. LC 93-15699. (gr. 4-7). 1993. SBE 13.95 (0-02-724495-4, Bradbury Pr) Macmillan Child Grp.
Cooper, Marva. Livingston's Vision. (Illus.). (gr. 1-7). write for info. (1-882185-08-0) Crnrstone Pub.
Cooper, Melrose. I Got a Family. Gottlieb, Dale, photos by. LC 92-1689. (Illus.). 32p. (ps-2). 1993. PLB 14.95 (0-8050-1965-0, Bks Young Read) H Holt & Co.
—I Got Community. 1994. write for info. (0-8050-3179-0) H Holt & Co.
—Life Riddles. 128p. (gr. 5-7). 1993. PLB 14.95 (0-8050-2613-4, Bks Young Read) H Holt & Co.
Cooper, Michael. Klondike Fever: The Famous Gold Rush of 1898. LC 89-+013. (Illus.). 80p. (gr. 4 up). 1989. 14.45 (0-89919-803-1, Clarion Bks) HM.
—Klondike Fever: The Famous Gold Rush of 1898. (gr. 4-7). 1990. pap. 5.70 (0-395-54784-9, Clarion Bks) HM.

—Racing Sled Dogs: An Original North American Sport. LC 87-25007. (Illus.). 96p. (gr. 4-7). 1988. 13.95 (0-89919-499-0, Clarion Bks) HM.
Cooper, Michael L. Playing America's Game: The Story of Negro League Baseball. (Illus.). 112p. (gr. 4-7). 1993. 15.99 (0-525-67407-1, Lodestar Bks) Dutton Child Bks.
Cooper, Myrtle E. From Tent Town to City: A Chronological History of Billings, Montana 1882-1935. Von Vogt, Janice, ed. Hulteng, Lee, illus. Wright, Kathryn, intro. by. (Illus.). 79p. (Orig.). (gr. 6-8). 1982. pap. 5.95 (0-9613224-0-3) Parmly Lib.
Cooper, Nancy, jt. auth. see Bin-Nun, Judy.
Cooper, Richard & Crary, Ryland. The Politics of Progress. (gr. 7-12). 1982. 9.95 (0-931992-42-7) Penns Valley.
Cooper, Rod. Journey Through Australia. Camm, Martin, illus. LC 91-46173. 32p. (gr. 3-5). 1993. PLB 11.89 (0-8167-2757-0); pap. text ed. 3.95 (0-8167-2758-9) Troll Assocs. Postponed.
Cooper, Susan. The Boggart. LC 92-15527. 208p. (gr. 4-7). 1993. SBE 14.95 (0-689-50576-0, M K McElderry) Macmillan Child Grp.
—Danny & the Kings. Smith, Joseph A., illus. LC 92-22744. 32p. (ps-3). 1993. SBE 14.95 (0-689-50577-9, M K McElderry) Macmillan Child Grp.
—The Dark Is Rising. Cober, Alan, illus. LC 72-85916. 232p. (gr. 5 up). 1973. SBE 14.95 (0-689-30317-3, M K McElderry) Macmillan Child Grp.
—The Dark Is Rising. LC 86-3647. 256p. (gr. 7 up). 1986. pap. 3.95 (0-689-71087-9, Aladdin) Macmillan Child Grp.
—The Dark Is Rising Sequence. 874p. (gr. 6 up). 1987. Boxed set incl. The Dark Is Rising, Greenwitch, The Grey King, & Silver on the Tree. pap. 13.95 (0-689-71155-7, Collier Young Ad) Macmillan Child Grp.
—The Dark Is Rising Sequence, 5 bks. (gr. 7 up). 1993. Boxed set. pap. 19.75 (0-02-042565-1, Aladdin) Macmillan Child Grp.
—Dawn of Fear. Gill, Margery, illus. LC 71-115755. 157p. (gr. 5 up). 1988. 14.95 (0-15-266201-4, HB Juv Bks) HarBrace.
—Dawn of Fear. Gill, Margery, illus. LC 89-6820. 224p. (gr. 5 up). 1989. pap. 3.95 (0-689-71327-4, Aladdin) Macmillan Child Grp.
—Greenwitch. Heslop, Michael, illus. LC 73-85319. 148p. (gr. 4-7). 1985. SBE 14.95 (0-689-30426-9, M K McElderry) Macmillan Child Grp.
—Greenwitch. LC 86-3324. 148p. (gr. 4-7). 1986. pap. 3.50 (0-689-71088-7, Collier Young Ad) Macmillan Child Grp.
—The Grey King. Heslop, Michael, illus. LC 75-8526. 224p. (gr. 4-8). 1975. SBE 14.95 (0-689-50029-7, M K McElderry) Macmillan Child Grp.
—The Grey King. LC 86-3613. 176p. (gr. 6 up). 1986. pap. 3.50 (0-689-71089-5, Collier Young Ad) Macmillan Child Grp.
—Matthew's Dragon. Smith, Jos. A., illus. LC 90-31532. 32p. (ps-3). 1991. SBE 13.95 (0-689-50512-4, M K McElderry) Macmillan Child Grp.
—Matthew's Dragon. Smith, Joseph A., illus. LC 93-26574. 32p. (gr. k-3). 1994. pap. 4.95 (0-689-71794-6, Aladdin) Macmillan Child Grp.
—Over Sea, Under Stone. Gill, Margery, illus. LC 66-11199. (gr. 5 up). 1966. 14.95 (0-15-259034-X, HB Juv Bks) HarBrace.
—Over Sea, under Stone. 256p. (gr. 5 up). 1989. pap. 3.50 (0-02-042785-9, Collier Young Ad) Macmillan Child Grp.
—Seaward. LC 83-7055. 180p. (gr. 5 up). 1983. SBE 14.95 (0-689-50275-3, M K McElderry) Macmillan Child Grp.
—Seaward. LC 86-23234. 180p. (gr. 5 up). 1987. pap. 3.95 (0-02-042190-7, Collier Young Ad) Macmillan Child Grp.
—The Selkie Girl. Hutton, Warwick, illus. LC 86-70147. 32p. (gr. k-4). 1986. SBE 14.95 (0-689-50390-3, M K McElderry) Macmillan Child Grp.
—The Selkie Girl. Hutton, Warwick, illus. LC 90-39982. 32p. 1991. pap. 4.95 (0-689-71467-X, Aladdin) Macmillan Child Grp.
—The Silver Cow: A Welsh Tale. Hutton, Warwick, illus. LC 82-13928. 32p. (gr. k-4). 1983. SBE 14.95 (0-689-50236-2, M K McElderry) Macmillan Child Grp.
—The Silver Cow: A Welsh Tale. Hutton, Warwick, illus. LC 91-234. 32p. (gr. k-3). 1991. pap. 4.95 (0-689-71512-9, Aladdin) Macmillan Child Grp.
—Silver on the Tree. LC 77-5361. 256p. (gr. 4-8). 1980. SBE 14.95 (0-689-50088-2, M K McElderry); 4.95 (0-689-70467-4) Macmillan Child Grp.
—Silver on the Tree. LC 86-3341. 288p. (gr. 6 up). 1987. pap. 3.95 (0-689-71152-2, Collier Young Ad) Macmillan Child Grp.
Cooper, Susan, retold by. Tam Lin. Hutton, Warwick, illus. LC 90-5571. 32p. (gr. k-4). 1991. SBE 14.95 (0-689-50505-1, M K McElderry) Macmillan Child Grp.
Cooper, Sydney. Meet Macauley Culkin. (Illus.). 64p. 1992. pap. 2.95 (1-56156-138-X) Kidsbks.
—Young Stars. (Illus.). 64p. (Orig.). 1991. pap. 2.95 (1-56156-080-4) Kidsbks.
Cooper, Timothy. Sonia. LC 91-73764. 304p. 1991. 19.95 (0-9619914-1-0) Americus Pr.
Cooper, Ursula. Mini Walks on the Mesa. Harroun, Dorothy, illus. LC 89-4448. 32p. (Orig.). (gr. 3-6). 1989. pap. 6.95 (0-86534-133-8) Sunstone Pr.

Cooper, William, ed. see Oana, Katherine.
Cooper, William H., ed. see Butrick, Lyn M.
Cooper, William H., ed. see Leonard, Mary K.
Cooper, William H., ed. see McCarthy, Donald.
Cooper, William H., ed. see McCarthy, Donald W.
Cooper, William H., ed. see Oana, Katherine.
Cooper, William H., ed. see Shuster, Albert H., et al.
Cooper, William H., ed. see Shuster, Albert H. & Miller, Russell R.
Cooper, William J., ed. see Barber, Lilian S.
Cooper, William R., ed. see Butrick, Lyn M.
Coopersmith, Harry, ed. More of the Songs We Sing. Oechsli, K., illus. (ENG & HEB.). 288p. (gr. 4-10). 1970. 9.50x (0-8381-0217-4) United Syn Bk.
Coords, Arthur E. The Space Story: The Children's Tribute to the Seven Challenger Astronauts. 32p. (gr. 2-6). 1992. PLB 7.70 (0-9631106-0-8) A E Coords.
Coote, Roger. Air Disasters. LC 93-6831. 48p. (gr. 4-6). 1993. 15.95 (1-56847-083-5) Thomson Lrning.
—The Anglo-Saxons. LC 93-34486. (Illus.). 32p. (gr. 4-6). 1994. 14.95 (1-56847-062-2) Thomson Lrning.
—The Egyptians. LC 93-8466. (Illus.). 32p. (gr. 4-6). 1993. 14.95 (1-56847-061-4) Thomson Lrning.
—First Voyage Around the World. (ps-3). 1990. PLB 11.90 (0-531-18302-5, Pub. by Bookwright Pr) Watts.
—Roman Cities. (Illus.). 24p. (gr. k-4). 1990. PLB 10.90 (0-531-18343-2, Pub. by Bookwright Pr) Watts.
—The Sailor Through History. Smith, Tony, illus. LC 92-43640. 48p. (gr. 5-8). 1993. 15.95 (1-56847-012-6) Thomson Lrning.
Coote, Roger, ed. see Raintree Steck-Vaughn Staff.
Cootes, R. J. Middle Ages. 2nd ed. 208p. (gr. 6-12). 1989. pap. text ed. 21.52 (0-582-31783-5, 78446) Longman.
Cootes, R. J. & Snellgrove, L. E. Ancient World. 2nd ed. (Illus.). 208p. (gr. 6-12). 1991. pap. text ed. 23.00 (0-582-31785-1, 79165); wkbk. 11.72 (0-582-36690-9, 72482) Longman.
Cope, Eddie. Don't Touch My Tutu. (Illus.). 40p. (Orig.). (gr. 4 up). 1985. pap. 4.00 (0-88680-242-3); royalty on application 40.00 (0-685-58020-2) I E Clark.
Cope, Wendy. The River Girl. Garland, Nicholas, illus. 64p. (gr. 7 up). 1991. 16.95 (0-571-16062-X); pap. 7.95 (0-571-16136-7) Faber & Faber.
—Twiddling Your Thumbs: Hand Rhymes by Wendy Cope. 32p. (ps-3). 1992. pap. 6.95 (0-571-16537-0) Faber & Faber.
Copeland, Colene. Little Prissy & T. C. Harrison, Edith, illus. LC 88-81916. 114p. (Orig.). (gr. 2 up). 1988. 8.95 (0-318-36004-7); pap. 3.95 (0-318-36005-5) Jordan Valley.
—Little Prissy & T. C. Harrison, Edith, illus. LC 88-81916. 1992. 8.95 (0-939810-07-7); pap. 3.95 (0-939810-08-5) Jordan Valley.
—Mystery in the Farrowing Barn. Harrison, Edith, illus. LC 91-62326. 150p. (Orig.). (gr. 3-7). 1991. 9.95 (0-939810-13-1); pap. 3.95 (0-939810-14-X) Jordan Valley.
—Priscilla. Harrison, Edith, illus. LC 81-80663. 212p. (Orig.). (gr. 3 up). 1981. 8.95 (0-939810-01-8); pap. 3.95 (0-939810-02-6) Jordan Valley.
—Priscilla. 1992. 8.95 (0-685-52575-9); pap. 3.95 (0-685-52576-7) Jordan Valley.
Copeland, Evelyn, tr. see Verne, Jules.
Copes, Wayne, et al. Graph Theory: Euler's Rich Legacy. (Illus.). 78p. (Orig.). (gr. 7-12). 1987. pap. text ed. 9.95 (0-939765-09-8, G106) Janson Pubns.
Copland, Aaron. What to Listen for in Music. rev. ed. Schuman, William. 192p. (RL 9). 1953. pap. 5.50 (0-451-62735-0, Ment) NAL-Dutton.
—What to Listen for in Music. rev. ed. 192p. (gr. 9-12). 1989. pap. 4.95 (0-451-62687-7, Ment) NAL-Dutton.
Coplans, Peta. Dottie. Coplans, Peta, illus. LC 92-41955. 1994. write for info. (0-395-66788-7) HM.
—Spaghetti for Suzy. Coplans, Peta, illus. LC 92-21611. 32p. (gr. k-3). 1993. 13.95 (0-395-65232-4) HM.
Coplon, Emily, et al. She'll Be Coming Round the Mountain. LC 93-20627. (Illus.). (gr. 4 up). Date not set. write for info. (0-553-09044-5); pap. write for info. (0-553-37340-4) Bantam.
Copping, Harold. Children's Stories from Dickens. Copping, Harold, illus. LC 92-37666. 1993. 8.99 (0-517-08485-6, Pub. by Derrydale Bks) Outlet Bk Co.
Coran, Pierre. The Crying Cat. (Illus.). 32p. (gr. k-2). 1991. 18.50 (0-89565-745-7); 12.95s.p. (0-685-55072-9) Childs World.
—The Lazy Beaver. (Illus.). 32p. (gr. k-2). 1991. 18.50 (0-89565-743-0); 12.95s.p. (0-685-55074-5) Childs World.
—Old Mr. Bennett's Carrots. (Illus.). 32p. (gr. 3-5). 1991. 18.50 (0-89565-749-X); 12.95s.p. (0-685-55089-3) Childs World.
—The Ranger Smokes Too Much. (Illus.). 32p. (gr. k-2). 1991. 18.50 (0-89565-748-1); 12.95s.p. (0-685-55078-8) Childs World.
—River at Risk. (Illus.). 32p. (gr. k-2). 1991. 18.50 (0-89565-747-3); 12.95s.p. (0-685-55079-6) Childs World.
—The Tree Poachers. (Illus.). 32p. (gr. k-2). 1991. 18.50 (0-89565-746-5); 12.95s.p. (0-685-55081-8) Childs World.
Corbalis, Judy. The Cuckoo Bird. Armitage, David, illus. LC 90-22576. 32p. (gr. 1-4). 1991. PLB 14.89 (0-06-021698-0) HarpC Child Bks.
—The Wrestling Princess & Other Stories. large type ed. Craig, Helen, illus. 208p. 1992. 13.95 (0-7451-1551-9, Galaxy Child Lrg Print) Chivers N Amer.

Corbeil, Jean-Claude. The Facts on File English - Spanish Visual Dictionary. (Illus.). 928p. 1992. 39.95 (0-8160-1546-5) Facts on File.

Corbett. The Mailbox Trick. 1993. pap. 2.75 (0-590-42750-4) Scholastic Inc.

Corbett, Julia. Sea Life at the Ocean's Edge. Warren, Hank & Moore, Shirley, eds. Kahler, Carole, illus. 24p. (gr. 4-6). 1984. pap. text ed. 3.95 (0-685-34734-6) NW Interpretive.

Corbett, Paula. Fantasy Fling. 56p. (gr. 4-6). 1984. 7.95 (0-88160-112-8, LW 247) Learning Wks.

Corbett, Pie. Playtime Treasury. 1990. 16.95 (0-385-26448-8) Doubleday.

Corbett, Pie & Emerson, Sally, eds. Dancing & Singing Games. Maclean, Moira & Maclean, Colin, illus. LC 92-28425. 1993. 4.95 (1-85697-902-4) Kingfisher Bks.

Corbett, Pie, jt. ed. see Emerson, Sally.

Corbett, Scott. Grave Doubts. LC 82-47916. 144p. (gr. 3-7). 1982. 14.95 (0-316-15659-0, Joy St Bks) Little.
—Jokes to Read in the Dark. Gusman, Annie, illus. LC 79-23129. 80p. (gr. 5-9). 1980. 12.95 (0-525-32796-7, 01063-320, DCB); (DCB) Dutton Child Bks.
—Jokes to Tell to Your Worst Enemy. Gusman, Annie, illus. LC 83-16564. 80p. (gr. 2-6). 1984. 10.95 (0-525-44082-8, DCB) Dutton Child Bks.
—The Lemonade Trick. Galdone, Paul, illus. 96p. (gr. 4-6). 1988. pap. 2.95 (0-590-32197-8, Apple Paperbacks) Scholastic Inc.
—Witch Hunt. 144p. (gr. 5 up). 1985. 14.95 (0-316-15750-3, Joy St Bks) Little.

Corbett, Sue. Our Riding Centre. (Illus.). 25p. (gr. 2-4). 1991. 12.95 (0-237-60145-1, Pub. by Evans Bros Ltd) Trafalgar.

Corbett, W. J. The Song Pentecost. (gr. k-6). 1985. pap. 3.25 (0-440-48092-2, YB) Dell.

Corbin, Carole L. Knights. 64p. (gr. 3-5). 1989. PLB 12.90 (0-531-10692-6) Watts.

Corbin, Linda & Dys, Pat. Jesus Helps Me Grow. Fieser, Stephen, illus. 28p. (Orig.). (gr. 1-6). 1986. pap. 5.99 (0-87509-374-4) Chr Pubns.
—Jesus Is God's Son. (Orig.). (gr. 1-6). 1988. pap. 5.99 (0-87509-404-X) Chr Pubns.
—Jesus Lights the Way. Fieser, Stephen, illus. 30p. (Orig.). (gr. 1-6). 1987. pap. 5.99 wkbk. (0-87509-385-X) Chr Pubns.
—Jesus Teaches Me. Fieser, Stephen, illus. 35p. (gr. 1-6). 1987. wkbk. 5.99 (0-87509-389-2) Chr Pubns.
—Jesus Wants Us to Obey. (Orig.). (gr. 1-6). 1987. pap. 5.99 (0-87509-400-7) Chr Pubns.
—Jesus Wins the Battle. (Illus., Orig.). (gr. 1-6). 1989. pap. 5.99 wkbk. (0-87509-410-4) Chr Pubns.

Corbin, Linda, jt. auth. see Dys, Pat.

Corbin, William. Me & the End of the World. LC 90-2355. 256p. (gr. 5-9). 1991. pap. 15.00 jacketed, 3-pc. bdg. (0-671-74223-X, S&S BFYR) S&S Trade.
—Me & the End of the World. (gr. 7). 1991. pap. write for info. (0-663-56251-1) Silver Burdett Pr.

Corbin, William G. Getting, Keeping, & Growing in a Job in the '90s. 136p. (gr. 10-12). 1994. pap. 9.95 (0-9634373-1-3) UN Communications.

Corbishley, Mike. Ancient Rome. (Illus.). 96p. 1989. 17.95 (0-8160-1970-3) Facts on File.
—The Ancient World. (Illus.). 60p. (gr. 5 up). 1993. 17.95 (0-87226-354-1) P Bedrick Bks.
—The Celts. (Illus.). (gr. 2-6). pap. 3.95 (0-7141-1387-5, Pub. by Brit Mus UK) Parkwest Pubns.
—Detecting the Past. LC 90-3234. (Illus.). 32p. (gr. 5-8). 1990. PLB 12.40 (0-531-17249-X) Watts.
—Everyday Life in Roman Times. LC 93-21191. 1994. write for info. (0-531-14288-4) Watts.
—Growing up in Ancient Rome. Molan, Chris, illus. LC 91-14851. 32p. (gr. 3-5). 1993. PLB 11.89 (0-8167-2721-X); pap. text ed. 3.95 (0-8167-2722-8) Troll Assocs. Postponed.
—The Medieval World. LC 92-31445. (Illus.). 60p. (gr. 5 up). 1993. PLB 17.95 (0-87226-362-2) P Bedrick Bks.
—Middle Ages. (Illus.). 96p. 1990. 17.95 (0-8160-1973-8) Facts on File.
—Rome & the Ancient World. (Illus.). 80p. (gr. 2-6). 1993. 17.95x (0-8160-2786-2) Facts on File.
—What Do We Know about the Romans? LC 91-28763. (Illus.). 40p. (gr. 3-7). 1992. PLB 16.95 (0-87226-352-5) P Bedrick Bks.

Corby, Ellen. The Pebble of Gibraltar. 1988. 13.95 (0-533-07623-4) Vantage.

Corby, Jane, jt. auth. see Webb, Phila H.

Corby, Jill, jt. auth. see Dwyer, Derek.

Corby, Jose, jt. auth. see Webb, Phila H.

Corcoran, Barbara. Annie's Monster. LC 89-28121. 192p. (gr. 3-7). 1990. SBE 14.95 (0-689-31632-1, Atheneum Child Bk) Macmillan Child Grp.
—Child of the Morning. large type ed. 120p. (gr. 6-9). 1984. Repr. of 1982 ed. 38.20 (0-317-01879-5, 4-03640-00) Am Printing Hse.
—Family Secrets. LC 91-13104. 176p. (gr. 3-7). 1992. SBE 13.95 (0-689-31744-1, Atheneum Child Bk) Macmillan Child Grp.
—The Hideaway. LC 86-28849. 128p. (gr. 5-9). 1987. SBE 13.95 (0-689-31353-5, Atheneum Child Bk) Macmillan Child Grp.
—The Hideaway. 128p. (Orig.). 1989. pap. 2.75 (0-380-70635-0, Flare) Avon.
—I am the Universe. LC 85-28726. 144p. (gr. 4-8). 1986. SBE 13.95 (0-689-31208-3, Atheneum Child Bk) Macmillan Child Grp.
—Mystery on Ice. LC 84-21559. 156p. (gr. 4-7). 1985. SBE 12.95 (0-689-31089-7, Atheneum Child Bk) Macmillan Child Grp.

—The Potato Kid. LC 89-14935. 192p. (gr. 3-7). 1989. SBE 14.95 (0-689-31589-9, Atheneum Child Bk) Macmillan Child Grp.
—The Potato Kid. 176p. 1993. pap. 3.50 (0-380-71213-X, Camelot) Avon.
—The Sky Is Falling. LC 87-33358. 192p. (gr. 3-7). 1988. SBE 14.95 (0-689-31388-8, Atheneum Child Bk) Macmillan Child Grp.
—The Sky Is Falling. 192p. 1990. pap. 2.95 (0-380-70837-X, Camelot) Avon.
—Stay Tuned. 192p. (gr. 3-7). 1991. SBE 14.95 (0-689-31673-9, Atheneum Child Bk) Macmillan Child Grp.
—Which Witch is Which? LC 91-45452. 128p. (gr. 3-7). 1992. pap. 3.95 (0-689-71572-2, Aladdin) Macmillan Child Grp.
—Wolf at the Door. LC 92-45108. 192p. (gr. 3-7). 1993. SBE 14.95 (0-689-31870-7, Atheneum Child Bk) Macmillan Child Grp.
—You Put up with Me, I'll Put up with You. 176p. (gr. 3-7). 1989. pap. 2.50 (0-380-70558-3, Camelot) Avon.

Corcoran, E. Meeting Basic Competencies in Mathematics: A Workstudy Book to Improve Math Skills. large type ed. 144p. (gr. 7-12). 1983. 25.91 (0-317-01910-4, 4-14720-00) Am Printing Hse.
—Meeting Basic Competencies in Practical Science & Health: A Workstudy Book to Improve Daily Living Skills. large type ed. 146p. (gr. 7-12). 1983. Repr. of 1979 ed. 25.91 (0-317-01911-2, 4-14710-00) Am Printing Hse.
—Meeting Basic Competencies in Reading: A Workstudy Book to Improve Reading Skills. large type ed. 132p. (gr. 7-12). 1983. 24.15 (0-317-01912-0, 4-14730-00) Am Printing Hse.

Corcoran, Eileen L., jt. auth. see Kranich, Roger E.

Corddry, Thomas. Kibby & the Red Elephant. Kock, Carl, illus. LC 72-13771. (gr. 3-6). 1973. 6.95 (0-87955-106-2) O'Hara.

Cordel, Betty, et al, eds. see Erickson, Sheldon, et al.

Cordell, Rose. Forget the ABC's until after Your Child Has Learned to Read. Ivins, Dorothy & Strait, Barbara, illus. 211p. (Orig.). (ps-3). 1983. 17.95 (0-940047-00-4); PLB 25.95 (0-940047-01-2); text ed. 17.95 (0-940047-02-0); pap. 14.95 (0-940047-03-9); tchr's guide for 6 yr. old 31.95 (0-940047-04-7); wkbk. level 1 words 7.00 (0-940047-05-5); tchr's guide for 5 yr. old (0-940047-06-3) Child Alphabet.

Corder, S. Scott, jt. auth. see Butts, Donna R.

Cordova, Laura. God Made Me Special. 64p. (ps-3). 1989. 8.95 (0-86653-496-2, SS1857, Shining Star Pubns) Good Apple.

Cordova, Loretta P. de see De Cordova, Loretta P.

Core, Earl L. & Ammons, Nelle P. Woody Plants in Winter. (Illus., Orig.). (gr. 9 up). 1958. pap. text ed. 9.95 (0-910286-02-7) Boxwood.

Corell, Brigitte. A Gift for You. LC 91-44377. (Illus.). 64p. PLB 19.93, Apr. 1992 (0-516-09260-X); pap. 8.95, Jul. 1992 (0-516-49260-8) Childrens.

Coren, Alan. Arthur the Kid. 80p. (gr. 4-6). 1984. pap. text ed. 2.25 (0-553-15169-X, Skylark) Bantam.

Corey, Deirdre. C U When the Snow Falls. 144p. 1991. pap. 2.75 (0-590-45109-X, Apple Paperbacks) Scholastic Inc.
—Friends 'til the Ocean Waves. 128p. (gr. 3-7). 1990. pap. 2.75 (0-590-44028-4) Scholastic Inc.
—Friends 'til the Thunder Claps. 144p. 1992. pap. 2.75 (0-590-45112-X, Apple Paperbacks) Scholastic Inc.
—Mysteriously Yours. (gr. 4-7). 1991. pap. 2.75 (0-590-44030-6, Apple Paperbacks) Scholastic Inc.
—Remember Me When This You See. (gr. 4-7). 1990. pap. 2.75 (0-590-44029-2) Scholastic Inc.

Corey, Donna. Manatee: A First Book. rev. ed. Corey, Donna, illus. Strykowski, Joe, photos by. LC 92-60557. 48p. (ps-6). 1993. pap. 5.00 (1-882533-15-1) Star Thrower.
—Manati: Un Libro Inicial. Strykowski, Joe, illus. LC 92-64397. 48p. (ps-6). 1992. pap. 4.95 (1-879488-01-9) Sundiver.
—Where is Manatee: A First Book. rev. ed. Corey, Donna, illus. Strykowski, Joe, photos by. LC 92-60557. 48p. (ps-6). 1992. pap. 4.95 (1-879488-00-0) Sundiver.

Corey, Dorothy. Will It Ever Be My Birthday? Fay, Ann, ed. LC 86-1565. (Illus.). 32p. (ps-3). 1986. PLB 13.95 (0-8075-9106-8) A Whitman.
—Will There Be a Lap for Me? Levine, Abby, ed. Poydar, Nancy, illus. LC 91-20324. 24p. (ps-1). 1992. PLB 11.95 (0-8075-9109-2) A Whitman.
—You Go Away. Rubin, Caroline & Axeman, Lois, illus. LC 75-33015. 32p. (ps-1). 1976. PLB 10.95 (0-8075-9441-5) A Whitman.

Corey, Melinda. Let's Visit a Spaghetti Factory. Emmerich, Donald, illus. LC 89-5110. 32p. (gr. 2-4). 1990. PLB 10.79 (0-8167-1741-9); pap. text ed. 2.95 (0-8167-1742-7) Troll Assocs.

Cork. Evolution. (Illus.). 32p. (gr. 4-8). 1985. PLB 13.96 (0-88110-219-9); pap. 6.95 (0-86020-867-2) EDC.
—Wild Animals. (gr. 2-5). 1982. (Usborne-Hayes); PLB 11.96 (0-88110-077-3); pap. 3.95 (0-86020-628-9) EDC.

Cork, jt. auth. see Cox.

Cork, B. & Bramwell, M. Rocks & Fossils. Jackson, I. & Suttie, A., illus. 32p. (gr. 5-8). 1983. PLB 13.96 (0-88110-159-1); pap. 6.95 (0-86020-765-X) EDC.

Cork, Barbara. Archaeology. McEwan, Joe, illus. 32p. (gr. 5-8). 1985. PLB 13.96 (0-88110-220-2, Pub. by Usborne); pap. 6.95 (0-86020-865-6) EDC.

—Plant Life. Jackson, Ian, illus. 32p. (gr. 6up). 1984. PLB 13.96 (0-88110-169-9); pap. 5.95 (0-86020-755-2) EDC.

Cork, Barbara & Morris, R. Mysteries & Marvels of Nature. Jackson, Ian & Quinn, David, illus. 192p. (gr. 3-6). 1983. 19.95 (0-7460-0421-4) EDC.

Cork, Barbara, ed. see Hill.

Cork, Sarah G. The Bottlestopper's Christmas Tree Farm. (Illus.). 50p. (gr. k-3). 1991. pap. 4.95 (0-943487-35-8) Sevgo Pr.

Corke, Philip. Handicrafts of the Arab World. (gr. 2-9). 1988. 7.95x (0-86685-496-7) Intl Bk Ctr.

Corke, Philip, illus. Rivers. 32p. (gr. 3-5). 1985. 7.95x (0-86685-452-5) Intl Bk Ctr.

Corkett, Anne. Norman Bethune: Doctor for the People. LC 89-49503. (Illus.). 64p. (gr. 5-6). 1990. PLB 18.60 (0-8368-0373-6) Gareth Stevens Inc.

Corkill, David, jt. auth. see Cubbit, David.

Corlett, William. The Gondolier's Cat. Turska, Krystyna, illus. 32p. (gr. s-1). 1994. 19.95 (0-340-54165-2, Pub. by Hodder & Stoughton UK) Trafalgar.

Corley, Elizabeth A. Tell Me about Death, Tell Me about Funerals. Pecoraro, Philip, intro. by. (Illus.). 36p. (Orig.). (gr. 3-6). 1973. pap. text ed. 2.00 (0-686-02638-1) Grammatical Sci.

Cormier, Larry. The Captain, the Gypsy & the Giant Bird. Bruni, Mary-Ann S., ed. Pressley, Ann, illus. 48p. (gr. k-8). 1986. 12.95 (0-935857-07-9); pap. write for info. (0-935857-08-7) Texart.

Cormier, Michael J. A Second Thought. Milone, Karen, illus. LC 91-41619. 32p. (gr. 2-6). 1992. PLB 17.96 (0-8114-3578-4) Raintree Steck-V.

Cormier, Robert. After the First Death. LC 78-11770. (Illus.). (gr. 7-12). 1979. 7.95 (0-394-84122-0); lib. bdg. 14.99 (0-394-94122-5) Pantheon.
—After the First Death. 1991. pap. 3.99 (0-440-20835-1, LFL) Dell.
—Beyond the Chocolate War. LC 84-22865. 288p. (gr. 9 up). 1985. 11.95 (0-394-87343-2); PLB 11.99 (0-394-97343-7) Knopf Bks Yng Read.
—Beyond the Chocolate War. (gr. 6 up). 1986. pap. 3.99 (0-440-90580-X, LFL) Dell.
—The Bumblebee Flies Anyway. 256p. (gr. 5 up). 1991. pap. 3.99 (0-440-90871-X, LFL) Dell.
—The Chocolate War. 192p. (gr. 6 up). 1986. pap. 3.99 (0-440-94459-7, LFL) Dell.
—The Chocolate War. LC 73-15109. 272p. (gr. 7-9). 1974. 20.00 (0-394-82805-4) Pantheon.
—Eight Plus One. 1991. pap. 3.99 (0-440-20838-6, LFL) Dell.
—Fade. LC 88-3540. (Illus.). (gr. 8 up). 1988. pap. 15.95 (0-440-50057-5) Delacorte.
—Fade. 1991. pap. 3.99 (0-440-21091-7, YB) Dell.
—I Am the Cheese. LC 76-55948. 224p. (gr. 7-12). 1977. 18.95 (0-394-83462-3) Pantheon.
—I Have Words to Spend: Confessions of a Small-Town Editor. (gr. 4-7). 1994. pap. 9.95 (0-385-31204-0) Delacorte.
—Little Raw on Monday Mornings. 1992. pap. 3.99 (0-440-21134-4) Dell.
—Now & at the Hour. 1991. pap. 3.99 (0-440-20882-3) Dell.
—Other Bells For Us to Ring. 1990. 15.00 (0-385-30245-2) Delacorte.
—Other Bells for Us to Ring. Ray, Deborah K., illus. 144p. (gr. 4-7). 1992. pap. 3.50 (0-440-40717-6, YB) Dell.
—Take Me Where the Good Times Are. 1991. pap. 3.99 (0-440-21096-8, YB) Dell.
—Tunes for Bears to Dance To. LC 92-2734. 112p. (gr. 5 up). 1992. 15.00 (0-385-30818-3) Delacorte.

Cornelia, Elizabeth. Australia. LC 78-56592. (Illus.). 48p. (gr. 5 up). 1978. PLB 16.98 (0-382-06182-9) Silver Burdett Pr.

Cornelius, James. The English Americans. (Illus.). 112p. (gr. 5 up). 1991. 17.95 (0-87754-874-9) Chelsea Hse.

Cornell, Donald. Ice Told Tales. Rosoff, Barbara, tr. Cornell, Donald, illus. (ENG & FRE). 58p. (Orig.). (ps-2). 1991. pap. 4.00 (0-9620738-1-4) D Cornell.

Cornell, Joseph & Deranja, Michael. Journey to the Heart of Nature: A Guided Exploration. (Illus.). 96p. (gr. 7-12). 1994. pap. 9.95 wkbk. (1-883220-06-8) Dawn CA.

Cornell, Pat. Search N Shade. Jacobs, Alan, ed. Haberer, Robert E., illus. (gr. 4-9). 1979. pap. 7.50 (0-918272-07-6) Jacobs.

Cornell, S. A. Flying Carrots. Jones, John, illus. LC 85-14093. 48p. (Orig.). (gr. 1-3). 1986. PLB 10.59 (0-8167-0640-9); pap. text ed. 3.50 (0-8167-0641-7) Troll Assocs.
—Little Eagle Learns to Fly. Jones, John, illus. LC 85-14086. 48p. (Orig.). (gr. 1-3). 1986. lib. bdg. 10.59 (0-8167-0618-2); pap. text ed. 3.50 (0-8167-0619-0) Troll Assocs.

Cornell, William A. Understanding Pennsylvania Civics. (gr. 7-12). 1987. 10.45 (0-931992-57-5); pap. 6.95 (0-931992-45-1) Penns Valley.

Cornell, William A. & Altland, Millard. Our Pennsylvania Heritage. LC 78-50430. (gr. 7-12). 1983. 15.95 (0-931992-21-4) Penns Valley.

Corning Museum of Glass Staff. Masterpieces of Glass from the Corning Museum: 24 Ready-to-Mail Full-Color. 12p. (Orig.). (gr. 7 up). 1984. pap. 3.95 (0-486-24526-8) Dover.

Cornish, Linda. Pong's Vists. LC 92-61596. (Illus.). 44p. (gr. k-3). 1993. 6.95 (1-55523-565-4) Winston-Derek.

Cornwell, Anita. The Girls of Summer. Caines, Kelly, illus. LC 88-64051. 100p. (Orig.). (gr. 6 up). 1989. pap. 12.95 (*0-938678-11-6*) New Seed.

Coronado, Rosa. Cooking the Mexican Way. LC 82-254. (Illus.). 48p. (gr. 5 up). 1982. PLB 14.95 (*0-8225-0907-5*) Lerner Pubns.

—Cooking the Mexican Way. (gr. 4-7). 1992. pap. 5.95 (*0-8225-9614-8*) Lerner Pubns.

Corpening, Gene S. I Love to Hear the Cold Wind Howl. James, Linda & Corpening, Gene S., illus. 40p. (Orig.). (gr. 1 up). 1993. pap. 7.95g (*0-9636775-9-4*) Alice Pub. A children's fairy tale that captures the wonderment of childhood in both verse & unforgettable illustrations. Told through the eyes of a little boy, it is the story of Dirty Ann (a reputed witch) & Farmer Plucket. Snuggle down into bed & pull the covers 'round your head, as you read about the strange doings of Dirty Ann & her disagreement with Plucket in a bygone time. Sixteen four-color illustrations. Volume discounts available from publisher--Alice Publishing, P.O. Box 257, Granite Falls, NC 28630; 704-396-7094. *Publisher Provided Annotation.*

Corral, Jeanie B. Scruffy 'n Me. 1994. 8.95 (*0-8062-4844-0*) Carlton.

Corrick, James A. Mars. (Illus.). 128p. (gr. 7-12). 1991. PLB 13.40 (*0-531-12528-9*) Watts.

—Muscular Dystrophy. LC 92-13772. (Illus.). 96p. (gr. 9-12). 1992. PLB 13.40 (*0-531-12540-8*) Watts.

Corrigan, Dorothy D. Watch Out for the Golly Whompers. McBride, Michael, illus. LC 88-50754. 35p. (gr. k-3). 1988. 6.95 (*1-55523-149-7*) Winston-Derek.

Corrigan, Robert J. Tracking Heroes: Thirteen Track & Field Champions. LC 89-51039. 163p. (gr. 4-9). 1990. 8.95 (*1-55523-236-1*) Winston-Derek.

Corrin, Ruth. Charlie Best. Moyes, Lesley, illus. LC 93-9229. 1994. write for info. (*0-383-03681-X*) SRA Schl Grp.

—It Always Rains for Jackie. Pye, Trevor, illus. 32p. (ps-2). 1990. bds. 8.95 (*0-19-558205-5*) OUP.

—Mr. Cat. Hurford, John, illus. LC 91-20236. 32p. (ps-3). 1991. 13.95 (*0-940793-89-X*, Crocodile Bks) Interlink Pub.

Corrin, Sara. Stories for Five-Year-Olds. (ps-3). 1989. pap. 9.95 (*0-571-12998-6*) Faber & Faber.

Corrin, Sara & Corrin, Sara, eds. A Time to Laugh: Funny Stories for Children. (Illus.). 142p. (ps) 1991. pap. 3.95 (*0-571-15499-9*) Faber & Faber.

Corrin, Sara & Corrin, Stephen, eds. The Faber Book of Christmas Stories. Bennet, Jill, illus. LC 84-13552. 150p. (gr. 3-7). 1984. pap. 9.95 (*0-571-13348-7*) Faber & Faber.

—Laugh out Loud: More Funny Stories for Children. Rose, Gerald, illus. 116p. (gr. k-2). 1991. pap. 2.95 (*0-571-14177-3*) Faber & Faber.

—More Stories for Under-Fives. Julian-Ottie, Vanessa, illus. 116p. (ps). 1990. pap. 9.95 (*0-571-12921-8*) Faber & Faber.

—Stories for Eight-Year-Olds. Hughes, Shirley, illus. 192p. (gr. 2-4). 1984. pap. 9.95 (*0-571-12969-2*) Faber & Faber.

—Stories for Nine-Year-Olds. Hughes, Shirley, illus. LC 79-670371. 160p. (gr. 2-5). 1979. pap. 10.95 (*0-571-12931-5*) Faber & Faber.

—Stories for Seven-Year-Olds. Hughes, Shirley, illus. 188p. (gr. 1-3). 1982. pap. 9.95 (*0-571-12910-2*) Faber & Faber.

—Stories for Six-Year-Olds. Hughes, Shirley, illus. 198p. (gr. k-2). 1984. pap. 9.95 (*0-571-12959-5*) Faber & Faber.

Corrin, Sara, jt. ed. see Corrin, Stephen.

Corrin, Sara, et al, eds. Stories for Under-Fives. Hughes, Shirley, illus. 158p. (ps-5). 1974. pap. 9.95 (*0-571-12920-X*) Faber & Faber.

Corrin, Sarah & Corrin, Stephen, eds. Round the Christmas Tree. (gr. 3-7). pap. 3.95 (*0-317-62263-3*, Puffin) Puffin Bks.

Corrin, Stephen & Corrin, Sara, eds. The Pied Piper of Hamelin. Le Cain, Errol, illus. 32p. (ps-5). 1989. 14.95 (*0-15-261596-2*, HB Juv Bks) HarBrace.

Corrin, Stephen, jt. ed. see Corrin, Sara.

Corrin, Stephen, jt. ed. see Corrin, Sarah.

Cortes, Jose L. The Roman Empire. LC 92-34595. (Illus.). 36p. (gr. 3 up). 1993. PLB 19.93 (*0-516-08382-1*); pap. 6.95 (*0-516-48382-X*) Childrens.

Cortesi, Wendy W. see National Geographic Society Staff.

Cortright, Sandy. Zoo Animals. Carroll, Marilee, illus. 80p. (ps). 1990. pap. 6.95 (*0-8120-4436-3*) Barron.

Corum, Ann K. Easy Cooking: The Island Way. LC 81-19881. (Illus.). 120p. (Orig.). (gr. 8 up). 1982. pap. 5.95 (*0-916630-24-2*) Pr Pacifica.

Corwin, Judith H. African Crafts. LC 90-12493. (Illus.). 48p. (gr. k-4). 1990. PLB 12.90 (*0-531-10846-5*) Watts.

—Asian Crafts. Rosoff, Iris, ed. LC 91-13500. (Illus.). 48p. (gr. 1-4). 1992. PLB 12.90 (*0-531-11013-3*) Watts.

—Birthday Fun. Corwin, Judith H., illus. 64p. (gr. 3 up). 1986. lib. bdg. 10.98 (*0-671-55519-7*, J Messner); lib. bdg. 5.95 (*0-671-60126-1*); PLB 7.71s.p. (*0-685-47048-2*); pap. 3.71s.p. (*0-685-47049-0*) S&S Trade.

—Christmas Around the World. LC 93-6567. (gr. 3 up). 1994. lib. bdg. 12.98 (*0-671-87239-7*, J Messner); lib. bdg. 6.95 (*0-671-87240-0*) S&S Trade.

—Christmas Crafts. LC 93-6366. 1994. write for info. (*0-531-11149-0*) Watts.

—Christmas Fun. Corwin, Judith H., illus. 64p. (gr. 3 up). 1983. lib. bdg. 10.98 (*0-671-45944-9*, J Messner); lib. bdg. 5.95 (*0-671-49583-6*); PLB 7.71s.p. (*0-685-47052-0*); pap. 4.46s.p. (*0-685-47053-9*) S&S Trade.

—Colonial American Crafts: The Home. LC 89-8958. (Illus.). 48p. (gr. 3-6). 1989. PLB 12.40 (*0-531-10713-2*) Watts.

—Colonial American Crafts: The School. LC 89-32542. (Illus.). 48p. (gr. 3-6). 1989. PLB 12.40 (*0-531-10714-0*) Watts.

—Colonial American Crafts: The Village. Corwin, Judith H., illus. LC 89-8966. 48p. (gr. 4-7). 1989. PLB 12.40 (*0-531-10715-9*) Watts.

—Cookie Fun. Corwin, Judith H., illus. 64p. (gr. 3 up). 1985. lib. bdg. 10.98 (*0-671-50797-4*, J Messner); lib. bdg. 5.95 (*0-671-55019-5*); PLB 7.71s.p. (*0-685-47050-4*); pap. 3.71s.p. (*0-685-47051-2*) S&S Trade.

—Easter Crafts. LC 93-21258. 1994. write for info. (*0-531-11145-8*) Watts.

—Easter Fun. Corwin, Judith H., illus. 64p. (gr. 3 up). 1984. (J Messner). lib. bdg. 5.95 (*0-671-53108-5*); PLB 7.71s.p. (*0-685-47054-7*); pap. 4.46s.p. (*0-685-47055-5*) S&S Trade.

—Halloween Crafts. LC 93-6367. 1994. write for info. (*0-531-11148-2*) Watts.

—Halloween Fun. Corwin, Judith H., illus. LC 83-8289. 64p. (gr. 3 up). 1983. (J Messner); lib. bdg. 5.95 (*0-671-49756-1*); PLB 7.71s.p. (*0-685-47056-3*); pap. 4.46s.p. (*0-685-47057-1*) S&S Trade.

—Jewish Holiday Fun. Corwin, Judith H., illus. LC 86-16201. 64p. (gr. 3 up). 1987. (J Messner); lib. bdg. 5.95 (*0-671-60127-X*); PLB 7.71s.p. (*0-685-47058-X*); pap. 4.46s.p. (*0-685-47059-8*) S&S Trade.

—Latin American & Caribbean Crafts. Rosoff, Iris, ed. LC 91-13466. (Illus.). 48p. (gr. 1-4). 1992. PLB 12.90 (*0-531-11014-1*) Watts.

—Messner Holiday Library, 9 bks. Corwin, Judith H., illus. (gr. 3 up). 1990. Set, 64p. ea. lib. bdg. 92.61 (*0-671-92641-1*, J Messner); Set, 64p. ea. pap. 49.55 (*0-671-92642-X*) S&S Trade.

—Papercrafts. Corwin, Judith H., illus. IRosoff, ed. LC 87-21611. (Illus.). 72p. (gr. 2-4). 1988. PLB 12.90 (*0-531-10465-6*) Watts.

—Patriotic Fun. Corwin, Judith H., illus. LC 85-18730. 64p. (gr. 3 up). 1986. lib. bdg. 10.98 (*0-671-50799-0*, J Messner); PLB 7.71s.p. (*0-685-47060-1*); pap. 3.71s.p. (*0-685-47061-X*) S&S Trade.

—Thanksgiving Crafts. LC 93-6369. 1994. write for info. (*0-531-11147-4*) Watts.

—Thanksgiving Fun. Corwin, Judith H., illus. 64p. (gr. 3 up). 1984. lib. bdg. 10.98 (*0-671-49422-8*, J Messner); lib. bdg. 5.95 (*0-671-50849-0*); PLB 7.71s.p. (*0-685-47062-8*); pap. 4.46s.p. (*0-685-47063-6*) S&S Trade.

—Valentine Crafts. LC 93-11970. 1994. write for info. (*0-531-11146-6*) Watts.

—Valentine Fun. Corwin, Judith H., illus. LC 82-6047. 64p. (gr. 3 up). 1983. (J Messner); lib. bdg. 5.95 (*0-671-49755-3*); PLB 7.71s.p. (*0-685-47064-4*); pap. 4.46s.p. (*0-685-47065-2*) S&S Trade.

Corwin, Marshall, jt. auth. see Nutkins, Terry.

Cory, Beverly. Dell & His Dot. Balkovek, James, illus. 64p. (Orig.). (ps-4). 1993. pap. 9.95 (*0-8449-4252-9*); FRE Translation Tool, "Trans-it" 4.95 (*0-8449-4281-2*); CHI Translation Tool, "Trans-it" 4.95 (*0-8449-4283-9*); GER Translation Tool, "Trans-it" 4.95 (*0-8449-4282-0*); SPA Translation Tool, "Trans-it" 4.95 (*0-8449-4280-4*) Good Morn Tchr.

—Gork & the Mop Tops. Balkovek, James, illus. 64p. (Orig.). (ps-4). 1993. pap. 9.95 (*0-8449-4251-0*); FRE Translation Tool, "Trans-it" 4.95 (*0-8449-4285-5*); CHI Translation Tool, "Trans-it" 4.95 (*0-8449-4287-1*); GER Translation Tool, "Trans-it" 4.95 (*0-8449-4286-3*); SPA Translation Tool, "Trans-it" 4.95 (*0-8449-4284-7*) Good Morn Tchr.

Cory, Fanny Y. The Fairy Alphabet of F. Y. Cory. Cory, Fanny Y., illus. 32p. 1991. 14.95 (*1-56037-006-8*) Am Wrld Geog.

Cory, Lynda. Boys Who Became Prophets. Mann, Paul, illus. LC 92-29812. 1992. 8.95 (*0-87579-664-8*) Deseret Bk.

Coryell, Susan. Eaglebait. 187p. (gr. 7 up). 1989. 14.95 (*0-15-200442-4*, Gulliver Bks) HarBrace.

Cosby, Bill, et al. Cambios: Descubriendo lo Mejor Que Hay en Ti. Callejas, Juan, et al, eds. Trevant, Pierre, tr. from ENG. Ordonez, Maria A. & Espada, Frank, illus. (SPA). 192p. (Orig.). (gr. 6-8). 1987. pap. text ed. 6.85 (*0-933419-21-X*) Quest Intl.

—Changes: Becoming the Best You Can Be. rev. ed. Barr, Linda & Wojcicki, Marba, eds. Robison, Don, et al, illus. 196p. (gr. 6-8). 1988. pap. text ed. 6.85 (*0-933419-24-4*) Quest Intl.

—Universal Spanish--Cambios: Descubriendo lo Mejor Que Hay en Ti. Callejas, Juan, et al, eds. Trevant, Pierre, tr. from ENG. Ordonez, Maria A. & Espada, Frank, illus. (SPA). 181p. (Orig.). (gr. 6-8). 1988. pap. text ed. 6.85 (*0-933419-44-9*) Quest Intl.

—You Are Somebody Special. 2nd ed. Shedd, Charlie W., ed. 205p. (gr. 9-12). 1989. Repr. of 1978 ed. text ed. 10.95 (*0-933419-50-3*) Quest Intl.

Cosby, Clair G. Junior High's a Jungle. LC 87-27040. 88p. (Orig.). (gr. 7-9). 1988. pap. 4.95 (*0-8361-3455-9*) Herald Pr.

—Lord, Help Me Love My Sister. LC 86-4831. 80p. (Orig.). (gr. 3-10). 1986. pap. 4.95 (*0-8361-3413-3*) Herald Pr.

Cosgrove, Brian. Weather. Shone, Karl & Percival, Keith, photos by. LC 90-4887. (Illus.). 64p. (gr. 5 up). 1991. 15.00 (*0-679-80784-5*); PLB 15.99 (*0-679-90784-X*) Knopf Bks Yng Read.

Cosgrove, Stephen. Balderdash. Gedrose, E. D., illus. 32p. (gr. 3-6). 1991. 14.95 (*1-55868-045-4*) Gr Arts Ctr Pub.

—Bangalee. (gr. 1-6). 1976. pap. 2.95 (*0-8431-0550-X*) Price Stern.

—Buttermilk. James, Robin, illus. 32p. (gr. 5-9). 1986. pap. 2.95 (*0-8431-1565-3*) Price Stern.

—Buttermilk-Bear. James, Robin, illus. 32p. (gr. 1-4). 1987. pap. 2.95 (*0-8431-1908-X*) Price Stern.

—Button Breaker. (ps-3). 1992. pap. 3.95 (*0-307-13450-4*) Western Pub.

—Button Breaker. Bonin, Diana R., illus. 32p. (gr. k-5). 1993. PLB 12.95 (*1-56674-043-6*, HTS Bks) Forest Hse.

—Catundra. James, Robin, illus. 32p. (gr. 1-4). 1978. pap. 2.95 (*0-8431-0571-2*) Price Stern.

—Crabby Gabby. James, Robin, illus. LC 85-14351. 32p. (Orig.). (gr. 1-4). 1985. pap. 2.95 (*0-8431-1441-X*) Price Stern.

—Crickle-Crack. James, Robin, illus. 32p. (gr. 1-4). 1987. pap. 2.95 (*0-8431-1909-8*) Price Stern.

—Dragolin. James, Robin, illus. LC 85-14400. (Orig.). (gr. k-5). 1978. pap. 2.95 (*0-8431-1165-8*) Price Stern.

—The Dream Stealer. Heyer, Carol, illus. LC 89-83843. 48p. (gr. 1-4). 1990. 16.95 (*1-55868-009-8*); pap. 5.95 (*1-55868-021-7*); pap. 12.95 incl. audio (*1-55868-042-X*) Gr Arts Ctr Pub.

—The Dream Tree. James, Robin, illus. (gr. 1-6). 1974. pap. 2.95 (*0-8431-0553-4*) Price Stern.

—Easter Bunnies. Edelson, Wendy, illus. 32p. (Orig.). (gr. k-4). 1992. pap. 4.95 (*0-8249-8538-9*, Ideals Child) Hambleton-Hill.

—Fanny. James, Robin, illus. 32p. (gr. 5-9). 1986. pap. 2.95 (*0-8431-1460-6*) Price Stern.

—Feather Fin. James, Robin, illus. LC 84-15057. 32p. (Orig.). (gr. k-4). 1983. pap. 2.95 (*0-8431-0593-3*) Price Stern.

—The Fine Family Farm. Steelhammer, Ilona, illus. 24p. (gr. k-2). 1990. PLB 10.95 (*1-878363-19-0*) Forest Hse.

—Flutterby Fly. James, Robin, illus. LC 85-14353. (Orig.). (gr. k-4). 1984. pap. 2.95 (*0-8431-1162-3*) Price Stern.

—Frazzle. 32p. 1990. pap. 2.95 (*0-8431-2838-0*) Price Stern.

—Glitterby Baby. James, Robin, illus. LC 85-14354. 32p. (Orig.). (gr. 1-4). 1978. pap. 2.95 (*0-8431-1166-6*) Price Stern.

—Gnome from Nome. James, Robin, illus. 32p. (gr. 1-6). 1974. pap. 2.95 (*0-8431-0555-0*) Price Stern.

—Grampa-Lop. James, Robin, illus. LC 84-15078. 32p. (Orig.). (gr. k-4). 1981. pap. 2.95 (*0-8431-0586-0*) Price Stern.

—The Grumpling. (Illus.). 32p. (Orig.). (gr. k-4). 1989. pap. 2.95 (*0-8431-2739-2*) Price Stern.

—Harmony. Casad, Michael, illus. LC 89-83842. 72p. (gr. 7 up). 1991. 24.95 (*1-55868-008-X*) Gr Arts Ctr Pub.

—Heidi's Rose. Edelson, Wendy, illus. LC 90-71079. 32p. (gr. 3-6). 1991. 14.95 (*1-55868-033-0*) Gr Arts Ctr Pub.

—Jalopy. 32p. 1990. 2.95 (*0-8431-2835-6*) Price Stern.

—Jingle Bear. James, Robin, illus. 32p. (Orig.). (gr. 1-4). 1985. pap. 2.95 (*0-8431-1440-1*) Price Stern.

—Kartusch. James, Robin, illus. (gr. k-4). 1978. pap. 2.95 (*0-8431-0568-2*) Price Stern.

—The Kind & Gentle Ladies. Steelhammer, Ilona, illus. 24p. (gr. k-2). 1990. PLB 10.95 (*1-878363-20-4*) Forest Hse.

—Kyomi. James, Robin, illus. (Orig.). (gr. k-4). 1984. pap. 2.95 (*0-8431-1164-X*) Price Stern.

—Lady Lonely. Steelhammer, Ilona, illus. 24p. (gr. k-2). 1990. PLB 10.95 (*1-878363-21-2*) Forest Hse.

—Lady Rose. 32p. 1990. pap. 2.95 (*0-8431-2837-2*) Price Stern.

—Leo the Lop: Tail Three. James, Robin, illus. 32p. (gr. k-4). 1978. pap. 2.95 (*0-8431-0577-1*) Price Stern.

—Leo the Lop: Tail Two. James, Robin, illus. 32p. (Orig.). (gr. k-6). 1978. pap. 2.95 (*0-8431-0572-0*) Price Stern.

—Little Mouse. James, Robin, illus. 32p. (gr. 1-4). 1978. pap. 2.95 (*0-8431-0569-0*) Price Stern.

—Maui-Maui. James, Robin, illus. 32p. (gr. k-6). 1979. pap. 2.95 (*0-8431-0573-9*) Price Stern.

—Memily. (Illus.). 32p. (gr. 1-4). pap. 2.95 (*0-8431-1907-1*) Price Stern.

—Ming Ling. James, Robin, illus. 32p. (Orig.). (gr. k-4). 1978. pap. 2.95 (*0-8431-0592-5*) Price Stern.
—Minikin. James, Robin, illus. (Orig.). (gr. k-4). 1984. pap. 2.95 (*0-8431-1163-1*) Price Stern.
—Morgan & Me. (Illus.). (gr. 1-6). 1975. pap. 2.95 (*0-8431-0560-7*) Price Stern.
—Morgan Morning. James, Robin, illus. 32p. (gr. 1-6). 1982. pap. 2.95 (*0-8431-0591-7*) Price Stern.
—Muffin Muncher. James, Robin, illus. 32p. (gr. 1-6). 1975. pap. 2.95 (*0-8431-0561-5*) Price Stern.
—Mumkin. James, Robin, illus. 32p. (gr. 5-9). 1986. pap. 2.95 (*0-8431-1431-2*) Price Stern.
—Nitter Pitter. James, Robin, illus. 32p. (gr. 1-4). 1978. pap. 2.95 (*0-8431-0570-4*) Price Stern.
—The Nosey Birds. Steelhammer, Ilona, illus. 24p. (gr. k-2). 1990. PLB 10.95 (*1-878363-22-0*) Forest Hse.
—Persnickety. James, Robin, illus. 32p. (gr. k-4). 1988. pap. 2.95 (*0-8431-2303-6*) Price Stern.
—Pish-Posh. James, Robin, illus. 32p. (gr. 5-9). 1986. pap. 2.95 (*0-8431-1449-5*) Price Stern.
—Poppyseed. (Illus.). 32p. (Orig.). (gr. k-4). 1989. pap. 2.95 (*0-8431-2738-4*) Price Stern.
—Prancer. Heyer, Carol, illus. LC 89-83843. 32p. (gr. k-7). 1990. 14.95 (*0-685-27179-X*); pap. 5.95 (*1-55868-020-9*); pap. 12.95 incl. audio (*1-55868-041-1*) Gr Arts Ctr Pub.
—Prancer: Christmas. (gr. k-7). 1989. 14.95 (*1-55868-019-5*) Gr Arts Ctr Pub.
—Raz-Ma-Taz. James, Robin, illus. 32p. (gr. 1-6). 1982. pap. 2.95 (*0-8431-0588-7*) Price Stern.
—Read Aloud Topsy-Turvy Library, 26 vols. Reasoner, Charles, illus. (ps-3). 1988. Set. 155.48 (*0-87475-600-6*) Stuttman.
—Read on Rita. Edelson, Wendy, illus. 32p. 1993. PLB 12.95 (*1-56674-042-8*, HTS Bks) Forest Hse.
—Rhubarb. James, Robin, illus. 32p. (gr. k-4). 1988. pap. 2.95 (*0-8431-2300-1*) Price Stern.
—Sassafras. James, Robin, illus. 32p. (gr. k-4). 1988. pap. 2.95 (*0-8431-2302-8*) Price Stern.
—Snicker Doodle. (ps-3). 1992. pap. 3.95 (*0-307-13452-0*) Western Pub.
—Snicker Doodle. Bonin, Diana R., illus. 32p. (gr. k-5). 1993. PLB 12.95 (*1-56674-044-4*, HTS Bks) Forest Hse.
—Sniffles. James, Robin, illus. 32p. (gr. k-4). 1988. pap. 2.95 (*0-8431-2301-X*) Price Stern.
—Squabbles. 32p. 1990. pap. 2.95 (*0-8431-2836-4*) Price Stern.
—Squeakers. James, Robin, illus. 32p. (Orig.). (gr. 1-4). 1985. pap. 2.95 (*0-8431-1442-8*) Price Stern.
—Tickle's Tail. (Illus.). 32p. (Orig.). (gr. k-4). 1989. pap. 2.95 (*0-8431-2736-8*) Price Stern.
—Tinkling. (ps-3). 1992. pap. 3.95 (*0-307-13451-2*) Western Pub.
—Tinkling. Bonin, Diana R., illus. 32p. (gr. k-5). 1993. PLB 12.95 (*1-56674-045-2*, HTS Bks) Forest Hse.
—Tizzy. (ps-3). 1992. pap. 3.95 (*0-307-13453-9*) Western Pub.
—Tizzy. Bonin, Diana R., illus. 32p. (gr. k-5). 1993. PLB 12.95 (*1-56674-046-0*, HTS Bks) Forest Hse.
—Trapper. James, Robin, illus. 32p. (gr. k-4). 1982. pap. 2.95 (*0-8431-0587-9*) Price Stern.
—Zippity Zoom. (Illus.). 32p. (Orig.). (gr. k-4). 1989. pap. 2.95 (*0-8431-2737-6*) Price Stern.
Cosgrove, Stephen & James, Robin. Misty Morgan. (Illus.). 32p. (gr. 1-4). pap. 2.95 (*0-8431-1910-1*) Price Stern.
Cosgrove, Stephen E. Derby Downs. Edelson, Wendy, illus. 32p. (ps-3). 1990. PLB 21.35 (*0-89565-659-0*); PLB 14.95s.p. (*0-685-58733-9*) Childs World.
—Fiddler. Edelson, Wendy, illus. 32p. (ps-3). 1990. PLB 21.35 (*0-89565-665-5*); PLB 14.95s.p. (*0-685-58735-5*) Childs World.
—Gigglesnitcher. James, Robin, illus. 48p. (gr. k-9). 1991. 12.95 (*1-55868-034-9*) Gr Arts Ctr Pub.
—Gossamer. Edelson, Wendy, illus. 32p. (ps-3). 1990. PLB 21.35 (*0-89565-662-0*); PLB 14.95s.p. (*0-685-58725-5*) Childs World.
—Hannah & Hickory. Edelson, Wendy, illus. 32p. (ps-3). 1990. PLB 21.35 (*0-89565-664-7*); PLB 14.95s.p. (*0-685-58729-8*) Childs World.
—Ira Wordworthy. Edelson, Wendy, illus. 32p. (ps-3). 1990. PLB 21.35 (*0-89565-658-2*); PLB 14.95s.p. (*0-685-58732-0*) Childs World.
—Persimmony. Edelson, Wendy, illus. 32p. (ps-3). 1990. PLB 21.35 (*0-89565-661-2*); PLB 14.95s.p. (*0-685-58736-3*) Childs World.
—Shadow Chaser. Edelson, Wendy, illus. 32p. (ps-3). 1990. PLB 21.35 (*0-89565-663-9*); PLB 14.95s.p. (*0-685-58734-7*) Childs World.
—T. J. Flopp. Edelson, Wendy, illus. 32p. (ps-3). 1990. PLB 14.95 (*0-89565-660-4*); PLB 14.95s.p. (*0-685-56224-7*) Childs World.
—Terrybrook Dragon. McNatt, Richard, illus. 32p. (gr. k-7). 1990. 14.95 (*1-55868-036-5*) Gr Arts Ctr Pub.
Cosman, Madeleine P. The Medieval Baker's Daughter: A Bilingual Adventure in Medieval Life with Costumes, Banners, Music, Food, & a Mystery Play. LC 84-71590. (ENG & SPA., Illus.). 112p. (gr. 3-12). 1984. pap. 7.95 (*0-916491-18-8*) Bard Hall Pr.
Cosner, Shaaron. Dinosaur Dinners. LC 90-47225. (Illus.). 48p. (gr. 2-4). 1991. PLB 12.90 (*0-531-20011-6*) Watts.
—The Light Bulb: Inventions That Changed Our Lives. LC 83-40398. 64p. (gr. 5 up). 1984. PLB 10.85 (*0-8027-6527-0*) Walker & Co.
—Lunar Bases. 1990. PLB 12.90 (*0-531-10894-5*) Watts.

—The Underground Railroad. LC 89-31171. (Illus.). 128p. (gr. 9-12). 1991. PLB 13.40 (*0-531-12505-X*) Watts.
—War Nurses. (gr. 7 up). 1988. 16.95 (*0-8027-6826-1*); 17.85 (*0-8027-6828-8*) Walker & Co.
Cossey, Ruth, et al. Quadice. Bergman, Lincoln & Fairwell, Kay, eds. Klofkorn, Lisa, illus. Hoyt, Richard, photos by. (Illus.). 44p. (Orig.). (gr. 4-8). 1987. pap. 8.50 (*0-912511-66-4*) Lawrence Science.
Cossi, Olga. Adventure on the Graveyard of the Wrecks. LC 90-20686. 144p. (Orig.). (gr. 9-12). 1991. pap. 5.95 (*0-88289-808-6*) Pelican.
—Fire Mate. 85p. (gr. 3 up). 1988. pap. 7.95 (*0-89992-116-7*) Coun India Ed.
—The Great Getaway. LC 89-42637. 32p. (gr. 1-2). 1991. PLB 18.60 (*0-8368-0107-5*) Gareth Stevens Inc.
—Harp Seals. (Illus.). 48p. (gr. 2-5). 1991. PLB 19.95 (*0-87614-437-7*) Carolrhoda Bks.
—Harp Seals. (ps-3). 1992. pap. 6.95 (*0-87614-567-5*) Carolrhoda Bks.
—The Magic Box. LC 89-8461. 192p. (gr. 12). 1990. 11.95 (*0-88289-748-9*) Pelican.
—Orlanda & the Contest of Thieves. Sarmo, Tom, illus. LC 89-15107. 32p. (gr. 1-6). 1989. 14.95 (*0-917665-32-5*) Pelican.
—Think Pink. Clarke, Lea A., illus. LC 93-5556. 1994. write for info. (*0-88289-995-3*) Pelican.
—Water Wars: The Fight to Control & Conserve Nature's Most Precious Resource. LC 92-43968. (Illus.). 144p. (gr. 6 up). 1993. RSBE 13.95 (*0-02-724595-0*, New Discovery Bks) Macmillan Child Grp.
—Wonderful, Wonder-Full Donkey. Porter, Sharon H., illus. LC 89-50142. 54p. (ps-4). 1989. pap. 10.95 (*0-932433-55-3*) Windswept Hse.
Costa, Gwen, ed. see Brashear, William.
Costa, Gwen, ed. see Miller, Leo.
Costa, Gwen, ed. see Stoltz, Donald R.
Costa, Nicoletta. My Poke & Look Busy Book. (Illus.). 44p. (ps-2). 1990. bds. 14.95 (*0-448-21034-7*, G&D) Putnam Pub Group.
Costa, Nicoletta, illus. My Poke & Look Busy Book Two. 32p. (ps-2). 1992. bds. 14.95 (*0-448-40390-0*, G&D) Putnam Pub Group.
Costabel, Eva D. The Early People of Florida. Costabel, Eva D., illus. LC 92-16283. 40p. (gr. 2-6). 1993. SBE 13.95 (*0-689-31500-7*, Atheneum Child Bk) Macmillan Child Grp.
—Jews of New Amsterdam. Costabel, Eva D., illus. LC 87-27873. 32p. (gr. 2-6). 1988. SBE 13.95 (*0-689-31351-9*, Atheneum Child Bk) Macmillan Child Grp.
Costa de Beauregard, Diane. Animals in Jeopardy. Bogard, Vicki, tr. from FRE. De Hugo, Pierre, illus. LC 90-50779. 38p. (gr. k-5). 1991. 4.95 (*0-944589-37-5*, 375) Young Discovery Lib.
Costantino, Maria. The Nineteen Thirties. Cumming, Valerie & Feldman, Elane, eds. (Illus.). 64p. (gr. 6-10). 1992. lib. bdg. 16.95x (*0-8160-2466-9*) Facts on File.
Costanzo, Christie. Learning New Roles. LC 91-11572. 64p. (gr. 6-12). 1991. 17.27 (*0-86593-117-8*); 12.95s.p. (*0-685-59202-2*) Rourke Corp.
—Volleyball. LC 93-27153. 1993. write for info. (*0-86593-344-8*) Rourke Corp.
Costa-Pace, Rosa. The City. LC 93-17918. (Illus.). 1994. 13.95 (*0-7910-2101-7*, Am Art Analog) Chelsea Hse.
—Conservation of the Sea. (Illus.). 1994. 13.95 (*0-7910-2103-3*, Am Art Analog) Chelsea Hse.
—The Junior Library of Ecology, 5 vols. (Illus.). 1994. Set. write for info. (*0-7910-2100-9*, Am Art Analog) Chelsea Hse.
—Protecting Our Forests. (Illus.). 1994. 13.95 (*0-7910-2104-1*, Am Art Analog) Chelsea Hse.
—Protecting Our Rivers & Lakes. (Illus.). 1994. 13.95 (*0-7910-2105-X*, Am Art Analog) Chelsea Hse.
Costas, jt. auth. see Switzer, Ellen.
Costas, Gloria, tr. see Lehman, Yvette K.
Coste, Marion. Honu. Gray, Cissy, illus. 32p. (ps-4). 1993. 9.95 (*0-8248-1507-6*) UH Pr.
—Nene. Gray, Cissy, illus. LC 92-36543. 32p. 1993. 9.95 (*0-8248-1389-8*, Kolowalu Bk) UH Pr.
Costello, Gwen. A Bible Way of the Cross for Children. Curley, Ed, illus. 32p. (Orig.). (gr. 4-6). 1988. pap. 1.95 (*0-89622-353-1*) Twenty-Third.
—Edna Eagle. Kendzia, Mary C., ed. McCall, Jeff, illus. 32p. (Orig.). 1992. pap. 4.95 (*0-89622-528-3*) Twenty-Third.
—Prayer Services for Religious Educators: Services for Catechists, Teachers, Parents, Children, Teenagers, & Parish Ministers. LC 88-51811. (Illus.). 80p. 1989. tchr's. ed. 9.95 (*0-89622-390-6*) Twenty-Third.
—Praying With Children: Twenty-Eight Services for Various Occasions. LC 90-70560. 96p. (Orig.). (gr. 2-6). 1990. pap. 9.95 (*0-89622-439-2*) Twenty-Third.
—Priscilla Tadpole. Kendzia, Mary C., ed. Read, Maryann, illus. 32p. (Orig.). 1992. pap. 4.95 (*0-89622-527-5*) Twenty-Third.
—Stations of the Cross for Teenagers. (Illus.). 32p. 1988. pap. 1.95 (*0-89622-386-8*) Twenty-Third.
Costello, Linda, designed by see Moore, Clement C.
Costello, Melina P. Tutti-Frutti Town: Blinky Blueberry Finds a Friend. Costello, Melina P., illus. 32p. (Orig.). (gr. k-3). 1991. pap. 6.50 (*1-878130-01-3*) Bang A Drum.
Coster, Charles T. De see De Coster, Charles T.
Costikyan, Greg. Another Day, Another Dungeon. 1990. pap. 3.95 (*0-8125-0140-3*) Tor Bks.
Cote. Curiosity, Reading Level 2. (Illus.). 32p. (gr. 1-4). 1989. PLB 15.94 (*0-86592-442-2*) Rourke Corp.

—Fairness, Reading Level 2. (Illus.). 32p. (gr. 1-4). 1989. PLB 15.94 (*0-86592-445-7*); lib. bdg. 11.95s.p. (*0-685-58780-0*) Rourke Corp.
—Hans Christian Andersen, Reading Level 2. (Illus.). 24p. (gr. 1-4). 1989. PLB 14.60 (*0-86592-430-9*); 10.95 (*0-685-58798-3*) Rourke Corp.
Cote, Elizabeth. Hans Christian Andersen, Vida de Cuento de Hadas. Lazzarino, Luciano & Palacios, Argentina, illus. LC 92-9534. (SPA). 1992. PLB 14.60 (*0-86593-186-0*); 10.95s.p. (*0-685-59299-5*) Rourke Corp.
Cote, Nancy. Palm Trees. Cote, Nancy, illus. LC 92-18938. 40p. (ps-2). 1993. RSBE 14.95 (*0-02-724760-0*, Four Winds) Macmillan Child Grp.
Cotera, Martha P., tr. see Hazen, Nancy.
Cothen, Joe. Come to Bethlehem: The Christmas Story. Seago, Robert, illus. LC 75-25503. 64p. (gr. 4 up). 1975. 7.95 (*0-88289-098-0*) Pelican.
Cothran, Betty. Destinations, Detours & Diversions: A Guide to Family Outings & Good Times. (Illus.). 75p. (Orig.). 1989. pap. 4.99 (*0-9625229-0-2*) Seaworthy Pubns.
Cothran, Jean, ed. Whang Doodle: Folk Tales from the Carolinas. LC 72-86904. (Illus.). (gr. 3-7). 1972. Repr. of 1989 ed. 5.95 (*0-87844-052-6*) Sandlapper Pub Co.
Cotler, Joanna. Sky Above Earth Below. Cotler, Joanna, illus. LC 89-26743. 32p. (ps-k). 1990. 14.95 (*0-06-021365-5*) HarpC Child Bks.
Cott, Jonathan, ed. see Dulac, Edmund.
Cottam, Clarence & Zim, Herbert S. Insects. Irving, James G., illus. 160p. 1987. pap. write for info. (*0-307-24055-X*, Pub. by Golden Bks) Western Pub.
Cotter, Joan A. Worksheets for the Abacus, Vol. 1. (Illus.). 192p. (gr. k-2). 1988. pap. 16.95 (*0-9609636-2-6*) Activities Learning.
—Worksheets for the Abacus, Vol. 2. (Illus.). 122p. (gr. 3-4). 1988. 16.95 (*0-9609636-5-0*) Activities Learning.
—Worksheets for the Abacus, Complete Volume. (Illus.). 320p. (gr. k-4). 1990. 24.95 (*0-9609636-6-9*) Activities Learning.
Cotter, Paulette & Johansen, Carol. Dream Scenes. 48p. (gr. 3-6). 1983. 5.95 (*0-88160-100-4*, LW 241) Learning Wks.
Cotton, Debie. Messy Marcy MacIntyre. LC 89-42629. 32p. (gr. 1-2). 1991. PLB 18.60 (*0-8368-0108-3*) Gareth Stevens Inc.
Cottonpaw. Buns Travels Across America. Love, David, photos by. (Illus.). 48p. (gr. k-5). 1992. pap. 7.95 (*1-881274-01-2*) Cotton Tale.
Cottonwood, Joe. The Adventures of Boone Barnaby. 224p. (gr. 4-7). 1990. 13.95 (*0-590-43546-9*) Scholastic Inc.
—The Adventures of Boone Barnaby. 1992. pap. 2.95 (*0-590-43547-7*, Apple Paperbacks) Scholastic Inc.
—Danny Ain't. (gr. 7 up). 1992. 13.95 (*0-590-45067-0*, 026, Scholastic Hardcover) Scholastic Inc.
Cottrell, Leonard. Up in a Balloon. LC 69-17423. (Illus.). (gr. 8 up). 1970. 24.95 (*0-87599-142-4*) S G Phillips.
Couch, Donna E. The Photograph. Kuchukian, J. Angele, illus. 40p. (gr. 1-6). 1992. 10.00g (*0-9634359-0-6*) Seabright Pr.
Couch, Frank. Children's Bible in Story. Codd, Michael, illus. 320p. 1989. 12.95 (*0-8249-8355-6*, Ideals Child) Hambleton-Hill.
Coucher, Helen. La Tigresa: Tigress. (ps-3). 1993. 16.00 (*0-374-37565-8*, Mirasol) FS&G.
Couderc, Agnes. The Amazing Fate of Raoul Raccoon, Vol. 1. Couderc, Agnes, illus. (ps-3). 1993. 12.95 (*0-316-15829-1*) Little.
Coudert, Allison, jt. auth. see Adams.
Coudert, Allison, jt. auth. see Adams, Laurie.
Coudron, Jill M. Alphabet Activities. (ps-3). 1982. pap. 11.95 (*0-8224-0297-1*) Fearon Teach Aids.
—Alphabet Fun & Games. LC 83-62563. (ps-3). 1984. pap. 11.95 (*0-8224-0295-5*) Fearon Teach Aids.
—Alphabet Puppets. LC 78-72077. (gr. k-3). 1979. pap. 9.95 (*0-8224-0298-X*) Fearon Teach Aids.
—Alphabet Stories. (ps-3). 1982. pap. 11.95 (*0-8224-0299-8*) Fearon Teach Aids.
Coughlan, John. Eco Cars: Earth-Friendly Electric Cars. 48p. (gr. 3-10). 1994. PLB 17.27 (*1-56065-211-X*) Capstone Pr.
—Experimental & Concept Cars. 48p. (gr. 3-10). 1994. PLB 17.27 (*1-56065-210-1*) Capstone Pr.
Coughlin, Elizabeth. Chester Pookins. 1993. 7.00 (*0-8062-4428-3*) Carlton.
Coughlin, Ramona, tr. see Green, Krister.
Coulter, Hope N. Uncle Chuck's Truck. Brown, Rick, illus. LC 91-42638. 32p. (ps-1). 1993. RSBE 13.95 (*0-02-724825-9*, Bradbury Pr) Macmillan Child Grp.
Coulter, Tony. Jacques Cartier, Samuel de Champlain, & the Explorers of Canada. Goetzmann, William H., ed. Collins, Michael, intro. by. (Illus.). 112p. (gr. 6-12). 1993. PLB 18.95 (*0-7910-1298-0*, Am Art Analog); pap. write for info. (*0-7910-1521-1*, Am Art Analog) Chelsea Hse.
—La Salle & the Explorers of the Mississippi. Goetzmann, William H., ed. Collins, Michael, intro. by. (Illus.). 112p. (gr. 5 up). 1991. lib. bdg. 18.95 (*0-7910-1304-9*); pap. 9.95 (*0-7910-1527-0*) Chelsea Hse.
Councell, Ruth T., jt. auth. see Yolen, Jane.
Council for Religion in Independent Schools Staff, ed. A Guide to Representative Community Service Programs. 135p. (gr. k up). 1987. pap. 15.00 (*1-881678-07-5*) CRIS.

Counhaye, Guy. The Chilly Bear. (Illus.). 32p. (gr. k-2). 1991. 18.50 (*0-89565-740-6*); 12.95s.p. (*0-685-55071-0*) Childs World.
Counihan, Claire. Twelve Days of Christmas. 1989. pap. 2.50 (*0-590-42918-3*) Scholastic Inc.
Coupe, Sheena. Sharks. 72p. (gr. 5-12). 1990. 17.95 (*0-8160-2270-4*) Facts on File.
Couper, H. & Henbest, N. The Space Atlas: A Pictorial Guide to our Universe. 1992. 16.95 (*0-15-200598-6*, HB Juv Bks) HarBrace.
Courington, D., as told to see Hayes, Bert.
Courlander, Harold & Herzog, George. The Cow-Tail Switch & Other West African Stories. Chastain, Madye L., illus. LC 47-30108. 160p. (gr. 2-4). 1988. 12.95 (*0-8050-0288-X*, Bks Young Read) H Holt & Co.
—The Cow-Tail Switch & Other West African Stories. LC 47-30108. 160p. (gr. 2-4). 1987. pap. 6.95 (*0-8050-0298-7*) H Holt & Co.
Coursen, H. R. The Search for Archerland. (Illus.). 245p. (Orig.). (gr. 8 up). 1993. pap. 12.50 (*1-880664-02-X*) E M Pr.
Courson, Diana. Let's Learn about Fairy Tales & Nursery Rhymes. 64p. (ps-2). 1988. wkbk. 7.95 (*0-86653-437-7*, GA1040) Good Apple.
—Let's Learn about Safety. Foster, Tom, illus. 64p. (ps-2). 1987. pap. 7.95 (*0-86653-382-6*, GA1011) Good Apple.
Courtalon, Corinne. On the Banks of the Pharaoh's Nile. Broutin, Christian, illus. LC 87-37195. 38p. (gr. k-5). 1988. 4.95 (*0-944589-07-3*, 073) Young Discovery Lib.
Courtault, Martine. Going West: Cowboys & Pioneers. Bogard, Vicki, tr. from FRE. Grant, Donald, illus. LC 89-5365. 38p. (gr. k-5). 1989. 4.95 (*0-944589-21-9*, 021) Young Discovery Lib.
Courtney, Dayle. The Great UFO Chase. rev. ed. 160p. (gr. 6-9). 1991. pap. 4.99 (*0-87403-833-2*, 24-03883) Standard Pub.
—The House That Ate People. rev. ed. 160p. (gr. 6-9). 1991. pap. 4.99 (*0-87403-832-4*, 24-03882) Standard Pub.
—Jaws of Terror. rev. ed. 160p. (gr. 6-9). 1991. pap. 4.99 (*0-87403-831-6*, 24-03881) Standard Pub.
—Secret of Pirates' Cave. rev. ed. 160p. (gr. 6-9). 1991. pap. 4.99 (*0-87403-834-0*, 24-03884) Standard Pub.
Courtney, Jane. Where Have All the Colours Gone? Lathwell, Alan, illus. 1990. 29.00x (*0-85439-407-9*, Pub. by St Paul Pubns UK) St Mut.
Courtney, Julia. Robert Baden Powell: The Man Who Created the International Scouting Movement That Gives Young People Opportunities to Excel. LC 90-30229. (Illus.). 64p. (gr. 5-6). 1990. PLB 18.60 (*0-8368-0214-4*) Gareth Stevens Inc.
—Sir Peter Scott: Champion for the Environment & Founder of the World Wildlife Fund. LC 88-2076. (Illus.). 68p. (gr. 5-6). 1989. PLB 19.93 (*1-55532-819-9*) Gareth Stevens Inc.
Courtney, Richard, illus. Dinosaurs: Giants of the Earth. Moseley, Keith, designed by. (Illus.). 12p. (ps-3). 1988. 6.95 (*0-448-19302-7*, G&D) Putnam Pub Group.
Cousins, Linda. Huggy Bean: A Desert Adventure. (Illus.). 28p. 1992. pap. 5.95 (*0-936073-12-8*) Gumbs & Thomas.
—Huggy Bean & the Origin of the Magic Kente Cloth. (Illus.). 28p. 1991. pap. 5.95 (*0-936073-11-X*) Gumbs & Thomas.
—Huggy Bean: We Happened upon a Beautiful Place. (Illus.). 28p. 1992. pap. 5.95 (*0-936073-13-6*) Gumbs & Thomas.
—Monica Made Me Promise. Webb, Jim, illus. 32p. (gr. 5-8). Date not set. pap. 3.99 (*0-912444-39-8*) DARE Bks.
Cousins, Lucy. Country Animals. Cousins, Lucy, illus. LC 90-35894. (ps). 1991. bds. 3.95 (*0-688-10070-8*, Tambourine Bks) Morrow.
—Farm Animals. Cousins, Lucy, illus. LC 90-35893. 1991. bds. 3.95 (*0-688-10071-6*, Tambourine Bks) Morrow.
—Flower in the Garden. Cousins, Lucy, illus. LC 91-71854. 8p. (ps). 1992. 4.95 (*1-56402-029-0*) Candlewick Pr.
—Garden Animals. Cousins, Lucy, illus. LC 90-36259. (ps). 1991. bds. 3.95 (*0-688-10072-4*, Tambourine Bks) Morrow.
—Hen on the Farm. Cousins, Lucy, illus. LC 91-71849. 8p. (ps). 1992. 4.95 (*1-56402-032-0*) Candlewick Pr.
—Kite in the Park. Cousins, Lucy, illus. LC 91-71842. 8p. (ps). 1992. 4.95 (*1-56402-031-2*) Candlewick Pr.
—Little Dog Laughed. (ps). (Illus.). 64p. (ps-k). 1990. 14.95 (*0-525-44573-0*, DCB) Dutton Child Bks.
—Maisy Goes Swimming. (ps). 1990. 12.95 (*0-316-15834-8*) Little.
—Maisy Goes to Bed. Cousins, Luch, illus. (ps). 1990. 12.95 (*0-316-15832-1*) Little.
—Maisy Goes to School. Cousins, Lucy, illus. LC 91-58743. 16p. (ps). 1992. 12.95 (*1-56402-085-1*) Candlewick Pr.
—Maisy Goes to the Playground. Cousins, Lucy, illus. LC 91-58742. 16p. (ps). 1992. 12.95 (*1-56402-084-3*) Candlewick Pr.
—Pet Animals. Cousins, Lucy, illus. LC 90-36260. (ps). 1991. bds. 3.95 (*0-688-10073-2*, Tambourine Bks) Morrow.
—Teddy in the House. Cousins, Lucy, illus. LC 91-71821. 8p. (ps). 1992. 4.95 (*1-56402-030-4*) Candlewick Pr.

—What Can Rabbit Hear? LC 90-21212. (Illus.). 16p. (ps up). 1991. 12.95 (*0-688-10455-X*, Tambourine Bks) Morrow.
—What Can Rabbit See? LC 90-21213. (Illus.). 16p. (ps up). 1991. 12.95 (*0-688-10454-1*, Tambourine Bks) Morrow.
Cousins, Lucy, retold by. & illus. Noah's Ark. LC 92-54589. 40p. (gr. 2 up). 1993. 14.95 (*1-56402-213-7*) Candlewick Pr.
Cousins, Margaret. Ben Franklin of Old Philadelphia. LC 81-806. 160p. (gr. 5-9). 1981. Repr. of 1981 ed. 4.95 (*0-394-84928-0*) Random Bks Yng Read.
—The Boy in the Alamo. Eggenhofer, Nicholas, illus. LC 83-72585. 180p. (gr. 5-7). 1983. pap. 5.95 (*0-931722-26-8*) Corona Pub.
—The Story of Thomas Alva Edison. LC 81-805. (Illus.). 160p. (gr. 5-9). 1981. pap. 3.95 (*0-394-84883-7*) Random Bks Yng Read.
Cousins, Michael. English Matters, Vol. 3. (gr. 8-10). 1985. pap. 8.95 (*0-7175-1201-0*) Dufour.
Cousteau Society Staff. Adventure in New Zealand. LC 91-3292. (gr. 3-7). 1992. pap. 14.00 (*0-671-77072-1*, S&S BFYR) S&S Trade.
—An Adventure in the Amazon. LC 91-34167. (Illus.). 48p. (gr. 3-7). 1992. pap. 14.00 jacketed (*0-671-77071-3*, S&S BFYR) S&S Trade.
—Albatross. LC 92-34179. (Illus.). (ps-1). 1993. pap. 3.95 POB (*0-671-86565-X*, Little Simon) S&S Trade.
—Corals: The Sea's Great Builders. LC 91-34458. 32p. (gr. 1-5). 1992. pap. 12.00 jacketed (*0-671-77068-3*, S&S BFYR) S&S Trade.
—Dolphins. LC 91-30589. (Illus.). 24p. (ps-1). 1992. pap. 3.95 (*0-671-77062-4*, Little Simon) S&S Trade.
—Garibaldi: Fish of the Pacific. LC 91-3512. (gr. 4-7). 1992. pap. 12.00 (*0-671-77069-1*, S&S BFYR) S&S Trade.
—Manatees. LC 92-34180. (Illus.). (ps-1). 1993. pap. 3.95 POB (*0-671-86566-8*, Little Simon) S&S Trade.
—Otters. LC 92-34177. (ps-1). 1993. pap. 3.95 POB (*0-671-86567-6*, Little Simon) S&S Trade.
—Penguins. LC 91-35229. (Illus.). 24p. (ps-1). 1992. pap. 3.95 (*0-671-77058-6*, Little Simon) S&S Trade.
—Seals. LC 91-34459. (Illus.). 24p. (ps-1). 1992. pap. 3.95 (*0-671-77061-6*, Little Simon) S&S Trade.
—Turtles. LC 91-32184. (Illus.). 24p. (ps-1). 1992. pap. 3.95 (*0-671-77059-4*, Little Simon) S&S Trade.
—Whales. LC 92-34176. (Illus.). (ps-1). 1993. pap. 3.95 POB (*0-671-86564-1*, Little Simon) S&S Trade.
Couture, Christin. The House on the Hill. (Illus.). 32p. (ps up). 1991. 13.95 (*0-374-33474-9*) FS&G.
Couture, Cristin. Walk in the Woods. 1993. 15.00 (*0-374-38227-1*) FS&G.
Couture, Susan A. Alfonso's Dream. LC 93-5784. 1994. write for info. (*0-02-724827-5*, Macmillan Child Bk) Macmillan Child Grp.
—The Block Book. Mathers, Petra, illus. LC 89-34504. 32p. (ps-3). 1990. HarpC Child Bks.
Couvillon, Alice & Moore, Elizabeth. Mimi's First Mardi Gras. Rougelot, Marilyn C., illus. LC 91-24006. 32p. (gr. 1-3). 1992. 14.95 (*0-88289-840-X*) Pelican.
Couvillon, Alice W., jt. auth. see Moore, Elizabeth B.
Coventry, Martha, tr. see Gallaz, Chrsitophe.
Cover, Arthur B. American Revolutionary. Martishuis, Walter & Nino, Alex, illus. 144p. (gr. 7-12). 1985. pap. 2.50 (*0-553-26773-6*) Bantam.
—Blade of the Guillotine. 144p. (Orig.). (gr. 7-12). 1986. pap. 2.50 (*0-553-26038-3*) Bantam.
—The Rings of Saturn. 144p. (gr. 5 up). 1985. pap. 2.25 (*0-553-25797-8*) Bantam.
Coville, Bruce. Aliens Ate My Homework. Coville, Katherine, illus. 160p. (gr. 3-6). 1993. 12.00 (*0-671-87249-4*, Minstrel Bks); pap. 3.50 (*0-671-72712-5*, Minstrel Bks) PB.
—Bruce Coville's Book of Monsters: Tales to Give You the Creeps. (gr. 4-7). 1993. pap. 2.95 (*0-590-46159-1*) Scholastic Inc.
—The Dinosaur That Followed Me Home. Pierard, John, illus. 160p. (Orig.). (gr. 3-6). 1990. pap. 2.99 (*0-671-64750-4*, Minstrel Bks) PB.
—The Foolish Giant. Coville, Katherine, illus. LC 77-18522. 48p. (ps-2). 1990. pap. 3.95 (*0-06-443229-7*, Trophy) HarpC Child Bks.
—Ghost in the Big Bed. Book. (gr. 4-7). 1991. pap. 3.50 (*0-553-15827-9*) Bantam.
—The Ghost Wore Grey. 128p. (Orig.). 1988. pap. 3.50 (*0-553-15610-1*, Skylark) Bantam.
—Goblins in the Castle. MacDonald, Pat, ed. Coville, Katherine, illus. 176p. (Orig.). 1992. pap. 3.50 (*0-671-72711-7*, Minstrel Bks) PB.
—Herds of Thunder: Manes of Gold. (gr. 4-7). 1991. pap. 9.00 (*0-385-41905-8*) Doubleday.
—Herds of Thunder, Manes of Gold: A Collection of Horse Stories & Poems. Lewin, Ted, illus. LC 88-34651. 176p. (gr. 5-10). 1989. 15.95 (*0-385-24642-0*) Doubleday.
—How I Survived My Summer Vacation. Newsom, Tom, illus. 96p. (Orig.). (gr. 3-5). 1988. pap. 2.99 (*0-671-68176-1*, Minstrel Bks) PB.
—Jennifer Murdley's Toad. Lippincott, G., illus. 1992. 16.95 (*0-15-200745-8*, HB Juv Bks) HarBrace.
—Jennifer Murdley's Toad. MacDonald, Pat, ed. Lippincott, Gary A., illus. 176p. 1993. pap. 3.50 (*0-671-79401-9*, Minstrel Bks) PB.
—Jeremy Thatcher, Dragon Hatcher. Yolen, Jane, ed. Lippincott, Gary, illus. 148p. (gr. 3-7). 1991. 16.95 (*0-15-200748-2*, J Yolen Bks) HarBrace.

—The Monster's Ring. Coville, Katherine, illus. LC 82-3436. 96p. (gr. 8-11). 1982. lib. bdg. 9.99 (*0-394-95320-7*) Pantheon.
—My Teacher Flunked the Planet. MacDonald, Pat, ed. Fisher, Steve, illus. 176p. (Orig.). 1992. pap. 3.50 (*0-671-75081-X*, Minstrel Bks) PB.
—My Teacher Fried My Brains. MacDonald, Patricia, ed. 128p. (Orig.). 1991. pap. 3.50 (*0-671-72710-9*, Minstrel Bks) PB.
—My Teacher Glows in the Dark. MacDonald, Patricia, ed. Pierard, John, illus. 144p. (Orig.). 1991. pap. 3.50 (*0-671-72709-5*, Minstrel Bks) PB.
—Space Brat. MacDonald, Pat, ed. Coville, Katherine, illus. 80p. (Orig.). 1992. pap. 3.50 (*0-671-74567-0*, Minstrel Bks) PB.
—Space Brat. MacDonald, Pat, ed. Coville, Katherine, illus. 1993. 12.00 (*0-671-87059-9*, Minstrel Bks) PB.
—Space Brat Two: Blork's Evil Twin. Coville, Bruce, illus. 80p. (Orig.). (gr. 2-4). 1993. 12.00 (*0-671-87038-6*, Minstrel Bks); pap. 3.50 (*0-671-77713-0*, Minstrel Bks) PB.
—Unicorn Treasury: Stories, Poems and Unicorn Lore. (gr. 4-7). 1991. pap. 9.00 (*0-385-41930-9*) Doubleday.
—Waiting Spirits. 160p. (Orig.). (gr. 8-10). 1984. pap. text ed. 2.25 (*0-553-26004-9*) Bantam.
Coville, Bruce & Coville, Katherine. The Foolish Giant. LC 77-18522. (Illus.). (gr. k-2). 1978. PLB 12.89 (*0-397-31800-6*, Lipp Jr Bks) HarpC Child Bks.
—Sarah's Unicorn. LC 79-2408. (Illus.). 48p. (ps-2). 1979. (Lipp Jr Bks); PLB 12.89 (*0-397-31873-1*) HarpC Child Bks.
—Sarah's Unicorn. Coville, Bruce & Coville, Katherine, illus. LC 85-42749. 48p. (gr. 1-4). 1985. 4.95 (*0-06-443084-7*, Trophy) HarpC Child Bks.
Coville, Bruce, compiled by. The Unicorn Treasury: Stories, Poems & Unicorn Lore. Hildebrandt, Tim, illus. LC 86-32919. 176p. (gr. 3 up). 1988. pap. 14.95 (*0-385-24000-7*) Doubleday.
Coville, Katherine, jt. auth. see Coville, Bruce.
Coville, Katherine, jt. auth. see San Souci, Robert D.
Covington, Dennis. Lizard. 1991. 9.00 (*0-385-30307-6*) Delacorte.
—Lizard. 1993. pap. 3.50 (*0-440-21490-4*) Dell.
Cowan, Catherine, retold by see Gogol, Nicolai.
Cowan, Dale. Deadly Sleep. 176p. (gr. 7 up). 1992. pap. 3.50 (*0-440-91961-4*, LFL) Dell.
Cowan, James. Emergency Rescue! Nightmare at Norton's Mills. (gr. 4-7). 1993. pap. 2.95 (*0-590-46019-6*) Scholastic Inc.
—Emergency Rescue: Trouble at Moosehead Lake. (gr. 4-7). 1993. pap. 2.95 (*0-590-46018-8*) Scholastic Inc.
—Kun-Man-Gur the Rainbow Serpent. Bancroft, Bronwyn, illus. LC 93-32319. 1994. 16.00 (*1-56957-906-7*) Barefoot Bks.
Cowcher, Helen. Antarctica. Red Grammer Staff, narrated by. Cowcher, Helen, illus. 32p. (ps-3). 1990. incl. audiocassette 19.95 (*0-924483-24-5*); incl. audio cass. tape & stuffed penguin toy 44.95 (*0-924483-65-2*) Soundprints.
—Antartida: Antarctica. (ps-3). 1993. 15.00 (*0-374-30370-3*) FS&G.
—El Bosque Tropical: Rain Forest. 1992. 15.00 (*0-374-30900-0*) FS&G.
—Rain Forest. (Illus.). 32p. (ps up). 1988. 14.95 (*0-374-36167-3*) FS&G.
—Rain Forest. Red Grammer Staff, narrated by. (Illus.). 32p. (ps-3). 1989. incl. audiocassette 19.95 (*0-924483-20-2*) Soundprints.
—La Tigresa. Marcuse, Aida, tr. (SPA.). 32p. (gr. 4-8). 1993. pap. 5.95 (*0-374-47779-5*) FS&G.
—La Tigresa: Tigress. (ps-3). 1993. pap. 5.95 (*0-374-47781-7*) FS&G.
—Tigress. (Illus.). 32p. (ps up). 1991. bds. 14.95 (*0-374-37567-4*) FS&G.
—Tigress. Thomas, Peter, narrated by. Cowcher, Helen, illus. 32p. (gr. k-4). incls. cassette 19.95 (*0-924483-33-4*, 3530) Soundprints.
—Whistling Thorns. LC 92-39533. (gr. 6 up). 1993. 14.95 (*0-590-47299-2*) Scholastic Inc.
Cowden, Diane, jt. auth. see Preece, Alison.

Cowden, Frances B. & Hatchett, Eve B. Of Butterflies & Unicorns: And Other Wonders of the Earth. Grove, Eric, illus. 52p. (gr. 7-12). 1993. pap. 7.95 (*1-884289-02-9*) Grandmother Erth. The words rich in visual & tactile imagery, sing of the need for preserving the beauty of our earth. They capture the magic of unicorns & butterflies in language suitable for middle school & high school students as well as young-at-heart adults. Both Memphis authors have taught poetry to children & young people in public schools & in workshops. Included are poems that have won prizes & have been previously published. The introduction by Patricia Garrett, principal of Lester Demonstration School, Memphis City Schools, shows how to use the book in reading lessons. Dr. Rosemary Stephens, President of the National League of American Pen Women, Chickasaw Branch in "About the Poets" gives insights into the work of the authors. The passages are illustrated with ink drawings by Memphis artist, Eric Grove. This edition is intended for all ages. However the material stresses the importance of teaching poetry to children & young people. Order directly from the publisher: Grandmother Earth Creations, 8463 Deerfield Lane, Germantown, TN 38138. *Publisher Provided Annotation.*

Cowell, Phyllis. A Hugga Bunch Hello. Kong, Emilie, illus. 40p. (ps). 1985. 4.00 (*0-910313-87-3*) Parker Bros.
Cowell, Phyllis F. The Baby Hugs Bear & Baby Tugs Bear Alphabet Book. (Illus.). 40p. (ps). 1984. 5.95 (*0-910313-72-5*) Parker Bros.
—Your Best Wishes Can Come True. Ewers, Joe, illus. 40p. (ps-3). 1984. 5.95 (*0-910313-18-0*) Parker Bros.
Cowen-Fletcher, Jane. Mama Zooms. Cowen-Fletcher, Jane, illus. LC 92-15553. 32p. (ps-1). 1993. 14.95 (*0-590-45774-8*) Scholastic Inc.
Cowger, Barry D. Family Dynamics & Astrology. Green, Jeff, intro. by. (Illus.). 175p. (Orig.). (gr. 12). 1990. pap. 9.95 (*0-685-29119-7*) Envision Pub.
Cowger, James F. Friction Ridge Skin: Comparison & Identification of Fingerprints. LC 93-24980. (gr. 7 up). 1993. write for info. (*0-8493-9502-X*) CRC PR.
Cowing, Renee. The Complete Book of Pet Names. LC 90-81851. 112p. 1990. 9.95 (*0-9626950-2-5*) Fireplug CA.
Cowley, Malcolm, ed. see Faulkner, William.
Cowley, Mert. Growing Up with Joey: A Fishing Trip for Joey - Joey & the Cabin in the Woods. (Illus.). 40p. (Orig.). (ps-2). 1991. pap. 3.29 (*0-9627867-2-1*) Banksiana.
Cowley, Stewart. Five Little Kittens: A Magic Window Board Book. Davies, Kate, illus. 22p. (ps). 1992. 6.99 (*0-89577-454-2*) RD Assn.
—Little Lost Rabbit. Slade, Catharine, illus. LC 92-60792. 22p. (ps). 1992. 6.99 (*0-89577-445-3*) RD Assn.
—Naughty Ducklings. Adams, Susi, illus. LC 92-60791. 22p. (ps). 1992. 6.99 (*0-89577-444-5*) RD Assn.
—Sleepy Bear. LC 93-77347. (ps-3). 1993. 6.99 (*0-89577-513-1*, Readers Digest Kids) RD Assn.
—Squirrel's Party. LC 93-77348. (ps-3). 1993. 6.99 (*0-89577-514-X*, Readers Digest Kids) RD Assn.
Cowley, Stewart & Davies, Kate. Hide-&-Seek Puppies. LC 92-60793. (Illus.). (ps). 1992. 6.99 (*0-89577-455-0*) RD Assn.
Cowling, Sue. What Is a Kumquat? And Other Poems. Edwards, Gunvor, illus. 64p. (Orig.). (gr. 2 up). 1991. pap. 6.95 (*0-571-16065-4*) Faber & Faber.
Cox & Cork. Birds. (gr. 2-5). 1980. (Usborne-Hayes); PLB 11.96 (*0-88110-072-2*); pap. 3.95 (*0-86020-475-8*) EDC.
—Butterflies & Moths. (gr. 2-5). 1980. PLB 11.96 (*0-88110-073-0*); pap. 3.95 (*0-86020-477-4*) EDC.
—First Book of Nature. (gr. 2-5). 1980. 12.95 (*0-86020-483-9*, Usborne-Hayes) EDC.
—Flowers. (gr. 2-5). 1980. (Usborne-Hayes); PLB 11.96 (*0-88110-074-9*); pap. 3.95 (*0-86020-479-0*) EDC.
Cox, Barry. Prehistoric Animals. (Illus.). (gr. 5 up). 1971. pap. 3.95 (*0-553-23610-5*) Bantam.
Cox, Bertha M. True Tales of Texas. Hendrick, Lura A., illus. LC 87-12091. 292p. (gr. 3-8). 1987. PLB 13.95 (*0-937460-28-1*); pap. 9.95 (*0-937460-77-X*) Hendrick Long.
Cox, Clinton. The Forgotten Heroes: The Story of the Buffalo Soldiers. LC 92-36622. 1993. write for info. (*0-590-45121-9*) Scholastic Inc.
—The Undying Glory. 176p. 1991. 14.95 (*0-590-44170-1*, Scholastic Hardcover) Scholastic Inc.
—Undying Glory: The Story of the Massachusetts Fifty-Fourth Regiment. (gr. 4-7). 1993. pap. 3.25 (*0-590-44171-X*) Scholastic Inc.
Cox, David. Captain Ding, the Double-Decker Pirate. Round, Graham, illus. 32p. (ps-1). 1993. 17.95 (*0-09-176365-1*). Pub. by Hutchinson UK) Trafalgar.
Cox, Gail, ed. see Flores, Kathy.
Cox, Gale R., jt. auth. see Price, Ray B.
Cox, Greg. The Pirate Paradox. 1991. pap. 3.50 (*0-06-106016-X*, Harp PBks) HarpC.
Cox, James A. Put Your Foot in Your Mouth & Other Silly Sayings. Weissman, Sam Q., illus. LC 80-12877. 72p. (gr. 2-5). 1980. bds. 3.95 (*0-394-84503-X*) Random Bks Yng Read.
Cox, Julia. The Adventures of Boo, Vol. 2: Circus. Ortland, Stephen, illus. 32p. 1992. write for info. (*0-9627586-2-0*) Mango Entrps.
Cox, Julie. The Adventures of Boo: The Journey Begins. Ortland, Stephen, illus. LC 90-62757. 32p. 1990. write for info. (*0-9627586-0-4*); write for info. audio cassette (*0-9627586-1-2*) Mango Entrps.

Cox, Kris, jt. auth. see Cox, Mike.
Cox, Lynn. Crazy Alphabet. McRae, Rodney, illus. LC 91-3734. 32p. (ps-1). 1992. 13.95 (*0-531-05966-9*); lib. bdg. 13.99 (*0-531-08566-X*) Orchard Bks Watts.
Cox, Mike. Texas Rangers. (Illus.). 144p. (gr. 6-9). 1992. 14.95 (*0-89015-818-5*) Eakin-Sunbelt.
Cox, Mike & Cox, Kris. Flowers. Wasserman, Dan, ed. Reese, Bob, illus. 1979. 7.95 (*0-89868-076-X*); pap. 2.95 (*0-89868-087-5*) ARO Pub.
Cox, Mike, et al. Fire Drill. Wasserman, Dan, ed. Reese, Bob, illus. (gr. k-1). 1979. 7.95 (*0-89868-071-9*); pap. 2.95 (*0-89868-082-4*) ARO Pub.
Cox, Nonie. Christopher Columbus. (Illus.). 48p. (gr. k-1). 1992. pap. 9.95 (*1-55799-240-1*) Evan-Moor Corp.
Cox, Palmer. The Brownies' Merry Adventures. Cox, Palmer, illus. LC 93-563. 224p. 1993. 6.00 (*1-56957-901-6*) Shambhala Pubns.
Cox, Paul. Case of the Botched Book. LC 91-3853. (ps-3). 1992. 16.00 (*0-671-77586-3*, Green Tiger) S&S Trade.
—Great Eucalyptus Mystery. LC 91-3853. (ps-3). 1992. 16.00 (*0-671-77574-X*, Green Tiger) S&S Trade.
—Riddle of the Floating Island. LC 91-3853. (ps-3). 1992. 16.00 (*0-671-77579-0*, Green Tiger) S&S Trade.
Cox, Rosemary C., jt. auth. see Cox, Willis F.
Cox, Sherri, jt. auth. see Cox, Tom.
Cox, Shirley. Earth Science. LC 92-9132. 1992. 16.67 (*0-86625-429-3*); 12.50s.p. (*0-685-59399-1*) Rourke Pubns.
Cox, Ted. Mario Lemieux (Super Mario) LC 93-19782. 1993. write for info. (*0-516-04378-1*) Childrens.
—Shaquille O'Neal: Shaq Attack. LC 93-19781. 1993. write for info. (*0-516-04379-X*) Childrens.
Cox, Thomas. Leaflets of the White Rose: A Filmplay. 125p. (Orig.). 1991. pap. 12.00 (*1-879710-02-1*) Riverside FL.
Cox, Tom & Cox, Sherri. School Records: Kindergarten - 12th Grade. Woodbury Graphics Design Staff, illus. 27p. (gr. k-12). 1990. comb. processing 9.95 (*0-9626932-0-0*) TCA Pub.
Cox, W. Miles. The Addictive Personality. (Illus.). 32p. (gr. 5 up). 1991. pap. 4.49 (*0-7910-0006-0*) Chelsea Hse.
—Addictive Personality. updated ed. (Illus.). (gr. 5 up). 1992. lib. bdg. 19.95 (*0-685-52233-4*) Chelsea Hse.
Cox, Willis F. & Cox, Rosemary C. Phillip's Daffodil. (Orig.). (gr. k-8). 1987. pap. 2.95 (*0-9610758-4-8*) W F Cox.
Coxe see Sohn, David A.
Coxe, Molly. Louella & the Yellow Balloon. Coxe, Molly, illus. LC 87-30379. 32p. (ps-2). 1988. (Crowell Jr Bks) HarpC Child Bks.
—Mirabel & Maxie. LC 92-26528. Date not set. 13.00 (*0-06-022868-7*); PLB 12.89 (*0-06-022869-5*) HarpC Child Bks. Postponed.
Coxon, Michele. The Cat Who Lost His Purr. Coxon, Michele, illus. 32p. (gr. k-3). 1991. 12.95 (*0-87226-453-X*, Bedrick Blackie) P Bedrick Bks.
Coxon, Michelle. Who Will Play with Me? Coxon, Michelle, illus. LC 91-40498. 32p. (gr. k-3). 1992. PLB 12.95 (*0-87226-469-6*, Bedrick Blackie) P Bedrick Bks.
Coy, John. Night Driving. 1994. write for info. (*0-8050-2931-1*) H Holt & Co.
Coy, Stanley C. Beaufort County: "Queen of the Carolina Sea Islands" Activity Book. 21p. (gr. 3-5). 1992. pap. 3.95 (*1-881459-00-4*) Eagle Pr SC.
Coyle, Neva & Chapian, Marie. Slimming Down & Growing Up. LC 85-15028. 160p. (Orig.). (gr. 4-7). 1985. pap. 5.99 (*0-87123-833-0*) Bethany Hse.
Coyle, Rena. My First Baking Book. Arnold, Tedd, illus. LC 87-40646. 144p. (gr. 1-5). 1988. pap. 9.95 (*0-89480-579-7*, 1579) Workman Pub.
—My First Cookbook. Joyner, Jerry, illus. LC 84-40683. 128p. (Orig.). (gr. 1-5). 1985. pap. 8.95 (*0-89480-846-X*, 846) Workman Pub.
Coynik, David. Film: Real to Reel. (Illus.). 273p. (Orig.). (gr. 10-12). 1976. pap. text ed. 11.73 (*0-88343-304-4*) McDougal-Littell.
Cozic, Charles, jt. auth. see Dudley, William.
Cozic, Charles & Swisher, Karin, eds. The AIDS Crisis. LC 91-30034. 200p. (gr. 10 up). 1991. PLB 16.95 (*0-89908-578-4*); pap. text ed. 9.95 (*0-89908-584-9*) Greenhaven.
—Chemical Dependency. LC 91-12228. (Illus.). 288p. (gr. 10 up). 1991. lib. bdg. 17.95 (*0-89908-179-7*); pap. text ed. 9.95 (*0-89908-154-1*) Greenhaven.
Cozic, Charles, jt. ed. see Polesetsky, Matthew.
Cozic, Charles P., ed. America's Cities: Opposing Viewpoints. (Illus.). 264p. (gr. 10 up). 1993. PLB 17.95 (*0-89908-195-9*); pap. text ed. 9.95 (*0-89908-170-3*) Greenhaven.
—Education in America: Opposing Viewpoints. LC 91-42495. (Illus.). 264p. (gr. 10 up). 1992. PLB 17.95 (*0-89908-188-6*); pap. text ed. 9.95 (*0-89908-163-0*) Greenhaven.
—Space Exploration: Opposing Viewpoints. LC 92-8149. (Illus.). 240p. (gr. 10 up). 1992. PLB 17.95 (*0-89908-197-5*); pap. text ed. 9.95 (*0-89908-172-X*) Greenhaven.
Cozic, Charles P. & Swisher, Karin L., eds. Nuclear Proliferation: Opposing Viewpoints. LC 92-23065. (Illus.). 240p. (gr. 10 up). 1992. PLB 17.95 (*1-56510-005-0*); pap. text ed. 9.95 (*1-56510-004-2*) Greenhaven.

Cozic, Charles P. & Tipp, Stacey, eds. Abortion: Opposing Viewpoints. LC 91-21279. (Illus.). 216p. (gr. 10 up). 1991. lib. bdg. 17.95 (*0-89908-181-9*); pap. 9.95 (*0-89908-156-8*) Greenhaven.
Cozic, Charles P., jt. ed. see Biskup, Michael D.
Cozic, Charles P., jt. ed. see Weksesser, Carol.
Crabtree, Cathy L. & Fowler, Joanne. Poor Me & the Magic of Christmas. rev. ed. Sanor, Peggy, illus. LC 89-84463. 20p. (gr. 2-3). 1989. pap. text ed. 5.95 (*0-9622719-0-X*) Lavender Pr.
Crabtree, Jack. Play It Safe. 210p. (Orig.). 1993. pap. 8.99 (*1-56476-110-X*, Victor Books) SP Pubns.
Crabtree, Paul. I Sincerely Doubt That This Old House Is Very Haunted: Musical. 1968. 4.50 (*0-87602-142-9*) Anchorage.
Cracchiolo, Rachelle. Holiday Cards. Darby's Designs, illus. 32p. (gr. 1-6). 1982. wkbk. 4.95 (*1-55734-031-5*) Tchr Create Mat.
Cracchiolo, Rachelle & Smith, Mary D. Christmas Activities. Crachiolo, Rachelle & Smith, Mary D., illus. 32p. (gr. 1-3). 1985. wkbk. 4.95 (*1-55734-013-7*) Tchr Create Mat.
—Halloween Activities. Crachiolo, Rachelle & Smith, Mary D., illus. 32p. (gr. 1-3). 1980. wkbk. 4.95 (*1-55734-011-0*) Tchr Create Mat.
—Holiday Hats. Cracchiolo, Rachelle & Smith, Mary D., illus. 16p. (gr. k-4). 1979. wkbk. 6.50 (*1-55734-002-1*) Tchr Create Mat.
—Quick Fun Art. (Illus.). 56p. (gr. k-3). 1977. wkbk. 5.95 (*1-55734-001-3*) Tchr Create Mat.
—Thanksgiving Activities. Crachiolo, Rachelle & Smith, Mary D., illus. 32p. (gr. 1-3). 1985. wkbk. 4.95 (*1-55734-012-9*) Tchr Create Mat.
Craft, Louise, jt. auth. see Harrast, Tracy.
Craft, Mary. Sea Otters Cruz & Slick. Craft, Mary, illus. 24p. (Orig.). (ps-4). 1991. pap. write for info. (*0-9624842-2-9*) M Craft.
Craft, Mary L. Little Orphan Otter. Craft, Mary L., illus. 20p. (Orig.). (gr. k-12). 1989. pap. text ed. 5.25 (*0-9624842-0-2*) M Craft.
Craft, Page, ed. see Roach, Margaret J.
Craft, Ruth. The Day of the Rainbow. Daly, Niki, illus. 32p. (ps-3). 1991. pap. 4.95 (*0-14-050935-6*, Puffin) Puffin Bks.
—The Winter Bear. Blegvad, Erik, illus. LC 74-18178. 32p. (ps-3). 1975. SBE 13.95 (*0-689-50017-3*, M K McElderry) Macmillan Child Grp.
—The Winter Bear. Blegvad, Erik, illus. LC 89-31866. 32p. (ps-3). 1989. pap. 3.95 (*0-689-71342-8*, Aladdin) Macmillan Child Grp.
Craig, A. Prehistoric Facts. (Illus.). 48p. (gr. 3-7). 1986. PLB 12.96 (*0-88110-228-8*); pap. 5.95 (*0-86020-973-3*) EDC.
Craig, A. & Rosney, C. Science Encyclopedia. (Illus.). 128p. 1989. lib. bdg. 16.96 (*0-88110-390-X*); pap. 12. 95 (*0-7460-0419-2*) EDC.
Craig, Diana. How to Draw & Paint Pets. 1991. 12.98 (*1-55521-716-8*) Bk Sales Inc.
—Making Models: Three-D Creations from Paper & Clay. LC 92-18413. (Illus.). 96p. (gr. 3 up). 1993. PLB 16.90 (*1-56294-204-2*); pap. 9.95 (*1-56294-710-9*) Millbrook Pr.
Craig, Dorothy, ed. see Ulrich, Cindy & Guild, Pat.
Craig, Helen. I See the Moon, & the Moon Sees Me. Craig, Helen, illus. LC 92-18996. 48p. (ps-2). 1993. 16.00 (*0-06-021453-8*); PLB 15.89 (*0-06-021454-6*) HarpC Child Bks.
—The Knight, the Princess & the Dragon. Craig, Helen, illus. LC 84-19419. 32p. (ps-2). 1985. lib. bdg. 8.99 (*0-394-97212-0*) Knopf Bks Yng Read.
—Night of the Paper Bag Monsters. LC 92-44610. (Orig.). (gr. 3 up). 1994. pap. 4.99 (*1-56402-120-3*) Candlewick Pr.
—Susie & Alfred in a Busy Day in Town. LC 93-21181. (Orig.). 1994. pap. write for info. (*1-56402-380-X*) Candlewick Pr.
Craig, Helen, jt. auth. see Hayes, Sarah.
Craig, Helen, retold by. & illus. The Town Mouse & the Country Mouse. LC 91-58761. 32p. (ps up). 1992. 13. 95 (*1-56402-102-5*) Candlewick Pr.
Craig, Janet. Amazing World of Night Creatures. Helmer, Jean, illus. LC 89-5002. 32p. (gr. 2-4). 1990. PLB 11.59 (*0-8167-1749-4*); pap. text ed. 2.95 (*0-8167-1750-8*) Troll Assocs.
—Amazing World of Spiders. Helmer, Jean, illus. LC 89-5005. 32p. (gr. 2-4). 1990. PLB 11.59 (*0-8167-1751-6*); pap. text ed. 2.95 (*0-8167-1752-4*) Troll Assocs.
—Ballet Dancer. Todd, Barbara, illus. LC 88-10043. 32p. (gr. k-3). 1989. PLB 10.89 (*0-8167-1434-7*); pap. text ed. 2.95 (*0-8167-1435-5*) Troll Assocs.
—Discovering Prehistoric Animals. Watling, James, illus. LC 89-4973. 32p. (gr. 2-4). 1990. PLB 11.59 (*0-8167-1755-9*); pap. text ed. 2.95 (*0-8167-1756-7*) Troll Assocs.
—Discovering Whales & Dolphins. Johnson, Pamela, illus. LC 89-5004. 32p. (gr. 2-4). 1990. PLB 11.59 (*0-8167-1759-1*); pap. text ed. 2.95 (*0-8167-1760-5*) Troll Assocs.
—Fisherman. Eitzen, Allan, illus. LC 88-10045. 32p. (gr. 1-3). 1989. PLB 10.89 (*0-8167-1438-X*); pap. text ed. 2.95 (*0-8167-1439-8*) Troll Assocs.
—Here Comes Winter. Karas, G. Brian, illus. LC 87-13738. 32p. (gr. k-2). 1988. PLB 7.89 (*0-8167-1225-5*); pap. text ed. 1.95 (*0-8167-1226-3*) Troll Assocs.

—Homer the Beachcomber. Mahan, Ben, illus. LC 87-10913. 32p. (gr. k-2). 1988. PLB 11.59 (0-8167-1085-6); pap. text ed. 2.95 (0-8167-1086-4) Troll Assocs.

—Joey the Jack-O'-Lantern. Miller, Susan, illus. LC 87-10845. 32p. (gr. k-2). 1988. PLB 11.59 (0-8167-1105-4); pap. text ed. 2.95 (0-8167-1106-2) Troll Assocs.

—Little Christmas Star. Miller, Susan, illus. LC 87-10936. 32p. (gr. k-2). 1988. PLB 11.59 (0-8167-1097-X); pap. text ed. 2.95 (0-8167-1098-8) Troll Assocs.

—Little Danny Dinosaur. Harvey, Paul, illus. LC 87-16228. 32p. (gr. k-2). 1988. PLB 7.89 (0-8167-1229-8); pap. text ed. 1.95 (0-8167-1230-1) Troll Assocs.

—Muffy & Fluffy: The Kittens Who Didn't Agree. Hall, Susan, illus. LC 87-16227. 32p. (gr. k-2). 1988. PLB 7.89 (0-8167-1227-1); pap. text ed. 1.95 (0-8167-1228-X) Troll Assocs.

—Santa's Cookie Surprise. Loh, Carolyn, illus. LC 88-19997. 32p. (gr. k-2). 1989. lib. bdg. 7.89 (0-8167-1538-6); pap. text ed. 1.95 (0-8167-1539-4) Troll Assocs.

—Thump, Bump. Paterson, Diane, illus. LC 87-10933. 32p. (gr. k-2). 1988. PLB 11.59 (0-8167-1077-5); pap. text ed. 2.95 (0-8167-1078-3) Troll Assocs.

—Turtles. Kelleher, Kathie, illus. LC 81-11448. 32p. (gr. k-2). 1982. PLB 11.59 (0-89375-664-4); pap. 2.95 (0-89375-665-2) Troll Assocs.

—What's It Like to Be a Newspaper Reporter. Kolding, Richard M., illus. LC 89-34384. 32p. (gr. k-3). 1989. lib. bdg. 10.89 (0-8167-1807-5); pap. text ed. 2.95 (0-8167-1808-3) Troll Assocs.

—What's under the Ocean. Harvey, Paul, illus. LC 81-11425. 32p. (gr. k-2). 1982. PLB 11.59 (0-89375-652-0); pap. 2.95 (0-89375-653-9) Troll Assocs.

—Windy Day. Durrell, Julie, illus. LC 87-10909. 32p. (gr. k-2). 1988. PLB 7.89 (0-8167-0982-3); pap. text ed. 1.95 (0-8167-0983-1) Troll Assocs.

—Wonders of the Rain Forest. Schindler, S. D., illus. LC 89-5001. 32p. (gr. 2-4). 1990. PLB 11.59 (0-8167-1763-X); pap. text ed. 2.95 (0-8167-1764-8) Troll Assocs.

Craig, Janet A. The Boo-Hoo Witch. Schories, Patricia L., illus. LC 93-2216. 32p. (gr. k-2). 1993. PLB 11.59 (0-8167-3186-1); pap. text ed. 2.95 (0-8167-3187-X) Troll Assocs.

—A Letter to Santa. Rader, Laura, illus. LC 93-2214. 32p. (gr. k-2). 1993. PLB 11.59 (0-8167-3252-3); pap. text ed. 2.95 (0-8167-3253-1) Troll Assocs.

—Valentine's Day Mess. Morse, Debby, illus. LC 93-2211. 32p. (gr. k-2). 1993. PLB 11.59 (0-8167-3254-X); pap. text ed. 2.95 (0-8167-3255-8) Troll Assocs.

Craig, Linda & Praytor, Phyllis. Criterion Referenced Test Kit: Math. Reed, Tom, illus. 54p. (gr. 4). 1978. write for info. (0-936394-01-3) Education Serv.

Craig, M. Jean. The Three Wishes. Salzman, Yuri, illus. 48p. (Orig.). (gr. k-3). 1986. pap. 2.50 (0-590-41744-4) Scholastic Inc.

Craig, Mary. Lech Walesa: The Leader of Solidarity & Campaigner for Freedom & Human Rights in Poland. LC 88-17732. (Illus.). 68p. (gr. 5-6). 1990. PLB 18.60 (1-55532-821-0) Gareth Stevens Inc.

—Mother Theresa. (Illus.). 64p. (gr. 5-9). 1991. 11.95 (0-237-60008-0, Pub. by Evans Bros Ltd) Trafalgar.

—Pope John Paul the Second. (Illus.). 64p. (gr. 5-9). 1991. 11.95 (0-237-60005-6, Pub. by Evans Bros Ltd) Trafalgar.

Craig, Stephanie, tr. see Reboul, Antoine.

Craighead, Charles. The Eagle & the River. Mangelsen, Tom, photos by. LC 92-23240. (Illus.). (gr. 1-5). 1994. RSBE 14.95 (0-02-762265-7, Macmillan Child Bk) Macmillan Child Grp.

Craighead-George, Jean. Julie & the Wolves: (Julie y los Lobos). (SPA.). (gr. 1-6). 9.95 (84-204-3206-7) Santillana.

Crain, Steve. Bible Fun Book, No. 7. 32p. (Orig.). (gr. k-4). 1981. oversized saddle stitched 1.19 (0-87123-766-0) Bethany Hse.

—Bible Fun Book, No. 8. 32p. (Orig.). (gr. k-4). 1981. pap. 1.19 oversized saddle stitched (0-87123-772-5) Bethany Hse.

Cram, Ralph A. Walled Towns. facsimile ed. LC 19-18459. 107p. 1987. bdg. 8.00 (0-942153-15-4) EntroCon.

Cramer, Alexander. A Night in Moonbeam County. 208p. (gr. 6-8). 1994. SBE 14.95 (0-684-19704-9, Scribners Young Read) Macmillan Child Grp.

Cramer, J. B. Fifty Selected Studies for Piano. Von Bulow, Hans, ed. 116p. 1946. pap. 12.00 (0-8258-0138-9, L 525) Fischer Inc NY.

Cramer, J. Grant, tr. see Grundtvig, Sven.

Crampton, Gertrude. Scuffy the Tugboat. Olson, Gordon, illus. 24p. (ps-k). 1993. 9.00 (0-307-74813-8, 64813, Golden Pr) Western Pub.

Crampton, Patricia, abridged by see Masefield, John.

Crampton, Patricia, tr. see Frank, Rudolf.

Crampton, Patricia, tr. see Kalas, Sybille.

Crampton, Patricia, tr. see Kalas, Sybille & Kalas, Klaus.

Crampton, Patricia, tr. see Prokofiev, Sergei.

Crampton, William. Flag. Plomer, Martin & Shone, Karl, illus. LC 88-27174. 64p. (gr. 5 up). 1989. 15.00 (0-394-82255-2); PLB 15.99 (0-394-92255-7) Knopf Bks Yng Read.

Cranberry, Nola, tr. see Shely, Patricia.

Cranberry, Nola, tr. see Woggon, Guillermo.

Cranch, Christopher P. Three Children's Novels. Little, Greta D. & Myerson, Joel, eds. LC 92-24894. (Illus.). 200p. (gr. 4 up). 1993. 30.00x (0-8203-1507-9) U of Ga Pr.

Crane, Barbara J. The Baby Jay. (Illus.). (gr. k-2). 1977. pap. 4.85 (0-89075-095-5) Bilingual Ed Serv.

—BS 1 Skillbooklet, No. I. (Illus.). (gr. k-2). 1982. pap. text ed. 2.49 ea. (0-89075-031-9) Bilingual Ed Serv.

Crane, Bob, jt. auth. see Golant, Mitch.

Crane, George. Red Badge of Courage. (gr. 4-7). 1993. pap. 4.95 (0-8114-6837-2) Raintree Steck-V.

Crane, Lucy, tr. see Grimm, Jacob & Grimm, Wilhelm K.

Crane, Margaret, ed. Rooms of Our Own: More Stories for Young Feminists. (Illus.). 160p. (gr. 8 up). 1993. 15.95 (0-8050-1616-3, Bks Young Read) H Holt & Co.

Crane, Stephen. Bride Comes to Yellow Sky. Johnson, V. C., illus. 40p. (gr. 6 up). 1982. PLB 13.95s.p. (0-87191-827-7) Creative Ed.

—Maggie & Other Stories. Gemme, F. R., intro. by. (gr. 11 up). 1968. pap. 2.75 (0-8049-0166-X, CL-166) Airmont.

—The Open Boat. Johnson, V. C., illus. 64p. (gr. 6 up). 1982. PLB 13.95s.p. (0-87191-826-9) Creative Ed.

—Reader's Digest Best Loved Books for Young Readers: The Red Badge of Courage. Ogburn, Jackie, ed. Barnett, Isa, illus. 120p. (gr. 4-12). 1989. 3.99 (0-945260-34-2) Choice Pub NY.

—Red Badge of Courage. (gr. 7 up). 1964. pap. 2.25 (0-8049-0003-5, CL-3) Airmont.

—The Red Badge of Courage. Shapiro, Irwin, ed. Cruz, E. R., illus. LC 73-75464. 64p. (Orig.). (gr. 5-10). 1973. pap. 2.95 (0-88301-101-8) Pendulum Pr.

—The Red Badge of Courage. Wright, Betty R., adapted by. Shaw, Charles, illus. LC 81-2611. 48p. (gr. 4 up). 1983. PLB 18.64 (0-8172-1670-7) Raintree Steck-V.

—The Red Badge of Courage. 1990. pap. 2.50 (0-8125-0479-8) Tor Bks.

—The Red Badge of Courage. (Illus.). 224p. 1991. 9.99 (0-517-66844-0) Outlet Bk Co.

—The Red Badge of Courage. (gr. 8). 1989. pap. write for info. (0-663-56259-7) Silver Burdett Pr.

—Red Badge of Courage & Other Writings. Chase, Richard, ed. (gr. 9 up). 1972. pap. 9.16 (0-395-05143-6, RivEd) HM.

Crane, Walter, illus. Favorite Poems of Childhood. LC 92-42770. 1993. 14.00 (0-671-86614-1, Green Tiger) S&S Trade.

Cranfield, Ingrid. Animal World. (Illus.). 64p. (gr. 4-6). 1991. PLB 14.90 (1-56294-008-2) Millbrook Pr.

Cranshaw, Peter. Australia. LC 88-18426. (Illus.). 48p. (gr. 4-8). 1988. PLB 14.98 (0-382-09511-1) Silver Burdett Pr.

Crapps, Joyce W. Who Made These Things? LC 86-18773. (ps). 1987. 5.95 (0-8054-4178-6) Broadman.

Crary, Elizabeth. Finders, Keepers. Strecker, Rebekah, illus. LC 87-60369. 64p. (Orig.). (gr. 2-6). 1987. PLB 16.95 (0-943990-39-4); pap. 5.95 (0-943990-38-6) Parenting Pr.

—I Can't Wait. Horosko, Marina M., illus. LC 82-6277. 32p. (Orig.). (ps-2). 1982. PLB 15.95 (0-9602862-6-8); pap. 4.95 (0-9602862-3-3) Parenting Pr.

—I Want It. Horosko, Marina M., illus. LC 82-2129. 32p. (Orig.). (ps-2). 1982. PLB 15.95 (0-9602862-5-X); pap. 4.95 (0-9602862-2-5) Parenting Pr.

—I Want to Play. Horosko, Marina M., illus. LC 82-3610. 32p. (Orig.). (ps-2). 1982. PLB 15.95 (0-9602862-7-6); pap. 4.95 (0-9602862-4-1) Parenting Pr.

—I'm Excited. Whitney, Jean, illus. LC 93-85378. 32p. (ps-4). 1993. lib. bdg. 16.95 (0-943990-92-0); pap. 5.95 (0-943990-91-2) Parenting Pr.

—I'm Frustrated. LC 90-63870. (ps-3). 1992. PLB 16.95 (0-943990-65-3); pap. 5.95 (0-943990-64-5) Parenting Pr.

—I'm Furious. Whitney, Jean, illus. LC 93-79529. 32p. (ps-4). 1993. lib. bdg. 16.95 (0-943990-94-7); pap. 5.95 (0-943990-93-9) Parenting Pr.

—I'm Lost. Megale, Marina, illus. LC 84-62128. 32p. (Orig.). (ps-2). 1985. PLB 15.95 (0-943990-08-4); pap. 4.95 (0-943990-09-2) Parenting Pr.

—I'm Mad. LC 90-63869. (ps-3). 1992. PLB 16.95 (0-943990-63-7); pap. 5.95 (0-943990-62-9) Parenting Pr.

—I'm Proud. LC 90-63871. (ps-3). 1992. PLB 16.95 (0-943990-67-X); pap. 5.95 (0-943990-66-1) Parenting Pr.

—I'm Scared. Whitney, Jean, illus. LC 93-85377. 32p. (Orig.). (ps-4). 1993. lib. bdg. 16.95 (0-943990-90-4); pap. 5.95 (0-943990-89-0) Parenting Pr.

—Mommy Don't Go. Megale, Marina, illus. LC 85-63759. 32p. (Orig.). (ps-2). 1986. lib. bdg. 15.95 (0-943990-27-0); pap. 4.95 (0-943990-26-2) Parenting Pr.

—My Name Is Not Dummy. Horosko, Marina M., illus. LC 83-24983. 32p. (Orig.). (ps-2). 1983. PLB 15.95 (0-9602862-9-2); pap. 4.95 (0-9602862-8-4) Parenting Pr.

Crary, Ryland, jt. auth. see Cooper, Richard.

Craven. Jaguar: The King of Cats. 1991. 12.50s.p. (0-86593-144-5); PLB 16.67 (0-685-59194-8) Rourke Corp.

—Rolls-Royce: Leader in Luxury. 1991. 12.50s.p. (0-86593-147-X); lib. bdg. 16.67 (0-685-59198-0) Rourke Corp.

Craven, Jerry, jt. auth. see Craven, Linda.

Craven, Linda. Stepfamilies: New Patterns of Harmony. LC 82-60652. (Illus.). 192p. (gr. 7 up). 1983. (J Messner) S&S Trade.

Craven, Linda & Craven, Jerry. Japanese Sports Cars. LC 93-14917. (Illus.). (gr. 5 up). 1993. write for info. (0-86593-256-5) Rourke Corp.

—Mustang: Ford's Wild Pony. LC 93-20243. (gr. 7-8). 1993. 17.26 (0-86593-255-7); 12.95s.p. (0-685-66591-7) Rourke Corp.

Craven, Margaret. I Heard the Owl Call My Name. (gr. 7 up). 1980. pap. 4.99 (0-440-34369-0, LE) Dell.

Craver, Mike. Beaver Ball at the Bug Club. Kaghan, Joan, illus. 32p. (ps-3). 1992. bds. 12.00 (0-374-30662-1) FS&G.

Crawford, A. F., ed. see Brooks, Rebecca.

Crawford, Ann F. Jane Long - Frontier Woman. Baxter, Rosario, illus. 64p. (gr. 4-7). 1990. lib. bdg. 12.95 (0-87443-090-9) Benson.

—Lizzie - Queen of the Cattle Trails. Fain, Cheryl G., illus. 64p. (gr. 4-7). 1990. lib. bdg. 12.95 (0-87443-091-7) Benson.

—New Life, New Land: Women in Early Texas. (Illus.). 48p. 1986. 9.95 (0-89015-560-7, Pub. by Panda Bks) Eakin-Sunbelt.

Crawford, Diane M. Comedy of Errors. (gr. 4-7). 1992. pap. 2.99 (0-553-29457-1) Bantam.

—Cowboy Kisses. 1993. pap. 2.99 (0-553-29984-0) Bantam.

Crawford, Elizabeth, tr. see Claverie, Jean.

Crawford, Elizabeth, tr. see Siegenthaler, Kathrin.

Crawford, Elizabeth D., tr. see Gehrts, Barbara.

Crawford, Elizabeth D., tr. see Grimm, Jacob & Grimm, Wilhelm K.

Crawford, Elizabeth D., tr. see Hartling, Peter.

Crawford, Elizabeth D., tr. see Kordon, Klaus.

Crawford, Elizabeth D., tr. see Mitgutsch, Ali.

Crawford, Elizabeth D., tr. see Prochazkova, Iva.

Crawford, F. Marion. Nightmare Ship. Richardson, I. M., adapted by. Toulmin-Rothe, Ann, illus. LC 81-21805. 32p. (gr. 5-10). 1982. PLB 10.79 (0-89375-632-6); pap. text ed. 2.95 (0-89375-633-4) Troll Assocs.

Crawford, Gail & Renna, Giani. Albert Schweitzer. (Illus.). 104p. (gr. 5-8). 1990. 16.98 (0-382-09976-1); pap. 8.95 (0-382-24003-0) Silver Burdett Pr.

Crawford, J., et al. Century Twenty-One Typewriting: Complete Course, 4 vols. 3rd, large type ed. 1008p. (gr. 9-12). 1982. Set. 125.00 (0-317-01878-7, J-03580-00) Am Printing Hse.

Crawford, Jane, jt. auth. see Veitch, Carol J.

Crawford, Jean, ed. Amazing Facts. LC 93-11599. (Illus.). 88p. (gr. k-3). 1994. write for info. (0-8094-9458-2); PLB write for info. (0-8094-9459-0) Time-Life.

Crawford, Jean B., ed. Pterodactyl Tunnel: Amusement Park Math. (Illus.). 64p. (gr. k-2). 1993. write for info. (0-8094-9990-8) Time-Life.

Crawford, Jean B., ed. see Time Life Inc. Editors.

Crawford, Jean B., et al, eds. see Time Life Inc. Editors.

Crawford, Jean B., et al, eds. see Time-Life Inc. Editors.

Crawford, Jearn, ed. Ecology. LC 93-28657. (Illus.). 88p. (gr. k-3). 1994. write for info. (0-8094-9466-3); PLB write for info. (0-8094-9467-1) Time-Life.

Crawford, Kenneth & Simmons, Paul. Growing up with Sex. 80p. (gr. 7-9). 1973. pap. 6.95 (0-8054-5312-1) Broadman.

Crawford, Lucy. Supervisory Skills in Marketing. Dorr, Eugene L., ed. (Illus.). (gr. 9-10). 1977. text ed. 12.28 (0-07-013471-5) McGraw.

Crawford, Marc, jt. auth. see Katz, William L.

Crawford, Maureen. Handmade Greeting Cards. LC 90-28753. (Illus.). 136p. (gr. 6 up). 1992. pap. 9.95 (0-8069-8327-2) Sterling.

Crawford, Ron. Bike. LC 92-42986. 1993. 12.00 (0-671-87002-5, Green Tiger); pap. 3.95 (0-671-87003-3, Green Tiger) S&S Trade.

—Pet. LC 92-18600. (gr. 1 up). 1993. POB 12.00 (0-671-79675-5, Green Tiger); pap. 3.95 (0-671-79335-7, Green Tiger) S&S Trade.

Crawford, Thomas. Pig Who Saved the Day. (Illus.). (gr. 3-4). 1972. pap. 1.95 (0-89375-049-2) Troll Assocs.

—Rooster Who Refused to Crow. (Illus.). (gr. 3-4). 1972. pap. 1.95 (0-89375-050-6) Troll Assocs.

Craycraft, Ken, jt. auth. see Warner, Laverne.

Craycraft, Kenneth, jt. auth. see Warner, Laverne.

Craymer, Sally. There's a Blue Square on My Brother's School Bus. LC 92-61768. (Illus.). 59p. (Orig.). (gr. k-2). 1992. pap. 4.95x (0-931563-12-7) Wishing Rm.

Creasy, Rosalind. Blue Potatoes, Orange Tomatoes: How to Grow a Rainbow Garden. Heller, Ruth, illus. LC 92-38800. (gr. 4 up). 1994. write for info. (0-87156-576-5) Sierra.

Crebbin, June. Fly by Night. Lambert, Stephen, illus. LC 92-53140. 32p. (ps-3). 1993. 14.95 (1-56402-149-1) Candlewick Pr.

Creech, Sharon. Walk Two Moons. LC 93-31277. 1994. 14.00 (0-06-023334-6, Festival); PLB 13.89 (0-06-023337-0, Festival) HarpC Child Bks.

Creedon, Sharon. A Look over the Edge. Waterline, Wendy, illus. 16p. (gr. k-4). 1987. pap. 5.95 (0-9620446-0-1) Sunset Mktg.

Creighton, J. Maybe a Monster. (Illus.). 24p. (ps-8). 1989. 12.95 (1-55037-037-5, Pub. by Annick CN); pap. 4.95 (1-55037-036-7, Pub. by Annick CN) Firefly Bks Ltd.

—One Day There Was Nothing to Do. (Illus.). 24p. (ps-8). 1990. PLB 14.95 (1-55037-091-X, Pub. by Annick CN); pap. 4.95 (1-55037-090-1, Pub. by Annick CN) Firefly Bks Ltd.

Creighton, Jill & Creighton, Robert. The Weaver's Horse. (gr. 2-4). 1991. 15.95 (*1-55037-181-9*, Pub. by Annick CN); pap. 5.95 (*1-55037-178-9*, Pub. by Annick CN) Firefly Bks Ltd.

Creighton, Robert, jt. auth. see Creighton, Jill.

Creighton, Susan. Funny Cars. LC 87-29016. (Illus.). 48p. (gr. 5-6). 1988. RSBE 11.95 (*0-89686-362-X*, Crestwood Hse) Macmillan Child Grp.

—The Giant Lizard. LC 88-16128. (Illus.). 48p. (gr. 5-6). 1988. RSBE 12.95 (*0-89686-394-8*, Crestwood Hse) Macmillan Child Grp.

—Greg Norman. LC 87-27565. (Illus.). 48p. (gr. 5-6). 1988. RSBE 11.95 (*0-89686-371-9*, Crestwood Hse) Macmillan Child Grp.

—A Hug from the Heart. (ps-3). 1985. 3.50 (*0-910313-92-X*) Parker Bros.

—Huggins & Kisses. Kong, Emilie, illus. 40p. (ps). 1985. 4.00 (*0-910313-94-6*) Parker Bros.

—Hugs from the Heart. Ewers, Joe, illus. 32p. (ps-3). 1985. pap. 0.99 (*0-87372-005-9*) Parker Bros.

Crelinsten, J. To the Limit. 1992. write for info. (*0-15-200616-8*, Gulliver Bks) HarBrace.

Crenshaw, Gwendolyn J., jt. auth. see AESOP Enterprises, Inc. Staff.

Crenson, Victoria, jt. auth. see Smith, Kathie B.

Crescenti, Peter. Alice Kramden's Guide to Handling a Hard-Headed Husband. 160p. (Orig.). 1992. pap. 5.95 (*1-55853-176-9*) Rutledge Hill Pr.

—Ed Norton's Secrets to the Meaning of Life. 160p. (Orig.). 1992. pap. 5.95 (*1-55853-177-7*) Rutledge Hill Pr.

—Hey, There, Ralphie Boy! (Illus.). 160p. (gr. 5 up). 1992. pap. 5.95 (*1-55853-178-5*) Rutledge Hill Pr.

Crespi, Frances. Christmas Decorations. 16p. 1992. pap. 7.95 (*0-8249-8529-X*, Ideals Child) Hambleton-Hill.

Crespo, George. How the Sea Began. Crespo, George, illus. 32p. (gr. k-3). 1993. 14.95 (*0-395-63033-9*, Clarion Bks) HM.

Cresswall, Helen. The Weather Cat. rev. ed. Walker, Barbara, illus. 32p. (gr. k-2). 1990. Repr. of 1989 ed. PLB 10.50 (*1-878363-06-9*) Forest Hse.

Cresswell, Helen. Bagthorpes Abroad: Being the Fifth Part of The Bagthorpe Saga. LC 84-7125. 180p. (gr. 5-9). 1984. SBE 14.95 (*0-02-725390-2*, Macmillan Child Bk) Macmillan Child Grp.

—Bagthorpes Haunted. (gr. 3-7). 1988. pap. 3.95 (*0-14-032172-1*, Puffin) Puffin Bks.

—Bagthorpes Haunted: Being the Sixth Part of the Bagthorpe Saga. LC 85-42798. 192p. (gr. 5-9). 1985. SBE 14.95 (*0-02-725380-5*, Macmillan Child Bk) Macmillan Child Grp.

—Bagthorpes Liberated. LC 89-2434. 192p. (gr. 5 up). 1989. SBE 14.95 (*0-02-725441-0*, Macmillan Child Bk) Macmillan Child Grp.

—Bagthorpes vs. the World: Being the Fourth Part of the Bagthorpe Saga. LC 79-13260. 204p. (gr. 5 up). 1979. SBE 14.95 (*0-02-725420-8*, Macmillan Child Bk) Macmillan Child Grp.

—Lizzie Dripping & the Witch. large type ed. Riddell, Chris, illus. 160p. 1993. 13.95 (*0-7451-1681-7*, Galaxy Child Lrg Print) Chivers N Amer.

—Meet Posy Bates. large type ed. Aldous, Kate, illus. 120p. 1991. 13.95 (*0-7451-1404-0*, Galaxy Child Lrg Print) Chivers N Amer.

—Meet Posy Bates. Aldous, Kate, illus. LC 91-24481. 96p. (gr. 1-4). 1992. SBE 12.95 (*0-02-725375-9*, Macmillan Child Bk) Macmillan Child Grp.

—Moondial. LC 87-5626. 208p. (gr. 5-9). 1987. SBE 14.95 (*0-02-725370-8*, Macmillan Child Bk) Macmillan Child Grp.

—The Night-Watchmen. large type ed. 168p. (gr. 3-7). 1990. 13.95 (*0-7451-1102-5*, Galaxy Child Lrg Print) Chivers N Amer.

—Ordinary Jack. (gr. 3-7). 1987. pap. 3.95 (*0-14-031176-9*, Puffin) Puffin Bks.

—Ordinary Jack: Being the First Part of the Bagthorpe Saga. LC 77-5146. 192p. (gr. 5 up). 1977. SBE 14.95 (*0-02-725540-9*, Macmillan Child Bk) Macmillan Child Grp.

—Posy Bates, Again! Aldous, Kate, illus. LC 93-5789. 112p. (gr. k-4). 1994. SBE 13.95 (*0-02-725372-4*, Macmillan Child Bk) Macmillan Child Grp.

—The Secret World of Polly Flint. Felts, Shirley, illus. LC 91-15531. 176p. (gr. 3-7). 1991. pap. 3.95 (*0-689-71532-3*, Aladdin) Macmillan Child Grp.

—Time Out. Elwell, Peter, illus. LC 89-36798. 80p. (gr. 2-5). 1990. SBE 13.95 (*0-02-725425-9*, Macmillan Child Bk) Macmillan Child Grp.

Cresswell, Helen & Brown, Judy. Almost Goodbye. LC 91-33464. (Illus.). 64p. (gr. 2-5). 1992. 11.00 (*0-525-44858-6*, DCB) Dutton Child Bks.

Creswick, Paul. Robin Hood. Wyeth, N. C., illus. LC 92-50796. 376p. (gr. 6 up). 1993. 16.95 (*1-56138-265-5*) Running Pr.

Cretan, Gladys. Joey's Head. Sims, Blanche, illus. LC 90-41592. 48p. (gr. 2-4). 1991. pap. 13.95 jacketed (*0-671-73201-3*, S&S BFYR) S&S Trade.

—Joey's Head. Sims, Blanche, illus. LC 90-41592. 48p. (gr. 2-4). 1993. pap. 2.95 (*0-671-86699-0*, Half Moon Bks) S&S Trade.

Crew, Gary. Strange Objects. LC 92-30519. 224p. (gr. 5-9). 1993. pap. 14.00 JR3 (*0-671-79759-X*, S&S BFYR) S&S Trade.

Crew, Linda. Children of the River. LC 88-20401. (gr. 7 up). 1989. 14.95 (*0-440-50122-9*) Delacorte.

—Children of the River. (gr. 7 up). 1991. pap. 3.50 (*0-440-21022-4*, LFL) Dell.

—Nekomah Creek. LC 90-49119. 192p. (gr. 4-5). 1991. 14.00 (*0-385-30442-0*) Delacorte.

—Nekomah Creek. (gr. 4-7). 1993. pap. 3.50 (*0-440-40788-5*) Dell.

—Someday I'll Laugh about This. 176p. (gr. 5-9). 1992. pap. 3.25 (*0-440-40679-X*, YB) Dell.

Crews, Donald. Award Puzzles: Freight Train. 1991. 5.95 (*0-938971-70-0*) JTG Nashville.

—Bicycle Race. LC 84-27912. (Illus.). 24p. (ps-1). 1985. 16.00 (*0-688-05171-5*); lib. bdg. 15.93 (*0-688-05172-3*) Greenwillow.

—Bigmama's. Crews, Donald, illus. LC 90-33142. 32p. (ps up). 1991. 15.00 (*0-688-09950-5*); PLB 13.88 (*0-688-09951-3*) Greenwillow.

—Bigmama's. Crews, Donald, illus. (gr. 4-4). 1993. text ed. 3.95 (*0-685-64817-6*); audio cass. 11.00 (*1-882869-75-3*) Read Advent.

—Carousel. Crews, Donald, illus. LC 82-3062. 32p. (ps-1). 1982. PLB 13.88 (*0-688-00909-3*) Greenwillow.

—Flying. Crews, Donald, illus. LC 85-27022. 32p. (ps-3). 1986. 14.95 (*0-688-04318-6*); PLB 14.88 (*0-688-04319-4*) Greenwillow.

—Flying. LC 85-27022. 32p. (ps-3). 1989. pap. 4.95 (*0-688-09235-7*, Mulberry) Morrow.

—Freight Train. LC 78-2303. (Illus.). 32p. (gr. k-3). 1978. 16.00 (*0-688-80165-X*); PLB 14.88 (*0-688-84165-1*) Greenwillow.

—Freight Train. LC 78-2303. (Illus.). 24p. (ps up). 1992. pap. 3.95 (*0-688-11701-5*, Mulberry) Morrow.

—Freight Train: Big Book Edition. (ps-3). 1993. pap. 18.95 (*0-688-12940-4*, Mulberry) Morrow.

—Harbor. Crews, Donald, illus. LC 81-6607. 32p. (ps-1). 1982. 11.75 (*0-688-00861-5*); PLB 14.93 (*0-688-00862-3*) Greenwillow.

—Harbor. LC 81-6607. (ps-1). 1987. pap. 3.95 (*0-688-07332-8*, Mulberry) Morrow.

—Light. LC 80-20273. (Illus.). 32p. (ps-1). 1981. PLB 13.88 (*0-688-00310-9*) Greenwillow.

—Parade. Crews, Donald, illus. LC 82-20927. 32p. (gr. k-3). 1983. 14.00 (*0-688-01995-1*); PLB 13.93 (*0-688-01996-X*) Greenwillow.

—Parade. LC 82-20927. (Illus.). (ps-3). 1986. 3.95 (*0-688-06520-1*, Mulberry) Morrow.

—School Bus. Crews, Donald, illus. LC 83-18681. 32p. (gr. k-3). 1984. 15.00 (*0-688-02807-1*); PLB 14.93 (*0-688-02808-X*) Greenwillow.

—School Bus. LC 85-576. (Illus.). 32p. (ps-1). 1985. pap. 3.99 (*0-14-050549-0*, Puffin) Puffin Bks.

—School Bus. LC 92-43766. (Illus.). 32p. (ps up). 1993. pap. text ed. 4.95 (*0-688-12267-1*, Mulberry) Morrow.

—Shortcut. LC 91-36312. (Illus.). 32p. (ps-6). 1992. 14.00 (*0-688-06436-1*); PLB 13.93 (*0-688-06437-X*) Greenwillow.

—Ten Black Dots. rev. ed. Crews, Donald, illus. LC 85-14871. 32p. (ps-3). 1986. 15.00 (*0-688-06067-6*); PLB 14.93 (*0-688-06068-4*) Greenwillow.

—Truck. LC 79-19031. (Illus.). 32p. (ps-2). 1980. 14.00 (*0-688-80244-3*); PLB 13.93 (*0-688-84244-5*) Greenwillow.

—Truck. LC 84-18137. (Illus.). 32p. (ps). 1985. pap. 3.95 (*0-14-050506-7*, Puffin) Puffin Bks.

—Truck. LC 79-19031. (Illus.). 32p. (ps-3). 1991. pap. 3.95 (*0-688-10481-9*, Mulberry) Morrow.

—Truck. enl. ed. Crews, Donald, illus. 32p. (ps up). 1993. pap. 18.95 (*0-688-12611-1*, Mulberry) Morrow.

—We Read: A to Z. Crews, Donald, illus. LC 83-25453. 64p. (ps-1). 1984. 15.95 (*0-688-03843-3*); PLB 15.88 (*0-688-03844-1*) Greenwillow.

Cribb, Joe. Money. British Museum, illus. LC 89-15589. 64p. (gr. 5 up). 1990. 13.95 (*0-679-80438-2*); PLB 15.99 (*0-679-90438-7*) Knopf Bks Yng Read.

Cribbs, Dianna G. A Kid's Guide to Fishing & Fun Things to Do! Cribbs, Dianna G., illus. 113p. (gr. 1-5). 1990. pap. 6.95 (*0-943487-27-7*) Sevgo Pr.

Crichton, Michael. Dinosaurs of Jurassic Park: An All Aboard Reading Book. (ps-3). 1993. pap. 3.50 (*0-448-40178-9*, Platt & Munk Pubs) Putnam Pub Group.

—Jurassic Park: The Movie Storybook. (Illus.). 1993. pap. 7.95 (*0-448-40173-8*, G&D) Putnam Pub Group.

—Jurassic Park: The Novelization. 96p. (Orig.). (gr. 4-7). 1993. pap. 3.95 (*0-448-40172-X*, G&D) Putnam Pub Group.

—Raptor Attack: A Three-D Storybook. (ps-3). 1993. pap. 6.95 (*0-448-40174-6*, Platt & Monk Pubs) Putnam Pub Group.

Crider, Bill. A Vampire Named Fred. Shaw, Charles, illus. Alter, Judy, intro. by. LC 89-14524. (Illus.). 176p. (Orig.). (gr. 4-9). 1990. pap. 5.95 (*0-936650-11-7*) E C Temple.

Crifasi, Kathleen. Woodley Rides the Subway Train. LC 87-62212. 54p. (ps-4). 1987. pap. 6.95 (*0-932433-30-8*) Windswept Hse.

Crikshank, G., tr. see Grimm, Jacob & Grimm, Wilhelm K.

Crillis, Carla, illus. I Can Help. 14p. (ps). 1991. Repr. bds. 5.50 (*0-86315-123-X*) Gryphon Hse.

Crilly, Eileen & Morris, Stephanie. Get Ready, Set, Grow. LC 84-60318. (ps). 1984. pap. 11.95 (*0-8224-5858-6*) Fearon Teach Aids.

Criminale, Ulrike & The Langauge School of the American Cultural Exchange. Springboard to German: Introduction to the German Language. Porter, Mary D., illus. 32p. (gr. k-4).

1991. Incl. cassettes. 19.95 (*1-880770-01-6*) ACE Pub.
SPRINGBOARD is a set of easy, encouraging foreign language lessons for young children ages 4-8. This popular series features two 90-minute cassette tapes on which a native speaker of the foreign language leads the child in short, playful sessions through a variety of actions by repeating simple commands both in the foreign language & in English. The child is not required to read or write the language. Instead, the language is absorbed almost effortlessly as the child enjoys a progression of music, games & activities. The program emphasizes well-planned lessons for the adult leader & can be enjoyed by anyone in the home setting as well as in class. Because the cassettes guide the activity, the adult is not required to know the language, but instead simply participates with the child. The accompanying Springboard books provide attractive illustrations & a word-for-word transcript of the cassettes along with a comprehensive Vocabulary Chart for review & an Activities Supplement with suggestions for further learning. The Series is available in French, German & Spanish, & will soon be available in Japanese.
Publisher Provided Annotation.

Criminale, Ulrike & The Language School of the American Cultural Exchange Staff. Springboard to French: Introduction to the French Language. rev. ed. Porter, Mary D., illus. 32p. (gr. k-4). 1991. Incl. cassettes. 19.95 (*1-880770-00-8*) ACE Pub.
SPRINGBOARD is a set of easy, encouraging foreign language lessons for young children ages 4-8. This popular series features two 90-minute cassettes on which a native speaker of the foreign language leads the child in short, playful sessions through a variety of actions by repeating simple commands in both the foreign language & in English. The child is not required to read or write the language. Instead, the language is absorbed almost effortlessly as the child enjoys a progression of music, games & activities. The program emphasizes well-planned lessons for the adult leader & can be enjoyed by anyone in the home setting as well as in class. Because the cassettes guide the activity, the adult is not required to know the language, but instead simply participates with the child. The accompanying Springboard books provide attractive illustrations & a word-for-word transcript of the cassettes along with a comprehensive Vocabulary Chart for review & an Activities Supplement with suggestions for further learning. The Series is available in French, German & Spanish, & will soon be available in Japanese.
Publisher Provided Annotation.

—Springboard to Spanish: Introduction to the Spanish Language. rev. ed.

Porter, Mary D., illus. (gr. k-4). 1991. Incl. cassettes. 19.95 (*1-880770-02-4*) ACE Pub. SPRINGBOARD is a set of easy, encouraging foreign language lessons for young children ages 4-8. This popular series features two 90-minute cassette tapes on which a native speaker of the foreign language leads the child in short, playful sessions through a variety of actions by repeating simple commands in both the foreign langauge & in English. The child is not required to read or write the language. Instead, the language is absorbed almost effortlessly as the child enjoys a progression of music, games & activities. The program emphasizes well-planned lessons for the adult leader & can be enjoyed by anyone in the home setting as well as in class. Because the cassettes guide the activity, the adult is not required to know the language, but instead simply participates with the child. The accompanying Springboard books provide attractive illustrations & a word-for-word transcript of the cassettes along with a comprehensive Vocabulary Chart for review & an Activities Supplement with suggestions for further learning. The Series is available in French, German & Spanish &, will soon be available in Japanese. *Publisher Provided Annotation.*

Cripwell, Kenneth. Language. Yapp, Malcolm, et al, eds. (Illus.). (gr. 6-11). 1980. pap. text ed. 3.45 (*0-89908-121-5*) Greenhaven.

Crisci, Elizabeth W. Five-Minute Bible Fun, Closing Activities. 96p. (ps-5). 1990. 10.95 (*0-86653-522-5*, SS1819, Shining Star Pubns) Good Apple.

Criscuolo, Nicholas P. & Herman, Barry. Fun With Words. (gr. 2-5). 1988. pap. 8.95 (*0-8224-3172-6*) Fearon Teach Aids.

Crisfield, Deborah. An Air Show Adventure. Emmerich, Donald, illus. LC 89-34372. 32p. (gr. 3-6). 1990. PLB 10.79 (*0-8167-1735-4*); pap. text ed. 2.95 (*0-8167-1736-2*) Troll Assocs.
—The Amityville Horror. LC 91-4528. (Illus.). 48p. (gr. 5-6). 1991. RSBE 13.95 (*0-89686-576-2*, Crestwood Hse) Macmillan Child Grp.
—Dysfunctional Families. LC 91-22088. (Illus.). 48p. (gr. 5-6). 1992. RSBE 11.95 (*0-89686-722-6*, Crestwood Hse) Macmillan Child Grp.
—Eating Disorders. LC 93-5538. 1994. write for info. (*0-89686-807-9*, Crestwood Hse) Macmillan Child Grp.
—Gambling. LC 90-47961. (Illus.). 48p. (gr. 5-6). 1991. RSBE 12.95 (*0-89686-607-6*, Crestwood Hse) Macmillan Child Grp.
—Jaws. LC 90-47941. (Illus.). 48p. (gr. 5-6). 1991. RSBE 13.95 (*0-89686-578-9*, Crestwood Hse) Macmillan Child Grp.
—Literacy. LC 91-39567. (Illus.). 48p. (gr. 5-6). 1992. RSBE 12.95 (*0-89686-750-1*, Crestwood Hse) Macmillan Child Grp.
—Sports Injuries. (Illus.). 48p. (gr. 5-6). 1991. RSBE 12.95 (*0-89686-663-7*, Crestwood Hse) Macmillan Child Grp.
—Travel. LC 93-15211. (Illus.). 48p. (gr. 5-6). 1994. RSBE 14.95 (*0-89686-790-0*, Crestwood Hse) Macmillan Child Grp.

Crisman, Ruth. Hot Off the Press: Getting the News into Print. (Illus.). 80p. (gr. 4 up). 1990. PLB 17.50 (*0-8225-1625-X*) Lerner Pubns.
—Racing the Iditarod Trail. LC 92-25870. (Illus.). 72p. (gr. 5 up). 1993. RSBE 14.95 (*0-87518-523-1*, Dillon) Macmillan Child Grp.
—Thomas Jefferson, Man with a Vision. (gr. 4-7). 1992. pap. 2.95 (*0-590-44553-7*) Scholastic Inc.

Crisp, George. Salvador Dali: Spanish Painter. (Illus.). (ps-3). 1994. PLB 18.95 (*0-7910-1778-8*, Am Art Analog) Chelsea Hse.

Crist, Harold L. Twice a Hero. 112p. (Orig.). 1990. pap. 5.95 (*0-9621743-1-9*) H L Crist.

Cristaldi, Kathryn. Babar in the Jungle. Fritz, Ronald, illus. LC 88-63342. 32p. (Orig.). (ps-3). 1989. pap. 1.50 (*0-679-80215-0*) Random Bks Yng Read.
—Baseball Ballerina. Carter, Abby, illus. LC 90-20234. 48p. (Orig.). (gr. 1-3). 1992. PLB 7.99 (*0-679-91734-9*); pap. 3.50 (*0-679-81734-4*) Random Bks Yng Read.
—The Secret Garden. (Illus.). (ps-3). 1993. pap. 2.95 (*0-590-47170-8*) Scholastic Inc.

Cristall, Barbara. Coping When a Parent Has Multiple Sclerosis. Rosen, Ruth, ed. (gr. 7-12). 1992. 13.95 (*0-8239-1406-2*) Rosen Group.

Cristini, Ermanno & Puricelli, Luigi. In My Garden. Cristini, Ermanno & Puricelli, Luigi, illus. LC 85-9402. 28p. (ps up). 1991. pap. 12.95 (*0-907234-05-4*) Picture Bk Studio.
—In the Pond. Cristini, Ermanno & Puricelli, Luigi, illus. LC 84-972. 28p. (ps up). 1991. pap. 12.95 (*0-907234-43-7*) Picture Bk Studio.
—In the Woods. Cristini, Ermanno & Puricelli, Luigi, illus. LC 83-8153. 28p. (ps up). 1991. pap. 12.95 (*0-907234-31-3*) Picture Bk Studio.

Croall, Stephen, tr. see Lindstrom, Eva.

Crocitto, Jane B., jt. auth. see Bullock, Gloria S.

Crocker, Chris. Cyndi Lauper. Arico, Diane, ed. (Illus.). 64p. (gr. 3-7). 1985. 9.29 (*0-685-09958-X*) S&S Trade.
—Wham! Arico, Diane, ed. (Illus.). 64p. (gr. 3-7). 1985. lib. bdg. 8.79 (*0-685-10386-2*); pap. 3.50 (*0-685-10387-0*) S&S Trade.

Crockett, Davy. Davy Crockett's Own Story: A Narrative of the Life of David Crockett of the State of Tennessee. LC 93-34222. (Illus.). 128p. 1993. pap. 12.95 (*1-55709-218-4*) Applewood.

Crofford, Emily. Born in the Year of Courage. 184p. (gr. 4-6). 1991. PLB 19.95 (*0-87614-679-5*) Carolrhoda Bks.
—Frontier Surgeons: A Story about the Mayo Brothers. Ritz, Karen, illus. 64p. (gr. 3-6). 1989. PLB 14.95 (*0-87614-381-8*) Carolrhoda Bks.
—Frontier Surgeons: A Story about the Mayo Brothers. (ps-3). 1991. pap. 4.95 (*0-87614-553-5*) Carolrhoda Bks.
—Great Auk. LC 89-31576. (Illus.). 48p. (gr. 5-6). 1989. RSBE 12.95 (*0-89686-459-6*, Crestwood Hse) Macmillan Child Grp.
—Healing Warrior: A Story about Sister Elizabeth Kenny. Ritz, Karen, illus. 64p. (gr. 3-6). 1989. PLB 14.95 (*0-87614-382-6*) Carolrhoda Bks.
—A Matter of Pride. LaMarche, Jim, illus. LC 81-387. 48p. (gr. 2-6). 1991. Repr. of 1981 ed. PLB 17.50 (*0-87614-171-8*, AACR2) Carolrhoda Bks.
—Opossum. LC 89-28269. (Illus.). 48p. (gr. 5 up). 1990. RSBE 12.95 (*0-89686-518-5*, Crestwood Hse) Macmillan Child Grp.
—A Place to Belong. LC 93-9289. 1993. 19.95 (*0-87614-808-9*) Carolrhoda Bks.
—Stories from the Blue Road. Nobens, C. A., illus. LC 81-21229. 168p. (gr. 4-8). 1981. PLB 13.50 (*0-87614-189-0*) Carolrhoda Bks.

Croft, Karen. Good for Me Cookbook. (Illus.). (gr. k-5). 1971. pap. 3.95 (*0-88247-177-5*) R & E Pubs.

Crofts, Trudy & Childers, Peggy, illus. The Hunter & the Quail. 32p. (gr. 1-6). 1993. pap. 7.95 (*0-89800-250-8*) Dharma Pub.

Croil, Marianne. Superfudge: A Study Guide. Friedland, Joyce & Kessler, Rikki, eds. (gr. 2-5). 1991. pap. text ed. 14.95 (*0-88122-574-6*) LRN Links.

Croix, Alice de La see De La Croix, Alice.

Croker, T. Crofton. Irish Folk Stories for Children. 1991. pap. 10.95 (*0-85342-919-7*) Dufour.

Croll, Carolyn. Too Many Babas. newly illus. ed. Croll, Carolyn, illus. LC 92-18779. 64p. (gr. k-3). 1979. 14.00 (*0-06-021383-3*); PLB 13.89 (*0-06-021384-1*) HarpC Child Bks.
—Too Many Babas. newly illus. ed. Croll, Carolyn, illus. LC 92-18779. 64p. (gr. k-4). 1994. pap. 3.50 (*0-06-444168-7*, Trophy) HarpC Child Bks.

Croll, Carolyn, adapted by. & illus. The Little Snowgirl. 32p. (ps-k). 1989. 14.95 (*0-39-21691-X*, Putnam) Putnam Pub Group.
—The Three Brothers: A German Folktale. (ps-3). 1991. 14.95 (*0-399-22195-6*, Whitebird Bks) Putnam Pub Group.

Cromack, Celeste, ed. see Renfro, Nancy.

Cromie, William. Skylab: The Story of Man's First Station in Space. LC 74-25983. (Illus.). 192p. (gr. 7 up). 1976. pap. 10.95 (*0-679-20300-1*) McKay.

Crompton, Anne E. The Snow Pony. 128p. (gr. 4-6). 1991. 14.95 (*0-8050-1573-6*, Bks Young Read) H Holt & Co.

Crompton, T., illus. The Good Samaritan: Retold by Catherine Storr. 32p. (gr. k-4). 1984. 14.65 (*0-8172-1988-9*, Raintree Childrens Books Belitha Press Ltd. - London) Raintree Steck-V.

Cron, Mary. Magic Penny Puzzlers, No. 4. (Illus.). 48p. 1990. pap. 2.95 (*0-8431-2754-6*) Price Stern.
—Monster Math Workbook. Cherbak, Yvonne, illus. 48p. (Orig.). (gr. 1-3). 1993. pap. 2.95 (*1-56565-030-1*) Lowell Hse.
—More Phonics Fun: Crossword Puzzles. McMahan, Kelly, illus. 48p. (Orig.). (gr. k-2). 1989. pap. 2.95 incl. chipboard (*0-8431-2358-3*) Price Stern.

Cronin, A. J. The Citadel. 1983. 16.45 (*0-316-16158-6*); pap. 9.95i (*0-316-16183-7*) Little.

Cronin, Gaynell B. The Forgiveness of the Lord. LC 93-72557. (Illus.). 64p. (Orig.). (gr. 2-3). 1993. pap. 4.50 (*0-87793-516-5*); 4.50 (*0-87793-518-1*); family bk. 3.50 (*0-87793-515-7*) Ave Maria.
—The Table of the Lord. LC 86-70131. (Illus., Orig.). (gr. 1-3). 1986. Child's Bk, 104 pgs. pap. text ed. 4.50 (*0-87793-299-9*); Director's Manual, 168 pgs. spiral 9.75 (*0-87793-325-1*); Family Bk., 96p. 3.50 (*0-87793-326-X*) Ave Maria.

Cronin, Gaynell B. & Bellina, Joan. Together at Mass. Murtagh, Betty, illus. LC 87-70417. 32p. (Orig.). (ps-2). 1987. pap. 2.95 (*0-87793-357-X*) Ave Maria.

Crook, Carol. Enter-Praise-Worship. (Illus.). 9p. (Orig.). (gr. 7 up). 1988. pap. 0.75x (*0-939399-03-2*) Bks of Truth.
—Overflowing with Love. 19p. (Orig.). (gr. 7 up). 1989. pap. 0.95x (*0-939399-06-7*) Bks of Truth.
—Thoughts Turn to Actions. 7p. (Orig.). (gr. 5 up). 1989. pap. 0.75x (*0-939399-10-5*) Bks of Truth.

Crook, Marion. Teenagers Talk about Adoption. 116p. (Orig.). (gr. 6 up). 1990. pap. 10.95 (*1-55021-047-5*, Pub. by NC Press CN) U of Toronto Pr.
—Teenagers Talk about Suicide. 128p. (gr. 7-12). 1988. pap. 12.95 (*1-55021-013-0*, Pub. by NC Press CN) U of Toronto Pr.
—Teenagers Talk about Suicide. 2nd ed. (gr. 9-12). 1989. pap. 10.95 (*1-55021-052-1*, Pub. by NC Pr Ltd) Seven Hills Bk Dists.

Croome, Angela. Hovercraft. Wilkinson, Gerald, illus. (gr. 5 up). 1962. 14.95 (*0-8392-3008-7*) Astor-Honor.

Crosbie, Karol. Mom & Me. (Illus., Orig.). (gr. 7-12). 1989. pap. 3.95 (*0-945485-13-1*) Comm Intervention.

Crosbie, Michael J. & Rosenthal, Steve. Architecture Colors. (Illus.). 26p. (ps). 1993. 6.95 (*0-89133-212-X*) Preservation Pr.
—Architecture Counts. (Illus.). 26p. (ps). 1993. 6.95 (*0-89133-213-8*) Preservation Pr.
—Architecture Shapes. (Illus.). 26p. (ps). 1993. 6.95 (*0-89133-211-1*) Preservation Pr.

Crosby, Harriet, ed. see Kelly, Karla, et al.

Crosby, Nina E. & Marten, Elizabeth H. Don't Teach Let Me Learn about Aerodynamics, Robots & Computers, Science Fiction & Astronomy. (Illus.). 80p. (Orig.). (gr. 3-10). 1979. pap. 8.95 (*0-914634-60-7*, 7902) DOK Pubs.
—Don't Teach! Let Me Learn about Fantasy, Magic, Monkeys & Monsters. Rossi, Richard, illus. 72p. (Orig.). (gr. 3-10). 1984. 8.95 (*0-88047-045-3*, 8410) DOK Pubs.
—Don't Teach Let Me Learn: About Mysteries, Mythology, Fairy Tales, Fables, Legends, the Supernatural. Zilliox, illus. 72p. (gr. 3-6). 1978. 8.95 (*0-88047-006-2*, 8209) DOK Pubs.
—Don't Teach Let Me Learn: About Nutrition, Chemistry, Medicine, Nursing. Sturckler, Joe, illus. 72p. (gr. 3-6). 1983. 8.95 (*0-88047-030-5*, 8313) DOK Pubs.
—Don't Teach Let Me Learn: About Opera, Ballet, American Theatre, Cinema. Zilliox, illus. 72p. (gr. 3-6). 1983. 8.95 (*0-88047-008-9*, 8210) DOK Pubs.
—Don't Teach Let Me Learn about Presidents, of the U. S. People, Genealogy, Immigrants. (Illus.). 80p. (Orig.). (gr. 3-9). 1979. pap. 8.95 tchr's. enrichment manual (*0-914634-67-4*, 7912) DOK Pubs.
—Don't Teach Let Me Learn: About the F.B.I., Firefighters, Felines, Futures. Rossi, Richard, illus. 72p. (gr. 3-6). 1983. tchr's. enrichment bk. 8.95 (*0-88047-029-1*, 8312) DOK Pubs.
—Don't Teach! Let Me Learn about World War II, Adventure, Dreams & Superstition. Rossi, Richard, illus. 72p. (Orig.). (gr. 3-10). 1984. 8.95 (*0-88047-044-5*, 8411) DOK Pubs.
—Know Your State. West, James A., illus. 32p. (Orig.). (gr. 4-7). 1984. pap. 5.95 (*0-88047-036-4*, 8401) DOK Pubs.

Crosby-Jones, Michael, tr. see Kaldhol, Marit.

Crose, Mark. Halloween. LC 90-45854. (Illus.). 48p. (gr. 5-6). 1991. 13.95 (*0-89686-577-0*, Crestwood Hse) Macmillan Child Grp.
—The Terminator. LC 90-28888. (Illus.). 48p. (gr. 5-6). 1991. RSBE 13.95 (*0-89686-580-0*, Crestwood Hse) Macmillan Child Grp.

Croser, Nigel. Help! Alder, George, illus. LC 89-35648. 28p. (gr. 1-2). 1989. PLB 15.93 (*0-8368-0223-3*) Gareth Stevens Inc.

Croser, Nigel, jt. auth. see Dodd, Lynley.

Crosher, Judith. Ancient Egypt. (Illus.). 48p. (gr. 3-7). 1993. 14.99 (*0-670-84755-0*) Viking Child Bks.

Cross, David & Morse, Sarah. Easy As One Two Three: Fifty Dulcimer Tunes for Beginners. (Illus.). 32p. (Orig.). (gr. 1-6). 1985. pap. text ed. 2.25 (*0-9614939-4-1*); tchr's. ed. 5.95 (*0-9614939-5-X*) Backyard Music.

Cross, Esther & Cross, Wilbur. Portugal. LC 85-26991. (Illus.). 127p. (gr. 5-6). 1986. PLB 26.60 (*0-516-02778-6*) Childrens.

Cross, Esther, jt. auth. see Cross, Wilbur.

Cross, Frank B. & Collins, Joseph T. Illustrated Guide to Fishes in Kansas. Robertson, Jeanne L., illus. 14p. (gr. 4-6). 1976. pap. 1.00 (*0-89338-000-8*) U of KS Mus Nat Hist.

Cross, Genevieve. The Engine That Lost Its Whistle. 10th ed. Cross, Genevieve, illus. 32p. (gr. 1-3). 1988. pap. 12.50 (*0-9621162-0-3*) Van Buren Cty Hist Soc.

Cross, Gilbert B. Mystery at Loon Lake. LC 92-42351. 144p. (gr. 3-7). 1993. pap. 3.95 (*0-689-71729-6*, Aladdin) Macmillan Child Grp.
—Terror Train! LC 93-25735. 128p. (gr. 3-7). 1994. pap. 3.95 (*0-689-71765-2*, Aladdin) Macmillan Child Grp.
—A Witch Across Time. LC 89-38474. 224p. (gr. 6-9). 1990. SBE 14.95 (*0-689-31602-X*, Atheneum Child Bk) Macmillan Child Grp.

Cross, Gillian. Born of the Sun. LC 84-3740. (Illus.). 240p. (gr. 7 up). 1984. 11.95 (*0-8234-0528-1*) Holiday.
—Born of the Sun. (gr. k-12). 1987. pap. 2.95 (*0-440-90710-1*, LFL) Dell.
—Chartbreaker. LC 86-46199. 184p. (gr. 7 up). 1987. 14.95 (*0-8234-0647-4*) Holiday.
—Chartbreaker. (gr. k-12). 1989. pap. 2.95 (*0-440-20312-0*, LFL) Dell.

—The Dark Behind the Curtain. 160p. (Orig.). (gr. k-12). 1988. pap. 2.95 (0-440-20207-8, LFL) Dell.
—The Dark Behind the Curtain. (Illus.). 160p. (gr. 1-5). 1987. 12.95 (0-19-271457-0) OUP.
—The Demon Headmaster. large type ed. 208p. (gr. 3 up). 1990. lib. bdg. 16.95x (0-7451-1150-5, Lythway Large Print) Hall.
—The Great American Elephant Chase. LC 92-54492. 160p. (gr. 4-7). 1993. 14.95 (0-8234-1016-1) Holiday.
—A Map of Nowhere. LC 88-24559. 160p. (gr. 4-7). 1989. 13.95 (0-8234-0741-1) Holiday.
—On the Edge. LC 84-48741. 176p. (gr. 7 up). 1985. 14.95 (0-8234-0559-1) Holiday.
—On the Edge. (gr. k-12). 1987. pap. 2.75 (0-440-96666-3, LFL) Dell.
—Roscoe's Leap. LC 87-45328. 160p. (gr. 7 up). 1987. 14.95 (0-8234-0669-5) Holiday.
—Twin & Super-Twin. Bradley, Maureen, illus. LC 90-55098. 176p. (gr. 3-7). 1990. 13.95 (0-8234-0840-X) Holiday.
—Wolf. LC 90-47040. 144p. 1991. 13.95 (0-8234-0870-1) Holiday.
—Wolf. 1993. pap. 3.25 (0-590-45608-3) Scholastic Inc.
Cross, Jeanne. Simple Printing Methods. Cross, Jeanne, illus. LC 72-39812. 48p. (gr. 6 up). 1972. 21.95 (0-87599-192-0) S G Phillips.
Cross, Luther. Object Lessons for Children. 99p. (Orig.). (gr. 2-5). 1967. pap. 4.99 (0-8010-2315-7) Baker Bk.
Cross, Molly. Wait for Me! Mathieu, Joe, illus. LC 87-12926. 40p. (ps-3). 1987. 4.95 (0-394-89135-X) Random Bks Yng Read.
—Wait for Me! Mathieu, Joe, illus. LC 87-12926. 40p. (ps-3). 1993. pap. 2.99 (0-679-83952-6) Random Bks Yng Read.
Cross, Peter. Trouble for Trumpets. Cross, Peter, illus. LC 83-43115. (gr. 3 up). 1984. 9.95 (0-394-86513-8) Random Bks Yng Read.
Cross, Peter, illus. & created by see Taylor, Judy.
Cross, Robin. Modern Military Weapons. (Illus.). 32p. (gr. 5-8). 1991. PLB 12.40 (0-531-11174-1); pap. 8.95 (0-531-15627-3) Watts.
—Roosevelt: And the Americans at War. (Illus.). 64p. (gr. 5-8). 1990. PLB 12.90 (0-531-17254-6, Gloucester Pr) Watts.
—Victims of War. LC 93-2252. (Illus.). 48p. (gr. 5-9). 1993. 14.95 (1-56847-081-9) Thomson Lrning.
Cross, Verda. Great-Grandma Tells of Threshing Day. Tucker, Kathleen, ed. Owens, Gail, illus. LC 90-28442. 40p. (gr. 1-6). 1992. 15.95 (0-8075-3042-5) A Whitman.
Cross, Wilbur. Brazil. LC 84-7602. (Illus.). 128p. (gr. 5-9). 1984. PLB 26.60 (0-516-02753-0) Childrens.
—Egypt. LC 82-9465. (Illus.). (gr. 5-9). 1982. PLB 26.60 (0-516-02762-X) Childrens.
Cross, Wilbur & Cross, Esther. Spain. LC 85-16588. 128p. (gr. 5-9). 1985. PLB 26.60 (0-516-02786-7) Childrens.
Cross, Wilbur, jt. auth. see Cross, Esther.
Crossley, Darry, tr. see Reynolds, Ralph V.
Crossley-Holland, Kevin. Beowulf. Keeping, Charles, illus. 48p. (gr. 5 up). 1988. 16.00 (0-19-279770-0); pap. 7.50 (0-19-272184-4) OUP.
—British Folk Tales: A Selection. large type ed. (gr. 1-8). 1993. 15.95 (0-7451-1911-5, Galaxy Child Lrg Print) Chivers N Amer.
Crosswhite, F. Joe, ed. Organizing for Mathematics Instruction: 1977 Yearbook. LC 77-23294. (Illus.). 256p. (gr. 5-8). 1977. 20.00 (0-87353-019-5) NCTM.
Crouch, Clifford. Cuba. (Illus.). 112p. (gr. 5 up). 1991. 14.95 (0-7910-1362-6) Chelsea Hse.
Crouch, Marcus. Ivan: Stories of Old Russia. Dewar, Bob, illus. 80p. (gr. 3-7). 1989. jacketed 18.95 (0-19-274135-7) OUP.
Crouch, Robin. The Americas: A Sticker Atlas of Exploration & Discovery. McRae, Patrick, illus. 16p. (Orig.). (gr. 1-3). 1993. pap. 5.95 (0-8249-8556-7, Ideals Child) Hambleton-Hill.
Crouch, Tom D. The National Aeronautics & Space Administration. (Illus.). 144p. (gr. 5 up). 1990. 14.95 (1-55546-120-4) Chelsea Hse.
Crouch, Tom D., jt. auth. see Embury, Barbara.
Crouse, Joan M., et al. Vietnam. LC 93-14939. 1993. write for info. (0-8013-0865-8) Longman.
Crouthamel, Thomas G., Sr. It's OK. 2nd ed. Hasty, Patti, illus. LC 86-27694. 36p. (gr. 6 up). 1990. pap. 6.95 (0-940701-18-9) Keystone Pr.
Crow, Faye. Ready Reading. Eisenhardt, Ann, illus. 135p. (Orig.). (ps-2). 1987. pap. 10.95 (0-9617529-0-4) Ready Work.
Crow, Lauri, ed. see Kohlenbert, Sherry.

Crow, Moses N. Hoksila & the Red Buffalo. Provincial, Bernard W., illus. 40p. (Orig.). (gr. 3 up). 1991. pap. 5.95 (1-877976-02-4, 406-0017) Tipi Pr.
Among the Lakota, this legend is called, Enya-hoksei. It is told differently by every story-teller of every clan. The outline of the legend remains the same as it travels with time. The whole story changes with the changing of times. The significance of it, as it goes through the ages, is that it

has no horses in it. The story has to be very old. But like all legends, it keeps in tune with the passing of time. When Hoksila the young warrior begins his long journey, his hunt to rescue his wife & to rid his tribe of the red buffalo with the ugly black spots. Then he could free all the young maidens. This is a story of the battle of good & evil, & how it's been handed down by the Lakota. An engaging story for the young & those not so young.
Publisher Provided Annotation.

—A Legend from Crazy Horse Clan. Flood, Renee S., ed. Long Soldier, Daniel, illus. 36p. (Orig.). (gr. 3 up). 1987. pap. 4.95 (1-877976-03-2, 406-0010) Tipi Pr.
A LEGEND FROM CRAZY HORSE CLAN is a story for children of all ages. Beautiful illustrations by Daniel Long Soldier keep the legend alive in the reader's eye. The historian or student of Indian ways will enjoy the book as much as the child of seven, in whose imagination the baby raccoon Mesu embodies all that is faithful & loving in a small furry pet. Listen carefully to the words of Tashia. The symbolic role of man & woman is evident throughout the legend. Although the story essentially describes the life of a girl, the narrator is male. Clearly, the legend describes the male viewpoint of manhood, religion, courtship, aging & death. The characters are gentle, yet there is a strong underlying theme of tribal identity. Without a doubt, we are looking at life through the eyes of a warrior. Indian oral narration is spoken American literature in its finest form. When Lakota children of the 1990s become grandparents themselves, they will tell the legends again. Thanks to Moses Big Crow, one of those legends may well be A LEGEND FROM CRAZY HORSE CLAN.
Publisher Provided Annotation.

Crow, Sherry R. Library Lightning. (Illus.). 128p. (gr. 3-6). 1990. pap. 12.95 (0-913839-72-8) Bk Lures.
Crowder, Dorothy. In the Land of the Wichitas: Stories about Burkburnett, Texas for the Young Reader. (Illus.). 48p. (Orig.). (gr. 3-4). 1986. pap. text ed. 7.50x (0-317-91365-4) Dorthenia Pubs.
Crowder, Jack L. & Hill, Faith. Stephanie & the Coyote. 3rd, rev. ed. Morgan, William, tr. Holm, Wayne, intro. by. (NAV & ENG., Illus.). 32p. (gr. 3 up). pap. 4.95 (0-9616589-0-8) Upper Strata.
—Tonibah & the Rainbow. Tohtsonie, Clara & Wilson, Joe, trs. Crowder, Jack L., photos by. (ENG & NAV., Illus.). 32p. (Orig.). (gr. 7 up). 1986. pap. 6.95 (0-9616589-1-6) Upper Strata.
Crowder, Susan. Daniel au Repaire des Lions. Crowder, Susan, illus. (FRE.). 36p. (Orig.). 1993. pap. 4.00x (0-912927-57-7, D018) St John Kronstadt.
—The Great Flood. Crowder, Susan, illus. 28p. (Orig.). 1988. pap. 2.50 (0-912927-27-5, X027) St John Kronstadt.
—The Three Children in the Furnace. Crowder, Susan, illus. 37p. (Orig.). 1984. pap. 2.50 (0-912927-11-9, X011) St John Kronstadt.
Crowder, Susan, illus. Daniel in the Lions' Den. 36p. (Orig.). 1984. pap. 3.00 (0-912927-08-9, X008) St John Kronstadt.
Crowdis, John. Disaster on Adonis Three. LaDell, Leo, ed. Ridge, Jeff & Midgette, Darrell, illus. 32p. (Orig.). (gr. 12). 1989. pap. 6.00 (1-55806-039-1, 9107) Iron Crown Ent Inc.
—Ghosts of the Southern Arduin. Ney, Jessica & Fenlon, Peter C., Jr., eds. McBride, Angus & Midgette, Darrell, illus. 32p. (Orig.). (gr. 12). 1989. pap. 6.00 (1-55806-030-8, 8109) Iron Crown Ent Inc.
—Hazards of the Harod Wood. Ney, Jessica, ed. McBride, Angus & Danforth, Liz, illus. 32p. (Orig.). (gr. 12). 1990. pap. 6.00 (1-55806-096-0, 8112) Iron Crown Ent Inc.

—Rogues of the Borderlands. Ney, Jessica, ed. McBride, Angus & Jermy, Paul, illus. 40p. (Orig.). (gr. 12). 1990. pap. 7.00 (1-55806-083-9, 8014) Iron Crown Ent Inc.
Crowdy, Deborah. Let's Take a Walk in the Park. Axeman, Lois, illus. LC 86-17598. 32p. (ps-2). 1986. PLB 21.35 (0-89565-357-5); PLB 14.95s.p. (0-685-55820-7) Childs World.
—Pride. McCallum, Jodie, illus. LC 89-48107. 32p. (gr. k-3). 1990. PLB 21.35 (0-89565-566-7); PLB 14.95s.p. (0-685-56200-X) Childs World.
Crowdy, Deborah, jt. auth. see Fiday, Beverly.
Crowdy, Deborah, jt. auth. see O'Connor, Karen.
Crowe, Elizabeth, tr. see Mori, Hana.
Crowe, Robert L. Clyde Monster. Chorao, Kay, illus. LC 76-10733. 32p. (ps-3). 1987. (DCB); pap. 3.95 (0-525-44289-8, DCB) Dutton Child Bks.
—Clyde Monster. (ps-3). 1993. pap. 4.99 (0-14-054743-6) Puffin Bks.
—Tyler Toad & the Thunder. Chorao, Kay, illus. LC 80-347. 32p. (ps-1). 1980. 9.95 (0-525-41795-8, DCB) Dutton Child Bks.
—Tyler Toad & the Thunder. Chorao, Kay, illus. LC 80-347. 32p. (ps-1). 1986. pap. 4.95 (0-525-44243-X, DCB) Dutton Child Bks.
Crowell, Robert L. The Lore & Legends of Flowers. Dowden, Anne O., illus. LC 79-7829. 88p. (gr. 7 up). 1982. (Crowell Jr Bks); (Crowell Jr Bks) HarpC Child Bks.

Crowl, Christine. The Hunter & the Woodpecker. (Illus.). 12p. (Orig.). (ps-6). 1990. pap. 2.50 (1-877976-09-1, 406-0015) Tipi Pr.
This children's book describes how the Sioux first discovered the flute, which makes magical music. The Red Headed Woodpecker tells a young brave of its powers to win over a beautiful maiden. A charming story, delightfully illustrated in four color. A story for children of all ages.
Publisher Provided Annotation.

—White Buffalo Women. (Illus.). 18p. (Orig.). (gr. 6). 1991. pap. 2.50 (1-877976-10-5, 406-0014) Tipi Pr.
This story is a core legend of the Sioux & how the Sioux received the Sacred Prayer Pipe. The pipe was an important religious symbol among the Sioux. It was a "moveable" altar which was used in prayer & ceremony. It was the most cherished thing a man could own. The legend of WHITE BUFFALO WOMEN & the pipe originated with the Brule Sioux & is a story that has been handed down through the centuries. Beautifully told & illustrated in four color, a charming story for children young & old.
Publisher Provided Annotation.

Crowley, Michael. New Kid on Spurwick Ave. Carter, Abby, illus. 32p. (gr. k-3). 1992. 14.95 (0-316-16230-2) Little.
—Shack & Back. (ps-3). 1993. 14.95 (0-316-16231-0) Little.
Crowley, Richard J., jt. auth. see Mills, Joyce C.
Crown, Bonnie & Atlas, Susan. D-I-V-O-R-C-E-S Spell Discover: A Kit to Help Children Express Their Feelings about Divorce. (Illus.). 52p. (Orig.). (gr. k-8). 1992. pap. 14.95 spiral bdg. (0-9633626-0-7) Courageous Kids.
Crowther, Jean D. Book of Mormon Puzzles & Pictures for Young Latter-Day Saints. LC 77-74495. (Illus.). 56p. (gr. 3 up). 1977. 5.95 (0-88290-080-3) Horizon Utah.
—Growing up in the Church: Gospel Principles & Practices for Children. rev. ed. Perry, Lucille R., illus. LC 67-25433. 84p. (gr. 2-6). 1973. Repr. of 1965 ed. 7.95 (0-88290-024-2) Horizon Utah.
—What Do I Do Now, Mom? Growing-up Guidance for Young Teen-age Girls. Bagley, Val C., illus. LC 80-82257. 86p. (gr. 9-12). 1980. 8.95 (0-88290-134-6) Horizon Utah.
Crowther, Robert. All the Fun of the Fair. Crowther, Robert, illus. LC 91-71863. 12p. (ps up) 1992. 15.95 (1-56402-001-0) Candlewick Pr.
—Animal Rap! Crowther, Robert, illus. LC 92-54586. 10p. (ps). 1993. 9.95 (1-56402-207-2) Candlewick Pr.
—Animal Snap! Crowther, Robert, illus. LC 92-54587. 10p. (ps). 1993. 9.95 (1-56402-208-0) Candlewick Pr.
—How Many Babies on the Farm? (Illus.). 10p. (ps-k). 1991. pap. 5.95 (0-671-73157-2, Little Simon) S&S Trade.

—The Most Amazing Hide-&-Seek Alphabet Book. LC 77-79334. (Illus.). (ps-1). 1978. pap. 13.95 (0-670-48996-4) Viking Child Bks.
—The Most Amazing Hide & Seek Counting Book. Crowther, Robert, illus. 14p. (ps-3). 1981. pap. 13.95 (0-670-48997-2) Viking Child Bks.
—Most Amazing Hide & Seek Opposites Book. Crowther, Robert, illus. LC 85-42757. 12p. (ps-3). 1985. pap. 12.95 pop-up (0-670-80121-6) Viking Child Bks.
—Pop Goes the Weasel! Twenty-Five Pop-Up Nursery Rhymes. (Illus.). (ps-3). 1987. Pop-Up ed. pap. 14.95 (0-670-81815-1) Viking Child Bks.
—Punchout Christmas Cards. 1989. pap. 5.95 (0-671-68401-9) S&S Trade.
—Punchout Christmas Decorations. 1989. pap. 5.95 (0-671-68400-0) S&S Trade.
—Robert Crowther's Most Amazing Pop-Up Book of Machines. (ps-3). 1988. pap. 14.95 (0-670-82339-2) Viking Child Bks.
—Who Lives in the Country? Crowther, Robert, illus. LC 91-58766. 10p. (ps). 1992. 6.95 (1-56402-090-8) Candlewick Pr.
—Who Lives in the Garden? Crowther, Robert, illus. LC 91-58767. 10p. (ps). 1992. 6.95 (1-56402-091-6) Candlewick Pr.
Croxton, William L. Amazing Card Tricks Made Easy to Do. rev. ed. (Illus.). 64p. (gr. 4 up). 1990. pap. 4.95 (0-9623230-0-4) WLC Enterprises.
Croy, Greg, ed. see Christophersen, Susan & Farr, J. Michael.
Croy, Greg, ed. see Farr, J. Michael & Pavlicko, Marie.
Crozat, Francois. I Am a Big Dinosaur. (Illus.). 24p. (ps-k). 1989. 8.95 (0-8120-6097-0) Barron.
—I Am a Big Dinosaur-Mini. 24p. (ps). 1990. 2.95 (0-8120-6193-4) Barron.
—I Am a Little Alligator. 28p. (ps-k). 1993. 8.95 (0-8120-6342-2); Miniature. 3.50 (0-8120-6343-0) Barron.
—I Am a Little Bear. (Illus.). 24p. (ps) 1989. 8.95 (0-8120-5903-4) Barron.
—I Am a Little Bear-Mini. 1990. 2.95 (0-8120-6191-8) Barron.
—I Am a Little Cat. (Illus.). 28p. (ps-k). 1992. 8.95 (0-8120-6277-9); Miniature version. 2.95 (0-8120-6287-6) Barron.
—I Am a Little Dog. (Illus.). 28p. (ps-k). 1992. 8.95 (0-8120-6276-0); Miniture version. 2.95 (0-8120-6286-8) Barron.
—I Am a Little Duck. (Illus.). 24p. (ps-k). 1989. 8.95 (0-8120-5904-2) Barron.
—I Am a Little Duck-Mini. 24p. (ps). 1990. 3.50 (0-8120-6192-6) Barron.
—I Am a Little Elephant. (Illus.). 28p. (ps-k). 1993. 8.95 (0-8120-6351-1); mini bk. 3.50 (0-8120-6353-8) Barron.
—I Am a Little Monkey. (Illus.). (ps-3). 1991. large 8.95 (0-8120-6149-7); miniature 2.95 (0-8120-6221-3) Barron.
—I Am a Little Panda. LC 92-30962. 28p. (ps-k). 1993. 8.95 (0-8120-6311-2); Miniature. 3.50 (0-8120-6312-0) Barron.
—I Am a Little Pig. (Illus.). (ps-3). 1991. large 8.95 (0-8120-6201-9); miniature 2.95 (0-8120-6222-1) Barron.
—I Am a Little Rabbit. (Illus.). 24p. (ps) 1989. 8.95 (0-8120-5905-0) Barron.
—I Am a Little Rabbit-Mini. 24p. (ps). 1990. 3.50 (0-8120-6194-2) Barron.
—I am a Little Tiger: Little Animal Stories. LC 92-21972. (ps). 1992. mini 3.50 (0-8120-6315-5); large 8.95 (0-8120-6316-3) Barron.
Cruickshank, Gordon. Cars & How They Work. LC 92-7623. (Illus.). 64p. (gr. 3 up). 1992. 11.95 (1-56458-142-X) Dorling Kindersley.
Cruickshank, Kathy. The Baby Book. Cruickshank, Kathy, illus. (ps-k). 1991. pap. 1.50 (0-307-10029-4, Golden Pr) Western Pub.
Cruickshank, Margrit. S.K.U.N.K. & the Ozone Conspiracy. 235p. 1990. pap. 8.95 (1-85371-067-9, Pub. by Poolbeg Pr ER) Dufour.
Cruise, Beth. Behind the Scenes at "Saved by the Bell" An Inside Look at TV's Hottest Teen Show. LC 91-27599. (Illus.). 64p. (Orig.). (gr. 5 up). 1992. pap. 6.95 (0-02-042778-6, Collier Young Ad) Macmillan Child Grp.
—Computer Confusion. 144p. (Orig.). (gr. 5 up). 1994. pap. 2.95 (0-02-042784-0, Collier Young Ad) Macmillan Child Grp.
—Kelly's Hero. (Illus.). 144p. (gr. 5 up). 1993. pap. 2.95 (0-02-042769-7, Collier Young Ad) Macmillan Child Grp.
—Saved by the Bell: Bayside Madness. LC 91-46070. 144p. (gr. 5 up). 1992. pap. 2.95 (0-02-042775-1, Collier Young Ad) Macmillan Child Grp.
—Saved by the Bell: California Scheming. LC 92-2739. 144p. (Orig.). (gr. 5 up). 1992. pap. 2.95 (0-02-042776-X, Collier Young Ad) Macmillan Child Grp.
—Saved by the Bell: Class Trip Chaos. LC 92-35523. 144p. (gr. 5 up). 1992. pap. 2.95 (0-02-042765-4, Collier Young Ad) Macmillan Child Grp.
—The Saved by the Bell Date Book. (Illus.). 96p. (gr. 5 up). 1993. pap. 8.95 (0-02-042768-9, Aladdin) Macmillan Child Grp.

—Saved by the Bell: Girls' Night Out. LC 92-24648. 144p. (gr. 5 up). 1992. pap. 2.95 (0-02-042766-2, Collier Young Ad) Macmillan Child Grp.
—Saved by the Bell Mario Lopez: High-Voltage Star. LC 91-27462. (Illus.). 120p. (Orig.). (gr. 5 up). 1992. pap. 2.95 (0-02-041851-5, Collier Young Ad) Macmillan Child Grp.
—Saved by the Bell Mark-Paul Gosselaar: Ultimate Gold. LC 91-27456. (Illus.). 120p. (Orig.). (gr. 5 up). 1992. pap. 2.95 (0-02-041841-8, Collier Young Ad) Macmillan Child Grp.
—Saved by the Bell: Zack Strikes Back. LC 92-5182. 144p. (Orig.). (gr. 5 up). 1992. pap. 2.95 (0-02-042777-8, Collier Young Ad) Macmillan Child Grp.
—Saved By the Bell: Zack's Last Scam. LC 92-31733. 144p. (gr. 5 up). 1992. pap. 2.95 (0-02-042767-0, Collier Young Ad) Macmillan Child Grp.
—Silver Spurs. 144p. (Orig.). (gr. 5 up). 1994. pap. 2.95 (0-02-042788-3, Collier Young Ad) Macmillan Child Grp.
Cruise, Beth & Schleifer, Jay. Dustin Diamond: Teen Star. (Illus.). 96p. (Orig.). (gr. 5 up). 1993. pap. 3.50 (0-02-044975-5, Collier Young Ad) Macmillan Child Grp.
Cruise, Beth & Schleifer, Laura. Impeach Screech. (Illus.). 144p. (Orig.). (gr. 5 up). 1993. pap. 2.95 (0-02-042762-X, Collier Young Ad) Macmillan Child Grp.
—One Wild Weekend. LC 93-2905. (Illus.). 144p. (Orig.). (gr. 5 up). 1993. pap. 2.95 (0-02-042763-8, Collier Young Ad) Macmillan Child Grp.
—That Old Zack Magic. (Illus.). 144p. (Orig.). (gr. 5 up). 1993. pap. 2.95 (0-02-042761-1, Collier Young Ad) Macmillan Child Grp.
Crum, John W. AP Exam in American History. 2nd ed. 320p. (gr. 9-12). 1990. pap. 10.95 (0-685-31171-6, Arco Test) P-H Gen Ref & Trav.
Crum, Thomas F. Magic of Conflict Workshop for Young People. Heffernan, Cheryl, illus. (gr. 6-12). 1989. multi-media kit 49.95 (1-877803-04-9) AIKI Works.
Crum, Wesley S. UFO Crash at Aztec: The Aztec Recovery, 25 March 1948. Stevens, Wendelle C., ed. (Illus.). 1p. (gr. 9-12). 1989. poster 3.95 (0-934269-16-5) UFO Photo.
Crumble, Mortimer. Madison Squid & the Ghost of Slapstick: Hilarious Children's Books for Grown-ups. D'Souza, Edgar, illus. LC 93-79348. 144p. 1994. 19.95 (0-9636606-1-6) Crumble Bks.
Crume, Vic. The Ghost That Came Alive. reissued ed. 1992. pap. 2.95 (0-590-46147-8, Apple Paperbacks) Scholastic Inc.
Crump, Courtni C. Jumping the Broom. Griffith, Gershom, illus. LC 92-45575. 32p. (gr. 4-8). 1994. 15.95 (0-8234-1042-0) Holiday.
Crump, Donald J. Creatures Small & Furry. LC 83-13456. 32p. (ps-3). 1983. Set of 4. 13.95 (0-87044-486-7); lib. bdg. 16.95 (0-87044-491-3) Natl Geog.
Crump, Donald J., ed. Adventures in Your National Parks. (gr. 3-8). 1989. 8.95 (0-87044-702-5); PLB 12.50 (0-87044-707-6) Natl Geog.
—Amazing Things Animals Do. (gr. 3-8). 1989. 8.95 (0-87044-709-2); PLB 12.50 (0-87044-704-1) Natl Geog.
—Animal Architects. LC 87-12198. (Illus.). 104p. (gr. 3-8). 1987. 8.95 (0-87044-612-6); PLB 12.50 (0-87044-617-7) Natl Geog.
—Animal Homes. No. 1. (Illus.). (ps-3). 1989. 21.95 (0-87044-758-0) Natl Geog.
—Animals at Play. (Illus.). (gr. k-4). 1988. Set. 13.95 (0-87044-739-4); Set. PLB 16.95 (0-87044-744-0) Natl Geog.
—Animals in Summer. (Illus.). (gr. k-4). 1988. Set. 13.95 (0-87044-738-6); Set. PLB 16.95 (0-87044-743-2) Natl Geog.
—Animals Showing Off. Chen, Tony, illus. (ps-5). 1988. Set. 21.95 (0-87044-724-6) Natl Geog.
—Books for Young Explorers, 4 vols, Set 13. Incl. Baby Bears & How They Grow. Buxton, Jane H; Saving Our Animal Friends. McGrath, Susan; Animals That Live in Trees. McCauley, Jane R; Animals & Their Hiding Places. McCauley, Jane R. 1986. Set. 13.95 (0-87044-638-X); Set. PLB 16.95 (0-87044-643-6) Natl Geog.
—Books for Young Explorers, 4 bks, Set 16. (gr. k-4). 1989. Set. 13.95 (0-87044-769-6); Set. PLB 16.95 (0-87044-774-2) No. 1: Cottontails - Little Rabbits of Field & Forest. No. 2: Amazing Otters. No. 3: Animals of the High Mountains. No. 4: Animal Clowns. Natl Geog.
—Books for Young Explorers: Along a Rocky Shore; Animal Families; Lions & Tigers & Leopards: The Big Cats; Our Amazing Animal Friends, 4 bks, Set 17. (gr. k-4). 1990. Set. 13.95 (0-87044-821-8); PLB 16.95 (0-87044-826-9) Natl Geog.
—Builders of the Ancient World: Marvels of Engineering. LC 86-5278. (Illus.). (gr. 8 up). 1986. 8.95 (0-87044-585-5) Natl Geog.
—Busy Beavers. (Illus.). (gr. k-4). 1988. Set. 13.95 (0-87044-740-8); Set. PLB 16.95 (0-87044-745-9) Natl Geog.
—Dolphins: Our Friends in the Sea. LC 86-18126. (Illus.). 104p. (gr. 4-5). 1986. 8.95 (0-87044-609-6); PLB 12.50 (0-87044-614-2) Natl Geog.
—The Emerald Realm: Earth's Precious Rain Forests. (Illus.). 1990. 9.95 (0-87044-790-4); deluxe ed. 12.95 (0-87044-795-5) Natl Geog.

—Excursion to Enchantment. (Illus.). 1988. 9.95 (0-87044-667-3); lib. bdg. 12.95 (0-87044-672-X) Natl Geog.
—Explore a Tropical Forest, No. 1. (Illus.). (ps-3). 1989. 21.95 (0-87044-757-2) Natl Geog.
—Exploring Your Solar System. (gr. 3-8). 1989. 8.95 (0-87044-703-3); PLB 12.50 (0-87044-708-4) Natl Geog.
—Exploring Your World. (Illus.). 1989. 31.95 (0-87044-726-2); deluxe ed. 41.95 (0-87044-728-9); lib. bdg. 34.95 (0-87044-727-0) Natl Geog.
—The Far-Out Fact Book. LC 79-1793. (Illus.). 104p. (gr. 3-8). 1980. 8.95 (0-87044-319-4); PLB 12.50 (0-87044-324-0) Natl Geog.
—Fun with Physics. LC 86-8501. (Illus.). 104p. (gr. 5 up). 1986. 8.95 (0-87044-576-6); lib. bdg. 12.50 (0-87044-581-2) Natl Geog.
—Geo-Whiz! 104p. (gr. 3-8). 1988. 8.95 (0-87044-657-6); PLB 12.50 (0-87044-662-2) Natl Geog.
—Giants from the Past. LC 81-47893. 104p. (gr. 3-8). 1983. 8.95 (0-87044-424-7); PLB 12.50 (0-87044-429-8) Natl Geog.
—Great American Journeys. (Illus.). 1989. 8.95 (0-87044-669-X); lib. bdg. 12.95 (0-87044-674-6) Natl Geog.
—Hidden Treasures of the Sea. 104p. (gr. 3-8). 1988. pap. 8.95 (0-87044-658-4); PLB 12.50 (0-87044-663-0) Natl Geog.
—Hidden Worlds. LC 79-3244. (Illus.). 104p. (gr. 3-8). 1981. 8.95 (0-87044-336-4); PLB 12.50 (0-87044-341-0) Natl Geog.
—Hidden Worlds of Wildlife. (Illus.). 1990. 9.95 (0-87044-791-2) Natl Geog.
—How Animals Behave. LC 84-989. (Illus.). 104p. (gr. 3-8). 1984. 8.95 (0-87044-500-6); PLB 12.50 (0-87044-505-7) Natl Geog.
—How Things Are Made. LC 79-3242. (Illus.). 104p. (gr. 3-8). 1981. 8.95 (0-87044-334-8); PLB 12.50 (0-87044-339-9) Natl Geog.
—How Things Work. LC 81-47894. (Illus.). 104p. (gr. 7 up). 1983. 8.95 (0-87044-425-5); PLB 12.50 (0-87044-430-1) Natl Geog.
—Let's Explore a River. (Illus.). (gr. k-4). 1988. Set. 13.95 (0-87044-741-6); Set. PLB 16.95 (0-87044-746-7) Natl Geog.
—New England: Land of Scenic Splendor. (Illus.). 1989. 9.95 (0-87044-715-7); lib. bdg. 12.95 (0-87044-720-3) Natl Geog.
—On the Brink of Tomorrow: Frontiers of Science. LC 81-48075. 200p. (gr. 7 up). 1982. 8.95 (0-87044-414-X) Natl Geog.
—Pathways to Discovery: Exploring America's National Trails. (Illus.). 1990. 9.95 (0-87044-792-0) Natl Geog.
—Secrets of Animal Survival. LC 81-47895. (Illus.). 104p. (gr. 3 up). 1983. 8.95 (0-87044-426-3); PLB 12.50 (0-87044-431-X) Natl Geog.
—Small Inventions That Make a Big Difference. LC 83-23770. 104p. (gr. 3-8). 1984. 8.95 (0-87044-498-0); PLB 12.50 (0-87044-503-0) Natl Geog.
—Surprising Lands Down Under. (Illus.). 1989. 9.95 (0-87044-714-9); lib. bdg. 12.95 (0-87044-719-X) Natl Geog.
—Whales, Bk. 2. (Illus.). (ps-3). 1990. Set. 21.95 (0-87044-810-2) Natl Geog.
—Wildlife: Making a Comeback. 104p. (gr. 3-8). 1987. 8.95 (0-87044-656-8); PLB 12.50 (0-87044-661-4) Natl Geog.
—Wonderful Animals of Australia, Bk. 1. (Illus.). (ps-3). 1990. Set. 21.95 (0-87044-809-9) Natl Geog.
—The World's Wild Shores. (Illus.). 1990. 9.95 (0-87044-716-5); lib. bdg. 12.95 (0-87044-721-1) Natl Geog.
—Yosemite: An American Treasure. (Illus.). 1990. 9.95 (0-87044-789-0); lib. bdg. 12.95 (0-87044-794-7) Natl Geog.
—You Won't Believe Your Eyes. LC 86-7637. (Illus.). 104p. (gr. 3-8). 1987. 8.95 (0-87044-611-8); PLB 12.50 (0-87044-616-9) Natl Geog.
—Your Wonderful Body. LC 81-47892. 104p. (gr. 4-8). 1982. 8.95 (0-87044-423-9); PLB 12.50 (0-87044-428-X) Natl Geog.
Crump, Donald J., ed. see Amos, William H.
Crump, Donald J., ed. see Barry, S. L., et al.
Crump, Donald J., ed. see Eugene, Toni.
Crump, Donald J., ed. see Fishbein, Seymour L.
Crump, Donald J., ed. see Fisher, Ron.
Crump, Donald J., ed. see Fisher, Ronald M.
Crump, Donald J., ed. see Gibson, Barbara & Pinkney, Jerry.
Crump, Donald J., ed. see Hirschland, Roger.
Crump, Donald J., ed. see Kostyal, Karen.
Crump, Donald J., ed. see McCauley, Jane.
Crump, Donald J., ed. see McCauley, Jane R.
Crump, Donald J., ed. see McGrath, Susan.
Crump, Donald J., ed. see McKelway, Margaret.
Crump, Donald J., ed. see Martin, Paul D.
Crump, Donald J., ed. see O'Neill, Catherine.
Crump, Donald J., ed. see Rinard, Judith E.
Crump, Donald J., ed. see Rinard, Judy.
Crump, Donald J., ed. see Stuart, Gene S.
Crump, Donald J., ed. see Urquhart, Jennifer C.
Crump, Donald J., ed. see Venino, Suzanne.
Crump, Donald J., ed. see Winston, Peggy D.
Crump, Fred. Afrotina & the Three Bears: (A Retold Story) Crump, Fred, illus. LC 88-51222. 44p. (gr. k-2). 1991. pap. 6.95 (1-55523-195-0) Winston-Derek.

—Little Red Riding Hood: (A Retold Story) Crump, Fred, illus. LC 88-51219. 44p. (gr. k-2). 1989. pap. 6.95 (1-55523-193-4) Winston-Derek.
—Mother Goose: A Retold Story. Crump, Fred, illus. LC 88-51224. 44p. (gr. k-2). 1989. pap. 6.95 (1-55523-194-2) Winston-Derek.
—Thumbelina: A Retold Story. Crump, Fred, illus. LC 88-51223. 44p. (gr. k-2). 1989. pap. 6.95 (1-55523-191-8) Winston-Derek.

Crump, Fred, Jr. Beauty & the Beast. Crump, Fred, Jr., illus. 44p. (gr. k-2). 1991. pap. 5.95 (1-55523-379-1) Winston-Derek.
—Cinderella: A Retold Story. Crump, Fred, Jr., illus. LC 89-51789. 44p. (gr. k-2). 1990. pap. 6.95 (1-55523-299-X) Winston-Derek.
—Ebony Duckling. Crump, Fred, Jr., illus. LC 91-75090. 44p. (gr. k-3). 1991. pap. 6.95 (1-55523-457-7) Winston-Derek.
—Hakim & Grenita: A Retold Story. Crump, Fred, Jr., illus. LC 89-51790. 44p. (gr. k-2). 1991. pap. 6.95 (1-55523-298-1) Winston-Derek.
—Jamako & the Beanstalk. Crump, Fred, illus. 44p. (gr. k-3). 1992. pap. 8.95 incl. cass. (1-55523-481-X) Winston-Derek.
—Jamako & the Beanstalk: A Retold Story. Crump, Fred, Jr., illus. LC 89-51792. 44p. (gr. k-2). 1990. pap. 6.95 (1-55523-296-5) Winston-Derek.
—MGambo & the Tiger. Crump, Fred, Jr., illus. 44p. (gr. k-2). 1991. pap. 6.95 (1-55523-410-0) Winston-Derek.
—The Other Little Angel. Crump, Fred, Jr., illus. LC 93-60369. 44p. (gr. k-3). 1993. pap. 6.95 (1-55523-624-3) Winston-Derek.
—Rapunzel. Crump, Fred, Jr., illus. 272p. (gr. k-2). 1991. pap. 6.95 (1-55523-408-9) Winston-Derek.
—Rapunzel. Crump, Fred, Jr., illus. LC 91-67499. 44p. (gr. k-3). 1992. pap. 8.95 incl. cass. (1-55523-482-8) Winston-Derek.
—Rumpelstiltskin. Crump, Fred, illus. 44p. (gr. k-2). 1991. pap. 6.95 (1-55523-409-7) Winston-Derek.
—Sleeping Beauty: A Retold Story. Crump, Fred, Jr., illus. LC 89-51788. 44p. (gr. k-2). 1991. pap. 6.95 (1-55523-300-7) Winston-Derek.
—Winston-Derek's Traditional Fairy Tales, 2 vols, Vols. I-II. (Illus.). (gr. k-3). 1992. PLB 39.95 ea. (1-55523-490-9) Vol. I, 224p (1-55523-491-7) Vol. II, 224p. Winston-Derek.

Crump, Patricia. Jesus' Stocking. Thomas, Ira, illus. 1990. 2.95 (0-8091-6591-0) Paulist Pr.

Cruse, Amy. The Book of Myths. LC 93-17341. 1993. 9.99 (0-517-09335-9, Pub. by Gramercy) Outlet Bk Co.

Crust, Linda. Melvin's Cold Feet. Brindle, John, illus. LC 90-47201. 32p. (gr. 2-3). 1991. PLB 18.60 (0-8368-0356-6) Gareth Stevens Inc.

Crutcher, Chris. Athletic Shorts. LC 91-4418. (gr. 12 up). 1991. 14.00 (0-688-10816-4) Greenwillow.
—Athletic Shorts: Six Short Stories. 160p. (gr. 7 up). 1992. pap. 3.50 (0-440-21390-8, LFL) Dell.
—Chinese Handcuffs. 1991. pap. 3.50 (0-440-20837-8, LFL) Dell.
—The Crazy Horse Electric Game. LC 86-14592. 160p. (gr. 7 up). 1987. 10.25 (0-688-06683-6) Greenwillow.
—The Crazy Horse Electric Game. (gr. k-12). 1988. pap. 3.50 (0-440-20094-6) Dell.
—Running Loose. LC 82-20935. 160p. (gr. 10 up). 1983. reinforced bdg. 13.95 (0-688-02002-X) Greenwillow.
—Running Loose. (gr. 7 up). 1986. pap. 3.50 (0-440-97570-0, LFL) Dell.
—Staying Fat for Sarah Byrnes. LC 91-40097. (gr. 7 up). 1993. 14.00 (0-688-11552-7) Greenwillow.
—Staying Fat for Sarah Byrnes. (gr. 9-12). 1993. 15.95 (0-7862-0062-6) Thorndike Pr.
—Stonan! (gr. k-12). 1988. pap. 3.50 (0-440-20080-6, LFL) Dell.
—Stotan! LC 85-12712. 192p. (gr. 7 up). 1986. reinforced trade ed. 12.00 (0-688-05715-2) Greenwillow.

Crutchfield, Charles. Brigands of Mirkwood. Fenlon, Peter C., Jr., ed. McBride, Angus, illus. 32p. (Orig.). (gr. 10-12). 1987. pap. 7.00 (0-915795-85-X, 8090) Iron Crown Ent Inc.
—Far Harad, the Scorched Land. Charlton, Coleman, ed. McBride, Angus, illus. 64p. (gr. 10-12). 1988. pap. 12.00 (1-55806-007-3, 8007) Iron Crown Ent Inc.
—Forest of Tears. Ney, Jessica, ed. McBride, Angus & Danforth, Liz, illus. 40p. (Orig.). (gr. 12). 1989. pap. 7.00 (1-55806-084-7, 8015) Iron Crown Ent Inc.
—Warlords of the Desert. Ney, Jessica, ed. McBride, Angus & Robin, Jeremy, illus. 40p. (Orig.). (gr. 12). 1989. pap. 7.00 (1-55806-058-8, 8012) Iron Crown Ent Inc.

Crutchfield, Charlie. Assassins of Dol Amroth. Fenlon, Peter C., Jr., ed. McBride, Angus, illus. (Orig.). (gr. 10-12). 1987. pap. 6.00 (0-915795-98-1, 8106) Iron Crown Ent Inc.

Crutsinger, Carla. Teenage Connection: A Tool for Effective Teenage Communication. LC 87-73063. 225p. (gr. 7-12). 1987. pap. 13.95x (0-944662-00-5) Brainworks Inc.

Cruz, Manuel & Cruz, Ruth. A Chicano Christmas Story. Cruz, Manuel, illus. LC 80-69444. (SPA.). 48p. (Orig.). (gr. ps-5). 1981. pap. text ed. 3.95 (0-86624-000-4, RM7) Bilingual Ed Serv.

Cruz, Ruth, jt. auth. see Cruz, Manuel.

Cryan-Hicks, Kathryn. W. E. B. Du Bois: Crusader for Peace. Hooks, Benjamin L. & Hooks, Benjamin L. contrib. by. LC 91-70820. (Illus.). 48p. (gr. 4-8). 1991. 14.95 (1-878668-05-6); pap. 7.95 (1-878668-09-9) Disc Enter Ltd.

Cryan-Hicks, Kathryn, intro. by. Pride & Promise: The Harlem Renaissance. (Illus.). 60p. (Orig.). (gr. 5-12). 1994. pap. 4.95 (1-878668-30-7) Disc Enter Ltd.

Cryer, Bruce, ed. see Childre, Doc L.

Crystal, Billy, read by see Dr. Seuss.

Crystal, David. Rediscover Grammar. 1987. pap. text ed. 10.47 (0-582-00258-3, 78071) Longman.

Crystal, Nancy, jt. auth. see Tytla, Milan.

Csaszar, Sonia, tr. see Garbarino, James.

Cubbit, David & Corkill, David. Ecuador. (Illus.). 130p. (gr. 11-12). 1988. pap. 7.50 (0-85345-760-3, Pub. by Lat Am Bur UK) Monthly Rev.

Cubley, Kathleen, ed. see Warren, Jean.

Cuellar, Carol, ed. The Complete Christmas Music Collection. 264p. (Orig.). 1993. pap. text ed. 16.95 (0-89898-642-7) CPP Belwin.
—The Complete Country Music Collection. 288p. (Orig.). 1992. pap. text ed. 16.95 (0-89898-584-6) CPP Belwin.
—The Complete Jazz Music Collection. 260p. (Orig.). 1993. pap. text ed. 16.95 (0-89898-587-0) CPP Belwin.
—The Complete Movie Music Collection. 330p. (Orig.). 1993. pap. text ed. 16.95 (0-89898-585-4) CPP Belwin.
—Country Showstoppers. 312p. (Orig.). 1992. pap. text ed. 18.95 (0-89898-595-1) CPP Belwin.
—Country Showstoppers, Vol. 2. 292p. (Orig.). 1993. pap. text ed. 18.95 (0-89898-596-X) CPP Belwin.
—Fifties & Sixties Showstoppers. 260p. (Orig.). 1990. pap. text ed. 18.95 (0-89898-594-3) CPP Belwin.
—Gospel & Inspirational Showstoppers. 316p. (Orig.). 1992. pap. text ed. 18.95 (0-89898-592-7) CPP Belwin.
—Todays' Kings of Country Music. 192p. (Orig.). 1991. pap. text ed. 12.95 (0-89898-589-7) CPP Belwin.
—Todays' Ladies of Country Music. 148p. (Orig.). 1991. pap. 12.95 (0-89898-591-9) CPP Belwin.
—Todays' Ladies of Country Music, Vol. 2. 138p. (Orig.). 1993. pap. text ed. 12.95 (0-89898-590-0) CPP Belwin.
—Wedding Showstoppers. 332p. (Orig.). 1992. pap. text ed. 18.95 (0-89898-593-5) CPP Belwin.

Cuellar, Carol, ed. see Brooks, Garth.

Cuellar, Carol, ed. see ZZ Top Staff.

Cuenca, Pilar de see Berenstain, Stan & Berenstain, Janice.

Cuenca, Pilar de see De Cuenca, Pilar.

Cuenca, Pilar de see Eastman, P. D.

Cuenca, Pilar de, tr. see Provensen, Alice & Provensen, Martin.

Cuevas, Gilbert J., jt. auth. see Coffland, Jack A.

Cuevas, Lou. Apache Legends: Songs of the Wind Dancer. Brown, Keven, ed. Cleveland, Fred, illus. 128p. (Orig.). 1990. 16.95 (0-87961-218-5); pap. text ed. 8.95 (0-87961-219-3) Naturegraph.

Culbreath, Myrna, jt. auth. see Marshak, Sondra.

Cullen, Alan. The Beeple. 1968. 4.50 (0-87602-108-9) Anchorage.
—The Golden Fleece. 74p. 1971. 4.50 (0-87602-130-5) Anchorage.
—The Man in the Moon. 1964. 4.50 (0-87602-153-4) Anchorage.
—Trudi & the Minstrel. (gr. 1-9). 1957. 4.50 (0-87602-214-X) Anchorage.

Cullen, Allan. Niccolo & Nicolette. (gr. 1-9). 1957. 4.50 (0-87602-162-3) Anchorage.

Cullen, C., et al. Fundamentals of Math, 2 vols. (gr. 9-12). 1982. Set. text ed. 19.95 (0-685-00708-1); Set. pap. text ed. 14.95 (0-685-67474-6) Vol. 1 (0-8120-2501-6) Vol. 2 (0-8120-2508-3) Barron.

Cullen, Countee, jt. auth. see Cat, Christopher.

Cullen, Countee, jt. auth. see Cat, Christopher.

Cullen, Lynn. The Backyard Ghost. LC 92-24580. 160p. (gr. 4-7). 1993. 13.95 (0-395-64527-1, Clarion Bks) HM.

Cullen, Ruth V. My Letter from Grandma. Antonucci, Emil, illus. LC 92-34381. 32p. 1993. pap. 4.95 (0-8091-6610-0) Paulist Pr.

Cullen-Dupont, Kathryn. Elizabeth Cady Stanton & Women's Liberty. (Illus.). 144p. (gr. 6-12). 1992. lib. bdg. 16.95x (0-8160-2413-8) Facts on File.

Culler, A., ed. see Arnold, Matthew.

Culleton, P., ed. see Barrett, Linda & Guengerich, Galen.

Culleton, P., ed. see Mayberry, Jodine.

Culliford, Pierre see Delporte, pseud.

Cullinan, Bernice E., jt. auth. see Hickman, Janet.

Cullison, Alan. The South Americans. Moynihan, Daniel P., intro. by. (Illus.). 112p. (gr. 5 up). 1991. lib. bdg. 17.95 (0-87754-863-3) Chelsea Hse.

Cullum, Albert. Aesop's Fables: Plays for Young Children. (gr. k-3). 1993. pap. 9.95 (0-86653-940-9) Fearon Teach Aids.
—Greek & Roman Plays for the Intermediate Grades. (gr. 4-8). 1993. pap. 16.95 (0-86653-941-7) Fearon Teach Aids.

Culton, Wilma. Down at the Billabong. Crossett, Warren, illus. LC 92-31951. 1993. 3.75 (0-383-03565-1) SRA Schl Grp.

Culver, Todd A. Discover Birds. (Illus.). 48p. (gr. 3-6). 1992. PLB 14.95 (1-878363-66-2, HTS Bks) Forest Hse.

Cumbaa, Stephen. The Bones Book & Skeleton. LC 90-50368. (Illus.). 64p. (Orig.). (gr. 1-7). 1991. pap. 14.95 (0-89480-860-5, 1860) Workman Pub.

Cumbaa, Stephen & Anderson, Karen C. The Bones & Skeleton Gamebook. (Illus.). 96p. (Orig.). 1993. pap. 7.95 (1-56305-497-3, 3497) Workman Pub.

Cumbow, Robert C., ed. see Hemphill, John A.

Cumming, David. The Ganges. LC 93-11987. (Illus.). 48p. (gr. 5-6). 1993. PLB 22.80 (0-8114-3105-3) Raintree Steck-V.
—India. (Illus.). 32p. (gr. k-4). 1991. 12.40 (0-531-18391-2, Pub. by Bookwright Pr) Watts.
—The Netherlands. LC 91-40478. (Illus.). 32p. (gr. k-4). 1992. PLB 12.40 (0-531-18423-4, Pub. by Bookwright Pr) Watts.
—Photography. LC 89-11534. (Illus.). 48p. (gr. 6-11). 1990. PLB 19.92 (0-8114-2360-3) Raintree Steck-V.
—Spain. LC 91-7340. (Illus.). 32p. (gr. 2-4). 1992. PLB 12.40 (0-531-18443-9, Pub. by Bookwright Pr) Watts.

Cumming, James T. & Moll, Hans G. And, God, What About...? 1980. 5.99 (0-570-03806-5, 12-2915) Concordia.

Cumming, Valerie, ed. see Baker, Patricia.

Cumming, Valerie, ed. see Carnegie, Vicky.

Cumming, Valerie, ed. see Connikie, Yvonne.

Cumming, Valerie, ed. see Costantino, Maria.

Cumming, Valerie, ed. see Feldman, Elane.

Cumming, Valerie, ed. see Herald, Jacqueline.

Cummings, Carol. I'm Always in Trouble. Howatson, Melody, illus. 24p. (ps-3). 1991. pap. 3.99 (0-9614574-5-7) Teaching WA.
—Sticks & Stones. Howatson, Melody, illus. 24p. (Orig.). (ps-3). 1992. pap. 4.99 (0-9614574-8-1) Teaching WA.
—Tattlin' Madeline. Howatson, Melody, illus. 24p. (Orig.). (ps-3). 1991. pap. 3.99 (0-9614574-4-9) Teaching WA.
—Win-Win Day. Howatson, Melody, illus. 24p. (Orig.). (ps-3). 1991. pap. 3.99 (0-9614574-6-5) Teaching WA.
—Won't You Ever Listen. Riddell, Russ, illus. 24p. (Orig.). (ps-3). 1992. pap. 5.99 (0-9614574-7-3) Teaching WA.

Cummings, Cynthia H. Christmas Joy. (Illus.). 84p. Repr. of 1986 ed. 8.00 (1-881811-05-0) H Peterson Pr.
—Christmas Spirit. (Illus.). 84p. Repr. of 1989 ed. 8.00 (1-881811-08-5) H Peterson Pr.
—Christmas Surprise. 2nd ed. (Illus.). 84p. 1990. Repr. of 1985 ed. 8.00 (1-881811-04-2) H Peterson Pr.

Cummings, e. e. Fairy Tales. Eaton, John, illus. LC 65-18727. 39p. (gr. k up). 1975. pap. 3.95 (0-15-629895-3, Voyager Bks) HarBrace.
—Hist Whist. Ray, Deborah K., illus. LC 89-596. 24p. (gr. k-4). 1989. 10.95 (0-517-57360-1) Crown Bks Yng Read.
—Hist Whist & Other Poems for Children. Firmage, George J., ed. (Illus.). (gr. 3 up). 1983. 12.95 (0-87140-640-3) Liveright.
—Little Tree. Ray, Deborah K., illus. LC 86-30940. 32p. (gr. k-4). 1988. PLB 10.95 (0-517-56598-6) Crown Bks Yng Read.

Cummings, e. e., et al. Spooky Poems. Bennett, Jill, compiled by. Rees, Mary, illus. (ps-3). 1989. 14.95 (0-316-08987-7, Joy St Bks) Little.

Cummings, Margaret A. Touched by AIDS. Butler, Cathy, ed. 22p. (Orig.). (gr. 7-12). 1992. pap. text ed. 1.95 (1-56309-024-4, Wrld Changers Res) Womans Mission Union.

Cummings, Pat. The Blue Lake. LC 92-24354. (Illus.). 64p. (gr. 1-5). 1995. 18.00 (0-06-021535-6); PLB 17.89 (0-06-021536-4) HarpC Child Bks.
—Carousel. Cummings, Pat, illus. LC 93-8708. 40p. (ps-3). 1994. RSBE 14.95 (0-02-725512-3, Bradbury Pr) Macmillan Child Grp.
—Clean Your Room, Harvey Moon! Cummings, Pat, illus. LC 89-23863. 32p. (ps-3). 1991. RSBE 13.95 (0-02-725511-5, Bradbury Pr) Macmillan Child Grp.
—Clean Your Room, Harvey Moon! Cummings, Pat, illus. LC 93-20571. 32p. (gr. k-3). 1994. pap. 4.95 (0-689-71798-9, Aladdin) Macmillan Child Grp.
—C.L.O.U.D.S. LC 85-9719. (Illus.). 32p. (ps-3). 1986. 12.95 (0-688-04682-7); PLB 12.88 (0-688-04683-5) Lothrop.
—Jimmy Lee Did It. LC 84-21322. (Illus.). (ps-3). 1985. 13.95 (0-688-04632-0); PLB 12.88 (0-688-04633-9) Lothrop.
—Petey Moroni's Camp Runamok Diary. Cummings, Pat, illus. LC 91-45774. 32p. (gr. k-5). 1992. SBE 14.95 (0-02-725513-1, Bradbury Pr) Macmillan Child Grp.
—Talking with Artists: Conversations with Victoria Chess, Pat Cummings, Leo & Diane Dillon, Richard Egielski, Lois Ehlert, Lisa Campbell Ernst, Tom Feelings, Steven Kellogg, Jerry Pinkney, Amy Schwartz, Lane Smith, Chris Van Allsburg, & David Wiesner. LC 91-9982. (Illus.). 96p. (gr. 4 up). 1992. SBE 18.95 (0-02-724245-5, Bradbury Pr) Macmillan Child Grp.

Cummings, Phil. Goodness Gracious! Smith, Craig, illus. LC 91-17473. 32p. (ps-1). 1992. 13.95 (0-531-05967-7); lib. bdg. 13.99 (0-531-08567-8) Orchard Bks Watts.

Cummings, Priscilla. Chadwick & the Garplegrungen. Cohen, A. R., illus. LC 87-71087. 32p. (gr. k-4). 1987. 8.95 (0-87033-377-1) Tidewater.
—The Chadwick Coloring Book. Cohen, A. R., illus. 32p. (Orig.). (gr. k-4). 1988. pap. 3.95 (0-87033-389-5) Tidewater.
—Chadwick Forever. Cohen, A. R., illus. 30p. (gr. 4-8). 1993. bds. 8.95 (0-87033-450-6) Tidewater.
—Chadwick the Crab. Cohen, A. R., illus. LC 85-41005. 32p. (gr. k-4). 1986. 8.95 (0-87033-347-X) Tidewater.
—Chadwick's Wedding. Cohen, A. R., illus. LC 88-51677. 30p. (gr. k-4). 1989. 8.95 (0-87033-390-9) Tidewater.
—Oswald the Timberdoodles. Cohen, A. R., illus. LC 90-70723. 30p. (gr. k-5). 1990. 8.95 (0-87033-411-5) Tidewater.

—Sid & Sal's Famous Channel Marker Diner. Cohen, A. R., illus. LC 91-65255. 30p. (gr. k-5). 1992. 8.95 (0-87033-423-9) Tidewater.

Cummings, Rhoda & Fisher, Gary. The School Survival Guide for Kids with LD (Learning Differences) Ways to Make Learning Easier & More Fun. LC 91-14489. (Illus.). 176p. (gr. 2 up). 1991. pap. 10.95 (0-915793-32-6) Free Spirit Pub.

—The Survival Guide for Teenagers with LD: (Learning Differences) Espeland, Pamela, ed. LC 93-6798. (Illus.). 200p. (Orig.). (gr. 7 up). 1993. pap. 11.95 (0-915793-51-2); pap. 28.90 incl. audiocassettes (0-915793-57-1); audiocassettes 19.95 (0-915793-56-3) Free Spirit Pub.

Cummings, Rhoda, jt. auth. see Fisher, Gary.

Cummings, Richard. Be Your Own Detective. (gr. 7 up). 1980. 7.95 (0-679-20682-5) McKay.

—Make Your Own Comics for Fun & Profit. (gr. 7 up). 1985. 8.95 (0-679-51208-X) McKay.

—Make Your Own Model Forts & Castles. Cummings, Richard, illus. (gr. 6 up). 1977. 8.95 (0-679-20400-8) McKay.

—Make Your Own Robots. 1985. 8.95 (0-679-20686-8) McKay.

Cummins, Lauren. Healthy Choices, Healthy Lives. (ps-k). 1993. pap. 9.95 (0-86653-935-2) Fearon Teach Aids.

Cummins, Ronald. Cuba. Lopez, Mercedes, illus. LC 89-43170. 64p. (gr. 5-6). 1991. PLB 19.93 (0-8368-0219-5) Gareth Stevens Inc.

Cummins, Ronnie. Guatemala. Welch, Rose, illus. LC 89-40246. 64p. (gr. 5-6). 1990. PLB 19.93 (0-8368-0120-2) Gareth Stevens Inc.

Cummins, Ronnie & Weber, Valerie. Children of the World: Costa Rica. Welch, Rose, photos by. LC 89-43138. 64p. (gr. 5-6). 1990. PLB 19.93 (0-8368-0222-5) Gareth Stevens Inc.

Cummins, Ronnie & Welch, Rose. Children of the World: El Salvador. Welch, Rose, photos by. LC 89-43137. (Illus.). 64p. (gr. 5-6). 1990. PLB 19.93 (0-8368-0220-9) Gareth Stevens Inc.

Cummins, Ronnie, jt. auth. see Peduzzi, Kelli.

Cumpiano, Ina. Homes Are for Living. (Illus.). 24p. (Orig.). (gr. 1-3). 1991. pap. text ed. 29.95 big bk. (1-56334-047-X); pap. text ed. 4.15 small bk. (1-56334-053-4) Hampton-Brown.

—Pan, Pan, Gran Pan (Big Book) Murdocca, Sal, illus. (SPA.). 16p. (Orig.). (gr. k-3). 1990. pap. text ed. 29.95 (0-917837-52-5) Hampton-Brown.

—Pan, Pan, Gran Pan (Small Book) Murdocca, Sal, illus. (SPA.). 16p. (Orig.). (gr. k-3). 1992. pap. text ed. 6.00 (1-56334-085-2) Hampton-Brown.

—Que Semana, Luchito! Halverson, Lydia, illus. (SPA.). 24p. (Orig.). (gr. 1-3). 1991. pap. text ed. 29.95 big bk. (1-56334-023-2); pap. text ed. 4.15 small bk. (1-56334-037-8) Hampton-Brown.

—Y Tu, Donde Vives? O'Neil, Sharron, illus. (SPA.). 24p. (Orig.). (gr. 1-3). 1992. pap. text ed. 29.95 big bk. (1-56334-045-3) Hampton-Brown.

Cundiff, Bette M. Little Lamb Project Book. (Illus.). 15p. (gr. k-5). 1981. pap. write for info. (1-880436-05-1) Miracle Exper.

Cuneo, Mary L. Anne Is Elegant. LC 92-42417. 176p. (gr. 4 up). 1993. 15.00 (0-06-022992-6); PLB 14.89 (0-06-022993-4) HarpC Child Bks.

—How to Grow a Picket Fence. Westcott, Nadine B., illus. LC 91-36444. 32p. (ps-3). 1993. 15.00 (0-06-020863-5); PLB 14.89 (0-06-020864-3) HarpC Child Bks.

—What Can a Giant Do? Huang, Benrei, illus. LC 92-8307. 32p. (ps-2). 1994. 14.00 (0-06-021214-4); PLB 13.89 (0-06-021217-9) HarpC Child Bks.

Cunliffe, John. Postman Pat & the Mystery Thief. (ps-5). 1993. pap. 2.50 (0-590-47099-X) Scholastic Inc.

—Postman Pat to the Rescue. (ps-5). 1993. pap. 2.50 (0-590-47098-1) Scholastic Inc.

Cunning, Peter. Out on the Ice in the Middle of the Bay. Priestley, Alice, illus. 32p. 1993. lib. bdg. 15.95 (1-55037-276-9, Pub. by Annick CN); pap. 6.95 (1-55037-277-7, Pub. by Annick CN) Firefly Bks Ltd.

Cunningham, A. Essential Chemistry. 64p. 1992. lib. bdg. 12.96 (0-88110-508-2, Usborne); pap. 5.95 (0-7460-0727-2) EDC.

Cunningham, Ann M., jt. auth. see White, Ryan.

Cunningham, Antonia. Rainforest Wildlife. (Illus.). 32p. (gr. 3-8). 1993. lib. bdg. 13.96 (0-88110-640-2, Usborne); pap. text ed. 6.95 (0-7460-0940-2, Usborne) EDC.

Cunningham, Beverly. Quick Thinking: Critical & Creative Thinking Challenges, Grades K-6. 80p. (gr. k-6). 1992. pap. text ed. 11.95 (0-944459-47-1) ECS Lrn Systs.

—Quick Thinking: Critical & Creative Thinking Challenges, Grades 7-12. 80p. (gr. 7-12). 1992. pap. text ed. 11.95 (0-944459-48-X) ECS Lrn Systs.

Cunningham, Beverly & Klar, Elizabeth. TAAS Quick Review Mathematics: Grade 7. (Illus.). 112p. (gr. 7). 1992. pap. text ed. 14.95 (0-944459-33-1) ECS Lrn Systs.

Cunningham, Beverly, jt. auth. see Klar, Elizabeth.

Cunningham, Carolyn. All Kinds of Separation. Mortenson, Bob, illus. 24p. (gr. k-6). 1988. wkbk. 3.95 (0-685-20040-X, 0494) Kidsrights.

Cunningham, Carolyn, jt. auth. see MacFarlane, Kee.

Cunningham, Colin. Building for the Victorians. (Illus.). 48p. (gr. 7 up). 1985. pap. 6.95 (0-521-23314-3) Cambridge U Pr.

Cunningham, Dale S., tr. see Pfluger, A.

Cunningham, Donald H., ed. see Stuart, Jesse.

Cunningham, Dru. The Most Wonderful Place to Live. LC 93-85310. (Illus.). 40p. (gr. k-3). 1994. pap. 5.95 (1-55523-644-8) Winston-Derek.

Cunningham, Elaine. Haldor Lillenas: The Marvelous Music Maker. (Illus.). 72p. (Orig.). (gr. 5-6). 1992. pap. 4.95 (0-8341-1443-7) Beacon Hill.

Cunningham, Julia. Viollet. Cober, Alan E., illus. (gr. 4-7). 1966. PLB 6.99 (0-394-91821-5) Pantheon.

Cunningham, Linda. The Copper Angel of Piper's Mill & How She Saved Her Town. Goldberg, Grace, illus. 4p. (gr. 3-5). 1989. 12.95 (0-89272-274-6) Down East.

Cunningham, Lowell. The Men in Black. Ulm, Chris, ed. Carruthers, Sandy, illus. 76p. 1990. pap. 7.95 (0-944735-60-6) Malibu Graphics.

Cunningham, Marilyn. Place of Power. Kratoville, Betty L., ed. (Illus.). 64p. (gr. 3-9). 1989. PLB 4.95 (0-87879-651-7) High Noon Bks.

Cunningham, Marilyn, jt. auth. see Scariano, Margaret.

Cunningham, Michael, jt. auth. see Denson, Wil.

Cunningham, Timothy. The Geode Kit. (Illus.). 64p. 1992. 16.95 (1-56138-144-6) Running Pr.

Cunnyngham, Jerry. Kamache & the Medicine Bead: An Apache Story. Gilliland, Hap, ed. Hardgrove, Tanya, illus. 48p. (gr. 4-10). 1991. pap. 5.95 (0-89992-123-X) Coun India Ed.

Cupo, Hortense. No Way Out but Through. LC 93-29519. 1993. 4.95 (0-8198-5130-2) St Paul Bks.

Cura, M. J., et al. A Path Through Advent for Children 1993. (Illus.). 48p. 1993. pap. 1.00 (0-915531-05-4) OR Catholic.

—A Path Through Easter - Pentecost for Children 1994. (Illus.). 48p. (gr. 3-7). 1994. pap. 1.00 (0-915531-10-0) OR Catholic.

—A Path Through Lent for Children 1994. (Illus.). 48p. (gr. 3-7). 1994. pap. 1.00 (0-915531-08-9) OR Catholic.

Curato, Guy, pseud. Batting One Thousand - Baseball's Leading Hitters: A Tribute to Lou Gehrig. LC 88-82916. 124p. (Orig.). (gr. 9). 1989. pap. write for info. (0-9621591-0-7) T Assicurato.

Curcio, Frances R., ed. see Geddes, Dorothy, et al.

Curen, Barbara Van see Van Curen, Barbara.

Curle, Jock. The Four Good Friends. Watts, Bernadette, illus. LC 86-62520. 32p. (gr. k-3). 1987. 14.95 (1-55858-062-X) North-South Bks NYC.

Curless, Alan, jt. auth. see Foster, John.

Curless, Maura R. Careers Without College: Kids. Hupping, Carol & Grimaldi, Alicia, eds. 96p. (Orig.). 1993. pap. 7.95 (1-56079-251-5) Petersons Guides.

Curran, Eileen. Birds Nests. Johnson, Pamela, illus. LC 84-8658. 32p. (gr. k-2). 1985. PLB 11.59 (0-8167-0341-8); pap. text ed. 2.95 (0-8167-0342-6) Troll Assocs.

—Easter Parade. Goodman, Joan E., illus. LC 84-8630. 32p. (gr. k-2). 1985. PLB 11.59 (0-8167-0353-1); pap. text ed. 2.95 (0-8167-0433-3) Troll Assocs.

—Hello, Farm Animals. Goldsborough, June, illus. LC 84-8657. 32p. (gr. k-2). 1985. PLB 11.59 (0-8167-0345-0); pap. text ed. 2.95 (0-8167-0346-9) Troll Assocs.

—Home for a Dinosaur. Karas, G. Brian, illus. LC 84-8627. 32p. (gr. k-2). 1985. lib. bdg. 11.59 (0-8167-0351-5); pap. text ed. 2.95 (0-8167-0431-7) Troll Assocs.

—Life in the Forest. Harvey, Paul, illus. LC 84-16455. 32p. (gr. k-2). 1985. PLB 11.59 (0-8167-0446-5); pap. text ed. 2.95 (0-8167-0447-3) Troll Assocs.

—Life in the Meadow. Watling, James, illus. LC 84-12384. 32p. (gr. k-2). 1985. PLB 11.59 (0-8167-0343-4); pap. text ed. 2.95 (0-8167-0344-2) Troll Assocs.

—Life in the Pond. Ellis, Elizabeth, illus. LC 84-16285. 32p. (gr. k-2). 1985. lib. bdg. 11.59 (0-8167-0452-X); pap. text ed. 2.95 (0-8167-0453-8) Troll Assocs.

—Life in the Sea. Snyder, Joel, illus. LC 84-16190. 32p. (gr. k-2). 1985. lib. bdg. 11.59 (0-8167-0448-1); pap. text ed. 2.95 (0-8167-0449-X) Troll Assocs.

—Little Christmas Elf. Page, Don, illus. LC 84-8628. 32p. (gr. k-2). 1985. PLB 11.59 (0-8167-0352-3); pap. text ed. 2.95 (0-8167-0432-5) Troll Assocs.

—Look at a Tree. Goldsborough, June, illus. LC 84-8843. 32p. (gr. k-2). 1985. PLB 11.59 (0-8167-0349-3); pap. text ed. 2.95 (0-8167-0350-7) Troll Assocs.

—Mountains & Volcanoes. Watling, James, illus. LC 84-8638. 32p. (gr. k-2). 1985. PLB 11.59 (0-8167-0347-7); pap. text ed. 2.95 (0-8167-0348-5) Troll Assocs.

Current, Andrew, jt. auth. see Lambert, David.

Currey, Anna, jt. auth. see Wilmer, Diane.

Currie, Quinn. Beautiful Joe. rev. & abr. ed. Heinonen, Susan, illus. Amory, Cleveland, intro. by. (Illus.). 72p. (gr. k-8). 1990. pap. 9.95 (0-9623072-1-1) S Ink WA.

—Black Beauty. rev. ed. Ryan, Donna, illus. 126p. (gr. k-8). 1990. pap. 10.95 (0-9623072-2-X) S Ink WA.

Currie, Robin. Mini Eater Activity Book. (Illus.). 48p. (gr. 1-5). 1993. pap. 1.49 (0-7459-2149-3) Lion USA.

Currie, Stephen. Music in the Civil War. LC 92-18102. (Illus.). 112p. (Orig.). (gr. 3-7). 1992. pap. 8.95 (1-55870-263-6) Shoe Tree Pr.

Currier, Mary. Bible Memory Activity Book. (Illus.). 96p. (ps-4). 1993. pap. 7.99 (0-8010-2578-8) Baker Bk.

—Christian Crafts from Paper Plates. 64p. (ps-5). 1989. 8.95 (0-86653-494-6, SS1880, Shining Star Pubns) Good Apple.

Curro, Ellen. No Need to Be Afraid...First Pelvic Exam: A Handbook for Young Women & Their Mothers. Piccirilli, Charles, illus. 80p. (gr. 9-12). 1991. pap. text ed. 4.95 (0-9629417-1-9) Linking Ed Med.

Curry, Jane L. Back in the Beforetime: Tales of the California Indians. Watts, James, illus. LC 86-21339. 144p. (gr. 3-7). 1987. SBE 13.95 (0-689-50410-1, M K McElderry) Macmillan Child Grp.

—The Big Smith Snatch. LC 89-8036. 192p. (gr. 4-7). 1989. SBE 14.95 (0-689-50478-0, M K McElderry) Macmillan Child Grp.

—The Christmas Knight. DiSalvo-Ryan, DyAnne, illus. LC 92-2277. 32p. (gr. k-4). 1993. SBE 14.95 (0-689-50572-8, M K McElderry) Macmillan Child Grp.

—The Daybreakers. Robinson, Charles, illus. (gr. 3-7). 1991. 20.50 (0-8446-6474-X) Peter Smith.

—The Great Flood Mystery. LC 85-1322. 180p. (gr. 3-6). 1985. SBE 13.95 (0-689-50306-7, M K McElderry) Macmillan Child Grp.

—The Great Smith House Hustle. LC 92-33073. 192p. (gr. 4-7). 1993. SBE 14.95 (0-689-50580-9, M K McElderry) Macmillan Child Grp.

—Little, Little Sister. Bleguad, Erik, illus. LC 88-13079. 32p. (ps-3). 1989. SBE 12.95 (0-689-50459-4, M K McElderry) Macmillan Child Grp.

—The Lotus Cup. LC 85-21467. 164p. (gr. 7 up). 1986. SBE 13.95 (0-689-50384-9, M K McElderry) Macmillan Child Grp.

—Me, Myself & I. LC 87-2681. 160p. (gr. 7 up). 1987. SBE 14.95 (0-689-50429-2, M K McElderry) Macmillan Child Grp.

—Mindy's Mysterious Miniature. (gr. 4-7). 19.75 (0-8446-6433-2) Peter Smith.

—What the Dickens! LC 90-26864. 160p. (gr. 4-7). 1991. SBE 13.95 (0-689-50524-8, M K McElderry) Macmillan Child Grp.

—What the Dickens! 160p. (gr. 5 up). 1993. pap. 3.99 (0-14-036284-3, Puffin) Puffin Bks.

Curry, Jennifer. Measles & Sneezles. (Illus.). 96p. (gr. 4-6). 1992. 15.95 (0-09-174082-7, Pub. by Hutchinson UK) Trafalgar.

Curry, Kathy J. Children of the Light - Level 1. (Illus.). 24p. (Orig.). (gr. k-3). 1991. pap. text ed. 9.95 (1-56322-025-3) V W Hensley.

—Children of the Light - Level 2. (Illus.). 24p. (Orig.). (gr. k-3). 1991. pap. text ed. 9.95 (1-56322-026-1) V W Hensley.

—Children of the Light - Level 3. (Illus.). 24p. (Orig.). (gr. k-3). 1991. pap. text ed. 9.95 (1-56322-027-X) V W Hensley.

Curson, Marjorie. Jonas Salk. Gallin, Richard, ed. (Illus.). 144p. (gr. 5-9). 1990. PLB 13.98 (0-382-09966-4); pap. 7.95 (0-382-09971-0) Silver Burdett Pr.

Curti, Anna. At Home. (Illus.). (ps-1). 1991. bds. 5.95 (0-316-16538-7) Little.

—Seasons. (ps-1). 1991. bds. 5.95 (0-316-16539-5) Little.

Curtin, Michael. The League Against Christmas. 256p. 1990. 21.95 (0-233-98382-1, Pub. by A Deutsch England) Trafalgar.

Curtis, A. & Hindley, J. Paper Fun. (Illus.). 32p. (gr. 3-6). 1977. pap. 5.95 (0-86020-001-9) EDC.

Curtis, Alice P. Every Cat Should Have a Home. (Illus.). 60p. (Orig.). 1992. pap. write for info. (0-9612126-0-8) A P Walmsley.

Curtis, Alice T. A Little Maid of New England. 1991. 7.99 (0-517-06494-4) Outlet Bk Co.

Curtis, Chara M. Fun Is a Feeling. Aldrich, Cynthia, illus. (ps-2). 1992. 14.95 (0-935699-04-X) Illum Arts.

—How Far to Heaven. (ps-3). 1993. 15.95 (0-935699-06-6) Illum Arts.

Curtis, David, et al. German Study-Aid. 1977. pap. 2.75 (0-87738-034-1) Youth Ed.

Curtis, Donald. New Age Understanding. LC 72-92276. 144p. 1990. pap. 7.95 (0-941992-23-5) Los Arboles Pub.

Curtis, Donald A. Fantasy on Sunset Mountain. LC 82-74122. 44p. (Orig.). (gr. 3-7). 1982. pap. 3.50 (0-9610284-0-8) D A Curtis.

Curtis, Dorris. Skammy: Prince of Troy. Curtis, Dorris, illus. 231p. (gr. 5-9). 1988. lib. bdg. 18.50 (0-944436-04-8) Univ Central AR Pr.

Curtis, Jamie L. When I Was Little: A Four-Year-Old's Memoir of Her Youth. Cornell, Laura, illus. LC 91-46188. 32p. (gr. k-3). 1993. 14.00 (0-06-021078-8); PLB 13.89 (0-06-021079-6) HarpC Child Bks.

Curtis, Neil & Greenland, Peter. How Bread Is Made. (Illus.). 24p. (gr. 1-3). 1992. PLB 13.50 (0-8225-2375-2) Lerner Pubns.

—How Paper Is Made. (Illus.). 24p. (gr. 1-3). 1992. PLB 13.50 (0-8225-2376-0) Lerner Pubns.

—How Steel Is Made. (Illus.). 24p. (gr. 1-3). 1992. PLB 13.50 (0-8225-2378-7) Lerner Pubns.

—How Tires Are Made. (Illus.). 24p. (gr. 1-3). 1992. PLB 13.50 (0-8225-2377-9) Lerner Pubns.

Curtis, Neil, et al. Planet Earth. LC 93-20103. (Illus.). 96p. (Orig.). (gr. 5 up). 1993. 15.95 (1-85697-848-6); pap. 9.95 (1-85697-847-8) Kingfisher Bks.

Curtis, Patricia. Animals & the New Zoos. (Illus.). 64p. (gr. 3-8). 1991. 15.95 (0-525-67347-4, Lodestar Bks) Dutton Child Bks.

—Aquatic Animals in the Wild & in Captivity. (Illus.). 64p. (gr. 3-8). 1992. 16.00 (0-525-67384-9, Lodestar Bks) Dutton Child Bks.

Curtis, Philip. Invasion of the Comet People: A Capers Book. Ross, Tony, illus. LC 82-9923. 128p. (gr. 3-5). 1983. lib. bdg. 5.99 (*0-394-95490-4*) Knopf Bks Yng Read.

Curtis, Robert H. Great Lives: Medicine. LC 92-5387. (Illus.). 336p. (gr. 4-6). 1992. SBE 22.95 (*0-684-19321-3*, Scribners Young Read) Macmillan Child Grp.

—Questions & Answers about Alcoholism. LC 76-7560. (Illus.). 1976. 10.95 (*0-13-748459-3*) P-H.

Curtis, Stefanie. Here's My Heart. 160p. (gr. 7 up). 1987. pap. 2.50 (*0-553-26566-0*) Bantam.

Curwood, James O. Baree, the Story of a Wolf-Dog. LC 90-37875. 256p. (gr. 3-11). 1992. 18.95 (*1-55704-075-3*); pap. 3.95 (*1-55704-132-6*) Newmarket.

—Bear. Annaud, Jean-Jacques, intro. by. LC 89-13247. 208p. (gr. 3-11). 1992. 16.95 (*1-55704-054-0*); pap. 3.95 (*1-55704-131-8*) Newmarket.

Cush, Cathie. Depression. LC 93-14252. (Illus.). (gr. 6-9). 1993. PLB 21.34 (*0-8114-3529-6*) Raintree Steck-V.

—Disasters That Shook the World. LC 93-10299. (Illus.). 48p. (gr. 5-7). 1993. PLB 22.80 (*0-8114-4929-7*) Raintree Steck-V.

—Pregnancy. LC 93-25155. (Illus.). (gr. 6-9). 1993. PLB 21.34 (*0-8114-3530-X*) Raintree Steck-V.

Cushman. Aunt Eaters Mystery Xmas. Date not set. 14. 00 (*0-06-023579-9*, Festival); PLB 13.89 (*0-06-023580-2*, Festival) HarpC Child Bks.

Cushman, Doug. ABC Mystery. Cushman, Doug, illus. LC 92-9621. 32p. (ps-2). 1993. 14.00 (*0-06-021226-8*); PLB 13.89 (*0-06-021227-6*) HarpC Child Bks.

—Aunt Eater Loves a Mystery. Cushman, Doug, illus. LC 87-73. 64p. (gr. k-3). 1987. 13.00 (*0-06-021326-4*); PLB 13.89 (*0-06-021327-2*) HarpC Child Bks.

—Aunt Eater Loves a Mystery. Cushman, Doug, illus. LC 87-73. 64p. (ps-3). 1989. pap. 3.50 (*0-06-444126-1*, Trophy) HarpC Child Bks.

—Aunt Eater Loves a Mystery. 15p. (gr. 2-4). 1987. pap. 1.20 (*0-685-66375-2*, BR8415) W A T Braille.

—Aunt Eater Loves a Mystery. 15p. 1991. text ed. 1.20 (*1-56956-189-3*) W A T Braille.

—Aunt Eater's Mystery Vacation. Cushman, Doug, illus. LC 91-25059. 64p. (gr. k-3). 1992. 13.00 (*0-06-020513-X*); PLB 13.89 (*0-06-020514-8*) HarpC Child Bks.

—Aunt Eater's Mystery Vacation. Cushman, Doug, illus. LC 91-25059. 64p. (gr. k-3). 1993. pap. 3.50 (*0-06-444169-5*, Trophy) HarpC Child Bks.

—Camp Big Paw. Cushman, Doug, illus. LC 89-26867. 64p. (gr. k-3). 1990. PLB 11.89 (*0-06-021368-X*) HarpC Child Bks.

—Camp Big Paw. LC 89-26867. (Illus.). 64p. (gr. k-3). 1993. pap. 3.50 (*0-06-444166-0*, Trophy) HarpC Child Bks.

—Possum Stew. LC 89-34481. (Illus.). 32p. (ps-1). 1990. 12.95 (*0-525-44566-8*, DCB) Dutton Child Bks.

—Uncle Foster's Hat Tree. Cushman, Doug, illus. LC 88-3573. 48p. (ps-3). 1988. 9.95 (*0-525-44410-6*, DCB) Dutton Child Bks.

Cushman, Doug, illus. The Pudgy Fingers Counting Book. 16p. (ps-3). 1983. pap. 2.95 (*0-448-10202-1*, G&D) Putnam Pub Group.

Cushman, Jack L. Math Flipper: A Guide to Basic Mathematics. (Illus.). 49p. (gr. 5 up). 1989. Repr. of 1975 ed. trade edition 5.95 (*1-878383-02-7*) C Lee Pubns.

—Punctuation & Capitalization Flipper. (Illus.). 49p. (gr. 5 up). 1989. Repr. of 1974 ed. trade edition 5.95 (*1-878383-00-0*) C Lee Pubns.

Cushman, Jean. Do You Wanna Bet? Your Chance to Find Out about Probability. Weston, Martha, illus. 112p. (gr. 3-7). 1991. 14.45 (*0-395-56516-2*, Clarion Bks) HM.

Cushman, Karen. Catherine, Called Birdy. 224p. (gr. 7 up). 1994. 14.95 (*0-395-68186-3*, Clarion Bks) HM.

Cushman, Kathleen. Circus Dreams: The Making of a Circus Artist. (gr. 4-7). 1990. 15.95 (*0-316-16561-1*, Joy St Bks) Little.

Cusick, Dawn. Fabric Lovers' Christmas Scrapcrafts. LC 93-10659. (Illus.). 128p. (gr. 10-12). 1993. 24.95 (*0-8069-0437-2*, Pub. by Lark Bks) Sterling.

Cusick, Dawn, jt. auth. see LaRose-Weaver, Diane.

Cusick, Richie. Buffy the Vampire Slayer. MacDonald, Pat, ed. 192p. 1992. pap. 3.99 (*0-671-79220-2*) PB.

Cusick, Richie T. Evil on the Bayou. 160p. (gr. 7 up). 1992. pap. 3.50 (*0-440-92431-6*, LFL) Dell.

—Help Wanted. 224p. (Orig.). (gr. 7 up). 1993. pap. 3.99 (*0-671-79403-5*, Archway) PB.

—The Lifeguard. 192p. (Orig.). (gr. 9 up). 1988. pap. 3.25 (*0-590-43203-6*) Scholastic Inc.

—The Mall. MacDonald, Pat, ed. 224p. (Orig.). 1992. pap. 3.75 (*0-671-70958-5*, Archway) PB.

—Teacher's Pet. 224p. (Orig.). (gr. 8-12). 1990. pap. 3.25 (*0-590-44331-5*) Scholastic Inc.

—Trick or Treat. 208p. (Orig.). (gr. 7 up). 1989. pap. 3.25 (*0-590-44235-X*) Scholastic Inc.

—Vampire. MacDonald, Patricia, ed. 224p. (Orig.). 1991. pap. 3.75 (*0-671-70956-9*, Archway) PB.

Custer, Elizabeth B. The Kid. Henry, Nadezhda, intro. by. (Illus.). 47p. (gr. 2-6). 1978. Repr. of 1900 ed. limited ed. 8.00x (*0-940696-05-3*) Monroe County Lib.

Custer, Jim, et al. The Best of the Jeremiah People: Humorous Sketches & Performance Tips by America's Leading Christian Repertory Group. LC 91-34195. 192p. (gr. 9 up). 1991. pap. 14.95 (*0-916260-81-X*, B117) Meriwether Pub.

Custer, Susan, et al. Smarts: A Study Skills Resource Guide. rev. ed. Oling, Tom, illus. (gr. 5-7). 1991. tchr's. ed. 11.95 (*0-944584-27-6*) Sopris.

Cutburth, Ronald W. Love from the Sea. Naumann, Cynthia E., ed. Witt, Hannelore, tr. Persels, Beth, illus. (GER.). 27p. (gr. 5-8). 1989. pap. write for info. (*1-878291-03-3*) Love From Sea.

—Love from the Sea. Naumann, Cynthia E., ed. Witt, Hannelore, tr. Persels, Beth, illus. (FRE.). 27p. (gr. 5-8). 1989. pap. write for info. (*1-878291-07-6*) Love From Sea.

—Love from the Sea. Naumann, Cynthia E., ed. Lander, Kerstin, tr. Persels, Beth, illus. (SWE.). 27p. (gr. 5-8). 1989. pap. write for info. (*1-878291-06-8*) Love From Sea.

—Love from the Sea. Naumann, Cynthia E., ed. Persels, Beth, illus. Tostado, Rocio G., tr. (SPA., Illus.). 27p. (gr. 5-8). 1990. pap. write for info. (*1-878291-09-2*) Love From Sea.

—Love from the Sea. Naumann, Cynthia E., ed. West, Bobbie, tr. Persels, Beth, illus. (CHI.). 27p. (gr. 5-8). 1990. pap. write for info. (*1-878291-11-4*) Love From Sea.

—Love from the Sea. Naumann, Cynthia E., ed. Persels, Beth, illus. 27p. (Orig.). (gr. 4-7). 1990. pap. 3.50 (*1-878291-01-7*) Love From Sea.

Cutchins, Judy & Johnston, Ginny. Animal Fathers. LC 93-27014. 1994. write for info. (*0-688-12255-8*); lib. bdg. write for info. (*0-688-12256-6*) Morrow JR Bks.

—The Crocodile & the Crane: Surviving in a Crowded World. LC 86-5339. (Illus.). 64p. (gr. 2-5). 1986. 12.95 (*0-688-06304-7*); lib. bdg. 12.88 (*0-688-06305-5*, Morrow Jr Bks) Morrow Jr Bks.

Cutchins, Judy, jt. auth. see Johnston, Ginny.

Cuthbert, Susan. Deep Sea Creatures. (Illus.). 16p. (gr. 1-6). 1992. pap. 1.99 activity bk. (*0-7459-2143-4*) Lion USA.

—Endangered Creatures. (Illus.). 16p. (gr. 1-6). 1992. pap. 1.99 activity bk. (*0-7459-2144-2*) Lion USA.

Cutler, C. Practice Your BASIC. Reed, Naomi, illus. 48p. (gr. 6 up). 1983. PLB 10.96 (*0-88110-142-7*); pap. 3.95 (*0-86020-743-9*) EDC.

Cutler, Ebbitt. I Once Knew an Indian Woman. Johnson, Bruce, illus. 72p. (gr. 5 up). 1985. (Dist. by U of Toronto Pr); pap. 6.95 (*0-88776-068-6*) Tundra Bks.

—If I Were a Cat I Would Sit in a Tree. Arnold, Rist, illus. 28p. (gr. k-4). 1985. text ed. 7.95 (*0-88776-177-1*, Dist. by U of Toronto Pr) Tundra Bks.

Cutler, Ebbitt, tr. see Nickl, Peter.

Cutler, Ivor. Doris. Munoz, Claudio, illus. LC 92-5923. 32p. (gr. k-3). 1992. PLB 14.00 (*0-688-11939-5*, Tambourine Bks) Morrow.

—Herbert: Five Stories. Benson, Patrick, illus. LC 88-2918. 48p. (ps-2). 1988. 13.00 (*0-688-08147-9*); PLB 12.88 (*0-688-08148-7*) Lothrop.

Cutler, Jane. Darcy & Gran Don't Like Babies. Ryan, Susannah, illus. LC 91-42214. 32p. (ps-2). 1993. 14.95 (*0-590-44587-1*, Scholastic Hardcover) Scholastic Inc.

—Family Dinner. Caswell, Philip, illus. 112p. (gr. 3 up). 1992. 13.95 (*0-374-32267-8*) FS&G.

—Mr. Carey's Garden. LC 93-13720. Date not set. 14.95 (*0-395-68191-X*) Ticknor & Fields.

—No Dogs Allowed. (gr. 4-7). 1992. 14.00 (*0-374-35526-6*) FS&G.

Cutlip, Glen W., jt. auth. see Shockley, Robert.

Cutlip, Ralph V. Mountain Massacres & Other Stories of Appalachia. Hallinan, Brenda C., illus. 167p. (Orig.). (gr. 8 up). 1986. pap. 6.50 (*0-317-47675-0*) B Cutlip.

Cutter, N., jt. auth. see Tatchell.

Cutting, Michael. The Little Crooked Christmas Tree. Broda, Ron, illus. 24p. 1990. 13.95 (*0-590-45204-5*, Scholastic Hardcover) Scholastic Inc.

Cutts, David. I Can Read About Creatures of the Night. LC 78-68468. (Illus.). (gr. 2-5). 1979. pap. 1.95 (*0-89375-202-9*) Troll Assocs.

—I Can Read About Reptiles. LC 72-96954. (Illus.). (gr. 2-4). 1973. pap. 1.95 (*0-89375-058-1*) Troll Assocs.

—I Can Read About Thunder & Lightning. LC 78-66273. (Illus.). (gr. 2-6). 1979. pap. 1.95 (*0-89375-217-7*) Troll Assocs.

—Look - a Butterfly. Conner, Eulala, illus. LC 81-11369. 32p. (gr. k-2). 1982. PLB 11.59 (*0-89375-662-8*); pap. text ed. 2.95 (*0-89375-663-6*) Troll Assocs.

—More about Dinosaurs. Wenzel, Gregory C., illus. LC 81-11432. 32p. (gr. k-2). 1982. PLB 11.59 (*0-89375-668-7*); pap. text ed. 2.95 (*0-89375-669-5*) Troll Assocs.

Cutts, David, ed. see Bros. Grimm.

Cutts, David, ed. see Grimm, Jacob & Grimm, Wilhelm K.

Cutts, David, adapted by see Jacobs, Joseph.

Cutts, David, retold by. Gingerbread Boy. Goodman, Joan E., illus. LC 78-18069. 32p. (gr. k-2). 1979. PLB 9.79 (*0-89375-122-7*); pap. 1.95 (*0-89375-100-6*) Troll Assocs.

—House That Jack Built. Silverstein, Don, illus. LC 78-18951. 32p. (gr. k-2). 1979. PLB 9.79 (*0-89375-127-8*); pap. 1.95 (*0-89375-105-7*) Troll Assocs.

Cutts, Grace. Let My People Go. 29p. (ps-2). 1991. 3.99 (*0-87509-450-3*) Chr Pubns.

—On Call. 30p. (ps-2). 1991. 3.99 (*0-87509-452-X*) Chr Pubns.

—To China & Back. 27p. (ps-2). 1991. 3.99 (*0-87509-453-8*) Chr Pubns.

Cutts, Gracie. Weak Thing in Moni Land. 29p. (ps-2). 1991. 3.99 (*0-87509-451-1*) Chr Pubns.

Cutts, William A. Weak Thing in Moni Land: The Story of Bill & Gracie Cutts. Richardson, Don, frwd. by. LC 90-80454. (Illus.). 168p. (Orig.). 1990. pap. 7.99 (*0-87509-429-5*) Chr Pubns.

Cuyler. Daisy Crazy Thanks. 1991. 14.95 (*0-8050-1557-4*) H Holt & Co.

Cuyler, Juliana & Walsh, Moira. I Is for Island - I Para Isla. Long, Rachel L., illus. (MAP & ENG.). 108p. (Orig.). (ps-2). 1992. pap. 10.00 (*0-9635260-0-6*) Alphabet.

Cuyler, Margery. Baby Dot: A Dinosaur Story. Weiss, Ellen, illus. 32p. (ps-1). 1990. 13.45 (*0-395-51934-9*, Clarion Bks) HM.

—Barry Bear & the Bad Guys. Stevens, Janet, illus. LC 92-11576. 1993. 14.45 (*0-395-59939-3*, Clarion Bks) HM.

—The Christmas Snowman. Westerman, Johanna, illus. 32p. (ps-3). 1992. 14.95 (*1-55970-066-1*) Arcade Pub Inc.

—Daisy's Crazy Thanksgiving. Kramer, Robin, illus. LC 90-4323. 32p. (ps-2). 1990. 14.95 (*0-8050-0559-5*, Owlet BYR) H Holt & Co.

—Daisy's Crazy Thanksgiving. Kramer, Robin, illus. LC 90-4323. 32p. (ps-2). 1992. pap. 4.95 (*0-8050-2348-8*, Owlet BYR) H Holt & Co.

—Fat Santa. LC 86-31962. 32p. (ps-2). 1987. 14.95 (*0-8050-0423-8*, Bks Young Read); pap. 4.95 (*0-8050-1167-6*, Bks Young Read) H Holt & Co.

—Freckles & Willie: A Valentine's Day Story. Winborn, Marsha, illus. LC 85-8646. 32p. (ps-2). 1986. 12.95 (*0-03-003772-7*, Bks Young Read) H Holt & Co.

—Freckles & Willie: A Valentine's Day Story. Winborn, Marsha, illus. LC 85-8646. 32p. (ps-2). 1989. pap. 4.95 (*0-8050-0949-3*, Bks Young Read) H Holt & Co.

—From Here to There. 1994. write for info. (*0-8050-3191-X*) H Holt & Co.

—Shadow's Baby. Weiss, Ellen, illus. LC 88-35257. 32p. (ps-1). 1989. 13.45 (*0-89919-831-7*, Clarion Bks) HM.

—Sir William & the Pumpkin Monster. Winborn, Marsha, illus. LC 84-610. 32p. (ps-2). 1989. pap. 4.95 (*0-8050-1017-3*, Bks Young Read) H Holt & Co.

—That's Good! That's Bad! Catrow, David, illus. LC 90-49353. 32p. (ps-2). 1991. 15.95 (*0-8050-1535-3*, Bks Young Read) H Holt & Co.

—That's Good! That's Bad! Catrow, David, illus. LC 90-49353. 32p. (ps-2). 1993. pap. 5.95 (*0-8050-2954-0*, Bks Young Read) H Holt & Co.

—Weird Wolf. Zimmer, Dirk, illus. LC 89-7541. 80p. (gr. 2-4). 1989. 12.95 (*0-8050-0835-7*, Bks Young Read) H Holt & Co.

—Weird Wolf. Zimmer, Dirk, illus. LC 89-1541. 80p. (gr. 2-4). 1991. pap. 4.95 (*0-8050-1643-0*, Bks Young Read) H Holt & Co.

Cvach, Milos, text by. Robert Delaunay: The Eiffel Tower: An Art Play Book. Curtil, Sophie. (Illus.). 32p. (gr. 2 up). 1988. 17.95 (*0-8109-1141-8*) Abrams.

Cvikota, Tom, jt. ed. see Albers, Maura.

Cwiklik, Robert. A. Philip Randolph & the Labor Movement. LC 92-32167. (Illus.). 32p. (gr. 2-4). 1993. PLB 12.40 (*1-56294-326-X*) Millbrook Pr.

—Albert Einstein. (Illus.). 144p. (gr. 3-6). 1987. pap. 5.95 (*0-8120-3921-1*) Barron.

—Bill Clinton: Our Forty-Second President. (Illus.). 48p. (gr. 2-4). 1993. PLB 12.40 (*1-56294-387-1*) Millbrook Pr.

—King Philip. Furstinger, Nancy, ed. (Illus.). 144p. (gr. 5-7). 1989. PLB 12.98 (*0-382-09573-1*); pap. 7.95 (*0-382-09762-9*) Silver Burdett Pr.

—Malcolm X & Black Pride. LC 92-23687. (Illus.). 32p. (gr. 2-4). 1991. PLB 12.40 (*1-56294-042-2*) Millbrook Pr.

—Sequoyah. Furstinger, Nancy, ed. (Illus.). 142p. (gr. 5-7). 1989. PLB 12.98 (*0-382-09570-7*); pap. 7.95 (*0-382-09759-9*) Silver Burdett Pr.

—Stokely Carmichael & Black Power. LC 92-11560. (Illus.). 32p. (gr. 2-4). 1993. PLB 12.40 (*1-56294-276-X*) Millbrook Pr.

—Tecumseh: Shawnee Rebel. (Illus.). 112p. (gr. 5 up). 1994. PLB 18.95 (*0-7910-1721-4*, Am Art Analog) Chelsea Hse.

Cymerman, Sandra, jt. auth. see Modest, Diane.

Cytron, Barry D. Fire! The Library Is Burning. (Illus.). 56p. (gr. 4 up). 1988. lib. bdg. 14.95 (*0-8225-0525-8*) Lerner Pubns.

Cytron, Phyllis. Myriam Mendilow: The Mother of Jerusalem. LC 93-15119. 1993. write for info. (*0-8225-4919-0*) Lerner Pubns.

Czaja, Paul C. Writing with Light: A Simple Workshop in Basic Photography. LC 72-93261. 96p. (gr. 6 up). 1973. 12.95 (*0-85699-068-X*) Chatham Pr.

Czajkowski, Alexandre M. Birds & Their Nests. (ps-3). 1993. 4.95 (*0-944589-49-9*) Young Discovery Lib.

Czarnecki, Lois R. The Six Wrinkled Woos. Almada, Laura, illus. 32p. (gr. k-3). 1992. 17.95 (*0-9627275-0-4*) Ohana Pr.

Czarra, Fred, jt. auth. see Collins, Thomas.

Czerkas, Stephen & Czerkas, Sylvia J. My Life with the Dinosaurs. (Illus.). 32p. (gr. 4-6). 1989. pap. 2.75 (*0-671-63454-2*, Minstrel Bks) PB.

Czerkas, Sylvia J., jt. auth. see Czerkas, Stephen.

Czernecki, Stefan. Bear in the Sky. LC 90-30224. (Illus.). 64p. (gr. 2-7). 1990. 14.95 (*0-920534-63-5*, Pub. by Hyperion Pr Ltd CN) Sterling.

—The Hummingbirds' Gift. (Illus.). 32p. (gr. k-4). 1994. 14.95 (*1-56282-604-2*); PLB 14.89 (*1-56282-605-0*) Hyprn Child.

Czernecki, Stefan & Rhodes, Timothy. Nina's Treasures.
LC 90-36592. (Illus.). 56p. (gr. 1-6). 1990. pap. 14.95
(0-920534-65-1) Sterling.
—Nina's Treasures. Czernecki, Stefan, illus. 40p. (gr. k-4).
1994. pap. 4.95 (1-56282-487-2) Hyprn Ppbks.
—Nina's Treasures. 1994. PLB write for info.
(1-56282-595-X) Hyprn Child.
—Pancho's Pinata. Czernecki, Stefan, illus. LC 92-7325.
40p. (gr. k-4). 1992. 14.95 (1-56282-277-2); PLB 14.
89 (1-56282-278-0) Hyprn Child.
—The Singing Snake. Czernecki, Stefan, illus. LC 92-
85515. 40p. (ps-2). 1993. 14.95 (1-56282-399-X); PLB
14.89 (1-56282-400-7) Hyprn Child.
—The Sleeping Bread. LC 91-75422. (Illus.). 40p. (gr.
k-4). 1992. 14.95 (1-56282-183-0); PLB 14.89
(1-56282-207-1) Hyprn Child.
—The Sleeping Bread. Czernecki, Stefan, illus. LC 91-
75422. 40p. (gr. k-4). 1993. pap. 4.95 (1-56282-519-4)
Hyprn Ppbks.
Czerneda, Julie. Great Careers for People Interested in
Living Things, 6 vols. LC 93-78080. (Illus.). 48p. (gr.
6-9). 1993. 16.95 (0-8103-9387-5, 102105, UXL)
Gale.
Czerny, Carl. One Hundred Practical Exercises for Piano,
Op. 139. 76p. 1905. pap. 8.95 (0-8258-0134-6) Fischer
Inc NY.
—School of Velocity for Piano, Op. 299, Complete
Edition. 101p. 1903. pap. 7.50 (0-8258-0108-7, L 338)
Fischer Inc NY.
—Thirty New Studies in Technique for Piano, Op. 849.
56p. 1907. pap. 6.75 (0-8258-0127-3, L 487) Fischer
Inc NY.

D

D. C. Cook Editors. The Big Picture Book about Jesus.
Hook, Richard & Hook, Frances, illus. LC 77-72722.
(gr. 3-7). 1977. 13.95 (0-89191-077-8, 08292, Chariot
Bks) Cook.
D, Lisa, ed. Stepping Stones to Recovery for Young
People. LC 91-8676. 240p. (Orig.). (gr. 9-12). 1991.
pap. 6.95 (0-934125-19-8) Glen Abbey Bks.
Daab, Marcia J. Science Fair Workshop. (gr. 4-8). 1990.
pap. 6.95 (0-8224-6374-1) Fearon Teach Aids.
Dabcovich. Busy Beavers. 1993. pap. 28.67
(0-590-72455-X) Scholastic Inc.
Dabcovich, Lydia. Ducks Fly. LC 89-38716. (Illus.). 32p.
(ps). 1990. 13.95 (0-525-44586-2, DCB) Dutton Child
Bks.
—Keys to My Kingdom: A Poem in Three Languages.
LC 90-4040. (ps-3). 1992. 14.00 (0-688-09774-X);
PLB 13.93 (0-688-09775-8) Lothrop.
—Mrs. Huggins & Her Hen Hannah. Dabcovich, Lydia,
illus. LC 85-4406. 24p. (ps-2). 1988. 12.95
(0-525-44203-0, DCB); pap. 3.95 (0-525-44368-1,
DCB) Dutton Child Bks.
—Sleepy Bear. Dabcovich, Lydia, illus. 32p. (ps-2). 1982.
12.95 (0-525-39465-6, DCB) Dutton Child Bks.
—Sleepy Bear. Dabcovich, Lydia, illus. 32p. (ps-2). 1985.
pap. 4.95 (0-525-44196-4, DCB) Dutton Child Bks.
—Sleepy Bear. Dabcovich. 32p. (ps-1). 1993. pap. 17.99
(0-14-054937-4, Puffin Unicorn) Puffin Bks.
Dabney, Gene. Swimming: A Step-By-Step Guide. LC 89-
27346. (Illus.). 64p. (gr. 4-8). 1990. PLB 9.79
(0-8167-1945-4); pap. 2.95 (0-8167-1946-2) Troll
Assocs.
Dabney, Joy, illus. A Book about Me. 32p. (gr. k-3).
1987. wkbk. 2.50 (0-939985-00-4) Creative
Dimensions.
Dace, Rosalind, ed. see Purves, Pamela.
Dackerman, Gerald, jt. auth. see Sohl, Marcia.
Dacquino, V. T. Kiss the Candy Days Good-Bye. LC 82-
70324. 160p. (gr. 4-6). 1982. pap. 11.95
(0-385-28532-9) Delacorte.
—Kiss the Candy Days Good-Bye. (gr. 5-9). 1986. pap.
2.25 (0-440-44369-5) Dell.
Dacquino, Vinny, jt. auth. see Messina, Kathlyn.
Dad-Burn. Adventures with Melvin, 6 vols. (Illus.). 85p.
(Orig.). (gr. 3-6). 1993. Set. pap. 32.95
(1-880310-35-X) Burnshire Hse.
—Melvin Meets the Kookamaroos. 85p. (gr. 3-6). 1992.
pap. write for info.; pap. 6.95 (1-880310-40-6)
Burnshire Hse.
—The Zany Peppermint Drop. rev. ed. 50p. (gr. 3-6).
1992. pap. 3.50 (1-880310-25-2) Burnshire Hse.
Dadey & Jones. Aliens Don't Wear Braces. 1993. pap.
2.95 (0-590-47070-1) Scholastic Inc.
Dadey, Debbie. Frankenstein Doesn't Plant Petunias. (gr.
9-12). 1993. pap. 2.75 (0-590-47071-X) Scholastic Inc.
Dadey, Debbie & Jones, Marcia. Leprechauns Don't Play
Basketball. 80p. 1992. pap. 2.75 (0-590-44822-6)
Scholastic Inc.
—Vampires Don't Wear Polka Dots. 96p. (Orig.). (gr.
2-5). 1990. pap. 2.50 (0-590-43411-X) Scholastic Inc.
—Werewolves Don't Go to Summer Camp. 128p. (gr.
2-5). 1991. pap. 2.50 (0-590-44061-6) Scholastic Inc.
Dadey, Debra & Jones, Marcia. Santa Claus Doesn't
Mop Floors. 80p. 1991. pap. 2.75 (0-590-44477-8)
Scholastic Inc.
Dadley, Debbie. Ghosts Don't Eat Potato Chips. (ps-3).
1992. pap. 2.75 (0-590-45854-X) Scholastic Inc.
Daffron, Carolyn. Edna St. Vincent Millay. Horner,
Matina S., intro. by. (Illus.). 112p. (gr. 5 up). 1990. 17.
95 (1-55546-668-0) Chelsea Hse.

—Gloria Steinem. Horner, Matina, intro. by. (Illus.).
112p. (gr. 5 up). 1988. lib. bdg. 17.95 (1-55546-679-6)
Chelsea Hse.
—Margaret Bourke-White. Horner, Matina, intro. by.
(Illus.). 112p. (Orig.). (gr. 5 up). 1988. 17.95
(1-55546-644-3); pap. 9.95 (0-7910-0411-2) Chelsea
Hse.
Dagavarian, Debra. Century of Children's Baseball
Stories. (gr. 4-7). 1990. pap. 7.95 (0-9625132-0-2)
Stadium Bks.
Dagavarian, Debra A., ed. A Century of Children's
Baseball Stories. 200p. 1992. lib. bdg. 16.95
(0-88736-832-8) Meckler Corp.
—A Century of Children's Baseball Stories, No. 2. 200p.
(Orig.). (gr. 5-8). 1993. 16.95 (0-9625132-2-9)
Meckler Corp.
—A Century of Children's Sports Stories. 200p. (gr. 5-8).
1993. lib. bdg. 16.95 (0-88736-852-2) Meckler Corp.
Daggett, John A. see Hall, Leo D.
Daggett, R. M., ed. & illus. see Kalakaua, David.
Daglish, Alice & Rhys, Ernest. Rock-a-Bye Rhymes:
Miniature Nursery Rhyme Books, 4 bks. Folkard,
Charles, illus. (ps-3). 1993. Repr. of 1932 ed. Set,
miniature bks. in rocking-horse slipcase. 16.95
(0-8118-0537-9) Chronicle Bks.
Dahl, Roald. The BFG. Blake, Quentin, illus. LC 85-566.
221p. (gr. 1 up). 1982. 16.00 (0-374-30469-6) FS&G.
—The BFG. Blake, Quentin, illus. 1989. pap. 4.50
(0-14-034019-X, Puffin) Puffin Bks.
—The BFG. LC 93-22605. 1993. 13.95 (0-679-42813-5,
Everymans Lib) Knopf.
—Boy: Tales of Childhood. LC 85-117335. (Illus.). 176p.
(gr. 3 up). 1984. 16.00 (0-374-37374-4) FS&G.
—Boy: Tales of Childhood. (gr. 4-6). 1986. pap. 4.99
(0-14-031890-9, Puffin) Puffin Bks.
—Charlie & Chocolate Factory, Vol. 1. (gr. 4-7). 1977.
pap. 2.75 (0-553-15248-3) Bantam.
—Charlie & the Chocolate Factory. Schindelman, Joseph,
illus. (gr. 5 up). 1964. 15.00 (0-394-81011-2); PLB 15.
99 (0-394-91011-7) Knopf Bks Yng Read.
—Charlie & the Chocolate Factory. 176p (ps up). 1988.
pap. 4.50 (0-14-032869-6, Puffin) Puffin Bks.
—Charlie & the Chocolate Factory. large type ed. 174p.
1989. Repr. of 1964 ed. lib. bdg. 13.95
(1-55736-154-1, Crnrstn Bks) BDD LT Grp.
—Charlie & the Chocolate Factory. 1984. pap. 2.75
(0-553-15454-0) Bantam.
—Charlie & the Chocolate Factory. (Illus.). 174p 1992.
Repr. PLB 14.95x (0-89966-904-2) Buccaneer Bks.
—Charlie & the Chocolate Factory - Charlie & the Great
Glass Elevator, 2 bks. (Illus.). 352p. (gr. 5 up). 1991.
Boxed set, slipcased. 30.00 (0-679-81940-1) Knopf Bks
Yng Read.
—Charlie & the Chocolate Factory: A Play. George,
Richard H., adapted by. 320p. (gr. 3-7). 1983. pap.
3.50 (0-14-031125-4, Puffin) Puffin Bks.
—Charlie & the Chocolate Factory: (Charlie y la Fabrica
de Chocolate) (SPA). 8.95 (968-6026-71-1) Santillana.
—Charlie & the Great Glass Elevator. 176p. 1988. pap.
4.50 (0-14-032870-X, Puffin) Puffin Bks.
—Charlie & the Great Glass Elevator. 1984. pap. 2.75
(0-553-15455-9) Bantam.
—Charlie & the Great Glass Elevator: The Further
Adventures of Charlie Bucket & Willie Wonka, the
Chocolate-Maker Extraordinaire. Schindelman,
Joseph, illus. (gr. k-7). 1972. 15.00 (0-394-82472-5);
lib. bdg. 15.99 (0-394-92472-X) Knopf Bks Yng Read.
—Charlie et la Chocolaterie. Simeon, Michel, illus.
(FRE.). 190p. (gr. 5-10). 1987. pap. 8.95
(0-685-60279-6) Schoenhof.
—Charlie et le Grand Ascenseur de Verre. Jacques, Faith,
illus. (FRE.). 151p. (gr. 5-10). 1978. pap. 7.95
(2-07-033065-6) Schoenhof.
—The Dahl Diary, 1992. Blake, Quentin, illus. 208p. (ps
up). 1991. pap. 8.95 (0-14-034647-3, Puffin) Puffin
Bks.
—Danny, Champion of the World. 1984. pap. 2.75
(0-553-15505-9) Bantam.
—Danny, the Champion of the World. 208p. 1988. pap.
4.50 (0-14-032873-4, Puffin) Puffin Bks.
—Danny: The Champion of the World. Bennett, Jill, illus.
208p. (gr. 3 up). 1975. 16.00 (0-394-83103-9); PLB
15.99 (0-394-93103-3) Knopf Bks Yng Read.
—Dirty Beasts. Blake, Quentin, illus. LC 85-594. 32p. (gr.
1 up). 1986. pap. 4.99 (0-14-050435-4, Puffin) Puffin
Bks.
—Doigt Magique. Galeron, Henri, illus. (FRE.). 63p. (gr.
1-5). 1989. pap. 9.95 (2-07-031185-6) Schoenhof.
—The Enormous Crocodile. 48p. (Orig.). (gr. 1-3). 1984.
pap. 2.95 (0-553-15243-2, Skylark) Bantam.
—The Enormous Crocodile. reissue ed. Blake, Quentin,
illus. LC 77-5081. 32p. (ps-3). 1978. 14.00
(0-394-83594-8); lib. bdg. 14.99 (0-394-93594-2)
Knopf Bks Yng Read.
—The Enormous Crocodile. Blake, Quentin, illus. 32p.
(gr. 1-5). 1993. pap. 3.99 (0-14-036556-7, Puffin)
Puffin Bks.
—Esio Trot. Blake, Quentin, illus. 1990. 14.95
(0-670-83424-3) Viking Child Bks.
—Esio Trot. Blake, Quentin, illus. LC 92-16931. 64p. (gr.
3-7). 1992. pap. 3.99 (0-14-036099-9) Puffin Bks.
—Fantastic Mr. Fox. (gr. 4-8). 1978. pap. 2.50
(0-553-15390-0, Skylark) Bantam.
—Fantastic Mr. Fox. Chaffin, Donald, illus. LC 74-
118704. 72p. (gr. 3-6). 1986. 14.95 (0-394-80497-X);
lib. bdg. 14.99 (0-394-90497-4) Knopf Bks Yng Read.
—Fantastic Mr. Fox. 96p. 1988. pap. 3.99
(0-14-032872-6, Puffin) Puffin Bks.

—Fantastique Maitre Renard. Ross, Tony, illus. (FRE.).
119p. (gr. 3-7). 1989. pap. 10.95 (2-07-031174-0)
Schoenhof.
—George's Marvelous Medicine. (gr. 2-4). 1987. pap.
2.75 (0-553-15394-3, Skylark) Bantam.
—George's Marvelous Medicine. Blake, Quentin, illus.
47p. (gr. k-7). 1991. pap.
3.99 (0-14-034641-4, Puffin) Puffin Bks.
—The Giraffe & the Pelly & Me. Blake, Quentin, illus.
LC 86-43079. 32p. (ps-3). 1987. pap. 4.99
(0-14-050566-0, Puffin) Puffin Bks.
—Going Solo. (Illus.). 208p. (gr. 8 up). 1986. 14.95
(0-374-16503-3) FS&G.
—Going Solo. 224p. (gr. 7 up). 1993. pap. 4.99
(0-14-032528-X, Puffin) Puffin Bks.
—James & the Giant Peach. Burkert, Nancy E., illus. (gr.
3 up). 1961. 15.00 (0-394-81282-4); PLB 15.99
(0-394-91282-9) Knopf Bks Yng Read.
—James & the Giant Peach. 112p. 1988. pap. 4.50
(0-14-032871-8, Puffin) Puffin Bks.
—James & the Giant Peach. large type ed. (gr. 4-7).
1989. lib. bdg. 14.95 (1-55736-155-X, Crnrstn Bks)
BDD LT Grp.
—James & the Giant Peach. 1993. Repr. of 1988 ed. lib. bdg.
19.95x (0-89966-702-3) Buccaneer Bks.
—James & the Giant Peach. 1984. pap. 2.95
(0-553-15317-X) Bantam.
—James & the Giant Peach: A Play. 128p. (gr. 3-7).
1983. pap. 3.50 (0-14-031464-4, Puffin) Puffin Bks.
—James et la Grosse Peche. Simeon, Michel, illus.
(FRE.). 174p. (gr. 5-10). 1988. pap. 8.95
(2-07-033517-8) Schoenhof.
—Magic Finger. Pene DuBois, William, illus. LC 66-
18657. 46p. (gr. 3-6). 1966. 15.00 (0-06-021381-7);
PLB 14.89 (0-06-021382-5) HarpC Child Bks.
—The Magic Finger. Ross, Tony, illus. LC 92-31443.
64p. (gr. 2-6). 1993. pap. 3.99 (0-14-036303-3) Puffin
Bks.
—Matilda. Blake, Quentin, illus. 240p. (gr. 3-7). 1988.
pap. 14.95 (0-670-82439-9) Viking Child Bks.
—Matilda. large type ed. 1989. Repr. of 1988 ed. lib. bdg.
15.95 (1-55736-123-1, Crnrstn Bks) BDD LT Grp.
—Matilda. 240p. (gr. 3-7). 1990. pap. 4.50
(0-14-034294-X, Puffin) Puffin Bks.
—The Minpins. 1991. 17.00 (0-670-84168-4) Viking
Child Bks.
—My Year. Blake, Quentin, illus. 64p. (gr. 4-7). 1994. 14.
99 (0-670-85397-6) Viking Child Bks.
—Potion Magique de Georges Bouillon. Blake, Quentin,
illus. (FRE.). 148p. (gr. 5-10). 1990. pap. 8.95
(2-07-033463-5) Schoenhof.
—Rhyme Stew. Blake, Quentin, illus. 80p. (gr. 4 up).
1990. pap. 14.95 (0-670-82916-1) Viking Child Bks.
—Roald Dahl Boxed Set: Includes; Charlie & the
Chocolate Factory; Charlie & the Great Glass
Elevator; the Big. (Illus.). (gr. 3-7). 1989. pap. 11.95
(0-14-095040-0) Viking Child Bks.
—Roald Dahl: Charlie & the Chocolate Factory, Charlie
& the Great Glass Elevator & The BFG, 3 bks. 1989.
Set. pap. 11.95 (0-685-30573-2) Viking Child Bks.
—Roald Dahl's Revolting Rhymes. Blake, Quentin, illus.
LC 82-15263. 48p. (gr. 3-6). 1983. 14.00
(0-394-85422-5); lib. bdg. 14.99 (0-394-95422-X)
Knopf Bks Yng Read.
—El Superzorro - Fantastic Mr. Fox. Buckley, Ramon, tr.
Elena, Horacio, illus. (SPA.). 153p. (gr. 2-4). 1992.
pap. write for info. (84-204-0013-0) Santillana.
—Three More from Roald Dahl: Includes The Witches,
James & the Giant Peach, & Danny the Champion of
the World. (gr. 3-7). 1991. 11.95 (0-14-095381-7)
Puffin Bks.
—The Twits. Blake, Quentin, illus. 96p. (gr. 2-6). 1991.
pap. 3.99 (0-14-034640-6, Puffin) Puffin Bks.
—The Vicar of Nibbleswicke. Blake, Quentin, illus. 24p.
1992. 12.50 (0-670-84384-9) Viking Child Bks.
—The Witches. Blake, Quentin, photos by. LC 83-14195.
(Illus.). 208p. (gr. 3-9). 1983. 16.00 (0-374-38457-6);
ltd. ed. o.s.i. 35.00 (0-374-38458-4) FS&G.
—The Witches. Blake, Quentin, illus. LC 85-519. 200p.
(gr. 3-7). 1985. pap. 3.95 (0-14-031730-9) Viking
Child Bks.
—The Wonderful Story of Henry Sugar & Six More. (gr.
4-8). 1979. pap. 2.95 (0-553-15445-1, Skylark Bk)
Bantam.
—The Wonderful Story of Henry Sugar & Six More.
224p. 1988. pap. 4.50 (0-14-032874-2, Puffin) Puffin
Bks.
—The Wonderful Story of Henry Sugar & Six More. large
type, rev. ed. 280p. 1989. lib. bdg. 14.95
(1-85089-984-3, Crnrstn Bks) BDD LT Grp.
—The Wonderful Story of Henry Sugar & Six More. LC
77-5354. 32p. (gr. 5 up). 1977. 15.00 (0-394-83604-9)
Knopf Bks Yng Read.
Dahl, Roald & Tannen, Mary. The Twits. Burgoyne,
John, illus. LC 80-18410. (ps-5). 1991. 12.00
(0-394-84599-4); lib. bdg. 12.99 (0-394-94599-9)
Knopf Bks Yng Read.
Dahl, Roald, ed. Roald Dahl's Book of Ghost Stories.
235p. (gr. 5 up). 1983. 19.00 (0-374-25131-2) FS&G.
—Roald Dahl's Book of Ghost Stories. 235p. (gr. 5 up).
1984. pap. 9.00 (0-374-51868-8) FS&G.
Dahl, Tessa. Babies, Babies, Babies. Dodds, Siobhan, illus.
32p. (ps-2). 1991. 12.95 (0-670-83921-3) Viking Child
Bks.
—The Same but Different. Robins, Arthur, illus. 32p.
(ps-3). 1993. pap. 3.99 (0-14-054823-8) Puffin Bks.
—School Can Wait. (gr. 4-7). 1991. 11.95
(0-670-84170-6) Viking Child Bks.

Dahlback, Helena. My Sister Lotta & Me. Ramel, Charlotte, illus. Lesser, Rika, tr. from SWE. (Illus.). 32p. (gr. k-3). 1993. PLB 15.95 (*0-8050-2558-8*, Bks Young Read) H Holt & Co.

Dahlen, Beverly. A Reading. 101p. (Orig.). (gr. 6-12). 1989. pap. 8.50 (*0-937013-33-1*) Potes Poets.

Dahlstedt, Marden A. The Terrible Wave: Memorial Edition. Robinson, Charles, illus. LC 72-76687. 125p. (gr. 7 up). 1988. pap. 5.00 (*0-9621827-0-2*) R R Dahlstedt.

Dahlstrom, Lorraine M. Doing the Days: A Year's Worth of Creative Journaling, Drawing, Listening, Reading, Thinking, Arts & Crafts Activities for Children Ages 8-12. Wallner, Rosemary, ed. 224p. (Orig.). (gr. 3-7). 1994. pap. 21.95 (*0-915793-62-8*) Free Spirit Pub.

—Writing down the Days: Three Hundred Sixty-Five Creative Journaling Ideas for Young People. LC 89-29616. (Illus.). 176p. (gr. 6 up). 1990. pap. 12.95 (*0-915793-19-9*) Free Spirit Pub.

Daiell, Saralyn, ed. see Dounuts, Kevin.

Daily, Robert. Earth. LC 93-6102. 1994. write for info. (*0-531-20158-9*) Watts.

Dairy Council of California Staff, jt. auth. see National Dairy Council Staff.

Daizovi, Lonnie G. & Saxon, Ed. Spanish Alive, Level I. (SPA., Illus.). 177p. (Orig.). (ps-3). 1990. Repr. of 1986 ed. songbook & cassette 11.95 (*0-935301-50-X*); tchr's. manual 18.95 (*0-935301-59-3*) Vibrante Pr.

Dakan, Peggy, jt. auth. see Bruno, Janet.

Dakenbing, William F. The Creation Book. Hendrickson, et al, illus. Von Braun, Wehrner. LC 75-39840. 70p. (gr. 3 up). 1976. 5.95 (*0-685-68397-4*); pap. 3.95 (*0-685-68398-2*) Triumph Pub.

Dakos, Kalli. Don't Read This Book Whatever You Do! More Poems about School. Karas, G. Brian, illus. LC 92-23236. 64p. (gr. 2-6). 1993. RSBE 13.95 (*0-02-725582-4*, Four Winds) Macmillan Child Grp.

—If You're Not Here, Please Raise Your Hand: Poems about School. Karas, G. Brian, illus. LC 89-71530. 64p. (gr. 2-6). 1990. SBE 12.95 (*0-02-725581-6*, Four Winds) Macmillan Child Grp.

DaLage, Ida. Beware! Beware! A Witch Won't Share. (Illus.). 48p. (gr. k-4). 1991. Repr. of 1972 ed. lib. bdg. 12.95 (*0-7910-1473-8*) Chelsea Hse.

—The Farmer & the Witch. Miret, Gil, illus. 48p. (gr. k-4). 1991. Repr. of 1966 ed. PLB 12.95 (*0-7910-1474-6*) Chelsea Hse.

Dalal-Clayton, Diksha. The Adventures of Young Krishna: The Blue God of India. LC 92-19072. 1992. 13.00 (*0-19-508113-7*) OUP.

Dalby, Judy N., jt. auth. see Hammond, Vicky L.

Dale. The Ivy. 1993. pap. 28.67 (*0-590-50128-3*) Scholastic Inc.

Dale, Alan T. The Crowd Is Waiting. 16p. (gr. 3-5). 1976. pap. 1.95 (*0-8192-1208-3*) Morehouse Pub.

—I've Found the Sheep. (Orig.). (gr. 3-5). 1976. pap. 1.95 (*0-8192-1206-7*) Morehouse Pub.

—Jesus Is Really Alive Again! (gr. 3-5). 1976. pap. 1.95 (*0-8192-1209-1*) Morehouse Pub.

—Paul the Traveler. 16p. (gr. 3-5). 1976. pap. 1.95 (*0-8192-1211-3*) Morehouse Pub.

—God Cares for Everybody, Everywhere. 16p. (Orig.). (gr. 3-5). 1978. pap. 1.95 (*0-8192-1237-7*) Morehouse Pub.

Dale, Bruce. Collection of Children's Stories. (Illus.). 88p. 1994. pap. 6.95 (*0-8059-3515-0*) Dorrance.

Dale, Delbert A. Trumpet Technique. Gorham, Charles, pref. by. (Illus.). 102p. (gr. 9 up). 1985. pap. 26.95 (*0-19-322128-4*) OUP.

Dale, E., jt. auth. see Alward, Edgar C.

Dale, Henry. Early Flying Machines. LC 92-21664. 1992. 16.00 (*0-19-520966-4*) OUP.

Dale, Henry, et al. The Industrial Revolution. LC 92-21663. 1992. 16.00 (*0-19-520967-2*) OUP.

Dale, Nora. The Best Trick of All. (Illus.). 32p. (gr. 1-4). 1989. PLB 15.96 (*0-8172-3505-1*); pap. 3.95 (*0-8114-6700-7*) Raintree Steck-V.

—Nan & the Sea Monster. (Illus.). 32p. (gr. 1-4). 1989. PLB 15.96 (*0-8172-3526-4*); pap. 3.95 (*0-8114-6728-7*) Raintree Steck-V.

Dale, Norman, tr. see Guillot, Rene.

Dale, Penny. All about Alice. Dale, Penny, illus. LC 92-52991. 32p. (ps-3). 1993. 13.95 (*1-56402-171-8*) Candlewick Pr.

—Bet You Can't. Dale, Penny, illus. LC 87-3780. 32p. (ps-1). 1988. (Lipp Jr Bks) HarpC Child Bks.

—The Elephant Tree. LC 90-38902. (Illus.). 32p. (gr. 3-6). 1991. 14.95 (*0-399-22282-0*, Putnam) Putnam Pub Group.

—Ten Out of Bed. LC 92-46116. 1994. write for info. (*1-56402-322-2*) Candlewick Pr.

—Wake up, Mr. B.! Dale, Penny, illus. LC 91-58763. 32p. (ps up). 1992. 14.95 (*1-56402-104-1*) Candlewick Pr.

Dale, Rodney. Early Cars. (Illus.). 64p. 1993. PLB 16.00 (*0-19-521002-6*) OUP.

—Early Railways. (Illus.). 64p. 1993. PLB 16.00 (*0-19-521003-4*) OUP.

—Timekeeping. LC 92-21661. 1992. 16.00 (*0-19-520968-0*) OUP.

Dale, Rodney & Weaver, Rebecca. Home Entertainment. (Illus.). 64p. 1993. PLB 16.00 (*0-19-521001-8*) OUP.

—Machines in the Office. (Illus.). 64p. 1993. PLB 16.00 (*0-19-521000-X*) OUP.

Dale, Rodney, jt. auth. see Weaver, Rebecca.

Dale, Rodney, ed. Discoveries & Inventions, 8 vols. (Illus.). 512p. 1994. Set. PLB 128.00 (*0-19-520973-7*) OUP.

D'Alelio, Jane. I Know That Building! Discovering Architecture with Activities & Games. (Illus.). 88p. (gr. 3-6). 1989. pap. 14.95 (*0-89133-133-6*) Preservation Pr.

Daley, Dan. A Song for Linda, No. 122. 144p. (Orig.). (gr. 7-12). 1987. pap. 2.50 (*0-553-26419-2*) Bantam.

Daley, Dennis, jt. auth. see Sinberg, Janet.

Daley, Dennis C., jt. auth. see Read, Edward M.

Daley, Maureen. Seventeenth Summer. (gr. 7-11). 1942. 10.95 (*0-396-02322-3*, Putnam) Putnam Pub Group.

Daley, William. The Chinese Americans. Moynihan, Daniel P., intro. by. (Illus.). 112p. (gr. 5 up). 1988. lib. bdg. 17.95 (*0-87754-867-6*) Chelsea Hse.

—Chinese Americans. (gr. 4-7). 1993. pap. 8.95 (*0-7910-0260-8*) Chelsea Hse.

Dalgiesh, Alice, jt. auth. see Milhous, Katherine.

Dalglieish, Alice. The Bears on Hemlock Mountain. Sewell, Helen, illus. LC 89-27651. 64p. (gr. 1-4). 1990. Repr. of 1952 ed. RSBE 13.95 (*0-684-19169-5*, Scribners Young Read) Macmillan Child Grp.

—The Bears on Hemlock Mountain. 2nd ed. Sewell, Helen, illus. LC 91-40166. 64p. (gr. 1-3). 1992. pap. 3.95 (*0-689-71604-4*, Aladdin) Macmillan Child Grp.

—The Courage of Sarah Noble. Weisgard, Leonard, illus. LC 54-5922. 64p. (gr. 1-5). 1987. Repr. of 1954 ed. SBE 13.95 (*0-684-18830-9*, Scribners Young Read) Macmillan Child Grp.

—The Courage of Sarah Noble. 2nd ed. Weisgard, Leonard, illus. LC 91-15531. 64p. (gr. 1-5). 1991. pap. 4.95 (*0-689-71540-4*, Aladdin) Macmillan Child Grp.

—Fourth of July Story. Nonnast, Marie, illus. LC 56-6138. 32p. (ps-3). 1972. RSBE 13.95 (*0-684-13164-1*, Scribners Young Read); (Scribner) Macmillan Child Grp.

—The Fourth of July Story. Nonnast, Marie, illus. LC 86-20662. 32p. (gr. k-4). 1987. pap. 3.95 (*0-689-71115-8*, Aladdin) Macmillan Child Grp.

—The Silver Pencil. Milhous, Katherine, illus. 248p. (gr. 7 up). 1991. pap. 4.99 (*0-14-034792-5*, Puffin) Puffin Bks.

—The Thanksgiving Story. Sewell, Helen, illus. LC 87-11471. 32p. (gr. k-3). 1985. pap. 4.95 (*0-689-71053-4*, Aladdin) Macmillan Child Grp.

—The Thanksgiving Story. Sewell, Helen, illus. LC 88-4448. 32p. (gr. k-3). 1988. Repr. of 1954 ed. RSBE 13.95 (*0-684-18999-2*, Scribners Young Read) Macmillan Child Grp.

Dallas I. S. D. Staff. The Bible Study Course of the New Treatment. 1993. pap. 4.95 (*0-925279-28-5*) Wallbuilders.

Dallinger, Jane. Grasshoppers. LC 80-27806. (Illus.). (gr. 4 up). 1981. PLB 19.95 (*0-8225-1455-9*) Lerner Pubns.

—Grasshoppers. Sato, Yuko, photos by. (Illus.). 48p. (gr. 4 up). pap. 5.95 (*0-8225-9568-0*) Lerner Pubns.

—Spiders. LC 80-27548. (Illus.). 48p. (gr. 4 up). 1981. PLB 19.95 (*0-8225-1456-7*, First Ave Edns); pap. 5.95 (*0-8225-9534-6*, First Ave Edns) Lerner Pubns.

Dallinger, Jane & Johnson, Sylvia A. Frogs & Toads. LC 80-27667. (Illus.). 48p. (gr. 4 up). 1982. PLB 19.95 (*0-8225-1454-0*, First Ave Edns); pap. 5.95 (*0-8225-9502-8*, First Ave Edns) Lerner Pubns.

Dalmais. Beaver, Reading Level 3-4. (Illus.). 28p. (gr. 2-5). 1983. PLB 16.67 (*0-86592-859-2*) Rourke Corp.

—Duck, Reading Level 3-4. (Illus.). 28p. (gr. 2-5). 1983. PLB 16.67 (*0-86592-862-2*); 12.50s.p. (*0-685-58816-5*) Rourke Corp.

—Kangaroo, Reading Level 3-4. (Illus.). 28p. (gr. 2-5). 1983. PLB 16.67 (*0-86592-864-9*); 12.50s.p. (*0-685-58820-3*) Rourke Corp.

—Penguin, Reading Level 3-4. (Illus.). 28p. (gr. 2-5). 1983. PLB 16.67 (*0-86592-854-1*); 12.50 (*0-685-58823-8*) Rourke Corp.

—Porcupine, Reading Level 3-4. (Illus.). 28p. (gr. 2-5). 1983. PLB 16.67 (*0-86592-852-5*); 12.50 (*0-685-58824-6*) Rourke Corp.

—Seal, Reading Level 3-4. (Illus.). 28p. (gr. 2-5). 1983. PLB 16.67 (*0-86592-867-3*); 12.50s.p. (*0-685-58825-4*) Rourke Corp.

—Squirrel, Reading Level 3-4. (Illus.). 28p. (gr. 2-5). 1983. PLB 16.67 (*0-86592-857-6*); 12.50 (*0-685-58826-2*) Rourke Corp.

Dalton, Anne. This Is the Way. (Illus.). (ps up). 1992. 14.95 (*0-590-45892-2*, 020, Scholastic Hardcover) Scholastic Inc.

Dalton, Annie. Out of the Ordinary. LC 89-39787. 256p. (gr. 7 up). 1992. pap. 3.95 (*0-06-447081-4*, Trophy) HarpC Child Bks.

—The Real Tilly Beany. large type ed. Aldous, Kate, illus. 1993. 15.95 (*0-7451-1807-0*, Galaxy Child Lrg Print) Chivers N Amer.

Dalton, Bill, ed. see Williams, George, III.

Dalton, Bill, ed. see Williams, George J., III.

Dalton, J. W. The Life Savers of Cape Cod. Ackerman, Frank, intro. by. (Illus.). 176p. 1991. pap. 8.95 (*0-940160-49-8*) Parnassus Imprints.

Dalton, Kathleen, jt. auth. see O'Leary, Daniel J.

Dalton, LeRoy C. & Snyder, Henry D. Topics for Mathematics Clubs. 2nd ed. LC 83-8296. 106p. (gr. 8-12). 1983. pap. 7.00 (*0-87353-208-2*) NCTM.

Dalton, Rosemary, jt. auth. see Barrett-Dragan, Patricia.

Daly, Jean, ed. see Anderson, Neil T. & Park, Dave.

Daly, John. Presenting S. E. Hinton. 1989. pap. 3.95 (*0-440-20482-8*, LFL) Dell.

Daly, Kathleen. Greek & Roman Mythology A to Z: A Young Reader's Companion. (Illus.). 128p. (gr. 4-10). 1992. lib. bdg. 19.95x (*0-8160-2151-1*) Facts on File.

Daly, Kathleen N. Big Golden Book of Backyard Birds. (gr. 3-6). 1990. write for info. (*0-307-15857-8*) Western Pub.

—Golden Book of Sharks & Whales. (Illus.). (gr. 2-6). 1989. write for info. (*0-307-15850-0*, Pub. by Golden Bks) Western Pub.

—The Macmillan Picture Wordbook. Wallner, John, illus. LC 82-6619. 80p. (ps-1). 1982. 7.95 (*0-02-725600-6*) Macmillan.

—Norse Mythology A to Z. (Illus.). 128p. 1990. 19.95x (*0-8160-2150-3*) Facts on File.

—The Shyest 'Kid in the 'Patch. Lace, Lynn, illus. 40p. (gr. 1-5). 1984. 5.95 (*0-910313-30-X*) Parker Bros.

—Strawberry Shortcake & Pets on Parade. Sustendal, Pat, illus. 40p. (ps-3). 1983. cancelled 5.95 (*0-910313-06-7*) Parker Bros.

Daly, Maureen. Acts of Love. LC 86-1863. 176p. (gr. 7 up). 1986. pap. 12.95 (*0-590-33873-0*) Scholastic Inc.

—Acts of Love. 192p. (gr. 7 up). 1987. pap. 2.75 (*0-590-43631-7*) Scholastic Inc.

—First a Dream. 224p. 1991. 3.25 (*0-590-40847-X*, Point) Scholastic Inc.

—Seventeenth Summer. (gr. 7-9). 1985. pap. 3.50 (*0-671-61931-4*, Archway) PB.

—Seventeenth Summer. 293p. 1981. Repr. PLB 23.95 (*0-89966-355-9*) Buccaneer Bks.

—Seventeenth Summer. 288p. 1981. Repr. PLB 19.95x (*0-89967-029-6*) Harmony Raine.

Daly, Niki. Ben's Gingerbread Man. LC 85-3327. (Illus.). 24p. (ps-1). 1985. 4.95 (*0-670-80806-7*) Viking Child Bks.

—Mama, Papa & Baby Joe. (ps-3). 1991. 14.95 (*0-670-84161-7*) Viking Child Bks.

—Mary Malloy & the Baby Who Wouldn't Sleep. (ps-3). 1991. 14.95 (*0-307-17501-4*, Artsts Writrs) Western Pub.

—Not So Fast, Songololo. Daly, Niki, illus. LC 85-70134. 32p. (gr. k-3). 1986. SBE 13.95 (*0-689-50367-9*, M K McElderry) Macmillan Child Grp.

—Not So Fast, Songololo. (ps-3). 1987. pap. 3.99 (*0-14-050715-9*, Puffin) Puffin Bks.

—Papa Lucky's Shadow. Daly, Niki, illus. LC 91-24283. 32p. (gr. k-3). 1992. SBE 14.95 (*0-689-50541-8*, M K McElderry) Macmillan Child Grp.

Daly, Niki, jt. auth. see Mennen, Ingrid.

Dalzel-Job, Patric. From Arctic Snow to Dust of Normandy. (Illus.). 224p. (gr. 9 up). 1991. 30.00 (*0-86299-842-5*) A Sutton Pub.

Dam, Eva Van see Van Dam, Eva.

Damaris, Gypsy. Pink Hair. 20p. (Orig.). (gr. 1). 1984. pap. 2.35 (*0-914917-00-5*) Folk Life.

Damashek, Sandy. Teeny-Tiny Train & Planes, 6 bks. Filippo, Margaret S., illus. (ps-k). 1992. bds. 14.95 (*1-56293-241-1*, Set, mini-board bks. in a tray) McClanahan Bk.

D'Amato, Alex, jt. auth. see D'Amato, Janet.

D'Amato, Janet & D'Amato, Alex. Cardboard Carpentry. D'Amato, Jane & D'Amato, Alex, illus. Thompson, Morton, intro. by. (gr. 2-5). PLB 13.95 (*0-87460-085-5*) Lion Bks.

—Handicrafts for Holidays. D'Amato, Janet & D'Amato, Alex, illus. (gr. 1-4). 1967. PLB 13.95 (*0-87460-086-3*) Lion Bks.

—Indian Crafts. D'Amato, Janet & D'Amato, Alex, illus. (gr. 2-5). PLB 13.95 (*0-87460-088-X*) Lion Bks.

D'Amato, Janet P. & Carter, Laurel S. How on Earth Do We Recycle Plastic? D'Amato, Janet P., illus. LC 91-22430. 64p. (gr. 4-6). 1992. PLB 12.90 (*1-56294-143-7*) Millbrook Pr.

D'Ambrosio, Bobbe, et al. Spell Well. (gr. 1-6). 1980. pap. 12.95 (*0-8224-6455-1*) Fearon Teach Aids.

Dambrosio, Monica & Barbieri, Roberto. The Americas in the Colonial Era. Ianni, Mary D., tr. from ITA. Berselli, Remo, illus. LC 92-19154. 72p. (gr. 5-6). 1992. PLB 17.97 (*0-8114-3326-9*) Raintree Steck-V.

—The Birth of Modern Europe. Di Ianni, Mary, tr. Berselli, Remo, illus. LC 92-22076. (ITA & ENG.). 72p. (gr. 5-6). 1992. PLB 17.97 (*0-8114-3325-0*) Raintree Steck-V.

Damjan, Mischa. Atuk. Wilkon, Josef, illus. LC 89-43728. 32p. (ps-3). 1990. 13.95 (*1-55858-091-3*) North-South Bks NYC.

—The Big Squirrel & the Little Rhinoceros. De Beer, Hans, illus. Hort, Lenny, tr. from GER. LC 91-17865. (Illus.). 32p. (gr. k-3). 1991. 14.95 (*1-55858-117-0*) North-South Bks NYC.

—Das Eichhorn und das Nashornchen. De Beer, Hans, illus. (GER.). 32p. (gr. k-3). 1992. 14.95 (*3-314-00538-5*) North-South Bks NYC.

—The False Flamingoes. Steadman, Ralph, illus. LC 70-105399. 32p. (ps-3). 7.95 (*0-87592-016-0*) Scroll Pr.

—La Foret Aux Milles Ombres. De Beer, Hans, illus. (FRE.). 32p. (gr. k-3). 1992. 14.95 (*3-314-20740-9*) North-South Bks NYC.

Damon, Dave, ed. see Damon, Valerie H.

Damon, Laura. Birthday Buddies. Aiello, Laurel, illus. LC 87-10866. 32p. (gr. k-2). 1988. PLB 11.59 (*0-8167-1091-0*); pap. text ed. 2.95 (*0-8167-1092-9*) Troll Assocs.

—Discovering Earthquakes & Volcanoes. Jones, John R., illus. LC 89-4974. 32p. (gr. 2-4). 1990. PLB 11.59 (*0-8167-1757-5*); pap. text ed. 2.95 (*0-8167-1758-3*) Troll Assocs.

—Fun in the Snow. Paterson, Diane, illus. LC 87-10843. 32p. (gr. k-2). 1988. PLB 11.59 (*0-8167-1081-3*); pap. text ed. 2.95 (*0-8167-1082-1*) Troll Assocs.
—Funny Fingers, Funny Toes. Kennedy, Anne, illus. LC 87-10915. 32p. (gr. k-2). 1988. PLB 11.59 (*0-8167-1089-9*); pap. text ed. 2.95 (*0-8167-1090-2*) Troll Assocs.
—Hide-&-Seek on the Farm. Kramer, Robin, illus. LC 87-13737. 32p. (gr. k-2). 1988. PLB 7.89 (*0-8167-1231-X*); pap. text ed. 1.95 (*0-8167-1232-8*) Troll Assocs.
—Secret Valentine. Kennedy, Anne, illus. LC 87-13736. 32p. (gr. k-2). 1988. PLB 11.59 (*0-8167-1101-1*); pap. text ed. 2.95 (*0-8167-1102-X*) Troll Assocs.
—Wonders of Plants & Flowers. Miyaki, Yoshi, illus. LC 89-5003. 32p. (gr. 2-4). 1990. PLB 11.59 (*0-8167-1761-3*); pap. text ed. 2.95 (*0-8167-1762-1*) Troll Assocs.
Damon, Valerie H. Grindle Lamfoon & the Procurnious Fleekers. Damon, Dave, ed. Damon, Valerie H., illus. LC 78-64526. (gr. 1-12). 1979. 12.95 (*0-932356-05-2*); fleeker ed. 14.95 (*0-932356-06-0*) Star Pubns MO.
—Tea with Adella Dine Crow. Damon, Dave, ed. LC 88-92261. (Illus.). 32p. (ps-5). 1990. 9.95 (*0-932356-15-X*) Star Pubns MO.
—Willo Mancifoot (and the Mugga Killa Whomps) Damon, Dave, ed. LC 83-50739. (Illus.). (gr. 2-6). 1985. 14.95 (*0-932356-07-9*); ltd. art ed. 100.00 (*0-932356-08-7*) Star Pubns Mo.
Dampier, Joseph H. Workbook on Christian Doctrine. 64p. (Orig.). (gr. 6 up). 1943. pap. 3.99 (*0-87239-072-1*, 3343) Standard Pub.
Damrell, Liz. With the Wind. Marchesi, Stephen, illus. LC 89-48942. 32p. (gr-2). 1991. 14.95 (*0-531-05882-4*); PLB 14.99 (*0-531-08482-5*) Orchard Bks Watts.
Dana, Barbara. Necessary Parties. LC 85-45267. 352p. (gr. 7 up). 1986. PLB 14.89 (*0-06-021409-0*) HarpC Child Bks.
—Necessary Parties. 320p. 1987. pap. 3.50 (*0-553-26984-4*, Starfire) Bantam.
—Young Joan. LC 90-39494. 384p. (gr. 7 up). 1991. 17.95 (*0-06-021422-8*); PLB 17.89 (*0-06-021423-6*) HarpC Child Bks.
—Zucchini. Christelow, Eileen, illus. LC 80-8448. 128p. (gr. 3-6). 1982. PLB 12.89 (*0-06-021395-7*) HarpC Child Bks.
—Zucchini. Christelow, Eileen, illus. 160p. (gr. 3-6). 1984. pap. 2.95 (*0-553-15437-0*, Skylark) Bantam.
—Zucchini. 1984. pap. 3.50 (*0-553-15608-X*) Bantam.
Dana, Katherine. Toodle D. Poodle. Shuster, Albert H., ed. LC 92-82386. (Illus.). 22p. (Orig.). 1992. pap. 5.52 (*0-914127-28-4*) Univ Class.
Dana, Maggie. If Wishes Were Horses. Ruff, Donna, illus. LC 87-16201. 128p. (gr. 4-8). 1988. PLB 9.89 (*0-8167-1197-6*); pap. text ed. 2.95 (*0-8167-1198-4*) Troll Assocs.
—Jumping into Trouble. Ruff, Donna, illus. LC 87-16248. 128p. (gr. 4-8). 1988. PLB 9.89 (*0-8167-1193-3*); pap. text ed. 2.95 (*0-8167-1194-1*) Troll Assocs.
—No Time for Secrets. Ruff, Donna, illus. LC 87-19027. 128p. (gr. 4-8). 1988. PLB 9.89 (*0-8167-1191-7*); pap. text ed. 2.95 (*0-8167-1192-5*) Troll Assocs.
—Racing for the Stars. Ruff, Donna, illus. LC 87-16246. 128p. (gr. 4-8). 1988. PLB 9.89 (*0-8167-1195-X*); pap. text ed. 2.95 (*0-8167-1196-8*) Troll Assocs.
Dana, Richard H. Two Years Before the Mast. Bennet, C. L., intro. by. (gr. 8 up). 1965. pap. 2.25 (*0-8049-0085-X*, CL-85) Airmont.
—Two Years Before the Mast. new & abr. ed. Fago, John N., ed. Cruz, Ernesto, illus. (gr. 4-12). 1977. pap. text ed. 2.95 (*0-88301-270-7*) Pendulum Pr.
Danaher, Kevin. Children's Book of Irish Folktales. Berson, Harold, illus. 108p. 1987. pap. 11.95 (*0-85342-718-6*, Pub. by Mercier Press Ltd Eire) Dufour.
D'Anard, Elizabeth. Cinderella Summer. (gr. 7 up). 1992. pap. 3.95 (*0-06-106776-8*, Harp PBks) HarpC.
Danby, Mary, compiled by. Rotten Riddles & Goofy Gags. Reading, Bryan, illus. LC 89-48859. 96p. (gr. 2-8). 1991. pap. 3.95 (*0-8069-7310-2*) Sterling.
Dando, Caroline Z., jt. auth. see Dando, William A.
Dando, Justin. Judo. rev. ed. (Illus.). 80p. (gr. 10-12). 1993. pap. 7.95 (*0-7137-2416-1*, Pub. by Blandford Pr UK) Sterling.
Dando, William A. & Dando, Caroline Z. A Reference Guide to World Hunger. LC 91-10733. 112p. (gr. 6 up). 1991. lib. bdg. 17.95 (*0-89490-326-8*) Enslow Pubs.
Dandola, John. Leif the Lucky. Lanawn-Shee Studios Staff, illus. 24p. (Orig.). (gr. k up). 1991. pap. 3.95 (*1-878452-05-3*) Tory Corner Editions.
—Rogers' Rangers. Dandola, John, illus. 24p. (Orig.). (gr. k-6). 1992. pap. 3.95 (*1-878452-08-8*) Tory Corner Editions.
Dandola, John, jt. auth. see Brice, Donald.
D'Andrade, Diane, ed. see Bunting, Eve.
D'Andrade, Diane, ed. see Grossman, Patricia.
D'Andrade, Diane, ed. see Hall, Lynn.
D'Andrade, Diane, ed. see Hayes, Ann.
D'Andrade, Diane, ed. see Johnson, Pamela.
D'Andrade, Diane, ed. see Lattimore, Eleanor.
D'Andrade, Diane, ed. see McPhail, David.
D'Andrade, Diane, ed. see Most, Bernard.
D'Andrade, Diane, ed. see Walsh, Ellen S.
D'Andrade, Diane, ed. see Wilbur, Richard.
D'Andrade, Diane, ed. see Willard, Nancy.

D'Andrea, Deborah. Count with Me 1,2,3. Ayers, Michael B., illus. 12p. (ps-k). 1991. 4.99 (*1-878338-07-2*) Picture Me Bks.
—If I Were a Firefighter: Or a Doctor, or an Astronaut, or... Ayers, Michael B., illus. 12p. (ps-k). 1991. 4.99 (*1-878338-04-8*) Picture Me Bks.
—If I Were a Reindeer. (Illus.). (ps-k). 1991. write for info. (*1-878338-03-X*) Picture Me Bks.
—Learn Letters with Me ABC. Ayers, Michael B., illus. 12p. (ps-k). 1991. 4.99 (*1-878338-06-4*) Picture Me Bks.
D'Andrea, Deborah B. Count with Me 1, 2, 3. Guenther, Luisa, tr. Ayers, Michael B., illus. (SPA.). 12p. (ps). 4.99 (*1-878338-35-8*) Picture Me Bks.
—Count With Me 1, 2, 3. Zavinski, Monique, tr. Ayers, Michael B., illus. (FRE.). 12p. (ps). 4.99 (*0-685-63815-4*) Picture Me Bks.
—If I Were a Bunny, Or a Panda, Or a Monkey, Or... Ayers, Michael B., illus. 12p. (ps-1). 1989. bds. 4.99 (*1-878338-00-5*) Picture Me Bks.
—If I Were a Bunny, Or a Panda, Or a Monkey, Or... Zavinski, Monique, tr. Ayers, Michael B., illus. (FRE.). 12p. (ps). 4.99 (*1-878338-30-7*) Picture Me Bks.
—If I Were a Bunny, Or a Panda, Or a Monkey, Or... Guenther, Luisa, tr. Ayers, Michael B., illus. (SPA.). 12p. (ps). 4.99 (*1-878338-36-6*) Picture Me Bks.
—If I Were a Fairy, Or a Ballerina, Or a Witch, Or... Ayers, Michael B., illus. 12p. (ps-1). 1989. bds. 4.99 (*1-878338-01-3*) Picture Me Bks.
—If I Were a Fairy, Or a Ballerina, Or a Witch, Or... Guenther, Luisa, tr. Ayers, Michael B., illus. (SPA.). 12p. (ps). 4.99 (*1-878338-38-2*) Picture Me Bks.
—If I Were a Fairy, Or a Ballerina, Or a Witch, Or... Zavinski, Monique, tr. Ayers, Michael B., illus. (FRE.). 12p. (ps). 4.99 (*1-878338-32-3*) Picture Me Bks.
—If I Were a Firefighter, Or a Doctor, Or an Astronaut, Or... Guenther, Luisa, tr. Ayers, Michael B., illus. (SPA.). 12p. (ps). 4.99 (*1-878338-39-0*) Picture Me Bks.
—If I Were a Firefighter, Or a Doctor, Or an Astronaut, Or... Zavinski, Monique, tr. Ayers, Michael B., illus. (FRE.). 12p. (ps). 4.99 (*1-878338-33-1*) Picture Me Bks.
—If I Were a Pirate, Or a Cowboy, Or a Knight, Or... Ayers, Michael B., illus. 12p. (ps-1). 1989. bds. 4.99 (*1-878338-02-1*) Picture Me Bks.
—If I Were a Pirate, Or a Cowboy, Or a Knight, Or... Guenther, Luisa, tr. Ayers, Michael B., illus. (SPA.). 12p. (ps). 4.99 (*1-878338-37-4*) Picture Me Bks.
—If I Were a Pirate, Or a Cowboy, Or a Knight, Or... Zavinski, Monique, tr. Ayers, Michael B., illus. (FRE.). 12p. (ps). 4.99 (*1-878338-31-5*) Picture Me Bks.
D'Andrea, Joseph. If I Played Baseball: Or Football, or Soccer, or... Ayers, Michael B., illus. 12p. (ps-k). 1991. 4.99 (*1-878338-05-6*) Picture Me Bks.
D'Andrea, Joseph C. If I Played Baseball, Or Football, Or Soccer, Or... Guenther, Luisa, tr. Ayers, Michael B., illus. (SPA.). 12p. (ps). 4.99 (*1-878338-40-4*) Picture Me Bks.
—If I Played Baseball, Or Football, Or Soccer, Or... Zavinski, Monique, tr. Ayers, Michael B., illus. (FRE.). 12p. (ps). 4.99 (*1-878338-34-X*) Picture Me Bks.
—If I Were a Boston Celtic. Wilson, Bill, illus. 24p. (Orig.). (gr. k-5). Date not set. pap. 5.95 (*1-878338-45-5*) Picture Me Bks.
—If I Were a Buffalo Bill. Wilson, Bill, illus. 24p. (Orig.). (ps-5). 1993. pap. 5.95 (*1-878338-51-X*) Picture Me Bks.
—If I Were a Charlotte Hornet. Wilson, Bill, illus. 24p. (Orig.). (ps-5). Date not set. pap. 5.95 (*1-878338-49-8*) Picture Me Bks.
—If I Were a Chicago Bear. Ayers, Michael B., illus. 28p. (ps-5). pap. 5.95 (*1-878338-08-0*) Picture Me Bks.
—If I Were a Chicago Bull. Wilson, Bill, illus. 24p. (Orig.). (ps-5). Date not set. pap. 5.95 (*1-878338-42-0*) Picture Me Bks.
—If I Were a Chicago Cub. Wilson, Bill, illus. 28p. (ps-5). pap. 5.95 (*1-878338-15-3*) Picture Me Bks.
—If I Were a Chicago White Sox. Wilson, Bill, illus. 28p. (ps-5). pap. 5.95 (*1-878338-16-1*) Picture Me Bks.
—If I Were a Cleveland Cavalier. Wilson, Bill, illus. 24p. (Orig.). (ps-5). Date not set. pap. 5.95 (*1-878338-50-1*) Picture Me Bks.
—If I Were a Colorado Rockie. Wilson, Bill, illus. 28p. (ps-5). pap. 5.95 (*1-878338-20-X*) Picture Me Bks.
—If I Were a Dallas Cowboy. Ayers, Michael B., illus. 28p. (ps-5). pap. 5.95 (*1-878338-11-0*) Picture Me Bks.
—If I Were a Florida Marlin. Wilson, Bill, illus. 28p. (ps-5). pap. 5.95 (*1-878338-21-8*) Picture Me Bks.
—If I Were a Green Bay Packer. Ayers, Michael B., illus. 28p. (ps-5). pap. 5.95 (*1-878338-29-3*) Picture Me Bks.
—If I Were a Kansas City Chief. Wilson, Bill, illus. 24p. (Orig.). (ps-5). 1993. pap. 5.95 (*1-878338-52-8*) Picture Me Bks.
—If I Were a Los Angeles Dodger. Wilson, Bill, illus. 28p. (ps-5). pap. 5.95 (*1-878338-16-1*) Picture Me Bks.
—If I Were a Los Angeles Laker. Wilson, Bill, illus. 24p. (Orig.). (ps-5). Date not set. pap. 5.95 (*1-878338-44-7*) Picture Me Bks.

—If I Were a Los Angeles Raider. Ayers, Michael B., illus. 28p. (ps-5). pap. 5.95 (*1-878338-10-2*) Picture Me Bks.
—If I Were a Miami Dolphin. Ayers, Michael B., illus. 28p. (ps-5). pap. 5.95 (*1-878338-24-2*) Picture Me Bks.
—If I Were a Minnesota Viking. Ayers, Michael B., illus. 28p. (ps-5). pap. 5.95 (*1-878338-27-7*) Picture Me Bks.
—If I Were a New Orleans Saint. Ayers, Michael B., illus. 28p. (ps-5). pap. 5.95 (*1-878338-13-7*) Picture Me Bks.
—If I Were a New York Giant. Ayers, Michael B., illus. 28p. (ps-5). pap. 5.95 (*1-878338-12-9*) Picture Me Bks.
—If I Were a New York Knick. Wilson, Bill, illus. 24p. (Orig.). (ps-5). Date not set. pap. 5.95 (*1-878338-43-9*) Picture Me Bks.
—If I Were a New York Yankee. Wilson, Bill, illus. 28p. (ps-5). pap. 5.95 (*1-878338-18-8*) Picture Me Bks.
—If I Were a Philadelphia Eagle. Ayers, Michael B., illus. 28p. (ps-5). pap. 5.95 (*1-878338-26-9*) Picture Me Bks.
—If I Were a Phoenix Sun. Wilson, Bill, illus. 24p. (Orig.). (ps-5). Date not set. pap. 5.95 (*1-878338-46-3*) Picture Me Bks.
—If I Were a Pittsburgh Steeler. Ayers, Michael B., illus. 28p. (ps-5). pap. 5.95 (*1-878338-28-5*) Picture Me Bks.
—If I Were a San Antonio Spur. Wilson, Bill, illus. 24p. (Orig.). (ps-5). Date not set. pap. 5.95 (*1-878338-48-X*) Picture Me Bks.
—If I Were a San Francisco 49er. Ayers, Michael B., illus. 28p. (ps-5). pap. 5.95 (*1-878338-23-4*) Picture Me Bks.
—If I Were a Toronto Blue Jay. Wilson, Bill, illus. 28p. (ps-5). pap. 5.95 (*1-878338-25-0*) Picture Me Bks.
—If I Were a Washington Redskin. Ayers, Michael B., illus. 28p. (ps-5). pap. 5.95 (*1-878338-22-6*) Picture Me Bks.
—If I Were an Atlanta Brave. Wilson, Bill, illus. 28p. (ps-5). pap. 5.95 (*1-878338-17-X*) Picture Me Bks.
—If I Were an Oakland Athletic. Wilson, Bill, illus. 28p. (ps-5). pap. 5.95 (*1-878338-19-6*) Picture Me Bks.
—If I Were an Orlando Magic. Wilson, Bill, illus. 24p. (Orig.). (ps-5). Date not set. pap. 5.95 (*1-878338-47-1*) Picture Me Bks.
Daneman, Meredith. Francie & the Boys. 192p. (gr. 6-9). 1989. 14.95 (*0-440-50137-7*) Delacorte.
Danforth, Helen H. A Tale of Two Cabins. (Illus.). 36p. (Orig.). (gr. 7 up). 1985. pap. 4.95 (*0-9614899-0-1*) Pioneer Farm.
Danforth, Kimberly, jt. auth. see Fassler, David.
Danhauser, Karen E., jt. auth. see Mumford, Amy.
Daniel, Alan. Good Families Don't. (ps-3). 1991. pap. 3.99 (*0-440-40565-3*) Dell.
Daniel, Amy. Bible Rebus Puzzles. 48p. (gr. 3 up). 1988. 6.95 (*0-86653-422-9*, SS886, Shining Star Pubns) Good Apple.
Daniel, Becky. Animals Love Their Alphabet. 32p. (ps-k). 1991. 7.95 (*0-86653-579-9*, GA1307) Good Apple.
—Christmas Story (Book & Frieze) 16p. (ps-3). 1990. incl. tchr's. guide 16.95 (*0-86653-555-1*, SS1876, Shining Star Pubns) Good Apple.
—Count on Your Friends. 32p. (ps-k). 1991. 7.95 (*0-86653-582-9*, GA1306) Good Apple.
—Following Directions Brain Boosters. (Illus.). 64p. (gr. 1-4). 1992. 7.95 (*0-86653-654-X*, GA1349) Good Apple.
—Hooray for Addition Facts! (Illus.). 80p. (gr. 1-3). 1990. 9.95 (*0-86653-517-9*, GA1133) Good Apple.
—Hooray for Division Facts! (Illus.). 80p. (gr. 2-4). 1990. 9.95 (*0-86653-520-9*, GA1135) Good Apple.
—Hooray for Fraction Facts! 80p. (gr. 2-5). 1990. 9.95 (*0-86653-568-3*, GA1165) Good Apple.
—Hooray for Multiplication Facts! (Illus.). 80p. (gr. 2-4). 1990. 9.95 (*0-86653-519-5*, GA1136) Good Apple.
—Hooray for Subtraction Facts! (Illus.). 80p. (gr. 1-3). 1990. 9.95 (*0-86653-518-7*, GA1134) Good Apple.
—Hooray for the Big Book of Math Facts! 288p. (gr. 1-4). 1990. 24.95 (*0-86653-533-0*, GA1148) Good Apple.
—Language Brain Boosters. (Illus.). 64p. (gr. 1-4). 1992. 7.95 (*0-86653-653-1*, GA1348) Good Apple.
—Logic Brain Boosters. (Illus.). 64p. (gr. 1-4). 1992. 7.95 (*0-86653-652-3*, GA1347) Good Apple.
—Logic Thinker Sheets. 64p. (gr. 4-8). 1989. 7.95 (*0-86653-505-5*, GA1099) Good Apple.
—Math Brainstorms. 80p. (gr. 1-4). 1990. 8.95 (*0-86653-565-9*, GA1170) Good Apple.
—Math Thinker Sheets. 64p. (gr. 4-8). 1988. wkbk. 7.95 (*0-86653-429-6*, GA1036) Good Apple.
—My Color Picnic. 32p. (ps-k). 1991. 7.95 (*0-86653-581-0*) Good Apple.
—Portraits in Black. (Illus.). 96p. (gr. 4-7). 1990. 9.95 (*0-86653-531-4*, GA1147) Good Apple.
—Reading Brainstorms. 80p. (gr. 1-4). 1990. 8.95 (*0-86653-560-8*, GA1171) Good Apple.
—Reading Thinker Sheets. 64p. (gr. 4-8). 1989. 7.95 (*0-86653-501-2*, GA1097) Good Apple.
—Spelling Thinker Sheets. 64p. (gr. 4-8). 1988. wkbk. 7.95 (*0-86653-423-7*, GA1035) Good Apple.
—Word Thinker Sheets. 64p. (gr. 4-8). 1988. wkbk. 7.95 (*0-86653-394-X*, GA1034) Good Apple.
—Writing Brainstorms. 80p. (gr. 1-4). 1990. 8.95 (*0-86653-569-1*, GA1172) Good Apple.

—Writing Thinker Sheets. 64p. (gr. 4-8). 1989. 7.95 (0-86653-490-3, GA1098) Good Apple.
Daniel, Becky & Daniel, Charlie. Arithmetrix. 64p. (gr. 5-8). 1980. 7.95 (0-916456-75-7, GA 188) Good Apple.
—Big Addition Book. 64p. (gr. k-3). 1979. 7.95 (0-916456-44-7, GA118) Good Apple.
—Big Subtraction Book. 64p. (gr. k-3). 1979. 7.95 (0-916456-43-9, GA117) Good Apple.
—Comprehension Zoo. 64p. (gr. 2-4). 1979. 6.95 (0-916456-40-4, GA113) Good Apple.
—The Division Book. 64p. (gr. 3-6). 1980. 7.95 (0-916456-77-3, GA 190) Good Apple.
—The Multiplication Book. 64p. (gr. 2-6). 1980. 7.95 (0-916456-76-5, GA 191) Good Apple.
—Strain Your Brain. 48p. (gr. 4-6). 1980. 5.95 (0-88160-032-6, LW 217) Learning Wks.
—Thinker Sheets. 64p. (gr. 2-6). 1978. 7.95 (0-916456-23-4, GA78) Good Apple.
—What's Next? 64p. (gr. k-6). 1979. 7.95 (0-916456-41-2, GA116) Good Apple.
Daniel, Becky, jt. auth. see Daniel, Charlie.
Daniel, Charlie & Daniel, Becky. Freaky Fractions. 48p. (gr. 1-5). 1978. 6.95 (0-916456-19-6, GA77) Good Apple.
—Super Spelling Fun. 64p. (gr. 2-6). 1978. 7.95 (0-916456-31-5, GA82) Good Apple.
—Writing about My Feelings. 64p. (gr. 1-4). 1978. 7.95 (0-916456-18-8, GA80) Good Apple.
Daniel, Charlie, jt. auth. see Daniel, Becky.
Daniel, Frank, illus. Chanukah. 20p. (ps). 1993. bds. 3.95 (0-689-71733-4, Aladdin) Macmillan Child Grp.
—Christmas. 20p. (ps). 1993. bds. 3.95 (0-689-71734-2, Aladdin) Macmillan Child Grp.
—Halloween. 20p. (ps). 1993. bds. 3.95 (0-689-71736-9, Aladdin) Macmillan Child Grp.
—Thanksgiving. 20p. (ps). 1993. bds. 3.95 (0-689-71735-0, Aladdin) Macmillan Child Grp.
Daniel, Jamie, adapted by. Nicaragua Is My Home. Welch, Rose, photos by. LC 92-17723. (Illus.). 1992. PLB 18.60 (0-8368-0850-9) Gareth Stevens Inc.
—South Africa Is My Home. Rogers, Stillman, photos by. LC 92-17722. (Illus.). 1992. PLB 18.60 (0-8368-0851-7) Gareth Stevens Inc.
Daniel, Jamie, jt. ed. see Bonar, Veronica.
Daniel, Jamie, tr. see Barkhausen, Annette & Geiser, Franz.
Daniel, Jennifer. Spin-a-Story, the Haunted Banana & Other Wacky Mysteries. Brown, Jean, illus. 24p. (Orig.). (gr. 4-7). 1990. pap. 2.95 (1-878890-02-6) Palisades Prodns.
—Spin-a-Story, Twenty Thousand French Fries under the Sea & Other Crazy Classics. Brown, Jean, illus. 24p. (gr. 4-7). 1990. pap. 2.95 (1-878890-01-8) Palisades Prodns.
Daniel, Kate. Babysitter's Nightmare. 1992. pap. 3.50 (0-06-106773-3, Harp PBks) HarpC.
—Running Scared. 1993. pap. 3.50 (0-06-106728-8, Harp PBks) HarpC.
—Sweet Dreams. 1992. pap. 3.50 (0-06-106720-2, Harp PBks) HarpC.
—Sweetheart. 1993. pap. 3.50 (0-06-106735-0, Harp PBks) HarpC.
—Teen Idol. 1992. pap. 3.50 (0-06-106779-2, Harp PBks) HarpC.
Daniel, Kira. Backyard Tent. Burns, Ray, illus. LC 85-14068. 48p. (Orig.). (gr. 1-3). 1986. PLB 10.59 (0-8167-0626-3); pap. text ed. 3.50 (0-8167-0627-1) Troll Assocs.
—Habits of Rabbits. Pellaton, Karen E., illus. LC 85-14122. 48p. (Orig.). (gr. 1-3). 1986. PLB 10.59 (0-8167-0632-8); pap. text ed. 3.50 (0-8167-0633-6) Troll Assocs.
—Home Builder. Smolinski, Dick, illus. LC 88-10354. 32p. (gr. k-3). 1989. PLB 10.89 (0-8167-1420-7); pap. text ed. 2.95 (0-8167-1421-5) Troll Assocs.
—The Magic Kite. Getchell, Marianne S., illus. LC 85-14015. 48p. (Orig.). (gr. 1-3). 1986. PLB 10.59 (0-8167-0614-X); pap. text ed. 3.50 (0-8167-0615-8) Troll Assocs.
—Teacher. Paterson, Diane, illus. LC 88-10041. 32p. (gr. k-3). 1989. PLB 10.89 (0-8167-1430-4); pap. text ed. 2.95 (0-8167-1431-2) Troll Assocs.
Daniel, Mark. Child's Treasury of Animal Verse. (ps up) 1989. 16.95 (0-8037-0606-5) Dial Bks Young.
Daniel, Mark, compiled by. Child's Christmas Treasury. LC 87-36527. (Illus.). 112p. (ps up). 1988. 15.95 (0-8037-0484-4) Dial Bks Young.
Daniel, Mark, ed. A Child's Treasury of Poems. LC 86-2194. (Illus.). 160p. (ps up). 1986. 17.00 (0-8037-0330-9) Dial Bks Young.
Daniel, Mark, compiled by. A Child's Treasury of Seaside Verse. LC 90-2819. (Illus.). 144p. (ps up). 1991. 16.95 (0-8037-0889-0) Dial Bks Young.
Daniel, Rebecca. Bible Teacher Time Savers. McClure, Nancee, illus. 48p. (gr. k-5). 1984. wkbk. 6.95 (0-86653-235-8, SS 817, Shining Star Pubns) Good Apple.
—Book I-His Birth. McClure, Nancee, illus. 32p. (gr. 2-7). 1984. wkbk. 5.95 (0-86653-213-7, SS 824, Shining Star Pubns) Good Apple.
—Book II-His Boyhood. McClure, Nancee, illus. 32p. (gr. 2-7). 1984. wkbk. 5.95 (0-86653-223-4, SS 825, Shining Star Pubns) Good Apple.
—Book III-Gathering His Disciples. McClure, Nancee, illus. 32p. (gr. 2-7). 1984. wkbk. 5.95 (0-86653-224-2, SS 826, Shining Star Pubns) Good Apple.
—Book IV-the Teacher. McClure, Nancee, illus. 32p. (gr. 2-7). 1984. wkbk. 5.95 (0-86653-225-0, SS 827, Shining Star Pubns) Good Apple.
—Book V-The Healer. McClure, Nancee, illus. 32p. (gr. 2-7). 1984. wkbk. 5.95 (0-86653-226-9, SS 828, Shining Star Pubns) Good Apple.
—Book VI-His Miracles. McClure, Nancee, illus. 32p. (gr. 2-7). 1984. wkbk. 5.95 (0-86653-227-7, SS 829, Shining Star Pubns) Good Apple.
—Book VII-His Parables. McClure, Nancee, illus. 32p. (gr. 2-7). 1984. wkbk. 5.95 (0-86653-228-5, SS 830, Shining Star Pubns) Good Apple.
—Book VIII-More Parables. McClure, Nancee, illus. 32p. (gr. 2-7). 1984. wkbk. 5.95 (0-86653-229-3, SS 831, Shining Star Pubns) Good Apple.
—Book X-His Last Days. McClure, Nancee, illus. 32p. (gr. 2-7). 1984. wkbk. 5.95 (0-86653-231-5, SS 833, Shining Star Pubns) Good Apple.
—Book XI-His Last Hours. McClure, Nancee, illus. 32p. (gr. 2-7). 1984. wkbk. 5.95 (0-86653-232-3, SS 834, Shining Star Pubns) Good Apple.
—Book XII-His Resurrection. McClure, Nancee, illus. 32p. (gr. 2-7). 1984. wkbk. 5.95 (0-86653-233-1, SS 835, Shining Star Pubns) Good Apple.
—Count God's Blessings. 48p. (ps-1). 1991. 9.95 (0-86653-626-4, SS1889, Shining Star Pubns) Good Apple.
—The Days of Creation. 16p. (ps-3). 1991. 16.95 (0-86653-633-7, SS1877, Shining Star Pubns) Good Apple.
—Famous Old Testament Heroes. 48p. (ps-6). 1990. 6.95 (0-86653-528-4, SS858, Shining Star Pubns) Good Apple.
—The First Easter. (Illus.). 48p. (ps-6). 1992. 6.95 (0-86653-641-8, SS1898, Shining Star Pubns) Good Apple.
—God's Colorful World. 48p. (ps-1). 1991. 9.95 (0-86653-630-2, SS1888, Shining Star Pubns) Good Apple.
—Goldilocks & the Three Bears. (Illus.). 16p. (ps-2). 1992. 16.95 (0-86653-667-1, GA1399) Good Apple.
—Jesus & His Miracles. 16p. (ps-3). 1991. 16.95 (0-86653-634-5, SS1879, Shining Star Pubns) Good Apple.
—Jesus: Birth to Ascension. (Illus.). 48p. (gr. k-6). 1992. 6.95 (0-86653-695-7, SS2825, Shining Star Pubns) Good Apple.
—Jesus' Life. 48p. (ps-6). 1988. 6.95 (0-86653-460-1, SS855, Shining Star Pubns) Good Apple.
—Moses & the Ten Commandments. (Illus.). 16p. (ps-3). 1992. 16.95 (0-86653-644-2, SS2810, Shining Star Pubns) Good Apple.
—The Three Little Pigs. (Illus.). 16p. (ps-2). 1992. 16.95 (0-86653-668-X, GA1397) Good Apple.
—Three-Minute Bible Skits & Songs. 96p. (gr. 1-7). 1991. 10.95 (0-86653-628-0, SS1885, Shining Star Pubns) Good Apple.
—Women of the Bible. 48p. (ps-6). 1989. 6.95 (0-86653-495-4, SS856, Shining Star Pubns) Good Apple.
Daniel, Rebecca & Hierstein, Judy. Easter Week. 16p. (ps-3). 1991. 16.95 (0-86653-575-6, SS1883, Shining Star Pubns) Good Apple.
—God's Animal Alphabet. 48p. (ps-1). 1991. 9.95 (0-86653-577-2, Shining Star Pubns) Good Apple.
—Noah's Story. 16p. (ps-3). 1991. 16.95 (0-86653-576-4, SS1878, Shining Star Pubns) Good Apple.
Daniel, Rebecca & Jones, Kathy. Night of Wonder Musical. (Illus.). 48p. (ps-7). 1992. incl. tape 16.95 (0-685-50800-5, SS2841, Shining Star Pubns); 6.95 (0-86653-705-8, SS2841, Shining Star Pubns); tape 9.95 (0-685-50801-3, SS2842, Shining Star Pubns) Good Apple.
—Noah & Company Musical. (Illus.). 48p. (ps-7). 1992. incl. tape 16.95 (0-685-50798-X, SS2839, Shining Star Pubns); 6.95 (0-86653-704-X, SS2839, Shining Star Pubns); tape 9.95 (0-685-50799-8, SS2840, Shining Star Pubns) Good Apple.
Daniel, Rebecca & Stegenga, Susan J. Christian Crafts from Cardboard Containers. (Illus.). 64p. (ps-5). 1992. 8.95 (0-86653-703-1, SS2833, Shining Star Pubns) Good Apple.
Daniel, Rebecca, compiled by. Biblical Christmas Performances. 96p. (ps-8). 1988. 10.95 (0-86653-461-X, SS1868, Shining Star Pubns) Good Apple.
—Biblical Christmas Plays & Musicals. 96p. (ps-8). 1989. 10.95 (0-86653-513-6, SS1871, Shining Star Pubns) Good Apple.
—Biblical Performances for Early Childhood. 96p. (ps-1). 1990. 10.95 (0-86653-548-9, SS1872, Shining Star Pubns) Good Apple.
Daniel, Sadie L. Women Builders. rev. & enl. ed. Perry, Thelma D., contrib. by. 1990. 12.95 (0-87498-084-4); pap. 10.95 (0-87498-085-2) Assoc Pubs DC.
Daniel, Sarah. Bible Rebus Quotes. 48p. (gr. 3 up). 1989. 6.95 (0-86653-512-8, SS890, Shining Star Pubns) Good Apple.
Daniells, Trenna. All Things Change: Maylene the Mermaid. Braille International, Inc. Staff & Henry, James, illus. (Orig.). (gr. 1). 1992. pap. 10.95 (1-56956-004-8) W A T Braille.
—All Things Change: Maylene the Mermaid. Braille International, Inc. Staff & Henry, James, illus. (Orig.). (gr. 2). 1992. pap. 10.95 (1-56956-029-3) W A T Braille.
—Be True to Yourself: I Don't Want to Be a Lion Anymore! 1992. incl. cassette 10.95 (0-685-63807-3, BI0003) W A T Braille.
—Be True to Yourself: I Don't Want to Be a Lion Anymore. Braille International, Inc. Staff & Henry, James, illus. 11p. (Orig.). (gr. 1). 1992. pap. 10.95 (1-56956-001-3) W A T Braille.
—Be True to Yourself: I Don't Want to Be a Lion Anymore. Braille International, Inc. Staff & Henry, James, illus. (Orig.). (gr. 2). 1992. pap. 10.95 (1-56956-026-9) W A T Braille.
—Don't Blame Others: Timothy Chicken Learns to Lead. Braille International, Inc. Staff & Henry, James, illus. (Orig.). (gr. 1). 1992. pap. 10.95 (1-56956-007-2) W A T Braille.
—Don't Blame Others: Timothy Chicken Learns to Lead. Braille International, Inc. Staff & Henry, James, illus. (Orig.). (gr. 2). 1992. pap. 10.95 (1-56956-016-1) W A T Braille.
—It's Okay to Be Different: Oliver's Adventures on Monkey Island. Braille International, Inc. Staff & Henry, James, illus. (Orig.). (gr. 1). 1992. pap. 10.95 (1-56956-008-0) W A T Braille.
—It's Okay to Be Different: Oliver's Adventures on Monkey Island. Braille International, Inc. Staff & Henry, James, illus. (Orig.). (gr. 2). 1992. pap. 10.95 (1-56956-017-X) W A T Braille.
—No More Nightmares: Keeper of the Dreams. Braille International, Inc. Staff & Henry, James, illus. (Orig.). (gr. 2). 1992. pap. 10.95 (1-56956-027-7) W A T Braille.

—**One to Grow On! Series.** James, Henry, tr. (Illus., Orig.). (gr. 1-2). 1992. Per vol., incl. audio cass. pap. 10.95 (1-56956-000-5) W A T Braille. Offered on audio-cassettes for several years, this popular children's series is now available in a format ideal for blind children who are developing their braille reading skills. Each of the 16 titles is produced in grade 1 & grade 2 braille plus print, so reading can be shared by blind & sighted children, parents & educators. The 30-minute audio-cassette, with music & sound effects, is included, allowing children to practice reading skills independently. The ONE TO GROW ON! series promotes self-responsibility & encourages high self-esteem. Children relate to & identify with the characters, which helps develop the determination & courage to approach life with a positive & successful attitude. Each adventure is filled with fun-loving characters, depicted in braille graphics to stimulate the imagination. Available in grade 1 & grade 2 braille. I Don't Want to Be a Lion Anymore!: Be True to Yourself. Gr. 1 ISBN 1-56956-001-3, Gr. 2 ISBN 1-56956-026-9; The Keeper of Dreams: No More Nightmares. Gr. 1, ISBN 1-56956-002-1, Gr. 2 ISBN 1-56956-027-7; When Jokes Aren't Fun: The Hyena Who Teased Too Much. Gr. 1 ISBN 1-56956-003-X, Gr. 2 ISBN 1-56956-028-5; Maylene the Mermaid: All Things Change. Gr. 1 ISBN 1-56956-004-8, Gr. 2 ISBN 1-56956-029-3; Travis & the Dragon: Accepting Others As They Are. Gr. 1 ISBN 1-56956-005-6, Gr. 2 ISBN 1-56956-030-7; Cody Caterpillar Turns Over a New Leaf: Taking the Problem Out of Bedtime. Gr. 1 ISBN 1-56956-006-4, Gr. 2 ISBN 1-56956-031-5; Timothy Chicken Learns to Lead: Don't Blame Others. Gr. 1 ISBN 1-56956-007-2, Gr. 2 ISBN 1-56956-016-1; Oliver's Adventures on Monkey Island: It's Okay to Be Different. Gr. 1 ISBN 1-56956-008-0, Gr. 2 ISBN 1-56956-017-X. To Order, contact Jeri Brubaker, Braille International, Inc., 3290 S.E. Slater St., Stuart, FL 34997;

1-800-336-3142.
Publisher Provided Annotation.

—Taking the Problems Out of Bedtime. Braille International, Inc. Staff & Henry, James, illus. (Orig.). (gr. 2). 1992. pap. 10.95 (*1-56956-031-5*) W A T Braille.
—Travis & the Dragon: Accepting Others As They Are. Braille International, Inc. Staff & Henry, James, illus. (Orig.). (gr. 1). 1992. pap. 10.95 (*1-56956-005-6*) W A T Braille.
—Travis & the Dragon: Accepting Others As They Are. Braille International, Inc. Staff & Henry, James, illus. (Orig.). (gr. 2). 1992. pap. 10.95 (*1-56956-030-7*) W A T Braille.
—When Jokes Aren't Fun: The Hyena Who Teased Too Much. Braille International, Inc. Staff & Henry, James, illus. 20p. (Orig.). (gr. 1). 1992. pap. 10.95 (*1-56956-003-X*) W A T Braille.
—When Jokes Aren't Fun: The Hyena Who Teased Too Much. Braille International, Inc. Staff & Henry, James, illus. (Orig.). (gr. 2). 1992. pap. 10.95 (*1-56956-028-5*) W A T Braille.
Daniels, Karen, ed. see Repp, Gloria.
Daniels, Lolee & Pollard, Rita. The Library Experience: Sharing the Responsibility. Sullivan-Szarek, Mary, illus. (gr. 6-8). 1987. Teacher's manual, 130pp. 64.95 (*0-935637-08-7*); Student workbook, 120pp. 11.99 (*0-935637-09-5*); Transparency Set. 85.00 (*0-935637-10-9*) Cambridge Strat.
Daniels, Neil, jt. auth. see Hudson, Anne.
Daniels, Patricia. Aladdin & the Magic Lamp. LC 79-27304. (Illus.). 24p. (gr. k-5). 1980. PLB 14.64 (*0-8393-0257-6*) Raintree Steck-V.
—Aladdin & the Magic Lamp. LC 79-27304. (Illus.). 24p. (gr. k-5). 1981. PLB 29.28 (*0-8393-1832-4*) Raintree Steck-V.
—Ali Baba & the Forty Thieves. LC 79-27042. (Illus.). 24p. (gr. k-5). 1981. PLB 29.28 (*0-8393-1837-5*); PLB 14.64 incl. cassette (*0-8393-0255-X*); cassette 14.00 (*0-685-42782-X*) Raintree Steck-V.
—Beauty & the Beast. Large, Annabel, illus. LC 79-28433. 24p. (gr. k-5). 1980. PLB 14.64 (*0-8393-0258-4*) Raintree Steck-V.
—Beauty & the Beast. LC 79-28433. (Illus.). 24p. (gr. k-5). 1981. PLB 29.28 incl. cassette (*0-8172-1833-5*); cassette 14.00 (*0-685-09554-1*) Raintree Steck-V.
—Cinderella. Read, Maggie, illus. LC 79-28526. 24p. (gr. k-5). 1980. PLB 29.28 incl. cassette (*0-8393-1834-0*); PLB 14.64 (*0-8393-0253-3*) Raintree Steck-V.
—Rumpelstiltskin. Nightingale, Sandy, illus. LC 79-27140. 24p. (gr. k-5). 1980. PLB 14.64 (*0-8393-0252-5*) Raintree Steck-V.
—Rumpelstiltskin. LC 79-27140. (Illus.). 24p. (gr. k-5). 1981. PLB 29.28 incl. cassette (*0-8393-1831-6*); cassette 14.00 (*0-685-09555-X*) Raintree Steck-V.
—Sinbad the Sailor. Webb, Roger, illus. LC 79-28588. 24p. (gr. k-5). 1980. PLB 14.64 (*0-8393-0256-8*) Raintree Steck-V.
—Sinbad the Sailor. LC 79-28588. (Illus.). 24p. (gr. k-5). 1980. PLB 29.28 incl. cassette (*0-8393-1835-9*) Raintree Steck-V.
—Sleeping Beauty. Tarrant, Carol, illus. LC 79-26974. 24p. (gr. k-5). 1980. PLB 14.64 (*0-8393-0254-1*) Raintree Steck-V.
—Sleeping Beauty. LC 79-26974. (Illus.). 24p. (gr. k-5). 1980. PLB 29.28 incl. cassette (*0-8393-1838-3*) Raintree Steck-V.
—Snow White & the Dwarfs. Spalding, Tony, illus. LC 79-28431. 24p. (gr. k-5). 1980. PLB 14.64 (*0-8393-0251-7*) Raintree Steck-V.
—Snow White & the Dwarfs. LC 79-28431. (Illus.). 24p. (gr. k-5). 1980. PLB 29.28 (*0-8393-1836-7*); cassette 14.00 (*0-685-09557-6*) Raintree Steck-V.
Daniels, Patricia, ed. Let's Discover Outer Space. (Illus.). 80p. (gr. k-6). 1986. pap. 23.32 (*0-8172-2595-1*) Raintree Steck-V.
Daniels, Patricia, adapted by see Melville, Herman.
Daniels, Patricia, ed. see Time Life Inc. Editors.
Daniels, Richard. The Heavy Guitar Bible. (Illus.). 104p. (gr. 8 up). 1979. pap. 12.95 (*0-89524-066-1*, 9105) Cherry Lane.
Danielson, Jan & Magoun, Christine. More Vocabulary to Go: Ready to Go, Ready to Teach Worksheets for Vocabulary Skills. (gr. 3-8). 1989. Set of 5. 27.95 (*1-55999-095-3*) LinguiSystems.
Danielson, Kathy. On My Honor: A Study Guide. Friedland, Joyce & Kessler, Rikki, eds. (gr. 3-6). 1991. pap. text ed. 14.95 (*0-88122-576-2*) LRN Links.
Danielson, Peter. The Golden Pharoah. 416p. (Orig.). 1986. pap. 4.95 (*0-553-26885-6*) Bantam.
Dank, Milton. The Dangerous Game. 144p. (gr. 7 up). 1986. pap. 1.50 (*0-440-91765-4*, LFL) Dell.
—Khaki Wings. LC 80-65832. 160p. (gr. 8-12). 1980. pap. 8.95 (*0-385-28523-X*) Delacorte.
—Khaki Wings. 160p. (gr. 7 up) 1983. pap. 1.95 (*0-317-00572-3*, LFL) Dell.
Danks, Hugh. The Bug Book & Bug Bottle. LC 86-40541. (Illus.). 64p. (Orig.). (gr. k-5). 1987. pap. 9.95 (*0-89480-314-X*, 1314) Workman Pub.
Danley, J. Useful Science. large type ed. 182p. (gr. 7-12). 1983. 32.76 (*0-317-01957-0*, 4-26770-00) Am Printing Hse.
Dann, Geoff & Gravett, Chris. Knight. LC 92-1590. 64p. (gr. 5 up). 1993. 15.00 (*0-679-83882-1*); PLB 15.99 (*0-679-93882-6*) Knopf Bks Yng Read.

Dann, Penny, compiled by. & illus. A Little Book of Friendship. LC 93-12918. 1993. write for info. (*1-56766-095-9*) Childs World.
Danner, Thomas. Lazy Cat. Crozat, Francois, illus. 28p. (ps-3). 1994. prepub. 12.95 (*1-56397-353-7*) Boyds Mills Pr.
Danskin, Elizabeth. Women's Gymnastics. (Illus.). 120p. (Orig.). (gr. 12). 1983. pap. 14.95 (*0-88839-045-9*) Hancock House.
Danson, Ted, narrated by see Dr. Seuss.
Dante & Sean. Echoes of Wolves. 30p. 1992. pap. write for info. (*0-9634867-3-X*) Peyto Pub.
Danwick, Chad. Marky Mark: Who's Hot! 48p. (gr. 4-7). 1992. pap. 1.49 (*0-440-21379-7*) Dell.
Danziger, Paula. Amber Brown Is Not a Crayon. LC 92-34678. 1994. write for info. (*0-399-22509-9*, Putnam) Putnam Pub Group.
—Can You Sue Your Parents for Malpractice? LC 78-72856. 266p. (gr. 7 up). 1979. 14.95 (*0-385-28112-9*) Delacorte.
—Can You Sue Your Parents for Malpractice? 144p. (gr. 7 up). 1980. pap. 3.99 (*0-440-91066-8*, LFL) Dell.
—The Cat Ate My Gymsuit. LC 74-5501. 128p. (gr. 7 up). 1974. 14.95 (*0-385-28183-8*); PLB 14.95 (*0-385-28194-3*) Delacorte.
—The Cat Ate My Gymsuit. 160p. (gr. 5 up). 1980. pap. 3.99 (*0-440-41612-4*, YB) Dell.
—Cat Ate My Gymsuit. large type ed. 184p. (gr. 3-7). 1987. Repr. of 1974 ed. lib. bdg. 14.95 (*1-55736-068-5*, Crnrstn Bks) BDD LT Grp.
—The Divorce Express. LC 82-70318. 144p. (gr. 7 up). 1982. 14.95 (*0-385-28217-6*) Delacorte.
—The Divorce Express. 160p. (gr. 7 up). 1983. pap. 3.50 (*0-440-92062-0*, LFL) Dell.
—Earth to Matthew. 160p. (gr. 4-7). 1992. pap. 3.50 (*0-440-40733-8*, YB) Dell.
—Everyone Else's Parents Said Yes. (gr. 3-7). 1989. 13.95 (*0-385-29805-6*) Delacorte.
—Everyone Else's Parents Said Yes. (gr. k-6). 1990. pap. 3.99 (*0-440-40333-2*, YB) Dell.
—Everyone Else's Parents Said Yes. large type ed. 160p. 1992. text ed. 13.95x (*0-7451-1550-0*, Lythway Large Print) Hall.
—It's an Aardvark-Eat-Turtle World. (gr. 5 up). 1986. pap. 3.50 (*0-440-94028-1*, LFL) Dell.
—It's an Aardvark-Eat-Turtle World. large type, unabr. ed. 145p. (gr. 4 up). 1989. lib. bdg. 13.95 (*0-8161-4704-3*) G K Hall.
—Make Like a Tree & Leave. (gr. 4-7). 1990. 13.95 (*0-385-30151-0*) Delacorte.
—Make Like a Tree & Leave. large type ed. (gr. 1-8). 1993. 15.95 (*0-7451-1912-3*, Galaxy Child Lrg Print) Chivers N Amer.
—Not for a Billion Gazillion Dollars. LC 92-2735. 127p. (gr. 4-6). 1992. 14.00 (*0-385-30819-1*) Delacorte.
—The Pistachio Prescription. LC 77-86330. 168p. (gr. 7 up). 1978. pap. 12.95 (*0-385-28784-4*) Delacorte.
—The Pistachio Prescription. 160p. (gr. 5 up). 1978. pap. 3.50 (*0-440-96895-X*, LFL) Dell.
—The Pistachio Prescription. (gr. k-12). 1988. pap. 2.95 (*0-317-67249-5*) Dell.
—Remember Me to Harold Square. LC 87-6844. 168p. (gr. 7 up). 1987. pap. 14.95 (*0-385-29610-X*) Delacorte.
—Remember Me to Harold Square. 144p. (gr. k-12). 1988. pap. 3.99 (*0-440-20153-5*, LFL) Dell.
—There's a Bat in Bunk Five. LC 80-64833. 160p. (gr. 7 up). 1980. pap. 10.95 (*0-385-29013-6*) Delacorte.
—There's a Bat in Bunk Five. 160p. (gr. 5-9). 1988. pap. 3.99 (*0-440-40098-8*, LE) Dell.
—There's a Bat in Bunk Five. large type ed. 200p. (gr. 5 up). 1988. Repr. of 1980 ed. lib. bdg. 15.95 (*1-55736-047-2*, Crnrstn Bks) BDD LT Grp.
—This Place Has No Atmosphere. LC 85-46070. 128p. (gr. 7 up). 1986. pap. 15.00 (*0-385-29489-1*) Delacorte.
—This Place Has No Atmosphere. (gr. k-12). 1987. pap. 3.99 (*0-440-98726-1*, LFL) Dell.
—This Place Has No Atmosphere. (gr. k-6). 1989. pap. 3.50 (*0-440-40205-0*, YB) Dell.
—This Place Has No Atmosphere. large type ed. 190p. 1989. Repr. of 1986 ed. lib. bdg. 15.95 (*1-55736-130-4*, Crnrstn Bks) BDD LT Grp.
Danzinger, Paula. Make Like a Tree & Leave. (gr. 4-7). 1992. pap. 3.50 (*0-440-40577-7*) Dell.
DaParma, Charles W., et al. Latin Study Aid. 1987. pap. 2.75 (*0-87738-035-X*) Youth Ed.
D'Apice, Mary. Pueblo. (Illus.). 32p. (gr. 5-8). 1990. lib. bdg. 15.94 (*0-86625-385-8*); lib. bdg. 11.95s.p. (*0-685-36390-2*) Rourke Corp.
D'Apice, Mary, jt. auth. see D'Apice, Rita.
D'Apice, R. Gamblers. (Illus.). 32p. (gr. 3-8). 1990. PLB 18.00 (*0-86625-371-8*); 13.50s.p. (*0-685-34711-7*) Rourke Corp.
D'Apice, Rita & D'Apice, Mary. Algonquian. (Illus.). 32p. (gr. 5-8). 1990. lib. bdg. 15.94 (*0-86625-388-2*); lib. bdg. 11.95s.p. (*0-685-36386-4*) Rourke Corp.
D'Apice, Rita, et al. Native American People, 6 bks, Set 11. (Illus.). 192p. (gr. 5-8). 1990. Set. lib. bdg. 95.64 (*0-86625-383-1*); Set. lib. bdg. 71.70s.p. (*0-685-36385-6*) Rourke Corp.
Darazs, Arpad & Jay, Stephen. Sight & Sound: Students' Manual. LC 64-25360. (gr. 3-6). 1965. pap. text ed. 5.00 (*0-913932-03-5*) Boosey & Hawkes.
Darby, Jean. Douglas MacArthur. (Illus.). 112p. (gr. 5 up). 1989. 21.50 (*0-8225-4901-8*) Lerner Pubns.
—Dwight D. Eisenhower. (Illus.). 112p. (gr. 5 up). 1989. 21.50 (*0-8225-4900-X*) Lerner Pubns.

—Martin Luther King, Jr. (Illus.). 112p. (gr. 5 up). 1990. PLB 21.50 (*0-8225-4902-6*) Lerner Pubns.
—Martin Luther King, Jr. (gr. 4-7). 1992. pap. 6.95 (*0-8225-9611-3*) Lerner Pubns.
—That's Me in Here. McCord, Kathi, illus. 43p. (Orig.). (gr. 1-2). 1989. pap. 4.95 (*0-8198-7345-4*) St Paul Bks.
Darin, Bobby & Murray, Jean. Splish Splash. Peterson, Bryan, illus. 24p. 1993. 12.95 (*0-7935-1841-5*, 00183010) H Leonard Pub Corp.
Darling, Abigail. Teddy Bear's Picnic Cookbook. (ps-3). 1991. 13.95 (*0-670-82947-1*) Viking Child Bks.
—Teddy Bears' Picnic Cookbook. Day, Alexandra, illus. LC 92-28174. 1993. 4.99 (*0-14-054157-8*) Puffin Bks.
Darling, Benjamin. Let's Be Safe: Containing Such Useful Information As the Avoidance of Strangers & Their Candy, How Not to Be Run over by a Car, & How Generally Not to Cut Oneself Open. LC 93-36103. 1994. write for info. (*0-8118-0545-X*) Chronicle Bks.
—Robert & the Balloon Machine. Solliday, Tim, illus. 32p. 1991. 11.95 (*0-88138-120-9*, Green Tiger) S&S Trade.
—Tips for Teens: Telephone Tactics, Petting Practices, & Other Milestones on the Road to Popularity. LC 93-35815. 1994. write for info. (*0-8118-0520-4*) Chronicle Bks.
—Valerie & the Silver Pear. Lane, Dan, illus. LC 90-24945. 32p. (gr. k-3). 1992. RSBE 14.95 (*0-02-726100-X*, Four Winds) Macmillan Child Grp.
Darling, David. Between Fire & Ice: The Science of Heat. LC 91-40966. (Illus.). 60p. (gr. 5 up). 1992. RSBE 13.95 (*0-87518-501-0*, Dillon) Macmillan Child Grp.
—Could You Ever Build a Time Machine? (Illus.). 60p. (gr. 5 up). 1991. RSBE 14.95 (*0-87518-456-1*, Dillon) Macmillan Child Grp.
—Could You Ever Dig a Hole to China? (Illus.). 60p. (gr. 5 up). 1991. RSBE 14.95 (*0-87518-449-9*, Dillon) Macmillan Child Grp.
—Could You Ever Fly to the Stars? (Illus.). 60p. (gr. 5 up). 1991. RSBE 14.95 (*0-87518-446-4*, Dillon) Macmillan Child Grp.
—Could You Ever Live Forever? (Illus.). 60p. (gr. 5 up). 1991. RSBE 14.95 (*0-87518-457-X*, Dillon) Macmillan Child Grp.
—Could You Ever Meet an Alien? (Illus.). 60p. (gr. 5 up). 1991. RSBE 14.95 (*0-87518-447-2*, Dillon) Macmillan Child Grp.
—Could You Ever Speak Chimpanzee? (Illus.). 60p. (gr. 5 up). 1991. RSBE 14.95 (*0-87518-448-0*, Dillon) Macmillan Child Grp.
—From Glasses to Gases: The Science of Matter. LC 91-38233. (Illus.). 60p. (gr. 5 up). 1992. RSBE 13.95 (*0-87518-500-2*, Dillon) Macmillan Child Grp.
—Making Light Work: The Science of Optics. LC 91-3999. (Illus.). 60p. (gr. 4-6). 1991. RSBE 13.95 (*0-87518-476-6*, Dillon) Macmillan Child Grp.
—Sounds Interesting: The Science of Acoustics. LC 91-4002. (Illus.). 60p. (gr. 4-6). 1991. RSBE 13.95 (*0-87518-477-4*, Dillon) Macmillan Child Grp.
—Spiderwebs to Skyscrapers: The Science of Structure. LC 91-4001. (Illus.). 60p. (gr. 4-6). 1991. RSBE 13.95 (*0-87518-478-2*, Dillon) Macmillan Child Grp.
—Up, up, & Away: The Science of Flight. LC 91-4000. (Illus.). 60p. (gr. 4-6). 1991. RSBE 13.95 (*0-87518-479-0*, Dillon) Macmillan Child Grp.
Darling, David J. The Stars: From Birth to Black Holes. Swofford, Jeanette, illus. LC 84-23067. 64p. (gr. 4 up). 1987. RSBE 12.95 (*0-87518-284-4*, Dillon) Macmillan Child Grp.
Darling, Harold. Happy Book. (Illus.). 48p. 1992. 6.95 (*0-9621131-5-8*) Blue Lantern Studio.
Darling, Harold, jt. ed. see Edens, Cooper.
Darling, Kathy. ABC Animal Crafts. 64p. (ps-2). 1988. 6.95 (*0-912107-77-4*, MM940) Monday Morning Bks.
—Alphabet Crafts. 64p. (gr. k-2). 1985. 6.95 (*0-912107-32-4*) Monday Morning Bks.
—Gift Crafts. (ps-2). 1988. 6.95 (*0-912107-75-8*, MM938) Monday Morning Bks.
—Kangaroos on Location. Darling, Tara, photos by. LC 92-38418. 1993. write for info. (*0-688-09728-6*); lib. bdg. write for info. (*0-688-09729-4*) Lothrop.
—Kids & Communities. (Illus.). 64p. (ps-2). 1989. 6.95 (*0-912107-94-4*, MM911) Monday Morning Bks.
—Kids & Seasons. (Illus.). 64p. (ps-2). 1989. 6.95 (*0-912107-93-6*, MM910) Monday Morning Bks.
—Manatee: On Location. (gr. 4-7). 1991. 14.95 (*0-688-09030-3*) Lothrop.
—Manatee: On Location. (ps). 1991. PLB 14.88 (*0-688-09031-1*) Lothrop.
—Preschool Bible Crafts. (Illus.). 96p. (ps-1). 1992. 10.95 (*0-86653-699-X*, SS2829, Shining Star Pubns) Good Apple.
—Preschool Christian Value Lessons. 96p. (ps-1). 1991. 10.95 (*0-86653-627-2*, SS1891, Shining Star Pubns) Good Apple.
—Safe Kids, Healthy Kids. (Illus.). 64p. (ps-2). 1989. 6.95 (*0-912107-92-8*, MM1909) Monday Morning Bks.
—Tasmanian Devil: On Location. Pearson, Susan, ed. Darling, Tara, photos by. LC 91-27561. (Illus.). 40p. (gr. 2 up). 1992. 15.00 (*0-688-09726-X*); PLB 14.93 (*0-688-09727-8*) Lothrop.
—Walrus: On Location. Darling, Tara, photos by. LC 90-33376. (Illus.). 40p. (gr. 2 up). 1991. 15.00 (*0-688-09032-X*); PLB 14.88 (*0-688-09033-8*) Lothrop.
Darling, Kathy & Sheridan, Terri. Nature Crafts. 64p. (ps-2). 1988. 6.95 (*0-912107-76-6*, MM939) Monday Morning Bks.
Darling, Kathy, jt. auth. see Cobb, Vicki.

Darlington, Joan R. Is It Poison Ivy? Darlington, Joan R., illus. 32p. (Orig.). (gr. 1-8). 1993. pap. 9.00g (*1-882291-53-0*) Oyster River Pr.

Darneille, Diane D. Season Science 1: Seasonal Mystery of Animal Coat Change. Porter, Robin A., illus. 32p. (Orig.). (gr. k-5). 1992. pap. 13.95 (*0-9634246-1-0*) Sci Passport. A National Literacy Foundation "Highly Recommended" Book. This non-fiction, early reader science book relates a child's experience changing his own coat to the seasonal coat changes animals make. Memorable verse & lifelike watercolor illustrations of children & animals fill the pages of SEASON SCIENCE (TM) 1. A rabbit ("showshoe hare") changes coat colors. A horse ("mustang") sheds its heavy coat for a lighter one. A reindeer (" barren-ground caribou") adds a fat lining to its coat for warmth & grows antlers for air conditioning. There's even a mystery to solve -- the way scientists do -- that leads to the discovery of a link between seasons & the earth's tilt relative to the sun. Included art activities, games & cards reinforce the learning in fun, age appropriate ways. *Publisher Provided Annotation.*

Darr, S. C., ed. see Henderson, Shelia & George, Bonnie S.
Darrow, Clarence see Jones, Mother.
Darrow, Paul. Avon: A Terrible Aspect. 192p. (gr. 5 up). 1991. pap. 4.50 (*0-8216-2503-9*, Carol Paperbacks) Carol Pub Group.
Darst, Shelia S., ed. see Barrett, Anna P.
Darst, Shelia S., ed. see Evey, Ethel L.
Dart, Alan, jt. auth. see Bird, Malcolm.
Dartez, Cecilia C. Jenny Giraffe & the Streetcar Party. Green, Andy, illus. LC 93-9924. 32p. (gr. k-3). 1993. 14.95 (*0-88289-962-7*) Pelican.
—Jenny Giraffe Discovers the French Quarter. Wilson, Shelby, illus. LC 90-48720. 32p. (ps-8). 1991. 12.95 (*0-88289-819-1*) Pelican.
—L Is for Louisiana. LC 92-44111. (Illus.). 32p. (gr. 3-7). 1993. 12.95 (*0-89658-182-9*) Voyageur Pr.
—The Louisiana Plantation Coloring Book. Arrigo, Joseph, illus. 32p. (Orig.). (ps-4). 1985. pap. 2.95 (*0-88289-473-0*) Pelican.
Dartford, Mark, jt. ed. see Clarke, Donald.
Darwin, Beatrice, illus. If You Lived with the Sioux Indians. 1992. pap. 4.95 (*0-590-45162-6*) Scholastic Inc.
Das, Manoj. Books Forever. Chatterji, Sukumar, illus. (gr. 2-8). 1979. pap. 2.50 (*0-89744-175-3*) Auromere.
Das, Prodeepta. India. (Illus.). 32p. (gr. 5-8). 1990. PLB 11.90 (*0-531-14045-8*) Watts.
Dasa, Yogesvara & Dasi, Jyotirmayi-Devi. A Gift of Love: The Story of Sudama Brahmin. Dasa, Puskar, illus. LC 82-8874. 32p. (gr. 5-8). 1982. PLB 7.00 (*0-89647-015-6*) Bala Bks.
Dasent, George W. East o' the Sun & West o' the Moon. LC 70-97214. (Illus.). xv, 418p. (gr. 1 up). 1970. pap. 8.95 (*0-486-22521-6*) Dover.
Dasent, George W., tr. East o' the Sun & West o' the Moon. Lynch, P. J., illus. LC 91-58727. 48p. (ps up). 1992. 15.95 (*1-56402-049-5*) Candlewick Pr.
Dash, Joan. The Triumph of Discovery: Women Scientists Who Won the Nobel Prize. 160p. (gr. 9 up). 1990. lib. bdg. 13.98 (*0-671-69332-8*, J Messner); pap. 8.95 (*0-671-69333-6*) S&S Trade.

Dashney, John. The Adventures of Walter the Weremouse. Somerville, Sheila, illus. 164p. (Orig.). (gr. 4-8). 1992. pap. 6.50x (*0-9633236-0-1*) J Dashney. A boy by day--a mouse by night! WALTER THE WEREMOUSE runs through town (& the suburbs & countryside too)--pursued by packs of dogs, the police, organized crime, an ex-Roller Derby star & the telephone company! This first book by award-winning international storyteller John Dashney is now triumphantly into its second printing &, like its author is gaining fans across America, Great Britain, Australia & New Zealand. "What fun to read about an underdog-- or should I say, an under-weremouse-- who finds a way to squeak his way to the top. A nice combination of fantasy & humor."--B.J. Quinlan, Youth Services Manager, Salem (OR) Public Library. "For children--& seekers--of all ages. This enchanting story will engage you from the start. Author/ storyteller John Dashney never lets you wander from Walter or the fabulous characters of his adventures."- -Oregon State Library for the Blind. *Publisher Provided Annotation.*

Dasi, Jyotirmayi-Devi, jt. auth. see Dasa, Yogesvara.
Dasmann, Raymond, jt. auth. see Yocom, Charles.
Dass, Baba H. Cat & Sparrow. Rich, Andrea, illus. LC 81-51915. 32p. (gr. k-3). 1982. 6.95 (*0-918100-06-2*) Sri Rama.
—The Magic Gem: A Story Coloring Book. Boratynski, Katrina & Giles, William B., illus. LC 76-10032. 32p. (Orig.). (ps-2). 1976. pap. 2.50 (*0-918100-07-0*) Sri Rama.
Dasso, Margaret & Skelly, Maryan. Dirt Busters. The Best Little Cleaning Book Ever. rev. ed. 130p. (gr. 5 up). 1991. pap. 7.95 (*0-9621757-1-4*) Peter & Thorton Pubs.
Dastrup, Linda. I Am a Child of God: My Gospel Principles Book. 14p. (gr. 1-7). 1985. wkbk. 3.95 (*0-9621898-2-0*) Creative Changes.
Data Notes Publishing Staff. Word Mapping for Educational Research Success: A Workbook. 14p. (gr. 11-12). 1988. pap. text ed. 9.95 (*0-911569-18-9*, Pub. by Data Notes) Prosperity & Profits.
Dauer, Rosamond. Bullfrog & Gertrude Go Camping. 64p. (gr. k-6). 1988. pap. 2.95 (*0-440-40074-0*) Dell.
—Bullfrog Grows Up. (gr. k-6). 1988. pap. 2.95 (*0-440-40007-4*) Dell.
Daugherty, Franklin. Postmodern Times. LC 87-71793. 280p. 1988. 14.95 (*0-944284-00-0*) T C DeLeon.
Daugherty, James. Andy & the Lion. Daugherty, James, illus. LC 38-27390. 80p. (gr. 1-4). 1938. pap. 13.95 (*0-670-12433-8*) Viking Child Bks.
—Andy & the Lion. (Illus.). 72p. (ps-3). 1989. pap. 4.99 (*0-14-050277-7*, Puffin) Puffin Bks.
—The Landing of the Pilgrims. LC 80-21430. (Illus.). 160p. (gr. 5-9). 1981. PLB 8.99 (*0-394-90302-1*); pap. 3.95 (*0-394-84697-4*) Random Bks Yng Read.
—Of Courage Undaunted: Across the Continent with Lewis & Clark. LC 90-49171. (Illus.). 168p. (gr. 6-10). 1991. PLB 13.95 (*1-55905-089-6*) Marshall Cavendish.
—Poor Richard. LC 90-49176. (Illus.). 160p. (gr. 6-10). 1991. PLB 13.95 (*1-55905-080-2*) Marshall Cavendish.
Daughters of St. Paul. Adventures of Peter & Paul. Gandolfo, C., illus. LC 84-26812. 120p. (gr. 5-9). 1984. 5.00 (*0-8198-0726-5*) St Paul Bks.
—Ahead of the Crowd. LC 78-145573. (gr. 3-7). 1970. 3.00 (*0-8198-0227-1*); pap. 2.00 (*0-8198-0715-X*) St Paul Bks.
—Bells of Conquest. LC 68-28105. (gr. 3-7). 1987. 3.00 (*0-8198-0228-X*); pap. 2.00 (*0-8198-1109-2*) St Paul Bks.
—The Bible for Young People. 142p. (gr. 4 up). 1988. pap. 5.00 (*0-8198-0212-3*) St Paul Bks.
—Boy with a Mission. (gr. 4-9). 1967. 3.00 (*0-8198-0229-8*); 2.00 (*0-8198-1116-5*) St Paul Bks.
—The Country Road Home. (gr. 3-7). 1987. 3.00 (*0-8198-0232-8*) St Paul Bks.
—Fifty-Seven Saints for Boys & Girls. (Illus.). (gr. 5-8). 1963. 16.95 (*0-8198-0044-9*); pap. 10.95 (*0-8198-0045-7*) St Paul Bks.
—The Fisher Prince. (gr. 3-7). 1984. 3.00 (*0-8198-0233-6*); pap. 2.00 (*0-8198-2610-3*) St Paul Bks.
—Flame in the Night. LC 67-25828. (gr. 4-9). 1967. 3.00 (*0-8198-0234-4*) St Paul Bks.
—Gamble for God. Mayer, Maxine, illus. LC 83-10087. 132p. (gr. 3-8). 1984. 3.00 (*0-8198-3033-X*) St Paul Bks.
—Gentle Revolutionary. LC 77-17206. (gr. 3 up). 1978. 3.00 (*0-8198-0358-8*) St Paul Bks.
—God Loves Me. (gr. 1-6). 1982. pap. 1.95 (*0-8198-3032-1*); tchr's. manual 3.95 (*0-8198-3031-3*) St Paul Bks.
—God's Secret Agent. LC 67-24026. (gr. 4-9). 1967. 3.00 (*0-8198-0236-0*); pap. 2.00 (*0-8198-3036-4*) St Paul Bks.
—Karol from Poland. (gr. 4-9). Date not set. write for info. St Paul Bks.
—No Place for Defeat. (gr. 3-9). 1987. 3.00 (*0-8198-0241-7*); 2.00 (*0-8198-5100-0*) St Paul Bks.
—Saints for Young People for Every Day, Vol. 1: January-June. (Illus.). 302p. (gr. 4-8). 1984. 6.00 (*0-8198-0143-7*); pap. 4.50 (*0-8198-0144-5*) St Paul Bks.
—Where's Grandma? (gr. k-2). 1982. pap. 1.75 (*0-8198-8204-6*) St Paul Bks.
Daughters of St. Paul Staff. The Holy Mass Coloring Book. rev. ed. Daughters of St. Paul Staff, illus. 16p. (gr. 1-4). 1993. pap. 0.95 (*0-8198-3343-6*) St Paul Bks.

—I Pray with Jesus. rev. ed. Smolinski, Dick, illus. 177p. (gr. 1-5). 1991. deluxe ed. 8.50 white (*0-8198-3630-3*); deluxe ed. 8.50 black (*0-8198-3631-1*) St Paul Bks.
—Saints of the Americas Coloring Book. Flanagan, Anne J., ed. Keating, Elizabeth A., illus. 18p. (Orig.). (gr. 1-4). 1993. pap. 0.95 (*0-8198-4768-2*) St Paul Bks.
Daughters of St. Paul Staff, compiled by see Alberione, James.
Daughters of St. Paul Staff, tr. see Paltro, Piera.
Daughters of St Paul. My Prayer Book. (gr. 3 up). 1978. plastic bdg. 2.00 (*0-8198-0359-6*); pap. 1.25 (*0-8198-0360-X*) St Paul Bks.
—Saints for Young People for Every Day of the Year, Vol. 2: July to December. (Illus.). 338p. (gr. 4 up). 1984. 6.00 (*0-8198-0647-1*); pap. 4.50 (*0-8198-0648-X*) St Paul Bks.
D'Aulaire, Edgar, jt. auth. see D'Aulaire, Ingri.
D'Aulaire, Edgar P., jt. auth. see D'Aulaire, Ingri.
D'Aulaire, Ingri. Abraham Lincoln. (ps-3). 1987. pap. 10. 00 (*0-440-40690-0*) Dell.
—D'Aulaire's Book of Greek Myths. (ps-3). 1992. pap. 14.95 (*0-440-40694-3*, YB) Dell.
—D'Aulaire's Trolls. (ps-3). 1993. pap. 8.00 (*0-440-40779-6*) Dell.
—Don't Count Your Chicks. (ps-3). 1993. pap. 4.99 (*0-440-40771-0*) Dell.
—Pocahontas. 1989. pap. 9.95 (*0-385-26607-3*) Doubleday.
D'Aulaire, Ingri & D'Aulaire, Edgar. Columbus. 64p. (gr. 2-5). 1992. pap. 8.00 (*0-440-40701-X*, YB) Dell.
D'Aulaire, Ingri & D'Aulaire, Edgar P. Abraham Lincoln. rev. ed. (gr. k-4). 1957. pap. 10.95 (*0-385-07669-X*) Doubleday.
—D'Aulaires' Book of Greek Myths. D'Aulaire, Ingri & D'Aulaire, Edgar P., illus. LC 62-15877. 1980. 20.00 (*0-385-01583-6*, Zephyr-BFYR); PLB 19.99 (*0-385-07108-6*); (Zephyr-BFYR) Doubleday.
—D'Aulaire's Norse Gods & Giants. LC 86-11677. (Illus.). 168p. (ps up). 1986. pap. 16.95 (*0-385-23692-1*, Pub. by Zephyr-BFYR) Doubleday.
—George Washington. D'Aulaire, Ingri & D'Aulaire, Edgar P., illus. LC 36-27417. 64p. (gr. 1-4). 1936. pap. 13.95 (*0-385-07306-2*) Doubleday.
—George Washington. LC 36-27417. (Illus.). 64p. (gr. 4-6). 1987. pap. 11.95 (*0-385-24107-0*) Doubleday.
D'Aulaire, Ingri & Parin, Edgar P. Benjamin Franklin. LC 50-10503. (Illus.). 48p. (gr. 4-6). 1987. pap. 11.95 (*0-385-24103-8*, Pub. by Zephyr-BFYR) Doubleday.
—Columbus. LC 86-24366. (Illus.). 64p. (gr. 4-6). 1987. pap. 8.95 (*0-385-24106-2*, Pub. by Zephyr-BFYR) Doubleday.
Dausereau, Raymond J. Tomorrow's Mission: World War II Diary of a Combat Aircrewman Aboard the U. S. S. Yorktown (CV-10), the Fighting Lady, During the Pacific War 1943-1945. LC 92-74143. (Illus.). 396p. (Orig.). (gr. 11-12). 1993. pap. 18.95 (*0-923687-24-6*) Celo Valley Bks.
Davenport, May. Blow Away Seaweeds. LC 89-92456. 212p. (gr. 7-12). 1993. 29.95 (*0-943864-60-7*) Davenport.
—Two Plays. LC 75-55603. (gr. 5-12). 1977. 2.50x (*0-9603118-0-7*) Davenport.
Davenport, May, ed. Courage: An Anthology of Short Stories, Articles & Poems. Kline, Gail, illus. LC 79-26261. (Orig.). (gr. 6-9). 1979. pap. text ed. 3.50x (*0-9603118-3-1*) Davenport.
—Involvement. Bd. with Casper the Cantankerous Cougar. Hall, Sherry; Dog Named Sleet. Humphrey, Sandra; Rock Little Flowers! Ross, Andrea. LC 82-70225. 80p. (Orig.). (gr. 5-12). 1984. pap. 3.50x (*0-943864-34-8*) Davenport.
—Watch Out, the Tide. LC 86-91602. 84p. (Orig.). (gr. 7-12). 1987. pap. 4.95x (*0-943864-27-5*) Pogosticks by Andrea Ross. Ginger: Poof! Bam! Growl! by Andrea Ross. Poems by Kay Garrard. Davenport.
Davenport, May, intro. by see McCoy, James C., et al.
Davenport, May, ed. see Zimelman, Nathan.
Davenport, May, illus. & intro. by see Dorio, Evelyn.
Davenport, Tom & Carden, Gary. From the Brothers Grimm: A Contemporary Retelling of American Folktales & Classic Stories. LC 92-30828. (Illus.). 105p. (gr. 2-12). 1993. pap. 12.95 (*0-917846-20-6*, 95526) Highsmith Pr.
Davenport-Powell, Darla. Here Comes Niya. rev. ed. Jenkins, Maurice M., illus. LC 87-410800. 22p. (Orig.). (ps-3). 1988. incl. cassette 12.95 (*0-945203-00-4*) Hi-Hopes Pub.
Daves, Prentiss V. The Strawberry Fox. Quintahlen, Patrique, ed. James, Nancy D., illus. LC 91-62065. 54p. (Orig.). 1992. pap. 3.95 (*0-9615560-9-9*) Scotjia Pub Co.
Davey, John. Mining Coal. (Illus.). 64p. (gr. 6 up). 1976. 15.95 (*0-7136-1596-6*) Dufour.
David, Alfred & Meek, Mary E. The Twelve Dancing Princesses & Other Fairy Tales. LC 73-16517. (Illus.). 320p. (gr. 1-6). 1974. 10.95x (*0-253-20173-X*, MB-173) Ind U Pr.
David C. Cook Publishing Staff. Awesome Real-Life Bible Devotions for Kids. (gr. 4-7). 1991. 9.95 (*1-55513-737-7*) Cook.
—Just for Kids Bible: Selected Readings for Active Kids. (gr. 4-7). 1992. 13.95 (*1-55513-713-X*) Cook.
—Lord Is My Shepherd: Bible Verses of Comfort & Encouragement for Children of All Ages. (ps-3). 1991. 8.99 (*1-55513-680-X*) Cook.
—My Own Little Bible: Storybook. (ps-3). 1991. 6.95 (*1-55513-682-6*) Cook.

—My Own Little Bible: Storybook. (ps-3). 1991. simulated leather, gift boxed 12.95 (1-55513-753-9) Cook.
David, Jo. Finishing Touches, Manners with Style. Richey, Donald, illus. LC 90-10888. 128p. (gr. 5-9). 1991. lib. bdg. 10.89 (0-8167-2179-3); pap. text ed. 2.95 (0-8167-2180-7) Troll Assocs.
David, Mark. Cartooning for Kids: A Step-by-Step Guide to Creating Your Own Cartoons. (gr. 4-7). 1993. pap. 3.95 (0-207-17144-0, Pub. by Angus & Robertson AT) HarpC.
David, Peter. Starfleet Academy, No. 2: Worf's Mission. 128p. (Orig.). (gr. 3-6). 1993. pap. 3.50 (0-671-87085-8, Minstrel Bks) PB.
—Survival. Fry, James, illus. 128p. (Orig.). 1993. pap. 3.50 (0-671-87086-6, Minstrel Bks) PB.
—Worf's First Adventure. 128p. (Orig.). (gr. 3-6). 1993. pap. 3.50 (0-671-87084-X, Minstrel Bks) PB.
David, Rosalie. Growing up in Ancient Egypt. McBride, Angus, illus. LC 91-40264. 32p. (gr. 3-5). 1993. PLB 11.89 (0-8167-2717-1); pap. text ed. 3.95 (0-8167-2718-X) Troll Assocs. Postponed.
David, Rosalie A. The Giant Book of the Mummy. Harris, Nick & Stewart, Roger, illus. LC 92-22734. 14p. (gr. 2-5). 1993. 24.95 (0-525-67413-6, Lodestar Bks) Dutton Child Bks.
David, Ward S. Ask Not for Victory. Grant, Wilda L., ed. Stein, August, illus. 234p. (Orig.). (gr. 8-12). 1991. pap. 9.95 (0-9630883-3-5) W S David.
Davidar, E. R. & Joshi, Jagadish. The Runaway Elephant Calf. (Illus.). 24p. (Orig.). (gr. k-3). 1980. pap. 2.75 (0-89744-216-4, Pub. by Childrens Bk Trust IA) Auromere.
Davidow, M. The Abacus Made Easy. 2nd, large type ed. 110p. (gr. 2-12). 1975. 9.69 (0-317-01865-5, 4-00100-00) Am Printing Hse.
Davids, Hollace & Davids, Paul. The Fires of Pele: Mark Twain's Legendary Lost Journal. (Illus.). 56p. (Orig.). (gr. 5-9). 1986. pap. 9.95 (0-939031-00-0) Pictorial Legends.
Davids, Hollace, jt. auth. see Davids, Paul.
Davids, Paul. The Fountain of Youth. Davids, Paul, photos by. (Illus.). 56p. (Orig.). (gr. 5-9). pap. text ed. 9.95 (0-939031-01-9) Pictorial Legends.
—Mission from Mount Yoda. (gr. 4-7). 1993. pap. 3.99 (0-553-15890-2) Bantam.
—Prophets of the Dark Side. (gr. 4-7). 1993. pap. 3.99 (0-553-15892-9) Bantam.
—Queen of the Empire. (gr. 4-7). 1993. pap. 3.99 (0-553-15891-0) Bantam.
Davids, Paul & Davids, Hollace. Glove of Darth Vader. (gr. 4-7). 1992. pap. 3.99 (0-553-15887-2, Starfire) Bantam.
—Jabba the Hutt's Revenge. 1992. pap. 3.99 (0-553-15889-9) Bantam.
—Lost City of the Jedi. (gr. 4-7). 1992. pap. 3.99 (0-553-15888-0, Starfire) Bantam.
Davids, Paul, jt. auth. see Davids, Hollace.
Davidson, Alan. The Bewitching of Alison Allbright. 160p. (gr. 5-9). 1991. pap. 3.95 (0-14-032520-4, Puffin) Puffin Bks.
Davidson, Alice J. Alice in Bibleland Storybooks: Prayers & Graces. Marshall, Victoria, illus. 32p. (gr. 3 up). 1986. 5.50 (0-8378-5078-9) Gibson.
—Alice in Bibleland Storybooks: Psalms & Proverbs. Marshall, Victoria, illus. 32p. (gr. 3 up). 1984. 5.50 (0-8378-5069-X) Gibson.
—Alice in Bibleland Storybooks: Story of David & Goliath. Marshall, Victoria, illus. 32p. (gr. 3 up). 1985. 5.50 (0-8378-5070-3) Gibson.
—Alice in Bibleland Storybooks: Story of Daniel & the Lions. Marshall, Victoria, illus. 32p. (gr. 3 up). 1986. 5.50 (0-8378-5079-7) Gibson.
—Alice in Bibleland Storybooks: Story of Baby Jesus. Marshall, Victoria, illus. 32p. (gr. 3 up). 1985. 5.50 (0-8378-5072-X) Gibson.
—Alice in Bibleland Storybooks: Story of Baby Moses. Marshall, Victoria, illus. 32p. (gr. 3 up). 1985. 5.50 (0-8378-5071-1) Gibson.
—Alice in Bibleland Storybooks: Story of Creation. Marshall, Victoria, illus. 32p. (gr. 3 up). 1984. 5.50 (0-8378-5066-5) Gibson.
—Alice in Bibleland Storybooks: Story of Easter. Marshall, Victoria, illus. 32p. (gr. 3 up). 1988. 5.50 (0-8378-1839-7) Gibson.
—Alice in Bibleland Storybooks: Story of Jonah. Marshall, Victoria, illus. 32p. (gr. 3 up). 1984. 5.50 (0-8378-5068-1) Gibson.
—Alice in Bibleland Storybooks: Story of Noah. Marshall, Victoria, illus. 32p. (gr. 3 up). 1984. 5.50 (0-8378-5067-3) Gibson.
—Alice in Bibleland Storybooks: Story of the Loaves & Fishes. Marshall, Victoria, illus. 32p. (ps-3). 1985. 5.50 (0-8378-5073-8) Gibson.
—Alice in Bibleland Storybooks: The Lord's Prayer. (Illus.). (gr. 3 up). 1989. 5.50 (0-8378-1868-0) Gibson.
—Alice in Bibleland Storybooks: The Story of Isaac & Rebeckah. (Illus.). (gr. 3 up). 1989. 5.50 (0-8378-1852-4) Gibson.
—Alice in Bibleland Storybooks: The Story of Jesus & His Disciples. (Illus.). (gr. 3 up). 1989. 5.50 (0-8378-1860-5) Gibson.
—Alice in Bibleland Storybooks: The Story of Ruth & Naomi. (Illus.). (gr. 3 up). 1989. 5.50 (0-8378-1855-9) Gibson.
—Alice in Bibleland Storybooks: The Story of Exodus. (Illus.). (gr. 3 up). 1989. 5.50 (0-8378-1849-4) Gibson.

—Alice in Bibleland Storybooks: The Story of Joshua. (Illus.). (gr. 3 up). 1989. 5.50 (0-8378-1850-8) Gibson.
—Alice in Bibleland Storybooks: The Story of Esther. (Illus.). (gr. 3 up). 1989. 5.50 (0-8378-1851-6) Gibson.
—Alice in Bibleland Storybooks: The Story of Paul. (Illus.). (gr. 3 up). 1989. 5.50 (0-8378-1853-2) Gibson.
—Alice in Bibleland Storybooks: The Story of the Good Samaritan. (Illus.). (gr. 3 up). 1989. 5.50 (0-8378-1854-0) Gibson.
—Alice in Bibleland Storybooks: The Story of the Lost Sheep. (Illus.). (gr. 3 up). 1989. 5.50 (0-8378-1865-6) Gibson.
—Alice in Bibleland Storybooks: The Story of the Prodigal Son. (Illus.). (gr. 3 up). 1989. 5.50 (0-8378-1848-6) Gibson.
—Alice in Bibleland Storybooks: The Story of the Tower of Babel. (Illus.). (gr. 3 up). 1989. 5.50 (0-8378-1866-4) Gibson.
Davidson, Alma & Pineda, Leonardo A. Kapampangan Newspaper Reader. Zorc, R. David, intro. by. LC 91-75539. 105p. 1992. 39.00 (0-931745-77-2); cassettes 20.00 (0-931745-85-3) Dunwoody Pr.
Davidson, Amanda. Teddy's Christmas Cut-Out. 16p. (gr. 4-7). 1990. pap. 2.50 (0-8167-2197-1) Troll Assocs.
—Teddy's Countdown to Christmas. 16p. (gr. 4-7). 1990. pap. 2.50 (0-8167-2198-X) Troll Assocs.
Davidson, Bob. Hillary & Tenzing Climb Everest. (Illus.). 32p. (gr. 5 up). 1993. RSBE 13.95 (0-87518-534-7, Dillon) Macmillan Child Grp.
Davidson, Diane, ed. see Shakespeare, William.
Davidson, Diane, ed. & illus. see Shakespeare, William.
Davidson, Doud P. Along the Endless Strip. 225p. (Orig.). 1992. pap. text ed. 5.95 (0-9630884-2-4) Team Effort.
Davidson, Jessica. Using the Cuisenaire Rods: A Photo-Text Guide for Teachers. (Illus.). 150p. (gr. 1-8). 1983. pap. text ed. 15.95 (0-914040-04-9) Cuisenaire.
Davidson, Josephine. The Old Testament: Ten Plays for Readers' Theater. Starr, Fiona, illus. LC 92-90957. 189p. (Orig.). (gr. 6-8). 1992. pap. text ed. write for info. (0-9628252-1-2) Right Bk.
Davidson, Linda. Cool Breezes. (gr. 10 up). 1989. pap. 2.95 (0-8041-0244-9) Ivy Books.
—Fast Forward. (gr. 10 up). 1989. pap. 2.95 (0-8041-0246-5) Ivy Books.
—On the Edge. (gr. 10 up). 1988. pap. 2.95 (0-8041-0243-0) Ivy Books.
—Treading Water. 192p. (gr. 10 up). 1988. pap. 2.95 (0-8041-0241-4) Ivy Books.
Davidson, Margaret. Five True Dog Stories. 1989. pap. 2.50 (0-590-42401-7) Five True Horse Stories. 1989. pap. 2.75 (0-590-42400-9) Scholastic Inc.
—Five True Horse Stories. 1989. pap. 2.75 (0-590-42400-9) Scholastic Inc.
—Frederick Douglass Fights for Freedom. 80p. (gr. 2-5). 1989. pap. 2.50 (0-590-42218-9, Apple Paperbacks) Scholastic Inc.
—Helen Keller. 1989. pap. 2.50 (0-590-42404-1) Scholastic Inc.
—Helen Keller's Teacher. 160p. 1992. pap. 2.95 (0-590-44652-5, Apple Paperbacks) Scholastic Inc.
—I Have a Dream: The Story of Martin Luther King. (gr. 4-7). 1991. pap. 2.75 (0-590-44230-9) Scholastic Inc.
—Louis Braille, l'Enfant de la Nuit. Dahar, Andre, illus. (FRE.). 103p. (gr. 3-7). 1990. pap. 10.95 (2-07-031225-9) Schoenhof.
—Louis Braille: The Boy Who Invented Books for the Blind. Compere, Janet, illus. 80p. 1991. pap. 2.75 (0-590-44350-X) Scholastic Inc.
—Nine True Dolphin Stories. 64p. (gr. 2-5). 1990. pap. 2.75 (0-590-42399-1) Scholastic Inc.
—The Story of Benjamin Franklin: Amazing American. (Orig.). (gr. k-6). 1988. pap. 3.25 (0-440-40021-X, YB) Dell.
—The Story of Jackie Robinson: Bravest Man in Baseball. (Orig.). (gr. k-6). 1988. pap. 3.50 (0-440-40019-8, YB) Dell.
—Story of Thomas Alva Edison: The Wizard of Menlo Park. 1990. pap. 2.75 (0-590-42403-3) Scholastic Inc.
Davidson, Margaret, jt. auth. see Bakoske, Sharon.
Davidson, Martine. Kevin & the School Nurse. Hafner, Marylin, illus. LC 91-30194. 32p. (Orig.). (ps-2). 1992. PLB 5.99 (0-679-91821-3); pap. 2.25 (0-679-81821-9) Random Bks Yng Read.
—Maggie & the Emergency Room. Hafner, Marylin, illus. LC 91-31413. 32p. (Orig.). (ps-2). 1992. PLB 5.99 (0-679-91818-3); pap. 2.25 (0-679-81818-9) Random Bks Yng Read.
—Rita Goes to the Hospital. Jones, John, illus. LC 91-43293. 32p. (Orig.). (ps-2). 1992. PLB 5.99 (0-679-91820-5); pap. 2.25 (0-679-81820-0) Random Bks Yng Read.
—Robby Visits the Doctor. Stevenson, Nancy, illus. LC 91-30193. 32p. (Orig.). (ps-2). 1992. PLB 5.99 (0-679-91819-1); pap. 2.25 (0-679-81819-7) Random Bks Yng Read.
Davidson, Mary R. Buffalo Bill: Wild West Showman. (Illus.). 80p. (gr. 2-6). 1993. Repr. of 1962 ed. lib. bdg. 12.95 (0-7910-1432-0) Chelsea Hse.
—Dolly Madison: Famous First Lady. (Illus.). 80p. (gr. 2-6). 1992. Repr. of 1966 ed. lib. bdg. 12.95 (0-7910-1446-0) Chelsea Hse.
Davidson, Nicole. Demon's Beach. 160p. (Orig.). (gr. 7-12). 1992. pap. 3.50 (0-380-76644-2, Flare) Avon.
—Fan Mail. 176p. (Orig.). 1993. pap. 3.50 (0-380-76995-6, Flare) Avon.
—Surprise Party. 192p. (Orig.). (gr. 5). 1993. pap. 3.50 (0-380-76996-4, Flare) Avon.

—Winterkill. 192p. (Orig.). 1991. pap. 2.95 (0-380-75965-9, Flare) Avon.
Davidson, Patricia. Idea Book: For Cuisenaire Rods at the Primary Level. (Illus.). 164p. (ps-2). 1977. pap. text ed. 15.95 (0-914040-18-9) Cuisenaire.
DAvidson, Patricia & Sellon, Jeffrey. Picture Puzzles with Cuisenaire Rods. 64p. (gr. 1-6). 1979. pap. text ed. 8.50 (0-914040-77-4) Cuisenaire.
Davidson, Patricia & Willcutt, Robert. Multiplication & Division with Rod Patterns & Graph Paper. (Illus.). 64p. (gr. 3-8). 1980. pap. text ed. 8.50 (0-914040-82-0) Cuisenaire.
—Spatial Problem Solving: With Cuisenaire Rods. 64p. (gr. 4-9). 1983. pap. text ed. 8.50 (0-914040-99-5) Cuisenaire.
Davidson, Patricia S. & Willcutt, Robert E. Spatial Problem Solving with Paper Folding & Cutting. 64p. (gr. 4-7). 1984. pap. text ed. 8.50 (0-914040-36-7) Cuisenaire.
Davidson, Robert G. God Doesn't Make Junk. (gr. 9-12). 1990. 8.00 (0-940754-93-2, 8242) Ed Ministries.
—Youth Programming Workbook. 40p. (Orig.). 1989. pap. 8.50 (0-940754-67-3) Ed Ministries.
Davidson, Ronnie, jt. auth. see Goldman, Kelly.
Davidson, Rosemary. Take a Look: An Introduction to the Experience of Art. (Illus.). 128p. (gr. 4-7). 1994. 18.99 (0-670-84478-0) Viking Child Bks.

Davidson, Sol M. Wild Jake Hiccup: The History of America's First Frontiersman. Davidson, Penny, illus. LC 91-19499. 160p. (Orig.). (gr. 2-9). 1992. 16.95 (1-56412-003-1); pap. 9.95 (1-56412-004-X); audio cassette 6.95 (1-56412-001-5) Hse Nine Muses. "The story of our tallest unknown folk hero, from his early days in colonial western "Pennsylvanny" to his epic battle with the young Paul Bunyan. Jacob grew up to play no small role in history: he is credited with single-handedly driving the French from Fort Duquense; suggesting a design for the U.S. flag based on George Washington's pajamas; making Mike Fink the victim of the first April Fool's joke; urging Audubon to add a few birds to his paintings; & inspiring John Chapman, later known as Johnny Peachfuzz - no, Johnny Peanutshell... Johnny Apricotpit something like that. The tale is told in "countrified" prose, illustrated with small, simple line drawings. Readers can absorb a fair dose of history while enjoying the droll adventures of this animal-loving, generally peacable giant."--KIRKUS REVIEWS, Aug. 1, 1992. "DELICIOUS!"--Mrs. M. Cunningham, 3rd grade teacher, Wash., D.C. "DELIGHTFUL!"--R. Messineo, Administrator, Passaic, N.J. Schools. "CHARMING!"--Mr. J. Wodden, Curriculum Dir., Des Moines, IA, Public Schools. "This book is funny & full of historical information. Overall, this book is very good & on a scale of one to ten, I would give it an eight & a half."--Megan Melamed, Age 12, The Gifted Child Today Magazine (GCT). Also ENJOYING AMERICAN HISTORY: Teacher's Guide to the Mining the Rich Vein of Ideas in Wild Jake Hiccup. Over 200 stimulating projects to make learning American History FUN! 80 pages. Illustrated. ISBN 1-56412-002-3. (softcover.) $5.95. For librarians, parents, grandparents to use with youngsters. Also THE BALLAD OF WILD JAKE HICCUP, audio cassette. Approx. 40 mins. Original words & music composed by John Deltenre & his Pioneer Band. $6.95. ISBN 1-56412-001-5. *Publisher Provided Annotation.*

Davidson, Wayne, jt. auth. see Brouwer, Sigmund.

Davie, Helen, illus. Sing with Me Christmas Carols. 24p. (ps up). 1987. pap. 5.95 incl. cassette (*0-394-89060-4*) Random Bks Yng Read.

Davie, John L. His Honor, the Buckaroo: The Autobiography of John L. Davie. rev. ed. LC 87-91072. (Illus.). 239p. (gr. 9-12). 1988. pap. 9.95 (*0-943077-12-5*) J Herzberg.

Davie, Sandy, jt. auth. see Lauffer, Butch.

Davies. Inside the Chip. Round, Grahm, illus. (gr. 6 up). 1984. pap. 4.95 (*0-86020-729-3*) EDC.

Davies, Andrew. Conrad's War. 144p. (gr. 5 up). 1986. pap. 1.95 (*0-440-91452-3*, LFL) Dell.

Davies, Andrew & Davies, Diana. Poonam's Pets. Dowling, Paul, illus. 32p. (ps-2). 1990. pap. 12.95 (*0-670-83321-5*) Viking Child Bks.

Davies, Benedict. Credo: A Catholic Catechism. 300p. 1984. pap. 11.00 (*0-86683-901-1*) Harper SF.

Davies, Diana, jt. auth. see Davies, Andrew.

Davies, Eryl. Transport: On Land, Road & Rail. Kline, Marjory, ed. (Illus.). 48p. (gr. 4-9). 1992. 13.95 (*0-531-15244-8*) Watts.

—Water Travel. LC 93-7074. 32p. (gr. 5-9). 1993. 14.95 (*1-56847-038-X*) Thomson Lrning.

Davies, Gillian. Why Worms? rev. ed. Kramer, Robin, illus. 32p. (gr. k-2). 1990. Repr. of 1989 ed. PLB 10.50 (*1-878363-07-7*) Forest Hse.

Davies, H. Beginner's French Dictionary. (Illus.). 128p. 1989. lib. bdg. 15.96 (*0-88110-346-2*); pap. 9.95 (*0-7460-0016-2*) EDC.

—Beginner's Italian Dictionary. (Illus.). 128p. (gr. 6 up). lib. bdg. 15.96 (*0-88110-423-X*, Usborne); pap. 9.95 (*0-7460-0764-7*) EDC.

Davies, H. & Whaton, M. Better BASIC. (Illus.). 48p. (gr. 6 up). 1983. lib. bdg. 10.96 (*0-88110-139-7*); pap. 3.95 (*0-86020-733-1*) EDC.

Davies, Kate. Play Mask Book - Wizard of Oz. 12p. (ps-3). 1991. pap. 5.95 (*0-8167-2373-7*) Troll Assocs.

Davies, Kate, jt. auth. see Cowley, Stewart.

Davies, Kath. Amelia Earhart Flies Around the World. (Illus.). 32p. (gr. 5). 1994. PLB 13.95 RSBE (*0-87518-531-2*, Dillon) Macmillan Child Grp.

—Wales. LC 90-10192. (Illus.). 96p. (gr. 6-12). 1990. PLB 19.92 (*0-8114-2437-5*) Raintree Steck-V.

Davies, Kay. My Balloon. (ps-3). 1990. pap. 6.95 (*0-385-41131-6*) Doubleday.

—My Mirror. 1990. pap. 6.95 (*0-385-41128-6*) Doubleday.

Davies, Kay & Oldfield, Wendy. Sound & Music. LC 91-23475. (Illus.). 32p. (gr. 2-5). 1991. PLB 17.28 (*0-8114-3003-0*); pap. 4.49 (*0-8114-1534-1*) Raintree Steck-V.

—The Super Science Book of Time. Lloyd, Frances, illus. LC 92-42131. 32p. (gr. 4-8). 1993. 14.95g (*1-56847-020-7*) Thomson Lrning.

—The Super Science Book of Weather. Lloyd, Frances, illus. LC 92-43298. 32p. (gr. 4-8). 1993. 14.95 (*1-56847-021-5*) Thomson Lrning.

Davies, Leah. Kelly Bear Beginnings, 5 bks. Hallett, Leah, illus. 176p. (ps-5). 1991. Set incl. Kelly Bear Feelings; Kelly Bear Behavior; Kelly Bear Health; Kelly Bear Activities; Kelly Bear Drug Awareness. pap. 29.95 (*0-9621054-7-3*) Kelly Bear Pr. The KELLY BEAR books teach children important life skills such as coping positively with emotions, learning appropriate behavior, making wholesome choices & accepting responsibility for their feelings, actions & bodies. Children identify with the green bear who is a positive role model. The INTERACTION books are to be read by an adult (teacher, librarian, counselor, parent) with a child or children. Throughout the books Kelly Bear asks questions that encourage children to share their thoughts & feelings, as Kelly Bear does. When adults listen with regard, children perceive themselves as valued & their self-esteem thrives. According to Dr. Kevin Swick, Univ. of South Carolina, the KELLY BEAR books have "exemplary situations"... which "have been used successfully with parents & children from every background & cultural orientation." A teacher, stated, "The books provide invaluable insights.. .a wonderful teaching tool." The acclaimed series is being used effectively with classrooms of children, in small groups, & with individuals, include high-risk & special education students. The KELLY BEAR books are the mainstay of an eight-week Drug Abuse Prevention Program (DAPP) $199.00. Kelly Bear Press, 4295 Co. Rd. 12, Lafayette, AL 36862. (205) 864-8991.
Publisher Provided Annotation.

Davies, Leah G. Drug Abuse Prevention Program Leader Guide. 56p. (ps-3). 1993. pap. write for info. (*0-9621054-5-7*) Kelly Bear Pr.

—Kelly Bear Activities. Hallett, Joy D., illus. LC 92-70013. 40p. (ps-3). 1992. pap. 10.95 (*0-9621054-4-9*) Kelly Bear Pr.

—Kelly Bear Behavior. Hallett, Joy D., illus. LC 88-82603. 28p. (Orig.). (ps-3). 1988. pap. 4.50 (*0-9621054-1-4*) Kelly Bear Pr.

—Kelly Bear Drug Awareness. Hallett, Joy D., illus. 40p. (ps-3). 1993. pap. 10.95 (*0-9621054-6-5*) Kelly Bear Pr.

—Kelly Bear Feelings. rev. ed. Davies, Joy D., illus. LC 88-82577. 28p. (ps-3). 1988. pap. 4.50 (*0-9621054-0-6*) Kelly Bear Pr.

—Kelly Bear Health. Davies, Joy D., illus. LC 89-85159. 28p. (Orig.). (ps-3). 1989. pap. 4.50 (*0-9621054-2-2*) Kelly Bear Pr.

Davies, Mark. Malcolm X: Another Side of the Movement. Gallin, Richard, ed. Young, Andrew, intro. by. (Illus.). 128p. (gr. 5 up). 1990. lib. bdg. 16.98 (*0-382-09925-7*); pap. 7.95 (*0-382-24063-4*) Silver Burdett Pr.

Davies, Nancy M. The Stock Market Crash of Nineteen Twenty-Nine. (Illus.). 96p. (gr. 6 up). 1994. PLB 14.95 RSBE (*0-02-726221-9*, New Discovery Bks) Macmillan Child Grp.

Davies, Valentine. Miracle on Thirty-Fourth Street. De Paola, Tomie, illus. (gr. k up). 1984. 16.95 (*0-15-254526-3*, HB Juv Bks) HarBrace.

Davis. Silk Ball. Date not set. 15.00 (*0-06-024279-5*, Festival); PLB 14.89 (*0-06-024288-4*) HarpC Child Bks.

Davis, Allison. Best Friends. Prebenna, David, illus. 32p. (ps-k). 1992. write for info. (*0-307-12008-2*, 12008) Western Pub.

Davis, Alvin G. A Day in the Life of a Cowboy. Moorhouse, Bob, photos by. LC 90-11130. (Illus.). 32p. (gr. 4-8). 1991. PLB 11.79 (*0-8167-2208-0*); pap. text ed. 2.95 (*0-8167-2209-9*) Troll Assocs.

Davis, Anita P. & Hall, Ed Y. Harriet Quimby - America's First Lady of the Air: An Activity Book for Children. (Illus.). 40p. (Orig.). (gr. 4-8). 1993. pap. 4.95 wkbk. (*0-9622166-6-6*) Honoribus Pr.

Davis, Arnold R. & Miller, Donald C. Science Games. (gr. 1-6). 1974. pap. 5.95 (*0-8224-6303-2*) Fearon Teach Aids.

Davis, Barbara, ed. see Mochnick, Beth R.

Davis, Bea. Cam Jansen & the Mystery of the Dinosaur Bones: A Study Guide. (gr. 1-3). 1986. tchr's. ed. & wkbk. 14.95 (*0-88122-068-X*) LRN Links.

Davis, Beatrice G. All of a Kind Family: A Study Guide. (gr. 3-6). 1984. tchr's. ed. & wkbk. 14.95 (*0-88122-072-8*) LRN Links.

Davis, Beatrice G., et al. Black Boy: A Study Guide. (gr. 9-12). 1984. tchr's. ed. & wkbk. 14.95 (*0-88122-105-8*) LRN Links.

Davis, Bertha. America's Housing Crisis. LC 89-37028. (gr. 9-12). 1990. PLB 13.40 (*0-531-10917-8*) Watts.

—Crisis in Industry. LC 88-38584. (Illus.). 128p. (gr. 10-12). 1990. 12.90 (*0-531-10659-4*) Watts.

—Gambling in America: A Growth Industry. LC 92-17591. 112p. (gr. 9-12). 1992. PLB 13.40 (*0-531-13021-5*) Watts.

—Poverty in America: What We Do About It. (Illus.). 144p. (gr. 9-12). 1991. PLB 13.90 (*0-531-13016-9*) Watts.

Davis, Burke. Black Heroes of the American Revolution. LC 75-44218. (Illus.). 80p. (gr. 5 up). 1976. 14.95 (*0-15-208560-2*, HB Juv Bks) HarBrace.

—Black Heroes of the American Revolution. (gr. 5 up). 1992. pap. 4.95 (*0-15-208561-0*, HB Juv Bks) HarBrace.

—Marine! The Life of Chesty Puller. 1991. pap. 4.99 (*0-553-27182-2*) Bantam.

Davis, Carolyn & Brown, Charlene. Painting Fun. (Illus.). 64p. (Orig.). (gr. k up). 1989. pap. 5.95 (*1-56010-034-6*, BA08) W Foster Pub.

Davis, Carolyn, jt. auth. see Brown, Charlene.

Davis, Cathy, ed. see Hansel, Tim.

Davis, Charles E. Creatures at My Feet. Neidigh, Sherry, illus. LC 92-81235. 32p. (ps-3). 1993. 14.95 (*0-87358-560-7*) Northland AZ.

Davis, Cos H., Jr. I'm Big Enough. LC 89-24027. (ps-3). 1991. 6.95 (*0-8054-4342-8*) Broadman.

Davis, D. G. American Spoken English in Real Life - Fast Natural, Urgent Survival, Foreign Accent Begone! The Phonology of General American Colloquial, Vol. 1. 300p. (Orig.). 1993. pap. 25.00 (*0-929350-01-4*) Spoken English Pubns.

—American Spoken English in Real Life, Basic Course: Learning to Understand Americans Talking Naturally & to Talk So They Readily Understand You, Vol. 2. 128p. (Orig.). 1993. pap. 10.00 (*0-929350-02-2*); 4 90-min. cass. 10.00 ea. Spoken English Pubns.

Davis, Dawn S. Fishing Buddies. LC 91-90919. (Illus.). 52p. (Orig.). (gr. 5-6). 1991. pap. 3.95 (*1-879318-03-2*) Wild Meadows.

—A Good Dog to Have Around the House. LC 90-90462. (Illus.). 52p. (Orig.). (gr. 1). 1990. pap. 3.95 (*1-879318-00-8*) Wild Meadows.

—Motorcycle Dog. LC 90-72039. (Illus.). 52p. (Orig.). (gr. 2-4). 1990. pap. 3.95 (*1-879318-01-6*) Wild Meadows.

Davis, Deborah. The Secret of the Seal. Davis, Deborah, illus. (gr. 2 up). 1988. 13.95 (*0-517-56725-3*) Crown Bks Yng Read.

Davis, Deena, ed. see Haidle, David & Haidle, Helen.

Davis, Deena, ed. see Sanford, Doris.

Davis, Diane. Something Is Wrong at My House. Megale, Marina, illus. LC 84-62129. 40p. (Orig.). (ps-6). 1985. PLB 15.95 (*0-943990-11-4*); pap. 4.95 (*0-943990-10-6*) Parenting Pr.

Davis, Donald. Jack Always Seeks His Fortune: Authentic Appalachian Jack Tales. Sodol, Joseph, intro. by. 176p. 1992. 21.95 (*0-87483-281-0*); pap. 11.95 (*0-87483-280-2*) August Hse.

Davis, Doris. The Mystery of Briar Rose Manor. LC 89-82583. (Illus.). 208p. (gr. 9-12). 1990. pap. 3.95 (*0-88243-652-X*, 02-0652) Gospel Pub.

Davis, Duane. Listen & Play with My Friends & Me Activity Manual. rev. ed. (ps-k). 1988. wkbk. 29.95 (*0-88671-331-5*, 4631) Am Guidance.

—My Friends & Me Activity Manual. rev. ed. (ps-k). 1988. pap. text ed. 64.95 (*0-88671-325-0*, 4601) Am Guidance.

—My Friends & Me Story Book. rev. ed. (ps-k). 1988. pap. text ed. 73.25 (*0-88671-326-9*, 4605) Am Guidance.

Davis, Emmett. Clues in the Desert. Downing, Julie, illus. LC 83-8626. 32p. (gr. 3-6). 1983. PLB 14.65 (*0-940742-29-2*) Raintree Steck-V.

Davis, G. J. Automotive Reference: A New Approach - to the World of Auto & Related Information. 470p. (Orig.). (gr. 7-12). 1987. 39.95 (*0-937591-01-7*); pap. 24.95 (*0-937591-00-9*) Whitehorse.

Davis, George. Multiple Choice Questions in Preparation for the AP Economics ("Macro" & "Micro") Examination. 124p. (gr. 11-12). 1992. wkbk. 15.95 (*1-878621-21-1*); tchr's. manual, 76p. avail. (*1-878621-22-X*) D & S Mktg Syst.

Davis, Gibbs. Christy's Magic Glove. (ps-3). 1992. pap. 3.25 (*0-553-15988-7*) Bantam.

—Lucky Socks. (gr. 4-7). 1991. pap. 2.99 (*0-553-15865-1*) Bantam.

—Major-League Melissa. (gr. 4-7). 1991. pap. 3.25 (*0-553-15866-X*) Bantam.

—Maud Flies Solo. (gr. 4-7). 1990. pap. 3.50 (*0-553-15786-8*) Bantam.

—Never Sink Nine, No. 5. 1992. pap. 2.99 (*0-553-15996-8*) Bantam.

—Olympics Otis. (ps-3). 1993. pap. 3.25 (*0-553-48078-2*) Bantam.

—The Other Emily. Shute, Linda, illus. LC 83-18913. 32p. (gr. k-3). 1984. 14.45 (*0-395-35482-X*, 5-84351) HM.

—The Other Emily. Shute, Linda, illus. 32p. (gr. k-3). 1990. pap. 4.95 (*0-395-54947-7*) HM.

—Pete the Magnificent. (ps-3). 1991. pap. 3.25 (*0-553-15896-1*) Bantam.

—Slugger Mike. (ps-3). 1991. pap. 3.25 (*0-553-15883-X*) Bantam.

—Swann Song. 176p. (gr. 7 up). 1989. pap. 2.50 (*0-380-75609-9*, Flare) Avon.

Davis, Harold. You'll Never Walk Alone: Dating from the Biblical Perspective. 108p. Date not set. pap. text ed. 10.00 (*0-9638553-0-1*) KJAC Pubng.

Davis, Hilda R., ed. Children's Church Time, No. 2: For Children's Church, Second Sunday School Sessions, & OT. 56p. (Orig.). (ps). 1992. pap. 19.95 (*0-687-08385-0*) Abingdon.

—Children's Church Time, No. 3: For Children's Church, Second Sunday School Sessions, & OT. 56p. (ps). 1993. pap. 19.95 (*0-687-08386-9*) Abingdon.

—Children's Church Time, No. 4: For Children's Church, Second Sunday School Sessions, & OT. 56p. (ps). 1993. pap. 19.95 (*0-687-08387-7*) Abingdon.

—Children's Church Times: Children's Church, Second Sunday School Sessions, & Other. 56p. (Orig.). (ps). 1992. pap. 19.95 (*0-687-08384-2*) Abingdon.

Davis, Hubert J. What Will the Weather Be?, No. 1: A Folk Weather Calendar. Turner, Erin, illus. LC 88-17869. 40p. (Orig.). (gr. k-12). 1988. pap. 4.95 (*0-936015-11-X*) Pocahontas Pr.

—What Will the Weather Be?, No. 2: Animal Signs. Turner, Erin, illus. LC 90-22327. 56p. (Orig.). (gr. k-12). 1991. pap. 5.95 (*0-936015-12-8*) Pocahontas Pr.

Davis, Inez T. Modestita's Gift - El Regalo de Modestita. LC 91-71032. (ENG & SPA.). 32p. (ps-3). 1991. pap. 4.99 (*0-8066-2532-5*, 9-2532) Augsburg Fortress.

Davis, J. Bradley. A Kid's Day Out: Eighty Four Ways to Spend Memorable Time with Your Child. 80p. 1992. pap. text ed. 7.95 (*1-881458-01-6*) Crazy Creat. Want to spend enjoyable, laughable, & memorable time with your child? Want some fascinating ideas for these memorable moments? Want to build

experiences that will be cherished for a life time? If this is your desire, or the desire of someone you know, this book is for you. This book contains 84 fantastic ideas on making memorable moments for both you & your child. There are ideas for every one of every age. You can select trips and outings that are educational, entertaining, sporting, and adventurous. To help you pick an outing that both you & your child will enjoy, there are icons (symbols & pictures) suggesting the cost, duration, & age for each outing. This book makes a wonderful reference for mothers, fathers, teachers, friends, & relatives. You will have fun just reading through the pages. To Order: Crazy Creations. P.O. Box 88154, Colorado Springs, Colorado 80908. Tel. (719) 495-0175. *Publisher Provided Annotation.*

Davis, J. E., ed. Ye Sylvan Archer, Vol. I. (Illus.). 336p. (gr. 10 up). 1993. Repr. of 1927 ed. 39.95 (*1-56416-100-5*) Derrydale Pr.
Davis, James. Our Communities & Others: Study Book. Hawke, Sharryl D. & Combs, Eunice A., eds. Carroll, Gary, illus. Calvin, Eunice, photos by. (Illus.). 57p. (gr. 3). 1983. pap. 4.50 (*0-943068-74-6*) Graphic Learning.
Davis, James A. Times Table Secrets. Davis, James A., illus. 12p. (gr. 3-5). 1994. incls. flash cards 10.00 (*0-9634088-1-X*) Simp Solns.
Davis, James E. Our Communities & Others: Manual. Hawke, Sharryl D. & Combs, Eunice A., eds. (Illus.). 323p. (gr. 3). 1983. duplication masters 69.00 (*0-943068-52-5*) Graphic Learning.
Davis, James E. & Hawke, Sharryl D. Chicago. (Illus.). 64p. (gr. 4-9). 1990. PLB 19.92 (*0-8172-3025-4*) Raintree Steck-V.
—London. (Illus.). 64p. (gr. 4-9). 1990. PLB 19.92 (*0-8172-3027-0*) Raintree Steck-V.
—Los Angeles. (Illus.). 64p. (gr. 4-9). 1990. PLB 19.92 (*0-8172-3028-9*) Raintree Steck-V.
—Mexico City. (Illus.). 64p. (gr. 4-9). 1990. PLB 19.92 (*0-8172-3029-7*) Raintree Steck-V.
—Moscow. (Illus.). 64p. (gr. 4-9). 1990. PLB 19.92 (*0-8172-3030-0*) Raintree Steck-V.
—Tokyo. (Illus.). 64p. (gr. 4-9). 1990. PLB 19.92 (*0-8172-3032-7*) Raintree Steck-V.
—Washington, D. C. (Illus.). 64p. (gr. 4-9). 1990. PLB 19.92 (*0-8172-3026-2*) Raintree Steck-V.
Davis, Jenine, jt. auth. see Buerger, Jane.
Davis, Jenny. Checking on the Moon. LC 91-8284. 224p. (gr. 6 up). 1991. 14.95 (*0-531-05960-X*); RLB 14.99 (*0-531-08560-0*) Orchard Bks Watts.
—Checking on the Moon. 1993. pap. 3.50 (*0-440-21491-2*) Dell.
—Good-bye & Keep Cold. LC 87-5794. 224p. (gr. 7 up). 1987. 12.95 (*0-531-05715-1*); PLB 12.99 (*0-531-08535-9*) Orchard Bks Watts.
—Sex Education. LC 87-30441. 160p. (gr. 7 up). 1988. 13.95 (*0-531-05756-9*); PLB 13.99 (*0-531-08356-X*) Orchard Bks Watts.
Davis, Jim. La Bonne Vie. (FRE.). 1988. 18.95 (*0-8288-4581-6*) Fr & Eur.
—La Diete, Jamais! (FRE.). 1987. 18.95 (*0-8288-4582-4*) Fr & Eur.
—La Faim Justifie Les Moyens. (FRE.). 1985. 18.95 (*0-8288-4583-2*, F91530) Fr & Eur.
—Faut Pas S'En Faire. (FRE.). 1984. 18.95 (*0-8288-4584-0*, F101551) Fr & Eur.
—Garfield Discovers America. 32p. 1992. 9.95 (*0-448-40257-2*, G&D) Putnam Pub Group.
—Garfield Prend Du Poids. (FRE.). 1984. 18.95 (*0-8288-4586-7*, F101550) Fr & Eur.
—Garfield, Tiens Bon la Rampe. (FRE.). 1989. 18.95 (*0-8288-4585-9*) Fr & Eur.
—Garfield's Night Before Christmas. (gr. 2 up). 1988. 8.95 (*0-448-09283-2*, G&D) Putnam Pub Group.
—The Great Christmas Contest. (Illus.). 48p. (ps up). 1988. bds. 7.95 (*0-553-34609-1*) Bantam.
—The Great Xmas Contest. 1988. pap. 6.95 (*0-553-05807-X*) Bantam.
—Let's Play Ball! 1989. pap. 2.50 (*0-553-34627-X*) Bantam.
—Moi, On M'Aime. (FRE.). 1986. 18.95 (*0-8288-4587-5*, M4211*) Fr & Eur.
—A Most Special Easter Egg. 1989. pap. 2.50 (*0-553-34628-8*) Bantam.
—Qui Dort Dine. (FRE.). 1988. 18.95 (*0-8288-4588-3*) Fr & Eur.
—Tiens Bon la Rampe. (FRE.). 1989. 18.95 (*0-8288-4589-1*) Fr & Eur.
—U. S. Acres Counts Its Chickens. (Illus.). 128p. (ps up). 1987. pap. 5.95 (*0-88687-314-2*, Pharos) F&W Inc NJ.
—U. S. Acres: Happy Birthday Sheldon! (ps-3). 1990. pap. 2.50 (*0-553-34873-6*) Bantam.

—Les Yeux Plus Gros Que le Ventre. (FRE.). 1985. 18.95 (*0-8288-4590-5*, F91520) Fr & Eur.
Davis, Jim & Hawke, Sherryl D. New York. (Illus.). 64p. (gr. 4-9). 1990. PLB 19.92 (*0-8172-3031-9*) Raintree Steck-V.
Davis, Julia A. African American History for Young Readers. 2nd ed. (Illus.). 336p. (gr. 5-9). 1992. 30.00 (*0-9631110-5-1*) Epps-Alford.
—The Children's Picture Book of African American History. 150p. (ps-5). 1992. 20.00 (*0-9631110-3-5*) Epps-Alford.
Davis, Julie N., jt. auth. see Blos, Sarah I.
Davis, Karen. Star Light, Star Bright. LC 92-17120. (ps-2). 1993. 15.00 (*0-671-79455-8*, Green Tiger) S&S Trade.
Davis, Kathleen & Mayes, Dave. Killer Bees. LC 92-46894. (Illus.). 60p. (gr. 5 up). 1993. RSBE 13.95 (*0-87518-582-7*, Dillon) Macmillan Child Grp.
Davis, Kay & Oldsfield, Wendy. Animals. LC 91-23413. (Illus.). 32p. (gr. 2-5). 1991. PLB 17.28 (*0-8114-3002-2*); PLB 4.49 (*0-8114-1528-7*) Raintree Steck-V.
—Electricity & Magnetism. LC 91-30069. (Illus.). 32p. (gr. 2-5). 1991. PLB 17.28 (*0-8114-3004-9*); pap. 4.49 (*0-8114-1532-5*) Raintree Steck-V.
—Floating & Sinking. LC 91-25756. (Illus.). 32p. (gr. 2-5). 1991. PLB 17.28 (*0-8114-3001-4*); pap. 4.49 (*0-8114-1529-5*) Raintree Steck-V.
—Food. LC 91-30068. (Illus.). 32p. (gr. 2-5). 1991. PLB 17.28 (*0-8114-3005-7*); pap. 4.49 (*0-8114-1533-3*) Raintree Steck-V.
—Light. LC 91-30067. (Illus.). 32p. (gr. 2-5). 1991. PLB 17.28 (*0-8114-3006-5*); pap. 4.49 (*0-8114-1530-9*) Raintree Steck-V.
—Waste. LC 91-23414. (Illus.). 32p. (gr. 2-5). 1991. PLB 17.28 (*0-8114-3000-6*); pap. 4.49 (*0-8114-1531-7*) Raintree Steck-V.
—Weather. LC 91-30066. (Illus.). 32p. (gr. 2-5). 1991. PLB 17.28 (*0-8114-3007-3*); pap. 4.49 (*0-8114-1535-X*) Raintree Steck-V.
Davis, Ken. How to Live with Your Parents Without Losing Your Mind. (gr. 7 up). 1988. pap. 7.99 (*0-310-32331-2*, 11791P, Pub. by Youth Spec) Zondervan.
Davis, Ken & Lambert, David. Jumper Fables. 192p. (gr. 5 up). 1993. pap. 8.99 (*0-310-40010-4*, Pub. by Youth Spec) Zondervan.

Davis, Kerry. The Swetsville Zoo. (Illus.). 44p. (gr. 1-6). 1993. 8.95 (*0-9635263-1-6*); It's More Than A Tree That You See, Bk. 1. pap. 4.95 (*0-9635263-0-8*); Set. 12.95 (*0-9635263-2-4*) Kerry Tales. A bizarre zoo of sculptures made of old farm machinery & junk auto parts. The story in rhyme is accompanied with bright colorful photos of two-headed winged dinosaurs, grasshoppers as big as cars, out of this world creatures. "The animals here are a motley crew, crazy critters at the Swetsville Zoo!" Davis, Kerry We're Baack! Swetsville Zoo Two. Color photo illus., 46 p., (J) April 1994, Hardcover $10.95. 0-9635263-4-0, Kerry Tales, Inc. Another zany adventure in rhyme with more great photos. This time a few of the critters borrow a spaceship & take a trip of their own. They are off to another planet to meet some incredibly weird creatures. There are lessons to learn along the way & a strange twist at the end. There's something new & exciting on the planet that you won't want to miss. It's More Than A Tree That You See, Color illus., 32p., (J) Sept. 1992, paperback $4.95, 0-9635263-0-8, Kerry Tales, Inc. A conservation story in rhyme, beautifully illustrated in watercolors. Life in the forest has always been fun for Timmy the Tree, but when the tree cutters come, Tim has a big problem. Since Tim can't run from the trouble at hand, he must use his mind to get out of his jam. Kerry Tales Picture Book Series, 0-9635263-2-4, $24.00, (3 books). 1995 Swetsville Zoo Calendar, 9 X 12, $9.95, 0-9635263-5-9, Kerry Tales Inc., Another colossal collection of colorful crazy critters from the Swetsville Zoo. Order from: Pacific Pipeline & Baker & Taylor. *Publisher Provided Annotation.*

Davis, Larry, jt. auth. see Quinn, Dan.
Davis, Lauren. Kidding Around Chicago: A Young Person's Guide. 2nd ed. Blakemore, Sally, illus. 64p. (gr. 3 up). 1993. pap. 9.95 (*1-56261-094-5*) John Muir.
Davis, Linda. A Purim Story. (Illus.). (ps-3). 1988. 7.95 (*0-317-68087-0*) Feldheim.
Davis, Lloyd S., photos by & text by. Penguin: A Season in the Life of the Adelie Penguin. LC 93-36407. 1994. 17.95 (*0-15-200070-4*, HB Juv Bks) HarBrace.
Davis, M. J. Beverly Hills, 90210: Exposed. 1991. pap. 4.50 (*0-06-106137-9*, Harp PBks) HarpC.
Davis, Maggie S. A Garden of Whales. O'Connell, Jennifer B., illus. LC 92-34411. 32p. 1993. 16.95 (*0-944475-36-1*); pap. 6.95 (*0-944475-35-3*) Camden Hse Pub.
—The Rinky-Dink Cafe. Sandford, John, illus. LC 87-35435. 32p. (ps-3). 1988. pap. 12.95 (*0-671-66408-5*) S&S Trade.
—Roots of Peace, Seeds of Hope: A Journey for Peacemakers. Davis, maggie S., illus. 60p. (gr. 5-12). 1994. pap. 8.95 (*0-9638813-0-2*) Heartsong Bks.
—Something Magic. LC 90-10062. (gr. k-3). 1991. pap. 13.95 (*0-671-69627-0*, S&S BFYR) S&S Trade.
Davis, Maria H., jt. auth. see Freeman, Marie E.
Davis, Marion M. Sam Predicts a Storm. Johnson, Anne, illus. 35p. (Orig.). 1991. pap. 6.95 (*0-9622221-1-9*) Starboard Cove.
—Sam the Royal Cat, No. 1. Starboard Cove Publishing Staff, ed. Johnston, Anne, illus. 35p. (Orig.). 1989. pap. 5.95x (*0-9622221-0-0*) Starboard Cove.
Davis, Martin M. The Gospel & the Twelve Steps: Developing a Closer Relationship with Jesus. LC 93-15977. 224p. (Orig.). (gr. 12 up). 1993. pap. 10.95 (*0-941405-31-1*) Recovery Pubns.
Davis, Mary P. Action Biology - Advanced Placement. (Illus.). 540p. (gr. 11-12). 1988. pap. text ed. 21.33 (*0-931054-18-4*) Clark Pub.
—Action Biology - for the First Year. (Illus.). 494p. (gr. 10). 1988. pap. text ed. 21.33 (*0-931054-19-2*) Clark Pub.
Davis, Michael. The Flower Princess. Luongo, Aldo, illus. 32p. (gr. k-12). 1989. write for info.; PLB write for info. R Bane Ltd.
Davis, Nancy M. Eskimos. Davis, Nancy M., illus. 32p. (Orig.). (ps-5). 1986. pap. 4.95 (*0-937103-06-3*) DaNa Pubns.
Davis, Nancy M. & Moon, Teresa. Indians. Davis, Nancy M., illus. 33p. (Orig.). (ps-5). 1986. pap. 4.95 (*0-937103-03-9*) DaNa Pubns.
Davis, Nancy M., et al. April & Easter. Davis, Nancy M., illus. 45p. (Orig.). (ps-2). 1986. pap. 5.95 (*0-937103-10-1*) DaNa Pubns.
—Colors. Davis, Nancy M., illus. (Orig.). (ps-2). 1986. pap. 4.95 (*0-937103-13-6*) DaNa Pubns.
—Fall & September. Davis, Nancy M., illus. 25p. (Orig.). (ps-2). 1986. pap. 4.95 (*0-937103-00-4*) DaNa Pubns.
—November & Thanksgiving. Davis, Nancy M., illus. 31p. (Orig.). (ps-2). 1986. pap. 4.95 (*0-937103-02-0*) DaNa Pubns.
—Numbers. Davis, Nancy M., illus. 26p. (Orig.). (ps-2). 1986. pap. 4.95 (*0-937103-14-4*) DaNa Pubns.
—Patriotism. Davis, Nancy M., illus. 34p. (Orig.). (ps-5). 1986. pap. 4.95 (*0-937103-19-5*) DaNa Pubns.
—St. Patrick's. Davis, Nancy M., illus. 29p. (Orig.). (ps-4). 1986. pap. 4.95 (*0-937103-08-X*) DaNa Pubns.
—Spring & May. Davis, Nancy M., illus. 46p. (Orig.). (ps-4). 1986. pap. 5.95 (*0-937103-11-X*) DaNa Pubns.
—Winter. Davis, Nancy M., illus. 29p. (ps-2). 1986. pap. 4.95 (*0-937103-05-5*) DaNa Pubns.
—February & Valentines. Davis, Nancy M., illus. 29p. (Orig.). (ps-2). 1986. pap. 4.95 (*0-937103-07-1*) DaNa Pubns.
Davis, Nancy M, et al. October & Halloween. Davis, Nancy M., illus. 28p. (Orig.). (ps-4). 1986. pap. 4.95 (*0-937103-01-2*) DaNa Pubns.
Davis, Natalie L. The Space Twin. Taylor, Neil, illus. 112p. (gr. 4-8). 1987. 7.95 (*1-55523-037-7*) Winston-Derek.
Davis, Nelle P. Stump Ranch Pioneer. Swetnam, Susan H., intro. by. LC 90-42417. 264p. (gr. 12). 1990. pap. 14.95 (*0-89301-141-X*) U of Idaho Pr.
Davis, Ossie. Escape to Freedom. (gr. 9-12). 1990. pap. 12.95 (*0-670-29775-5*) Viking Child Bks.
—Escape to Freedom: A Play about Young Frederick Douglass. (gr. 4-7). 1990. pap. 3.99 (*0-14-034355-5*, Puffin) Puffin Bks.
—Just Like Martin. LC 91-4672. 1992. pap. 14.00 (*0-671-73202-1*, S&S BFYR) S&S Trade.
—Langston: A Play. LC 82-70314. 144p. (gr. 7 up). 1982. pap. 11.95 (*0-385-28543-4*) Delacorte.
Davis, Pat. Play the Game: Badminton. (Illus.). 80p. (gr. 10-12). 1991. pap. 6.95 (*0-7063-6663-8*, Pub. by Ward Lock UK) Sterling.
Davis, Pat, jt. auth. see Hargreaves, Margaret.

Davis, R. Dell. Ashes & Sparks. LC 89-81718. (Illus.). 172p. (gr. 1-8). 1989. Set. text ed. 24.95 incl. audiotape & slipcase (*0-9616736-1-3*) J Franklin. ASHES & SPARKS "Tales of the Indian Territory" is a series of stories

told chronologically of a young girl growing up in Indian Territory circa 1902. Her fresh approach to her family & friends makes this a fascinating "read" for adults as well as children. Autobiographical in nature, authentic in nature & environmental details, it is best as a read aloud book as it conjures memories of one's own family with tales to be passed on. Teachers have found the audiotape stories told by the author to fascinate children. The chapbook which is encased in a drawstring "domestic" cloth bag with the audiotape describes customs & artifacts depicted in the arresting illustrations. The slipcased two volumes designed by Carol Harolson has been nominated for several design awards. It is an heirloom to be passed down to future generations. *Publisher Provided Annotation.*

Davis, Ray J. American Government: Law in Action. 464p. (Orig.). (gr. 11-12). 1991. pap. text ed. 18.67 (*0-931054-23-0*) Clark Pub.

Davis, Rebecca H. With Daring Faith. 187p. (Orig.). 1987. pap. 4.95 (*0-89084-414-3*) Bob Jones Univ Pr.

Davis, Rebecca J. A Sunnybrook Garden Tale. Kvarnes, Davette L., illus. LC 92-97014. 32p. (gr. 3-5). 1993. PLB 12.00 (*0-9634032-0-6*) R J Davis. Filled with bright, colorful language & accompanied by vivid illustrations A SUNNYBROOK GARDEN TALE thoughtfully addresses the consequences of irresponsible use of pesticides through two unlikely, but very effective characters. By personifying a bad beetle--Buster Beetle, & a very insecure thistle--Missile Thistle, the story conveys the message that all living beings must live harmoniously if our planet & all that live on it are to remain healthy. Review Quotes: "All the wonderful characters, human & otherwise, weave a story that can enter a child's imagination & find a home there."--Donna Aquaviva, writer. "It carries a gentle environmental message that children should hear when they're very young."--Bob Naylor, editor. "A very pleasant story from an interesting point of view, & the scale of the story makes ecology more approachable for children."--Anita Trout, librarian. "A SUNNYBROOK GARDEN TALE has brought back the goodness that children need to read about."--JoAnn Overington, teacher. "Delightful, charming--fun for all ages." --Felicia Cogan, professor. "With exquisite illustrations & charming personifications of thistles, beetles & other plants & creatures the story delivers an ecological messsage."--Rana Harmon, The Shepherdstown Chronicle (5/28/93). "Award-winner, Children's Literature, 1991 Shenandoah Valley Writers' Guild Creative Writing Conference."--Author. Rebecca J. Davis, P.O. Box 144, Route 1/13, Summit Point, WV 25446-0144, (304) 725-1609. *Publisher Provided Annotation.*

Davis, Rhonda K. Purnell the Curious Ant, Vol. I. (Illus.). 30p. (Orig.). (ps-1). 1992. pap. 3.00 (*1-881967-15-8*) Express In Writing.
—Purnell the Curious Ant. 16p. (ps-5). 1992. pap. 3.00 (*1-881967-01-8*) Express In Writing.
—Seven-Series Educational Value Pak. (Illus.). (ps up). 1992. Set. 21.00 (*1-881967-07-7*) Express In Writing.

—Sons & Daughters. 16p. (ps-5). 1992. pap. 3.00 (*1-881967-00-X*) Express In Writing.
—Sons & Daughters of Autumn, Vol. I. Davis, Rhonda K. & Beck, Arthello, illus. 32p. (Orig.). (ps-4). 1992. pap. 3.00 (*1-881967-14-X*) Express In Writing.
Davis, Richard C., et al. Rational Numbers Study Aid. 1976. pap. 3.00 (*0-87738-039-2*) Youth Ed.
Davis, Richard H. Ranson's Folly & Other Stories. (gr. 9 up). 1968. pap. 1.95 (*0-8049-0192-9*, CL-192) Airmont.
Davis, Robert. Kimura. 224p. 1989. 18.95 (*0-8027-5736-7*) Walker & Co.
Davis, Robert B. Discovery in Mathematics: A Text for Teachers. 274p. (gr. 4-8). 1980. pap. text ed. 14.95 (*0-914040-86-3*) Cuisenaire.
Davis, Robert C. The E-waa, Vol. 1. Tremblay, Martin, illus. LC 91-61838. 28p. (Orig.). 1991. pap. 5.50g (*0-9629949-0-1*) Across the Road.
Davis, Ruby, ed. see Clark, Barbara R.
Davis, Russell B. & Ashabranner, Brent K. The Choctaw Code. (Illus.). 152p. (gr. 3-6). 1994. Repr. of 1961 ed. lib. bdg. 16.00 (*0-208-02377-1*, Pub. by Linnet) Shoe String.
Davis, Russell H. Black Americans in Cleveland. (Illus.). 1990. pap. 10.00 (*0-87498-075-5*) Assoc Pubs DC.
Davis, S. K. Bible Crossword Puzzle Book. (gr. k-3). 1969. pap. 3.99 (*0-8010-2812-4*) Baker Bk.
Davis, Sandra P. That Special Touch. LC 89-92544. (Illus.). 140p. 1990. 39.95 (*0-9625232-0-8*) Special Touch.
Davis, Sharon, ed. see Billac, Pete.
Davis, Sharon K., ed. see Billac, Pete.
Davis, Susan. Password to Heaven. 32p. (gr. k-3). 1980. pap. 2.50 (*0-8127-0298-0*) Review & Herald.
—When God Lived in a Tent. (Illus.). (ps-1). 1978. 1.95 (*0-8127-0181-X*) Review & Herald.
Davis, T. Frederick. History of Jacksonville, Florida & Vicinity 1513 to 1924. 3rd ed. (Illus.). 513p. (gr. 8 up). 1990. Repr. of 1925 ed. 22.50 (*0-935259-06-6*) San Marco Bk.
Davis, Terry. If Rock & Roll Were a Machine. LC 91-41807. 224p. (gr. 7 up). 1992. 15.00 (*0-385-30762-4*) Delacorte.
Davis, Wesley, ed. see Hodgson, Karen.
Davis, William S. Day in Old Athens. LC 60-16707. (Illus.). (gr. 7 up). 1965. 20.00 (*0-8196-0111-X*) Biblo.
—Day in Old Rome. LC 61-24993. (Illus.). (gr. 7 up). 1963. 20.00 (*0-8196-1206-5*) Biblo.
Davison, Katherine. Moon Magic: Stories from Asia. Rosborough, Thomas A., illus. LC 92-44504. 1993. 18. 95 (*0-87614-751-1*) Carolrhoda Bks.
Davison, Kenneth E., jt. auth. see Burke, James L.
Davison, Rebecca & Mesner, Susan, eds. The Treasury of Religious & Spiritual Quotations: Words to Live By. LC 93-28016. (gr. 5 up). 1994. 22.00 (*0-89577-549-2*) RD Assn.
Davis Pinkney, Andrea. Alvin Ailey. Pinkney, Brian, illus. LC 92-54865. 32p. (gr. 1-4). 1993. 13.95 (*1-56282-413-9*); PLB 13.89 (*1-56282-414-7*) Hyprn Child.
Davis-Thompson, Helen. Let's Celebrate Kwanzaa: An Activity Book for Young Readers. Hall, Chris A., illus. 32p. (ps-5). 1993. pap. 5.95 (*0-936073-07-1*) Gumbs & Thomas.
Davol, Marguerite. Black, White, Just Right. Trivas, Irene, illus. LC 93-19932. 1993. write for info. (*0-8075-0785-7*) A Whitman.
Davol, Marguerite W. Heart of the Wood. LC 91-3374. (ps-3). 1992. pap. 14.00 (*0-671-74778-9*, S&S BFYR) S&S Trade.
Davoll, Barbara. Ashley's Yellow Ribbon. (gr. 4-7). 1991. pap. 5.99 (*0-8024-0815-X*) Moody.
—The Camping Caper. Hockerman, Dennis, illus. 24p. 1993. 6.99 (*1-56476-162-2*, Victor Books) SP Pubns.
—The Christopher Churchmouse Treasury. Hockerman, Dennis, illus. (Orig.). 1992. pap. 12.99 (*0-89693-078-5*, Victor Books) SP Pubns.
—Dusty Mole Private Eye. Hockerman, Dennis, illus. (gr. 2-6). 1992. pap. 5.99 (*0-8024-2700-6*) Moody.
—Foul Play at Moler Park. (gr. 4-7). 1993. pap. 6.99 (*0-8024-2703-0*) Moody.
—Grandpa's Secret. Hockerman, Dennis, illus. 24p. 1993. 6.99 (*1-56476-161-4*, Victor Books) SP Pubns.
—Hare-Brained Habit. (gr. 4-7). 1993. pap. 6.99 (*0-8024-2705-7*) Moody.
—A Load of Trouble. Hockerman, David, illus. 24p. 1988. pap. 6.99 (*0-89693-407-1*, Victor Books); cassette 9.99 (*0-89693-618-X*) SP Pubns.
—Molehole Mysteries Upstairs Connection. (gr. 4-7). 1993. pap. 6.99 (*0-8024-2704-9*) Moody.
—A Pack of Lies. Hockerman, Dennis, illus. 24p. 1989. pap. 6.99 (*0-89693-497-7*, Victor Books); cassette 9.99 (*0-89693-030-0*) SP Pubns.
—The Potluck Supper. Hockerman, Dennis, illus. 1988. 4.95 (*0-685-22774-X*); book & cassette 7.95 (*0-685-22775-8*) Zondervan.
—The Potluck Supper. Hockerman, Dennis, illus. 24p. 1988. 6.99 (*0-89693-406-3*, Victor Books); cassette 9.99 (*0-89693-617-1*) SP Pubns.
—Rainy Day Rescue. Hockerman, Dennis, illus. 24p. 1988. 6.99 (*0-89693-408-X*, Victor Books); cassette 9.99 (*0-89693-619-6*) SP Pubns.
—Saved by the Bell. Hockerman, Dennis, illus. 24p. 1988. text ed. 6.99 (*0-89693-403-9*, Victor Books); cassette 9.99 (*0-89693-614-7*) SP Pubns.
—Secret at Mossy Root Mansion. Hockerman, Dennis, illus. (gr. 2-7). 1992. 5.99 (*0-8024-2701-4*) Moody.

—The Shiny Red Sled. Hockerman, Dennis, illus. 24p. 1989. text ed. 6.99 (*0-89693-498-5*, Victor Books); cassette 9.99 (*0-89693-031-9*) SP Pubns.
—A Sticky Mystery. Hockerman, Dennis, illus. 24p. 1989. 6.99 (*0-89693-485-3*); cassette 9.99 (*0-89693-033-5*) SP Pubns.
—A Sunday Surprise. Hockerman, Dennis, illus. 24p. 1988. 6.99 (*0-89693-405-5*, Victor Books); cassette 9.99 (*0-89693-616-3*) SP Pubns.
—The White Trail. Hockerman, Dennis, illus. 24p. 1988. 6.99 (*0-89693-404-7*, Victor Books); cassette 9.99 (*0-89693-615-5*) SP Pubns.
Davoll, Barbara & Hockerman, Dennis. A Short Tail. 24p. 1989. 6.99 (*0-89693-499-3*); cassette 9.99 (*0-89693-032-7*) SP Pubns.
DaVolls, Linda. Tano & Binti: Two Chimpanzees Return to the Wild. DaVolls, Andy, illus. LC 93-25403. 1994. write for info. (*0-395-68701-2*, Clarion Bks) HM.
Dawe, Karen. The Beach Book & Beach Bucket. LC 87-40648. (Illus.). (gr. k-5). 1988. pap. 7.95 incl. bucket (*0-89480-590-8*, 1590) Workman Pub.
Dawe, Karen, jt. auth. see Dawe, Neil.
Dawe, Neil & Dawe, Karen. Bird Book & the Bird Feeder. LC 88-40225. (gr. k-7). 1988. pap. 10.95 (*0-89480-614-9*, 1614) Workman Pub.
Dawnay-Timms, Romayne. The Champions of Appleby Magna. Dawnay-Timms, Romayne, illus. 160p. (gr. 3-7). 1994. SBE 14.95 (*0-02-789355-3*, Four Winds) Macmillan Child Grp.
Dawood, N. J. Aladdin: And Other Tales from the Arabian Nights. 176p. (gr. 4 up). 1990. pap. 2.99 (*0-14-035105-1*, Puffin) Puffin Bks.
Dawood, N. J., retold by. Sinbad the Sailor & Other Tales from the Arabian Nights. 176p. (gr. 2 up). 1991. pap. 2.99 (*0-14-035106-X*, Puffin) Puffin Bks.
Dawson, Imogen. Food & Feasts in the Middle Ages. LC 93-27200. (Illus.). 32p. (gr. 6 up). 1994. PLB 14.95 RSBE (*0-02-726324-X*, New Discovery Bks) Macmillan Child Grp.
Dawson, Linda. Basketball. 1990. 7.95x (*0-86685-477-0*) Intl Bk Ctr.
—Tennis. 1990. 7.95x (*0-86685-476-2*) Intl Bk Ctr.
Dawson, Mildred L. Over Here It's Different: Carolina's Story. Ancona, George, photos by. LC 92-44515. (Illus.). 48p. (gr. 3-7). 1993. RSBE 13.95 (*0-02-726328-2*, Macmillan Child Bk) Macmillan Child Grp.
Dawson, Pam, ed. see Messent, Jan.
Dawson, Steve, ed. see Blaisdell, Frank.
Day, Adrienne. In Search of a Song, Vol. 4. Fisher, Barbara & Spiegel, Richard, eds. (Illus.). 27p. (Orig.). (gr. 3 up). 1983. pap. 2.00 (*0-934830-29-0*) Ten Penny.
Day, Alexandra. Carl Goes Shopping. (Illus.). (gr. 3 up). 1989. 11.95 (*0-374-31110-2*) FS&G.
—Carl Goes Shopping. Day, Alexandra, illus. (ps). 1992. 6.00x (*0-374-31101-3*) FS&G.
—Carl Goes to Daycare. (ps). 1993. 12.95 (*0-374-31093-9*) FS&G.
—Carlito en el Parque una Tarde: Carl's Afternoon in the Park. (SPA., Illus.). 32p. 1992. bds. 11.95 (*0-374-31100-5*, Mirasol) FS&G.
—Carl's Afternoon in the Park. (Illus.). 32p. 1991. bds. 11.95 (*0-374-31109-9*) FS&G.
—Carl's Afternoon in the Park. Day, Alexandra, illus. (ps). 1992. 6.00x (*0-374-31104-8*) FS&G.
—Carl's Christmas. Day, Alexandra, illus. 32p. 1990. bds. 11.95 (*0-374-31114-5*) FS&G.
—Carl's Christmas. Day, Alexandra, illus. (ps). 1992. 6.00 (*0-374-31102-1*) FS&G.
—Carl's Masdquerade. (ps). 1993. 5.95 (*0-374-31090-4*) FS&G.
—Carl's Masquerade. 1992. 12.95 (*0-374-31094-7*) FS&G.
—Frank & Ernest. Day, Alexandra, illus. 40p. (gr. k-3). 1988. 13.95 (*0-590-41557-3*, Pub. by Scholastic Hardcover) Scholastic Inc.
—Frank & Ernest. Day, Alexandra, illus. 1991. pap. 3.95 (*0-590-41556-5*, Blue Ribbon Bks) Scholastic Inc.
—Frank & Ernest on the Road. (Illus.). 48p. (ps-3). 1994. 14.95 (*0-590-45048-4*, Scholastic Hardcover) Scholastic Inc.
—Frank & Ernest Play Ball. Day, Alexandra, illus. LC 89-10312. (gr. k-3). 1990. 12.95 (*0-590-42548-X*) Scholastic Inc.
—Good Dog, Carl. Day, Alexandra, illus. 36p. (Orig.). (ps up) 1991. 11.95 (*0-88138-062-8*, Green Tiger) S&S Trade.
—Good Dog, Carl. LC 91-25274. (Illus.). 36p. (Orig.). (ps up). 1991. 11.95 (*0-671-75204-9*, Green Tiger) S&S Trade.
—Paddy's Pay Day. Day, Alexandra, illus. (ps-3). 1989. 14.00 (*0-670-82598-0*, Puffin) Puffin Bks.
—Paddy's Pay-Day. Day, Alexandra, illus. (ps-3). 1991. pap. 4.00x (*0-14-050963-1*, Puffin) Puffin Bks.
—River Parade. (Illus.). 32p. (ps-2). 1990. pap. 12.95 (*0-670-82946-3*) Viking Child Bks.
—River Parade. (Illus.). 32p. (gr. 3-7). 1992. pap. 3.99 (*0-14-054158-6*, Puffin) Puffin Bks.
Day, Alexandra, jt. auth. see Edens, Cooper.
Day, Betsy. Stefan & Olga. Day, Betsy, illus. LC 89-23647. 32p. (ps-3). 1991. 12.95 (*0-8037-0816-5*); PLB 12.89 (*0-8037-0817-3*) Dial Bks Young.
Day, Dan. I've Got This Problem with Sex... 32p. (gr. 9 up). 1973. pap. 0.99 (*0-8163-0012-7*, 09790-7) Pacific Pr Pub Assn.
Day, David. Aska's Animals. 1991. PLB 15.99 (*0-385-42126-5*) Doubleday.

—Aska's Animals. 1991. 15.00 (*0-385-25315-X*) Doubleday.
—Aska's Birds. 1992. pap. 15.00 (*0-385-25388-5*) Doubleday.
—The King of the Woods. Brown, Ken, illus. LC 93-9410. 32p. (ps-2). 1993. Repr. of 1993 ed. RSBE 13.95 (*0-02-726361-4*, Four Winds) Macmillan Child Grp.
—The Walking Catfish. Entwisle, Mark, illus. LC 91-9144. 32p. (gr. k-3). 1992. 13.95 (*0-02-726360-6*, Macmillan Child Bk) Macmillan Child Grp.
Day, Edward C. John Tabor's Ride. Zimmer, Dirk, illus. LC 88-9065. 40p. (ps-3). 1989. PLB 13.99 (*0-394-98577-X*) Knopf Bks Yng Read.
Day, Jon. Let's Make Magic: Over Forty Tricks You Can Do. Fisher, Chris, illus. LC 92-53093. 96p. (Orig.). (gr. 2-6). 1992. 14.95 (*1-85697-834-6*); pap. 9.95 (*1-85697-806-0*) Kingfisher Bks.
Day, Lara. My Brother & I. 15p. (ps-k). 1992. pap. text ed. 23.00 big bk. (*1-56843-004-3*); pap. text ed. 4.50 (*1-56843-054-X*) BGR Pub.
Day, M. H. Fossil History of Man. 3rd ed. Head, J. J., ed. LC 84-70785. (Illus.). 16p. (gr. 10 up). 1984. pap. 2.75 (*0-89278-432-6*, 45-9632) Carolina Biological.
Day, Marie. Dragon in the Rocks: A Story Based on the Childhood of the Early Paleontologist, Mary Anning. Day, Marie, illus. 32p. (ps up). 1992. 12.95 (*0-920775-76-4*, Pub. by Greey de Pencier CN) Firefly Bks Ltd.
Day, Michael, jt. auth. see Tivers, Jacqueline.
Day, Nancy. The Horseshoe Crab. LC 92-9772. (Illus.). 60p. (gr. 4 up). 1992. RSBE 13.95 (*0-87518-545-2*, Dillon) Macmillan Child Grp.
Day, O. M. ABC's of Bugs & Beasts. Day, O. M., illus. 31p. (Orig.). (gr. 3-12). 1991. pap. 11.95 (*0-9629795-1-1*) Klar-Iden Pub.
Day, Rachel, jt. auth. see Hofer, Grace.
Day, Rachel, tr. see Hofer, Grace & Day, Rachel.
Day, Rhonda, ed. see Garcia, Joseph G.
Day, Russell E. Hoot-U-Ee. 1991. 6.95 (*0-533-09279-5*) Vantage.
Day, S. Monica's Mother Said No. (Illus.). 24p. (ps-8). 1987. pap. 4.95 (*0-88753-158-X*, Pub. by Annick CN) Firefly Bks Ltd.
Day, Trevor. The Random House Book of One Thousand One Questions & Answers about the Human Body. LC 93-6386. 1994. write for info. (*0-679-85432-0*) Random Hse Yng Read.
Dayee, Frances S. Babysitting. LC 89-24773. (gr. 4-7). 1990. PLB 12.90 (*0-531-10908-9*) Watts.
—Smart Plays: A Story about Safety for Young People. (Illus.). 80p. (gr. 3-7). 1989. pap. 9.95 (*0-89106-039-1*, 7383) Consulting Psychol.
Dayrell, Elphinstone. Why the Sun & Moon Live in the Sky. Lent, Blair, illus. 32p. (gr. k-3). 1990. pap. 4.80 (*0-395-53963-3*) HM.
DC Comics Staff. Black Egg of Atlantis. (gr. 4-7). 1992. 3.95 (*0-316-17768-7*) Little.
—I, Werewolf. (gr. 4-7). 1992. pap. 3.95 (*0-316-17769-5*) Little.
—Six Deadly Demons. (gr. 4-7). 1992. pap. 3.95 (*0-316-17767-9*) Little.
—Terror on the High Skies. (gr. 4-7). 1992. pap. 3.95 (*0-316-17765-2*) Little.
Deacon, John. The Drawing Book. (Illus.). 64p. (gr. 4 up). 1989. pap. 5.95 (*0-590-42142-5*) Scholastic Inc.
Deal, Borden. The Least One. Davis, Sara D., intro. by. 368p. 1992. pap. 19.95t (*0-8173-0673-0*) U of Ala Pr.
Deal, Tara, jt. ed. see Swisher, Karin.
De Amicis, Edmondo. Coure: The Heart of a Boy. Hartley, Desmond, tr. from ITA. LC 87-60487. 253p. 1986. 30.00 (*0-7206-0657-8*, Pub. by P Owen Ltd UK) Dufour.
Dean, Anabel. Strange Partners: The Story of Symbiosis. Matte, L'Enc, illus. LC 75-38479. 96p. (gr. 3-6). 1976. lib. bdg. 9.50 (*0-8225-1100-2*) Lerner Pubns.
Dean, Bessie. Aprendamos el Plan de Dios. Balderas, Eduardo, tr. Dean, Bessie, illus. LC 80-82256. (SPA.). 64p. (gr. k-3). 1980. pap. text ed. 5.95 (*0-88290-135-4*) Horizon Utah.
—God Hears My Prayers. (Illus.). 24p. (ps-3). 1993. pap. 3.98 (*0-88290-110-9*) Horizon Utah.
—I'm Happy When I'm Good. (Illus.). 24p. (ps-3). 1979. pap. 3.95 (*0-88290-109-5*) Horizon Utah.
—Lessons Jesus Taught. Dean, Bessie. 72p. (Orig.). (gr. k-5). 1980. pap. 5.95 (*0-88290-146-X*) Horizon Utah.
—Let's Go to Church. Dean, Bessie, illus. LC 76-3995. 63p. (ps-3). 1993. pap. 3.98 (*0-88290-062-5*) Horizon Utah.
—Let's Learn about Jesus: A Child's Coloring Book of the Life of Christ. (Illus.). 72p. (ps-6). 1988. pap. 5.95 (*0-88290-131-1*) Horizon Utah.
—Let's Learn of God's Love. LC 79-89367. (Illus.). 64p. (ps-3). 1979. pap. 5.95 (*0-88290-124-9*) Horizon Utah.
—Let's Learn the First Principles. LC 78-70366. (Illus.). 64p. (ps-3). 1993. pap. 3.98 (*0-88290-104-4*) Horizon Utah.
—Let's Love One Another. LC 77-74492. (Illus.). 64p. (ps-3). 1993. pap. 3.98 (*0-88290-077-3*) Horizon Utah.
—Living the Articles of Faith. Dean, Bessie, illus. 88p. (gr. k-4). 1988. pap. 6.95 (*0-88290-336-5*) Horizon Utah.
—Paul, God's Special Missionary. 72p. (Orig.). (gr. k-5). 1980. pap. 5.95 (*0-88290-152-4*) Horizon Utah.
—Paul's Letters of Love. (Illus.). 72p. (Orig.). (gr. k-5). 1981. pap. 5.95 (*0-88290-170-2*) Horizon Utah.

—Stories Jesus Told. 72p. 1979. pap. 5.95 (*0-88290-132-X*) Horizon Utah.
Dean, John. Games Make Spelling Fun: Activities for Better Spelling. rev. ed. (gr. 4-8). 1973. pap. 5.95 (*0-8224-3255-2*) Fearon Teach Aids.
Dean, John F. Writing Well. (gr. 5-12). 1985. pap. 8.95 (*0-8224-7530-8*) Fearon Teach Aids.
Dean, Julia. The Life Cycle of Monhegan Island. LC 93-24534. 1994. 16.95 (*0-395-66476-4*) Ticknor & Fields.
Dean, Karen S. Cammy Takes a Bow. (gr. 3-7). 1988. pap. 2.50 (*0-380-75400-2*, Camelot) Avon.
Dean, Leonard F., ed. Shakespeare: Modern Essays in Criticism. 2nd ed. (Illus.). (gr. 9 up). 1967. pap. 15. 95x (*0-19-500688-7*) OUP.
Dean, Lois. Fox in a Fix. 1959. 4.00 (*0-87602-128-3*) Anchorage.
Dean, Robyn. A Black Cat Named Smokey: On Vacation. Dean, Robyn, illus. LC 92-93502. 64p. (Orig.). (gr. k-3). 1992. pap. 7.95 (*0-9633466-0-1*) Zyxalon Pr.
Dean, Theresa & Lucadamo, Rhonda. Pocket Full of School Memories. Dean, Theresa, illus. 26p. (ps-8). 1992. 18.95 (*1-881511-00-6*) Pockets Pr.
Dean, Wayne. The Incredible, Spreadable, Magic, Drawing Book. Harryman, Diana L. & Leatherbury, Leven C., eds. Dean, Wayne, illus. 56p. (gr. 3-9). 1983. pap. 9.95 (*0-9616161-0-5*) W Dean Editions.
Deane, Bill. Bob Gibson. (Illus.). 64p. (gr. 3 up). 1994. PLB 14.95 (*0-7910-1177-1*, Am Art Analog) Chelsea Hse.
De Angeli, Marguerite. Book of Nursery & Mother Goose Rhymes. De Angeli, Marguerite, illus. (gr. k-5). 1954. Doubleday.
—Copper-Toed Boots. LC 88-34417. (Illus.). 96p. (gr. 4 up). 1989. Repr. of 1938 ed. 14.95x (*0-8143-1922-X*) Wayne St U Pr.
—The Door in the Wall: Story of Medieval London. De Angeli, Marguerite, illus. LC 64-7025. 111p. (gr. 3-6). 1989. pap. 14.95 (*0-385-07283-X*) Doubleday.
—The Lion in the Box. De Angeli, Marguerite, illus. 80p. (gr. 2-5). 1992. pap. 3.50 (*0-440-40740-0*, YB) Dell.
—Marguerite De Angeli's Book of Nursery & Mother Goose Rhymes. De Angeli, Marguerite, illus. LC 54-9838. (gr. k-5). 1979. pap. 18.95 (*0-685-01499-1*, Zephyr BFYR); pap. 7.95 (*0-385-15291-4*) Doubleday.
—Thee, Hannah! (Illus.). 96p. (gr. 2-5). 1970. 15.95 (*0-385-07525-1*, Zephyr-BFYR) Doubleday.
De Angeli, Marguerite see Angeli, Marguerite de.
De Angulo, Jaime see Angeli, Marguerite de.
De Angulo, Jaime. Indian Tales. De Angulo, Jaime, illus. 256p. (gr. 5 up). 1984. 10.95 (*0-374-52163-8*, Am Century) FS&G.
Deans, Sis B. Blazing Bear. Comyns, Nantz, illus. LC 92-60478. 40p. (gr. 3-7). 1992. pap. 9.95 (*0-932433-94-4*) Windswept Hse.
De Aragon, Ray J. Dodo the Bird & Other Stories. Calles, Rosa M., illus. 105p. (Orig.). (gr. 1-12). pap. 5.95 (*0-932906-21-4*) Pan-AM Publishing Co.
Dearden, Carmen D., tr. see Gutierrez, Douglas.
De Armond, Dale. Berry Woman's Children. De Armond, Dale, illus. LC 84-29760. 40p. (gr. 1 up). 1985. 10.25 (*0-688-05814-0*); lib. bdg. 10.88 (*0-688-05815-9*) Greenwillow.
DeArmond, Dale. The Seal Oil Lamp. DeArmond, Dale, illus. 48p. (gr. k-4). 1988. 14.95 (*0-316-17786-5*) Little.
Deaton, Wendy. My Own Thoughts: A Growth & Recovery Workbook for Young Boys. 32p. (gr. 2-6). 1993. wkbk. 5.95 (*0-89793-131-9*); practitioner packs 15.95 (*0-89793-134-3*) Hunter Hse.
—My Own Thoughts: A Growth & Recovery Workbook for Young Girls. 32p. (gr. 2-6). 1993. wkbk. 5.95 (*0-89793-130-0*); practitioner packs 15.95 (*0-89793-133-5*) Hunter Hse.
—My Own Thoughts on Stopping the Hurt. 32p. (gr. 2-6). 1993. wkbk. 5.95 (*0-89793-132-7*); write for info. practitioner packs 15.95 (*0-89793-135-1*) Hunter Hse.
Deaton, Wendy & Johnson, Kendall. Living with My Family. 32p. (gr. 4-6). 1991. wkbk. 5.95 (*0-89793-084-3*); practitioner packs 15.95 (*0-89793-086-X*) Hunter Hse.
—No More Hurt. 32p. (gr. 4-6). 1991. wkbk. 5.95 (*0-89793-083-5*); practitioner packs 15.95 (*0-89793-085-1*) Hunter Hse.
Deaux, John. The Saints Joke Book. (Illus.). 48p. (Orig.). (gr. 6 up). 1981. pap. 2.95 (*0-937552-08-9*) Quail Ridge.
Deaver, Julie R. First Wedding, Once Removed. LC 90-4184. 224p. (gr. 5-9). 1990. PLB 13.89 (*0-06-021427-9*) HarpC Child Bks.
—First Wedding, Once Removed. LC 90-4184. 224p. (gr. 5-9). 1993. pap. 4.95 (*0-06-440402-1*, Trophy) HarpC Child Bks.
—Say Goodnight, Gracie. LC 87-45278. 224p. (gr. 7 up). 1988. 13.00 (*0-06-021418-X*); PLB 12.89 (*0-06-021419-8*) HarpC Child Bks.
—Say Goodnight Gracie. LC 87-45278. 224p. (gr. 7 up). 1989. pap. 3.95 (*0-06-447007-5*, Trophy) HarpC Child Bks.
—You Bet Your Life. LC 92-28211. 224p. (gr. 7 up). 1993. 15.00 (*0-06-021516-X*); PLB 14.89 (*0-06-021517-8*) HarpC Child Bks.
De Backker, Vera. En Cuerpo y Alma. (Illus.). 32p. 1993. pap. 5.95 (*0-8120-1743-9*) Barron.
—Through Thick & Thin. (Illus.). 32p. 1993. 12.95 (*0-8120-6361-9*); pap. 4.95 (*0-8120-1727-7*) Barron.
De Balzac, Honore. La Grande Bretche. 48p. (gr. 6). 1990. PLB 13.95s.p. (*0-88682-306-4*) Creative Ed.

—Passion in the Desert. LC 83-71790. 48p. (gr. 6 up). 1983. PLB 13.95s.p. (*0-87191-965-6*) Creative Ed.
—Pere Goriot. Canon, R. R., intro. by. (gr. 10 up). 1965. pap. 1.50 (*0-8049-0084-1*, CL-84) Airmont.
—Le Pere Goriot. (gr. 7-12). pap. 5.95 (*0-88436-043-1*, 40280) EMC.
De Beaumont, de Leprince see De Leprince de Beaumont.
De Beaumont, Madame. Beauty & the Beast. Shumate, Mark, adapted by. Hicks, Russell, illus. 26p. (ps). 1987. Packaged with pre-programmed audio cass. tape. 9.95 (*0-934323-66-6*) Alchemy Comms.
De Beaumont, Marie Leprince see Leprince de Beaumont's, Marie.
De Beauregard, Diane C. The Blue Planet: Seas & Oceans. Bogard, Vicki, tr. from FRE. Lepagnol, Cyril, illus. LC 89-8912. 38p. (gr. k-5). 1989. 4.95 (*0-944589-22-7*, 022) Young Discovery Lib.
De Beauregard, Diane Costa see Costa de Beauregard, Diane.
De Beauvoir, Simone. Tous les Hommes Sont Mortels. (FRE.). 544p. 1974. 12.95 (*2-07-036533-6*) Schoenhof.
De Beer, Hans. Ahoy There, Little Polar Bear. De Beer, Hans, illus. LC 88-42533. 32p. (gr. k-3). 1988. 13.95 (*1-55858-028-X*) North-South Bks NYC.
—Ahoy There, Little Polar Bear. De Beer, Hans, illus. 32p. (gr. k-3). 1991. pap. 2.95 (*1-55858-109-X*) North-South Bks NYC.
—Kleiner Eisbar, Komm Bald Wieder! De Beer, Hans, illus. (GER.). 32p. (gr. k-3). 1992. 13.95 (*3-85825-316-2*) North-South Bks NYC.
—Kleiner Eisbar, Nimm Mich Mit! De Beer, Hans, illus. (GER.). 320p. (gr. k-3). 1992. 22.50 (*3-314-00344-7*, Bradford Bks) North-South Bks NYC.
—Kleiner Eisbar, Wohin Fahrst Du? De Beer, Hans, illus. (GER.). 32p. (gr. k-3). 1992. 13.95 (*3-85825-290-5*) North-South Bks NYC.
—Little Polar Bear. De Beer, Hans, illus. LC 86-33208. 32p. (gr. k-3). 1989. 13.95 (*1-55858-024-7*); pap. 2.95 (*1-55858-030-1*) North-South Bks NYC.
—Little Polar Bear Address Book. De Beer, Hans, illus. 128p. 1990. 7.95 (*1-55858-080-8*) North-South Bks NYC.
—Little Polar Bear & the Brave Little Hare. De Beer, Hans, illus. James, J. Alison, tr. from GER. LC 92-9803. (Illus.). 32p. (gr. k-3). 1992. 12.95 (*1-55858-179-0*); PLB 12.88 (*1-55858-180-4*) North-South Bks NYC.
—Little Polar Bear Birthday Book. De Beer, Hans, illus. 120p. 1990. 7.95 (*1-55858-081-6*) North-South Bks NYC.
—Little Polar Bear Finds a Friend. De Beer, Hans, illus. LC 89-43727. (ps-3). 1990. 13.95 (*1-55858-092-1*) North-South Bks NYC.
—Little Polar Bear Finds a Friend. De Beer, Hans, illus. 32p. (gr. k-3). 1992. pap. 2.95 (*1-55858-144-8*) North-South Bks NYC.
—Plume en Bateau. De Beer, Hans, illus. (FRE.). 32p. (gr. k-3). 1992. 13.95 (*3-85539-647-7*) North-South Bks NYC.
—Plume S'Echappe. De Beer, Hans, illus. (FRE.). 32p. (gr. k-3). 1992. 13.95 (*3-314-20719-0*) North-South Bks NYC.
—Le Voyage de Plume. De Beer, Hans, illus. (FRE.). 32p. (gr. k-3). 1992. 13.95 (*3-314-20619-4*) North-South Bks NYC.
De Beer, Hans & De Beer, Hans. Little Polar Bear: A Pop-up Book. (Illus.). 32p. (gr. k-3). 1993. 14.95 (*1-55858-226-6*) North-South Bks NYC.
DeBeer, Liz. Ming's Monster. Fahey, Cathy, illus. LC 92-70985. 44p. (gr. k-3). 1993. 7.95 (*1-55523-521-2*) Winston-Derek.
De Bello, Rosario. Gina's Saturday Adventure. De Bello, Rosario, illus. LC 93-5845. 32p. (ps-3). 1994. pap. 4.95 (*0-8091-6612-7*) Paulist Pr.
DeBiase, Louis A. How to Break into Politics on a Shoestring. Lyon, Lucinda, illus. 61p. (Orig.). (gr. 9-12). 1981. pap. 4.95 (*0-686-31571-5*) Louvin Pub.
De Bie, Catherine F. Multiplication & Division Made Easy. Weigand, Betty, ed. (Illus.). 72p. (Orig.). 1990. pap. 10.95 (*0-9627585-0-7*) M & D Made Easy.
Debnam, Betty. Rookie Cookie Cookbook: Everyday Recipes for Kids. (Illus.). 128p. (Orig.). 1989. pap. 7.95 (*0-8362-4206-8*) Andrews & McMeel.
De Boe, David C. Sponsors' Handbook: Junior Historian & Walter Prescott Webb Historical Society. rev. ed. iv, 86p. pap. 5.00 (*0-87611-120-7*) Tex St Hist Assn.
De Bosschere, Jean see Bosschere, Jean de & Morris, M. C.
De Bourgoing, Pascale. Cats. (Illus.). 1992. bds. 10.95 (*0-590-45269-X*, 039, Cartwheel) Scholastic Inc.
—Colors. Valat, P. M. & Perols, Sylvie, illus. 1991. pap. 10.95 (*0-590-45236-3*, Cartwheel) Scholastic Inc.
—Egg. Valat, P. M. & Perols, Sylvie, illus. 24p. 1992. pap. 10.95 (*0-590-45266-5*, Cartwheel) Scholastic Inc.
—Fruit. (Illus.). 24p. 1991. pap. 10.95 (*0-590-45233-9*, Cartwheel) Scholastic Inc.
—Ladybug & Other Insects. Perols, Sylvie, illus. 24p. 1991. pap. 10.95 (*0-590-45235-5*, Cartwheel) Scholastic Inc.
—Tree. Valat, P. M. & Perols, Sylvie, illus. 24p. 1992. pap. 10.95 (*0-590-45265-7*, Cartwheel) Scholastic Inc.
—Weather. Kniffke, Sophie, illus. 24p. 1991. pap. 10.95 (*0-590-45234-7*, Cartwheel) Scholastic Inc.
De Brebeuf, Jean. Huron Carol. Tyrrell, Frances, illus. LC 91-35965. 32p. (ps-6). 1992. 15.00 (*0-525-44909-4*, DCB) Dutton Child Bks.
De Brincat, Matthew see Brincat, Matthew De.

De Brissac, Elvire. Grabuge et l'Indomptable Amelie. Lapointe, Claude, illus. (FRE.). 144p. (gr. 3-7). 1990. pap. 11.95 (2-07-031212-7) Schoenhof.

DeBruin, Jerry. Creative Hands-on Science Cards & Activities. 336p. (gr. 3-9). 1990. 19.95 (0-86653-538-1, GA1150) Good Apple.

—Creative, Hands-on Science Experiences. 256p. (gr. k-6). 1980. 15.95 (0-916456-87-0, GA 165) Good Apple.

—Look to the Sky. 160p. (gr. 4-12). 1988. wkbk. 12.95 (0-86653-440-7, GA1051) Good Apple.

—Rocks & Minerals. Swemba, Jeane, illus. 32p. (gr. 4 up). 1986. wkbk. 5.95 (0-86653-341-9, GA 689) Good Apple.

—School Yard-Backyard, Cycles of Science. 160p. (gr. 3-9). 1989. 12.95 (0-86653-489-X, GA1084) Good Apple.

—Science Fairs with Style. 336p. (gr. 5-12). 1991. 19.95 (0-86653-606-X, GA1325) Good Apple.

—Scientists Around the World. Junkasem, Rochana, illus. 160p. (gr. 4-12). 1987. pap. 12.95 (0-86653-416-4, GA1005) Good Apple.

—Young Scientists Explore: Inner & Outer Space. Czernick, Charlene, illus. 32p. (gr. 4 up). 1983. wkbk. 5.95 (0-86653-152-1, GA 457) Good Apple.

—Young Scientists Explore: The Weather. Czerniak, Jerry, illus. 32p. (gr. 4 up). 1983. wkbk. 5.95 (0-86653-129-7, GA 456) Good Apple.

De Brunhoff, Jean. Babar & Father Christmas. De Brunhoff, Jean, illus. 40p. (gr. k-3). 1987. 16.95 (0-394-89265-8) Random Bks Yng Read.

Debrunhoff, Jean. Babar & Father Christmas. 1949. 7.95 (0-394-80578-X) Random Bks Yng Read.

De Brunhoff, Jean. Babar & Father Christmas. De Brunhoff, Jean, illus. LC 90-61863. 48p. 1991. 4.95 (0-679-81483-3) Random Bks Yng Read.

—Babar & His Children. Haas, Merle, tr. (Illus.). (ps). 1969. 11.00 (0-394-80577-1); lib. bdg. 11.99 (0-394-90577-6) Random Bks Yng Read.

—Babar & Zephir. Haas, Merle, tr. (Illus.). (ps). 1969. 9.95 (0-394-80579-8) Random Bks Yng Read.

Debrunhoff, Jean. Babar the King. 1937. 11.00 (0-394-80580-1); lib. bdg. 11.99 (0-394-90580-6) Random Bks Yng Read.

De Brunhoff, Jean. Babar the King: (El Rey Babar) (SPA.). 11.50 (84-204-3038-2) Santillana.

—Meet Babar & His Family. (Illus.). (gr.-1). 1973. pap. 2.25 (0-394-82682-5) Random Bks Yng Read.

—The Pop-up Travels of Babar. De Brunhoff, Laurent, illus. LC 91-60192. 12p. (ps-1). 1991. 13.00 (0-679-82151-1) Random Bks Yng Read.

—The Story of Babar. (Illus.). (ps). 1937. 9.95 (0-394-80575-5); PLB 10.99 (0-394-90575-X) Random Bks Yng Read.

—The Story of Babar. De Brunhoff, Jean, illus. 48p. (ps-1). 1984. Oversized Facsimile ed. 19.00 (0-394-86823-4) Random Bks Yng Read.

—The Story of Babar. De Brunhoff, Jean, illus. LC 90-61704. 48p. 1991. miniature ed. 4.95 (0-679-81049-8) Random Bks Yng Read.

—Travels of Babar. (Illus.). (ps). 1967. 9.95 (0-394-80576-3); lib. bdg. 11.99 (0-394-90576-8) Random Bks Yng Read.

—The Travels of Babar. De Brunhoff, Jean, illus. LC 85-2236. 48p. (gr. up). 1985. 18.95 (0-394-87453-6) Random Bks Yng Read.

—Le Voyage de Babar. (FRE & SPA., Illus.). bds. 15.95 (0-685-11626-3) Fr & Eur.

De Brunhoff, Jean & De Brunhoff, Laurent. Babar's Anniversary Album. reissued ed. De Brunhoff, Jean & De Brunhoff, Laurent, illus. Sendak, Maurice, intro. by. LC 81-5182. 144p. (ps-3). 1993. 18.00 (0-394-84813-6); lib. bdg. 16.99 (0-394-94813-0) Random Bks Yng Read.

De Brunhoff, L. La Fete de Celesteville. (gr. 4-6). 15.95 (0-685-33969-6) Fr & Eur.

De Brunhoff, Laurent. Babar a la Mer. (FRE.). (gr. 2-3). 15.95 (0-685-11023-0) Fr & Eur.

—Babar a New York. (Illus.). (gr. 4-6). bds. 15.95 (0-685-11024-9) Fr & Eur.

—Babar & the Ghost. De Brunhoff, Laurent, illus. LC 80-5753. 32p. (gr. k-3). 1981. PLB 11.99 (0-394-94660-X) Random Bks Yng Read.

—Babar & the Ghost: An Easy-to-Read Version: A Step Two Book. De Brunhoff, Laurent, illus. LC 85-11841. 48p. (gr. 1-3). 1986. pap. 2.95 (0-394-87908-2) Random Bks Yng Read.

—Babar Artiste Peintre. (FRE.). (gr. 2-3). 15.95 (0-685-28424-7) Fr & Eur.

—Babar Chez le Docteur. (FRE.). (gr. 2-3). 15.95 (0-685-28425-5) Fr & Eur.

—Babar en Ballon. (FRE.). (gr. 2-3). 15.95 (0-685-28422-0) Fr & Eur.

—Babar en Promenade. (FRE.). (gr. 2-3). 15.95 (0-685-11026-5) Fr & Eur.

—Babar et ce coquin d'Arthur. (FRE., Illus.). (gr. 4-6). bds. 15.95 (0-685-11027-3) Fr & Eur.

—Babar et le Prof. Grifaton. (FRE.). (gr. 2-4). 15.95 (0-685-28434-4) Fr & Eur.

—Babar et ses Enfants. (FRE.). (gr. 2-3). 15.95 (0-685-28436-0) Fr & Eur.

—Babar Fait Du Ski. (FRE.). (gr. 2-3). 14.95 (0-685-11029-X) Fr & Eur.

—Babar Jardinier. (FRE.). (gr. 2-3). 15.95 (0-685-11030-3) Fr & Eur.

—Babar Learns to Cook. De Brunhoff, Laurent, illus. LC 78-11769. (ps-3). 1979. 2.25 (0-394-84108-5) Random Bks Yng Read.

—Babar Loses His Crown. De Brunhoff, Laurent, illus. LC 67-21918. 72p. (gr. k-3). 1967. lib. bdg. 7.99 (0-394-90045-6) Beginner.

—Babar's ABC. LC 83-2987. (Illus.). 36p. (gr. k-1). 1983. pap. 12.00 (0-394-85920-0) Random Bks Yng Read.

—Babar's Bath Book. De Brunhoff, Laurent, illus. 10p. (ps). 1992. vinyl bdg. 3.99 (0-679-83434-6) Random Bks Yng Read.

—Babar's Battle. De Brunhoff, Laurent, illus. LC 91-53169. 36p. (ps-3). 1992. 10.00 (0-679-81068-4); PLB 10.99 (0-679-91068-9) Random Bks Yng Read.

—Babar's Birthday Surprise. LC 74-123071. (Illus.). 36p. (ps-2). 1970. Repr. of 1970 ed. 10.95 (0-394-80591-7); lib. bdg. 11.99 (0-394-90591-1) Random Bks Yng Read.

—Babar's Book of Color. De Brunhoff, Laurent, illus. LC 84-42737. 36p. (ps-2). 1984. 12.00 (0-394-86896-X); lib. bdg. 10.99 (0-394-96896-4) Random Bks Yng Read.

—Babar's Busy Year: a Book about Seasons: Just Right for 2's & 3's. De Brunhoff, Laurent, illus. LC 88-35726. 24p. (ps). 1989. 6.00 (0-394-82882-8) Random Bks Yng Read.

—Babar's Car. De Brunhoff, Laurent, illus. 14p. (ps-k). 1992. bds. 3.99 (0-679-83242-4) Random Bks Yng Read.

—Babar's Counting Book. De Brunhoff, Laurent, illus. LC 85-19652. 36p. (ps). 1986. 10.00 (0-394-87517-6); PLB 10.99 (0-394-97517-0) Random Bks Yng Read.

—Babar's Family Album: Five Favorite Stories. De Brunhoff, Laurent, illus. LC 90-8748. 112p. (ps-3). 1991. 17.00 (0-679-81167-2); lib. bdg. 17.99 (0-679-91167-7) Random Bks Yng Read.

—Babar's French & English Word Book. LC 93-27873. 1994. write for info. (0-679-83644-6) Random Bks Yng Read.

—Babar's French Lessons. (Illus.). (ps). 1963. 11.00 (0-394-80587-9); lib. bdg. 5.99 (0-394-90587-3) Random Bks Yng Read.

—Babar's Little Circus Star. De Brunhoff, Laurent, illus. LC 87-14149. 32p. (Orig.). (ps-1). 1988. lib. bdg. 7.99 (0-394-98959-7); pap. 3.50 (0-394-88959-2) Random Bks Yng Read.

—Babar's Little Girl. De Brunhoff, Laurent, illus. LC 68-42962. 36p. (ps-3). 1987. 11.00 (0-394-88689-5); lib. bdg. 9.99 (0-394-98689-X) Random Bks Yng Read.

—Babar's Little Library: Stories About Earth, About Fire, About Air, About Water, 4 bks. De Brunhoff, Laurent, illus. (ps-2). 1992. Set of mini-bks. in slipcase incls. Air, Water, 48 pgs. ea. & Earth & Fire, 32 pgs. ea. 8.99 (0-394-84365-7) Random Bks Yng Read.

—Babar's Paint. 1989. pap. 0.71 (0-394-82281-1) Random Bks Yng Read.

—Babar's Peekaboo Fair. De Brunhoff, Laurent, illus. LC 92-64269. 14p. (ps). 1993. bds. 3.99 (0-679-83935-6) Random Bks Yng Read.

—Babar's Picnic. De Brunhoff, Laurent, illus. LC 90-61349. 24p. (Orig.). (ps-2). 1991. pap. 2.25 (0-679-81245-8) Random Bks Yng Read.

—Babar's Trunk, 4 bks. Incl. Babar at the Seashore; Babar the Gardener; Babar Goes Skiing; Babar on a Picnic. (ps-2). 1969. Set. slipcased 9.95 (0-394-80585-2) Random Bks Yng Read.

—Chateau du Roi Babar. (FRE.). (gr. 3-8). 15.95 (0-685-11078-8) Fr & Eur.

—Le Couronnement de Babar. (FRE.). (gr. 2-3). 4.95 (0-685-28420-4) Fr & Eur.

—Enfance de Babar. (FRE.). (gr. 2-3). 4.95 (0-685-28421-2) Fr & Eur.

—Gregory & the Turtle. 1971. 3.95 (0-394-82321-4) Pantheon.

—Hello, Babar! De Brunhoff, Laurent, illus. 12p. (ps). 1991. foam filling 3.99 (0-679-81073-0) Random Bks Yng Read.

—Histoire de Babar. (FRE.). (gr. 2-4). 15.95 (0-685-28435-2) Fr & Eur.

—Isabelle's New Friend: A Babar Book. De Brunhoff, Laurent, illus. LC 89-3727. 32p. (ps-1). 1990. PLB 5.99 (0-394-92880-6); pap. 2.25 (0-394-82880-1) Random Bks Yng Read.

—Je Parle Allemand avec Babar. (FRE., Illus.). (gr. 4-6). 15.95 (0-685-11271-3) Fr & Eur.

—Je Parle Anglais avec Babar. (FRE., Illus.). (gr. 4-6). 15.95 (0-685-11272-1) Fr & Eur.

—Je Parle Espagnol avec Babar. (FRE., Illus.). (gr. 4-6). 15.95 (0-685-11273-X) Fr & Eur.

—Je Parle Italien avec Babar. (FRE.). (gr. 4-6). 7.95 (0-685-11274-8) Fr & Eur.

—Meet Babar & His Family. De Brunhoff, Laurent, illus. 32p. (ps-1). 1985. pap. 5.95 incl. cassette (0-394-87653-9) Random Bks Yng Read.

—The One Pig with Horns. Howard, Richard, tr. from FRE. De Brunhoff, Laurent, illus. LC 78-4917. (gr. k-3). 1979. Pantheon.

—The Rescue of Babar. De Brunhoff, Laurent, illus. LC 92-50958. 36p. (ps-3). 1993. 20.00 (0-679-83897-X) Random Bks Yng Read.

—Roi Babar. (FRE.). (gr. 4-6). 1975. 15.95 (0-685-11533-X) Fr & Eur.

—Vive le Roi Babar. (FRE.). (gr. 2-3). 4.95 (0-685-28423-9) Fr & Eur.

De Brunhoff, Laurent, jt. auth. see De Brunhoff, Jean.

De Brunhoff, Laurent, illus. Babar's Busy Week. LC 89-64400. 22p. (ps). 1990. bds. 2.95 (0-679-80664-4) Random Bks Yng Read.

De Brunoff, Laurent. Babar Saves the Day. LC 76-11684. (Illus.). (gr. 3-6). 1976. 2.25 (0-394-83341-4) Random Bks Yng Read.

Dec, Myra & Dec, Sam. Wilderness Tails: A Book to Color, Poetry to Share. 32p. (ps-3). 1993. pap. 3.50 (0-9638192-0-8) Quinn Pubng. WILDERNESS TAILS: A BOOK TO COLOR, POETRY TO SHARE is designed for the very young, ages 2-6. A delightful collection of poems about animals & their lives. The combined effect of poetry & pictures will help the very young child develop a sense of wonder about the natural world. The interrelatedness of nature & diversity of life are exemplified by easily identified animals. WILDERNESS TAILS will inspire curiosity & challenge the young to learn more about their natural world. The author, Myra Dec, has been a National Park Ranger (Interpreter-Educator) for ten years & is the recipient of the 1993 Southwest Regional FREEMAN TILDEN AWARD, given for outstanding service in the field of interpretation in the National Park Service. "Tails, tails in the air, Tails, tales everywhere. Tails long & tails short, tails of nearly every sort." Order from: Quinn Publishing Co., P.O. Box 9452, Asheville, NC 28815; 714-668-4622, FAX 704-668-4622. *Publisher Provided Annotation.*

Dec, Sam, jt. auth. see Dec, Myra.

De Camp, L. Sprague. The Undesired Princess & the Enchanted Bunny. Orig. pap. 4.99 (0-671-69875-3) Baen Bks.

De Castro, C. Fernandez. The Life of the Very Noble King of Castile & Leon, Saint Ferdinand III. Foundation for a Christian Civilization, Inc. Staff, tr. from SPA. LC 86-83054. (Illus.). 280p. (Orig.). (gr. 8). 1987. pap. 14.95 (1-877-90509-7) TFFACC.

De Castro, Rogelio, tr. see Bruni, Mary-Ann S.

Decell, Florri, jt. auth. see Weston, Marti.

De Cervantes, Miguel. Don Quixote. (gr. 11 up). 1967. pap. 2.75 (0-8049-0153-8, CL-153) Airmont.

—Don Quixote. abr. ed. Starkie, Walter, tr. (RL 7). 1957. pap. 5.99 (0-451-62484-2, Ment) NAL-Dutton.

De Cervantes, Miguel Saavedra. Don Quixote. Cohen, John M., tr. (Orig.). (gr. 9 up). 1979. pap. 7.95 (0-14-044010-0) Viking Child Bks.

DeCesare, Ruth. Myth, Music & Dance of the American Indian. Feldstein, Sandy, et al, eds. Seckler, Judy & Shelly, Walt, illus. 80p. (gr. 4-12). 1988. tchr's. ed. 12.95 (0-88284-371-0, 3518); student, 16p 3.95 (0-88284-372-9, 3520); Student Songbk., 24p 4.95 (0-88284-373-7, 3519); tchr's ed. with cassette 19.95 (0-88284-383-4, 3534) Alfred Pub.

—Songs of Hispanic Americans. O'Reilly, John & Wilson, Patrick, eds. (gr. 4-12). 1991. tchr's. ed. 12.95 (0-88284-486-5, 3569); wkbk. 5.50 (0-88284-487-3, 3568); tchr's ed. & cassette 19.95 (0-88284-488-1, 3570) Alfred Pub.

DeChancie, John. Juan Peron. Schlesinger, Arthur M., Jr., intro. by. (Illus.). 112p. (gr. 5 up). 1987. lib. bdg. 17.95 (0-87754-548-0) Chelsea Hse.

De Christopher, Marlowe. Greencoat & the Swanboy. De Christopher, Marlowe, illus. 32p. (ps-3). 1991. 14.95 (0-399-22165-4, Philomel) Putnam Pub Group.

Decker, Barbara, ed. A Coloring Book of Bible Verses from Proverbs. NIV ed. Clark, Penny, illus. 32p. (Orig.). (ps-8). 1991. 2.50 (0-9618608-6-3) Lynn's Bookshelf.

—A Coloring Book of Bible Verses from the Epistles. Clark, Penny, illus. 32p. (Orig.). 1989. coloring bk 2.50 (0-9618608-4-7) Lynn's Bookshelf.

—A Coloring Book of Bible Verses from the Epistles. Clark, Penny, illus. 32p. (ps-5). 1992. 2.50 (0-9618608-9-8) Lynn's Bookshelf.

Decker, DeLynn. The Power of Patriotism. LC 81-50387. (gr. k-7). lib. bdg. write for info. (0-911712-84-4) Eagle Mktg Corp.

Decker, Marjorie. Christian Mother Goose Humpty Dumpty. (ps). 1989. 3.99 (0-529-06683-1) World Bible.

—Christian Mother Goose Little Bo Peep. (ps). 1989. 3.99 (0-529-06687-4) World Bible.

—Christian Mother Goose Little Miss Muffet. (ps). 1989. 3.99 (0-529-06686-6) World Bible.

—Christian Mother Goose: Little Tommy Tucker. (ps). 1989. 3.99 (0-529-06685-8) World Bible.

—Christian Mother Goose Piano Book. (gr. k-4). 1989. 8.99 (0-529-06692-0) World Bible.

—Christian Mother Goose Pop-Up Animal Friends. (ps). 1989. 6.99 (*0-685-31140-6*) World Bible.
—Christian Mother Goose Pop-Up Bedtime Rhymes. (ps). 1989. 6.99 (*0-529-06688-2*) World Bible.
—Christian Mother Goose Pop-Up Favorite Rhymes. (ps). 1989. 6.99 (*0-529-06691-2*) World Bible.
—Christian Mother Goose Pop-Up Happy Rhymes. (ps). 1989. 6.99 (*0-529-06690-4*) World Bible.
Decker, Marjorie A. Christian Mother Goose - Rock-a-Bye-Bible. (Illus.). 96p. (ps-k). 1987. text ed. 7.99 (*0-529-06481-2*) World Bible.
—Christian Mother Goose Big Book. Sparr, Theanna, et al, illus. LC 92-60502. 304p. (ps-4). 1992. 14.99 (*0-529-07315-3*) World Bible.
—Rock-a-Bye Prayers: Christian Mother Goose. 1990. 7.99 (*0-529-06843-5*) World Bible.
—Rock-a-Bye Stories of Jesus. (ps-3). 1993. 7.99 (*0-529-10003-7*) World Bible.
Decker, Nan. The Caption Workbook. Drescher, Joan, illus. 27p. (gr. 5-8). 1984. pap. text ed. 1.95 (*0-913072-61-3*) Natl Assn Deaf.
Deckert, Frank J., ed. see Rudig, Doug.
DeClements, Barthe. The Bite of the Gold Bug: A Story of the Alaskan Gold Rush. Andreasen, Dan, illus. 64p. (gr. 2-6). 1992. 13.00 (*0-670-84495-0*) Viking Child Bks.
—Breaking Out. (gr. 4-7). 1993. pap. 3.50 (*0-440-40802-4*) Dell.
—Five-Finger Discount. (gr. 4-7). 1989. 13.95 (*0-440-50166-0*) Delacorte.
—Five-Finger Discount, Bk. I. 1990. pap. 3.25 (*0-440-40321-9*, YB) Dell.
—The Fourth Grade Master Wizards. 144p. (gr. 3-7). 1988. pap. 12.95 (*0-670-82290-6*) Viking Child Bks.
—Fourth Grade Wizards. large type ed. 144p. 1989. lib. bdg. 15.95 (*1-55736-111-8*, Crnrstn Bks) BDD LT Grp.
—The Fourth Grade Wizards. 144p. (gr. 3 up). 1990. pap. 3.99 (*0-14-032760-6*, Puffin) Puffin Bks.
—How Do You Lose Ninth Grade Blues? 144p. (gr. 5 up). 1993. pap. 3.99 (*0-14-036333-5*, Puffin) Puffin Bks.
—Monkey See, Monkey Do. 160p. (gr. 4-7). 1992. pap. 3.50 (*0-440-40675-7*, YB) Dell.
—No Place for Me. (gr. 5-9). 1987. pap. 12.95 (*0-670-81908-5*) Viking Child Bks.
—Nothing's Fair in Fifth Grade. LC 80-54195. 144p. (gr. 3-7). 1981. pap. 12.95 (*0-670-51741-0*) Viking Child Bks.
—Nothing's Fair in Fifth Grade. 144p. (gr. 3 up). 1990. pap. 3.50 (*0-14-034443-8*, Puffin) Puffin Bks.
—Nothing's Fair in the Fifth Grade. large type ed. 190p. (gr. 3-7). 1987. Repr. of 1981 ed. lib. bdg. 15.95 (*1-55736-072-3*, Crnrstn Bks) BDD LT Grp.
—The Pickle Song. 160p. (gr. 3-7). 1993. 13.99 (*0-670-85101-9*) Viking Child Bks.
—Seventeen & In-Between. 180p. (gr. 7-9). 1984. pap. 13. 95 (*0-670-63615-0*) Viking Child Bks.
—Seventeen & In-Between: A Novel. LC 92-37596. 176p. (gr. 7 up). 1993. pap. 3.99 (*0-14-036475-7*, Puffin) Puffin Bks.
—Sixth Grade Can Really Kill You. LC 85-40382. 146p. (gr. 5-8). 1985. pap. 12.95 (*0-670-80656-0*) Viking Child Bks.
—Sixth Grade Can Really Kill You. large type ed. 163p. 1989. lib. bdg. 15.95 (*1-55736-108-8*, Crnrstn Bks) BDD LT Grp.
—Sixth Grade Can Really Kill You. (gr. 3-7). 1986. pap. 2.95 (*0-590-42883-7*, Apple Paperbacks) Scholastic Inc.
—Wake Me at Midnight. (gr. 4-7). 1991. 13.95 (*0-670-84038-6*) Viking Child Bks.
—Wake Me at Midnight. 160p. (gr. 3-7). 1993. pap. 3.99 (*0-14-036486-2*, Puffin) Puffin Bks.
DeCloux, Tina. Tina's Science Adventures. Werges, Rosanne, ed. Sullivan, Tara, illus. 80p. (ps-3). 1992. pap. 12.95 spiral bdg. (*0-9615903-3-5*) Symbiosis Bks.
DeCloux, Tina & Werges, Rosanne. Tina's Science Notebook. Sullivan, Tara, illus. 80p. (gr. k-3). 1985. pap. 12.95 (*0-9615903-0-0*) Symbiosis Bks.
De Coccola, Raymond see Coccola, Raymond de & King, Paul.
De Cordova, Loretta P. Five Centuries in Puerto Rico: Portraits & Eras. 2nd, rev. ed. (Illus.). 140p. (gr. 7 up). 1993. pap. 19.95 (*0-89825-006-4*) Pub Resces PR.
De Coster, Charles T. Flemish Legends. Taylor, Harold, tr. Delstanche, Albert, illus. LC 78-74513. (gr. 7 up). 1979. Repr. of 1920 ed. 18.75x (*0-8486-0217-X*) Roth Pub Inc.
DeCremer, Shirley. Freddie the Frog. Overton, Amy, illus. LC 92-33094. 16p. Date not set. 14.95 (*0-935343-03-2*) Peartree.
De Cuenca, Pilar. Cinco Ciento Palabras Nuevas Para Ti. Alvarez, Ines, tr. McNaught, Harry, illus. LC 81-13766. 32p. (ps-3). 1982. lib. bdg. 5.99 (*0-394-95145-X*); pap. 2.25 (*0-394-85145-5*) Random Bks Yng Read.
De Cuenca, Pilar, tr. see Berenstain, Stan & Berenstain, Janice.
De Cuenca, Pilar, tr. see Eastman, P. D.
Dede, Vivian. Jesus' First Miracle. LC 59-1445. (Illus.). 24p. (ps-4). 1990. pap. 1.89 (*0-570-09022-9*) Concordia.
Dede, Vivian H. Elizabeth's Christmas Story. LC 59-1430. (Illus.). 24p. (gr. k-4). 1987. pap. 1.89 (*0-570-09002-4*, 59-1430) Concordia.

Dedieu, Thierry. The Little Christmas Soldier. Dedieu, Thierry, illus. LC 92-40172. 32p. (ps-2). 1993. PLB 15.95 (*0-8050-2612-6*, Bks Young Read) H Holt & Co.
Dee, Abbie & Scott, Annie. Betsy's Riddles. 11p. (ps-1). 1991. pap. text ed. 21.00 big bk. (*1-56843-035-3*); pap. text ed. 4.25 (*1-56843-083-3*) BGR Pub.
—Brittany the Brontosaurus. 8p. (ps-1). 1991. pap. text ed. 21.00 big bk. (*1-56843-032-9*); pap. text ed. 4.25 (*1-56843-080-9*) BGR Pub.
—Four Seasons. 9p. (ps-1). 1991. pap. text ed. 21.00 big bk. (*1-56843-026-4*); pap. text ed. 4.25 (*1-56843-074-4*) BGR Pub.
—Nature Hike. 18p. (ps-1). 1991. pap. text ed. 21.00 big bk. (*1-56843-028-0*); pap. text ed. 4.25 (*1-56843-076-0*) BGR Pub.
—Opposites at the Zoo. 12p. (ps-1). 1991. pap. text ed. 21.00 big bk. (*1-56843-029-9*); pap. text ed. 4.25 (*1-56843-077-9*) BGR Pub.
—Pets on Parade. 14p. (ps-1). 1991. pap. text ed. 21.00 big bk. (*1-56843-027-2*); pap. text ed. 4.25 (*1-56843-075-2*) BGR Pub.
—Sea Horse, Sea Horse. 10p. (ps-1). 1991. pap. text ed. 21.00 big bk. (*1-56843-031-0*); pap. text ed. 4.25 (*1-56843-079-5*) BGR Pub.
Dee, M. M. Adventures of Dusty. LC 84-81557. (Illus.). 48p. (gr. k-4). 1985. 9.95 (*0-937460-14-1*) Hendrick-Long.
Dee, Ruby. Tower to Heaven. Bent, Jennifer, illus. LC 90-34131. 32p. (ps-2). 1991. 14.95 (*0-8050-1460-8*, Bks Young Read) H Holt & Co.
—Two Ways to Count to Ten. Meddaugh, Susan, illus. LC 86-33513. 32p. (ps-2). 1990. pap. 5.95 (*0-8050-1314-8*, Owlet BYR) H Holt & Co.
Dee, Ruby, ed. Glowchild & Other Poems. Davis, Ossie, frwd. by. LC 72-77858. 112p. (gr. 7 up). 1972. 12.95 (*0-89388-040-X*) Okpaku Communications.
Deedat, Ahmed. Was Jesus Crucified. Obaba, Al I., ed. 49p. (Orig.). 1991. pap. text ed. 2.00 (*0-916157-72-5*) African Islam Miss Pubns.
—What Is His Name. Obaba, Al I., ed. (Illus.). 49p. (Orig.). 1991. pap. text ed. 4.00 (*0-916157-74-1*) African Islam Miss Pubns.
Deedy, Carmen A. Agatha's Feather Bed: Not Just Another Wild Goose Story. Seeley, Laura L., illus. 32p. (ps-5). 1991. 14.95 (*1-56145-008-1*) Peachtree Pubs.
—Tree Man. Ponte, Douglas J., illus. LC 93-1667. 1993. 16.95 (*1-56145-077-4*) Peachtree Pubs.
Deegan, Paul. Clarence Thomas. Italia, Bob, ed. LC 92-13717. 1992. PLB 13.99 (*1-56239-088-0*) Abdo & Dghtrs.
—Fights over Rights. Abbott, Phyllis, et al, eds. Wadsworth, Elaine, illus. LC 87-71091. 48p. (gr. 4). 1987. lib. bdg. 10.95 (*0-939179-21-0*) Abdo & Dghtrs.
—Harvard University. LC 88-71725. (Illus.). 48p. (gr. 4 up). 1988. lib. bdg. 10.95 (*0-939179-50-4*) Abdo & Dghtrs.
—The Masters. (gr. 5 up). 1992. PLB 14.95 (*0-88682-535-0*) Creative Ed.
—A Revolutionary Idea. Abbott, Phyllis, et al, eds. Wadsworth, Elaine, illus. LC 87-71092. 48p. (gr. 4). 1987. lib. bdg. 10.95 (*0-939179-20-2*) Abdo & Dghtrs.
—Rice University. LC 88-71729. (Illus.). 48p. (gr. 4 up). 1988. lib. bdg. 10.95 (*0-939179-52-0*) Abdo & Dghtrs.
—Right to Bear Arms. Abbott, Phyllis, et al, eds. Wadsworth, Elaine, illus. LC 87-71088. 32p. (gr. 4). 1987. lib. bdg. 10.95 (*0-939179-24-5*) Abdo & Dghtrs.
—The Rose Bowl. (gr. 5 up). 1992. PLB 14.95 (*0-88682-534-2*) Creative Ed.
—Sandra Day O'Connor. Italia, Bob, ed. LC 92-13716. 1992. PLB 13.99 (*1-56239-089-9*) Abdo & Dghtrs.
—Search & Seizure. Abbott, Phyllis, et al, eds. Wadsworth, Elaine, illus. LC 87-71090. 32p. (gr. 4). 1987. lib. bdg. 10.95 (*0-939179-23-7*) Abdo & Dghtrs.
—Stanford University. LC 88-71728. (Illus.). 48p. (gr. 4 up). 1988. lib. bdg. 10.95 (*0-939179-53-9*) Abdo & Dghtrs.
—Supreme Court Book. Italia, Bob, ed. LC 92-13715. 1992. lib. bdg. 13.99 (*1-56239-097-X*) Abdo & Dghtrs.
—University of California of Los Angeles. LC 88-71727. (Illus.). 48p. (gr. 4 up). 1988. lib. bdg. 10.95 (*0-939179-48-2*) Abdo & Dghtrs.
—University of Chicago. LC 88-71726. (Illus.). 48p. (gr. 4 up). 1988. lib. bdg. 10.95 (*0-939179-49-0*) Abdo & Dghtrs.
—University of Notre Dame. LC 88-71724. (Illus.). 48p. (gr. 4 up). 1988. lib. bdg. 10.95 (*0-939179-51-2*) Abdo & Dghtrs.
Deegan, Paul, jt. auth. see Italia, Bob.
Deegan, Paul, ed. see Italia, Bob.
Deegan, Paul, ed. see Wheeler, Jill.
Deegan, Paul J. The Arab-Israeli Conflict. LC 91-73073. 202p. (gr. 4 up). 1991. 13.99 (*1-56239-028-7*) Abdo & Dghtrs.
—George Bush. Wallner, Rosemary, ed. LC 91-73077. (gr. 4 up). 1991. 13.99 (*1-56239-024-4*) Abdo & Dghtrs.
—Michael Jordan, Basketball's Soaring Star. LC 87-29669. (Illus.). 64p. (gr. 4-9). 1988. 13.50 (*0-8225-0492-8*, First Ave Edns); pap. 4.95 (*0-8225-9548-6*, First Ave Edns) Lerner Pubns.
—Operation Desert Storm. LC 91-73078. (gr. 4 up). 1991. 13.99 (*1-56239-023-6*) Abdo & Dghtrs.
—Persian Gulf Nations. LC 91-73072. (gr. 4 up). 1991. 13.99 (*1-56239-029-5*) Abdo & Dghtrs.

—Saddam Hussein. Wallner, Rosemary, ed. LC 91-73076. (gr. 4 up). 1991. 13.99 (*1-56239-025-2*) Abdo & Dghtrs.
Deem, James. How to Travel Through Time. 128p. (Orig.). 1993. pap. 3.50 (*0-380-76681-7*, Camelot) Avon.
Deem, James M. Ghost Hunters. Biegel, Michael D., illus. 128p. (Orig.). 1992. pap. 3.50 (*0-380-76682-5*, Camelot) Avon.
—How to Catch a Flying Saucer. Kelley, True, illus. LC 90-4931. 192p. (gr. 5-9). 1991. 16.45 (*0-395-51958-6*) HM.
—How to Catch a Flying Saucer. Kelley, True, illus. 192p. 1993. pap. 3.50 (*0-380-71898-7*, Camelot) Avon.
—How to Find a Ghost. Kelley, True, illus. 144p. (gr. 5-9). 1988. 13.45 (*0-395-46846-9*) HM.
—How to Find a Ghost. 144p. 1990. pap. 3.25 (*0-380-70829-9*, Camelot) Avon.
—How to Hunt Buried Treasure. Kelley, True, illus. LC 91-21749. 192p. (gr. 3-7). 1992. 15.45 (*0-395-58799-9*) HM.
—How to Read Your Mother's Mind. Kelley, True, illus. LC 92-41351. 1994. write for info. (*0-395-62426-6*) HM.
Deery, Ruth. Earthquakes & Volcanoes. Miller-Ray, Sue E., illus. 48p. (gr. 4-8). 1985. wkbk. 6.95 (*0-86653-272-2*, GA 630) Good Apple.
—Tornadoes & Hurricanes. Micallef, Mary, illus. 48p. (gr. 4-8). 1985. wkbk. 6.95 (*0-86653-318-4*, GA 631) Good Apple.
Dees, Susan C. Allergy. Head, J. J., ed. Imrick, Ann T., illus. LC 86-72199. 16p. (Orig.). (gr. 10 up). 1988. pap. text ed. 2.75 (*0-89278-169-6*, 45-9769) Carolina Biological.
Deeter, C., jt. auth. see Walker, A.
Deeter, Catherine. Seymour Bleu: A Space Odyssey. LC 92-24525. Date not set. 15.00 (*0-06-021524-0*); PLB 14.89 (*0-06-021525-9*) HarpC Child Bks. Postponed.
De Fajardo, Vilma, ed. La Biblia Me Ensena. 96p. (ps). 1988. pap. 5.95 (*0-311-11454-7*) Casa Bautista.
DeFelice, Cynthia. Devil's Bridge. LC 92-7497. 96p. (gr. 5 up). 1992. SBE 12.95 (*0-02-726465-3*, Macmillan Child Bk) Macmillan Child Grp.
—The Light on Hogback Hill. 144p. (gr. 3-7). 1993. SBE 13.95 (*0-02-726453-X*, Macmillan Child Bk) Macmillan Child Grp.
—Lostman's River. 160p. (gr. 5 up). 1994. SBE 13.95 (*0-02-726466-1*, Macmillan Child Bk) Macmillan Child Grp.
—The Strange Night Writing of Jessamine Colter. LC 88-4325. 56p. (gr. 5 up). 1988. SBE 12.95 (*0-02-726451-3*, Macmillan Child Bk) Macmillan Child Grp.
—Weasel. LC 89-37794. 128p. (gr. 5 up). 1990. SBE 13. 95 (*0-02-726457-2*, Macmillan Child Bk) Macmillan Child Grp.
—Weasel. 128p. (gr. 5). 1991. pap. 3.50 (*0-380-71358-6*, Camelot) Avon.
DeFelice, Cynthia C. The Dancing Skeleton. Parker, Robert Andrew, illus. LC 88-30245. 32p. (gr. k-3). 1989. RSBE 13.95 (*0-02-726452-1*, Macmillan Child Bk) Macmillan Child Grp.
—When Grampa Kissed His Elbow. Swanson, Karl, illus. LC 90-6696. 32p. (gr. k-3). 1992. RSBE 13.95 (*0-02-726455-6*, Macmillan Child Bk) Macmillan Child Grp.
DeFina, Anthony V. Bioscience II: An Advanced Biology Course Manual. rev. ed. DeSalvo, Antonio, illus. 396p. (gr. 12). 1993. tchr's. ed. 27.50 (*0-916209-10-5*); wkbk. student's ed. 25.00 (*0-916209-11-3*) Owlet Pubns.
Defoe, Daniel. Moll Flanders. (gr. 11 up). 1969. pap. 1.95 (*0-8049-0200-3*, CL-200) Airmont.
—Moll Flanders. Sutherland, James, ed. LC 59-16265. (gr. 9 up). 1972. pap. 7.96 (*0-395-05129-0*, 3-47665, RivEd) HM.
—Reader's Digest Best Loved Books for Young Readers: The Life & Strange Surprising Adventures of Robinson Crusoe. Ogburn, Jackie, ed. Foster, Robert, illus. 168p. (gr. 4-12). 1989. 3.99 (*0-945260-27-X*) Choice Pub NY.
—Robinson Crusoe. (gr. 6 up). 1964. pap. 2.25 (*0-8049-0022-1*, CL-22) Airmont.
—Robinson Crusoe. Ward, Lynd, illus. (gr. 4-6). 1952-63. 13.95 (*0-448-06021-3*, G&D) Putnam Pub Group.
—Robinson Crusoe. 320p. (RL 6). 1961. pap. 2.50 (*0-451-52236-2*, Sig Classics) NAL-Dutton.
—Robinson Crusoe. Ross, Angus, ed. (gr. 9 up). 1966. pap. 3.95 (*0-14-043007-5*, Penguin Classics) Viking Penguin.
—Robinson Crusoe. Dolch, Edward W., et al, eds. (gr. k-3). 1988. pap. 2.95 (*0-590-41841-6*) Scholastic Inc.
—Robinson Crusoe. (Illus.). (gr. 3-6). 1981. 4.50 (*0-86020-554-1*, Usborne-Hayes); PLB 11.96 (*0-88110-062-5*); pap. 3.95 (*0-86020-553-3*) EDC.
—Robinson Crusoe. 1990. 12.99 (*0-517-01757-1*) Outlet Bk Co.
—Robinson Crusoe. (gr. 4-7). 1990. pap. 3.50 (*0-590-43285-0*) Scholastic Inc.
—Robinson Crusoe. rev. & abr. ed. De Graaf, Anne, ed. Ruyer, Francois, illus. 64p. (gr. 1-5). 1991. 8.95 (*0-89107-601-8*) Good News.
—Robinson Crusoe. (Illus.). 1992. write for info. (*0-89434-126-X*) Ferguson.
—Robinson Crusoe. Lindskoog, Kathryn, ed. (gr. 3-7). 1991. pap. 4.99 (*0-88070-438-1*, Gold & Honey) Questar Pubs.
—Robinson Crusoe. Larsen, Dan, adapted by. (gr. 3 up). 1992. 9.95 (*1-55748-277-2*) Barbour & Co.

—Robinson Crusoe. Wyeth, N. C., illus. LC 90-84707. 370p. (gr. 7 up). 1993. Repr. of 1990 ed. 16.95 (*1-56138-263-9*) Running Pr.
—Robinson Crusoe. 1993. 13.95 (*0-679-42819-4*, Everymans Lib) Knopf.
DeFord, Deborah. I Wonder Why Skunks Are So Smelly & Other Neat Facts about Mammals. (Illus.). 36p. (ps-3). 1992. write for info. (*0-307-11323-X*, 11323) Western Pub.
DeFord, Deborah H. & Stout, Harry S. An Enemy among Them. 208p. (gr. 5-9). 1987. 13.45 (*0-395-44239-7*) HM.
Defrates, Joanna. What Do We Know about the Aztecs? Shone, Rob, illus. LC 92-16997. 40p. (gr. 3-6). 1993. 16.95 (*0-87226-357-6*) P Bedrick Bks.
—What Do We Know about the Egyptians? LC 91-25175. (Illus.). 40p. (gr. 3-7). 1992. PLB 16.95 (*0-87226-353-3*) P Bedrick Bks.
De Frisching, Sacha. Let's Learn about America. (Illus.). 32p. (gr. 4 up). 1988. pap. 4.95 (*0-8442-7629-4*, Passport Bks) NTC Pub Grp.
—Let's Learn about France. (Illus.). 32p. (gr. 4 up). 1988. pap. 4.95 (*0-8442-1403-5*, Passport Bks) NTC Pub Grp.
—Let's Learn about Germany. (Illus.). 32p. (gr. 4 up). 1988. pap. 4.95 (*0-8442-2162-7*, Passport Bks) NTC Pub Grp.
—Let's Learn about Italy. (Illus.). 32p. (gr. 4 up). 1988. pap. text ed. 4.95 (*0-8442-8061-5*, Passport Bks) NTC Pub Grp.
—Let's Learn about Spain. (Illus.). 32p. (gr. 4 up). 1988. pap. 4.95 (*0-8442-7631-6*, Passport Bks) NTC Pub Grp.

DeGaetano, Gloria M. Television & the Lives of Our Children: A Manual for Teachers & Parents. Grimsley, Kent, et al, illus. 128p. 1993. pap. text ed. 10.95 (*0-9638737-0-9*) Train Thought.
This book addresses the ways habitual viewing significantly impacts children's attention, thinking, creativity, self-concept as learners, & emotional well-being. Eight chapters cover the topics: TV Time: How Much Is Too Much?, TV Impact on Brain Development, TV & Creativity, TV & Classroom Learning, Stimulus Addiction & Video Games, Media Violence, TV & Teens, & Students & Advertising. Each chapter is divided into three sections: information, reproducible parent handouts & reproducible student activities (Grades 1-8) totaling 50 reproducible pages. Many useful ideas are given for raising & educating children in a video age - ways to protect children from the effects of media misuse & ways to educate them about wise use. This is a valuable resource for all teachers & parents. Strongly endorsed & welcomed by parent educators & experts in media literacy. Dr. Jane Healy, author of Endangered Minds, has stated, "If we want to rescue the brains of the next generation, we should pay attention to this important & practical book. Gloria doesn't mince words on the dangers of media - but she tells us how to manage it constructively. Parents & teachers, take note!" Available from the publisher, Train of Thought, P.O. Box 311, Redmond, WA 98073-0311, (206) 883-1544.
Publisher Provided Annotation.

De Gale, Ann. Island Encounter. (Orig.). (gr. 6 up). 1986. pap. 2.50 (*0-440-94026-5*, LFL) Dell.
DeGarmo, Eddie, et al. Go to the Top - Leave the Crowd Behind: 49 Readings Based on the Bible & DeGarmo & Key Lyrics. 88p. 1991. pap. 4.99 (*0-8307-1504-5*, S185202) Regal.
De Gasztold, Carmen B. Creature's Choir. (FRE., Illus.). (gr. 3-8). 29.95 (*0-8288-9331-4*, F140841) Fr & Eur.
—Prayers from the Ark. (FRE.). (gr. 3-8). 29.95 (*0-685-11511-9*) Fr & Eur.
De Gasztold, Carmen Bernos see Bernos de Gasztold, Carmen.
Degen, Bruce. Jamberry. Degen, Bruce, illus. (gr. k-3). 1986. incl. cassette 19.95 (*0-87499-028-9*); pap. 12.95 incl. cassette (*0-87499-026-2*); 4 paperbacks, cassette & guide 27.95 (*0-87499-027-0*) Live Oak Media.

—Jamberry. Degen, Bruce, illus. LC 82-47708. 32p. (ps-1). 1983. 14.00 (*0-06-021416-3*) HarpC Child Bks.
—Jamberry. 1983. PLB 13.89 (*0-06-021417-1*) HarpC Child Bks.
—Jamberry: Big Book. Degen, Bruce, illus. LC 82-47708. 32p. (ps-3). 1992. pap. 19.95 (*0-06-443311-0*, Trophy) HarpC Child Bks.
—The Little Witch & the Riddle. Degen, Bruce, illus. LC 78-19475. 64p. (gr. k-3). 1988. pap. 3.50 (*0-06-444125-3*, Trophy) HarpC Child Bks.
—Teddy Bear Towers. Degen, Bruce, illus. LC 90-31937. 32p. (ps-1). 1991. 14.00 (*0-06-021420-1*); PLB 13.89 (*0-06-021430-9*) HarpC Child Bks.
Degen, Bruce, jt. auth. see Cole, Joanna.
Degens, T. Transport 7-41-R. 176p. (gr. 7 up). 1991. pap. 3.95 (*0-14-034789-5*, Puffin) Puffin Bks.
De Gerez, Toni. Louhi, Witch of North Farm. Cooney, Barbara, illus. LC 84-21600. 32p. (ps-3). 1986. 13.95 (*0-670-80556-4*) Viking Child Bks.
De Gerez, Toni see Gerez, Toni de.
De Goscinny, Rene. Asterix & Caesar's Gift. 1977. pap. 4.95x (*0-317-00093-4*) Intl Lang.
—Asterix & Cleopatra. Uderzo, illus. 1976. pap. 9.95 (*0-340-17220-7*) Intl Lang.
—Asterix & the Big Fight. Uderzo, illus. 1976. pap. 9.95 (*0-340-19167-8*) Intl Lang.
—Asterix & the Cauldron. Uderzo, illus. 1976. pap. 9.95 (*0-340-22711-7*) Intl Lang.
—Asterix & the Chieftain's Shield. (Illus.). 1977. pap. 9.95 (*0-340-22710-9*) Intl Lang.
—Asterix & the Golden Sickle. Uderzo, illus. 1976. pap. 9.95 (*0-340-21209-8*) Intl Lang.
—Asterix & the Goths. Uderzo, illus. 1976. pap. 9.95 (*0-917201-54-X*) Intl Lang.
—Asterix & the Great Crossing. Uderzo, illus. 1976. pap. 9.95 (*0-340-21589-5*) Intl Lang.
—Asterix & the Laurel Wreath. Uderzo, illus. 1976. pap. 9.95 (*0-340-20699-3*) Intl Lang.
—Asterix & the Roman Agent. Uderzo, illus. 1976. pap. 9.95 (*0-340-19168-6*) Intl Lang.
—Asterix & the Soothsayer. Uderzo, illus. 1976. pap. 9.95 (*0-340-20697-7*) Intl Lang.
—Asterix at the Olympic Games. Uderzo, illus. 1976. pap. 9.95 (*0-340-19169-4*) Intl Lang.
—Asterix aux Jeux Olympiques. (FRE.). (gr. 7-9). 1990. 19.95 (*0-8288-5109-3*, FC884) Fr & Eur.
—Asterix Chez les Bretons. (FRE.). (gr. 7-9). 1990. 19.95 (*0-8288-5108-5*, FC880) Fr & Eur.
—Asterix Chez les Helvetes. (FRE., Illus.). (gr. 7-9). 1990. 19.95 (*0-8288-5110-7*, FC889) Fr & Eur.
—Asterix en Hispanie. (FRE., Illus.). (gr. 7-9). 1990. 19.95 (*0-8288-5111-5*, FC887) Fr & Eur.
—Asterix et Cleopatre. (FRE.). (gr. 7-9). 1990. 19.95 (*0-8288-5112-3*, FC878) Fr & Eur.
—Asterix et le Chaudron. (FRE., Illus.). (gr. 7-9). 1990. 19.95 (*0-8288-5113-1*, FC885) Fr & Eur.
—Asterix et les Goths. (FRE.). (gr. 7-9). 1990. 19.95 (*0-8288-5114-X*, FC875) Fr & Eur.
—Asterix et les Normands. (FRE.). (gr. 7-9). 1990. 19.95 (*0-8288-5115-8*, FC881) Fr & Eur.
—Asterix Gladiateur. (FRE.). (gr. 7-9). 1990. 19.95 (*0-8288-5116-6*, FC876) Fr & Eur.
—Asterix in Britain. Uderzo, illus. 1976. pap. 9.95 (*0-340-17221-5*) Intl Lang.
—Asterix in Spain. Uderzo, illus. 1976. pap. 9.95 (*0-340-18326-8*) Intl Lang.
—Asterix in Switzerland. Uderzo, illus. 1976. pap. 9.95 (*0-340-19270-4*) Intl Lang.
—Asterix la Zizanie. (FRE., Illus.). (gr. 7-9). 1990. 19.95 (*0-8288-5117-4*, FC888) Fr & Eur.
—Asterix le Gaulois. (FRE.). (gr. 7-9). 1990. 19.95 (*0-8288-5118-2*, FC873) Fr & Eur.
—Asterix Legionnaire. (FRE.). (gr. 7-9). 1990. 19.95 (*0-8288-5119-0*, FC882) Fr & Eur.
—Asterix the Gladiator. Uderzo, illus. 1976. pap. 9.95 (*0-340-18320-9*) Intl Lang.
—Asterix the Legionary. Uderzo, illus. 1976. pap. 9.95 (*0-340-18321-7*) Intl Lang.
—Le Bouclier Arverne. (FRE.). (gr. 7-9). 1990. 19.95 (*0-8288-5120-4*, FC883) Fr & Eur.
—Le Combat des Chefs. (FRE.). (gr. 7-9). 1990. 19.95 (*0-8288-5121-2*, FC879) Fr & Eur.
—Le Devin. (FRE.). (gr. 7-9). 1990. 19.95 (*0-8288-5122-0*, FC890) Fr & Eur.
—The Mansion of the Gods. Uderzo, illus. 1976. pap. 9.95 (*0-340-19269-0*) Intl Lang.
—La Serpe d'Or. (FRE.). (gr. 7-9). 1990. 19.95 (*0-8288-5126-3*, FC874) Fr & Eur.
De Goscinny, Rene & Uderzo, M. Domaine des Dieux. (FRE., Illus.). (gr. 7-9). 1990. 19.95 (*0-8288-5123-9*, FC886) Fr & Eur.
—La Gran Travesia. (SPA., Illus.). 19.95 (*0-8288-5124-7*) Fr & Eur.
—Der Seher. (GER., Illus.). 19.95 (*0-8288-5125-5*) Fr & Eur.
DeGouy, L. P. The Derrydale Cook Book of Fish & Game, Vol. I. 308p. (gr. 10 up). 1992. Repr. of 1950 ed. 40.00 (*1-56416-041-6*) Derrydale Pr.
—The Derrydale Cook Book of Fish & Game, Vol. II. 330p. (gr. 10 up). 1992. Repr. of 1950 ed. 40.00 (*1-56416-042-4*) Derrydale Pr.
De Graaf, Anne. Believing the Truth. (Illus.). 32p. 1989. 4.95 (*0-310-52770-8*) Zondervan.
—The Early Years of Jesus. (Illus.). 32p. 1989. 4.95 (*0-310-52720-1*) Zondervan.
—Following the Messiah. (Illus.). 32p. 1989. 4.95 (*0-310-52740-6*) Zondervan.

—Healing Minds & Bodies. (Illus.). 32p. 1989. 4.95 (*0-310-52730-9*) Zondervan.
—Jesus Touches People. (Illus.). 32p. 1989. 4.95 (*0-310-52750-3*) Zondervan.
—The Two Greatest Commandments. (Illus.). 32p. 1989. 4.95 (*0-310-52760-0*) Zondervan.
De Graaf, Anne, ed. see Defoe, Daniel.
De Graaf, Anne, ed. see Spyri, Johanna.
DeGraf, Anna. Pioneering on the Yukon, 1892-1917. Brown, Roger S., ed. LC 92-14808. (Illus.). ix, 128p. 1992. lib. bdg. 19.50 (*0-208-02362-3*, Pub. by Archon Bks) Shoe String.
De Graff, John, jt. auth. see Anker, Debby.
De Gree, Melvin. Brickhouse Dreams: Young Benjamin E. Mays. Davis, Beverly, illus. 140p. (Orig.). (gr. 3-10). 1992. pap. 11.95 (*0-9632895-0-0*) Trail of Success.
Degroat, Diane. Annie Pitts, Artichoke. LC 91-759108. (gr. 4-7). 1992. pap. 12.00 (*0-671-75910-8*, S&S BFYR) S&S Trade.
—Annie Potts, Swamp Monster. LC 93-2474. 1994. pap. 12.00 (*0-671-87004-1*, S&S BFYR) S&S Trade.
DeGroat, Florence. Animal Stories. Wilson, Patricia, illus. 88p. (gr. 2-6). 1983. pap. 2.95 (*0-87516-509-5*) DeVorss.
—A Fairy's Workday. Wilson, Patricia, illus. 65p. (gr. 1-6). 1983. pap. 2.25 (*0-87516-508-7*) DeVorss.
—Tales from Galilee. 96p. (Orig.). (gr. 4 up). 1982. pap. 4.50 (*0-87516-485-4*) DeVorss.
DeGrote, Barbara. Take the Pizza & Run: And Other Stories for Children about Stewardship. Martens, Ray, illus. 32p. 1992. pap. 5.99 (*0-8066-2599-6*, 10-25996) Augsburg Fortress.
DeGrote-Sorensen, Barbara. Everybody Needs a Friend: A Young Christian Book for Girls. LC 86-32152. 112p. (Orig.). (gr. 3-7). 1987. pap. 5.99 (*0-8066-2247-4*, 10-2120, Augsburg) Augsburg Fortress.
De Grote-Sorensen, Barbara. Who's That in My Mirror? LC 89-49097. 112p. (Orig.). (gr. 3-7). 1990. pap. 5.99 (*0-8066-2441-8*, 9-2441) Augsburg Fortress.
De Grummond, Lena & Delaune, Lynn. Jeb Stuart. LC 62-16298. (Illus.). 160p. (gr. 4-6). 1979. pap. 5.95 (*0-88289-247-9*) Pelican.
De Hamel, Joan. Hemi's Pet. LC 86-26905. (ps-2). 1987. 13.95 (*0-395-43665-6*) HM.
DeHart, Jack. So You Want to Serve. Caito, Mike, illus. 189p. (Orig.). 1990. pap. 6.95 (*0-932581-77-3*) Word Aflame.
De Haven, Tom. Joe Gosh. Reese, Ralph, illus. (gr. 7 up). 1988. 15.95 (*0-8027-6824-5*) Walker & Co.
De Hieronymis, Elve F. Beach. (ps). 1992. 4.50 (*1-56397-204-2*) Boyds Mills Pr.
—A Night at the Circus. (Illus.). 16p. 1989. 8.95 (*0-8120-5995-6*) Barron.
Dehnbostel, Nancy L. & Hartman, Mary E. Space. Sturckler, Joe, illus. 44p. (gr. 1-6). 1982. 6.50 (*0-88047-010-0*, 8205) DOK Pubs.
Dehr, Roma & Bazar, Ronald. Good Planets Are Hard to Find: An Environmental Information Guide for Kids. Johnson, Nola, illus. 40p. (Orig.). (gr. 4 up). 1990. pap. 4.95 (*0-919597-09-2*) Firefly Bks Ltd.
Deibert, Alvin N. B. J. & the Language of the Woodland. Joy, Carol, illus. LC 82-24422. 48p. (Orig.). (gr. 2-6). 1983. pap. 7.50 (*0-87743-701-7*, 353-019, Pub. by Bellwood Pr) Bahai.
Deich, Joy. J. P.'s Pumpkin Patch: Too Many Pumpkins. 32p. (gr. k-4). 1993. pap. 2.95 (*0-9629698-5-0*) Aaron Lake Pub.
Deihl, Edna G. The Teddy Bear That Prowled at Night. Russell, Mary L., illus. 24p. (gr. k-3). 1991. pap. 7.95 (*0-88138-079-2*, Green Tiger) S&S Trade.
Deitch, Kenneth M. Leonard Bernstein: America's Maestro, With a Message from Issac Stern. Foley, Sheila, illus. Stern, Isaac, intro. by. LC 91-70821. (Illus.). 48p. (gr. 5-12). 1991. PLB 14.95 (*1-878668-03-X*); pap. 7.95 (*1-878668-07-2*) Disc Enter Ltd.
Deitch, Kenneth M. & Weisman, JoAnne B. Dwight D. Eisenhower: Man of Many Hats; With a Message from John S. D. Eisenhower. Connolly, Jay, illus. Eisenhower, John S., intro. by. LC 90-82588. (Illus.). 48p. (gr. 5-12). 1990. PLB 14.95 (*1-878668-02-1*) Disc Enter Ltd.
Deitch, Kenneth M., jt. auth. see Weisman, JoAnne B.
Deitrick, David R., illus. Tales from the Ether. 64p. (Orig.). (gr. 9-12). 1989. pap. 8.00 (*1-55878-011-4*) Game Designers.
Deitz, Lawrence. Jimmy Coon Story Book, No. 1. McCoy, Beverly, illus. 34p. (Orig.). 1985. pap. 2.95 (*0-934750-79-3*) Mntn Memories Bks.
—Jimmy Coon Story Book, No. 2. McCoy, Beverly, illus. 37p. 1985. pap. 2.95 (*0-934750-42-4*) Mntn Memories Bks.
—Jimmy Coon Story Book, No. 3. 37p. 1986. pap. 2.95 (*0-934750-85-8*) Mntn Memories Bks.
—Jimmy Coon Story Book, No. 4. McCoy, Beverly, illus. 30p. 1986. pap. 2.95 (*0-934750-14-9*) Mntn Memories Bks.
—Jimmy Coon Story Book, No. 5. (Illus.). 40p. (Orig.). (ps up). 1986. pap. 2.95 (*0-938985-02-7*) Mntn Memories Bks.
De Jenkins, Lyll B. The Honorable Prison. LC 87-25197. 192p. (gr. 7 up). 1988. 14.95 (*0-525-67238-9*, Lodestar Bks) Dutton Child Bks.
—The Honorable Prison. 208p. (gr. 7 up). 1989. pap. 3.95 (*0-14-032952-8*, Puffin) Puffin Bks.
De Jenkins, Lyll Becerra see Becerra de Jenkins, Lyll.

DeJong, Meindert. Along Came a Dog. Sendak, Maurice, illus. LC 57-9265. 192p. (gr. 3-6). 1958. PLB 15.89 (0-06-021421-X) HarpC Child Bks.
—Along Came a Dog. Sendak, Maurice, illus. LC 57-9265. 192p. (gr. 4-7). 1980. pap. 4.95 (0-06-440114-6, Trophy) HarpC Child Bks.
—The Easter Cat. Hoban, Lillian, illus. LC 90-24407. 128p. (gr. 3-7). 1991. pap. 3.95 (0-689-71468-8, Aladdin) Macmillan Child Grp.
—House of Sixty Fathers. Sendak, Maurice, illus. LC 56-8148. 192p. (gr. 5-8). 1956. PLB 13.89 (0-06-021481-3) HarpC Child Bks.
—The House of Sixty Fathers. Sendak, Maurice, illus. LC 56-8148. 192p. (gr. 5-8). 1987. pap. 3.95 (0-06-440200-2, Trophy) HarpC Child Bks.
—Hurry Home, Candy. Sendak, Maurice, illus. LC 53-8536. 224p. (gr. 4-7). 1953. PLB 14.89 (0-06-021486-4) HarpC Child Bks.
—Hurry Home, Candy. LC 53-8536. (Illus.). 244p. (gr. 4-7). 1972. pap. 3.50 (0-06-440025-5, Trophy) HarpC Child Bks.
—Shadrach. Sendak, Maurice, illus. LC 53-5250. 192p. (gr. 3-6). 1953. PLB 14.89 (0-06-021546-1) HarpC Child Bks.
—Shadrach. Sendak, Maurice, illus. LC 53-5250. 192p. (gr. 3-6). 1980. pap. 3.95 (0-06-440115-4, Trophy) HarpC Child Bks.
—Wheel on the School. Sendak, Maurice, illus. LC 54-8945. 256p. (gr. 4-7). 1954. 15.00 (0-06-021585-2); PLB 14.89 (0-06-021586-0) HarpC Child Bks.
—Wheel on the School. LC 54-8945. (Illus.). (gr. 4-7). 1972. pap. 3.95 (0-06-440021-2, Trophy) HarpC Child Bks.
De Jonge, Joanne. All Nature Sings. (Illus.). 144p. 1992. pap. 8.99 (0-8028-5065-0) Eerdmans.
—My Listening Ears. (Illus.). 144p. (Orig.). 1992. pap. 8.99 (0-8028-5066-9) Eerdmans.
—Of Skies & Seas. (Illus.). 144p. (gr. 5-12). 1991. pap. 8.99 (0-8028-5068-5) Eerdmans.
—The Rustling Grass. (gr. 5-12). 1991. pap. 8.99 (0-8028-5067-7) Eerdmans.
—Trash Can Review. Foley, Timothy, illus. 64p. (Orig.). 1992. pap. 7.99 (0-8028-5071-5) Eerdmans.
De Kay, James T. Left-Handed Kids. LC 89-36893. (Illus.). 96p. 1989. pap. 5.95 (0-87131-591-2) M Evans.
—Meet Christopher Columbus. Edens, John, illus. LC 88-19068. 72p. (gr. 2-4). 1989. PLB 6.99 (0-394-91963-7); pap. 2.99 (0-394-81963-2) Random Bks Yng Read.
—Meet Martin Luther King, Jr. LC 88-26383. (Illus.). 72p. (gr. 2-4). 1989. PLB 6.99 (0-394-91962-9); pap. 2.99 (0-394-81962-4) Random Bks Yng Read.
DeKay, James T. Meet Martin Luther King, Jr. rev. ed. (Illus.). 112p. (gr. 3-5). 1993. 2.99 (0-679-85411-8); PLB 9.99 (0-679-95411-2) Random Bks Yng Read.
DeKeles, Jon C., ed. Video Game Secrets: A Top Secret Guide to One Thousand Tips, Tricks & Codes. (Illus.). 192p. (Orig.). (gr. 6 up). 1990. pap. 9.95 (0-9625057-3-0) DMS ID.
Dekker, Thomas see Bald, Robert C.
De la Bedoyere, C., tr. see Johnson, Peter D.
Delacre, Lulu. Arroz Con Leche. Delacre, Lulu, illus. 1992. pap. 3.95 (0-590-41886-6, Blue Ribbon Bks); cassette 4.95 (0-590-60035-4, Blue Ribbon Bks) Scholastic Inc.
—Arroz Con Leche: Popular Songs & Rhymes from Latin America. (Illus.). (ps-3). 1989. pap. 13.95 (0-590-41887-4) Scholastic Inc.
—Nathan's Fishing Trip. (ps-2). 1989. pap. 2.50 (0-590-41282-5) Scholastic Inc.
—Peter Cottontail's Easter Book. Delacre, Lulu, illus. 32p. (ps-1). 1991. 12.95 (0-590-43338-5, Scholastic Hardcover) Scholastic Inc.
—Peter Cottontail's Easter Book. 32p. 1992. pap. 2.50 (0-590-43337-7) Scholastic Inc.
—Time for School for, Nathan! 1989. pap. 12.95 (0-590-41942-0) Scholastic Inc.
—Time for School, Nathan! Delacre, Lulu, illus. 32p. (ps-2). 1991. pap. 2.50 (0-590-45688-1) Scholastic Inc.
—Vejigantes Masquerade. LC 92-15480. (ENG. & SPA., Illus.). 40p. (gr. k-3). 1993. 14.95 (0-590-45776-4) Scholastic Inc.
Delacre, Lulu, illus. Sing with Me Mother Goose. (ps-1). 1987. incl. cassette 5.95 (0-394-88812-X) Random Bks Yng Read.
De La Croix, Alice. Mattie's Whisper. LC 91-73885. 128p. (gr. 3-7). 1992. 14.95 (1-56397-036-8) Boyds Mills Pr.
De la Cruz Aymes, Maria, et al. Growing with God's Forgiveness & I Celebrate Reconcilation. 72p. (gr. 1-3). 1985. pap. text ed. 5.25 (0-8215-2371-6); tchr's. ed. 7.41 (0-8215-2373-2); parent pack (10 booklets) 15.39 (0-8215-2377-5) Sadlier.
—Growing with the Bread of Life & My Mass Book. 72p. (gr. 1-3). 1985. pap. text ed. 5.25 (0-8215-2370-8); tchr's. ed. 7.41 (0-8215-2372-4); parent pack (10 booklets) 15.39 (0-8215-2376-7) Sadlier.
De la Fontaine, Jean. Dame Renard et Dame Cigogne - Mrs. Fox & Mrs. Stork. 2nd ed. Calamaro, Emanuel, adapted by. Nofziger, Edward, illus. (FRE.). 19p. (gr. k-12). 1993. pap. 2.95 (0-922852-20-0) AIMS Intl.
Delafosse, Claude. Musical Instruments. Grant, Donald, illus. 24p. (ps-2). 1994. 11.95 (0-590-47729-3, Cartwheel) Scholastic Inc.
Delafosse, Claude & Prunier, James. Dinosaurs. (Illus.). (gr. 4 up). 1993. 10.95 (0-590-46358-6) Scholastic Inc.

DeLage, Ida. The Old Witch & Her Magic Basket. Sloan, Ellen, illus. 48p. (gr. k-4). 1991. Repr. of 1978 ed. lib. bdg. 12.95 (0-7910-1475-4) Chelsea Hse.
—The Old Witch & the Crows. Smith, Marianne, illus. 48p. (gr. k-4). 1991. Repr. of 1983 ed. lib. bdg. 12.95 (0-7910-1476-2) Chelsea Hse.
—The Old Witch & the Dragon. Unada, illus. 48p. (gr. k-4). 1991. Repr. of 1979 ed. lib. bdg. 12.95 (0-7910-1477-0) Chelsea Hse.
—The Old Witch & the Ghost Parade. Taylor, Jody, illus. 48p. (gr. k-4). 1991. Repr. of 1978 ed. lib. bdg. 12.95 (0-7910-1478-9) Chelsea Hse.
—The Old Witch & the Snores. Miret, Gil, illus. 48p. (gr. k-4). 1991. Repr. of 1970 ed. lib. bdg. 12.95 (0-7910-1479-7) Chelsea Hse.
—The Old Witch & the Wizard. Korach, Mimi, illus. 48p. (gr. k-4). 1991. Repr. of 1974 ed. lib. bdg. 12.95 (0-7910-1480-0) Chelsea Hse.
—The Old Witch Finds a New House. Paris, Pat, illus. 48p. (gr. k-4). 1991. Repr. of 1979 ed. lib. bdg. 12.95 (0-7910-1481-9) Chelsea Hse.
—The Old Witch Gets a Surprise. Sloan, Ellen, illus. 48p. (gr. k-4). 1991. Repr. of 1981 ed. lib. bdg. 12.95 (0-7910-1482-7) Chelsea Hse.
—The Old Witch Goes to the Ball. Nebel, Gustave E., illus. 48p. (gr. k-4). 1991. Repr. of 1969 ed. lib. bdg. 12.95 (0-7910-1483-5) Chelsea Hse.
—The Old Witch's Party. Korach, Mimi, illus. 48p. (gr. k-4). 1991. Repr. of 1976 ed. lib. bdg. 12.95 (0-7910-1484-3) Chelsea Hse.
—Weeny Witch. Oechsli, Kelli, illus. 48p. (gr. k-4). 1991. Repr. of 1966 ed. lib. bdg. 12.95 (0-7910-1485-1) Chelsea Hse.
—What Does a Witch Need? Schroeder, Ted, illus. 48p. (gr. k-4). 1991. Repr. of 1971 ed. PLB 12.95 (0-7910-1486-X) Chelsea Hse.
—The Witchy Broom. Peaver, Walt, illus. 48p. (gr. k-4). 1991. Repr. of 1969 ed. lib. bdg. 12.95 (0-7910-1487-8) Chelsea Hse.
Delamare, David. The Christmas Secret. LC 91-12779. (Illus.). 40p. (ps-2). 1991. jacketed, reinforced bdg. 15.00 (0-671-74822-X, Green Tiger) S&S Trade.
—Cinderella. LC 92-25126. 1993. 15.00 (0-671-76944-8, S&S BFYR) S&S Trade.
Delamare, David, illus. Nutcracker. 48p. (gr. 1-5). 1992. 12.95 (0-88101-235-1) Unicorn Pub.
—Nutcracker. 48p. (ps-3). 1992. 4.95 (0-88101-244-0) Unicorn Pub.
—Steadfast Tin Soldier. Ingram, John W., ed. Delamare, David, illus. LC 90-10927. 48p. (gr. 1-5). 1990. 9.95 (0-88101-077-4) Unicorn Pub.
—Steadfast Tin Soldier. 48p. (ps-3). 1992. 4.95 (0-88101-245-9) Unicorn Pub.
—Steadfast Tin Soldier. 48p. (ps-3). 1990. 12.95 (0-88101-237-8) Unicorn Pub.
—Twelve Days of Christmas. 48p. 1992. 12.95 (0-88101-236-6) Unicorn Pub.
—Twelve Days of Christmas. 48p. 1993. 5.95 (0-88101-264-5) Unicorn Pub.
—Twelve Days of Christmas (Fairy Tale Classic) 48p. 1992. 9.95 (0-88101-228-9) Unicorn Pub.
De la Mare, Walter. Peacock Pie: A Book of Rhymes. LC 89-1828. (Illus.). (gr. 2-4). 1989. 17.95 (0-8050-1124-2, Bks Young Read) H Holt & Co.
—Rhymes & Verses: Collected Poems for Young People. Blaisdell, Elinore, illus. LC 88-45278. 370p. (gr. 2-4). 1988. 15.95 (0-8050-0847-0, Bks Young Read); pap. 7.95 (0-8050-0848-9) H Holt & Co.
—Songs of Childhood. 106p. (gr. 3 up) pap. 4.50 (0-486-21972-0) Dover.
—Stories from the Bible: From the Garden of Eden to the Promised Land. Ardizzone, Edward, illus. 418p. (gr. 3 up). 1985. pap. 8.95 (0-571-11086-X) Faber & Faber.
—The Three Sillies. 1991. PLB 13.95s.p. (0-88682-467-2) Creative Ed.
—The Turnip. Hawkes, Kevin, illus. LC 92-6191. 1992. 18.95 (0-87923-934-4) Godine.
—Visitors. LC 86-6244. 40p. (gr. 4 up). 1986. PLB 13.95s.p. (0-88682-070-7) Creative Ed.
De la Martre, Audrey, ed. Chemical Abuse Assessment Workbook for Adolescents. rev. ed. Payne, William J., intro. by. 34p. (gr. 6-12). 1989. Repr. of 1981 ed. wkbk. 7.00 (0-317-92294-7) New Connect Pub.
Delaney, Antoinette. The Gunnywolf. Delaney, Antoinette, illus. LC 87-29351. 32p. (ps-3). 1992. pap. 4.95 (0-06-443304-8, Trophy) HarpC Child Bks.
Delaney, Frank. Legends of the Celts. (Illus.). 272p. (gr. 10-12). 1992. pap. 14.95 (0-8069-8351-5) Sterling.
Delany, Martin R. Origin of Races & Color: With an Archeological Compendium of Ethiopian & Egyptian Civilization. LC 90-82685. 100p. 1991. 19.95 (0-933121-51-2); pap. 8.95 (0-933121-50-4) Black Classic.
Delany, Mary M. Of Irish Ways. (gr. k-3). 1993. pap. 10.00 (0-06-092421-7, PL) HarpC.
De La Paz, Myrna J. Abadeha: The Philippine Cinderella. De Leon, Romeo, illus. 28p. (gr. k-7). 1991. 13.95 (0-9629255-0-0) Pazific Queen.
Dela Pena, Alba. Milas, the Innkeeper of Harvest Tree. Hough, Bonnie J. & Cook, Allen, illus. 28p. 1993. saddle stitched 8.95 (1-56167-119-3) Am Literary Pr.
De la Ramee, Marie Louise see Ouida, pseud.
De Larramendi, Alberto Ruiz see Ruiz de Larramendi, Alberto.

De Larramendi Ruis, Alberto. Tropical Rain Forests of Central America. LC 92-35062. (Illus.). 36p. (gr. 3 up). 1993. PLB 19.93 (0-516-08383-X); pap. 6.75 (0-516-48383-8) Childrens.
De la Sota, Ann. Amazing Animals. (Illus.). 32p. (gr. 3 up). 1986. incl. hand held Decoder 5.95 (0-88679-457-9) Educ Insights.
Delaune, Lynn, jt. auth. see De Grummond, Lena.
Delavan, Elizabeth. Peter & George & Uncle Henry. (Illus.). 48p. (gr. 3-4). 1988. pap. 2.95 (1-55787-020-9, NY75041) Heart of the Lakes.
Delbridge, Joyce, et al, eds. Northwest Ferry Tales: Stories, Poems & Anecdotes from Washington, British Columbia & Alaska. Delbridge, Joyce, frwd. by. LC 88-50264. (Illus.). 128p. (Orig.). (gr. 5 up). 1989. pap. 8.95 (0-9616103-8-7) Vashon PT Prod.
Del Carmen Blazquez, Maria, tr. see Gomez-Navarro, Maria J., et al.
Del Carmen Blazquez, Maria, tr. see Puncel, Maria.
Del Castillo, Bernal Diaz see Castillo, Bernal D. de.
Del Castillo Bernal, Diaz see Bernal-Diaz, Del Castillo.
Delcher, Eden, compiled by. Mother Goose Animal Rhymes. 1993. 2.98 (1-55521-834-2) Bk Sales Inc.
—Mother Goose Counting Rhymes. 1993. 2.98 (1-55521-832-6) Bk Sales Inc.
—Mother Goose Favorite Rhymes. (gr. k up). 1993. 2.98 (1-55521-835-0) Bk Sales Inc.
—Mother Goose Rhymes about Children. 1993. 2.98 (1-55521-833-4) Bk Sales Inc.
Delderfield, Eric. Eric Delderfield's Bumper Book of Animal Stories. large type ed. 224p. 1993. 24.95 (1-85695-036-0, Pub. by ISIS UK) Transaction Pubs.
DeLeeuw, Adele. The Boy with Wings. LC 74-15860. (gr. 1-6). 1971. 8.95 (0-87874-001-5, Nautilus) Galloway.
—George Rogers Clark: Frontier Fighter. (Illus.). 80p. (gr. 2-6). 1993. Repr. of 1967 ed. lib. bdg. 12.95 (0-7910-1456-8) Chelsea Hse.
—Richard E. Byrd: Adventurer to the Poles. (Illus.). 80p. (gr. 2-6). 1992. Repr. of 1963 ed. PLB 12.95 (0-7910-1455-X) Chelsea Hse.
De Leeuw, Hendrik, et al. Fireproof Children Education Kit. (Illus.). 308p. (gr. k-6). 1990. 99.95 (0-9626076-1-4) Natl Fire Serv Support Systs.
DeLeon, Thomas C. Four Years in Rebel Capitals. LC 83-9280. (gr. 7 up). 1983. Kivar binding 26.60 (0-8094-4462-3) Time-Life.
De Leprince de Beaumont. Belle et la Bete. Glaseur, Willi, illus. (FRE.). 87p. (gr. 1-5). 1989. pap. 10.95 (2-07-031188-0) Schoenhof.
Delessert, Etienne. Ashes, Ashes. LC 89-28586. (Illus.). 32p. 1990. PLB 14.95 (1-55670-137-3) Stewart Tabori & Chang.
—Ashes, Ashes. Delessert, Etienne, illus. 32p. (gr. 1-12). Date not set. lib. bdg. 16.95 RLB smythe-sewn (0-88682-628-4, 97855-098) Creative Ed.
—At Home. Delessert, Etienne, illus. LC 93-27456. 1993. write for info. (0-88682-646-2) Creative Ed.
—Best Friends. Delessert, Etienne, illus. LC 93-27461. 1993. write for info. (0-88682-639-X) Creative Ed.
—Dance! Delessert, Etienne, illus. 32p. (gr. 1-8). Date not set. RLB smythe-sewn 16.95 (0-88682-627-6, 97938-098) Creative Ed.
—For the Birds. Delessert, Etienne, illus. LC 93-27462. 1993. write for info. (0-88682-638-1) Creative Ed.
—Let's Play. Delessert, Etienne, illus. LC 93-27459. 1993. write for info. (0-88682-649-7) Creative Ed.
—A Long Long Song. LC 87-73491. (Illus.). 32p. (ps up). 1988. 13.95 (0-374-34638-0) FS&G.
—Magic Tricks. Delessert, Etienne, illus. LC 93-31972. 1993. write for info. (0-88682-642-X) Creative Ed.
—Moonlight. Delessert, Etienne, illus. LC 93-27458. 1993. write for info. (0-88682-648-9) Creative Ed.
—Nonsense. Delessert, Etienne, illus. LC 93-27464. 1993. write for info. (0-88682-641-1) Creative Ed.
—Nuts! Delessert, Etienne, illus. LC 93-27454. 1993. write for info. (0-88682-644-6) Creative Ed.
—Snowflakes. Delessert, Etienne, illus. LC 93-27457. 1993. write for info. (0-88682-647-0) Creative Ed.
—Surprises. Delessert, Etienne, illus. LC 93-27453. 1993. write for info. (0-88682-643-8) Creative Ed.
—Weird? Delessert, Etienne, illus. LC 93-27455. 1993. write for info. (0-88682-645-4) Creative Ed.
—What a Circus! Delessert, Etienne, illus. LC 93-27463. 1993. write for info. (0-88682-640-3) Creative Ed.
Delessert, Etienne, ed. see Gallaz, Chrsitophe.
Delf, Brian, illus. Picture Atlas of the World. LC 92-37056. 1992. write for info. (0-528-83564-5) Rand McNally.
Delgado, Jose, jt. auth. see Clemens, Peter.
Delis-Abrams, Alexandra. ABC Feelings: A Coloring - Learning Book. rev. ed. Follendore, Joan, ed. Gurstein, Shari, illus. 64p. (gr. 3-8). 1991. pap. text ed. 7.95 (1-879889-00-5) Adage Pubns.
Delisle, James & Galbraith, Judy. The Gifted Kids Survival Guide II. Espeland, Pamela, ed. LC 87-80584. (Illus.). 160p. (gr. 6-12). 1987. pap. 9.95 (0-915793-09-1) Free Spirit Pub.
Delisle, James R. Gifted Kids Speak Out: Hundreds of Kids Ages 6-13 Talk about School, Friends, Their Families & the Future. Espeland, Pamela, ed. Urbanovic, Jackie, illus. LC 87-25139. 120p. (Orig.). (gr. 2-7). 1987. pap. 9.95 (0-915793-10-5) Free Spirit Pub.
Delisle, Jim. Kidstories: Biographies of Twenty Young People You'd Like to Know. Espeland, Pamela, ed. LC 91-18363. 176p. (Orig.). (gr. 3 up). 1991. pap. 9.95 (0-915793-34-2) Free Spirit Pub.
Deliz, Osdila O., ed. see Ronnholm, Ursula O.

Deliz, Osdila O., ed. see Ronnholm, Ursula O.

Deliz, Wenceslao S. Adios Falcon. Marichal, Poli, illus. LC 85-1116. (SPA.). 15p. (ps-3). 1985. pap. 2.00 (0-8477-3530-3) U of PR Pr.

Dell, Catherine. Horses & Ponies. Bissex, Thelma & Turner, Elizabeth, illus. LC 88-17652. 24p. (Orig.). (gr. 2-5). 1989. PLB 5.99 (0-394-99987-8) Random Bks Yng Read.

Dell, Pamela. Hotscopes: Aquarius 1994: Day-by-Day Horoscopes for Teens. 1993. pap. 3.95 (0-307-22460-0, Golden Pr) Western Pub.
—Hotscopes: Aries 1994: Day-by-Day Horoscopes for Teens. 1993. pap. 3.95 (0-307-22450-3, Golden Pr) Western Pub.
—Hotscopes: Cancer 1994: Day-by-Day Horoscopes for Teens. 1993. pap. 3.95 (0-307-22453-8, Golden Pr) Western Pub.
—Hotscopes: Capricorn 1994: Day-by-Day Horoscopes for Teens. 1993. pap. 3.95 (0-307-22459-7, Golden Pr) Western Pub.
—Hotscopes: Gemini 1994: Day-By-Day Horoscopes for Teens. 1993. pap. 3.95 (0-307-22452-X, Golden Pr) Western Pub.
—Hotscopes: Leo 1994: Day-by-Day Horoscopes for Teens. 1993. pap. 3.95 (0-307-22454-6, Golden Pr) Western Pub.
—Hotscopes: Libra 1994: Day-by-Day Horoscopes for Teens. 1993. pap. 3.95 (0-307-22456-2, Golden Pr) Western Pub.
—Hotscopes: Pisces 1994: Day-by-Day Horoscopes for Teens. 1993. pap. 3.95 (0-307-22461-9, Golden Pr) Western Pub.
—Hotscopes: Sagittarius 1994: Day-by-Day Horoscopes for Teens. 1993. pap. 3.95 (0-307-22458-9, Golden Pr) Western Pub.
—Hotscopes: Scorpio 1994: Day-by-Day Horoscopes for Teens. 1993. pap. 3.95 (0-307-22457-0, Golden Pr) Western Pub.
—Hotscopes: Taurus 1994: Day-by-Day Horoscopes for Teens. 1993. pap. 3.95 (0-307-22451-1, Golden Pr) Western Pub.
—Hotscopes: Virgo 1994: Day-by-Day Horoscopes for Teens. 1993. pap. 3.95 (0-307-22455-4, Golden Pr) Western Pub.
—I. M. Pei, Designer of Dreams. LC 92-36903. (Illus.). 32p. (gr. 2-4). 1993. PLB 15.27 (0-516-04186-X) Childrens.
—Michael Chang: Tennis Champion. LC 92-6384. (Illus.). 32p. (gr. 2-5). 1992. PLB 14.60 (0-516-04185-1); pap. 3.95 (0-516-44185-X) Childrens.

Dell Staff. Story of Bill Clinton & Al Gore. (gr. 4-7). 1993. pap. 3.50 (0-440-40843-1) Dell.

Dellinger, A. & Fletcher, S. Family Devotions. (ps-3). 1983. pap. 0.69 (0-570-08313-3, 56HH1445) Concordia.
—Favorite Bible Verses. (ps-3). 1983. pap. 0.69 (0-570-08310-9, 56HH1442) Concordia.
—N. T. Stories. (ps-3). 1983. pap. 0.69 (0-570-08312-5, 56HH1444) Concordia.
—O. T. Heroes. (ps-3). 1983. pap. 0.69 (0-570-08311-7, 56HH1443) Concordia.
—Proverbs. 16p. (ps-3). 1983. pap. 0.69 (0-570-08309-5, 56HH1441) Concordia.
—Table Prayers. (ps-3). 1983. pap. 0.69 (0-570-08316-8, 56HH1448) Concordia.

Dellinger, Annetta. Ann Elizabeth Signs With Love. (ps-2). 1991. 8.99 (0-570-04192-9, 56-1651) Concordia.
—The Jesus Tree. Morris, Susan S., illus. 32p. (ps-2). 1991. 7.99 (0-570-04191-0) Concordia.

Dellinger, Annetta E. Adopted & Loved Forever. (Illus.). (ps-2). 1987. 5.99 (0-570-04167-8, 56-1624) Concordia.
—Angels Are My Friends. LC 85-7858. 32p. (gr. 5-9). 1985. 5.99 (0-570-04120-1, 56-1531) Concordia.
—Good Manners for God's Children. (ps-k). 1984. pap. 4.99 (0-570-04093-0, 56-1461) Concordia.
—Hugging. Williams, Jenny, illus. LC 84-21505. 32p. (gr. k-3). 1985. PLB 21.35 (0-89565-301-X); PLB 14.95s.p. (0-685-57947-6) Childs World.
—My First Easter Book. Hohag, Linda, illus. LC 84-21512. 32p. (ps-2). 1985. PLB 15.00 (0-516-02904-5); pap. 3.95 (0-516-42904-3) Childrens.

Deloch-Hughes, Edye. I Like Gym Shoe Soup. Hughes, Darryl, illus. 16p. (gr. k-3). 1991. 10.25 (0-941484-11-4) Urban Res Pr.

Delp, Debra. Packing for Heaven. Zoglio, Suzanne, ed. Larsen, Rob, illus. 32p. (Orig.). (gr. k-5). 1991. pap. text ed. 8.95 (0-941668-03-7) Tower Hill Pr.

Delporte, pseud. Romeo & Smurfette & Twelve Other Smurfy Stories. Peyo, illus. LC 82-60258. 48p. (gr. 4-7). 1983. 2.95 (0-394-85618-X) Random Bks Yng Read.

Del Real, Maria E., ed. see Editorial America, S. A., Staff.

Del Real, Maria E., ed. see Editorial America, S. A. Staff.

Del Real, Maria E. Alvarez see Alvarez del Real, Maria E.

Del Rosario Marquez, Nieves. Raices y Alas (Poesias Para Ninos y Jovenes) Montes, Jesus, illus. LC 81-65415. (Orig.). (gr. 6). 1981. pap. 5.00 (0-89729-289-8) Ediciones.

Delton & McCue. Mom Made Me Go to School. 1993. pap. 2.99 (0-440-40841-5) Dell.

Delton, Alan T., illus. Huckleberry Hash. 1990. pap. 2.95 (0-440-40325-1, YB) Dell.

Delton, Judy. Angel in Charge. Morrill, Leslie, illus. LC 84-27862. 152p. (gr. 2-5). 1985. 13.45 (0-395-37488-X) HM.
—Angel in Charge. (gr. k-6). 1990. pap. 2.95 (0-440-40264-6, YB) Dell.
—Angel's Mother's Baby. Apple, Margot, illus. 144p. (gr. 2-5). 1989. 13.45 (0-395-50926-2) HM.
—Angel's Mother's Baby. (gr. 4-7). 1992. pap. 3.25 (0-440-40586-6) Dell.
—Angel's Mother's Boyfriend. Apple, Margot, illus. LC 82-27054. 176p. (gr. 2-5). 1986. 12.95 (0-395-39968-8) HM.
—Angel's Mother's Boyfriend. (gr. k-6). 1990. pap. 2.95 (0-440-40275-1, YB) Dell.
—Angel's Mother's Wedding. 128p. (gr. 3-7). 1987. 13.45 (0-395-44470-5) HM.
—Angel's Mother's Wedding. (gr. k-6). 1990. pap. 2.95 (0-440-40281-6, YB) Dell.
—Back Yard Angel. Morrill, Leslie, illus. 112p. (gr. 2-5). 1983. 14.45 (0-395-33883-2) HM.
—Back Yard Angel. Morrill, Leslie, illus. 112p. (gr. k up). 1990. pap. 3.25 (0-440-40445-2, YB) Dell.
—Bad, Bad Bunnies. (gr. k-6). 1990. pap. 2.99 (0-440-40278-6, YB) Dell.
—Birthday Bike for Brimhall. (ps-3). 1991. pap. 2.99 (0-440-40461-4) Dell.
—Birthday Bike for Brimhall. LC 83-21025. (Illus.). 56p. (gr. k-4). 1985. 14.95 (0-87614-256-0) Carolrhoda Bks.
—Blue Skies, French Fries. 80p. (Orig.). (gr. k-6). 1988. pap. 2.99 (0-440-40064-3, YB) Dell.
—Brimhall Turns Detective. LC 82-9582. (Illus.). 48p. (gr. k-4). 1983. 14.95 (0-87614-203-X) Carolrhoda Bks.
—Camp Ghost-Away. 80p. (Orig.). (gr. k-6). 1988. pap. 3.25 (0-440-40062-7, YB) Dell.
—Cookies & Crutches. 80p. (Orig.). (gr. k-6). 1988. pap. 2.99 (0-440-40010-4, YB) Dell.
—Fishey Wishes. (ps-3). 1993. pap. 3.25 (0-440-40850-4) Dell.
—Greedy Groundhogs. (ps-3). 1994. pap. 3.25 (0-440-40931-4) Dell.
—Grumpy Pumpkins. 80p. (Orig.). (gr. k-6). 1988. pap. 2.99 (0-440-40065-1, YB) Dell.
—Hello Huckleberry Heights. Tiegreen, Alan, illus. (Orig.). 1990. pap. 2.95 (0-440-40304-9) Dell.
—Hired Help for Rabbit. McCue, Lisa, illus. LC 91-15551. 32p. (gr. k-3). 1992. pap. 4.50 (0-689-71522-6, Aladdin) Macmillan Child Grp.
—I Never Win! Gilchrist, Cathy, illus. LC 80-27618. 32p. (gr. k-4). 1981. PLB 14.95 (0-87614-139-4) Carolrhoda Bks.
—I Never Win. (ps-3). 1991. pap. 2.95 (0-440-40414-2) Dell.
—I'll Never Love Anything Ever Again. Fay, Ann, ed. Daniel, Alan, illus. LC 84-17271. 32p. (gr. k-3). 1985. PLB 11.95 (0-8075-3521-4) A Whitman.
—Kitty from the Start. LC 86-21481. (gr. 3-5). 1987. 13.95 (0-395-42847-5) HM.
—Lights, Action, Land-Ho! Tiegreen, Alan, illus. 80p. (Orig.). (gr. 1-4). 1992. pap. 3.25 (0-440-40732-X, YB) Dell.
—Lucky Dog Days. 80p. (gr. k-3). 1988. pap. 2.99 (0-440-40063-5, YB) Dell.
—Merry Merry Huckleberry. Tiegreen, Alan, illus. (Orig.). 1990. pap. 2.95 (0-440-40365-0, Pub. by Yearling Classics) Dell.
—Mom Made Me Go to Camp. 1993. pap. 2.99 (0-440-40838-5) Dell.
—My Mom Hates Me in January. Faulkner, John, illus. LC 77-5749. (gr. 1-3). 1977. PLB 11.95 (0-8075-5356-5) A Whitman.
—My Mom Made Me Go to Camp. (gr. 1-3). 1993. pap. 2.99 (0-553-37251-3) Bantam.
—My Mom Made Me Go to School. (gr. 1-3). 1993. pap. 2.99 (0-553-37252-1) Bantam.
—My Mom Made Me Take Piano Lessons. LC 92-45661. (gr. 4 up). 1994. 13.95 (0-385-31091-9) Doubleday.
—The Mystery of the Haunted Cabin. O'Brien, Anne S., illus. LC 86-7723. 128p. (gr. 2-5). 1986. 13.45 (0-395-41917-4) HM.
—The New Girl at School. Hoban, Lillian, illus. LC 79-11409. (gr. k-3). 1979. 12.95 (0-525-35780-7, DCB) Dutton Child Bks.
—No Time for Christmas. Mitchell, Anastasia, illus. 48p. (gr. k-4). 1988. PLB 14.95 (0-87614-327-3) Carolrhoda Bks.
—No Time for Christmas. Mitchell, Anastasia, illus. 48p. (gr. k-4). 1989. pap. 5.95 (0-87614-503-9, First Ave Edns) Lerner Pubns.
—Peanut Butter Pilgrims. 80p. (Orig.). (gr. k-6). 1988. pap. 2.50 (0-440-40066-X, YB) Dell.
—A Pee Wee Christmas. 80p. (Orig.). (gr. k-6). 1988. pap. 2.99 (0-440-40067-8, YB) Dell.
—The Pee Wee Jubilee. (gr. k-6). 1989. pap. 2.99 (0-440-40226-3, YB) Dell.
—Pee Wee Scout Backpack, 6 vols. (gr. 4-7). 1990. pap. 15.00 (0-440-36014-5) Dell.
—Pee Wees on Parade. Tiegreen, Alan, illus. 80p. (ps-3). 1992. pap. 2.99 (0-440-40700-1, YB) Dell.
—Pee Wee's on Skis. 1993. pap. 3.25 (0-440-40885-7) Dell.
—The Perfect Christmas Gift. McCue, Lisa, illus. LC 91-6549. 32p. (gr. k-3). 1992. RSBE 13.95 (0-02-728471-9, Macmillan Child Bk) Macmillan Child Grp.
—Piles of Pets. (ps-3). 1993. pap. 3.25 (0-440-40792-3) Dell.

—The Pooped Troop. Tiegreen, Alan, illus. 80p. (ps-3). 1989. pap. 3.25 (0-440-40184-4, YB) Dell.
—Rabbit's New Rug. Brown, Marc, illus. LC 79-16639. 40p. (ps-3). 1980. 5.95 (0-8193-1009-3); PLB 5.95 (0-8193-1010-7) Parents.
—Rabbit's New Rug. Brown, Marc, illus. 48p. (ps-2). 1992. pap. 2.95 (0-448-40318-8, G&D) Putnam Pub Group.
—Rabbit's New Rug. Brown, Marc, illus. LC 93-15453. 1993. write for info. (0-8368-0972-6) Gareth Stevens Inc.
—Rosy Noses, Freezing Toes. Tiegreen, Alan, illus. (Orig.). 1990. pap. 2.99 (0-440-40384-7) Dell.
—Scary, Scary Huckleberry. Tiegreen, Alan, illus. (Orig.). (gr. k-6). 1990. pap. 2.95 (0-440-40336-7, YB) Dell.
—Sky Babies. (ps-3). 1991. pap. 2.99 (0-440-40530-0, YB) Dell.
—Sonny's Secret. (ps-3). 1991. pap. 2.99 (0-440-40429-0) Dell.
—Spring Sprouts. Tiegreen, Alan, illus. 80p. (Orig.). (gr. k-6). 1989. pap. 3.25 (0-440-40160-7, YB) Dell.
—Summer Showdown. Tiegreen, Alan, illus. (Orig.). 1990. pap. 2.95 (0-440-40307-3) Dell.
—That Mushy Stuff. (Orig.). (gr. k-6). 1989. pap. 2.99 (0-440-40176-3, YB) Dell.
—Trash Bash. (ps-3). 1992. pap. 3.25 (0-440-40592-0, YB) Dell.

Delton, Judy & Tucker, Dorothy. My Grandma's in a Nursing Home. Tucker, Kathleen, ed. Robinson, Charles, illus. LC 86-1640. 32p. (gr. 2-5). 1986. PLB 11.95 (0-8075-5333-6) A Whitman.

DeLuca, June M. The Lily Pad Four & Friends. Faycheux, Wallace P., Jr., illus. 32p. (gr. k-2). 1992. pap. 2.95 (0-8198-4431-4) St Paul Bks.

De Luca, Sam. Junior Football Playbook. LC 73-80413. (Illus.). 128p. (gr. 4-8). 1973. 5.95 (0-8246-0150-5) Jonathan David.

DeLuise, Dom. Charlie the Caterpillar. Santoro, Christopher, illus. LC 90-31557. 40p. (ps-1). 1990. pap. 13.95 jacketed (0-671-69358-1, S&S BFYR) S&S Trade.
—Charlie the Caterpillar. Santoro, Christopher, illus. LC 90-31557. 40p. (ps-1). 1993. pap. 4.95 (0-671-79607-0, S&S BFYR) S&S Trade.
—Goldilocks. LC 91-2021. (ps-3). 1992. pap. 14.00 (0-671-74690-1, S&S BFYR) S&S Trade.

Delval, Marie-Helene. The Apple-Tree Canoe. (Illus.). 48p. (gr. k-4). 1990. 12.75 (0-89565-805-4); 8.95s.p. (0-685-55095-8) Childs World.
—The Seven Witches. (Illus.). (gr. 1-8). 1992. PLB 8.95 (0-89565-897-6); Resale. 12.75 (0-685-60995-2) Childs World.

DelVecchio, Ellen, jt. auth. see Maestro, Betsy.

DelVecchio, Valentine. Cadet Gray: Your Guidebook to Military Schools, Military Colleges, & Cadet Programs. (Illus.). 212p. (Orig.). (gr. 7-12). 1990. pap. 11.95 (0-9625749-0-2) Ref Desk Bks.

Delvin, Harry, jt. auth. see Devlin, Wende.

De Lyman, Alicia G., jt. auth. see Sheldon, Dyan.

DeMaio, Toni. How to Wrestle a Summer Dream. Teasley, Jamie, ed. LC 89-51760. 238p. 1990. pap. 7.95 (1-55523-291-4) Winston-Derek.

Deman, Barry A. Van see Van Deman, Barry A. & McDonald, Ed.

Demarest, Chris. Kitman & Willy at Sea. (gr. k-3). 1991. pap. 13.95 (0-671-65696-1, S&S BFYR) S&S Trade.
—Kitman & Willy at Sea. LC 90-46837. (Illus.). 32p. (ps-1). 1993. pap. 7.95 (0-671-79849-9, S&S BYR) S&S Trade.

Demarest, Chris L. Lindbergh. Demarest, Chris L., illus. LC 92-41845. 40p. (ps-4). 1993. 15.99 (0-517-58718-1); PLB 15.99 (0-517-58719-X) Crown Bks Yng Read.
—The Lunatic Adventure of Kitman & Willy. (gr. 2). 1991. write for info. (0-663-56217-1) Silver Burdett Pr.
—Morton & Sidney. Demarest, Chris L., illus. LC 92-44153. 32p. (gr. k-2). 1993. pap. 4.95 (0-689-71740-7, Aladdin) Macmillan Child Grp.
—My Little Red Car. Demarest, Chris L., illus. 32p. (ps-1). 1992. PLB 14.95 (1-878093-86-X) Boyds Mills Pr.
—No Peas for Nellie. LC 87-14167. (Illus.). 32p. (ps-2). 1988. RSBE 13.95 (0-02-728460-3, Macmillan Child Bk) Macmillan Child Grp.
—No Peas for Nellie. Demarest, Chris L., illus. LC 90-39986. 32p. (gr. k-3). 1991. pap. 3.95 (0-689-71474-2, Aladdin) Macmillan Child Grp.

Demarest, Dorothy E. Mrs. Cooderberry's Nine Grandchildren. 1992. text ed. 8.95 (0-533-10117-4) Vantage.

De Marolles, Chantal. The Farmer's Three Sons. (Illus.). 48p. (gr. k-4). 1990. 12.75 (0-89565-816-X); 8.95s.p. (0-685-55099-0) Childs World.
—The Lonely Wolf. Schmid, Eleonore, illus. LC 86-2511. 32p. (gr. k-3). 1986. 14.95 (1-55858-073-5) North-South Bks NYC.

De Martinez, Luz M., tr. see Hooker, Irene H. & Brindle, Susan A.

De Martinez, Violeta S., tr. see Stowell, Gordon.

Demas-Bliss, C. Matthew's Meadow. Lewin, T., illus. 1992. 14.95 (0-15-200759-8, HB Juv Bks) HarBrace.

De Masco, Steve & Simmons, Alex. We Want to Win! Tiegreen, Alan, illus. LC 91-40935. 64p. (gr. 1-4). 1993. text ed. 9.59 (0-8167-3100-4); tchr's. ed. 2.50 (0-8167-3101-2) Troll Assocs.

DeMattos, Jack. Masterson & Roosevelt. Earle, James H., illus. DeArment, Robert K., photos by. LC 84-17591. (Illus.). 151p. (gr. 9 up). 1984. 18.95 (0-932702-31-7) Creative Texas.

De Maupassant, Guy. Best Short Stories of Guy de Maupassant. Canon, R. R., intro. by. (gr. 9 up). 1968. pap. 2.75 (0-8049-0161-9, CL-161) Airmont.
—The Devil. (gr. 5 up). 1992. PLB 13.95 (0-88682-504-0) Creative Ed.
—The Hand. (gr. 5 up). 1992. PLB 13.95 (0-88682-502-4) Creative Ed.
—In the Country. (gr. 5 up). 1992. PLB 13.95 (0-88682-503-2) Creative Ed.
—The Necklace. rev. ed. Weissenhorn, Mathilde, tr. from FRE. (gr. 9-12). 1989. Repr. of 1907 ed. multi-media kit 35.00 (0-685-31124-4) Balance Pub.
—The Necklace. Kelley, Gary, illus. (gr. 5 up). 1992. PLB 19.95 (0-88682-489-3) Creative Ed.
—The String. 32p. (gr. 6). 1990. PLB 13.95s.p. (0-88682-297-1) Creative Ed.
—Two Friends. Redpath, Ann, ed. Delessert, Etienne, illus. (gr. 4 up). 1985. PLB 13.95s.p. (0-88682-003-0) Creative Ed.

De Medeiros, Selene. This Is How I Love You. 67p. (gr. 9-12). 1990. pap. 6.00 perfect bdg. (0-916418-76-6) Lotus.

De Mejo, Oscar. La Bella Magellona: And the Little Cavalier. De Mejo, Oscar, illus. 32p. (gr. k-4). 1992. PLB 14.95 (0-399-22138-7, Philomel Bks) Putnam Pub Group.
—Oscar de Mejo's ABC. De Mejo, Oscar, illus. LC 91-28768. 32p. (ps up). 1992. 17.00 (0-06-020516-4); PLB 16.89 (0-06-020517-2) HarpC Child Bks.
—The Professor of Etiquette. (Illus.). 32p. (gr up). 1992. 14.95 (0-399-21866-1, Philomel Bks) Putnam Pub Group.

DeMello, Vianna F. The Pocket Dictionary. large type ed. 392p. (gr. 10 up). 1985. Repr. of 1978 ed. 95.08 (0-317-01921-X, 4-21900-00) Am Printing Hse.

De Mello Vianna, Fernando, ed. see Webster's New World Dictionaries Staff.

Demerath, N. J., 3rd see Pope, Liston.

DeMers, Ella see Stuart, Jesse.

Demers, Paul. Oliver & Ophelia: A Tale of Opossums. Delaney, Jacqueline K., illus. LC 85-6020. 20p. (Orig.). (gr. 1-6). 1986. pap. 2.95 (0-916897-04-4) Andrew Mtn Pr.

Demertzis, Strati. The Power of Modern Greek: Basic Course I. 136p. (Orig.). (gr. 7-12). 1986. pap. text ed. 11.00 (0-9618466-0-7) Expressway Pubs.
—The Power of Modern Greek: Basic Course II. 164p. (Orig.). (gr. 7-12). 1986. pap. text ed. 12.00 (0-9618466-1-5) Expressway Pubs.

Demi. The Artist & the Architect. Demi, illus. LC 90-40936. 32p. (gr. 2-5). 1991. 15.95 (0-8050-1580-9, Bks Young Read); PLB 15.89 (0-8050-1685-6) H Holt & Co.
—Chingis Khan. Demi, illus. LC 90-28807. 64p. (gr. 3-5). 1991. 19.95 (0-8050-1708-9, Bks Young Read) H Holt & Co.
—Cuddly Chick. Demi, illus. 12p. (ps). 1987. bds. 6.95 (0-448-19154-7, G&D) Putnam Pub Group.
—Demi's Count the Animals One-Two-Three. Demi, illus. LC 85-81653. 48p. (ps-2). 1986. PLB 12.95 (0-448-19081-8, G&D) Putnam Pub Group.
—Demi's Count the Animals 1 2 3. (Illus.). 48p. 1990. pap. 5.95 (0-448-19166-0, G&D) Putnam Pub Group.
—Demi's Dozen Dinos. (gr. 4 up). 1994. write for info. (0-8050-2783-1) H Holt & Co.
—Demi's Dozen Farm Friends, 12 bks. Demi, illus. (ps-2). 1991. Set. 9.95 (0-8050-1956-1, Bks Young Read) H Holt & Co.
—Demi's Dozen Good Eggs, 12 bks. (Illus.). 1993. Set, 12p. per bk. boxed 9.95 (0-8050-2552-9) H Holt & Co.
—Demi's Dozen Winter. 1992. 9.95 (0-8050-2202-3) H Holt & Co.
—Demi's Dozen X-Mas. 1994. pap. write for info. (0-8050-3245-2) H Holt & Co.
—Demi's Dragons & Fantastic Creatures. Demi, illus. 50p. (ps-2). 1993. PLB 19.95 (0-8050-2564-2, Bks Young Read) H Holt & Co.
—Demi's Find the Animal A B C. (Illus.). 48p. 1990. pap. 5.95 (0-448-19165-2, G&D) Putnam Pub Group.
—Demi's Find the Animal ABC. Demi, illus. LC 85-70285. 48p. (ps up). 1985. 12.95 (0-448-18970-4, G&D) Putnam Pub Group.
—Demi's Opposites: An Animal Game Book. Demi, illus. (ps-2). 1990. 10.95 (0-448-18995-X, G&D) Putnam Pub Group.
—Downy Duckling. Demi, illus. 12p. (ps). 1987. bds. 6.95 (0-448-19153-9, G&D) Putnam Pub Group.
—Dragon Kites & Dragonflies: A Collection of Chinese Nursery Rhymes. LC 86-7637. (Illus.). 32p. (ps-3). 1986. 14.95 (0-15-224199-X, HB Juv Bks) HarBrace.
—The Empty Pot. Demi, illus. LC 89-39062. 32p. (ps-2). 1990. 15.95 (0-8050-1217-6, Bks Young Read) H Holt & Co.
—Find Demi's Baby Animals. Demi, illus. LC 89-82234. (Illus.). 48p. 1990. 13.95 (0-448-19169-5, G&D) Putnam Pub Group.
—Find Demi's Dinosaurs: An Animal Game Book. Demi, illus. 50p. (ps-3). 1989. 15.95 (0-448-19020-6, G&D) Putnam Pub Group.
—Find Demi's Sea Creatures. Demi, illus. 1991. 14.95 (0-399-22112-3) Putnam Pub Group.
—The Firebird. 1994. write for info. (0-8050-3244-4) H Holt & Co.

—Fleecy Lamb. Demi, illus. 12p. (gr. 4 up). 1987. 6.95 (0-448-19152-0, G&D) Putnam Pub Group.
—Liang & the Magic Paintbrush. Demi, illus. LC 80-11351. 32p. (ps-2). 1988. pap. 5.95 (0-8050-0801-2, Bks Young Read) H Holt & Co.
—Little Baby Lamb. Demi, illus. 12p. (ps). 1993. bds. 3.95 (0-448-40580-6, G&D) Putnam Pub Group.
—Little Bitty Bunny. Demi, illus. LC 90-85828. 12p. (ps). 1992. 3.95 (0-448-41089-3, G&D) Putnam Pub Group.
—Little Chick Chick. Demi, illus. LC 90-85829. 12p. (ps). 1992. 3.95 (0-448-41090-7, G&D) Putnam Pub Group.
—Little Lucky Ducky. Demi, illus. 12p. (ps). 1993. bds. 3.95 (0-448-40581-4, G&D) Putnam Pub Group.
—The Magic Boat. Demi, illus. LC 90-4425. 32p. (ps-2). 1990. 15.95 (0-8050-1141-2, Bks Young Read) H Holt & Co.
—Sequel to Empty Pot. 1994. write for info. (0-8050-3243-6) H Holt & Co.
—So Soft Kitty. Demi, illus. 12p. (ps). 1986. pap. 6.95 (0-448-18986-0, G&D) Putnam Pub Group.
—Watch Harry Grow! Demi, illus. LC 84-60109. 26p. (ps-1). 1984. bds. 3.50 (0-394-86857-9) Random Bks Yng Read.
—Where Is Willie Worm? Demi, illus. LC 80-53680. 24p. (ps-1). 1981. 3.95 (0-394-84759-8) Random Bks Yng Read.

Demi, compiled by. & illus. Demi's Secret Garden. LC 92-27204. 50p. (ps-2). 1993. PLB 19.95 (0-8050-2553-7, Bks Young Read) H Holt & Co.

Demi, selected by. & illus. In the Eyes of the Cat. Tze-Si Huang, tr. from JPN. LC 91-27729. 80p. (gr. 1-3). 1992. 15.95 (0-8050-1955-3, Bks Young Read) H Holt & Co.

Demi, retold by. & illus. The Magic Tapestry: A Chinese Folktale. LC 93-11426. 1994. write for info. (0-8050-2810-2) H Holt & Co.

Demi, illus. A Chinese Zoo: Fables & Proverbs. LC 86-33562. 32p. (ps-3). 1987. 14.95 (0-15-217510-5, HB Juv Bks) HarBrace.

Deming, A. G. Who Is Tapping at My Window? Wellington, Monica, illus. 24p. (ps). 1994. pap. 4.99 (0-14-054553-0, Puffin Unicorn) Puffin Bks.
—Who Is Tapping at My Window? Wellington, Monica, illus. 24p. (ps). 1994. pap. 17.99 giant format (0-14-050303-X) Puffin Bks.

Deming, Susan. The Desert: A Nature Panorama. Deming, Susan, illus. 7p. (ps-3). 1991. bds. 5.95 (0-8118-0291-4) Chronicle Bks.
—The Forest: A Nature Panorama Board Book. (Illus.). (ps-3). 1991. bds. 5.95 (0-87701-815-4) Chronicle Bks.
—The Ocean: A Nature Panorama. Deming, Susan, illus. 7p. (ps-3). 1992. bds. 5.95 (0-8118-0158-6) Chronicle Bks.
—The River: A Nature Panorama. Deming, Susan, illus. 7p. (ps-3). 1991. bds. 5.95 (0-87701-812-X) Chronicle Bks.

DeMoor, Robert. Quest of Faith. 149p. (Orig.). (gr. 9 up). 1989. pap. text ed. 5.75 (0-930265-74-2) CRC Pubns.

Demos, John. The Tried & True: Native American Women Confronting Colonization. (Illus.). 144p. 1994. 20.00 (0-19-508142-0) OUP.

Demou, Doris B. More to Give. Meredith, Mary, ed. (Orig.). 1991. pap. 6.00 (0-685-40721-7) Doris Demou.
—A Part of Myself: I Give to You. 2nd, rev. ed. Meredith, Mary, ed. (Illus.). (gr. 6 up). 1990. pap. text ed. 6.00 (0-9604794-0-6); tchr's. ed. 8.00 (0-9604794-1-4) Doris Demou.

Dempsey, Michael. Student Atlas. Miles, John C. & Novis, Constance, eds. LC 90-675152. (Illus.). 128p. (gr. 3-7). 1991. lib. bdg. 14.89 (0-8167-2253-6); pap. 9.95 (0-8167-2254-4) Troll Assocs.

Dempsey, Michael, ed. Growing up with Science: The Illustrated Encyclopedia of Invention, 26 vols. rev. ed. LC 82-63047. (Illus.). (gr. 5-10). 1987. Set. 181.48 (0-87475-841-6) Stuttman.
—Growing up with Science: The Illustrated Encyclopedia of Invention. (Illus.). 2496p. (gr. 3-10). 1990. 239.95 (0-87475-839-4) Marshall Cavendish.

Dempsey, Michael W. Children's First Geography Encyclopedia. 1985. 6.98 (0-671-07746-5) S&S Trade.
—Children's First Science Encyclopedia. 1987. 6.98 (0-671-07745-7) S&S Trade.

Dempsey, Michael W. & Lye, Keith. Student Encyclopedia. LC 90-11116. (Illus.). 128p. (gr. 3-7). 1991. lib. bdg. 14.89 (0-8167-2257-9); pap. text ed. 9.95 (0-8167-2258-7) Troll Assocs.

Dempsey, Walter. Children's First Encyclopedia. 1985. 6.98 (0-671-07744-9) S&S Trade.

Demsky, Andrew. Five Hundred Degrees in the Shade: Every Teen Feels the Heat. LC 93-15564. 1993. write for info. (0-8163-1162-5) Pacific Pr Pub Assn.

De Muth, Jillian. Blue Skies, Green Days. Gamble, Kim, illus. 48p. (gr. 1-6). 1993. 16.95 (1-86373-062-1, Pub. by Allen & Unwin Aust Pty AT) IPG Chicago.

Demuth, Patricia. Inside Your Busy Body. Billin-Frye, Paige, illus. LC 92-44173. 32p. (ps-3). 1993. pap. 2.25 (0-448-40189-4, G&D) Putnam Pub Group.

Demuth, Patricia B. Ants. Schnidler, S. D., illus. LC 93-1769. 1994. text ed. 14.95 (0-02-728467-0) Macmillan.
—Cradles in the Trees: The Story of Bird Nests. Barnes, Susan, ed. LC 93-9114. (Illus.). write for info. (0-02-728466-2) Macmillan Child Grp.

—Max, the Bad-Talking Parrot. Zaunders, Bo, illus. LC 89-26015. 32p. (gr. k-4). 1990. 12.95 (0-525-44613-3, DCB); pap. 3.95 (0-525-44595-1, DCB) Dutton Child Bks.
—Ornery Morning. Brown, Craig M., illus. LC 90-40188. 24p. (ps-1). 1991. 13.95 (0-525-44688-5, DCB) Dutton Child Bks.
—Pick up Your Ears, Henry. Barner, Bob, illus. LC 91-27162. 32p. (ps-1). 1992. RSBE 13.95 (0-02-728465-4, Macmillan Child Bk) Macmillan Child Grp.

Denan, Corinne. Dragon & Monster Tales. new ed. LC 79-66329. (Illus.). 48p. (gr. 3-6). 1980. PLB 9.89 (0-89375-326-2); pap. 2.95 (0-89375-325-4) Troll Assocs.
—Giant Tales. LC 79-66330. (Illus.). 48p. (gr. 3-6). 1980. lib. bdg. 9.89 (0-89375-328-9); pap. 2.95 (0-89375-327-0) Troll Assocs.
—Goblin Tales. LC 79-66326. (Illus.). 48p. (gr. 3-6). 1980. lib. bdg. 9.89 (0-89375-320-3); pap. 2.95 (0-89375-319-X) Troll Assocs.
—Hair-Raising Tales. LC 79-66334. (Illus.). 48p. (gr. 5-7). 1980. PLB 9.89 (0-89375-334-3); pap. 2.95 (0-89375-333-5) Troll Assocs.
—Haunted House Tales. Toulmin-Rothe, Ann, illus. LC 79-66335. 48p. (gr. 5-7). 1980. PLB 9.89 (0-89375-336-X); pap. text ed. 2.95 (0-89375-335-1); cassette avail. Troll Assocs.
—Once upon a Time Tales. LC 79-66337. (Illus.). 48p. (gr. 2-6). 1980. lib. bdg. 9.89 (0-89375-340-8); pap. 2.95 (0-89375-339-4) Troll Assocs.
—Strange & Eerie Tales. new ed. LC 79-66336. (Illus.). 48p. (gr. 4-6). 1980. lib. bdg. 9.89 (0-89375-338-6); pap. 2.95 (0-89375-337-8) Troll Assocs.
—Tales of Magic & Spells. Watling, James, illus. LC 79-66325. 48p. (gr. 3-6). 1980. PLB 9.89 (0-89375-318-1); pap. text ed. 2.95 (0-89375-317-3); cassette avail. Troll Assocs.
—Tales of the Ugly Ogres. Craft, Kinuko Y., illus. LC 79-66333. 48p. (gr. 3-6). 1980. PLB 9.89 (0-89375-332-7); pap. text ed. 2.95 (0-89375-331-9) Troll Assocs.
—Troll Tales. new ed. LC 79-66327. (Illus.). 48p. (gr. 3-6). 1980. lib. bdg. 9.89 (0-89375-322-X); pap. 2.95 (0-89375-321-1); cassette avail. Troll Assocs.
—Witch Tales. new ed. LC 79-66328. (Illus.). 48p. (gr. 3-6). 1980. lib. bdg. 9.89 (0-89375-324-6); pap. 2.95 (0-89375-323-8) Troll Assocs.
—Wizard Tales. new ed. LC 79-66331. (Illus.). 48p. (gr. 3-6). 1980. lib. bdg. 9.89 (0-89375-330-0); pap. 2.95 (0-89375-329-7) Troll Assocs.

Denan, Jay. Burnout: Funny Car Races. LC 79-64700. (Illus.). 32p. (gr. 4-9). 1980. PLB 10.79 (0-89375-256-8); pap. 2.95 (0-89375-257-6) Troll Assocs.
—The Glory Ride, Road Racing. LC 79-52179. (Illus.). 32p. (gr. 4-9). 1980. PLB 10.79 (0-89375-254-1); pap. 2.95 (0-89375-255-X) Troll Assocs.
—Hot on Wheels: The Rally Scene. LC 79-64701. (Illus.). 32p. (gr. 4-9). 1980. PLB 10.79 (0-89375-258-4) Troll Assocs.
—Start Your Engines: Racing the Championship Trail. LC 79-64702. (Illus.). 32p. (gr. 4-9). 1980. PLB 10.79 (0-89375-260-6); pap. 2.95 (0-89375-261-4) Troll Assocs.

DenBoer, Helen. Please Don't Cry, Mom. Goldstein, Janice G., illus. LC 93-14699. 1993. 13.50 (0-87614-805-4) Carolrhoda Bks.

Deneberg, Barry. The True Story of J. Edgar Hoover & The F.B.I. LC 91-8021. 208p. (gr. 5 up). 1993. 13.95 (0-590-43168-4) Scholastic Inc.

DeNee, JoAnne & Hand, Julia. Exploring the Secrets of the Meadow-Thicket. Peduzzi, Carolyn, illus. 275p. (Orig.). (gr. 1-4). 1993. page. write for info. (1-884430-02-3) Food Works.

Denenberg, Barry. John Fitzgerald Kennedy: America's 35th President. 128p. (gr. 5-8). 1988. pap. 2.95 (0-590-41344-9) Scholastic Inc.
—Nelson Mandela. (gr. 4-7). 1991. pap. 2.95 (0-590-44154-X) Scholastic Inc.
—Nelson Mandela: "No Easy Walk to Freedom" 160p. (gr. 3-9). 1991. 12.95 (0-590-44163-9, Scholastic Hardcover) Scholastic Inc.
—Stealing Home Story of Jackie. (gr. 5-7). 1990. pap. 2.95 (0-590-42560-9) Scholastic Inc.
—The Story of Muhammad Ali, Heavyweight Champion of the World. (Illus.). 96p. (gr. 3-5). 1990. pap. 3.25 (0-440-40259-X, YB) Dell.

Denend, G. Van see Van Denend, G.
Denend, G. Van see Van Denend, G. & Vreeman, J.

Dengler, Sandra. Code of Honor. LC 88-18729. 272p. (Orig.). (gr. 11-12). 1988. pap. 7.99 (0-87123-994-9) Bethany Hse.

Dengler, Sandy. Fanny Crosby: Writer of Eight Thousand Songs. (Orig.). (gr. 2-7). 1985. pap. 4.50 (0-8024-2529-1) Moody.
—John Bunyan: Writer of Pilgrim's Progress. (Orig.). (gr. 2-7). 1986. pap. text ed. 4.50 (0-8024-4352-4) Moody.
—Smokey, a Simple Country Bear Who Made Good. Dengler, Sandy, illus. 31p. (gr. 3-5). 1987. pap. text ed. 3.00 (0-914019-15-5) NW Interpretive.
—Susanna Wesley. Date not set. pap. text ed. 4.99 (0-8024-8414-X) Moody.

Denholtz, Roni S. The Day the T. V. Broke. Fontalvo, Nelsy, illus. LC 86-81371. 32p. (gr. k-2). 1986. PLB 7.59 (0-87386-016-0); pap. 1.95 (0-87386-012-8) Jan Prods.

—The Ghost in the New House. Fontalvo, Nelsy, illus. LC 86-81369. 32p. (gr. k-2). 1986. PLB 7.59 (0-87386-017-9); pap. 1.95 (0-87386-013-6) Jan Prods.

Denim, Sue. The Dumb Bunnies. Pilkey, Dav, illus. LC 93-2255. 32p. (ps-3). 1994. 12.95 (0-590-47708-0, Blue Sky Press) Scholastic Inc.

De Ninojosa, Ida N., tr. see Georgiady, Nicholas P. & Romano, Louis G.

Denis-Huot, Christine & Denis-Huot, Michel. The Elephant. (Illus.). 28p. (gr. 3-8). 1992. pap. 6.95 (0-88106-427-0) Charlesbridge Pub.
—The Giraffe. 28p. (ps-3). 1993. pap. 6.95 (0-88106-431-9) Charlesbridge Pub.

Denis-Huot, Michel, jt. auth. see Denis-Huot, Christine.

Denman, Cherry. The Little Peacock's Gift: A Folk Tale from China. Denman, Cherry, illus. LC 87-17504. 32p. (gr. k-3). 1988. PLB 14.95 (0-87226-175-1, Bedrick Blackie) P Bedrick Bks.

Denn, Jon. Rack 'em Daddy! By the Pied Piper of Pool. Denn, et al, illus. LC 92-73955. 128p. (Orig.). (gr. 3). 1992. pap. 13.95 (0-9634187-5-0) Colburn Pr.

Dennard, Deborah. Can Elephants Drink Through Their Noses? The Strange Things People Say about Animals at the Zoo. Boles, Terry, illus. LC 92-9956. 1992. 19.95 (0-87614-720-1) Carolrhoda Bks.
—Do Cats Have Nine Lives? The Strange Things People Say about Animals Around the House. Urbanovic, Jackie, illus. LC 92-10353. 1992. 19.95 (0-87614-773-2) Carolrhoda Bks.
—How Wise Is an Owl? The Strange Things People Say about Animals in the Woods. Neavill, Michelle, illus. LC 92-10354. 1992. 19.95 (0-87614-721-X) Carolrhoda Bks.

Dennee, JoAnne. Exploring the Forest with Grandforest Tree. Peduzzi, Carolyn, illus. 275p. (gr. 1-4). 1993. pap. write for info. (1-884430-03-1) Food Works.
—In the Three Sisters Garden. 350p. (gr. 1-2). 1994. pap. write for info. (1-884430-01-5) Food Works.

Denner, Patricia. Language Through Play. LC 72-84851. (Illus.). (ps-1). 1969. pap. 8.95 (0-405-00118-5) Ayer.

Denney, Robert. Civil War Years: A Daily Account of the Life of a Nation. Urwin, Gregory J., frwd. by. LC 92-28956. (Illus.). 608p. (gr. 10-12). 1992. 24.95 (0-8069-8519-4) Sterling.

Dennie, Joseph & Weathers, Joseph. Smarty's New Friend. Bonnette, Charlotte A., ed. Williams, Vanessa R. & Washington, Mariama K., illus. 22p. (Orig.). (gr. k-3). 1993. pap. 6.95 (1-877971-11-1) Mid Atl Reg Pr.

Dennis, Anne T. Marshall Yesterday: An Adventure Back in Time for Children & Adults. 36p. (gr. 4 up). 1991. pap. 5.00 (1-879703-00-9) Marshall Regnl Arts.

Dennis, J. Richard. Fractions Are Parts of Things. LC 73-127603. (Illus.). 40p. (gr. 2-4). 1972. PLB 12.89 (0-690-31521-X, Crowell Jr Bks) HarpC Child Bks.

Dennis, John J. The Boy Who Could Not Fly. 64p. (gr. 4-8). pap. 7.95 (0-9629036-0-4) Grow Up Hlthy.

Dennis, Martin C. Will Arnold See Christmas? 1993. 7.95 (0-533-10404-1) Vantage.

Dennis, Wesley. Flip. Dennis, Wesley, illus. (ps-1). 1977. pap. 3.95 (0-14-050203-3, Puffin) Puffin Bks.
—Flip & the Cows. LC 88-39705. (Illus.). 64p. (ps-2). 1989. Repr. of 1942 ed. lib. bdg. 16.00 (0-208-02240-6, Linnet) Shoe String.
—Flip & the Morning. Dennis, Wesley, illus. LC 51-13521. (ps-1). 1977. pap. 3.95 (0-14-050204-1, Puffin) Puffin Bks.

Dennison, George. And Then a Harvest Feast. (gr. 4-7). 1992. pap. 4.50 (0-374-40377-5) FS&G.

Denny, Don. Kid Valley. LC 90-72113. 165p. (gr. 5 up). 1991. 8.95 (1-55523-423-2) Winston-Derek.

Denny, Kevin M. A Teenager's Guide How to Manipulate Your Way to Happiness: Thirty-Seven Easy Steps in the Care & Feeding of Your Parents. Winton, Andrea, illus. LC 92-81556. 240p. (Orig.). (gr. 8-12). 1992. pap. 13.95 (0-9633108-0-1) Warthog Pub.

Denny, Roz. A Taste of France. (Illus.). 48p. (gr. 3-5). 1994. 14.95 (1-56847-163-7) Thomson Lrning.
—A Taste of India. (Illus.). 48p. (gr. 3-5). 1994. 14.95 (1-56847-164-5) Thomson Lrning.
—Thirty-Six Strange Little Animals Waiting to Eat: With Simple Little Recipes to Make. Percy, Graham, illus. LC 92-358. 32p. (Illus.). 1992. 12.95 (1-55670-272-8) Stewart Tabori & Chang.

Denslow, Sharon P. At Taylor's Place. Carpenter, Nancy, illus. LC 89-23898. 32p. (ps-2). 1990. RSBE 13.95 (0-02-728685-1, Bradbury Pr) Macmillan Child Grp.
—Bus Riders. Carpenter, Nancy, illus. LC 92-14109. 32p. (ps-2). 1993. RSBE 14.95 (0-02-728682-7, Four Winds) Macmillan Child Grp.
—Hazel's Circle. McGinley-Nally, Sharon, illus. LC 91-18182. 32p. (ps-3). 1992. RSBE 14.95 (0-02-728683-5, Four Winds) Macmillan Child Grp.
—Night Owls. Kastner, Jill, illus. LC 89-33937. 32p. (ps-2). 1990. RSBE 12.95 (0-02-728681-9, Bradbury Pr) Macmillan Child Grp.
—Radio Boy. Gillman, Alec, photos by. LC 93-36281. 1994. write for info. (0-02-728684-3, Four Winds) Macmillan Child Grp.
—Riding with Aunt Lucy. Carpenter, Nancy, illus. LC 90-37803. 32p. (ps-2). 1991. RSBE 13.95 (0-02-728686-X, Bradbury Pr) Macmillan Child Grp.

Denslow, W. W., illus. Denslow's Picture Book Treasury. 80p. (ps-2). 1990. 17.95 (1-55970-071-8) Arcade Pub Inc.

Denson, Wil. Artie. (Illus.). 32p. (Orig.). (gr. 7-12). 1988. pap. 3.50 (0-88680-292-X); royalty on application 40.00 (0-685-58400-3) I E Clark.
—Welcome to Carnie. (Illus., Orig.). (gr. 7-12). 1989. pap. 3.75 (0-88680-315-2); royalty on application 50.00 (0-685-58564-6) I E Clark.

Denson, Wil & Cunningham, Michael. Aladdin McFaddin. (Illus.). 44p. (gr. 2 up). 1977. pap. 3.50 (0-88680-004-8); royalty on application 60.00 (0-317-03621-1); Piano-Vocal Score 7.50 (0-88680-005-6) I E Clark.

Dent, Anne, jt. auth. see Ceccerallo, Julius.

Dent, Tom. Blue Lights & River Songs. Ward, Jerry, intro. by. LC 81-82659. 75p. (gr. 9-12). 1982. pap. 4.50x perfect bd. (0-916418-31-6) Lotus.

Dentemaro, Christine & Kranz, Rachel. Straight Talk about Student Life. Ryan, Elizabeth A., ed. 128p. (gr. 9-12). Date not set. 16.95x (0-685-63076-5) Facts on File.
—Straight Talk about Surviving in School. LC 92-31488. 1993. write for info. (0-8160-2735-8) Facts on File.

Denton, Kady M. Christmas Boot. (ps). 1990. 12.95 (0-316-18091-2) Little.
—Granny Is a Darling. LC 87-22635. (Illus.). 32p. (ps-3). 1988. SBE 13.95 (0-689-50452-7, M K McElderry) Macmillan Child Grp.
—Granny Is a Darling. Denton, Kady M., illus. LC 89-18397. 32p. (ps-2). 1990. pap. 4.95 (0-689-71207-3, Aladdin) Macmillan Child Grp.
—Janet's Horses. Denton, Kady M., illus. 32p. (ps-2). 1991. 12.70 (0-395-51601-3, Clarion Bks) HM.

Denton, Terry. Home Is the Sailor. Denton, Terry, illus. 32p. (gr. k-3). 1989. 13.45 (0-395-51525-4) HM.
—The School for Laughter. Denton, Terry, illus. 32p. (gr. k-3). 1990. 13.45 (0-395-53353-8) HM.

DeNure, Dennis. The Age of the Video Athlete. (Illus.). 1984. write for info. (0-915659-00-X) Video Athlete.

Denzel, Justin. Boy of the Painted Cave. 160p. (gr. 3-7). 1988. 14.95 (0-399-21559-X, Philomel Bks) Putnam Pub Group.
—Hunt for the Last Cat. (gr. 5 up). 1991. 14.95 (0-399-22101-8, Philomel) Putnam Pub Group.
—Land of the Thundering Herds. Watkinson, Brent, illus. LC 92-26222. 176p. (gr. 5 up). 1993. 14.95 (0-399-21894-7, Philomel Bks) Putnam Pub Group.

Denzer, Ron. Anti-Helicopter Warfare Manual. (Illus.). 60p. (Orig.). 1985. pap. text ed. 8.95 (0-9616331-0-7) Ron Denzer.

DeOld, Alan R. & Judge, Joseph W. Space Travel: A Technological Frontier. (Illus.). 144p. (Orig.). (gr. 7-12). 1990. pap. text ed. 13.81 (0-87192-206-1) Delmar.

De Paola, Tomie. Andy: That's My Name. 32p. (ps-2). 1991. 10.95 (0-13-036731-1, S&S BFYR); pap. 6.00 (0-671-66465-4, S&S BFYR) S&S Trade.
—The Art Lesson. De Paola, Tomie, illus. 32p. (ps-3). 1989. 13.95 (0-399-21688-X, Putnam) Putnam Pub Group.
—Baby's First Christmas. (Illus.). 12p. (ps). 1988. bds. 4.95 (0-399-21591-3, Putnam) Putnam Pub Group.
—Big Anthony & the Magic Ring. De Paola, Tomie, illus. LC 78-23631. 32p. (gr. k up). 1979. 14.95 (0-15-207124-5); pap. 4.95 (0-15-611907-2) HarBrace.
—Bill & Pete. De Paola, Tomie, illus. LC 78-5330. (gr. k-2). 1978. 14.95 (0-399-20646-9, Putnam); pap. 5.95 (0-399-20650-7, Putnam) Putnam Pub Group.
—Bill & Pete. (ps-1). 1992. pap. 5.95 (0-399-22402-5, Sandcastle Bks) Putnam Pub Group.
—Bill & Pete Go Down the Nile. De Paola, Tomie, illus. 32p. (ps-1). 1987. 14.95 (0-399-21395-3, Putnam) Putnam Pub Group.
—Bill & Pete Go down the Nile. (Illus.). 32p. (ps-3). 1990. pap. 5.95 (0-399-22003-8, Sandcastle Bks) Putnam Pub Group.
—Charlie Needs a Cloak. LC 73-16365. (Illus.). 32p. (gr. k-4). 1982. pap. 14.00 (0-671-66466-2, S&S BFYR); pap. 5.95 (0-671-66467-0, S&S BFYR) S&S Trade.
—The Cloud Book. De Paola, Tomie, illus. LC 74-34493. 32p. (ps-3). 1975. reinforced bdg. 14.95 (0-8234-0259-2); pap. 5.95 (0-8234-0531-1) Holiday.
—The Clown of God. De Paola, Tomie, illus. LC 78-3845. (gr. k up). 1978. 13.95 (0-15-219175-5, HB Juv Bks) HarBrace.
—The Clown of God. De Paola, Tomie, illus. LC 78-3845. 45p. (gr. k up). 1978. pap. 5.95 (0-15-618192-4, Voyager Bks) HarBrace.
—The Comic Adventures of Old Mother Hubbard & Her Dog. LC 80-19270. (Illus.). 32p. (ps-3). 1981. 13.95 (0-15-219541-6, HB Juv Bks); pap. 3.95 (0-15-219542-4, PL) HarBrace.
—An Early American Christmas. De Paola, Tomie, illus. LC 86-3102. 32p. (ps-3). 1987. reinforced bdg. 15.95 (0-8234-0617-2); pap. 5.95 (0-8234-0979-1) Holiday.
—The Family Christmas Tree Book. LC 80-12081. (Illus.). 32p. (ps-3). 1980. reinforced bdg. 14.95 (0-8234-0416-1); pap. 5.95 (0-8234-0535-4) Holiday.
—Fin M'Coul, the Giant of Knockmany Hill. LC 80-2254. (Illus.). 32p. (ps-3). 1981. reinforced bdg. 15.95 (0-8234-0384-X); pap. 5.95 (0-8234-0385-8) Holiday.
—The First Christmas. (Illus.). 6p. (ps-1). 1984. 16.95 (0-399-21070-9, Putnam) Putnam Pub Group.
—Four Stories for Four Seasons. De Paola, Tomie, illus. LC 76-8837. (ps-3). 1977. PLB 9.95 o. p. (0-13-330175-3, Pub. by Treehouse); pap. 3.95 (0-13-330100-1) P-H.
—Four Stories for Four Seasons. LC 76-8837. (Illus.). 48p. (gr. 5 up). 1987. 12.95 (0-13-330119-2) P-H.

—Four Stories for Four Seasons. LC 76-8837. (Illus.). 48p. (ps-2). 1987. pap. 15.00 jacketed (0-671-66686-X, Little Simon) S&S Trade.
—Four Stories for Four Seasons. (ps-3). 1994. pap. 5.95 (0-671-88633-9, Half Moon Bks) S&S Trade.
—Francis: The Poor Man of Assisi. De Paola, Tomie, illus. LC 81-6984. 48p. (ps-3). 1982. reinforced bdg. 16.95 (0-8234-0435-8); pap. 6.95 (0-8234-0812-4) Holiday.
—The Friendly Beasts: An Old English Christmas Carol. De Paola, Tomie, illus. 32p. (ps-2). 1981. (Putnam); pap. 7.95 (0-399-20777-5, Putnam) Putnam Pub Group.
—Haircuts for the Woolseys. De Paola, Tomie, illus. 24p. (ps-1). 1989. 5.95 (0-399-21662-6, Putnam) Putnam Pub Group.
—Helga's Dowry. De Paola, Tomie, illus. LC 76-54953. 32p. (gr. k-3). 1977. 15.95 (0-15-233701-6, HB Juv Bks) HarBrace.
—Helga's Dowry. De Paola, Tomie, illus. LC 76-54953. 32p. (gr. k-3). 1977. pap. 4.95 (0-15-640010-3, Voyager Bks) HarBrace.
—The Hunter & the Animals: A Wordless Picture Book. LC 81-2875. (Illus.). 32p. (ps-3). 1981. reinforced bdg. 15.95 (0-8234-0397-1); pap. 5.95 (0-8234-0428-5) Holiday.
—Jamie O'Rourke & the Big Potato: An Irish Folktale. 32p. (ps-3). 1992. 14.95 (0-399-22257-X, Whitebird Bks) Putnam Pub Group.
—Jingle the Christmas Clown. (Illus.). 40p. (ps-3). 1992. 15.95 (0-399-22338-X, Putnam) Putnam Pub Group.
—The Kids' Cat Book. LC 79-2090. (Illus.). 32p. (ps-3). 1979. reinforced bdg. 14.95 (0-8234-0365-3); pap. 5.95 (0-8234-0534-6) Holiday.
—The Knight & the Dragon. (Illus.). 32p. (gr. k-2). 1980. 14.95 (0-399-20707-4, Sandcastle Bks); pap. 6.95 (0-399-20708-2, Sandcastle Bks) Putnam Pub Group.
—The Knight & the Dragon. (Illus.). (ps-k). 1992. pap. 6.95 (0-399-22401-7, Sandcastle Bks) Putnam Pub Group.
—The Lady of Guadalupe. De Paola, Tomie, illus. LC 79-19610. 48p. (ps-4). 1980. reinforced bdg. 16.95 (0-8234-0373-4); pap. 6.95 (0-8234-0403-X) Holiday.
—The Legend of Old Befana. De Paola, Tomie, illus. LC 80-12293. 32p. (gr. 1-5). 1980. 14.95 (0-15-243816-5, HB Juv Bks) HarBrace.
—The Legend of Old Befana. De Paola, Tomie, illus. LC 80-12293. 32p. (gr. 1-5). 1980. pap. 3.95 (0-15-243817-3, Voyager Bks) HarBrace.
—Legend of the Bluebonnet. (SPA., Illus.). 32p. (ps-3). 1993. pap. 6.95 (0-399-22441-6, Putnam) Putnam Pub Group.
—The Legend of the Indian Paintbrush. (Illus.). 32p. (ps-3). 1991. pap. 5.95 (0-399-21777-0, Sandcastle Bks) Putnam Pub Group.
—The Legend of the Persian Carpet. Ewart, Claire, illus. 32p. (ps-3). 1993. 14.95 (0-399-22415-7, Putnam-Whitebird) Putnam Pub Group.
—The Legend of the Poinsettia. LC 92-20459. 1993. write for info. (0-399-21692-8, Putnam) Putnam Pub Group.
—La Leyenda Del Pincel Indio: The Legend of the Indian Paintbrush. DePaola, Tomie, illus. 32p. (ps-3). 1993. pap. 5.95 (0-399-22604-4, Putnam) Putnam Pub Group.
—El Libro de las Arenas Movedizas. (ps-3). 1993. 14.95 (0-8234-1056-0); pap. 5.95 (0-8234-1057-9) Holiday.
—El Libro de las Nubes. (ps-3). 1993. 14.95 (0-8234-1054-4); pap. 5.95 (0-8234-1055-2) Holiday.
—El Libro de las Palomitas de Maiz. (ps-3). 1993. 14.95 (0-8234-1058-7); pap. 5.95 (0-8234-1059-5) Holiday.
—Little Grunt & the Big Egg. DePaola, Tomie, illus. (ps-3). 1993. pap. 5.95 (0-8234-1027-7) Holiday.
—Little Grunt & the Big Egg: A Prehistoric Fairy Tale. De Paola, Tomie, illus. LC 88-17009. 32p. (ps-3). 1990. reinforced bdg. 14.95 (0-8234-0730-6) Holiday.
—Marianna May & Nursey. De Paola, Tomie, illus. LC 82-9364. 32p. (ps-3). 1983. reinforced bdg. 14.95 (0-8234-0473-0); pap. 5.95 (0-8234-0623-7) Holiday.
—Merry Christmas, Strega Nona. De Paola, Tomie, illus. LC 86-4639. 32p. (ps-3). 1986. 14.95 (0-15-253183-1, HB Juv Bks) HarBrace.
—Merry Christmas, Strega Nona. (ps-3). 1991. pap. 4.95 (0-15-253184-X, HB Juv Bks) HarBrace.
—Michael Bird-Boy. De Paola, Tomie, illus. LC 74-23563. 32p. (gr. 4 up). 1987. 12.95 (0-317-63504-2) P-H.
—Michael Bird Boy. LC 74-23563. (Illus.). 32p. (gr. k-4). 1987. 12.95 jacketed (0-671-66468-9, S&S BFYR); pap. 5.95 (0-671-66469-7, S&S BFYR) S&S Trade.
—Michael Bird-Boy. (gr. 2). 1990. pap. write for info. (0-663-56216-3) Silver Burdett Pr.
—The Miracles of Jesus. De Paola, Tomie, illus. LC 86-18297. 32p. (gr. k-4). 1987. reinforced bdg. 15.95 (0-8234-0635-0) Holiday.
—My First Chanukah. De Paola, Tomie, illus. 12p. (ps-k). 1989. 5.95 (0-399-21780-0, Putnam) Putnam Pub Group.
—My First Easter. (Illus.). 12p. 1991. 5.95 (0-399-21783-5, Putnam) Putnam Pub Group.
—My First Halloween. LC 90-62401. 12p. 1991. 5.95 (0-399-21785-1, Putnam) Putnam Pub Group.
—My First Passover. (Illus.). 12p. 1991. 5.95 (0-399-21784-3, Putnam) Putnam Pub Group.
—My First Thanksgiving. (Illus.). 12p. (ps). 1992. 5.95 (0-399-22327-4, Putnam) Putnam Pub Group.

—The Mysterious Giant of Barletta. De Paola, Tomie, illus. LC 83-18445. 32p. (ps-3). 1988. pap. 3.95 (0-15-256349-0, Voyager Bks) HarBrace.
—Nana Upstairs & Nana Downstairs. (Illus.). (gr. 1-3). 1978. pap. 4.99 (0-14-050290-4, Puffin) Puffin Bks.
—Nana Upstairs & Nana Downstairs. De Paola, Tomie, illus. 32p. (ps-3). 1973. 13.95 (0-399-21417-8, Putnam) Putnam Pub Group.
—Noah & the Ark. De Paola, Tomie, illus. 40p. (Orig.). (ps-4). 1985. pap. 5.95 (0-685-07222-3) Harper SF.
—Now One Foot, Now the Other. De Paola, Tomie, illus. 48p. (gr. 3-7). 1981. 13.95 (0-399-20774-0, Putnam); pap. 5.95 (0-399-20775-9) Putnam Pub Group.
—Now One Foot, Now the Other. (gr. k-4). 1992. pap. 5.95 (0-399-22400-9, Sandcastle Bks) Putnam Pub Group.
—Nuestra Senora de Guadalupe. LC 79-19609. (SPA., Illus.). 48p. (gr. k-4). 1980. reinforced bdg. 16.95 (0-8234-0374-2); pap. 6.95 (0-8234-0404-8) Holiday.
—Oliver Button Is a Sissy. De Paola, Tomie, illus. LC 78-12624. 48p. (gr. k-3). 1979. 11.95 (0-15-257852-8, HB Juv Bks) HarBrace.
—Oliver Button Is a Sissy. De Paola, Tomie, illus. LC 78-12624. 46p. (ps-3). 1979. pap. 4.95 (0-15-668140-4, Voyager Bks) HarBrace.
—Pancakes for Breakfast. De Paola, Tomie, illus. LC 77-15523. 32p. (ps-2). 1978. 14.95 (0-15-259455-8, HB Juv Bks) HarBrace.
—Pancakes for Breakfast. De Paola, Tomie, illus. LC 77-15523. 32p. (ps-3). 1978. pap. 4.95 (0-15-670768-3, Voyager Bks) HarBrace.
—The Parables of Jesus. De Paola, Tomie, illus. LC 86-18323. 32p. (gr. k-4). 1987. reinforced bdg. 15.95 (0-8234-0636-9) Holiday.
—Patrick: Patron Saint of Ireland. De Paola, Tomie, illus. LC 91-19417. 32p. (ps-3). 1992. reinforced bdg. 15.95 (0-8234-0924-4) Holiday.
—The Popcorn Book. De Paola, Tomie, illus. LC 77-21456. (Illus.). 32p. (ps-3). 1978. reinforced bdg. 14.95 (0-8234-0314-9); pap. 5.95 (0-8234-0533-8) Holiday.
—The Prince of the Dolomites. De Paola, Tomie, illus. LC 79-18524. 46p. (gr. 1-5). 1980. pap. 4.50 (0-15-674432-5, Voyager Bks) HarBrace.
—The Quicksand Book. De Paola, Tomie, illus. LC 76-28762. (Illus.). 32p. (ps-3). 1977. reinforced bdg. 14.95 (0-8234-0291-6); pap. 5.95 (0-8234-0532-X) Holiday.
—Sing, Pierrot, Sing. LC 83-8403. (Illus.). 32p. (Orig.). (ps-3). 1987. pap. 3.95 (0-15-274989-6, Voyager Bks) HarBrace.
—Sing, Pierrot, Sing: A Picture Book in Mime. De Paola, Tomie, illus. LC 83-8403. 32p. (ps-3). 1983. 12.95 (0-15-274988-8, HB Juv Bks) HarBrace.
—Strega Nona. LC 75-11565. (Illus.). 32p. (ps-4). 1979. pap. 13.95 (0-671-66283-X, S&S BFYR); pap. 6.95 (0-671-66606-1, S&S BFYR) S&S Trade.
—Strega Nona. (gr. 3). 1992. pap. 19.95 (0-590-72625-0) Scholastic Inc.
—Strega Nona. (gr. 3). 1991. pap. write for info. (0-663-56227-9) Silver Burdett Pr.
—Strega Nona Meets Her Match. LC 92-8199. (Illus.). 32p. (gr. 5 up). 1993. 14.95 (0-399-22421-1, Putnam) Putnam Pub Group.
—Strega Nona Meets Her Match. DePaola, Tomie, illus. 32p. (ps-3). 1993. 14.95 (0-685-66576-6, Putnam) Putnam Pub Group.
—Strega Nona's Magic Lessons. De Paola, Tomie, illus. LC 80-28260. 32p. (gr. k up). 1982. 13.95 (0-15-281785-9, HB Juv Bks) HarBrace.
—Strega Nona's Magic Lessons. De Paola, Tomie, illus. 32p. (gr. k up). 1984. pap. 4.95 (0-15-281786-7, Voyager Bks) HarBrace.
—Tom. (Illus.). 32p. (ps-3). 1993. PLB 14.95 (0-399-22417-3, Putnam) Putnam Pub Group.
—Tomie De Paola's Book of Bible Stories. 128p. 1990. 19.95 (0-399-21690-1, Putnam) Putnam Pub Group.
—Tomie DePaola's Book of Christmas Carols. DePaola, Tomie, illus. 82p. (gr. 1 up). 1987. 19.95 (0-399-21432-1, Putnam) Putnam Pub Group.
—Tony's Bread. De Paola, Tomie, illus. 32p. (ps-3). 1989. 14.95 (0-399-21693-6, Whitebird Bks) Putnam Pub Group.
—Too Many Hopkins. De Paola, Tomie, illus. 24p. (ps-1). 1989. 5.95 (0-399-21661-8, Putnam) Putnam Pub Group.
—The Walking Coat. LC 81-7395. (Illus.). 32p. (gr. k-4). 1987. pap. 4.95 (0-13-944314-2) P-H.
—Watch Out for the Chicken Feet in Your Soup. LC 74-8201. (Illus.). 32p. (gr. k-4). 1974. 12.95 (0-685-35587-X, S&S BFYR); pap. 5.95 (0-685-35588-8, S&S BFYR) S&S Trade.
De Paola, Tomie see Keller, Charles & Baker, Richard.
De Paola, Tomie, jt. auth. see Lear, Edward.
De Paola, Tomie, retold by. & illus. The Legend of the Bluebonnet: An Old Tale of Texas. LC 82-12391. 32p. (ps-3). 1983. 14.95 (0-399-20937-9, Putnam); pap. 5.95 (0-399-20938-7, Putnam) Putnam Pub Group.
De Paola, Tomie, retold & illus. The Legend of the Indian Paintbrush. LC 87-20160. 40p. (ps-2). 1988. 14.95 (0-399-21534-4, Putnam) Putnam Pub Group.
De Paola, Tomie, selected by. & illus. Tomie de Paola's Favorite Nursery Tales. 128p. (gr. 1 up). 1986. 18.95 (0-399-21319-8, Putnam) Putnam Pub Group.
De Paola, Tomie, illus. Hey Diddle Diddle: And Other Mother Goose Rhymes. (gr. 1 up). 1988. pap. 5.95 (0-399-21589-1, Putnam) Putnam Pub Group.

De Paolo, Paula. Rosie & the Yellow Ribbon. Wolf, Janet, illus. 32p. (ps-3). 1992. 14.95 (0-316-18100-5, Joy St Bks) Little.

Department of Classical Art. Greek Gods & Heroes. (Illus.). 105p. (gr. 3-6). 1981. pap. 5.95 (0-87846-215-5) Mus Fine Arts Boston.

Department of Geography, Lerner Publications. Egypt in Pictures. (Illus.). 64p. (gr. 5 up). 1988. PLB 17.50 (0-8225-1840-6) Lerner Pubns.
—Ethiopia in Pictures. (Illus.). 64p. (gr. 5 up). 1988. PLB 17.50 (0-8225-1836-8) Lerner Pubns.
—Israel in Pictures. (Illus.). 64p. (gr. 5 up). 1988. PLB 17.50 (0-8225-1833-3) Lerner Pubns.
—Jordan in Pictures. (Illus.). 64p. (gr. 5 up). 1988. PLB 17.50 (0-8225-1834-1) Lerner Pubns.
—Liberia in Pictures. (Illus.). 64p. (gr. 5 up). 1988. PLB 17.50 (0-8225-1837-6) Lerner Pubns.
—Madagascar in Pictures. (Illus.). 64p. (gr. 5 up). 1988. PLB 17.50 (0-8225-1841-4) Lerner Pubns.
—Malawi in Pictures. (Illus.). 64p. (gr. 5 up). 1988. PLB 17.50 (0-8225-1842-2) Lerner Pubns.

Department of Geography, Lerner Publications Company Staff. Mexico in Pictures. (Illus.). 64p. (gr. 5 up). 1988. PLB 17.50 (0-8225-1821-5) Lerner Pubns.
Department of Geography, Lerner Publications. Nigeria in Pictures. (Illus.). 64p. (gr. 5 up). 1988. 17.50 (0-8225-1826-0) Lerner Pubns.
—Senegal in Pictures. (Illus.). 64p. (gr. 5 up). 1988. 17.50 (0-8225-1827-9) Lerner Pubns.
—South Africa in Pictures. (Illus.). 64p. (gr. 5 up). 1988. PLB 17.50 (0-8225-1835-X) Lerner Pubns.
—Sudan in Pictures. (Illus.). 64p. (gr. 5 up). 1988. PLB 17.50 (0-8225-1839-2) Lerner Pubns.
—Tanzania in Pictures. (Illus.). 64p. (gr. 5 up). 1988. PLB 17.50 (0-8225-1838-4) Lerner Pubns.
—Turkey in Pictures. (Illus.). 64p. (gr. 5 up). 1988. PLB 17.50 (0-8225-1831-7) Lerner Pubns.
—Zimbabwe in Pictures. (Illus.). 64p. (gr. 5 up). 1988. 17.50 (0-8225-1825-2) Lerner Pubns.
DePaul, Don. Caterfly. Cofer, Camilla, illus. LC 76-39691. (gr. 7 up). 1977. pap. 4.25 (0-8356-0490-X, Quest) Theos Pub Hse.
DePauw, Debbie. In the Rainforest. (Illus.). 48p. (gr. k-1). 1993. pap. text ed. 9.95 incl. poster (1-55799-255-X) Evan-Moor Corp.
De Pauw, Linda G. Founding Mothers: Women of America in the Revolutionary Era. (Illus.). 228p. (gr. 7 up). 1975. 16.95 (0-395-21896-9) HM.
—Seafaring Women. (gr. 7 up). 1982. 13.45 (0-395-32434-3) HM.
De Poix, Carol. Jo, Flo & Yolanda. (SPA & ENG., Illus.). 35p. (Orig.). (gr. 1). 1973. pap. 4.95 (0-914996-04-5) Lollipop Power.
De Ponce, Blanca N. La Aventura de Estudiar: Programa para Desarrollar Destrezas de Estudio e Informacion en el nivel Elemental e Intermedio. Figueroa, Ivelisse, illus. (SPA.). 100p. (Orig.). (gr. 5-9). 1984. write for info. B Ponce.
Deranja, Michael, jt. auth. see Cornell, Joseph.

Derby, Janice. Are You My Friend? Keenan, Joy D., illus. 32p. (ps-3). 1993. 11.95 (0-8361-3609-8) Herald Pr.
The expressive watercolors of Joy Dunn Keenan dance across these pages as a boy & his grandfather spend a day at the park. Throughout the day they meet many people & the boy observes how they are different from him. He also notices that they are like him in the things they enjoy seeing & doing. He asks each one, "Are you my friend?" At the end, all the friends gather at the carousel. This book written by Janice Derby allows children to acknowledge characteristics such as language, skin color, being physically or mentally challenged, or having a different economic status that can separate us. By observing that others enjoy the same kinds of activities, children learn that the differences are minor compared to the many similarities we share. For children ages 4-to-8 & the adults who love them.
Publisher Provided Annotation.

Derby, Pat. Goodbye Emily, Hello. (gr. 7 up). 1989. 15.00 (0-374-32744-0) FS&G.
—Grams, Her Boyfriend, My Family, & Me. 256p. (gr. 12 up). 1994. 16.00 (0-374-38131-3) FS&G.
—Visiting Miss Pierce. LC 86-7559. 144p. (gr. 6 up). 1986. 14.00 (0-374-38162-3) FS&G.
—Visiting Miss Pierce. 144p. (gr. 3 up). 1989. pap. 3.50 (0-374-48156-3, Sunburst) FS&G.

Derby, Sally. Jacob & the Stranger. Gore, Leonid, illus. LC 93-11022. 1994. 13.95 (0-395-66897-2) Ticknor & Fields.
—The Mouse Who Owned the Sun. Henstra, Friso, illus. LC 91-40965. 32p. (ps-3). 1993. pap. 14.95 RSBE (0-02-766965-3, Four Winds) Macmillan Child Grp.
De Regniers, B Schenk see Schenk de Regniers, Beatrice.
De Regniers, Beatrice S. Going for a Walk. newly illus ed. Knox, Robert, illus. LC 91-43177. 32p. (ps-1). 1993. 15.00 (0-06-022954-3); PLB 14.89 (0-06-022957-8) HarpC Child Bks.
—How Joe the Bear & Sam the Mouse Got Together. Myers, Bernice, illus. LC 89-12110. 32p. (ps-2). 1990. 12.95 (0-688-09079-6); lib. bdg. 12.88 (0-688-09080-X) Lothrop.
—It Does Not Say Meow. Galdone, Paul, illus. LC 72-75704. 40p. (ps-3). 1979. 14.95 (0-395-28822-3, Clarion Bks) HM.
—Jack & the Beanstalk: Retold in Verse for Boys & Girls to Read Themselves. Wilsdorf, Anne, illus. LC 89-18663. 48p. (ps-2). 1990. pap. 4.95 (0-689-71421-1, Aladdin) Macmillan Child Grp.
—Jack the Giant Killer. Wilsdorf, Anne, illus. LC 86-3606. 32p. (gr. k-3). 1987. 13.95 (0-689-31218-0, Atheneum Child Bk) Macmillan Child Grp.
—Little Sister & the Month Brothers. Tomes, Margot, illus. LC 75-4594. 48p. (ps-3). 1976. 8.95 (0-8164-3147-7, Clarion Bks) HM.
—May I Bring a Friend? Montresor, Beni, illus. LC 64-19562. 48p. (ps-2). 1971. RSBE 14.95 (0-689-20615-1, Atheneum Child Bk) Macmillan Child Grp.
—May I Bring a Friend? Montresor, Beni, illus. LC 89-15087. 48p. (gr. k-3). 1989. pap. 4.95 (0-689-71353-3, Aladdin) Macmillan Child Grp.
—Red Riding Hood: Retold in Verse for Boys & Girls to Read Themselves. 2nd ed. LC 89-38024. (Illus.). 48p. (gr. k-3). 1990. pap. 4.95 (0-689-71373-8, Aladdin) Macmillan Child Grp.
—The Snow Party. Myers, Bernice, illus. LC 88-13332. 32p. (ps-3). 1989. 12.95 (0-688-08570-9); PLB 12.88 (0-688-08571-7) Lothrop.
—So Many Cats. Weiss, Ellen, illus. LC 85-3739. 32p. (ps-3). 1985. (Clarion Bks); pap. 4.95 (0-89919-700-0, Clarion Bks) HM.
—The Way I Feel... Sometimes. Meddaugh, Susan, illus. LC 87-18245. 48p. (gr. 1-4). 1988. 13.95 (0-89919-647-0, Clarion Bks) HM.
—A Week in the Life of Best Friends: And Other Poems of Friendship. Doyle, Nancy, illus. LC 85-28680. 48p. (gr. 3-7). 1986. SBE 12.95 (0-689-31179-6, Atheneum Child Bk) Macmillan Child Grp.
—What Can You Do with a Shoe? Sendak, Maurice, illus. LC 55-6429. 32p. (ps-k). 1955. PLB 11.89 (0-06-024850-5) HarpC Child Bks.
De Regniers, Beatrice S. & Haas, Irene. Little House of Your Own. Haas, Irene, illus. LC 86-27013. 32p. (ps-3). 1955. 9.95 (0-15-245787-9, HB Juv Bks) HarBrace.
De Regniers, Beatrice S., et al, eds. Sing a Song of Popcorn: Every Child's Book of Poems. (Illus.). 160p. (gr. k up). 1988. pap. 18.95 (0-590-43974-X, Scholastic Hardcovers) Scholastic Inc.
Dereske, Jo. The Lone Sentinel. LC 88-36254. 176p. (gr. 4-8). 1989. SBE 13.95 (0-689-31552-X, Atheneum Child Bk) Macmillan Child Grp.
—My Cousin, the Poodle. LC 90-25294. 128p. (gr. 3-9). 1991. SBE 12.95 (0-689-31732-8, Atheneum Child Bk) Macmillan Child Grp.
Der Laan, Carrie van see Van der Laan, Carrie.
Derman, Karen. The Magic Hole in the Sky. Neel, Jennifer & Williams, Roger, illus. 48p. (Orig.). 1992. pap. 14.95 (0-9630026-0-0) Childlight Pr.
Derman, Martha. Tales from Academy Street. (gr. 4-7). 1992. pap. 2.95 (0-590-43704-6) Scholastic Inc.
Der Manuelian, Peter. Hieroglyphs from A to Z: A Rhyming Book with Ancient Egyptian Stencils for Kids. (Illus.). 48p. (gr. 2 up). 1993. 19.95 (0-8478-1701-6) Rizzoli Intl.
Der Meer, Ron van see Van der Meer, Ron.
Der Meer Ron, Van see Van der Meer, Ron.
DeRoo, Sally. Exploring Our Environment: A Resource Guide-Manual: Animals. DeRoo, Sally, illus. 207p. (gr. 3-6). 1979. tchr's. ed. 5.00 (0-87879-827-7, Ann Arbor Div) Acad Therapy.
—Exploring Our Environment: Animals Student Materials One. DeRoo, Sally, illus. 22p. (gr. 3-6). 1979. wkbk. 1.00 (0-87879-828-5, Ann Arbor Div) Acad Therapy.
—Exploring Our Environment: Animals Student Materials Two. DeRoo, Sally, illus. 22p. (gr. 3-6). 1979. wkbk. 1.00 (0-87879-829-3, Ann Arbor Div) Acad Therapy.
—Exploring Our Environment: Plants-Student Materials 1. (Illus.). 32p. (gr. 3-6). 1977. wkbk 1.00 (0-87879-825-0, Ann Arbor Div) Acad Therapy.
—Exploring Our Environment: Plants-Student Materials 2. 32p. (gr. 3-6). 1977. wkbk 1.00 (0-87879-826-9, Ann Arbor Div) Acad Therapy.
DeRosa, jt. auth. see Leonard, Marcia.
DeRosemond, Peggy. A Royal Romance Paper Dolls. (gr. 8-12). 1984. pap. 4.00 (0-914510-14-2) Evergreen.
Derrig, Leslie A. & Westdyk, Roxanne H. Mommy in the Sky. Murphy, Anne, illus. LC 83-73248. 32p. (Orig.). (gr. k-5). 1983. pap. 6.95 (0-915479-68-0) Cottage Pub Co.
Derrydale. Animals. 1989. 2.49 (0-517-67588-9) Outlet Bk Co.

—Machines. (ps-1). 1989. 2.49 *(0-517-67587-0)* Outlet Bk Co.

—Playtime. (ps-1). 1989. 2.49 *(0-517-67589-7)* Outlet Bk Co.

Derrydale Press Staff, jt. auth. see Clark, Roland.

Dershem, Kurt. The Olympians. Bell, Rob, ed. Perez, George & Sutherland, Jackie, illus. 48p. (Orig.). (gr. 12). 1990. pap. 9.00 *(1-55806-114-2,* 414) Iron Crown Ent Inc.

Deru, Myriam & Alen, Paule. The Birthday Surprise. (SPA & ENG., Illus.). 32p. (ps-1). 1991. 5.99 *(0-517-65556-X)* Outlet Bk Co.

—The Busy Day. (SPA & ENG., Illus.). 32p. (ps-1). 1991. 5.99 *(0-517-65558-6)* Outlet Bk Co.

—My First Day at School. (SPA & ENG., Illus.). 32p. (ps-1). 1991. 5.99 *(0-517-65557-8)* Outlet Bk Co.

De Ruiz, Dana C. To Fly with the Swallows: A Story of Old California. Heller, Debbe, illus. LC 92-14416. 53p. (gr. 2-5). 1992. PLB 21.34 *(0-8114-7234-5)* Raintree Steck-V.

De Ruiz, Dana C. & Larios, Richard. La Causa: The Migrant Farmworkers' Story. Gutierrez, Rudy, illus. LC 92-12806. 92p. (gr. 2-5). 1992. PLB 21.34 *(0-8114-7231-0)* Raintree Steck-V.

Derwent, Lavinia. The Boy from Sula. 158p. (gr. 5-7). 1989. pap. 6.95 *(0-86241-111-4,* Pub. by Cnngt Pub Ltd) Trafalgar.

—Return to Sula. 128p. (gr. 5-8). 1989. pap. 6.95 *(0-86241-073-8,* Pub. by Cnngt Pub Ltd) Trafalgar.

—Song of Sula. 128p. (gr. 5-7). 1989. pap. 6.95 *(0-86241-135-1,* Pub. by Cnngt Pub Ltd) Trafalgar.

—Sula. 160p. (gr. 5-7). 1989. pap. 6.95 *(0-86241-068-1,* Pub. by Cnngt Pub Ltd) Trafalgar.

Derwingham, Richard, jt. auth. see Emerson, Roger.

De Saint-Beauguat, Henri. The First People. LC 86-42657. (Illus.). 77p. (gr. 7 up). 1986. 17.98 *(0-382-09212-0)*; 13.49s.p. *(0-685-17548-0)* Silver Burdett Pr.

De Saint-Beauquet, Henri. The First Settlements. LC 86-42659. (Illus.). 77p. (gr. 7 up). 1987. 17.98 *(0-382-09213-9)*; 13.49s.p. *(0-685-17549-9)* Silver Burdett Pr.

De Saint-Exupery, Antoine. The Little Prince. 1992. Repr. lib. bdg. 18.95x *(0-89968-299-5)* Lightyear.

—The Little Prince. Woods, Katherine, tr. LC 92-37907. (gr. 4 up). 1993. 50.00 *(0-15-243820-3)* HarBrace.

—Petit Prince. (FRE.). 123p. (gr. 5-10). 1987. pap. 9.95 *(2-07-033453-8)* Schoenhof.

—Petit Prince. (FRE.). 93p. (gr. 5-10). 1988. pap. 29.95 incl. cassette *(2-07-032267-X)* Schoenhof.

De Saint-Exupery, Antoine see Saint-Exupery, Antoine de.

De Saint Mars, Dominique. Lily Fights with Max. LC 92-18000. (gr. 1-8). 1992. PLB 8.95 *(0-89565-980-8)*; Resale. 12.75 *(0-685-60107-2)* Childs World.

—Lily Is in Love. Bloch, Serge, illus. LC 93-10988. 1993. write for info. *(1-56766-101-7)* Childs World.

—Max Doesn't Like School. Bloch, Serge, illus. LC 93-23773. 1993. write for info. *(1-56766-103-3)* Childs World.

—Max Doesn't Like to Read. LC 92-17998. (gr. 1-8). 1992. PLB 8.95 *(0-89565-979-4)*; Resale. 12.75 *(0-685-60115-3)* Childs World.

—Max Is Crazy about Video Games. Bloch, Serge, illus. LC 93-10987. 1993. write for info. *(1-56766-102-5)* Childs World.

—Max Is Shy. LC 92-17996. (gr. 1-8). 1992. 12.75 *(0-685-60114-5)*; Resale. PLB 8.95 *(0-89565-977-8)* Childs World.

—Zoe's Parents Are Getting Divorced. Bloch, Serge, illus. LC 93-19767. 1993. write for info. *(1-56766-104-1)* Childs World.

De Sairigne, Catherine. Animals in Winter. Matthews, Sarah, tr. from FRE. Mathieu, Agnes, illus. LC 87-34086. 38p. (gr. k-5). 1988. 4.95 *(0-944589-05-7,* 057) Young Discovery Lib.

Desaix, Deborah D. In the Back Seat. (ps-3). 1993. 14.00 *(0-374-33639-3)* FS&G.

DeSaix, Frank. The Girl Who Danced with Dolphins. DeSaix, Debbi D., illus. 32p. (gr. k-3). 1991. 14.95 *(0-374-32626-6)* FS&G.

—Hilary & the Lions. (gr. 4-8). 1990. 15.00 *(0-374-33237-1)* FS&G.

De Sales, R. de Roussy see Roussy de Sales, R. de.

DeSantis, Kenny. A Dentist's Tools. Ayre, Patricia A., photos by. LC 87-36505. (Illus.). 48p. (gr. k-3). 1988. 10.99 *(0-396-09043-5,* Putnam); (Putnam) Putnam Pub Group.

De Sart, Jean. Birds of the Night. Winants, Jean-Marie, illus. LC 93-31749. 1994. 14.95 *(0-88106-671-0)* Charlesbridge Pub.

—Scary Animals. Winants, Jean-Marie, illus. LC 93-20963. 1994. 14.95 *(0-88106-674-5)* Charlesbridge Pub.

De Saules, Janet. Getting to Know Spain. Wooley, Kim, illus. 32p. (gr. 3-7). 1993. pap. 12.95 incl. 60 min. cassette *(0-8120-8127-7)* Barron.

De Saulles, Janet, jt. auth. see Watson, Carol.

De Souza, James, as told by. Brother Anansi & the Cattle Ranch: (El Hermano Anansi y el Rancho) Zubizarreta, Rosalma, tr. Rohmer, Harriet, adapted by. Von Mason, Stephen, illus. LC 88-37091. (SPA & ENG.). 32p. (ps-7). 1989. 13.95 *(0-89239-044-1)* Childrens Book Pr.

Descamps-Lequime, Sophie & Vernerey, Denise. The Ancient Greeks: In the Land of the Gods. LaRose, Mary K., tr. from FRE. Martin, Annie-Claude, illus. LC 91-35941. 64p. (gr. 4-6). 1992. PLB 14.90 *(1-56294-069-4)* Millbrook Pr.

Deschaine, Scott. Monster Love. Donovan, Bob, illus. 36p. 1993. pap. 2.50 *(1-878181-05-X)* Discovery Comics.

—Popcorn! Donovan, Bob, illus. 68p. 1993. pap. 4.95 *(1-878181-06-8)* Discovery Comics.

—Screaming Eagle. Roy, Mike, illus. 296p. 1993. pap. 11. 95 *(1-878181-04-1)* Discovery Comics.

Deschaine, Scott & Bonno, Chris. Head On. Deschaine, Scott & Bonno, Chris, illus. 36p. 1990. pap. 2.00 *(1-878181-02-5)* Discovery Comics.

Deschaine, Scott & Weisberg, Lynette. A Bug's Gift. Deschaine, Scott & Weisberg, Lynette, illus. 20p. 1991. pap. 1.95 *(1-878181-01-7)* Discovery Comics.

De Segur. Francois le Bossu. Bayard, Emile, illus. (FRE.). 250p. (gr. 5-10). 1981. pap. 8.95 *(2-07-033196-2)* Schoenhof.

—General Dourakine. Bayard, Emile, illus. (FRE.). 220p. (gr. 5-10). 1979. pap. 8.95 *(2-07-033092-3)* Schoenhof.

—Nouveaux Contes de Fees. Dore, G. & Didier, J., illus. (FRE.). 216p. (gr. 5-10). 1980. pap. 8.95 *(2-07-033149-0)* Schoenhof.

DeShay, Bernice A., jt. auth. see DeShay, Samuel L.

DeShay, Samuel L. & DeShay, Bernice A. Plus Fifteen: Fifteen Days to Lower Blood Pressure & Cholesterol. rev. ed. (gr. 10). 1992. 14.95 *(0-945460-16-3)* Upward Way.

De Shazo, Jerry, ed. see Porter, Patrick K.

Desimini, Lisa. I Am Running Away Today. Desimini, Lisa, illus. LC 91-25341. 32p. (ps-3). 1992. 13.95 *(1-56282-120-2)*; PLB 13.89 *(1-56282-121-0)* Hyprn Child.

—Moon Soup. Desimini, Lisa, illus. LC 92-55041. 32p. (ps-3). 1993. 14.95 *(1-56282-463-5)*; PLB 14.89 *(1-56282-464-5)* Hyprn Child.

—My Heart Is Like a Zoo. 1994. write for info. *(0-8050-3144-8)* H Holt & Co.

DeSimone, James. The Official G. I. Joe Collectors Guide to Completing & Collating Your G. I. Joes & Accessories. 1993. pap. 11.94 *(0-9635956-0-1)* GI Joe Collect.

Desmond, Theresa, jt. auth. see Almonte, Paul.

Desnos, Robert. Chantefables. Annen, Sharon, tr. from FRE. Annen, Charles, illus. LC 84-61257. 60p. (gr. 1-6). 1988. 17.95 *(0-9613938-0-7)* Penstemon Pr.

DeSomma, Vince. The Mission to Mars & Beyond. (Illus.). 112p. (gr. 5 up). 1992. lib. bdg. 18.95 *(0-7910-1325-1)* Chelsea Hse.

De Souza, Chris. Listening to Music. LC 89-7119. (Illus.). 48p. (gr. 4-8). 1990. 13.95 *(1-85435-104-4)* Marshall Cavendish.

DeSpain, Andrew. The Dating Journal. 66p. (gr. 10 up). 1993. 13.95 *(0-963791-0-9)* A&D Pub.

DeSpain, Pleasant L. Twenty-Two Splendid Tales to Tell from Around the World, Vol. 1. 2nd ed. Lyttle, Kirk, illus. LC 90-62095. 96p. (gr. 1-6). 1990. pap. 10.95x *(0-9627239-0-8)* Merrill Ct Pr.

—Twenty-Two Splendid Tales to Tell from Around the World, Vol. 2. 2nd ed. Lyttle, Kirk, illus. LC 90-62095. 96p. (gr. 1-6). 1990. pap. 10.95x *(0-9627239-1-6)* Merrill Ct Pr.

Despins, Cindy R., illus. see Kaopuiki, Stacey S.

Des Pres, Francois Turenne see Turenne des Pres, Francois & California Afro-American Museum Foundation, Los Angeles Staff.

Despres, Joseph & Blumenthal, Richard. Major Decisions: A Guide to College Majors. 2nd ed. 168p. (gr. 12). pap. text ed. 15.00x *(1-878172-20-4)* Orchard Hse MA.

Desputeaux, Helene. Lollypop's Animals. (Illus.). 8p. (ps). 1993. bds. 4.95 *(2-921198-41-X,* Pub. by Les Edits Herit CN) Adams Inc MA.

—Lollypop's Colors. (Illus.). 8p. (ps). 1993. bds. 4.95 *(2-921198-38-X,* Pub. by Les Edits Herit CN) Adams Inc MA.

—Lollypop's Numbers. (Illus.). 8p. (ps). 1993. bds. 4.95 *(2-921198-39-8,* Pub. by Les Edits Herit CN) Adams Inc MA.

—Lollypop's Playtime. (Illus.). (ps). 1993. bath bk. 4.95 *(2-921198-40-1,* Pub. by Les Edits Herit CN) Adams Inc MA.

—My Clothes. (Illus.). 26p. (ps). 1993. bds. 2.95 *(2-921198-25-8,* Pub. by Les Edits Herit CN) Adams Inc MA.

—My Food. (Illus.). 26p. (ps). 1993. bds. 2.95 *(2-921198-27-4,* Pub. by Les Edits Herit CN) Adams Inc MA.

—My House. (Illus.). 26p. (ps). 1993. bds. 2.95 *(2-921198-24-X,* Pub. by Les Edits Herit CN) Adams Inc MA.

—My Toys. (Illus.). 26p. (ps). 1993. bds. 2.95 *(2-921198-26-6,* Pub. by Les Edits Herit CN) Adams Inc MA.

Destang, Francoise, jt. auth. see Paschos, Jacqueline.

DeStefano, Susan. Chico Mendes: Fight for the Forest. Raymond, Larry, illus. 76p. (gr. 4-7). 1992. PLB 14.95 *(0-8050-2887-0)* TFC Bks NY.

—Drugs & the Family. Raymond, Larry, illus. 88p. (gr. 5-8). 1991. PLB 14.95 *(0-941477-61-4)* TFC Bks NY.

—Focus on Medicines. (Illus.). 64p. (gr. 2-4). 1991. PLB 14.95 *(0-941477-94-0)* TFC Bks NY.

—Focus on Opiates. (Illus.). 68p. (gr. 2-4). 1991. PLB 14. 95 *(0-941477-91-6)* TFC Bks NY.

—Theodore Roosevelt: Conservation President. Castro, Antonio, illus. 80p. (gr. 4-7). 1993. PLB 14.95 *(0-8050-2122-1)* TFC Bks NY.

De Tagyos, Paul Ratz see Ratz de Tagyos, Paul.

Determined Productions. Pet Snoopy. Schulz, Charles, illus. (ps). 1983. pap. 4.95 *(0-915696-72-X)* Determined Prods.

Dethier, Vincent G. Newbery: The Life & Times of a Maine Clam. LC 81-66267. (Illus.). (gr. 1-4). 1981. pap. 6.95 *(0-89272-085-9)* Down East.

Detorie, Rick. Ghost in the Closet. 24p. (gr. k-3). 1989. pap. 1.95 *(0-8167-1457-6)* Troll Assocs.

—Haunted Elevator. 24p. (gr. k-3). 1989. pap. 1.95 *(0-8167-1459-2)* Troll Assocs.

—Haunted Tool Shed. 24p. (gr. k-3). 1989. pap. 1.95 *(0-8167-1456-8)* Troll Assocs.

—Red-Headed Gooseberry Ghost. 24p. (gr. k-3). 1989. pap. 1.95 *(0-8167-1458-4)* Troll Assocs.

DeTreville, Stan, jt. auth. see DeTreville, Susan.

DeTreville, Susan & DeTreville, Stan. Butterflies & Moths. (Illus.). 32p. (Orig.). 1981. pap. 4.50 *(0-8431-1731-1)* Price Stern.

De Trevino, Elizabeth B. El Guero. Bowman, Leslie W., illus. 112p. (gr. 3 up). 1989. 14.00 *(0-374-31995-2)* FS&G.

—El Guero. (Illus.). 112p. (gr. 3 up). 1991. pap. 3.95 *(0-374-42028-9)* FS&G.

—I, Juan De Pareja. LC 65-19330. 192p. (gr. 7 up). 1965. 16.00 *(0-374-33531-1)*; pap. 3.95, 1987 *(0-374-43525-1,* Sunburst) FS&G.

De Trevino, Elizabeth Borton. Yo, Juan de Pareja. Borton, Enrique R. Trevino, tr. from ENG. (SPA.). 192p. (gr. 12 up). 1994. 16.00 *(0-374-38699-4)* FS&G.

Dettre, Judith. One, Two, Three, Read! LC 79-52661. (gr. 3-12). 1980. pap. 9.95 *(0-8224-5788-1)* Fearon Teach Aids.

Detz, Joan. You Mean I Have to Stand Up & Say Something? Marshall, David, illus. 96p. (gr. 5-9). 1986. SBE 13.95 *(0-689-31221-0,* Atheneum Child Bk) Macmillan Child Grp.

Detzer, David. An Asian Tragedy: America & Vietnam. LC 91-37228. (Illus.). 160p. (gr. 7 up). 1992. PLB 16. 90 *(1-56294-066-X)* Millbrook Pr.

Deuker, Carl. Heart of a Champion. LC 92-37231. 1993. 15.95 *(0-316-18166-8,* Joy St Bks) Little.

—On the Devil's Court. 208p. (gr. 7 up). 1989. 15.95 *(0-316-18147-1,* Joy St Bks) Little.

—On the Devil's Court. 256p. 1991. pap. 3.50 *(0-380-70879-5,* Flare) Avon.

Deutsch, Evelyn, jt. auth. see Drutman, Ave D.

Deutsch, Sarah J. From Ballots to Breadlines: American Women, 1920-1940. LC 93-30664. 1994. write for info. *(0-19-508063-7)* OUP.

Deutschman, Alan. Winning Money for College: A High School Student's Guide to Scholarship Contests. 3rd ed. LC 92-21967. 224p. (gr. 10-12). 1992. pap. 10.95 *(1-56079-059-8)* Petersons Guides.

DeVaney, Janet S. Speech Stations: The One-Stop Speech Book. DeVaney, Janet S., illus. 205p. (ps-5). 1987. 24.95 *(0-937857-03-3,* 1552) Speech Bin.

Devaney, John. America Fights the Tide, 1942. 192p. (gr. 12 up). 1991. 17.95 *(0-8027-6997-7)*; lib. bdg. 18.85 *(0-8027-6998-5)* Walker & Co.

—America Goes to War, 1941. 192p. (gr. 12 up). 1991. 16.95 *(0-8027-6979-9)*; lib. bdg. 17.85 *(0-8027-6980-2)* Walker & Co.

—America on the Attack, 1943. LC 92-8993. 1992. cancelled 17.95 *(0-8027-8194-2)*; PLB 18.85 *(0-8027-8195-0)* Walker & Co.

—America Storms the Beaches, 1944. LC 92-47057. 1993. 17.95 *(0-8027-8244-2)*; PLB 18.85 *(0-8027-8245-0)* Walker & Co.

—Bo Jackson: A Star for All Seasons. 132p. 1992. 14.95 *(0-8027-8178-0)*; PLB 15.85 *(0-8027-8179-9)* Walker & Co.

—Franklin Delano Roosevelt, President. LC 86-46254. (Illus.). 76p. (gr. 5-9). 1987. 12.95 *(0-8027-6713-3)*; PLB 13.85 *(0-8027-6714-1)* Walker & Co.

—Lyndon Baines Johnson, President. LC 85-31751. 128p. (gr. 5 up). 1986. 12.95 *(0-8027-6638-2)*; PLB 13.85 *(0-8027-6639-0)* Walker & Co.

—Ronald Reagan. (Illus.). (gr. 7 up). 1990. 13.95 *(0-8027-6931-4)*; lib. bdg. 14.85 *(0-8027-6932-2)* Walker & Co.

—Sports Great Roger Clemens. LC 89-7874. (Illus.). 64p. (gr. 4-10). 1990. lib. bdg. 15.95 *(0-89490-284-9)* Enslow Pubs.

—The Vietnam War. (Illus.). 64p. (gr. 5-8). 1992. PLB 12.90 *(0-531-20046-9)* Watts.

—The Vietnam War. (Illus.). 64p. (gr. 5-8). 1993. pap. 5.95 *(0-531-15658-3)* Watts.

—Winners of the Heisman Trophy. 2nd ed. (Illus.). (gr. 5 up). 1990. 14.95 *(0-8027-6906-3)*; lib. bdg. 15.85 *(0-8027-6907-1)* Walker & Co.

De Varona, Frank. Benito Juarez, President of Mexico. LC 92-19349. (Illus.). 32p. (gr. 2-4). 1993. PLB 12.40 *(1-56294-279-4)* Millbrook Pr.

—Bernardo De Galvez. Redman, Tom, illus. (SPA & ENG.). 32p. (gr. 3-6). 1990. PLB 15.96 *(0-8172-3379-2)* Raintree Steck-V.

—Miguel Hidalgo y Costilla - Father of Mexican Independence. LC 92-36562. (Illus.). 32p. (gr. 2-4). 1993. PLB 12.40 *(1-56294-370-7)* Millbrook Pr.

—Simon Bolivar: Latin American Liberator. LC 92-19459. (Illus.). 32p. (gr. 2-4). 1993. PLB 12.40 *(1-56294-278-6)* Millbrook Pr.

De Varona, Frank, intro. by see Codye, Corinn.

De Varona, Frank, intro. by see Gleiter, Jan.

DeVasure, John, jt. auth. see **Champlin, Connie.**

DeVault, Christine, jt. auth. see **Strong, Bryan.**

De Veaux, Alexis. Don't Explain (A Song of Billie Holiday) LC 78-19471. (Illus.). 160p. (gr. 7 up). 1980. PLB 12.89 (0-06-021630-1) HarpC Child Bks.

—Don't Explain: A Song of Billie Holiday. 151p. (gr. 9 up). 1988. pap. 7.95 (0-86316-132-4) Writers & Readers.

—An Enchanted Hair Tale. Hanna, Cheryl, illus. LC 85-45824. 40p. (gr. k-3). 1987. 15.00 (0-06-021623-9); PLB 14.89 (0-06-021624-7) HarpC Child Bks.

—An Enchanted Hair Tale. Hanna, Cheryl, illus. LC 85-45824. 40p. (gr. k-3). 1991. pap. 4.95 (0-06-443271-8, Trophy) HarpC Child Bks.

DeVenzio, Richard. Smart Moves: How Young Adults Can Succeed in School, Sports, Career & Life. 300p. (gr. 6-12). 1989. pap. 13.95 (0-87975-546-6) Prometheus Bks.

Dever, Joe. Joe Dever's Legends of Lone Wolf, No. 3: The Tides of Treachery. 1991. pap. 3.50 (0-425-12551-3, Berkley-Pacer) Berkley Pub.

—Lone Wolf, No. 13: The Plague Lords of Ruel. 1992. pap. 3.50 (0-425-13245-5) Berkley Pub.

Dever, Joe & Chalk, Gary. Lone Wolf, No. 6: Kingdoms of Terror. 240p. (gr. 7 up). 1987. pap. 3.99 (0-425-08446-9, Berkley-Pacer) Berkley Pub.

—Lone Wolf, No. 9: The Cauldron of Fear. 256p. (gr. 10 up). 1988. pap. 3.99 (0-425-10848-1, Berkley-Pacer) Berkley Pub.

De Vere, Charles. Motorcycles. LC 92-346. (Illus.). 32p. (gr. k-4). 1992. PLB 11.90 (0-531-17379-8, Gloucester Pr) Watts.

Deverell, Catherine. Grandma Told Me So. (ps-k). 1988. 1.59 (0-87403-386-1, 2016) Standard Pub.

—Grandpa Told Me So. Petach, Heidi, illus. LC 87-62600. 20p. (ps). 1988. pap. 1.59 (0-87403-387-X, 24-02017) Standard Pub.

—Stradivari's Singing Violin. (ps-3). 1992. 14.95 (0-87614-732-5) Carolrhoda Bks.

—Stradivari's Singing Violin. (ps-3). 1992. pap. 5.95 (0-87614-583-7) Carolrhoda Bks.

Deverell, Gweneth. Follow the Sun...to Tahiti, to Western Samoa, to Fiji, to Melanesia, to Micronesia. (gr. 1-3). 1982. 3.95 (0-377-00120-1) Friendship Pr.

Devereux, Frederick L., Jr. Famous American Horses. LC 75-13347. (Illus.). 128p. (gr. 8 up). 1975. 24.95 (0-8159-5512-X) Devin.

Devi-Doolin, Daya. Dabney, Dormck & Wiggle's Slakadunan Adventure. Devi-Doolin, Daya & Joiner, Eddie, illus. 50p. (gr. 4-8). 1989. pap. text ed. 6.50 (1-877945-02-1) Padaran Pubns.

—Dormck. Devi-Doolin, Daya, illus. LC 89-8613. 10p. (Orig.). (gr. 2-5). 1989. pap. 4.50 (1-877945-01-3) Padaran Pubns.

—Dormck & the Temple of the Healing Light. LC 89-63461. (Illus.). 50p. (Orig.). (gr. 4-8). 1989. pap. text ed. 6.50 incl. cassette (1-877945-05-6) Padaran Pubns.

Devilleres, David L. The Rescuers. (gr. 3 up). 1993. 7.95 (0-8062-4724-X) Carlton.

De Vinck, Christopher. Augusta & Trab. 128p. (gr. 3-7). 1993. pap. 13.95 SBE (0-02-729945-7, Four Winds) Macmillan Child Grp.

DeVito, Cara. Where I Want to Be. LC 92-15038. 192p. (gr. 7 up). 1993. 13.95 (0-395-64592-1) HM.

DeVito, Pam. Lydia & the Purple Paint. Weinberger, Jane, ed. DeVito, Pam, illus. LC 89-50681. 52p. (ps-4). 1989. pap. 5.95 (0-932433-59-6) Windswept Hse.

Devlin, Harry & Devlin, Wende. Cranberry Moving Day. LC 93-36279. (gr. 3 up). 1994. 2.95 (0-689-71777-6) MacMillan Child Grp.

Devlin, Harry, jt. auth. see **Devlin, Wende.**

Devlin, Wende & Devlin, Harry. Cranberry Trip to the Dentist. LC 93-36280. (gr. 3 up). 1994. write for info. (0-689-71779-2) MacMillan Child Grp.

Devlin, Wende & Devlin, Harry. Cranberry Autumn. LC 92-23237. (Illus.). 40p. (gr. k-3). 1993. RSBE 13.95 (0-02-729936-8, Four Winds) Macmillan Child Grp.

—Cranberry Birthday. Devlin, Wende & Devlin, Harry, illus. LC 88-294. 40p. (gr. k-3). 1988. RSBE 13.95 (0-02-729210-X, Four Winds) Macmillan Child Grp.

—Cranberry Birthday. Devlin, Harry, illus. LC 92-23541. 40p. (ps-3). 1993. pap. 4.95 (0-689-71697-4, Aladdin) Macmillan Child Grp.

—Cranberry Christmas. Devlin, Harry, illus. LC 80-16971. 40p. (ps-3). 1984. Repr. of 1976 ed. RSBE 13. 95 (0-02-729900-7, Four Winds) Macmillan Child Grp.

—Cranberry Christmas. Devlin, Wende & Devlin, Harry, illus. LC 91-9188. 40p. (gr. k-3). 1991. pap. 3.95 (0-689-71510-2, Aladdin) Macmillan Child Grp.

—Cranberry Easter. Devlin, Harry, illus. LC 88-21370. 40p. (gr. k-3). 1990. RSBE 13.95 (0-02-729935-X, Four Wind) Macmillan Child Grp.

—Cranberry Easter. Devlin, Harry, illus. LC 92-23537. 40p. (ps-3). 1993. Repr. of 1990 ed. 4.95 (0-689-71698-2, Aladdin) Macmillan Child Grp.

—Cranberry Halloween. LC 81-22134. (Illus.). 32p. (gr. k-3). 1982. RSBE 13.95 (0-02-729910-4, Four Winds) Macmillan Child Grp.

—Cranberry Halloween. Devlin, Wende & Devlin, Harry, illus. LC 89-18666. 40p. (gr. k-3). 1990. pap. 3.95 (0-689-71428-9, Aladdin) Macmillan Child Grp.

—Cranberry Mystery. LC 85-16015. (Illus.). 40p. (ps-3). 1984. Repr. of 1978 ed. RSBE 13.95 (0-02-729920-1, Four Winds) Macmillan Child Grp.

—Cranberry Summer. Devlin, Harry, illus. LC 90-24560. 40p. (gr. k-3). 1992. RSBE 13.95 (0-02-729181-2, Four Winds) Macmillan Child Grp.

—Cranberry Thanksgiving. Devlin, Harry, illus. LC 80-17070. 48p. (ps-3). 1984. Repr. of 1971 ed. RSBE 13. 95 (0-02-729930-9, Four Winds) Macmillan Child Grp.

—Cranberry Thanksgiving. Devlin, Wende & Devlin, Harry, illus. LC 89-18642. 40p. (gr. k-3). 1990. pap. 3.95 (0-689-71429-7, Aladdin) Macmillan Child Grp.

—Cranberry Valentine. Devlin, Wende & Devlin, Harry, illus. LC 85-24047. 32p. (gr. k-3). 1986. SBE 13.95 (0-02-729200-2, Four Winds) Macmillan Child Grp.

—Cranberry Valentine. Devlin, Wende & Devlin, Harry, illus. LC 91-6915. 40p. (gr. k-3). 1992. pap. 3.95 (0-689-71509-9, Aladdin) Macmillan Child Grp.

—Old Black Witch. Devlin, Wende & Devlin, Harry, illus. LC 91-42133. 32p. (gr. k-3). 1992. pap. 3.95 (0-689-71636-2, Aladdin) Macmillan Child Grp.

—Old Black Witch. 2nd ed. Devlin, Harry, illus. LC 92-19897. 32p. (gr. k-3). 1992. RSBE 13.95 (0-02-729185-5, Four Winds) Macmillan Child Grp.

—The Trouble with Henriette. Date not set. write for info. (0-02-729937-6, Four Winds) Macmillan Child Grp.

Devlin, Wende, jt. auth. see **Devlin, Harry.**

DeVoe, Howard. Communities of Molecules: A Physical Chemistry Module. Gardner, Marjorie, intro. by. (Illus.). 106p. (Orig.). (gr. 9-12). 1991. pap. text ed. 8.20 (1-879827-04-2) Vistas.

Devon, Gary. Bad Desire. LC 89-43415. 326p. 1990. pap. write for info. (0-679-73304-3) Random Bks Yng Read.

Devonshire, H., et al. Christmas Crafts. (Illus.). 48p. (gr. 5-8). 1990. PLB 12.40 (0-531-14073-3) Watts.

Devonshire, Hilary. Air. LC 91-34421. (Illus.). 32p. (gr. 5-8). 1992. PLB 12.40 (0-531-14134-9) Watts.

—Color. LC 91-11871. (Illus.). 32p. (gr. 5-8). 1992. PLB 12.40 (0-531-14221-3) Watts.

—Drawing. (ps-3). 1990. PLB 12.40 (0-531-10855-4) Watts.

—Flight. LC 92-6077. (Illus.). 32p. (gr. 5-8). 1993. PLB 12.40 (0-531-14234-5) Watts.

—Greeting Cards & Gift Wrap. LC 91-39594. (Illus.). 48p. (gr. 5-8). 1992. PLB 12.40 (0-531-14219-1) Watts.

—Light. Kline, Marjory, ed. (Illus.). 32p. (gr. 5-7). 1992. PLB 12.40 (0-531-14126-8) Watts.

—Movement. LC 92-7837. (Illus.). 32p. (gr. 5-8). 1993. PLB 12.40 (0-531-14229-9) Watts.

—Moving Art. (Illus.). 48p. (gr. 5-8). 1990. PLB 12.40 (0-531-14076-8) Watts.

—Water. Kline, Marjory, ed. (Illus.). 32p. (gr. 5-7). 1992. PLB 12.40 (0-531-14125-X) Watts.

Devore, Cynthia D. Breakfast for Dinner. LC 93-13066. 32p. (gr. 5 up). 1993. 14.96 (1-56239-245-X) Abdo & Dghtrs.

—Do Rainbows Last Forever? LC 93-7720. (gr. 5 up). 1993. 14.96 (1-56239-248-4) Abdo & Dghtrs.

—A Week Past Forever. LC 93-7722. 1993. 14.96 (1-56239-246-8) Abdo & Dghtrs.

—The Wind Before It Blows. LC 93-7723. (Illus.). 1993. 14.96 (1-56239-247-6) Abdo & Dghtrs.

DeVore, Dixon, II. Mortimer the Very Rich Mouse. (Illus.). 32p. (gr. k-5). 1991. tchr's. ed. 125.00 (0-9614998-1-8) Cricket Power.

DeVries, Betty. One Hundred One Bible Activity Sheets. 144p. (ps up) 1983. pap. 8.99 (0-8010-2931-7) Baker Bk.

De Vries, C. M. On the Way to Bethlehem. Vilain, Frederic, tr. from DUT. Muller, Anna-Hermine, illus. LC 90-43765. 16p. (Orig.). 1990. pap. 1.50 (0-8198-5415-8) St Paul Bks.

De Vries, David. Home at Last. (gr. 4-7). 1992. pap. 3.25 (0-440-40621-8) Dell.

DeVries, Douglas. Matilda & the Twins. (Illus.). 32p. (Orig.). (ps-3). 1990. pap. text ed. 8.00 (1-877721-02-8) Jade Ram Pub.

—Muscles, the Moose Calf. Parker, Patricia, illus. LC 89-84651. 32p. (Orig.). (ps-3). 1989. 8.00 (1-877721-00-X) Jade Ram Pub.

—Muscles Visits Anchorage. Parker, Patricia, illus. LC 90-61154. 32p. (Orig.). (ps-3). 1990. pap. text ed. 8.00 (1-877721-01-8) Jade Ram Pub.

De Vries, Maggie, jt. auth. see **Little, Jean.**

Dewaard, John. History of NASA: America's Voyage to the Stars. 1984. 12.98 (0-671-06983-7) S&S Trade.

Dewan, Ted. Inside the Whale & Other Animals. (ps) 1992. pap. 16.00 (0-385-30651-2) Doubleday.

De Warren, Shaun. The Harris Visits the Garden of Everything. Coupland, Gill, illus. 32p. (ps-3). 1985. cloth 12.95 (0-913299-21-9, Dist. by PGW) Stillpoint.

Dewazien, Karl. Fundamental Soccer Goalkeeping. Lavery, Vincent J., ed. (Illus.). 128p. (Orig.). (gr. 6). 1986. pap. 7.95 (0-9619139-1-6) Fun Soccer Ent.

—Fundamental Soccer Practice. Lavery, Vincent J., ed. Garcia, Joseph G., illus. 128p. (gr. 6). 1985. pap. 7.95 (0-9619139-0-8) Fun Soccer Ent.

—FUNdamental Soccer Series. Maher, Alan, ed. Garcia, Joe, illus. 128p. (gr. 1 up). 1991. pap. 4.95 (0-9619139-4-0) Fun Soccer Ent.

—Fundamental Soccer Tactics. Lavery, Vincent J., ed. (Illus.). 128p. (Orig.). (gr. 6). 1987. pap. 7.97 (0-9619139-2-4) Fun Soccer Ent.

De Weese, Gene. The Calvin Nullifier. (gr. k-6). 1989. pap. 2.95 (0-440-40214-X, YB) Dell.

—The Dandelion Caper. (gr. k-6). 1989. pap. 2.95 (0-440-40202-6, YB) Dell.

De Wetering, Janwillem Van see **Van de Wetering, Janwillem.**

Dewey, Ariane. Gib Morgan, Oilman. Dewey, Ariane, illus. LC 86-284. 48p. (gr. 1-3). 1987. 11.75 (0-688-06566-X); PLB 11.88 (0-688-06567-8) Greenwillow.

—Gib Morgan, Oilman. LC 92-43779. (Illus.). 48p. (gr. 1 up). 1993. pap. text ed. 4.95 (0-688-04583-9, Mulberry) Morrow.

—Lafitte, the Pirate. LC 92-43787. (Illus.). 48p. (gr. 1 up). 1993. pap. 4.95 (0-688-04578-2, Mulberry) Morrow.

—Naming Colors. LC 93-2635. (gr. 1-8). 1995. write for info. (0-06-021291-8, Festival); lib. bdg. write for info. (0-06-021292-6) HarpC Child Bks.

—The Narrow Escapes of Davy Crockett. Dewey, Ariane, illus. LC 88-34902. (gr. 1 up). 1990. 13.95 (0-688-08914-3); PLB 13.88 (0-688-08915-1) Greenwillow.

—The Narrow Escapes of Davy Crockett. LC 92-24586. (Illus.). 48p. (gr. 2 up). 1993. pap. 4.95 (0-688-12269-8, Mulberry) Morrow.

—Pecos Bill. LC 82-9229. (Illus.). 56p. (gr. k-3). 1983. 14.95 (0-688-01410-0) Greenwillow.

—Pecos Bill. Dewey, Ariane, illus. 56p. (gr. 1 up). 1994. pap. 4.95 (0-688-13108-5, Mulberry) Morrow.

—The Tea Squall. LC 87-14868. (Illus.). 40p. (gr. 1-4). 1988. 11.95 (0-688-07492-8); lib. bdg. 11.88 (0-688-07493-6) Greenwillow.

—The Tea Squall. Dewey, Ariane, illus. 40p. (gr. 1 up). 1994. pap. 4.95 (0-688-04582-0, Mulberry) Morrow.

Dewey, Ariane, jt. auth. see **Aruego, Jose.**

Dewey, Charles R. see **Uncle Hyggly, pseud.**

Dewey, Jennifer. Mammals on the Rise: A Prehistoric Southwest Coloring Book. (ps-3). 1992. pap. 4.95 (0-89013-238-0) Museum NM Pr.

—Spiders near & Far. (Illus.). 48p. (gr. 5 up). 1993. 14.99 (0-525-44979-5, DCB) Dutton Child Bks.

Dewey, Jennifer & Lyon, Lucy. Prehistoric Swimmers & Flyers of the Southwest. (Illus.). 32p. (gr. 4 up). 1990. pap. text ed. 4.95 (0-89013-195-3) Museum NM Pr.

Dewey, Jennifer O. The Adelie Penguin. Dewey, Jennifer O., illus. LC 88-13010. 48p. (gr. 3-6). 1989. 15.95 (0-316-18207-9) Little.

—Animal Architecture. LC 90-43010. (Illus.). 72p. (gr. 3-6). 1991. 14.95 (0-531-05930-8); PLB 14.99 (0-531-08530-9) Orchard Bks Watts.

—At the Edge of the Pond. Dewey, Jennifer O., illus. 48p. (gr. 1-5). 1987. 14.95 (0-316-18208-7) Little.

—Night & Day in the Desert, Vol. 1. (ps-3). 1991. 15.95 (0-316-18210-9) Little.

—The Wandering Albatross. Dewey, Jennifer O., illus. LC 88-31419. 48p. (gr. 3-6). 1989. 15.95 (0-316-18209-5) Little.

DeWeyer, Robert Van see **Van DeWeyer, Robert & Spenceley, Annabel.**

Dewhirst, Carin & Dewhirst, Joan. My Tricks & Treats: Halloween Stories, Songs, Poems, Recipes, Crafts & Fun for Kids. Barnes-Murphy, Rowan, illus. 80p. (ps-3). 1993. 9.98 (0-8317-5172-X) Smithmark.

Dewhirst, Joan, jt. auth. see **Dewhirst, Carin.**

Dewhurst, William. Your First Aquarium Plants. (Illus.). 34p. (Orig.). (gr. 9-12). 1991. pap. 1.95 (0-86622-112-3, YF-101) TFH Pubns.

De Wijs, Ivo. Donde Esta Springer? Van Den Hurk, Nicolle, illus. (SPA.). (ps-2). 1993. pap. 5.95 (0-8120-1747-1) Barron.

—Where Is Springer? Van Den Hurk, Nicolle, illus. 32p. (ps-2). 1993. 12.95 (0-8120-6360-0); pap. 4.95 (0-8120-1728-5) Barron.

DeWitt, Jamie. Jamie's Turn. LC 84-13973. (Illus.). 32p. (gr. 3-6). 1984. PLB 17.96 (0-940742-37-3) Raintree Steck-V.

DeWitt, Jim. The En-Dec System of Writing & Reading. DeWitt, Jim, illus. 52p. (Orig.). (gr. 9-12). 1987. pap. 6.95 (0-915199-74-2) Pen-Dec.

—Fingernail Souffle. Cole, Bradley, illus. 136p. (Orig.). (gr. 4-12). 1987. pap. 6.00 (0-915199-03-3) Pen Dec.

—Jammy Donuts a Season After. LC 83-90481. (Illus.). 64p. (Orig.). (gr. 4-12). 1984. pap. text ed. 5.95 (0-915199-04-1) Pen-Dec.

—Means Something Else--"The Doubles" Figures of Speech Writing Book, No. 2. Gleissner, Alex & Nordgren, Steve, illus. 64p. (Orig.). (gr. 6-12). 1987. wkbk. 6.00 (0-915199-51-3) Pen-Dec.

—Quiet-Time Thoughts. LC 83-90474. (Illus.). 64p. (Orig.). (gr. 3-10). 1984. pap. text ed. 5.95 (0-915199-00-9) Pen-Dec.

—Sharpshooting at Kinkajous. Cole, Bradley, illus. 136p. (gr. 4-12). 1987. pap. 6.00 (0-915199-06-8) Pen Dec.

—Twin Talk: Vocabulary Study Writing Book, Bk. 1. Hall, Christine, et al, illus. 76p. (Orig.). (gr. 4-12). 1987. pap. 6.00 wkbk. (0-915199-25-4) Pen-Dec.

DeWitt, Lisa F. Nobel Prize Winners: Biographical Sketches for Listening & Reading. (Illus.). 142p. (gr. 8 up). 1991. 12.95x (0-86647-047-6); three cassette tapes 26.95x (0-86647-049-2) Pro Lingua.

DeWitt, Lynda. What Will the Weather Be? Croll, Carolyn, illus. LC 90-1446. 32p. (gr. k-4). 1991. 13.95 (0-06-021596-8); PLB 13.89 (0-06-021597-6) HarpC Child Bks.

—What Will the Weather Be? Croll, Carolyn, illus. LC 90-1446. 32p. (gr. k-4). 1993. pap. 4.50 (0-06-445113-5, Trophy) HarpC Child Bks.

Dewitt, Sorena. String Figures from Around the World. Michel, Robin, illus. 32p. (gr. 2-6). 1992. pap. 4.95 (0-89346-356-6) Heian Intl.

De Witt, Sorena, jt. auth. see **Peaslee, Ann.**

DeWolf, Carol. The Candy Heart. LC 92-82937. (Illus.). 56p. (ps-3). 1993. pap. 3.50 (*0-943864-67-4*) Davenport.
—Object Talks from A to Z. Rigo, Russell, illus. 64p. (gr. k-4). 1987. 7.99 (*0-87403-237-7*, 2867) Standard Pub.
Dewoody, Betty N., jt. auth. see Dewoody, Darrel W.
Dewoody, Darrel W. & Dewoody, Betty N. C. T. the Living Christmas Tree. Plunkett, Kathleen, illus. (gr. k-6). 1989. write for info. Old Amer Pr.
Dexter, Alison. Grandma. Dexter, Alison, illus. LC 92-6473. 32p. (ps-2). 1993. 15.00 (*0-06-021143-1*); PLB 14.89 (*0-06-021144-X*) HarpC Child Bks.
Dexter, Catherine. Gerties's Green Thumb. (gr. 4-7). 1988. pap. 2.75 (*0-440-40018-X*, YB) Dell.
—The Gilded Cat. 208p. (gr. 4 up). 1992. 14.00 (*0-688-09425-2*) Morrow Jr Bks.
—Mazemaker. Ingraham, Erick, illus. LC 88-32349. 224p. (gr. 5-9). 1989. 11.95 (*0-688-07383-2*) Morrow Jr Bks.
—The Oracle Doll. (gr. k-6). 1988. pap. 2.95 (*0-440-40114-3*, YB) Dell.
Dexter, Harriet, contrib. by. The Nuremberg Stove. (Illus.). 40p. (gr. 3 up). 1981. pap. 3.00 (*0-88680-142-7*); royalty on application 35.00 (*0-317-03607-6*) I E Clark.
DeYoung, Donald B. Weather & the Bible: One Hundred Questions & Answers. Morris, Henry M., frwd. by. LC 92-6248. 144p. 1992. pap. 7.99 (*0-8010-3013-7*) Baker Bk.
DeYoung, Lorie. Beginning Addition & Subtraction. Hoffman, Joan, ed. (Illus.). 32p. (gr. 2). 1993. wkbk. 1.99 (*0-938256-32-7*) Sch Zone Pub Co.
—Time, Money & Fractions. Hoffman, Joan, ed. (Illus.). 32p. (gr. 1-2). 1993. wkbk. 1.99 (*0-938256-44-0*) Sch Zone Pub Co.
DeZinno, Ted. Christopher Columbus: The Dream That Changed the World. (Illus.). 1992. pap. 12.50 (*0-9632182-0-4*) McClain.
De Zutter, Hank. Who Says a Dog Goes Bow-Wow? LC 92-4232. (ps-3). 1993. pap. 15.00 (*0-385-30659-8*) Doubleday.
Dhanjal, Beryl. Amritsar. LC 93-31445. (Illus.). 48p. (gr. 5). 1994. PLB 13.95 RSBE (*0-87518-571-1*, Dillon) Macmillan Child Grp.
—Ranjit & the Fire Engines. (Illus.). 25p. (gr. 2-4). 1991. 15.95 (*0-237-60156-7*, Pub. by Evans Bros Ltd) Trafalgar.
—Sarah's Birthday Surprise. (Illus.). 25p. (gr. 2-4). 1991. 15.95 (*0-237-60158-3*, Pub. by Evans Bros Ltd) Trafalgar.
Dharma Realm Buddhist University Faculty. Human Roots: Buddhist Stories for Young Readers, Vol. 2. (Illus.). 140p. (Orig.). (gr. 3 up). 1984. pap. 5.00 (*0-88139-017-8*) Buddhist Text.
Dhondy, Farrukh. Black Swan. LC 92-30425. 208p. (gr. 6 up). 1993. 14.95 (*0-395-66076-9*) HM.
Dhuibhne, Eilis N. Hugo & the Sunshine Girl. Betera, Carol, illus. 129p. (Orig.). (gr. 5-9). 1991. pap. 7.95 (*1-85371-160-8*, Pub. by Poolbeg Pr ER) Dufour.
Diagram Group & Lambert, David. The Field Guide to Geology. (Illus.). 256p. (gr. 8-12). 1988. 24.95x (*0-8160-1697-6*) Facts on File.
Diagram Group Staff. Family Fun & Games. LC 92-21169. (Illus.). 800p. (gr. 6 up). 1992. 24.95 (*0-8069-8776-6*) Sterling.
—Junior Science on File Collection. 288p. (gr. 4-6). 1991. 201.50 (*0-8160-2706-4*) Facts on File.
Diagram Group Staff & Lambert, David. The Field Guide to Early Man. (Illus.). 256p. (gr. 8-12). 1988. 24.95x (*0-8160-1517-1*) Facts on File.
—The Field Guide to Geology. (Illus.). 256p. (gr. 8-12). 1989. pap. 14.95 (*0-8160-2032-9*) Facts on File.
—A Field Guide to Prehistoric Life. (Illus.). 256p. (gr. 8-12). 1986. 24.95x (*0-8160-1125-7*) Facts on File.
Diamantes, Kitty, illus. Favorite Tales from Grimm. 96p. (gr. 3 up). 1988. 9.95 (*0-02-689060-7*) Checkerboard.
Diamond, Arthur. Alcoholism. LC 92-23601. (Illus.). 112p. (gr. 5-8). 1992. PLB 14.95 (*1-56006-136-7*) Lucent Bks.
—The Bhopal Chemical Leak. LC 90-6011. (Illus.). 64p. (gr. 5-8). 1990. PLB 11.95 (*1-56006-009-3*) Lucent Bks.
—Egypt: Land of Mysteries. LC 91-43105. (Illus.). 128p. (gr. 4 up). 1992. RSBE 14.95 (*0-87518-511-8*, Dillon) Macmillan Child Grp.
—Jackie Robinson. LC 92-19871. (Illus.). 112p. (gr. 5-8). 1992. PLB 14.95 (*1-56006-029-8*) Lucent Bks.
—Malcolm X: A Voice for Black America. LC 93-8431. (gr. 8 up). 1994. write for info. (*0-89490-435-3*) Enslow Pubs.
—Prince Hall. King, Coretta Scott, intro. by. (Illus.). (gr. 5 up). 1992. 17.95 (*1-55546-588-9*) Chelsea Hse.
—The Romanian Americans. Moynihan, Daniel P., intro. by. (Illus.). 112p. (gr. 5 up). 1988. lib. bdg. 17.95 (*0-87754-898-6*) Chelsea Hse.
—Smallpox & the American Indian. LC 91-23066. (Illus.). 96p. (gr. 5-8). 1991. PLB 11.95 (*1-56006-018-2*) Lucent Bks.
Diamond, Bert. Technology You Can Build. (Illus.). 92p. (Orig.). 1990. pap. text ed. 13.81 (*0-87192-215-0*) Delmar.
Diamond, Judith. Laos. LC 89-34279. 128p. (gr. 5-9). 1989. PLB 26.60 (*0-516-02713-1*) Childrens.
Diamond, Laurie. Anastasia Krupnik: A Study Guide. Friedland, Joyce & Kessler, Rikki, eds. 26p. (gr. 9-12). 1990. pap. text ed. 14.95 (*0-88122-402-2*) Lrn Links.
—The Chalk Box Kid: A Study Guide. Friedland, Joyce & Kessler, Rikki, eds. 23p. (gr. 9-12). 1990. pap. text ed. 14.95 (*0-88122-398-0*) Lrn Links.

—The Hundred Dresses: A Study Guide. Friedland, Joyce & Kessler, Rikki, eds. 21p. (gr. 9-12). 1990. pap. text ed. 14.95 (*0-88122-404-9*) Lrn Links.
—Jacob Two-Two Meets the Hooded Fang: A Study Guide. Friedland, Joyce & Kessler, Rikki, eds. (gr. 2-5). 1991. pap. text ed. 14.95 (*0-88122-568-1*) LRN Links.
—Little Soup's Hayride: A Study Guide. Friedland, J. & Kessler, R., eds. 20p. (gr. 1-3). 1992. pap. text ed. 14.95 (*0-88122-699-8*) Lrn Links.
—Next Spring an Oriole: A Study Guide. Friedland, Joyce & Kessler, Rikki, eds. (gr. 1-4). 1991. pap. text ed. 14.95 (*0-88122-565-7*) LRN Links.
—O'Diddy: A Study Guide. Friedland, Joyce & Kessler, Rikki, eds. (gr. 2-4). 1991. pap. text ed. 14.95 (*0-88122-570-3*) LRN Links.
—The One in the Middle Is the Green Kangaroo: A Study Guide. Friedland, Joyce & Kessler, Rikki, eds. 16p. (gr. 9-12). 1990. pap. text ed. 14.95 (*0-88122-408-1*) Lrn Links.
—Rip-Roaring Russell: A Study Guide. Friedland, Joyce & Kessler, Rikki, eds. 20p. (gr. 9-12). 1990. pap. text ed. 14.95 (*0-88122-405-7*) Lrn Links.
Diamond, Lynell. Let's Discover Bryce & Zion National Parks. (Illus.). 32p. (gr. 1-6). 1990. pap. 4.95 (*0-89886-253-1*) Mountaineers.
Diamond, Lynnell. Let's Discover Capitol Reef, Arches, & Canyonlands National Parks: A Children's Activity Book for Ages 6-11. (Illus.). 32p. (gr. 1-6). 1991. pap. 4.95 (*0-89886-285-X*) Mountaineers.
—Let's Discover Petrified Forest National Park: A Children's Activity Book for Ages 6-11. (Illus.). 32p. (gr. 1-6). 1991. pap. 4.95 (*0-89886-286-8*) Mountaineers.
—Let's Discover the Grand Canyon. 32p. (gr. 1-6). 1990. pap. 3.95 (*0-89886-252-3*) Mountaineers.
Diamond, Lynnell & Mueller, Marge. Let's Discover the San Juan Islands. Diamond, Lynnell & Mueller, Marge, illus. 48p. (Orig.). 1989. pap. 4.95 (*0-89886-220-5*) Mountaineers.
Diamond, Troy. Rings, Springs, & Thingamajigs: How to Discover Your Power & How Not to Abuse It: What Every Child Needs to Know to Survive. LC 90-61384. (Illus.). 100p. 1990. 9.95 (*0-945437-08-0*) MacDonald-Sward.
Diamonstein, Barbaralee. Landmarks: Eighteen Wonders of the New York World. Lorenz, Albert, illus. 160p. 1992. 35.00 (*0-8109-3565-1*) Abrams.
Diane, James. Knitting. Baker, Wendy, illus. LC 93-21217. 48p. (gr. 3-7). 1994. 16.95 (*1-56847-146-7*) Thomson Lrning.
Diaz, Jorge. The Rebellious Alphabet. Jorfald, Ivind S., illus. Fox, Geoffrey, tr. LC 93-12697. (Illus.). 32p. (gr. 7 up). 1993. PLB 14.95 (*0-8050-2765-3*, Bks Young Read) H Holt & Co.
Diaz, Jorge A. Pablo Recuerda: La Fiesta del Dia de los Muertos. (SPA.). 48p. (gr. 5 up). 1993. 15.00 (*0-688-12894-7*) Lothrop.
Diaz, Olimpia, tr. see McPhee, John.
Diaz Del Castillo, Bernal see Castillo, Bernal D. de.
Dibble, Lisa. Food & Farming. LC 93-19073. (gr. 4 up). 1993. write for info. (*1-56458-387-2*) Dorling Kindersley.
DiBello, P., jt. auth. see Amery, H.
Dibner, Ellen J. & Gustafson, Ronald. Book Finders for Kids: The "Easy to Use" Subject Guide to Finding Non-fiction Books in a Library. Dibner, Ellen J. & Gustafson, Ronald, illus. LC 88-61646. 16p. (Orig.). (gr. 2-8). 1988. pap. 2.95 (*0-9620888-0-3*) Point Publications.
DiCarlo, Joseph, Jr. Following Christ. Puccetti, Patricia I., illus. 142p. (Orig.). (gr. 6). 1985. pap. 6.80 (*0-89870-065-5*) Ignatius Pr.
DiCerto, Joseph J. The Pony Express: Hoofbeats in the Wilderness. LC 88-34548. (Illus.). 64p. (gr. 3-5). 1989. PLB 12.90 (*0-531-10751-5*) Watts.
Dichmann, Kurt. Operations East Africa. Brown, Bill, ed. (Illus.). 96p. (Orig.). (gr. 9-12). 1989. pap. write for info. Ceise Corp.
Dick, Jean. Bomb Squads & Swat Teams. LC 88-15907. (Illus.). 48p. (gr. 5-6). 1988. RSBE 11.95 (*0-89686-401-4*, Crestwood Hse) Macmillan Child Grp.
—Mental & Emotional Disabilities. LC 88-21555. (Illus.). 48p. (gr. 5-6). 1988. RSBE 12.95 (*0-89686-418-9*, Crestwood Hse) Macmillan Child Grp.
Dick, K. & Sylvester, D. Victory. (gr. 4-7). 1987. 6.95 (*0-88160-104-7*, LW 244) Learning Wks.
Dick, Lois H. Discovering with God. Espe, Marvin, illus. 22p. (gr. k-6). 1984. pap. text ed. 4.25 (*1-55976-143-1*) CEF Press.
—I Dare. Lombard, Lynette, illus. 42p. (gr. k-6). 1971. pap. text ed. 9.45 (*1-55976-034-6*) CEF Press.
—Run Ma Run. Butcher, Sam, illus. 57p. (gr. k-6). 1978. pap. text ed. 8.99 (*1-55976-055-9*) CEF Press.
Dickens, Charles. The Bagman's Story. 48p. (gr. 4 up). 1983. PLB 13.95s.p. (*0-87191-922-2*) Creative Ed.
—The Baron of Grogzwig. Greenway, Shirley, ed. Barnes-Murphy, Rowan, illus. LC 93-18627. 1993. write for info. (*1-879085-81-X*) Whsprng Coyote Pr.
—Bleak House. Zabel, Morton D., ed. LC 84-25543. (gr. 9 up). 1956. pap. 9.16 (*0-395-05104-5*, RivEd) HM.
—Charles Dickens' A Christmas Carol. Richardson, I. M., ed. Kendall, Jane F., illus. LC 87-11270. 32p. (gr. 2-6). 1988. PLB 9.79 (*0-8167-1053-5*); pap. text ed. 1.95 (*0-8167-1054-6*) Troll Assocs.
—Christmas Books. Glancy, Ruth, intro. by. 520p. 1989. pap. 7.95 (*0-19-281790-6*) OUP.

—Christmas Carol. LC 85-15815. (gr. 7 up). 1963. pap. 2.25 (*0-8049-0026-4*, CL-26) Airmont.
—A Christmas Carol. LC 85-15815. 191p. 1981. Repr. PLB 15.95x (*0-89966-344-3*) Buccaneer Bks.
—A Christmas Carol. LC 85-15815. 150p. 1980. Repr. PLB 15.95 (*0-89967-017-2*) Harmony Raine.
—A Christmas Carol. Hyman, Trina S., illus. LC 85-15815. 128p. (gr. 4-6). 1983. 16.95 (*0-8234-0486-2*) Holiday.
—A Christmas Carol. Hildebrandt, Gregory, illus. LC 85-15815. 128p. 1983. pap. 14.95 (*0-671-45599-0*, S&S BFYR) S&S Trade.
—A Christmas Carol. Imsand, Marcel, illus. LC 85-15815. 78p. (gr. 4 up). 1984. PLB 13.95s.p. (*0-87191-955-9*) Creative Ed.
—A Christmas Carol. LC 85-15815. 176p. (gr. 7). 1984. pap. 3.95 (*0-14-035027-6*, Puffin) Puffin Bks.
—A Christmas Carol. Kennedy, Pam, ed. Flint, Russ, illus. 32p. (gr. k-6). 1985. pap. 2.95 (*0-8249-8099-9*, Ideals Child) Hambleton-Hill.
—A Christmas Carol. abr. ed. Wendt, Michael & Pizar, Kathleen, eds. Sturrock, Walt, illus. 80p. (gr. 2-5). 1988. 5.95 (*0-88101-087-1*) Unicorn Pub.
—A Christmas Carol. Zwerger, Lisbeth, illus. LC 88-15161. 60p. (gr. 5 up). 1991. pap. 19.95 (*0-88708-069-3*) Picture Bk Studio.
—A Christmas Carol. Innocenti, Roberto, illus. LC 90-1335. 152p. 1990. 30.00 (*1-55670-161-6*) Stewart Tabori & Chang.
—A Christmas Carol. abr. ed. Cook, Scott, illus. LC 89-24076. 72p. (gr. 2 up). 1990. 14.95 (*0-394-82239-0*); PLB 15.99 (*0-394-92239-5*) Random Bks Yng Read.
—A Christmas Carol. Rice, James, illus. & retold by. 48p. 14.95 (*0-88289-812-4*) Pelican.
—A Christmas Carol. 128p. (gr. 4-7). 1987. pap. 2.75 (*0-590-43527-2*) Scholastic Inc.
—Christmas Carol. Sturrock, Walt, illus. 1990. 11.95 (*0-88101-108-8*) Unicorn Pub.
—A Christmas Carol. 1990. pap. 2.50 (*0-8125-0434-8*) Tor Bks.
—A Christmas Carol. Boddy, Joe, illus. LC 91-9054. 48p. (ps-2). 1991. Animal version. 6.95 (*0-88101-160-6*) Unicorn Pub.
—Christmas Carol. 1992. pap. 10.70 (*0-395-60726-4*) HM.
—A Christmas Carol. Innocenti, Roberto, illus. 152p. (gr. 1-12). Date not set. lib. bdg. 25.00 RLB smythe-sewn (*0-88682-327-7*, 97200-098) Creative Ed.
—A Christmas Carol: A Changing Picture & Lift-the-Flap Book. Taylerson, Kareen, illus. 32p. (ps-3). 1989. pap. 14.95 (*0-670-82694-4*) Viking Child Bks.
—Christmas Carol: Xmas Treasury Pop-Ups. 1993. pap. 4.99 (*0-517-08787-1*) Outlet Bk Co.
—David Copperfield. (gr. 9 up). 1965. pap. 3.95 (*0-8049-0065-5*, CL-65) Airmont.
—David Copperfield. Ford, G. H., ed. LC 58-14706. (gr. 7 up). 1958. pap. 9.16 (*0-395-05122-3*, RivEd) HM.
—David Copperfield. 880p. (RL 7). 1988. pap. 4.95 (*0-451-52292-3*, Sig Classics) NAL-Dutton.
—David Copperfield. Blount, Trevor, ed. (Orig.). (gr. 9 up). 1979. pap. 5.00 (*0-14-043008-3*) Viking Child Bks.
—Dombey & Son. (ps-8). 1990. Repr. lib. bdg. 29.95x (*0-89966-678-7*) Buccaneer Bks.
—Great Expectations. Threapleton, M. M., intro. by. (gr. 9 up). 1965. pap. 3.95 (*0-8049-0068-X*, CL-68) Airmont.
—Great Expectations. Calder, Angus, ed. (Orig.). (gr. 9 up). 1965. pap. 4.95 (*0-14-043003-2*) Viking Child Bks.
—Great Expectations. (Illus.). 48p. (gr. 4 up). 1988. PLB 18.64 (*0-8172-2762-8*) Raintree Steck-V.
—Great Expectations. rev. ed. Klischer, Beth, ed. Weikel, Cheryl, illus. 587p. (Orig.). (gr. 10 up). 1989. pap. 6.95 (*0-89084-504-2*) Bob Jones Univ Pr.
—Great Expectations. 536p. (RL 9). 1961. pap. 3.95 (*0-451-52524-8*, Sig Classics) NAL-Dutton.
—Great Expectations. abr. ed. (Illus.). 172p. 1950. pap. text ed. 4.46 (*0-582-53003-2*) Longman.
—Great Expectations. 464p. (gr. 5 up). 1992. pap. 3.50 (*0-14-035130-2*, Puffin) Puffin Bks.
—Great Expectations. LC 92-50184. 536p. 1992. 5.98 (*1-56138-170-5*) Courage Bks.
—Hard Times. Spector, Robert D., intro. by. 304p. (gr. 9-12). 1981. pap. 2.50 (*0-553-21016-5*, Bantam Classics) Bantam.
—Hard Times. Adams, Richard, ed. (gr. 7 up). 1988. pap. text ed. 5.72 (*0-582-24396-3*, 78095) Longman.
—The Life of Our Lord. 128p. 1991. 15.99 (*0-8407-9126-7*); audio cassette 12.99 (*0-8407-9965-9*) Oliver-Nelson.
—Little Dorrit. (ps-8). 1990. Repr. lib. bdg. 39.95x (*0-89966-680-9*) Buccaneer Bks.
—Mystery of Edwin Drood. Budgey, N. F., intro. by. (gr. 10 up). 1966. pap. 1.50 (*0-8049-0114-7*, CL-114) Airmont.
—Nicholas Nickleby. Johnson, Edgar, intro. by. 816p. (gr. 10-12). 1983. pap. 5.95 (*0-553-21265-6*, Bantam Classics) Bantam.
—Oliver Twist. (gr. 9 up). 1964. pap. 3.50 (*0-8049-0009-4*, CL-9) Airmont.
—Oliver Twist. abridged ed. Martin, Les, adapted by. Zallinger, Jean, illus. LC 89-24279. 96p. (Orig.). (gr. 2-6). 1990. PLB 5.99 (*0-679-90391-7*); pap. 2.95 (*0-679-80391-2*) Random Bks Yng Read.
—Oliver Twist. 496p. (gr. 7). 1961. pap. 3.50 (*0-451-52351-2*, Sig Classics) NAL-Dutton.

—Oliver Twist. (Illus.). (gr. 3-5). 3.50 (0-7214-0823-0) Ladybird Bks.
—Oliver Twist. abr. ed. 137p. 1962. pap. text ed. 4.46 (0-582-53014-8) Longman.
—Oliver Twist. Nyborg, Randy, illus. 373p. 1992. Repr. PLB 29.95 (1-87776-769-7) Regal Pubns.
—Oliver Twist: In Arabic. (gr. 8-12). 1982. pap. 12.00x (0-86685-138-0) Intl Bk Ctr.
—Our Mutual Friend. (RL 8). 1964. pap. 5.95 (0-451-52250-8, CE1863, Sig Classics) NAL-Dutton.
—The Oxford Illustrated Dickens, 21 vols. Incl. The Old Curiosity Shop. Cattermole, George & Phiz, illus. 1951. 10.95 (0-19-254506-X); Our Mutual Friend. Stone, Marcus, illus. 1952. 10.95 (0-19-254510-8); The Personal History of David Copperfield. 10.95 (0-19-254502-7); The Posthumous Papers of the Pickwick Club. Dickens, Charles. (Illus.). 1947. 10.95 (0-19-254501-9); Sketches by Boz: Illustrative of Every-Day Life & Every-Day People. Cruickshank, George, illus. 1957. 10.95 (0-19-254518-3); A Tale of Two Cities. 1949. 10.95 (0-19-254504-3); The Uncommercial Traveller, & Reprinted Pieces. Dickens, Charles. 1958. 10.95 (0-19-254521-3); The Adventures of Oliver Twist. Cruickshank, George, illus. House, Humphy, intro. by. 1949. 10.95 (0-19-254505-1); American Notes & Pictures from Italy. Stone, Marcus, et al, illus. Sitwell, Sacheverell, intro. by. 1987. 10.95 (0-19-254519-1); Barnaby Rudge: A Tale of the Riots of 'Eighty. Dickens, Charles. 1954. 10.95 (0-19-254513-2); Bleak House. Phiz, illus. Sitwell, Osbert, intro. by. 1948. 10.95 (0-19-254503-5); Christmas Books. Farjeon, Eleanor, intro. by. (Illus.). 1954. 10.95 (0-19-254514-0); Christmas Stories. Dickens, Charles. (Illus.). 774p. 1956. 10.95 (0-19-254517-5); Dealings with the Firm of Dombey, & Son, Wholesale, Retail, & for Exploration. Phiz, illus. Garrod, H. W., intro. by. 1950. 10.95 (0-19-254507-8); Great Expectations. Dickens, Charles. (Illus.). 460p. 1987. 10.95 (0-19-254511-6); Hard Times for These Times. Walker, F. & Greiffenhagen, Maurice, illus. Foot, Dingle, intro. by. 1955. 10.95 (0-19-254515-9); The Life & Adventures of Martin Chuzzlewit. Phiz, illus. Russell, Geoffrey, intro. by. 1951. 10.95 (0-19-254509-4); The Life & Adventures of Nicholas Nickleby. Phiz, illus. Thorndike, Dame S., intro. by. 1950. 10.95 (0-19-254508-6); Little Dorrit. Dickens, Charles. (Illus.). 826p. 1953. 10.95 (0-19-254512-4); Master Humphrey's Clock & a Child's History of England. Dickens, Charles. (Illus.). 544p. 1958. 10.95 (0-19-254520-5); The Mystery of Edwin Drood. Fildes, Luke & Collins, Charles, illus. Roberts, S. C., intro. by. 294p. 1956. 10.95 (0-19-254516-7). 1987. Set. 200.00 (0-19-254522-1) OUP.
—Pickwick Papers. (gr. 10 up). 1968. pap. 2.95 (0-8049-0191-0, CL-191) Airmont.
—Pickwick Papers. (RL 9). 1964. pap. 5.95 (0-451-51756-3, CE1756, Sig Classics) NAL-Dutton.
—The Signalman. Richardson, I. M., adapted by. Ashmead, Hal, illus. LC 81-19819. 32p. (gr. 5-10). 1982. PLB 10.79 (0-89375-630-X); pap. text ed. 2.95 (0-89375-631-8) Troll Assocs.
—Tale of Two Cities. (gr. 9 up). 1964. pap. 2.95 (0-8049-0021-3, CL-21) Airmont.
—Tale of Two Cities. 384p. (RL 7). 1960. pap. 2.95 (0-451-52441-1, Sig Classics) NAL-Dutton.
—A Tale of Two Cities. Shaw, Charles, illus. Krapesh, Patti, adapted by. LC 79-24746. (Illus.). (gr. 4 up). 1983. PLB 18.64 (0-8172-1658-8) Raintree Steck-V.
—Tale of Two Cities. 384p. 1989. pap. 2.50 (0-8125-0506-9) Tor Bks.
Dickens, Estelle & Sellon, Jeffrey. Cuisenaire Roddles: Games & Puzzles to Measure Thinking Skills. (Illus.). 28p. 1981. pap. text ed. 9.95 (0-914040-90-1) Cuisenaire.
Dickens, Frank. Albert Herbert Hawkins: The Naughtiest Boy in the World. Dickens, Frank. (Illus.). LC 72-149044. 32p. (gr. ps-3). 7.95 (0-87592-000-4) Scroll Pr.
Dickens, Lucy. At the Beach. (Illus.). 10p. (ps-1). 1991. bds. 4.95 (0-670-83927-2) Viking Child Bks.
—Dancing Class. Dickens, Lucy, illus. 32p. (ps-3). 1992. 14.00 (0-670-84484-5) Viking Child Bks.
—Dirty Henry. (Illus.). 32p. (ps-1). 1991. 13.95 (0-670-83578-1) Viking Child Bks.
—Go Fish. (ps-3). 1991. 13.95 (0-670-84164-1) Viking Child Bks.
—Our Day. (Illus.). 10p. (ps-1). 1991. bds. 4.95 (0-670-83929-9) Viking Child Bks.
—Outside. (Illus.). 10p. (ps-1). 1991. bds. 4.95 (0-670-83928-0) Viking Child Bks.
—Playtime. (Illus.). 10p. (ps-1). 1991. bds. 4.95 (0-670-83926-4) Viking Child Bks.
Dickenson, Celia. Too Many Boys. 160p. (Orig.). (gr. 5-6). 1984. pap. 2.50 (0-553-26615-2) Bantam.
Dickenson, Gill. Children's Costume. 1993. 12.98 (1-55521-919-5) Bk Sales Inc.
—Face Painting: Art for Children. 1993. 12.98 (1-55521-918-7) Bk Sales Inc.
Dicker, Eva B., jt. auth. see Greene, Laura.
Dickerson, Beverly, jt. auth. see Short, J. Rodney.
Dickerson, Donald, ed. see Thompson, David.
Dickerson, Karle. Forgotten Fifty. (gr. 4-7). 1993. pap. 3.50 (0-06-106732-6, Harp PBks) HarpC.
Dickert, Barbara K. I Love You More. (gr. 5 up). 1993. 7.95 (0-8062-4716-9) Carlton.
Dickey, Glenn. Sports Great Jerry Rice. LC 93-19997. (Illus.). 64p. (gr. 4-10). 1993. lib. bdg. 15.95 (0-89490-419-1) Enslow Pubs.

—Sports Great Kevin Mitchell. LC 92-24159. (Illus.). 64p. (gr. 4-10). 1993. lib. bdg. 15.95 (0-89490-388-8) Enslow Pubs.
Dickey, James. Bronwen, the Traw, & the Shape-Shifter. Watson, Richard J., illus. LC 85-27082. 32p. (gr. k-3). 1986. 13.95 (0-15-212580-9, HB Juv Bks) HarBrace.
Dickey, Kate, ed. see Berry, Joy W.
Dickey, Terry P., ed. see Yarber, Yvonne & Choy, Carol E.
Dickins, Roberts, jt. auth. see Brown, Hayden.
Dickinson, Dan & Dickinson, Kieran. Major League Stadiums: A Vacation Planning Reference to the 26 Baseball Parks. LC 91-52509. 320p. (gr. 9-12). 1991. pap. 24.95x (0-89950-610-0) McFarland & Co.
Dickinson, Dof. Write from the Start. (Illus.). 136p. (Orig.). (gr. 3 up). 1988. pap. 19.95 (0-333-47822-3, Macmillan Ed UK) Players Pr.
Dickinson, Emily. A Brighter Garden. Ackerman, Karen, compiled by. Tudor, Tasha, illus. 63p. 1990. 17.95 (0-399-21490-9, Philomel Bks) Putnam Pub Group.
—I'm Nobody! Who Are You? Poems of Emily Dickinson for Children. Schneider, Rex, illus. Sewall, Richard, intro. by. LC 78-6828. (Illus.). 96p. (gr. 1 up). 1978. 21.95 (0-916144-21-6); pap. 14.95 (0-916144-22-4) Stemmer Hse.
Dickinson, Jane. All about Trees. D'Adamo, Anthony, illus. LC 82-17382. 32p. (gr. 3-6). 1983. PLB 10.59 (0-89375-892-2); pap. text ed. 2.95 (0-89375-893-0) Troll Assocs.
—Wonders of Water. Schneider, Rex, illus. LC 82-17388. 32p. (gr. 3-6). 1983. PLB 10.59 (0-89375-874-4); pap. text ed. 2.95 (0-89375-875-2) Troll Assocs.
Dickinson, Kieran, jt. auth. see Dickinson, Dan.
Dickinson, Lavona & Watts, Ramona. Come Learn with Me. (ps). 1989. page. 12.95 (0-8224-1377-9) Fearon Teach Aids.
—Storytime Learning. (ps). 1989. pap. 15.95 (0-8224-6277-X) Fearon Teach Aids.
Dickinson, Peter. AK. 1992. 15.00 (0-385-30608-3) Doubleday.
—The Blue Hawk. (gr. 5-9). 1991. 21.50 (0-8446-6478-2) Peter Smith.
—A Bone from a Dry Sea. LC 92-20491. 1993. 16.00 (0-385-30821-3) Delacorte.
—A Box of Nothing. LC 87-25660. 128p. (gr. 3-6). 1988. pap. 14.95 (0-385-29664-9) Delacorte.
—The Changes: A Trilogy, 3 vols. Incl. The Devil's Children. 192p. 1986. pap. 14.95 (0-385-29449-2); Heartsease. 192p. 1986. pap. 14.95 (0-385-29451-4); The Weathermonger. 244p. 1986. pap. 14.95 (0-385-29450-6). (gr. 7 up). 1986. pap. Delacorte.
—City of Gold. Foreman, Michael, illus. 192p. (gr. 5 up). 1992. pap. 13.45 (0-395-63173-4) HM.
—The Devil's Children. (gr. k-12). 1988. pap. 2.95 (0-440-20082-2, LFL) Dell.
—Emma Tupper's Diary. 224p. (gr. 3 up). 1988. pap. 3.25 (0-440-40080-5, YB) Dell.
—Eva. (gr. 7 up). 1989. 14.95 (0-440-50129-6) Delacorte.
—Heartease. (gr. 7 up). 1988. pap. 2.95 (0-317-69490-1, LFL) Dell.
—Heartsease. (gr. k-10). 1988. pap. 2.95 (0-440-20096-2, LFL) Dell.
—Merlin Dreams. Lee, Alan, illus. LC 88-3985. 160p. (gr. k-12). 1988. 19.95 (0-440-50067-2) Delacorte.
—Seventh Raven. 1991. pap. 3.50 (0-440-20836-X, LFL) Dell.
—Time & the Clock Mice, Etcetera. Chichester-Clark, Emma, illus. LC 93-11434. 1994. write for info. (0-385-32038-8) Delacorte.
—The Weathermonger. (gr. k-12). 1988. pap. 2.95 (0-440-20003-2) Dell.
Dickinson, Pter. AK. 1994. pap. 3.99 (0-440-21897-7) Dell.
Dickinson, Rebecca. Animal Babies. Bonforte, Lisa, illus. LC 87-81765. 22p. (ps). 1988. write for info. (0-307-12116-X, Pub. by Golden Bks) Western Pub.
Dickinson, Susan. Brer Rabbit & the Peanut Patch. rev. ed. Frankland, David, illus. 32p. (gr. k-2). 1990. Repr. of 1985 ed. PLB 10.50 (1-878363-18-2) Forest Hse.
Dickinson, Terence. Exploring the Night Sky: The Equinox Astronomy Guide for Beginners. Bianchi, John, illus. 72p. (Orig.). (gr. 5 up). 1989. 17.95 (0-920656-64-1, Pub. by Camden Hse CN); pap. 9.95 (0-920656-66-8, Pub. by Camden Hse CN) Firefly Bks Ltd.
Dickman, Charaleen. Memories of Me Baby, 18 vols. Hungerford, La Farne G., illus. (ps). Date not set. pap. text ed. 34.95 (1-882237-01-3) Life Time Pubs.
Dickmeyer, Lowell A. Skateboarding Is for Me. LC 78-54361. (Illus.). 48p. (gr. 2-5). 1978. PLB 13.50 (0-8225-1081-2) Lerner Pubns.
Dicks, Brian. Greece. (Illus.). (gr. 4-6). 1991. 17.95 (0-237-60192-3, Pub. by Evans Bros Ltd) Trafalgar.
—Lanzarote: Fire Island of the Canaries. (Illus.). 62p. (gr. 7-9). 1988. 22.95 (0-85219-727-6, Pub. by Batsford UK) Trafalgar.
Dicks, Ian. Them Bones. 1993. pap. 13.95 (0-385-31045-5) Dell.
Dicks, Terrance. A Cat Called Max: Magnificent Max. Goffe, Toni, illus. 64p. (gr. 3-6). 1990. pap. 2.95 (0-8120-4427-4) Barron.
—A Cat Called Max: Max & the Quiz Kids. Goffe, Toni, illus. 64p. (gr. 2-5). 1990. pap. 2.95 (0-8120-4501-7) Barron.
—A Cat Called Max: Max's Amazing Summer. Goffe, Toni, illus. 52p. (gr. 3-6). 1992. pap. 3.50 (0-8120-4819-9) Barron.

—Goliath & the Burglar. Littlewood, Valerie, illus. 64p. (gr. k-4). 1987. 7.95 (0-8120-5823-2); pap. 3.50 (0-8120-3820-7) Barron.
—Goliath & the Buried Treasure. Littlewood, Valerie, illus. (gr. k-4). 1987. 7.95 (0-8120-5822-4); pap. 2.95 (0-8120-3819-3) Barron.
—Goliath & the Cub Scouts. Littlewood, Valerie, illus. 64p. (gr. 2-4). 1990. pap. 2.95 (0-8120-4493-2) Barron.
—Goliath at the Dog Show. Littlewood, Valerie, illus. 64p. (gr. k-4). 1987. 7.95 (0-8120-5821-6); pap. 3.50 (0-8120-3818-5) Barron.
—Goliath at the Seaside. Littlewood, Valerie, illus. 52p. (gr. 2-4). 1989. pap. 2.95 (0-8120-4209-3) Barron.
—Goliath Goes to Summer School. Littlewood, Valerie, illus. 52p. (gr. 2-4). 1989. pap. 2.95 (0-8120-4210-7) Barron.
—Goliath on Vacation. Littlewood, Valerie, illus. 64p. (gr. k-4). 1987. 7.95 (0-8120-5824-0); pap. 3.50 (0-8120-3821-5) Barron.
—Goliath's Birthday. Littlewood, Valerie, illus. 52p. (gr. 2-5). 1992. pap. 3.50 (0-8120-4821-0) Barron.
—Goliath's Christmas. Littlewood, Valerie, illus. 64p. (gr. 2-4). 1987. PLB 7.95 (0-8120-5843-7); pap. 2.95 (0-8120-3878-9) Barron.
—The MacMagics: A Spell for My Sister. Canning, Celia, illus. 96p. (gr. 3-6). 1992. pap. 3.50 (0-8120-4881-4) Barron.
—The MacMagics: My Brother the Vampire. Canning, Celia, illus. 96p. (ps-3). 1992. pap. 3.50 (0-8120-4883-0) Barron.
—Meet the MacMagics. Canning, Celia, illus. 96p. (gr. 3-6). 1992. pap. 3.50 (0-8120-4882-2) Barron.
—Nurse Sally Ann. Sims, Blanche, illus. LC 92-22075. 1994. pap. 14.00 (0-671-79428-0, S&S BYFR) S&S Trade.
—On Their Own. Littlewood, Valerie, illus. 64p. (gr. 2-5). 1993. pap. 3.50 (0-8120-1675-0) Barron.
—Sally Ann & the Mystery Picnic. Sims, Blanche, illus. LC 92-22074. (gr. 1-3). 1993. pap. 14.00 JRT (0-671-79427-2, S&S BYFR) S&S Trade.
—Sally Ann & the School Show. LC 91-1541. (ps-3). 1992. pap. 14.00 (0-671-74513-1, S&S BYFR) S&S Trade.
—Sally Ann on Her Own. Sims, Blanche, illus. LC 91-15379. 64p. (gr. k-3). 1992. pap. 14.00 jacketed (0-671-74512-3, S&S BYFR) S&S Trade.
—Teacher's Pet. Littlewood, Valerie, illus. 52p. (gr. 2-5). 1992. pap. 3.50 (0-8120-4820-2) Barron.
Dickson, Anna H. Oh, I Am So Embarrassed! Cooke, Tom, illus. LC 87-81782. 32p. (ps-1). 1988. write for info. (0-307-12027-9) Western Pub.
Dickson, Anna H. See You Later Mashed Potater. (ps). 1990. write for info. (0-307-12042-2) Western Pub.
Dickson, Anna H. Where's My Blankie? Nicklalus, Carol, illus. LC 83-83278. 32p. (ps). 1984. write for info. (0-307-12013-9, 12013, Golden Bks) Western Pub.
Dickson, Charles. Beating the Chemical Cop-Out. Nelson, Becky, ed. 22p. (Orig.). (gr. 7-12). 1992. pap. text ed. 1.95 (1-56309-036-8, Wrld Changers Res) Womans Mission Union.
—Please Help Me Hold On. Nelson, Becky, ed. 22p. (Orig.). (gr. 7-12). 1992. pap. text ed. 1.95 (1-56309-037-6, Wrld Changers Res) Womans Mission Union.
Dickson, Edward & Galan, Mark. The Immigration & Naturalization Service. (Illus.). 112p. (gr. 5 up). 1990. 14.95 (1-55546-113-1) Chelsea Hse.
Dickson, Sandy L. The Story of Smartworms: The Journey Begins. Barrow, Madeline H., ed. Dixon, David, illus. 34p. (gr. k-5). 1989. write for info.; PLB write for info.; pap. write for info. Smartworm Corp.
Dickson, Sue. Complete Classroom Kit. rev. ed. Portadino, Norma, illus. 7968p. (gr. k-3). 1984. pap. 533.00 (1-55574-006-6, KC 510) CBN Publishing.
—Off We Go. rev. ed. Portadino, Norma, illus. 112p. (gr. k-3). 1985. pap. 4.97 (1-55574-001-4, WB-130) CBN Publishing.
—Phonetic Storybook Readers, 17 vols. rev. ed. Portadino, Norma, illus. 960p. (gr. k-3). 1984. pap. 48.00 (1-55574-003-0, SR-310) CBN Publishing.
—Raceway. rev. ed. Portadino, Norma, illus. 96p. (gr. k-3). 1984. pap. 4.97 (1-55574-002-2, WB-140) CBN Publishing.
Did You Know Publishings Staff. Rosa Parks. LC 92-71756. 32p. 1992. text ed. 8.50 (0-9633151-0-2) Did You Know Pub.
Diebel, Anne, jt. auth. see Newbold, Patt.
Diebert, Linda. Motivational Magic. (Illus.). 128p. (ps-2). 1990. 10.95 (0-86653-535-7, GA1137) Good Apple.
—Science for Me. 112p. (ps-2). 1991. 11.95 (0-86653-597-7, GA1318) Good Apple.
Diehl, Harold S., et al. Health & Safety for You. 5th ed. 1980. text ed. 29.52 (0-07-016863-6) McGraw.
Diehn, Gwen & Krautwurst, Terry. Nature Crafts for Kids. LC 91-36387. (Illus.). 144p. 1992. 19.95 (0-8069-8372-8) Sterling.
Diener, Carolyn S., et al. Energy: A Curriculum Unit for Three, Four & Five Year Olds. LC 81-83050. (Illus.). 112p. (ps-k). 1982. pap. 9.95 (0-89334-069-3) Humanics Ltd.
Diep, Bridgette. Trip Through Cambodia. Vaing, Jocelang, illus. LC 73-159478. 32p. (ps-3). 8.95 (0-87592-054-3) Scroll Pr.
Dierbeck, Jim. The Rock Witch. (gr. 5-9). 1988. pap. text ed. 8.00 (0-910303-10-X) Writers Pub Serv.
Dierks, Carrie, jt. auth. see Asimov, Isaac.

Diestel-Feddersen, Mary. Try Again, Sally Jane. Ashley, Yvonne, illus. LC 86-42810. 30p. (gr. 2-3). 1987. PLB 18.60 (*1-55532-150-X*) Gareth Stevens Inc.

Dieterich, Michele. Skiing. (Illus.). 48p. (gr. 4-12). 1992. PLB 17.50 (*0-8225-2478-3*) Lerner Pubns.

Dietl, Ulla. The Plant-and-Grow Project Book. LC 93-24788. (Illus.). 48p. (gr. 2-10). 1993. 12.95 (*0-8069-0456-9*) Sterling.

Dietrich, Helen R., ed. see Janssen, James S.

Dietrich, Wilson G. Muckwa: The Adventures of a Chippewa Indian Boy. Graves, Helen, ed. LC 89-52120. (Illus.). 71p. (gr. 3-10). 1990. pap. 6.95 (*1-55523-304-X*) Winston-Derek.

Dietz, ed. Prayers for Children. (Illus.). (gr. k-6). 1990. booklet .99 (*0-87509-121-0*) Chr Pubns.

Dietz, Lew. The Story of Andre. Shevis, Stell, illus. (gr. 2-3). 1979. pap. 9.95 (*0-89272-052-2*) Down East.

Dievart, Roger. Teeth, Tusks & Fangs. Bogard, Vicki, tr. from FRE. Valat, Pierre-Marie, illus. LC 90-50778. 38p. (gr. k-5). 1991. 4.95 (*0-944589-35-9*, 359) Young Discovery Lib.

Diffenderfer, Susan. Ecology: Learning to Love Our Planet. 115p. (gr. k-8). 1984. 19.95 (*0-913705-01-2*) Zephyr Pr AZ.

Diffenderfer, Terri. Me & My Puppy. Frame, Paul, illus. 24p. (Orig.). (gr. k-1). 1990. pap. 0.99 (*1-878624-41-5*) McClanahan Bk.

DiFiori, Larry. Muffin Mouse's New House. DiFiori, Larry, illus. (ps-k). 1991. pap. write for info. (*0-307-10028-6*, Golden Pr) Western Pub.

DiFiori, Lawrence. The Truck Book. DiFiori, Lawrence, illus. LC 83-83106. (ps). 1984. write for info. (*0-307-12299-9*, Golden Bks) Western Pub.

Di Franco, J. Philip. The Italian Americans. Moynihan, Daniel P., intro. by. 112p. (Orig.). (gr. 5 up). 1988. 17.95 (*0-87754-886-2*); pap. 9.95 (*0-7910-0268-3*) Chelsea Hse.

Diggle, Giles. Roosters. 192p. (gr. 7 up). 1992. 18.95 (*0-571-16512-5*) Faber & Faber.

Diggs, Lucy. Everyday Friends. (gr. 5 up). 1987. pap. 2.95 (*0-8167-1047-3*) Troll Assocs.

Diggs, Richard N. Let's Talk about Sex: Facts, Statistics & Information Which May Help You Avoid...Screwin up Your Life! Clancey, Eleanor, ed. (Illus.). 96p. (Orig.). (gr. 8-10). 1992. pap. 5.95 (*0-937157-11-2*) Progressive Pubns.

DiGiovanni, Pauline G. The Golden Key to Reading: The Paula Di Intensive Phonics Method of Reading-Writing-Spelling - Student's Writing Booklet - Program 2. 50p. (gr. k-1). 1982. wkbk. 4.99 (*0-936543-03-5*) Paula Di Ed.

—The Golden Key to Reading: The Paula Di Intensive Phonics Method of Reading-Writing-Spelling - Student's Writing Booklet - Program 1. 46p. (gr. k-1). 1982. wkbk. 4.99 (*0-9613130-5-6*) Paula Di Ed.

—The Golden Key to Reading: The Paula Di Intensive Phonics Method of Reading-Writing-Spelling - Reading Supplement A. (Illus.). 56p. (gr. k-2). 1982. pap. text ed. 4.99 (*0-9613130-4-8*); tchr's. ed. 4.99 (*0-685-11931-9*) Paula Di Ed.

—The Golden Key to Reading: The Paula Di Intensive Phonics Method of Reading-Writing-Spelling, Bk. 1. 2nd, rev. ed. (Illus.). 60p. (Orig.). (gr. k-1). 1985. pap. text ed. 6.99 (*0-9613130-7-2*); tchr's. ed. 7.99 (*0-936543-00-0*) Paula Di Ed.

—The Golden Key to Reading: The Paula Di Intensive Phonics Method of Reading-Writing-Spelling, 3 bks, Bks. 1-3. 2nd, rev. ed. (gr. k-3). 1985. Set. pap. text ed. write for info. (*0-9613130-6-4*) Paula Di Ed.

—The Golden Key to Reading: The Paula Di Intensive Phonics Method of Reading-Writing-Spelling, Bk. 2. 2nd, rev. ed. (Illus.). 158p. (Orig.). (gr. k-2). 1985. pap. text ed. 10.99 (*0-9613130-8-0*); tchr's. ed. 11.99 (*0-936543-01-9*) Paula Di Ed.

—The Golden Key to Reading: The Paula Di Intensive Phonics Method of Reading-Writing-Spelling, Bk. 3. 2nd, rev. ed. (Illus.). 238p. (Orig.). (gr. 1-3). 1985. pap. text ed. 13.99 (*0-9613130-9-9*); tchr's. ed. 14.99 (*0-936543-02-7*) Paula Di Ed.

DiGirolamo, Vincent. Whispers under the Wharf. LC 90-331073. 144p. (Orig.). 1990. pap. 8.95 (*0-931832-52-7*) Fithian Pr.

Di Ianni, Mary, tr. see Dambrosio, Monica & Barbieri, Roberto.

Dijs, Carla. Are You My Daddy? Dijs, Carla, illus. 12p. (ps). 1990. pap. 5.95 casebound, pop-up (*0-671-70227-0*, Little Simon) S&S Trade.

—Are You My Mommy? Dijs, Carla, illus. 12p. (ps). 1990. pap. 5.95 casebound, pop-up (*0-671-70226-2*, Little Simon) S&S Trade.

—Cinderella Pop-up Book. (ps). 1991. 4.99 (*0-440-40535-1*, YB) Dell.

—A Giraffe Needs to Laugh: Pop-up Book. Dijs, Carla, illus. 10p. (gr. k-2). 1993. 7.99 (*0-8431-3480-1*) Price Stern.

—Hansel & Gretel Pop-up Book. (ps). 1991. 4.99 (*0-440-40538-6*, YB) Dell.

—Little Red Riding Hood Pop-up Book. (ps). 1991. 4.99 (*0-440-40536-X*, YB) Dell.

—Pretend You're a Hippo. (Illus.). 14p. (ps). 1992. pap. 6.95 pop-up bk. (*0-671-76057-2*, Little Simon) S&S Trade.

—Pretend You're a Whale. (Illus.). 14p. (ps). 1992. pap. 6.95 pop-up bk. (*0-671-75980-9*, Little Simon) S&S Trade.

—Three Little Pigs Pop-up Book. (ps). 1991. 4.99 (*0-440-40537-8*, YB) Dell.

—What Do I Do at Eight O'Clock? (Illus.). 22p. (ps). 1993. pap. 8.95 casebound (*0-671-79526-0*, S&S BFYR) S&S Trade.

—Who Sees You? at the Ocean. (ps-2). 1987. 5.95 (*0-448-34350-9*, G&D) Putnam Pub Group.

—Who Sees You? At the Pond. (Illus.). 12p. (ps-k). 1992. 5.95 (*0-448-40309-9*, G&D) Putnam Pub Group.

—Who Sees You? at the Zoo. (ps-2). 1987. 5.95 (*0-448-34353-3*, G&D) Putnam Pub Group.

—Who Sees You? in the Forest. (ps-2). 1987. 5.95 (*0-448-34351-7*, G&D) Putnam Pub Group.

—Who Sees You? In the Jungle. (Illus.). 12p. (ps-k). 1992. 5.95 (*0-448-40310-2*, G&D) Putnam Pub Group.

—Who Sees You? on the Farm. (ps-3). 1987. 5.95 (*0-448-34352-5*, G&D) Putnam Pub Group.

Dijs, Carla & Moerbeek, Kees. Bee Says Buzz. (gr. 3 up). 1990. 9.95 (*0-85953-222-4*) Childs Play.

—Hiding Places. (gr. 4 up). 1990. 9.95 (*0-85953-223-2*) Childs Play.

—Let's Play. (gr. 3 up). 1990. 9.95 (*0-85953-224-0*) Childs Play.

Dijs, Carla, jt. auth. see Moerbeek, Kees.

Dijs, Carla, illus. Who Sees You? At Night. 12p. (ps). 1993. 5.95 (*0-448-40079-0*, G&D) Putnam Pub Group.

—Who Sees You? Underground. 12p. (ps). 1993. 5.95 (*0-448-40080-4*, G&D) Putnam Pub Group.

Dikis, Eloise. The Twelve Powers of Animals. Wortman, Mary, ed. Ford, Phyllis, illus. 44p. (ps-5). 1989. comb bdg. 7.95 (*0-939339-06-4*) AFCOM Pub.

Diller, Harriett. Grandaddy's Highway. 22p. (ps-3). 1993. 14.95 (*1-878093-63-0*) Boyds Mills Pr.

Dillon, Barbara. A Mom by Magic. Lindberg, Jeffrey, illus. LC 89-29410. 144p. (gr. 3-7). 1990. (Lipp Jr Bks); PLB 13.89 (*0-397-32449-9*, Lipp Jr Bks) HarpC Child Bks.

—Mrs. Tooey & the Terrible Toxic Tar. LC 87-45985. 96p. (gr. 3-7). 1988. (Lipp Jr Bks); PLB 10.89 (*0-397-32277-1*, Lipp Jr Bks) HarpC Child Bks.

—My Stepfather Shrank! LC 91-23901. (Illus.). 128p. (gr. 3-7). 1992. 13.00 (*0-06-021574-7*); PLB 12.89 (*0-06-021581-X*) HarpC Child Bks.

—My Stepfather Shrank! Casale, Paul, illus. LC 91-23901. 128p. (gr. 3-6). 1994. pap. 3.95 (*0-06-440459-5*, Trophy) HarpC Child Bks.

—The Teddy Bear Tree. MacDonald, Patricia, ed. Rose, David, illus. 80p. (gr. 2-5). 1990. pap. 2.95 (*0-671-68432-9*, Minstrel Bks) PB.

Dillon, Eilis. Children of Bach. LC 91-45432. 176p. (gr. 5-8). 1992. SBE 13.95 (*0-684-19440-6*, Scribners Young Read) Macmillan Child Grp.

—The Cruise of the Santa Maria. (Illus.). (gr. 3-7). 1991. pap. 9.95 (*0-86278-263-5*, Pub. by OBrien Pr IE) Dufour.

—The Five Hundred. (Illus.). 87p. (gr. 2-6). 1991. pap. 8.95 (*0-86278-262-7*, Pub. by OBrien Pr IE) Dufour.

—Living in Imperial Rome. (Illus.). 176p. (gr. 4-8). 1991. pap. 10.95 (*0-86278-264-3*, Pub. by OBrien Pr IE) Dufour.

—Lost Island. 204p. 1987. pap. 8.95 (*0-86278-118-3*, Pub. by O'Brien Press Ltd Eire) Dufour.

—The Singing Cave. 259p. (gr. 4-6). 1992. pap. 7.95 (*1-85371-153-5*, Pub. by Poolbeg Pr ER) Dufour.

Dillon, Ellis. The Island of Ghosts. LC 89-31265. 160p. (gr. 5-7). 1989. SBE 13.95 (*0-684-19107-5*, Scribners Young Read) Macmillan Child Grp.

Dillon, Jacquelyn, et al. Strictly Strings - Piano, Bk. 1: A Comprehensive String Method. (Illus.). 64p. (Orig.). (gr. 4-6). 1992. pap. 11.95 (*0-88284-535-7*, 5298) Alfred Pub.

—Strictly Strings: A Comprehensive String Method, Bk. 1: Bass. (Illus.). 40p. (Orig.). (gr. 4-6). 1992. pap. 4.95 (*0-88284-533-0*, 5296) Alfred Pub.

—Strictly Strings: A Comprehensive String Method, Bk. 1: Cello. (Illus.). 40p. (Orig.). (gr. 4-6). 1992. pap. 4.95 (*0-88284-532-2*, 5295) Alfred Pub.

—Strictly Strings: A Comprehensive String Method, Bk. 1: Score. (Illus.). 216p. (gr. 4-6). 1992. pap. 19.95 (*0-88284-534-9*, 5297) Alfred Pub.

—Strictly Strings: A Comprehensive String Method, Bk. 1: Violin. (Illus.). 40p. (Orig.). (gr. 4-6). 1992. pap. 4.95 (*0-88284-530-6*, 5293) Alfred Pub.

—Strictly Strings: A Comprehensive String Method, Bk. 1: Viola. (Illus.). 40p. (Orig.). (gr. 4-6). 1992. pap. 4.95 (*0-88284-531-4*, 5294) Alfred Pub.

Dillon, Jana. Jeb Scarecrow's Pumpkin Patch. Dillon, Jana, illus. LC 91-16423. 32p. (ps-3). 1992. 14.45 (*0-395-57578-8*) HM.

Dillon, L. D., jt. auth. see Willard, N.

Dillow, John, illus. Baby's Day: Board Books. 10p. (ps). 1991. bds. 3.50 (*0-7214-9136-7*) Ladybird Bks.

—Baby's Toys: Little Ladybird Board Book. 8p. (ps). 1991. bds. 3.50 (*0-7214-9137-5*, S851-15) Ladybird Bks.

—Picture Atlas of the World. 45p. 1993. 11.95 (*0-7214-5354-6*) Ladybird Bks.

Dils, Tracey. George Washington, Country Boy, Country Gentleman. (Illus.). 32p. (gr. 1-3). 1992. pap. 3.50 (*0-87406-629-8*) Willowisp Pr.

—The Girl Talk Guide to Boytalk. 96p. (gr. 3-7). 1992. pap. 2.95 (*0-307-22104-0*, 22104, Golden Pr) Western Pub.

Dils, Tracey E. The Scariest Stories You've Ever Heard, Pt. III. 96p. (gr. 4-8). 1991. pap. 2.99 (*0-87406-515-1*) Willowisp Pr.

Dilts, Susan & Stokes, Chris, eds. Peterson's Guide to Colleges in New England 1994. 10th, rev. ed. 150p. (gr. 11-12). 1995. pap. 13.95 (*1-56079-274-4*) Petersons Guides.

—Peterson's Guide to Colleges in New York 1994. 10th, rev. ed. 140p. (gr. 11-12). 1993. pap. 13.95 (*1-56079-273-6*) Petersons Guides.

—Peterson's Guide to Colleges in the Middle Atlantic States 1994. 10th, rev. ed. 230p. (gr. 11-12). 1993. pap. 13.95 (*1-56079-278-7*) Petersons Guides.

—Peterson's Guide to Colleges in the Midwest 1994. 10th, rev. ed. 350p. (gr. 11-12). 1993. pap. 13.95 (*1-56079-275-2*) Petersons Guides.

—Peterson's Guide to Colleges in the South 1994. 9th, rev. ed. 300p. (gr. 11-12). 1993. pap. 13.95 (*1-56079-276-0*) Petersons Guides.

—Peterson's Guide to Colleges in the West 1994. 8th, rev. ed. 200p. (gr. 11-12). 1993. pap. 13.95 (*1-56079-277-9*) Petersons Guides.

DiMatteo, Richard, tr. see Parker, Roberta N. & Parker, Harvey C.

Dimino, Frank. Amazing Aircraft Coloring Book. (Illus.). 32p. (Orig.). (gr. 6-12). 1989. pap. 4.50 (*0-8431-1958-6*) Price Stern.

—Hot Rods. DiMino, Frank, illus. 32p. (Orig.). (gr. k-2). 1993. pap. 3.99 (*0-8431-3514-X*) Troubador Pr.

Di Mino, Frank. Hot Trucks. Di Mino, Frank, illus. (gr. k-2). 1993. pap. 4.50 (*0-8431-3515-8*) Price Stern.

Dimino, Frank. Monster Trucks Coloring Book. (Illus.). 32p. (Orig.). (gr. 6-12). 1989. pap. 4.50 (*0-8431-1957-8*) Price Stern.

Dimond, Jasper. Dinosaurs. Dimond, Jasper, illus. 48p. (gr. 3-7). 1985. pap. 10.95 (*0-13-214628-2*) P-H.

—Noah's Ark. (Illus.). 48p. (gr. k-3). 1983. 8.95 (*0-13-622951-4*) P-H.

Dimont, Max I. The Amazing Adventures of the Jewish People. LC 84-16806. 175p. (gr. 8 up). 1984. 5.95 (*0-87441-391-5*) Behrman.

Dinan, Carolyn. Alfred Mouse. Dinan, Carolyn, illus. 80p. (ps). 1992. laminated bds. 15.95 (*0-571-16500-1*) Faber & Faber.

Dinardo, Jeffrey. Henry's Bunny Hop. (ps-3). 1993. pap. 3.25 (*0-440-40769-9*) Dell.

—Henry's Christmas, No. 4. 1993. pap. 3.25 (*0-440-40873-3*) Dell.

—Henry's Halloween. (ps-3). 1993. pap. 3.25 (*0-440-40754-7*) Dell.

—Henry's Secret Valentine. (ps-3). 1993. pap. 3.25 (*0-440-40758-3*) Dell.

—Timothy & the Christmas Gift. 1989. pap. 12.95 (*0-671-67959-7*, S&S BFYR) S&S Trade.

—Timothy & the Night Noises. Dinardo, Jeffrey, illus. LC 86-9383. 32p. (gr. 2-5). 1986. 11.95 (*0-13-922048-8*) P-H.

—Timothy & the Night Noises. LC 86-9383. 1990. pap. 11.95 (*0-671-66807-2*, Little Simon); pap. 2.25 (*0-671-70298-X*, Little Simon) S&S Trade.

Dineen, Jacqueline. The Aztecs. LC 91-36169. (Illus.). 64p. (gr. 6 up). 1992. RSBE 14.95 (*0-02-730652-6*, New Discovery) Macmillan Child Grp.

—Chocolate. (Illus.). 32p. (gr. 1-4). 1991. PLB 14.95 (*0-87614-657-4*) Carolrhoda Bks.

—The Greeks. LC 91-512. (Illus.). 64p. (gr. 6 up). 1992. RSBE 14.95 (*0-02-730650-X*, New Discovery) Macmillan Child Grp.

—Hurricanes & Typhoons. LC 91-11302. (Illus.). 32p. (gr. 5-8). 1991. PLB 12.40 (*0-531-17339-9*, Gloucester Pr) Watts.

—The Romans. LC 91-511. (Illus.). 64p. (gr. 6 up). 1992. RSBE 14.95 (*0-02-730651-8*, New Discovery) Macmillan Child Grp.

—Volcanoes. LC 91-11303. (Illus.). 32p. (gr. 5-8). 1991. PLB 12.40 (*0-531-17338-0*, Gloucester Pr) Watts.

Dineen, Jacqueline, jt. auth. see Wilkinson, Philip.

Dineen, John. Marbles, Hopscotch & Jacks. (gr. 4-7). 1992. pap. 3.95 (*0-207-17719-8*, Pub. by Angus & Robertson AT) HarpC.

Dinero, G. Who's Hot! Malcolm X. 1993. pap. 1.49 (*0-440-21480-7*) Dell.

—Who's Hot! Vanessa Williams. (gr. 4-7). 1993. pap. 1.49 (*0-440-21479-3*) Dell.

Dines, Carol. Best Friends Tell the Best Lies. LC 88-29433. (gr. 7 up). 1989. 14.95 (*0-385-29704-1*) Delacorte.

Dines, Glen. Sir Cecil & the Bad Blue Beast. Dines, Glen, illus. LC 70-125868. (gr. k-2). 1970. 20.95 (*0-87599-175-0*) S G Phillips.

Dingerkus, Guido. The Shark Watcher's Guide. Burkel, Dietrich, illus. 176p. (gr. 7 up). 1989. lib. bdg. 10.98 (*0-671-50234-4*, J Messner); lib. bdg. 5.95 (*0-671-68815-4*) S&S Trade.

Dinges, Susan & Thomas, Sue. Curtain II: Creative Drama for Children 9-12. (ps-7). 1986. 15.00 (*0-89824-168-5*) Trillium Pr.

Dinges, Susan, jt. auth. see Thomas, Sue.

Dingus, Lowell. What Color Is That Dinosaur? Questions, Answers, & Mysteries. Quinn, Stephen C., illus. LC 93-10664. 72p. (gr. 4-6). 1994. PLB 14.90 (*1-56294-365-0*) Millbrook Pr.

Dinkmeyer, Don, Sr. & Dinkmeyer, Don, Jr. Developing Understanding of Self & Others (DUSO) Storybook, No. 1. (gr. k-4). 1982. pap. text ed. 42.75 (*0-88671-278-5*, 5505) Am Guidance.

Dinkmeyer, Don, Sr., et al. PREP for Effective Family Living. (gr. 7 up). 1985. 129.95 (*0-88671-225-4*) Am Guidance.

Dinneen, John. Marbles, Hopscotch & Jacks. (gr. 4-7). 1992. pap. 3.95 (*0-207-15536-4*, Pub. by Angus & Robertson AT) HarpC.

Dinner, Sherry H. Nothing to Be Ashamed Of: Growing up with Mental Illness in Your Family. LC 88-13244. 160p. (gr. 5 up). 1989. pap. 7.95 (*0-688-08493-1*, Pub. by Beech Tree Bks) Morrow.
—Nothing to Be Ashamed Of: Growing up with Mental Illness in Your Family. 160p. (ps-3). 1989. PLB 12.88 (*0-688-08482-6*) Lothrop.
Dinter, B. Tell Me about Jesus. (Illus.). 80p. (ps). 1991. 3.95 (*0-8146-1881-2*) Liturgical Pr.
Dionetti, Michelle. Coal Mine Peaches. Riggio, Anita, illus. LC 90-28693. 32p. (ps-2). 1991. 14.95 (*0-531-05948-0*); RLB 14.99 (*0-531-08548-1*) Orchard Bks Watts.
Dionne, Wanda. The Couturiere of Galvez. LC 92-46147. (Illus.). (gr. 6-9). 1993. 15.95 (*0-89015-860-6*) Eakin-Sunbelt.
Diop, Birago. Mother Crocodile: "Maman-Caiman" LC 80-393. (ps-3). 1993. 15.00 (*0-385-30803-5*) Doubleday.
Diorio, MaryAnn L. Dating Etiquette for Christian Teens. Crescenzo, Phil, illus. 48p. (Orig.). (gr. 6-12). 1984. pap. 3.95 (*0-930037-00-6*) Daystar Comm.
Di Piazza, Domenica. Arkansas. LC 93-33391. 1994. PLB write for info. (*0-8225-2742-1*) Lerner Pubns.
Di Raimondo, P. Domenico, tr. see Hart, Corinne.
Di Raimondo, P. Domenico, tr. see Shannon, Ellen & Hart, Corinne.
Direct, R. F. Art Distribution Manual. (gr. 10). 1989. pap. write for info. (*0-945661-03-7*) PASE Pubns.
—Brochure Distribution Manual. rev. ed. (gr. 12). 1989. pap. text ed. 45.00 (*0-945661-14-2*) PASE Pubns.
—Doing Basic Research for Pay. 130p. (gr. 10). 1988. pap. text ed. 39.95x (*0-945661-01-0*) PASE Pubns.
—Handwriting Analysis for Pay. rev. ed. (gr. 12). 1989. pap. text ed. 45.00 (*0-945661-13-4*) PASE Pubns.
—Mailing Letters for Pay. rev. ed. (gr. 12). 1989. pap. text ed. 45.00 (*0-945661-12-6*) PASE Pubns.
—Reading Books for Pay. rev. ed. 192p. (gr. 12). 1989. pap. text ed. 45.00 (*0-945661-09-6*) PASE Pubns.
DiSalvo-Ryan, DyAnne. This Lot. LC 93-27117. 1994. write for info. (*0-688-12786-X*); PLB write for info. (*0-688-12787-8*) Morrow Jr Bks.
—Uncle Willie & the Soup Kitchen. DiSalvo-Ryan, Dyanne, illus. LC 90-6375. 32p. (gr. 1 up). 1991. 13. 95 (*0-688-09165-2*); PLB 13.88 (*0-688-09166-0*, Morrow Jr Bks) Morrow Jr Bks.
Disch, Thomas. Brave Little Toaster. 1986. pap. 12.95 (*0-385-23050-8*) Doubleday.
Disch, Thomas M. The Tale of Dan De Lion. McClun, Rhonda, illus. 32p. (ps up) 1986. 9.95 (*0-918273-30-7*) Coffee Hse.
Disher, Garry. The Bamboo Flute. LC 92-39787. 1993. 10.95 (*0-395-66595-7*) Ticknor & Fields.
Di Silvestro, Frank. Kid Wise Talks to Kids about Drugs. Berlin, Rosemary, illus. 22p. (gr. 1-8). 1990. pap. write for info. (*0-934591-02-4*) Songs & Stories.
DiSilvestro, Frank. Sing Along with Me. Likht, Marina, illus. 52p. (gr. 8-10). 1985. pap. 7.95 (*0-934591-00-8*) Songs & Stories.
Diskavich, Laura & Woods, Samuel, Jr. Everything You Need to Know about STD (Sexually Transmitted Diseases) Rosen, Ruth, ed. (gr. 7-12). 1990. PLB 13. 95 (*0-8239-1010-5*) Rosen Group.
Disney. Prince & the Pauper. 1990. 6.98 (*0-8317-2433-1*) Viking Child Bks.
—Rudolph the Red Nosed Reindeer. (ps-3). Date not set. 2.95 (*0-307-10849-X*) Western Pub.
Disney Staff. Disney's Beauty & the Beast. 1991. 6.98 (*0-8317-2434-X*) Viking Child Bks.
—Snow White Play Set. (Illus.). (gr. 1-6). 1993. 7.99 (*0-8431-3531-X*) Troubador Pr.
—Walt Disney Fairy Tale Treasury: Blue. 1991. 9.98 (*0-8317-9291-4*) Viking Child Bks.
—Walt Disney Fairy Tale Treasury: Red. 1991. 9.98 (*0-8317-9292-2*) Viking Child Bks.
Disney, Walt. Aladdin Junior Graphic Novel. (gr. 4-7). 1993. pap. 3.95 (*0-8167-3062-8*) Troll Assocs.
—Aristocats. 1988. 5.99 (*0-517-66195-0*) Outlet Bk Co.
—Disney's Aladdin en Espanol. 1993. 6.98 (*0-453-03164-1*) Mouse Works.
—Disney's Aladdin: Little Library. (ps). 1993. 5.98 (*0-453-03170-6*) Mouse Works.
—Disney's Aladdin: The Genie Gets Wet Bath Book. (ps). 1993. 5.98 (*0-453-03169-2*) Mouse Works.
—Disney's Aladdin: Travels with Genie. (ps-3). 1993. 6.98 (*0-453-03138-2*) Mouse Works.
—Disney's Beauty & the Beast: Be Our Guest Bath Book. (ps). 1993. 5.98 (*0-453-03171-4*) Mouse Works.
—Disney's Silly Songs. (ps-3). 1993. pap. 9.95 (*0-7935-1829-6*, 0290187) H Leonard Pub Corp.
—Disney's the Little Mermaid: A Visit with Friends Storyboard; Ariel's Story, Sebastian's Story. (ps-3). 1993. 6.98 (*0-453-03127-7*) Mouse Works.
—Disney's the Little Mermaid: Makes a Splash Bath Book. (ps). 1993. 5.98 (*0-453-03172-2*) Mouse Works.
—Dumbo. 1988. 5.99 (*0-517-66197-7*) Outlet Bk Co.
—Getting to Know You: Mickey & His Friends. (ps). 1993. 6.98 (*0-453-03126-9*) Mouse Works.
—Goof Troop Graphic Novel. (gr. 4-7). 1993. pap. 3.95 (*0-8167-3063-6*) Troll Assocs.
—Goofy Family Mix Up: A Mix & Match Book. (ps-3). 1993. 6.98 (*0-453-03125-0*) Mouse Works.
—Great Mouse Detective. (ps-3). 1988. 6.98 (*0-453-03188-9*) NAL-Dutton.
—Lady & the Tramp. (Illus.). 48p. (ps-6). 1988. 5.99 (*0-517-66194-2*) Outlet Bk Co.
—Little Mermaid under the Sea. (gr. 4-7). 1991. pap. 2.25 (*0-307-21805-8*, Golden Pr) Western Pub.

—Little Treasury of Walt Disney: Favorite Stories, 6 vols. in 1. 1988. boxed 5.99 (*0-517-61630-0*) Outlet Bk Co.
—Mickey's Costume Party: A Mix & Match Book. (ps-3). 1993. 6.98 (*0-453-03124-2*) Mouse Works.
—Mighty Ducks Junior Novelization. (gr. 4-7). 1993. pap. 3.50 (*1-56282-505-4*) Disney Pr.
—Oliver & Company. 1988. 5.99 (*0-517-67004-6*) Outlet Bk Co.
—Oliver & Company. (ps-3). 1990. 6.98 (*0-8317-6574-7*) Viking Child Bks.
—Perils of Mickey: The Mail Must Go Through. (ps-3). 1993. 6.98 (*0-453-03096-3*) Mouse Works.
—Pinocchio. 1988. 5.99 (*0-517-66198-5*) Outlet Bk Co.
—Pinocchio. (ps-3). 1986. 2.95 (*0-307-10381-1*) Western Pub.
—Snow White. (ps-3). 1993. 6.98 (*0-453-03166-8*) Mouse Works.
—Snow White & Seven Dwarfs. (Illus.). 1988. 5.99 (*0-517-66196-9*) Outlet Bk Co.
—Speak up, Patch! With One Hundred & One Dalmations. (ps). 1993. 6.98 (*0-453-03131-5*) Mouse Works.
—Three Musketeers Junior Novelization. (gr. 4-7). 1993. pap. 3.50 (*1-56282-590-9*) Disney Pr.
—Walt Disney the Rescuers. (ps-3). 1993. 6.98 (*0-453-03010-6*) Mouse Works.
—Walt Disney's Cinderella. (ps-3). 1993. 6.98 (*0-453-03167-6*) Mouse Works.
—Walt Disney's One Hundred & One Dalmations: Spotless Puppies Bath Book. (ps). 1993. 5.98 (*0-453-03173-0*) Mouse Works.
—Walt Disney's Sleeping Beauty. (ps-3). 1993. 6.98 (*0-453-03168-4*) Mouse Works.
Disney, Walt, Productions Staff. Adventures with Letters & Numbers. LC 85-43076. 80p. (Orig.). 1985. pap. 5.95 (*0-553-05533-X*) Bantam.
—All about People. LC 85-43075. 80p. (Orig.). 1985. pap. 5.95 (*0-553-05536-4*) Bantam.
—The Aristocats. LC 73-15626. (Illus.). 48p. (ps-2). 1974. 6.95 (*0-394-82553-5*) Random Bks Yng Read.
—The Book of Tall Tales: Featuring "The Shaggy Dog" LC 77-74466. (Illus.). (gr. 2-6). 1978. lib. bdg. 4.99 (*0-394-93596-9*) Random Bks Yng Read.
—Colors, Shapes, & Sizes. LC 85-43077. 80p. (Orig.). 1985. pap. 5.95 (*0-553-05534-8*) Bantam.
—Goofy's Book of Colors. LC 82-18630. (Illus.). 32p. (ps-1). 1983. lib. bdg. 4.99 (*0-394-95734-2*) Random Bks Yng Read.
—How Do You Do? I'm Winnie the Pooh. Disney, Walt, Productions Staff, tr. (Illus.). 10p. (ps). 1985. vinyl 3.95 (*0-394-87029-8*) Random Bks Yng Read.
—How It Works in the City. (gr. 4-6). 1982. write for info. (*0-89434-046-8*) Ferguson.
—How It Works in the Country. (gr. 4-6). 1982. write for info. (*0-89434-047-6*) Ferguson.
—How It Works in the Home. (gr. 4-6). 1982. write for info. (*0-89434-048-4*) Ferguson.
—The Mickey Mouse Birthday Book. LC 78-55911. (Illus.). (ps-3). 1978. 3.95 (*0-394-83963-3*); lib. bdg. 4.99 (*0-394-93963-8*) Random Bks Yng Read.
—The Mickey Mouse Magic Book. LC 74-16420. (Illus.). 48p. (gr. 1-2). 1975. 6.95 (*0-394-82567-5*) Random Bks Yng Read.
—Mickey's Pop-Up Book of Opposites. (Illus.). 14p. (ps-1). 1985. 6.95 (*0-394-87347-5*) Random Bks Yng Read.
—Simple Science. 1986. 5.95 (*0-553-05415-5*) Bantam.
—The Sorcerer's Apprentice. LC 73-9891. (Illus.). 48p. (ps-2). 1974. 6.95 (*0-394-82551-9*); lib. bdg. 4.99 (*0-394-92551-3*) Random Bks Yng Read.
—Walt Disney Productions Presents "The Black Hole" LC 79-10622. (Illus.). (ps-3). 1979. 4.95 (*0-394-84279-0*); lib. bdg. 4.99 (*0-394-94279-5*) Random Bks Yng Read.
—Walt Disney Productions Presents "The Haunted House" LC 75-16430. (Illus.). 48p. (ps-3). 1976. 6.95 (*0-394-82570-5*); lib. bdg. 4.99 (*0-394-92570-X*) Random Bks Yng Read.
—Walt Disney Productions Presents Tod & Copper from The Fox & the Hound. LC 81-2619. (Illus.). 48p. (ps-3). 1981. 4.95 (*0-394-84819-5*) Random Bks Yng Read.
—Walt Disney Productions Presents Tod & Vixey from The Fox & the Hound. LC 81-5209. (Illus.). 48p. (ps-3). 1981. 4.95 (*0-394-84904-3*) Random Bks Yng Read.
—Walt Disney's Cinderella. LC 74-22325. (Illus.). 48p. (ps-3). 1974. 3.95 (*0-394-82552-7*); lib. bdg. 4.99 (*0-394-92552-1*) Random Bks Yng Read.
—Walt Disney's One Hundred & One Dalmatians. LC 74-10829. (Illus.). 48p. (ps-3). 1975. 6.95 (*0-394-82571-3*); lib. bdg. 4.99 (*0-394-92571-8*) Random Bks Yng Read.
—Walt Disney's Pinocchio. (Illus.). (ps-3). 1973. 6.95 (*0-394-82626-4*); lib. bdg. 4.99 (*0-394-92626-9*) Random Bks Yng Read.
—Walt Disney's Snow White & the Seven Dwarfs. (Illus.). (ps-3). 1973. 6.95 (*0-394-82625-6*); lib. bdg. 5.99 (*0-394-92625-0*) Random Bks Yng Read.
—Walt Disney's Story Land. (Illus.). 320p. (gr. 1-5). 1987. write for info. (*0-307-16547-7*, Golden Bks) Western Pub.
—Walt Disney's the Adventures of Mr. Toad Adapted from the Wind in the Willows. LC 81-2783. (Illus.). 48p. (ps-3). 1981. 4.95 (*0-394-84818-7*) Random Bks Yng Read.

—Walt Disney's Winnie the Pooh & Tigger Too. LC 75-20349. (Illus.). 48p. (ps-3). 1976. 6.95 (*0-394-82569-1*); lib. bdg. 4.99 (*0-394-92569-6*) Random Bks Yng Read.
—Words, Riddles, & Stories. LC 85-43074. 80p. 1985. pap. 5.95 (*0-553-05535-6*) Bantam.
Disney, Walt, Studios Staff. The Pop-up Mickey Mouse: Story & Illustrations. facsimile ed. LC 93-31910. (Illus.). 32p. 1994. Repr. of 1933 ed. 9.95 (*1-55709-210-9*); 100.00 (*1-55709-215-X*) Applewood.
Ditmore, Shirley, tr. see Neighbour, Ralph W., Jr.
Dittberner-Jax, Norita, ed. The Ragged Heart. Wood, Marce, illus. 164p. (Orig.). 1989. pap. 8.00 (*0-927663-14-7*) COMPAS.
Dittenhaver, Sarah L., et al. Tune Time, 2 pts. rev. ed. Goss, Louise, ed. 48p. (gr. k-6). 1973. pap. text ed. 6.95 pt. A (*0-87487-194-8*); pap. text ed. 6.95 pt. B (*0-87487-195-6*) Summy-Birchard.
Diuguid, Norah M., et al. The History of the Helping Hand Club. 1990. 8.95 (*0-87498-010-0*) Assoc Pubs DC.
DiVito, Anna. Elephants on Ice. LC 90-22392. (Illus.). 32p. (ps-4). 1991. 12.95 (*0-8037-0797-5*); PLB 12.89 (*0-8037-0798-3*) Dial Bks Young.
Dixey, Kay. Judar & His Two Brothers. (gr. 2-8). 1990. 7. 95x (*0-86685-483-5*) Intl Bk Ctr.
—Khaled & Aida. 1991. write for info. (*0-86685-571-8*) Intl Bk Ctr.
Dixon. Ice Age Explorer. (ps-7). 1987. pap. 2.50 (*0-553-27049-4*) Bantam.
Dixon, Ann, retold by. How Raven Brought Light to People. Watts, James, illus. LC 90-28948. 32p. (gr. k-4). 1992. SBE 13.95 (*0-689-50536-1*, M K McElderry) Macmillan Child Grp.
Dixon, Annabelle. Clay. Stefoff, Rebecca, ed. Barber, Ed, photos by. LC 90-40369. (Illus.). 22p. (gr. 3-5). 1990. PLB 15.93 (*0-944483-69-0*) Garrett Ed Corp.
—Paper. Stefoff, Rebecca, ed. Barber, Ed, photos by. LC 91-18188. (Illus.). 32p. (gr. 3-5). 1991. PLB 15.93 (*1-56074-003-5*) Garrett Ed Corp.
—Wool. Stefoff, Rebecca, ed. Barber, Ed, photos by. LC 90-40366. (Illus.). 32p. (gr. 3-5). 1990. PLB 15.93 (*0-944483-73-9*) Garrett Ed Corp.
Dixon, Debra S. & Henry, Susan V. Our Earth: The Water Planet, Vol. 1: An Introduction. Spence, Lundie & San Jose, Christine, eds. (Illus.). 45p. (Orig.). (gr. 3-7). 1992. pap. 14.95 (*0-9609506-2-1*) Prescott Durrell & Co.
Dixon, Delores. The Tooth Fairy. 1991. 7.95 (*0-533-09433-X*) Vantage.
Dixon, Doris N. Rumpelstiltskin. Fox, Neal, illus. 24p. (ps-2). 1993. pap. 9.95 (*1-882171-01-2*) Confetti Ent.
Dixon, Dorothy A. Teaching Young Children to Care: Thirty-Seven Activities for Developing Self-Esteem. LC 90-70418. 88p. (Orig.). (gr. k-3). 1990. pap. 9.95 (*0-89622-436-8*) Twenty-Third.
—Teaching Young Children to Care: Thirty-Seven Activities for Developing Concern for Others. LC 90-70417. (Illus.). 88p. (Orig.). (gr. k-3). 1990. pap. 9.95 (*0-89622-437-6*) Twenty-Third.
Dixon, Dougal. Be a Dinosaur Detective. Lings, Steve, illus. 36p. (gr. k-4). 1988. 18.95 (*0-8225-0894-X*); pap. 4.95 (*0-8225-9538-9*) Lerner Pubns.
—The Changing Earth. LC 93-6829. (Illus.). 32p. (gr. 4-6). 1993. 14.95 (*1-56847-052-5*) Thomson Lrning.
—Dino Dots. LC 88-28583. 96p. 1988. pap. 4.95 (*0-88166-122-8*) Meadowbrook.
—Dougal Dixon's Dinosaurs. (Illus.). 160p. (gr. 4-7). 1993. 17.95 (*1-56397-261-1*) Boyds Mills Pr.
—Explore the World of Prehistoric Life. Hayward, Tim, illus. 48p. (gr. 3-7). 1992. write for info. (*0-307-15607-9*, 15607, Golden Pr) Western Pub.
—The First Dinosaurs. Burton, Jane, illus. LC 87-6460. 32p. (gr. 2-3). 1987. PLB 15.93 (*1-55532-258-1*) Gareth Stevens Inc.
—The First Dinosaurs. (Orig.). 1990. pap. 4.95 (*0-440-40373-1*, Pub. by Yearling Classics) Dell.
—Hunting the Dinosaurs. Burton, Jane, illus. LC 87-6461. 32p. (gr. 2-3). 1987. PLB 15.93 (*1-55532-259-X*) Gareth Stevens Inc.
—Jungles. (Illus.). 32p. (gr. 4-6). 1991. 13.95 (*0-237-60161-3*, Pub. by Evans Bros Ltd) Trafalgar.
—The Jurassic Dinosaurs. Burton, Jane, illus. LC 87-6462. 32p. (gr. 2-3). 1987. PLB 15.93 (*1-55532-260-3*) Gareth Stevens Inc.
—The Last Dinosaurs. Burton, Jane, illus. LC 87-6463. 32p. (gr. 2-3). 1987. PLB 15.93 (*1-55532-261-1*) Gareth Stevens Inc.
—The Last Dinosaurs. (Orig.). 1990. pap. 4.95 (*0-440-40377-4*, Pub. by Yearling Classics) Dell.
Dixon, Douglas. Be a Fossil Detective. 40p. (gr. 2 up). 1989. 3.99 (*0-517-68022-X*) Outlet Bk Co.
—Hunting the Dinosaurs. (Orig.). 1990. pap. 4.95 (*0-440-40372-3*, Pub. by Yearling Classics) Dell.
—The Jurassic Dinosaurs. (Orig.). 1990. pap. 4.95 (*0-440-40375-8*, Pub. by Yearling Classics) Dell.
—The New Dinosaur Library, 4 vols. Burton, Jene, illus. 128p. (gr. 2-3). 1988. Set. PLB 63.73 (*1-55532-262-X*) Gareth Stevens Inc.
Dixon, Franklin W. The Alien Factor. Greenberg, Anne, ed. 224p. (Orig.). 1993. pap. 3.99 (*0-671-79532-5*, Archway) PB.
—Bad Rap. Greenberg, Ann, ed. 160p. (Orig.). (gr. 6 up). 1993. pap. 3.99 (*0-671-73109-2*, Archway) PB.
—The Baseball Card Conspiracy. Winkler, Ellen, ed. 160p. (Orig.). (gr. 3-6). 1992. pap. 3.99 (*0-671-73064-9*, Minstrel Bks) PB.

—Beyond the Law. Greenberg, Anne, ed. 160p. (Orig.). 1991. pap. 12.95 (0-671-73091-6, Archway) PB.
—Blood Money. 160p. (Orig.). 1991. pap. 3.50 (0-671-74665-0, Archway) PB.
—The Borgia Dagger. 160p. (Orig.). (gr. 7 up). 1991. pap. 3.50 (0-671-73676-0, Archway) PB.
—The Case of the Cosmic Kidnapping. Winkler, Ellen, ed. 160p. (Orig.). 1993. pap. 3.99 (0-671-79310-1, Minstrel Bks) PB.
—Case of the Counterfeit Criminals. Winkler, Ellen, ed. 160p. (Orig.). 1992. pap. 3.99 (0-671-73061-4, Minstrel Bks) PB.
—Cast of Criminals. (Orig.). (gr. 7 up). 1989. pap. 3.50 (0-671-66307-0, Minstrel Bks) PB.
—Castle Fear. Greenberg, Anne, ed. 160p. (Orig.). (gr. 7 up). 1991. pap. 3.75 (0-671-74615-4, Archway) PB.
—Cold Sweat. Greenberg, Anne, ed. 160p. (Orig.). 1992. pap. 3.75 (0-671-73099-1) PB.
—Collision Course. 160p. 1991. pap. 3.50 (0-671-74666-9, Archway) PB.
—The Crowning Terror. 160p. (Orig.). (gr. 7 up). 1991. pap. 3.50 (0-671-73670-1, Archway) PB.
—The Crowning Terror: Casefiles Six. large type ed. 154p. (gr. 5-10). 1988. Repr. of 1987 ed. 9.50 (0-942545-47-8); PLB 10.50 (0-942545-57-5, Dist. by Gareth Stevens) Grey Castle.
—Cult of Crime. (gr. 7 up). 1989. pap. 3.75 (0-671-68726-3, Archway) PB.
—Cult of Crime: Casefiles Three. large type ed. LC 88-21493. 151p. (gr. 5-10). 1988. Repr. of 1987 ed. 9.50 (0-942545-44-3); PLB 10.50 (0-942545-54-0, Dist. by Gareth Stevens) Grey Castle.
—Danger on the Air. (Orig.). (gr. 3-7). 1989. pap. 3.50 (0-671-66305-4, Minstrel Bks) PB.
—Danger on the Diamond. Greenberg, Anne, ed. 160p. (gr. 3-6). 1988. pap. 3.99 (0-671-63425-9, Minstrel Bks) PB.
—Danger Unlimited. Greenberg, Anne, ed. 160p. (Orig.). (gr. 6 up). 1993. pap. 3.99 (0-671-79463-9, Archway) PB.
—Dead on Target: Casefiles One. large type ed. 153p. (gr. 5-10). 1988. Repr. of 1987 ed. 9.50 (0-942545-42-7); PLB 10.50 (0-942545-52-4, Dist. by Gareth Stevens) Grey Castle.
—The Dead Season. 160p. 1991. pap. 3.50 (0-671-74105-5, Archway) PB.
—Deadfall. 160p. (Orig.). 1992. pap. 3.75 (0-671-73096-7) PB.
—The Deadliest Dare. (Orig.). (gr. 7 up). 1991. pap. 3.50 (0-671-74613-8, Archway) PB.
—Deathgame. 160p. (Orig.). (gr. 7 up). 1991. pap. 3.99 (0-671-73672-8, Archway) PB.
—Deathgame: Casefiles Seven. large type ed. 151p. (gr. 7-10). 1988. Repr. of 1987 ed. 9.50 (0-942545-48-6); PLB 10.50 (0-942545-58-3, Dist. by Gareth Stevens) Grey Castle.
—Deep Trouble. Greenberg, Anne, ed. 160p. (Orig.). 1991. pap. 3.50 (0-671-73090-8, Archway) PB.
—The Demolition Mission. Greenberg, Ann, ed. 160p. (Orig.). 1992. pap. 3.99 (0-671-73058-4) PB.
—Edge of Destruction. 160p. (Orig.). (gr. 7 up). 1991. pap. 3.50 (0-671-73669-8, Archway) PB.
—Edge of Destruction: Casefiles Five. large type ed. LC 88-21402. 153p. (gr. 5-10). 1988. Repr. of 1987 ed. 9.50 (0-942545-46-X); PLB 10.50 (0-942545-56-7, Dist. by Gareth Stevens) Grey Castle.
—Endangered Species. Greenberg, Anne, ed. 160p. (Orig.). 1992. pap. 3.75 (0-671-73100-9, Archway) PB.
—Evil, Inc. (Orig.). (gr. 7 up). 1991. pap. 3.75 (0-671-73668-X, Archway) PB.
—Evil, Inc. Casefiles Two. large type ed. 153p. (gr. 5-10). 1988. Repr. of 1987 ed. 9.50 (0-942545-43-5); PLB 10.50 (0-942545-53-2, Dist. by Gareth Stevens) Grey Castle.
—Fear on Wheels. Greenberg, Anne, ed. 160p. (Orig.). 1991. pap. 3.99 (0-671-69277-1, Minstrel Bks) PB.
—Final Gambit. Greenberg, Anne, ed. 160p. (Orig.). 1992. pap. 3.75 (0-671-73098-3) PB.
—Flight into Danger. Greenberg, Ann, ed. 160p. (Orig.). 1991. pap. 3.75 (0-671-70044-8, Archway) PB.
—Foul Play. Greenberg, Ann, ed. 160p. (Orig.). (gr. 7 up). 1990. pap. 3.75 (0-671-70043-X, Archway) PB.
—The Four-Headed Dragon. 176p. (ps). 1988. pap. 3.50 (0-671-65797-6, Minstrel Bks) PB.
—The Genius Thieves. 1991. pap. 3.50 (0-671-73674-4, Archway) PB.
—The Genius Thieves: Casefiles Nine. large type ed. 153p. (gr. 5-10). 1988. Repr. of 1987 ed. 9.50 (0-942545-50-8); PLB 10.50 (0-942545-60-5, Dist. by Gareth Stevens) Grey Castle.
—The Hardy Boys Casefiles, No. 80: Dead of the Night. 160p. (Orig.). (gr. 6 up). 1993. pap. 3.99 (0-671-79464-7, Archway) PB.
—The Hardy Boys: Demon's Den. Barish, Wendy, ed. Frame, Paul, illus. 208p. (gr. 3 up). 1984. 9.95 (0-685-09177-5) S&S Trade.
—Hardy Boys Digest. 1987. Boxed. pap. 14.00 (0-671-91514-2, Minstrel Bks) PB.
—Hardy Boys Ghost Stories. Greenberg, Ann, ed. 144p. (gr. 3-7). 1989. pap. 3.99 (0-671-69133-3, Minstrel Bks) PB.
—The Hardy Boys Gift Set, 3 vols. Boxed Set. pap. 8.55 (0-317-12424-2) S&S Trade.
—Hardy Boys, No. 1: Tower Treasure. LC 91-46833. 1991. 12.95 (1-55709-144-7) Applewood.
—The Hardy Boys, No. 122: Carnival of Crime. 160p. (Orig.). (gr. 3-7). 1993. pap. 3.99 (0-671-79312-8, Minstrel Bks) PB.

—Hardy Boys, No. 2: The House on the Cliff. LC 91-46733. 1991. pap. 12.95 (1-55709-145-5) Applewood.
—Hardy Boys, No. 3: The Secret of the Old Mill. LC 91-46349. 1991. 12.95 (1-55709-146-3) Applewood.
—Hardy Boys: The Apeman's Secret. (Illus.). 192p. (Orig.). (gr. 3-7). 1980. S&S Trade.
—Hardy Boys: The Demon's Den. 1984. 8.95 (0-685-08794-8); pap. 2.95 (0-685-08795-6) S&S Trade.
—Hardy Boys: The Infinity Clue. Morrill, Leslie, illus. 192p. (Orig.). (gr. 3-7). 1981. S&S Trade.
—Hardy Boys: The Outlaw's Silver. Morrill, Leslie, illus. 192p. (Orig.). (gr. 3-7). 1981. S&S Trade.
—Hardy Boys: The Submarine Caper. Morrill, Leslie, illus. 192p. (Orig.). (gr. 3-7). 1981. S&S Trade.
—Height of Danger. Greenberg, Anne, ed. 160p. (Orig.). 1991. pap. 3.50 (0-671-73092-4, Archway) PB.
—Highway Robbery. Greenberg, Ann, ed. 160p. (Orig.). 1990. pap. 3.75 (0-671-70038-3, Archway) PB.
—Hostage of Hate: Casefiles Ten. large type ed. 153p. (gr. 5-10). 1988. Repr. of 1987 ed. 9.50 (0-942545-51-6); PLB 10.50 (0-942545-61-3, Dist. by Gareth Stevens) Grey Castle.
—In Self-Defense. Greenberg, Ann, ed. 160p. (Orig.). (gr. 7 up). 1990. pap. 3.75 (0-671-70042-1, Archway) PB.
—Last Laugh. Greenberg, Ann, ed. 160p. (gr. 7 up). 1991. pap. 3.50 (0-671-74614-6, Archway) PB.
—The Lazarus Plot: Casefiles Four. large type ed. 152p. (gr. 5-10). 1988. Repr. of 1987 ed. 9.50 (0-942545-45-1); PLB 10.50 (0-942545-55-9, Dist. by Gareth Stevens) Grey Castle.
—Lethal Cargo. Greenberg, Anne, ed. 160p. (Orig.). 1992. pap. 3.75 (0-671-73103-3, Archway) PB.
—Mayhem in Motion. Greenberg, Anne, ed. 160p. (Orig.). (gr. 7 up). 1992. pap. 3.75 (0-671-73105-X, Archway) PB.
—Melted Coins. 1944. 4.50 (0-448-08923-8, Platt & Munk Pubs) Putnam Pub Group.
—The Million Dollar Nightmare. Greenberg, Ann, ed. 160p. (Orig.). (gr. 4-7). 1990. pap. 3.99 (0-671-69272-0, Minstrel Bks) PB.
—The Money Hunt. Greenberg, Ann, ed. 160p. 1990. pap. 3.99 (0-671-69451-0, Minstrel Bks) PB.
—The Mummy Case. 192p. (gr. 3-6). 1987. pap. 3.99 (0-671-64289-8, Minstrel Bks) PB.
—The Mystery in the Old Mine. 160p. (Orig.). (gr. 5 up). 1993. pap. 3.99 (0-671-79311-X, Minstrel Bks) PB.
—Mystery of Chinese Junk. 1959. 4.50 (0-448-08939-4, Platt & Munk Pubs) Putnam Pub Group.
—Mystery of Smugglers Cove. 176p. (Orig.). (gr. 3-6). 1988. pap. 3.50 (0-671-66229-5, Minstrel Bks) PB.
—Mystery of the Desert Giant. 1960. 4.50 (0-448-08940-8, Platt & Munk Pubs) Putnam Pub Group.
—Mystery of the Samurai Sword. (gr. 2-7). 1984. 8.85 (0-685-09393-X) S&S Trade.
—Mystery of the Samurai Sword. 192p. (gr. 3-7). 1988. pap. 3.99 (0-671-67302-5, Minstrel Bks) PB.
—The Mystery of the Silver Star. (gr. 3-6). 1987. pap. 3.50 (0-671-64374-6, Minstrel Bks) PB.
—Mystery on Makatunk Island. 1994. pap. 3.99 (0-671-79315-2, Minstrel Bks) PB.
—Night of the Werewolf. (gr. 2-7). 1984. 8.85 (0-685-09390-5, Little Simon) S&S Trade.
—Night of the Werewolf. Greenberg, Anne, ed. 192p. 1990. pap. 3.99 (0-671-70993-3, Minstrel Bks) PB.
—No Mercy. Greenberg, Anne, ed. 160p. (Orig.). 1992. pap. 3.75 (0-671-73101-7, Archway) PB.
—No Way Out. Greenberg, Anne, ed. 160p. (Orig.). 1993. pap. 3.99 (0-671-73111-4, Archway) PB.
—Panic on Gull Island. 160p. (Orig.). 1991. pap. 3.99 (0-671-69276-3, Minstrel Bks) PB.
—The Pentagon Spy. (gr. 2-7). 1984. 8.85 (0-685-42775-7) S&S Trade.
—The Pentagon Spy. reissued ed. Greenberg, Anne, ed. 192p. (gr. 3-7). 1988. pap. 3.99 (0-671-67221-5, Minstrel Bks) PB.
—The Phoenix Equation. Greenberg, Anne, ed. 160p. (Orig.). 1992. pap. 3.99 (0-671-73102-5, Archway) PB.
—Poisoned Paradise. Greenberg, Anne, ed. 160p. (Orig.). 1993. pap. 3.99 (0-671-79466-3, Archway) PB.
—Power Play. Greenberg, Anne, ed. 160p. (Orig.). (gr. 6 up). 1991. pap. 3.50 (0-671-70047-2, Archway) PB.
—Program for Destruction. Greenberg, Ann, ed. (gr. 3-6). 1987. pap. 3.99 (0-671-64895-0, Minstrel Bks) PB.
—Radical Moves. Winkler, Ellen, ed. 160p. (Orig.). 1992. pap. 3.99 (0-671-73060-6) PB.
—Real Horror. Greenberg, Anne, ed. 160p. (Orig.). 1993. pap. 3.75 (0-671-73107-6, Archway) PB.
—Rigged for Revenge. Greenberg, Anne, ed. 160p. (Orig.). (gr. 7 up). 1992. pap. 3.75 (0-671-73106-8, Archway) PB.
—The Ring of Evil, No. 1: Tagged for Terror. Greenberg, Anne, ed. 160p. (Orig.). 1993. pap. 3.99 (0-671-73112-2, Archway) PB.
—The Ring of Evil, No. 2: Survival Run. Greenberg, Ann, ed. 160p. (Orig.). 1993. pap. 3.99 (0-671-79461-2, Archway) PB.
—The Ring of Evil, No. 3: The Pacific Conspiracy. 160p. (Orig.). 1993. pap. 3.99 (0-671-79462-0, Archway) PB.
—The Roaring River Mystery. Schwartz, Betty, ed. (Orig.). (gr. 3-7). 1991. pap. 3.50 (0-671-73004-5) S&S Trade.
—The Robot's Revenge. Winkler, Ellen, ed. 160p. (Orig.). 1993. pap. 3.99 (0-671-79313-6, Minstrel Bks) PB.
—Rock 'n' Roll Renegades. Winkler, Ellen, ed. 160p. (Orig.). 1992. pap. 3.99 (0-671-73063-0, Minstrel Bks) PB.

—Rough Riding. Greenberg, Anne, ed. 160p. (Orig.). 1992. pap. 3.99 (0-671-73104-1, Archway) PB.
—Sabotage at Sports City. Winkler, Ellen, ed. 160p. (Orig.). 1992. pap. 3.99 (0-671-73062-2, Minstrel Bks) PB.
—Scene of the Crime. (gr. 7 up). 1989. pap. 2.95 (0-671-69377-8, Archway) PB.
—Screamers. Greenberg, Anne, ed. 160p. (Orig.). 1993. pap. 3.75 (0-671-73108-4, Archway) PB.
—The Secret of Sigma Seven. 160p. (Orig.). 1991. pap. 3.99 (0-671-72717-6, Minstrel Bks) PB.
—See No Evil. (gr. 7 up). 1991. pap. 3.50 (0-671-73673-6, Archway) PB.
—See No Evil: Casefiles Eight. large type ed. 152p. (gr. 5-10). 1988. Repr. of 1987 ed. 9.50 (0-942545-49-4); PLB 10.50 (0-942545-59-1, Dist. by Gareth Stevens) Grey Castle.
—The Shadow Killers. 1988. pap. 3.99 (0-671-66309-7, Minstrel Bks) PB.
—Sheer Terror. Greenberg, Anne, ed. 160p. (Orig.). 1993. pap. 3.99 (0-671-79465-5, Archway) PB.
—The Sky Blue Frame. 160p. (gr. 3-6). 1988. pap. 3.50 (0-671-64974-4, Minstrel Bks) PB.
—The Smoke Screen Mystery. Greenberg, Ann, ed. 160p. (Orig.). (gr. 3-6). 1990. pap. 3.99 (0-671-69274-7, Minstrel Bks) PB.
—Spark of Suspicion. Greenberg, Ann, ed. 160p. (Orig.). 1989. pap. 3.99 (0-671-66304-6, Minstrel Bks) PB.
—Spiked! Greenberg, Anne, ed. 160p. (Orig.). 1991. pap. 3.50 (0-671-73094-0, Archway) PB.
—Terminal Shock. Greenberg, Anne, ed. 160p. (gr. 6 up). 1990. pap. 3.99 (0-671-69288-7, Minstrel) PB.
—Thick As Thieves. (Orig.). (gr. 7 up). 1991. pap. 3.50 (0-671-74663-4, Archway) PB.
—Three-Ring Terror. Greenberg, Anne, ed. 160p. (Orig.). 1991. pap. 3.99 (0-671-73057-6, Minstrel Bks) PB.
—Time Bomb. Greenberg, Anne, ed. 224p. (Orig.). 1992. pap. 3.75 (0-671-75661-3, Archway) PB.
—Too Many Traitors. 160p. (Orig.). (gr. 7 up). 1991. pap. 3.50 (0-671-73677-9, Archway) PB.
—Track of the Zombie. 1986. pap. 3.50 (0-671-62623-X) PB.
—Tricks of the Trade. Greenberg, Ann, ed. 160p. (Orig.). (gr. 3-6). 1990. pap. 3.99 (0-671-69273-9, Minstrel Bks) PB.
—Tricky Business. Greenberg, Ann, ed. 160p. (gr. 3-6). 1988. pap. 3.99 (0-671-64973-6, Minstrel Bks) PB.
—Uncivil War. Greenberg, Anne, ed. 160p. (Orig.). 1991. pap. 3.50 (0-671-70049-9, Archway) PB.
—Virtual Villainy. 1994. pap. 3.99 (0-671-79470-1, Archway) PB.
—Web of Horror. Greenberg, Ann, ed. 160p. (Orig.). 1991. pap. 3.50 (0-671-73089-4, Archway) PB.
—Wipeout. (Orig.). (gr. 7 up). 1989. pap. 3.50 (0-671-66306-2, Minstrel Bks) PB.
Dixon, Franklin W. & Greenberg, Anne. Terror on Track. 160p. (Orig.). 1991. pap. 3.99 (0-671-73093-2, Archway) PB.
Dixon, Franklin W. & Link, Sheila. Hardy Boys Handbook: Seven Stories of Survival. (Illus.). 144p. (gr. 3-7). 1980. PLB 8.95 (0-671-95705-8); pap. 3.95 (0-671-95602-7) S&S Trade.
Dixon, Franklin W., jt. auth. see Keene, Carolyn.
Dixon, Jim. The Zoo Is Blue: And Should Be Read. Dixon, Jim, illus. 36p. (gr. k-2). 1991. 12.95 (1-880453-01-0) J Hefty Pub.
Dixon, Jim, jt. auth. see Sullivan, Jem.
Dixon, Malcolm. Communications. (Illus.). 48p. (gr. 5-8). 1991. 12.90 (0-531-18411-0, Pub. by Bookwright Pr) Watts.
—Flight. LC 90-38122. (Illus.). 48p. (gr. 3-7). 1991. PLB 12.90 (0-531-18380-7) Watts.
—Land Transportation. (Illus.). 48p. (gr. 5-8). 1991. 12.90 (0-531-18412-9, Pub. by Bookwright Pr) Watts.
—Structures. (Illus.). 48p. (gr. 3-7). 1991. PLB 12.90 (0-531-18379-3, Pub. by Bookwright Pr) Watts.
Dixon, Michael B. & Cole, Jan. Tales from the Arabian Nights. (Illus.). 52p. (Orig.). (gr. k up). 1985. pap. 4.00 (0-88680-239-3); piano & vocal score 5.00 (0-88680-240-7); royalty on application 75.00 (0-685-58023-7) I E Clark.
Dixon, Michael B., et al. Striking Out! (Orig.). (gr. k up). 1984. pap. 4.50 (0-87602-252-2) Anchorage.
Dixon, Peter W., intro. by. Great Tales of Old. LC 87-83338. (Illus.). 312p. (gr. k-3). 1988. text ed. 15.95 (0-945161-01-8); pap. 9.95 (0-945161-00-X) Lantern Bks.
Dixon, Rachel. The Witch's Ring. (Illus.). 128p. 1994. write for info. (1-56282-545-3); PLB write for info. (1-56282-546-1) Hyprn Child.
Dixon, Sarah. Advanced Puzzle Adventure. (Illus.). 48p. (gr. 6 up). pap. 9.95 (0-7460-0753-1, Usborne) EDC.
—Cobra Consignment. (Illus.). 48p. (gr. 6 up). PLB 10.96 (0-88110-516-3, Usborne); pap. 4.50 (0-7460-0751-5, Usborne) EDC.
—Codename Quicksilver. (Illus.). 48p. (gr. 6 up). 1992. PLB 11.96 (0-88110-517-1, Usborne); pap. 4.95 (0-7460-0688-8, Usborne) EDC.
—Map & Maze Puzzles. (Illus.). 48p. (gr. 4-8). 1993. PLB 12.96 (0-88110-525-2, Usborne); pap. 6.95 (0-7460-1579-8, Usborne) EDC.
—Murder on Main Street. (Illus.). 48p. (gr. 6 up). PLB 10.96 (0-88110-518-X, Usborne); pap. 4.50 (0-7460-0660-8, Usborne) EDC.
—The Vanishing Village. (Illus.). 48p. 1990. PLB 11.96 (0-88110-405-1); pap. 4.95 (0-7460-0330-7) EDC.

Dixon, William C. Pointed Tales. LC 80-81102. 98p. (Orig.). (gr. 1-4). 1980. pap. 5.95 (*0-8192-1270-9*) Morehouse Pub.
Dixon, Lolita. Exercises in English Conversation, 2 Bks. (Illus., Orig.). (gr. 7 up). 1987. Bk. 1. pap. text ed. 8.00 (*0-13-294646-7*, 18011); Bk. 2. pap. text ed. 7.00 (*0-13-294679-3*, 18012); Tape 1 (Set of 4) 64.00 (*0-13-294654-8*); Tape 2 (Set of 4) 64.00 (*0-13-294695-5*) Prentice ESL.
Dizeno, Patricia. Why Me? The Story of Jenny. (gr. 7 up). 1976. pap. 3.50 (*0-380-00563-8*, Flare) Avon.
Dlugokinski, Eric. The Boys' & Girls' Book of Dealing with Feelings. 31p. (gr. k-6). 1988. pap. 10.95 (*1-882801-02-4*) Feelings Factory.
Dlugokinski, Eric, jt. auth. see Allen, Sandra.
Do, Le, tr. see La Fonatine, Jean de.
Doane, Jim. North Carolina: From the Mountains to the Sea. LC 80-80955. (ps-12). 1980. 72p. 2.95, (*0-936672-02-1*) Aerial Photo.
Doane, Jim, Jr. Aerial America: From Sea to Shining Sea. (ps-12). 1981. 2.95 (*0-936672-11-0*) Aerial Photo.
—America: An Aerial View. (ps-12). 1986. 5.00 (*84-599-7121-X*) Aerial Photo.
Doane, Nancy L. Indian Doctor Book. 54p. (ps-12). pap. text ed. 2.00 (*0-936672-15-3*) Aerial Photo.
Dobak, Annelies, tr. see Waechter, Friederich K.
Dobbs, Katy. My First Gamebook. Joyner, Jerry, illus. LC 85-40524. (ps-2). 1986. 6 bds. 5.95 (*0-89480-945-8*, 945) Workman Pub.
Dobkin, Bonnie. Collecting. (Illus.). 32p. (ps-2). 1993. PLB 13.27 (*0-516-02015-3*) Childrens.
—Everybody Says. (Illus.). 32p. (ps-2). 1993. PLB 13.27 (*0-516-02019-6*) Childrens.
—Go-with Words. (Illus.). 32p. (ps-2). 1993. PLB 13.27 (*0-516-02016-1*) Childrens.
—The Great Bug Hunt. Dunnington, Tom, illus. LC 93-10333. 32p. (ps-2). 1993. PLB 11.93 (*0-516-02017-X*) Childrens.
—I Love Fishing. Dunnington, Tom, illus. LC 92-38506. 32p. (ps-2). 1993. PLB 11.93 (*0-516-02013-7*); pap. 2.95 (*0-516-42013-5*) Childrens.
—Just a Little Different. Martin, Clovis, illus. LC 93-13024. 1993. write for info. (*0-516-02018-8*) Childrens.
Dobkins, Lucy M. Daddy, There's a Hippo in the Grapes. Botero, Kirk, illus. LC 92-20321. 64p. (gr. 3-7). 1992. 12.95 (*0-88289-889-2*) Pelican.
Dobrin, Arnold. Josephine's 'Magination. 48p. (gr. 2-5). 1991. pap. 4.95 (*0-590-43494-2*) Scholastic Inc.
Dobrin, Peter. Start Exploring Architecture: A Fact-Filled Coloring Book. (Illus.). 128p. (Orig.). (gr. 3 up). 1993. pap. 8.95 (*1-56138-237-X*) Running Pr.
Dobrow, Vicki. Johnny Tremain - Study Guide. Friedland, Joyce & Kessler, Rikki, eds. (gr. 7-10). Date not set. pap. text ed. 14.95 (*0-88122-025-6*) Lrn Links.
Dobson, Clive. Fred's TV. Dobson, Clive, illus. 32p. (ps-5). 1989. 12.95 (*0-920668-60-7*); pap. 4.95 (*0-920668-59-3*) Firefly Bks Ltd.
Dobson, Danae. Forest Friends Help Each Other. Morales, Cuitlahuac, illus. 32p. (ps-k). 1993. 7.99 (*0-8499-0986-4*) Word Inc.
—Forest Friends Learn to Be Kind. Morales, Cuitlahuac, illus. 32p. 1993. 7.99 (*0-8499-1016-1*) Word Inc.
—Forest Friends Learn to Share. Morales, Cuitlahuac, illus. 32p. (ps-k). 1993. 7.99 (*0-8499-0985-6*) Word Inc.
—Forest Friends Play Fair. Morales, Cuitlahuac, illus. 32p. (ps-k). Date not set. 7.99 (*0-8499-0987-2*) Word Inc.
—Woof & the Big Fire. 32p. 1990. write for info. (*0-8499-8362-2*) Word Inc.
—Woof, the Seeing-Eye Dog. 32p. 1990. write for info. (*0-8499-8363-0*) Word Inc.
Dobson, Eileen. The First Maths Games File. 40p. (ps-4). 1986. pap. 7.50 (*0-906212-42-1*, Pub. by Tarquin UK) Parkwest Pubns.
Dobson, James. Preparing for Adolescence. rev. ed. Mills, Kathi, ed. LC 89-30455. 175p. 1989. pap. 7.99 (*0-8307-1258-5*, 5419314); 4.99 (*0-8307-1384-0*, 5018928) Regal.
—Preparing for Adolescence. 248p. (gr. 5-8). 1978. 19.84 (*0-685-63799-9*, BR7895) W A T Braille.
Dobyns, Henry F. The Pima-Maricopa. (Illus.). 112p. (gr. 5 up). 1989. 17.95 (*1-55546-724-5*) Chelsea Hse.
Docekal, Eileen M. Nature Detective: How to Solve Outdoor Mysteries. LC 89-31387. (Illus.). 128p. (gr. 4-12). 1989. 14.95 (*0-8069-6844-3*) Sterling.
—Nature Detective: How to Solve Outdoor Mysteries. Eames, David, illus. LC 89-31387. 128p. (gr. 3-10). 1991. pap. 7.95 (*0-8069-6845-1*) Sterling.
—Sky Detective. (Illus.). 128p. (gr. 9-12). 1992. 14.95 (*0-8069-8404-X*) Sterling.
Dockery, Della. Cami & Other Familiar Friends. Dockery, Della, illus. 20p. (ps-1). 1987. pap. 2.95 (*0-943487-05-6*) Sevgo Pr.
Dockrey, Karen. Dating: Making Your Own Choices. LC 86-30985. (Orig.). (gr. 7-12). 1987. pap. 4.95 (*0-8054-5345-8*) Broadman.
—Getting to Know God. LC 84-1702. (Orig.). (gr. 9-12). 1984. pap. 4.95 (*0-8054-5341-5*, 4253-41) Broadman.
—Getting to Know God: Study Guide. LC 86-8272. (Orig.). (gr. 9-12). 1986. pap. 2.95 (*0-8054-3240-X*) Broadman.
—It's Not Fair! Through Grief to Healing. Nelson, Becky, ed. (gr. 7-12). 1992. pap. text ed. 1.95 (*1-56309-035-X*, Wrld Changers Res) Womans Mission Union.

—What's a Kid Like Me Doing in a Family Like This? Leader's Book. 72p. (gr. 7-9). 1992. pap. 4.99 (*0-89693-113-7*) SP Pubns.
—What's Your Problem? 96p. (gr. 7 up). 1987. pap. 12.99 (*0-89693-381-4*, Victor Books); pap. 2.99 student bk. (*0-317-60085-0*) SP Pubns.
—Will I Ever Feel Good Again? When You're Overwhelmed by Grief & Loss. 160p. (Orig.). 1993. pap. 7.99 (*0-8007-5475-1*) Revell.
Dodd, Anne W. Footprints & Shadows. LC 91-4661. (ps-3). 1992. pap. 14.00 (*0-671-78716-0*, S&S BFYR) S&S Trade.
Dodd, Lynley. The Apple Tree. Dodd, Lynley, illus. LC 85-9774. 26p. (gr. 1-2). 1985. PLB 15.93 (*0-918831-08-3*) Gareth Stevens Inc.
—Dragon in a Wagon. Sherwood, Rhoda, ed. Dodd, Lynley, illus. LC 88-42925. 32p. (gr. 1-2). 1988. PLB 15.93 (*1-55532-911-X*) Gareth Stevens Inc.
—Find Me a Tiger. LC 91-50553. (Illus.). 32p. (gr. 1-2). 1992. PLB 15.93 (*0-8368-0762-6*) Gareth Stevens Inc.
—Hairy Maclary from Donaldson's Dairy. Dodd, Lynley, illus. LC 85-9773. 38p. (gr. 1-2). 1988. 15.93 (*0-918831-05-9*) Gareth Stevens Inc.
—Hairy Maclary-Scattercat. Dodd, Lynley, illus. LC 86-42797. 32p. (gr. 1-2). 1988. PLB 15.93 (*1-55532-123-2*) Gareth Stevens Inc.
—Hairy Maclary's Bone. Dodd, Lynley, illus. LC 85-9772. 32p. (gr. 1-2). 1985. PLB 15.93 (*0-918831-06-7*) Gareth Stevens Inc.
—Hairy Maclary's Caterwaul Caper. Dodd, Lynley, illus. LC 88-42926. 32p. (ps-2). 1989. PLB 15.93 (*1-55532-910-1*) Gareth Stevens Inc.
—Hairy Maclary's Rumpus at the Vet. Dodd, Lynley, illus. LC 89-43120. 28p. (gr. 1-2). 1989. PLB 15.93 (*0-8368-0126-1*) Gareth Stevens Inc.
—Hairy Maclary's Show Business. LC 91-50554. (Illus.). 32p. (gr. 1-2). 1992. PLB 15.93 (*0-8368-0763-4*) Gareth Stevens Inc.
—The Minister's Cat. LC 93-36139. 1994. write for info. (*0-8368-1073-2*) Gareth Stevens Inc.
—Slinky Malinki. Dodd, Lynley, illus. LC 90-44686. 32p. (gr. 1-2). 1991. PLB 15.93 (*0-8368-0197-0*) Gareth Stevens Inc.
—Slinky Malinki, Open the Door. LC 93-21180. 1994. write for info. (*0-8368-1074-0*) Gareth Stevens Inc.
—Smallest Turtle. Dodd, Lynley, illus. LC 85-9771. 29p. (gr. 1-2). 1985. PLB 15.93 (*0-918831-07-5*) Gareth Stevens Inc.
—Wake Up Bear. Dodd, Lynley, illus. LC 86-42798. 32p. (gr. 1-2). 1988. PLB 15.93 (*1-55532-124-0*) Gareth Stevens Inc.
Dodd, Lynley & Croser, Nigel. Gold Star First Readers, 14 vols. Aldridge, George, illus. 360p. (gr. 1-2). 1989. Set. PLB 223.02 (*0-8368-0775-8*) Gareth Stevens Inc.
Dodds, Bill. Bedtime Parables, Vol. 1. LC 92-61549. (Illus.). 32p. (gr. 5-6). 1993. 9.95 (*0-87973-570-8*, 570); pap. 6.95 (*0-87973-569-4*, 569) Our Sunday Visitor.
—The Hidden Fortune. LC 91-60944. 128p. (Orig.). (gr. 9-12). 1991. pap. text ed. 4.95 (*0-89243-346-9*) Liguori Pubns.
—My Sister Annie. 96p. (gr. 4-7). 1993. 14.95 (*1-56397-114-3*) Boyds Mills Pr.
Dodds, Dayle A. The Color Box. Laroche, Giles, illus. 32p. (ps-1). 1992. 12.95 (*0-316-18820-4*) Little.
—Do Bunnies Talk? Dubanevich, Arlene, illus. LC 91-13434. 32p. (ps-k). 1992. 15.00 (*0-06-020248-3*); PLB 14.89 (*0-06-020249-1*) HarpC Child Bks.
—On Our Way to Market. Gurney, John, illus. LC 91-6436. 40p. (ps-k). 1991. pap. 13.95 jacketed (*0-671-73567-5*, S&S BFYR) S&S Trade.
—Wheel Away! Hurd, Thacher, illus. LC 87-27091. 32p. (ps-1). 1989. PLB 13.89 (*0-06-021689-1*) HarpC Child Bks.
—Wheel Away! Hurd, Thacher, illus. LC 87-27091. 32p. (ps-1). 1991. pap. 4.95 (*0-06-443267-X*, Trophy) HarpC Child Bks.
Dodds, George. Voice Placing & Training Exercise, 2 vols. Incl. Contralto & Baritone. 10.95 (*0-19-322141-1*); Soprano & Tenor. 10.95 (*0-19-322140-3*). (gr. 9 up). 1927. OUP.
Dodds, Siobhan. Charles Tiger. Dodds, Siobhan, illus. (ps-3). 1988. 9.95 (*0-316-18817-4*, Joy Street Bks) Little.
—Elizabeth Hen. Dodds, Siobhan, illus. (ps-3). 1988. 9.95 (*0-316-18818-2*, Joy Street Bks) Little.
—Grandpa Bud. Dodds, Siobhan, illus. LC 92-53135. 32p. (ps-3). 1993. 13.95 (*1-56402-175-0*) Candlewick Pr.
—Words & Pictures: Reading with Clues. LC 91-71817. (ps-3). 1994. 4.99 (*1-56402-285-4*) Candlewick Pr.
—Words & Pictures: Reading with Picture Clues. Dodds, Siobhan, illus. LC 91-71817. 32p. (ps). 1992. 14.95 (*1-56402-042-8*) Candlewick Pr.
Dodge, Howard. How to Prepare for SAT II: Mathematics, Level IIC. 5th ed. LC 93-30068. 1994. pap. 11.95 (*0-8120-1704-8*) Barron.
Dodge, Mary M. Hans Brinker. (gr. k-6). 1985. pap. 4.95 (*0-440-43446-7*, Pub. by Yearling Classics) Dell.
—Hans Brinker. Betts, Louise, adapted by. Elwell, Peter, illus. LC 87-15472. 48p. (gr. 3-6). 1988. PLB 12.89 (*0-8167-1205-0*); pap. text ed. 3.95 (*0-8167-1206-9*) Troll Assocs.
—Hans Brinker, or, The Silver Skates. 1993. pap. 2.50 (*0-8125-3342-9*) Tor Bks.

—Hans Brinker: Or The Silver Skates. (gr. 4 up). 1993. pap. 4.99 (*0-88070-528-0*, Gold & Honey) Questar Pubs.
—Hans Brinker: The Silver Skates. LC 54-14472. (gr. 5 up). 1966. pap. 1.50 (*0-8049-0099-X*, CL-99) Airmont.
—Hans Brinker: The Silver Skates. 332p. (gr. 6 up). 1985. pap. 3.99 (*0-14-035042-X*, Puffin) Puffin Bks.
Dodge, Nancy C. El Cuento de Thumpy: Un Cuento que Comparte Amor y Pena por Thumpy, el Conejito. rev., 2nd ed. (SPA., Illus.). 24p. (gr. k-12). 1986. pap. 5.95 (*0-918533-44-9*) Prairie Lark.
—Thumpy's Story: A Story of Love & Grief Shared. Veara, Kevin, illus. LC 84-61293. 24p. (gr. k-12). 1985. pap. 5.95 (*0-918533-00-7*) Prairie Lark.
Dodge, Steven C. Christopher Columbus & the First Voyages to the New World. Goetzmann, William H., ed. Collins, Michael, intro. by. (Illus.). 112p. (gr. 5 up). 1991. lib. bdg. 18.95 (*0-7910-1299-9*); pap. 9.95 (*0-7910-1522-X*) Chelsea Hse.
Dodgson, Charles, pseud. Alice in Wonderland. (Illus.). 1992. write for info. (*0-89434-121-9*) Ferguson.
Dodson, Benjamin C. The Promise of Oregon. Dodson, O. Ray, intro. by. 118p. (Orig.). (gr. 7-12). 1989. pap. 6.75 (*0-9620550-3-4*) Dodson Assocs.
Dodson, Bert, illus. Lazy Jack. LC 78-18070. 32p. (gr. k-4). 1979. PLB 9.79 (*0-89375-123-5*); pap. 1.95 (*0-89375-101-4*) Troll Assocs.
Dodson, Lamar. Be My Daddy. 1992. 12.95 (*0-533-10200-6*) Vantage.
Dodson, Peter. Discover Dinosaurs. (Illus.). 48p. (gr. 3-6). 1992. PLB 14.95 (*1-878363-68-9*, HTS Bks) Forest Hse.
Dodson, Susan. The Eye of the Storm. (gr. 7 up) pap. 2.25 (*0-317-62893-3*) S&S Trade.
—Shadows Across the Sand. (gr. 7 up). 1984. pap. 2.25 (*0-449-70114-X*, Juniper) Fawcett.
Doerken, Nan. The First Family Car. 59p. (gr. 1-4). 1986. pap. 3.95 (*0-919797-53-9*) Kindred Pr.
Doerksen, Nan. Bears for Breakfast: The Thiessen Family Adventures. Penner, Kathy, illus. 34p. (ps-k). 1983. pap. 2.50 (*0-919797-07-5*) Kindred Pr.
Doerr, Cathy A. Student Organizational Planbook. 112p. (gr. 3-12). 1992. pap. 5.95 (*0-9632893-0-6*) Skills For Lrn.
Doggett, Clinton & Doggett, Lois. The U. S. Information Agency. (Illus.). 112p. (gr. 5 up). 1990. lib. bdg. 14.95 (*1-55546-124-7*) Chelsea Hse.
Doggett, Clinton L. Equal Employment Opportunities Commission. (Illus.). 112p. (gr. 5 up). 1990. lib. bdg. 14.95 (*1-55546-106-9*) Chelsea Hse.
Doggett, Lois, jt. auth. see Doggett, Clinton.
Dogin, Yvette. Teen-Agers at Work. 64p. (gr. 8 up). 1988. pap. text ed. 3.75 (*0-88323-244-8*, 164); tchr's key 1.25 (*0-318-33412-7*, 277) Pendergrass Pub.
Doheny, Catherine, ed. see Anderson, Jill & Weinman, Susan.
Doherty, Berlie. Dear Nobody. 192p. (gr. 6-12). 1992. 14.95 (*0-531-05461-6*); PLB 14.99 (*0-531-08611-9*) Orchard Bks Watts.
—Dear Nobody. LC 93-9626. 192p. (gr. 8 up). 1994. pap. 3.95 (*0-688-12764-9*, Pub. by Beech Tree Bks) Morrow.
—Dear Nobody. large type ed. LC 93-13531. (gr. 6 up). 1993. Alk. paper. 15.95 (*1-56054-769-3*) Thorndike Pr.
—Granny Was a Buffer Girl. LC 87-25080. 160p. (gr. 5 up). 1988. 12.95 (*0-531-05754-2*); PLB 12.99 (*0-531-08354-3*) Orchard Bks Watts.
—Granny Was a Buffer Girl. LC 92-24594. (Illus.). 144p. (gr. 8 up). 1993. pap. 3.95 (*0-688-11863-1*, Pub. by Beech Tree Bks) Morrow.
—Granny Was a Buffer Girl. large type ed. (gr. 1-8). 1991. 13.95 (*0-7451-0725-7*, Galaxy Child Lrg Print) Chivers N Amer.
—Snowy. Bowen, Keith, illus. LC 91-47519. 32p. (ps-3). 1993. 14.00 (*0-8037-1343-6*) Dial Bks Young.
—White Peak Farm. LC 89-23060. 128p. (gr. 5 up). 1990. 13.95 (*0-531-05867-0*); PLB 13.99 (*0-531-08467-1*) Orchard Bks Watts.
Doherty, Berlie, retold by see Ewing, Juliana H.
Doherty, Bertie. White Peak Farm. LC 92-43778. 112p. (gr. 8 up). 1993. pap. 3.95 (*0-688-11864-X*, Pub. by Beech Tree Bks) Morrow.
Doherty, Craig. Arnold Schwarzenegger. (gr. 4-7). 1993. 14.95 (*0-8027-8236-1*); PLB 15.85 (*0-8027-8238-8*) Walker & Co.
Doherty, Craig A. & Doherty, Katherine M. The Apaches & Navajos. LC 89-9079. (Illus.). 64p. (gr. 3-5). 1989. PLB 12.90 (*0-531-10743-4*) Watts.
—The Apaches & Navajos. (Illus.). 64p. (gr. 1 up). 1991. pap. 5.95 (*0-531-15602-8*) Watts.
—The Cahuilla. LC 93-31863. (gr. 4 up). 1994. write for info. (*0-86625-527-3*) Rourke Corp.
—The Huron. LC 93-32667. 1994. write for info. (*0-86625-528-1*) Rourke Pubns.
—The Iroquois. LC 89-33055. (Illus.). 64p. (gr. 3-5). 1989. PLB 12.90 (*0-531-10747-7*) Watts.
—The Iroquois. (Illus.). 64p. (gr. 3 up). 1991. pap. 5.95 (*0-531-15603-6*) Watts.
—The Narragansett. LC 93-32669. 1994. write for info. (*0-86625-525-7*) Rourke Pubns.
Doherty, Craig A., jt. auth. see Doherty, Katherine M.
Doherty, Jim & O'Donnell, Joe. Journey to the Bay. 160p. (Orig.). (gr. 4-8). 1991. pap. 7.95 (*0-86322-136-X*, Pub. by Brandon Bk Pubs ER) Irish Bks Media.

Doherty, Katherine M. & Doherty, Craig A. The Crow. LC 93-35660. 1994. write for info. (0-86625-529-X) Rourke Pubns.
—The Zunis. LC 93-18372. 1993. lib. bdg. 12.90 (0-531-20157-0) Watts.

Doherty, Katherine M., jt. auth. see Doherty, Craig A.

Doherty, Paul. King Arthur. Schlesinger, Arthur M., Jr., intro. by. (Illus.). 112p. (gr. 5 up). 1987. lib. bdg. 17.95 (0-87754-506-5) Chelsea Hse.

Doherty, William T. West Virginia: Our Land - Our People. Buckalew, Marshall, ed. Harvey, Eve S. & Harvey, Cliff, illus. 320p. (gr. 8). 1990. 25.00 (0-914498-07-X); punched for 3-ring binder tchr's. manual 25.00 (0-914498-10-X) WV Hist Ed Found.

Doherty, William T. & Conley, Phil. West Virginia History. (Illus.). 494p. (gr. 8). 1974. 10.25 (0-914498-00-2) WV Hist Ed Found.

Dolan, Edward F. America after Vietnam: Legacies of a Hated War. LC 89-8982. (Illus.). 160p. (gr. 7-12). 1989. PLB 13.90 (0-531-10793-0) Watts.
—America in World War II: 1941. (gr. 4-7). 1992. pap. 6.70 (0-395-65944-2) HM.
—America in World War II: 1943. (gr. 4-7). 1992. pap. 6.70 (0-395-62463-0) HM.
—America in World War II: 1944. (Illus.). 72p. (gr. 4-6). 1993. PLB 15.90 (1-56294-221-2) Millbrook Pr.
—America in World War II: 1945. (Illus.). 72p. (gr. 4-6). 1994. 15.90 (1-56294-320-0) Millbrook Pr.
—America in World War Two: Nineteen Forty-Three. LC 91-30808. (Illus.). 72p. (gr. 4-6). 1992. PLB 15.90 (1-56294-113-5) Millbrook Pr.
—America in World War Two: 1941. LC 91-30808. (Illus.). 72p. (gr. 4-6). 1991. PLB 15.90 (1-878841-05-X) Millbrook Pr.
—America in World War Two: 1942. LC 91-30808. (Illus.). 72p. (gr. 4-6). 1991. PLB 15.90 (1-56294-007-4) Millbrook Pr.
—The American Wilderness & Its Future: Conservation Versus Use. Roxas, Reni, ed. LC 91-33440. (Illus.). 160p. (gr. 9-12). 1992. PLB 14.40 (0-531-11062-1) Watts.
—Child Abuse. rev. ed. LC 92-11355. 128p. (gr. 9-12). 1992. PLB 13.90 (0-531-11042-7) Watts.
—Communications. 1995. write for info. (0-8050-2861-7) H Holt & Co.
—Drought: The Past, Present, & Future Enemy. LC 89-25016. (gr. 9-12). 1990. PLB 13.90 (0-531-10900-3) Watts.
—Drugs in Sports. rev. ed. Roxas, Reni, ed. LC 91-36794. (Illus.). 144p. (gr. 9-12). 1992. PLB 14.40 (0-531-11041-9) Watts.
—Electricity. (gr. 4 up). 1995. PLB write for info. (0-8050-2862-5) H Holt & Co.
—Famous Firsts in Space. LC 89-811. (Illus.). 144p. (gr. 4-7). 1989. 13.95 (0-525-65007-5, Cobblehill Bks) Dutton Child Bks.
—Military. 1995. PLB write for info. (0-8050-2865-X) H Holt & Co.
—Our Poisoned Sky. LC 90-14031. (Illus.). 144p. (gr. 7 up). 1991. 15.00 (0-525-65056-3, Cobblehill Bks) Dutton Child Bks.
—Panama & the United States: Their Canal, Their Stormy Years. 1990. PLB 14.40 (0-531-10911-9) Watts.
—The Police in American Society. Rasof, Henry, ed. LC 88-14265. (Illus.). 160p. (gr. 7-12). 1988. PLB 14.40 (0-531-10608-X) Watts.
—Science. 1995. PLB write for info. (0-8050-2863-3) H Holt & Co.
—Space. 1995. PLB write for info. (0-8050-2864-1) H Holt & Co.
—Teenagers & Compulsive Gambling. LC 93-31956. 1994. write for info. (0-531-11100-8) Watts.
—Transportation. 1995. write for info. (0-8050-2860-9) H Holt & Co.

Dolan, Edward F. & Scariano, Margaret M. Nuclear Waste: The Ten Thousand-Year Challenge. LC 90-34586. (Illus.). 128p. (gr. 9-12). 1990. PLB 14.40 (0-531-10943-7) Watts.

Dolan, Edward F., Jr. Bicycle Touring & Camping. American, Youth Hostels, intro. by. LC 81-21962. 192p. (gr. 7 up). 1982. (J Messner); pap. 5.75 (0-685-05841-7) S&S Trade.
—Protect Your Legal Rights: A Handbook for Teenagers. LC 83-8162. 128p. (gr. 7 up). 1983. (J Messner) S&S Trade.

Dolan, Ellen M. Susan Butcher & the Iditarod Trail. LC 92-36837. 1993. 14.95 (0-8027-8211-6); PLB 15.85 (0-8027-8212-4) Walker & Co.

Dolan, Ellen M. & Bolinske, Janet L., eds. Aladdin & the Magic Lamp. Lie, Eula, illus. LC 87-61661. 32p. (Orig.). (gr. 1-3). 1987. text ed. 8.95 (0-88335-564-7); pap. text ed. 4.95 (0-88335-584-1) Milliken Pub Co.
—Casey at the Bat. LC 87-61667. (Illus.). 32p. (Orig.). (gr. 1-3). 1987. text ed. 8.95 (0-88335-558-2); pap. text ed. 4.95 (0-88335-578-7) Milliken Pub Co.
—The Coming of the Sun. Nichol, Bee, illus. LC 87-61659. 32p. (Orig.). (gr. 1-3). 1987. text ed. 8.95 (0-88335-566-3); pap. text ed. 4.95 (0-88335-586-8) Milliken Pub Co.
—Drakestail. LC 87-61663. (Illus.). 32p. (Orig.). (gr. 1-3). 1987. text ed. 8.95 (0-88335-562-0); pap. text ed. 4.95 (0-88335-582-5) Milliken Pub Co.
—Hansel & Gretel. Nichol, Bee, illus. LC 87-61670. 32p. (Orig.). (gr. 1-3). 1987. text ed. 8.95 (0-88335-555-8); 4.95 (0-88335-545-0); pap. text ed. 3.95 (0-88335-575-2) Milliken Pub Co.

—Henny Penny. Lie, Eula, illus. LC 87-61674. 32p. (Orig.). (gr. 1-3). 1987. spiral bdg. 14.95 (0-88335-541-8); text ed. 8.95 (0-88335-551-5); pap. text ed. 4.95 (0-88335-571-X) Milliken Pub Co.
—Jack & the Beanstalk. LC 87-61662. (Illus.). 32p. (Orig.). (gr. 1-3). 1987. text ed. 8.95 (0-88335-563-9); pap. text ed. 4.95 (0-88335-583-3) Milliken Pub Co.
—The Leaves of Autumn. Nichol, Bee, illus. LC 87-61658. 32p. (Orig.). (gr. 1-3). 1987. text ed. 8.95 (0-88335-567-1); pap. text ed. 4.95 (0-88335-587-6) Milliken Pub Co.
—The Legend of Sleepy Hollow. Lie, Eula, illus. LC 87-61665. 32p. (Orig.). (gr. 1-3). 1987. text ed. 8.95 (0-88335-560-4); pap. text ed. 4.95 (0-88335-580-9) Milliken Pub Co.
—Little Red Riding Hood. LC 87-61673. (Illus.). 32p. (Orig.). (gr. 1-3). 1987. spiral bdg. 14.95 (0-88335-543-4); text ed. 8.95 (0-88335-553-1); pap. text ed. 4.95 (0-88335-573-6) Milliken Pub Co.
—The Nightingale. Lie, Eula, illus. LC 87-61666. 32p. (Orig.). (gr. 1-3). 1987. text ed. 8.95 (0-88335-559-0); pap. text ed. 4.95 (0-88335-579-5) Milliken Pub Co.
—Paul Bunyan. LC 87-61664. (Illus.). 32p. (Orig.). (gr. 1-3). 1987. text ed. 8.95 (0-88335-561-2); pap. text ed. 4.95 (0-88335-581-7) Milliken Pub Co.
—Peter Rabbit. Lie, Eula, illus. LC 87-61672. 32p. (Orig.). (gr. 1-3). 1987. spiral bdg. 14.95 (0-88335-542-6); text ed. 8.95 (0-88335-552-3); pap. text ed. 4.95 (0-88335-572-8) Milliken Pub Co.
—The Robin's Red Breast. Nichol, Bee, illus. LC 87-61657. 32p. (Orig.). (gr. 1-3). 1987. text ed. 8.95 (0-88335-568-X); pap. text ed. 4.95 (0-88335-588-4) Milliken Pub Co.
—The Snow Queen. LC 87-61668. 32p. (Orig.). (gr. 1-3). 1987. text ed. 8.95 (0-88335-557-4); pap. text ed. 4.95 (0-88335-577-9) Milliken Pub Co.
—Thumbelina. LC 87-61669. (Illus.). 32p. (Orig.). (gr. 1-3). 1987. spiral bdg. 14.95 (0-88335-546-9); text ed. 8.95 (0-88335-556-6); pap. text ed. 4.95 (0-88335-576-0) Milliken Pub Co.
—The Ugly Duckling. Lie, Eula, illus. LC 87-61671. 32p. (Orig.). (gr. 1-3). 1987. spiral bdg. 14.95 (0-88335-544-2); text ed. 8.95 (0-88335-554-X); pap. text ed. 4.95 (0-88335-574-4) Milliken Pub Co.
—Why the Loon Calls. Nichol, Bee, illus. LC 87-61660. 32p. (Orig.). (gr. 1-3). 1987. text ed. 8.95 (0-88335-565-5); pap. text ed. 4.95 (0-88335-585-X) Milliken Pub Co.

Dolan, Sean. Chiang Kai-Shek. Schlesinger, Arthur M., Jr., intro. by. (Illus.). 112p. (gr. 5 up). 1989. lib. bdg. 17.95 (0-87754-517-0) Chelsea Hse.
—Earvin "Magic" Johnson. King, Coretta Scott, intro. by. (Illus.). 112p. (gr. 5 up). 1993. PLB 17.95 (0-7910-1774-5) Chelsea Hse.
—Gabriel Garcia Marquez: Colombian Writer. LC 93-9478. (Illus.). 1994. 18.95 (0-7910-1243-3, Am Art Analog); pap. write for info. (0-7910-1270-0) Chelsea Hse.
—James Beckwourth. (Illus.). (gr. 5 up). 1992. lib. bdg. 17.95 (0-7910-1120-8) Chelsea Hse.
—Junipero Serra. (Illus.). 112p. (gr. 5 up). 1991. lib. bdg. 17.95 (0-7910-1255-7) Chelsea Hse.
—Junipero Serra: Hispanics of Achievement. (gr. 4-7). 1992. pap. 7.95 (0-7910-1282-4) Chelsea Hse.
—Magic Johnson, Basketball Great. LC 92-21378. (Illus.). (gr. 5 up). 1994. PLB 18.95 (0-7910-1975-6, Am Art Analog); pap. write for info. (0-7910-1976-4, Am Art Analog) Chelsea Hse.
—Matthew Henson. (Illus.). 72p. (gr. 3-5). 1991. lib. bdg. 12.95 (0-7910-1568-8) Chelsea Hse.
—Michael Jordan, Basketball Great. LC 93-16714. (Illus.). (gr. 5 up). 1994. PLB 18.95 (0-7910-2150-5, Am Art Analog); pap. write for info. (0-7910-2151-3, Am Art Analog) Chelsea Hse.
—West Germany: On the Road to Reunification. (Illus.). 128p. (gr. 5 up). 1991. 14.95 (0-7910-1367-7) Chelsea Hse.

Dolan, Terrance. The Kiowa Indians. LC 93-17696. (Illus.). (gr. 2-5). 1993. PLB 13.95 (0-7910-1663-3, Am Art Analog); pap. write for info. (0-7910-2028-2, Am Art Analog) Chelsea Hse.
—Probing Deep Space. Goetzmann, William H., ed. Collins, Michael, intro. by. (Illus.). 112p. (gr. 6-12). 1993. PLB 19.95 (0-7910-1326-X, Am Art Analog); pap. write for info. (0-7910-1550-5, Am Art Analog) Chelsea Hse.
—The Teton Sioux Indians. (Illus.). 1994. 13.95 (0-7910-1680-3, Am Art Analog) Chelsea Hse.

Dolb, K. Danger at Demon's Cove. (Illus.). 48p. (gr. 4-9). 1988. PLB 11.96 (0-88110-333-0); pap. 4.95 (0-7460-0179-7) EDC.

Dolby, K. The Ghost in the Mirror. (Illus.). 48p. 1989. PLB 11.96 (0-88110-369-1); pap. 4.95 (0-7460-0334-X) EDC.
—Ghostly Puzzle Adventures. (gr. 4-7). 1990. pap. 9.95 (0-7460-0336-6, Usborne) EDC.
—The Incredible Dinosaur Expedition. (Illus.). 48p. (gr. 3-5). 1987. PLB 11.96 (0-88110-300-4); pap. 4.95 (0-7460-0149-5) EDC.

Dolby, K., et al. Second Usborne Book of Puzzle Adventures. (Illus.). 144p. (gr. 3-8). 1990. pap. 9.95 (0-7460-0310-2, Usborne) EDC.

Dolby, Karen. House of Shadows. (Illus.). 48p. (gr. 3 up). 1993. PLB 11.96 (0-88110-520-1, Usborne); pap. 4.95 (0-7460-0679-9, Usborne) EDC.

Dolce, J. Ellen, illus. Baby's Mother Goose. LC 87-81921. 12p. (ps). 1988. write for info. (0-307-06066-7, Pub. by Golden Bks) Western Pub.

Dolce, Laura. Australia. (Illus.). 128p. (gr. 5 up). 1990. 14.95 (0-7910-1105-4) Chelsea Hse.
—Mental Retardation. (Illus.). (gr. 6-12). 1994. 19.95 (0-7910-0050-8, Am Art Analog); pap. write for info. (0-7910-0530-5, Am Art Analog) Chelsea Hse.
—Suicide. (Illus.). 112p. (gr. 6-12). 1992. 18.95 (0-7910-0053-2) Chelsea Hse.

Dolch, Edward W., et al, eds. see Defoe, Daniel.

Dole, Helen B., tr. see Spyri, Johanna.

Doleski, Teddi. The Hurt. (Illus.). 32p. (gr. 2-5). 1983. pap. 3.95 (0-8091-6551-1) Paulist Pr.
—Silvester & the Oogaloo Boogalo. 1990. 2.95 (0-8091-6596-1) Paulist Pr.

Dolin, Eric J. The U. S. Fish & Wildlife Service. Schlesinger, Arthur M., Jr., intro. by. (Illus.). 112p. (gr. 5 up). 1989. lib. bdg. 14.95 (1-55546-128-X) Chelsea Hse.

Doll, F., et al. Preparing Young Children for Christmas 1993. (Illus.). 48p. 1993. pap. 1.00 (0-915531-06-2) OR Catholic.
—Preparing Young Children for Easter 1994. (Illus.). 48p. (ps-2). 1994. pap. 1.00 (0-915531-07-0) OR Catholic.

Dollinger, Peter, ed. see Conservation Treaty Support Group Staff.

Dolmetsch, Paul & Mauriette, Gail, eds. Teens Talk about Alcohol & Alcoholism. LC 86-16616. 144p. 1987. pap. 7.95 (0-385-23084-2) Doubleday.

Dolphin, Laurie. Georgia to Georgia: Making Friends in the U. S. S. R. McGee, E. Alan, illus. LC 90-47494. 40p. (gr. 2 up). 1991. 13.95 (0-688-09896-7, Tambourine Bks); PLB 13.88 (0-688-09897-5, Tambourine Bks) Morrow.

Dolson, Bobbie J. Van see Jones, Lucile.

Dolson, Gina, ed. Lisa & the Magic Doll: Russian & Ukrainian Fairy Tales. Mandeville, Jerry & Brodsky, Anna, trs. from RUS & UKR. Mawolski, Stanley M., illus. 56p. (Orig.). (gr. 1-4). 10). 1986. pap. 4.50x (0-914265-07-5) New Eng Pub MA.

Doman, Bruce K. Goodbye, Mommy. Melton, David, illus. LC 77-79632. 86p. (ps-2). 1982. 8.95 (0-936676-00-0) Better Baby.

Domanska, Janina. A Was an Angler. LC 88-35589. (Illus.). 32p. (ps up). 1991. 13.95 (0-688-06990-8); PLB 13.88 (0-688-06991-6) Greenwillow.
—Busy Monday Morning. Domanska, Janina, illus. LC 83-25362. 32p. (ps-1). 1985. 13.00 (0-688-03833-6); PLB 14.93 (0-688-03834-4) Greenwillow.

Domanska, Janina, illus. The First Noel. LC 85-27084. 24p. (ps up). 1986. 11.75 (0-688-04324-0); PLB 11.88 (0-688-04325-9) Greenwillow.
—If All the Seas Were One Sea. reissued ed. LC 73-146621. 32p. (ps-2). 1987. SBE 14.95 (0-02-732540-7, Macmillan Child Bk) Macmillan Child Grp.

Dombey, Moshe, tr. see Fuchs, Yitzchak Y.

Dombrower, Jan. Getting to Know Your Feelings. Stricklin, Patricia, illus. Johnson, Debbie, ed. 32p. (Orig.). (ps-3). 1990. pap. text ed. 5.95 (0-9626348-0-8) Heartwise Pr.

Domhoff, G. William. Who Rules America Now? A View for the Eighties. 230p. (Orig.). (gr. 9-12). 1983. (Spec); pap. 7.95 (0-13-958405-6, Spec) P-H.

Dominguez, Joseph F., tr. see Jimenez, Juan R.

Dominick, Bayard. Joe, a Porpoise. (Illus.). (gr. 3-5). 1968. 10.95 (0-8392-3067-2) Astor-Honor.
—Sam, a Goat. (Illus.). (gr. 3-5). 1968. 9.95 (0-8392-3062-1) Astor-Honor.

Dominques, Manuel, jt. auth. see Laycock, Mary.

Dominquez, Angel. Diary of a Victorian Mouse. Dominquez, Angel, illus. 32p. (sp up). 1991. 14.95 (1-55970-121-8) Arcade Pub Inc.

Dominy, Jeannine. Katherine Dunham. (Illus.). 112p. (gr. 5 up). 1992. lib. bdg. 17.95 (0-7910-1123-2) Chelsea Hse.
—Leontyne Price. (Illus.). (gr. 5 up). 1992. PLB 17.95 (0-7910-1135-6) Chelsea Hse.

Domke, Lonnie. Kids Cook Too! Creative Cookery for Children & Teens. Domke, Tim, ed. LC 90-84362. (Illus.). 100p. (gr. k up). 1991. 12.95 (0-9627795-2-0); pap. 10.95 spiral bdg. (0-9627795-1-2) Carolina Cnslts Network.

Domke, Tim, ed. see Domke, Lonnie.

Domke, Todd. Grounded. LC 81-14267. 192p. (gr. 4-7). 1982. pap. 9.95 (0-394-85163-3) Knopf Bks Yng Read.

Donahue, A. K. Four by Fours & Pickups. 48p. (gr. 3-4). 1991. PLB 11.95 (1-56065-075-3) Capstone Pr.

Donahue, Bob & Donahue, Marilyn. The Right Way to Eat Spaghetti. (Illus.). 128p. (Orig.). (gr. 9-12). 1988. pap. 4.95 (0-8423-5597-9) Tyndale.

Donahue, David M. & Flowers, Nancy. The Uprooted: Refugees & the United States - A Resource Curriculum. (Illus.). 224p. (Orig.). (gr. 7-12). 1993. pap. 15.95x (0-89793-122-X) Hunter Hse.

Donahue, Marilyn. A Place to Belong. LC 88-14808. 1988. pap. 4.49 (1-55513-757-1, Chariot Bks) Cook.
—Reach with All Your Heart. LC 88-14807. 1988. pap. 4.49 (1-55513-755-5, Chariot Bks) Cook.
—Somebody Special to Love. LC 88-14809. 1988. pap. 4.49 (0-89191-360-2, Chariot Bks) Cook.

Donahue, Marilyn, jt. auth. see Donahue, Bob.

Donahue, Marilyn C. The Valley in Between. (gr. 5 up). 1987. 14.95 (0-8027-6731-1); PLB 15.85 (0-8027-6733-8) Walker & Co.

Donahue, Michael & Strawn, Janice. The Grandpa Tree. 24p. (gr. 1-3). 1988. pap. 4.95 (0-911797-42-4) R Rinehart.

Donahue, Shiobhan. Kristi Yamaguchi: Artist on Ice. LC 92-38272. 1993. 13.50 (0-8225-0522-3) Lerner Pubns.

Donaldson, Joan. The Real Pretend. Tudor, Tash, illus. 32p. (ps-3). 1992. 12.95 (*1-56288-158-2*) Checkerboard.

Donaldson, Judith E. Doodles, Diddles, Puzzles, Quizzies & Fun Stuff, Vol. 2. Peters, Robert, illus. 144p. (Orig.). (gr. 2 up). 1981. pap. 2.25 (*0-939942-00-3*) Larkspur.

—Travel Games: Vol. 2, Five to Ten Years. Brown, George H., ed. Donaldson, Judith E., illus. 36p. (gr. k-5). pap. text ed. 1.50 (*0-939942-06-2*) Larkspur.

Donaldson, Julia. A Squash & a Squeeze. Scheffler, Axel, illus. LC 92-16507. 32p. (ps-3). 1993. SBE 14.95 (*0-689-50571-X*, M K McElderry) Macmillan Child Grp.

Donaldson, Stephen E. & Myers, William A. Rails Through the Orange Groves, Vol. 2. LC 89-7619. (Illus.). 144p. (gr. 11). 1990. 34.95 (*0-87046-094-3*, Pub. by Trans-Anglo) Interurban.

Donatelli, Betty. A Good Book to Toot About. Donatelli, Betty, illus. 11p. (Orig.). (gr. 1-2). 1984. pap. 2.00 (*0-912981-10-5*) Hse BonGiovanni.

—Growing in Reading. Donatelli, Betty, illus. 11p. (Orig.). (gr. 1-2). 1984. pap. 2.00 (*0-912981-07-5*) Hse BonGiovanni.

—Merry Words for You. Donatelli, Betty, illus. 11p. (Orig.). (gr. 1-2). 1984. pap. 2.00 (*0-912981-09-1*) Hse BonGiovanni.

—Sounding Words with Roy & Joy. Donatelli, Betty, illus. 11p. (Orig.). (gr. k-2). 1984. pap. 1.00 (*0-912981-06-7*) Hse BonGiovanni.

—Sunny, Funny Stories. Donatelli, Betty, illus. 11p. (Orig.). (gr. 1-2). 1984. pap. 1.00 (*0-912981-08-3*) Hse BonGiovanni.

Donati, Annabelle. I Wonder If Dragons Are Real & Other Neat Facts about Reptiles & Amphibians. (Illus.). (ps-3). 1992. write for info. (*0-307-11321-3*, 11321) Western Pub.

—I Wonder If Sea Cows Give Milk & Other Neat Facts about Unusual Animals. (ps-3). 1993. pap. 4.95 (*0-307-11327-2*, Golden Pr) Western Pub.

—I Wonder What a Rain Forest Is & Other Neat Facts about Plants. (Illus.). 36p. (ps-3). 1992. write for info. (*0-307-11322-1*, 11322) Western Pub.

—I Wonder Why Fish Don't Drown & Other Neat Facts about Underwater Animals. (Illus.). 36p. (ps-3). 1992. write for info. (*0-307-11325-6*, 11325) Western Pub.

—Wonder Which Snake Is the Longest & Other Neat Facts about Animal Records. (ps-3). 1993. pap. 4.95 (*0-307-11326-4*, Golden Pr) Western Pub.

Donauer, Friedrich. Swords Against Carthage. Cooper, F. T., tr. LC 61-12878. (Illus.). (gr. 7-11). 1932. 20.00 (*0-8196-0112-8*) Biblo.

Doncaster, Islay. Traditional China. Killingray, Margaret & O'Connor, Edmund, eds. (Illus.). (gr. 6-11). 1980. pap. text ed. 3.45 (*0-89908-007-3*) Greenhaven.

Dondiego, Barbara L. After-School Crafts. Cawley, Jacqueline, illus. 144p. 1992. 22.95 (*0-8306-3868-7*, 4138); pap. 12.95 (*0-8306-3869-5*, 4138) TAB Bks.

Donegan, Maureen. The Bedside Book of Irish Fables & Legends. reissued ed. 117p. (gr. 5 up). 1993. pap. 11.95 (*1-85635-063-0*, Pub. by Mercier Pr ER) Dufour.

Donehower, Bruce. Miko: Little Hunter of the North. Pohrt, Tom, illus. (gr. 2-7). 1990. 12.95 (*0-374-34970-3*) FS&G.

Doney, Mary K. & Doney, Stef. Acts of Courage. Anderian, Kaffi & Johannsen, Rob, illus. 48p. (gr. 5-9). 1985. pap. 5.95 (*0-88625-091-9*) Durkin Hayes Pub.

Doney, Stef. Amazing Adventures. Hughes, Mark, illus. 48p. (gr. 5-9). 1985. pap. 5.95 (*0-88625-093-5*) Durkin Hayes Pub.

Doney, Stef, jt. auth. see Doney, Mary K.

Doney. All in the Ark. 1992. write for info. (*1-55513-766-0*, Chariot Bks) Cook.

Doney, Malcolm & Doney, Meryl. Who Made Me? Butterworth, Nick & Inkpen, Mick, illus. 38p. (ps-3). 1987. 9.99 (*0-310-55660-0*, 19064) Zondervan.

Doney, Meryl. Away in a Manger. (Illus.). 8p. (gr. 1-2). 1991. 5.99 (*0-8407-9608-0*) Oliver-Nelson.

—Discovering Out of Doors. (Illus.). 28p. (ps-3). 1979. pap. 2.99 (*0-85648-175-0*) Lion USA.

—Discovering the City. (Illus.). 32p. (gr. k-2). pap. 2.99 (*0-85648-259-5*) Lion USA.

—The Green Activity Book. (Illus.). 32p. (Orig.). (gr. p-8). 1991. pap. 4.99 (*0-7459-1901-4*) Lion USA.

—How the Bible Came to Us. (Illus.). 48p. (gr. 8 up). 1985. 13.95 (*0-85648-574-8*) Lion USA.

—Jesus: The Man Who Changed History. (Illus.). 48p. (gr. 4 up). 1988. text ed. 13.95 (*0-7459-1050-5*) Lion USA.

—Lion for the King. (ps up). 1990. 9.99 (*0-7459-1834-4*) Lion USA.

—Lion for the King. (ps-3). 1993. pap. 4.99 (*0-7459-2260-0*) Lion USA.

—Look What I've Found! Acorn. (ps). 1990. bds. 4.99 (*0-7459-1923-5*) Lion USA.

—Look What I've Found! Bulb. (ps). 1990. bds. 4.99 (*0-7459-1937-5*) Lion USA.

—Look What I've Found! Cocoon. (ps). 1990. bds. 4.99 (*0-7459-1936-7*) Lion USA.

—Look What I've Found! Egg. (ps). 1990. bds. 4.99 (*0-7459-1935-9*) Lion USA.

—The Ninety-Ninth Sheep. (Illus.). 1991. 8.99 (*0-8423-4740-2*) Tyndale.

—The Very Worried Sparrow. Geldart, William, illus. 32p. (ps-6). 1991. 11.95 (*0-7459-1919-7*) Lion USA.

Doney, Meryl, jt. auth. see Doney, Malcolm.

Doney, Meryl, jt. auth. see Vesey, Susan.

Dongarra, Kathryn, ed. see Stuart, Sally E. & Young, Woody.

Donington, Margaret & Donington, Robert. Scales, Arpeggios, & Exercises for the Recorder. (gr. 9 up). 1961. 19.95 (*0-19-322160-8*) OUP.

Donington, Robert, jt. auth. see Donington, Margaret.

Donnelly, Elfie. A Package for Miss Marshwater. Krause, Ute, illus. (gr. 2-5). 1987. Dial Bks Young.

Donnelly, Judy. All Around the World. Kelley, True, illus. 1991. 13.95 (*0-448-40137-1*, G&D) Putnam Pub Group.

—Moonwalk: The First Trip to the Moon. Davidson, Dennis, illus. LC 88-23668. 48p. (Orig.). (gr. 2-4). 1989. PLB 7.99 (*0-394-92457-6*); pap. 3.50 (*0-394-82457-1*) Random Bks Yng Read.

—The Titanic: Lost...& Found. Kohler, Keith, illus. LC 86-20402. 48p. (gr. 1-3). 1987. lib. bdg. 7.99 (*0-394-98669-5*); pap. 3.50 (*0-394-88669-0*) Random Bks Yng Read.

—True-Life Treasure Hunts. La Padula, Thomas, illus. 48p. (gr. 2-4). 1993. PLB 7.99 (*0-679-93980-6*); pap. 3.50 (*0-679-83980-1*) Random Bks Yng Read.

—Tut's Mummy: Lost & Found. Watling, James, illus. LC 87-20790. (Illus.). (gr. 2-3). 1988. lib. bdg. 7.99 (*0-394-99189-3*); pap. 2.95 (*0-394-89189-9*) Random Bks Yng Read.

—A Wall of Names: The Story of the Vietnam Veterans Memorial A Step 4 Book - Grades 2-4. Wenzel, Paul, illus. LC 90-30275. 48p. (gr. 2-4). 1991. PLB 7.99 (*0-679-90169-8*); pap. 2.95 (*0-679-80169-3*) Random Bks Yng Read.

—Who Shot the President? The Death of John F. Kennedy. LC 88-4418. (Illus.). 48p. (Orig.). (gr. 2-4). 1988. lib. bdg. 7.99 (*0-394-99944-4*); pap. 3.50 (*0-394-89944-X*) Random Bks Yng Read.

Donnelly, Judy & Kramer, Sydelle. Space Junk: Pollution Beyond the Earth. LC 89-13544. (Illus.). 112p. (gr. 4-7). 1990. 12.95 (*0-688-08678-0*); PLB 12.88 (*0-688-08679-9*, Morrow Jr Bks) Morrow Jr Bks.

—Survive! Could You? 96p. (Orig.). (gr. 2-10). 1993. PLB 9.99 (*0-679-94363-3*); pap. 2.99 (*0-679-84363-9*) Random Bks Yng Read.

Donnelly, Judy, ed. see Cole, Joanna.

Donnelly, Judy, ed. see Krensky, Stephen.

Donnelly, Judy, ed. see Penner, Lucille R.

Donnelly, Liza. Dinosaur Beach. Donnelly, Liza, illus. 32p. (Orig.). 1991. 2.50 (*0-590-42176-X*); pap. 2.50 (*0-685-43744-2*) Scholastic Inc.

—Dinosaur Day. 32p. (ps-3). 1987. pap. 2.50 (*0-590-41800-9*) Scholastic Inc.

—Dinosaur Garden. (Illus.). 32p. (ps-3). 1991. pap. 2.50 (*0-590-43172-2*) Scholastic Inc.

—Dinosaurs' Christmas. 32p. (ps-3). 1991. 12.95 (*0-590-44797-1*, Scholastic Hardcover) Scholastic Inc.

—Dinosaurs' Halloween. (ps-3). 1988. 12.95 (*0-590-41025-3*); pap. 2.50 (*0-590-41006-7*) Scholastic Inc.

Donnelly, Loraine B. California State Capitol Time Machine Coloring Book. Wolf, Billy, illus. 23p. (Orig.). (gr. 4-9). 1989. pap. text ed. 3.50 (*0-9626304-0-3*) Capital Enter.

Donnelly, Mary L. Genealogy: A Step-by-Step Approach for Beginners, Ages 10 to 80. LC 83-71116. (Illus.). 64p. (gr. 4 up). 1983. 4.00 (*0-939142-08-2*) MLD Geog.

Donnely, Marcus. Guffy the Bear. (Illus.). 32p. (ps). 1986. 4.50 (*0-938715-00-3*) Toy Works Pr.

—Squeak the Dinosaur. Young, Debby, illus. 32p. (ps-2). 1987. 9.00 (*0-938715-02-X*) Toy Works Pr.

D'Onofrio, Carol N., jt. auth. see Rich, Ruth.

Donohue, Julie. Fancy Fish Coloring Book. 22p. (gr. 3-5). 1990. 3.95 (*0-943864-61-5*) Davenport.

Donojue, Shiobhan. Kristi Yamaguchi: Artist on Ice. (gr. 4-7). 1993. pap. 4.95 (*0-8225-9649-0*) Lerner Pubns.

Donovan, Frank. Let's Go Metric. (Illus.). 192p. 1974. 6.95 (*0-679-40057-5*, Weybright) McKay.

Donovan, Mary L. Papa's Bedtime Story. Root, Kimberly B., illus. LC 91-27792. 40p. (ps-3). 1993. 15.00 (*0-679-81790-5*); PLB 15.99 (*0-679-91790-X*) Knopf Bks Yng Read.

Donovan, Melanie, selected by. The Mother Goose Word Book. Schweninger, Ann, illus. LC 86-81489. 22p. (ps). 1987. write for info. (*0-307-12119-4*, Pub. by Golden Bks) Western Pub.

Donovan, Melanie, ed. see Moss, Marissa.

Donovan, Melissa. Research Challanges. Schneider, Al, illus. 168p. (gr. 4-8). 1985. wkbk. 12.95 (*0-86653-271-4*, GA 660) Good Apple.

—Teaching Creative Writing. 144p. (gr. 3-8). 1990. 12.95 (*0-86653-559-4*, GA1156) Good Apple.

Donovan, Michael, ed. see Kipling, Rudyard.

Donovan, Pete. Carol Johnston: The One-Armed Gymnast. LC 82-4449. (Illus.). (gr. 2-8). 1982. PLB 13.27 (*0-516-04323-4*) Childrens.

Donovan, Richard X. Black Scientists of America. Sorrels, Judith, illus. 134p. (gr. 6 up). 1990. pap. 10.95 (*0-89420-265-0*, 297000) Natl Book.

Donze, Mary T. I Can Pray the Mass! (Illus.). 48p. 1992. pap. text ed. 2.95 (*0-89243-449-X*) Liguori Pubns.

—I Can Pray the Mass. (SPA & ENG., Illus.). 48p. (gr. 2-4). 1993. pap. text ed. 2.95 (*0-89243-513-5*) Liguori Pubns.

—I Can Pray the Rosary! Donze, Mary T., illus. 48p. (Orig.). (gr. 2-4). 1991. pap. 2.95 (*0-89243-335-3*) Liguori Pubns.

—I Can Pray the Rosary: Spanish - English Edition. (SPA & ENG.). 48p. (gr. 7-9). 1992. pap. text ed. 2.95 (*0-89243-457-0*) Liguori Pubns.

—I Can Pray with the Saints! (Illus.). 32p. 1992. pap. text ed. 2.95 (*0-89243-441-4*) Liguori Pubns.

—I Can Pray with the Saints. (SPA & ENG., Illus.). 64p. (gr. 2-4). 1993. pap. text ed. 2.95 (*0-89243-514-3*) Liguori Pubns.

—In My Heart Room, Bk. 2: More Love Prayers for Children. LC 90-70810. (Illus.). 80p. (Orig.). (gr. 1-5). 1990. pap. 3.95 (*0-89243-329-9*) Liguori Pubns.

—Jesus Forgives My Sins. 32p. (Orig.). 1993. pap. text ed. 2.95 (*0-89243-480-5*) Liguori Pubns.

Doohan, Julie, ed. see Kerrins, Joseph & Jacobs, George W.

Dooley, Kevin, ed. see Giffen, Keith & Jones, Gerard.

Dooley, Norah. Everybody Cooks Rice. Thornton, Peter, illus. 32p. (ps-3). 1991. PLB 18.95 (*0-87614-412-1*) Carolrhoda Bks.

—Everybody Cooks Rice. (ps-3). 1992. pap. 6.95 (*0-87614-591-8*) Carolrhoda Bks.

Doolittle, Eileen. The Ark in the Attic: An Alphabet Adventure. Ockenga, Starr, photos by. LC 86-45534. (ps up). 1987. 19.95 (*0-87923-684-1*) Godine.

Doolittle, Hilda. The Hedgehog. Schaffner, Perdita, intro. by. Plank, George, illus. LC 88-3927. 96p. 1988. 12.95 (*0-8112-1069-3*) New Directions.

Doolittle, Robert. Be Alive in Christ. Stamschror, Robert P., ed. St. George, Carolyn, illus. 188p. (Orig.). (gr. 9-12). 1991. pap. 16.95 (*0-88489-246-8*) St Marys.

—Create Community with Christ. Stamschror, Robert P., ed. St. George, Carolyn, illus. 168p. (Orig.). (gr. 9-12). 1991. pap. 16.95 (*0-88489-247-6*) St Marys.

—Homemade Youth Retreats. Stamschror, Robert, ed. (Illus.). 54p. (gr. 7-12). 1992. stitched 7.95 (*0-88489-291-3*) St Marys.

—Searching Young Hearts: Adolescent Sexuality & Spirituality. Stamschror, Robert, ed. (Illus.). 72p. (gr. 7-12). 1993. stitched 8.95 (*0-88489-292-1*) St Marys.

Doran, Madeleine, ed. see Shakespeare, William.

Doray, Andrea. Boris Bear Remembers His Manners. Gress, Jonna C., ed. Claflin, Dale, illus. LC 91-78098. 18p. (Orig.). (gr. k-3). 1992. pap. 11.60 (*0-944943-06-3*) Current Inc.

—Friends. Gress, Jonna, ed. LC 92-72842. (Illus.). 12p. (ps-2). 1992. pap. text ed. 11.60 (*0-944943-13-6*) Current Inc.

Doray, S. J. Gateway to Islam, 4. pap. 10.00 (*1-56744-019-3*) Kazi Pubns.

Doren, Liz Van see Anglund, Joan W.

Doren, Liz Van see Kaye, Marilyn.

Doren, Liz van see Woolf, Virginia.

Doren, Marion. Nell of Blue Harbor. 153p. (gr. 3-7). 1990. 15.95 (*0-15-256889-1*) HarBrace.

—A Pony in the Field. 160p. (gr. 3-7). 1991. pap. 2.75 (*0-590-43663-5*, Apple Paperbacks) Scholastic Inc.

Dorer, Ann. Mother Makes a Mistake. LC 89-42638. 32p. (gr. 1-2). 1991. PLB 18.60 (*0-8368-0109-1*) Gareth Stevens Inc.

Dorio, Evelyn. Pigalee Pink & Other Stories. Davenport, May, illus. & intro. by. LC 79-56540. 95p. (gr. 3-6). 1979. 4.50x (*0-9603118-5-8*); pap. text ed. 1.25 (*0-9603118-4-X*) Davenport.

Dorling Kindersley Staff. Insects & Crawly Creatures. LC 92-12356. (Illus.). 24p. (ps-k). 1992. POB 7.95 (*0-689-71645-1*, Aladdin) Macmillan Child Grp.

—My Very First Word Book. LC 93-1112. 1993. write for info. (*1-56458-375-9*, D Kindersley) HM.

Dorman, Michael. Second Man: The Changing Role of the Vice Presidency. LC 67-19765. (gr. 7 up). 1968. pap. 6.95 (*0-440-07703-6*) Delacorte.

Dorman, N. B. Petey & Miss Magic. LC 92-11265. (Illus.). 99p. (gr. 2-6). 1992. lib. bdg. 14.95 (*0-208-02345-3*, Pub. by Linnet) Shoe String.

Dorn, Bethea ver see Ver Dorn, Bethea.

Dorner, Terrence, jt. auth. see Scarpa, Ron.

Dorr, Eugene L., ed. see Crawford, Lucy.

Dorr, Eugene L., ed. see Ely, Vivian K. & Barnes, Michael.

Dorris, Michael. Morning Girl. LC 92-52989. 80p. (gr. 3 up). 1992. 12.95 (*1-56282-284-5*); PLB 12.89 (*1-56282-285-3*) Hyprn Child.

Dorros, Arthur. Abuela. Kleven, Elisa, illus. LC 90-21459. 40p. (ps-2). 1991. 14.00 (*0-525-44750-4*, DCB) Dutton Child Bks.

—Alligator Shoes. Dorros, Arthur, illus. LC 82-2409. (ps-k). 1982. 3.95 (*0-525-44001-1*, Dutton) NAL-Dutton.

—Alligator Shoes. Dorros, Arthur, illus. LC 82-2409. 24p. (ps-k). 1988. pap. 3.95 (*0-525-44428-9*) Dutton Child Bks.

—Animal Tracks. 40p. 1991. 13.95 (*0-590-43367-9*, Scholastic Hardcover) Scholastic Inc.

—Ant Cities. Dorros, Arthur, illus. LC 85-48244. 32p. (ps-3). 1987. (Crowell Jr Bks); PLB 14.89 (*0-690-04570-0*, Crowell Jr Bks) HarpC Child Bks.

—Ant Cities. Dorros, Arthur, illus. LC 85-48244. 32p. (gr. k-3). 1988. pap. 4.95 (*0-06-445079-1*, Trophy) HarpC Child Bks.

—Elephant Families. LC 92-38972. 1994. 14.00 (*0-06-022948-9*); PLB 13.89 (*0-06-022949-7*) HarpC Child Bks.

—Feel the Wind. Dorros, Arthur, illus. LC 88-18961. 32p. (ps-3). 1989. (Crowell Jr Bks); PLB 13.89 (*0-690-04741-X*, Crowell Jr Bks) HarpC Child Bks.

—Feel the Wind. Dorros, Arthur, illus. LC 88-18961. 32p. (ps-3). 1990. pap. 4.50 (*0-06-445095-3*, Trophy) HarpC Child Bks.

—Follow the Water from Brook to Ocean. Dorros, Arthur, illus. LC 90-1438. 32p. (gr. k-4). 1991. 15.00 (0-06-021598-4); PLB 14.89 (0-06-021599-2) HarpC Child Bks.
—Follow the Water from Brook to Ocean. LC 90-1438. (Illus.). 32p. (gr. k-4). 1993. pap. 4.50 (0-06-445115-1, Trophy) HarpC Child Bks.
—Las Huellas de los Animales: Animal Tracks. Dorros, Sandra M., tr. from ENG. (SPA., Illus.). (ps-2). 1993. pap. 4.95 (0-590-46847-2) Scholastic Inc.
—Me & My Shadow. (ps-3). 1990. pap. 12.95 (0-590-42772-5) Scholastic Inc.
—Por Fin Es Carnaval. Dorros, Sandra M., tr. Club de Madres Virgen del Carmen Staff, illus. LC 90-36222. (SPA.). 32p. (ps-3). 1991. 13.95 (0-525-44690-7, DCB) Dutton Child Bks.
—Radio Man - Don Radio: A Story in English & Spanish. Dorros, Sandra M., tr. LC 92-28369. (Illus.). 40p. (gr. 1-5). 1993. 16.00 (0-06-021547-X); PLB 15. 89 (0-06-021548-8) HarpC Child Bks.
—Rainforest Secrets. 1990. 14.95 (0-590-43369-5, Scholastic Hardcover) Scholastic Inc.
—This is My House. (Illus.). (ps). 1992. 14.95 (0-590-45302-5, 019, Scholastic Hardcover) Scholastic Inc.
—Tonight Is Carnaval. Club De Madres Virgen Del Carmen Staff, illus. LC 90-32391. 32p. (gr. k-3). 1991. 13.95 (0-525-44641-9, DCB) Dutton Child Bks.
Dorros, Sandra M., tr. see Dorros, Arthur.
Dorsey, Marilyn M. Rhymin' Simon's Small Talk: Self Discovery Stress Management. Dorsey, Kim, illus. 83p. (gr. 4 up). 1991. pap. 6.95 (0-916369-18-8) Magnolia Pr.
Doss, Michael P. Plenty Coups. Viola, Herman, intro. by Miyake, Yoshi, illus. 32p. (gr. 3-6). 1990. PLB 17.96 (0-8172-3409-8); pap. 4.95 (0-8114-4089-3) Raintree Steck-V.
Dossenbach, Hans D. Horses. LC 92-10658. 48p. (gr. 4 up). 1992. PLB 17.27 (0-8368-0841-X) Gareth Stevens Inc.
Dostoyevsky, Fyodor. Brothers Karamazov. Rudzik, O. H., intro. by. (gr. 11 up). 1966. pap. 3.95 (0-8049-0128-7, CL-128) Airmont.
—Brothers Karamazov. Garnett, Constance, tr. Slonim, M., intro. by. 1951. pap. text ed. 12.10 (0-07-553575-0, T12) McGraw.
—Crime & Punishment. Canon, R. R., intro. by. (Illus.). (gr. 11 up). 1967. pap. 3.95 (0-8049-0145-7, CL-145) Airmont.
—The Heavenly Christmas Tree. (gr. 5 up). 1992. PLB 13.95 (0-88682-492-3) Creative Ed.
Dotson, Williette D. Visions: The Story of a Black Girl Determined to Make It Despite the Odds. 190p. (gr. 9 up). 1993. text ed. 18.95 (0-9635032-0-0) SAC Pr.
Dott, A. Eric. Hide a book: They Meet. Talbot, Jim, illus. 22p. (ps-1). 1987. PLB 5.95 (0-939871-00-9) Monarch Toy.
Dotts, M. Franklin, ed. see Halverson, Delia T.
Dotts, Maryann. When Jesus Was Born. 32p. (Orig.). 1994. pap. 0.95 (0-687-45019-5) Abingdon.
Doty, Jean S. Dark Horse. Chhuy, Dorothy H., illus. LC 82-21651. 122p. (gr. 4-6). 1983. 12.95 (0-688-01703-7) Morrow Jr Bks.
Doty, Randall. Ents of Fangorn. Fenlon, Peter C., Jr., ed. McBride, Angus, illus. 60p. (Orig.). (gr. 10-12). 1987. pap. 12.00 (0-915795-84-1, 3500) Iron Crown Ent Inc.
Doty, Roy. Fleet of Nursery Rhymes. (Illus.). (ps) 1991. pap. 4.95 punch-outs (0-671-72843-1, S&S BFYR) S&S Trade.
—Wonderful Circus Parade. (ps). 1991. pap. 4.95 (0-671-72842-3, Little Simon) S&S Trade.
—Words around the Year. Murdocca, Sal, illus. LC 92-19312. 1994. pap. 11.00 (0-671-77836-6, S&S BFYR) S&S Trade.
Doubilet, Anne. Under the Sea from A to Z. Doubilet, David, photos by. LC 90-1355. (Illus.). 32p. (gr. k-6). 1991. 15.00 (0-517-57836-0); PLB 15.00 (0-517-57837-9) Crown Bks Yng Read.
Doubleday, Veronica. Salt Lake City. (Illus.). 48p. (gr. 5). 1994. PLB 13.95 RSBE (0-87518-574-6, Dillon) Macmillan Child Bks.
Doucet, Daisy J. Can You Imagine. (gr. k-5). 1991. 7.95 (0-533-08961-1) Vantage.
Doud, Guy. God Loves Me - So What! 192p. (Orig.). 1992. pap. 6.99 (0-570-04572-X) Concordia.
Doud, Guy R. Stuff You Gotta Know: Straight Talk about Real-Life. LC 93-25113. (Illus.). 160p. (Orig.). (gr. 8-12). 1993. pap. 6.99 (0-570-04622-X) Concordia.
Doudt, Kenny. Surfing with the Great White Shark. LC 92-90967. (Orig.). Date not set. pap. 8.95 (0-9633342-7-1) Shark-Bite.
Dougall, Alan, ed. see Jwing-Ming, Yang.
Dougall, Alan, ed. see Ywing-Ming, Yang.
Dougherty, Karla. The Willowisp Book of Jewish Holidays. (Illus.). 32p. (gr. 3 up). 1992. pap. 3.50 (0-87406-639-5) Willowisp Pr.
Dougherty, Mary A., ed. see Reese, Lyn.
Doughty, Bix L. Noah & the Great Auk. (gr. k up). 1978. 5.50 (0-87602-163-1) Anchorage.
Doughty, Carolyn & McGrath, Jim. The Winning Edge: A Guide for College Bound Athletes. 112p. (Orig.). (gr. 9-12). 1988. pap. 9.95 (0-317-91054-X) Sports Plan Consult.
Doughty, Robin W. The Mockingbird. LC 88-736. (Illus.). 80p. (gr. 10-12). 1988. 14.95 (0-292-75099-4) U of Tex Pr.

Douglas, Barbara. Good As New! Brewster, Patience, illus. LC 80-21406. (ps). 1989. pap. 3.95 (0-688-08739-6, Mulberry) Morrow.
Douglas, Eileen. Rachel & the Upside down Heart. (Illus.). 32p. 1990. pap. 6.95 (0-8431-2734-1) Price Stern.
Douglas, Ellen. The Magic Carpet & Other Tales. Anderson, Walter, illus. LC 87-10434. (ps up). 1987. 35.00 (0-87805-327-1) U Pr of Miss.
Douglas, Jeannine G. Don't Drown in the Mainstream. rev. ed. 66p. (gr. k-12). 1986. pap. text ed. 5.50 (0-9607872-1-6) Vail Pub.
Douglas, Jim, ed. Contentment or, the Compleat Nutmeg-State Songster. (Illus.). 128p. (gr. 10-12). 1988. pap. text ed. 12.95x (0-318-23884-5, Dist. by Legacy Bks); LP of songs in book 9.50x (0-318-23885-3) Pedlar Pr.
Douglas, Robert W. John Paul II: The Pilgrim Pope. LC 79-24930. (Illus.). 32p. (gr. k up). 1980. PLB 14.60 (0-516-03563-0) Childrens.
Douglas, Vincent. Math. Robison, Don, illus. 48p. (Orig.). (gr. 4). 1993. wkbk. 1.99 (1-56189-074-X) Amer Educ Pub.
—Math. Robison, Don, illus. 48p. (Orig.). (gr. 5). 1993. wkbk. 1.99 (1-56189-075-8) Amer Educ Pub.
—Math. Robison, Don, illus. 48p. (Orig.). (gr. 6). 1993. wkbk. 1.99 (1-56189-076-6) Amer Educ Pub.
Douglas, Vincent & Way, Voldi. Brighter Child Software: Math. Robison, Don, et al, illus. 32p. (gr. 1). 1993. wkbk., incl. software 9.95 (1-561894-15-X) Amer Educ Pub.
—Brighter Child Software: Math. Robison, Don, et al, illus. 32p. (gr. 3). 1993. wkbk., incl. software 9.95 (1-561894-17-6) Amer Educ Pub.
—Brighter Child Software: Math. Robison, Don, et al, illus. 32p. (gr. 2). 1993. wkbk., incl. software 9.95 (1-561894-16-8) Amer Educ Pub.
—Brighter Child Software: Reading. Robison, Don, et al, illus. 32p. (gr. 1). 1993. wkbk., incl. software 9.95 (1-561894-11-7) Amer Educ Pub.
—Brighter Child Software: Reading. Robison, Don, et al, illus. 32p. (gr. 2). 1993. wkbk., incl. software 9.95 (1-561894-12-5) Amer Educ Pub.
—Brighter Child Software: Reading. Robison, Don, et al, illus. 32p. (gr. 3). 1993. wkbk., incl. software 9.95 (1-561894-13-3) Amer Educ Pub.
Douglas, William O. Muir of the Mountains. San Souci, Daniel, illus. 112p. (gr. 4-7). Date not set. 15.95 (0-87156-505-6) Sierra.
Douglas-Hamilton, Oria. The Elephant Family Book. Douglas-Hamilton, Iain, photos by. LC 89-77319. (Illus.). 56p. (ps up). 1991. pap. 15.95 (0-88708-126-6) Picture Bk Studio.
Douglass, Barbara. Good As New. Brewster, Patience, illus. LC 80-21406. 32p. (ps-1). 1982. 13.00 (0-688-41983-6); PLB 12.88 (0-688-51983-0) Lothrop.
Douglass, Frederick. Escape from Slavery: The Boyhood of Frederick Douglass in His Own Words. McCurdy, Michael, ed & illus. King, Coretta S., intro. by. LC 93-19239. 64p. (gr. 4 up). 1994. 15.00 (0-679-84652-2); pap. 5.99 (0-679-84651-4) Knopf Bks Yng Read.
—Narrative of the Life of Frederick Douglass: An American Slave. Garrison, W. L., pref. by. 128p. (RL 7). 1968. pap. 4.99 (0-451-16188-2, Sig) NAL-Dutton.
—Why Is the Negro Lynched. Obaba, Al I., ed. 49p. (Orig.). 1991. pap. text ed. 7.95 (0-916157-78-4) African Islam Miss Pubns.
Douglass, Herbert E. The Faith of Jesus: Saying Yes to God's Love. 96p. (gr. 10). 1991. pap. 6.95 (0-945460-12-0) Upward Way.
—Why Jesus Waits: How the Sanctuary Message Explains the Mission of the Seventh-Day Adventist Church. rev. ed. LC 76-10925. 96p. (gr. 10 up). 1987. pap. 3.95 (0-945460-00-7) Upward Way.
Douglas-Wiggins, Kate. Rebecca of Sunnybrook Farm. Hinkle, Don, ed. Elwell, Peter, illus. LC 87-15475. 48p. (gr. 3-6). 1988. PLB 12.89 (0-8167-1217-4); pap. text ed. 3.95 (0-8167-1218-2) Troll Assocs.
Douglis, Marjie. Peace Porridge. Peterson, Pete, ed. French, Ed, illus. 122p. (gr. 3-6). 1986. pap. 3.99 (0-934998-22-1) Bethel Pub.
Douillard, Jeanne, ed. Chansons de Chez-Nous. Snow, Suzanne. Blais, Lise M. Albert, Julie D., illus. (FRE.). 61p. (gr. k-6). 1978. pap. text ed. 1.00 (0-911409-01-7) Natl Mat Dev.
Dounuts, Kevin. Doomed to Die: A Lonely Walk. Anderson, Mignon, ed. 70p. (Orig.). 1993. pap. 9.95 (0-9636006-3-X) Old Cntry Bks.
—Sensational Beauty, Vol. 1: Universal Controversy. Daiell, Saralyn, ed. LC 92-82046. (Illus.). 50p. (Orig.). (gr. 7 up). 1993. pap. write for info. (0-9636006-2-1) Old Cntry Bks.
Dow, Lesley. Alligators & Crocodiles. 72p. 1990. 17.95 (0-8160-2273-9) Facts on File.
—Whales. 72p. (gr. 5-12). 1990. 17.95 (0-8160-2271-2) Facts on File.
Doward, Jan S. Finding the Right Path. 96p. (gr. 5 up). 1990. pap. 6.95 (0-8163-0938-8) Pacific Pr Pub Assn.
Dowd, John. Ring of Tall Trees. 128p. (gr. 2-7). 1992. 14. 95 (0-88240-398-2) Alaska Northwest.
Dowd, Ned. That's a Wrap: How Movies Are Made. Horenstein, Henry, photos by. Mamet, David, frwd. by. LC 91-6435. (Illus.). 64p. (gr. 3-7). 1991. pap. 15. 00 jacketed (0-671-70972-0, S&S BFYR) S&S Trade.

Dowd, Tom & Kubasik, Chris. Virtual Realities: A Shadowrun Sourcebook. Ippolito, Donna & Mulvihill, Sharon T., eds. Nelson, Jim & Biske, Joel, illus. 160p. (gr. 7 up). 1991. pap. 15.00 (1-55560-144-8, 7107) FASA Corp.
Dowdell, D. Secrets of the ABCs. LC 65-22301. (Illus.). 64p. (gr. 2 up). 1968. PLB 10.95 (0-87783-035-5) Oddo.
Dowden, Anne O. The Blossom on the Bough: A Book of Trees. LC 93-22726. (gr. 4 up). 1994. 13.95 (0-395-68375-0) Ticknor & Fields.
—The Clover & the Bee: A Book of Pollination. Dowden, Anne O., illus. LC 87-30116. 96p. (gr. 5 up). 1990. 18. 00 (0-690-04677-4, Crowell Jr Bks); PLB 17.89 (0-690-04679-0, Crowell Jr Bks) HarpC Child Bks.
—Plants That Harm & Heal. LC 92-9518. 1994. 15.00 (0-06-020861-9); PLB 14.89 (0-06-020862-7) HarpC Child Bks.
—State Flowers. Reissue. ed. Dowden, Anne O., illus. LC 78-41927. 96p. (gr. 5 up). 1978. PLB 14.89 (0-690-03884-4, Crowell Jr Bks) HarpC Child Bks.
Dowdy, Linda. Barney Goes to the Zoo. (ps). 1993. 4.95 (1-57064-011-4) Barney Pub.
—Barney Goes to the Zoo. Hartley, Linda, ed. McGlophlin, David, illus. 20p. (ps-k). 1993. 4.95 (0-7829-0371-1) Barney Pub.
Dowell, Olivia S. The First Adventure of Peter Nelson Panda. West, Linnea F., illus. 16p. (gr. 2-4). 1986. pap. 5.95 (0-9617624-0-3) Bear Tracks Pub.
Dowell, Ruth I. Alphabet-ter Letter Rhymes. 32p. (Orig.). (ps-2). 1987. pap. 6.00 (0-945842-05-8) Pollyanna Prodns.
—Alphabet-ter Letter Rhymes Activity Book. (ps-2). 1991. pap. 6.00 (0-945842-14-7) Pollyanna Prodns.
—Busy Being Me: Fitness, Fun & Fundamentals. Johnson, Pete, illus. 40p. (Orig.). (ps-3). 1988. pap. 6.00 (0-945842-07-4) Pollyanna Prodns.
—I Say...You Say! Cantwell, Jim, illus. 104p. (ps-2). 1991. pap. 9.95 (0-945842-12-0) Pollyanna Prodns.
—Jiggle on the Doorknob. Johnson, Pete, illus. 70p. (Orig.). (gr. 2-6). 1984. pap. 4.00 (0-945842-01-5) Pollyanna Prodns.
—Let's Talk! Cantwell, Jim, illus. 24p. (ps-6). 1986. 6.00 (0-945842-03-1) Pollyanna Prodns.
—Mother Ruth's Rhymes. Cantwell, Jim, illus. 104p. (ps-6). 1991. pap. 9.95 (0-945842-13-9) Pollyanna Prodns.

—Move Over, Mother Goose Series. Doolittle, Jerry, et al, illus. (Orig.). (ps-6). 1991. pap. write for info. (0-945842-24-4) Pollyanna Prodns. Move Over Mother Goose!, ISBN 0-945842-00-7 $6.00; Jiggle on the Doorknob, ISBN 0-945842-01-5 $4.00; Watch Out, Pollyanna!, ISBN 0-945842-02-3 $4.00; Let's Talk!, ISBN 0-945842-03-1 $6.00; Think About It, ISBN 0-945842-04-X $3.00; Alphabet-ter Letter Rhymes, ISBN 0-945842-05-8 $6.00; Busy Being Me, ISBN 0-945842-07-4 $6.00; Pollyanna Herself, ISBN 0-945842-08-2 $6.00; I Say...You Say!, ISBN 0-945842-12-0 $9.95; Mother Ruth's Rhymes, ISBN 0-945842-13-9 $12.00; Alphabet-ter Letter Rhymes Activity Book, ISBN 0-945842-14-7 $6.00. Fingerplays, action verses & a wide subject range of rhymes to grow by. Indexed for concepts & the curriculum: story rhymes that "grab children & hold on!" *Publisher Provided Annotation.*

—Pollyanna Herself. Doolittle, Jerry, illus. 44p. (ps-6). 1988. pap. 6.00 (0-945842-08-2) Pollyanna Prodns.
—Think about It! Johnson, Pete, illus. 36p. (Orig.). (ps-6). 1987. pap. 3.00 (0-945842-04-X) Pollyanna Prodns.
—Watch Out, Pollyanna! Johnson, Pete, illus. 40p. (gr. 2-6). 1986. pap. 4.00 (0-945842-02-3) Pollyanna Prodns.
Dowling, Pat. The Hungry Anteater. (Illus.). 32p. (ps-2). 1992. 15.95 (0-86264-345-7, Pub. by Andersen Pr UK) Trafalgar.
Dowling, Paul. Are You Sleepy, Puff? Dowling, Paul, illus. LC 92-72934. 32p. (ps-k). 1993. 9.95 (1-56282-393-0) Hyprn Child.
—Happy Birthday, Owl. Dowling, Paul, illus. LC 91-45660. 32p. (ps-k). 1992. text ed. 9.95 (1-56282-253-5) Hyprn Child.
—Meg & Jack Are Moving. Dowling, Paul, illus. 32p. (ps-3). 1990. 10.70 (0-395-53514-X) HM.
—Meg & Jack's New Friends. Dowling, Paul, illus. 32p. (ps-3). 1990. 10.70 (0-395-53513-1) HM.
—Splodger. Dowling, Paul, illus. 32p. (ps). 1991. 13.45 (0-395-57443-9, Sandpiper) HM.

—Where Are You Going, Jimmy? LC 92-27206. (Illus.). 24p. (ps-3). 1993. 12.95 (*1-56566-026-9*) Thomasson-Grant.

—You Can Do It, Rabbit. Dowling, Paul, illus. LC 91-48352. 32p. (ps-k). 1992. Repr. text ed. 9.95 (*1-56282-252-7*) Hyprn Child.

—You Need a Bath, Mustard. Dowling, Paul, illus. LC 92-72933. 32p. (ps-k). 1993. 9.95 (*1-56282-392-2*) Hyprn Child.

Down, Mike. Bear. McAllister, David, illus. LC 91-44726. 32p. (gr. 4-6). 1993. text ed. 11.59 (*0-8167-2765-1*); tchr's. ed. 3.95 (*0-8167-2766-X*) Troll Assocs. Postponed.

Downer, Ann. The Books of the Keepers. LC 92-30131. 256p. (gr. 7 up). 1993. SBE 15.95 (*0-689-31519-8*, Atheneum Child Bk) Macmillan Child Grp.

—Don't Blink Now! Capturing the Hidden World of Sea Creatures. (Illus.). 40p. (gr. 5-8). 1991. 14.95 (*0-531-15225-1*); PLB 14.90 (*0-531-11072-9*) Watts.

—Spring Pool: A Guide to the Ecology of Temporary Ponds. LC 92-19269. (Illus.). 56p. (gr. 5-8). 1992. 15.95 (*0-531-15251-0*); PLB 15.90 (*0-531-11150-4*) Watts.

Downes, P. G. The Story of Chakapas. 32p. (ps-8). 1987. 7.95 (*0-920806-91-0*, Pub. by Penumbra Pr CN) U of Toronto Pr.

Downes, Paul, ed. C-LECT Jr. rev. ed. (gr. 7-10). 1992. write for info. instr's. guide, 6p. (*1-55631-201-6*); wkbk., 12p. 1.25 (*1-55631-202-4*) Chron Guide.

—Career Profile Guide. 250p. (gr. 7-10). 1992. pap. text ed. 48.50 (*1-55631-199-0*) Chron Guide.

Downes, Paul A., ed. Modular C-LECT College Module User's Guide, 1993-94. rev. ed. 32p. (gr. 9-12). 1993. pap. text ed. 10.50 (*1-55631-213-X*, CLCMG) Chron Guide.

—Modular C-LECT Financial Aid Module User's Guide, 1993-94. 16p. (gr. 9-12). 1993. pap. text ed. 11.00 (*1-55631-214-8*, CLFAG) Chron Guide.

—Modular C-LECT Occupational Modules User's Guide, 1993-94. rev. ed. 32p. (gr. 9-12). 1993. pap. text ed. 19.00 (*1-55631-211-3*, CLOG) Chron Guide.

—Modular C-LECT Vocational School Module User's Guide, 1993-94. rev. ed. 32p. (gr. 9-12). 1993. pap. text ed. 12.00 (*1-55631-212-1*, CLVSG) Chron Guide.

Downey, Cynthia. ed. see Downey, Tiffany.

Downey, Douglas W., et al, eds. see Standard Educational Corporation Staff.

Downey, John, ed. see MacHovec, et al.

Downey, Melissa C. & Lingo, Susan L. Early Life of Jesus. Hayes, Theresa, ed. Green, Roy, illus. 32p. (Orig.). (gr. 1-5). 1994. wkbk. 3.99 (*0-7847-0140-7*) Standard Pub.

—Miracles of Jesus. Hayes, Theresa, ed. Green, Roy, illus. 32p. (Orig.). (gr. 1-5). 1994. wkbk. 3.99 (*0-7847-0141-5*) Standard Pub.

—New Life in Jesus. Hayes, Theresa, ed. Green, Roy, illus. 32p. (Orig.). (gr. 1-5). 1994. wkbk. 3.99 (*0-7847-0143-1*) Standard Pub.

—Parables of Jesus. Hayes, Theresa, ed. Green, Roy, illus. 32p. (Orig.). (gr. 1-5). 1994. wkbk. 3.99 (*0-7847-0142-3*) Standard Pub.

Downey, Melissa C., jt. auth. see Lingo, Susan L.

Downey, Michael. Tall Boys: The Rock-n-Roll Musical That Explores Teen-Age Drinking & Driving. Schultz, Paul, contrib. by. (Illus.). 68p. (Orig.). (gr. 7-12). 1990. pap. 4.25 (*0-88680-338-1*); guitar/percussion/vocal score 15.00 (*0-88680-339-X*); royalty on application 75.00 (*0-685-58902-1*) I E Clark.

Downey, Tiffany. Spelling Fitness: One Thousand One of the Most Frequently Misspelled Words. Downey, Cynthia, ed. 102p. (Orig.). (gr. 7-12). 1988. 29.95 (*0-685-22519-4*) Infini Educ.

Downie, Jill. Alphabet Puzzle. Downie, Jill, illus. LC 88-80278. 64p. (ps-1). 1988. 16.00 (*0-688-08044-8*) Lothrop.

—Follow the Wind. (Illus.). 32p. (ps-2). 1992. 15.95 (*0-86264-287-6*, Pub. by Andersen Pr UK) Trafalgar.

Downing, Charles. Armenian Folk-Tales & Fables. Papas, William, illus. 240p. 1993. pap. 10.95 (*0-19-274155-1*) OUP.

—Russian Tales & Legends. Kiddell-Monroe, Joan, illus. 224p. (gr. 4 up). 1990. pap. 10.95 (*0-19-274144-6*) OUP.

Downing, Joan. Baseball Is Our Game. LC 82-4418. (Illus.). (gr. k-3). 1982. pap. 3.95 (*0-516-43402-0*) Childrens.

—El Beisbol Es Nuestro Juego (Baseball's Our Game) Kratky, Lada, tr. from ENG. Freeman, Tony, illus. LC 82-4418. (SPA.). 32p. (gr. k-3). 1984. PLB 15.93 (*0-516-33402-6*); pap. 3.95 (*0-516-53402-5*) Childrens.

Downing, Johnette. A Squirrel Jumped Out of the Tree. Downing, Johnette, illus. (ps). 1990. pap. 2.50 (*0-938991-57-4*) Colonial Pr AL.

Downing, Julie. Mozart Tonight. Downing, Julie, illus. LC 90-34479. 40p. 1991. RSBE 15.95 (*0-02-732881-3*, Bradbury Pr) Macmillan Child Grp.

—Mozart Tonight. Downing, Julie, illus. LC 93-27445. 40p. 1994. pap. 5.95 (*0-685-68187-4*, Aladdin) Macmillan Child Grp.

—Mozart Tonight. LC 93-27445. 1994. write for info. (*0-689-71808-X*, Aladdin) Macmillan Child Grp.

—White Snow - Blue Feather. Downing, Julie, illus. LC 89-815. 32p. (ps-1). 1989. RSBE 13.95 (*0-02-732530-X*, Bradbury Pr) Macmillan Child Grp.

Downing, Sybil & Barker, Jane. Crown of Life: The Story of Mary Roberts Rinehart. (Illus.). 192p. 1992. 19.50 (*1-879373-13-0*); pap. 9.95 (*1-879373-18-1*) R Rinehart.

Downing, Sybil & Barker, Jane V. Happy Harvest. (Illus.). 43p. pap. text ed. 3.95 (*1-878611-02-X*) Silver Rim Pr.

—Mesas to Mountains. (Illus.). 47p. (ps-8). pap. 3.95 (*1-878611-04-6*) Silver Rim Pr.

Downing, Sybil, jt. auth. see Barker, Jane V.

Downing, Sybil ed. see Barker, Jane V.

Downing, Warwick. Kid Curry's Last Ride. 176p. (gr. 5-7). 1989. 12.95 (*0-531-05802-6*); PLB 12.99 (*0-531-08402-7*) Orchard Bks Watts.

—Kid Curry's Last Ride. 176p. (gr. 5-7). 1992. pap. 3.95 (*0-06-440421-8*, Trophy) HarpC Child Bks.

Downswell, P., jt. auth. see Claridge, M.

Doyle, A. C. Bimbo the Bumble Bee & Rose the Rose Bud. 20p. (gr. 4-7). 1982. 3.50 (*0-939476-74-6*, Pub. by Biblio Pr GA) Prosperity & Profits.

—Posie the Positive Train: Illustrated Edition. 60p. (gr. 4-9). 1990. pap. 19.95 (*0-939476-96-7*, Pub. by Biblio Pr GA) Prosperity & Profits.

—Story Rhyme Journal. 60p. (Orig.). (gr. 6-9). 1991. pap. text ed. 15.95 (*0-317-04222-X*, Pub. by Biblio Pr GA) Prosperity & Profits.

Doyle, Arthur Conan. The Adventure of the Solitary Cyclist. 1991. PLB 13.95 s.p. (*0-88682-472-9*) Creative Ed.

—The Adventure of the Speckled Band. 64p. (gr. 6). 1990. PLB 13.95 s.p. (*0-88682-301-3*) Creative Ed.

—The Adventures of Sherlock Holmes. 304p. (gr. 10 up). 1985. pap. 3.50 (*0-425-09838-9*) Berkley Pub.

—Adventures of Sherlock Holmes. 272p. (gr. 9-12). 1989. pap. 2.50 (*0-8125-0424-0*) Tor Bks.

—The Adventures of Sherlock Holmes. Moser, Barry, illus. Glassman, Peter, afterword by. LC 91-39632. (Illus.). 352p. 1992. 20.00 (*0-688-10782-6*) Morrow Jr Bks.

—The Adventures of Sherlock Holmes, Bk. 1. Glass, Andrew, illus. Sadler, Catherine E., adapted by. (Illus.). 140p. (Orig.). (gr. 4-7). 1981. pap. 3.50 (*0-380-78089-5*, Camelot) Avon.

—The Adventures of Sherlock Holmes, Bk. 2. Glass, Andrew, illus. Sadler, Catherine E., adapted by. (Illus.). 156p. (Orig.). (gr. 4-7). 1981. pap. 2.95 (*0-380-78097-6*, Camelot) Avon.

—The Adventures of Sherlock Holmes, Bk. 3. Glass, Andrew, illus. Sadler, Catherine E., frwd by. (Illus.). 112p. (Orig.). (gr. 4-7). 1981. pap. 2.95 (*0-380-78105-0*, Camelot) Avon.

—The Adventures of Sherlock Holmes, Bk. 4. Glass, Andrew, illus. Sadler, Catherine E., adapted by. (Illus.). 112p. (Orig.). (gr. 4-7). 1988. pap. 3.50 (*0-380-78113-1*, Camelot) Avon.

—Complete Sherlock Holmes. LC 65-6074. 1960. Two vols. 19.95 (*0-385-04591-3*); pap. 25.00 (*0-385-00689-6*) Doubleday.

—The Great Adventures of Sherlock Holmes. (Illus.). 256p. (gr. 5 up). 1991. pap. 2.95 (*0-14-035116-7*, Puffin) Puffin Bks.

—Great Stories of Sherlock Holmes. 287p. (gr. 5 up). 1962. pap. 1.75 (*0-440-93190-8*, LFL) Dell.

—Hound of the Baskervilles. (gr. 8 up). 1965. pap. 2.50 (*0-8049-0062-0*, CL-62) Airmont.

—Hound of the Baskervilles. new & abr. ed. Fago, John N., ed. Cruz, E. R., illus. (gr. 4-12). 1977. pap. text ed. 2.95 (*0-88301-264-2*) Pendulum Pr.

—The Hound of the Baskervilles. (gr. 10 up). 1983. pap. 3.50 (*0-425-10405-2*) Berkley Pub.

—The Hound of the Baskervilles. Busch, Frederick, afterword by. (gr. 7 up). 1986. pap. 3.50 (*0-451-52478-0*, Sig Classics) (Sig Classics) NAL-Dutton.

—The Hound of the Baskervilles. (gr. 4-6). 1986. pap. 2.25 (*0-14-035064-0*, Puffin) Puffin Bks.

—The Hound of the Baskervilles. Martinez, Sergio & Paget, Sidney, illus. 272p. (gr. 4 up). 1992. 12.99 (*0-517-07770-1*, Child Classics) Outlet Bk Co.

—The Hound of the Baskervilles. (Illus.). 272p. 1991. 9.99 (*0-517-67028-3*) Outlet Bk Co.

—The Lost World. (Illus.). 272p. (gr. 5 up). 1991. pap. 2.95 (*0-14-035013-6*, Puffin) Puffin Bks.

—The Lost World. 256p. 1993. pap. 4.99 (*0-8125-3468-9*) Tor Bks.

—Memoirs of Sherlock Holmes. (gr. 10 up). 1984. pap. 2.75 (*0-425-10402-8*) Berkley Pub.

—Mysteries of Sherlock Holmes. Conaway, Judith, ed. LC 81-15751. (Illus.). 96p. (gr. 3-7). 1988. pap. 2.95 (*0-394-85086-6*) Random Bks Yng Read.

—Reader's Digest Best Loved Books for Young Readers: Great Cases of Sherlock Holmes. Ogburn, Jackie, ed. Deel, Guy, illus. 184p. (gr. 4-12). 1989. 3.99 (*0-945260-22-9*) Choice Pub NY.

—The Red-Headed League. 64p. (gr. 6). 1990. PLB 13.95 s.p. (*0-88682-300-5*) Creative Ed.

—Sherlock Holmes. Toht, Don, illus. Stewart, Diana, adapted by. LC 79-24106. (Illus.). 48p. (gr. 4 up). 1983. PLB 18.64 (*0-8172-1657-X*) Raintree Steck-V.

—Silver Blaze. 64p. 1990. PLB 13.95 s.p. (*0-88682-302-1*) Creative Ed.

—A Study in Scarlet & the Sign of the Four. 256p. (gr. 10 up). 1985. pap. 3.50 (*0-425-10240-8*) Berkley Pub.

—The White Company. Wyeth, N. C., illus. Glassman, Peter, afterword by. LC 87-62625. (Illus.). 362p. (ps up). 1988. 17.00 (*0-688-07817-6*) Morrow Jr Bks.

Doyle, Brian. Angel Square. 128p. (gr. 4-7). 1991. pap. 4.95 (*0-88899-070-7*, Pub. by Groundwood-Douglas & McIntyre CN) Firefly Bks Ltd.

—Easy Avenue. 128p. (gr. 4-7). 1991. pap. 4.95 (*0-88899-124-X*, Pub. by Groundwood-Douglas & McIntyre CN) Firefly Bks Ltd.

—Up to Low. 116p. (gr. 4-7). 1991. pap. 4.95 (*0-88899-088-X*, Pub. by Groundwood-Douglas & McIntyre CN) Firefly Bks Ltd.

—You Can Pick Me up at Peggy's Cove. 120p. (gr. 4-7). 1991. pap. 4.95 (*0-88899-116-9*, Pub. by Groundwood-Douglas & McIntyre CN) Firefly Bks Ltd.

Doyle, Charlotte. Freddie's Spaghetti. Reilly, Nicholas, illus. LC 90-61003. 24p. (Orig.). (ps-2). 1991. pap. 2.25 (*0-679-81160-5*) Random Bks Yng Read.

Doyle, Debra. Bad Blood: The Moon Is Full Beware the Beast. 1993. pap. 3.99 (*0-425-13953-0*) Berkley Pub.

—Timecrime Inc. (gr. 9-12). 1991. pap. 3.50 (*0-06-106014-3*, PL) HarpC.

Doyle, Debra & Macdonald, James. The City by the Sea. Mitchell, Judy, illus. LC 89-5213. 144p. (gr. 5-9). 1990. PLB 9.89 (*0-8167-1830-X*); pap. text ed. 2.95 (*0-8167-1831-8*) Troll Assocs.

—The Prince's Players. Mitchell, Judy, illus. LC 89-5244. 144p. (gr. 5-9). 1990. PLB 9.89 (*0-8167-1832-6*); pap. text ed. 2.95 (*0-8167-1833-4*) Troll Assocs.

—School of Wizardry. Mitchell, Judy, illus. LC 89-33882. 144p. (gr. 5-9). 1990. PLB 9.89 (*0-8167-1826-1*); pap. text ed. 2.95 (*0-8167-1827-X*) Troll Assocs.

—Tournament & Tower. Mitchell, Judy, illus. LC 89-33881. 144p. (gr. 5-9). 1990. PLB 9.89 (*0-8167-1828-8*); pap. text ed. 2.95 (*0-8167-1829-6*) Troll Assocs.

Doyle, Debra & Macdonald, James M. The Knight's Wyrd. LC 92-53789. 1992. write for info. (*0-15-200764-4*, J Yolen Bks) HarBrace.

Doyle, Elizabeth. Strawberry Shortcake & the Birthday Surprise. Sustendal, Pat, illus. 48p. (ps-3). 1983. cancelled 5.95 (*0-910313-11-3*) Parker Bros.

Doyle, Sharon E. In Other Words. 1976. 4.00 (*0-87602-141-0*) Anchorage.

Doyle, Tara. All about the Seasons Activity Book. (ps-3). 1993. pap. 1.95 (*0-590-46296-2*) Scholastic Inc.

—Little Bunny's Easter Surprise. (ps-3). 1993. pap. 4.95 (*0-590-46262-8*) Scholastic Inc.

—Trick-or-Treat Books, 4 vol. set. Kalish, Lionel & Weissman, Bari, illus. 16p. (ps-1). 1993. pap. 2.75 (*0-590-66583-9*, Cartwheel) Scholastic Inc.

Drabble, Margaret. The Millstone. (Illus.). 144p. (gr. 9-12). 1989. pap. 7.95 (*0-452-26126-0*, Plume) NAL-Dutton.

Dragonwagon, Crescent. Alligator Arrived with Apples: A Potluck Alphabet Feast. Aruego, Jose & Dewey, Ariane, illus. LC 86-37. 40p. (gr. k-3). 1987. RSBE 15.95 (*0-02-733090-7*, Macmillan Child Bk) Macmillan Child Grp.

—Alligator Arrived with Apples: A Potluck Alphabet Feast. Aruego, Jose & Dewey, Ariane, illus. LC 91-38490. 40p. (gr. k-3). 1992. pap. 4.95 (*0-689-71613-3*, Aladdin) Macmillan Child Grp.

—Alligators & Others All Year Long! A Book of Months. Aruego, Jose & Dewey, Ariane, illus. LC 91-2831. 32p. (ps-3). 1993. RSBE 14.95 (*0-02-733091-5*, Macmillan Child Bk) Macmillan Child Grp.

—Always, Always. Zeldich, Arieh, illus. LC 83-22199. 32p. (gr. 1-4). 1984. RSBE 12.95 (*0-02-733080-X*, Macmillan Child Bk) Macmillan Child Grp.

—Annie Flies the Birthday Bike. McCully, Emily A., illus. LC 90-42861. 32p. (gr. k-3). 1993. RSBE 14.95 (*0-02-733155-5*, Macmillan Child Bk) Macmillan Child Grp.

—Half a Moon & One Whole Star. Pinkney, Jerry, illus. LC 85-13818. 32p. (gr. k-3). 1986. RSBE 14.95 (*0-02-733120-2*, Macmillan Child Bk) Macmillan Child Grp.

—Half a Moon & One Whole Star. Pinkney, Jerry, illus. LC 89-18643. 32p. (gr. k-3). 1990. pap. 3.95 (*0-689-71415-7*, Aladdin) Macmillan Child Grp.

—Home Place. Pinkney, Jerry, illus. LC 89-32911. 40p. (gr. k-3). 1990. SBE 14.95 (*0-02-733190-3*, Macmillan Child Bk) Macmillan Child Grp.

—Home Place. Pinkney, Jerry, illus. LC 92-46366. 40p. (gr. k-3). 1993. pap. 4.95 (*0-689-71758-X*, Aladdin) Macmillan Child Grp.

—I Hate My Sister Maggie. Morrill, Leslie, illus. LC 88-8197. 32p. (gr. k-3). 1989. RSBE 12.95 (*0-02-733150-4*, Macmillan Child Bk) Macmillan Child Grp.

—The Itch Book. Mahler, Joseph, illus. LC 89-2695. 32p. (gr. k-3). 1990. RSBE 13.95 (*0-02-733121-0*, Macmillan Child Bk) Macmillan Child Grp.

—Margaret Ziegler Is Horse Crazy. Elwell, Peter, illus. LC 87-23975. 32p. (gr. 1-4). 1988. RSBE 12.95 (*0-02-733230-6*, Macmillan Child Bk) Macmillan Child Grp.

—This Is the Bread I Baked for Ned. Seltzer, Isadore, illus. LC 88-22619. 32p. (gr. k-3). 1989. RSBE 13.95 (*0-02-733220-9*, Macmillan Child Bk) Macmillan Child Grp.

—Winter Holding Spring. Himler, Ronald, illus. LC 88-13747. 32p. (gr. 2-5). 1990. RSBE 11.95 (*0-02-733122-9*, Macmillan Child Bk) Macmillan Child Grp.

Dragonwagon, Crescent & Zindel, Paul. To Take a Dare. 240p. (gr. 7-12). 1984. pap. 2.95 (*0-553-26601-2*) Bantam.

Draimin, Barbara H. Coping When a Parent Has AIDS. LC 93-5070. 1993. 13.95 (*0-8239-1664-2*) Rosen Group.

Drake, Ann. Quigby Captures His Dream. Caroland, Mary, ed. LC 90-71142. 79p. (gr. 4-8). 1991. 6.95 (*1-55523-368-6*) Winston-Derek.

Drake, Jane & Love, Ann. The Kids Cottage Book. Collins, Heather, illus. LC 93-2524. 1994. 13.95 *(0-395-68711-X)*; pap. 10.95 *(0-395-68709-8)* Ticknor & Fields.

Drake, Jane, jt. auth. see Love, Ann.

Drake, John. The Beginning of the River: Herman's Quest. Kortekaas, Kelly, illus. 48p. (gr. k-5). 1992. 16.95 *(0-9633574-0-9)* Little Turtle.

Drake, Samuel A. Book of New England Legends & Folk Lore. LC 76-157254. (Illus.). 502p. (gr. 9 up). 1971. pap. 14.95 *(0-8048-0990-9)* C E Tuttle.

Dramer, Dan. Monsters. (Illus.). 160p. (gr. 6 up). 1985. pap. text ed. 7.75x *(0-89061-451-2)* Jamestown Pubs.

Dramer, Dan, jt. auth. see Kravitz, Alvin.

Dramer, Kim. Kublai Khan. (Illus.). (gr. 5 up). 1990. 17.95 *(1-55546-812-8)* Chelsea Hse.

Drane, John. Christians. (Illus.). 48p. (gr. 3-6). 1993. 14.95 *(0-7459-2516-2)* Lion USA.

Draper & Bailey. Steps in Clothing Skills. (gr. 7-9). 1978. text ed. 20.80 *(0-02-665710-4)*; tchr's guide 2.00 *(0-02-665720-1)* Bennett IL.

Draper, David K. Cody: A Novel That Motivates Towards Success. 88p. (Orig.). (gr. 9-12). 1990. pap. 8.95 *(0-88290-409-4)* Horizon Utah.

Draper, Edythe. Cool: How a Kid Should Live. (gr. 3-5). 1974. kivar 9.99 *(0-8423-0435-5)* Tyndale.

—Wonder. 448p. (gr. 1-4). 1984. 8.99 *(0-8423-8385-9)* Tyndale.

Draper, Kathy. Sunny or Stormy? The Kid's Guide to Mastering the Stress Mess. 83p. (gr. 2-6). 1993. pap. 10.95 *(1-883771-00-5)* Except Educ.

Draper, Tani, illus. Peanut Butter & Jelly Big Book. (ps-2). 1988. pap. text ed. 14.00 *(0-922053-10-3)* N Edge Res.

Drath, Viola & Moeller, Jack R. Noch Dazu! LC 79-64140. (gr. 9-12). 1980. pap. 11.28 *(0-395-27930-5)* HM.

Dravecky, Dave & Stafford, Tim. Dave Dravecky. 112p. (gr. 3-9). 1992. pap. 4.99 *(0-310-58651-8, Youth Bks)* Zondervan.

Drayton, Grace G. Adventures of Dolly Dingle Paper Dolls. 1985. pap. 3.95 *(0-486-24809-7)* Dover.

Dreamer, Sue. A Teddy Bear Christmas. Dreamer, Sue, illus. 10p. (ps-1). 1992. bds. 7.95 *(1-56397-121-6)* Boyds Mills Pr.

Drechsler, Lawrence. The Pirates. LC 85-52401. (Illus., Orig.). (gr. 6 up). pap. write for info. *(0-935143-01-7)* Treadle Pr.

Dreher, Barbara S. Sounds of Science. LC 89-52116. (Illus.). 44p. (gr. k-3). 1990. 5.95 *(1-55523-310-4)* Winston-Derek.

Dreher, Jean. Iron Horses-Iron Men. (Illus.). 130p. (gr. 10 up). 1984. 12.95 *(0-912113-20-0)*; pap. 5.95 *(0-912113-21-9)* Railhead Pubns.

Dreiser, Theodore. Sister Carrie. Andrews, C. A., intro. by. (gr. 11 up). pap. 2.95 *(0-8049-0147-3, CL-147)* Airmont.

—Sister Carrie. Simpson, Claude, ed. LC 59-1819. (gr. 9 up). 1972. pap. 9.16 *(0-395-05134-7, RivEd)* HM.

Dreizler, Loch A. Princess Pickle Head. Mallord, Lauri, illus. LC 88-80123. 42p. (Orig.). (ps-4). 1988. pap. 2.95 *(0-9620053-0-4)* LAD Redondo Beach.

Drenchko, John D. A True Story about Button. 1989. 6.95 *(0-533-07972-1)* Vantage.

Drescher, Henrik. Pat the Beastie: A Pull-&-Poke Book. Drescher, Henrik, illus. 18p. (ps). 1993. 9.95 *(1-56282-407-4)* Hyprn Child.

—Simon's Book. LC 82-24931. (Illus.). 32p. (gr. k-3). 1983. 14.95 *(0-688-02085-2)*; lib. bdg. 14.88 *(0-688-02086-0)* Lothrop.

—Simon's Book. LC 82-24931. (Illus.). 40p. (ps-3). 1991. pap. 3.95 *(0-688-10484-3, Mulberry)* Morrow.

—Whose Furry Nose? Drescher, Henrik, illus. LC 87-45151. 32p. (gr. k-3). 1987. (Lipp Jr Bks) HarpC Child Bks.

—Whose Scaly Tail? Drescher, Henrik, illus. LC 87-45152. 32p. (gr. k-3). 1987. (Lipp Jr Bks) HarpC Child Bks.

—The Yellow Umbrella. LC 87-70157. (Illus.). 40p. (ps-2). 1987. RSBE 12.95 *(0-02-733240-3, Bradbury Pr)* Macmillan Child Grp.

Drescher, Joan. The Birth-Order Blues. Drescher, Joan, illus. 32p. (gr. k-3). 1993. RB 13.99 *(0-670-83621-4)* Viking Child Bks.

—I'm in Charge. Drescher, Joan, illus. (gr. 1-3). 1981. 9.95 *(0-316-19330-5, Pub. by Atlantic Pr)* Little.

—Max & Rufus. Drescher, Joan, illus. (gr. k-3). 1982. write for info. HM.

—My Mother's Getting Married. Drescher, Joan, illus. LC 84-18642. 32p. (ps-3). 1986. PLB 10.89 *(0-8037-0176-4)* Dial Bks Young.

—My Mother's Getting Married. Drescher, Joan, illus. LC 84-18642. 32p. (ps-3). 1989. pap. 4.95 *(0-8037-0642-1)* Dial Bks Young.

—Your Doctor, My Doctor. 32p. (gr. 1-3). 1987. 10.95 *(0-8027-6668-4)*; PLB 11.85 *(0-8027-6669-2)* Walker & Co.

—Your Family, My Family. Drescher, Joan, illus. 32p. (gr. 2-5). 1980. PLB 13.85 *(0-8027-6383-9)* Walker & Co.

Dresser, Ginny, ed. see Linse, Barbara & Knight, Marilyn.

Dresser, Norine. I Felt Like I Was from Another Planet: Writing from Personal Experience. (gr. 4-7). 1993. pap. 14.95 *(0-201-86058-9)* Addison-Wesley.

Dressman, John. On the Cliffs of Acoma. Ortega, Pedro R., tr. from SPA. LC 83-20177. (Illus.). 32p. (gr. 2-4). 1984. pap. 5.95 *(0-86534-021-8)* Sunstone Pr.

Drew, Bonnie & Drew, Noel. Fast Cash for Kids: One Hundred-One Moneymaking Projects for Young Entrepreneurs. rev. ed. (Illus.). 184p. (gr. 3-12). 1991. pap. 9.95 *(0-934829-99-3)* Career Pr Inc.

Drew, Bonnie J. & Drew, O. Noel. Fast Cash for Kids. (Illus.). 168p. (Orig.). (gr. 4-9). 1987. pap. 9.95 *(0-939445-01-8)* Homeland Pubns.

Drew, David. Ah, Treasure! Tulloch, Coral, illus. LC 92-21455. 1993. 3.75 *(0-383-03611-9)* SRA Schl Grp.

—The Big Brown Box. Ruth, Trevor, illus. LC 92-30673. 1993. 2.50 *(0-383-03619-4)* SRA Schl Grp.

—Does a Duck Eat Honey? Fleming, Leanne, illus. LC 92-31917. 1993. 4.25 *(0-383-03563-5)* SRA Schl Grp.

—How Many Legs? Stewart, Chantal, illus. LC 92-34268. 1993. 4.25 *(0-383-03631-3)* SRA Schl Grp.

—Jock Jerome. Culio, Ned, illus. LC 92-31133. 1993. 2.50 *(0-383-03636-4)* SRA Schl Grp.

—Make a Salad Face. Robertson, Ian, illus. LC 92-34335. 1993. 2.50 *(0-383-03640-2)* SRA Schl Grp.

—My House. Wood, Bill, illus. LC 92-30424. 1993. 2.50 *(0-383-03586-4)* SRA Schl Grp.

—Nibbly Mouse. Newman, Penny, illus. LC 92-21397. 1993. 4.25 *(0-383-03587-2)* SRA Schl Grp.

—The Python Caught the Eagle. Reynolds, Pat, illus. LC 92-31134. 1993. 2.50 *(0-383-03648-8)* SRA Schl Grp.

—The Seesaw. Forss, Ian, illus. LC 92-21394. (gr. 2 up). 1993. 2.50 *(0-685-69191-8)* SRA Schl Grp.

—Senses. Strahan, Heather, illus. LC 92-34162. 1993. 3.75 *(0-383-03651-8)* SRA Schl Grp.

—Something Silver, Something Blue. Roennfeldt, Robert, illus. LC 92-34256. 1993. 4.25 *(0-383-03654-2)* SRA Schl Grp.

—The Storm. Costeloe, Brenda, illus. LC 92-30671. 1993. write for info. *(0-383-03656-9)* SRA Schl Grp.

—Toenails. Fleming, Leanne, illus. LC 92-31135. 1993. 2.50 *(0-383-03661-5)* SRA Schl Grp.

—Two More. Jacobs, Elizabeth, illus. LC 92-31957. 1993. 3.75 *(0-383-03600-3)* SRA Schl Grp.

—When I Turned Six. Gouldthorpe, Peter, illus. LC 93-26929. 1994. 4.25 *(0-383-03784-0)* SRA Schl Grp.

Drew, Helen. My First Baking Book. LC 91-10239. (Illus.). 48p. (gr. 2-6). 1991. 12.00 *(0-679-81545-7)*; lib. bdg. 13.99 *(0-679-91545-1)* Knopf Bks Yng Read.

—My First Music Book. (Illus.). 48p. (gr. k-3). 1993. 12.95 *(1-56458-215-9)* Dorling Kindersley.

Drew, James. Rackstraw: The Magical Thoughts & Adventures of A Brilliant Young Art Mouse. George, Mary G., ed. Drew, James, illus. LC 93-71718. 168p. (gr. 2-9). 1994. 18.95 *(0-9625023-9-1)* Art Pr Intl.

In this world of Art Mice, magic & art shape the lives of Rackstraw & his family, leading to mysterious & exciting adventures that include a ghost, hornets, menacing hawks, & dancing spiders. Woven into the fabric of this multilayered, humorous fantasy are some of the world's greatest artists, real & imagined, from Bach to Picasso to the Art Mouse in Prague known simply as Bela - all supported by the values & traditions that are essential for the survival of our culture. RACKSTRAW celebrates children's dreams, their aspirations, & their imaginations & it reflects the best qualities in all of us. In the words of concert pianist Lorin Hollander, "RACKSTRAW is deeply sensitive & very moving; it captures the interest & heart of those who enter in on its journey." Noted educators Frances Clark & Louise Goss declare that "RACKSTRAW surely deserves to become a children's classic." Pulitzer Prize winner Donald Martino states, "RACKSTRAW should be required reading for all of us - young & old." Adults will enjoy reading this story to the young child; junior readers (ages 9-13) will read RACKSTRAW themselves, & will find encouragement for their own artistic adventures, for this is an Art Mouse's spiritual odyssey. Order from: Artistry Press International, P.O. Box 741111, Orange City, FL 32774-1111; 904-775-6407.

Publisher Provided Annotation.

Drew, Margaret, ed. Holocaust & Human Behavior: Annotated Bibliography. 124p. 1989. lib. bdg. 15.85 *(0-8027-9411-4)* Walker & Co.

Drew, Naomi. Learning the Skills of Peacemaking. Lovelady, Janet, ed. Gandhi, Yogesh K., frwd. by. LC 87-81609. 224p. (Orig.). (gr. k-8). 1987. pap. 21.95 *(0-915190-46-X, JP9046-X)* Jalmar Pr.

Drew, Noel, jt. auth. see Drew, Bonnie.

Drew, O. Noel, jt. auth. see Drew, Bonnie J.

Drew-Bernstein, Charlotte, jt. auth. see Garrett, Dan.

Drews, Mark. New Ears: The Audio Career & Education Handbook. 2nd, rev. ed. Pohlmann, Ken, intro. by. LC 93-92640. 320p. 1993. pap. 24.95 *(0-9623502-1-4)* New Ear Prodns.

Dreyer, Ellen. Wild Animals. Hall, Douglas & Dennison, Graham, illus. LC 90-11163. 96p. (gr. 2-5). 1991. PLB 14.89 *(0-8167-2242-0)*; pap. text ed. 6.95 *(0-8167-2243-9)* Troll Assocs.

Dreyer, Ellen, retold by. Raggedy Ann & Andy Second Giant Treasury. Gruelle, Johnny, illus. 80p. 1989. 5.99 *(0-517-66719-3)* Outlet Bk Co.

Driemen, J. E. Robert Oppenheimer: Atomic Dawn: A Biography of Robert Oppenheimer. LC 88-18968. (Illus.). 160p. (gr. 5 up). 1988. RSBE 13.95 *(0-87518-397-2, Dillon)* Macmillan Child Grp.

—Winston Churchill: An Unbreakable Spirit. LC 89-26029. (Illus.). 128p. (gr. 5 up). 1990. RSBE 13.95 *(0-87518-434-0, Dillon)* Macmillan Child Grp.

Driemen, John E. Clarence Darrow. (Illus.). 112p. (gr. 5 up). 1992. lib. bdg. 17.95 *(0-7910-1624-2)* Chelsea Hse.

Drighi, Laura. Children of the World: Italy. LC 87-42640. (Illus.). 64p. (gr. 5-6). 1988. PLB 19.93 *(1-55532-404-5)* Gareth Stevens Inc.

Drimmer, Frederick. Born Different: The Amazing Stories of Some Very Special People. LC 87-33354. (Illus.). 192p. (gr. 5-9). 1988. SBE 14.95 *(0-689-31360-8, Atheneum Child Bk)* Macmillan Child Grp.

Drimmer, Fredrick. Born Different: Amazing Stories of Very Special People. 1991. pap. 3.50 *(0-553-15897-X)* Bantam.

Drinkwater, Carol. The Haunted School. (gr. 5-9). 1988. pap. 3.95 *(0-317-69631-9, Puffin)* Puffin Bks.

Driscoll, Debbie. Baby Comes Home. Samuels, Barbara, illus. LC 91-2414. 40p. (ps-k). 1993. pap. 14.00 JRT *(0-671-75540-4, S&S BFYR)* S&S Trade.

—Three Two One Day. Cravath, Lynne, illus. LC 92-23420. 1994. pap. 14.00 *(0-671-79330-6, S&S BFYR)* S&S Trade.

Driscoll, Edwin. Alf & the Red-Eyed Yellow Monster. (gr. k-4). 1985. 3.50 *(0-89536-942-7, 7559)* CSS OH.

Driscoll, Jack. Skylight. LC 91-10593. 192p. (gr. 7 up). 1991. 14.95 *(0-531-05961-8)*; RLB 14.99 *(0-531-08561-9)* Orchard Bks Watts.

Driscoll, William, et al. Problem Solving Connections. (gr. 3-6). 1992. write for info. Charlesbridge Pub.

Driskill, J. Lawrence. Mission Adventures in Many Lands. Jackson, Russ, illus. LC 92-15689. (gr. 3-6). 1992. PLB 17.95 *(0-932727-57-3)*; pap. 11.95 *(0-932727-56-5)* Hope Pub Hse.

—Mission Stories from Around the World. 192p. (gr. 4-8). 1994. PLB 19.95 *(0-932727-72-7)*; pap. 11.95 *(0-932727-71-9)* Hope Pub Hse.

Dr. Oetker. Let's Bake. (Illus.). 48p. (gr. 4-10). 1993. pap. 5.95 *(0-8069-8535-6)* Sterling.

—Let's Cook. (Illus.). 48p. (gr. 4-10). 1993. pap. 5.95 *(0-8069-8533-X)* Sterling.

Drogues, Valerie. Battleship Missouri. LC 93-10423. (Illus.). 48p. (gr. 5-6). 1994. RSBE 13.95 *(0-89686-825-7, Crestwood Hse)* Macmillan Child Grp.

Dromgoole, Dick, ed. see Stopple, Libby.

Droscher, Elke. The Victorian Sticker Postcard Book. (Illus.). 64p. (Orig.). pap. 7.95 *(0-89471-384-1)* Running Pr.

Dr. Seuss. And to Think That I Saw It on Mulberry Street. LC 88-38411. (Illus.). 32p. (ps-3). 1989. Repr. of 1937 ed. 11.95 *(0-394-84494-7)*; lib. bdg. 11.99 *(0-394-94494-1)* Random Bks Yng Read.

—Bartholomew & the Oobleck. Dr. Seuss, illus. (gr. k-3). 1949. 11.00 *(0-394-80075-3)*; lib. bdg. 11.99 *(0-394-90075-8)* Random Bks Yng Read.

—The Butter Battle Book. Dr. Seuss, illus. LC 83-21286. 48p. (gr. 5 up). 1984. 12.00 *(0-394-86580-4)*; lib. bdg. 12.99 *(0-394-96580-9)* Random Bks Yng Read.

—Cat in the Hat. Dr. Seuss, illus. LC 56-5470. 72p. (gr. 1-2). 1957. 6.95 *(0-394-80001-X)*; lib. bdg. 7.99 *(0-394-90001-4)* Random Bks Yng Read.

—The Cat in the Hat. Dr. Seuss, illus. 64p. (ps-1). 1987. book & cassette 6.95 *(0-394-89218-6)* Random Bks Yng Read.

—The Cat in the Hat - el Gato Ensombrerado. Dr. Seuss, illus. (ENG & SPA.). 72p. (ps-3). 1993. incl. cass. 6.95 *(0-679-84329-9)* Random Bks Yng Read.

—Cat in the Hat Comes Back. Dr. Seuss, illus. LC 58-9017. 72p. (gr. k-3). 1958. 6.95 *(0-394-80002-8)*; lib. bdg. 7.99 *(0-394-90002-2)* Random Bks Yng Read.

—The Cat in the Hat Comes Back. (ps-1). 1986. pap. 6.95 incl. cassette *(0-394-88327-6)* Random Bks Yng Read.

—The Cat in the Hat in English & Spanish. Dr. Seuss, illus. Rivera, Carlos, tr. LC 67-19013. (Illus.). 72p. (gr. 1-2). 1967. 6.95 *(0-394-81626-9)* Beginner.

—Cat in the Hat Songbook. reissued ed. LC 67-21921. (Illus.). 72p. (k up). 1993. 12.00 *(0-394-81695-1)* Random Bks Yng Read.

—The Cat's Quizzer. LC 92-17409. (Illus.). (gr. k-3). 1993. 6.95 (0-394-83296-5) Random Bks Yng Read.
Dr. Seuss, pseud. Cat's Quizzer. (ps-3). 1993. 6.95 (0-679-84024-9) Knopf Bks Yng Read.
Dr. Seuss. Did I Ever Tell You How Lucky You Are? Dr. Seuss, illus. (ps-4). 1973. 11.00 (0-394-82719-8); PLB 11.99 (0-394-92719-2) Random Bks Yng Read.
—Did I Ever Tell You How Lucky You Are? Dr. Seuss, illus. 64p. (Orig.). (ps up) 1993. incl. cass. 13.00 (0-679-84993-9) Random Bks Yng Read.
—Dr. Seuss Beginner Book Classics, 5 bks. Dr. Seuss, illus. (ps-3). 1992. Boxed set incls. The Cat in the Hat, Dr. Seuss's ABC, Fox in Socks, Green Eggs & Ham & One Fish Two Fish Red Fish Blue Fish, 72 pgs. ea. 50.00 (0-679-83846-5) Random Bks Yng Read.
—Dr. Seuss's ABC. Dr. Seuss, illus. LC 63-9810. 72p. (gr. k-3). 1963. 6.95 (0-394-80030-3); lib. bdg. 7.99 (0-394-90030-8) Random Bks Yng Read.
—Dr. Seuss's ABC. (Illus.). 64p. (ps-1). 1988. pap. 6.95 bk. & cassette pkg. (0-394-89784-6) Random Bks Yng Read.
—Dr. Seuss's Sleep Book. Dr. Seuss, illus. (gr. 3-7). 1962. 13.00 (0-394-80091-5); lib. bdg. 13.99 (0-394-90091-X) Random Bks Yng Read.
—The Five Hundred Hats of Bartholomew Cubbins. LC 88-38412. (Illus.). 48p. (ps-3). 1989. Repr. of 1938 ed. 11.00 (0-394-84484-X); lib. bdg. 10.99 (0-394-94484-4) Random Bks Yng Read.
—Foot Book. Dr. Seuss, illus. LC 68-28462. (ps-1). 1968. 6.95 (0-394-80937-8); lib. bdg. 7.99 (0-394-90937-2) Random Bks Yng Read.
—Fox in Socks. Dr. Seuss, illus. LC 65-10484. 72p. (gr. k-3). 1965. 6.95 (0-394-80038-9); lib. bdg. 7.99 (0-394-90038-3) Random Bks Yng Read.
—Fox in Socks. (ps-1). 1986. pap. 6.95 incl. cassette (0-394-88322-5) Random Bks Yng Read.
—Great Day for Up! Blake, Quentin, illus. LC 74-5517. 36p. (ps-1). 1974. 6.95 (0-394-82913-1); lib. bdg. 7.99 (0-394-92913-6) Random Bks Yng Read.
—Green Eggs & Ham. Dr. Seuss, illus. LC 60-13493. 72p. (gr. 1-2). 1960. 6.95 (0-394-80016-8); lib. bdg. 7.99 (0-394-90016-2) Random Bks Yng Read.
—Green Eggs & Ham. Dr. Seuss, illus. 64p. (ps-1). 1987. pap. 6.95 incl. cassette (0-394-89220-8) Random Bks Yng Read.
—Happy Birthday to You. Dr. Seuss, illus. (gr. 1-5). 1959. 13.00 (0-394-80076-1); PLB 13.99 (0-394-90076-6) Random Bks Yng Read.
—Hop on Pop. Dr. Seuss, illus. LC 63-9810. 72p. (gr. 1-2). 1963. 6.95 (0-394-80029-X); lib. bdg. 7.99 (0-394-90029-4) Random Bks Yng Read.
—Hop on Pop. Dr. Seuss, illus. 64p. (ps-1). 1987. pap. 6.95 incl. cassette (0-394-89222-4) Random Bks Yng Read.
—Horton Hatches the Egg. Dr. Seuss, illus. (gr. k-3). 1940. 11.95 (0-394-80077-X); lib. bdg. 13.99 (0-394-90077-4) Random Bks Yng Read.
—Horton Hatches the Egg. reissued ed. Crystal, Billy, read by. Dr. Seuss, illus. LC 40-27753. 64p. (ps up) 1991. pap. 10.95 incls. cassette (0-394-82956-5) Random Bks Yng Read.
—Horton Hears a Who. Dr. Seuss, illus. (gr. k-3). 1954. 12.00 (0-394-80078-8); PLB 12.99 (0-394-90078-2) Random Bks Yng Read.
—Horton Hears a Who! Hoffman, Dustin, narrated by. LC 54-7012. (Illus.). 72p. (ps-1). 1990. pap. 10.95 incl. cassette (0-679-80003-4) Random Bks Yng Read.
—How the Grinch Stole Christmas. Dr. Seuss, illus. (gr. k-3). 1957. 9.95 (0-394-80079-6); PLB 9.99 (0-394-90079-0) Random Bks Yng Read.
—How the Grinch Stole Christmas! Dr. Seuss, illus. Matthau, Walter, contrib. by. (Illus.). 64p. (ps-1). 1988. bk. & cassette pkg. 10.00 (0-394-81339-1) Random Bks Yng Read.
—Huevos Verdes Con Jamon. Marcuse, Aida, tr. (Illus.). 62p. (gr. 2-3). 1992. 8.95 (1-880507-01-3) Lectorum Pubns.
—Hunches in Bunches. Dr. Seuss, illus. 48p. (gr. 1-5). 1982. lib. bdg. 10.99 (0-394-95502-1); pap. 10.95 (0-394-85502-7) Random Bks Yng Read.
—I Am Not Going to Get up Today! Stevenson, James, illus. LC 87-11466. 48p. (gr. k-3). 1987. 6.95 (0-394-89217-8); lib. bdg. 7.99 (0-394-99217-2) Random Bks Yng Read.
—I Am Not Going to Get up Today! Stevenson, James, illus. 32p. (ps-1). 1990. pap. 6.95 (0-679-80307-6); cass. incl. Random Bks Yng Read.
—I Can Draw It Myself: By Me, Myself with a Little Help from My Friend Dr. Seuss. Dr. Seuss, illus. LC 75-117541. 48p. (ps-4). 1987. pap. 9.00 (0-394-80097-4) Beginner.
—I Can Lick Thirty Tigers Today & Other Stories. Dr. Seuss, illus. (gr. k-3). 1969. 13.00 (0-394-80094-X) Random Bks Yng Read.
—I Can Read with My Eyes Shut! Dr. Seuss, illus. LC 78-7193. (gr. 1-3). 1978. 6.95 (0-394-83912-9); lib. bdg. 7.99 (0-394-93912-3) Random Bks Yng Read.
—I Can Read with My Eyes Shut! Dr. Seuss, illus. 40p. (ps-1). 1987. Incl. cassette. 6.95 (0-394-88767-0) Random Bks Yng Read.
—I Had Trouble in Getting to Solla Sollew. Dr. Seuss, illus. LC 65-23994. 64p. (gr. 1-4). 1992. 13.00 (0-394-80092-3) Random Bks Yng Read.
—If I Ran the Circus. Dr. Seuss, illus. (gr. k-3). 1956. 13. 00 (0-394-80080-X); lib. bdg. 10.99 (0-394-90080-4) Random Bks Yng Read.

—If I Ran the Zoo. Dr. Seuss, illus. (gr. k-3). 1950. 13.00 (0-394-80081-8); lib. bdg. 13.99 (0-394-90081-2) Random Bks Yng Read.
—King's Stilts. Dr. Seuss, illus. (gr. k-3). 1939. 9.95 (0-394-80082-6); lib. bdg. 9.99 (0-394-90082-0) Random Bks Yng Read.
—Lorax. Dr. Seuss, illus. (gr. 2-3). 1971. 12.00 (0-394-82337-0); lib. bdg. 12.99 (0-394-92337-5) Random Bks Yng Read.
—The Lorax. Danson, Ted, narrated by. Dr. Seuss, illus. 64p. (ps up). 1992. incl. cassette 13.00 (0-679-82273-9) Random Bks Yng Read.
—El Lorax. Marcuse, Aida E., tr. (Illus.). 64p. (gr. 3-6). 1993. 13.95 (1-880507-04-8) Lectorum Pubns.
—McElligot's Pool. Dr. Seuss, illus. (gr. k-3). 1947. 11.00 (0-394-80083-4); lib. bdg. 11.99 (0-394-90083-9) Random Bks Yng Read.
—Marvin K. Mooney, Will You Please Go Now. Dr. Seuss, illus. (ps-2). 1972. 6.95 (0-394-82490-3); lib. bdg. 7.99 (0-394-92490-8) Random Bks Yng Read.
—Mister Brown Can Moo, Can You. Dr. Seuss, illus. (ps-1). 1970. 6.95 (0-394-80622-0); lib. bdg. 7.99 (0-394-90622-5) Random Bks Yng Read.
—Mr. Brown Can Moo! Can You? - The Foot Book, 2 bks. reissue ed. Dr. Seuss, illus. (ps-1). 1991. Set, 32p. ea. incl. 2 20-min. cassette 8.95 (0-679-82036-1) Random Bks Yng Read.
—My Book about Me. (gr. k-8). 1969. 8.95 (0-394-80093-1) Random Bks Yng Read.
—Oh, Cuan Lejos Llegaras. Marcuse, Aida, tr. (Illus.). (gr. 4-6). 1993. 13.95 (1-880507-05-6) Lectorum Pubns.
—Oh, Say Can You Say? Dr. Seuss, illus. LC 78-20716. (gr. 1-4). 1979. 6.95 (0-394-84255-3, BYR); lib. bdg. 7.99 (0-394-94255-8) Beginner.
—Oh Say Can You Say? Dr. Seuss, illus. 40p. (ps-1). 1987. Incl. cassette. 6.95 (0-394-88769-7) Random Bks Yng Read.
—Oh, the Places You'll Go. 11p. 1991. Braille. 0.88 (1-56590-292-X) W A T Braille.
—Oh, the Places You'll Go! LC 89-36892. (gr. k-3). 1990. 13.00 (0-679-80527-3); PLB 13.99 (0-679-90527-8) Random Bks Yng Read.
—Oh, the Places You'll Go! Dr. Seuss, illus. LC 89-36892. 48p. (gr. k up). 1993. 20.00 (0-679-84736-7) Random Bks Yng Read.
—Oh, the Places You'll Go! 11p. 1990. pap. 0.88 (0-685-63785-9, BR8247) W A T Braille.
—Oh! The Thinks You Can Think! Dr. Seuss, illus. LC 75-1602. 48p. (ps-1). 1975. 6.95 (0-394-83129-2); lib. bdg. 7.99 (0-394-93129-7) Beginner.
—On Beyond Zebra. Dr. Seuss, illus. (ps-3). 1955. 12.00 (0-394-80084-2); lib. bdg. 12.99 (0-394-90084-7) Random Bks Yng Read.
—One Fish Two Fish Red Fish Blue Fish. Dr. Seuss, illus. LC 60-7180. 72p. (gr. 1-2). 1960. 6.95 (0-394-80013-3); PLB 7.99 (0-394-90013-8) Random Bks Yng Read.
—One Fish Two Fish Red Fish Blue Fish. Dr. Seuss, illus. 64p. (ps-1). 1987. pap. 6.95 incl. cassette (0-394-89224-0) Random Bks Yng Read.
—Scrambled Eggs Super! Dr. Seuss, illus. (gr. k-3). 1953. lib. bdg. 13.99 (0-394-90085-5) Random Bks Yng Read.
—Scrambled Eggs Super! Dr. Seuss, illus. LC 53-5013. 64p. (gr. 1-4). 1992. 13.00 (0-394-80085-0) Random Bks Yng Read.
—Shape of Me & Other Stuff. Dr. Seuss, illus. (ps-1). 1973. 6.95 (0-394-82687-6); lib. bdg. 7.99 (0-394-92687-0) Random Bks Yng Read.
—Six by Seuss: A Treasury of Dr. Seuss Classics. Dr. Seuss, illus. LC 91-6311. 352p. 1991. 25.00 (0-679-82148-1) Random Bks Yng Read.
—Sneetches & Other Stories. Dr. Seuss, illus. (gr. k-4). 1961. 9.95 (0-394-80089-3); lib. bdg. 13.99 (0-394-90089-8) Random Bks Yng Read.
—There's a Wocket in My Pocket! Dr. Seuss, illus. LC 74-5516. 36p. (ps-1). 1974. 6.95 (0-394-82920-4); lib. bdg. 7.99 (0-394-92920-9) Random Bks Yng Read.
—There's a Wocket in My Pocket & Marvin K. Mooney Will You Please Go Now! Dr. Seuss, illus. (ps-1). 1989. bk. & cassette 7.95 (0-394-82954-9) Random Bks Yng Read.
—Thidwick, the Big-Hearted Moose. Dr. Seuss, illus. (gr. k-3). 1948. 11.00 (0-394-80086-9); lib. bdg. 11.99 (0-394-90086-3) Random Bks Yng Read.
—Thidwick the Big-Hearted Moose. Dr. Seuss, illus. 48p. (ps-6). 1993. incl. cass. 12.00 (0-679-84338-8) Random Bks Yng Read.
—Yertle the Turtle & Other Stories. Dr. Seuss, illus. (gr. k-3). 1958. 13.00 (0-394-80087-7); PLB 13.99 (0-394-90087-1) Random Bks Yng Read.
—Yertle the Turtle & Other Stories. reissue ed. Lithgow, John, narrated by. Dr. Seuss, illus. 80p. (ps). 1992. pap. 14.00 incl. cass. (0-679-83229-7) Random Bks Yng Read.
Druce, Arden. Witch, Witch. LC 91-29763. 1991. 11.95 (0-85953-780-3); pap. 5.95 (0-685-52311-X) Childs Play.
Drucker, M. Grandma's Latkes. Chwast, E., ed. 1992. write for info. (0-15-200468-8, Gulliver Bks) HarBrace.
—A Jewish Holiday ABC. Pocock, R., illus. 1992. 13.95 (0-15-200482-3, HB Juv Bks) HarBrace.
Drucker, Malka. The Family Treasury of Jewish Holidays. Patz, Nancy, illus. LC 93-7549. Date not set. 21.95 (0-316-19343-7) Little.

—Frida Kahlo: Torment & Triumph in Her Life & Art. 1991. 16.50 (0-553-07165-3); pap. 7.00 (0-553-35408-6) Bantam.
—Hanukkah: Eight Nights, Eight Lights. Hoban, Brom, illus. LC 80-15852. 96p. (gr. 4 up). 1980. reinforced bdg. 14.95 (0-8234-0377-7) Holiday.
Drucker, Malka & Halperin, Michael. Jacob's Rescue: A Holocaust Story. LC 92-30523. (gr. 4-7). 1993. 15.00 (0-553-08976-5, Skylark) Bantam.
Drucker, Olga L. Kindertransport. LC 92-14121. (gr. 5-8). 1992. 14.95 (0-8050-1711-9, Bks Young Read) H Holt & Co.
Druist, Miriam. Wildlife on the Farm. (gr. 2 up). 1977. 6.55 (0-686-23334-4) Rod & Staff.
Drum & Spear Collective Staff. Children of Africa: A Coloring Book. Drum & Spear Collective Staff, illus. LC 92-63013. 24p. (ps-3). 1993. pap. 5.95 (0-88378-076-3) Third World.
Drum, William, jt. auth. see Clark, James.
Drummond, Allan. The Willow Pattern Story. Drummond, Allan, illus. LC 91-46239. 32p. (gr. k-3). 1992. 14.95 (1-55858-171-5); PLB 14.88 (1-55858-172-3) North-South Bks NYC.
Drummond, H. & Hughes. Our World Today Series. large type ed. Incl. The Eastern Hemisphere, 5 vols. 996p. Set. 252.77 (0-317-02421-3, 4-05230-00) Am Printing Hse.
(4-05230-00) Am Printing Hse.
1981 (4-05230-00) Am Printing Hse.
Drumtra, Stacy. Face-off. 128p. (Orig.). 1992. pap. 3.50 (0-380-76863-1, Flare) Avon.
Drury, John, tr. see Biffi, Inos.
Drury, John, tr. see Biffi, Inos.
Drury, Keith. Your Life As a Disciple. 48p. (Orig.). (gr. 9-12). 1990. pap. 7.99 (1-55945-204-8) Group Pub.
Drutman, Ava & Zuckerman, Susan. Protecting Our Planet (Intermediate) 144p. (gr. 4-8). 1991. 12.95 (0-86653-589-6, GA1302) Good Apple.
Drutman, Ava D. Land (Primary) (Illus.). 48p. (gr. 1-3). 1992. wkbk. 7.95 (0-86653-599-3, 1406) Good Apple.
—Protecting Our Planet - Primary Grades. 144p. (gr. 1-3). 1991. 12.95 (0-86653-619-1, GA1338) Good Apple.
—Water (Primary) (Illus.). 48p. (gr. 1-3). 1992. wkbk. 7.95 (0-86653-604-3, 1407) Good Apple.
Drutman, Ave D. & Deutsch, Evelyn. Protecting Our Planet (Early Childhood Version) (Illus.). 128p. (ps-1). 1992. 11.95 (0-86653-665-5, GA1400) Good Apple.
Dryden, John see Wilson, John H.
Dryden, John, tr. see Virgil.
Dryden, Pamela. Riding Home. 144p. (gr. 3-7). 1988. pap. 2.95 (0-553-15591-1) Bantam.
Dryer, Bonnie J. Steggie Saurus: Kindergartener in Korea. LC 92-60813. 44p. (gr. k-3). 1993. pap. 5.95 (1-55523-547-6) Winston-Derek.
Duane, Diane E. Deep Wizardry. LC 84-15566. 288p. (gr. 7 up). 1985. 15.95 (0-385-29373-9) Delacorte.
—Deep Wizardry. 288p. (gr. 4-7). 1992. pap. 3.50 (0-440-40658-7, YB) Dell.
—High Wizardry. 1990. 14.95 (0-385-29983-4) Delacorte.
—High Wizardry. 272p. (gr. 5-9). 1992. pap. 3.50 (0-440-40680-3, YB) Dell.
—So You Want to be a Wizard. LC 83-5216. 288p. (gr. 7 up). 1983. 14.95 (0-385-29305-4) Delacorte.
—So You Want to Be a Wizard. (gr. 5-8). 1986. pap. 2.75 (0-440-98252-9, LFL) Dell.
—So You Want to Be a Wizard. (gr. 5 up). 1992. 3.50 (0-440-40638-2, YB) Dell.
Dubanevich, Arlene. Calico Cows. (Illus.). 32p. (ps-3). 1993. PLB 13.50 (0-670-84436-5) Viking Child Bks.
—Pig William. Dubanevich, Arlene, illus. LC 85-5776. 32p. (ps-2). 1985. RSBE 13.95 (0-02-733200-4, Bradbury Pr) Macmillan Child Grp.
—Pig William. LC 85-5776. (Illus.). 32p. (gr. k-3). 1990. pap. 3.95 (0-689-71372-X, Aladdin) Macmillan Child Grp.
—Pigs at Christmas. Dubanevich, Arlene, illus. LC 86-6891. 32p. (ps-2). 1986. RSBE 13.95 (0-02-733160-1, Bradbury Pr) Macmillan Child Grp.
—Pigs at Christmas. Dubanevich, Arlene, illus. LC 89-32229. 32p. (ps-3). 1989. pap. 3.95 (0-689-71344-4, Aladdin) Macmillan Child Grp.
—Pigs in Hiding. Dubanevich, Arlene, illus. LC 83-1409. 32p. (ps-1). 1983. RSBE 13.95 (0-02-732140-1, Four Winds) Macmillan Child Grp.
—Pigs in Hiding. Dubanevich, Arlene, illus. 32p. (gr. k-3). 1989. pap. 3.95 (0-590-44503-0) Scholastic Inc.
—Tom's Tail. (ps-3). 1990. 13.95 (0-670-83021-6) Viking Child Bks.
—Tom's Tail. LC 92-8615. (gr. 4 up). 1992. 4.50 (0-14-054177-2) Puffin Bks.
Dubay, Brenda, adapted by. Just So Stories: Adapted from the Book by Rudyard Kipling. Dubay, Bren, contrib. by. (Illus.). 36p. (Orig.). (ps-7). 1990. pap. 3.50 (0-88680-333-0); royalty on application 40.00 (0-685-58897-1) I E Clark.
Dubelaar, Thea. Looking for Vincent. Bruijn, Ruud, illus. 56p. (gr. 2-8). 1992. 9.95 (1-56288-300-3) Checkerboard.
Dubin, Arthur D. More Classic Trains. LC 73-92249. (Illus.). 512p. (gr. 11). 1991. Repr. of 1974 ed. 85.95 (0-916374-85-8) Interurban.
Dubin, Debbie I., jt. auth. see Block, Linda F.
Dubin, Stephen. Biospherians, the New Pioneers. 40p. (gr. 2 up). 1994. pap. 6.95 (1-882428-05-6) Biosphere Pr.
DuBois, Jill. Colombia. LC 90-22468. (Illus.). 128p. (gr. 5-9). 1991. PLB 21.95 (1-85435-384-5) Marshall Cavendish.
—Israel. LC 92-10208. 1992. 21.95 (1-85435-531-7) Marshall Cavendish.

—South Korea. LC 93-4381. 1993. 21.95 (*1-85435-582-1*) Marshall Cavendish.

—Women in Society: Mexico. Siow, Eric, illus. LC 92-34402. 1993. 22.95 (*1-85435-557-0*); Set. write for info. Marshall Cavendish.

Du Bois, William P. Bear Party. (ps-1). 1987. pap. 3.99 (*0-14-050793-0*, Puffin) Puffin Bks.

—The Giant. (Orig.). (gr. k-6). 1987. pap. 4.95 (*0-440-42994-3*, Pub. by Yearling Classics) Dell.

—The Twenty-One Balloons. Du Bois, William P., illus. 184p. (gr. 5-9). 1986. pap. 3.99 (*0-14-032097-0*, Puffin) Puffin Bks.

Du Bois, William Pene see Newbery Library Award Staff.

Du Bois, William Pene see Pene Du Bois, William.

Du Bois, William Pene see Pene Du Bois, William.

DuBosque, D. C. How Do You Draw Dinosaurs? 64p. (Orig.). (gr. 3-9). 1989. pap. 6.95 (*0-939217-10-4*) Peel Prod.

—Learn to Draw Now! DuBosque, D. C., illus. 64p. (Orig.). (gr. 3-9). 1991. pap. 7.95 (*0-939217-16-3*) Peel Prod.

DuBosque, Doug. Draw! Cars. (Illus.). 80p. (Orig.). (gr. 3-9). 1993. pap. 8.95 (*0-939217-19-8*) Peel Prod.

—Draw! Dinosaurs. (Illus.). 80p. (ps-4). 1993. pap. 8.95 (*0-939217-20-1*) Peel Prod.

—Draw! Monsters, Aliens & Robots. (Illus.). 80p. (gr. 3-9). 1994. pap. 8.95 (*0-939217-22-8*) Peel Prod.

—Learn to Draw 3-D. (Illus.). 80p. (gr. 3-9). 1992. pap. 8.95 (*0-939217-17-1*) Peel Prod.

Dubov, Christine. Aleksandra, Where Are Your Toes? Schnieder, Josef, photos by. (Illus.). 14p. (ps). 1986. 3.95 (*0-312-01717-0*) St Martin.

—Aleksandra, Where Is Your Nose. Schneider, Josef, photos by. (Illus.). 12p. (ps). 1986. 3.95 (*0-312-01719-7*) St Martin.

Dubov, Christine S. Ding Dong! & Other Sounds. Hathon, Elizabeth, photos by. LC 90-47301. (Illus.). 12p. (ps). 1991. bds. 3.95 (*0-688-10162-3*, Tambourine Bks) Morrow.

—Knock! & Other Sounds. Hathon, Elizabeth, photos by. LC 90-47302. (Illus.). 12p. (ps). 1991. bds. 3.95 (*0-688-10161-5*, Tambourine Bks) Morrow.

—Oink! & Other Sounds. Hathon, Elizabeth, photos by. LC 90-47303. (Illus.). 12p. (ps). 1991. bds. 3.95 (*0-688-10102-X*, Tambourine Bks) Morrow.

Dubowski, Cathy, adapted by see Barrie, J. M.

Dubowski, Cathy E. An American Tail: The Illustrated Story. Lazor-Bahr, Beverly, illus. LC 91-70104. 48p. (ps-3). 1991. 9.95 (*0-448-40211-4*, G&D) Putnam Pub Group.

—An American Tail, The Novelization. LC 91-70103. (Illus.). 64p. (gr. 2-6). 1991. pap. 2.95 (*0-448-40210-6*, G&D) Putnam Pub Group.

—Carla the Carpenter. Speirs, John, illus. 28p. (ps-2). 1992. 3.95 (*0-7214-5339-2*) Ladybird Bks.

—Cave Boy. Dubowski, Mark, illus. LC 87-23427. 32p. (ps-1). 1988. lib. bdg. 7.99 (*0-394-99571-6*); pap. 2.95 (*0-394-89571-1*) Random Bks Yng Read.

—The Christmas Santa Almost Missed. Pollard, Nan, illus. 24p. (Orig.). (gr. k-1). 1990. pap. 0.99 (*1-878624-48-2*) McClanahan Bk.

—Clara Barton: Healing the Wounds. (Illus.). 160p. (gr. 5 up). 1990. lib. bdg. 18.98 (*0-382-09940-0*); pap. 8.95 (*0-382-24049-9*) Silver Burdett Pr.

—Dumpy the Dump Truck. Samuels, Mark, illus. 24p. (Orig.). (gr. k-1). 1990. pap. 0.99 (*1-878624-32-6*) McClanahan Bk.

—Ernie the Electrician. Speirs, John, illus. 28p. (ps-2). 1992. 3.95 (*0-7214-5340-6*) Ladybird Bks.

—Fire Engine to the Rescue. Beckes, Shirley, illus. 24p. (Orig.). (gr. k-1). 1990. pap. 0.99 (*1-878624-37-7*) McClanahan Bk.

—The Littlest Angel. Pollard, Nan, illus. 24p. (ps-2). 1991. pap. 0.99 (*1-56293-116-4*) McClanahan Bk.

—Milo the Mechanic. Speirs, John, illus. 28p. (ps-2). 1992. 3.95 (*0-7214-5341-4*) Ladybird Bks.

—Paulina the Plummer. Speirs, John, illus. 28p. (ps-2). 1992. 3.95 (*0-7214-5342-2*) Ladybird Bks.

—Robert E. Lee & the Rise of the South. (Illus.). 160p. (gr. 5 up). 1990. lib. bdg. 18.98 (*0-382-09942-7*); pap. 8.95 (*0-382-24051-0*) Silver Burdett Pr.

—We're Back! The Novelization. (Illus.). 64p. (gr. 2-6). 1993. pap. 3.95 (*0-448-40445-1*, G&D) Putnam Pub Group.

Dubowski, Cathy E., ed. see Burnett, Frances H.

Dubowski, Cathy W. Pretty Good Magic. Dubowski, Mark, illus. LC 87-4784. 48p. (gr. 1-3). 1987. lib. bdg. 7.99 (*0-394-99068-4*); 3.50 (*0-394-89068-X*) Random Bks Yng Read.

Dubrovin, Vivian. Storytelling for the Fun of It: A Handbook for Children. LC 93-93694. 160p. (gr. 4-7). 1994. pap. 14.95 (*0-9638339-0-1*) Storycraft Pub.

Dubuc, Suzanne. How to Make Your Own Gifts. (Illus.). 32p. (gr. 3-7). 1993. 7.95 (*2-7625-7159-6*, Pub. by Les Edits Herit CN) Adams Inc MA.

—Make up Funny Masks. (Illus.). 32p. (gr. 3-7). 1993. 7.95 (*2-7625-6740-8*, Pub. by Les Edits Herit CN) Adams Inc MA.

—Paper Costumes. (Illus.). 32p. (gr. 3-7). 1993. 7.95 (*2-7625-6739-4*, Pub. by Les Edits Herit CN) Adams Inc MA.

Duch, Mabel. Easy-to-Make Puppets: Step-by-Step Instructions. Mohrmann, Gary, illus. LC 93-15320. 64p. (gr. 3-8). 1993. pap. 8.95 (*0-8238-0300-7*) Plays.

Duchess of York. The Adventures of Budgie. Richardson, John, illus. LC 92-11218. 1992. ltd. ed. 60.00 (*0-685-59711-3*, S&S BFYR); incls. cassettes 20.00 (*0-685-59712-1*) S&S Trade.

—Budgie at Bendick's Point. Richardson, John, illus. (ps-1). 1989. pap. 11.95 jacketed (*0-671-67684-9*, S&S BFYR) S&S Trade.

—Budgie the Little Helicopter. Richardson, John, illus. (ps-1). 1989. pap. 11.95 jacketed (*0-671-67683-0*, S&S BFYR) S&S Trade.

Duckert, Mary J., ed. see Fogle, Jeanne S.

Ducket, Mary Jean, ed. see Fogle, Jeanne S.

Duckett, Alfred, jt. auth. see Robinson, Jackie.

Duckett, Barbara, jt. auth. see Webb, Jane C.

Duckett, Gary. The Return of Talatu'u. LC 86-40285. 150p. (gr. 4-6). 1987. 7.95 (*1-55523-022-9*) Winston-Derek.

Duck of Beauford, ed. see Longman, C. J. & Walrond, H.

Duckworth. Environmental Lawyer. Date not set. PLB write for info. (*0-8050-2280-5*) H Holt & Co.

Duckworth, John. The School Zone. 96p. (gr. 7-9). 1986. pap. 2.99 student bk. (*0-89693-558-2*, Victor Books); tchr's. ed. 12.99 (*0-89693-198-6*) SP Pubns.

Duckworth, John, et al. Muhammad & the Arab Empire. Yapp, Malcolm & Killingray, Margaret, eds. (Illus.). (gr. 6-11). 1980. pap. text ed. 3.45 (*0-89908-011-1*) Greenhaven.

Duckworth, Marion. BJ Bernard Grows up. Chase, Andra, illus. 28p. (ps-k). 1993. 4.99 (*0-7847-0065-6*, 24-03845) Standard Pub.

Duckworth, Rita L. see Lucy, Reda, pseud.

Duco, Joyce. Workbook for Self Image Is the Key. LC 89-92547. 69p. (gr. 7-12). 1990. Set. pap. 5.00 (*0-9612896-2-7*) J Duco.

Duden, Jane. Animal Handlers & Trainers. LC 89-31125. (Illus.). 48p. (gr. 4 up). 1989. RSBE 11.95 (*0-89686-427-8*, Crestwood Hse) Macmillan Child Grp.

—Baseball. LC 91-7365. (Illus.). 48p. (gr. 5-6). 1991. RSBE 11.95 (*0-89686-625-4*, Crestwood Hse) Macmillan Child Grp.

—Christmas. LC 89-28520. (Illus.). 48p. (gr. 4-5). 1990. RSBE 12.95 (*0-89686-497-9*, Crestwood Hse) Macmillan Child Grp.

—Ferret. LC 89-28268. (Illus.). 48p. (gr. 5 up). 1990. RSBE 12.95 (*0-89686-517-7*, Crestwood Hse) Macmillan Child Grp.

—Great Moments in Sports. LC 91-23791. (Illus.). 48p. (gr. 5-6). 1992. RSBE 11.95 (*0-89686-726-9*, Crestwood Hse) Macmillan Child Grp.

—Gymnastics. LC 91-24682. (Illus.). 48p. (gr. 5-6). 1992. RSBE 11.95 (*0-89686-727-7*, Crestwood Hse) Macmillan Child Grp.

—Harp Seal. LC 89-28274. (Illus.). 48p. (gr. 5 up). 1990. RSBE 12.95 (*0-89686-516-9*, Crestwood Hse) Macmillan Child Grp.

—Nineteen Fifties. LC 89-34400. (Illus.). 48p. (gr. 4-5). 1989. RSBE 11.95 (*0-89686-476-6*, Crestwood Hse) Macmillan Child Grp.

—Nineteen Forties. LC 89-34401. (Illus.). 48p. (gr. 4-5). 1989. RSBE 11.95 (*0-89686-475-8*, Crestwood Hse) Macmillan Child Grp.

—Nineteen Ninety. LC 92-72890. (Illus.). 48p. (gr. 5). 1992. RSBE 12.95 (*0-89686-769-2*, Crestwood Hse) Macmillan Child Grp.

—Nineteen Ninety-One. LC 92-72889. (Illus.). 48p. (gr. 5). 1992. RSBE 12.95 (*0-89686-770-6*, Crestwood Hse) Macmillan Child Grp.

—Nineteen Ninety-Two. (Illus.). 48p. (gr. 5 up). 1993. lib. bdg. 12.95 RSBE (*0-89686-852-4*, Crestwood Hse) Macmillan Child Grp.

—Nineteen Seventies. LC 89-34630. (Illus.). 48p. (gr. 4-5). 1989. RSBE 11.95 (*0-89686-478-2*, Crestwood Hse) Macmillan Child Grp.

—Nineteen Sixties. LC 89-34399. (Illus.). 48p. (gr. 4-5). 1989. RSBE 11.95 (*0-89686-477-4*, Crestwood Hse) Macmillan Child Grp.

—The Olympics. (Illus.). 48p. (gr. 5-6). 1991. RSBE 11.95 (*0-89686-624-6*, Crestwood Hse) Macmillan Child Grp.

—The Ozone Layer. LC 90-36297. (Illus.). 48p. (gr. 5-6). 1990. RSBE 12.95 (*0-89686-546-0*, Crestwood Hse) Macmillan Child Grp.

—Shirley Muldowney. LC 87-27570. (Illus.). 48p. (gr. 5-6). 1988. RSBE 11.95 (*0-89686-369-7*, Crestwood Hse) Macmillan Child Grp.

—The Super Bowl. LC 91-24692. (Illus.). 48p. (gr. 5-6). 1992. RSBE 11.95 (*0-89686-725-0*, Crestwood Hse) Macmillan Child Grp.

—Thanksgiving. LC 89-25397. (Illus.). 48p. (gr. 5 up). 1990. RSBE 12.95 (*0-89686-503-7*, Crestwood Hse) Macmillan Child Grp.

—The World Series. LC 91-23790. (Illus.). 48p. (gr. 5-6). 1992. RSBE 11.95 (*0-89686-724-2*, Crestwood Hse) Macmillan Child Grp.

Duden, Jane & Osberg, Susan. Basketball. LC 90-28515. (Illus.). 48p. (gr. 5-6). 1991. RSBE 11.95 (*0-89686-627-0*, Crestwood Hse) Macmillan Child Grp.

—Football. LC 90-26338. (Illus.). 48p. (gr. 5-6). 1991. RSBE 11.95 (*0-89686-626-2*, Crestwood Hse) Macmillan Child Grp.

Duden, Jane & Stewart, Gail B. Nineteen Eighties. LC 90-46827. (Illus.). 48p. (gr. 5-6). 1991. RSBE 11.95 (*0-89686-599-1*, Crestwood Hse) Macmillan Child Grp.

Duder, Tessa. Alex in Rome. LC 91-41275. 166p. (gr. 6 up). 1992. 13.95 (*0-395-62879-2*) HM.

—In Lane Three, Alex Archer. 1991. pap. 3.50 (*0-553-29020-7*) Bantam.

—Journey to Olympia, the Story of the Ancient Olympics. (Illus.). 1992. pap. 3.95 (*0-590-45796-9*) Scholastic Inc.

Dudko, Mary A. Baby Bop Discovers Shapes. (ps). 1993. 4.95 (*1-57064-010-6*) Barney Pub.

—Baby Bop's ABC's. (ps). 1993. pap. 2.25 (*1-57064-008-4*) Barney Pub.

—Tent Too Full. (ps-3). 1993. pap. 2.25 (*1-57064-009-2*) Barney Pub.

Dudko, Mary A. & Larsen, Margie. Baby Bop's Counting Book. Hartley, Linda, ed. 22p. (ps). 1993. 3.95 (*0-7829-0374-6*) Barney Pub.

—Barney's Color Surprise. Hartley, Linda, ed. 20p. (ps). 1993. 3.95 (*0-7829-0373-8*) Barney Pub.

—Barney's Hats. Hartley, Linda, ed. 24p. (ps-k). 1993. pap. 2.25 (*0-7829-0376-2*) Barney Pub.

—Where Are My Shoes? Hartley, Linda, ed. Daste, Larry, illus. 24p. (ps-k). 1993. pap. 2.25 (*0-7829-0375-4*) Barney Pub.

Dudley, Art. Word Processing Basics: An Introduction for Young People. Petronella, Michael, illus. LC 84-22315. 48p. (gr. 4-9). 1985. 9.95 (*0-13-963513-0*) P-H.

Dudley, Dick. What Do You Give a Sick Tyrannosaurus Rex? 12p. (ps-3). 1992. 5.95 (*1-56288-179-5*) Checkerboard.

—Why Does a Brachiosaurus Have Such a Long Neck? (ps-3). 1992. 5.95 (*1-56288-178-7*) Checkerboard.

Dudley, Dick & Kong, Emilie. When Are Pteranodons Sad? (Illus.). 12p. (ps-2). 1992. 5.95 (*1-56288-180-9*) Checkerboard.

—Why Does an Apatosaurus Get Its Way? (Illus.). 12p. 1992. 5.95 (*1-56288-181-7*) Checkerboard.

Dudley, Elizabeth. Start Exploring Forests: A Fact-Filled Coloring Book. (Illus., Orig.). 1989. pap. 8.95 (*0-89471-782-0*) Running Pr.

Dudley, Lynn. Farm Animals. 12p. (gr. 4-7). 1990. pap. 5.95 (*0-8167-2087-8*) Troll Assocs.

—Forest Animals. 12p. (gr. 4-7). 1990. pap. 5.95 (*0-8167-2084-3*) Troll Assocs.

Dudley, Mark. An Eye to the Sky. LC 91-33880. (Illus.). 48p. (gr. 5-6). 1992. RSBE 12.95 (*0-89686-691-2*, Crestwood Hse) Macmillan Child Grp.

Dudley, Mark E. Brown v. Board of Education (1954) School Desegregation. LC 93-32712. 1994. write for info. (*0-02-736271-X*, New Discovery Bks) Macmillan Child Grp.

Dudley, William. The Environment: Distinguishing Between Fact & Opinion. (Illus.). 32p. (gr. 3-6). 1990. PLB 10.95 (*0-89908-603-9*) Greenhaven.

—The U. S. Constitution: Locating the Author's Main Idea. LC 90-42328. (Illus.). 32p. (gr. 3-6). 1990. PLB 10.95 (*0-89908-601-2*) Greenhaven.

Dudley, William & Cozic, Charles. Racism in America: Opposing Viewpoints. LC 91-14293. (Illus.). 240p. (gr. 10 up). 1991. lib. bdg. 17.95 (*0-89908-182-7*); pap. 9.95 (*0-89908-157-6*) Greenhaven.

Dudley, William, ed. The American Revolution: Opposing Viewpoints. LC 92-21795. 288p. 1992. lib. bdg. 17.95 (*1-56510-011-5*); pap. 9.95 (*1-56510-010-7*) Greenhaven.

—The Cold War: Opposing Viewpoints. LC 92-21797. 288p. 1992. lib. bdg. 17.95 (*1-56510-009-3*); pap. 9.95 (*1-56510-008-5*) Greenhaven.

—Crime & Criminals: Opposing Viewpoints. LC 89-2155. (Illus.). 240p. (gr. 10 up). 1989. lib. bdg. 17.95 (*0-89908-441-9*); pap. text ed. 9.95 (*0-89908-416-8*) Greenhaven.

—Death & Dying: Opposing Viewpoints. LC 92-6667. (Illus.). 240p. (gr. 10 up). 1992. PLB 17.95 (*0-89908-192-4*); pap. text ed. 9.95 (*0-89908-167-3*) Greenhaven.

—Genetic Engineering: Opposing Viewpoints. LC 89-25765. (Illus.). 264p. (gr. 10 up). 1990. lib. bdg. 17.95 (*0-89908-477-X*); pap. text ed. 9.95 (*0-89908-452-4*) Greenhaven.

—Homosexuality: Opposing Viewpoints. (Illus.). 264p. (gr. 10 up). 1993. PLB 17.95 (*0-89908-481-8*); pap. text ed. 9.95 (*0-89908-456-7*) Greenhaven.

—Immigration: Opposing Viewpoints. LC 90-13854. (Illus.). 240p. (gr. 10 up). 1990. PLB 17.95 (*0-89908-485-0*); pap. text ed. 9.95 (*0-89908-460-5*) Greenhaven.

—Japan: Opposing Viewpoints. LC 89-36620. (Illus.). 240p. (gr. 10 up). 1989. PLB 17.95 (*0-89908-444-3*); pap. 9.95 (*0-89908-419-2*) Greenhaven.

—The Middle East: Opposing Viewpoints. LC 91-43280. (Illus.). 264p. (gr. 10 up). 1992. PLB 17.95 (*0-89908-185-1*); pap. text ed. 9.95 (*0-89908-160-6*) Greenhaven.

—Police Brutality. LC 91-22818. 200p. (gr. 10 up). 1991. PLB 16.95 (*0-89908-580-6*); pap. text ed. 9.95 (*0-89908-586-5*) Greenhaven.

—Slavery: Opposing Viewpoints. LC 92-21796. 288p. 1992. lib. bdg. 17.95 (*1-56510-013-1*); pap. 9.95 (*1-56510-012-3*) Greenhaven.

—Trade: Opposing Viewpoints. LC 90-24087. (Illus.). 264p. (gr. 10 up). 1991. PLB 17.95 (*0-89908-176-2*); pap. 9.95 (*0-89908-151-7*) Greenhaven.

—The Vietnam War: Opposing Viewpoints. rev. ed. LC 90-39794. (Illus.). 240p. (gr. 10 up). 1990. PLB 17.95 (*0-89908-478-8*); pap. text ed. 9.95 (*0-89908-453-2*) Greenhaven.

Dudley, William & Swisher, Karin, eds. China. LC 88-24296. (Illus.). 250p. (gr. 10 up). 1988. lib. bdg. 17.95 *(0-89908-439-7)*; pap. text ed. 9.95 *(0-89908-414-1)* Greenhaven.

Dudley, William & Szumski, Bonnie, eds. America's Future: Opposing Viewpoints. LC 89-25885. (Illus.). 312p. (gr. 10 up). 1990. lib. bdg. 17.95 *(0-89908-448-6)*; pap. text ed. 9.95 *(0-89908-423-0)* Greenhaven.

Dudley, William & Tipp, Stacey, eds. Iraq. LC 91-30036. 200p. (gr. 10 up). 1991. PLB 16.95 *(0-89908-575-X)*; pap. text ed. 9.95 *(0-89908-581-4)* Greenhaven.

Dudley, William, jt. ed. see Polesetsky, Matthew.

Dudley-Smith, Timothy. The Lion Book of Stories of Jesus. (Illus.). 96p. (gr. 1-5). 1989. 11.95 *(0-85648-906-9)* Lion USA.

Dudman, J. Division of Berlin. (Illus.). 80p. (gr. 7 up). 1988. PLB 18.60 *(0-86592-037-0)*; 13.95s.p. *(0-685-58321-X)* Rourke Corp.

Dudman, John. Earthquake. LC 92-41510. 32p. (gr. 4-6). 1993. 14.95 *(1-56847-000-2)* Thomson Lrning.

—Volcano. LC 92-41511. 32p. (gr. 4-6). 1993. 14.95 *(1-56847-001-0)* Thomson Lrning.

Duel, Debra. William's Story. Ryan, Donna, illus. 72p. (Orig.). (gr. k-8). 1992. pap. 9.95 *(1-880812-02-9)* S Ink WA.

Duel, John. Wide Awake in Dreamland. Burton, Bruce, illus. LC 91-66837. 239p. (gr. 4-8). 1992. 15.95 *(0-9630923-0-8)* Stargaze Pub.

Dueland, Joy. Barn Kitten, House Kitten. (Illus.). (gr. 2-8). 1978. pap. 3.50 *(0-931942-00-4)* Phunn Pubs.

—Dear Tabby. (Illus.). (gr. 4-8). 1978. pap. 2.50 *(0-931942-02-0)* Phunn Pubs.

—Filled up Full. (Illus.). 30p. (Orig.). (gr. k-3). 1974. pap. 4.95 *(0-87510-100-3)* Christian Sci.

—God's Great Adventure. (Illus.). 111p. (ps up). 1980. 8.95 *(0-685-08285-7)* Phunn Pubs.

—Kitten in the Manger. (Illus.). 32p. (gr. 2-8). 1981. pap. 6.95 *(0-685-08286-5)* Phunn Pubs.

—My Best Friend. (Illus.). 27p. (Orig.). (gr. k-3). 1972. pap. 4.95 *(0-87510-081-3)* Christian Sci.

Duell, jt. auth. see Leonard, Marcia.

Duerrstein, Richard, illus. In - Out: A Disney Book of Opposites. LC 91-58979. 12p. (ps). 1992. bds. 5.95 *(1-56282-266-7)* Disney Pr.

—Mickey Is Happy: A Disney Book of Feelings. LC 92-52974. 12p. (ps). 1992. bds. 5.95 *(1-56282-267-5)* Disney Pr.

Duerstein, Richard, illus. One Mickey Mouse: A Disney Book of Numbers. LC 92-52973. 12p. (ps). 1992. 5.95 *(1-56282-251-9)* Disney Pr.

Duey, Kathleen. Double-Yuck Magic. 144p. (Orig.). 1991. pap. 2.99 *(0-380-76116-5,* Camelot) Avon.

—Mr. Stumpguss Is a Third Grader. Fiammenghi, Gioia, illus. 80p. (Orig.). 1992. pap. 3.50 *(0-380-76939-5,* Camelot Young) Avon.

—The Third Grade's Skinny Pig. 80p. (Orig.). (gr. 1). 1993. pap. 3.50 *(0-380-76730-9,* Camelot Young) Avon.

Duffey, Betsy. Boy in the Doghouse. LC 90-47751. (Illus.). 96p. 1991. pap. 12.00 jacketed *(0-671-73618-3,* S&S BFYR) S&S Trade.

—A Boy in the Doghouse. Morrill, Leslie, illus. LC 90-47751. 96p. (gr. 2-6). 1993. pap. 2.95 *(0-671-86698-2,* Half Moon Bks) S&S Trade.

—Gadget War. (gr. 4-7). 1991. 12.00 *(0-670-84152-8)* Viking Child Bks.

—How to Be Cool in the Third Grade. Wilson, Janet, illus. 80p. (gr. 2-5). 1993. 12.99 *(0-670-84798-4)* Viking Child Bks.

—Lucky in Left Field. LC 91-4579. (ps-3). 1992. pap. 13.00 *(0-671-74687-1,* S&S BFYR) S&S Trade.

—Lucky on the Loose. Morrill, Leslie, illus. LC 92-21421. 1993. pap. 13.00 *(0-671-86424-6,* S&S BFYR) S&S Trade.

—The Math Wiz. (gr. 4-7). 1990. 12.00 *(0-670-83422-X)* Viking Child Bks.

—The Math Wiz. Wilson, Janet, illus. 80p. (gr. 2-5). 1993. pap. 3.99 *(0-14-034477-2)* Puffin Bks.

—Puppy Love. Natti, Susanna, illus. LC 92-12705. 64p. (gr. 2-6). 1992. 13.00 *(0-670-84346-6)* Viking Child Bks.

—Throw-Away Pets. Natti, Susanna, illus. 80p. (gr. 2-6). 1993. 12.99 *(0-670-84348-2)* Viking Child Bks.

—The Wild Things. Natti, Susanna, illus. LC 92-25938. 80p. (gr. 2-6). 1993. 12.99 *(0-670-84347-4)* Viking Child Bks.

Duffield, Francesca, illus. ABC Rhymes. LC 92-75611. 10p. (ps). 1993. bds. 5.95 *(1-85697-941-5)* Kingfisher Bks.

—A Bedtime Story. LC 92-75613. 10p. 1993. 5.95 *(1-85697-915-6)* Kingfisher Bks.

—Lullabies. LC 92-75609. (ps-k). 1993. 5.95 *(1-85697-916-4)* Kingfisher Bks.

—Nursery Rhymes. LC 92-75584. 10p. (ps-k). 1993. 5.95 *(1-85697-917-2)* Kingfisher Bks.

—One-Two-Three Rhymes. LC 92-75610. 10p. (ps). 1993. bds. 5.95 *(1-85697-942-3)* Kingfisher Bks.

—A Teddy Tale. LC 92-75612. 10p. (ps). 1993. 5.95 *(1-85697-918-0)* Kingfisher Bks.

Duffy, Carol A. I Wouldn't Thank You for a Valentine: Poems for Young Feminists. Rafferty, Trisha, illus. 112p. (gr. 7 up). 1994. PLB 14.95 *(0-8050-2756-4,* Bks Young Read) H Holt & Co.

Duffy, Carol A., ed. I Wouldn't Thank You for a Valentine: Poems for Young Feminists. Rafferty, Trisha, illus. LC 93-3172. 1993. write for info. H Holt & Co.

Duffy, Deborah. Barnyard Tracks. Marshall, Janet P., illus. LC 91-72973. 32p. (ps up). 1992. 12.95 *(1-878093-66-5)* Boyds Mills Pr.

Duffy, James. Be Kind to Animals! Lattimer, Evan, illus. LC 88-80281. 24p. (gr. k-3). 1988. *(0-307-10285-8)* Western Pub.

—The Christmas Gang. 80p. 1991. pap. 2.99 *(0-380-71149-4,* Camelot) Avon.

—Cleaver & Company. LC 91-9932. 144p. (gr. 4-6). 1991. SBE 13.95 *(0-684-19371-X,* Scribners Young Read) Macmillan Child Grp.

—Cleaver of the Good Luck Diner. LC 88-29906. (Illus.). 128p. (gr. 3-6). 1989. SBE 13.95 *(0-684-18969-0,* Scribners Young Read) Macmillan Child Grp.

—The Graveyard Gang. LC 92-30990. 192p. (gr. 5-7). 1993. SBE 14.95 *(0-684-19449-X,* Scribners Young Read) Macmillan Child Grp.

—The Man in the River. LC 89-10200. 176p. (gr. 5-7). 1990. SBE 13.95 *(0-684-19161-X,* Scribners Young Read) Macmillan Child Grp.

—Missing. LC 87-25295. 144p. (gr. 4-7). 1988. SBE 13.95 *(0-684-18912-7,* Scribners Young Read) Macmillan Child Grp.

—Radical Red. 160p. (gr. 4-7). 1993. SBE 13.95 *(0-684-19533-X,* Scribners Young Read) Macmillan Child Grp.

—Uncle Shamus. LC 91-19217. 144p. (gr. 4-6). 1992. SBE 13.95 *(0-684-19434-1,* Scribners Young Read) Macmillan Child Grp.

Duffy, Karen & Lokenvitz, Judith. Angel, Devils, Mermaids, & Monsters. Katz, Kathleen, illus. 1989. pap. 4.95 *(0-89013-187-2)* Museum NM Pr.

Duffy, Robert. The American Quiz Book. 134p. (gr. 7 up). 1993. pap. 6.95 *(1-85371-187-X,* Pub. by Poolbeg Pr ER) Dufour.

—Children's Quiz Book. 132p. 1988. pap. 5.95 *(1-85371-020-2,* Pub. by Poolbeg Pr UK) Dufour.

Duffy, Trent. The Vanishing Wetlands. LC 93-26332. 1994. write for info. *(0-531-13034-7)* Watts.

Duffy, William G., Jr. The Adventures of Grubber Bug. LC 82-71946. 45p. (ps-3). 1984. 3.50x *(0-943864-33-X)* Davenport.

Dufort, Anthony. Ballet Steps. rev. & enlarged ed. LC 89-37078. (Illus.). 176p. (gr. 7 up). 1990. 18.00 *(0-517-57770-4)* Crown Bks Yng Read.

Dufton, Jo S., jt. auth. see Johnson, Liliane.

Dugan, Barbara. Good-Bye, Hello. (gr. 6 up). 1994. write for info. *(0-688-12447-X)* Greenwillow.

—Leaving Home with a Pickle Jar. Baker, Karen L., illus. LC 91-48256. 32p. (gr. k up). 1993. 14.00 *(0-688-10836-9)*; PLB 13.93 *(0-688-10837-7)* Greenwillow.

—Loop the Loop. Stevenson, James, illus. LC 90-21727. 32p. (gr. k up). 1992. 14.00 *(0-688-09647-6)*; PLB 13.93 *(0-688-09648-4)* Greenwillow.

—Loop the Loop. Stevenson, James, illus. LC 92-40168. 32p. (ps-3). 1993. pap. 4.99 *(0-14-054904-8,* Puffin) Puffin Bks.

Dugan, Karen. Fly Away Home. Dugan, Karen, illus. 26p. (gr. up). 1994. 11.95 *(0-8431-3687-1)* Price Stern.

Dugan, Michael. The Emu Who Wanted to Be a Horse. Smith, Craig, illus. LC 93-11736. 1994. 4.25 *(0-383-03743-3)* SRA Schl Grp.

Dugan, Robert, ed. see Highlights Editors.

DuGan, Thomas K. & Green, Susan L. Through the Eyes: A Venture Through America. (Illus.). 436p. (Orig.). (gr. 12). 1990. pap. 5.50 *(1-878342-07-X)* Bentwerth Pr.

Dugas-Bonds, Pat. Due Season. rev. ed. Mitchell, Sarah, ed. 110p. (Orig.). 1988. 15.00 *(0-317-93048-6)* BDB Unlimited.

Duggan, Alice. Violet's Finest Hour. Stevenson, Harvey, illus. LC 91-52588. 64p. (gr. 1 up). 1991. text ed. 10. *(0-688-09456-2)* Lothrop.

Duggan, Maureen H. Mommy Doesn't Live Here Anymore. Liberman, Jane, illus. 48p. (Orig.). (ps-7). 1987. pap. 8.95 *(0-944453-01-5)* B Brae. MOMMY DOESN'T LIVE HERE ANYMORE - a sensitive chronicle of a mother's alcoholism & how it affected her children. It has successfully captured the essence of life within an alcoholic family: the stresses, tensions, pressures & pains. Most importantly, it has done so from the vantage point of the child, as the child reflects upon the total experience. No other work has presented such a realistic portrayal of the magnitude of suffering, emotional pain & psychic turmoil of young children within alcoholic families. It reveals the thoughts, reasoning, feelings & behaviors of children in alcoholic homes, & yet, accomplishes such spirit of understanding & sympathy within an overall message of hope & help for our children. MOMMY DOESN'T LIVE HERE ANYMORE is an inspirational work, revealing that the tragedies of familial alcoholism & tragic consequences for our youth need to be dealt with in a personal & delicate manner. "Maureen Duggan has always been regarded highly for her thoughtful & gentle manner, compassionate understanding, & her acute sensitivity towards alcoholics & family needs. Her own serenity & spirituality are guides for many seeking their own honesty & fulfillment."--Nelson C. Acquilano, Executive Director, Council on Alcoholism of The Finger Lakes, N.Y. *Publisher Provided Annotation.*

Duggleby, John. Doomed Expeditions. LC 89-25459. (Illus.). 48p. (gr. 5 up). 1990. RSBE 11.95 *(0-89686-506-1,* Crestwood Hse) Macmillan Child Grp.

—Impossible Quests. LC 89-28988. (Illus.). 48p. (gr. 5 up). 1990. RSBE 11.95 *(0-89686-509-6,* Crestwood Hse) Macmillan Child Grp.

—Pesticides. LC 90-35496. (Illus.). 48p. (gr. 5-6). 1990. RSBE 12.95 *(0-89686-540-1,* Crestwood Hse) Macmillan Child Grp.

—Saber-Tooth Cat. LC 89-31574. (Illus.). 48p. (gr. 5-6). 1989. RSBE 12.95 *(0-89686-462-6,* Crestwood Hse) Macmillan Child Grp.

Dugin, Andrej & Dugina, Olga. Dragon Feathers. (Illus.). 24p. 1993. 14.95 *(1-56566-047-1)* Thomasson-Grant.

Dugina, Olga, jt. auth. see Dugin, Andrej.

Duin, Edgar C., tr. see Bachmann, Bertha.

Duitsman, Dominique. Understanding the Horse. Splane, Lily & Duitsman, Penny, illus. 64p. (gr. 6-9). 1989. pap. text ed. 8.95 *(0-945962-02-9)* Anaphase II.

Duke, Dulcie. The Growth of a Medieval Town. 2nd ed. (Illus.). 48p. (gr. 7 up). 1988. pap. 7.50 *(0-521-33725-9)* Cambridge U Pr.

Duke, Jerry. Clog Dance in the Appalachians. (Illus.). 96p. (Orig.). 1984. pap. 7.95 *(0-9613727-0-2)* Duke Pub Co.

Duke, Kate. Aunt Isabel Tells a Good One. Duke, Kate, illus. LC 91-14598. 32p. (ps-2). 1992. 14.00 *(0-525-44685-7,* DCB) Dutton Child Bks.

—Bedtime. Duke, Kate, illus. LC 84-73140. 12p. (ps). 1986. bds. 2.95 *(0-525-44207-3,* DCB) Dutton Child Bks.

—Clean-Up Day. Duke, Kate, illus. LC 84-73139. 12p. (ps). 1986. bds. 2.95 *(0-525-44208-1,* DCB) Dutton Child Bks.

—The Guinea Pig ABC. Duke, Kate, illus. LC 83-1410. 32p. (ps-1). 1983. 12.95 *(0-525-44058-5,* DCB) Dutton Child Bks.

—Guinea Pigs Far & Near. Duke, Kate, illus. LC 84-1580. 24p. (ps-1). 1984. 9.95 *(0-525-44112-3,* DCB) Dutton Child Bks.

—Guinea Pigs Far & Near. Duke, Kate, illus. LC 84-1580. 24p. (ps-1). 1989. 3.95 *(0-525-44480-7,* DCB) Dutton Child Bks.

—If You Walk Down This Road. Duke, Kate, illus. LC 92-27685. 32p. (ps-k). 1993. 13.99 *(0-525-45072-6,* DCB) Dutton Child Bks.

—The Playground. Duke, Kate, illus. LC 84-73141. 12p. (ps). 1986. bds. 2.95 *(0-525-44206-5,* DCB) Dutton Child Bks.

—Roseberry's Great Escape. LC 89-37847. (Illus.). 24p. (ps-1). 1990. 12.95 *(0-525-44597-8,* DCB) Dutton Child Bks.

—What Bounces? Duke, Kate, illus. LC 84-73138. 12p. (ps). 1986. 2.95 *(0-525-44209-X,* DCB) Dutton Child Bks.

Duke, Kate, illus. Tingalayo. (ps-2). 1988. 9.95 *(0-517-56926-4)* Crown Bks Yng Read.

Duke, Mary A. Victoria Scarlett Jones. LC 93-70815. (Illus.). 55p. (Orig.). (gr. 3-5). 1993. Incls. Victoria Scarlett & the Big Black Bear; Victoria Scarlett & Clara at Christmas; Victoria Scarlett Says, "Recess Was a Mess!" pap. 5.95 *(1-883241-05-7)* Cognitive Pr.

—Writing for "Real World" Reasons: A Ten Week Step-by-Step Outline for Writing, Producing & Performing Student's Original Works. LC 93-70816. (Illus.). 100p. (Orig.). (gr. 3-7). 1993. pap. 18.95 *(1-883241-06-5)* Cognitive Pr.

DuKore, Jesse. Long Distance Love. (gr. 7-12). 1983. pap. 2.25 *(0-553-17853-9)* Bantam.

Dulac, Colette. Shortcut to French. (gr. 9 up). 1977. pap. text ed. 5.45 *(0-88345-300-2,* 18441); cassettes 25.00 *(0-685-79306-0,* 58442) Prentice ESL.

Dulac, Edmund. Fairy Tales of the World. Cott, Jonathan, ed. Dulac, Edmund, illus. LC 93-24486. 200p. 1994. 15.00 *(1-56957-914-8)* Barefoot Bks.

Dulac, Glen. The Color Coded Alphabet: The Best Coloring Book Ever. Fischer, Robert, et al, illus. (gr. k-3). 1991. pap. 5.00 *(0-9628227-4-4)* Desert Bks.

Dulac, Glen J. The Color Coded Alphabet, an Alphabet for Easy Reading: The Best Coloring Book as It Has Never Been Seen Before. Dulac, Glen J. & Dulac, John J., illus. (ps-2). 1990. 49.50 *(0-9628227-2-8)* Desert Bks.

Dumas, Alexandre. Georges. Rivers, W. Napoleon, et al, eds. (FRE.). 1990. 7.95 *(0-87498-082-8)*; pap. 5.95 *(0-87498-083-6)* Assoc Pubs DC.

—Man in the Iron Mask. Hillerich, R., intro. by. (gr. 9 up). 1967. pap. 2.75 (0-8049-0150-3, CL-150) Airmont.
—Three Musketeers. (gr. 8 up). 1966. pap. 3.95 (0-8049-0127-9, CL-127) Airmont.
—Three Musketeers. Price, Norman & Van Swearingen, E. C., illus. (gr. 4-6). 1953-59. (G&D); deluxe ed. 13. 95 (0-448-06024-8) Putnam Pub Group.
—The Three Musketeers. abr. ed. Hochman, Eleanor, rev. by. & tr. Flanagan, Thomas, afterword by. 608p. (RL 7). 1991. pap. 5.95 (0-451-52547-7, W8107, Sig Classics) NAL-Dutton.
—The Three Musketeers. unabridged ed. Bair, Lowell, tr. from FRE. 560p. 1984. pap. 5.95 (0-553-21337-7, Bantam Classics) Bantam.
—The Three Musketeers. 1994. pap. 4.99 (0-8125-3602-9) Tor Bks.

Dumas, Philippe. The Lippizaners: And the Spanish Riding School of Vienna. (gr. 3-7). 1981. 10.95 (0-13-537068-X) P-H.
Dumbleton, Mike. Dial-a-Croc. James, Ann, illus. LC 90-25385. 32p. (ps-2). 1991. 14.95 (0-531-05945-6); RLB 14.99 (0-531-08545-7) Orchard Bks Watts.
Dumelle, Grace. The Lord's Prayer: Explained for Little Ones. Williams, Abbie, illus. 24p. (Orig.). 1990. pap. text ed. 4.95 (0-937739-08-1) Roman IL.
Dumelle, Graci. Saints O'Lore: Our Shining Examples. Lloyd, John R., illus. 32p. (Orig.). (gr. k-6). 1992. pap. 5.95 (0-937739-12-X) Roman IL.
Dummer, H. Boylston. Adventures of the Animal Town Aviators, Bk. I. Dummer, H. Boylston, illus. 118p. (ps-3). 1989. 17.95 (0-87510-198-4) Monitor Bks.
—Adventures of the Animal Town Aviators, Bk. II. Dummer, H. Boylston, illus. 118p. (ps-3). 1989. 17.95 (0-87510-199-2) Monitor Bks.
Dumond, Michael. Coping with Life after High School. Rosen, Roger, ed. (gr. 7 up). 1988. PLB 13.95 (0-8239-0781-3) Rosen Group.
—Dad Is Leaving Home. 196p. (gr. 7-12). 1987. PLB 12. 95 (0-8239-0699-X) Rosen Group.
Dumond, Val. Visiting Olympia. Ballman, Jean, illus. 24p. (Orig.). (gr. 1-4). 1983. pap. 2.75 (0-933992-39-4) Coffee Break.
Dumpleton, John. Law & Order: The Story of the Police. (Illus.). (gr. 3-7). 1983. Repr. of 1963 ed. 14.95 (0-7136-1079-4) Dufour.
Duna, Bill & Duna, Lois. Let's Play--Right Away with Play-Along Tape, Bk. 1. Guthrie, Ruth, illus. 32p. (Orig.). (gr. k up). 1981. pap. 12.95 (0-942928-00-8) Duna Studios.
—Let's Play--Right Away with Play-Along Tape, Bk. 2. Guthrie, Ruth, illus. 30p. (Orig.). (gr. k-9). 1981. pap. 12.95 (0-942928-01-6) Duna Studios.
—Let's Play & Play & Play... Practice & Assignment Book. (Illus.). 56p. (gr. up). 1983. pap. 6.95 (0-942928-02-4) Duna Studios.
Duna, Lois, jt. auth. see Duna, Bill.
Dunbar, C., jt. auth. see Harte, J. P.
Dunbar, James, jt. auth. see Dunbar, Joyce.
Dunbar, Joyce. A Cake for Barney. Boon, Emilie, illus. LC 87-15294. 32p. (ps-2). 1988. 12.95 (0-531-05735-6); PLB 12.99 (0-531-08335-7) Orchard Bks Watts.
—I Want a Blue Banana. Dunbar, James, illus. 32p. (ps). 1991. 13.45 (0-395-57579-6, Sandpiper) HM.
—Lollopy. Varley, Susan, illus. LC 91-26212. 32p. (ps-1). 1992. SBE 14.95 (0-02-733195-4, Macmillan Child Bk) Macmillan Child Grp.
—Ten Little Mice. 24p. (ps-1). 1990. 13.95 (0-15-200601-X) HarBrace.
—Ten Little Mice. (ps). 1992. 19.95 (0-15-284614-X) HarBrace.
—Why Is the Sky Up? Dunbar, James, illus. 32p. (ps). 1991. 13.45 (0-395-57580-X, Sandpiper) HM.
Dunbar, Joyce & Dunbar, James. Jugg. 1980. 15.00 (0-85967-596-3, Pub. by Scolar Pr UK) Ashgate Pub Co.
Dunbar, Joyce, et al. Read-Aloud Storybook for Young Children. LC 92-29125. 1993. 14.95 (1-85697-911-3) Kingfisher Bks.
Dunbar, Robert E. Guide to Military Careers. LC 92-10921. 128p. (gr. 9-12). 1992. PLB 13.40 (0-531-11118-0) Watts.
—How to Debate. 2nd ed. LC 93-11959. 1994. write for info. (0-531-11122-9) Watts.
—Making Your Point. LC 89-25088. 1990. PLB 13.90 (0-531-10905-4) Watts.
—Mental Retardation. LC 91-18513. (Illus.). 96p. (gr. 9-12). 1991. PLB 13.40 (0-531-12502-5) Watts.
Duncan. Nature Search. Date not set. 15.00 (0-06-023596-9, Festival); PLB 14.89 (0-06-023597-7, Festival) HarpC Child Bks.
Duncan, Beverly K. Christmas in the Stable. (Illus.). 32p. (ps up). 1990. 14.95 (0-15-217758-2) HarBrace.
Duncan, Jane. Brave Janet Reachfar. Hedderwick, Mairi, illus. LC 74-8693. 32p. (ps-3). 1975. 7.95 (0-8164-3130-2, Clarion Bks) HM.
—Janet Reachfar and the Kelpie. Hedderwick, Mairi, illus. LC 75-44166. 32p. (ps-3). 1976. 7.50 (0-685-02316-8, Clarion Bks) HM.
Duncan, Jane C. Careers in Veterinary Medicine. (Illus.). (gr. 7-12). 1988. PLB 13.95 (0-8239-1678-2); pap. 9.95 (0-8239-1719-3) Rosen Group.
Duncan, Janie L., jt. auth. see Clark, Raymond C.
Duncan, Jim. Practical Math Skills - Intermediate Level. Tom, Darcy, illus. 64p. (gr. 4-6). 1989. wkbk. 7.95 (0-86653-465-2, GA1070) Good Apple.

—Practical Math Skills - Junior High Level. Tom, Darcy, illus. 64p. (gr. 7-9). 1989. wkbk. 7.95 (0-86653-466-0, GA1071) Good Apple.
—Practical Math Skills - Primary Level. Tom, Darcy, illus. 64p. (gr. 1-3). 1989. wkbk. 7.95 (0-86653-464-4, GA1069) Good Apple.
Duncan, Kyle, ed. see Johnson, Greg & Shellenberger, Susie.
Duncan, Leonard C. Greek Roots. Bigelow, Holly, illus. 82p. (Orig.). (gr. 6-12). 1982. pap. 10.00 (0-941414-01-9) LCD.
—Learn to Read with Phonetic & Non-Phonetic Words. Incl. Bk. 1. 97p; Bk. 2. 85p (0-941414-12-4); Bk. 3. 99p (0-941414-13-2); Bk. 4. 110p (0-941414-14-0); Bk. 5. Nursery Rhymes. 109p. (Illus., Orig.). (gr. 1-3). pap. 10.00 (0-317-11632-0) LCD.
Duncan, Lois. Birthday Moon. Davis, Susan, illus. 32p. (ps-3). 1989. 13.95 (0-670-82238-8) Viking Child Bks.
—Birthday Moon. (ps-3). 1991. pap. 3.95 (0-14-050876-7, Puffin) Puffin Bks.
—Chapters: My Growth As a Writer. 276p. (gr. 7 up). 1982. 15.95 (0-316-19552-9) Little.
—The Circus Comes Home. Steinmetz, Joseph J., photos by. LC 92-7481. (Illus.). 1993. 16.95 (0-385-30689-X) Doubleday.
—Daughters of Eve. 1990. pap. 3.50 (0-440-91864-2) Dell.
—Don't Look Behind You. (gr. 7 up). 1989. 14.95 (0-385-29793-4) Delacorte.
—Don't Look Behind You. 1990. pap. 3.99 (0-440-20729-0, LFL) Dell.
—Down a Dark Hall. 192p. (gr. 7 up). 1974. 15.95 (0-316-19547-2) Little.
—Down a Dark Hall. 192p. (gr. 5-9). 1990. pap. 3.99 (0-440-91805-7, LFL) Dell.
—A Gift of Magic. (gr. 5-7). 1990. pap. 3.50 (0-671-72649-8, Archway) PB.
—A Gift of Magic. Stewart, Arvis, illus. (gr. 4-6). 1971. 15.95 (0-316-19545-6) Little.
—Horses of Dreamland. Diamond, Donna, illus. 32p. (ps-3). 1986. 12.95 (0-316-19554-5) Little.
—Hotel for Dogs. (gr. 4-7). 1991. pap. 3.25 (0-440-40435-5) Dell.
—I Know What You Did Last Summer. (gr. 7 up). 1973. 15.95 (0-316-19546-4) Little.
—Killing Mr. Griffin. 224p. (gr. 7 up). 1990. pap. 3.99 (0-440-94515-1, LFL) Dell.
—Killing Mr. Griffin. (gr. 7 up). 1978. 15.95 (0-316-19549-9) Little.
—Locked in Time. 240p. (gr. 7 up). 1985. 15.95 (0-316-19555-3) Little.
—Locked in Time. (gr. 6 up). 1986. pap. 3.50 (0-440-94942-4, LFL) Dell.
—Ransom. 144p. (gr. 7-12). 1990. pap. 3.50 (0-440-97292-2, LFL) Dell.
—Stranger with My Face. (gr. 8 up). 1981. 15.95 (0-316-19551-0) Little.
—Stranger with My Face. 176p. (gr. 7 up). 1990. pap. 3.99 (0-440-98356-8, LFL) Dell.
—Summer of Fear. 224p. (gr. 7 up). 1977. pap. 3.99 (0-440-98324-X, LFL) Dell.
—Summer of Fear. 252p. (gr. 7-12). 1976. 15.95 (0-316-19548-0) Little.
—The Third Eye. (gr. 7up). 1984. 15.95 (0-316-19553-7) Little.
—The Third Eye. 224p. (gr. 6-12). 1991. pap. 3.99 (0-440-98720-2, LFL) Dell.
—The Twisted Window. LC 86-29054. 192p. (gr. 7 up). 1987. pap. 14.95 (0-385-29566-9) Delacorte.
—The Twisted Window. 192p. (gr. k-12). 1988. pap. 3.99 (0-440-20184-5, LFL) Dell.
—Wonder Kid Meets the Evil Lunch Snatcher. Sanfilippo, Margaret, illus. LC 87-26490. 76p. (gr. 7-10). 1988. 9.95 (0-316-19558-8) Little.
—Wonder Kid Meets the Evil Lunch Snatcher. (gr. 2-4). 1990. 2.95 (0-316-19561-8) Little.
Duncan, Patsy G. Know America Activity & Coloring Book. 72p. (gr. 2-6). 1989. 2.95 (0-925449-00-8) D&M Pubns.
—Know America Coloring & Activity Book. (Illus.). 64p. (Orig.). (gr. 1-6). 1988. pap. text ed. 2.95 (0-685-25274-4) D&M Pubns.
Duncan, Riana. A Nutcracker in a Tree: A Book of Riddles. Duncan, Riana, illus. LC 80-67492. 32p. (gr. k-3). 1981. PLB 8.95 (0-385-28733-X); pap. 8.95 (0-385-28732-1) Delacorte.
—When Emily Woke up Angry. Duncan, Riana, illus. 32p.(ps-1). 1989. incl. dust jacket 9.95 (0-8120-5985-9) Barron.
Duncan, Shirley E. The Tree That Would Not Grow But Did. Reid, Nancy G., ed. Gibson, Judy, illus. 1991. 12.95 (1-878647-02-4) Duncan & Duncan. Postponed.
Duncanson, Neil. Sports Technology. LC 91-17570. (Illus.). 48p. (gr. 5-9). 1992. PLB 12.90 (0-531-18401-3, Pub. by Bookwright Pr) Watts.
Dunford, Elizabeth P. The Hawaiians of Old. rev. ed. Kudlak, Aimee A., illus. 220p. (gr. 4 up). 1990. text ed. 25.95 (0-935848-43-6); pap. text ed. 15.95 (0-935848-01-0); wkbk. 5.95 (0-935848-08-8); tchr's. manual 5.00 (0-935848-09-6) Bess Pr.
Dunham, Katharine. Kasamance: A Fantasy. LC 73-92612. (gr. 4 up). 1974. 25.00 (0-89388-128-7) Okpaku Communications.
Dunham, Meredith. Colors: How Do You Say It? Dunham, Meredith, illus. LC 86-27739. 24p. (ps up). 1987. 9.25 (0-688-06948-7); PLB 9.88 (0-688-06949-5) Lothrop.

—Shapes: How Do You Say It? Dunham, Meredith, illus. LC 86-27740. 24p. (ps up). 1987. PLB 9.88 (0-688-06953-3) Lothrop.
Dunham, Montrew. Langston Hughes: Young Poet. LC 93-21128. 1994. 3.95 (0-689-71787-3, Aladdin) Macmillan Child Grp.
—Mahalia Jackson: Young Gospel Singer. LC 93-34072. 1994. 3.95 (0-689-71786-5, Aladdin) Macmillan Child Grp.
Dunham, Steve, ed. see Sadiku, Matthew N.
Dunhill, Priscilla, jt. auth. see Grossman, John.
Dunkle, Sidney W. Damselflies of Florida, Bermuda, & the Bahamas. (Illus.). 148p. (gr. 9-12). 1990. 19.95 (0-945417-86-1); pap. 14.95 (0-945417-85-3) Sci Pubs.
Dunlap, Hope. The Little Lame Prince. Dunlap, Hope, illus. LC 92-37665. 1993. 8.99 (0-517-08484-8, Pub. by Derrydale Bks) Outlet Bk Co.
Dunlap, Julie. Aldo Leopold: Living with the Land. (Illus.). 64p. (gr. 4-7). 1993. PLB 14.95 (0-8050-2501-4) TFC Bks NY.
Dunlavy, Kathy. Learn & Grow from A to Z: Learning Centers & Activities for Young Children. Terrill, Veronica, illus. 160p. (ps-2). 1992. Wkbk. 12.95 (0-86653-682-5, GA1416) Good Apple.
Dunlavy, Kathy, jt. auth. see Carroll, Jeri.
Dunlea, Nancy. The Courtesy Book. Saunders, Dorothy, illus. Hubalek, Linda K. & Rex, Margeryintro. by. LC 93-80030. (Illus.). 128p. (gr. 4-8). pap. 7.95 (1-882420-07-1) Hearth KS.
Dunlop, Beverly. The Poetry Girl. 216p. (gr. 6-8). 1989. 13.45 (0-395-49679-9) HM.
Dunlop, Eileen. Clementina. LC 86-22913. 160p. (gr. 7 up). 1987. 12.95 (0-8234-0642-3) Holiday.
—Finn's Island. LC 91-55027. 128p. (gr. 5-9). 1992. 13. 95 (0-8234-0910-4) Holiday.
—Green Willow. LC 92-33402. 160p. (gr. 5-9). 1993. 14. 95 (0-8234-1021-8) Holiday.
—The House on the Hill. LC 87-388. 160p. (gr. 4 up). 1987. 13.95 (0-8234-0658-X) Holiday.
—House on the Hill. 160p. (gr. 2-9). 1989. pap. 2.95 (0-8167-1323-5) Troll Assocs.
—Tales of St. Columba. 136p. (gr. 4 up). 1992. pap. 6.95 (1-85371-134-9, Pub. by Poolbeg Pr ER) Dufour.
—The Valley of Deer. LC 89-1931. 152p. (gr. 4-7). 1989. 13.95 (0-8234-0766-7) Holiday.
Dunmire, Marj. Mountain Wildlife. Dunmire, Marj, illus. 48p. (gr. 2 up). 1986. 3.95 (0-942559-03-7) Pegasus Graphics.
—National Parks of Alaska. (Illus.). 48p. (gr. 2-8). 1991. pap. 4.95 (0-942559-07-X) Pegasus Graphics.
—Not Even Footprints. Dunmire, Marj, illus. 72p. (Orig.). (gr. 2-7). 1987. pap. 4.95 (0-942559-04-5) Pegasus Graphics.
—Water Birds. Dunmire, Marj, illus. 48p. (gr. 2-8). 1990. pap. 3.95 (0-942559-06-1) Pegasus Graphics.
—Wildlife of Cactus & Canyon Country. Dunmire, Marj, illus. 48p. (gr. 2-6). 1988. pap. 3.95 (0-942559-05-3) Pegasus Graphics.
Dunn, Allison B., jt. auth. see Dunn, Kathryn B.
Dunn, Andrew. Alexander Graham Bell. (Illus.). 48p. (gr. 5-7). 1991. PLB 12.40 (0-531-18418-8, Pub. by Bookwright Pr) Watts.
—Bridges. LC 93-6832. 32p. (gr. 5-8). 1993. 13.95 (1-56847-028-2) Thomson Lrning.
—Dams. LC 93-6835. 32p. (gr. 5-8). 1993. 13.95 (1-56847-029-0) Thomson Lrning.
—Heat. LC 93-7518. (Illus.). 32p. (gr. 3-6). 1993. 13.95 (1-56847-018-5) Thomson Lrning.
—It's Electric. LC 93-7520. (Illus.). 32p. (gr. 3-6). 1993. 13.95 (1-56847-019-3) Thomson Lrning.
—Lifting by Levers. Carr, Ed, illus. LC 93-6828. 32p. (gr. 3-6). 1993. 13.95 (1-56847-016-9) Thomson Lrning.
—Marie Curie. LC 90-37563. (Illus.). 48p. (gr. 5-8). 1991. PLB 12.40 (0-531-18375-0, Pub. by Bookwright Pr) Watts.
—The Power of Pressure. LC 92-41512. 32p. (gr. 3-6). 1993. 13.95 (1-56847-015-0) Thomson Lrning.
—Simple Slopes. Carr, Ed, illus. LC 93-6836. 32p. (gr. 3-6). 1993. 13.95 (1-56847-017-7) Thomson Lrning.
—Skyscrapers. LC 92-43944. (Illus.). 32p. (gr. 5-8). 1993. PLB 13.95 (1-56847-027-4) Thomson Lrning.
—Tunnels. LC 92-43945. (Illus.). 32p. (gr. 5-8). 1993. 13. 95 (1-56847-026-6) Thomson Lrning.
—Wheels at Work. LC 92-41513. 32p. (gr. 3-6). 1993. 13. 95 (1-56847-014-2) Thomson Lrning.
Dunn, Ben. Ninja High School, Vol. 1: Graphic Album. 2nd ed. Castro, Carlos & Dunn, Ben, illus. 126p. (gr. 10). 1990. pap. 9.95 (0-944735-13-4) Malibu Graphics.
—Ninja High School, Vol. 2: Beware of Dog. Ulm, Chris, ed. Dunn, Ben, illus. 121p. 1990. pap. 9.95 (0-944735-59-2) Malibu Graphics.
Dunn, Bill, jt. auth. see Stafford, Greg.
Dunn, Bill, ed. see Stafford, Greg.
Dunn, Cynthia T. If You Squint at a Rhinoceros... Lopez, Stella, illus. LC 90-30384. 32p. (gr. 2-5). 1990. 12.95 (0-943173-67-1) Harbinger AZ.
Dunn, Gary. Descubre Mariposas. University of Mexico City Staff, tr. from SPA. O'Neill, Pablo M. & Robare, Lorie, illus. 48p. (gr. 3-8). 1993. PLB 16.95 (1-56674-048-7, HTS Bks) Forest Hse.
Dunn, Joyce E. Riding on a School Bus. rev. ed. Dunn, Joyce E., illus. Doyle, James M., intro. by. (Illus.). 56p. (gr. k-1). 1989. pap. 4.95 (0-9624280-0-0) SPI Pub.
Dunn, Judy. The Little Duck. Dunn, Phoebe, photos by. LC 75-36467. (Illus.). 32p. (ps-1). 1976. pap. 2.25 (0-394-83247-7) Random Bks Yng Read.

—The Little Goat. Dunn, Phoebe, illus. LC 77-91658. (ps-1). 1979. lib. bdg. 5.99 (*0-394-93872-0*); pap. 2.25 (*0-394-83872-6*) Random Bks Read.
—The Little Kitten. Dunn, Phoebe, photos by. LC 82-16711. (Illus.). (ps-4). 1983. lib. bdg. 5.99 (*0-394-95818-7*); 2.25 (*0-394-85818-2*) Random Bks Yng Read.
—The Little Lamb. Dunn, Phoebe, illus. LC 76-24167. (ps-2). 1978. lib. bdg. 5.99 (*0-394-93455-5*); pap. 2.25 (*0-394-83455-0*) Random Bks Yng Read.
—The Little Pig. Dunn, Phoebe, photos by. LC 86-42956. (Illus.). 32p. (ps-3). 1987. pap. 2.25 (*0-394-88774-3*) Random Bks Yng Read.
—The Little Puppy. Dunn, Phoebe, illus. LC 84-2031. 32p. (ps-3). 1984. lib. bdg. 5.99 (*0-394-96595-7*); saddle-stitched 2.25 (*0-394-86595-2*) Random Bks Yng Read.
—The Little Rabbit. Dunn, Phoebe, illus. LC 79-5241. 32p. (ps). 1980. lib. bdg. 5.99 (*0-394-94377-5*); pap. 2.25 (*0-394-84377-0*) Random Bks Yng Read.
Dunn, Kathryn B. & Dunn, Allison B. Trouble with School: A Family Story about Learning Disabilities. Stromoski, Rick, illus. 32p. (Orig.). (gr. 1-5). 1993. 9.95 (*0-933149-57-3*) Woodbine House.
Dunn, Lois, tr. see Freeman, Lory.
Dunn, Lynne. The Department of Justice. (Illus.). 112p. (gr. 5 up). 1990. 14.95 (*0-87754-843-9*) Chelsea Hse.
Dunn, Opal. Butterfly Match & Patch Book. (ps). 1992. 4.99 (*0-440-40613-7*, YB) Dell.
—Duck Match & Patch Book. (ps). 1992. 4.99 (*0-440-40610-2*) Dell.
—Rabbit Match & Patch Book. (ps). 1992. 4.99 (*0-440-40607-2*) Dell.
—Teddy Match & Patch Book. (ps). 1992. 4.99 (*0-440-40604-8*) Dell.
Dunn, Patricia. Children's Book of Irish Fairy Tales. 1988. pap. 9.95 (*0-85342-843-3*) Dufour.
—Math Trivial Pursuit - Intermediate Level. Dunn, Patricia, illus. 64p. (gr. 4-6). 1989. wkbk. 12.95 (*0-86653-468-7*, GA1073) Good Apple.
—Math Trivial Pursuit - Junior High Level. Dunn, Patricia, illus. 64p. (gr. 7-9). 1989. wkbk. 12.95 (*0-86653-469-5*, GA1074) Good Apple.
—Math Trivial Pursuit - Primary Level. Dunn, Patricia, illus. 64p. (gr. 1-3). 1989. wkbk. 12.95 (*0-86653-492-X*, GA1072) Good Apple.
Dunn, Phoebe. Baby's Busy Year. LC 89-51127. (Illus.). 28p. (ps). 1990. 2.95 (*0-679-80260-6*) Random Bks Yng Read.
—Busy Busy Toddlers. LC 86-62247. (Illus.). 14p. (ps). 1987. 2.99 (*0-394-88604-6*) Random Bks Yng Read.
Dunn, Phoebe, photos by. Baby's Animal Friends. LC 87-61462. (Illus.). 28p. (ps). 1988. bds. 2.95 (*0-394-89583-5*) Random Bks Yng Read.
—I'm a Baby! LC 86-61904. (Illus.). 14p. 1987. 2.99 (*0-394-88605-4*) Random Bks Yng Read.
Dunn, Phoebe & Lee, Vincent B., photos by. How Many? A Matchem Couunting Bk. LC 87-61521. (Illus.). 18p. (ps). 1988. bds. 4.95 (*0-394-89388-3*) Random Bks Yng Read.
Dunn, Richard, ed. see Bronte, Emily.
Dunn, Sandra. A Walk Through Biosphere 2: Coloring Book. (Illus.). 16p. 1993. pap. 4.00 (*1-882428-00-5*) Biosphere Pr.
Dunn, Wendy, jt. auth. see Morey, Janet.
Dunn, Wendy, jt. auth. see Morey, Janet N.
Dunnahoo, Terry. How to Survive High School: A Student's Guide. LC 92-41700. (Illus.). 112p. (gr. 7-12). PLB 13.40 (*0-531-11135-0*) Watts.
—How to Win a School Election. Rosenbloom, Richard, illus. LC 88-30341. 96p. (gr. 10-12). 1990. 12.90 (*0-531-10695-0*) Watts.
—The Lost Parrots of America. LC 89-7846. (Illus.). 48p. (gr. 5-6). 1989. RSBE 12.95 (*0-89686-461-8*, Crestwood Hse) Macmillan Child Grp.
—Pearl Harbor: America Enters the War. LC 90-13035. (Illus.). 144p. (gr. 7-12). 1991. PLB 13.90 (*0-531-11010-9*) Watts.
—U. S. Territories Freely Associated States. Rakos, Jennie, ed. LC 88-16982. (Illus.). 96p. 1988. PLB 13. 40 (*0-531-10605-5*) Watts.
Dunnahoo, Terry J., jt. auth. see Silverstein, Herma.
Dunnan, Nancy. Banking. Easton, Emily, ed. (Illus.). 128p. (gr. 4 up). 1990. lib. bdg. 14.98 (*0-382-09917-6*); pap. 7.95 (*0-382-24028-6*) Silver Burdett Pr.
—Barcelona. (Illus.). 64p. (gr. 3-7). PLB 14.95 (*1-56711-018-5*) Blackbirch.
—Collectibles. Raston, Emily, ed. (Illus.). 128p. (gr. 7 up). 1990. PLB 14.98 (*0-382-09918-4*); PLB 11.24s.p. (*0-685-47044-X*); pap. 7.95 (*0-382-24029-4*); pap. 5. 96s.p. (*0-685-47045-8*) Silver Burdett Pr.
—Entrepreneurship. (Illus.). 128p. (gr. 7-10). 1990. lib. bdg. 14.98 (*0-382-09916-8*); pap. 7.95 (*0-382-24027-8*) Silver Burdett Pr.
—Inside Track Library, 4 bks. (Illus.). (gr. 7-10). 1990. Set. lib. bdg. 59.92 (*0-382-09913-3*); pap. 31.80 (*0-382-24024-3*) Silver Burdett Pr.
—One Europe. LC 91-30083. (Illus.). 64p. (gr. 5-8). 1992. PLB 15.90 (*1-56294-105-4*) Millbrook Pr.
—One Europe. 1992. pap. 4.95 (*0-395-62470-3*) HM.
—The Stock Market. (Illus.). 128p. (gr. 7-10). 1990. lib. bdg. 14.98 (*0-382-09914-1*); pap. 7.95 (*0-382-24025-1*) Silver Burdett Pr.
Dunnigan, Alice A. The Fascinating Story of Black Kentuckians: Their Heritage & Tradition. 1990. 29.45 (*0-87498-088-7*); index 8.00 (*0-87498-089-5*) Assoc Pubs DC.

Dunning, David, jt. auth. see Dunning, Mary.
Dunning, Jack. Future Computer Opportunities: Business Ideas into the Year 2000. Lingham, Gretchen & Steward-Shahan, Leah, eds. 200p. (Orig.). 1991. pap. text ed. 8.95 (*0-945776-24-1*) Comptr Pub Enterprises.
—How to Make Money with Computers. Lingham, Gretchen & Shahan, Leah S., eds. 208p. (Orig.). 1991. pap. 8.95 (*0-945776-18-7*) Comptr Pub Enterprises.
Dunning, Mary & Dunning, David. Good Apple & Wonderful Word Games. 144p. (gr. 3-7). 1981. 11.95 (*0-86653-053-3*, GA 254) Good Apple.
Dunning, Stephen & Stafford, William. Getting the Knack: Twenty Poetry Writing Exercises. LC 92-36710. 1992. 11.95 (*0-8141-1848-8*) NCTE.
Dunning, Stephen, et al, eds. Reflections on a Gift of Watermelon Pickle & Other Modern Verse. LC 66-8763. (Illus.). 144p. (gr. 7 up). 1966. 14.95 (*0-688-41231-9*); PLB 13.88 (*0-688-51231-3*) Lothrop.
Dunnington, Tom, jt. auth. see Punnett, Dick.
Dunnington, Tom, illus. Animals. LC 83-25213. 32p. (gr. k-3). 1984. PLB 21.35 (*0-89565-264-1*); PLB 14.95s.p. (*0-685-55699-9*) Childs World.
Dunphy, Madeleine. Here Is the Arctic Winter. Robinson, Alan J., illus. LC 92-72022. 32p. (ps-3). 1993. 14.95 (*1-56282-336-1*); PLB 14.89 (*0-685-59361-4*) Hyprn Child.
—Here is the Tropical Rainforest. Rothman, Michael, illus. LC 93-24850. 32p. (ps-3). 1994. 14.95 (*1-56282-636-0*); PLB 14.89 (*1-56282-637-9*) Hyprn Child.
Dunrea, Olivier. The Broody Hen. LC 91-29377. (Illus.). 32p. (ps-3). 1992. 15.00 (*0-385-30597-4*) Doubleday.
—Deep Down Underground. Dunrea, Olivier, illus. LC 88-13534. 32p. (ps-2). 1989. RSBE 13.95 (*0-02-732861-9*, Macmillan Child Bk) Macmillan Child Grp.
—Deep down Underground. Dunrea, Olivier, illus. LC 92-45273. 32p. (gr. k-3). 1993. pap. 4.95 (*0-689-71756-3*, Aladdin) Macmillan Child Grp.
—Eppie M. Says... Dunrea, Olivier, illus. LC 89-8134. 32p. (ps-2). 1990. RSBE 13.95 (*0-02-733205-5*, Macmillan Child Bk) Macmillan Child Grp.
—Fergus & Bridey. Dunrea, Olivier, illus. 32p. (ps-3). 1992. pap. 3.99 (*0-440-40691-9*, YB) Dell.
—Mogwogs on the March. Dunrea, Olivier, illus. LC 85-5493. 32p. (ps-1). 1985. pap. 5.95 (*0-8234-0845-0*) Holiday.
—Ravena. 1992. 3.99 (*0-440-40645-5*, YB) Dell.
—Skara Brae: The Story of a Prehistoric Village. Dunrea, Olivier, illus. LC 85-42882. 40p. (gr. 3-7). 1986. reinforced bdg. 13.95 (*0-8234-0583-4*) Holiday.
Dunsany. The Ghosts. (gr. 5 up). 1992. PLB 13.95 (*0-88682-494-X*) Creative Ed.
Dunster, Mark. Archpriest. 11p. (Orig.). 1994. pap. 4.00 (*0-89642-241-0*) Linden Pubs.
—Chimney. 14p. (Orig.). 1990. pap. 4.00 (*0-89642-180-5*) Linden Pubs.
—Doricio. 11p. (Orig.). 1989. pap. 4.00 (*0-89642-170-8*) Linden Pubs.
—Emily, Pt. 3: Gib. 29p. (Orig.). 1994. pap. 5.00 (*0-89642-239-9*) Linden Pubs.
—Marsh King. 10p. (Orig.). 1990. pap. 4.00 (*0-89642-184-8*) Linden Pubs.
—Moon. 10p. (Orig.). 1993. pap. 4.00 (*0-89642-220-8*) Linden Pubs.
—Nutcrack. 11p. (Orig.). (gr. 1-7). 1990. pap. 4.00 (*0-89642-190-2*) Linden Pubs.
—Zond. 45p. (Orig.). 1989. pap. 5.00 (*0-89642-168-6*) Linden Pubs.
Duntze, Dorothee. The Twelve Days of Christmas. Duntze, Dorothee, illus. LC 91-32359. 32p. (gr. k-3). 1992. 14.95 (*1-55858-151-0*); PLB 14.88 (*1-55858-152-9*) North-South Bks NYC.
Duntze, Dorothee, illus. The Life of Jesus. LC 93-28776. 1993. write for info. (*0-8146-2303-4*) Liturgical Pr.
Dupas, Alain. Voyagers in Space. (ps-3). 1994. 4.95 (*0-944589-47-2*) Young Discovery Lib.
Dupasquier, Philippe. Andy's Pirate Ship. 1994. write for info. (*0-8050-3154-5*) H Holt & Co.
—Dear Daddy. (ps-3). 1988. pap. 3.95 (*0-14-050822-8*, Puffin) Puffin Bks.
—I Can't Sleep. LC 89-26599. (Illus.). 40p. (ps-1). 1990. 13.95 (*0-531-05874-3*); PLB 13.99 (*0-531-08474-4*) Orchard Bks Watts.
—Jack at Sea. (Illus.). 32p. (gr. 2-6). 1987. 12.95 (*0-13-509209-4*) P-H.
—Our House on the Hill. (Illus.). 32p. (ps-3). 1990. pap. 3.95 (*0-14-054227-2*, Puffin) Puffin Bks.
Duplex, Mary. Trouble with a Capital T. 96p. 1992. pap. 7.95 (*0-8163-1057-2*) Pacific Pr Pub Assn.
Duplex, Mary H., et al. Quiet Times with Jesus. LC 92-20278. (ps). 1992. pap. 9.95 (*0-8280-0678-4*) Review & Herald.
Dupont, Marie. Your First Kitten. (Illus.). 36p. (Orig.). 1991. pap. 1.95 (*0-86622-061-5*, YF-118) TFH Pubns.
Dupont, Philippe & Tracqui, Valerie. The Cheetah: Animal Close-Ups. (Illus.). 28p. (ps-3). 1992. pap. 6.95 (*0-88106-425-4*) Charlesbridge Pub.
DuPrau, Jeanne. Adoption: The Facts, Feelings & Issues of a Double Heritage. rev. ed. Steltenpohl, Jane, ed. 128p. (gr. 7 up). 1990. lib. bdg. 12.98 (*0-671-69328-X*, J Messner); lib. bdg. 5.95 (*0-671-69329-8*) S&S Trade.
Dupre, Jean-Paul. The Barron's Junior Fact-Finder: An Illustrated Encyclopedia for Children. (Illus.). 296p. (gr. 2-6). 1989. 19.95 (*0-8120-6072-5*) Barron.
Dupre, Jean-Paul, et al. Enciclopedia Mega-Junior. (SPA., Illus.). 296p. (gr. 1-4). 1993. Repr. of 1989 ed. 19.95 (*970-607-104-0*) CKG Pubs.

Dupre, Judith. The Mouse Bride: A Mayan Folktale. Vanden Broeck, Fabricio, illus. LC 92-15275. (ps-3). 1993. 8.99 (*0-679-83273-4*); PLB 9.99 (*0-679-93273-9*) Knopf Bks Yng Read.
Dupre, Rick. Agassu: Legend of the Leopard King. Dupre, Rick, illus. 40p. (gr. 1-4). 1993. 18.95 (*0-87614-764-3*) Carolrhoda Bks.
—The Wishing Chair. LC 92-38880. 1993. 18.95 (*0-87614-774-0*) Carolrhoda Bks.
Dupree, Herbert & Dupree, Sherry. Busy Bookworm: Good Conduct Book. (Illus.). (gr. k-5). 1980. pap. 2.25 (*0-686-70919-5*) Displays Sch.
Dupree, Sherry, jt. auth. see Dupree, Herbert.
DuPree, Sherry S. What You Always Wanted to Know about the Card Catalog But Was Afraid to Ask. rev. 1988 ed. LC 77-87133. (Illus.). (gr. k-6). 1988. pap. 6.95 (*0-9600962-3-X*) Displays Sch.
Duprez, Martine. Animals That Wear Disguises. Appell-Mertiny, Helene, illus. LC 93-20967. 1994. 14.95 (*0-88106-673-7*) Charlesbridge Pub.
Duque, Sarah. Sally & Fr. Serra. (Illus.). 104p. (gr. 4-8). 1987. 9.95 (*0-89505-504-X*, 21105) Tabor Pub.
DuQuette, Keith. Hotel Animal. DuQuette, Keith, illus. LC 93-14531. 32p. (ps-3). 1994. PLB 13.99 (*0-670-85056-X*) Viking Child Bks.
Duran, Gloria. Malinche: Slave Princess of Cortez. LC 92-31776. (Illus.). 248p. (gr. 6-12). 1992. PLB 17.50 (*0-208-02343-7*, Pub. by Linnet) Shoe String.
Durant. Prize-Winning Science Fair Projects. 1992. pap. 2.95 (*0-590-44019-5*) Scholastic Inc.
Durant, Charlotte, ed. see Ceasor, Ebraska D.
Durant, Charlotte T. Miss Mary McLeod Bethune: The Life of a Beautiful African American Woman. Pye, Ethel, ed. Durant, Charlotte T., illus. 40p. (Orig.). (ps-1). 1992. pap. 4.00 (*0-913678-21-X*) New Day Pr.
Durant, Penny R. Make A Splash! Science Activities with Liquids. Huehnergarth, John, illus. LC 90-34063. 32p. (gr. 1-4). 1991. PLB 12.90 (*0-531-10971-2*) Watts.
—When Heroes Die. LC 91-48267. 144p. (gr. 5 up). 1992. SBE 13.95 (*0-689-31764-6*, Atheneum Child Bk) Macmillan Child Grp.
Durbin, Carolyn. Houston Handbook. 4th ed. Vanderwater, Jeanette, ed. (Illus.). 28p. (gr. 8-12). 1988. pap. 5.00x (*0-939903-01-6*) LWV Houston Ed Fund.
Durbin, Chris. The European Community. LC 93-12513. 1994. write for info. (*0-531-14261-2*) Watts.
Durell, Ann, compiled by. The Diane Goode Book of American Folk Tales & Songs. Goode, Diane, illus. LC 89-1097. 64p. (ps-5). 1989. 14.95 (*0-525-44458-0*, DCB) Dutton Child Bks.
Durell, Ann & Sachs, Marilyn, eds. The Big Book for Peace. LC 89-37595. (Illus.). 128p. (gr. 7-12). 1990. 17.50 (*0-525-44605-2*, DCB) Dutton Child Bks.
Durell, Ann, et al, eds. The Big Book for Our Planet. LC 92-33433. 144p. (gr. k-12). 1993. 17.99 (*0-525-45119-6*, DCB) Dutton Child Bks.
Durepo, Martha. Our Bible. LC 86-17571. (ps). 1987. 5.95 (*0-8054-4175-1*) Broadman.
Durham, Jackie. In Search of Energy. Pennington, Celeste, ed. Stevens, Bill, illus. LC 93-13575. (Illus.). (gr. 4-6). 1984. pap. 1.75 (*0-937170-27-5*) Home Mission.
Durham, Jamie A. Little Airplane. Pittman, Dockery, illus. 32p. (ps). 1989. write for info. Magpie AL.
Durham, Quentin. Minigroup Science. (Illus.). 230p. (gr. 7-12). 1980. pap. 20.00 (*0-87879-244-9*) Acad Therapy.
Durhan, Robert. My Giant Picture Dictionary. (Illus.). 1988. 5.99 (*0-517-65715-5*) Outlet Bk Co.
Durkin, John F. & Newton, Joe. Running to the Top of the Mountain. Cudworth, Chris, illus. 350p. (Orig.). (gr. 9-12). 1988. pap. text ed. 24.95 (*0-9621313-0-X*) J & J Win Edge.
Durkin, Pat. The Kaua'i Guide to Beaches & Water Activities with Safety Tips. rev. ed. Ida, Gerald, et al, illus. 80p. pap. 2.50 (*0-942255-08-9*, G4-2) Magic Fishes Pr.
—The Kaua'i Guide to Beaches, Water Activities & Safety. Kauai County Planning Dept. Staff, illus. 64p. (Orig.). 1988. pap. 2.50 (*0-942255-05-4*, G4) Magic Fishes Pr.
Durkin, Peter, jt. auth. see Ferguson, Virginia.
Durlacher, Ed, ed. The Play Party Book: Singing Games for Children. Bare, Arnold E., illus. 38p. (ps-5). 1945. 9.50 (*0-8159-6505-2*) Devin.
Durnin, Michael. Learn to Play Mozart. (Illus.). 64p. (gr. 5-12). 1993. pap. 8.95 (*0-7460-0964-X*, Usborne) EDC.
Duroska, Lud & Schiffer, Don. Football Rules in Pictures. rev. ed. (Illus.). 80p. 1991. pap. 7.95 (*0-399-51689-1*, Perigee Bks) Putnam Pub Group.

Durr, W., et al. Houghton Mifflin Reading Program. large type ed. Incl. Level B--Bears. 56p. (gr. 1). 1982. 10.44 (*0-317-04440-0*, 4-33310-00); Level C--Balloons. 56p. (gr. 1). 1982. 10.44 (*0-317-04441-9*, 4-33320-00); Level D--Boats. 72p. (gr. 1). 1981. 18.50 (*0-317-04442-7*, J-33330-00); Level B, C, D--Bears, Balloons, Boats Practice Book, 2 vols. 268p. (gr. 1). 1981. 73.00 (*0-317-04443-5*, J-33340-00); Level E--Sunshine. 200p. (gr. 1). 1981. 50.50 (*0-317-04444-3*, J-33350-00); Practice bk. 200p. 55.00 (*0-317-04445-1*, J-33360-00); Level F--Moonbeams. 232p. (gr. 2). 1982. 61.00 (*0-317-04446-X*, J-33370-00); Practice bk., 204p. 56.00 (*0-317-04447-8*, J-33380-00); Level G--Skylights, 2 vols. 290p. (gr. 2). 1981. Set. 81.50 (*0-317-04448-6*, J-33390-00); practice bk., 2 vols., 264p. 63.00 (*0-317-04449-4*, J-33400-00); Level I--Spinners, 2 vols. 390p. (gr. 3). 1981. Set. 81.50 (*0-317-04450-8*, J-33430-00); practice bk., 2 vols., 240p. 58.00 (*0-317-04451-6*, J-33440-00); Level J--Weavers, 2 vols. 394p. (gr. 3). 1982. Set. 95.50 (*0-317-04452-4*, J-33450-00); practice bk., 2 vols., 212p. 59.00 (*0-317-04453-2*, J-33500-00); Level K--Gateways, 3 vols. 594p. (gr. 4). 1981. Set. 151.00 (*0-317-03500-2*, J-33470-00); practice bk., 2 vols., 240p. 59.00 (*0-317-04454-0*, J-33480-00). (gr. 1-6) Am Printing Hse.

Durrell, Dennis, illus. Lady & the Tramp: Pop-up Book. LC 93-71380. 12p. (ps-3). 1994. 11.95 (*1-56282-612-3*) Disney Pr.

Durrell, Gerald. The Fantastic Dinosaur Adventure. Percy, Graham, illus. LC 89-49099. 96p. (gr. 2-5). 1990. pap. 16.95 (*0-671-70871-6*) S&S Trade.
—The Fantastic Flying Journey. (gr. 4). 1991. write for info. (*0-663-56238-4*) Silver Burdett Pr.
—Keeper. West, Keith, illus. LC 90-55612. 32p. (gr. 1-4). 1991. 13.95 (*1-55970-122-6*) Arcade Pub Inc.
—Toby the Tortoise. West, Keith, illus. 32p. (ps-3). 1991. 14.95 (*1-55970-145-5*) Arcade Pub Inc.

Durrell, Julie. Mouse Tails. Durrell, Julie, illus. LC 84-12638. 32p. (ps-1). 1985. 6.95 (*0-517-55592-1*) Crown Bks Yng Read.
—Peek-a-Boo. Bahr, Amy C. & Klimo, Kate, eds. Durrell, Julie, illus. 8p. (ps). 1982. pap. 3.95 (*0-671-45546-X*, Little Simon) S&S Trade.

Durrell, Julie, illus. The Pudgy Book of Farm Animals. 16p. (gr. k). 1984. 2.95 (*0-448-10211-0*, G&D) Putnam Pub Group.
—The Pudgy Book of Toys. 16p. (ps-3). 1983. pap. 2.95 (*0-448-10201-3*, G&D) Putnam Pub Group.

Durrett, Deanne. Organ Transplants. (Illus.). 112p. (gr. 5-8). 1993. PLB 14.95 (*1-56006-137-5*) Lucent Bks.

Durst, Russel K., jt. ed. see Newell, George E.

Durwood, Thomas A. Andrew Johnson: Rebuilding the Union. Gallin, Richard, ed. Steele, Henry, intro. by. (Illus.). 160p. (gr. 4-8). 1990. PLB 18.98 (*0-382-09945-1*); PLB 12.74s.p. (*0-685-47042-3*); pap. 8.95 (*0-382-24054-5*); pap. 5.96s.p. (*0-685-54163-0*) Silver Burdett Pr.
—John C. Calhoun & the Roots of War. (Illus.). 160p. (gr. 5 up). 1990. lib. bdg. 18.99 (*0-382-09936-2*); pap. 8.95 (*0-382-24045-6*) Silver Burdett Pr.

Durwood, Thomas A., et al. The History of the Civil War Series, 10 vols. (Illus.). 1600p. (gr. 5 up). 1990. Set. PLB 189.80 (*0-382-09935-4*); Set. pap. 89.50 (*0-382-24044-8*) Silver Burdett Pr.

Dusseault, Melissa A. The Secrets of the Wee People. 1991. 6.95 (*0-8062-4168-3*) Carlton.

Dutch, R. Roget's Thesaurus of English Words & Phrases, 12 vols. new, rev., large type ed. 2672p. (gr. 7 up). 1968. Repr. of 1962 ed. Set. 668.00 (*0-317-01931-7*, J-22420-00) Am Printing Hse.

Duthie, Dorothy B., ed. see Ford, Beatrice.

Dutro, Jack. Night Light: A Story for Children Afraid of the Dark. Boyle, Kenneth, illus. LC 91-19612. 32p. (ps-4). 1991. 16.95 (*0-945354-37-1*); pap. 6.95 (*0-945354-38-X*) Magination Pr.
—Night Light: A Story for Children Afraid of the Dark. Boyle, Kenneth, illus. LC 92-56873. 1993. PLB 17.26 (*0-8368-0934-3*) Gareth Stevens Inc.

Dutta, S. & Hemalata. Harishchandra. Wheaton, Jaya, illus. (gr. 1-8). 1979. pap. 3.00 (*0-89744-155-9*) Auromere.

Dutton, Bertha P. Southwest Indians, Bk. 2: Hopi, Acoma, Tewa, Zuni. (gr. 1-9). 1992. pap. 3.95 (*0-88388-062-8*) Bellerophon Bks.

Dutton, Bertha P., jt. auth. see Olin, Caroline.

Dutton, Cheryl. Not in Here, Dad! Smith, Wendy, illus. 32p. (ps-2). 1989. 10.95 (*0-8120-6105-5*) Barron.

Dutton, June. Fourth Adventure of the S. S. Happiness Crew: Visit to a Magic Mountain. Hill, Eric, illus. 1983. 5.95 (*0-915696-64-9*) Determined Prods.

Dutton, June & Schulz, Charles M. Snoopy & the Gang Out West. LC 82-71284. (Illus.). 1983. 6.95 (*0-915696-55-X*); pap. 4.95 (*0-915696-82-7*) Determined Prods.

Dutton, Roderic. An Arab Family. LC 85-10272. (Illus.). 32p. (gr. 2-5). 1985. PLB 13.50 (*0-8225-1660-8*) Lerner Pubns.

Dutton, Sandra. The Magic of Myrna C. Waxweather. Clark, Matthew, illus. LC 86-20579. 96p. (gr. 2-5). 1987. SBE 12.95 (*0-689-31273-3*, Atheneum Child Bk) Macmillan Child Grp.
—The Magic of Myrna C. Waxweather. (gr. 2-6). 1990. pap. 2.75 (*0-553-15788-4*, Skylark) Bantam.

Duva, Nicholas, compiled by. Somebody Real. (Illus.). 192p. (Orig.). (gr. 5-12). 1973. 6.95 (*0-912834-01-3*); pap. 3.95 (*0-912834-04-8*) Am Faculty Pr.

Duvall, Jill. The Mohawk. LC 90-21166. (Illus.). 48p. (gr. k-4). 1991. PLB 15.27 (*0-516-01115-4*); pap. 4.95 (*0-516-41115-2*) Childrens.
—The Penobscot. (Illus.). 48p. (gr. k-4). 1993. PLB 16.60 (*0-516-01194-4*) Childrens.
—The Seneca. LC 90-21150. (Illus.). 48p. (gr. k-4). 1991. PLB 15.27 (*0-516-01119-7*); pap. 4.95 (*0-516-41119-5*) Childrens.

Duvall, Jill D. The Cayuga. LC 91-3038. 48p. (gr. k-4). 1991. PLB 15.27 (*0-516-01123-5*); pap. 4.95 (*0-516-41123-3*) Childrens.
—The Oneida. LC 91-8893. 48p. (gr. k-4). 1991. PLB 15.27 (*0-516-01125-1*); pap. 4.95 (*0-516-41125-X*) Childrens.
—The Onondaga. LC 91-8894. 48p. (gr. k-4). 1991. PLB 15.27 (*0-516-01126-X*); pap. 4.95 (*0-516-41126-8*) Childrens.
—The Tuscarora. LC 91-3037. 48p. (gr. k-4). 1991. PLB 15.27 (*0-516-01128-6*); pap. 4.95 (*0-516-41128-4*) Childrens.

Duvall, Shelley. Merry Christmas. 8p. 1992. pap. 11.98 incl. CD (*1-56668-147-2*, 70506-2); pap. 7.98 incl. audio cass. (*1-56668-145-6*, 70406-4) Rincon Child Ent.
—Sweet Dreams. 8p. 1992. pap. 11.98 incl. CD (*1-56668-144-8*, 70505-2); pap. 7.98 incl. audio cass. (*1-56668-142-1*, 70405-4) Rincon Child Ent.

Duvoisin, Roger. Petunia. Duvoisin, Roger, illus. (gr. k-3). 1962. lib. bdg. 9.99 (*0-394-90865-1*) Knopf Bks Yng Read.
—Petunia, Beware! Duvoisin, Roger, illus. (gr. 1-3). 1964. lib. bdg. 12.99 (*0-394-90867-8*) Knopf Bks Yng Read.
—Petunia, Beware! Duvoisin, Roger, illus. LC 72-580009. 32p. (ps-2). 1990. pap. 3.95 (*0-679-80334-3*) Knopf Bks Yng Read.
—Petunia the Silly Goose Stories: Five Read-Aloud Classics. Duvoisin, Roger, illus. LC 86-2783. 160p. (ps-3). 1987. PLB 15.99 (*0-394-98292-4*) Knopf Bks Yng Read.
—Petunia's Christmas. Duvoisin, Roger, illus. (gr. k-3). 1963. lib. bdg. 12.99 (*0-394-90868-6*) Knopf Bks Yng Read.

Duyff, Roberta L. Big Bug Book of Exercise. McKissack, Patricia & McKissack, Fredrick, eds. Bartholomew, illus. LC 87-61656. 24p. (Orig.). (gr. k-1). 1987. spiral bdg. 14.95 (*0-88335-761-5*); pap. text ed. 4.95 (*0-88335-771-2*) Milliken Pub Co.
—The Bread That Grew. McKissack, Patricia & McKissack, Fredrick, eds. Dorenkamp, Michelle, illus. LC 87-61646. 32p. (Orig.). (gr. 1-3). 1987. text ed. 8.95 (*0-88335-725-9*); pap. text ed. 4.95 (*0-88335-745-3*) Milliken Pub Co.
—Smiles for Smiles. McKissack, Patricia & McKissack, Fredrick, eds. Dorenkamp, Michelle, illus. LC 88-60386. 32p. (Orig.). (gr. 1-3). 1988. text ed. 8.95 (*0-88335-780-1*); pap. text ed. 4.95 (*0-88335-792-5*) Milliken Pub Co.

D'Vincent, Cynthia. The Whale Family Book. LC 91-41145. (Illus.). 60p. (gr. 5 up). 1992. pap. 15.95 (*0-88708-148-7*) Picture Bk Studio.

Dvir, Azriel & Mashat, Mazal. My Little Siddur. 68p. 8.95 (*0-915361-87-6*) Modan-Adama Bks.

Dvorah-Leah. Lost in the Zoo on Erev Shabbat. rev. ed. (ps-1). 1987. 8.95 (*0-685-18057-3*); pap. 6.95 (*0-685-18058-1*) Judaica Pr.

Dvorak, David, Jr. A Sea of Grass: The Tallgrass Prairie. Dvorak, David, Jr., illus. LC 93-19507. 32p. (gr. 1-4). 1994. RSBE 14.95 (*0-02-733245-4*, Macmillan Child Bk) Macmillan Child Grp.

Dwiggins, Gwen, jt. auth. see Hughes, Barbara.

Dwight, John A. & Peel, William J. Video Reading Technics, Bks. 1. (gr. 7). 1976. pap. text ed. 8.95 (*0-934902-00-3*); tchr's ed. 15.00 (*0-934902-04-6*) Learn Concepts OH.

Dwight, Laura. We Can Do It! (Illus.). 32p. (ps-4). 1992. 7.95 (*1-56288-301-1*) Checkerboard.

Dwight, Laura, photos by. All My Things. (Illus.). 28p. (ps). 1992. bds. 2.95 (*1-56288-185-X*) Checkerboard.
—Babies All Around. (Illus.). 28p. (ps). 1992. bds. 2.95 (*1-56288-184-1*) Checkerboard.

Dworski, Susan, jt. auth. see Thum, Robert.

Dwyer, Chris. Chile. (Illus.). 128p. (gr. 5 up). 1990. 14.95 (*0-7910-1102-X*) Chelsea Hse.

Dwyer, Christopher. The Dominican Americans. Moynihan, Daniel P., intro. by. (Illus.). 112p. (gr. 5 up). 1991. lib. bdg. 17.95 (*0-87754-872-2*) Chelsea Hse.
—Robert Peary & the Quest for the North Pole. (Illus.). 112p. (gr. 5 up). 1992. lib. bdg. 18.95 (*0-7910-1316-2*); pap. write for info. (*0-7910-1540-8*) Chelsea Hse.

Dwyer, Christopher, jt. auth. see Smith, Alan.

Dwyer, Christopher, Jr. The Small Business Administration. (Illus.). 112p. (gr. 5 up). 1991. 14.95 (*1-55546-122-0*) Chelsea Hse.

Dwyer, Derek & Corby, Jill. More Fun with Science: Practice at Home. Lobban, John, illus. 24p. (Orig.). (gr. 3-5). 1992. pap. 2.95 wkbk. (*0-7214-3240-9*, S9115-3) Ladybird Bks.

Dwyer, Frank. George-Jacques Danton. Schlesinger, Arthur M., Jr., intro. by. (Illus.). 112p. (gr. 5 up). 1987. lib. bdg. 17.95 (*0-87754-519-7*) Chelsea Hse.
—Henry VIII. Schlesinger, Arthur M., Jr., intro. by. (Illus.). 112p. (gr. 5 up). 1988. lib. bdg. 17.95 (*0-87754-530-8*) Chelsea Hse.
—James the First. Schlesinger, Arthur M., Jr., intro. by. (Illus.). 112p. (gr. 5 up). 1988. 17.95 (*1-55546-811-X*) Chelsea Hse.

—John Adams. (Illus.). (gr. 5 up). 1989. 17.95 (*1-55546-801-2*) Chelsea Hse.

Dwyer, Kathleen M. What Do You Mean I Have a Learning Disability? (Illus.). (gr. 5-9). 1991. 14.95 (*0-8027-8102-0*); PLB 15.85 (*0-8027-8103-9*) Walker & Co.

Dwyer, Paulinus, jt. auth. see MacKenthun, Carole.

Dyches, Richard W. & Shaw, Jean M. First Math Dictionary. Czeslaw, illus. LC 91-7527. 104p. (gr. k-4). 1991. 15.95 (*0-531-15238-3*); PLB 15.90 (*0-531-11111-3*) Watts.
—Primer Diccionario de Matematica. Sornat, Czeslaw, illus. (SPA.). 104p. (gr. k-4). 1991. 15.95 (*0-531-15236-7*); PLB 15.90 (*0-531-07926-0*) Watts.

Dyches, Richard W., jt. auth. see Shaw, Jean M.

Dyck, Peter J. Shalom at Last. Neidigh, Sherry, illus. 128p. (Orig.). 1992. pap. 5.95 (*0-8361-3615-2*) Herald Pr.

Dyer, Jane. Moo, Moo Peekaboo. Dyer, Jane, illus. LC 85-61530. (ps). 1986. 3.99 (*0-394-87883-3*) Random Bks Yng Read.

Dyer, Jane, selected by. & illus. Babyland: A Book for Babies. LC 93-4244. 1994. 17.95 (*0-316-19766-1*) Little.

Dyer, Jane, illus. Goldilocks & the Three Bears. 16p. (ps). 1984. 3.95 (*0-448-10213-7*, G&D) Putnam Pub Group.

Dyer, Ruth. Sam's Easy Reader Stories. LC 93-60261. (Illus.). 44p. (ps-3). 1994. pap. 4.95 (*1-55523-614-6*) Winston-Derek.
—Starlights. LC 89-51255. 50p. (gr. k-3). 1992. pap. 5.95 (*1-55523-258-2*) Winston-Derek.

Dyer, T. A. Way of His Own. 1990. pap. 4.80 (*0-395-54969-8*) HM.

Dygard, Thomas J. Backfield Package. LC 92-6315. 208p. (gr. 7 up). 1992. 14.00 (*0-688-11471-7*) Morrow Jr Bks.
—Backfield Package. LC 93-7721. 208p. (gr. 5 up). 1993. pap. 3.99 (*0-14-036348-3*, Puffin) Puffin Bks.
—Forward Pass. LC 89-33427. (Illus.). 192p. (gr. 7 up). 1989. 11.95 (*0-688-07961-X*) Morrow Jr Bks.
—Forward Pass. (gr. 4 up). 1990. pap. 3.99 (*0-14-034562-0*, Puffin) Puffin Bks.
—Game Plan. LC 92-47252. 224p. (gr. 7 up). 1993. 14.00 (*0-688-12007-5*) Morrow Jr Bks.
—Halfback Tough. LC 85-25987. 224p. (gr. 7 up). 1986. 12.95 (*0-688-05925-2*) Morrow Jr Bks.
—Halfback Tough. 224p. (gr. 5 up). 1989. pap. 3.99 (*0-14-034113-7*, Puffin) Puffin Bks.
—Outside Shooter. (Illus.). 192p. (gr. 5 up). 1991. pap. 3.99 (*0-14-034671-6*, Puffin) Puffin Bks.
—Point Spread. (gr. 4-7). 1991. pap. 3.95 (*0-14-034591-4*, Puffin) Puffin Bks.
—Quarterback Walk-On. LC 81-18715. 224p. (gr. 7-9). 1982. 13.65 (*0-688-01065-2*) Morrow Jr Bks.
—Quaterback Walk-On. 224p. (gr. 5 up). 1989. pap. 3.99 (*0-14-034115-3*, Puffin) Puffin Bks.
—Rebound Caper. LC 82-18821. 176p. (gr. 7 up). 1983. 12.95 (*0-688-01707-X*) Morrow Jr Bks.
—Rebound Caper. 176p. (gr. 5 up). 1992. pap. 3.99 (*0-14-034913-8*) Puffin Bks.
—The Rookie Arrives. LC 87-26238. 208p. (gr. 7 up). 1988. 12.95 (*0-688-07598-3*) Morrow Jr Bks.
—The Rookie Arrives. 176p. (gr. 5-9). 1989. pap. 3.95 (*0-14-034112-9*, Puffin) Puffin Bks.
—Running Scared. 192p. (gr. 5 up). 1992. pap. 3.99 (*0-14-034914-6*, Puffin) Puffin Bks.
—Soccer Duel. 224p. (gr. 4 up). 1990. pap. 3.99 (*0-14-034116-1*, Puffin) Puffin Bks.
—Tournament Upstart. LC 83-25039. 208p. (gr. 7 up). 1984. 9.50 (*0-688-02761-X*) Morrow Jr Bks.
—Tournament Upstart. 208p. (gr. 5-9). 1989. pap. 3.99 (*0-14-034114-5*, Puffin) Puffin Bks.
—Wilderness Peril. LC 84-25577. 208p. (gr. 7 up). 1985. 12.95 (*0-688-04146-9*) Morrow Jr Bks.
—Wilderness Peril. 238p. (gr. 5 up). 1991. pap. 3.99 (*0-14-034785-2*, Puffin) Puffin Bks.
—Winning Kicker. 192p. (gr. 4 up). 1990. pap. 3.99 (*0-14-034117-X*, Puffin) Puffin Bks.

Dygert, Janice. Red Horse & the Buffalo Robe Man. Gilliland, Hap, ed. (Illus.). (gr. 4-8). 1978. 1.95 (*0-89992-074-8*) Coun India Ed.

Dyjak, Elisabeth. Bertha's Garden. Wilkins, Janet, illus. LC 93-28594. 1994. write for info. (*0-395-68715-2*) HM.
—I Should Have Listened to Moon. LC 89-26739. 130p. (gr. 4-6). 1990. 13.45 (*0-395-52279-X*) HM.

Dyke, Henry van see Van Dyke, Henry.

Dyke, Henry Van see Van Dyke, Henry.

Dyke, Henry van see Wells, Ruth & Van Dyke, Henry.

Dykes, Tomoko T., tr. see Tsuchiya, Yukio.

Dykstra, Darrell I. Egypt in the Nineteenth Century: The Impact of Europe Upon a Non-Western Society. (Orig.). (gr. 10-12). 1979. pap. text ed. 5.00x (*0-932098-15-0*) UM Ctr MENAS.

Dykstra, Mary A. The Best Color of All. Chandler, Jean, illus. 24p. (ps-k). 1993. 9.00 (*0-307-74816-2*, 64816, Golden Pr) Western Pub.

D'yley, Enid F. Animal Fables & Other Tales Retold: Africa in the New World. LC 87-73226. 40p. (Orig.). (gr. 1-7). 1989. 12.95 (*0-86543-075-6*); pap. 5.95 (*0-86543-076-4*) Africa World.

Dys, Pat & Corbin, Linda. He Obeyed God: A Child's Life of A. B. Simpson. LC 86-71048. 55p. (gr. 1-5). 1986. pap. 3.99 (*0-87509-382-5*) Chr Pubns.

Dys, Pat, jt. auth. see Corbin, Linda.

Dyson, Betty, jt. auth. see Dyson, Clegg.

Dyson, Clegg & Dyson, Betty. Follow Me. 44p. (Orig.). (gr. 3-7). Date not set. pap. 4.99 (*1-884553-15-X*) Discipleshp.
Dyson, John. Westward with Columbus. Marschall, Ken, illus. Christopher, Peter, photos by. LC 90-15566. (Illus.). 64p. (gr. 4-7). 1991. 6.95 (*0-590-43847-6*) Scholastic Inc.
—Westward with Columbus: A Time Quest Book. 64p. 1991. 15.95 (*0-590-43846-8*, Scholastic Hardcover) Scholastic Inc.
Dyson, Sue. Wood. LC 93-216572. 32p. (gr. 3-6). 1993. 13.95 (*1-56847-043-6*) Thomson Lrning.
Dyson, Sue, jt. auth. see Hoare, Stephen.
Dziuba, Mark. Stand Alone Fusion. 32p. pap. 9.95 (*0-88284-542-X*, 4429) Alfred Pub.

E

Eaarl, Archie W., Sr. What Every Prospective College Student Should Know. 85p. (gr. 11-12). 1994. lib. bdg. 25.95 (*1-884169-04-X*); pap. text ed. 13.95 (*1-884169-05-8*) Intl Educ Improve.
Eades, Jo A. A New Salem Primer. (Illus.). 80p. (Orig.). (gr. 5-8). 1989. pap. text ed. 5.95 (*0-685-26274-X*) J A Eades.
Eads, Ed. The Bloody Harlanite, Vol. I. 418p. 1989. 19. 95 (*0-9623752-0-9*) Three E GA.
Eads, Sandra & Post, Beverly. Digging into Logic. (gr. 5-12). 1987. pap. 6.95 (*0-8224-4458-5*) Fearon Teach Aids.
—Logic in the Round. (gr. 5 up). 1989. pap. 8.95 (*0-8224-4206-X*) Fearon Teach Aids.
Eads, Sandra, jt. auth. see Post, Beverly.
Eagan, Andrea B. Why Am I So Miserable If These Are the Best Years of My Life? (gr. 7 up). 1979. pap. 2.95 (*0-380-46136-6*, Flare) Avon.
Eagen, Jane & McGinnis, Jeanne. Our Maryland. (Illus.). 288p. (gr. 4). 1987. 22.00 (*0-685-24530-6*, Peregrine Smith) Gibbs Smith Pub.
Eager, Edward. Half Magic. Bodecker, N. M., illus. LC 54-5153. 217p. (gr. 3-7). 1954. 14.95 (*0-15-233078-X*, HB Juv Bks) HarBrace.
—Half Magic. Treherne, Katie T. & Bodecker, N. M., illus. 192p. (gr. 3-7). 1989. pap. 4.95 (*0-15-233081-X*, Odyssey) HarBrace.
—Knight's Castle. Bodecker, N. M., illus. (gr. 4-6). 16.75 (*0-8446-6232-1*) Peter Smith.
—Knight's Castle. Treherne, Katie T. & Bodecker, N. M., illus. 198p. (gr. 3-7). 1989. pap. 3.95 (*0-15-243105-5*, Odyssey) HarBrace.
—Magic by the Lake. Treherne, Katie T. & Bodecker, N. M., illus. 190p. (gr. 3-7). 1989. pap. 3.95 (*0-15-250044-3*, Odyssey) HarBrace.
—Magic or Not? Bodecker, N. M., illus. (gr. 4-6). 1984. 16.75 (*0-8446-6154-6*) Peter Smith.
—Magic or Not? Treherne, Katie T. & Bodecker, N. M., illus. 197p. (gr. 3-7). 1989. pap. 3.95 (*0-15-251160-1*, Odyssey) HarBrace.
—Seven-Day Magic. (gr. 4-6). 16.75 (*0-8446-6381-6*) Peter Smith.
—Seven-Day Magic. Treherne, Katie T. & Bodecker, N. M., illus. 190p. (gr. 3-7). 1989. pap. 3.95 (*0-15-272916-X*, Odyssey) HarBrace.
—The Time Garden. Bodecker, N. M., illus. (gr. 4-6). 17. 50 (*0-8446-6233-X*) Peter Smith.
—The Time Garden. Treherne, Katie T. & Bodecker, N. M., illus. 193p. (gr. 3-7). 1990. pap. 4.95 (*0-15-288193-X*, Odyssey) HarBrace.
—The Well-Wishers. (gr. 3-7). 17.50 (*0-8446-6382-4*) Peter Smith.
—The Well Wishers. Treherne, Katie T. & Bodecker, N. M., illus. 220p. (gr. 3-7). 1990. pap. 4.95 (*0-15-294994-1*, Odyssey) HarBrace.
Eager, George B. Dating: What to Do...What Not to Do. Philbrook, Diana, illus. 29p. (Orig.). (gr. 6-12). 1993. pap. 3.00x (*1-879224-09-7*) Mailbox.
—Love, Dating & Marriage. Wetmore, Gordon, et al, illus. LC 86-90552. 136p. (Orig.). (gr. 6-12). 1987. pap. 6.95 (*0-9603752-5-2*) Mailbox.
—Love, Dating & Sex: What Teens Want to Know. Philbrook, Diana, illus. 208p. (gr. 7-12). 1989. PLB 14.95 (*0-9603752-9-5*); pap. text ed. 9.95 (*0-9603752-8-7*) Mailbox.
—Peer Pressure: How to Handle It. Philbrook, Diana, illus. 29p. (Orig.). 1993. pap. 3.00x (*1-879224-10-0*) Mailbox.
—Relationships: How to be a Winner! Philbrook, Diana, illus. (Orig.). (gr. 6-12). 1993. pap. 3.00x (*1-879224-08-9*) Mailbox.
—Save Sex. 2nd ed. Philbrook, Diana, illus. 29p. 6-12). 1993. pap. 3.00x (*1-879224-97-6*) Mailbox.
—Understanding Your Sex Drive. Philbrook, Diana, illus. 29p. (Orig.). (gr. 6-12). 1993. pap. 3.00x (*1-879224-05-4*) Mailbox.
—Understanding Your Sex Drive. rev. ed. Philbrook, Diana, illus. 96p. (gr. 6-12). 1993. pap. 5.95 (*1-879224-12-7*) Mailbox.
—What Is Real Love? Philbrook, Diana, illus. (Orig.). (gr. 6-12). 1993. pap. 3.00x (*1-879224-06-2*) Mailbox.
Eagle, Ellen. Gypsy's Cleaning Day. Eagle, Ellen, illus. LC 89-34315. 32p. (gr. ps up). 1990. 13.95 (*0-688-07391-3*); PLB 13.88 (*0-688-07392-1*, Morrow Jr Bks) Morrow Jr Bks.

Eagles, Douglas A. Nutritional Diseases. LC 87-8124. (Illus.). (gr. 4-8). 1987. PLB 10.90 (*0-531-10391-9*) Watts.
Eakin, Ed, ed. see Kerr, Rita.
Eakin, Ed, ed. see Wheatly, Mark.
Eakin, Ed, ed. see Zappler, Liz.
Eakin, Edwin M., ed. see Eytcheson, Pat.
Eakin, Edwin M., ed. see Ferguson, Joe.
Eakin, Edwin M., ed. see Grimmer, Glenna.
Eakin, Edwin M., ed. see Kerr, Rita.
Eakin, Edwin M., ed. see Munson, Sammye.
Eakin, Edwin M., ed. see Richardson, Jean.
Eakin, Edwin M., ed. see Shefelman, Janice J.
Eakin, Edwin M., ed. see Teague, Wells.
Eakin, Edwin M., ed. see Townsend, Tom.
Eames, Marion, ed. The Dark Land. 59p. 1991. pap. 23. 00x (*0-86383-741-7*, Pub. by Gomer Pr UK) St Mut.
Eannace, Maryrose. The Pizza Problem: Democracy in Action. 70p. (Orig.). (gr. 6-10). 1990. pap. text ed. 8. 75x (*0-936826-35-5*) PS Assocs Croton.
Earle, Ann. Bats: Let's Read & Find Out About Science Ser. Cole, Henry, illus. LC 93-11052. (gr. 4 up). 1994. 15.00 (*0-06-023479-2*); PLB 14.89 (*0-06-023480-6*) HarpC Child Bks.
Earle, Vana. Honesty. (Illus.). 64p. (gr. 7-12,RL 4-6). 1990. 13.95 (*0-8239-1109-8*) Rosen Group.
Earley, Lawrence S., intro. by. North Carolina Wild Places: A Closer Look. Runyon, Anne & Brown, Jim, illus. LC 92-81998. (Orig.). (gr. 8 up). 1993. pap. 8.50 (*0-9628949-1-5*) NC Wildlife.
Early, Margaret, retold by. & illus. William Tell. 32p. 1991. 17.95 (*0-8109-3854-5*) Abrams.
Early, Theresa S. New Mexico. LC 92-13364. 1993. PLB 17.50 (*0-8225-2748-0*) Lerner Pubns.
Earring, Monica F., et al. Prairie Legends. Robinson, Pat, illus. (gr. 6-9). 1978. 1.95 (*0-89992-069-1*) Coun India Ed.
Earth Works Project Staff. Fifty Simple Things You Can Do to Save the Earth. (gr. 9 up). 1990. pap. 4.95 (*0-929634-06-3*) Grnleaf Pubs.
Earthbooks, Inc. Staff. The National Wildlife Federation's Book of Dinosaurs & Other Pre-Historic Animals. Aaestas, Ken, illus. 64p. (Orig.). (gr. 4). 1991. pap. 5.95 (*1-877731-16-1*) Earthbooks Inc.
—National Wildlife Federation's Book of Endangered Species. Maestis, Ken, illus. 64p. (Orig.). (gr. 4-6). 1991. pap. 5.95 (*1-877731-17-X*) Earthbooks Inc.
Earthbound Environmental Creations, Inc. Staff. Rescue the Reef! A Coloring-Activities Book. Miller, Susan L., illus. Stec, Ruth E., intro. by. (Illus.). 40p. (ps-4). 1993. pap. text ed. write for info. (*0-9632284-3-9*) R M S Pub.
Earthbound Environmental Creations Staff. Protecting Forest Habitat: A Coloring-Activities Book. 40p. (ps-4). 1992. pap. write for info. (*0-9632284-1-2*) R M S Pub.
—Saving the Sea Creatures: A Coloring-Activities Book. 40p. (ps-4). 1992. pap. text ed. write for info. (*0-9632284-2-0*) R M S Pub.
Earthworks Group Staff. Fifty Simple Things Kids Can Do to Recycle. (gr. 2-12). 1993. pap. 5.95 (*1-879682-00-1*) Earth Works.
—Kid Heroes of the Environment: Simple Things Real Kids Are Doing to Save the Earth. (gr. 3-12). 1991. pap. 4.95 (*1-879682-12-5*) Earth Works.
Eason, Lowell E. Thou Art a Wonderful God. (Illus.). (gr. k-6). 1957. visualized song 5.99 (*3-90117-006-5*) CEF Press.
Easson, Roger, ed. see Weiss, Clarence B.
Easson, Roger R., ed. see Awiakta, Marilou.
Easson, Roger R., ed. see Jones, Margaret W.
East, Ben. Frozen Terror. LC 79-53747. (Illus.). 48p. (gr. 3-4). 1980. RSBE 9.95 (*0-89686-049-3*, Crestwood Hse) Macmillan Child Grp.
East, Ben & Nentl, Jerolyn. Trapped in Devil's Hole. Dahl, Jack, illus. LC 79-53773. (gr. 3 up). 1989. RSBE o.p. 9.95 (*0-89686-048-5*, Crestwood Hse) Macmillan Child Grp.
East, Helen, compiled by. The Singing Sack. Currie, Mary, illus. 80p. (gr. 2 up). 16.95 (*0-7136-3115-5*, Pub. by A&C Black UK) Talman.
Easterling, Bill. Prize in the Snow. Owens, Mary B., illus. LC 92-23411. 1993. 15.95 (*0-316-22489-8*) Little.
Eastern, Anne G. The Picolinis. 160p. (Orig.). (gr. 2-5). 1988. pap. 2.75 (*0-553-15566-0*, Skylark) Bantam.
Eastman, Charles A. Indian Boyhood. Blumenschein, E. L., illus. LC 68-58282. (gr. 3-7). 4.95 (*0-486-22037-0*) Dover.
—Indian Boyhood. (Illus.). (gr. 4-9). 16.25 (*0-8446-0085-5*) Peter Smith.
Eastman, David. I Can Read About Bees & Wasps. LC 78-57373. (Illus.). (gr. 2-5). 1979. pap. 1.95 (*0-89375-203-7*) Troll Assocs.
—I Can Read About My Own Body. LC 72-96958. (Illus.). (gr. 2-4). 1973. pap. 1.95 (*0-89375-057-3*) Troll Assocs.
—I Can Read About Prehistoric Animals. Nodel, Norman, illus. LC 76-54492. (gr. 2-4). 1977. pap. 1.95 (*0-89375-039-5*) Troll Assocs.
—Peter & the Wolf. Atkinson, Allen, illus. LC 87-11275. 32p. (gr. k-3). 1988. PLB 9.79 (*0-8167-1057-0*); pap. text ed. 1.95 (*0-8167-1058-9*) Troll Assocs.
—The Sorcerer's Apprentice. Jones, John, illus. LC 87-13767. 32p. (gr. k-4). 1988. PLB 9.79 (*0-8167-1067-8*); pap. text ed. 1.95 (*0-8167-1068-6*) Troll Assocs.

—Story of Dinosaurs. LC 81-11363. PLB 11.59 (*0-89375-648-2*); pap. 2.95 (*0-89375-649-0*) Troll Assocs.
—What Is a Fish? Sweat, Lynn, illus. LC 81-11373. 32p. (gr. k-2). 1982. lib. bdg. 11.59 (*0-89375-660-1*); pap. text ed. 2.95 (*0-89375-661-X*) Troll Assocs.
Eastman, David, adapted by. Aladdin & the Wonderful Lamp. Waldman, Bryna, illus. LC 87-13756. 32p. (gr. 1-4). 1988. PLB 9.79 (*0-8167-1073-2*); pap. text ed. 1.95 (*0-8167-1074-0*) Troll Assocs.
—Sherlock Holmes: The Adventure of the Empty House. Eitzen, Allan, illus. LC 81-11673. 32p. (gr. 5-9). 1982. PLB 10.79 (*0-89375-616-4*); pap. 2.95 (*0-89375-617-2*) Troll Assocs.
—Sherlock Holmes: The Adventure of the Speckled Band. Eitzen, David, illus. LC 81-11694. 32p. (gr. 5-9). 1982. PLB 10.79 (*0-89375-618-0*); pap. 2.95 (*0-89375-619-9*); cassettes avail. Troll Assocs.
—Sherlock Holmes: The Final Problem. Eitzen, Allan, illus. LC 81-11609. 32p. (gr. 5-9). 1982. PLB 10.79 (*0-89375-612-1*); pap. 2.95 (*0-89375-613-X*) Troll Assocs.
—Sherlock Holmes: The Red-Headed League. Eitzen, Allan, illus. LC 81-11619. 32p. (gr. 5-9). 1982. PLB 10.79 (*0-89375-614-8*); pap. 2.95 (*0-89375-615-6*) Troll Assocs.
Eastman, David, ed. see Williams, Margery.
Eastman, Elizabeth. Fly Beyond the Mountain. Large, Hazel, illus. ii, 18p. (Orig.). (gr. k-4). 1985. pap. 1.49 (*0-9615959-0-6*) JAARS Inc.
Eastman, Kevin & Laird, Peter. Teenage Mutant Ninja Turtles. Dooney, Michael, illus. (gr. 2-6). 1989. bk. & cassette 5.95 (*0-394-84169-7*) Random Bks Yng Read.
—Teenage Mutant Ninja Turtles in Intergalactic Wrestling & Other Adventures. Eastman, Kevin & Laird, Peter, illus. 96p. (Orig.). (gr. 2-8). 1991. pap. 6.95 incls. cassette (*0-679-81747-6*) Random Bks Yng Read.
Eastman Kodak Company Staff, ed. Hot Shots: AC-210. LC 91-71095. 48p. (Orig.). (gr. 7-12). text ed. 2.00 (*0-87985-745-5*) Eastman Kodak.
Eastman, P. D. Are You My Mother? (ps-1). 1986. pap. 6.95 incl. cassette (*0-394-88325-X*) Random Bks Yng Read.
—Are You My Mother? - Eres Tu Mi Mama? Eastman, P. D., illus. (ENG & SPA.). 64p. (ps-3). 1993. incl. cass. 6.95 (*0-679-84430-9*) Random Bks Yng Read.
—Corre, Perro, Corre! Mlawer, Teresa, tr. (Illus.). 64p. (gr. 1-2). 1992. 8.95 (*1-880507-02-1*) Lectorum Pubns.
—Flap Your Wings. (Illus.). 64p. 1991. pap. 2.99 incl. cass. (*0-517-05445-0*) Outlet Bk Co.
—Go, Dog, Go! (ps-1). 1986. pap. 6.95 incl. cassette (*0-394-88328-4*) Random Bks Yng Read.
—Perro Grande...Perro Pequeno: (Big Dog...Little Dog) De Cuenca, Pilar & Alvarez, Ines, trs. Eastman, P. D., illus. LC 81-12070. (SPA.). 32p. (ps-3). 1982. lib. bdg. 5.99 (*0-394-95142-5*); pap. 2.25 (*0-394-85142-0*) Random Bks Yng Read.
Eastman, P. D., jt. tr. see Rivera, Carlos.
Eastman, Patricia. Sometimes Things Change. LC 83-10090. (Illus.). 32p. (ps-2). 1983. PLB 11.93 (*0-516-02044-7*); pap. 2.95 (*0-516-42044-5*) Childrens.
—Sometimes Things Change Big Book. 32p. (ps-2). 1988. PLB 30.60 (*0-516-49509-7*) Childrens.
—A Veces las Cosas Cambian-Libro Grande: Sometimes Things Change-Big Book. (Illus.). 32p. (ps-2). 1988. PLB 30.60 (*0-516-59509-1*) Childrens.
—A Veces las Cosas Cambian (Sometimes Things Change) Fleishman, Seymour, illus. LC 83-10090. (SPA.). 32p. (ps-2). 1988. PLB 11.93 (*0-516-32044-0*); pap. 2.95 (*0-516-52044-4*) Childrens.
Eastman, Philip D. The Alphabet Book. Eastman, Philip D., illus. LC 73-16859. 32p. (ps-3). 1974. pap. 2.25 (*0-394-82818-6*) Random Bks Yng Read.
—Are You My Mother? LC 60-13495. (Illus.). 64p. (gr. 1-2). 1960. 6.95 (*0-394-80018-4*); lib. bdg. 7.99 (*0-394-90018-9*) Beginner.
—Best Nest. Eastman, Philip D., illus. LC 68-28459. 72p. (gr. k-3). 1968. 6.95 (*0-394-80051-6*); lib. bdg. 7.99 (*0-394-90051-0*) Beginner.
—Big Dog, Little Dog: A Bedtime Story. (Illus.). (ps-1). 1973. pap. 2.25 (*0-394-82669-8*) Random Bks Yng Read.
—Cat in the Hat Beginner Book Dictionary. LC 64-1157. (Illus.). 144p. (gr. k-6). 1984. 8.95 (*0-394-81009-0*); lib. bdg. 9.99 (*0-394-91009-5*) Random Bks Yng Read.
—The Cat in the Hat Beginner Book Dictionary in French & English. LC 65-22650. (Illus.). 144p. (gr. 2-3). 1965. 15.95 (*0-394-81063-5*) Beginner.
—Cat in the Hat Beginner Book Dictionary in Spanish & English. LC 66-10688. (SPA & ENG., Illus.). 144p. (gr. k-3). 1966. 16.00 (*0-394-81542-4*) Beginner.
—Flap Your Wings. Eastman, P. D., illus. 32p. (ps-1). 1985. pap. 4.95 incl. cassette (*0-394-87655-5*) Random Bks Yng Read.
—Go, Dog, Go. LC 61-7069. (Illus.). 72p. (gr. 1-3). 1966. 6.95 (*0-394-80020-6*); lib. bdg. 7.99 (*0-394-90020-0*) Random Bks Yng Read.
—Sam & the Firefly. LC 58-11966. (Illus.). 72p. (gr. 1-2). 1958. 6.95 (*0-394-80006-0*); lib. bdg. 7.99 (*0-394-90006-5*) Beginner.
Eastman, Philip D., jt. auth. see McKie, Roy.
Easton, Emily, ed. see Brown, Gene.
Easton, Emily, ed. see Dunnan, Nancy.
Easton, Emily, ed. see Odijk, Pamela.
Easton, Emily, ed. see Shuker, Nancy.
Easton, Patricia H. Rebel's Choice. 153p. (gr. 7 up). 1989. 14.95 (*0-15-200571-4*, Gulliver Bks) HarBrace.

—Stable Girl: Working for the Family. Ferguson, Herb, illus. 44p. (gr. 1-7). 1991. 18.95 (0-15-278340-7) HarBrace.

—Summer's Chance. LC 87-17728. 150p. (gr. 7 up). 1988. 13.95 (0-15-200591-9, Gulliver Bks) HarBrace.

—Summer's Chance. LC (gr. 4-7). 1992. pap. 4.95 (0-15-282493-6) HarBrace.

Easton, Samantha. Beauty & the Beast. Sanderson, Ruth, illus. 32p. (ps-3). 1992. 6.95 (0-8362-4919-4) Andrews & McMeel.

Easton, Samantha, retold by. Cinderella. Bywaters, Lynn, illus. 32p. (ps-3). 1992. 6.95 (0-8362-4905-4) Andrews & McMeel.

—Peter & the Wolf. Bernal, Richard, illus. 32p. (ps-3). 1992. 6.95 (0-8362-4921-6) Andrews & McMeel.

—Puss in Boots. Dieneman, Debbie, illus. (ps-3). 1992. 6.95 (0-8362-4932-1) Andrews & McMeel.

—Sleeping Beauty. Bywaters, Lynn, illus. 32p. (ps-3). 1992. 6.95 (0-8362-4915-1) Andrews & McMeel.

Easton, Samantha, retold by see Andersen, Hans Christian.

Easton, Samantha, retold by see Grimm, Jacob & Grimm, Wilhelm K.

Easton-Wickham, Randi, jt. auth. see Spinal-Robinson, Phyllis.

Eastwick, Ivy O. In & Out the Windows: Happy Poems for Children. Barth, Gillian, illus. Swinger, Marlys. LC 73-90841. (Illus.). 80p. (ps-3). 1969. 8.00 (0-87486-007-5) Plough.

Easy, Brenda A. How Hope Grew. (Illus.). 16p. (gr. 1-6). 1994. saddle-stitched 7.95 (0-8059-3456-1) Dorrance.

Eaton, Joi, jt. auth. see George, J. Carroll.

Eaton, Seymour. The Roosevelt Bears Go to Washington. Campbell, V. Floyd & Culver, R. K., illus. 192p. (gr. 6 up). 1981. pap. 4.50 (0-486-24163-7) Dover.

—The Roosevelt Bears: Their Travels & Adventures. Campbell, V. Floyd, illus. 192p. (gr. 1 up). 1979. pap. 5.95 (0-486-23819-9) Dover.

Eavey, Louise. A Child's Shining Pathway. Murphy, Emmy L., illus. (ps-1). 1976. pap. 1.95 (0-915374-08-0, 08-0) Rapids Christian.

—Happiness Rhymes for Children. Murphy, Emmy L., illus. (ps-1). 1969. pap. 1.95 (0-915374-09-9, 09-0) Rapids Christian.

Ebeling, Jean. Waldo, the Goat Dog. Roberts, Melissa, ed. Arlitt, Nancy, illus. 48p. (gr. 4-7). 1987. 8.95 (0-89015-588-7, Pub. by Panda Bks) Eakin-Sunbelt.

Eberhardt, Lorraine, jt. auth. see Sanborn, Laura.

Eberle, Bob. Imagin-Action. (Illus.). 20p. (Orig.). (gr. 4-12). 1984. 4.50 (0-88047-048-8, 8414) DOK Pubs.

—Warm-Up to Creativity. Weber, June Kern, illus. 64p. (gr. 5 up). 1985. wkbk. 7.95 (0-86653-275-7, GA 667) Good Apple.

Eberle, Irmengarde. Picture Stories for Children. (gr. k-6). 1988. pap. 2.95 (0-440-40031-7, YB) Dell.

Eberle, Jean F. The Incredible Owen Girls. (gr. 7 up). 1977. pap. 4.50 (0-932114-00-8) Boars Head.

Ebersapacher, Margy, ed. see Zeplin, Zeno & Jones, Judy.

Eberspacher, Jeff, ed. see Brown, Bernice.

Eberts, Marjorie & Gisler, Margaret. Careers for Good Samaritans: And Other Humanitarian Types. LC 90-50724. 160p. (Illus.). (gr. 7 up). 1991. pap. 8.95 (0-8442-8126-3, VGM Career Bks) NTC Pub Grp.

—Pancakes, Crackers & Pizza: A Book of Shapes. Hayes, Steven, illus. LC 84-7699. 32p. (ps-2). 1984. lib. bdg. 11.93 (0-516-02063-3); pap. 2.95 (0-516-42063-1) Childrens.

Eble, Diane. Personal Best. 160p. 1991. pap. 7.99 (0-310-71141-X, Campus Life) Zondervan.

Ebner, Adeline R. see Great Aunt Adeline, pseud.

Ebo, Runett N. A Brand New Flavor. Byrd, N. Kalomo, illus. 28p. (Orig.). (gr. 9-12). 1993. pap. 8.00 (1-883753-02-3) Jwand Ent.

Ebon, Martin. Nikita Khrushchev. (Illus.). 112p. (gr. 5 up). 1986. lib. bdg. 17.95 (0-87754-562-6) Chelsea Hse.

Eccles, Anne. Colorado Activity & Coloring Book. Eccles, Anne, illus. 32p. (ps-8). 1986. pap. 2.95 (0-9618555-0-9) Anne M Eccles.

Eccles, Anne M. New Mexico Activity & Coloring Book. (Illus.). 32p. (ps-8). 1987. activity & coloring book 2.95 (0-9618555-1-7) Anne M Eccles.

—United States Activity & Coloring Book. Eccles, Anne M., illus. 36p. (ps-8). 1992. activity/coloring bk. 3.95 (0-9618555-2-5) Anne M Eccles.

Eccles, Jane. Maxwell's Birthday. LC 91-16290. (Illus.). 32p. (ps-3). 1992. 14.00 (0-688-11036-3, Tambourine Bks); PLB 13.93 (0-688-11037-1, Tambourine Bks) Morrow.

Echewa, T. O. How Tables Came to Umu Madu. LC 88-83368. (Illus.). 90p. (gr. 5 up). 1993. 19.95 (0-86543-127-2); pap. 7.95 (0-86543-128-0) Africa World.

Echewa, T. Obinkaram. The Ancestor Tree. Hale, Christy, illus. Date not set. write for info. (0-525-67467-5, Lodestar Bks) Dutton Child Bks.

Echo-Hawk, Roger C. & Echo-Hawk, Walter R. Battlefields & Burial Grounds: The Indian Struggle to Protect Ancestral Graves & Human Remains in the United States. LC 92-39893. 1993. 19.95 (0-8225-2663-8) Lerner Pubns.

Echo-Hawk, Walter R., jt. auth. see Echo-Hawk, Roger C.

Echols, Jean C. Animal Defenses. Bergman, Lincoln & Fairwell, Kay, eds. Bevilacqua, Carol, illus. Barrett, Reginald & Craig, Rose, photos by. (Illus.). 27p. (Orig.). (ps-k). 1987. pap. 7.50 (0-912511-09-5) Lawrence Science.

—Buzzing a Hive. Bergman, Lincoln & Fairwell, Kay, eds. Baker, Lisa H., illus. Curtis, Elizabeth, et al, photos by. (Illus.). 97p. (Orig.). (gr. 1-3). 1987. pap. 12.00 (0-912511-12-5) Lawrence Science.

—Hide a Butterfly. Bergman, Lincoln & Fairwell, Kay, eds. Baker, Lisa H. & Klofkorn, Lisa, illus. Callaway, Jane, et al, photos by. 28p. (Orig.). (gr. 1-3). 1986. pap. 7.50 (0-912511-23-0) Lawrence Science.

Ecke, Wolfgang. The Bank Holdup. Rettich, Rolf & Langenfass, Hansjorg, illus. 144p. (gr. 3-7). 1985. pap. 5.95 (0-13-056474-5) P-H.

—The Castle of the Red Gorillas. Rettich, Rolf, illus. LC 82-23122. 120p. (gr. 5-9). 1983. 9.95 (0-13-120360-6) P-H.

—The Castle of the Red Gorillas. Rettich, Rolf, illus. 120p. (gr. 5-9). 1986. pap. 5.95 (0-13-120387-8) P-H.

—The Face at the Window. Ecke, Wolfgang, illus. LC 79-15628. (gr. 5-9). 1979. 9.95 (0-13-299115-2) P-H.

—The Midnight Chess Game. Rettich, Rolf, illus. LC 84-26564. 144p. (gr. 5 up). 1985. 10.95 (0-13-582826-0) P-H.

Eckert, Allan W. Blue Jacket: War Chief of Shawnees. LC 69-10656. 177p. (gr. 7 up). 1983. pap. 6.95 (0-913428-36-1) Landfall Pr.

—Incident at Hawk's Hill. Schoenherr, John, illus. 173p. (gr. 7 up). 1971. 15.95 (0-316-20866-3) Little.

Eckhart, Mary L. Columbus' Dictionary. 100p. (Orig.). (gr. 5-10). 1992. pap. 11.95 (0-8283-1993-6) Branden Pub Co.

Eckhouse, Morris. Bob Feller. (Illus.). 64p. (gr. 3 up). 1990. 14.95 (0-7910-1174-7) Chelsea Hse.

Eckles, Melita Z. The Horse That Blew Up. LC 89-52188. (Illus.). 35p. (gr. 2-5). 1990. pap. 4.95 (1-55523-319-8) Winston-Derek.

Eckstein, Joan & Gleit, Joyce. The Best Joke Book for Kids, No. 1. Behr, J., illus. 48p. (gr. 7-12). 1977. pap. 2.99 (0-380-01734-2, Camelot) Avon.

—The Best Joke Book for Kids, No. 2. Kohl, Joe, illus. 64p. (gr. 3 up). 1987. pap. 2.99 (0-380-75209-3, Camelot) Avon.

—The Best Joke Book for Kids, No. 3. 64p. 1990. pap. 2.99 (0-380-75872-5, Camelot) Avon.

—The Best Joke Book for Kids, No. 4. 64p. (Orig.). 1991. pap. 2.95 (0-380-76263-3, Camelot) Avon.

—Fun in the Kitchen. rev. ed. 160p. 1990. pap. 2.95 (0-380-75919-5, Camelot) Avon.

—Fun with Making Things. 160p. 1991. pap. 2.99 (0-380-76213-7, Camelot) Avon.

Eckstein, Maxwell, ed. Let Us Have Music for Piano: Seventy-Four Famous Melodies, Vol. 2. 111p. pap. 9.95 (0-8258-0048-X, 03127) Fischer Inc NY.

—Let Us Have Music for Piano: Seventy-Four Melodies, Vol. 1. 112p. pap. 9.95 (0-8258-0047-1, 02942) Fischer Inc NY.

Eco, Umberto. The Bomb & the General. Weaver, William, tr. Carmi, Eugenio, illus. 40p. (gr. up). 1989. 12.95 (0-15-209700-7) HarBrace.

—The Three Astronauts. Carmi, Eugenio, illus. (gr. 1 up). 1989. 12.95 (0-15-286383-4, HB Juv Bks) HarBrace.

Economos, Chris. Let's Take the Bus. (Illus.). 32p. (gr. 1-4). 1989. PLB 15.96 (0-8172-3500-0); pap. 3.95 (0-8114-6702-3) Raintree Steck-V.

—The New Kid. (Illus.). 32p. (gr. 1-4). 1989. PLB 15.96 (0-8172-3512-4); pap. 3.95 (0-8114-6715-5) Raintree Steck-V.

Edades, Jean. An Animal ABC. Garibay, U. N., illus. (gr. 3-5). 1979. pap. 3.50 (0-686-25221-7, Pub. by New Day Pub PI) Cellar.

Edades, Jean, jt. auth. see Hashimoto, Yasuko.

EDC Staff. Language of Numbers: Seeing & Thinking Mathematically in Middle School. Date not set. pap. text ed. write for info. (0-435-08349-X) Heinemann.

Edeen, Susan & Flatt, Carol. Instant Graphics. LC 84-60319. 1984. pap. 16.95 (0-8224-3821-6) Fearon Teach Aids.

Edel, Leon, ed. see James, Henry.

Edelheit, Jami, jt. auth. see Wonders, Allison.

Edelman, Elaine. I Love My Baby Sister: Most of the Time. Watson, Wendy, illus. LC 85-574. 24p. (ps-3). 1985. pap. 3.95 (0-14-050547-4, Puffin) Puffin Bks.

Edelman, Heinz, illus. Prince Ring: Icelandic Fairy Tale. 32p. (gr. 6 up). 1983. PLB 13.95 s.p. (0-87191-951-6) Creative Ed.

Edelman, Lily. Sukkah & the Big Wind. Kessler, Leonard, illus. (gr. k-2). 1956. 5.95 (0-8381-0716-8) United Syn Bk.

Edelson, Ed. Clean Air. (Illus.). (gr. 5 up) 1992. lib. bdg. 19.95 (0-7910-1582-3) Chelsea Hse.

Edelson, Edward. Aging. (Illus.). 112p. (gr. 6-12). 1991. 18.95 (0-7910-0035-4) Chelsea Hse.

—Allergies. Koop, C. Everett, intro. by. (Illus.). 96p. (gr. 6-12). 1989. 18.95 (0-7910-0055-9); pap. 9.95 (0-7910-0482-1) Chelsea Hse.

—Genetics & Heredity. (Illus.). 112p. (gr. 6-12). 1991. 18.95 (0-7910-0018-4) Chelsea Hse.

—The Immune System. (Illus.). 104p. (gr. 6-12). 1990. 18.95 (0-7910-0021-4) Chelsea Hse.

—Nervous System. (Illus.). 112p. (gr. 6-12). 1989. 18.95 (0-7910-0023-0) Chelsea Hse.

—Sleep. (Illus.). 112p. (gr. 6-12). 1992. lib. bdg. 18.95 (0-7910-0092-3) Chelsea Hse.

—Sports Medicine. (Illus.). 112p. (gr. 6-12). 1988. 18.95 (0-7910-0030-3); pap. 9.95 (0-7910-0470-8) Chelsea Hse.

Edelstein, Terese, tr. see Vos, Ida.

Eden, Cooper, intro. by. Goldilocks. abr. ed. (Illus.). 48p. (gr. 9-12). 1991. 14.95 (0-88138-135-7, Green Tiger) S&S Trade.

Eden Toys Staff, ed. Toys & Designs from the World of Beatrix Potter. Menchini, Pat, et al. (Illus.). 128p. 1992. 18.00 (0-7232-4005-1) Warne.

Edens, Cooper. Caretakers of Wonder. Edens, Cooper, illus. LC 91-24035. 40p. (gr. 3 up). 1991. 11.95 (0-671-75193-X, Green Tiger) S&S Trade.

—Caretakers of Wonder. 1987. pap. 4.95 (0-671-97231-6, Green Tiger) S&S Trade.

—Day & Night & Other Dreams. LC 91-3977. (Illus.). 1991. incl. cassette 19.95 (0-671-75590-0, Green Tiger) S&S Trade.

—Hansel & Gretel. (Illus.). 48p. (gr. 9-12). 1991. 14.95 (0-88138-154-3, Green Tiger) S&S Trade.

—Hugh's Hues. (Illus.). 1991. pap. 5.95 (0-88138-108-X, Green Tiger) S&S Trade.

—If You're Afraid of the Dark, Remember the Night Rainbow. Edens, Cooper, illus. LC 91-15823. 1991. 11.95 (0-671-74952-8, Green Tiger) S&S Trade.

—If You're Afraid of the Dark, Remember the Night Rainbow. 2nd, smaller ed. (Illus.). 40p. (gr. 9-12). 1991. pap. 4.95 (0-671-76053-X, Green Tiger) S&S Trade.

—Jack & the Beanstalk. (Illus.). 48p. (gr. 9-12). 1991. 14.95 (0-88138-139-X, Green Tiger) S&S Trade.

—Nineteen Hats, Ten Teacups, an Empty Birdcage, & the Art of Longing. LC 91-25277. (Illus.). 40p. 1992. signed & numbered 20.00 (0-671-75592-7, Green Tiger); pap. 8.00 (0-671-74968-4, Green Tiger) S&S Trade.

—Now Is the Moon's Eyebrow. (Orig.). (gr. 7-12). 1991. pap. 4.95 (0-88138-070-9, Green Tiger) S&S Trade.

—A Present for Rose. Hashimoto, Molly, illus. 32p. (gr. 4 up). 1993. 15.95 (0-912365-89-7) Sasquatch Bks.

—Santa Cow Island Vacation. Lane, Daniel, illus. LC 93-30899. 1994. write for info. (0-671-88319-4, Green Tiger) S&S Trade.

—Santa Cows. Lane, Daniel, illus. LC 91-57. 40p. (gr. 2 up). 1991. jacketed, reinforced bdg. 14.00 (0-671-74863-7, Green Tiger) S&S Trade.

—The Starcleaner Reunion. Edens, Cooper, illus. 1991. (Green Tiger); pap. 8.95 (0-671-74969-2) S&S Trade.

—The Story Cloud. Grant, Kenneth L., illus. LC 91-13315. 48p. (ps-1). 1991. jacketed, reinforced bdg. 16.00 (0-671-74823-8, Green Tiger) S&S Trade.

—Three Princesses: The Ultimate Illustrated Edition. (Illus.). (ps-3). 1991. 22.50 (0-553-07368-0) Bantam.

—With Secret Friends. LC 91-23642. (Illus.). 48p. (gr. 7-12). 1992. signed & numbered 20.00 (0-671-75593-5, Green Tiger); pap. 8.00 (0-671-74970-6, Green Tiger) S&S Trade.

—The Wonderful Counting Clock. Kimball, Katherine, illus. LC 93-14404. 1994. 14.00 (0-671-88334-8, Green Tiger) S&S Trade.

Edens, Cooper & Day, Alexandra. Children of Wonder. 14p. (Orig.). (ps-2). 1991. pap. 3.95 (0-88138-083-0, Green Tiger) S&S Trade.

Edens, Cooper, ed. & intro. by. Beauty & the Beast. abr. ed. LC 88-81988. (Illus.). 48p. (gr. 9-12). 1991. 14.95 (0-88138-115-2, Green Tiger) S&S Trade.

Edens, Cooper, compiled by. The Glorious ABC. LC 90-30566. (Illus.). 40p. 1990. SBE 15.95 (0-689-31605-4, Atheneum Child Bk) Macmillan Child Grp.

Edens, Cooper, selected by. The Glorious Mother Goose. LC 87-35491. (Illus.). 96p. 1988. SBE 15.95 (0-689-31434-5, Atheneum Child Bk) Macmillan Child Grp.

Edens, Cooper, intro. by. Little Red Riding Hood. (Illus.). 48p. (gr. 9-12). 1991. 14.95 (0-88138-128-4, Green Tiger) S&S Trade.

Edens, Cooper & Darling, Harold, eds. Favorite Fairy Tales: A Classic Illustrated Edition. Rackham, Arthur, et al, illus. 128p. (ps up). 1991. 16.95 (0-87701-848-0) Chronicle Bks.

Edens, Cooper, compiled by see Carroll, Lewis.

Edens, David. The Changing Me. 48p. (gr. 4-6). 1991. pap. 9.95 (0-8054-4411-4) Broadman.

Eder, Enelle G. & Pulham, Grace. Growing in God's Garden - the Greatest Show on Earth: Four Theme-Related Programs to Use with Children, 2 vols. in 1. LC 88-83338. (Illus.). 112p. (gr. 3-6). 1989. tchr's. ed. 9.50 (0-88243-555-8, 02-0555) Gospel Pub.

Eder, James M. How to Prepare for the Advanced Placement Examination: AP European History. LC 93-21094. 1994. pap. 11.95 (0-8120-1623-8) Barron.

Edgar, George. Words & Pictures. LC 90-46583. 1989. 13.95 (0-85953-235-6) Childs Play.

Edgar, Pamela & Matz, Dale. Adventures of Jason: Mythical Magical Journey into Self-Discovery. LC 85-9695. (Illus.). 64p. (Orig.). (gr. 1-5). 1985. pap. 7.95 (0-941992-05-5) Los Arboles Pub.

Edge, Denzil, jt. auth. see Peebles, Catherine.

Edge, Nellie. I Can Read Colors Big Book. Saylor, Melissa, illus. (ps-2). 1988. pap. text ed. 14.00 (0-922053-03-0) N Edge Res.

—Kindergarten Cooks. Leitz, Pierr M., illus. LC 76-48558. 165p. (gr. k-6). 1975. pap. 9.95 (0-918146-00-3) Peninsula WA.

—Se Leer Colores. Zamora-Pearson, Marissa, tr. from ENG. Saylor, Melissa, illus. (SPA.). (ps-2). 1993. pap. text ed. 15.00 (0-922053-28-6) N Edge Res.

Edge, Nellie & Leitz, Pierr M. Kids in the Kitchen. LC 76-48558. (Illus.). 165p. (gr. k-6). 1979. 9.95 (0-918146-18-6) Peninsula WA.

Edge, Nellie, adapted by. La Cancion De Opuestos. Zamora-Pearson, Marissa, tr. from ENG. Nicholas, Barry, illus. (SPA.). (ps-2). 1993. pap. text ed. 15.00 (0-922053-25-1) N Edge Res.

—I've Got a Cat Big Book. Saylor, Melissa, illus. (ps-2). 1988. pap. text ed. 14.00 (*0-922053-13-8*) N Edge Res.

Edge, Nellie, compiled by. Make Friends with Mother Goose, Vol. II. Saylor, Melissa, illus. (ps-2). 1991. text ed. 15.00 (*0-922053-24-3*) N Edge Res.

—Make Friends with Mother Goose Big Book, Vol. I. Saylor, Melissa, illus. (ps-2). 1988. pap. text ed. 15.00 (*0-922053-11-1*) N Edge Res.

Edge, Nellie, adapted by. Opposite Song Big Book. Nichols, Barry, illus. (ps-2). 1988. pap. text ed. 14.00 (*0-922053-06-5*) N Edge Res.

—Osito, Osito. Zamora-Pearson, Marissa, tr. from ENG. Somerville, Sheila, illus. (SPA.). (ps-2). 1993. pap. text ed. 15.00 (*0-922053-26-X*) N Edge Res.

Edge, Nellie, compiled by. Songs & Rhymes for a Rainy Day Big Book. Saylor, Melissa, illus. (ps-2). 1988. pap. text ed. 15.00 (*0-922053-07-3*) N Edge Res.

Edge, Nellie, adapted by. Teddy Bear, Teddy Bear Big Book. Somerville, Sheila, illus. (ps-2). 1988. pap. text ed. 14.00 (*0-922053-04-9*) N Edge Res.

—Yo Tengo un Gato. Zamora-Pearson, Marissa, tr. from ENG. Saylor, Melissa, illus. (SPA.). (ps-2). 1993. pap. text ed. 15.00 (*0-922053-29-4*) N Edge Res.

Edge, Terry. Double Crossing Duo. 135p. (gr. 6-9). 1990. pap. 9.95 (*0-233-98319-8*, Pub. by A Deutsch England) Trafalgar.

—Fanfare for a Teenage Warrior in Love. 141p. (gr. 6-9). 1990. pap. 9.95 (*0-233-98080-6*, Pub. by A Deutsch England) Trafalgar.

Edgerton, Jean & Rolff, Ray. The Year of Our Lord: A Primer. Edgerton, Jean, illus. 102p. (Orig.). 1989. pap. 15.95 wkbk. (*0-9624794-0-3*) Lilium Pr.

Edison, June. Clavinova Sampler Pack Software. Schulz, Charles, illus. 12p. (Orig.). (gr. 1-6). 1992. pap. 19.95 (*1-56516-014-2*) Houston IN.

—Peanuts, Bk. 1. Schulz, Charles, illus. 40p. (Orig.). (gr. 1-6). 1989. pap. 5.50 (*1-56516-038-X*) Houston IN.

—Peanuts, Bk. 2. Schulz, Charles, illus. 38p. (Orig.). (gr. 1-6). 1989. pap. 5.50 (*1-56516-039-8*) Houston IN.

—Peanuts, Bk. 3. Schulz, Charles, illus. 40p. (Orig.). (gr. 1-6). 1989. pap. 5.50 (*1-56516-040-1*) Houston IN.

—Peanuts, Bk. 4. Schulz, Charles, illus. 40p. (Orig.). (gr. 1-6). 1989. pap. 5.50 (*1-56516-041-X*) Houston IN.

—Peanuts, Bk. 5. Schulz, Charles, illus. 40p. (Orig.). (gr. 1-6). 1989. pap. 5.50 (*1-56516-042-8*) Houston IN.

—Peanuts, Bk. 6. Schulz, Charles, illus. 38p. (Orig.). (gr. 1-6). 1989. pap. 5.50 (*1-56516-043-6*) Houston IN.

—Peanuts Christmas Album. Schulz, Charles, illus. 58p. (Orig.). (gr. 1-6). 1989. pap. 5.50 (*1-56516-049-5*) Houston IN.

—Peanuts First Program Book. Schultz, Charles, illus. 30p. (Orig.). (gr. 1-6). 1989. pap. 5.50 (*1-56516-044-4*) Houston IN.

—Peanuts First Program Book: Clavinova Software. Schulz, Charles, illus. 30p. (Orig.). (gr. 1-6). 1992. pap. 34.95 (*1-56516-018-5*) Houston IN.

—Peanuts Piano, Bk. 1: Clavinova Software. Schulz, Charles, illus. 40p. (Orig.). (gr. 1-6). 1992. pap. 34.95 (*1-56516-015-0*) Houston IN.

—Peanuts Piano, Bk. 2: Clavinova Software. Schulz, Charles, illus. 38p. (Orig.). (gr. 1-6). 1992. pap. 34.95 (*1-56516-016-9*) Houston IN.

—Peanuts Second Program Book. Schulz, Charles, illus. 36p. (Orig.). (gr. 1-6). 1989. pap. 5.50 (*1-56516-045-2*) Houston IN.

—Snoopy's Very First Christmas Songs. Schulz, Charles, illus. 32p. (Orig.). (gr. 1-6). 1989. pap. 5.50 (*1-56516-046-0*) Houston IN.

—Snoopy's Very First Christmas Songs: Clavinova Software. Schulz, Charles, illus. 32p. (Orig.). (gr. 1-6). 1992. pap. 34.95 (*1-56516-020-7*) Houston IN.

Editorial America, S. A. Staff. Los Cuentos Infantiles Mas Famosos Del Mundo. Del Real, Maria E., ed. (SPA., Illus.). 464p. (Orig.). (ps-8). 1990. pap. write for info. (*0-944499-93-7*) Editorial Amer.

Editorial America, S. A., Staff. Manual Del Filatelista. Del Real, Maria E., ed. (SPA., Illus.). 256p. (Orig.). 1990. pap. 4.95 (*0-944499-51-1*) Editorial Amer.

Edler, Timothy. Crawfish-Man Rescues Ron Guidry. (Illus.). (gr. k-8). 1980. lea. 6.00 (*0-931108-05-5*) Little Cajun Bks.

—Crawfish-Man Rescues the Ol' Beachcomber. (Illus.). 32p. (gr. k-8). 1985. leather 10.00 (*0-931108-13-6*) Little Cajun Bks.

Edler, Timothy J. The Adventures of Crawfish-Man. Edler, Timothy J., illus. 40p. (gr. k-8). 1979. pap. 6.00x (*0-931108-04-7*) Little Cajun Bks.

—Coocan: Boy of the Swamp. (Illus.). (gr. k-8). 1983. pap. 6.00 (*0-931108-09-8*) Little Cajun Bks.

—Crawfish-Man's Fifty Ways to Keep Your Kids from Using Drugs. (Illus.). 52p. (gr. k-8). 1982. pap. 6.00 (*0-931108-08-X*) Little Cajun Bks.

—Crawfish-Man's Night Befo' Christmas. (Illus.). 40p. (gr. k-8). 1984. pap. 10.00 (*0-931108-12-8*) Little Cajun Bks.

—Dark Gator. (Illus.). 48p. (gr. k-8). 1980. pap. 6.00 (*0-931108-06-3*) Little Cajun Bks.

—Maurice the Snake & Gaston the Near-Sighted Turtle: Tim Edler's Tales from the Atchafalaya. (Illus.). 36p. (gr. k-8). 1977. pap. 6.00 (*0-931108-00-4*) Little Cajun Bks.

—Rhombus: The Cajun Unicorn. (Illus.). 40p. (gr. k up). 1984. pap. 10.00 (*0-931108-10-1*) Little Cajun Bks.

—Santa's Cajun Christmas Adventure. (Illus.). 48p. (gr. k-8). 1981. pap. 6.00 (*0-931108-07-1*) Little Cajun Bks.

—T-Boy & the Trial for Life. (Illus.). 36p. (gr. k-8). 1978. pap. 6.00 (*0-931108-02-0*) Little Cajun Bks.

—T-Boy in Mossland. (Illus.). 48p. (gr. k-8). 1978. pap. 6.00 (*0-931108-03-9*) Little Cajun Bks.

—T-Boy the Little Cajun. Judice, Van, illus. 36p. (gr. k-8). 1978. pap. 6.00 (*0-931108-01-2*) Little Cajun Bks.

Edmark, Tomima. Kissing: Everything You Ever Wanted to Know. (Illus.). 144p. (Orig.). 1991. pap. 6.95 (*0-671-70883-X*, Fireside) S&S Trade.

Edmisten, Donald D. Every Wheel That Turns: Spinning True Tales of California Rails. Rockefeller, Ruth, frwd. by. (Illus.). 53p. (Orig.). 1989. pap. write for info. (*0-9626263-0-9*) DonSyl Pubns.

Edmiston, Jim. Huff Puff & Ruffly. Burgess, Mark, illus. 96p. (gr. 2-4). 1993. 18.95 (*0-460-88123-X*, Pub. by J M Dent & Sons) Trafalgar.

—Little Eagle Lots of Owls. Ross, Jane, illus. LC 92-22683. 32p. (gr. k-3). 1993. 13.95 (*0-395-65564-1*) HM.

—Mizzy & the Tigers. (ps-3). 1992. pap. 5.95 (*0-8120-4828-8*) Barron.

Edmiston, Margaret. Merlin Book of Logic Puzzles. LC 91-24019. (Illus.). 128p. (gr. 4-11). 1991. 12.95 (*0-8069-8220-9*) Sterling.

Edmiston, Margaret C. Merlin Book of Logic Puzzles. Williams, Jack, illus. LC 91-24019. 128p. (gr. 8 up). 1992. pap. 4.95 (*0-8069-8221-7*) Sterling.

Edmonds, I. G. Ooka the Wise: Tales of Old Japan. Yamazaki, Sanae, illus. 96p. (gr. 3 up). 1994. Repr. of 1961 ed. PLB 14.95 (*0-208-02379-8*, Pub. by Linnet) Shoe String.

Edmonds, Walter. Matchlock Gun. 50p. (gr. 3-6). 1991. pap. 4.95 (*0-8167-2367-2*) Troll Assocs.

Edmonds, Walter D. Bert Breen's Barn. 280p. 1991. pap. 9.95 (*0-8156-0255-3*) Syracuse U Pr.

—The Matchlock Gun. (Illus.). 64p. (gr. 3-7). 1941. 14.95 (*0-399-21911-0*, Putnam) Putnam Pub Group.

Edmonds, William. Big Book of Time. Marsden, Helen, illus. LC 93-35709. 1994. write for info. (*0-89577-579-4*) RD Assn.

Edmondson, Amy. Success Through Algebra. (gr. 8-12). 1989. 24.95 (*0-945525-12-5*) Supercamp.

Edmondson, Elizabeth. The Trojan War. LC 91-31860. (Illus.). 32p. (gr. 6 up). 1992. RSBE 13.95 (*0-02-733273-X*, New Discovery) Macmillan Child Grp.

Edney, Andrew. ASPCA Complete Cat Care Manual. LC 92-52783. (Illus.). 192p. 1992. 24.95 (*1-56458-064-4*) Dorling Kindersley.

Edom, H. Homes & Houses. (Illus.). 24p. (gr. 2-4). 1989. lib. bdg. 11.96 (*0-88110-398-5*, Usborne); pap. 3.95 (*0-7460-0450-8*, Usborne) EDC.

—Science Activities. (Illus.). 72p. (gr. 1-4). 1992. 12.95 (*0-7460-0698-5*, Usborne) EDC.

—Science with Light & Mirrors. (Illus.). 24p. (gr. 1-4). 1992. PLB 12.96 (*0-88110-545-7*, Usborne); pap. 4.50 (*0-7460-0696-9*, Usborne) EDC.

—Science with Magnets. (Illus.). 24p. (gr. 1-4). 1991. PLB 12.96 (*0-88110-629-1*, Usborne); pap. 4.50 (*0-7460-1259-4*, Usborne) EDC.

—Science with Water. (Illus.). 24p. (gr. 1-4). 1991. lib. bdg. 12.96 (*0-88110-630-5*, Usborne); pap. 4.50 (*0-7460-1261-6*, Usborne) EDC.

—Starting Ballet. (Illus.). 32p. (gr. k-3). 1993. PLB 12.96 (*0-88110-634-8*); pap. 4.95 (*0-7460-0982-8*) EDC.

—Starting Riding. (Illus.). 32p. (gr. k-3). 1992. PLB 12.96 (*0-88110-022-6*); pap. 4.95 (*0-7460-0980-1*) EDC.

—Travel & Transport. (Illus.). 24p. (gr. 2-4). 1990. lib. bdg. 11.96 (*0-88110-401-9*); pap. 3.95 (*0-7460-0446-X*) EDC.

Edom, H. & Brooks, F. Living Long Ago (B - U) (Illus.). 96p. (gr. 1-5). 1993. pap. 10.95 (*0-7460-1109-1*) EDC.

Edom, H., et al. Where Things Come from & How Things Are Made. (Illus.). 72p. (gr. 2-4). 1989. 11.95 (*0-7460-0282-3*, Usborne) EDC.

Edson, Ann & Insel, Eunice. Reading Maps, Globes, Charts, Graphs. (gr. 4-6). 1982. wkbk. 2.69 (*0-89525-175-2*) Ed Activities.

Edson, Ann, jt. auth. see Insel, Eunice.

Educational Assessment Publishing Company Staff. Discover: Skills for Life, Level 8: Student Book. (Illus.). 240p. (gr. 8). 1991. text ed. 16.60 (*0-942277-32-5*) Educ Assess Pub.

—Life Skills Handbook. (SPA., Illus.). 48p. (gr. 9-12). 1993. text ed. 6.00 wkbk. (*1-56269-090-6*); tchr's. manual, 72p. 9.00 (*1-56269-091-4*) Educ Assess Pub.

—Parent - Child Learning Library: Communication English Big Book. (Illus.). 32p. (gr. k-3). 1991. text ed. 16.95 (*0-942277-75-9*) Educ Assess Pub.

—Parent - Child Learning Library: Communication Spanish Big Book. (SPA., Illus.). 32p. (gr. k-3). 1991. text ed. 16.95 (*0-942277-76-7*) Educ Assess Pub.

—Parent - Child Learning Library: Communication Spanish Edition. (SPA.). 32p. (ps). 1991. text ed. 9.95 (*0-942277-93-7*) Educ Assess Pub.

—Parent - Child Learning Library: Communication. (Illus.). 32p. (ps). 1991. text ed. 9.95 (*0-942277-61-9*) Educ Assess Pub.

—Parent - Child Learning Library: Courtesy English Big Book. (Illus.). 32p. (gr. k-3). 1991. text ed. 16.95 (*0-942277-77-5*) Educ Assess Pub.

—Parent - Child Learning Library: Courtesy Spanish Big Book. (SPA., Illus.). 32p. (gr. k-3). 1991. text ed. 16. 95 (*0-942277-78-3*) Educ Assess Pub.

—Parent - Child Learning Library: Courtesy Spanish Edition. (SPA.). 32p. 1991. text ed. 9.95 (*0-942277-94-5*) Educ Assess Pub.

—Parent - Child Learning Library: Courtesy. (Illus.). 32p. (ps). 1991. text ed. 9.95 (*0-942277-62-7*) Educ Assess Pub.

—Parent - Child Learning Library: Drug Information. (Illus.). 32p. (gr. k-3). 1991. text ed. 9.95 (*0-942277-54-6*) Educ Assess Pub.

—Parent - Child Learning Library: Drug Information English Big Book. (Illus.). 32p. (gr. k-3). 1991. text ed. 16.95 (*0-942277-48-1*) Educ Assess Pub.

—Parent - Child Learning Library: Drug Information Spanish Big Book. (SPA., Illus.). 32p. (gr. k-3). 1991. text ed. 16.95 (*0-942277-49-X*) Educ Assess Pub.

—Parent - Child Learning Library: Drug Information Spanish Edition. (SPA., Illus.). 32p. (ps). 1991. text ed. 9.95 (*0-942277-90-2*) Educ Assess Pub.

—Parent - Child Learning Library: Healthy Relationships. (Illus.). 32p. (gr. k-3). 1991. text ed. 9.95 (*0-942277-55-4*) Educ Assess Pub.

—Parent - Child Learning Library: Healthy Relationships English Big Book. (Illus.). 32p. (gr. k-3). 1991. text ed. 16.95 (*0-942277-73-2*) Educ Assess Pub.

—Parent - Child Learning Library: Health Relationships Spanish Big Book. (SPA., Illus.). 32p. (gr. k-3). 1991. text ed. 16.95 (*0-942277-74-0*) Educ Assess Pub.

—Parent - Child Learning Library: Healthy Relationships Spanish Edition. (SPA.). 32p. (ps). 1991. text ed. 9.95 (*0-942277-91-0*) Educ Assess Pub.

—Parent - Child Learning Library: Honesty English Big Book. (Illus.). 32p. (gr. k-3). 1991. text ed. 16.95 (*0-942277-42-2*) Educ Assess Pub.

—Parent - Child Learning Library: Honesty Spanish Big Book. (SPA., Illus.). 32p. (gr. k-3). 1991. text ed. 16. 95 (*0-942277-41-4*) Educ Assess Pub.

—Parent - Child Learning Library: Honesty Spanish Edition. (SPA., Illus.). 32p. (ps). 1991. text ed. 9.95 (*0-942277-87-2*) Educ Assess Pub.

—Parent - Child Learning Library: Honesty. (Illus.). 32p. (ps-k). 1991. text ed. 9.95 (*0-942277-59-7*) Educ Assess Pub.

—Parent - Child Learning Library: Responsibility English Big Book. (Illus.). 32p. 1991. text ed. 16.95 (*0-942277-44-9*) Educ Assess Pub.

—Parent - Child Learning Library: Responsibility. (Illus.). 32p. (gr. k-3). 1991. text ed. 9.95 (*0-942277-58-9*) Educ Assess Pub.

—Parent - Child Learning Library: Responsibility Spanish Big Book. (SPA., Illus.). 32p. (gr. k-3). 1991. text ed. 16.95 (*0-942277-45-7*) Educ Assess Pub.

—Parent - Child Learning Library: Responsibility Spanish Edition. (SPA.). 32p. (ps). 1991. text ed. 9.95 (*0-942277-92-9*) Educ Assess Pub.

—Parent - Child Learning Library: Self-Esteem. (Illus.). 40p. 1991. text ed. 9.95 (*0-942277-53-8*) Educ Assess Pub.

—Parent - Child Learning Library: Self-Esteem English Big Book. (Illus.). 40p. (gr. k-3). 1991. text ed. 16.95 (*0-942277-46-5*) Educ Assess Pub.

—Parent - Child Learning Library: Self-Esteem Spanish Big Book. (SPA., Illus.). 40p. (gr. k-3). 1991. text ed. 16.95 (*0-942277-47-3*) Educ Assess Pub.

—Parent - Child Learning Library: Self-Esteem Spanish Edition. (SPA.). 40p. (ps). 1991. text ed. 9.95 (*0-942277-89-9*) Educ Assess Pub.

—Parent - Child Learning Library: Your Uniqueness. (Illus.). 32p. (ps-k). 1991. text ed. 9.95 (*0-942277-63-5*) Educ Assess Pub.

—Parent - Child Learning Library: Your Uniqueness English Big Book. (Illus.). 32p. (gr. k-3). 1991. text ed. 16.95 (*0-942277-79-1*) Educ Assess Pub.

—Parent - Child Learning Library: Your Uniqueness Spanish Big Book. (SPA., Illus.). 32p. (gr. k-3). 1991. text ed. 16.95 (*0-942277-80-5*) Educ Assess Pub.

—Parent - Child Learning Library: Your Uniqueness Spanish Edition. (SPA.). 32p. (ps). 1991. text ed. 9.95 (*0-942277-95-3*) Educ Assess Pub.

—Skills for Life. (Illus.). (gr. 9-12). 1993. text ed. 18.50 (*1-56269-050-7*); tchr's. ed. 39.25 (*1-56269-051-5*); Total tchr. support system. 208.75 (*1-56269-052-3*) Educ Assess Pub.

—Skills for Life. (Illus.). 48p. (gr. 1). 1992. Spanish. text ed. 10.60 (*1-56269-000-0*); Spanish big bk. text ed. 76. 95 (*1-56269-035-3*); Bilingual tchr's. ed., 80p. 31.21 (*1-56269-001-9*); Bilingual total tchr. support system, 168p. 92.35 (*1-56269-003-5*) Educ Assess Pub.

—Skills for Life. (Illus.). 48p. (gr. 1). 1992. Spanish. text ed. 10.60 (*1-56269-005-1*); Spanish big bk., 64p. text ed. 76.95 (*1-56269-036-1*); Bilingual tchr's. ed., 96p. 31.21 (*1-56269-006-X*); Total tchr. support system, 168p. 92.35 (*1-56269-008-6*) Educ Assess Pub.

—Skills for Life. (Illus.). 64p. (gr. 2). 1992. Spanish. text ed. 10.60 (*1-56269-010-8*); Bilingual tchr's. ed., 112p. 31.21 (*1-56269-011-6*); Bilingual total tchr. support system, 168p. 92.35 (*1-56269-013-2*) Educ Assess Pub.

—Skills for Life. (Illus.). 80p. (gr. 3). 1992. Spanish. text ed. 11.45 (*1-56269-015-9*); Bilingual tchr's. ed., 112p. 34.18 (*1-56269-016-7*); 93.75 (*0-685-57572-1*) Bilingual total tchr. support system, 186p (*1-56269-018-3*) Educ Assess Pub.

—Skills for Life. (Illus.). 116p. (gr. 4). 1992. Spanish. text ed. 11.45 (*1-56269-020-5*); Bilingual tchr's. ed., 116p. 34.18 (*1-56269-021-3*); Bilingual total tchr. support system, 216p. 93.75 (*0-685-57573-X*) Educ Assess Pub.

—Skills for Life. (Illus.). 128p. (gr. 5). 1992. Spanish. text ed. 12.65 (*1-56269-025-6*); Bilingual tchr's. ed., 168p. 34.18 (*1-56269-026-4*); Bilingual total tchr. support system, 216p. 93.75 (*1-56269-028-0*) Educ Assess Pub.

—Skills for Life. (Illus.). 144p. (gr. 6). 1992. Spanish. text ed. 13.65 (*1-56269-030-2*); Bilingual tchr's. ed., 168p. 34.18 (*1-56269-031-0*); Bilingual total tchr. support system, 224p. 93.75 (*1-56269-033-7*) Educ Assess Pub.

Educational Assessment Publishing Co. Staff. Skills for Life. (Illus.). 240p. (gr. 7). 1992. Spanish. text ed. 16.60 (*1-56269-042-6*); Bilingual tchr's. ed., 256p. 39.25 (*1-56269-043-4*); Bilingual total tchr. support system, 396p. 208.15 (*1-56269-044-2*) Educ Assess Pub.

Educational Assessment Publishing Company Staff. Skills for Life. (Illus.). 240p. (gr. 8). 1992. Spanish. text ed. 16.60 (*1-56269-045-0*); Bilingual tchr's. ed., 256p. 39.25 (*1-56269-046-9*); Bilingual total tchr. support system, 396p. 208.15 (*1-56269-047-7*) Educ Assess Pub.

Edward, S. S. Miracle of the Shoebox Baby. 104p. (gr. 5-12). 1993. 11.95 (*1-883500-22-2*); pap. 8.95 (*1-883500-23-0*) RAMSI Bks.

Edwards, Amelia B. The Phantom Coach. Richardson, I. M., adapted by. Ashmead, Hal, illus. LC 81-19862. 32p. (gr. 5-10). 1982. PLB 10.79 (*0-89375-634-2*); pap. text ed. 2.95 (*0-89375-635-0*) Troll Assocs.

Edwards, Anne, jt. auth. see Steen, Shirley.

Edwards, Archibald C. Charlotte. Musser, Rebecca F., illus. LC 90-63680. 112p. (Orig.). (gr. 7 up). 1990. pap. 11.95 (*0-9626413-0-8*) Rosedale Pr.

Edwards, Don. Cartooning. Stieglitz, Cliff, ed. Edwards, Don, illus. 64p. (Orig.). (gr. 7 up). 1993. pap. 12.95 (*0-9637336-0-5*) Airbrush Act.

Edwards, Dorothy. My Naughty Little Sister & Bad Harry's Rabbit. Hughes, Shirley, illus. (ps-2). 1981. 8. 95x (*0-13-608935-6*) P-H.

Edwards, E. Dean. The American Pioneer. (Illus.). 36p. (Orig.). (gr. 1 up). 1988. pap. 2.95 (*0-685-44554-2*) E D Edwards.

Edwards, E. W. Exploring Careers Using Foreign Languages. rev. ed. Rosen, Ruth, ed. (gr. 7-12). 1990. PLB 13.95 (*0-8239-0968-9*) Rosen Group.

Edwards, Elsy. Sandy's Suitcase. Webb, Philip, illus. LC 92-34269. 1993. 14.00 (*0-383-03650-X*) SRA Schl Grp.

Edwards, Frank & Bianchi, John. Melody Mooner Stayed up All Night. (Illus.). 24p. (Orig.). (ps-3). 1991. PLB 14.95 (*0-921285-03-5*, Pub. by Bungalo Bks CN); pap. 4.95 (*0-921285-01-9*, Pub. by Bungalo Bks CN) Firefly Bks Ltd.

Edwards, Frank B. Close Up: Microscopic Photographs of Everyday Stuff. (Illus.). 48p. 1992. lib. bdg. 17.95 (*0-921285-25-6*, Pub. by Bungalo Bks CN); pap. 6.95 (*0-921285-24-8*, Pub. by Hedgehog Prods CN) Firefly Bks Ltd.

Edwards, Frank B. & Bianchi, John. Mortimer Mooner Stopped Taking a Bath. (Illus.). 24p. (ps-2). 1990. 14. 95 (*0-921285-21-3*, Pub. by Bungalo Bks CN); pap. 4.95 (*0-921285-20-5*, Pub. by Bungalo Bks CN) Firefly Bks Ltd.

Edwards, Frank B., jt. auth. see Aziz, Laurel.

Edwards, Frank B., jt. auth. see Bianchi, John.

Edwards, Gabrielle. Drugs on Your Streets. rev. ed. (gr. 7-12). 1993. PLB 14.95 (*0-8239-1682-0*) Rosen Group.

Edwards, Gabrielle I. Coping with Drug Abuse. rev. ed. Rosen, Roger, ed. (gr. 7 up). 1990. PLB 13.95 (*0-8239-1144-6*) Rosen Group.

Edwards, Hazel. Snail Mail. Clement, Rod, illus. 32p. (gr. k-3). 1991. pap. 7.95 (*0-7322-7206-8*, Pub. by Angus & Robertson AT) HarpC.

—Stickybeak. Sherwood, Rhoda, ed. Wilson, Rosemary, illus. LC 88-42915. 32p. (gr. 2-3). 1988. PLB 18.60 (*1-55532-932-2*) Gareth Stevens Inc.

Edwards, Jane, adapted by see Stevenson, Robert Louis.

Edwards, Juanita, ed. see Hall, Judy A.

Edwards, Judith. Colter's Run. Potter, John, illus. 32p. (Orig.). 1993. pap. 5.95 (*1-56044-178-X*) Falcon Pr MT.

Edwards, Julie. Last of the Really Great Whangdoodles. LC 73-5482. 288p. (gr. 3-7). 1989. pap. 3.95 (*0-06-440314-9*, Trophy) HarpC Child Bks.

—Mandy. Brown, Judith G., illus. LC 76-157901. 224p. (gr. 3-6). 1989. pap. 3.95 (*0-06-440296-7*, Trophy) HarpC Child Bks.

—Mandy. reissued ed. Brown, Judith G., illus. LC 76-157901. 192p. (gr. 4-7). 1990. PLB 13.89 (*0-06-021803-7*) HarpC Child Bks.

Edwards, Lillie. Denmark Vesey. King, Coretta Scott, intro. by. (Illus.). (gr. 5 up). 1990. 17.95 (*1-55546-614-1*) Chelsea Hse.

Edwards, Linda S. The Downtown Day. Edwards, Linda S., illus. LC 82-4645. 48p. (gr. k-3). 1983. 9.95 (*0-394-85407-1*) Pantheon.

Edwards, Lisa. Disney Babies Look at Babies. Hundelman, Dorothy & Handelman, Dorothy, photos by. LC 91-71346. (Illus.). 24p. (ps). 1991. 6.95 (*1-56282-053-2*) Disney Pr.

Edwards, Lois. Great Careers for People Interested in the Human Body, 6 vols. LC 93-78078. (Illus.). 48p. (gr. 6-9). 1993. 16.95 (*0-8103-9386-7*, 102104, UXL) Gale.

Edwards, Margaret B. Little Stitch. Pennanen, Judi, illus. 24p. (ps-8). 1986. 7.95 (*0-920806-69-4*, Pub. by Penumbra Pr CN) U of Toronto Pr.

Edwards, Michelle. Alef-Bet: A Hebrew Alphabet Book. Pearson, Susan, ed. Edwards, Michelle, illus. LC 91-31011. 32p. (ps-3). 1992. 15.00 (*0-688-09724-3*); PLB 14.93 (*0-688-09725-1*) Lothrop.

—A Baker's Portrait. LC 90-41926. (Illus.). 32p. (gr. k up). 1991. 13.95 (*0-688-09712-X*); PLB 13.88 (*0-688-09713-8*) Lothrop.

—Blessed Are You: Traditional Everyday Hebrew Prayers. LC 92-1666. (ps-3). 1993. 14.93 (*0-688-10760-5*) Lothrop.

—Blessed Are You: Traditional Jewish Prayers for Children. LC 92-1666. 1993. write for info. (*0-688-10759-1*) Lothrop.

—Chicken Man. (ps-3). 1991. PLB 13.88 (*0-688-09709-X*) Lothrop.

—Chicken Man. (Illus.). (gr. k-3). 1991. 13.95 (*0-688-09708-1*) Lothrop.

—Chicken Man. Edwards, Michelle, illus. 32p. (ps up). 1994. pap. 4.95 (*0-688-13106-9*, Mulberry) Morrow.

—Dora's Book. Edwards, Michelle, illus. 32p. (gr. k-4). 1990. PLB 19.95 (*0-87614-411-3*) Carolrhoda Bks.

—Dora's Book. (gr. 4-7). 1993. pap. 6.95 (*0-87614-535-7*) Carolrhoda Bks.

—Eve & Smithy. LC 92-44166. (gr. 4 up). 1995. write for info. (*0-688-11825-9*); lib. bdg. write for info. (*0-688-11826-7*) Lothrop.

—Misha the Minstrel. LC 84-62336. (Illus.). 32p. (gr. 3-7). 1985. 8.95 (*0-930100-19-0*) Holy Cow.

Edwards, Mildred & Latham, Joy. We Sing & Play. (Illus.). 48p. (ps-3). Date not set. 3.50 (*0-685-68205-6*, BCMB-225) Lillenas.

Edwards, Nicholas. Stand & Deliver. 1989. pap. 3.25 (*0-590-42831-4*) Scholastic Inc.

Edwards, Paul M. Our Legacy of Faith: A Brief History of the Reorganized Church of Jesus Christ of Latter Day Saints. 360p. 1991. text ed. 27.50 (*0-8309-0594-4*) Herald Hse.

Edwards, R. International Terrorism. (Illus.). 48p. (gr. 5 up). 1988. PLB 18.60 (*0-86592-285-3*); 13.95s.p. (*0-685-58316-3*) Rourke Corp.

—Korean War. (Illus.). 80p. (gr. 7 up). 1988. PLB 18.60 (*0-86592-036-2*); 13.95 (*0-685-58322-8*) Rourke Corp.

Edwards, R. G. Beginnings of Human Life. Head, J. J., ed. LC 79-208. (Illus.). 16p. (gr. 10 up). 1981. pap. 2.75 (*0-89278-217-X*, 45-9735) Carolina Biological.

Edwards, Richard. Moles Can Dance. Anstey, Caroline, illus. LC 93-2462. 1994. write for info. (*1-56402-361-3*) Candlewick Pr.

—Moon Frog. Fox-Davies, Sarah, illus. LC 92-53014. 48p. (ps-3). 1993. 16.95 (*1-56402-116-5*) Candlewick Pr.

—A Mouse in My Roof. Venice, illus. (ps up). 1990. write for info. Delacorte.

—A Mouse in My Roof. 1990. 13.95 (*0-385-30035-2*) Doubleday.

—A Mouse in My Roof. 1990. PLB 14.99 (*0-385-30127-8*) Dell.

—Ten Tall Oak Trees. Crossland, Caroline, illus. LC 92-41771. 32p. (ps up). 1993. 15.00 (*0-688-04620-7*, Tambourine Bks); PLB 14.93 (*0-688-04621-5*, Tambourine Bks) Morrow.

—Vietnam War, Reading Level 8. LC 86-20295. (Illus.). 77p. (gr. 7 up). 1987. PLB 18.60 (*0-86592-031-1*); PLB 13.95s.p. (*0-685-58244-2*) Rourke Corp.

—The Word Party. Lawrence, John, illus. LC 91-26919. 80p. (gr. k-3). 1992. 13.50 (*0-385-30620-2*) Delacorte.

Edwards, Roberta, retold by. Five Silly Fishermen: A Step One Book. Wickstrom, Sylvie, illus. LC 89-42508. 32p. (Orig.). (ps-1). 1989. PLB 7.99 (*0-679-90092-6*); pap. 3.50 (*0-679-80092-1*) Random Bks Yng Read.

Edwards, Roger. Max Science & the Glowing Firefly. Sanchez, Brenda L., ed. Beard, Derrick, illus. 26p. (gr. k-5). 1991. pap. 3.95 (*1-879350-01-7*) Max Sci Pub.

Edwards, Roland. Tigers. Riches, Judith, illus. LC 91-40098. 32p. (ps-2). 1992. 15.00 (*0-688-11685-X*, Tambourine Bks); PLB 14.93 (*0-688-11686-8*, Tambourine Bks) Morrow.

Edwards, Ronald R. Problem Solving Through Critical Thinking. (gr. 4-7). 1990. pap. 7.95 (*0-201-48024-7*) Addison-Wesley.

Edwards, Ronald R. & Cook, Wanda D. Problem Solving Through Critical Thinking. 48p. (gr. 5-8). 1990. pap. text ed. 7.95 (*0-938587-13-7*) Cuisenaire.

Edwards, S., jt. auth. see Edwards, W.

Edwards, S., jt. ed. see Edwards, W.

Edwards, Sarah, see Sturkie, Joan.

Edwards, Susan, jt. auth. see Ann Arbor Publishers Editorial Staff.

Edwards, W. & Edwards, S. Symbol Discrimination & Sequencing. (gr. 2). 1976. wkbk. black on reusable 9.00 (*0-87879-730-0*, Ann Arbor Div); wkbk. red on reusable 9.00 (*0-87879-731-9*) Acad Therapy.

Edwards, W. & Edwards, S., eds. Cursive Tracking: Reusable Edition. (gr. 3). 1972. wkbk. 9.00 (*0-87879-751-3*, Ann Arbor Div) Acad Therapy.

—Cursive Writing: Letters, Level 1: Reusable Edition. (gr. 1-3). 1975. Level 1. wkbk. 6.50 (*0-87879-793-9*, Ann Arbor Div) Acad Therapy.

—Cursive Writing: Letters, Level 2: Reusable Edition. 52p. (gr. 3-6). 1975. Level 2. wkbk. 6.50 (*0-87879-794-7*, Ann Arbor Div) Acad Therapy.

—Cursive Writing Words, Book 2: Reusable Edition. (gr. 1). 1972. Bk. 2. wkbk. 6.50 (*0-87879-792-0*, Ann Arbor Div) Acad Therapy.

—Letter Tracking, Bk. 1. large type ed. 40p. (gr. 1 up). 1975. 9.00 (*0-87879-851-X*) Acad Therapy.

—Letter Tracking, Bks. 1-2: Reusable Edition. (gr. 3-8). 1975. black on reusable, bk. 1 9.00 (*0-87879-736-X*, Ann Arbor Div); black on reusable, bk. 2 9.00 (*0-87879-868-4*, Ann Arbor Div); red on reusable, bk. 1 9.00 (*0-87879-737-8*, Ann Arbor Div); red on reusable, bk. 2 9.00 (*0-87879-883-8*, Ann Arbor Div); red 7.00 (*0-87879-866-8*, Ann Arbor Div); red/green 7.00 (*0-87879-865-X*, Ann Arbor Div); bk. 1 7.00 (*0-87879-735-1*, Ann Arbor Div) Acad Therapy.

—Letter Tracking: Reusable Edition. (gr. k-1). 1973. wkbk. 5.00 (*0-89039-019-3*, Ann Arbor Div) Acad Therapy.

—Manuscript Tracking: Reusable Edition. (gr. k-1). 1975. 5.00 (*0-89039-017-7*, Ann Arbor Div) Acad Therapy.

Edwards, William H. Fretboard Logic, Vol. 1: The Reasoning Behind the Guitar's Unique Tuning System. rev. ed. (Illus.). 34p. (gr. 7-12). 1983. pap. 9.95 spiral bdg. (*0-685-29425-0*) Edwards Music Pub.

Effendi, Shoghi. Your True Brother. Weinberg, Robert & Weinberg, Robertcompiled by. (Illus.). 24p. (Orig.). (gr. 8-10). 1991. pap. 7.50 (*0-85398-324-0*) G Ronald Pub.

Effinger, Marta. Bunker & Me: Summer Adventures of Best Friends, Vol. I. Lawrence & Penny, ed. Effinger, Michael, illus. Washington, Pat, intro. by. (Illus.). 30p. (gr. 3-5). 1990. 12.95x (*0-929917-02-2*) Magnolia PA.

Efflandt, Lloyd H. The Black Hawk War, Why? Pate, Dorothy, illus. 25p. pap. 1.25 (*0-9617938-0-5*, 5M) Rock Isl Arsenal Hist Soc.

Efron, Marshall & Olsen, Alfa-Betty. Really Scared Stiff: Three Creepy Tales. Medley, Linda, illus. 48p. (gr. 2-4). 1992. pap. write for info. (*0-307-11469-4*, 11469, Golden Pr) Western Pub.

Efron, Marshall, jt. auth. see Olsen, Alfa-Betty.

Egan, Frank. Uninvited Guest. (Illus.). 45p. (ps-8). 1985. 10.95 (*0-86327-082-4*, Pub. by Wolfhound Press Eire) Dufour.

Egan, Joseph, as told to see Fendler, Donn.

Egan, L. Betts, ed. see Grimm, Jacob & Grimm, Wilhelm K.

Egan, Louise. Thomas A. Edison. (Illus.). 144p. (gr. 3-6). 1987. pap. 5.95 (*0-8120-3922-X*) Barron.

Egan, Louise B. Santa's Christmas Ride: A Storybook with Real Presents. Officer, Robyn, illus. 52p. 1993. incl. gifts 16.95 (*0-8362-4505-9*) Andrews & McMeel.

Egan, Louise B., ed. The Classic Treasury of Children's Poetry. LC 89-83327. (Illus.). 56p. (gr. 1 up). 1990. 9.98 (*0-89471-802-9*) Courage Bks.

Egan, Louise B., retold by. The Easter Bunny. Dieneman, Debbie, illus. LC 92-32435. 1993. 6.95 (*0-8362-4935-6*) Andrews & McMeel.

Egan, Patricia. Saint Patrick & the Snakes. (Illus.). 28p. (gr. 1-8). 1990. 9.95 (*1-85390-059-1*, Pub. by Veritas Pubns ER) Irish Bks Media.

Egan, Terry, et al. Macmillan Book of Baseball Stories. LC 92-6447. (Illus.). 128p. (gr. 3 up). 1992. SBE 14.95 (*0-02-733280-2*, Macmillan Child Bk) Macmillan Child Grp.

Egan, Tim. Friday Night at Hodges' Cafe. LC 93-11290. 1994. write for info. (*0-395-68076-X*) HM.

Egbert, Barbara. Cheerleading & Songleading. LC 80-52322. (Illus.). 128p. (gr. 9 up). 1980. pap. 9.95 (*0-8069-8950-5*) Sterling.

Egbert, Rebecca A. The Vision of the Spokane Prophet. Gilliland, Hap, ed. Hardgrove, Tanya, illus. 36p. (Orig.). (gr. 5-10). 1989. pap. 5.95 (*0-89992-118-3*) Coun India Ed.

Ege, Christine. Words for the World: Including God's Word for the World. Herbert, Janet, illus. LC 91-90681. 136p. (gr. k-8). 1992. text ed. 35.00 incl. 1 8-cass. tape album (*1-884161-01-4*) Comprehen Lang.

Egermeier, Elsie E. Egermeier's Bible Story Book. 5th ed. Uptton, Clive, illus. LC 68-23397. (gr. k-6). 1969. 14. 95 (*0-87162-006-5*, D2005); deluxe ed. 15.95 (*0-87162-007-3*, D2006); pap. 8.95 (*0-87162-229-7*, D2008) Warner Pr.

—Egermeier's Favorite Bible Stories. (gr. k-1). 1965. 9.95 (*0-87162-014-6*, D3695) Warner Pr.

—Egermeier's Picture-Story Life of Jesus. Inns, Kenneth, illus. (gr. k-6). 1969. 7.95 (*0-87162-008-1*, D2015) Warner Pr.

—Picture Story Bible ABC Book. rev. ed. (Illus.). (ps-1). 1963. 9.95 (*0-87162-262-9*, D1703) Warner Pr.

Egertson, Eric. Developing Computer Skills: Operating Principles for Apple IIc, IIe & IIgs. 212p. (Orig.). (gr. 7-10). 1989. pap. text ed. 14.95 (*0-8134-2791-6*); 2.95 (*0-8134-2792-4*) Interstate.

Eggleston, Edward. The Hoosier Schoolboy. 1988. Repr. of 1883 ed. lib. bdg. 59.00x (*0-7812-1178-6*) Rprt Serv.

—Mister Blake's Walking Stick. 1988. Repr. of 1870 ed. lib. bdg. 59.00x (*0-7812-1170-0*) Rprt Serv.

—The Schoolmaster's Stories for Boys & Girls. 1988. Repr. of 1874 ed. lib. bdg. 59.00x (*0-7812-1176-X*) Rprt Serv.

Egielski. Buz. Date not set. 15.00 (*0-06-023566-7*, Festival); PLB 14.89 (*0-06-023567-5*, Festival) HarpC Child Bks.

Egloff, Keith & Woodward, Deborah, eds. First People: The Early Indians of Virginia. (Illus.). 48p. (gr. 5-8). 1992. pap. 11.95 (*0-8139-1474-4*) U Pr of Va.

Eglsaer, Marie-Therese. Further Adventures of Figaro. Eglsaer, Robert J., ed. Root, Joseph, illus. LC 89-61954. 108p. (Orig.). (gr. 8-10). 1989. pap. write for info. (*0-88100-061-2*) Natl Writ Pr.

Eglsaer, Robert J., ed. see Eglsaer, Marie-Therese.

Egner, Thorbjorn. Karius & Baktus. Sevig, Mike, tr. from NOR. LC 86-62750. (gr. 1-4). 1986. write for info. *(0-9615394-1-0)* Skandisk.
—People & Robbers of Cardemon Town: Musical. 1968. 4.50 *(0-87602-172-0)* Anchorage.
Egsgard, John, et al. Making Connections: With Mathematics. (Illus.). 102p. (gr. 9-12). 1989. pap. 19. 95 *(0-939765-27-6,* G116) Janson Pubns.
Ehlers, Sabine. The Bossy Hawaiian Moon. Kiyabu, Walter H., illus. 32p. (ps-1). 1980. pap. 2.95 *(0-930492-15-3)* Hawaiian Serv.
Ehlert, L. Moon Rope: Un Lazo a la Luna. 1992. 14.95 *(0-15-255343-6,* HB Juv Bks) HarBrace.
Ehlert, Lois. Award Puzzles: Color Zoo. 1991. 5.95 *(0-938971-66-2)* JTG Nashville.
—Circus. Ehlert, lois, illus. LC 91-12067. 40p. (ps-1). 1992. 15.00 *(0-06-020252-1);* PLB 14.89 *(0-06-020253-X)* HarpC Child Bks.
—Color Farm. Ehlert, Lois, illus. LC 89-13561. 40p. (ps-k). 1990. 12.95 *(0-397-32440-5,* Lipp Jr Bks); PLB 12.89 *(0-397-32441-3,* Lipp Jr Bks) HarpC Child Bks.
—Color Zoo. Ehlert, Lois, illus. LC 87-17065. 32p. (ps-1). 1989. 14.00 *(0-397-32259-3,* Lipp Jr Bks); PLB 13.89 *(0-397-32260-7)* HarpC Child Bks.
—Eating the Alphabet. LC 88-10906. (gr. 2 up). 1993. pap. 4.95 *(0-15-224436-0,* HB Juv Bks) HarBrace.
—Eating the Alphabet: Fruits & Vegetables from A to Z. 32p. (ps-3). 1989. 14.95 *(0-15-224435-2)* HarBrace.
—Feathers for Lunch. 33p. (ps-3). 1990. 13.95 *(0-15-230550-5)* HarBrace.
—Feathers for Lunch. LC 89-29459. (ps-3). 1993. pap. 19.95 *(0-15-230551-3)* HarBrace.
—Fish Eyes: A Book You Can Count On. Ehlert, Lois, illus. 32p. (ps-1). 1990. 14.95 *(0-15-228050-2)* HarBrace.
—Fish Eyes: A Book You Can Count On. LC 89-1535. (ps-3). 1992. pap. 4.95 *(0-15-228051-0,* Voyager Bks) HarBrace.
—Growing Vegetable Soup. 40p. (ps-2). 1990. pap. 4.95 *(0-15-232580-8,* Voyager Bks) HarBrace.
—Growing Vegetable Soup. Ehlert, Lois, illus. 32p. (ps-3). 1991. pap. 19.95 *(0-15-232581-6)* HarBrace.
—Growing Vegetable Soup. (ps-3). 1987. 13.95 *(0-15-232575-1,* HB Juv Bks) HarBrace.
—Mole's Hill: A Woodland Tale. LC 93-31151. 1994. PLB 14.95 *(0-15-255116-6,* HB Juv Bks) HarBrace.
—Nuts to You! LC 92-19441. (Illus.). 32p. (ps-3). 1993. 14.95 *(0-15-257647-9,* HB Juv Bks) HarBrace.
—Planting a Rainbow. 32p. (ps-3). 1988. 14.95 *(0-15-262609-3)* HarBrace.
—Planting a Rainbow. (ps-3). 1992. pap. 19.95 *(0-15-262611-5);* pap. 4.95 *(0-15-262610-7)* HarBrace.
—Red Leaf, Yellow Leaf. 32p. (ps-3). 1991. 14.95 *(0-15-266197-2,* HB Juv Bks) HarBrace.
Ehrenhaft, George. How to Prepare for SAT II: Writing. (Orig.). 1994. pap. 11.95 *(0-8120-1477-4)* Barron.
—Write Your Way into College. 2nd, rev. ed. LC 93-13380. 120p. (gr. 9 up). 1993. pap. 8.95 *(0-8120-1415-4)* Barron.
—The Writer's Survival Guide. 124p. (Orig.). (gr. 9-12). 1988. pap. text ed. 14.99, 8.99 per book for classroom sets *(0-87438-047-2);* tchr's. ed. 14.99 *(0-87438-048-0)* Media Devel.
Ehrlich, Amy. Buck-Buck the Chicken. Alley, R. W., illus. LC 86-31639. 48p. (gr. 1-3). 1987. lib. bdg. 7.99 *(0-394-98804-3);* pap. 2.95 *(0-394-88804-9)* Random Bks Yng Read.
—Bunnies All Day Long. Henry, Marie H., illus. LC 84-20031. (ps-2). 1989. (Dial Pied Piper) Puffin Bks.
—Bunnies at Christmastime. Henry, Marie, illus. LC 86-2202. 32p. (ps-2). 1989. 11.95 *(0-8037-0321-X)* Dial Bks Young.
—Bunnies on Their Own. LC 85-20467. (Illus.). 32p. (ps-2). 1992. pap. 3.99 *(0-8037-1138-7,* Dial Pied Piper) Puffin Bks.
—The Dark Card. 1991. 13.95 *(0-670-83733-4)* Viking Child Bks.
—The Dark Card. 180p. (gr. 7 up). 1993. pap. 3.99 *(0-14-036332-7)* Puffin Bks.
—Leo, Zack & Emmie. Kellogg, Steven, illus. LC 81-2604. 64p. (ps-3). 1981. PLB 9.89 *(0-8037-4761-6)* Dial Bks Young.
—Leo, Zack & Emmie. Kellogg, Steven, illus. 64p. (ps-3). 1981. pap. 4.95 *(0-8037-4760-8,* Dial Easy to Read) Puffin Bks.
—Leo, Zack & Emmie Together Again. LC 86-16810. (Illus.). 56p. (ps-3). 1987. 9.95 *(0-8037-0381-3);* PLB 9.89 *(0-8037-0382-1)* Dial Bks Young.
—Leo, Zack, & Emmie Together Again. LC 86-16810. (Illus.). 56p. (ps-3). 1990. pap. 3.95 *(0-8037-0837-8)* Dial Bks Young.
—Lucy's Winter Tale. Howell, Troy, illus. LC 88-25740. 32p. (gr. k). 1992. 14.00 *(0-8037-0659-6);* PLB 13.89 *(0-8037-0661-8)* Dial Bks Young.
—Parents in the Pigpen, Pigs in the Tub. Kellogg, Steven, illus. LC 91-15601. 40p. (ps-3). 1993. 14.99 *(0-8037-0933-1);* lib. bdg. 14.89 *(0-8037-0928-5)* Dial Bks Young.
—Pome & Peel. Gal, Laszlo, illus. 32p. (ps-3). 1993. pap. 4.99 *(0-14-054587-5)* Puffin Bks.
—Rapunzel. Waldherr, Kris, illus. LC 88-25918. 32p. (ps-3). 1989. 12.95 *(0-8037-0654-5);* PLB 12.89 *(0-8037-0655-3)* Dial Bks Young.
—Story of Hanukkah. Sherman, Ori, illus. (ps up) 1989. 14.95 *(0-8037-0615-4);* PLB 14.89 *(0-8037-0616-2)* Dial Bks Young.

—Where It Stops, Nobody Knows. LC 88-4095. 192p. (gr. 6 up). 1988. 14.95 *(0-8037-0575-1)* Dial Bks Young.
—Where It Stops, Nobody Knows. 224p. (gr. 6 up). 1990. pap. 3.95 *(0-14-034266-4,* Puffin) Puffin Bks.
—Zeek Silver Moon. Parker, Robert A., illus. LC 70-181787. 32p. (ps-3). 1972. Dial Bks Young.
Ehrlich, Amy, adapted by. The Random House Book of Fairy Tales. Goode, Diane, illus. LC 83-13833. 224p. (gr. k-4). 1985. bds. 17.00 *(0-394-85693-7);* lib. bdg. 17.99 *(0-394-95693-1)* Random Bks Yng Read.
Ehrlich, Amy, adapted by see Brown, Dee.
Ehrlich, Doris. Animal Alphabet. 2nd ed. O'Rourke, Dawn M., illus. 36p. (ps-k). 1988. pap. text ed. 80.00 classroom pack *(0-932957-90-0);* tchr's. ed. 4.50 *(0-932957-91-9);* wkbk. 3.90 *(0-932957-89-7);* wall posters 17.50 *(0-932957-96-X)* Natl School.
Ehrlich, Doris, ed. see Krampe, Leesa.
Ehrlich, Elizabeth. Nellie Bly. Horner, Matina S., intro. by. (Illus.). 112p. (gr. 5 up). 1989. 17.95 *(1-55546-643-5)* Chelsea Hse.
Ehrlich, Fred. A Class Play with Ms. Vanilla. Gradisher, Martha, illus. 32p. (ps-3). 1992. 9.00 *(0-670-84651-1)* Viking Child Bks.
—A Class Play with Ms. Vanilla. Gradisher, Martha, illus. 32p. (ps-3). 1992. pap. 3.50 *(0-14-054580-8)* Puffin Bks.
—Lunch Boxes. Gradisher, Martha, illus. 32p. (ps-3). 1991. 8.95 *(0-670-83860-8)* Viking Child Bks.
—Lunch Boxes. Gradisher, Martha, illus. 32p. (ps-3). 1991. pap. 3.50 *(0-14-054393-7,* Puffin) Puffin Bks.
—Lunch Boxes. Gradisher, Martha, illus. LC 93-2724. (gr. k-3). 1993. pap. 3.25 *(0-14-036555-9,* Puffin) Puffin Bks.
—A Valentine for Ms. Vanilla. Gradisher, Martha, illus. 32p. (ps-3). 1992. 8.95 *(0-670-84274-5)* Viking Child Bks.
Ehrlich, Robert. The Cosmological Milkshake: A Semi-Serious Look at the Size of Things. Ehrlich, Gary, illus. LC 93-28135. 1994. 29.95 *(0-8135-2045-2);* pap. 14.95 *(0-8135-2046-0)* Rutgers U Pr.
Ehrlich, Susanne. Es War Einmal. (GER., Illus.). 96p. 1991. pap. 9.95 incl. 60-min. cassette *(0-8442-2426-X,* Passport Bks); pap. 6.95 bk. only *(0-8442-2433-2,* Passport Bks) NTC Pub Grp.
—Das Ratselheft. (GER., Illus.). 72p. (gr. 5 up). 1983. pap. 6.95 *(0-8442-2227-5,* Passport Bks) NTC Pub Grp.
Eichel, C. & Sanders, E. Question Collection. (gr. 5-12). 1988. 7.95 *(0-88160-153-5,* LW 271) Learning Wks.
Eichenberg, Fritz. Ape in a Cape: An Alphabet of Odd Animals. Eichenberg, Fritz, illus. LC 52-6908. 26p. (ps-3). 1952. 15.95 *(0-15-203722-5,* HB Juv Bks) HarBrace.
—Ape in a Cape: An Alphabet of Odd Animals. Eichenberg, Fritz, illus. LC 52-6908. 32p. (ps-3). 1988. pap. 4.95 *(0-15-607830-9,* Voyager Bks) HarBrace.
—Dancing in the Moon: Counting Rhymes. Eichenberg, Fritz, illus. LC 75-8154. 25p. (gr. k-1). 1975. pap. 3.95 *(0-15-623811-X,* Voyager Bks) HarBrace.
Eichhorn, Dennis P. Hammer. (Illus.). 96p. (Orig.). (gr. 8-12). 1993. pap. 3.25 *(0-89872-219-5,* 217) Turman Pub.
Eicholz, Robert, et al. Extending the Ideas Enrichment Workbook. 2nd ed. (gr. 4). 1980. pap. text ed. write for info. *(0-201-16035-8);* pap. text ed. write for info. *(0-201-16045-5);* Grade 4. write for info. tchr's. ed. *(0-201-16046-3)* Addison-Wesley.
—Extending the Ideas Enrichment Workbook. 2nd ed. (gr. 5-6). 1980. pap. text ed. write for info. *(0-201-16055-2);* Grade 5. write for info. tchr's ed. *(0-201-16056-0);* pap. text ed. write for info. *(0-201-16065-X);* Grade 6. write for info. tchr's ed. *(201-16066)* Addison-Wesley.
Eickschen, Connie. Yestergames. 28p. (ps-7). 1991. pap. 4.95 *(0-9631442-0-0)* YesterCo.
Eide, Lorraine. Robert Mugabe. Schlesinger, Arthur M., intro. by. (Illus.). 112p. (gr. 5 up). 1989. 17.95 *(1-55546-845-4)* Chelsea Hse.
Eide, Lucille. My UFO. Eide, Lucille, illus. LC 81-90261. 84p. (Orig.). 1980. pap. 4.95 *(0-9610668-1-4)* L Eide.
Eidenier, Betty. Warp Zone Shakespeare! Active Learning Lessons for the Gifted. (gr. 6-12). 1990. 12. 00 *(0-910609-23-3)* Gifted Educ Pr.
Eidsmoe, John. Columbus & Cortez: Conquerors for Christ. LC 92-81425. 304p. (Orig.). 1992. pap. 9.95 *(0-89221-223-3)* New Leaf.
Eige, Lillian. Cady. Wentworth, Janet, illus. LC 85-45818. 192p. (gr. 3-7). 1987. HarpC Child Bks.
Eimon, Mina H. Why Cats Chase Mice: A Story of the 12 Zodiac Signs. Eimon, Mina H., illus. 32p. (gr. k-6). 1993. 11.95 *(0-89346-533-X)* Heian Intl.
Einhorn, Franne, jt. auth. see Bin-Nun, Judy.
Einstein, Albert. Albert Einstein. Redpath, Ann, ed. Delessert, Etienne, illus. 32p. (gr. 9 up). 1986. PLB 12.95.s.p. *(0-88682-011-1)* Creative Ed.
Einstein, Stephen J. & Kukoff, Lydia. Every Person's Guide to Judaism. 196p. 1989. pap. 8.95 *(0-8074-0434-9,* 142610) UAHC.
Eires, Anita. Summer Awakening. (gr. 6 up). 1986. pap. 2.50 *(0-440-98369-X,* LFL) Dell.
Eisemann, Henry. His-Her, The Shy Serpent. O'Grady-Steinberg, Chrissy, illus. 32p. (Orig.). (gr. k-6). 1992. pap. 6.95 *(0-938129-05-8)* Emprise Pubns.
—Hump-Free Goes to Galapagos. Campbell, Jay, illus. 26p. (Orig.). (gr. k-6). 1990. pap. 7.95g *(0-938129-04-X)* Emprise Pubns.

—Hump-Free Heads for Hawaii. Campbell, Jay, illus. 24p. (gr. k-6). 1989. pap. 6.95 *(0-938129-02-3)* Emprise Pubns.
—Hump-Free Visits Vancouver Expo. Campbell, Jay, illus. (Orig.). (gr. k-6). 1986. pap. 6.95 *(0-938129-01-5)* Emprise Pubns.
—Su-Su, the Fremont School Panda. Steinberg, Chris, illus. 22p. (Orig.). (gr. k-6). 1987. pap. 6.95 *(0-938129-03-1)* Emprise Pubns.
Eisen, Armand. Treasury of Children's Literature. LC 92-2847. (Illus.). 304p. (gr. 3-7). 1992. 24.45 *(0-395-53349-X)* HM.
—A Visit to Christmasland: A Storybook with a Real Charm Bracelet. Lisi, Victoria, illus. 32p. 1993. incl. bracelet 12.95 *(0-8362-4506-7)* Andrews & McMeel.
—Wish upon a Star: A Tale of Bedtime Magic. (Illus.). 32p. 1993. 14.95 *(0-8362-4937-2)* Andrews & McMeel.
Eisen, Armand, ed. The Classic Christmas Treasury for Children. LC 89-43004. (Illus.). 56p. (gr. 3 up). 1990. 9.98 *(0-89471-769-3)* Courage Bks.
—Classic Poems for Children. Dieneman, Debbie, illus. LC 92-13078. 32p. 1992. 6.95 *(0-8362-4909-7)* Andrews & McMeel.
Eisen, David. Fun with Architecture: From the Metropolitan Museum of Art. 64p. 1992. shrink-wrapped incl. 32 r 22.50 *(0-670-84684-8)* Viking Child Bks.
Eisenberg, A. & Globe, Leah A. Secret Weapon & Other Stories of Faith & Valor. (Illus.). (gr. 4-6). 1971. 9.95x *(0-685-01035-X)* Bloch.
Eisenberg, Ann. Bible Heroes I Can Be. Schanzer, Roz, illus. LC 89-48188. 24p. (ps). 1990. 12.95 *(0-929371-09-7);* pap. 4.95 *(0-929371-10-0)* Kar Ben.
—I Can Celebrate. Schanzer, Roz, illus. LC 88-83567. 12p. (ps). 1988. bds. 4.95 *(0-930494-93-8)* Kar Ben.
Eisenberg, Azriel. Fill a Blank Page: A Biography of Solomon Schechter. (Illus.). (gr. 6-11). 3.75 *(0-8381-0730-3,* 10-730) United Syn Bk.
Eisenberg, Azriel & Robinson, Jessie B. My Jewish Holidays. 208p. (gr. 5-6). 3.95x *(0-8381-0176-3,* 10-176) United Syn Bk.
Eisenberg, Joyce. Grenada. (Illus.). 88p. (gr. 5 up). 1988. lib. bdg. 14.95 *(1-55546-777-6)* Chelsea Hse.
Eisenberg, Lisa. Brain Builders...Not! (gr. 4-7). 1993. pap. 1.95 *(0-590-47295-X)* Scholastic Inc.
—Happy Birthday, Lexie. 144p. (gr. 3-7). 1991. 12.95 *(0-670-83553-6)* Viking Child Bks.
—Happy Birthday, Lexie. 144p. (gr. 3-7). 1993. pap. 3.99 *(0-14-034568-X)* Puffin Bks.
—Leave It to Lexie. 144p. (gr. 2-7). 1989. pap. 11.95 *(0-670-82844-0)* Viking Child Bks.
—Leave It to Lexie. 144p. (gr. 3-7). 1991. 3.95 *(0-14-034181-1)* Puffin Bks.
—Lexie on Her Own. 128p. (gr. 3-7). 1992. 13.00 *(0-670-84489-6)* Viking Child Bks.
—Mystery at Camp Windingo. 144p. (gr. 4-7). 1991. 14. 95 *(0-8037-0950-1)* Dial Bks Young.
—Mystery at Snowshoe Mountain Lodge. LC 86-11535. 176p. (gr. 5 up). 1987. 12.95 *(0-8037-0359-7)* Dial Bks Young.
—Mystery at Snowshoe Mountain Lodge. 176p. (gr. 2-9). 1988. pap. 2.95 *(0-8167-1322-7)* Troll Assocs.
—One Hundred One Hopelessly Hilarious Jokes. 1990. pap. 1.95 *(0-590-43636-8)* Scholastic Inc.
—The Story of Babe Ruth. (gr. k-6). 1990. pap. 2.95 *(0-440-40274-3,* YB) Dell.
—Story of Sitting Bull. (gr. 4-7). 1991. pap. 2.99 *(0-440-40508-4)* Dell.
Eisenberg, Lisa & Hall, Katy. One Hundred One Ghost Jokes. Orehek, Don, illus. (gr. 3-7). 1988. pap. 1.95 *(0-590-41811-4)* Scholastic Inc.
—Quickie Comebacks. 1992. pap. 1.95 *(0-590-44998-2)* Scholastic Inc.
Eisenberg, Lisa, jt. auth. see Hall, Katy.
Eisenberg, Phyllis R. You're My Nikki. Kastner, Jill, illus. LC 91-2670. 32p. (ps-3). 1992. 14.00 *(0-8037-1127-1);* PLB 13.89 *(0-8037-1129-8)* Dial Bks Young.
Eisenberg, Ruth P., jt. ed. see Fischer, Sophia M.
Eisenhower, Julie N. Special People. (Illus.). 208p. 1990. pap. text ed. 7.95 *(0-939631-24-5)* Thomas Publications.
Eisler, Colin. Cats Know Best. Ivory, Lesley A., illus. LC 87-15653. 32p. (ps up). 1988. 13.95 *(0-8037-0503-4);* PLB 13.89 *(0-8037-0560-3)* Dial Bks Young.
—Cats Know Best. LC 87-15653. (Illus.). 32p. 1992. pap. 4.99 *(0-8037-1139-5,* Dial Pied Piper) Puffin Bks.
Eisler, Colin, compiled by. David's Songs: His Psalms & Their Story. Pinkney, Jerry, illus. Eisler, Bolin, intro. by. LC 90-25459. (Illus.). 64p. 1992. 17.00 *(0-8037-1058-5);* PLB 16.89 *(0-8037-1059-3)* Dial Bks Young.
Eitan, Ora. A Veces Grande, a Veces Pequeno. Writer, C. C. & Nielsen, Lisa C., trs. Elchanan, illus. (SPA.). 24p. (Orig.). (ps). 1992. pap. text ed. 3.00x *(1-56134-149-5)* Dushkin Pub.
—Sometimes Big, Sometimes Small. Kriss, David, tr. from HEB. Elcanan, illus. 24p. (Orig.). (ps). 1992. pap. text ed. 3.00 *(1-56134-139-8)* Dushkin Pub.
Eitzen, Ruth. The White Feather. Eitzen, Allan, illus. LC 86-31786. 64p. (gr. 3-4). 1987. 12.95 *(0-8361-3439-7)* Herald Pr.

Ekberg, Susan. Pink Stars & Angel Wings. Neavill, Michelle, illus. LC 91-91216. 32p. (ps up). 1992. 16.95

(0-9630419-0-8) Spiritseeker. "Wish, whoosh, Kari swooshed through the window..." Kari's magical journey to her special star reveals much about herself & the world. Through a delightful tale of faith & love, we share Kari's adventure, her hopes & joy as she learns that she will never be alone in this big world -- we all have someone protecting us, watching us, & loving us. This is a story for children of all ages, about peace found through self-awareness & trust in the universe. This book focuses on children's spirituality, & deals with issues about God, guardian angels, our inner voice, & believing in things we can't always see with our eyes. "The gentle guidance & reassurance that Kate gives Kari is so healing & nurturing to a child's questioning mind...this story is a delightful trail to the heart...it is indeed a journey to one's inner voice of love & self-acceptance...so needed in these days of rapid change & growth..." Illustrated by Michelle Neavill. Published by: Spiritseeker Publishing, Inc. PO Box 2441, Fargo, ND, 58108-2441; 1-800-538-6415. T-shirts, posters, buttons & stickers also available. Call or write for brochure. *Publisher Provided Annotation.*

Ekey, Robert. Fire! in Yellowstone. Mayer, Larry, illus. LC 89-43156. 32p. (gr. 2-4). 1989. PLB 15.93 (0-8368-0226-8) Gareth Stevens Inc.

Eko, Paul M. Cry Cry My Beloved People. Scalist, Paula, ed. 286p. 1990. 18.95x (0-685-28130-2) Backwards & Backwards.

—Water Finds Its Own Level. Scalist, Paula, ed. 105p. 1990. pap. 8.95 (0-685-28132-9) Backwards & Backwards.

Ekoomiak, Normee. Arctic Memories. LC 89-39194. (Illus.). 32p. (gr. 3 up). 1990. 15.95 (0-8050-1254-0, Bks Young Read) H Holt & Co.

—Arctic Memories. LC 89-39194. (Illus.). 32p. (gr. 3 up). 1992. 5.95 (0-8050-2347-X, Bks Young Read) H Holt & Co.

Elam, Richard M., ed. Teen-Age Suspense Stories. (gr. 6-10). 1963. PLB 7.19 (0-8313-0047-7) Lantern.

Elbek, Gail. What Every Child Must Know about Grownups. Jaworski, Jo, ed. Taylor, Neil, illus. LC 86-40333. 65p. (gr. k-4). 1990. 5.95 (1-55523-015-6) Winston-Derek.

Elbert, Elizabeth, pseud. Camp Adventure. LC 92-59948. 108p. (gr. 4-8). 1993. pap. 5.95 (1-55523-576-X) Winston-Derek.

Elbl, Martin. Tales of the Amazon. Neubacher, Gerda, illus. 32p. (gr. k-3). 1985. 10.95 (0-88625-127-3) Durkin Hayes Pub.

Elchoness, Monte. Why Can't Anyone Hear Me? A Guide for Surviving Adolescence. 2nd, rev. ed. Elchoness, Monte, illus. LC 86-737. 200p. (gr. 6-12). 1989. pap. 10.95 (0-936781-06-8, Dist. by Publishers Group West) Monroe Pr.

—Why Do Kids Need Feelings? A Guide to Healthy Emotions. (Illus.). (gr. 3 up). 1992. pap. 9.95 (0-936781-07-6) Monroe Pr.

Eldadah, Basil. The Greatest Act. 84p. 1989. pap. 5.95 (0-915957-05-1) Amana Corp.

Elden, Lucky. Jazz Guitar Lines. Stang, Aaron, ed. (Orig.). 1992. pap. text ed. 17.95 (0-89898-577-3) CPP Belwin.

Eldin, Peter. The Magic Handbook. Colville, Jeane, et al, illus. LC 85-171061. 192p. (gr. 4 up). 1985. lib. bdg. 9.79 (0-671-55040-3, J Messner); pap. 6.95 (0-685-42988-1) S&S Trade.

—Spookster's Handbook. LC 89-32659. (Illus.). 96p. (Orig.). (gr. 4 up). 1990. 12.95 (0-8069-5742-5); pap. 3.95 (0-8069-5743-3) Sterling.

—Trickster's Handbook. LC 89-32073. (Illus.). 96p. (gr. 10-12). 1989. 12.95 (0-8069-5740-9) Sterling.

—The Trickster's Handbook. Smith, Roger, illus. LC 89-32073. 96p. (gr. 3-10). 1991. pap. 3.95 (0-8069-5741-7) Sterling.

Eldredge, Niles, et al. Fossil Factory: A Kid's Guide to Digging up Dinosaurs, Exploring Evolution & Finding Fossils. Kelley, True & Lindblom, Steve, illus. 111p. (gr. 2-7). 1989. pap. 8.61 (0-201-18599-7) Addison-Wesley.

Eldrid, Brenda. Pershey the Rabbit. County Studio Staff, illus. 24p. (ps-2). 1993. pap. text ed. 0.99 (1-56293-342-6) McClanahan Bk.

—Teddy's Day in the Forest. Bates, Louise, illus. 24p. (ps-2). 1993. pap. text ed. 0.99 (1-56293-341-8) McClanahan Bk.

Eldrid, Brenda M. The Little School Bus That Talked. Beckes, Shirley, illus. 24p. (ps-2). 1992. pap. 0.99 (1-56293-113-X) McClanahan Bk.

Eldridge, David. Flying Dragons, Ancient Reptiles That Ruled the Air. Nodel, Norman, illus. LC 79-87965. 32p. (gr. 3-6). 1980. PLB 10.79 (0-89375-241-X); pap. 2.95 (0-89375-245-2) Troll Assocs.

—The Giant Dinosaurs, Ancient Reptiles That Ruled the Land. Nodel, Norman, illus. LC 79-87967. 32p. (gr. 3-6). 1980. PLB 10.79 (0-89375-242-8); pap. 2.95 (0-89375-246-0) Troll Assocs.

—Last of the Dinosaurs, the End of an Age. Nodel, Norman, illus. LC 79-64636. 32p. (gr. 3-6). 1980. PLB 10.79 (0-89375-243-6); pap. 2.95 (0-89375-247-9) Troll Assocs.

—Sea Monsters, Ancient Reptiles That Ruled the Sea. Nodel, Norman, illus. LC 79-87964. 32p. (gr. 3-6). 1980. PLB 10.79 (0-89375-240-1); pap. 2.95 (0-89375-244-4) Troll Assocs.

Eldridge, Melinda. Salcott, the Indian Boy. (Illus.). 32p. 1989. PLB 29.28 (0-8172-2462-9); pap. 17.96 (0-8172-2778-4) Raintree Steck-V.

Eleanor Roosevelt Institute Staff. War or Peace in the Twentieth Century. Roff, Sue R., ed. (Illus.). 270p. (gr. 8-12). 1984. binder 59.95 (0-89908-502-4) Greenhaven.

Electric Company Staff. Tickle Yourself Again with Riddles. Smollin, Michael J., illus. LC 78-19699. (gr. 1-5). 1988. pap. 2.95 (0-394-84152-2) Random Bks Yng Read.

—Tickle Yourself with Riddles. Smollin, Mike, illus. LC 77-90197. 96p. (gr. 1-5). 1988. pap. 2.99 (0-394-83783-5) Random Bks Yng Read.

Elementary School Children of California. The Poetry Express, Nineteen Eighty-Eight: A Collection of Poetry by the Children of California. Reed, John M. & Gillman, Lillian E., eds. Hayden, Jaime, contrib. by. 192p. (ps-6). 1988. 8.95 (0-317-93373-6) Other Eye.

Elementary School Children of Oregon. Rhyme Time, Nineteen Eighty-Eight: A Collection of Poetry by the Children of Oregon. Reed, John M. & Gillman, Lillian E., eds. Hayden, Jaime, contrib. by. 104p. (Orig.). (ps-6). 1988. 6.95 (0-317-93374-4) Other Eye.

Elementary School Children of Washington State. A Child's Eye View: A Collection of Poetry by the Children of Washington State, Vol. 1. Reed, John M. & Gillman, Lillian E., eds. Hayden, Jaime, contrib. by. 143p. (ps-6). 1987. 7.95 (0-317-93371-X) Other Eye.

—A Child's Eye View: A Collection of Poetry by the Children of Washington State, Vol. 2. Reed, John M. & Gillman, Lillian E., eds. Hayden, Jaime, contrib. by. 200p. (ps-6). 1988. 7.95 (0-317-93372-8) Other Eye.

Eley, Janet. Understanding Your Horse's Health: A Practical Guide. (Illus.). 144p. (gr. 2 up). 1992. 24.95 (0-7063-6963-7, Pub. by Ward Lock UK) Sterling.

Elfman, Blossom. Love Me Deadly. (gr. 7 up). 1989. pap. 2.95 (0-449-70298-7, Juniper) Fawcett.

Elfman, Eric. The Very Scary Almanac. Suckow, Will, illus. 80p. (Orig.). (gr. 4-7). 1993. pap. 4.99 (0-679-84401-5) Random Bks Yng Read.

Elford, George R. Recall to Inferno: Devil's Guard Two. (Orig.). 1988. pap. 3.95 (0-440-20199-3) Dell.

Elgaard, Elin, tr. see Andersen, Maria.

Elgin, Kathleen & Osterritter, John F. Twenty-Eight Days. LC 73-77779. (Illus.). 64p. (gr. 5 up). 1973. pap. 5.95 (0-679-51382-5) McKay.

Elgorriaga, Jose A., adapted by see La Fonatine, Jean de.

Elias, Joyce. Whose Toes Are Those? Sturm, Cathy, illus. LC 92-8603. (ps). 1992. 11.95 (0-8120-6215-9) Barron.

Elias, Miriam. Families. Erie. 1991. 12.95 (0-87306-576-X) Feldheim.

—Goodbye, My Friends. (gr. 6-9). 1989. 10.95 (0-87306-491-7); pap. 8.95 (0-87306-492-5) Feldheim.

Elias, Miriam L. Special Days Are Wonderful: A Guessing Game Book. Leff, Tova, illus. 32p. (ps). 1993. English ed. 9.95 (0-922613-46-X); Russian ed. 9.95 (0-922613-49-4) Hachai Pubns.

Elias, Susan C. Strong & Safe: A Children's Guide to Self Protection. Wise, Caroline, illus. 60p. (Orig.). (gr. 1-3). 1989. pap. 8.95 (0-317-93904-1) Womansource.

Eliason, Peter. The Comeuppance of Dipsey Dolan. 162p. (Orig.). (gr. 2-10). 1984. pap. 5.95 (0-916777-34-0) W P Allen.

Elinsky, Stephen E. Innovations in Cooking. 2nd ed. Summy, Barbara L., illus. 85p. (gr. 7 up). 1988. pap. 17.95 (0-9620526-0-4) Elins Laboratories.

Eliot, Carol, et al. Values in Action: A Middle-School Ethics Course. 162p. (gr. 5-8). 1991. curriculum guide 22.00 (1-881678-39-3) CRIS.

Eliot, Chip. The Clintons: Meet the First Family. LC 93-14027. (Illus.). 24p. (gr. 2-6). 1993. pap. text ed. 1.95 (0-8167-3243-4) Troll Assocs.

—Ivan Lendl. LC 88-1829. (Illus.). 48p. (gr. 5-6). 1988. RSBE 11.95 (0-89686-380-8, Crestwood Hse) Macmillan Child Grp.

Eliot, George. Adam Bede. Paterson, John, ed. LC 68-5227. (gr. 9 up). 1968. pap. 9.16 (0-395-05204-1, RivEd) HM.

—Middlemarch. Haight, G. S., ed. LC 56-13878. (gr. 9 up). 1956. pap. 9.16 (0-395-05105-3, RivEd) HM.

—Mill on the Floss. (gr. 9 up). 1964. pap. 2.95 (0-8049-0043-4, CL-43) Airmont.

—Mill on the Floss. Haight, G. S., ed. LC 62-16032. (gr. 9 up). 1972. 9.16 (0-395-05151-7, RivEd) HM.

—Silas Marner. (gr. 9 up). 1964. pap. 2.50 (0-8049-0014-0, CL-14) Airmont.

—Silas Marner. 192p. (gr. 7 up). 1960. pap. 2.50 (0-451-52427-6, Sig Classics) NAL-Dutton.

Eliot, T. S. Growltiger's Last Stand & Other Poems. Le Cain, Errol, illus. 32p. (ps up). 1987. 14.00 (0-374-32809-9, Co-pub. by HarBraceJ) FS&G.

—Growltigers Last Stand & Other Poems. Le Cain, Errol, illus. (ps up). 1990. pap. 4.95 (0-374-42811-5) FS&G.

—Mr. Mistoffelees with Mungojerrie & Rumpelteazer. Howton, Louise, ed. Le Cain, Errol, illus. 32p. (ps up). 1991. 13.95 (0-15-256230-3) HarBrace.

—Selected Poems. LC 67-23064. 127p. (gr. 7-12). 1967. pap. 6.95 (0-15-680647-9, Harvest Bks) HarBrace.

Elish, Dan. The Great Squirrel Uprising. Cazet, Denys, illus. LC 91-27145. 128p. (gr. 4 up). 1992. 14.95 (0-531-05995-2); lib. bdg. 14.99 (0-531-08595-3) Orchard Bks Watts.

—Harriet Tubman & the Underground Railroad. LC 92-9562. (Illus.). 32p. (gr. 2-4). 1993. PLB 12.40 (1-56294-273-5) Millbrook Pr.

—James Meredith & School Desegregation. LC 93-9383. (Illus.). 32p. (gr. 2-4). 1994. PLB 12.40 (1-56294-379-0) Millbrook Pr.

—Jason & the Baseball Bear. Shafter, John, illus. LC 89-23102. 160p. (gr. 3-5). 1990. 13.95 (0-531-05868-9); PLB 13.99 (0-531-08468-X) Orchard Bks Watts.

—Jason & the Bear. 1992. pap. 3.50 (0-553-15878-3) Bantam.

—My Christmas Stocking: Stories, Songs, Poems, Recipes, Crafts & Fun for Kids. Bernardin, James, illus. Palubniak, Nancy, photos by. (Illus.). 80p. (ps-3). 1993. 9.98 (0-8317-5173-8) Smithmark.

—The Transcontinental Railroad: Triumph of a Dream. LC 92-39995. (Illus.). 64p. (gr. 4-6). 1993. PLB 14.90 (1-56294-337-5) Millbrook Pr.

—The Worldwide Dessert Contest. Gurney, John, illus. LC 87-24694. 208p. (gr. 4-6). 1988. 13.95 (0-531-05752-6); PLB 13.99 (0-531-08352-7) Orchard Bks Watts.

—Worldwide Dessert Contest. (gr. 4 up). 1990. pap. 3.50 (0-553-15820-1) Bantam.

Elitzig, Francis. Sea Girl. (Orig.). 1993. pap. 4.50 playscript (0-87602-318-9) Anchorage.

Elkan, Betty, intro. by see Yulin, Betty.

Elkin, Benjamin. Money. LC 83-7436. (Illus.). 48p. (gr. k-4). 1983. PLB 15.27 (0-516-01697-0) Childrens.

—Seis Pescadores Disparatados - Six Foolish Fisherman. LC 86-21611. (Illus.). 32p. (gr. k-3). 1986. PLB 15.00 (0-516-33601-0); pap. 3.95 (0-516-53601-X) Childrens.

Elkin, Judith. A Family in Japan. (Illus.). 32p. (gr. 2-5). 1987. PLB 13.50 (0-8225-1672-1) Lerner Pubns.

Elkington, John, et al. Going Green: A Kid's Handbook to Saving the Planet. Ross, Tony, illus. 96p. (gr. 3 up). 1990. 16.00 (0-670-83611-7) Viking Child Bks.

—Going Green: A Kid's Handbook to Saving the Planet. (Illus.). 96p. (gr. 3 up). 1990. pap. 8.95 (0-14-034597-3, Puffin) Puffin Bks.

Elkins, Dov P. Shepherd of Jerusalem. LC 75-39436. (Illus.). (gr. 8-12). 1976. 11.95 (0-88400-045-1) Shengold.

Elkins, Stephen. Stories That End with a Hug. Menck, Kevin, illus. 32p. (gr. k-8). 1993. 12.98 (1-56919-021-X) Wonder Wkshop.

—Stories That End with a Prayer. Menck, Kevin, illus. 32p. (gr. k-8). Date not set. 12.98 (1-56919-003-8) Wonder Wkshop.

—Stories That End with a Song. Menck, Kevin, illus. 32p. (gr. k-8). Date not set. 12.98 (0-685-68095-9) Wonder Wkshop.

Elledge, Scott, ed. Wider Than the Sky: Poems to Grow up With. LC 90-4135. 368p. (gr. 5 up). 1990. 20.00 (0-06-021786-3); PLB 19.89 (0-06-021787-1) HarpC Child Bks.

Ellenberger, W., et al. Atlas of Animal Anatomy for Artists. rev. ed. Brown, Lewis S., ed. Weinbaum, Helen, tr. (Illus.). 192p. (gr. 9-12). 1956. pap. 8.95 (0-486-20082-5) Dover.

Ellenby, J. Anglo-Saxon Household. (Illus.). 32p. (gr. 1-5). 1986. 6.95 (0-521-30379-6) Cambridge U Pr.

Eller, Scott. The Johnson Boys: The Football Wars. 1992. pap. 2.95 (0-590-42828-4, 060, Apple Paperbacks) Scholastic Inc.

—That Soccer Season. (gr. 4-7). 1993. pap. 2.95 (0-590-42829-2) Scholastic Inc.

—Twenty-First Century Fox. 1990. pap. 2.95 (0-590-41938-2) Scholastic Inc.

Ellerbusch, Kristin. Jump-Rope Rap. LC 92-18794. (Illus.). (gr. 1-8). 1992. PLB 14.95 (0-89565-973-5); Resale. 21.35 (0-685-60109-9) Childs World.

Ellerby, Leona. King Tut's Game Board. LC 79-91279. 120p. (gr. 4 up). 1980. 13.50 (0-8225-0765-X) Lerner Pubns.

Ellinger, Marko. Fun Food to Tickle Your Mood: A Cookbook for Children Who Cherish the Earth. Krone, Mike & Panek, Judy, illus. 96p. (gr. 2-6). 1992. pap. 9.95 (0-9630147-5-7) Piccadilly TX.

Elliot, David. An Alphabet of Rotten Kids! (Illus.). 32p. (ps up). 1991. 14.95 (0-399-22260-X, Philomel Bks) Putnam Pub Group.

Elliot, Irene. Dragonsong. (Orig.). 1991. Playscript. pap. 5.00 (0-87602-294-8) Anchorage.

Elliot, J. Children's Encyclopedia. King, Colin, illus. 128p. (gr. 3-6). 1987. PLB 12.95 (0-88110-265-2); pap. 6.95 (0-7460-0000-6) EDC.

Elliott, Allison. The Cowboy Cookbook. LC 88-51042. (Illus.). 120p. (Orig.). (gr. 1-8). 1989. 8.95x (0-941099-02-4) Tourmaline Pub.

—Humpty Dumpty Was an Egg: A Coloring Cookbook. (Illus.). 64p. (gr. k-6). 1989. 8.95x (0-941099-03-2) Tourmaline Pub.

Elliott, Brian. Strawberry Shortcake & Baby Needs a Name. Gatie, John, illus. 40p. (ps-3). 1984. cancelled 5.95 (0-910313-21-0) Parker Bros.

Elliott, Dan. The Adventures of Ernie & Bert at the South Pole. Cooke, Tom, illus. LC 84-60187. 32p. (ps-3). 1984. pap. 1.50 (0-394-86299-6) Random Bks Yng Read.

—The Adventures of Ernie & Bert in Twiddlebug Land. LC 83-61719. (Illus.). 32p. (ps-3). 1984. pap. 1.50 (0-394-85925-1) Random Bks Yng Read.

—Ernie's Little Lie. Mathieu, Joe, illus. LC 82-7574. 40p. (ps-3). 1992. 4.95 (0-394-85440-3); pap. 2.99 (0-679-82401-4) Random Bks Yng Read.

—Grover Goes to School. Chartier, Normand, illus. LC 81-15398. 40p. (ps-3). 1992. pap. 2.99 (0-679-82397-2) Random Bks Yng Read.

—Grover Learns to Read. Chartier, Normand, illus. LC 84-27692. 40p. (ps-3). 1985. 4.95 (0-394-87498-6) Random Bks Yng Read.

—Grover Learns to Read. Chartier, Normand, illus. LC 84-27692. 40p. (ps-3). 1993. pap. 2.99 (0-679-83949-6) Random Bks Yng Read.

—My Doll Is Lost! Manthieu, Joe, illus. LC 83-11211. 40p. (ps-3). 1984. 3.95 (0-394-86251-1); lib. bdg. 6.99 (0-394-96251-6) Random Bks Yng Read.

—My Doll Is Lost! Mathieu, Joe, illus. LC 83-11211. 40p. (ps-3). 1993. pap. 2.99 (0-679-83953-4) Random Bks Yng Read.

—Oscar's Rotten Birthday. Chartier, Normand, illus. LC 81-2398. 40p. (ps-3). 1992. pap. 2.99 (0-679-82400-6) Random Bks Yng Read.

—Two Wheels for Grover. Mathieu, Joe, illus. LC 84-4732. 40p. (ps-3). 1984. 4.95 (0-394-86586-3); lib. bdg. 6.99 (0-394-96586-8) Random Bks Yng Read.

—A Visit to the Sesame Street Firehouse. Mathieu, Joe, illus. LC 83-44616. 32p. (ps-3). 1983. lib. bdg. 5.99 (0-394-96029-7); pap. 2.25 (0-394-86029-2) Random Bks Yng Read.

—Una Visita a la Estacion de Bomberos de Sesame Street. Miro, Norma S. & Saunders, Paola B., trs. from ENG. Mathieu, Joe, illus. LC 92-3814. (SPA.). 32p. (ps-3). 1992. pap. 2.25 (0-679-83499-0) Random Bks Yng Read.

Elliott, David W. Listen to the Silence. 224p. (gr. 7 up). 1971. pap. 4.99 (0-451-06588-3, Y6588, Sig) NAL-Dutton.

Elliott, Deborah. Making a Book. LC 93-38569. (Illus.). 48p. (gr. 2-4). 1994. 15.95 (1-56847-103-3) Thomson Lrning.

Elliott, Donald. Alligators & Music. Arrowood, Clinton, illus. LC 84-13862. (gr. 8). 1984. (Pub. by Gambit); pap. 8.95 (0-87645-118-0, Pub. by Gambit) Harvard Common Pr.

—Frogs & Ballet. Arrowood, Clinton, illus. LC 78-19566. (gr. 1 up). 1979. smythe sewn 12.95 (0-87645-099-0, Pub. by Gambit); pap. 8.95 (0-87645-119-9) Harvard Common Pr.

Elliott, Ingrid G. Hospital Roadmap: A Book to Help Explain the Hospital Experience to Young children. LC 82-80226. (Illus.). 36p. (Orig.). (gr. k-2). 1984. pap. 8.95 (0-9608150-0-7) Resources Children.

—Hospital Roadmap Manual: A Curriculum Guide to Explain the Hospital Experience to Young Children. 100p. (Orig.). (gr. k-2). 1986. pap. 11.95 (0-9608150-1-5) Resources Children.

Elliott, Joey. Beezle's Bravery. Chapin, Tom, narrated by. Buzzanco, Eileen M., illus. 32p. (gr. k-4). 1989. 11.95 (0-924483-17-2); incl. audiocassette 16.95 (0-924483-15-6); incl. audiocassette & toy combination 39.95 (0-924483-13-X); incl. audiocassette & small toy combination 25.95 (0-924483-35-0); write for info. audiocassette (0-924483-19-9) Soundprints.

—Scamp's New Home. Chapin, Tom, narrated by. Buzzanco, Eileen M., illus. 32p. (gr. k-4). 1989. 11.95 (0-924483-16-4); incl. audiocassette 16.95 (0-924483-14-8); incl. audiocassette & toy combination 39.95 (0-924483-12-1); incl. audiocassette & small toy combination 25.95 (0-924483-39-3); write for info. audiocassette (0-924483-18-0) Soundprints.

Elliott, Lisa E. Old Friends & New Friends, Old Kitties & New Kitties. Caroland, Mary, ed. LC 90-71002. 44p. (gr. k-3). 1991. 5.95 (1-55523-364-3) Winston-Derek.

Elliott, Paula. Every Day Can Feel Like Christmas: Color Your World with Love. Royall, Sandra, illus. 32p. (Orig.). 1991. pap. 4.95 (1-879052-02-4) Planetary Pubns.

—Fluffy & Sparky: A Story about True Buddies. Royall, Sandy, illus. 32p. (ps up). 1991. 12.95 (1-879052-00-8) Planetary Pubns.

Elliott, Robert C., ed. see Bellamy, Edward.

Elliott, Tony. High Country Wildlife. Elliott, Tony, illus. LC 86-2218. 64p. (Orig.). (gr. 1-6). 1988. pap. 2.50 (0-914565-20-6, 20-6) Capstan Pubns.

—Texas Outdoors: Read 'n Color Book. Elliott, Tony, illus. (gr. 1-8). 1986. pap. 3.95 (0-914565-24-9, 24-9, Timbertrails) Capstan Pubns.

—This Is Wyoming: Read 'n Color Book. Elliott, Tony, illus. LC 89-469. (gr. 3-6). 1989. pap. 3.95 (0-914565-39-7, 39-7, Timbertrails) Capstan Pubns.

Ellis. My Secret Admirer. 1993. pap. 3.25 (0-590-44768-8) Scholastic Inc.

Ellis, Anne L. Dabble Duck. Truesdell, Sue, illus. LC 83-47692. 32p. (ps-2). 1984. 13.00i (0-06-021817-7); PLB 12.89 (0-06-021818-5) HarpC Child Bks.

—Dabble Duck. Truesdell, Sue, illus. LC 83-47692. 32p. (ps-3). 1984. pap. 3.95 (0-06-443153-3, Trophy) HarpC Child Bks.

—The Dragon of Middlethorpe. (Illus.). 192p. (gr. 4-7). 1991. 14.95 (0-8050-1713-5, Bks Young Read) H Holt & Co.

Ellis, Carol. Camp Fear. 1993. pap. 3.25 (0-590-46411-6) Scholastic Inc.

—Stepdaughter. 1993. pap. 3.25 (0-590-46044-7) Scholastic Inc.

—There's a Troll in My Closet. 1994. pap. 2.99 (0-671-87161-7, Minstrel Bks) PB.

—There's a Troll in My Popcorn. 1994. pap. 3.50 (0-671-87162-5, Minstrel Bks) PB.

—The Window. 1992. pap. 2.99 (0-590-44916-8, Point) Scholastic Inc.

Ellis, Cathy. The Adventures of Gilly, the Guitar, Bk. 1. Moya, Patricia, illus. 40p. (ps-2). 1991. wkbk. incl. audiotape 15.95 (1-879542-04-8) Ellis Family Mus.

—Complete Guide for the Guitar. rev. ed. Lee, et al. (Illus.). 255p. (gr. 6-12). 1990. tchr's ed. 34.95 (1-879542-01-3); wkbk., student ed., spiral bd. 29.95 (1-879542-00-5) Ellis Family Mus.

—Holiday Guitar: Songs for Christmas & Hanukah. rev. ed. 48p. 1992. Repr. of 1985 ed. lab manual 18.95 (1-879542-11-0); audiotape 14.95 (1-879542-12-9) Ellis Family Mus.

—More Adventures of Gilly, the Guitar, Bk. 3. (Illus.). 48p. (ps-2). 1993. wkbk. 12.95 (1-879542-26-9); audiotape 14.95 (1-879542-27-7) Ellis Family Mus.

—More Adventures with Gilly, the Guitar, Bk. 2. Moya, Patricia, illus. 48p. (ps-2). 1992. wkbk. 12.95 (1-879542-08-0); audiotape 14.95 (1-879542-14-5) Ellis Family Mus.

Ellis, Chris. Water. (Illus.). 48p. (gr. 7-9). 1992. 13.95 (0-563-34756-2, BBC-Parkwest); pap. 6.95 (0-563-34616-7, BBC-Parkwest) Parkwest Pubns.

Ellis, David, ed. see Carroll, Lewis.

Ellis, David M. New York State: Gateway to America. (Illus.). 400p. (gr. 7 up). 1988. 24.95 (0-89781-246-8) Windsor Pubns Inc.

Ellis, Ella T. The Boy Who Loved Whales. 1995. write for info. (0-8050-3306-8) H Holt & Co.

Ellis, Franklin F. Untold Millions. (gr. k-6). 1972. visualized song 4.50 (3-90117-007-3) CEF Press.

Ellis, Jana. The Best of Everything. LC 88-12380. 160p. (gr. 7 up). 1988. pap. text ed. 2.50 (0-8167-1356-1) Troll Assocs.

—Better Than the Truth. LC 88-15881. 160p. (gr. 7 up). 1988. pap. text ed. 2.50 (0-8167-1362-6) Troll Assocs.

—Hometown Hero. LC 89-34374. 160p. (gr. 7 up). 1989. pap. text ed. 2.50 (0-8167-1609-9) Troll Assocs.

—Junior Weekend. LC 88-19988. 160p. (gr. 7 up). 1988. pap. text ed. 2.50 (0-8167-1364-2) Troll Assocs.

—Lost & Found. LC 89-36350. 160p. (gr. 7 up). 1989. pap. text ed. 2.50 (0-8167-1675-7) Troll Assocs.

—Never Say Good-Bye. LC 89-34376. 160p. (gr. 7 up). 1989. pap. text ed. 2.50 (0-8167-1618-8) Troll Assocs.

—Never Stop Smiling. LC 88-12390. 160p. (gr. 7 up). 1988. pap. text ed. 2.50 (0-8167-1360-X) Troll Assocs.

—Perfect Strangers. LC 89-36349. 160p. (gr. 7 up). 1989. pap. text ed. 2.50 (0-8167-1674-9) Troll Assocs.

—Playing Games. LC 88-12389. 160p. (gr. 7 up). 1988. pap. text ed. 2.50 (0-8167-1358-8) Troll Assocs.

—Slave for a Day. LC 89-34375. 160p. (gr. 7 up). 1989. pap. text ed. 2.50 (0-8167-1610-2) Troll Assocs.

—Sweet Success. LC 89-36348. 160p. (gr. 7 up). 1989. pap. text ed. 2.50 (0-8167-1673-0) Troll Assocs.

—Two for One. LC 88-12384. 160p. (gr. 7 up). 1988. pap. text ed. 2.50 (0-8167-1354-5) Troll Assocs.

Ellis, John S., ed. My Play a Tune Book: All Time Disney Classics. (Illus.). 26p. 1988. 15.95 (0-938971-07-7) JTG Nashville.

Ellis, John S. & Leary, Mary B., eds. My Play a Tune Book: Children's Songs. Trebing, Tom, illus. 26p. (ps up). 1985. 14.95 (0-938971-00-X) JTG Nashville.

Ellis, Joseph, jt. auth. see Pringle, Mary L.

Ellis, Joyce. Tiffany. LC 86-70910. 160p. (Orig.). (gr. 9-12). 1986. pap. 3.99 (0-87123-893-4) Bethany Hse.

Ellis, Joyce & Lynn, Claire. Bible Bees. Lautermilch, John, illus. 36p. (gr. k). 1981. 2.95 (0-89323-049-9) Bible Memory.

Ellis, Joyce K., compiled by. Saved by a Broken Pole & Other Stories. 75p. (Orig.). (gr. 2-6). 1980. pap. 1.25 (0-89323-007-3, 096) Bible Memory.

Ellis, Julie L. Handbook of Creative Problem Solving Techniques. 60p. (Orig.). (gr. 8-12). 1987. pap. text ed. 7.99 (0-89824-067-0) Trillium Pr.

Ellis, Karen S., intro. by. Domino: Traditional Children's Songs, Proverbs & Culture from the American Virgin Islands. Arpino, Alaria, illus. 96p. (Orig.). (gr. 1-6). 1990. Set. pap. 21.50 (0-9625560-7-6); pap. text ed. 14.50 (0-9625560-3-3); incl. audio tape 10.00 (0-9625560-0-9) Guavaberry Bks.

Ellis, Lucy. American Gladiators. (Illus.). 48p. 1993. 1.49 (0-440-21436-X) Dell.

—Fielder's Choice: Pink Parrots, No. 3. 120p. (gr. 3-6). 1991. PLB 17.50 (0-8225-3113-5) Lerner Pubns.

—Mixed Signals: Pink Parrots, No. 4. 121p. (gr. 3-6). 1991. PLB 17.50 (0-8225-3112-7) Lerner Pubns.

—Pink Parrots - The Girls Strike Back: The Making of the Pink Parrots. (gr. 4-7). 1990. pap. 3.50 (0-316-71967-6, Spts Illus Kids) Little.

—Pink Parrots, No. 3: Mixed Signals. (gr. 4-7). 1991. pap. 3.50 (0-316-18566-3, Spts Illus Kids) Little.

—Pink Parrots, No. 4: Fielder's Choice. (gr. 4-7). 1991. pap. 3.50 (0-316-12447-8, Spts Illus Kids) Little.

Ellis, Neil C. The Power of the Blood. 48p. (Orig.). 1991. pap. text ed. 7.95 (0-925783-01-3) Natl BIE Pub.

Ellis, Rafaela. Dwight D. Eisenhower: Thirty-Fourth President of the United States. Young, Richard G., ed. LC 88-24538. (Illus.). (gr. 5-9). 1989. PLB 17.26 (0-944483-13-5) Garrett Ed Corp.

—Martin Van Buren: Eighth President of the United States. Young, Richard G., ed. LC 88-24535. (Illus.). (gr. 5-9). 1989. PLB 17.26 (0-944483-12-7) Garrett Ed Corp.

Ellis, Richard. Physty: The True Story of a Young Whale's Life. LC 92-54937. (Illus.). 56p. (gr. 3 up). 1993. 9.98 (1-56138-271-X) Courage Bks.

Ellis, Rob, jt. auth. see Schmidt, Mike.

Ellis, Sarah. A Family Project. LC 87-22818. 144p. (gr. 4-7). 1988. SBE 13.95 (0-689-50444-6, M K McElderry) Macmillan Child Grp.

—A Family Project. (Orig.). (gr. k-6). 1991. pap. 3.25 (0-440-40397-9, Pub. by Yearling Classics) Dell.

—Next-Door Neighbors. LC 89-37923. 160p. (gr. 4-7). 1990. SBE 13.95 (0-689-50495-0, M K McElderry) Macmillan Child Grp.

—Next-Door Neighbors. (gr. 4-7). 1992. pap. 3.25 (0-440-40620-X) Dell.

—Pick-up Sticks. Chan, Harvey, contrib. by. LC 91-26585. 128p. (gr. 7 up). 1992. SBE 13.95 (0-689-50550-7, M K McElderry) Macmillan Child Grp.

—Pick-Up Sticks. LC 93-7759. 128p. (gr. 5 up). 1993. pap. 3.99 (0-14-036340-8, Puffin) Puffin Bks.

Ellis, Terry. Explorers from Willow Wood Springs. LC 85-63827. (Illus.). 180p. (Orig.). (gr. 4 up). 1989. pap. 4.75 (0-915677-31-8) Roundtable Pub.

—The Invasion of Willow Wood Springs. LC 85-63826. (Illus.). 168p. (Orig.). (gr. 4 up). 1989. pap. 4.75 (0-915677-32-6) Roundtable Pub.

—The Legend of Willow Wood Springs. LC 85-63828. (Illus.). 180p. (Orig.). (gr. 4 up). 1989. pap. 4.75 (0-915677-30-X) Roundtable Pub.

Ellis, Toni. My Play a Tune Book: Nintendo. Nintendo, illus. 26p. 1989. 15.95 (0-938971-21-2) JTG Nashville.

Ellis, Toni, ed. My Play a Tune Book: American Songs. (Illus.). 26p. 1988. PLB 15.95 (0-938971-12-3) JTG Nashville.

Ellis, Veronica F. Afro-Bets Activity & Enrichment Guide: First Book about Africa. (gr. 1-4). 1989. pap. 7.95 (0-940975-07-6) Just Us Bks.

—Afro-Bets First Book about Africa. Ford, George, illus. LC 89-85157. 32p. (Orig.). (gr. 1-4). 1990. PLB 13.95 (0-940975-12-2); pap. 6.95 (0-940975-03-3) Just Us Bks.

—Land of the Four Winds. Walker, Sylvia, illus. LC 92-72001. 32p. (gr. 1-4). 1993. 14.95 (0-940975-38-6); pap. 6.95 (0-940975-39-4) Just Us Bks.

Ellison, Don, jt. auth. see Goodwin, Jude.

Ellison, Douglas W. David Lant: The Vanished Outlaw. 232p. (Orig.). 1988. pap. text ed. write for info. (0-929918-01-0) Midstates Pub.

Ellison, Harold. Santa's Gone Away. LC 88-51034. 44p. (gr. k-3). 1988. 6.95 (1-55523-201-9) Winston-Derek.

Ellison, Jean F. Justine...It's Time. Collier, Bobbie, contrib. by. LC 93-83722. (Illus.). 24p. (Orig.). (gr. 2-8). 1993. 12.95 (0-9637825-1-7); pap. 10.00 (0-9637825-0-9); pap. 8.00 ea. 6 or more copies Spotlght News.

Ellison, Virginia. The Pooh Cook Book. 1991. pap. 3.50 (0-440-47300-4) Dell.

—Pooh Get-Well Book. 1991. pap. 3.50 (0-440-46971-6) Dell.

—Pooh Party Book. 1991. pap. 3.50 (0-440-47299-7) Dell.

—Pooh's Alphabet Book. 1991. pap. 3.50 (0-440-40630-7) Dell.

Elmer, Robert. Target Archery: With a History of the Sport in America. St. Charles, Glenn, frwd. by. (Illus.). 524p. (gr. 10 up). 1992. Repr. of 1946 ed. 39.95 (1-56416-090-4) Derrydale Pr.

Elmer, Robert, ed. see Thompson, Maurice.

Elmer, Robert P. American Archery: A Vade Mecum of the Art of Shooting with the Long Bow. McMeek, Samuel G., intro. by. (Illus.). 312p. (gr. 10 up). 1993. Repr. of 1917 ed. 39.95 (1-56416-099-8) Derrydale Pr.

—Archery by Elmer. (Illus.). 458p. (gr. 10 up). 1993. Repr. of 1927 ed. 39.95 (1-56416-097-1) Derrydale Pr.

Elmore, Patricia. Susannah & the Poison Green Halloween. Schick, Joel, illus. LC 82-2493. 128p. (gr. 4-7). 1982. 9.95 (0-525-44019-4, DCB) Dutton Child Bks.

—Susannah & the Purple Mongoose Mystery. LC 91-43643. (Illus.). 120p. (gr. 3-7). 1992. 15.00 (0-525-44907-8, DCB) Dutton Child Bks.

Elmshauser, John, ed. I'm in Junior High, but It's Not My Fault. Koehler, Ed, illus. 127p. (Orig.). (gr. 7-9). 1992. pap. 6.99 (0-570-04723-4) Concordia.

Elovson, Allana. The Kindergarten Survival Handbook: The Before School Checklist & a Guide for Parents. rev. ed. Elovson, Andrea K., illus. 96p. (Orig.). (gr. k). 1993. Spanish ed. pap. text ed. 12.95 perfect bdg. (1-879888-07-6); English ed. pap. text ed. 12.95 (1-879888-06-8) Parent Ed.

"SMALLER THAN A BOX OF RICE KRISPIES, THE KINDERGARTEN SURVIVAL HANDBOOK IS WORTH ITS WEIGHT IN GOLD!"-- The Harrisburg, PA Patriot News. Coming to school ready to learn is crucial to children's self-esteem, attitude toward school & subsequent school achievement & is the Number One goal of Education 2000, our national education strategy. Written in simple language accessible to parents of every socio-economic level & cultural backround, the charmingly illustrated KINDERGARTEN SURVIVAL HANDBOOK & its Spanish language version EL MANUAL DE COMO SOBRE VIVIR EL JARDIN DE NINOS, present the whys, the whats & the hows of kindergarten readiness. First, THE BEFORE SCHOOL CHECKLIST identifies the skills & information that prepare children to THRIVE as well as survive in kindergarten. Then, A GUIDE FOR PARENTS & THE NEXT STEP offer simple, enjoyable, inexpensive ways to use everyday experiences to transform a child's world into an exciting learning environment & establish a beneficial relationship with school & teachers. An invaluable resource for all parents including teens & immigrant parents; teachers, pre-schools, schools, parent educators, & for community & training programs of all kinds. Strongly endorsed by educators, teachers, child-care professionals, parents & reviewers throughout the country: "THE KINDERGARTEN SURVIVAL HANDBOOK IS FABULOUS, & HAS BEEN NEEDED FOR A LONG, LONG TIME!" says Cherry Belanger, Kindergarten Teacher, L.A. Available from major wholesalers & Publishers' Services, P. O. Box 2510, Novato, CA 94948.
Publisher Provided Annotation.

Els. Silver Elephant, No. 2. 1987. 4.95 (*0-02-970370-0*) Macmillan.
Els, Betty Vander see Vander Els, Betty.
Elsant, Martin. Bar Mitzvah Lessons. LC 93-628. 1993. write for info. (*1-88128-301-1*) Alef Design.
Elsasser, Albert B., ed. see Brown, Vinson.
Else, JoAnn, jt. auth. see Cera, Mary J.

Elsemann, Henry. Hump-Free: The Wrong Way Whale. (Illus., Orig.). (gr. k-6). 1985. pap. 6.95 (*0-938129-00-7*) Emprise Pubns.
One of a series of stories about the lone humpback whale that visited the San Francisco Bay & the Sacramento River in October 1985. This free-spirited whale shared his adventures with a concerned world. As one of the earth's endangered species, the whale occupies a special place in the heart of his fellow mammal--Man. Each book in the series has been highly acclaimed & been used in schools throughout the country. Teachers find the stories helpful in environmental studies, geography, science & for inspiring student story-writing. The appealing bright & colorful illustrations highlight the lively text which provides insight into the undersea world. The story has been a consistent favorite on TV's "Reading Rainbow". Other books in the series find Hump-Free in Canada

meeting his cousins, the dolphins & killer whales; in Hawaii with his family; & in the Galapagos Archipelago seeing the unique animals living there. The books are meant to teach as they entertain. Readers or listeners are equally enthralled with the whales & their adventures. Order From: Empire Publns., 1000 S. Main St., Salinas, CA 93901; 408/422-0415.
Publisher Provided Annotation.

Elting, Mary. The Big Golden Book of Dinosaurs. Santoro, Christopher, illus. LC 87-81784. 64p. (gr. 3-6). pap. text ed. write for info. (*0-307-15567-6*, Golden Pr) Western Pub.
—Macmillan Book of Dinosaurs & Other Prehistoric Creatures. Hamberger, John, illus. LC 84-4372. 80p. (gr. 2-7). 1984. SBE 16.95 (*0-02-733430-9*, Macmillan Child Bk) Macmillan Child Grp.
—The Macmillan Book of Dinosaurs & Other Prehistoric Creatures. LC 84-4944. (Illus.). 80p. (gr. 3-7). 1984. pap. 8.95 (*0-02-043000-0*, Aladdin) Macmillan Child Grp.
—The Macmillan Book of the Human Body. Moldoff, Kirk, illus. LC 85-24204. 80p. (gr. 3-7). 1986. pap. 8.95 (*0-02-043080-9*, Aladdin) Macmillan Child Grp.
—Macmillan Book of the Human Body. LC 85-24204. (Illus.). 80p. (gr. 3-7). 1986. SBE 16.95 (*0-02-733440-6*, Macmillan Child Bk) Macmillan Child Grp.
—Snakes & Other Reptiles. Santoro, Christopher, illus. (gr. 3-7). 1987. pap. 8.95 (*0-671-61835-0*, S&S BFYR) S&S Trade.
—Volcanoes & Earthquakes. Courtney, illus. LC 89-37107. 48p. (gr. 3-7). 1990. pap. 9.95 (*0-671-67217-7*, S&S BFYR) S&S Trade.
Elting, Mary & Folsom, Michael. Q Is for Duck. Kent, Jack, illus. LC 80-13854. 64p. (ps-3). 1980. 13.95 (*0-395-29437-1*, Clarion Bks); pap. 5.70 (*0-395-30062-2*) HM.
Elting, Mary, jt. auth. see Wyler, Rose.
Eltinge, et al. The Staffordshire Bull Terrier in America. Eltinge, Steve, ed. Epps, Sarah, illus. Eltinge, Steve, intro. by. 140p. (gr. 4 up). 1986. pap. 24.95 (*0-9617204-0-9*) MIP Pub.
Eltinge, Steve, ed. see Eltinge, et al.
Elvidge, Vivian, jt. ed. see Johnston, Helen.
Elwell, Marty. Searching for Treasure Coloring Book. Rose, Steve, illus. 1992. 5.00 (*0-923463-85-2*) Noble Pub Assocs.
Elwell, Sharon. Jeremy & the Wappo. Gentry, Debra, illus. 126p. (Orig.). (gr. 3-4). 1991. pap. 15.95 (*0-9626210-0-5*) Rattle OK Pubns.
Elwood, Ann & Madigan, Carol O. The Macmillan Book of Fascinating Facts: An Almanac for Kids. Martin, Dick, illus. LC 88-22844. 448p. (gr. 4 up). 1989. SBE 16.95 (*0-02-733461-9*, Macmillan Child Bk) Macmillan Child Grp.
Elwood, Ann, et al. Macmillan Illustrated Almanac for Kids. Barrett, Lindsey, illus. LC 81-82099. 400p. (gr. 4 up). 1984. SBE 12.95 (*0-02-535420-5*, Macmillan Child Bk); pap. 7.95 (*0-02-043040-X*) Macmillan Child Grp.
—Macmillan Illustrated Almanac for Kids. Barrett, Lindsey, illus. LC 83-26296. 448p. (gr. 4 up). 1986. pap. 10.95 (*0-02-043100-7*, Aladdin) Macmillan Child Grp.
Elwood, Roger. Angelwalk. LC 87-70456. 192p. (Orig.). 1988. pap. 8.99 (*0-89107-440-6*, Crossway Bks) Good News.
—Forbidden River. (gr. 3-7). 1991. pap. 4.99 (*0-8499-3304-8*) Word Inc.
—The Frankenstein Project. (gr. 3-7). 1991. pap. 4.99 (*0-8499-3303-X*) Word Inc.
—Nightmare at Skull Junction. LC 92-7295. 128p. (gr. 3-9). 1992. pap. 4.99 (*0-8499-3361-7*) Word Pub.
Ely, Vivian K. & Barnes, Michael. Starting Your Own Marketing Business. 2nd ed. Dorr, Eugene L., ed. (Illus.). (gr. 11-12). 1978. text ed. 12.28 (*0-07-019307-X*) McGraw.
Elzbieta. Dikou & the Baby Star. Elzbieta, illus. LC 88-302. 32p. (ps-3). 1989. (Crowell Jr Bks) HarpC Child Bks.
—Dikou & the Mysterious Moon Sheep. Elzbieta, illus. LC 87-13587. 32p. (ps-3). 1988. (Crowell Jr Bks) HarpC Child Bks.
—Flon Flon & Musette. 1994. write for info. (*0-8050-3299-1*) H Holt & Co.
—Mimi's Scary Theater: A Play in Nine Scenes for Seven Chartacters & an Egg. Elzbieta, illus. LC 92-54868. 18p. (ps-3). 1993. 14.95 (*1-56282-415-5*) Hyprn Child.
Emanuel, James A. Whole Grain: Collected Poems 1958-1989. Anderson, Keith O., illus. LC 90-61082. 400p. (gr. 9-12). 1991. 25.00 (*0-916418-79-0*) Lotus.
Emanuel, Sr. M. Dic Mihi Latine. (ENG & LAT.). 50p. 1.70 (*0-939507-05-6*, B2) Amer Classical.
Emanuels, George. California Indians: An Illustrated Guide. (Illus.). 172p. (gr. 4-8). incl. study guide 19.95 (*0-9607520-5-6*); pap. 14.95 (*0-9607520-3-X*) Diablo Bks.

Emberley, Barbara. Drummer Hoff. Emberley, Ed E., illus. LC 74-8201. 32p. (gr. k-4). 1985. pap. 12.95 jacketed (*0-671-66682-7*, S&S BFYR); pap. 5.95 (*0-671-66745-9*, S&S BFYR) S&S Trade.
—The Story of Paul Bunyan. Emberley, Ed, illus. LC 93-11791. 1994. pap. 14.00 (*0-671-88557-X*, S&S BFYR) S&S Trade.
Emberley, Barbara, adapted by. One Wide River to Cross. Emberley, Ed, illus. 32p. (ps-3). 1992. pap. 4.95 (*0-316-23445-1*) Little.
Emberley, Ed. Ed Emberley's Drawing Book: Make a World. (ps-3). 1991. pap. 6.95 (*0-316-23644-6*) Little.
—Ed Emberley's Drawing Book of Faces. (Illus.). (ps-3). 1992. pap. 4.95 (*0-316-23655-1*) Little.
—Ed Emberley's Thumbprint Drawing Box. 32p. (ps-3). 1992. 14.95 (*0-316-23648-9*) Little.
—Go Away, Big Green Monster! (ps-3). 1993. 12.95 (*0-316-23653-5*) Little.
Emberley, Ed E. Ed Emberley's A. B. C. (Illus.). 56p. (gr. k-2). 1978. lib. bdg. 15.95 (*0-316-23408-7*) Little.
—Ed Emberley's Big Green Drawing Book. Emberley, Ed E., illus. LC 79-16247. (gr. k up). 1979. 15.95 (*0-316-23595-4*); pap. 8.95 (*0-316-23596-2*) Little.
—Ed Emberley's Big Orange Drawing Book. (Illus.). 96p. (gr. 1-5). 1980. 15.95 (*0-316-23418-4*); pap. 8.95 (*0-316-23419-2*) Little.
—Ed Emberley's Big Purple Drawing Book. Emberley, Ed E., illus. (gr. 1 up). 1981. 14.95 (*0-316-23422-2*); pap. 8.95 (*0-316-23423-0*) Little.
—Ed Emberley's Christmas Drawing Book, Vol. 1. 1989. pap. 4.95 (*0-316-23438-9*) Little.
—Ed Emberley's Drawing Book: Make a World. Emberley, Ed E., illus. LC 70-154962. (gr. 2 up). 1972. lib. bdg. 14.95 (*0-316-23598-9*) Little.
—Ed Emberley's Drawing Book of Faces. Emberley, Ed E., illus. 32p. (gr. k-3). 1975. lib. bdg. 14.95 (*0-316-23609-8*) Little.
—Ed Emberley's Drawing Box. 1988. Incl. 4 colored pens, 4 drawing bks. & drawing pad. pap. 14.95 (*0-316-23436-2*) Little.
—Ed Emberley's Great Thumbprint Drawing Book. Emberley, Ed E., illus. (gr. 1 up). 1977. lib. bdg. 14.95 (*0-316-23613-6*) Little.
—Ed Emberley's Make-It-Yourself Christmas Tree Kit, Vol. 1. 1989. 10.95 (*0-316-23641-1*) Little.
—Ed Emberley's Picture Pie: A Book of Circle Art. Emberley, Ed E., illus. 48p. 1984. 15.95 (*0-316-23425-7*); pap. 7.95 (*0-316-23426-5*) Little.
—Ed Emberley's Second Drawing Box. (ps-3). 1990. pap. 14.95 (*0-316-23412-5*) Little.
—Green Says Go. LC 68-21165. (Illus.). (ps-3). 1972. lib. bdg. 14.95 (*0-316-23599-7*) Little.
—The Wing on a Flea: A Book about Shapes. Emberley, Ed E., illus. (ps-3). 1988. lib. bdg. 14.95 (*0-316-23600-4*) Little.
Emberley, Ed E. & Emberley, Rebecca. Ed Emberley's Big Red Drawing Book, Vol. 1. Emberley, Ed E. & Emberley, Rebecca, illus. 96p. (gr. 1-5). 1987. 14.95 (*0-316-23434-6*); pap. 8.95 (*0-316-23435-4*) Little.
Emberley, Ed E., illus. First Words: Animals. (ps). 1987. pap. 3.50 (*0-316-23428-1*) Little.
—First Words: Cars, Boats, & Planes. (ps). 1987. pap. 3.50 (*0-316-23430-3*) Little.
—First Words: Home. (ps). 1987. pap. 3.50 (*0-316-23433-8*) Little.
Emberley, Michael. Dinosaurs! A Drawing Book. Emberley, Michael, illus. 48p. (gr. 3 up). 1985. pap. 5.95 (*0-316-23631-4*) Little.
—Dinosaurs!, Vol. 1. A Drawing Book. 1980. 14.95 (*0-316-23417-6*) Little.
—More Dinosaurs! And Other Prehistoric Beasts. Emberley, Michael, illus. LC 83-9822. 64p. (gr. 3 up). 1983. 13.95 (*0-316-23424-9*) Little.
—More Dinosaurs! & Other Prehistoric Beasts. Emberley, Michael, illus. 64p. (ps-3). 1992. pap. 5.95 (*0-316-23441-9*) Little.
—Present, Vol. 1. (ps-3). 1991. 14.95 (*0-316-23411-7*) Little.
—Ruby. (ps-3). 1992. pap. 4.95 (*0-316-23660-8*) Little.
—Ruby, Vol. 1. (ps-3). 1990. 14.95 (*0-316-23643-8*) Little.
—Welcome Back, Sun. LC 92-9786. (gr. 4 up). 1993. 14.95 (*0-316-23647-0*) Little.
Emberley, Rebecca. City Sounds. Emberley, Rebecca, illus. 32p. (ps-1). 1989. 15.95 (*0-316-23635-7*) Little.
—Drawing with Numbers & Letters. (gr. 6 up). 1981. 12.95 (*0-316-23406-0*) Little.
—Jungle Sounds. Emberley, Rebecca, illus. 32p. (ps-1). 1989. 13.95 (*0-316-23636-5*) Little.
—Let's Go in Two Languages - Vamos: un Libro en Dos Lenguas. LC 92-37278. (ENG & SPA.). 1993. 15.95 (*0-316-23450-8*) Little.
—My Day: A Book in Two Languages - Mi Dia: un Libro En Dos Lenguas. LC 92-37277. (ENG & SPA.). 1993. 15.95 (*0-316-23454-0*) Little.
—My House Mi Casa. (ps-3). 1993. pap. 5.95 (*0-316-23448-6*) Little.
—My House, Mi Casa: A Book in Two Languages. Emberley, Rebecca, illus. LC 89-12893. (ps-2). 1990. 15.95 (*0-316-23637-3*) Little.
—Rebecca Emberley's Cut-Ups: A Book to Cut & Glue. (ps-3). 1992. pap. 12.95 (*0-316-23645-4*) Little.
—Taking a Walk Caminando. (ps-3). 1990. 14.95 (*0-316-23640-3*) Little.
Emberley, Rebecca, jt. auth. see Emberley, Ed E.
Embry, Lynn. Rx for the Classroom Blahs. Filkins, Vanessa, illus. 64p. (gr. 4-8). 1983. wkbk. 7.95 (*0-86653-104-1*, GA 462) Good Apple.

—Scientific Encounters of the Curious Kind. McClure, Nancee, illus. 64p. (gr. 4-7). 1984. wkbk. 7.95 (0-86653-176-9, GA 550) Good Apple.
—Scientific Encounters of the Endangered Kind. McClure, Nancee, illus. 64p. (gr. 4-7). 1986. wkbk. 7.95 (0-86653-353-2, GA 694) Good Apple.
—Scientific Encounters of the Insect World. 64p. (gr. 4-7). 1988. wkbk. 7.95 (0-86653-424-5, GA 1039) Good Apple.
—Scientific Encounters of the Mysterious Sea. McClure, Nancee, illus. 64p. (gr. 4-7). 1987. pap. 7.95 (0-86653-407-5, GA1013) Good Apple.
Embry, Lynn & Bobo, Betty. Math America. Skiles, Janet, illus. 128p. (gr. 4-6). 1987. pap. 11.95 (0-86653-378-8, GA1015) Good Apple.
—Math Around the World. 144p. (gr. 4-6). 1991. 11.95 (0-86653-600-0, GA1319) Good Apple.
Embry, Margaret. The Blue-Nosed Witch. Rose, Carl, illus. 48p. (gr. 2-5). 1984. pap. 2.75 (0-553-15435-4) Bantam.
Embury, Barbara & Crouch, Tom D. The Dream Is Alive: A Flight of Discovery Aboard the Space Shuttle. LC 90-55194. (Illus.). 64p. (gr. 3-7). 1991. 14.95 (0-06-021813-4) HarpC Child Bks.
Emecheta, Buchi. The Joys of Motherhood. 224p. (Orig.). 1989. pap. 8.95 (0-435-90684-4, 90684) Heinemann.
—The Moonlight Bride. LC 82-17816. 77p. (gr. 6-10). 1983. pap. 6.95 (0-8076-1063-1) Braziller.
—The Wrestling Match. LC 82-17750. 74p. (gr. 6-10). 1983. pap. 4.95 (0-8076-1061-5) Braziller.
Emekwulu, Paul C. The Magic of Numbers: Supplementary Text for High Schools. Saleh, Umaru, ed. Coppedge, Floyd, intro. by. LC 89-91024. (Orig.). (gr. 9-12). 1989. pap. text ed. write for info. (0-9623353-3-9) Novelty Bks.
Emerman, Ellen. Is It Shabbos Yet? Vegh, Toby, illus. 32p. (ps-1). 1990. 8.95 (0-922613-21-4); pap. 6.95 (0-922613-22-2) Hachai Pubns.
Emerson, Karen L. Nellie Bly: Making Headlines: A Biography of Nellie Bly. LC 88-35910. (Illus.). 112p. (gr. 5 up). 1989. RSBE 13.95 (0-87518-406-5, Dillon) Macmillan Child Grp.
Emerson, Kathy L. The Mystery of the Missing Bagpipes. 128p. (Orig.). (gr. 5). 1991. pap. 2.95 (0-380-76138-6, Camelot) Avon.
Emerson, Mark. The Mean Lean Weightlifting Queen. 120p. (gr. 9-12). 1992. 17.95 (0-936389-26-5) Tudor Pubs.
Emerson, Ralph Waldo. Selections from Ralph Waldo Emerson. Whicher, Stephen, ed. LC 61-16166. (gr. 9 up). 1972. pap. 9.16 (0-395-05112-6, RivEd) HM.
Emerson, Roger & Derwingson, Richard. On My Own. (gr. 5-8). 1989. singer's ed., 3 pts. 2.95 (0-931205-50-6); singer's ed., 2 pts. 2.95 (0-931205-49-2); tchr's ed. 12.95 (0-931205-48-4) Jenson Pubns.
Emerson, Sally. Nursery Rhyme Songbook: With Easy Music to Play for Piano & Guitar. Maclean, Colin & Maclean, Moira, illus. LC 92-53106. 72p. (ps-k). 1992. 16.95 (1-85697-823-0) Kingfisher Bks.
Emerson, Sally, selected by. ABCs & Other Learning Rhymes. Maclean, Moira & Maclean, Colin, illus. LC 92-32576. 1993. pap. 4.95 (1-85697-899-0) Kingfisher Bks.
—Baby Games & Lullabies. Maclean, Moira & Maclean, Colin, illus. LC 92-27488. 1993. 4.95 (1-85697-901-6) Kingfisher Bks.
Emerson, Sally, compiled by. Nursery Rhymes. Maclean, Moira & Maclean, Colin, illus. LC 92-26446. 32p. (ps-k). 1993. pap. 4.95 (1-85697-905-9) Kingfisher Bks.
—The Nursery Treasury: A Collection of Rhymes, Poems, Lullabies & Games. Maclean, Moira & Maclean, Colin, illus. 128p. 1988. pap. 17.95 (0-385-24650-1) Doubleday.
Emerson, Sally & Corbett, Pie, eds. Action Rhymes. Maclean, Moira & Maclean, Colin, illus. LC 92-26445. 32p. (ps-k). 1993. pap. 4.95 (1-85697-900-8) Kingfisher Bks.
Emerson, Sally, jt. ed. see Corbett, Pie.
Emerson, Zack. Hill Five Hundred Sixty-Eight. 1991. pap. 2.95 (0-590-44592-8) Scholastic Inc.
—Stand Down. 128p. 1992. pap. 2.95 (0-590-44594-4, Point) Scholastic Inc.
—'Tis the Season. 256p. 1991. pap. 2.95 (0-590-44593-6) Scholastic Inc.
—Welcome to Vietnam. 1991. pap. 2.95 (0-590-44591-X) Scholastic Inc.
Emert, Phyllis. Fun with Paints: Little Crafters. 1992. pap. 3.99 (0-517-09276-4) Outlet Bk Co.
—Fun with Paper: Little Crafters. 1992. pap. 3.99 (0-517-08277-2) Outlet Bk Co.
Emert, Phyllis R. Fighter Planes. (Illus.). 64p. (gr. 5-9). 1990. lib. bdg. 12.98 (0-671-68959-2, J Messner); lib. bdg. 5.95 (0-671-68964-9) S&S Trade.
—Ghosts, Hauntings, & Mysterious Happenings. 128p. 1992. pap. 2.50 (0-8125-2057-2) Tor Bks.
—Ghosts, Hauntings, & Mysterious Happenings. 1994. pap. 2.50 (0-8125-2038-6) Tor Bks.
—Guide Dogs. LC 85-12756. (Illus.). 48p. (gr. 5-6). 1985. RSBE 11.95 (0-89686-282-8, Crestwood Hse) Macmillan Child Grp.
—Hearing-Ear Dogs. LC 85-12841. (Illus.). 48p. (gr. 5-6). 1985. RSBE 11.95 (0-89686-283-6, Crestwood Hse) Macmillan Child Grp.
—Helicopters. (Illus.). 64p. (gr. 5-9). 1990. lib. bdg. 12.98 (0-671-68962-2, J Messner); pap. 5.95 (0-671-68967-3) S&S Trade.

—Law Enforcement Dogs. LC 85-21351. (Illus.). 48p. (gr. 5-6). 1985. RSBE 11.95 (0-89686-284-4, Crestwood Hse) Macmillan Child Grp.
—Military Dogs. LC 85-17488. (Illus.). 48p. (gr. 5-6). 1985. RSBE 11.95 (0-89686-286-0, Crestwood Hse) Macmillan Child Grp.
—Monsters, Strange Dreams, & UFO's. 1990. pap. 2.50 (0-8125-9425-8) Tor Bks.
—Mysteries of People & Places. 128p. 1992. pap. 2.50 (0-8125-2056-4) Tor Bks.
—Mysteries of Ships & Planes. 128p. 1990. pap. 2.50 (0-8125-9427-4) Tor Bks.
—Search & Rescue Dogs. LC 85-18967. (Illus.). 48p. (gr. 5-6). 1985. RSBE 11.95 (0-89686-285-2, Crestwood Hse) Macmillan Child Grp.
—Sled Dogs. LC 85-14967. (Illus.). 48p. (gr. 5-6). 1985. RSBE 11.95 (0-89686-288-7, Crestwood Hse) Macmillan Child Grp.
—Special Task Aircraft. (Illus.). 64p. (gr. 5-9). 1990. lib. bdg. 12.98 (0-671-68963-0, J Messner) S&S Trade.
—Transports & Bombers. (Illus.). 64p. (gr. 5-9). 1990. lib. bdg. 12.98 (0-671-68961-4, J Messner) S&S Trade.
—Wild Wings Series, 4 bks. (Illus.). 256p. (gr. 5-9). 1990. Set. lib. bdg. 51.92 (0-671-31238-3, J Messner); Set. lib. bdg. 23.80 (0-671-31239-1); Set. PLB 38.94s.p. (0-685-47009-1); Set. pap. 17.85s.p. (0-685-47010-5) S&S Trade.
Emery, jt. auth. see King.
Emery, C. F. Horny. Le Blanc, L., illus. LC 68-17304. 48p. (gr. 2 up). 1967. PLB 9.26 (0-87783-017-7) Oddo.
Emil, Jane. All about Rivers. LC 83-4868. (Illus.). 32p. (gr. 3-6). 1984. lib. bdg. 10.59 (0-89375-979-1); pap. text ed. 2.95 (0-89375-980-5) Troll Assocs.
Emma Kemp Books. Rudolph the Red-Nosed Reindeer: Musical Board Book. Bushell, Isobel, illus. 12p. (ps). 1993. 5.95 (0-694-00564-9) HarpC Child Bks.
Emmanuel, Sr. M. Via Latina. (ENG & LAT.). 50p. 1.70 (0-939507-13-7, B3) Amer Classical.
Emmence, Lew. Running. LC 91-15143. (Illus.). 32p. (gr. 2-5). 1992. PLB 11.90 (0-531-18464-1, Pub. by Bookwright Pr) Watts.
Emmens, Carol A. The Abortion Controversy. 128p. 1987. lib. bdg. 12.98 (0-671-64209-X, J Messner); lib. bdg. 12.98 (0-671-62284-6) S&S Trade.
—The Abortion Controversy. rev. ed. LC 86-28532. 144p. (gr. 7 up). 1991. lib. bdg. 13.98 (0-671-74539-5, J Messner); lib. bdg. 6.95 (0-671-74967-6, J Messner) S&S Trade.
Emmens, Cliff W. A Step-by-Step Book about Tropical Fish. (Illus.). 64p. (gr. 9-12). 1988. pap. 3.95 (0-86622-471-8, SK-018) TFH Pubns.
Emmerich, Elsbeth & Hull, Robert. My Childhood in Nazi Germany. (Illus.). 96p. (gr. 4-9). 1992. PLB 13.90 (0-531-18429-3, Pub. by Bookwright Pr) Watts.
Emmert, Michelle. I'm the Big Sister Now. Levine, Abby, ed. Owens, Gail, illus. LC 89-5534. 32p. (gr. 2-6). 1989. PLB 13.95 (0-8075-3458-7) A Whitman.
Emmet, E. R. Brain Puzzler's Delight. LC 93-8555. (Illus.). 96p. (gr. 10-12). 1993. pap. 4.95 (0-8069-8816-9) Sterling.
Emmond, Ken. Manitoba. LC 91-951136. (Illus.). 144p. (gr. 4 up). 1992. PLB 26.60 (0-516-06612-9) Childrens.
Emsden, Katharine N. Voices from the West: Life along the Trail. (Illus.). 60p. (Orig.). (gr. 5-12). 1992. pap. 4.95 (1-878666-18-8) Disc Enter Ltd.
Emsden, Katharine N., intro. by. Coming to America: A New Life in a New Land. (Illus.). 64p. (Orig.). (gr. 5-12). 1993. pap. 4.95 (1-878666-23-4) Disc Enter Ltd.
Encyclopaedia Britannica Publishers, Inc. Staff, et al. Enciclopedia Hispanica. (Illus.). 7792p. 1995. write for info. (1-56409-007-8) EBP Latin Am.
Encyclopaedia Britannica Publishers, Inc. Staff. Hombre, Ciencia y Tecnologia. (SPA., Illus.). 3160p. 1992. write for info. (1-56409-005-1) EBP Latin Am.
—Libro del Ano, 1992. (SPA., Illus.). 416p. 1992. write for info. (1-56409-004-3) EBP Latin Am.
Endacott, Geoff. Inventions & Discoveries. 1991. 15.95 (0-670-84177-3) Viking Child Bks.
—Oceans. 1991. 15.95 (0-670-84176-5) Viking Child Bks.
Ende, Michael. Jim Button: And Luke the Engine Driver. Dodd, Maurice, illus. Bell, Anthea, tr. (Illus.). 244p. (gr. 3 up). 1990. 13.95 (0-87951-391-8) Overlook Pr.
—The Neverending Story. Manheim, Ralph, tr. 448p. (gr. 5 up). 1993. pap. 4.99 (0-14-031793-7) Puffin Bks.
—The Night of Wishes. Schwarzbauer, Heike & Takvorian, Rick, trs. Kehn, Regina, illus. 244p. (gr. 5 up). 1992. 16.00 (0-374-19594-3) FS&G.
—Ophelia's Shadow Theater. Hechelmann, Friedrich, illus. 32p. (gr. 1 up). 1989. 14.95 (0-87951-371-3) Overlook Pr.
Enderle, Judith R. & Tessler, Stephanie G. The Good-for-Something Dragon. Gray, Les, illus. 32p. (ps-3). 1993. pap. 14.95 (1-56397-214-X) Boyds Mills Pr.
—Pile of Pigs. 24p. (ps-3). 1993. pap. 10.95 (1-878009-88-6) Boyds Mills Pr.
—Six Creepy Sheep. O'Brien, John, illus. 24p. (ps-1). 1992. PLB 12.95 (1-56397-092-9) Boyds Mills Pr.
—Six Creepy Sheep. O'Brien, John, illus. LC 93-7140. 26p. (ps-1). 1993. pap. 4.99 (0-14-054994-3, Puffin) Puffin Bks.
Endersby, Frank. The Baby Sitter. (gr. 4 up). 1981. 3.95 (0-85953-279-8) Childs Play.
—The Boy & the Horse. Endersby, Frank, illus. LC 90-46601. 16p. (ps-2). 1976. 11.95 (0-85953-098-1, Pub. by Child's Play England) Childs Play.

—Jasmine & the Cat. (Illus.). 12p. (ps). 1984. 3.95 (0-85953-183-X, Child's Play England) Childs Play.
—Jasmine & the Flowers. 12p. (ps). 1984. 3.95 (0-85953-184-8, Child's Play England) Childs Play.
—Jasmine's Bath Time. 12p. (ps). 1984. 3.95 (0-85953-185-6, Child's Play England) Childs Play.
—Jasmine's Bed Time. 12p. (ps). 1984. 3.95 (0-85953-186-4, Child's Play England) Childs Play.
—Let's Talk Together. (Illus.). 32p. (ps-k). 1993. 15.95 (0-460-88059-4, Pub. by J M Dent & Sons) Trafalgar.
—Man's Work. (gr. 4 up). 1981. 3.95 (0-85953-270-4) Childs Play.
—The Nuisance. (gr. 4 up). 1981. 3.95 (0-85953-233-X) Childs Play.
—Our New Baby. (gr. 4 up). 1981. 3.95 (0-85953-231-3) Childs Play.
—The Plumber. (gr. 4 up). 1981. 3.95 (0-85953-272-0) Childs Play.
—Waiting for Baby. (gr. 4 up). 1981. 3.95 (0-85953-230-5) Childs Play.
—Wash Day. (gr. 4 up). 1981. 3.95 (0-85953-273-9) Childs Play.
—What about Me? (gr. 4 up). 1981. 3.95 (0-85953-232-1) Childs Play.
Endo, Kimio. The Pheasant. Pohl, Kathy, ed. LC 85-28207. (Illus.). 32p. (gr. 3-7). 1986. PLB 17.96 (0-8172-2549-8) Raintree Steck-V.
Endo, Terry, ed. Children's Yellow Pages: Orange County, 1986-87 Edition. Goldstein, Howard, illus. 200p. (Orig.). (gr. k up). 1986. pap. 6.95 (0-938789-00-7) Teruko Ent.
Endore, Guy. Babouk. rev. ed. Kincaid, Jamaica & Trouillot, Michel-Rolphintro. by. 352p. (gr. 9-12). 28.00 (0-85345-759-X); pap. 9.00 (0-85345-745-X) Monthly Rev.
Enell, Trinka. Roll Over, Rosie. Gackenbach, Dick, illus. 32p. (ps-3). 1992. 13.45 (0-395-59340-9, Clarion Bks) HM.
Enerson, Laura. Our Library Lives in a Bus. Robin, illus. LC 77-71462. (gr. 3-5). 1977. 3.50 (0-930480-01-5) R H Barnes.
Engdahl, Sylvia. Enchantress from the Stars. Shackell, Rodney, illus. 288p. (gr. 7 up). 1989. pap. 3.95 (0-02-043031-0, Collier Young Ad) Macmillan Child Grp.
—Enchantress from the Stars. (gr. 6-10). 1991. 16.75 (0-8446-6448-0) Peter Smith.
—The Far Side of Evil. Cufari, Richard, illus. 288p. (gr. 7 up). 1989. pap. 3.95 (0-02-043041-8, Collier Young Ad) Macmillan Child Grp.
Engebrecht, P. A. Under the Haystack. (gr. 5-12). 1991. 19.75 (0-8446-6473-1) Peter Smith.
Engel, Diana. Eleanor, Arthur, & Claire. Engel, Diana, illus. LC 91-21781. 32p. (gr. k-3). 1992. RSBE 14.95 (0-02-733462-7, Macmillan Child Bk) Macmillan Child Grp.
—Fishing. Engel, Diana, illus. LC 91-47705. 32p. (gr. k-3). 1993. RSBE 14.95 (0-02-733463-5, Macmillan Child Bk) Macmillan Child Grp.
—Gino Badino. Engel, Diana, illus. LC 90-36456. 32p. (ps up). 1991. 13.95 (0-688-09502-X); PLB 13.88 (0-688-09503-8, Morrow Jr Bks) Morrow Jr Bks.
—Josephina Hates Her Name. Engel, Diana, illus. LC 88-1500. 32p. (ps-2). 1989. 13.95 (0-688-07795-1); PLB 13.88 (0-688-07796-X, Morrow Jr Bks) Morrow Jr Bks.
—Josephina, the Great Collector. Engel, Diana, illus. LC 87-20358. 32p. (ps-2). 1988. 12.95 (0-688-07542-8); PLB 12.88 (0-688-07543-6, Morrow Jr Bks) Morrow Jr Bks.
—The Little Lump of Clay. Engel, Diana, illus. LC 88-22049. 32p. (ps up). 1989. 13.95 (0-688-08969-0); PLB 13.88 (0-688-08407-9, Morrow Jr Bks) Morrow Jr Bks.
—The Shelf-Paper Jungle. Engel, Diana, illus. LC 93-21772. 32p. (gr. k-3). 1994. RSBE 14.95 (0-02-733464-3, Macmillan Child Bk) Macmillan Child Grp.
Engel, Lorenz. Among the Plains Indians. Catlin, George & Bodmer, Karl, illus. LC 74-102895. 108p. (gr. 5 up). 1970. PLB 14.95 (0-8225-0564-9) Lerner Pubns.
Engelhardt, John, compiled by. Geometry in Our World. (Illus.). 20p. (gr. k-12). 1987. 3 ring notebk. 200 slides 80.00 (0-87353-243-0) NCTM.
Engelhart, Margaret S., jt. auth. see Kurelek, William.
Engelmann, Jeanne. My Body Is My House: A Coloring Book about Alcohol, Drugs & Health. Barton, Patrice, illus. 16p. (gr. k-5). 1990. pap. 1.50 (0-89486-735-0) Hazelden.
—Rule of the Szak King: A Smoke-Free Adventure on the Planet Quark. Hanson, Eric, illus. 23p. (gr. 5-9). 1991. pap. 1.75 (0-89486-748-2) Hazelden.
—The Sweet Air of Starship Orr: Rescue from the Inhalant Planet. Hanson, Eric, illus. 27p. (gr. 5-9). 1991. pap. 1.75 (0-89486-749-0) Hazelden.
—Wonder What I Feel Today? A Coloring Book about Feelings. Barton, Patrice, illus. 16p. (gr. k-5). 1991. pap. 1.50 (0-89486-744-X) Hazelden.
Engelmann, Siegfried & Silbert, Jerome. Expressive Writing, No. 2. (gr. 4 up). 1985. tchr's ed., 210 p 55.00, (0-574-41850-4); student wkbk. (pkg. of 5), 182 pgs. 28.50, (0-574-51852-5) SRA.
Engelsman, Alan & Engelsman, Penny. Theatre Arts Two - Student Handbook: On Stage & Off Stage Roles. 170p. (gr. 6-12). 1991. pap. text ed. 18.50 (1-879692-00-7) Alpen & Jeffries.
Engelsman, Penny, jt. auth. see Engelsman, Alan.
Engen, Kari, tr. see Arpi, Erik.

Engfer, LeeAnne. Maine. (Illus.). 72p. (gr. 3-6). 1991. PLB 17.50 (*0-8225-2701-4*) Lerner Pubns.

Engh, M. J. House in the Snow. 144p. 1990. pap. 2.75 (*0-590-42658-3*) Scholastic Inc.

Engholm, Christopher. The Armenian Earthquake. LC 89-33555. (Illus.). 64p. (gr. 5-8). 1989. PLB 11.95 (*1-56006-004-2*) Lucent Bks.

England, Beth. The Bible. LC 85-24332. 198p. (ps). 1986. 4.99 (*0-8054-4169-7*) Broadman.

England, Kathleen. Why We Are Baptized. LC 78-19180. (Illus.). 27p. (gr. 2-5). 1978. pap. 5.95 (*0-87747-893-7*) Deseret Bk.

Englander, Lois, et al. The Jewish Holiday Do-Book. new ed. (gr. 3 up). 1977. 12.95x (*0-685-76976-3*) Bloch.

Englander, Roger. Opera! What's All the Screaming About? LC 82-23742. (Illus.). 192p. (gr. 6 up). 1983. 12.95 (*0-8027-6491-6*) Walker & Co.

Englebardt, Stanley L. Kids & Alcohol, the Deadliest Drug. LC 75-20327. 64p. (gr. 5 up). 1975. PLB 12.88 (*0-688-51717-X*) Lothrop.

Englehart, Steve. Christmas Countdown: A Story a Day for 25 Days for Everyone Who Just Can't Wait 'til Christmas. Waldman, Bryna, illus. 64p. (Orig.). 1992. pap. 5.99 (*0-380-76842-9*, Camelot Young) Avon.

Engler, Dan, jt. auth. see Urbide, Fernando.

Engler, Dan, jt. auth. see Urbide, Fernando.

Engler, Dan, jt. auth. see Uribe, Fernando.

Englin, A., tr. see Rosenfeld, Dina.

English, Betty L. Women at Their Work. English, Betty L., illus. LC 76-42924. 48p. (gr. k-4). 1988. pap. 4.95 (*0-8037-0496-8*) Dial Bks Young.

English, Billy J., jt. auth. see Calhoun, Sharon C.

English, Gayla I., jt. auth. see English, Timothy M.

English, Timothy M. & English, Gayla I. Science Fun Centers. (Illus.). 48p. (Orig.). (gr. 3-5). 1990. pap. text ed. 4.69 (*1-878931-00-8*, 3B90-001) English Enterprises.

English, Tracey. Old Macdonald Had a Farm: A Lift & Look Counting Book. (ps-3). 1993. 9.95 (*0-307-17601-0*, Artsts Writrs) Western Pub.

Engman, Suzy, jt. auth. see Grossman, Cheryl S.

Engvick, William, ed. Lullabies & Night Songs. Sendak, Maurice, illus. LC 65-22880. (ps-3). 1965. 26.00 (*0-06-021820-7*) HarpC Child Bks.

Enk, Jean & Hendricks, Meg. Shortcuts for Teachers: Strategies for Reducing Classroom Workload. LC 81-81392. (gr. k-6). 1981. pap. 9.95 (*0-8224-6373-3*) Fearon Teach Aids.

Enloe, Walter, et al. We've Got the Power: Skills for Democracy. Garton, Marcia, intro. by. (Illus.). 87p. (gr. 7-12). 1992. pap. text ed. 15.00 (*1-877889-03-2*) League Wmn Voters MN.

Ennes, Phyllis L., ed. see Feller, Ron L. & Feller, Marsha Y.

Enns, Peter. Drugs - a Dead End Street: The Dangers of Substance Abuse. Wolverton, Lock, illus. 40p. (Orig.). (ps-6). 1992. pap. 5.98 incl. cassette (*0-943593-98-0*) Kids Intl Inc.

—God Is Good. Ligon, Terry, illus. 24p. (ps-5). 1985. 4.95 (*0-936215-21-6*); cassette incl. STL Intl.

—Jesus Loves Me. Ligon, Terry, illus. 24p. (ps-5). 1985. 4.95 (*0-936215-23-2*); cassette incl. STL Intl.

—The Pollution Solution: Keeping Earth a Beautiful Place. Wolverton, Lock, illus. 40p. (Orig.). (ps-6). 1992. pap. 5.98 incl. cassette (*0-943593-76-X*) Kids Intl Inc.

—Putting the Brakes on AIDS: The Story of Macho McKar. Wolverton, Lock, illus. 40p. (Orig.). (ps-6). 1992. pap. 5.98 incl. cassette (*0-943593-97-2*) Kids Intl Inc.

—Special Friends. Ligon, Terry, illus. 24p. (ps-5). 4.95 (*0-936215-22-4*); cassette incl. STL Intl.

—Stories to Remember: David, God's Champion. Ligon, Terry, illus. 32p. (ps-5). 1987. pap. 2.98 (*0-943593-04-2*); cassette 5.98 (*0-943593-06-9*); coloring bk. 0.98 (*0-943593-05-0*) Kids Intl Inc.

—Stories to Remember: Here Comes Jesus. Ligon, Terry, illus. 32p. (ps-5). 1987. pap. 2.98 (*0-943593-12-3*); coloring bk. 0.98 (*0-943593-13-1*); cassette 5.98 (*0-943593-14-X*) Kids Intl Inc.

—Stories to Remember: Walking with Jesus. Ligon, Terry, illus. 32p. (ps-5). 1987. pap. 2.98 (*0-943593-08-5*); coloring bk. 0.98 (*0-943593-09-3*) Kids Intl Inc.

—Street Smarts! The Rewards of a Good Education. Wolverton, Lock, illus. 40p. (Orig.). (ps-6). 1992. pap. 5.98 incl. cassette (*0-943593-75-1*) Kids Intl Inc.

Enns, Peter & Forsberg, Glen. Adam & Eve & Five Other Stories. Friesen, John H., illus. 24p. (ps-5). 1985. book & Cassette 4.95 (*0-936215-01-1*) STL Intl.

—Daniel & the Lions & Five Other Stories. Friesen, John H., illus. 24p. (ps-5). 1985. book & cassette 4.95 (*0-936215-04-6*) STL Intl.

—David & Goliath & Five Other Stories. Friesen, John H., illus. 24p. (ps-5). 1985. book & Cassette 4.95 (*0-936215-03-8*) STL Intl.

—Jesus Is Alive! & Five Other Stories. Friesen, John H., illus. 24p. (ps-5). 1985. book & cassette 4.95 (*0-936215-06-2*) STL Intl.

—Joseph the Dreamer & Five Other Stories. Friesen, John H., illus. 24p. (ps-5). 1985. book & cassette 4.95 (*0-936215-02-X*) STL Intl.

—Six Stories of Jesus. Friesen, John H., illus. 24p. (ps-5). 1985. 4.95 (*0-936215-07-0*); cassette incl. STL Intl.

—Stories That Live, 6 vols. Friesen, John H., illus. 144p. (ps-5). 1985. books & cassettes 29.70 (*0-936215-00-3*) STL Intl.

Enns, Peter & Ligon, Terry. Stories to Remember: Look What God Made. (Illus.). 32p. (ps-5). 1987. pap. 2.98 (*0-943593-00-X*); coloring bk. 0.98 (*0-943593-01-8*); cassette 5.98 (*0-943593-02-6*) Kids Intl Inc.

Enright, Elizabeth. A Christmas Tree for Lydia. Zimdars, Berta, illus. 32p. (gr. 4 up). 1986. PLB 13.95s.p. (*0-88682-063-4*) Creative Ed.

—Gone-Away Lake. Dyer, Jane & Krush, Beth, illus. 256p. (gr. 3-7). 1990. pap. 4.95 (*0-15-231649-3*, Odyssey) HarBrace.

—Return to Gone-Away. (gr. 3-7). 1988. 17.25 (*0-8446-6357-3*) Peter Smith.

—Return to Gone-Away. Dyer, Jane & Krush, Beth, illus. 212p. (gr. 3-7). 1990. pap. 4.95 (*0-15-266377-0*, Odyssey) HarBrace.

—The Saturdays. Enright, Elizabeth. (gr. 4-6). 1988. 12.95 (*0-8050-0291-X*, Bks Young Read) H Holt & Co.

—Spiderweb for Two. (gr. k-6). 1987. pap. 2.95 (*0-440-48204-8*, YB) Dell.

—Tatsinda. Johnston, Allyn, ed. Treherne, Katie T., illus. 65p. (gr. k-5). 1991. 16.95 (*0-15-284280-2*) HarBrace.

—Then There Were Five. Enright, Elizabeth, illus. (gr. k-6). 1987. pap. 2.95 (*0-440-48806-0*, YB) Dell.

—Thimble Summer. (gr. k-6). 1987. pap. 3.50 (*0-440-48681-5*, YB) Dell.

—Thimble Summer. Enright, Elizabeth, illus. LC 38-27586. 124p. (gr. 6 up). 1938. 15.95 (*0-8050-0306-1*, Bks Young Read) H Holt & Co.

—Zeee. LC 92-29611. (ps-3). 1993. 15.95 (*0-15-299958-2*) HarBrace.

Enriquez, Edmund C. The Golden Gospel: A Pictorial History of the Restoration. Enriquez, Edmund C., illus. 96p. (gr. 6-12). 1989. pap. 7.95 (*0-88290-198-2*) Horizon Utah.

Enscoe, Andrea, jt. auth. see Enscoe, Lawrence.

Enscoe, Andrea J., jt. ed. see Enscoe, Lawrence G.

Enscoe, Lawrence & Enscoe, Andrea. Get a Grip! A Year 'Round Drama-Rama of Scenes & Monologs for Christian Teens. Zapel, Arthur L., ed. LC 91-37422. 128p. (Orig.). (gr. 9-12). 1992. pap. 9.95 (*0-916260-82-8*, B128) Meriwether Pub.

Enscoe, Lawrence G. & Enscoe, Andrea J., eds. You Can Get There from Here. Date not set. 8.95 (*0-685-68697-3*, BCMP-655) Lillenas.

Enselek, Patricia & Griffin, Susan. Eighth Grade Math TAAS Instructional Packet. 73p. (gr. 8). 1991. 19.95 (*1-883396-16-6*) Educ Etc.

—Eighth Grade Reading TAAS Instructional Packet. 68p. (gr. 8). 1992. 19.95 (*1-883396-14-X*) Educ Etc.

—Eighth Grade Writing TAAS Instructional Packet. 73p. (gr. 8). 1991. 19.95 (*1-883396-15-8*) Educ Etc.

—Exit Level Math TAAS Instructional Packet. 83p. (gr. 10). 1991. 19.95 (*1-883396-22-0*) Educ Etc.

—Exit Level Reading TAAS Instructional Packet. 66p. (gr. 10). 1991. 19.95 (*1-883396-20-4*) Educ Etc.

—Exit Level Writing TAAS Instructional Packet. 55p. (gr. 10). 1991. 19.95 (*1-883396-21-2*) Educ Etc.

—Fifth Grade Math TAAS Instructional Packet. 60p. (gr. 5). 1991. 19.95 (*1-883396-07-7*) Educ Etc.

—Fifth Grade Reading & Writing TAAS Instructional Packet. 76p. (gr. 5). 1991. 19.95 (*1-883396-06-9*) Educ Etc.

—Fourth Grade Math TAAS Instructional Packet. 132p. (gr. 4). 1990. 26.95 (*1-883396-05-0*) Educ Etc.

—Fourth Grade Reading & Writing TAAS Instructional Packet. 156p. (gr. 4). 1990. 26.95 (*1-883396-04-2*) Educ Etc.

—Ninth Grade Math TAAS Instructional Packet. 73p. (gr. 9). 1991. 19.95 (*1-883396-19-0*) Educ Etc.

—Ninth Grade Reading TAAS Instructional Packet. 76p. (gr. 9). 1991. 19.95 (*1-883396-17-4*) Educ Etc.

—Ninth Grade Writing TAAS Instructional Packet. 73p. (gr. 9). 1991. 19.95 (*1-883396-18-2*) Educ Etc.

—Second Grade Math TAAS Instructional Packet. 127p. (gr. 2). 1990. 26.95 (*1-883396-01-8*) Educ Etc.

—Second Grade Reading & Writing TAAS Instructional Packet. 134p. (gr. 2). 1990. 26.95 (*1-883396-00-X*) Educ Etc.

—Seventh Grade Math TAAS Instructional Packet. 72p. (gr. 7). 1991. 19.95 (*1-883396-13-1*) Educ Etc.

—Seventh Grade Reading TAAS Instructional Packet. 73p. (gr. 7). 1991. 19.95 (*1-883396-11-5*) Educ Etc.

—Seventh Grade Writing TAAS Instructional Packet. 71p. (gr. 7). 1991. 19.95 (*1-883396-12-3*) Educ Etc.

—Sixth Grade Math TAAS Instructional Packet. 91p. (gr. 6). 1991. 19.95 (*1-883396-10-7*) Educ Etc.

—Sixth Grade Reading TAAS Instructional Packet. 68p. (gr. 6). 1991. 19.95 (*1-883396-08-5*) Educ Etc.

—Sixth Grade Writing Instructional Packet. 67p. (gr. 6). 1990. 19.95 (*1-883396-09-3*) Educ Etc.

—Third Grade Math TAAS Instructional Packet. 72p. (gr. 3). 1991. 19.95 (*1-883396-03-4*) Educ Etc.

—Third Grade Reading & Writing TAAS Instructional Packet. 72p. (gr. 3). 1991. 19.95 (*1-883396-02-6*) Educ Etc.

Ensminger, M. E. Poultry Science. 3rd ed. (Illus.). (gr. 9-12). 1992. 59.95 (*0-8134-2929-3*, 2087); text ed. 44.95 (*0-685-51895-7*) Interstate.

Ensor, Wendy-Ann. Heroes & Heroines in Music. (Illus.). (gr. 1-4). 1981. cassette 18.00x (*0-685-06116-7*) OUP.

Entz, Angeline J. Elijah: Brave Prophet. Fields, Don, illus. (gr. 1-6). 1978. 5.95 (*0-8054-4244-8*, 4242-44) Broadman.

Epes, William. Muhammad Ali. (Illus.). 80p. (gr. 3-5). 1993. PLB 12.95 (*0-7910-1760-5*); pap. write for info. (*0-7910-1966-7*) Chelsea Hse.

Ephron, Delia. The Girl Who Changed the World. LC 92-42444. (gr. 9-12). 1993. 13.95 (*0-395-66139-0*) Ticknor & Fields.

Epinal. Antique Paperdolls of the Edwardian Era. 1983. pap. 3.95 (*0-486-23175-5*) Dover.

Epler, Doris. The Berlin Wall: How It Rose & Why It Fell. LC 91-20610. (Illus.). 128p. (gr. 7 up). 1992. PLB 15.90 (*1-56294-114-3*) Millbrook Pr.

Epperley, Mike. Buckethead Bunch: Bossy, Loser, Show-off & Angry. Erb, Sherry, illus. LC 92-85592. 40p. (Orig.). (gr. k-6). 1992. pap. 5.98x (*1-882183-24-X*) Computer Pr.

—The Buckethead Families: Givers & Takers. rev. ed. Erb, Sherry, illus. LC 92-85597. 32p. (gr. k-6). 1992. pap. 5.98 (*1-882183-23-1*) Computer Pr.

—The Three Bucketeers: Commander, Thinker, Player. Erb, Sherry, illus. 40p. (Orig.). (gr. k-6). 1993. pap. 5.98 (*1-882183-22-3*) Computer Pr.

Eppinga, Jane. Kids Can Cook with Billy the Kid. Eppinga, Jane, illus. 67p. (gr. 4-6). 1979. pap. 4.95x (*0-9618890-0-4*) BK Pubns.

Epple, Wolfgang. Barn Owls. Rogl, Manfred, photos by. (Illus.). 48p. (gr. 2-5). 1992. 19.95 (*0-87614-742-2*) Carolrhoda Bks.

Epstein, Beryl, jt. auth. see Epstein, Sam.

Epstein, Beryl, jt. auth. see Epstein, Samuel D.

Epstein, June. The Name. Power, Margaret, illus. LC 92-34161. 1993. 3.75 (*0-383-03643-7*) SRA Schl Grp.

Epstein, Lawrence. Exploring Careers in Computer Sales. Rosen, Roger, ed. 64p. (gr. 7-12). 1990. PLB 13.95 (*0-8239-0667-1*) Rosen Group.

Epstein, Melvin H. The Young Musician's Series. Darrell, Gail O., illus. LC 92-80357. (Orig.). (gr. 4-9). 1992. Five vol. set. pap. text ed. 65.00 (*1-881136-00-0*) Vol. 1: The Basics of Music (*1-881136-01-9*) Vol. 2: Melody. pap. text ed. 14.95 (*1-881136-02-7*); Vol. 3: Harmony. pap. text ed. 14.94 (*1-881136-03-5*); Vol. 4: Time & Rhythm. pap. text ed. 12.95 (*1-881136-04-3*); Vol. 5: Special Effects. pap. text ed. 12.95 (*1-881136-05-1*) Worth Hse.

Epstein, Rachel. Careers in Health Care. Koop, C. Everett, intro. by. (Illus.). 112p. (gr. 6-12). 1989. 18.95 (*0-7910-0081-8*) Chelsea Hse.

—Eating Habits & Disorders. (Illus.). 112p. (gr. 6-12). 1990. 18.95 (*0-7910-0048-6*) Chelsea Hse.

Epstein, Sam & Epstein, Beryl. Bugs for Dinner? The Eating Habits of Neighborhood Creatures. Gaffney-Kessell, Walter, illus. LC 88-26654. 48p. (gr. 1-5). 1989. RSBE 13.95 (*0-02-733501-1*, Macmillan Child Bk) Macmillan Child Grp.

—George Washington Carver. (Illus.). (gr. k-6). 1991. pap. 3.25 (*0-440-40404-5*, Pub. by Yearling Classics) Dell.

—You Call That a Farm? Raising Leeches, Alligators, Weeds, & Other Unusual Things. (Illus.). 64p. (gr. 2-5). 1991. 13.95 (*0-374-38705-2*) FS&G.

Epstein, Samuel, et al. What's for Lunch? The Eating Habits of Seashore Creatures. Gaffney-Kessell, Walter, illus. LC 85-4964. 48p. (gr. 1-4). 1985. RSBE 13.95 (*0-02-733500-3*, Macmillan Child Bk) Macmillan Child Grp.

Epstein, Samuel D. & Epstein, Beryl. Tunnels. (Illus.). 128p. (gr. 5 up). 1985. 14.95 (*0-316-24573-9*) Little.

Epstein, Sylvia. How the Rosh Hashanah Challah Became Round. Migron, Hagit, illus. 28p. 1993. 8.95 (*965-229-095-5*, Pub. by Gefen Pub Hse IS) Gefen Bks.

Epstein, Vivian S. History of Women Artists for Children. (Illus.). 32p. (ps-6). 1987. 12.95 (*0-9601002-5-3*); pap. 6.95 (*0-9601002-6-1*) V S Epstein.

—History of Women for Children. Epstein, Vivian S., illus. 32p. (ps-5). 1984. 12.95 (*0-9601002-4-5*); pap. 5.95 (*0-9601002-3-7*) V S Epstein.

—History of Women in Science for Young People. Epstein, Vivian S., illus. 40p. (Orig.). (gr. 4-9). 1993. 14.95 (*0-9601002-8-8*); pap. 7.95 (*0-9601002-7-X*) V S Epstein.

Epstin, Vivian S. The ABCs of What a Girl Can Be. (Illus.). 32p. (ps-3). 1980. 5.95 (*0-9601002-2-9*) V S Epstein.

Erben, Karel J. Listen, Kids... Czech Fairy Tales. Ciuffreda, Lillian, ed. Kalnoky, Julius, tr. Jelinek, Otakar, illus. LC 87-83652. 65p. (gr. 3-8). 1988. 13.95 (*0-9619982-0-2*) Kalnoky Pr.

Erbsen, Wayne. The Complete & Painless Guide to the Guitar for Young Beginner. (Illus.). 64p. 1979. pap. 6.95 (*0-8258-0002-1*, PCB 111) Fischer Inc NY.

Erdogan, Haydar & Halasi-kun, George. Hazardous Waste. Head, J. J., ed. (Illus.). 16p. (Orig.). (gr. 10 up). 1993. pap. text ed. 2.75 (*0-89278-174-2*, 45-9774) Carolina Biological.

Erdrich, Heidi E. Maria Tallchief. Whipple, Rick, illus. LC 92-12256. 32p. (gr. 3-6). 1992. PLB 17.96 (*0-8114-6577-2*); pap. 4.95 (*0-8114-4099-0*) Raintree Steck-V.

Erdtmann, Greta. The Path to Math. Erdtmann, Greta, illus. Doman, Glenn, intro. by. (Illus.). 60p. (ps). 1981. 8.95 (*0-936676-11-6*) Better Baby.

Ericksen, Claire, ed. A Monster is Bigger than Nine. Ericksen, Mary, illus. 48p. (gr. 1-3). 1991. pap. 8.95 (*0-88138-099-7*, Green Tiger) S&S Trade.

Erickson, Carol. Kingdom Come. (ps-3). 1990. 12.95 (*1-55503-175-7*) Covenant Comms.

Erickson, Dean. Seven Days to Care for God's World: Rupert Learns What It Means to Take Care of God's Earth. LC 91-8875. 48p. 1991. pap. 6.99 (*0-8066-2533-3*, 9-2533) Augsburg Fortress.

Erickson, Gina C. Alphabet Tails. Foster, Kelli C., ed. Russell, Kerri G., illus. 73p. (gr. k-4). 1989. pap. 6.95 (*0-927971-00-3*) OnTrack Inc.

Erickson, Gina C. & Foster, Kelli C. The Best Pets Yet. Gifford-Russell, Kerri, illus. 24p. (ps-2). 1992. pap. 3.50 (*0-8120-4857-1*) Barron.

—Bub & Chub. Gifford-Russell, Kerri, illus. 24p. (ps-2). 1992. pap. 3.50 (*0-8120-4859-8*) Barron.

—The Bug Club. Russell, Kerri G., illus. 24p. (ps-2). 1991. pap. 3.50 (*0-8120-4730-3*) Barron.

—Dwight & the Trilobite. Gifford, Kerri, illus. 24p. (ps-3). 1994. pap. 3.50 (*0-8120-1839-7*) Barron.

—Find Nat. Russell, Kerri G., illus. 24p. (ps-2). 1991. pap. 3.50 (*0-8120-4678-1*) Barron.

—Frog Knows Best. Gifford-Russell, Kerri, illus. 24p. (ps-2). 1992. pap. 3.50 (*0-8120-4855-5*) Barron.

—Jake & the Snake. Russell, Kerri G., illus. 24p. (ps-3). 1993. pap. 3.50 (*0-8120-1732-3*) Barron.

—Jeepers, Creepers. Gifford, Kerri, illus. 24p. (ps-3). 1994. pap. 3.50 (*0-8120-1841-9*) Barron.

—A Mop for Pop. Russell, Kerri G., illus. 24p. (ps-2). 1991. pap. 3.50 (*0-8120-4680-3*) Barron.

—Pip & Kip. Russell, Kerri G., illus. LC 92-29864. 24p. (ps-2). 1993. pap. 3.50 (*0-8120-1454-5*) Barron.

—The Sled Surprise. Russell, Kerri G., illus. 24p. (ps-2). 1991. pap. 3.50 (*0-8120-4677-3*) Barron.

—Sometimes I Wish. Russell, Kerri G., illus. 24p. (ps-2). 1991. pap. 3.50 (*0-8120-4681-1*) Barron.

—The Tan Can. Gifford-Russell, Kerri, illus. 24p. 1992. pap. 3.50 (*0-8120-4856-3*) Barron.

—A Valentine That Shines. Gifford, Kerri, illus. 24p. (ps-3). 1994. pap. 3.50 (*0-8120-1838-9*) Barron.

—What a Day for Flying! Russell, Kerri G., illus. LC 92-42078. 32p. (ps-2). 1993. pap. 3.95 (*0-8120-1557-6*) Barron.

—What Rose Doesn't Know. Gifford, Kerri, illus. LC 93-36071. 24p. (ps-3). 1994. pap. 3.50 (*0-8120-1672-6*) Barron.

—Whiptale of Blackshale Trail. Russell, Kerri G., illus. 24p. (ps-3). 1993. pap. 3.50 (*0-8120-1733-1*) Barron.

Erickson, Gina C. & Goster, Kelli C. Tall & Small. Gifford, Kerri, illus. 24p. (ps-3). 1994. pap. 3.50 (*0-8120-1840-0*) Barron.

Erickson, Gina K. Bat's Surprise. (ps-3). 1993. pap. 3.95 (*0-8120-1735-8*) Barron.

—Something of My Own. (ps-3). 1993. pap. 3.50 (*0-685-67782-6*) Barron.

Erickson, John. The Case of the Missing Cat: Discover the Land of Enchantment. (Illus.). 144p. 1990. 11.95 (*0-87719-186-7*); pap. 6.95 (*0-87719-185-9*); 2 cass. 15.95 (*0-87719-187-5*) Gulf Pub.

Erickson, John, tr. Hank el Perro Vaquero, No. 1. (SPA.). 112p. (gr. 3 up). 1992. pap. 6.95 (*0-87719-216-2*) Gulf Pub.

—Hank el Perro Vaquero, No. 2. 116p. 1992. pap. 6.95 (*0-87719-217-0*) Gulf Pub.

Erickson, John R. Alkali County Tales. Holmes, Gerald, illus. 100p. (Orig.). (gr. 3up). 1984. 9.95 (*0-916941-06-X*); pap. 5.95 (*0-9608612-8-9*) Maverick Bks.

—The Case of the Car-Barkaholic Dog. (Illus.). 118p. 1991. 11.95 (*0-87719-198-0*, 9198); pap. 6.95 (*0-87719-199-9*, 9199); incls. 2 cass. 15.95 (*0-87719-200-6*) Gulf Pub.

—Cowboys Are Partly Human. Holmes, Gerald L., illus. 110p. (Orig.). (gr. 3 up). 1983. 9.95 (*0-9608612-6-2*); pap. 5.95 (*0-9608612-4-6*) Maverick Bks.

—The Further Adventures of Hank the Cowdog. Holmes, Gerald L., illus. 93p. (Orig.). (gr. 3). 1983. 9.95 (*0-9608612-7-0*); pap. 6.95 (*0-9608612-5-4*); tape 13.95 (*0-916941-02-7*) Maverick Bks.

—Hank the Cowdog: Faded Love. (gr. 3 up). 1985. 9.95 (*0-916941-11-6*); pap. 6.95 (*0-916941-10-8*); 13.95 (*0-916941-12-4*) Maverick Bks.

—Hank the Cowdog: It's a Dog's Life. (Illus.). 100p. (Orig.). (gr. 3 up). 1986. 9.95 (*0-916941-04-3*); pap. 5.95 (*0-9608612-9-7*); talking book 13.95 (*0-916941-03-5*) Maverick Bks.

—Hank the Cowdog: Let Sleeping Dogs Lie. Holmes, Gerald, illus. 19p. (gr. 3 up). 1986. 9.95 (*0-916941-15-9*); pap. 6.95 (*0-916941-14-0*); talking book 13.95 (*0-916941-16-7*) Maverick Bks.

—Hank the Cowdog: Murder in the Middle Pasture. Holmes, Gerald L., illus. 91p. (Orig.). (gr. 3 up). 1985. 9.95 (*0-916941-08-6*); pap. 6.95 (*0-916941-07-8*); talking book 13.95 (*0-916941-09-4*) Maverick Bks.

—Hank the Cowdog: The Case of the Hooking Bull, No. 18. 118p. 1992. 11.95 (*0-87719-213-8*); pap. 6.95 (*0-87719-212-X*); 2 cassettes 15.95 (*0-87719-214-6*) Gulf Pub.

—Hank the Cowdog, Vol. 19: The Case of the Midnight Rustler. Holmes, Gerald, illus. 116p. (Orig.). (gr. 4-6). 1992. 11.95 (*0-87719-219-7*); pap. 6.95 (*0-87719-218-9*); tape 15.95 (*0-87719-220-0*) Gulf Pub.

Erickson, Jon. Target Earth! Asteroid Collisions Past & Future. (Illus.). 176p. (gr. 7 up). 1991. incl. 4-pg. insert 23.95 (*0-8306-8673-8*, 3673); pap. 14.95 incl. 4-pg. insert (*0-8306-7673-2*) TAB Bks.

Erickson, Judith. The Directory of American Youth Organizations, 1992-93 Edition: A Guide to 500 Clubs, Groups, Troops, Teams, Societies, Lodges, & More for Young People. Espeland, Pamela, ed. 184p. (gr. k up). 1992. pap. 18.95 (*0-915793-36-9*) Free Spirit Pub.

Erickson, Laura L., jt. auth. see Rapp, George, Jr.

Erickson, Mary. God Can Do Anything. LC 92-33128. 1993. write for info. (*0-7814-0001-5*, Chariot Bks) Cook.

—I Can Make God Glad! LC 93-33070. (gr. 3 up). 1994. write for info. (*0-7814-0102-X*, Chariot Bks) Cook.

—Six Busy Days. LC 88-11803. (Illus.). 32p. (ps-2). 1988. 9.99 (*1-55513-699-0*, Chariot Bks) Cook.

Erickson, Mary E. Christmas Star Sight & Sound. (ps-3). 1992. 12.99 (*0-87403-990-8*, 24-03690) Standard Pub.

—Miracle in the Morning: The Wonderful Story of Easter. LC 92-20260. 1993. write for info. (*0-7814-0779-6*, Chariot Bks) Cook.

Erickson, P. C. Stand Tall. Pugh, Kayleen, illus. (Orig.). (gr. 4-8). 1978. pap. 2.95 (*0-89036-111-8*) Hawkes Pub Inc.

Erickson, Paul, jt. auth. see Segaloff, Nat.

Erickson, Russell. A Toad for Tuesday. Di Fiori, Lawrence, illus. LC 73-19900. 64p. (gr. k-4). 1974. PLB 12.88 (*0-688-51569-X*) Lothrop.

Erickson, Russell E. A Toad for Tuesday. Di Fiori, Lawrence, photos by. LC 92-24595. (Illus.). 64p. (gr. 3 up). 1993. pap. 3.95 (*0-688-12276-0*, Pub. by Beech Tree Bks) Morrow.

—Warton & the Contest. Di Fiori, Lawrence, illus. LC 86-102. 96p. (ps-4). 1986. 11.95 (*0-688-05818-3*); PLB 11.88 (*0-688-05819-1*) Lothrop.

Erickson, Sheldon, et al. Machine Shop: Simple Machines. Cordel, Betty, et al, eds. (Illus.). 169p. (Orig.). (gr. 5-9). 1993. pap. text ed. 14.95 (*1-881431-39-8*, 1311) AIMS Educ Fnd.

Erickson, Tim. Get It Together: Math Problems for Groups Grades 4-12. Craig, Rose & Noll, Sally, illus. 180p. (Orig.). (gr. 4-12). 1989. pap. 15.00 (*0-912511-53-2*) Lawrence Science.

Ericson, Anton. Super Bowl Heroes. (Illus.). 24p. (Orig.). 1991. pap. 2.50 (*1-56156-081-2*) Kidsbks.

Ericson, Carolyn R., jt. auth. see Ericson, Joe E.

Ericson, Joe E. & Ericson, Carolyn R. Spoiling for a Fight: John S. Roberts & Early Nacogdoches (Texas) LC 86-82813. (Illus.). 250p. 1989. PLB 17.95 (*0-911317-41-4*) Ericson Bks.

Ericson, Marc. Hockey Superstars. (Illus.). 48p. (Orig.). 1991. pap. 3.95 (*1-56156-082-0*) Kidsbks.

Ericsson, Jennifer A. No Milk! Eitan, Ora, illus. LC 92-21806. 32p. (ps up) 1993. 14.00 (*0-688-11306-0*, Tambourine Bks); PLB 13.93 (*0-688-11307-9*, Tambourine Bks) Morrow.

Erie Art Museum Staff. Commodore Perry & Other Paper Dolls of the Flagship Niagara. Macie, Edward, illus. 10p. (Orig.). (gr. 1-3). 1988. pap. 6.00 (*0-9616623-4-4*) Erie Art Mus.

Eriksson, Ake. Joel, Jesper, & Julia. Eriksson, Ake, illus. LC 89-25116. 32p. (ps-4). 1990. PLB 18.95 (*0-87614-419-9*) Carolrhoda Bks.

Erkel, Cynthia R. The Farmhouse Mouse. Erkel, Michael, illus. LC 92-27040. 1993. write for info. (*0-399-22444-0*, Putnam) Putnam Pub Group.

Erlanger, Ellen. Eating Disorders: A Question & Answer Book about Anorexia Nervosa & Bulimia Nervosa. LC 87-15311. (gr. 6-10). 1988. 15.95 (*0-8225-0038-8*) Lerner Pubns.

—Isaac Asimov: Scientist & Storyteller. LC 86-10675. (Illus.). 56p. (gr. 4 up). 1986. PLB 13.50 (*0-8225-0482-0*) Lerner Pubns.

—Jane Fonda: More Than a Movie Star. LC 83-27542. (Illus.). 56p. (gr. 4 up). 1984. PLB 13.50 (*0-8225-0485-5*) Lerner Pubns.

Erlbach, Arlene. Bicycles. LC 93-34457. 1994. 17.50 (*0-8225-2388-4*) Lerner Pubns.

—Dropout Blues. (gr. 6 up). 1988. write for info. (*0-373-98020-5*) S&S Trade.

—Hurricanes. LC 92-37811. (Illus.). 48p. (gr. k-4). 1993. PLB 15.27 (*0-516-41333-3*); pap. 4.95 (*0-685-63236-9*) Childrens.

—Peanut Butter. LC 93-20217. (gr. 3-7). 1993. 17.50 (*0-8225-2387-6*) Lerner Pubns.

—Soda Pop. LC 93-20106. 1993. 17.50 (*0-8225-2386-8*) Lerner Pubns.

—Videogames. LC 93-36086. 1994. 17.50 (*0-8225-2389-2*) Lerner Pubns.

Erlbruch, Wolf, jt. auth. see Holzwarth, Werner.

Ernest Benn Ltd. Staff, tr. see Beskow, Elsa.

Ernst, Donna B. Sundance, My Uncle. (Illus.). 170p. (gr. 9). 1992. 21.95 (*0-932702-96-1*) Creative Texas.

Ernst, John. Jesse James. Miller, Ted, illus. LC 76-10206. (gr. 4-7). 1976. 9.95 (*0-13-509695-2*) P-H.

Ernst, Kathryn F. Danny & His Thumb. De Paola, Tomie, illus. (ps-3). 1975. (Pub. by Treehouse); pap. 4.95 (*0-13-196808-4*) P-H.

Ernst, Kenneth, Jr. Fossils, Frogs, Fish & Friends. LC 82-71243. (Illus.). (gr. 2-3). 1984. pap. 4.95 (*0-932766-15-3*, Inst Creation) Master Bks.

Ernst, Lee, jt. auth. see Ernst, Lisa C.

Ernst, Lisa C. Ginger Jumps. Ernst, Lisa C., illus. LC 89-38706. 32p. (ps-2). 1990. RSBE 14.95 (*0-02-733565-8*, Bradbury Pr) Macmillan Child Grp.

—The Luckiest Kid on the Planet. 1994. write for info. (*0-02-733566-6*, Bradbury Pr) Macmillan Child Grp.

—Miss Penny & Mr. Grubbs. Ernst, Lisa C., illus. LC 90-43175. 40p. (ps-4). 1991. RSBE 14.95 (*0-02-733563-1*, Bradbury Pr) Macmillan Child Grp.

—Nattie Parsons' Good-Luck Lamb. LC 87-13700. (Illus.). 32p. (ps-3). 1988. pap. 11.95 (*0-670-81778-3*) Viking Child Bks.

—Nattie Parsons' Good-Luck Lamb. (Illus.). 32p. (ps-3). 1990. pap. 3.95 (*0-14-050772-8*, Puffin) Puffin Bks.

—Sam Johnson & the Blue Ribbon Quilt. LC 82-9980. (Illus.). 32p. (gr. k-3). 1983. lib. bdg. 12.88 (*0-688-01517-4*) Lothrop.

—Sam Johnson & the Blue Ribbon Quilt. LC 82-9980. (Illus.). 32p. (gr. k up). 1992. pap. 3.95 (*0-688-11505-5*, Mulberry) Morrow.

—Squirrel Park. Ernst, Lisa C., illus. LC 92-27920. 40p. (ps-2). 1993. RSBE 15.95 (*0-02-733562-3*, Bradbury Pr) Macmillan Child Grp.

—Up to Ten & down Again. LC 84-21852. (Illus.). 40p. (ps). 1986. 13.95 (*0-688-04541-3*); PLB 13.88 (*0-688-04542-1*) Lothrop.

—Walter's Tail. Ernst, Lisa C., illus. LC 91-19948. 40p. (ps-2). 1992. RSBE 14.95 (*0-02-733564-X*, Bradbury Pr) Macmillan Child Grp.

—When Bluebell Sang. Ernst, Lisa C., illus. LC 88-22262. 32p. (ps-1). 1989. RSBE 13.95 (*0-02-733561-5*, Bradbury Pr) Macmillan Child Grp.

—When Bluebell Sang. Ernst, Lisa C., illus. LC 91-15552. 40p. (ps-1). 1992. pap. 4.95 (*0-689-71584-6*, Aladdin) Macmillan Child Grp.

—Zinnia & Dot. (Illus.). 32p. (ps-3). 1992. 14.00 (*0-670-83091-7*) Viking Child Bks.

Ernst, Lisa C. & Ernst, Lee. The Tangram Magician. (Illus.). 24p. 1990. 19.95 (*0-8109-3851-0*) Abrams.

Erskine, Jim. Bedtime Story. Schweninger, Ann, illus. LC 81-3163. 32p. (ps-1). 1981. PLB 8.95 (*0-517-54540-3*) Crown Bks Yng Read.

Erson, Tim. Courageous Pacers: The Complete Guide to Running, Walking & Fitness for Kids (Ages 8-108) Diaz, Michael A., illus. 250p. (Orig.). (gr. 2 up). 1993. Incl. logbook & journal. 18.95 (*0-9636547-0-5*) PRO-ACTIV Pubns.

Courage, Confidence, Fitness & Friendship are the themes of this book which introduces children to life skills of fun & athletics through running & walking. Inspiring & humorous, it includes 20 delightfully illustrated chapters & teaches the Courageous Pacer philosophy of respect for oneself, respect for others, & respect for the community. It also emphasizes goal setting & working through the ups & downs of goal completion. Practical advice about getting started, training, how & where to enter events, nutrition, & injury care are neatly folded into true stories of sports heroes, courageous dreamers, communities, winners & more. Excellent source for youth & adults interested in combining sports, fitness & personal growth. It's the book parents have been waiting for that will inspire champions & everyday heroes alike. Author Tim Erson, M.S., P.T., is a graduate of Columbia University's Program in Physical Therapy & a returned Peace Corps Volunteer. He has been recognized for positive & motivational leadership in youth fitness programs since 1981. Timely & intergenerational. A book for families, individuals, or groups. To order, call: (512) 884-8351, or write: PRO-ACTIV Publications, P.O. Box 331186, Corpus Christi, TX 78463-1186. *Publisher Provided Annotation.*

Ertner, James D. Super Silly Animal Riddles. Sinclair, Jeff, illus. LC 92-41919. 96p. 1993. 12.95 (*0-8069-0333-3*) Sterling.

—Super Silly Animal Riddles. Sinclair, Jeff, illus. 96p. (gr. 2-7). 1993. pap. 3.95 (*0-8069-0334-1*) Sterling.

Ervin, Timothy S., jt. auth. see Mallett, Jerry J.

Erwin, Carolyn M. What Makes Danny Run? (Illus.). 32p. (Orig.). (gr. k-6). 1991. pap. 8.95 (*0-9630903-0-5*) Little Gems.

Erwin, Vicki B. Mystery of the Secret Dolls. (gr. 4-7). 1993. pap. 2.95 (*0-590-44412-3*) Scholastic Inc.

Esbensen, Barbara J. Baby Whales Drink Milk. Davis, Lambert, illus. LC 92-30375. 32p. (ps-1). 1994. 15.00 (*0-06-021551-8*); PLB 14.89 (*0-06-021552-6*) HarpC Child Bks.

—Baby Whales Drink Milk. Davis, Lambert, illus. LC 92-30375. 32p. (ps-2). 1994. pap. 4.95 (*0-06-445119-4*, Trophy) HarpC Child Bks.

—Cold Stars & Fireflies: Poems for the Four Seasons. Bonners, Susan, illus. LC 83-45051. 80p. (gr. 3-7). 1984. PLB 14.89 (0-690-04363-5, Crowell Jr Bks) HarpC Child Bks.

—Ladder to the Sky: How the Gift of Healing Came to the Ojibway Nation. Davie, Helen K., illus. (ps-3). 1989. 15.95 (0-316-24952-1) Little.

—Playful Slider: The North American River Otter. Brown, Mary B., illus. LC 92-13783. 1993. 15.95 (0-316-24977-7) Little.

—Sponges Are Skeletons. Keller, Holly, illus. LC 92-9740. 32p. (gr. k-4). 1993. 15.00 (0-06-021034-6); PLB 14.89 (0-06-021037-0) HarpC Child Bks.

—The Star Maiden: An Ojibway Tale. Davie, Helen K., illus. (ps-3). 1988. 14.95 (0-316-24951-3) Little.

—The Star Maiden: An Ojibway Tale. Davie, Helen K., illus. (ps-3). 1991. pap. 4.95 (0-316-24955-6) Little.

—Tiger with Wings: The Great Horned Owl. Brown, Mary B., illus. LC 90-23034. 32p. (gr. 2-4). 1991. 14.95 (0-531-05940-5); RLB 14.99 (0-531-08540-6) Orchard Bks Watts.

—Who Shrank My Grandmother's House? Poems of Discovery. Beddows, Eric, illus. LC 90-39631. 48p. (gr. 3-7). 1992. 15.00 (0-06-021827-4); PLB 14.89 (0-06-021828-2) HarpC Child Bks.

—Words with Wrinkled Knees. Stadler, John, illus. LC 85-47886. 48p. (gr. 2-7). 1987. (Crowell Jr Bks); PLB 14.89 (0-690-04505-0, Crowell Jr Bks) HarpC Child Bks.

Esbensen, Barbara J., retold by. The Great Buffalo Race: How the Buffalo Got His Hump: a Seneca Tale. David, Helen K., illus. LC 92-23410. 1994. 14.95 (0-316-24982-3) Little.

Escabar, URias, tr. see Thomas, Mary A.

Escamill, Edna. Daughter of the Mountain: Un Cuento. LC 91-9754. 192p. (gr. 5 up). 1991. lib. bdg. 18.95 (1-879960-08-7); pap. 8.95 (1-879960-07-9) Aunt Lute Bks.

Eschele, Lou. The Curse of Tutankhamen. (gr. 5 up). 1994. 14.95 (1-56006-152-9) Lucent Bks.

Escott, John. Crime Is a Five Letter Word: A Detective Puzzle. (Illus.). 64p. (gr. 2-5). 1994. 5.95 (0-340-56910-7, Pub. by Hodder & Stoughton UK) Trafalgar.

Escoula, Yvonne. Six Blue Horses. LC 70-103044. (gr. 5-9). 1970. 21.95 (0-87599-162-9) S G Phillips.

Escovito, Pete. Viva la Musica. (gr. 4-7). 1991. pap. 9.95 (0-930647-09-2) Lancaster Prodns.

Escudie, Rene. Little John's Fears. (Illus.). (gr. 1-8). 1992. PLB 8.95 (0-89565-886-0); Resale. 12.75 (0-685-60989-8) Childs World.

—Paul & Sebastian. Townley, Roderick, tr. from FRE. Wensell, Ulises, illus. LC 88-12768. 32p. (ps-3). 1988. 11.95 (0-916291-19-7) Kane-Miller Bk.

—Paul & Sebastian. (Illus.). 48p. (gr. k-4). 1990. 12.75 (0-89565-806-2); 8.95s.p. (0-685-55103-2) Childs World.

—Paul & Sebastian. Townley, Roderick, tr. Wensell, Ulises, illus. (FRE.). 32p. (ps-3). 1994. pap. 6.95 (0-916291-49-9) Kane-Miller Bk.

Esh, Olivia. The Fence Was Too High. Childress, Rhonda, illus. LC 93-34499. 1994. write for info. (0-8114-4460-0) Raintree Steck-V.

Es'Kia Mphahlele see Kumalo, Alf.

Esko, Edward. Healing Planet Earth. 64p. (Orig.). (gr. 8 up). 1992. pap. 5.95 (0-9628528-5-6) One Peaceful World.

Eskow, Dennis. Lyndon Baines Johnson. LC 92-43687. (Illus.). 160p. (gr. 9-12). 1993. PLB 14.40 (0-531-13019-3) Watts.

Esparza, Esther L. & Esparza, Thomas, Jr. Humpty Dumpty & Friends in the Southwest, Bk. I. Esparza, Thomas, Jr., illus. 28p. (Orig.). (ps-9). 1991. pap. text ed. 6.95 (1-879817-05-5); pap. text ed. 12.95 incl. cassette (1-879817-15-2); cassette 9.95 (1-879817-10-1) Star Light Pr.

—Humpty Dumpty & Friends in the Southwest, Bk. II. Esparza, Thomas, Jr., illus. 28p. (Orig.). (ps-9). 1991. pap. text ed. 6.95 (1-879817-06-3); pap. text ed. 12.95 incl. cassette (1-879817-16-0); cassette 9.95 (1-879817-11-X) Star Light Pr.

—Humpty Dumpty & Friends in the Southwest, Bk. III. Esparza, Thomas, Jr., illus. 28p. (Orig.). (ps-9). 1991. pap. text ed. 6.95 (1-879817-07-1); pap. text ed. 12.95 incl. cassette (1-879817-17-9); cassette 9.95 (1-879817-12-8) Star Light Pr.

—Humpty Dumpty & Friends in the Southwest, 3 vols, Bks. I, II & III. Esparza, Thomas, Jr., illus. (Orig.). (ps-9). 1991. Set. pap. text ed. 19.95 (1-879817-08-X); Set. pap. text ed. 35.95 incl. cassettes (1-879817-14-4); Set. cassettes 24.95 (1-879817-13-6) Star Light Pr.

Esparza, Thomas, Jr., jt. auth. see Esparza, Esther L.

Espeland, Pamela & Wallner, Rosemary. Making the Most of Today: Daily Readings for Young People on Self-Awareness, Creativity & Self-Esteem. LC 91-14494. 392p. (Orig.). (gr. 5 up). 1991. pap. 8.95 (0-915793-33-4) Free Spirit Pub.

Espeland, Pamela, ed. see Adderholdt-Elliott, Miriam.

Espeland, Pamela, ed. see Barrett, Susan L.

Espeland, Pamela, ed. see Cummings, Rhoda & Fisher, Gary.

Espeland, Pamela, ed. see Delisle, James & Galbraith, Judy.

Espeland, Pamela, ed. see Delisle, James R.

Espeland, Pamela, ed. see Delisle, Jim.

Espeland, Pamela, ed. see Erickson, Judith.

Espeland, Pamela, ed. see Gootman, Marilyn E.

Espeland, Pamela, ed. see Heacox, Diane.

Espeland, Pamela, ed. see Johnson, Lee & Johnson, Sue K.

Espeland, Pamela, ed. see Kimeldorf, Martin.

Espeland, Pamela, ed. see Kincher, Jonni.

Espeland, Pamela, ed. see Lewis, Barbara A.

Espeland, Pamela, ed. see Packer, Alex J.

Espeland, Pamela, ed. see Roberts, Gail C. & Guttormson, Lorraine.

Espeland, Pamela, ed. see Schumm, Jeanne S. & Radencich, Marguerite.

Espeland, Pamela, ed. see Simmons, Cassandra W.

Espinassous, Louis. Little Lost Fox Cub, on the Trail of Little Fox. Routiaux, Claudine, illus. LC 92-27116. 1993. PLB 18.60 (0-8368-0927-0) Gareth Stevens Inc.

Esquinaldo, Virginia. Newton, Nell, & Barney: Someday I Want to Be - LC 93-13322. (Illus.). (ps-6). 1993. 8.95 (0-8120-1621-1) Barron.

—The Someday Game. (Illus.). 32p. (ps-2). 1993. 12.95 (0-8120-6405-4); pap. text ed. 5.95 (0-8120-1746-3) Barron.

Essley, Roger. Paul's Fantastic Photos. LC 93-12035. (ps-6). 1994. 15.00 (0-671-86722-9, S&S BFYR) S&S Trade.

Esslinger, Jessica. Discover Dinosaurs: Activity Book. Belcher, Cynthia, illus. (Illus.). 20p. (gr. 1-6). 1988. wkbk. 2.95 (0-911239-26-X) Carnegie Mus.

—Discover Dinosaurs at the Carnegie. (Illus.). 20p. (gr. 1-6). 1988. wkbk. 2.95 (0-911239-25-1) Carnegie Mus.

Estalella, Robert. Galaxies. Ferron, Miquel, illus. LC 93-24596. (gr. 4-8). 1994. 12.95 (0-8120-6367-8); pap. 6.95 (0-8120-1742-0) Barron.

—Our Planet: Earth. Socias, Marcel, illus. LC 93-24597. (gr. 4-8). 1994. 12.95 (0-8120-6368-6); pap. write for info. (0-8120-1741-2) Barron.

—Our Satellite: The Moon. Ferron, Miquel, illus. LC 93-19897. (gr. 4-8). 1994. 12.95 (0-8120-6369-4); pap. 6.95 (0-8120-1740-4) Barron.

—Our Star: The Sun. (Illus.). 32p. (gr. 4-8). 1993. 12.95 (0-8120-6370-8); pap. 6.95 (0-8120-1739-0) Barron.

—Planets & Satellites. (Illus.). 32p. (gr. 4-8). 1993. 12.95 (0-8120-6372-4); pap. 6.95 (0-8120-1737-4) Barron.

—The Stars. (Illus.). 32p. (gr. 4-8). 1993. 12.95 (0-8120-6371-6); pap. 6.95 (0-8120-1738-2) Barron.

Estep, Don. Cat & Kittens. Dubin, Jill, illus. 28p. (ps) 1990. 2.95 (0-02-689487-4) Checkerboard.

—Lucy's Early Day. Dubin, Jill, illus. 28p. (ps). 1990. 2.95 (0-02-689489-0) Checkerboard.

Esterl, Arnica. The Fine Round Cake. Hejl, Pauline, tr. from GER. Dugin, Andrej & Dugina, Olga, illus. LC 91-6411. 24p. (ps-2). 1991. SBE 14.95 (0-02-733568-2, Four Winds) Macmillan Child Grp.

Esterman, M. M. A Fish That's a Box: Folk Art from the National Museum of American Art, Smithsonian Institution. LC 90-3802. (Illus.). 32p. (gr. k-5). 1990. 12.95 (0-915556-21-9) Great Ocean.

Estern, Anne G. Letters from Philippa. (gr. 4-7). 1991. pap. 3.50 (0-553-15941-0) Bantam.

—The Picolinis & the Haunted House. Frenck, Hal, illus. 115p. (gr. 3-5). 1989. pap. 2.95 (0-553-15771-X, Skylark) Bantam.

Estes, Eleanor. Los Cien Vestidos. Slobodkin, Louis, illus. 96p. (gr. 4). 1993. 13.95 (1-880507-06-4) Lectorum Pubns.

—The Curious Adventures of Jimmy McGee. O'Brien, John, illus. LC 86-31793. 160p. (gr. 3-7). 1987. 14.95 (0-15-221075-X, HB Juv Bks) HarBrace.

—Ginger Pye. Estes, Eleanor, illus. LC 51-10446. (gr. 3-7). 1950. 13.95 (0-15-230930-6, HB Juv Bks) HarBrace.

—Ginger Pye. large type ed. (Illus.). 300p. (gr. 3-7). 1987. Repr. of 1951 ed. lib. bdg. 14.95 (1-55736-056-1, Crnrstn Bks) BDD LT Grp.

—Ginger Pye. Schwartz, Amy, contrib. by. 306p. (gr. 3-7). 1990. pap. 3.95 (0-15-230933-0, Odyssey) HarBrace.

—Hundred Dresses. Slobodkin, Louis, illus. LC 44-8963. 32p. (gr. 1-5). 1944. 14.95 (0-15-237374-8, HB Juv Bks) HarBrace.

—The Hundred Dresses. Slobodkin, Louis, illus. LC 73-12940. 80p. (gr. 1-5). 1974. pap. 4.95 (0-15-642350-2, Voyager Bks) HarBrace.

—Middle Moffat. 1989. pap. 3.25 (0-440-70028-0) Dell.

—The Middle Moffats. (gr. k-6). 1989. pap. 3.25 (0-440-40180-1, YB) Dell.

—The Moffat Museum. Estes, Eleanor, illus. LC 83-8427. 262p. (gr. 3-7). 1983. 10.95 (0-15-255086-0, HB Juv Bks) HarBrace.

—The Moffat Museum. (gr. k-6). 1989. pap. 3.25 (0-440-40201-8, YB) Dell.

—Moffat Museum. 1989. pap. 3.25 (0-440-70029-9) Dell.

—Moffats. Slobodkin, Louis, illus. LC 41-51893. 32p. (gr. 3-7). 1941. 14.95 (0-15-255095-X, HB Juv Bks) HarBrace.

—The Moffats. 1989. pap. 3.25 (0-440-70026-4) Dell.

—Pinky Pye. Ardizzone, Edward, illus. LC 58-5708. (gr. 3-7). 1958. 10.95 (0-15-262076-1, HB Juv Bks) HarBrace.

—Pinky Pye. Ardizzone, Edward, illus. LC 75-31581. 192p. (gr. 3-7). 1976. pap. 1.75 (0-15-671840-5, Voyager Bks) HarBrace.

—Rufus M. Slobodkin, Louis, illus. LC 43-51239. (gr. 3-7). 1943. 15.95 (0-15-269415-3, HB Juv Bks) HarBrace.

—Rufus M. 1989. pap. 3.25 (0-440-70027-2) Dell.

—The Witch Family. Hewitt, Kathryn & Ardizzone, Edward, illus. 223p. (gr. 3-7). 1990. pap. 4.95 (0-15-298572-7, Odyssey) HarBrace.

Estes, James L. Alabama's Youngest Admirals. Krauel, Mary E., ed. Christian, Releta, illus. 132p. (Orig.). (gr. 4-12). 1991. pap. 8.95 (0-9628634-0-8) J L Estes.

Estes, Rose. The Case of the Dancing Dinosaur. Vincente, illus. LC 83-63444. 128p. (gr. 4-7). 1985. pap. 2.95 (0-394-86431-X) Random Bks Yng Read.

—The Mystery of the Turkish Tattoo. Fanelli, Jenny, ed. Gowing, Toby, illus. LC 85-62805. 128p. (gr. 4-7). 1986. pap. 2.95 (0-394-86434-4) Random Bks Yng Read.

Estes, Sherrill Y. Sell Like a Pro! The Secrets of Consultative Selling. (Illus.). 192p. (gr. 7 up). 1988. 18.95 (0-87491-917-7) Acropolis.

Estoril, Jean. Drina's Dancing Year, No. 2. 1989. pap. 2.75 (0-590-42192-1) Scholastic Inc.

Estrada, Zilia C. If I Were a Bird. Estrada, Zilia C., illus. (Orig.). (gr. 1 up). 1988. pap. write for info. Blue Flame Pr.

Estrem, Paul. ATV's. LC 87-19900. (Illus.). 48p. (gr. 5-6). 1987. RSBE 11.95 (0-89686-348-4, Crestwood Hse) Macmillan Child Grp.

—BMX's. LC 87-15554. (Illus.). 48p. (gr. 5-6). 1987. RSBE 11.95 (0-89686-349-2, Crestwood Hse) Macmillan Child Grp.

—Motocross Cycles. LC 87-16115. (Illus.). 48p. (gr. 5-6). 1987. RSBE 11.95 (0-89686-354-9, Crestwood Hse) Macmillan Child Grp.

—Rocket-Powered Cars. LC 87-22374. (Illus.). 48p. (gr. 5-6). 1987. RSBE 11.95 (0-89686-352-2, Crestwood Hse) Macmillan Child Grp.

Estrin, Leibel. The Man Who Rode with Eliyahu Haravi. Stern, Ayala, illus. 32p. (ps-3). 1990. 9.95 (0-922613-23-0); pap. 7.95 (0-922613-24-9) Hachai Pubns.

—The Story of Danny Three Times. Zelcer, Amir, illus. 32p. (ps-1). 1989. 8.95 (0-922613-10-9); pap. 6.95 (0-922613-11-7) Hachai Pubns.

Estvanik, Nicole B. Snowman Who Wanted to See July. (Illus.). 32p. 1989. PLB 17.96 (0-8172-2779-2) Raintree Steck-V.

—The Snowman Who Wanted to See July. (Illus.). 32p. 1989. PLB 29.28 (0-8172-2463-7) Raintree Steck-V.

—Snowman Who Wanted to See July. (ps-3). 1993. pap. 3.95 (0-8114-5210-7) Raintree Steck-V.

Etheredge, Warren. The All-New Ultimate Football Quiz Book. 176p. (Orig.). 1993. pap. 3.99 (0-451-17616-2, Sig) NAL-Dutton.

Etherege, George see Wilson, John H.

Ethridge, Kenneth. Toothpick. 128p. (gr. 7 up). 1988. pap. 2.50 (0-8167-1316-2) Troll Assocs.

Ethridge, Kenneth E. Toothpick. LC 85-42883. 128p. (gr. 7 up). 1985. 13.95 (0-8234-0585-0) Holiday.

—Viola, Furgy, Bobbi & Me. LC 88-28429. 166p. 1989. 13.95 (0-8234-0746-2) Holiday.

Etkin, Linda & Willoughby, Bebe, eds. America's Children: Stories, Poems, & Real-Life Adventures of Children Through Our Nation's History. (Illus.). 96p. (gr. 2-7). 1992. write for info. (0-307-15876-4, 15876, Golden Pr) Western Pub.

Etow, Carole, illus. What Goes Inside? 8p. (ps). 1992. 5.95 (0-8431-2998-0) Price Stern.

—Where Does It Come From? 8p. (ps). 1992. 5.95 (0-8431-2999-9) Price Stern.

—Whose Footprints Are These? 8p. (ps). 1992. 5.95 (0-8431-3358-9) Price Stern.

ETR Associates. No, No, Annette. Paley, Nina, illus. LC 93-16478. (gr. 5 up). 1993. write for info. ETR Assocs.

—When Momma Got Her Bonus. LC 93-16476. (gr. 4 up). 1993. write for info. ETR Assocs.

ETR Associates Staff. Ellie's Birthday. Paley, Nina, illus. LC 92-8358. 1992. write for info. (1-56071-106-X) ETR Assocs.

—A Family That Fits. Paley, Nina, illus. LC 92-8361. 1992. write for info. (1-56071-103-5) ETR Assocs.

—The Golden Treasure. Paley, Nina, illus. LC 92-8360. 1992. write for info. (1-56071-104-3) ETR Assocs.

—A Helmet for Harry. Paley, Nina, illus. LC 92-8357. 1992. write for info. (1-56071-102-7) ETR Assocs.

—In My Shoes. Paley, Nina, illus. LC 92-8359. 1992. write for info. (1-56071-105-1) ETR Assocs.

—Messages from the Zoo. Paley, Nina, illus. LC 93-16477. 1993. write for info. ETR Assocs.

—Who Likes That Stuff? Paley, Nina, illus. LC 92-8356. 1992. write for info. (1-56071-101-9) ETR Assocs.

Etra, Jon & Spinner, Stephanie. Aliens for Lunch. Bjorkman, Steve, illus. LC 90-39417. 64p. (Orig.). (gr. 2-4). 1991. PLB 6.99 (0-679-91056-5); pap. 2.50 (0-679-81056-0) Random Bks Yng Read.

Etra, Jonathan & Spinner, Stephanie. Aliens for Breakfast. Bjorkman, Steve, illus. LC 88-6653. 64p. (Orig.). (gr. 2-4). 1988. lib. bdg. 6.99 (0-394-92093-7); pap. 2.50 (0-394-82093-2) Random Bks Yng Read.

Ets, Marie H. Gilberto & the Wind. Ets, Marie H., illus. LC 63-8527. (gr. k-3). 1978. pap. 3.99 (0-14-050276-9, Puffin) Puffin Bks.

—Gilberto & the Wind. Ets, Marie H., illus. (ps-1). 1963. pap. 14.00 (0-670-34025-1) Viking Child Bks.

—In the Forest. (Illus.). (ps-2). 1976. pap. 3.95 (0-14-050180-0, Puffin) Puffin Bks.

—Just Me. (Illus.). (gr. k-2). 1978. pap. 4.99 (0-14-050325-0, Puffin) Puffin Bks.

—Just Me. Ets, Marie H., illus. (ps-2). 1965. pap. 14.95 (0-670-41109-4) Viking Child Bks.

—Just Me. Ets, Marie H., illus. (gr. k-3). 1985. bk. & cassette 19.95 (0-941078-75-2); pap. 12.95 bk. & cassette (0-941078-73-6); cassette, 4 paperbacks & guide 27.95 (0-941078-74-4) Live Oak Media.

—Nine Days to Christmas. Labastida, Aurora, illus. 48p. (ps-3). 1991. 4.95 (*0-14-054442-9*, Puffin) Puffin Bks.
—Nueve Dias Para Navidad. Labastida, Aurora, illus. 48p. (ps-3). 1991. 4.95 (*0-14-054441-0*, Puffin) Puffin Bks.
—Play with Me. (ps-k). 1976. pap. 3.95 (*0-14-050178-9*, Puffin) Puffin Bks.
—Play with Me. Ets, Marie H., illus. (ps-1). 1955. pap. 13.95 (*0-670-55977-6*) Viking Child Bks.
Ets, Marie H. & Labastida, Aurora. Nine Days to Christmas. Ets, Marie H., illus. (ps-2). 1959. pap. 13. 95 (*0-670-51350-4*) Viking Child Bks.
Ettah, Geneieve, ed. see Otumokala, Jean & Okon, Bern.
Ettinger, Tom & Jaspersohn, Bill. My Ballet Book. (Illus.). 48p. (gr. 3-7). 1993. 10.95 (*0-694-00477-4*, Festival) HarpC Child Bks.
—My Baseball Book: A Write-in-Me Book for Young Players. (Illus.). 48p. (gr. 3-7). 1993. 10.95 (*0-694-00466-9*, Festival) HarpC Child Bks.
—My Riding Book: A Write-in-Me Bk. for Young Riders. (Illus.). 48p. (gr. 3-7). 1993. 10.95 (*0-694-00465-0*, Festival) HarpC Child Bks.
—My Soccer Book. (Illus.). 48p. (gr. 3-7). 1993. 10.95 (*0-694-00478-2*, Festival) HarpC Child Bks.
Eubank, Mary G. & Hollingsworth, Mary. King's Alphabet. (ps-3). 1990. write for info. (*0-8499-0713-6*) Word Inc.
—King's Manners. (ps-3). 1990. write for info. (*0-8499-0826-4*) Word Inc.
—King's Workers. 1990. write for info. (*0-8499-0827-2*) Word Inc.
Eubanks, Sandra S. Slow-Go. 1992. 6.95 (*0-533-08763-5*) Vantage.
Eugene, Toni. Animal Acrobats. Cremins, Robert, illus. LC 93-9768. (Illus.). 1993. write for info. (*0-87044-955-9*) Natl Geog.
—Descubre Estrellas y Planetas. University of Mexico City Staff, tr. from SPA. O'Neill, Pablo M. & Robare, Lorie, illus. 48p. (gr. 3-8). 1993. PLB 16.95 (*1-56674-052-5*, HTS Bks) Forest Hse.
—Discover Stars & Planets. (Illus.). 48p. (gr. 3-6). 1992. PLB 14.95 (*1-87836-3-71-9*, HTS Bks) Forest Hse.
—Koalas & Kangaroos: Strange Animals of Australia. Crump, Donald J., ed. LC 81-607859. 32p. (ps-3). 1981. Set. 13.95 (*0-87044-403-4*); PLB 16.95 (*0-87044-408-5*) Natl Geog.
Eugene, Toni see National Geographic Society Staff.
Eugene, Toni. Beyond the Horizon: Adventures in Faraway Lands. (Illus.). 1992. 9.95 (*0-87044-831-5*) Natl Geog.
Eure, Wesley. Red Wings of Christmas. Paolillo, Ronald G., illus. LC 92-5457. 160p. (gr. 3-7). 1992. 19.95 (*0-88289-902-3*) Pelican.
Euretig, Mary. I'm in the Spotlight! A Journal of Discovery for Young Writers. Bacchini, Lisa, illus. 160p. (gr. 1-5). 1993. pap. 11.95 (*0-9628216-1-6*) Dream Tree Pr.
Euretig, Mary & Kreisberg, Darlene. Rainbow Writing: A Journal with Activities for Budding Young Writers. Bacchini, Lisa, illus. (Orig.). (gr. 1-3). 1990. pap. 11.95 (*0-9628216-0-8*) Dream Tree Pr.
Euripides see Lind, Levi R.
Eustaquio, Roque B. Islas: A Social Studies Workbook. 98p. (gr. 9-12). 1989. write for info wkbk. Marianas Red Pub.
Eustis, Helen. The Redheaded Woman. Reinhard, Michl, illus. LC 84-145828. 36p. (Orig.). (gr. 7 up). 1991. pap. 2.95 (*0-88138-013-X*, Green Tiger) S&S Trade.
Euvremer, Teryl. The Thieves of Peck's Pocket. Euvremer, Teryl, illus. LC 89-23845. 32p. (ps-2). 1990. PLB 13.99 (*0-517-57538-8*) Crown Bks Yng Read.
—Triple Whammy. Euvremer, Teryl, illus. LC 91-44240. 32p. (gr. k-4). 1993. 15.00 (*0-06-021060-5*); PLB 14. 89 (*0-06-021061-3*) HarpC Child Bks.
Evans & Millard. Greek Myths & Legends. (Illus.). 64p. (gr. 6-10). 1986. PLB 14.96 (*0-88110-224-5*); pap. 8.95 (*0-86020-946-6*) EDC.
Evans, A. J. & Palmer, Marilyn. More Writing about Pictures: Using Pictures to Develop Language & Writing Skills. (gr. 1-3). 1982. Bk. 1: Familiar Places. pap. 3.95x (*0-8077-6037-4*); Bk. 2: Action & Activity. pap. 3.95x (*0-8077-6038-2*); Bk. 3: Supplement-Fables. pap. 3.95x (*0-8077-6039-0*); tchr's. manual 2.95x (*0-8077-6040-4*) Tchrs Coll.
Evans, Art. First Photos: How Kids Can Take Great Pictures. LC 92-50482. (Illus.). 64p. (Orig.). (gr. 3-12). 1993. pap. 9.95 perfect bdg. (*0-9626508-7-0*) Photo Data Res.
Evans, Arthur N. The Automobile. (Illus.). 52p. (gr. 5 up). 1985. PLB 13.50 (*0-8225-1232-7*) Lerner Pubns.
—The Motor Car. LC 82-9713. (Illus.). 48p. (gr. 7 up). 1983. pap. 6.95 (*0-521-28416-3*) Cambridge U Pr.
—The Railways. (Illus.). 48p. (gr. 7 up). 1988. pap. 6.95 (*0-521-26918-0*) Cambridge U Pr.
Evans, Bob, ed. see Evans, Inez.
Evans, C. Acting & Theater. (Illus.). 64p. (gr. 6 up). 1992. lib. bdg. 13.96 (*0-88110-505-8*, Usborne); pap. 7.95 (*0-7460-0699-3*) EDC.
—Calligraphy. (Illus.). 48p. (gr. 6 up). 1990. PLB 14.96 (*0-88110-432-9*, Usborne); pap. 7.95 (*0-7460-0426-5*) EDC.
Evans, C. & Keable-Elliott, I. Complete Book of Magic. (Illus.). 64p. 1989. PLB 13.96 (*0-88110-383-7*); pap. 7.95 (*0-7460-0300-5*) EDC.
Evans, C. & Millard, A. Greek & Norse Legends. (Illus.). 112p. (gr. 6-10). 1987. pap. 12.95 (*0-7460-0240-8*) EDC.

Evans, C., jt. auth. see Tatchell, J.
Evans, C., et al. Complete Book of Magic & Magic Tricks. (Illus.). 128p. 1992. 15.95 (*0-7460-0742-6*) EDC.
Evans, C. S. Cinderella. 1993. 12.95 (*0-679-42313-3*, Everymans Lib) Knopf.
—Sleeping Beauty. 1993. 12.95 (*0-679-42814-3*, Everymans Lib) Knopf.
Evans, Carol, ed. see Schnell, Louise.
Evans, D. R. Palindor. LC 93-20220. (Illus.). 1993. write for info. (*0-7814-0117-8*, Chariot Bks) Cook.
Evans, David. The Famous Hooper Brothers. Labby, Sherman, illus. 101p. (Orig.). 1988. pap. 15.95 (*0-929422-00-7*) Jonah Pr.
—Fishing for Angels: The Magic of Kites. D'Arcy, Adele, illus. 88p. (Orig.). (gr. 5 up). 1991. pap. 12.95 (*1-55037-162-2*, Pub. by Annick CN) Firefly Bks Ltd.
—How We Used to Live: Victorians Early & Late. (Illus.). 48p. (gr. 4-8). 1995. 14.95 (*0-7136-3310-7*, Pub. by A&C Black UK) Talman.
Evans, David & Williams, Claudette. Air & Flying. (Illus.). 32p. (gr. k-4). 1993. 9.95 (*1-56458-343-0*) Dorling Kindersley.
—Building Things. LC 93-7066. (Illus.). 32p. (gr. k-4). 1993. 9.95 (*1-56458-344-9*) Dorling Kindersley.
—Color & Light. LC 92-53480. (Illus.). 24p. (gr. k-3). 1993. 9.95 (*1-56458-207-8*) Dorling Kindersley.
—Living Things. LC 93-7073. (Illus.). 32p. (gr. k-3). 1993. 9.95 (*1-56458-345-7*) Dorling Kindersley.
—Magnets & Batteries. (Illus.). 32p. (gr. k-4). 1993. 9.95 (*1-56458-346-5*) Dorling Kindersley.
—Make It Balance. LC 92-52814. (Illus.). 32p. (gr. k-3). 1992. 9.95 (*1-56458-118-7*) Dorling Kindersley.
—Make It Change. LC 92-52815. (Illus.). 32p. (gr. k-3). 1992. 9.95 (*1-56458-119-5*) Dorling Kindersley.
—Make It Go. LC 92-52816. (Illus.). 32p. (gr. k-3). 1992. 9.95 (*1-56458-120-9*) Dorling Kindersley.
—Me & My Body. LC 92-52817. (Illus.). 32p. (gr. k-3). 1992. 9.95 (*1-56458-121-7*) Dorling Kindersley.
—Rocks & Soil. LC 92-53478. (Illus.). 24p. (gr. k-3). 1993. 9.95 (*1-56458-209-4*) Dorling Kindersley.
—Sound & Music. LC 92-53481. (Illus.). 24p. (gr. k-3). 1993. 9.95 (*1-56458-206-X*) Dorling Kindersley.
—Water & Floating. LC 92-53479. (Illus.). 24p. (gr. k-3). 1993. 9.95 (*1-56458-208-6*) Dorling Kindersley.
Evans, Dilys. Monster Soup. (Illus.). 1992. 14.95 (*0-590-45208-8*, 001, Scholastic Hardcover) Scholastic Inc.
Evans, Eugene. Bremen Town Musicians. Boddy, Joe & Boddy, Joe, illus. LC 90-10974. 48p. (gr. 1-5). 1990. 5.95 (*0-88101-102-9*) Unicorn Pub.
Evans, Gillian, ed. see Rogerson, John.
Evans, Helen K. Jesus Is Born. 64p. (ps-3). 1990. 8.95 (*0-86653-551-9*, SS894, Shining Star Pubns) Good Apple.
—Jesus, My Friend. 64p. (ps-3). 1988. 8.95 (*0-86653-428-8*, SS1856, Shining Star Pubns) Good Apple.
Evans, Inez. Spent Arrow. Evans, Robley & Evans, Bob, eds. 306p. (gr. 7-12). 1987. 15.95 (*0-934188-24-6*) Evans Pubns.
Evans, J. Edward. Freedom of Religion. (Illus.). 88p. (gr. 4 up). 1990. PLB 14.95 (*0-8225-1754-X*) Lerner Pubns.
—Freedom of Speech. (Illus.). 88p. (gr. 4 up). 1990. PLB 14.95 (*0-8225-1753-1*) Lerner Pubns.
—Freedom of the Press. (Illus.). 72p. (gr. 5 up). 1990. PLB 14.95 (*0-8225-1752-3*) Lerner Pubns.
—Jerry Rice: Touchdown Talent. (gr. 4-7). 1993. pap. 4.95 (*0-8225-9634-2*) Lerner Pubns.
Evans, Jack, ed. see Barklow, Irene.
Evans, Jeremy. Camping & Survival. LC 91-39143. (Illus.). 48p. (gr. 6). 1992. RSBE 12.95 (*0-89686-686-6*, Crestwood Hse) Macmillan Child Grp.
—Hiking & Climbing. LC 91-4061. (Illus.). 48p. (gr. 6). 1992. RSBE 12.95 (*0-89686-684-X*, Crestwood Hse) Macmillan Child Grp.
—Horseback Riding. LC 91-23340. (Illus.). 48p. (gr. 6). 1992. RSBE 12.95 (*0-89686-683-1*, Crestwood Hse) Macmillan Child Grp.
—Motocross & Trials. LC 93-9385. (Illus.). 48p. (gr. 5-6). 1994. RSBE 13.95 (*0-89686-821-4*, Crestwood Hse) Macmillan Child Grp.
—Off-Road Biking. LC 91-13629. (Illus.). 48p. (gr. 6). 1992. RSBE 12.95 (*0-89686-687-4*, Crestwood Hse) Macmillan Child Grp.
—Sailing. LC 91-12321. (Illus.). 48p. (gr. 6). 1992. RSBE 12.95 (*0-89686-682-3*, Crestwood Hse) Macmillan Child Grp.
—Skateboarding. LC 93-18165. (Illus.). 48p. (gr. 5-6). 1994. RSBE 13.95 (*0-89686-822-2*, Crestwood Hse) Macmillan Child Grp.
—Skiing. LC 91-32025. (Illus.). 48p. (gr. 5-6). 1992. RSBE 12.95 (*0-89686-681-5*, Crestwood Hse) Macmillan Child Grp.
—Surfing. LC 92-43227. (Illus.). 48p. (gr. 5-6). 1994. RSBE 13.95 (*0-89686-824-9*, Crestwood Hse) Macmillan Child Grp.
—Whitewater Kayaking. LC 91-39142. (Illus.). 48p. (gr. 5-6). 1992. RSBE 12.95 (*0-89686-685-8*, Crestwood Hse) Macmillan Child Grp.
—Windsurfing. LC 91-7886. (Illus.). 48p. (gr. 6). 1992. RSBE 12.95 (*0-89686-680-7*, Crestwood Hse) Macmillan Child Grp.
Evans, Jerry. Karate Master. LC 89-62355. 206p. (Orig.). (gr. 11 up). 1989. pap. 7.95 (*0-9623698-0-2*) Magnum Pr.

Evans, Jo & Moore, Jo E. Conociendome a Mi Mismo. Wolfe, Liz & Ficklin, Dora, trs. from ENG. (SPA., Illus.). 24p. (gr. 1-3). 1990. pap. text ed. 4.95 (*1-55799-182-0*) Evan-Moor Corp.
Evans, Joy. The Big Book of Art Centers. (Illus.). 64p. (gr. 1-4). 1992. pap. 11.95 (*1-55799-221-5*) Evan-Moor Corp.
—Consonants. (Illus.). 32p. (gr. k-2). 1987. pap. text ed. 4.95 (*1-55799-109-X*) Evan-Moor Corp.
—Creative Thinking Through Art, Vol. 1: Mixed Media. (Illus.). 64p. (gr. 2-5). 1993. pap. text ed. 11.95 (*1-55799-263-0*) Evan-Moor Corp.
—Creative Thinking Through Art, Vol. 2: Drawing. (Illus.). 64p. (gr. 2-5). 1993. pap. text ed. 11.95 (*1-55799-264-9*) Evan-Moor Corp.
—Draw Animals Around the World. Shipman, Gary, illus. 36p. (gr. 2-6). 1992. pap. 7.95 (*1-55799-223-1*) Evan-Moor Corp.
Evans, Joy & Moore, Jo E. Actividades De Ciencia Para Pomer En Secuencia. Mayer, Jan, et al, trs. from ENG. (SPA., Illus.). 32p. (gr. 1-3). 1990. pap. text ed. 4.95 (*1-55799-188-X*) Evan-Moor Corp.
—Barnyard Babies. (Illus.). 48p. (gr. 1-3). 1990. pap. text ed. 9.95 (*1-55799-169-3*) Evan-Moor Corp.
—Casas De Animales. Wolfe, Liz & Ficklin, Dora, trs. from ENG. (SPA., Illus.). 20p. (gr. 1-3). 1990. pap. text ed. 4.95 (*1-55799-189-8*) Evan-Moor Corp.
—Ciclos De La Vida Animal: Aves, Anfibios, e Insectos. Wolfe, Liz & Ficklin, Dora, trs. from ENG. (SPA., Illus.). 16p. (gr. 1-3). 1992. pap. text ed. 5.95 incl. poster (*1-55799-232-0*) Evan-Moor Corp.
—Ciclos De La Vida Animales: Mamiferos y Reptiles. Wolfe, Liz & Ficklin, Dora, trs. from ENG. (SPA., Illus.). 16p. (gr. 1-3). 1992. pap. text ed. 5.95 incl. poster (*1-55799-231-2*) Evan-Moor Corp.
—Dibuja... Luego, Escribe. Wolfe, Liz & Ficklin, Dora, trs. from ENG. (SPA., Illus.). 32p. (gr. 1-3). 1990. pap. text ed. 4.95 (*1-55799-181-2*) Evan-Moor Corp.
—En Mi Patio. Mayer, Jan, et al, trs. from ENG. (SPA., Illus.). 32p. (gr. 1-3). 1990. pap. text ed. 4.95 (*1-55799-187-1*) Evan-Moor Corp.
—El Esqueleto y los Musculos. Wolfe, Liz & Ficklin, Dora, trs. from ENG. (SPA., Illus.). 16p. (gr. 1-3). 1992. pap. text ed. 5.95 incl. poster (*1-55799-236-3*) Evan-Moor Corp.
—Formas Para Reportes De Libros. Mayer, Jan et al, trs. from ENG. (SPA., Illus.). 32p. (gr. 1-6). 1990. pap. text ed. 4.95 (*1-55799-186-3*) Evan-Moor Corp.
—Habitaculos - Oceanos & Charcas. Wolfe, Liz & Ficklin, Dora, trs. from ENG. (SPA., Illus.). 16p. (gr. 1-3). 1992. pap. text ed. 5.95 incl. poster (*1-55799-231-2*) Evan-Moor Corp.
—How to Make Books with Children, Vol. II. (Illus.). 96p. (gr. 1-6). 1991. pap. 9.95 (*1-55799-212-6*) Evan-Moor Corp.
—Lee, Piensa, Corta y Pega. Wolfe, Liz & Ficklin, Dora, trs. from ENG. (SPA., Illus.). 20p. (gr. 1-3). 1990. pap. text ed. 4.95 (*1-55799-183-9*) Evan-Moor Corp.
—Mis Cinco Sentidos. Wolfe, Liz & Ficklin, Dora, trs. from ENG. (SPA., Illus.). 16p. (gr. 1-3). 1992. pap. text ed. 5.95 incl. poster (*1-55799-233-9*) Evan-Moor Corp.
—Los Planetas. Wolfe, Liz & Ficklin, Dora, trs. from ENG. (SPA., Illus.). 16p. (gr. 1-3). 1992. pap. text ed. 5.95 incl. poster (*1-55799-237-1*) Evan-Moor Corp.
—Las Plantas. Wolfe, Liz & Ficklin, Dora, trs. from ENG. (SPA., Illus.). 16p. (gr. 1-3). 1992. pap. text ed. 5.95 incl. poster (*1-55799-230-4*) Evan-Moor Corp.
—Pon un Cuentito En Orden. Wolfe, Liz & Ficklin, Dora, trs. from ENG. (SPA., Illus.). 20p. (gr. 1-2). 1990. pap. text ed. 4.95 (*1-55799-184-7*) Evan-Moor Corp.
—Quien? Que? Donde? Cuando? Wolfe, Liz & Ficklin, Dora, trs. from ENG. (SPA., Illus.). 20p. (gr. 2-3). 1990. pap. text ed. 4.95 (*1-55799-185-5*) Evan-Moor Corp.
—Read & Do. (Illus.). 32p. (gr. k-2). 1987. pap. text ed. 4.95 (*1-55799-111-1*) Evan-Moor Corp.
—Short & Long Vowels. (Illus.). 32p. (gr. k-2). 1987. pap. text ed. 4.95 (*1-55799-110-3*) Evan-Moor Corp.
—Siguiendo Instrucciones A. Mayer, Jan, et al, trs. from ENG. (SPA., Illus.). 32p. (gr. ps-1). 1990. pap. text ed. 4.95 (*1-55799-179-0*) Evan-Moor Corp.
—Siguiendo Instrucciones B. Mayer, Jan, et al, trs. from ENG. (SPA., Illus.). 32p. (gr. 1-3). 1990. pap. text ed. 4.95 (*1-55799-178-2*) Evan-Moor Corp.
—El Sol, la Luna, y las Estrellas. Wolfe, Liz & Ficklin, Dora, trs. from ENG. (SPA., Illus.). 16p. (gr. 1-3). 1992. pap. text ed. 5.95 incl. poster (*1-55799-235-5*) Evan-Moor Corp.
Evans, Joy & Tryon, Leslie. Bob & Sam. (Illus.). 32p. (gr. k-2). 1987. pap. text ed. 4.95 (*1-55799-162-X*) Evan-Moor Corp.
—Maps of the U. S. A. (Illus.). 64p. (gr. 1-6). 1989. pap. text ed. 6.95 (*1-55799-148-0*) Evan-Moor Corp.
Evans, Joy, jt. auth. see Moore, Jo E.
Evans, Joy, et al. Making Big Books with Children. (Illus.). 64p. (gr. k-2). 1989. pap. 11.95 (*1-55799-165-0*) Evan-Moor Corp.
Evans, June B. Ancestors Coloring Book. LC 84-71724. (Illus.). 32p. (gr. 1-12). 1984. pap. 6.00x (*0-9611114-2-9*) Bryn Ffyliaid.
Evans, Karen. Beginning to Subtract. Nayer, Judith E., ed. McCarthy, Kathleen, illus. 32p. (gr. k-1). 1991. wkbk. 1.95 (*1-878624-56-3*) McClanahan Bk.
—Subtraction. Nayer, Judith E., ed. Kennedy, Anne & Wilson, Ann, illus. 32p. (gr. k-1). 1991. wkbk. 1.95 (*1-878624-58-X*) McClanahan Bk.

Evans, Katie. Hunky Dory Ate It. Stoeke, Janet M., illus. LC 91-13992. 32p. (ps-1). 1992. 13.50 (0-525-44847-0, DCB) Dutton Child Bks.
—Hunky Dory Found It. Stoeke, Janet M., illus. LC 93-15826. 32p. (ps-k). 1994. 13.99 (0-525-45192-7, DCB) Dutton Child Bks.
Evans, Larry. Gross & Gruesome Games & Puzzles. (gr. 4-7). 1992. pap. 3.99 (0-8431-3443-7) Price Stern.
—Invisibles Two. (Illus.). 40p. (Orig.). 1981. pap. 3.50 (0-8431-1711-7) Price Stern.
—Three-D Mazes, Vol. 1. (Illus.). 40p. 1976. pap. 3.95 (0-8431-1744-3) Price Stern.
—World of Nature Invisibles: Hidden Picture Book. 40p. (gr. 4-6). 1993. pap. 3.50 (0-8431-3490-9) Troubador Pr.
Evans, Lee. Basic Pen & Ink Sketching for Pathfinders III: A Y. E. S. Book. Gattis, L. S., ed. (Illus.). 20p. (Orig.). (gr. 5-6). 1987. tchrs. ed 5.00 (0-936241-34-9) Cheetah Pub.
Evans, Lisa G. An Elephant Never Forgets Its Snorkel: How Animals Survive Without Tools & Gadgets. De Groat, Diane, illus. LC 91-31828. 40p. (gr. 1-5). 1992. 10.00 (0-517-58401-8); PLB 10.99 (0-517-58404-2) Crown Bks Yng Read.
Evans, Lynn. Richmond, Virginia: The Travel Guide for Kids. 1991. pap. 5.00 (0-945600-07-0) Colormore Inc.
Evans, Mari. I Look at Me. (ps-2). 1974. pap. 2.50 (0-88378-038-0) Third World.
Evans, Mariam, ed. see Yushij, Nima.
Evans, Mariam, tr. see Yushij, Nima.
Evans, Marilyn. Guided Report Writing. (Illus.). 64p. (gr. 3-6). 1987. pap. 6.95 (1-55799-075-1) Evan-Moor Corp.
Evans, Mark. Fish. Caras, Roger, intro. by. LC 92-53476. (Illus.). 48p. (gr. 3-7). 1993. 9.95 (1-56458-222-1) Dorling Kindersley.
—Guinea Pigs. LC 92-52826. (Illus.). 48p. (gr. 2 up). 1992. 9.95 (1-56458-125-X) Dorling Kindersley.
—Hamster. Caras, Roger, intro. by. LC 92-53475. (Illus.). 48p. (gr. 3-7). 1993. 9.95 (1-56458-223-X) Dorling Kindersley.
—Kitten. LC 92-52827. (Illus.). 48p. (gr. 2 up). 1992. 9.95 (1-56458-126-8) Dorling Kindersley.
—Pepito: The Little Dancing Dog. Cugat, Xavier, illus. LC 78-65354. (gr. k-4). 1979. 6.95 (0-87592-063-2) Scroll Pr.
—Puppy. LC 92-52828. (Illus.). 48p. (gr. 2 up). 1992. 9.95 (1-56458-127-6) Dorling Kindersley.
—Rabbit. LC 92-52829. (Illus.). 48p. (gr. 2 up). 1992. 9.95 (1-56458-128-4) Dorling Kindersley.
Evans, Marla D. This Is Me & My Single Parent: A Discovery Workbook for Children & Single Parents to Work on Together. (Illus.). 80p. (Orig.). (gr. 2-6). 1989. pap. 13.95 (0-945354-17-7) Magination Pr.
—This Is Me & My Two Families: An Awareness Scrapbook - Journal for Children Living in Stepfamilies. (Illus.). 88p. (gr. 2-6). 1988. pap. 14.95 (0-945354-06-1) Magination Pr.
Evans, Mary A., adapted by see Wells, H. G.
Evans, Mary J. & Anderson, Deborah. Tales from Hans Christian Andersen. (gr. k up). 1983. pap. 4.50 (0-87602-257-3) Anchorage.
Evans, Max. My Pardner. Bjorklund, Lorence, illus. LC 75-187421. 104p. (gr. 5-9). 1972. 3.95 (0-395-13725-X) HM.
Evans, Michael. Nativity Press-Out. Evans, Michael, illus. 12p. (ps-5). 1993. pap. 7.95 (0-8249-8635-0, Ideals Child) Hambleton-Hill.
—Noah's Ark: With Press-Out Model Ark, Animals, People & More. Evans, Michael, illus. 16p. (Orig.). (gr. k-4). 1993. pap. 7.95 (0-8249-8600-8, Ideals Child) Hambleton-Hill.
Evans, Michael, jt. auth. see Greenway, Shirley.
Evans, Nancy, jt. auth. see Banks, Ann.
Evans, Nate. The Mixed-up Zoo of Professor Yahoo. Gibson, Kate & Sundeen, Ann, eds. LC 92-71679. (Illus.). 32p. (ps-3). 1993. 14.95 (0-9607076-3-8) Jr League KC.
Evans, Olive. Secrets of the Forest. (gr. 3-12). 1985. pap. 6.00 play script (0-88734-502-6) Players Pr.
Evans, Patrick, jt. auth. see Black, John.
Evans, Pearl. Dancing with the Times: What's a Young Adult to Believe! Taylor, Richard, illus. 160p. (Orig.). (gr. 8 up). 1993. pap. 4.99 (0-938453-05-X) Small Helm Pr.
Evans, Peter. Technology Two Thousand. (Illus.). 64p. (gr. 7 up). 1986. 14.95x (0-8160-1155-9) Facts on File.
Evans, Phillip. City. (ps). 1990. 14.60 (0-8172-3668-6) Raintree Steck-V.
—Doing. (ps). 1990. 14.60 (0-8172-3651-1) Raintree Steck-V.
Evans, Phyllis R. The Sea World Book of Seals & Sea Lions. LC 85-27100. (Illus.). (gr. 4-7). 1986. 15.95 (0-15-271954-7, HB Juv Bks); pap. 9.95 (0-15-271955-5) HarBrace.
Evans, R. E. The War of American Independence. (Illus.). 48p. (gr. 7 up). 1976. pap. 7.50 (0-521-20903-X) Cambridge U Pr.
Evans, Robley, ed. see Evans, Inez.
Evans, Sanford. Naomi's Geese. Chabrian, Deborah, illus. LC 92-44109. (gr. 5 up). 1993. pap. 15.00 (0-671-75623-0, S&S BFYR) S&S Trade.
Evans, Shirlee. Tree Tall & the Horse Race. Ponter, James, illus. LC 86-7659. 136p. (Orig.). (gr. 3-8). 1986. pap. 3.95 (0-8361-3414-1) Herald Pr.
—Tree Tall & the Whiteskins. LC 85-13952. (Illus.). 112p. (gr. 9 up). 1985. pap. 3.95 (0-8361-3402-8) Herald Pr.

—Tree Tall to the Rescue. Ponter, James, illus. LC 87-8615. 144p. (Orig.). (gr. 4-9). 1987. pap. 4.50 (0-8361-3444-3) Herald Pr.
Evans, Thomas W. Mentors: Making a Difference in our Public Schools. 256p. (Orig.). 1993. pap. 9.95 (1-56079-325-2) Petersons Guides.

Evans, Vicki. Be Like the Sun & Shine. (ENG, FRE & SPA., Illus.). 32p. (ps-5). 1993. pap. 9.00 (0-9636367-0-7) V Evans.
Unique children's book in English, Spanish & French. Read an imaginative children's story, then participate in two innovative educational activities. Develop abilities in art & creative writing, enhancing self-esteem by stimulating the imagination. Become familiar with two other languages besides your own as you read this book. This book provides opportunities for the child to both develop creativity & become exposed to other languages. CHILDREN'S STORY: Did you ever want to be something else instead of being you? A boy named Leroy loves nature & wishes he were the Sun. He's sent to his room to clean up & wishes he were the Sun so he could play more. A magical bird comes to his bedroom window & tells him how he can be the Sun. Read this book to see if Leroy becomes the Sun & what he learns in this process. ART & CREATIVE WRITING ACTIVITY: "INSIDE THE WORLD OF YOUR IMAGINATION": Eleven trilingual activities stimulate the imagination & encourage self-expression through creative art & writing utilizing guided imagery. Draw & write about your experiences from these activities to express your thoughts & feelings. "WORDS IN THREE LANGUAGES": Practice saying & learning two pages of familiar words from the story in other languages. To order: Vicki Evans, P.O. Box 20141, Houston, TX 77225-0141. Telephone: 713-667-7359.
Publisher Provided Annotation.

Evans-Smith, Deborah. The Whale's Tale. Evans, Valeria, illus. LC 85-51791. 25p. (gr. 2-6). 1986. 8.95 (0-917507-02-9) Sea Fog Pr.
Evans-Tiller, Jan. Around the Church, Around the Year: Unitarian Universalism for Children. Lewis, Kathryn, et al, eds. Conteh-Morgan, Jane, illus. 144p. (Orig.). (gr. k-3). 1990. pap. text ed. 29.95 (1-55896-174-7) Unitarian Univ.
Evarts, Hal. Jay-Jay & the Peking Monster. (gr. 5-9). 1984. 15.25 (0-8446-6166-X) Peter Smith.
Evelyn-Marie. Daniel Scott & the Monster. Lang, Irene, illus. LC 83-13369. 32p. (gr. k-3). 1985. 7.95 (0-9614746-1-0); PLB 9.95 (0-9614746-2-9); bk. & cassette 11.95 (0-9614746-0-2); pap. 3.00 (0-9614746-4-5) Berry Bks.
—Pick Your Own Strawberries. rev. ed. Evelyn-Marie, illus. 32p. (gr. k-3). 1983. pap. 3.00 (0-9614746-3-7) Berry Bks.
Evenhouse, Bill. Reasons One, Sects & Cults with Non-Christian Roots. rev. ed. 120p. 1991. 5.75 (0-930265-97-1); tchr's. manual, 60p. 5.75 (1-56212-007-7) CRC Pubns.
—Reasons Two, Sects & Cults with Christian Roots. (Orig.). (gr. 10-12). 1981. pap. text ed. 5.75 (0-933140-25-8); tchr's. manual, 70p. 5.75 (0-933140-26-6) CRC Pubns.
Evens, Lori H. Movin' Mountains. 176p. (Orig.). 1991. pap. 7.95 (0-929292-21-9) Hannibal Bks.
Everding, Maria P. Pretty As a Picture: A Guide to Manners, Poise & Appearance. 138p. (Orig.). (gr. 4-7). 1986. pap. 14.95 (0-9617665-0-6) GME Pub Co.
Everett, Betty S. I Want to Be Like You, Lord: Bible Devotion for Girls. LC 84-21563. 112p. (Orig.). (gr. 7-10). 1984. pap. 5.99 (0-8066-2112-5, 10-3196, Augsburg) Augsburg Fortress.
—Who Am I, Lord? LC 82-72645. 112p. (Orig.). (gr. 3-6). 1983. pap. 5.99 (0-8066-1951-1, 10-7072, Augsburg) Augsburg Fortress.
Everett, F. Explorers. (Illus.). 48p. (gr. 4 up). 1991. PLB 14.96 (0-88110-504-X, Usborne); pap. 7.95 (0-7460-0514-8) EDC.

—Farm Animals. (Illus.). 32p. (gr. k-1). 1993. lib. bdg. 13.96 (0-88110-648-8, Usborne); pap. 5.95 (0-7460-1022-2, Usborne) EDC.
—Fashion Design. (Illus.). (gr. 6 up). 1988. PLB 14.96 (0-88110-307-1); pap. 8.95 (0-7460-0187-8) EDC.
—Jewelry. (Illus.). (gr. 6 up). 1987. PLB 13.96 (0-88110-243-1); pap. 5.95 (0-7460-0077-4) EDC.
—Make-up. (Illus.). 32p. (gr. 6 up). 1987. PLB 13.96 (0-88110-242-3); pap. 5.95 (0-7460-0075-8) EDC.
Everett, F. & Garbera, C. Making Clothes. (Illus.). 48p. (gr. 6 up). 1986. PLB 14.96 (0-88110-321-7); pap. 6.95 (0-86020-981-4) EDC.
Everett, F. & Woods, P., eds. Decorate Your Room. (Illus.). 48p. (gr. 6 up). 1989. lib. bdg. 13.96 (0-88110-392-6, Usborne); pap. 7.95 (0-7460-0438-9) EDC.

Everett, Gwen. John Brown: One Man Against Slavery. Lawrence, Jacob, illus. LC 92-41973. 32p. (gr. 5 up). 1993. 15.95 (0-8478-1702-4) Rizzoli Intl.
JOHN BROWN is the story of the famous abolitionist told from the viewpoint of his young daughter, Annie. John Brown's legendary fight against slavery electrified the nation & moved it closer to Civil War on the night of October 16, 1859, when he led a raid on the U.S. Government Arsenal in Harper's Ferry, Virginia. Gwen Everett, author of award winning LI'L SIS & UNCLE WILLIE (Rizzoli, 1992), recounts Brown's sincere conviction that all people are equal, regardless of skin color. By capturing the events through Annie's eyes, Everett allows young readers to explore contemporary issues & to examine questions of might versus morality. Was it right for one man to seek a positive change through murder & bloodshed? Were there alternatives? Can one person fight a corrupt system? A stunning series of gouache paintings created in 1941 by renowned African-American artist Jacob Lawrence illustrates this valuable new book. Throughout his career, he has often worked in series dealing with historical & social issues, recording the triumphs & tragedies of African-Americans. The JOHN BROWN sequence is featured here for the first time in book format. His dramatic compositions radiate with the intensity & intrigue of this riveting chapter in American history. "A powerful presentation...the gouaches are captivating."--Kirkus Reviews (Pointer.)
Publisher Provided Annotation.

—Lil Sis & Uncle Willie. (Illus.). 32p. 1994. pap. write for info. (1-56282-593-3) Hyprn Ppbks.
Everett, Gwen & National Museum of American Art Staff. Li'l Sis & Uncle Willie: A Story Based on the Life & Paintings of William H. Johnson. Johnson, William H., illus. LC 91-14800. 32p. (ps-3). 1992. Repr. of 1991 ed. 13.95 (0-8478-1462-9) Rizzoli Intl.
Everett, Karen H., jt. auth. see Herman, Ethel.
Everett, Louise. Amigo Means Friend. Radinowitz, Sandy, illus. LC 87-11274. 32p. (gr. k-2). 1988. PLB 7.89 (0-8167-1000-7); pap. text ed. 1.95 (0-8167-1001-5) Troll Assocs.
—Bubble Gum in the Sky. Harvey, Paul, illus. LC 86-30859. 32p. (gr. k-2). 1988. PLB 7.89 (0-8167-0998-X); pap. text ed. 1.95 (0-8167-0999-8) Troll Assocs.
—More Fun Crosswords. (ps). 1991. pap. 1.95 (0-8167-0884-3) Troll Assocs.
—Skating on Thin Ice. Kolding, Richard M., illus. LC 86-30857. 32p. (gr. k-2). 1988. PLB 7.89 (0-8167-0992-0); pap. text ed. 1.95 (0-8167-0993-9) Troll Assocs.
Everett, Mimi, illus. Cinderella. 24p. 1991. pap. 1.25 (0-7214-5300-7, S9016-1 SER.) Ladybird Bks.
—Snow White & the Seven Dwarfs. 24p. (ps-1). 1991. pap. 1.25 (0-7214-5306-6, S9016-7) Ladybird Bks.
Everett, Percival. The One That Got Away. Zimmer, Dirk, illus. 32p. (gr. 1-4). 1992. PLB 14.95 (0-685-52550-3, Clarion Bks) HM.
—The One That Got Away. Zimmer, Dirk, illus. (gr. 1-4). 1992. 14.45 (0-395-56437-9, Clarion Bks) HM.

—One That Got Away. (ps-3). 1992. 14.95 (0-395-56427-1, Clarion Bks) HM.
Ever-Hadani, Yoram. The Man & His Line. LC 91-70733. 64p. 1991. 10.00 (0-449-90627-2, Columbine) Fawcett.
Everitt, B. Mean Soup. 1992. 13.95 (0-15-253146-7, HB Juv Bks) HBrace.
Everitt, Betsy. Frida the Wondercat. 32p. (ps-3). 1990. 13.95 (0-15-229540-2) HarBrace.
—Fride the Wondercat. (ps-3). pap. 4.95 (0-15-229541-0, HB Juv Bks) HarBrace.
—TV Dinner. LC 93-19159. 1994. write for info. (0-15-283950-X, HB Juv Bks) HarBrace.
Everitt-Stewart, Andy, jt. auth. see Moseley, Keith.
Everix, Nancy. Ethnic Celebrations Around the World. 160p. (gr. 3-8). 1991. 12.95 (0-86653-607-8, GA1326) Good Apple.
—More Windows to the World. Everix, Nancy, illus. 128p. (gr. 2-8). 1985. wkbk. 11.95 (0-86653-316-8, GA 640) Good Apple.
—Windows to the World. Everix, Nancy, illus. 128p. (gr. 2-8). 1984. wkbk. 11.95 (0-86653-173-4, GA 527) Good Apple.
Everly, Kathleen & Gordon, Sol. How Can You Tell If You're Really in Love? Cohen, Vivien, illus. 20p. (gr. 7-12). 1983. pap. 1.95 (0-934978-06-9) Ed-U Pr.
Evernden, Margery, jt. auth. see Hodges, Margaret.
Evers, June V., ed. & illus. The Original Book of Recipes for Horses. 1994. 19.95 (0-9638814-1-8) Horse Hollow.
Eversole, Robyn H. The Magic House. Palagonia, Peter, illus. LC 91-17824. 32p. (ps-2). 1992. 13.95 (0-531-05924-3); lib. bdg. 13.99 (0-531-08524-4) Orchard Bks Watts.
Everston, Jonathan. Colin Powell. (gr. 4-7). 1991. pap. 3.50 (0-553-15966-6) Bantam.
Everts, Tammy, jt. auth. see Kalman, Bobbie.
Evey, Ethel L. Stowaway to Texas. Darst, Shelia S., ed. 201p. (gr. 4-7). 1986. 9.95 (0-89896-102-5, Post Oak Pr); pap. 6.95 (0-89896-101-7, Post Oak Pr) Larksdale.
Evitts, William J. Early Immigration in the United States. LC 88-34544. (Illus.). 64p. (gr. 3-5). 1989. PLB 12.90 (0-531-10744-2) Watts.
Evslin, et al. Heroes & Monsters of Greek Myth. (gr. 4 up). pap. 2.95 (0-590-43440-3) Scholastic Inc.
Evslin, Bernard. The Adventures of Ulysses. 1989. pap. 3.25 (0-590-42599-4) Scholastic Inc.
—Fentis: Monsters of Mythology. 1992. 19.95 (1-55546-248-0) Chelsea Hse.
—Greek Gods. (gr. 4-7). 1984. pap. 2.95 (0-590-44110-8) Scholastic Inc.
—Hercules. Smith, Joseph A., illus. LC 83-23834. 160p. (gr. 5up). 1984. 14.95 (0-688-02748-2) Morrow Jr Bks.
—Heroes, Gods & Monsters of Greek Myths. (gr-7). 1984. pap. 4.99 (0-553-25920-2) Bantam.
—Jason & the Argonauts. Dodson, Bert, illus. LC 86-32114. 176p. (gr. 5 up). 1986. 13.00 (0-688-06245-8) Morrow Jr Bks.
—The Trojan War. 160p. (gr. 5 up). 1988. pap. 2.95 (0-590-41626-X) Scholastic Inc.
Ewart, Claire. One Cold Night. (Illus.). 32p. (ps-1). 1992. 14.95 (0-399-22341-X, Putnam) Putnam Pub Group.
Ewart, Gavin. Caterpillar Stew: A Feast of Animal Poems. Ferns, Ronald, illus. 80p. (gr. 3-5). 1992. 15.95 (0-09-174097-5, Pub. by Hutchinson UK) Trafalgar.
Ewen, Patricia B., jt. auth. see Quatmann, Gail R.
Ewers, Joe, illus. Little Yellow School Bus. 14p. (ps-k). 1992. bds. 3.99 (0-679-83243-2) Random Bks Yng Read.
Ewing. A Really Popular Girl. 1993. pap. 2.75 (0-590-43202-8) Scholastic Inc.
Ewing, C. S., jt. auth. see Penn, Audrey.
Ewing, Carolyn, illus. Jingle Bells: A Holiday Book with Lights & Music. 10p. (ps-1). 1990. 10.95 (0-689-71431-9, Aladdin) Macmillan Child Grp.
Ewing, Juliana H. Old Father Christmas: Based on a Story by Juliana Horatia Ewing. Doherty, Berlie, retold by. Meloni, Maria T., illus. LC 92-43820. 42p. (ps-3). 1993. 12.95 (0-8120-6354-6) Barron.
—Our Field. LC 85-31445. 32p. (gr. 4 up). 1986. PLB 13.95s.p. (0-88682-074-X) Creative Ed.
Ewing, Kathryn. Family Karate. Henderson, Dave, illus. 96p. (gr. 5 up). 1992. PLB 13.95 (1-56397-117-8) Boyds Mills Pr.
Exley, Helen. What It's Like to Be Me. 2nd ed. (Illus.). 127p. (gr. 4-11). 1984. pap. 10.95 (0-377-00144-9) Friendship Pr.
Exum, Cheryl, jt. auth. see Bach, Alice.
Exum, J. Cheryl, jt. auth. see Bach, Alice.
Eyles, Heather. Into the Night House. Gon, Adriano, illus. 64p. (gr. 4-7). 1990. pap. 2.95 (0-8120-4423-1) Barron.
—Well, I Never! Ross, Tony, illus. 32p. (ps-3). 1990. 11.95 (0-87951-383-7) Overlook Pr.
Eynon, Dana. Daniel. (Illus.). 16p. 1992. 8.99 (9-5032-0570-0, 14-02240) Standard Pub.

Eyre, Sue, ed. Best Kids Love the Earth Activity Book. Forrest, Sandy, illus. 96p. (Orig.). (gr. 4-7). 1993. pap. 11.99 (0-376-04010-6) Sunset Pub. This lively & colorful book helps kids discover the earth & develop an appreciation for the environment. The

bright & whimsical illustrations & color photographs throughout highlight dozens of hands-on projects & simple experiments, from gardening to attract butterflies to making a solar snack. Nature activities ranging from special hikes to crafts projects show kids how they can help the earth through their own actions. Basic earth systems are explained simply to help kids understand how each of us affects the rest of the earth's family. Specific, positive, action-oriented suggestions inspire & empower children, giving them a feeling that "I can do it!" Also available in this kid-tested & approved series are the BEST KIDS COOK BOOK. 112p. 1992. $9.99 (0-376-02083-0), BEST KIDS GARDEN BOOK. 96p. 1992. $9.99 (0-376-03076-3), & BEST KIDS COOKIE BOOK. 112p. 1993. $11.99 (0-376-02388-0). These innovative books capture a child's imagination & give him or her a sense of accomplishment. Sunset Publishing Corporation, 80 Willow Rd., Menlo Park, CA 94025; 800-227-7346, in CA 800-321-0372. *Publisher Provided Annotation.*

Eytcheson, Pat. Catch a Winner. Eakin, Edwin M., ed. Peacock, Joe, illus. 48p. (gr. 2-3). 1989. 10.95 (0-89015-704-9, Pub. by Panda Bks) Eakin-Sunbelt.
—Catch a Winner Leaves the Ranch. Peacock, Joe, illus. 48p. (gr. 1-3). 1991. 10.95 (0-89015-828-2) Eakin-Sunbelt.
Ezekiel, Karen. Zoot Zoot Zaggle Splot: Or, What to Do with a Scary Dream. Ezekiel, Karen, illus. LC 89-35425. 40p. (ps-3). 1989. 14.95 (0-943173-50-7) Harbinger AZ.
Ezell, Elaine & Newhouse, George. Cruets Cruets Cruets, Vol. 1. (Illus.). 200p. (Orig.). 1991. 37.95 (0-915410-73-7, 4004); pap. 29.92 (0-915410-72-9, 4003) Antique Pubns.

F

Faber. Smithsonian Ladies. 1994. write for info. (0-8050-3015-8) H Holt & Co.
Faber, Betty L. Discover Butterflies. (Illus.). 48p. (gr. 3-6). 1992. PLB 14.95 (1-878363-67-0, HTS Bks) Forest Hse.
Faber, Donald, jt. auth. see Faber, Doris.
Faber, Doris. Amish. (gr. 4-7). 1991. pap. 12.95 (0-385-26130-6) Doubleday.
—Calamity Jane: Her Life & Her Legend. LC 91-40050. (Illus.). 80p. (gr. 5-9). 1992. 14.45 (0-395-56396-8) HM.
—Eleanor Roosevelt: First Lady of the World. Ruff, Donna, photos by. LC 84-20861. (Illus.). 64p. (gr. 2-6). 1985. pap. 10.95 (0-670-80551-3) Viking Child Bks.
—Eleanor Roosevelt: First Lady of the World. Ruff, Doris, illus. 64p. (gr. 2-6). 1986. pap. 4.50 (0-14-032103-9, Puffin) Puffin Bks.
—Smithsonian Book of the First Ladies. (gr. 4-7). 1993. 19.95 (0-8050-1751-8) H Holt & Co.
Faber, Doris & Faber, Donald. Martin Luther King, Jr. LC 90-49172. (Illus.). 128p. (gr. 6-10). 1991. PLB 13.95 (1-55905-086-1) Marshall Cavendish.
Faber, Doris & Faber, Harold. The Birth of a Nation: The Early Years of the United States. LC 88-30805. (Illus.). 208p. (gr. 7 up). 1989. SBE 14.95 (0-684-19007-9, Scribners Young Read) Macmillan Child Grp.
—Great Lives: American Government. LC 88-4968. (Illus.). 288p. (gr. 4-6). 1988. SBE 22.95 (0-684-18521-0, Scribners Young Read) Macmillan Child Grp.
—Great Lives: Nature & the Environment. LC 90-8847. (Illus.). 304p. (gr. 4-6). 1991. SBE 22.95 (0-684-19047-8, Scribners Young Read) Macmillan Child Grp.
—Mahatma Gandhi. LC 86-8734. (Illus.). 128p. (gr. 5 up). 1986. lib. bdg. 10.98 (0-671-60176-8, J Messner) S&S Trade.
Faber, Doris, jt. auth. see Faber, Harold.
Faber, Gail & Lasagna, Michele. Pasquala: The Story of a California Indian Girl. Faber, Gail, illus. 95p. (Orig.). (gr. 4-8). 1990. 12.95 (0-936480-07-6); pap. 9.95 (0-936480-06-8); tchr's. guide 8.95 (0-936480-08-4) Magpie Pubns.

Faber, Harold. The Discoverers of America. LC 91-17001. (Illus.). 304p. (gr. 9 up). 1992. SBE 17.95 (0-684-19217-9, Scribners Young Read) Macmillan Child Grp.
—From Sea to Sea: The Growth of the United States. LC 91-43728. (Illus.). 256p. (gr. 7 up). 1992. SBE 15.95 (0-684-19442-2, Scribners Young Read) Macmillan Child Grp.
Faber, Harold & Faber, Doris. We the People: The Story of the United States Constitution since 1787. LC 86-31404. 256p. (gr. 7 up). 1987. SBE 15.95 (0-684-18753-1, Scribners Young Read) Macmillan Child Grp.
Faber, Harold, jt. auth. see Faber, Doris.
Faber, Nancy & Faber, Randall. ChordTime Piano Hymns: Level 2 - I, IV, V7 Chords in Keys of C,G & F. McLean, Edwin, ed. Terpstra, Gwen, illus. 24p. (gr. 2-4). 1988. pap. 4.95 (0-929666-03-8) FJH Music Co Inc.
—PlayTime Piano Christmas: Level 1 - Five Finger Melodies. McLean, Edwin, ed. Terpstra, Gwen, illus. 24p. (gr. 1-3). 1988. pap. 4.95 (0-929666-02-X) FJH Music Co Inc.
—PlayTime Piano Hymns: Level One - Five Finger Melodies. McLean, Edwin, ed. Terpstra, Gwen, illus. 24p. (gr. 1-3). 1988. pap. 4.95 (0-929666-00-3) FJH Music Co Inc.
—PlayTime Piano Popular: Level One - Five Finger Melodies. McLean, Edwin, ed. Terpstra, Gwen, illus. 24p. (gr. 1-3). 1988. pap. 4.95 (0-929666-01-1) FJH Music Co Inc.
Faber, Randall, jt. auth. see Faber, Nancy.
Faber, Roger A. Birds on a Wire. Faber, Roger A., illus. (ps-1). Date not set. pap. write for info. (1-880122-06-5) White Stone.
—Peter Pig Likes to Dig. Faber, Roger A., illus. 32p. (gr. 1-2). Date not set. 12.00 (1-880122-05-7) White Stone.
—The Return. 64p. (gr. 9-12). 1992. pap. 7.00 (1-880122-03-0) White Stone.
—What Happened to Milly? Monroe, John, illus. (gr. 3 up). Date not set. pap. write for info. (1-880122-07-3) White Stone.
Fabian, Margaret W. My Friend Luke, the Stenciller. Fabian, Margaret W., illus. LC 83-50689. 35p. (gr. 3-4). 1987. pap. 8.95 over boards (0-931474-25-6) TBW Bks.
Fabian, Stella. A Handful of Magic. Mejia, Roger, illus. 125p. (gr. 2-6). 1988. pap. 3.25 (0-922434-36-0) Brighton & Lloyd.
—Is Your Heart Happy? Is Your Body Strong? (Orig.). (gr. 6). 1992. pap. 3.75 (0-685-52888-X) Brighton & Lloyd.
—The Opal Mystery. LC 90-83465. (Illus.). 192p. (Orig.). (gr. 3-7). 1992. pap. 3.25 (0-922434-39-5) Brighton & Lloyd.
—A Pocketful of Dreams. (Illus.). (gr. 3-6). 1989. write for info. (0-922434-37-9) Brighton & Lloyd.
Fabian, William M. Fiction Finder Manual. (gr. 4-12). 1984. 6.95 (0-916625-08-7) Computer Assis.
Fabo, J. A. Perez, illus. Paso a Paso, Nivel 4. 3rd ed. 256p. (Orig.). (gr. 4). 1991. pap. text ed. 7.95 (1-56328-014-0) Edit Plaza Mayor.
Facklam, Howard & Facklam, Margery. Avalanche! LC 90-45622. (Illus.). 48p. (gr. 5-6). 1991. RSBE 12.95 (0-89686-598-3, Crestwood Hse) Macmillan Child Grp.
—Plants: Extinction or Survival? LC 89-17038. (Illus.). 96p. (gr. 6 up). 1990. lib. bdg. 16.95 (0-89490-248-2) Enslow Pubs.
Facklam, Howard, jt. auth. see Facklam, Margery.
Facklam, Margery. And Then There Was One, Vol. 1. (gr. 4-7). 1990. 14.95 (0-316-25984-5, Joy St Bks) Little.
—And Then There Was One: The Mysteries of Extinction. Johnson, Pamela, illus. 45p. (gr. 3-6). 1993. pap. 6.95 (0-316-25982-9) Sierra.
—Bees Dance & Whales Sing: The Mysteries of Animal Communication. Johnson, Pamela, illus. 48p. (gr. 3-6). 1992. 14.95 (0-87156-573-0) Sierra.
—The Biggest Bug Book. Facklam, Paul, illus. LC 92-24517. 1993. write for info. (0-316-27389-9) Little.
—But Not Like Mine. Bassett, Jeni, illus. LC 86-33588. 18p. (gr. 3-5). 1988. 6.95 (0-15-200585-4, Gulliver Bks) HarBrace.
—Do Not Disturb: The Mysteries of Animal Hibernation & Sleep. Johnson, Pamela, illus. LC 88-10921. 48p. (gr. 3-6). 1989. 15.95 (0-316-27379-1) Little.
—I Eat Dinner. Riggio, Anita, illus. LC 91-76020. 6p. (ps). 1992. bds. 3.95 (1-56397-031-7); Set of 3 bks. bds. 11.85 (1-56397-077-5) Boyds Mills Pr.
—I Go to Sleep. Riggio, Anita, illus. LC 91-76018. 6p. (ps). 1992. bds. 3.95 (1-56397-030-9); Set of 3 bks. bds. 11.85 (1-56397-076-7) Boyds Mills Pr.
—Partners for Life: The Mysteries of Animal Symbiosis. Johnson, Pamela, illus. 48p. (gr. 3-6). 1989. 12.95 (0-316-25983-7) Sierra.
—So Can I. Bassett, Jeni, illus. LC 86-33720. 28p. (ps-k). 1988. 6.95 (0-15-200419-X, Gulliver Bks) HarBrace.
—The Trouble with Mothers. Grassy S. 1991. pap. 2.95 (0-380-71139-7, Camelot) Avon.
—What Does the Crow Know? The Mysteries of Animal Intelligence. Johnson, Pamela, illus. LC 93-17811. 48p. (gr. 3-6). 1993. 14.95 (0-87156-544-7) Sierra.
—Who Harnessed the Horse? The Story of Animal Domestication. Parton, Steven, illus. 176p. (gr. 2-5). 1992. 15.95 (0-316-27381-3) Little.

Facklam, Margery & Facklam, Howard. The Brain: Magnificent Mind Machine. Facklam, Paul, illus. LC 81-47529. 118p. (gr. 7 up). 1982. 12.95 (0-15-211388-6, HB Juv Bks) HarBrace.
—Changes in the Wind: The Earth's Shifting Climate. Facklam, Paul, illus. LC 85-5475. 128p. (gr. 7 up). 1986. 14.95 (0-15-216115-5, HB Juv Bks) HarBrace.
—Pharmacology: The Good Drugs. LC 92-9198. (Illus.). 128p. 1992. PLB 17.95x (0-8160-2627-0) Facts on File.
—Spare Parts for People. (Illus.). 143p. (gr. 7 up). 1987. 15.95 (0-15-277410-6, HB Juv Bks) HarBrace.
Facklam, Margery & Thomas, Margaret. The Kids' World Almanac of Amazing Facts about Numbers, Math, & Money. (Illus.). 256p. (Orig.). 1992. 14.95 (0-88687-635-4, World Almanac); pap. 7.95 (0-88687-634-6, World Almanac) F&W Inc NJ.
Facklam, Margery, jt. auth. see Facklam, Howard.
Facklan, Howard. Bacteria. 1994. PLB write for info. (0-8050-2857-9) H Holt & Co.
—Insects. 1994. PLB write for info. (0-8050-2859-5) H Holt & Co.
—Parasites. 1994. PLB write for info. (0-8050-2858-7) H Holt & Co.
—Viruses. 1994. PLB write for info. (0-8050-2856-0) H Holt & Co.
Fadiman, Clifton. Wally the Wordworm. Atherton, Lisa, illus. LC 83-9181. (gr. 3 up). 1984. 12.95 (0-88045-038-X); cassette & bk. 21.90 (0-88045-101-7); cassette only 8.95 (0-88045-098-3) Stemmer Hse.
Fagan, Elizabeth, ed. see Rand McNally Staff.
Fagan, Elizabeth G. Rand McNally Children's Atlas of World Wildlife. Wills, Jan, illus. LC 93-503. 1993. write for info. (0-528-83581-5) Rand McNally.
Fagan, Margaret. The Fight Against Homelessness. LC 90-3214. (Illus.). 64p. (gr. 5-8). 1990. PLB 12.40 (0-531-17251-1) Watts.
Fager, Charles. Life, Death & Two Chickens. 100p. (gr. 3-6). 1990. pap. 10.95 (0-945177-04-6) Kimo Pr.
—The Magic Quilts. Lewis, Charlotte, illus. 100p. (gr. 3-6). 1990. pap. 12.95 (0-945177-03-8) Kimo Pr.
Faggella, Kathy. My Christmas: A Photolog Book. (ps-3). 1993. 9.95 (1-55670-330-9) Stewart Tabori & Chang.
Faggella, kathy, jt. auth. see Horowitz, Janet.
Faggella, kathy, jt. auth. see Horowitz, Janet.
Fago, John N. Vincent Lombardi-Pele. Caravana, Tony & Cruz, Nardo, illus. (gr. 4-12). 1979. text ed. 7.50 (0-88301-370-3); pap. text ed. 2.95 (0-88301-358-4); wkbk. 1.25 (0-88301-382-7) Pendulum Pr.
Fago, John N. & Farr, Naunerle C. Jim Thorpe - Althea Gibson. Redondo, Frank & Carrillo, Fred, illus. (gr. 4-12). 1979. pap. text ed. 2.95 (0-88301-360-6); wkbk. 1.25 (0-88301-384-3) Pendulum Pr.
Fago, John N. & Toan, Debbie. Houdini - Walt Disney. Cruz, E. R. & Henson, Tenny, illus. (gr. 4-12). 1979. pap. text ed. 2.95 (0-88301-350-9); wkbk 1.25 (0-88301-374-6) Pendulum Pr.
Fago, John N., jt. auth. see Farr, Naunerle C.
Fago, John N., ed. see Dana, Richard H.
Fago, John N., ed. see Doyle, Arthur Conan.
Fago, John N., ed. see Kipling, Rudyard.
Fago, John N., ed. see Porter, William S.
Fago, John N., ed. see Twain, Mark.
Fahs, Sophia L. Jesus - the Carpenter's Son. rev. ed. Baldridge, Cyrus L., illus. 160p. 1990. pap. 14.95 (1-55896-191-7) Unitarian Univ.
Fahs, Sophia L. & Cobb, Alice. Old Tales for a New Day. 2nd ed. Stair, Gobin, illus. 201p. (gr. 4-9). 1992. pap. 14.95 (0-87975-730-2) Prometheus Bks.
—Old Tales for a New Day: Early Answers to Life's Eternal Questions. Stair, Gobin, illus. LC 80-84076. (gr. 3-9). 1980. 17.95 (0-87975-138-X); tchr's manual o.p. 9.95 (0-87975-131-2) Prometheus Bks.
Fahy, Mary. The Tree That Survived the Winter. Antonucci, Emil, illus. 64p. (gr. 8-12). 1989. pap. 8.95 (0-8091-0432-6) Paulist Pr.
Fain, James W. Rodeos. LC 82-23460. (SPA.). 48p. (gr. k-4). 1987. PLB 15.27 (0-516-31685-0); pap. 4.95 (0-516-51685-X) Childrens.
Fain, Kathleen. Handsigns: An Animal Alphabet. LC 92-32103. 1993. 13.95 (0-8118-0310-4) Chronicle Bks.
Fain, Max M. Toward Polaris. 2nd, rev. ed. 171p. 1990. 8.95 (0-9618960-4-3) M M Fain.
Fair, Jan. Tangram Treasury, Bk. C. 48p. (gr. 5-10). 1987. pap. text ed. 7.95 (0-914040-55-3) Cuisenaire.
—Tangram Treasury, Bk. B. 48p. (gr. 3-6). 1987. pap. text ed. 7.95 (0-914040-54-5) Cuisenaire.
—Tangram Treasury, Bk. A. 48p. (gr. 1-4). 1987. pap. text ed. 7.95 (0-914040-53-7) Cuisenaire.
Fair, Jeff. Bears for Kids. 48p. 1991. 14.95 (1-55971-119-1); pap. 6.95 (1-55971-134-5) NorthWord.
—Black Bear Magic for Kids. LC 91-50551. (Illus.). 48p. (gr. 3-4). 1992. PLB 18.60 (0-8368-0760-X) Gareth Stevens Inc.
—Moose for Kids. (ps-3). 1992. 14.95 (1-55971-187-6) Northword.
Fair, Phillip, jt. auth. see Rabold, Ted.
Fair, Ronald. Rufus. LC 79-38743. 58p. (gr. 7-12). 1980. pap. 4.00x perf. bound (0-916418-21-9) Lotus.
Fair, Sharon, jt. auth. see Upton, Richard.
Fair, Sylvia. The Bedspread. Fair, Sylvia, illus. LC 81-11152. 32p. (gr. k-3). 1982. 14.95 (0-688-00877-1) Morrow Jr Bks.

Fairbank, Anna. Lucky Me! An Adoption Story. Weston, Martha, illus. LC 88-60649. 32p. (Orig.). (ps-1). 1988. pap. 8.95 (0-945436-01-7) Mariah Pr.
Fairbanks, Ellen & Bodman, D. Middle East Master Map Kit: Their Lands & Ours. 39p. (gr. 5 up). 1989. 14.95 (0-930141-25-3) World Eagle.
Fairbanks, Eugene B., jt. auth. see McCabe, Ann C.
Fairbanks, Mary Jo, ed. see New York State League of Women Voters Staff.
Fairclough, Chris, jt. auth. see Ball, John.
Fairhall, Winnifred, ed. see Beauzile, Anthony L. & Beauzile, Gerard, Jr.
Fairman, Tony. Bury My Bones But Keep My Words: African Tales for Retelling. Asare, Meshack, illus. 192p. 1993. 15.95 (0-8050-2333-X, Bks Young Read) H Holt & Co.
Fairwell, Kay, ed. see Agler, Leigh.
Fairwell, Kay, ed. see Ahouse, Jeremy J.
Fairwell, Kay, ed. see Barber, Jacqueline.
Fairwell, Kay, ed. see Barrett, Katharine.
Fairwell, Kay, ed. see Barrett, Katharine, et al.
Fairwell, Kay, ed. see Buegler, Marion E.
Fairwell, Kay, ed. see Cossey, Ruth, et al.
Fairwell, Kay, ed. see Echols, Jean C.
Fairwell, Kay, ed. see Goodman, Jan M.
Fairwell, Kay, ed. see Gould, Alan.
Fairwell, Kay, ed. see Hocking, Colin, et al.
Fairwell, Kay, ed. see Kopp, Jaine.
Fairwell, Kay, ed. see Sneider, Cary & Gould, Alan.
Fairwell, Kay, ed. see Sneider, Cary I.
Fairwell, Kay, ed. see Sneider, Cary I., et al.
Fairwell, Kay, ed. see Sneider, Cary I.
Fairwell, Kay, ed. see Sneider, Cary I. & Barber, Jacqueline.
Fairwell, Kay, ed. see Sneider, Cary I. & Gould, Alan.
Faithful, Denise, jt. auth. see Knapp, Elsie M.
Fajardo, David, compiled by. Pero...Debo Dejarlo Todo? But...Should I Give up Everything? (SPA.). 64p. (Orig.). (gr. 11 up). 1990. pap. text ed. 2.50 (0-311-12340-6) Casa Bautista.
Fajardo, Vilma de see De Fajardo, Vilma.
Fakih, Kimberly O. Grandpa Putter & Granny Hoe. Pearson, Tracy C., illus. 128p. (gr. 2-5). 1992. 13.00 (0-374-32762-9) FS&G.
Falcone, Vincent J. Great Thinkers, Great Ideas: An Introduction to Western Thought. LC 88-1639. 274p. (Orig.). (gr. 11-12). 1988. pap. text ed. 17.50 (0-88427-075-0) North River.
—Great Thinkers, Great Ideas: An Introduction to Western Thought. 2nd ed. LC 92-7554. 288p. (gr. 12 up). 1992. pap. text ed. 9.95 (0-9629323-1-0) Cranbury Pubns.
Falconer, Elizabeth. The House That Jack Built. Falconer, Elizabeth, illus. 32p. 1990. 13.95 (0-8249-8459-5, Ideals Child) Hambleton-Hill.
—A Treasury of Mother Goose: A Pop-up Book. (Illus.). 18p. (ps-1). 1992. POB 11.95 (0-689-71505-6, Aladdin) Macmillan Child Grp.
Falk, Aaron. The Torah for Children. Nodel, Norman, illus. LC 92-28623. 1992. write for info. (1-880582-06-6); pap. write for info. (1-880582-07-4) Judaica Pr.
Falk, Barbara B. Grusha. Falk, Barbara B., illus. LC 92-14980. 32p. (ps-3). 1993. 15.00 (0-06-021299-3); PLB 14.89 (0-06-021300-0) HarpC Child Bks.
Falk, Bonnie H. Forget-Me-Not. Huber, Nancy D., illus. LC 84-90501. 192p. (gr. 4-8). 1984. pap. 7.95 (0-9614108-0-9) BHF Memories.
Falken, Linda C. Kitty's First Airplane Trip. Adams, Lynn, illus. 32p. (ps-2). 1993. pap. 2.50 (0-590-45788-8) Scholastic Inc.
Falkenberg, P. R. Fifteen Days to Study Power. 2nd ed. (Illus.). 378p. (Orig.). (gr. 7 up). 1985. pap. 12.95 (0-939800-01-2) Greencrest.
Falkof, Lucille. George Washington: First President of the United States. (Illus.). (gr. 5-9). 1989. PLB 17.26 (0-944483-19-4) Garrett Ed Corp.
—Helen Gurley Brown: The Queen of Cosmopolitan. Young, Richard G., ed. LC 91-32053. (Illus.). 64p. (gr. 4-8). 1992. PLB 17.26 (1-56074-013-2) Garrett Ed Corp.
—John F. Kennedy: 35th President of the United States. Young, Richard G., ed. LC 87-35954. (Illus.). (gr. 5-9). 1988. PLB 17.26 (0-944483-03-8) Garrett Ed Corp.
—John H. Johnson: The Man from Ebony. Young, Richard G., ed. LC 91-32073. (Illus.). 64p. (gr. 4-8). 1992. PLB 17.26 (1-56074-018-3) Garrett Ed Corp.
—John Tyler: Tenth President of the United States. Young, Richard G., ed. LC 89-39951. (Illus.). 128p. (gr. 5-9). 1990. PLB 17.26 (0-944483-60-7) Garrett Ed Corp.
—Lyndon B. Johnson: Thirty-Sixth President of the United States. Young, Richard G., ed. LC 88-31003. (Illus.). (gr. 5-9). 1989. PLB 17.26 (0-944483-20-8) Garrett Ed Corp.
—Ulysses S. Grant: 18th President of the United States. Young, Richard G., ed. LC 87-32817. (Illus.). (gr. 5-9). 1988. PLB 17.26 (0-944483-02-X) Garrett Ed Corp.
—William H. Taft: Twenty-Seventh President of the United States. Young, Richard G., ed. LC 89-39947. (Illus.). 128p. (gr. 5-9). 1990. PLB 17.26 (0-944483-56-9) Garrett Ed Corp.
Fall, Thomas. Canal Boat to Freedom. 2nd ed. Cellini, Joseph, illus. (Illus.). (gr. 4-6). pap. write for info. (0-9636532-0-2) Neversink Valley.

Fallow, Allan, ed. see Time Life Inc. Editors.
Falls, Gregory A. The Forgotten Door. (Orig.). (gr. 4 up). 1985. pap. 5.00 (0-87602-242-5) Anchorage.
—The Pushcart War. (Orig.). (gr. 4 up). 1985. pap. 4.50 (0-87602-248-4) Anchorage.
Falls, Gregory A. & Beattie, Kurt. The Odyssey. 1978. 5.00 (0-87602-238-7) Anchorage.
Falwell, Catherine. Nicky & Grandpa. Falwell, Cathryn, illus. 32p. (ps). 1991. 5.70 (0-395-56917-6, Clarion Bks) HM.
—Nicky's Walk. Falwell, Cathryn, illus. 32p. (ps). 1991. 5.70 (0-395-56914-1, Clarion Bks) HM.
Falwell, Cathryn. Clowning Around. LC 90-29064. (Illus.). 32p. (ps-1). 1991. 13.95 (0-531-05952-9); RLB 13.99 (0-531-08552-X) Orchard Bks Watts.
—Feast for Ten. Falwell, Cathryn, illus. LC 92-35512. 32p. (ps-3). 1993. 14.95 (0-395-62037-6, Clarion Bks) HM.
—The Letter Jesters: A Kids' Guide to Letterforms. LC 93-22739. 1994. 14.95 (0-395-66898-0) Ticknor & Fields.
—Nicky & Alex. Falwell, Cathryn, illus. 32p. (ps). 1992. 5.95 (0-395-56915-X, Clarion Bks) HM.
—Nicky Loves Daddy. Falwell, Cathryn, illus. 32p. (ps). 1992. 5.70 (0-395-60820-1, Clarion Bks) HM.
—Nicky, 1-2-3. Briley, Dorthy, ed. Falwell, Cathryn, illus. 24p. (ps). 1991. 5.70 (0-395-56913-3, Clarion Bks) HM.
—Shape Space. Falwell, Cathryn, illus. 32p. (ps-2). 1992. 13.45 (0-395-61305-1, Clarion Bks) HM.
—We Have a Baby. LC 92-40268. 1993. 13.45 (0-395-62038-4, Clarion Bks) HM.
—Where's Nicky? Briley, Cathryn, ed. Falwell, Cathryn, illus. 24p. (ps). 1991. 5.70 (0-395-56936-2, Clarion Bks) HM.
Family of the America's Staff & Sincro Communications Staff. If You Love Me...Show Me! CCC of America Staff, illus. 41p. (gr. 5-7). 1992. incl. video 21.95 (1-56814-400-8); pap. text ed. 6.95 book (0-685-62406-4) CCC of America.
FamilyVision Press Staff. Dino Mites Declare War! (Illus.). 80p. 1993. pap. 8.95 (1-56969-100-2) FamilyVision.
—Kidnapped to the Center of the Earth. (Illus.). 48p. 1993. 14.95 (1-56969-125-8) FamilyVision.
Fanelli, Jenny, ed. see Estes, Rose.
Fanelli, Jenny, ed. see Tanaka, Shelley.
Fanidi, Theo, jt. auth. see Berger, Sidney L.
Fanning, Jim. Walt Disney. (Illus.). 1994. 18.95 (0-7910-2331-1, Am Art Analog); pap. write for info. (0-7910-2356-7, Am Art Analog) Chelsea Hse.
Fanning, Margaret & Bak, Linda. The Famished Fox. 18p. (Orig.). (gr. k-1). 1992. pap. text ed. 6.00 set of 2 scripts (1-882063-23-6) Cottage Pr MA.
—The Greedy Pup. Bak, Linda, illus. 18p. (Orig.). 1992. Set of 2 scripts. pap. text ed. 6.00 (1-882063-25-2) Cottage Pr MA.
—The Lad & the Fib. 18p. (Orig.). 1992. pap. text ed. 18.00 set of 6 scripts (1-882063-24-4) Cottage Pr MA.
—The Three Little Pigs. 24p. (gr. k-1). 1992. pap. text ed. 18.00 set of 6 scripts (1-882063-22-8) Cottage Pr MA.
Fanning, Odom. Opportunities in Environmental Careers. rev. ed. LC 90-50734. 160p. (gr. 7 up). 1991. 13.95 (0-8442-8161-1, VGM Career Bks); pap. 10.95 (0-8442-8163-8, VGM Career Bks) NTC Pub Grp.
Fannon. Around the World. 1991. 12.95s.p. (0-86593-119-4) Rourke Corp.
Fannon, Cecilia. Leaders. LC 91-11570. 64p. (gr. 5-7). 1991. 17.27 (0-86593-118-6); 12.95s.p. (0-685-59201-4) Rourke Corp.
—Soviet Union. (Illus.). 64p. (gr. 7 up). 1990. lib. bdg. 17.27 (0-86593-092-9); lib. bdg. 12.95s.p. (0-685-36367-8) Rourke Corp.
Fant, Louie J., Jr. Intermediate Sign Language. LC 78-61003. (Illus.). 225p. (gr. 7 up). 1980. text ed. 24.95 (0-917002-54-7) Joyce Media.
—Noah. new ed. Castillo, Romulo & Paul, Frank A., illus. 14p. (gr. 3-4). 1973. pap. text ed. 5.00 (0-917002-70-9) Joyce Media.
Fantini, Alvino E., ed. see Hawkinson, Annie.
Fara, P., jt. auth. see Reid, S.
Faraday, Michael. Faraday's Chemical History of a Candle. (Illus.). (gr. 7-11). 1988. pap. 9.95 (1-55652-035-2) Chicago Review.
Farber, Betty, jt. auth. see Knoepfel, Marilyn.
Farber, Norma. As I Was Crossing Boston Common. Lobel, Arnold, illus. LC 75-6520. 32p. (ps-2). 1991. Repr. 14.95 (0-525-25960-0, DCB) Dutton Child Bks.
—As I Was Crossing Boston Common. Lobel, Arnold, illus. LC 75-6520. 32p. (ps-2). 1991. pap. 3.95 (0-525-44781-4, Puffin) Puffin Bks.
—How Does It Feel to Be Old? Hyman, Trina S., illus. LC 79-11516. 32p. (gr. 4-8). 1988. (DCB); pap. 4.99 (0-525-44367-3, DCB) Dutton Child Bks.
—Return of the Shadows. Baruffi, Andrea, illus. LC 91-27517. 40p. (gr. k-3). 1992. 15.00 (0-06-020518-0); PLB 14.89 (0-06-020519-9) HarpC Child Bks.
—When It Snowed That Night. Mathers, Petra, illus. LC 92-27414. 40p. (gr. k up). 1993. 16.00 (0-06-021707-3); PLB 15.89 (0-06-021708-1) HarpC Child Bks.
Farber, Norma & Livingston, Myra C., eds. These Small Stones. Livingston, Myra C., intro. by. LC 87-264. 128p. (gr. 3-7). 1987. PLB 12.89 (0-06-024014-8) HarpC Child Bks.

Farcot, Kimberly I. Imagine: A Journey Through the Child's Imagination. Farcot, Kimberly I., illus. LC 92-90202. 32p. (Orig.). (gr. k-4). 1992. pap. 8.95 (0-9632372-2-5) Custom Artwk.

Farentinos, Robert. Winter's Orphans: The Search for a Family of Mountain Lion Cubs, a True Story. (Illus.). 64p. (gr. 4-6). 1993. 19.95 (1-879373-54-8); pap. 13.95 (1-879373-53-X) R Rinehart.

Farge, Sheila La see Haugen, Tormod.

Farha, Mary N. Fairy Tale Jewels. rev. & expanded ed. Lantz, Carol, illus. 110p. (gr. 2-10). 1991. 10.95 (1-55914-522-6); pap. 8.95 (1-55914-523-4) ABBE Pubs Assn.

Farish, Terry. Shelter for a Seabird. LC 89-25776. (gr. 7 up). 1990. 12.95 (0-688-09627-1) Greenwillow.
—Why I'm Already Blue. LC 89-2051. 176p. (gr. 7 up). 1989. 12.95 (0-688-09096-6) Greenwillow.

Farjam, Farideh. The Crystal Flower & the Sun. new & rev. ed. Jabbari, Ahmad, ed. & tr. from PER. Nojoomi, Nikzad, illus. LC 83-60453. 24p. (Orig.). (gr. k up). 1983. pap. 4.95 (0-939214-16-4) Mazda Pubs.

Farjam, Farideh & Azaad, Meyer. Uncle Noruz (Uncle New Year) Jabbari, Ahmad, ed. & tr. from PER. Mesqali, Farshid, illus. LC 83-60450. 24p. (Orig.). (gr. k up). 1983. pap. 4.95 (0-939214-14-8) Mazda Pubs.

Farjeon, Eleanor. Eleanor Farjeon's Poems for Children. LC 51-11164. 256p. (gr. 4 up). 1984. PLB 12.89 (0-685-17657-6, Lipp Jr Bks); PLB 12.89 (0-397-32091-4) HarpC Child Bks.
—The Glass Slipper. 159p. 1981. Repr. PLB 16.95x (0-89966-360-5) Buccaneer Bks.
—The Glass Slipper. 108p. 1981. Repr. PLB 16.95x (0-89967-034-2) Harmony Raine.

Farley, Carol. The Case of the Haunted Health Club. 112p. 1991. pap. 2.95 (0-380-75918-7, Camelot) Avon.
—The Case of the Lost Lookalike. 112p. 1988. pap. 2.50 (0-380-75450-9, Camelot) Avon.
—The Case of the Vanishing Villain. 80p. (gr. 3-7). 1986. pap. 2.95 (0-380-89959-0, Camelot) Avon.
—King Sejong's Secret. Cooper, Floyd, illus. LC 93-12967. 1995. write for info. (0-688-12776-2); lib. bdg. write for info. (0-688-12777-0) Lothrop.
—Korea: Land of the Morning Calm. (Illus.). 128p. (gr. 5 up). 1991. RSBE 14.95 (0-87518-465-0, Dillon) Macmillan Child Grp.

Farley, Karin C. Harry Truman: The Man from Independence. Steltenpohl, Jane, ed. (Illus.). 160p. (gr. 5-9). 1989. lib. 11.98 (0-671-65853-0, J Messner) S&S Trade.
—Robert H. Goddard. (Illus.). 144p. (gr. 5-9). 1992. PLB 13.98 (0-382-24171-1); pap. 7.95 (0-382-24177-0) Silver Burdett Pr.
—Thomas Paine. LC 92-17662. (Illus.). 128p. (gr. 7-10). 1992. PLB 22.80 (0-8114-2329-8) Raintree Steck-V.

Farley, Steven, jt. auth. see Farley, Walter.

Farley, Walter. Black Stallion. Ward, Keith, illus. LC 85-19927. (gr. 3-7). 1977. 3.95 (0-394-80601-8); lib. bdg. 11.99 (0-394-90601-2); pap. 3.95 (0-394-83609-X) Random Bks Yng Read.
—The Black Stallion: An Easy-to-Read Adaptation. Rabinowitz, Sandy, illus. LC 85-19927. 48p. (ps-3). 1986. lib. bdg. 7.99 (0-394-96876-X) Random Bks Yng Read.
—Black Stallion & Flame. LC 60-10029. (Illus.). (gr. 5 up). 1980. pap. 3.95 (0-394-84372-X) Random Bks Yng Read.
—The Black Stallion & the Girl. (gr. 4 up). 1977. lib. bdg. 10.99 (0-394-92145-3); pap. 3.95 (0-394-83614-6) Knopf Bks Yng Read.
—Black Stallion Challenged. LC 64-15094. (Illus.). (gr. 5-9). 1980. pap. 3.95 (0-394-84371-1) Random Bks Yng Read.
—The Black Stallion: Golden Anniversary Edition. D'Andrea, Domenick, illus. LC 90-53670. 224p. (gr. 4 up). 1991. Repr. of 1941 ed. gift ed. 15.00 (0-679-81349-7); lib. bdg. 15.99 gift ed. (0-679-91349-1) Random Bks Yng Read.
—The Black Stallion Legend. LC 83-1870. (Illus.). 224p. (gr. 5-9). 1983. lib. bdg. 10.99 (0-394-96026-2) Random Bks Yng Read.
—The Black Stallion Legend. LC 83-1870. 192p. (gr. 5-8). 1985. pap. 3.95 (0-394-87500-1) Random Bks Yng Read.
—The Black Stallion Mystery. (gr. 4-6). 1977. pap. 3.95 (0-394-83611-1) Random Bks Yng Read.
—The Black Stallion Revolts. LC 53-6284. (gr. 4-9). 1977. pap. 3.95 (0-394-83613-8) Random Bks Yng Read.
—Black Stallion's Filly. LC 52-7216. (Illus.). (gr. 4-6). 1978. pap. 3.95 (0-394-83916-1) Random Bks Yng Read.
—Black Stallion's Ghost. Draper, Angie, illus. (gr. 5-9). 1978. lib. bdg. 10.99 (0-394-90618-7); pap. 3.95 (0-394-83919-6) Random Bks Yng Read.
—Black Stallion's Sulky Colt. (Illus.). (gr. 4-6). 1978. pap. 3.95 (0-394-83917-X) Random Bks Yng Read.
—Blood Bay Colt. (Illus.). (gr. 4-6). 1978. pap. 3.95 (0-394-83915-3) Random Bks Yng Read.
—The Great Dane Thor. 192p. (gr. 4-7). 1980. pap. 1.50 (0-440-93095-2, LFL) Dell.
—The Horse-Tamer. LC 58-9030. 160p. (gr. 5-8). 1980. pap. 3.95 (0-394-84374-6) Random Bks Yng Read.
—Island Stallion. (Illus.). (gr. 5-6). 1980. pap. 3.95 (0-394-84376-2) Random Bks Yng Read.
—Island Stallion Races. (Illus.). (gr. 4-6). 1980. pap. 3.95 (0-394-84375-4) Random Bks Yng Read.

—Island Stallion's Fury. (Illus.). (gr. 5-6). 1980. pap. 3.95 (0-394-84373-8) Random Bks Yng Read.
—Little Black, a Pony. LC 61-7789. (Illus.). 62p. (gr. 1-2). 1961. lib. bdg. 7.99 (0-394-90021-9) Beginner.
—Man O' War. LC 62-9000. (Illus.). 352p. (gr. 5-9). 1983. 4.99 (0-394-86015-2) Knopf Bks Yng Read.
—Walter Farley's Black Stallion Books, 4 bks. Incl. The Black Stallion. LC 41-21882; The Black Stallion Returns. LC 45-8763; The Black Stallion & Satan. LC 49-6117; The Black Stallion Mystery. LC 57-7527. (gr. 4-9). 1979. Boxed Set. pap. 11.80 (0-394-84176-X) Random Bks Yng Read.

Farley, Walter & Farley, Steven. The Young Black Stallion. LC 89-42763. 192p. (gr. 5-9). 1989. 10.95 (0-394-84562-5); lib. bdg. 11.99 (0-394-94562-X) Random Bks Yng Read.

Farlow, James O. On the Tracks of Dinosaurs: A Study of Dinosaur Footprints. Tischler, Doris, illus. 64p. (gr. 4-6). 1991. 15.95 (0-531-15220-0); PLB 15.90 (0-531-10991-7) Watts.

Farlow, James O. & Molnar, Ralph E. The Great Hunters: Meat-Eating Dinosaurs. Franczak, Brian, illus. LC 93-29844. 1994. write for info. (0-531-11180-6) Watts.

Farmer, Lucile. A Willing Heart. Loudermick, Mary, pref. by Judd, Edwin, frwd. by. 246p. (Orig.). Date not set. pap. 7.95 (1-877917-10-9) Alpha Bible Pubns.

Farmer, Lynne, jt. auth. see Farmer, Tony.

Farmer, Lynne, illus. First Animal Words. 26p. 1993. 3.50 (0-7214-1521-0) Ladybird Bks.

Farmer, Nancy. Do You Know Me. Jackson, Shelley, illus. LC 92-34068. 112p. (gr. 3-5). 1993. 15.95 (0-531-05474-8); PLB 15.99 (0-531-08624-0) Orchard Bks Watts.
—The Ear, the Eye & the Arm. LC 93-11814. 320p. (gr. 7 up). 1994. 16.95 (0-531-06829-3); lib. bdg. 16.99 RLB (0-531-08679-8) Orchard Bks Watts.

Farmer, Patti. What Do You Think I Am... Crazy? Veno, Joe, illus. 32p. (ps-3). 1991. 10.95 (0-8120-5979-4) Barron.

Farmer, Penelope. Charlotte Sometimes. (Orig.). (gr. k-6). 1987. pap. 4.95 (0-440-41261-7, Pub. by Yearling Classics) Dell.
—Emma in Winter. (gr. k-6). 1987. pap. 2.95 (0-440-42308-2, YB) Dell.
—The Summer Birds. (Orig.). (gr. k-6). 1987. pap. 2.50 (0-440-47737-9, YB) Dell.
—The Summer Birds. large type ed. 176p. (gr. 3 up). 1990. lib. bdg. 14.95x (0-7451-1066-5, Lythway Large Print) Hall.
—Thicker Than Water. LC 92-53133. 208p. (gr. 5-10). 1993. 14.95 (1-56402-178-5) Candlewick Pr.

Farmer, Tony. How Small Is an Ant? (ps-3). 1990. 3.95 (0-85953-518-5) Childs Play.

Farmer, Tony & Farmer, Lynne. How BIG Is an Elephant? LC 91-285. (gr. 3 up). 1991. 2.95 (0-85953-516-9) Childs Play.
—How HIGH Is the Moon? LC 91-9350. (gr. 4 up). 1991. 2.95 (0-85953-517-7) Childs Play.

Farmer, Wesley M. Seashore Discoveries. Hamann, Jeff, illus. 124p. (Orig.). (gr. 9 up). 1986. pap. text ed. 7.95x (0-937772-01-X) W M Farmer.

Farnagle, A. E. The Not So Goody Gum Drop Shop: A Play in One Act. 32p. (gr. 3-8). 1984. pap. 3.50 (0-916565-06-8) Whitehall Pr.

Farnagle, A. E. & Smith, W. Hovey. Farnagle's Fables for Children & Adults. Crawford, Kimberly Ann, illus. 64p. (Orig.). (gr. 1-5). 1984. pap. 4.25 (0-916565-04-1) Whitehall Pr.

Farnan, Nancy J., jt. auth. see Goldman, Elizabeth.

Farndon, John. How the Earth Works: One Hundred Ways Parents & Kids Can Share the Secrets of the Earth. LC 91-45004. (Illus.). 192p. (gr. 3 up). 1992. 23.50 (0-89577-411-9, Dist. by Random) RD Assn.

Farnes, C. Survive in Five Languages. (Illus.). 64p. (gr. 8 up). 1993. PLB 12.96 (0-88110-623-2); pap. 5.95 (0-7460-1034-6) EDC.

Farnette, Cherrie, et al. I've Got Me & I'm Glad. rev. ed. 80p. (gr. 4-7). 1989. pap. text ed. 7.95 (0-86530-069-0, IP 52-8) Incentive Pubns.
—People Need Each Other. rev. ed 80p. (gr. 4-7). 1989. pap. text ed. 7.95 (0-86530-070-4, IP 63-3) Incentive Pubns.

Farnham, Willard, ed. see Shakespeare, William.

Farnsworth, Bill, illus. The Illustrated Children's Bible. LC 93-16222. (gr. 1-8). 1993. 19.95 (0-15-232876-9) HarBrace.

Farquhar, George see Wilson, John H.

Farquhar, Kristin. Voices of the Earth: Florida's Environmental Storybook, Vol. 1: Coastal Creatures. Wright, Betty & Griffin, Kimbra, eds. Farquhar, Kristin, illus. 48p. (Orig.). (gr. 2-3). 1992. pap. 7.95 (0-9632064-0-4) ECO-ALERT Pubns.

Farr, J. Michael. The Right Job for You: An Interactive Career Planning Guide. 1991. pap. text ed. 7.95 (0-942784-73-1, RJ) JIST Works.

Farr, J. Michael & Amore, JoAnn. Exploring Careers: The World of Work & You. Reader, Spring D., photos by. (Illus.). 32p. (gr. 6-12). 1989. wkbk. 1.95 (0-942784-28-6, EXPAB) JIST Works.

Farr, J. Michael & Christophersen, Susan. The Skills Advantage: Identify Your Skills for School, Work, & Life. Adams, Sara, ed. (Illus.). 64p. (gr. 6 up). 1993. pap. 6.95 wkbk. (1-56370-093-X, SKAD) JIST Works.

Farr, J. Michael & Pavlicko, Marie. The JIST Job Search Course: A Young Person's Guide to Getting & Keeping a Good Job. Croy, Greg, ed. Kreffel, Mike, et al, illus. (gr. 7-12). 1990. pap. 6.95 121p. (0-942784-34-0, YP); data minder, 22p. 1.00 (0-942784-35-9, DM) JIST Works.
—The JIST Job Search Course: A Young Person's Guide to Getting & Keeping a Good Job. Croy, Greg, ed. Kreffel, Mike, et al, illus. 138p. (gr. 7-12). 1990. pap. 12.95 instr's. guide (0-942784-36-7, YPTM) JIST Works.

Farr, J. Michael, jt. auth. see Christophersen, Susan.

Farr, J. Michael, ed. see U. S. Department of Labor, Employment & Training Administration Staff.

Farr, Naunerle. America Becomes a World Power, 1890-1920. Calhoun, D'Ann & Bloch, Lawrence W., eds. Ronguillo, Resty, illus. (gr. 4-12). 1977. pap. text ed. 2.95 (0-88301-199-9); student book 1.25 (0-88301-236-7) Pendulum Pr.
—America Today: Nineteen Forty-Five to Nineteen Eighty-One. Calhoun, D'Ann & Bloch, Lawrence W., eds. (Illus.). (gr. 4-12). 1976. pap. text ed. 2.95 (0-88301-234-0); 1.25wkbk (0-88301-246-4) Pendulum Pr.
—Americans Move Westward, 1800-1850. Calhoun, D'Ann & Bloch, Lawrence W., eds. Redondo, Frank, illus. (gr. 4-12). 1977. pap. text ed. 2.95 (0-88301-227-8); wkbk. 1.25 (0-88301-239-1) Pendulum Pr.
—Madame Curie - Albert Einstein. Leonidez, Nestor & Redondo, Nestor, illus. (gr. 4-12). 1979. pap. text ed. 2.95 (0-88301-356-8); wkbk. 1.25 (0-88301-380-0) Pendulum Pr.
—The New World, 1500-1750. Calhoun, D'Ann & Bloch, Lawrence W., eds. Cruz, E. R., illus. (gr. 4-12). 1977. Pendulum Pr.

Farr, Naunerle, ed. see Bronte, Charlotte.

Farr, Naunerle, ed. see Bronte, Emily.

Farr, Naunerle, ed. see Clemens, Samuel.

Farr, Naunerle, ed. see Cooper, James Fenimore.

Farr, Naunerle, ed. see Hawthorne, Nathaniel.

Farr, Naunerle, ed. see London, Jack.

Farr, Naunerle, ed. see Poe, Edgar Allan.

Farr, Naunerle, ed. see Sewell, Anna.

Farr, Naunerle, ed. see Stoker, Bram.

Farr, Naunerle C. Abraham Lincoln - Franklin D. Roosevelt. Redondo, Nestor & LoFamia, Jun, illus. (gr. 4-12). 1979. pap. text ed. 2.95 (0-88301-354-1); wkbk. 1.25 (0-88301-378-9) Pendulum Pr.
—Babe Ruth-Jackie Robinson. Caravana, Tony & Cruz, Nardo, illus. (gr. 4-12). 1979. pap. text ed. 2.95 (0-88301-359-2); wkbk 1.25 (0-88301-383-5) Pendulum Pr.
—Davy Crockett-Daniel Boone. Carrillo, Fred & Redondo, Nestor, illus. (gr. 4-12). 1979. pap. text ed. 2.95 (0-88301-351-7); wkbk. 1.25 (0-88301-375-4) Pendulum Pr.
—George Washington-Thomas Jefferson. Carrillo, Fred & Cruz, E. R., illus. (gr. 4-12). 1979. pap. text ed. 2.95 (0-88301-355-X); wkbk. 1.25 (0-88301-379-7) Pendulum Pr.
—Thomas Edison - Alexander Graham Bell. Taloac, Gerry & Trinidad, Angel, illus. (gr. 4-12). 1979. pap. text ed. 2.95 (0-88301-357-6); wkbk. 1.25 (0-88301-381-9) Pendulum Pr.

Farr, Naunerle C. & Fago, John N. Amelia Earhart - Charles Lindbergh. Vicatan, illus. (gr. 4-12). 1979. pap. text ed. 2.95 (0-88301-349-5); wkbk. 1.25 (0-88301-373-8) Pendulum Pr.

Farr, Naunerle C., jt. auth. see Fago, John N.

Farrand, Brent, jt. auth. see Farrand, Vernell C.

Farrand, Vernell C. & Farrand, Brent. Afro-Bets Activity & Enrichment Guide: Book of Black Heroes from A to Z. 1989. pap. 7.95 (0-940975-05-X) Just Us Bks.

Farrant, Don. Lure & Lore of the Golden Isles. (Illus.). 192p. (Orig.). (gr. 10 up). 1993. pap. 8.95 (1-55853-262-5) Rutledge Hill Pr.

Farrant, Don W. Real Ghosts Don't Wear Sheets. Kusmierz, James P., illus. 80p. (Orig.). 1985. pap. 7.00 (0-935604-02-2) Ivystone.

Farrar, Susan C. Emily & Her Cavalier. Weinberger, Jane & Little, Carl, eds. LC 90-71373. (Illus.). 124p. 1991. 12.95g (0-932433-76-6); pap. 9.95 (0-932433-77-4) Windswept Hse.
—Samantha on Stage. Sanderson, Ruth, illus. 164p. (gr. 3 up). 1990. pap. 3.95 (0-14-034328-8, Puffin) Puffin Bks.

Farre, Marie. Crocodiles & Alligators. Matthews, Sarah, tr. from FRE. Wallis, Diz, illus. LC 87-31804. 38p. (gr. k-5). 1988. 4.95 (0-944589-01-4, 014) Young Discovery Lib.
—Long Ago in a Castle. Matthews, Sarah, tr. from FRE. Thibault, Dominique, illus. LC 87-33996. 38p. (gr. k-5). 1988. 4.95 (0-944589-06-5, 065) Young Discovery Lib.

Farrell, Don A. Liberation Nineteen Forty-Four: The Pictorial History of Guam. Koontz, Phyllis, ed. Dimalanta, Ariel, illus. (gr. 8-12). 1984. Repr. 15.95 (0-930839-00-5) Micronesian.

Farrell, Edward. Young Jackie Robinson, Baseball Hero. Stuart, Dennis, illus. LC 91-24680. 32p. (gr. k-2). 1992. text ed. 11.59 (0-8167-2536-5); pap. text ed. 2.95 (0-8167-2537-3) Troll Assocs.

Farrell, Kate, jt. auth. see Koch, Kenneth.

Farrell, Lee, ed. see Leahy, Barbara H.

Farrell, Vivian. Robert's Tall Friend: A Story of the Fire Island Lighthouse. Edwards, Christy, illus. LC 87-35246. 64p. (gr. 4-7). 1988. write for info. (0-9619832-0-5) Island-Metro Pubns.

Farrell, William R. Characters in Mythology. Chapman, Bettina B., illus. 60p. (gr. k-10). 1992. spiral bdg. 9.25 (0-939507-38-2, B423) Amer Classical.

Farrington, Liz & McGuire, Leslie. Nightmares in the Mist. Farrington, Liz, created by. LC 92-46876. (Illus.). 40p. (gr. k-4). 1994. 14.95 (1-56844-003-0) Enchante Pub.

Farrington, Liz & Rubin, Susan G. The Rainbow Fields. Farrington, Liz, created by. LC 92-46875. (Illus.). 40p. (gr. k-4). 1993. 14.95 (1-56844-004-9) Enchante Pub.

Farrington, Liz & Sherwood, Jonathan. Painting the Fire. Moran, J. Douglas, illus. Farrington, Liz, created by. LC 92-76022. (Illus.). 40p. (gr. k-4). 1993. 14.95 (1-56844-001-4) Enchante Pub.

Farrington, Liz & Weil, Jennifer C. And Peter Said Goodbye. Scardova, Jaclyne, illus. Farrington, Liz, created by. LC 92-35977. (Illus.). 40p. (gr. k-4). 1993. 14.95 (1-56844-000-6) Enchante Pub.

Farrington, Liz, created by see Sherwood, Jonathan.

Farrington, Liz, created by see Weil, Jennifer C.

Farrington, S. Kip. Tony the Tuna. (gr. 4-5). 1976. 6.95 (0-911660-25-9) Yankee Peddler.

Farris, Diane. In Dolphin Time. Farris, Diane, illus. LC 92-42512. 32p. 1994. RSBE 14.95 (0-02-734365-0, Four Winds) Macmillan Child Grp.

Farris, John. The Dust Bowl. LC 89-33557. (Illus.). 64p. (gr. 5-8). 1989. PLB 11.95 (1-56006-005-0) Lucent Bks.

—Hiroshima. McGovern, Brian, illus. LC 90-34064. 64p. (gr. 5-8). 1990. PLB 11.95 (1-56006-015-8) Lucent Bks.

Farris, Katherine, ed. Let's Speak French! A First Book of Words. rev. ed. Hendry, Linda, illus. LC 92-41737. (ENG & FRE.). 48p. (ps-5). 1993. 11.99 (0-670-85042-X) Viking Child Bks.

—Let's Speak Spanish! A First Book of Words. Hendry, Linda, illus. 48p. (ps-5). 1993. 11.99 (0-670-84994-4) Viking Child Bks.

Farrow, Peter & Lampert, Diane. Twyllyp. (Illus.). (gr. 3-7). 1963. 10.95 (0-8392-3040-0) Astor-Honor.

Farry, Liane. Frank & Sam's Summer at Aramoana. Wells, Gregory, illus. LC 93-11733. 1994. 4.25 (0-383-03744-1) SRA Schl Grp.

Fasco, Rudolph. In Quest of the Zohar. Frades, Ernesto, ed. Pereira, Ernesto, illus. 275p. (Orig.). 1990. pap. write for info. (0-9624929-0-6) Little Great Whale.

Fass, Bernie & Caggiano, Rosemary. Children Are People. 48p. (gr. 2-10). 1977. pap. 14.95 (0-86704-003-3) Clarus Music.

—The Four Seasons. 48p. (gr. k-6). 1976. pap. 14.95 (0-86704-001-7) Clarus Music.

—Happy Birthday Party Time. 48p. (gr. k-6). 1976. pap. 14.95 (0-86704-002-5) Clarus Music.

—The Power Is You. 48p. (gr. 2-12). 1979. pap. 14.95 (0-86704-005-X) Clarus Music.

—The Weather Company. 48p. (gr. k-8). 1978. pap. 14.95 (0-86704-004-1) Clarus Music.

Fass, Bernie & Wolfson, Mack. Christmas on Main Street. 48p. (gr. 3-12). 1986. pap. 16.95 (0-86704-036-X); student bk. 2.95 (0-86704-037-8) Clarus Music.

—The Halloween Machine. (gr. k-9). 1984. pap. 15.95, 48 pgs. 3.25 student's ed, 32 pgs. (0-86704-009-2); student ed, 32 pgs. (0-86704-010-6) Clarus Music.

—United Santas of America. 48p. (gr. 3-12). 1987. pap. 16.95 (0-86704-038-6); student bk. 2.95 (0-86704-039-4) Clarus Music.

Fass, Bernie, et al. Old MacDonald Had a Farm. 32p. (gr. k-4). 1981. pap. 14.95 (0-86704-007-6) Clarus Music.

Fassler, David & Danforth, Kimberly. Coming to America: The Kids' Book about Immigration. (Illus.). 160p. (Orig.). 1992. pap. text ed. 12.95 (0-914525-23-9); tchr's. ed. plastic comb spiral bdg. 16.95 (0-914525-24-7) Waterfront Bks.

Fassler, David & McQueen, Kelly. Que Es Un Virus? Un Libro Para Ninos Sobre el SIDA. Quinones, Wanda M., tr. from ENG. LC 90-24631. (Illus.). 70p. (Orig.). (ps-5). 1991. pap. 8.95 (0-914525-17-4); pap. 12.95 plastic comb. (0-685-47790-8) (0-914525-16-6) Waterfront Bks.

—What's a Virus, Anyway? The Kids' Book about AIDS. LC 89-40719. (Illus.). 85p. (Orig.). (ps-6). 1990. plastic comb spiral 10.95 (0-914525-14-X); pap. 8.95 (0-914525-15-8) Waterfront Bks.

Fassler, David, jt. auth. see McQueen, Kelly.

Fassler, Joan. All Alone with Daddy: A Young Girl Plays the Role of Mother. Gregory, Dorothy L., illus. LC 76-80120. 32p. (ps-3). 1975. 16.95 (0-87705-009-0) Human Sci Pr.

—The Boy with a Problem: Johnny Learns to Share His Troubles. LC 78-147125. (Illus.). 32p. (ps-3). 1971. 16.95 (0-87705-054-6) Human Sci Pr.

—Don't Worry Dear. Kranz, Stewart, illus. LC 74-147124. 32p. (ps-3). 1971. 16.95 (0-87705-055-4) Human Sci Pr.

—Howie Helps Himself. Lasker, Joe, illus. LC 74-12284. 32p. (gr. 1-3). 1975. PLB 13.95 (0-8075-3422-6) A Whitman.

—The Man of the House. Landa, Peter, illus. LC 73-80122. 32p. (ps-3). 1975. 16.95 (0-87705-010-4) Human Sci Pr.

—My Grandpa Died Today. Kranz, Stewart, illus. LC 71-147126. 32p. (ps-3). 1983. 14.95 (0-87705-053-8); pap. 9.95 (0-89885-174-2) Human Sci Pr.

—One Little Girl. Smyth, M. Jane, illus. LC 76-80120. 32p. (ps-3). 1969. 16.95 (0-87705-008-2) Human Sci Pr.

Fast, Freda. Anna. LC 90-67768. 63p. (Orig.). 1992. pap. 7.00 (1-56002-169-1, Univ Edtns) Aegina Pr.

Fast, Jonathan, adapted by. Newsies. LC 91-73973. (Illus.). 136p. (Orig.). (gr. 2-6). 1992. pap. 3.50 (1-56282-115-6) Disney Pr.

Fast, Suellen M. America's Daughters. Fast, Suellen M., photos by. 100p. (Orig.). (gr. k up). pap. 19.00 (0-935281-13-4) Daughter Cult.

—Celebrations of Daughterhood. Serman, Gina L., ed. LC 85-72281. 68p. (Orig.). (gr. 1 up). 1985. pap. 8.00 (0-935281-06-1) Daughter Cult.

—Celebrations of Daughterhood. 2nd, rev. ed. Serman, Gina L., ed. 70p. (Orig.). (gr. k up). 1988. pap. 8.00 (0-317-57532-5) Daughter Cult.

—Golden-Brown Baby Bear & the Three Sisters. Serman, Gina L., ed. 30p. (Orig.). (ps up). pap. 4.00 (0-935281-11-8) Daughter Cult.

Father Gander, pseud. Father Gander Nursery Rhymes. Blattel, Carolyn & Blair, Janice, illus. LC 85-72785. 47p. (ps up). 1985. 15.95 (0-911655-12-3, Dist. by Ingram Bookpeople) Advocacy Pr.

Father Robert J. Fox. The Day the Sun Danced: The True Story of Fatima. CCC of America Staff, illus. 60p. (Orig.). (gr. k-6). 1989. incl. video 21.95 (1-56814-001-0); book 4.95 (0-685-62401-3) CCC of America.

Faucher. Surviving. 1993. pap. 2.95 (0-590-43731-3) Scholastic Inc.

Faucher, Elizabeth. Charles in Charge. 128p. (Orig.). (gr. 7 up). 1984. pap. 2.25 (0-590-33550-2, Point) Scholastic Inc.

Faul, Michael. Africa & Her Flags. (gr. 1-9). 1992. pap. 3.95 (0-88388-160-8) Bellerophon Bks.

Faulk, Diane, jt. auth. see Howard, Esther.

Faulk, Tim. What Causes Our Teens to Take Their Lives? Dying to Live. 80p. (Orig.). (gr. 9 up). 1989. pap. text ed. 5.95 (0-685-29873-6) T Faulk Ministries.

Faulkner, Hal, jt. auth. see Perry, Cheryl.

Faulkner, Keith. Boastful Bullfrog. Lambert, Jonathan, illus. 22p. (gr. 1-3). 1991. 5.95 (0-681-41051-5) Longmeadow Pr.

—Butterfly. Lambert, Jonathan, illus. 12p. (ps-2). 1993. 4.95 (0-694-00463-4, Festival) HarpC Child Bks.

—David Dreaming of Dinosaurs. Lambert, Jonathan, illus. (ps-3). 1992. 13.00 (1-56021-182-2) W J Fantasy.

—Dracula. Lambert, Jonathan, illus. 16p. (ps-2). 1993. 10.95 (0-694-00559-2, Festival) HarpC Child Bks.

—Elephant & the Rainbow. Lambert, Jonathan, illus. 22p. (gr. 1-3). 1990. 5.95 (0-681-40977-0) Longmeadow Pr.

—Fisherman's Tale. Lambert, Jonathan, illus. 16p. (gr. 1-4). 1994. 11.95 (0-8431-3646-4) Price Stern.

—Frog. Lambert, Jonathan, illus. 12p. (ps-2). 1993. 4.95 (0-694-00464-2, Festival) HarpC Child Bks.

—Good Night, Tom. Lambert, Jonathan, illus. LC 92-82912. 20p. (ps). 1993. 4.95 (0-590-46924-X, Cartwheel) Scholastic Inc.

—I Can Count. 1994. pap. 7.95 (0-671-88027-6, Little Simon) S&S Trade.

—Kittens Who Didn't Share. Lambert, Jonathan, illus. 16p. (gr. 1-4). 1992. 5.95 (0-681-41412-X) Longmeadow Pr.

—Monster in My Bathroom. Lambert, Tony, illus. 16p. (gr. 1-4). 1993. text ed. 4.99 (0-8431-3482-8) Price Stern.

—Monster in My Toybox. Lambert, Tony, illus. 16p. (gr. 1-4). 1993. text ed. 4.99 (0-8431-3481-X) Price Stern.

—My First One Hundred Words in French & English. (Illus.). 14p. (ps-3). 1993. pap. 11.00 casebound (0-671-86447-5, S&S BFYR) S&S Trade.

—My First Phrases in Spanish & English. Johnson, Paul, illus. 14p. (ps-4). 1993. pap. 11.00 casebound (0-671-86595-1, S&S BFYR) S&S Trade.

—My New Neighbors. Lambert, Jonathan, illus. 24p. (ps-2). 1992. 9.95 (0-694-00426-X, Festival) HarpC Child Bks.

—Oh No! A Giant Flap Book. Lambert, Jonathan, illus. 16p. (ps-1). 1991. pap. 14.95 (0-671-74747-9, S&S BFYR) S&S Trade.

—Runaway Whale. Lambert, Jonathan, illus. 22p. (gr. 1-3). 1990. 5.95 (0-681-41014-0) Longmeadow Pr.

—Simple Sums. (ps-3). 1994. 11.00 (0-671-88555-3, S&S BFYR) S&S Trade.

—This Is Me. Lambert, Jonathan, illus. 10p. (ps-k). 1987. 5.95 (0-312-00967-4) St Martin.

—Tom's Friends. Lambert, Jonathan, illus. LC 92-82910. 20p. (ps). 1993. 4.95 (0-590-46949-5, Cartwheel) Scholastic Inc.

—Tom's Picnic. Lambert, Jonathan, illus. LC 92-82911. 20p. (ps). 1993. 4.95 (0-590-46947-9, Cartwheel) Scholastic Inc.

—Tom's School Day. Lambert, Jonathan, illus. LC 92-82909. 20p. (ps). 1993. 4.95 (0-590-46948-7, Cartwheel) Scholastic Inc.

—Two by Two. Lambert, Tony, illus. 16p. (gr. 1-4). 1993. 12.99 (0-8431-3477-1) Price Stern.

Faulkner, Keith, jt. auth. see MacKay-Robinson, Christina.

Faulkner, Linda M. The Young Christian's Puzzle Book: For Becoming a Grown-up Christian. (Illus.). 40p. (gr. 5-7). 1992. pap. 3.50 (0-88243-828-X, 02-0828) Gospel Pub.

Faulkner, Matt. The Amazing Voyage of Jackie Grace. Faulkner, Matt, illus. 1991. pap. 3.95 (0-590-44860-9) Scholastic Inc.

—Jack & the Beanstalk. (Illus.). 48p. (Orig.). (gr. k-3). 1986. pap. 2.50 (0-590-40164-5) Scholastic Inc.

—The Moon Clock. Faulkner, Matt, illus. 56p. 1991. 14.95 (0-590-41593-X, Scholastic Hardcover) Scholastic Inc.

Faulkner, William. Collected Stories of William Faulkner. (gr. 9 up). 1977. pap. 18.00 (0-394-72257-4) Random Bks Yng Read.

—Portable Faulkner. rev. ed. Cowley, Malcolm, ed. (gr. 10 up). 1977. pap. 9.95 (0-14-015018-8, Penguin Bks) Viking Penguin.

Fauquez, Arthur. Don Quixote of La Mancha. 1967. 4.50 (0-87602-121-6) Anchorage.

—The Man Who Killed Time. 1964. 4.50 (0-87602-154-2) Anchorage.

—Reynard the Fox. 1962. 5.50 (0-87602-187-9) Anchorage.

Faurot, Chip, jt. auth. see Gonzales, Rod.

Faust, Naomi F. All Beautiful Things. 2nd ed. LC 82-83853. 104p. (gr. 7-12). 1983. pap. 5.00 perf. bnd. (0-916418-49-9) Lotus.

—And I Travel by Rhythms & Words: New & Selected Poems. LC 89-63039. 318p. (gr. 7-12). 1990. pap. 18.00 perfect bdg. (0-916418-77-4) Lotus.

Faville, Barry. Stanley's Aquarium. 160p. (gr. 7 up). 1990. jacketed 14.95 (0-19-558197-0) OUP.

Favors, Jean. Tough Choices. 112p. (Orig.). (gr. 4-9). 1992. pap. 2.95 (0-448-40492-3, G&D) Putnam Pub Group.

—Waters Dark & Deep. 1993. pap. 3.50 (0-06-106736-9, Harp PBks) HarpC.

Favors, John & Favors, Kathryne. John Quincy Adams & the Amistad: A President Who Fought for the Rights of Africans. Dellums, Ronald, intro. by. (Illus.). 28p. (Orig.). (gr. 12). 1974. write for info. (1-878794-02-7) Jonka Enter.

—White Americans Who Cared Kit. 26p. (gr. 4 up). 1990. Repr. of 1978 ed. 299.95 (1-878794-01-9) Jonka Enter.

Favors, Kathryne, jt. auth. see Favors, John.

Faxton, Carlita. A's with Ease. 52p. Date not set. pap. write for info. (0-9636553-3-7) C Faxton.

—Be Beautiful from Your Head to Your Feet. 52p. (Orig.). 1994. pap. write for info. (0-9636553-4-5) C Faxton.

—Business Sense: For Budding Entrepreneurs. 64p. (Orig.). 1994. pap. write for info. (0-9636553-6-1) C Faxton.

—The Key to Success in the Corporate World. 52p. Date not set. pap. write for info. (0-9636553-5-3) C Faxton.

Fay, Ann, ed. see Addy, Sharon H.

Fay, Ann, ed. see Aylesworth, Jim.

Fay, Ann, ed. see Bernstein, Joanne & Cohen, Paul.

Fay, Ann, ed. see Bernstein, Joanne E. & Cohen, Paul.

Fay, Ann, ed. see Broekel, Ray & White, Laurence B., Jr.

Fay, Ann, ed. see Christian, Mary B.

Fay, Ann, ed. see Corey, Dorothy.

Fay, Ann, ed. see Delton, Judy.

Fay, Ann, ed. see Hong, Lily T.

Fay, Ann, ed. see Kline, Suzy.

Fay, Ann, ed. see Kline, Suzy W.

Fay, Ann, ed. see Levine, Abby.

Fay, Ann, ed. see Limmer, Milly J.

Fay, Ann, ed. see Mueller, Virginia.

Fay, Ann, ed. see Newton, Laura.

Fay, Ann, ed. see Nims, Bonnie L.

Fay, Ann, ed. see Nixon, Joan L.

Fay, Ann, ed. see Rosner, Ruth.

Fay, Ann, ed. see Seltzer, Meyer.

Fay, Ann, ed. see Sills, Leslie.

Fay, Ann, ed. see Stanek, Muriel.

Fay, Ann, ed. see Vigna, Judith.

Fay, Ann, ed. see White, Larry & Broekel, Ray.

Fay, Anne, ed. see Broekel, Ray & White, Laurence B., Jr.

Fay, Anne, ed. see Latta, Richard.

Fayerweather Street School Staff. The Kids' Book about Death & Dying. Rofes, Eric E., ed. 119p. (gr. 5 up). 1985. 16.95 (0-316-75390-4) Little.

Feagan, Mary. Questions to Ask a Cat When It Comes Home from a Trip. (Illus.). 24p. (gr. k-3). 1988. 3.95 (0-929986-63-6) Rainbow Cat Pubs.

—The Rainbow Child. (Illus.). 20p. (gr. 1-4). 1988. 8.95 (0-929986-06-7) Rainbow Cat Pubs.

Feagles, Anita. Casey, the Utterly Impossible Horse. Wilson, Dagmar W., illus. LC 88-13871. 96p. (gr. 3-7). 1989. Repr. of 1960 ed. lib. bdg. 16.00 (0-208-02239-2, Linnet) Shoe String.

—The Tooth Fairy. (Illus.). 32p. (gr. k-2). 1993. Repr. of 1962 ed. PLB write for info. (0-208-02323-2, Linnet) Shoe String.

Fearing, Kelly, et al. The Way of Art: Inner Vision-Outer Expression. (Illus.). (gr. 7-8). 1986. Vol. I, 160 pages. pap. 17.79 (0-87443-066-6); Vol. II, 166 pages. text ed. 17.79 (0-87443-067-4); Tchr's manual, 80 pages. 6.00 (0-87443-068-2) Benson.

Fearn, Leif. Developmental Writing & the Writing Kabyn. 70p. (gr. 2-9). 1981. 1.00 (0-940444-07-0) Kabyn.

—The Fear. 178p. (gr. 2 up). 1983. 6.95 (0-940444-20-8) Kabyn.

—The First First I Think. 91p. (gr. 1-3). 1981. 6.95 (0-940444-14-3) Kabyn.

—First I Think: Then I Write My Think. 160p. (gr. 3-12). 1981. 6.95 (*0-940444-13-5*) Kabyn.
—Reading in the Mind. 41p. (gr. 1-7). 1984. 25.00 (*0-940444-22-4*) Kabyn.
Fearn, Leif & Garner, Irene A. The Alpha Cards. 54p. (gr. 2-9). 1982. card pack 14.00 (*0-940444-12-7*) Kabyn.
—Maneras de Divertirme con Mi Mente. (Illus.). 182p. (gr. 3-9). 1982. 6.50 (*0-940444-16-X*) Kabyn.
Fearn, Leif & Goldman, Elizabeth. Writing Kabyn: Assessment & Editing. 96p. (gr. 2-9). 1981. classroom kit 27.50 (*0-940444-11-9*) Kabyn.
—Writing Kabyn: Products. 148p. (gr. 2-9). 1982. classroom kit 48.00 (*0-940444-09-7*) Kabyn.
—Writing Kabyn: Sentences-Paragraphs. 125p. (gr. 2-9). 1982. classroom kit 69.00 (*0-940444-08-9*) Kabyn.
—Writing Kabyn: Technology. 76p. (gr. 2-9). 1981. classroom Kit 49.00 (*0-940444-10-0*) Kabyn.
Fearn, Leif & Goliaz-Benson, Ursula. Forty-Two Ways to Have Fun with My Mind. Curtner, Rondi L., illus. 58p. (ps-6). 1976. 5.00 (*0-940444-00-3*) Kabyn.
Fearn, Leif & Golisz-Benson, Ursula. Fifty-Two Ways to Have Fun with My Mind. Emmet, Mary, illus. 62p. (gr. 1-3). 1975. 5.00 (*0-940444-01-1*) Kabyn.
—Seventy-Two Ways to Have Fun with My Mind. Curtner, Rondi, illus. 80p. (Orig.). (gr. 4-6). 1976. 5.00 (*0-940444-03-8*) Kabyn.
—Sixty-Two Ways to Have Fun with My Mind. (Illus.). 72p. (Orig.). (gr. 3-6). 1982. 5.00 (*0-940444-02-X*) Kabyn.
Fearnehaugh, Mary E. see Elbert, Elizabeth, pseud.
Fearon, Mike. Martin Luther. 144p. 1993. 4.99 (*1-55661-306-7*) Bethany Hse.
Featherstone, Vaughn J. The Aaronic Priesthood & You. LC 87-15731. 99p. (gr. 7-12). 1987. 9.95 (*0-87579-085-2*) Deseret Bk.
—The Aaronic Priesthood & You. LC 87-15731. 99p. (gr. 8-12). 1993. pap. 8.95 (*0-87579-755-5*) Deseret Bk.
Feczko, Kathy. The Great Bunny Race. Jones, John, illus. LC 84-8634. 32p. (gr. k-2). 1985. PLB 11.59 (*0-8167-0357-4*); pap. text ed. 2.95 (*0-8167-0437-6*) Troll Assocs.
—Halloween Party. Sims, Blanche, illus. LC 84-8635. 32p. (gr. k-2). 1985. PLB 11.59 (*0-8167-0354-X*); pap. text ed. 2.95 (*0-8167-0434-1*) Troll Assocs.
—Three Little Chicks. Harvey, Paul, illus. LC 84-8629. 32p. (gr. k-2). 1985. PLB 11.59 (*0-8167-0355-8*); pap. text ed. 2.95 (*0-8167-0435-X*) Troll Assocs.
—Umbrella Parade. Borgo, Deborah C., illus. LC 84-8650. 32p. (gr. k-2). 1985. PLB 11.59 (*0-8167-0356-6*); pap. text ed. 2.95 (*0-8167-0436-8*) Troll Assocs.
Feder, Chris W. Brain Quest: Grade 1. (gr. 1). 1992. pap. 9.95 (*1-56305-258-X*, 3258) Workman Pub.
—Brain Quest: Grade 2. (gr. 2). 1992. pap. 9.95 (*1-56305-259-8*, 3259) Workman Pub.
—Brain Quest: Grade 3. (gr. 3). 1992. pap. 9.95 (*1-56305-260-1*, 3260) Workman Pub.
—Brain Quest: Grade 4. (gr. 4). 1992. pap. 9.95 (*1-56305-261-X*, 3261) Workman Pub.
—Brain Quest: Grade 5. (gr. 5). 1992. pap. 9.95 (*1-56305-262-8*, 3262) Workman Pub.
—Brain Quest: Grade 6. (gr. 6). 1992. pap. 9.95 (*1-56305-263-6*, 3263) Workman Pub.
—Brain Quest: Grade 7. (gr. 7). 1992. pap. 9.95 (*1-56305-264-4*, 3264) Workman Pub.
—Brain Quest (Kindergarten) (gr. k-1). 1993. pap. 10.95 (*1-56305-352-7*, 3352) Workman Pub.
—Brain Quest (Preschool) (ps-3). 1993. pap. 10.95 (*1-56305-351-9*, 3351) Workman Pub.
Feder, Harriet. What Can You Do with a Bagel? Springer, Sally, illus. LC 91-60591. 12p. (ps). 1992. bds. 4.95 (*0-929371-59-3*) Kar Ben.
Feder, Harriet K. It Happened in Shushan: A Purim Story. Schanzer, Roz, illus. LC 88-2676. (Orig.). (ps-3). 1990. pap. 3.95 (*0-930494-75-X*) Kar Ben.
—Judah Who Always Said, "No!" Kahn, Katherine J., illus. LC 90-4854. 32p. (ps-2). 1990. 12.95 (*0-929371-13-5*); pap. 4.95 (*0-929371-14-3*) Kar Ben.
—Mystery in Miami Beach: A Vivi Hartman Adventure. 176p. (gr. 5-12). 1992. PLB 17.50 (*0-8225-0733-1*) Lerner Pubns.
Feder, Jane. Table, Chair, Bear: A Room in Many Languages. LC 92-40529. 1993. 13.95 (*0-395-65938-8*) Ticknor & Fields.
Feder, Paula K. Did You Lose the Car Again? Hayashi, Nancy, illus. 64p. (gr. 2-5). 1991. pap. 3.50 (*0-14-034800-X*, Puffin) Puffin Bks.
—Where Does the Teacher Live? Hoban, Lillian, illus. LC 78-13157. 48p. (gr. 1-3). 1979. 12.95 (*0-525-42586-1*, DCB) Dutton Child Bks.
—Where Does the Teacher Live? Hoban, Lillian, illus. LC 78-13157. 48p. (gr. 1-3). 1992. pap. 3.99 (*0-525-44889-6*, Unicorn Pbks) Dutton Child Bks.
Fedotousky, Alex. Dingle Dorts vs Dingle Saurs. Fedotousky, Alex, illus. 32p. 1993. pap. text ed. 2.75 (*0-9638756-0-4*) Skylght Studios.
Feehan, Mary. Book of Children's Jokes. 1990. pap. 5.95 (*0-85342-495-0*) Dufour.
Feelings, Muriel. Jambo Means Hello: Swahili Alphabet Book. Feelings, Tom, illus. LC 73-15441. 56p. (gr. k-3). 1985. Repr. of 1974 ed. 15.00 (*0-8037-4346-7*); PLB 13.89 (*0-8037-4350-5*) Dial Bks Young.
—Moja Means One: A Swahili Counting Book. Feelings, Tom, illus. LC 76-134856. (ps-3). 1987. 13.95 (*0-8037-5776-X*); PLB 13.89 (*0-8037-5777-8*) Dial Bks Young.

—Moja Means One: A Swahili Counting Book. LC 76-134856. (Illus.). 32p. (gr. k up). 1976. pap. 4.95 (*0-8037-5711-5*) Dial Bks Young.
Feelings, Muriel & Feelings, Tom. Jambo Means Hello: Swahili Alphabet Book. (Illus.). 56p. (gr. k-3). 1985. pap. 4.99 (*0-8037-4428-5*, Dial Pied Piper) Puffin Bks.
Feelings, Tom. Soul Looks Back in Wonder. Angelou, Maya, et al. LC 93-824. (Illus.). 40p. 1994. 15.99 (*0-8037-1001-1*, Dial Pr) Doubleday.
—Tommy Traveller in the World of Black History. (Illus.). 48p. (gr. 3-6). 1991. 13.95 (*0-86316-202-9*) Writers & Readers.
Feelings, Tom, jt. auth. see Feelings, Muriel.
Feeney, Mary. Shawn Learns about Drugs. 1990. 7.95 (*0-533-08640-X*) Vantage.
Feeney, Stephanie. A Is for Aloha. Reese, Jeff, photos by. LC 85-50569. (Illus.). 64p. (ps-3). 1985. 8.95 (*0-8248-0722-7*) UH Pr.
—Hawaii Is a Rainbow. Hammid, Hella, illus. LC 80-5462. 64p. (ps-k). 1980. 12.95 (*0-8248-1007-4*) UH Pr.
Feeney, Stephanie & Fielding, Ann. Sand to Sea: Marine Life of Hawaii. LC 88-38669. 1989. 12.95 (*0-8248-1180-1*, Kolowalu Bk) UH Pr.
Feest, Christian F. The Powhatan Tribes. (Illus.). 112p. (gr. 5 up). 1990. 17.95 (*1-55546-726-1*) Chelsea Hse.
Feghali, Habaka J. Arabic Hijazi Reader. Murphy, John D., ed. LC 91-70530. 193p. 1991. 44.00 (*0-931745-72-1*); cassettes avail. (*0-931745-87-X*) Dunwoody Pr.
Fehiner, Paul. Dog & Cat. LC 90-30164. (Illus.). 28p. (ps-2). 1990. PLB 12.33 (*0-516-05353-1*); pap. 3.95 (*0-516-45353-X*) Childrens.
Fehlauer, Adolph. Catechism Lessons: Pupil's Book. Grunze, Richard, ed. May, Lawrence, illus. 336p. (gr. 5-6). 1981. 6.95 (*0-938272-09-8*) WELS Board.
—Catechism Lessons-Teacher's Book. Grunze, R., ed. 392p. (gr. 5-6). 1978. 3-ring binder 9.95 (*0-938272-08-X*) WELS Board.
—Life & Faith of Martin Luther. (gr. 6-9). 1981. pap. 6.95 (*0-8100-0125-X*, 15N0376) Northwest Pub.
Fehling, Roberta H. Thinking Speech: A Blueprint for Carryover. 112p. (gr. 3 up). 1991. 16.95 (*0-937857-28-9*, 1593) Speech Bin.
Fehlner, Paul. The Story of Christmas. (Illus.). 24p. (ps-3). 1989. pap. write for info. (*0-307-11710-3*, Pub. by Golden Bks) Western Pub.
Fehr, Barbara. Yankee Denim Dandies. Eschweiler, Jane, contrib. by. LC 74-79127. (Illus.). 96p. (gr. 6 up). 1984. 15.00 (*0-87832-014-8*) Piper.
Feierabend, John. Music for Little People. Kramer, Gary, illus. 74p. (Orig.). (ps). 1989. pap. 11.95 (*0-913932-46-9*); pap. 14.95 incl. tape (*0-913932-48-5*) Boosey & Hawkes.
Feierabend, John M. Music for Very Little People. Kramer, Gary M., illus. 74p. (ps). 1986. pap. 14.95 (*0-685-14607-3*); pap. write for info. incl. tape (*0-913932-13-2*); cassette avail. Boosey & Hawkes.
Feiffer, Jules. The Man in the Ceiling. Feiffer, Jules, illus. LC 92-59953. 192p. (gr. 3-7). 1993. 15.00 (*0-06-205035-4*); PLB 14.89 (*0-06-205036-2*) HarpC Child Bks.
Feig, Barbara K. Now You're Cooking: A Guide to Cooking for Boys & Girls. Haney, Elizabeth M., illus. LC 75-10991. 144p. (gr. 7 up). 1975. pap. 4.95 (*0-916836-01-0*) J B Pal.
Feigen, Roberta, jt. auth. see Males, Carolyn.
Feild, William B., Jr. & Stassun, Peter G. Perils on the Sea of Rhun. Ney, Jessica, ed. Hook, Richard & Danforth, Liz, illus. 32p. (Orig.). (gr. 12). 1989. pap. 6.00 (*0-685-37962-0*, 8110) Iron Crown Ent Inc.
Feinberg, Anna. Wiggy & Boa. James, Ann, illus. 112p. (gr. 3-7). 1990. 13.95 (*0-395-53704-5*) HM.
Feinberg, Barbara S. American Political Scandals Past & Present. (Illus.). 160p. (gr. 9-12). 1992. PLB 13.90 (*0-531-11126-1*) Watts.
—Harry S. Truman. LC 93-30895. 1994. write for info. (*0-531-13036-3*) Watts.
—Local Governments. LC 92-27366. 1993. lib. bdg. 12.90 (*0-531-20153-8*) Watts.
—The National Government. LC 92-25915. 1993. lib. bdg. 12.90 (*0-531-20155-4*) Watts.
—State Governments. LC 92-27368. 1993. lib. bdg. 12.90 (*0-531-20154-6*) Watts.
—Watergate: Scandal in the White House. LC 90-34726. (Illus.). 144p. (gr. 9-12). 1990. PLB 13.90 (*0-531-10963-1*) Watts.
Feinberg, Brian. The Musculoskeletal System. Garell, Dale C. & Snyder, Solomon H., eds. (Illus.). 112p. (gr. 7-12). 1994. 19.95 (*0-7910-0028-1*, Am Art Analog) Chelsea Hse.
—The Musculoskeletal System. Koop, C. Everett, intro. by. LC 92-21956. 1993. pap. write for info. (*0-7910-0463-5*) Chelsea Hse.
—Nelson Mandela. (Illus.). 72p. (gr. 3-5). 1991. lib. bdg. 12.95 (*0-7910-1569-6*) Chelsea Hse.
Feinberg, Jeremy R. Reading the Sports Page: A Guide to Understanding Sports Statistics. LC 92-18972. (Illus.). 80p. (gr. 6 up). 1992. RSBE 12.95 (*0-02-734420-7*, New Discovery) Macmillan Child Grp.
Feingold, Marilyn N., jt. auth. see Feingold, S. Norman.
Feingold, S. Norman & Feingold, Marilyn N. The Complete Job & Career Handbook: One Hundred One Ways to Get from Here to There. LC 92-39716. (Illus.). 179p. (Orig.). (gr. 9 up). 1993. pap. 15.00 (*1-880774-01-1*) Garrett Pk.
Feinman, Joel, jt. auth. see Feldman, Robert S.

Feinstein, Morley. Jewish Law Review, Vol. 1 Mishnah: The Mishnah on Damages. (Illus.). 64p. (gr. 6 up). 1987. pap. text ed. 4.95 (*0-933873-08-5*) Torah Aura.
Feirer, John L., jt. auth. see Groneman, Chris H.
Feistmantl, Eric, jt. auth. see Maran, Richard.
Feitlowitz, Marguerite, tr. see Calders, Pere.
Fekete, Irene & Ward, Peter D. Disease & Medicine. 64p. 1987. 15.95x (*0-8160-1060-9*) Facts on File.
Feldbaum, Carl B. & Bee, Ronald J. Looking the Tiger in the Eye: Confronting the Nuclear Threat. LC 85-48253. (Illus.). 320p. (gr. 7 up). 1988. 14.95 (*0-06-020414-1*) HarpC Child Bks.
Felder, Deborah G. The Kids' World Almanac of Animals & Pets. Lane, John, illus. 1990. 14.95 (*0-88687-556-0*, World Almanac); pap. 6.95 (*0-88687-555-2*, World Almanac) F&W Inc NJ.
—The Kids' World Almanac of History. Lane, John, illus. 288p. (Orig.). 1991. 14.95 (*0-88687-496-3*, World Almanac); pap. 6.95 (*0-88687-495-5*, World Almanac) F&W Inc NJ.
Felder, Pamela T. I'm Black & I'm Beautiful. Slade, John, ed. Rice, Kendrick, illus. 14p. (Orig.). 1993. pap. 3.50 (*0-9638310-0-3*) Pams Unique.
Feldman, Annette & Leavitt, Nancy. To Grandma & Grandpa with Love. (Illus.). 1990. 7.95 (*0-8378-2062-6*) Gibson.
Feldman, B. Going, Going. (Illus.). 24p. (ps-8). 1989. 12.95 (*1-55037-045-6*, Pub. by Annick CN); pap. 4.95 (*1-55037-046-4*, Pub. by Annick CN) Firefly Bks Ltd.
Feldman, Barbara. Stephen's Frog. Feldman, Barbara, illus. 24p. (ps-1). 1991. PLB 14.95 (*1-55037-200-9*, Pub. by Annick CN); pap. 4.95 (*1-55037-201-7*, Pub. by Annick CN) Firefly Bks Ltd.
Feldman, Elane. The Nineteen Nineties. Cumming, Valerie, ed. (Illus.). 64p. (gr. 7-12). 1992. bds. 16.95x (*0-8160-2472-3*) Facts on File.
Feldman, Elane, ed. see Baker, Patricia.
Feldman, Elane, ed. see Carnegie, Vicky.
Feldman, Elane, ed. see Connikie, Yvonne.
Feldman, Elane, ed. see Costantino, Maria.
Feldman, Elane, ed. see Herald, Jacqueline.
Feldman, Enid. Freaky Friday: A Study Guide. (gr. 4-7). 1988. tchr's. ed. & wkbk. 14.95 (*0-88122-083-3*) LRN Links.
Feldman, Eva B. Seymour, the Formerly Fearful. LC 89-35668. 160p. (gr. 3-6). 1990. SBE 13.95 (*0-02-734371-5*, Four Winds Press) Macmillan Child Grp.
Feldman, Eve. Get Set & Go! (Illus.). 32p. (gr. 1-4). 1989. PLB 15.96 (*0-8172-3501-9*); pap. 3.95 (*0-8114-6701-5*) Raintree Steck-V.
—A Giant Surprise. (Illus.). 32p. (gr. 1-4). 1989. PLB 15.96 (*0-8172-3527-2*); pap. 3.95 (*0-8114-6724-4*) Raintree Steck-V.
—The Squire Takes a Wife. Weissman, Barry, illus. 24p. (ps-2). 1990. PLB 14.60 (*0-8172-3580-9*); PLB 10.95 pkg. of 3 (*0-685-58551-4*) Raintree Steck-V.
—We Are Friends. (Illus.). 32p. (gr. 1-4). 1989. PLB 15.96 (*0-8172-3517-5*); pap. 3.95 (*0-8114-6716-3*) Raintree Steck-V.
Feldman, Eve B. Animals Don't Wear Pajamas: A Book about Sleeping. Owens, Mary B., illus. LC 91-25192. 32p. (ps-3). 1992. 14.95 (*0-8050-1710-0*, Bks Young Read) H Holt & Co.
—Benjamin Franklin: Scientist & Inventor. (Illus.). 64p. (gr. 5-8). 1990. PLB 12.90 (*0-531-10867-8*) Watts.
—Dog Crazy. Nones, Eric J., illus. LC 91-11083. 112p. (gr. 2 up). 1992. 13.00 (*0-688-10819-9*, Tambourine Bks) Morrow.

Feldman, Jacqueline. The Lavender Box. Hoffman, Nannette, illus. LC 89-85206. 41p. (ps-6). 1992. 11.95 (*0-9623903-0-5*) Ellicott Pr.
A small boy disappears into a very large hat; a child silently shares poignant feelings with a chipmunk; a little girl preaches the rules of etiquette to a bee. Poems dealing with nature & the pleasures of domestic life transform childhood experiences into rhythmic images. And in the final offering, a lavender box becomes a metaphor for the entire book. Although these poems were written for children aged 3 to 11, Ms. Feldman's awareness of & wonder at the workings of a child's mind give readers of all ages an exhilarating & joyous experience. The poems are beautifully complemented by Nannette Hoffman's whimsical black & white drawings. "A resonant voice is gently in tune with the imagination of children in this poetry collection...the imagery reverberates on every page." -- SCHOOL LIBRARY JOURNAL. "In rhythmical, memorable verse, she recreates-- for children & adult readers

alike-- a child's sense of wonder." -- Anne Whitehouse, poet & reviewer for THE NEW YORK TIMES. "Quite a treasure box of a book." --THE BOOK READER. THE LAVENDER BOX is now in its second printing. *Publisher Provided Annotation.*

Feldman, Jay. Hitting. (Illus.). 96p. (gr. 5 up). 1991. pap. 12.95 (*0-671-73318-4*, S&S BFYR); pap. 5.95 (*0-671-70442-7*, S&S BFYR) S&S Trade.
Feldman, Judy. The Alphabet in Nature. LC 90-22315. (Illus.). 32p. (ps-2). 1991. PLB 17.27 (*0-516-05101-6*) Childrens.
—Shapes in Nature. LC 90-23091. (Illus.). 32p. (ps-2). 1991. PLB 17.27 (*0-516-05102-4*) Childrens.
Feldman, Robert S. Understanding Stress. Cohn, Tom, ed. (Illus.). 96p. (gr. 7-12). 1992. PLB 12.90 (*0-531-12531-9*) Watts.
Feldman, Robert S. & Feinman, Joel. Who You Are: Personality & Its Development. (Illus.). 128p. (gr. 9-12). 1992. PLB 13.40 (*0-531-12544-0*) Watts.
Feldman, Thea, ed. see Ryder, Joanne.
Feldscher, Sharla. The Kidfun Activity Book. LC 89-46088. 160p. (Orig.). (ps-3). 1990. pap. 9.00 (*0-06-096495-2*, HarpT) HarpC.
Feldstein, Sandy. Practical Theory, Vol. 1. 1992. pap. text ed. 4.50 (*0-88284-216-1*, 2280) Alfred Pub.
—Practical Theory, Vol. 2. 1992. pap. 4.95 (*0-88284-217-X*, 2281) Alfred Pub.
—Practical Theory, Vol. 3. 1992. pap. text ed. 4.95 (*0-88284-218-8*, 2282) Alfred Pub.
—Practical Theory: Complete. 1992. pap. text ed. 9.95 (*0-88284-225-0*, 1998) Alfred Pub.
Feldstein, Sandy, et al, eds. see DeCesare, Ruth.
Feldstein, Sandy, et al, eds. see Nash, Grace C. & Rapley, Janice.
Felix, Monique. Alphabet: Mouse Books. (Illus.). 32p. (ps). 1993. pap. 2.95 (*1-56189-094-4*) Amer Educ Pub.
—The Boat. (Illus.). 32p. (gr. 4-7). 1993. 7.95 (*1-56846-080-5*) Creat Editions.
—The Colors. Felix, Monique, illus. LC 91-4478. (gr. k-3). 1991. 8.95 (*1-55670-227-2*) Stewart Tabori & Chang.
—The Colors. 1992. PLB 10.95s.p. (*0-88682-404-4*) Creative Ed.
—Colors. (ps). 1993. 5.95 (*1-56846-075-9*) Creat Editions.
—Colors: Mouse Books. (Illus.). 32p. (ps). 1993. pap. 2.95 (*1-56189-093-6*) Amer Educ Pub.
—The House. Felix, Monique, illus. LC 91-281. 32p. (gr. k-3). 1991. 8.95 (*1-55670-225-6*) Stewart Tabori & Chang.
—The House. 1992. PLB 10.95s.p. (*0-88682-405-2*) Creative Ed.
—House. (ps). 1993. 5.95 (*1-56846-074-0*) Creat Editions.
—House: Mouse Books. (Illus.). 32p. (ps). 1993. pap. 2.95 (*1-56189-096-0*) Amer Educ Pub.

—Mouse Book Series, 6 bks. Felix, Monique, illus. 32p. (Orig.). (ps-k). 1993. Set. pap. 17.70 (*1-56189-077-4*) Amer Educ Pub.
Almost everyone has heard of a mouse in an attic, or a mouse in a garage, but a mouse trapped in a book? Never! That is, until now. Within the wonderfully illustrated pages of the Mouse Books, Swiss illustrator Monique Felix has created six unique adventures. Each story begins with the mouse innocently eating her way into a book & from there the fun begins. Where will she go? What will she do? How will she escape? These are all the questions that only the mouse can answer. But you can be sure that no matter where the mouse goes, an exciting adventure will closely follow. So come, enter the pages of these visual escapades--there are no words--& explore the world of a little mouse trapped in a book. Titles include: Numbers, ISBN 1-56189-091-X, $2.95; Opposites, ISBN 1-56189-092-8, $2.95; Colors, ISBN 1-56189-093-6, $2.95; Alphabet, ISBN 1-56189-094-4, $2.95; Wind, ISBN 1-56189-095-2, $2.95; House, ISBN 1-56189-096-0, $2.95. *Publisher Provided Annotation.*

—Numbers: Mouse Books. (Illus.). 32p. (ps). 1993. pap. 2.95 (*1-56189-091-X*) Amer Educ Pub.
—Opposites: Mouse Books. (Illus.). 32p. (ps). 1993. 2.95 (*1-56189-092-8*) Amer Educ Pub.
—The Plane. Felix, Monique, illus. LC 92-44058. 1993. PLB 10.95s.p. (*0-88682-604-7*) Creative Ed.
—The Plane. (Illus.). 32p. (gr. 4-7). 1993. 7.95 (*1-56846-079-1*) Creat Editions.
—The Wind. Felix, Monique, illus. LC 91-277. 32p. (gr. k-3). 1991. 8.95 (*1-55670-226-4*) Stewart Tabori & Chang.
—The Wind. 1992. PLB 10.95s.p. (*0-88682-406-0*) Creative Ed.
—Wind. (ps). 1993. 5.95 (*1-56846-073-2*) Creat Editions.
—Wind: Mouse Books. (Illus.). 32p. (ps). 1993. pap. 2.95 (*1-56189-095-2*) Amer Educ Pub.
Felix, Monique, illus. & created by. The Alphabet. (gr. 5 up). 1992. PLB 10.95 (*0-88682-563-6*) Creative Ed.
—The Numbers. (gr. 5 up). 1992. PLB 10.95 (*0-88682-562-8*) Creative Ed.
Felix, Monique, illus. The Opposites. LC 92-16357. (gr. 5 up). 1992. PLB 10.95 (*0-88682-569-5*) Creative Ed.
Feller, Marsha Y., jt. auth. see Feller, Ron L.
Feller, Robyn M. Everything You Need to Know about Peer Pressure. Rosen, Ruth, ed. (gr. 7-12). 1993. PLB 13.95 (*0-8239-1528-X*) Rosen Group.
Feller, Ron L. & Feller, Marsha Y. Fanciful Faces & Handbound Books: Fairy Tales. Ennes, Phyllis L., ed. Hastings, Kathryn K., illus. Smith, Andrew P., photos by. LC 88-34952. (Illus.). 72p. (Orig.). (gr. 2-9). 1989. pap. 9.95 (*0-9615873-1-8*) Arts Factory.
—Paper Masks & Puppets for Stories, Songs & Plays. Hastings, Kathryn K., illus. Joyner, Hermon, photos by. Graves, Jan, frwd. by. LC 85-72952. (Illus.). 104p. (Orig.). (gr. 2-9). 1986. pap. 14.95 (*0-9615873-0-X*) Arts Factory.
Fellers, Pat & Gritzmacher, Kathy. Intermediate Aphabet Soup: A Curriculum for Your First Week of School. Marson, Ron, ed. Marson, Peg, illus. 112p. (gr. 3-8). 1985. tchr's ed. 13.95 (*0-941008-62-2*) Tops Learning.
Felloney, Nanette. Meet Me on the Mayflower. (Illus.). 21p. (gr. 3 up). 1992. pap. 3.95 (*1-882684-00-1*) True Tales.
Fellows, Bob. Easily Fooled: New Insights & Techniques for Resisting Manipulation. rev. ed. Gray, Steve, illus. 64p. (Orig.). (gr. 7 up). 1989. pap. 5.95 (*0-9622879-0-3*) Mind Matters.
Fellows, Marian & Parkhurst, Christine. Script Ease: Manuscript of Calligraphy. Gaus, Helen, illus. 61p. (gr. 2-6). 1982. pap. text ed. 9.95 (*0-317-62675-2*) Kino Pubns.
Felman, Yehudi M. Genital Herpes. Head, J. J., ed. Steffen, Ann T. & Whitely, Derek, illus. LC 84-71142. 16p. (Orig.). (gr. 10 up). 1987. pap. text ed. 2.75 (*0-89278-153-X*, 45-9753) Carolina Biological.
Felsen, Henry G. Boy Gets Car. (Illus.). (gr. 7-11). 1968. lib. bdg. 5.39 (*0-394-90976-3*) Random Bks Yng Read.
—Crash Club. 208p. (gr. 9-12). 1990. pap. 25.00 slipcase, ltd. ed. (*0-917473-06-X*) G P Pub MI.
—Fever Heat. 224p. (gr. 9-12). 1990. pap. 25.00 slipcase, ltd. ed. (*0-917473-09-4*) G P Pub MI.
—Hot Rod. 160p. (gr. 9-12). 1990. pap. 25.00 slipcase, ltd. ed. (*0-917473-11-6*) G P Pub MI.
—Rag Top. 160p. (gr. 9-12). 1990. pap. 25.00 slipcase, ltd. ed. (*0-917473-08-6*) G P Pub MI.
—Road Rocket. 216p. (gr. 9-12). 1990. pap. 25.00 slipcase, ltd. ed. (*0-917473-07-8*) G P Pub MI.
—Street Rod. 160p. (gr. 9-12). 1990. pap. 25.00 slipcase, ltd. ed. (*0-917473-10-8*) G P Pub MI.
Felt, Freddi. My Going to Camp Book. Fredman, Foan, illus. 40p. (gr. 1-6). 1988. 5.95 (*0-9616875-2-5*) F & F Pub.
—My Going to School Book. Fredman, Joan, illus. 48p. (gr. k-3). 1987. pap. 5.95 wkbk. (*0-9616875-1-7*) F & F Pub.
Feltenberger, Myles. Mr. Everybody's Musical Apartment, Bk. 1. Dominiak, Dana M., et al, illus. LC 92-96919. 40p. 1993. pap. 9.95 (*0-9634218-0-8*) Myles Music.
Felts, Shirley, jt. auth. see Bailey, Jill.
Feltwell, John. Butterflies & Moths. LC 92-54313. (Illus.). 64p. (gr. 3 up). 1993. 9.95 (*1-56458-227-2*) Dorling Kindersley.
Fender, Kay. Odette: A Springtime in Paris. Dumas, Philippe, illus. 32p. (ps-3). 1991. 10.95 (*0-916291-33-2*) Kane-Miller Bk.
Fendler, Donn. Lost on a Mountain in Maine. Egan, Joseph, as told to. LC 77-99178. (Illus.). 128p. (gr. 4 up). 1992. pap. 3.95 (*0-688-11573-X*, Pub. by Beech Tree Bks) Morrow.
Fenlon, Peter, ed. see Sochard, Ruth.
Fenlon, Peter, ed. see Staplehurst, Graham.
Fenlon, Peter, ed. see Willner, Carl.
Fenlon, Peter C. Moria. (Illus.). 72p. (gr. 10-12). 1984. 12.00 (*0-915795-27-2*, 2900) Iron Crown Ent Inc.
Fenlon, Peter C. & Colborn, Mark. Lords of Middle-Earth, Vol 1. McBride, Angus, illus. 96p. (Orig.). 1986. pap. 12.00 (*0-915795-26-4*, 8002) Iron Crown Ent Inc.
Fenlon, Peter C., Jr., jt. auth. see McKeage, Jeff.
Fenlon, Peter C., Jr., ed. Lords of Middle-Earth, Vol. 2: The Mannish Races. McBride, Angus, illus. 112p. (Orig.). (gr. 10-12). 1987. pap. 12.00 (*0-915795-32-9*, 8003) Iron Crown Ent Inc.
Fenlon, Peter C., Jr., ed. see Amthor, Terry K.
Fenlon, Peter C., Jr., ed. see Crowdis, John.
Fenlon, Peter C., Jr., ed. see Crutchfield, Charles.
Fenlon, Peter C., Jr., ed. see Crutchfield, Charlie.
Fenlon, Peter C., Jr., ed. see Doty, Randall.
Fenlon, Peter C., Jr., ed. see McKeage, Jeff.
Fenlon, Peter C., Jr., ed. see Morin, John B.
Fenlon, Peter C., Jr., ed. see Sochard, Ruth.
Fenlon, Peter C., Jr., ed. see Staplehurst, Graham.
Fennell, Francis. Addition Skills, Level 3: Rainbow Skill Builders. (ps-3). pap. 2.95 (*0-8431-2503-9*) Price Stern.
Fenner, Carol. Randall's Wall. LC 90-46490. 96p. (gr. 4-7). 1991. SBE 12.95 (*0-689-50518-3*, M K McElderry) Macmillan Child Grp.
—Randall's Wall. 1992. pap. 3.50 (*0-553-48021-9*) Bantam.
—The Skates of Uncle Richard. Forberg, Ati, illus. LC 78-55910. (gr. 2-5). 1978. lib. bdg. 7.99 (*0-394-93553-5*) Random Bks Yng Read.
—A Summer of Horses. LC 88-45878. 144p. (Orig.). (gr. 3-6). 1989. lib. bdg. 7.99 (*0-394-90480-X*); pap. 2.95 (*0-394-80480-5*) Knopf Bks Yng Read.

Fennoy, Thelma R. Kristina & Diabetes: How Kristina Faced the Disease. Durant, Charlotte T., illus. 56p. (Orig.). (gr. 2 up). 1993. pap. text ed. 5.00 (*0-9637350-0-4*) T R Fennoy.
This book is designed for young children, especially those who have diabetes. It depicts real-life episodes in the life of Kristina, a ten-year old diabetic, & gives fresh & personal view of how it feels to have this disease as a young person. This information is both vital & accurate. It explains what happens to the body when diabetes occurs & what role the child can play in coping with the disease. This is a book filled with hope, encouragement & courage. "This book should be very helpful to children who have been recently diagnosed with diabetes."--Carl R. Turner, M.D., F.A.A.P. "I enjoyed reading Mrs. Fennoy's KRISTINA & DIABETES, & I feel that this booklet helps to fill a void in instructive literature for those children affected with juvenile diabetes. I feel that the booklet will be of benefit to both the child & the child's parents."--Peter Pappas, Jr., M.D. KRISTINA & DIABETES-HOW KRISTINA FACED THE DISEASE, Cost $5.00 plus $3.00 shipping & handling. Order from: T.R. Fennoy, Publisher, Route 2, Box 173, Jefferson, TX 75657. *Publisher Provided Annotation.*

Fenske, S. H. My Life in Christ: A Momento of My Confirmation. LC 76-5729. (gr. 8 up). 1976. pap. 2.95 (*0-8100-0056-3*, 16N0514) Northwest Pub.
Fenton, Ann D., jt. auth. see Peterson, Carolyn S.
Fenton, Edward. Duffy's Rocks. (gr. k-12). 1989. pap. 3.25 (*0-440-20242-6*, LFL) Dell.
—The Refugee Summer. LC 81-12593. 272p. (gr. 7 up). 1982. pap. 10.95 (*0-385-28854-9*) Delacorte.
Fenton, Stephen H., jt. auth. see Molnar, Dorothy E.
Fentz, Mike, jt. auth. see Kraft, Jim.
Ferarro, Bonita. Colors & Shapes. Robison, Don, illus. 32p. (Orig.). (ps). 1993. wkbk. 1.99 (*1-56189-058-8*) Amer Educ Pub.
—Letters & Sounds. Robison, Don, illus. 32p. (Orig.). (ps). 1993. wkbk. 1.99 (*1-56189-059-6*) Amer Educ Pub.
—Numbers & Counting. Robison, Don, illus. 32p. (Orig.). (ps). 1993. wkbk. 1.99 (*1-56189-057-X*) Amer Educ Pub.
Ferguson, Alane. Cricket & the Crackerbox Kid. LC 89-39291. 192p. (gr. 3-7). 1990. SBE 14.95 (*0-02-734525-4*, Bradbury Pr) Macmillan Child Grp.
—Cricket & the Crackerbox Kid. 192p. (gr. 5). 1992. pap. 3.50 (*0-380-71341-1*, Camelot) Avon.
—Overkill. LC 92-11426. 176p. (gr. 7 up). 1992. SBE 13.95 (*0-02-734523-8*, Bradbury Pr) Macmillan Child Grp.
—The Practical Joke War. LC 90-45578. 144p. (gr. 3-7). 1991. SBE 12.95 (*0-02-734526-2*, Bradbury Pr) Macmillan Child Grp.
—The Practical Joke War. 96p. (gr. 4-8). 1993. pap. 3.50 (*0-380-71721-2*, Camelot) Avon.
—Show Me the Evidence. LC 88-39203. 160p. (gr. 7 up). 1989. SBE 13.95 (*0-02-734521-1*, Bradbury Pr) Macmillan Child Grp.
—Stardust. LC 92-33011. 160p. (gr. 3-7). 1993. SBE 13.95 (*0-02-734527-0*, Bradbury Pr) Macmillan Child Grp.

Ferguson, David L. Cookbook for Kids: The Kids Can Cook, Too, Cookbook. Ferguson, Jane, ed. Cheney, Glenn L., illus. LC 90-86154. 56p. (Orig.). (gr. 3-6). 1991. cerlox bound 9.95 (0-9628148-0-6) Abigail Pubns.

Ferguson, Don. Disney's Winnie the Pooh's A to Zzzz. Langley, Bill & Wakeman, Diana, illus. LC 91-73812. 32p. 1992. 12.95 (1-56282-015-X) Disney Pr.

Ferguson, Donald L. Journalism Today! 4th ed. 448p. (gr. 9-12). 1993. text ed. 23.95 (0-685-62760-8, C5675-7, Natl Textbk); tchr's. manual, 153p. 10.95 (0-685-62761-6, C5676-5, Natl Textbk); tchr's. resource bk., 3-ring looseleaf vinyl binder, 430p. 79.95 (0-685-62762-4, C5651-X, Natl Textbk); student wkbk., 168p. 6.95 (0-685-62763-2, C5677-3, Natl Textbk); tchr's. ed. wkbk. 14.95 (0-685-62764-0, C5678-1, Natl Textbk) NTC Pub Grp

Ferguson, Donald L. & Patten, Jim. Modern Journalism Workbook. 160p. (gr. 7-12). 1993. pap. 7.95 student wkbk. (0-685-62766-7, C5706-0, Natl Textbk); tchr's. guide 4.95 (0-685-62767-5, C5707-9, Natl Textbk) NTC Pub Grp

Ferguson, Dorothy. A Bunch of Balloons: A Book - Workbook for Grieving Children. Enbody, Shari B., illus. (Orig.). (gr. 1-6). 1992. pap. 5.95 (1-56123-054-5) Centering Corp.

Ferguson, Dwayne. Afro-Bets A B C Coloring & Activity Book. 1989. pap. 3.95 (0-940975-13-0) Just Us Bks.

—Afro-Bets Kids Christmas Fun: An Activity & Coloring Book. Ferguson, Dwayne, illus. LC 92-72003. 48p. (gr. k-3). 1992. pap. 2.95 (0-940975-41-6) Just Us Bks.

—Captain Africa & the Fury of Anubis: The Graphic Novel. Ferguson, Dwayne, illus. 96p. (gr. 4-11). 1993. 29.95 (0-86543-397-6); pap. 9.95 (0-86543-398-4) Africa World.

Ferguson, Dwayne J. Captain Africa: The Battle for Egyptica. Ferguson, Dwayne J., illus. LC 92-78316. 156p. (gr. 7-10). 1992. 24.95 (0-86543-335-6); pap. 9.95 (0-86543-336-4) Africa World.

Ferguson, Elva S. They Carried the Torch: The Story of Oklahoma's Pioneer Newspapers. Griffis, Molly L., ed. Ferguson, Benton, illus. Johnson, Edith, intro. by. LC 89-80347. (Illus.). 84p. (gr. 8 up). 1989. pap. 5.00 (0-9618634-8-X) Levite Apache.

Ferguson-Florissant Early Education Teachers Staff. Home Activities for Fours. Wilson, Marion M., ed. (Illus.). 110p. (Orig.). (ps). 1990. pap. text ed. 15.00 (0-939418-60-6) Ferguson-Florissant.

Ferguson, Gary, jt. auth. see Ferguson, Jane.

Ferguson, Jane & Ferguson, Gary. Narrow Gauge Fun. Kirkeeide, Deborah, illus. 24p. (ps-6). 1987. pap. 1.98 (0-9624846-1-X) J & G Ferguson.

—Sawtooth Mountain Fun. Jenney, David, illus. 24p. (ps-6). 1982. pap. 1.98 (0-9624846-0-1) J & G Ferguson.

Ferguson, Jane, ed. see Ferguson, David L.

Ferguson, Joe. The Deathless White Stallion & Other Tales. Sky Rivers & Eakin, Edwin M., eds. Morris, Aaron, illus. 64p. (gr. 4-6). 1989. 10.95 (0-89015-702-2, Pub. by Panda Bks); pap. 3.95 (0-89015-712-X) Eakin-Sunbelt.

Ferguson, Kathleen M. Musical Mysteries. Melton, Gerald, illus. 144p. (gr. 4-8). 1985. wkbk. 11.95 (0-86653-282-X, GA 684) Good Apple.

Ferguson, Kitty. Black Holes in Space-Time. LC 91-2111. (Illus.). 128p. (gr. 7-9). 1991. PLB 13.40 (0-531-12524-6) Watts.

—Stephen Hawking: Quest for a Theory of the Universe. (Illus.). 240p. (gr. 9-12). 1991. PLB 15.40 (0-531-11067-2) Watts.

Ferguson, Kurt. I Just Got Saved: A Follow-up for Young Converts. (Illus.). 29p. (gr. 2). 1993. coloring bk. 1.25 (0-9635644-0-4) K&C Pubns.

Ferguson, Marvin. Boys on the Gold Coast. 247p. (gr. 7-12). 1993. pap. 9.95 (1-882286-00-6) Parker Pub IL.

Ferguson, Susan Y. Uncle Lester's Lemonade Lure. Ferguson, Susan Y., illus. 15p. (Orig.). 1988. lib. bdg. write for info. (0-9621556-0-8) SYF Enter.

Ferguson, Tom, jt. auth. see Allison, Linda.

Ferguson, Virginia & Durkin, Peter. Autumn Leaves. Swan, Susan, illus. LC 92-34253. 1993. 3.75 (0-383-03615-1) SRA Schl Grp.

—I Went to Visit a Friend One Day. Fleming, Leanne, illus. LC 92-31926. 1993. 4.25 (0-383-03575-9) SRA Schl Grp.

—Waiting. Fleming, Leanne, illus. LC 92-34336. 1993. 3.75 (0-383-03663-1) SRA Schl Grp.

Ferman, Arlene, et al. Better Than Our Best - Women of Valor in American History. (Illus.). 150p. (Orig.). (gr. 6-9). 1990. pap. 9.95 (0-8283-1941-3) Branden Pub Co.

Fern, Eugene. Pepito's Story. Fern, Eugene, illus. LC 90-23639. 52p. (gr. 3-5). 1991. Repr. of 1960 ed. smythe sewn 14.95 (1-878274-04-X) Yarrow Pr.

—Pepito's Story. LC 90-23639. (ps-3). 1993. pap. 4.99 (0-553-37163-0) Bantam.

Fern, Tami L. Project Funny Bone. Himmelstein, Virginia, illus. 40p. (gr. 3-6). 1990. pap. 9.95 (0-936386-56-8) Creative Learning.

Fernandes, Eugenie, illus. One Light, One Sun. 32p. (ps-2). 1988. PLB 9.95 (0-517-56785-7) Crown Bks Yng Read.

Fernandes, Kim. Visiting Granny. Fernandes, Kim, illus. Lacroix, Pat, photos by. (Illus.). 24p. (ps-k). 1990. 12.95 (1-55037-077-4, Pub. by Annick CN); pap. 4.95 (1-55037-084-7, Pub. by Annik CN) Firefly Bks Ltd.

Fernandes, Kim & Lacroix, Pat. Zebo & the Dirty Planet. (ps-1). 1991. 14.95 (1-55037-183-5, Pub. by Annick CN); pap. 4.95 (1-55037-180-0, Pub. by Annick CN) Firefly Bks Ltd.

Fernandez, Brenda. My Life. Iscaro, Nancy L., ed. West Side High School Students, illus. 50p. (Orig.). (gr. 10-12). 1989. pap. text ed. write for info. West Side Pubns.

Fernandez, Joaquin, tr. see George, Jean C.

Fernandez, Jose B. Jose de San Martin: Latin America's Quiet Hero. LC 93-9735. (Illus.). 32p. (gr. 2-4). 1994. PLB 12.40 (1-56294-383-9) Millbrook Pr.

Fernyhough, Frances, jt. auth. see Richards, Elspeth.

Ferraris, L. E. The Adventures of Kitten & Pachyderm. 1992. 11.95 (0-533-10132-8) Vantage.

Ferraro, Bonita. Saving Our Planet. Robinson, Don, illus. 40p. (gr. 3). 1991. wkbk. 3.95 (1-561894-03-6) Amer Educ Pub.

—Saving Our Planet. Robinson, Don, illus. 40p. (gr. 2). 1991. wkbk. 3.95 (1-561894-02-8) Amer Educ Pub.

—Saving Our Planet. Robinson, Don, illus. 40p. (gr. 1). 1991. wkbk. 3.95 (1-561894-01-X) Amer Educ Pub.

Ferrell, John M. Playing Flag Football. 32p. (gr. 1-6). 1983. pap. 3.00 (0-88035-052-0, 3029, Pub. by YMCA USA) Human Kinetics.

Ferrell, Keith. George Orwell: The Political Pen. LC 84-25932. 192p. (gr. 7 up). 1984. 11.95 (0-87131-444-4) M Evans.

Ferrell, Nancy W. The U. S. Air Force. (Illus.). 72p. (gr. 5 up). 1990. PLB 22.95 (0-8225-1433-8) Lerner Pubns.

—The U. S. Coast Guard. (Illus.). 72p. (gr. 5 up). 1989. 22.95 (0-8225-1431-1) Lerner Pubns.

Ferrell, Robert, intro. by see Simons, Frank D.

Ferrer, Gabriel, jt. auth. see Boone, Debby.

Ferrier, Lucy. Diving the Great Barrier Reef. new ed. LC 75-23411. (Illus.). 32p. (gr. 5-10). 1976. PLB 10.79 (0-89375-005-0) Troll Assocs.

Ferris, Helen, ed. Favorite Poems Old & New. Weisgard, Leonard, illus. LC 57-11418. 598p. (gr. 3-7). 1957. pap. 19.95 (0-385-07696-7) Doubleday.

Ferris, Jean. Across the Grain. 212p. 1990. 15.00 (0-374-30030-5) FS&G.

—Across the Grain. (ps-3). 1993. pap. 3.95 (0-374-40057-1) FS&G.

—Invincible Summer. 176p. (gr. 7 up). 1989. pap. 3.50 (0-380-70619-9, Flare) Avon.

—Looking for Home. 176p. (gr. 8 up). 1989. 15.00 (0-374-34649-6) FS&G.

—Looking for Home. 1993. pap. 3.95 (0-374-44566-4) FS&G.

—Relative Strangers. 1993. 16.00 (0-374-36243-2) FS&G.

—The Stainless Steel Rule. LC 85-45731. 192p. (gr. 7 up). 1986. 15.00 (0-374-37212-8) FS&G.

Ferris, Jeri. Arctic Explorer: The Story of Matthew Henson. (Illus.). 80p. (gr. 3-6). 1989. PLB 17.50 (0-87614-370-2); pap. 5.95 (0-87614-507-1) Carolrhoda Bks.

—Go Free or Die: A Story about Harriet Tubman. Ritz, Karen, illus. 64p. (gr. 3-6). 1988. lib. bdg. 14.95 (0-87614-147-5) Carolrhoda Bks.

—Go Free or Die: A Story about Harriet Tubman. Ritz, Karen, illus. 64p. (gr. 3-6). 1989. pap. 5.95 (0-87614-504-7, First Ave Edns) Lerner Pubns.

—Native American Doctor: The Story of Susan LaFlesche Picotte. (Illus.). 80p. (gr. 3-6). 1991. PLB 17.50 (0-87614-443-1) Carolrhoda Bks.

—Native American Doctor: The Story of Susan Laflesche Picotte. (gr. 4-7). 1991. pap. 6.95 (0-87614-548-9) Carolrhoda Bks.

—Walking the Road to Freedom: A Story about Sojourner Truth. Hanson, Peter E., illus. 64p. (gr. 3-6). 1988. lib. bdg. 14.95 (0-87614-318-4) Carolrhoda Bks.

—Walking the Road to Freedom: A Story about Sojourner Truth. Hanson, Peter E., illus. 64p. (gr. 3-6). 1989. pap. 5.95 (0-87614-505-5, First Ave Edns) Lerner Pubns.

—What Are You Figuring Now? A Story about Benjamin Banneker. Johnson, Amy, illus. LC 88-7267. 56p. (gr. 3-6). 1988. PLB 14.95 (0-87614-331-1); pap. 4.95 (0-685-19616-X) Carolrhoda Bks.

—What Are You Figuring Now? A Story about Benjamin Banneker. Johnson, Amy, illus. 64p. (gr. 3-6). Repr. of 1988 ed. 4.95 (0-87614-521-7) Carolrhoda Bks.

—What Do You Mean? A Story about Noah Webster. Michaels, Steve, illus. 56p. (gr. 3-6). 1988. PLB 14.95 (0-87614-330-3) Carolrhoda Bks.

—What I Had Was Singing: The Story of Marian Anderson. LC 93-28502. (gr. 4 up). Date not set. 17.50 (0-87614-818-6) Carolrhoda Bks.

Ferris, Lynn B., retold by. & illus. Goldilocks & the Three Bears. LC 86-46154. 24p. (gr. k up). 1987. 9.95 (0-394-55882-0) Knopf Bks Yng Read.

Ferris, Lynn B., illus. A Classic Treasury of Christmas. 48p. 1991. 13.95 (0-8249-8524-9, Ideals Child); incl. cassette 17.95 (0-8249-7453-0) Hambleton-Hill.

Ferris, Sean. Children of the Great Muskeg. (Illus.). 84p. (gr. 3-5). 1991. pap. 12.95 (0-88753-128-8, Pub. by Black Moss Pr CN) Firefly Bks Ltd.

Ferriss, Lloyd. Secrets of a Mountain. Jack, Susan, ed. Sakaka, Donna, illus. 76p. (Orig.). (gr. 4-10). 1982. pap. 3.95 (0-930096-18-5) G Gannett.

Ferroa, Peggy. China. LC 91-15865. (Illus.). 128p. (gr. 5-9). 1991. PLB 21.95 (1-85435-399-3) Marshall Cavendish.

Ferroli, Stephen J. Disciple of a Master (How to Hit a Baseball to Your Potential) Dickenson, Ken, illus. 200p. (Orig.). (gr. 7-12). 1986. pap. 9.95 (0-939905-00-0) Line Drive.

Ferrone, John M. Ghost Warriors. Ney, Jessica, ed. McBride, Angus & Danforth, Liz, illus. (Orig.). (gr. 12). 1990. pap. 10.00 (1-55806-107-X, 8016) Iron Crown Ent Inc.

Ferry, Charles. Binge. LC 92-93408. 94p. (Orig.). (gr. 7 up). 1992. pap. 8.95 (0-9632799-0-4) DaisyHill Pr.
"A VITALLY IMPORTANT BOOK... This is an incredibly powerful, mesmerizing, tragic, read-in-one-sitting little book with an authenticity & understanding rare in adolescent literature...It pulls no punches, offers no pat endings, just describes a kid mired in his own alcohol denial...It is an absolutely superb book, highly readable, & relentlessly constructed to make its point, without being a tract... We have needed a book like this for a very long time."--Mary K. Chelton, VOYA (Voice of Youth Advocates). *Publisher Provided Annotation.*

—Raspberry One. LC 82-25476. 224p. (gr. 7 up). 1983. 13.45 (0-395-34069-1) HM.

Fersen-Osten, Renee. Don't They Know the World Stopped Breathing? Reminiscences of a Child During the Holocaust Years. 280p. (gr. 5-8). 1990. 16.95 (1-56171-019-9) Shapolsky Pubs.

Fetterolf, Michele, ed. Internships, 1994: On-the-Job Training Opportunities for Students & Adults. 14th ed. 460p. 1993. pap. 29.95 (1-56079-286-8) Petersons Guides.

—Summer Jobs, 1994. 43rd ed. 310p. 1993. pap. 15.95 (1-56079-280-9) Petersons Guides.

Fetterolf, Michele & Colton, Kitty, eds. Peterson's Guide to Vocational & Technical Schools East: Accredited Institutions Offering Career Training Programs. 936p. 1993. pap. 34.95 (1-56079-261-2) Petersons Guides.

—Peterson's Guide to Vocational & Technical Schools West: Accredited Institutions Offering Career Training Programs. 528p. 1993. pap. 34.95 (1-56079-262-0) Petersons Guides.

Fetterolf, Michele, jt. auth. see Schneider, Terry.

Fettig, Art. The Pos Activity Book. Carpenter, Joe, illus. LC 86-83237. 48p. (gr. k-7). 1984. pap. 5.95 (0-9601334-5-3) Growth Unltd.

—The Pos Just Say "Yes" Activity Book. LC 86-83236. (Illus.). 64p. (gr. k-7). 1987. pap. 5.95 (0-916927-06-7) Growth Unltd.

—Remembering. LC 81-90188. (Illus.). (gr. k-7). 1982. pap. 3.95 (0-9601334-2-9) Growth Unltd.

—The Three Robots Discover Their Pos-Abilities: A Lesson in Goal Setting. Carpenter, Joe, illus. LC 84-81461. (gr. k-7). 1984. pap. 3.95 (0-916927-00-8) Growth Unltd.

—The Three Robots Find a Grandpa. Carpenter, Joe, illus. LC 84-80378. 96p. (Orig.). (gr. k-7). 1984. pap. 3.95 (0-9601334-8-8); cassette incl. Growth Unltd.

—The Three Robots Learn about Drugs. Carpenter, Joe, illus. LC 86-83041. 96p. (gr. k-7). 1987. pap. 3.95 (0-916927-04-0) Growth Unltd.

Fetting, Art. The Three Robots & the Sandstorm. LC 82-90993. (Illus.). 96p. (gr. k-7). 1983. pap. 3.95 (0-9601334-3-7) Growth Unltd.

Fettke, Tom & Rebuck, Linda. Miracle after Miracle. Date not set. 4.50 (0-685-68201-3, BCMB-505); cassette 9.98 (0-685-68202-1, BCTA-9032C) Lillenas.

Fettke, Tom, jt. auth. see Rebuck, Linda.

Feuer, Elizabeth. One Friend to Another. LC 87-45363. 192p. (gr. 6 up). 1987. 15.00 (0-374-35642-4) FS&G.

Feund, Chanie. Read Me Berashis. Leff, Tora, illus. LC 90-83948. 32p. (ps-2). 1990. 9.95 (0-685-46905-0) CIS Comm.

Few, Roger. Macmillan Animal Encyclopedia for Children. LC 91-3982. (Illus.). 120p. (gr. 2 up). 1991. 16.95 (0-02-762425-0, Macmillan Child Bks) Macmillan Child Grp.

—Macmillan Children's Guide to Endangered Animals. Pringle, Laurence, frwd. by. LC 92-41433. (Illus.). 96p. (gr. 2 up). 1993. SBE 17.95 (0-02-734545-9, Macmillan Child Bk) Macmillan Child Grp.

Fiarotta, Noel & Fiarotta, Phyllis. Music Crafts for Kids: The How-to Book of Music Dicovery. LC 93-24114. (Illus.). 160p. (gr. 3 up). 1993. 17.95 (0-8069-0406-2) Sterling.

Fiarotta, Noel, jt. auth. see Fiarotta, Phyllis.

Fiarotta, Phyllis. Snips & Snails & Walnut Whales. LC 75-9574. (Illus.). 288p. (gr. 1-5). 1975. pap. 8.95 (0-911104-49-6, 065) Workman Pub.

—Sticks & Stones & Ice Cream Cones. LC 74-160843. (Illus.). 322p. (gr. 1-5). 1973. pap. 10.95 (0-911104-30-5, 011) Workman Pub.

Fiarotta, Phyllis & Fiarotta, Noel. Cups & Cans & Paper Plate Fans: Craft Projects from Recycled Materials. (Illus.). 200p. (gr. 2 up). 1993. pap. 9.95 (0-8069-8529-1) Sterling.

—Cups, Cans & Paper Plate Fans. LC 91-41825. (Illus.). 192p. (gr. 9-12). 1992. 19.95 (*0-8069-8528-3*) Sterling.

Fiarotta, Phyllis, jt. auth. see Fiarotta, Noel.

Fichter, George S. American Indian Music & Musical Instruments. (gr. 5-10). 1978. 8.95 (*0-679-20443-1*) McKay.

—Bees, Wasps, & Ants. Kest, Kristin, illus. 36p. (gr. k-3). 1993. 4.95 (*0-307-11434-1*, 11434, Golden Pr) Western Pub.

—Butterflies & Moths. Kest, Kristin, illus. 36p. (gr. k-3). 1993. 4.95 (*0-307-11435-X*, 11435, Golden Pr) Western Pub.

—First Steamboat down the Mississippi. Boddy, Joe, illus. LC 88-30308. 112p. (gr. 4-6). 1989. 9.95 (*0-88289-715-2*) Pelican.

—Floridians All. Cardin, George, illus. LC 91-9858. 96p. (ps-8). 1991. 15.95 (*0-88289-804-3*) Pelican.

—Insect Pests. Strekalovsky, Nicholas, illus. (gr. 5 up). 1966. pap. write for info. (*0-307-24016-9*, Golden Pr.) Western Pub.

—Poisonous Animals. LC 91-3794. (Illus.). 64p. (gr. 5-8). 1991. PLB 12.90 (*0-531-20050-7*) Watts.

—Snakes & Lizards: A Golden Junior Guide. (ps-3). 1993. 4.95 (*0-307-11432-5*, Golden Pr) Western Pub.

—Starfish, Seashells, & Crabs. Sandstrom, George, illus. 36p. (gr. k-3). 1993. 4.95 (*0-307-11430-9*, 11430, Golden Pr) Western Pub.

—Turtles, Toads, & Frogs. Ambler, Barbara H., illus. 36p. (gr. k-3). 1993. 4.95 (*0-307-11433-3*, 11433, Golden Pr) Western Pub.

—Whales & Other Marine Mammals. 1990. pap. write for info. (*0-307-24075-4*) Western Pub.

Fichter, George S., ed. see Brockman, C. Frank.

Fichter, George S., ed. see Levi, Herbert W. & Levi, Lorna R.

Ficklin, Dora, tr. see Evans, Jo & Moore, Jo E.

Ficklin, Dora, tr. see Evans, Joy & Moore, Jo E.

Ficklin, Dora, tr. see Moore, Jo E. & Evans, Joy.

Fidanque, Ann, et al. MECC Keyboard Success: Keyboard Primer Version. 131p. (Orig.). (gr. 3-8). 1987. pap. 25.00 tchr.'s guide (*0-924667-37-0*) Intl Society Tech Educ.

—PAWS Keyboard Success: PAWS Microtype Version. 135p. (Orig.). (gr. 3-8). 1987. pap. 25.00 (*0-924667-36-2*) Intl Society Tech Educ.

Fiday, Beverly. Patience. Rigo, Christina L., illus. LC 86-12984. 32p. (gr. k-3). 1986. PLB 21.35 (*0-89565-358-3*); PLB 14.95s.p. (*0-685-55833-9*) Childs World.

Fiday, Beverly & Crowdy, Deborah. Respect. Hutton, Kathryn, illus. LC 87-36981. 32p. (gr. k-3). 1988. PLB 21.35 (*0-89565-417-2*); PLB 14.95s.p. (*0-685-55932-7*) Childs World.

Fiday, Beverly & Fiday, David. Time to Go. Allen, Thomas B., illus. 30p. (ps-3). 1990. 14.95 (*0-15-200608-7*) HarBrace.

Fiday, David, jt. auth. see Fiday, Beverly.

Fidell, David. More Silly Signs. 1992. pap. 1.95 (*0-590-44837-4*) Scholastic Inc.

Fidler, Kathleen. The Desperate Journey. (Illus.). 158p. (gr. 5-8). 1989. pap. 6.95 (*0-86241-056-8*, Pub. by Cnngt Pub Ltd) Trafalgar.

—Flash the Sheepdog. (Illus.). 164p. (gr. 5-8). 1989. pap. 6.95 (*0-86241-071-1*, Pub. by Cnngt Pub Ltd) Trafalgar.

—Haki the Shetland Pony. 142p. (gr. 5-8). 1989. pap. 6.95 (*0-86241-075-4*, Pub. by Cnngt Pub Ltd) Trafalgar.

—Turk the Border Collie. 160p. (gr. 5-7). 1989. pap. 6.95 (*0-86241-130-0*, Pub. by Cnngt Pub Ltd) Trafalgar.

Fiedler, Hal, jt. auth. see Fiedler, Jean.

Fiedler, Jean & Fiedler, Hal. Be Smart about Sex: Facts for Young People. LC 89-7919. (Illus.). 128p. (gr. 6 up). 1990. lib. bdg. 17.95 (*0-89490-168-0*) Enslow Pubs.

Field, Arthur W. Cisco & the Twin Foals. Cosgrove, Colleen B., illus. LC 83-61713. 160p. (gr. 8 up). 1983. 12.00 (*0-935356-06-1*) Mills Pub Co.

Field, Elliot, jt. auth. see Field, Mary.

Field, Eugene. Dibdin's Ghost. 1992. Repr. of 1893 ed. lib. bdg. 75.00 (*0-7812-2649-X*) Rprt Serv.

—The Gingham Dog & the Calico Cat. Street, Janet, illus. 32p. 1990. 14.95 (*0-399-22151-4*, Philomel Bks) Putnam Pub Group.

—The Gingham Dog & the Calico Cat. Street, Janet, illus. 32p. (ps up). 1993. pap. 5.95 (*0-399-22517-X*, Philomel Bks) Putnam Pub Group.

—A Little Book of Western Verse. 1992. Repr. of 1889 ed. lib. bdg. 75.00 (*0-7812-2642-2*) Rprt Serv.

—Love Songs of Children. 1992. Repr. of 1894 ed. lib. bdg. 75.00 (*0-7812-2645-7*) Rprt Serv.

—Lullaby Land. 1992. Repr. of 1897 ed. lib. bdg. 75.00 (*0-7812-2646-5*) Rprt Serv.

—Poems of Childhood. (Illus.). (gr. 4 up). 1969. pap. 2.95 (*0-8049-0211-9*, CL-211) Airmont.

—Second Book of Verse. 1992. Repr. of 1892 ed. lib. bdg. 75.00 (*0-7812-2644-9*) Rprt Serv.

—Wynken, Blynken & Nod. Jeffers, Susan, illus. LC 82-2434. 32p. (ps-1). 1982. 13.50 (*0-525-44022-4*, DCB) Dutton Child Bks.

—Wynken, Blynken, & Nod. Beckett, Sheilah, illus. 18p. (ps). 1986. 3.95 (*0-448-10225-0*, G&D) Putnam Pub Group.

—Wynken, Blynken & Nod. Hague, Michael. 1989. pap. 2.95 (*0-590-42422-X*) Scholastic Inc.

—Wynken, Blynken & Nod. Looney, Barbara, illus. 32p. 1991. Repr. of 1964 ed. 9.95 (*0-8038-9333-7*) Hastings.

—Wynken, Blynken, & Nod. 1993. pap. 28.67 (*0-590-71588-7*) Scholastic Inc.

Field, Mary & Elliot. A Loving Guide to the World As a Two Year-Old Says It. Taklender, Sharon, illus. 14p. (Orig.). (ps up). 1983. pap. 5.95 (*0-914445-00-6*) Palm Springs Pub.

Field, Mary B. All about Divorce. Forbes, Alex, illus. Shapiro, Lawrence, intro. by. (Illus.). 150p. (Orig.). (gr. k-6). 1992. pap. 16.95 (*1-882732-00-6*) Ctr Applied Psy.

Field, Nancy & Karasov, Corliss. Discovering Wolves. Hunkel, Cary, illus. 40p. (Orig.). (gr. 3-6). 1991. pap. 4.95 (*0-941042-10-3*) Dog Eared Pubns.

Field, Nancy & Machlas, Sally. Discovering Endangered Species. (Illus.). 40p. (Orig.). (gr. 3-6). 1990. pap. 3.95 (*0-941042-09-X*) Dog Eared Pubns.
This book is part of the NATURE DISCOVERY LIBRARY, a series designed to involve children's minds in learning about the natural world & environmental problems. The authors seek to hook children on science & help them grow up with an environmental ethic. Written by science educators & based on current research, they are reviewed prior to publication by notable scientists. These interactive books enhance learning retention for children in grades 3 to 6, adaptable to other grade levels. All softbound, 8 1/2 x 11", books are printed on recycled paper. Series titles at $3.95: DISCOVERING... * ENDANGERED SPECIES (ISBN 0-941042-09-X); * MARINE MAMMALS (ISBN 0-941042-06-5); * SALMON (ISBN 0-941042-05-7); * NORTHWEST VOLCANOES (ISBN 0-941042-03-2); * CRATER LAKE (ISBN 0-941042-08-1); * MOUNT RANIER, revised (ISBN 0-941042-13-8; * SEATTLE AQUARIUM (ISBN 0-941042-07-3). At $4.95: * DISCOVERING WOLVES (ISBN 0-941042-10-3); * NEW EARLY IN 1994: - ANCIENT FORESTS (ISBN 0-941042-14-6); - DISCOVERING EARTHQUAKES (ISBN 0-941042-11-1); NATURE DISCOVERY LIBRARY (for all above books) $42.50 (ISBN 0-941042-15-4). Contact: Dog-Eared Publications, P.O. Box 620863, Middleton, WI 53562, Phone & FAX (608) 831-1410.
Publisher Provided Annotation.

Field, Nancy & Machlis, Sally. Discovering Crater Lake. Machlis, Sally, illus. 32p. (Orig.). (gr. 1-6). 1989. pap. 3.50 (*0-941042-08-1*) Dog Eared Pubns.

—Discovering Marine Mammals. (Illus.). 32p. (Orig.). (gr. 1-6). 1987. pap. 3.50 (*0-941042-06-5*) Dog Eared Pubns.

—Discovering Mount Rainier. Machlis, Sally, illus. 28p. (Orig.). (gr. 1-6). 1980. pap. 3.50 (*0-941042-02-2*) Dog Eared Pubns.

—Discovering Northwest Volcanoes. rev. ed. Machlis, Sally, illus. 32p. (gr. 2-6). 1980. pap. 3.50 (*0-941042-03-0*) Dog Eared Pubns.

—Discovering Salmon. Machlis, Sally, illus. 32p. (Orig.). (gr. k-6). 1984. pap. 3.50 (*0-941042-05-7*) Dog Eared Pubns.

—Discovery Book for the Seattle Aquarium. rev. & abr. ed. Machlis, Sally, illus. 32p. (gr. 1-6). 1987. pap. 3.50 (*0-941042-07-3*) Dog Eared Pubns.

Field, Nancy & Maehlis, Sally. Discovering Mount Rainier. rev. ed. Maehlis, Sally, illus. 32p. (gr. 1-6). 1992. pap. 3.95 (*0-941042-13-8*) Dog Eared Pubns.

Field, Nancy & Schepige, Adele. Discovering Earthquakes. Gillham, Andrew, illus. 40p. (Orig.). (gr. 3-6). 1994. pap. 4.95 Dog Eared Pubns.

Field, Nancy, et al. Ancient Forests. Torvik, Sharon, illus. 40p. (Orig.). (gr. 3-6). 1994. pap. 4.95 (*0-941042-14-6*) Dog Eared Pubns.

—Nature Discovery Library. Machlis, Sally & Torvik, Sharon, illus. (gr. 3-6). 1990. Set. pap. text ed. 42.50 (*0-941042-15-4*) Dog Eared Pubns.

The **NATURE DISCOVERY LIBRARY is a series designed to involve children's minds in learning about the natural world & environmental problems. The authors seek to hook children on science & help them grow up with an environmental ethic. Written by science educators & based on current research, they are reviewed prior to publication by notable scientists. These interactive books enhance learning retention for children grades 3 to 6, adaptable to other grade levels. All softbound, 8 1/2 X 11", books are printed on recycled paper. SERIES TITLES AT $3.95: DISCOVERING... * ENDANGERED SPECIES (ISBN 0-941042-09-X); * MARINE MAMMALS (ISBN 0-941042-06-5); * SALMON (ISBN 0-941042-05-7); * NORTHWEST VOLCANOES (ISBN 0-941042-05-7); * CRATER LAKE (ISBN 0-941042-08-1); * MOUNT RANIER, revised, (ISBN 0-941042-13-8); * SEATTLE AQUARIUM (ISBN 0-941042-07-3). AT $4.95: * DISCOVERING WOLVES (0-941042-10-3); * New early in 1994: - ANCIENT FORESTS (ISBN 0-941042-14-6); - DISCOVERING EARTHQUAKES (ISBN 0-941042-11-1); NATURE DISCOVERY LIBRARY (for all above books) $2.50 (ISBN 0-941042-15-4). Contact: Dog-Eared Publications, P.O. Box 620863, Middleton, WI 53562, Phone & FAX (608) 831-1410.**
Publisher Provided Annotation.

Field, Rachael. Calico Bush. (gr. 4-8). 1988. pap. 3.50 (*0-440-40100-3*, YB) Dell.

Field, Rachel. Calico Bush. reissued ed. Lewis, Allen, illus. LC 66-19095. 224p. (gr. 5-9). 1987. SBE 14.95 (*0-02-734610-2*, Macmillan Child Bk) Macmillan Child Grp.

—Calico Bush. 1990. pap. 3.50 (*0-440-40368-5*, Pub. by Yearling Classics) Dell.

—General Store. Parker, Nancy W., illus. LC 87-21641. 24p. (ps-1). 1988. 11.95 (*0-688-07353-0*); lib. bdg. 11. 88 (*0-688-07354-9*) Greenwillow.

—General Store. Laroche, Giles, illus. LC 87-37218. (ps-3). 1988. 15.95 (*0-316-28163-8*) Little.

—Hitty: Her First Hundred Years. Lathrop, Dorothy P., illus. LC 29-22704. 208p. (gr. 4-6). 1969. SBE 14.95 (*0-02-734840-7*, Macmillan Child Bk) Macmillan Child Grp.

—Hitty, Her First Hundred Years. (gr. k-6). 1990. pap. 3.95 (*0-440-40307-5*, YB) Dell.

—If Once You Have Slept on an Island. 32p. (ps-3). 1993. 14.95 (*1-56397-106-2*) Boyds Mills Pr.

—Prayer for a Child. Jones, Elizabeth O., illus. LC 44-47191. 32p. (ps-1). 1968. SBE 11.95 (*0-02-735190-4*, Macmillan Child Bk) Macmillan Child Grp.

—Prayer for a Child. Jones, Elizabeth O., illus. LC 84-70991. 32p. (ps-k). 1984. pap. 3.95 (*0-02-043070-1*, Aladdin) Macmillan Child Grp.

—Road Might Lead to Anywhere, Vol. 1. LC 89-32815. (ps-3). 1990. 14.95 (*0-316-28178-6*) Little.

Field, Sally. Career Opportunities in Theater & the Performing Arts. 240p. (gr. 9-12). 1993. 27.50 (*0-8160-2580-0*); pap. 14.95 (*0-8160-2579-7*) Facts on File.

Field, Shelly. Career Opportunities in the Sports Industry. 264p. (gr. 9-12). 1992. pap. 14.95 (*0-8160-2672-6*) Facts on File.

—Careers As an Animal Rights Activist. Rosen, Ruth, ed. (gr. 7-12). 1993. PLB 13.95 (*0-8239-1465-8*); pap. 9.95 (*0-8239-1722-3*) Rosen Group.

Field, Shirley. Fire! 128p. (gr. 7-10). 1990. pap. 4.99 (*0-7459-1851-4*) Lion USA.

Field, Susan. The Sun, the Moon, & the Silver Baboon. Field, Susan, illus. LC 92-44496. 32p. (ps-2). 1993. 14. 00 (*0-06-022990-X*); PLB 13.89 (*0-06-022991-8*) HarpC Child Bks.

Field, William T., Jr., jt. auth. see Martinello, Marian.

Field Drake, Christin. The Sleepy Baker: A Collection of Stories & Recipes for Children. Eldridge, Alexandra, illus. LC 92-56509. 56p. (gr. k-5). 1993. 14.95 (*0-87358-551-8*) Northland AZ.

Fielding, Ann, jt. auth. see Feeney, Stephanie.

Fielding, Henry. Joseph Andrews. Battestin, Martin C., ed. Bd. with Shamela. LC 61-16166. (gr. 9up). 1961. pap. 9.16 (*0-395-05150-9*, RivEd) HM.

—Tom Jones. Rowland, B., intro. by. (gr. 11 up). 1967. pap. 2.50 (0-8049-0135-X, CL-135) Airmont.
Fielding, Joy. Good Intentions. 336p. 1993. pap. 4.99 (0-451-40230-8, Onyx) NAL-Dutton.
Fields, Doug. If Life Is a Piece of Cake, Why Am I Still Hungry? (Orig.). (gr. 7-9). 1989. pap. 5.99 (0-89081-718-9) Harvest Hse.
Fields, Frever. Frumpy McDoogle: The Boy Who Made a Poem. 32p. (gr. 1-3). 1992. 12.95 (0-9632675-0-7) Kimberlite.

Fields, Harriette. Phonics for the New Reader: Step-by-Step. Cox, Anne, illus. LC 90-70334. 128p. (Orig.). (ps-2). 1991. 17.95x (0-9625802-0-1); pap. 8.95 (0-9625802-1-X) Words Pub CO. "The author provides a ready-to-use blueprint for helping young children understand phonics & provides the necessary tools for that understanding," says former President of the National Association of State Boards of Education, Roseann Bentley. "This book provides clear, well-organized directions," & "I think this would be an excellent book for people striving to learn English as a second language." TABLE OF CONTENTS: Lesson 1-Letter Names, Shapes & Sounds; Lesson 2- Short Vowels; Lesson 3-Long Vowels; Lesson 4- Special Words & Letters; Lesson 5- Reading Consonant Combinations; Lesson 6-Reading Vowel Combinations; Lesson 7- Special Vowel Combinations; Lesson 8- Reading Vowel-Consonant Combinations. *Publisher Provided Annotation.*

Fields, Harvey J. A Torah Commentary for Our Times, Vol. 2: Exodus & Leviticus. Carmi, Giora, illus. LC 89-28478. (gr. 7-9). 1991. pap. text ed. 12.00x (0-8074-0334-2, 164010) UAHC.
—A Torah Commentary for Our Times, Vol. 3: Numbers & Deuteronomy. Cormi, Giora, illus. & 89-28478. (Orig.). (gr. 7-9). 1993. pap. text ed. 12.00x (0-8074-0511-6, 164020) UAHC.
Fields, Harvey J., ed. A Torah Commentary for Our Times: Genesis, Vol. I. Carmi, Giora, illus. LC 89-28478. (gr. 7 up). 1990. pap. text ed. 12.00 (0-8074-0308-3, 164000) UAHC.
Fields, Julia. The Green Lion of Zion Street. Pinkney, Jerry, illus. LC 87-15519. 32p. (gr. k-4). 1988. SBE 14.95 (0-689-50414-4, M K McElderry) Macmillan Child Grp.
—The Green Lion of Zion Street. Pinkney, Jerry, illus. LC 92-24571. 32p. (gr. k-3). 1993. pap. 4.95 (0-689-71693-1, Aladdin) Macmillan Child Grp.
Fields, Richard L. Haiku Animal World. Lam, Fahn, illus. 80p. (Orig.). (gr. 6-12). 1989. pap. 7.95 (0-927256-00-2) ELF Assocs.
—Haiku Fin & Fathom World. (Illus.). 86p. (Orig.). (gr. 6-12). 1989. pap. 7.95 (0-317-93460-0) ELF Assocs.
—Haiku Wing & Feather World. (Illus.). 108p. (Orig.). (gr. 6-12). 1989. pap. 7.95 (0-317-93461-9) ELF Assocs.
—Haiku Zing & Sting World. (Illus.). 70p. (Orig.). (gr. 6-12). 1989. pap. 7.95 (0-317-93459-7) ELF Assocs.
Fields, Sadie. Whose Coat? Hawcock, David, illus. 10p. (ps). 1993. pap. 4.95 (0-671-79163-X, Little Simon) S&S Trade.
—Whose Home? Hawcock, David, illus. 10p. (ps). 1993. pap. 4.95 (0-671-79164-8, Little Simon) S&S Trade.
—Whose Nose? Hawcock, David, illus. 10p. (ps). 1993. pap. 4.95 (0-671-79162-1, Little Simon) S&S Trade.
Fields, Terri. Day the Fifth Grade Disappeared. (gr. 4-7). 1992. pap. 2.95 (0-590-45403-X) Scholastic Inc.
—The Other Me. 160p. (Orig.). (gr. 7-12). 1987. pap. 2.50 (0-553-26196-7) Bantam.
Fienberg, Anna. The Magnificent Nose: And Other Marvels. Gamble, Kim, illus. (ps-3). 1992. 13.95 (0-316-28195-6, Joy Street) Little.
Fierstein, Jeff. Kid Contracts. 32p. (gr. 4-8). 1982. 5.95 (0-86653-091-6, GA 442) Good Apple.
Fife, Dale H. The Empty Lot. Arnosky, Jim, illus. 32p. (gr. k-4). 1991. 14.95 (0-316-28167-0) Sierra.
Fifth Period LEAP & Honors English Classes. The Cure: A World in Distress. Hames, Karen & Martin, Peggy, eds. Arroyo, John, illus. 142p. (Orig.). (gr. 6-8). 1990. pap. 3.00 (0-9623607-9-1) BRAT Pubns.
Figh, Margaret G., jt. auth. see Windham, Kathryn T.
Figtree, Dale. Eat Smart: A Guide to Good Health for Kids. LC 92-4550. 128p. 1992. 10.95 (0-8329-0465-1) New Win Pub.
Figueroa, Mariano. Experience. Figueroa, Mariano, illus. Terry, Sarah, frwd. by. (Illus.). 50p. (Orig.). (gr. 9-12). 1989. pap. text ed. write for info. West Side Pubns.
Filbin, Dan. Arizona. (Illus.). 72p. (gr. 3-6). 1990. PLB 17.50 (0-8225-2705-7) Lerner Pubns.

Filichia, Peter. Girls Can't Do It. 224p. (Orig.). 1990. pap. 2.95 (0-380-75784-2, Flare) Avon.
—The Most Embarrassing Mother in the World. 192p. 1991. pap. 3.50 (0-380-76084-3, Flare) Avon.
—What's in a Name? 224p. (gr. 7 up). 1988. pap. 2.75 (0-380-75536-X, Flare) Avon.
Filisky, Michael. Living Lights: Creatures That Glow in the Dark. Brown-Wing, Katherine, illus. LC 90-27880. 24p. (gr. k-4). 1991. 15.00 (0-517-58162-0); lib. bdg. 15.99 (0-517-58163-9) Crown Bks Yng Read.
Filisky, Michael, jt. auth. see White, Sandra.
Filkins, Vanessa. Early Learning Bulletin Boards. 144p. (ps-2). 1990. 11.95 (0-86653-529-2, GA1141) Good Apple.
—Gifts for Giving. 144p. (gr. k-5). 1991. 11.95 (0-86653-611-6, GA1330) Good Apple.
Fillingham, David, tr. see Brodmann, Aliana.
Fillipo, Patrick R. San see San Fillipo, Patrick R.
Filson, Brent. Famous Experiments & How to Repeat Them. Fuhrmann, Brigita, illus. LC 85-22259. 64p. (gr. 4 up). 1986. lib. bdg. 12.98 (0-671-55687-8, J Messner) S&S Trade.
—Superconductors & Other New Breakthroughs in Science. (Illus.). 128p. (gr. 5-9). 1989. lib. bdg. 13.98 (0-671-65857-3, J Messner); PLB 9.74s.p. (0-685-24680-9) S&S Trade.
Filson, Henry J. Little Hands with First Drawing Practice. (Illus.). 28p. (gr. 10 up). 1978. plasctic bdg. 2.75 (0-918554-01-2) Old Violin.
Filtness, Charles. Play the Game: Chess. (Illus.). 80p. (gr. 10-12). 1991. pap. 6.95 (0-7063-6855-X, Pub. by Ward Lock UK) Sterling.
Fina, James. English Skills by Objectives, Bk. 1. 192p. (gr. 7-9). 1988. pap. text ed. 5.25 (0-8428-0213-4) Cambridge Bk.
—English Skills by Objectives, Bk. 3. 352p. (gr. 7-9). 1988. pap. text ed. write for info. (0-8428-0215-0) Cambridge Bk.

Finch, Carolyn B. Socks Says! Barrows, Jack, illus. 40p. (Orig.). 1993. pap. 8.95 (1-882956-00-1) Bogart Comm. SOCKS SAYS!, another book by Carolyn Finch, professional speaker noted for UNIVERSAL HANDTALK & PORTRAITS OF SOUNDS, has written this poetic plea for a positive self-image. The story narrated by the President Clinton family cat is for ages one to one hundred & one. Cartoon illustrations & calligraphy give uniqueness to this delightful poetic plea for a positive self-image. Cartoon illustrations by artist Jack Barrows make the story come alive. Steve Allen, author, musician, & entertainer writes: "Thank you for permitting me to see a pre-publication copy of your charming book SOCKS SAYS! I plan to take it home this evening & share it with my grandchildren. I'm sure they'll enjoy it as much as I did." The book with black & white drawings is $8.95 or (pkg. B) with Crayola pencils in a zip lock bag for travel, $10.95. The book is available through not-for-profit groups & organizations who need to help themselves & wish to use the books as a fund raiser. This is especially good for schools, hospitals & health care organizations. It is also available in book stores & gift shops. ORDER FROM: Bogart Communications, Inc., 51 Cedar Drive, Danbury CT 06811. 203-792-4833, FAX: 203-794-0945. *Publisher Provided Annotation.*

Finch, Margo. Christmas Cookies. 20p. 1989. bds. 2.95 (0-8167-1892-X) Troll Assocs.
—Christmas Mix-Up. 1989. bds. 2.95 (0-8167-1893-8) Troll Assocs.
Finch, Max. The A, B, C of the Biosphere. 32p. 1993. pap. 7.95 (1-882428-03-X) Biosphere Pr.
Fincher, E. B. Mexico & the United States: Their Linked Destinies. LC 82-45581. (Illus.). 224p. (gr. 7 up). 1983. (Crowell Jr Bks); (Crowell Jr Bks) HarpC Child Bks.
Finck, Lila, jt. auth. see Hayes, John.
Finckel, Edwin A. Now We'll Make the Rafters Ring: Classic & Contemporary Rounds for Everyone. Morice, David, illus. LC 92-43866. 144p. (Orig.). (gr. k-12). 1993. pap. 11.95 (1-55652-186-3) A Cappella Bks.

Findlay, Lois P. The Enchanted Cowboy. Roberts, Anne F., ed. Williams, Exin R., illus. 99p. (Orig.). (gr. 1 up). 1988. pap. 5.00 (0-317-89520-6) Libr Commns Servs.
Findley, Nigel D. Native American Nations: A Shadowrun Sourcebook, Vol. 1. Ippolito, Donna & Mulvihill, Sharon T., eds. Laubenstein, Jeff & Bradstreet, Tim, illus. 136p. (gr. 7 up). 1991. pap. 12.00 (1-55560-130-8, 7202) FASA Corp.
Findly, Ian, jt. auth. see Beasant, Pam.
Fine, Anne. Alias Madame Doubtfire. (gr. 7 up). 1988. 12.95 (0-316-28313-4, Joy Street Bks) Little.
—Alias Madame Doubtfire. (gr. 5 up). 1990. pap. 3.50 (0-553-28189-5, Starfire) Bantam.
—Alias Madame Doubtfire. 1990. pap. 3.99 (0-553-56615-6) Bantam.
—The Book of the Banshee. LC 91-23715. (gr. 7 up). 1992. 13.95 (0-316-28315-0) Little.
—Madame Doubtfire. Pena, Flora, tr. (SPA.). 165p. (gr. 5-8). 1992. pap. write for info. (84-204-4680-7) Santillana.
—My War with Goggle-Eyes. 160p. (gr. 5 up). 1989. 13.95 (0-316-28314-2, Joy St Bks) Little.
—Poor Monty. Vulliamy, Clara, illus. 32p. (ps-1). 1992. 14.45 (0-395-60472-9, Clarion Bks) HM.
—The True Story of Harrowing Farm. Fisher, Cynthia, illus. LC 92-33935. 1993. 12.95 (0-316-28316-9, Joy St Bks) Little.
Fine, Edith & Josephson, Judith. Big on Bugs. 24p. (ps). 1982. 2.95 (0-88160-089-X, LW 128) Learning Wks.
Fine, Edith H. The Python & Anaconda. LC 88-5421. (Illus.). 48p. (gr. 5-6). 1988. RSBE 12.95 (0-89686-391-3, Crestwood Hse) Macmillan Child Grp.
Fine, John C. The Boy & the Dolphin. Weinberger, Jane, ed. Kardas, Aleksander, intro. by. LC 90-70094. (Illus.). 34p. (gr. 4-6). 1990. 15.95 (0-932433-60-X); pap. 9.95 (0-932433-79-0) Windswept Hse.
—Creatures of the Sea. LC 89-34. (Illus.). 32p. (ps-3). 1989. RSBE 14.95 (0-689-31420-5, Atheneum Child Bk) Macmillan Child Grp.
—Free Spirits in the Sky. (Illus.). 32p. (gr. 2-5). 1994. SBE 14.95 (0-689-31705-0, Atheneum Child Bk) Macmillan Child Grp.
—The Hunger Road. Fine, John C., illus. LC 87-27794. 144p. (gr. 5 up). 1988. SBE 13.95 (0-689-31361-6, Atheneum Child Bk) Macmillan Child Grp.
—Oceans in Peril. Fine, John C., illus. LC 86-26546. 128p. (gr. 5 up). 1987. SBE 15.95 (0-689-31328-4, Atheneum Child Bk) Macmillan Child Grp.
—Racket Squad. LC 92-5199. (Illus.). 144p. (gr. 5 up). 1993. SBE 14.95 (0-689-31569-4, Atheneum Child Bk) Macmillan Child Grp.
—Sunken Ships & Treasures. LC 86-3652. (Illus.). 128p. (gr. 3 up). 1987. SBE 16.95 (0-689-31280-6, Atheneum Child Bk) Macmillan Child Grp.
Fine, Judylaine. Afraid to Ask: A Book for Families to Share about Cancer. LC 85-28386. (Illus.). 172p. 1986. pap. 6.95 (0-688-06196-6, Pub. by Beech Tree Bks) Morrow.
Finger, Bill & Schwartz, Alvin. Batman: The Sunday Classics. Kitchen, Dennis, ed. Kane, Bob, et al, illus. Schwartz, Alvin, intro. by. 208p. (Orig.). 1991. pap. 19.95 (0-930289-95-1) DC Comics.
Finger, Charles J. Tales from Silver Lands. Honore, Paul, illus. 225p. (gr. 7 up). 1965. 16.95 (0-685-01496-7) Doubleday.
—Tales from Silver Lands. 1989. pap. 3.25 (0-590-42447-5) Scholastic Inc.
Fingert, Howard J. Cancer Therapy. Head, J. J., ed. Steffen, Ann T., illus. LC 86-72194. 16p. (gr. 10 up). 1987. pap. text ed. 2.75 (0-89278-370-2, 45-9770) Carolina Biological.
Fink, Dale B. Mr. Silver & Mrs. Gold. Chan, Shirley, illus. LC 79-15924. 32p. (ps-3). 1980. 16.95 (0-87705-447-9) Human Sci Pr.
Fink, Joanne, adapted by see Aschenbrenner, Gerald.
Fink, Joanne, ed. see Parker, Steve.
Finke, Blythe F. Aleksandr Solzhenitsyn: Beleaguered Literary Giant of the U. S. S. R. Rahmas, D. Steve, ed. 32p. (gr. 7-12). 1973. lib. bdg. 4.95 incl. catalog cards (0-87157-560-4) SamHar Pr.
—Angela Davis: Traitor or Martyr of the Freedom of Expression? Rahmas, D. Steve, ed. LC 77-190246. 32p. (Orig.). (gr. 7-12). 1972. lib. bdg. 4.95 incl. catalog cards (0-87157-528-0) SamHar Pr.
—Anwar Sadat, Egyptian Ruler & Peace Maker. 32p. (gr. 7-12). 1986. lib. bdg. 4.95 (0-87157-596-5) SamHar Pr.
—Assassination: Case Studies. Rahmas, Sigurd C., ed. 32p. (gr. 7-12). 1982. lib. bdg. 4.95 (0-87157-818-2) SamHar Pr.
—Bernard M. Baruch: Speculator & Statesman. Rahmas, D. Steve, ed. LC 78-190249. 32p. (Orig.). (gr. 7-12). 1972. lib. bdg. 4.95 incl. catalog cards (0-87157-532-9) SamHar Pr.
—Charlie Chaplin: Famous Silent Movie Actor & Comic. Rahmas, D. Steve, ed. LC 7-12. 32p. 1973. lib. bdg. 4.95 incl. catalog cards (0-87157-539-6) SamHar Pr.
—General Patton: Fearless Military Leader. Rahmas, D. Steve, ed. LC 76-190251. 32p. (gr. 7-12). 1972. lib. bdg. 4.95 incl. catalog cards (0-87157-534-5) SamHar Pr.
—Howard R. Hughes: Twentieth Century Multi-Millionaire & Recluse. Rahmas, D. Steve, ed. 32p. (Orig.). (gr. 7-12). 1974. lib. bdg. 4.95 incl. catalog cards (0-87157-569-8) SamHar Pr.

—John Foster Dulles: Master of Brinksmanship & Diplomacy. Ramas, D. Steve, ed. LC 77-185666. 32p. (Orig.). (gr. 7-12). 1972. lib. bdg. 4.95 incl. catalog cards (0-87157-510-8) SamHar Pr.

—Konrad Adenauer: Architect of the New Germany. Rahmas, D. Steve, ed. LC 79-190241. 32p. (Orig.). (gr. 7-12). 1972. lib. bdg. 4.95 incl. catalog cards (0-87157-523-X) SamHar Pr.

—W. C. Fields: Renowned Comedian of the Early Motion Picture Industry. Rahmas, D. Steve, ed. 32p. (Orig.). (gr. 7-12). 1972. lib. bdg. 4.95 incl. catalog cards (0-87157-552-3) SamHar Pr.

Finkel, LeRoy, et al. Microsoft Works Through Applications: IBM PC Version 2.0. LC 90-38911. (Illus.). 352p. (gr. 7 up). 1991. text ed. 27.95 (0-941681-23-8); pap. text ed. 21.95 spiral bdg. (0-941681-18-1); tchr's. ed. 34.95 (0-941681-19-X); 5.25 in. disk 19.95 (0-941681-22-X); tchr's. guide 14.95 (0-941681-24-6) Computer Lit Pr.

—Microsoft Works Through Applications: Macintosh Version 3.0. LC 92-38337. (Illus.). 416p. (gr. 7-12). 1993. text ed. 27.95 (0-941681-38-6); pap. text ed. 21.95 spiral bdg. (0-941681-37-8); tchr's. ed. 34.95 (0-941681-39-4); tchr's. guide 14.95 (0-941681-40-8); 3.5" disk 19.95 (0-941681-41-6) Computer Lit Pr.

Finkelman, S. The Story of Reb Yosef Chaim: The Life & Times of Rabbi Yosef Chaim Sonnefield, the Guardian of Jerusalem. Dershowitz, Y., illus. 160p. (gr. 6-12). 1984. 11.95 (0-89906-779-4); pap. 8.95 (0-89906-780-8) Mesorah Pubns.

Finkelman, Shimon. The Story of Reb Elchonon: The Life of Rabbi Elchonon Wasserman. Dershowitz, Yosef, illus. 160p. (gr. 6-12). 1984. 11.95 (0-89906-770-0); pap. 8.95 (0-89906-771-9) Mesorah Pubns.

—The Story of Reb Nachum'ke: The Nineteenth Century Tzaddik - A Legend in His Time. Dershowitz, Yosef, illus. 144p. (gr. 6-12). 1985. 11.95 (0-89906-781-6); pap. 8.95 (0-89906-782-4) Mesorah Pubns.

—The Story of Reb Yisrael Salanter: The Legendary Founder of the Mussar Movement. Dershowitz, Y., illus. 96p. (gr. 6-12). 1986. 11.95 (0-89906-797-2); pap. 8.95 (0-89906-798-0) Mesorah Pubns.

—The Story of the Sha'agas Aryeh: The Man Behind the Legend. Dershowitz, Yosef, illus. 96p. (gr. 4-12). 1986. 11.95 (0-89906-793-X); pap. 8.95 (0-89906-794-8) Mesorah Pubns.

Finkelstein, Chaim. Cheery Bim Band 1. 204p. 1993. 9.95 (1-56062-189-3) CIS Comm.

—Cheery Bim Band 2: Let's Do It Again. LC 93-72269. 204p. (gr. 5-6). 1993. write for info. (1-56062-209-1) CIS Comm.

Finkelstein, Norman. Captain of Innocence. LC 90-27845. 160p. (gr. 6 up). 1991. 15.95 (0-399-22243-X, Putnam) Putnam Pub Group.

—Douglas MacArthur: The Emperor General: A Biography of Douglas MacArthur. LC 88-22863. (Illus.). 128p. (gr. 5 up). 1989. RSBE 13.95 (0-87518-396-4, Dillon) Macmillan Child Grp.

Finkelstein, Norman H. The Other Fourteen Ninety-Two: Jewish Settlement in the New World. LC 89-6253. (Illus.). 96p. (gr. 5-9). 1989. SBE 13.95 (0-684-18913-5, Scribners Young Read) Macmillan Child Grp.

—The Other Fourteen Ninety-Two: Jewish Settlement in the New World. LC 89-6253. (Illus.). 100p. (gr. 6 up). 1992. pap. 4.95 (0-688-11572-1, Pub. by Beech Tree Bks) Morrow.

—Remember Not to Forget: A Memory of the Holocaust. Hokanson, Lois & Hokanson, Lars, illus. LC 92-24603. 32p. (gr. 2 up). 1993. pap. 4.95 (0-688-11802-X, Mulberry) Morrow.

—Sounds in the Air: The Golden Age of Radio. LC 92-25354. 144p. (gr. 7 up). 1993. SBE 14.95 (0-684-19271-3, Scribners Young Read) Macmillan Child Grp.

Finkelstein, Ruth. Baila Wants a Bicycle Bell. Dinkels, Rochel, illus. 24p. (ps-4). 1992. 8.95 (0-9628157-1-3) Feldheim.

—Do You Know What I'm Going to Be? I'm Going to Be a Yeshiva Bochur. Cohen, Toby M., illus. 16p. (Orig.). (ps-k). 1991. pap. 4.50 (0-9628157-0-5) R Finkelstein.

Finkelstien, Aurohom. Tzvi Tells the Truth. Friedman, Aaron, illus. 64p. 1991. 10.95 (1-56062-094-3) CIS Comm.

Finlay, Alice S. A Gift from the Sea for Laura Lee. 48p. (gr. k-2). 1993. pap. 3.99 (0-310-59871-0, Pub. by Youth Spec) Zondervan.

—Laura Lee & the Little Pine Tree. 48p. (gr. k-2). 1993. pap. 3.99 (0-310-59861-3, Pub. by Youth Spec) Zondervan.

—Laura Lee & the Monster Sea. 48p. (gr. k-2). 1993. pap. 3.99 (0-310-59841-9, Pub. by Youth Spec) Zondervan.

—A Victory for Laura Lee. LC 93-3501. 48p. (gr. k-2). 1993. pap. 3.99 (0-310-59851-6, Pub. by Youth Spec) Zondervan.

Finlay, Winifred. Danger at Black Dyke. (Illus.). (gr. 7-12). 1968. 21.95 (0-87599-150-5) S G Phillips.

Finley, Dean, compiled by. Handbook for Youth Evangelism. LC 88-4350. 240p. (Illus.). (gr. 7-12). 1991. pap. 7.95 (0-8054-6256-2) Broadman.

Finley, Martha. Elsie at Nantucket. 301p. 1981. Repr. PLB 25.95x (0-89966-333-8) Buccaneer Bks.

—Elsie at Nantucket. 302p. 1980. Repr. PLB 17.95x (0-89967-011-3) Harmony Raine.

—Elsie Dinsmore. LC 74-15737. (Illus.). 342p. (gr. 7 up). 1975. Repr. of 1896 ed. 24.00x (0-405-06372-5) Ayer.

—Elsie Dinsmore. 332p. 1987. Repr. PLB 25.95x (0-89966-332-X) Buccaneer Bks.

—Elsie Dinsmore. 332p. 1980. Repr. lib. bdg. 25.95x (0-89967-010-5) Buccaneer Bks.

—Elsie's Children. 243p. 1981. Repr. PLB 25.95x (0-89966-336-2) Buccaneer Bks.

—Elsie's Girlhood. 273p. 1981. Repr. PLB 25.95x (0-89966-334-6) Buccaneer Bks.

—Elsie's Motherhood. 243p. 1981. Repr. PLB 25.95x (0-89966-335-4) Buccaneer Bks.

Finley, Mary Pearce. Soaring Eagle. LC 92-38263. (gr. 6 up). 1993. pap. 14.00 (0-671-75598-6, S&S BFYR) S&S Trade.

Finley, Tom. Ecclesiastes: Survival in the 21st Century. (gr. 9-12). 1989. pap. 6.99 (0-8307-1305-0, S185108) Regal.

—The World Is Not Enough. Parrish, Annette, ed. LC 86-22049. 239p. (Orig.). (gr. 7-12). 1986. pap. 5.99 (0-8307-1151-1, S183329) Regal.

Finn, Donna M., jt. auth. see Finn, Thomas.

Finn, Felicity. Jeremy & the Aunties. 156p. (Orig.). (gr. 5-7). 1992. pap. 6.95 (0-929005-40-6, Pub. by Second Story Pr CN) InBook.

Finn, James K., jt. auth. see Groten, Frank J., Jr.

Finn, Jeffrey. Health Care Delivery. (Illus.). (gr. 6-12). 1993. 18.95 (0-7910-0084-2) Chelsea Hse.

Finn, Jeffrey, jt. auth. see Marshall, Eliot.

Finn, Thomas & Finn, Donna M. Love & Relationships: God's Plan for Human Sexuality. 70p. (Orig.). 1991. facilitator manual 18.95 (0-937997-20-X) Hi-Time Pub.

Finn, Tony. Waterskiboarding - An Illustrated Guide to Learning & Mastering the Sport. Robertson, Jo, ed. LC 88-50675. (Illus.). 113p. (Orig.). 1988. pap. 14.95 (0-944406-04-1) World Pub FL.

Finne, Martha, jt. auth. see Anderson, Deborah.

Finnegan, Thomas J., et al. Mathematics Study Aid. 1975. pap. 2.50 (0-87738-036-8) Youth Ed.

—Metric System Study Aid. 1976. pap. 2.50 (0-87738-042-2) Youth Ed.

Finney Company Staff. Occupational Guidance Series, 5 units. Incl. Unit 1F. 1989 (0-912486-53-8); Unit 2F. 1990; Unit 3F. 1991 (0-912486-56-2); Unit 4F. 1992 (0-912486-57-0); Unit 5F. 1993 (0-912486-68-6). LC 75-20074. (gr. 7 up). Set. 522.50 (0-912486-16-3); 104.50 ea.; index 1.00 ea. Finney Co.

Finney, La Rhue. Things Magical. Finney, La Rhue, illus. 22p. (Orig.). (gr. 2-4). 1992. pap. text ed. 6.95 (0-9635276-0-6) Taffey Apple.

Finney, Shan. Geared for Romance. 192p. (Orig.). (gr. 7-12). 1987. pap. 2.50 (0-553-26902-X) Bantam.

Finney, Susan. The Soviet Union. 64p. (gr. 4-8). 1991. 7.95 (0-86653-580-2, GA1311) Good Apple.

Finney, Susan & Kindle, Patricia. China: Then & Now. 64p. (gr. 4-8). 1988. wkbk. 7.95 (0-86653-458-X, GA1062) Good Apple.

Finney, Susan, jt. auth. see Kindle, Pat.

Finney, Susan, jt. auth. see Kindle, Patricia.

Finnigan, Dave. The Complete Juggler. 2nd, rev. ed. Edwards, Bruce, illus. Strong, Todd, contrib. by. LC 91-61138. (Illus.). 576p. (gr. 9-12). 1991. lib. bdg. 19.95 (0-9615521-1-5); pap. 14.95 (0-9615521-0-7) Jugglebug.

—The Joy of Juggling. rev. ed. Edwards, Bruce, illus. 100p. (gr. 4-9). 1993. pap. 6.00 (0-9615521-3-1, 09001) Jugglebug.

—Scarf Juggling. Edwards, Bruce, illus. 24p. (Orig.). (gr. 2-7). 1991. pap. 7.95 (0-9615521-8-2, 04000) Jugglebug.

Finnigan, Joan. The Dog Who Wouldn't Be Left Behind. Beinicke, Steve, illus. 32p. (ps-2). 1991. 12.95 (0-88899-057-X, Pub. by Groundwood-Douglas & McIntyre CN) Firefly Bks Ltd.

Finocchiaro, Mary, ed. Children's Living Spanish. (Illus.). 1988. manual, incl. cassette 17.95 (0-517-56333-9, Crown); dictionary 5.00 (0-517-56336-3); pap. 5.00 manual (0-517-56335-5) Crown Pub Group.

Finsand, Mary J. The Town That Moved. 1991. pap. 2.99 (0-440-40489-4) Dell.

Finton, Esther. Bulletin Boards Should Be More Than Something to Look At. 64p. (gr. k-6). 1979. 7.95 (0-916456-32-3, GA97) Good Apple.

Finzel, Julia. Large As Life. LC 90-49816. (Illus.). 32p. (ps up). 1991. 14.95 (0-688-10652-8); PLB 14.88 (0-688-10653-6) Lothrop.

Fiore, Carmen A. The Snakeskin. Ferri, Penny J., illus. 112p. (gr. 3-7). 1991. 14.95 (0-939219-07-7) Townhouse Pub.

Fiorilla, Sal J., jt. auth. see Hoffman, Beverly.

Firer, Benzion. Saadiah Weissman. 140p. (gr. 5-12). 1982. 9.95 (0-87306-294-9); pap. 6.95 (0-685-07830-2) Feldheim.

—The Twins. Scae, Bracha, tr. from HEB. 230p. (gr. 4-8). 1983. 10.95 (0-87306-279-5); pap. 7.95 (0-87306-340-6) Feldheim.

Fireside, Bryna, jt. auth. see Bernstein, Joanne E.

Fireside, Bryna J. Is There a Woman in the House - or Senate? Levine, Abby, ed. LC 92-28286. (Illus.). 144p. (gr. 4-9). 1993. PLB 14.95 (0-8075-3662-8) A Whitman.

Firestone, Allan L. Mr. Luckypennys Magic Book. Katz, Deborah, illus. LC 77-71450. (gr. 2-7). 1977. pap. 4.95 (0-934682-01-1) Emmett.

Firmage, George J., ed. see Cummings, e. e.

Firman, Mary, jt. auth. see Chattington, Jenny.

Firmin, Peter. Boastful Mr. Bear. Firmin, Peter, illus. (ps-1). 1989. 8.95 (0-440-50083-4) Delacorte.

—Boastful Mr. Bear. 1990. pap. 2.95 (0-440-40371-5, YB) Dell.

—Foolish Miss Crow. Firmin, Peter, illus. (ps-1). 1989. 8.95 (0-440-50082-6) Delacorte.

—Foolish Miss Crow. 1990. pap. 2.95 (0-440-40332-4, YB) Dell.

—Happy Miss Rat. Firmin, Peter, illus. (ps-1). 1989. 8.95 (0-440-50081-8) Delacorte.

—Happy Miss Rat. 1990. pap. 2.95 (0-440-40382-0, YB) Dell.

—Hungry Mr. Fox. Firmin, Peter, illus. (ps-1). 1989. 8.95 (0-440-50034-6) Delacorte.

—Hungry Mr. Fox. (gr. k-6). 1990. pap. 2.95 (0-440-40340-5, YB) Dell.

Firmin, Peter, illus. Day & Night. 16p. (ps-1). 1986. 4.50 (0-7460-0795-7) EDC.

—Summer & Winter. 16p. (ps-1). 1986. 4.50 (0-7460-0793-0) EDC.

—Then & Now. 16p. (ps-1). 1986. 4.50 (0-7460-0794-9) EDC.

First Graders of A. R. Shepherd Washington, D. C. A Caterpillar's Wish. (Illus.). 24p. (Orig.). (ps-2). 1988. pap. 3.50 (0-87406-307-8) Willowisp Pr.

First, Ruth. One Hundred Seventeen Days. Sachs, Albie & Lodge, Tomfrwd. by. 192p. (gr. 11-12). 1989. 24.00 (0-85345-789-1); pap. 9.00 (0-85345-790-5) Monthly Rev.

Firth, Lesley, ed. When Did It Happen. (Illus.). 128p. (gr. 3-7). 1990. (S&S BFYR); pap. 7.95 (0-671-72497-5, S&S BFYR) S&S Trade.

Fisch, Arnold G., Jr. Department of the Army. Schlesinger, Arthur M., intro. by. (Illus.). 96p. (gr. 5 up). 1988. lib. bdg. 14.95 (0-87754-835-8) Chelsea Hse.

Fischel, E. Midnight Ghosts. (Illus.). 48p. (gr. 5 up). 1992. PLB 11.96 (0-88110-521-X, Usborne); pap. 4.95 (0-7460-0651-9, Usborne) EDC.

—Swimming & Diving Skills. (Illus.). 48p. (gr. 6-12). 1989. (Usborne); pap. 5.95 (0-7460-0171-1) EDC.

Fischel, Emma. Murder Unlimited. (Illus.). 48p. (gr. 4-7). 1993. PLB 11.96 (0-88110-522-8, Usborne); pap. 4.95 (0-7460-0610-1, Usborne) EDC.

Fischer, Christy, et al. National Parks: A Kid's-Eye View: The Rocky Mountains. (Illus.). 24p. (Orig.). (gr. 4-6). 1988. pap. 5.95 (0-945710-00-3) Starword Bks.

Fischer, David M. Ted Turner. LC 92-44761. 1993. 19.93 (0-86625-496-X); 14.95s.p. (0-685-66547-X) Rourke Pubns.

Fischer, Elyse. The Silver Coach: A Study Guide. Friedland, Joyce & Kessler, Rikki, eds. (gr. 3-5). 1991. pap. text ed. 14.95 (0-88122-577-0) LRN Links.

Fischer, John. Saint Ben. 288p. (Orig.). 1993. pap. 7.99 (1-55661-259-1) Bethany Hse.

—True Believers Don't Ask Why. 192p. (Orig.). (gr. 11-12). 1989. 12.99 (1-55661-055-6) Bethany Hse.

Fischer, Kathleen M., jt. auth. see Levine, Gloria.

Fischer, Lee, ed. Colorado Is for Kids! An Activity Book for Kids! Parker, Steve, illus. 32p. (gr. 1-6). 1990. pap. 2.95 (0-929526-05-8) Double B Pubns.

Fischer, Louis. Gandhi: His Life & Message for the World. 192p. (gr. 9-12). 1982. pap. 4.50 (0-451-62742-3, Ment) NAL-Dutton.

Fischer, Marsha. Miami. LC 89-25694. (Illus.). 60p. (gr. 3 up). 1990. RSBE 13.95 (0-87518-428-6, Dillon) Macmillan Child Grp.

Fischer, Maureen. Little Mary. Haley, Patrick & Haley, Irene, eds. LC 85-82197. 106p. (gr. 7-12). 1986. 14.00 (0-9605738-3-6); pap. 6.00 (0-9605738-4-4) East Eagle.

Fischer, Max W. American History Simulations. Apodaca, Blanca, illus. 96p. (gr. 5-8). 1993. wkbk. 9.95 (1-55734-480-9) Tchr Create Mat.

—World History Simulations. Buhler, Cheryl, illus. 96p. (gr. 5-8). 1993. wkbk. 9.95 (1-55734-481-7) Tchr Create Mat.

Fischer, Richard, et al. Little Biddle Riddle Book. 32p. 1991. 3.95 (0-935284-89-3) Patrice Pr.

Fischer, Sara, jt. auth. see Kiebanow, Barbara.

Fischer, Sharon G. Lucy & the Leprechaun's Rainbow. 1991. 7.95 (0-533-09513-1) Vantage.

Fischer, Sophia M. & Eisenberg, Ruth P., eds. Reflections on the March of the Living: April 26 - May 10, 1992. Greenzweig, Gene, intros. by. 164p. (Orig.). (gr. 11-12). 1993. pap. 18.00 (0-930029-07-0) Central Agency.

Fischer, Steven. There's a Blue Dog under My Bed. Fischer, Thomas, ed. Fischer, Steven, illus. LC 90-84006. 64p. (Orig.). (gr. k-6). 1991. pap. 2.95 (0-9627367-0-8) Blue Dog Prodns.

Fischer, Susan, jt. auth. see Gravelle, Karen.

Fischer, Thomas, ed. see Fischer, Steven.

Fischer, William E., ed. see Aderman, James.

Fischer, William E., ed. see Stadler, Richard H.

Fischer, William E., ed. see Wendland, Ernst H.

Fischer-Nagel, Andreas & Fischer-Nagel, Heiderose. Life of the Honeybee. Fischer-Nagel, Andreas & Fischer-Nagel, Heiderose, illus. 48p. (gr. 2-5). 1986. pap. 6.95 (0-87614-470-9) Carolrhoda Bks.

—Life of the Ladybug. Fischer-Nagel, Andreas & Fischer-Nagel, Heiderose, illus. LC 85-25467. 48p. (gr. 2-5). 1986. lib. bdg. 19.95 (0-87614-240-4) Carolrhoda Bks.

Fischer-Nagel, Andreas, jt. auth. see Fischer-Nagel, Heiderose.

Fischer-Nagel, Heiderose & Fischer-Nagel, Andreas. An Ant Colony. Fischer-Nagel, Andreas & Fischer-Nagel, Heiderose, illus. 48p. (gr. 2-5). 1989. PLB 19.95 (0-87614-333-8); pap. 6.95 (0-87614-519-5) Carolrhoda Bks.

—Fir Trees. Fischer-Nagel, Heiderose & Fischer-Nagel, Andreas, photos by. (Illus.). 48p. (gr. 2-5). 1989. 19.95 (0-87614-340-0) Carolrhoda Bks.

—The Housefly. Fischer-Nagel, Heiderose & Fischer-Nagel, Andreas, illus. 48p. (gr. 2-6). 1990. PLB 19.95 (0-87614-374-5) Carolrhoda Bks.

—Inside the Burrow: The Life of the Golden Hamster. LC 86-2591. (Illus.). 48p. (gr. 2-5). 1986. PLB 19.95 (0-87614-286-2); pap. 6.95 (0-87614-478-4) Carolrhoda Bks.

—Life of the Butterfly. Simon, Noel, tr. from GER. Fischer-Nagel, Heiderose & Fischer-Nagel, Andreas, photos by. (Illus.). 48p. (gr. 2-5). 1987. lib. bdg. 19.95 (0-87614-244-7); pap. 6.95 (0-87614-484-9) Carolrhoda Bks.

—Life of the Honeybee. (Illus.). 48p. (gr. 2-5). 1987. pap. 6.95 (0-685-18832-9, First Ave Edns) Lerner Pubns.

—A Look Through the Mouse Hole. Fischer-Nagel, Heiderose & Fischer-Nagel, Andreas, illus. 48p. (gr. 2-5). 1989. lib. bdg. 19.95 (0-87614-326-5) Carolrhoda Bks.

Fischer-Nagel, Heiderose, jt. auth. see Fischer-Nagel, Andreas.

Fischetto, Laura. All Pigs on Deck: Christopher Columbus's Second Marvelous Voyage. (ps-3). 1991. PLB 15.99 (0-385-30440-4) Delacorte.

—The Jungle Is My Home. Galli, Letizia, illus. 32p. (ps-3). 1991. 13.95 (0-670-83550-1) Viking Child Bks.

—The Jungle Is My Home. Galli, Letitzia, illus. 32p. (ps-3). 1993. pap. 4.99 (0-14-054324-4, Puffin) Puffin Bks.

Fischgrund, Tom, ed. Barron's Top Fifty: An Inside Look at America's Best Colleges. 2nd ed. LC 92-39776. (gr. 9 up). 1993. pap. 12.95 (0-8120-1447-2) Barron.

Fischman, Joyce. Bible Work & Play, Vol. 1. rev. ed. Steinberger, Heidi, illus. 80p. (Orig.). (gr. 1-3). 1985. pap. text ed. 5.00 (0-8074-0304-0, 103620) UAHC.

—Holiday Work & Play. rev. ed. (Illus.). 64p. (gr. 1-3). 1986. pap. 5.00 (0-8074-0315-6, 101961) UAHC.

Fischman, Sheila, tr. see Carrier, Roch.

Fish, Helen D. When the Root Children Wake Up. Von Olfers, Sibylle, illus. LC 91-22577. 24p. 1991. Repr. of 1906 ed. 12.95 (0-671-75216-2, Green Tiger) S&S Trade.

Fish, Helen D., selected by see Lathrop, Dorothy B.

Fishbein, Seymour L. Yellowstone Country: The Enduring Wonder. Crump, Donald J., ed. (Illus.). 1989. 9.95 (0-87044-713-0); PLB 12.95 (0-87044-718-1) Natl Geog.

Fisher, Aileen. Always Wondering: Some Favorite Poems of Aileen Fisher. Sandin, Joan, illus. LC 90-23069. 96p. (gr. 2-6). 1991. 13.95 (0-06-022851-2); PLB 13.89 (0-06-022858-X) HarpC Child Bks.

—The House of a Mouse. Sandin, Joan, illus. LC 87-24947. 32p. (ps-3). 1988. HarpC Child Bks.

—Rabbits, Rabbits. Niemann, Gail, illus. LC 82-48849. 32p. (gr. k-3). 1983. 12.95i (0-06-021896-7) HarpC Child Bks.

Fisher, Aileen, ed. Holiday Programs for Boys & Girls. 393p. (gr. 2-6). 1986. pap. 13.95 (0-8238-0277-9) Plays.

Fisher, Aileen L. My First Hanukkah Book. Kiedrowski, Priscilla, illus. LC 84-21510. 32p. (ps-2). 1985. PLB 15.00 (0-516-02905-3); pap. 3.95 (0-516-42905-1) Childrens.

Fisher, Ann. Perplexing Puzzlers. (Illus.). 80p. (gr. 4-8). 1992. wkbk. 9.95 (0-86653-677-9, 1411) Good Apple.

Fisher, Anne B. Bears, Pirates & Silver Lace. (Illus.). 146p. (gr. 3-7). 1975. pap. 5.95 (0-8323-0255-4) Binford Mort.

Fisher, Barbara. Big Harold & Tiny Enid. (Illus.). 26p. (Orig.). (gr. 1-3). 1975. pap. 2.00 (0-934830-01-0) Ten Penny.

—Car Boy. Fisher, Barbara, illus. 29p. (Orig.). (gr. k-2). 1977. pap. 2.00 (0-934830-02-9) Ten Penny.

—Dan. Fisher, Barbara, illus. 20p. (Orig.). (gr. k-5). 1981. pap. 2.00 (0-934830-19-3) Ten Penny.

—Harmony Hurricane Muldoon. Fisher, Barbara, illus. 22p. (Orig.). (gr. 3-5). 1979. pap. 2.00 (0-934830-09-6) Ten Penny.

—Jolly Molly Molar. Fisher, Barbara, illus. 44p. (Orig.). (gr. 1-3). 1979. pap. 2.00 (0-934830-10-X) Ten Penny.

—Linkups. (Illus., Orig.). (ps-3). 1977. pap. 2.00 slipcased (0-934830-05-3) Ten Penny.

—Philpin's Tree. (Illus.). 12p. (Orig.). (gr. 1-3). 1977. pap. 2.00 (0-934830-00-2) Ten Penny.

Fisher, Barbara & Spiegel, Richard, eds. Bibliomania Three, Vol. 1. 47p. (Orig.). (gr. k-6). 1993. pap. 3.00 (0-685-65120-7) Ten Penny.

—Bibliomania Three, Vol. 2. 47p. (Orig.). (gr. 7-12). 1993. pap. 3.00 (0-934830-54-1) Ten Penny.

—In Search of a Song: Jefferson Market Library, Vol. 3. (Illus.). 64p. (Orig.). (gr. 1-6). 1982. pap. 2.00 (0-934830-27-4) Ten Penny.

—In Search of a Song: PS-114, Vol. 1. (Illus.). 90p. (Orig.). (gr. k-6). 1981. pap. 2.00 (0-934830-25-8) Ten Penny.

—In Search of a Song: PS-276, Vol. 2. (Illus.). 90p. (Orig.). (gr. k-6). 1981. pap. 2.00 (0-934830-26-6) Ten Penny.

—More Poetry Hunter. (Illus.). 92p. (Orig.). (gr. 3 up). 1981. pap. 2.00 (0-934830-23-1) Ten Penny.

—Poetry Hunter, No. 1. (Illus.). 92p. (Orig.). (gr. k-6). 1981. pap. 2.00 (0-934830-21-5) Ten Penny.

—Still More Poetry Hunter. (Illus.). 36p. (Orig.). (gr. k-6). 1981. pap. 2.00 (0-934830-24-X) Ten Penny.

—Streams. (Illus.). 138p. (Orig.). (gr. 9-12). 1987. pap. 5.00 (0-934830-39-8) Ten Penny.

—Streams, No. 2. (Illus.). 142p. (gr. 9-12). 1988. pap. 5.00 (0-934830-42-8) Ten Penny.

—Streams, No. 3. (Illus.). (gr. 9-12). 1989. pap. 5.00 (0-934830-43-6) Ten Penny.

—Streams Four. (Illus.). 150p. (Orig.). (gr. 9-12). 1990. pap. 5.00 (0-934830-44-4) Ten Penny.

—Streams Seven. 150p. (Orig.). (gr. 7-12). 1993. pap. 5.00 (0-934830-53-3) Ten Penny.

—Subway Slams. (Illus.). 48p. (Orig.). (gr. k-8). 1981. pap. 2.00 (0-934830-22-3) Ten Penny.

—Yearning to Breathe Free. 32p. (Orig.). (gr. 4-9). 1984. pap. 2.00 (0-934830-33-9) Ten Penny.

Fisher, Barbara, ed. see Day, Adrienne.

Fisher, Barbara, ed. see Mennella, Roxanna.

Fisher, Barbara, jt. ed. see New York Book Fair Staff.

Fisher, Barbara, jt. ed. see Spiegel, Richard.

Fisher, Barbara, ed. see Spiegel, Richard.

Fisher, Barbara, jt. ed. see Spiegel, Richard.

Fisher, Barbara, jt. ed. see Spiegel, Richard A.

Fisher, Barbara, ed. see Wilkins, Sarah.

Fisher, Barbara, ed. see Wilkins, Sarah & Mennella, Roxanna.

Fisher, Betty J., ed. see Abdu'l-Baha.

Fisher, Bill. Thirty Years over Donner. LC 90-22185. (Illus.). 198p. (Orig.). (gr. 11). 1991. (Pub. by Trans-Anglo); pap. 19.95 (0-87046-102-8, Pub. by Trans-Anglo) Interurban.

Fisher, Bubbles. Candy Apple New York for Kids. 2nd ed. 1989. pap. 12.95 (0-13-114976-8) P-H.

Fisher, Clayton P. The Stock Market Explained for Young Investors: Young Investors Ser. 175p. 1993. 17.95 (0-931133-02-5) Busn Class.

Fisher, Cyrus. The Avion My Uncle Flew. Floethe, Richard, illus. 254p. (gr. 5 up). 1993. pap. 4.99 (0-14-036487-0, Puffin) Puffin Bks.

Fisher, David E. The Origin & Evolution of Our Own Particular Universe. LC 88-14108. (Illus.). 192p. (gr. 7 up). 1988. SBE 14.95 (0-689-31368-3, Atheneum Child Bk) Macmillan Child Grp.

Fisher, Dorothy C. Our Independence & the Constitution. LC 87-4656. 192p. (gr. 5-9). 1964. pap. 2.95 (0-394-89175-9, Random Juv) Random Bks Yng Read.

—Understood Betsy. (gr. k-6). 1987. pap. 4.95 (0-440-49179-7, Pub. by Yearling Classics) Dell.

—Understood Betsy. (gr. 4-7). 1991. pap. 3.50 (0-440-40796-6) Dell.

Fisher, Gary & Cummings, Rhoda. The Survival Guide for Kids with LD: Learning Differences. Nielsen, Nancy, ed. Urbanovic, Jackie, illus. LC 89-37084. 104p. (Orig.). (gr. 5 up). 1990. pap. 16.95 incl. audiocassette (0-915793-21-0); pap. 9.95 (0-915793-18-0); audiocassette 10.00 (0-915793-20-2) Free Spirit Pub.

Fisher, Gary, jt. auth. see Cummings, Rhoda.

Fisher, Iris L. Katie-Bo: An Adoption Story. Schaer, Miriam, illus. (ps-3). 1988. 12.95 (0-915361-91-4) Modan-Adama Bks.

Fisher, John. John Fisher's Magic Book. De Paola, Tomie, illus. (gr. 5-8). 1975. pap. 1.95 (0-13-510222-7, Pub. by Treehouse) P-H.

Fisher, Juliet. Juliet Fisher & the Foolproof Plan. 96p. 1994. pap. 3.50 (0-380-72066-3, Camelot) Avon.

Fisher, Leonard E. The ABC Exhibit. LC 90-6639. (Illus.). 32p. (ps up). 1991. SBE 15.95 (0-02-735251-X, Macmillan Child Bk) Macmillan Child Grp.

—The Alamo. Fisher, Leonard E., illus. LC 86-46204. 64p. (gr. 3-7). 1987. reinforced bdg. 14.95 (0-8234-0646-6) Holiday.

—Alphabet Art: Thirteen ABC's from Around the World. LC 84-28752. (Illus.). 64p. (gr. 3-7). Repr. of 1978 ed. SBE 14.95 (0-02-735230-7, Four Winds) Macmillan Child Grp.

—Calendar Art: Thirteen Days, Weeks, Months, Years from Around the World. Fisher, Leonard E., illus. LC 86-25835. 64p. (ps up). 1987. SBE 14.95 (0-02-735350-8, Four Winds) Macmillan Child Grp.

—Cyclops. Fisher, Leonard E., illus. LC 90-29317. 32p. (ps-3). 1991. reinforced bdg. 15.95 (0-8234-0891-4) Holiday.

—Cyclops. Fisher, Leonard E., illus. 1993. pap. 5.95 (0-8234-1062-5) Holiday.

—Ellis Island: Gateway to the New World. Fisher, Leonard E., illus. LC 86-2286. 64p. (gr. 3-7). 1986. reinforced 13.95 (0-8234-0612-1) Holiday.

—Galileo. Fisher, Leonard E., illus. LC 91-31146. 32p. (gr. 2-6). 1992. SBE 14.95 (0-02-735235-8, Macmillan Child Bk) Macmillan Child Grp.

—The Great Wall of China. Fisher, Leonard E., illus. LC 85-15324. 32p. (gr. 1-5). 1986. RSBE 14.95 (0-02-735220-X, Macmillan Child Bk) Macmillan Child Grp.

—Gutenberg. Fisher, Leonard E., illus. LC 92-26991. 32p. (gr. 2-6). 1993. 14.95 (0-02-735238-2, Macmillan Child Bk) Macmillan Child Grp.

—Jason & the Golden Fleece. Fisher, Leonard E., illus. LC 89-20074. 32p. (gr. k-4). 1990. reinforced bdg. 14.95 (0-8234-0794-2) Holiday.

—Kinderdike. Fisher, Leonard E., illus. LC 93-8140. 32p. (gr. k-3). 1994. RSBE 15.95 (0-02-735365-6, Macmillan Child Bk) Macmillan Child Grp.

—Monticello. LC 87-25219. (Illus.). 64p. (gr. 3-7). 1988. reinforced bdg. 14.95 (0-8234-0688-1) Holiday.

—Number Art: Thirteen 1 2 3s from Around the World. Fisher, Leonard E., illus. LC 82-5050. 64p. (gr. 3-7). 1982. SBE 14.95 (0-02-735240-4, Four Winds) Macmillan Child Grp.

—Olympians: Great Gods & Goddesses of Ancient Greece. Fisher, Leonard E., illus. LC 84-516. 32p. (gr. 1-4). 1984. reinforced bdg. 15.95 (0-8234-0522-2); pap. 5.95 (0-8234-0740-3) Holiday.

—The Oregon Trail. LC 90-55103. (Illus.). 64p. (gr. 3-7). 1990. reinforced 14.95 (0-8234-0833-7) Holiday.

—Prince Henry the Navigator. Fisher, Leonard E., illus. LC 89-28068. 32p. (gr. 2-6). 1990. 14.95 (0-02-735231-5, Macmillan Child Bk) Macmillan Child Grp.

—Pyramid of the Sun - Pyramid of the Moon. Fisher, Leonard E., illus. LC 88-1410. 32p. (gr. 1-5). 1988. SBE 14.95 (0-02-735300-1) Macmillan Child Grp.

—Sailboat Lost. Fisher, Leonard E., illus. LC 90-21504. 32p. (ps up). 1991. 15.95 (0-02-735351-6, Macmillan Child Bk) Macmillan Child Grp.

—Stars & Stripes. LC 93-20176. (Illus.). 32p. 1993. reinforced bdg. 15.95 (0-8234-1053-6) Holiday.

—The Statue of Liberty. Fisher, Leonard E., illus. LC 85-42878. 64p. (gr. 3-7). 1985. reinforced bdg. 14.95 (0-8234-0586-9) Holiday.

—Symbol Art: Thirteen Squares, Circles & Triangles from Around the World. Fisher, Leonard E., illus. LC 85-42805. 64p. (gr. 4-6). 1986. SBE 14.95 (0-02-735270-6, Four Winds) Macmillan Child Grp.

—The Tanners. Fisher, Leonard E., illus. LC 66-10136. 48p. (gr. 3 up). 1986. pap. 5.95 (0-87923-609-4) Godine.

—The Tower of London. Fisher, Leonard E., illus. LC 87-1629. 32p. (gr. 1-5). 1987. SBE 14.95 (0-02-735370-2, Macmillan Child Bk) Macmillan Child Grp.

—Tracks Across America: The Story of the American Railroad, 1825-1900. LC 91-28441. (Illus.). 192p. (gr. 5 up). 1992. 17.95 (0-8234-0945-7) Holiday.

—The Wailing Wall. Fisher, Leonard E., illus. LC 88-27192. 32p. (gr. 1-5). 1989. SBE 15.95 (0-02-735310-9, Macmillan Child Bk) Macmillan Child Grp.

—The White House. LC 89-1990. (Illus.). 96p. (gr. 3-7). 1989. reinforced bdg. 15.95 (0-8234-0774-8) Holiday.

Fisher, Leonard E., adapted by. & illus. David & Goliath. LC 92-24063. 32p. (ps-3). 1993. reinforced bdg. 15.95 (0-8234-0997-X) Holiday.

Fisher, Leonard E., retold by. & illus. Theseus & the Minotaur. LC 88-1970. 32p. (gr. 1-4). 1988. reinforced bdg. 15.95 (0-8234-0703-9); pap. 5.95 (0-8234-0954-6) Holiday.

Fisher, Leonard E., illus. & adapted by. The Seven Days of Creation. LC 81-2952. 32p. (ps-3). 1981. reinforced bdg. 14.95 (0-8234-0398-X); pap. 5.95 (0-8234-0757-8) Holiday.

Fisher, Lucretia. The Butterfly & the Stone. Jardine, Thomas, illus. LC 80-29260. 48p. (Orig.). (ps up). 1981. pap. 3.95 (0-916144-69-0) Stemmer Hse.

—Two Monsters: A Fable. Jardine, Thomas, illus. LC 76-21684. 48p. (ps up). 1976. pap. 3.95 (0-916144-08-9) Stemmer Hse.

Fisher, Margaret & Fowler, Mary J., eds. Colonial America: English Colonies. rev. ed. LC 87-81353. (Illus.). 128p. (gr. 4 up). 1988. 1-4 copies 14.95 ea. (0-934291-23-3); 5 or more copies 11.95 (0-317-91141-4) Gateway Pr MI.

Fisher, Margaret, jt. ed. see Fowler, Mary J.

Fisher, Marshall. The Ozone Layer. (Illus.). 111p. (gr. 5 up). 1992. lib. bdg. 19.95 (0-7910-1576-9) Chelsea Hse.

Fisher, Mary P. Remember the Light. Janus, Donna, illus. 32p. (Illus.). (gr. k-4). 1986. pap. 4.50 (0-9615149-7-3) Fenton Valley Pr.

Fisher, Maxine P. The Country Mouse & the City Mouse: "Christmas Is Where the Heart Is" Smath, Jerry, illus. LC 93-26488. 1994. write for info. (0-679-84684-0) Random Bks Yng Read.

—The Walt Disney Story. Sporn, Michael, illus. Rakos, Jennie, ed. (Illus.). 72p. (gr. 7 up). 1988. PLB 10.90 (0-531-10493-1) Watts.

Fisher, Nell. A Handbell for Hans. 1990. 2.95 (0-8378-1885-0) Gibson.

—My Brother's Drum. 1990. 2.95 (0-8378-1886-9) Gibson.

Fisher, Pam, jt. ed. see Chaney, Sky.

Fisher, R. L. The Prince of Whales. 160p. 1988. pap. 2.95 (0-8125-6637-8) Tor Bks.

—The Prince of Whales. Satter, Denise, illus. 160p. (gr. 3 up). 1987. pap. 2.50 (0-8125-6635-1) Tor Bks.

Fisher, Richard E., tr. see Cohen, Peter.

Fisher, Richard E., tr. see Landstrom, Olof & Landstrom, Lena.

Fisher, Richard E., tr. see Lindgren, Barbro.

Fisher, Richard E., tr. see Proysen, Alf.

Fisher, Richard E., tr. see Sundvall, Viveca.

Fisher, Richard E., tr. see Widerberg, Siv.

Fisher, Robert, ed. Amazing Monsters: Verses to Thrill & Chill. Allen, Rowena, illus. 96p. (gr. k-5). 1982. pap. 5.95 (0-571-13925-6) Faber & Faber.

—Funny Folk: Poems about People. Dann, Penny, illus. 80p. (ps-3). 1992. pap. 5.95 (0-571-16214-2) Faber & Faber.

—Minibeasts: Poems about Little Creatures. Widdowson, Kay, illus. 96p. (gr. 2 up). 1992. 13.95 (0-571-16511-7) Faber & Faber.

—Pet Poems. (Illus.). (gr. 1-6). 1989. bds. 12.95 laminated (*0-571-15248-1*) Faber & Faber.
—Pet Poems. Kindberg, Sally. illus. 96p. (gr. 1 up). 1993. pap. 4.95 (*0-571-16830-2*) Faber & Faber.
—Witch Words: Poems of Magic & Mystery. Felts, Shirley, illus. 80p. (gr. 3-6). 1987. laminated boards 9.95 (*0-571-14559-0*) Faber & Faber.
—Witch Words: Poems of Magic & Mystery. Felts, Shirley, illus. 70p. (gr. 2 up). 1991. pap. 4.95 (*0-571-16319-X*) Faber & Faber.
Fisher, Ron. Mountain Adventure: Exploring the Appalachian Trail. Crump, Donald J., ed. (Illus.). 1988. 9.95 (*0-87044-673-8*) Natl Geog.
Fisher, Ronald K. Beyond the Rockies: A Narrative History of Idaho. LC 89-83506. (Illus.). (gr. 4-9). 1989. text ed. 14.85 (*0-941734-00-5*); write for info. tchr's. ed. Alpha Om ID.
Fisher, Ronald M. Animals in Winter. Crump, Donald J., ed. LC 82-47859. 32p. (gr. 3-8). 1982. Set. 13.95 (*0-87044-453-0*); lib. bdg. 16.95 (*0-87044-466-2*) Natl Geog.
Fisher, Ronald M. see National Geographic Society Staff.
Fisher, Rosemarie, tr. see Beauchamp, Andre.
Fisher, Sally. The Christmas Journey. Sardo, Douglas, illus. 40p. (ps-7). 1993. 19.99 (*0-670-85039-X*) Viking Child Bks.
Fisher, Trevor. Portrait of a Decade: Nineteen Ten to Nineteen Nineteen. (Illus.). 72p. (gr. 7-11). 1990. 19. 95 (*0-7134-6071-7*, Pub. by Batsford UK) Trafalgar.
—Portrait of a Decade: The Nineteen Sixties. (Illus.). 72p. (gr. 7-9). 1988. 19.95 (*0-7134-5603-5*, Pub. by Batsford UK) Trafalgar.
Fishlock, Trevor. Indira Gandhi. (Illus.). 64p. (gr. 5-9). 1991. 11.95 (*0-237-60025-0*, Pub. by Evans Bros Ltd) Trafalgar.
Fishman, Cathy. On Passover. Baskin, Leonard, illus. LC 91-43110. 32p. (gr. k up). 1994. RSBE 14.95 (*0-02-735320-6*, Macmillan Child Bk) Macmillan Child Grp.
Fishman, Isidore. Remember the Days of Old. LC 79-100058. (Illus.). (gr. 4-9). 1969. 4.95 (*0-87677-000-6*) Hartmore.
Fishman, Priscilla. Learn Mishnah Notebook. 128p. (gr. 7-8). 1983. pap. 3.50x (*0-87441-369-9*) Behrman.
Fishman, Priscilla, ed. see Frankel, Max & Hoffman, Judy.
Fishman, Richard A. The Sandlot Summit. Sutter, Richard, illus. LC 85-63032. 197p. (Orig.). (gr. 4-9). 1985. pap. 3.95 (*0-9615884-0-3*) Sunlakes Pub.
Fishman, Ross. Alcohol & Alcoholism. updated ed. (Illus.). (gr. 5 up). 1992. lib. bdg. 19.95 (*0-685-52234-2*) Chelsea Hse.
Fishman, Sylvia E., jt. auth. see Bauman, Chris.
Fisk, George W. Benny, the Lazy Beaver. Barker, Scott J., illus. LC 90-45200. 32p. 1991. 10.99 (*0-9620507-1-7*) Cosmic Concepts Pr.
Fisk, Pauline. Midnight Blue. 220p. (gr. 6-10). 1992. pap. text ed. 4.99 (*0-7459-1925-1*) Lion USA.
—Telling the Sea. 256p. (gr. 6-10). 1992. text ed. 11.95 (*0-7459-2061-6*) Lion USA.
Fiske, Roger. Score Reading, 4 vols. Incl. Vol. 1. Orchestration. 1958. 11.95x (*0-19-321301-X*); Vol. 2. Musical Form. 1958. 11.95x (*0-19-321302-8*); Vol. 3. Concertos. 1960. 11.95x (*0-19-321303-6*); Vol. 4. Oratorios. 1955. (gr. 9up) OUP.
Fissel, Alma M. Cat Tales. 1991. 6.95 (*0-533-09252-3*) Vantage.
Fitch, Marguerite. Samuel Francis Smith: My Country 'tis of Thee. (Illus.). (gr. 3-6). 1987. pap. 6.95 (*0-88062-049-8*) Mott Media.
Fitch, Sheree. Sleeping Dragons All. 1991. PLB 14.99 (*0-385-42001-3*) Doubleday.
—Toes in My Nose: And Other Poems. Bobak, Molly, illus. 48p. (gr. 1-5). 1993. pap. 6.95 (*1-56397-127-5*, Wordsong) Boyds Mills Pr.
Fittro, Charlene C. Hoppy the Easter Bunny. Kaye, Sz-71919. (Illus.). 20p. (Orig.). (ps-3). 1992. pap. 7.95 (*0-9633053-4-4*) Child Bks & Mus.
Fittro, Pat, ed. Adventures with God: A Year of Devotional Activities for Kids, 2 bks. (Illus.). (gr. 8 up). 1993. pap. 5.99 ea. Bk. 1, 88p (*0-7847-0083-4*, 12-02823) Bk. 2, 88p (*0-7847-0084-2*, 12-02829) Standard Pub.
Fittro, Pat, compiled by. Standard Easter Program Book, No. 41. 48p. 1990. pap. 2.50 (*0-87403-717-4*, 21-08711) Standard Pub.
Fittro, Pat, ed. see Ison, Colleen.
Fitzgerald, Annie. Dear God, Bless Our Food. LC 84-71372. 16p. (Orig.). (ps-4). 1984. pap. 1.99 (*0-8066-2108-7*, 10-1859, Augsburg) Augsburg Fortress.
—Dear God, Good Morning. LC 84-71377. 16p. (Orig.). (ps-4). 1984. pap. 1.99 (*0-8066-2104-4*, 10-1860, Augsburg) Augsburg Fortress.
—Dear God, Good Night. LC 84-71374. 16p. (ps-4). 1984. pap. 1.99 (*0-8066-2105-2*, 10-1861, Augsburg) Augsburg Fortress.
—Dear God, I Just Love Birthdays. LC 84-71371. 16p. (Orig.). (ps-4). 1984. pap. 1.99 (*0-8066-2107-9*, 10-1862, Augsburg) Augsburg Fortress.
—Dear God, Let's Play. LC 83-70495. 16p. (Orig.). (gr. 3-6). 1983. pap. 1.99 (*0-8066-2001-3*, 10-1852, Augsburg) Augsburg Fortress.
—Dear God, Thanks for Friends. LC 84-71873. 16p. (Orig.). (ps-4). 1984. pap. 1.99 (*0-8066-2109-5*, 10-1863, Augsburg) Augsburg Fortress.

—Dear God, Thanks for Making Me Me. LC 83-71368. 16p. (Orig.). (ps-4). 1984. pap. 1.99 (*0-8066-2106-0*, 10-1864, Augsburg) Augsburg Fortress.
—Dear God, Thanks for Thinking up Love. LC 83-70499. 16p. (gr. 3-6). 1983. pap. 1.99 (*0-8066-2005-6*, 10-1853, Augsburg) Augsburg Fortress.
—Dear God, Thanks for Your Help. LC 83-70496. 16p. (gr. 3-6). 1983. pap. 1.99 (*0-8066-2002-1*, 10-1854, Augsburg) Augsburg Fortress.
—Dear God, We Just Love Christmas. LC 83-70494. 16p. (Orig.). (gr. 3-6). 1983. pap. 1.99 (*0-8066-2000-5*, 10-1855, Augsburg) Augsburg Fortress.
—Dear God, Where Do You Live? LC 83-70497. 16p. (gr. 3-6). 1983. pap. 1.99 (*0-8066-2003-X*, 10-1856, Augsburg) Augsburg Fortress.
—Dear God, Your World Is Wonderful. LC 83-70498. 16p. (gr. 3-6). 1983. pap. 1.99 (*0-8066-2004-8*, 10-1857, Augsburg) Augsburg Fortress.
Fitzgerald, Bridget. Little Dark Cloud. Alston, Virgil, illus. Harman, Sandra L., intro. by. LC 78-189877. (Illus.). 44p. (gr. 1-2). 1973. 2.50 (*0-87884-012-5*) Unicorn Ent.
—Winkie, the Cross-Eyed Witch. LC 71-189878. (Illus.). (gr. 1-2). 1973. 2.50 (*0-87884-020-6*) Unicorn Ent.
Fitz-Gerald, C. William Henry Harrison. LC 87-16842. (Illus.). 100p. (gr. 3 up). 1987. PLB 17.27 (*0-516-01392-0*) Childrens.
Fitz-Gerald, Christine A. Meriwether Lewis & William Clark: The Northwest Expedition. LC 90-20696. (Illus.). 128p. (gr. 3 up). 1991. PLB 26.60 (*0-516-03061-2*); pap. 9.95 (*0-516-43061-0*) Childrens.
Fitz-Gerald, Christine M. I Can Be a Mother. LC 87-35189. (Illus.). 32p. (gr. k-3). 1988. pap. 3.95 (*0-516-41914-5*) Childrens.
—I Can Be a Reporter. LC 86-9614. (Illus.). 32p. (gr. k-3). 1986. pap. 3.95 (*0-516-41899-8*) Childrens.
—James Monroe. LC 86-33436. (Illus.). 100p. (gr. 3 up). 1987. PLB 17.27 (*0-516-01383-1*); pap. 6.95 (*0-516-41383-X*) Childrens.
Fitzgerald, Edward, tr. see Khayyam, Omar.
Fitzgerald, Frank. Where's Kevin? LC 92-33058. (gr. 4-7). 1992. pap. 7.99 (*0-553-37199-1*) Bantam.
Fitzgerald, Janet. Autumn in the Wood. (Illus.). 32p. (gr. 1-3). 1991. 15.95 (*0-237-60216-4*, Pub. by Evans Bros Ltd) Trafalgar.
—Autumn on the Farm. (Illus.). 32p. (gr. 1-3). 1991. 15. 95 (*0-237-60222-9*, Pub. by Evans Bros Ltd) Trafalgar.
—Spring in the Wood. (Illus.). 32p. (gr. 1-3). 1991. 15.95 (*0-237-60218-0*, Pub. by Evans Bros Ltd) Trafalgar.
—Summer in the Wood. (Illus.). 32p. (gr. 1-3). 1991. 15. 95 (*0-237-60217-2*, Pub. by Evans Bros Ltd) Trafalgar.
—Summer on the Farm. (Illus.). 32p. (gr. 1-3). 1991. 15. 95 (*0-237-60221-0*, Pub. by Evans Bros Ltd) Trafalgar.
—Winter in the Wood. (Illus.). 32p. (gr. 1-3). 1991. 15.95 (*0-237-60215-6*, Pub. by Evans Bros Ltd) Trafalgar.
—Winter on the Farm. (Illus.). 32p. (gr. 1-3). 1991. 15.95 (*0-237-60219-9*, Pub. by Evans Bros Ltd) Trafalgar.
Fitzgerald, Jean. The Golden Gate Bridge Troll. Donovan, Karen, illus. 48p. (Orig.). (gr. k-2). 1978. pap. 6.95x (*0-9618225-0-3*) Bridge Troll Pr.
Fitzgerald, John & Fitzgerald, Lyn. Barnaby's Birthday. Posey, Pam, illus. LC 92-34275. 1993. 14.00 (*0-383-03618-6*) SRA Schl Grp.
Fitzgerald, John D. Great Brain. (gr. k-6). 1972. pap. 3.99 (*0-440-43071-2*, YB) Dell.
—The Great Brain. Mayer, Mercer, illus. LC 67-22252. (gr. 4-8). 1985. 12.95 (*0-8037-3074-8*); PLB 11.89 (*0-8037-3076-4*) Dial Bks Young.
—The Great Brain. large type ed. (Illus.). 219p. 1989. lib. bdg. 15.95 (*1-55736-102-9*, Crnrstn Bks) BDD LT Grp.
—The Great Brain at the Academy. 164p. (gr. k-6). 1982. pap. 3.50 (*0-440-43113-1*, YB) Dell.
—The Great Brain at the Academy. Mayer, Mercer, illus. LC 72-712. 176p. (gr. 4-7). 1985. 12.95 (*0-8037-3039-X*); PLB 11.89 (*0-8037-3040-3*) Dial Bks Young.
—The Great Brain Does It Again. (gr. 3-7). 1976. pap. 3.50 (*0-440-42983-8*, YB) Dell.
—The Great Brain Does It Again. Mayer, Mercer, illus. LC 74-18600. (gr. 4-7). 1975. PLB 11.89 (*0-8037-5066-8*) Dial Bks Young.
—The Great Brain Reforms. 176p. (gr. k-6). 1975. pap. 3.50 (*0-440-44841-7*, YB) Dell.
—The Great Brain Reforms. LC 72-7601. (Illus.). 176p. (gr. 4-7). 1973. PLB 11.89 (*0-8037-3068-3*) Dial Bks Young.
—Me & My Little Brain. 144p. (gr. 4-7). 1972. 3.25 (*0-440-45533-2*, YB) Dell.
—Me & My Little Brain. Mayer, Mercer, illus. LC 71-153732. (gr. 4-7). 1985. PLB 11.89 (*0-8037-5532-5*) Dial Bks Young.
—More Adventures of the Great Brain. 144p. (gr. k-6). 1971. pap. 3.50 (*0-440-45822-6*, YB) Dell.
—More Adventures of the Great Brain. Mayer, Mercer, illus. LC 73-85547. (gr. 4-8). 1985. 12.95 (*0-8037-5819-7*, 01160-350) Dial Bks Young.
—The Return of the Great Brain. 180p. (gr. 3-5). 1975. pap. 3.50 (*0-440-45941-9*, YB) Dell.
—The Return of the Great Brain. Mayer, Mercer, illus. LC 73-15443. 176p. (gr. 4-7). 1985. 12.95 (*0-8037-7403-6*) Dial Bks Young.
Fitzgerald, Julie. Spring on the Farm. (Illus.). 32p. (gr. 1-3). 1991. 15.95 (*0-237-60220-2*, Pub. by Evans Bros Ltd) Trafalgar.
Fitzgerald, Lyn, jt. auth. see Fitzgerald, John.
Fitzgerald, Phyllis. Alphabets. LC 87-51494. (Illus.). 30p. (gr. k-2). 1988. 6.95 (*1-55523-130-6*) Winston-Derek.

Fitzgerald, Rick. Helen & the Great Quiet. MacGregor, Marilyn, illus. LC 88-5095. 32p. (ps-2). 1989. 13.95 (*0-688-07723-4*); PLB 13.88 (*0-688-07724-2*, Morrow Jr Bks) Morrow Jr Bks.
Fitzgerald, Sharon. Harriet Tubman, Patriot. 1992. pap. 3.95 (*0-685-59550-1*, Melrose Sq) Holloway.
Fitzhugh, Louise. Harriet the Spy. 304p. (gr. 5 up). 1978. pap. 3.25 (*0-440-93447-8*, LFL) Dell.
—Harriet the Spy. 304p. (gr. 5 up). 1979. pap. 3.50 (*0-440-43447-5*, YB) Dell.
—Harriet the Spy. Fitzhugh, Louise, illus. LC 64-19711. 224p. (gr. 4-7). 1964. 15.00 (*0-06-021910-6*); PLB 14. 89 (*0-06-021911-4*) HarpC Child Bks.
—Harriet the Spy. large type ed. Fitzhugh, Louise, illus. 282p. (gr. 2-6). 1987. Repr. of 1964 ed. lib. bdg. 13.95 (*1-55736-012-X*, Crnrstn Bks) BDD LT Grp.
—Harriet the Spy. Fitzhugh, Louise, illus. LC 64-19711. 304p. (gr. 3-7). 1990. pap. 3.95 (*0-06-440331-9*, Trophy) HarpC Child Bks.
—I Am Five. Fitzhugh, Louise, illus. LC 78-50404. (ps-2). 1978. PLB 5.47 (*0-440-03953-3*); pap. 5.95 (*0-440-03952-5*) Delacorte.
—I Am Four. Bonners, Susan, illus. LC 82-70309. 48p. (ps-k). 1982. pap. 8.95 (*0-385-28444-6*); pap. 8.89 (*0-385-28445-4*) Delacorte.
—I Am Three. Natti, Sussans, illus. LC 81-15218. 48p. (ps). 1982. 8.95 (*0-440-04035-3*); PLB 8.89 (*0-440-04039-6*) Delacorte.
—I Know Everything about John & He Knows Everything about Me. Hoban, Lillian, illus. LC 92-28028. 1993. 13.95 (*0-385-30802-7*) Doubleday.
—Long Secret. Fitzhugh, Louise, illus. LC 65-23370. (gr. 5 up). 1965. 15.00i (*0-06-021410-4*); PLB 14.89 (*0-06-021411-2*) HarpC Child Bks.
—The Long Secret. Fitzhugh, Louise, illus. LC 65-23370. 288p. (gr. 3-7). 1990. pap. 3.95 (*0-06-440332-7*, Trophy) HarpC Child Bks.
—Nobody's Family Is Going to Change. 224p. (gr. 3-7). 1975. pap. 1.75 (*0-440-46454-4*, YB) Dell.
—Nobody's Family Is Going to Change. (Illus.). 221p. (gr. 5-9). 1986. pap. 4.50 (*0-374-45523-6*) FS&G.
—Sport. LC 78-72861. 250p. (gr. 4-6). 1979. pap. 8.95 (*0-385-28908-1*) Delacorte.
—Sport. 224p. (gr. 7 up) 1980. pap. 1.75 (*0-440-98350-9*, LFL) Dell.
Fitzmahan, Don. The Roller Coaster: A Story of Alcoholism & the Family. Cocklin-Ray, Christine, illus. Black, Claudia, intro. by. LC 88-63798. (Illus.). 36p. (Orig.). (gr. 6). 1986. pap. 8.00 (*0-935529-11-X*) Comprehen Health Educ.
Fitzpatrick, Julie. Bounce, Stretch & Spring. (Illus.). 30p. (gr. 3-5). 1991. 11.95 (*0-237-60212-1*, Pub. by Evans Bros Ltd) Trafalgar.
—In the Air. LC 84-40839. (Illus.). 32p. (gr. 2-5). PLB 9.96 (*0-382-09060-8*) Silver Burdett Pr.
—In the Air. (Illus.). 30p. (gr. 3-5). 1991. 11.95 (*0-237-60207-5*, Pub. by Evans Bros Ltd) Trafalgar.
—Magnets. (Illus.). 30p. (gr. 3-5). 1991. 11.95 (*0-237-60208-3*, Pub. by Evans Bros Ltd) Trafalgar.
—Mirrors. (Illus.). 30p. (gr. 3-5). 1991. 11.95 (*0-237-60209-1*, Pub. by Evans Bros Ltd) Trafalgar.
—On the Water. (Illus.). 30p. (gr. 3-5). 1991. 11.95 (*0-237-60210-5*, Pub. by Evans Bros Ltd) Trafalgar.
—Towers & Bridges. (Illus.). 30p. (gr. 3-5). 1991. 11.95 (*0-237-60213-X*, Pub. by Evans Bros Ltd) Trafalgar.
—Wheels. (Illus.). 30p. (gr. 3-5). 1991. 11.95 (*0-237-60214-8*, Pub. by Evans Bros Ltd) Trafalgar.
Fitzpatrick, Michael. Apes. (Illus.). 32p. (gr. 4-6). 1991. 13.95 (*0-237-60176-1*, Pub. by Evans Bros Ltd) Trafalgar.
—Your Move: A Chess Adventure for Young Beginners. Kelly, Andy, illus. 64p. (gr. 3-6). 1990. 12.95 (*0-86278-196-5*, Pub. by OBrien Pr IE) Dufour.
Fitzpatrick, Regina D. It Wasn't the Truth They Told. Graves, Helen, ed. LC 88-50112. 80p. (gr. 4-8). 1988. 6.95 (*1-55523-142-X*) Winston-Derek.
Fitz-Randolph, Jane, jt. auth. see Jespersen, James.
Fitzrandolph, Joyce. Learn to Paint with the Alexander Brush Club. (Illus.). 24p. (gr. 4-6). Date not set. pap. text ed. write for info. (*1-883576-32-6*, KT-220B) Alexander Art.
FitzSimmons, Joyce. Hide & Seek. FitzSimmons, Joy, illus. LC 91-38246. 32p. (ps). 1992. PLB 9.95 (*0-87226-467-X*, Bedrick Blackie) P Bedrick Bks.
Fix, Philippe. Not So Very Long Ago: Life in a Small Country Village. Fix, Philippe, illus. LC 93-8428. 40p. (gr. 2 up). 1994. 16.99 (*0-525-44594-3*, DCB) Dutton Child Bks.
—A Village Christmas. 1991. 8.95 (*0-525-44748-2*) Dutton Child Bks.
Fixico, Donald L. Urban Indians. (Illus.). 104p. (gr. 5 up). 1991. 17.95 (*1-55546-732-6*) Chelsea Hse.
Fjelde, Rolf, tr. see Ibsen, Henrik.
Flack, Jerry. Destinations: Grand Visions. 112p. (gr. 5-9). 1993. pap. text ed. 13.95 (*0-944459-67-6*) ECS Lrn Systs.
—Voyages: Expanding Horizons. 112p. (gr. 5-9). 1993. pap. text ed. 13.95 (*0-944459-66-8*) ECS Lrn Systs.
Flack, Jerry D. Odysseys: Personal Discoveries. 96p. (gr. 5-9). 1993. pap. text ed. 13.95 (*0-944459-63-3*) ECS Lrn Systs.
Flack, Marjorie. Angus & the Cat. 1989. (Zephyr-BFYR) Doubleday.
Flack, Marjorie. Angus & the Cat. 40p. (ps-k). 1989. PLB 13.99 (*0-685-01488-6*); pap. 12.95 (*0-685-01489-4*) Doubleday.

—Ask Mr. Bear. Flack, Marjorie, illus. LC 58-8370. 32p. (ps-1). 1971. pap. 3.95 (0-02-043090-6, Aladdin) Macmillan Child Grp.
—Ask Mr. Bear. Flack, Marjorie, illus. LC 58-8370. 32p. (gr. k-1). 1968. RSBE 12.95 (0-02-735390-7, Macmillan Child Bk) Macmillan Child Grp.
—Ask Mr. Bear. Flack, Marjorie, illus. (ps-3). 1990. incl. cass. 19.95 (0-87499-044-0); pap. 12.95 incl. cass. (0-87499-043-2); Set; incl. 4 bks., cass., & guide. pap. 27.95 (0-87499-045-9) Live Oak Media.
—Boats on the River. Barnum, Jay H., illus. 32p. (ps-3). 1991. 14.95 (0-670-83918-3) Viking Child Bks.
—The Story about Ping. Wiese, Kurt, illus. (gr. k-2). 1977. pap. 3.99 (0-14-050241-6, Puffin) Puffin Bks.
—Story about Ping. Wiese, Kurt, illus. LC 33-29356. (ps-2). 1933. pap. 14.00 (0-670-67223-8) Viking Child Bks.
Flack, Marjorie & Wiese, Kurt. The Story about Ping. (Illus.). 1993. pap. 6.99 incl. cassette (0-14-095117-2, Puffin) Puffin Bks.
Flagenheimer-Riggle, Ellen, jt. auth. see Chapin, Laurie.
Flagg, Isaac, ed. see Autenrieth, Georg.
Flaherty, Leo & Goetzmann, William H. Roald Amundsen & the Quest for the South Pole. Collins, Michael, intro. by. (Illus.). 112p. (gr. 6-12). 1993. PLB 18.95 (0-7910-1308-1) Chelsea Hse.
Flamm, Jackie, ed. see Claire, Elizabeth.
Flanagan, Anne J. Children's Way of the Cross. Smolinski, Dick, illus. 39p. (Orig.). (gr. 2-6). 1992. pap. 1.50 (0-8198-6954-6) St Paul Bks.
Flanagan, Anne J., ed. see Daughters of St. Paul Staff.
Flanagan, Anne J., tr. see Quaglini, Juliana.
Flanagan, James M. Builders of Maine. LC 91-58091. 400p. 1994. 19.95 (0-932433-87-1) Windswept Hse.
Flanagan, Joan. Mr. Shanahan's Secret. Seal, Bob, illus. LC 88-42914. 32p. (gr. 2-3). 1988. PLB 18.60 (1-55532-930-6) Gareth Stevens Inc.
Flanagan, John. Kids 'n Values: A Handbook for Helping Kids Discover Christian Values. LC 91-62268. (Illus.). 144p. (gr. 2-7). 1992. pap. text ed. 11.95 (0-89243-411-2) Liguori Pubns.
Flanagan, Mary I. Me at Five: A Religion Readiness Program. (Illus.). 64p. (gr. k). 1993. pap. text ed. 9.51 (1-55944-037-6) Franciscan Comns.
—Me At Three: A Religion Readiness Program. (Illus.). 64p. (ps). 1989. pap. text ed. 9.51 (1-55944-028-7) Franciscan Comns.
Flanagan, Mike. Westward Ho! (Orig.). 1992. pap. 4.50 playscript (0-87602-307-3) Anchorage.
Flanders, Carl N. Abortion. 256p. (gr. 9-12). 1990. 22.95x (0-8160-1908-8) Facts on File.
Flanders, Carl N., jt. auth. see Flanders, Stephen A.
Flanders, Michael & Swann, Donald. The Hippopotamus Song: A Muddy Love Story. Westcott, Nadine B., illus. (ps-3). 1991. 14.95 (0-316-28557-9) Little.
Flanders, Stephen A. Capital Punishment. 240p. (gr. 9-12). 1991. 22.95x (0-8160-1912-6) Facts on File.
—Suicide. 240p. (gr. 9-12). 1991. 22.95x (0-8160-1909-6) Facts on File.
Flanders, Stephen A. & Flanders, Carl N. AIDS. 240p. (gr. 9-12). 1990. 22.95x (0-8160-1910-X) Facts on File.
Flashinski, Linda. Just As We Are. Flashinski, Todd, illus. 120p. (gr. k-8). 1987. spiral bdg. 11.95 (0-9619625-0-X); lib. bdg. 14.95 (0-9619625-1-8) Lavinia Pub.
Flatt, Carol, jt. auth. see Edeen, Susan.
Flaubert, Gustave. Madame Bovary. (gr. 11 up). 1965. pap. 1.95 (0-8049-0089-2, CL-89) Airmont.
Flaxman, J., jt. auth. see Hall, K.
Fleckenstein, Henry A., Jr. Decoys of the Mid-Atlantic Region. LC 79-52438. (Illus.). 256p. (gr. 9-12). 1989. pap. 19.95 (0-88740-174-0) Schiffer.
Fleet, Matthew Van see Van Fleet, Matthew.
Fleetwood, Jenni. While Shepherds Watched. Pearson, Susan, ed. Melnyczuk, Peter, illus. LC 91-38779. 32p. (gr. k up). 1992. 14.00 (0-688-11598-5); PLB 13.93 (0-688-11599-3) Lothrop.
Fleetwood, Jennie. Happy Birthday: Nine Birthday Stories. Willow, illus. 96p. (gr. 2-4). 1993. 16.95 (0-460-88050-0, Pub. by J M Dent & Sons) Trafalgar.
Fleetwood, Wade B. The Case of the Pelican's Feather: An Ocean City, Maryland Novel. Boren, James H., illus. LC 91-77403. 296p. 1992. pap. 5.95 (0-9631466-0-2) W B Fleetwood.
Flegenheimer-Riggle, Ellen, jt. auth. see Chapin, Laurie.
Flegg, Jim. Animal Builders. (Illus.). 32p. (gr. 4-6). 1991. PLB 11.90 (1-878137-05-0) Newington.
—Animal Communication. (Illus.). 32p. (gr. 4-6). 1991. PLB 11.90 (1-878137-23-9) Newington.
—Animal Families. (Illus.). 32p. (gr. 4-6). 1991. PLB 11.90 (1-878137-20-4) Newington.
—Animal Helpers. (Illus.). 32p. (gr. 4-6). 1991. PLB 11.90 (1-878137-06-9) Newington.
—Animal Hunters. (Illus.). 32p. (gr. 4-6). 1991. PLB 11.90 (1-878137-04-2) Newington.
—Animal Movement. (Illus.). 32p. (gr. 4-6). 1991. PLB 11.90 (1-878137-22-0) Newington.
—Animal Senses. (Illus.). 32p. (gr. 4-6). 1991. PLB 11.90 (1-878137-21-2) Newington.
—Animal Travelers. (Illus.). 32p. (gr. 4-6). 1991. PLB 11.90 (1-878137-19-0) Newington.
Flegler, Daniel, jt. auth. see Conrad, Steven R.
Fleischer, Jane. Pontiac, Chief of the Ottawas. LC 78-18050. (Illus.). 48p. (gr. 4-6). 1979. PLB 10.59 (0-89375-156-1); pap. 3.50 (0-89375-146-4); cassette avail. Troll Assocs.

—Sitting Bull, Warrior of the Sioux. new ed. LC 78-18047. (Illus.). 48p. (gr. 4-6). 1979. PLB 10.59 (0-89375-154-5); pap. 3.50 (0-89375-144-8) Troll Assocs.
—Tecumseh, Shawnee War Chief. new ed. LC 78-18046. (Illus.). 48p. (gr. 4-6). 1979. PLB 10.59 (0-89375-153-7); pap. 3.50 (0-89375-143-X) Troll Assocs.
Fleischhacker, Daniel J. The Merry Pranks of Tyll. 46p. 1961. 4.50 (0-87602-157-7) Anchorage.
Fleischman, Paul. The Birthday Tree. Sewall, Marcia, illus. LC 78-22155. (gr. k-3). 1979. PLB 13.89 (0-06-021916-5) HarpC Child Bks.
—The Birthday Tree. Sewall, Marcia, illus. LC 78-22155. 32p. (gr. k-3). 1991. pap. 4.50 (0-06-443246-7, Trophy) HarpC Child Bks.
—The Borning Room. LC 91-4432. 80p. (gr. 6 up). 1991. 14.00 (0-06-023762-7); PLB 13.89 (0-06-023785-6) HarpC Child Bks.
—The Borning Room. LC 91-4432. 112p. (gr. 7 up). 1993. pap. 3.95 (0-06-447099-7, Trophy) HarpC Child Bks.
—Bull Run. Frampton, David, illus. LC 92-14745. 112p. (gr. 5 up). 1993. 14.00 (0-06-021446-5); PLB 13.89 (0-06-021447-3) HarpC Child Bks.
—Coming-&-Going Men: Four Tales. Gaul, Randy, illus. LC 84-48336. 160p. (gr. 6 up). 1985. PLB 12.89 (0-06-021884-3) HarpC Child Bks.
—Copier Creations. LC 91-45413. (Illus.). 128p. (gr. 3-9). 1993. pap. 8.95 (0-06-446152-1, Trophy) HarpC Child Bks.
—Copier Creations: Using Copy Machines to Make Decals, Silhouettes, Flip Books, Films, & Much More! Cain, David, illus. LC 91-45413. 128p. (gr. 3 up). 1993. 14.00 (0-06-021052-4); PLB 13.89 (0-06-021053-2) HarpC Child Bks.
—Finzel the Farsighted. Sewall, Marcia, illus. LC 83-1416. 48p. (gr. 1-5). 1983. 11.95 (0-525-44057-7, DCB) Dutton Child Bks.
—Graven Images. LC 81-48649. (Illus.). 96p. (gr. 6 up). 1982. 14.00 (0-06-021906-8); PLB 13.89 (0-06-021907-6) HarpC Child Bks.
—Graven Images. Glass, Andrew, illus. LC 81-48649. 96p. (gr. 6 up). 1987. pap. 3.50 (0-06-440186-3, Trophy) HarpC Child Bks.
—The Half-a-Moon Inn. Jacobi, Kathy, illus. LC 79-2010. 96p. (gr. k-4). 1980. PLB 12.89 (0-06-021918-1) HarpC Child Bks.
—The Half-a-Moon Inn. Jacobi, Kathy, illus. LC 79-2010. 96p. (gr. 3-7). 1991. pap. 3.95 (0-06-440364-5, Trophy) HarpC Child Bks.
—I Am Phoenix. LC 85-24615. (Illus.). 64p. (gr. 2 up). 1989. pap. 3.95 (0-06-446092-4, Trophy) HarpC Child Bks.
—I Am Phoenix: Poems for Two Voices. Nutt, Ken, illus. LC 85-24615. 64p. (gr. 3-8). 1985. 12.00 (0-06-021881-9); PLB 11.89 (0-06-021882-7) HarpC Child Bks.
—Joyful Noise: Poems for Two Voices. Beddows, Eric, illus. LC 87-45280. 64p. (gr. 3-8). 1988. 14.00 (0-06-021852-5); PLB 13.89 (0-06-021853-3) HarpC Child Bks.
—Joyful Noise: Poems for Two Voices. Beddows, Eric, illus. LC 87-45280. 64p. (gr. 3 up). 1992. pap. 3.95 (0-06-446093-2, Trophy) HarpC Child Bks.
—Path of the Pale Horse. LC 82-48611. 160p. (gr. 6 up). 1983. PLB 12.89 (0-06-021905-X) HarpC Child Bks.
—Path of the Pale Horse. LC 82-48611. 160p. (gr. 5 up). 1992. pap. 3.95 (0-06-440442-0, Trophy) HarpC Child Bks.
—Rear-View Mirrors. LC 85-45387. 128p. (gr. 7 up). 1986. 12.95 (0-06-021866-5); PLB 12.89 (0-06-021867-3) HarpC Child Bks.
—Rondo in C. Wentworth, Janet, illus. LC 87-29375. 32p. (gr. k-3). 1988. PLB 13.89 (0-06-021857-6) HarpC Child Bks.
—Saturnalia. LC 89-36380. 128p. (gr. 7 up). 1990. 14.00 (0-06-021912-2); PLB 13.89 (0-06-021913-0) HarpC Child Bks.
—Saturnalia. LC 89-36380. 128p. (gr. 7 up). 1992. pap. 3.95 (0-06-447089-X, Trophy) HarpC Child Bks.
—Shadow Play. Beddows, Eric, illus. LC 89-26874. 48p. (gr. 2 up). 1990. PLB 14.89 (0-06-021865-7) HarpC Child Bks.
—Time Train. Ewart, Claire, illus. LC 90-27357. 32p. (gr. k-4). 1991. 15.00 (0-06-021709-X); PLB 14.89 (0-06-021710-3) HarpC Child Bks.
—Time Train. Ewart, Claire, illus. LC 90-27357. 32p. (gr. k-4). 1994. pap. 4.95 (0-06-443351-X, Trophy) HarpC Child Bks.
—Townsend's Warbler. LC 91-26836. (Illus.). 64p. (gr. 3-7). 1992. 13.00 (0-06-021874-6); PLB 12.89 (0-06-021875-4) HarpC Child Bks.
Fleischman, Sid. By the Great Horn Spoon. Von Schmidt, Eric, illus. (gr. 4-6). 1988. 15.95 (0-316-28577-3, Joy St Bks); pap. 4.95 (0-316-28612-5, Joy St Bks) Little.
—Chancy & the Grand Rascal. Von Schmidt, Eric, illus. 190p. (gr. 3-7). 1989. 14.95 (0-316-28575-7, Joy St Bks); pap. 4.95 (0-316-26012-6, Joy St Bks) Little.
—The Ghost in the Noonday Sun. Sis, Peter, illus. LC 88-11066. (gr. 5 up). 1989. 11.95 (0-688-08410-9) Greenwillow.
—The Ghost in the Noonday Sun. 144p. (gr. 3-7). 1991. pap. 2.75 (0-590-43662-7, Apple Paperbacks) Scholastic Inc.

—The Ghost on Saturday Night. Von Schmidt, Eric, illus. 64p. (gr. 4-6). 1974. 14.95 (0-316-28583-8, Joy St Bks) Little.
—The Ghost on Saturday Night. 32p. (gr. 3-6). 1974. pap. 2.56 (0-685-63795-6, BR8553) W A T Braille.
—Ghost on Saturday Night. 32p. 1992. pap. text ed. 2.56 (1-56956-241-5) W A T Braille.
—Here Comes McBroom. Blake, Quentin, illus. LC 91-32689. 80p. (gr. 1 up). 1992. 14.00 (0-688-11160-2) Greenwillow.
—Humbug Mountain. Von Schmidt, Eric, illus. (gr. 3-7). 1988. pap. 4.95 (0-316-28613-3, Joy St Bks) Little.
—Jim Ugly. Sewall, Marcia, illus. LC 91-14392. 144p. (gr. 3 up). 1992. 14.00 (0-688-10886-5) Greenwillow.
—Jim Ugly. (gr. 4-7). 1993. pap. 3.50 (0-440-40803-2) Dell.
—McBroom & the Big Wind. Lorraine, Walter H., illus. 48p. (gr. 3 up). 1982. (Pub. by Atlantic Monthly Pr); pap. 3.95 (0-316-28544-7) Little.
—McBroom & the Great Race. Lorraine, Walter H., illus. 64p. (gr. 3-7). 1980. 13.95 (0-316-28568-4, Joy St Bks) Little.
—McBroom Tells the Truth. Lorraine, Walter H., illus. LC 81-1035. 48p. (gr. 3-7). 1981. 12.45i (0-316-28550-1, Pub. by Atlantic Pr) Little.
—McBroom's Almanac. Lorraine, Walter H., illus. (gr. 3-7). 1984. 14.95 (0-316-26009-6, Joy St Bks) Little.
—McBroom's Wonderful One-Acre Farm. Blake, Quentin, illus. LC 91-31906. 64p. (gr. 1 up). 1992. 14.00 (0-688-11159-9) Greenwillow.
—The Midnight Horse. Sis, Peter, illus. LC 89-23441. 84p. (gr. 3 up). 1990. 13.00 (0-688-09441-4) Greenwillow.
—Midnight Horse. (gr. 4-7). 1992. pap. 3.50 (0-440-40614-5) Dell.
—The Scarebird. Sis, Peter, illus. LC 87-4099. 32p. (gr. k-3). 1988. 15.00 (0-688-07317-4); lib. bdg. 14.93 (0-688-07318-2) Greenwillow.
—The Scarebird. Sis, Peter, illus. 32p. (ps up). 1994. pap. 4.95 (0-688-13105-0, Mulberry) Morrow.
—The Whipping Boy. Sis, Peter, illus. LC 85-17555. 96p. (gr. 2-6). 1986. PLB 15.00 (0-688-06216-4) Greenwillow.
—The Whipping Boy. Sis, Peter, illus. (gr. 2-5). 1987. pap. 2.95 (0-8167-1038-4) Troll Assocs.
—The Whipping Boy. large type ed. (Illus.). 104p. 1989. lib. bdg. 15.95 (1-55736-115-0, Crnrstn Bks) BDD LT Grp.
—The Whipping Boy. 95p. 1992. text ed. 7.60 (1-56956-123-0) W A T Braille.
Fleischman, Susan. Boy Who Looked for Spring. LC 90-36819. (gr. 4-7). 1993. 15.95 (0-15-210699-5) HarBrace.
Fleisher, Gila M. Dan Goes to First Grade. Kriss, David, tr. from HEB. Eagle, Mike, illus. 24p. (Orig.). (ps). 1992. pap. text ed. 3.00x (1-56134-166-5) Dushkin Pub.
—Daniel Entra Al Primer Grado. Writer, C. C. & Nielsen, Lisa C., trs. Eagle, Mike, illus. (SPA.). 24p. (Orig.). (ps). 1992. pap. text ed. 3.00x (1-56134-176-2) Dushkin Pub.
Fleisher, Paul. Ecology A to Z. LC 93-13623. (Illus.). 192p. (gr. 5). 1994. RSBE 14.95 (0-87518-561-4, Dillon) Macmillan Child Grp.
—The Master Violinmaker. Saunders, David, photos by. LC 92-28050. (Illus.). 1993. 14.95 (0-395-65365-7) HM.
—Secrets of the Universe: Discovering the Universal Laws of Science. Keeler, Patricia, illus. LC 86-14001. 224p. (gr. 5-9). 1987. SBE 17.95 (0-689-31266-0, Atheneum Child Bk) Macmillan Child Grp.
—Write Now! 80p. (gr. 5-8). 1989. 8.95 (0-86653-493-8, GA1088) Good Apple.
Fleisher, Paul & Keeler, Patricia. Looking Inside: Machines & Constructions. LC 90-743. (Illus.). 40p. (gr. 2-7). 1991. RSBE 13.95 (0-689-31483-3, Atheneum Child Bk) Macmillan Child Grp.
Fleischmann, Devorah E., jt. auth. see Fleishmann, Hedy.
Fleischmann, Hedy & Fleischmann, Devorah E. Bittersweet Beginnings. LC 92-76096. 140p. 1992. write for info. (1-56062-125-7); pap. write for info. (1-56062-126-5) CIS South.
Fleissner, Else M. Herman N. Hesse: Modern German Poet & Writer. Rahmas, D. Steve, ed. LC 70-190244. 32p. (Orig.). (gr. 7-12). 1972. lib. bdg. 4.95 incl. catalog cards (0-87157-526-4) SamHar Pr.
—Inflation. Rahmas, D. Steve, ed. LC 72-89225. 32p. (Orig.). (gr. 7-12). 1973. lib. bdg. 4.95 incl. catalog cards (0-87157-803-4) SamHar Pr.
Fleming, Alice. George Washington Wasn't Always Old. (gr. 4-7). 1991. pap. 11.95 jacketed (0-671-69557-6, Little Simon) S&S Trade.
—George Washington Wasn't Always Old. (gr. 5). 1991. pap. write for info. (0-663-56243-0) Silver Burdett Pr.
—The King of Prussia & a Peanut Butter Sandwich. Himler, Ronald, illus. LC 88-18244. 48p. (gr. 2-4). 1988. SBE 13.95 (0-684-18880-5, Scribners Young Read) Macmillan Child Grp.
—P. T. Barnum. (gr. 4-7). 1993. PLB 15.85 (0-8027-8235-3) Walker & Co.
—P. T. Barnum: The World's Greatest Showman. LC 93-14720. 1993. 14.95 (0-8027-8234-5) Walker & Co.
—What, Me Worry? How to Hang in When Your Problems Stress You Out. LC 91-31678. 96p. (gr. 7 up). 1992. SBE 12.95 (0-684-19277-2, Scribners Young Read) Macmillan Child Grp.

—What to Say When You Don't Know What to Say. LC 82-5782. 128p. (gr. 7 up). 1982. SBE 13.95 (*0-684-17626-2*, Scribners Young Read) Macmillan Child Grp.

Fleming, Beatrice J. & Pryde, Marion J. Distinguished Negroes Abroad. rev. ed. (Illus.). (gr. 1-6). 1990. 21.95 (*0-87498-002-X*) Assoc Pubs DC.

Fleming, Beverly A. Scott the Dot: A Self-Esteem Tale for Children. Fleming, Beverly A., illus. LC 91-44898. 32p. (Orig.). (ps-3). 1992. pap. 3.95 (*0-915166-73-9*) Impact Pubs Cal.

Fleming, Bill, jt. auth. see Petersen-Fleming, Judy.

Fleming, Candace. Professor Fergus Fahrenheit & His Wonderful Weather Machine. Weller, Don, illus. LC 93-4432. 1994. pap. 14.00 (*0-671-87047-5*, S&S BFYR) S&S Trade.

Fleming, Denise. Barnyard Banter. LC 93-11032. 1994. write for info. (*0-8050-1957-X*) H Holt & Co.

—Count! Fleming, Denise, illus. LC 91-25686. 32p. (ps-1). 1992. 14.95 (*0-8050-1595-7*, Bks Young Read) H Holt & Co.

—In the Small, Small Pond. Fleming, Denise, illus. LC 92-25770. 32p. (ps-1). 1993. PLB 15.95 (*0-8050-2264-3*, Bks Young Read) H Holt & Co.

—In the Tall, Tall Grass. Fleming, Denise, illus. LC 90-26444. 32p. (ps-1). 1991. 15.95 (*0-8050-1635-X*, Bks Young Read) H Holt & Co.

—In the Tall, Tall Grass. Fleming, Denise, illus. 32p. (ps-1). 1993. pap. 19.95 (*0-8050-2950-8*, Bks Young Read) H Holt & Co.

—Lunch. LC 92-178. (Illus.). 32p. (ps-2). 1992. 14.95 (*0-8050-1636-8*, Bks Young Read) H Holt & Co.

Fleming, Ian. Chitty Chitty Bang Bang. 159p. (gr. 5-6). Repr. of 1964 ed. lib. bdg. 15.95 (*0-88411-983-1*, Pub. by Aeonian Pr) Amereon Ltd.

—Chitty-Chitty-Bang-Bang. Burningham, John, illus. LC 64-21282. 112p. (gr. 3-7). 1989. pap. 2.95 (*0-394-81948-9*) Knopf Bks Yng Read.

Fleming, Joyce C. The Tale of Lovable, the Baby Walrus. 1993. 6.95 (*0-8062-4703-7*) Carlton.

Fleming, Ray. Diplomatic Relations. LC 81-82660. 59p. (gr. 9-12). 1982. pap. 4.00x perfect bd. (*0-916418-34-0*) Lotus.

Fleming, Red. Recollections of a Mountain Boy Plus Stories of Sudden Death. Rose, Jennifer, ed. Rose, Krystal, illus. 112p. (Orig.). 1992. pap. 9.95 (*0-930401-55-7*) Artex Pub.

Fleming, Robert A. Fleming's One Thousand: Top College Merit Scholarships. 71p. (gr. 9-12). 1992. pap. 19.95 (*0-9637250-3-3*) Coll News Parents.

Fleming, Ronald L., jt. auth. see Von Tscharner, Renata.

Fleming, Stuart. The Egyptians. LC 91-41198. (Illus.). 64p. (gr. 6 up). 1992. RSBE 14.95 (*0-02-730654-2*, New Discovery) Macmillan Child Grp.

Fleming, Thomas. Band of Brothers. (gr. 8 up). 1988. 13.95 (*0-8027-6740-0*); PLB 14.85 (*0-8027-6741-9*) Walker & Co.

—Behind the Headlines. (gr. 5 up). 1989. 14.95 (*0-8027-6890-3*); PLB 15.85 (*0-8027-6891-1*) Walker & Co.

—First in Their Hearts: A Biography of George Washington. LC 90-48979. (Illus.). 176p. (gr. 6-10). 1991. PLB 13.95 (*1-55905-099-3*) Marshall Cavendish.

—Harry S Truman. LC 93-153. 1993. 14.95 (*0-8027-8267-1*); lib. bdg. 15.85 (*0-8027-8269-8*) Walker & Co.

Fleming, Virginia. Be Good to Eddie Lee. Cooper, Floyd, illus. 32p. (ps-3). 1993. write for info. (Philomel Bks) Putnam Pub Group.

—Be Good to Eddie Lee. Cooper, Floyd, illus. 32p. (ps-3). 1993. PLB 14.95 (*0-399-21993-5*, Philomel Bks) Putnam Pub Group.

Flesch, Carl. The Art of Violin Playing, Bk. 1. rev. ed. Martens, Frederick H., tr. (Illus.). 188p. 1924. pap. 24.95 (*0-8258-0135-4*, 01317) Fischer Inc NY.

—The Art of Violin Playing: Artistic Realization & Instruction, Book 2. Martens, Frederick H., tr. 237p. 1930. pap. 24.95 (*0-8258-0136-2*, 0 2046) Fischer Inc NY.

Fletcher, Bill & Fletcher, Sally. The Universe is My Home: A Children's Adventure Story. Fletcher, Bill & Fletcher, Sally, illus. 34p. (gr. k-5). 1993. 14.95 (*0-9634622-0-2*) Sci & Art Prods.

Fletcher, Cynthia H. My Jesus Pocketbook of ABC's. Sherman, Erin, illus. LC 81-80218. 32p. (Orig.). (ps-3). 1981. pap. 0.69 (*0-937420-01-8*) Stirrup Assoc.

—My Jesus Pocketbook of Nursery Rhymes. Sherman, Erin, illus. LC 80-52041. 32p. (Orig.). (ps-3). 1980. pap. 0.69 (*0-937420-00-X*) Stirrup Assoc.

Fletcher, Guy, jt. auth. see Flett, Douglas.

Fletcher, Helen J. & Groves, Seli. How on Earth Do We Recycle Paper? Seiden, Art, illus. LC 91-24404. 64p. (gr. 4-6). 1992. PLB 12.90 (*1-56294-140-2*) Millbrook Pr.

Fletcher, James. Exploring Geography: Using the Atlas. 80p. (Orig.). (gr. 5-8). 1986. pap. text ed. 20.00 (*0-528-17782-6*) Rand McNally.

Fletcher, John see Bald, Robert C.

Fletcher, Ralph. I Am Wings. Baker, Joe, illus. 48p. (gr. 5-9). 1994. SBE 12.95 (*0-02-735395-8*, Bradbury Pr) Macmillan Child Grp.

—Water Planet. 48p. (Orig.). (ps-3). 1991. pap. 5.95x (*0-9628238-5-6*) Language Lrn Assocs.

Fletcher, S., jt. auth. see Dellinger, A.

Fletcher, Sally, jt. auth. see Fletcher, Bill.

Fletcher, Sarah. My Bible Story Book. LC 73-91810. (Illus.). 72p. (ps-3). 1974. 9.99 (*0-570-03423-X*, 56-1171) Concordia.

—My Stories about God's People. Kueker, Don, illus. 32p. (ps-3). 1974. pap. 2.89 (*0-570-03426-4*, 56-1181) Concordia.

—My Stories about Jesus. Kueker, Don, illus. 32p. (ps-3). 1974. pap. 2.89 (*0-570-03427-2*, 56-1182) Concordia.

—Prayers for Little People. Kueker, Don, illus. 32p. (gr. 3-7). 1974. pap. 2.89 (*0-570-03429-9*, 56-1184) Concordia.

—Teen Manners--Why Bother: Showing You Care Helps Others to Like you. (Illus.). 64p. (gr. 7-12). 1987. pap. 3.99 (*0-570-04449-9*, 12-3060) Concordia.

Fletcher, Susan. Dragon's Milk. LC 88-35059. 224p. (gr. 6 up). 1989. SBE 15.95 (*0-689-31579-1*, Atheneum Child Bk) Macmillan Child Grp.

—Dragon's Milk. LC 91-31358. 256p. (gr. 3-7). 1992. pap. 3.95 (*0-689-71623-0*, Aladdin) Macmillan Child Grp.

—Flight of the Dragon Kyn. LC 92-44787. 224p. (gr. 5-9). 1993. SBE 15.95 (*0-689-31880-4*, Atheneum Child Bk) Macmillan Child Grp.

—The Stuttgart Nanny Mafia. LC 90-23225. 160p. (gr. 3-7). 1991. SBE 14.95 (*0-689-31709-3*, Atheneum Child Bk) Macmillan Child Grp.

Flett, Douglas & Fletcher, Guy. The Goose That Laid the Golden Egg. 38p. (gr. 3-6). 1991. pap. 69.95 (*1-56516-003-7*) Houston IN.

—The Hare & the Tortoise. 38p. (gr. 3-6). 1991. pap. 69.95 (*1-56516-004-5*) Houston IN.

Flettrich, Terry. House in the Bend of Bourbon Street. Lo-An, illus. (gr. 1-6). 1974. pap. 2.95 (*0-88289-015-8*) Pelican.

Flewellyn, Valada S. Poetically, Just Us. 128p. (gr. 5-12). 1992. text ed. 24.95 (*1-880997-01-0*) Parker Init Pubns.

Flick, Pauline. Discovering Toys & Toy Museums. 2nd ed. (Illus.). 72p. (Orig.). (gr. 6 up). 1977. pap. 3.00 (*0-913714-38-0*) Legacy Bks.

Flieger, Pat. The Fog's Net. Gamper, Ruth, illus. LC 93-31512. 1994. write for info. (*0-395-68194-4*) HM.

Flier, Michael S., jt. auth. see Stepanoff, N. C.

Fling, Helen. Marionettes: How to Make & Work Them. Forbell, Charles, illus. (gr. 6 up). 16.50 (*0-8446-4736-5*) Peter Smith.

Fling, Paul N. & Puterbaugh, Donald L. The Basic Manual of Fly Tying: Fundamentals of Imitation. rev. ed. LC 92-25346. (Illus.). 232p. (gr. 10-12). 1992. pap. 16.95 (*0-8069-8654-9*) Sterling.

Flinn, Lisa, jt. auth. see Younger, Barbara.

Flint, David. Canada. LC 92-43923. (Illus.). 32p. (gr. 3-4). 1993. PLB 19.24 (*0-8114-2939-3*) Raintree Steck-V.

—China. LC 93-15794. (Illus.). 32p. (gr. 3-4). 1993. PLB 19.24 (*0-8114-3421-4*) Raintree Steck-V.

—Egypt. LC 93-10995. (Illus.). 32p. (gr. 3-4). 1993. PLB 19.24 (*0-8114-3420-6*) Raintree Steck-V.

—Germany. LC 93-631. (Illus.). 32p. (gr. 3-4). 1993. PLB 19.24 (*0-8114-3418-4*) Raintree-Steck V.

—Germany. LC 93-26534. 1993. write for info. (*0-8114-1845-6*) Raintree Steck-V.

—Japan. LC 92-43189. (gr. 5 up). 1992. write for info. Raintree Steck-V.

—Japan. LC 92-43189. (Illus.). 32p. (gr. 3-4). 1992. PLB 19.24 (*0-8114-2940-7*) Raintree Steck-V.

—The Mediterranean & Its People. (Illus.). 48p. (gr. 5-8). 1994. 15.95 (*1-56847-166-1*) Thomson Lrning.

—Mexico. LC 93-7529. (Illus.). 32p. (gr. 3-4). 1993. PLB 19.24 (*0-8114-3419-2*) Raintree Steck-V.

—The Prairies & Their People. (Illus.). 48p. (gr. 5-8). 1994. 15.95 (*1-56847-154-8*) Thomson Lrning.

—Russia. LC 92-43190. (gr. 5 up). 1992. write for info. Raintree Steck-V.

—Russia. LC 92-43190. (Illus.). 32p. (gr. 3-4). 1992. PLB 19.24 (*0-8114-2941-5*) Raintree Steck-V.

—The Russian Federation. LC 92-5737. (Illus.). 32p. (gr. 4-6). 1992. PLB 13.90 (*1-56294-305-7*) Millbrook Pr.

—The United Kingdom. LC 93-13610. 1994. write for info. (*0-8114-1849-9*) Raintree Steck-V.

—Weather & Climate: Projects with Geography. (Illus.). 32p. (gr. 5-8). 1991. PLB 12.40 (*0-531-17321-6*, Gloucester Pr) Watts.

—West Indies. LC 92-43914. (Illus.). 32p. (gr. 3-4). 1993. PLB 19.24 (*0-8114-2942-3*) Raintree Steck-V.

—The World's Weather. LC 93-6827. (Illus.). 32p. (gr. 4-6). 1993. 14.95 (*1-56847-053-3*) Thomson Lrning.

Flint, David C. The Baltic States. LC 92-2240. (Illus.). 32p. (gr. 4-6). 1992. PLB 13.90 (*1-56294-310-3*) Millbrook Pr.

Flint, S. Jane. Viruses. Head, J. J., ed. Imrick, Ann T., illus. LC 87-70987. 16p. (Orig.). (gr. 10 up). 1988. pap. text ed. 2.75 (*0-89278-094-0*, 45-9794) Carolina Biological.

Flippo, Rona. Test Wise. (gr. 7-12). 1988. pap. 13.95 (*0-8224-6939-1*) Fearon Teach Aids.

Flodin, Mickey. Signing for Kids: The Fun Way for Anyone to Learn American Sign Language. (Illus.). 144p. (gr. 3-9). 1991. pap. 9.95 (*0-399-51672-7*, Perigee Bks) Putnam Pub Group.

Flodin, Mickey, jt. auth. see Butterworth, Rod R.

Floding, Matthew, jt. auth. see Nystrom, Carolyn.

Flood, E. L. The Fly. LC 91-7376. (Illus.). 48p. (gr. 5-6). 1991. RSBE 13.95 (*0-89686-574-6*, Crestwood Hse) Macmillan Child Grp.

—A Nightmare on Elm Street. LC 90-47425. (Illus.). 48p. (gr. 5-6). 1991. RSBE 13.95 (*0-89686-579-7*, Crestwood Hse) Macmillan Child Grp.

Flood, Renee S., ed. see Crow, Moses N.

Flora. Feathers Like a Rainbow: An Amazon Indian Tale. Flora, illus. LC 88-26788. 32p. (gr. k-3). 1989. PLB 14.89 (*0-06-021838-X*) HarpC Child Bks.

Flora, James. The Fabulous Firework Family. Flora, James, illus. LC 93-11472. (SPA.). 32p. (gr. k-4). 1994. SBE 14.95 (*0-689-50596-5*, M K McElderry) Macmillan Child Grp.

—Grandpa's Ghost Stories. LC 78-51999. (Illus.). 32p. (gr. k-4). 1980. SBE 13.95 (*0-689-50112-9*, M K McElderry) Macmillan Child Grp.

Flor Ada, Alma, tr. see Rohmer, Harriet.

Flores, Anthony. Awards, Rewards & Marvelous Messages. (gr. 1-6). 1985. pap. 8.95 (*0-8224-0535-0*) Fearon Teach Aids.

—From the Hands of a Child. (ps-4). 1987. pap. 8.95 (*0-8224-3167-X*) Fearon Teach Aids.

—Instant Borders. (gr. k-6). 1979. pap. 9.95 (*0-8224-3899-2*) Fearon Teach Aids.

—Instant Bulletin Boards: Month by Month Classroom Graphics. (gr. k-6). 1983. pap. 12.95 (*0-8224-3900-X*) Fearon Teach Aids.

Flores, Kathy. Beauty for Ashes. Cox, Gail, ed. Gobble, Janice, illus. Malvido, Lalo, photos by. 37p. (Orig.). 1990. pap. 3.98 (*0-9626862-0-4*) K Flores Min.

Florian, D. Vegetable Garden. 1991. 13.95 (*0-15-293383-2*, HB Juv Bks) HarBrace.

Florian, Douglas. At the Zoo. LC 89-77727. 32p. (ps up). 1992. 14.00 (*0-688-09628-X*); PLB 13.93 (*0-688-09629-8*) Greenwillow.

—An Auto Mechanic. LC 90-48809. (Illus.). 24p. (ps up). 1991. 13.95 (*0-688-10635-8*); PLB 13.88 (*0-688-10636-6*) Greenwillow.

—An Auto Mechanic. Florian, Douglas, illus. 24p. (ps up). 1994. pap. 3.95 (*0-688-13104-2*, Mulberry) Morrow.

—Beach Day. LC 89-1933. (Illus.). 32p. (ps up). 1990. 12.95 (*0-688-09104-0*); lib. bdg. 12.88 (*0-688-09105-9*) Greenwillow.

—Beast Feast. LC 93-10720. (gr. 5 up). 1994. write for info. (*0-15-295178-4*) HarBrace.

—A Carpenter. LC 90-30752. (Illus.). 24p. (ps up). 1991. 13.95 (*0-688-09760-X*); PLB 13.88 (*0-688-09761-8*) Greenwillow.

—A Chef. LC 91-29545. (Illus.). 32p. (ps-3). 1992. 14.00 (*0-688-11108-4*); PLB 13.93 (*0-688-11109-2*) Greenwillow.

—City Street. Florian, Douglas, illus. LC 89-28694. 32p. (ps up). 1990. 12.95 (*0-688-09543-7*); PLB 12.88 (*0-688-09544-5*) Greenwillow.

—Discovering Butterflies. LC 89-37816. 32p. (ps-2). 1990. pap. 3.95 (*0-689-71376-2*, Aladdin) Macmillan Child Grp.

—Discovering Frogs. Florian, Douglas, illus. LC 86-6731. 32p. (ps-3). 1986. SBE 13.95 (*0-684-18688-8*, Scribners Young Read) Macmillan Child Grp.

—Discovering Seashells. Florian, Douglas, illus. LC 86-11903. 32p. (ps-2). 1986. SBE 13.95 (*0-684-18740-X*, Scribners Young Read) Macmillan Child Grp.

—Discovering Trees. LC 89-37817. 32p. (ps-2). 1990. pap. 3.95 (*0-689-71377-0*, Aladdin) Macmillan Child Grp.

—A Fisher. LC 93-26515. 1994. write for info. (*0-688-13129-8*); PLB write for info. (*0-688-13130-1*) Greenwillow.

—Monster Motel. LC 92-7309. (ps-3). 1993. 13.99 (*0-15-255320-7*) HarBrace.

—Nature Walk. LC 88-39430. (Illus.). 32p. (ps up). 1989. 12.95 (*0-688-08266-1*); PLB 12.88 (*0-688-08269-6*) Greenwillow.

—A Painter. LC 92-29583. (Illus.). 32p. (ps up). 1993. 14.00 (*0-688-11872-0*); PLB 13.93 (*0-688-11873-9*) Greenwillow.

—A Potter. LC 90-33940. (Illus.). 24p. (ps up). 1991. 13.95 (*0-688-10100-3*); PLB 13.88 (*0-688-10101-1*) Greenwillow.

—A Summer Day. LC 87-8484. (Illus.). 24p. (ps-1). 1988. 11.95 (*0-688-07564-9*); lib. bdg. 11.88 (*0-688-07565-7*) Greenwillow.

—Turtle Day. Florian, Douglas, illus. LC 88-30321. 32p. (ps-2). 1989. (Crowell Jr Bks); PLB 13.89 (*0-690-04745-2*, Crowell Jr Bks) HarpC Child Bks.

—A Winter Day. LC 86-33524. (Illus.). 24p. (ps-1). 1987. 11.75 (*0-688-07351-4*); lib. bdg. 11.88 (*0-688-07352-2*) Greenwillow.

—A Year in the Country. LC 88-16026. (Illus.). 32p. (ps up). 1989. 12.95 (*0-688-08186-X*); lib. bdg. 12.88 (*0-688-08187-8*) Greenwillow.

Flory, Jane. The Great Bamboozlement. Flory, Jane, illus. 160p. (gr. 5-9). 1982. 13.45 (*0-395-31859-9*) HM.

Flournoy, Valerie. The Best Time of Day. Ford, George, illus. LC 77-91641. 32p. (ps-1). 1992. PLB 5.99 (*0-394-93799-6*); 2.25 (*0-394-83799-1*) Random Bks Yng Read.

—The Patchwork Quilt. Pinkey, Jerry, illus. LC 84-1711. (gr. 4-8). 1985. 14.00 (*0-8037-0097-0*); PLB 13.89 (*0-8037-0098-9*) Dial Bks Young.

Flowers, Nancy, jt. auth. see Donahue, David M.

Flowers, Sandra H. Leslie: Maybe I'll Be. Allred, David & Leonard, Camille, eds. Maudsley, Kenith, illus. 24p. (Orig.). (gr. 1-4). Date not set. pap. 1.00 (*0-9630029-4-5*) Community Comm.

Floyd, James C. Some Gentle Moving Thing. 2nd ed. McBride, Michael, illus. LC 82-60198. 70p. (gr. 7-9). 1982. 6.95 (*0-938232-11-8*) Winston-Derek.

Flucke, Paul. The Secret of the Gifts. Yoe, Craig, illus. LC 92-5679. 32p. 1992. 11.99 (*0-8308-1841-3*, 1841) InterVarsity.

Fluek, Toby. Passover As I Remember It. Fluek, Toby, illus. 42p. (gr. k-5). 1994. 14.00 (0-679-83876-7) Knopf Bks Yng Read.

Flumiani, C. M. Teenager's Guide to Economics & Finance, 2 vols. in one. LC 72-91789. (Illus.). 70p. (gr. 10-12). 1973. Set. 97.75 (0-913314-16-1) Am Classical Coll Pr.

—The Wall Street Manual for Teenagers. LC 72-89684. (Illus.). 80p. (gr. 7-12). 1973. 47.00 (0-913314-24-2) Am Classical Coll Pr.

Flyn, Jean. James Butler Bonham: The Rebel Hero. 64p. (gr. 5-7). 1984. 10.95 (0-89015-511-9) Eakin-Sunbelt.

Flynn, Amy, illus. Teddy's Busy Night. 24p. (ps). 1993. bds. 2.95 (0-448-40557-1, G&D) Putnam Pub Group.

Flynn, Jean. Jim Bowie: A Texas Legend. (gr. 4-7). 1980. 10.95 (0-89015-241-1, Pub. by Panda Bks) Eakin-Sunbelt.

—Lady: The Story of Claudia Alta (Lady Bird) Johnson. 144p. (gr. 8-12). 1992. 14.95 (0-89015-821-5) Eakin-Sunbelt.

—Stephen F. Austin: The Father of Texas. Mullin, Buddy, illus. 84p. (gr. 4-7). 1981. 10.95 (0-89015-285-5) Eakin-Sunbelt.

—William Barret Travis. (gr. 4-7). 1982. 10.95 (0-89015-348-5, Pub. by Panda Bks) Eakin-Sunbelt.

Flynn, Kristee, compiled by. A Little Book of Courage. Dann, Penny, illus. LC 93-6640. 1993. write for info. (1-56706-094-0) Childs World.

Flynn, Mary. Cornelius in Charge. Myler, Terry, illus. (Orig.). (gr. 1-6). 1990. 10.95 (0-947962-53-0, Pub. by Anvil Bks Ltd Ireland); pap. 7.95 (0-947962-54-9, Pub. by Anvil Bks Ltd Ireland) Irish Bks Media.

Flynn, Mary J. The Blue Kangaroo. Flynn, Mary J., illus. 24p. (ps-k). 1992. pap. text ed. 5.95 (1-880812-03-7) S Ink WA.

—If a Seahorse Wore a Saddle. Flynn, Mary J., illus. 48p. (Orig.). (ps-1). 1991. pap. 10.95 (0-9623072-3-8) S Ink WA.

—The Lost & Found Puppy. Flynn, Mary J., illus. 48p. (Orig.). (gr. k-1). 1991. pap. 10.95 (0-9623072-6-2) S Ink WA.

Flynn, Nigel. Orwell. (Illus.). 112p. (gr. 7 up). 1990. lib. bdg. 19.94 (0-86593-018-X); lib. bdg. 14.95s.p. (0-685-46452-0) Rourke Corp.

Fobes, Jacqueline. A Papago Boy & His Friends. (gr. 1-4). 1980. pap. 1.50 (0-686-32641-5) Impresora Sahuaro.

Fochman, Joyce. Bible Work & Play, Vol. 3. rev. ed. Lemelman, Martin, illus. 80p. 1986. pap. 5.00 wkbk. (0-8074-0305-9, 103640) UAHC.

Focus on the Family Staff & Myers, Bill. McGee & Me No. 5: Twister & Shout. 1989. pap. 3.99 (0-8423-4166-8); video 19.95 (0-8423-4156-0) Tyndale.

Fodor, R. V. Gold, Copper, Iron: How Metals Are Formed, Found, & Used. LC 87-24464. (Illus.). 96p. (gr. 6 up). 1989. lib. bdg. 16.95 (0-89490-138-9) Enslow Pubs.

—The Strange World of Deep-Sea Vents. LC 89-71442. (Illus.). 64p. (gr. 6 up). 1991. lib. bdg. 15.95 (0-89490-249-0) Enslow Pubs.

Foehl, Jamie L. Trick or Treat Taffy. Foehl, Barbara B., illus. LC 89-92436. 40p. (Orig.). (ps-6). 1989. write for info. (0-9625337-0-X); PLB write for info.; pap. write for info. B Bk Pub Co.

Fogartie, Arthur F. The Sixteenth Manger. 64p. 1987. pap. 7.00 (0-8170-1119-6) Judson.

Fogelman, Phyllis J., ed. see Barracca, Sal & Barracca, Debra.

Fogelman, Phyllis J., ed. see Kellogg, Steven.

Fogelman, Phyllis J., ed. see Kitchen, Bert.

Fogelman, Phyllis J., jt. ed. see Lester, Julius.

Fogelman, Phyllis J., ed. see Lewis, Patrick.

Fogelman, Phyllis J., ed. see Luttrell, Ida.

Fogelman, Phyllis J., ed. see Mahy, Margaret.

Fogelman, Phyllis J., ed. see Marshall, James.

Fogelman, Phyllis J., ed. see Marzollo, Jean.

Fogelman, Phyllis J., ed. see San Souci, Robert D.

Fogelman, Phyllis J., ed. see Selberg, Ingrid.

Fogelman, Phyllis J., ed. see Taylor, Mildred D.

Fogelman, Phyllis J., ed. see Wood, Audrey.

Fogelson, Genia. Charity Memorial Hospital: The Rope. (Orig.). (ps-12). 1986. pap. 2.95 (0-87067-719-5) Holloway.

—Harry Belafonte. rev. ed. (ps up) 1991. pap. 3.95 (0-87067-571-0, BH571) Holloway.

Fogelson, Gina. Charity Memorial Hospital: The Fire. (ps-12). 1985. pap. 2.95 (0-87067-716-0, BH716) Holloway.

Foghorn Press Staff. Fantasies & Monsters. (gr. 4-7). 1993. pap. 12.95 (0-685-67901-2) Foghorn Pr.

Fogle, Jeanne S. Seasons of God's Love: The Church Year. Duckert, Mary J. & Lane, Ben, eds. Widener, Bea, illus. LC 88-6414. 32p. 1988. pap. 7.99 (0-664-25032-7, Geneva Pr) Westminster John Knox.

—Signs of God's Love: Baptism & Communion. Duckert, Mary J. & Lane, W. Ben, eds. Weidner, Bea, illus. 32p. (Orig.). (gr. 3-8). 1984. pap. 7.99 (0-664-24636-2, Geneva Pr) Westminster John Knox.

—Symbols of God's Love: Codes & Passwords. Ducket, Mary Jean & Lane, W. Ben, eds. Weidner, Bea, illus. LC 86-12014. 32p. (Orig.). (gr. k-3). 1986. pap. 7.99 (0-664-24050-X, Westminster) Westminster John Knox.

—Teaching the Bible with Puppets. LC 89-50563. (Illus.). 1989. tchr's ed. 9.95 (0-89622-405-8) Twenty-Third.

Foglio, Phil, jt. auth. see Pollotta, Nick.

Folder, M. Michael, ed. see Rockefeller, R. D. & Chen, Gerald H.

Foley, jt. auth. see Bagley.

Foley, Bernice W. Spaceships of the Ancients. Hoffman, Lee, illus. LC 78-59116. (gr. 3-6). 1978. 6.95 (0-915964-04-X) Veritie Pr.

Foley, Diane. My Big Box. Quinn, Annie, illus. LC 92-31910. 1993. 3.75 (0-383-03584-8) SRA Schl Grp.

Foley, Jack, jt. auth. see MisKowski, Mike.

Foley, June. Falling in Love Is No Snap. LC 86-1990. 144p. (gr. 7 up). 1986. pap. 14.95 (0-385-29490-5) Delacorte.

—Falling in Love Is No Snap. 144p. (gr. 6 up). 1989. pap. 2.95 (0-440-20349-X, LFL) Dell.

—It's No Crush, I'm in Love. LC 81-15214. 224p. (gr. 7 up). 1982. 12.95 (0-385-28465-9) Delacorte.

—Love by Any Other Name. LC 82-72752. 224p. (gr. 7 up). 1983. pap. 13.95 (0-385-29245-7) Delacorte.

—Susanna Siegelbaum Gives up Guys. 160p. 1991. 13.95 (0-590-43699-6, Scholastic Hardcover) Scholastic Inc.

—Susanna Siegelbaum Gives up Guys. 1992. pap. 3.25 (0-590-43700-3) Scholastic Inc.

Foley, Kathryn, et al. The Good Apple Guide to Creative Drama. 128p. (gr. 2-6). 1981. 11.95 (0-86653-030-4, GA 258) Good Apple.

Foley, Leonard M., III. When Our Days Go to the Dogs: We Don't Have to Step in Their S..t! 64p. (gr. 9-12). 1992. pap. 1.95 (0-9630314-2-2) One World SC.

Foley, Louise. Australia: Find the Flying Foxes. LC 88-16911. 112p. 1989. pap. text ed. 3.95 (0-07-047996-8) McGraw.

Foley, Louise M. The Cobra Connection. 1990. pap. 3.25 (0-553-28574-2) Bantam.

—Danger at Anchor Mine. 128p. (gr. 4). 1985. pap. 2.25 (0-553-25496-0) Bantam.

—Ghost Train. (gr. 4-7). 1992. pap. 3.25 (0-553-29358-3) Bantam.

—In Search of the Hidden Statue. Miller, Cliff, illus. (gr. 2-6). 1993. incl. puzzle 12.95 (0-922242-46-1) Lombard Mktg.

—The Lost Tribe, No. 23. (Illus.). 128p. 1984. pap. 2.25 (0-553-26182-7) Bantam.

—The Mardi Gras Mystery. 128p. (Orig.). (gr. 4). 1987. pap. 2.25 (0-553-26291-2) Bantam.

—The Mystery of Echo Lodge. 128p. (gr. 4 up) 1985. pap. 2.25 (0-553-26313-7) Bantam.

—The Mystery of the Highland Crest. (gr. 4 up) 1984. pap. 1.95 (0-553-24344-6) Bantam.

—Mystery of the Sacred Stones: Choose Your Own Adventure, No. 79. 128p. (Orig.). (gr. 7 up) 1988. pap. 2.50 (0-553-26950-X) Bantam.

—Poison! Said the Cat, No. 3. 192p. 1992. pap. 3.50 (0-425-12898-9) Berkley Pub.

—Tackle Twenty-Two. Heinly, John, illus. 48p. (ps-3). 1981. pap. 1.75 (0-440-48484-7, YB) Dell.

—Thief! Said the Cat, No. 1. 1992. pap. 3.50 (0-425-12732-X) Berkley Pub.

Foley, Pat. Edge. (Illus.). 19p. (Orig.). (gr. k-1). 1989. pap. 5.00 (0-9624315-0-8) Pajari Pr.

—Seismo & Ellie. 2nd ed. Foley, Pat, illus. 14p. (gr. k-1). 1990. pap. 6.00 (0-9624315-1-6) Pajari Pr.

Foley, Patricia. John & the Fiddler. Sewall, Marcia, illus. LC 89-34514. 64p. (gr. 1-5). 1990. PLB 12.89 (0-06-021842-8) HarpC Child Bks.

Foley, Red. Red Foley's Best Baseball Book. (gr. 4-7). 1994. pap. 8.95 (0-671-87577-9, Little Simon) S&S Trade.

—Red Foley's Best Baseball Book Ever. 6th, rev. & updated ed. (Illus.). 96p. (gr. 1 up). 1992. pap. 8.95 (0-671-75426-2, Little Simon) S&S Trade.

—Red Foley's Best Baseball Book Ever, 1993. (Illus.). 80p. (gr. 1 up). 1993. pap. 8.95 (0-671-79732-8, Little Simon) S&S Trade.

—Red Foley's Cartoon History of Baseball. Whitehead, S. B., illus. 96p. (gr. 3 up). 1992. pap. 8.95 (0-671-73627-2, Little Simon) S&S Trade.

Foley, Sheila, intro. by. Faith Unfurled: The Pilgrims' Quest for Freedom. (Illus.). 64p. (Orig.). (gr. 5-12). 1993. pap. 4.95 (1-878668-24-2) Disc Enter Ltd.

Foley, Tod. Beyond the Core: Frontier Zone 5. Amthor, Terry K., ed. 64p. (Orig.). (gr. 10-12). 1987. pap. 12.00 (0-915795-83-3, 9600, Dist. by Berkley Pub Group) Iron Crown Ent Inc.

—Tales from Deep Space. Amthor, Terry K., ed. McKie, Angus, illus. 32p. (Orig.). (gr. 10-12). 1988. pap. 6.00 (1-55806-006-5, 9103) Iron Crown Ent Inc.

—War on a Distant Moon. LaDell, Leo, ed. Velez, Waller & Waltrip, Jason, illus. 32p. (Orig.). (gr. 12). 1988. pap. 6.00 (1-55806-020-0, 9104) Iron Crown Ent Inc.

Foley, Tom, illus. Sakshi Gopal: A Witness for the Wedding. Greene, Joshua, retold by. (Illus.). 16p. (gr. 1-4). 1981. pap. 2.00 (0-89647-036-9) Bala Bks.

Foley, William A., jt. auth. see Richardson, Ben.

Foley, William E., jt. auth. see McCandless, Perry.

Foling, Debra & Sherbondy, Sharon. Super Sketches for Youth Ministry: Thirty Creative Topical Dramas from Willow Creek Community Church. 192p. 1991. pap. 12.99 (0-310-53411-9, Pub. by Youth Spec) Zondervan.

Folk, Betsy E., jt. auth. see Myrick, Robert D.

Follendore, Joan, ed. see Delis-Abrams, Alexandra.

Follett, Ken. The Key to Rebecca. 352p. (gr. 9-12). 1981. pap. 4.95 (0-451-15510-6, Sig) NAL-Dutton.

—The Mystery Hideout. Marchesi, Stephen, illus. LC 89-39961. 96p. (gr. 5 up). 1990. Repr. of 1976 ed. 12.95 (0-688-08721-3) Morrow Jr Bks.

—Mystery Hideout. (gr. 4-7). 1991. pap. 2.75 (0-590-42506-4, Apple Paperbacks) Scholastic Inc.

—The Power Twins. Marchesi, Stephen, illus. LC 90-35367. 96p. (gr. 5 up). 1990. 12.95g (0-688-08723-X) Morrow Jr Bks.

—Power Twins. (gr. 4-7). 1991. pap. 2.75 (0-590-42507-2) Scholastic Inc.

Folliet, A. P., jt. auth. see Watson.

Folmer, A. P. Barnabys First Christmas. 1989. pap. 5.95 (0-590-42892-6) Scholastic Inc.

—Fabulous Christmas Fun Book. (gr. 4-7). 1993. pap. 3.95 (0-590-46476-0) Scholastic Inc.

—Fabulous Easter Fun Book. (gr. k-3). 1986. pap. 3.95 (0-590-40207-2) Scholastic Inc.

—Fabulous Halloween Fun Book. (gr. 4-7). 1993. pap. 4.95 (0-590-47348-4) Scholastic Inc.

—Fabulous Valentine Fun Book. (Illus.). 16p. (gr. k-3). 1989. pap. 3.95 (0-590-41669-3) Scholastic Inc.

—Super Eggs Easter Fun Book. (ps-3). 1992. pap. 2.95 (0-590-45557-5) Scholastic Inc.

—Valentine Pop-up Cards to Make. (ps-3). 1991. pap. 3.95 (0-590-44033-0) Scholastic Inc.

Folsom, Franklin. Black Cowboy: The Life & Legend of George McJunkin. 3rd ed. (Illus.). 162p. 1992. pap. 7.95 (1-879373-14-9) R Rinehart.

—Red Power on the Rio Grande. Ortiz, Alfonso, intro. by. 144p. (gr. 4 up). 1989. 12.95 (0-89992-421-2); pap. 9.95 (0-89992-121-3) Coun India Ed.

—Sand Dune Pony. (Illus.). 250p. (gr. 3-6). 1991. pap. 8.95 (0-911799-99-8) R Rinehart.

Folsom, Marcia & Folsom, Michael. Easy As Pie: A Guessing Game of Sayings. Kent, Jack, illus. LC 84-14978. 64p. (ps-3). 1985. 13.95 (0-89919-303-X, Clarion Bks); pap. 5.95 (0-89919-351-X, Clarion Bks) HM.

Folsom, Marcia, jt. auth. see Folsom, Michael.

Folsom, Michael & Folsom, Marcia. The Macmillan Book of How Things Work. Hammann, Brad, illus. LC 86-23761. 80p. (gr. 3-7). 1987. SBE 16.95 (0-02-735360-5, Macmillan Child Bk) Macmillan Child Grp.

—The Macmillan Book of How Things Work. Hammann, Brad, illus. LC 86-23761. 80p. (gr. 3-7). 1987. pap. 8.95 (0-689-71139-5, Aladdin) Macmillan Child Grp.

Folsom, Michael, jt. auth. see Elting, Mary.

Folsom, Michael, jt. auth. see Folsom, Marcia.

Foltzer, Monica. Alphabet Picture Key Word Cards. Hoffman, Jo-Ann, illus. 38p. 1987. 38 cards 4.60 (0-9607918-5-X, A 505419) St Ursula.

—A Sound Track to Reading. 3rd ed. 52p. (gr. 3 up). 1985. pap. text ed. 3.80 (0-9607918-4-1, 764921) St Ursula.

—Spelling Phonics Gives Sound Advice. 5th ed. 16p. 1984. pap. text ed. 1.20x (*0-9607918-2-5*, 801878) St Ursula.

Fontaine Jean de, La see De la Fontaine, Jean.

Fontana, A. I Draw, I Paint: Animals. (Illus.). 48p. (gr. 3 up). 1993. pap. 7.95 (*0-8120-1706-4*) Barron.

—I Draw, I Paint: Collage. (Illus.). 48p. (gr. 3 up). 1993. pap. 7.95 (*0-8120-1707-2*) Barron.

Fontane, Theodor. Nick Ribbeck of Ribbeck of Havelland. Bell, Anthea, tr. from GER. Koci, Marta, illus. LC 90-7164. 32p. (gr. k up). 1991. pap. 14.95 (*0-88708-149-5*) Picture Bk Studio.

Fontanel, Beatrice. Cats, Big & Little. Bogard, Vicki, tr. from FRE. Logvinoff, Anne, illus. LC 90-50772. 38p. (gr. k-5). 1991. 4.95 (*0-944589-27-8*, 278) Young Discovery Lib.

Fontanel, Beatrice & Tracqui, Valerie. The Penguin: Animal Close-Ups. (Illus.). 28p. (ps-3). 1992. pap. 6.95 (*0-88106-426-2*) Charlesbridge Pub.

Fontenot, Mary A. Clovis Crawfish & Batiste Bete Puante. Blazek, Scott R., illus. LC 93-1249. 32p. (gr. k-3). 1993. 14.95 (*0-88289-952-X*) Pelican.

—Clovis Crawfish & Bertile's Bon Voyage. Blazek, Scott R., illus. LC 90-22160. 32p. (ps-3). 1991. 12.95 (*0-88289-825-6*) Pelican.

—Clovis Crawfish & Etienne Escargot. Blazek, Scott R., illus. LC 91-26896. 32p. (ps-3). 1992. 12.95 (*0-88289-826-4*) Pelican.

—Clovis Crawfish & His Friends. rev. ed. Graves, Keith, illus. LC 85-16994. 32p. (ps-3). 1985. 12.95 (*0-88289-479-X*) Pelican.

—Clovis Crawfish & His Friends: French Edition. Graves, Keith, illus. (FRE.). 32p. (ps-3). 1994. write for info. Pelican.

—Clovis Crawfish & Michelle Mantis. Blazek, Scott R., illus. LC 88-30305. 32p. (ps-3). 1989. 12.95 (*0-88289-730-6*) Pelican.

—Clovis Crawfish & Petit Papillon. Graves, Keith, illus. LC 83-27325. 52p. (ps-3). 1985. Repr. 12.95 (*0-88289-448-X*) Pelican.

—Clovis Crawfish & Simeon Suce-Fleur. Blazek, Scott R., illus. LC 89-35370. 32p. (ps-3). 1990. 12.95 (*0-88289-751-9*) Pelican.

—Clovis Crawfish & the Curious Crapaud. Kidder, Christine, illus. LC 86-4997. 32p. (ps-3). 1986. 12.95 (*0-88289-610-5*) Pelican.

—Clovis Crawfish & the Orphan Zo Zo. Vincent, Eric, illus. LC 81-17740. 32p. (ps-3). 1983. 12.95 (*0-88289-312-2*) Pelican.

—Clovis Crawfish & the Singing Cigales. Vincent, Eric, illus. LC 81-5608. 32p. (ps-3). 1981. 12.95 (*0-88289-270-3*) Pelican.

—Clovis Crawfish & the Spinning Spider. LC 86-23778. (Illus.). 32p. (ps-3). 1987. 12.95 (*0-88289-644-X*) Pelican.

—Star Seed. Cregan, Nannette, illus. LC 86-12171. 32p. (gr. k-4). 1986. Repr. 7.95 (*0-88289-628-8*) Pelican.

Fontes, Ron & Korman, Justine. Annie Oakley in the Wild West Extravaganza! Shaw, Charlie, illus. LC 93-70937. 80p. (gr. 1-4). 1993. PLB 12.89 (*1-56282-492-9*); pap. 2.95 (*1-56282-491-0*) Disney Pr.

—Calamity Jane at Fort Sanders. LC 92-52972. (Illus.). 80p. (gr. 1-4). 1992. PLB 12.89 (*1-56282-265-9*); pap. 2.95 (*1-56282-264-0*) Disney Pr.

—Davy Crockett & the Highwaymen. LC 92-52975. (Illus.). 80p. (gr. 1-4). 1992. PLB 12.89 (*1-56282-261-6*); pap. 2.95 (*1-56282-260-8*) Disney Pr.

—Davy Crockett Meets Death Hug. Shaw, Charlie, illus. LC 93-71032. 80p. (gr. 1-4). 1993. PLB 12.89 (*1-56282-496-1*); pap. 2.95 (*1-56282-495-3*) Disney Pr.

—Wild Bill Hickok & the Rebel Raiders. Shaw, Charlie & Bill Smith Studios Staff, illus. LC 92-56159. 80p. (Orig.). (gr. 1-4). 1993. PLB 12.89 (*1-56282-494-5*); pap. 2.95 (*1-56282-493-7*) Disney Pr.

Fontes, Ron, jt. auth. see Korman, Justine.

Fontes, Ron, adapted by. Rocketeer. (gr. 4-7). 1991. pap. 2.95 (*1-56282-056-7*) Disney Pr.

Fonteyn, Margot. Swan Lake. Hyman, Trina S., illus. 1991. incl. cassette 19.95 (*0-15-200602-8*, HB Juv Bks) HarBrace.

Foon, Dennis. The Short Tree & the Bird That Could Not Sing. Bianchi, John, illus. 32p. (ps-2). 1991. pap. 4.95 (*0-88899-120-7*, Pub. by Groundwood-Douglas & McIntyre CN) Firefly Bks Ltd.

Foord, Jo, photos by. The Book of Babies: A First Picture Book of All the Things That Babies Do. LC 90-39490. (Illus.). 32p. (ps). 1991. 10.95 (*0-679-80955-4*); PLB 12.99 (*0-679-90955-9*) Random Bks Yng Read.

Foote, Margaret, jt. auth. see Jenkins, Sarah.

Foran, Eileen, adapted by. Costa Rica Is My Home. Welch, Rose, photos by. LC 92-17727. (Illus.). 1992. PLB 18.60 (*0-8368-0847-9*) Gareth Stevens Inc.

—El Salvador Is My Home. Welch, Rose, photos by. LC 92-17724. (Illus.). 1992. PLB 18.60 (*0-8368-0849-5*) Gareth Stevens Inc.

—The Wonder of Bald Eagles. Leeson, Tom & Leeson, Pat, photos by. LC 92-16943. (Illus.). 1992. PLB 18.60 (*0-8368-0854-1*) Gareth Stevens Inc.

Forbes, Esther. America's Paul Revere. (Illus.). 48p. (gr. 3-5). 1990. pap. 5.70 (*0-395-24907-4*) HM.

—America's Paul Revere. LC 90-484984. (Illus.). 88p. (gr. 6-10). 1991. PLB 13.95 (*1-55905-093-4*) Marshall Cavendish.

—Johnny Tremain. Ward, Lynd, illus. 272p. (gr. k-6). 1969. pap. 3.99 (*0-440-94250-0*, YB) Dell.

—Johnny Tremain. Ward, Lynd, illus. (gr. 7-9). 1943. 13. 45 (*0-395-06766-9*) HM.

—Johnny Tremain. large type ed. 354p. (gr. 3-7). 1987. lib. bdg. 14.95 (*1-55736-023-5*, Crnrstn Bks) BDD LT Grp.

—Johnny Tremain. 1987. pap. 3.99 (*0-440-44250-8*) Dell.

—Johnny Tremain. Ward, Lynd, illus. 1992. 16.50 (*0-8446-6600-9*) Peter Smith.

—Paul Revere & the World He Lived In. (Illus.). 528p. (gr. 4-8). 1972. pap. 10.70 (*0-395-08370-2*) HM.

Forbes, Esther see Newbery Library Award Staff.

Forbes, Milton L. Out of the Mists of Time: Who Wrote the Bible & Why. LC 91-91561. 125p. 1992. pap. 4.95 (*0-9623700-2-9*) Mtntop Bks.

Forbis, Judith E. Hoofbeats along the Tigris. Forbis, Judith E., illus. Forbis, Donald L., intro. by. (Illus.). 146p. (gr. 8 up). 1990. Repr. 34.95 (*0-9625644-1-9*) Ansata Pubns.

Force, Eden. John Muir. Gallin, Richard, ed. (Illus.). 144p. (gr. 5-9). 1990. PLB 13.98 (*0-382-09965-6*); pap. 7.95 (*0-382-09970-2*) Silver Burdett Pr.

Force, Roland W. The American Indians. Moynihan, Daniel P., intro. by. (Illus.). 112p. (gr. 5 up). 1991. 17. 95 (*0-87754-860-9*) Chelsea Hse.

—American Indians. (gr. 4-7). 1992. pap. 7.95 (*0-7910-0280-2*) Chelsea Hse.

Forcier, Mitchell D. Strange Planes: A Collection of Unusual Paper Airplanes. Ziba Design Staff, illus. 32p. (Orig.). (gr. k up). 1989. pap. 5.95 (*0-9618419-4-X*) Paper Press.

Ford, Adam. Weather Watch. LC 81-637. (Illus.). 48p. (gr. 3-7). 1982. 11.95 (*0-688-00959-X*) Lothrop.

Ford, B. G. Do You Know? One Hundred Fascinating Facts. McNaught, Harry, illus. LC 78-62132. (ps-1). 1979. pap. 2.25 (*0-394-84070-4*) Random Bks Yng Read.

Ford, Barbara. The Automobile: Inventions That Changed Our Lives. (gr. 3-7). 1987. 10.95 (*0-8027-6724-9*); PLB 11.85 (*0-8027-6725-7*) Walker & Co.

—The Eagles' Child. LC 90-5633. 160p. (gr. 3-7). 1990. SBE 13.95 (*0-02-735405-9*, Macmillan Child Bk) Macmillan Child Grp.

—The Elevator. LC 82-70440. (Illus.). 64p. (gr. 4-6). 1982. 7.95 (*0-8027-6450-9*); PLB 8.85 (*0-8027-6451-7*) Walker & Co.

—St. Louis. LC 88-35912. (Illus.). 60p. (gr. 3 up). 1989. RSBE 13.95 (*0-87518-402-2*, Dillon) Macmillan Child Grp.

—Walt Disney: A Biography. (Illus.). 160p. (gr. 4-7). 1989. 15.95 (*0-8027-6864-4*); PLB 16.85 (*0-8027-6865-2*) Walker & Co.

—Wildlife Rescue. Tucker, Kathleen, ed. Ross, Steve, illus. LC 87-6133. 48p. (gr. 3-7). 1987. PLB 11.95 (*0-8075-9099-1*) A Whitman.

Ford, Beatrice. The Great Asparagus War. Duthie, Dorothy B., ed. Brown, Elizabeth, illus. 1991. pap. write for info. (*1-88017-250-X*) Storyteller.

—Royal Eggplant. Duthie, Dorothy B., ed. (Illus.). 1991. pap. write for info. (*1-880172-52-6*) Storyteller.

Ford, Bernette. The Hunter Who Was King & Other African Tales. Ford, George, illus. LC 93-10278. 16p. (ps-3). 1994. 14.95 (*1-56282-585-2*) Hyprn Child.

Ford, Bernette G., jt. auth. see Hudson, Cheryl W.

Ford, G. H., ed. see Dickens, Charles.

Ford, George. Baby's First Picture Book. Ford, George, illus. LC 79-62941. (ps). 1979. 3.50 (*0-394-84245-6*) Random Bks Yng Read.

Ford, George, jt. auth. see Williamson, Mel.

Ford, Gillian. The Inside Story. 123p. (Orig.). 1985. pap. text ed. 6.95 (*1-883619-05-X*) D Ford Pubns.

Ford, Hildegard. My Go to Bed Book. (Illus.). (ps). 1976. 6.95 (*0-8054-4151-4*, 4241-51) Broadman.

Ford, Horace, jt. auth. see Asham, Roger.

Ford, Jerry. The Grand Slam Collection: Have Fun Collecting Baseball Cards. (Illus.). 64p. (gr. 5-12). 1992. 15.95 (*0-8225-2350-7*); pap. 6.95 (*0-8225-9598-2*) Lerner Pubns.

Ford, John see Bald, Robert C.

Ford, Lauren. Little Book about God. Ford, Lauren, illus. LC 81-43749. 48p. (ps-3). 1985. pap. 9.95 (*0-385-17691-0*) Doubleday.

Ford, M. Roxanne, jt. auth. see Green, Carl R.

Ford, M. Thomas. Paula Abdul: Straight Up. LC 91-40231. (Illus.). 72p. (gr. 3 up). 1992. RSBE 12.95 (*0-87518-508-8*, Dillon) Macmillan Child Grp.

—Who's Hot -- Clint Black. (gr. 4-7). 1993. pap. 1.49 (*0-440-21598-6*) Dell.

Ford, Marianne. Copycats & Artifacts. Pugh, Anna, illus. LC 86-45532. 96p. 1986. 9.95 (*0-87923-645-0*) Godine.

Ford, Michael. One Hundred Questions & Answers about AIDS: A Guide for All People. 208p. (gr. 7 up). 1993. pap. 4.95 (*0-688-12697-9*, Pub. by Beech Tree Bks) Morrow.

Ford, Michael T. One Hundred Questions & Answers about AIDS: A Guide for Young People. LC 92-15072. (Illus.). 208p. (gr. 6 up). 1992. RSBE 14.95 (*0-02-735424-5*, New Discovery Bks) Macmillan Child Grp.

Ford, Miela. Little Elephant. Hoban, Tana, photos by. LC 93-25208. (Illus.). 1994. write for info. (*0-688-13140-9*); PLB write for info. (*0-688-13141-7*) Greenwillow.

Ford, Noel. An Earful of Aliens. 64p. (gr. 2-4). 1994. 5.95 (*0-340-56914-X*, Pub. by Hodder & Stoughton UK) Trafalgar.

Ford, Paul L. Janice Meredith. Teitel, N. R., intro. by. (gr. 11 up). 1967. pap. 0.95 (*0-8049-0148-1*, CL-148) Airmont.

Forell, Betty & Wind, Betty. Little Benjamin & the First Christmas. (Illus.). (ps-3). 1964. laminated bdg. 1.89 (*0-570-06005-2*, 59-1113) Concordia.

Forelle, Helen. Mortimer Meets Melody. Leih, Janet, ed. Stevens, Barbara, illus. 20p. (gr. 1-3). 1981. pap. 3.00 (*1-877649-02-3*) Tesseract SD.

Foreman, Donna. Story of the Christmas Bear. Blonski, Maribeth, illus. 40p. (gr. k-3). 1992. 7.95 (*1-880851-02-4*) Greene Bark Pr.

Foreman, Gloria. Busy Hands. (Illus.). (gr. 3-8). 1959. pap. 1.00 (*0-915198-01-0*) G Foreman.

Foreman, M. Jack's Fantastic Voyage. 1992. write for info. (*0-15-239496-6*, HB Juv Bks) HarBrace.

Foreman, Marcey G. The Russian in the Attic. LC 88-50755. 119p. (gr. 5-8). 1988. 7.95 (*1-55523-160-8*) Winston-Derek.

Foreman, Mark. Scraps. (Illus.). 32p. (ps-2). 1991. 15.95 (*0-86264-306-6*, Pub. by Andersen Pr UK) Trafalgar.

—Sid the Kitten. (Illus.). 32p. (ps-2). 1989. 13.95 (*0-86264-218-3*, Pub. by Andersen Pr UK) Trafalgar.

Foreman, Mary M., tr. from ENG. Encuentralo con Elena. King, Ed, illus. (SPA.). 24p. 1992. pap. 3.95 (*1-56288-238-4*) Checkerboard.

—Investiga con Ines. King, Ed, illus. (SPA.). 24p. 1992. pap. 3.95 (*1-56288-239-2*) Checkerboard.

—Paseate con Paco. King, Ed, illus. (SPA.). 24p. 1929. pap. 3.95 (*1-56288-240-6*) Checkerboard.

—Viaja con Victor. King, Ed, illus. (SPA.). 24p. 1992. pap. 3.95 (*1-56288-237-6*) Checkerboard.

Foreman, Michael. The Boy Who Sailed with Columbus. Foreman, Michael, illus. 80p. (gr. 1-4). 1992. 16.95 (*1-55970-178-1*) Arcade Pub Inc.

—Cat & Canary. LC 84-9568. (Illus.). 32p. (ps-3). 1987. pap. 5.99 (*0-8037-0133-0*) Dial Bks Young.

—Grandfather's Pencil & the Room of Stories. Foreman, Michael, illus. LC 93-6266. 1994. 14.95 (*0-15-200061-5*) HarBrace.

—Michael Foreman's Mother Goose. 152p. (ps up). 1991. 19.95 (*0-15-255820-9*, HB Juv Bks) HarBrace.

—One World. Foreman, Michael, illus. 32p. (gr. 2-5). 1991. 14.95 (*1-55970-108-0*) Arcade Pub Inc.

—War Boy: A Country Childhood. Foreman, Michael, illus. 96p. (gr. 3 up). 1990. 16.95 (*1-55970-049-1*) Arcade Pub Inc.

Foreman, Michael & Gray, Nigel. I'll Take You to Mrs. Cole. (Illus.). 32p. (gr. k-3). 1986. 11.95 (*0-930267-21-4*) Bergh Pub.

Foreman, Michael, jt. auth. see Newman, Nanette.

Foreman, Michael, jt. auth. see Wright, Friere.

Foreman, Michael, ed. & illus. Michael Foreman's World of Fairy Tales. 144p. (gr. 1 up). 1991. 18.95 (*1-55970-164-1*) Arcade Pub Inc.

Foreman, Michael, illus. Over in the Meadow. 20p. (ps-2). 1992. pap. 13.00 casebound, pop-up (*0-671-75109-3*, S&S BFYR) S&S Trade.

Foreman, Ronald, ed. see Murphy, Daniel O.

Foreman, Ronald J., ed. see Brugge, David.

Foreman, Ronald J., ed. see Gardner, Mark.

Foreman, Ronald J., ed. see Gnesios, Gregory.

Foreman, Ronald J., ed. see Lamb, Susan.

Foreman, Ronald J., ed. see Parent, Laurence E.

Foreman, Ronald J., ed. see Torres, Luis.

Foreman, Ronald J., ed. see Utley, Robert.

Foreman, Ronald J., et al. eds. see Calderazzo, John.

Foreman, Ronald J., et al, eds. see Jablonsky, Alice.

Foreman, Rosmarie. God Created. 32p. 1986. pap. text ed. 1.25 (*1-882449-12-6*) Messenger Pub.

Forest, Heather. Baker's Dozen: A Colonial American Tale. (Illus.). 1993. pap. 4.95 (*0-15-200587-4*, HB Juv Bks) HarBrace.

—The Woman Who Flummoxed the Fairies. Gaber, Susan, illus. 28p. (ps-3). 1990. 14.95 (*0-15-299150-6*) HarBrace.

Forest, Heather, retold by. The Baker's Dozen: A Colonial American Tale. Gaber, Susan, illus. 28p. (ps-3). 1988. 14.95 (*0-15-200412-2*, Gulliver Bks) HarBrace.

Forester, Anne & Reinhard, Margaret. Learners' Way. 300p. (Orig.). (gr. k-3). 1989. pap. 17.95 (*0-920541-96-8*) Peguis Pubs Ltd.

Forester, C. S. Commodore Hornblower. (gr. 7 up). 1989. 17.95 (*0-316-28894-2*); pap. 9.95 (*0-316-28938-8*) Little.

—Lieutenant Hornblower. (gr. 7 up). 1984. 17.95 (*0-316-28907-8*); pap. 9.95 (*0-316-28921-3*) Little.

—Lord Hornblower, Vol. 1. (gr. 7 up). 1989. 17.95 (*0-316-28908-6*); pap. 9.95 (*0-316-28943-4*) Little.

—Mr. Midshipman Hornblower. (gr. 7 up). 1950. 17.95 (*0-316-28909-4*) Little.

Forester, Frank. My Shooting Box. 2nd ed. Ball, Robert, illus. 187p. (gr. 10 up). 1990. Repr. of 1941 ed. 35.00 (*1-56416-014-9*) Derrydale Pr.

—Warwick Woodlands. 2nd ed. Ball, Robert, illus. 200p. (gr. 10 up). 1990. Repr. of 1934 ed. 35.00 (*1-56416-015-7*) Derrydale Pr.

Forker, Dom. Baseball Brain Teasers: Major League Puzzles. Hoffman, Sandy, illus. LC 85-27955. 128p. (Orig.). (gr. 5-9). 1986. pap. 4.95 (*0-8069-6284-4*) Sterling.

Forman, James. Code Name Valkyrie: Count Claus von Stauffenberg & the Plot to Kill Hitler. LC 72-12581. (Illus.). 296p. (gr. 9-12). 1973. PLB 24.95 (*0-87599-188-2*) S G Phillips.

Forman, James D. Becca's Story. LC 92-1375. 192p. (gr. 7 up). 1992. SBE 14.95 (*0-684-19332-9*, Scribners Young Read) Macmillan Child Grp.

—Fascism: The Meaning & Experience of Reactionary Revolution. 156p. (gr. 7 up). 1976. pap. 1.25 (0-440-94707-3, LFL) Dell.
—Prince Charlie's Year. LC 90-26898. 144p. (gr. 7 up). 1991. SBE 13.95 (0-684-19242-X, Scribners Young Read) Macmillan Child Grp.
Forman-Hitt, Kathy & Young, Janet. Beginning Reading Five. Wheeler, Sharon, ed. Richesson, Robin, illus. (ps). 1986. wkbk. 1.95 (0-916119-22-X) Creat Teach Pr.
—Beginning Reading Four. Wheeler, Sharon, ed. Koeller, Neena, illus. (ps). 1986. wkbk. 1.95 (0-916119-21-1) Creat Teach Pr.
—Beginning Reading One. Wheeler, Sharon, ed. Richesson, Robin, illus. (ps). 1986. wkbk. 1.95 (0-916119-18-1) Creat Teach Pr.
—Beginning Reading Six. Wheeler, Sharon, ed. Richesson, Robin, illus. (ps). 1986. wkbk. 1.95 (0-916119-23-8) Creat Teach Pr.
—Beginning Reading Three. Wheeler, Sharon, ed. Koeller, Neena, illus. (ps). 1986. wkbk. 1.95 (0-916119-20-3) Creat Teach Pr.
—Beginning Reading Two. Wheeler, Sharon, ed. Richesson, Robin, illus. (ps). 1986. wkbk. 1.95 (0-916119-19-X) Creat Teach Pr.
Forrest, Wendy. Rosa Luxemburg. (Illus.). 64p. (gr. 6-10). 1991. 15.95 (0-237-60040-4, Pub. by Evans Bros Ltd) Trafalgar.
Forrestal, Julienne, ed. see Mast, Coleen K.
Forrester, Maureen, selected by. Joy to the World! Tyrrell, Frances, illus. Heller, Charles, contrib. by. (Illus.). 32p. 1993. reinforced bdg. 14.99 (0-525-45169-2, DCB) Dutton Child Bks.
Forrester, Victoria. Poor Gabriella: A Christmas Story. Boulet, Susan B., illus. LC 86-3607. 32p. 1986. SBE 14.95 (0-689-31265-2, Atheneum Child Bk) Macmillan Child Grp.
Forsberg, Glen, jt. auth. see Enns, Peter.
Forse, Ken, ed. see Baron, Phil.
Forshay-Lunsford, Lin. Walk Through Cold Fire. (gr. 6 up). 1986. pap. 2.95 (0-440-99322-9, LFL) Dell.
Forsse, Ken. The Airship. High, David, et al, illus. 26p. (ps). 1985. incl. audio-cassette 9.95 (0-934323-00-3) Alchemy Comms.
—Teddy Ruxpin Lullabies II. Hicks, Russell, et al, illus. 26p. (ps). 1988. 21.00 (0-934323-68-2); pre-programmed audiocassette incl. Alchemy Comms.
—Teddy Ruxpin's Lullabies. High, David, et al, illus. 26p. (ps). 1985. incl. audio-cassette 9.95 (0-934323-01-1) Alchemy Comms.
Forsse, Ken & Hughes, Margaret. The Little Red Hen. Becker, Mary, ed. (Illus.). 26p. (ps). 1986. packaged with pre-programmed audio cass. tape 9.95 (0-934323-22-4) Alchemy Comms.
—The Tortoise & the Hare. Becker, Mary, ed. (Illus.). 26p. (ps). 1986. incl. pre-programmed audio cass. tape 9.95 (0-934323-21-6) Alchemy Comms.
Forsse, Ken, ed. see Baron, Phil.
Forsse, Ken, ed. see Hughes, Margaret A.
Forsse, Ken, jt. ed. see Hughes, Margaret A.
Forsten, Charlene. The Indian in the Cupboard: A Study Guide. Friedland, Joyce & Kessler, Rikki, eds. 23p. (gr. 9-12). 1990. pap. text ed. 14.95 (0-88122-406-5) Lrn Links.
—The Littles: A Study Guide. Friedland, Joyce & Kessler, Rikki, eds. 21p. (gr. 9-12). 1990. pap. text ed. 14.95 (0-88122-412-X) Lrn Links.
—The Wish Giver: A Study Guide. Friedland, Joyce & Kessler, Rikki, eds. 24p. (gr. 9-12). 1990. pap. text ed. 14.95 (0-88122-401-4) Lrn Links.
Forsten, Charlene A. Cobblestone Companion: A Teacher's Activity Guide. (Illus.). 128p. (gr. 4-9). 1985. pap. 8.95 (0-9607638-4-8) Cobblestone Pub.
Forster, John, jt. auth. see Chapin, Tom.
Forster, Leonard, ed. Penguin Book of German Verse. (GER). 512p. (gr. 9 up). 1988. pap. 10.00 (0-14-058546-X, Penguin Bks) Viking Penguin.
Forsthoefel, John. Utilizing Problem Solving in Math. Zilliox, Elaine, illus. 40p. (Orig.). (gr. 3-8). 1984. 5.95 (0-88047-039-9, 8405) DOK Pubs.
Forsthoefel, John & Ransick, Gary. Discovering Botany. Sellers, Marci, illus. 84p. (gr. 3-6). 1982. 9.95 (0-88047-005-4, 8206) DOK Pubs.
Forsyth, Adrian. Architecture of Animals. 72p. (gr. 8 up). 1989. 15.95 (0-920656-16-1, Pub. by Camden Hse CN); pap. 9.95 (0-920656-08-0, Pub. by Camden Hse CN) Firefly Bks Ltd.
—Exploring the World of Insects: The Equinox Guide to Insect Behavior. Folkens, Pieter, illus. 64p. (gr. 5 up). 1992. PLB 17.95 (0-921820-47-X, Pub. by Camden Hse CN); pap. 9.95 (0-921820-49-6, Pub. by Camden Hse CN) Firefly Bks Ltd.
Forsyth, Adrian & Aziz, Laurel. Exploring the World of Birds: An Equinox Guide to Avian Life. (Illus.). 72p. (gr. 4 up). 1990. 15.95 (0-920656-98-6, Pub. by Camden Hse CN); pap. 9.95 (0-920656-94-3, Pub. by Annick CN) Firefly Bks Ltd.
Forsyth, Andrian. Journey Through a Tropical Jungle. LC 88-14683. (gr. 3-7). 1989. pap. 15.95 jacketed (0-671-66262-7, S&S BFYR) S&S Trade.
Forsyth, Elizabeth, jt. auth. see Hyde, Margaret O.
Forsyth, Elizabeth H., jt. auth. see Hyde, Margaret O.
Fort, Donny. Church Camp. 144p. 1992. pap. 6.99 (0-310-54861-6, Pub. by Zondervan Bks) Zondervan.
Fort, Patrick. Redbird. LC 87-23591. (Illus.). 18p. (ps-5). 1988. 19.95 (0-531-05746-1) Orchard Bks Watts.

Forte, Imogene. Arts & Crafts: From Things Around the House. LC 83-80961. (Illus.). 80p. (gr. k-6). 1983. pap. text ed. 3.95 (0-86530-090-9, IP909) Incentive Pubns.
—Box Crafts: Over 50 Things to Make & Do with Boxes of Every Size. LC 86-82933. (Illus.). 80p. (gr. k-6). 1987. pap. text ed. 3.95 (0-86530-123-9, IP 942) Incentive Pubns.
—Cookbook: A No Cook & Learn Book. LC 83-80962. (Illus.). 80p. (gr. k-6). 1983. pap. text ed. 3.95 (0-86530-089-5, IP-895) Incentive Pubns.
—Crayons & Markers: Artistic Creations, One of a Kind & Made By You. LC 86-82934. (Illus.). 80p. (gr. k-6). 1987. pap. text ed. 3.95 (0-86530-162-X, IP 943) Incentive Pubns.
—December Patterns, Projects & Plans. 80p. (ps-1). 1989. pap. text ed. 7.95 (0-86530-128-X, IP 167-0) Incentive Pubns.
—Dinosaur Learning Fun. (Illus.). 48p. (ps-3). 1987. pap. 2.95 (0-86530-145-X, IP 100-6) Incentive Pubns.
—Dinosaurs: Facts Fun, & Fantastic Crafts. LC 86-82932. (Illus.). 80p. (gr. k-6). 1987. pap. text ed. 3.95 (0-86530-149-2, IP 944) Incentive Pubns.
—Early Learning Bulletin Boards. (Illus.). 64p. (ps-1). 1987. pap. text ed. 6.95 (0-86530-166-2, IP 112-7) Incentive Pubns.
—Fairy Tale Learning Fun. (Illus.). 48p. (ps-3). 1987. pap. 2.95 (0-86530-146-8, IP 100-7) Incentive Pubns.
—Fall Bulletin Boards. (Illus.). 64p. (gr. k-6). 1987. pap. text ed. 6.95 (0-86530-167-0, IP 112-8) Incentive Pubns.
—Holiday & Seasonal Bulletin Boards. (Illus.). 64p. (gr. k-6). 1986. pap. text ed. 6.95 (0-86530-137-9, IP 112-6) Incentive Pubns.
—I'm Ready to Learn about Beginning Consonants. (Illus.). 64p. (ps-1). 1987. pap. text ed. 1.95 (0-86530-155-7, IP 111-4) Incentive Pubns.
—I'm Ready to Learn about Beginning Math. (Illus.). 64p. (ps-1). 1986. pap. text ed. 1.95 (0-86530-119-0, 110-1) Incentive Pubns.
—I'm Ready to Learn about Beginning Reading. (Illus.). 64p. (ps-1). 1986. pap. text ed. 1.95 (0-86530-110-7, 110-2) Incentive Pubns.
—I'm Ready to Learn about Beginning Science. (Illus.). (ps-1). 1986. pap. text ed. 1.95 (0-86530-116-6, IP 110-3) Incentive Pubns.
—I'm Ready to Learn about Colors. (Illus.). (ps-1). 1986. pap. text ed. 1.95 (0-86530-111-5, IP 110-4) Incentive Pubns.
—I'm Ready to Learn about Dot-to-Dot. (Illus.). (ps-1). 1987. pap. text ed. 1.95 (0-86530-156-5, 111-6) Incentive Pubns.
—I'm Ready to Learn about Following Directions. (Illus.). (ps-1). 1986. pap. text ed. 1.95 (0-86530-109-3, IP 110-5) Incentive Pubns.
—I'm Ready to Learn about Kindergarten Skills. (Illus.). (ps-1). 1987. pap. text ed. 1.95 (0-86530-157-3, IP 111-7) Incentive Pubns.
—I'm Ready to Learn about Mazes & Puzzles. (Illus.). (gr. k-1). 1987. pap. text ed. 1.95 (0-86530-158-1, IP 111 3) Incentive Pubns.
—I'm Ready to Learn about Money. (Illus.). (gr. k-1). 1987. pap. text ed. 1.95 (0-86530-159-X, IP 111-5) Incentive Pubns.
—I'm Ready to Learn about My First Words. (Illus.). (gr. k-1). 1987. pap. text ed. 1.95 (0-86530-154-9, IP 111-8) Incentive Pubns.
—I'm Ready to Learn about Numbers. (Illus.). (gr. k-1). 1986. pap. text ed. 1.95 (0-86530-108-5, IP 110-6) Incentive Pubns.
—I'm Ready to Learn about Preschool Skills. (Illus.). (gr. k-1). 1986. pap. text ed. 1.95 (0-86530-113-1, IP 110-7) Incentive Pubns.
—I'm Ready to Learn about Safety. (Illus.). (gr. k-1). 1986. pap. text ed. 1.95 (0-86530-120-4, IP 110-8) Incentive Pubns.
—I'm Ready to Learn about Shapes. (Illus.). (gr. k-1). 1986. pap. text ed. 1.95 (0-86530-112-3, IP 110-9) Incentive Pubns.
—I'm Ready to Learn about Telling Time. (Illus.). (gr. k-1). 1986. pap. text ed. 1.95 (0-86530-118-2, IP-111-0) Incentive Pubns.
—I'm Ready to Learn about Thinking Skills. (Illus.). 64p. (ps-1). 1986. pap. text ed. write for info. (0-86530-117-4, IP 111-1) Incentive Pubns.
—I'm Ready to Learn about Visual Perception. (gr. k-1). 1986. pap. text ed. 1.95 (0-86530-114-X, IP-1112) Incentive Pubns.
—The Kids' Stuff: Book of Patterns, Projects & Plans to Perk Up Early Learning Programs. LC 82-83051. (Illus.). 200p. (ps-1). 1982. pap. text ed. 12.95 (0-86530-054-2, IP 54-2) Incentive Pubns.
—Library & Reference Bulletin Boards. 64p. (gr. k-6). 1986. pap. text ed. 6.95 (0-86530-136-0, IP-112-5) Incentive Pubns.
—Monster Learning Fun. (Illus.). 48p. (ps-3). 1987. pap. 2.95 (0-86530-147-6, IP 100-8) Incentive Pubns.
—Mother Goose Learning Fun. (Illus.). 48p. (ps-3). 1987. pap. 2.95 (0-86530-148-4, IP 100-5) Incentive Pubns.
—Nature Crafts. LC 84-62931. (Illus.). 80p. (gr. k-6). 1985. 3.95 (0-86530-098-4, IP 91-2) Incentive Pubns.
—November Patterns, Projects & Plans. 80p. (ps-1). 1989. pap. text ed. 7.95 (0-86530-127-1, IP 166-9) Incentive Pubns.
—October Patterns, Projects & Plans. 80p. (ps-1). 1989. pap. text ed. 7.95 (0-86530-126-3, IP 166-8) Incentive Pubns.
—Paper Capers. LC 84-62932. (Illus.). 80p. (gr. k-6). 1985. 3.95 (0-86530-097-6, IP 91-1) Incentive Pubns.

—Private "I" LC 84-62921. (Illus.). 80p. (gr. k-6). 1985. wkbk 3.95 (0-86530-096-8, IP 91-0) Incentive Pubns.
—Puppets. LC 84-62934. (Illus.). 80p. (gr. k-6). 1985. pap. text ed. 3.95 (0-86530-101-8, IP 91-5) Incentive Pubns.
—Rainbow Fun: Rainbows to Keep, Share & Give Away. LC 86-82873. 80p. (gr. k-6). 1987. pap. text ed. 3.95 (0-86530-161-1, IP-94-5) Incentive Pubns.
—Rainy Day: Magic for Wonderful Wet Weather. LC 83-82332. (Illus.). 80p. (gr. k-6). 1983. pap. text ed. 3.95 (0-86530-094-1, IP94-1) Incentive Pubns.
—Read about It: Beginning Readers. LC 82-81720. (Illus.). 80p. (gr. k-1). 1982. pap. text ed. 7.95 (0-86530-005-4, IP 05-4) Incentive Pubns.
—Read about It: Middle Grades. LC 82-80502. (Illus.). 80p. (gr. 4-6). 1982. pap. text ed. 7.95 (0-86530-007-0, IP 070) Incentive Pubns.
—Read about It: Primary. LC 82-80499. (Illus.). 80p. (gr. 2-4). 1982. pap. text ed. 7.95 (0-86530-006-2, IP-062) Incentive Pubns.
—Science Fun. LC 84-62935. (Illus.). 80p. (gr. k-6). 1985. pap. text ed. 3.95 (0-86530-100-X, IP 91-4) Incentive Pubns.
—September Patterns, Projects & Plans. 80p. (ps-1). 1989. pap. text ed. 7.95 (0-86530-125-5, IP 166-7) Incentive Pubns.
—Spring Bulletin Boards. 64p. (gr. k-6). 1987. pap. text ed. 6.95 (0-86530-169-7, IP-113-0) Incentive Pubns.
—Think about It! Kindergarten. (Illus.). 80p. (ps-k). 1981. pap. text ed. 7.95 (0-913916-96-X, IP-96X) Incentive Pubn.
—Think about It! Middle Grades. (Illus.). 80p. (gr. 4-6). 1981. pap. text ed. 7.95 (0-913916-98-6, IP 98-6) Incentive Pubn.
—Think about It! Primary. (Illus.). 80p. (gr. 1-3). 1981. pap. text ed. 7.95 (0-913916-97-8, IP 97-8) Incentive Pubn.
—Winter Bulletin Boards. (Illus.). 64p. (gr. k-6). 1987. pap. text ed. 6.95 (0-86530-168-9, IP 112-9) Incentive Pubns.
—Write about It Series, 3 vols. Incl. Beginning Writers. (gr. k-1). 1983. pap. text ed. 7.95 (0-86530-044-5, IP 44-5); Primary. (gr. 2-4). 1983. pap. text ed. 7.95 (0-86530-045-3, IP 45-3); Middle Grades. (gr. 4-6). 1983. pap. text ed. 7.95 (0-86530-046-1, IP 46-1). (Illus., 80 pgs. ea. volume). (gr. k-6). 1983. pap. text ed. 23.50 (0-685-06165-5, IP 43-7) Incentive Pubns.
Forte, Imogene & Frank, Marge. Puddles & Wings & Grapevine Swings. LC 81-85014. (Illus.). 304p. (ps-6). 1982. pap. text ed. 16.95 (0-86530-004-6, IP-046) Incentive Pubns.
Forte, Imogene & MacKenzie, Joy. Composition & Creative Writing for the Middle Grades. Lewis, Sherri Y., intro. by. Bullock, Kathleen, illus. 80p. (Orig.). (gr. 5-8). 1991. pap. text ed. 7.95 (0-86530-176-X, IP 192-1) Incentive Pubns.
—The Kids' Stuff: Book of Reading & Language Arts for the Primary Grades. (Illus.). 240p. (gr. 1-3). 1989. pap. text 14.95 (0-86530-121-2, IP 01-3) Incentive Pubns.
Forte, Imogene & Pangle, Mary Ann. Reading Bulletin Boards. (Illus.). 64p. (gr. k-6). 1986. pap. text ed. 6.95 (0-86530-134-4, IP-112-3) Incentive Pubns.
—Science Bulletin Boards. 64p. (gr. k-6). 1986. pap. text ed. 6.95 (0-86530-131-X, IP 112-1) Incentive Pubns.
Forte, Imogene & Schurr, Sandra. Science Mind Stretchers. (Illus.). 128p. (gr. 4-7). 1987. pap. text ed. 9.95 (0-86530-165-4, 165-4) Incentive Pubns.
Forte, Imogene, et al. The Kids Stuff: TM Book of Reading & Language Arts for the Middle Grades. 240p. (gr. 4-7). 1987. pap. text ed. 14.95 (0-86530-122-0, IP 122-0) Incentive Pubns.
Fortescue, J. W. The Story of a Red Deer. 160p. (gr. 5-8). 1989. pap. 6.95 (0-86241-174-2, Pub. by Cnngt Pub Ltd) Trafalgar.
Fortey, Richard. Dinosaur's Alphabet. (gr. 4-8). 1990. 14. 95 (0-8120-6202-7) Barron.
Fortier, E. H. Judas Maccabeus. Schlesinger, Arthur M., Jr., intro. by. (Illus.). 112p. (gr. 5 up). 1988. lib. bdg. 17.95 (0-87754-539-1) Chelsea Hse.
Fortier, Ron, jt. auth. see Mayhar, Ardath.
Fortman, Jan. Creatures of Mystery. LC 77-24705. (Illus.). 48p. (gr. 4 up). 1983. PLB 18.64 (0-8172-1063-6) Raintree Steck-V.
Fortson, Walter. Amazing Animal Facts. Starver, Randy, et al, illus. LC 89-80109. 128p. (Orig.). (gr. 5). 1989. pap. 6.95 (0-685-29400-5) Fortson Pubs.
Fortunato, Pat. A Colonial Williamsburg Activities Book: Fun Activities for Young Visitors. Wallner, John, illus. 48p. (Orig.). (gr. 1-4). 1982. pap. 3.95 (0-87935-062-8) Williamsburg.
Fortune, J. J. Revenge in the Silent Tomb. 160p. (Orig.). (gr. 7-12). 1984. pap. 2.25 (0-440-97707-X, LFL) Dell.
Fortune, Marie M., jt. auth. see Reid, Kathryn G.
Forward, Toby. Traveling Backwards. Cornell, Laura, illus. LC 93-32514. 1994. write for info. RTE (0-688-13076-3, Tambourine Bks) Morrow.
Fosburgh, Liza. Bella Arabella. Stock, Catherine, illus. LC 85-42809. 128p. (gr. 4-7). 1986. SBE 12.95 (0-02-735430-X, Four Winds) Macmillan Child Grp.
—Bella Arabella. 112p. 1987. pap. 2.50 (0-553-15484-2, Skylark) Bantam.
—Cruise Control. 224p. (gr. 7 up). 1988. 13.95 (0-553-05491-0, Starfire) Bantam.
—Mrs. Abercorn & the Bunce Boys. 128p. (gr. k-6). 1989. pap. 2.75 (0-440-40154-2, YB) Dell.
—Wrong Way Home. 1990. 14.95 (0-553-05883-5) Bantam.

Foslien, Dagmar. The Fantastic Fashion Show. Paris, Pat & Shackelford, Jeane, illus. 40p. (ps-3). 1984. 5.95 (*0-910313-50-4*) Parker Bros.
—A Garden of Love to Share. Paris, Pat & Williams, Karin, illus. 1984. incl. cassette 7.95 (*0-910313-63-6*) Parker Bros.

Foss, Allen J. Living in God's Grace: Apostles' Creed - Sacraments. Rinden, David, ed. 266p. (gr. 6-8). 1989. pap. 5.95 (*0-943167-06-X*) Faith & Fellowship Pr.
—Walking in God's Truth: Ten Commandments-Lord's Prayer. rev. ed. Rinden, David, intro. by. Heiman, Lori, illus. 276p. (gr. 6-8). 1989. pap. text ed. 5.95 (*0-943167-04-3*) Faith & Fellowship Pr.

Fossey, Keith R. The Football Scholarship Guide: How to Maximize Scholarship Potential. Thomas, Roger, frwd. by. LC 92-90842. (Illus.). 309p. (Orig.). (gr. 9-12). 1992. pap. 24.95 (*0-9633495-0-3*) Pigskin Pr.

Fosten, Tom, tr. see LuBin, Deanna R.

Foster, Cass. Shakespeare for Children: The Story of Romeo & Juliet. Molyneux, Lisa, illus. LC 89-80371. 105p. (gr. 2 up). 1989. pap. 9.95 (*0-9619853-3-X*) Five Star AZ.
—The Sixty-Minute Shakespeare: Romeo & Juliet. Hawkins, Mary E., ed. LC 89-82072. 136p. 1990. pap. 3.95 (*0-9619853-8-0*); 5.00 (*1-877749-00-1*) Five Star AZ.

Foster, Elizabeth. Gigi in America: The Further Adventures of a Merry-Go-Round Horse. Cote, Phyllis N., illus. 130p. (gr. 4-8). pap. 9.95 (*0-913028-69-X*) North Atlantic.
—Gigi: The Story of a Merry-Go-Round Horse. Birchoff, Ilse, illus. 124p. (gr. 4-8). pap. 9.95 (*0-913028-55-X*) North Atlantic.
—Gigi: The Story of a Merry-Go-Round Horse. Bischoff, Ilse, illus. Israel, Nancy M., intro. by. (Illus.). 118p. (gr. 2-6). 1990. Repr. of 1943 ed. 14.95 (*0-9626165-0-8*) Paper Memories.

Foster, Elizabeth S. Tutoring: Learning by Helping: A Student Handbook for Training Peer & Cross Age Tutors. rev. ed. McKee, Mary M., illus. LC 92-71011. 140p. (gr. 8-12). 1992. pap. text ed. 12.95x (*0-932796-44-3*) Ed Media Corp.

Foster, Elizabeth V. Lyrico. 2nd ed. Buba, Joy, illus. 230p. (gr. 6-8). 1991. pap. 10.95 (*0-930407-21-0*) Parabola Bks.

Foster, Frances, ed. see Hendershot, Judith.

Foster, Frances, ed. see Richler, Mordecai.

Foster, Janet. A Cabin Full of Mice. (Illus.). 36p. (gr. 2 up). 1992. pap. 4.95 (*0-919872-66-2*, Pub. by Greey de Pencier CN) Firefly Bks Ltd.
—Journey to the Top of the World. Foster, Janet, photos by. (Illus.). (gr. 3-7). 1988. 14.95 (*0-13-511445-4*) P-H.
—The Wilds of Whip-Poor-Will-Farm. Kassian, Olena, illus. 112p. (gr. 3 up). 1992. pap. 7.95 (*0-919872-79-4*, Pub. by Greey de Pencier CN) Firefly Bks Ltd.

Foster, Joanna. Cartons Cans & Orange Peels. (gr. 4-7). 1993. pap. 7.95 (*0-395-66504-3*, Clarion Bks) HM.
—Cartons, Cans, & Orange Peels: Where Does Our Garbage Go? (Illus.). 64p. (gr. 3-6). 1991. 15.45 (*0-395-56436-0*, Clarion Bks) HM.

Foster, John. Let's Celebrate: Festival Poems. (Illus.). 112p. (gr. 3 up). 1990. 15.00 (*0-19-276083-1*) OUP.
—Never Say Boo to a Ghost. Paul, Korky, illus. 96p. 1991. pap. 2.75 (*0-590-45127-8*) Scholastic Inc.

Foster, John & Curless, Alan. A Second Poetry Book. White, Martin & Wright, Joseph, illus. 128p. (gr. 4-6). 1987. 11.95 (*0-19-918137-3*); pap. 5.95 (*0-19-918136-5*) OUP.

Foster, John, compiled by. Another Fifth Poetry Book. (Illus.). 128p. (gr. 5-7). 1989. bds. 11.95 laminated (*0-19-917128-9*); pap. 5.95 (*0-19-917127-0*) OUP.
—Another First Poetry Book. (Illus.). 128p. (ps-6). 1988. pap. 5.95 (*0-19-917119-X*) OUP.
—Another Fourth Poetry Book. (Illus.). 128p. (gr. 5-7). 1989. bds. 11.95 laminated (*0-19-917126-2*); pap. 5.95 (*0-19-917125-4*) OUP.
—Another Second Poetry Book. (Illus.). 128p. (ps-6). 1988. pap. 5.95 (*0-19-917121-1*) OUP.
—Another Third Poetry Book. (Illus.). 128p. (ps-6). 1988. pap. 5.95 (*0-19-917123-8*) OUP.

Foster, John, ed. Dragon Poems. Paul, Corky, illus. 32p. (gr. 1 up). 1992. bds. 12.95 laminated (*0-19-276096-3*); pap. 2.95 (*0-19-916425-8*) OUP.
—Egg Poems. (Illus.). 16p. (gr. 1 up). 1992. pap. 2.95 (*0-19-916422-3*) OUP.

Foster, John, compiled by. A Fifth Poetry Book. (Illus.). 128p. 1987. 11.95 (*0-19-916054-6*); pap. 5.95 (*0-19-916053-8*) OUP.
—A First Poetry Book. Orr, Chris, et al, illus. 128p. (gr. 1-3). 1980. 11.95 (*0-19-918113-6*); pap. 5.95 (*0-19-918112-8*) OUP.
—A Fourth Poetry Book. Benton, Peter, et al, illus. 128p. 1987. 11.95 (*0-19-918152-7*); pap. 5.95 (*0-19-918151-9*) OUP.

Foster, John, ed. Fox Poems. (Illus.). 16p. (gr. 1 up). 1992. pap. 2.95 (*0-19-916423-1*) OUP.
—Ghost Poems. (Illus.). 16p. (gr. 1 up). 1992. pap. 2.95 (*0-19-916429-0*) OUP.
—Horse Poems. (Illus.). 16p. (gr. 1 up). 1992. pap. 2.95 (*0-19-916421-5*) OUP.
—Mouse Poems. (Illus.). 16p. (gr. 1 up). 1992. pap. 2.95 (*0-19-916430-4*) OUP.
—Pocket Poetry: Horse Poems, Egg Poems, Fox Poems, Sea Poems, Dragon Poems, Seed Poems, Snow Poems, Sports Poems, Ghost Poems, Mouse Poems, 10 vols. (Illus.). (gr. 1 up). 1992. Set. pap. 29.50 (*0-19-501516-9*) OUP.

—Sea Poems. (Illus.). 16p. (gr. 1 up). 1992. pap. 2.95 (*0-19-916424-X*) OUP.
—Seed Poems. (Illus.). 16p. (gr. 1 up). 1992. pap. 2.95 (*0-19-916426-6*) OUP.
—Snow Poems. (Illus.). 16p. (gr. 1 up). 1992. pap. 2.95 (*0-19-916427-4*) OUP.

Foster, John, compiled by. Spaceways: An Anthology of Space Poetry. Curless, Allan, et al, illus. 128p. 1987. bds. 14.00 (*0-19-276056-4*) OUP.

Foster, John, ed. Sports Poems. (Illus.). 16p. (gr. 1 up). 1992. pap. 2.95 (*0-19-916428-2*) OUP.

Foster, John, compiled by. A Third Poetry Book. Curless, Allan, et al, illus. 128p. 1987. 11.95 (*0-19-918140-3*); pap. 5.95 (*0-19-918139-X*) OUP.
—A Very First Poetry Book. (Illus.). 128p. 1987. bds. 11.95 laminated (*0-19-916051-1*); pap. 5.95 (*0-19-916050-3*) OUP.

Foster, Karen. Rattles, Bells, & Chiming Bars. LC 92-5163. (Illus.). 48p. (gr. 2-6). 1992. PLB 13.90 (*1-56294-284-0*) Millbrook Pr.

Foster, Karen, jt. ed. see Bingham, Caroline.

Foster, Kelli C., jt. auth. see Erickson, Gina C.

Foster, Kelli C., ed. see Erickson, Gina C.

Foster, Kim, ed. see Hart, Rhonda M.

Foster, Leila M. Bhutan. LC 88-37375. (Illus.). 128p. (gr. 5-9). 1989. PLB 26.60 (*0-516-02709-3*) Childrens.
—David Glasgow Farragut: Courageous Naval Officer. LC 91-8031. (Illus.). 152p. (gr. 4 up). 1991. PLB 18.60 (*0-516-03273-9*); pap. 5.95 (*0-516-43273-7*) Childrens.
—Iraq. LC 90-2174. (Illus.). 128p. (gr. 5-9). 1991. PLB 26.60 (*0-516-02723-9*) Childrens.
—Jordan. LC 91-8888. 128p. (gr. 5-9). 1991. PLB 26.60 (*0-516-02603-8*) Childrens.
—Lebanon. LC 91-32230. 128p. (gr. 5-9). 1992. PLB 26.60 (*0-516-02612-7*) Childrens.
—Margaret Thatcher: First Woman Prime Minister of Great Britain. LC 90-2209. (Illus.). 152p. (gr. 4 up). 1990. PLB 18.60 (*0-516-03269-0*) Childrens.
—Nien Cheng: Courage in China. LC 92-9333. (Illus.). 152p. (gr. 4 up). 1992. PLB 18.60 (*0-516-03279-8*); pap. 5.95 (*0-516-43279-6*) Childrens.
—Saudi Arabia. LC 92-8890. (Illus.). 128p. (gr. 5-9). 1993. PLB 26.60 (*0-516-02611-9*) Childrens.
—The Story of Rachel Carson & the Environmental Movement. LC 90-2208. (Illus.). 32p. (gr. 3-6). 1990. PLB 13.27 (*0-516-04753-1*); pap. 3.95 (*0-516-44753-X*) Childrens.
—The Story of the Cold War. LC 90-2175. (Illus.). 32p. (gr. 3-6). 1990. pap. 3.95 (*0-516-44750-5*) Childrens.
—The Story of the Great Society. LC 90-22445. (Illus.). 32p. (gr. 3-6). 1991. PLB 13.27 (*0-516-04755-8*); pap. 3.95 (*0-516-44755-6*) Childrens.
—The Story of the Persian Gulf War. LC 91-4037. (Illus.). 32p. (gr. 3-6). 1991. PLB 13.27 (*0-516-04762-0*); pap. 3.95 (*0-516-44762-9*) Childrens.
—The Sumerians. LC 90-12132. (Illus.). 64p. (gr. 5-8). 1990. PLB 12.90 (*0-531-10874-0*) Watts.

Foster, Erin & Gitchel, Sam. Hablemos Acerca del...S-E-X-O: Un Libro para Toda la Familia Acerca de la Pubertad. (SPA & ENG., Illus.). 90p. (gr. 4-8). 1985. pap. 4.95 (*0-9610122-1-8*) Plan Par Ctrl CA.

Foster, Lorri, jt. auth. see Gitchel, Sam.

Foster, Lucile. Lucy the Cat. 1993. 7.95 (*0-8062-4774-6*) Carlton.

Foster, Lynne. Exploring the Grand Canyon: Adventures of Yesterday & Today. (Illus.). 160p. (gr. 4 up). 1990. pap. 15.95 (*0-938216-33-3*) GCNHA. A lively yet comprehensive look at the natural & cultural history of the Grand Canyon -- its geology (a trip back in time via time machine to see geologic forces at work), the first people (Anasazi) to inhabit it, explorers & pioneer settlers, early tourists & river runners, & a cross-canyon hike to learn about plants & animals. Colorful illustrations & maps. EXTRAS: timeline (5 million years ago to present), activities suitable for classroom use, annotated reading list, hiking guide & checklist, glossary & index. WINNER: National Park Service Award of Excellence in Children's Publications. "...clear, readable...engaging."--BOOKLIST. "... easy reading but not at all simplistic, this book tackles the complex problem of explaining the Canyon, & succeeds admirably."--BOOKS OF THE SOUTHWEST. *Publisher Provided Annotation.*

—Take a Hike. (gr. 4-7). 1991. pap. 8.95 (*0-316-28948-5*, Joy St Bks) Little.

—Take a Hike! The Sierra Club Beginner's Guide to Hiking & Backpacking. Weston, Martha, illus. (gr. 4-7). 1990. write for info. Sierra.

Foster, P. Painting. (Illus.). (gr. 5-10). 1981. PLB 13.96 (*0-88110-026-9*); pap. 6.95 (*0-86020-546-0*) EDC.

Foster, Patience. Drawing. (gr. 2-5). 1981. (Usborne-Hayes); PLB 13.96 (*0-88110-025-0*); pap. 6.95 (*0-86020-540-1*) EDC.
—One Windy Day. (Illus.). 32p. (ps-2). 1990. 15.95 (*0-434-93860-2*, Pub. by W Heinemann Ltd) Trafalgar.

Foster, Sally. The Private World of Smith Island. Foster, Sally, photos by. LC 92-17975. (Illus.). (gr. 3-7). 1993. 14.99 (*0-525-65122-5*, Cobblehill Bks) Dutton Child Bks.
—Simon Says...Let's Play. Foster, Sally, photos by. LC 89-9776. (Illus.). 48p. (gr. 1-6). 1990. 13.95 (*0-525-65019-9*, Cobblehill Bks) Dutton Child Bks.

Foster, Sharon. Stormy Leigh. 368p. (Orig.). (gr. 9 up). 1988. pap. 6.95 (*1-56292-535-0*) Honor Bks Ok.

Foster, Stephanie. A Chance at Love, No. 6. 192p. (gr. 5 up). 1988. pap. 2.95 (*0-553-27017-6*, Sweet Dreams) Bantam.
—A Penny for Your Dreams. 192p. (Orig.). (gr. 6-12). 1982. pap. 1.95 (*0-8439-1116-6*) Dorchester Pub Co.

Foster, Susan Q. The Hummingbird among the Flowers. Oxford Scientific Films Ser., photos by. LC 89-31912. (Illus.). 32p. (gr. 4-6). 1989. PLB 15.93 (*0-8368-0115-6*) Gareth Stevens Inc.

Foster, Tom. Color to Read, Vol. Aleph. LuBin, L., ed. Foster, Tom, illus. 72p. (ps-1). 1990. lib. bdg. write for info.; pap. write for info.; write for info. tchr's. ed. Lubin Pr.

Foundation for a Christian Civilization, Inc. Staff, tr. see De Castro, C. Fernandez.

Fourie, Denise K. Hawks, Owls & Other Birds of Prey. Leon, Vicki, ed. (Illus.). 40p. (Orig.). (gr. 5 up). 1989. pap. 7.95 (*0-918303-18-4*) Blake Pub.

Fournier. Le Grand Meaulnes. (gr. 7-12). pap. 5.95 (*0-88436-110-1*, 40272) EMC.

Fournier, Jude D., jt. auth. see Vos Wezeman, Phyllis.

Foust, Sylvia. Beginning Book of Letters & Consonant Sounds. (gr. k-2). 1986. pap. 6.95 (*0-8224-0692-6*) Fearon Teach Aids.
—Beginning Book of Vowel Sounds. (gr. k-2). 1986. pap. 6.95 (*0-8224-0693-4*) Fearon Teach Aids.

Foust, Sylvia J. Dictionary Skills. Foust, Sylvia J., illus. 48p. (gr. 2-6). 1986. wkbk. 5.95 (*1-55734-339-X*) Tchr Create Mat.
—Parts of Speech. Foust, Sylvia J., illus. 48p. (gr. 2-6). 1986. wkbk. 5.95 (*1-55734-337-3*) Tchr Create Mat.
—Reading Comprehension. (Illus.). 48p. (gr. 2-6). 1986. wkbk. 5.95 (*1-55734-340-3*) Tchr Create Mat.

Fowke, Edith. Ring Around the Moon: Two Hundred Songs, Tongue Twisters, Riddles & Rhymes for Children. Brown, Judith G., illus. 160p. (gr. k-5). 1987. pap. 12.95 (*1-55021-006-8*, Pub. by NC Press CN) U of Toronto Pr.

Fowke, Edith, ed. Paul Bunyan: Superhero of the Lumberjacks. (Illus.). 112p. (Orig.). Date not set. pap. 6.95 (*0-919601-63-4*, Pub. by NC Press CN) U of Toronto Pr.

Fowler, Allan. All along the River. LC 93-39646. 1994. write for info. (*0-516-06019-8*) Childrens.
—El Animal Mas Grande Del Mundo - The Biggest Animal Ever. LC 92-9410. (SPA., Illus.). 32p. (ps-2). 1993. big bk. 30.60 (*0-516-59628-4*); pap. 12.60 (*0-685-63237-7*); pap. 3.95 (*0-685-63238-5*) Childrens.
—The Biggest Animal Ever. LC 92-9410. (Illus.). 32p. (ps-2). 1992. PLB 12.60 (*0-516-06001-5*); big bk. 30.60 (*0-516-49628-X*) Childrens.
—The Biggest Animal Ever. LC 92-9410. (Illus.). 32p. (ps-2). 1993. pap. 3.95 (*0-516-46001-3*) Childrens.
—Caballos, Caballos, Caballos: Horses, Horses, Horses. LC 91-35063. (SPA., Illus.). 32p. (ps-2). 1992. PLB 12.60 (*0-516-34921-X*); pap. 3.95 (*0-516-54921-9*); big bk. 30.60 (*0-516-59622-5*) Childrens.
—The Chicken or the Egg? LC 92-35054. (Illus.). 32p. (ps-2). 1993. write for info. (*0-516-06008-2*); pap. 3.95 (*0-516-46008-0*); big bk. 30.60 (*0-516-49639-5*) Childrens.
—Como Sabes Que Es Otono? How Do You Know It's Fall? LC 91-35060. (SPA., Illus.). 32p. (ps-2). 1992. PLB 12.60 (*0-516-34922-8*); pap. 3.95 (*0-516-54922-7*); big bk. 30.60 (*0-516-59623-3*) Childrens.
—Como Sabes Que Es Verano? How Do You Know It's Summer? LC 91-35061. (SPA., Illus.). 32p. (ps-2). 1992. PLB 12.60 (*0-516-34923-6*); pap. 3.95 (*0-516-54923-5*); big bk. 30.60 (*0-516-59624-1*) Childrens.
—Cua, Cua, Gra, Gra! (Quack & Honk) LC 92-35056. (SPA., Illus.). 32p. (ps-2). 1993. PLB 13.93 (*0-516-36012-4*) Childrens.
—Cual es Tu Flor Favorita? - What's Your Favorite Flower? LC 92-7404. (SPA., Illus.). 32p. (ps-2). 1993. big bk. 30.60 (*0-516-59634-9*); PLB 12.60 (*0-516-36007-8*); pap. 3.95 (*0-516-56007-7*) Childrens.
—Cubs & Colts & Calves & Kittens. LC 91-3140. 32p. (ps-2). 1991. PLB 12.60 (*0-516-04913-5*); PLB 30.60 big bk. (*0-516-49473-2*); pap. 3.95 (*0-516-44913-3*) Childrens.
—Es Mejor Dejar en Paz a las Serpientes: It's Best to Leave a Snake Alone. LC 91-39245. (SPA., Illus.). 32p. (ps-2). 1992. PLB 12.60 (*0-516-34926-0*); pap. 3.95 (*0-516-54926-X*); big bk. 30.60 (*0-516-59627-6*) Childrens.

—Feeling Things. LC 90-22526. (Illus.). 32p. (ps-2). 1991. PLB 12.60 (*0-516-04908-9*); pap. 3.95 (*0-516-44908-7*) Childrens.
—Feeling Things Big Book. 32p. (ps-2). 1991. PLB 30.60 (*0-516-49468-6*) Childrens.
—Frogs & Toads, & Tadpoles, Too. LC 91-42178. (Illus.). 32p. (ps-2). 1992. PLB 12.60 (*0-516-04925-9*); PLB 30.60 big bk. (*0-516-49626-3*); pap. 3.95 (*0-516-44925-7*) Childrens.
—Gracias a las Vacas: Thanks to Cows. LC 91-35062. (SPA., Illus.). 32p. (ps-2). 1992. PLB 12.60 (*0-516-34924-4*); pap. 3.95 (*0-516-54924-3*); big bk. 30.60 (*0-516-59625-X*) Childrens.
—El Gusto de las Cosas: Tasting Things. LC 90-21647. (SPA., Illus.). 32p. (ps-2). PLB 12.60, Apr. 1992 (*0-516-34911-2*); pap. 3.95, Jul. 1992 (*0-516-54911-1*) Childrens.
—Hearing Things. LC 90-22524. (Illus.). 32p. (ps-2). 1991. PLB 12.60 (*0-516-04909-7*); pap. 3.95 (*0-516-44909-5*) Childrens.
—Hearing Things Big Book. (Illus.). 32p. (ps-2). 1991. PLB 30.60 (*0-516-49469-4*) Childrens.
—Horses, Horses, Horses. LC 91-35063. (Illus.). 32p. (ps-2). 1992. PLB 12.60 (*0-516-04921-6*); PLB 30.60 big bk. (*0-516-49622-0*); pap. 3.95 (*0-516-44921-4*) Childrens.
—How Do You Know It's Fall? LC 91-35060. (Illus.). 32p. (ps-2). 1992. PLB 12.60 (*0-516-04922-4*); PLB 30.60 big bk. (*0-516-49623-9*); pap. 3.95 (*0-516-44922-2*) Childrens.
—How Do You Know It's Spring? LC 91-12760. 32p. (ps-2). 1991. PLB 12.60 (*0-516-04914-3*); PLB 30.60 big bk. (*0-516-49474-0*); pap. 3.95 (*0-516-44914-1*) Childrens.
—How Do You Know It's Summer? LC 91-35061. (Illus.). 32p. (ps-2). 1992. PLB 12.60 (*0-516-04923-2*); PLB 30.60 big bk. (*0-516-49624-7*); pap. 3.95 (*0-516-44923-0*) Childrens.
—How Do You Know It's Winter? LC 91-3129. 32p. (ps-2). 1991. PLB 12.60 (*0-516-04915-1*); PLB 30.60 big bk. (*0-516-49475-9*); pap. 3.95 (*0-516-44915-X*) Childrens.
—El Huevo O la Gallina? (The Chicken or the Egg?) LC 92-35054. (SPA., Illus.). 32p. (ps-2). 1993. PLB 13.93 (*0-516-36008-6*) Childrens.
—If It Weren't for Farmers. LC 92-35055. (Illus.). 32p. (ps-2). 1993. PLB 13.93 (*0-516-36009-4*) Childrens.
—It Could Still Be a Bird. LC 90-2206. (Illus.). 32p. (ps-2). 1990. PLB 12.60 (*0-516-04901-1*); pap. 30.60 big bk. (*0-516-49461-9*); pap. 3.95 (*0-516-44901-X*) Childrens.
—It Could Still Be a Cat. (Illus.). 32p. (ps-2). 1993. PLB 13.93 (*0-516-06015-5*) Childrens.
—It Could Still Be a Dog. LC 93-880. 1993. write for info. (*0-516-06016-3*) Childrens.
—It Could Still Be a Fish. LC 90-2203. (Illus.). 32p. (ps-2). 1990. PLB 12.60 (*0-516-04902-X*); pap. 30.60 big bk. (*0-516-49462-7*); pap. 3.95 (*0-516-44902-8*) Childrens.
—It Could Still Be a Leaf. LC 93-882. 1993. write for info. (*0-516-06017-1*) Childrens.
—It Could Still Be a Mammal. LC 90-2161. (Illus.). 32p. (ps-2). 1990. PLB 12.60 (*0-516-04903-8*); pap. 30.60 big bk. (*0-516-49463-5*); pap. 3.95 (*0-516-44903-6*) Childrens.
—It Could Still Be a Rock. LC 92-39260. (Illus.). 32p. (ps-2). 1993. big bk. 30.60 (*0-516-49641-7*); PLB 12.60 (*0-516-06010-4*); pap. 3.95 (*0-516-46010-2*) Childrens.
—It Could Still Be a Tree. LC 90-2207. (Illus.). 32p. (ps-2). 1990. PLB 12.60 (*0-516-04904-6*); pap. 30.60 big bk. (*0-516-49464-3*); pap. 3.95 (*0-516-44904-4*) Childrens.
—It Could Still Be Water. LC 92-7402. (Illus.). 32p. (ps-2). 1992. PLB 12.60 (*0-516-06003-1*); big bk. 30.60 (*0-516-49630-1*) Childrens.
—It Could Still Be Water. LC 92-7402. (Illus.). 32p. (ps-2). 1993. pap. 3.95 (*0-516-46003-X*) Childrens.
—It's a Good Thing There Are Insects. LC 90-2205. (Illus.). 32p. (ps-2). 1990. PLB 12.60 (*0-516-04905-4*); pap. 30.60 big bk. (*0-516-49465-1*); pap. 3.95 (*0-516-44905-2*) Childrens.
—It's Best to Leave a Snake Alone. LC 91-39245. (Illus.). 32p. (ps-2). 1992. PLB 12.60 (*0-516-04926-7*); PLB 30.60 big bk. (*0-516-49627-1*); pap. 3.95 (*0-516-44926-5*) Childrens.
—Los Limpios e Inteligentes Cerdos: (Smart, Clean Pigs) LC 92-36365. (SPA., Illus.). 32p. (ps-2). 1993. PLB 13.93 (*0-516-36013-2*) Childrens.
—Lo Que Escuchas - Libro Grande: (Hearing Things Big Book) LC 90-22524. (SPA., Illus.). 32p. (ps-2). 1993. 30.60 (*0-516-59469-9*) Childrens.
—Lo Que Escuchas: Hearing Things. LC 90-22524. (SPA., Illus.). 32p. (ps-2). PLB 12.60, Apr. 1992 (*0-516-34909-0*); pap. 3.95, Jul. 1992 (*0-516-54909-X*) Childrens.
—Lo Que Sientes Al Tocar: Feeling Things. LC 90-22526. (SPA., Illus.). 32p. (ps-2). PLB 12.60, Apr. 1992 (*0-516-34908-2*); pap. 3.95, Jul. 1992 (*0-516-54908-1*) Childrens.
—Lo Que Ves - Libro Grande: (Seeing Things Big Book) LC 90-22527. (SPA., Illus.). 32p. (ps-2). 1993. 30.60 (*0-516-59470-2*) Childrens.
—Lo Que Ves: Seeing Things. LC 91-22527. (SPA., Illus.). 32p. (ps-2). PLB 12.60, Apr. 1992 (*0-516-34910-3*) Childrens.

—Norte, Sur, Este & Oeste: (North, South, East, & West) LC 92-39261. (SPA., Illus.). 32p. (ps-2). 1993. PLB 13.93 (*0-516-36011-6*) Childrens.
—North, South, East, & West. LC 92-39261. (Illus.). 32p. (ps-2). 1993. big bk. 30.60 (*0-516-59642-5*); PLB 12.60 (*0-516-06011-2*); pap. 3.95 (*0-516-46011-0*) Childrens.
—Nos Gusta la Fruta! - We Love Fruit! LC 92-13312. (SPA., Illus.). 32p. (ps-2). 1993. big bk. 30.60 (*0-516-59633-0*); PLB 12.60 (*0-516-36006-X*); pap. 3.95 (*0-516-56006-9*) Childrens.
—El Olor De las Cosas: Smelling Things. LC 90-22123. (SPA., Illus.). 32p. (ps-2). PLB 12.60, Apr. 1992 (*0-516-34912-0*); pap. 3.95, Jul. 1992 (*0-516-54912-X*) Childrens.
—Ovejas Lanudas y Cabras Hambrientas: (Woolly Sheep & Hungry Goats) LC 92-36366. (SPA., Illus.). 32p. (ps-2). 1993. PLB 13.93 (*0-516-36014-0*) Childrens.
—Los Planetas Del Sol - The Sun's Family of Planets. LC 92-7405. (SPA., Illus.). 32p. (ps-2). 1993. big bk. 30.60 (*0-516-59631-4*); PLB 12.60 (*0-516-36004-3*); pap. 3.95 (*0-516-56004-2*) Childrens.
—Please Don't Feed the Bears. LC 91-3130. 32p. (ps-2). 1991. PLB 12.60 (*0-516-04916-X*); PLB 30.60 big bk. (*0-516-49476-7*); pap. 3.95 (*0-516-44916-8*) Childrens.
—Podria Ser un Arbol - Libro Grande: (It Could Still Be a Tree Big Book) LC 90-2207. (SPA., Illus.). 32p. (ps-2). 1993. 30.60 (*0-516-59464-8*) Childrens.
—Podria Ser un Arbol: It Could Still Be a Tree. LC 90-2207. (SPA., Illus.). 32p. (ps-2). 1991. PLB 12.60 (*0-516-34904-X*); pap. 3.95 (*0-516-54904-9*) Childrens.
—Podria Ser un Mamifero - Libro Grande: (It Could Still Be a Mammal Big Book) LC 90-2161. (SPA., Illus.). 32p. (ps-2). 1993. 30.60 (*0-516-59463-X*) Childrens.
—Podria Ser un Mamifero: It Could Still Be a Mammal. LC 90-2161. (SPA., Illus.). 32p. (ps-2). 1991. PLB 12.60 (*0-516-34903-1*); pap. 3.95 (*0-516-54903-0*) Childrens.
—Podria Ser un Pajaro: It Could Still Be a Bird. LC 90-2206. (SPA., Illus.). 32p. (ps-2). 1991. PLB 12.60 (*0-516-34901-5*); pap. 3.95 (*0-516-54901-4*) Childrens.
—Podria Ser un Pez - Libro Grande: (It Could Still Be a Fish Big Book) LC 90-2203. (SPA., Illus.). 32p. (ps-2). 1993. 30.60 (*0-516-59462-1*) Childrens.
—Podria Ser un Pez: It Could Still Be a Fish. LC 90-2203. (SPA., Illus.). 32p. (ps-2). 1991. PLB 12.60 (*0-516-34902-3*); pap. 3.95 (*0-516-54902-2*) Childrens.
—Podria Ser una Roca: (It Could Still Be a Rock) LC 92-39260. (SPA., Illus.). 32p. (ps-2). 1993. PLB 13.93 (*0-516-36010-8*) Childrens.
—Podria Sr un Pajaro - Libro Grande: (It Could Still Be a Bird Big Book) LC 90-2206. (SPA., Illus.). 32p. (ps-2). 1993. 30.60 (*0-516-59461-3*) Childrens.
—Quack & Honk. LC 92-36365. (Illus.). 32p. (ps-2). 1993. big bk. 30.60 (*0-516-49643-3*); PLB 12.60 (*0-516-06012-0*); pap. 3.95 (*0-516-46012-9*) Childrens.
—Que Bueno Que Haya Insectos! It's a Good Thing There Are Insects. LC 90-2205. (SPA.). 32p. (ps-2). 1991. PLB 12.60 (*0-516-34905-8*); pap. 3.95 (*0-516-54905-7*) Childrens.
—Ranas, Sapos y Renacuajos! Frogs & Toads, & Tadpoles, Too. LC 91-42178. (SPA., Illus.). 32p. (ps-2). 1992. PLB 12.60 (*0-516-34925-2*); pap. 3.95 (*0-516-54925-1*); big bk. 30.60 (*0-516-59626-8*) Childrens.
—Seeing Things. LC 90-22527. (Illus.). 32p. (ps-2). 1991. PLB 12.60 (*0-516-04910-0*); pap. 3.95 (*0-516-44910-9*) Childrens.
—Seeing Things Big Book. (Illus.). 32p. (ps-2). 1991. PLB 30.60 (*0-516-49470-8*) Childrens.
—Smart, Clean Pigs. LC 92-36365. (Illus.). 32p. (ps-2). 1993. big bk. 30.60 (*0-516-49644-1*); PLB 12.60 (*0-516-06013-9*); pap. 3.95 (*0-516-46013-7*) Childrens.
—Smelling Things. LC 90-22123. (Illus.). 32p. (ps-2). 1991. PLB 12.60 (*0-516-04912-7*); pap. 3.95 (*0-516-44912-5*) Childrens.
—Smelling Things Big Book. (Illus.). 32p. (ps-2). 1991. PLB 30.60 (*0-516-49472-4*) Childrens.
—So That's How the Moon Changes Shape. LC 91-3142. 32p. (ps-2). 1991. PLB 12.60 (*0-516-04917-8*); PLB 30.60 big bk. (*0-516-49477-5*); pap. 3.95 (*0-516-44917-6*) Childrens.
—El Sol Siempre Brilla En Alguna Parte: The Sun Is Always Shining Somewhere. LC 90-2176. (SPA., Illus.). 32p. (ps-2). PLB 12.60, Apr. 1992 (*0-516-34906-6*); pap. 3.95, Jul. 1992 (*0-516-54906-5*) Childrens.
—Sound-a-Likes One: One, Won. Cafferata, Sue, illus. 32p. (gr. k-2). 1993. PLB 10.95 (*1-878363-97-2*) Forest Hse.
—Sound-a-Likes Two: Two, To, Too. Cafferata, Sue, illus. 32p. (gr. 2-4). 1993. PLB 10.95 (*1-878363-98-0*) Forest Hse.
—The Sun Is Always Shining Somewhere. (Illus.). 32p. (ps-2). 1991. PLB 12.60 (*0-516-04906-2*); pap. 3.95 (*0-516-44906-0*) Childrens.
—The Sun Is Always Shining Somewhere Big Book. (Illus.). 32p. (ps-2). 1991. PLB 30.60 (*0-516-49466-X*) Childrens.
—The Sun's Family of Planets. LC 92-7405. (Illus.). 32p. (ps-2). 1992. PLB 12.60 (*0-516-06004-X*); big bk. 30. 60 (*0-516-49631-X*) Childrens.
—The Sun's Family of Planets. LC 92-7405. (Illus.). 32p. (ps-2). 1993. pap. 3.95 (*0-516-46004-8*) Childrens.
—Tasting Things. LC 90-21647. (Illus.). 32p. (ps-2). 1991. PLB 12.60 (*0-516-04911-9*); pap. 3.95 (*0-516-44911-7*) Childrens.
—Tasting Things Big Book. (Illus.). 32p. (ps-2). 1991. PLB 30.60 (*0-516-49471-6*) Childrens.

—Thanks to Cows. LC 91-35062. (Illus.). 32p. (ps-2). 1992. PLB 12.60 (*0-516-04924-0*); PLB 30.60 big bk. (*0-516-49625-5*); pap. 3.95 (*0-516-44924-9*) Childrens.
—Las Tortugas So Se Apuran - Turtles Take Their Time. LC 92-7403. (SPA., Illus.). 32p. (ps-2). 1993. big bk. 30.60 (*0-516-59632-2*); PLB 12.60 (*0-516-36005-1*); pap. 3.95 (*0-516-56005-0*) Childrens.
—Turtles Take Their Time. LC 92-7403. (Illus.). 32p. (ps-2). 1992. PLB 12.60 (*0-516-06005-8*); big bk. 30. 60 (*0-516-49632-8*) Childrens.
—Turtles Take Their Time. LC 92-7403. (Illus.). 32p. (ps-2). 1993. pap. 3.95 (*0-516-46005-6*) Childrens.
—The Upside-Down Sloth. LC 93-18981. (Illus.). 32p. (ps-2). 1993. PLB 13.93 (*0-516-06018-X*) Childrens.
—What's the Weather Today? LC 91-3125. 32p. (ps-2). 1991. PLB 12.60 (*0-516-04918-6*); PLB 30.60 big bk. (*0-516-49478-3*); pap. 3.95 (*0-516-44918-4*) Childrens.
—What's Your Favorite Flower? LC 92-7404. (Illus.). 32p. (ps-2). 1992. PLB 12.60 (*0-516-06007-4*); big bk. 30.60 (*0-516-49634-4*) Childrens.
—What's Your Favorite Flower? LC 92-7404. (Illus.). 32p. (ps-2). 1993. pap. 3.95 (*0-516-46007-2*) Childrens.
—Woolly Sheep & Hungry Goats. LC 92-36366. (Illus.). 32p. (ps-2). 1993. big bk. 30.60 (*0-516-49645-X*); PLB 12.60 (*0-516-06014-7*); pap. 3.95 (*0-685-62937-6*) Childrens.
—World's Fairs & Expos. LC 91-8891. 48p. (gr. k-4). 1991. PLB 15.27 (*0-516-01130-8*); pap. 4.95 (*0-516-41130-6*) Childrens.
—Y Aun Podria Ser Agua - It Could Still Be Water. LC 92-7402. (SPA., Illus.). 32p. (ps-2). 1993. big bk. 30.60 (*0-516-59630-6*); PLB 12.60 (*0-516-36003-5*); pap. 3.95 (*0-516-56003-4*) Childrens.
Fowler, H. Seymour, rev. by see Palmer, E. Lawrence.
Fowler, Joanne, jt. auth. see Crabtree, Cathy L.
Fowler, Loretta. The Arapaho. (Illus.). 128p. (gr. 5 up). 1989. 17.95 (*1-55546-690-7*) Chelsea Hse.
Fowler, Mary J. & Fisher, Margaret, eds. Great Americans. rev. ed. LC 87-81352. (Illus.). 160p. (gr. 4 up). 1988. 1-4 copies 14.95 ea. (*0-934291-25-X*); 5 or more copies 11.95 (*0-317-91143-0*) Gateway Pr MI.
Fowler, Mary J., jt. ed. see Fisher, Margaret.
Fowler, R. Ted & Dolly's Submarine. (Illus.). 20p. 1991. text ed. 9.95 (*0-88110-569-4*, Usborne) EDC.
Fowler, Richard. Honeybee's Busy Day. LC 93-31152. 1994. 12.95 (*0-15-200055-0*, Gulliver Bks) HarBrace.
—Ladybug on the Move. LC 92-19740. 1993. write for info. (*0-15-200475-0*) HarBrace.
—Let's Make It Go from Side to Side. Fowler, Richard, illus. 8p. (ps). 1990. Repr. of 1985 ed. bds. 4.95 (*0-88335-898-0*, AT03) Milliken Pub Co.
—Let's Make It Go In & Out. Fowler, Richard, illus. 8p. (ps). 1990. Repr. of 1984 ed. bds. 4.95 (*0-88335-737-2*, AT01) Milliken Pub Co.
—Let's Make It Go Round. Fowler, Richard, illus. 8p. (ps). 1990. Repr. of 1984 ed. bds. 4.95 (*0-88335-738-0*, AT02) Milliken Pub Co.
—Let's Make It Go up & Down. (Illus.). (ps). 1990. bds. 4.95 (*0-88335-899-9*, AT04) Milliken Pub Co.
—Mr. Little's Noisy Car. Fowler, Richard, illus. LC 85-80381. 20p. (ps-1). 1986. 11.95 (*0-448-18977-1*, G&D) Putnam Pub Group.
—Mr. Little's Noisy Fire Engine. (Illus.). 20p. 1990. 11.95 (*0-448-40042-1*, G&D) Putnam Pub Group.
—Mr. Little's Noisy Plane: A Lift-the-Flap Book. Fowler, Richard, illus. 20p. (ps-1). 1988. 11.95 (*0-448-19007-9*, G&D) Putnam Pub Group.
—Mr. Little's Noisy Truck: A Life-the-Flap Book. Fowler, Richard, illus. 20p. (ps-1). 1989. 11.95 (*0-448-19021-4*, G&D) Putnam Pub Group.
—Squirrel's Tale. 24p. (ps-3). 1984. 9.95 (*0-88110-157-5*) EDC.
—Ted & Dolly Fairytale Flight. (Illus.). 24p. (ps-3). 1984. 9.95 (*0-88110-190-7*) EDC.
—Ted & Dolly's Magic Carpet Ride. 24p. (ps-1). 1984. 9.95 (*0-88110-155-9*) EDC.
—There's a Mouse about the House. (Illus.). 24p. (ps-1). 1984. 9.95 (*0-88110-154-0*) EDC.
—Time Travellers. Fowler, Richard, illus. 22p. (p up). 1994. 10.95 (*0-8431-3594-8*) Price Stern.
Fowler, Ruth. Lights! Camera! Love in Action! Smothers, Mark, illus. 64p. (Orig.). (gr. 4-6). 1989. pap. text ed. 3.95 (*0-936625-68-6*) Womans Mission Union.
Fowler, Susi G. Fog. Fowler, Jim, illus. LC 91-28509. 32p. (ps-8). 1992. 14.00 (*0-688-10593-9*); PLB 13.93 (*0-688-10594-7*) Greenwillow.
—I'll See You When the Moon Is Full. Fowler, Jim, illus. LC 91-47667. 24p. (ps up). 1994. write for info. (*0-688-10830-X*); PLB write for info. (*0-688-10831-8*) Greenwillow.
—When Joel Comes Home. Fowler, Jim, illus. LC 92-7979. 24p. (ps up). 1993. 14.00 (*0-688-11064-9*); PLB 13.93 (*0-688-11065-7*) Greenwillow.
—When Summer Ends. Russo, Marisabina, illus. LC 87-14937. 32p. (ps up). 1989. 11.95 (*0-688-07605-X*); PLB 11.88 (*0-688-07606-8*) Greenwillow.
—When Summer Ends. Russo, Marisabina, illus. 32p. (ps-3). 1992. pap. 4.50 (*0-14-054472-0*, Puffin) Puffin Bks.
Fowler, Virginia. Christmas Crafts & Customs Around the World. Fowler, Virginia, illus. LC 84-9770. 180p. (gr. 5 up). 1988. (S&S BFYR); hpc. 5.95 (*0-671-67057-3*, S&S BFYR) S&S Trade.
Fowler, Virginie. Clayworks: Colorful Crafts from Around the World. Fowler, Virginie, illus. (gr. 5 up). 1986. 11.95 (*0-13-136417-0*) P-H.

—Folk Arts Around the World. Fowler, Virginie, illus. 168p. (gr. 5 up). 1984. pap. 6.95 (0-13-322975-0) P-H.
—Folk Arts Around the World: And How to Make Them. (gr. 5 up). 1981. 7.95 (0-13-323014-7) P-H.
—Folk Toys Around the World & How to Make Them. 160p. 1984. 10.95 (0-13-323148-8) P-H.
—Paperworks: Colorful Crafts from Picture Eggs to Fish Kites. Fowler, Virginie, illus. 162p. (Orig.). (gr. 5 up). 1982. 10.95 (0-13-648543-X) P-H.
Fowler, Zinita. Ghost Stories of Old Texas. (Illus.). 68p. (gr. 4-7). 1983. 10.95 (0-89015-407-4, Pub. by Panda Bks) Eakin-Sunbelt.
—Ghost Stories of Old Texas II. Fowler, Jack, illus. LC 92-19263. 80p. (gr. 4-7). 1992. 10.95 (0-89015-868-1) Eakin-Sunbelt.
—The Last Innocent Summer. LC 89-20417. 144p. (gr. 6-9). 1990. pap. 11.95 (0-87565-045-7) Tex Christian.
Fox. Easter, Reading Level 4. (Illus.). 48p. (gr. 3-8). 1989. PLB 15.94 (0-86592-985-8); 11.95 (0-685-58772-X) Rourke Corp.
Fox, Alan. Kayaking. LC 92-5548. 1993. 17.50 (0-8225-2482-1) Lerner Pubns.
Fox, Bernice, tr. see White, E. B.
Fox, C. Lynn. Handicapped...How Does It Feel: Activity Packet. Lovelady, Janet, ed. Button, Mary, illus. 48p. (gr. k-12). 1982. pap. 5.95 (0-935266-13-5, BW6613-5) B L Winch.
Fox, Cecil H. AIDS & HIV Diseases. Head, J. J., ed. Botzis, Ka, illus. 16p. (Orig.). (gr. 10 up). 1991. pap. text ed. 2.75 (0-89278-120-3, 45-9620) Carolina Biological.
Fox, Dan. We Wish You a Merry Christmas: Songs of the Season for Young People. Metropolitan Museum of Art Staff, illus. 80p. 1989. 16.95 (1-55970-043-2) Arcade Pub Inc.
Fox, F. Earle. Biblical Sexuality & the Battle for Science. LC 88-80409. 208p. (Orig.). (gr. 9-12). 1988. pap. 5.45 (0-945778-00-7) Emmaus Ministries.
Fox, Fiona. How to Reach Your Favorite Star. LC 92-17291. (Illus.). 64p. (gr. 4-8). 1992. pap. 3.95 (1-56288-330-5) Checkerboard.
—How to Reach Your Favorite Star, No. 2. (gr. 4-7). 1993. pap. 2.95 (0-307-22550-X, Golden Pr) Western Pub.
Fox, Frances M. The Little Cat That Could Not Sleep. Hughes, Shirley, illus. LC 72-89335. 32p. (gr. k-4). 1973. 7.95 (0-87592-030-6) Scroll Pr.
Fox, Geoffrey. The Land & People of Argentina. LC 89-37811. (Illus.). 256p. (gr. 6 up). 1990. 16.95 (0-397-32380-8, Lipp Jr Bks); PLB 18.89 (0-397-32381-6, Lipp Jr Bks) HarpC Child Bks.
—The Land & People of Venezuela. LC 90-20431. (Illus.). 208p. (gr. 6 up). 1991. 17.95 (0-06-022476-2); PLB 17.89 (0-06-022477-0) HarpC Child Bks.
Fox, Geoffrey, tr. see Diaz, Jorge.
Fox, George & Puffer, Lela. Okemos: Story of a Fox Indian in His Youth. (gr. 3-9). 1976. 1.50 (0-89992-036-5) Coun India Ed.
Fox, Greg, ed. see Lupo, Ann.
Fox, Ken. Everything You Need to Know about Your Legal Rights. (gr. 7-12). 1992. PLB 13.95 (0-8239-1322-8) Rosen Group.
Fox, Larry. Football Basics. Gow, Bill, illus. (gr. 3-7). 1981. 9.95 (0-13-323998-5) P-H.
—Sports Great John Elway. LC 89-28465. (Illus.). 64p. (gr. 4-10). 1990. lib. bdg. 15.95 (0-685-59059-3) Enslow Pubs.
Fox, Lori M. The Craziest Riddle Book in the World. Hoffman, Sanford, illus. LC 91-13209. 96p. (gr. 3-9). 1992. 12.95 (0-8069-8406-6); pap. 3.95 (0-8069-8407-4) Sterling.
—Oodles of Riddles. LC 89-4549. (Illus.). 96p. (gr. 2-8). 1989. 12.95 (0-8069-6880-X); PLB 15.69 (0-8069-6881-8) Sterling.
—Riddlemania. Hoffman, Sanford, illus. LC 90-43230. 96p. (gr. 2-7). 1991. 12.95 (0-8069-7352-8) Sterling.
—Riddlemania. Hoffman, Sanford, illus. LC 90-43230. 96p. (gr. 1-7). 1992. pap. 3.95 (0-8069-7353-6) Sterling.
—Shake, Riddle & Roll. LC 89-26235. (Illus.). 96p. (gr. 2-8). 1990. 12.95 (0-8069-7252-1); PLB 15.69 (0-8069-7253-X) Sterling.
—Shake, Riddle & Roll. Hoffman, Sanford, illus. 96p. (gr. 3-9). 1991. pap. 3.95 (0-8069-7251-3) Sterling.
Fox, Mary V. About Martin Luther King Day. LC 88-23230. (Illus.). 64p. (gr. 4-7). 1989. lib. bdg. 15.95 (0-89490-200-8) Enslow Pubs.
—Bahrain. (Illus.). 128p. (gr. 5-9). 1992. PLB 26.60 (0-516-02608-9) Childrens.
—Bette Bao Lord: Novelist & Chinese Voice for Change. LC 92-36805. (Illus.). 152p. (gr. 4 up). 1993. PLB 18.60 (0-516-03291-7); pap. 5.95 (0-516-43291-5) Childrens.
—Chief Joseph of the Nez Perce Indians: Champion of Liberty. LC 92-35053. (Illus.). 152p. (gr. 4 up) 1992. PLB 18.60 (0-516-03275-5) Childrens.
—Chief Joseph of the Nez Perce Indians: Champion of Liberty. LC 92-35053. (Illus.). 152p. (gr. 4 up) 1993. pap. 5.95 (0-516-43275-3) Childrens.
—Cyprus. LC 93-755. (Illus.). 128p. (gr. 5-9). 1993. PLB 26.60 (0-516-02617-8) Childrens.
—Iran. LC 90-21264. (Illus.). 128p. (gr. 5-9). 1991. PLB 26.60 (0-516-02727-1) Childrens.
—New Zealand. LC 90-20010. (Illus.). 128p. (gr. 5-9). 1991. PLB 26.60 (0-516-02728-X) Childrens.
—Papua New Guinea. LC 93-35493. 1994. write for info. (0-516-02621-6) Childrens.

—Princess Diana. LC 86-4451. (Illus.). 128p. (gr. 6 up). 1986. lib. bdg. 17.95 (0-89490-129-X) Enslow Pubs.
—A Queen Named King: Henrietta of the King Ranch. 96p. (gr. 4-7). 1986. 9.95 (0-89015-562-3, Pub. by Panda Bks) Eakin-Sunbelt.
—The Story of Women Who Shaped the West. LC 90-21444. (Illus.). 32p. (gr. 3-6). 1991. PLB 13.27 (0-516-04757-4); pap. 3.95 (0-516-44757-2) Childrens.
—Tunisia. LC 90-2199. (Illus.). 128p. (gr. 5-9). 1990. PLB 26.60 (0-516-02724-7) Childrens.
—Women Astronauts: Aboard the Space Shuttle. rev. ed. LC 87-10814. (Illus.). 144p. (gr. 7 up). 1987. lib. bdg. 13.98 (0-671-64840-3, J Messner); lib. bdg. 5.95 (0-671-64841-1) S&S Trade.
Fox, Mem. Guess What? Goodman, Vivienne, illus. LC 90-4127. 28p. (ps up). 1990. 13.95 (0-15-200452-1, Gulliver Bks) HarBrace.
—Hattie & the Fox. Mullins, Patricia, illus. LC 86-18849. 32p. (ps-2). 1988. RSBE 13.95 (0-02-735470-9, Bradbury Pr); pap. 16.95 big book (0-02-735471-7) Macmillan Child Grp.
—Hattie & the Fox. Mullins, Patricia, illus. LC 91-41727. 32p. (ps-2). 1992. pap. 4.95 (0-689-71611-7, Aladdin) Macmillan Child Grp.
—Koala Lou. 28p. (ps-1). 1989. 13.95 (0-15-200502-1) HarBrace.
—Night Noises. 30p. (ps-2). 1989. 13.95 (0-15-200543-9) HarBrace.
—Night Noises. LC 89-216. (ps-3). 1992. pap. 4.95 (0-15-257421-2, Voyager Bks) HarBrace.
—Possum Magic. Vivas, Julie, illus. 32p. (ps-2). 1990. 13. 95 (0-15-200572-2, Gulliver Bks) HarBrace.
—Possum Magic. 32p. (ps-3). 1991. pap. 4.95 (0-15-263224-7, HB Juv Bks) HarBrace.
—Shoes from Grandpa. Mullins, Patricia, illus. LC 89-35401. 32p. (ps-1). 1990. 13.95 (0-531-05848-4); PLB 13.99 (0-531-08448-5) Orchard Bks Watts.
—Shoes from Grandpa. Mullins, Patricia, illus. LC 89-35401. 32p. (ps-1). 1992. pap. 4.95 (0-531-07031-X) Orchard Bks Watts.
—Time for Bed. Dyer, Jane, illus. LC 92-19771. 1993. 13. 95 (0-15-288183-2) HarBrace.
—Wilfrid Gordon McDonald Partridge. Vivas, Julie, illus. LC 85-14720. 32p. (gr. k-5). 1985. 13.95 (0-916291-04-9) Kane Miller Bk.
—Wilfrid Gordon McDonald Partridge. Vivas, Julie, illus. 32p. (gr. k-4). 1989. pap. 7.95 (0-916291-26-X) Kane-Miller Bk.
—With Love, at Christmas. Lippincott, Gary, illus. LC 88-6332. (gr. 2 up). 1988. 12.95 (0-687-45863-3) Abingdon.
Fox, Naomi. A Christmas Carol. Fox, Neal, illus. 24p. (ps-2). 1993. pap. 9.95 (1-882179-06-4) Confetti Ent.
—A Difficult Kind of Christmas. Fox, Neal, illus. 24p. (ps-2). 1993. pap. text ed. 9.95 (1-882179-04-8) Confetti Ent.

—**The Frog Prince.** Fox, Neal, illus. 24p. (ps-1). 1992. Incl. cassette. pap. 9.95 (1-882179-11-0) Confetti Ent.
The Confetti Company Books & Tapes are special adaptations of well-known fairy tales which feature non-violence, happy family settings & show that children can make a difference. Narrated by Robert Guillaume, the characters come to life as a cast of children & act out the scenes. The addition of original music makes for an entertaining & magical experience. In this fun-filled tale, children will learn responsibility, the value of friendship & the importance of keeping a promise. When Ivy loses her mother's ring, she receives the help of a lonely frog. He dives for the ring in the dark pond & Ivy promises she will continue to visit him. Busy in school & with her friends, she neglects the frog. When Ivy realizes she has not kept her promise, she enlists her friends' help. When they find the frog, Ivy excitedly kisses him on his cheek & he becomes their new friend, the Frog Prince. To order: The Confetti Entertainment Company, 15250 Ventura Blvd., Suite 800, Sherman Oaks, CA 91403. (818) 783-6253. FAX: (818) 783-6518.
Publisher Provided Annotation.

—**Hansel & Gretel.** Fox, Neal, illus. 24p. (ps-1). 1992. Incl. cassette. pap. 9.95 (1-882179-12-9) Confetti Ent.
The Confetti Company Books & Tapes are special adaptations of well-known fairy tales which feature non-violence, happy family settings & show that children can make a difference. Narrated by Robert Guillaume, the characters come to life as a cast of children act out the scenes. The addition of original music makes for an entertaining & magical experience. Desperately wanting to help their parents, Hansel & Gretel embark on an adventure in the woods to search for food. Instead they encounter an evil witch. In the end, the resourceful children manage to out-smart the witch & become heroes. In a non-violent approach, this story confirms that witches are not real people, thus leaving children with a restful night's sleep. An exciting & suspenseful story for all. To order: The Confetti Entertainment Company, 15250 Ventura Blvd., Suite 800, Sherman Oaks, CA 91403. (818) 783-6253. FAX: (818) 783-6518.
Publisher Provided Annotation.

—Little Red Riding Hood. Fox, Neal, illus. 24p. (ps-1). 1993. Incl. cassette. pap. 9.95 (1-882179-14-5) Confetti Ent.

—**The Shoemaker & the Elves.** Fox, Neal, illus. 24p. (ps-1). 1993. Incl. cassette. pap. 9.95 (1-882179-15-3) Confetti Ent.
The Confetti Company Books & Tapes are special adaptations of well-known fairy tales, which feature non-violence, happy family settings & show that children can make a difference. Narrated by Robert Guillaume, the characters come to life as a cast of children act out the scenes. The addition of original music makes for an entertaining & magical experience. This is the magical tale of three children that save the shop of a kind-hearted shoemaker named Kwame & his loving wife Neema. Mysteriously, the children enter the shop at night & make beautifully well-crafted shoes. After discovering that their "elves" are really homeless children, Kwame & Neema offer them a new home. This warm & caring story shows children being helpful without asking for anything in return. The story ends allowing the reader to draw their own conclusions on how the elves (children) manage to get locked into the shop. To order: The Confetti Entertainment Company, 15250 Ventura Blvd., Suite 800, Sherman Oaks, CA 91403. (818) 783-6253, FAX: (818) 783-6518.
Publisher Provided Annotation.

—**Sleeping Beauty.** Fox, Neal, illus. 24p. (ps-1). 1992. Incl. cassette. pap. 9.95 (1-882179-13-7) Confetti Ent.
The Confetti Company Books & Tapes are special adaptations of well-known fairy tales which feature non-violence, happy family endings & show that children can make a difference. Narrated by Robert Guillaume, the characters come to life as a cast of children act out the scenes. The addition of original music makes for an entertaining & magical experience. This charming adaptation of Sleeping Beauty emphasizes how good prevails over evil. Although the witch places a

curse on the Princess, the good fairies use a magic spell to protect her. Though the Prince awakens Sleeping Beauty from an eternal slumber, it is the gift of a "good heart" that truly saves her life. This delightful story of love, family & friends is a favorite with children everywhere. To order: The Confetti Entertainment Company, 15250 Ventura Blvd., Suite 800, Sherman Oaks, CA 91403. (818) 783-6253. FAX: (818) 783-6518. *Publisher Provided Annotation.*

Fox, Paula. Amzat & His Brothers: Three Italian Folktales. McCully, Emily, illus. LC 92-19494. 80p. (gr. 3-5). 1993. 15.95 *(0-531-05462-4)*; PLB 15.99 *(0-531-08612-7)* Orchard Bks Watts.
—Blowfish Live in the Sea. 128p. (gr. 6-8). 1986. pap. 3.95 *(0-689-71092-5,* Aladdin) Macmillan Child Grp.
—Blowfish Live in the Sea. (gr. 6-8). 1991. 16.75 *(0-8446-6449-9)* Peter Smith.
—How Many Miles to Babylon? Giovanopoulos, Paul, illus. LC 79-25802. 128p. (gr. 5-7). 1982. SBE 13.95 *(0-02-735590-X,* Bradbury Pr) Macmillan Child Grp.
—A Likely Place. Ardizzone, Edward, illus. LC 87-5542. 64p. (gr. 2-6). 1987. Repr. SBE 13.95 *(0-02-735761-9,* Macmillan Child Bk) Macmillan Child Grp.
—Lily & the Lost Boy. LC 87-5778. 160p (gr. 6-8). 1987. 12.95 *(0-531-05720-8)*; PLB 12.99 *(0-531-08320-9)* Orchard Bks Watts.
—Lily & the Lost Boys. large (gr. k-6). 1989. pap. 3.50 *(0-440-40235-2,* YB) Dell.
—Lily & the Lost Boys. large type, unabr. ed. 230p. (gr. 5-7). 1989. lib. bdg. 13.95x *(0-8161-4725-6)* G K Hall.
—Maurice's Room. reissued ed. Fetz, Ingrid, illus. LC 85-7200. 64p. (gr. 2-6). 1985. SBE 13.95 *(0-02-735490-3,* Macmillan Child Bk) Macmillan Child Grp.
—Maurice's Room. Fetz, Ingrid, illus. LC 87-19504. 64p. (gr. 2-6). 1988. pap. 3.95 *(0-689-71216-2,* Aladdin) Macmillan Child Grp.
—Monkey Island. LC 91-7460. 160p. (gr. 5 up). 1991. 14.95 *(0-531-05962-6)*; RLB 14.99 *(0-531-08562-7)* Orchard Bks Watts.
—Monkey Island. 1993. pap. 3.99 *(0-440-40770-2)* Dell.
—The Moonlight Man. LC 85-26907. 192p. (gr. 7 up). 1986. SBE 14.95 *(0-02-735480-6,* Bradbury Pr) Macmillan Child Grp.
—The Moonlight Man. (gr. k-12). 1988. pap. 3.50 *(0-440-20079-2,* LFL) Dell.
—One-Eyed Cat. Trivas, Irene, illus. LC 84-10964. 192p. (gr. 6-8). 1984. SBE 14.95 *(0-02-735540-3,* Bradbury Pr) Macmillan Child Grp.
—One-Eyed Cat. (gr. k-6). 1985. pap. 3.99 *(0-440-46641-5,* YB) Dell.
—One-Eyed Cat. large type ed. 300p. (gr. 3-7). 1987. Repr. of 1984 ed. lib. bdg. 15.95 *(1-55736-071-5,* Crnrstn Bks) BDD LT Grp.
—One Eyed Cat. (gr. 4-7). 1993. pap. 1.99 *(0-440-21625-7)* Dell.
—A Place Apart. 192p. (gr. 7 up). 1982. pap. 2.25 *(0-451-14338-8,* Sig) NAL-Dutton.
—Place Apart. 1993. pap. 3.95 *(0-374-45868-5)* FS&G.
—Portrait of Ivan. reissue ed. Lambert, Saul, illus. LC 74-93085. 144p. (gr. 5-7). 1985. SBE 13.95 *(0-02-735510-1,* Bradbury Pr) Macmillan Child Grp.
—Portrait of Ivan. Lambert, Saul, illus. LC 87-1109. 144p. (gr. 6-8). 1987. pap. 3.95 *(0-689-71167-0,* Aladdin) Macmillan Child Grp.
—The Slave Dancer. Eros, Keith, illus. LC 73-80642. 192p. (gr. 5-8). 1982. SBE 14.95 *(0-02-735560-8,* Bradbury Pr) Macmillan Child Grp.
—Slave Dancer. large type ed. (gr. 3-7). 1988. Repr. of 1973 ed. lib. bdg. 15.95 *(1-55736-029-4,* Crnrstn Bks) BDD LT Grp.
—The Slave Dancer. (Orig.). (gr. k-6). 1991. pap. 3.99 *(0-440-40402-9,* Pub. by Yearling Classics) Dell.
—The Stone-Faced Boy. Mackay, Donald A., illus. LC 68-9053. 112p. (gr. 4-6). 1982. SBE 13.95 *(0-02-735570-5,* Bradbury Pr) Macmillan Child Grp.
—The Stone-Faced Boy. LC 86-22204. 112p. (gr. 4-6). 1987. pap. 3.95 *(0-689-71127-1,* Aladdin) Macmillan Child Grp.
—The Village by the Sea. LC 88-60099. 160p. (gr. 5-7). 1988. 13.95 *(0-531-05788-7)*; PLB 13.99 *(0-531-08388-8)* Orchard Bks Watts.
—The Village by the Sea. (gr. k-6). 1990. pap. 3.50 *(0-440-40299-9,* Pub. by Yearling Classics) Dell.
—Western Wind. LC 93-9629. 208p. (gr. 5 up). 1993. 14.95 *(0-531-06802-1)*; PLB 14.99 *(0-531-08652-6)* Orchard Bks Watts.
Fox, Robert B. The Land of the Long White Cloud. LC 92-60489. 169p. (gr. 7 up). 1993. 7.95 *(1-55523-532-8)* Winston-Derek.
—Walks Two Worlds. LC 83-513. (Illus.). 62p. (Orig.). (gr. 4-6). 1983. pap. 6.95 *(0-86534-015-3)* Sunstone Pr.
Fox, Robert J. Catholic Truth for Youth. Mary Loretta, illus. Luther, Ben, intro. by. LC 78-104309. (Illus.). 448p. (gr. 5-12). 1978. pap. 5.95 *(0-911988-05-X)* AMI Pr.

—The Gift of Sexuality: A Guide for Young People. LC 88-63528. (Orig.). (gr. 9 up). 1989. pap. 7.95 *(0-87973-425-6,* 425) Our Sunday Visitor.
—A Prayer Book for Young Catholics. LC 82-81318. 168p. (gr. 4-8). 1982. pap. 4.95 leatherette *(0-87973-370-5,* 370) Our Sunday Visitor.
Fox, Robin. Poulet: A Rooster Who Laid Eggs. (FRE., Illus.). 3.50 *(0-685-11509-7)* Fr & Eur.
Fox, Stacey. Totally Cool California Dreams Scrapbook. (gr. 4-7). 1993. pap. 4.95 *(0-590-47450-2)* Scholastic Inc.
Fox, Terry. A Little Miracle: A Hanukah Story. Fox, David A., illus. LC 85-51615. 52p. (Orig.). (ps up) 1985. pap. 5.95 *(0-9615397-0-4)* Tenderfoot Pr.
Foxton, David. Ivan & the Firebird. (Orig.). 1991. Playscript. 5.00 *(0-87602-297-2)* Anchorage.
—Sepia & Song. (Illus.). 96p. (Orig.). 1990. pap. 14.95 *(0-333-40923-X,* McMillan Ed UK) Players Pr.
Fradera, Narcis, tr. see Babbitt, Natalie.
Frades, Ernesto. The Happy Valley of the Elves: A Terry Turtle Adventure. Frades, Ernesto, illus. 48p. (Orig.). (gr. k-3). 1990. pap. write for info. *(0-9624929-1-4)* Little Great Whale.
Frades, Ernesto, ed. see Fasco, Rudolph.
Fradin, Dennis. Alabama: In Words & Pictures. Wahl, Richard, illus. LC 80-15135. 48p. (gr. 2-5). 1980. PLB 17.27 *(0-516-03901-6)* Childrens.
—Alaska: In Words & Pictures. Ulm, Robert, illus. LC 77-4353. 48p. (gr. 2-5). 1977. PLB 17.27 *(0-516-03902-4)* Childrens.
—Arizona: In Words & Pictures. LC 79-21480. (Illus.). 48p. (gr. 2-5). 1980. PLB 17.27 *(0-516-03903-2)*; pap. 4.95 *(0-516-43903-0)* Childrens.
—Arkansas: In Words & Pictures. Wahl, Richard, illus. LC 80-11995. 48p. (gr. 2-5). 1980. PLB 17.27 *(0-516-03904-0)* Childrens.
—California en Palabras y Fotos: California: In Words & Pictures. LC 86-21526. (Illus.). 48p. (gr. 2-6). 1986. PLB 15.93 *(0-516-33905-2)*; pap. 4.95 *(0-516-53905-1)* Childrens.
—California: In Words & Pictures. Ulm, Robert, illus. LC 76-50600. 48p. (gr. 2-5). 1977. PLB 17.27 *(0-516-03905-9)* Childrens.
—Cancer. (gr. 5-9). 1988. 15.27 *(0-516-01210-X)*; pap. 4.95 *(0-516-41210-8)* Childrens.
—Colorado: In Words & Pictures. Wahl, Richard, illus. LC 80-15778. 48p. (gr. k-4). 1980. PLB 17.27 *(0-516-03906-7)*; pap. 4.95 *(0-516-43906-5)* Childrens.
—Connecticut: In Words & Pictures. Wahl, Richard & Meents, Len, illus. LC 79-23292. 48p. (gr. 2-5). 1980. PLB 17.27 *(0-516-03907-5)* Childrens.
—Continents. LC 86-9580. (Illus.). 48p. (gr. k-4). 1986. PLB 15.27 *(0-516-01291-6)*; pap. 4.95 *(0-516-41291-4)* Childrens.
—Delaware: In Words & Pictures. LC 80-5842. (Illus.). 48p. (gr. 2-5). 1980. PLB 17.27 *(0-516-03908-3)* Childrens.
—Explorers. LC 84-7077. (Illus.). 48p. (gr. k-4). 1984. PLB 15.27 *(0-516-01926-0)* Childrens.
—Florida: In Words & Pictures. Wahl, Richard, illus. LC 80-16681. 48p. (gr. 2-5). 1980. PLB 17.27 *(0-516-03909-1)* Childrens.
—Georgia. LC 91-12101. 64p. (gr. 3-5). 1991. PLB 19.93 *(0-516-03810-9)* Childrens.
—Georgia: In Words & Pictures. Wahl, Richard, illus. LC 80-26768. 48p. (gr. 2-5). 1981. PLB 17.27 *(0-516-03910-5)* Childrens.
—Hawaii: In Words & Pictures. LC 79-25605. (Illus.). 48p. (gr. 2-5). 1980. PLB 17.27 *(0-516-03913-X)*; pap. 4.95 *(0-516-43913-8)* Childrens.
—Heredity. LC 87-831. (Illus.). 48p. (gr. k-4). 1987. PLB 15.27 *(0-516-01233-9)* Childrens.
—Idaho: In Words & Pictures. LC 80-14660. (Illus.). 48p. (gr. 2-5). 1980. PLB 17.27 *(0-516-03914-8)* Childrens.
—Illinois. LC 91-13510. 64p. (gr. 3-5). 1991. PLB 19.93 *(0-516-03813-3)* Childrens.
—Illinois: In Words & Pictures. LC 76-7389. (Illus.). 48p. (gr. 2-5). 1976. PLB 17.27 *(0-516-03911-3)* Childrens.
—Indiana: In Words & Pictures. LC 79-21383. (Illus.). 48p. (gr. 2-5). 1980. PLB 17.27 *(0-516-03912-1)* Childrens.
—Iowa: In Words & Pictures. LC 79-19399. (Illus.). 48p. (gr. 2-5). 1980. PLB 17.27 *(0-516-03915-6)* Childrens.
—Kansas: In Words & Pictures. Wahl, Richard, illus. LC 80-12576. 48p. (gr. 2-5). 1980. PLB 17.27 *(0-516-03916-4)* Childrens.
—Kentucky: In Words & Pictures. Wahl, Richard, illus. LC 80-25810. 48p. (gr. 2-5). 1981. PLB 17.27 *(0-516-03917-2)* Childrens.
—Louisiana: In Words & Pictures. Wahl, Richard, illus. LC 80-28609. 48p. (gr. 2-5). 1981. PLB 17.27 *(0-516-03918-0)*; pap. 3.95 *(0-516-43918-9)* Childrens.
—Maine: In Words & Pictures. LC 79-25122. (Illus.). 48p. (gr. 2-5). 1980. PLB 17.27 *(0-516-03919-9)* Childrens.
—Maryland: In Words & Pictures. LC 80-15185. (Illus.). 48p. (gr. 2-5). 1980. PLB 17.27 *(0-516-03920-2)* Childrens.
—Massachusetts. LC 91-541. 64p. (gr. 3-5). 1991. PLB 19.93 *(0-516-03811-7)* Childrens.
—Massachusetts: In Words & Pictures. Wahl, Richard, illus. LC 80-26161. 48p. (gr. 2-5). 1981. PLB 17.27 *(0-516-03921-0)* Childrens.
—Michigan: In Words & Pictures. LC 79-225356. (Illus.). 48p. (gr. 2-5). 1980. PLB 17.27 *(0-516-03922-9)* Childrens.

—Minnesota: In Words & Pictures. LC 79-21543. (Illus.). 48p. (gr. 2-5). 1980. PLB 17.27 *(0-516-03923-7)* Childrens.
—Mississippi: In Words & Pictures. Wahl, Richard, illus. LC 80-36855. 48p. (gr. 2-5). 1980. PLB 17.27 *(0-516-03924-5)* Childrens.
—Missouri: In Words & Pictures. Wahl, Richard, illus. LC 80-12249. 48p. (gr. 2-5). 1980. PLB 17.27 *(0-516-03925-3)* Childrens.
—Montana: In Words & Pictures. Wahl, Richard, illus. LC 80-25023. 48p. (gr. 2-5). 1981. PLB 17.27 *(0-516-03926-1)* Childrens.
—Moon Flights. LC 84-23154. (Illus.). 48p. (gr. k-4). 1985. PLB 15.27 *(0-516-01940-6)* Childrens.
—Nebraska: In Words & Pictures. LC 79-19456. (Illus.). 48p. (gr. 2-5). 1980. PLB 17.27 *(0-516-03927-X)* Childrens.
—Nevada: In Words & Pictures. Wahl, Richard, illus. LC 80-24179. 48p. (gr. 2-6). 1981. PLB 17.27 *(0-516-03928-8)* Childrens.
—New Hampshire: In Words & Pictures. Wahl, Richard, illus. LC 80-25421. 48p. (gr. 2-5). 1981. PLB 17.27 *(0-516-03929-6)* Childrens.
—The New Jersey Colony. LC 90-22437. (Illus.). (gr. 4 up). 1991. PLB 23.93 *(0-516-00395-X)* Childrens.
—New Jersey: In Words & Pictures. Wahl, Richard, illus. LC 80-19688. 48p. (gr. 2-5). 1980. PLB 17.27 *(0-516-03930-X)* Childrens.
—New Mexico: In Words & Pictures. Wahl, Richard, illus. LC 81-298. 48p. (gr. 2-5). 1981. PLB 17.27 *(0-516-03931-8)* Childrens.
—New York: In Words & Pictures. Wahl, Richard, illus. LC 81-28366. 48p. (gr. 2-5). 1981. PLB 17.27 *(0-516-03932-6)* Childrens.
—North Carolina Colony. LC 91-13314. 190p. (gr. 4 up). 1991. PLB 23.93 *(0-516-00396-8)* Childrens.
—North Carolina: In Words & Pictures. LC 79-25291. (Illus.). 48p. (gr. 2-5). 1980. PLB 17.27 *(0-516-03933-4)* Childrens.
—North Dakota: In Words & Pictures. Wahl, Richard, illus. LC 80-26480. 48p. (gr. 2-5). 1981. PLB 17.27 *(0-516-03934-2)* Childrens.
—Nuclear Energy. (Illus.). (gr. k-4). 1987. PLB 15.27 *(0-516-01237-1)* Childrens.
—Ohio: In Words & Pictures. Ulm, Robert, illus. LC 76-46941. 48p. (gr. 2-5). 1977. PLB 17.27 *(0-516-03935-0)*; pap. 3.95 *(0-516-43935-9)* Childrens.
—Oklahoma: In Words & Pictures. Wahl, Richard, illus. LC 80-26961. 48p. (gr. 2-5). 1981. PLB 17.27 *(0-516-03936-9)* Childrens.
—Oregon: In Words & Pictures. Wahl, Richard, illus. LC 80-15183. 48p. (gr. 3-8). 1980. PLB 17.27 *(0-516-03937-7)* Childrens.
—Pennsylvania: In Words & Pictures. LC 79-24942. (Illus.). 48p. (gr. 2-5). 1980. PLB 17.27 *(0-516-03938-5)*; pap. 4.95 *(0-516-43938-3)* Childrens.
—Pioneers. LC 84-9418. (Illus.). 48p. (gr. k-4). 1984. PLB 15.27 *(0-516-01927-9)* Childrens.
—The Republic of Ireland. LC 83-20960. (Illus.). 128p. (gr. 5-9). 1984. PLB 26.60 *(0-516-02767-0)* Childrens.
—Rhode Island: In Words & Pictures. Wahl, Len, illus. LC 80-22497. 48p. (gr. 2-5). 1981. PLB 17.27 *(0-516-03939-3)* Childrens.
—Search for Extraterrestrial Intelligence. LC 87-14618. (Illus.). 48p. (gr. k-4). 1987. pap. 4.95 *(0-516-41242-6)* Childrens.
—South Carolina: In Words & Pictures. LC 79-22550. (Illus.). 48p. (gr. 2-5). 1980. PLB 17.27 *(0-516-03940-7)* Childrens.
—South Dakota: In Words & Pictures. Wahl, Richard, illus. LC 80-25349. 48p. (gr. 2-5). 1981. PLB 17.27 *(0-516-03941-5)* Childrens.
—Spacelab. LC 84-12702. (Illus.). 48p. (gr. k-4). 1984. PLB 15.27 *(0-516-01930-9)*; pap. 4.95 *(0-516-41930-7)* Childrens.
—Tennessee: In Words & Pictures. LC 79-19218. (Illus.). 48p. (gr. 2-5). 1980. PLB 17.27 *(0-516-03942-3)*; pap. 4.95 *(0-516-43942-1)* Childrens.
—Texas en Palabras y Fotos: Texas: In Words & Pictures. 48p. (gr. 2-6). 1986. PLB 15.93 *(0-516-33943-5)*; pap. 4.95 *(0-516-53943-4)* Childrens.
—Texas: In Words & Pictures. Wahl, Richard, illus. LC 80-27497. 48p. (gr. 2-5). 1981. PLB 17.27 *(0-516-03943-1)*; pap. 3.95 *(0-516-43943-X)* Childrens.
—Utah: In Words & Pictures. LC 80-15177. (Illus.). 48p. (gr. 2-5). 1980. PLB 17.27 *(0-516-03944-X)* Childrens.
—Vermont: In Words & Pictures. LC 79-22069. (Illus.). 48p. (gr. 2-5). 1980. PLB 17.27 *(0-516-03946-6)* Childrens.
—Virginia in Words & Pictures. LC 76-7387. (Illus.). 48p. (gr. 2-5). 1976. PLB 17.27 *(0-516-03945-8)* Childrens.
—The Voyager Space Probes. LC 84-23250. (Illus.). 48p. (gr. k-4). 1985. PLB 15.27 *(0-516-01944-9)* Childrens.
—Washington: In Words & Pictures. Wahl, Richard, illus. LC 80-14745. 48p. (gr. 2-5). 1980. PLB 17.27 *(0-516-03947-4)* Childrens.
—West Virginia: In Words & Pictures. Wahl, Richard, illus. LC 80-12133. 48p. (gr. 2-5). 1980. PLB 17.27 *(0-516-03949-0)* Childrens.
—Wisconsin: In Words & Pictures. Ulm, Robert, illus. LC 77-5330. 48p. (gr. 2-5). 1977. PLB 17.27 *(0-516-03948-2)* Childrens.
—Wyoming: In Words & Pictures. LC 79-26511. (Illus.). 48p. (gr. 2-5). 1980. PLB 17.27 *(0-516-03950-4)* Childrens.
Fradin, Dennis B. Abigail Adams: Adviser to a President. LC 88-31331. (Illus.). 48p. (gr. 3-6). 1989. lib. bdg. 14.95 *(0-89490-228-8)* Enslow Pubs.

—Alabama. LC 92-37047. (Illus.). 64p. (gr. 3-5). 1993. PLB 19.93 (*0-516-03801-X*) Childrens.
—Alaska - From Sea to Shining Sea. (Illus.). 64p. (gr. 3-5). 1993. PLB 21.27 (*0-516-03802-8*) Childrens.
—Amerigo Vespucci. LC 91-14748. (Illus.). 64p. (gr. 5-8). 1991. PLB 12.90 (*0-531-20035-3*) Watts.
—Anne Hutchinson: Fighter for Religious Freedom. LC 88-31329. (Illus.). 48p. (gr. 3-6). 1990. lib. bdg. 14.95 (*0-89490-229-6*) Enslow Pubs.
—Archaeology. LC 83-7309. 48p. (gr. k-4). 1983. PLB 15.27 (*0-516-01691-1*); pap. 4.95 (*0-516-41691-X*) Childrens.
—Arizona - From Sea to Shining Sea. (Illus.). 64p. (gr. 3-5). 1993. PLB 21.27 (*0-516-03803-6*) Childrens.
—Arkansas. LC 93-32677. 1994. write for info. (*0-516-03804-4*) Childrens.
—Astronomy. LC 82-19722. (Illus.). 48p. (gr. k-4). 1983. PLB 15.27 (*0-516-01673-3*); pap. 4.95 (*0-516-41673-1*) Childrens.
—California - De Mar a Mar: (California - From Sea to Shining Sea) LC 92-12944. (SPA., Illus.). 64p. (gr. 3-5). 1993. PLB 21.27 (*0-516-33805-6*) Childrens.
—California - from Sea to Shining Sea. LC 92-12944. (Illus.). 64p. (gr. 3-5). 1992. PLB 19.93 (*0-516-03805-2*) Childrens.
—The Cheyenne. LC 87-33792. (Illus.). 48p. (gr. k-4). 1988. PLB 15.27 (*0-516-01211-8*); pap. 4.95 (*0-516-41211-6*) Childrens.
—Christmas. LC 89-25634. (Illus.). 48p. (gr. 1-4). 1990. lib. bdg. 14.95 (*0-89490-258-X*) Enslow Pubs.
—Colonial Profiles Series, 5 bks. (Illus.). (gr. 3-6). Set, 48p. ea. lib. bdg. 74.75 (*0-89490-341-1*) Enslow Pubs.
—Colorado - From Sea to Shining Sea. LC 93-2648. (Illus.). 64p. (gr. 3-5). 1993. PLB 21.27 (*0-516-03806-0*) Childrens.
—Columbus Day. LC 89-7663. (Illus.). 48p. (gr. 1-4). 1990. lib. bdg. 14.95 (*0-89490-233-4*) Enslow Pubs.
—Comets, Asteroids & Meteors. LC 83-23231. (Illus.). 48p. (gr. k-4). 1984. PLB 15.27 (*0-516-01723-3*); pap. 4.95 (*0-516-41723-1*) Childrens.
—The Connecticut Colony. LC 89-29205. (Illus.). 160p. (gr. 4 up). 1990. PLB 23.93 (*0-516-00393-3*) Childrens.
—The Declaration of Independence. LC 88-11870. (Illus.). 48p. (gr. k-4). 1988. PLB 15.27 (*0-516-01153-7*); pap. 4.95 (*0-516-41153-5*) Childrens.
—The Delaware Colony. LC 92-10467. (Illus.). 190p. (gr. 4 up). 1992. PLB 23.93 (*0-516-00398-4*) Childrens.
—Drug Abuse. LC 87-33789. (Illus.). 48p. (gr. k-4). 1988. PLB 15.27 (*0-516-01212-6*); pap. 4.95 (*0-516-41212-4*) Childrens.
—Earth. LC 89-9982. 48p. (gr. k-4). 1989. PLB 15.27 (*0-516-01172-3*); pap. 4.95 (*0-516-41172-1*) Childrens.
—Ethiopia. LC 88-10882. (Illus.). 128p. (gr. 5-9). 1988. PLB 26.60 (*0-516-02706-9*) Childrens.
—The Flag of the United States. LC 88-15436. (Illus.). 48p. (gr. k-4). 1988. PLB 15.27 (*0-516-01158-8*); pap. 4.95 (*0-516-41158-6*) Childrens.
—Florida. LC 91-32918. (Illus.). 64p. (gr. 3-5). 1992. PLB 19.93 (*0-516-03809-5*) Childrens.
—The Georgia Colony. LC 89-34954. 160p. (gr. 4 up). 1989. PLB 23.93 (*0-516-00392-5*) Childrens.
—Halley's Comet. LC 85-17067. (Illus.). 48p. (gr. k-4). 1985. PLB 15.27 (*0-516-01275-4*) Childrens.
—Halloween. LC 89-7681. (Illus.). 48p. (gr. 1-4). 1990. lib. bdg. 14.95 (*0-89490-234-2*) Enslow Pubs.
—Hanukkah. LC 89-25643. (Illus.). 48p. (gr. 1-4). 1990. lib. bdg. 14.95 (*0-89490-259-8*) Enslow Pubs.
—Hiawatha: Messenger of Peace. Jacobs, Arnold, illus. LC 90-26312. 48p. (gr. 2-6). 1992. SBE 14.95 (*0-689-50519-1*, M K McElderry) Macmillan Child Grp.
—Iowa - From Sea to Shining Sea. LC 93-16331. (Illus.). 64p. (gr. 3-5). 1993. PLB 21.27 (*0-516-03815-X*) Childrens.
—John Hancock: First Signer of the Declaration of Independence. LC 88-31332. (Illus.). 48p. (gr. 3-6). 1989. lib. bdg. 14.95 (*0-89490-230-X*) Enslow Pubs.
—Jupiter. LC 89-9983. 48p. (gr. k-4). 1989. PLB 15.27 (*0-516-01173-1*); pap. 4.95 (*0-516-41173-X*) Childrens.
—Kentucky. LC 92-38810. (Illus.). 64p. (gr. 3-5). 1993. PLB 19.93 (*0-516-03817-6*) Childrens.
—King Philip: Indian Leader. LC 88-31344. (Illus.). 48p. (gr. 3-6). 1990. lib. bdg. 14.95 (*0-89490-231-8*) Enslow Pubs.
—Lincoln's Birthday. LC 89-7665. (Illus.). 48p. (gr. 1-4). 1990. lib. bdg. 14.95 (*0-89490-250-4*) Enslow Pubs.
—Maine. LC 93-32680. 1994. write for info. (*0-516-03819-2*) Childrens.
—Mars. LC 88-39122. (Illus.). 48p. (gr. k-4). 1989. PLB 15.27 (*0-516-01164-2*); pap. 4.95 (*0-516-41164-0*) Childrens.
—The Maryland Colony. LC 90-2210. (Illus.). 160p. (gr. 4 up). 1990. PLB 23.93 (*0-516-00394-1*) Childrens.
—The Massachusetts Colony. LC 86-9753. (Illus.). 160p. (gr. 4 up). 1986. PLB 23.93 (*0-516-00386-0*) Childrens.
—Medicine: Yesterday, Today, & Tomorrow. LC 88-15336. 194p. (gr. 4 up). 1989. PLB 34.60 (*0-516-00538-3*) Childrens.
—Mercury. LC 89-25359. (Illus.). 48p. (gr. k-4). 1990. PLB 15.27 (*0-516-01186-3*); pap. 4.95 (*0-516-41186-1*) Childrens.
—Michigan. LC 91-32920. 64p. (gr. 3-5). 1992. PLB 19.93 (*0-516-03822-2*) Childrens.
—Missouri. LC 93-32675. 1994. write for info. (*0-516-03825-7*) Childrens.

—Montana. LC 91-37958. 64p. (gr. 3-5). 1992. PLB 19.93 (*0-516-03826-5*) Childrens.
—Neptune. LC 89-71174. (Illus.). 48p. (gr. k-4). 1990. PLB 15.27 (*0-516-01187-1*); pap. 4.95 (*0-516-41187-X*) Childrens.
—The Netherlands. LC 82-17896. (Illus.). 128p. (gr. 5-9). 1983. PLB 26.60 (*0-516-02779-4*) Childrens.
—New Hampshire. LC 92-9216. (Illus.). 64p. (gr. 3-5). 1992. PLB 19.93 (*0-516-03829-X*) Childrens.
—The New Hampshire Colony. LC 87-14619. (Illus.). 190p. (gr. 4 up). 1987. PLB 23.93 (*0-516-00388-7*) Childrens.
—New Jersey. LC 92-34601. (Illus.). 64p. (gr. 3-5). 1993. PLB 19.93 (*0-516-03830-3*) Childrens.
—New Mexico - From Sea to Shining Sea. LC 93-799. (Illus.). 64p. (gr. 3-5). 1993. PLB 21.27 (*0-516-03831-1*) Childrens.
—New York - From Sea to Shining Sea. (Illus.). 64p. (gr. 3-5). 1993. PLB 21.27 (*0-516-03832-X*) Childrens.
—The New York Colony. LC 87-35803. (Illus.). 160p. (gr. 4 up). 1988. PLB 23.93 (*0-516-00389-5*) Childrens.
—The Nina, the Pinta, & the Santa Maria. LC 91-4664. (Illus.). 64p. (gr. 5-8). 1991. PLB 12.90 (*0-531-20034-5*) Watts.
—North Carolina. LC 91-35576. 64p. (gr. 3-5). 1992. PLB 19.93 (*0-516-03833-8*) Childrens.
—Ohio. (Illus.). 64p. (gr. 3-5). 1993. PLB 19.93 (*0-516-03835-4*) Childrens.
—Olympics. LC 83-7214. (Illus.). 48p. (gr. k-4). 1983. PLB 15.27 (*0-516-01703-9*); pap. 4.95 (*0-516-41703-7*) Childrens.
—Patrick Henry: "Give Me Liberty or Give Me Death!" LC 88-31330. (Illus.). 48p. (gr. 3-6). 1990. lib. bdg. 14. 95 (*0-89490-232-6*) Enslow Pubs.
—The Pawnee. LC 88-11820. (Illus.). 48p. (gr. k-4). 1988. PLB 15.27 (*0-516-01155-3*); pap. 4.95 (*0-516-41155-1*) Childrens.
—Pennsylvania. LC 93-32757. 1994. write for info. (*0-516-03838-9*) Childrens.
—The Pennsylvania Colony. LC 88-11975. 160p. (gr. 4 up). 1988. PLB 23.93 (*0-516-00390-9*) Childrens.
—Pluto. LC 89-9925. 48p. (gr. k-4). 1989. PLB 15.27 (*0-516-01175-8*); pap. 4.95 (*0-516-41175-6*) Childrens.
—Remarkable Children: Twenty Who Made History. 208p. (gr. 4-7). 1987. 15.95 (*0-316-29126-9*) Little.
—The Rhode Island Colony. LC 89-744. (Illus.). 160p. (gr. 4 up). 1989. PLB 23.93 (*0-516-00391-7*) Childrens.
—Saturn. LC 88-39117. (Illus.). 48p. (gr. k-4). 1989. PLB 15.27 (*0-516-01166-9*); pap. 4.95 (*0-516-41166-7*) Childrens.
—The Shoshoni. LC 88-11821. (Illus.). 48p. (gr. k-4). 1988. PLB 15.27 (*0-516-01156-1*); pap. 4.95 (*0-516-41156-X*) Childrens.
—Skylab. LC 83-23180. (Illus.). 48p. (gr. k-4). 1984. PLB 15.27 (*0-516-01727-6*) Childrens.
—South Carolina. LC 91-32921. 64p. (gr. 3-5). 1992. PLB 19.93 (*0-516-03840-0*) Childrens.
—The South Carolina Colony. LC 91-32330. (Illus.). 190p. (gr. 4 up). 1992. PLB 23.93 (*0-516-00397-6*) Childrens.
—Space Colonies. LC 85-7722. (Illus.). 48p. (gr. k-4). 1985. pap. 4.95 (*0-516-41273-6*) Childrens.
—Tennessee - from Sea to Shining Sea. LC 92-6385. (Illus.). 64p. (gr. 3-5). 1992. PLB 19.93 (*0-516-03842-7*) Childrens.
—Texas. LC 92-9189. (Illus.). 64p. (gr. 3-5). 1992. PLB 19.93 (*0-516-03843-5*) Childrens.
—Texas - De Mar a Mar: (Texas - From Sea to Shining Sea) LC 92-9189. (SPA., Illus.). 64p. (gr. 3-5). 1993. PLB 21.27 (*0-516-33843-9*) Childrens.
—Thanksgiving Day. LC 89-7680. (Illus.). 48p. (gr. 1-4). 1990. lib. bdg. 14.95 (*0-89490-236-9*) Enslow Pubs.
—The Thirteen Colonies. LC 88-11827. (Illus.). 48p. (gr. k-4). 1988. PLB 15.27 (*0-516-01157-X*); pap. 4.95 (*0-516-41157-8*) Childrens.
—Uranus. LC 89-9984. 48p. (gr. k-4). 1989. PLB 15.27 (*0-516-01177-4*); pap. 4.95 (*0-516-41177-2*) Childrens.
—Utah. LC 92-36370. (Illus.). 64p. (gr. 3-5). 1993. PLB 19.93 (*0-516-03844-3*) Childrens.
—Valentine's Day. LC 89-7682. (Illus.). 48p. (gr. 1-4). 1990. lib. bdg. 14.95 (*0-89490-237-7*) Enslow Pubs.
—Venus. LC 88-39121. (Illus.). 48p. (gr. k-4). 1989. PLB 15.27 (*0-516-01168-5*); pap. 4.95 (*0-516-41168-3*) Childrens.
—Vermont. LC 92-36371. (Illus.). 64p. (gr. 3-5). 1993. PLB 19.93 (*0-516-03845-1*) Childrens.
—Virginia. LC 92-6386. (Illus.). 64p. (gr. 3-5). 1992. PLB 19.93 (*0-516-03846-X*) Childrens.
—The Virginia Colony. LC 86-13639. (Illus.). 160p. (gr. 4 up). 1986. PLB 23.93 (*0-516-00387-9*) Childrens.
—Voting & Elections. LC 85-7715. (Illus.). 45p. (gr. k-4). 1985. PLB 15.27 (*0-516-01274-6*); pap. 4.95 (*0-516-41274-4*) Childrens.
—Washington, D. C. LC 91-32919. 64p. (gr. 3-5). 1992. PLB 19.93 (*0-516-03851-6*) Childrens.
—Washington's Birthday. LC 89-7664. (Illus.). 48p. (gr. 1-4). 1990. lib. bdg. 14.95 (*0-89490-235-0*) Enslow Pubs.
—Wisconsin - From Sea to Shining Sea. LC 92-8135. (Illus.). 64p. (gr. 3-5). 1992. PLB 19.93 (*0-516-03849-4*) Childrens.
Fradin, Dennis B. & Fradin, Judith B. Wyoming. LC 93-39880. 1994. write for info. (*0-516-03850-8*) Childrens.
Fradin, Judith B., jt. auth. see Fradin, Dennis B.

Fradken, Ada. The Enormous Egg: A Study Guide. (gr. 4-6). 1986. tchr's. ed. & wkbk. 14.95 (*0-685-31133-3*) LRN Links.
Fradon, Dana. Harold the Herald: A Book about Heraldry. Fradon, Dana, illus. LC 89-49479. 40p. (gr. 4-7). 1990. PLB 14.95 (*0-525-44634-6*, DCB) Dutton Child Bks.
—The King's Fool: A Book about Medieval & Renaissance Fools. Fradon, Dana, illus. LC 92-43836. 40p. (gr. 3-7). 1993. 14.99 (*0-525-45074-2*, DCB) Dutton Child Bks.
—Sir Dana - A Knight: As Told by His Trusty Armor. Fradon, Dana, illus. LC 88-3968. 32p. (gr. 3-7). 1988. 13.95 (*0-525-44424-6*, DCB) Dutton Child Bks.
Fradsen, Karen. Hoy Fue Mi Primer Dia de Escuela: I Started School Today. LC 86-21623. (Illus.). 32p. (gr. k-3). 1986. PLB 13.93 (*0-516-33495-6*); pap. 3.95 (*0-516-53495-5*) Childrens.
Fraenkel, Eran, ed. see Miller, Miamon.
Frame, Janet. Mona Minium & the Smell of the Sun. 96p. (gr. 4-7). 1993. 17.95 (*0-8076-1334-7*) Braziller.
Frame, Paul. Drawing Cats & Kittens. (ps-3). 1990. pap. 3.95 (*0-531-15198-0*) Watts.
—Drawing Dogs & Puppies. (ps-3). 1990. pap. 3.95 (*0-531-15199-9*) Watts.
Frances, Marian. Mr. Mac-A-Doodle. (Illus.). (gr. 1). 1972. pap. 1.95 (*0-89375-045-X*) Troll Assocs.
—Witch on a Motorcycle. new ed. (Illus.). (gr. 3-4). 1972. pap. 1.95 (*0-89375-047-6*) Troll Assocs.
Franchere, Ruth. Cesar Chavez. Thollander, Earl, illus. LC 85-42999. 48p. (gr. 2-5). 1986. pap. 4.95 (*0-06-446023-1*, Trophy) HarpC Child Bks.
—Cesar Chavez. LC 78-101927. (Illus.). 40p. (gr. 2-5). 1970. PLB 14.89 (*0-690-18384-4*, Crowell Jr Bks) HarpC Child Bks.
Francis, Carolyn. Music Reading & Theory Skills, Level 1 & 2: A Sequential Method for Practice & Mastery. 226p. (gr. 4-12). 1986. incl. reproducible curriculum pkg. 179.95 (*0-931303-04-4*); 3-ring binder, black line masters avail. (*0-931303-02-8*) Innovative Learn.
Francis, Dorothy. Computer Crime. LC 87-4190. 128p. (gr. 7 up). 1987. 12.95 (*0-525-67192-7*, Lodestar Bks) Dutton Child Bks.
Francis, Dorothy B. Suicide, a Preventable Tragedy. LC 88-26856. 144p. (gr. 7 up). 1989. 13.95 (*0-525-67279-6*, Lodestar Bks) Dutton Child Bks.
Francis, Francis. A Book on Angling: Being a Complete Treatise on the Art of Angling with Explanatory Plates. (Illus.). 529p. (gr. 10 up). 1993. Repr. of 1985 ed. 42.90 (*1-56416-115-3*) Derrydale Pr.
Francis, Lynnrae & Francis, Steven. The Shape of Good Nutrition. Nick, Christopher, illus. Birch, Gail, intro. by. (Illus.). 20p. (Orig.). 1993. saddlestitched 2.50 (*0-9638754-0-X*) Providers Pr.
Francis, Neil. Super Flyers. LC 88-19336. 1988. pap. 6.68 (*0-201-14933-8*) Addison-Wesley.
Francis, Steven, jt. auth. see Francis, Lynnrae.
Franck, jt. ed. see Brownstone.
Franck, Eddie see Cooke, Frank E.
Franck, Irene, jt. auth. see Brownstone, David.
Franck, Irene M. The German-American Heritage. (Illus.). 160p. 1988. 16.95x (*0-8160-1629-1*) Facts on File.
—Irish-American Heritage. (Illus.). 160p. (gr. 5 up). 1989. 16.95x (*0-8160-1630-5*) Facts on File.
Franck, Irene M. & Brownstone, David M. Communicators. (Illus.). 240p. (gr. 7 up). 1986. 17.95x (*0-8160-1443-4*) Facts on File.
—Performers & Players. (Illus.). 208p. (gr. 7 up). 1988. 17.95x (*0-8160-1448-5*) Facts on File.
—Restaurateurs & Innkeepers. (Illus.). 176p. 1988. 17.95x (*0-8160-1451-5*) Facts on File.
—Scholars & Priests. (Illus.). 208p. (gr. 7 up). 1988. 17. 95x (*0-8160-1449-3*) Facts on File.
Franck, Irene M., jt. auth. see Brownstone, David M.
Franco, Betsy. Around the World, Vol. 1: Mexico. (Illus.). 48p. (gr. 1-3). 1993. pap. text ed. 7.95 (*1-55799-256-8*) Evan-Moor Corp.
—Around the World, Vol. 2: Japan. (Illus.). 48p. (gr. 1-3). 1993. pap. text ed. 7.95 (*1-55799-257-6*) Evan-Moor Corp.
—Around the World, Vol. 3: Russia. (Illus.). 48p. (gr. 1-3). 1993. pap. text ed. 7.95 (*1-55799-258-4*) Evan-Moor Corp.
Franco, Eloise. Little Stories. Bredius, Rein, illus. (gr. k-5). 1979. pap. 4.50 (*0-87516-384-X*) DeVorss.
—The Young Look. (Illus.). (gr. 3-7). 1979. pap. 5.95 (*0-87516-294-0*) DeVorss.
Franco, Eloise & Franco, Johan. Making Music. (Illus.). (gr. 1-5). 1976. pap. 4.95 (*0-87516-212-6*) DeVorss.
Franco, J. Philip di see Di Franco, J. Philip.
Franco, Jean, ed. Spanish Short Stories. (gr. 9 up). 1966. pap. 9.00 (*0-14-002500-6*, Penguin Bks) Viking Penguin.
Franco, Johan, jt. auth. see Franco, Eloise.
Frandsen, Karen G. I Started School Today. LC 83-23169. (Illus.). 32p. (ps-2). 1984. PLB 13.93 (*0-516-03495-2*); pap. 3.95 (*0-516-43495-0*) Childrens.
—I'd Rather Get a Spanking Than Go to the Doctor. Frandsen, Karen G., illus. LC 86-11735. 32p. (ps-3). 1987. pap. 3.95 (*0-516-43498-5*) Childrens.
—Michael's New Haircut. Frandsen, Karen G., illus. LC 86-11696. 32p. (ps-3). 1986. pap. 3.95 (*0-516-43545-0*) Childrens.
Frane-Nohain, Marie M. Baby's Journal. (Illus.). 156p. 1978. 13.95 (*0-684-15979-1*, Scribners Young Read) Macmillan Child Grp.

Frank, Anne. Anne Frank: The Diary of a Young Girl. rev. ed. Mooyaart, B. M., tr. Roosevelt, Eleanor, intro. by. LC 52-6355. 312p. (gr. 7 up). 1967. 24.00 (0-385-04019-9) Doubleday.
—Anne Frank: The Diary of a Young Girl. (gr. 4-7). 1988. lib. bdg. 15.95 (1-55736-098-7, Crnrstn Bks) BDD LT Grp.
—Diary of a Young Girl. large type ed. 1989. Repr. of 1947 ed. 15.95 (0-685-47378-3, Crnrstn Bks) BDD LT Grp.
Frank, Elizabeth B. Cooder Cutlas. LC 85-45822. 320p. (gr. 7 up). 1987. 13.95i (0-685-17655-X) HarpC Child Bks.
Frank, Herta, jt. auth. see Gipson, Morrell.
Frank, John. Erin's Voyage. Schutzer, Dena, illus. LC 92-31783. 1994. pap. 14.00 (0-671-79585-6, S&S BFYR) S&S Trade.
—Odds 'N Ends Alvy. Karas, G. Brian, illus. LC 92-27151. 32p. (gr. k-4). 1993. RSBE 14.95 (0-02-735675-2, Four Winds) Macmillan Child Grp.
Frank, Josette, ed. Poems to Read to the Very Young. Wilkin, Eloise, illus. LC 82-518. 48p. (ps-3). 1982. 7.95 (0-394-85188-9) Random Bks Yng Read.
—Poems to Read to the Very Young. Wilson, Dagmar W., illus. LC 87-23234. 32p. (ps-1). 1988. pap. 2.25 (0-394-89768-4) Random Bks Yng Read.
Frank, Josette, selected by. Snow Toward Evening, a Year in a River Valley. Locker, Thomas, illus. LC 89-48307. 32p. 1990. 16.00 (0-8037-0810-6); PLB 15.89 (0-8037-0811-4) Dial Bks Young.
Frank, Josette, adapted by see Barrie, James M.
Frank, Julia. Alzheimer's Disease: The Silent Epidemic. (Illus.). 80p. (gr. 5 up). 1985. PLB 13.50 (0-8225-1578-4) Lerner Pubns.
Frank, Marge. If You're Trying to Teach Kids How to Write, You've Gotta Have This Book! LC 78-70901. (Illus.). 232p. (gr. 2 up). 1979. pap. 12.95 (0-913916-62-5, IP625) Incentive Pubns.
Frank, Marge, jt. auth. see Forte, Imogene.
Frank, Marjorie. Complete Writing Lessons for the Middle Grades. (Illus.). 128p. (gr. 4-6). 1987. pap. text ed. 9.95 (0-86530-160-3, IP 1603) Incentive Pubns.
—Complete Writing Lessons for the Primary Grades. (Illus.). 128p. (gr. 1-3). 1987. pap. text ed. 9.95 (0-86530-163-8, IP1638) Incentive Pubns.
—I Can Make a Rainbow. LC 76-506. (Illus.). 300p. (gr. k-6). 1976. pap. 16.95 (0-913916-19-6, IP 19-6) Incentive Pubns.
—The Kids' Stuff: Book of Math for the Middle Grades. (Illus.). 240p. (gr. 4-6). 1988. pap. text ed. 14.95 (0-86530-012-7, IP 13-1) Incentive Pubns.
—The Kids' Stuff: Book of Math for the Primary Grades. (Illus.). 240p. (gr. 1-3). 1988. pap. text ed. 14.95 (0-86530-040-2, IP 13-0) Incentive Pubns.
—Math Bulletin Boards. (Illus.). 64p. (gr. k-6). 1986. pap. text ed. 6.95 (0-86530-133-6, IP 112-2) Incentive Pubns.
Frank, Marjorie, ed. see Ozaeta, Pablo.
Frank, Michael, ed. see Benanti, Carol.
Frank, Mike. Young Stamp Collector. Benanti, Carol, ed. 48p. (Orig.). (gr. 3-7). 1991. pap. 2.95 (1-880592-00-2) Pace Prods.
Frank, Pat. Alas, Babylon. 320p. (gr. 8 up). 1976. pap. 3.95 (0-553-26314-5) Bantam.
Frank, Penny. Abraham, Friend of God. (ps-3). 1984. 3.99 (0-85648-729-5) Lion USA.
—Adam & Eve. (ps-3). 1988. 3.99 (0-85648-727-9) Lion USA.
—Adam & Eve. Haysom, John & Morris, Tony, illus. Burow, Daniel, contrib. by. LC 92-29470. 1992. 6.95 (0-7459-2609-6) Lion USA.
—A Baby Called John. Morris, Tony, et al, illus. 24p. (ps-3). 1988. 3.99 (0-85648-756-2) Lion USA.
—The Battle of Jericho. (Illus.). 24p. (gr. 1 up). 1986. 3.99 (0-85648-748-3) Lion USA.
—Come Down, Zacchaeus! Morris, Tony, et al, illus. 24p. (ps-3). 3.99 (0-85648-764-0) Lion USA.
—Daniel in the Lion's Den. (Illus.). 24p. (gr. 1 up). 1987. 3.99 (0-85648-752-X) Lion USA.
—David & Goliath. (Illus.). 24p. (gr. 1 up). 1986. 3.99 (0-85648-743-0) Lion USA.
—David & Goliath. Haysom, John & Morris, Tony, illus. Burow, Daniel, contrib. by. LC 92-20481. (gr. 5 up). 1992. 5.95 (0-7459-2606-1) RD Assn.
—Elijah & the Prophets of Baal. (Illus.). 24p. (gr. 1-4). 1987. 3.99 (0-85648-747-3) Lion USA.
—Elijah Asks for Bread. Morris, Tony, et al, illus. 24p. (ps-3). 3.99 (0-85648-746-5) Lion USA.
—Enemies All Around. (Illus.). 24p. (gr. 1 up). 1986. 3.99 (0-85648-749-X) Lion USA.
—The First Christmas. (Illus.). 24p. (gr. 1 up). 1986. 3.99 (0-85648-757-0) Lion USA.
—The First Christmas. Haysom, John & Morris, Tony, illus. Burow, Daniel, contrib. by. LC 92-20479. (gr. 4 up). 1992. 5.95 (0-7459-2603-7) RD Assn.
—The First Easter. (ps-3). 1987. 3.99 (0-85648-773-2) Lion USA.
—The First Easter. Haysom, John & Morris, Tony, illus. Burow, Daniel, contrib. by. LC 92-31640. 1992. 6.95 (0-7459-2607-X) Lion USA.
—Gideon Fights for God. (Illus.). 24p. (gr. 1-4). 1987. 3.99 (0-85648-738-4) Lion USA.
—God Speaks to Samuel. Morris, Tony, et al, illus. 24p. (ps-3). 3.99 (0-85648-741-4) Lion USA.
—Good News for Everyone. Morris, Tony, et al, illus. 24p. (ps-3). 3.99 (0-85648-774-0) Lion USA.
—In the Beginning. (ps-3). 1988. 3.99 (0-85648-726-0) Lion USA.

—In the Beginning. Haysom, John, illus. LC 92-31617. 1992. 6.95 (0-7459-2608-8) Lion USA.
—Isaac Finds a Wife. Morris, Tony, et al, illus. 24p. (ps-3). 3.99 (0-85648-730-9) Lion USA.
—Jacob & Esau. (ps-3). 1988. 3.99 (0-85648-731-7) Lion USA.
—Jeremiah & the Great Disaster. (Illus.). 24p. (gr. 1-4). 1987. 3.99 (0-85648-750-3) Lion USA.
—Jesus Gives the People Food. (ps-3). 1988. 3.99 (0-85648-761-9) Lion USA.
—Jesus on Trial. (Illus.). 24p. (gr. 1 up). 1987. 3.99 (0-85648-772-4) Lion USA.
—Jesus on Trial. Haysom, John & Morris, Tony, illus. Burow, Daniel, contrib. by. LC 92-31641. 1992. 6.95 (0-7459-2610-X) RD Assn.
—Jesus' Special Friends. Morris, Tony, et al, illus. 24p. (ps-3). 3.99 (0-85648-759-7) Lion USA.
—Jesus the King. (ps-3). 1984. 3.95 (0-85648-771-6) Lion USA.
—Jesus the Teacher. (Illus.). 24p. (gr. 1 up). 1987. 3.99 (0-85648-760-0) Lion USA.
—Jonah Runs Away. (Illus.). 24p. (gr. 1-4). 1987. 3.99 (0-85648-755-4) Lion USA.
—Joseph & the King of Egypt. Morris, Tony, et al, illus. 24p. (ps-3). 3.99 (0-85648-733-3) Lion USA.
—Joseph the Dreamer. Morris, Tony, et al, illus. 24p. (ps-3). 3.99 (0-85648-732-5) Lion USA.
—Journey to the Promised Land. (Illus.). 24p. (gr. 1 up). 1986. 3.99 (0-85648-736-8) Lion USA.
—King David. (Illus.). 24p. (gr. 1 up). 1987. 3.99 (0-85648-744-9) Lion USA.
—A King for Israel. Morris, Tony, et al, illus. 24p. (ps-3). 3.99 (0-85648-742-2) Lion USA.
—King Nebuchadnezzar's Golden Statue. Morris, Tony, et al, illus. 24p. (ps-3). 3.99 (0-85648-751-1) Lion USA.
—Let My People Go! Morris, Tony, et al, illus. 24p. (ps-3). 3.99 (0-85648-735-X) Lion USA.
—Mary, Martha & Lazarus. (Illus.). 24p. (gr. 1-4). 1987. 3.99 (0-85648-769-4) Lion USA.
—Naaman's Dreadful Secret. (Illus.). 24p. (gr. 1 up). 1987. 3.99 (0-85648-748-1) Lion USA.
—Nehemiah's Greatest Day. (Illus.). (gr. 1 up). 1987. pap. 3.99 (0-85648-754-6) Lion USA.
—Noah & the Great Flood. (ps-3). 1988. 3.99 (0-85648-728-7) Lion USA.
—Paul & Friends. (Illus.). 24p. (gr. 1 up). 1987. 3.99 (0-85648-776-7) Lion USA.
—Paul at Damascus. (Illus.). 24p. (gr. 1 up). 1986. 3.99 (0-85648-775-9) Lion USA.
—Paul the Prisoner. (Illus.). 24p. (gr. 1-4). 1987. 3.99 (0-85648-777-5) Lion USA.
—People Jesus Met. Morris, Tony, et al, illus. 24p. (ps-3). 3.99 (0-85648-770-8) Lion USA.
—The Princess & the Baby. (ps-3). 1988. 3.99 (0-85648-734-1) Lion USA.
—Queen Esther Saves Her People. Morris, Tony, et al, illus. 24p. (ps-3). 3.99 (0-85648-753-8) Lion USA.
—Ruth's New Family. Morris, Tony, et al, illus. 24p. (ps-3). 3.99 (0-85648-740-6) Lion USA.
—Samson the Strong Man. (ps-3). 1985. 3.99 (0-85648-739-2) Lion USA.
—Secrets Jesus Told. (Illus.). 24p. (ps-4). 1982. 3.99 (0-85648-762-7) Lion USA.
—Solomon's Golden Temple. (Illus.). 24p. (ps-4). 1987. 3.99 (0-85648-745-7) Lion USA.
—Story of the Good Samaritan. (ps-3). 1985. 3.99 (0-85648-763-5) Lion USA.
—The Story of the Great Feast. Morris, Tony, et al, illus. 24p. (ps-3). 3.99 (0-85648-766-X) Lion USA.
—The Story of the Lost Sheep. Morris, Tony, et al, illus. 24p. (ps-3). 3.99 (0-85648-767-8) Lion USA.
—The Story of the Sower. Morris, Tony, et al, illus. 24p. (ps-3). 3.99 (0-85648-768-6) Lion USA.
—The Story of the Two Brothers. (Illus.). 24p. (gr. 4 up). 1987. 3.99 (0-85648-765-1) Lion USA.
—When Jesus Was Young. (Illus.). 24p. (gr. 1 up). 1986. 3.99 (0-85648-758-9) Lion USA.
—When Jesus Was Young. Haysom, John & Morris, Tony, illus. Burow, Daniel, contrib. by. LC 92-20482. 1992. 5.95 (0-7459-2604-5) RD Assn.
Frank, Penny & Burow, Daniel. Noah & the Great Flood. Haysom, John & Morris, Tony, illus. LC 92-20480. 1992. 5.95 (0-7459-2605-3) RD Assn.
Frank, Raymond. God Looked Down & Saw a Baby. 69p. (Orig.). (ps). 1984. pap. 2.00 (0-932588-07-7) Jesus Bks.
Frank, Rudolf. No Hero for the Kaiser. Crampton, Patricia, tr. from GER. Steffans, Klaus, illus. 224p. (gr. 7 up). 1986. Repr. of 1931 ed. 13.00 (0-688-06093-5) Lothrop.
Frank, Tenney. Life & Literature in the Roman Republic. (gr. 9-12). 1930. pap. 11.00x (0-520-00428-0) U CA Pr.
Frankel, Alona. Mi Bacinica y Yo (Once upon a Potty) (SPA.). 36p. (ps). 1986. Hers. 4.95 (0-8120-5751-1); His. (0-8120-5750-3) Barron.
—Once upon a Potty: His. LC 79-53769. (Illus.). (ps-3). 1980. 5.50 (0-8120-5371-0); pkg., 1987 13.95 (0-8120-7457-2) Barron.
Frankel, Alona, jt. auth. see Cashman, Greer F.
Frankel, B. Tertius & Pliny. Clark, E., ed. 1992. 13.95 (0-15-200604-4, Gulliver Bks) HarBrace.
Frankel, Bruce, jt. ed. see Sheffield, Anne.

Frankel, Julie. Hare & Bear. McKissack, Patricia & McKissack, Fredrick, eds. Smith, Ted, illus. LC 87-61647. 32p. (Orig.). (gr. 1-3). 1987. text ed. 8.95 (0-88335-724-0); pap. text ed. 4.95 (0-88335-744-5) Milliken Pub Co.
—Hare & Bear Go Shopping. McKissack, Patricia & McKissack, Fredrick, eds. Smith, Ted, illus. LC 88-60394. 32p. (Orig.). (gr. 1-3). 1990. text ed. 8.95 (0-88335-778-X); pap. text ed. 4.95 (0-88335-790-9) Milliken Pub Co.
Frankel, Julie E. Mice! Venezia, Mike, illus. LC 86-1008. 32p. (ps-2). 1986. PLB 11.93 (0-516-02070-6); pap. 2.95 (0-516-42070-4) Childrens.
—Oh No, Otis! Martin, Clovis, illus. LC 91-15328. 32p. (ps-2). 1991. PLB 11.93 (0-516-02009-9); pap. 2.95 (0-516-42009-7) Childrens.
Frankel, Marvin & Saideman, Ellen. Out of the Shadows of Night: The Struggle for International Human Rights. (gr. 9 up). 1989. pap. 8.95 (0-385-29820-X) Delacorte.
Frankel, Marvin E. International Human. 1989. pap. 16.95 (0-440-50145-8) Dell.
Frankel, Max & Hoffman, Judy. I Live in Israel. Fishman, Priscilla, ed. LC 79-12833. (Illus.). (gr. 3-4). 1979. pap. text ed. 5.95x (0-87441-317-6) Behrman.
Frankhausen, Edward, jt. auth. see Savary, Louis.
Frankl, Ron. Bruce Springsteen. LC 93-1850. (gr. 7 up). 1994. 18.95 (0-7910-2327-3, Am Art Analog); pap. write for info. (0-7910-2352-4, Am Art Analog) Chelsea Hse.
—Charlie Parker. King, Coretta Scott, intro. by. (Illus.). 112p. (gr. 5 up). 1992. lib. bdg. 17.95 (0-7910-1134-8); pap. write for info. (0-7910-1159-3) Chelsea Hse.
—Duke Ellington. King, Coretta Scott, intro. by. (Illus.). 112p. (Orig.). (gr. 5 up). 1988. 17.95 (1-55546-584-6); pap. 9.95 (0-7910-0208-X) Chelsea Hse.
Franklin, Benjamin. Autobiography & Other Writings. Nye, Russel B., ed. LC 85-12061. (gr. 9 up). 1958. pap. 7.96 (0-395-05130-4, RivEd) HM.
—Autobiography of Benjamin Franklin. Bigoness, J. W., intro. by. LC 80-26312. (gr. 8 up). 1965. pap. 2.75 (0-8049-0071-X, CL-71) Airmont.
—Poor Richard's Almanack. (gr. 7 up). 1952. dust jacket 9.95 (0-88088-918-7) Peter Pauper.
Franklin, Harold L. see Alimayo, Chikuyo, pseud.
Franklin, Herb. Fireman Fred's, Fire Safety Coloring Book. Miller, Jackie, illus. 8p. (gr. 1-5). 1990. pap. 0.50 (0-945145-02-0) Miller Family Pubns.
Franklin, Jonathan. Don't Wake the Baby. (Illus.). 32p. (ps-1). 1991. bds. 13.95 jacketed (0-374-31826-3) FS&G.
Franklin, Kristine L. The Old, Old Man & the Very Little Boy. Shaffer, Terea, illus. LC 91-2611. 32p. (ps-1). 1992. SBE 14.95 (0-689-31735-2, Atheneum Child Bk) Macmillan Child Grp.
—The Shepherd Boy: El Nino Pastor. Ada, Alma F., tr. Kastner, Jill, illus. LC 92-33441. (ENG & SPA.). 40p. (ps-1). 1994. English ed. SBE 14.95 (0-689-31809-X, Atheneum Child Bk); Spanish ed. SBE 14.95 (0-689-31918-5, Atheneum Child Bk) Macmillan Child Grp.
—When the Monkeys Came Back. Roth, Robert, illus. LC 92-33684. 1994. text ed. 15.95 (0-689-31807-3, Atheneum) Macmillan.
Franklin, Lance. Double Play. 144p. (gr. 6 up). 1987. pap. 2.50 (0-553-26526-1, Starfire) Bantam.
Franklin, Paula A., jt. auth. see Katz, William L.
Franklin, Robert J., jt. auth. see Bunte, Pamela A.
Franklin Watts Ltd., ed. see Barrett, Norman.
Franklin Watts Ltd., ed. see Bender, Lionel.
Franklin Watts Ltd., ed. see Jennings, Terry.
Franklin Watts Ltd., ed. see Langley, Andrew.
Franklin Watts Ltd., ed. see Pope, Joyce.
Franklin Watts Ltd., ed. see Versfield, Ruth.

Frank-Mosenson, Sandra. Earth Day Lessons from Planet Mars. Carlos, Christina, illus. 72p. (Orig.). (gr. 4 up). 1991. Perfect bdg. 10.95 (0-9629607-3-X) Wisdom Pr IL. 1993 NATIONAL BOOK AWARD recipient for the "BEST CHILDREN'S BOOK OF THE YEAR" from the Writer's Foundation of America. Chosen to represent the United States at the International Children's Book Fair, it is currently a part of a thirty-month state-wide tour of all Illinois libraries. New age fairy tales told in poem with clear lyrical quality & sense of purpose. A review by HEARTLAND JOURNAL: "This is a book of poetic imagery, emotion & gentle wisdom, with a mission, stimulating children to a commitment to their Earth, helping them to realize the importance of all families of all species to live in a non-violent world." Accompanied by intriguing black & white illustrations, printed with soy-based ink on acid-free 100% recycled 80lb. text paper. "Small frogs golden/ living in harmony beneath the mimosa/ Lonely cheetah crying his mornful song/ as man grows closer." The reviewer continues, "As a mother of four, I loved this book, including the glossary & environmental resource list. I encourage you to add this book to your children's collection, & by all means, share the message & the moments." To order, call WISDOM PRESS, (312) 477-3737 or BAKER & TAYLOR, (800) 775-1800. *Publisher Provided Annotation.*

Franks, Tom. Born to Raze Hell. 112p. (Orig.). 1989. pap. 5.95 (*1-877717-00-2*) Mercedes Ministries.
Franz, Wanda K., jt. auth. see Redfield, Robert.
Frascino, Edward. Nanny Noony & the Dust Queen. Frascino, Edward, illus. 32p. (gr. k-3). 1990. PLB 14.95 (*0-945912-09-9*) Pippin Pr.
—Nanny Noony & the Magic Spell. Frascino, Edward, illus. 32p. (gr. k-3). 1988. 14.95 (*0-945912-00-5*) Pippin Pr.
Frascino, Edward, jt. auth. see Warren, William E.
Frase, Marianne, jt. auth. see Hunt, Linda.
Fraser. Mystery at Deepwood Bay. 1992. write for info. (*1-55513-717-2*, Chariot Bks) Cook.
Fraser, Alison. Walter White. King, Coretta Scott, intro. by. (Illus.). 112p. (gr. 5 up). 1991. 17.95 (*1-55546-617-6*); pap. 9.95 (*0-7910-0253-5*) Chelsea Hse.
Fraser, Antonia. Quiet As a Nun. large type ed. LC 93-17965. (gr. 5 up). 1993. 20.95 (*0-7927-1690-6*, Curley Lrg Print); pap. 18.95 (*0-7927-1689-2*, Curley Lrg Print) Chivers N Amer.
Fraser, Betty. First Things First. Fraser, Betty, illus. LC 86-42993. 32p. (gr. k-3). 1994. pap. 4.95 (*0-06-443300-5*, Trophy) HarpC Child Bks.
—First Things First: An Illustrated Collection of Sayings Useful & Familiar for Children. Fraser, Betty, illus. LC 86-42993. 32p. (gr. k-3). 1990. PLB 12.89 (*0-06-021855-X*) HarpC Child Bks.
Fraser, Judith & Herman, Jon. Careful Campers Coloring Book: A Children's Guide to Caring for Nature's Wonders. (Illus.). 32p. (Orig.). (gr. 1-3). 1990. pap. text ed. 2.00 (*0-914019-26-0*) NW Interpretive.
Fraser, K. & Collyer, J. Word Processing. (Illus.). 48p. (gr. 6 up). 1992. pap. 6.95 (*0-86020-930-X*) EDC.
Fraser, K. & Tatchell, J. Fitness & Health. (Illus.). 48p. (gr. 6-10). 1987. PLB 13.96 (*0-88110-234-2*); pap. 6.95 (*0-7460-0040-9*) EDC.
Fraser, K., jt. auth. see Tatchell, J.
Fraser, Mary A. On Top of the World: The Conquest of Mount Everest. Fraser, Mary A., illus. LC 90-48988. 40p. (gr. 2-5). 1991. 14.95 (*0-8050-1578-7*, Bks Young Read) H Holt & Co.
—One Giant Leap. Fraser, Mary A., illus. LC 92-41044. 40p. (gr. 3-7). 1993. PLB 15.95 (*0-8050-2295-3*) H Holt & Co.
—Ten Mile Day: The Building of the Transcontinental Railroad. Fraser, Mary A., illus. LC 92-3007. 40p. (gr. 3-7). 1993. PLB 15.95 (*0-8050-1902-2*, Bks Young Read) H Holt & Co.
Fraser, Mary Ann. Sanctuary. 1994. write for info. (*0-8050-2920-6*) H Holt & Co.
Fraser, Sheila. I Can Play Soccer. Kopper, Lisa, illus. 24p. (ps-3). 1991. 5.95 (*0-8120-6225-6*) Barron.
—I Can Ride a Bike. Kopper, Lisa, illus. 24p. (ps-3). 1991. 5.95 (*0-8120-6227-2*) Barron.
—I Can Roller Skate. Kopper, Lisa, illus. 24p. (ps-3). 1991. 5.95 (*0-8120-6228-0*) Barron.
—I Can Swim. Kopper, Lisa, illus. 24p. (ps-3). 1991. 5.95 (*0-8120-6226-4*) Barron.
Fraser, W. Courage on Mirror Mountain. 128p. (gr. 3-7). 1989. pap. 4.49 (*1-55513-039-9*, Chariot Bks) Cook.
—Mystery on Mirror Mountain. 112p. (gr. 3-7). 1989. pap. 4.49 (*1-55513-588-9*, Chariot Bks) Cook.
Fraser, Wynnette. Invasion on Mirror Mountain. LC 93-32678. (gr. 3 up). 1994. write for info. (*0-7814-0104-6*, Chariot Bks) Cook.
Fraser-Simon, H., jt. auth. see Milne, A. A.
Frasier, Debra. On the Day You Were Born. Johnston, Allyn, ed. Frasier, Debra, illus. 32p. (ps up). 1991. 13.95 (*0-15-257995-8*) HarBrace.
Frasier, Elizabeth. Wow! What a Wonderful World. Black, Robert, illus. 32p. (Orig.). (gr. k-4). 1990. pap. 4.50 (*1-879253-00-3*) Apex Creat.
Fratti, Mario, et al. Thank You, Gorbachev! 70p. (Orig.). 1990. pap. write for info. (*0-9626427-0-3*) Wall to Wall.
Frauman-Prickel, Maxine. Action English Pictures. Takahashi, Noriko, illus. 120p. (gr. 7 up). 1985. pap. text ed. 19.95 (*0-13-009077-8*) Alemany Pr.
Frazee, Charles & Yopp, Hallie K. Ancient Europe. Frazee, Kathleen & Lumba, Eric, illus. (gr. 6). 1990. pap. text ed. write for info. Delos Pubns.
—The Ancient World. Frazee, Kathleen & Lumba, Eric, illus. (gr. 6). 1990. text ed. 21.08 (*1-878473-51-4*); tchr's. ed. 27.08 (*1-878473-54-9*); wkbk. 3.00 (*1-878473-55-7*) Delos Pubns.

—Medieval & Early Modern Europe. Frazee, Kathleen & Lumba, Eric, illus. (gr. 7). 1990. pap. text ed. 5.50 wkbk. (*0-685-44932-7*) Delos Pubns.
—Medieval & Early Modern Times. Frazee, Kathleen & Lumba, Eric, illus. (gr. 7). 1990. pap. text ed. 24.77 (*1-878473-56-5*); tchr's. ed. 30.77 (*1-878473-58-1*); wkbk. 3.00 (*0-685-58493-3*) Delos Pubns.
Frazee, Charles & Yopp, Hallie Kay. Early People & the First Civilizations. Frazee, Kathleen & Lumba, Eric, illus. (gr. 6). 1990. write for info. Delos Pubns.
Frazer, Linda, jt. auth. see Kramer, Patricia.
Frazier, Nancy. Frida Kahlo: Mysterious Painter. (Illus.). 64p. (gr. 3-7). 1992. PLB 14.95 (*1-56711-012-6*) Blackbirch.
Frazier, Nancy, jt. auth. see Renfro, Nancy.
Frazier, Neta L. Stout-Hearted Seven. 174p. (gr. 4-6). 1984. pap. text ed. 4.95 (*0-914019-22-8*) NW Interpretive.
Fredeen, Charles. Kansas. Lerner Geography Department Staff, ed. (Illus.). 72p. (gr. 4-7). 1992. 17.50 (*0-8225-2716-2*) Lerner Pubns.
—New Jersey. LC 92-13363. 1993. PLB 17.50 (*0-8225-2732-4*) Lerner Pubns.
—South Carolina. 72p. (gr. 3-6). 1991. PLB 17.50 (*0-8225-2712-X*) Lerner Pubns.
Fredeking, Jean T. Gertrude: A Goose on the Loose. Weinberger, Jane, ed. LC 91-65295. (Illus.). 40p. 1991. 7.95 (*0-932433-81-2*) Windswept Hse.
—My Trip On a Ship. 16p. 1987. pap. 20.00x (*0-317-59267-X*, Pub. by A H Stockwell England) St Mut.
—The Snuffling Hedgehog. 1987. pap. 20.00x (*0-317-59264-5*, Pub. by A H Stockwell England) St Mut.
Frederick, Ruth. A Surprise for Miss Van. O'Connell, Ruth A., illus. 32p. (gr. 1-2). 1991. pap. 3.99 (*0-87403-805-7*, 24-03895) Standard Pub.
—Where's Tommy? O'Connell, Ruth A., illus. 32p. (gr. 1-2). 1991. pap. 3.99 saddle stitch (*0-87403-806-5*, 24-03896) Standard Pub.
Fredericks & Lipner. Barron's How to Prepare for the Regents Competency Examination: Reading. (gr. 11-12). 1982. pap. 12.95 (*0-8120-2287-4*) Barron.
Fredericks, Anthony D. The Integrated Curriculum: Books for Reluctant Readers, Grades 2-5. (Illus.). 175p. (gr. 2-5). 1992. pap. text ed. 21.00 (*0-87287-994-1*) Libs Unl.
—Letters to Parents in Science. (Illus.). 152p. (Orig.). (gr. 3-6). 1993. pap. 9.95 (*0-673-36079-2*) GdYrBks.
Fredlee. Magic of Sea Shells. rev. ed. (Illus.). 36p. (gr. 1-3). 1985. pap. 3.50 (*0-685-47437-2*) Windward Pub.
Fredman, Lionel E. & Kurland, Gerald. John Adams: American Revolutionary Leader & President. Rahmas, D. Steve, ed. LC 73-87627. 32p. (gr. 7-12). 1973. lib. bdg. 4.95 incl. catalog cards (*0-87157-565-5*) SamHar Pr.
Fredman, Shelly. Creeps. LC 89-50957. 208p. (gr. 7-12). 1989. 16.95x (*0-943864-55-0*) Davenport.
Fredricks, Faye, et al. Children's Bulletin Idea Book. 240p. (gr. 5-10). 1987. pap. 19.99 (*0-8010-3536-8*) Baker Bk.
Free, John Da see John, Da Free.
Freeberg, Dolores. Graph Paper Art. Freeberg, Dolores, illus. 48p. (gr. 2-6). 1986. wkbk. 5.95 (*1-55734-052-8*) Tchr Create Mat.
Freeberg, Dolores, jt. auth. see Freeberg, Erling.
Freeberg, Erling & Freeberg, Dolores. Challenging Graph Art. Freeberg, Erling & Freeberg, Dolores, illus. 48p. (gr. 2-6). 1987. wkbk. 5.95 (*1-55734-096-X*) Tchr Create Mat.
—Holiday Graph Art. Freeberg, Erling & Freeberg, Dolores, illus. 48p. (gr. 2-6). 1987. wkbk. 5.95 (*1-55734-093-5*) Tchr Create Mat.
—Patriotic Graph Art. Freeberg, Erling & Freeberg, Dolores, illus. 48p. (gr. 2-6). 1987. wkbk. 5.95 (*1-55734-094-3*) Tchr Create Mat.
—Simple Graph Art. Freeberg, Erling & Freeberg, Dolores, illus. 48p. (gr. k-1). 1987. wkbk. 5.95 (*1-55734-095-1*) Tchr Create Mat.
Freebies Staff. The Official Freebies for Kids. (Illus.). 80p. (Orig.). 1993. pap. 4.95 (*1-56565-044-1*) Lowell Hse.
Freed, Alvyn M. T. A. for Tots: (& Other Prinzes) rev. ed. Dick, Jo A. & Ferreri, Donna, illus. 144p. (ps-5). 1991. pap. 14.95 (*0-915190-73-7*, JP9073-7) Jalmar Pr.
—TA for Teens (& Other Important People) Faul-Jansen, Regina, illus. LC 76-19651. (gr. 8-12). 1976. pap. 18.95 (*0-915190-03-8*, JP9003-6) Jalmar Pr.
—TA for Tots Coloring Book. (ps-3). 1976. pap. 1.95 (*0-915190-33-8*, JP9033-8) Jalmar Pr.
Freed, Alvyn M. & Freed, Margaret. TA for Kids (& Grownups Too) 3rd rev ed. Hackney, Rick, illus. LC 77-81761. (gr. 4-7). 1977. pap. 9.95 (*0-915190-09-5*, JP9009-5) Jalmar Pr.
Freed, Carol. Let's Visit a Television Station. LC 87-3461. (Illus.). 32p. (gr. 2-4). 1988. PLB 10.79 (*0-8167-1165-8*); pap. text ed. 2.95 (*0-8167-1166-6*) Troll Assocs.
Freed, Margaret, jt. auth. see Freed, Alvyn M.
Freed, Rita E. Egypt's Golden Age: A Picture Book. (Illus.). 68p. (Orig.). (gr. 3-6). 1982. pap. 4.95 (*0-87846-208-2*) Mus Fine Arts Boston.
Freedland, Sara. Hanukkah! A Three-Dimensional Celebration. 1991. 15.95 (*0-670-84092-0*) Viking Child Bks.

—Passover! A Three-Dimensional Celebration. Clarke, Sue, illus. LC 93-34026. 8p. (ps-3). 1994. 15.99 (*0-670-85111-6*) Viking Child Bks.
Freedman, Benedict & Freedman, Nancy. Mrs. Mike. (gr. 7 up). 1984. pap. 3.95 (*0-425-10328-5*) Berkley Pub.
Freedman, E. B. What Does Being Jewish Mean? 1991. pap. 7.95 (*0-13-962747-2*) P-H.
Freedman, Florence B. Two Tickets to Freedom: The True Story of Ellen & William Craft, Fugitive Slaves. Keats, Ezra J., illus. 96p. (gr. 4 up). 1989. 12.95 (*0-87226-330-4*); pap. 5.95 (*0-87226-221-9*) P Bedrick Bks.
Freedman, Nancy, jt. auth. see Freedman, Benedict.
Freedman, Robin L. Open-Ended Questioning: A Handbook for Educators. (ps-3). 1993. pap. 16.20 (*0-201-81958-9*) Addison-Wesley.
Freedman, Russell. Animal Superstars: Biggest, Strongest, Fastest, Smartest. (Illus.). 112p. (gr. 5 up). 1984. pap. 5.95 (*0-13-037615-9*) P-H.
—Buffalo Hunt. LC 87-35303. (Illus.). 52p. (gr. 3-7). 1988. reinforced bdg. 18.95 (*0-8234-0702-0*) Holiday.
—Can Bears Predict Earthquakes? Unsolved Mysteries of Animal Behavior. (Illus.). 96p. (gr. 5 up). 1982. 10.95 (*0-13-114009-4*) P-H.
—Children of the Wild West. LC 83-5133. (Illus.). 128p. (gr. 3-6). 1983. 14.95 (*0-89919-143-6*, Clarion Bks) HM.
—Children of the Wild West. (Illus.). (gr. 4-7). 1990. pap. 5.70 (*0-395-54785-7*, Clarion Bks) HM.
—Cowboys of the Wild West. LC 85-4200. (Illus.). 128p. (gr. 3-7). 1985. 14.95 (*0-89919-301-3*, Clarion Bks) HM.
—Cowboys of the Wild West. LC 85-4200. (Illus.). 128p. (gr. 3-6). 1990. pap. 5.70 (*0-395-54800-4*, Clarion Bks) HM.
—Dinosaurs & Their Young. Morrill, Leslie, illus. LC 83-6160. 32p. (gr. 1-4). 1983. reinforced bdg. 13.95 (*0-8234-0496-X*) Holiday.
—Franklin Delano Roosevelt. (Illus.). 208p. (gr. 4 up). 1990. 16.95 (*0-89919-379-X*, Clarion Bks) HM.
—Immigrant Kids. LC 79-20060. 64p. (gr. 3-7). 1980. 16.95 (*0-525-32538-7*, DCB) Dutton Child Bks.
—Indian Chiefs. Freedman, Russell, photos by. LC 86-46198. (Illus.). 160p. (gr. 4 up). 1987. reinforced bdg. 18.95 (*0-8234-0625-3*); pap. 9.95 (*0-8234-0971-6*) Holiday.
—An Indian Winter. Bodmer, Karl, illus. LC 91-24205. 96p. (gr. 5 up). 1992. 21.95 (*0-8234-0930-9*) Holiday.
—Kids at Work: Lewis Hine & the Crusade Against Child Labor. Hine, Lewis, photos by. LC 93-5989. (Illus.). Date not set. write for info. (*0-395-58703-4*, Clarion Bks) HM.
—Killer Fish. LC 81-85089. (Illus.). 40p. (gr. 1-4). 1982. reinforced bdg. 13.95 (*0-8234-0449-8*) Holiday.
—Killer Snakes. LC 82-80821. (Illus.). 40p. (gr. 1-4). 1982. reinforced bdg. 13.95 (*0-8234-0460-9*) Holiday.
—Lincoln: A Photobiography. 160p. (gr. 4 up). 1987. 15.95 (*0-89919-380-3*, Clarion Bks) HM.
—Lincoln: A Photobiography. (Illus.). 160p. Pub. 1989. pap. 7.70 (*0-395-51848-2*, Clarion Bks) HM.
—Rattlesnakes. Freedman, Russell, illus. LC 84-4602. 40p. (gr. 1-4). 1984. reinforced bdg. 13.95 (*0-8234-0536-2*) Holiday.
—Sharks. Freedman, Russell, illus. LC 85-24881. 40p. (gr. 1-4). 1985. reinforced bdg. 13.95 (*0-8234-0582-6*) Holiday.
—The Wright Brothers: How They Invented the Airplane. Wright, Orville & Wright, Wilbur, photos by. LC 90-48440. (Illus.). 132p. (gr. 5 up). 1991. 18.95 (*0-8234-0875-2*) Holiday.
Freedman, Sally. Devin's New Bed. Levine, Abby, ed. LC 86-15823. (Illus.). 32p. (ps-k). 1986. PLB 13.95 (*0-8075-1565-5*) A Whitman.
Freedman, Suzanne. Ida B. Wells-Barnett & the Antilynching Crusade. LC 92-45855. (Illus.). 32p. (gr. 2-4). 1994. PLB 12.40 (*1-56294-377-4*) Millbrook Pr.
Freehof, Lillian S. Bible Legends: An Introduction to Midrash, Vol. 1: Genesis. Schwartz, Howard, ed. (gr. 4-6). 1987. pap. text ed. 6.95 (*0-8074-0357-1*, 123050) UAHC.
—Bible Legends: An Introduction to Midrash, Vol. 2: Exodus. Schwartz, Howard, ed. Tarlow, Phyllis, illus. 160p. (gr. 4-6). 1988. pap. text ed. 6.95 (*0-8074-0412-8*, 123060) UAHC.
Freeley, James. Are You an Entrepreneur? The Characteristics & Skills Needed to Start Your Own Business. LC 89-50287. (Illus.). 112p. (Orig.). (gr. 12). 1989. pap. text ed. 9.95 (*0-9619860-1-8*) Busn Resc Network.
Freeman. Baby's Lullabies. (ps). 1965. bds. 4.95 (*0-448-03088-8*, G&D) Putnam Pub Group.
Freeman, Aaron E. Astro Blue: A Member of Our Family. LC 83-73197. (Illus.). 144p. (gr. 6 up). 1984. lib. bdg. 9.95x (*0-915509-00-8*); pap. 6.95x (*0-915509-01-6*) Argos Pub Co.
Freeman, Ann, tr. see Zimmerman, H. Werner.
Freeman, Charles. Portrait of a Decade: Nineteen Thirties. (Illus.). 72p. (gr. 7-10). 1990. 19.95 (*0-7134-6073-3*, Pub. by Batsford UK) Trafalgar.
—Terrorists. (Illus.). 72p. (gr. 7-10). 1990. 19.95 (*0-7134-6076-8*, Pub. by Batsford UK) Trafalgar.
—U. S. A. - U. S. S. R. The Superpowers. (Illus.). 72p. (gr. 7-10). 1990. 19.95 (*0-7134-6077-6*, Pub. by Batsford UK) Trafalgar.
Freeman, Charlotte M. A Day in the Life of a Horse Trainer. Jann, Gayle, illus. LC 87-10681. 32p. (gr. 4-8). 1988. PLB 11.79 (*0-8167-1111-9*); pap. text ed. 2.95 (*0-8167-1112-7*) Troll Assocs.

Freeman, Chester D. & McGuire, John E. Runaway Bear. Kuper, Rachel, illus. LC 93-16893. 32p. (gr. k-3). 1993. 14.95 (*0-88289-956-2*); ltd. boxed signed ed. 29.95 (*1-56554-016-6*) Pelican.

Freeman, Don. Beady Bear. (Illus.). (gr. 3-6). 1977. pap. 4.99 (*0-14-050197-5*, Puffin) Puffin Bks.

—Beady Bear. Freeman, Don, illus. LC 54-12295. 48p. (ps-1). 1954. 13.95 (*0-670-15056-8*) Viking Child Bks.

—Bearymore. (Illus.). (ps-3). 1979. pap. 3.95 (*0-14-050279-3*, Puffin) Puffin Bks.

—Bearymore. LC 76-94. (Illus.). 40p. (gr. k-3). 1976. 14.95 (*0-670-15174-2*) Viking Child Bks.

—Un Bosillo Para Corduroy: A Pocket for Corduroy. Freeman, Don, illus. (ENG & SPA.). 32p. (ps-3). 1992. RB 13.00 (*0-670-84483-7*) Viking Child Bks.

—Corduroy. (Illus.). (gr. k-1). 1993. pap. 3.99 (*0-14-050173-8*, Puffin); StoryTape 6.99 (*0-14-095114-8*, Puffin) Puffin Bks.

—Corduroy. Freeman, Don, illus. LC 68-16068. 32p. 1968. 12.99 (*0-670-24133-4*) Viking Child Bks.

—Corduroy. Freeman, Don, illus. (gr. k-3). 1988. incl. cass. 19.95 (*0-941078-08-6*); pap. 12.95 incl. cass. (*0-941078-06-X*); user's guide incl. 4 pbs. & cass. 27.95 (*0-941078-07-8*) Live Oak Media.

—Corduroy, Edicion Espanola. Freeman, Don, illus. (SPA.). 32p. (ps-3). 1988. 11.95 (*0-670-82265-5*) Viking Child Bks.

—Corduroy: Edicion Espanola. (Illus.). 32p. (ps-3). 1990. pap. 4.50 (*0-14-054252-3*, Puffin) Puffin Bks.

—Corduroy: (Edicion Espanola) Freeman, Don, illus. (SPA.). (ps-3). 1990. incl. cass. 19.95 (*0-87499-192-7*); pap. 12.95 incl. cass. (*0-87499-213-3*); Set; incl. 4 bks., guide, & cass. pap. 27.95 (*0-87499-193-5*) Live Oak Media.

—Corduroy's Busy Street & Corduroy Goes to the Doctor. 2 bks. McCue, Lisa, illus. (ps-k). 1989. Repr. of 1987 ed. bds. 12.95 incl. cass. (*0-87499-133-1*) Live Oak Media.

—Dandelion. Freeman, Don, illus. LC 64-21472. (ps-2). 1977. pap. 4.50 (*0-14-050218-1*, VS4, Puffin) Puffin Bks.

—Dandelion. Freeman, Don, illus. LC 64-21472. 48p. (ps-2). 1964. pap. 14.00 (*0-670-25532-7*) Viking Child Bks.

—Dandelion. Freeman, Don, illus. (gr. k-3). 1982. incl. cassette 19.95 (*0-941078-11-6*); pap. 12.95 incl. cassette (*0-941078-09-4*); user's guide incl. 4 pbs. & cassette 27.95 (*0-941078-10-8*) Live Oak Media.

—Hattie the Backstage Bat. (Illus.). 32p. (Orig.). (ps-3). 1988. pap. 4.99 (*0-14-050893-7*, Puffin) Puffin Bks.

—Mop Top. Freeman, Don, illus. (ps-1). 1955. pap. 13.95 (*0-670-48882-8*) Viking Child Bks.

—Mop Top. Freeman, Don, illus. (gr. k-3). 1982. incl. cass. 19.95 (*0-941078-14-0*); pap. 12.95 incl. cass. (*0-941078-12-4*); user's guide incl. 6 pbs. & cass. 27.95 (*0-941078-13-2*) Live Oak Media.

—Norman the Doorman. Freeman, Don, illus. (ps-3). 1989. pap. 4.99 (*0-14-050288-2*, Puffin) Puffin Bks.

—Norman the Doorman. Freeman, Don, illus. (ps-2). 1959. pap. 15.95 (*0-670-51515-9*) Viking Child Bks.

—The Paper Party. (Illus.). (gr. 1 up). 1977. pap. 3.95 (*0-14-050212-2*, Puffin) Puffin Bks.

—A Pocket for Corduroy. (Illus.). (ps). 1993. pap. 3.99 (*0-14-050352-8*, Puffin); StoryTape 6.99 (*0-14-095124-5*) Puffin Bks.

—A Pocket for Corduroy. LC 77-16123. (Illus.). (gr. 3-5). 1978. 11.95 (*0-670-56172-X*) Viking Child Bks.

—A Pocket for Corduroy. Freeman, Don, illus. (gr. k-3). 1982. incl. cass. 19.95 (*0-941078-17-5*); pap. 12.95 incl. cass. (*0-941078-15-9*); user's guide incl. 4 pbs. & cass. 27.95 (*0-941078-16-7*) Live Oak Media.

—A Pocket for Corduroy. (Illus.). (ps-3). 1989. pap. 6.95 (*0-14-095036-2*, Puffin) Puffin Bks.

—Quiet! There's a Canary in the Library. Freeman, Dan, illus. LC 69-15398. 48p. (gr. k-3). 1969. 15.00 (*0-516-08737-1*); pap. 3.95 (*0-516-48737-X*) Childrens.

—A Rainbow of My Own. 32p. (ps-2). 1978. pap. 3.95 (*0-14-050328-5*, Puffin) Puffin Bks.

—Rainbow of My Own. (Illus.). (gr. k-3). 1966. pap. 13.95 (*0-670-58928-4*) Viking Child Bks.

—A Rainbow of My Own. Freeman, Don, illus. (gr. k-3). 1982. incl. cass. 19.95 (*0-941078-20-5*); pap. 12.95 incl. cass. (*0-941078-18-3*); user's guide incl. 4 pbs. & cass. 27.95 (*0-941078-19-1*) Live Oak Media.

—Space Witch. (Illus.). (gr. k-3). 1979. pap. 4.99 (*0-14-050346-3*, Puffin) Puffin Bks.

—Tilly Witch. (ps-k). 1978. pap. 3.95 (*0-14-050262-9*, Puffin) Puffin Bks.

—Tilly Witch. Freeman, Don, illus. (gr. k-3). 1969. pap. 13.95 (*0-670-71303-1*) Viking Child Bks.

Freeman, Don, jt. auth. see Freeman, Lydia.

Freeman, Dorothy, jt. auth. see MacMillan, Dianne.

Freeman, Dorothy R. St. Patrick's Day. LC 91-43098. (Illus.). 48p. (gr. 1-4). 1992. lib. bdg. 14.95 (*0-89490-383-7*) Enslow Pubs.

Freeman, Dorothy R. & MacMillan, Dianne M. Kwanzaa. LC 91-43100. (Illus.). 48p. (gr. 1-4). 1992. lib. bdg. 14.95 (*0-89490-381-0*) Enslow Pubs.

Freeman, Florence B. It Happened in Chelm: A Story of the Legendary Town of Fools. Krevitsky, Nik, illus. 64p. (gr. 3-8). 1990. pap. text ed. 9.95 (*0-933503-22-9*) Shapolsky Pubs.

Freeman, Grace & Sugarman, Joan. Inside the Synagogue. rev. ed. Mass, Ronald, photos by. (Illus.). 64p. (gr. 3-5). 1984. pap. 6.00 (*0-8074-0268-0*, 301785) UAHC.

Freeman, Hobart E. Biblical Thinking & Confession: The Key to Victorious Living 365 Days a Year. (Orig.). 1990. pap. write for info (*1-878725-36-X*) Faith Min & Pubns.

Freeman, Ira M., jt. auth. see Freeman, Mae B.

Freeman, J. W. Discovering Surnames: Their Origins & Meanings. 4th ed. 72p. (gr. 6 up). 1979. pap. 4.95 (*0-913714-36-4*) Legacy Bks.

Freeman, Jodi L., jt. auth. see Brian, J.

Freeman, Lory. It's My Body. Deach, Carol, illus. 32p. (ps-3). 1983. lib. bdg. 15.95 (*0-943990-02-5*); pap. 4.95 (*0-943990-03-3*) Parenting Pr.

—Loving Touches. Deach, Carol, illus. LC 85-62434. 32p. (Orig.). (ps). 1985. PLB 15.95 (*0-943990-21-1*); pap. 4.95 (*0-943990-20-3*) Parenting Pr.

—Mi Cuerpo Es Mio. Dunn, Lois, tr. from ENG. Deach, Carol, illus. LC 85-62435. (SPA.). 32p. (Orig.). (ps). 1985. pap. 4.95 (*0-943990-19-X*) Parenting Pr.

Freeman, Lydia. Corduroy's Day. McCue, Lisa, illus. LC 84-40477. 14p. (ps). 1985. pap. 3.99 (*0-670-80521-1*) Viking Child Bks.

—Corduroy's Party. McCue, Lisa, illus. LC 84-40476. 14p. (ps). 1985. pap. 3.99 (*0-670-80520-3*) Viking Child Bks.

—Corduroy's Toys. McCue, Lisa, illus. LC 84-40478. 24p. 1985. pap. 3.50 (*0-670-80522-X*) Viking Child Bks.

Freeman, Lydia & Freeman, Don. Pet of the Met. (Illus.). 64p. (Orig.). (ps-3). 1988. pap. 4.95 (*0-14-050892-9*, Puffin) Puffin Bks.

—Pet of the Met. (Illus.). 64p. (ps-3). 1953. pap. 13.95 (*0-670-54875-8*) Viking Child Bks.

Freeman, Mae B. & Freeman, Ira M. The Sun, the Moon, & the Stars. rev. ed. Martin, Rene, illus. LC 78-64604. (gr. 2-4). 1979. 8.95 (*0-394-80110-5*); lib. bdg. 5.99 (*0-394-90110-X*) Random Bks Yng Read.

Freeman, Marie E. & Davis, Maria H. Alpine to Alkali. Delany, Dan & Walker, Jan, illus. LC 83-80807. 150p. (Orig.). (gr. 7-12). 1983. pap. text ed. 7.95 (*0-913205-01-X*) Grace Dangberg.

Freeman, Marji. Creative Graphing. (gr. 4-7). 1992. pap. 7.95 (*0-201-48026-3*) Addison-Wesley.

—Creative Graphing. 48p. (gr. 4-8). 1986. pap. text ed. 7.95 (*0-914040-47-2*) Cuisenaire.

Freeman, Mark. Big League Break. 144p. (gr. 4 up). 1989. pap. 2.95 (*0-345-35904-6*) Ballantine.

—Big League Play. 1989. 3.99 (*0-345-35905-4*) Ballantine.

—Halfcourt Hero. 1989. 3.99 (*0-345-35911-9*) Ballantine.

—Play Ball. 144p. (gr. 4 up). 1989. pap. 2.95 (*0-345-35902-X*) Ballantine.

—Squeeze Play. 144p. (gr. 7-9). 1989. pap. 3.99 (*0-345-35903-8*) Ballantine.

Freeman, Mary E. The Revolt of Mother. (gr. 5 up). 1992. PLB 13.95 (*0-88682-495-8*) Creative Ed.

Freeman, Peggy P. Swept Back to a Texas Future. Haas, Holly, illus. 40p. (gr. 4-7). 1991. pap. 7.95 (*0-937460-72-9*) Hendrick-Long.

Freeman, Ron. Makeup Art. LC 90-38305. (Illus.). 48p. (gr. 5-8). 1991. PLB 12.90 (*0-531-14133-0*) Watts.

Freeman, Warren S., jt. auth. see Barbour, Harriot B.

Freidman, Rita, jt. auth. see Reiss, Elayne.

Freifeld, Art. One Thousand Plus Picture Dictionary: One Hundred One Activities. Leung, Paul, illus. 90p. (Orig.). (gr. 5 up). 1988. pap. text ed. 6.95 (*0-916177-06-8*); tchr's. ed. 1.45 (*0-916177-24-6*) Am Eng Pubns.

Freisner, Esther M. Wishing Season. Freas, Frank K., illus. LC 93-71527. 144p. (gr. 7 up). 1993. SBE 14.95 (*0-689-31574-0*, Atheneum Child Bk) Macmillan Child Grp.

Freitas, F. Bapu. Freitas, F., illus. (gr. 1-9). 1979. Pt. I. pap. 2.50 (*0-89744-173-7*); Pt. II. pap. 2.50 (*0-89744-174-5*) Auromere.

Frekko, Janet, jt. auth. see Katz, Phyllis.

Frem, Margie, illus. Conversation Games: Vol. III, Solutions. Rev. ed. Freeman, Harold, Jr., intro. by. (Illus.). 134p. (ps-6). 1981. pap. 17.00 (*0-939632-23-3*) ILM.

Fremantle, Anne. Island of Cats. Sapieha, Christine, illus. (gr. 1-4). 1964. 12.95 (*0-8392-3011-7*) Astor-Honor.

Fremon, David. The Trail of Tears. (Illus.). 96p. (gr. 6 up). 1994. PLB 14.95 RSBE (*0-02-735745-7*, New Discovery Bks) Macmillan Child Grp.

Fremont, Eleanor. Jokes from the Crypt. LC 92-4056. (Illus.). 96p. (Orig.). (gr. 4-7). 1992. pap. 2.99 (*0-679-83168-1*) Random Bks Yng Read.

—Tales from the Crypt: Introduced by the Crypt-Keeper, Vol. 4. LC 90-23916. (Illus.). 96p. (Orig.). (gr. 4-7). 1992. pap. 2.99 (*0-679-83073-1*) Random Bks Yng Read.

—Tales from the Crypt: Introduced by the Old Witch, Vol. 5. LC 90-23916. (Illus.). 96p. (Orig.). (gr. 4-7). 1992. pap. 2.99 (*0-679-83074-X*) Random Bks Yng Read.

Fremont, Eleanor, adapted by. Tales from the Crypt, Vol. 1: Introduced by the Crypt-Keeper. Davis, Jack, illus. LC 90-23916. 96p. (Orig.). (gr. 4-7). 1991. pap. 2.99 (*0-679-81799-9*) Random Bks Yng Read.

—Tales from the Crypt, Vol. 2: Introduced by the Old Witch. Davis, Jack, illus. LC 90-23916. 96p. (Orig.). (gr. 4-7). 1991. pap. 2.99 (*0-679-81800-6*) Random Bks Yng Read.

French, Alice. My Name Is Masak. (Illus.). 110p. (gr. 7-8). 1992. pap. 9.95 (*0-919566-56-1*) Peguis Pubs Ltd.

French, Allen. The Story of Rolf: And the Viking Bow. Reynolds, Lydia, intro. by. 256p. (gr. 6-12). 1994. pap. 12.95 (*1-883937-01-9*) Bethlehem WA.

French, Barbara. Coping with Bulimia. (Illus.). 160p. (Orig.). (gr. 10 up). 1984. pap. 8.95 (*0-7225-1380-1*) Thorsons SF.

French, Dorothy K. Pioneer Saddle Mystery. LC 75-12428. 192p. (gr. 5-10). 1975. PLB 7.19 (*0-8313-0113-9*) Lantern.

French, Fiona. Anancy & Mr. Dry-Bone. (Illus.). (ps-3). 1991. 14.95 (*0-316-29298-2*) Little.

—King of Another Country. LC 92-12661. (Illus.). 32p. (ps-3). 1993. 14.95 (*0-590-46369-1*) Scholastic Inc.

—The Magic Vase. (Illus.). 32p. (gr. 2 up). 1991. bds. 13.95 laminated (*0-19-279875-8*) OUP.

—Snow White in New York. (Illus.). 32p. (gr. 1-4). 1987. bds. 14.95 (*0-19-279808-1*) OUP.

—Snow White in New York. (Illus.). 32p. 1990. pap. 6.95 (*0-19-272210-7*) OUP.

French, Michael. Circle of Revenge. LC 88-19340. 160p. (gr. 6 up). 1988. 13.95 (*0-553-05495-3*, Starfire) Bantam.

—Pursuit. LC 82-70319. 192p. (gr. 7 up). 1982. 9.95 (*0-385-28781-X*) Delacorte.

—Pursuit. 192p. (gr. 9 up). 1983. pap. 2.95 (*0-440-96665-5*, LFL) Dell.

—Soldier Boy. (gr. 7 up). 1990. pap. 2.95 (*0-553-28609-9*, Starfire) Bantam.

—Split Image. (gr. 7 up). 1990. 14.95 (*0-553-07021-5*, Starfire) Bantam.

—The Throwing Season. LC 79-53598. (gr. 9-12). 1980. 8.95 (*0-440-08600-0*) Delacorte.

—Us Against Them. (gr. 7-12). 1989. pap. 2.95 (*0-553-27647-6*, Starfire) Bantam.

—Us Against Them. 1987. 13.95 (*0-553-05440-6*) Bantam.

French, P. M. & Taylor, J. W. How Lasers Are Made. (Illus.). 32p. (gr. 5-12). 1987. 12.95x (*0-8160-1690-9*) Facts on File.

French, Simon. Change the Locks. LC 92-30194. 112p. (gr. 3-7). 1993. 13.95 (*0-590-45593-1*) Scholastic Inc.

French, Susan M. Dressing up Like Mommy. Hu, Ying-Hwa, illus. 24p. (Orig.). (gr. k-1). 1990. pap. 0.99 (*1-878624-35-0*) McClanahan Bk.

—The Magic Train. Lynn, Patty, illus. 24p. (Orig.). (gr. k-1). 1990. pap. 0.99 (*1-878624-33-4*) McClanahan Bk.

French, Vivian. Caterpillar, Caterpillar. Voake, Charlotte, illus. LC 92-544006. 32p. (ps-up). 1993. 14.95 (*1-56402-206-4*) Candlewick Pr.

—It's a Go-to-the-Park Day. Scruton, Clive, illus. LC 90-28506. 40p. (ps-1). 1992. jacketed 14.00 (*0-671-74477-1*, S&S BFYR) S&S Trade.

—One Ballerina Two. Ormerod, Jan, illus. LC 90-45969. 32p. (ps up). 1991. 13.95 (*0-688-10333-2*); PLB 13.88 (*0-688-10334-0*) Lothrop.

—Under the Moon. Fisher, Chris, illus. LC 93-877. Date not set. write for info. (*1-56402-330-3*) Candlewick Pr.

French, Vivian, abridged by. Charles Dicken's "A Christmas Carol" 1st U.S. ed. Benson, Patrick, illus. LC 93-54577. 48p. (gr. 4 up). 1993. 15.95 (*1-56402-204-8*) Candlewick Pr.

French, Vivian, retold by. Why the Sea Is Salt. Aggs, Patrice, illus. LC 92-53138. 32p. (ps-3). 1993. 14.95 (*1-56402-183-1*) Candlewick Pr.

Frenck, Hal, illus. The Tale of Benjamin Bunny. LC 87-40283. (ps up). 1990. incl. audio cassettes 6.95 (*1-55782-016-3*, Pub. by Warner Juvenile Bks) Little.

Freniere, Annette La see Warren, Betsy.

Freschet, Bernice. Furlie Cat. Lewin, Betsy, illus. LC 85-11656. 32p. (ps-3). 1986. 12.95 (*0-688-05917-1*) Lothrop.

Fretz, Clarence Y. Story of God's People. (gr. 7). 1978. pap. 5.90x (*0-87813-900-1*); tchr's. guide 8.75x (*0-87813-901-X*) Christian Light.

—You & Your Bible-You & Your Life. (gr. 8). 1968. pap. 4.10x (*0-87813-902-8*); tchr's. guide 16.00x (*0-87813-903-6*) Christian Light.

Freudberg, Judy & Geiss, Tony. Susan & Gordon Adopt a Baby. Mathieu, Joe, illus. LC 86-2951. 24p. (ps-2). 1992. 5.99 (*0-394-88341-1*) Random Bks Yng Read.

Freund, Chavie. Read Me the Haggadah. Ieff, Tova, illus. (ps-2). 1990. 10.95 (*1-56062-021-8*) CIS Comm.

Frick, Dumas F. The Adventures of Phineous. Shauck, Chuck, illus. 96p. (gr. 1-3). 1993. 21.95 (*1-56167-112-6*) Noble Hse MD.

Friddle, Sue. Jake Art. Friddle, Jacob, illus. (Orig.). (gr. k-7). 1989. pap. 5.00 (*0-9623308-1-7*) Anyones Pub.

Friedenberg, Daniel M. Life, Liberty & the Pursuit of Land: The Plunder of Early America. (Illus.). 380p. 1992. 27.95 (*0-87975-722-1*) Prometheus Bks.

Friedhoffer. More Magic Tricks, Science Facts. Kaufman, Richard, illus. White, Timothy, photos by. (Illus.). 128p. (gr. 5-8). 1990. PLB 12.90 (*0-531-10969-0*) Watts.

Friedhoffer & Brown, Harriet. How to Haunt a House for Halloween. Kaufman, Richard, illus. White, Timothy, photos by. (Illus.). 96p. (gr. 3 up). 1989. pap. 6.95 (*0-531-15122-0*) Watts.

Friedhoffer, Bob. Magic Tricks, Science Facts. 1990. PLB 12.90 (*0-531-10902-X*) Watts.

—Magic Tricks, Science Facts. 1990. pap. 6.95 (*0-531-15186-7*) Watts.

—Walt Disney's Sorcerer's Apprentice Storybook & Magic Tricks. Slater, Teddy, retold by. Mateu, Franc & Kaufman, Richard, illus. LC 91-73813. 64p. (gr. 1-7). 1993. 12.95 (*1-56282-144-X*) Disney Pr.

Friedhoffer, Robert. Forces, Motion, & Energy. Kaufman, Richard & Eisenberg, Linda, illus. White, Timothy, photos by. LC 92-16625. 112p. (gr. 5-8). 1992. PLB 13.40 (0-531-11052-4) Watts.
—Light. Kaufman, Richard & Eisenberg, Linda, illus. White, Timothy, photos by. LC 92-19522. (gr. 5-8). 1992. PLB 13.40 (0-531-11082-6) Watts.
—Magnetism & Electricity. Kaufman, Richard & Eisenberg, Linda, illus. White, Timothy, photos by. LC 92-19223. (gr. 5-8). 1992. PLB 13.40 (0-531-11084-2) Watts.
—Matter & Energy. Kaufman, Richard & Eisenberg, Linda, illus. White, Timothy, photos by. LC 92-16623. (gr. 5-8). 1992. PLB 13.40 (0-531-11051-6) Watts.
—Molecules & Heat. Kaufman, Richard & Eisenberg, Linda, illus. White, Timothy, photos by. LC 92-16960. (gr. 5-8). 1992. PLB 13.40 (0-531-11053-2) Watts.
—More Magic Tricks, Science Facts. 1993. pap. 6.95 (0-531-15669-9) Watts.
—Sound. Kaufman, Richard & Eisenberg, Linda, illus. White, Timothy, photos by. LC 92-16961. (gr. 5-8). 1992. PLB 13.90 (0-531-11083-4) Watts.

Friedl, Michael. Ah...To Be A Kid: Three Dozen Aikido Games for Children of All Ages. Ransom, Stefan P., illus. 82p. (Orig.). 1994. pap. 9.95 (0-9638530-1-5, Castle Capers) Magical Michael. AH...TO BE A KID is a must for those of you teaching children or adults about conflict resolution. This book introduces a variety of games which teach people how to harmonize with each other & to interact in a noncompetitive manner. Using movement principles of Aikido, the author explains the importance of blending & redirecting movement instead of competing with it. As children (& adults) actually play the games described, they gain skills that help them to assess situations & react quickly, to think clearly, & to remain relaxed. One teacher sums it up this way: "Noncompetitive games are important tools for teaching children how to cooperate & succeed. This book provides educators with several ideas for helping children learn harmony among themselves & with their environment." Whether you are four years old or forty, if you enjoy the "kid" in you, then these games will create laughter, giggles & a joy for physical interaction. AH...TO BE A KID is an excellent resource for teaching conflict resolution skills in a fun & interactive manner. *Publisher Provided Annotation.*

Friedland, Bruce. Childhood. (Illus.). 112p. (gr. 7-12). 1993. 18.95 (0-7910-0036-2) Chelsea Hse.
—Personality Disorders. (Illus.). 112p. (gr. 6-12). 1991. 18.95 (0-7910-0051-6) Chelsea Hse.
Friedland, Helen, jt. auth. see Strauss, Barbara.
Friedland, J., ed. see Christopher, Garrett.
Friedland, J., ed. see Diamond, Laurie.
Friedland, J., ed. see Golden, Michael.
Friedland, J., ed. see Spencer, Anne.
Friedland, Joyce. From Books to Film: A Study Guide. (gr. 6-10). 1991. pap. text ed. 14.95 (0-88122-690-4) LRN Links.
Friedland, Joyce & Kessler, Rikki. The Big Wave: A Study Guide. LC 82-196. 1982. tchr's ed. & wkbk. 14.95 (0-88122-000-0) LRN Links.
—Bless the Beasts & the Children: A Study Guide. 1983. tchr's ed. & wkbk. 14.95 (0-88122-023-X) LRN Links.
—Bridge to Teribithia: A Study Guide. (gr. 4-6). 1982. tchr's ed. & wkbk. 14.95 (0-88122-001-9) LRN Links.
—Busybody Nora: A Study Guide. (gr. 2-4). 1982. tchr's ed. & wkbk. 14.95 (0-88122-002-7) LRN Links.
—Charlotte's Web: A Study Guide. (gr. 2-5). 1983. tchr's ed. & wkbk. 14.95 (0-88122-015-9) LRN Links.
—Girl Who Owned a City: A Study Guide. (gr. 4-6). 1982. tchr's ed. & wkbk. 14.95 (0-88122-003-5) LRN Links.
—Maggie Marmelstein for President: A Study Guide. (gr. 4-6). 1982. tchr's ed. & wkbk. 14.95 (0-88122-006-X) LRN Links.
—The Pearl - Study Guide. Reeves, Barbara, ed. (gr. 6-10). Date not set. pap. text ed. 14.95 (0-88122-031-0) Lrn Links.
—A Separate Peace - Study Guide. (gr. 7-10). Date not set. pap. text ed. 14.95 (0-88122-022-1) Lrn Links.
—A Wrinkle in Time - Study Guide. (gr. 6-10). Date not set. pap. text ed. 14.95 (0-88122-014-0) Lrn Links.
Friedland, Joyce, ed. see Albert, Toni.
Friedland, Joyce, ed. see Bachelder, Marvin.
Friedland, Joyce, ed. see Christopher, Garrett.
Friedland, Joyce, ed. see Claydon, Dina.
Friedland, Joyce, ed. see Croil, Marianne.
Friedland, Joyce, ed. see Danielson, Kathy.
Friedland, Joyce, ed. see Diamond, Laurie.
Friedland, Joyce, ed. see Dobrow, Vicki.
Friedland, Joyce, ed. see Fischer, Elyse.
Friedland, Joyce, ed. see Forsten, Charlene.
Friedland, Joyce, ed. see Gluzband, Cheryl.
Friedland, Joyce, ed. see Golden, Michael.
Friedland, Joyce, ed. see Goldish, Meish.
Friedland, Joyce, ed. see Halverson, Patricia A.
Friedland, Joyce, ed. see Hanus, Karen.
Friedland, Joyce, ed. see Klitzner, Carol.
Friedland, Joyce, ed. see Levine, Gloria.
Friedland, Joyce, ed. see Levine, Gloria & Fischer, Kathleen M.
Friedland, Joyce, ed. see McGee, Brenda.
Friedland, Joyce, ed. see McGee, Brenda H.
Friedland, Joyce, ed. see Marsh, Norma.
Friedland, Joyce, ed. see Medland, Mary.
Friedland, Joyce, ed. see Murphy, Michael.
Friedland, Joyce, ed. see Norris, Crystal.
Friedland, Joyce, ed. see Peitz, Mary.
Friedland, Joyce, ed. see Pilar, Arlene.
Friedland, Joyce, ed. see Reeves, Barbara.
Friedland, Joyce, ed. see Snodgrass, Mary E.
Friedland, Joyce, ed. see Sussman, Linda.
Friedland, Joyce, ed. see Tretler, Marcia.
Friedland, Joyce, ed. see Villanella, Rosemary.
Friedland, Joyce, ed. see Witt, Sandi & Petrovich, Janice.
Friedman, jt. auth. see Weimann.
Friedman, Aileen, ed. see Burns, Marilyn.
Friedman, Alice, jt. auth. see Schmidt, Fran.
Friedman, Arthur, illus. The Three Sillies. LC 80-27636. 32p. (gr. k-4). 1981. PLB 9.79 (0-89375-486-2); pap. text ed. 1.95 (0-89375-487-0) Troll Assocs.
Friedman, Audrey M. & Zwerin, Raymond. High Holy Day Do It Yourself Dictionary. Ruten, Marlene L., illus. 32p. (gr. k-3). 1983. pap. 5.00 (0-8074-0162-5, 101100) UAHC.
Friedman, Barbara, jt. auth. see Loomar, Jane.
Friedman, David. Focus on Drugs & the Brain. Neuhaus, David, illus. 64p. (gr. 2-4). 1990. PLB 14.95 (0-941477-95-9) TFC Bks NY.
Friedman, Donna, jt. auth. see Hill, Tom.
Friedman, Frieda. Dot for Short. 173p. 1981. Repr. PLB 14.95x (0-686-73781-4) Buccaneer Bks.
—Dot for Short. 168p. 1981. Repr. PLB 10.95x (0-89967-038-5) Harmony Raine.
—Dot for Short. Haywood, Carolyn, illus. (gr. 5-7). 1988. pap. 3.95 (0-317-69653-X, Puffin) Puffin Bks.
Friedman, Herbert & Zuber, Sharon. Doing Your Best on the S. A. T. 4th ed. 64p. (gr. 12). 1990. pap. text ed. 7.50x (0-9606824-6-5) Medfd Pr.
Friedman, Ina R. How My Parents Learned to Eat. Say, Allen, illus. LC 84-18553. 32p. (gr. k-3). 1987. 13.45 (0-395-35379-3); pap. 4.80 (0-395-44235-4) HM.
—The Other Victims: First-Person Stories of Non-Jews Persecuted by the Nazis. 224p. (gr. 5-9). 1990. 14.45 (0-395-50212-8) HM.
Friedman, Judi. Operation Siberian Crane: The Story Behind the International Effort to Save an Amazing Bird. LC 92-13775. (Illus.). 96p. (gr. 5 up). 1992. RSBE 13.95 (0-87518-515-0, Dillon) Macmillan Child Grp.
Friedman, Judith & Sonnenblick, Carol. Attack Pack. 128p. (gr. 4-12). 1982. write for info. (0-9609616-0-7) New Dir Pr.
Friedman, M., jt. auth. see Weiss, E.
Friedman, Mel, jt. auth. see Weiss, Ellen.
Friedman, Michael J. Star Trek: The Next Generation - The Star Lost. Kahan, Bob, ed. (Illus.). 144p. (Orig.). 1993. pap. 14.95 (1-56389-084-4) DC Comics.
Friedman, Rita, jt. auth. see Reiss, Elayne.
Friedman, Rita, jt. auth. see Weimann.
Friedman, Rita, jt. auth. see Weimann, Elaine.
Friedman, Rita, jt. auth. see Weimann, Elayne.
Friedman, Sharon, jt. auth. see Shere, Irene.
Friedman, Susan L., jt. auth. see Conlin, Susan.
Friedrich, Elizabeth. The Story of God's Love. 144p. (gr. 6-9). 1985. 9.99 (0-570-04122-8, 56-1533) Concordia.
Friedrich, Liz. Teen Guide to Married Life. (Illus.). 64p. (gr. 7-12). 1989. PLB 13.40 (0-531-10836-8) Watts.
—Teen Guide to Married Life. 1990. pap. 4.95 (0-531-15209-X) Watts.
Friedrich, Otto, jt. auth. see Friedrich, Priscilla.
Friedrich, Priscilla & Friedrich, Otto. The Easter Bunny That Overslept. Adams, Adrienne, illus. LC 82-13013. 1987. pap. 4.95 (0-688-07038-8, Mulberry) Morrow.
—The Easter Bunny That Overslept. Adams, Adrienne, illus. 40p. (ps up). 1993. Repr. text ed. 4.95 (0-688-12667-7, Tupelo Bks) Morrow.
Friend, Catherine. My Head Is Full of Colors. (Illus.). 32p. (ps-3). 1994. 14.95 (1-56282-360-4); PLB 14.89 (1-56282-361-2) Hyprn Child.
—Sawfin Stickleback. (Illus.). 32p. 1994. 13.95 (1-56282-473-2); PLB 13.89 (1-56282-474-0) Hyprn Child.
Friend, David. Baseball, Football, Daddy & Me. Brown, Rick, illus. 32p. (ps-3). 1990. 12.95 (0-670-82420-8) Viking Child Bks.
—Baseball, Football, Daddy & Me. Brown, Rick, illus. 32p. (ps-3). 1992. pap. 3.99 (0-14-050914-3) Puffin Bks.
Friend, Janet. To Grow by Storybook Phonics Readers. Capezio, Betsy, illus. (gr. k-3). 1990. Set. pap. text ed. 44.95 (0-910311-69-2) Huntington Hse.
Friend, Mari. Discovering Nature's Secrets: An All-Year-Round Activity Book. (Illus.). 80p. (gr. 3-7). 1992. 15.95 (0-87663-638-5) Universe.
Friendly, Alfred. Dragomir. Weinberger, Jane & Black, Albert, eds. DeVito, Pamela, illus. LC 88-50316. 46p. (ps up). 1988. pap. 9.95 (0-932433-44-8) Windswept Hse.
Friends in Recovery & Jerry S. Prayers for the Twelve Steps - A Way Out. LC 93-11016. 128p. (Orig.). (gr. 12 up). 1993. pap. 7.95 (0-941405-29-X) Recovery CA.
—Prayers for the Twelve Steps: A Spiritual Journey. LC 93-15978. 128p. (Orig.). (gr. 12). 1993. pap. 7.95 (0-941405-28-1) Recovery Pubns.
Friese, Kai. Tenzin Gyatso. (Illus.). 112p. (gr. 5 up). 1990. 17.95 (1-55546-836-5) Chelsea Hse.
Friese, Kai J. Rosa Parks: The Movement Organizes. Gallin, Richard, ed. Young, Andrew, intro. by. (Illus.). 128p. (gr. 5 up). 1990. lib. bdg. 16.98 (0-382-09927-3); pap. 7.95 (0-382-24065-0) Silver Burdett Pr.
Friesel, Uwe. Tim, the Peacemaker. Wilkon, Jozef, illus. LC 72-145822. 32p. (ps-3). 8.95 (0-87592-052-7) Scroll Pr.
Friggens, Myriam. Tales, Trails & Tommyknockers: Stories from Colorado's Past. Coulter, Gene, illus. LC 79-84876. 144p. (gr. 6 up). 1979. pap. 7.95 (0-933472-01-3) Johnson Bks.
Frinks, Donna. All about Me. (gr. k). 1989. text incl. activity program 160.00 (0-318-41077-X) Southwinds Pr.
Friou, Deborah. Rodgers & Hammerstein for the Harp. 48p. (Orig.). 1990. pap. 15.95 (0-9628120-0-5) Friou Music.
Frisbee, Lucy P. John Fitzgerald Kennedy: America's Youngest President. Fiorentinl, Al, illus. LC 86-10965. 192p. (gr. 2-6). 1986. pap. 3.95 (0-02-041990-2, Aladdin) Macmillan Child Grp.
Frisch. Ducks. 1981. 11.95s.p. (0-86625-192-8) Rourke Pubns.
—Hamsters. 1991. 11.95s.p. (0-86625-191-X) Rourke Pubns.
—Horses. 1991. 11.95s.p. (0-86625-189-8) Rourke Pubns.
—Parrots. 1991. 11.95s.p. (0-86625-190-1) Rourke Pubns.
—Pigeons. 1991. 11.95s.p. (0-86625-193-6) Rourke Pubns.
—Responsible Pet Care Series, 6 bks, Set II. 1991. s.p. 71.70 (0-86625-195-2) Rourke Pubns.
—Turtles. 1991. 11.95s.p. (0-86625-194-4) Rourke Pubns.
Frisch, C. Advertising. (Illus.). 48p. (gr. 4-8). 1989. lib. bdg. 17.27 (0-86592-078-8); lib. bdg. 12.95s.p. (0-685-58626-X) Rourke Corp.
Frisch, Carlienne. Destinations: How to Use All Kinds of Maps. LC 93-10577. 1993. 12.95 (0-8239-1607-3) Rosen Group.
—Wyoming. LC 93-23098. (gr. 5 up). 1994. lib. bdg. write for info. (0-8225-2736-7) Lerner Pubns.
Frisch, Carlienne & Balcziak, Bill. Communications, Reading Level 5: Today & Tomorrow, 6 bks. (Illus.). 288p. (gr. 4-8). 1989. Set. PLB 103.60 (0-685-54148-7); lib. bdg. 77.70s.p. (0-86592-055-9) Rourke Corp.
Frisch, Vern A. & Handal, Joan S. Applied Office Typewriting. 4th ed. (Illus.). (gr. 11-12). 1977. text ed. 14.24 (0-07-022504-4) McGraw.
Frisching, Sacha de see De Frisching, Sacha.
Friskey, Margaret. Birds We Know. LC 81-7745. (Illus.). 48p. (gr. k-4). 1981. PLB 15.27 (0-516-01609-1); pap. 4.95 (0-516-41609-X) Childrens.
—Chicken Little Count-To-Ten. Evans, K., illus. 32p. (gr. k-3). 1946. PLB 15.00 (0-516-03431-6) Childrens.
—Indian Two Feet & His Horse. (Illus.). 64p. (gr. k-3). 1959. 15.93 (0-516-03501-0) Childrens.
—Indian Two Feet & the Wolf Cubs. Hawkinson, John, illus. 64p. (gr. k-3). 1971. PLB 15.93 (0-516-03506-1) Childrens.
—Indian Two Feet Rides Alone. Hankinson, John, illus. LC 80-12688. 32p. (gr. k-3). 1980. PLB 15.00 (0-516-03523-1) Childrens.
—Lanzaderas Espaciales (Space Shuttles) Kratky, Lada, tr. from ENG. LC 81-11648. (SPA., Illus.). 48p. (gr. k-4). 1984. pap. 4.95 (0-516-51655-8) Childrens.
—The Perky Little Pumpkin. Dunnington, Tom, illus. LC 90-38376. 32p. (ps-3). 1990. PLB 15.00 (0-516-03564-9); pap. 4.95 (0-516-43564-7) Childrens.
—Pollito Pequenito Cuenta hasta Diez - Chicken Little Count-to-Ten. Kratky, Lada, tr. from ENG. Evans, K., illus. (SPA.). (gr. k-3). 1984. PLB 15.00 (0-516-33431-X); pap. 3.95 (0-516-53431-9) Childrens.
—Seven Diving Ducks. Morey, Jean, illus. LC 65-20889. 32p. (gr. k-3). 1965. PLB 15.00 (0-516-03605-X) Childrens.
—Space Shuttles. LC 81-11648. (Illus.). 48p. (gr. k-4). 1982. PLB 15.27 (0-516-01655-5); pap. 4.95 (0-516-41655-3) Childrens.
Frith, Julia. Pelican Sketchbook. Frith, Julia, illus. LC 93-29013. 1994. 4.25 (0-383-03769-7) SRA Schl Grp.
Frith, Michael. Autographs! I Collect Them! Frith, Michael, illus. LC 89-63064. 48p. (gr. 1-5). 1990. pap. 4.95 (0-679-80691-1) Random Bks Yng Read.
—I'll Teach My Dog One Hundred Words. (Illus.). (ps-1). 1973. 6.95 (0-394-82692-2); lib. bdg. 7.99 (0-394-92692-7) Random Bks Yng Read.

Fritz & Angel. Light Bears, Bk. 2: Planting the Seeds. Berthon, Prue, illus. 38p. (Orig.). (ps-1). 1991. pap. 17.95 (0-9629140-1-0) Fritz & Angel.

Fritz & Clute. Champion Dog Prince Tom. large type ed. (gr. 3-5). Repr. of 1958 ed. write for info. NAVH.

Fritz, Jean. And Then What Happened, Paul Revere? Tomes, Margot, illus. 48p. (gr. 2-6). 1973. 13.95 (0-698-20274-0, Coward); pap. 6.95 (0-698-20541-3) Putnam Pub Group.

—Around the World in a Hundred Years: Henry the Navigator - Magellan. Venti, Anthony B., illus. LC 92-27042. 128p. (gr. 2-6). 1994. 17.95 (0-399-22527-7, Putnam) Putnam Pub Group.

—Brady. Ward, Lynd, illus. (gr. 5-9). 1987. pap. 4.99 (0-14-032258-2, Puffin) Puffin Bks.

—Brendan the Navigator. Arno, Enrico, illus. LC 78-13247. (gr. 2-5). 1979. 14.95 (0-698-20473-5, Coward) Putnam Pub Group.

—Bully for You, Teddy Roosevelt! (Illus.). 128p. 1991. 15.95 (0-399-21769-X, Putnam) Putnam Pub Group.

—The Cabin Faced West. Rojankovsky, Feodor, illus. (gr. 4-7). 1958. 13.95 (0-698-20016-0, Coward) Putnam Pub Group.

—The Cabin Faced West. Rojanovsky, Feodor, illus. (gr. 1-7). 1987. pap. 3.99 (0-14-032256-6, Puffin) Puffin Bks.

—Can't You Make Them Behave, King George? De Paolo, Tomie, illus. 48p. (gr. 3-6). 1982. 13.95 (0-698-20315-1, Coward); pap. 6.95 (0-698-20542-1) Putnam Pub Group.

—China Homecoming. Fritz, Michael, photos by. LC 84-24775. (Illus.). 144p. (gr. 5 up). 1985. 15.95 (0-399-21132-9, Putnam) Putnam Pub Group.

—China's Long March: 6000 Miles of Danger. Cheng, Yang Zhr, illus. LC 87-31171. 128p. (gr. 7 up). 1988. 15.95 (0-399-21512-3, Putnam) Putnam Pub Group.

—The Double Life of Pocahantas. Rojanovsky, Feodor, illus. (gr. 1-7). 1987. pap. 3.99 (0-14-032257-4, Puffin) Puffin Bks.

—The Double Life of Pocahontas. LC 90-48977. (Illus.). 128p. (gr. 6-10). 1991. PLB 13.95 (1-55905-092-6) Marshall Cavendish.

—Early Thunder. Ward, Lynd, illus. (gr. 5-9). 1987. pap. 4.99 (0-14-032259-0, Puffin) Puffin Bks.

—George Washington's Breakfast. Galdone, Paul, illus. (gr. 2-6). 1984. (Coward); pap. 6.95 (0-698-20616-9, Coward) Putnam Pub Group.

—George Washington's Mother. DiSalvo-Ryan, DyAnne, illus. 48p. (gr. 2-4). 1992. 3.50 (0-448-40385-4, G&D) (G&D) Putnam Pub Group.

—The Good Giants & The Bad Pukwudgies. De Paola, Tomie, illus. 40p. (gr. 3-7). 1982. (Sandcastle Bks); pap. 5.95 (0-399-21732-0, Sandcastle Bks) Putnam Pub Group.

—The Great Adventure of Christopher Columbus. De Paola, Tomie, illus. 1992. 15.95 (0-399-22113-1, Putnam) Putnam Pub Group.

—The Great Little Madison. (Illus.). 160p. (gr. 5 up). 1989. 15.95 (0-399-21768-1, Putnam) Putnam Pub Group.

—Harriet Beecher Stowe & the Beecher Preachers. LC 93-6408. 1994. write for info. (0-399-22666-4, Putnam) Putnam Pub Group.

—Homesick: My Own Story. Tomes, Margot, illus. 160p. (gr. 3-7). 1982. 14.95 (0-399-20933-6, Putnam) Putnam Pub Group.

—Homesick: My Own Story. (gr. k-6). 1984. pap. 3.99 (0-440-43683-4, YB) Dell.

—Homesick: My Own Story. large type ed. (Illus.). 184p. (gr. 3-9). 1987. Repr. of 1982 ed. lib. bdg. 15.95 (1-55736-070-7, Crnrstn Bks) BDD LT Grp.

—Just a Few Words, Mr. Lincoln: The Story of the Gettysburg Address. Robinson, Charles, illus. LC 92-35319. 48p. (gr. 2-3). 1993. 7.99 (0-448-40171-1, G&D); pap. 3.50 (0-448-40170-3, G&D) Putnam Pub Group.

—Make Way for Sam Houston. Primavera, Elise, illus. LC 85-25601. 109p. (gr. 4-6). 1986. 13.95 (0-399-21303-1, Putnam); pap. 6.95 (0-399-21304-X) Putnam Pub Group.

—Shh! We're Writing the Constitution. De Paola, Tomie, illus. 64p. (gr. 3-7). 1987. 14.95 (0-399-21403-8, Putnam); pap. 6.95 (0-399-21404-6, Putnam) Putnam Pub Group.

—Stonewall. (Illus.). (gr. 3-7). 1979. 15.95 (0-399-20698-1, Putnam) Putnam Pub Group.

—Stonewall. Gammell, Stephen, illus. 160p. (gr. 5-9). 1989. pap. 4.99 (0-14-032937-4, Puffin) Puffin Bks.

—Traitor: The Case of Benedict Arnold. Andre, John, illus. (gr. 3-7). 1981. 15.95 (0-399-20834-8, Putnam) Putnam Pub Group.

—Traitor: The Case of Benedict Arnold. 192p. (gr. 5-9). 1989. pap. 4.99 (0-14-032940-4, Puffin) Puffin Bks.

—What's the Big Idea, Ben Franklin? (Illus.). 48p. (gr. 2-6). 1982. 13.95 (0-698-20365-8, Coward); pap. 6.95 (0-698-20543-X, Coward) Putnam Pub Group.

—Where Do You Think You're Going, Christopher Columbus? Tomes, Margot, illus. 80p. (gr. 3-7). 1981. (Putnam); pap. 7.95 (0-399-20734-1, Putnam) Putnam Pub Group.

—Where Was Patrick Henry on the 29th of May? Tomes, Margot, illus. 48p. (gr. 3-5). 1982. 13.95 (0-698-20307-0, Coward); pap. 6.95 (0-698-20544-8, Coward) Putnam Pub Group.

—Who's That Stepping on Plymouth Rock? Handelsman, J. B., illus. LC 74-30593. 32p. (gr. 2-6). 1975. 13.95 (0-698-20325-9, Coward) Putnam Pub Group.

—Why Don't You Get a Horse, Sam Adams? Hyman, Trina S., illus. 48p. (gr. 2-6). 1982. 13.95 (0-698-20292-9, Coward); pap. 6.95 (0-698-20545-6, Coward) Putnam Pub Group.

—Will You Sign Here, John Hancock? Hyman, Trina S., illus. LC 75-33243. 48p. (gr. 2-6). 1982. 13.95 (0-698-20308-9, Coward); pap. 6.95 (0-698-20539-1, Coward) Putnam Pub Group.

Fritz, Jean, et al. The World in 1492. (Illus.). 160p. (gr. 6-9). 1992. 19.95 (0-8050-1674-0, Bks Young Read) H Holt & Co.

Fritz, Ron. Let's Have a Party! Scott, Dennis, illus. LC 92-28560. 32p. (gr. k-2). 1992. PLB 11.89 (0-8167-2984-0); pap. text ed. 3.95 (0-8167-2985-9) Troll Assocs.

Frohlich, Margaret, jt. auth. see Niederhauser, Hans R.

Frois, Jeanne. Louisianians All. Carley, Nathan B., illus. LC 92-19208. 96p. 1991. 11.95 (0-88289-824-8) Pelican.

Froissart, Benedicte. Uncle Henry's Dinner Guests. Pratt, Pierre, illus. 32p. (ps-2). 1990. 14.95 (1-55037-141-X, Pub. by Annick CN); pap. 4.95 (1-55037-140-1, Pub. by Annick CN) Firefly Bks Ltd.

Frolick, S. J. Once There Was a President. rev. ed. LC 80-69972. 64p. (gr. 3-7). 1980. pap. 6.95 (0-9605426-0-4) Black Star Pub.

Frome, Shelly. Sun Dance for Andy Horn. 124p. (gr. 9-12). 1990. 14.95 (0-89992-324-0); pap. 9.95 (0-89992-124-8) Coun India Ed.

Fromer, Julie. Jane Goodall: Living with the Chimps. Castro, Antonio, illus. 72p. (gr. 4-7). 1992. PLB 14.95 (0-8050-2116-7) TFC Bks NY.

Fromer, Margaret & Nystrom, Carolyn. Acts 13-28: Missions Accomplished. DeVelasco, Joe, illus. 93p. (gr. 7-12). 1979. saddle-stitched tchr's. ed. 4.99 (0-87788-011-5); saddle- stitched student ed. 3.99 (0-87788-010-7) Shaw Pubs.

Fromm, Pete. Monkey Tag. LC 93-34593. 1994. 14.95 (0-590-46525-2) Scholastic Inc.

Frommer, Harvey. A Hundred & Fiftieth Anniversary Album of Baseball. Solomon, Maury, ed. (Illus.). 96p. (gr. 7 up). 1988. PLB 13.90 (0-531-10588-1) Watts.

Frontier Press Company Staff. Lincoln Library of Sports Champions, 20 vols. 5th ed. LC 88-82571. (Illus.). 2560p. (gr. 4 up). 1989. Set. 439.00 (0-912168-13-7) Frontier Pr Co.

Frost. Two Frost Poems. 1993. 13.95 (0-8050-1493-4) H Holt & Co.

Frost, Abigail. The Age of Chivalry. LC 89-17396. (Illus.). 48p. (gr. 4-8). 1990. PLB 13.95 (1-85435-235-0) Marshall Cavendish.

—The Amazon. LC 89-17357. (Illus.). 48p. (gr. 4-8). 1990. PLB 13.95 (1-85435-236-9) Marshall Cavendish.

—Ancient Egypt. LC 89-25410. (Illus.). 48p. (gr. 4-8). 1990. PLB 13.95 (1-85435-234-2) Marshall Cavendish.

—Elizabeth I. (Illus.). 32p. (gr. 3-8). 1989. PLB 10.95 (1-85435-113-3) Marshall Cavendish.

—The Wolf. LC 89-17445. (Illus.). 48p. (gr. 4-8). 1990. PLB 13.95 (1-85435-237-7) Marshall Cavendish.

Frost, Dorothy R. Dad! Why'd You Leave Me? (Illus.). 96p. (Orig.). (gr. 3-6). 1992. pap. 4.95 (0-8361-3592-X) Herald Pr.

Frost, Ed & Frost, Roon. Just for Kids: The New England Guide & Activity Book for Young Travelers. Leach, Carol, illus. 150p. (Orig.). (gr. ps-5). 1989. pap. 7.95 (0-9618806-2-7) Glove Compart Bks.

—The Kids' Holiday Book: Activities Through the Seasons. Leach, Carol, illus. 176p. (Orig.). (gr. ps-7). 1990. pap. 11.95 (0-9618806-3-5) Glove Compart Bks.

Frost, Erica. Case of the Missing Chick. new ed. Harvey, Paul, illus. LC 78-18036. 48p. (gr. 2-4). 1979. PLB 10.89 (0-89375-092-1); pap. 3.50 (0-89375-080-8) Troll Assocs.

—Harold & the Dinosaur Mystery. new ed. Sims, Deborah, illus. LC 78-60123. 48p. (gr. 2-4). 1979. PLB 10.89 (0-89375-088-3); pap. 3.50 (0-89375-076-X) Troll Assocs.

—I Can Read about Ballet. LC 74-24927. (Illus.). (gr. 2-4). 1975. pap. 1.95 (0-89375-063-8) Troll Assocs.

—I Can Read about Ghosts. LC 74-24964. (Illus.). (gr. 2-4). 1975. pap. 1.95 (0-89375-065-4) Troll Assocs.

—I Can Read about Good Manners. LC 74-24878. (Illus.). (gr. 1-2). 1975. pap. 1.95 (0-89375-059-X) Troll Assocs.

—Jonathan's Amazing Adventure. Hall, Susan, illus. LC 85-14129. 48p. (Orig.). (gr. 1-3). 1986. PLB 10.59 (0-8167-0662-X); pap. text ed. 3.50 (0-8167-0663-8) Troll Assocs.

—A Kitten for Rosie. Fiammenghi, Gioia, illus. LC 85-14126. 48p. (Orig.). (gr. 1-3). 1986. PLB 10.59 (0-8167-0650-6); pap. text ed. 3.50 (0-8167-0651-4) Troll Assocs.

—The Littlest Pig. Paterson, Diane, illus. LC 85-14121. 48p. (Orig.). (gr. 1-3). 1986. PLB 10.59 (0-8167-0654-9); pap. text ed. 3.50 (0-8167-0655-7) Troll Assocs.

—Mr. Lion Goes to Lunch. Epstein, Len, illus. LC 85-14012. 48p. (Orig.). (gr. 1-3). 1986. PLB 10.59 (0-8167-0638-7); pap. text ed. 3.50 (0-8167-0639-5) Troll Assocs.

—Mystery of the Midnight Visitors. Gamache, Ann, illus. LC 78-18038. 48p. (gr. 2-4). 1979. PLB 10.89 (0-89375-094-8); pap. 3.50 (0-89375-082-4) Troll Assocs.

—Mystery of the Runaway Sled. Grant, Leigh, illus. LC 78-60124. 48p. (gr. 2-4). 1979. PLB 10.89 (0-89375-089-1); pap. 3.50 (0-89375-077-8) Troll Assocs.

—The Story of Matt & Mary. Schumacher, Claire, illus. LC 85-14011. 48p. (Orig.). (gr. 1-3). 1986. PLB 10.59 (0-8167-0602-6); pap. text ed. 3.50 (0-8167-0603-4) Troll Assocs.

Frost, Joan. Art, Books & Children: Art Activities Based on Children's Literature. (Illus.). 88p. (gr. 1-6). 1984. spiral bdg. 13.95 (0-938594-03-6) Spec Lit Pr.

—Exceptional Art--Exceptional Children: Fostering Creativity & Developing Independence. (Illus.). 140p. (gr. 1-8). 1985. spiral bdg. 16.95 (0-938594-07-9) Spec Lit Pr.

Frost, Lesley. Digging Down to China. Hudnut, R., illus. 64p. (gr. 1-4). 1968. 9.95 (0-8159-5306-2) Devin.

—Really, Not Really. Remington, Barbara, illus. 64p. (ps-3). 1966. 10.00 (0-8159-6702-0) Devin.

Frost, Robert. Birches. Young, Ed, illus. LC 87-46359. 32p. (gr. 2-4). 1988. 13.95 (0-8050-0570-6, Bks Young Read) H Holt & Co.

—Christmas Trees. Rand, Ted, illus. LC 89-48899. 32p. (gr. 2-4). 1990. 14.95 (0-8050-1208-7, Bks Young Read) H Holt & Co.

—Stopping by Woods on a Snowy Evening. Jeffers, Susan, illus. LC 78-8134. (gr. 3 up). 1978. 13.00 (0-525-40115-6, 01063-320, DCB) Dutton Child Bks.

—A Swinger of Birches: Poems of Robert Frost for Young People. Koeppen, Peter, illus. Fadiman, Clifton, intro. by. LC 82-5517. (Illus.). 80p. (gr. 4 up). 1982. 21.95 (0-916144-92-5); pap. 9.95 (0-916144-93-3); cass. & bk. 23.90 (0-685-05629-5, 102-5); cassette only 8.95 (0-88045-099-1) Stemmer Hse.

Frost, Roon, jt. auth. see Frost, Ed.

Frost, T. Olly on Safari. (Illus.). 32p. (ps-3). 1987. PLB 14.65 (0-88625-189-3); pap. 4.95 (0-88625-187-7) Durkin Hayes Pub.

Fry, Annette R. The Orphan Trains. (Illus.). 96p. (gr. 6 up). 1994. PLB 14.95 RSBE (0-02-735721-X, New Discovery Bks) Macmillan Child Grp.

Fry, Ed. Paseo en Barco de Vela - Sailboat Ride. (ENG & SPA., Illus.). 24p. (gr. k-1). 1992. pap. 23.75 (0-89061-721-X) Jamestown Pubs.

—El Viento Fuerte - the Big Wind. (ENG & SPA., Illus.). 24p. (gr. k-1). 1992. pap. 23.75 (0-89061-722-8) Jamestown Pubs.

Fry, Edward B. Computer Keyboarding for Children. rev. ed. (gr. 3-6). 1984. pap. text ed. 9.95x (0-8077-2754-7) Tchrs Coll.

Fry, Fiona S. Horses. (Illus.). (gr. 6up). 1981. 14.95 (0-7136-2114-1) Dufour.

Fry, Janice, jt. auth. see Haener, Donald R.

Fry, Janice K., jt. auth. see Haener, Donald R.

Fry, Ron. Your First Resume: The Essential, Comprehensive Guide for Anyone Entering or Reentering the Job Market. 3rd ed. LC 92-13494. 160p. (gr. 9 up). 1992. pap. 8.95 (1-56414-018-0) Career Pr Inc.

Fry, Varian. Assignment Rescue: An Autobiography. 04/1993 ed. (gr. 7 up). pap. 3.50 (0-590-46970-3) Scholastic Inc.

Fry, William R. & Hoopes, Roy. Legal Careers & the Legal System. LC 87-9298. (Illus.). 64p. (gr. 6 up). 1988. lib. bdg. 15.95 (0-89490-142-7) Enslow Pubs.

Fryar, Jane. The Easter Day Surprise. (Illus.). 24p. (Orig.). (ps-4). 1993. pap. 1.89 (0-570-09033-4) Concordia.

—Jesus Enters Jerusalem. (Illus.). 24p. (Orig.). (ps-4). 1993. pap. 1.89 (0-570-09032-6) Concordia.

—The Locked-in Friend. Wilson, Deborah, illus. 32p. (ps-2). 1991. 7.99 (0-570-04195-7) Concordia.

—Lost at the Mall: Morris the Mouse Adventure Ser. Wilson, Deborah, illus. 32p. (ps-1). 1991. 7.99 (0-570-04196-1, 56-1655) Concordia.

Fryatt, Evelyn H. Festive Gingerbreads. LC 92-14950. (Illus.). 80p. (gr. 10-12). 1992. 14.95 (1-89556-904-4, Pub. by Tamos Bks CN) Sterling.

Frydenborg, Kay. They Dreamed of Horses: Careers for Horse Lovers. Wood, Tanya, photos by. LC 93-33023. (Illus.). 1994. write for info. (0-8027-8283-3); PLB write for info. (0-8027-8284-1) Walker & Co.

Frye, Chad. The Fun Bible Search Book...Find Rupert. Frye, Chad, illus. 32p. 1992. 12.95 (1-55748-309-4) Barbour & Co.

Frye, Judy. Teddy Bear Connection Color-Me Calendar. 1992. write for info. (0-9632316-1-8) Teddy Bear Connect.

Frye, Keith. Roadside Geology of Virginia. Alt, David & Hyndman, Donald, eds. Venkatakrishnan, Rames, illus. Milici, Robert C., frwd. by. LC 86-8755. (Illus.). 256p. (Orig.). (gr. 5 up). 1986. pap. 12.00 (0-87842-199-8) Mountain Pr.

Frye, Tom. The Jewel Folk. Hammond, Lee, illus. (Orig.). 1993. pap. 8.95 (1-881663-17-5) Advent Mean Pr.

—The Kid, the Cop, & the Con. 256p. (Orig.). (gr. 6 up). 1993. pap. 9.95 (1-881663-18-3) Advent Mean Pr.

—Scratchin' on the Eight Ball. 240p. (gr. 6 up). 1993. pap. 9.95 (1-881663-16-7) Advent Mean Pr.

Fryer, Lee & Bradford, Leigh. A Child's Organic Garden. Albert, Eddie, frwd. by. 96p. 1989. 9.95 (0-87491-963-0); pap. 9.95 (0-685-28260-0) Acropolis.

Frykman, John. The Hassle Handbook. rev. ed. LC 84-6851. (Illus.). 108p. 1988. 9.95 (0-916147-02-9) Regent Pr.

Fryman, Alice J. Nobody Sees Tomorrow. 1992. 7.95 (0-533-10017-8) Vantage.

FS-Aladdin Staff, ed. see Gamlin, Linda.

FS-Aladdin Staff, ed. see Hemming, Judith.

FS-Aladdin Staff, ed. see Mohun, Janet.

FS-Ltd Staff, ed. see Healey, Tim.

FS Staff, ed. see Alexander, Sue.

FS Staff, ed. see Barrett, N. S.
FS Staff, ed. see Barrett, Norman S.
FS Staff, ed. see Binney, Don.
FS Staff, ed. see Larsen, Rebecca.
FS Staff, ed. see Thomson, Ruth.
FS-Watts Staff, ed. see Bender, Lionel.
Fuchs. Bear for All Seasons. 1993. 14.95 (*0-8050-2139-6*) H Holt & Co.
Fuchs, Carol. Disappearances. 48p. (gr. 3-4). 1991. PLB 11.95 (*1-56065-041-9*) Capstone Pr.
—Jackie Joyner-Kersee: Track-&-Field Star. LC 92-45244. 1993. 14.60 (*0-86593-261-1*); 10.95s.p. (*0-685-66421-X*) Rourke Corp.
—Jane Goodall: The Chimpanzee's Friend. LC 93-6506. 1993. 14.60 (*0-86593-262-X*); 10.95s.p. (*0-685-66546-1*) Rourke Corp.
Fuchs, M., et al. Top Twenty ESL Word Games. 1990. incl. blackline masters 29.95 (*0-8013-0365-6*, 78138) Longman.
Fuchs, Marjorie S., et al. Families: Ten Card Games for Language Learners. Burrows, Arthur A., ed. (Illus.). 26p. (Orig.). (gr. 4 up). 1986. pap. text ed. 8.50x (*0-86647-016-6*) Pro Lingua.
Fuchs, Yitzchak Y. Halichos Bas Yisroel, Vol. 1. Dombey, Moshe, tr. from HEB. (gr. 7-12). 1986. 14.95 (*0-87306-397-X*) Feldheim.
Fuchshuber, Annegert. The Cuckoo-Clock Cuckoo. 32p. (gr. k-4). 1988. lib. bdg. 18.95 (*0-87614-320-6*) Carolrhoda Bks.
—The Cuckoo-Clock Cuckoo. (Illus.). 32p. (gr. k-4). 1989. pap. 5.95 (*0-87614-499-7*, First Ave Edns) Lerner Pubns.
—From Dinosaurs to Fossils. Fuchshuber, Annegert, illus. LC 80-28596. 24p. (gr. k-3). 1981. PLB 10.95 (*0-87614-152-1*) Carolrhoda Bks.
—Giant Story - Mouse Tale: A Half Picture Book. (Illus.). 32p. (gr-3). 1988. lib. bdg. 18.95 (*0-87614-319-2*) Carolrhoda Bks.
Fuchshuber, Annegert, illus. Augsburg Story Bible. LC 92-2527. 272p. (gr. 3-7). 1992. lib. bdg. 19.99 (*0-8066-2607-0*, 9-2607, Augsburg) Augsburg Fortress.
Fuda, Siri, jt. ed. see Walsh, Joy.
Fuentes, Vilma M. The Fairy of Masara. Inis, Ninabeth R., illus. 24p. (Orig.). (gr. k-3). 1984. pap. 3.50 (*971-10-0211-6*, Pub by New Day Philippines) Cellar.
—Kimod & the Swan Maiden. Inis, Ninabeth R., illus. 36p. (Orig.). (gr. k-3). 1984. pap. 3.50 (*971-10-0135-7*, Pub. by New Day Pub PI) Cellar.
—Manggob & His Golden Top. Inis, Ninabeth R., illus. 48p. (Orig.). (gr. k-3). 1985. pap. 4.00 (*971-10-0218-3*, Pub. by New Day Pub PI) Cellar.
—Pearl Makers: Six Stories about Children in the Philippines. (Illus., Orig.). (gr. 1-6). 1989. 4.95 (*0-377-00191-0*) Friendship Pr.
Fugate, Clara T. The Legend of Natural Tunnel: La Leyenda del Tunel Natural. Calvera, Elizabeth C., ed. Socarras-Roufagalas, Gilda, tr. Ertmann, Caren L. & Read, Jacqueline P., illus. LC 85-30068. (SPA & ENG). 80p. (Orig.). (gr. 6-12). 1986. pap. 5.95 (*0-936015-02-0*) Pocahontas Pr.
Fuge, Charles & Hayles, Karen. Whale Is Stuck. LC 92-34078. (ps-1). 1993. pap. 14.00 JRT (*0-671-86587-0*, S&S BFYR) S&S Trade.
Fugii, Satoru, et al, trs. see Koike, Kazuo.
Fugitt, Douglas & Fugitt, Elizabeth. A Bird's-Eye View of Birds. Thomas, DeVoe M., illus. 190p. (Orig.). (gr. 6). 1986. PLB 17.95 (*0-9617159-0-1*); pap. 11.95 (*0-9617159-1-X*) Willow Pr.
Fugitt, Elizabeth, jt. auth. see Fugitt, Douglas.
Fugitt, Eva D. He Hit Me Back First! Creative Visualization Activities for Parenting & Teaching--Self-Esteem Through Self-Discipline. Houston, Jean, intro. by. LC 82-83063. (Illus.). 106p. (Orig.). (gr. 1-8). 1982. pap. 12.95 (*0-915190-36-2*, JP9036-2) Jalmar Pr.
Fuhler, Carol. Caddie Woodlawn: A Study Guide. (gr. 4-7). 1988. tchr's. ed. & wkbk. 14.95 (*0-88122-079-5*) Lrn Links.
Fuhr, U. & Sautai, R., illus. Baleine. (FRE.). (ps-1). 1991. 17.95 (*2-07-035729-5*) Schoenhof.
Fujii, Satoru, tr. see Asamiya, Kia.
Fujii, Satoru, tr. see Koike, Kazuo.
Fujii, Satoru, et al, trs. see Koike, Kazuo.
Fujikawa, Gyo. Babes of the Wild. Fujikawa, Gyo, illus. 16p. (ps). 1989. Repr. bds. 6.95 (*1-55987-008-7*, Sunny Bks) J B Comns.
—Betty Bear's Birthday. Fujikawa, Gyo, illus. 16p. (ps). 1989. Repr. bds. 6.95 (*1-55987-011-7*, Sunny Bks) J B Comns.
—Can You Count? Fujikawa, Gyo, illus. 16p. (ps). 1989. Repr. of 1977 ed. bds. 6.95 (*1-55987-003-6*, Sunny Bks) J B Comns.
—Gyo Fujikawa's Oh, What a Busy Day! Fujikawa, Gyo, illus. 80p. 1989. 13.95 (*0-448-04304-1*, G&D) Putnam Pub Group.
—Let's Eat. Fujikawa, Gyo, illus. 16p. (ps). 1989. Repr. of 1975 ed. bds. 6.95 (*1-55987-005-2*, Sunny Bks) J B Comns.
—Let's Grow a Garden. Fujikawa, Gyo, illus. 16p. (ps). 1989. Repr. bds. 6.95 (*1-55987-010-9*, Sunny Bks) J B Comns.
—Let's Play. Fujikawa, Gyo, illus. 16p. (ps). 1989. Repr. of 1975 ed. bds. 6.95 (*0-317-93045-1*, Sunny Bks) J B Comns.
—Millie's Secret. Fujikawa, Gyo, illus. 16p. (ps). 1989. bds. 6.95 (*1-55987-006-0*, Sunny Bks) J B Comns.

—My Favorite Thing. Fujikawa, Gyo, illus. 16p. (ps). 1989. Repr. of 1978 ed. bds. 6.95 (*1-55987-004-4*, Sunny Bks) J B Comns.
—Our Best Friends. Fujikawa, Gyo, illus. 16p. (ps). 1989. Repr. bds. 6.95 (*1-55987-009-5*, Sunny Bks) J B Comns.
—Puppies, Pussycats & Other Friends. Fujikawa, Gyo, illus. 16p. (ps). 1989. Repr. of 1977 ed. bds. 6.95 (*1-55987-000-1*, Sunny Bks) J B Comns.
—Sleepy Time. Fujikawa, Gyo, illus. 16p. (ps). 1989. Repr. of 1975 ed. bds. 6.95 (*1-55987-001-X*, Sunny Bks) J B Comns.
—Sunny Books - Four-Favorite Tales, 4 bks, No. 1. Fujikawa, Gyo, illus. (ps). 1989. Repr. of 1975 ed. Boxed set, 4 books, 16 pgs. ea. bds. write for info. (*1-55987-040-0*, Sunny Bks) J B Comns.
—Sunny Books - Four-Favorite Tales, 4 bks, No. 2. Fujikawa, Gyo, illus. (ps). 1989. Repr. Boxed set, four bks., 16 pgs. ea. bds. write for info. (*1-55987-041-9*, Sunny Bks) J B Comns.
—Sunny Books - Four-Favorite Tales, 4 bks, No. 3. Fujikawa, Gyo, illus. (ps). 1989. Repr. Boxed set, four bks., 16 pgs. ea. bds. write for info. (*1-55987-042-7*, Sunny Bks) J B Comns.
—Surprise! Surprise! Fujikawa, Gyo, illus. 16p. (ps). 1989. Repr. bds. 6.95 (*1-55987-007-9*, Sunny Bks) J B Comns.
—Ten Little Babies. Fujikawa, Gyo, illus. LC 88-60966. 24p. (ps-1). 1989. pap. 4.95 (*0-394-89033-7*) Random Bks Yng Read.
Fujikawa, Gyo, illus. Babies. (ps). 1963. bds. 4.95 (*0-448-03084-5*, G&D) Putnam Pub Group.
—Baby Animals. (ps). 1963. bds. 4.95 (*0-448-03083-7*, G&D) Putnam Pub Group.
—Good Night, Sleep Tight, Shh... 22p. (ps). 1990. bds. 2.95 (*0-679-80845-0*) Random Bks Yng Read.
Fukami, Haruo. An Orange for a Bellybutton. Fukami, Haruo, illus. 32p. (ps-3). 1990. PLB 18.95 (*0-87614-429-6*) Carolrhoda Bks.
Fukijawa, Gyo, illus. Gyo Fujikawa's a Child's Book of Poems. 80p. (gr. k up). 1989. 13.95 (*0-448-04302-5*, G&D) Putnam Pub Group.
Fulbright, Robert G. Old Testament Friends: Men of Courage. McPheeters, William N., illus. (gr. 1-6). 1979. 5.95 (*0-8054-4251-0*, 4242-51) Broadman.
Fulk, Penny. Children's Parties Made Easy. Durdee, Becky, illus. 142p. (Orig.). pap. 6.00 (*0-941951-00-6*) JJJ Pubs.
Fullen, Dave. Lessons Learned: Students with Learning Disabilities, Ages 7-19, Share What They've Learned about Life & Learning. Farley, Brendon, illus. 40p. (Orig.). (gr. 1 up). 1993. pap. 4.95 (*1-881650-02-2*) Mntn Bks.
—The Mountain Song. Farley, Brendon, illus. Oremus, Earl, contrib. by. 20p. (gr. 1-6). 1992. pap. 14.95 incl. cass. (*1-881650-00-6*) Mntn Bks.
—A Nest in the Gale. Farley, Brendon, illus. 80p. (Orig.). (gr. 2-6). 1993. incl. audio cassette 24.95 (*1-881650-03-0*); pap. 18.95 incl. audio cassette (*1-881650-01-4*) Mntn Bks.
Fullen, M. K. Pathblazers: Eight People Who Made a Difference. Waldman, Selma, illus. 64p. (Orig.). (gr. 3-10). 1992. 12.95 (*0-940880-35-0*); pap. 6.95 (*0-940880-36-9*) Open Hand.
Fuller. Garth Owen Smith. 1993. PLB write for info. (*0-8050-2306-2*) H Holt & Co.
Fuller, Barbara. Germany. LC 92-13447. 1992. 21.95 (*1-85435-530-9*) Marshall Cavendish.
Fuller, Bob. God Made Big & Little Things. 12p. 1992. bds. 2.99 (*0-89693-139-0*) SP Pubns.
—God Made Quiet & Loud Things. 12p. 1992. bds. 2.99 (*0-89693-140-4*) SP Pubns.
—God Made Warm & Cool Things. 12p. 1992. bds. 2.99 (*0-89693-142-0*) SP Pubns.
—God Made Wild & Tame Things. 12p. 1992. bds. 2.99 (*0-89693-141-2*) SP Pubns.
—Why Is There War? (Illus.). 23p. 1989. pap. 3.99 (*0-89693-989-8*, Victor Bks) SP Pubns.
Fuller, Elizabeth, jt. auth. see Bishop, Conrad.
Fuller, Joy. The Glorious Presence. Russell, Marjorie H., ed. & illus. LC 81-65753. 176p. (gr. 9-12). 1989. pap. 7.98x (*0-9614745-1-3*) Arcadia Corp.
Fuller, Melvin L. & Weisberg, Maggie. Student Inventors Lesson Plan. Christensen, Don, illus. 75p. (Orig.). (gr. 4-12). 1989. pap. 14.95x (*0-685-25993-5*) M&M Assocs.
Fuller, Rose & Asato, Andrew. I'm in Charge of the FACTS. 60p. (gr. 7-9). 1993. wkbk. 3.50 (*1-880220-06-7*) NW Family Srvs.
Fuller, Rose, et al. FACTS & Reasons. Williams, Sarah, illus. 70p. (gr. 10-11). 1993. wkbk. 3.50 (*1-880220-07-5*) NW Family Srvs.
Fuller, Ted. Barney the Bus. Weinberger, Jane, ed. DeVito, Pamela, illus. LC 88-51276. 48p. (ps-4). 1989. pap. 7.95 (*0-932433-49-9*) Windswept Hse.
Fulop, Scott, intro. by. Archie Americana, Vol. 1: The 1940's. King, Stephen, frwd by. (Illus.). 128p. 1991. pap. 8.95 (*1-879794-00-4*, Archie Comics) Archie Comic.
Fulton, Eleanor & Smith, Pat. Let's Slice the Ice: A Collection of Black Children's Ring Games & Chants. Leissner, John, Jr., illus. 56p. (ps-k). 1978. pap. 7.95 (*0-918812-02-X*) MMB Music.
Fulton, Ginger A. Good Manners & Me. (Illus.). (ps-2). pap. 3.25 (*0-8024-3083-X*) Moody.
—When I'm a Mommy: A Little Girl's Paraphrase of Proverbs 31. (Illus.). (gr. 1-4). 1984. pap. 3.25 (*0-8024-0367-0*) Moody.

Fulton, Mary J. Too Many Jellybeans! Gleeson, Kate, illus. 24p. (ps-k). 1993. pap. 1.45 (*0-307-11539-9*, 11539, Golden Pr) Western Pub.
Fulves, Karl. The Children's Magic Kit: Sixteen Easy-to-Do Tricks Complete with Cardboard Cutouts. Schmidt, Joseph K., illus. 32p. (Orig.). (gr. 3-6). 1981. pap. 3.95 (*0-486-24019-3*) Dover.
—Easy-to-Do Magic Tricks for Children. Schmidt, Joseph K., illus. 32p. (Orig.). (gr. 4-6). 1993. pap. 2.95 (*0-486-27613-9*) Dover.
—More Self-Working Card Tricks: 88 Fool-Proof Card Miracles for the Amateur Magician. 96p. (Orig.). (gr. 6up). 1984. pap. 3.95 (*0-486-24580-2*) Dover.
—Self-Working Table Magic: Ninety-Seven Foolproof Tricks with Everyday Objects. Schmidt, Joseph K., illus. 128p. (Orig.). 1981. pap. 3.95 (*0-486-24116-5*) Dover.
Fun Group Staff. Make Your Own...Videos, Commercials, Radio. Sasaki, Ellen J., illus. LC 90-86409. 96p. (gr. 2-6). 1992. pap. 2.95 (*0-448-40201-7*, G&D) Putnam Pub Group.
Fun, J. J. The Partners & the Dolphins Who Moved In. 24p. (gr. k-8). 1992. pap. write for info. (*0-9632622-1-1*) J J Fun.
Funakoshi, Canna. One Christmas. Izawa, Yohji, illus. LC 90-7445. 40p. (gr. k up). 1991. pap. 12.95 (*0-88708-140-1*) Picture Bk Studio.
—One Evening. Izawa, Yohji, illus. LC 87-29243. (ps up). 1991. pap. 11.95 (*0-88708-063-4*) Picture Bk Studio.
—One Morning. LC 86-91538. (Illus.). 34p. (ps-3). 1991. pap. 11.95 (*0-88708-033-2*) Picture Bk Studio.
Funes, Marilyn & Lazarus, Alan. Popular Careers. Piltch, Benjamin, ed. Bartick, Robert, illus. 64p. (gr. 7 up). 1980. 3.95 (*0-934618-01-1*) Learning Well.
Funk, Nancy C., tr. see Bradbury, Thomas E.
Funston, Sylvia. Eastern Cougar. Kassian, Elena, illus. 32p. (gr. 1-5). 1992. 4.95 (*0-920775-95-0*, Pub. by Greey de Pencier CN) Firefly Bks Ltd.
—Leatherback Turtle. Kassian, Olena, illus. 32p. (gr. 1-5). 1992. 4.95 (*0-920775-97-7*, Pub. by Greey de Pencier CN) Firefly Bks Ltd.
—Peregrine Falcon. Owl Magazine Staff, ed. Kassian, Olena, illus. 32p. (gr. 1 up). 1992. 4.95 (*0-920775-99-3*, Pub. by Greey de Pencier CN) Firefly Bks Ltd.
—St. Lawrence Beluga. Kassian, Olena, illus. 32p. (gr. 1-5). 1992. 4.95 (*0-920775-93-4*, Pub. by Greey de Pencier CN) Firefly Bks Ltd.
Furlong, Kaye & Casolaro, Nancy. Gifted & Talented Puzzles & Games for Reading & Math. Whitten, Leesa, illus. 96p. (gr. 1-3). 1993. pap. 3.95 (*1-56565-065-4*) Lowell Hse.
Furlong, Monica. Juniper. LC 90-9800. 192p. (gr. 5-9). 1991. PLB 13.99 (*0-394-93220-X*) Knopf Bks Yng Read.
—Wise Child. LC 87-3063. 192p. (gr. 5 up). 1987. lib. bdg. 12.99 (*0-394-99105-2*) Knopf Bks Yng Read.
Furlong, Nicholas. A Foster Son for a King. (Illus.). 128p. (Orig.). (gr. 5-8). 1986. 9.95 (*0-947962-03-4*, Pub. by Childrens Pr); pap. 5.95 (*0-947962-04-2*, Pub. by Childrens Pr) Irish Bks Media.
Furlong, Philip. The Old World & America. LC 82-51247. 371p. (gr. 6). 1984. pap. 16.50 (*0-89555-202-7*) TAN Bks Pubs.
Furlow. Paul Keene. 1993. PLB 13.95 (*0-8050-2213-9*) H Holt & Co.
Furman, Abraham L., ed. Everygirls Adventure Stories. (Illus.). (gr. 6-10). PLB 7.19 (*0-8313-0053-1*) Lantern.
—Everygirls Career Stories. (Illus.). (gr. 6-10). PLB 7.19 (*0-8313-0049-3*) Lantern.
—Everygirls Companion. LC 68-11184. (gr. 5-9). 1968. PLB 7.19 (*0-685-13773-2*) Lantern.
—Everygirls Detective Stories. (Illus.). (gr. 6-10). PLB 7.19 (*0-8313-0060-4*) Lantern.
—More Teen-Age Ghost Stories. (gr. 6-10). 1963. PLB 7.19 (*0-8313-0052-3*) Lantern.
—More Teen-Age Haunted Stories. (gr. 5-10). 1967. PLB 7.19 (*0-8313-0057-4*) Lantern.
Furniss, Cathy, jt. auth. see Lipman, Michel.
Furniss, Tim. Exploitation of Space. (Illus.). 48p. (gr. 5 up). 1990. lib. bdg. 18.60 (*0-86592-097-4*); lib. bdg. 13.95s.p. (*0-685-36377-5*) Rourke Corp.
—The First Men on the Moon. Bull, Peter, illus. LC 88-24166. 32p. (gr. 4-6). 1989. PLB 11.90 (*0-531-18240-1*, Pub. by Bookwright Pr) Watts.
Furstinger, Nancy, ed. see Barnes, Jeremy.
Furstinger, Nancy, ed. see Black, Sheila.
Furstinger, Nancy, ed. see Booth, Basil.
Furstinger, Nancy, ed. see Bowman, John.
Furstinger, Nancy, ed. see Cwiklik, Robert.
Furstinger, Nancy, ed. see Glassman, Bruce.
Furstinger, Nancy, ed. see Lambert, David.
Furstinger, Nancy, ed. see Lye, Keith.
Furstinger, Nancy, ed. see McClard, Megan & Ypsilantis, George.
Furstinger, Nancy, ed. see Penny, Malcolm.
Furstinger, Nancy, ed. see Shorto, Russell.
Furstinger, Nancy, ed. see Shuker, Nancy.
Furtado, Jo. Sorry, Miss Folio! Joos, Frederic, illus. 32p. (ps-3). 1988. 10.95 (*0-916291-18-9*) Kane-Miller Bk.
—Sorry, Miss Folio! Joos, Frederic, illus. (ps-3). 1992. pap. 6.95 (*0-916291-41-3*) Kane-Miller Bk.
Fusako Ishinabe. Hiro's Pillow. Young, Richard G., ed. Kaisei - Sha, tr. LC 89-11768. (Illus.). 32p. (gr. 1-3). 1989. PLB 14.60 (*0-944483-44-5*) Garrett Ed Corp.
Fusonie, Donna J. Wicca, Flicka & JJ: The Night of the Poachers Moon. LC 92-72679. 125p. (gr. 7-9). 1993. 13.95 (*1-880851-05-9*) Greene Bark Pr.

Fussenegger, Gertrud. Noah's Ark. Fuchshuber, Annegert, illus. LC 87-45153. 32p. (gr. k-3). 1987. (Lipp Jr Bks) HarpC Child Bks.
Fustec, Fabienne. Plants. (Illus.). 128p. (ps-3). 1993. 10. 00 (0-679-84161-X); PLB 11.99 (0-679-94161-4) Random Bks Yng Read.
Futcher, Jane. Promise Not to Tell. 192p. (Orig.). (gr. 4-5). 1991. pap. 2.95 (0-380-76037-1, Flare) Avon.
Fuzellier, Michel. Rufus & the Paper. LC 93-13933. (Illus.). 1993. write for info. (1-56766-105-X) Childs World.
—Rufus Recycles Trash. LC 93-35706. (Illus.). 1993. write for info. (1-56766-106-8) Childs World.
Fyleman, Rose. Fairy Went A-Marketing. Henterly, Jamichael, illus. LC 86-4468. 24p. (ps-1). 1986. 11.95 (0-525-44258-8, DCB) Dutton Child Bks.
—Fairy Went A-Marketing. LC 86-4468. (Illus.). 24p. (ps-1). 1990. pap. 3.95 (0-525-44556-0, DCB) Dutton Child Bks.
Fynes-Clinton, Michael, ed. see Shakespeare, William.
Fyson, Nance L. Growing up in the Second World War. (Illus.). 72p. (gr. 6 up). 1981. 19.95 (0-7134-3574-7, Pub. by Batsford UK) Trafalgar.
—Hong Kong. LC 89-26247. (Illus.). 96p. (gr. 6-12). 1990. PLB 19.92 (0-8114-2433-2) Raintree Steck-V.
—Indonesia. LC 89-26283. (Illus.). 96p. (gr. 6-12). 1990. PLB 19.92 (0-8114-2435-9) Raintree Steck-V.
—People at Work in Sri Lanka. (gr. 6 up). 1988. 19.95 (0-7134-5479-2, Pub. by Batsford UK) Trafalgar.
—Portrait of a Decade: The 1940s. (Illus.). 72p. (gr. 7-10). 1989. 19.95 (0-7134-5628-0, Pub. by Batsford UK) Trafalgar.
—Portrait of a Decade: The 1950s. (Illus.). 72p. (gr. 7-11). 1990. 19.95 (0-7134-6070-9, Pub. by Batsford UK) Trafalgar.
—Sri Lanka. (Illus.). 64p. (gr. 7-9). 1988. 19.95 (0-85219-729-2, Pub. by Batsford UK) Trafalgar.
Fyson, Nance L. & Greenhill, Richard. A Family in China. LC 84-19426. (Illus.). 32p. (gr. 2-5). 1985. PLB 13.50 (0-8225-1653-5) Lerner Pubns.

G

Gaban, Jesus. Harry Dresses Himself. Colorado, Nani, illus. 16p. (ps-1). 1992. PLB 13.27 (0-8368-0715-4) Gareth Stevens Inc.
—Harry the Hippo, 4 vols. Colorado, Nani, illus. 16p. (ps-1). 1992. Set. PLB 53.08 (0-8368-0714-6) Gareth Stevens Inc.
—Harry's Mealtime Mess. Colorado, Nani, illus. 16p. (ps-1). 1992. PLB 13.27 (0-8368-0717-0) Gareth Stevens Inc.
—Harry's Sandbox Surprise. Colorado, Nani, illus. 16p. (ps-1). 1992. PLB 13.27 (0-8368-0716-2) Gareth Stevens Inc.
—Tub Time for Harry. Colorado, Nani, illus. 16p. (ps-1). 1992. PLB 13.27 (0-8368-0718-9) Gareth Stevens Inc.
Gabany, Steve G. The Working Person's Survival Guide - Instructor's Guide. (Illus.). 36p. (gr. 9-12). 1991. 5.95 (0-9624583-1-7) Hunt & Peck Pub.
Gabb, Michael. Creatures Great & Small. LC 79-64386. (Illus.). 36p. (gr. 3-6). 1980. PLB 13.50 (0-8225-1178-9, First Ave Edns); pap. 4.95 (0-8225-9540-0, First Ave Edns) Lerner Pubns.
—Everyday Science. LC 79-64387. (Illus.). 36p. (gr. 3-6). 1980. PLB 13.50 (0-8225-1179-7, First Ave Edns); pap. 4.95 (0-8225-9508-7, First Ave Edns) Lerner Pubns.
—The Human Body. LC 91-2560. (Illus.). 48p. (gr. 5-8). 1991. PLB 13.90 (0-531-19145-1, Warwick) Watts.
—The Human Body. LC 92-53092. (Illus.). 48p. (Orig.). (gr. 3-8). 1992. pap. 5.95 (1-85697-812-5) Kingfisher Bks.
Gabel, Rya, tr. see Panova, V.
Gabel, Susan. Filling in the Blanks: A Guided Look at Growing up Adopted. Seregny, Julie, illus. 160p. (gr. 5-10). 1988. wkbk. 15.00 (0-9609504-8-6) Perspect Indiana.
Gabel, Susan L. Where the Sun Kisses the Sea. Bowring, Joanne, illus. LC 89-16296. 32p. (ps-5). 1989. 12.95 (0-944934-00-5) Perspect Indiana.
Gaber, Susan. Favorite Poems for Children Coloring Book. (Illus.). 48p. (Orig.). (ps-3). 1980. pap. 2.95 (0-486-23923-3) Dover.
Gabet, Marcia. Bulletin Boards for Holidays & Everyday. Gabet, Marcia, illus. 64p. (gr. k-6). 1985. wkbk. 6.95 (1-55734-060-9) Tchr Create Mat.
—Fun with Science. Gabet, Marcia, illus. 48p. (gr. k-3). 1985. wkbk. 5.95 (1-55734-036-6) Tchr Create Mat.
—Fun with Social Studies. Gabet, Marcia, illus. 48p. (gr. k-3). 1985. wkbk. 5.95 (1-55734-037-4) Tchr Create Mat.
Gabhart, Ann. Bridge to Courage. 160p. (gr. 6). 1993. pap. 3.50 (0-380-76051-7, Flare) Avon.
—For Sheila. 160p. (Orig.). 1991. pap. 2.95 (0-380-75920-9, Flare) Avon.
—The Gifting. (gr. 6 up). 1987. 2.25 (0-373-98008-6) S&S Trade.
—Only in Sunshine. (gr. 7 up). 1988. pap. 2.95 (0-380-75395-2, Flare) Avon.
—Two of a Kind. (gr. 4-7). 1992. pap. 3.50 (0-380-76153-X, Camelot) Avon.
—Wish Come True. 160p. (gr. 7 up). 1988. pap. 2.50 (0-380-75653-6, Flare) Avon.

Gabin, Martin. Your First Parrot. (Illus.). 36p. (Orig.). 1991. pap. 1.95 (0-86622-070-4, YF-113) TFH Pubns.
Gabler, Mirko. Alphabet Soup. LC 92-1127. (Illus.). 32p. (ps-3). 1992. 14.95 (0-8050-2049-7, Bks Young Read) H Holt & Co.
—Brackus, Krakus. Gabler, Mirko, illus. LC 92-25819. 32p. (ps-3). 1993. PLB 14.95 (0-8050-1963-4, Bks Young Read) H Holt & Co.
Gabriel, Diane & Cohen, Judith. To Puedes Ser una Paleontologa. Yanez, Juan, tr. from ENG. Katz, David, illus. (SPA.). 40p. (gr. 3-7). 1993. pap. text ed. 6.00 (1-880599-13-9) Cascade Pass.
—You Can Be a Woman Paleontologist. Katz, David, illus. LC 93-21349. 40p. (gr. 3-6). 1993. pap. 6.00 (1-880599-12-0) Cascade Pass.
Gabriel, Howard W., III. Growing up with Character: Character Building Stories for Children, Vol. 1. Hasting, Christine Q., illus. 112p. (Orig.). (gr. k-8). 1986. pap. 7.95 (0-936997-00-1, 038601) M & H Enter.
—Loving Memories from Dog to Dog. House, David J., illus. 32p. (Orig.). (gr. k-6). 1987. pap. 2.95 (0-936997-01-X) M & H Enter.
Gabriel, Ingrid. Herb Identifier & Handbook. (Illus.). 128p. (gr. 10-12). 1992. pap. 12.95 (0-8069-8550-X) Sterling.
Gabriel, Nancy, jt. auth. see Barber, Linda.
Gabriel, Suellen, jt. auth. see Beck, Ray.
Gabriele. ABCs. 1985. pap. 1.95 (0-911211-65-9) Penny Lane Pubns.
—Astronauts & Spacecraft. 1985. pap. 1.95 (0-911211-62-4) Penny Lane Pubns.
—Bears. 1985. pap. 1.95 (0-911211-68-3) Penny Lane Pubns.
—Christmas Arts & Crafts. 1985. pap. 1.95 (0-911211-76-4) Penny Lane Pubns.
—Christmas Traditions. 1985. pap. 1.95 (0-911211-78-0) Penny Lane Pubns.
—Last Days of the Dinosaurs. 1984. pap. 1.50 (0-911211-06-3) Penny Lane Pubns.
—Nativity Story. 1985. pap. 1.95 (0-911211-75-6) Penny Lane Pubns.
—The Night Before Christmas. 1985. pap. 1.95 (0-911211-77-2) Penny Lane Pubns.
—One Two Threes. 1985. pap. 1.95 (0-911211-66-7) Penny Lane Pubns.
—Planets. 1986. pap. 1.95 (0-911211-61-6) Penny Lane Pubns.
—Shapes. 1985. pap. 1.95 (0-911211-67-5) Penny Lane Pubns.
—Statue of Liberty & Ellis Island. 1986. pap. 1.95 (0-911211-79-9) Penny Lane Pubns.
—Trains. 1986. pap. 1.95 (0-911211-63-2) Penny Lane Pubns.
—Wild Animals. 1986. pap. 1.95 (0-911211-60-8) Penny Lane Pubns.
Gabriele, Joseph. The First Days of the Dinosaurs: Text Edition. Hurst, Marageret, illus. 32p. (Orig.). (gr. 1-3). pap. 1.95 (0-911211-55-1, Pub. by Know & Show Bks) Penny Lane Pubns.
—The Great Age of the Dinosaurs. Hurst, Margaret, illus. 32p. (Orig.). (gr. 1-3). 1985. pap. text ed. 1.95 (0-911211-56-X, Pub. by Know & Show Bks) Penny Lane Pubns.
—The Last Days of the Dinosaurs: Text Editions. Hurst, Maragaret, illus. 32p. (Orig.). (gr. 1-3). 1985. pap. 1.95 (0-911211-57-8, Pub. by Know & Show Bks) Penny Lane Pubns.
—Prehistoric Reptiles of the Sea & Air: Text Editions. Hurst, Maragaret, illus. 32p. (gr. 1-3). 1985. pap. 1.95 (0-911211-58-6, Pub. by Know & Show Bks) Penny Lane Pubns.
Gabrielson, Ira N., jt. auth. see Zim, Herbert S.
Gackenbach, D. Mighty Tree. 1992. 13.95 (0-15-200519-6, HB Juv Bks) HarBrace.
Gackenbach, Dick. A Bag Full of Pups. LC 80-23230. 32p. (gr. k-3). 1983. pap. 4.95 (0-89919-179-7, Clarion Bks) HM.
—Beauty, Brave & Beautiful. Gackenbach, Dick, illus. LC 89-17418. 32p. (ps-3). 1990. 14.95 (0-395-52000-2) HM.
—Claude Has a Picnic. Gackenbach, Dick, illus. LC 92-8242. 32p. (ps-1). 1993. 14.95 (0-395-61161-X, Clarion Bks) HM.
—Claude the Dog. Gackenbach, Dick, illus. LC 74-3403. 32p. (ps-2). 1982. pap. 4.95 (0-89919-124-X, Clarion Bks) HM.
—Claude the Dog. LC 74-3403. 32p. (ps-2). 1979. 13.45 (0-395-28792-8, Clarion Bks) HM.
—Dog for a Day. Gackenbach, Dick, illus. LC 86-17514. 32p. (ps-1). 1987. (Clarion Bks); pap. 4.95 (0-89919-851-1, Clarion Bks) HM.
—Harry & the Terrible Whatzit. Gackenbach, Dick, illus. LC 76-40205. 32p. (ps-3). 1979. 14.45 (0-395-28795-2, Clarion Bks) HM.
—Harry & the Terrible Whatzit. Gackenbach, Dick, illus. LC 76-40205. 32p. (ps-3). 1984. pap. 4.95 (0-89919-223-8, Clarion Bks) HM.
—Harry y el Terrible Quiensabeque. (ps-3). pap. 2.95 (0-590-41820-3) Scholastic Inc.
—Harvey the Foolish Pig. Gackenbach, Dick, illus. LC 87-15691. 32p. (gr. k-3). 1988. 13.95 (0-89919-540-7, Clarion Bks) HM.
—Hattie Be Quiet, Hattie Be Good. LC 76-58697. (Illus.). 32p. (ps-3). 1977. PLB 13.89 (0-06-021952-1) HarpC Child Bks.
—Hattie Rabbit. LC 75-37018. (Illus.). 32p. (ps-3). 1976. PLB 13.89 (0-06-021940-8) HarpC Child Bks.

—Hattie Rabbit. Gackenbach, Dick, illus. LC 75-37018. 32p. (ps-2). 1990. pap. 2.95 (0-06-444133-4, Trophy) HarpC Child Bks.
—Hattie, Tom, & the Chicken Witch. Gackenbach, Dick, illus. LC 79-2742. 64p. (gr. k-3). 1980. PLB 13.89 (0-06-021959-9) HarpC Child Bks.
—Mag the Magnificent. Gackenbach, Dick, illus. LC 85-2645. 32p. (ps-3). 1987. 12.95 (0-89919-339-0, Clarion Bks); pap. 4.95 (0-89919-522-9, Clarion Bks) HM.
—Poppy the Panda. Gackenbach, Dick, illus. LC 84-4952. 32p. (ps-3). 1984. 14.45 (0-89919-276-9, Pub. by Clarion); pap. 4.80 (0-89919-492-3, Pub. by Clarion) HM.
—Supposes. Gackenbach, Dick, illus. 103p. (ps-3). 1989. 12.95 (0-15-200594-3, Gulliver Bks) HarBrace.
—Timid Timothy's Tongue Twisters. Gackenbach, Dick, illus. (gr. k-3). 1989. bk. & cassette 19.95 (0-87499-128-5); bk. & cassette 12.95 (0-87499-127-7); 4 cassettes & guide 27.95 (0-87499-129-3) Live Oak Media.
—Tiny for a Day. Gackenbach, Dick, illus. LC 92-37580. 1993. 14.45 (0-395-65616-8, Clarion Bks) HM.
—What's Claude Doing? LC 83-14983. (Illus.). 32p. (ps-3). 1986. pap. 4.95 (0-89919-464-8, Clarion Bks) HM.
—With Love from Gran. Gackenbach, Dick, illus. LC 88-35248. 32p. (ps). 1989. 13.45 (0-89919-842-2, Clarion Bks) HM.
Gackenbach, Dick, adapted by. & illus. Timid Timothy's Tongue Twisters. LC 85-30531. 32p. (ps-3). 1986. reinforced bdg. 14.95 (0-8234-0610-5) Holiday.
Gackenbash, Dick. With Love from Gran. (ps-3). 1990. pap. 5.70 (0-395-54775-X, Clarion Bks) HM.
Gacono, Carl B. & Meloy, J. Reid. The Rorschach Assessment of Aggressive & Psychopathic Personalities. 250p. 1994. text ed. 40.00 (0-8058-0980-5) L Erlbaum Assocs.
Gad, Carol L., jt. auth. see Null, Cheryl J.
Gadler, Steve & Adamson, Wendy. Sun Power: Facts About Solar Energy. LC 77-92290. (Illus.). 104p. (gr. 5 up). 1978. PLB 11.95 (0-8225-0643-2) Lerner Pubns.
Gadzella, Bernadette, jt. auth. see Brown, William F.
Gaeddart, Louann. Your Former Friend, Matthew. 80p. 1985. pap. 2.25 (0-553-15345-5, Skylark) Bantam.
Gaeddert, John, jt. ed. see Hartzler, Arlene.
Gaeddert, LouAnn. Breaking Free. LC 93-22600. 144p. (gr. 3-7). 1994. SBE 14.95 (0-689-31883-9, Atheneum Child Bk) Macmillan Child Grp.
—A Summer Like Turnips. LC 88-37380. 80p. (gr. 2-4). 1989. 13.95 (0-8050-0839-X, Bks Young Read) H Holt & Co.
Gaelen, Nina. The Hebrew Primer: Script Writing Workbook. 63p. (gr. 4-7). 1987. pap. text ed. 2.95x (0-87441-416-4) Behrman.

Gaes, Jason. My Book for Kids with Cansur: A Child's Autobiography of Hope. LC 87-60794. (Illus.). 32p. (gr. 1-7). 1987. 12.95 (0-937603-04-X) Melius Pub.
The basis for an Academy Award winning documentary, MY BOOK FOR KIDS WITH CANSUR has been translated into French, German & Japanese. Seven-year-old Jason was in the midst of a battle with cancer when he wrote this book. Jason survived & his book is a stunning legacy for the children & parents who must face the terror of cancer. Jason wrote this book for his peers, but his words inspire young & old. "A touching work. All ages."--PUBLISHER'S WEEKLY. A valuable resource, MY BOOK FOR KIDS WITH CANSUR is used by teachers & health care professionals to help children, their schoolmates & their parents deal with the onset of a child's cancer. "The true strength of this story for children is that Jason honestly & openly shares his experiences & fears & continues to supply hope. Young readers know that they are truly sharing an experience with a peer."--JOURNAL OF THE AMERICAN MEDICAL ASSOCATION. "A moving source of hope."--LOS ANGELES TIMES. Melius Publishing, 118 River Road, Pierre, SD 57501. 1-800-882-5171. *Publisher Provided Annotation.*

—My Book for Kids with Cansur: A Child's Autobiography of Hope. Gaes, Adam & Gaes, Tim, illus. LC 90-63822. 34p. (gr. 1-8). 1991. pap. 6.95 (0-937603-09-0) Melius Pub.

Gaetano, Ronald J. & Masterson, James J. Teenage Drug Abusers: One Hundred Most Commonly Asked Questions about Adolescent Substance Abuse. 128p. (gr. 9 up). 1988. write for info. Union Hosp Found.

Gaff, Jackie. Buildings, Bridges & Tunnels. Fisher, Michael, et al, illus. LC 91-212. 40p. (Orig.). (gr. 2-5). 1991. pap. 3.99 (0-679-80865-5) Random Bks Yng Read.

—Guide to France. LC 93-39008. 1994. 3.95 (1-85697-958-X) Kingfisher Bks.

Gaff, Sha. Bunny Butz Sings the Blues. Geurts, Kelly, illus. LC 91-67753. 70p. 1993. pap. 7.00 (1-56002-161-6, Univ Edtns) Aegina Pr.

Gaffigan, Catherine, ed. By Kids, for Kids. LC 93-31562. 64p. (Orig.). (gr. 4-6). 1994. pap. 7.95 (0-9627226-8-5) Excalibur Publishing.

Gaffney, Eugene S. Dinosaurs. (gr. 3 up). 1990. pap. write for info. (0-307-24076-2) Western Pub.

Gaffney, T. Kennedy Space Center. LC 85-11317. 48p. (gr. k-4). 1985. pap. 4.95 (0-516-01244-7) Childrens.

Gaffney, Timothy R. Chuck Yeager: First Man to Fly Faster than Sound. LC 86-9555. (Illus.). 128p. (gr. 4 up). 1986. PLB 18.60 (0-516-03223-2) Childrens.

—Edmund Hillary: First to Climb Mt. Everest. LC 89-28624. (Illus.). 128p. (gr. 3 up). 1990. PLB 26.60 (0-516-03052-3) Childrens.

Gaffron, Norma. The Bermuda Triangle: Opposing Viewpoints. LC 87-7502. (Illus.). 96p. (gr. 5-8). 1988. lib. bdg. 14.95 (0-89908-055-3) Greenhaven.

—Bigfoot: Opposing Viewpoints. (Illus.). 112p. (gr. 5-8). 1989. PLB 14.95 (0-89908-058-8) Greenhaven.

—Dealing with Death. LC 89-37592. (Illus.). 96p. (gr. 5 up). 1989. PLB 14.95 (1-56006-108-1) Lucent Bks.

—El Dorado, Land of Gold: Opposing Viewpoints. LC 90-3838. (Illus.). 112p. (gr. 5-8). 1990. PLB 14.95 (0-89908-086-3) Greenhaven.

—Unicorns: Opposing Viewpoints. LC 89-11660. (Illus.). 112p. (gr. 5-8). 1989. PLB 14.95 (0-89908-063-4) Greenhaven.

Gafney, Leo, ed. see Gurau, Peter K. & Lieberthal, Edwin M.

Gag, Wanda. ABC Bunny. Gag, Wanda, illus. LC 33-27359. (gr. k-2). 1978. 14.95 (0-698-20000-4, Coward); (Coward); pap. 6.95 (0-698-20683-5, Coward) Putnam Pub Group.

—The Funny Thing. (Illus.). 32p. (ps-3). 1991. pap. 4.95 (0-698-20676-2, Sandcastle) Putnam Pub Group.

—Millions of Cats. Gag, Wanda, illus. 112p. (gr. k-3). 1977. 9.95 (0-698-20091-8, Coward) Putnam Pub Group.

—Millions of Cats. (Illus.). 112p. (gr. k-3). 1977. pap. 4.95 (0-698-20637-1, Sandcastle) Putnam Pub Group.

Gage, Rodney. Let's Talk about AIDS & Sex. LC 92-30853. 1992. 5.99 (0-8054-6073-X) Broadman.

Gage, Wilson. Cully Cully & the Bear. Stevenson, James, illus. LC 82-11715. (ps-3). 1988. pap. 7.95 incl. cassette (0-688-08401-X, Mulberry) Morrow.

—Cully Cully & the Bear. LC 82-11715. (Illus.). (ps-3). 1983. PLB 14.93 (0-688-01769-X); pap. 3.95 (0-688-07043-4) Greenwillow.

—The Ghost of Five Owl Farm. (gr. 4-8). 1986. pap. 2.50 (0-671-56085-9, Archway) PB.

—Mike's Toads. Rounds, Glen, illus. LC 88-34907. 96p. (gr. 3 up). 1990. 12.95 (0-688-08834-1) Greenwillow.

—Mike's Toads. Rounds, Glen, illus. LC 88-34907. 96p. (gr. 4-6). 1991. pap. 3.95 (0-688-10977-2, Pub. by Beech Tree Bks) Morrow.

—Mrs. Gaddy & the Ghost. Hafner, Marylin, illus. LC 78-16366. 56p. (gr. 1-3). 1979. 14.95 (0-688-80179-X) Greenwillow.

Gage, Wilson, pseud. Mrs. Gaddy & the Ghost. Hafner, Marilyn, illus. LC 78-16366. 56p. (gr. 1-3). 1991. pap. 4.95 (0-688-10996-9, Mulberry) Morrow.

Gage, Wilson. My Stars, It's Mrs. Gaddy! Hafner, Marylin, illus. LC 90-478577. 96p. (gr. 1 up). 1991. 15.95 (0-688-10514-9) Greenwillow.

Gagnon, Constance. Help! for Preschoolers. 64p. (ps). 1982. 5.95 (0-86653-061-4, GA 412) Good Apple.

Gagnon, Daniel & Morningstar, Amadea. Breathe Free: Nutritional & Herbal Care for Your Respiratory System. LC 90-24413. 180p. (Orig.). 1991. pap. 14.95 (0-914955-07-1) Lotus Light.

Gaidar. Cyk i Gek. (gr. 7-12). pap. 5.95 (0-88436-051-2, 65250) EMC.

Gaige, Amity. We Are a Thunderstorm. Thatch, Nancy R., ed. Melton, David, intro. by. LC 90-5922. (Illus.). 26p. 1990. PLB 14.95 (0-933849-27-3) Landmark Edns.

Gaige, Grace, ed. Recitations for Younger Children. LC 78-74816. (gr. 3-8). 1979. Repr. of 1927 ed. 19.50x (0-89609-134-1) Roth Pub Inc.

Gainer, Cindy, jt. auth. see Kohl, MaryAnn F.

Gaines, Ann. Alexander von Humboldt, Colossus of Exploration. Goetzmann, William H., ed. Collins, Michael, intro. by. (Illus.). 112p. (gr. 5 up). 1991. lib. bdg. 18.95 (0-7910-1313-8) Chelsea Hse.

—Herodotus & the Explorers of the Classical Age. Goetzmann, William H., ed. Collins, Michael, intro. by. (Illus.). 112p. (gr. 6-12). 1993. PLB 19.95 (0-7910-1293-X) Chelsea Hse.

—John Wesley Powell & the Great Surveys of the American West. 112p. (gr. 5 up). 1992. lib. bdg. 18.95 (0-7910-1318-9) Chelsea Hse.

Gaines, Charles, jt. auth. see Schwarzenegger, Arnold.

Gaines, Charles K. By the Will of Apollo. Wilcoxon, Reba, intro. by. LC 76-3310. (gr. 6 up). 1976. 12.95 (0-8265-1204-6) Vanderbilt U Pr.

—Gorgo: A Romance of Old Athens. LC 76-3311. (gr. 6 up). 1976. Repr. of 1903 ed. 12.95 (0-8265-1203-8) Vanderbilt U Pr.

Gaines, Edith, jt. auth. see Ceasor, Frank, Sr.

Gaines, Edith, jt. auth. see Shepard, Mary L.

Gaines, Edith M. Freedom Train: Underground Railroad Stories from Ripley, Ohio. Clay, Cliff, illus. (Orig.). (gr. 5-8). 1991. pap. 6.95 (0-913678-20-1) New Day Pr.

Gaines, Edith M., et al. Black Image Makers. Adrine-Robinson, Kenyette, ed. Belanger, Ray, et al, illus. Gregory, Dick, frwd. by. (Orig.). (gr. 5-9). 1988. pap. 5.00 (0-913678-17-1) New Day Pr.

Gaines, M. C., ed. Picture Stories from the Bible: The New Testament in Full-Color Comic-Strip Form. Cameron, Don, illus. LC 80-51593. 144p. (gr. 3-10). 1980. Repr. of 1946 ed. 12.95 (0-934386-02-1) Scarf Pr.

—Picture Stories from the Bible: The Old Testament in Full-Color Comic-Strip Form. Cameron, Don, illus. LC 79-66064. 222p. (gr. 3-10). 1979. Repr. of 1943 ed. 12.95 (0-934386-01-3) Scarf Pr.

Gaines, Richard. The Explorers of the Undersea World. Goetzmann, William H., ed. Collins, Michael, intro. by. (Illus.). 112p. (gr. 6-12). 1994. PLB 19.95 (0-7910-1323-5, Am Art Analog) Chelsea Hse.

Gair, Angela. How to Draw & Paint People. 1991. 12.98 (1-55521-717-6) Bk Sales Inc.

Gajadin, Chitra & Tagore, Rabindranath, eds. Amal & the Letter from the King: Adapted from a Play by Rabindranath Tagore. Ong, Helen, illus. 40p. 1992. PLB 14.95 (1-56397-120-8) Boyds Mills Pr.

Gajewski, N. & Mayo, P. POW! Personal Power! (gr. 5-12). 1992. 39.00 (0-930599-76-4) Thinking Pubns.

Gajewski, Nancy & Mayo, Patty. SSS: Social Skill Strategies, Bk. A: A Curriculum for Adolescents, Bk. A. 336p. (gr. 5-12). 1989. pap. 33.00 (0-930599-51-9) Thinking Pubns.

Gajewski, Nancy, jt. auth. see Mayo, Patty.

Gakken Co. Ltd. Editors. Famous Places. Time-Life Books Inc. Editors, tr. 90p. (gr. k-3). 1989. write for info. (0-8094-4893-9); PLB write for info. (0-8094-4894-7) Time-Life.

Gakken Co. Ltd. Editors, ed. Things to Do. Time-Life Books Inc. Editors, tr. 90p. (gr. k-3). 1989. write for info. (0-8094-4897-1); PLB write for info. (0-8094-4898-X) Time-Life.

—Wheels & Wings. Time-Life Books Inc. Editors, tr. (Illus.). 90p. (gr. k-3). 1988. 15.93 (0-8094-4861-0); PLB 21.27 (0-8094-4862-9) Time-Life.

—World We Live In. Time-Life Books Inc Editors, tr. 90p. (gr. k-3). 1989. write for info. (0-8094-4885-8); PLB write for info. (0-8094-4886-6) Time-Life.

Gakken Co. Ltd., Staff, ed. Our Bodies. Time-Life Books Inc., Staff, tr. (Illus.). 90p. (gr. k-3). 1991. write for info. (0-8094-9450-7); lib. bdg. write for info. (0-8094-9451-5); text ed. write for info. (0-8094-9452-3); pap. write for info. (0-8094-9453-1) Time-Life.

Gakken Co. Ltd. Staff, ed. Wind & Weather. Time-Life Books Inc. Editors, tr. (Illus.). 90p. (gr. k-3). 1989. 15.93 (0-8094-4829-7); PLB 21.27 (0-8094-4830-0) Time-Life.

Gal, Laszlo. East of the Sun & West of the Moon. 1993. 16.95 (1-895565-29-4) Firefly Bks Ltd.

—Prince Ivan & the Firebird. Gal, Laszlo, illus. 40p. 1992. text ed. 14.95 (0-920668-98-4) Firefly Bks Ltd.

Galan, Mark, jt. auth. see Dickson, Edward.

Galas, Judith. Anesthetics: Surgery Without Pain. LC 92-27852. (Illus.). 96p. (gr. 5-8). 1992. PLB 15.95 (1-56006-224-X) Lucent Bks.

Galbraith, Catherine A. & Mehta, Rama. India Now & Through Time. 160p. (gr. 6 up). 1980. 16.45 (0-395-29207-7) HM.

Galbraith, Judy. The Gifted Kids Survival Guide (For Ages 10 & Under) LC 83-83015. (Illus.). 72p. (Orig.). (gr. k-5). 1984. pap. 7.95 (0-915793-00-8) Free Spirit Pub.

—The Gifted Kids Survival Guide (for ages 11-18) LC 84-80997. (Illus.). 144p. (Orig.). (gr. 5-12). 1983. pap. 8.95 (0-915793-01-6) Free Spirit Pub.

Galbraith, Judy, jt. auth. see Delisle, James.

Galbraith, Kathryn. Laura Charlotte. Cooper, Floyd, illus. 32p. (ps-3). 1990. 14.95 (0-399-21613-8, Philomel Bks) Putnam Pub Group.

Galbraith, Kathryn O. Laura Charlotte. Cooper, Floyd, illus. 32p. (ps up). 1993. pap. 5.95 (0-399-22514-5, Philomel Bks) Putnam Pub Group.

—Look! Snow! Montezinos, Nina, illus. LC 91-28250. 32p. (gr. k-3). 1992. SBE 13.95 (0-689-50551-5, M K McElderry) Macmillan Child Grp.

—Roommates. LC 89-33434. (Illus.). 48p. (gr. 1-4). 1990. SBE 12.95 (0-689-50487-X, M K McElderry) Macmillan Child Grp.

—Roommates. 48p. (gr. 1). 1991. pap. 2.99 (0-380-71357-8, Camelot) Avon.

—Roommates Again. Graham, Mark, illus. LC 93-8709. 1994. write for info. (0-689-50592-2, M K McElderry) Macmillan Child Grp.

—Roommates Again. Graham, Mark, illus. LC 93-8709. 48p. (gr. 1-4). 1994. SBE 13.95 (0-689-50597-3, M K McElderry) Macmillan Child Grp.

—Roommates & Rachel. Graham, Mark, illus. LC 90-34768. 48p. (gr. 1-4). 1991. SBE 12.95 (0-689-50520-5, M K McElderry) Macmillan Child Grp.

—Roommates & Rachel. 48p. (gr. 1). 1993. pap. 3.50 (0-380-71762-X, Camelot Young) Avon.

—Something Suspicious. 128p. (gr. 3 up). 1987. pap. 2.50 (0-380-70253-3, Camelot) Avon.

Galbreath, Bob. Tennessee Red Berry Tales. Garrett, Deborah G., ed. 97p. (Orig.). (gr. 3 up). 1986. pap. 7.95 (0-9616918-0-8) Whites Creek Pr.

Galchutt, David. There Was Magic Inside. LC 91-44107. (Illus.). 40p. (ps-2). 1993. pap. 14.00 JRT (0-671-75978-7, S&S BFYR) S&S Trade.

Galdone, Joanna. The Tailypo. LC 77-23289. (Illus.). 48p. (ps-4). 1979. 14.45 (0-395-28809-6, Clarion Bks) HM; pap. 4.80 (0-395-30084-3) HM.

Galdone, Paul. The Amazing Pig. LC 80-16990. (Illus.). 32p. (ps-3). 1981. 14.45 (0-395-29101-1, Clarion Bks) HM.

—Cat Goes Fiddle-i-Fee. Galdone, Paul, illus. LC 85-2686. 32p. (ps-3). 1985. 13.95 (0-89919-336-6, Clarion Bks) HM.

—Cat Goes Fiddle-I-Fee. LC 85-2686. (Illus.). (ps-1). 1988. pap. 4.95 (0-89919-705-1, Clarion Bks) HM.

—The Elves & the Shoemaker. Galdone, Paul, illus. LC 83-14979. 32p. (ps-3). 1986. 13.95 (0-89919-226-2, Clarion Bks); pap. 4.95 (0-89919-422-2, Clarion Bks) HM.

—Henny Penny. Galdone, Paul, illus. LC 68-24735. 32p. (ps-3). 1979. 13.45 (0-395-28800-2, Clarion Bks) HM.

—Henny Penny. Galdone, Paul, illus. LC 68-24735. 32p. (ps-3). 1984. pap. 4.95 (0-89919-225-4, Clarion Bks) HM.

—Jack & the Beanstalk. Galdone, Paul, illus. LC 73-9726. 32p. (ps-3). 1982. pap. 4.95 (0-89919-085-5, Clarion Bks) HM.

—King of the Cats: A Ghost Story. Galdone, Paul, illus. LC 79-16659. (gr. k-3). 1985. pap. 4.95 (0-89919-400-1, Clarion Bks) HM.

—The Little Red Hen. LC 72-97770. (Illus.). 32p. (ps-2). 1979. 13.45 (0-395-28803-7, Clarion Bks) HM.

—The Little Red Hen. LC 84-4311. (Illus.). 48p. (ps-3). 1985. pap. 4.95 (0-89919-349-8, Clarion Bks) HM.

—Little Red Hen. (ps-3). 1987. incl. cass. 6.95 (0-317-64569-2) HM.

—Little Tuppen. Galdone, Paul, illus. LC 67-10364. 32p. (ps-3). 1976. 14.45 (0-395-28040-5, Clarion Bks) HM.

—Little Tuppen: An Old Tale. Galdone, Paul, illus. 32p. (ps-2). 1991. pap. 5.70 (0-395-58104-4, Clarion Bks) HM.

—The Magic Porridge Pot. Galdone, Paul, illus. LC 76-3531. 32p. (ps-3). 1979. 13.45 (0-395-28805-3, Clarion Bks) HM.

—Monkey & The Crocodile. Galdone, Paul, illus. LC 78-79939. 32p. (ps-3). 1987. 13.45 (0-395-28806-1, Pub. by Clarion); pap. 4.80 (0-89919-524-5, Pub. by Clarion) HM.

—Nightmare in History: The Holocaust 1933-1945. (ps). 1992. pap. 5.70 (0-395-61579-8, Clarion Bks) HM.

—Over in the Meadow. (gr. 1). 1991. pap. write for info. (0-663-56210-4) Silver Burdett Pr.

—Puss in Boots. Galdone, Paul, illus. LC 75-25505. 32p. (ps-4). 1979. 13.45 (0-395-28808-8, Clarion Bks) HM.

—Puss in Boots. LC 75-25505. 32p. (gr. k-3). 1983. pap. 4.95 (0-89919-192-4, Clarion Bks) HM.

—Puss 'N Boots. (ps-3). 1987. incl. cass. 6.95 (0-317-64571-4) HM.

—Rumpelstiltskin. Galdone, Paul, illus. LC 84-12741. 32p. (ps-3). 1985. 13.95 (0-89919-266-1, Clarion Bks) HM.

—The Teeny Tiny Woman. Galdone, Paul, illus. LC 84-4311. 32p. (ps-3). 1984. 14.95 (0-89919-270-X, Pub. by Clarion); pap. 4.95 (0-89919-463-X, Pub. by Clarion) HM.

—The Teeny-Tiny Woman. Galdone, Paul, illus. 1993. Incl. cassette. 7.70 (0-395-52602-7, Clarion Bks) HM.

—Three Aesop Fox Fables. Galdone, Paul, illus. LC 79-133061. 32p. (ps-2). 1979. 13.45 (0-395-28810-X, Clarion Bks) HM.

—The Three Bears. Galdone, Paul, illus. LC 78-158833. 32p. (ps-3). 1985. pap. 5.95 (0-89919-401-X, Clarion Bks) HM.

—The Three Billy Goats Gruff. Galdone, Paul, illus. 32p. (ps-3). 1981. pap. 4.95 (0-89919-035-9, Clarion Bks) HM.

—Three Little Kittens. Galdone, Paul, illus. LC 86-2655. 32p. (ps-3). 1986. 13.95 (0-89919-426-5, Clarion Bks); pap. 4.95 (0-89919-796-5, Clarion Bks) HM.

—Three Little Pigs. Galdone, Paul, illus. LC 75-123456. (ps-3). 1979. 13.45 (0-395-28813-4, Clarion Bks) HM.

—The Three Little Pigs. Galdone, Paul, illus. LC 75-123456. 40p. (Orig.). 1984. pap. 4.95 (0-89919-275-0, Clarion Bks) HM.

—Three Little Pigs. (gr. 1 up). 1987. incl. cass. 6.95 (0-317-64579-X) HM.

—The Turtle & the Monkey. Galdone, Paul, illus. 32p. (ps-3). 1990. pap. 4.80 (0-395-54425-4, Clarion Bks) HM.

—What's in Fox's Sack. Galdone, Paul, illus. 32p. (ps-1). 1982. 13.95 (0-89919-062-6, Clarion Bks) HM.

—What's in Fox's Sack? LC 81-10251. (Illus.). (gr. 1-3). 1987. pap. 4.95 (0-89919-491-5, Clarion Bks) HM.

Galdone, Paul, jt. auth. see Titus, Eve.

Galdone, Paul, retold by. & illus. The Gingerbread Boy. LC 74-11461. 40p. (ps-3). 1983. 14.45 (0-395-28799-5, Clarion Bks) HM; pap. 4.95 (0-89919-163-0, Clarion) HM.

—The Monster & the Tailor. LC 82-1246. 32p. (ps-1). 1988. pap. 5.70 (*0-89919-795-7*, Clarion Bks) HM.
Galdone, Paul, adapted by. & illus. Over in the Meadow. (ps-1). 1989. (S&S BFYR); pap. 5.95 (*0-671-67837-X*, S&S BFYR) S&S Trade.
Galdone, Paul, ed. & illus. The Three Bears. LC 78-158833. 32p. (ps-3). 1979. 14.45 (*0-395-28811-8*, Clarion Bks) HM.
Galdone, Paul, retold by. & illus. The Three Billy Goats Gruff. LC 72-85338. 32p. (ps-3). 1979. 14.95 (*0-395-28812-6*, Clarion Bks) HM.
Galdone, Paul, illus. Little Red Riding Hood. LC 74-6426. 32p. (gr. k-3). 1974. text ed. 14.95 (*0-07-022732-2*) McGraw.
Galdston, Olive. Play with Puppets. rev. ed. Galdston, Olive, illus. 52p. (Orig.). (ps up) 1971. pap. 1.50x (*0-686-01100-7*); pap. text ed. 1.50x (*0-936426-07-1*) Play Schs.
Gale, Ann De see De Gale, Ann.
Gale, Clarice W., jt. auth. see Gale, Frank C.
Gale, David, ed. Don't Give up the Ghost: The Delacorte Book of Original Ghost Stories. LC 92-47088. 1993. 14.95 (*0-385-31109-5*) Delacorte.
Gale, Frank C. & Gale, Clarice W. Experiences with Plants for Young Children. Solis-Navarro, Kelly, illus. Durett, Mary E., frwd. by. LC 78-88376. (Illus.). (ps-3). 1975. 12.95x (*0-87015-211-4*) Pacific Bks.
Gale, Jay. A Young Man's Guide to Sex. (Illus.). 256p. 1988. pap. 9.95 (*0-89586-691-9*, Body Pr-Perigee) Putnam Pub Group.
Gale, Wendy, illus. Jack-O-Faces Big Book. (ps-2). 1988. pap. text ed. 14.00 (*0-922053-23-5*) N Edge Res.
Galeone, Victor. The Great Drama of Jesus: A Life of Christ for Teens Who Want to Be Challenged. Reid, James, illus. 207p. (Orig.). (gr. 7-8). 1979. pap. 7.95 (*0-913382-31-0*, 101-28) Prow Bks-Franciscan.
Galeoti, Mike. Among the Dead. 80p. (Orig.). 1992. pap. 10.00 (*1-55878-107-2*) Game Designers.
Galeron, Henri, illus. Chat. (FRE.). (ps-1). 1989. 8.95 (*2-07-035703-1*) Schoenhof.
Gales, Donald M. Handbook of Wildflowers, Weeds, Wildlife & Weather of the South Bay & Palos Verdes (California) 3rd, rev. ed. 240p. (gr. 8 up). 1988. pap. 12.00 (*0-317-89904-X*) D M Gales.
Galicich, Anne. The German Americans. Moynihan, Daniel P. (Illus.). 112p. (gr. 5 up). 1989. lib. bdg. 17.95 (*1-55546-141-7*); pap. 9.95 (*0-7910-0265-9*) Chelsea Hse.
—Samantha Smith: A Journey for Peace. LC 87-13614. (Illus.). 64p. (gr. 3 up). 1988. RSBE 13.95 (*0-87518-367-0*, Dillon) Macmillan Child Grp.
Gallagher, I. J. The Case of the Ancient Astronauts. LC 77-10822. (Illus.). 48p. (gr. 4 up). 1977. PLB 18.64 (*0-8172-1059-8*) Raintree Steck-V.
Gallagher, Matthew P., Jr. Hans & the Gold Nugget. 16p. (gr. 3). 1993. pap. 6.95 (*0-9636119-0-9*) Gallagher & Assocs.
Gallagher, Patricia C., ed. see Mohan, Claire J.
Gallagher, Rosemary R. Reinforcing Reference Skills. (gr. 4-6). 1987. pap. 8.95 (*0-8224-4672-3*) Fearon Teach Aids.
Gallant, Janet. My Brother's Bar Mitzvah. Avishai, Susan, illus. LC 90-4879. 32p. (ps-3). 1990. 12.95 (*0-929371-20-8*); pap. 4.95 (*0-929371-21-6*) Kar Ben.
Gallant, Morrie. The Nuttiest Riddle Book in the World. Hoffman, Sanford, illus. LC 93-7871. 96p. (gr. 2-10). 1993. 12.95 (*0-8069-0420-8*) Sterling.
Gallant, Roy. The Planets: Exploring the Solar System. rev. ed. LC 84-29725. (Illus.). 192p. (gr. 7 up). 1990. Repr. of 1985 ed. SBE 15.95 (*0-02-735773-2*, Four Winds) Macmillan Child Grp.
Gallant, Roy A. Ancient Indians: The First Americans. LC 87-36526. (Illus.). 128p. (gr. 6 up). 1989. lib. bdg. 17.95 (*0-89490-187-7*) Enslow Pubs.
—Before the Sun Dies: The Story of Evolution. LC 88-8284. (Illus.). 224p. (gr. 5 up). 1989. SBE 15.95 (*0-02-735771-6*, Macmillan Child Bk) Macmillan Child Grp.
—The Constellations: How They Came to Be. rev. ed. LC 84-28755. (Illus.). 224p. (gr. 7 up). 1991. SBE 15.95 (*0-02-735776-7*, Four Winds) Macmillan Child Grp.
—Earth's Changing Climate. Gallant, Roy A., illus. LC 78-22124. 240p. (gr. 7 up). 1984. SBE 14.95 (*0-02-736840-8*, Four Winds) Macmillan Child Grp.
—Earth's Vanishing Forests. LC 91-2624. (Illus.). 176p. (gr. 5-9). 1992. SBE 14.95 (*0-02-735774-0*, Macmillan Child Bk) Macmillan Child Grp.
—The Macmillan Book of Astronomy. Miller, Ron, et al, illus. LC 86-24158. 80p. (gr. 3-7). 1986. pap. 8.95 (*0-02-043230-5*, Aladdin) Macmillan Child Grp.
—Macmillan Book of Astronomy. LC 85-24158. (Illus.). 80p. (gr. 3-7). 1986. SBE 15.95 (*0-02-738040-8*, Macmillan Child Bk) Macmillan Child Grp.
—Memory: How It Works & How to Improve It. LC 85-4471. (Illus.). 128p. (gr. 7 up). 1984. Repr. of 1980 ed. SBE 12.95 (*0-02-736850-5*, Four Winds) Macmillan Child Grp.
—National Geographic Picture Atlas of Our Universe. Sedeen, Margaret, ed. Collins, Michael, frwd. by. (Illus.). 276p. (gr. 6 up). 1980. 23.95 (*0-87044-356-9*); lib. bdg. 18.95 (*0-87044-357-7*) Natl Geog.
—One Hundred & One Questions & Answers about the Universe. LC 84-7875. (Illus.). 96p. (gr. 1-5). 1984. SBE 13.95 (*0-02-736750-9*, Macmillan Child Bk) Macmillan Child Grp.

—The Peopling of Planet Earth: Human Population Growth Through the Ages. LC 89-34575. (Illus.). 128p. (gr. 3-7). 1990. SBE 15.95 (*0-02-735772-4*, Macmillan Child Bk) Macmillan Child Grp.
—Private Lives of the Stars. LC 86-5338. (Illus.). 128p. (gr. 5 up). 1986. SBE 15.95 (*0-02-737350-9*, Macmillan Child Bk) Macmillan Child Grp.
—Rainbows, Mirages, & Sundogs. LC 86-23728. (Illus.). 112p. (gr. 3-7). 1987. SBE 14.95 (*0-02-737010-0*, Macmillan Child Bk) Macmillan Child Grp.
—A Young Person's Guide to Science: Ideas That Change the World. LC 92-12332. (Illus.). 256p. (gr. 5 up). 1993. SBE 16.95 (*0-02-735775-9*, Macmillan Child Bk) Macmillan Child Grp.
Gallardo, Evelyn. Among the Orangutans: The Birute Galdikas Story. LC 92-25777. 1993. 12.95 (*0-8118-0031-8*) Chronicle Bks.
—Among the Orangutans: The Birute Galdikas Story. (gr. 4-7). 1993. pap. 6.95 (*0-8118-0408-9*) Chronicle Bks.
Gallaz, Christophe. Threadbear. Vincent, Gabrielle, illus 40p. (ps-3). 1993. 14.95 (*1-56846-085-6*) Creat Editions.
—Threadbear. Vincent, Gabrielle, illus. Sokolinsky, Martin, tr. from FRE. LC 93-14581. (Illus.). 1993. 14.95 (*0-88682-630-6*) Creative Ed.
Gallaz, Chrsitophe. Rose Blanche: Based on the Original Idea of Roberto Innocenti. Delessert, Etienne & Redpath, Ann, eds. Coventry, Martha, tr. from FRE. LC 85-70219. (Illus.). 32p. (gr. 6 up). 1986. PLB 17.95s.p. (*0-87191-994-X*) Creative Ed.
Gallenkamp, Charles, jt. auth. see Meyer, Carolyn.
Gallez, Christophe. Mozart. 32p. (gr. 4). 1990. PLB 14.95s.p. (*0-88682-322-6*) Creative Ed.
Gallico, P. Flowers for Mrs. Harris. abr. ed. (Illus.). 118p. 1964. pap. text ed. 5.95 (*0-582-53024-5*) Longman.
Gallico, Paul. Snow Goose. (gr. 9 up). 1941. 12.00 (*0-394-44593-7*) Knopf Bks Yng Read.
—The Snow Goose. 50th anniversary ed. Peck, Beth, illus. LC 90-46880. 48p. 1992. 16.00 (*0-679-80683-0*); PLB 16.99 (*0-679-90683-5*) Knopf Bks Yng Read.
Gallienne, Eva Le see Andersen, Hans Christian.
Gallienne, Eva Le see Andersen, Hans Christian.
Gallin, Richard, ed. see Brophy, Ann.
Gallin, Richard, ed. see Curson, Marjorie.
Gallin, Richard, ed. see Davies, Mark.
Gallin, Richard, ed. see Durwood, Thomas A.
Gallin, Richard, ed. see Force, Eden.
Gallin, Richard, ed. see Friese, Kai J.
Gallin, Richard, ed. see Gray, James M.
Gallin, Richard, ed. see Hess, Debra.
Gallin, Richard, ed. see Johnson, Jacqueline.
Gallin, Richard, ed. see Potter, Robert R.
Gallin, Richard, ed. see Rowland, Della.
Gallin, Richard, ed. see Rubel, David.
Gallin, Richard, ed. see Wheeler, Leslie A.
Gallin, Richard, ed. see Wilkinson, Brenda.
Gallina, Jill, jt. auth. see Gallina, Michael.
Gallina, Michael & Gallina, Jill. The Inside Pitch. Singer's ed. (gr. k-6). 1989. 2.95 (*0-931205-47-6*); tchr's ed. (gr. k-6). 1989. 14.95 (*0-931205-46-8*) Jenson Pubns.
—Movin' Right along with Me. (gr. k-6). 1989. 14.95 (*0-931205-51-4*) Jenson Pubns.
Gallivan, Marion F. Fun for Kids II: An Index to Craft Books. LC 92-16667. 483p. (Illus.). 1992. 42.50 (*0-8108-2546-5*) Scarecrow.
Gallo, Donald. Presenting Richard Peck. LC 89-32346. 176p. (gr. 8 up). 1989. text ed. 19.95x (*0-8057-8209-5*, Twayne) Macmillan.
Gallo, Donald R. Presenting Richard. 1993. pap. 4.99 (*0-440-21888-8*) Dell.
—Short Circuits. 1993. pap. 4.99 (*0-440-21889-6*) Dell.
—Within Reach: Ten Stories. LC 92-29378. 192p. (gr. 4 up). 1993. 15.00 (*0-06-021440-6*); PLB 14.89 (*0-06-021441-4*) HarpC Child Bks.
Gallo, Donald R., ed. Authors' Insights: Turning Teenagers into Readers & Writers. 131p. (gr. 9-12). 1992. pap. 14.95 (*0-86709-294-7*, 0294) Boynton Cook Pubs.
—Center Stage: One-Act Plays for Teenage Readers & Actors. LC 90-4050. 384p. (gr. 7 up). 1990. 17.00 (*0-06-022170-4*); PLB 16.89 (*0-06-022171-2*) HarpC Child Bks.
—Center Stage: One-Act Plays for Teenage Readers & Actors. LC 90-4050. 384p. (gr. 7 up). 1991. pap. 4.95 (*0-06-447078-4*, Trophy) HarpC Child Bks.
—Join In: Multiethnic Short Stories by Outstanding Writers for Young Adults. LC 92-43169. 1993. 15.95 (*0-385-31080-3*) Delacorte.
—Short Circuits: Thirteen Shocking Stories by Outstanding Writers for Young Adults. LC 91-46164. 192p. (gr. 6 up). 1992. 16.00 (*0-385-30785-3*) Delacorte.
—Sixteen: Short Stories by Outstanding Writers for Young Adults. LC 84-3250. 208p. (gr. 7 up). 1984. 16.95 (*0-385-29346-1*) Delacorte.
—Sixteen: Short Stories by Outstanding Young Adult Writers. 192p. (gr. 5-12). 1985. pap. 3.99 (*0-440-97757-6*, LFL) Dell.
Gallo, Donald R., intro. by. Speaking for Ourselves, Too: More Autobiographical Sketches by Notable Authors of Books for Young Adults. 256p. (Orig.). (gr. 7-12). 1992. pap. 14.50 (*0-8141-4623-6*) NCTE.
Gallo, Donald R., ed. Visions: Nineteen Short Stories by Outstanding Writers for Young Adults. (gr. k-12). 1988. pap. 3.99 (*0-440-20208-6*, LFL) Dell.
—Visions: 19 Short Stories by Outstanding Writers for Young Adults. LC 87-6787. 240p. (gr. 7 up) 1987. pap. 16.95 (*0-385-29588-X*) Delacorte.

Galloway, Anne. Tovangar. 1978. 3.00 (*0-939046-25-3*) Malki Mus Pr.
Galloway, Mary R. & Chiltosky, Mary U. Aunt Mary, Tell Me a Story: A Collection of Cherokee Legends & Tales. Galloway, John B., et al, illus. (Orig.). 1991. pap. 3.00 (*0-9628630-0-9*) Cherokee Comn.

Galloway-Blake, Jacqueline. My African Roots: A Child's Create Your Own Keepsake Book of Family History & African-Awareness. 32p. (ps-7). 1992. Wkbk. 5.95 (*0-9637243-6-3*) Brwn Sug & Spice.
MY AFRICAN ROOTS is a 32-page activity book designed to grow with children ages 4-12 years, who want to record their family history & to learn more about Africa. The book helps families who want to research their genealogy & to get the children involved in the project. There are pages for family reunion photos, autographs, self-portraits & African history. Each year the child adds more information to this unique keepsake book & personalizes the pages with his own drawings & family data. Knowing one's history is a boost to self-esteem. MY AFRICAN ROOTS is an aid to a child's self-discovery & should help him feel better about himself. To enhance academic performance, children need more opportunities for creative thinking & independent study. This book gives the child a constructive personal project to work on. By completing many pages of activities the child sharpens his writing, interviewing & research skills while learning more about himself & his own family. The author, Jacqueline Galloway-Blake is an educational specialist who has spent many years assisting parents, children & teachers in selecting multicultural literature. Exciting activities, informative fill-in pages... this new book encourages research skills, family interaction & artistic expression while increasing the child's self-esteem as he learns more about himself & his African heritage. The 8 1/2" X 11" softcover edition (ISBN 0-9637243-6-3) is available at the Henry Ford Museum-Greenfield Village shops, Dearborn, Michigan or at the wholesale discount (10-24 books at 40% off) from BROWN SUGAR & SPICE, 8584 Whitehorn, Romulus, MI 48174, (313) 729-0501. SRP $5.95. Request COD or prepay. Add 5% shipping. Satisfaction is guaranteed. *Publisher Provided Annotation.*

Gallup, Beth, ed. see Norberg, Jon.
Gallup, Beth, ed. see Pranzo, Donard.
Galperin, Ann. Gynecological Disorders. (Illus.). 112p. (gr. 6-12). 1991. 18.95 (*0-7910-0075-3*) Chelsea Hse.
Galperin, Anne. Nutrition. (Illus.). 120p. (gr. 6-12). 1991. 18.95 (*0-7910-0024-9*) Chelsea Hse.
—Stroke & Heart Disease. (Illus.). 112p. (gr. 6-12). 1991. 18.95 (*0-7910-0077-X*) Chelsea Hse.
Galperin, Anne L. Nuclear Energy - Nuclear Waste. (Illus.). 112p. (gr. 5 up). 1992. PLB 19.95 (*0-7910-1585-8*) Chelsea Hse.
Galt, Hugh. Horse Thief. 208p. (gr. 5-10). 1993. pap. 9.95 (*0-86278-278-3*, Pub. by OBrien Pr IE) Dufour.
Galt, Margot F. The Story in History: Writing Your Way into the American Experience. (Illus.). 280p. (Orig.). 1992. 24.95 (*0-915924-38-2*); pap. 15.95 (*0-915924-39-0*) Tchrs & Writers Coll.
Galton, Grace C., jt. auth. see Bloom, Marjorie W.
Galvin, Irene F. Chile: Land of Poets & Patriots. LC 89-28747. (Illus.). 128p. (gr. 5 up). 1990. RSBE 14.95 (*0-87518-421-9*, Dillon) Macmillan Child Grp.
Galvin, Matthew R. Clouds & Clocks: A Story for Children Who Soil. Ferraro, Sandra, illus. LC 89-12278. 48p. 1989. 16.95 (*0-945354-18-5*); pap. 6.95 (*0-945354-15-0*) Magination Pr.

—Ignatius Finds Help: A Story About Psychotherapy for Children. Ferraro, Sandra, illus. LC 87-34899. 48p. (ps-6). 1988. 16.95 (0-945354-01-0); pap. 6.95 (0-945354-00-2) Magination Pr.
—Robby Really Transforms: A Story About Grown-ups Helping Children. Ferraro, Sandra, illus. LC 87-34883. 48p. (ps-6). 1988. lib. bdg. 16.95 (0-945354-05-3); pap. 6.95 (0-945354-02-9) Magination Pr.
Galway, Bonnie, tr. see Geller, Norman.
Gambill, Henrietta. Are You Listening? Axeman, Lois, illus. LC 85-10349. 32p. (gr. k-2). 1985. PLB 21.35 (0-89565-332-X); PLB 14.95s.p. (0-685-55764-2) Childs World.
—Self-Control. Hutton, Kathryn, illus. LC 82-1201. 32p. (gr. k-3). 1982. PLB 21.35 (0-89565-225-0); PLB 14.95s.p. (0-685-55648-4) Childs World.
Gambill, Henrietta, ed. see Lysne, Mary E.
Gambill, Henrietta G. The First Zoo. Boddy, Joe, illus. 32p. (gr. k-2). 1989. pasted 2.50 (0-87403-592-9, 3852) Standard Pub.
Gambill, Hentietta D. Bible Learning Games. Wimmer, Sandy, illus. 16p. (gr. 1-7). 1993. 8.99 (9-5032-0569-7, 14-02259) Standard Pub.
Gamble, Donna T. Games to Go, 5 bklets. (ps-5). 1989. 27.95 (1-55999-041-4) LinguiSystems.
—Homework to Go: Ready to Go, Ready to Use Worksheets for Communication Practice at Home, 5 bklts. (ps-5). 1990. Set. vinyl 27.95 (1-55999-106-2) LinguiSystems.
Gamboli, Mario. What Else Could It Be? Gamboli, Mario, illus. LC 91-70423. 12p. (ps-k). 1991. bds. 3.95 (1-878093-72-X) Boyds Mills Pr.
—What Is Hiding? Gamboli, Mario, illus. LC 91-70422. 12p. (ps-k). 1991. bds. 3.95 (1-878093-92-4); Set of 3 bks. bds. 11.95 (0-685-66071-0) Boyds Mills Pr.
—What Will It Be? Gamboli, Mario, illus. LC 91-70413. 12p. (ps-k). 1991. bds. 3.95 (1-878093-73-8) Set of 3 bks. 11.85. Boyds Mills Pr.
Gambrell, Jamey, tr. see Kharms, Daniil.
Gamec, Hazel S. The Disappearing ABC Game Book. Gamec, Hazel S., illus. 12p. write for info. (0-938042-02-5) Printek.
—Looking Out of the Window. Gamec, Hazel S., illus. 12p. 1980. write for info. (0-938042-01-7) Printek.
—The Magic Pencil Counting Book. Gamec, Hazel S., illus. 12p. 1980. write for info. (0-938042-00-9) Printek.
Gameillo, Elvira. Kids Word Find Puzzles. (Illus.). 64p. (Orig.). (gr. 4-6). 1988. pap. 1.95 (0-942025-43-1) Kidsbks.
Gamepro Magazine Staff. The Official Street Fighter Two Strategy Guide. 164p. (gr. 7-12). 1992. 9.95 (1-882455-00-2) Gamepro Pub.
Gamgee, John, ed. Journey Through France. Forsey, Chris, illus. LC 91-46175. 32p. (gr. 3-5). 1993. PLB 11.89 (0-8167-2759-7); pap. text ed. 3.95 (0-8167-2760-0) Troll Assocs. Postponed.
Gamiello, Elvira. A-Maze-Ing Chiller Word Search Puzzles. (Illus., Orig.). (gr. 4-6). 1987. pap. 1.95 (0-942025-05-9) Kidsbks.
—A-Maze-Ing Monster Crack-Up Puzzles. (Illus., Orig.). (gr. 4-6). 1987. pap. 1.95 (0-942025-02-4) Kidsbks.
—America's Presidents Activity & Fun Book. (Illus., Orig.). (gr. 4-6). 1989. pap. 1.95 (0-942025-51-2) Kidsbks.
—Crossword Crack-Up Puzzles. (Illus., Orig.). (gr. 4-6). 1987. pap. 1.95 (0-942025-04-0) Kidsbks.
—Dinosaurs Trivia Fun Book. (Illus., Orig.). 32p. (Orig.). 1989. pap. 1.50 (0-942025-09-1) Kidsbks.
—Fun to Find Word Search Puzzles. (Illus., Orig.). (gr. 4-6). 1988. pap. 1.95 (0-942025-37-7) Kidsbks.
—Giant Word Find Dinosaurs Poster Book. (Illus., Orig.). 1988. pap. 1.95 (0-942025-49-0) Kidsbks.
—Haunted Mazes. (Illus.). 96p. (Orig.) 1988. pap. 1.95 (0-942025-29-6) Kidsbks.
—Hidden Messages You Can Solve. (Illus., Orig.). (gr. 4-6). 1989. pap. 1.95 (0-942025-41-5) Kidsbks.
—Maze Madness. (Illus.). 64p. (Orig.). (gr. 4-6). 1988. pap. 1.95 (0-942025-93-8) Kidsbks.
—Monster Activity & Game Book. (Illus., Orig.). (gr. 4-6). 1988. pap. 1.95 (0-942025-28-8) Kidsbks.
—More Fun to Find Word Search. (Illus.). 64p. (Orig.). 1991. pap. 1.95 (1-56156-000-6) Kidsbks.
—Scary Search a Word Puzzles. (Illus., Orig.). (gr. 4-6). 1988. pap. 1.95 (0-942025-39-3) Kidsbks.
—Search-A-Picture Puzzles. (Illus., Orig.). (gr. 4-6). 1987. pap. 1.95 (0-942025-07-5) Kidsbks.
—Secret Codes & Other Word Games. (Illus., Orig.). (gr. 4-6). 1988. pap. 1.95 (0-942025-45-8) Kidsbks.
—Secret Jokes & Hidden Riddles Activity & Fun Book. (Illus., Orig.). (gr. 4-6). 1989. pap. 1.95 (0-942025-25-3) Kidsbks.
—Sharks Activity & Game Book. (Illus., Orig.). (gr. 4-6). 1988. pap. 1.95 (0-942025-46-6) Kidsbks.
—Silly Jokes & Riddles. (Illus.). 96p. (Orig.) 1988. pap. 1.95 (0-942025-32-6) Kidsbks.
—Snowy Days Activity & Game Book. (Illus., Orig.). (gr. 4-6). 1989. pap. 1.95 (0-942025-36-9) Kidsbks.
—Space Age Mazes. (Illus., Orig.). (gr. 4-6). 1989. pap. 1.95 (0-942025-94-6) Kidsbks.
—Spooky Haunted House Puzzles. (Illus., Orig.). (gr. 4-6). 1987. pap. 1.95 (0-942025-06-7) Kidsbks.
—Summertime Puzzle & Fun Book. (Illus., Orig.). (gr. 4-6). 1988. pap. 1.95 (0-942025-62-8) Kidsbks.
—Sunny Days Word Games & Mazes. (Illus., Orig.). (gr. 4-6). 1988. pap. 1.95 (0-942025-40-7) Kidsbks.
—Super Secret Codes & Jokes. (Illus., Orig.). (gr. 4-6). 1990. pap. 1.95 (0-942025-44-X) Kidsbks.

—Vacation Puzzle & Fun Book. (Illus., Orig.). (gr. 4-6). 1989. pap. 1.95 (0-942025-63-6) Kidsbks.
—Wacky Word Search Puzzles. (Illus., Orig.). (gr. 4-6). 1987. pap. 1.95 (0-942025-03-2) Kidsbks.
—Weird & Wacky Word Search Puzzles. (Illus., Orig.). (gr. 4-6). 1988. pap. 1.95 (0-942025-42-3) Kidsbks.
—What's Wrong Here. (Illus., Orig.). (gr. 4-6). 1989. pap. 1.95 (0-942025-91-1) Kidsbks.
—Word Find Puzzles for Kids. (Illus.). 64p. (Orig.). 1988. pap. 1.95 (0-942025-58-X) Kidsbks.
Gamiello, Nina, illus. Funtime Stencils: Animals. 16p. 1992. pap. 2.95 (1-56156-153-3) Kidsbks.
—Funtime Stencils: Cars. 16p. Date not set. pap. 2.95 (1-56156-154-1) Kidsbks.
Gamlin, Linda. The Deer in the Forest. Oxford Scientific Film Staff, illus. LC 87-9916. 32p. (gr. 4-6). 1987. PLB 15.93 (1-55532-273-5) Gareth Stevens Inc.
—Evolution. LC 92-54478. (Illus.). 64p. (gr. 7 up). 1993. 15.95 (1-56458-233-7) Dorling Kindersley.
—The Human Body. FS-Aladdin Staff, ed. Hayward, Ron, illus. LC 88-17792. (Illus.). 32p. (gr. 4-9). 1988. PLB 12.40 (0-531-17117-5) Gloucester Pr) Watts.
—The Human Race. FS-Aladdin Staff, ed. Hayward, Ron, illus. LC 88-50506. 40p. (gr. 1-6). 1988. PLB 12.40 (0-531-17118-3, Gloucester Pr) Watts.
—Life on Earth. FS-Aladdin Staff, ed. Hayward, Ron, illus. 40p. (gr. 4-9). 1988. PLB 12.40 (0-531-17120-5, Gloucester Pr) Watts.
—Origins of Life. FS-Aladdin Staff, ed. Hayward, Ron, illus. 40p. (gr. 4-9). 1988. PLB 12.40 (0-531-17119-1, Gloucester Pr) Watts.
—Trees. LC 92-54310. (Illus.). 64p. (gr. 3 up). 1993. 9.95 (1-56458-230-2) Dorling Kindersley.
Gamlin, Linda, jt. auth. see Staple, Michele.
Gammell, Stephen. Award Puzzles: Song & Dance Man. 1991. 5.95 (0-938971-61-1) JTG Nashville.
—Once upon MacDonald's Farm. Gammell, Stephen, illus. LC 84-29356. 32p. (gr. k-3). 1984. Repr. of 1981 ed. RSBE 13.95 (0-02-737210-3, Four Winds) Macmillan Child Grp.
—Once upon Macdonald's Farm. LC 89-17792. (Illus.). 32p. (gr. k-3). 1990. pap. 3.95 (0-689-71379-7, Aladdin) Macmillan Child Grp.
—Wake up, Bear...It's Christmas! Gammell, Stephen, illus. LC 81-5019. 32p. (ps-3). 1981. PLB 12.88 (0-688-00693-0) Lothrop.
—Wake up, Bear...It's Christmas! LC 81-5019. (Illus.). 32p. (ps-2). 1990. pap. 4.95 (0-688-09934-3, Mulberry) Morrow.
Gamsey, Wayne, ed. see Koenig, Herbert G., et al.
Gamsey, Wayne, ed. see Osborne, John, et al.
Gamsey, Wayne, ed. see Stich, Paul, et al.
Gamsey, Wayne H., ed. see Koenig, Herbert G., et al.
Gamsey, Wayne H., ed. see McCabe, Ann C. & Fairbanks, Eugene B.
Gander, Terry. Artillery. Gibbons, Tony, et al, illus. 48p. (gr. 5 up). 1987. PLB 14.95 (0-8225-1380-3) Lerner Pubns.
Gandhi, Mahatma. Mahatma Gandhi. Redpath, Ann, ed. Delessert, Etienne, illus. 32p. (gr. 4 up). 1985. PLB 12.95s.p. (0-88682-010-3) Creative Ed.
Gandiol-Coppin, Brigitte. Cathedrals: Stone upon Stone. Bogard, Vicki, tr. from FRE. Thibault, Dominique, illus. LC 89-5361. 38p. (gr. k-5). 1989. 4.95 (0-944589-24-3, 024) Young Discovery Lib.
Ganeri, A. Amazing Feats. (Illus.). 48p. (gr. 3-7). 1992. PLB 12.96 (0-88110-584-8); pap. 5.95 (0-7460-0946-1) EDC.
—Animal Facts. (Illus.). 48p. (gr. 3-7). 1988. PLB 12.96 (0-88110-317-9); pap. 5.95 (0-86020-971-7) EDC.
—Bird Facts. (Illus.). 48p. (gr. 3-7). 1991. lib. bdg. 12.96 (0-88110-530-9, Usborne); pap. 5.95 (0-7460-0619-5, Usborne) EDC.
—Body Facts. (Illus.). 48p. (gr. 3-7). 1993. PLB 12.96 (0-88110-599-6); pap. 5.95 (0-7460-0948-8) EDC.
—Nature Facts & Lists. (Illus.). 144p. (gr. 3-7). 1993. pap. 10.95 (0-7460-0645-4, Usborne) EDC.
—Tennis Skills. (Illus.). 48p. (gr. 6-12). (Usborne); pap. 5.95 (0-7460-0173-8) EDC.
—Weather Facts. (Illus.). 48p. (gr. 3-7). 1987. PLB 12.96 (0-88110-241-5); pap. 5.95 (0-86020-975-X) EDC.
Ganeri, Anita. Ancient Egyptians. (Illus.). 32p. (gr. 5-7). 1993. PLB 12.40 (0-531-17373-9, Gloucester Pr) Watts.
—Ancient Greeks. LC 93-11178. (Illus.). (gr. 5 up). 1993. PLB 12.40 (0-531-17369-0, Gloucester Pr) Watts.
—And Now...the Weather. Wingham, Peter, illus. LC 91-26682. 32p. (gr. 5-2). 1992. pap. 5.95 (0-689-71583-8, Aladdin) Macmillan Child Grp.
—Animal Babies. Taylor, Kate, illus. 32p. (ps-1). 1991. 6.95 (0-8120-6241-8) Barron.
—Animal Behavior. Taylor, Kate, illus. 32p. (ps-1). 1992. 6.95 (0-8120-6301-5) Barron.
—Animal Camouflage. Taylor, Kate, illus. 32p. (ps-1). 1991. 6.95 (0-8120-6236-1) Barron.
—Animal Families. Taylor, Kate, illus. 32p. (ps-1). 1992. 6.95 (0-8120-6274-4) Barron.
—Animal Food. Taylor, Kate, illus. 32p. (ps-1). 1992. 6.95 (0-8120-6302-3) Barron.
—Animal Movements. Taylor, Kate, illus. 32p. (ps-1). 1991. 6.95 (0-8120-6238-8) Barron.
—Animal Records. Taylor, Kate, illus. 32p. (ps-1). 1992. 6.95 (0-8120-6300-7) Barron.
—Animal Science. LC 92-25342. (Illus.). 48p. (gr. 5 up). 1993. RSBE 13.95 (0-87518-575-4, Dillon) Macmillan Child Grp.
—Animal Talk. Taylor, Kate, illus. 32p. (ps-1). 1991. 6.95 (0-8120-6239-6) Barron.

—Benares. (Illus.). 48p. (gr. 5 up). 1993. lib. bdg. 13.95 RSBE (0-87518-573-8, Dillon) Macmillan Child Grp.
—Biggest & Smallest: Questions & Answers about Record Breakers. West, David, illus. LC 92-12497. (ps-3). 1992. 6.95 (0-8120-6291-4) Barron.
—Birds. Kline, Marjory, ed. (Illus.). 32p. (gr. 5-8). 1993. PLB 12.40 (0-531-17362-3) Watts.
—Body Science. LC 92-22722. (Illus.). 48p. (gr. 5 up). 1993. RSBE 13.95 (0-87518-576-2, Dillon) Macmillan Child Grp.
—Earth Science. LC 93-16753. (Illus.). 48p. (gr. 5 up). 1993. RSBE 13.95 (0-87518-577-0, Dillon) Macmillan Child Grp.
—Explore the World of Exotic Rainforests. Morton, Robert, illus. 48p. (gr. 3-7). 1992. write for info. (0-307-15606-0, 15606, Golden Pr) Western Pub.
—Families. LC 92-6798. (Illus.). 32p. (gr. 5-8). 1992. PLB 12.40 (0-531-17364-X, Gloucester Pr) Watts.
—Fastest & Slowest: Questions & Answers about Record Breakers. West, David, illus. LC 92-10077. (ps-3). 1992. 6.95 (0-8120-6290-6) Barron.
—First & Last: Questions & Answers about Record Breakers. (ps-3). 1992. 6.95 (0-8120-6292-2) Barron.
—France & the French. (Illus.). 32p. (gr. 5-8). 1993. PLB 12.40 (0-531-17401-8) Watts.
—Germany & the Germans. LC 92-37091. (Illus.). 32p. (gr. 5-8). 1993. PLB 12.40 (0-531-17402-6, Gloucester Pr) Watts.
—Giant Book of Animal Worlds. Butler, John, illus. 14p. (gr. 2-5). 1992. 19.95 (0-525-67369-5, Lodestar Bks) Dutton Child Bks.
—I Wonder Why Camels Have Humps & Other Questions about Animals: And Other Questions about Animals. Holmes, Stephen & Kenyon, Tony, illus. LC 92-44260. 32p. (gr. k-3). 1993. 8.95 (1-85697-873-7) Kingfisher Bks.
—Indoor Science. (Illus.). 48p. (gr. 5 up). 1993. lib. bdg. 13.95 RSBE (0-87518-578-9, Dillon) Macmillan Child Grp.
—Insects. (Illus.). 32p. (gr. 5-7). 1993. PLB 11.90 (0-531-14225-6) Watts.
—Journey Through India. Burns, Robert, illus. LC 91-46176. 32p. (gr. 3-5). 1993. PLB 11.89 (0-8167-2761-9); pap. text ed. 3.95 (0-8167-2762-7) Troll Assocs. Postponed.
—Jungle Birds. Lings, Steve & Weston, Steve, illus. LC 93-19869. 32p. (gr. 4-6). 1993. PLB 19.97 (0-8114-6160-2) Raintree Steck-V.
—Longest & Shortest: Questions & Answers about Record Breakers. LC 92-12502. (ps-3). 1992. 6.95 (0-8120-6293-0) Barron.
—The Oceans Atlas. Corbella, Luciano, illus. LC 93-28724. 1994. write for info. (1-56458-475-5) Dorling Kindersley.
—Outdoor Science. LC 93-13125. (Illus.). 48p. (gr. 5 up). 1993. lib. bdg. 13.95 RSBE (0-87518-579-7, Dillon) Macmillan Child Grp.
—Plant Science. LC 92-36738. (Illus.). 48p. (gr. 5 up). 1993. RSBE 13.95 (0-87518-580-0, Dillon) Macmillan Child Grp.
—Plants. (Illus.). 32p. (gr. 5-8). 1992. PLB 11.90 (0-531-14194-2) Watts.
—Ponds & Pond Life. (Illus.). 32p. (gr. 5-7). 1993. PLB 11.90 (0-531-14226-4) Watts.
—Ponds, Rivers, & Lakes. LC 91-5039. (Illus.). 48p. (gr. 5 up). 1992. RSBE 13.95 (0-87518-497-9, Dillon) Macmillan Child Grp.
—Romans. LC 92-15000. (Illus.). 32p. (gr. 5-8). 1992. PLB 12.40 (0-531-17387-9, Gloucester Pr) Watts.
—Sea Mammals. Ovendon, Dennis & McGregor, Malcolm, illus. LC 93-19706. 32p. (gr. 4-6). 1993. PLB 19.97 (0-8114-6159-9) Raintree Steck-V.
—Small Mammals. LC 92-32706. 1993. 11.90 (0-531-14249-3) Watts.
—Trees. Kline, Marjory, ed. (Illus.). 32p. (gr. 4-7). 1993. PLB 12.90 (0-531-17317-8, Gloucester Pr) Watts.
—Vikings. LC 92-15001. (Illus.). 32p. (gr. 5-8). 1992. PLB 12.40 (0-531-17388-7, Gloucester Pr) Watts.
—The Weather. LC 92-26987. 1993. 11.90 (0-531-14250-7) Watts.
Ganeri, Anita & Butterfield, Maira. Natural World. Bull, Peter & Johnson, Paul, illus. LC 89-11349. 48p. (gr. 4-5). 1989. PLB 17.27 (0-8368-0133-4) Gareth Stevens Inc.
Ganeri, Anita & Wright, Rachel. France. LC 92-27136. 1993. 11.90 (0-531-14256-6) Watts.
Gang, Philip S. Our Planet, Our Home: A Gaia Learning Material. 60p. (gr. 1-9). 1989. Incl. card material. tchr's ed. 30.00 (0-685-27868-9); wkbk. 5.00 (0-685-27869-7) Dagaz Pr.
Gangelhoff, Jeanne M. & Belk, Bradford. A Walk Through the Minnesota Zoo. Gangelhoff, Gene, illus. 32p. Date not set. 9.95 (0-9635006-1-9) G J & B Pub.
Gangwer, Rosalie M. Jesus Calms the Storm: Matthew 8, 23-27 & Mark 4, 35-41 for the Beginning Reader. Mitter, Kathryn, illus. LC 93-17472. 32p. (ps-3). 1993. 6.50 (0-8198-3955-8) St Paul Bks.
Gannett, Ruth S. The Dragons of Blueland. Gannett, Ruth C., illus. LC 86-27480. 96p. (gr. 2-5). 1963. 3.99 (0-394-89050-7) Knopf Bks Yng Read.
—Elmer & the Dragon. Gannett, Ruth C., illus. LC 86-27479. 96p. (gr. 2-5). 1987. PLB 3.99 (0-394-89049-3) Knopf Bks Yng Read.
—My Father's Dragon. gift edition ed. Gannett, Ruth S., illus. LC 48-6527. 88p. (gr. 2-5). 1986. 14.95 (0-394-88460-4); PLB 14.99 (0-394-91438-4) Random Bks Yng Read.

—My Father's Dragon. Gannett, Ruth C., illus. LC 86-27635. 96p. (gr. 2-5). 1987. pap. 3.99 (0-394-89048-5) Knopf Bks Yng Read.
Gannon, Charles E. Darktek Equipment Handbook. 104p. (Orig.). 1991. pap. 12.00 (1-55878-084-X) Game Designers.
Gano, Lila. Hazardous Waste. LC 90-23528. (Illus.). 112p. (gr. 5-8). 1991. PLB 14.95 (1-56006-117-0) Lucent Bks.
—Smoking. LC 89-12650. (Illus.). 96p. (gr. 5-8). 1989. PLB 14.95 (1-56006-103-0) Lucent Bks.
—Television: Electronic Pictures. LC 90-6470. (Illus.). 96p. (gr. 5-8). 1990. PLB 15.95 (1-56006-202-9) Lucent Bks.
Gans, Roma. Caves. Maestro, Giulio, illus. LC 76-4881. 40p. (gr. k-3). 1962. PLB 14.89 (0-690-01070-2, Crowell Jr Bks) HarpC Child Bks.
—Danger--Icebergs! Revised Edition of Icebergs. Rosenblum, Richard, illus. LC 87-45143. 32p. (ps-3). 1987. pap. 4.50 (0-06-445066-X, Trophy) HarpC Child Bks.
—Rock Collecting. 2nd ed. Keller, Holly, illus. LC 83-46170. 32p. (gr. k-3). 1984. PLB 13.89 (0-690-04266-3, Crowell Jr Bks) HarpC Child Bks.
—Rock Collecting. Keller, Holly, illus. LC 83-46170. 32p. (ps-3). 1987. pap. 4.50 (0-06-445063-5, Trophy) HarpC Child Bks.
—Water for Dinosaurs & You. LC 78-158691. (Illus.). (gr. k-3). 1973. PLB 11.89 (0-690-87027-2, Crowell Jr Bks); (TYC-J) HarpC Child Bks.
—When Birds Change Their Feathers. Bond, Felicia, illus. LC 78-20627. 40p. (gr. k-3). 1980. PLB 13.89 (0-690-03948-4, Crowell Jr Bks) HarpC Child Bks.
Gansberger, Christine. Unicorn Color & Story Album. (gr. 2 up). pap. 3.99 (0-8431-1755-9) Troubador Pr.
Gantos, Jack. Happy Birthday, Rotten Ralph. Rubel, Nicole, illus. 32p. (ps-3). 1990. 13.45 (0-395-53766-5) HM.
—Not So Rotten Ralph. Rubel, Nicole, illus. LC 93-759. (gr. 4 up). 1994. write for info. (0-395-62302-2) HM.
—Rotten Ralph. Rubel, Nicole, illus. LC 75-34101. 48p. (gr. k-3). 1976. 13.95 (0-395-24276-2); pap. 4.50 (0-685-02307-9) HM.
—Rotten Ralph. Rubel, Nicole, illus. (gr. k-3). 1980. pap. 4.80 (0-395-29202-6, Sandpiper) HM.
—Rotten Ralph. Rubel, Nicole, illus. 1988. Incl. cass. pap. 7.70 (0-395-48873-7) HM.
—Rotten Ralph's Rotten Christmas. Rubel, Nicole, illus. LC 84-664. 32p. (ps-3). 1984. 13.95 (0-395-35380-7); pap. 17.95 incl. doll (0-395-45346-1); pap. 4.80 (0-395-45685-1) HM.
—Rotten Ralph's Show & Tell. Rubel, Nicole, illus. 32p. (ps-3). 1989. 13.45 (0-395-44312-1) HM.
—Rotten Ralph's Show & Tell. Rubel, Nicole, illus. 32p. (gr. k-3). 1991. pap. 4.80 (0-395-60285-8, Sandpiper) HM.
—Rotten Ralph's Trick or Treat. Rubel, Nicole, illus. LC 86-7276. 32p. (gr. k-3). 1986. 13.45 (0-395-38943-7) HM.
—Rotten Ralph's Trick or Treat. Rubel, Nicole, illus. 32p. (gr. k-3). 1988. pap. 4.80 (0-395-48655-6, Sandpiper) HM.
—Worse Than Rotten, Ralph. Rubel, Nicole, illus. (gr. k-3). 1982. 13.95 (0-395-27106-1); pap. 5.70 (0-395-32919-1) HM.
Gantschev, Ivan. The Christmas Teddy Bear. Clements, Andrew, adapted by. LC 93-20121. (gr. 4 up). 1993. write for info. (0-88708-333-1) Picture Bk Studio.
—Good Morning, Good Night. Clements, Andrew, tr. Gantschev, Ivan, illus. LC 91-3603. 28p. (gr. k up). 1991. pap. 14.95 (0-88708-183-5) Picture Bk Studio.
—Moon Lake. (ps-3). 1991. pap. 14.95 (0-907234-08-9) Picture Bk Studio.
—The Moon Lake. (Illus.). 28p. (gr. k). 1993. Repr. Mini-bk. 4.95 (0-88708-304-8) Picture Bk Studio.
—The Train to Grandma's. LC 87-13899. (Illus.). 36p. (ps up). 1991. pap. 16.95 (0-88708-053-7) Picture Bk Studio.
—Where Is Mr. Mole? Clements, Andrew, tr. Gantschev, Ivan, illus. LC 89-8778. 28p. (ps up). 1991. pap. 15.95 (0-88708-109-6) Picture Bk Studio.
Gantschev, Ivan, jt. auth. see Aoki, Hisako.
Gantz, David. The Biggest Christmas Tree. 32p. 1991. pap. 2.50 (0-590-44026-8) Scholastic Inc.
—The Biggest Thanksgiving Turkey Ever. 32p. 1991. pap. 2.50 (0-590-45132-4) Scholastic Inc.
—Biggest Valentine. 1990. pap. 2.50 (0-590-43329-6) Scholastic Inc.
—Davey's Hanukkah Golem. Gantz, David, illus. LC 91-2328. 32p. (gr. k-3). 1991. 13.95 (0-8276-0380-0) JPS Phila.
—The Spookiest Day. Gantz, David, illus. 32p. (Orig.). (gr. k-3). 1986. pap. 2.50 (0-590-40325-7) Scholastic Inc.
Ganz, Y. Chanukah. Date not set. 7.95 (0-89906-979-7) Mesorah Pubns.
—Pesach. Date not set. 7.95 (0-89906-981-9) Mesorah Pubns.
—Purim. Date not set. 7.95 (0-89906-980-0) Mesorah Pubns.
—Rosh Hashanah. Date not set. 7.95 (0-89906-976-2) Mesorah Pubns.
—Shavuos. Date not set. 7.95 (0-89906-982-7) Mesorah Pubns.
—Succos. Date not set. 7.95 (0-89906-978-9) Mesorah Pubns.
—Tisha B'Av. Date not set. 7.95 (0-89906-983-5) Mesorah Pubns.

—Yom Kippur. Date not set. 7.95 (0-89906-977-0) Mesorah Pubns.
Ganz, Yaffa. Alef To Tav. Horen, Michael, illus. 48p. (gr. 1-6). 1989. 11.95 (0-89906-962-2); pap. 7.95 (0-89906-963-0) Mesorah Pubns.
—Follow the Moon: A Journey Through the Jewish Year. Klineman, Harvey, illus. (gr. k-4). 1984. 8.95 (0-87306-369-4) Feldheim.
—Hello Heddy Levi. (gr. 4-7). 1989. 8.95 (0-87306-480-1) Feldheim.
—The Jewish Fact-Finder: A Bookful of Important Jewish Facts & Handy Information. (gr. 5-9). 1988. 12.95 (0-87306-447-X); pap. 9.95 (0-87306-470-4) Feldheim.
—The Little Old Lady Who Couldn't Fall Asleep. Ben-Yosef, Yisrael, illus. 32p. (gr. k-6). 1989. 6.95 (0-89906-501-5) Mesorah Pubns.
—Our Jerusalem. (Illus.). (gr. k-2). 1979. pap. 4.25x (0-87441-308-7) Behrman.
—Savta Simcha & the Cinnamon Tree. Gewirtz, Bina & Poppins, Jewish M., illus. (gr. 6-10). 11.95 (0-87306-354-6) Feldheim.
—Savta Simcha, Uncle Nechemya, & the Very Strange Stone in the Garden. Gewirtz, Bina, illus. LC 92-26165. 1992. write for info. (0-87306-618-9) Feldheim.
—Sharing a Sunshine Umbrella: A Mimmy & Simmy Story. Klineman, Harvey, illus. 1989. 9.95 (0-87306-496-8) Feldheim.
—Shukis Upsidedown Dream. Gewirtz, Bina, illus. (gr. k-3). 1986. 6.95 (0-87306-384-8) Feldheim.
—Tali's Slippers, Tova's Shoes. Ariel, Liat B., illus. 32p. (gr. k-6). 1989. 6.95 (0-89906-502-3) Mesorah Pubns.
—Who Knows One? A Book of Jewish Numbers. Klineman, Harvey, illus. (gr. k-4). 1981. 10.95 (0-87306-285-X) Feldheim.
—The Wonderful World We Live In. Ariel, Liat B., illus. 48p. (gr. k-6). 1989. 10.95 (0-89906-964-9); pap. 6.95 (0-89906-965-7) Mesorah Pubns.
Gao, R. L., tr. from CHI. The Adventures of Monkey King. Allen, Rita, illus. 132p. (Orig.). (gr. 2-5). 1989. pap. 6.95 (0-9620765-1-1) Victory Press.
Gapper, Joe, illus. Colors. 6p. (ps). 1993. bds. 5.99 (0-8431-3624-3) Price Stern.
—Mommy & Baby. 12p. (ps). 1993. bds. 5.99 (0-8431-3625-1) Price Stern.
—Opposites. 12p. (ps). 1993. bds. 5.99 (0-8431-3626-X) Price Stern.
—Togethers. 12p. (ps). 1993. bds. 5.99 (0-8431-3627-8) Price Stern.
Garafalo, Lorraine. I'm Growing Up. Wheeler, Sharon, ed. Richesson, Robin, illus. (ps). 1985. wkbk. 1.95 (0-916119-16-5) Creat Teach Pr.
—I'm Starting School. Wheeler, Sharon, ed. Richesson, Robin, illus. (ps). 1985. wkbk. 1.95 (0-916119-15-7) Creat Teach Pr.
—I'm Staying Healthy. Wheeler, Sharon, ed. Richesson, Robin, illus. (ps). 1985. wkbk. 1.95 (0-916119-17-3) Creat Teach Pr.
—Making Friends. Wheeler, Sharon, ed. Richesson, Robin, illus. (ps). 1985. wkbk. 1.95 (0-916119-13-0) Creat Teach Pr.
—My Family & Me. Wheeler, Sharon, ed. Richesson, Robin, illus. (ps). 1985. pap. 1.95 wkbk. (0-916119-12-2) Creat Teach Pr.
—My Own Feelings. Wheeler, Sharon, ed. Richesson, Robin, illus. (ps). 1985. pap. 1.95 wkbk. (0-916119-14-9) Creat Teach Pr.
Garaway, Margaret K. Ashkii & His Grandfather. Warren, Harry, illus. LC 89-50604. 32p. (Orig.). (gr. k-6). 1989. pap. 5.95 (0-918080-41-X) Treasure Chest.
—Dezbah & the Dancing Tumbleweeds. Lowmiller, Cathie, illus. 175p. (Orig.). (gr. 3-5). 1990. pap. 7.95 (0-918080-50-9) Treasure Chest.
Garay, Julio. Quiet Thoughts. Cohen, Mel & Iscaro, Nancy L., eds. West Side High School Students, illus. 38p. (Orig.). (gr. 10-12). 1989. pap. text ed. write for info. West Side Pubns.
Garbarino, James. Let's Talk about Living in a World with Violence: An Activity Book for School-Age Children. Csaszar, Sonia, tr. Green, Phillip M., illus. (SPA.). 48p. (gr. k-8). 1993. wkbk. 10.00 (0-9639159-0-8) Erikson Inst.
Garbarino, Merwyn S. The Seminole. Potter, Frank W., intro. by. (Illus.). 112p. (Orig.). (gr. 5 up). 1989. 17.95 (1-55546-729-6); pap. 9.95 (0-7910-0367-1) Chelsea Hse.
Garber, Barbara J. Me & Daffodil. Garber, Barbara J., illus. LC 92-61375. 66p. 1993. pap. 8.00 (1-56002-212-4, Univ Edtns) Aegina Pr.
Garber, Marianne D., jt. auth. see Spizman, Robyn F.
Garber, S. David, ed. see Travis, Lucille.
Garbera, C., jt. auth. see Everett, F.
Garbera, C., jt. auth. see Wilkes, A.
Garces, David F., compiled by. Ideas Para Actividade Especiales - Ideas for Special Activities. (SPA.). 64p. (Orig.). (gr. 12 up). 1992. pap. 3.50 (0-311-12251-5) Casa Bautista.
Garchik, Morton. Art Fundamentals. LC 78-10336. (Illus.). (gr. 9-12). 1979. 19.95 (0-87396-082-3) Stravon.
Garcia, Conrad. Thinking in Poetry. 65p. (Orig.). (gr. 10-12). 1988. pap. 7.50 (0-9621124-0-2) C Garcia.
Garcia, Edward & Pellegrini, Nina. Homer the Homely Hound Dog. (Illus.). (gr. 2-6). 1974. 3.95 (0-917476-02-6) Inst Rational-Emotive.
Garcia, Gloria. Be My Friend. LC 90-49243. (ps). 1990. 9.95 (0-85953-421-9) Childs Play.

—Flying High. LC 90-49238. 1990. 9.95 (0-85953-424-3) Childs Play.
—I Can't Stop Now. LC 90-49239. (ps). 1990. 9.95 (0-85953-423-5) Childs Play.
—Life on the Ocean Wave. LC 90-49237. (ps). 1990. 9.95 (0-85953-422-7) Childs Play.
Garcia, Joseph G. Jump for the Apple! The Story of Lily Pond, a Soccer-Playing Frog with Long, Long Legs. Day, Rhonda, ed. Garcia, Joseph G., illus. 28p. (gr. 4up). 1983. pap. 5.95 (0-9612350-0-4) Goal Ent.
Garcia, Lola. A Girlfriend at Acoma, Siyu, & an Invitation to Supper. Aragon, Sherry, illus. 14p. (Orig.). (ps-7). 1981. pap. 3.75 (0-915347-09-1) Pueblo Acoma Pr.
Garcia, Maria. The Adventures of Connie & Diego (Los aventuras de Connie y Diego) LC 86-17132. (ENG & SPA., Illus.). 32p. (gr. 2-9). 1987. 13.95 (0-89239-028-X) Childrens Book Pr.
—The Adventures of Connie & Diego Read-Along. 1988. incl. audiocassette 22.95 (0-89239-033-6) Childrens Book Pr.
Garcia, Mary H. & Gonzalez-Mena, Janet. English All Around Us: Learning Package One. Ragan, Lise B., ed. LC 75-27579. (Prog. Bk.). (gr. 1-2). 1976. tchr's. manual 21.95 (0-8325-0464-5, Natl Textbk); student wkbk. 6.60 (0-8325-0465-3, Natl Textbk) program pkg 107.25 (0-685-57740-6, Natl Textbk) NTC Pub Grp.
Garcia, Richard. My Aunt Otilia's Spirits: Los espiritus de mi Tia Otilia. Guerrero Rea, Jesus, tr. Cherin, Robin & Reyes, Roger I., illus. LC 86-17129. (ENG & SPA.). 24p. (gr. 2-9). 1987. 13.95 (0-89239-029-8) Childrens Book Pr.
Garcia, Santos, intro. by see Ortiz, Lucio.
Garcia, Vince. Quest of the Ancients. Cabuco, et al, illus. 224p. (Orig.). (gr. 9-12). 1990. pap. 23.00 (0-9628003-0-9) Unicorn Game Pubns.
Garcia, Vince, ed. see Unicorn Game Pubs. Staff.
Garcia, Yolanda. Celebremos. (SPA., Illus.). (gr. 1-6). 10.95 (0-935303-03-0) Victory Pub.
—Celebremos con Numeros. (SPA., Illus.). 60p. (gr. k-2). 1986. pap. text ed. 7.95 (0-935303-01-4) Victory Pub.
—Espanol Divertido: Spanish Fun. LC 86-90286. (Illus.). (gr. 1-6). 1986. pap. 7.95 (0-935303-00-6) Victory Pub.
Garcia, Yolanda P. Spanish in a Taco Shell. Garcia, Veronica J., illus. (ENG & SPA., Orig.). (gr. 4-9). 1991. pap. 10.95 (0-935303-04-9) Victory Pub.

Garcia Sanchez, J. L. El Nino Gigante (The Giant Child) Sole, Carme, illus. (SPA.). 32p. (gr. k-2). 1988. 9.95 (84-372-1346-0) Santillana. **An outstanding selection from the DERECHOS DEL NINO series (The Rights of Children). Each book portrays one of the rights of children declared by the United Nations General Assembly. In this selection, a young boy becomes separated from his parents. In searching for them, he encounters a town of tiny people who abuse him until the children of the town come to his rescue. Young readers will enjoy this heartwarming story & its message. Simplistic illustrations by Carme Sole. To order: Santillana, 901 West Walnut, Compton, CA 90220. Telephone 1-310-763-0455.** *Publisher Provided Annotation.*

Gardam, Catharine. The Animals' Christmas. Rowe, Gavin, illus. LC 90-5538. 32p. (gr. k-4). 1990. SBE 13.95 (0-689-50502-7, M K McElderry) Macmillan Child Grp.
Gardam, Jane. A Few Fair Days. LC 88-5477. 128p. (gr. 5 up). 1988. 11.95 (0-688-07602-5) Greenwillow.
—The Hollow Land. Rawlings, Janet, illus. LC 81-6620. 160p. (gr. 5-9). 1982. 10.25 (0-688-00873-9) Greenwillow.
—Through the Dolls' House Door. LC 87-200. (Illus.). 128p. (gr. 5 up). 1987. 10.25 (0-688-07447-2) Greenwillow.
—Through the Dolls' House Door. (gr. 4-7). 1991. pap. 3.25 (0-440-40433-9) Dell.
Gardella, Tricia. Just Like My Dad. Apple, Margot, illus. LC 90-4403. 32p. (ps-3). 1993. 15.00 (0-06-021937-8); PLB 14.89 (0-06-021938-6) HarpC Child Bks.
Garden, Nancy. Annie on My Mind. 1992. pap. 3.95 (0-374-40414-3) FS&G.
—Annie on My Mind. LC 82-9189. 232p. (gr. 7 up). 1984. pap. 3.95 (0-374-40413-5) FS&G.
—The Door Between. LC 87-8778. 192p. (gr. 5 up). 1987. 15.00 (0-374-31833-6) FS&G.
—Fours Crossing. LC 80-21854. 199p. (gr. 5 up). 1981. 15.00 (0-374-32451-4) FS&G.
—The Kid's Code & Cipher Book. LC 91-30453. (Illus.). 163p. (gr. 6-12). 1991. Repr. of 1981 ed. PLB 17.50 (0-208-02341-0, Linnet) Shoe String.
—Lark in the Morning. 288p. (gr. 9-12). 1991. 14.95 (0-374-34338-1) FS&G.

—The Mystery of the Night Raiders. LC 87-45829. 144p. (gr. 4-6). 1987. 14.00 (0-374-35221-6) FS&G.
—Mystery of the Secret Marks. 192p. (gr. 3 up). 1989. 15.00 (0-374-35021-3) FS&G.
—Peace, O River. 245p. (gr. 7 up). 1986. 15.00 (0-374-35763-3) FS&G.
—Prisoner of Vampires. (gr. 2-6). 1986. pap. 2.95 (0-440-47194-X, YB) Dell.
—Prisoner of Vampires. (gr. 4-7). 1993. pap. 3.95 (0-374-46018-3) FS&G.
—Watersmeet. LC 83-11512. 202p. (gr. 5 up). 1983. 15.00 (0-374-38244-1) FS&G.
Gardener, Beau. The Look Again...& Again, & Again, & Again Book. LC 84-748. (Illus.). 32p. (ps-3). 1983. 11.00 (0-688-03805-0); lib. bdg. 10.08 (0-688-03806-9) Lothrop.

Gardenier, George E. Statistical Methods: Games & Songs. Gardenier, T. K., ed. Gardenier, Jason C., illus. 99p. (gr. 3 up). 1989. 89.00 (0-685-29043-3) Teka Trends. This series provides a unique method of teaching mathematics without fear by combining poetry, music, & three-dimensional games. It introduces principles of statistical methods to early ages, & simplifies advanced concepts used by scientists & industrial engineers. Media familiar to children are used through an experiment in planting & growth. The series consists of the following individual booklets, each accompanied by a tape of the melody, evaluation form, & optional math-manipulatives oriented game kits. OVERVIEW: FUN WITH NUMBERS (ISBN 0-685-29038-7, 0002) presents objectives & overview of terms such as "matrix," "run," & "factor." MODULE I: BRANCHING TREES (ISBN 0-685-29039-5,0003) teaches how to use the "factorial" design & the Latin Square through an experiment in planting. MODULE II COMPUTER MODELS (ISBN 0-685-29040-9,0004) designs a "metamodel" equation & plots it in 3-D form. MODULE III: TIME (ISBN 0-685-29041-7,0005) traces changes over time & relates it to quality control concepts with examples in environmental monitoring. MODULE IV: TWO-BY-TWO (ISBN 0-685-29042-5,0006) includes templates for "stem-&-leaf" charts, an innovation in statistical histograms, & presents methods to statistically test the difference between two sets of data. The series provides a bridge between mathematics & science. Knowledge of music theory is not essential. Teamwork is emphasized by presenting dexterity oriented tasks to groups, or sets of two children. A class exercise component, which can be duplicated, has been incorporated. Options exist for purchasing individual modules with introductory overview & components of math manipulative games. Series is distributed through Pragmatica Corporation.
Publisher Provided Annotation.

Gardenier, George H., jt. auth. see Kumbaraci, Turkan.
Gardenier, T. K., ed. see Gardenier, George E.
Gardenier, Turkan K. Songs for Computing & Marching: Adapted from Turkish Melodies. LC 89-90942. (Illus.). (gr. 7-12). 1989. 20.00 (0-685-67706-0, 0007) Teka Trends.
Gardiner, Brian. Nuclear Waste. (Illus.). 32p. (gr. 2-4). 1992. PLB 11.90 (0-531-17351-8, Gloucester Pr) Watts.
Gardiner, Harold C. Edmund Campion: Hero of God's Underground. Goudket, Rose, illus. LC 91-76073. 180p. 1992. pap. 9.95 (0-89870-387-5) Ignatius Pr.
Gardiner, John R. General Butterfingers. Smith, Catherine B., illus. 96p. (gr. 3-7). 1986. 13.45 (0-395-41853-4) HM.

—General Butterfingers. Smith, Cat B., illus. LC 92-44487. 96p. (gr. 3-7). 1993. pap. 3.99 (0-14-036355-6, Puffin) Puffin Bks.
—Stone Fox. Sewall, Marcia, illus. LC 79-7895. 96p. (gr. 2-6). 1980. 14.00 (0-690-03983-2, Crowell Jr Bks); PLB 13.89 (0-690-03984-0, Crowell Jr Bks) HarpC Child Bks.
—Stone Fox. Sewall, Marcia, illus. LC 79-7895. 96p. (gr. 2-6). 1983. pap. 3.95 (0-06-440132-4, Trophy) HarpC Child Bks.
—Top Secret. Simont, Marc, illus. 129p. (gr. 3-7). 1985. 15.95 (0-316-30368-2) Little.
Gardner, Beau. Guess What? LC 85-242. (Illus.). 48p. (ps-3). 1985. 13.95 (0-688-04982-6); PLB 13.88 (0-688-04983-4) Lothrop.
—The Turn about, Think about, Look about Book. Gardner, Beau, illus. LC 80-12885. 32p. (gr. k-6). 1980. 13.95 (0-688-41969-0); PLB 13.88 (0-688-51969-5) Lothrop.
Gardner, James. Illustrated Soccer Dictionary for Young People. Ross, David, illus. 125p. (gr. 4 up). 1978. pap. 2.50 (0-13-451146-8, Pub. by Treehouse) P-H.
Gardner, Jane M. A Gift to America. Bolduc, Susan, illus. 32p. (Orig.). (gr. k-3). 1986. pap. 3.95 (0-9617183-0-7) Gardner Pub.
—Henry Moore: From Bones & Stones to Sketches & Sculptures. (Illus.). 32p. (gr. k-2). 1993. RSBE 15.95 (0-02-735812-7, Four Winds) Macmillan Child Grp.
Gardner, Karen A. My Life As a Hand. rev. ed. (Illus.). 37p. (ps-2). 1984. Set of 1-4. PLB 1.70 (0-931421-03-9) Psychol Educ Pubns.
—My Life As a Nose. rev. ed. (Illus.). 37p. (ps-2). 1984. Set of 1-4. PLB 1.70 (0-931421-04-7) Psychol Educ Pubns.
—My Life As a Tongue. rev. ed. (Illus.). 37p. (ps-2). 1984. Set of 1-4. PLB 1.70 (0-931421-05-5) Psychol Educ Pubns.
—My Life As an Ear. rev. ed. (Illus.). 37p. (ps-2). 1984. Set of 1-4. PLB 1.70 (0-931421-01-2) Psychol Educ Pubns.
—My Life As an Eye. rev. ed. (Illus.). 37p. (ps-2). 1984. Set of 1-4. PLB 1.70 (0-931421-02-0) Psychol Educ Pubns.
Gardner, Katherine L., tr. see Yost, Carolyn K.
Gardner, Mark. Santa Fe Trail. Foreman, Ronald J. & Priehs, T. J., eds. 16p. (Orig.). 1992. pap. 2.95 (1-877856-20-7) SW Pks Mnmts.
Gardner, Martin. Entertaining Science Experiments with Everyday Objects. Ravielli, Anthony, illus. (gr. 5 up). 16.50 (0-8446-5888-X) Peter Smith.
—The Snark Puzzle Book. Holiday, Henry & Tenniel, John, illus. 124p. (gr. 3 up). 1990. Repr. of 1973 ed. PLB 14.95 (0-87975-583-0) Prometheus Bks.
Gardner, Mary, jt. auth. see Landin, Les.
Gardner, Richard. Boys & Girls of Divorce. 1985. pap. 4.99 (0-553-27619-0) Bantam.
Gardner, Richard A. Boys & Girls Book about Divorce. LC 84-2815. (Illus.). 160p. (gr. 7 up). 1992. Repr. of 1983 ed. 25.00 (0-87668-664-1) Aronson.
—The Boys & Girls Book about Divorce. (Illus.). (gr. 4 up). 1971. pap. 3.50 (0-553-25310-7) Bantam.
—The Boys & Girls Book about One-Parent Families. LC 78-18388. (Illus.). 122p. (gr. k-8). 1983. pap. 4.99 (0-933812-16-7) Creative Therapeutics.
—The Boys & Girls Book about Stepfamilies. Lowenheim, Alfred, illus. 180p. (gr. 3-10). 1985. pap. 4.99 (0-933812-13-2) Creative Therapeutics.
—Dr. Gardner's Fables for Our Times. Myers, Robert, illus. LC 80-26098. 125p. (gr. k-6). 1981. 14.95 (0-933812-06-X) Creative Therapeutics.
—Dr. Gardner's Fairy Tales for Today's Children. Lowenheim, Alfred, illus. LC 80-16187. 96p. (gr. 1-6). 1978. Repr. of 1974 ed. PLB 14.95 (0-933812-02-7) Creative Therapeutics.
—Dr. Gardner's Modern Fairy Tales. Lowenheim, Al, illus. LC 83-40149. 106p. (gr. 2-6). Repr. 14.95 (0-933812-09-4) Creative Therapeutics.
—Dr. Gardner's Stories About the Real World, Vol. I. Lowenheim, Alfred, illus. LC 80-16542. 127p. (gr. k-6). 1980. Repr. of 1972 ed. PLB 14.95 (0-933812-04-3) Creative Therapeutics.
—Dr. Gardner's Stories About the Real World, Vol. II. Myers, Robert, illus. LC 80-16592. 95p. (gr. k-6). 1983. 14.95 (0-933812-05-1) Creative Therapeutics.
—Dr. Gardner's Stories about the Real World, Vol. I. LC 80-16542. (Illus.). 127p. (gr. k-6). 1980. pap. 4.99 (0-933812-07-8) Creative Therapeutics.
—Dorothy & the Lizard of Oz. Richmond, Frank, illus. LC 80-12787. 108p. (gr. 1-6). 1980. 14.95 (0-933812-03-5) Creative Therapeutics.
—The Girls & Boys Book about Good & Bad Behavior. Lowenheim, Al, illus. LC 90-31241. 221p. (gr. 2-6). 1990. 17.00 (0-933812-21-3) Creative Therapeutics.
Gardner, Robert. Architecture. 1994. PLB write for info. (0-8050-2855-2) H Holt & Co.
—Celebrating Earth Day: A Sourcebook of Activities & Experiments. LC 91-38297. (Illus.). 96p. (gr. 5 up). 1992. PLB 15.90 (1-56294-070-8) Millbrook Pr.
—Communication. 1994. PLB write for info. (0-8050-2854-4) H Holt & Co.
—Crime Lab. 101: Experimenting with Crime Detection. 123p. (gr. 6-9). 1992. 13.95 (0-8027-8158-6); lib. bdg. 14.85 (0-8027-8159-4) Walker & Co.
—Electricity. LC 92-34075. (gr. 4 up). 1993. lib. bdg. 14.98 (0-671-69039-6, J Messner) S&S Trade.
—Electricity & Magnetism. 1994. PLB write for info. (0-8050-2850-1) H Holt & Co.

—Energy Projects. LC 86-32433. (Illus.). 128p. (gr. 7-12). 1987. PLB 13.90 (0-531-10338-2) Watts.
—Energy Projects for Young Scientists. 1989. pap. 6.95 (0-531-15129-8) Watts.
—Experimenting with Energy Conservation. (Illus.). 128p. (gr. 9-12). 1992. PLB 13.40 (0-531-12538-6) Watts.
—Experimenting with Illusions. LC 89-24780. (gr. 4-7). 1990. PLB 13.40 (0-531-10909-7) Watts.
—Experimenting with Inventions. LC 89-24788. (gr. 4-7). 1990. PLB 12.90 (0-531-10910-0) Watts.
—Experimenting with Light. LC 90-48496. (Illus.). 144p. (gr. 7-12). 1991. PLB 13.90 (0-531-12520-3) Watts.
—Experimenting with Science in Sports. (Illus.). 128p. (gr. 7-12). 1993. pap. 6.95 (0-531-15682-6) Watts.
—Experimenting with Sound. LC 91-4012. (Illus.). 128p. (gr. 9-12). 1991. PLB 13.40 (0-531-12503-3) Watts.
—Experimenting with Water. (Illus.). 144p. (gr. 7-12). 1993. PLB 13.40 (0-531-12549-1) Watts.
—Famous Experiments You Can Do. LC 90-34043. (Illus.). 144p. (gr. 9-12). 1990. PLB 13.90 (0-531-10883-X) Watts.
—Forces & Machines. (Illus.). 136p. (gr. 7 up). 1991. lib. bdg. 14.98 (0-671-69041-8, J Messner); pap. 9.95 (0-671-69046-9) S&S Trade.
—Ideas for Science Projects. LC 86-9238. (Illus.). 144p. (gr. 7-12). 1989. PLB 13.90 (0-531-10246-7); pap. 6.95 (0-531-15125-5) Watts.
—Kitchen Chemistry: Science Experiments to Do at Home. Steltenpohl, Jane, ed. (Illus.). 136p. (gr. 4-8). 1989. lib. bdg. 13.98 (0-671-67776-4, J Messner); lib. bdg. 5.95 (0-671-67576-1); PLB 8.99s.p. (0-685-47082-2); pap. 3.71s.p. (0-685-47083-0) S&S Trade.
—Light. (Illus.). 136p. (gr. 7 up). 1990. lib. bdg. 14.98 (0-671-69037-X, J Messner); pap. 9.95 (0-671-69042-6) S&S Trade.
—More Ideas for Science Projects. 1989. pap. 6.95 (0-531-15126-3) Watts.
—Optics. 1994. PLB write for info. (0-8050-2852-8) H Holt & Co.
—Projects in Space Science. (Illus.). 136p. (gr. 4-8). 1988. lib. bdg. 11.98 (0-671-63639-1, J Messner); lib. bdg. 5.95 (0-671-65993-6); PLB 8.99s.p. (0-685-47085-7); pap. 3.71s.p. (0-685-47086-5) S&S Trade.
—Robert Gardner's Challenging Science Experiments. LC 92-21116. (Illus.). 176p. (gr. 9-12). 1993. PLB 12.40 (0-531-11090-7); pap. 6.95 (0-531-15671-0) Watts.
—Robert Gardner's Favorite Science Experiments. LC 92-17579. (Illus.). 128p. (gr. 5-8). 1992. PLB 12.90 (0-531-11038-9); pap. 6.95 (0-531-15255-3) Watts.
—Robert Gardner's Science Activity Books, 4 vols. (Illus.). 544p. (gr. 4-8). 1990. Set. PLB 47.92 (0-671-94217-4, J Messner); Set. PLB 35.94s.p. (0-685-47080-6); Set. pap. 19.80 (0-671-94218-2); Set. pap. 14.84s.p. (0-685-47081-4) S&S Trade.
—Science Around the House. (Illus.). 136p. (gr. 4-8). 1989. lib. bdg. 11.98 (0-671-54663-5, J Messner); pap. 4.95 (0-671-68139-7); 8.99s.p. (0-685-47084-9) S&S Trade.
—Science Experiments. Rasof, Henry, ed. LC 87-19880. (Illus.). 72p. (gr. 5-7). 1988. PLB 10.90 (0-531-10484-2) Watts.
—Science Projects about the Human Body. LC 92-43802. (Illus.). 104p. (gr. 6 up). 1993. lib. bdg. 17.95 (0-89490-443-4) Enslow Pubs.
—Space. 1994. PLB write for info. (0-8050-2851-X) H Holt & Co.
—Transportation. 1994. PLB write for info. (0-8050-2853-6) H Holt & Co.
—The Whale Watchers' Guide. Sineti, Don, illus. LC 83-17425. 170p. (gr. 7 up). 1984. lib. bdg. 10.98 (0-671-45811-6, J Messner); pap. 5.95 (0-671-49807-X) S&S Trade.
Gardner, Robert & Kemer, Eric. Making & Using Scientific Models. LC 92-21124. (Illus.). 144p. (gr. 9-12). 1993. PLB 13.90 (0-531-10986-0); pap. 6.95 (0-531-15662-1) Watts.
—Temperature & Heat. LC 92-32367. (gr. 3-7). 1993. lib. bdg. 14.98 (0-671-69040-X, J Messner); pap. 9.95 (0-671-69045-0, J Messner) S&S Trade.
Gardner, Robert & Shortelle, Dennis. The Forgotten Players: The Story of Black Baseball in America. LC 92-29618. 128p. (gr. 6 up). 1993. 12.95 (0-8027-8248-5); PLB 13.85 (0-8027-8249-3) Walker & Co.
—The Future & the Past. Steltenpohl, Jane, ed. (Illus.). 176p. (gr. 6-10). 1989. lib. bdg. 14.98 (0-671-65742-9, J Messner) S&S Trade.
Gardner, Robert & Webster, David. Science in Your Backyard. (Illus.). 136p. (gr. 4-8). 1987. lib. bdg. 11.98 (0-671-55565-0, J Messner); lib. bdg. 4.95 (0-671-63835-1); PLB 8.99s.p. (0-685-47087-3); pap. 3.71s.p. (0-685-47088-1) S&S Trade.
Gardner, Sally. The Little Nut Tree. Gardner, Sally, illus. LC 93-26714. 32p. 1994. 14.00 (0-688-13297-9, Tambourine Bks); PLB write for info. (0-688-13298-7, Tambourine Bks) Morrow.
Gardner, Sandra. Street Gangs in America. Herz, Cary, photos by. LC 92-16618. (Illus.). 112p. (gr. 9-12). 1992. PLB 13.40 (0-531-11037-0) Watts.
Gardner, Sandra & Rosenberg, Gary. Teenage Suicide. LC 85-14277. 160p. (gr. 7 up). 1986. lib. bdg. 11.98 (0-671-49975-0, J Messner); pap. 4.95 (0-671-63241-8) S&S Trade.

Gardner, Sandra & Rosenberg, Gary B. Teenage Suicide. rev. ed. (Illus.). 128p. (gr. 7 up). 1990. lib. bdg. 13.98 *(0-671-70200-9,* J Messner); pap. 5.95 *(0-671-70201-7)* S&S Trade.

Gardner, Theodroe R., II. Something Nice to See. Hamlin, Peter, illus. LC 93-61121. 32p. (gr. 4 up). Date not set. 15.00 *(0-9627297-6-0)* A A Knoll Pubs.

Gardner-Loulan, JoAnn, et al. Period. updated ed. Quackenbush, Marcia, illus. & LC 90-46065. 95p. (gr. 4-8). 1991. pap. 9.95 incl. removable parents' guide *(0-912078-88-X)* Volcano Pr.

Garee, Betty. Ideas for Kids on the Go. Franch, Julie, illus. Cheever, Raymond, intro. by. LC 84-73366. (Illus., Orig.). (ps up). 1984. pap. 6.95 *(0-915708-17-5)* Cheever Pub.

Garee, Betty, ed. see Winston, Lynn.

Garehime, Ed. Mr. Jelly Bean, No. 1. 2nd ed. American Red Cross Staff, tr. Garehime, Marianne, illus. LC 77-82261. 64p. (ps-4). 1979. 9.95 *(0-918822-01-7)* Deem Corp.

Garelick, May, jt. auth. see Brenner, Barbara.

Garell, Dale C. & Snyder, Solomon H., eds. Arthritis. (Illus.). (gr. 6-12). 1992. 18.95 *(0-7910-0057-5)* Chelsea Hse.

—Compulsive Behavior. (Illus.). 112p. (gr. 7-12). 1993. 18.95 *(0-7910-0044-3)*; pap. write for info. *(0-7910-0510-0)* Chelsea Hse.

—Delinquency & Criminal Behavior. (Illus.). 112p.(gr. 7-12). 1989. 18.95 *(0-7910-0045-1)* Chelsea Hse.

—The Encyclopedia of Health, 79 vols. (Illus.). 8848p. (gr. 5 up). 1988. Set. lib. bdg. 1497.05 *(0-7910-0007-9)* Chelsea Hse.

—Medical Disorders & Their Treatment Series, 27 vols. (Illus.). 2542p. (gr. 6-12). 1994. Set. 511.65x *(0-7910-0011-7,* Am Art Analog) Chelsea Hse.

—Medical Issues Series, 8 vols. (Illus.). 756p. (gr. 6-12). 1994. Set. PLB 208.45x *(0-7910-0012-5,* Am Art Analog) Chelsea Hse.

—Medical Technology. (Illus.). (gr. 6-12). 1993. 18.95 *(0-7910-0087-7)* Chelsea Hse.

—Psychological Disorders & Their Treatment, 13 vols. (Illus.). 1248p. (gr. 6-12). 1994. Set. 246.35x *(0-7910-0010-9,* Am Art Analog) Chelsea Hse.

Garell, Dale C., ed. see Carson-Finnerty, LaVonne.

Garell, Dale C., ed. see Feinberg, Brian.

Garell, Dale C., ed. see Murphy, Wendy & Murphy, Jack.

Garell, Dale C., ed. see Siegel, Dorothy S.

Garell, Dale C., ed. see Wax, Nina.

Garfield, Curtis F., jt. auth. see Ridley, Alison.

Garfield, James B. Follow My Leader. Greiner, Robert, illus. LC 57-1611. 192p. (gr. 4-6). 1957. pap. 13.95 *(0-670-32332-2)* Viking Child Bks.

Garfield, Leon. The Apprentices. (gr. 7 up). 1988. pap. 4.95 *(0-14-031595-0,* Puffin) Puffin Bks.

—The December Rose. 208p. (gr. 5-9). 1988. pap. 3.99 *(0-14-032070-9,* Puffin) Puffin Bks.

—Devil in the Fog. (gr. k-6). 1988. pap. 3.25 *(0-440-40095-3,* YB) Dell.

—Devil-in-the-Fog. (gr. 6-10). 1991. 15.00 *(0-8446-6452-9)* Peter Smith.

—The Empty Sleeve. LC 87-37580. 216p. (gr. 5 up). 1988. pap. 14.95 *(0-440-50049-4)* Delacorte.

—Empty Sleeve. 1988. 14.95 *(0-385-29817-X)* Delacorte.

—Footsteps. (gr. k-6). 1988. pap. 3.25 *(0-440-40102-X,* YB) Dell.

—Footsteps: A Novel. LC 80-65834. 192p. (gr. 7 up). 1980. 12.95 *(0-385-28294-X)* Delacorte.

—John Diamond. large type ed. (Illus.). 272p. (gr. 5 up). 1988. 13.95 *(0-7451-0757-5,* Galaxy Child Lrg Print) Chivers N Amer.

—The Night of the Comet. LC 79-50670. (gr. 7 up). 1979. 8.95 *(0-685-01396-0)*; pap. 7.45 *(0-385-28753-4)* Delacorte.

—The Night of the Comet. (gr. k-6). 1988. pap. 3.25 *(0-440-40070-8,* YB) Dell.

—The Saracen Maid. O'Brien, John, illus. LC 93-6612. 1994. pap. 13.00 *(0-671-86646-X,* S&S BFYR) S&S Trade.

—Shakespeare Stories. Foreman, Michael, illus. LC 85-1971. 288p. (gr. 5 up). 1991. 24.45 *(0-395-56397-6)* HM.

—Smith. large type ed. (gr. 1-8). 1991. 13.95 *(0-7451-0448-7,* Galaxy Child Lrg Print) Chivers N Amer.

—The Strange Affair of Adelaide Harris. (gr. k-6). 1988. pap. 3.25 *(0-440-40057-0,* YB) Dell.

—The Wedding Ghost. Keeping, Charles, illus. 66p. (gr. 6 up). 1987. bds. 16.00 laminated *(0-19-279779-4)* OUP.

—The Wedding Ghost. Keeping, Charles, illus. 64p. (gr. 4 up). 1992. pap. 6.95 *(0-19-272246-8)* OUP.

—Young Nick & Jubilee. Lewin, Ted, illus. (gr. 1-2). 1989. 13.95 *(0-385-29777-7)* Delacorte.

Garfield, Leon, abridged by. Hamlet. Orlova, Natalia, et al, illus. LC 92-14525. 48p. (gr. 5 up). 1993. PLB 11.99 *(0-679-83871-0)*; pap. 6.99 *(0-679-83871-6)* Knopf Bks Yng Read.

—Macbeth. Serebriakov, Nikolai, illus. LC 92-14521. 48p. (gr. 5 up). 1993. PLB 11.99 *(0-679-83875-3)*; pap. 6.99 *(0-679-83875-9)* Knopf Bks Yng Read.

—A Midsummer Night's Dream. Prorokova, Elena, illus. LC 92-14522. 48p. (gr. 5 up). 1993. PLB 11.99 *(0-679-83870-2)*; pap. 6.99 *(0-679-83870-8)* Knopf Bks Yng Read.

—Romeo & Juliet. Makarov, Igor, illus. LC 92-14523. 48p. (gr. 5 up). 1993. PLB 11.99 *(0-679-83874-5)*; pap. 6.99 *(0-679-83874-0)* Knopf Bks Yng Read.

—The Tempest. Livanova, Elena, illus. LC 92-14526. 48p. (gr. 5 up). 1993. PLB 11.99 *(0-679-83873-7)*; pap. 6.99 *(0-679-83873-2)* Knopf Bks Yng Read.

—Twelfth Night. Prytkova, Ksenia, illus. LC 92-14524. 48p. (gr. 5 up). 1993. PLB 11.99 *(0-679-83872-9)*; pap. 6.99 *(0-679-83872-4)* Knopf Bks Yng Read.

Garfield, Richard. Magic: The Gathering. 36p. 1993. incl. cards 7.95 *(1-880992-22-1)*; booster pack cards 2.45 *(1-880992-23-X)* Wizards Coast.

Garfield, Vivien & Alcock, Vivien. The Sylvia Game. (gr. k-6). 1990. pap. 2.95 *(0-440-40266-2,* YB) Dell.

Garfinkel, Bernard. Margaret Thatcher. (Illus.). 112p. (gr. 5 up). 1985. lib. bdg. 17.95 *(0-87754-552-9)*; pap. 9.95 *(0-7910-0603-4)* Chelsea Hse.

Garfunkel, Debby. Baker's Dozen: Through Thick & Thin. 144p. (Orig.). (gr. 4-9). 1993. pap. 7.95 *(1-56871-024-0)* Targum Pr.

Garibaldi, Louis E., jt. auth. see Bernstein, Louis.

Garigan, Elizabeth & Urbanski, Michael. Living with Divorce - Middle School. 64p. (gr. 5-9). 1991. 7.95 *(0-86653-596-9,* GA1315) Good Apple.

—Living with Divorce - Primary. 64p. (gr. 1-4). 1991. 7.95 *(0-86653-595-0,* GA1314) Good Apple.

Garinger, Alan. Water Monsters: Opposing Viewpoints. LC 91-15174. (Illus.). 112p. (gr. 5-8). 1991. PLB 14.95 *(0-89908-087-1)* Greenhaven.

Garis, Howard R. Uncle Wiggily to the Rescue. Chambless-Rigie, Jane, illus. LC 92-14551. 32p. (ps-2). 1987. pap. 1.95 *(0-448-34305-3,* G&D) Putnam Pub Group.

—Uncle Wiggily's Storybook. (Illus.). 260p. (ps-4). 1987. 10.95 *(0-448-40090-1,* G&D) Putnam Pub Group.

Garland, Hamlin. The Long Trail. 1988. Repr. of 1907 ed. lib. bdg. 59.00x *(0-7812-1236-7)* Rprt Serv.

—Main-Travelled Roads. 1987. Repr. lib. bdg. 18.95x *(0-89966-551-1)* Buccaneer Bks.

—The Return of a Private. LC 92-44051. 1994. write for info. *(0-88682-583-0)* Creative Ed.

Garland, Michael. Circus Girl. Garland, Michael, illus. LC 92-22270. 32p. (ps-3). 1993. 14.99 *(0-525-45069-6,* DCB) Dutton Child Bks.

Garland, S. Song of the Buffalo Boy. 1992. 15.95 *(0-15-277107-7,* HB Juv Bks) HarBrace.

Garland, Sara. All Gone! (ps). 1991. pap. 3.95 *(0-14-054409-7,* Puffin) Puffin Bks.

Garland, Sarah. Billy & Belle. Garland, Sarah, illus. 32p. (ps-3). 1992. 13.00 *(0-670-84396-2)* Viking Child Bks.

—Doing the Garden. (Illus.). (ps-1). 1993. 15.95 *(0-370-31635-5,* Pub. by Bodley Head UK) Trafalgar.

—Going to Playschool. (Illus.). 32p. (gr. k-2). 1992. 13.95 *(0-370-31539-1,* Pub. by Bodley Head UK) Trafalgar.

—Oh, No! (Illus.). 32p. (ps-1). 1990. pap. 8.95 *(0-670-83075-5)* Viking Child Bks.

—Oh, No! (ps). 1991. pap. 3.95 *(0-14-054411-9,* Puffin) Puffin Bks.

—Polly's Puffin. LC 88-24348. (Illus.). 24p. (ps up). 1989. 11.95 *(0-688-08748-5)*; PLB 13.88 *(0-688-08749-3)* Greenwillow.

Garland, Sherry. Best Horse on the Force. 112p. (gr. 4-6). 1991. 13.95 *(0-8050-1658-9,* Bks Young Read) H Holt & Co.

—Lotus Seed. LC 92-2913. (gr. 4-7). 1993. 14.95 *(0-15-249465-0)* HarBrace.

—Shadow of the Dragon. 1993. 10.95 *(0-15-273530-5,* HB Juv Bks). pap. 3.95 *(0-15-273532-1)* HarBrace.

—The Silent Storm. LC 92-33690. 1992. write for info. *(0-15-274170-4)* HarBrace.

—Vietnam: Rebuilding a Nation. LC 89-29212. (Illus.). 130p. (gr. 5 up). 1990. RSBE 14.95 *(0-87518-422-7,* Dillon) Macmillan Child Grp.

—Why Ducks Sleep on One Leg. Tseng, Jean & Tseng, Mou-sien, illus. LC 92-9709. 32p. (ps-3). 1993. 14.95 *(0-590-45697-0)* Scholastic Inc.

Garlie, Gina. Mount St. Helens Is My Home. Elfstrand, Elizabeth, illus. 40p. (gr. k-3). 1993. pap. 5.95 *(0-9637878-0-2,* 574180)* Lupine Pr.

Garlits, Don & Yates, Brock. Big Daddy: The Autobiography of Don Garlits. 2nd, rev., enl. & updated ed. Smith, Donna G., ed. (Illus.). 354p. 1990. 50.00 *(0-685-35751-1)*; pap. 9.95 *(0-9626565-0-X)* D Garlits.

Garlow, Willa R. Jesus Is a Special Person. LC 85-24361. (Illus.). (ps). 1986. 4.95 *(0-8054-4166-2)* Broadman.

Garman, Dave, ed. see Tucker, Paul.

Garne, S. T. One White Sail. Etre, Lisa, illus. LC 91-24662. 32p. 1992. 14.00 *(0-671-75579-X,* Green Tiger) S&S Trade.

Garner, Alan. A Bag of Moonshine. Lynch, Patrick J., illus. LC 86-13362. 160p. (gr. k-5). 1986. pap. 15.95 *(0-385-29517-0)* Delacorte.

—Elidor. (gr. 4-7). 1993. pap. 3.99 *(0-440-40763-X)* Dell.

—Jack & the Beanstalk. Heller, Julek, illus. LC 91-36717. 32p. (gr. k-3). 1992. 14.00 *(0-385-30693-8)* Doubleday.

—Once upon a Time. Messenger, Norman, illus. LC 93-9686. 32p. (gr. k-4). 1993. 12.95 *(1-56458-381-3)* Dorling Kindersley.

—The Owl Service. 160p. (gr. 5 up). 1992. pap. 3.50 *(0-440-40735-4,* YB) Dell.

—The Stone Book Quartet. (gr. k-12). 1988. pap. 4.95 *(0-440-40049-X,* Pub by Yearning Classics) Dell.

Garner, Alan, retold by. Once upon a Time. Messenger, Norman, illus. LC 93-9686. 32p. (gr. 2-6). 1993. 12.95 *(1-56458-380-5)* Dorling Kindersley.

Garner, Irene A., jt. auth. see Fearn, Leif.

Garnett, C. G. Great Adaptations in Life: Adapt to Life & Thrive: Children's Version, Vol. 1. (Illus., Orig.). (gr. k-6). 1993. pap. write for info. *(1-883709-21-0)* Gold Crest Pubns.

—Great Adaptations in Life: Adapt to Life & Thrive: Young Adult Version, Vol. 1. (Illus., Orig.). (gr. 7-12). 1993. pap. write for info. *(1-883709-11-3)* Gold Crest Pubns.

Garnett, Constance, tr. see Dostoyevsky, Fyodor.

Garnett, Constance, tr. see Turgenev, Ivan S.

Garnett, Paul D. Investigating Morals & Values in Today's Society. 160p. (gr. 5-10). 1988. wkbk. 12.95 *(0-86653-443-1,* GA1053) Good Apple.

Garrett, B. J. Who's on What? Basketball Trading Cards Reference Book, 1990-1991. Taylor, David S., illus. 100p. (Orig.). (gr. 3 up). 1993. pap. write for info. *(1-882816-00-5)* Eyes of August.

Garrett, Beatrice. A Bite of Black History: A Collective of Narrative & Short Poems of Afro-American History for Juveniles & Young Adults. LC 91-74117. 72p. (gr. 6 up). 1991. 14.95 *(0-9629887-1-5)*; pap. 9.95 *(0-9629887-0-7)* Bosck Pub Hse.

Garrett, Dan. Australia. LC 89-21726. (Illus.). 96p. (gr. 6-12). 1990. PLB 19.92 *(0-8114-2429-4)* Raintree Steck-V.

—Scandinavia. LC 91-6422. (Illus.). 96p.(gr. 6-11). 1991. PLB 19.92 *(0-8114-2444-8)* Raintree Steck-V.

Garrett, Dan & Drew-Bernstein, Charlotte. Germany. LC 91-20790. (Illus.). 96p. (gr. 6-12). 1992. PLB 19.92 *(0-8114-2446-4)* Raintree Steck-V.

Garrett, Dan, ed. Friends & Neighbors. (Illus.). 96p. (Orig.). 1990. pap. 14.95 *(0-333-36054-0,* McMillan Ed UK) Players Pr.

—Girls. (Illus.). 96p. (Orig.). 1990. pap. 14.95 *(0-333-46708-6,* McMillan Ed UK) Players Pr.

—Masks & Faces. (Illus.). 96p. (Orig.). 1990. pap. 14.95 *(0-333-36056-7,* McMillan Ed UK) Players Pr.

—Scapegoats. (Illus.). 96p. (Orig.). 1990. pap. 14.95 *(0-333-36055-9,* McMillan Ed UK) Players Pr.

—Taking Issue. (Illus.). 96p. (Orig.). 1990. pap. 14.95 *(0-333-46709-4,* McMillan Ed UK) Players Pr.

—Upheavals. (Illus.). 96p. (Orig.). 1990. pap. 14.95 *(0-333-36057-5,* McMillan Ed UK) Players Pr.

Garrett, Deborah G., ed. see Galbreath, Bob.

Garrett, Michael. The Seventies. LC 89-27177. (Illus.). 48p. (gr. 5-9). 1990. PLB 19.92 *(0-8114-4214-4)* Raintree Steck-V.

Garrett, Norman A. Great Bread Machine Recipes. LC 92-16781. 128p. (gr. 10-12). 1992. pap. 6.95 *(0-8069-8724-3)* Sterling.

—Quick & Delicious Bread Machine Recipes. LC 91-37674. 128p. (gr. 10-12). 1993. pap. 6.95 *(0-8069-8812-6)* Sterling.

Garrett, Romeo B. The Presidents & the Negro. 1990. 24.45 *(0-87498-013-5)* Assoc Pubs DC.

Garrett, Sandra G. & Williams, Philip C. The Blanket Burgler. LC 93-31883. 1994. write for info. *(0-86625-503-6)* Rourke Pubns.

—The Candy Bandit. LC 93-31882. 1994. write for info. *(0-86625-502-8)* Rourke Pubns.

—The Smuggler's Secret. LC 93-31884. (gr. 6 up). 1994. write for info. *(0-86625-501-X)* Rourke Pubns.

Garrett, Sean. The Suez Canal. Yapp, Malcolm, et al, eds. (Illus.). 32p. (gr. 6-11). 1980. pap. text ed. 3.45 *(0-89908-205-X)* Greenhaven.

Garrett-Goodyear, Joan H., et al. Writing Papers: A Handbook for Students at Smith College. 2nd, rev. ed. 60p. (gr. 9-12). 1986. pap. 2.95 *(0-88741-098-7)* Sundance Pubs.

Garrick, Elizabeth. Camelot World: The Mysterious Cat. 128p. (Orig.). 1990. pap. 2.95 *(0-380-76038-X,* Camelot) Avon.

Garrick, Liz. Quest for King Arthur, No. 23. Best, Charles, illus. 144p. (ps-6). 1988. pap. 2.50 *(0-553-27126-1)* Bantam.

Garrigue, Sheila. The Eternal Spring of Mr. Ito. LC 85-5687. 176p. (gr. 5-7). 1985. SBE 13.95 *(0-02-737300-2,* Bradbury Pr) Macmillan Child Grp.

—The Eternal Spring of Mr. Ito. 176p. (gr. 3-7). 1994. pap. 3.95 *(0-689-71809-8,* Aladdin) Macmillan Child Grp.

Garrison, Christian. The Dream Eater. Goode, Diane, illus. LC 85-26671. 32p. (ps-2). 1986. pap. 3.95 *(0-689-71058-5,* Aladdin) Macmillan Child Grp.

Garrison, Edward T., Jr. Short Stories about States & Capitals. (Illus.). 1986. 4.95 *(0-9634033-0-3)* E G Photoprint.

Garrison, Eileen & Albanese, Gayle. Eucharistic Manual for Children. Dickinson, Charles, illus. LC 84-60217. 28p. (gr. 1-8). 1984. pap. 4.75 *(0-8192-1343-8)* Morehouse Pub.

Garrison, Thomas S., ed. Annual Directory of World Leaders, 1991, Vol. 3. 200p. (Orig.). (gr. 9-12). 1991. pap. 39.95 *(0-9610590-5-2)* IASB Enviro.

Garrison, Webb. Civil War Trivia & Fact Book. (Illus.). 240p. (Orig.). 1992. pap. 9.95 *(1-55853-160-2)* Rutledge Hill Pr.

—Great Stories of the American Revolution. LC 90-33127. (Illus.). 256p. (gr. 8 up). 1990. 16.95 *(1-55853-072-X)* Rutledge Hill Pr.

—Great Stories of the American Revolution. (Illus.). 288p. (gr. 9 up). 1993. pap. 12.95 *(1-55853-270-6)* Rutledge Hill Pr.

—A Treasury of Ohio Tales. (Illus.). 192p. (gr. 9 up). 1993. 9.95 *(1-55853-249-8)* Rutledge Hill Pr.

Garrity, Leslie & Schecter, Teri. Colorado Geography. (Orig.). (gr. k-5). 1988. pap. text ed. 8.95 s.p. *(0-87108-278-0)*; tchr's. guide pap. 8.95 *(0-87108-281-0)* Pruett.

Garrity, Robert K. The Twentieth Century: An Epic of American History. 208p. (Orig.). (gr. 9-12). 1991. pap. write for info. R K Garrity.

Garry-McCord, Kathleen, illus. Dick Whittington. LC 80-28171. 32p. (gr. k-4). 1981. PLB 9.79 (0-89375-482-X); pap. text ed. 1.95 (0-89375-483-8) Troll Assocs.

Gars, Lissa, ed. The Lost Child & Other Stories. (Illus.). 80p. (gr. 4-9). 1993. pap. 9.95 (1-882427-02-5) Aspasia Pubns.

—The Tree Elf & Other Folktales: Illustrated Tales for Children. (Illus.). 60p. (gr. 2-6). 1993. pap. 9.95 (1-882427-01-7) Aspasia Pubns.

Garside, Alice H. The Ant & the Duck. Meeks, Catherine F., illus. 30p. (Orig.). (gr. k-2). 1990. pap. 2.10 (1-882063-07-4) Cottage Pr MA.

—The Dog & the Bone. Meeks, Catherine F., illus. 20p. (Orig.). (gr. k-2). 1990. pap. 2.10 (1-882063-11-2) Cottage Pr MA.

—The Dog & the Wolf. Meeks, Catherine F., illus. 20p. (Orig.). (gr. k-2). 1990. pap. 2.10 (1-882063-08-2) Cottage Pr MA.

—The Fox & the Stork. Meeks, Catherine F., illus. 40p. (Orig.). (gr. k-2). 1990. pap. 2.10 (1-882063-10-4) Cottage Pr MA.

—The Fox & the Thrush. Meeks, Catherine F., illus. 20p. (Orig.). (gr. k-2). 1990. pap. 2.10 (1-882063-09-0) Cottage Pr MA.

—The Garside Readers, 6 vols. Meeks, Catherine F., illus. 1990. Set. pap. 6.25 (1-882063-18-X) Cottage Pr MA.

—The Man, the Fox & the Skunk. Meeks, Catherine F., illus. 24p. (Orig.). (gr. k-2). 1989. pap. text ed. 2.10 (1-882063-06-6) Cottage Pr MA.

Garson, Eugenia, ed. The Laura Ingalls Wilder Songbook: Favorite Songs from the "Little House" Books. reissued ed. Williams, Garth, illus. LC 68-24327. 160p. (gr. 4 up). 1968. 19.00 (0-06-021933-5); PLB 18.89 (0-06-021934-3) HarpC Child Bks.

Garson, Mike. A New Age Christmas. Roed, Tom, ed. 56p. (Orig.). 1992. pap. text ed. 14.95 (0-89898-648-6) CPP Belwin.

Garst, Hitjo. From Mountain to Mountain: Stories about Baha'u'llah. McKinley, Olive, tr. from DUT. Parsons, Brian, illus. 138p. (gr. 3-4). 1988. 20.95 (0-85398-265-1) G Ronald Pub.

Garten, Jan. The Alphabet Tale. Batherman, Muriel, illus. (ps up). 1994. write for info. (0-688-12702-9); PLB write for info. (0-688-12703-7) Greenwillow.

Gartenhaus, Alan. Start Exploring Masterpieces of American Art: A Fact-Filled Coloring Book. Driggs, Helen, illus. 128p. (Orig.). 1992. pap. 8.95 (1-56138-083-0) Running Pr.

Garth, Maureen. Starbright: Meditations for Children. LC 90-56458. 96p. (Orig.). 1991. pap. 8.95 (0-06-250398-7) Harper SF.

Gartner, Bob. Exploring Careers in the National Park Service. Rosen, Ruth, ed. (gr. 7-12). 1993. 13.95 (0-8239-1414-3); pap. 9.95 (0-8239-1726-6) Rosen Group.

Garver, Susan & McGuire, Paula. From Mexico, Cuba, & Puerto Rico. (gr. 7-11). pap. 2.50 (0-317-13311-X, LFL) Dell.

Garvy, Helen. Bingo Book, No. 4: Spanish. 80p. (Orig.). 1994. pap. 6.00 (0-918828-15-5) Shire Pr.

—Bingo Book, No. 5: French. 80p. 1994. pap. 6.00 (0-918828-16-3) Shire Pr.

—The Immune System: Your Magic Doctor. Bessie, Dan, illus. LC 91-91575. 76p. (gr. 4 up). 1992. lib. bdg. 15. 00 (0-918828-09-0); pap. 10.00 (0-918828-10-4) Shire Pr.

Gary Grimm & Associates Staff. Chicago for Kids: Of All Ages. rev. ed. Filkins, Vanessa, illus. 32p. (gr. k-8). Repr. of 1985 ed. wkbk. 4.00 (1-56490-001-0) G Grimm Assocs.

—Let's Color Chicago. Filkins, Vanessa, illus. 40p. (Orig.). (ps-6). 1993. wkbk. 4.00 (1-56490-000-2) G Grimm Assocs.

Garza, Carmen Lomas see Lomas Garza, Carmen.

Garza, Hedda. Francisco Franco. Schlesinger, Arthur M., Jr., intro. by. (Illus.). 112p. (gr. 5 up). 1987. lib. bdg. 17.95 (0-87754-524-3) Chelsea Hse.

—Frida Kahlo: Mexican Painter. (Illus.). (ps-3). 1994. PLB 18.95 (0-7910-1698-6, Am Art Analog); pap. 7.95 (0-7910-1699-4, Am Art Analog) Chelsea Hse.

—Joan Baez. (Illus.). 120p. (gr. 5 up). 1991. lib. bdg. 17. 95 (0-7910-1233-6) Chelsea Hse.

—Joan Baez: Hispanics of Achievement. (gr. 4-7). 1992. pap. 7.95 (0-7910-1260-3) Chelsea Hse.

—Mao Zedong. (Illus.). 112p. (gr. 5 up). 1988. lib. bdg. 17.95 (0-87754-564-2) Chelsea Hse.

—Pablo Casals. (gr. 4-7). 1992. pap. 7.95 (0-7910-1261-1) Chelsea Hse.

Gascoigne, Toss, et al, eds. Dream Time. Honey, Elizabeth, illus. 192p. 1991. 13.45 (0-395-57434-X, Sandpiper) HM.

Gaskill, Rebecca, jt. auth. see Stevens, Jill.

Gaskin, Carol. Camelot World: Secrets of the Samurai. 128p. (Orig.). 1990. pap. 2.95 (0-380-76040-1, Camelot) Avon.

—Caravan to China. (gr. 5 up). 1987. pap. 2.50 (0-317-65091-2) Bantam.

—A Day in the Life of a Circus Clown. Klein, John F., illus. LC 87-10954. 32p. (gr. 4-8). 1988. PLB 11.79 (0-8167-1107-0); pap. text ed. 2.95 (0-8167-1108-9) Troll Assocs.

—A Day in the Life of a Racing Car Mechanic. Klein, John F., illus. LC 84-2430. 32p. (gr. 4-8). 1985. PLB 11.79 (0-8167-0091-5); pap. 2.95 (0-8167-0092-3) Troll Assocs.

—The Forbidden Towers. Price, T. Alexander, illus. LC 84-16219. 128p. (gr. 3-7). 1985. lib. bdg. 9.49 (0-8167-0324-8) Troll Assocs.

—Legend of Hiawatha, No. 2. 80p. (Orig.). 1986. pap. 2.50 (0-553-15450-8) Bantam.

—The Magician's Ring. Price, T. Alexander, illus. LC 84-8499. 128p. (gr. 3-7). 1985. PLB 9.49 (0-8167-0320-5); pap. text ed. 2.95 (0-8167-0321-3) Troll Assocs.

—Master of Mazes. Price, T. Alexander, illus. LC 84-24015. 128p. (gr. 3-7). 1985. PLB 9.49 (0-8167-0322-1) Troll Assocs.

—Secret of the Royal Treasure. 144p. (Orig.). 1986. pap. 2.50 (0-553-25729-3) Bantam.

—The War of the Wizards. Price, T. Alexander, illus. LC 84-2663. 128p. (gr. 3-7). 1985. PLB 9.49 (0-8167-0318-3); pap. text ed. 2.95 (0-8167-0319-1) Troll Assocs.

Gaskin, Carol, jt. auth. see Klein, John F.

Gaspar, Tomas R. La Aventura de Yolanda; Yolanda's Hike. (ENG & SPA., Illus.). (ps-3). 1974. 5.95 (0-938678-03-5) New Seed.

Gaspard, Helen. Doctor Dan the Bandage Man. reissued ed. Malvern, Corinne, illus. (ps-k). 1992. write for info. (0-307-00142-3, 312-07, Golden Pr) Western Pub.

Gaspari, Claudia. Food in Italy. LC 88-33269. (Illus.). 32p. (gr. 3-6). 1989. lib. bdg. 15.94 (0-86625-342-4); 11.95s.p. (0-685-58498-4) Rourke Corp.

Gasperini, Jim. The Mystery of Atlantis. 144p. (Orig.). (gr. 5 up). 1985. pap. 2.50 (0-553-25073-6) Bantam.

—Sail with Pirates. Pierard, John & Nino, Alex, illus. 144p. (gr. 4 up). 1984. pap. 2.50 (0-553-26497-4) Bantam.

—Secrets of the Pyramids. (ps-7). 1984. pap. 2.50 (0-553-26960-7) Bantam.

Gasperini, Jim, jt. auth. see Preiss, Byron.

Gasque, Pratt. Rum Gully Tales from Tuck'em Inn. (Illus.). 148p. 1990. 14.95 (0-87844-094-1); pap. 8.95 (0-87844-095-X) Sandpaper Pub Co.

Gast, Natalie. Universal Speaking Pictures, No. 2. Capello, Joe, illus. (Orig.). 1984. wkbk., 36 p. 7.45 (0-916177-01-7); pap. 1.45 ans. key, 8 p. (0-685-50631-2) Am Emp Pubns.

Gastineau, Jerrel, jt. auth. see Quackenbush, Ross.

Gastman, Joseph W. Creatrivia. 112p. (gr. 4-8). 1989. 9.95 (0-86653-482-2, GA1087) Good Apple.

Gaston, Blanche P. I Like Me, Vol. I. Kerns, Aaron, illus. 24p. (Orig.). (gr. k-3). 1982. 6.95x (0-9608516-0-7); pap. 4.95x (0-9608516-1-5) I Like Me Pub.

—I Like Me. (Illus.). 25p. (gr. k-3). 1984. 7.95 (0-941484-04-1) Urban Res Pr.

Gaston, I. Carlos. El Derecho a Vivir con Dignidad: A Traves del Sistema Empresarial Cooperativo. (SPA.). 192p. (Orig.). (gr. 9-12). 1989. pap. 8.00 (0-917049-44-6) Saeta.

Gaston, Jane. Safari: A Lift-the-Flaps Adventure. Gaston, Jane, illus. LC 92-80525. 24p. (ps-1). 1993. 7.99 (0-679-83044-8) Random Bks Yng Read.

Gasztold, Carmen B. De see De Gasztold, Carmen B.
Gasztold, Carmen Bernos De see Bernos de Gasztold, Carmen.

Gatch, Jean. School Makes Sense...Sometimes. Turnbull, Jean, illus. LC 80-10281. 32p. (gr. k-5). 1980. 16.95 (0-87705-494-0) Human Sci Pr.

Gately, George. Heathcliff: The Good Life. 128p. (Orig.). 1992. pap. 3.50 (0-8125-1745-8) Tor Bks.

Gates, Doris. Blue Willow. Lantz, Paul, illus. LC 40-32435. (gr. 4-6). 1976. pap. 3.99 (0-14-030924-1, VS30, Puffin) Puffin Bks.

—Blue Willow. Lantz, Paul, illus. LC 40-32435. 176p. (gr. 4-7). 1940. pap. 14.00 (0-670-17557-9) Viking Child Bks.

—A Fair Wind for Troy. Mikolaycak, Charles, illus. 96p. (gr. 4-6). 1984. pap. 4.95 (0-14-031718-X, Puffin) Puffin Bks.

—The Golden God: Apollo. CoConis, Constantine, illus. 110p. (gr. 3-7). 1983. pap. 4.99 (0-14-031647-7, Puffin) Puffin Bks.

—Lord of the Sky: Zeus. Handville, Robert, illus. (gr. 3-7). 1982. pap. 4.99 (0-14-031532-2, Puffin) Puffin Bks.

—Mightiest of Mortals: Heracles. Cuffari, Richard, illus. 96p. (gr. 3-7). 1984. pap. 4.95 (0-14-031531-4, Puffin) Puffin Bks.

—Two Queens of Heaven: Aphrodite & Demeter. CoConis, Constantine, illus. 94p. (gr. 3-7). 1983. pap. 4.99 (0-14-031646-9, Puffin) Puffin Bks.

—The Warrior Goddess: Athena. Bolognese, Don, illus. (gr. 3-7). 1982. pap. 4.99 (0-14-031530-6, Puffin) Puffin Bks.

Gates, Fay C. Judaism. (Illus.). 128p. (gr. 7-12). 1991. 17. 95x (0-8160-2444-8) Facts on File.

Gates, Frieda. Easy-to-Make Monster Masks & Disguises. (Illus.). (gr. 1-3). 1981. pap. 3.95 (0-13-222794-0, Pub. by Treehouse) P-H.

—North American Indian Masks. Gates, Frieda, illus. 64p. (gr. 5 up). 1982. 8.95 (0-8027-6462-2); lib. bdg. 9.85 (0-8027-6463-0) Walker & Co.

Gates, Richard. Conservation. LC 81-38482. (Illus.). 48p. (gr. k-4). 1982. PLB 15.27 (0-516-01618-0) Childrens.

Gathings, Evelyn. Cut & Make Cat Masks in Full Color. 32p. (gr. 1 up). 1988. pap. 4.95 (0-486-25804-1) Dover.

Gathorne-Hardy, Jonathan. Jane's Adventures In & Out of the Book. Hill, Nicholas, illus. LC 80-29185. 192p. (gr. 5 up). 1981. 13.95 (0-87951-122-2) Overlook Pr.

Gatland, K. Spaceflight. 32p. (gr. 4-8). 1976. lib. bdg. 13. 96 (0-88110-436-1, Usborne); pap. 6.95 (0-86020-049-3) EDC.

Gattegno, Caleb. Words in Color. rev. ed. (Orig.). (gr. k-12). 1977. mini-charts 8.75 (0-87825-143-X); Word Charts. 100.00 (0-87825-131-6); Phonic Code Charts. 40.00 (0-87825-132-4); Book R-0. 0.25 (0-87825-127-8); Book R-1. 0.65 (0-87825-128-6); Book R-2. 1.50 (0-87825-129-4); Book R-3. 1.50 (0-87825-130-8); Worksheets 1-7. 3.65 (0-87825-178-2); Worksheets 8-14. 1.65 (0-87825-059-X) Ed Solutions.

Gatti, Anne. Isabella Bird Bishop. (Illus.). 64p. (gr. 6-10). 1991. 13.95 (0-237-60035-8, Pub. by Evans Bros Ltd) Trafalgar.

Gatti, Maria N., tr. see Mann, Peggy.

Gattis, L. S. ed. see Evans, Lee.

Gattis, L. S., III. Animal Tracking for Pathfinders: A Basic Youth Enrichment Skill Honor Packet. (Illus.). 26p. (Orig.). (gr. 5 up). 1989. pap. 5.00 tchr's. ed. (0-936241-48-9) Cheetah Pub.

—Butterflies & Moths for Pathfinders: A Basic Youth Enrichment Skill Honor Packet. (Illus.). 20p. (Orig.). (gr. 5 up). 1987. pap. 5.00 tchr's. ed. (0-936241-31-4) Cheetah Pub.

—Cats for Pathfinders: A Basic Youth Enrichment Skill Honor Packet. (Illus.). 20p. (Orig.). (gr. 5 up). 1987. pap. 5.00 tchr's ed (0-936241-25-X) Cheetah Pub.

—Computer for Pathfinders: A Basic Youth Enrichment Skill Honor Packet. (Illus.). 20p. (Orig.). (gr. 5 up). 1987. pap. 5.00 tchr's. ed. (0-936241-11-X) Cheetah Pub.

—Cooking for Pathfinders: A Basic & Advanced Youth Enrichment Skill Honor Packet. (Illus.). 24p. (Orig.). (gr. 5 up). 1989. pap. 5.00 tchr's. ed. (0-936241-49-7) Cheetah Pub.

—Crime Prevention for Pathfinders: A Basic Youth Enrichment Skill Honor Packet. (Illus.). 20p. (Orig.). (gr. 5 up). 1987. pap. 5.00 tchr's. ed. (0-936241-27-6) Cheetah Pub.

—Crystals for Pathfinders: A Basic Youth Enrichment Skill Honor Packet. (Illus.). 20p. (Orig.). (gr. 5 up). 1987. pap. 5.00 tchr's. ed. (0-936241-22-5) Cheetah Pub.

—Cycling for Pathfinders: A Basic Youth Enrichment Skill Honor Packet. (Illus.). 20p. (Orig.). (gr. 5 up). 1987. pap. 5.00 tchr's. ed. (0-936241-15-2) Cheetah Pub.

—Dogs for Pathfinders: A Basic Youth Enrichment Skill Honor Packet. (Illus.). 20p. (Orig.). (gr. 5 up). 1987. pap. 5.00 tchr's. ed. (0-936241-24-1) Cheetah Pub.

—Fossil Collecting for Pathfinders: A Basic Youth Enrichment Skill Honor Packet. (Illus.). 20p. (Orig.). (gr. 5 up). 1987. pap. 5.00 tchr's. ed. (0-936241-16-0) Cheetah Pub.

—Fungi for Pathfinders: A Basic Youth Enrichment Skill Honor Packet. (Illus.). 20p. (Orig.). (gr. 5 up). 1987. pap. 5.00 tchr's. ed. (0-936241-20-9) Cheetah Pub.

—Houseplants for Pathfinders: A Basic Youth Enrichment Skill Honor Packet. (Illus.). 24p. (Orig.). (gr. 5 up). 1989. pap. 5.00 tchr's. ed. (0-936241-50-0) Cheetah Pub.

—Insects for Pathfinders: A Basic Youth Enrichment Skill Honor Packet. (Illus.). 24p. (Orig.). (gr. 5 up). 1987. pap. 5.00 tchr's. ed. (0-936241-30-6) Cheetah Pub.

—Junior Witnessing for Pathfinders: A Basic Youth Enrichment Skill Honor Packet. (Illus.). 20p. (Orig.). (gr. 5 up). 1987. pap. 5.00 tchr's. ed. (0-936241-18-7) Cheetah Pub.

—Kites (Barriletes Papalotes) for Pathfinders: A Basic Youth Enrichment Skill Honor Packet. (SPA., Illus.). 20p. (Orig.). (gr. 5 up). 1987. pap. 5.00 tchr's. ed. (0-936241-32-2) Cheetah Pub.

—Kites for Pathfinders: A Basic Youth Enrichment Skill Honor Packet. Gattis, L. S., III, illus. 18p. (Orig.). (gr. 5 up). 1986. pap. 5.00 tchr's. ed. (0-936241-07-1) Cheetah Pub.

—Laundering for Pathfinders: A Basic Youth Enrichment Skill Honor Packet. (Illus.). 20p. (Orig.). (gr. 5 up). 1988. pap. 5.00 tchr's. ed. (0-936241-38-1) Cheetah Pub.

—Leathercraft for Pathfinders: A Basic Youth Enrichment Skill Honor Packet. Gattis, L. S., III, illus. 20p. (Orig.). (gr. 5 up). 1987. pap. 5.00 tchr's. ed. (0-936241-09-8) Cheetah Pub.

—Leathercraft for Pathfinders: An Advanced Youth Enrichment Skill Honor Packet. Gattis, L. S., III, illus. 20p. (Orig.). (gr. 5 up). 1987. pap. 5.00 tchr's. ed. (0-936241-10-1) Cheetah Pub.

—Rocks & Minerals for Pathfinders: A Basic Youth Enrichment Skill Honor Packet. (Illus.). 22p. (Orig.). (gr. 5 up). 1987. pap. 5.00 tchr's. ed. (0-936241-29-2) Cheetah Pub.

—Shells for Pathfinders: A Basic Youth Enrichment Skill Honor Packet. (Illus.). 26p. (Orig.). (gr. 5 up). 1989. pap. 5.00 tchr's. ed. (0-936241-47-0) Cheetah Pub.

—Shrubs for Pathfinders: A Basic Youth Enrichment Skill Honor Packet. (Illus.). 20p. (Orig.). (gr. 5 up). 1989. pap. 5.00 tchr's. ed. (0-936241-41-1) Cheetah Pub.

—Small Engine Repair for Pathfinders: A Basic Youth Enrichment Skill Honor Packet. (Illus.). 20p. (Orig.). (gr. 5 up). 1987. pap. 5.00 tchr's. ed. (0-936241-19-5) Cheetah Pub.

—Trailblazer Fun Honors I: Birds, Buttons, Computers, Dress, Kites & Stamps. (Illus.). 20p. (Orig.). (ps-5). 1986. pap. 5.00 tchr's. ed. (0-936241-08-X) Cheetah Pub.

—Trailblazer Fun Honors II: Cooking, Dogs, Flowers, Hiking, Seeds & Trees. (Illus.). 20p. (Orig.). (ps-5). 1987. pap. 5.00 tchr's. ed. (*0-936241-43-8*) Cheetah Pub.

—Trees for Pathfinders: A Basic Youth Enrichment Skill Honor Packet. (Illus.). 20p. (Orig.). (gr. 5 up). 1988. pap. 5.00 tchr's. ed. (*0-936241-36-5*) Cheetah Pub.

—Wood Handicraft for Pathfinders: A Basic Youth Enrichment Skill Honor Packet. (Illus.). 20p. (Orig.). (gr. 5 up). 1987. pap. 5.00 tchr's. ed. (*0-936241-28-4*) Cheetah Pub.

Gatto, Joseph A. Emphasis: A Design Principle. LC 75-21112. (Illus.). 80p. (gr. 7-12). 1975. 10.95 (*0-87192-075-1*) Davis Mass.

Gauarino, Deborah. Is Your Mama a Llama? (ps-3). 1992. pap. 19.95 (*0-590-72525-4*) Scholastic Inc.

Gauch, Patricia. Uncle Magic. Ray, Deborah K., illus. LC 91-22356. 32p. (ps-3). 1992. reinforced bdg. 14.95 (*0-8234-0937-6*) Holiday.

Gauch, Patricia L. Bravo, Tanya. Ichikawa, Satomi, illus. 40p. (ps-3). 1992. PLB 14.95 (*0-399-22145-X*, Philomel Bks) Putnam Pub Group.

—C. K. & the Time She Quit the Family. Primavera, Elise, illus. 32p. (ps-3). 1992. pap. 5.95 (*0-399-22405-X*, Putnam) Putnam Pub Group.

—Christina Katerina & the Box. Burn, Doris, illus. 48p. 1980. pap. 6.95 (*0-698-20524-3*, Coward) Putnam Pub Group.

—Christina Katerina & the Great Bear Train. Primavera, Elise, illus. 32p. 1990. 14.95 (*0-399-21623-5*, Putnam) Putnam Pub Group.

—Christina Katerina & the Time She Quit the Family. Primavera, Elise, illus. 32p. (ps-3). 1987. 14.95 (*0-399-21408-9*, Putnam) Putnam Pub Group.

—Dance, Tanya. Ichikawa, Satomi, illus. 32p. (ps-3). 1989. 13.95 (*0-399-21521-2*, Philomel Bks) Putnam Pub Group.

—Tanya & Emily in a Pas De Deux. Ichikawa, Satomi, illus. LC 93-5354. 1994. write for info. (*0-399-22688-5*, Philomel Bks) Putnam Pub Group.

—This Time, Tempe Wick? Tomes, Margot, illus. 48p. (gr. 1-4). 1992. 12.95 (*0-399-21880-7*, Putnam) Putnam Pub Group.

—Thunder at Gettysburg. Gammell, Stephen, illus. 48p. (gr. 3-6). 1990. 14.95 (*0-399-22201-4*, Putnam) Putnam Pub Group.

—Thunder at Gettysburg. (ps-3). 1991. pap. 2.99 (*0-553-15951-8*) Bantam.

Gauch, Patricia Lee. Noah. Green, Jonathan, illus. LC 92-44283. 1994. write for info. (*0-399-22548-X*, Philomel Bks) Putnam Pub Group.

Gaudiano, Andrea. Azteca: The Story of a Jaguar Warrior. (SPA & ENG., Illus.). 160p. 1992. pap. 14.95 (*1-879373-05-X*) R Rinehart.

—Azteca: The Story of a Jaguar Warrior. (Illus.). 80p. 1992. pap. 7.95 (*1-879373-32-7*) R Rinehart.

Gaudrat, Marie-Agnes. Hello, God. (Illus.). 48p. (ps-4). 1991. 6.99 (*0-7459-1959-6*) Lion USA.

—Here I Am, God. (Illus.). 48p. (ps-4). 1991. 6.99 (*0-7459-1960-X*) Lion USA.

Gaudreau, Carmen. Bernard et Bridget: a la cabane a sucre. LeBlanc, Lorraine, illus. (FRE.). 40p. (gr. k-1). 1979. pap. text ed. 1.50 (*0-911409-47-5*); of 53 2x2 slides 13.25 set (*0-686-42727-0*) Natl Mat Dev.

Gauduchon, Michaele. French Grammar Flipper. 49p. (gr. 5 up). 1989. trade edition 5.95 (*1-878383-12-4*) C Lee Pubns.

Gaughenbaugh, Michael & Camburn, Herbert. Old House, New House. Camburn, Herbert, illus. 56p. (gr. 4-6). 1993. 16.95 (*0-89133-236-7*) Preservation Pr.

Gault. The Home Run Kings. 1993. pap. 2.75 (*0-590-45530-3*) Scholastic Inc.

Gauthier, Bertrand. Zachary in Camping Out. Sylvestre, Daniel, illus. LC 93-15457. 1993. write for info. (*0-8368-1012-0*) Gareth Stevens Inc.

—Zachary in I'm Zachary! Sylvestre, Daniel, illus. LC 93-1168. 1993. 21.27 (*0-8368-1007-4*) Gareth Stevens Inc.

—Zachary in the Championship. Sylvestre, Daniel, illus. LC 93-1169. 1993. 21.27 (*0-8368-1008-2*) Gareth Stevens Inc.

—Zachary in the Present. Sylvestre, Daniel, illus. LC 93-7719. 1993. 21.27 (*0-8368-1010-4*) Gareth Stevens Inc.

—Zachary in the Wawabongbong. Sylvestre, Daniel, illus. LC 93-15456. 1993. write for info. (*0-8368-1011-2*) Gareth Stevens Inc.

—Zachary in the Winner. Sylvestre, Daniel, illus. LC 93-7718. 1993. 21.27 (*0-8368-1009-0*) Gareth Stevens Inc.

Gauthier, Don, illus. Jack & the Beanstalk: European Folk Tales. 24p. (ps-2). 1992. pap. 3.50 (*0-88625-287-3*) Durkin Hayes Pub.

Gautier, Bertrand. Just Me & My Dad, 6 titles. Sylvestre, Daniel, illus. (gr. 2 up). 1993. Set. PLB 95.60 (*0-8368-1006-6*); PLB 15.93 ea. Gareth Stevens Inc.

Gautier, Dick. The Career Cartoonist: A Step-by-Step Guide to Presenting & Selling Your Artwork. 128p. (Orig.). 1992. pap. 10.95 (*0-399-51732-4*, Perigee Bks) Putnam Pub Group.

—A Child's Garden of Weirdness: Illustrations, Verse, & Worse. LC 92-43033. 1993. 14.95 (*0-8048-1825-8*) C E Tuttle.

Gauz, Yaffa. From Head to Toe: A Book About You. (gr. 5-8). 1988. 11.95 (*0-87306-446-1*) Feldheim.

—Me & My Bubby, My Zeidy & Me. 1991. 9.95 (*0-87306-543-3*) Feldheim.

—Savta Simcha & the Seven Splendid Gifts. Gewirtz, Bina, illus. LC 87-3643. (gr. 4-7). 1987. 12.95 (*0-87306-437-2*) Feldheim.

Gavan, Terrence. The Barons of Newport: A Guide to the Gilded Age. (Illus.). 88p. (Orig.). 1988. pap. 7.50 (*0-929249-01-1*) Pineapple Pubns.

—Complete Guide to Newport. (Illus.). 64p. (Orig.). 1988. pap. 5.95 (*0-929249-00-3*) Pineapple Pubns.

Gave, Marc. Disney's Goof Troop: Max's Treasure Hunt. (Illus.). 24p. (ps-3). 1992. pap. write for info. (*0-307-12762-1*, 12762, Golden Pr) Western Pub.

—Monkey See, Monkey Do. Rogers, Jackie, illus. 32p. (ps-2). 1993. pap. 2.95 (*0-590-45801-9*) Scholastic Inc.

—Tess & Tim. Carter, Abby, illus. LC 88-12418. 48p. (ps-3). 1988. 5.95 (*0-8193-1185-5*) Parents.

—Travels with Tess & Tim. Carter, Abby, illus. LC 89-16401. 48p. (ps-3). 1990. 5.95 (*0-8193-1192-8*) Parents.

—Walt Disney's Pinocchio: Fun with Shapes & Sizes. Kurtz, John, illus. 14p. (ps-k). 1992. bds. write for info. (*0-307-12332-4*, 12332, Golden Pr) Western Pub.

Gavin, Peggy, compiled by. Meet the Real Me. Kinnealy, Janice, illus. LC 92-21644. 32p. (gr. 2-8). 1992. pap. text ed. 2.50 (*0-8167-2939-5*) Troll Assocs.

Gaw, Robyn. Chick-in-a-Box. Cooper-Brown, Jean, illus. LC 93-11735. 1994. 4.25 (*0-383-03799-9*) SRA Schl Grp.

—Ducks. Lee, Connell, illus. LC 92-31915. 1993. 4.25 (*0-383-03567-8*) SRA Schl Grp.

Gawr, Rhuddlwm. The Triads: The Wisdom of the Welsh Witches. Gawr, Rhuddlwm, illus. LC 85-73755. 140p. (Orig.). 1989. 14.95 (*0-931760-45-3*, CP 10123); pap. 10.95 (*0-931760-23-2*) Camelot GA.

—The Way: The Discovery of the Grail of Immortality. Gawr, Rhuddlwm, et al, illus. LC 85-73759. (Orig.). 1987. 18.95 (*0-931760-50-X*, CP 10128); pap. 15.95 (*0-931760-28-3*) Camelot GA.

Gawron, Marlene. Busy Bodies: Finger Plays & Action Rhymes. rev. ed. (Illus.). 72p. (ps-1). 1985. pap. 5.50 (*0-913545-12-0*) Moonlight FL.

Gawron, Marlene E. Ten Little Bunnies. Sterchele, Christina L., illus. (ps-1). 1981. 3.50 (*0-913545-06-6*) Moonlight FL.

Gay, David. Voyage to Freedom: Story of the Pilgrim Fathers. 149p. 1984. pap. 8.95 (*0-85151-384-0*) Banner of Truth.

Gay, Kathlyn. Adoption & Foster Care. LC 89-36476. (Illus.). 128p. (gr. 6 up). 1990. lib. bdg. 17.95 (*0-89490-239-3*) Enslow Pubs.

—Air Pollution. LC 91-17780. (Illus.). 144p. (gr. 9-12). 1991. PLB 13.90 (*0-531-13002-9*) Watts.

—Bigotry. LC 88-30428. (Illus.). 144p. (gr. 6 up). 1989. lib. bdg. 18.95 (*0-89490-171-0*) Enslow Pubs.

—Breast Implants: Making Safe Choices. LC 92-35095. (Illus.). 128p. (gr. 6 up). 1993. RSBE 13.95 (*0-02-737955-8*, New Discovery) Macmillan Child Grp.

—Caretakers of the Earth. LC 92-23048. (Illus.). 104p. (gr. 6 up). 1993. lib. bdg. 17.95 (*0-89490-397-7*) Enslow Pubs.

—Caution: This May Be an Advertisement: A Teen Guide to Advertising. Roxas, Reni, ed. LC 91-38159. (Illus.). 208p. (gr. 9-12). 1992. PLB 14.90 (*0-531-11039-7*) Watts.

—Church & State: Government & Religion in the United States. LC 91-34753. (Illus.). 128p. (gr. 7 up). 1992. PLB 14.90 (*1-56294-063-5*) Millbrook Pr.

—Civil War. (gr. 6 up). 1995. PLB write for info. (*0-8050-2845-5*) H Holt & Co.

—Cleaning Nature Naturally. 144p. (gr. 7-9). 1991. 15.95 (*0-8027-8118-7*); PLB 16.85 (*0-8027-8119-5*) Walker & Co.

—Day Care: Looking for Answers. LC 91-18141. (Illus.). 128p. (gr. 6 up). 1992. lib. bdg. 17.95 (*0-89490-324-1*) Enslow Pubs.

—Ergonomics: Making Products & Places Fit People. LC 85-20634. (Illus.). 128p. (gr. 6 up). 1986. lib. bdg. 17.95 (*0-89490-118-4*) Enslow Pubs.

—Garbage & Recycling. LC 91-7130. (Illus.). 128p. (gr. 6 up). 1991. lib. bdg. 17.95 (*0-89490-321-7*) Enslow Pubs.

—Getting Your Message Across. LC 92-41820. (Illus.). 128p. (gr. 6 up). 1993. RSBE 13.95 (*0-02-735815-1*, New Discovery Bks) Macmillan Child Grp.

—Ozone. LC 89-9031. (Illus.). 128p. (gr. 7 up). 1989. PLB 13.90 (*0-531-10777-9*) Watts.

—Revolutionary War. 1995. PLB write for info. (*0-8050-2844-7*) H Holt & Co.

—The Right to Die: Public Controversy, Private Matter. LC 92-32201. (Illus.). 128p. 1993. PLB 15.90 (*1-56294-325-1*) Millbrook Pr.

—Science in Ancient Greece. Rasof, Henry, ed. LC 87-23747. (Illus.). 96p. (gr. 5-8). 1988. PLB 10.90 (*0-531-10487-7*) Watts.

—Silent Killers: Radon & Other Hazards. Kline, M., ed. LC 88-5549. (Illus.). (gr. 6-12). 1988. PLB 13.40 (*0-531-10598-9*) Watts.

—Spanish American War. 1995. PLB write for info. (*0-8050-2847-1*) H Holt & Co.

—They Don't Wash Their Socks! (Illus.). (gr. 4-7). 1990. 13.95 (*0-8027-6916-0*); lib. bdg. 14.85 (*0-8027-6917-9*) Walker & Co.

—They Don't Wash Their Socks! 112p. 1991. pap. 3.50 (*0-380-71302-0*, Camelot) Avon.

—War of 1812. 1995. PLB write for info. (*0-8050-2846-3*) H Holt & Co.

—Water Pollution. LC 90-376. (Illus.). 144p. (gr. 9-12). 1990. PLB 13.90 (*0-531-10949-6*) Watts.

—World War One. 1995. PLB write for info. (*0-8050-2848-X*) H Holt & Co.

—World War Two. 1995. PLB write for info. (*0-8050-2849-8*) H Holt & Co.

Gay, Kristin. Herschel's Special Dream. Matsumoto, Allen, illus. 60p. (Orig.). 1986. pap. 5.95 (*0-945265-08-5*) Accord Comm.

Gay, Marie-Louise. Rainy Day Magic. Tucker, Kathy, ed. Gay, Marie-Louise, illus. LC 89-5380. 32p. (ps-2). 1989. PLB 13.95 (*0-8075-6767-1*) A Whitman.

—Willy Nilly. Levine, Abby, ed. Gay, Marie-Louise, illus. LC 90-12376. 32p. (gr. 1-3). 1990. 13.95 (*0-8075-9119-X*) A Whitman.

Gay, Michel. Bibi Takes Flight. Gay, Michel, illus. LC 87-28262. 40p. (ps-1). 1988. 12.95 (*0-688-06828-6*); PLB 12.88 (*0-688-06829-4*, Morrow Jr Bks) Morrow Jr Bks.

Gay, Tanner O. Dinosaurs & Their Relatives in Action. Cassels, Jean, illus. 16p. (ps-3). 1990. POB 7.95 (*0-689-71434-3*, Aladdin) Macmillan Child Grp.

—Sharks in Action. Cassels, Jean, illus. 16p. (ps-4). 1990. POB 7.95 (*0-689-71435-1*, Aladdin) Macmillan Child Grp.

—Snakes & Other Reptiles in Action. Cassels, Jean, illus. 16p. (gr. k-4). 1991. POB 7.95 (*0-689-71536-6*, Aladdin) Macmillan Child Grp.

—Whales & Dolphins in Action. Cassels, Jean, illus. 16p. (gr. k-4). 1991. POB 7.95 (*0-689-71535-8*, Aladdin) Macmillan Child Grp.

Gaydos, Janine, jt. auth. see Stoker, Richard G.

Gayle, Addison. Claude McKay: The Black Poet at War. LC 77-180040. (gr. 12 up). 1972. pap. 3.00 (*0-910296-76-6*) Broadside Pr.

Gaylord, Gloria L. & Ried, Glenda E. Careers in Accounting. LC 90-50729. 128p. (gr. 9 up). 1991. 16.95 (*0-8442-8140-9*, VGM Career Bks); pap. 12.95 (*0-8442-8141-7*, VGM Career Bks) NTC Pub Grp.

Gaynor, Brigid. Back Yard Attractions. Rollins, Nancy O., illus. (ps). 1992. 15.95 (*1-56828-018-1*) Red Jacket Pr.

—Backyard Attractions. Rollins, Nancy O., illus. (ps). 1993. Gift box set of 4 bks., 12p. ea. incl. seed packs. bds. 14.95 (*1-56828-043-2*) Red Jacket Pr.

—The Flower Garden. Rollins, Nancy O., illus. 12p. (ps). 1992. 4.95 (*1-56828-014-9*) Red Jacket Pr.

—The Home Zoo. Rollins, Nancy O., illus. 12p. (ps). 1992. 4.95 (*1-56828-017-3*) Red Jacket Pr.

—Things to Do. Rollins, Nancy O., illus. 12p. (ps). 1992. 4.95 (*1-56828-015-7*) Red Jacket Pr.

—The Vegetable Garden. Rollins, Nancy O., illus. 12p. (ps). 1992. 4.95 (*1-56828-016-5*) Red Jacket Pr.

Gayu, Kathlyn. Global Garbage: Exporting Trash & Toxic Waste. (Illus.). 144p. (gr. 9-12). 1992. PLB 13.90 (*0-531-13009-6*) Watts.

Gearhart, Susan W. Opportunities in Modeling Careers. rev. ed. LC 90-50733. 160p. (gr. 7 up). 1991. 13.95 (*0-8442-8156-5*, VGM Career Bks); pap. 10.95 (*0-8442-8157-3*, VGM Career Bks) NTC Pub Grp.

Geary, Joe, jt. auth. see Geary, Susan.

Geary, Rosemary J., jt. auth. see Blustein, Lotte.

Geary, Susan & Geary, Joe. Best Friends Forever. Geary, Jennifer, illus. 100p. (Orig.). (gr. 2-4). 1991. pap. write for info. (*0-9629760-0-8*) Bear Paw Bks.

Geary, Susan R. The Black Bear: El Oso Negro. Geary, Jennifer, illus. 100p. (Orig.). (gr. 3-4). 1991. pap. write for info. (*0-9629760-1-6*) Bear Paw Bks.

Gebhardt, Catherine. A Perfect Christmas for Kate Leary. LC 90-70222. 44p. (gr. k-3). 1990. pap. 5.95 (*1-55523-331-7*) Winston-Derek.

Gebhart, Leslie, et al. Have You Ever Been a Child? (Hints for Helping When Life Seems Complicated) LC 93-60305. (Illus.). 1993. pap. 10.00 (*0-9636399-8-6*) Trinehrt Pubs.
Here is the book that connects the cord of communication among children, adults & therapists. The book has been praised by business leaders, religious leaders & therapists as well as moms & dads. HAVE YOU EVER BEEN A CHILD? (HINTS FOR HELPING WHEN LIFE SEEMS COMPLICATED) is a fully illustrated guide that facilitates the busy person's conversations with those people who matter most. Dr. K.C. Reilly, California State University has said, "..add this book to the collection of helping resources. Its messages, size & layout will appeal to all children." Sharon Wegscheider-Cruse & Joseph Cruse, MD say, "HAVE YOU EVER BEEN A CHILD? is a valuable tool for family & therapy sessions alike. It's the ice breaker that children & many adults need to gain confidence & freedom to voice concerns." HAVE

YOU EVER BEEN A CHILD? may be read cover to cover or open & experienced just one special page at a time. You will gain insight that will guide your decision making process. It is a feelings book. The emphasis is on the fact that EACH of us IS capable of creating change. A reader reacts: "For the adult child its wondrous; for the child child it's so safe." To order contact: Trineheart Publishers, P.O. Box 600E, Palm Springs, CA 92263. Telephone (619) 320-2688. *Publisher Provided Annotation.*

Geddes, Dorothy, et al. Geometry in the Middle Grades. Curcio, Frances R., ed. LC 92-15551. (Illus.). 88p. (Orig.). (gr. 5-8). 1992. pap. 15.00 (0-87353-323-2) NCTM.

Gedye, Jane. Dinner's Ready! A Pig's Book of Table Manners. 1989. 9.95 (0-385-26083-0) Doubleday.

Gee, John. Hidden Pictures: Favorites by John Gee. (Illus.). 32p. (gr. 1-6). 1981. pap. 2.95 (0-87534-230-2) Highlights.

—Timbertoes. (Illus.). 32p. (gr. k-2). 1967. pap. 2.95 (0-87534-133-0) Highlights.

Gee, Maurice. The Champion. LC 92-37670. 1993. pap. 14.00 (0-671-86561-7, S&S BFYR) S&S Trade.

—The Fire-Raiser. LC 92-8017. 150p. (gr. 5-9). 1992. 13.45 (0-395-62428-2) HM.

—The Fire-Raiser. large type ed. LC 93-31871. (gr. 9-12). 1993. 15.95 (0-7862-0065-0) Thorndike Pr.

Gee, R. Babies. 48p. (gr. 5-10). 1986. PLB 13.96 (0-88110-336-5); pap. 6.95 (0-86020-839-7) EDC.

Gee, R. & Bryant-Mole, K. Adding & Subtraction Puzzles. (Illus.). 32p. (gr. 2-6). 1993. pap. 4.95 (0-7460-1074-5) EDC.

Gee, R. & Inglis, L. Television. (Illus.). 32p. (gr. 3-9). 1992. PLB 13.96 (0-88110-586-4); pap. 6.95 (0-7460-1057-5) EDC.

Gee, R. & Meredith, S. Facts of Life (B - U) (Illus.). 96p. (gr. 5-9). pap. 12.95 (0-86020-851-6) EDC.

—Growing Up: Adolescence, Body Changes & Sex. 48p. 1986. PLB 13.96 (0-88110-337-3); pap. 6.95 (0-86020-837-0) EDC.

Gee, R., jt. auth. see Chisholm, J.

Gee, R., jt. auth. see Gibson, K.

Gee, R., jt. auth. see Gibson, K.

Gee, R., jt. auth. see Tyler, J.

Gee, Robyn, jt. auth. see Bryant-Mole, Karen.

Gee, Robyn, ed. Castle Times. McCaig, Rob & Ashman, Iain, illus. 24p. (gr. 3-6). 1982. lib. bdg. 11.96 (0-88110-106-0); pap. 4.50 (0-86020-621-1) EDC.

Geehan, Wayne. Captain Blackwell's Treasure. Geehan, Wayne, illus. (gr. 2-6). 1993. incl. puzzle 12.95 (0-922242-47-X) Lombard Mktg.

—ComputerSleuths. Sullivan, Suzanne, illus. (gr. 2-6). 1993. incl. puzzle 12.95 (0-922242-45-3) Lombard Mktg.

Geelan, Agnes. The Dakota Maverick. (Illus.). 186p. (gr. 9-12). 1983. pap. 7.95 (0-911007-03-2) Prairie Hse.

Gehman, Christian. Riders of Rohan. (Illus.). 48p. (gr. 10-12). 1985. pap. 12.00 (0-915795-29-9, 3100) Iron Crown Ent Inc.

Gehret, Jeanne. The Don't-Give-up Kid & Learning Differences: Learning Differences. 2nd ed. DePauw, Sandra A., illus. 40p. (gr. 1-5). 1992. 13.95 (0-9625136-3-6); pap. 8.95 (0-9625136-2-8) Verbal Images Pr.

—Eagle Eyes: A Child's Guide to Paying Attention. 2nd ed. Covert, Susan, illus. 40p. (gr. 1-5). 1991. 13.95 (0-9625136-5-2); pap. 8.95 perfect bdg. (0-9625136-4-4) Verbal Images Pr.

—I'm Somebody Too. 159p. (gr. 4-7). 1992. text ed. 16.00 (0-9625136-7-9); pap. 12.00 (0-9625136-6-0) Verbal Images Pr.

—Susan B. Anthony: And Justice for All. (Illus.). 100p. (gr. 4 up). 1993. write for info. (0-9625136-9-5); pap. write for info. (0-9625136-8-7) Verbal Images Pr. This engaging biography personalizes the struggle for female suffrage through the experience of its most famous advocate. It shows how woman suffrage grew out of the temperance & abolition movements, chronicling the development of these reforms through the Civil War & into the 20th century. Behind Susan B. Anthony's stern face was a warm, quick-witted organizer whom friends nicknamed "Napoleon." Her collaboration with other reformers of the day is carefully documented for students of American history. Other study aids include photographs, illustrations, a detailed chronology & index. Author Jeanne Gehert is a native of Rochester, New York, which Anthony called home. She has served as a docent at Anthony's house & published dozens of historical pieces about the region. Gehret has researched primary sources (some never published) as well as the most recent writings on Anthony & her contemporaries. She brings to this work the same eyewitness quality of her previous popular books: EAGLE EYES; THE DON'T-GIVE-UP KID; & I'M SOMEBODY TOO. The result: the most up-to-date, easy-to-read biography of American history's most famous woman. For grades 4 & up. $14.95 hardcover, $6.95 softcover. Fully-reproducible teacher handbook (50pp.) $19.95. *Publisher Provided Annotation.*

Gehrt, Vicky E. A Matter of Music. Paris, Pat & Thornley, Jean, illus. 1984. incl. cassette 7.95 (0-910313-64-4) Parker Bros.

Gehrts, Barbara. Don't Say a Word. Crawford, Elizabeth D., tr. LC 86-7248. 192p. (gr. 7 up). 1986. SBE 13.95 (0-689-50412-8, M K McElderry) Macmillan Child Grp.

Geier, Marguerite E. Rama, the Holy Family Dog. 1991. 11.95 (0-533-09441-0) Vantage.

Geiger, Eve. Two Hundred & Ninety-Two Activities for Literature & Language Arts. (gr. 1-6). 1990. pap. 8.95 (0-8224-6746-1) Fearon Teach Aids.

Geiger, John & Beattie, Owen. Buried in Ice: The Mystery of a Lost Arctic Expedition. (gr. 8-12). 1993. pap. 6.95 (0-590-43849-2) Scholastic Inc.

Geiger, John, jt. auth. see Beattie, Owen.

Geiger, Mary J., tr. see Neighbour, Ralph W., Jr.

Geiger, Michael. Alphabet in Signs: ABC's in Fingerspelling. Bartusch, Nancy, illus. 60p. (Orig.). (ps-3). 1984. pap. 5.00 (0-916708-13-6) Modern Signs.

Geis, Arthur. One Quiet Voice. (Illus.). 20p. (Orig.). (gr. 12). 1988. pap. 4.95 (0-317-93130-X) Artisan IL.

Geis, Arthur, ed. Glimpses of the Gods. 20p. (Orig.). (gr. 12). 1988. pap. text ed. 4.95 (0-317-93129-6) Artisan IL.

Geis, Darlene. Dinosaurs. Shannon, Kenyon, illus. (Orig.). (gr. 4-6). 1960. pap. 2.95 (0-8431-4250-2) Wonder.

Geis, Darlene, ed. Walt Disney's Treasury of Children's Classics. (Illus.). (gr. 5 up). 1978. 29.95 (0-8109-0812-3) Abrams.

Geis, Jacqueline, adapted by. & illus. Where the Buffalo Roam. 32p. (gr. k-3). 1992. 13.95 (0-8249-8570-2, Ideals Child); PLB 14.00 (0-8249-8584-2) Hambleton-Hill.

Geisel, Theodore see Dr. Seuss, pseud.

Geiser, Franz, jt. auth. see Barkhausen, Annette.

Geiser, Gary. Because. LC 88-50833. (Illus.). 72p. (gr. 3-5). 1988. pap. 6.95 (1-55523-164-0) Winston-Derek.

Geisert, Arthur. After the Flood. LC 93-758. 1994. write for info. (0-395-66611-2) HM.

—Alphabet Book. (ps-1). 1985. write for info. HM.

—The Ark. Geisert, Arthur, illus. LC 88-15889. 48p. (ps up). 1988. 15.45 (0-395-43078-X) HM.

—The Building of Noah's Ark. (Illus.). 1988. write for info. HM.

—Oink. Geisert, Arthur, illus. LC 90-46123. 32p. 1991. 13.45 (0-395-55329-6) HM.

—Oink, Oink. Geisert, Arthur, illus. LC 92-31778. 32p. (gr. k-3). 1993. 13.45 (0-395-64048-2) HM.

—Pa's Balloon & Other Pig Tales. Geisert, Arthur, illus. LC 83-18552. 96p. (gr. k-3). 1984. 13.95 (0-395-35381-5, 5-86480) HM.

—Pigs from A to Z. Geisert, Arthur, illus. LC 86-18542. 64p. (gr. 2 up). 1986. 16.45 (0-395-38509-1) HM.

—Pigs from One to Ten. Geisert, Arthur, illus. LC 92-5097. 32p. (gr. k-3). 1992. 14.45 (0-395-58519-8) HM.

Geiss, Tony, jt. auth. see Freudberg, Judy.

Geiss, Tony, et al. The Sesame Street Bedtime Storybook. Cooke, Tom, et al, illus. LC 77-93774. (ps-2). 1978. 10.00 (0-394-83843-2); lib. bdg. 7.99 (0-394-93843-7) Random Bks Yng Read.

Geissler, Darry, ed. see Reynolds, Ralph V.

Geissler, Kimberly, ed. see Reynolds, Ralph V.

Geistdoefer, Patrick. Undersea Giants. Boucher, Joelle, illus. LC 87-34531. 38p. (gr. k-5). 1988. 4.95 (0-944589-02-2, 022) Young Discovery Lib.

Geitler, Jan & Thompson, Kathleen. Sequoya. (Illus.). 32p. (Orig.). (gr. 2-5). 1988. PLB 17.96 (0-8172-2678-8) Raintree Steck-V.

Gela, Darlene. Dinosaurs & Other Prehistoric Animals. Peterson, Russell F., illus. 108p. (gr. 3-8). 1982. 9.95 (0-448-02882-4, G&D) Putnam Pub Group.

Gelb, Alan. Live From New York. 208p. 1991. pap. 2.95 (0-380-75745-1, Flare) Avon.

Gelbart, Ofra. Sonidos Que Oigo. Writer, C. C. & Nielsen, Lisa C., trs. Eagle, Mike, illus. (SPA.). 24p. (Orig.). (ps). 1992. pap. text ed. 3.00x (1-56134-148-7) Dushkin Pub.

—Sounds I Hear. Kriss, David, tr. from HEB. Eagle, Mike, illus. 24p. (Orig.). (ps). 1992. pap. text ed. 3.00x (1-56134-138-X) Dushkin Pub.

Gelber, Carol. Masks Tell Stories. LC 92-15595. (Illus.). 72p. (gr. 4-6). 1993. PLB 14.90 (1-56294-224-7) Millbrook Pr.

Gelbert, Ofra. Otra Cosa. Writer, C. C. & Nielsen, Lisa C., trs. Elchanan, illus. (SPA.). 24p. (Orig.). (ps). 1992. pap. text ed. 3.00x (1-56134-175-4) Dushkin Pub.

—Something Else. Kriss, David, tr. from HEB. Elchanan, illus. 24p. (Orig.). (ps). 1992. pap. text ed. 3.00x (1-56134-165-7) Dushkin Pub.

Gelder, L. van, et al. Enciclopedia Juvenil Labor: Encyclopedia of Child Labor, 3 vols. (SPA.). 592p. 1977. 99.50 (0-8288-5411-4, S50474) Fr & Eur.

Gelder, Richard G. van see Bancroft, Henrietta & Van Gelder, Richard G.

Gelhay, Patrick & Marcantel, David E. Notre Langue Louisianaise: Our Louisiana Language, Bk. 1. Graeff, Benny, et al, illus. LC 85-81018. (ENG & FRE.). 180p. (gr. 4). 1985. text ed. 14.95 (0-935085-00-9); Tchr's ed. 14.95 (0-935085-01-7); write for info. Dialogue Booklet (0-935085-03-3); Cassette Tape Set 49.95 (0-935085-02-5) Ed Francaises.

Gelinas, Paul J. Coping with Weight Problems. 131p. (gr. 7-12). 1983. PLB 13.95 (0-8239-0598-5) Rosen Group.

Geller, Mark. My Life in the Seventh Grade. LC 85-45265. 160p. (gr. 5-7). 1986. PLB 11.89 (0-06-021982-3) HarpC Child Bks.

—My Life in the Seventh Grade. LC 85-45265. 128p. (gr. 5 up). 1988. pap. 3.50 (0-06-440276-2, Trophy) HarpC Child Bks.

—The Strange Case of the Reluctant Partners. LC 89-29409. 96p. (gr. 5-9). 1990. 13.95 (0-06-021972-6); PLB 13.89 (0-06-021973-4) HarpC Child Bks.

—What I Heard. LC 86-45494. 128p. (gr. 5 up). 1987. HarpC Child Bks.

—Who's on First? LC 91-46184. 64p. (gr. 6 up). 1992. 14.00 (0-06-021084-2); PLB 13.89 (0-06-021085-0) HarpC Child Bks.

Geller, Norman. Color Me Happy It's Passover. Gruchow, Jane, illus. 23p. (gr. k-2). pap. 2.95 (0-915753-14-6) N Geller Pub.

—Color Me Happy: It's Rosh Hashannah & Yom Kippur. Cruchow, Jane C., illus. 36p. (gr. k-4). 1986. pap. 2.95 (0-915753-10-3) N Geller Pub.

—Farfel, the Cat That Left Egypt. Gruchow, Jane C., illus. 31p. (Orig.). (gr. 3-7). 1987. pap. text ed. 6.95 (0-915753-12-X) N Geller Pub.

—The First Seven Days. (Illus.). 32p. (gr. 1-4). 1983. pap. 6.95 (0-915753-00-6) N Geller Pub.

—I Don't Want to Visit Grandma Anymore. Tomlinson, Albert J., illus. 28p. (gr. 1-4). 1984. pap. 4.95 (0-915753-05-7) N Geller Pub.

—It's Not the Jewish Christmas. Gruchow, Jane C., illus. 20p. (gr. 3-6). 1985. pap. 4.95 (0-915753-09-X) N Geller Pub.

—The Last Teenage Suicide. Canter, Barbara, illus. (Orig.). (gr. 6-12). 1988. pap. 7.95 (0-915753-13-8) N Geller Pub.

—Talk to God... I'll Get the Message: Black Version. Tomlinson, Albert J., illus. 23p. (gr. 1-4). 1985. pap. 4.95 (0-915753-08-1) N Geller Pub.

—Talk to God... I'll Get the Message: Catholic Version. Tomlinson, Albert, illus. 23p. (gr. 1-4). 1983. pap. 4.95 (0-915753-03-0) N Geller Pub.

—Talk to God... I'll Get the Message: Jewish Version. Tomlinson, Albert J., illus. 23p. (gr. 1-4). 1983. pap. 4.95 (0-915753-02-2) N Geller Pub.

—Talk to God... I'll Get the Message: Protestant Version. Tomlinson, Albert J., illus. 23p. (gr. 1-4). 1983. pap. 4.95 (0-915753-04-9) N Geller Pub.

—Talk to God... I'll Get the Message: Spanish Version. Galway, Bonnie, tr. from ENG. Tomlinson, Albert J., illus. 23p. (gr. 1-4). 1985. pap. 4.95 (0-915753-07-3) N Geller Pub.

—Unto Dust You Shall Return. Grant, Larry & Jalbert, Marc, illus. 16p. (gr. 6-10). 1986. pap. 4.95 (0-915753-11-1) N Geller Pub.

Gellman, Ellie. It's Rosh-Hashanah. Kahn, Katherine J., illus. LC 85-80783. 12p. (ps). 1985. bds. 4.95 (0-930494-50-4) Kar Ben.

—Shai's Shabbat Walk. McLean, Chari, illus. LC 85-80780. 12p. (ps). 1985. bds. 4.95 (0-930494-49-0) Kar Ben.

—Tamar's Sukkah. Kahn, Katherine J., illus. LC 88-23388. 32p. (ps-2). 1988. pap. 4.95 (0-930494-79-2) Kar Ben.

Gellman, Marc. Does God Have a Big Toe? Stories about Stories in the Bible. De Mejo, Oscar, illus. LC 89-1893. 96p. (gr. 4 up). 1989. 16.00 (0-06-022432-0); PLB 15.89 (0-06-022433-9) HarpC Child Bks.

—Does God Have a Big Toe? Stories about Stories in the Bible. De Mejo, Oscar, illus. LC 89-1893. 96p. (gr. 4-6). 1993. pap. 7.95 (0-06-440453-6, Trophy) HarpC Child Bks.

Gelman. Hello Cat You Need a Hat. 1993. pap. 28.67 (0-590-71915-7) Scholastic Inc.

—Why Can't I Fly? 1993. pap. 28.67 (0-590-71580-1) Scholastic Inc.

Gelman, Amy. Connecticut. (Illus.). 72p. (gr. 3-6). 1991. PLB 17.50 (0-8225-2709-X) Lerner Pubns.

—New York. Lerner Geography Department Staff, ed. (Illus.). 72p. (gr. 3-6). 1992. PLB 17.50 (0-8225-2720-0) Lerner Pubns.
Gelman, Rita G. Body Battles. (ps-3). 1992. pap. 3.95 (0-590-44973-7) Scholastic Inc.
—Cats & Mice. Gurney, Eric, illus. 48p. (gr. k-3). 1989. Big Book. 28.67 (0-590-64644-3); pap. 1.95 (0-590-71593-3) Scholastic Inc.
—Dawn to Dusk in the Galapagos, Vol. 1. 1991. 16.95 (0-316-30739-4) Little.
—I Went to the Zoo. Kovalski, Maryann, illus. LC 92-27671. 1993. 14.95 (0-590-45882-5) Scholastic Inc.
—A Koala Grows Up. Fiammenghi, Gioia, illus. 32p. (Orig.). (gr. k-3). 1986. pap. 3.95 (0-590-41869-6) Scholastic Inc.
—Monsters of the Sea, Vol. 1. (gr. 3-7). 1990. 12.95 (0-316-30738-6, Joy St Bks) Little.
—More Spaghetti, I Say! Gerberg, Mort, illus. 32p. (ps-3). 1993. pap. 2.95 (0-590-45783-7) Scholastic Inc.
—More Spaghetti, I Say. (ps-3). 1993. pap. 19.95 (0-590-71439-2) Scholastic Inc.
—Panda Grows Up. (ps-3). 1993. pap. 3.95 (0-590-43612-0) Scholastic Inc.
—What Are Scientists? What Do They Do? Let's Find Out. (ps-3). 1991. pap. 3.95 (0-590-43184-0) Scholastic Inc.
Gemme, Leila B. El Futbol es Nuestro Juego: Soccer Is Our Game. LC 79-13245. 32p. (gr. k-3). 1990. PLB 15.93 (0-516-33615-0); pap. 3.95 (0-516-53615-X) Childrens.
—Soccer Is Our Game. Caliger, Roberta, illus. LC 79-13245. 32p. (gr. k-3). 1979. PLB 15.93 (0-516-03615-7); pap. 3.95 (0-516-43615-5) Childrens.
—T-Ball Is Our Game. Marshall, Richard, photos by. LC 77-17173. (Illus.). 32p. (gr. k-3). 1978. PLB 15.93 (0-516-03630-0) Childrens.
Gemmell, Kathy & Tyler, Jenny. First French at Home. (Illus.). 32p. (gr. 1-6). 1993. lib. bdg. 12.96 (0-88110-643-7, Usborne); pap. 5.95 (0-7460-1049-4, Usborne) EDC.
—First German at Home. (Illus.). 32p. (gr. 1-6). 1993. lib. bdg. 12.96 (0-88110-644-5, Usborne); pap. 5.95 (0-7460-1051-6, Usborne) EDC.
Gendusa, Sam. Carving Jack-O-Lanterns. rev. ed. Ruse, Arnold, ed. Gendusa, Sam, illus. Ruse, Arnold, intro. by. LC 89-92605. (Illus.). 80p. 1989. pap. 9.95x (0-9621071-1-5) SG Prodns.
Gene, jt. auth. see Joan.
Genee, Gloria, ed. see Kelley, Shirley.
Genet, Barbara. Ta-Poo-Ach Means Apple. Genet, Barbara, illus. LC 85-60009. 46p. (ps-3). 1985. 8.00 (0-86705-015-2) A R E Pub.
Gennings, S. Atocha Treasure. (Illus.). 32p. (gr. 4 up). 1988. PLB 17.27 (0-86592-874-6); PLB 12.95s.p. (0-685-58293-0) Rourke Corp.
Gentile, Gennaro L. The Mouse in the Manger. McKissack, Vernon, illus. LC 78-72944. 80p. (gr. k-4). 1978. pap. 5.95 (0-87793-165-8) Ave Maria.
Gentle, Mary. Golden Witchbreed. (gr. 9-12). 1990. pap. 3.95 (0-451-13606-3, Sig) NAL-Dutton.
Gentry, Linnea. Inside Biosphere Two: The Ocean & Its Reef. 64p. (gr. 3 up). 1993. pap. 8.95 (1-882428-02-1) Biosphere Pr.
Gentry, Linnea & Liptak, Karen. The Glass Ark. 80p. (gr. 3-7). 1991. 7.95 (0-14-034928-6) Puffin Bks.
—The Glass Ark: The Story of Biosphere Two. LC 81-25328. (Illus.). 94p. (gr. 5-8). 1991. 15.95 (0-670-84173-0) Viking Child Bks.
Gentry, Roosevelt. Fun with Calculators While Learning. LC 86-72013. 120p. (Orig.). (gr. k-7). 1987. pap. 20.00 (0-938991-04-3) Colonial Pr AL.
Gentry, Tony. Alice Walker. King, Coretta Scott. (Illus.). 112p. (gr. 5 up). 1993. PLB 17.95 (0-7910-1884-9) Chelsea Hse.
—Alice Walker: Black Americans of Achievement. (gr. 4-7). 1992. pap. 7.95 (0-7910-1913-6) Chelsea Hse.
—Dizzy Gillespie: Musician. King, Coretta Scott, intro. by. (Illus.). 112p. (gr. 5 up). 1994. PLB 18.95 (0-7910-1127-5, Am Art Analog); pap. write for info. (0-7910-1152-6, Am Art Analog) Chelsea Hse.
—Elvis Presley. LC 93-28486. (Illus.). 1994. 18.95 (0-7910-2329-X, Am Art Analog); pap. write for info. (0-7910-2354-0, Am Art Analog) Chelsea Hse.
—Jesse Owens. King, Coretta Scott, intro. by. (Illus.). (gr. 5 up). 1990. 17.95 (1-55546-603-6); pap. 9.95 (0-7910-0247-0) Chelsea Hse.
—Paul L. Dunbar. King, Coretta Scott, intro. by. (Illus.). 112p. (Orig.). (gr. 5 up). 1989. 17.95 (1-55546-583-8); pap. 9.95 (0-7910-0223-3) Chelsea Hse.
Geo. A. Jackson School Staff. The Literary Lion. (Illus.). 148p. (Orig.). 1992. pap. text ed. 10.00 (0-940429-10-1) M B Glass Assocs.
Geoffrion, Sondra. Power Study to up Your Grades & Grade Point Average. LC 88-61283. 60p. (gr. 11 up). 1989. pap. 3.95 (0-88247-787-0) R & E Pubs.
—Power Study to up Your Grades in English. LC 88-61276. 60p. (Orig.). 1989. pap. text ed. 3.95 (0-88247-784-6) R & E Pubs.
—Power Study to up Your Grades in Math. LC 88-61284. 60p. (gr. 11 up). 1989. pap. text ed. 3.95 (0-88247-783-8) R & E Pubs.
—Power Study to up Your Grades in Science. LC 88-61275. 60p. (gr. 11 up). 1989. pap. text ed. 3.95 (0-88247-785-4) R & E Pubs.
—Power Study to up Your Grades in Social Studies. LC 88-61277. 60p. (gr. 11 up). 1989. pap. text ed. 3.95 (0-88247-786-2) R & E Pubs.
Geoghegan, Judy, jt. auth. see Hegarty, Sue.

Geography Department. Hungary--in Picture. LC 93-3179. 1993. 17.50 (0-8225-1883-X) Lerner Pubns.
Geography Department Staff. Vietnam: In Pictures. LC 93-21343. 1994. write for info. (0-8225-1909-7) Lerner Pubns.
Geok-Lin Lim, Shirley & Tsutakawa, Mayumi, eds. The Forbidden Stitch: An Asian-American Women's Anthology. LC 88-8117. 290p. (Orig.). (gr. 9-12). 1989. 32.00 (0-934971-10-2); pap. 16.95 (0-934971-04-8) Calyx Bks.
George. Jean George Spotted Owl. Date not set. 15.00 (0-06-023641-8, Festival); PLB 14.89 (0-06-023640-X, Festival) HarpC Child Bks.
—Jean George Volcanoes Book. Date not set. 15.00 (0-06-023628-0, Festival); PLB 14.89 (0-06-023629-9, Festival) HarpC Child Bks.
George A. Jackson School Students. The Literary Lion, 1993. (Illus.). 164p. (Orig.). 1993. pap. 10.00 (0-940429-11-X) M B Glass Assocs.
George, Alan. First Christians. Butcher, Sam, illus. 56p. (gr. k-6). 1991. pap. text ed. 9.45 (1-55976-023-0) CEF Press.
—My Wonderful Lord. Butcher, Sam & Hilterbrand, Greg, illus. 61p. (gr. k-6). 1987. pap. text ed. 8.99 (1-55976-029-X) CEF Press.
—Paul, God's Servant. (Illus.). 88p. (gr. k-6). 1992. pap. text ed. write for info. (1-55976-036-2) CEF Press.
George, B., ed. Volume International Discography of the New Wave, Vol. 1. Meyer, Pam, illus. 264p. (Orig.). (gr. 8 up). 1980. pap. 7.95 (0-9605778-0-7) One Ten Records.
George, Barbara. The Popples' Book of Jokes & Riddles. Henry, Barb, illus. LC 86-62222. 32p. (ps-3). 1987. pap. 1.25 (0-394-88757-3) Random Bks Yng Read.
George, Bonnie S., jt. auth. see Henderson, Shelia.
George, Diann. The Peanut Butter Witch. (ps-3). 1992. 6.95 (0-8062-4179-9) Carlton.
George, Elly-Kree. Please Don't Step on Me. Kennedy, Faye W., illus. 20p. (gr. 1-3). 1981. 3.50 (0-935741-07-0) Cherokee Pubns.
George, Gail. The Popples' Pajama Party. Sustendal, Pat, illus. LC 85-19403. 32p. (ps-3). 1986. pap. 1.95 (0-394-88041-2) Random Bks Yng Read.
George, J. Carroll & Eaton, Joi. Divorcing Daddy. 125p. (gr. 7-12). 1992. pap. 5.95 (1-881223-01-9) Zulema Ent.
George, Jean C. The Cry of the Crow. LC 79-2016. 160p. (gr. 5 up). 1980. PLB 12.89 (0-06-021957-2) HarpC Child Bks.
—The Cry of the Crow. reissue ed. LC 79-2016. 160p. (gr. 5 up). 1992. pap. 3.95 (0-06-440131-6, Trophy) HarpC Child Bks.
—Dear Rebecca, Winter Is Here. Krupinski, Loretta, illus. LC 92-9515. 32p. (ps-3). 1993. 15.00 (0-06-021139-3); PLB 14.89 (0-06-021140-7) HarpC Child Bks.
—The Everglades. Minor, Wendell, illus. LC 92-9517. 1992. 15.00 (0-06-021228-4); PLB 14.89 (0-06-021229-2) HarpC Child Bks. Postponed.
—Famous Animals. Merrill, Christine, photos by. LC 92-28326. (Illus.). 1993. 15.00 (0-06-021543-7); PLB 14.89 (0-06-021544-5) HarpC Child Bks.
—The Fire Bug Connection: An Ecological Mystery. LC 92-18005. 160p. (gr. 3-7). 1993. 14.00 (0-06-021490-2); PLB 13.89 (0-06-021491-0) HarpC Child Bks.
—First Thanksgiving. Locker, Thomas, illus. LC 91-46643. 32p. (ps up). 1993. PLB 15.95 (0-399-21991-9, Philomel Bks) Putnam Pub Group.
—The Grizzly Bear with the Golden Ears. Schoenherr, John, illus. LC 80-7908. 32p. (ps-3). 1982. PLB 13.89 (0-06-021966-1) HarpC Child Bks.
—Julie of the Wolves. Schoenherr, John, illus. LC 72-76509. 180p. (gr. 7 up). 1974. 15.00i (0-06-021943-2); PLB 14.89 (0-06-021944-0); pap. 3.95 (0-06-440058-1) HarpC Child Bks.
—Julie of the Wolves. large type ed. (Illus.). 260p. (gr. 3-7). 1987. lib. bdg. 14.95 (1-55736-053-7, Crnrstn Bks) BDD LT Grp.
—Julie's Choice. Minor, Wendell, illus. LC 93-27738. 1994. write for info. (0-06-023528-4); lib. bdg. write for info. (0-06-023529-2) HarpC Child Bks.
—The Missing 'Gator of Gumbo Limbo. LC 91-20779. 160p. (gr. 3-7). 1993. pap. 3.95 (0-06-440434-X, Trophy) HarpC Child Bks.
—The Missing 'Gator of Gumbo Limbo: An Ecological Mystery. LC 91-20779. 176p. (gr. 3-7). 1992. 14.00 (0-06-020396-X); PLB 13.89 (0-06-020397-8) HarpC Child Bks.
—The Moon of the Alligators. new ed. Rothman, Michael, illus. LC 90-38169. 48p. (gr. 3-7). 1991. 15.00 (0-06-022427-4); PLB 14.89 (0-06-022428-2) HarpC Child Bks.
—The Moon of the Bears. Parker, Ron, illus. LC 91-22557. 48p. (gr. 3-7). 1993. 15.00 (0-06-022791-5); PLB 14.89 (0-06-022792-3) HarpC Child Bks.
—The Moon of the Chickarees. new ed. Rodell, Don, illus. LC 90-22409. 48p. (gr. 3-7). 1992. 15.00 (0-06-022507-6); PLB 14.89 (0-06-022508-4) HarpC Child Bks.
—The Moon of the Deer. Catalano, Sal, illus. LC 91-14607. 48p. (gr. 3-7). 1992. 15.00 (0-06-020261-0); PLB 14.89 (0-06-020262-9) HarpC Child Bks.
—The Moon of the Fox Pups. new ed. Adams, Norman, illus. LC 90-22386. 48p. (gr. 3-7). 1992. 15.00 (0-06-022859-8); PLB 14.89 (0-06-022860-1) HarpC Child Bks.

—The Moon of the Gray Wolves. new ed. Catalano, Sal, illus. LC 90-38166. 48p. (gr. 3-7). 1991. 15.00 (0-06-022442-8); PLB 14.89 (0-06-022443-6) HarpC Child Bks.
—The Moon of the Moles. Rothman, Michael, illus. LC 91-14535. 48p. (gr. 3-7). 1992. 15.00 (0-06-020258-0); PLB 14.89 (0-06-020259-9) HarpC Child Bks.
—The Moon of the Monarch Butterflies. Mak, Kam, illus. LC 91-33152. 48p. (gr. 3-7). 1993. 15.00 (0-06-020816-3); PLB 14.89 (0-06-020817-1) HarpC Child Bks.
—The Moon of the Mountain Lions. new ed. Parker, Ron, illus. LC 90-39451. 48p. (gr. 3-7). 1991. 15.00 (0-06-022429-0); PLB 14.89 (0-06-022438-X) HarpC Child Bks.
—The Moon of the Owls. Minor, Wendell, illus. LC 91-2735. 48p. (gr. 3-7). 1993. 15.00 (0-06-020192-4); PLB 14.89 (0-06-020193-2) HarpC Child Bks.
—The Moon of the Salamanders. new ed. Werner, Marlene H., illus. LC 90-25591. 48p. (gr. 3-7). 1992. 15.00 (0-06-022609-9); PLB 14.89 (0-06-022694-3) HarpC Child Bks.
—The Moon of the Wild Pigs. Mirocha, Paul, illus. LC 91-3495. 48p. (gr. 3-7). 1992. 15.00 (0-06-020263-7); PLB 14.89 (0-06-020264-5) HarpC Child Bks.
—The Moon of the Winter Bird. Nasta, Vincent, illus. LC 91-1537. 48p. (gr. 3-7). 1992. 15.00 (0-06-020267-X); PLB 14.89 (0-06-020268-8) HarpC Child Bks.
—My Side of the Mountain. George, Jean C., illus. LC 87-27556. 176p. (gr. 3-7). 1988. 15.00 (0-525-44392-4, 01258-370, DCB); pap. 4.95 (0-525-44395-9, 0481-140, DCB) Dutton Child Bks.
—My Side of the Mountain. 1991. pap. 4.95 (0-14-034810-7) Puffin Bks.
—On the Far Side of the Mountain. LC 89-25988. 176p. (gr. 3-7). 1990. 15.00 (0-525-44563-3, DCB) Dutton Child Bks.
—On the Far Side of the Mountain. 144p. (gr. 3-7). 1991. pap. 4.99 (0-14-034248-6, Puffin) Puffin Bks.
—One Day in the Alpine Tundra. Gaffney-Kessel, Walter, illus. LC 82-45590. 48p. (gr. 5-7). 1984. (Crowell Jr Bks); PLB 13.89 (0-690-04326-0, Crowell Jr Bks) HarpC Child Bks.
—One Day in the Desert. Brenner, Fred, illus. LC 82-45924. 48p. (gr. 5-7). 1983. PLB 13.89 (0-690-04341-4, Crowell Jr Bks) HarpC Child Bks.
—One Day in the Prairie. Marstall, Bob, illus. LC 85-48254. 48p. (gr. 5-7). 1986. PLB 13.89 (0-690-04566-2, Crowell Jr Bks) HarpC Child Bks.
—One Day in the Tropical Rain Forest. Allen, Gary, illus. LC 89-36583. 64p. (gr. 4-7). 1990. 14.00 (0-690-04767-3, Crowell Jr Bks); PLB 13.89 (0-690-04769-X, Crowell Jr Bks) HarpC Child Bks.
—One Day in the Woods. Allen, Gary, illus. LC 87-21712. 48p. (gr. 4-7). 1988. (Crowell Jr Bks); PLB 13.89 (0-690-04724-X, Crowell Jr Bks) HarpC Child Bks.
—Pescar un Pez, Conquistar una Montana - Hook a Fish, Catch a Mountain. Fernandez, Joaquin, tr. (SPA.). 141p. (gr. 9-12). 1989. pap. write for info. (84-204-4642-4) Santillana.
—Shark Beneath the Reef. LC 88-25194. 192p. (gr. 7 up). 1989. 13.00 (0-06-021992-0); PLB 12.89 (0-06-021993-9) HarpC Child Bks.
—Shark Beneath the Reef. LC 88-25194. 192p. (gr. 7 up). 1991. pap. 3.95 (0-06-440308-4, Trophy) HarpC Child Bks.
—The Summer of the Falcon. George, Jean C., illus. LC 62-16543. 153p. (gr. 5 up). 1979. pap. 3.95 (0-06-440095-6, Trophy) HarpC Child Bks.
—The Talking Earth. LC 82-48850. 160p. (gr. 6 up). 1983. PLB 13.89 (0-06-021976-9) HarpC Child Bks.
—The Talking Earth. LC 82-48850. 160p. (gr. 5 up). 1987. pap. 3.95 (0-06-440212-6, Trophy) HarpC Child Bks.
—Water Sky. George, Jean C., illus. LC 86-45496. 224p. (gr. 6 up). 1987. 13.00 (0-06-022198-4); PLB 12.89 (0-06-022199-2) HarpC Child Bks.
—Water Sky. George, Jean C., illus. LC 86-45496. 224p. (gr. 5 up). 1989. pap. 3.95 (0-06-440202-9, Trophy) HarpC Child Bks.
—Who Really Killed Cock Robin? An Ecological Mystery. LC 90-38659. 176p. (gr. 3-7). 1991. 15.00 (0-06-021980-7); PLB 14.89 (0-06-021981-5) HarpC Child Bks.
—Who Really Killed Cock Robin? An Ecological Mystery. LC 90-38659. 192p. (gr. 3-7). 1992. pap. 3.95 (0-06-440405-6, Trophy) HarpC Child Bks.
—The Wounded Wolf. Schoenherr, John, illus. LC 76-58711. (ps-3). 1978. PLB 14.89 (0-06-021950-5) HarpC Child Bks.
George, Jean C. & Locker, Thomas. To Climb a Waterfall. LC 93-5841. 1994. write for info. (0-399-22673-7, Philomel Bks) Putnam Pub Group.
George, Jean G. Julie of the Wolves. 190p. 1992. text ed. 15.20 (1-56956-117-6) W A T Braille.
George, Jon & Kraehenbuehl, David. Supplementary Solos: Levels 3 & 4. Clark, Francis & Goss, Louise, eds. 48p. (gr. k-12). 1974. pap. 7.95 (0-87487-140-9) Summy-Birchard.
George, Judith St. see St. George, Judith.
George, Linda C. The Hallelujah Corn Cobs. Verreaux, V. Carlin, illus. LC 90-71549. 41p. (Orig.). (gr. k-6). 1991. pap. 4.95 (1-56002-027-X) Aegina Pr.
George, Lindsay B. In the Woods: Who's Been Here? LC 93-16244. (Illus.). 40p. (ps up). 1994. write for info. (0-688-12318-X); PLB write for info. (0-688-12319-8) Greenwillow.

—William & Boomer. George, Lindsay B., illus. LC 86-9789. 24p. (ps-1). 1987. 15.00 (0-688-06640-2); PLB 14.93 (0-688-06641-0) Greenwillow.
—William & Boomer. Red Grammer Staff, narrated by. George, Lindsay B., illus. 24p. (ps-3). 1990. incl. audiocassette 19.95 (0-924483-23-7) Soundprints.
George, Lindsay B., jt. auth. see George, William T.
George, Lonnie. Star, Little Star. Abbatiello, illus. 24p. (ps). 1992. spiral bdg. 9.95 (0-448-40487-7, G&D) Putnam Pub Group.
George, Mary. Kinder Bakker. (Illus.). 167p. (gr. 3-9). 1983. Set of 12. spiral 84.00 (0-9612710-1-9, Pub. by Steketee-Van Huis) Holland Jr Welfare.
George, Mary G., ed. see Drew, James.
George, Maureen. The Neighbor from Outer Space. 96p. (gr. 2-5). 1992. pap. 2.75 (0-590-44583-9, Little Apple) Scholastic Inc.
George, Michael. Alligators & Crocodiles. 32p. 1991. 22.75 (0-89565-720-1); 15.95s.p. (0-685-55044-3) Childs World.
—Antarctica. LC 93-18281. 1993. PLB 18.95 (0-88682-600-4) Creative Ed.
—Bats. 32p. 1991. 22.75 (0-89565-712-0); 15.95s.p. (0-685-55047-8) Childs World.
—Birds. 32p. 1991. 22.75 (0-89565-702-3); 15.95s.p. (0-685-55048-6) Childs World.
—Cells. (gr. 5 up). 1992. PLB 18.95 (0-88682-437-0) Creative Ed.
—Cells. (gr. 4-7). 1993. 14.95 (1-56846-057-0) Creat Editions.
—Clouds. 1992. PLB 18.95s.p. (0-88682-435-4) Creative Ed.
—Coral Reef. (gr. 5 up). 1992. PLB 18.95 (0-88682-430-3) Creative Ed.
—Coral Reef. (gr. 4-7). 1993. 14.95 (1-56846-059-7) Creat Editions.
—Deserts. (gr. 5 up). Date not set. PLB 18.95 (0-88682-434-6) Creative Ed.
—Deserts. (gr. 4-7). 1993. 14.95 (1-56846-054-6) Creat Editions.
—Fish. 32p. 1991. 22.75 (0-89565-701-5); 15.95s.p. (0-685-55053-2) Childs World.
—Galaxies. (gr. 5 up). 1993. PLB 18.95 (0-88682-433-8) Creative Ed.
—Galaxies. (gr. 4-7). 1993. 14.95 (1-56846-053-8) Creat Editions.
—Glaciers. LC 90-22068. (Illus.). 40p. (gr. 3-5). 1992. PLB 18.95s.p. (0-88682-401-X) Creative Ed.
—Glaciers. (gr. 4-7). 1993. 14.95 (1-56846-061-9) Creat Editions.
—Insects. 32p. 1991. 22.75 (0-89565-703-1); 15.95s.p. (0-685-55055-9) Childs World.
—Life. LC 93-12205. (gr. 4 up). 1993. PLB 18.95s.p. (0-88682-602-0) Creative Ed.
—Mammals. (gr. 1-8). 1992. PLB 15.95 (0-89565-846-1); Resale. 22.75 (0-685-61007-1) Childs World.
—Mars. (gr. 5 up). 1992. PLB 18.95 (0-88682-432-X) Creative Ed.
—Mars. (gr. 1-8). 1992. PLB 15.95 (0-89565-852-6); Resale. 22.75 (0-685-61001-2) Childs World.
—The Moon. LC 92-8411. (gr. 1-8). 1992. PLB 15.95 (0-89565-853-4); Resale. 22.75 (0-685-59392-4) Childs World.
—The Moon. (gr. 5 up). 1993. PLB 18.95 (0-88682-436-2) Creative Ed.
—Moon. (gr. 4-7). 1993. 14.95 (1-56846-056-2) Creat Editions.
—Musk-Oxen. 32p. 1991. 22.75 (0-89565-721-X); 15.95s.p. (0-685-55059-1) Childs World.
—Owls. (gr. 1-8). 1992. PLB 15.95 (0-89565-837-2); Resale. 22.75 (0-685-61015-2) Childs World.
—Rain Forest. 1992. PLB 18.95s.p. (0-88682-483-4) Creative Ed.
—Rain Forest. (gr. 4-7). 1993. 14.95 (1-56846-062-7) Creat Editions.
—Rhinoceroses. (gr. 1-8). 1992. PLB 15.95 (0-89565-838-0); Resale. 22.75 (0-685-66169-5) Childs World.
—Sequoias. (gr. 5 up). 1992. PLB 18.95 (0-88682-482-6) Creative Ed.
—Sequoias. (gr. 4-7). 1993. 14.95 (1-56846-055-4) Creat Editions.
—Space Exploration. (gr. 5 up). 1993. PLB 18.95 (0-88682-481-8) Creative Ed.
—Space Exploration. (gr. 4-7). 1993. 14.95 (1-56846-058-9) Creat Editions.
—Stars. 1992. PLB 18.95s.p. (0-88682-400-1) Creative Ed.
—Stars. (gr. 4-7). 1993. 14.95 (1-56846-063-5) Creat Editions.
—The Sun. 1992. PLB 18.95s.p. (0-88682-402-8) Creative Ed.
—The Sun. LC 92-8413. (gr. 1-8). 1992. PLB 15.95 (0-89565-855-0); Resale. 22.75 (0-685-66122-9) Childs World.
—Tundra. LC 93-18275. 1993. PLB 18.95 (0-88682-601-2) Creative Ed.
—Volcanoes. LC 90-22064. (Illus.). 40p. (gr. 3-5). 1992. PLB 18.95s.p. (0-88682-403-6) Creative Ed.
—Volcanoes. (gr. 4-7). 1993. 14.95 (1-56846-065-1) Creat Editions.
George, Nelson. Malcolm Then & Now. 1992. write for info. (0-8050-2387-9) H Holt & Co.
George, Richard R., adapted by see Dahl, Roald.
George, Sally. Bad Dog, George! Mancini, Rob, illus. LC 92-34258. 1993. 4.25 (0-383-03616-X) SRA Schl Grp.

George, William T. Beaver at Long Pond. Red Grammer Staff, narrated by. George, Lindsay B., illus. 24p. (ps-3). 1989. incl. audiocassette 19.95 (0-924483-22-9) Soundprints.
—Box Turtle at Long Pond. George, Lindsay B., illus. LC 88-18787. 24p. (ps-1). 1989. 14.00 (0-688-08184-3); PLB 13.93 (0-688-08185-1) Greenwillow.
—Box Turtle at Long Pond. Grammer, Red, narrated by. Barrett George, Lindsay, illus. 24p. (ps-3). 1989. incl. audiocassette 19.95 (0-924483-21-0) Soundprints.
—Christmas at Long Pond. George, Lindsay B., illus. LC 91-31475. 32p. (ps-8). 1992. 14.00 (0-688-09214-4); PLB 13.93 (0-688-09215-2) Greenwillow.
George, William T. & George, Lindsay B. Beaver at Long Pond. LC 87-281. (Illus.). 24p. (ps-3). 1988. 14.00 (0-688-07106-6); lib. bdg. 13.88 (0-688-07107-4) Greenwillow.
—Fishing at Long Pond. LC 89-77514. (Illus.). 24p. (ps up). 1991. 13.95 (0-688-09401-5); PLB 13.88 (0-688-09402-3) Greenwillow.
Georges, D. V. Africa. LC 86-9586. (Illus.). 48p. (gr. k-4). 1986. LC 15.27 (0-516-01287-8); pap. 4.95 (0-516-41287-6) Childrens.
—Asia. LC 86-9631. (Illus.). 48p. (gr. k-4). 1986. PLB 15.27 (0-516-01288-6); pap. 4.95 (0-516-41288-4) Childrens.
—Australia. LC 86-9587. (Illus.). 48p. (gr. k-4). 1986. PLB 15.27 (0-516-01290-8); pap. 4.95 (0-516-41290-6) Childrens.
—Europe. LC 86-9585. (Illus.). 48p. (gr. k-4). 1986. PLB 15.27 (0-516-01292-4); pap. 4.95 (0-516-41292-2) Childrens.
—Glaciers. LC 85-30884. (Illus.). 48p. (gr. k-4). 1986. PLB 15.27 (0-516-01281-9); pap. 4.95 (0-516-41281-7) Childrens.
—North America. LC 86-9638. (Illus.). 48p. (gr. k-4). 1986. PLB 15.27 (0-516-01294-0); pap. 4.95 (0-516-41294-9) Childrens.
—South America. LC 86-9584. (Illus.). 48p. (gr. k-4). 1986. PLB 15.27 (0-516-01296-7); pap. 4.95 (0-516-41296-5) Childrens.
Georgiady, Nicholas P. & Romano, Louis G. Gertie the Duck. Wilson, Dagmar, illus. (gr. 1-3). 1982. lib. ed. 2.97 (0-89564-43363-6); pap. 1.50 (0-685-10942-9) Follett Pr.
—Gertie the Duck: Look! I-Can-Read Book. (Illus.). 32p. (gr. k-4). 1988. pap. 3.00 (0-695-83363-4) Argee Pubs.
—Trudi La Cane. Thorne, Patrice, tr. Wilson, Dagmar W., illus. 32p. (gr. 1-4). 1982. pap. 5.00 (0-317-05572-0) Argee Pubs.
—Trudi La Cane. Thorne, Patrice, tr. from ENG. Wilson, Dagmar W., illus. (FRE.). 27p. (gr. k-4). pap. 5.00 (0-317-03037-X) Argee Pubs.
—Tulita la Patita. De Ninojosa, Ida N., tr. Wilson, Dagmar W., illus. 32p. (gr. 1-4). 1984. pap. 3.00 (0-317-03352-2) Argee Pubs.
Georgiou, Constantine. Proserpina, the Duck That Came to School. (gr. 3-6). 1992. pap. write for info. (0-9637111-0-5) C Georgiou.
Geraghty, Helen M. Chris Burke: Actor. (Illus.). 1994. 18.95 (0-7910-2081-9, Am Art Analog); pap. write for info. (0-7910-2094-0, Am Art Analog) Chelsea Hse.
Geraghty, Paul. The Great Knitting Needle Hunt. (Illus.). 32p. (ps-2). 1992. 14.95 (0-09-173749-4, Pub. by Hutchinson UK) Trafalgar.
—The Hunter. LC 93-22730. (gr. k-4). 1994. write for info. (0-517-59692-X); PLB write for info. (0-517-59693-8) Crown Bks Yng Read.
—Look Out, Patrick! Geraghty, Paul, illus. LC 89-77850. 32p. (ps-1). 1990. 13.95 (0-02-735822-4, Macmillan Child Bk) Macmillan Child Grp.
—Over the Steamy Swamp. Geraghty, Paul, illus. 28p. (ps-1). 1989. 13.95 (0-15-200561-7, Gulliver Bks) HarBrace.
—Slobcat. Geraghty, Paul, illus. LC 90-27577. 32p. (ps-1). 1991. 13.95 (0-02-735825-9, Macmillan Child Bk) Macmillan Child Grp.
—Stop That Noise! Geraghty, Paul, illus. LC 92-6608. 32p. (ps-2). 1992. 13.00 (0-517-59158-8); PLB 13.99 (0-517-59159-6) Crown Bks Yng Read.
Geraghty, Paul, jt. auth. see Bush, John.
Gerardi, Robert. Opportunities in Music Careers. rev. ed. LC 90-50739. 160p. (gr. 7 up). 1991. 13.95 (0-8442-8154-9, VGM Career Bks); pap. 10.95 (0-8442-8155-7, VGM Career Bks) NTC Pub Grp.
Geras, Adele. Golden Windows & Other Stories of Jerusalem. LC 92-39885. 160p. (gr. 3-7). 1993. 14.00 (0-06-022941-1); PLB 13.89 (0-06-022942-X) HarpC Child Bks.
—Happy Endings. Grove, Karen, ed. 173p. (gr. 7 up). 1991. 14.95 (0-15-233375-4) HarBrace.
—My Grandmother's Stories: A Collection of Jewish Folk Tales. Jordan, Jael, illus. LC 90-4309. 96p. (gr. 3-7). 1990. 17.95 (0-679-80910-4); PLB 18.99 (0-679-90910-9) Knopf Bks Yng Read.
—Pictures of the Night. LC 92-27425. 1993. write for info. (0-15-261588-1) HarBrace.
—The Tower Room. 1992. 15.95 (0-15-289627-9, HB Juv Bks) HarBrace.
—Watching the Roses. LC 92-8160. 1992. write for info. (0-15-294816-3, HB Juv Bks) HarBrace.
Gerber, Carole. Master Comprehension Workbook Grade One. (ps-3). 1990. pap. 4.95 (1-56189-041-3) Amer Educ Pub.
—Master Comprehension Workbook Grade Three. (ps-3). 1990. pap. 4.95 (1-56189-043-X) Amer Educ Pub.
—Master Comprehension Workbook Grade Two. (ps-3). 1990. pap. 4.95 (1-56189-042-1) Amer Educ Pub.

—Master Math Workbook Grade Five. (gr. 4-7). 1990. pap. 4.95 (1-56189-015-4) Amer Educ Pub.
—Master Math Workbook Grade Four. (gr. 4-7). 1990. pap. 4.95 (1-56189-014-6) Amer Educ Pub.
—Master Math Workbook Grade K. (ps-3). 1990. pap. 4.95 (1-56189-010-3) Amer Educ Pub.
—Master Math Workbook Grade One. (ps-3). 1990. pap. 4.95 (1-56189-011-1) Amer Educ Pub.
—Master Math Workbook Grade Six. (gr. 4-7). 1990. pap. 4.95 (1-56189-016-2) Amer Educ Pub.
—Master Math Workbook Grade Three. (ps-3). 1990. pap. 4.95 (1-56189-013-8) Amer Educ Pub.
—Master Math Workbook Grade Two. (ps-3). 1990. pap. 4.95 (1-56189-012-X) Amer Educ Pub.
—Master Reading Workbook Grade Five. (gr. 4-7). 1990. pap. 4.95 (1-56189-005-7) Amer Educ Pub.
—Master Reading Workbook Grade Four. (gr. 4-7). 1990. pap. 4.95 (1-56189-004-9) Amer Educ Pub.
—Master Reading Workbook Grade K. (ps-3). 1990. pap. 4.95 (1-56189-000-6) Amer Educ Pub.
—Master Reading Workbook Grade One. (ps-3). 1990. pap. 4.95 (1-56189-001-4) Amer Educ Pub.
—Master Reading Workbook Grade Six. (gr. 4-7). 1990. pap. 4.95 (1-56189-006-5) Amer Educ Pub.
—Master Reading Workbook Grade Three. (ps-3). 1990. pap. 4.95 (1-56189-003-0) Amer Educ Pub.
—Master Reading Workbook Grade Two. (ps-3). 1990. pap. 4.95 (1-56189-002-2) Amer Educ Pub.
—Master Study Skills Workbook Grade One. (ps-3). 1990. pap. 4.95 (1-56189-051-0) Amer Educ Pub.
—Master Study Skills Workbook Grade Three. (ps-3). 1990. pap. 4.95 (1-56189-053-7) Amer Educ Pub.
—Master Study Skills Workbook Grade Two. (ps-3). 1990. pap. 4.95 (1-56189-052-9) Amer Educ Pub.
—Weird, Wacky, & Totally True: Strange Tales about Animals. (Illus.). 32p. (gr. 2 up). 1992. pap. 2.99 (0-87406-632-8) Willowisp Pr.
Gerber, Carole, ed. English. 2nd ed. Robison, Don, illus. 40p. (gr. 2). 1992. wkbk. 1.99 (1-56189-082-0) Amer Educ Pub.
—English. Robison, Don, illus. 40p. (gr. 3). 1992. wkbk. 1.99 (1-56189-083-9) Amer Educ Pub.
—English & Phonics. Robison, Don, illus. 32p. (gr. k). 1992. wkbk. 1.99 (1-56189-080-4) Amer Educ Pub.
—English & Phonics. Robison, Don, illus. 40p. (gr. 1). 1992. wkbk. 1.99 (1-56189-081-2) Amer Educ Pub.
Gerber, Merrill J. Also Known As Sadzia! The Belly Dancer! LC 86-45484. 192p. (gr. 7 up). 1987. HarpC Child Bks.
—Handsome As Anything. 1990. 13.95 (0-590-43019-X) Scholastic Inc.
—Handsome As Anything. 176p. 1992. pap. 2.95 (0-590-43020-3, Point) Scholastic Inc.
Gerber, Will, et al. The Rings on Woot-Kew's Tail: Indian Legends of the Origin of the Sun, Moon & Stars. (gr. 3-9). 1973. 1.50 (0-89992-059-4) Coun India Ed.
Gerberg, Mort. Geographunny: A Book of Global Riddles. Gerberg, Mort, illus. 64p. (gr. 3 up). 1991. 14.45 (0-395-52449-0, Clarion Bks); pap. 7.70 (0-395-60312-9, Clarion Bks) HM.
Gerbi, Susan A. From Genes to Proteins. Head, J. J., ed. Steffen, Ann T., illus. LC 84-45830. 16p. (Orig.). (gr. 10 up). 1993. pap. text ed. 2.75 (0-89278-358-3, 45-9758) Carolina Biological.
Gerbino, Mary, jt. auth. see Sanchez, Gail J.
Gere, Bill. The Truck Book. LaPadula, Tom, illus. 24p. (ps-k). 1987. pap. write for info. (0-307-10051-0, Pub. by Golden Bks) Western Pub.
Gerez, Toni de see De Gerez, Toni.
Gerez, Toni de, retold by. Louhi, Witch of North Farm: A Finnish Tale. Cooney, Barbara, illus. (ps-3). 1988. pap. 4.99 (0-14-050529-6, Puffin) Puffin Bks.
Gergely, Tibor, illus. Three Best-Loved Tales: Tootle; The Happy Man & His Dump Truck; Scuffy the Tugboat. 80p. (ps-2). 1992. write for info. (0-307-15633-8, 15633, Golden Pr) Western Pub.
Gergen, Joe. World Series Heroes & Goats: The Men Who Made History in America's October Classics. LC 82-611. (Illus.). 160p. (gr. 5-9). 1982. pap. 1.95 (0-394-85018-1) Random Bks Yng Read.
Geringer, Laura. The Cow Is Mooing Anyhow. Zimmer, Dirk, illus. LC 85-45251. 40p. (ps-4). 1991. PLB 14.89 (0-06-021987-4) HarpC Child Bks.
—The Cow Is Mooing Anyhow. Zimmer, Dirk, illus. LC 85-45251. 40p. (ps-4). 1993. pap. 4.95 (0-06-443332-3, Trophy) HarpC Child Bks.
—Look Out, Look Out, It's Coming! Truesdell, Sue, illus. LC 91-4707. 40p. (ps-2). 1992. 15.00 (0-06-021711-1); PLB 14.89 (0-06-021712-X) HarpC Child Bks.
—Molly's New Washing Machine. Mathers, Petra, illus. LC 85-45839. 32p. (gr. k-3). 1986. HarpC Child Bks.
—Silverpoint. LC 91-6648. 160p. (gr. 5 up). 1991. 13.95 (0-06-023849-6); PLB 13.89 (0-06-023850-X) HarpC Child Bks.
—A Three Hat Day. Lobel, Arnold, illus. LC 85-42640. 32p. (ps-3). 1985. PLB 14.89 (0-06-021989-0) HarpC Child Bks.
—A Three Hat Day. Lobel, Arnold, illus. LC 85-42640. 32p. (ps-3). 1987. pap. 4.95 (0-06-443157-6, Trophy) HarpC Child Bks.
—Yours 'Til the Ice Cracks: A Book of Valentines. Baruffi, Andrea, illus. LC 91-22687. 32p. (gr. 1-7). 1992. 10.00 (0-06-020399-4) HarpC Child Bks.
Geringer, Laura, retold by. The Seven Ravens. Gazsi, Edward S., illus. LC 93-8161. Date not set. 15.00 (0-06-023552-7); PLB 14.89 (0-06-023553-5) HarpC.

Germaine, Elizabeth & Burckhardt, Ann. Cooking the Australian Way. Wolfe, Bob & Wolfe, Diane, photos by. (Illus.). 48p. (gr. 5 up). 1990. PLB 14.95 (0-8225-0923-7) Lerner Pubns.

German Craftsmen Staff, illus. King Winter: Treasures from the Library of Congress. 16p. 1992. Repr. of 1859 ed. saddle wired 3.95 (1-55709-168-4) Applewood.

German, Norman. No Other World. rev. ed. (Illus.). 175p. 1992. pap. 10.95 (0-9621724-2-1) Blue Heron LA.

Gernand, Renee. The Cuban Americans. Moynihan, Daniel P., intro. by. (Illus.). 112p. (gr. 5 up). 1989. lib. bdg. 17.95 (0-87754-869-2) Chelsea Hse.

Geronimi, Clyde. Chips Quips. Geronimi, Clyde, illus. LC 83-72694. 55p. (gr. 4 up). 1983. pap. 3.95 (0-939126-09-5) Back Bay.

Gerrard, Anne. The Adventures of Christopher Bear & His Friends. (Illus.). 32p. (gr. 3). 1993. pap. 8.95 (0-8059-3329-8) Dorrance.

Gerrard, Jean. Matilda Jane. Gerrard, Roy, illus. LC 83-48082. 32p. (ps-3). 1983. 15.00 (0-374-34865-0) FS&G.

Gerrard, Roy. The Favershams. (Illus.). 32p. (gr. 2 up). 1987. pap. 3.95 (0-374-42293-1) FS&G.
—The Favershams. Gerrard, Roy, illus. 32p. (gr. 1-9). 1983. 15.00 (0-374-32292-9) FS&G.
—Jocasta Carr, Movie Star. LC 92-6751. 1992. 15.00 (0-374-33654-7) FS&G.
—Mik's Mammoth. (Illus.). 32p. (gr. k-3). 1990. 15.00 (0-374-31891-3) FS&G.
—Mik's Mammoth. (ps-3). 1992. pap. 4.95 (0-374-44843-4) FS&G.
—A Pocket Full of Posies. (Illus.). 32p. 1991. bds. 9.95 (0-374-36032-4) FS&G.
—Rosie & the Rustlers. 32p. (ps up). 1989. 15.00 (0-374-36345-5) FS&G.
—Rosie & the Rustlers. (Illus.). 32p. (ps up). 1991. pap. 4.95 (0-374-46339-5) FS&G.
—Sir Cedric. LC 84-6111. (Illus.). 32p. (ps up). 1984. 14.95 (0-374-36959-3) FS&G.
—Sir Cedric. (Illus.). 32p. (gr. k up). 1986. pap. 4.95 (0-374-46659-9) FS&G.
—Sir Cedric Rides Again. (Illus.). 32p. (ps up). 1988. pap. 4.95 (0-374-46662-9, Sunburst) FS&G. Postponed.
—Sir Francis Drake: His Daring Deeds. (Illus.). 32p. (gr. 3 up). 1988. 15.00 (0-374-36962-3) FS&G.

Gerrold, David. Voyage of Star Wolf. 240p. 1990. pap. 4.99 (0-553-26466-4, Spectra) Bantam.
—When Harlie Was One. 288p. 1988. pap. 3.95 (0-553-26465-6, Spectra) Bantam.

Gersbach, Jo R. The Case of the Buried Money Bags. (gr. 5-8). 1978. 6.50 (0-87881-065-X) Mojave Bks.

Gersh, Harry. Talmud: Law & Commentary. 64p. (gr. 9 up). 1986. pap. text ed. 4.95x (0-87441-434-2); By Derek J. Penslar. tchr's. ed. 9.95 (0-87441-435-0) Behrman.
—When a Jew Celebrates. Weihs, Erika, illus. LC 70-116678. 256p. (gr. 5-6). 1971. pap. text ed. 7.95x (0-87441-091-6); tchr's guide 14.95 (0-685-41997-5); student activity bk. 3.95 (0-685-41998-3); tchr's cassette 5.95 (0-685-00740-5) Behrman.

Gershator, David. Bread Is for Eating. Date not set. write for info. (0-8050-3173-1) H Holt & Co.

Gershator, Phillis. Honi's Circle of Trees. Green, Mim, illus. LC 93-29748. 1994. write for info. (0-8276-0511-0) JPS Phila.
—Rata-Pata-Scata-Fata: A Caribbean Story. Meade, Holly, illus. LC 92-40695. 1993. 14.95 (0-316-30470-0, Joy St Bks) Little.

Gershator, Phyllis, retold by. The Iroko-Man: A Yoruba Folktale. Kim, Holly C., illus. LC 93-4888. 32p. (ps-2). 1994. 14.95 (0-531-06810-2); PLB 14.99 (0-531-08660-7) Orchard Bks Watts.

Gersoh, Harry. Kabbalah. (gr. 9 up). 1989. pap. text ed. 4.95 (0-318-42862-8) Behrman.

Gerson, Corinne. My Grandfather the Spy. 1990. 14.95 (0-8027-6955-1) Walker & Co.
—Passing Through. 208p. (gr. 8 up). 1980. pap. 1.50 (0-440-96958-1, LFL) Dell.
—Tread Softly. LC 78-72199. (gr. 4-7). 1979. Dial Bks Young.

Gerson, Mary-Joan. Why the Sky Is Far Away: A Nigerian Folktale. (ps-3). 1992. 15.95 (0-316-30852-8, Joy St Bks) Little.

Gerson, Mary-Joan, retold by. How Night Came from the Sea: A Story from Brazil. Golembe, Carla, illus. LC 93-20054. 1992. 15.95 (0-316-30855-2, Joy St Bks) Little.

Gerson, Trina. Holiday Crafts. Gerson, Janice, illus. 80p. (ps-7). 1983. pap. text ed. write for info. (0-9605878-1-0) Anirt Pr.
—Holiday Songs. Gerson, Ivan, illus. 84p. (ps-7). 1984. pap. text ed. write for info. (0-9605878-2-9) Anirt Pr.
—Poetic Shapes. Gerson, Janice, illus. 52p. (ps-7). 1981. pap. text ed. 2.95 (0-9605878-0-2) Anirt Pr.

Gerstein, Mordicai. Arnold of the Ducks. Gerstein, Mordicai, illus. LC 82-47735. 64p. (gr. k-3). 1983. PLB 14.89 (0-06-022003-1) HarpC Child Bks.
—The Gigantic Baby. Levin, Arnie, illus. LC 90-35537. 32p. (gr. k-3). 1991. PLB 14.89 (0-06-022106-2) HarpC Child Bks.
—The Mountains of Tibet. Gerstein, Mordicai, illus. LC 85-45684. 32p. (gr. 2 up). 1987. 14.00 (0-06-022144-5) HarpC Child Bks.
—The Mountains of Tibet. LC 85-45684. (Illus.). 32p. (gr. 2 up). 1989. pap. 5.95 (0-06-443211-4, Trophy) HarpC Child Bks.

—The New Creatures. LC 90-4128. (Illus.). 32p. (ps-3). 1991. PLB 14.89 (0-06-022167-4) HarpC Child Bks.
—Roll Over! LC 83-18884. (Illus.). 32p. (ps-1). 1988. 11.00 (0-517-55209-4) Crown Bks Yng Read.
—The Seal Mother. Gerstein, Mordicai, illus. LC 82-29295. 32p. (ps-3). 1986. PLB 10.89 (0-8037-0303-1) Dial Bks Young.
—The Seal Mother. (ps-3). 1990. pap. 3.95 (0-8037-0743-6) Dial Bks Young.
—The Story of May. Gerstein, Mordicai, illus. LC 90-22410. 48p. (ps-3). 1993. 16.00 (0-06-022288-3); PLB 15.89 (0-06-022289-1) HarpC Child Bks.
—The Sun's Day. LC 88-24738. (Illus.). 32p. (ps-1). 1989. 13.00 (0-06-022404-5); PLB 12.89 (0-06-022405-3) HarpC Child Bks.

Gerstein, Mordicai & Harris, Susan Y. Guess What? Gerstein, Mordicai & Harris, Susan Y., illus. LC 90-47318. 32p. (ps-2). 1991. 8.00 (0-517-58217-1) Crown Bks Yng Read.

Gerstein, Mordicai, retold by. & illus. Beauty & the Beast. 48p. (ps-2). 1989. (DCB); bk. & cassette 17.95 (0-525-44511-0) Dutton Child Bks.

Gerstein, Mordicai, tr. see Levy, Elizabeth.

Gerstenfeld, Sheldon. Zoo Clues: Making the Most of Your Visit to the Zoo. Doty, Eldon C., illus. 120p. (gr. 2 up). 1993. pap. 4.99 (0-14-032813-0, Puffin) Puffin Bks.

Gerstenfeld, Sheldon L. The Aquarium Take-Along Book. Harvey, Paul, illus. LC 93-23059. 128p. (gr. 2-5). 1994. 14.99 (0-670-84386-5) Viking Child Bks.
—The Aquarium Take-along Book. Harvey, Paul, illus. 128p. (gr. 2-5). 1994. pap. 6.99 (0-14-036019-0) Puffin Bks.
—Zoo Clues: Making the Most of Your Visit to the Zoo. Doty, Eldon C., illus. 128p. (gr. 2-5). 1991. 13.95 (0-670-82362-7) Viking Child Bks.

Gerstung, Estella, ed. see Clark, Barbara R.

Gertz, Susan E. Hanukkah & Christmas at My House. Gertz, Susan E., illus. LC 91-73702. 32p. (ps-6). 1992. pap. 6.95 (0-9630934-0-1) Willow & Laurel. As seen in WORKING MOTHER & CHILD magazines. "Young children enjoy hearing tales of their parents' childhoods, & this delightful book uses a Jewish mommy's recollections of Hanukkah & a Christian daddy's memories of Christmas as the framework for presenting the stories, foods, songs, decorations, & special customs unique to each holiday. Several features which add to the value of this book are the recipes for the holiday foods, the historical background material, & the charming illustrations which can help young children visualize unfamiliar objects & events from both holidays. "Ms. Gertz has provided an EXCELLENT RESOURCE FOR FAMILIES & RELIGIOUS EDUCATION CLASSES."--District Curriculum Librarian, Unitarian Universalist Association. "For the young children for whom this book is intended, & for their parents for whom the author has provided a more detailed history & some good traditional recipes, THIS BOOK IS A MUST. It may be one of the few publications available through which to deal with a child's confusion in having a mom & dad of different religious backgrounds."--Small Press Magazine. "Potato latkes & Christmas cookies, a menorah & a Christmas angel, 'I Had a Little Dreidle' & 'Deck the Halls' all coexist in a suprisingly simple & logical manner in this extraordinary book."--All About Kids. "...A BOOK THAT ALL CHILDREN SHOULD READ, so they may better understand...families which celebrate both holidays."--B'nai Brith Messenger. Distributed by Children's Small Press Collection (800) 221-8056. *Publisher Provided Annotation.*

Gerver, Jane E. Happy Bear, Christmas Star. Barto, Bobbi, illus. LC 90-60174. 32p. (Orig.). (ps-3). 1990. pap. 2.25 (0-679-80858-2) Random Bks Yng Read.

Gesch, Roy C. Confirmed in Christ. (gr. 7 up). 1983. pap. 2.99 (0-570-03911-8, 12-2852) Concordia.

Geser, Ingrid. TV & Video. Stefoff, Rebecca, ed. LC 90-13868. (Illus.). 32p. (gr. 4-8). 1991. PLB 17.26 (0-944483-99-2) Garrett Ed Corp.

Gesme, Carole & Peterson, Larry. Help for Kids: Understanding Your Feelings about Moving. Schmoker, Lisa, ed. Lindstrom, Jack, illus. 56p. (gr. 1-12). 1992. spiral bound wkbk. 12.95 (0-9633761-0-1); spiral bound 8.95 (0-9633761-1-X) Pine Tr Pr MN.

Gess, Denise. Togo. (Illus.). 96p. (gr. 5 up). 1988. lib. bdg. 14.95x (1-55546-190-5) Chelsea Hse.

Gess, Diane, jt. auth. see Rothstein, Evelyn.

Gess, Diane, ed. see Rothstein, Evelyn.

Gessner, Lynne. Malcolm Yucca Seed. rev. ed. Bock, William S. & Jensen, Debbie, illus. 64p. (gr. 3-8). pap. 5.95 (0-918080-63-0) Treasure Chest.

Gettinger, Shifrah. A Very Special Gift. Leff, Tova, illus. 32p. (ps-3). 1993. 8.95 (0-922613-52-4); pap. text ed. 6.95 (0-922613-53-2) Hachai Pubns.

Getz, David. Almost Famous. 192p. (gr. 4-7). 1993. 13.95 (0-8050-1940-5, Bks Young Read) H Holt & Co.
—The Frozen Man. 1994. write for info. (0-8050-3261-4) H Holt & Co.
—Thin Air. LC 90-34137. 128p. (gr. 6 up). 1990. 14.95 (0-8050-1379-2, Bks Young Read) H Holt & Co.
—Thin Air. LC 90-34137. 128p. (gr. 3-7). 1992. pap. 3.95 (0-06-440422-6, Trophy) HarpC Child Bks.

Getzel. The Stone Cutter Who Wanted to Be Rich. LC 90-82970. (Illus.). 48p. (gr. 1-5). 1990. 9.95 (0-685-45648-X) CIS Comm.

Getzoff, Ann & McClenahan, Carolyn. Stepkids: A Survival Guide for Teenagers in Stepfamilies...& for Stepparents Doubtful of Their Own Survival. 171p. (gr. 5 up). 1985. pap. 9.95 (0-8027-7236-6) Walker & Co.

Gevirtz, Eliezer. The Mystery of the Missing Bar Mitzvah Gift. (gr. 4-7). 1987. 9.95 (0-317-57109-5); pap. 7.95 (0-317-57110-9) Feldheim.
—The Mystery of the Missing Pushke. Mazal, Chanan, illus. 200p. (gr. 5-7). 1982. 8.95 (0-87306-291-4); pap. 6.95 (0-685-07004-2) Feldheim.

Gevirtz, Eliezer, jt. auth. see Scherman, Nosson.

Gewing, Lisa. Mama, Daddy, Baby & Me. Larimer, Donna, illus. 30p. (ps). 1989. 12.95 (0-944296-04-1) Spirit Pr.

Gewirtz, Gladys, jt. auth. see Grossman, Roz.

Gewirtz, Herman & Martin, David S. How to Prepare for SAT II: Physics. 6th ed. 1994. pap. 11.95 (0-8120-1705-6) Barron.

Geyer, Waldon M. Santa & Friends. 32p. 1991. 14.95 (1-880695-01-4); incl. cassette 23.95 (1-880695-03-0); pap. 8.95 (1-880695-02-2); pap. 15.95 incl. cassette (1-880695-04-9); cassette 7.95 (1-880695-00-6) Santa & Friends.

Gezi, Kal & Bradford, Ann. The Mystery at Misty Falls. McLean, Mina G., illus. LC 80-15708. 32p. (gr. k-4). 1980. PLB 18.50 (0-89565-147-5); PLB 12.95s.p. (0-685-55525-9) Childs World.
—The Mystery in the Secret Club House. McLean, Mina G., illus. LC 78-6418. 32p. (gr. k-3). 1978. PLB 18.50 (0-89565-027-4); PLB 12.95s.p. (0-685-55527-5) Childs World.
—The Mystery of the Blind Writer. McLean, Mina G., illus. LC 80-12395. 32p. (gr. k-4). 1980. PLB 18.50 (0-89565-145-9); PLB 12.95s.p. (0-685-55528-3) Childs World.
—The Mystery of the Live Ghosts. McLean, Mina G., illus. LC 78-8142. 32p. (gr. k-3). 1978. PLB 18.50 (0-89565-026-6); PLB 12.95s.p. (0-685-55529-1) Childs World.
—The Mystery of the Square Footprints. McLean, Mina G., illus. LC 80-10437. 32p. (gr. k-4). 1980. PLB 18.50 (0-89565-144-0); PLB 12.95s.p. (0-685-55532-1) Childs World.

Gezi, Kal, jt. auth. see Bradford, Ann.

Ghanoonparvar, Mohammad R., tr. see Azaad, Meyer.

Ghazi, Abidullah. Grandfather's Orchard. Ghazi, Tasneema, et al, eds. Van Patten, Michele, illus. 15p. Date not set. text ed. 14.95 (1-56316-307-1) Iqra Intl Ed Fdtn.

Ghazi, Tasneema, et al, eds. see Ghazi, Abidullah.

Gherman, Beverly. Agnes De Mille: Dancing off the Earth. LC 89-6888. (Illus.). 160p. (gr. 4 up). 1990. SBE 13.95 (0-689-31441-8, Atheneum Child Bk) Macmillan Child Grp.
—Agnes de Mille: Dancing off the Earth. LC 93-26606. 160p. 1994. pap. 5.95 (0-02-043240-2, Collier Young Ad) Macmillan Child Grp.
—E B White - Some Writer! (Illus.). 144p. (gr. 5 up). 1994. pap. 3.95 (0-688-12826-2, Pub. by Beech Tree Bks) Morrow.
—E. B. White: Some Writer! LC 91-19012. (Illus.). 144p. (gr. 3-7). 1992. SBE 13.95 (0-689-31672-0, Atheneum Child Bk) Macmillan Child Grp.
—Georgia O'Keefe: The "Wideness & Wonder" of Her World. LC 85-26860. (Illus.). 144p. (gr. 4 up). 1986. SBE 13.95 (0-689-31164-8, Atheneum Child Bk) Macmillan Child Grp.
—Georgia O'Keeffe: The "Wideness & Wonder" of Her World. 144p. (gr. 7 up). 1994. pap. 5.95 (0-02-040388-7, Collier Young Ad) Macmillan Child Grp.
—The Mysterious Rays of Dr. Roentgen. Marchesi, Stephen, illus. LC 92-38966. 32p. (gr. 2-5). 1994. SBE 14.95 (0-689-31839-1, Atheneum Child Bk) Macmillan Child Grp.

—Sandra Day O'Connor. (gr. 4-7). 1991. 10.95 (0-670-82756-8) Viking Child Bks.
—Sandra Day O'Connor: Justice for All. Masheris, Robert, illus. LC 92-42464. 64p. (gr. 2-6). 1993. pap. 3.99 (0-14-034100-5, Puffin) Puffin Bks.

Ghigna, Charles. Father Goose: A Treasury of Poems for Children. (Illus.). 40p. 1994. 14.95 (1-56282-481-3); PLB 14.89 (1-56282-482-1) Hyprn Child.
—Good Cats, Bad Cats. Catrow, David, illus. LC 92-52984. 40p. 1992. 7.95 (1-56282-292-6); PLB 10.89 (1-56282-293-4) Hyprn Child.
Ghinga, Charles. Good Dogs, Bad Dogs. Catrow, David, illus. LC 92-52985. 32p. 1992. 7.95 (1-56282-290-X); PLB 10.89 (1-56282-291-8) Hyprn Child.
Ghosh, A. Chanakya. Vilas, Anil, illus. (gr. 1-8). 1979. pap. 3.00 (0-89744-152-4) Auromere.
—Legends from Indian History. Mukerji, Debrabrata, illus. (gr. 1-8). 1979. pap. 3.00 (0-89744-157-5); 4.50 (0-685-00594-1) Auromere.
Ghrist, Julie, illus. Taelly's Counting Adventures. (ps). 1993. Gift box set of 4 bks., 12p. ea. incl. counting flash cards. bds. 14.95 (1-56828-042-4) Red Jacket Pr.
—Taelly's Counting Adventures: At Sea. 12p. (ps). 1993. 4.95 (1-56828-027-0) Red Jacket Pr.
—Taelly's Counting Adventures: Down on the Farm. 12p. (ps). 1993. 4.95 (1-56828-029-7) Red Jacket Pr.
—Taelly's Counting Adventures: In the Neighborhood. 12p. (ps). 1993. 4.95 (1-56828-030-0) Red Jacket Pr.
—Taelly's Counting Adventures: On Mars. 12p. (ps). 1993. 4.95 (1-56828-028-9) Red Jacket Pr.
Giampa, Linda. Jesus & Me, ABC Activity Book. (Illus.). 32p. (Orig.). (ps-2). 1991. pap. 2.99 (0-570-04198-8) Concordia.
—New Testament Activity Book. Giampa, Linda, illus. 32p. (Orig.). (gr. k-3). 1992. pap. 2.99 (0-570-04725-0) Concordia.
—Old Testament Activity Book. Giampa, Linda, illus. 32p. (gr. k-3). 1992. pap. 2.99 (0-570-04724-2) Concordia.
Giannini, Enzo. Zorina Ballerina. LC 91-21970. (Illus.). 40p. (gr. ps-1). 1993. 14.00 JRT (0-671-74776-2, S&S BFYR) S&S Trade.
Gibala-Broxholm, Janice. Let Me Do It! Paterson, Diane, illus. LC 92-12856. 32p. (ps-k). 1994. RSBE 14.95 (0-02-735827-5, Bradbury Pr) Macmillan Child Grp.
Gibb, Christopher. The Dalai Lama: The Leader of the Exiled People of Tibet & Tireless Worker for World Peace. LC 89-43119. (Illus.). 68p. (gr. 5-6). 1990. PLB 18.60 (0-8368-0224-1) Gareth Stevens Inc.
—Food or Famine. (Illus.). 48p. (gr. 5 up). 1987. PLB 18.60 (0-86592-279-9); 13.95 (0-685-67571-8) Rourke Corp.
Gibb, George, ed. see Lam, Roger.
Gibbons, Dave. Batman Versus Predator: The Collected Edition. Kahan, Bob, ed. O'Neil, Dennis, intros. by. (Illus.). 128p. (Orig.). 1992. pap. 5.95 (1-56389-092-5) DC Comics.
—War Machine. Burton, Richard, ed. Simpson, Will, illus. 80p. 1993. text ed. 14.95 (1-56862-018-7) Tundra MA.
Gibbons, Faye. King Shoes & Clown Pockets. LC 89-33429. 240p. (gr. 4 up). 1989. 12.95 (0-688-06592-9) Morrow Jr Bks.
Gibbons, Gail. Beacons of Light: Lighthouses. Gibbons, Gail, illus. LC 89-33884. 32p. (gr. 1 up). 1990. 12.95 (0-688-07379-4); PLB 12.88 (0-688-07380-8, Morrow Jr Bks) Morrow Jr Bks.
—Boat Book. Gibbons, Gail, illus. LC 82-15851. 32p. (ps-3). 1983. reinforced bdg. 14.95 (0-8234-0478-1); pap. 5.95 (0-8234-0709-8) Holiday.
—Catch the Wind! All about Kites. Gibbons, Gail, illus. LC 88-28820. (gr. k-3). 1989. 14.95 (0-316-30955-9) Little.
—Caves & Caverns. LC 92-760. (gr. 4-7). 1993. 14.95 (0-15-226820-0, HB Juv Bks) HarBrace.
—Check It Out: The Book about Libraries. Gibbons, Gail, illus. LC 85-5414. 32p. (ps-3). 1985. 12.95 (0-15-216400-6, HB Juv Bks) HarBrace.
—Check It Out! The Book about Libraries. Gibbons, Gail, illus. 32p. (ps-3). 1988. pap. 3.95 (0-15-216401-4, Voyager Bks) HarBrace.
—Christmas Time. LC 82-1038. (Illus.). 32p. (ps-3). 1982. reinforced bdg. 14.95 (0-8234-0453-6); pap. 5.95 (0-8234-0575-3) Holiday.
—Christmas Time. Gibbons, Gail, illus. (gr. k-3). 1985. PLB incl. cassette 19.95 (0-941078-84-1); pap. 12.95 incl. Cassette (0-941078-82-5); PLB 27.95 incl. cassette, 4 paperbacks, guide (0-317-40160-2) Live Oak Media.
—Country Fair. LC 93-30289. 1994. 14.95 (0-316-30951-6) Little.
—Deadline! From News to Newspaper. Gibbons, Gail, illus. LC 86-47654. 32p. (gr. 1-4). 1987. PLB 14.89 (0-690-04602-2, Crowell Jr Bks) HarpC Child Bks.
—Dinosaurs. Gibbons, Gail, illus. LC 87-364. 32p. (ps-3). 1987. reinforced bdg. 14.95 (0-8234-0657-1); pap. 5.95 (0-8234-0708-X) Holiday.
—Dinosaurs, Dragonflies & Diamonds: All About Natural History Museums. Gibbons, Gail, illus. LC 88-38831. 32p. (gr. k-3). 1988. RSBE 13.95 (0-02-737240-5, Four Winds) Macmillan Child Grp.
—Easter. Gibbons, Gail, illus. LC 88-23292. 32p. (ps-3). 1989. reinforced bdg. 14.95 (0-8234-0737-3); pap. 5.95 (0-8234-0866-3) Holiday.
—Farming. Gibbons, Gail, illus. LC 87-21254. 32p. (ps-3). 1988. PLB 14.95 reinforced bdg. (0-8234-0682-2); pap. 5.95 (0-8234-0797-7) Holiday.

—Fill It Up! Gibbons, Gail, illus. LC 84-45345. 32p. (gr. k-4). 1985. (Crowell Jr Bks); PLB 14.89 (0-690-04440-2) HarpC Child Bks.
—Fill It Up! LC 84-45345. (Illus.). 32p. (gr. k-4). 1986. pap. 4.95 (0-06-446051-7, Trophy) HarpC Child Bks.
—Fire! Fire! Gibbons, Gail, illus. LC 84-45345. 40p. (gr. k-4). 1984. (Crowell Jr Bks); PLB 14.89 (0-690-04416-X) HarpC Child Bks.
—Fire! Fire! Gibbons, Gail, illus. LC 83-46162. 40p. (gr. k-4). 1987. pap. 5.95 (0-06-446058-4, Trophy) HarpC Child Bks.
—Flying. Gibbons, Gail, illus. LC 85-22027. 32p. (ps-3). 1986. reinforced bdg. 14.95 (0-8234-0599-0); pap. 5.95 (0-8234-0977-5) Holiday.
—Frogs. (Illus.). 1993. reinforced bdg. 15.95 (0-8234-1052-8) Holiday.
—From Path to Highway: The Story of the Boston Post Road. Gibbons, Gail, illus. LC 85-47897. 32p. (gr. 1-4). 1986. (Crowell Jr Bks); PLB 14.89 (0-690-04514-X) HarpC Child Bks.
—From Seed to Plant. Gibbons, Gail, illus. LC 90-47037. 32p. (ps-3). 1991. reinforced 14.95 (0-8234-0872-8) Holiday.
—From Seed to Plant. Gibbons, Gail, illus. (ps-3). 1993. pap. 5.95 (0-8234-1025-0) Holiday.
—The Great St. Lawrence Seaway. Gibbons, Gail, illus. LC 91-9851. 40p. (gr. 1 up). 1992. 15.00 (0-688-06984-3); PLB 14.93 (0-688-06985-1) Morrow Jr Bks.
—Halloween. Gibbons, Gail, illus. LC 84-519. 32p. (ps-3). 1984. reinforced bdg. 14.95 (0-8234-0524-9); pap. 5.95 (0-8234-0577-X) Holiday.
—Halloween. Gibbons, Gail, illus. (gr. k-3). 1985. incl. cassette 19.95 (0-941078-87-6); pap. 12.95 incl. cassette (0-941078-85-X); incl. cassette, 4 paperbacks guide 27.95 (0-941078-86-8) Live Oak Media.
—Happy Birthday! LC 86-297. (Illus.). 32p. (ps-3). 1986. reinforced bdg. 14.95 (0-8234-0614-8) Holiday.
—How a House Is Built. Gibbons, Gail, illus. LC 90-55107. 32p. (ps-3). 1990. reinforced bdg. 14.95 (0-8234-0841-8) Holiday.
—Lights! Camera! Action!: How a Movie Is Made. Gibbons, Gail, illus. LC 85-47536. 32p. (gr. 1-4). 1985. (Crowell Jr Bks); PLB 13.89 (0-690-04477-1) HarpC Child Bks.
—Lights! Camera! Action! How a Movie Is Made. Gibbons, Gail, illus. LC 85-47536. 32p. (gr. 1-4). 1989. pap. 4.95 (0-06-446088-6, Trophy) HarpC Child Bks.
—Marge's Diner. Gibbons, Gail, illus. LC 88-26789. 32p. (gr. 1-4). 1989. (Crowell Jr Bks); PLB 12.89 (0-690-04606-5, Crowell Jr Bks) HarpC Child Bks.
—The Milk Makers. LC 84-20081. (Illus.). 32p. (gr. k-3). 1985. RSBE 13.95 (0-02-736640-5, Macmillan Child Bk) Macmillan Child Grp.
—The Milk Makers. Gibbons, Gail, illus. LC 86-22148. 32p. (gr. k-3). 1987. pap. 3.95 (0-689-71116-6, Aladdin) Macmillan Child Grp.
—Monarch Butterfly. Gibbons, Gail, illus. LC 89-1880. 32p. (ps-3). 1989. reinforced bdg. 14.95 (0-8234-0773-X) Holiday.
—Monarch Butterfly. Gibbons, Gail, illus. LC 89-1880. 32p. (ps-3). 1991. pap. 5.95 (0-8234-0909-0) Holiday.
—Nature's Green Umbrella: Tropical Rain Forests. LC 93-17569. (gr. 4-8). 1994. write for info. (0-688-12353-8); PLB write for info. (0-688-12354-6) Morrow Jr Bks.
—New Road! Gibbons, Gail, illus. LC 82-45917. (Illus.). 32p. (gr. k-4). 1983. (Crowell Jr Bks); PLB 14.89 (0-690-04343-0) HarpC Child Bks.
—New Road! Gibbons, Gail, illus. LC 82-45917. 32p. (gr. k-4). 1987. pap. 4.95 (0-06-446059-2, Trophy) HarpC Child Bks.
—Paper, Paper Everywhere. Gibbons, Gail, illus. LC 82-3109. 32p. (gr. 1-5). 1983. 10.95 (0-15-259488-4, HB Juv Bks) HarBrace.
—Pirates: Robbers of the High Seas. LC 92-18375. 1993. 14.95 (0-316-30975-3) Little.
—The Planets. LC 92-44429. (Illus.). 32p. (ps-3). 1993. reinforced bdg. 15.95 (0-8234-1040-4) Holiday.
—Playgrounds. Gibbons, Gail, illus. LC 84-19285. 32p. (ps-3). 1985. reinforced bdg. 14.95 (0-8234-0553-2) Holiday.
—The Post Office Book. Gibbons, Gail, illus. LC 81-43888. 32p. (gr. k-3). 1982. (Crowell Jr Bks); PLB 14.89 (0-690-04199-3) HarpC Child Bks.
—The Post Office Book: Mail & How It Moves. Gibbons, Gail, illus. LC 85-45397. 32p. (gr. k-4). 1986. pap. 4.95 (0-06-446029-0, Trophy) HarpC Child Bks.
—The Pottery Place. Gibbons, Gail, illus. LC 86-32790. 32p. (ps-3). 1987. 12.95 (0-15-263265-4, HB Juv Bks) HarBrace.
—Prehistoric Animals. Gibbons, Gail, illus. LC 88-4661. 32p. (ps-3). 1988. reinforced bdg. 14.95 (0-8234-0704-7) Holiday.
—Puff - Flash - Bang! A Book about Signals. LC 92-13170. (ps up). 1993. 15.00 (0-688-07377-8); PLB 14.93 (0-688-07378-6) Morrow Jr Bks.
—The Puffins Are Back! Gibbons, Gail, illus. LC 90-30525. 32p. (gr. 3-5). 1991. 14.00 (0-06-021603-4); PLB 13.89 (0-06-021604-2) HarpC Child Bks.
—Recycle! A Handbook for Kids. Gibbons, Gail, illus. 32p. (ps-3). 1992. 14.95 (0-316-30971-0) Little.
—St. Patrick's Day. Gibbons, Gail, illus. LC 93-29570. 32p. (gr. 4-8). 1994. 15.95 (0-8234-1119-2) Holiday.

—Say Woof! The Day of a Country Veterinarian. Gibbons, Gail, illus. LC 91-48270. 32p. (gr. k-3). 1992. RSBE 13.95 (0-02-736781-9, Macmillan Child Bk) Macmillan Child Grp.
—The Seasons of Arnold's Apple Tree. LC 84-4484. (Illus.). 32p. (ps-3). 1984. 14.95 (0-15-271246-1, HB Juv Bks) HarBrace.
—Sharks. LC 91-31524. (Illus.). 32p. (ps-3). 1992. reinforced bdg. 14.95 (0-8234-0960-0) Holiday.
—Sharks. (Illus.). 1993. pap. 5.95 (0-8234-1068-4) Holiday.
—Spiders. LC 92-54414. (Illus.). 32p. (ps-3). 1993. reinforced bdg. 14.95 (0-8234-1006-4) Holiday.
—Stargazers. Gibbons, Gail, illus. LC 92-52713. 32p. (ps-3). 1992. reinforced bdg. 14.95 (0-8234-0983-X) Holiday.
—Sun up, Sun Down. Gibbons, Gail, illus. LC 82-23420. 32p. (gr. 1-5). 1983. 14.95 (0-15-282781-1, HB Juv Bks) HarBrace.
—Sun up, Sun Down. LC 82-23420. (Illus.). 32p. (Orig.). (ps-3). 1987. pap. 4.95 (0-15-282782-X, Voyager Bks) HarBrace.
—Sunken Treasure. Gibbons, Gail, illus. LC 87-30114. 32p. (gr. 1-5). 1988. 14.00 (0-690-04734-7, Crowell Jr Bks); PLB 13.89 (0-690-04736-3) HarpC Child Bks.
—Sunken Treasure. Gibbons, Gail, illus. LC 87-30114. 32p. (gr. 1-5). 1990. pap. 4.95 (0-06-446097-5, Trophy) HarpC Child Bks.
—Surrounded by Sea: Life on a New England Fishing Island. (ps-3). 1991. 14.95 (0-316-30961-3) Little.
—Thanksgiving Day. Gibbons, Gail, illus. LC 83-175. 32p. (ps-3). 1983. reinforced bdg. 14.95 (0-8234-0489-7); pap. 5.95 (0-8234-0576-1) Holiday.
—Thanksgiving Day. Gibbons, Gail, illus. (gr. k-3). 1984. incl. cassette 19.95 (0-941078-61-2); pap. 12.95 incl. cassette (0-941078-63-9); pap. 27.95 4 bks., cassette & guide (0-941078-62-0); sound filmstrip 22.95 (0-941078-60-4) Live Oak Media.
—Tool Book. Gibbons, Gail, illus. LC 81-13386. 32p. (ps-3). 1982. reinforced bdg. 14.95 (0-8234-0444-7); pap. 5.95 (0-8234-0694-6) Holiday.
—Trains. LC 86-19595. (Illus.). 32p. (ps-3). 1987. reinforced bdg. 14.95 (0-8234-0640-7); pap. 5.95 (0-8234-0699-7) Holiday.
—Trucks. Gibbons, Gail, illus. LC 81-43039. 32p. (ps-2). 1981. (Crowell Jr Bks); PLB 14.89 (0-690-04119-5) HarpC Child Bks.
—Trucks. Gibbons, Gail, illus. LC 81-43039. 32p. (ps-2). 1985. pap. 4.95 (0-06-443069-3, Trophy) HarpC Child Bks.
—Tunnels. Gibbons, Gail, illus. LC 83-18589. 32p. (ps-3). 1984. reinforced bdg. 14.95 (0-8234-0507-9); pap. 5.95 (0-8234-0670-9) Holiday.
—Up Goes the Skyscraper! Gibbons, Gail, illus. LC 85-16245. 32p. (gr. k-3). 1986. RSBE 13.95 (0-02-736780-0, Four Winds) Macmillan Child Grp.
—Up Goes the Skyscraper! Gibbons, Gail, illus. LC 90-31777. 32p. (gr. k-3). 1990. pap. 4.95 (0-689-71411-4, Aladdin) Macmillan Child Grp.
—Valentine's Day. Gibbons, Gail, illus. LC 85-916. 32p. (ps-3). 1986. reinforced bdg. 14.95 (0-8234-0572-9); pap. 5.95 (0-8234-0764-0) Holiday.
—Weather Forecasting. Gibbons, Gail, illus. LC 86-7602. 32p. (gr. k-3). 1987. RSBE 13.95 (0-02-737250-2, Four Winds) Macmillan Child Grp.
—Weather Forecasting. Gibbons, Gail, illus. LC 92-22264. 32p. (ps-3). 1993. pap. 3.95 (0-689-71683-4, Aladdin) Macmillan Child Grp.
—Weather Words & What They Mean. Gibbons, Gail, illus. LC 89-39515. 32p. (ps-3). 1994. 14.95 (0-8234-0805-1); pap. 5.95 (0-8234-0952-X) Holiday.
—Whales. Gibbons, Gail, illus. LC 91-4507. 32p. (ps-3). 1991. reinforced 14.95 (0-8234-0900-7) Holiday.
—Whales. Gibbons, Gail, illus. (ps-3). 1993. pap. 5.95 (0-8234-1030-7) Holiday.
—Zoo. Gibbons, Gail, illus. LC 87-582. 32p. (ps-3). 1987. 15.00 (0-690-04631-6, Crowell Jr Bks); PLB 14.89 (0-690-04633-2) HarpC Child Bks.
—Zoo. Gibbons, Gail, illus. LC 87-582. 32p. (ps-3). 1991. pap. 4.95 (0-06-446096-7, Trophy) HarpC Child Bks.
Gibbons, Maurice & Keating, Barb. How to Become an Expert: Discover, Research, & Build a Project in Your Chosen Field. rev. ed. (Illus.). 145p. (gr. 5-8). 1991. pap. text ed. 19.95 (0-913705-55-1) Zephyr Pr AZ.
Gibbons, Ted. Amen! An Interrupted Prayer. 6p. 1990. pap. text ed. 1.95 (0-929985-00-1) Sonos.
—Daniel Webster & the Blacksmith's Fee. 8p. (Orig.). 1988. pap. 1.95 stiched with dustcover (0-929985-03-6) Sonos.
—I Witnessed the Carthage Massacre: The Testimony of Willard Richards. 64p. (Orig.). (gr. 8 up). 1988. pap. 3.95 (0-929985-06-0) Sonos.
—Lincoln & the Lady. 21p. 1989. pap. text ed. 2.50 (0-929985-11-7) Sonos.
Gibbons, Tony. Submarines. Gibbons, Tony, et al, illus. 48p. (gr. 5 up). 1987. PLB 14.95 (0-8225-1383-8, First Ave Edns); pap. 4.95 (0-8225-9542-7, First Ave Edns) Lerner Pubns.
Gibbons Plummer, Jeanne, ed. see Kirkwood, Tim.
Gibbs, Alfred P. Four Letter Words. (Illus.). (gr. k-6). 1989. visualized song 4.50 (3-90117-000-6) CEF Press.
Gibbs, B. Ocean Facts. (Illus.). 48p. (gr. 3-7). 1991. lib. bdg. 12.96 (0-88110-531-7, Usborne); pap. 5.95 (0-7460-0621-7, Usborne) EDC.
Gibbs, Bridget. Mommy & Baby in the Wild. Gatt, Elizabeth, illus. 12p. 1992. 4.95 (0-681-41553-3) Longmeadow Pr.

—Mommy & Baby on the Farm. Gatt, Elizabeth, illus. 12p. 1992. 4.95 (*0-681-41554-1*) Longmeadow Pr.
—What's in the Bag? 1990. 9.95 (*1-55782-333-2*, Pub. by Warner Juvenile Bks) Little.
—What's in the Box? 1990. 9.95 (*1-55782-334-0*, Pub. by Warner Juvenile Bks) Little.
Gibbs, C. Jeanean, ed. see Bathersfield, Arnold, et al.
Gibbs, Carrol R. Friends of Frederick Douglass. Williams, Robert M., illus. 23p (Orig.). (gr. 5-12). 1992. pap. 5.00 (*1-877835-50-1*); pap. text ed. 3.75 (*1-877835-51-X*) TD Pub.
Gibbs, Greg. Willowby's World of Unicorns "Activity Book" 14p. (Orig.). (gr. 2-6). 1984. pap. 4.00x (*0-910349-03-7*) Cloud Ten.
Gibbs, Jeanne, ed. see Kling, Imogene.
Giblin, James. The Riddle of the Rosetta Stone. Tobin, Patricia, illus. LC 89-29289. 96p. (gr. 3-7). 1993. pap. 5.95 (*0-06-446137-8*, Trophy) HarpC Child Bks.
Giblin, James, ed. see Bunting, Eve.
Giblin, James, ed. see Chorao, Kay.
Giblin, James, ed. see Christelow, Eileen.
Giblin, James, ed. see Hahn, Mary D.
Giblin, James, ed. see Hines, Anna G.
Giblin, James, ed. see Hotze, Sollace.
Giblin, James, ed. see Perl, Lila.
Giblin, James, ed. see Willis, Patricia C.
Giblin, James C. Be Seated: A Book about Chairs. LC 92-25073. (Illus.). 144p. (gr. 3-7). 1993. 15.00 (*0-06-021537-2*); PLB 14.89 (*0-06-021538-0*) HarpC Child Bks.
—Chimney Sweeps. Tomes, Margot, illus. LC 81-43878. 64p. (gr. 4-8). 1982. (Crowell Jr Bks); (Crowell Jr Bks) HarpC Child Bks.
—Chimney Sweeps: Yesterday & Today. Tomes, Margot, illus. LC 81-43878. 64p. (gr. 4-7). 1987. pap. 5.95 (*0-06-446061-4*, Trophy) HarpC Child Bks.
—Edith Wilson: The Woman Who Ran the United States. Laporte, Michele, illus. 64p. (gr. 2-6). 1992. RB 11.00 (*0-670-83005-4*) Viking Child Bks.
—Edith Wilson: The Woman Who Ran the United States. Laporte, Michele, illus. LC 93-15139. 64p. (gr. 2-5). 1993. pap. 3.99 (*0-14-034249-4*, Puffin) Puffin Bks.
—Fireworks, Picnics, & Flags: The Story of the Fourth of July Symbols. Arndt, Ursula, illus. LC 82-9612. 96p. (gr. 3-6). 1983. 14.95 (*0-89919-146-0*, Clarion Bks); pap. 4.95 (*0-89919-174-6*, Clarion Bks) HM.
—From Hand to Mouth: Or, How We Invented Knives, Forks, Spoons, & Chopsticks, & the Table Manners To Go with Them. LC 86-29341. (Illus.). 96p. (gr. 3-7). 1987. (Crowell Jr Bks); PLB 12.89 (*0-690-04662-6*, Crowell Jr Bks) HarpC Child Bks.
—George Washington: A Picture Book Biography. (Illus.). (ps up) 1992. 14.95 (*0-590-42550-1*, 017, Scholastic Hardcover) Scholastic Inc.
—Milk: The Fight for Purity. LC 85-48252. (Illus.). 128p. (gr. 3-7). 1986. (Crowell Jr Bks); PLB 12.89 (*0-690-04574-3*, Crowell Jr Bks) HarpC Child Bks.
—The Riddle of the Rosetta Stone: Key to Ancient Egypt. LC 89-29289. (Orig.). 96p. (gr. 3-7). 1990. 15.00 (*0-690-04797-5*, Crowell Jr Bks); PLB 14.89 (*0-690-04799-1*, Crowell Jr Bks) HarpC Child Bks.
—The Skyscraper Book. Kramer, Anthony, illus. Anderson, David, photos by. LC 81-43038. (Illus.). 96p. (gr. 3-6). 1981. (Crowell Jr Bks); PLB 14.89 (*0-690-04155-1*, Crowell Jr Bks) HarpC Child Bks.
—Thomas Jefferson: A Picture Book Biography. Dooling, Michael, illus. LC 93-23340. 1994. 14.95 (*0-590-44838-2*) Scholastic Inc.
—The Truth about Santa Claus. LC 85-47541. (Illus.). 96p. (gr. 3-7). 1985. (Crowell Jr Bks); PLB 15.89 (*0-690-04484-4*, Crowell Jr Bks) HarpC Child Bks.
—The Truth about Unicorns. McDermott, Michael, illus. LC 90-47233. 128p. (gr. 3-7). 1991. 15.00 (*0-06-022478-9*); PLB 14.89 (*0-06-022479-7*) HarpC Child Bks.
Giblin, James C., retold by. The Dwarf, the Giant, & the Unicorn: A Tale of King Arthur. Ewart, Claire, illus. LC 92-34031. 1994. write for info. (*0-395-60520-2*, Clarion Bks) HM.
Giblin, Peter, ed. Mathematical Challenges: Puzzles & Problems in Secondary School Mathematics. 59p. (gr. 9-12). 1989. pap. 17.50 (*0-939765-28-4*, G118) Janson Pubns.
Gibson, Andrew. The Abradizil. Riddell, Chris, illus. 164p. (gr. 3-7). 1992. pap. 4.95 (*0-571-16508-7*) Faber & Faber.
—Ellis & the Hummells. Riddell, Chris, illus. 132p. (gr. 3-6). 1990. pap. 3.95 (*0-571-14412-8*) Faber & Faber.
—Jemima, Grandma & the Great Lost Zone. Riddell, Chris, illus. 128p. (gr. 3-7). 1992. 15.95 (*0-571-16455-2*) Faber & Faber.
—Jemima, Grandma & the Great Lost Zone. Riddell, Chris, illus. 128p. (gr. 3-7). 1992. pap. 6.95 (*0-571-16737-3*) Faber & Faber.
—The Rollickers & Other Stories. (Illus.). 160p. (gr. 3 up). 1993. 10.95 (*0-571-16687-3*) Faber & Faber.
Gibson, Arrell M., jt. auth. see Hale, Duane.
Gibson, Barbara & Pinkney, Jerry. Creatures of the Desert World & Strange Animals of the Sea, 2 bks. Crump, Donald J., ed. (Illus.). 20p. (gr. 3-8). 1987. Set. 21.95 (*0-87044-688-6*) Natl Geog.
Gibson, Betty. Story of Little Quack. (ps-3). 1991. 12.95 (*0-316-30966-4*, Joy St Bks) Little.
Gibson, Charles E. Handbook of Knots & Splices: & Other Work with Hempen & Wire Rope. (Illus.). (gr. 7 up). 12.95 (*0-87523-146-2*) Emerson.

Gibson, Christine R. & Hargrave, J. Michael. The Tator Tales: A Guide to Substance Abuse Prevention for Youth & Adults. Majewski, Chuck, illus. (Orig.). (gr. 4-8). 1989. pap. write for info. Tator Enterprises.
—The Tator Tales: A Story & Activity Book on Handling Peer Pressure. Majewski, Chuck, illus. 51p. (gr. 3-5). 1988. pap. 6.95 (*0-9624285-0-7*) Tator Enterprises.
Gibson, Christine R., jt. auth. see Hargrave, J. Michael.
Gibson, Eva. Laina. LC 85-73423. 150p. (Orig.). (gr. 9-12). 1986. pap. 3.99 (*0-87123-896-9*) Bethany Hse.
—Listening to My Heart. 160p. (Orig.). 1990. special spiral bdg. 10.99 (*1-55661-132-3*) Bethany Hse.
—Marty. LC 86-72529. 176p. (Orig.). (gr. 6-9). 1987. pap. 3.99 (*0-87123-915-9*) Bethany Hse.
—Sara. LC 84-71717. 144p. (Orig.). (gr. 8-12). 1984. pap. 3.99 (*0-87123-598-6*) Bethany Hse.
Gibson, K. & Gee, R. Christmas. (Illus.). 32p. (ps-3). 1992. pap. 5.95 (*0-7460-1030-3*) EDC.
Gibson, Kate, ed. see Evans, Nate.
Gibson, Katherine. The Tall Book of Bible Stories. reissued ed. Chaiko, Ted, illus. LC 57-10952. 128p. (ps-3). 1957. 9.95 (*0-06-021935-1*) HarpC Child Bks.
Gibson, Litzkah R. How to Read Palms. Adelman, Sherri, ed. (Illus.). 184p. (gr. 10-12). 1989. pap. 8.95 (*0-8119-0033-9*) Lifetime.
Gibson, Michael. The Energy Crisis. (Illus.). 48p. (gr. 5 up). 1987. PLB 18.60 (*0-86592-277-2*); 13.95 (*0-685-67573-4*) Rourke Corp.
—The War in Vietnam. (Illus.). 64p. (gr. 7-12). 1992. PLB 13.40 (*0-531-18408-0*, Pub. by Bookwright Pr) Watts.
Gibson, Paul. How to Be Your Own Astrologer. (Illus.). 28p. (gr. 7 up). 1987. pap. text ed. 13.20 (*0-9619757-0-9*) Astor Pubns.
Gibson, R. Odds & Ends. (Illus.). 32p. (ps-2). 1990. lib. bdg. 13.96 (*0-88110-488-4*, Usborne); pap. 5.95 (*0-7460-0633-0*, Usborne) EDC.
—Paperplay. (Illus.). 32p. (ps-3). 1989. lib. bdg. 13.96 (*0-88110-422-1*, Usborne); pap. 5.95 (*0-7460-0466-4*) EDC.
—Reading Games. (Illus.). 32p. (ps-9). 1993. lib. bdg. 13. 96 (*0-88110-645-3*, Usborne); pap. 5.95 (*0-7460-1292-6*, Usborne) EDC.
Gibson, R. & Gee, R. Paint Fun. (Illus.). 32p. (ps-3). 1992. PLB 13.96 (*0-88110-285-7*); pap. 5.95 (*0-7460-1085-0*) EDC.
Gibson, R. & Tyler, J. Playdough. (Illus.). 32p. (ps-3). 1989. lib. bdg. 13.96 (*0-88110-413-2*, Usborne); pap. 5.95 (*0-7460-0465-6*) EDC.
Gibson, R., jt. auth. see Somerville, L.
Gibson, Ray. Learning Games. (Illus.). 64p. (ps-1). 1993. pap. 8.95 (*0-7460-1296-9*, Usborne) EDC.
—Number Games. (Illus.). 32p. (ps-9). 1993. pap. 13.96 (*0-88110-651-8*, Usborne); pap. text ed. 5.95 (*0-7460-1294-2*, Usborne) EDC.
Gibson, Rex, ed. see Shakespeare, William.
Gibson, Robert O. The Chumash. (Illus.). (gr. 5 up). 1991. 17.95 (*1-55546-700-8*) Chelsea Hse.
—The Chumash. (Illus.). 104p. (Orig.). (gr. 5 up). 1991. pap. 9.95 (*0-7910-0376-0*) Chelsea Hse.
Gibson, Robert W. Captain Harlock Returns. Ulm, Chris, ed. Duke, Pat, et al, illus. 86p. 1991. pap. 9.95 (*0-944735-75-4*) Malibu Graphics.
Gibson, Roxie C. Hey, God! Hurry! Gibson, James, illus. Harvey, Paul, intro. by. LC 82-60193. (Illus.). 52p. (gr. 3-5). 1982. 4.95 (*0-938232-08-8*, 32534) Winston-Derek.
—Hey, God! Listen! Gibson, James, illus. Harvey, Paul, intro. by. LC 82-60195. (Illus.). 68p.(gr. 3-5). 1982. 4.95 (*0-938232-06-1*, 32466) Winston-Derek.
—Hey, God! What Is America? Gibson, James, illus. Harvey, Paul, intro. by. LC 81-71025. (Illus.). 52p. (gr. 3-5). 1982. 4.95 (*0-938232-05-3*, 32795) Winston-Derek.
—Hey, God! What Is Christmas. Gibson, James, illus. LC 82-60192. 64p. (gr. 3-5). 1982. 4.95 (*0-938232-09-6*, 32752) Winston-Derek.
—Hey! God! What Is Death? LC 90-70219. (Illus.). 50p. (gr. k-5). 1990. 4.95 (*1-55523-329-5*) Winston-Derek.
—Hey, God! Where Are You? Gibson, James, illus. Harvey, Paul, intro. by. LC 82-60194. (Illus.). 64p. (gr. 3-5). 1982. 4.95 (*0-938232-07-X*, 32485) Winston-Derek.
Gibson, Sylvia S. Latawnya, the Naughty Horse, Learns to Say "No" to Drugs. 1990. 6.95 (*0-533-09102-0*) Vantage.
Gibson, W., ed. see Howells, William Dean.
Gibson, William. The Miracle Worker. (gr. 6-9). 1984. pap. 3.99 (*0-553-24778-6*) Bantam.
Gick, Georg J. & Swinger, Marlys. Shepherd's Pipe Songs from the Holy Night: A Christmas Cantata for Children's Voices or Youth Choir. Choral ed. Maendel, Maria A. & Maendel, Maria M., illus. Clement, J. T., intro. by. LC 71-85805. 64p. (gr. k up). 1969. pap. 3.50 (*0-87486-011-3*); cassette 7.00 (*0-87486-049-0*) Plough.
Gieck, Charlene. Bald Eagle Magic for Kids. LC 91-50552. (Illus.). 48p. (gr. 3-4). 1992. PLB 18.60 (*0-8368-0761-8*) Gareth Stevens Inc.
—Eagles for Kids. 48p. 1991. 14.95 (*1-55971-120-5*); pap. 6.95 (*1-55971-133-7*) NorthWord.
Giegling, John. Snowflake Come Home: A Wolf's Story. Oliver, Bryan, illus. LC 92-10746. 32p. (gr. 7-9). 1992. pap. 4.95 (*0-912661-12-7*) Woodsong Graph.
Giesen, Rosemary, jt. auth. see Caveney, Sylvia.
Giesen, Rosemary, jt. auth. see Thompson, Brenda.

Gifaldi, David. The Boy Who Spoke Colors. Greger, C. Shana, illus. LC 92-11301. 32p. (gr. 2-5). 1993. 14.95 (*0-395-65025-9*) HM.
—Gregory, Maw, & the Mean One. Glass, Andrew, illus. 144p. (gr. 7 up). 1992. 13.45 (*0-395-60821-X*, Clarion Bks) HM.
—One Thing for Sure. LC 86-2677. 160p. (gr. 4-7). 1986. 13.95 (*0-89919-462-1*, Clarion Bks) HM.
—Toby Scudder, Ultimate Warrior. LC 92-39532. 1993. 13.95 (*0-395-66400-4*, Clarion Bks) HM.
Giff, Patricia R. Advent: Molly Maguire, No. 2. 1994. write for info. (*0-670-81410-5*) Viking Child Bks.
—All about Stacy. Sims, Blanche, illus. 80p. (Orig.). (gr. k-6). 1988. pap. 3.25 (*0-440-40088-0*, YB) Dell.
—The Almost Awful Play. Natti, Susanna, illus. LC 84-17922. 32p. (ps-3). 1985. pap. 3.95 (*0-14-050530-X*, Puffin) Puffin Bks.
—The Almost Awful Play. Natti, Susanna, illus. (gr. 2-4). 1989. bk. & cassette 19.95 (*0-87499-116-1*); bk. & cassette 12.95 (*0-87499-115-3*); pap. 27.95 4 cassettes & guide (*0-87499-117-X*) Live Oak Media.
—B-E-S-T Friends. 80p. (Orig.). (gr. k-6). 1988. pap. 2.99 (*0-440-40090-2*, YB) Dell.
—Beast & the Halloween Horror. Sims, Blanche, illus. (Orig.). (gr. k-6). 1990. pap. 2.99 (*0-440-40335-9*, YB) Dell.
—The Beast in Ms. Rooney's Room. 80p. (Orig.). (gr. 1-4). 1984. pap. 3.25 (*0-440-40485-1*, YB) Dell.
—The Candy Corn Contest. 80p. (Orig.). (ps-6). 1984. pap. 3.25 (*0-440-41072-X*, YB) Dell.
—The Case of the Cool-Itch Kid. (gr. k-6). 1989. pap. 3.25 (*0-440-40199-2*) Dell.
—Columbus Circle. (Orig.). (gr. k-6). 1988. pap. 2.75 (*0-440-40036-8*, YB) Dell.
—Count Your Money with the Polk Street School. (ps-3). 1994. pap. 3.50 (*0-440-40929-2*) Dell.
—December Secrets. Sims, Blanche, illus. 80p. (gr. k-6). 1984. pap. 3.25 (*0-440-41795-3*, YB) Dell.
—Diana: Twentieth-Century Princess. (gr. 4-7). 1991. 10. 95 (*0-670-83806-3*) Viking Child Bks.
—Diana: Twentieth-Century Princess. Laporte, Michelle, illus. 64p. (gr. 3-5). 1992. pap. 3.99 (*0-14-034707-0*, Puffin) Puffin Bks.
—Emily Arrow Promises to Do Better This Year. (Orig.). 1990. pap. 2.99 (*0-440-40369-3*, Pub. by Yearling Classics) Dell.
—Fish Face. Sims, Blanche, illus. 80p. (Orig.). (gr. 1-4). 1984. pap. 3.25 (*0-440-42557-3*, YB) Dell.
—The Fourth Grade Celebrity. 128p. (gr. k-6). 1989. pap. 3.50 (*0-440-42676-6*, YB) Dell.
—Fourth Grade Celebrity. Morrill, Leslie, illus. 128p. (gr. 4-6). 1984. 8.95 (*0-385-28308-3*) Delacorte.
—Fourth Grade Celebrity. Morrill, Leslie, illus. LC 79-50678. (gr. 4-6). 1979. 8.95 (*0-440-02725-X*); PLB 8.89 (*0-440-02726-8*) Delacorte.
—Garbage Juice for Breakfast. (gr. 1-4). 1989. pap. 2.99 (*0-440-40207-7*, YB) Dell.
—The Gift of the Pirate Queen. Rutherford, Jenny, illus. 160p. (gr. 4-8). 1983. pap. 3.25 (*0-440-43046-1*, Pub. by Yearling Classics) Dell.
—The Gift of the Pirate Queen. Rutherford, Jenny, illus. LC 82-70310. 160p. (gr. 4-6). 1982. 11.95 (*0-385-28338-5*); PLB 11.95 (*0-385-28339-3*) Delacorte.
—The Gift of the Pirate Queen. Rutherford, Jenny, illus. LC 82-70310. 160p. (gr. 4-8). 1982. 9.95 (*0-440-02970-8*); PLB 9.89 (*0-440-02972-4*) Delacorte.
—The Girl Who Knew It All. 128p. (gr. k-6). 1989. pap. 3.25 (*0-440-42855-6*, YB) Dell.
—The Girl Who Knew It All. Morrill, Leslie, illus. (gr. 4-6). 1984. 6.95 (*0-385-28362-8*); PLB 6.95 (*0-385-28363-6*) Delacorte.
—The Girl Who Knew It All. Morrill, Leslie, illus. LC 79-50677. (gr. 4-6). 1979. 6.95 (*0-440-03137-0*); PLB 6.89 (*0-440-03138-9*) Delacorte.
—The Great Shamrock Disaster. (ps-3). 1993. pap. 3.25 (*0-440-40778-8*) Dell.
—Happy Birthday, Ronald Morgan! Natti, Susanna, illus. LC 85-32303. 32p. (ps-4). 1986. pap. 10.95 (*0-670-80741-9*) Viking Child Bks.
—Happy Birthday, Ronald Morgan! Natti, Susanna, illus. 32p. (ps-3). 1988. pap. 4.99 (*0-14-050668-3*, Puffin) Puffin Bks.
—Happy Birthday, Ronald Morgan. Natti, Susanna, illus. (gr. 2-4). 1989. bk. & cassette 19.95 (*0-87499-122-6*); bk. & cassette 12.95 (*0-87499-121-8*); 4 cassettes & guide 27.95 (*0-87499-123-4*) Live Oak Media.
—Have You Seen Hyacinth Macaw? 128p. (gr. k-6). 1982. pap. 3.25 (*0-440-43450-5*, YB) Dell.
—Have You Seen Hyacinth Macaw? Kramer, Anthony, illus. (gr. 4-6). 1981. 11.95 (*0-385-28389-X*); pap. 12. 95 (*0-385-28390-3*) Delacorte.
—Have You Seen Hyacinth Macaw: A Mystery. Kramer, Anthony, illus. LC 80-68729. 128p. (gr. 4-7). 1981. 9.95 (*0-440-03467-1*); PLB 9.89 (*0-440-03472-8*) Delacorte.
—I Love Saturday. Remkiewicz, Frank, illus. 32p. (ps-3). 1991. pap. 3.99 (*0-14-050653-5*) Puffin Bks.
—If the Shoe Fits. (Orig.). (gr. k-6). 1988. pap. 3.25 (*0-440-40086-4*, YB) Dell.
—In the Dinosaur's Paw. Sims, Blanche, illus. 80p. (gr. k-6). 1985. pap. 3.25 (*0-440-44150-1*, YB) Dell.
—The Jingle Bells Jam. McCully, Emily A., illus. 80p. (Orig.). (gr. 1-4). 1992. pap. 3.25 (*0-440-40534-3*, YB) Dell.

—The Kids of the Polk Street School, 6 bks. Incl. The Beast in Ms. Rooney's Room; The Candy Corn Contest; December Secrets; Fish Face; In the Dinosaur's Paw; The Valentine Star. (gr. k-6). 1988. Boxed Set. pap. 14.10 (0-440-44385-7) Dell.
—Laura Ingalls Wilder: Growing Up in the Little House. McKeating, Eileen, illus. (gr. 2-6). 1987. pap. 10.95 (0-670-81072-X) Viking Child Bks.
—Lazy Lions, Lucky Lambs. Sims, Blanche, illus. 80p. (gr. k-6). 1985. pap. 3.25 (0-440-44640-6, YB) Dell.
—Left-Handed Shortstop. Morrill, Leslie, illus. 128p. (gr. k-6). 1989. pap. 2.95 (0-440-44672-4, YB) Dell.
—Left-Handed Shortstop. Morrill, Leslie, illus. (gr. 4-6). 1980. pap. 11.95 (0-385-28533-7); pap. 11.95 (0-385-28534-5) Delacorte.
—Loretta P. Sweeny, Where Are You? Kramer, Anthony, illus. 144p. (gr. 4-8). 1990. pap. 3.25 (0-440-44926-X, YB) Dell.
—Love, from the Fifth-Grade Celebrity. (gr. k-6). 1987. pap. 3.50 (0-440-44948-0, YB) Dell.
—Love, from the Fifth-Grade Celebrity. Morrill, Leslie, illus. LC 85-46075. 144p. (gr. 4-6). 1986. 13.95 (0-385-29486-7) Delacorte.
—Matthew Jackson Meets the Wall. 1990. 13.95 (0-385-29972-9) Delacorte.
—Matthew Jackson Meets the Wall. (gr. 4-7). 1991. pap. 3.25 (0-440-40547-5, YB) Dell.
—Meet the Lincoln Lions Band. McCully, Emily A., illus. 80p. (gr. 1-4). 1992. pap. 3.25 (0-440-40516-5, YB) Dell.
—Monster Rabbit Runs. (gr. 4-7). 1991. pap. 2.95 (0-440-40424-X) Dell.
—Mother Teresa: A Sister to the Poor. Lewin, Ted, illus. LC 85-40885. 64p. (gr. 2-6). 1986. pap. 10.95 (0-670-81096-7) Viking Child Bks.
—Mother Teresa: Sister to the Poor. Lewin, Ted, illus. (gr. 2-6). 1987. pap. 4.50 (0-14-032225-6, Puffin) Puffin Bks.
—The Mystery of the Blue Ring. (Orig.). (gr. k-6). 1987. pap. 3.25 (0-440-45998-2, YB) Dell.
—The Mystery of the Blue Ring. (gr. 1-4). 16.25 (0-8446-6375-1) Peter Smith.
—New Kids of the Polk Street School, 6 vols. (gr. 4-7). 1990. pap. 16.50 boxed set (0-440-36029-3) Dell.
—Next Year I'll Be Special. Hafner, Marylin, photos by. LC 92-20749. 1993. 13.95 (0-385-30903-1, Zephyr-BFYR) Doubleday.
—Pickle Puss. (Orig.). (gr. k-3). 1986. pap. 3.25 (0-440-46844-2, YB) Dell.
—Pickle Puss. Sims, Blanche, illus. (ps-3). 1986. pap. 8.95 (0-385-29477-8) Delacorte.
—Poopsie Pomerantz, Pick up Your Feet. (gr. k-6). 1990. pap. 2.95 (0-440-40287-5, YB) Dell.
—The Powder Puff Puzzle. (Orig.). (gr. k-6). 1987. pap. 3.25 (0-440-47180-X, YB) Dell.
—Purple Climbing Days. Sims, Blanche, illus. 80p. (gr. 5 up). 1985. pap. 3.25 (0-440-47309-8, YB) Dell.
—Purple Climbing Days. Sims, Blanche, illus. (ps-3). 1986. pap. 8.95 (0-385-29500-6) Delacorte.
—Rat Teeth. Morrill, Leslie, illus. LC 83-16601. 144p. (gr. 4-6). 1984. 12.95 (0-385-29339-9); PLB 12.95 (0-385-29309-7) Delacorte.
—Rat Teeth. (gr. k-6). 1990. pap. 3.25 (0-440-47457-4, YB) Dell.
—The Red, White, & Blue Valentine. (ps-3). 1993. pap. 3.25 (0-440-40768-0) Dell.
—The Riddle of the Red Purse. (Orig.). (gr. k-6). 1987. pap. 3.25 (0-440-47534-1, YB) Dell.
—The Riddle of the Red Purse. (gr. 1-4). 16.00 (0-8446-6374-3) Peter Smith.
—Ronald Morgan Goes to Bat. Natti, Susanna, illus. 32p. (gr. k-4). 1988. pap. 10.95 (0-670-81457-1) Viking Child Bks.
—Ronald Morgan Goes to Bat. Natti, Susanna, illus. 32p. (ps-3). 1990. pap. 3.99 (0-14-050669-1, Puffin) Puffin Bks.
—The Rootin' Tootin' Bugle Boy. (ps-3). 1993. pap. 3.25 (0-440-40757-5) Dell.
—Say "Cheese" Sims, Blanche, illus. 28p. 1986. pap. 8.95 (0-385-29501-4) Delacorte.
—Say "Cheese, No. 10. Sims, Blanche, illus. (gr. 6-9). 1985. pap. 3.25 (0-440-47639-9, YB) Dell.
—The Secret at the Polk Street School. (Orig.). (gr. k-6). 1987. pap. 3.25 (0-440-47696-8, YB) Dell.
—Show Time at the Polk Street School: Plays You Can Do Yourself. Sims, Blanche, illus. LC 91-46163. 80p. (gr. 1-4). 1992. 14.00 (0-385-30794-2) Delacorte.
—Snaggle Doodles. Sims, Blanche, illus. 80p. (gr. 1-4). 1985. pap. 3.25 (0-440-48068-X, YB) Dell.
—Spectacular Stone Soup. 80p. (Orig.). (gr. k-6). 1989. pap. 3.25 (0-440-40134-8, YB) Dell.
—Stacy Says Good-Bye. Sims, Blanche, illus. 80p. (gr. k-3). 1989. pap. 3.25 (0-440-40135-6, YB) Dell.
—Sunny Side Up. (Orig.). (gr. k-3). 1986. pap. 2.99 (0-440-48406-5, YB) Dell.
—Today Was a Terrible Day. Natti, Suzanna, illus. (gr. k-3). 1984. incl. cassette 19.95 (0-941078-50-7); pap. 12.95 incl. cassette (0-941078-48-5); pap. 27.95 4 bks, cassette, & guide (0-941078-49-3); sound fimlstrip 22. 95 (0-941078-47-7) Live Oak Media.
—Today Was a Terrible Day. Natti, Susanna, illus. 1980. 11.95 (0-670-71830-0) Viking Child Bks.
—Today Was a Terrible Day. Natti, Susanna, illus. 32p. (ps-k). 1984. pap. 3.99 (0-14-050453-2) Viking Child Bks.
—Today Was a Terrible Day. Natti, Susanna, illus. 32p. (ps-k). 1984. pap. 3.95 incl. cassette (0-685-54175-4, Penguin Bks) Viking Penguin.
—Today Was a Terrible Day. Natti, Susanna, illus. 1993. pap. 6.99 incl. cassette (0-14-095119-9, Puffin) Puffin Bks.
—Tootsie Tanner, Why Don't You Talk. (gr. k-6). 1990. pap. 2.95 (0-440-40239-5, YB) Dell.
—Tootsie Tanner, Why Don't You Talk? An Abby Jones, Junior Detective, Mystery. Kramer, Anthony, illus. LC 86-32910. 144p. (gr. 4-6). 1987. pap. 13.95 (0-385-29579-0) Delacorte.
—The Valentine Star. Sims, Blanche, illus. 80p. (Orig.). (gr. k-6). 1985. pap. 3.25 (0-440-49204-1, YB) Dell.
—Wake Up Its Mothers Day. (ps-3). 1991. pap. 3.25 (0-440-40455-X) Dell.
—War Began at Supper: Letters to Miss Loria. (gr. 4-7). 1991. pap. 2.95 (0-440-40572-6) Dell.
—Watch Out! Man-Eating Snake. 80p. (Orig.). (gr. k-6). 1988. pap. 2.99 (0-440-40085-6, YB) Dell.
—Watch Out! Man-Eating Snake. (gr. 1-4). 17.50 (0-8446-6378-6) Peter Smith.
—Watch Out, Ronald Morgan. Natti, Susanna, illus. LC 84-19623. 24p. (gr. k-3). 1985. pap. 10.95 (0-670-80433-9) Viking Child Bks.
—Watch Out, Ronald Morgan. Natti, Susanna, illus. 32p. (gr. k-4). 1986. pap. 4.99 (0-14-050638-1, Puffin) Puffin Bks.
—The Winter Worm Business. Morrill, Leslie, illus. 144p. (gr. k-6). 1983. pap. 3.50 (0-440-49259-9, YB) Dell.
—The Winter Worm Business. Morrill, Leslie, illus. (gr. 4-6). 1981. pap. 8.95 (0-385-29152-3); pap. 8.89 (0-385-29154-X) Delacorte.
—Write up a Storm. 1993. pap. 3.50 (0-440-40882-2) Dell.
—Yankee Doodle Drumsticks. McCully, Emily A., illus. 80p. (Orig.). (gr. 1-4). 1992. pap. 3.25 (0-440-40518-1, YB) Dell.

Giff, Patricia R. & Kramer, Anthony. Loretta P. Sweeny, Where Are You? LC 83-5164. (Illus.). 144p. (gr. 4-6). 1983. 11.95 (0-385-29298-8); PLB 11.95 (0-385-29299-6) Delacorte.
Giff, Patricia R. & Sims, Blanche. The Trail of the Screaming Teenager. (Orig.). 1990. pap. 3.25 (0-440-40312-X) Dell.
Giffard, Hannah. Fast Car. Giffard, Hannah, illus. LC 92-62422. 12p. (ps). 1993. bds. 3.95 (0-688-12444-5, Tambourine Bks) Morrow.
—Hens Say Cluck. Giffard, Hannah, illus. LC 92-62425. 12p. (ps). 1993. bds. 3.95 (0-688-12442-9, Tambourine Bks) Morrow.
—Red Bus. Giffard, Hannah, illus. LC 92-62424. 12p. (ps). 1993. bds. 3.95 (0-688-12443-7, Tambourine Bks) Morrow.
—Red Fox. Giffard, Hannah, illus. LC 90-2807. 36p. (ps-3). 1991. 12.95 (0-8037-0869-6) Dial Bks Young.
—Red Fox on the Move. Giffard, Hannah, illus. LC 90-25646. 36p. (ps-3). 1992. 14.00 (0-8037-1057-7) Dial Bks Young.
—Striped Zebra. Giffard, Hannah, illus. LC 92-62423. 12p. (ps). 1993. bds. 3.95 (0-688-12441-0, Tambourine Bks) Morrow.
Giffen, Keith & Jones, Gerard. Green Lantern: Emerald Dawn (TPB) Dooley, Kevin, ed. Tanghal, Romeo & Bright, M. D., illus. Dooley, Kevin, intro. by. 144p. (Orig.). 1991. pap. 4.95 (0-930289-88-9) DC Comics.
Gifford, Douglas. Warriors, Gods & Spirits from Central & South American Mythology. Sibbeck, John & Dew, Heather, illus. LC 93-1013. 128p. (gr. 6 up). 1993. 22. 50 (0-87226-914-0); pap. 14.95 sewn (0-87226-915-9) P Bedrick Bks.
Gifford, George E., Jr., ed. Dear Jeffie: Being the Letters from Jeffries Wyman to His Son Jeffries Wyman, Jr. LC 78-58830. (gr. 6 up). 1978. 15.00x (0-87365-796-9) Peabody Harvard.
Gifford, Griselda. Miranda's Monster. (Illus.). 28p. (gr. k-2). 1988. 15.95 (0-340-41156-2, Pub. by Hodder & Stoughton UK) Trafalgar.
—Revenge of the Wildcat. (Illus.). 106p. (gr. 3-6). 1991. pap. 6.95 (0-86241-334-6, Pub. by Cnngt Pub Ltd) Trafalgar.
—The Story of Ranald. 104p. (gr. 5-8). 1990. pap. 6.95 (0-86241-094-0, Pub. by Cnngt Pub Ltd) Trafalgar.
Gifford, James M., ed. see Clark, Billy C.
Gifford, James M., ed. see Goode, James B.
Gifford, James M., ed. see Stuart, Jesse.
Gifford, James M., intro. by see Stuart, Jesse.
Gifford, James M., et al, eds. see Clark, Billy C.
Gifford, James M., et al, eds. see Lowe, Jimmy.
Gifford, James M., et al, eds. see Pace, Mildred M.
Gifford, James M., et al, eds. see Stuart, Jesse.
Gifford, Scott. The Call of the Wild: A Study Guide. (gr. 9-12). 1990. pap. text ed. 14.95 (0-88122-411-1) Lrn Links.
Giganti, Paul, Jr. Each Orange Had Eight Slices: A Counting Book. Crews, Donald, illus. LC 90-24167. 24p. (ps up). 1992. 14.00 (0-688-10428-2); PLB 13.93 (0-688-10429-0) Greenwillow.
—Each Orange Has Eight Slices. Crews, Donald, illus. 32p. (ps up). 1994. pap. 18.95 (0-688-13116-6, Mulberry) Morrow.
—How Many Snails? LC 87-26281. (Illus.). 24p. (ps-1). 1988. 15.00 (0-688-06369-1); lib. bdg. 14.93 (0-688-06370-5) Greenwillow.
Gikow, Louise. Baby Kermit & the Magic Trunk. Spahr, Kathy, illus. 26p. (ps up). 1987. 12.95 (1-55578-601-4) Worlds Wonder.
—Baby Kermit's Christmas. (ps-3). 1993. 5.95 (0-307-13722-8, Golden Pr) Western Pub.
—Baby Piggy at the Bat. Chauhan, Manhar, illus. LC 86-62182. 32p. (ps-3). 1987. 1.25 (0-394-88783-2) Random Bks Yng Read.
—Baby Rowlf & the Boomtown Bandits. Cooke, Tom, illus. 26p. (ps up). 1987. 12.95 (1-55578-600-6) Worlds Wonder.
—Bye-Bye, Pacifier. Cooke, Tom, illus. 18p. (ps). 1992. bds. 3.50 (0-307-12330-8, 12330, Golden Pr) Western Pub.
—I Am Kermit. (ps). 1993. 4.95 (0-307-12170-4, Golden Pr) Western Pub.
—Meet Jim Henson. LC 92-30225. 1993. pap. 2.99 (0-679-82691-2) Random Bks Yng Read.
—Meet Jim Henson. LC 92-30225. 80p. (Orig.). (gr. 2-6). 1993. pap. 2.99 (0-679-84642-5) Random Bks Yng Read.
—Muppet Babies & the Magic Garden. Attinello, Lauren, illus. 26p. (ps up). 1987. 12.95 (1-55578-608-1) Worlds Wonder.
—Muppet Christmas Carol. (ps-3). 1993. pap. 2.25 (0-307-12795-8, Golden Pr) Western Pub.
—Muppet Kids in Frogs Only! Cooke, Tom, illus. 32p. (ps-3). 1992. 1.95 (0-307-12651-X, 12651, Golden Pr) Western Pub.
—Muppet Kids in Help! We're Lost! Leigh, Tom, illus. (ps-3). 1991. pap. 1.95 (0-307-12659-5, Golden Pr) Western Pub.
—Muppet Kids in I'm Mad at You! Chauhan, Manhar, illus. 24p. (ps-3). 1992. 1.95 (0-307-12648-X, 12648) Western Pub.
—Muppet Kids in Mom's Having a Baby. Cooke, Tom, illus. (ps-3). 1991. pap. 1.95 (0-307-12661-7, Golden Pr) Western Pub.
—Piggy & the Missing Penny. (ps-3). 1993. pap. 3.50 (0-307-11569-0, Golden Pr) Western Pub.
—There's a Bear in the Woods. (ps-3). 1993. pap. 3.50 (0-307-11568-2, Golden Pr) Western Pub.
Gikow, Louise & Weiss, Ellen. For Every Child, a Better World. McNally, Bruce, illus. (Illus.). 48p. (gr. k-4). 1993. 9.95 (0-307-15628-1, 15628, Golden Pr) Western Pub.
Gikow, Louise, retold by. Muppet Babies Classic Children's Tales. (Illus.). 32p. 1990. 14.95 (0-88363-690-5) H L Levin.
Gikow, Louise, et al. My First Muppet Dictionary. Cooke, Tom, illus. 112p. (ps-2). 1992. 9.95 (0-307-15610-9, 15610, Golden Pr) Western Pub.
Gil, Eliana. I Told My Secret. (SPA., Illus.). 16p. (Orig.). (gr. 3 up). 1986. pap. 2.00 (1-877872-01-6) Launch Pr.
Gil, Eliana M. I Told My Secret: A Book for Kids Who Were Abused. Haskell, Sally, illus. 16p. (Orig.). (gr. 3 up). 1986. pap. 2.00 (0-9613205-1-6) Launch Pr.
Gil, Yvonne. Professor Curious & the Mystery of the Hiking Dinosaurs. Timmons, Bonnie, illus. LC 90-42592. 24p. (gr. 1-5). 1991. 13.95 (0-517-58025-X, Clarkson Potter); PLB 14.99 (0-517-58178-7, C N Potter Bks) Crown Bks Yng Read.
Gilabert, Frank. Business Career Planning Series, 5 bks. (Orig.). (gr. 12). 1993. Set. pap. 55.00 (1-884194-05-2); The Biz Careers Finance Guide: How to Improve Your Business Knowledge about Finance, 100p. pap. 14.95 (1-884194-02-8); The Biz Careers Accounting Guide: How to Improve Your Business Knowledge about Accounting, 100p. pap. 14. 95 (1-884194-01-X); The Biz Careers Planning Guide: How to Prepare for Your Business Career, 70p. pap. 9.95 (1-884194-00-1); The Business Careers Information Systems Guide: How to Improve Your Business Knowledge about Information Systems, 100p. pap. 14.95 (1-884194-03-6); The Biz Careers Marketing Guide: How to Improve Your Business Knowledge about Marketing, 100p. pap. 14.95 (1-884194-04-4) Biz Careers.
Gilbar, Annie, jt. auth. see Brokaw, Meredith.
Gilbert, Ann. Seig the Magnificent. Martin, Jan, ed. Setoda, C. Dodie, illus. 110p. (Orig.). (gr. 6-12). 1994. pap. 12.95 (0-944875-32-7) Doral Pub. Postponed.
Gilbert, Carol, ed. see Miller, Arlene D.
Gilbert, Charles E., Jr. Flags of Texas. Rice, James, illus. LC 88-34511. 96p. (gr. 6 up). 1989. 14.95 (0-88289-721-7) Pelican.
Gilbert, Jane. Grouchy Old Fuddley. 1991. 6.95 (0-533-09110-1) Vantage.
Gilbert, Jeanette. Seaside Stories. Barta, Beverly, ed. Feldmann, Susan, illus. 16p. (Orig.). (gr. 1-4). 1990. pap. write for info. (0-9623503-0-3) Palm Pub.
Gilbert, Mariana. Your First Goldfish. 36p. (Orig.). 1991. pap. 1.95 (0-86622-065-8, YF-108) TFH Pubns.
Gilbert, Miriam. Rosie: The Oldest Horse in St. Augustine. Roch, J., illus. LC 67-30409. (FRE, SPA & ENG.). (gr. k-6). 1974. 6.95 (0-87208-105-2); pap. 5.95 (0-87208-007-2) Island Pr Pubs.
Gilbert, Nancy. The Special Olympics. 32p. (gr. 4). 1990. PLB 14.95s.p. (0-88682-311-0) Creative Ed.
Gilbert, Ray. We Think the World Is Round. (Illus.). 24p. (Orig.). (ps-7). 1992. pap. 6.95 incl. cassette (0-943351-56-1, XE 2001) Astor Bks.
Gilbert, Sara. How to Live with a Single Parent. LC 81-12413. 128p. (gr. 7 up). 1982. PLB 12.88 (0-688-00633-7) Lothrop.
—Lend a Hand: The How, Where & Why of Volunteering. LC 87-32077. 176p. (gr. 5 up). 1988. 12. 95 (0-688-07247-X) Morrow Jr Bks.
—You Can Speak up in Class. Doty, Roy, illus. 64p. (gr. 3 up). 1991. pap. 6.95 (0-688-10304-9, Pub. by Beech Tree Bks) Morrow.

—You Can Speak up in Class. Doty, Roy, illus. LC 90-19268. 64p. (gr. 3 up). 1991. PLB 12.88 (0-688-09867-3) Morrow Jr Bks.
Gilbert, Steve, jt. auth. see Harrison, Maureen.
Gilbert, Susan. Medical Fakes & Frauds. Koop, C. Everett, intro. by. (Illus.). 112p. (gr. 6-12). 1989. 18.95 (0-7910-0090-7) Chelsea Hse.
Gilbert, Thomas W. Lee Trevino. (Illus.). 112p. (gr. 5 up). 1992. lib. bdg. 17.95 (0-7910-1256-5) Chelsea Hse.
—Roberto Clemente. (Illus.). 112p. (gr. 5 up). 1991. lib. bdg. 17.95 (0-7910-1240-9) Chelsea Hse.
Gilbert, Tom. Roberto Clemente. (gr. 4-7). 1993. pap. 7.95 (0-7910-1267-0) Chelsea Hse.
Gilbert, Yvonne. Baby's Book of Lullabies & Cradle Songs. LC 89-25898. (Illus.). 48p. (ps). 1990. 12.95 (0-8037-0794-0); PLB 12.89 (0-8037-0795-9) Dial Bks Young.
Gilbo, Patrick F. American Red Cross. Schlesinger, Arthur M., Jr., intro. by. (Illus.). 96p. (gr. 5 up). 1987. lib. bdg. 14.95 (0-87754-827-7) Chelsea Hse.
Gilbreth, Frank B. & Carey, Ernestine G. Cheaper by the Dozen. rev. ed. Vasiliy, illus. LC 63-20411. 256p. (gr. 7 up). 1963. 20.00 (0-690-18632-0, Crowell Jr Bks) HarpC.
Gilbreth, Frank B., Jr. & Carey, Ernestine G. Cheaper by the Dozen. (gr. 6 up). 1984. pap. 3.50 (0-553-25018-3) Bantam.
—Cheaper by the Dozen. (gr. 6 up). 1984. pap. 3.99 (0-553-27250-0, Starfire) Bantam.
—Cheaper by the Dozen, 2 vols. large type ed. (gr. 7 up). write for info. NAVH.
Gilchrest, Guy. My Mom's Okay. Gilchrest, Guy, illus. LC 91-10722. 24p. (ps-3). 1991. 5.95 (1-56288-088-8) Checkerboard.
Gilchrist, Brad, jt. auth. see Gilchrist, Guy.
Gilchrist, Cherry, retold by. Prince Ivan & the Firebird. Troshkov, Andrei, illus. 1994. 15.00 (1-56957-920-2) Barefoot Bks.
Gilchrist, Ellen. Muppets, No. 3: Froggy Mountain Breakdown. 128p. (Orig.). 1985. pap. 2.50 (0-8125-7380-3) Tor Bks.
—Muppets, No. 4: Chickens Are People Too. 128p. (Orig.). 1985. pap. 1.95 (0-8125-7369-2) Tor Bks.
—Muppets, No. 5: On the Town. 128p. (Orig.). 1986. pap. 1.95 (0-8125-7371-4) Tor Bks.
Gilchrist, Guy. Tiny Dinos Fun at the Beach: A Book of Actions. Gilchrist, Guy, illus. LC 87-40337. (ps-1). 1988. 4.95 (1-55782-013-9, Pub. by Warner Juvenile Bks) Little.
Gilchrist, Guy & Gilchrist, Brad. Muppets, No. 3: Froggy Mountain Breakdown. 128p. (Orig.). 1985. pap. 1.95 (0-8125-7367-6, Dist. by Warner Pub Services & St. Martin's Press) Tor Bks.
Gilchrist, Jan S. Indigo & Moonlight Gold. Gilchrist, Jan S., illus. 32p. 1992. 13.95 (0-86316-210-X) Writers & Readers.
Gildemeister, Jerry. Around the Cat's Back. Gildemeister, Jerry, illus. 128p. (gr. 4-12). 1989. 32.50 (0-936376-06-6) Bear Wallow Pub.
—Avian Dreamers. Gildemeister, Jerry & Larson, Tim, illus. LC 90-85397. (gr. 9-12). 1991. 45.00 (0-936376-07-4) Bear Wallow Pub.
—A Letter Home. Gildemeister, Jerry & Gray, Don, illus. LC 87-1151. 120p. (gr. 4-12). 1987. 24.50 (0-936376-04-X) Bear Wallow Pub.
Gilden, Mel. Beverly Hills, 90210. 1991. pap. 3.99 (0-06-100417-0, Harp PBks) HarpC.
—Beverly Hills, 90210: No Secrets. (gr. 7 up). 1992. pap. 3.99 (0-06-106136-0, Harp PBks) HarpC.
—Beverly Hills 90210: 'Tis the Season. 1992. pap. 3.99 (0-06-106786-5, Harp PBks) HarpC.
—Beverly Hills, 90210: Where the Boys Are. (gr. 9-12). 1993. pap. 3.99 (0-06-106145-X, Harp PBks) HarpC.
—Beverly Hills, 90210: Which Way to the Beach? 1992. pap. 3.99 (0-06-106768-7, Harp PBks) HarpC.
—Fifth Grade Monsters, No. 12: Werewolf Come Home. 1990. pap. 2.75 (0-380-75908-X, Camelot) Avon.
—Fifth Grade Monsters, No. 14: Troll Patrol. 96p. (Orig.). 1991. pap. 2.95 (0-380-76306-0, Camelot) Avon.
—Fifth Grade Monsters, No. 15: The Secret of Dinosaur Bog. 96p. (Orig.). (gr. 5). 1991. pap. 2.99 (0-380-76308-7, Camelot) Avon.
—How to Be a Vampire in One Easy Lesson. 1990. pap. 2.75 (0-380-75906-3, Camelot) Avon.
—Island of the Weird. 96p. 1990. pap. 2.95 (0-380-75907-1, Camelot) Avon.
—M Is for Monster. 96p. 1987. pap. 2.75 (0-380-75423-1, Camelot) Avon.
—The Monster in Creeps Head Bay. 96p. 1990. pap. 2.75 (0-380-75905-5, Camelot) Avon.
—Monster Mashers. 96p. (Orig.). (gr. 5 up). 1989. pap. 2.75 (0-380-75785-0, Camelot) Avon.
—More Than Words. 1993. pap. 3.99 (0-06-106146-8, Harp PBks) HarpC.
—Outer Space & All That Junk. LaVigne, Daniel, illus. LC 88-37110. 176p. (gr. 5-9). 1989. (Lipp Jr Bks); PLB 12.89 (0-397-32307-7, Lipp Jr Bks) HarpC Child Bks.
—The Pet of Frankenstein. 96p. (gr. 3-7). 1988. pap. 2.50 (0-380-75185-2, Camelot) Avon.
—The Planetoid of Amazement. LC 91-7261. 224p. (gr. 5-9). 1991. PLB 14.89 (0-06-021714-6) HarpC Child Bks.
—Pokey to the Rescue. Couman, Carol & Codor, Dick, illus. (gr. k-3). 1988. pap. 2.25 (0-671-63900-5) S&S Trade.
—The Return of Captain Conquer. (gr. 5-8). 1985. 12.95 (0-685-11811-8) HM.

—RV & the Haunted Garage. Bouman, Carol & Codor, Dick, illus. (gr. k-3). 1988. pap. 2.25 (0-671-63901-3) S&S Trade.
—Summer Love. 1993. pap. 3.99 (0-06-106756-3, Harp PBks) HarpC.
—Things That Go Bark in the Park. 96p. 1989. pap. 2.75 (0-380-75786-9, Camelot) Avon.
—Two Hearts. 1993. pap. 3.99 (0-06-106144-1, Harp PBks) HarpC.
—Yuckers. 96p. 1989. pap. 2.95 (0-380-75787-7, Camelot) Avon.
—Z Is for Zombie. 96p. (gr. 3-7). 1988. pap. 2.75 (0-380-75686-2, Camelot) Avon.
Gile, John. The First Forest. Heflin, Tom, illus. LC 89-91458. 40p. (gr. k up). 1989. 13.95 (0-910941-01-7) J Gile Comm.
—Footsteps in the Forest. (gr. 3 up). 1992. 14.95 (0-910941-03-3) J Gile Comm.
Giles, Lucille. Color Me Brown. rev. ed. Holmes, Louis F., illus. 47p. (gr. k-6). 1974. pap. 5.00 (0-87485-017-7) Johnson Chi.
Giles, Nancy. Creative Food Box Crafts. Petty, Melissa, illus. 64p. (ps-2). 1989. wkbk. 7.95 (0-86653-475-X, GA1076) Good Apple.
—Creative Milk Carton Crafts. Petty, Melissa, illus. 64p. (ps-2). 1989. wkbk. 7.95 (0-86653-462-8, GA1075) Good Apple.
Gilfond, Henry & Blevins, George. Holiday Plays for Reading. (Illus.). 160p. (gr. 4 up). 1985. PLB 10.85 (0-8027-6601-3) Walker & Co.
Gilgallon, Barbara & Seddon, Sue. Travel Games. (Illus.). 96p. (gr. 3-10). 1991. pap. 4.95 (0-7063-6643-3, Pub. by Ward Lock UK) Sterling.
Gilgallon, Barbara, jt. auth. see Seddon, Sue.
Gili, Phillida. The Nutcracker: A Pop-Up Book. LC 91-77288. (Illus.). 12p. (ps up). 1992. 14.95 (0-694-00414-6, Festival) HarpC Child Bks.
Gilks, Helen. Bears. Bale, Andrew, illus. LC 92-37693. (gr. 3 up). 1993. 15.45 (0-395-66899-9) Ticknor & Fields.
Gill, Bob. What Color Is Your World. Gill, Bob, illus. (gr. k-3). 1963. 10.95 (0-8392-3042-7) Astor-Honor.
Gill, Madelaine. The Spring Hat. LC 91-30556. (Illus.). 40p. (ps-1). 1993. pap. 13.00 (0-671-75666-4, S&S BYR) S&S Trade.
Gill, Madelaine & Pliska, Greg. Praise for the Singing: Song for Children. (Illus.). 1993. 18.95 (0-316-52627-4) Little.
Gill, Nancy. Electing Our President. rev. ed. (gr. 5-8). 1991. pap. 8.95 (0-86653-953-0) Fearon Teach Aids.
—Using Cereal Boxes. McGinnity, Molly, illus. 13p. (gr. 4-6). 1980. pap. 3.95 (0-8431-2574-8) Enrich.
—Vocabulary Boosters I. (gr. 3-6). 1985. pap. 6.95 (0-8224-7280-5) Fearon Teach Aids.
—Vocabulary Boosters II. (gr. 3-6). 1985. pap. 6.95 (0-8224-7281-3) Fearon Teach Aids.
Gill, Peter. Birds. Hargreaves, Anglea & Bowring, Isabel, illus. LC 89-20306. 32p. (gr. 3-6). 1990. PLB 11.59 (0-8167-1959-4); pap. text ed. 3.95 (0-8167-1960-8) Troll Assocs.
Gill, Roma, ed. see Shakespeare, William.
Gill, Shelley R. Alaska Mother Goose. Cartwright, Shannon, illus. 36p. (Orig.). (gr. k-6). 1987. 13.95 (0-934007-05-5); pap. 8.95 (0-934007-02-0) Charlesbridge Pub.
—Kiana's Iditarod. Cartwright, Shannon, illus. 52p. (Orig.). (gr. 2-6). 1984. pap. 8.95 (0-934007-00-4) Paws Four Pub.
—Mammoth Magic. Cartwright, Shannon, illus. 36p. (Orig.). (gr. k-6). 1986. pap. 7.95 (0-934007-01-2) Paws Four Pub.
—Thunderfeet, Alaska's Dinosaurs & Other Prehistoric Critters. (Illus.). 36p. (Orig.). (gr. k-4). 1988. pap. 11. 95 incl. cass. (0-934007-03-9) Paws Four Pub.
Gill, Shelly. Alaska's Three Bears. Cartwright, Shannon, illus. 32p. (ps-3). 1992. 13.95 (0-934007-10-1); pap. 7.95 (0-934007-11-X) Paws Four Pub.
Gillen, Patricia B. My Signing Book of Numbers. LC 87-28758. (Illus.). 59p. (ps up). 1987. 13.95 (0-930323-37-8, Kendall Green Pubns) Gallaudet Univ Pr.
Gilleo, Alma. Prince Charles. Endres, Helen, illus. LC 78-18938. (gr. k-4). 1978. PLB 19.95 (0-89565-029-0); PLB 13.95s.p. (0-685-55540-2) Childs World.
Gillespie, Bill. Because I Care. 24p. (Orig.). 1985. pap. 5.95 (0-940859-01-7) Snd Dollar Pub.
—Boat Ride. Poe, Janice, illus. 24p. 1988. pap. 3.50 (0-940859-05-X) Snd Dollar Pub.
—Butterflies' Wings & Beautiful Things. Poe, Janice, illus. 24p. 1986. pap. 3.50 (0-940859-02-5) Snd Dollar Pub.
—Peter Potter Teeter Totter. Poe, Janice, illus. 22p. (Orig.). 1987. pap. 3.50 (0-940859-06-8) Snd Dollar Pub.
—Spotty Spotty Jones. Poe, Janice, illus. 22p. (Orig.). 1986. pap. 3.50 (0-940859-03-3) Snd Dollar Pub.
Gillespie, Bonita. Peggy's Problem. Cover, Marilyn, illus. 35p. (gr. 3-8). 1987. 6.95 (1-55523-058-X) Winston-Derek.
Gillespie, John T. & Lembo, Diana L. Introducing Books: A Guide for the Middle Grades. LC 74-94512. 318p. (gr. 4-6). 1970. 29.95 (0-8352-0215-1) Bowker.
Gillespie, Mike. Caring for God's Creation. (Illus.). 48p. (gr. 6-8). 1991. pap. 7.99 (1-55945-121-1) Group Pub.
—Making Good Decisions. (Illus.). 48p. (gr. 9-12). 1991. pap. 7.99 (1-55945-209-9) Group Pub.
Gillet, David. Mystery Rider at Thunder Ridge. LC 87-27846. 22p. (gr. 3-7). 1988. pap. 4.49 (1-55513-398-3, Chariot Bks) Cook.

Gillett. The Great Reptile Race. 1992. write for info. (1-55513-538-2, Chariot Bks) Cook.
Gillette, J. Lynett. The Search for Seismosaurus. Hallett, Mark, photos by. LC 92-28199. (Illus.). 1993. 14.99 (0-8037-1358-4) Dial Bks Young.
Gillette, J. Lynette. Search for Seismosaurus: The World's Longest Dinosaur. LC 92-28199. (gr. 4-7). 1994. 14.89 (0-8037-1359-2) Dial Bks Young.
Gillette, Lynett. Dinosaur Diary: My Triassic Homeland. Larkin, Catherine, illus. 32p. (gr. 4). 1988. pap. 2.95 (0-945695-00-4) Petrified Forest Mus Assn.
Gillham, Bill. The First Words Picture Book. Grainger, Sam, photos by. LC 81-12452. (Illus.). 32p. (gr. 1-5). 1982. 7.95 (0-698-20560-X, Coward) Putnam Pub Group.
Gilliam, Terry & McKeown, Charles. The Adventures of Baron Munchausen: The Novel. Gilliam, Terry, illus. 192p. (Orig.). 1989. pap. 12.95 (1-55783-039-8) Applause Theatre Bk Pubs.
Gillianti, Simone. Rick Springfield. 1984. lib. bdg. write for info. (0-671-53104-2) S&S Trade.
Gillies, John. The New Russia. LC 93-25380. (Illus.). 128p. (gr. 4). 1994. RSBE 14.95 (0-87518-481-2, Dillon) Macmillan Child Grp.
Gillies, Patrick. Conflicts in Somalia & Ethiopia. (Illus.). 48p. (gr. 6 up). 1994. PLB 13.95 RSBE (0-02-792528-5, New Discovery Bks) Macmillan Child Grp.
Gillig, jt. auth. see Montgomery.
Gilligan, Alison. Earthquake! (gr. 4-7). 1992. pap. 3.25 (0-553-29299-4) Bantam.
—The Treasure of the Onyx. 1990. pap. 3.25 (0-553-28610-2) Bantam.
Gilligan, Shannon. The Case of the Missing Formula. (gr. 4-7). 1991. pap. 2.95 (0-553-15864-3) Bantam.
—The Case of the Silk King. large type ed. Bolle, Frank, illus. 114p. (gr. 3-7). 1987. Repr. of 1986 ed. 8.95 (0-942545-14-1); PLB 9.95 (0-942545-19-2, Dist. by Grolier) Grey Castle.
—Case of the Silk King. (gr. 5-12). 1986. pap. 3.25 (0-553-25489-8) Bantam.
—The Clue in the Clock Tower. (gr. 4-7). 1991. pap. 2.95 (0-553-15855-4) Bantam.
—The Fairy Kidnap. 64p. (Orig.). (gr. 2 up). 1985. pap. 2.25 (0-553-15488-5) Bantam.
—The Haunted Swamp. (gr. 4-7). 1991. pap. 2.95 (0-553-15856-2) Bantam.
—The Locker Thief. (gr. 4-7). 1991. pap. 2.99 (0-553-15895-3) Bantam.
—Mona Is Missing. 64p. (Orig.). 1984. pap. 2.25 (0-553-15441-9) Bantam.
—The Mystery of Ura Senke. 128p. (Orig.). (gr. 5). 1985. pap. 2.25 (0-553-25499-5) Bantam.
—Our Secret Gang, No. 6. 1992. pap. 2.99 (0-553-15994-1) Bantam.
—Project U. F. O. No. 143. 1994. pap. 3.50 (0-553-56003-4) Bantam.
—Science Lab Sabotage. (gr. 4-7). 1991. pap. 2.99 (0-553-15913-5) Bantam.
—The Search for Champ. Kramer, Anthony, illus. 50p. (gr. 4). 1983. pap. 2.25 (0-553-15442-7) Bantam.
—Showdown. 1992. pap. 3.25 (0-553-29297-8) Bantam.
Gilligan, Shannon, pseud. Terror in Australia. 128p. (Orig.). 1988. pap. 2.50 (0-553-27277-2) Bantam.
Gilligan, Shannon. The Three Wishes. 64p. (Orig.). (gr. 1-3). 1984. pap. text ed. 2.25 (0-553-15444-3, Skylark) Bantam.
Gilligan, W. Doyle. The Penny Catechism: Three Hundred & Seventy Fundamental Questions & Answers on the Catholic Faith. 74p. (Orig.). (gr. 5-8). 1982. pap. 1.75 (0-913382-48-5, 103-12) Prow Bks-Franciscan.
Gilliland, Hap. Broken Ice. (gr. 1-8). 1972. 5.95 (0-89992-024-1) Coun India Ed.
—Coyote's Pow-Wow. (gr. 1-6). 1972. 4.95 (0-89992-022-5) Coun India Ed.
—How the Dogs Saved the Cheyenne. 32p. 1972. 4.95 (0-89992-017-9) Coun India Ed.
—No One Like a Brother. (gr. 4-12). 1970. 4.95 (0-89992-003-9) Coun India Ed.
—O'kohome: The Coyote Dog. Hardgrove, Tanya, illus. 47p. (Orig.). (gr. 4-9). 1989. pap. 5.95 (0-89992-102-7) Coun India Ed.
Gilliland, Hap & Kovach, Tom. The Dark Side of the Moon. Hardgrove, Tanya, illus. 32p. (gr. 1-4). 1984. pap. 4.95 (0-89992-086-1) Coun India Ed.
Gilliland, Hap, jt. auth. see Bullshows, Harry.
Gilliland, Hap, ed. see Bryant, Martha F.
Gilliland, Hap, ed. see Chandonnet, Ann.
Gilliland, Hap, ed. see Cunnyngham, Jerry.
Gilliland, Hap, ed. see Dygert, Janice.
Gilliland, Hap, ed. see Egbert, Rebecca A.
Gilliland, Hap, ed. see Holland, Royce Q.
Gilliland, Hap, ed. see Van Ahnan, Katherine & Young Bear, Joan A.
Gilliland, Hap, et al. When We Went to the Mountains. (ENG, SPA, NAV, CRO & CHY.). 36p. (gr. 1-9). 1991. pap. 5.95 (0-89992-103-5) Coun India Ed.
Gilliland, Judith H. River. (ps-3). 1993. 14.95 (0-395-55963-4, Clarion Bks) HM.
Gilliland, Judith H., jt. auth. see Heide, Florence P.
Gillis, Everett A. Goldie. Gillis, Paul, illus. (gr. 3-7). 1982. pap. 8.00 (0-938328-02-6) Pisces Pr TX.
Gillis, Jennifer S. An Apple a Day! Over Twenty Apple Projects for Kids. Delmonte, Patti, illus. 64p. (Orig.). (gr. k-4). 1993. pap. 8.95 (0-88266-849-8, Garden Way Pub) Storey Comm Inc.

—Hearts & Crafts: Over Twenty Projects for Fun-Loving Kids. Steege, Gwen, ed. Delmonte, Patti, illus. LC 93-4841. 64p. (gr. k-4). 1994. pap. 9.95 (0-88266-844-7) Storey Comm Inc.
—In a Pumpkin Shell: Over Twenty Pumpkin Projects for Kids. Delmonte, Patti, illus. LC 91-50604. 64p. (gr. k-4). 1992. (Garden Way Pub); pap. 8.95 (0-88266-771-8, Garden Way Pub) Storey Comm Inc.
Gillman, Lillian E., ed. see Elementary School Children of California.
Gillman, Lillian E., ed. see Elementary School Children of Oregon.
Gillman, Lillian E., ed. see Elementary School Children of Washington State.
Gillon, Edmund. Cut & Assemble a Western Frontier Town. 1950. pap. 5.95 (0-486-23736-2) Dover.
—Cut & Assemble an Early New England Village. 1950. pap. 5.95 (0-486-23536-X) Dover.
Gillon, Edmund V. Cut & Assemble-Victorian Houses. 1980. pap. 5.95 (0-486-23849-0) Dover.
—Cut & Assemble Victorian Seaside Resort. 1986. pap. 5.95 (0-486-25097-0) Dover.
Gillsepie, Bill. Giraffes. Poe, Janice, illus. 12p. (Orig.). 1985. pap. 3.00 (0-940859-00-9) Snd Dollar Pub.
Gillum, Perry & Allen, Rob. Improving Your Grip. 33p. (Orig.). (gr. 8 up). 1987. pap. 3.95 (0-934942-66-8); 2.95 (0-934942-67-6) White Wing Pub.
Gillum, Perry & Allen, Rob, eds. Getting a Grip: Bible Study for Young Teens. 41p. (Orig.). (gr. 7-9). 1986. pap. 3.95 (0-934942-55-2); tchr's. ed. 2.95 (0-934942-56-0) White Wing Pub.
Gilman. Grandma & the Pirates. 1992. pap. 3.95 (0-590-43425-X) Scholastic Inc.
—Jillian Jiggs. 1993. pap. 28.67 (0-590-71823-1) Scholastic Inc.
—Little Blue Hen. 1993. pap. 28.67 (0-590-73273-0) Scholastic Inc.
Gilman, Alma B. & Gilman, Clarence R. Revelations in a Schoolroom: And Other Recollections As Remembered in the Year 1984. Custard Paste Art Staff & Loweree, Paul, illus. Kelley, Win, intro. by. 56p. (Orig.). 1984. pap. 3.75 (0-9613914-0-5) A B Gilman.
Gilman, Clarence R., jt. auth. see Gilman, Alma B.
Gilman, Dorothy. Girl in Buckskin. 144p. (gr. 7 up). 1990. pap. 3.50 (0-449-70380-0, Juniper) Fawcett.
—Maze in the Heart of the Castle. 1991. pap. 3.99 (0-449-70398-3) Fawcett.
Gilman, Michael. Matthew Henson. King, Coretta Scott, intro. by. (Illus.). 112p. (Orig.). (gr. 5 up). 1988. 17.95 (1-55546-590-0); pap. 9.95 (0-7910-0207-1) Chelsea Hse.
Gilman, Phoebe. Jillian Jiggs. Gilman, Phoebe, illus. 40p. (Orig.). (gr. k-3). 1988. pap. 2.50 (0-590-41340-6) Scholastic Inc.
—Wonderful Pigs of Jillian Jiggs. 1989. pap. 2.50 (0-590-41341-4) Scholastic Inc.
Gilman, Phoebe, adapted by. Something from Nothing. LC 92-37587. 1993. write for info. (0-590-47280-1) Scholastic Inc.
Gilman, Rhoda R. The Story of Minnesota's Past. LC 91-11189. (Illus.). 231p. 1991. pap. 22.50 (0-87351-267-7) Minn Hist Soc.
Gilmartin, Thelma. What Happens to Me When I Fish the Sea & a Fish Catches me. Barton, Kent, illus. LC 76-12929. 36p. (Orig.). (gr. 1-3). 1976. pap. 3.50 (0-89317-009-7) Windward Pub.
Gilmore, Jackie. Welcome to Grand Teton: An Explosion of Life & Color. NPS Staff, ed. Wordmill Staff, tr. Stark, Jack, intro. by. 24p. 1991. German. pap. 4.95 ea. (0-931895-15-4) Spanish (0-931895-18-9) Japanese (0-931895-16-2) French (0-931895-17-0) Grand Teton NHA.
—Welcome to Grand Teton National Park: An Explosion of Life & Color. NPS Staff, ed. (Illus.). 24p. 1991. pap. 4.95 (0-931895-19-7) Grand Teton NHA.
—A Year at Elk Meadow. Strawn, Susan, illus. 16p. (ps-3). 1986. pap. 4.95 (0-911797-24-6) R Rinehart.
Gilmore, Kate. Enter Three Witches. 216p. (gr. 5-9). 1990. 13.45 (0-395-50213-6) HM.
—Enter Three Witches. 1992. pap. 2.95 (0-590-44494-8, Point) Scholastic Inc.
—Jason & the Bard. LC 92-2680. 240p. (gr. 7 up). 1993. 14.45 (0-395-62472-X) HM.
Gilmore, Rachna. Aunt Fred Is a Witch. (Illus.). (gr. k-4). 1991. pap. 5.95 (0-929005-23-6, Pub. by Second Story Pr CN) InBook.
Gilow, Betty & Tickle, Phyllis. It's No Fun to Be Sick by Paula & Her Friends. (Illus.). (gr. 2-6). 1976. 3.95 (0-918518-02-4) St Lukes Pr.
Gilroy, Mark. Christine Leadership. (Illus.). 48p. (gr. 9-12). 1993. pap. 7.99 (1-55945-231-5) Group Pub.
—Exploring Ethical Issues. (Illus.). 48p. (gr. 9-12). 1992. pap. 7.99 (1-55945-225-0) Group Pub.
—Sharing My Faith: A Teen's Guide to Evangelism. (Illus.). 104p. 1991. pap. 5.95 (0-8341-1384-8) Beacon Hill.
—Spending Time with God: A Teen's Guide to Devotions. 72p. (Orig.). 1987. pap. 3.95 (0-8341-1197-7) Beacon Hill.
Gilroy, Mark K. Step by Step: Twenty-Eight Devotionals for Christian Teens. 36p. (Orig.). 1993. pap. 1.95 saddlestitched (0-8341-1468-2) Beacon Hill.
Gilson, Jamie. Can't Catch Me, I'm the Gingerbread Man. LC 80-39748. 192p. (gr. 5-9). 1981. 12.95 (0-688-00435-0); PLB 12.88 (0-688-00436-9) Lothrop.
—Can't Catch Me, I'm the Gingerbread Man. 128p. (gr. 4-7). 1989. pap. 2.75 (0-671-69160-0, Minstrel Bks) PB.
—Do Bananas Chew Gum? LC 80-11414. 160p. (gr. 5-9). 1980. 12.95 (0-688-41960-7); PLB 12.88 (0-688-51960-1) Lothrop.
—Double Dare Dog. Primavera, Elise, illus. LC 87-37855. 126p. (gr. 3-5). 1988. 12.95 (0-688-07969-5) Lothrop.
—Double Dog Dare. (Illus.). 1989. pap. 2.75 (0-671-67898-1, Minstrel Bks) PB.
—Four-B Goes Wild. Edwards, Linda S., illus. LC 83-948. 160p. (gr. 4-6). 1983. 12.95 (0-688-02236-7) Lothrop.
—Four-B Goes Wild. MacDonald, Pat, ed. Edwards, Linda S., illus. (gr. 3-6). 1989. pap. 2.99 (0-671-68063-3, Minstrel Bks) PB.
—Harvey, the Beer Can King. Wallner, John, illus. LC 78-1807. 128p. (gr. 4-6). 1983. 13.95 (0-688-02382-7) Lothrop.
—Harvey, the Beer Can King. (Illus.). (gr. 4-6). 1988. pap. 2.50 (0-671-67423-4, Minstrel Bks) PB.
—Hello, My Name Is Scrambled Eggs. Wallner, John, illus. LC 84-10075. 160p. (gr. 4-6). 1985. 12.95 (0-688-04095-0) Lothrop.
—Hello, My Name Is Scrambled Eggs. Wallner, John, illus. (gr. 3-6). 1991. pap. 2.99 (0-671-74104-7, Minstrel Bks) PB.
—Hobie Hanson, Greatest Hero of the Mall. Riggio, Anita, illus. LC 89-2343. 160p. (gr. 3-6). 1989. 12.95 (0-688-08968-2) Lothrop.
—Hobie Hanson, Greatest Hero of the Mall. Riggio, Anita, illus. 160p. (gr. 3-6). 1990. pap. 2.95 (0-671-70646-2, Minstrel Bks) PB.
—Hobie Hanson, You're Weird. LC 86-15241. 170p. (gr. 4-7). 1987. 12.95 (0-688-06700-X) Lothrop.
—Hobie Hanson, You're Weird. MacDonald, Pat, ed. Primavera, Elise, illus. 176p. (gr. 3-6). 1988. pap. 2.99 (0-671-73752-X, Minstrel Bks) PB.
—Itchy Richard. De Groat, Diane, illus. 64p. (gr. 1-5). 1991. 13.45 (0-395-59282-8, Clarion Bks) HM.
—Overnight at the Pennywise Motel. LC 92-9716. 1993. write for info. (0-688-12021-0) Lothrop.
—Sticks & Stones & Skeleton Bones. DeRosa, Dee, illus. (gr. 3-6). 1991. 12.95 (0-688-10098-8) Lothrop.
—Thirteen Ways to Sink a Sub. Edwards, Linda S., illus. (gr. 3-7). 1982. 12.95 (0-688-01304-X) Lothrop.
—Thirteen Ways to Sink a Sub. large type ed. 260p. (gr. 5 up). 1988. Repr. lib. bdg. 15.95 (1-55736-049-9, Crnrstn Bks) BDD LT Grp.
—You Cheat! Chambliss, Maxie, illus. LC 91-13886. 64p. (gr. 1-4). 1992. SBE 13.95 (0-02-735993-X, Bradbury Pr) Macmillan Child Grp.
—You Don't Know Beans about Bats. De Groat, Diane, illus. LC 93-559. 1994. write for info. (0-395-67063-2, Clarion Bks) HM.
Gilsvik, Bob. The Complete Book of Trapping. Gilsvik, David, illus. 172p. (gr. 7). Repr. of 1976 ed. 10.95 (0-936622-29-6) A R Harding Pub.
Gimbel, Cheryl & Maners, Wendelin. Why Does Santa Celebrate Christmas? Lovelady, J., ed. (Illus.). 36p. (gr. k up). 1990. 12.95 (0-915190-67-2, JP9067-2) Jalmar Pr.
Gimmestad, Nancy, jt. auth. see Rivlin, Asher E.
Gingras, Louie & Rainboldt, Jo. Coyote & Kootenai. (gr. 2-6). 1977. 1.95 (0-89992-067-5) Coun India Ed.
Ginns, P. C. Ghostwriter: The Big Book of Kid's Puzzles Mystery Issue. (ps-3). 1992. pap. 1.25 (0-553-37074-X) Bantam.
Ginolfi, Arthur. Tiny Star. Schories, Pat, illus. 32p. 1989. 6.95 (1-56288-134-5) Checkerboard.
Ginsberg, Daniel. Whales & Dolphins: An Educational Coloring Book. Ginsberg, Daniel, illus. 32p. (Orig.). (gr. 1-4). 1989. pap. 2.95 (0-9623284-0-5) R Rinehart.
Ginsberg, Mirra. Three Kittens. (ps-1). 1992. pap. 3.50 (0-679-83254-8) Random Bks Yng Read.
Ginsburg, Marvell. Tattooed Torah. (Illus.). 32p. (gr. k-3). 1983. 6.95 (0-8074-0252-4, 104030) UAHC.
Ginsburg, Max, jt. auth. see San Souci, Robert D.
Ginsburg, Mirra. Across the Stream. Tafuri, Nancy, illus. LC 81-20306. 24p. (ps-1). 1982. 15.95 (0-688-01204-3); PLB 15.88 (0-688-01206-X) Greenwillow.
—Across the Stream. Tafuri, Nancy, illus. LC 81-20306. 24p. (ps-3). 1991. pap. 3.95 (0-688-10477-0, Mulberry) Morrow.
—Asleep, Asleep. Tafuri, Nancy, illus. LC 91-14393. 24p. (ps up). 1992. 14.00 (0-688-09153-9); PLB 13.93 (0-688-09154-7) Greenwillow.
—The Chick & the Duckling. Suteyev, V., tr. from RUS. Aruego, Jose & Dewey, Ariane, illus. LC 74-188773. 32p. (ps-1). 1972. RSBE 14.95 (0-02-735940-9, Macmillan Child Bk) Macmillan Child Grp.
—The Chick & the Duckling. Aruego, Jose & Dewey, Ariane, illus. 32p. (ps-1). 1988. pap. 4.95 (0-689-71226-X, Aladdin) Macmillan Child Grp.
—Chinese Mirror. (Illus.). 1992. pap. 4.95 (0-15-217508-3, HB Juv Bks) HarBrace.
—Clay Boy. Henwood, Simon, illus. 32p. (ps-3). 1993. PLB 14.95 (0-399-21988-9, Philomel Bks) Putnam Pub Group.
—Four Brave Sailors. Tafuri, Lynn, illus. LC 86-7555. 24p. (ps-1). 1987. 11.75 (0-688-06514-7); PLB 11.88 (0-688-06515-5) Greenwillow.
—Good Morning, Chick. Barton, Byron, illus. LC 80-11352. 32p. (ps). 1980. PLB 12.88 (0-688-84284-4) Greenwillow.
—Good Morning, Chick. LC 80-11352. (Illus.). (gr. 1 up). 1989. pap. 3.95 (0-688-08741-8, Mulberry) Morrow.
—Good Morning Chick. Barton, Byron, illus. 32p. (ps up). 1993. Repr. text ed. 4.95 (0-688-12666-9, Tupelo Bks) Morrow.
—The King Who Tried to Fry an Egg on His Head. Hillenbrand, Will, illus. LC 91-10099. 32p. (gr. k-3). 1994. RSBE 14.95 (0-02-736242-6, Macmillan Child Bk) Macmillan Child Grp.
—Merry-Go-Round: Four Stories. Aruego, Jose & Dewey, Ariane, illus. LC 90-30439. 48p. 1992. 15.00 (0-688-09256-X); PLB 14.93 (0-688-09257-8) Greenwillow.
—Mushroom in the Rain. Aruego, Jose & Dewey, Ariane, illus. LC 72-92438. 32p. (ps-1). 1987. RSBE 13.95 (0-02-736241-8, Macmillan Child Bk) Macmillan Child Grp.
—Mushroom in the Rain. Ginsburg, Mirra, illus. LC 90-31814. 32p. (ps-1). 1990. pap. 3.95 (0-689-71441-6, Aladdin) Macmillan Child Grp.
—The Sun's Asleep Behind the Hill. Zelinsky, Paul O., illus. LC 81-6615. 32p. (ps-1). 1982. 12.95 (0-688-00824-0); PLB 12.88 (0-688-00825-9) Greenwillow.
—Two Greedy Bears. LC 76-8819. (Illus.). 32p. (ps-3). 1990. pap. 3.95 (0-689-71392-4, Aladdin) Macmillan Child Grp.
—Two Greedy Bears: Adapted from a Hungarian Folk Tale. Aruego, Jose & Dewey, Ariane, illus. LC 76-8819. 32p. (ps-2). 1976. RSBE 13.95 (0-02-736450-X, Macmillan Child Bk) Macmillan Child Grp.
—Where Does the Sun Go at Night? Aruego, Jose & Dewey, Ariane, illus. LC 79-16151. 32p. (gr. k-3). 1980. 10.95 (0-688-80245-1); PLB 10.88 (0-688-84245-3) Greenwillow.
—Where Does the Sun Go at Night? Aruego, Jose & Dewey, Ariane, illus. LC 79-16151. 32p. (ps-3). 1987. pap. 4.95 (0-688-07041-8, Mulberry) Morrow.
Ginsburg, Mirra, ed. The Chinese Mirror. Zemach, Margot, illus. LC 86-22940. 26p. (ps-3). 1988. 15.95 (0-15-200420-3, Gulliver Bks) HarBrace.
Ginsburg, Mirra, adapted by. The Old Man & His Birds. Ruff, Donna, illus. LC 93-26705. 1994. write for info. (0-688-04603-7); PLB write for info. (0-688-04604-5) Greenwillow.
Ginsburg, Mirra, tr. Last Door to Aiya: A Selection of the Best New Science Fiction from the Soviet Union. LC 68-16347. (gr. 10 up). 1968. 21.95 (0-87599-135-1) S G Phillips.
Gintzler, A. S. Rough & Ready Cowboys. 48p. (gr. 4-7). 1994. text ed. 12.95 (1-56261-152-6) John Muir.
—Rough & Ready Homesteaders. 48p. (gr. 4-7). 1994. text ed. 12.95 (1-56261-154-2) John Muir.
—Rough & Ready Prospectors. 48p. (gr. 4-7). 1994. text ed. 12.95 (1-56261-153-4) John Muir.
Giombi, Gary. Paths of Prayer: A Textbook of Prayer & Meditation. 160p. (Orig.). (gr. 9-12). pap. text ed. 9.95 (0-937997-27-7); tchr's. ed. 23.95 (0-937997-29-3) HI-Time Pub.
Giono, Jean. Homme qui Plantait des Arbres. Glaseur, Willi, illus. (FRE.). 71p. (Orig.). 1990. pap. 12.95 (2-07-031180-5) Schoenhof.
Giorda. William the Last. (Illus.). (gr. 1-8). 1992. PLB 8.95 (0-89565-884-4); Resale. 12.75 (0-685-60985-5) Childs World.
Giovanni. The Maiden Voyage. Schumake, John P., ed. (Orig.). (gr. 4-6). 1992. pap. 9.95 (0-9616789-5-X) Earnest Pubns.
Giovanni, Nikki. Ego-Tripping & Other Poems for Young People. Ford, George, illus. LC 73-81745. 37p. (gr. 2-7). 1974. 7.95 (1-55652-062-X) L Hill Bks.
—Ego-Tripping & Other Poems for Young People. 2nd, rev. ed. Ford, George, illus. LC 93-29578. 72p. (gr. 5-12). 1993. 14.95 (1-55652-188-X); pap. 9.95 (1-55652-189-8) L Hill Bks.
—Grand Mothers. 1994. write for info. (0-8050-2766-1) H Holt & Co.
—Knoxville, Tennessee. Johnson, Larry, illus. LC 93-8877. 32p. 1994. 14.95 (0-590-47074-4) Scholastic Inc.
—Spin a Soft Black Song. rev. ed. Martins, George, illus. LC 84-19287. 64p. (gr. 2 up). 1985. 11.95 (0-8090-8796-0) Hill & Wang.
—Spin a Soft Black Song. rev. ed. Martins, George, illus. (gr. k up). 1987. pap. 3.95 (0-374-46469-3, Sunburst) FS&G.
—Vacation Time: Poems for Children. Russo, Marisabina, illus. LC 79-91643. 32p. (gr. 7 up). 1981. pap. 6.00 (0-688-00507-1, Quill) Morrow.
Gipe, George. Gremlins. (Illus.). 77p. (gr. 3-7). 1984. pap. 2.95 (0-380-89003-8, Camelot) Avon.
Gipson, Fred. Curly & the Wild Boar. Himler, Ronald, illus. LC 77-25644. 96p. (gr. 5 up) 1979. HarpC Child Bks.
—Old Yeller. LC 56-8780. (Illus.). (gr. 7-9). 1956. 22.00i (0-06-011545-9, HarpT) HarpC.
—Old Yeller. LC 56-8780. 176p. (gr. 5 up). 1990. pap. 3.95 (0-06-440382-3, Trophy) HarpC Child Bks.
—Old Yeller. 192p. 1992. Repr. PLB 15.95x (0-899966-906-9) Buccaneer Bks.
—Savage Sam. (gr. 1-5). 1976. pap. 5.50 (0-06-080377-0, P377, PL) HarpC.
—The Trail-Driving Rooster. Lich, Glen, intro. by. (Illus.). 88p. (gr. 4-7). 1987. Repr. of 1955 ed. 9.95 (0-89015-620-4, Pub. by Panda Bks) Eakin-Sunbelt.
Gipson, Morrell. Rip Van Winkle. San Souci, Daniel, illus. LC 83-20624. 32p. (gr. k-3). 1987. pap. 4.95 (0-385-23965-3, Pub. by Zephyr-BFYR) Doubleday.

Gipson, Morrell & Frank, Herta. Tom's Lucky Quarter. Stefoff, Rebecca, ed. LC 90-13796. (Illus.). 24p. (gr. k-3). 1990. PLB 14.60 (0-944483-89-5) Garrett Ed Corp.

Gipson, Morrell & Hansson, Peter. Clumsy Clown Willie. Stefoff, Rebecca, ed. LC 90-13793. (Illus.). 24p. (gr. k-3). 1990. PLB 14.60 (0-944483-90-9) Garrett Ed Corp.

Gipson, Morrell & Mangold, Paul. Walkers Go Hiking. LC 90-13797. (Illus.). 24p. (gr. k-3). 1990. PLB 14.60 (0-944483-91-7) Garrett Ed Corp.

—Whose Tracks Are These? Stefoff, Rebecca, ed. LC 90-13798. (Illus.). 24p. (gr. k-3). 1990. PLB 14.60 (0-944483-93-3) Garrett Ed Corp.

Gipson, Morrell & Mann, Marek. Easter with Friends. Stefoff, Rebecca, ed. LC 90-13794. (Illus.). 24p. (gr. k-3). 1990. PLB 14.60 (0-944483-88-7) Garrett Ed Corp.

Gipson, Morrell & Mayer, Lene. Let's Be Friends. Stefoff, Rebecca, ed. LC 90-13795. (Illus.). 24p. (gr. k-3). 1990. PLB 14.60 (0-944483-92-5) Garrett Ed Corp.

Girard, Linda. You Were Born on Your Very First Birthday. Tucker, Kathy, ed. LC 82-13700. (Illus.). 32p. (ps-3). 1983. PLB 13.95 (0-8075-9455-5); pap. 5.95 (0-8075-9456-3) A Whitman.

Girard, Linda W. Adoption Is for Always. Levine, Abby, ed. LC 86-15843. (Illus.). 32p. (gr. 1-5). 1986. PLB 11.95 (0-8075-0185-9); pap. 4.95 (0-8075-0187-5) A Whitman.

—Alex, the Kid with AIDS. Levine, Abby, ed. Sims, Blanche, illus. LC 89-77592. 32p. (gr. 2-5). 1991. PLB 13.95 (0-8075-0245-6); pap. 5.95 (0-8075-0247-2) A Whitman.

—At Daddy's on Saturdays. Levine, Abby, ed. LC 87-2126. (Illus.). 32p. (gr. k-3). 1987. PLB 13.95 (0-8075-0475-0); pap. 5.95 (0-8075-0473-4) A Whitman.

—My Body Is Private. Tucker, Kathleen, ed. LC 84-17220. (Illus.). 32p. (ps-3). 1984. PLB 11.95 (0-8075-5320-4); pap. 4.95 (0-8075-5319-0) A Whitman.

—We Adopted You, Benjamin Koo. Levine, Abby, ed. LC 88-23653. (Illus.). 32p. (gr. 2-6). 1989. 13.95 (0-8075-8694-3); pap. 5.95 (0-8075-8695-1) A Whitman.

—Who Is a Stranger & What Should I Do? Levine, Abby, ed. Cogancherry, Helen, illus. LC 84-17313. 32p. (gr. 2-6). 1985. PLB 11.95 (0-8075-9014-2); pap. 4.95 (0-8075-9016-9) A Whitman.

—Young Frederick Douglass: The Slave Who Learned to Read. Bootman, Collin, illus. LC 93-28245. 1994. write for info. (0-8075-9463-6) A Whitman.

Giraud, Robert, jt. auth. see Asimov, Isaac.

Giraudy, Daniele, text by. Pablo Picasso: The Minotaur, An Art Play Book. (Illus.). 32p. (gr. 2 up). 1988. 17.95 (0-8109-1471-9) Abrams.

Gire, Judy. A Boy & His Baseball: The Dave Dravecky Story. Zp. 1992. 14.99 (0-310-58630-5, Youth Bks) Zondervan.

Gire, Ken. Adventures in the Big Thicket. (Illus.). 112p. (gr. k-5). 1990. 14.99 (0-929608-72-0) Focus Family.

—Treasure in an Oatmeal Box. LC 90-61790. 144p. (gr. 4-7). 1990. pap. 6.00 (0-89109-367-2) NavPress.

Girgis, Nazih. The Arabic Alphabet. Lowry-Elks, C., illus. (ENG & ARA.). 57p. (gr. k-12). 1983. pap. 15.00 incl. cass. (0-86685-340-5) Intl Bk Ctr.

Girion, Barbara. Front Page Exclusive. (gr. 7 up). 1987. pap. 2.50 (0-440-92663-7) Dell.

—A Handful of Stars. 192p. (gr. 7 up). 1986. pap. 2.95 (0-440-93642-X, LFL) Dell.

—Indian Summer. (gr. 4-7). 1993. pap. 2.95 (0-590-42637-0) Scholastic Inc.

—Misty & Me. LC 90-31675. 144p. (gr. 3-7). 1990. pap. 3.95 (0-689-71442-4, Aladdin) Macmillan Child Grp.

—Portfolio to Fame. (Orig.). (gr. k-12). 1987. pap. 2.50 (0-440-97148-9, LFL) Dell.

—Prescription for Success. (gr. 7 up). 1987. pap. 2.50 (0-440-97165-9) Dell.

—Prime Time Attraction. (Orig.). (gr. k-12). 1987. pap. 2.50 (0-440-97179-9, LFL) Dell.

Girl Scouts of the U. S. A. Staff. Brownies' Own Songbook. Roos, Ann, et al. 48p. (gr. 1-3). 1968. pap. 4.00 (0-88441-351-9, 23-130) Girl Scouts USA.

—Girl Scout Pocket Songbook: For Juniors, Cadettes, Seniors, & Leaders. 56p. (gr. 3 up). 1973. pap. 1.00 (0-88441-306-3, 20-192) Girl Scouts USA.

—Sing Together: A Girl Scout Songbook. (Illus.). 192p. (gr. 1-12). 1973. spiral bdg. 8.00 (0-88441-309-8, 20-206) Girl Scouts USA.

—Wide World of Girl Guiding & Girl Scouting. (Illus.). 88p. (gr. 1-6). 1980. pap. text ed. 7.00 (0-88441-143-5, 19-713) Girl Scouts USA.

Girst, Jack A. Renfro Would Rather Rest. Girst, Jack A., illus. 32p. (gr. k-2). 1989. pap. 1.99 (0-87403-633-X, 3972) Standard Pub.

Girzone, Joseph F. Joshua & the Children, 2 Vols. 1991. pap. 17.95 (0-02-019891-4, Collier Young Rd) Macmillan Child Grp.

—Kara: The Lonely Falcon. Molloy, Eideen, illus. LC 78-63393. 52p. (gr. 2 up). 1985. Repr. of 1979 ed. 8.95 (0-911519-05-X) Richelieu Court.

Gise, Joanne. A Picture Book of Birds. Pistolesi, Roseanna, illus. LC 89-37328. 24p. (gr. 1-4). 1990. lib. bdg. 9.59 (0-8167-1898-9); pap. text ed. 2.50 (0-8167-1899-7) Troll Assocs.

—A Picture Book of Desert Animals. Pistolesi, Roseanna, illus. LC 90-40436. 24p. (gr. 1-4). 1991. lib. bdg. 9.59 (0-8167-2148-3); pap. text ed. 2.50 (0-8167-2149-1) Troll Assocs.

—A Picture Book of Dogs. Pistolesi, Roseanna, illus. LC 89-39430. 24p. (gr. 1-4). 1990. PLB 9.59 (0-8167-1902-0); pap. text ed. 2.50 (0-8167-1903-9) Troll Assocs.

—A Picture Book of Forest Animals. Pistolesi, Roseanna, illus. LC 89-37329. 24p. (gr. 1-4). 1990. lib. bdg. 9.59 (0-8167-1904-7); pap. text ed. 2.50 (0-8167-1905-5) Troll Assocs.

—A Picture Book of Horses. Pistolesi, Roseanna, illus. LC 90-40437. 24p. (gr. 1-4). 1991. lib. bdg. 9.59 (0-8167-2152-1); pap. text ed. 2.50 (0-8167-2153-X) Troll Assocs.

—A Picture Book of Wild Animals. Pistolesi, Roseanna, illus. LC 89-37334. 24p. (gr. 1-4). 1990. lib. bdg. 9.59 (0-8167-1908-X); pap. text ed. 2.50 (0-8167-1909-8) Troll Assocs.

Gise, Joanne, adapted by see Twain, Mark.

Gish, Lillian & Lanes, Selma. An Actor's Life for Me! Lincoln, Patricia H., illus. 64p. (gr. 2-5). 1987. pap. 15.00 (0-670-80416-9) Viking Child Bks.

Gisler, David. Addition Annie. Dunnington, Tom, illus. LC 91-17654. 32p. (ps-2). 1991. PLB 11.93 (0-516-02007-2); pap. 2.95 (0-516-42007-0) Childrens.

Gisler, Margaret, jt. auth. see Eberts, Marjorie.

Gissendanner, Rainah. Choices. 1992. 9.95 (0-8062-4208-6) Carlton.

Gitchel, Sam & Foster, Lorri. Let's Talk about...S-E-X: A Read & Discuss Guide for People 9 to 12 & Their Parents. Cooper, Andrea, illus. 59p. (gr. 4-8). 1983. pap. 4.95 (0-9610122-0-X) Plan Par Ctrl CA.

Gitchel, Sam, jt. auth. see Foster, Lorri.

Gitenstein, Judy. Summer Camp. 64p. (Orig.). (gr. 2-4). 1984. pap. 2.75 (0-553-15562-8, Skylark) Bantam.

Gitkin, Lisa S., jt. auth. see Radlauer, Ruth.

Gittelsohn, Roland B. How Do I Decide? (Orig.). (gr. 7-9). 1989. pap. text ed. 8.95x (0-87441-488-1) Behrman.

—Love in Your Life: A Jewish View of Teenage Sexuality. (gr. 7-9). 1991. pap. 9.95 (0-8074-0460-8, 142685) UAHC.

Gittins, Anne. Tales from the South Pacific Islands. LC 76-5411. (Illus.). 96p. (gr. 3 up). 1977. 7.95 (0-916144-02-X) Stemmer Hse.

Giuliani, Alfred, illus. The Little Engine That Could: A Story to Color. 48p. (ps-2). 1992. pap. 0.42 (0-448-40377-3, Platt & Munk Pubs) Putnam Pub Group.

Givens, Bill. Film Flubs: Not-So-Great Moments from the Movies. 1990. pap. 6.95 (0-8065-1161-3, Citadel Pr) Carol Pub Group.

Givens, Terryl. Dragon Scales & Willow Leaves. Portwood, Andrew, illus. LC 93-665. Date not set. write for info. (0-399-22619-2, Putnam) Putnam Pub Group.

Gjelfriend, George E. High Island Treasure. Little, Carl, ed. LC 91-58093. (Illus.). 120p. (gr. 4-8). 1992. pap. 9.95 (0-932433-84-7) Windswept Hse.

Gjovaag, Eric, jt. auth. see Carlson, Karyl.

Glancy, Ruth, intro. by see Dickens, Charles.

Glaser, Byron, jt. auth. see Neumeier, Marty.

Glaser, Elizabeth & Biel, Timothy L. The Ethiopian Famine. LC 90-6247. (Illus.). 64p. (gr. 5-8). 1990. PLB 11.95 (1-56006-014-X) Lucent Bks.

Glaser, Linda. Keep Your Socks on, Albert! Ward, Sally G., illus. LC 91-19387. 48p. (ps-2). 1992. 11.00 (0-525-44838-1, DCB) Dutton Child Bks.

—Tanya's Big Green Dream. McGinnis, Susan, illus. LC 93-9968. 48p. (gr. 1-5). 1994. RSBE 13.95 (0-02-735994-8, Macmillan Child Bk) MacMillan Child Grp.

—Wonderful Worms. Krupinski, Loretta, illus. LC 91-38752. 32p. (gr. k-3). 1992. 14.95 (1-56294-703-6); PLB 14.90 (1-56294-062-7) Millbrook Pr.

Glaser, Michael. Does Anyone Know Where a Hermit Crab Goes? Glaser, Michael, illus. LC 82-84341. 32p. (Orig.). (ps-3). 1983. pap. 3.95 (0-911635-00-9) Knickerbocker.

—Driftwood. LC 85-50601. (Illus.). 32p. (ps-3). 1985. pap. 3.95 (0-911635-01-7) Knickerbocker.

—The Nature of the Seashore. Glaser, Michael, illus. 16p. (Orig.). (gr. 1-6). 1986. pap. 4.95 (0-911635-02-5) Knickerbocker.

Glaspell, Susan. A Jury of Her Peers. (gr. 5). 1992. PLB 13.95 (0-88682-496-6) Creative Ed.

Glass, Andrew. Charles T. McBiddle. LC 91-29026. (ps-3). 1993. 15.00 (0-385-30554-0) Doubleday.

Glass, Brent D. The Textile Industry in North Carolina: A History. (Illus.). xiv, 119p. (Orig.). (gr. 8-12). 1992. pap. 6.00 (0-86526-256-X) NC Archives.

Glass, Don, ed. Why You Can Never Get to the End of the Rainbow & Other Moments of Science. Singh, Paul, contrib. by. LC 92-34770. 1993. write for info. (0-253-32591-9); pap. write for info. (0-253-20780-0) Ind U Pr.

Glass, Eli. The Perfect Touch. rev. ed. (gr. 9-12). 1989. Repr. of 1983 ed. multi-media kit 35.00 (0-685-31129-5) Balance Pub.

Glass, Malcolm, jt. auth. see Brown, Bill.

Glasscock, Paula, jt. auth. see Weber, Sally.

Glassman, Bruce. The Crash of Twenty-Nine & the New Deal. (Illus.). 64p. (gr. 5 up). 1985. PLB 16.98 (0-382-06831-9); pap. 8.95 (0-382-06978-1) Silver Burdett.

—Everything You Need to Know about Stepfamilies. rev. ed. (Illus.). 64p. (gr. 7-12). 1993. 13.95 (0-8239-1798-3) Rosen Group.

—J. Paul Getty. Furstinger, Nancy, ed. (Illus.). 112p. (gr. 7-10). 1989. PLB 13.98 (0-382-09584-7) Silver Burdett Pr.

—New York. (Illus.). 64p. (gr. 3-7). PLB 14.95 (1-56711-024-X) Blackbirch.

—Wilma Mankiller: Chief of the Cherokee Nation. (Illus.). 64p. (gr. 3-7). PLB 14.95 (1-56711-032-0) Blackbirch.

Glassman, Bruce, jt. auth. see McNear, Robert.

Glassman, Bruce S. Arthur Miller. (Illus.). 128p. (gr. 7-9). 1990. 17.98 (0-382-09904-4); pap. 14.95 (0-382-24032-4) Silver Burdett Pr.

—Mikhail Baryshnikov. (Illus.). 128p. (gr. 7-9). 1990. 14.95 (0-382-24035-9); 11.21s.p. (0-685-47027-X) PLB 17.98 (0-382-09907-9) Silver Burdett Pr.

Glassman, Judy. The Morning Glory War. LC 90-3831. 160p. (gr. 5 up). 1990. 13.95 (0-525-44637-0, DCB) Dutton Child Bks.

—Morning Glory War. (gr. 4-7). 1993. pap. 3.50 (0-440-40765-6) Dell.

Glassman, Peter. My Working Mom. Arnold, Tedd, illus. LC 93-22036. 1994. write for info. (0-688-12259-0); PLB write for info. (0-688-12260-4) Morrow Jr Bks.

—The Wizard Next Door. Kellogg, Steven, illus. LC 92-21562. 40p. (gr. k up). 1993. 15.00 (0-688-10645-5); PLB 14.93 (0-688-10646-3) Morrow Jr Bks.

Glatzer. Quest for the Cities of Gold, No. 16. 144p. (Orig.). (ps-6). 1987. pap. 2.50 (0-553-26295-5) Bantam.

Glatzer, David & Glatzer, Joyce. The Casio SL-450: A Tool for Teaching Mathematics. Sobel, Max, ed. (Illus.). 72p. (gr. k-6). 1993. wkbk. 9.95 (1-878532-05-7) Casio Inc.

Glatzer, Joyce, jt. auth. see Glatzer, David.

Glavich, Kathleen. Acting Out the Miracles & Parables: 52 Five-Minute Plays for Education & Worship. LC 88-50330. (Illus., Orig.). (gr. 4-6). 1988. pap. 12.95 (0-89622-363-9) Twenty-Third.

Glavich, Mary K. Gospel Plays for Students: Thirty-Six Scripts for Education & Worship. LC 89-50562. (Illus.). 112p. 1989. 12.95 (0-89622-407-4) Twenty-Third.

Glazer, Susan M. & Brown, Carol S. Portfolios & Beyond: Collaborative Assessment in Reading & Writing. (Illus.). 216p. (Orig.). (gr. k-12). 1993. pap. text ed. 18.95 (0-926842-25-0) CG Pubs Inc.

Glazer, Tom. America the Beautiful. 1987. pap. 12.95 (0-385-24074-0) Doubleday.

—Do Your Ears Hang Low? Lazarevich, Mila, illus. LC 78-20072. 96p. (gr. 1-3). 1980. 12.95 (0-385-12602-6) Doubleday.

—Eye Winker, Tom Tinker, Chin Chopper. Himler, Ron, illus. LC 72-97497. (ps-3). 1973. pap. 11.95 (0-385-08200-2, Zephyr) Doubleday.

—Mother Goose Songbook. 1990. pap. 12.95 (0-385-24631-5) Doubleday.

—Music for Ones & Twos: Songs & Games for the Very Young Child. Weinhaus, Karen T., illus. LC 82-45199. 96p. (ps). 1983. pap. 12.00 (0-385-14252-8, Pub. by Zephyr-BFYR) Doubleday.

—Tom Glazer's Christmas Songbook. Corrigan, Barbara, illus. 1989. 16.00 (0-685-29548-6) Doubleday.

—Tom Glazer's Christmas Songbook. Corrigan, Barbara, illus. 128p. (gr. 3 up). 1989. pap. 16.00 (0-385-24641-2, Zephyr-BFYR) Doubleday.

Glazer, Tom, ed. Tom Glazer's Treasury of Songs for Children. (Illus.). (gr. 1-6). 1988. 12.95 (0-686-74302-4) J R Pubns.

Glazier, Lyle. Summer for Joey. LC 86-63092. 256p. 1987. pap. 9.95 (0-912395-08-7) Millers River Pub Co.

Gleasner, Bill. Rock Climbing. 1980. 7.95 (0-679-20925-5) McKay.

Gleasner, Diana. The Movies. (Illus.). (gr. 4-6). 1983. lib. bdg. 8.85 (0-8027-6483-5) Walker & Co.

Gleason, Karan. Factivities. 144p. (gr. k-5). 1991. 11.95 (0-86653-601-9, GA1320) Good Apple.

—Rainy Day Fun. Filkins, Vanessa, illus. 112p. (gr. k-4). 1987. pap. 9.95 (0-86653-408-3, GA1002) Good Apple.

Gleason, Norma. Fun with Word Puzzles. 1991. pap. 2.95 (0-486-26923-X) Dover.

Gleason, Richard. Sprout. LC 86-51074. (Illus.). 84p. (gr. 3-8). 1987. 7.95 (1-55523-052-0) Winston-Derek.

Gleason, Roger. Seeing for Yourself: Techniques & Projects for Beginning Photographers. (Illus.). 176p. (gr. 9-12). 1992. pap. 14.95 (1-55652-159-6) Chicago Review.

Gleeson, Brian. Anansi. Guarnaccia, Steven, illus. LC 91-40671. 36p. (gr. k up). 1992. pap. 14.95 (0-88708-230-0, Rabbit Ears); incl. cass. 19.95 (0-88708-231-9, Rabbit Ears) Picture Bk Studio.

—Finn McCoul. De Seve, Peter, illus. 40p. (gr. k up). 1993. incl. cass. 19.95 (0-88708-272-6, Rabbit Ears); 14.95 (0-88708-271-8, Rabbit Ears) Picture Bk Studio.

—Koi & the Kola Nuts. Reynold, illus. LC 92-7094. 40p. 1992. pap. 14.95 (0-88708-281-5, Rabbit Ears); pap. 19.95 incl. cass. (0-88708-282-3, Rabbit Ears) Picture Bk Studio.

—Paul Bunyan. Meyerowitz, Rick, illus. LC 90-8558. 32p. (gr. k up). 1991. pap. 14.95 (0-88708-142-8, Rabbit Ears); pap. 19.95 incl. cass. (0-88708-143-6, Rabbit Ears) Picture Bk Studio.

—Paul Bunyan. Meyerowitz, Rick, illus. 64p. 1993. Repr. of 1990 ed. incl. cass. 9.95 (0-88708-303-X, Rabbit Ears); 5.95 (0-88708-302-1, Rabbit Ears) Picture Bk Studio.
—The Savior Is Born. Van Nutt, Robert, illus. LC 92-4577. 40p. 1992. pap. 14.95 (0-88708-283-1, Rabbit Ears); pap. 19.95 incl. cass. (0-88708-284-X, Rabbit Ears) Picture Bk Studio.
—The Tiger & the Brahmin. Vargo, Kurt, illus. 40p. (gr. k up). 1992. pap. 14.95 (0-88708-232-7, Rabbit Ears); incl. cass. 19.95 (0-88708-233-5, Rabbit Ears) Picture Bk Studio.
Gleeson, Brian, as told by. Pecos Bill. Raglin, Tim, illus. LC 88-11581. 36p. (ps up). 1991. pap. 14.95 (0-88708-081-2, Rabbit Ears); bk. & cass. pkg. 19.95 (0-88708-086-3, Rabbit Ears) Picture Bk Studio.
Gleeson, Brian & Winters, Jonathan, eds. Paul Bunyan. Meyerowitz, Rick, illus. Kottke, Leo, contrib. by. (Illus.). 32p. (ps up). 1992. pap. write for info. slipcase pkg., incl. cassette (0-307-14325-2, 14325, Golden Pr) Western Pub.
Gleeson, Kate. Kate Gleeson's Three Little Kittens. (ps). 1993. bds. 2.25 (0-307-06122-1, Pub. by Golden Bks) Western Pub.
Gleeson, Libby. Eleanor, Elizabeth. LC 89-36009. 136p. (gr. 5-9). 1990. 13.95 (0-8234-0804-3) Holiday.
—The Great Big Scary Dog. Greder, Armin, illus. LC 93-13398. 32p. (ps up). 1994. 15.00 (0-688-11293-5, Tambourine Bks); PLB 14.93 (0-688-11294-3, Tambourine Bks) Morrow.
—Hurry Up! Vane, Mitch, illus. LC 92-21448. 1993. 3.75 (0-383-03632-1) SRA Schl Grp.
—I Am Susannah. LC 88-24568. 128p. (gr. 4-7). 1989. 12.95 (0-8234-0742-X) Holiday.
—I Am Susannah. ALC Staff, ed. 128p. (gr. 7-12). 1992. pap. 3.95 (0-688-11636-1, Pub. by Beech Tree Bks) Morrow.
—Uncle David. Greder, Armin, illus. & photos by LC 92-18155. 32p. (ps up). 1993. 15.00 (0-688-12417-8, Tambourine Bks); PLB 14.93 (0-688-12418-6, Tambourine Bks) Morrow.
—Walking to School. McClelland, Linda, illus. LC 92-31945. 1993. 2.50 (0-383-03602-X) SRA Schl Grp.
Gleit, Joyce, jt. auth. see Eckstein, Joan.
Gleiter, Jan. Benito Juarez. De Varona, Frank, intro. by. (SPA & ENG., Illus.). 32p. (gr. 3-6). 1990. PLB 15.96 (0-8172-3381-4) Raintree Steck-V.
—Color Rhymes. (Illus.). 32p. (ps-3). 1986. PLB 13.31 (0-8172-2441-6); pap. 9.27 (0-8172-2446-7) Raintree Steck-V.
—Counting Rhymes. (Illus.). 32p. (ps-3). 1986. PLB 13.31 (0-8172-2442-4); pap. 9.98 (0-8172-2447-5) Raintree Steck-V.
—Legend of Sleepy Hollow. (ps-3). 1993. pap. 3.95 (0-8114-8351-7) Raintree Steck-V.
Gleiter, Jan & Thompson, Kathleen. Annie Oakley. Miyake, Yoshi, illus. 32p. (gr. 2-5). 1986. PLB 17.96 (0-8172-2641-9) Raintree Steck-V.
—Booker T. Washington. LC 87-26325. (Illus.). 32p. (Orig.). (gr. 2-5). 1987. PLB 17.96 (0-8172-2663-X) Raintree Steck-V.
—Casey Jones. Balistreri, Francis, illus. 32p. (gr. 2-5). 1987. PLB 17.96 (0-8172-2653-2); pap. 9.27 (0-685-67542-4) Raintree Steck-V.
—Christopher Columbus. Whipple, Rick, illus. 32p. (gr. 2-5). 1986. PLB 17.96 (0-8172-2643-5); pap. text ed. 9.27 (0-8172-2647-8) Raintree Steck-V.
—Daniel Boone. LC 84-9816. (Illus.). (gr. 2-5). 1984. PLB 17.96 (0-8172-2120-4); PLB 29.28 incl. cassette (0-8172-2242-1); pap. 23.95 incl. cassette (0-8172-2273-1) Raintree Steck-V.
—Elizabeth Cady Stanton. (Illus.). 32p. (Orig.). (gr. 2-5). 1988. PLB 17.96 (0-8172-2677-X) Raintree Steck-V.
—Jack London. LC 87-23578. (Illus.). 32p. (Orig.). (gr. 2-5). 1987. PLB 17.96 (0-8172-2661-3) Raintree Steck-V.
—Jane Addams. (Illus.). 32p. (Orig.). (gr. 2-5). 1987. PLB 17.96 (0-8172-2662-1) Raintree Steck-V.
—John J. Audubon. (Illus.). 32p. (gr. 2-5). 1987. PLB 17. 96 (0-8172-2675-3) Raintree Steck-V.
—Kit Carson. Whipple, Rick, illus. 32p. (gr. 2-5). 1987. PLB 17.96 (0-8172-2650-8) Raintree Steck-V.
—Matthew Henson. (Illus.). 32p. (Orig.). (gr. 2-5). 1988. PLB 17.96 (0-8172-2676-1) Raintree Steck-V.
—Molly Pitcher. Shaw, Charles, illus. 32p. (gr. 2-5). 1987. PLB 17.96 (0-8172-2652-4) Raintree Steck-V.
—Paul Bunyan & Babe the Blue Ox. LC 84-9786. (Illus.). 32p. (gr. k-5). 1984. PLB 17.96 (0-8172-2119-0); PLB 29.28 incl. cassette (0-8172-2241-3); pap. 23.95 incl. cassette (0-8172-2272-3) Raintree Steck-V.
—Paul Revere. Balistreri, Francis, illus. 32p. (gr. 2-5). 1986. PLB 17.96 (0-8172-2644-3) Raintree Steck-V.
—Pocahontas. LC 84-9819. (Illus.). 32p. (gr. 2-5). 1984. PLB 17.96 (0-8172-2118-2); PLB 29.28 incl. cassette (0-8172-2240-5); cassette 14.00 (0-685-09501-0) Raintree Steck-V.
—Sacagawea. Miyake, Yoshi, illus. 32p. (gr. 2-5). 1987. PLB 17.96 (0-8172-2651-6) Raintree Steck-V.
—Sam Houston. LC 87-24161. (Illus.). 32p. (Orig.). (gr. 2-5). 1987. PLB 17.96 (0-8172-2660-5) Raintree Steck-V.
Gleiter, Jan, retold by. The Legend of Sleepy Hollow. Thompson, Kathleen, retold by. LC 84-9931. (Illus.). (gr. 2-5). 1984. PLB 17.96 (0-8172-2117-4); PLB 29.28 incl. cassette (0-8172-2239-1); pap. 23.95 incl. cassette (0-8172-2270-7) Raintree Steck-V.
Gleitzman, Morris. Misery Guts. LC 92-22570. 1993. 12.95 (0-15-254768-1) HarBrace.

—Two Weeks with the Queen. 144p. 1991. 14.95 (0-399-22249-9, Putnam) Putnam Pub Group.
—Two Weeks with the Queen. Bacha, Andy, illus. 144p. (gr. 3-7). 1993. pap. 3.95 (0-06-440482-X, Trophy) HarpC Child Bks.
—Worry Warts. LC 92-22631. 1993. 12.95 (0-15-299666-4) HarBrace.
Glen, Maggie. Ruby. (Illus.). 32p. (ps-3). 1991. 14.95 (0-399-22281-2, Putnam) Putnam Pub Group.
—Ruby to the Rescue. (Illus.). 32p. (ps-3). 1992. 15.95 (0-399-22149-2, Putnam) Putnam Pub Group.
Glenard East Echo Staff & Spanogle, Howard, eds. Voices of Hope: Teenagers Themselves, Pt. III. (Illus.). (gr. 7 up). 1988. 16.95 (1-55774-012-7, Dist. by Watts) Modan-Adama Bks.
Glenbard East Echo Staff, compiled by. Teenagers Themselves. Spanogle, Howard, pref. by. Spanogla, Howard, ed. LC 83-26568. (Illus.). 272p. (gr. 9-12). 1985. 16.95 (0-915361-04-3); pap. 9.95 (0-915361-33-7, 09734-X) Modan-Adama Bks.
Glendinning, Richard & Glendinning, Sally. The Ringling Brothers: Circus Family. Hutchinson, William, illus. 80p. (gr. 2-6). 1991. Repr. of 1972 ed. lib. bdg. 12.95 (0-7910-1468-1) Chelsea Hse.
Glendinning, Sally, jt. auth. see Glendinning, Richard.
Glenn, Albert. Reflections. 20p. (gr. 9-12). 1991. pap. text ed. 4.95 (1-877860-08-5) Eula Intl Pub.
Glenn, Eula M. The Struggle Continues. (Illus.). 20p. (Orig.). (gr. 5 up). 1991. pap. text ed. 4.95 (1-877860-11-5) Eula Intl Pub.
—The Struggle for Survival. 42p. (Orig.). (gr. 5 up). 1989. pap. text ed. 10.00 (1-877860-02-6) Eula Intl Pub.
—The Student Survival Handbook. 2nd ed. (Illus.). 30p. (gr. 1-12). 1990. pap. text ed. 3.95 (1-877860-06-9) Eula Intl Pub.
Glenn, George S., Jr. Start Exploring Insects: A Fact-Filled Coloring Book. Driggs, Helen, illus. 128p. (Orig.). (gr. 3 up). 1991. pap. 8.95 (1-56138-043-1) Running Pr.
Glenn, Mel. Back to Class: Poems by Mel Glenn. Bernstein, Michael J., photos by. LC 88-2835. (Illus.). 112p. (gr. 7 up). 1988. 13.95 (0-89919-656-X, Clarion Bks) HM.
—Class Dismissed! High School Poems. Bernstein, Michael, illus. LC 81-38441. 112p. 1991. pap. 5.70 (0-395-58111-7, Clarion Bks) HM.
—Class Dismissed Two: More High School Poems. Bernstein, Michael J., photos by. LC 86-2671. (Illus.). 96p. (gr. 8 up). 1986. 13.95 (0-89919-443-5, Clarion Bks) HM.
—My Friend's Got This Problem, Mr. Candler. (gr. 4-7). 1991. 14.95 (0-89919-833-3) HM.
—My Friend's Got This Problem, Mr. Chandler. 1992. write for info. (Clarion Bks) HM.
—Play-by-Play. LC 85-13990. 112p. (gr. 3-7). 1986. 12.95 (0-89919-392-7, Clarion Bks) HM.
Glenn, Monica, jt. auth. see Morrow, Roger.
Glenn, Particia B. Under Every Roof: A Kid's Study & Field Guide to the Architecture of American Houses. Stites, Joe, illus. 112p. (gr. 3-6). 1993. 16.95 (0-89133-214-6) Preservation Pr.
Glennon, Karen M. Miss Eva & the Red Balloon. Poppel, Hans, illus. LC 89-32515. 32p. (ps-3). 1990. pap. 13. 95 jacketed (0-671-68854-5, S&S BFYR) S&S Trade.
Glicksburg, Joy B. Crosswords for Language Arts. (gr. 1-5). 1985. pap. 9.95 (0-8224-2353-7) Fearon Teach Aids.
Gligor, Adrian & Strauss, Karen. Romanian Traditions & Customs. Strauss, Karen, illus. 32p. (Orig.). (gr. 4-). 1993. pap. 11.95 (0-9634797-1-7) K Strauss & A Gligor.
Gligor, Adrian, jt. auth. see Reynolds-Strauss, Karen.
Glines, Edna L. A Turtle on Her Toe. Pierpoint, Marsha W., illus. LC 83-17870. 66p. (ps up). 1984. 9.95 (0-9612160-0-X) Tumbleweed Pub Co.
Gliori, Debi. My Little Brother. Gliori, Debi, illus. LC 91-58748. 32p. (ps up). 1992. 13.95 (1-56402-079-7) Candlewick Pr.
—New Big House. Gliori, Debi, illus. LC 91-71829. 32p. (ps up). 1992. 13.95 (1-56402-036-3) Candlewick Pr.
—New Big Sister. Gliori, Debi, illus. LC 90-49272. 32p. (ps-3). 1991. SBE 12.95 (0-02-735995-6, Bradbury Pr) Macmillan Child Grp.
—When I'm Big. LC 92-43346. 1994. 3.99 (1-56402-241-2) Candlewick Pr.
Glisan, Ellen M. U. S. Constitution Text. rev. ed. (Illus.). 41p. (gr. 7-12). 1989. pap. text ed. write for info. (0-944791-92-1, SS505) Peekan Pubns.
Globe, Leah A., jt. auth. see Eisenberg, A.
Glore, John. Folktales Too. (Illus.). 52p. (Orig.). (ps up). 1991. pap. 3.50 (0-88680-352-7); royalty on application 40.00 (0-685-59140-9) I E Clark.
—Teenage Parents. (Illus.). 64p. (gr. 7 up). 1990. lib. bdg. 17.27 (0-86593-080-5); lib. bdg. 12.95.s.p. (0-685-36219-X) Rourke Corp.
Glossop, Pat. Cardinal Richelieu. (Illus.). 112p. (gr. 5 up). 1990. 17.95 (1-55546-822-5) Chelsea Hse.
Glotzbach, Gerri. Adoption. (Illus.). 64p. (gr. 7 up). 1990. lib. bdg. 17.27 (0-86593-078-3); lib. bdg. 12.95s.p. (0-685-36294-9) Rourke Corp.
Glotzbach, Gerri, et al. The Family, 6 bks. (Illus.). 384p. (gr. 7 up). 1990. Set. lib. bdg. 103.62 (0-86593-075-9); lib. bdg. 77.70s.p. (0-685-58753-3) Rourke Corp.
Glovach, Linda. The Little Witch's Birthday Book. (gr. 1-4). 1981. 7.95 (0-13-537977-6) P-H.
—Little Witch's Black Magic Book of Disguises. (gr. 1-4). 1977. (Pub. by Treehouse) pap. 3.95 (0-13-537944-X) P-H.

—Little Witch's Black Magic Book of Games. (gr. 1-4). 1973. 7.95 (0-13-537928-8) P-H.
—Little Witch's Black Magic Cookbook. Glovach, Linda, illus. (gr. 1-4). 1975. pap. 3.95 (0-13-537936-9, Pub. by Treehouse) P-H.
—The Little Witch's: Books of Toys. Glovach, Linda, illus. 48p. (gr. 2-5). 1986. 10.95 (0-13-537879-6) P-H.
—The Little Witch's Cat Book. Glovach, Linda, illus. LC 85-6513. 48p. (gr. 1-3). 1985. 9.95 (0-13-537697-1) P-H.
—The Little Witch's Christmas Book. Glovach, Linda, illus. 48p. (gr. 1-4). 1982. pap. 4.95 (0-13-538090-1, Pub. by Treehouse) P-H.
—Little Witch's Halloween Book. Glovach, Linda, illus. LC 75-11713. (gr. 1-4). 1975. 7.95 (0-13-537985-7) P-H.
—The Little Witch's Halloween Book. (Illus.). 32p. (gr. 1-4). 1983. pap. 4.95 (0-13-538116-9, Pub. by Treehouse Bks) P-H.
—The Little Witch's Summertime Book. (Illus.). 48p. (gr. 1-4). 1986. 10.95 (0-13-538018-9) P-H.
—The Little Witch's Valentine Book. (Illus.). 48p. 1984. 9.95 (0-13-538026-X) P-H.
Glovach, Linda & Glovach, Linda. The Little Witch's Dinosaur Book. (Illus.). 48p. (gr. 1-4). 1984. 8.95 (0-13-537739-0) P-H.
Glover, Danny, read by see Kipling, Rudyard.
Glover, David. Batteries, Bulbs & Wires. LC 92-40215. 32p. (gr. 1-4). 1993. 10.95 (1-85697-837-0); pap. 5.95 (1-85697-933-4) Kingfisher Bks.
—Flying & Floating. LC 92-40212. 32p. (gr. 1-4). 1993. 10.95 (1-85697-843-5); pap. 5.95 (1-85697-937-7) Kingfisher Bks.
—Solids & Liquids. LC 92-40214. 32p. (gr. 1-4). 1993. 10.95 (1-85697-845-1); pap. 5.95 (1-85697-934-2) Kingfisher Bks.
—Sound & Light. LC 92-40213. 32p. (gr. 1-4). 1993. 10. 95 (1-85697-839-7); pap. 5.95 (1-85697-935-0) Kingfisher Bks.
—The Super Science Book of Sound. Lloyd, Frances, illus 32p. 1994. 14.95 (1-56847-156-4) Thomson Lrning.
Glover, Janice. Katharine Lee Bates: Author of "America the Beautiful" Howard, Susie, illus. (Orig.). (gr. 3-7). 1993. pap. 7.95 (1-883613-00-0) Byte Size.
Glover, Susanne & Grewe, Georgeann. Bone up on Book Reports. 64p. (gr. 3-8). 1981. 7.95 (0-86653-001-0, GA 228) Good Apple.
—Bulletin Board Smorgasbord. (gr. 2-6). 1982. 9.95 (0-88160-091-1, LW 233) Learning Wks.
—Holiday Happenings. (gr. 1-4). 1982. 9.95 (0-88160-046-6, LW 231) Learning Wks.
—A Splash of Fall. Grewe, Georgeann, illus. 128p. (gr. 2-5). 1987. 11.95 (0-86653-410-5, GA1024) Good Apple.
—A Splash of Spring. Grewe, Georgeann, illus. 128p. (gr. 2-5). 1987. 11.95 (0-86653-412-1, GA1026) Good Apple.
—A Splash of Winter. Grewe, Georgeann, illus. 128p. (gr. 2-5). 1987. 11.95 (0-86653-411-3, GA1025) Good Apple.
Glover, Susanne, jt. auth. see Grewe, Georgeann.
Glover, Susanne, et al. A Bulletin Board Book for All Seasons. 64p. (gr. k-6). 1980. 7.95 (0-916456-79-X, GA 160) Good Apple.
Glover, Zebrena M., jt. auth. see Singletary, Helen P.
Glubok, Shirley. Painting. LC 93-8319. (Illus.). 256p. (gr. 4-6). 1994. SBE 24.95 (0-684-19052-4, Scribners Young Read) Macmillan.
Glubok, Shirley & Tamarin, Alfred. Olympic Games in Ancient Greece. LC 75-25408. (Illus.). 128p. (gr. 5-9). 1976. PLB 15.89 (0-06-022048-1) HarpC Child Bks.
Gluchowsky, Paul M. The Mind Program: How to Raise Your Mental Age. rev. ed. Rudd, Betty, ed. 342p. 1993. 23.95 (1-878398-13-X) Blue Note Pubns.
Glugg, Professor. The Blue Skidoo Crew. Glugg, Professor, illus. LC 92-75278. 32p. (Orig.). (ps up). 1993. pap. 3.95 (1-881905-03-9) Glue Bks.
—Flip & the Magic Wando Whip. Glugg, Professor, illus. LC 92-73552. 32p. (Orig.). (ps up). 1993. pap. 3.95 (1-881905-01-2) Glue Bks.
—Glugg-A-Lug Bug. Glugg, Professor, illus. LC 92-74768. 32p. (Orig.). (ps up). 1993. pap. 3.95 (1-881905-02-0) Glue Bks.
—Who Took Apple Frapple's Cookbook? Glugg, Professor, illus. LC 92-73242. 32p. (Orig.). (ps up). 1992. pap. 3.95 (1-881905-00-4) Glue Bks.
Gluklikh, Alexander. The Classical Collection for Guitar Tab. Stang, Aaron, ed. 48p. (Orig.). 1992. pap. text ed. 17.95 (0-89898-581-1) CPP Belwin.
Glut, D. F. The Dinosaur Dictionary. Romer, A. S. & Techter, Donald, intro. by. (Illus.). (gr. 2-6). 1985. pap. 5.98 (0-517-45589-7) Outlet Bk Co.
Glut, Donald F. The Dinosaur Dictionary. Romer, Alfred S., intro. by. (gr. 9 up). 1972. 12.50 (0-8065-0283-5, Pub. by Citadel Pr) Carol Pub Group.
Glutterbuck, Mary, illus. Man Who Never Laughed. 1987. 7.95x (0-86685-567-X) Intl Bk Ctr.
Gluzband, Cheryl. Rumble Fish - Study Guide. Friedland, Joyce & Kessler, Rikki, illus. (gr. 6-9). Date not set. pap. text ed. 14.95 (0-88122-128-7) Lrn Links.
Glyman, Caroline A. All Around the World: A Bedtime Book. (Illus.). 32p. (gr. k-3). 1994. PLB 12.95 (1-878363-77-8) Forest Hse.
—The Birthday Present. Biser, Dee, illus. 32p. (gr. k-3). 1992. PLB 12.95 (1-878363-79-4) Forest Hse.

—Learning Your ABC's of Nutrition. Biser, Dee, illus. 32p. (gr. k-3). 1992. PLB 12.95 (*1-878363-75-1*) Forest Hse.

—What's above the Sky? A Book about the Planets. Biser, Dee, illus. 32p. (gr. k-3). 1992. PLB 12.95 (*1-878363-76-X*) Forest Hse.

Gnam, Rosemarie. Let's Get to Know the Bahama Parrot. (Illus.). 20p. (gr. 1-3). 1991. write for info. (*0-9629613-0-2*) Isld Conser Effort.

Gnesios, Gregory. Whiskeytown National Recreation Area. Foreman, Ronald J. & Priehs, T. J., eds. (Illus.). 16p. (Orig.). 1993. pap. 2.95 (*1-877856-23-1*) SW Pks Mnmts.

Goaman. Animal World. Quinn, David, illus. 32p. (gr. 6up). 1984. 13.96 (*0-88110-168-0*); PLB 5.95 (*0-86020-751-X*) EDC.

Goaman, Karen, ed. see Hill.

Goble, Paul. Award Puzzles: The Girl Who Loved Wild Horses. 1991. 5.95 (*0-938971-65-4*) JTG Nashville.

—Beyond the Ridge. Goble, Paul, illus. LC 87-33113. 32p. (ps-3). 1989. RSBE 14.95 (*0-02-736581-6*, Bradbury Pr) Macmillan Child Grp.

—Beyond the Ridge. Goble, Paul, illus. LC 92-39786. 32p. (gr. k-3). 1993. pap. 4.95 (*0-689-71731-8*, Aladdin) Macmillan Child Grp.

—Brave Eagle's Account of the Fetterman Fight. LC 91-23198. (Illus.). 64p. 1992. pap. 9.95 (*0-8032-7032-1*, Bison Books) U of Nebr Pr.

—Buffalo Woman. LC 83-15704. (Illus.). 32p. (gr. k up). 1984. RSBE 14.95 (*0-02-737720-2*, Bradbury Pr) Macmillan Child Grp.

—Buffalo Woman. Goble, Paul, illus. LC 86-20573. 32p. (gr. k up). 1987. pap. 4.95 (*0-689-71109-3*, Aladdin) Macmillan Child Grp.

—Crow Chief: A Plains Indian Story. Goble, Paul, illus. LC 90-28457. 32p. (ps-2). 1992. 14.95 (*0-531-05947-2*); lib. bdg. 14.99 (*0-531-08547-3*) Orchard Bks Watts.

—Death of the Iron Horse. Goble, Paul, illus. LC 85-28011. 32p. (gr. k-3). 1987. SBE 14.95 (*0-02-737830-6*, Bradbury Pr) Macmillan Child Grp.

—Death of the Iron Horse. Goble, Paul, illus. LC 92-1723. 32p. (ps-3). 1993. pap. 4.95 (*0-689-71686-9*, Aladdin) Macmillan Child Grp.

—Dream Wolf. Goble, Paul, illus. LC 89-687. 32p. (gr. 3 up). 1990. RSBE 14.95 (*0-02-736585-9*, Bradbury Pr) Macmillan Child Grp.

—The Gift of the Sacred Dog. Goble, Paul, illus. LC 80-15843. 32p. (gr. k-2). 1982. Repr. of 1980 ed. SBE 14.95 (*0-02-736560-3*, Bradbury Pr) Macmillan Child Grp.

—Gift of the Sacred Dog. LC 87-14817. (gr. k-3). 1984. pap. 4.95 (*0-02-043280-1*, Aladdin) Macmillan Child Grp.

—The Girl Who Loved Wild Horses. Goble, Paul, illus. LC 77-20500. 32p. (gr. k-3). 1982. SBE 14.95 (*0-02-736570-0*, Bradbury Pr) Macmillan Child Grp.

—The Girl Who Loved Wild Horses. Goble, Paul, illus. LC 92-29560. 32p. (ps-3). 1993. pap. 4.95 (*0-689-71696-6*, Aladdin) Macmillan Child Grp.

—The Great Race. LC 85-4202. (Illus.). 32p. (ps-2). 1985. RSBE 14.95 (*0-02-736950-1*, Bradbury Pr) Macmillan Child Grp.

—The Great Race. LC 90-39983. (Illus.). 32p. (gr. k-3). 1991. pap. 4.95 (*0-689-71452-1*, Aladdin) Macmillan Child Grp.

—Her Seven Brothers. LC 86-31776. (Illus.). 32p. 1988. RSBE 14.95 (*0-02-737960-4*, Bradbury Pr) Macmillan Child Grp.

—Her Seven Brothers. Goble, Paul, illus. LC 92-40562. 32p. (gr. k-3). 1993. pap. 4.95 (*0-689-71730-X*, Aladdin) Macmillan Child Grp.

—I Sing for the Animals. Goble, Paul, illus. LC 90-19812. 32p. 1991. 9.95 (*0-02-737725-3*, Bradbury Pr) Macmillan Child Grp.

—The Lost Children. Goble, Paul, illus. LC 91-44283. 40p. (gr-12). 1993. SBE 14.95 (*0-02-736555-7*, Bradbury Pr) Macmillan Child Grp.

—The Love Flute. Goble, Paul, illus. LC 91-19716. 32p. (ps up). 1992. SBE 14.95 (*0-02-736261-2*, Bradbury Pr) Macmillan Child Grp.

—Love Flute. Goble, Paul, illus. (gr. k-4). 1993. 14.95 (*0-685-64813-3*); audiocassette 11.00 (*1-882869-80-X*) Read Advent.

—Red Hawk's Account of Custer's Last Battle. Goble, Paul, illus. LC y1-231701. 64p. 1992. pap. 9.95 (*0-8032-7033-X*, Bison Books) U of Nebr Pr.

—Star Boy. Goble, Paul, illus. LC 82-20599. 32p. (gr. k up). 1983. SBE 14.95 (*0-02-722660-3*, Bradbury Pr) Macmillan Child Grp.

—Star Boy. Goble, Paul, illus. LC 91-8694. 32p. (gr. k-3). 1991. pap. 4.95 (*0-689-71499-8*, Aladdin) Macmillan Child Grp.

Goble, Paul, retold by. & illus. Iktomi & the Berries: A Plains Indian Story. LC 88-23353. 32p. (ps-2). 1989. 14.95 (*0-531-05819-0*); PLB 14.99 (*0-531-08419-1*) Orchard Bks Watts.

—Iktomi & the Berries: A Plains Indian Story. LC 88-23353. 32p. (ps-2). 1992. pap. 5.95 (*0-531-07029-8*) Orchard Bks Watts.

—Iktomi & the Boulder: A Plains Indian Story. LC 87-35789. 32p. (ps-2). 1988. 14.95 (*0-531-05760-7*); PLB 14.99 (*0-531-08360-8*) Orchard Bks Watts.

—Iktomi & the Boulder: A Plains Indian Story. LC 87-35789. 32p. (ps-2). 1991. pap. 4.95 (*0-531-07023-9*) Orchard Bks Watts.

Goble, Paul, as told by. & illus. Iktomi & the Buffalo Skull: A Plains Indian Story. LC 90-7716. 32p. (ps-2). 1991. 14.95 (*0-531-05911-1*); PLB 14.99 (*0-531-08511-2*) Orchard Bks Watts.

Goble, Paul, retold by. Iktomi & the Buzzard: A Plains Indian Story. LC 93-24872. (Illus.). 1994. write for info. (*0-531-06812-9*); PLB write for info. (*0-531-08662-3*) Orchard Bks Watts.

Goble, Paul, retold by. & illus. Iktomi & the Ducks: A Plains Indian Story. LC 89-71025. 32p. (ps-1). 1990. 14.95 (*0-531-05883-2*); PLB 14.99 (*0-531-08483-3*) Orchard Bks Watts.

—Iktomi & the Ducks: A Plains Indians Story. LC 89-71025. 32p. (ps-1). 1994. pap. 5.95 (*0-531-07044-1*) Orchard Bks Watts.

Goble, Paul, illus. Adopted by the Eagles. LC 93-24247. 1994. write for info. (*0-02-736575-1*, Bradbury Pr) Macmillan Child Grp.

Goc, Michael J. Stewards of the Wisconsin, the Wisconsin Valley Improvement Company. (Illus.). 152p. 1993. 29.95 (*0-938627-19-8*) New Past Pr.

Gockel, Herman W. & Saleska, Edward J., eds. Child's Garden of Prayer. (Illus.). (gr. k-2). 1981. pap. 2.99 (*0-570-03412-4*, 56-1016) Concordia.

Godbeer, Deardre. Somalia. (Illus.). 96p. (gr. 5 up). 1988. LC 91-70919. 4.95 (*0-7910-0119-9*) Chelsea Hse.

Goddard, Carrie L. My Jesus Storybook. 32p. (Orig.). 1994. 5.95 (*0-687-19924-7*) Abingdon.

Goddard, Jerome. Mystery at Eastport Cove. LC 91-61636. 130p. (gr. 4-8). 1991. pap. 3.50 (*0-9630609-0-2*) Robins Cliff.

Godden, Rumer. Candy Floss. Hogrogian, Nonny, illus. 64p. (ps-3). 1991. 16.95 (*0-399-21807-6*, Philomel) Putnam Pub Group.

—The Doll's House. LC 62-18693. (ps-3). 1976. pap. 3.99 (*0-14-030942-X*, Puffin) Puffin Bks.

—An Episode of Sparrows. 208p. (gr. 7 up). 1989. pap. 4.95 (*0-14-034024-6*, Puffin) Puffin Bks.

—Four Dolls. Baynes, Pauline, illus. LC 83-14157. 144p. (gr. 4-6). 1984. reinforced 13.00 (*0-688-02801-2*) Greenwillow.

—Four Dolls. (gr. 3-7). 1986. pap. 4.95 (*0-440-42568-9*) Dell.

—Fu-Dog. Littlewood, Valerie, illus. 64p. (ps-2). 1990. pap. 14.95 (*0-670-82300-7*) Viking Child Bks.

—Great Grandfather's House. Littlewood, Valerie, illus. LC 91-48030. 80p. (gr. 1 up). 1993. 18.00 (*0-688-11319-2*) Greenwillow.

—Greengage Summer. 206p. (gr. 7 up). 1986. pap. 3.95 (*0-14-031982-4*, Puffin) Puffin Bks.

—Listen to the Nightingale. 192p. (gr. 5 up). 1992. 15.00 (*0-670-84517-5*) Viking Child Bks.

—Little Plum. LC 86-43078. (Illus.). 112p. (gr. 2-6). 1987. pap. 3.95 (*0-14-030737-0*, Puffin) Puffin Bks.

—Miss Happiness & Miss Flower. LC 86-43077. (Illus.). 88p. (gr. 2-6). 1987. pap. 3.95 (*0-14-030273-5*, Puffin) Puffin Bks.

—The Peacock Spring. 286p. (gr. 7 up). 1986. pap. 3.95 (*0-14-032005-9*, Penguin Bks) Viking Penguin.

—The Rocking Horse Secret. Smith, Juliet S., photos by. (gr. 3-7). 1988. pap. 3.95 (*0-317-69650-5*, Puffin) Puffin Bks.

—The Rocking Horse Secret. (gr. 2-6). 1992. 16.50 (*0-8446-6568-1*) Peter Smith.

—The Story of Holly & Ivy. Cooney, Barbara, illus. LC 84-25799. 32p. (ps-5). 1985. pap. 15.00 (*0-670-80622-6*) Viking Child Bks.

—The Story of Holly & Ivy. Cooney, Barbara, illus. (gr. k-5). 1987. pap. 4.99 (*0-14-050723-X*, Puffin) Puffin Bks.

—Thursday's Children. (gr. k-12). 1987. pap. 3.25 (*0-440-98790-3*, LFL) Dell.

Godden, Rumer, tr. see Bernos de Gasztold, Carmen.

Godfrey, Martyn. Fire! Fire! 96p. (gr. 7-12). 1986. pap. text ed. 4.50 (*0-8219-0233-4*, 35360); 1.20 (*0-8219-0234-2*, 35719) EMC.

—Ice Hawk. 96p. (gr. 7-12). 1986. pap. text ed. 4.50 (*0-8219-0235-0*, 35361); 1.20 (*0-8219-0236-9*, 35720) EMC.

—The Last War. LC 88-11459. (Illus.). 96p. (Orig.). (gr. 5 up). 1989. pap. 2.95 (*0-02-041791-8*, Collier Young Ad) Macmillan Child Grp.

—Please Remove Your Elbow from My Ear. 128p. (Orig.). 1993. pap. 3.50 (*0-380-76580-2*, Flare) Avon.

Godfrey, Martyn N. The Great Science Fair Disaster. 1992. pap. 2.95 (*0-590-44081-0*, Apple Paperbacks) Scholastic Inc.

Godfrey, Neale S. The Kid's Money Book. Novak, Justin, illus. 128p. (gr. 3 up). 1991. 12.95 (*1-56288-002-0*) Checkerboard.

Godkin, Celia. What About Ladybugs. LC 93-4202. (gr. 1-8). 1994. write for info. (*0-87156-549-8*) Sierra.

—Wolf Island. (ps-3). 1993. 15.95 (*0-7167-6513-6*) W H Freeman.

Godlewski, Lorraine, et al. Preparing for the Science RCT. (Illus., Orig.). 1987. wkbk. 3.45 (*0-937323-08-X*) United Pub Co.

Godlington, Douglas. Skiing. (Illus.). 80p. (gr. 7 up). 1991. pap. 6.95 (*0-7063-6823-1*, Pub. by Ward Lock UK) Sterling.

—Skiing. rev. ed. (Illus.). 80p. (gr. 10-12). 1993. pap. 7.95 (*0-7137-2411-0*, Pub. by Blandford Pr UK) Sterling.

Godman, Arthur. Energy Supply A-Z. LC 90-34909. 144p. (gr. 6 up). 1991. lib. bdg. 18.95 (*0-89490-262-8*) Enslow Pubs.

—Illustrated Dictionary of Science in English with English-Arabic & Arabic-English Glossaries. (gr. 8-12). 1982. 15.00x (*0-86685-354-5*) Intl Bk Ctr.

Godreau, Cecile. Call Me Jonathan for Short. Peterson, Mary J., illus. 64p. (gr. 4-5). 1991. pap. 2.95 (*0-8198-1463-6*) St Paul Bks.

Godsey, Kyle. Object Lessons about God. 96p. (Orig.). (gr. 3-6). 1991. pap. 5.99 (*0-8010-3841-3*) Baker Bk.

Godwin, Jeff. Dancing with Demons: The Music's Real Master. LC 88-90860. (Illus.). 352p. (Orig.). (gr. 7-12). 1988. pap. 10.50 (*0-937958-28-X*) Chick Pubns.

—What's Wrong with Christian Rock? LC 90-85347. (Illus.). (gr. 7-12). 1990. pap. 8.95 (*0-937958-36-0*) Chick Pubns.

Godwin, Patricia. I Feel Orange Today. Macaulay, Kitty, illus. 24p. 1993. lib. bdg. 14.95 (*1-55037-284-X*, Pub. by Annick CN); pap. 4.95 (*1-55037-285-8*, Pub. by Annick CN) Firefly Bks Ltd.

Goedecke, Christopher J. The Wind Warrior: The Training of a Karate Champion. Hauserr, Rosmarie, illus. LC 91-6405. 64p. (gr. 4-5). 1992. RSBE 15.95 (*0-02-736262-0*, Four Winds) Macmillan Child Grp.

Goennel, Heidi. The Circus. LC 91-448. (Illus.). 32p. (ps-3). 1992. 15.00 (*0-688-10883-0*, Tambourine Bks); PLB 14.93 (*0-688-10884-9*, Tambourine Bks) Morrow.

—Colors, Vol. 1. (ps-4). 1990. 15.95 (*0-316-31843-4*) Little.

—Heidi's Zoo: An Un-Alphabet Book. Goennel, Heidi, illus. LC 92-16367. 32p. (gr. 1 up). 1993. 16.00 (*0-688-12109-8*, Tambourine Bks); PLB 15.93 (*0-688-12110-1*, Tambourine Bks) Morrow.

—It's My Birthday. Goennel, Heidi, illus. LC 91-30231. 32p. (ps-1). 1992. 14.00 (*0-688-11421-0*, Tambourine Bks); PLB 13.93 (*0-688-11422-9*, Tambourine Bks) Morrow.

—My Dog. LC 88-38706. (Illus.). 32p. (ps-1). 1989. 14.95 (*0-531-05834-4*); PLB 14.99 (*0-531-08434-5*) Orchard Bks Watts.

—Odds & Evens: A Numbers Book. Goennel, Heidi, illus. LC 93-15420. 32p. 1994. 15.00 (*0-688-12918-8*, Tambourine Bks); PLB 14.93 (*0-688-12919-6*, Tambourine Bks) Morrow.

—Sometimes I Like to Be Alone. Goennel, Heidi, illus. LC 88-30780. (gr. k-2). 1989. 14.95 (*0-316-31842-6*) Little.

—While I Am Little. Goennel, Heidi, illus. LC 92-36795. 32p. (ps up). 1993. 14.00 (*0-688-12371-6*, Tambourine Bks); PLB 13.93 (*0-688-12372-4*, Tambourine Bks) Morrow.

Goepfert, Laura P. Re Tell Stories: From Words to Conversation with Meaning. Goepfert, Laura P., illus. 50p. (ps-2). 1986. 16.95 (*0-937857-02-5*, 1441) Speech Bln.

Goes. Das Brandopfer. (gr. 7-12). pap. 5.95 (*0-88436-057-1*, 45274) EMC.

Goetz, Bracha. Nicanor Knew the Secret. Zakutinsky, Ruth, ed. Nodel, Norman, illus. 32p. (gr. 3). 1992. PLB 6.95 (*0-911643-14-1*) Aura Bklyn.

—Noah's Noisy Ark. Zakutinsky, Ruth, ed. Friedman, Aaron, illus. 32p. (gr. 1-4). 1992. PLB 6.95 (*0-911643-13-3*) Aura Bklyn.

Goetzmann, William H., jt. auth. see Flaherty, Leo.

Goetzmann, William H., ed. World Explorers Series, 32 vols. Collins, Michael, intro. by. (Illus.). 3696p. (gr. 5 up). 1993. Set lib. bdg. 625.35 (*0-7910-1290-5*, Am Art Analog) Chelsea Hse.

Goetzmann, William H., ed. see Allen, John L.

Goetzmann, William H., ed. see Bernhard, Brendan.

Goetzmann, William H., ed. see Brown, Warren.

Goetzmann, William H., ed. see Cavan, Seamus.

Goetzmann, William H., ed. see Coulter, Tony.

Goetzmann, William H., ed. see Dodge, Steven C.

Goetzmann, William H., ed. see Dolan, Terrance.

Goetzmann, William H., ed. see Gaines, Ann.

Goetzmann, William H., ed. see Gaines, Richard.

Goetzmann, William H., ed. see Haney, David.

Goetzmann, William H., ed. see Harris, Edward D.

Goetzmann, William H., ed. see Kennedy, Gregory P.

Goetzmann, William H., ed. see Moulton, Gary.

Goetzmann, William H., ed. see Smith, Alice.

Goetzmann, William H., ed. see Stallones, Jared.

Goetzmann, William H., ed. see Stefoff, Rebecca.

Goetzmann, William H., ed. see Whitman, Sylvia.

Goetzmann, William H., ed. see Wolfe, Cheri.

Gofen, Ethel C. Argentina. LC 90-23159. (Illus.). 128p. (gr. 5-9). 1991. PLB 21.95 (*1-85435-381-0*) Marshall Cavendish.

Goff, Beth. Where Is Daddy? The Story of a Divorce. Perl, Susan, illus. LC 69-14608. 32p. (ps-k). 1969. pap. 4.95 (*0-8070-2305-1*, BP 694) Beacon Pr.

Goff, Denise. Early China. (Illus.). 32p. (gr. 4-6). 1991. 13.95 (*0-237-60169-9*, Pub. by Evans Bros Ltd) Trafalgar.

Goff, Georgeanna, jt. auth. see Guth, Phyllis.

Goffe, Toni. Bully for You. LC 91-9891. (gr. 4 up). 1991. 7.95 (*0-85953-365-4*); pap. 3.95 (*0-85953-355-7*) Childs Play.

—Charm School. LC 91-32061. 1992. 7.95 (*0-85953-367-0*); pap. 3.95 (*0-85953-357-3*) Childs Play.

—Giant That Sneezed. (ps-3). 1993. pap. 11.95 (*0-85953-927-X*) Childs Play.

—Joe Giant's Missing Boot. 32p. 1990. 12.95 (*0-688-09532-1*); PLB 12.88 (*0-688-09533-X*) Lothrop.

—Ma, You're Driving Me Crazy! LC 92-40565. 1993. 5.95 (*0-85953-401-4*) Childs Play.

—The President. LC 92-259. 1992. 7.95 (*0-85953-787-0*); pap. 3.95 (*0-85953-788-9*) Childs Play.

—Relax. (ps-3). 1993. 7.95 (*0-85953-789-7*) Childs Play.

—War & Peace. LC 91-18197. (gr. 4 up). 1991. 7.95 (*0-85953-366-2*); pap. 3.95 (*0-85953-356-5*) Childs Play.

Goffe, Toni, illus. How to Be Rich. LC 93-9575. 1993. 5.95 (*0-85953-405-7*) Childs Play.
—The Monster. LC 93-21862. (ps-3). 1993. 5.95 (*0-85953-406-5*) Childs Play.
—No Smoking: Do You Mind If I Don't Smoke? LC 92-10849. 1992. 7.95 (*0-85953-782-X*, Pub. by Child's Play UK); pap. 3.95 (*0-85953-783-8*, Pub. by Childs Play UK) Childs Play.
—President Citizen. LC 92-10848. 1992. 7.95 (*0-85953-368-9*); pap. 3.95 (*0-85953-369-7*) Childs Play.

Goffin, Jeffrey. My Gun Is Pink. (Illus.). 32p. (Orig.). (gr. 6 up). 1987. pap. 3.50 (*0-88680-280-6*); royalty on application 35.00 I E Clark.
Goffin, Josse. OH! (Illus.). 28p. 1991. 14.95 (*0-8109-3660-7*) Abrams.
—Who Is the Boss? Goffin, Josse, illus. 32p. (gr. k-3). 1992. 13.45 (*0-395-61192-X*, Clarion Bks) HM.
—Yes. LC 92-54430. (ps-3). 1993. 13.00 (*0-688-12375-9*) Lothrop.

Goffin, Josse, illus. Silent Christmas. LC 90-83430. 32p. (ps-k). 1991. 14.95 (*1-878093-08-8*) Boyds Mills Pr.

Goffstein, Brooke. An Actor. Goffstein, Brooke, illus. LC 87-165. 32p. (ps up). 1987. HarpC Child Bks.

Goffstein, M. B. An Artists Album. Goffstein, M. B., illus. LC 85-42612. 48p. (ps up). 1985. HarpC Child Bks.
—Fish for Supper. LC 75-27598. (Illus.). 32p. (gr. k-2). 1976. PLB 9.89 (*0-8037-2572-8*) Dial Bks Young.
—Fish for Supper. Goffstein, M. B., illus. LC 75-27598. 32p. (ps-2). 1986. pap. 3.95 (*0-8037-0284-1*) Dial Bks Young.
—Goldie the Dollmaker. LC 79-85369. (Illus.). 64p. (ps up). 1985. pap. 3.45 (*0-374-42740-2*) FS&G.
—Our Snowman. LC 85-45836. (Illus.). 32p. (ps up). 1986. HarpC Child Bks.

Gogol, Nicolai. The Nose. Cowan, Catherine, retold by. Hawkes, Kevin, illus. LC 93-4975. 1995. write for info. (*0-688-10464-9*); PLB write for info. (*0-688-10465-7*) Lothrop.

Gogol, Nikolai V. Dead Souls. Girling, Z., intro. by. (gr. 11 up). 1966. pap. 1.75 (*0-8049-0122-8*, CL-122) Airmont.

Gogol, Sara. Vatsana's Lucky New Year. LC 92-11243. 1992. 18.95 (*0-8225-0734-X*) Lerner Pubns.

Gohier, Francois. Humpback Whales. Leon, Vicki, ed. (Illus.). 40p. (Orig.). (gr. 5 up). 1990. pap. 7.95 (*0-918303-26-5*) Blake Pub.
—A Pod of Gray Whales. (Illus.). 40p. (Orig.). (gr. 5 up). 1987. pap. 7.95 (*0-918303-14-1*) Blake Pub.

Goin, Kenn, et al. Bugs to Bunnies: Hands-on Animal Science Activities for Young Children. (Illus.). 192p. (Orig.). (gr. k-2). 1989. pap. text ed. 14.95 (*0-943129-03-6*) Chatterbox Pr.

Going, Nancy. Boosting Self-Esteem. 48p. (Orig.). (gr. 6-8). 1990. pap. 7.99 (*1-55945-100-9*) Group Pub.
—Materialism. (Illus.). 48p. (gr. 6-8). 1992. pap. 7.99 (*1-55945-130-0*) Group Pub.

Goins, Barbara L. Penny Pinching Art. Goldfluss, Karen J., ed. Fullam, Sue, illus. 96p. (gr. k-6). 1993. PLB 9.95 wkbk. (*1-55734-139-7*) Tchr Create Mat.

Golant, Mitch & Crane, Bob. It's O.K. to Be Different. 128p. (gr. 1-5). 1988. pap. 4.95 (*0-8125-9462-2*) Tor Bks.

Golay, Michael. The Civil War. Bowman, John, ed. (Illus.). 192p. (gr. 6-12). 1992. lib. bdg. 17.95x (*0-8160-2514-2*) Facts on File.

Gold, Auner. The Marrano Prince. Hinlicky, Gregg, illus. 286p. (gr. 9-12). 1988. 13.95 (*0-935063-39-0*); text ed. 10.95 (*0-935063-40-4*) CIS Comm.
—The Purple Ring. Hinlicky, Gregg, illus. 191p. (gr. 9-12). 1986. 10.95 (*0-935063-16-1*); pap. 8.95 (*0-935063-15-3*) CIS Comm.

Gold, Avie. The ArtScroll Youth Pirkei Avos, 2 vols. Halasz, Andras & Horen, Michael, illus. 48p. (gr. 3-12). 1989. 15.95 ea. (*0-89906-244-X*); 12.95 ea. (*0-89906-245-8*) Mesorah Pubns.

Gold, Avie, ed. see Scherman, Nosson & Zlotowitz, Meir.

Gold, Avner. The Dream. Reinman, Y. Y., ed. Hinlicky, G., illus. 112p. (gr. 7-11). 1983. pap. 7.95 (*0-935063-01-3*) CIS Comm.
—Envoy from Vienna. Hinlicky, Gregg, contrib. by. 185p. (gr. 9-12). 1986. 10.95 (*0-935063-22-6*); pap. 8.95 (*0-935063-21-8*) CIS Comm.
—The Impostor. Reinman, Y. Y., ed. LC 85-72405. 192p. (gr. 5 up). 1985. 9.95 (*0-935063-14-5*); pap. 7.95 (*0-935063-13-7*) CIS Comm.
—The Promised Child. Reinman, Y. Y., ed. Hinlicky, G., illus. LC 85-72493. 128p. (gr. 7-11). 1985. 9.95 (*0-935063-10-2*); pap. 7.95 (*0-935063-00-5*) CIS Comm.
—Twilight. Reinman, Y. Y., ed. Hinklicky, G., illus. LC 85-72404. 128p. (gr. 7-11). 1985. 9.95 (*0-935063-11-0*); pap. 7.95 (*0-935063-03-X*) CIS Comm.
—The Year of the Sword. Reinman, Y. Y., ed. Hinlicky, G., illus. 112p. (gr. 5 up). 1984. pap. 7.95 (*0-935063-02-1*) CIS Comm.

Gold, John C. Board of Education vs. Pico (1982) Book Banning. LC 93-23487. 1994. write for info. (*0-02-736272-8*, New Discovery Bks) Macmillan Child Grp.

Gold, Maria, jt. auth. see Gold, Stephen.

Gold, Mary C. Teaching Reading in the Social Studies: A Global Approach for K-5. rev. ed. (Illus.). 106p. (Orig.). (gr. k-5). 1991. pap. 21.95 (*0-943804-29-9*) U of Denver Teach.

Gold, Mike, ed. see Kane, Bob, et al.

Gold, Phyllis. Please Don't Say Hello: Living with Childhood Autism. Baker, Carl, photos by. LC 74-13185. (Illus.). 48p. (gr. 1-5). 1975. 14.95 (*0-87705-211-5*); pap. 9.95 (*0-89885-199-8*) Human Sci Pr.

Gold, Porter. Who's There? (Illus.). 32p. (gr. 1-4). 1989. PLB 15.96 (*0-8172-3514-0*); pap. 3.95 (*0-8114-6717-1*) Raintree Steck-V.

Gold, Robert S. Point of Departure. (gr. 7-12). 1981. pap. 2.75 (*0-685-01409-6*, LE) Dell.
—Stepping Stones: Seventeen Powerful Stories of Growing Up. 320p. (gr. 7 up). 1981. pap. 3.25 (*0-440-98269-3*, LFL) Dell.

Gold, Sharlya & Caspi, Mishael M. The Answered Prayer: And Other Yemenite Folktales. Wunsch, Marjory, illus. 80p. (gr. 3-5). 1990. 13.95 (*0-8276-0354-1*) JPS Phila.

Gold, Stephen & Gold, Maria. Earthquakes! LC 92-18190. (Illus.). 32p. (Orig.). (gr. k-4). 1992. pap. 4.95 (*0-89334-155-X*) Humanics Ltd.

Gold, Susan D. Countdown to the Moon. LC 91-30360. (Illus.). 48p. (gr. 5-6). 1992. RSBE 12.95 (*0-89686-689-0*, Crestwood Hse) Macmillan Child Grp.
—The Kennedy Space Center: Gateway to Space. LC 91-42566. (Illus.). 48p. (gr. 5-6). 1992. RSBE 12.95 (*0-89686-690-4*, Crestwood Hse) Macmillan Child Grp.
—Pharaohs Curse. LC 89-25424. (Illus.). 48p. (gr. 5 up). 1990. RSBE 11.95 (*0-89686-511-8*, Crestwood Hse) Macmillan Child Grp.
—To Space & Back: The Story of the Shuttle. LC 91-42565. (Illus.). 48p. (gr. 5-6). 1992. RSBE 12.95 (*0-89686-688-2*, Crestwood Hse) Macmillan Child Grp.
—Toxic Waste. LC 90-36295. (Illus.). 48p. (gr. 5-6). 1990. RSBE 12.95 (*0-89686-542-8*, Crestwood Hse) Macmillan Child Grp.

Gold, Yeshara. Hurry, Friday's a Short Day: One Boy's Erev Shabbat in Jerusalem's Old City. (Illus.). 32p. (gr. 3-8). 1986. 10.95 (*0-89906-800-6*); pap. 7.95 (*0-89906-801-4*) Mesorah Pubns.
—Just a Week to Go: One Boy's Pesach Preparations in Jerusalem's Old City. (Illus.). 32p. (gr. 3-8). 1987. 10.95 (*0-89906-802-2*); pap. 7.95 (*0-89906-803-0*) Mesorah Pubns.

Goldberg, Bob. Diving Basics. Seiden, Art, illus. 48p. (gr. 3-7). 1986. 10.95 (*0-13-215963-5*) P-H.

Goldberg, Jake. Economics & the Environment. (Illus.). 112p. (gr. 5 up). 1993. PLB 19.95 (*0-7910-1594-7*); pap. write for info. (*0-7910-1619-6*) Chelsea Hse.
—Hispanics of Achievement, 33 vols. (Illus.). 1993. Set. PLB write for info. (Am Art Analog) Chelsea Hse.
—Rachel Carson. (Illus.). 72p. (gr. 3-5). 1991. lib. bdg. 12.95 (*0-7910-1566-1*) Chelsea Hse.

Goldberg, Larry. Dear Mr. Rainbows, 1994. Wolf, Barbara & Waldron, Shirley, illus. LC 93-72611. 112p. (Orig.). (gr. 2-6). 1993. pap. 9.95 (*0-9638457-0-5*) Blue-Black.

Goldberg, Michael. Breaking New Ground: American Women, 1800-1848. (Illus.). 144p. 1994. PLB 20.00 (*0-19-508202-8*) OUP.

Goldberg, Minerva J., jt. auth. see Jones, William E.

Goldberg, Moses. Aladdin: A Participation Play. 1977. 4.50 (*0-87602-001-1*) Anchorage.
—The Analysis of Mineral Number Four. (Orig.). (gr. 4 up). 1982. playscript 4.50 (*0-87602-234-4*) Anchorage.
—The Men's Cottage. (Orig.). (gr. 4 up). 1980. playscript 4.50 (*0-87602-229-8*) Anchorage.
—The Outlaw Robin Hood. 1967. 4.50 (*0-87602-168-2*) Anchorage.
—Puss in Boots: (A Participation Play) (Orig.). 1991. Playscript. pap. 4.50 (*0-87602-299-9*) Anchorage.
—Rumpelstiltskin: A Participation Play. (gr. k-3). 1987. pap. 4.50 playscript (*0-87602-269-7*) Anchorage.
—The Wind in the Willows. (gr. 1-7). 1974. 4.50 (*0-87602-220-4*) Anchorage.

Goldberg, Nathan. The New Illustrated Hebrew-English Dictionary for Young Readers. (HEB & ENG., Illus.). (gr. 4-7). 1958. pap. 6.95x (*0-87068-370-5*) Ktav.

Goldberg, Steve. Pholdit. (gr. 3 up). 1972. 6.50 (*0-918932-67-X*) Activity Resources.

Goldberg, Sue & Altman, Joyce. Dear Bronx Zoo. Falk, Douglas, frwd. by. LC 89-28226. (Illus.). 144p. (gr. 3 up). 1990. SBE 14.95 (*0-02-700640-9*, Macmillan Child Bk) Macmillan Child Grp.

Goldberg, Sue, jt. auth. see Altman, Joyce.

Goldberg, Whoopi. Alice. Rocco, John, illus. LC 92-15935. 48p. 1992. 15.00 (*0-553-08990-0*) Bantam.

Goldberg, Whoopi, narrated by see Jones, Malcolm.

Golden, Joseph. Johnny Moonbeam & the Silver Arrow. 1962. 4.50 (*0-87602-144-5*) Anchorage.

Golden, Michael. Celebrating Cultural Diversity: A Study Guide. (gr. 5-8). 1991. pap. text ed. 19.95 (*0-88122-689-0*) LRN Links.
—The Devil's Arithmetic: A Study Guide. Friedland, J. & Kessler, K., eds. 29p. (gr. 4-7). 1992. pap. text ed. 14.95 (*0-88122-697-1*) Lrn Links.
—Interstellar Pig: A Study Guide. Friedland, Joyce & Kessler, Rikki, eds. (gr. 6-9). 1991. pap. text ed. 14.95 (*0-88122-584-3*) LRN Links.

—Journeying Through the Middle Ages: A Study Guide. (gr. 5-8). 1991. pap. text ed. 19.95 (*0-88122-687-4*) LRN Links.
—Traveling Through Time & Space: A Study Guide. (gr. 5-8). 1991. pap. text ed. 19.95 (*0-88122-563-0*) LRN Links.
—Where the Red Fern Grows - Study Guide. Friedland, Joyce & Kessler, Rikki, eds. (gr. 6-8). Date not set. pap. text ed. 14.95 (*0-88122-034-5*) Lrn Links.

Golden, N., retold by see Gruelle, Johnny.

Golden, Nora. Comical Celtic Cat. (gr. 1 up). 1984. 13.95 (*0-85105-901-5*, Pub. by Colin Smythe Ltd Britain) Dufour.

Golden, Silvia. The King's Forest. Eichenauer, Gabriele G., illus. 1988. 14.95 (*0-86315-085-3*, 20247) Gryphon Hse.

Goldenman, Gretta, ed. see Rifas, Leonard.

Goldentyer, Debra. Dropping Out of School. LC 93-14251. (Illus.). 80p. (gr. 6-9). 1993. PLB 21.34 (*0-8114-3526-1*) Raintree Steck-V.
—Gangs. LC 93-14227. (Illus.). 80p. (gr. 6-9). 1993. PLB 21.34 (*0-8114-3527-X*) Raintree Steck-V.

Golder, Stephen & Memling, Lise. Buffy's Orange Leash. Ramsey, Marcy, illus. 32p. (gr. k-3). 9.95 (*1-878363-23-9*) Forest Hse.

Goldfarb, Mace. Fighters, Refugees, Immigrants: A Story of the Hmong. LC 82-4370. (Illus.). 48p. (gr. 4 up). 1982. lib. bdg. 13.50 (*0-87614-197-1*) Carolrhoda Bks.

Goldfluss, Karen, ed. see Hollis, Barbara.

Goldfluss, Karen J. & Sima, Patricia M. Inventions. Vasconcelles, Keith, et al, illus. 80p. (gr. 4-6). 1993. wkbk. 7.95 (*1-55734-232-6*) Tchr Create Mat.

Goldfluss, Karen J., ed. see Goins, Barbara L.

Goldfluss, Karen J., et al, eds. see Guerette, Doris J.

Goldhagen, Nancy P. Parole Crociate Per Gli Studenti. (ITA., Illus.). 48p. (gr. 3 up). 1983. 6.50 (*0-8442-8021-6*, Passport Bks) NTC Pub Grp.

Goldin, Augusta. Ducks Don't Get Wet. new ed. Kessler, Leonard, illus. LC 88-18073. 32p. (ps-3). 1989. (Crowell Jr Bks); PLB 13.89 (*0-690-04782-7*, Crowell Jr Bks) HarpC Child Bks.
—Ducks Don't Get Wet. rev. ed. Kessler, Leonard, illus. LC 88-18073. 32p. (ps-3). 1989. pap. 4.95 (*0-06-445082-1*, Trophy) HarpC Child Bks.
—Small Energy Sources: Choices That Work. LC 87-167. (Illus.). 178p. (gr. 7 up). 1988. 17.95 (*0-15-276215-9*, HB Juv Bks) HarBrace.
—Straight Hair, Curly Hair. Emberley, Ed E., illus. LC 66-12669. 40p. (gr. k-3). 1966. PLB 13.89 (*0-690-77921-6*, Crowell Jr Bks) HarpC Child Bks.

Goldin, Barbara. A Child's Book of Midrash: Fifty-Two Jewish Stories from the Sages. LC 90-39598. 124p. 1992. 25.00 (*0-87668-837-7*) Aronson.

Goldin, Barbara D. Cakes & Miracles: A Purim Tale. Weihs, Erika, illus. LC 92-25848. 1993. pap. 4.99 (*0-14-054871-8*) Puffin Bks.
—Cakes & Miracles: A Purin Tale. Weihs, Erika, illus. (ps-3). 1991. 15.00 (*0-670-83047-X*) Viking Child Bks.
—Fire! The Beginnings of the Labor Movement. Watling, James, illus. 64p. (gr. 2-6). 1992. RB 13.00 (*0-670-84475-6*) Viking Child Bks.
—Just Enough Is Plenty: A Hannukah Tale. Chwast, Seymour, illus. (ps-3). 1988. pap. 12.95 (*0-670-81852-6*) Viking Child Bks.
—Just Enough Is Plenty, a Hanukkah Tale. (ps-3). 1990. pap. 3.95 (*0-14-050787-6*, Puffin) Puffin Bks.
—The Magician's Visit: A Passover Tale. Parker, Robert A., illus. LC 92-22903. 34p. 1993. 14.99 (*0-670-84840-9*) Viking Child Bks.
—The Passover Journey: A Seder Companion. Waldman, Neil, illus. LC 93-5133. 64p. 1994. 15.99 (*0-670-82421-6*) Viking Child Bks.
—Red Means Good Fortune: A Story of San Francisco's Chinatown. Ma, Wenhai, illus. 64p. (gr. 2-6). 1994. PLB 12.99 (*0-670-85352-6*) Viking Child Bks.
—World's Birthday. LC 89-29208. 28p. (ps-3). 1990. 13.95 (*0-15-299648-6*) HarBrace.

Goldin, Stephen & Mason, Mary. Jade Darcy & the Zen Pirates. (gr. 9-12). 1993. pap. 3.95 (*0-451-16157-2*, Sig) NAL-Dutton.

Golding, Goldie. Arrogant Ari Learns a Lesson. Snowden, Linda & Horen, Michael, illus. 32p. (gr. k-6). 1988. 6.95 (*0-89906-500-7*) Mesorah Pubns.

Golding, Leila P. Rachel. LC 88-71304. 176p. (Orig.). (gr. 10-12). 1988. pap. 3.99 (*0-87123-963-9*) Bethany Hse.
—Shelly. LC 85-73424. 150p. (Orig.). (gr. 9-12). 1986. pap. 3.99 (*0-87123-867-5*) Bethany Hse.

Goldish. Immigration. 1994. PLB write for info. (*0-8050-3182-0*) H Holt & Co.

Goldish, Meish. Does the Moon Change Shape? (Illus.). 32p. (gr. 1-4). 1989. PLB 15.96 (*0-8172-3518-3*); pap. 3.95 (*0-8114-6718-X*) Raintree Steck-V.
—How Plants Get Food. (Illus.). 32p. (gr. 1-4). 1989. PLB 15.96 (*0-8172-3507-8*); pap. 3.95 (*0-8114-6708-2*) Raintree Steck-V.
—Journey to Jo'burg: A Study Guide. Friedland, Joyce & Kessler, Rikki, eds. (gr. 5-8). 1991. pap. text ed. 14.95 (*0-88122-573-8*) LRN Links.
—Levi Strauss. LC 93-11997. (gr. 1-8). 1993. 15.93 (*0-86592-070-2*); 11.95s.p. (*0-685-66542-9*) Rourke Enter.
—The Paper Party. 16p. (ps-2). 1992. pap. 14.95 (*1-56784-054-X*) Newbridge Comms.
—The Same But Different. (Illus.). 32p. (gr. 1-4). 1989. PLB 15.96 (*0-8172-3528-0*); pap. 3.95 (*0-8114-6729-5*) Raintree Steck-V.

—What is a Fossil? (Illus.). 32p. (gr. 1-4). 1989. PLB 15.
96 (0-8172-3535-3); pap. 3.95 (0-8114-6734-1)
Raintree Steck-V.
Goldman, Alex J. The Greatest Rabbis Hall of Fame. (gr.
7 up). 1987. 14.95 (0-933503-11-3); pap. 7.95
(0-933503-14-8) Shapolsky Pubs.
Goldman, Bonnie, ed. see Lehmann, Asher.
Goldman, Bonnie, ed. see Winkler, Gershon.
Goldman, David. A Is for Ox. (Illus.). 64p. (gr. 4-6).
1994. PLB 12.95 (1-881889-41-6) Silver Moon.
Goldman, E. M. Money to Burn. LC 93-14584. 212p. (gr.
5-9). 1994. 14.99 (0-670-85339-9) Viking Child Bks.
Goldman, Edwin F., ed. see Arban, Jean B.
Goldman, Elizabeth & Farnan, Nancy J. Developing
Writers in Grades 7-12. 294p. (gr. 7-12). 1985. 44.90
(0-940444-23-2) Kabyn.
Goldman, Elizabeth, jt. auth. see Fearn, Leif.
Goldman, Elizabeth, jt. auth. see McCabe, Robert E.
Goldman, Kelly & Davidson, Ronnie. Sherlick Hound &
the Valentine Mystery. Levine, Abby, ed. Madden,
Don, illus. LC 88-20561. 32p. (gr. 1-4). 1989. 8.95
(0-8075-7335-3) A Whitman.
Goldman, Margaret F. My A, B, C, D, E Thinking,
Feeling & Doing Book. Era, Diane, illus. Ellis, Albert,
intro. by. LC 83-90397. (Illus.). 48p. (ps up). 11.95
(0-914237-00-4) L & M Bks.
Goldman, Martin S. Nat Turner: And the Southampton
Revolt of 1831. Roxas, Reni, ed. LC 91-36618. (Illus.).
160p. (gr. 9-12). 1992. PLB 14.40 (0-531-13011-8)
Watts.
Goldman, Meredith & Lissauer, T. Human Body.
Ashman, Iain, illus. 32p. (gr. 6 up). 1983. lib. bdg. 13.
96 (0-88110-150-8); pap. 6.95 (86020-747-1) EDC.
Goldman, Phyllis, ed. Monkeyshines on How the Fifty
States Were Named. Grigni, John, illus. 116p. (Orig.).
1993. pap. 11.95 (0-9620900-4-2) NC Learn Inst
Fitness.
Goldman, Phyllis B. Monkeyshines on Strange &
Wonderful Facts. Grigni, John, illus. 116p. (Orig.).
(ps-8). 1991. pap. 8.95 (0-9620900-2-6) NC Learn Inst
Fitness.
Goldman, Phyllis B., ed. Monkeyshines on the United
States Presidents: Games, Puzzles, & Trivia. Rubin,
97p. (gr. 4 up). 1990. pap. 12.95x (0-9620900-1-8) NC
Learn Inst Fitness.
Goldman, Ronald & Lynch, Martha E. High Hat Early
Reading Program. (ps-1). 1986. 309.95
(0-88671-242-4, 7930) Am Guidance.
—High Hat One Lesson Guide. (ps-1). 1986. pap. text ed.
39.49 (0-88671-243-2, 7931) Am Guidance.
—High Hat Story: Book One. (ps-1). 1986. text ed. 24.49
(0-88671-244-0, 7941) Am Guidance.
—High Hat Story: Book Two. (ps-1). 1986. 24.49
(0-88671-245-9, 7942); lesson guide 7.50
(0-88671-248-3, 7932); wkbk. 7.00 (0-88671-249-1)
Am Guidance.
Goldman, Russ. Learning the Bible Through Puzzles. 38p.
1992. pap. write for info. (1-882185-00-5) Crnrstone
Pub.
Goldman, Susan. Grandma Is Somebody Special. Rubin,
Caroline, ed. Golden, Susan, illus. LC 76-18980. 32p.
(ps-1). 1976. PLB 9.95 (0-8075-3034-4) A Whitman.
Goldner, Kathryn A., jt. auth. see Vogel, Carole G.
Goldner, Marian see Grandma, Marian, pseud.
Goldner, Marian see Grandma Marian, pseud.
Goldsboro, Bobby. Bobby Goldsboro's A Cat Named
Bob. 16p. (ps-2). 1993. write for info. (1-883366-33-X)
YES Ent.
—Bobby Goldsboro's The Boy Who Became a Frog. 16p.
(ps-2). 1993. write for info. (1-883366-12-7) YES Ent.
Goldsborough, June. What's in the Woods? LC 76-10271.
(Illus.). 32p. 1981. pap. 2.95 (0-13-955047-X) P-H.
Goldshlag-Cooks, Roberta. Gittel & the Bell. Martz,
Susan, illus. LC 87-2828. (gr. k-4). 1987. 10.95
(0-930494-68-7) Kar Ben.
**Goldsmith, Evelyn, rev. by see Smith, David & Newton,
Derek.**
Goldsmith, Howard. Toto the Timid Turtle. LC 80-
15096. (Illus.). 32p. (ps-3). 1980. 16.95
(0-87705-525-4) Human Sci Pr.
Goldsmith, Ilse. Human Anatomy for Children. Krause,
William, illus. (gr. 5-8). 1969. pap. 2.95
(0-486-22355-8) Dover.
Goldsmith, Melissa. A Cat State of Mind. Goldsmith,
Melissa, illus. LC 90-403394. 120p. (Orig.). (gr. 2-11).
1990. 17.95 (0-938921-06-1); pap. text ed. 6.95
(0-938921-07-X) Tigertail Ent.
Goldsmith, Oliver. Vicar of Wakefield. (gr. 10 up). 1964.
pap. 1.25 (0-8049-0052-3, CL-52) Airmont.
Goldstein, Bobbye. Bear in Mind: A Book of Bear Poems.
DuBois, William P., illus. 32p. (ps-3). 1989. 12.95
(0-670-81007-7) Viking Child Bks.
Goldstein, Bobbye S. Birthday Rhymes, Special Times.
(ps-3). 1993. 15.00 (0-385-30419-6) Doubleday.
Goldstein, Bobbye S., compiled by. Bear in Mind: A
Book of Bear Poems. Pene du Bois, William, illus. 32p.
(ps-3). 1991. pap. 3.95 (0-14-050799-X, Puffin) Puffin
Bks.
Goldstein, Bobbye S., ed. Inner Chimes: Poems on
Poetry. Zalben, Jane B., illus. (ps-7). 1992. PLB
14.95 (1-56397-040-6) Boyds Mills Pr.
Goldstein, Bobbye S., compiled by. What's on the Menu?
Demarest, Chris L., illus. 32p. (ps-3). 1992. PLB 12.50
(0-670-83031-3) Viking Child Bks.
Goldstein, Eleanor. What Citizens Need to Know about
Government. rev. ed. LC 93-30248. 1994. 16.00
(0-89777-146-X) Soc Issues.

Goldstein, Ernest. Grant Wood: American Gothic.
(Illus.). 52p. (gr. 7-12). 1984. pap. 9.95
(0-317-02721-2) NAL-Dutton.
Goldstein, Frances. Children's Treasure Hunt Travel
Guide to Britain. LC 78-71424. (Illus.). (gr. 1-12).
1979. pap. 6.95 (0-933334-00-1, Dist. by Hippocrene)
Paper Tiger Pap.
—Children's Treasure Hunt Travel Guide to Italy.
Goldstein, Frances, illus. LC 79-67280. (Orig.). (gr. k-
12). 1980. pap. 6.95 (0-933334-01-X, Dist. by
Hippocrene) Paper Tiger Pap.
—Children's Treasure Hunt Travel to Belgium & France.
Goldstein, Frances, illus. LC 80-85012. 230p. (Orig.).
(gr. k-12). 1981. pap. 6.95 (0-933334-02-8, Dist. by
Hippocrene) Paper Tiger Pap.
Goldstein, Helen H. Kids' Cuisine. Bolch, Judy, ed.
Pittman, Jackie, illus. LC 83-60306. 64p. (Orig.). (gr.
k-7). 1983. pap. 5.95 (0-935400-09-5) News &
Observer.
Goldstein, Jody, jt. auth. see Goldstein, Ray.
Goldstein, Lynn, ed. see Kolkmeyer, Alexandra.
Goldstein, Margaret J. Brett Hull: Hockey's Top Gun.
(Illus.). 64p. (gr. 4-7). 1992. PLB 13.50
(0-8225-0544-4); pap. 3.95 (0-8225-9599-0) Lerner
Pubns.
—Jennifer Capriati: Tennis Sensation. LC 92-38867.
1993. 13.50 (0-8225-0519-3) Lerner Pubns.
—Jennifer Capriati: Tennis Sensation. (gr. 4-7). 1993.
pap. 4.95 (0-8225-9645-8) Lerner Pubns.
Goldstein, Margaret J. & Larson, Jennifer. Jackie
Joyner-Kersee: Super Woman. LC 93-2976. 1993. 13.
50 (0-8225-0524-X) Lerner Pubns.
Goldstein, Nancy, ed. see Sauer, Sue, et al.
Goldstein, Nettie & Warner, Norma. How Hip Are You,
Bk 1. (Illus.). (gr. 5-12). 1977. wkbk. 5.95
(0-87594-160-5) Book-Lab.
Goldstein, Peggy. Long Is a Dragon: Chinese Writing for
Children. LC 90-81148. (Illus.). 32p. (gr. 3-7). 1990.
15.95 (1-881896-01-3) China Bks.
—Peng & You Are Friends: Chinese Writing for
Children. 32p. (gr. 2-8). 1993. 15.95 (1-881896-09-9)
Pacific View Pr.
Goldstein, Philip. Genetics Is Easy. rev. ed. (Illus.). (gr. 9
up). 8.05 (0-8313-1539-3) Lantern.
Goldstein, Ray & Goldstein, Jody. Where's Jess? Borum,
Shari, illus. 24p. (Illus.). (ps). 1982. pap. 3.25
(1-56123-009-X) Centering Corp.
Goldstein, Rebecca. The Mind-Body Problem. 304p. (gr.
5 up). 1985. pap. 4.95 (0-440-35651-2, LE) Dell.
Goldstein, Rose B. Songs to Share. Schloss, E., illus.
(HEB & ENG). 64p. (ps-5). 2.95x (0-8381-0720-6,
10-720) United Syn Bk.
Goldstein, Toby. Waking from the Dream: America in
the Sixties. LC 87-14016. (Illus.). 160p. (gr. 7-12).
1988. (J Messner). pap. 5.95 (0-671-66051-9) S&S
Trade.
Goldstein-Alpern, Neva. Beginning of the World. Gray,
Heather, illus. 12p. (ps). 1987. 4.95 (0-910818-73-8)
Judaica Pr.
—Ying-Ling Does Mitzvot. Gray, Heather, illus. 12p.
(ps). 1987. 4.95 (0-910818-72-X) Judaica Pr.
Goldstein-Alpern, Neva, ed. see Lehmann, Asher.
Goldstein-Alpern, Neva, ed. see Lepon, Shoshana.
Gold-Vukson, Marji & Gold-Vukson, Michael. Imagine
Exploring Israel: Creative Drawing Adventures. Gold-
Vukson, Michael, illus. 48p. (Orig.). (gr. k-4). 1993.
wkbk. 3.95 (0-929371-64-X) Kar Ben.
Gold-Vukson, Marji & Gold-Vukson, Micheal. Can You
Imagine? Creative Drawing Adventures for the Jewish
Holidays. LC 91-42842. 48p. (ps-5). pap. 3.95
(0-929371-3-3) Kar Ben.
Gold-Vukson, Michael, jt. auth. see Gold-Vukson, Marji.
Gold-Vukson, Micheal, jt. auth. see Gold-Vukson, Marji.
Goldwurm, Hersh & Holder, Meir. History of the Jewish
People, Vol. I: The Second Temple Era. (Illus.). 226p.
(gr. 7-8). 1993. 18.95 (0-89906-454-X); pap. 15.95
(0-89906-455-8) Mesorah Pubns.
Goldwurm, Hersh, ed. see Holder, Meir.
Goldwurm, Hersh, ed. & intro. by see Teich, Shmuel.
Golenbock, Peter. Teammates. Bacon, Paul, illus. (gr.
1-4). 1990. 15.95 (0-15-200603-6) HarBrace.
—Teammates. LC 89-3816. (gr. 1-3). 1992. pap. 4.95
(0-15-284286-1, HB Juv Bks) HarBrace.
Goley. Cooperation, Reading Level 2. (Illus.). 32p. (gr.
1-4). 1989. PLB 15.94 (0-86592-390-6) Rourke Corp.
—Determination, Reading Level 2. (Illus.). 32p. (gr. 1-4).
1989. PLB 15.94 (0-86592-389-2); 11.95s.p.
(0-685-58779-7) Rourke Corp.
—Faith, Reading Level 2. (Illus.). 32p. (gr. 1-4). 1989.
PLB 15.94 (0-86592-386-8); lib. bdg. 11.95s.p.
(0-685-58781-9) Rourke Corp.
—Giving, Reading Level 2. (Illus.). 32p. (gr. 1-4). 1989.
PLB 15.94 (0-86592-392-2); 11.95s.p. (0-685-58782-7)
Rourke Corp.
—Joy, Reading Level 2. (Illus.). 32p. (gr. 1-4). 1989. PLB
15.74 (0-86592-393-0); 11.95s.p. (0-685-58784-3)
Rourke Corp.
—Learning, Reading Level 2. (Illus.). 32p. (gr. 1-4). 1989.
PLB 15.94 (0-86592-396-5); 11.95s.p. (0-685-58785-1)
Rourke Corp.
—Manners, Reading Level 2. (Illus.). 32p. (gr. 1-4). 1989.
PLB 15.94 (0-86592-395-7); 11.95 (0-685-58787-8)
Rourke Corp.
—Respect, Reading Level 2. (Illus.). 32p. (gr. 1-4). 1989.
PLB 14.60 (0-86592-387-6); 11.95 (0-685-58788-6)
Rourke Corp.

—Responsibility, Reading Level 2. (Illus.). 32p. (gr. 1-4).
1989. PLB 14.60 (0-86592-394-9); 11.95s.p.
(0-685-58789-4) Rourke Corp.
—Self Control, Reading Level 2. (Illus.). 32p. (gr. 1-4).
1989. PLB 15.94 (0-86592-397-3); 11.95s.p.
(0-685-58790-8) Rourke Corp.
—Sharing, Reading Level 2. (Illus.). 32p. (gr. 1-4). 1989.
PLB 15.94 (0-86592-388-4); 11.95 (0-685-58791-6)
Rourke Corp.
Goley, Elaine. Believing in Yourself, Reading Level 2.
(Illus.). 32p. (gr. 1-4). 1989. PLB 15.94
(0-86592-398-1); 11.95s.p. (0-685-58777-0) Rourke
Corp.
—Caring. (Illus.). 32p. (gr. 1-4). 1987. PLB 15.94
(0-86592-381-7); 11.95 (0-685-67587-4) Rourke Corp.
—Courage. (Illus.). 32p. (gr. 1-4). 1987. PLB 15.94
(0-86592-377-9); lib. bdg. 11.95 (0-685-67576-9)
Rourke Corp.
—Friendship. (Illus.). 32p. (gr. 1-4). 1987. PLB 15.94
(0-86592-376-0); 11.95s.p. (0-685-67575-0) Rourke
Corp.
—Helping. (Illus.). 32p. (gr. 1-4). 1987. PLB 15.94
(0-86592-384-1); 11.95s.p. Rourke Corp.
—Honesty. (Illus.). 32p. (gr. 1-4). 1987. PLB 15.74
(0-86523-857-X); 11.95s.p. (0-685-58144-6) Rourke
Corp.
—Kindness. (Illus.). 32p. (gr. 1-4). 1987. PLB 15.74
(0-86592-383-3); 11.95s.p. (0-685-67579-3) Rourke
Corp.
—Learn the Value, 10 bks, Set I, Reading Level 2.
(Illus.). 320p. (gr. 1-4). 1987. PLB 119.50s.p.
(0-685-58775-4) Rourke Corp.
—Love. (Illus.). 32p. (gr. 1-4). 1987. PLB 132.66 10 bk.
set (0-317-60299-7); PLB 15.94 (0-86592-380-9); 11.
95s.p. (0-685-67578-5) Rourke Corp.
—Patience. (Illus.). 32p. (gr. 1-4). 1987. PLB 15.94
(0-86592-379-5); 11.95 (0-685-67574-2) Rourke Corp.
—Trust. (Illus.). 32p. (gr. 1-4). 1987. PLB 15.94
(0-86592-378-7); PLB 11.95s.p. (0-685-67577-7)
Rourke Corp.
—Understanding Others. (Illus.). 32p. (gr. 1-4). 1987.
PLB 15.94 (0-86592-382-5); PLB 11.95s.p.
(0-685-67588-2) Rourke Corp.
Goley, Elaine, et al. Learn the Value, 18 bks, Set II,
Reading Level 2. (Illus.). 576p. (gr. 1-4). 1989. Set.
PLB 286.92 (0-86592-391-4); 215.10s.p.
(0-685-58776-2) Rourke Corp.
Goliaz-Benson, Ursula, jt. auth. see Fearn, Leif.
Golisz-Benson, Ursula, jt. auth. see Fearn, Leif.
Goliwas, Ruth M., jt. auth. see Mackintosh, William H.
Golland, Derrick. Pressures on the Countryside. (Illus.).
48p. (gr. 7-12). 1986. 19.95 (0-85219-625-3, Pub. by
Batsford UK) Trafalgar.
Gollub, Matthew. The Moon Was at a Fiesta. Martinez,
Leovigildo, illus. LC 93-14750. 32p. 1994. 15.00
(0-688-11637-X, Tambourine Bks); PLB 14.93
(0-688-11638-8) Morrow.
—The Twenty-Five Mixtec Cats. Martinez, Leovigildo,
illus. LC 92-13585. 32p. (gr. 1 up). 1993. 14.00
(0-688-11639-6, Tambourine Bks); PLB 13.93
(0-688-11640-X, Tambourine Bks) Morrow.
Golomb, Morris. Know Jewish Living & Enjoy It. LC 78-
54569. (Illus.). (gr. 5-9). 1981. 14.95 (0-88400-054-0)
Shengold.
Golomb, Morris, rev. by. Know Your Festivals & Enjoy
Them. (Illus.). 189p. (gr. 3-7). 1993. 15.95
(0-88400-035-4) Shengold.
Golub, Jane see Rabinowitz, Jan.
Goma, Eulalia. Diccionario Magico Infantil. 7th ed.
(SPA). 50p. 1978. 19.95 (0-8288-5141-7, S26065) Fr
& Eur.
—Diccionario Magico Infantil en Seis Lenguas. 2nd ed.
(SPA, CAT, FRE & ENG). 96p. 1978. 29.95
(0-8288-5140-9, S50028) Fr & Eur.
Gomboli, Mario. What Are You Touching? Gomboli,
Mario, illus. 10p. (ps-k). 1992. bds. 3.95
(1-56397-150-X); Set of 3 bks. bds. 11.85
(1-56397-155-0) Boyds Mills Pr.
—What Shape Is This? Gomboli, Mario, illus. 10p. (ps-k).
1992. bds. 3.95 (1-56397-149-6); Set of 3 bks. bds. 11.
85 (1-56397-157-7) Boyds Mills Pr.
—What's in Disguise? Gomboli, Mario, illus. 10p. (ps-k).
1992. bds. 3.95 (1-56397-151-8); Set of 3 bks. bds. 11.
85 (1-56397-156-9) Boyds Mills Pr.
Gomez, Cruz, jt. ed. see Rohmer, Harriet.
Gomez, Paolo. Food in Mexico. LC 88-31529. (Illus.).
32p. (gr. 6-9). 1989. lib. bdg. 15.94 (0-86625-341-6);
11.95s.p. (0-685-58499-2) Rourke Corp.
Gomez-Navarro, Maria J., et al, eds. Plantas - Plants.
Del Carmen Blazquez, Maria, tr. End, Simone &
Woodcock, John, illus. (SPA). 64p. (gr. 5-12). 1993.
write for info. (84-372-4529-X) Santillana.
Gomi, Taro. The Big Book of Boxes. Gomi, Taro, illus.
12p. (ps up). 1991. pap. 14.95 (0-8118-0067-9)
Chronicle Bks.
—Bus Stops. Gomi, Taro, illus. 32p. (ps-1).
1988. 10.95 (0-87701-551-1) Chronicle Bks.
—Coco Can't Wait. Gomi, Taro, illus. (ps-1). 1985. pap.
3.95 (0-14-050522-9, Puffin) Puffin Bks.
—Everyone Poops. Stinchecum, Amanda M., tr. from
JPN. 32p. (ps). 1993. 11.95 (0-916291-45-6) Kane-
Miller Bk.
—Guess What? A Peek-a-Boo Book. Chronicle Books, tr.
from JPN. Gomi, Taro, illus. 16p. (ps-k). 1992. bds.
4.95 (0-8118-0015-6) Chronicle Bks.
—Guess Who? A Peek-A-Boo Book. Gomi, Taro, illus.
16p. (ps-k). 1991. bds. 4.95 (0-8118-0021-0) Chronicle
Bks.

—Hide & Seek. Young, Richard G., ed. Kaisei-sha, tr. LC 89-12049. (Illus.). 32p. (gr. 1-3). 1989. PLB 14.60 (0-944483-45-3) Garrett Ed Corp.

—My Friends. LC 89-23940. (Illus.). 40p. (ps-1). 1990. 9.95 (0-87701-688-7) Chronicle Bks.

—Seeing, Saying, Doing, Playing: A Big Book of Action Words. (Illus.). 32p. (ps-3). 1991. 13.95 (0-87701-859-6) Chronicle Bks.

—Spring Is Here. (Illus.). 32p. (ps-1). 1989. 11.95 (0-87701-626-7) Chronicle Bks.

—There's a Mouse in the House. Chronicle Books, tr. from JPN. Gomi, Taro, illus. 16p. (ps-k). 1991. bds. 4.95 (0-8118-0024-5) Chronicle Bks.

—Where's the Fish? Gomi, Taro, illus. LC 85-15282. 32p. (ps-k). 1986. 11.95 (0-688-06241-5); lib. bdg. 11.88 (0-688-06242-3, Morrow Jr Bks) Morrow Jr Bks.

—Who Ate It? (Illus.). 24p. (ps). 1991. PLB 8.40 (1-56294-301-4); pap. 6.95 (1-56294-706-0) Millbrook Pr.

—Who Ate It? (ps). 1992. pap. 4.80 (0-395-65834-9) HM.

—Who Hid It? (Illus.). 24p. (ps). 1992. PLB 8.40 (1-56294-011-2); pap. 6.95 (1-56294-707-9) Millbrook Pr.

—Who Hid It? (ps). 1992. pap. 4.80 (0-395-65835-7) HM.

Gompertz, Helen. First Prayers. (Illus.). 32p. (ps-3). 1983. 7.00 (0-8170-1013-0) Judson.

Gondosch, Linda. Brutus the Wonder Poodle. Dann, Penny, illus. LC 89-39377. 64p. (Orig.). (gr. 2-4). 1990. PLB 5.99 (0-679-90573-1); pap. 1.95 (0-679-80573-7) Random Bks Yng Read.

—Camp Kickapoo. Lincoln, Patricia H., illus. LC 92-28060. 128p. (gr. 4-6). 1993. 13.99 (0-525-67373-3, Lodestar Bks) Dutton Child Bks.

—The Monsters of Marble Avenue. (Illus.). (gr. 2-4). 1988. 10.95 (0-316-31991-0) Little.

—Monsters of Marble Avenue. (gr. 4-7). 1990. pap. 2.95 (0-316-31992-9, Joy St Bks) Little.

—The Strawberryland Choo-Choo. Sustendal, Pat, illus. 40p. (ps-3). 1984. cancelled 5.95 (0-910313-24-5) Parker Bros.

—Who's Afraid of Haggerty House. 1989. pap. 2.99 (0-671-67237-1, Minstrel Bks) PB.

—The Witches of Hopper Street. (Illus.). (gr. 3-6). 1990. pap. 2.99 (0-671-72468-1, Archway) PB.

Gonen, Rivka. Charge! Weapons & Warfare in Ancient Times. LC 92-36772. 1993. lib. bdg. 22.95 (0-8225-3201-8, Runestone Pr) Lerner Pubns.

—Fired Up! How Ancient Pottery Was Made. LC 92-41748. 1993. PLB 22.95 (0-8225-3202-6, Runestone Pr) Lerner Pubns.

Gonick, Larry & Wheelis, Mark. The Cartoon Guide to Genetics. rev. ed. 1991. pap. 11.00 (0-06-273099-1, Harper Ref) HarpC.

Gonsalves, Carol. Sermon on the Mountain. (gr. k-4). 1981. pap. 1.89 (0-570-06149-0, 59-1304) Concordia.

Gonyea, James. College-Vocational Selector Guide. (Illus.). 44p. (Orig.). (gr. 12). 1991. pap. write for info. wkbk. (0-933510-81-0) Orchard Hse MA.

Gonzales, Doreen. Madeleine L'Engle: Author of "A Wrinkle in Time" LC 91-3883. (Illus.). 112p. (gr. 4-6). 1991. RSBE 13.95 (0-87518-485-5, Dillon) Macmillan Child Grp.

Gonzales, Jose L. Puerto Rico: The Four-Storyed Country. Guinness, Gerald, tr. from SPA. & intro. by. LC 92-45619. 164p. 1993. pap. text ed. 12.95 (1-55876-072-5) Wiener Pubs Inc.

Gonzales, Linda, jt. auth. see Kiraithe, Jackie.

Gonzales, Linda, ed. see Kiraithe, Jackie.

Gonzales, Rod & Faurot, Chip. To the Summit. McDonald, Mike, ed. Gonzales, Rod, illus. 32p. (Orig.). (gr. 5-10). 1993. pap. 3.95 (1-882724-00-3) Alaska Comics.
TO THE SUMMIT is the story of a 12-year-old kid who climbs Mt. McKinley. It was June 23, 1991, solstice day, that he summited, making him the youngest mountaineer to do so. Taras lives within the "shadows" of Mt. McKinley in beautiful Talkeetna, Alaska. He is the son of the late & legendary Ray Genet who perished 12 years earlier on the upper-Mt. Everest slope. It was back then that the promise was made - "...some day I'm gonna take you up Denali." That day, he was a special guest member of a guided expedition led by Fantasy Ridge Expedition, Inc. AK. Comics artist Rod Gonzalez worked closely with chief guide Chip Faurot, Taras & his mother on this project. We feel that we have produced a clean & inspirational story & are anxious to share it with you. TO THE SUMMIT is a 32-page B/W production with UV coating on the cover...printed on bookpaper (making it a great coloring book). Alaska Comics uses Capitol City Distribution, Inc., P.O. Box 8156, Madison, WI 53708. For direct contact: Max North Alaska Comics, 316 Price Street, Anchorage, AK 99508, 907/279-4913. ISBN 1-882724-00-3, $3.95. *Publisher Provided Annotation.*

Gonzalez, Catherine T. Jane Long, Mother of Texas. (gr. 4-7). 1982. 10.95 (0-89015-299-3, Pub. by Panda Bks) Eakin-Sunbelt.

—Lafitte: Terror of the Gulf. (Illus.). 64p. (gr. 4-7). 1981. 10.95 (0-89015-284-5, Pub. by Panda Bks) Eakin-Sunbelt.

Gonzalez, Christina. Inca Civilization. LC 92-37021. (Illus.). 36p. (gr. 3 up). 1993. PLB 19.93 (0-516-08380-5); pap. 6.95 (0-516-48380-3) Childrens.

Gonzalez, Fernando. Gloria Estefan, Cuban-American Singing Star. LC 92-39798. (Illus.). 32p. (gr. 2-4). 1993. PLB 12.40 (1-56294-371-5) Millbrook Pr.

Gonzalez, Gloria. A Deadly Rhyme. (Orig.). (gr. 5-8). 1986. pap. 2.50 (0-440-91866-9, LFL) Dell.

Gonzalez, Inez, tr. see Robinson, Lafayette.

Gonzalez, Lucia M., retold by. The Bossy Gallito: A Traditional Cuban Folk Tale. Delacre, Lulu, illus. LC 93-15541. 32p. (ps-2). 1994. 14.95 (0-590-46843-X) Scholastic Inc.

Gonzalez-Mena, Janet. English Experiences. Walner, Hari, illus. LC 75-5307. (ps). 1975. Program Package Set. 87.25 (0-685-02507-1, Natl Textbk); wkbk. 6.60 (0-8325-0682-6, Natl Textbk); tchr's. manual 21.25 (0-8325-0681-8, Natl Textbk); Spanish. wkbk. 6.60 (0-8325-9639-6, Natl Textbk); Spanish. tchr's. manual 21.25 (0-8325-9638-8, Natl Textbk) NTC Pub Grp.

Gonzalez-Mena, Janet, jt. auth. see Garcia, Mary H.

Gooc, Van. Goldilocks & the Three Bears. (Illus.). 48p. (ps-1). 1989. 5.99 (0-517-69318-6) Outlet Bk Co.

Good, Alice. Magic Squares Puzzle Book. 48p. 1991. pap. 2.95 (0-8431-2870-4) Price Stern.

Good, Bertha. Carlos of North Road Camp: And Other Stories & Poems. 2nd ed. 167p. (gr. 2-4). 1993. pap. 5.50 (0-9627643-6-1) Green Psturs Pr.

Good, C. Edward. Does Your Resume Wear Blue Jeans? High School Edition. 139p. (Orig.). (gr. 9-12). 1989. pap. 6.95 (0-934961-05-0) Blue Jeans Pr.

Good, Elaine. It's Summertime! LC 89-28895. (Illus.). 32p. (ps-1). 1990. 12.95 (0-934672-68-7) Good Bks PA.

Good, Elaine W. Fall Is Here! I Love It! Wenger, Susie S., illus. LC 90-71115. 32p. (ps-1). 1990. text ed. 12.95 (1-56148-007-X) Good Bks PA.

—That's What Happens When It's Spring. Shenks, Susie, illus. LC 87-14964. 32p. (ps-1). 1987. 12.95 (0-934672-53-9) Good Bks PA.

—White Wonderful Winter. Wenger, Susie S., illus. LC 91-74052. 32p. (ps-1). 1991. 12.95 (1-56148-018-5) Good Bks PA.

Good Little Books for Good Little Children Staff. God Made Me. 12p. (ps). 1986. 3.25 (0-8378-5207-2) Gibson.

—The Little Lost Lamb. 12p. (ps). 1986. 3.25 (0-8378-5206-4) Gibson.

—Noah's Ark. 12p. (ps). 1986. 3.25 (0-8378-5205-6) Gibson.

Good, Merle. Amos & Susie: An Amish Story. Benner, Cheryl A., illus. 24p. (ps-3). 1993. 12.95 (1-561480-88-6); pap. 4.95 (0-934672-46-6) Good Bks PA.

—Reuben & the Fire. Moss, P. Buckley, illus. LC 93-1798. 32p. (ps-3). 1993. PLB 14.95 (1-56148-091-6) Good Bks Pa.

Good, Sharon. Alpha, Beta & Gamma: A Small Story. LC 90-86292. (Illus.). 48p. 1991. pap. 6.95 (0-9627226-1-8) Excalibur Publishing.

Goodacres, Selwyn H. see Carroll, Lewis.

Goodale, Katherine D. Pas de Trois, Fun with Ballet Words. Goodale, Kit, illus. Houlton, Loyce, intro. by. (Illus.). 25p. (Orig.). (gr. k-7). 1982. pap. 5.95 (0-9609662-0-X) Goodale Pub.

Goodall, Jane. The Chimpanzee Family Book. Neugebauer, Michael, illus. LC 88-33359. 72p. (up). 1991. pap. 17.95 (0-88708-090-1) Picture Bk Studio.

—Jane Goodall's Animal World: Elephants. LC 89-78128. (Illus.). 32p. (gr. 3-7). 1990. pap. 3.95 (0-689-71395-9, Aladdin) Macmillan Child Grp.

—Jane Goodall's Animal World: Gorillas. LC 89-78064. (Illus.). 32p. (gr. 3-7). 1990. pap. 3.95 (0-689-71396-7, Aladdin) Macmillan Child Grp.

—Jane Goodall's Animal World: Sea Otters. LC 89-78133. (Illus.). 32p. (gr. 3-7). 1990. pap. 3.95 (0-689-71394-0, Aladdin) Macmillan Child Grp.

—Jane Goodall's Animal World: Tigers. LC 89-78130. (Illus.). 32p. (gr. 3-7). 1990. pap. 3.95 (0-689-71393-2, Aladdin) Macmillan Child Grp.

—My Life with Chimpanzees. (Illus.). 128p. (gr. 4-6). 1988. pap. 2.99 (0-671-66095-0, Minstrel Bks) PB.

—My Life with the Chimpanzees. (gr. 5). 1990. pap. write for info. (0-663-56245-7) Silver Burdett Pr.

Goodall, Jane & Van Lawick-Goodall, Hugo. Grub the Bush Baby. 80p. (ps up). 1988. 13.45 (0-395-48696-3, Sandpiper); (Sandpiper) HM.

Goodall, John S. Great Days of a Country House. Goodall, John S., illus. LC 91-62147. 64p. (ps up). 1992. SBE 15.95 (0-689-50545-0, M K McElderry) Macmillan Child Grp.

—Lavinia's Cottage: A Pop-Up Story. LC 82-71160. (Illus.). 16p. (gr. 1-4). 1983. SBE 14.95 (0-689-50257-5, M K McElderry) Macmillan Child Grp.

—Little Red Riding Hood. LC 87-34245. (Illus.). 60p. (ps-3). 1988. SBE 14.95 (0-689-50457-8, M K McElderry) Macmillan Child Grp.

—Paddy Under Water. reissue ed. Goodall, John S., illus. LC 83-71901. 32p. 1991. SBE 12.95 (0-689-50297-4, M K McElderry) Macmillan Child Grp.

—Puss in Boots. Goodall, John S., illus. LC 90-38606. 56p. (ps-3). 1990. SBE 14.95 (0-689-50521-3, M K McElderry) Macmillan Child Grp.

—The Story of a Castle. Goodall, John S., illus. LC 86-70130. 60p. 1986. SBE 14.95 (0-689-50405-5, M K McElderry) Macmillan Child Grp.

—The Story of a Farm. Goodall, John S., illus. LC 88-3398. (gr. 4 up). 1989. RSBE 14.95 (0-689-50479-9, M K McElderry) Macmillan Child Grp.

—The Story of a Main Street. Goodall, John S., illus. LC 87-60644. 60p. 1987. SBE 14.95 (0-689-50436-5, M K McElderry) Macmillan Child Grp.

—The Story of an English Village. Goodall, John S., illus. LC 78-56242. 60p. 1979. SBE 14.95 (0-689-50125-0, M K McElderry) Macmillan Child Grp.

—The Story of the Seashore. LC 89-8328. (Illus.). 54p. 1990. SBE 14.95 (0-689-50491-8, M K McElderry) Macmillan Child Grp.

Goodchild, Peter. The Spark in the Stone: Skills & Projects from the Native American Tradition. LC 90-27324. (Illus.). 144p. (Orig.). (gr. 5 up). 1991. pap. 11.95 (1-55652-102-2) Chicago Review.

Goode, Diane. Diane Goode's American Christmas. Goode, Diane, illus. LC 89-70727. 80p. (ps-up). 1990. 14.95 (0-525-44620-6, DCB) Dutton Child Bks.

—Diane Goode's Book of Silly Stories & Songs. LC 91-38192. (Illus.). 64p. (ps-6). 1992. 15.00 (0-525-44967-1, DCB) Dutton Child Bks.

—I Hear a Noise. Goode, Diane, illus. LC 87-3060. 32p. (ps-1). 1988. 12.95 (0-525-44353-3, DCB) Dutton Child Bks.

—I Hear a Noise. Goode, Diane, illus. LC 87-3060. 32p. (ps-1). 1992. pap. 3.99 (0-525-44884-5, Puffin) Puffin Bks.

—Where's Our Mama? Goode, Diane, illus. LC 91-2158. 32p. (ps-2). 1991. 13.95 (0-525-44770-9, DCB) Dutton Child Bks.

Goode, Diane, adapted by. & illu see Andersen, Hans Christian.

Goode, Diane, tr. from FRE see Perrault, Charles.

Goode, Diane, illus. Christmas Carols. LC 82-62169. 32p. (ps up). 1988. pap. 1.25 (0-394-81940-3) Random Bks Yng Read.

—Diane Goode's Book of Scary Stories & Songs. LC 93-32610. (gr. 3 up). 1994. write for info. 0-525-45175-7, DCB) Dutton Child Bks.

—Diane Goode's Christmas Magic: Poems & Carols. LC 92-6366. 32p. (Orig.). (ps-3). 1992. PLB 5.99 (0-679-92427-2); pap. 2.25 (0-679-82427-8) Random Bks Yng Read.

—Diane Goode's Little Library of Christmas Classics. 32p. (gr. 1 up). 1983. boxed set 7.95 (0-394-85229-X) Random Bks Yng Read.

—The Little Books of Nursery Animals: The Little Book of Cats; The Little Book of Farm Friends; The Little Book of Mice; The Little Book of Pigs. (ps). 1993. Boxed set, 24p. ea. 11.99 (0-525-45122-6, DCB) Dutton Child Bks.

—The Nutcracker: The Story Based on the Ballet. LC 82-62170. 32p. 1988. pap. 1.25 (0-394-81939-X) Random Bks Yng Read.

Goode, James B. Up from the Mines: Images of the Appalachian Mining Experience. Gifford, James M., ed. (Illus.). 144p. (gr. 8 up). 1993. 19.95 (0-945084-37-4) J Stuart Found.

Gooden, Kimberly W. Coping with Family Stress. Rosen, Ruth, ed. (gr. 7-12). 1989. PLB 13.95 (0-8239-0980-8) Rosen Group.

Goodenough, J. E. Animal Communication. Head, John J., ed. LC 83-70598. (Illus.). 16p. (gr. 10 up). 1984. pap. 2.75 (0-89278-343-5, 45-9743) Carolina Biological.

Goodfellow, E. J., jt. auth. see Rook, Lizzie.

Goodheart, Barbara. Diabetes. LC 90-31328. (Illus.). 128p. (gr. 9-12). 1990. PLB 13.40 (0-531-10882-1) Watts.

Goodhue, Horace R. Indian Bead-Weaving Patterns: Chain Weaving Designs & Bead Loom Weaving-An Illustrated "How-To" Guide. Barich, Mike, et al, illus. LC 84-71456. 64p. (gr. 3 up). 1984. pap. 4.95 (0-9613503-0-X) Bead Craft.

Goodin, Evelyn. The Greatest Living Scientist. Van Treese, James B., ed. 128p. 1993. pap. 7.95 (1-56901-004-8) NW Pub.

Gooding, Margaret K. A Growing-up Year. 70p. (gr. 6-7). 1992. 19.95 (0-933840-34-9) Unitarian Univ.

Goodman, Ailene S. Abe Lincoln in Song & Story. LC 88-753827. (gr. 4-12). 1989. incl. audio cass. & guidebook 11.98 (0-9620704-0-8) A S Goodman.

Goodman, Beth. Fun with the Norfin Trolls: A Coloring & Activity Book. (ps-8). 1992. pap. 1.95 (*0-590-45926-0*) Scholastic Inc.
—Meet Crystal Starr: A Coloring Activity Book. (ps-3). 1993. pap. 1.95 (*0-590-46605-4*) Scholastic Inc.
—The Norfin Trolls Laugh Out Loud. (Illus.). 1992. 2.50 (*0-590-45925-2*, 046) Scholastic Inc.
—Super Saved by the Bell Scrapbook. (gr. 4-7). 1993. pap. 4.95 (*0-590-47168-6*) Scholastic Inc.
Goodman, Billy. Animal Homes & Societies. Goodman, Billy, illus. 96p. (gr. 3-7). 1992. 17.95 (*0-316-32018-8*) Little.
—Camelot World: A Kid's Guide to How to Save the Planet. 128p. (Orig.). 1990. pap. 2.95 (*0-380-76041-X*, Camelot) Avon.
—Natural Wonders & Disasters. Goodman, Billy, illus. (gr. 3-7). 1991. 17.95 (*0-316-32016-1*) Little.
—The Rain Forest. Goodman, Billy, illus. 96p. (gr. 3-7). 1992. 17.95 (*0-316-32019-6*) Little.
—Taking Care of the Earth. Gleeson, Kate, illus. 24p. (ps-k). 1992. write for info. (*0-307-11532-1*, 11532) Western Pub.
Goodman, Burton. After Shocks. 151p. (gr. 5). 1994. pap. 9.00 (*0-89061-751-1*) Jamestown Pubs.
—More Conflicts. 160p. (gr. 8). 1993. pap. 9.50 (*0-89061-718-X*) Jamestown Pubs.
—More Surprises. 144p. (gr. 4). 1990. pap. 7.75 (*0-89061-676-0*) Jamestown Pubs.
—More Twists. 120p. (gr. 6). 1988. pap. text ed. 8.00x (*0-89061-502-0*) Jamestown Pubs.
—Shocks. 151p. (gr. 5). 1994. pap. 9.00 (*0-89061-750-3*) Jamestown Pubs.
—Sudden Twists. 120p. (gr. 6). 1988. pap. text ed. 8.00x (*0-89061-501-2*) Jamestown Pubs.
—Surprises. 144p. (gr. 4). 1990. pap. 7.75 (*0-89061-675-2*) Jamestown Pubs.
Goodman, Burton, et al. Conflicts. 160p. (gr. 8). 1993. pap. 9.50 (*0-89061-717-1*) Jamestown Pubs.
Goodman, Charles, ed. see Graham, Billy, et al.
Goodman, David R. The Mitzvah Mouse. 24p. 1992. 8.95 (*965-229-069-6*, Pub. by Gefen Pub Hse IS) Gefen Bks.
Goodman, Deborah L. The Magic of the Unicorn. 128p. (Orig.). (gr. 4). 1985. pap. 2.25 (*0-553-25242-9*) Bantam.
—The Throne of Zeus. 128p. 1985. pap. 2.25 (*0-553-26265-3*) Bantam.
—The Trumpet of Terror. 128p. (Orig.). (gr. 4). 1986. pap. 2.25 (*0-553-25491-X*) Bantam.
—Vanished! 128p. (Orig.). (gr. 4). 1986. pap. 2.25 (*0-553-25941-5*) Bantam.
Goodman, Florence J. A Young Person's Philosophical Dictionary. (gr. 5-12). 1978. pap. 9.95x (*0-917232-06-2*) Gee Tee Bee.
Goodman, Frances B., ed. see Barrett, Anna P.
Goodman, Jan M. Group Solutions. Bergman, Lincoln & Fairwell, Kay, eds. (Illus.). 144p. (gr. k-4). 1992. pap. 15.00 (*0-912511-81-8*) Lawrence Science.
Goodman, Jim. Thailand. LC 91-17719. (Illus.). 128p. (gr. 5-9). 1991. PLB 21.95 (*1-85435-402-7*) Marshall Cavendish.
Goodman, Joan E. Hush Little Darling. 1992. 4.95 (*0-590-45247-9*, Cartwheel) Scholastic Inc.
Goodman, Joe, ed. see Hardgrove, Nelle.
Goodman, Julius. The Magic Path. 64p. (Orig.). (gr. 2). 1985. pap. 2.25 (*0-553-15482-6*) Bantam.
—Space Patrol, No. 22. (Illus.). 128p 1983. pap. 2.50 (*0-553-27520-8*) Bantam.
—Treasure Diver. 128p. (gr. 5-9). 1984. pap. 2.25 (*0-553-25764-1*) Bantam.
Goodman, Louise. Ida's Doll. Carter, Debby L., illus. LC 87-25085. 32p. (ps-3). 1989. HarpC Child Bks.
Goodman, Marlene, illus. Let's Learn Japanese Picture Dictionary: Elementary Through Junior High. (JPN.). 80p. 1993. pap. 9.95 (*0-685-62858-2*, F8494-7, Natl Textbk); pap. 8.46 ea. 10 or more copies (F8494-7, Natl Textbk) NTC Pub Grp.
—Let's Learn Portuguese Picture Dictionary: Elementary. (POR.). 72p. 1993. 9.95 (*0-685-62862-0*, F4699-9, Natl Textbk); 10 or more copies 8.46 ea. (F4699-9, Natl Textbk) NTC Pub Grp.
Goodman, Michael. Atlanta Braves. 48p. (gr. 4-10). 1992. PLB 14.95s.p. (*0-88682-460-5*) Creative Ed.
—Chicago Cubs. 48p. (gr. 4-10). 1992. PLB 14.95s.p. (*0-88682-464-8*) Creative Ed.
—Cincinnati Reds. 48p. (gr. 4-10). 1992. PLB 14.95s.p. (*0-88682-462-1*) Creative Ed.
—Dallas Mavericks. (Illus.). 32p. (gr. 4 up). 1993. PLB 14.95 (*0-88682-528-8*) Creative Ed.
—Houston Astros. (gr. 4-10). 1992. PLB 14.95s.p. (*0-88682-459-1*) Creative Ed.
—Los Angeles Dodgers. 48p. (gr. 4-10). 1992. PLB 14.95s.p. (*0-88682-458-3*) Creative Ed.
—Montreal Expos. 48p. (gr. 4-10). 1992. PLB 14.95s.p. (*0-88682-457-5*) Creative Ed.
—New York Mets. 48p. (gr. 4-10). 1992. PLB 14.95s.p. (*0-88682-456-7*) Creative Ed.
—Philadelphia Phillies. 48p. (gr. 4-10). 1993. PLB 14.95s.p. (*0-88682-455-9*) Creative Ed.
—Pittsburgh Pirates. 48p. (gr. 4-10). 1992. PLB 14.95s.p. (*0-88682-454-0*) Creative Ed.
—St. Louis Cardinals. 48p. (gr. 4-10). 1992. PLB 14.95s.p. (*0-88682-461-3*) Creative Ed.
—San Diego Padres. 48p. (gr. 4-10). 1992. PLB 14.95s.p. (*0-88682-463-X*) Creative Ed.
—San Francisco Giants. 48p. (gr. 4-10). 1993. PLB 14.95s.p. (*0-88682-453-2*) Creative Ed.

—Seattle Mariners. 48p. (gr. 4-10). 1992. PLB 14.95s.p. (*0-88682-452-4*) Creative Ed.
—The World Cup (Soccer) 32p. (gr. 4). 1990. PLB 14.95s.p. (*0-88682-320-X*) Creative Ed.
Goodman, Michael E. Boston Celtics. rev. ed. (Illus.). 32p. (gr. 4 up). 1993. PLB 14.95 (*0-88682-530-X*) Creative Ed.
—Cars & Trucks. (Illus.). 24p. (ps-k). 1989. pap. write for info. (*0-307-11753-7*, Pub. by Golden Bks) Western Pub.
—Denver Nuggets. rev. ed. (Illus.). 32p. (gr. 4 up). 1993. PLB 14.95 (*0-88682-546-6*) Creative Ed.
—Houston Rockets. 32p. (gr. 4). 1993. PLB 14.95s.p. (*0-88682-529-6*) Creative Ed.
—Lawrence Taylor. LC 87-29023. (Illus.). 48p. (gr. 5-6). 1988. RSBE 11.95 (*0-89686-365-4*, Crestwood Hse) Macmillan Child Grp.
—Los Angeles Lakers. rev. ed. (Illus.). 32p. (gr. 4 up). 1993. PLB 14.95 (*0-88682-542-3*) Creative Ed.
—Magic Johnson. LC 88-20982. (Illus.). 48p. (gr. 5-6). 1988. RSBE 11.95 (*0-89686-382-4*, Crestwood Hse) Macmillan Child Grp.
—Model Railroading. LC 91-15853. (Illus.). 48p. (gr. 5 up). 1993. lib. bdg. 12.95 RSBE (*0-89686-620-3*, Crestwood Hse) Macmillan Child Grp.
—New York Knicks. (Illus.). 32p. (gr. 4 up). 1993. PLB 14.95 (*0-88682-515-6*) Creative Ed.
—Philadelphia 76ers. rev. ed. (Illus.). 32p. (gr. 4 up). 1993. PLB 14.95 (*0-88682-544-X*) Creative Ed.
—Radio Control Models. LC 91-47750. (Illus.). 48p. (gr. 5 up). 1993. lib. bdg. 12.95 RSBE (*0-89686-622-X*, Crestwood Hse) Macmillan Child Grp.
—Sacramento Kings. (Illus.). 32p. (gr. 4 up). 1993. PLB 14.95 (*0-88682-540-7*) Creative Ed.
—Seattle Supersonics. rev. ed. (Illus.). 32p. (gr. 4 up). 1993. PLB 14.95s.p. (*0-88682-543-1*) Creative Ed.
Goodman, Mike. Astronauts. LC 89-31222. (Illus.). 48p. (gr. 4-5). 1989. RSBE 11.95 (*0-89686-430-8*, Crestwood Hse) Macmillan Child Grp.
Goodman, Robert & Spicer, Robert. Urashima Taro. 2nd ed. Suyeoka, George, illus. 72p. Date not set. 15.95 (*0-89610-276-9*, 24019-000) Island Heritage.
Goodman, Roberta L. God's Top Ten: The Meaning of the Ten Commandments. Steinberger, Heidi, illus. 32p. (Orig.). (gr. 4-6). 1992. pap. text ed. 1.85 (*0-933873-73-5*) Torah Aura.
Goodman, Roger B. The Statue of Liberty & Ellis Island. (Illus.). 74p. (Orig.). (gr. 9 up). 1990. pap. 6.50 (*0-9632191-0-3*); pap. text ed. 6.50 (*0-9632191-1-1*); tchr's. ed. 6.50 (*0-9632191-2-X*); wkbk. 3.00 (*0-685-57051-7*) Pulitzer-Goodman.
Goodman, Sarah. Shani Plus Three. 176p. (gr. 6-9). Date not set. 9.95 (*1-56871-028-3*) Targum Pr.
Goodman, Sharon L., ed. see Philadelphia Schools Students.
Goodman, Susan. Amazing Biofacts. (Illus.). 160p. (gr. 7 up). 1993. PLB 18.00 (*0-87226-364-9*); pap. 9.95 (*0-87226-256-1*) P Bedrick Bks.
—Amazing Spacefacts. LC 92-40112. (Illus.). 144p. (gr. 7 up). 1993. PLB 18.00 (*0-87226-365-7*); pap. 8.95 (*0-87226-257-X*) P Bedrick Bks.
Goodman, Victor, jt. auth. see Zimet, Susan.
Goodnight, Lynn. Getting Started in Debate. 2nd ed. 160p. (gr. 7-12). 1993. pap. text ed. 8.95 (*0-685-62773-X*, C5288-3, Natl Textbk); tchr's. manual 7.95 (*0-685-62774-8*, C5289-1, Natl Textbk) NTC Pub Grp.
Goodnough, David. Christopher Columbus. new ed. LC 78-18052. (Illus.). 48p. (gr. 4-7). 1979. PLB 10.59 (*0-89375-170-7*); pap. 3.50 (*0-89375-162-6*) Troll Assocs.
—Francis Drake. LC 78-18056. (Illus.). 48p. (gr. 4-7). 1979. PLB 10.50 (*0-89375-173-1*); pap. 3.50 (*0-89375-165-0*) Troll Assocs.
—John Cabot & Son. LC 78-18054. (Illus.). 48p. (gr. 4-7). 1979. PLB 10.50 (*0-89375-172-3*); pap. 3.50 (*0-89375-164-2*) Troll Assocs.
Goodrich, Beatrice. Happy Hollow Stories, Bk. 1. LC 86-51204. (Illus.). 54p. (gr. k-6). 1987. pap. 5.95 (*0-932433-20-0*) Windswept Hse.
Goodrich, Charles A. A Child's History of the United States. 1992. Repr. of 1846 ed. lib. bdg. 75.00 (*0-7812-2935-9*) Rprt Serv.
Goodrich, Norma L. Medieval Myths. rev. ed. 224p. (RL 9). 1961. pap. 5.99 (*0-451-62661-3*, Ment) NAL-Dutton.
Goodrich, Patricia. Barefeet & Bellybuttons: Poems & Activities to Tickle a Child. Boytin, Michael, illus. 46p. (gr. k-4). 1989. pap. 5.00 (*0-9625348-1-1*) P Goodrich.
Goodrum, Don. Lettres Acadiennes. LC 92-5124. (Illus.). 32p. (gr. k-3). 1992. 14.95 (*0-88289-899-X*) Pelican.
Goodsmith, Lauren. The Children of Mauritania: Days in the Desert and At the River Shore. LC 92-46145. (gr. 3 up). 1993. 19.95 (*0-87614-782-1*) Carolrhoda bks.
Goodspeed, Antonia. The First Woman Doctor. LC 92-45996. 1993. 9.95 (*0-8380-3820-4*, Marek) Putnam Pub Group.
Goodspeed, Edgar J., jt. auth. see Owen, William B.
Goodspeed, Peter. A Rhinoceros Wakes Me up in the Morning. Panek, Dennis, illus. 32p. (ps-k). 1984. pap. 3.95 (*0-14-050455-9*, Puffin) Puffin Bks.
Goodwin, Bob & Hayes, Dympna. Famous Lives. Kelly, Teri, ed. (Illus.). 48p. (gr. 4). 1987. PLB 14.65 (*0-88625-171-0*); pap. 5.95 (*0-88625-150-8*) Durkin Hayes Pub.

Goodwin, Irene & Silvers, Ruth. Polka Dotted Pencil Pushers: Math. Goodwin, Irene, illus. LC 79-63129. 156p. (Orig.). 1979. pap. 8.95 tchr's. guide (*0-932970-08-7*) Prinit Pr.
Goodwin, Irene, ed. see Jenkins, Sheila.
Goodwin, Jean. Mischief & Mercy: Tales of the Saints. (Illus.). 228p. (gr. 9 up). 1993. pap. 9.95 (*1-883672-02-3*) Tricycle Pr.
Goodwin, Jude & Ellison, Don. Teach Me to Play: A First Book of Bridge. (gr. 3-9). 1988. PLB 10.95 (*0-944705-03-0*); pap. 10.95 (*0-944705-01-4*) Pando Pubns.
Goodwin, Mary T. & Pollen, Gerry. Creative Food Experiences for Children. 2nd rev. ed. Versel, Lauren, illus. 256p. (gr. k-6). 1980. pap. 7.95 (*0-89329-027-0*) Ctr Sci Public.
Goodwin, Peter. Engineering Projects for Young Scientists. LC 86-32528. 1989. PLB 13.90 (*0-531-10339-0*); pap. 4.95 (*0-531-15130-1*) Watts.
—Physics Projects for Young Scientists. LC 91-17822. (Illus.). 128p. (gr. 9-12). 1991. PLB 13.90 (*0-531-11070-2*) Watts.
Gool, Van. The Emperor's New Clothes. (Illus.). 48p. 1989. 5.99 (*0-517-69316-X*) Outlet Bk Co.
—Puss in Boots. (Illus.). 48p. (ps-1). 1989. 5.99 (*0-517-69319-4*) Outlet Bk Co.
Goold, I. The Rutan Voyager. (Illus.). 32p. (gr. 4 up). 1988. PLB 17.27 (*0-86592-869-X*); lib. bdg. 12.95 (*0-685-58288-4*) Rourke Corp.
Goom, Bridget. A Family in Singapore. (Illus.). 32p. (gr. 2-5). 1986. lib. bdg. 13.50 (*0-8225-1663-2*) Lerner Pubns.
Goor, Nancy, jt. auth. see Goor, Ron.
Goor, Ron & Goor, Nancy. Heads. Goor, Ron, illus. LC 87-30262. 64p. (gr. 2-6). 1988. SBE 13.95 (*0-689-31400-0*, Atheneum Child Bk) Macmillan Child Grp.
—Insect Metamorphosis: From Egg to Adult. LC 89-15144. (Illus.). 32p. (gr. 2-6). 1990. SBE 14.95 (*0-689-31445-0*, Atheneum Child Bk) Macmillan Child Grp.
—Pompeii: Exploring a Roman Ghost Town. Goor, Ron & Goor, Nancy, illus. LC 85-47895. 128p. (gr. 5-9). 1986. 15.00 (*0-690-04515-8*, Crowell Jr Bks); PLB 14.89 (*0-690-04516-6*, Crowell Jr Bks) HarpC Child Bks.
—Shadows: Here, There, & Everywhere. Goor, Ron, photos by. LC 81-43036. (Illus.). 48p. (gr. k-3). 1981. PLB 13.89 (*0-690-04133-0*, Crowell Jr Bks) HarpC Child Bks.
Gootman, Marilyn E. When a Friend Dies: A Book for Teens about Grieving & Healing. Espeland, Pamela, ed. 112p. (Orig.). (gr. 5 up). 1994. pap. 7.95 (*0-915793-66-0*) Free Spirit Pub.
Gorbaty, Norman. Dump Truck. Gorbaty, Norman, illus. 12p. (ps). 1993. bds. 6.95 (*0-448-40594-6*, G&D) Putnam Pub Group.
—Good Morning, Little Bert. 1987. 1.10 (*0-394-88504-X*) Random Bks Yng Read.
—Little Dinosaur. Gorbaty, Norman, illus. LC 87-61420. 24p. (ps-1). 1988. bk. & doll pkg. 4.95 (*0-394-89575-4*) Random Bks Yng Read.
—Little Ernie's Animal Friends. 1987. 1.10 (*0-394-88508-2*) Random Bks Yng Read.
—School Bus: A Baby Fast Rolling Book. (ps). 1993. 6.95 (*0-448-40596-2*, G&D) Putnam Pub Group.
—Sesame Street: At the Playground. 1987. 1.10 (*0-394-88503-1*) Random Bks Yng Read.
—Sesame Street: Goodnight Little Grover. 1987. 1.10 (*0-394-88506-6*) Random Bks Yng Read.
—Sesame Street: Playtime with Bigbird. 1987. 1.10 (*0-394-88507-4*) Random Bks Yng Read.
—Sesame Street: Tubbie Time with Little Ernie. 1987. 1.10 (*0-394-88505-8*) Random Bks Yng Read.
—Tow Truck: A Baby Fast Rolling Book. (ps). 1993. 6.95 (*0-448-40597-0*, G&D) Putnam Pub Group.
Gorbaty, Norman, tr. Baby in the Park. (Illus.). 12p. (ps). 1988. 2.95 (*0-394-81925-X*) Random Bks Yng Read.
Gorbaty, Norman, illus. Baby Animals Say Hello. 12p. (ps). 1986. 3.99 (*0-394-88241-5*) Random Bks Yng Read.
—Baby at Home. 12p. (ps). 1988. 2.95 (*0-394-81924-1*) Random Bks Yng Read.
—Ducky Colors. 12p. (ps). 1991. pap. 3.95 (*0-671-74435-6*, Little Simon) S&S Trade.
—Fire Engine. 12p. (ps). 1993. bds. 6.95 (*0-448-40595-4*, G&D) Putnam Pub Group.
—Get up & Go, Little Dinosaur! LC 89-64282. 22p. (ps). 1990. bds. 2.95 (*0-679-80693-8*) Random Bks Yng Read.
—Kitty in & Out. 12p. (ps). 1991. pap. 3.95 (*0-671-74437-2*, Little Simon) S&S Trade.
—Puppy Round & Square. 12p. (ps). 1991. pap. 3.95 (*0-671-74436-4*, Little Simon) S&S Trade.
—Turtle Count. 12p. (ps). 1991. pap. 3.95 (*0-671-74434-8*, Little Simon) S&S Trade.
—What Do You See on Sesame Street? 12p. (ps). 1988. 3.99 (*0-394-80594-1*) Random Bks Yng Read.
Gorden, Charles L. Van see Van Gorden, Charles L.
Gordner, Brad, jt. auth. see Molyneux, Lynn.
Gordon. Pierced by a Ray of Sun. Date not set. 15.00 (*0-06-023613-2*, Festival); PLB 14.89 (*0-06-023614-0*, Festival) HarpC Child Bks.
Gordon, Alvin J. Tortillas. DeGrazia, Ted, illus. 20p. (Orig.). (gr. 1-3). 1971. pap. 6.95 (*0-916955-06-0*) ARCUS Pub.
Gordon, April, ed. see Jackson, Bobby L.

Gordon, Christine W. Mee Glows with Health & Happiness. Gordon, Christine W., illus. LC 87-90587. 32p. (Orig.). (ps-2). 1987. pap. 5.00 (0-9618854-1-6) Mee Enterp.
—Mee, Who Is Hardly Any Size at All. Gordon, Christine W., illus. LC 87-90588. (Orig.). (ps-k). 1987. pap. 4.00 (0-9618854-0-8) Mee Enterp.
Gordon, Erica, retold by. The Rabbi's Wisdom: A Jewish Folk Tale from Eastern Europe. Ambrus, Victor, illus. LC 90-44375. 32p. (gr. k-3). 1991. PLB 14.95 (0-87226-446-7, Bedrick Blackie) P Bedrick Bks.
Gordon, Gaelyn. Duckat. (ps). 1992. 13.95 (0-590-45455-2, Scholastic Hardcover) Scholastic Inc.
Gordon, Ginger. My Two Worlds. Cooper, Martha, photos by. LC 92-39271. (gr. 5 up). 1993. 14.45 (0-395-58704-2, Clarion Bks) HM.
Gordon, Glen. The Delicate Balance: An Environmental Chemistry Module. Gardner, Marjorie, intro. by. (Illus.). 138p. (Orig.). (gr. 9-12). 1991. pap. text ed. 8.20 (1-879827-06-9) Vistas.
Gordon, Henry. It's Magic. (Illus.). 92p. (gr. 5 up). 1989. pap. 9.95 (0-87975-545-8) Prometheus Bks.
Gordon, James. Stress Management. (Illus.). 112p. (gr. 6-12). 1990. 18.95 (0-7910-0042-7) Chelsea Hse.
Gordon, James S. Holistic Medicine. (Illus.). 120p. (gr. 6-12). 1988. lib. bdg. 18.95x (0-7910-0085-0) Chelsea Hse.
Gordon, Jeanie. If My Parents Are Getting Divorced, Why Am I the One Who Hurts? 144p. (gr. 9-12). 1993. pap. 7.99 (0-310-59311-5, Pub. by Youth Spec) Zondervan.
Gordon, Jeffie R. Hide & Shriek: Riddles about Ghosts & Goblins. (Illus.). 32p. (gr. 1-4). 1991. PLB 11.95 (0-8225-2336-1); pap. 3.95 (0-8225-9594-X) Lerner Pubns.
—Muriel & Ruth: A Book about Friendship. Yerkes, Lane, illus. LC 91-728718. 24p. (ps-3). 1992. 8.95 (1-878093-18-5) Boyds Mills Pr.
—Six Sleepy Sheep. O'Brien, John, illus. LC 90-85728. 24p. (ps-1). 1991. 12.95 (1-878093-06-1) Boyds Mills Pr.
—Six Sleepy Sheep. O'Brien, John, illus. 24p. (ps-1). 1993. pap. 4.99 (0-14-054848-3, Puffin) Puffin Bks.
—Two Badd Babies. Demarest, Chris L., illus. LC 91-72869. 32p. (ps-3). 1992. 13.95 (1-878093-85-1) Boyds Mills Pr.
Gordon, Jo W. Recycling. LC 92-9788. 1992. 12.40 (0-531-17332-1, Gloucester Pr) Watts.
Gordon, John. The Burning Baby & Other Ghosts. LC 92-54579. 192p. (gr. 7-11). 1993. 14.95 (1-56402-067-3) Candlewick Pr.
Gordon, Judith, jt. auth. see Gordon, Sol.
Gordon, Karen E. The Well-Tempered Sentence: A Punctuation Handbook for the Innocent, the Eager & the Doomed. LC 82-19704. (Illus.). 96p. (gr. 7 up). 1983. 9.70 (0-89919-170-3, Clarion Bks) HM.
Gordon, M. Typing Tips. large type ed. (gr. 6 up). 1972. 4.28 (0-317-01952-X, 4-26550-00) Am Printing Hse.
Gordon, Maria, jt. auth. see Gordon, Mike.
Gordon, Matthew. Hafez al-Assad. (Illus.). (gr. 5 up). 1989. 17.95 (1-55546-827-6) Chelsea Hse.
Gordon, Matthew S. The Gemayels. Schlesinger, Arthur M., Jr., intro. by. (Illus.). 112p. (gr. 5 up). 1988. 17.95 (1-55545-834-9) Chelsea Hse.
—Islam. (Illus.). 128p. (gr. 7-12). 1991. 17.95x (0-8160-2443-X) Facts on File.
Gordon, Michael. I Would If I Could: A Teenager's Guide to ADHD-Hyperactivity. Jimco, Janet, illus. 34p. (Illus.). (gr. 6-12). 1992. pap. 12.50 (0-9627701-3-2) GSI Pubns.
—My Brother's a World-Class Pain: A Sibling's Guide to ADHD-Hyperactivity. Thomas, Sandra F., intro. by. Junco, Janet H., illus. 40p. (gr. 4 up). 1992. pap. 11.00 (0-9627701-2-4) GSI Pubns.
Gordon, Mike & Gordon, Maria. Haunted House Glow in the Dark Sticker Book. (Illus.). 12p. (gr. 2-6). 1990. pap. 5.99 (0-517-03356-9) Outlet Bk Co.
Gordon, Nayvin. A Family Visits the Doctor. LC 93-60740. 140p. (gr. 2-8). 1993. pap. 5.95 (1-55523-631-6) Winston-Derek.
Gordon, Pat, jt. auth. see Robinson, Betty.
Gordon, Patricia & Snow, Reed C. Kids Learn America! Bringing Geography to Life with People, Places, & History. Williamson, Susan, ed. LC 91-27245. (Illus.). 176p. (Orig.). (gr. 1 up). 1991. pap. 12.95 (0-913589-58-6) Williamson Pub Co.
Gordon, Richard D. Martin & the Mountaintop: An Illustrated Tribute to Dr. Martin Luther King, Jr. Gordon, Richard D., illus. LC 88-92651. 85p. (gr. 7 up). 1988. 14.95 (0-9621308-0-X) CMark Pr.
Gordon, Ruth. Feathers. Dabcovich, Lydia, illus. LC 92-26164. 32p. (gr. k-3). 1993. RSBE 14.95 (0-02-736511-5, Macmillan Child Bk) Macmillan Child Grp.
Gordon, Ruth, selected by. Peeling the Onion: An Anthology of Poems Selected by Ruth Gordon. LC 92-571. 192p. (gr. 5 up). 1993. 15.00 (0-06-021727-8); 14.89 (0-06-021728-6) HarpC Child Bks.
Gordon, Ruth, ed. Time Is the Longest Distance. LC 90-4947. 96p. (gr. 7 up). 1991. 13.95 (0-06-022297-2); PLB 13.89 (0-06-022424-X) HarpC Child Bks.
—Under All Silences: The Many Shades of Love (An Anthology of Poems Selected by Ruth Gordon) LC 85-45845. 128p. (gr. 7 up). 1987. 13.00 (0-06-022154-2) HarpC Child Bks.
Gordon, Sharon. Christmas Surprise. Magine, John, illus. 32p. (gr. k-2). 1980. PLB 7.89 (0-89375-373-4); pap. 1.95 (0-89375-273-8) Troll Assocs.
—Dinosaur in Trouble. Harvey, Paul, illus. 32p. (gr. k-2). 1980. PLB 7.89 (0-89375-374-2); pap. 1.95 (0-89375-274-6) Troll Assocs.
—Un Dinosauro en Peligro. Havey, Paul, illus. (SPA.). 32p. (gr. k-2). 1981. PLB 7.89 (0-89375-554-0); pap. 1.95 (0-685-42386-7) Troll Assocs.
—Dolphins & Porpoises. Goldsborough, June, illus. LC 84-8594. 32p. (gr. k-2). 1985. PLB 11.59 (0-8167-0340-X); pap. text ed. 2.95 (0-8167-0443-0) Troll Assocs.
—Drip Drop. Page, Don, illus. LC 81-5112. 32p. (gr. k-2). 1981. PLB 11.59 (0-89375-507-9); pap. 2.95 (0-89375-508-7) Troll Assocs.
—Easter Bunny's Lost Egg. Magine, Sharon, illus. 32p. (gr. k-2). 1980. PLB 7.89 (0-89375-375-0); pap. 1.95 (0-89375-275-4) Troll Assocs.
—First Day of Spring. Willis, Christine, illus. LC 81-2750. 32p. (gr. k-2). 1981. PLB 11.59 (0-89375-531-1); pap. text ed. 2.95 (0-89375-532-X) Troll Assocs.
—Friendly Snowman. Magine, John, illus. 32p. (gr. k-2). 1980. PLB 7.89 (0-89375-377-7); pap. 1.95 (0-89375-277-0) Troll Assocs.
—Home for a Puppy. Wheeler, Jody, illus. LC 86-30853. 32p. (gr. k-2). 1988. PLB 7.89 (0-8167-0978-5); pap. text ed. 1.95 (0-8167-0979-3) Troll Assocs.
—The Jolly Monsters. Cushman, Doug, illus. LC 87-10867. 32p. (gr. k-2). 1988. PLB 11.59 (0-8167-1079-1); pap. text ed. 2.95 (0-8167-1080-5) Troll Assocs.
—Maxwell Mouse. Rosenberg, Amye, illus. LC 81-4653. 32p. (gr. k-2). 1981. PLB 11.59 (0-89375-501-X); pap. 2.95 (0-89375-502-8) Troll Assocs.
—Mike's First Haircut. Fiammenghi, Gioia, illus. LC 87-10911. 32p. (gr. k-2). 1988. PLB 7.89 (0-8167-1113-5); pap. text ed. 1.95 (0-8167-1114-3) Troll Assocs.
—Pete the Parakeet. Harvey, Paul, illus. 32p. (gr. k-2). 1980. PLB 7.89 (0-89375-384-X); pap. 1.95 (0-89375-284-3) Troll Assocs.
—Play Ball, Kate! Page, Don, illus. LC 81-4855. 32p. (gr. k-2). 1981. pap. text ed. 11.59 (0-89375-525-7); pap. 2.95 (0-89375-526-5) Troll Assocs.
—Playground Fun. Karas, G. Brian, illus. LC 86-30854. 32p. (gr. k-2). 1988. lib. bdg. 7.89 (0-8167-0990-4); pap. text ed. 1.95 (0-8167-0991-2) Troll Assocs.
—Sam the Scarecrow. Silverstein, Don, illus. 32p. (gr. k-2). 1980. PLB 7.89 (0-89375-387-4); pap. 1.95 (0-89375-287-8) Troll Assocs.
—Samuel el Espantapajaros. Silverstein, Don, illus. (SPA.). 32p. (gr. k-2). 1981. PLB 7.89 (0-89375-556-7); pap. 1.95 (0-89375-958-9) Troll Assocs.
—Show & Tell. Kolding, Richard M., illus. LC 86-30855. 32p. (gr. k-2). 1988. PLB 7.89 (0-8167-0994-7); pap. text ed. 1.95 (0-8167-0995-5) Troll Assocs.
—The Spelling Bee. Garcia, Tom, illus. LC 81-4648. 32p. (gr. k-2). 1981. PLB 11.59 (0-89375-535-4); pap. 2.95 (0-89375-536-2) Troll Assocs.
—Surprise Party. Hall, Susan, illus. LC 81-4869. 32p. (gr. k-2). 1981. PLB 11.59 (0-89375-521-4); pap. 2.95 (0-89375-522-2) Troll Assocs.
—Three Little Witches. Sims, Deborah, illus. 32p. (gr. k-2). 1980. PLB 7.89 (0-89375-390-4); pap. 1.95 (0-89375-290-8) Troll Assocs.
—Tick Tock Clock. LC 81-11393. 1982. PLB 11.59 (0-89375-676-8); pap. 2.95 (0-89375-677-6) Troll Assocs.
—Trees. Trivas, Irene, illus. LC 82-20291. 32p. (gr. k-2). 1983. lib. bdg. 11.59 (0-89375-901-5); pap. text ed. 2.95 (0-8167-0879-7) Troll Assocs.
—What a Dog. Sims, Deborah, illus. 32p. (gr. k-2). 1980. PLB 7.89 (0-89375-393-9); pap. 1.95 (0-89375-293-2) Troll Assocs.
Gordon, Sheila. Middle of Somewhere: A Story of South Africa. LC 90-30625. 160p. (gr. 4-6). 1990. 13.95 (0-531-05908-1); PLB 13.99 (0-531-08508-2) Orchard Bks Watts.
—Middle of Somewhere: A Story of South Africa. (gr. 4-7). 1992. pap. 3.50 (0-553-15991-7) Bantam.
—Waiting for the Rain. LC 87-7638. 224p. (gr. 7 up). 1987. 12.95 (0-531-05726-7); PLB 12.99 (0-531-08326-8) Orchard Bks Watts.
—Waiting for the Rain. (gr. 7 up). 1989. pap. 3.99 (0-553-27911-4, Starfire) Bantam.
Gordon, Shirley. The Boy Who Wanted a Family. 96p. (gr. 1-4). 1982. pap. 2.95 (0-440-40786-9, YB) Dell.
—Crystal's Christmas Carol. Frascino, Edward, illus. LC 87-33487. 40p. (gr. k-3). 1989. PLB 12.89 (0-06-022239-5) HarpC Child Bks.
—Me & the Bad Guys. Frascino, Edward, illus. 80p. (gr. 3-7). 1984. pap. 2.25 (0-440-45520-0, YB) Dell.
Gordon, Sol. Better Safe Than Sorry Book. (ps-3). 1992. pap. 8.95 (0-87975-768-X) Prometheus Bks.
—Facts about Sex: For Today's Youth. Cohen, Vivien, illus. 50p. (gr. 2-5). 1992. pap. 8.95 (0-934978-01-8) Prometheus Bks.
—Girls Are Girls & Boys Are Boys: So What's the Difference? Cohen, Vivien, illus. 48p. (Orig.). (gr. 3-7). 1991. pap. 9.95 (0-87975-686-1) Prometheus Bks.
—Protect Yourself from Becoming an Unwanted Parent. (Illus.). (gr. 9-12). 1983. pap. 1.95 (0-934978-08-5) Ed U Pr.
Gordon, Sol & Cohen, Judith. Did the Sun Shine Before You Were Born: A Sex Education Primer. LC 74-82733. (ps-2). 1974. 12.00 (0-89388-179-1) Okpaku Communications.
Gordon, Sol & Gordon, Judith. A Better Safe Than Sorry Book: A Family Guide for Sexual Assault Prevention. Cohen, Vivien, illus. 44p. (gr. 2-7). 1992. pap. 8.95 (0-934978-13-1) Prometheus Bks.
—Did the Sun Shine Before You Were Born? A Sex Education Primer. (ps-3). 1982. pap. 7.95 (0-934978-03-4) Ed-U Pr.
—Did the Sun Shine Before Your Were Born? Cohen, Vivien, illus. 48p. (Orig.). (gr. k-5). 1992. pap. 8.95 (0-87975-723-X) Prometheus Bks.
Gordon, Sol, jt. auth. see Everly, Kathleen.
Gordon, Susan. Asian Indians. Daniels, Roger, contrib. by. LC 90-12275. (Illus.). 64p. (gr. 5-8). 1990. PLB 13.40 (0-531-10976-3) Watts.
Gordon, Vivian V. & Smith-Owens, Lois. Prisons & the Criminal Justice System. 160p. (gr. 7 up). 1992. PLB 15.85 (0-8027-8121-7); pap. 9.95 (0-8027-7370-2) Walker & Co.
Gordon, Yosi. In the Beginning God Created the Alef-Bet. Grishaver, Joel L., illus. (Orig.). (gr. 3-5). 1991. pap. 3.75 wkbk. (0-933873-61-1) Torah Aura.
—Ot La-Ba'ot, 5 bks. Urbanovic, Jacki, illus. 120p. (gr. 3-4). 1991. Set. wkbk. 6.95 (0-933873-54-9) Torah Aura.
Gore, Sheila. My Shadow. 1990. pap. 6.95 (0-385-41130-8) Doubleday.
—Swamps. Burns, Robert, illus. LC 91-45081. 32p. (gr. 4-6). 1993. PLB 11.59 (0-8167-2755-4); pap. text ed. 3.95 (0-8167-2756-2) Troll Assocs. Postponed.
Gore, Willma W. Earth Day. LC 92-43199. (Illus.). 48p. (gr. 1-4). 1992. lib. bdg. 14.95 (0-89490-380-2) Enslow Pubs.
—Independence Day. LC 92-18946. (Illus.). 48p. (gr. 1-4). 1993. lib. bdg. 14.95 (0-89490-403-5) Enslow Pubs.
—Mother's Day. LC 92-32675. (Illus.). 48p. (gr. 1-4). 1993. lib. bdg. 14.95 (0-89490-404-3) Enslow Pubs.
Gorey, Edward. The Bug Book. (Illus.). (gr. 4 up). 1987. 8.95 (0-915361-69-8) Modan-Adama Bks.
—Cat E Gory. LC 86-10938. (ps up). 1986. 8.95 (0-915361-55-8) Modan-Adama Bks.
—The Wuggly Ump. Gorey, Edward, illus. LC 86-11273. (ps up). 1986. 6.95 (0-915361-56-6, Dist. by Watts) Modan-Adama Bks.
Gorey, Edward, illus. Category. LC 86-10938. (ps up). 1986. Repr. 8.95 (0-685-13444-X) Modan-Adama Bks.
Gorham, Kelly, ed. see Burgess, Joe.
Gorham, Kelly, ed. see Marchetti, Tony.
Gorham, Zoe. ABC I Can Be. (ps-3). 1993. pap. 3.95 (0-85953-129-5) Childs Play.
Gorman, Carol. Biggest Bully in Brookdale. (Illus.). 80p. (gr. 2-4). 1992. pap. 3.99 (0-570-04713-7) Concordia.
—Brian's Footsteps. LC 93-38322. 1994. PLB 3.99 (0-570-04629-7) Concordia.
—Chelsea & the Green-Haired Kid. Ashby, Ruth, ed. 128p. (gr. 7 up). 1992. pap. 2.99 (0-671-78713-6, Archway) PB.
—Chelsey & the Green-Haired Kid. (gr. 5 up). 1987. 13.45 (0-395-41854-2) HM.
—Chelsey & the Green-Haired Kid. 1992. pap. 12.95 (0-395-44767-4) HM.
—Die for Me. 144p. (Orig.). (gr. 7-12). 1992. pap. 3.50 (0-380-76686-8, Flare) Avon.
—The Great Director. Nappi, Rudi, illus. LC 93-20228. 60p. (Orig.). (gr. 2-4). 1993. pap. 3.99 (0-570-04746-3) Concordia.
—It's Not Fair. (Illus.). 80p. (Orig.). (gr. 2-4). 1992. pap. 3.99 (0-570-04714-5) Concordia.
—Jennifer the Jerk Is Missing. LC 93-11474. 1994. write for info. (0-671-86578-1, S&S BFYR) S&S Trade.
—Nobody's Friend. Nappi, Rudy, illus. LC 92-24936. 60p. (Orig.). (gr. 1-4). 1993. pap. 3.99 (0-570-04729-3) Concordia.
—The Richest Kid in the World. Nappi, Rudy, illus. LC 92-24935. 60p. (Orig.). (gr. 1-4). 1993. pap. 3.99 (0-570-04728-5) Concordia.
—Skin Deep. Nappi, Rudy, illus. LC 93-20230. 60p. (gr. 2-4). 1993. pap. 3.99 (0-570-04747-1) Concordia.
—The Taming of Roberta Parsley. LC 93-38312. 1994. pap. 3.99 (0-570-04628-9) Concordia.
Gorman, Cinda. Growing up Christian in a Sexy World. 50p. (Orig.). (gr. 5-6). 1989. pap. 8.50 (0-940754-78-9) Ed Ministries.
Gorman, James, jt. auth. see Horner, John.
Gorman, Michael J. Texts & Contexts: A Guide to Careful Thinking & Writing about the Bible. 51p. (gr. 9-12). 1990. pap. 13.50 (1-881678-04-0) CRIS.
Gorman, Michael J., jt. ed. see Sands, Catherine D.
Gorman, S. S. Goal Maker. Clancy, Lisa, ed. 128p. (Orig.). (gr. 4-6). 1993. pap. 2.99 (0-671-78905-8, Minstrel Bks) PB.
—High-Fives: Slam Dunk. MacDonald, Patricia, ed. 128p. (Orig.). (gr. 3-6). 1990. pap. 2.99 (0-671-70381-1, Minstrel Bks) PB.
—Quarterback Sneak. MacDonald, Pat, ed. 144p. (gr. 4-6). 1991. pap. 2.95 (0-671-70383-8, Minstrel Bks) PB.
—Soccer Is a Kick. MacDonald, Patricia, ed. 144p. (Orig.). (gr. 4-7). 1990. pap. 2.99 (0-671-70380-3, Minstrel Bks) PB.
—Survive! Clancy, Lisa, ed. 128p. 1992. pap. 2.99 (0-671-74503-4, Minstrel Bks) PB.
Gorman, Susan. The Game of Love. (gr. 6 up). 1988. pap. 2.50 (0-553-27476-7) Bantam.
—This Time for Real. 192p. (Orig.). (gr. 7 up). 1988. pap. 2.50 (0-553-27175-X) Bantam.

Gorman-Gard, Kathleen. Figurative Language: A Comprehensive Program. LC 91-44747. 240p. (gr. 5-12). 1992. pap. 31.00 (*0-930599-72-1*) Thinking Pubns.

Gormley, Beatrice. Best Friend Insurance. McCully, Emily A., illus. LC 83-5713. 160p. (gr. 3-6). 1983. 10.95 (*0-525-44066-6*, DCB) Dutton Child Bks.
—Best Friend Insurance. McCully, Emily A., illus. 160p. (gr. 3-7). 1985. pap. 2.50 (*0-380-69854-4*, Camelot) Avon.
—Ellie's Birthstone Ring. (Illus.). (gr. 2-4). 1992. 14.00 (*0-525-44969-8*, DCB) Dutton Child Bks.
—Fifth Grade Magic. McCully, Emily A., illus. 128p. (gr. 3-7). 1984. 3.50 (*0-380-67439-4*, Camelot) Avon.
—The Ghastly Glasses. McCully, Emily A., illus. LC 85-10112. 128p. (gr. 2-6). 1985. 12.95 (*0-525-44215-4*, DCB) Dutton Child Bks.
—The Magic Mean Machine. McCully, Emily A., illus. 128p. (Orig.). (gr. 5 up). 1989. pap. 2.95 (*0-380-75519-X*, Camelot) Avon.
—Mail-Order Wings. McCully, Emily A., illus. 164p. (gr. 3-7). 1984. pap. 2.95 (*0-380-67421-1*, Camelot) Avon.
—More Fifth Grade Magic. 112p. 1990. pap. 3.50 (*0-380-70883-3*, Camelot) Avon.
—Paul's Volcano. Smith, Catherine B., illus. LC 86-27543. (gr. 4-6). 1987. 13.95 (*0-395-43079-8*) HM.
—Paul's Volcano. 160p. 1988. pap. 2.50 (*0-380-70562-1*, Camelot) Avon.
—Sky Guys to White Cat. McCully, Emily A., illus. LC 91-364. 144p. (gr. 3-6). 1991. 12.95 (*0-525-44743-1*, DCB) Dutton Child Bks.
—Wanted: UFO. LC 89-26017. (Illus.). 128p. (gr. 3-6). 1990. 12.95 (*0-525-44593-5*, DCB) Dutton Child Bks.
—Wanted: UFO. 128p. 1992. pap. 2.99 (*0-380-71313-6*, Camelot) Avon.
Gorney, jt. auth. see Jones.
Gorney, Janifer, ed. see Christensen, Kathryn.
Gorog, Judith. In a Messy, Messy Room: And Other Strange Stories. Root, Kim, illus. 48p. (gr. 4-7). 1990. 14.95 (*0-399-22218-9*, Philomel Bks) Putnam Pub Group.
—No Swimming in Dark Pond & Other Stories. LC 86-22586. 1987. 14.95 (*0-399-21418-6*, Philomel) Putnam Pub Group.
—On Meeting Witches at Wells. (gr. 3 up). 1991. 14.95 (*0-399-21803-3*, Philomel) Putnam Pub Group.
—Three Dreams & a Nightmare. 160p. (gr. 7-9). 1992. pap. 2.50 (*0-8167-1822-9*) Troll Assocs.
—Three Dreams & a Nightmare: And Other Tales of the Dark. 160p. (gr. 4 up). 1988. 14.95 (*0-399-21578-6*, Philomel Bks) Putnam Pub Group.
—When Nobody's Home: Thirteen Tales for Tonight. LC 93-34595. 1994. 13.95 (*0-590-46862-6*) Scholastic Inc.
—Winning Scheherazade. LC 90-1134. 112p. (gr. 5 up). 1991. SBE 12.95 (*0-689-31648-8*, Atheneum Child Bk) Macmillan Child Grp.
Gorsline, Douglas, jt. auth. see Gorsline, Marie.
Gorsline, Marie & Gorsline, Douglas. Cowboys. Gorsline, Douglas, illus. LC 78-1131. 32p. (ps-2). 1980. lib. bdg. 5.99 (*0-394-93935-2*); pap. 2.25 (*0-394-83935-8*) Random Bks Yng Read.
—North American Indians. Gorsline, Douglas, illus. LC 77-79843. (ps-2). 1978. pap. 2.25 (*0-394-83702-9*) Random Bks Yng Read.
—The Pioneers. reissued ed. Gorsline, Marie & Gorsline, Douglas, illus. LC 78-54960. 32p. (gr. k-4). 1982. pap. 2.25 (*0-394-83905-6*) Random Bks Yng Read.
Gorsline, Marie, ed. Nursery Rhymes. reissue ed. Gorsline, Douglas, illus. LC 76-24168. 32p. (ps-1). 1992. pap. 2.25 (*0-394-83550-6*) Random Bks Yng Read.
Goscinny, R. & Uderzo, M. (SPA., Illus.). 14.95 (*0-8288-6082-3*, S26630) Fr & Eur.
—Der Arvernerschild. (GER., Illus.). 19.95 (*0-8288-4914-5*) Fr & Eur.
—Asterix & Operation Getafix. 1990. 19.95 (*0-8288-8570-2*) Fr & Eur.
—Asterix & Son. 1990. 19.95 (*0-8288-8568-0*) Fr & Eur.
—Asterix & the Banquet. 1990. 19.95 (*0-8288-8590-7*) Fr & Eur.
—Asterix & the Big Fight. (Illus.). (gr. 7-10). 1990. 19.95 (*0-8288-8917-X*) Fr & Eur.
—Asterix & the Black Gold. 1990. 19.95 (*0-8288-8592-3*) Fr & Eur.
—Asterix & the Great Divide. 1990. 19.95 (*0-8288-8567-2*) Fr & Eur.
—Asterix & the Magic Carpet. 1990. 19.95 (*0-8288-8569-9*) Fr & Eur.
—Asterix Chez Rahazade. (FRE.). 1990. 19.95 (*0-8288-8572-9*) Fr & Eur.
—Asterix: Comment Obelix est Tombe dans la Marmite du Druide Quand Il Etait Petit. (FRE.). 1990. 19.95 (*0-8288-8597-4*) Fr & Eur.
—Asterix el Galo. (SPA., Illus.). (gr. 7-10). 19.95 (*0-8288-4933-1*) Fr & Eur.
—Asterix et la Rose et le Glaive. (FRE.). 1990. 19.95 (*0-8288-8573-7*) Fr & Eur.
—Asterix: How Obelix Fell into the Magic Cauldron When He Was a Little Boy. 1990. 19.95 (*0-8288-8594-X*) Fr & Eur.
—Asterix in Belgium. 1990. 19.95 (*0-8288-8591-5*) Fr & Eur.
—Asterix in Corsica. 1990. 19.95 (*0-8288-8566-4*) Fr & Eur.
—Asterix, Obelix & Company. 1990. 19.95 (*0-8288-8565-6*) Fr & Eur.
—Asterix vs Caesar. 1990. 19.95 (*0-8288-8593-1*) Fr & Eur.

—Le Cadeau de Cesar. (FRE., Illus.). 1990. 19.95 (*0-8288-4959-5*) Fr & Eur.
—The Caldron. (Illus.). 1990. 19.95 (*0-8288-4960-9*) Fr & Eur.
—La Cizana. (SPA., Illus.). 19.95 (*0-8288-4961-7*) Fr & Eur.
—El Combate de los Jefes. (SPA., Illus.). 19.95 (*0-8288-4962-5*) Fr & Eur.
—Les Douze Travaux d'Asterix. (FRE., Illus.). 1990. 19.95 (*0-8288-4964-1*) Fr & Eur.
—El Escudo Arverno. (SPA., Illus.). 19.95 (*0-8288-4965-X*) Fr & Eur.
—Falx Aurea. (LAT., Illus.). 19.95 (*0-8288-4966-8*) Fr & Eur.
—Fils d'Asterix. (FRE.). 1990. 19.95 (*0-8288-8571-0*) Fr & Eur.
—Das Geschenk Casars. (GER., Illus.). 19.95 (*0-8288-4967-6*) Fr & Eur.
—Die Goldene Sichel. (GER., Illus.). 19.95 (*0-8288-4969-2*) Fr & Eur.
—Grand Fosse. (FRE.). 1990. 19.95 (*0-8288-8595-8*) Fr & Eur.
—La Grande Traversee. (FRE., Illus.). 1990. 19.95 (*0-8288-4970-6*) Fr & Eur.
—The Great Crossing. (Illus.). 1990. 19.95 (*0-8288-4971-4*) Fr & Eur.
—Die Grosse Uberfahrt. (GER., Illus.). 19.95 (*0-8288-4972-2*) Fr & Eur.
—La Hoz de Oro. (SPA., Illus.). 19.95 (*0-8288-4973-0*) Fr & Eur.
—Der Kampf der Hauptlinge. (GER., Illus.). 19.95 (*0-8288-4974-9*) Fr & Eur.
—Der Kupferkessel. (GER., Illus.). 19.95 (*0-8288-4975-7*) Fr & Eur.
—Los Laureles del Cesar. (SPA., Illus.). 19.95 (*0-8288-4976-5*) Fr & Eur.
—Les Lauriers de Cesar. (FRE., Illus.). 1990. 19.95 (*0-8288-4977-3*) Fr & Eur.
—Die Lorbeeren des Casar. (GER., Illus.). 19.95 (*0-8288-4978-1*) Fr & Eur.
—The Mansions of the Gods. (Illus.). 1990. 19.95 (*0-8288-4979-X*) Fr & Eur.
—Die Normannen. (GER., Illus.). 19.95 (*0-8288-4980-3*) Fr & Eur.
—Obelix et Compagnie. (FRE., Illus.). 1990. 19.95 (*0-8288-5479-3*) Fr & Eur.
—Odyssee d'Asterix. (FRE.). 1990. 19.95 (*0-8288-8596-6*) Fr & Eur.
—El Regalo del Cesar. (SPA., Illus.). 19.95 (*0-8288-4900-5*) Fr & Eur.
—La Residencia de los Dioses. (SPA., Illus.). 19.95 (*0-8288-4901-3*) Fr & Eur.
—La Serpe d'Or. (FRE., Illus.). 1990. 19.95 (*0-8288-4904-8*) Fr & Eur.
—The Soothsayer. (Illus.). 1990. 19.95 (*0-8288-4905-6*) Fr & Eur.
—Streit Um Asterix. (GER., Illus.). 19.95 (*0-8288-4906-4*) Fr & Eur.
—Tour de France. (GER., Illus.). 1990. 19.95 (*0-8288-4907-2*) Fr & Eur.
—Le Tour de Gaulle. (FRE., Illus.). 1990. 19.95 (*0-8288-4908-0*) Fr & Eur.
—Die Trabantenstadt. (GER., Illus.). 19.95 (*0-8288-4910-2*) Fr & Eur.
—La Vuelta a la Galia. (SPA., Illus.). 19.95 (*0-8288-4911-0*) Fr & Eur.
—La Zizanie. (FRE., Illus.). 1990. 19.95 (*0-8288-4912-9*) Fr & Eur.
Goscinny, R., jt. auth. see Sempe, Jean-Jacques.
Goscinny, Rene. Le Tour de Gaulle. (FRE., Also avail. in Span.). (gr. 3-8). 1990. 19.95 (*0-8288-4909-9*) Fr & Eur.
Goscinny, Rene & Uderzo, M. The Golden Sickle. (Illus.). 1990. 19.95 (*0-8288-4968-4*) Fr & Eur.
Goscinny, Rene de Asterix a la Serpe d'or. (FRE., Illus.). (gr. 3-8). 1990. 19.95 (*0-8288-4939-0*) Fr & Eur.
Goscinny, Rene de & Uderzo, M. Asterix als Gladiator. (GER., Illus.). (gr. 7-10). 1992. 19.95 (*0-8288-4923-4*)
—Asterix als Legionar. (GER., Illus.). (gr. 7-10). 1992. 19.95 (*0-8288-4924-2*) Fr & Eur.
—Asterix & Caesar's Gift. (Illus.). (gr. 7-10). 1990. 19.95 (*0-8288-4915-3*) Fr & Eur.
—Asterix & Cleopatra. (Illus.). (gr. 7-10). 1990. 19.95 (*0-8288-4916-1*) Fr & Eur.
—Asterix & the Chieftain's Shield. (Illus.). (gr. 7-10). 1990. 19.95 (*0-8288-4918-8*) Fr & Eur.
—Asterix & the Goths. (Illus.). (gr. 7-10). 1990. 19.95 (*0-8288-4919-6*) Fr & Eur.
—Asterix & the Laurel Wreath. (Illus.). (gr. 7-10). 1990. 19.95 (*0-8288-4920-X*) Fr & Eur.
—Asterix & the Normans. (Illus.). (gr. 7-10). 1990. 19.95 (*0-8288-4921-8*) Fr & Eur.
—Asterix & the Roman Agent. (Illus.). (gr. 7-10). 1990. 19.95 (*0-8288-4922-6*) Fr & Eur.
—Asterix apud Gothos. (LAT., Illus.). (gr. 7-10). 1990. PLB 19.95 (*0-8288-4925-0*) Fr & Eur.
—Asterix at the Olympic Games. (Illus.). (gr. 7-10). 1990. 19.95 (*0-8288-4926-9*) Fr & Eur.
—Asterix auf Korsika. (GER., Illus.). (gr. 7-10). 1990. PLB 19.95 (*0-8288-4927-7*) Fr & Eur.
—Asterix bei den Briten. (GER., Illus.). (gr. 7-10). 1990. PLB 19.95 (*0-8288-4928-5*) Fr & Eur.
—Asterix bei den Olympischen Spielen. (GER., Illus.). (gr. 7-10). 1990. PLB 19.95 (*0-8288-4929-3*) Fr & Eur.

—Asterix bei den Schweizern. (GER., Illus.). (gr. 7-10). 1990. PLB 19.95 (*0-8288-4930-7*) Fr & Eur.
—Asterix chez les Belges. (FRE., Illus.). (gr. 7-10). 1990. 19.95 (*0-8288-4931-5*) Fr & Eur.
—Asterix der Gallier. (GER., Illus.). (gr. 7-10). 1990. PLB 19.95 (*0-8288-4932-3*) Fr & Eur.
—Asterix en Bretana. (SPA., Illus.). (gr. 7-10). 1990. PLB 19.95 (*0-8288-4934-X*) Fr & Eur.
—Asterix en Corcega. (SPA., Illus.). (gr. 7-10). 1990. PLB 19.95 (*0-8288-4935-8*) Fr & Eur.
—Asterix en Corse. (FRE., Illus.). (gr. 7-10). 1990. 19.95 (*0-8288-4936-6*) Fr & Eur.
—Asterix en Helvecia. (SPA., Illus.). (gr. 7-10). 1990. PLB 19.95 (*0-8288-4937-4*) Fr & Eur.
—Asterix en los Juegos Olimpicos. (SPA., Illus.). (gr. 7-10). 1990. PLB 19.95 (*0-8288-4938-2*) Fr & Eur.
—Asterix Gallus. (LAT., Illus.). (gr. 7-10). 1990. lib. bdg. 19.95 (*0-8288-4941-2*) Fr & Eur.
—Asterix Gladiador. (SPA., Illus.). (gr. 7-10). 1990. PLB 19.95 (*0-8288-4942-0*) Fr & Eur.
—Asterix Gladiator. (LAT., Illus.). 1990. 19.95 (*0-8288-4943-9*) Fr & Eur.
—Asterix in Britain. (Illus.). 1990. 19.95 (*0-8288-4944-7*) Fr & Eur.
—Asterix in Spain. (Illus.). 1990. 19.95 (*0-8288-4945-5*) Fr & Eur.
—Asterix in Spanien. (GER., Illus.). 1990. PLB 19.95 (*0-8288-4946-3*) Fr & Eur.
—Asterix in Switzerland. (Illus.). 1990. PLB 19.95 (*0-8288-4947-1*) Fr & Eur.
—Asterix iter Gallicum. (LAT., Illus.). 1990. PLB 19.95 (*0-8288-4948-X*) Fr & Eur.
—Asterix Legionario. (SPA., Illus.). 1990. PLB 19.95 (*0-8288-4949-8*) Fr & Eur.
—Asterix the Gaul. (Illus.). 1990. 19.95 (*0-8288-4950-1*) Fr & Eur.
—Asterix the Gladiator. (Illus.). 1990. 19.95 (*0-8288-4951-X*) Fr & Eur.
—Asterix the Legionary. (Illus.). 1990. 19.95 (*0-8288-4952-8*) Fr & Eur.
—Asterix und die Goten. (GER., Illus.). 1990. PLB 19.95 (*0-8288-4953-6*) Fr & Eur.
—Asterix und Kleopatra. (GER., Illus.). 1990. PLB 19.95 (*0-8288-4954-4*) Fr & Eur.
—Asterix y Cleopatra. (SPA., Illus.). 1990. PLB 19.95 (*0-8288-4955-2*) Fr & Eur.
—Asterix y el Caldero. (SPA., Illus.). 1990. PLB 19.95 (*0-8288-4956-0*) Fr & Eur.
—Asterix y los Godos. (SPA., Illus.). 1990. PLB 19.95 (*0-8288-4957-9*) Fr & Eur.
—Asterix y los Normandos. (SPA., Illus.). 1990. PLB 19.95 (*0-8288-4958-7*) Fr & Eur.
Goscinny, Rene De see De Goscinny, Rene.
Goscinny, Rene de see De Goscinny, Rene.
Goscinny, Rene de see De Goscinny, Rene & Uderzo, M.
Goshorn, Bill, ed. see Mackie, Dan.
Gosnell, Kelvin. Belarus, Ukraine, & Moldavia. Channon, John, contrib. by. LC 92-2241. (Illus.). 32p. (gr. 4-6). 1992. PLB 13.90 (*1-56294-306-5*) Millbrook Pr.
—Nuclear Power Stations. LC 91-34406. (Illus.). 32p. (gr. 5-8). 1992. PLB 12.40 (*0-531-17331-3*, Gloucester Pr) Watts.
Goss, Clay, jt. auth. see Goss, Linda.
Goss, Linda & Goss, Clay. The Baby Leopard: An African Folktale. Bailey-Jones, Suzanne & Jones, Michael R., illus. 32p. (ps-3). 1989. audiocassette 7.95 (*0-318-42071-5*) Bantam.
—It's Kwanzaa Time! LC 92-30380. 1993. write for info. (*0-399-22505-6*, Philomel Bks) Putnam Pub Group.
Goss, Louise & McArtot, Marion. Technic Time, Pt. A. 48p. (Orig.). (gr. k-6). 1974. pap. text ed. 6.95 (*0-87487-189-1*) Summy-Birchard.
Goss, Louise, jt. auth. see Clark, Frances.
Goss, Louise, ed. Themes from Masterworks, 3 bks. 16p. (Orig.). (gr. k-12). 1970. pap. text ed. 5.95 Bk. 1 (*0-87487-191-3*); pap. text ed. 5.95 Bk. 2 (*0-87487-192-1*); pap. text ed. 5.95 Bk. 3 (*0-87487-193-X*) Summy-Birchard.
Goss, Louise, ed. see Dittenhaver, Sarah L., et al.
Goss, Louise, ed. see George, Jon & Kraehenbuehl, David.
Goss, Louise, ed. see Kraehenbuehl, David, et al.
Goss, Louise, ed. see Pearce, Elvina T.
Goss, Louise see Clark, Frances.
Goss, Marilyn. Maggie Suzanne, Star of Christmas. Goss, Marilyn, illus. 36p. (gr. 3 up). 1988. 15.95 (*0-9620766-0-0*) Art Room Pubns.
Goster, Kelli C., jt. auth. see Erickson, Gina C.
Gothard, Bill. The Eagle Story. LC 81-85536. (Illus.). 64p. (gr. 3-12). 1982. 8.00 (*0-916888-07-X*) Inst Basic Youth.
Gotta, K. L. Teach Me How to Pray. 72p. (Orig.). 1993. pap. 6.00 (*0-9628819-0-2*) LWMM.
Gottesman, Meir U. Chaimkel the Dreamer. Scheinberg, Shepsil, illus. 157p. (gr. 3-5). 1987. 9.95 (*0-935063-26-9*); pap. 7.95 (*0-935063-27-7*) CIS Comm.
—A Face at the Window. Hinlicky, Gregg, illus. 140p. (gr. 6-8). 1990. 10.95 (*1-56062-017-X*); pap. 7.95 (*1-56062-018-8*) CIS Comm.
—Shpeter: Book One. (Illus.). (gr. 1-3). 1981. 5.95 (*0-910818-35-5*); pap. 4.95 (*0-910818-36-3*) Judaica Pr.
—Shpeter: Book Two. (Illus.). (gr. 1-3). 1981. 5.95 (*0-910818-39-8*); pap. 4.95 (*0-910818-40-1*) Judaica Pr.

Gottfredson, Floyd. Walt Disney's Mickey Mouse Comic Album. Gottfredson, Floyd, illus. Blum, Geoffrey, intro. by. (Illus.). 48p. (Orig.). (ps up). 1987. pap. 5.95 (*0-944599-03-6*) Gladstone Pub.
—Walt Disney's Mickey Mouse Comic Album. Gottfredson, Floyd, illus. Blum, Geoffrey, intro. by. (Illus.). 48p. (Orig.). (ps up). 1988. pap. 5.95 (*0-944599-07-9*) Gladstone Pub.
—Walt Disney's Mickey Mouse Comic Album. Gottfredson, Floyd, illus. Blum, Geoff, intro. by. (Illus.). 48p. (Orig.). 1989. pap. 5.95 (*0-944599-17-6*) Gladstone Pub.
—Walt Disney's Mickey Mouse Comic Album. Gottfredson, Floyd, illus. Blum, Geoff, intro. by. (Illus.). 48p. (Orig.). 1989. pap. 5.95 (*0-944599-21-4*) Gladstone Pub.
—Walt Disney's Mickey Mouse Giant Album. Blum, Geoffrey, intro. by. (Illus.). 72p. (Orig.). 1989. pap. 8.95 (*0-944599-25-7*) Gladstone Pub.
Gottfried, Ted. Enrico Fermi. (Illus.). 128p. (gr. 5 up). 1992. PLB 16.95x (*0-8160-2623-8*) Facts on File.
—Georges Clemenceau. Schlesinger, Arthur M., Jr., intro. by. (Illus.). 112p. (gr. 5 up). 1987. lib. bdg. 17.95 (*0-87754-518-9*) Chelsea Hse.
—Gun Control: Public Safety & the Right to Bear Arms. LC 92-32775. (Illus.). 128p. (gr. 7 up). 1993. PLB 15.90 (*1-56294-342-1*) Millbrook Pr.
—Libya: Desert Land in Conflict. LC 93-15096. (Illus.). 160p. (gr. 7 up). 1994. PLB 16.90 (*1-56294-351-0*) Millbrook Pr.
—Muammar El-Qaddafi. Sclesinger, Arthur M., Jr., intro. by. (Illus.). 112p. (gr. 5 up). 1987. lib. bdg. 17.95 (*0-87754-598-7*) Chelsea Hse.
Gottlieb, Dale. Big Dog. Gottlieb, Dale, illus. LC 88-5295. 32p. (ps-1). 1989. 11.95 (*0-688-07381-6*); PLB 11.88 (*0-688-07382-4*, Morrow Jr Bks) Morrow Jr Bks.
—Big Dog. (Illus.). 32p. (ps-3). 1992. pap. 3.99 (*0-14-054431-3*) Puffin Bks.
—My Stories by Hildy Calpurnia Rose. Gottlieb, Dale, illus. LC 90-46096. 40p. (ps-4). 1991. 14.00 (*0-679-81150-8*); lib. bdg. 14.99 (*0-679-91150-2*) Knopf Bks Yng Read.
—Seeing Eye Willie. Gottlieb, Dale, illus. LC 91-18606. 40p. (gr. 1-4). 1992. 15.00 (*0-679-82449-9*); PLB 15.99 (*0-679-92449-3*) Knopf Bks Yng Read.
Gottlieb, Gerald. The Adventures of Ulysses. Savage, Steele, illus. LC 88-19232. xii, 170p. (gr. 6-12). 1988. Repr. of 1959 ed. lib. bdg. 16.50 (*0-208-02222-8*, Linnet) Shoe String.
Gottlieb, Jane, photos by. Garden Tales: Classic Stories from Favorite Writers. LC 89-40643. (Illus.). 112p. 1990. 12.95 (*0-670-83173-5*, Viking Studio) Studio Bks.
Gottlieb, T., tr. see Cole, Brock.
Gottlieb, Yaffa L. My Upsheren Book. Bindel, Binah T., illus. 32p. (ps-1). 1991. 8.95 (*0-922613-37-0*); pap. 6.95 (*0-922613-38-9*) Hachai Pubns.
—The Shushan Chronicle: The Story of Purim. Barkman, Aidel, illus. 56p. (gr. k-4). 1991. 11.95 (*0-922613-39-7*); pap. 9.95 (*0-922613-40-0*) Hachai Pubns.
Gottschalk, Alfred. To Learn & to Teach Your Life as a Rabbi. (Illus.). (gr. 7-12). 1988. lib. bdg. 12.95 (*0-8239-0700-7*) Rosen Group.
Gottschalk, Louis A. The Tree of Knowledge. LC 85-71701. (Illus.). 236p. (gr. 8 up). 1985. text ed. 12.50x (*0-939373-01-7*) Eden Press.
Gouck, Maura M. The Great Barrier Reef. LC 93-85. (gr. 1-8). 1993. write for info. (*1-56766-008-8*) Childs World.
—Mountain Lions. LC 93-16250. (ps-6). 1993. write for info. (*1-56766-057-6*) Childs World.
—The Solar System. LC 93-17027. (SPA & ENG.). 1993. 22.75 (*1-56766-061-4*) Childs World.
—Whales. 32p. 1991. 22.75 (*0-89565-717-1*); 15.95s.p. (*0-685-55065-6*) Childs World.
Goudge, Eileen. Against the Rules. (Orig.). (gr. 6 up). 1986. pap. 2.25 (*0-440-90096-4*, LFL) Dell.
—Deep-Sea Summer. (Orig.). (gr. k-12). 1988. pap. 2.95 (*0-440-20123-3*) Dell.
—Don't Say Goodbye. 153p. (Orig.). (gr. 6-12). 1985. pap. 2.25 (*0-440-92108-2*, LFL) Dell.
—Hawaiian Christmas. (gr. 6 up). 1986. pap. 2.95 (*0-440-93649-7*, LFL) Dell.
—Heart for Sale. (Orig.). (gr. 7-12). 1986. pap. 2.25 (*0-440-93382-X*, LFL) Dell.
—Kiss & Make Up. 154p. (Orig.). (gr. 6-12). 1986. pap. 2.25 (*0-440-94514-3*, LFL) Dell.
—Looking for Love. (Orig.). 1986. pap. 2.25 (*0-440-94730-8*, LFL) Dell.
—Night after Night. (gr. 6-12). 1986. pap. 2.25 (*0-440-96369-9*, LFL) Dell.
—Old Enough: Super Seniors, No. 1. (gr. 6 up). 1986. pap. 2.95 (*0-440-96118-1*, LFL) Dell.
—Presenting Superhunk. (Orig.). (gr. 6-12). 1985. pap. 2.25 (*0-440-97172-1*, LFL) Dell.
—Smart Enough to Know. (Orig.). (gr. 7-12). 1984. pap. 2.25 (*0-440-98168-9*, LFL) Dell.
—Something Borrowed, Something Blue. (Orig.). (gr. k-12). 1988. pap. 2.95 (*0-440-20055-5*, LFL) Dell.
—Sweet Talk. (Orig.). (gr. k-12). 1986. pap. 2.25 (*0-440-98411-4*, LFL) Dell.
—Sweet Talk. 160p. 1986. pap. 2.95 (*0-553-17220-4*) Bantam.
—Too Hot to Handle. 192p. (gr. 7 up). 1987. pap. 2.25 (*0-440-98812-8*, YB) Dell.
—Too Much Too Soon. 160p. (gr. 7-12). 1984. pap. 2.25 (*0-440-98974-4*) Dell.
—A Touch of Ginger. (Orig.). (gr. 7-12). 1985. pap. 2.25 (*0-440-98816-0*, LFL) Dell.
—Treat Me Right. (Orig.). (gr. 6 up). 1986. pap. 2.25 (*0-440-98845-4*, LFL) Dell.
—Winner All the Way. 160p. (Orig.). (gr. 7-12). 1984. pap. 2.25 (*0-440-99480-2*, LFL) Dell.
Goudge, Elizabeth. I Saw Three Ships. (Orig.). 1990. pap. 2.95 (*0-440-40367-7*, Pub. by Yearling Classics) Dell.
—The Little White Horse. 1976. 25.95 (*0-89966-474-1*) Buccaneer Bks.
—The Little White Horse. 272p. (gr. 5 up). 1992. pap. 3.50 (*0-440-40734-6*, YB) Dell.
Gouffe, Marie A. Treasures Beyond the Snows. Sellon, Michael B., illus. LC 77-95392. (gr. 3-9). 1970. 3.75 (*0-8356-0026-2*, Quest) Theos Pub Hse.
Gouge, Betty, et al. KidSkills Interpersonal Skill Series, Choices! Choices! Choices! Responsibility: Making & Living with Choices. Morse, J. Thomas, ed. Bleck, Linda & Bleck, Cathie, illus. LC 86-45001. 45p. (ps). 1986. PLB 8.95 (*0-934275-09-2*); bk. & cassette 11.95 (*0-934275-23-8*) Fam Skills.
—KidSkills Interpersonal Skill Series, Let's Share: Friendship: Sharing. Morse, J. Thomas, et al, eds. Bleck, Linda & Bleck, Cathie, illus. LC 86-81270. 48p. (ps). 1986. PLB 8.95 (*0-934275-13-0*); bk. & cassette 11.95 (*0-934275-27-0*) Fam Skills.
—KidSkills Interpersonal Skill Series, My Feelings & Me: Feelings: Experiencing Feelings. Morse, J. Thomas, et al, eds. Bleck, Linda & Bleck, Cathie, illus. LC 85-81270. 44p. (ps). 1986. 8.95 (*0-934275-10-6*); bk. & cassette 11.95 (*0-934275-24-6*) Fam Skills.
—KidSkills Interpersonal Skill Series, The Rules at My House: Responsibility: Understanding & Accepting Limits. Morse, J. Thomas, et al, eds. Bleck, Linda & Bleck, Cathie, illus. 44p. (ps). 1986. PLB 8.95 (*0-934275-11-4*); bk. & cassette 11.95 (*0-934275-25-4*) Fam Skills.
—KidSkills Interpersonal Skill Series, Wonderful You: Self-Awareness: Accepting & Knowing Myself. Morse, J. Thomas, et al, eds. Bleck, Linda & Bleck, Cathie, illus. LC 85-81270. 42p. (ps). 1986. PLB 8.95 (*0-934275-12-2*); bk. & cassette 11.95 (*0-934275-26-2*) Fam Skills.
Gouge, Betty, et al, eds. see Morse, J. Thomas, et al.
Gouge, Elizabeth. Linnets & Valerians. (gr. 4-7). 1992. pap. 3.50 (*0-440-40590-4*, YB) Dell.
Gough, Kristeen. Be Happy Not Sad, 2 bks. (ps-3). 1989. Set. pap. 8.50 (*0-685-26502-1*) Children's storybook in sign language, 16p (*0-916708-19-5*) Colorbook, 16p (*0-916708-20-9*) Modern Signs.
Gould, Alan. Convection: A Current Event. Bergman, Lincoln & Fairwell, Kay, eds. Klofkorn, Lisa, illus. Hoyt, Richard, photos by. (Illus.). 38p. (Orig.). (gr. 6-9). 1988. pap. 8.50 (*0-912511-15-X*) Lawrence Science.
—Hot Water & Warm Homes from Sunlight. Bergman, Lincoln & Fairwell, Kay, eds. Baker, Lisa H. & Byal, Chris, illus. Sneider, Cary I., photos by. 40p. (Orig.). (gr. 4-8). 1986. pap. 8.50 (*0-912511-24-9*) Lawrence Science.
Gould, Alan, jt. auth. see Sneider, Cary.
Gould, Alan, jt. auth. see Sneider, Cary I.
Gould, Alberta. First Lady of the Senate: A Life of Margaret Chase Smith, U. S. Senator. Weinberger, Jane, ed. LC 89-51315. (Illus.). 150p. (gr. 5-10). 1990. 15.95 (*0-932433-64-2*) Windswept Hse.
Gould, Bette, jt. auth. see Madsen, Sheila.
Gould, Deborah. Aaron's Shirt. Harness, Cheryl, illus. LC 88-10414. 32p. (ps-3). 1989. SBE 13.95 (*0-02-736351-1*, Bradbury Pr) Macmillan Child Grp.
—Camping in the Temple of the Sun. Paterson, Diane, illus. LC 91-16358. 32p. (gr-k-5). 1992. RSBE 13.95 (*0-02-736355-4*, Bradbury Pr) Macmillan Child Grp.
—Grandpa's Slide Show. Harness, Cheryl, illus. LC 86-20981. 32p. (ps-3). 1987. 13.95 (*0-688-06972-X*); PLB 13.88 (*0-688-06973-8*) Lothrop.
—Terry's Creature. Ivanov, Anatoly, illus. LC 88-13297. 32p. (gr. k-3). 1989. 13.95 (*0-688-07570-3*); PLB 13.88 (*0-688-07571-1*) Lothrop.
Gould, Dennis E. Botswana. (Illus.). 96p. (gr. 5 up). 1988. 14.95 (*0-222-01101-7*) Chelsea Hse.
Gould, Ellen. The Blue Number Counting Book. Kelly, Cathy, illus. 13p. (ps-2). pap. 6.00 (*0-938017-01-2*) Learn Tools.
—The Red Letter Alphabet Book. Kelley, Cathy, illus. 29p. (gr. k up). 1983. pap. 7.00 (*0-938017-00-4*) Learn Tools.
Gould, Marilyn. Friends True & Periwinkle Blue. 160p. (Orig.). 1992. pap. 2.99 (*0-380-76484-9*, Camelot) Avon.

—Golden Daffodils. LC 84-40758. 17p. (gr. 4 up). 1991. PLB 12.95 (*0-397-32164-3*); pap. 6.95 (*0-9632305-1-4*) Allied Crafts.
In GOLDEN DAFFODILS, Janis, a ten-year-old with cerebral palsy, finds the work at her new school hard & the kids mean--especially Cheryl & Garth who challenge her & Barney (her not too athletic friend) to a handball match. But through her struggles, Janis learns that even "normal" kids can be handicapped by a lack of confidence & insensitivity. "Appealing & readable." (SLJ) "Clearly portrayed" (Booklist) with "humor, caring, & love." (PW) "that makes you want to laugh & cry." (U. of Mo.) In the sequel, THE TWELFTH OF JUNE, Janis is in seventh grade having problems growing up. No one understands that having a disability doesn't keep her from having the same sexual fantasies & desires as other teen-agers--like having a boyfriend. Of course, there's Barney, but he has his own problems, pressured with schoolwork, violin lessons, Bar Mitzvah preparation, & threats from gang members--he wants to split--run away on June 12th--& he wants Janis to go with him. "A treasure! Well done!" (LA Times) "Fast reading" (SLJ) "Highly recommended." "A must buy." (Md. U).
Publisher Provided Annotation.

—Graffiti Wipeout. LC 91-90783. 112p. (gr. 5 up). 1992. pap. 6.95 (*0-9632305-0-6*) Allied Crafts.
ELGAR lives in a little house on the roof of a factory building where his father is custodian. It's Elgar's job to paint out graffiti sprayed on the building. RISK sprays graffiti all over downtown, but his favorite is the building Elgar paints. That's why he lurks in the background waiting for Elgar to finish so he can "tag" it again. MORGAN, the kooky daughter of a senator, thinks graffiti looks a lot like the "way out" art her father collects, but she hangs around to help Elgar because she's lonesome & has nothing to do--until the two of them decide to catch RISK, set a trap for him once & for all to wipe out graffiti--& the chase is on! "Interesting facts about graffiti (who does it, why, the cost of removing it, the risks)." "Readers are left to come to their own conclusions." "Gould handles another serious problem with compassion, humor & suspense."
Publisher Provided Annotation.

—Playground Sports: A Book of Ball Games. (Illus.). 62p. (gr. 2 up). 1991. 10.95 (*0-9632305-2-2*) Allied Crafts.
PLAYGROUND SPORTS gives rules, techniques, & tips for ball games most loved & played on elementary school playgrounds in a book children will find helpful & fun to read. "Tips, simple rules, & techniques are clearly described in a breezy enthusiastic style." (Kirkus). "Well-illustrated action photographs, diagrams, & cartoons that are not only appealing to young people, but teachers will welcome the demonstrations & explanations." (Booklist). Kids, group leaders, & sports buffs of all ages will find PLAYGROUND SPORTS AN INVALUABLE SOURCE BOOK FOR PLAYGROUND, SUMMER CAMP, PARK & BACKYARD FUN. "A well-illustrated & clearly written guide." (SLJ).
Publisher Provided Annotation.

—Skateboarding. 48p. (gr. 3-4). 1991. PLB 11.95 (*1-56065-048-6*) Capstone Pr.

—The Twelfth of June. LC 85-45173. 192p. (gr. 4-7). 1986. 12.95 (*0-397-32130-9*) Allied Crafts.

Gould, Toni. The Adventures of Mel & Tess. (Illus.). (gr. 1-3). 1984. pap. text ed. 12.95x (*0-8027-9189-1*) Walker & Co.

—Fun with the Fumble Families. LC 83-5928. (Illus.). (gr. 1-3). 1984. pap. 12.95x (*0-8027-9191-3*) Walker & Co.

—Fun with Water & Ice. LC 83-5938. (Illus.). (gr. 1-3). 1984. pap. text ed. 12.95x (*0-8027-9194-8*) Walker & Co.

Gould, Toni S. & Warnke, Marie. Learn to Read Program. (gr. 1-3). 1985. 59.95x (*0-8027-9244-8*) Walker & Co.

Goulding, George. Azar: The Writings of the Mantira, Vol. 1. 225p. (Orig.). 1989. pap. write for info. Azalar Pub.

Goulet, Rosalina M. Poems of Childhood: Mga Tula ng Kabataan. (TAG & ENG., Illus.). 106p. (Orig.). (gr. k-2). 1989. pap. 7.50x (*971-10-0349-X*, Pub. by New Day Pub PI) Cellar.

Gounaud, Karen J. A Very Mice Joke Book. Munsinger, Lynn, illus. (gr. 2-5). 1981. HM.

Gourley, Pamela R., ed. Careers to Think About: A Young Person's Guide to Future Job Opportunities. (Illus.). 315p. (Orig.). (gr. 5-9). 1987. PLB 12.95 (*0-943621-21-6*) TechWest Pubns.

Gourse, Leslie. Dizzy Gillespie & the Birth of Bebop. LC 93-30222. (Illus.). 160p. (gr. 7 up). 1994. SBE 14.95 (*0-689-31869-3*, Atheneum Child Bk) Macmillan Child Grp.

Gouverneur, Aisha, jt. auth. see Azzam, Leila.

Gove, Doris. Miracle at Egg Rock: A Puffin's Story. Bishop, Bonnie, illus. LC 85-7050. 48p. (Orig.). (gr. 1-4). 1985. pap. 6.95 (*0-89272-205-3*) Down East.

—One Rainy Night. Krudop, Walter L., illus. LC 93-13900. 32p. (gr. 2-5). 1994. SBE 14.95 (*0-689-31800-6*, Atheneum Child Bk) Macmillan Child Grp.

—Red-Spotted Newt. Duncan, Beverly, illus. LC 91-34497. 1993. write for info. (*0-689-31697-6*, Aladdin) Macmillan Child Grp.

—A Water Snake's Year. Duncan, Beverly, illus. LC 90-673. 40p. (gr. 2-6). 1991. SBE 13.95 (*0-689-31597-X*, Atheneum Child Bk) Macmillan Child Grp.

Govier, Heather. Buildings. Young, Richard, ed. LC 91-19816. (Illus.). 32p. (gr. 3-5). 1991. PLB 15.93 (*1-56074-007-8*) Garrett Ed Corp.

—Clothes. Young, Richard, ed. LC 91-20533. (Illus.). 32p. (gr. 3-5). 1991. PLB 15.93 (*1-56074-009-4*) Garrett Ed Corp.

Gowdey, David. Basketball Super Stars. Whitehead, Sam, illus. 64p. (gr. 1-4). 1994. pap. 8.95 (*0-448-40542-3*, G&D) Putnam Pub Group.

Gowell, Elizabeth T. Sea Jellies: Rainbows in the Sea. (Illus.). 56p. (gr. 5-8). 1993. 15.95 (*0-531-15259-6*); PLB 15.90 (*0-531-11152-0*) Watts.

Gowing, Toby, tr. see Lawlor, Laurie.

Goyallon, Jerome. Drawing Dinosaurs. LC 93-2809. (Illus.). 80p. (gr. 3 up). 1993. 12.95 (*0-8069-8742-1*) Sterling.

Goyette, Ron, tr. see Bradbury, Thomas E.

GP Publications Staff. Game Players Encyclopedia of Nintendo Games, Vol. 1. (Illus.). 272p. (ps-12). 1990. pap. 10.95 (*0-929307-11-9*) GP Pubns.

Graaf, Anne de see Defoe, Daniel.

Graaf, Anne de see De Graaf, Anne.

Graaf, Anne de see Spyri, Johanna.

Grabarits, Anna C. Kathy Needs Comfort & Timmy's New Outlook. (Illus.). 16p. 1993. saddlestitched 4.95 (*0-8059-3424-3*) Dorrance.

Graber. Prouty & Me. Date not set. 15.00 (*0-06-024251-5*, Festival); PLB 14.89 (*0-06-024252-3*, Festival) HarpC Child Bks.

Graboff, Abner. In a Cat's Eye. (Illus.). (gr. 7 up). 1976. pap. 5.00 (*0-912846-25-9*) Bookstore Pr.

Grabowski, John. Jackie Robinson. Murray, Jim, intro. by. (Illus.). 64p. (gr. 3 up). 1991. lib. bdg. 14.95 (*0-7910-1188-7*) Chelsea Hse.

—Sandy Koufax. Murray, Jim, intro. by. (Illus.). 64p. (gr. 3 up). 1992. lib. bdg. 14.95 (*0-7910-1180-1*) Chelsea Hse.

—Willie Mays. (Illus.). 64p. (gr. 3 up). 1990. 14.95 (*0-7910-1183-6*) Chelsea Hse.

Grabowski, John F. Stan Musial. (Illus.). 1994. 14.95 (*0-7910-1184-4*, Am Art Analog) Chelsea Hse.

Grace, Eileen, illus. Three Little Pigs. LC 80-27483. 32p. (gr. k-2). 1981. PLB 9.79 (*0-89375-462-5*); pap. text ed. 1.95 (*0-89375-463-3*) Troll Assocs.

Grace, Eric S. Seals. Bruemmer, Fred, illus. (gr. 3-6). 1991. 15.95 (*0-316-32279-2*) Little.

Grace, Eric S., text by. Elephants. LC 92-32835. 1993. 15.95 (*0-87156-538-2*) Sierra.

Grace, Harry A. Improving - Peacefully. 100p. (Orig.). (gr. 11). 1991. pap. write for info. (*0-9618083-4-9*) Vyoupoint.

—My Selves & I. 110p. (Orig.). (gr. 12). 1991. pap. write for info. (*0-9618083-2-2*) Vyoupoint.

Grace, John. A Busy Day. Trotter, Stuart, illus. 28p. (ps-1). 1991. 3.95 (*0-7214-5333-3*, S914-2) Ladybird Bks.

—A Quiet Walk. Trotter, Stuart, illus. 28p. (ps-1). 1991. 3.95 (*0-7214-5332-5*, S914-1 SER.) Ladybird Bks.

Grace, Theresa. A Picture Book of Flowers. Pistolesi, Roseanna, illus. LC 92-8716. 24p. (gr. 1-4). 1992. PLB 9.59 (*0-8167-2836-4*); pap. text ed. 2.50 (*0-8167-2837-2*) Troll Assocs.

—A Picture Book of Swamp & Marsh Animals. Pistolesi, Roseanna, illus. LC 91-16034. 24p. (gr. 1-4). 1992. lib. bdg. 9.59 (*0-8167-2434-2*); pap. text ed. 2.50 (*0-8167-2435-0*) Troll Assocs.

—A Picture Book of Underwater Life. Pistolesi, Roseanna, illus. LC 89-37330. 24p. (gr. 1-4). 1990. lib. bdg. 9.59 (*0-8167-1906-3*); pap. text ed. 2.50 (*0-8167-1907-1*) Troll Assocs.

Gracey, Kirsten, tr. see Arpi, Erik.

Gracia, Debbie. My Birthday on Christmas Day. Aragon, Hilda, illus. 30p. (Orig.). (ps-7). 1980. pap. 3.75 (*0-915347-05-9*) Pueblo Acoma Pr.

Graczyk, Ed. Aesop's Falables: Musical. 1969. 4.50 (*0-87602-100-3*) Anchorage.

—Appleseed. 1971. 4.50 (*0-87602-106-2*) Anchorage.

—Livin' de Life. 1970. 4.50 (*0-87602-151-8*) Anchorage.

—The Rude Mechanicals. (gr. 4-12). 1970. 4.50 (*0-87602-194-1*) Anchorage.

—Runaway: Musical. (gr. 7-12). 1973. 4.50 (*0-87602-196-8*) Anchorage.

Gradisher, Martha, jt. auth. see Ziefert, Harriet.

Grady, Kitten S. Jiggsy's Necklace. Grady, Kitten S., illus. LC 87-62211. 40p. (gr. 1-6). 1987. 5.95 (*0-932433-34-0*) Windswept Hse.

Grady, Sean M. Marie Curie. LC 92-21031. (Illus.). 112p. (gr. 5-8). 1992. PLB 14.95 (*1-56006-033-6*) Lucent Bks.

—Plate Tectonics: Earth's Shifting Crust. LC 91-16714. (Illus.). 96p. (gr. 5-8). 1991. PLB 15.95 (*1-56006-217-7*) Lucent Bks.

—Ships: Crossing the World's Oceans. LC 92-9162. (Illus.). 96p. (gr. 5-8). 1992. 15.95 (*1-56006-220-7*) Lucent Bks.

Graeber, Charlotte. The Fluff Puff Farm. French, Marty & Lamb, Jim, illus. 26p. (ps up). 1988. incl. cassette 7.95 (*1-55578-917-X*) Worlds Wonder.

—Mustard. Diamond, Donna, illus. 64p. 1988. pap. 2.75 (*0-553-15674-8*, Skylark) Bantam.

Graeber, Charlotte T. Fudge. Harness, Cheryl, illus. LC 86-7353. 128p. (gr. 1-4). 1987. 12.95 (*0-688-06735-2*) Lothrop.

—Fudge. 1989. pap. 2.99 (*0-671-70288-2*, Minstrel Bks) PB.

—Grey Cloud. Bloom, Lloyd, illus. LC 79-14673. 128p. (gr. 3-7). 1984. SBE 12.95 (*0-02-736910-2*, Four Winds) Macmillan Child Grp.

Graeber, Laurel. Are You Dying for a Drink? Teenagers & Alcohol Abuse. LC 85-8880. (Illus.). 128p. (gr. 7 up). 1986. lib. bdg. 12.98 (*0-671-50818-0*, J Messner); lib. bdg. 5.95 (*0-671-63180-2*) S&S Trade.

Graeker, Charlotte. The Fluff Puff Farm. French, Marty, et al, illus. 26p. (ps up). 1986. Book & Cassette. 7.95 (*1-55578-110-1*) Worlds Wonder.

Graf, Mike. National Parks Projects. (gr. 3-8). 1993. pap. 13.95 (*0-86653-934-4*) Fearon Teach Aids.

—The Weather Report. (gr. 3-6). 1989. pap. 13.95 (*0-8224-7511-1*) Fearon Teach Aids.

Graf, Rosanna & Graf, Virginia. Beary, Beary, Quite Contrary. Lawson, Laura, illus. (Orig.). Date not set. pap. 9.50 (*1-882788-02-8*) VanGar Pubs.

Graf, Virginia, jt. auth. see Graf, Rosanna.

Graf, Virginia, ed. The Friendship Tree & Other Stories for Children by Children. Yourell, Pamela, illus. (Orig.). (gr. 3-8). Date not set. pap. 9.50 (*1-882788-03-6*) VanGar Pubs.

Graff, Charles G., jt. auth. see Benoit, David.

Graff, John de see Anker, Debby & De Graff, John.

Graff, Nancy P. The Call of the Running Tide: A Portrait of an Island Family. Howard, Richard, illus. (gr. 3-7). 1991. 16.95 (*0-316-32278-4*) Little.

—Where the River Runs: A Portrait of a Refugee Family. Howard, Richard, photos by. LC 92-24184. (Illus.). 1993. 16.95 (*0-316-32287-3*) Little.

Graff, Nancy Price. The Strength of the Hills: A Portrait of a Family Farm, Vol. 1. Howard, Richard, illus. 1989. 14.95 (*0-316-32277-6*) Little.

Graff, Polly A., jt. auth. see Graff, Stewart.

Graff, Stewart. George Washington: Father of Freedom. (Illus.). 80p. (gr. 2-6). 1993. Repr. of 1964 ed. lib. bdg. 12.95 (*0-7910-1451-7*) Chelsea Hse.

—Helen Keller. (ps-3). 1991. pap. 3.25 (*0-440-40439-8*) Dell.

—John Paul Jones: Sailor Hero. (Illus.). 80p. (gr. 2-6). 1993. Repr. of 1961 ed. lib. bdg. 12.95 (*0-7910-1460-6*) Chelsea Hse.

Graff, Stewart & Graff, Polly A. Helen Keller. Frame, Paul, illus. 80p. (gr. 2-7). 1980. pap. 2.95 (*0-440-43566-8*, YB) Dell.

—Helen Keller: Toward the Light. (Illus.). 80p. (gr. 2-6). 1992. Repr. of 1965 ed. lib. bdg. 12.95 (*0-7910-1412-6*) Chelsea Hse.

Graft, Janine. TAAS Quick Review Mathematics: Exit Level. (Illus.). 112p. (gr. 11). 1992. pap. text ed. 14.95 (*0-944459-35-8*) ECS Lrn Systs.

Grafton, Allison, jt. auth. see Levine, Shar.

Grafton, Carol B. Children's Bookmarks in Full Color. (ps-3). 1985. pap. 3.50 (*0-486-24794-5*) Dover.

—Cut & Use Stencil Alphabet. 1984. pap. 4.95 (*0-486-24623-X*) Dover.

Grafton, Carol B., ed. Victorian Spot Illustrations, Alphabets & Ornaments from Porret's Type Catalog. (Illus.). 96p. (gr. 5 up). 1982. pap. 5.95 (*0-486-24271-4*) Dover.

Graham. Wind in the Willows. 1988. pap. 2.99 (*0-14-035087-X*, Puffin) Puffin Bks.

Graham, Ada & Graham, Frank. Bears in the Wild. Tyler, D. D., illus. LC 80-68732. 128p. (gr. 4-7). 1981. 8.95 (*0-440-00532-9*); PLB 8.44 (*0-440-00538-8*) Delacorte.

—Bears in the Wild. Tyler, D. D., illus. 176p. (gr. 4-8). 1983. pap. 2.25 (*0-440-40897-0*, YB) Dell.

—Whale Watch. Tyler, D. D., illus. LC 77-20531. (gr. 5 up). 1978. 7.95 (*0-440-09505-0*); pap. 6.46 (*0-440-09506-9*) Delacorte.

Graham, Alastair. Full Moon Soup: Or Fall of the Hotel Splendile. (ps-3). 1991. 14.95 (*0-8037-1045-3*) Dial Bks Young.

Graham, Amanda. Always Arthur. Gynell, Donna, illus. LC 89-4474. 32p. (gr. 2-3). 1990. PLB 18.60 (*0-8368-0096-6*) Gareth Stevens Inc.

—Educating Arthur. Gynell, Donna, illus. LC 87-42756. 32p. (gr. 2-3). 1988. PLB 18.60 (*1-55532-411-8*) Gareth Stevens Inc.

—Picasso the Green Tree Frog. Siow, John, illus. LC 86-42809. 1987p. (gr. 2-3). 1987. PLB 18.60 (*1-55532-152-6*) Gareth Stevens Inc.

—Who Wants Arthur? Gynell, Donna, illus. LC 86-42812. 32p. (gr. 2-3). 1987. PLB 18.60 (*1-55532-868-7*) Gareth Stevens Inc.

Graham, Andrew, jt. auth. see Hutchinson, Robert.

Graham, Bill. The Balloon Ride. 18p. (ps-2). 1987. 9.95 (*1-879680-02-5*) About You.

—A Birthday Mystery. 18p. (ps). 1991. 9.95 (*1-879680-05-X*) About You.

—The Circus Star. 18p. (ps). 1987. 9.95 (*1-879680-00-9*) About You.

—God's Promise. Wyrick, Monica, illus. 18p. (ps). 1991. 9.95 (*1-879680-11-4*) About You.

—The Hanukkah Rescue. 18p. (ps). 1990. 9.95 (*1-879680-07-6*) About You.

—If I Could Be... 18p. (ps). 1989. 9.95 (*1-879680-03-3*) About You.

—Imagine That! 18p. (ps). 1990. 9.95 (*1-879680-04-1*) About You.

—The Lost Dinosaur. 18p. (gr. 2). 1989. 9.95 (*1-879680-01-7*) About You.

—My ABC's Crayon Book. 18p. (ps). 1989. 4.95 (*1-879680-08-4*) About You.

—My Book of Zoo Rhymes. Horton, Vicki M., illus. 18p. (ps). 1991. 9.95 (*1-879680-10-6*) About You.

—Santa's Secret Helper. 18p. (ps). 1987. 9.95 (*1-879680-06-8*) About You.

Graham, Billy, et al. Church Humor Digest. Ingram, William R. & Goodman, Charles, eds. Chambers, Alma, et al, illus. 106p. (Orig.). 1991. pap. 7.95 (*0-916693-15-5*) Castle Bks.

Graham, Bob. Grandad's Magic. Graham, Bob, illus. LC 88-83007. (gr. k-2). 1989. 13.95 (*0-316-32321-7*) Little.

—Greetings from Sandy Beach. Graham, Bob, illus. 32p. (ps-3). 1992. 12.95 (*0-916291-40-5*) Kane-Miller Bk.

—Pete & Roland. (ps-3). 1988. pap. 3.95 (*0-318-32773-2*, Puffin) Puffin Bks.

—The Red Woolen Blanket. 32p. (ps-3). 1988. 10.95 (*0-316-32310-1*) Little.

—Rose Meets Mr. Wintergarten. Graham, Bob, illus. LC 91-71824. 32p. (ps up). 1992. 14.95 (*1-56402-039-8*) Candlewick Pr.

Graham, Carolyn. The Electric Elephant & Other Stories. (Illus., Orig.). (gr. 7-12). 1982. pap. text ed. 7.95x (*0-19-503229-2*) OUP.

Graham, Dennis, et al. Culture Trek. (Illus.). 32p. (gr. 3 up). 1989. incl. hand held Decoder 5.95 (*0-88679-572-9*) Educ Insights.

—Exploring America. (Illus.). 32p. (gr. 3 up). 1989. incl. hand held Decoder 5.95 (*0-88679-573-7*) Educ Insights.

—Prehistoric Life. (Illus.). 32p. (gr. 3 up). 1989. incl. hand held Decoder 5.95 (*0-88679-571-0*) Educ Insights.

—Undersea Adventures. (Illus.). 32p. (gr. 3 up). 1989. incl. hand held Decoder 5.95 (*0-88679-574-5*) Educ Insights.

Graham, Evelyn P. Where the Laurel Grows. LC 86-51075. 96p. (gr. 7 up). 1987. 6.95 (*1-55523-056-3*) Winston-Derek.

Graham, Frank, jt. auth. see Graham, Ada.

Graham, Gail B. The Beggar in the Blanket. Bryan, Brigitte, illus. LC 77-85548. 96p. (gr. 1-5). 1988. PLB 12.89 (*0-8037-0663-4*) Dial Bks Young.

Graham, Heather X. Sweet Savage Eden. (Orig.). 1989. pap. 4.99 (*0-440-20235-3*) Dell.

Graham, I., jt. auth. see Myring, L.

Graham, Ian. Astronomer. (Illus.). 32p. (gr. 5-8). 1991. PLB 12.40 (*0-531-17314-3*, Gloucester Pr) Watts.

—Boats, Ships, Submarines, & Other Floating Machines. LC 92-33588. (Illus.). 40p. (Orig.). (gr. 3-8). 1993. PLB 10.95 (*0-85697-868-0*); pap. 5.95 (*1-85697-867-2*) Kingfisher Bks.

—Cameras. LC 90-43982. (Illus.). 32p. (gr. 4-7). 1991. PLB 12.40 (*0-531-17280-5*, Gloucester Pr) Watts.

—Cars. Gillah, Mick, illus. LC 93-19707. 32p. (gr. 4-6). 1993. PLB 19.97 (*0-8114-6162-9*) Raintree Steck-V.

—Cars, Bikes, Trains, & Other Land Machines. LC 92-33587. (Illus.). 40p. (Orig.). (gr. 3-8). 1993. PLB 10.95 (*1-85697-872-9*); pap. 5.95 (*1-85697-871-0*) Kingfisher Bks.

—Communications. LC 91-10008. (Illus.). 48p. (gr. 5-8). 1991. PLB 19.92 (*0-8114-2803-6*) Raintree Steck-V.

—Computer Games. (gr. 5-9). 1982. pap. 3.95 (*0-86020-681-5*, Usborne-Hayes); PLB 10.96 (*0-88110-010-2*) EDC.

—Computers. LC 91-34405. (Illus.). 32p. (gr. 5-8). 1992. PLB 12.40 (*0-531-17330-5*, Gloucester Pr) Watts.

—Helicopters. Hayward, Ron & Khan, Aziz, illus. 32p. (gr. 5-6). 1989. PLB 12.40 (*0-531-17171-X*, Gloucester Pr) Watts.

—Lasers & Holograms. LC 91-10827. (Illus.). 32p. (gr. 5-8). 1991. PLB 12.40 (*0-531-17264-3*, Gloucester Pr) Watts.
—Salvage at Sea. (Illus.). 32p. (gr. 5-8). 1990. PLB 12.40 (*0-531-17177-9*) Watts.
—Space Science. LC 92-18319. 48p. (gr. 5). 1992. PLB 22.80 (*0-8114-2806-0*) Raintree Steck-V.
—Television & Video. Kline, M., ed. LC 90-43983. (Illus.). 32p. (gr. 4-7). 1991. PLB 12.40 (*0-531-17281-3*, Gloucester Pr) Watts.
—Transportation. LC 92-20740. 48p. (gr. 5 up). 1992. lib. bdg. 19.92 (*0-8114-2807-9*) Raintree Steck-V.
—Transportation. LC 92-20740. (Illus.). 48p. (gr. 5). Date not set. PLB 22.80 (*0-685-68787-2*) Raintree Steck-V.
—Trucks. (Illus.). 32p. (gr. 5-8). 1990. PLB 12.40 (*0-531-51240-6*, Gloucester Pr) Watts.
Graham, John. I Love You, Mouse. De Paola, Tomie, illus. LC 76-8022. (ps-2). 1976. 12.95 (*0-15-238005-1*, HB Juv Bks) HarBrace.
—I Love You, Mouse. De Paola, Tomie, illus. LC 78-6214. 32p. (ps-2). 1990. pap. 3.95 (*0-15-644106-3*, Voyager Bks) HarBrace.
Graham, Kenneth. Wind in the Willows. 224p. 1989. pap. 2.50 (*0-8125-0510-7*) Tor Bks.
Graham, Lorenz. Every Man Heart Lay Down. Browning, Colleen, illus. 48p. (gr. 3 up). 1993. 15.95 (*1-56397-184-4*) Boyds Mills Pr.
—I, Momolu. Biggers, John, illus. LC 87-82944. 240p. (gr. 7-12). 1988. pap. 9.95 (*0-9619521-0-5*) Graham Bks.
Graham, Margaret B. Be Nice to Spiders. Graham, Margaret B., illus. LC 67-17101. 32p. (gr. k-3). 1967. PLB 14.89 (*0-06-022073-2*) HarpC Child Bks.
Graham, Rhonda. Yesterday's Tears. 94p. (gr. 5 up). 1991. pap. 6.95 (*0-8163-1023-8*) Pacific Pr Pub Assn.
Graham, Richard. Jack & the Monster. Varley, Susan, illus. (ps-3). 1989. 13.45 (*0-395-49680-2*) HM.
Graham, Rickard. Norman Castles. LC 89-34447. 1990. PLB 10.90 (*0-531-18323-8*, Pub. by Bookwright Pr) Watts.
Graham, Terry. Let Loose on Mother Goose. LC 81-80248. (Illus.). 96p. (gr. k-1). 1982. pap. text ed. 7.95 (*0-86530-030-5*, IP 30-5) Incentive Pubns.
Graham, Terry L. Fingerplays & Rhymes for Always & Sometimes. LC 84-10937. (Illus.). 160p. (ps). 1984. pap. text ed. 14.95 (*0-89334-083-9*) Humanics Ltd.
—Listening Is a Way of Loving. LC 92-5801. (Illus.). 160p. (Orig.). (gr. k-3). 1992. pap. 17.95 (*0-89334-156-8*) Humanics Ltd.
Graham, Tether. Fudge Dream Supreme. Kock, Carl, illus. LC 73-16815. (ps-2). 1975. 6.95 (*0-87955-109-7*); PLB 5.95 (*0-686-57941-0*) O'Hara.
Graham, Thomas. Mr. Bear's Boat. LC 87-24466. (Illus.). 32p. (ps-2). 1991. pap. 3.95 (*0-525-44739-3*, Puffin) Puffin Bks.
—Mr. Bear's Chair. Graham, Thomas, illus. LC 86-19920. 32p. (ps-2). 1990. 10.95 (*0-525-44300-2*, DCB); pap. 3.95 (*0-525-44651-6*, DCB) Dutton Child Bks.
Graham-Barber, Lynda. Confusable Creatures: And Other Look-Alikes in Nature. Gillman, Alec, illus. LC 92-35398. 48p. (gr. k-3). 1994. RSBE 15.95 (*0-02-736931-5*, Four Winds) Macmillan Child Grp.
—Doodle Dandy! The Complete Book of Independence Day Words. Lewin, Betsy, illus. LC 91-19409. 128p. (gr. 4-10). 1992. SBE 13.95 (*0-02-736675-8*, Bradbury Pr) Macmillan Child Grp.
—Gobble! The Complete Book of Thanksgiving Words. Lewin, Betsy, illus. LC 90-22770. 128p. (gr. 4-10). 1991. SBE 13.95 (*0-02-708332-2*, Bradbury Pr) Macmillan Child Grp.
—Ho! Ho! Ho! The Complete Book of Christmas Words. Lewin, Betsy, illus. LC 92-6715. 128p. (gr. 4-7). 1993. pap. 14.95 SBE (*0-02-736933-1*, Bradbury Pr) Macmillan Child Grp.
—Mushy! The Complete Book of Valentine Words. Lewin, Betsy, illus. LC 90-33047. 128p. (gr. 4-10). 1990. 13.95 (*0-02-736941-2*, Bradbury Pr) Macmillan Child Grp.
—Mushy! The Complete Book of Valentine Words. 144p. 1993. pap. 3.50 (*0-380-71650-X*, Camelot) Avon.
Grahame. Wind in the Willows. 1993. pap. 3.25 (*0-590-44774-2*) Scholastic Inc.
—Wind in the Willows. 1991. 19.95 (*0-8050-1664-3*) H Holt & Co.
Grahame, jt. auth. see Hague.
Grahame, Kenneth. Dream Days. Parrish, Maxfield, illus. LC 92-44589. 1993. 18.95 (*0-89815-546-0*) Ten Speed Pr.
—The Golden Age. Parrish, Maxfield, illus. LC 92-44992. 1993. 18.95 (*0-89815-545-2*) Ten Speed Pr.
—Little Treasury of the Wind in the Willows, 6 vols. in 1. 1988. boxed 5.99 (*0-517-65353-2*) Outlet Bk Co.
—Mole's Christmas. Gooding, Beverly, illus. 32p. (gr. k-3). 1986. pap. 4.95 (*0-13-599747-X*) P-H.
—Mole's Christmas: Or Home Sweet Home. Gooding, Beverly, illus. LC 82-12333. 32p. (gr. k-3). 1983. 10. 95 (*0-13-599738-0*) P-H.
—Reluctant Dragon. Shepard, Ernest H., illus. LC 89-1658. 58p. (gr. 3-6). 1938. 12.95 (*0-8234-0093-X*); pap. 4.95 (*0-8234-0755-1*) Holiday.
—The Reluctant Dragon. Hague, Michael, illus. LC 83-209. 48p. (gr. 2-4). 1983. 14.95 (*0-8050-1112-9*, Bks Young Read) H Holt & Co.
—The Reluctant Dragon. Richardson, I. M., ed. Ekman, Marlene, illus. LC 87-10906. 32p. (gr. k-4). 1988. lib. bdg. 9.79 (*0-8167-1059-7*); pap. text ed. 1.95 (*0-8167-1060-0*) Troll Assocs.

—The Reluctant Dragon. Hague, Michael, illus. LC 83-209. 48p. (gr. 2-4). 1988. pap. 5.95 (*0-8050-0802-0*, Bks Young Read) H Holt & Co.
—The Wind in the Willows. LC 80-12509. 224p. (gr. 4-6). 1980. 19.95 (*0-8050-0213-8*, Bks Young Read) H Holt & Co.
—Wind in the Willows. (gr. 4 up). 1966. pap. 2.75 (*0-8049-0105-8*, CL-105) Airmont.
—The Wind in the Willows. 253p. (gr. 5-6). Repr. of 1908 ed. lib. bdg. 19.95x (*0-88411-877-0*, Pub. by Aeonian Pr) Amereon Ltd.
—Wind in the Willows. 234p. 1981. Repr. lib. bdg. 17.95 (*0-89966-305-2*) Buccaneer Bks.
—Wind in the Willows. Tsao, Alex, illus. Ellman, M., intro. by. (Illus.). 224p. (Orig.). (RL 4). 1989. pap. 2.95 (*0-451-52164-1*, Sig Classics) NAL-Dutton.
—The Wind in the Willows. Morrill, Les, illus. Sale, Roger, intro. by. (Illus.). 256p. (gr. 4-12). 1983. pap. 1.95 (*0-553-21129-3*, Bantam Classics) Bantam.
—The Wind in the Willows. Burningham, John, illus. 240p. (gr. 1 up). 1983. 15.75 (*0-670-77120-1*) Viking Child Bks.
—The Wind in the Willows. Green, Peter, ed. (gr. 5 up). 1983. pap. 2.95 (*0-19-281640-3*) OUP.
—The Wind in the Willows. 75th Anniversary ed. Shepard, Ernest H., illus. Hodges, Margaret, pref. by. LC 83-11573. (Illus.). 256p. (gr. 3 up). 1983. SBE 18. 95 (*0-684-17957-1*, Scribners Young Read) Macmillan Child Grp.
—The Wind in the Willows. Burningham, John, illus. 240p. (gr. 4-6). 1984. pap. 2.95 (*0-14-031544-6*) Viking Child Bks.
—The Wind in the Willows. Flax, Zena, illus. LC 85-13538. 224p. (gr. 2 up). 1985. 12.95 (*0-915361-32-9*, Dist. by Watts) Modan-Adama Bks.
—The Wind in the Willows. Lee, Robert J., illus. 256p. (gr. 1 up). 1969. pap. 3.25 (*0-440-49555-5*, YB) Dell.
—The Wind in the Willows. Shepard, Ernest H., illus. LC 88-8046. 272p. (ps up). 1989. pap. 4.95 (*0-689-71310-X*, Aladdin) Macmillan Child Grp.
—Wind in the Willows. LC 87-15818. 1988. 12.99 (*0-517-63230-6*) Outlet Bk Co.
—The Wind in the Willows. Morrill, Les, illus. Sale, Roger, intro. by. (Illus.). 256p. 1983. pap. 2.95 (*0-553-21368-7*, Bantam Classics Spectra) Bantam.
—Wind in the Willows. 1988. 7.99 (*0-517-49284-9*) Outlet Bk Co.
—Wind in the Willows. 1987. 3.98 (*0-671-08895-5*) S&S Trade.
—The Wind in the Willows. (Illus.). (gr. 3-5). 3.50 (*0-7214-0757-9*) Ladybird Bks.
—The Wind in the Willows. Shepard, Ernest H., illus. LC 90-64091. 264p. (gr. 8 up). 1991. SBE 24.95 (*0-684-19345-0*, Scribners Young Read) Macmillan Child Grp.
—Wind in the Willows. 256p. 1992. 9.49 (*0-8167-2562-4*); pap. 2.95 (*0-8167-2563-2*) Troll Assocs.
—Wind in the Willows. 1991. pap. 12.70 (*0-395-60728-0*) HM.
—The Wind in the Willows. Percy, Graham, illus. 192p. (gr. 3-6). 1992. 24.95 (*1-85145-603-1*, Pub. by Pavilion UK) Trafalgar.
—Wind in the Willows. 1990. pap. 3.50 (*0-440-40385-5*, Pub. by Yearling Classics) Dell.
—The Wind in the Willows. Ashachik, Diane M., retold by. Lydecker, Laura, illus. LC 92-13203. 48p. (gr. 3-6). 1992. 12.89 (*0-8167-2870-4*); pap. text ed. 3.95 (*0-8167-2871-2*) Troll Assocs.
—The Wind in the Willows. Daily, Don, illus. 56p. (gr. 2 up). 1993. 9.98 (*0-685-65070-7*) Courage Bks.
—The Wind in the Willows. (gr. 5 up). 1993. 13.95 (*0-679-41802-4*, Everymans Lib Childs) Knopf.
—Wind in the Willows, Vol. 1. 272p. (gr. 8 up). 1972. RSBE 13.95 (*0-684-12819-5*, Scribners Young Read) Macmillan Child Grp.
—Wind in the Willows: (El Viento en los Sauces I, II) (SPA). 9.50 ea. Vol. I (*84-372-1882-9*) Vol. II (*84-372-1883-7*) Santillana.
Grama, Shimon. Students' Yoman. (ENG & HEB.). 112p. (gr. 4-12). 1993. pap. text ed. 10.00 (*0-9635739-0-X*) Innovat NY.
Gramatky, Dorothea C., jt. auth. see Gramatky, Hardie.
Gramatky, Hardie. Little Toot. Gramatky, Hardie, illus. LC 78-4801. (gr. k-3). 1978. (Putnam); (Putnam); pap. 7.95 (*0-399-20649-3*, Putnam) Putnam Pub Group.
—Little Toot. (ps-3). 1992. 14.95 (*0-399-22419-X*) Putnam Pub Group.
—Little Toot. Long, Laurie, illus. 12p. (ps). 1993. bds. 4.95 (*0-448-40585-7*, G&D) Putnam Pub Group.
Gramatky, Hardie & Gramatky, Dorothea C. Little Toot & the Loch Ness Monster. Gramatky, Hardie, illus. 48p. (ps-3). 1989. 13.95 (*0-399-21684-7*, Putnam) Putnam Pub Group.
Grambling, Lois. An Alligator Named...Alligator. Cushman, Doug, illus. 32p. (ps-1). 1991. lib. bdg. 12. 95 (*0-8120-6224-8*); pap. 5.95 (*0-8120-4756-7*) Barron.
—Elephant & Mouse Celebrate Halloween. Maze, Deborah, illus. (ps-1). 1991. 12.95 (*0-8120-6186-1*); pap. 5.95 (*0-8120-4761-3*) Barron.
Grambling, Lois G. Elephant & Mouse Get Ready for Christmas. Maze, Deborah, illus. 32p. 1990. with dust jacket 12.95 (*0-8120-6185-3*) Barron.
—Elephant & Mouse Get Ready for Easter. Maze, Debrah, illus. 32p. (ps-3). 1991. 12.95 (*0-8120-6200-0*) Barron.

—Hundred Million Reasons for Owning an Elephant: Or at Least a Dozen That I Can Think of Right Now. Learner, Vickie M., illus. 32p. (ps). 1990. 6.95 (*0-8120-6189-6*) Barron.
Gramfors, Bo. Coloring MAPBOOK - Countries & Flags, Bk. I. 39p. (gr. 2-7). 1992. pap. 7.95 (*1-879856-15-8*) Interarts.
—Coloring MAPBOOK - The Living Earth, Bk. II. 39p. (gr. 2-6). 1992. pap. 7.95 (*1-879856-16-6*) Interarts.
Grammer, Maurine. The Bear That Turned White & Other Native Tales. Herrera, Joe, illus. Smith, Laurence C., frwd. by. LC 90-53590. (Illus.). 108p. (Orig.). (gr. 4 up). 1991. pap. 11.95 (*0-87358-515-1*) Northland AZ.
—The Navajo Brothers & the Stolen Herd. Cleveland, Fred, illus. Rushing, Jack, frwd. by. LC 92-15018. (Illus.). 120p. (gr. 6-8). 1992. pap. 9.95 (*1-878610-23-6*) Red Crane Bks.
Grammer, Red, narrated by see George, William T.
Granbeck, M., et al. Sprint Library Three: High-Interest, Low Vocabulary Textbooks Ser. large type ed. Incl. The Hidden Box Mystery. 100p. 1981. 18.98 (*0-317-04583-0*, 4-23170-00); Lily the Lovable Lion. 100p. 1981. 18.98 (*0-317-03695-5*, 4-23180-00); Sealab 2020. 100p. 1981. 25.00 (*0-317-03696-3*, J-23190-00); Secret Radio Messages. 100p. 1981. 18.98 (*0-317-03697-1*, 4-23200-00); The Trail Blazers. 100p. 1981. 18.98 (*0-317-02594-5*, 4-23210-00); Teacher's Guide. 28p. 1981. 5.24 (*0-317-02595-3*, 4-23300-00). (gr. 4-6). 1982. Repr. of 1975 ed. 18.98 (*0-317-04582-2*, 4-23170-00) Am Printing Hse.
Granberry, Nola, tr. see Shely, Patricia.
Granberry, Nola, tr. see Woggon, Guillermo.
Grancell-Frank, Barbara. The Oldest Mommy in the Park. Frank, Barbara, illus. Thomas, R. David, frwd. by. (Illus.). 64p. (Orig.). (gr. 6-12). 1993. pap. 8.95 (*1-56883-022-X*) Colonial Pr AL.
Grand, Gordon. Col. Weatherford & His Friends. Twachtman, J. Alden, illus. 242p. (gr. 10 up). 1991. Repr. of 1933 ed. 40.00 (*1-56416-026-2*) Derrydale Pr.
—Colonel Weatherford's Young Entry: Being an Account of the South Dorchester Ratters & Other Genteel Diversions Suitable for Children. Brown, Paul, illus. 214p. (gr. 10 up). 1991. Repr. of 1935 ed. 40.00 (*1-56416-028-9*) Derrydale Pr.
—Old Man: And Other Colonel Weatherford Stories. Hays, William J., illus. 239p. (gr. 10 up). 1991. Repr. of 1934 ed. 40.00 (*1-56416-027-0*) Derrydale Pr.
—Silver Horn: And Other Sporting Tales of John Weatherford. Twachtman, J. Alden, illus. 229p. (gr. 10 up). 1991. Repr. of 1932 ed. 40.00 (*1-56416-025-4*) Derrydale Pr.
Grandma, Marian, pseud. Georgie the Jovial Giraffe. Sott, Donna, illus. LC 85-71331. 32p. (gr. 3 up). 1985. text ed. write for info. (*0-9614989-0-0*) Banmar Inc.
Grandma Marian, pseud. Beni the Bashful Beaver. Kmiecik, Anne, illus. LC 87-71490. 32p. 1988. 6.95 (*0-9614989-1-9*) Banmar Inc.
—Mrs. Pam Polar Bear. Sullo, Lorraine T., illus. 32p. (gr. k-2). 1989. 7.95 (*0-9614989-9-4*) Banmar Inc.
Grandpa. Sir Reginald's Meeting. 1993. pap. 10.95 (*0-533-10487-4*) Vantage.
Grandpa Bill. Let It Snow: Three Snow Stories for Children. 1992. 7.95 (*0-533-10159-X*) Vantage.
Graner, Carl E. Who Is Who at the Zoo. Long, J. O., ed. Wright, Evelyn M., illus. k-1). 1989. pap. text ed. 3.95 (*0-685-27226-5*) Word & Image Pr.
Granfield, Linda. Cowboy: An Album. LC 93-11027. (gr. 4 up). 1994. 17.95 (*0-395-68430-7*) Ticknor & Fields.
—Extra! Extra! The Who, What, Where, When & Why of Newspapers. Slavin, Bill, illus. LC 93-11807. 1994. write for info. (*0-531-06833-1*); lib. bdg. write for info. (*0-531-08683-6*) Orchard Bks Watts.
Granfield, Linda, jt. auth. see Von Konigslow, Andrea.
Grange, Wallace B. Those of the Forest. Petrie, Chuck, ed. Murie, Olaus J., illus. Johnson, Dan, intro. by. (Illus.). 336p. (gr. 6 up). 1989. Repr. of 1953 ed. 19.50 (*0-932558-49-6*) Willow Creek Pr.
Granger, Judith. Amazing World of Dinosaurs. Baldwin-Ford, Pamela, illus. LC 81-7476. 32p. (gr. 2-4). 1982. PLB 11.59 (*0-89375-562-1*); pap. text ed. 2.95 (*0-89375-563-X*) Troll Assocs.
Granger, Michele. Eliza, the Hypnotizer: And Other Eliza & Francie Stories. (gr. 4-7). 1993. pap. 2.75 (*0-590-45506-0*) Scholastic Inc.
Granowsky, Alvin. Dinosaur Fossils. Herring, Lee, illus. LC 91-23407. 32p. (gr. 1-4). 1992. PLB 15.96 (*0-8114-3253-X*); pap. 3.95 (*0-8114-6228-5*) Raintree Steck-V.
—The Dinosaurs' Last Days. Lopez, Paul, illus. LC 91-23408. 32p. (gr. 1-4). 1992. PLB 15.96 (*0-8114-3250-5*); pap. 3.95 (*0-8114-6225-0*) Raintree Steck-V.
—Dinosaurs of All Sizes. Lopez, Paul, illus. LC 91-22343. 32p. (gr. 1-4). 1992. PLB 15.96 (*0-8114-3251-3*); pap. 3.95 (*0-8114-6229-3*) Raintree Steck-V.
—Hungry Dinosaurs. Inouye, Carol, illus. LC 91-23405. 32p. (gr. 1-4). 1992. PLB 15.96 (*0-8114-3252-1*); pap. 3.95 (*0-8114-6226-9*) Raintree Steck-V.
—Meat-Eating Dinosaurs. Inouye, Carol, illus. LC 91-23406. 32p. (gr. 1-4). 1992. PLB 15.96 (*0-8114-3254-8*); pap. 3.95 (*0-8114-6227-7*) Raintree Steck-V.
Grant, Alan, jt. auth. see Wagner, John.
Grant, Amy. Heart to Heart. 96p. 1989. 10.99 (*0-8499-0710-1*) Word Inc.

Grant, Bruce. Concise Encyclopedia of the American Indian. (Illus.). 352p. 1989. 8.99 (*0-517-69310-0*) Outlet Bk Co.
Grant, Charles. Fire Mask. (gr. 7 up). 1992. pap. 3.99 (*0-553-29673-6*, Starfire) Bantam.
Grant, Charles L. Fire Mask. (gr. 7 up). 1991. 14.95 (*0-553-07167-X*, Starfire) Bantam.
Grant, Christy, ed. see Gregg, Andy.
Grant, Christy, ed. see Levine, Caroline.
Grant, Christy, ed. see Roberts, Bethany.
Grant, Christy, ed. see Robinson, Fay.
Grant, Christy, ed. see Shute, Linda.
Grant, Cynthia D. Keep Laughing. LC 91-6816. 192p. (gr. 7 up). 1991. SBE 14.95 (*0-689-31514-7*, Atheneum Child Bk) Macmillan Child Grp.
—Kumquat May, I'll Always Love You. (gr. 7-12). 1987. pap. 2.95 (*0-553-26416-8*, Starfire) Bantam.
—Phoenix Rising: or How to Survive Your Life. LC 88-7370. 160p. 1989. SBE 13.95 (*0-689-31458-2*, Atheneum Child Bk) Macmillan Child Grp.
—Phoenix Rising: or How to Survive Your Life. 160p. (gr. 7 up). 1991. pap. 3.50 (*0-06-447060-1*, Trophy) HarpC Child Bks.
—Shadow Man. LC 91-36054. 160p. (gr. 7 up). 1992. SBE 13.95 (*0-689-31772-7*, Atheneum Child Bk) Macmillan Child Grp.
—Uncle Vampire. LC 92-44455. 160p. (gr. 8 up). 1993. SBE 13.95 (*0-689-31852-9*, Atheneum Child Bk) Macmillan Child Grp.
Grant, Donald, illus. Airplanes & Flying Machines. (ps). 1992. bds. 10.95 (*0-590-45267-3*, 037, Cartwheel) Scholastic Inc.
Grant, E. A. Kids' Book of Secret Codes, Signals, & Ciphers. (Illus., Orig.). (gr. 2 up). 1989. pap. 6.95 (*0-89471-781-2*) Running Pr.
Grant, Edgar. Exploring Careers in the Travel Industry. rev. ed. Rosen, Ruth, ed. (gr. 7-12). 1989. PLB 13.95 (*0-8239-0961-1*) Rosen Group.
Grant, Elaine. Critter Crafts. Grant, Elaine, illus. 30p. (gr. 4-7). 1991. pap. 9.95 spiral bdg. (*0-9632722-0-9*) Arteg Creations.
Grant, Eva. I Hate My Name. Mayo, Gretchen, illus. Hollingsworth, Charles, intro. by. LC 80-14428. (Illus.). 32p. (gr. k-6). 1980. PLB 17.96 (*0-8172-1362-7*) Raintree Steck-V.
—I Hate My Name. (ps-3). 1993. pap. 3.95 (*0-8114-5204-2*) Raintree Steck-V.
—Will I Ever Be Older? Lexa, Susan, illus. Hollingsworth, Charles E., intro. by. LC 80-24782. (Illus.). (gr. k-6). 1981. PLB 17.96 (*0-8172-1363-5*) Raintree Steck-V.
—Will I Ever Be Older? (ps-3). 1993. pap. 3.95 (*0-8114-5206-9*) Raintree Steck-V.
Grant, Janet E. Young Person's Guide to Becoming a Writer. LC 91-19473. 152p. (Orig.). (gr. 6 up). 1991. pap. 8.95 (*1-55870-215-6*) Shoe Tree Pr.
Grant, Joan. The Blue Faience Hippopotamus. Day, Alexandra, illus. LC 91-17133. 32p. (Orig.). (gr. 7-9). 1991. Repr. of 1942 ed. 11.95 (*0-671-74977-3*, Green Tiger) S&S Trade.
—The Monster That Grew Small. Schwarz, Jill K., illus. LC 86-15302. 32p. (ps-4). 1987. 12.95 (*0-688-06808-1*); PLB 12.88 (*0-688-06809-X*) Lothrop.
Grant, Lesley. Great Careers for People Concerned About the Environment, 6 vols. LC 93-78077. (Illus.). 48p. (gr. 6-9). 1993. 16.95 (*0-8103-9388-3*, 102106, UXL) Gale.
Grant, Matthew G. Paul Revere. LC 73-18076. 1988. PLB 14.95s.p. (*0-88682-186-X*) Creative Ed.
Grant, Matthew G. & Zadra, Dan. Chief Joseph. LC 73-9816. 1987. PLB 14.95s.p. (*0-88682-158-4*) Creative Ed.
Grant, Myrna Ivan & the American Journey. LC 88-71170. (gr. 3-7). 1988. 4.99 (*0-88419-221-0*, Creation Hse) Strang Comms Co.
—Ivan & the Daring Escape. LC 89-80820. (Illus.). 167p. (gr. 1-8). 1989. pap. 4.99 (*0-88419-257-1*, Creation Hse) Strang Comms Co.
—Ivan & the Hidden Bible. LC 88-71169. (gr. 3-7). 1988. 4.99 (*0-88419-222-9*, Creation Hse) Strang Comms Co.
—Ivan & the Informer. LC 89-80819. (Illus.). 108p. (gr. 1-8). 1989. pap. 4.99 (*0-88419-256-3*, Creation Hse) Strang Comms Co.
—Ivan & the Secret in the Suitcase. LC 88-71168. (gr. 3-7). 1988. 4.99 (*0-88419-223-7*, Creation Hse) Strang Comms Co.
Grant, Neil. The Great Atlas of Discovery. Morter, Peter, illus. LC 91-29668. 64p. 1992. 20.00 (*0-679-81660-7*); PLB 21.99 (*0-679-91660-1*) Knopf Bks Yng Read.
—Heroes of World War Two. LC 90-9468. (Illus.). 48p. (gr. 4-8). 1990. PLB 19.92 (*0-8114-2754-4*) Raintree Steck-V.
—Ireland. (Illus.). 48p. (gr. 4-8). 1989. lib. bdg. 14.98 (*0-382-09819-6*) Silver Burdett Pr.
—Roman Conquests. (Illus.). 32p. (gr. 3-9). 1991. PLB 10.95 (*1-85435-262-8*) Marshall Cavendish.
—United Kingdom. LC 88-18315. (Illus.). 48p. (gr. 4-8). 1988. PLB 14.98 (*0-382-09513-8*) Silver Burdett Pr.
—The World of Odysseus. (Illus.). 48p. (gr. 7-9). 1992. 13.95 (*0-563-34414-8*, BBC-Parkwest); pap. 6.95 (*0-563-34415-6*, BBC-Parkwest) Parkwest Pubns.
Grant, Robin R., Sr. RobinSays Try Manhood Before Fatherhood. 16p. 1993. pap. 2.25 (*0-9638384-1-5*) RobinSays.

—RobinSays Try Womanhood Before Motherhood. 10p. 1992. pap. 2.25 (*0-9638384-0-7*, TX 3 303 786) RobinSays.
Grant, Roy E., jt. auth. see Jordan, Myra J.
Grant, Wilda L., ed. see David, Ward S.
Granville, Katherine H. Let's Go See. (gr. 4 up). 1981. 6.50 (*0-9623897-1-4*) Catalyst Pr.
Grasmick, Alta C. U'n I Read a Note. Rust, Thomas O., illus. 68p. (gr. k-1). 1989. pap. 15.95 (*0-9621909-0-X*) A C Grasmick.
Grassli, Michaelene, et al. All I Really Need Is My Mom. 1993. pap. 1.50 (*0-88494-877-3*) Bookcraft Inc.
Grater, Lindsay. Runaway Row. Grater, Lindsay, illus. 24p. (ps-3). 1992. PLB 15.95 (*1-55037-213-0*, Pub. by Annick CN); pap. 5.95 (*1-55037-210-6*, Pub. by Annick CN) Firefly Bks Ltd.
Grater, Michael. Cut & Fold Extraterrestrial Invaders That Fly. 1983. pap. 2.95 (*0-486-24478-4*) Dover.
—Cut & Fold Paper Spaceships. 1981. pap. 2.95 (*0-486-23978-0*) Dover.
—Cut & Make Monster Masks in Full Color. 1978. pap. 4.95 (*0-486-23576-9*) Dover.
—Make It in Paper: Creative Three-Dimensional Paper Projects. (Illus.). 96p. (gr. 5 up). 1983. pap. 4.95 (*0-486-24468-7*) Dover.
Graube, Ireta S. Seasons - a Thematic Unit. Apodaca, Blanqui, illus. 80p. (ps-1). 1990. wkbk. 7.95 (*1-55734-251-2*) Tchr Create Mat.
—Using Big Books with Children. Fullam, Sue & Vasconcelles, Keith, illus. 80p. (ps-2). 1991. wkbk. 7.95 (*1-55734-131-1*) Tchr Create Mat.
Grauer, Neil. Drugs & the Law. Mendelson, Jack H. & Mello, Nancyintro. by. (Illus.). 120p. (gr. 5 up). 1988. lib. bdg. 19.95 (*1-55546-230-8*) Chelsea Hse.
—Medicine & the Law. (Illus.). 120p. (gr. 6-12). 1990. 18.95 (*0-7910-0088-5*) Chelsea Hse.
Grauer, Rita & Urquhart, John. Gold Fever. 46p. (Orig.). 1992. pap. 4.50 playscript (*0-87602-302-2*) Anchorage.
Gravatt, Glenn. Fifty Modern Card Tricks You Can Do! 50p. (Orig.). (gr. 7 up). 1977. pap. 3.00 (*0-915926-07-5*) Magic Ltd.
—Fifty More Modern Card Tricks. Walker, Barbara, ed. 60p. (gr. 7 up). 1979. 4.00 (*0-915926-33-4*) Magic Ltd.
Gravel, Fern, pseud. Oh Millersville! Andrews, Clarence A., tr. LC 41-3646. (Illus.). 128p. (gr. 3 up). 1981. PLB 8.95 (*0-934582-01-7*); pap. 5.95 (*0-685-42267-4*) Midwest Heritage.
Gravelle, Karen. Animal Societies. LC 92-35877. (Illus.). 96p. (gr. 7-12). 1993. PLB 13.40 (*0-531-12530-0*) Watts.
—Lizards. LC 91-4665. (Illus.). 64p. (gr. 5-8). 1991. PLB 12.90 (*0-531-20026-4*) Watts.
—Teenage Fathers. LC 91-2967. 1992. lib. bdg. 11.98 (*0-671-72850-4*, J Messner); lib. bdg. 5.95 (*0-671-72851-2*, J Messner) S&S Trade.
—Understanding Birth Defects. LC 90-32658. (Illus.). 126p. (gr. 7-12). 1990. PLB 13.40 (*0-531-10955-0*) Watts.
Gravelle, Karen & Bertram, John. Teenagers Face-to-Face with Cancer. LC 86-8608. 96p. (gr. 7 up). 1986. lib. bdg. 12.98 (*0-671-54549-3*, J Messner) S&S Trade.
Gravelle, Karen & Fischer, Susan. Where Are My Birth Parents? A Guide for Teenage Adoptees. LC 92-34586. 112p. (gr. 5 up). 1993. 14.95 (*0-8027-8257-4*); PLB 15.85 (*0-8027-8258-2*) Walker & Co.
Gravelle, Karen & Haskins, Charles. Teenagers Face to Face with Bereavement. Steltenpohl, Jane, ed. 128p. (gr. 7 up). 1989. lib. bdg. 12.98 (*0-671-65856-5*, J Messner); pap. 5.95 (*0-671-65975-8*) S&S Trade.
Gravelle, Karen & Squire, Ann. Animal Talk. LC 87-14016. (Illus.). 128p. (gr. 4-7). 1987. lib. bdg. 12.98 (*0-671-63726-6*, J Messner) S&S Trade.
Graver, Fred. The Journey to Stonehenge. (gr. 4 up). 1984. pap. 2.25 (*0-553-25961-X*) Bantam.
Graver, Jane. How You Are Changing. 64p. (gr. 3-6). 1988. 7.99 (*0-570-08483-0*, 14-1623) Concordia.
Graver, Jane, jt. auth. see Ameiss, Bill.

Graves, Carolyn. Skip-a-Star: The Legend of the Christmas Snow. 2nd ed. (Illus.). 32p. (gr. 2-4). 1993. Set, audio cass. & bk. 9.95 (*1-882716-03-5*); Bk. pap. text ed. 4.95 (*1-882716-05-1*); write for info. audio cassette (*1-882716-04-3*) PAVE. A magical dancing fairy living on a star longs to share his joy with others. When he accidentally tumbles off his star, he begins an adventure that leads him to Christmasland. But Christmasland is in crisis. Santa, & Mrs. Claus, the elves & even the reindeer are very worried. No snow has fallen! The reindeer won't be able to pull the heavy sleigh. How will Santa deliver all the toys & gifts on time? Skip-A-Star saves the spirit-of-Christmas for the world in a charming & magical way. The audio tape--narrated by the author--is complete with music & sound effects that create a theatre for the mind. SKIP-A-STAR will delight young & old alike. His story is certain to become part of everyone's Christmas tradition. Reading level: grades 2-4; Cassette running time: 17 min. Published by Prosperity Audio-Visual Enterprises (PAVE): STORY-CARD ENTERPRISES DIVISION. TO ORDER: 33049 35TH SW, FEDERAL WAY, WA 98023. (206) 927-2639 INFORMATION & FAX. Trade discounts: Libraries/ bookstores 40%; wholesalers/ distributors 50%. Libraries receive discounts on replacement books & cassettes. FREE SHIPPING TO LIBRARIES. 10% discount on shipping charges for orders of 100 plus. *Publisher Provided Annotation.*

Graves, Charles P. Annie Oakley: The Shooting Star. (Illus.). 80p. (gr. 2-6). 1991. Repr. of 1961 ed. lib. bdg. 12.95 (*0-7910-1448-7*) Chelsea Hse.
—Benjamin Franklin: Man of Ideas. (Illus.). 80p. (gr. 2-6). 1993. Repr. of 1960 ed. lib. bdg. 12.95 (*0-7910-1422-3*) Chelsea Hse.
—Henry Morton Stanley. (Illus.). 96p. (gr. 3-5). 1991. Repr. of 1967 ed. lib. bdg. 12.95 (*0-7910-1507-6*) Chelsea Hse.
—John F. Kennedy: New Frontiersman. (Illus.). 80p. (gr. 2-6). 1992. Repr. of 1965 ed. PLB 12.95 (*0-7910-1444-4*) Chelsea Hse.
—John Smith. (Illus.). 96p. (gr. 3-5). 1991. Repr. of 1965 ed. PLB 12.95 (*0-7910-1499-1*) Chelsea Hse.
—Marco Polo. (Illus.). 96p. (gr. 3-5). 1991. Repr. of 1963 ed. lib. bdg. 12.95 (*0-7910-1505-X*) Chelsea Hse.
—Paul Revere: Rider for Liberty. (Illus.). 80p. (gr. 2-6). 1991. Repr. of 1964 ed. lib. bdg. 12.95 (*0-7910-1419-3*) Chelsea Hse.
—Robert E. Lee: Hero of the South. (Illus.). 80p. (gr. 2-6). 1991. Repr. of 1964 ed. lib. bdg. 12.95 (*0-7910-1462-2*) Chelsea Hse.
Graves, Helen, ed. see Armstrong, Velma.
Graves, Helen, ed. see Armstrong, William.
Graves, Helen, ed. see Borden, Margie.
Graves, Helen, ed. see Dietrich, Wilson G.
Graves, Helen, ed. see Fitzpatrick, Regina D.
Graves, Helen, ed. see Hines, Jane B.
Graves, Helen, ed. see Keathley, Jean.
Graves, Helen, ed. see Mitchell, Tucker.
Graves, Helen, ed. see Ritch, Ronald.
Graves, Helen, ed. see Smith, Martha.
Graves, Helen, ed. see Van Antwerp, T. Cooper.
Graves, Helen, ed. see Weck, Thomas.
Graves, Helen, tr. see Hol, Coby.
Graves, Helen, tr. see Sopko, Eugen.
Graves, Helen, tr. see Wilkon, Piotr.
Graves, Jack A. What Is a California Gray Whale? Daines, Cameron K., illus. 48p. (gr. 1-4). 1991. pap. 4.95 (*0-929526-13-9*) Double B Pubns.
—What Is a California Sea Otter? Cooke, Ralph W., illus. (gr. 3 up). 1977. pap. 3.95 (*0-910286-61-2*) Boxwood.
Graves, Robert. An Ancient Castle. Graves, Elizabeth, illus. Thomas, William P., afterword by. LC 81-17204. (Illus.). 72p. (gr. 7 up). 1981. 13.95 (*0-935576-06-1*); pap. 8.95 (*0-935576-33-9*) Kesend Pub Ltd.
—The Big Green Book. reissued ed. Sendak, Maurice, illus. LC 84-42972. 64p. (gr. 1-4). 1985. RSBE 14.95 (*0-02-736810-6*, Macmillan Child Bk) Macmillan Child Grp.
—Big Green Book. (Illus.). 64p. (gr. 1-4). 1990. pap. 4.95 (*0-689-71402-5*, Aladdin) Macmillan Child Grp.
—Greek Gods & Heroes. 125p. 1965. pap. 3.99 (*0-440-93221-1*, LFL) Dell.
—Greek Myths, 2 Vols. (Orig.). (gr. 9 up). 1955. Vol. 1. pap. 4.95 (*0-14-020508-X*, Penguin Bks); Vol. 2. pap. 4.95 (*0-14-020509-8*) Viking Child Bks.
Gravett, Chris, jt. auth. see Dann, Geoff.
Gravett, Christopher. Castle. LC 93-32594. (Illus.). 1994. 15.00 (*0-679-86000-2*); PLB 15.99 (*0-679-96000-7*) Knopf Bks Yng Read.
Gravitz, Herbert see Mansmann, Patricia A. & Neuhausel, Patricia A.
Gravois, Jeanne M. Quickly, Quigley. Hill, Alison, illus. LC 93-1990. 32p. 1994. 14.00 (*0-688-13047-X*, Tambourine Bks); PLB 13.93 (*0-688-13048-8*, Tambourine Bks) Morrow.
Gray, Anne. The Wonderful World of San Diego. 2nd ed. LC 74-76733. (Illus.). (gr. 4 up). 1975. pap. 3.95 (*0-88289-081-6*) Pelican.
Gray, Barbara J. Problem Solving for Teens: An Interactive Approach to Real-Life Problem Solving. (Illus.). (gr. 7-12). 1990. spiral bdg. 27.95 (*1-55999-113-5*) LinguiSystems.
Gray, Carole, illus. Christmas Nativity Diorama. (ps-1). 1992. page 13.00 case, shrinkwrapped (*0-671-78513-3*, S&S BFYR) S&S Trade.
Gray, Catherine. One, Two, Three & Four: No More? Moss, Marissa, illus. 32p. (gr. k-3). 1988. 13.45 (*0-395-48293-3*) HM.

Gray, Catherine & Gray, James. Tammy & the Gigantic Fish. Joyce, William, illus. LC 82-47732. 32p. (ps-1). 1991. pap. 3.95 (0-06-443263-7, Trophy) HarpC Child Bks.
Gray, Charlotte. Bob Geldof: The Rock Star Who Raised 140 Million Dollars for Famine Relief in Ethiopia. Sherwood, Rhoda, ed. LC 88-2231. (Illus.). 68p. (gr. 5-6). 1988. PLB 18.60 (1-55532-814-8) Gareth Stevens Inc.
—Florence Nightingale: The Determined English Woman Who Founded Modern Nursing & Reformed Military Medicine. Sherwood, Rhoda, ed. LC 88-4913. (Illus.). 68p. (gr. 5-6). 1989. PLB 18.60 (1-55532-860-1) Gareth Stevens Inc.
—Henry Dunant: Founder of the Red Cross, the Relief Organization Dedicated to Helping Suffering People All over the World. Sherwood, Rhoda, ed. LC 88-4917. (Illus.). 68p. (gr. 5-6). 1989. PLB 18.60 (1-55532-824-5) Gareth Stevens Inc.
—Mother Teresa. LC 88-2226. (Illus.). 68p. (Orig.). (gr. 5-6). 1990. pap. 7.95 (0-8192-1523-6) Morehouse Pub.
—Mother Teresa: Her Mission to Serve God by Caring for the Poor. Sherwood, Rhoda, ed. LC 88-2226. (Illus.). 68p. (gr. 5-6). 1988. PLB 18.60 (1-55532-816-4) Gareth Stevens Inc.
—Mother Teresa: Servant to the World's Suffering People. Ullstein, Susan, adapted by. LC 89-49750. (Illus.). 64p. (gr. 3-4). 1990. PLB 18.60 (0-8368-0393-0) Gareth Stevens Inc.
Gray, Elizabeth J. Adam of the Road. Lawson, Robert, illus 320p. (gr. 4-8). 1942. pap. 15.95 (0-670-10435-3) Viking Child Bks.
—Adam of the Road. Lawson, Robert, illus. (gr. 3-7). 1987. pap. 4.99 (0-14-032464-X, Puffin) Puffin Bks.
Gray, Genevieve. How Far, Felipe? Grifalconi, Ann, illus. LC 77-11846. 64p. (gr. k-3). 1978. PLB 11.89 (0-06-022108-9) HarpC Child Bks.
Gray, Harold. Little Orphan Annie. (Illus.). 64p. (gr. 2 up). 1982. pap. 2.95 (0-486-24420-2) Dover.
—Little Orphan Annie in the Great Depression. Gray, Harold, illus. 58p. (Orig.). (gr. 5 up). 1979. pap. 3.95 (0-486-23737-0) Dover.
Gray, Ian. Birds of Prey. LC 90-33768. (Illus.). 32p. (gr. 2-4). 1991. PLB 12.40 (0-531-18367-X, Pub. by Bookwright Pr) Watts.
Gray, James, jt. auth. see Gray, Catherine.
Gray, James M. George Washington Carver. Gallin, Richard, ed. (Illus.). 144p. (gr. 5-9). 1990. PLB 13.98 (0-382-09964-8); pap. 7.95 (0-382-09969-9) Silver Burdett Pr.
Gray, Libba M. Dear Willie Rudd. Fiore, Peter, illus. LC 92-25064. 1993. pap. 14.00 (0-671-79774-3, S&S BFYR) S&S Trade.
—Fenton's Leap. Bosson, Jo-Ellen, illus. LC 92-19648. 1994. pap. 14.00 (0-671-79196-6, S&S BFYR) S&S Trade.
—Miss Tizzy. Rowland, Jada, illus. LC 92-8409. (ps-2). 1993. pap. 14.00 JRT (0-671-77590-1, S&S BFYR) S&S Trade.
Gray, Mattie E. Images: A Workbook for Enhancing Self-esteem & Promoting Career Preparation. (Illus.). 186p. (gr. 6-12). 1992. pap. 10.00 (0-8011-0782-2) Calif Education.

Gray, Milton. Cartoon Animation: Introduction to a Career. LC 90-63934. (Illus.). 124p. 1991. pap. 12.95 (0-9628444-5-4, Dist. by Samuel French Trade) Lion's Den.
An up-to-date guide to securing employment in the Hollywood animation industry, at the entry & advanced levels, where production is presently booming & the studios are actively seeking new qualified artists. The author is currently an animator/producer who has worked at the Walt Disney Studio, Warner Bros. & other Hollywood studios for 25 years. This book is also a uniquely insightful how-to on animation, direction, writing & producing cartoon animation films, with special emphasis on high quality production. Illustrated, with bibliography & index. "A major step forward in learning how to animate & make cartoon films. I highly recommend it!"--Eddie Fitzgerald, Instructor, Animation Department, California Institute of the Arts, & Director, Warner Bros. Cartoons. Available through: Lion's Den Publications, Inc., PO Box 7368-W, Northridge CA 91327-7368. Telephone (818) 783-2713.
Publisher Provided Annotation.

Greegor, Katherine. Trouble - of the Northwest Territory. Cummins, Lisa, illus. LC 92-61031. 100p. (Orig.). (gr. 3-8). 1992. pap. 5.95 (0-9633091-7-X) Promise Land Pubs.
An ornery pet raccoon named Trouble & twelve-year-old Jeremiah find plenty of adventure in TROUBLE--OF THE NORTHWEST TERRITORY. The setting is in Ohio before it became a

Gray, Nigel. A Balloon for Grandad. Ray, Jane, illus. LC 87-27867. 32p. (ps-2). 1988. 13.95 (0-531-05755-0); PLB 13.99 (0-531-08355-1) Orchard Bks Watts.
—A Country Far Away. LC 88-22360. (Illus.). 32p. (ps-1). 1988. 14.95 (0-531-05792-5); PLB 14.99 (0-531-08392-6) Orchard Bks Watts.
—A Country Far Away. LC 88-22360. (Illus.). 32p. (ps-1). 1991. pap. 5.95 (0-531-07024-7) Orchard Bks Watts.
—I'll Take You to Mrs. Cole! Foreman, Michael, illus. 32p. (ps-3). 1992. 12.95 (0-916291-39-1) Kane-Miller Bk.
—The One & Only Robin Hood. Craig, Helen, illus. LC 87-2680. 32p. (ps-3). 1987. 12.95 (0-316-32578-3, Joy St Bks) Little.
—Pigs Can't Fly. Vendrell, Carme S., illus. 32p. (ps-1). 1991. 15.95 (0-86264-272-8, Pub. by Andersen Pr UK) Trafalgar.
Gray, Nigel, jt. auth. see Foreman, Michael.
Gray, Patricia. What a Haircut! Webb, Philip, illus. LC 93-26931. 1994. 4.25 (0-383-03783-2) SRA Schl Grp.
Gray, Prentiss N. Records of North American Big Game. 2nd ed. Rungius, Carl & Knight, C. W., illus. 178p. (gr. 10 up). 1990. Repr. of 1932 ed. 39.95 (1-56416-011-4) Derrydale Pr.
Gray, Ronald D. Christopher Wren & St. Paul's Cathedral. LC 81-13696. (Illus.). 48p. (gr. 7 up). 1980. pap. 6.95 (0-521-21666-4) Cambridge U Pr.
—Hitler & the Germans. LC 81-3913. (Illus.). 48p. (gr. 7 up). 1982. pap. 7.50 (0-521-22702-X) Cambridge U Pr.
Gray, Virginia. The Write Tool to Teach Algebra. 104p. (gr. 9-12). 1993. pap. 12.95 (1-55953-064-2) Key Curr Pr.
Graymont, Barbara. The Iroquois. Porter, Frank, intro. by. (Illus.). 128p. (Orig.). (gr. 5 up). 1988. 17.95 (1-55546-709-1); pap. 9.95 (0-7910-0361-2) Chelsea Hse.
Grayson, Marion. Let's Do Fingerplays. Weyl, Nancy, illus. LC 62-10217. (ps-3). 1962. 12.95 (0-88331-003-1) Luce.
Greanias, Francis. More Pasting Penguins. 24p. (gr. k-3). 1980. 3.95 (0-88160-060-1, LW 608) Learning Wks.
—Pasting Penguin. 24p. (gr. k-3). 1980. 3.95 (0-88160-059-8, LW 607) Learning Wks.
Great Aunt Adeline, pseud. The Legend of Sinter Klaas. (Illus.). 32p. (Orig.). (gr. k-4). 1992. pap. text ed. 5.95 (0-9632863-0-7) Ebner & Steffes.
Greathead, Susan D., ed. see Popkin, Michael H.
Greaves, John. Henrietta the Clumsy Hippo. McLachlan, Edward, illus. (ps-3). 1988. 7.95 (0-8120-6090-3) Barron.
Greaves, Margaret. Amanda & the Star Child. Catchpole, Diane, illus. 32p. (ps-1). 1993. pap. 8.95 (0-460-88138-8, Pub. by J M Dent & Sons) Trafalgar.
—Henry's Wild Morning. O'Brien, Teresa, illus. LC 90-3554. 40p. (ps-3). 1991. 13.95 (0-8037-0907-2) Dial Bks Young.
—The Ice Journey. Darke, Alison C., illus. 32p. (ps-1). 1994. 22.95 (0-460-88133-7, Pub. by J M Dent & Sons) Trafalgar.
—The Lost Ones. De Lacey, Honey, illus. 96p. (gr. 4-6). 1993. 16.95 (0-460-88053-5, Pub. by J M Dent & Sons) Trafalgar.
—The Lucky Coin. Underhill, Liz, illus. LC 89-19718. 12p. 1990. 14.95 (1-55670-129-2) Stewart Tabori & Chang.
—The Naming. Baynes, Pauline, illus. 32p. (ps-3). 1993. 14.95 (0-15-200534-X) HarBrace.
—Sarah's Lion. (ps-3). 1992. 13.95 (0-8120-6279-5) Barron.
—The Serpent Shell. Nesbitt, Jan, illus. 32p. (ps-3). 1993. 13.95 (0-8120-6350-3) Barron.
—Star Horse. (ps-3). 1992. 13.95 (0-8120-6294-9) Barron.
—Tattercoats. Chamberlain, Margaret, illus. LC 90-6919. 32p. (ps-2). 1990. 13.95 (0-517-58026-8) Crown Bks Yng Read.
Greaves, Nick. When Hippo Was Hairy & Other Tales from Africa. Clement, Rod, illus. 144p. (gr. 3-12). 1988. 12.95 (0-8120-4131-3) Barron.
—When Hippo Was Hairy & Other Tales from Africa. Clement, Rod, illus. 144p. (gr. k up). 1991. pap. 8.95 (0-8120-4548-3) Barron.
—When Lion Could Fly: And Other Tales from Africa. Clement, Rod, illus. LC 93-21841. 144p. (gr. 3 up). 1993. 13.95 (0-8120-6344-9); pap. 8.95 (0-8120-1625-4) Barron.
Greco, Gail. The Romance of Country Inns: A Decorating Book for Your Home. Bagley, Tom, photos by. (Illus.). 288p. (gr. 10 up). 1993. 29.95 (1-55853-175-0) Rutledge Hill Pr.
Greder, Armin, illus. & photos by see Gleeson, Libby.
Gree, Melvin de see De Gree, Melvin.

state, near the place where missionary David Zesiberger established a settlement of converted Indians & taught them how to live a Christian life. While Jeremiah struggles with acceptance of his parents' Christian values & the loss of his friends back East, Trouble's antics lead Jeremiah to a terrifying meeting with one of those Indians. It's all complicated by the fact that the new neighbor, sixteen-year-old Jedd, hates all Indians. There's plenty of excitement in the forests of Ohio & along the rivers as the boys learn about the spirit of forgiveness & other Christian principles. Even adults enjoy & learn from this book. Book review: There is a happy balance achieved by the author, making the spiritual elements of the story to be conspicuously evident without detracting from the exciting adventures that form the developing plot of the book. The book fulfills a real need for high-quality Christian reading for children & young people. We recommend it gladly.--THE SWORD OF THE LORD.
Publisher Provided Annotation.

Greeley, Sheila. S.T.A.R. Junior First Aid. Strong, Susan, illus. 32p. (gr. k-5). 1989. write for info. spiral bdg. FAFCTPC.
—S.T.A.R. Patrol. 30p. (Orig.). 1993. pap. text ed. 7.95 (0-9622812-1-2) FAFCTPC.
Greeley, Valerie. Animals. (Illus.). 12p. (gr. k-2). 1990. bds. 5.95 (0-87226-435-1, Bedrick Blackie) P Bedrick Bks.
—Animals at Home. 12p. (gr. k-2). 1992. 5.95 (0-87226-473-4, Bedrick Blackie) P Bedrick Bks.
—Where's My Share? Greeley, Valerie, illus. LC 89-13299. 32p. (ps-1). 1990. SBE 12.95 (0-02-736761-4, Macmillan Child Bk) Macmillan Child Grp.
—White Is the Moon. Greeley, Valerie, illus. LC 90-40522. 32p. (ps-1). 1991. 12.95 (0-02-736915-3, Macmillan Child Bk) Macmillan Child Grp.
Greeley, Valerie, illus. Field Animals. LC 83-22507. 12p. (gr. k-2). 1984. bds. 3.95 (0-911745-23-8, Bedrick Blackie) P Bedrick Bks.
Green, Alan, jt. auth. see Jones, Davy.
Green, Barbara, ed. see Bingham, Mindy, et al.
Green, Barbara-Marie. Dream No Small Dreams: An Autobiography. (Orig.). (gr. 7 up). 1993. pap. write for info. (1-883414-03-2) Bar JaMae.
—A Success Design. (Orig.). (gr. 7 up). 1994. pap. write for info. (1-883414-04-0) Bar JaMae.
Green, Barbara-Marie, et al. Emerging Poets of Hampton Roads, Virginia: An Anthology. (Orig.). (gr. 7 up). 1994. pap. write for info. (1-883414-02-4) Bar JaMae.
—More Poetic Thoughts: By Love Pain Hope Poet, Barbara-Marie Green & Others. 70p. (Orig.). 1993. pap. 5.50 (1-883414-01-6) Bar JaMae.
Green, Belva. How the Robin Got Its Red Breast. Beitler, Stanley, ed. White, Monica, illus. LC 90-80399. 32p. (ps-3). 1990. 12.95 (0-945740-01-8) Indp Pubs.
Green, Bill. Alcoholism. Rahmas, Sigurd C., ed. 32p. (Orig.). (gr. 7-12). 1982. lib. bdg. 4.95 incl. catalog cards (0-87157-820-4) SamHar Pr.
Green, Carl & Sanford, Bill. Dodo. LC 89-7867. (Illus.). 48p. (gr. 5-6). 1989. RSBE 12.95 (0-89686-455-3, Crestwood Hse) Macmillan Child Grp.
—Woolly Mammoth. LC 89-31575. (Illus.). 48p. (gr. 5-6). 1989. RSBE 12.95 (0-89686-456-1, Crestwood Hse) Macmillan Child Grp.
Green, Carl & Sanford, William. Congress. (Illus.). 96p. (gr. 7 up). 1990. lib. bdg. 18.60 (0-86593-083-X); lib. bdg. 13.95 s.p. (0-685-46455-5) Rourke Corp.
—Judiciary. (Illus.). 96p. (gr. 7 up). 1990. lib. bdg. 18.60 (0-86593-086-4); lib. bdg. 13.95 s.p. (0-685-46457-1) Rourke Corp.
—Movie Monsters, 10 Bks. (Illus.). 48p. (gr. 3-5). 1991. Set. RSBE 119.40 (0-89686-753-6, Crestwood Hse) Macmillan Child Grp.
—Presidency. (Illus.). 96p. (gr. 7 up). 1990. lib. bdg. 18.60 (0-86593-084-8); lib. bdg. 13.95 s.p. (0-685-36360-0) Rourke Corp.
—Tarantula. LC 84-20067. (Illus.). 48p. (gr. 3-5). 1985. RSBE 10.95 (0-89686-264-X, Crestwood Hse) Macmillan Child Grp.
—Werewolf of London. LC 84-19910. (Illus.). 48p. (gr. 3-5). 1985. RSBE 10.95 (0-89686-265-8, Crestwood Hse) Macmillan Child Grp.
Green, Carl, jt. auth. see Sanford, Bill.
Green, Carl, jt. auth. see Sanford, William.

Green, Carl, et al. American Government, 4 bks. (Illus.). 384p. (gr. 7 up). 1990. Set. lib. bdg. 74.40 (*0-86593-082-1*); Set. lib. bdg. 55.80s.p. (*0-685-46454-7*) Rourke Corp.
Green, Carl R. Jackie Joyner-Kersee. LC 93-456. (Illus.). 48p. (gr. 5-6). 1994. RSBE 13.95 (*0-89686-838-9*, Crestwood Hse) Macmillan Child Grp.
—Orel Hershiser. LC 93-28044. (gr. 5 up). 1994. text ed. 13.95 (*0-89686-836-2*, Crestwood Hse) Macmillan.
—Troy Aikman. LC 93-17480. (Illus.). 48p. (gr. 5-6). 1994. RSBE 13.95 (*0-89686-833-8*, Crestwood Hse) Macmillan Child Grp.
Green, Carl R. & Ford, M. Roxanne. David Robinson. LC 93-4976. (Illus.). 48p. (gr. 5-6). 1994. RSBE 13.95 (*0-89686-839-7*, Crestwood Hse) Macmillan Child Grp.
—Deion Sanders. LC 93-951. (Illus.). 48p. (gr. 5-6). 1994. RSBE 13.95 (*0-89686-840-0*, Crestwood Hse) Macmillan Child Grp.
Green, Carl R. & Green, Roxanne. Brett Hull. LC 93-23424. 1994. write for info. (*0-89686-837-0*) Macmillan Child Grp.
Green, Carl R. & Sanford, William R. African Lion. LC 87-13648. (Illus.). 48p. (gr. 5-6). 1987. RSBE 12.95 (*0-89686-328-X*, Crestwood Hse) Macmillan Child Grp.
—The African Rhinos. (Illus.). 48p. (gr. 4-5). 1987. RSBE 12.95 (*0-89686-327-1*, Crestwood Hse) Macmillan Child Grp.
—Asiatic Elephant. LC 87-20200. (Illus.). 48p. (gr. 5-6). 1987. RSBE 12.95 (*0-89686-333-6*, Crestwood Hse) Macmillan Child Grp.
—Babe Ruth. LC 91-21639. (Illus.). 48p. (gr. 5-6). 1992. RSBE 11.95 (*0-89686-741-2*, Crestwood Hse) Macmillan Child Grp.
—The Badger. LC 85-19486. (Illus.). 48p. (gr. 4-5). 1986. RSBE 12.95 (*0-89686-290-9*, Crestwood Hse) Macmillan Child Grp.
—Bat Masterson. LC 91-29857. (Illus.). 48p. (gr. 4-10). 1992. lib. bdg. 14.95 (*0-89490-362-4*) Enslow Pubs.
—Belle Starr. LC 91-22310. (Illus.). 48p. (gr. 4-10). 1992. lib. bdg. 14.95 (*0-89490-363-2*) Enslow Pubs.
—The Bengal Tiger. LC 85-31411. (Illus.). 48p. (gr. 5-6). 1986. RSBE 12.95 (*0-89686-270-4*, Crestwood Hse) Macmillan Child Grp.
—Billy the Kid. LC 91-18124. (Illus.). 48p. (gr. 4-10). 1992. lib. bdg. 14.95 (*0-89490-364-0*) Enslow Pubs.
—The Bison. LC 85-6624. (Illus.). 48p. (gr. 4-5). 1985. RSBE 12.95 (*0-89686-275-5*, Crestwood Hse) Macmillan Child Grp.
—The Bottlenose Dolphin. LC 87-19420. (Illus.). 48p. (gr. 5-6). 1987. RSBE 12.95 (*0-89686-329-8*, Crestwood Hse) Macmillan Child Grp.
—The Camel. LC 88-5957. (Illus.). 48p. (gr. 5-6). 1988. RSBE 12.95 (*0-89686-385-9*, Crestwood Hse) Macmillan Child Grp.
—The Cobra. LC 85-14969. (Illus.). 48p. (gr. 5-6). 1986. RSBE 11.95 (*0-89686-266-6*, Crestwood Hse) Macmillan Child Grp.
—The Elephant Seal. LC 87-22349. (Illus.). 48p. (gr. 5-6). 1987. RSBE 12.95 (*0-89686-330-1*, Crestwood Hse) Macmillan Child Grp.
—Exploring the Unknown Series. (Illus.). 48p. (gr. 4-10). 1993. Set. lib. bdg. 89.70 (*0-89490-475-2*) Enslow Pubs.
—Fortune Telling. Robinson, Keith, illus. LC 93-12029. 48p. (gr. 4-10). 1993. lib. bdg. 14.95 (*0-89490-456-6*) Enslow Pubs.
—The Giant Panda. LC 87-14002. (Illus.). 48p. (gr. 5-6). 1987. RSBE 12.95 (*0-89686-331-X*, Crestwood Hse) Macmillan Child Grp.
—The Giraffes. LC 87-1363. (Illus.). 48p. (gr. 5-6). 1987. RSBE 12.95 (*0-89686-332-8*, Crestwood Hse) Macmillan Child Grp.
—The Gorilla. LC 85-9991. (Illus.). 48p. (gr. 5-6). 1986. RSBE 12.95 (*0-89686-269-0*, Crestwood Hse) Macmillan Child Grp.
—The Great White Shark. LC 85-14936. (Illus.). 48p. (gr. 5-6). 1986. RSBE 12.95 (*0-89686-281-X*, Crestwood Hse) Macmillan Child Grp.
—The Hippopotamus. LC 88-1830. (Illus.). 48p. (gr. 5-6). 1988. RSBE 12.95 (*0-89686-383-2*, Crestwood Hse) Macmillan Child Grp.
—The Humpback Whale. LC 85-9645. (Illus.). 48p. (gr. 5-6). 1985. RSBE 12.95 (*0-89686-274-7*, Crestwood Hse) Macmillan Child Grp.
—The Hyena. LC 88-5876. (Illus.). 48p. (gr. 5-6). 1988. RSBE 12.95 (*0-89686-384-0*, Crestwood Hse) Macmillan Child Grp.
—Jackie Robinson. LC 91-23921. (Illus.). 48p. (gr. 5). 1992. RSBE 11.95 (*0-89686-743-9*, Crestwood Hse) Macmillan Child Grp.
—Jesse James. LC 91-18123. (Illus.). 48p. (gr. 4-10). 1992. lib. bdg. 14.95 (*0-89490-365-9*) Enslow Pubs.
—Jesse Owens. LC 91-27185. (Illus.). 48p. (gr. 5). 1992. RSBE 11.95 (*0-89686-742-0*, Crestwood Hse) Macmillan Child Grp.
—Jim Thorpe. LC 91-32900. (Illus.). 48p. (gr. 5). 1992. RSBE 11.95 (*0-89686-740-4*, Crestwood Hse) Macmillan Child Grp.
—The Koala. LC 85. 48p. (gr. 5-6). 1987. RSBE 12.95 (*0-89686-334-4*, Crestwood Hse) Macmillan Child Grp.
—The Little Brown Bat. LC 85-22345. (Illus.). 48p. (gr. 4-5). 1986. RSBE 12.95 (*0-89686-267-4*, Crestwood Hse) Macmillan Child Grp.

—Mysterious Mind Powers. Robinson, Keith, illus. LC 92-44678. 48p. (gr. 4-10). 1993. PLB 14.95 (*0-89490-455-8*) Enslow Pubs.
—The Mystery of Dreams. LC 93-6539. (Illus.). 48p. (gr. 4-10). 1993. PLB 14.95 (*0-89490-453-1*) Enslow Pubs.
—The Orangutan. LC 87-19811. (Illus.). 48p. (gr. 5-6). 1987. RSBE 12.95 (*0-89686-335-2*, Crestwood Hse) Macmillan Child Grp.
—The Ostrich. LC 87-20175. (Illus.). 48p. (gr. 5-6). 1987. RSBE 12.95 (*0-89686-336-0*, Crestwood Hse) Macmillan Child Grp.
—Out-of-Body Experiences. (Illus.). 48p. (gr. 4-10). 1993. lib. bdg. 14.95 (*0-89490-457-4*) Enslow Pubs.
—Outlaws & Lawmen of the Wild West Series, 6 bks. (Illus.). (gr. 4-10). 1992. Set, 48p. ea. lib. bdg. 89.70 (*0-89490-391-8*) Enslow Pubs.
—The Pelicans. LC 87-22251. (Illus.). 48p. (gr. 5-6). 1987. RSBE 12.95 (*0-89686-337-9*, Crestwood Hse) Macmillan Child Grp.
—The Peregrine Falcon. LC 86-2670. (Illus.). 48p. (gr. 4-5). 1986. RSBE 12.95 (*0-89686-271-2*, Crestwood Hse) Macmillan Child Grp.
—The Porcupine. LC 85-7899. (Illus.). 48p. (gr. 5-6). 1985. RSBE 12.95 (*0-89686-280-1*, Crestwood Hse) Macmillan Child Grp.
—The Rabbit. LC 88-9601. (Illus.). 48p. (gr. 5-6). 1988. RSBE 12.95 (*0-89686-387-5*, Crestwood Hse) Macmillan Child Grp.
—Recalling Past Lives. Robinson, Keith, illus. 48p. (gr. 4-10). 1993. lib. bdg. 14.95 (*0-89490-458-2*) Enslow Pubs.
—Seeing the Unseen. Robinson, Keith, illus. LC 92-44677. 48p. (gr. 4-10). 1993. lib. bdg. 14.95 (*0-89490-454-X*) Enslow Pubs.
—The Striped Skunk. LC 87-6652. (Illus.). 48p. (gr. 5-6). 1987. RSBE 12.95 (*0-89686-338-7*, Crestwood Hse) Macmillan Child Grp.
—The Tarantulas. LC 87-22342. (Illus.). 48p. (gr. 5-6). 1987. RSBE 12.95 (*0-89686-339-5*, Crestwood Hse) Macmillan Child Grp.
—The Walrus. LC 85-17509. (Illus.). 48p. (gr. 4-5). 1986. RSBE 12.95 (*0-89686-273-9*, Crestwood Hse) Macmillan Child Grp.
—Wild Bill Hickok. LC 91-29856. (Illus.). 48p. (gr. 4-10). 1992. lib. bdg. 14.95 (*0-89490-366-7*) Enslow Pubs.
—The Wild Horses. LC 85-13276. (Illus.). 48p. (gr. 5-6). 1986. RSBE 12.95 (*0-89686-291-7*, Crestwood Hse) Macmillan Child Grp.
—Wyatt Earp. LC 91-29855. (Illus.). 48p. (gr. 4-10). 1992. lib. bdg. 14.95 (*0-89490-367-5*) Enslow Pubs.
—The Zebra. LC 88-1831. (Illus.). 48p. (gr. 5-6). 1988. RSBE 12.95 (*0-89686-388-3*, Crestwood Hse) Macmillan Child Grp.
Green, Carl R., jt. auth. see Sanford, Willam R.
Green, Carl R., jt. auth. see Sanford, William R.
Green, Carl R., jt. auth. see Sanford, William R.
Green, Carl R., jt. auth. see Sanford, William R.
Green, Cecile. Tale of Theodore Bear. LC 68-56812. (Illus.). 32p. (gr. 1-2). 1968. PLB 9.95 (*0-87783-038-X*) Oddo.
—The Tale of Theodore Bear. Lysaker, Gene, illus. (gr. 1-2). 1978. pap. 1.25 (*0-89508-060-5*) Rainbow Bks.
Green, Connie J. Emmy. Crofut, bob, illus. LC 92-1513. 160p. (gr. 5-9). 1992. SBE 13.95 (*0-689-50556-6*, M K McElderry) Macmillan Child Grp.
—The War at Home. LC 88-26663. 160p. (gr. 5-9). 1989. SBE 13.95 (*0-689-50470-5*, M K McElderry) Macmillan Child Grp.
Green, George W. Halloween Book & Masks. Hatter, Laurie, illus. (ps) 1993. Gift box set of 4 bks., 12p. ea. bds. 14.95 (*1-56828-040-8*) Red Jacket Pr.
Green, Harriet & Martin, Sue. Sprouts. 144p. (gr. 3-8). 1981. 11.95 (*0-86653-028-2*, GA256) Good Apple.
Green, Harriet, jt. auth. see Martin, Susan.
Green, Harriet H. & Martin, Sue G. Treasure Hunts. 144p. (gr. 4-7). 1983. wkbk. 11.95 (*0-86653-115-7*, GA 469) Good Apple.
Green, I. Conservation from A to Z. LC 66-11443. (Illus.). 64p. (gr. 4 up). 1968. PLB 10.95 (*0-87783-009-6*); pap. 3.94 deluxe ed. (*0-87783-088-6*) Oddo.
—Where Is Duckling Three? Le Blanc, L., illus. LC 68-16402. 32p. (gr. 1-2). 1967. PLB 9.95 (*0-87783-048-7*) Oddo.
Green, I., et al. Double Action Library One-A. large type ed. Incl. Anything for a Friend. 134p. 1979. 24.15 (*0-317-02186-9*, 4-23310-00); Buckaroo. 134p. 1982. 24.15 (*0-317-02187-7*, 4-23320-00); The Firefighter. 134p. 1982. 24.15 (*0-317-02188-5*, 4-23330-00); The Hotel Mystery. 134p. 1982. 24.15 (*0-317-02189-3*, 4-23340-00); (gr. 7-12) An Printing Hse.
Green, Ivah. Splash & Trickle. LC 68-56818. (Illus.). 32p. (gr. 2-3). 1968. PLB 9.95 (*0-87783-037-1*); pap. 3.94 deluxe ed. (*0-87783-109-2*); cassette o.s.i. 7.94x (*0-87783-226-9*) Oddo.
—Splash & Trickle. Connor, Bil, illus. (gr. 2-3). 1978. pap. 1.25 (*0-89508-062-1*) Rainbow Bks.
Green, Ivah J. Loon. LC 65-22310. (Illus.). 32p. (gr. 4 up). 1968. PLB 9.95 (*0-87783-025-8*) Oddo.
Green, Janice. Who Hides Here? Gapper, Jo, illus. 12p. 1992. 4.95 (*0-681-41552-5*) Longmeadow Pr.
—Who Lives Here? Gapper, Jo, illus. 12p. 1992. 4.95 (*0-681-41551-7*) Longmeadow Pr.
Green, Jeffrey M., jt. auth. see Birger, Trudy.
Green, Jen. Making Crazy Animals. LC 91-33868. (Illus.). 32p. (gr. 2-4). 1992. PLB 12.40 (*0-531-17324-0*, Gloucester Pr) Watts.

—Making Fantastic Aliens & Spaceships. LC 92-9814. 1992. 12.40 (*0-531-17366-6*, Gloucester Pr) Watts.
—Making Mad Machines. (Illus.). 32p. (gr. 2-4). 1992. PLB 12.40 (*0-531-17326-7*, Gloucester Pr) Watts.
—Making Masks & Crazy Faces. LC 92-9813. 1992. 12. 40 (*0-531-17365-8*, Gloucester Pr) Watts.
Green, John F. There Are Trolls. rev. ed. White, Kenneth R., illus. 24p. (gr. k-3). 1975. 7.95 (*0-919566-38-3*) Peguis Pubs Ltd.
Green, Julian. The War at Sixteen: Autobiography, Vol. 2. Cameron, Euan, tr. from FRE. LC 93-656. 224p. 1993. 24.95 (*0-7145-2969-9*) M Boyars Pubs.
Green, Kate. Between Friends. (Illus.). 32p. 1992. 22.75 (*0-89565-780-5*); 15.95s.p. (*0-685-55129-6*) Childs World.
—Buddy Rock's Race. (Illus.). 32p. 1992. 22.75 (*0-89565-781-3*); 15.95s.p. (*0-685-55130-X*) Childs World.
—Everything a Dinosaur Could Want. (Illus.). 32p. 1992. 22.75 (*0-89565-739-2*); 15.95s.p. (*0-685-55131-8*) Childs World.
—Grumble Day. Mark, Steve, illus. (gr. 1-8). 1992. PLB 15.95 (*0-89565-870-4*); Resale. 22.75 (*0-685-60968-5*) Childs World.
—Just about Perfect. Mark, Steve, illus. (gr. 1-8). 1992. PLB 15.95 (*0-89565-871-2*); Resale. 22.75 (*0-685-60967-7*) Childs World.
—Little Bookmobile. 1986. pap. 7.95 (*0-385-23633-6*) Doubleday.
—T-Bone's Tent. (Illus.). 32p. 1992. 22.75 (*0-89565-782-1*); 15.95s.p. (*0-685-55132-6*) Childs World.
Green, Kate, jt. auth. see Wormell, Christopher.
Green, Krister. Lisi & the Kittens. Coughlin, Ramona, tr. from SWE. Martin, Lisi, illus. 28p. (gr. 3-5). 1990. 12. 95g (*0-940607-07-7*) Pictura NJ.
Green, Laurel & Beck, Trudy. My Birthday Memories. Nebeker, Kinde, illus. (ps-12). 1985. 5.00 (*0-9613079-1-9*) Greenbeck.
Green, Lucinda. The Young Rider. LC 93-22103. (Illus.). 64p. (gr. 3-6). 1993. 15.45 (*1-56458-320-1*) Dorling Kindersley.
Green, Martha G. Grampa's in Heaven. LC 90-71356. (Illus.). 44p. (gr. 3-8). 1991. pap. 5.95 (*1-55523-399-6*) Winston-Derek.
Green, Mary A. Projects for Christmas. Young, Richard G., ed. Marffy, Janos, illus. LC 89-35285. 32p. (gr. 3-5). 1989. PLB 15.93 (*0-944483-43-7*) Garrett Ed Corp.
Green, Michael D. The Creeks. Porter, Frank, intro. by. (Illus.). 128p. (gr. 5 up). 1990. lib. bdg. 17.95x (*1-55546-703-2*) Chelsea Hse.
Green, Michelle Y. Willie Pearl. (gr. 4-7). 1991. pap. 9.95 (*0-9627697-0-3*) W Ruth Co.

—**Willie Pearl Series. 1992. write for info. (*0-9627697-6-2*) W Ruth Co.**
An historical fiction for families, set in a Depression-era coal-mining town in Eastern Kentucky. The series centers around a 10-year-old Black girl who is raised in a poor, but loving, whole family environment. Willie Pearl will serve as the first-ever literature series featuring a Black central character. The goal of the Willie Pearl literature series is to create a positive self-image & role model for Black youth, to stress a return to basic family values, & to fill a void in the children's book market with regard to minority readers. Additionally, it is a model of whole language literature. UNDER THE MOUNTAIN involves a daring adventure in which Willie Pearl falls into a mining break days before the coal company is due to seal off a mining chamber. Thematically, the book deals with the challenge we all have, children as well as adults, of confronting our fears. WILLIE PEARL: UNDER THE MOUNTAIN (ISBN 0-9627697-1-1) is the second in the six-part Willie Pearl book series for families, written by Michelle Y. Green, & published by William Ruth & Company (301-899-3434). The first book in the series, WILLIE PEARL (ISBN 0-9627697-0-3) is also available. Order from: William Ruth & Co., 3202 Brinkley Rd., Temple Hills, MD 20748-6302. 301-899-3434.
Publisher Provided Annotation.

—Willie Pearl: Under the Mountain. McCracken, Steve, illus. Green, Oliver W., contrib. by. (Illus., Orig.). (gr. 4-6). 1992. pap. 9.95 (0-9627697-1-1) W Ruth Co.
Green, Nancy S. Curious & Creative: Critical Thinking & Language Development. (ps-3). pap. 32.00 (0-201-55420-8) Addison-Wesley.
Green, Norma. The Hole in the Dyke. Carle, Eric, illus. LC 74-23562. 32p. (gr. k-3). 1975. (Crowell Jr Bks); PLB 15.89 (0-690-00676-4) HarpC Child Bks.
Green, Norma, retold by. The Hole in the Dike. Carle, Eric, illus. 32p. (ps-2). 1993. pap. 4.95 (0-590-46146-X) Scholastic Inc.
Green, Paul & Abbott, Abbe. I Am Eskimo: Aknik My Name. Ahgupuk, George, illus. LC 59-15891. (Orig.). 1959. pap. 12.95 (0-88240-001-0) Alaska Northwest.
Green, Peter, ed. see Grahame, Kenneth.
Green, Phyllis. Chucky Bellman Was So Bad. Mathews, Judith, ed. Fragomenghi, Gioia, illus. LC 90-26823. 32p. (gr. k-3). 1991. 13.95 (0-8075-1156-0) A Whitman.
—Eating Ice Cream with a Werewolf. Stern, Patti, illus. LC 82-47727. 128p. (gr. 3-7). 1983. HarpC Child Bks.
—Eating Ice Cream with a Werewolf. (gr. 4-6). 1985. pap. 2.95 (0-440-42182-9, YB) Dell.
—A New Mother for Martha. Luks, Margaret. LC 78-16731. (Illus.). 32p. (gr. k-3). 1978. 16.95 (0-87705-330-8) Human Sci Pr.
Green, R. L. The Tale of Thebes. LC 76-22979. (Illus.). 1977. Cambridge U Pr.
Green, Rayna. Women in American Indian Society. (Illus.). (gr. 5 up). 1992. 17.95 (1-55546-734-2) Chelsea Hse.
Green, Richard G. Sing, Like a Hermit Thrush. Longboat, Dianne, ed. Green, Richard, illus. Doxtater, Michael, intro. by. (Illus.). 112p. (Orig.). (gr. 6). 1990. pap. 7.95x (0-911737-01-4) Ricara Features.
Green, Richard L. Myths of the Norsemen. Wildsmith, Brian, illus. (gr. 4-6). 1970. pap. 3.50 (0-14-030464-9) Viking Child Bks.
Green, Robyn & Scarffe, Bronwen. Black & White. Sofilas, Mark, illus. LC 92-21393. (gr. 4 up). 1993. 2.50 (0-383-03555-4) SRA Schl Grp.
Green, Roger J. The Throttlepenny Murder. 206p. (gr. 7 up). 1989. jacketed 14.95 (0-19-271601-8) OUP.
Green, Roger L. Adventures of Robin Hood. (Orig.). (gr. 2-5). 1984. pap. 2.99 (0-14-035034-9, Puffin) Puffin Bks.
—King Arthur & His Knights of the Round Table. (Orig.). (gr. 5-7). 1974. pap. 2.95 (0-14-030073-2) Viking Child Bks.
—King Arthur & His Knights of the Round Table. (gr. 5 up). 1990. pap. 3.99 (0-14-035100-0) Puffin Bks.
—King Arthur & His Knights of the Round Table. (gr. 5 up). 1993. 13.95 (0-679-42311-7, Everymans Lib Childs) Knopf.
—The Luck of Troy. 176p. (gr. 5 up). 1993. pap. 2.25 (0-14-035103-5) Puffin Bks.
—Myths of the Norsemen. (gr. 5 up). 1970. pap. 3.50 (0-14-035098-5) Puffin Bks.
—Tale of Troy. (Illus., Orig.). (gr. 5-7). 1974. pap. 3.95 (0-14-030120-8, Puffin) Puffin Bks.
—Tales of Ancient Egypt. (gr. k-3). 1990. pap. 3.50 (0-14-035101-9, Puffin) Puffin Bks.
—Tales of Greek Heroes. (Orig.). (gr. 5-7). 1989. pap. 2.99 (0-14-035099-3, Puffin) Puffin Bks.
Green, Roxanne, jt. auth. see Green, Carl R.
Green, Sharon W. & Siemon, Michael. How to Prepare for the CHSPE - California High School Proficency Exam. 4th ed. 380p. (gr. 9 up). 1993. pap. 11.95 (0-8120-1439-1) Barron.
Green, Susan L., jt. auth. see DuGan, Thomas K.
Green, Suzanne. The Little Choo-Choo: Sounds, Sights & Opposites. Fujita, Miho, illus. 14p. (ps-k). 1988. pap. 8.95 incl. pull toy (0-385-24426-6) Doubleday.
Green, Timothy. Mystery of Navajo Moon. Green, Timothy, illus. LC 91-52600. 48p. (ps-4). 1991. 14.95 (0-87358-523-2) Northland AZ.
Green, Yvonne. Rising Star: Kelly Blake, Teen Model, No. 2. 176p. (gr. 7-12). 1986. pap. 2.50 (0-553-25639-4) Bantam.
Greenaway, Elizabeth. Cat Nap. Greenaway, Elizabeth, illus. 14p. (ps). 1994. bds. 2.99 (0-679-83958-5) Random Bks Yng Read.
—Rabbit Food. Greenaway, Elizabeth, illus. 14p. (ps). 1994. bds. 2.99 (0-679-83959-3) Random Bks Yng Read.
Greenaway, Frank. Amazing Bats. Young, Jerry & Greenaway, Frank, photos by. LC 91-6517. (Illus.). 32p. (Orig.). (gr. 1-5). 1991. lib. bdg. 9.99 (0-679-91518-4); pap. 7.99 (0-679-81518-X) Knopf Bks Yng Read.
Greenaway, Kate. A Apple Pie. 1993. 4.99 (0-517-09302-2) Outlet Bk Co.
—Kate Greenaway Nursery Rhymes. 1993. 9.99 (0-517-08782-0) Outlet Bk Co.
—Kate Greenaway's Book of Games. (Illus.). 64p. (gr. 2 up). 1987. 9.95x (0-312-01175-X) St Martin.
Greenaway, Kate, illus. Mother Goose. 12p. (ps-5). 1973. pap. 3.25 (0-914510-04-5) Evergreen.
Greenaway, Theresa. Amazing Bears. King, Dave, photos by. LC 92-910. (Illus.). 32p. (Orig.). (gr. 1-5). 1992. PLB 9.99 (0-679-92769-7); pap. 7.99 (0-679-82769-2) Knopf Bks Yng Read.
—Fir Trees. LC 90-9640. (Illus.). 48p. (gr. 5-9). 1990. PLB 19.92 (0-8114-2727-7) Raintree Steck-V.
—First Plants. LC 90-10003. (Illus.). 48p. (gr. 5-9). 1990. PLB 19.92 (0-8114-2734-X) Raintree Steck-V.

—Grasses & Grains. LC 90-9563. (Illus.). 48p. (gr. 5-9). 1990. PLB 19.92 (0-8114-2729-3) Raintree Steck-V.
—Mosses & Liverworts. LC 91-14936. (Illus.). 48p. (gr. 5-9). 1992. PLB 19.92 (0-8114-2738-2) Raintree Steck-V.
—Woodland Trees. LC 90-37227. (Illus.). 48p. (gr. 5-9). 1990. PLB 19.92 (0-8114-2732-3) Raintree Steck-V.
Greenbacker, Liz. Bugs: Stingers, Suckers, Sweeties, Swingers. LC 92-24963. (Illus.). 64p. (gr. 5-8). 1993. PLB 12.90 (0-531-20072-8) Watts.
—Bugs: Stingers, Suckers, Sweeties, Swingers. (Illus.). 64p. (gr. 5-8). 1993. pap. 5.95 (0-531-15673-7) Watts.
Greenbaum, David & Wasser, Edward. My First Health & Nutrition Coloring Book: Mr. Carrots Coloring Book. Puglisi, Lou, illus. 40p. (Orig.). (gr. 2). 1988. pap. 0.99 (0-9621833-0-X) D Greenbaum.
Greenberg. Family Abuse. 1994. PLB write for info. (0-8050-3183-9) H Holt & Co.
—Hurricanes, Tornadoes, & Cyclones. 1994. PLB write for info. (0-8050-3095-6) H Holt & Co.
Greenberg, Ann, ed. see Appleton, Victor.
Greenberg, Ann, ed. see Dixon, Franklin W.
Greenberg, Ann, ed. see Hope, Laura L.
Greenberg, Ann, ed. see Keene, Carolyn.
Greenberg, Ann, ed. see Seigel, Barbara & Seigel, Scott.
Greenberg, Anne, jt. auth. see Dixon, Franklin W.
Greenberg, Anne, ed. see Appleton, Victor.
Greenberg, Anne, ed. see Dixon, Franklin W.
Greenberg, Anne, ed. see Hope, Laura L.
Greenberg, Anne, ed. see Keene, Carolyn.
Greenberg, Bernice, jt. auth. see Lipson, Greta.
Greenberg, Daniel & Siembieda, Kevin. Turtles Go Hollywood. Marciniszyn, Alex, ed. Long, Kevin, illus. 48p. (Orig.). (gr. 8 up). 1990. pap. 7.95 (0-916211-46-0, 510) Palladium Bks.
Greenberg, Daniel A. The Great Baseball Card Hunt. Dodson, Bert, illus. Lewis, Glenn. (Illus.). 112p. (gr. 2-6). 1992. pap. 12.00 (0-671-72927-6, S&S BFYR); pap. 2.95 (0-671-72931-4, S&S BFYR) S&S Trade.
—The Missing Championship Ring. Dodson, Bert, illus. Lewis, Glenn. (Illus.). 112p. (gr. 2-6). 1992. (Little Simon); pap. 2.95 (0-671-72933-0, Little Simon) S&S Trade.
Greenberg, David. Slugs. Chase, Victoria, illus. LC 82-10017. 32p. (gr. k-5). 1983. 13.95 (0-316-32658-5, Joy St Bks); pap. 4.95i (0-316-32659-3, Joy St Bks) Little.
—Your Dog Might Be a Werewolf, Your Toes Could All Explode. (ps-3). 1992. pap. 2.99 (0-553-15909-7) Bantam.
Greenberg, Eliezer, jt. ed. see Howe, Irving.
Greenberg, Harvey R. Emotional Illness in Your Family: Helping Your Relatives, Helping Yourself. LC 89-31042. 304p. (gr. 6 up). 1989. SBE 16.95 (0-02-736921-8, Macmillan Child Bk) Macmillan Child Grp.
Greenberg, Jan. Bye, Bye, Miss American Pie. LC 85-47590. 150p. (gr. 7 up). 1985. 14.00 (0-374-31012-2) FS&G.
—Exercises of the Heart. LC 86-11977. 160p. (gr. 6 up). 1986. 14.00 (0-374-32237-6) FS&G.
—The Iceberg & Its Shadow. LC 80-20060. 132p. (gr. 7 up). 1980. 13.00 (0-374-33624-5) FS&G.
—Just the Two of Us. LC 88-45330. 128p. (gr. 5 up). 1988 14.00, (0-374-36198-3) FS&G.
—Just the Two of Us. LC 88-45330. 128p. (gr. 5 up). 1991. pap. 3.95 (0-374-43982-6) FS&G.
—No Dragons to Slay. LC 83-17200. 152p. (gr. 7 up). 1983. 14.00 (0-374-35528-2) FS&G.
—No Dragons to Slay. LC 83-17200. 152p. (gr. 7 up). 1984. pap. 3.50 (0-374-45509-0) FS&G.
—Painter's Eye: Learning to Look at Contemporary American Art. 1991. 20.00 (0-385-30319-X) Delacorte.
—The Pig-Out Blues. LC 82-2552. 121p. (gr. 7 up). 1982. 14.00 (0-374-35937-7) FS&G.
—A Season In-Between. LC 79-17997. 120p. (gr. 5 up). 1979. 14.00 (0-374-36564-4) FS&G.
Greenberg, Jan & Jordan, Sandra. The Sculptor's Eye: Looking at Contemporary American Art. LC 92-16323. 1993. 19.95 (0-385-30902-5) Delacorte.
Greenberg, Judith & Carey, Helen. Election Special. (gr. 7-12). 1988. Set incl. 10 texts & 1 tchr's. guide (updated annually) pap. text ed. 24.95 (0-941342-18-2) Entry Pub.
Greenberg, Judith E. & Carey, Helen H. Caves. Miyake, Yoshi, illus. 32p. (gr. 2-4). 1990. PLB 17.96 (0-8172-3750-X) Raintree Steck-V.
—Dinosaurs. Birmingham, Lloyd, illus. 32p. (gr. 2-4). 1990. PLB 17.96 (0-8172-3751-8) Raintree Steck-V.
—The Moon. Corvi, Donna, illus. 32p. (gr. 2-4). 1990. PLB 17.96 (0-8172-3752-6) Raintree Steck-V.
—The Rain Forest. Masheris, Bob, illus. 32p. (gr. 2-4). 1990. PLB 17.96 (0-8172-3753-4) Raintree Steck-V.
—Space. Karpinski, Rick, illus. 32p. (gr. 2-4). 1990. 17.96 (0-8172-3754-2) Raintree Steck-V.
—Under the Sea. Tachiera, Andrea, illus. 32p. (gr. 2-4). 1990. 17.96 (0-8172-3755-0) Raintree Steck-V.
—Volcanoes. Shaw, Charles, illus. 32p. (gr. 2-4). 1990. 17.96 (0-8172-3756-9) Raintree Steck-V.
—Whales. Fujiwara, Kim, illus. 32p. (gr. 2-4). 1990. PLB 17.96 (0-8172-3757-7) Raintree Steck-V.
Greenberg, Keith. Nolan Ryan. LC 92-40311. 1993. 15.93 (0-86592-002-8); 11.95s.p. (0-685-66273-X) Rourke Enter.
—Sam Walton. LC 92-45123. 1993. 15.93 (0-86592-047-8); 11.95s.p. (0-685-66419-8) Rourke Enter.

—Terrorism: The New Menace. LC 93-23565. 1994. write for info. (1-56294-488-6) Millbrook Pr.
Greenberg, Keith E. Ben & Jerry: Ice Cream for Everybody! (Illus.). 48p. (gr. 2-5). 1994. PLB 12.95 (1-56711-064-9) Blackbirch.
—Bill & Hillary: Working Together in the White House. (Illus.). 48p. (gr. 2-5). 1994. PLB 12.95 (1-56711-067-3) Blackbirch.
—Erik Is Homeless. Halebian, Carol, photos by. (Illus.). 40p. (gr. 4-8). 1992. PLB 17.50 (0-8225-2551-8) Lerner Pubns.
—John Johnson. LC 92-41751. (gr. 3 up). 1993. 15.93 (0-86592-033-8); 11.95s.p. (0-685-66329-9) Rourke Enter.
—Madonna. LC 85-18030. (Illus.). 40p. (gr. 4-9). 1986. lib. bdg. 13.50 (0-8225-1606-3) Lerner Pubns.
—Magic Johnson: Champion with a Cause. (Illus.). 64p. (gr. 4-9). 1992. PLB 13.50 (0-8225-0546-0) Lerner Pubns.
—Magic Johnson: Champion with a Cause. (gr. 4-7). 1992. pap. 4.95 (0-8225-9612-1) Lerner Pubns.
—Michael J. Fox. (Illus.). 32p. (gr. 4-9). 1986. PLB 13.50 (0-8225-1611-X) Lerner Pubns.
—New Kids on the Block. (Illus.). 32p. (gr. 4-9). 1991. PLB 13.50 (0-8225-1620-9) Lerner Pubns.
—Out of the Gang. (Illus.). 40p. (gr. 4-8). 1992. PLB 17.50 (0-8225-2553-4) Lerner Pubns.
—Rap. (Illus.). 40p. (gr. 4-9). 1988. 13.50 (0-8225-1617-9) Lerner Pubns.
—Whitney Houston. (Illus.). 32p. (gr. 4-9). 1988. lib. bdg. 13.50 (0-8225-1619-5) Lerner Pubns.
Greenberg, Kenneth R. The Adventures of Tusky & His Friends: A Christmas Mystery. Pearson, Allison K., illus. 63p. (gr. k-3). 1991. PLB 14.95 (1-879100-01-0) Tusky Enterprises.
—The Adventures of Tusky & His Friends, Bk. 1: A Jungle Adventure. Pearson, Allison K., illus. (gr. k-3). 1991. 13.95 (1-879100-00-2) Tusky Enterprises.
—The Adventures of Tusky & His Friends, Bk. 3: Tusky Gets Mad at Tusky. Pearson, Allison K., illus. 52p. (gr. k-4). 1992. 15.50 (1-879100-02-9) Tusky Enterprises.

**—The Adventures of Tusky & His Friends Series, Bk. I. Pearson, Allison K., illus. (gr. k-3). 1992. PLB write for info. (1-879100-49-5) Tusky Enterprises.
THE ADVENTURES OF TUSKY & HIS FRIENDS. Book I. A JUNGLE ADVENTURE. ISBN 1-879100-00-2 $13.95.** The introductory book of an educational "Snuggle-Up" & read-to series of picture story books for ages 6-8 that encourages interaction between child & reader. Tusky & his friend Packy meet Hooty, an owl, who becomes their mentor. Negative & positive thinking, reacting to "labels" people give us, showing sensitivity & thinking ahead are discussed. **A CHRISTMAS MYSTERY: A HOLIDAY SPECIAL ISBN 1-879100-01-0 $14.95.** While the animals are decorating the jungle for Christmas, someone poisons the elephant herd. Hooty solves the mystery & Santa Claus calls Tusky & his friends heroes for saving the herd. Book 2: **TUSKY MEETS THE GREEN-EYED MONSTER ISBN 1-879100-03-7 (Approx. $15.50).** Tusky is jealous of Ellie, his sister. In anger, he runs away from home. He talks to a stranger & is kidnapped. Hooty devises a plan to free him & later explains jealousy & how to overcome it. Tusky returns home & gets a big surprise. Book 3: **TUSKY GETS MAD AT TUSKY. ISBN 1-879100-02-9 (Approx. $15.50).** Tusky is mad at himself because there are too many things he can't do. Hooty helps him feel better about himself. There is a thunder & lightning storm & when Tusky saves the life of a doe, his self-concept is improved. Discussion questions have been prepared for each story.
Publisher Provided Annotation.

—The Adventures of Tusky & His Friends, Vol. 2: Tusky Meets the Green-Eyed Monster. Pearson, Allison K., illus. 66p. (gr. k-4). 1992. 15.95 (1-879100-03-7) Tusky Enterprises.

Greenberg, Lorna. AIDS: How It Works in the Body. Mathews, V., ed. LC 91-28620. (Illus.). 64p. (gr. 3-6). 1992. PLB 12.90 (0-531-20074-4) Watts.

Greenberg, Lorna, ed. see Brandt, Sue R.

Greenberg, Lorna, ed. see Claypool, Jane.

Greenberg, Lorna, ed. see Mischel, Florence.

Greenberg, Martin. Newbery Christmas. (gr. 4-7). 1991. 16.00 (0-385-30485-4) Delacorte.

Greenberg, Martin, jt. auth. see Waugh, Charles.

Greenberg, Martin H. & Waugh, Charles G., eds. A Newbery Halloween: Thirteen Scary Stories by Newbery Award-Winning Authors. LC 92-43877. 1993. pap. 16.95 (0-385-31028-5) Doubleday.

Greenberg, Martin H., jt. ed. see Asimov, Isaac.

Greenberg, Martin H., jt. ed. see Yolen, Jane.

Greenberg, Melanie H. At the Beach. Greenberg, Melanie H., illus. LC 88-29995. 24p. (ps-2). 1989. 11.95 (0-525-44474-2, DCB) Dutton Child Bks.

—Celebrations: Our Jewish Holidays. Greenberg, Melanie H., illus. LC 91-12744. 32p. (ps-3). 1991. 14.95 (0-8276-0396-7); pap. 9.95 (0-8276-0505-6) JPS Phila.

—My Father's Luncheonette. Greenberg, Melanie H., illus. LC 90-45586. 32p. (ps-2). 1991. 12.95 (0-525-44725-3, DCB) Dutton Child Bks.

Greenberg, Morrie. American Adventures: True Stories from America's Past, 1770-1870. Long, Laurel, illus. LC 90-2652. 96p. (Illus.). (gr. 4-9). 1991. pap. text ed. 9.95 (0-9622652-1-7) Brooke-Richards.

—Harry Truman: The Buck Stops Here. LC 88-20264. (Illus.). 128p. (gr. 5 up). 1991. RSBE 13.95 (0-87518-394-8, Dillon) Macmillan Child Grp.

Greenberg, Polly. I Know I'm Myself Because... Barrett, Jennifer, illus. 32p. (ps-3). 1986. 16.95 (0-89885-045-2); pap. 9.95 (0-89885-200-5) Human Sci Pr.

Greenberg, Robert B. Tyrannosaurus Tex. Zady, Mary, illus. LC 89-4225. 64p. (gr. k-4). 1989. pap. 5.95 (0-938349-38-4) State House Pr.

—Tyrannosaurus Tex: First Grade. LC 90-9749. (Illus.). 64p. (gr. k-4). 1991. pap. 5.95 (0-938349-56-2) State House Pr.

Greenberg, Russell. El Sur de Mexico: Cruce de Caminos para los Pajaros Migratorios: Southern Mexico: Crossroads for Migratory Birds. Zickefoose, Julie, et al, illus. (ENG & SPA.). 32p. 1990. pap. 3.00 (1-881230-01-5) Smiths Migratory.

Greenberg, Russell & Lumpkin, Susan. Birds over Troubled Forests. Zickefooser, Julie, illus. 32p. (Orig.). 1991. pap. 5.00 (1-881230-00-7) Smiths Migratory.

Greenberg, Sidney & Silverman, Morris. Siddurenu. (gr. 3-7). 8.95x (0-87677-099-5) Prayer Bk.

Greenberger, Bob, ed. see Barr, Mike, et al.

Greenblat, Rodney A. Aunt Ippy's Museum of Junk. Greenblat, Rodney A., illus. LC 90-44939. 32p. (gr. k-4). 1991. 14.95 (0-06-022511-4); PLB 14.89 (0-06-022512-2) HarpC Child Bks.

—Slombo the Gross. LC 91-31235. (Illus.). 32p. (ps-3). 1993. 15.00 (0-06-020775-2); PLB 14.89 (0-06-020776-0) HarpC Child Bks.

—Uncle Wizzmo's New Used Car. Greenblat, Rodney A., illus. LC 89-36577. 32p. (ps-3). 1990. 13.95 (0-06-022097-X); PLB 13.89 (0-06-022098-8) HarpC Child Bks.

—Uncle Wizzmo's New Used Car. LC 89-36577. (Illus.). 32p. (ps-3). 1992. pap. 4.95 (0-06-443305-6, Trophy) HarpC Child Bks.

Greenblatt, Miriam. Franklin D. Roosevelt: Thirty-Second President of the United States. Young, Richard G., ed. LC 87-36121. (Illus.). (gr. 5-9). 1989. PLB 17.26 (0-944483-06-2) Garrett Ed Corp.

—James K. Polk: 11th President of the United States. Young, Richard G., ed. LC 87-35981. (Illus.). (gr. 5-9). 1988. PLB 17.26 (0-944483-04-6) Garrett Ed Corp.

—John Quincy Adams: Sixth President of the United States. Young, Richard G., ed. LC 89-39950. (Illus.). 128p. (gr. 5-9). 1990. PLB 17.26 (0-944483-21-6) Garrett Ed Corp.

Greenburg, Dan. Jumbo the Boy & Arnold the Elephant. Perl, Susan, illus. LC 87-24931. 48p. (gr. 2-4). 1989. Repr. of 1969 ed. HarpC Child Bks.

—Young Santa. Miller, Warren, illus. 80p. 1991. 13.95 (0-670-83905-1) Viking Child Bks.

—Young Santa. Miller, Warren, illus. LC 93-7482. 80p. 1993. pap. 4.99 (0-14-034773-9, Puffin) Puffin Bks.

Greenburg, Joanne. Jack in the Beanstalk. Walsh, Michael S., illus. 48p. (gr. 3 up). 1980. 16.50 (0-8299-1033-6) West Pub.

Greene, A. C. The Last Captive. (Illus.). 185p. (gr. 6-9). 1972. 25.00 (0-88426-004-6) Encino Pr.

Greene, Barbara, ed. see Bingham, Mindy, et al.

Greene, Bette. Drowning of Stephan Jones. 1991. 16.00 (0-553-07437-7) Bantam.

—Drowning of Stephan Jones. 1992. pap. 3.99 (0-553-29793-3) Bantam.

—Get out out of Here, Philip Hall. 144p. (gr. 4-7). 1984. pap. 2.75 (0-440-43038-0, YB) Dell.

—Philip Hall Likes Me, I Reckon, Maybe. Lilly, Charles, illus. 144p. 1975. pap. 3.50 (0-440-45755-6, YB) Dell.

—Philip Hall Likes Me, I Reckon Maybe. large type ed. (Illus.). 158p. 1989. PLB 15.95 (1-55736-106-1, Crnrstn Bks) BDD LT Grp.

—Summer of My German. 1993. pap. 3.99 (0-440-21892-6) Dell.

—Summer of My German Soldier. 208p. (gr. 7-12). 1984. pap. 3.50 (0-553-27247-0) Bantam.

—Summer of My German Soldier. 224p. (gr. 7 up). 1973. 14.95 (0-8037-8321-3) Dial Bks Young.

—The Summer of My German Soldier. large type ed. 272p. 1989. Repr. of 1973 ed. lib. bdg. 15.95 (1-55736-134-7, Crnrstn Bks) BDD LT Grp.

Greene, C. The Golden Locket. Sewall, M., illus. 1992. 13.95 (0-15-231220-X, HB Juv Bks) HarBrace.

Greene, Carol. Abraham Lincoln: President of a Divided Country. Dobson, Steven, illus. LC 89-33845. 48p. (gr. k-3). 1989. PLB 15.93 (0-516-04206-8); pap. 4.95 (0-516-44206-6) Childrens.

—Albert Schweitzer: Friend of All Life. LC 93-12975. (Illus.). 48p. (gr. k-3). 1993. PLB 16.60 (0-516-04258-0) Childrens.

—Astronauts. LC 83-23142. (Illus.). 48p. (gr. k-4). 1984. PLB 15.27 (0-516-01722-5); pap. 4.95 (0-516-41722-3) Childrens.

—Austria. LC 85-27994. (Illus.). 126p. (gr. 5-6). 1986. PLB 26.60 (0-516-02756-5) Childrens.

—Beggars, Beasts & Easter Fire: Stories of Early Saints. Klausmeier, Robert, ed. Root, Kimberly B., illus. LC 92-31408. 128p. (gr. 3-6). 1993. 15.95 (0-7459-2221-X) Lion USA.

—Benjamin Franklin: A Man with Many Jobs. Dobson, Steven, illus. LC 88-15011. 48p. (gr. k-3). 1988. PLB 15.93 (0-516-04202-5); pap. 4.95 (0-516-44202-3) Childrens.

—Black Elk: A Man with a Vision. LC 90-39480. (Illus.). 48p. (gr. k-3). 1990. PLB 15.93 (0-516-04213-0); pap. 4.95 (0-516-44213-9) Childrens.

—Blue Ben. McKissack, Patricia & McKissack, Fredrick, eds. Boddy, Joe, illus. LC 87-61649. 32p. (Orig.). (gr. 1-3). 1987. text ed. 8.95 (0-88335-722-4); pap. text ed. 4.95 (0-88335-742-9) Milliken Pub Co.

—Caring for Our Air. LC 91-9236. (Illus.). 32p. (gr. k-3). 1991. lib. bdg. 12.95 (0-89490-351-9) Enslow Pubs.

—Caring for Our Animals. LC 91-9237. (Illus.). 32p. (gr. k-3). 1991. lib. bdg. 12.95 (0-89490-352-7) Enslow Pubs.

—Caring for Our Earth Series, 6 bks. (Illus.). (gr. k-3). Set, 32p. ea. lib. bdg. 77.70 (0-89490-377-2) Enslow Pubs.

—Caring for Our Forests. LC 91-4703. (Illus.). 32p. (gr. k-3). 1991. lib. bdg. 12.95 (0-89490-353-5) Enslow Pubs.

—Caring for Our Land. LC 91-10613. (Illus.). 32p. (gr. k-3). 1991. lib. bdg. 12.95 (0-89490-354-3) Enslow Pubs.

—Caring for Our People. LC 91-9235. (Illus.). 32p. (gr. k-3). 1991. lib. bdg. 12.95 (0-89490-355-1) Enslow Pubs.

—Caring for Our Water. LC 91-2683. (Illus.). 32p. (gr. k-3). 1991. lib. bdg. 12.95 (0-89490-356-X) Enslow Pubs.

—Christopher Columbus: A Great Explorer. Dobson, Steven, illus. LC 88-37943. 48p. (gr. k-3). 1989. PLB 15.93 (0-516-04204-1); pap. 4.95 (0-516-44204-X) Childrens.

—Columbus & Frankie the Cat. Dunnington, Tom, illus. LC 88-33067. 32p. (ps-2). 1989. pap. 3.95 (0-516-43462-4) Childrens.

—Congress. LC 84-23243. (Illus.). 48p. (gr. k-4). 1985. PLB 15.27 (0-516-01939-2); pap. 4.95 (0-516-41939-0) Childrens.

—Daniel Boone: Man of the Forests. Dobson, Steven, illus. LC 89-25346. 48p. (gr. k-3). 1990. PLB 15.93 (0-516-04210-6); pap. 4.95 (0-516-44210-4) Childrens.

—Desmond Tutu: Bishop of Peace. LC 86-9582. (Illus.). 32p. (gr. 2-5). 1986. PLB 14.60 (0-516-03634-3); pap. 3.95 (0-516-43634-1) Childrens.

—Diana, Princess of Wales. LC 85-12751. (Illus.). 32p. (gr. 2-4). 1985. PLB 14.60 (0-516-03538-X); pap. 3.95 (0-516-43538-8) Childrens.

—The Easter Women. (Illus.). 24p. (gr. k-4). 1987. pap. 1.89 (0-570-09003-2, 59-1431) Concordia.

—Elie Wiesel: Messenger from the Holocaust. LC 87-6341. (Illus.). 32p. (gr. 2-5). 1987. PLB 14.60 (0-516-03490-1) Childrens.

—Elizabeth Blackwell: First Woman Doctor. Dobson, Steven, illus. LC 90-20001. 48p. (gr. k-3). 1991. PLB 15.93 (0-516-04217-3); pap. 4.95 (0-516-44217-1) Childrens.

—Elizabeth the First: Queen of England. Dobson, Steven, illus. LC 90-2204. 48p. (gr. k-3). 1990. PLB 15.93 (0-516-04214-9); pap. 4.95 (0-516-44214-7) Childrens.

—England. LC 82-4471. (Illus.). (gr. 5-9). 1982. PLB 26.60 (0-516-02763-8) Childrens.

—Friends in Danger Series, 6 bks. (Illus.). 32p. (gr. k-3). 1993. Set. lib. bdg. 83.70 (0-89490-447-7) Enslow Pubs.

—George Washington Carver: Scientist & Teacher. Dobson, Steven, illus. LC 92-7374. 48p. (gr. k-3). 1992. PLB 15.93 (0-516-04250-5) Childrens.

—George Washington Carver: Scientist & Teacher. Dobson, Steven, illus. LC 92-7374. 48p. (gr. k-3). 1993. pap. 4.95 (0-516-44250-3) Childrens.

—George Washington: First President of the United States. Dobson, Steven, illus. LC 90-22195. 48p. (gr. k-3). 1991. PLB 15.93 (0-516-04218-1); pap. 4.95 (0-516-44218-X) Childrens.

—Hans Christian Andersen: Prince of Storytellers. Dobson, Steven, illus. LC 90-19998. 48p. (gr. k-3). 1991. PLB 15.93 (0-516-04219-X); pap. 4.95 (0-516-44219-8) Childrens.

—Hans Christian Andersen: Teller of Tales. LC 85-27991. (Illus.). 128p. (gr. 4-7). 1986. PLB 18.60 (0-516-03216-X); pap. 4.95 (0-685-67523-8) Childrens.

—Hi, Clouds. Sharp, Gene, illus. LC 82-19854. 32p. (ps-2). 1983. PLB 11.93 (0-516-02036-6); pap. 2.95 (0-516-42036-4) Childrens.

—Holidays Around the World. LC 82-9734. (Illus.). (gr. k-4). 1982. PLB 15.93 (0-516-01624-5); pap. 4.95 (0-516-41624-3) Childrens.

—How a Book Is Made. (gr. 5-9). 1988. PLB 15.27 (0-516-01216-9); pap. 4.95 (0-516-41216-7) Childrens.

—I Can Be a Baseball Player. LC 84-23222. (Illus.). 32p. (gr. k-3). 1985. PLB 14.60 (0-516-01845-0); pap. 3.95 (0-516-41845-9) Childrens.

—I Can Be a Football Player. LC 84-9609. (Illus.). 32p. (gr. k-3). 1984. PLB 14.60 (0-516-01839-6); pap. 3.95 (0-516-41839-4) Childrens.

—I Can Be a Forest Ranger. LC 88-37717. (Illus.). 32p. (gr. k-3). 1989. PLB 14.60 (0-516-01924-4); pap. 3.95 (0-516-41924-2) Childrens.

—I Can Be a Librarian. LC 87-35537. (Illus.). 32p. (gr. k-3). 1988. PLB 14.60 (0-516-01913-9) Childrens.

—I Can Be a Model. LC 85-9676. 32p. (gr. k-3). 1985. PLB 14.60 (0-516-01887-6) Childrens.

—I Can Be a Salesperson. LC 89-15848. 32p. (gr. k-3). 1989. pap. 3.95 (0-516-41959-5) Childrens.

—Ice Is...Whee! Sharp, Paul, illus. LC 82-19855. 32p. (ps-2). 1983. PLB 11.93 (0-516-02037-4); pap. 2.95 (0-516-42037-2) Childrens.

—The Insignificant Elephant. Gantner, Susan, illus. LC 84-1531. 32p. (gr. k-3). 1985. 13.95 (0-15-238730-7, HB Juv Bks) HarBrace.

—Jackie Robinson: Baseball's First Black Major Leaguer. Dobson, Steven, illus. LC 89-28816. 48p. (gr. k-3). 1990. PLB 15.93 (0-516-04211-4); pap. 4.95 (0-516-44211-2) Childrens.

—Jacques Cousteau: Man of the Oceans. Dobson, Steven, illus. LC 90-2162. 48p. (gr. k-3). 1990. PLB 15.93 (0-516-04215-7); pap. 4.95 (0-516-44215-5) Childrens.

—Japan. LC 83-7603. (Illus.). 128p. (gr. 5-9). 1983. PLB 26.60 (0-516-02769-7) Childrens.

—The Jenny Summer. Eagle, Ellen, illus. LC 87-45283. 80p. (gr. 1-4). 1988. PLB 12.89 (0-06-022209-3) HarpC Child Bks.

—Johann Sebastian Bach: Great Man of Music. Dobson, Steven, illus. LC 92-7373. 48p. (gr. k-3). 1992. PLB 15.93 (0-516-04251-3) Childrens.

—Johann Sebastian Bach: Great Man of Music. Dobson, Steven, illus. LC 92-7373. 48p. (gr. k-3). 1993. pap. 4.95 (0-516-44251-1) Childrens.

—John Chapman: The Man Who Was Johnny Appleseed. LC 91-12649. (Illus.). 48p. (gr. k-3). 1991. PLB 15.93 (0-516-04223-8); pap. 4.95 (0-516-44223-6) Childrens.

—John Muir: Man of the Wild Places. Dobson, Steven, illus. LC 90-19993. 48p. (gr. k-3). 1991. PLB 15.93 (0-516-04220-3); pap. 4.95 (0-516-44220-1) Childrens.

—John Philip Sousa: The March King. LC 91-37891. (Illus.). 48p. (gr. k-3). 1992. PLB 15.93 (0-516-04226-2); pap. 4.95, Jul. 1992 (0-516-44226-0) Childrens.

—Katherine Dunham: Black Dancer. Dobson, Steven, illus. LC 92-8769. 48p. (gr. k-3). 1992. PLB 15.93 (0-516-04252-1) Childrens.

—Katherine Dunham: Black Dancer. Dobson, Steven, illus. LC 92-8769. 48p. (gr. k-3). 1993. pap. 4.95 (0-516-44252-X) Childrens.

—Kiri & the First Easter. (Illus.). 32p. (ps-4). 1972. pap. 1.89 (0-570-06064-8, 59-1182) Concordia.

—Language. LC 83-7421. (Illus.). 48p. (gr. k-4). 1983. PLB 15.27 (0-516-01694-6) Childrens.

—Laura Ingalls Wilder: Author of the Little House Books. Dobson, Steven, illus. LC 89-25362. 48p. (gr. k-3). 1990. PLB 15.93 (0-516-04212-2); pap. 4.95 (0-516-44212-0) Childrens.

—Lewis Carroll: Author of Alice in Wonderland. LC 91-37821. (Illus.). 48p. (gr. k-3). 1992. PLB 15.93 (0-516-04227-0); pap. 4.95 (0-516-44227-9) Childrens.

—Louis Pasteur: Enemy of Disease. Dobson, Steven, illus. LC 90-2197. 48p. (gr. k-3). 1990. PLB 15.93 (0-516-04216-5); pap. 4.95 (0-516-44216-3) Childrens.

—Louisa May Alcott: Author, Nurse, Suffragette. LC 84-5902. (Illus.). 112p. (gr. 4 up). 1984. PLB 18.60 (0-516-03208-9) Childrens.

—Ludwig Van Beethoven: Musical Pioneer. Dobson, Steven, illus. LC 89-15849. 48p. (gr. k-3). 1989. PLB 15.93 (0-516-04208-4); pap. 4.95 (0-516-44208-2) Childrens.

—Marco Polo: Voyager to the Orient. LC 86-29977. (Illus.). 112p. (gr. 4 up). 1987. PLB 18.60 (0-516-03229-1) Childrens.

—Margaret Wise Brown: Author of Goodnight Moon. LC 92-34471. (Illus.). 48p. (gr. k-3). 1993. 16.60 (0-516-04254-8) Childrens.

—Margarete Steiff: Toy Maker. LC 93-16855. (Illus.). 48p. (gr. k-3). 1993. PLB 16.60 (0-516-04257-2) Childrens.

—Marie Curie: Pioneer Physicist. LC 83-26273. (Illus.). 112p. (gr. 4 up). 1984. PLB 18.60 (0-516-03203-8) Childrens.

—Mark Twain: Author of Tom Sawyer. LC 91-40829. (Illus.). 48p. (gr. k-3). 1992. PLB 15.93 (0-516-04228-9); pap. 4.95 (0-516-44228-7) Childrens.

—Martin Luther King, Jr. A Man Who Changed Things. Dobson, Steven, illus. LC 88-37714. 48p. (gr. k-3). 1989. PLB 15.93 (0-516-04205-X); pap. 4.95 (0-516-44205-8) Childrens.

—Mary McLeod Bethune: Champion for Education. LC 92-37013. (Illus.). 48p. (gr. k-3). 1993. PLB 15.93 (0-516-04255-6) Childrens.

—Miss Apple's Hats. McKissack, Patricia & McKissack, Fredrick, eds. Martin, Clovis, illus. LC 88-60395. 32p. (Orig.). (gr. 1-3). 1988. text ed. 8.95 (0-88335-779-8); pap. text ed. 4.95 (0-88335-791-7) Milliken Pub Co.

—Mother Teresa: Friend of the Friendless. LC 83-7386. (Illus.). 32p. (gr. 2-5). 1983. PLB 14.60 (0-516-03559-2) Concordia.

—My Bible Stories: The Hop-Aboard Handbook & Sing-along Cassette. (Illus.). 64p. (Orig.). (ps). 1993. pap. 13.99 (0-570-04752-8) Concordia.

—The Old Ladies Who Liked Cats. Krupinski, Loretta, illus. LC 90-4443. 32p. (gr. k-3). 1991. 15.00 (0-06-022104-6); PLB 14.89 (0-06-022105-4) HarpC Child Bks.

—The Old Ladies Who Liked Cats. Krupinski, Loretta, illus. LC 90-4443. 32p. (gr. k-3). 1994. pap. 4.95 (0-06-443354-4, Trophy) HarpC Child Bks.

—The Pilgrims Are Marching. Dunnington, Tom, illus. LC 88-20219. 32p. (ps-2). 1988. PLB 15.00 (0-516-08234-5); pap. 3.95 (0-516-48234-3) Childrens.

—Please, Wind? LC 82-4548. (Illus.). (ps-2). 1982. PLB 11.93 (0-516-02033-1); pap. 2.95 (0-516-42033-X) Childrens.

—Pocahontas: Daughter of a Chief. Dobson, Steven, illus. LC 88-11978. 48p. (gr. k-3). 1988. PLB 15.93 (0-516-04203-3); pap. 4.95 (0-516-44203-1) Childrens.

—Poland. LC 82-19737. (Illus.). 128p. (gr. 5-9). 1983. PLB 26.60 (0-516-02783-2) Childrens.

—Los Presidentes (Presidents) Kratky, Lada, tr. LC 85-31848. (SPA., Illus.). 48p. (gr. k-4). 1986. PLB 15.27 (0-516-31928-0); pap. 4.95 (0-516-51928-X) Childrens.

—Presidents. LC 84-7719. (Illus.). 48p. (gr. k-4). 1984. PLB 15.27 (0-516-01928-7); pap. 4.95 (0-516-41928-5) Childrens.

—Puedo Ser Jugador de Beisbol (I Can Be a Baseball Player) Kratky, Lada, tr. LC 86-996. (SPA., Illus.). 32p. (gr. k-3). 1986. PLB 13.93 (0-516-31845-4); pap. 3.95 (0-516-51845-3) Childrens.

—Rachel Carson: Friend of Nature. Dobson, Steven, illus. LC 91-39446. 48p. (gr. k-3). 1992. PLB 15.93 (0-516-04229-7) Childrens.

—Rachel Carson: Friend of Nature. Dobson, Steven, illus. LC 91-39446. 48p. (gr. k-3). 1993. pap. 4.95 (0-516-44229-5) Childrens.

—Rain! Rain! LC 82-9509. (Illus.). (ps-2). 1982. PLB 11.93 (0-516-02034-X); pap. 2.95 (0-516-42034-8) Childrens.

—Reading about the Gray Wolf. LC 92-26800. (Illus.). 32p. (gr. k-3). 1993. lib. bdg. 13.95 (0-89490-427-2) Enslow Pubs.

—Reading about the Grizzly Bear. LC 92-26803. (Illus.). 32p. (gr. k-3). 1993. lib. bdg. 13.95 (0-89490-423-X) Enslow Pubs.

—Reading about the Humpback Whale. LC 92-26805. (Illus.). 32p. (gr. k-3). 1993. lib. bdg. 13.95 (0-89490-426-4) Enslow Pubs.

—Reading about the Manatee. LC 92-26811. (Illus.). 32p. (gr. k-3). 1993. lib. bdg. 13.95 (0-89490-424-8) Enslow Pubs.

—Reading about the Peregrine Falcon. LC 92-26804. (Illus.). 32p. (gr. k-3). 1993. lib. bdg. 13.95 (0-89490-422-1) Enslow Pubs.

—Reading about the River Otter. LC 92-26801. (Illus.). 32p. (gr. k-3). 1993. lib. bdg. 13.95 (0-89490-425-6) Enslow Pubs.

—Robert E. Lee: Leader in War & Peace. Dobson, Steven, illus. LC 89-33749. 48p. (gr. k-3). 1989. PLB 15.93 (0-516-04209-2); pap. 4.95 (0-516-44209-0) Childrens.

—Roberto Clemente: Baseball Superstar. LC 91-12664. (Illus.). 48p. (gr. k-3). 1991. PLB 15.93 (0-516-04222-X); pap. 4.95 (0-516-44222-8) Childrens.

—Robots. LC 82-17872. (Illus.). 48p. (gr. k-4). 1983. PLB 15.27 (0-516-01684-9); pap. 4.95 (0-516-41684-7) Childrens.

—Roy Campanella, Major League Champion. LC 93-37878. 1994. write for info. Childrens.

—Sandra Day O'Connor: First Woman on the Supreme Court. LC 81-18038. (Illus.). 32p. (gr. 1-4). 1982. PLB 14.60 (0-516-03618-1) Childrens.

—Shine, Sun! Sharp, Gene, illus. LC 82-19853. 32p. (ps-2). 1983. PLB 11.93 (0-516-02038-2); pap. 2.95 (0-516-42038-0) Childrens.

—Simon Bolivar: South American Liberator. LC 89-34663. (gr. 4 up). 1989. PLB 18.60 (0-516-03267-4) Childrens.

—Snow Joe. LC 82-9403. (Illus.). (ps-2). 1982. PLB 11.93 (0-516-02035-8); pap. 2.95 (0-516-42035-6) Childrens.

—The Supreme Court. LC 84-23230. (Illus.). 48p. (gr. k-4). 1985. PLB 15.27 (0-516-01943-0) Childrens.

—The Thirteen Days of Halloween. LC 83-7347. (Illus.). 32p. (ps-2). 1983. PLB 15.00 (0-516-08231-0); pap. 3.95 (0-516-48231-9) Childrens.

—Thomas Alva Edison: Bringer of Light. LC 84-23247. (Illus.). 128p. (gr. 4 up). 1985. PLB 18.60 (0-516-03213-5) Childrens.

—Thomas Jefferson: Author, Inventor, President. LC 91-16363. (Illus.). 48p. (gr. k-3). 1991. PLB 15.93 (0-516-04224-6); pap. 4.95 (0-516-44224-4) Childrens.

—Thurgood Marshall: First Black Supreme Court Justice. LC 91-4798. (Illus.). 48p. (gr. k-3). 1991. PLB 15.93 (0-516-04225-4); pap. 4.95 (0-516-44225-2) Childrens.

—The United Nations. LC 83-10068. (Illus.). 48p. (gr. k-4). 1983. PLB 15.27 (0-516-01710-1); pap. 4.95 (0-516-41710-X) Childrens.

—Waiting for Christmas: Stories & Activities for Advent. Swisher, Elizabeth, illus. LC 87-70474. 32p. (Orig.). (ps-5). 1987. pap. 5.99 (0-8066-2264-4, 10-6915, Augsburg) Augsburg Fortress.

—Wendy & the Whine. (Illus.). 32p. (gr. 1-4). 1987. pap. 4.99 (0-570-04157-0, 56-1615) Concordia.

—Why Boys & Girls Are Different. 32p. (ps up). 1988. 7.99 (0-570-08481-4, 14-1621) Concordia.

—Wolfgang Amadeus Mozart: Musical Genius. LC 92-36879. (Illus.). 48p. (gr. k-3). 1993. PLB 15.93 (0-516-04256-4) Childrens.

—Wolfgang Amadeus Mozart: Musician. LC 87-13824. (Illus.). 152p. (gr. 4 up). 1987. PLB 18.60 (0-516-03261-5) Childrens.

—The World's Biggest Birthday Cake. LC 85-16664. (Illus.). 32p. (ps-2). 1985. PLB 15.00 (0-516-08233-7) Childrens.

—Yugoslavia. LC 83-21049. (Illus.). 128p. (gr. 5-9). 1984. PLB 26.60 (0-516-02791-3) Childrens.

Greene, Constance C. Al(exandra) the Great. LC 81-16058. 144p. (gr. 5-9). 1982. pap. 13.95 (0-670-11197-X) Viking Child Bks.

—Al(exandra) the Great. 144p. (gr. 5-9). 1983. pap. 2.95 (0-440-40350-2, YB) Dell.

—Al(exandra) the Great. 144p. (gr. 5-9). 1991. 3.95 (0-14-034883-2) Puffin Bks.

—Al's Blind Date. Barton, Byron, illus. 128p. (gr. 5-9). 1991. pap. 3.95 (0-14-034171-4, Puffin) Puffin Bks.

—Ask Anybody. 160p. (gr. k-6). 1984. pap. 2.75 (0-440-40330-8, YB) Dell.

—Ask Anybody. Barton, Byron, illus. 160p. (gr. 5-9). 1991. pap. 3.95 (0-14-034787-9, Puffin) Puffin Bks.

—Beat the Turtle Drum. 128p. (gr. 5-8). 1979. pap. 3.25 (0-440-40875-X, YB) Dell.

—Beat the Turtle Drum. large type ed. 215p. (gr. 5 up). 1988. Repr. of 1976 ed. 15.95 (1-55736-039-1, Crnrstn Bks) BDD LT Grp.

—Beat the Turtle Drum. (gr. 5-8). 1992. 16.25 (0-8446-6598-3) Peter Smith.

—Beat the Turtle Drum. 1128p. (gr. 5 up). 1994. pap. 3.99 (0-14-036850-7) Puffin Bks.

—Dotty's Suitcase. 144p. (gr. 3-7). 1982. pap. 1.95 (0-440-42108-X, YB) Dell.

—Dotty's Suitcase. 160p. (gr. 5-9). 1991. 3.95 (0-14-034882-4) Puffin Bks.

—Double-Dare O'Toole. 176p. (gr. 4-7). 1983. pap. 3.25 (0-440-41982-4, YB) Dell.

—Double-Dare O'Toole. (gr. 4 up). 1990. pap. 3.95 (0-14-034541-8, Puffin) Puffin Bks.

—A Girl Called Al. 128p. (gr. 5-9). 1977. pap. 2.95 (0-440-42810-6, YB) Dell.

—A Girl Called Al. Barton, Byron, illus. (gr. 6-8). 1969. pap. 15.00 (0-670-34153-3) Viking Child Bks.

—A Girl Called Al. large type ed. 1989. Repr. of 1969 ed. lib. bdg. 15.95 (1-55736-145-2, Crnrstn Bks) BDD LT Grp.

—A Girl Called Al. Barton, Byron, illus. 128p. (gr. 5-9). 1991. pap. 3.99 (0-14-034786-0, Puffin) Puffin Bks.

—I & Sproggy. McCully, Emily A., illus. 144p. (gr. 5 up). 1981. pap. 1.95 (0-440-43986-8, YB) Dell.

—I Know You, Al. (gr. k-6). 1977. pap. 2.95 (0-440-44123-4, YB) Dell.

—I Know You, Al. 128p. (gr. 5-9). 1991. pap. 3.95 (0-14-034884-0, Puffin) Puffin Bks.

—Isabelle & Little Orphan Frannie. (gr. 4 up). 1990. pap. 3.95 (0-14-032916-1, Puffin) Puffin Bks.

—Isabelle Shows Her Stuff. (gr. 4-6). 1986. pap. 2.95 (0-440-44152-8, YB) Dell.

—Isabelle Shows Her Stuff. 144p. (gr. 3-7). 1992. pap. 3.99 (0-14-036029-8) Puffin Bks.

—Isabelle the Itch. 128p. (gr. 3-7). 1992. pap. 3.99 (0-14-036028-X) Puffin Bks.

—Just Plain Al. LC 86-5516. 144p. (gr. 5-9). 1986. pap. 12.95 (0-670-81250-1) Viking Child Bks.

—Just Plain Al. (gr. k-6). 1988. pap. 2.95 (0-440-40073-2, YB) Dell.

—The Love Letters of J. Timothy Owen. LC 85-45846. 192p. (gr. 7 up). 1986. HarpC Child Bks.

—The Love Letters of J. Timothy Owen. LC 85-45846. 192p. (gr. 7 up). 1988. pap. 2.75 (0-06-447026-1, Trophy) HarpC Child Bks.

—Nora: Maybe a Ghost Story. (gr. 4-7). 1993. pap. 3.95 (0-15-276895-5) HarBrace.

—Odds on Oliver. Schindler, S. D., illus. LC 92-25932. 64p. (gr. 2-5). 1993. PLB 12.99 (0-670-84549-3) Viking Child Bks.

—Star Shine. (gr. k-6). 1987. pap. 2.75 (0-440-47920-7, YB) Dell.

—Your Old Pal, Al. 160p. (gr. k-6). 1981. pap. 2.95 (0-440-49862-7, YB) Dell.

—Your Old Pal, Al. LC 79-12350. (gr. 5-9). 1979. pap. 13.95 (0-670-79575-5) Viking Child Bks.

Greene, Elizabeth. Turtle Soup. LC 91-67766. (Illus.). 64p. 1993. pap. 7.00 (1-56002-166-7, Univ Edtns) Aegina Pr.

Greene, Ellin. Legend of the Cranberry. (ps-6). 1993. pap. 15.00 (0-671-75975-2, S&S BFYR) S&S Trade.

Greene, Ellin, retold by. Billy Beg & His Bull: An Irish Tale. Root, Kimberly B., illus. LC 93-7730. 32p. (gr. 4-8). 1994. 15.95 (0-8234-1100-1) Holiday.

Greene, George W. Christmas Books & Ornaments. Hatter, Laurie, illus. (ps). 1993. Gift box set of 4 bks., 12p. ea. bds. 14.95 (1-56828-041-6) Red Jacket Pr.

—Gardening Storybox. Hatter, Laurie, illus. (ps). 1993. Activity kit incl. 2 bks., 12p. ea. 16.95 (1-56828-045-9) Red Jacket Pr.

—Hamlet Trims His Tree. Hatter, Laurie, illus. 12p. (ps). 1993. 4.95 (1-56828-023-8) Red Jacket Pr.

—The Legend of Jack O'Lantern. Hatter, Laurie, illus. 12p. (ps). 1992. 4.95 (1-56828-000-9) Red Jacket Pr.

—Margaret's Christmas Stocking. Hatter, Laurie, illus. 12p. (ps). 1993. 4.95 (1-56828-022-X) Red Jacket Pr.

—Me & My Snowman. Hatter, Laurie, illus. (ps). 1993. 4.95 (1-56828-020-3) Red Jacket Pr.

—Sal's Garden Trowell. Hatter, Laurie, illus. 12p. (ps). 1993. 4.95 (1-56828-031-9) Red Jacket Pr.

—Sam's Watering Can. Hatter, Laurie, illus. 12p. (ps). 1993. 4.95 (1-56828-032-7) Red Jacket Pr.

—Santa's Hat. Hatter, Laurie, illus. (ps). 1993. 4.95 (1-56828-021-1) Red Jacket Pr.

—What Haunts Hamlet's House? Hatter, Laurie, illus. 12p. (ps). 1992. 4.95 (1-56828-003-3) Red Jacket Pr.

—Why Ghosts Like Halloween. Hatter, Laurie, illus. 12p. (ps). 1992. 4.95 (1-56828-002-5) Red Jacket Pr.

—Witch's Brew. Hatter, Laurie, illus. 12p. (ps). 1992. 4.95 (1-56828-001-7) Red Jacket Pr.

Greene, Graham. The Destructors. (gr. 4-9). Date not set. 13.95 (0-88682-348-X, 97213-098) Creative Ed.

—The End of the Party. (gr. 5 up). 1992. PLB 13.95 (0-88682-497-4); Resale. 19.95s.p. (0-685-60909-X) Creative Ed.

Greene, Ida. Self Esteem - the Essence of You. (Illus.). 30p. (Orig.). 1992. pap. text ed. 4.95 (1-881165-15-9) People Skills.

Greene, Jack. The Mudgrump. Florman, Lisa, illus. LC 80-68130. 56p. (Orig.). (gr. k-6). 1980. pap. text ed. 3.95 perfect binding (0-9601258-3-3) Golden Owl Pub.

Greene, Jacqueline. One Foot Ashore. LC 93-22961. 1994. 16.95 (0-8027-8217-1) Walker & Co.

Greene, Jacqueline D. The Chippewa. LC 93-18371. (Illus.). 64p. (gr. 4-6). 1993. PLB 12.90 (0-531-20122-8) Watts.

—The Hanukah Tooth. Ouellet, Pauline A., illus. LC 81-90033. 28p. (ps-2). 1981. pap. 3.00 (0-938836-02-1) Pascal Pubs.

—The Maya. Rosoff, Iris, ed. LC 91-29433. (Illus.). 64p. (gr. 3-5). 1992. PLB 12.90 (0-531-20067-1) Watts.

—The Maya. (Illus.). 64p. (gr. 5-8). 1992. pap. 5.95 (0-531-15638-9) Watts.

—Out of Many Waters. (gr. 5 up). 1988. 16.95 (0-8027-6811-3) Walker & Co.

—Out of Many Waters. 208p. (Orig.). (gr. 5 up). 1993. pap. 8.95 (0-8027-7401-6) Walker & Co.

—What His Father Did. O'Brien, John, illus. 32p. (gr. k-3). 1992. 13.45 (0-395-55042-4) HM.

Greene, Jane F. & Woods, Judy F. J & J Language Readers: Level I. Ranson, Peggy, illus. (gr. 2-3). 1992. Set of 18 units, 45p. ea. pap. text ed. 49.00 (0-944584-86-1) Sopris.

—J & J Language Readers: Level II. Ranson, Peggy, illus. (gr. 2-4). 1992. Set of 18 units, 45p. ea. pap. text ed. 49.00 (0-944584-87-X) Sopris.

—J & J Language Readers: Level III. Ranson, Peggy, illus. (gr. 3-5). 1992. Set of 18 units, 45p. ea. pap. text ed. 49.00 (0-944584-88-8) Sopris.

Greene, Janice, et al. Our Century: 1900-1910. LC 93-11445. (gr. 4 up). 1993. Repr. of 1989 ed. PLB 21.27 (0-8368-1032-5) Gareth Stevens Inc.

Greene, Joshua, retold by. Krishna, Master of All Mystics. Amendola, Dominique, illus. 16p. (gr. 1-4). 1981. 4.00 (0-89647-035-0) Bala Bks.

Greene, Joshua, ed. see Wilson, Karen.

Greene, Karen. Once upon a Recipe: Delicious, Healthy Foods for Kids of all Ages. Heinz, Anna M. & Greene, Karen, illus. LC 92-9666. 96p. 1992. pap. 12.95 (0-399-51784-7, Perigee Bks) Putnam Pub Group.

Greene, Laura. Change: Getting to Know about Ebb & Flow. Mayo, Gretchen, illus. LC 80-81081. 32p. (gr. k-3). 1981. 16.95 (0-87705-401-0) Human Sci Pr.

—Help: Getting to Know about Needing & Giving. Mayo, Gretchen, illus. LC 80-81082. 32p. (ps-3). 1981. 16.95 (0-87705-402-9) Human Sci Pr.

Greene, Laura & Dicker, Eva B. Discovering Sign Language. LC 88-24609. (Illus.). 96p. (gr. 5-12). 1988. pap. 4.95 (0-930323-48-3, Kendall Green Pubns) Gallaudet Univ Pr.

—Interpreting Sign Language. (Illus.). 96p. (gr. 5-9). 1990. PLB 12.90 (0-531-10773-6) Watts.

—Sign Language Talk. Solomon, Maury, ed. Caraway, Caren, illus. 96p. (gr. 5 up). 1989. PLB 11.90 (0-531-10597-0) Watts.

—Sign-Me-Fine: Experiencing American Sign Language. Caraway, Caren, illus. LC 90-5148. 120p. (gr. 7-12). 1989. pap. 5.95 (0-930323-76-9, Pub. by K Green Pubns) Gallaudet Univ Pr.

Greene, Laura O. Child Labor: Then & Now. LC 92-17721. 1992. 13.40 (0-531-13008-8) Watts.

Greene, Leia A. The Angel Told Me to Tell You Good-Bye. Greene, Leia A., illus. 24p. (gr. k-12). 1991. pap. text ed. 4.95 (1-880737-06-X) Crystal Jrns.

—The Bridge Between Two Worlds. Greene, Leia A., illus. 36p. (gr. k-12). 1992. pap. text ed. 4.95 (1-880737-08-6) Crystal Jrns.

—Crystals R for Kids. Greene, Leia A., illus. 40p. (gr. k-12). 1991. wkbk. 4.95 (1-880737-04-3) Crystal Jrns.

—Exploring the Chakras. Greene, Leia A., illus. 32p. (gr. k-12). 1991. wkbk. 4.95 (1-880737-03-5) Crystal Jrns.

—Happy Feet: A Child's Guide to Foot Reflexology. Greene, Leia A., illus. 38p. (gr. k-12). 1992. wkbk. 4.95 (1-880737-10-8) Crystal Jrns.

—I Am Special Too: Circle of Angels Workbook. Green, Leia A., illus. 99p. (gr. k-9). 1991. 18.95 (1-880737-00-0) Crystal Jrns.

—Mommy! Why Is Everyone Staring at Me? Greene, Leia A., illus. (gr. k-12). 1992. wkbk. 4.95 *(1-880737-11-6)* Crystal Jrns.
—One Red Rose. Greene, Leia A., illus. (gr. k-12). 1992. pap. text ed. 4.95 *(1-880737-07-8)* Crystal Jrns.
—When the Earth Was New: An Experience in Healing Our Planet. Green, Leia A., illus. 20p. (gr. k-9). 1991. wkbk. 4.95 *(1-880737-02-7)* Crystal Jrns.
—Where Is God? Greene, Leia A., illus. 40p. (gr. k-12). 1991. pap. text ed. 4.95 *(1-880737-05-1)* Crystal Jrns.
—Who's Afraid of the Dark? Greene, Leia A., illus. 32p. (gr. k-12). 1992. pap. text ed. 4.95 *(1-880737-09-4)* Crystal Jrns.
Greene, Michael. Where's the Green Pea? Ringston, Ray, illus. LC 91-91536. 32p. (ps-1). 1992. PLB 19.95 incl. audiocassette *(1-881134-00-8)* Tues Child.
Greene, Patricia B. The Sabbath Garden. (Illus.). 192p. (gr. 7 up). 1993. 15.99 *(0-525-67430-6,* Lodestar Bks) Dutton Child Bks.
Greene, Richard, jt. auth. see Barrett, Katherine.
Greene, Shelley. Teenage Mutant Ninja Turtles Totally Awesome Activity Book. Lawson, Jim & Burger, Dan, illus. 96p. (gr. 1-5). 1990. pap. 3.95 *(0-679-81108-7)* Random Bks Yng Read.
Greene, Shep. The Boy Who Drank Too Much. 144p. (gr. 7 up). 1980. pap. 3.50 *(0-440-90493-5,* LFL) Dell.
Greene, Yvonne. Double Trouble. 160p. (Orig.). (gr. 7-12). 1986. pap. 2.50 *(0-553-26154-1)* Bantam.
—Hard to Get-Kelly Blake. 176p. (Orig.). (gr. 7-12). 1986. pap. 2.50 *(0-553-26037-5)* Bantam.
—Headliners-Kelly Blake. 160p. (Orig.). (gr. 7-12). 1986. pap. 2.50 *(0-553-26112-6)* Bantam.
—Little Sister. (gr. 11 up). 1981. pap. 2.50 *(0-553-26613-6)* Bantam.
—The Love Hunt. 192p. (Orig.). (gr. 5 up). 1985. pap. 2.25 *(0-553-25070-1)* Bantam.
—Paris Nights, No. 6. 160p. (Orig.). (gr. 7-12). 1987. pap. 2.50 *(0-553-26199-1)* Bantam.
Greenes, Carole, et al. Mathletics: Gold Medal Problems. (Illus.). 149p. (gr. 8-10). 1989. pap. 19.95 *(0-939765-31-4,* G119) Janson Pubns.
Greenewalt, Crawford H. Hummingbirds. (gr. 5 up). 1990. pap. 15.95 *(0-486-26431-9)* Dover.
Greenfeld, Howard. The Hidden Children. LC 93-20326. (gr. 1-8). 1993. 15.95 *(0-395-66074-2)* Ticknor & Fields.
—Marc Chagall. (Illus.). 80p. (gr. 7 up). 1990. 19.95 *(0-8109-3152-4)* Abrams.
—Paul Gauguin. LC 93-9454. 1993. 19.95 *(0-8109-3376-4)* Abrams.
Greenfield, Eloise. Aaron & Gayla's Alphabet Book. Gilchrist, Jan S., illus. 20p. 1992. 9.95 *(0-86316-208-8)* Writers & Readers.
—Aaron & Gayla's Counting Book. Gilchrist, Jan S., illus. 20p. 1992. 9.95 *(0-86316-209-6)* Writers & Readers.
—Africa Dream. Byard, Carole, illus. LC 77-5080. 32p. (ps-3). 1989. PLB 13.89 *(0-690-04776-2,* Crowell Jr Bks) HarpC Child Bks.
—Africa Dream. Byard, Carole, illus. LC 77-5080. 32p. (ps-3). 1990. pap. 4.95 *(0-06-443277-7,* Trophy) HarpC Child Bks.
—Big Friend, Little Friend. Gilchrist, Jan S., illus. 12p. (ps-1). 1991. bds. 4.95 *(0-86316-204-5)* Writers & Readers.
—Childtimes: A Three-Generation Memoir. Little, Lessie J., illus. LC 77-26581. 192p. (gr. 4-6). 1993. pap. 5.95 *(0-06-446134-3,* Trophy) HarpC Child Bks.
—Daydreamers. Feelings, Tom, illus. (gr. k up). 1981. 13.95 *(0-8037-2137-4)* Dial Bks Young.
—Daydreamers. Feelings, Tom, illus. LC 80-27262. (gr. k up). 1985. pap. 4.95 *(0-8037-0167-5)* Dial Bks Young.
—First Pink Light. Gilchrist, Jan S., illus. 32p. (ps-4). 1991. 13.95 *(0-86316-207-X)* Writers & Readers.
—Grandmama's Joy. Byard, Carole, illus. LC 79-11403. 32p. (gr. 2-5). 1980. 13.95 *(0-399-21064-4,* Philomel) Putnam Pub Group.
—Grandpa's Face. Cooper, Floyd, illus. LC 87-16729. 32p. (ps-2). 1988. 14.95 *(0-399-21525-5,* Philomel Bks) Putnam Pub Group.
—Grandpa's Face. Cooper, Floyd, illus. 32p. (ps-3). 1991. pap. 5.95 *(0-399-22106-9,* Sandcastle Bks) Putnam Pub Group.
—Grandpa's Face. Cooper, Floyd, illus. (SPA.). 32p. (ps up). 1993. pap. 5.95 *(0-399-22511-0,* Philomel Bks) Putnam Pub Group.
—Honey, I Love: And Other Love Poems. Dillon, Diane & Dillon, Leo, illus. LC 77-2845. 48p. (gr. 1-3). 1978. 13.00 *(0-690-01334-5,* Crowell Jr Bks); PLB 12.89 *(0-690-03845-3)* HarpC Child Bks.
—Honey, I Love & Other Love Poems. Dillon, Diane & Dillon, Leo, illus. LC 85-45398. 48p. (gr. 1-4). 1986. pap. 3.95 *(0-06-443097-9,* Trophy) HarpC Child Bks.
—I Make Music. Gilchrist, Jan S., illus. 12p. (ps-1). 1991. bds. 4.95 *(0-86316-205-3)* Writers & Readers.
—Koya Delaney & the Good Girl Blues. 176p. 1992. 13.95 *(0-590-43300-8,* Scholastic Hardcover) Scholastic Inc.
—Mary McLeod Bethune. Pinkney, Jerry, illus. LC 76-11522. 40p. (gr. 2-5). 1977. PLB 14.89 *(0-690-01129-6,* Crowell Jr Bks) HarpC Child Bks.
—Me & Neesie. Barnett, Moneta, illus. LC 74-23078. 40p. (gr. 1-4). 1975. PLB 13.89 *(0-690-00715-9,* Crowell Jr Bks) HarpC Child Bks.
—Me & Neesie. Barnett, Moneta, illus. LC 74-23078. 40p. (gr. k-3). 1984. pap. 4.95 *(0-06-443057-X,* Trophy) HarpC Child Bks.
—My Daddy & I. Gilchrist, Jan S., illus. 12p. 1991. bds. 4.95 *(0-86316-206-1)* Writers & Readers.

—My Doll, Keshia. Gilchrist, Jan S., illus. 12p. (ps-1). 1991. bds. 5.95 *(0-86316-203-7)* Writers & Readers.
—Nathaniel Talking. Gilchrist, Jan S., illus. 32p. (gr. k-5). 1988. 12.95 *(0-86316-200-2)* Writers & Readers.
—Night on Neighborhood Street. (ps-3). 1991. 14.00 *(0-8037-0777-0)*; PLB 13.89 *(0-8037-0778-9)* Dial Bks Young.
—Paul Robeson. Ford, George, illus. LC 74-13663. 40p. (gr. 1-5). 1975. PLB 15.89 *(0-690-00660-8,* Crowell Jr Bks) HarpC Child Bks.
—Rosa Parks. Marlow, Eric, illus. LC 72-83782. 40p. (gr. 1-5). 1973. PLB 14.89 *(0-690-71211-1,* Crowell Jr Bks) HarpC Child Bks.
—She Come Bringing Me That Little Baby Girl. Steptoe, John, illus. LC 74-8104. 32p. (gr. k-3). 1990. 14.00 *(0-397-31586-4,* Lipp Jr Bks); PLB 13.89 *(0-397-32478-2)* HarpC Child Bks.
—She Come Bringing Me That Little Baby Girl. Steptoe, John, illus. LC 74-8104. 32p. (ps-3). 1993. pap. 4.95 *(0-06-443296-3,* Trophy) HarpC Child Bks.
—Sister. Barnett, Moneta, illus. LC 73-22182. 96p. (gr. 5-12). 1974. 15.00 *(0-690-00497-4,* Crowell Jr Bks) HarpC Child Bks.
—Sister. Barnett, Moneta, illus. LC 73-22182. 96p. (gr. 5-8). 1987. pap. 3.95 *(0-06-440199-5,* Trophy) HarpC Child Bks.
—Sweet Baby Coming. Gilchrist, Jan S., illus. 14p. (ps). 1994. 4.95 *(0-694-00578-9,* Festival) HarpC Child Bks.
—Talk about a Family. reissued ed. Calvin, James, illus. LC 77-16423. 64p. (gr. 2-5). 1991. PLB 12.89 *(0-397-32504-5,* Lipp Jr Bks) HarpC Child Bks.
—Talk about a Family. LC 77-16423. (Illus.). 64p. (gr. 2-5). 1993. pap. 3.95 *(0-06-440444-7,* Trophy) HarpC Child Bks.
—Under the Sunday Tree. Ferguson, Amos, illus. LC 87-29373. 48p. (ps-1). 1988. PLB 14.89 *(0-06-022257-3)* HarpC Child Bks.
—Under the Sunday Tree. Ferguson, Amos, illus. LC 87-29373. 48p. (gr. 1 up). 1991. pap. 5.95 *(0-06-443257-2,* Trophy) HarpC Child Bks.
—William and the Good Old Days. Gilchrist, Jan S., illus. LC 91-47030. 32p. (gr. k-3). 1993. 15.00 *(0-06-021093-1)*; PLB 14.89 *(0-06-021094-X)* HarpC Child Bks.
Greenfield, Eloise & Little, Lessie J. Childtimes: A Three-Generation Memoir. Pinkney, Jerry, illus. LC 77-26581. 160p. (gr. 5 up). 1979. (Crowell Jr Bks); PLB 13.89 *(0-690-03875-5,* Crowell Jr Bks) HarpC Child Bks.
Greenfield, Eloise, jt. auth. see Little, Lessie J.
Greenfield, Karen R. Sister Yessa's Story. Ewart, Claire, illus. LC 91-15634. 32p. (gr. k-4). 1992. 15.00 *(0-06-020278-5)*; PLB 14.89 *(0-06-020279-3)* HarpC Child Bks.
Greenfield, Monica. Baby. Gilchrist, Jan S., illus. 14p. (ps). 1994. 4.95 *(0-694-00577-0,* Festival) HarpC Child Bks.
Greenhaven. Teacher's Guide to Opposing Viewpoints. 1988. pap. 6.95 *(0-89908-301-3)* Greenhaven.
Greenhaven Press, Inc. Staff, ed. What Weapons Would Strengthen America's Defense? (Illus.). 50p. (gr. 10 up). 1991. pap. text ed. 3.45 *(0-89908-645-4)* Greenhaven.
Greenhill, Richard, jt. auth. see Fyson, Nance L.
Greenland, Peter, jt. auth. see Curtis, Neil.
Greenlaw, M. Jean. Ranch Dressing: The Story of Western Wear. (Illus.). 64p. (gr. 3-7). 1993. 15.99 *(0-525-67432-2,* Lodestar Bks) Dutton Child Bks.
Greenleaf, Ann. Max & Molly's Fall. 1993. 4.99 *(0-517-09155-0)* Outlet Bk Co.
—Max & Molly's Spring. 1993. 4.99 *(0-517-09153-4)* Outlet Bk Co.
—Max & Molly's Summer. 1993. 4.99 *(0-517-09154-2)* Outlet Bk Co.
—Max & Molly's Winter. 1993. 4.99 *(0-517-09152-6)* Outlet Bk Co.
—Too Many Monsters. 1993. 4.99 *(0-517-09158-5)* Outlet Bk Co.
Greenleaf, Ann G. Emily's New Ghost. LC 93-17779. (Illus.). 1993. 4.99 *(0-517-01959-0,* Pub. by Derrydale Bks) Outlet Bk Co.
—The Goblins Did It! LC 93-19746. (Illus.). 1993. 4.99 *(0-517-09157-7)* Outlet Bk Co.
Greenleaf, E. Pricky, a Pet Porcupine. LC 65-22311. (Illus.). 48p. (gr. 2-5). 1968. PLB 10.95 *(0-87783-031-2)*; pap. 3.94 deluxe ed. *(0-87783-158-0)* Oddo.
—Who Wants to Nap? LC 68-56820. (Illus.). 32p. (gr. 2-3). PLB 9.95 *(0-87783-050-9)* Oddo.
Greenlee, Sharon. When Someone Dies. Drath, Bill, illus. 40p. (gr. 1-7). 1992. 12.95 *(1-56145-044-8)* Peachtree Pubs.
Greenman, Joseph & Joachim, Ann, eds. Educational Film Guide for Middle Eastern Studies. xxxvii, 126p. (gr. 10-12). 1980. pap. text ed. 6.00x *(0-932098-16-9)* UM CTR MENAS.
Greenspan, Alice. Helping Is Fun. Hoha, Linda, illus. 32p. (gr. k-2). 1990. pasted 2.50 *(0-87403-027-7,* 24-03912) Standard Pub.
Greenspun, Adele A. Daddies. Greenspun, Adele A., illus. 48p. 1991. 15.95 *(0-399-22259-6,* Philomel Bks) Putnam Pub Group.
Greenstein, Elaine. Emily & the Crows. Greenstein, Elaine, illus. LC 91-39917. 28p. (gr. k up). 1992. pap. 14.95 *(0-88708-238-6)* Picture Bk Studio.
—Mrs. Rose's Garden. Greenstein, Elaine, illus. 28p. (gr. k up). 1993. 14.95 *(0-88708-264-5)* Picture Bk Studio.

Greenwald, Dorothy. Coping with Moving. Rosen, Ruth, ed. 128p. (gr. 7 up). 1987. PLB 13.95 *(0-8239-0683-3)* Rosen Group.
Greenwald, Sheila. All the Way to Wit's End. (gr. k-6). 1987. pap. 2.75 *(0-440-40188-7,* YB) Dell.
—Alvin Webster's Surefire Plan for Success (& How It Failed) Greenwald, Sheila, illus. 96p. (gr. 3-6). 1987. 12.95 *(0-316-32706-9,* Joy St Bks) Little.
—The Atrocious Two. (Orig.). (gr. k-6). 1989. pap. 2.95 *(0-440-40141-0,* YB) Dell.
—Give Us a Great Big Smile, Rosy Cole. Greenwald, Sheila, illus. 80p. (gr. 3 up). 1981. 12.95 *(0-316-32672-0,* Joy St Bks) Little.
—Give Us a Great Big Smile, Rosy Cole. 80p. (gr. 5-7). 1982. pap. 2.50 *(0-440-42923-4,* YB) Dell.
—Here's Hermione: A Rosy Cole Production. (Illus.). (gr. 3-7). 1991. 13.95 *(0-316-32715-8)* Little.
—It All Began with Jane Eyre: Or, the Secret Life of Franny Dillman. 128p. (gr. 5 up). 1981. pap. 1.75 *(0-440-94136-9,* LE) Dell.
—The Mariah Delaney Lending Library Disaster. (Illus.). (gr. 4-6). 1977. 14.45 *(0-395-25836-7)* HM.
—The Mariah Delany Lending Library Disaster. (gr. k-6). 1986. pap. 2.75 *(0-440-45327-5,* YB) Dell.
—Mat Pit & the Tunnel Tenants. Greenwald, Sheila, illus. 128p. (gr. k-6). 1989. pap. 2.75 *(0-440-40155-0,* YB) Dell.
—Move Over, Columbus, Rosy Cole Discovers America! LC 92-12480. 1992. 13.95 *(0-316-32721-2,* Joy St Bks) Little.
—My Fabulous New Life. LC 92-44928. 160p. (gr. 3-7). 1993. 10.95 *(0-15-277693-1,* Browndeer Pr)*; pap. 3.95 *(0-15-276716-9,* Browndeer Pr) HarBrace.
—Rosy Cole's Great American Guilt Club. Greenwald, Sheila, illus. LC 85-47876. 96p. (gr. 3-7). 1985. 12.95 *(0-316-32709-3,* Joy St Bks) Little.
—Rosy's Romance. Greenwald, Sheila, illus. 96p. (gr. 3-6). 1989. 12.95 *(0-316-32704-2,* Joy St Bks) Little.
—The Secret in Miranda's Closet. (gr. k-6). 1989. pap. 2.95 *(0-440-40128-3,* YB) Dell.
—The Secret Museum. Greenwald, Sheila, illus. 128p. (gr. k-6). 1989. pap. 2.95 *(0-440-40148-8,* YB) Dell.
—Valentine Rosy. (gr. 3-7). 1986. pap. 2.50 *(0-440-49203-3,* YB) Dell.
—Will the Real Gertrude Hollings Please Stand Up? 176p. (gr. k-6). 1985. pap. 2.95 *(0-440-49553-9,* YB) Dell.
—Write on, Rosy! A Young Author in Crisis. Greenwald, Sheila, illus. 128p. (gr. 3-6). 1988. 13.95 *(0-316-32705-0,* Joy St Bks) Little.
Greenway, Jennifer. A Real Little Bunny: A Sequel to The Velveteen Rabbit. Officer, Robyn, illus. LC 92-37149. 40p. 1993. 14.95 *(0-8362-4936-4)* Andrews & McMeel.
Greenway, Jennifer, retold by. Goldilocks & the Three Bears. Miles, Elizabeth, illus. 1991. 6.95 *(0-8362-4900-3)* Andrews & McMeel.
—Jack & the Beanstalk. Bernal, Richard, illus. 1991. 6.95 *(0-8362-4903-8)* Andrews & McMeel.
—The Three Billy Goats Gruff. Lustig, Loretta, illus. 1991. 6.95 *(0-8362-4913-5)* Andrews & McMeel.
—The Three Little Pigs. Dieneman, Debbie, illus. 1991. 6.95 *(0-8362-4904-6)* Andrews & McMeel.
Greenway, Jennifer, retold by see Grimm, Jacob & Grimm, Wilhelm K.
Greenway, Shirley. Burrows. (Illus.). 24p. (gr. k-4). 1991. PLB 9.90 *(1-878137-11-5)* Newington.
—Can You See Me? (Illus.). 32p. (ps-2). 1992. PLB 11.00 *(0-8249-8575-3,* Ideals Child); pap. 3.95 *(0-8249-8560-5)* Hambleton-Hill.
—Color Me Bright. Oxford Scientific Films Staff, photos by. (Illus.). 16p. (ps-6). 1992. bds. 3.95 *(1-879085-53-4)* Whsprng Coyote Pr.
—Here's Ears. Oxford Scientific Films Staff, photos by. (Illus.). 16p. (ps-k). 1992. bds. 3.95 *(1-879085-50-X)* Whsprng Coyote Pr.
—How Big Am I? Oxford Scientific Films Staff, photos by. LC 93-18593. (Illus.). 32p. (ps-1). 1993. PLB 11.00 *(0-8249-8625-3,* Ideals Child); pap. 3.95 *(0-8249-8601-6)* Hambleton-Hill.
—How Do I Move? (Illus.). 32p. (ps-2). 1992. PLB 11.00 *(0-8249-8578-8,* Ideals Child); pap. 3.95 *(0-8249-8563-X)* Hambleton-Hill.
—Legs & All. Oxford Scientific Films Staff, photos by. (Illus.). 16p. (ps-k). 1992. bds. 3.95 *(1-879085-52-6)* Whsprng Coyote Pr.
—A Tale of Tails. Oxford Scientific Films Staff, photos by. (Illus.). 16p. (ps-6). 1992. bds. 3.95 *(1-879085-51-8)* Whsprng Coyote Pr.
—Water. (Illus.). 24p. (gr. k-4). 1991. PLB 9.90 *(1-878137-10-7)* Newington.
—What Do I Eat? Oxford Scientific Films Staff, photos by. LC 93-18592. (Illus.). 32p. (ps). 1993. PLB 11.00 *(0-8249-8627-X,* Ideals Child); pap. 3.95 *(0-8249-8602-4)* Hambleton-Hill.
—Where Do I Live? (Illus.). 32p. (ps-2). 1992. PLB 11.00 *(0-8249-8576-1,* Ideals Child); pap. 3.95 *(0-8249-8561-3)* Hambleton-Hill.
—Whose Baby Am I? 32p. (ps-2). 1992. 11.00 *(0-8249-8577-X,* Ideals Child); pap. 3.95 *(0-8249-8562-1)* Hambleton-Hill.
Greenway, Shirley & Evans, Michael. Dragons, Dolphins & Dinosaurs. LC 93-20397. (Illus.). 32p. (ps-12). 1993. smythe sewn reinforced 13.95 *(1-879085-83-6)* Whsprng Coyote Pr.
Greenway, Shirley, ed. see Dickens, Charles.
Greenway, Shirley, jt. ed. see Trotman, Felicity.

Greenway, Theresa. Ferns. LC 91-14935. (Illus.). 48p. (gr. 5-9). 1992. PLB 19.92 (*0-8114-2735-8*) Raintree Steck-V.

—Swamp Life. Taylor, Kim & Burton, Jane, photos by. LC 92-53489. (Illus.). 32p. (gr. 2-5). 1993. 9.95 (*1-56458-211-6*) Dorling Kindersley.

—Tree Life. Taylor, Kim, photos by. LC 92-52824. (Illus.). 32p. (gr. 2-5). 1992. 9.95 (*1-56458-132-2*) Dorling Kindersley.

Greenwood, Donald J. Advanced Squad Leader: WWII Tactical Warfare. Keebler, Charlie, illus. 200p. (gr. 9 up). 1989. 45.00 (*0-911605-50-9*) Avalon Hill.

Greenwood, Pamela D. I Found Mouse. Plecas, Jennifer, illus. LC 93-46427. (ps). 1994. write for info. (*0-395-65478-5*, Clarion Bks) HM.

—What about My Goldfish? Barrett-Plecas, Jennifer, illus. LC 92-11281. 1993. 14.95 (*0-395-64337-6*, Clarion Bks) HM.

Greer, Blanche. The Black Swan & the Green See Saw. Sarnoff, Arthur, illus. LC 75-261399. (gr. 5 up). 1977. 4.50 (*0-930422-07-4*) Dennis-Landman.

Greer, Gary & Ruddick, Bob. This Island Isn't Big Enough for the Four of Us! LC 86-47750. 160p. (gr. 3-7). 1989. pap. 3.95 (*0-06-440203-7*, Trophy) HarpC Child Bks.

Greer, Gery & Ruddick, Bob. Jason & the Aliens down the Street. Sims, Blanche L., illus. LC 90-47386. 96p. (gr. 2-5). 1991. 12.95 (*0-06-021761-8*); PLB 12.89 (*0-06-021762-6*) HarpC Child Bks.

—Jason & the Aliens Down the Street. LC 90-47386. (Illus.). 96p. (gr. 2-5). 1992. pap. 3.95 (*0-06-440446-3*, Trophy) HarpC Child Bks.

—Jason & the Escape from Bat Planet. Sims, Blanche L., illus. LC 92-41169. 96p. (gr. 2-5). 1993. 14.00 (*0-06-021221-7*); PLB 13.89 (*0-06-021222-5*) HarpC Child Bks.

—Jason & the Lizard Pirates. Sims, Blanche L., illus. LC 91-14327. 96p. (gr. 2-5). 1993. pap. 3.95 (*0-06-440481-1*, Trophy) HarpC Child Bks.

—Let Me off This Spaceship! Sims, Blanche C., illus. LC 90-32045. 64p. (gr. 2-5). 1991. 12.95 (*0-06-021605-0*); PLB 12.89 (*0-06-021606-9*) HarpC Child Bks.

—Let Me off This Spaceship! Sims, Blanche L., illus. LC 90-47386. 80p. (gr. 2-5). 1992. pap. 3.95 (*0-06-440436-6*, Trophy) HarpC Child Bks.

—Max & Me & the Time Machine. LC 82-48762. 140p. (gr. 4-7). 1983. 13.95 (*0-15-253134-3*, HB Juv Bks) HarBrace.

—Max & Me & the Time Machine. LC 87-45284. 128p. (gr. 3-7). 1988. pap. 3.95 (*0-06-440222-3*, Trophy) HarpC Child Bks.

—Max & Me & the Wild West. LC 87-12066. 138p. (gr. 4-7). 1988. 12.95 (*0-15-253136-X*) HarBrace.

—This Island Isn't Big Enough for the Four of Us. LC 86-47750. 160p. (gr. 3-7). 1987. 14.00 (*0-690-04612-X*, Crowell Jr Bks); PLB 13.89 (*0-690-04614-6*, Crowell Jr Bks) HarpC Child Bks.

Greer, Gery & Ruddick, Robert. Jason & the Lizard Pirates. Sims, Blanche L., illus. LC 91-14327. 96p. (gr. 2-5). 1992. 14.00 (*0-06-022721-4*); PLB 13.89 (*0-06-022722-2*) HarpC Child Bks.

Greeson, Janet. An American Army of Two. Mulvihill, Patricia, illus. 48p. (gr. k-4). 1991. PLB 14.95 (*0-87614-664-7*) Carolrhoda Bks.

—An American Army of Two. (ps-3). 1991. pap. 5.95 (*0-87614-547-0*) Carolrhoda Bks.

—Kenny Wild's Hair. LC 89-31167. 140p. (gr. 3-6). 1989. 13.95 (*0-531-15118-2*); PLB 13.90 (*0-531-10792-2*) Watts.

—The Stingy Baker. LaRochelle, David, illus. 32p. (ps-3). 1989. PLB 18.95 (*0-87614-378-8*) Carolrhoda Bks.

Greger, C. Shana. The Fifth & Final Sun. LC 93-11159. (Illus.). (ps-6). 1994. write for info. (*0-395-67438-7*) HM.

Gregg, Andy. Great Rabbit & the Long-Tailed Wildcat. Grant, Christy, ed. Smith, Cat B., illus. LC 92-22950. 32p. (gr. 1-5). 1993. PLB 13.95 (*0-8075-3047-6*) A Whitman.

Gregorich, B. Vocabulary Vampire. (gr. 7-12). 1982. 5.95 (*0-88160-083-0*, LW 1001) Learning Wks.

Gregorich, Barbara. Addition & Subtraction: First Grade. Hoffman, Joan, ed. Koontz, Robin M., illus. (gr. 1). 1990. wkbk. 2.29 (*0-88743-182-8*) Sch Zone Pub Co.

—Addition & Subtraction: Second Grade. Hoffman, Joan, ed. Koontz, Robin M., illus. 32p. (gr. 2). 1990. wkbk. 2.29 (*0-88743-188-7*) Sch Zone Pub Co.

—Adjectives & Adverbs. Pape, Richard, illus. 24p. (gr. 3-4). 1980. wkbk. 2.95 (*0-89403-596-7*) EDC.

—El Alfabeto: Minusculas: Alphabet: Lowercase. Hoffman, Joan, ed. Shepherd-Bartram, tr. from ENG. Pape, Richard, illus. (SPA.). 32p. (Orig.). (ps). 1987. wkbk. 1.99 (*0-938256-76-9*) Sch Zone Pub Co.

—Alike-Not Alike & Go-Togethers: Kindergarten. Hoffman, Joan, ed. Koontz, Robin M., illus. 32p. (gr. k). 1990. wkbk. 2.29 (*0-88743-176-3*) Sch Zone Pub Co.

—Alphabet Avalanche. Hoffman, Joan, ed. Alexander, Barbara, et al, illus. 32p. (Orig.). (ps-1). wkbk. 1.99 (*0-88743-128-3*) Sch Zone Pub Co.

—Alphabet: Lowercase. Hoffman, Joan, ed. Pape, Richard, illus. 32p. (ps). 1983. wkbk. 1.99 (*0-938256-66-1*) Sch Zone Pub Co.

—Alphabet Skills: Kindergarten. Hoffman, Joan, ed. Koontz, Robin M., illus. 32p. (gr. k). 1990. wkbk. 2.29 (*0-88743-177-1*) Sch Zone Pub Co.

—Alphabet: Uppercase. Hoffman, Joan, ed. Pape, Richard, illus. 32p. (ps). 1983. wkbk. 1.99 (*0-938256-65-3*) Sch Zone Pub Co.

—Apostrophe, Colon, Hyphen. Pape, Richard, illus. 24p. (gr. 3-4). 1980. wkbk. 2.95 (*0-89403-593-2*) EDC.

—Basic Math: First Grade. Hoffman, Joan, ed. Koontz, Robin M., illus. 32p. (gr. 1). 1990. wkbk. 2.29 (*0-88743-181-X*) Sch Zone Pub Co.

—Basic Math: Second Grade. Hoffman, Joan, ed. Koontz, Robin M., illus. 32p. (gr. 2). 1990. wkbk. 2.29 (*0-88743-187-9*) Sch Zone Pub Co.

—Beep, Beep. Hoffman, Joan, ed. Taber, Ed, illus. 16p. (Orig.). (gr. k-2). 1984. pap. 2.25 (*0-88743-007-4*, 06007) Sch Zone Pub Co.

—Beep, Beep. Hoffman, Joan, ed. (Illus.). 32p. (gr. k-2). 1992. pap. 3.95 (*0-88743-405-3*, 06057) Sch Zone Pub Co.

—Beginning Sounds. Hoffman, Joan, ed. Pape, Richard, illus. 32p. (ps). 1983. wkbk. 1.99 (*0-938256-54-8*) Sch Zone Pub Co.

—Blends. Hoffman, Joan, ed. Cook, Chris, illus. 32p. (gr. 1-3). 1981. wkbk. 1.99 (*0-938256-39-4*) Sch Zone Pub Co.

—Capital Letters. Pape, Richard, illus. 24p. (gr. 3-4). 1980. wkbk. 2.95 (*0-89403-604-1*) EDC.

—Chicken Scratch. Hoffman, Joan, ed. Alexander, Barbara, et al, illus. 32p. (Orig.). (ps-1). 1986. wkbk. 1.99 (*0-88743-127-5*) Sch Zone Pub Co.

—Los Colores. Hoffman, Joan, ed. Shepherd-Bartram, tr. from ENG. Pape, Richard, illus. (SPA.). 32p. (Orig.). (ps). 1987. wkbk. 1.99 (*0-938256-78-5*) Sch Zone Pub Co.

—Colors. Hoffman, Joan, ed. Pape, Richard, illus. 32p. (ps). 1983. wkbk. 1.99 (*0-938256-64-5*) Sch Zone Pub Co.

—Comma. Pape, Richard, illus. 24p. (gr. 3-4). 1980. wkbk. 2.95 (*0-89403-595-9*) EDC.

—The Comprehension Adventure. 48p. (gr. 7-12). 1984. 5.95 (*0-88160-109-8*, LW 1004) Learning Wks.

—Connect the Dots. Hoffman, Joan, ed. Pape, Richard, illus. 32p. (ps). 1983. wkbk. 1.99 (*0-938256-58-0*) Sch Zone Pub Co.

—Consonants. Hoffman, Joan, ed. Cook, Chris, illus. 32p. (gr. 1-3). 1981. wkbk. 1.99 (*0-938256-37-8*) Sch Zone Pub Co.

—Contando del 1 al 10: Counting 1 to 10. Hoffman, Joan, ed. Shepherd-Bartram, tr. from ENG. Pape, Richard, illus. (SPA.). 32p. (Orig.). 1987. wkbk. 1.99 (*0-938256-79-3*) Sch Zone Pub Co.

—Context Clues. Pape, Richard, illus. 24p. (gr. 3-4). 1980. wkbk. 2.95 (*0-89403-602-5*) EDC.

—Counting Caterpillars. Hoffman, Joan, ed. Alexander, Barbara, et al, illus. 32p. (Orig.). (ps-1). 1986. wkbk. 1.99 (*0-88743-126-7*) Sch Zone Pub Co.

—Counting One to Ten. Hoffman, Joan, ed. Pape, Richard, illus. 32p. (ps). 1983. wkbk. 1.99 (*0-938256-56-4*) Sch Zone Pub Co.

—Dictionary Skills. Pape, Richard, illus. 24p. (gr. 3-4). 1980. wkbk. 2.95 (*0-89403-605-X*) EDC.

—A Different Tune. Hoffman, Joan, ed. (Illus.). 16p. (Orig.). (gr. k-2). 1991. pap. 2.25 (*0-88743-028-7*, 06028) Sch Zone Pub Co.

—Does It Belong? Hoffman, Joan, ed. Pape, Richard, illus. 32p. (ps). 1983. wkbk. 1.99 (*0-938256-59-9*) Sch Zone Pub Co.

—El Alfabeto: Mayusculas: Alphabet: Uppercase. Hoffman, Joan, ed. Shepherd-Bartram, tr. from ENG. Pape, Richard, illus. (SPA.). 32p. (Orig.). (ps). 1987. wkbk. 1.99 (*0-938256-75-0*) Sch Zone Pub Co.

—Elephant & Envelope. Hoffman, Joan, ed. (Illus.). 16p. (Orig.). (gr. k-2). 1985. pap. 2.25 (*0-88743-017-1*, 06017) Sch Zone Pub Co.

—Figures of Speech. Pape, Richard, illus. 24p. (gr. 3-4). 1980. wkbk. 2.95 (*0-89403-601-7*) EDC.

—Following Directions. Hoffman, Joan, ed. Pape, Richard, illus. 32p. (ps). 1983. wkbk. 1.99 (*0-938256-62-9*) Sch Zone Pub Co.

—The Fox on the Box. Hoffman, Joan, ed. Masheris, Robert, illus. 16p. (Orig.). (gr. k-2). 1984. pap. 2.25 (*0-88743-005-8*, 06005) Sch Zone Pub Co.

—The Fox on the Box. Hoffman, Joan, ed. (Illus.). 32p. (gr. k-2). 1992. pap. 3.95 (*0-88743-403-7*, 06055) Sch Zone Pub Co.

—The Fox, the Goose & the Corn: Reading Workbook. Hoffman, Joan, ed. Laurent, Richard & Pape, Richard, illus. 32p. (Orig.). (gr. k-2). 1988. 1.99 (*0-88743-107-0*) Sch Zone Pub Co.

—The Great Ape Trick. Hoffman, Joan, ed. Lewin, Betsy, illus. 32p. (gr. k-2). 1987. wkbk. 1.99 (*0-88743-105-4*, 02605) Sch Zone Pub Co.

—The Gum on the Drum. Hoffman, Joan, ed. Sandford, John, illus. 16p. (Orig.). (gr. k-2). 1984. pap. 2.25 (*0-88743-004-X*, 06004) Sch Zone Pub Co.

—The Gum on the Drum. Hoffman, Joan, ed. (Illus.). 32p. (gr. k-2). 1992. pap. 3.95 (*0-88743-402-9*, 06054) Sch Zone Pub Co.

—Hidden Pictures. Hoffman, Joan, ed. Pape, Richard, illus. 32p. (ps). 1983. wkbk. 1.99 (*0-938256-50-5*) Sch Zone Pub Co.

—I Want a Pet. Hoffman, Joan, ed. Schneider, Rex, illus. 16p. (Orig.). (gr. k-2). 1984. pap. 2.25 (*0-88743-003-1*, 06003) Sch Zone Pub Co.

—I Want a Pet. Hoffman, Joan, ed. (Illus.). 32p. (gr. k-2). 1992. pap. 3.95 (*0-88743-401-0*, 06053) Sch Zone Pub Co.

—Igual O Diferente: Same or Different. Hoffman, Joan, ed. Shepherd-Bartram, tr. from ENG. Pape, Richard, illus. (SPA.). 32p. (Orig.). (ps). 1987. wkbk. 1.99 (*0-938256-80-7*) Sch Zone Pub Co.

—It's Magic. Hoffman, Joan, ed. Pape, Richard, illus. 32p. (gr. k-2). 1987. 1.99 (*0-88743-104-6*, 02604) Sch Zone Pub Co.

—It's Magic. Hoffman, Joan, ed. (Illus.). 16p. (Orig.). (gr. k-2). 1991. pap. 2.25 (*0-88743-029-5*, 06029) Sch Zone Pub Co.

—Jace, Mace, & the Big Race. Hoffman, Joan, ed. (Illus.). 16p. (Orig.). (gr. k-2). 1985. pap. 2.25 (*0-88743-018-X*, 06018) Sch Zone Pub Co.

—Jace, Mace, & the Big Race. Hoffman, Joan, ed. (Illus.). 32p. (gr. k-2). 1992. pap. 3.95 (*0-88743-416-9*, 06068) Sch Zone Pub Co.

—Jog, Frog, Jog. Hoffman, Joan, ed. Schneider, Rex, illus. 16p. (Orig.). (gr. k-2). 1984. pap. 2.25 (*0-88743-006-6*, 06006) Sch Zone Pub Co.

—Jog, Frog, Jog. Hoffman, Joan, ed. (Illus.). 32p. (gr. k-2). 1992. pap. 3.95 (*0-88743-404-5*, 06056) Sch Zone Pub Co.

—Letters & Words: Kindergarten. Hoffman, Joan, ed. Koontz, Robin M., illus. 32p. (gr. k). 1990. wkbk. 2.29 (*0-88743-179-8*) Sch Zone Pub Co.

—Logical Logic. (Illus.). 48p. (gr. 7-12). 1986. 5.95 (*0-88160-123-3*, LW 1003) Learning Wks.

—Long Vowels. Hoffman, Joan, ed. Cook, Chris, illus. 32p. (gr. 1-3). 1981. wkbk. 1.99 (*0-938256-41-6*) Sch Zone Pub Co.

—Mazes. Hoffman, Joan, ed. Pape, Richard, illus. 32p. (ps). 1983. wkbk. 1.99 (*0-938256-57-2*) Sch Zone Pub Co.

—Mouse & Owl. Hoffman, Joan, ed. (Illus.). 16p. (Orig.). (gr. k-2). 1991. pap. 2.25 (*0-88743-025-2*, 06025) Sch Zone Pub Co.

—My Friend Goes Left. Hoffman, Joan, ed. John, Joyce, illus. 16p. (Orig.). (gr. k-2). 1984. pap. 2.25 (*0-88743-008-2*, 06008) Sch Zone Pub Co.

—My Friend Goes Left. Hoffman, Joan, ed. (Illus.). 32p. (gr. k-2). 1992. pap. 3.95 (*0-88743-406-1*, 06058) Sch Zone Pub Co.

—Nicole Digs a Hole. Hoffman, Joan, ed. Brooks, Nan, illus. 32p. (gr. k-2). 1987. wkbk. 1.99 (*0-88743-101-1*, 02601) Sch Zone Pub Co.

—Nicole Digs a Hole. Hoffman, Joan, ed. (Illus.). 16p. (Orig.). (gr. k-2). 1991. pap. 2.25 (*0-88743-026-0*, 06026) Sch Zone Pub Co.

—Nine Men Chase a Hen. Hoffman, Joan, ed. Sandford, John, illus. 16p. (Orig.). (gr. k-2). 1984. pap. 2.25 (*0-88743-009-0*, 06009) Sch Zone Pub Co.

—Nine Men Chase a Hen. Hoffman, Joan, ed. (Illus.). 32p. (gr. k-2). 1992. pap. 3.95 (*0-88743-407-X*, 06059) Sch Zone Pub Co.

—Noise in the Night. Hoffman, Joan, ed. (Illus.). 16p. (Orig.). (gr. k-2). 1991. pap. 2.25 (*0-88743-027-9*, 06027) Sch Zone Pub Co.

—Period, Question Mark, Exclamation Mark. Pape, Richard, illus. 24p. (gr. 3-4). 1980. wkbk. 2.95 (*0-89403-592-4*) EDC.

—Positional Words & Opposite Words: Kindergarten. Hoffman, Joan, ed. Koontz, Robin M., illus. 32p. (gr. k). 1990. wkbk. 2.29 (*0-88743-180-1*) Sch Zone Pub Co.

—Prefixes, Bases, & Suffixes. Pape, Richard, illus. 24p. (gr. 3-4). 1980. wkbk. 2.95 (*0-89403-600-9*) EDC.

—Prepositions & Conjunctions. Pape, Richard, illus. 24p. (gr. 3-4). 1980. wkbk. 2.95 (*0-89403-597-5*) EDC.

—The Raccoon on the Moon. Hoffman, Joan, ed. (Illus.). 16p. (Orig.). (gr. k-2). 1991. pap. 2.25 (*0-88743-024-4*, 06024) Sch Zone Pub Co.

—Reading: First Grade. Hoffman, Joan, ed. Koontz, Robin M., illus. 32p. (gr. 1). 1990. wkbk. 2.29 (*0-88743-183-6*) Sch Zone Pub Co.

—Reading Railroad. Hofman, Joan, ed. Alexander, Barbara, et al, illus. 32p. (ps-1). 1986. wkbk. 1.99 (*0-88743-130-5*, 02506) Sch Zone Pub Co.

—Reading: Second Grade. Hoffman, Joan, ed. Koontz, Robin M., illus. 32p. (gr. 2). 1990. wkbk. 2.29 (*0-88743-189-5*) Sch Zone Pub Co.

—Reading Survival Skills. (Illus.). 72p. (gr. 7-12). 1982. 7.95 (*0-88160-084-9*, LW 1002) Learning Wks.

—Rhyming Families. Hoffman, Joan, ed. Cook, Chris, illus. 32p. (gr. 1-3). 1981. wkbk. 1.99 (*0-938256-38-6*) Sch Zone Pub Co.

—Rhyming Pictures. Hoffman, Joan, ed. Pape, Richard, illus. 32p. (ps). 1983. wkbk. 1.99 (*0-938256-53-X*) Sch Zone Pub Co.

—Same or Different. Hoffman, Joan, ed. Pape, Richard, illus. 32p. (ps). 1983. wkbk. 1.99 (*0-938256-52-1*) Sch Zone Pub Co.

—Say Good Night. Hoffman, Joan, ed. Stasiak, Krystyna, illus. 16p. (Orig.). (gr. k-2). 1984. pap. 2.25 (*0-88743-010-4*, 06010) Sch Zone Pub Co.

—Say Good Night. Hoffman, Joan, ed. (Illus.). 32p. (gr. k-2). 1992. pap. 3.95 (*0-88743-408-8*, 06060) Sch Zone Pub Co.

—School Time Fun. Hoffman, Joan, ed. Pape, Richard, illus. 32p. (ps). 1983. wkbk. 1.99 (*0-938256-67-X*) Sch Zone Pub Co.

—Shapes. Hoffman, Joan, ed. Pape, Richard, illus. 32p. (ps). 1983. wkbk. 1.99 (*0-938256-63-7*) Sch Zone Pub Co.

—Short Vowels. Hoffman, Joan, ed. Cook, Chris, illus. 32p. (gr. 1-3). 1981. wkbk. 1.99 (*0-938256-40-8*) Sch Zone Pub Co.

—Los Sonidos para Empezar: Beginning Sounds. Hoffman, Joan, ed. Shepherd-Bartram, tr. from ENG. Pape, Richard, illus. (SPA.). 32p. (Orig.). (ps) 1987. wkbk. 1.99 (*0-938256-77-7*, 02077) Sch Zone Pub Co.
—Story Problems: Grades 1-2 Math. Hoffman, Joan, ed. Cook, Chris, illus. 32p. (gr. 1-2). 1982. wkbk. 1.99 (*0-938256-45-9*) Sch Zone Pub Co.
—Story Problems: Grades 3-4 Math. Hoffman, Joan, ed. Cook, Chris, illus. 32p. (gr. 3-4). 1982. wkbk. 1.99 (*0-938256-46-7*) Sch Zone Pub Co.
—Sue Likes Blue. Hoffman, Joan, ed. John, Joyce, illus. 16p. (Orig.). (gr. k-2). 1984. pap. 2.25 (*0-88743-011-2*, 06011) Sch Zone Pub Co.
—Sue Likes Blue. Hoffman, Joan, ed. (Illus.). 32p. (gr. k-2). 1992. pap. 3.95 (*0-88743-409-6*, 06061) Sch Zone Pub Co.
—Trouble Again: Reading Workbook. Hoffman, Joan, ed. Murdocca, Sal & Pape, Richard, illus. 32p. (Orig.). (gr. k-2). 1988. 1.99 (*0-88743-110-0*) Sch Zone Pub Co.
—Up Went the Goat. Hoffman, Joan, ed. Masheris, Robert, illus. 16p. (Orig.). (gr. k-2). 1984. pap. 2.25 (*0-88743-002-3*, 06002) Sch Zone Pub Co.
—Up Went the Goat. Hoffman, Joan, ed. (Illus.). 32p. (gr. k-2). 1992. pap. 3.95 (*0-88743-400-2*, 06052) Sch Zone Pub Co.
—Word Skills: First Grade. Hoffman, Joan, ed. Koontz, Robin M., illus. 32p. (gr. 1). 1990. wkbk. 2.29 (*0-88743-184-4*) Sch Zone Pub Co.
—Word Skills: Second Grade. Hoffman, Joan, ed. Koontz, Robin M., illus. 32p. (gr. 2). 1990. wkbk. 2.29 (*0-88743-190-9*) Sch Zone Pub Co.
—Word Wagon. Hoffman, Joan, ed. Alexander, Barbara, et al, illus. 32p. (Orig.). (ps-1). wkbk. 1.99 (*0-88743-129-1*) Sch Zone Pub Co.
Gregorich, Barbara & Zack, Carol. The Newspaper: Reading Skills. Henebry, John, Jr., illus. LC 78-730963. (gr. 7-9). 1978. Incl. 4 filmstrips, 4 cass., 24 worksheets, & guide. pap. text ed. 165.00 (*0-89290-114-4*, A160) Soc for Visual.
Gregorich, Barbara, jt. auth. see Witty, Bruce.
Gregorich, Barbara, ed. see Antle, Nancy.
Gregorich, Barbara, ed. see Hoffman, Jennifer.
Gregorich, Barbara, ed. see Hoffman, Joan.
Gregorich, Barbara, ed. see Johnson, Sharon S.
Gregorich, Barbara, ed. see Schneider, Rex.
Gregorich, Barbara, ed. see Simon, Shirley.
Gregorie, Caroline. Patate Horreur. 1994. write for info. (*0-8050-3300-9*) H Holt & Co.
Gregorio, Frank, ed. see Vuillequez, Richard J. & Veslocki, Matthew.
Gregorowski, Christopher. Bible for Young People. (gr. 3 up). 1990. 6.98 (*1-55521-588-2*) Bk Sales Inc.
Gregory, Cynthia. Cynthia Gregory Dances Swan Lake. Swope, Martha, illus. 48p. (gr. 3-7). 1990. pap. 14.95 jacketed (*0-671-68786-7*, S&S BFYR) S&S Trade.
Gregory, David. The Chappell Recorder Book. (gr. 4-12). 1992. pap. 11.95 (*0-237-60280-6*, Pub. by Evans Bros Ltd) Trafalgar.
Gregory, Diana. Two's a Crowd. 144p. (Orig.). (gr. 6 up). 1985. pap. 2.25 (*0-553-24992-4*) Bantam.
Gregory, Elizabeth. Alfred's Alphabet Antics. (Illus.). 1981. 6.95 (*0-933184-07-7*); pap. 4.95 (*0-933184-08-5*) Flame Intl.
—Beach Colors & Beach Creatures. (Illus.). 1981. 6.95 (*0-933184-17-4*); pap. 5.50 (*0-933184-18-2*) Flame Intl.
—Blinky & the Blends. (Illus.). 1981. 6.95 (*0-933184-11-5*); pap. 4.95 (*0-933184-12-3*) Flame Intl.
—The Short & Long. (Illus.). 1981. 6.95 (*0-933184-09-3*); pap. 4.95 (*0-933184-10-7*) Flame Intl.
Gregory, G., et al, eds. see Jagen, Edward J.
Gregory, Hugh. Soul Music A-Z. (Illus.). 288p. (gr. 10-12). 1992. pap. 14.95 (*0-7137-2183-9*, Pub. by Blandford Pr UK) Sterling.
Gregory, Isabella. Irish Legends for Children. (Illus.). 90p. (ps-8). 1983. pap. 5.95 (*0-85342-691-0*, Pub. by Mercier Press Ltd Eire) Dufour.
Gregory, Isabella A. Irish Legends for Children. 1991. pap. 10.95 (*0-85342-920-0*) Dufour.
Gregory, Justina, tr. see Levine, David.
Gregory, K. Earthquake at Dawn. 1992. 15.95 (*0-15-200446-7*, HB Juv Bks) HarBrace.
Gregory, Kim. Case at Hand. Marks, Theresa, illus. LC 91-93065. 36p. (Orig.). (ps-3). 1992. pap. text ed. 10.98 incl. wristband with interchangeable snap-on theme lids (*9-6630898-0-3*) K T Kids.
Gregory, Kristiana. Legend of Jimmy Spoon. 182p. (gr. 3-7). 1991. pap. 4.95 (*0-15-243812-2*, HB Juv Bks) HarBrace.
Gregory, Kristiana. Jenny of the Tetons. 119p. (gr. 3-7). 1989. 13.95 (*0-15-200480-7*) HarBrace.
—Legend of Jimmy Spoon. 165p. (gr. 3-7). 1990. 15.95 (*0-15-200506-4*) HarBrace.
Gregory, Kristina. Jenny of the Tetons. 140p. (gr. 3-7). 1991. pap. 4.95 (*0-15-200481-5*, HB Juv Bks) HarBrace.
Gregory, Patrick, tr. see Levine, David.
Gregory, Paul. Baseball & Softball. (Illus.). 80p. (gr. 10-12). 1992. pap. 6.95 (*0-7063-6667-0*, Pub. by Ward Lock UK) Sterling.
Gregory, Philippa. Florizella & the Wolves. Aggs, Patrice, illus. LC 92-52998. 80p. (gr. 3-6). 1993. 13.95 (*1-56402-126-2*) Candlewick Pr.
Gregory, Ross. America 1914 to 1945. Balkin, Rick, ed. (Illus.). 300p. (gr. 5-10). 1994. 35.00 (*0-8160-2532-0*) Facts on File.

Gregory, Stephen. Bobsledding: Down the Chute! new ed. LC 75-23407. (Illus.). 32p. (gr. 5-10). 1976. PLB 10.79 (*0-89375-002-6*); pap. 2.95 (*0-89375-018-2*) Troll Assocs.
—Racing to Win: The Salt Flats. new ed. LC 75-21845. (Illus.). (gr. 5-10). 1976. PLB 10.79 (*0-89375-010-7*) Troll Assocs.
Gregory, Tony. The Dark Ages. LC 91-43093. (Illus.). 80p. (gr. 2-6). 1993. 17.95x (*0-8160-2787-0*) Facts on File.
Gregory, Valiska. Babysitting for Benjamin. Munsinger, Lynn, illus. LC 92-18373. 32p. (ps-3). 1993. 13.95 (*0-316-32785-9*) Little.
—Happy Burpday, Maggie McDougal! Porter, Pat, illus. 64p. (gr. 2-4). 1992. 11.95 (*0-316-32777-8*) Little.
—Through the Mickle Woods. (ps-3). 1992. 15.95 (*0-316-32779-4*) Little.
—The Words Like Angels Come. 40p. (Orig.). (gr. 7 up). 1987. o. p. 25.00 (*1-55780-093-6*); pap. 6.00 (*1-55780-095-2*) Juniper Pr WI.
Gregson, Bob. Incredible Indoor Games Book: One Hundred & Sixty Group Projects, Games, & Activities. LC 82-81983. (gr. k-12). 1982. pap. 14.95 (*0-8224-0765-5*) Fearon Teach Aids.
—Outrageous Outdoor Games. LC 83-62564. (gr. k-12). 1984. pap. 14.95 (*0-8224-5099-2*) Fearon Teach Aids.
—Take Part Art. (gr. 3-6). 1990. pap. 14.95 (*0-8224-6781-X*) Fearon Teach Aids.
Grehan, Ida. Irish Family Names. Bailey, Karen, illus. 96p. (Orig.). 1985. pap. 7.95 (*0-86281-133-3*, Pub. by Appletree Pr ER) Irish Bks Media.
Greidanus, Aad. Two Pails of Water. (gr. 1-7). 1965. 4.50 (*0-87602-215-8*) Anchorage.
Greinke, Pamylle & King, Lise. Jacqueline & the Beanstalk. LC 83-63250. (Illus.). 64p. (ps-7). 1984. pap. 5.95 (*0-932966-52-7*) Permanent Pr.
Greisman, Joan. First Dictionary. (ps-3). 1990. pap. write for info. (*0-307-15853-5*) Western Pub.
Greisman, Joan, jt. auth. see Wittels, Harriet.
Greisman, Joan, jt. auth. see Wittles, Harriet.
Greison, Betty, et al. Black Hawk & Jim Thorp: Super Heroes; Sauk Indian Stories for Children. (gr. 5-12). 1983. pap. 4.95 (*0-89992-085-3*) Coun India Ed.
Grejniec, Michael. Good Morning, Good Night. Grejniec, Michael, illus. LC 92-23530. 32p. (gr. k-3). 1993. 14.95 (*1-55858-173-1*); lib. bdg. 14.88 (*1-55858-174-X*) North-South Bks NYC.
—Look. Grejniec, Michael, illus. LC 93-16066. 32p. (gr. k-3). 1993. 14.95 (*1-55858-212-6*); PLB 14.88 (*1-55858-213-4*) North-South Bks NYC.
—What Do You Like? Grejniec, Michael, illus. LC 92-3481. 32p. (gr. k). 1992. 14.95 (*1-55858-175-8*); PLB 14.88 (*1-55858-176-6*) North-South Bks NYC.
Grenier, Nicolas. Following Indian Trails. Grant, Donald, illus. LC 87-34597. 38p. (gr. k-5). 1988. 4.95 (*0-944589-09-X*, 09X) Young Discovery Lib.
Grenquist, Barbara. Cubans. LC 90-12984. (Illus.). 64p. (gr. 5-10). 1991. 13.40 (*0-531-11107-5*) Watts.
Gresko, Bernatta. How Do You Spell...? English Only. Gresko, Bernetta, illus. 44p. (gr. 2-8). 1987. pap. 4.95 (*0-939755-11-4*); wkbk. act sheets 4.95 (*0-939755-14-9*); wkbk. crossword puzzles 4.95 (*0-939755-06-8*) Sunset Prods.
—How Do You Spell...? English to Spanish. Gresko, Bernetta, tr. & illus. 44p. (gr. 2-8). 1987. pap. 4.95 (*0-939755-12-2*); wkbk. 4.95 (*0-939755-13-0*) Sunset Prods.
—One-a-Day Writeamins. Gresko, Beinetta, illus. 34p. 1987. pap. 4.95 (*0-939755-15-7*) Sunset Prods.
—Sound It Out. Gresko, Bernetta, illus. 75p. (gr. 2-8). 1985. pap. 8.95 (*0-939755-10-6*) Sunset Prods.
—Writing Verbs. Gresko, Bernetta, illus. 48p. 1982. wkbk. 4.95 (*0-939755-09-2*) Sunset Prods.
Gress, Jonna, ed. see Arkow, Phil.
Gress, Jonna, ed. see Doray, Andrea.
Gress, Jonna, ed. see Kuyper, Vicki J.
Gress, Jonna, ed. see McConnell, Nancy P.
Gress, Jonna, ed. see Rayburn, Cherie.
Gress, Jonna, ed. see Rhoda, Michael D.
Gress, Jonna C., ed. see Doray, Andrea.
Gretchen, Sylvia, ed. & tr. from TIB. Hero of the Land of Snow. Witwer, Julia, illus. LC 89-25603. vi, 32p. (gr. 5-8). 1990. 14.95 (*0-89800-201-X*); pap. 7.95 (*0-89800-202-8*) Dharma Pub.
Gretz, Susanna. Duck Takes Off. Gretz, Susanna, illus. LC 90-3846. 32p. (ps-1). 1991. RSBE 12.95 (*0-02-737472-6*, Four Winds) Macmillan Child Grp.
—Frog, Duck & Rabbit. Gretz, Susanna, illus. LC 91-16364. 32p. (ps-1). 1992. SBE 12.95 (*0-02-737327-4*, Four Winds) Macmillan Child Grp.
—Frog in the Middle. Gretz, Susanna, illus. LC 90-3842. 32p. (ps-1). 1991. RSBE 12.95 (*0-02-737471-8*, Four Winds) Macmillan Child Grp.
—Rabbit Rambles On. Gretz, Susanna, illus. LC 91-17069. 32p. (ps-1). 1992. SBE 12.95 (*0-02-737325-8*, Four Winds) Macmillan Child Grp.
—Roger Loses His Marbles. Gretz, Susanna, illus. LC 88-3753. 32p. (ps-2). 1988. 11.95 (*0-8037-0565-4*) Dial Bks Young.
—Roger Loses His Marbles! Gretz, Susanna, illus. 32p. (ps-2). 1991. pap. 3.95 (*0-8037-0986-2*, Dial Pied Piper) Puffin Bks.
—Roger Takes Charge! LC 86-24061. (Illus.). 32p. (ps-2). 1987. 12.95 (*0-8037-0121-7*) Dial Bks Young.
—Roger Takes Charge. 1990. pap. 3.95 (*0-8037-0742-8*, Dial Pied Piper) Puffin Bks.

—Teddy Bears ABC. Gretz, Susanna, illus. LC 86-4742. 32p. (ps-k). 1986. RSBE 13.95 (*0-02-738130-7*, Four Winds) Macmillan Child Grp.
—Teddy Bears Cure a Cold. Sage, Alison, illus. LC 84-4015. 40p. (gr. k-3). 1985. RSBE 13.95 (*0-02-736960-9*, Four Winds) Macmillan Child Grp.
—Teddy Bears Cure a Cold. Sage, Alison, illus. 32p. (ps-2). 1986. pap. 3.95 (*0-590-43495-0*) Scholastic Inc.
—Teddy Bears Go Shopping. Gretz, Susanna, illus. LC 85-4494. 32p. (gr. k-3). 1984. RSBE 13.95 (*0-02-737310-X*, Four Winds) Macmillan Child Grp.
—Teddy Bears' Moving Day. Gretz, Susanna, illus. LC 88-10365. 32p. (gr. k-3). 1988. pap. 3.95 (*0-689-71269-3*, Aladdin) Macmillan Child Grp.
—Teddy Bears Stay Indoors. Gretz, Susanna, illus. LC 86-19511. 32p. (gr. k-3). 1987. SBE 13.95 (*0-02-738150-1*, Four Winds) Macmillan Child Grp.
—Teddy Bears Take the Train. Gretz, Susanna, illus. LC 87-8572. 32p. (gr. k-3). 1988. SBE 13.95 (*0-02-738170-6*, Four Winds) Macmillan Child Grp.
—Teddy Bears 1 to 10. Gretz, Susanna, illus. LC 86-4795. 32p. (ps-k). 1986. RSBE 13.95 (*0-02-738140-4*, Four Winds) Macmillan Child Grp.
Gretz, Susanna & Sage, Alison. Teddy Bears at the Seaside. Gretz, Susanna, illus. LC 88-11280. 32p. (gr. k-3). 1989. SBE 12.95 (*0-02-738141-2*, Four Winds) Macmillan Child Grp.
Greuel, David P., ed. Anthology of Advanced Placement French Literature: For the 1992 Exam. (FRE.). 408p. (Orig.). (gr. 11-12). 1991. pap. text ed. 17.27 (*1-877653-14-4*) Wayside Pub.
Greve, Andreas. Christopher's Dream Car. Greve, Andreas, illus. 32p. (gr. 1-3). 1991. PLB 15.95 (*1-55037-169-X*, Pub. by Annick CN); pap. 5.95 (*1-55037-166-5*, Pub. by Annick CN) Firefly Bks Ltd.
Grewar, Mindy, ed. see AIT Staff.
Grewe, Georgeann & Glover, Susanne. Calendar Companions for Fall. Grewe, Georgeann, illus. 128p. (gr. 1-6). 1984. wkbk. 11.95 (*0-317-43005-X*, GA 534) Good Apple.
—Calendar Companions for Spring. Grewe, Georgeann, illus. 128p. (gr. 1-6). 1984. wkbk. 11.95 (*0-86653-171-8*, GA 536) Good Apple.
—Calendar Companions for Winter. Grewe, Georgeann, illus. 128p. (gr. 1-6). 1984. wkbk. 11.95 (*0-86653-168-8*, GA 535) Good Apple.
—Motivational Units for Fall. 144p. (gr. 2-6). 1990. 11.95 (*0-86653-543-8*, GA1146) Good Apple.
—Motivational Units for Spring. (Illus.). 144p. (gr. 2-6). 1990. 11.95 (*0-86653-524-1*, GA1145) Good Apple.
Grewe, Georgeann, jt. auth. see Glover, Susanne.
Grey, Alan. Sitting Bull. Hagar, Ashley, illus. 64p. (gr. k-6). 1993. pap. 9.95 (*1-56883-015-7*) Colonial Pr AL.
—Sitting Bull. Hagar, Ashley, illus. 64p. Date not set. pap. 9.95 (*1-56883-031-9*) Colonial Pr AL.
Grey, Charlotte. Bob Geldof: Champion of Africa's Hungry People. Adrian-Vallance, D'Arcy, adapted by. LC 89-77588. (Illus.). 64p. (gr. 3-4). 1990. PLB 18.60 (*0-8368-0391-4*) Gareth Stevens Inc.
Grey, Edward. The Eighties. LC 89-27178. (Illus.). 48p. (gr. 5-9). 1990. PLB 19.92 (*0-8114-4215-2*) Raintree Steck-V.
—The Sixties. LC 89-21618. (Illus.). 48p. (gr. 5-9). 1990. PLB 19.92 (*0-8114-4213-6*) Raintree Steck-V.
Grey, Harry. The Hoods. 1987. Repr. lib. bdg. 35.95x (*0-89966-549-7*) Buccaneer Bks.
Grey, J. The Turtle Who Wanted to Run. LC 68-56813. (Illus.). 32p. (gr. 1-3). 1968. PLB 9.95 (*0-87783-045-2*) Oddo.
Grey, Judith. Mud Pies. Sims, Deborah, illus. LC 81-4042. 32p. (gr. k-2). 1981. PLB 11.59 (*0-89375-541-9*); pap. 2.95 (*0-89375-542-7*) Troll Assocs.
—What Time Is It? Hall, Susan, illus. LC 81-5113. 32p. (gr. k-2). 1981. PLB 11.59 (*0-89375-509-5*); pap. text ed. 2.95 (*0-89375-510-9*) Troll Assocs.
—Yummy, Yummy. Goodman, Joan E., illus. LC 81-2360. 32p. (gr. k-2). 1981. PLB 11.59 (*0-89375-543-5*); pap. 2.95 (*0-89375-544-3*) Troll Assocs.
Grey, Zane. The Shortstop. Thorn, John, frwd. by. LC 91-24034. 240p. (gr. 7 up). 1992. Repr. of 1909 ed. 13.00 (*0-688-11088-6*) Morrow Jr Bks.
—The Shortstop. LC 91-24034. 240p. (gr. 7 up). 1992. pap. 4.95 (*0-688-11261-7*, Pub. by Beech Tree Bks) Morrow.
—The Young Pitcher. Thorn, John, frwd. by. LC 91-23670. 256p. (gr. 7 up). 1992. Repr. of 1911 ed. 13.00 (*0-688-11090-8*) Morrow Jr Bks.
—The Young Pitcher. LC 91-23670. 256p. (gr. 7 up). 1992. pap. 4.95 (*0-688-11262-5*, Pub. by Beech Tree Bks) Morrow.
—Zane Grey Famous Fishing Library. 2nd ed. (gr. 10 up). 1991-92. Set. 350.00 (*1-56416-075-0*) Tales of Tahitian Waters, 303p (*1-56416-076-9*) Tales of Fishing Virgin Seas, 216p (*1-56416-077-7*) Tales of Fresh Water Fishing (*1-56416-078-5*) Tales of Angler's Eldorado (*1-56416-079-3*) Tales of Swordfish & Tuna (*1-56416-080-7*) Derrydale Pr.
Greydanus, Rose. Animals at the Zoo. Hall, Susan T., illus. 32p. (gr. k-2). 1980. PLB 7.89 (*0-89375-371-8*); pap. 1.95 (*0-89375-271-1*) Troll Assocs.
—Bedtime Story. Cushman, Doug, illus. LC 86-30858. 32p. (gr. k-2). 1988. PLB 7.89 (*0-89375-0996-3*); pap. text ed. 1.95 (*0-8167-0997-1*) Troll Assocs.
—Big Red Fire Engine. Harvey, Paul, illus. 32p. (gr. k-2). 1980. PLB 7.89 (*0-89375-372-6*); pap. 1.95 (*0-89375-272-X*) Troll Assocs.

—Un Carro De Bomberos Grande y Rojo. Harvey, Paul, illus. (SPA.). 32p. (gr. k-2). 1981. PLB 7.89 *(0-89375-555-9)*; pap. 1.95 *(0-685-04944-2)* Troll Assocs.
—Changing Seasons. Hall, Susan, illus. LC 82-19959. 32p. (gr. k-2). 1983. PLB 11.59 *(0-89375-902-3)*; pap. 2.95 *(0-8167-1478-9)* Troll Assocs.
—Climb Aboard. Ulrich, George, illus. LC 87-19150. 32p. (gr. k-2). 1988. PLB 11.59 *(0-8167-1099-6)*; pap. text ed. 2.95 *(0-8167-1100-3)* Troll Assocs.
—Double Trouble. Rodegast, Roland, illus. LC 81-2358. 32p. (gr. k-2). 1981. PLB 11.59 *(0-89375-529-X)*; pap. 2.95 *(0-89375-530-3)* Troll Assocs.
—Federiquito el Sapo. Garcia, Tom, illus. (SPA.). 32p. (gr. k-2). 1981. PLB 7.89 *(0-89375-549-4)*; pap. 1.95 *(0-685-04947-7)* Troll Assocs.
—Freddie the Frog. (Illus.). 32p. (gr. k-2). 1980. PLB 7.89 *(0-89375-376-9)*; pap. 1.95 *(0-89375-276-2)* Troll Assocs.
—Hocus Pocus, Magic Show! Goodman, Joan, illus. LC 81-2637. 32p. (gr. k-2). 1981. PLB 11.59 *(0-89375-539-7)*; pap. text ed. 2.95 *(0-89375-540-0)* Troll Assocs.
—Horses. Snyder, Joel, illus. LC 82-20296. 32p. (gr. k-2). 1983. lib. bdg. 11.59 *(0-89375-900-7)*; pap. 2.95 *(0-8167-1479-7)* Troll Assocs.
—Let's Get a Pet. Sweat, Lynn, illus. LC 87-10938. 32p. (gr. k-2). 1988. PLB 7.89 *(0-8167-0986-6)*; pap. text ed. 1.95 *(0-8167-0987-4)* Troll Assocs.
—Let's Pretend. Winborn, Marsha, illus. LC 81-2357. 32p. (gr. k-2). 1981. PLB 11.59 *(0-89375-545-1)*; pap. text ed. 2.95 *(0-89375-546-X)* Troll Assocs.
—Mike's New Bike. Sims, Deborah, illus. 32p. (gr. k-2). 1980. PLB 7.89 *(0-89375-382-3)*; pap. 1.95 *(0-89375-282-7)* Troll Assocs.
—My Secret Hiding Place. Harvey, Paul, illus. 32p. (gr. k-2). 1980. PLB 7.89 *(0-89375-383-1)*; pap. 1.95 *(0-89375-283-5)* Troll Assocs.
—Susie Goes Shopping. Apple, Margot, illus. 32p. (gr. k-2). 1980. PLB 7.89 *(0-89375-389-0)*; pap. 1.95 *(0-89375-289-4)* Troll Assocs.
—Tree House Fun. Demarest, Chris, illus. 32p. (gr. k-2). 1980. PLB 7.89 *(0-89375-391-2)*; pap. 1.95 *(0-89375-291-6)* Troll Assocs.
—Trouble in Space. Page, Don, illus. LC 81-5114. 32p. (gr. k-2). 1981. PLB 11.59 *(0-89375-517-6)*; pap. text ed. 2.95 *(0-89375-518-4)* Troll Assocs.
—Valentine's Day Grump. Page, Don, illus. LC 81-4712. 32p. (gr. k-2). 1981. PLB 11.59 *(0-89375-515-X)*; pap. text ed. 2.95 *(0-89375-516-8)* Troll Assocs.
—Willie the Slowpoke. Eberbach, Andrea, illus. 32p. (gr. k-2). 1980. PLB 7.89 *(0-89375-394-7)*; pap. 1.95 *(0-89375-294-0)*; cassette 8.95 *(0-685-04954-X)* Troll Assocs.
Griego, Margo C., et al. Tortillitas Para Mama: And Other Nursery Rhymes, Spanish & English. LC 81-4823. (Illus.). 32p. (ps-2). 1981. pap. 5.95 *(0-8050-0317-7, Owlet BYR)* H Holt & Co.
—Tortillitas Para Mama: And Other Nursery Rhymes, Spanish & English. Cooney, Barbara, illus. LC 81-4823. 32p. (ps-2). 1981. 14.95 *(0-8050-0285-5, Bks Young Read)* H Holt & Co.
Grier, Paula. The Early Mexicans. (Illus.). 47p. (Orig.). (gr. 6-8). 1982. pap. text ed. 14.95 *(1-878550-03-9)* Inter Dev Res Assn.
Griesbach, Ellen & Taylor, Jerry. The Prentice-Hall Encyclopedia of Mathematics. Taylor, Louis, ed. (Illus., Orig.). (gr. 6 up). 1982. 39.50 *(0-13-696013-8)* P-H.
Grifalcon, Ann. Flyaway Girl. (ps-3). 1992. 15.95 *(0-316-32866-9)* Little.
Grifalconi, Ann. Darkness & the Butterfly. Grifalconi, Ann, illus. 32p. (ps-3). 1987. 15.95 *(0-316-32863-4)* Little.
—Kinda Blue. Grifalconi, Ann, illus. (ps-3). 1993. 15.95 *(0-316-32869-3)* Little.
—Osa's Pride, Vol. 1. Grifalconi, Ann, illus. (ps-3). 1990. 15.95 *(0-316-32865-0)* Little.
—Village of Round & Square Houses. Grifalconi, Ann, illus. 32p. (gr. k-3). 1986. lib. bdg. 15.95 *(0-316-32862-6)* Little.
Griffey, Harriet. Birthday Time: Toddler's World. King, Colin, illus. 28p. (ps-1). 1992. 3.50 *(0-7214-1479-6, 928-2)* Ladybird Bks.
Griffin. Building English Skills. large type ed. Incl. Pink Level, 2 vols. 332p. (gr. 1). 1984. 64.59 *(0-317-02117-6, 4-03210-00)*; Plum Level, 2 vols. 442p. (gr. 2). 1985. 79.32 *(0-317-02118-4, 4-03220-00)*. Am Printing Hse.
Griffin, Arthur E., ed. Ah Mo: Indian Legends from Washington State. Malin, Edward, illus. 75p. (Orig.). (gr. 2-5). 1989. pap. write for info. Bainbridge Pr.
—The Legend of Tom Pepper & Other Stories. Malin, Edward, illus. 100p. (Orig.). (gr. 2-5). 1989. pap. write for info. Bainbridge Pr.
—Spelyi & Other Indian Legends. Malin, Edward, illus. (gr. 2-5). 1989. write for info. Bainbridge Pr.
Griffin, Clive. Classical Music. (Illus.). 64p. (gr. 7-9). 1988. 19.95 *(0-85219-756-X, Pub. by Batsford UK)* Trafalgar.
Griffin, Elizabeth, jt. auth. see Griffin, Steven.
Griffin, Frank W., jt. auth. see Smith, Sanderson M.
Griffin, Gail. An Afternoon at Emmi's. Eagle, Mike, illus. 24p. (Orig.). (ps). 1992. pap. text ed. 3.00x *(1-56134-163-0)* Dushkin Pub.

Griffin, Gail M. Una Tarde en la Casa de Emmi. Writer, C. C. & Nielsen, Lisa C., trs. Eagle, Mike, illus. (SPA.). 24p. (Orig.). (ps) 1992. pap. text ed. 3.00x *(1-56134-173-8)* Dushkin Pub.
Griffin, Georgene, illus. How to Draw Fantasy Creatures. 48p. 1992. pap. 2.95 *(1-56156-144-4)* Kidsbks.
Griffin, Henry W. Jesus for Children. Swisher, Elizabeth, illus. 132p. 1986. 12.95 *(0-685-43036-7)*; pap. 7.95 *(0-86683-866-X)* Harper SF.
Griffin, James D., Jr., ed. see Bailey, John B.
Griffin, Jeannie. Seven Key Scriptures to Lead Someone to the Lord. 128p. (Orig.). (gr. 12). 1990. pap. 5.00 *(0-9625016-3-8)* Jeannie Griffin.
Griffin, John H. Black Like Me. 160p. (gr. 8). 1962. pap. 3.95 *(0-451-15530-0, Sig)* NAL-Dutton.
—Black Like Me. 160p. (gr. 9-12). 1962. pap. 4.99 *(0-451-16317-6, Sig)* NAL-Dutton.
Griffin, John Q. Motorcycles on the Move. LC 75-17435. (Illus.). 52p. (gr. 4-9). 1976. PLB 14.95 *(0-8225-0414-6)* Lerner Pubns.
Griffin, Judith B. Phoebe the Spy. (gr. 4-6). 1979. pap. 1.50 *(0-590-05758-8)* Scholastic Inc.
—Phoebe the Spy. 48p. (gr. 3-6). 1991. pap. 2.75 *(0-590-42432-7)* Scholastic Inc.
Griffin, Kimbra, ed. see Farquhar, Kristin.
Griffin, Michael. A Family in Kenya. (Illus.). 32p. (gr. 2-5). 1988. lib. bdg. 13.50 *(0-8225-1680-2)* Lerner Pubns.
Griffin, Peggy A. The Big Ten. 1986. write for info. wkbk. *(1-884056-00-8)* Scribes Pubns.
—Uphill Downhill. 1993. pap. text ed. write for info. *(1-884056-01-6)* Scribes Pubns.
Griffin, Peni R. The Brick House Burglars. LC 93-22914. 144p. (gr. 4-7). 1994. SBE 14.95 *(0-689-50579-5, M K McElderry)* Macmillan Child Grp.
—A Dig in Time. LC 90-47388. 192p. (gr. 4-7). 1991. SBE 14.95 *(0-689-50525-6, M K McElderry)* Macmillan Child Grp.
—A Dig in Time. LC 92-18958. 160p. (gr. 3-7). 1992. pap. 3.99 *(0-14-036001-8)* Puffin Bks.
—Hobkin LC 91-24079. 208p. (gr. 4-7). 1992. SBE 14.95 *(0-689-50539-6, M K McElderry)* Macmillan Child Grp.
—Hobkin. 93-7758. 208p. (gr. 3-7). 1993. pap. 3.99 *(0-14-036356-4, Puffin)* Puffin Bks.
—Otto from Otherwhere. LC 89-38026. (ps). 1990. SBE 14.95 *(0-689-50500-0, M K McElderry)* Macmillan Child Grp.
—The Switching Well. LC 92-38442. 224p. (gr. 5-9). 1993. SBE 15.95 *(0-689-50581-7, M K McElderry)* Macmillan Child Grp.
—The Treasure Bird. Gowing, Toby, illus. LC 91-42773. 144p. (gr. 4-7). 1992. SBE 13.95 *(0-689-50554-X, M K McElderry)* Macmillan Child Grp.
Griffin, Ralph G., ed. see Church, J. R.
Griffin, Robert J., Jr. The Department of Commerce. (Illus.). 104p. (gr. 5 up). 1991. 14.95 *(0-87754-836-6)* Chelsea Hse.
Griffin, Sandi Z. Becca Bumbum Bunny, Vol. 3: Tails with a Moral. Griffin, Sandi Z., illus. 28p. (ps-2). 1993. write for info. *(1-883838-03-7)* S Z Griffin.
—Curly Pig, Vol. 2: Tails with a Moral. Griffin, Sandi Z., illus. 28p. (ps-2). 1993. write for info. *(1-883838-02-9)* S Z Griffin.
—Lumpa Lou Elephant, Vol. I: Tails with a Moral. Griffin, Sandi Z., illus. 28p. (ps-2). 1993. write for info. *(1-883838-01-0)* S Z Griffin.
Griffin, Sandra U. Earth Circles. Griffin, Sandra U., illus. 32p. (ps-3). 1989. 12.95 *(0-8027-6843-1)*; PLB 13.85 *(0-8027-6845-8)* Walker & Co.
Griffin, Steve. Children's Guitar Hymnal. 32p. (gr. 4-10). 1978. wkbk. 2.95 *(0-89228-052-2)* Impact Bks MO.
Griffin, Steven & Griffin, Elizabeth. Fishing for Kids. Linder, Greg, illus. (ps-6). 1993. pap. 6.95 *(1-55971-145-0)* NorthWord.
Griffin, Susan, jt. auth. see Enselek, Patricia.
Griffin, Ted, ed. see Rue, Nancy.
Griffin, Ted, ed. see Stahl, Hilda.
Griffis, Molly L., ed. see Ferguson, Elva S.
Griffis, Molly L., ed. see Jackson, Robert B.
Griffith, Connie. Mysterious Rescuer. LC 93-8421. 1993. write for info. *(0-8010-3865-0)* Baker Bk.
—Secret Behind Locked Doors. LC 93-8420. 1993. write for info. *(0-8010-3864-2)* Baker Bk.
—Surprise at Logan School. 128p. (Orig.). (gr. 6-9). 1993. pap. 4.99 *(0-8010-3866-1)* Baker Bk.
—The Unexpected Weapon. 128p. (Orig.). (gr. 6-9). 1993. pap. 4.99 *(0-8010-3858-8)* Baker Bk.
Griffith, Helen. Georgia Music. Stevenson, James, illus. LC 85-24918. (Illus.). 32p. (ps-3). 1986. 13.95 *(0-688-06071-4)*; PLB 13.88 *(0-688-06072-2)* Greenwillow.
Griffith, Helen V. Alex & the Cat. Low, Joseph, illus. LC 81-11608. 64p. (gr. 1-3). 1982. 13.95 *(0-688-00420-2)*; PLB 13.88 *(0-688-00421-0)* Greenwillow.
—Caitlin's Holiday. Lamb, Susan C., illus. LC 89-27228. 96p. (gr. 1 up). 1990. 12.95 *(0-688-09470-8)* Greenwillow.
—Doll Trouble. Lamb, Susan C., illus. LC 92-31510. 128p. (gr. 3 up). 1993. 13.00 *(0-688-12421-6)* Greenwillow.
—Dream Meadow. Barnet, Nancy, illus. LC 93-18175. 24p. (ps up). 1994. write for info. *(0-688-12293-0)*; PLB write for info. *(0-688-12294-9)* Greenwillow.
—Emily & the Enchanted Frog. Lamb, Susan C., illus. LC 88-16511. 32p. (gr. 1 up). 1989. 12.95 *(0-688-08483-4)*; PLB 12.88 *(0-688-08484-2)* Greenwillow.

—Foxy. LC 83-16392. 144p. (gr. 5-9). 1984. reinforced 11.95 *(0-688-02567-6)* Greenwillow.
—Georgia Music. Stevenson, James, illus. LC 85-24918. 24p. (ps-2). 1990. pap. 3.95 *(0-688-09931-9, Mulberry)* Morrow.
—Grandaddy & Janetta. Stevenson, James, illus. LC 91-47707. 32p. (gr. k up). 1993. 14.00 *(0-688-11226-9)*; PLB 13.93 *(0-688-11227-7)* Greenwillow.
—Grandaddy's Place. Stevenson, James, illus. LC 86-19573. 40p. (gr. 1-4). 1987. 13.95 *(0-688-06253-9)*; PLB 13.88 *(0-688-06254-7)* Greenwillow.
—Grandaddy's Place. Stevenson, James, illus. LC 86-19573. 40p. (ps-3). 1991. pap. 4.95 *(0-688-10491-6, Mulberry)* Morrow.
—Journal of a Teenage Genius. (gr. 3-7). 1987. 11.75 *(0-688-07226-7)* Greenwillow.
—Journal of a Teenage Genius. 128p. (gr. 7 up). 1988. pap. 2.50 *(0-8167-1325-1)* Troll Assocs.
—Mine Will, Said John. Smith, J. A., illus. LC 91-32476. 32p. (ps-8). 1992. 14.00 *(0-688-10957-8)*; PLB 13.93 *(0-688-10958-6)* Greenwillow.
—Plunk's Dreams. LC 88-34905. (Illus.). 32p. (ps up). 1990. 12.95 *(0-688-08812-0)*; lib. bdg. 12.88 *(0-688-08813-9)* Greenwillow.
Griffith, Linda. Sleeping Beauty: Perform Your Very Own Ballet a Book, Tiara, Poster, & Audiotape. (Illus.). 36p. 1993. incl. 90-min. audiotape 16.95 *(0-8362-4215-7)* Andrews & McMeel.
Griffith, Neysa. The Magic of Green. Duarte, Steven, illus. LC 93-34811. 1994. 4.95 *(1-56844-028-6)* Enchante Pub.
—The Magic of Orange. Duarte, Steven, illus. LC 93-35439. 1994. 4.95 *(1-56844-026-X)* Enchante Pub.
—The Magic of Red. Duarte, Steven, illus. LC 93-34813. 1994. 4.95 *(1-56844-025-1)* Enchante Pub.
—The Magic of Yellow. Duarte, Steven, illus. LC 93-34812. 1994. 4.95 *(1-56844-027-8)* Enchante Pub.
Griffith, Reva. This Song's for You. LC 92-74144. (Illus.). 240p. (Orig.). (gr. 9-12). 1993. pap. 14.95 *(0-923687-23-8)* Celo Valley Bks.
Griffiths, Barbara. Frankenstein's Hamster: Ten Spine-Tingling Tales. (gr. 4-7). 1992. 15.00 *(0-8037-0952-8)* Dial Bks Young.
Griffiths, I. Crisis in South Africa. (Illus.). 80p. (gr. 7 up). 1988. PLB 18.60 *(0-86592-035-4)* Rourke Corp.
Griffiths, J. Conflict in Afghanistan. (Illus.). 80p. (gr. 7 up). 1988. PLB 18.60 *(0-86592-039-7)* Rourke Corp.
—Crisis in Central America. (Illus.). 80p. (gr. 7 up). 1988. PLB 18.60 *(0-86592-034-6)* Rourke Corp.
Griffiths, John. The Caribbean. LC 88-28782. (Illus.). 48p. (gr. 5-6). 1989. PLB 13.90 *(0-531-18274-6)* Watts.
—The Last Day in Saigon. 64p. (gr. 6-8). 1987. 19.95 *(0-85219-671-7, Pub. by Batsford UK)* Trafalgar.
—Take a Trip to Panama. LC 89-8929. (Illus.). 32p. (gr. 3-5). 1989. PLB 10.90 *(0-531-10736-1)* Watts.
Grifoni, Maria C., tr. see Mahoney, Judy.
Grigas, Denise. Articu-ACTION. Grigas, Denise, illus. 144p. (ps-6). 1993. tchr's. ed. 14.95 *(0-937857-37-8, 1524)* Speech Bin.
Griggs, John & Barbosa-Lima, Carlos. Christmas Album. Stang, Aaron, ed. 40p. (Orig.). 1993. pap. text ed. 9.95 *(0-89898-641-9)* CPP Belwin.
Grillis, Carla. Animals. (Illus.). (ps). 1988. bds. 5.50 *(0-86315-072-1, 20232)* Gryphon Hse.
—Flowers of the Seasons. (Illus.). 12p. (ps). 1990. bds. 5.95 *(0-86315-088-8, 1362, Pub. by Floris Bks UK)* Anthroposophic.
Grimaldi, Alicia, ed. Education for the Earth: A Guide to the Top Environmental Studies Programs. LC 92-33025. 192p. (Orig.). 1992. pap. 10.95 *(1-56079-164-0)* Petersons Guides.
—Internships 1993: Fifty-Thousand-on-the-Job Training Opportunities for Students & Adults. 13th, rev. ed. 416p. 1992. pap. 28.95 *(1-56079-149-7)* Petersons Guides.
Grimaldi, Alicia, ed. see Curless, Maura R.
Grimaldi, Alicia, ed. see Peterson, Linda.
Grimbol, William R. Why Should I Care? Honest Answers to the Questions That Trouble Teens. LC 88-7503. 144p. (Orig.). (gr. 8 up). 1988. pap. 9.99 *(0-8066-2363-2, 10-7176, Augsburg)* Augsburg Fortress.
Grimes, Bobbie M. The Parable of Jesus & Santa. Cooley, Nance, illus. LC 84-90331. 40p. (ps-5). 1984. 14.95 *(0-9613328-0-8)* B & D Pub.
Grimes, Frances H. Sweet Dreams: Love Lines, No. 154. (gr. 6 up). 1988. pap. 2.50 *(0-318-37112-X)* Bantam.
Grimes, Harriette H. & Knack, John W., Sr. Visual Aural Games Book. Reusable ed. (gr. 1-8). 1976. wkbk. 9.00 *(0-87879-756-4, Ann Arbor Div)* Acad Therapy.
Grimes, N. Oh, Bother! Someone's Baby-Sitting! Disney's Winnie the Pooh Helping Hands Book. DiCiccio, Sue, illus. 24p. (ps-k). 1991. pap. write for info. *(Golden Pr)* Western Pub.
Grimes, Nikki. From a Child's Heart. Joysmith, Brenda, illus. LC 93-79000. 32p. (gr. 2-6). 1993. 15.95 *(0-940975-44-0)*; pap. 7.95 *(0-940975-43-2)* Just Us Bks.
—Malcolm X: A Force for Change. (gr. 7 up). 1992. pap. 4.00 *(0-449-90803-8)* Fawcett.
—Meet Danitra Brown. Cooper, Floyd, illus. LC 92-43707. (gr. 4 up). 1995. write for info. *(0-688-12073-3)* *(0-688-12074-1)* Lothrop.
—Something on My Mind. Feelings, Tom, illus. LC 77-86266. 32p. (gr. k-4). 1986. pap. 4.95 *(0-8037-0273-6)* Dial Bks Young.

Grimes, Nikki, retold by. Walt Disney's Cinderella. Williams, Don & Story, Jim, illus. 24p. (ps-3). 1993. pap. 1.95 (*0-307-12684-6*, 12684, Golden Pr) Western Pub.

Grimes, Rich. Satchel Stories: Ammon's Courage. Hiller, Annie, ed. Grimes, Rich, illus. 4p. (ps) 1992. text ed. 8.95 (*0-9623915-0-6*) Jackson Pub.

—Satchel Stories: David & Goliath. Hiller, Annie, ed. Grimes, Rich, illus. 4p. (ps) 1992. text ed. 8.95 (*1-56713-002-X*) Jackson Pub.

—Satchel Stories: Dinosaurs. Hiller, Annie, ed. Grimes, Rich, illus. 4p. (ps) 1992. text ed. 8.95 (*1-56713-003-8*) Jackson Pub.

—Satchel Stories: Jesus Blessing the Children. Hiller, Annie, ed. Grimes, Rich, illus. 4p. (ps) 1992. text ed. 8.95 (*1-56713-001-1*) Jackson Pub.

—Satchel Stories: Laban's Sword. Hiller, Annie, ed. Grimes, Rich, illus. 4p. (ps) 1992. text ed. 8.95 (*0-9623915-8-1*) Jackson Pub.

—Satchel Stories: Nephi's Broken Bow. Hiller, Annie, ed. Grimes, Rich, illus. 4p. (ps) 1992. text ed. 8.95 (*1-56713-000-3*) Jackson Pub.

—Satchel Stories: The Brother of Jared. Hiller, Annie, ed. Grimes, Rich, illus. 4p. (ps) 1992. text ed. 8.95 (*0-9623915-9-X*) Jackson Pub.

—Satchel Stories: Whales. Hiller, Annie, ed. Grimes, Rich, illus. 4p. (ps). 1992. text ed. 8.95 (*1-56713-004-6*) Jackson Pub.

Grimley, Mildred H. Mattie Loves All. Wine, Jeanine M., illus. 22p. (gr. 1-5). 1985. 5.95 (*0-87178-552-8*) Brethren.

Grimm. Grimm's Fairy Tales. 1994. write for info. (*0-8050-3127-8*) H Holt & Co.

Grimm, Carol & Montgomery, Becky. T Is for Touching. (gr. k up). 1985. manual & 3-filmstrip series o.p. 79.00 (*0-317-40553-5*); manual & videotape one half inch 79.95 (*0-914633-09-0*); manual & videotape three quarter inch o.p. 95.00 (*0-914633-08-2*); write for info. manual *0-914633-05-8*) Rape Abuse Crisis.

Grimm, Gary & Mitchell, Don. Good Apple Creative Writing Book. 112p. (gr. 3-8). 1976. 9.95 (*0-916456-04-8*, GA61) Good Apple.

—Good Apple Math Book. 220p. (gr. 3-8). 1975. 14.95 (*0-916456-00-5*, GA59) Good Apple.

Grimm, Jacob. King Grisly-Beard. (ps-3). 1987. pap. 2.95 (*0-374-44049-2*) FS&G.

—The Shoemaker & the Elves. Adams, Adrienne, illus. Grimm, Wilhelm K. LC 60-12607. (Illus.). 32p. (ps-3). 1972. RSBE 13.95 (*0-684-12982-5*, Scribners Young Read) Macmillan Child Grp.

Grimm, Jacob & Grimm, Wilhelm K. About Wise Men & Simpletons: Twelve Tales from Grimm. Shub, Elizabeth, tr. Hogrogian, Nonny, illus. LC 85-15330. 128p. (gr. 4-6). 1986. SBE 14.95 (*0-02-737450-5*, Macmillan Child Bk) Macmillan Child Grp.

—Anno's Twice Told Tales: The Fisherman & His Wife & The Four Clever Brothers. Anno, Mitsumasa, retold by. & illus. LC 92-25307. 64p. (ps up) 1993. PLB 17.95 (*0-399-22005-4*, Philomel Bks) Putnam Pub Group.

—The Bear & the Bird King. Byrd, Robert, retold by. & illus. LC 93-15741. 32p. (ps-3). 1994. 14.99 (*0-525-45118-8*, DCB) Dutton Child Bks.

—Brave Little Tailor. Corcoran, Mark, illus. LC 78-18075. 32p. (gr. 1-4). 1979. PLB 9.79 (*0-89375-137-5*); pap. 1.95 (*0-89375-115-4*) Troll Assocs.

—The Brave Little Tailor. Bell, Anthea, tr. Tharlet, Eve, illus. LC 88-33367. 28p. (ps up). 1991. pap. 14.95 (*0-88708-091-X*) Picture Bk Studio.

—The Brave Little Tailor: A Classic Tale. Jose, Eduard, adapted by. Moncure, Jane B., tr. Rovira, Francesc, illus. LC 88-35311. 32p. (gr. 1-4). 1988. PLB 19.95 (*0-89565-460-1*); PLB 13.95s.p. (*0-685-56032-5*) Childs World.

—Bremen Town Musicians. Ford, Pamela B., illus. LC 78-18064. 32p. (gr. k-3). 1979. PLB 9.79 (*0-89375-133-2*); pap. 1.95 (*0-89375-111-1*) Troll Assocs.

—Bremen Town Musicians. Bell, Anthea, tr. Palecek, Josef, illus. LC 88-15179. 32p. (ps up). 1991. pap. 13.95 (*0-88708-071-5*) Picture Bk Studio.

—The Bremen Town Musicians. Easton, Samantha, retold by. Corcoran, Mark, illus. 1991. 6.95 (*0-8362-4925-9*) Andrews & McMeel.

—The Bremen Town Musicians. Watts, Bernadette, illus. Bell, Anthea, tr. from GER. LC 91-30375. (Illus.). 32p. (gr. k-3). 1992. 14.95 (*1-55858-140-5*); lib. bdg. 14.88 (*1-55858-148-0*) North-South Bks NYC.

—The Bremen Town Musicians. Stevens, Janet, retold by. & illus. LC 91-815. 32p. (gr. k-3). 1992. reinforced bdg. 15.95 (*0-8234-0939-2*) Holiday.

—Children's Classics: Grimm's Fairy Tales. 1989. 5.98 (*0-671-08756-8*) S&S Trade.

—Cinderella: A Classic Tale. Jose, Eduard, adapted by. Moncure, Jane B., tr. Asensio, Augusti, illus. LC 88-35317. 32p. (gr. 1-4). 1988. PLB 19.95 (*0-89565-483-0*); PLB 13.95s.p. (*0-685-56029-5*) Childs World.

—The Classic Grimm's Fairy Tale. Egan, L. Betts, ed. LC 89-43005. (Illus.). 56p. (gr. 1-8). 1989. 9.98 (*0-89471-768-5*) Courage Bks.

—Complete Brothers Grimm Fairy Tale. 1986. 9.99 (*0-517-45374-6*) Outlet Bk Co.

—The Devil with the Three Golden Hairs. Hogrogian, Nonny, illus. LC 82-12735. 40p. (gr. k-3). 1983. PLB 10.99 (*0-394-95560-9*) Knopf Bks Yng Read.

—The Elves & the Shoemaker. LC 80-27634. (Illus.). 32p. (gr. k-3). 1981. PLB 9.79 (*0-89375-472-2*); pap. text ed. 1.95 (*0-89375-473-0*) Troll Assocs.

—The Elves & the Shoemaker. Watts, Bernadette, illus. LC 85-63306. 32p. (gr. k-2). 1986. 14.95 (*1-55858-035-2*) North-South Bks NYC.

—Fairy Tales. Rackham, Arthur, illus. LC 92-53180. 224p. 1992. 12.95 (*0-679-41796-6*, Evrymans Lib Childs Class) Knopf.

—The Falling Stars. Sopko, Eugen, illus. LC 85-7193. (gr. k-3). 1988. 14.95 (*1-55858-041-7*) North-South Bks NYC.

—The Fisherman & His Wife. Howe, John, illus. 32p. (gr. 6 up). 1983. PLB 13.95s.p. (*0-87191-937-0*) Creative Ed.

—The Fisherman & His Wife. Jarrell, Randall, tr. from GER. Zemach, Margot, illus. 32p. (ps up). 1987. pap. 4.95 (*0-374-42326-1*) FS&G.

—The Fisherman & His Wife. Richardson, I. M., ed. Lippincott, Gary, illus. LC 87-10902. 32p. (gr. k-4). 1988. PLB 9.79 (*0-8167-1075-9*); pap. text ed. 1.95 (*0-8167-1076-7*) Troll Assocs.

—The Fisherman & His Wife. Bell, Anthea, tr. Marks, Alan, illus. LC 88-15165. 28p. (ps up). 1991. pap. 14.95 (*0-88708-072-3*) Picture Bk Studio.

—The Fisherman & His Wife. Metaxas, Eric, tr. from GER. Bryan, Diana, illus. LC 89-28445. 32p. (ps up). 1991. pap. 14.95 (*0-88708-122-3*, Rabbit Ears); includes cassette 19.95 (*0-88708-123-1*) Picture Bk Studio.

—Fisherman & His Wife. Miles, Elizabeth, illus. 32p. (ps-3). 1992. 6.95 (*0-8362-4930-5*) Andrews & McMeel.

—Fitcher's Bird. Arisman, Marshall, illus. 32p. (gr. 9 up). 1983. PLB 13.95s.p. (*0-87191-942-7*) Creative Ed.

—The Frog King & Other Tales of the Brothers Grimm. 315p. (gr. k-8). 1989. pap. 2.95 (*0-451-52379-2*, Sig Classics) NAL-Dutton.

—Frog Prince. Baxter, Robert, illus. LC 78-18073. 32p. (gr. k-4). 1979. PLB 9.79 (*0-89375-126-X*); pap. 1.95 (*0-89375-104-9*) Troll Assocs.

—The Frog Prince. Alchemy II, Inc. Staff, illus. 26p. (ps) 1988. incl. cassette 9.95 (*1-55578-900-5*) Worlds Wonder.

—The Frog Prince. Lewis, Naomi, tr. from GER. Schroeder, Binette, illus. LC 89-24613. (GER.). 32p. (gr. k-3). 1989. 15.95 (*1-55858-015-8*) North-South Bks NYC.

—The Frog Prince. Black, Fiona, retold by. Parmenter, Wayne, illus. 1991. 6.95 (*0-8362-4920-8*) Andrews & McMeel.

—The Frog Prince & The Pear Tree. (Illus.). 48p. (gr. 1-4). 1985. 5.95 (*0-88110-251-2*) EDC.

—Der Froschkonig. Schroeder, Binette, illus. (GER.). 32p. (gr. k-3). 1992. 15.95 (*3-314-00336-6*) North-South Bks NYC.

—The Golden Goose. Paterson, Diane, illus. LC 80-29207. 32p. (gr. k-3). 1981. PLB 9.79 (*0-89375-476-5*); pap. 1.95 (*0-89375-477-3*) Troll Assocs.

—The Golden Goose. Duntze, Dorothee, illus. Bell, Anthea, tr. LC 87-32108. (Illus.). 32p. (gr. k-3). 1988. 13.95 (*1-55858-047-6*) North-South Bks NYC.

—The Goose Girl. Perret, Paul, illus. 32p. (gr. 4 up). 1984. PLB 13.95s.p. (*0-87191-934-6*) Creative Ed.

—The Goose Maiden. Archipowa, Anastassija, illus. 24p. 1990. 5.99 (*0-517-05388-8*) Outlet Bk Co.

—Grimms' Fairy Tales. Gotlieb, Jules, illus. (gr. 3 up). 1968. pap. 2.50 (*0-8049-0168-6*, CL-168) Airmont.

—Grimm's Fairy Tales. (SPA & FRE.). Span. ed. 8.95 (*0-685-23350-2*); fr. ed 5.50 (*0-685-23351-0*) Fr & Eur.

—Grimms' Fairy Tales. (Illus.). 1981. (G&D); deluxe ed. 13.95 (*0-448-06009-4*, G&D) Putnam Pub Group.

—Grimm's Fairy Tales. Crikshank, G., tr. (Illus.). (gr. 7 up). 1985. pap. 3.50 (*0-14-035070-5*, Puffin) Puffin Bks.

—Grimm's Fairy Tales. Carter, Peter, ed. & tr. Richardson, Peter, illus. 238p. (ps-6). 1987. 18.95 (*0-19-274529-8*) OUP.

—Grimm's Tales for Young & Old: The Complete Stories. Manheim, Ralph, tr. LC 76-56318. 648p. (gr. k-12). 1983. 14.95 (*0-385-11005-7*); pap. 15.95 (*0-385-18950-8*) Doubleday.

—Hansel & Gretel. Jeffers, Susan, illus. LC 80-15079. 32p. (gr. k up) 1980. 16.00 (*0-8037-3492-1*); PLB 14.89 (*0-8037-3491-3*) Dial Bks Young.

—Hansel & Gretel. Felix, Monique, illus. 32p. (gr. 6 up). 1983. PLB 13.95s.p. (*0-87191-935-4*) Creative Ed.

—Hansel & Gretel. LC 85-6286. (Illus.). 32p. (gr. k-3). 1985. 11.95 (*0-13-383654-1*) P-H.

—Hansel & Gretel. Jeffers, Susan, illus. LC 80-15079. 32p. (gr. k up). 1986. pap. 4.95 (*0-8037-0318-X*) Dial Bks Young.

—Hansel & Gretel. Becker, Lois & Stratton, Mark, eds. (Illus.). 26p. (ps). 1987. Packaged with pre-programmed audio cass. tape. 9.95 (*0-934323-64-X*) Alchemy Comms.

—Hansel & Gretel. LC 87-32833. 1991. pap. 14.95 (*0-88708-068-5*) Picture Bk Studio.

—Hansel & Gretel. Zwerger, Lisbeth, illus. 32p. (ps-2). 1991. pap. 3.95 (*0-590-44459-X*, Blue Ribbon Bks) Scholastic Inc.

—Hansel & Gretel. Black, Fiona, retold by. Gurney, John, illus. 1991. 6.95 (*0-8362-4912-7*) Andrews & McMeel.

—Hansel & Gretel. 2nd, abd. ed. Crawford, Elizabeth D., tr. LC 91-40656. (Illus.). 28p. (gr. k up). 1992. pap. 4.95 (*0-88708-225-4*) Picture Bk Studio.

—Hansel & Gretel: A Classic Tale. Jose, Eduard, adapted by. Riehecky, Janet, tr. Asensio, Augusti, illus. LC 88-35212. 32p. (gr. 1-4). 1988. PLB 19.95 (*0-89565-480-6*); PLB 13.95s.p. (*0-685-56039-2*) Childs World.

—Household Stories of the Brothers Grimm. Crane, Lucy, tr. Crane, Walter, illus. x, 269p. (gr. 3-9). 1886. pap. 4.95 (*0-486-21080-4*) Dover.

—Iron Hans. Heyer, Marilee, illus. LC 93-14662. 32p. 1993. 14.99 (*0-670-81741-4*) Viking Child Bks.

—Jack in Luck. Bell, Anthea, tr. Tharlet, Eve, illus. LC 92-7102. 28p. (ps up). 1992. pap. 14.95 (*0-88708-249-1*) Picture Bk Studio.

—Jorinda & Joringel. Cutts, David, ed. Rickman, David, illus. LC 87-10937. 32p. (gr. k-4). 1988. PLB 9.79 (*0-8167-1065-1*); pap. text ed. 1.95 (*0-8167-1066-X*) Troll Assocs.

—King Grisly-Beard. Sendak, Maurice, illus. Taylor, Edgar, tr. from GER. LC 73-77911. (Illus.). (ps-3). 1973. 14.00 (*0-374-34133-8*) FS&G.

—Little Red Cap. Crawford, Elizabeth D., tr. from GER. Zwerger, Lisbeth, illus. LC 82-14211. 24p. (ps-3). 1983. PLB 11.88 (*0-688-01716-9*) Morrow Jr Bks.

—Little Red Cap: A Fairy Tale. Bell, Anthea, tr. from GER. Laimgruber, Monika, illus. LC 93-19923. 32p. (gr. k-3). 1993. 14.95 (*1-55858-167-7*); PLB 14.88 (*1-55858-168-5*) North-South Bks NYC.

—Little Red Riding Hood. Mahan, Benton, illus. LC 80-27684. 32p. (gr. k-3). 1981. PLB 9.79 (*0-89375-488-9*); pap. 1.95 (*0-89375-489-7*) Troll Assocs.

—Little Red Riding Hood. Hyman, Trina S., retold by. & illus. LC 82-7700. 32p. (ps-3). 1983. reinforced bdg. 15.95 (*0-8234-0470-6*); pap. 5.95 (*0-8234-0653-9*) Holiday.

—Little Red Riding Hood. Schmidt, Karen, illus. 32p. (Orig.). (gr. k-2). 1986. pap. 2.50 (*0-590-41881-5*) Scholastic Inc.

—Little Red Riding Hood. Alchemy II, Inc. Staff, illus. 26p. (ps). 1988. incl. cassette 9.95 (*1-55578-903-X*) Worlds Wonder.

—Little Red Riding Hood. (Illus.). 32p. (ps-3). 1992. 6.95 (*0-8362-4901-1*) Andrews & McMeel.

—Musicians of Bremen: European Folk Tales. Rodgers, Gregg, illus. 24p. 1992. pap. 3.50 (*0-88625-286-5*) Durkin Hayes Pub.

—Les Nains. Watts, Bernadette, illus. (FRE.). 32p. (gr. k-3). 1992. 14.95 (*3-85539-581-0*) North-South Bks NYC.

—Le Prince Grenouille. Schroeder, Binette, illus. (FRE.). 32p. (gr. k-3). 1992. 15.95 (*3-314-20666-6*) North-South Bks NYC.

—The Queen Bee. Dumas, Phillipe, illus. 32p. (gr. 4 up). 1984. PLB 13.95s.p. (*0-87191-939-7*) Creative Ed.

—Ragamuffins. Watts, Bernadette, illus. LC 89-42609. 32p. (gr. k-3). 1989. 13.95 (*1-55858-014-X*) North-South Bks NYC.

—Rapunzel. Dodson, Bert, illus. LC 78-18066. 32p. (gr. k-3). 1979. PLB 9.79 (*0-89375-135-9*); pap. 1.95 (*0-89375-113-8*) Troll Assocs.

—Rapunzel. Rogasky, Barbara, retold by. Hyman, Trina S., illus. LC 81-6419. 32p. (ps-3). 1982. Reinforced bdg. 14.95 (*0-8234-0454-4*); pap. 5.95 (*0-8234-0652-0*) Holiday.

—Rapunzel. Hague, Michael, illus. 32p. (gr. 6 up). 1986. PLB 13.95s.p. (*0-87191-936-2*) Creative Ed.

—Rapunzel. Heyer, Carol, illus. 32p. (gr. k-3). 1992. 14.95 (*0-8249-8558-3*, Ideals Child); PLB 15.00 (*0-8249-8585-0*) Hambleton-Hill.

—Rapunzel. Black, Fiona, retold by. Lisi, Victoria, illus. LC 92-14259. 32p. 1992. 6.95 (*0-8362-4924-0*) Andrews & McMeel.

—Rapunzel, & The Seven Ravens. Archipowa, Anastassija, illus. 24p. 1990. 3.99 (*0-517-05386-1*) Outlet Bk Co.

—Rumpelstiltskin. Hockerman, Dennis, illus. LC 78-18079. 32p. (gr. k-3). 1979. PLB 9.79 (*0-89375-140-5*); pap. 1.95 (*0-89375-118-9*) Troll Assocs.

—Rumpelstiltskin. Zelinsky, Paul O., retold by. & illus. LC 86-4482. 40p. (gr. k up). 1986. 14.00 (*0-525-44265-0*, DCB) Dutton Child Bks.

—Rumpelstiltskin. Alchemy II, Inc. Staff, illus. 26p. 1988. incl. cassette 9.95 (*1-55578-910-2*) Worlds Wonder.

—Rumpelstiltskin. Sage, Alison, retold by. Spirin, Gennady, illus. 32p. (ps-3). 1991. 12.95 (*0-8037-0908-0*) Dial Bks Young.

—Rumpelstiltskin. (Illus.). 20p. (ps up). 1992. write for info. incl. long-life batteries (*0-307-74711-5*, 64711, Golden Pr) Western Pub.

—Rumpelstiltskin. Cooley, Gary, illus. 32p. (ps-3). 1992. 6.95 (*0-8362-4922-4*) Andrews & McMeel.

—Rumpelstiltskin: A Classic Tale. Moncure, Jane B., tr. from SPA. Asensio, Augusti, illus. LC 88-35315. 32p. (gr. 1-4). 1988. PLB 19.95 (*0-89565-463-6*); PLB 13.95s.p. (*0-685-56025-2*) Childs World.

—Rumpelstiltskin: A Fairy Tale. Watts, Bernadette, illus. Bell, Anthea, tr. LC 92-31331. (Illus.). 32p. (gr. k-3). 1993. 14.95 (*1-55858-188-X*); PLB 14.88 (*1-55858-189-8*) North-South Bks NYC.

—The Seven Ravens. Zwerger, Lisbeth, illus. LC 83-61777. 28p. (gr. k up). 1991. pap. 14.95 (*0-88708-092-8*); pap. 5.95 (*0-685-24951-4*) Picture Bk Studio.

—The Seven Ravens. Zwerger, Lisbeth, illus. Bell, Anthea, tr. LC 93-20122. (Illus.). (ps-8). 1993. 4.95 (0-88708-326-9) Picture Bk Studio.
—Shoemaker & the Elves. Roman, Barbara J., illus. 32p. (ps-3). 1992. 6.95 (0-8362-4923-2) Andrews & McMeel.
—The Sleeping Beauty. Alchemy II, Inc. Staff, illus. 26p. (ps). 1988. incl. cassette 9.95 (1-55578-908-0) Worlds Wonder.
—Sleeping Beauty & Other Fairy Tales. (Illus.). 96p. (Orig.). 1992. pap. 1.00t (0-486-27084-X) Dover.
—Sleeping Beauty & The Frog Prince. Archipowa, Anastassija, illus. 24p. 1990. 5.99 (0-517-05385-3) Outlet Bk Co.
—Snow White. Hyman, Trina S., illus. Heins, Paul, tr. (Illus.). (ps-3). 1979. lib. bdg. 14.95 (0-316-35450-3, Joy St Bks); pap. 6.95 (0-316-35451-1, Joy St Bks) Little.
—Snow White. Greenway, Jennifer, retold by. Augestine, Erin, illus. 1991. 6.95 (0-8362-4906-2) Andrews & McMeel.
—Snow White. Poole, Josephine, ed. LC 91-18411. (Illus.). 32p. 1991. 15.00 (0-679-82656-4); PLB 16.99 (0-679-92656-9) Knopf Bks Yng Read.
—Snow White & Rose Red. Weren, James, illus. LC 78-18074. 32p. (gr. k-3). 1979. PLB 9.79 (0-89375-136-7); pap. 1.95 (0-89375-114-6) Troll Assocs.
—Snow White & Rose Red. Topor, Roland, illus. 32p. (gr. 6 up). 1984. PLB 13.95s.p. (0-87191-938-9) Creative Ed.
—Snow White & Rose Red. Wallner, John, illus. LC 84-4910. 32p. (gr. k-3). 1984. 10.95 (0-13-815234-9) P-H.
—Snow White & Rose Red. Watts, Bernadette, illus. LC 87-72036. 32p. (gr. k-3). 1988. 14.95 (1-55858-054-9) North-South Bks NYC.
—Snow White & Rose Red. Spirin, Gennady, illus. 32p. (ps up). 1992. 14.95 (0-399-21873-4, Philomel Bks) Putnam Pub Group.
—Snow White & the Seven Dwarfs. (FRE., Illus.). (gr. 3-8). 8.95 (0-685-11566-6) Fr & Eur.
—Snow-White & the Seven Dwarfs. Jarrell, Randall, tr. from GER. Burkert, Nancy E., illus. LC 28-1489. 32p. (ps up). 1972. 17.00 (0-374-37099-0) FS&G.
—Snow White & the Seven Dwarfs. Iwasaki, Chihiro, illus. LC 85-12158. 40p. (gr. 1 up). 1991. pap. 15.95 (0-88708-012-X) Picture Bk Studio.
—Snow-White & the Seven Dwarfs. Jarrell, Randall, tr. from GER. Burkert, Nancy E., illus. 32p. (ps up). 1987. pap. 5.95 (0-374-46868-0, Sunburst) FS&G.
—Snow White & the Seven Dwarfs. Kassier, Sue, retold by. May, Darcy, illus. LC 92-44516. 32p. (gr. 2 up). 1993. pap. 2.25 (0-679-84347-7) Random Bks Yng Read.
—The Table, the Donkey & the Stick. Galdone, Paul, illus. (ps-3). 1976. PLB 7.95 (0-07-022701-2) McGraw.
—Tales from the Brothers Grimm. 1987. 1.98 (0-671-08490-9) S&S Trade.
—Three Feathers. Schmid, Eleanor, illus. 32p. (gr. 4 up). 1984. PLB 13.95s.p. (0-87191-941-9) Creative Ed.
—Three Languages. Chermayeff, Ivan, illus. 32p. (gr. 4 up). 1984. PLB 13.95s.p. (0-87191-940-0) Creative Ed.
—Twelve Dancing Princesses. Hockerman, Dennis, illus. LC 78-18077. 32p. (gr. k-4). 1979. PLB 9.79 (0-89375-139-1); pap. 1.95 (0-89375-117-0) Troll Assocs.
—The Twelve Dancing Princesses. Carter, Anne, retold by. Dalton, Anne, illus. LC 88-13794. 32p. (ps-4). 1989. (Lipp Jr Bks); (Lipp Jr Bks) HarpC Child Bks.
—Die Wichtelmanner. Watts, Bernadette, illus. (GER.). 32p. (gr. k-3). 1992. 14.95 (3-85825-256-5) North-South Bks NYC.
—Wolf & the Seven Kids. new ed. Craft, Kinuko Y., illus. LC 78-18076. 32p. (gr. 1-4). 1979. PLB 9.79 (0-89375-138-3); pap. 1.95 (0-89375-116-2) Troll Assocs.
Grimm, Jacob, et al. Jan Pienkowski Fairy Tale Library, 4 bks. Walser, David, tr. Pienkowski, Jan, illus. 48p. 1992. Slipcase set incls. miniature eds. of Cinderella, Puss-in-Boots, The Sleeping Beauty, & Snow White. 15.00 (0-679-82270-4) Knopf Bks Yng Read.
Grimm, Rosemary. Stunt Planes. LC 87-29020. (Illus.). 48p. (gr. 5-6). 1988. RSBE 11.95 (0-89686-363-8, Crestwood Hse) Macmillan Child Grp.
—Truck & Tractor Pullers. LC 87-30592. (Illus.). 48p. (gr. 5-6). 1988. RSBE 11.95 (0-89686-358-1, Crestwood Hse) Macmillan Child Grp.
Grimm, Wilhelm K. Dear Mili. Sendak, Maurice, illus. Manheim, Ralph, tr. (Illus.). 40p. 1990. gift ed. 18.95 (0-374-31766-6); ltd. ed. 750.00 (0-374-31763-1); 1988 16.95, (0-374-31762-3) FS&G.
—Hansel & Gretel. Zelinsky, Paul O. & Lesser, Rika, eds. (Illus.). 48p. (gr. k-3). 1985. 14.95 (0-399-21733-9, Putnam) Putnam Pub Group.
Grimm, Wilhelm K., jt. auth. see Grimm, Jacob.
Grimm, Wilhelm K. see Grimm, Jacob.
Grimm, Wilhelm K., jt. auth. see Grimm, Jacob.
Grimmer, Glenna. ABCs of Texas Wildflowers. Roberts, M, ed. Laughlin, Mary J, illus. 64p. (gr. 2-5). 1982. 9.95 (0-89015-358-2) Eakin-Sunbelt.
—Things That Swim in Texas Waters Alphabetically Speaking: And in Other Coastal States of the Gulf of Mexico. Eakin, Edwin M., ed. Hoese, H. Dickson, illus. 48p. (gr. 4-6). 1989. 11.95 (0-89015-694-8, Pub. by Panda Bks) Eakin-Sunbelt.
Grimsdell, Jeremy. Kalinzu. LC 92-45573. (Illus.). 32p. (ps-3). 1993. 14.95 (1-85697-886-9) Kingfisher Bks.

Grindley, Sally. The Big Crocodile Book. (Illus.). 80p. (gr. 2-5). 1993. 19.95 (0-09-176382-7, Pub. by Hutchinson UK) Trafalgar.
—A Day with Alice & Sam. Galvani, Maureen, illus. LC 92-29124. 1993. 10.95 (1-85697-912-1) Kingfisher Bks.
—I Don't Want To! LC 89-85798. (ps-3). 1990. 13.95 (0-316-32893-6, Joy St Bks) Little.
—Knock, Knock! Who's There? Browne, Anthony, illus. LC 86-112. 32p. (ps-2). 1986. PLB 7.95 (0-394-88400-0) Knopf Bks Yng Read.
—Reader's Digest Children's Book of Animals. Trotter, Stuart, illus. LC 92-15234. 48p. 1992. 13.00 (0-89577-443-7, Readers Digest Kids) RD Assn.
—Shhh! A Lift the Flap Book. Utton, Peter, illus. 32p. (ps-3). 1992. 13.95 (0-316-32899-5, Joy St Bks) Little.
—Stories for Christmas. 1991. 6.98 (0-8317-1282-1) Smithmark.
—Wake up, Dad! 1989. 12.95 (0-385-26017-2) Doubleday.
Gringhuis, Dirk. Young Voyageur: Trade & Treachery at Michilimackinac. rev. ed. (Illus.). 202p. (gr. 9 up). 1969. pap. 6.00 (0-911872-34-5) Mackinac Island.
Grinney, Ellen. The Hospital. (Illus.). 112p. (gr. 6-12). 1991. 18.95 (0-7910-0065-6) Chelsea Hse.
Grinstead, Wayne. The Ross Hannas: Living, Laughing, Loving. LC 86-6807. (gr. 4-6). 1986. 5.95 (0-8054-4325-8) Broadman.
Gripari, Pierre. Gentil Petit Diable et Autres Contes de la Rue Broca. Rosado, Puig, illus. (FRE.). 157p. (gr. 5-10). 1988. pap. 7.95 (2-07-033451-1) Schoenhof.
—Sorciere de la Rue Mouffetard et Autre Contes de la Rue Broca. Rosado, Puig, illus. (FRE.). 153p. (gr. 5-10). 1987. pap. 7.95 (2-07-033440-6) Schoenhof.
Gripe, Maria. Elvis & His Secret. Gripe, Harald, illus. 208p. (gr. 3-7). 1979. pap. 1.50 (0-440-42434-8, YB) Dell.

Griscom, Bailey & Griscom, Pam. Why Can't I Be the Leader? (Illus.). 24p. (Orig.). (ps up). 1992. pap. 4.95 (0-9633705-2-9) Share Pub CA.

WHY CAN'T I BE THE LEADER? grew out of conversations that two-year old Bailey initiated during the Persian Gulf War. Her mother, Pam Griscom, edited Bailey's refreshing insights into an 8" x 8" picturebook about sharing - a resource which encourages children of all ages to actively engage in improving their world. She believes that children are acutely aware of the complex things happening around them, & that what they IMAGINE about an undiscussed subject is likely to be much more frightening than honest, empowering communication could ever be. "I hope your book's message is heard again & again."--Rev. Robert McAfee Brown."...a pioneer effort to present the topic of war & public policy to the 3-7 year age group... ingeniously clarified by Scot Halpin's illustrations."--"Peaceworks"-Oct. '92, Palo Alto, CA. "...she learns that she can indeed become a leader, but that to be a good leader requires sharing."--" Feminist Bookstore News"-Nov./Dec. '92. "I would also recommend it to adults as a model of ways to talk to children..."--"CEASE News"-Winter '93. Share Publishing, 3130 Alpine Road, Suite 200-1009, Portola Valley, CA 94028. (415-854-0294).
Publisher Provided Annotation.

Griscom, Laura & Griscom, Pam. Who Would Want Those Apples Anyway? Halpin, Scot, illus. 24p. (Orig.). (ps-5). 1993. pap. 4.95 (0-9633705-3-7) Share Pub CA.

WHO WOULD WANT THOSE APPLES ANYWAY? is an enchanting picture book based on three-year-old Laura Griscom's questions about agricultural pesticides, boldly illustrated by T. Scot Halpin. A bug problem in Laura's garden sends her to a commercial farm in search of advice. A friendship with a farm worker's child

leads to discussions about what shoppers support with their decisions at the marketplace. Laura wonders why so many farmers & consumers make unhealthy choices. By deciding that bugs "have very TEENY little teeth," this curious child reframes a dilemma, & avoids the use of pesticides on her tiny crop. She & her sister decide that the perfect looking CONVENTIONAL produce isn't attractive after all; they want the same pear that the bug tasted, because "bugs are very smart" & "it's OK to share." From ecology to aesthetics to economics, this book is an excellent resource for parents & teachers; a non-threatening way to introduce the hidden consequences of food production to future consumers. "...Strikes just the right note, makes all the points & is beautifully written."-- Dr. Marion Moses. Share Publishing, 3130 Alpine Road, Suite 200-1009, Portola Valley, CA 94028. (415-851-0731) FAX: 415-854-8202.
Publisher Provided Annotation.

Griscom, Pam, jt. auth. see Griscom, Bailey.
Griscom, Pam, jt. auth. see Griscom, Laura.
Grisewood, John. Fun to Learn French. Sleight, Katy, illus. 48p. (gr. 2-5). 1992. 12.95 (0-531-15241-3, Warwick); PLB 12.90 (0-531-19120-6, Warwick) Watts.
—Fun to Learn Spanish. Sleight, Katy, illus. 48p. (gr. 2-5). 1992. 12.95 (0-531-15242-1, Warwick); PLB 12.90 (0-531-19112-5, Warwick) Watts.
Grisham, Noel & Warren, Betsy. Buffalo & Indians on the Great Plains. (Illus.). (gr. k-4). 1985. 12.95 (0-89015-470-8, Pub. by Panda Bks) Eakin-Sunbelt.
Grisham, Sharon M. Gregory Flies Again. LC 89-62750. 16p. (Orig.). (ps-6). 1989. pap. 4.95 (0-9624673-1-6) Picture This Bks.
—Gregory's First Flight. 16p. (Orig.). (ps-6). 1989. pap. 4.95 (0-9624673-0-8) Picture This Bks.
Grishaver, Joel, jt. auth. see Alper, Janis.
Grishaver, Joel see Rabinowitz, Jan.
Grishaver, Joel L. Alef Bet Gimmel Dalet: Ox House Camel Door. (Illus.). 96p. (gr. 2-3). 1989. wkbk. 5.25 (0-933873-45-X) Torah Aura.
—Being Torah Student Commentary, 2 Vols. (Illus.). 72p. (Orig.). (gr. 2-4). 1986. pap. text ed. 4.95 ea. Vol. 1 (0-933873-09-3) Vol. 2 (0-933873-10-7) Torah Aura.
—Building Jewish Life: Hanukkah Activity Book. (Illus.). 31p. 1988. pap. 1.85 (0-933873-32-8) Torah Aura.
—Building Jewish Life: High Holy Days. LC 87-13949. (Illus.). 48p. (gr. k-3). 1988. pap. text ed. 4.95 (0-933873-17-4) Torah Aura.
—Building Jewish Life Passover Haggadah. (HEB & ENG., Illus.). 48p. (Orig.). (gr. 4-8). 1989. pap. 2.95 (0-933873-41-7) Torah Aura.
—Building Jewish Life: Rosh Ha-Shanah & Yom Kippur Activity Book. (Illus.). 48p. (gr. 1-2). 1988. wkbk. 1.85 (0-933873-26-3) Torah Aura.
—Building Jewish Life: Shabbat Activity Book. (Illus.). 32p. (gr. 1-2). 1990. wkbk. 1.85 (0-933873-50-6) Torah Aura.
—Building Jewish Life: Siddur Commentary. Torah Aura Staff, photos by. (Illus.). 48p. (Orig.). (gr. 2-4). 1992. pap. text ed. 2.45 (0-933873-74-3) Torah Aura.
—Building Jewish Life: Sukkot & Simhat Torah. (Illus.). 48p. 1988. pap. text ed. 4.95 (0-933873-13-1) Torah Aura.
—Building Jewish Life: Sukkot & Simhat Torah Activity Book. (Illus.). 32p. (gr. 1-2). 1988. wkbk. 1.85 (0-933873-27-1) Torah Aura.
—Building Jewish Life: Synagogue Activity Book. (Illus.). (gr. 1-2). 1991. pap. text ed. 1.85 (0-933873-59-X) Torah Aura.
—Nineteen Out of Eighteen. Steinberger, Heidi, illus. (Orig.). (gr. 5-8). 1991. pap. 5.95 wkbk. (0-685-50246-5) Torah Aura.
—Shema & Company. rev. ed. Steinberger, Heidi, illus. (gr. 5-8). 1991. wkbk. 5.95 (0-933873-62-X) Torah Aura.
—Tanta Teva & the Magic Booth. Bleicher, David, illus. LC 93-13193. 1993. 11.95 (1-881283-00-3) Alef Design.
—Torah Toons I. (Illus.). 115p. (Orig.). (gr. 4 up). 1985. pap. text ed. 5.50 (0-933873-01-8) Torah Aura.
—Torah Toons II. (Illus.). 114p. (Orig.). (gr. 6 up). 1985. pap. text ed. 5.50 (0-933873-02-6) Torah Aura.
—The Words Know the Way. Grishaver, Joel L., illus. 64p. (gr. 3-4). 1990. wkbk. 4.95 (0-933873-53-0) Torah Aura.
Grishaver, Joel L., jt. auth. see Wise, Ira J.
Grishaver, Joel L., et al. When I Stood on Mt. Sinai. Grishaver, Joel L., illus. 32p. (Orig.). (gr. 6 up). 1992. pap. text ed. 2.45 (0-933873-70-0) Torah Aura.
Griswold, David H., jt. auth. see Merriss, William E.

Griswold, Millie H. Promises to Keep: Simplified Edition. 24p. 1985. write for info. wkbk. (*1-881909-14-X*) Advent Christ Gen Conf.

Gritzmacher, Kathy, jt. auth. see Fellers, Pat.

Groat, Diane de see Bunting, Eve.

Groat, Diane de see Gilson, Jamie.

Groat, Diane de see Nickman, Steven L.

Groat, Diane de see Roth, Kevin.

Groat, Diane de see Simon, Seymour.

Grode, Phyllis A. Sophie's Name. Haas, Shelly O., illus. LC 90-4833. 32p. (gr. k-3). 1990. 12.95 (*0-929371-18-6*); pap. 4.95 (*0-929371-19-4*) Kar Ben.

Grodin, Charles. Freddie the Fly. Murdocca, Sal, illus. LC 92-5234. 32p. (ps-2). 1993. 12.00 (*0-679-83847-3*) Random Bks Yng Read.

Groening, Maggie, jt. auth. see Groening, Matt.

Groening, Matt & Groening, Maggie. Maggie Simpson's Alphabet Book. LC 91-2867. (Illus.). 32p. (ps-1). 1991. PLB 11.89 (*0-06-020236-X*) HarpC Child Bks.

—Maggie Simpson's Book of Animals. LC 91-2866. (Illus.). 32p. (ps-1). 1991. 2.95 (*0-694-00321-2*); PLB 11.89 (*0-06-020237-8*) HarpC Child Bks.

—Maggie Simpson's Book of Colors & Shapes. LC 91-2864. (Illus.). 32p. (ps-1). 1991. PLB 11.89 (*0-06-020235-1*) HarpC Child Bks.

—Maggie Simpson's Counting Book. LC 91-2865. (Illus.). 32p. (ps-1). 1991. PLB 11.89 (*0-06-020238-6*) HarpC Child Bks.

Grofe, Anne C., jt. auth. see Seymour, Ruth G.

Groff, Phylis. The Christmas Nightingale. 1935. 4.50 (*0-87602-115-1*) Anchorage.

Groff, Richard L., Jr. Ic Spraece Angel-Seax: A Beginning Anglo-Saxon Grammar for Children. Groff, Richard L., illus. 36p. (Orig.). (gr. 2-6). 1991. pap. 10.98 incl. audio tape (*0-9630718-1-5*) New Dawn NY.

Grohmann, Susan. The Dust under Mrs. Merriweather's Bed. Grohmann, Susan, illus. LC 93-21804. 1993. 13.95 (*1-879085-82-8*) Whsprng Coyote Pr.

Grollman, Earl A. Straight Talk about Death for Teenagers: How to Cope with Losing Someone You Love. LC 92-34540. 144p. 1993. 22.50 (*0-8070-2500-3*); pap. 7.95 (*0-8070-2501-1*) Beacon Pr.

—Talking about Death: A Dialogue Between Parent & Child; With Parent's Guide & Recommended Resources. 3rd ed. Heau, Gisela, illus. LC 89-46061. 128p. (gr. k-4). 1990. 18.95 (*0-8070-2364-7*, BP531) Beacon Pr.

—Talking about Divorce & Separation: A Dialogue Between Parent & Child. Cann., Alison, illus. LC 75-5289. (gr. k-4). 1990. 9.00 (*0-8070-2375-2*, BP524) Beacon Pr.

Groneman, C. General Woodworking. 4 vols. 4th, large type ed. 848p. (gr. 7-12). 1971. Set. 103.30 (*0-317-01890-6*, 4-07930-00) Am Printing Hse.

Groneman, Chris H. & Feirer, John L. Getting Started in Electricity & Electronics. LC 78-19120. (Illus.). (gr. 7-9). 1979. text ed. 9.52 (*0-07-024999-7*) McGraw.

—Getting Started in Metalworking. (Illus.). 1979. text ed. 9.52 (*0-07-024949-9*) McGraw.

Groner, Judye & Wikler, Madeline. All about Hanukkah. Schanzer, Rosalyn, illus. LC 88-13435. (gr. k-5). 1988. 10.95 (*0-930494-81-4*); pap. 4.95 (*0-930494-82-2*) Kar Ben.

—Hanukkah Fun: For Little Hands. Kahn, Katherine J., illus. 32p. (ps-2). 1992. pap. 3.95 (*0-929371-62-3*) Kar Ben.

—Shabbat Shalom. Yaffa, illus. LC 88-83568. 12p. (ps). 1989. bds. 4.95 (*0-930494-91-1*) Kar Ben.

—Where is the Afikomen. Schanzer, Roz, illus. LC 89-63254. 12p. (ps). 1989. bds. 4.95 (*0-929371-06-2*) Kar Ben.

Groner, Judye, jt. auth. see Wikler, Madeline.

Groner, Judyth & Wikler, Madeline. Let's Build a Sukkah. Kahn, Katherine J., illus. LC 86-81717. 12p. (ps). 1986. bds. 4.95 (*0-930494-58-X*) Kar Ben.

Groner, Judyth & Wikler, Madeline. Thank You, God: A Jewish Child's Book of Prayers. Haas, Shelly O., illus. (HEB & ENG.). 32p. (ps-2). 1993. 14.95 (*0-929371-65-8*) Kar Ben.

Groomer, Vera. Dibe Yahzi. (ps). 1980. pap. 1.95 (*0-8127-0260-3*) Review & Herald.

—Quiet Because. (ps). 1979. pap. 2.15 (*0-8127-0253-0*) Review & Herald.

Grooters, Jeff, jt. auth. see Tanis, Joel E.

Groscost, Connie A. Letter Creatures...from A to Z. (Illus.). 1992. 7.95 (*0-533-10047-X*) Vantage.

Grosman, Ernesto L., tr. see Bemelmans, Ludwig.

Gross, Alan. I Don't Want to Go to School Book. LC 81-17034. (Illus.). (ps-3). 1982. pap. 3.95 (*0-516-43496-9*) Childrens.

—What If the Teacher Calls on Me? Venezia, Mike, illus. LC 79-18560. 32p. (ps-3). 1980. pap. 3.95 (*0-516-43671-6*) Childrens.

Gross, Arthur W. & Jahsmann, Allan H. Little Children Sing to God. (gr. k-1). 1960. 8.95 (*0-570-03471-X*, 56-1036) Concordia.

Gross, Cheryl & Werz, Ed. The Sock Club: Angry Feelings - Smart Choices. 16p. (gr. k-4). 1992. 0.95 (*1-56688-053-X*) Bur For At-Risk.

—The Sock Club: Drugs Make You Do Bad Things. 16p. (gr. k-4). 1992. 0.95 (*1-56688-050-5*) Bur For At-Risk.

—The Sock Club: How to Say No to Drugs? 16p. (gr. k-4). 1992. 0.95 (*1-56688-052-1*) Bur For At-Risk.

—The Sock Club: Real & Fake. 16p. (gr. k-4). 1992. 0.95 (*1-56688-049-1*) Bur For At-Risk.

—The Sock Club: What Could Happen. 16p. (gr. k-4). 1992. 0.95 (*1-56688-051-3*) Bur For At-Risk.

Gross, Cynthia S. The New Biotechnology: Putting Microbes to Work. LC 88-18823. (Illus.). 96p. (gr. 5 up). 1988. PLB 21.50 (*0-8225-1583-0*) Lerner Pubns.

Gross, David C. Why Remain Jewish? 224p. (gr. 8 up). 1993. pap. 9.95 (*0-7818-0216-4*) Hippocrene Bks.

Gross, Edward. The Alien Nation Companion. (Illus.). 112p. (gr. 9-12). 1991. pap. 12.95 (*0-9627508-1-6*) Image NY.

Gross, Edward, ed. Above & Below: A Guide to Beauty & the Beast. (Illus.). 112p. (Orig.). (gr. 9-12). 1990. pap. 12.95 (*0-9627508-0-8*) Image NY.

Gross, Gwen. Knights of the Round Table. Green, Norman, illus. LC 85-2176. 96p. (gr. 2-6). 1993. lib. bdg. 5.99 (*0-394-97579-0*); pap. 2.99 (*0-394-87579-6*) Random Bks Yng Read.

Gross, Judith. Celebrate: A Book of Jewish Holidays. Weissman, Bari, illus. LC 91-29867. (gr. k-3). 1992. PLB 7.99 (*0-448-40303-X*, Platt & Munk Pubs); pap. 2.25 (*0-448-40302-1*, Platt & Munk Pubs) Putnam Pub Group.

Gross, Karen, ed. see Becker, Melissa.

Gross, Karen, ed. see Branson, Mary.

Gross, Karen, ed. see Compher, Catherine.

Gross, Karen, ed. see Hughes, Ann K.

Gross, Karen, ed. see Kizer, Kathryn.

Gross, Karen, ed. see Owen, Barbara.

Gross, Karen, ed. see Sledge, Sharlande.

Gross, Karen, ed. see Smith, Marjorie.

Gross, Karen, ed. see Strawn, Kathy.

Gross, Karen, ed. see Thomason, Kendra.

Gross, Lisa. The Half & Half Dog. Gross, Lisa, illus. LC 88-9347. 26p. (gr. k-6). 1988. PLB 14.95 (*0-933849-13-3*) Landmark Edns.

Gross, Philip. The All-Nite Cafe. (gr. 4 up). 1993. pap. 5.95 (*0-571-16753-5*) Faber & Faber.

Gross, Ruth B. A Book about Pandas. (Illus.). 32p. (gr. k-3). 1991. pap. 2.50 (*0-590-43492-6*) Scholastic Inc.

—The Bremen-Town Musicians. Kent, Jack, illus. 32p. (Orig.). 1985. pap. 2.50 (*0-590-42364-9*) Scholastic Inc.

—The Emperor's New Clothes. Kent, Jack, illus. 32p. (Orig.). 1991. pap. 2.50 (*0-590-43267-2*) Scholastic Inc.

—If You Grew up with George Washington. (gr. 4-7). 1993. pap. 4.95 (*0-590-45155-3*) Scholastic Inc.

—Snakes. reissued ed. LC 89-38254. (Illus.). 64p. (ps-3). 1990. Repr. of 1973 ed. RSBE 14.95 (*0-02-737022-4*, Four Winds Press) Macmillan Child Grp.

—Snakes. 64p. (gr. 1-4). 1989. pap. 2.50 (*0-590-44090-X*) Scholastic Inc.

—True Stories about Abraham Lincoln. Kastner, Jill, illus. LC 89-45899. 48p. (gr. k-3). 1989. 12.95 (*0-688-08797-3*); lib. bdg. 12.88 (*0-688-08798-1*) Lothrop.

—True Stories about Abraham Lincoln. (gr. 4-7). 1991. pap. 2.50 (*0-590-43879-4*) Scholastic Inc.

—What's on My Plate? Seltzer, Isadore, illus. LC 87-22057. 32p. (gr. k-3). 1990. RSBE 13.95 (*0-02-737000-3*, Macmillan Child Bk) Macmillan Child Grp.

—You Don't Need Words. Ryan, Susannah, illus. 48p. 1991. 13.95 (*0-590-43897-2*, Scholastic Hardcover) Scholastic Inc.

Gross, Sukey. The Whispering Wind. Shiman, Hedy, illus. 128p. (gr. 6-8). 1991. 10.95 (*1-56062-068-4*); pap. 7.95 (*1-56062-069-2*) CIS Comm.

Gross, Sukey S. The Golden Gate. Shiman, Hedy, illus. 172p. (gr. 5-8). 1989. 11.95 (*1-56062-002-1*); pap. 8.95 (*1-56062-003-X*) CIS Comm.

—Passport to Russia. Backman, Aidel, illus. 158p. (gr. 5-8). 1989. 10.95 (*0-935063-59-5*); pap. 7.95 (*0-935063-60-9*) CIS Comm.

—The Secret Diary. Backman, Aidel, illus. (gr. 5-8). 1989. 10.95 (*0-935063-67-6*); pap. 7.95 (*0-935063-68-4*) CIS Comm.

—The Silent Summer. Shiman, Hedy, illus. 139p. (gr. 7-9). 1989. 10.95 (*1-56062-004-8*); pap. 7.95 (*1-56062-005-6*) CIS Comm.

Gross, Theodore F. Everyone Asked about You. Samton, Sheila W., illus. 32p. (ps-3). 1990. 14.95 (*0-399-21727-4*, Philomel Bks) Putnam Pub Group.

Gross, Virginia. The President Is Dead: A Story of the Kennedy Assassination. Andreasen, Dan, illus. 64p. (gr. 2-6). 1993. reinforced bdg. 12.99 (*0-670-84516-6*) Viking Child Bks.

Gross, Virginia T. The Day It Rained Forever: A Story of the Johnstown Flood. Himler, Ronald, illus. 64p. (gr. 2-6). 1991. 11.95 (*0-670-83552-8*) Viking Child Bks.

—The Day It Rained Forever: The Story of the Johnstown Flood. Himler, Ronald, illus. LC 92-44712. 64p. (gr. 2-6). 1993. pap. 3.99 (*0-14-034567-1*, Puffin Puffin Bks.

—It's Only Goodbye. (gr. 4-8). 1990. 11.95 (*0-670-83289-8*) Viking Child Bks.

—It's Only Goodbye: An Immigrant Story. Raymond, Larry, illus. LC 92-18959. 64p. (gr. 2-6). 1992. pap. 3.99 (*0-14-034409-8*) Puffin Bks.

Grosseck, Joyce & Atwood, Elizabeth, eds. Great Explorers. rev. ed. LC 87-81354. (Illus.). 160p. (gr. 4 up). 1988. 1-4 copies 14.95 ea. (*0-934291-22-5*); 5 or more copies 11.95 (*0-317-91140-6*) Gateway Pr MI.

Grosser, Morton. The Fabulous Fifty. LC 89-77999. 224p. (gr. 7 up). 1990. SBE 14.95 (*0-689-31656-9*, Atheneum Child Bk) Macmillan Child Grp.

Grosset & Dunlap Staff. I'm So Big! (Illus.). 18p. (ps). 1991. bds. 2.95 (*0-448-40122-3*, G&D) Putnam Pub Group.

—Wheels on the Bus. Smath, Jerry, illus. 18p. (ps). 1991. bds. 2.95 (*0-448-40124-X*, G&D) Putnam Pub Group.

—Who Says Quack? (Illus.). 18p. (ps). 1991. bds. 2.95 (*0-448-40123-1*, G&D) Putnam Pub Group.

Grosshandler, Henry & Grosshandler, Janet. Everyone Wins at Tee Ball. Grosshandler, Henry & Grosshandler, Janet, illus. LC 89-7875. 32p. (gr. k-3). 1990. 12.95 (*0-525-65016-4*, Cobblehill Bks) Dutton Child Bks.

Grosshandler, Janet. Coping with Drinking & Driving. rev. ed. Rosen, Ruth, ed. (gr. 7-12). 1993. PLB 13.95 (*0-8239-1603-0*) Rosen Group.

—Coping with Verbal Abuse. Rosen, Ruth, ed. (gr. 7-12). 1989. PLB 13.95 (*0-8239-0979-4*) Rosen Group.

—Drugs & Driving. Rosen, Ruth, ed. (gr. 7-12). 1992. 14.95 (*0-8239-1417-8*) Rosen Group.

—Drugs & the Law. Rosen, Ruth, ed. (gr. 7-12). 1993. 14.95 (*0-8239-1463-1*) Rosen Group.

—The Value of Generosity. (gr. 7-12). 1991. PLB 15.95 (*0-8239-1287-6*) Rosen Group.

—Winning Ways in Soccer. Grosshandler, Janet, photos by. LC 90-48620. (Illus.). 32p. (gr. k-3). 1991. 13.95 (*0-525-65064-4*, Cobblehill Bks) Dutton Child Bks.

Grosshandler, Janet, jt. auth. see Grosshandler, Henry.

Grossman, Bill. Cowboy Ed. Wint, Florence, illus. LC 92-23393. 32p. (ps-2). 1993. 15.00 (*0-06-021570-4*); PLB 14.89 (*0-06-021571-2*) HarpC Child Bks.

—Donna O'Neeshuck Was Chased by Some Cows. Truesdell, Sue, illus. LC 85-45823. 40p. (gr. k-3). 1988. PLB 12.89 (*0-06-022159-3*) HarpC Child Bks.

—Donna O'Neeshuck Was Chased by Some Cows. Truesdell, Sue, illus. LC 85-45823. 40p. (gr. k-3). 1991. pap. 5.95 (*0-06-443255-6*, Trophy) HarpC Child Bks.

—The Guy Who Was Five Minutes Late. Glasser, Judy, illus. LC 89-36336. 32p. (ps-3). 1990. PLB 13.89 (*0-06-022269-7*) HarpC Child Bks.

—Tommy at the Grocery Store. Chess, Victoria, illus. LC 88-35756. 32p. (ps-2). 1989. 13.00 (*0-06-022408-8*); PLB 12.89 (*0-06-022409-6*) HarpC Child Bks.

—Tommy at the Grocery Store. Chess, Victoria, illus. LC 88-35756. 32p. (ps-2). 1991. pap. 4.95 (*0-06-443266-1*, Trophy) HarpC Child Bks.

—Tommy at the Grocery Store Big Book. Chess, Victoria, illus. LC 88-35756. 32p. (ps-1). 1992. 19.95 (*0-694-00387-5*) HarpC Child Bks.

Grossman, Cheryl S. & Engman, Suzy. Jewish Literature for Children: A Teaching Guide. LC 85-70543. 230p. (Orig.). (gr. 4 up). 1985. text ed. 19.00 (*0-86705-018-7*); pap. text ed. 15.00 (*0-685-10172-X*) A R E Pub.

Grossman, Florence. Getting from Here to There: Writing & Reading Poetry. LC 82-4319. 171p. (gr. 10-12). 1982. pap. text ed. 14.50x (*0-86709-033-2*) Boynton Cook Pubs.

—Listening to the Bells: Learning to Read Poetry by Writing Poetry. 133p. (Orig.). (gr. 8-9). 1991. pap. text ed. 13.50x (*0-86709-274-2*, 0274) Boynton Cook Pubs.

Grossman, Joan A., jt. auth. see Isaacman, Clara.

Grossman, John & Dunhill, Priscilla. Nonsense & Commonsense: A Child's Book of Victorian Verse. 128p. 1992. 17.95 (*1-56305-313-6*, 3313) Workman Pub.

Grossman, Miriam. The Wonder of Becoming You: How a Jewish Girl Grows Up. (gr. 6-8). 1988. 8.95 (*0-87306-438-0*) Feldheim.

Grossman, Patricia. The Night Ones. D'Andrade, Diane, ed. Dabcovich, Lydia, illus. 32p. (ps-3). 1991. 13.95 (*0-15-257438-7*) HarBrace.

Grossman, Ronald P. Italians in America. LC 92-31325. 1993. lib. bdg. 15.95 (*0-8225-0244-5*); pap. 5.95 (*0-8225-1040-5*) Lerner Pubns.

Grossman, Roz & Gewirtz, Gladys. Let's Play Dreidel. Springer, Sally, illus. LC 89-34892. 16p. (ps-3). 1989. incl. tape & dreidel 6.95 (*0-929371-00-3*) Kar Ben.

Grossman, Susan. Piranhas. LC 93-1772. (Illus.). 60p. (gr. 4). 1994. RSBE 13.95 (*0-87518-593-2*, Dillon) Macmillan Child Grp.

Grossman, Virginia. Ten Little Rabbits. Long, Sylvia, illus. 32p. (ps-3). 1991. 12.95 (*0-87701-552-X*) Chronicle Bks.

Grosvenor, Carol. Once upon a Forest. (ps-3). 1993. 12.95 (*1-878685-87-2*) Turner Pub GA.

Grosvenor, Donna K. see National Geographic Society Staff.

Grosvenor, Richard. An Airplane Ride over Newport. 8p. (gr. k-2). 1993. pap. write for info. (*1-882563-02-6*) Lamont Bks.

—Geronimo. 8p. (gr. k-2). 1993. pap. write for info. (*1-882563-06-9*) Lamont Bks.

Grosvenor, Rick. Fishing in Narragansett Bay. 8p. (gr. k-2). 1993. pap. write for info. (*1-882563-04-2*) Lamont Bks.

Groten, Frank J., Jr. & Finn, James K. A Basic Course for Reading Attic Greek. LC 85-234367. 284p. (gr. 9-12). 1990. Repr. of 1983 ed. 19.90x (*0-942573-50-1*) Hill School.

Groten, Frank J., Jr., jt. auth. see Anderson, John A.

Grote-Sorensen, Barbara De see De Grote-Sorensen, Barbara.

Groth, J. L. Prayer: Learning How to Talk to God. LC 56-1395. (gr. 1 up). 1983. pap. 3.99 (*0-570-07799-0*) Concordia.

Groth, Lynn. God Cares for Me. 8p. (Orig.). (ps). 1985. pap. 1.25 (*0-938272-75-6*) Wels Board.

—Jesus Loves Children. 16p. (Orig.). (ps). 1985. pap. 1.25 (*0-938272-78-0*) Wels Board.

—Reaching Tender Hearts, 3 vols. Grunze, R., ed. May, Lawrence & Steele, illus. (Orig.). (ps-k). 1988. Set. pap. text ed. write for info. (*0-938272-45-4*) WELS Board.
—Reaching Tender Hearts, Vol. 1. Grunze, Richard, ed. May, Lawrence & Steele, Loren, illus. 157p. (ps-k). 1987. pap. 7.95 (*0-938272-42-X*) WELS Board.
—Reaching Tender Hearts, Vol. 2. Grunze, Richard, ed. May, Lawrence & Steele, Loren, illus. 176p. (ps-k). 1988. pap. 8.95 (*0-938272-43-8*) WELS Board.
—Reaching Tender Hearts, Vol. 3. Grunze, R., ed. May, Lawrence & Steele, Lawrence, trs. (Illus.). 163p. (Orig.). (gr. k). 1988. pap. text ed. 8.95 (*0-938272-44-6*) WELS Board.
—A Very Special Baby-Jesus. 8p. (Orig.). (ps). 1985. pap. 1.25 (*0-938272-76-4*) Wels Board.
—With You, Dear Child, in Mind. 16p. (Orig.). (ps). 1985. pap. 1.25 (*0-938272-77-2*) Wels Board.
Group for Environmental Education, Inc. Staff. Our Man-Made Environment, Book 7. (gr. 7). 1973. pap. 7.95x (*0-262-07050-2*) MIT Pr.
Group Publishing, Inc. Editors. Angels, Demons, Miracles & Prayer. (Illus.). 48p. (gr. 9-12). 1993. pap. 8.99 (*1-55945-235-8*) Group Pub.
—Dealing with Life's Pressures. (Illus.). 48p. (gr. 9-12). 1993. pap. 8.99 (*1-55945-232-3*) Group Pub.
—Doing Your Best. (Illus.). 48p. (gr. 6-8). 1993. pap. 8.99 (*1-55945-142-4*) Group Pub.
—The Miracle of Easter. (Illus.). 48p. (gr. 6-8). 1993. pap. 8.99 (*1-55945-143-2*) Group Pub.
—Psalms. (Illus.). 48p. (gr. 9-12). 1993. pap. 8.99 (*1-55945-234-X*) Group Pub.
—The Thirteen Most Important Bible Lessons for Teenagers. LC 93-13436. 100p. 1993. pap. 12.99 (*1-55945-261-7*) Group Pub.
Group Publishing, Inc. Staff. Hands-on Bible Curriculum. Incl. (gr. 1-2). 1993. learning lab 34.99 (*1-55945-325-7*); tchr's. guide 14.99 (*1-55945-324-9*); (gr. 1-2). 1993. learning lab 34.99 (*1-55945-327-3*); tchr's. guide 14.99 (*1-55945-326-5*); (gr. 3-4). 1993. learning lab 34.99 (*1-55945-339-7*); tchr's. guide 14.99 (*1-55945-338-9*); (gr. 3-4). 1993. learning lab 34.99 (*1-55945-341-9*); tchr's. guide 14.99 (*1-55945-340-0*); (gr. 5-6). 1993. learning lab 34.99 (*1-55945-315-X*); tchr's. guide 14.99 (*1-55945-314-1*); (gr. 5-6). 1993. learning lab 34.99 (*1-55945-317-6*); tchr's. guide 14.99 (*1-55945-316-8*). Group Pub.
Group Publishing, Inc. Staff, ed. Ten-Minute Devotions, Vol. III. LC 93-7811. 1993. 10.99 (*1-55945-171-8*) Group Pub.
Grout, Harry & Grout, Susan. Fun & Easy Guide to San Francisco. Hardin, Harry, illus. 32p. (Orig.). (gr. 2). 1991. pap. 5.95 (*0-9626868-4-0*) Locations Plus.
Grout, Susan, jt. auth. see Grout, Harry.
Groutage, Cor. The Dog Walkers. LC 93-32597. (gr. 4 up). 1995. write for info. (*0-679-85439-8*); PLB write for info. (*0-679-95439-2*) Knopf Bks Yng Read.
Grove, Karen, ed. see Geras, Adele.
Grove, Karen, ed. see Koller, Jackie F.
Grove, Karen, ed. see Rinaldi, Ann.
Grove, Karen, ed. see Spurr, Elizabeth.
Grove, Roger. Riches of Rag. 16p. (Orig.). (gr. k-12). 1976. pap. text ed. 5.95 (*0-87487-188-3*) Summy-Birchard.
Grove, Vicki. The Fastest Friend in the West. 176p. (gr. 4-8). 1990. 14.95 (*0-399-22184-0*, Putnam) Putnam Pub Group.
—Fastest Friend in the West. 176p. 1992. pap. 2.95 (*0-590-44338-0*, Apple Paperbacks) Scholastic Inc.
—Good-bye, My Wishing Star. 128p. (gr. 3-7). 1988. 13. 95 (*0-399-21532-8*, Putnam) Putnam Pub Group.
—Goodbye My Wishing Star. 1989. pap. 2.95 (*0-590-42152-2*) Scholastic Inc.
—He Gave Her Roses. 144p. (Orig.). (gr. 7-12). 1989. pap. 6.99 (*0-931529-92-1*) Group Pub.
—Junglerama. (gr. 4-7). 1991. pap. 2.75 (*0-590-43163-3*, Apple Paperbacks) Scholastic Inc.
—Rimwalkers. LC 92-36091. 224p. (gr. 5 up). 1993. 14. 95 (*0-399-22430-0*, Putnam) Putnam Pub Group.
Grover, Max. The Accidental Zucchini: An Unexpected Alphabet. LC 93-24881. 1993. write for info. (*0-15-277695-8*, Browndeer Pr) HarBrace.
Grover, Teddi. Buttons: The Foster Bunny. Iverson, Diane, illus. Martone, Frederick A., intro. by. (Illus.). 48p. (Orig.). (ps-5). 1992. pap. 8.95 (*0-9623349-3-6*) MS Assoc.
Grover, Wayne. Ali & the Golden Eagle. LC 91-43736. (Illus.). 160p. (gr. 7 up). 1993. 13.00 (*0-688-11385-0*) Greenwillow.
—Dolphin Adventure: A True Story. Fowler, Jim, illus. LC 89-27226. 48p. (gr. 3 up). 1990. 12.00 (*0-688-09442-2*) Greenwillow.
—Dolphin Adventure: A True Story. Fowler, Jim, illus. LC 92-25545. 48p. (gr. 4 up). 1993. pap. 3.95 (*0-688-12277-9*, Pub. by Beech Tree Bks) Morrow.
Groves, Richard. Surprise, Surprise, Queen Loonia! Burgess, Mark, illus. 32p. (ps-1). 1992. pap. 5.95 (*0-8120-4582-3*) Barron.
Groves, Seli, jt. auth. see Fletcher, Helen J.
Groves, Seli, jt. auth. see Rott, Joanna R.
Grubbs, J. Angle Iron: Basketball. Abell, J., illus. 20p. (Orig.). 1992. pap. 18.00 (*1-56611-008-4*) Jones.
—Angle Iron: The Junior High Team. Abell, J., ed. 50p. (gr. 6-8). 1988. lib. bdg. 15.00 (*1-56611-003-3*) Jones.
—Muscle Building. Abel, J., illus. 36p. 1992. pap. 18.00 (*1-56611-010-6*) Jones.
—Socks, the Cat Who Moved to Washington. Abell, J., ed. Grubbs, J., illus. 50p. (gr. 1-4). 1993. 22.00x (*1-56611-022-X*); pap. 10.00 (*0-685-63570-8*) Jones.
—The Survival Kit. rev. ed. Abell, ed. & illus. (gr. 7-8). Date not set. lib. bdg. 25.00 (*1-56611-011-4*); pap. 10. 00 (*0-685-66203-9*) Jones.
Grubbs, J. & Abell, J. Henry the Cop. Grubbs, J., illus. 50p. (Orig.). (gr. 2-5). 1993. text ed. 18.00 (*1-56611-020-3*); pap. 7.00 (*0-685-63577-5*) Jones.
Grubbs, J., ed. Where Do the Birds Go When It Storms. Abell, J. & Abell, J., illus. (gr. 1-3). 1992. lib. bdg. 20. 00 (*1-56611-012-2*); pap. 10.00 (*0-685-66201-2*) Jones.
Grubbs, J., et al. Running for Ribbons. 32p. (gr. 1-5). 1984. lib. bdg. 15.00 (*1-56611-001-7*) Jones.
Grubbs, Joan. A Sweet Potato: A Christmas Story. Abell, J., ed. (Orig.). (gr. 2-5). 1993. text ed. 18.00 (*1-56611-021-1*); pap. 7.00 (*0-685-63583-X*) Jones.
Grubbs, Joan & Grubbs, Tori. PH - Little Leaguer: Little League Peewee Baseball. Abel, J., illus. 17p. (Orig.). (gr. 1-3). 1992. pap. 10.00 (*1-56611-009-2*) Jones.
Grubbs, Joan, et al. The Big Fish Tale. (Illus.). 30p. (Orig.). 1993. PLB 22.00 (*1-56611-023-8*); pap. text ed. 18.00 (*1-56611-027-0*) Jones.
—C Little Leaguer: (A Little League Baseball Story) Abell, ed. & illus. 50p. (gr. 1-4). 1993. 18.00 (*0-685-66007-9*); pap. 10.00 (*0-685-66008-7*) Jones.
—Possessive Pronouns. rev. ed. Abell, ed. Grubbs, Joan, illus. 50p. (gr. 3-6). 1993. 23.00 (*0-685-65773-6*); PLB 23.00 (*0-685-65774-4*); pap. 11.00 (*0-685-65775-2*) Jones.
Grubbs, Joan J., et al. Books for Young Gentlemen. rev. ed. Grubbs, Joan, illus. 50p. (gr. 6-8). 1993. 22.00 (*1-56611-024-6*); PLB 22.00 (*0-685-65769-8*); pap. 10. 00 (*0-685-65770-1*) Jones.
Grubbs, Joan P. The Cat Who Returned Nine Times. Abell, ed. & illus. 50p. (Orig.). (gr. 1-4). 1993. 25.00 (*1-56611-060-2*); pap. 15.00 (*0-685-68773-2*) Jones.
Grubbs, T. Tori Had the Chicken-Pox: Halloween. Abell, J., ed. & illus. 36p. (Orig.). (gr. k-3). 1991. pap. 10.00 software looseleaf (*1-56611-002-5*) Jones.
Grubbs, Tab & Abell, J., illus. Light Industrial. (gr. 1-3). 1993. pap. 7.00 spiral (*0-685-62313-0*) Jones.
Grubbs, Tabitha & McQueen, Tiffany. Different Types of Stories & Poems. (Illus.). 52p. (gr. k-3). 1983. PLB 15. 00 (*1-56611-000-9*) Jones.
Grubbs, Tori, jt. auth. see Grubbs, Joan.
Grube, Karl W. Cribbage d'Etroit. Grube, Karl W., illus. 129p. (gr. 3 up). Date not set. 29.95 (*0-685-63059-5*); tchr's. ed. 49.95 (*0-685-63060-9*) Intl Gamester.
—Cribbage in Schools Program. Grube, Karl W., illus. 29p. (gr. 3 up). Date not set. pap. text ed. 10.00 tchr's. guide (*0-685-63061-7*) Intl Gamester.
—Lake Huron Poker. Grube, Karl W., illus. 124p. (gr. 3 up). Date not set. pap. text ed. 29.95 (*0-685-63062-5*); tchr's. ed. 49.95 (*0-685-63063-3*) Intl Gamester.
—Lake Michigan Poker. Grube, Karl W., illus. 132p. (gr. 3 up). Date not set. pap. text ed. 29.95 (*0-685-63064-1*); tchr's. ed. 49.95 (*0-685-63065-X*) Intl Gamester.
Grube, Karl W. & Grube, Kathryn. Lake Superior Cribbage. Grube, Kathryn, illus. 112p. (gr. 3 up). Date not set. pap. text ed. 29.95 (*0-685-63057-9*); tchr's. ed. 49.95 (*0-685-63058-7*) Intl Gamester.
Grube, Kathryn, jt. auth. see Grube, Karl W.
Grube, Karl W., intro. by see Wergin, Joseph P. & Smith, Beatrice S.
Gruber, Barbara. Building Literacy. (Illus.). 64p. (gr. k-6). 1992. 7.95 (*0-86734-139-4*, FS-8323) Schaffer Pubns.
Gruber, Gary R. Dr. Gary Gruber's Essential Guide to Test Taking for Kids. LC 86-8655. 120p. (Orig.). (gr. 3-5). 1986. pap. text ed. 7.95 (*0-688-06350-0*, Quill) Morrow.
—Dr. Gary Gruber's Essential Guide to Test-Taking for Kids. Guarnaschelli, Maria D., ed. LC 86-9392. 120p. (Orig.). (gr. 6-9). 1986. pap. text ed. 7.95 (*0-688-06351-9*, Quill) Morrow.
—Gruber's Complete Preparation for the SAT - Featuring Critical Thinking Skills. (Orig.). (gr. 10-12). 1992. pap. 12.95 (*0-935475-00-1*) Critical Book.
Gruber, Suzanne. Chatty Chipmunk's Nutty Day. Cushman, Doug, illus. LC 84-8665. 32p. (gr. k-2). 1985. PLB 11.59 (*0-8167-0360-4*); pap. text ed. 2.95 (*0-8167-0440-6*) Troll Assocs.
—Monster under My Bed. Bret, Stephanie, illus. LC 84-45687. 32p. (gr. k-2). 1985. PLB 10.89 (*0-8167-0456-2*); pap. text ed. 2.95 (*0-8167-0457-0*) Troll Assocs.
Gruelle, Johnny. Original Adventures of Raggedy Andy. LC 88-3704. 1988. 8.99 (*0-517-66582-4*) Outlet Bk Co.
—Original Adventures of Raggedy Ann. LC 88-3684. (Illus.). 64p. 1988. 7.99 (*0-517-66581-6*) Outlet Bk Co.
—Orphan Annie Story Book. 2nd ed. LC 89-80852. 100p. (gr. k-5). 1989. Repr. of 1921 ed. 14.95 (*0-9617367-9-8*) Guild Pr IN.
—Raggedy Andy Stories. Gruelle, Johnny, illus. 96p. (ps up). 1987. Repr. PLB 25.95x (*0-89966-618-3*) Buccaneer Bks.
—Raggedy Andy Stories: Introducing the Little Rag Brother of Raggedy Ann. reissued ed. Gruelle, Johnny, illus. Gruelle, Kim, afterword by. LC 93-21967. (Illus.). 96p. (gr. k up). 1993. SBE 16.95 (*0-02-737586-2*, Macmillan Child Bk) Macmillan Child Grp.
—Raggedy Ann & Andy & the Camel with the Wrinkled Knees. (gr. 1-4). 1977. pap. 1.95 (*0-440-47390-X*) Dell.
—Raggedy Ann & Andy Giant Treasury: Four Adventures Plus 12 Short Stories. Golden, N., retold by. Nash, C., frwd. by. (Illus.). 96p. (ps-1). 1985. 5.99 (*0-517-45594-3*) Outlet Bk Co.
—Raggedy Ann Stories. reissued ed. Gruelle, Johnny, illus. Gruelle, Kim, afterword by. LC 93-630. (Illus.). 96p. (gr. k up). 1993. SBE 16.95 (*0-02-737585-4*, Macmillan Child Bk) Macmillan Child Grp.
—The Raggedy Ann Stories. Facsimile ed. LC 93-8698. 1994. 6.99 (*0-517-10037-1*, Pub. by Derrydale Bks) Outlet Bk Co.
Gruelle, Johny. Original Adventures of Raggedy Ann & Raggedy Andy. (Illus.). 128p. 1991. 9.99 (*0-517-06631-9*, Pub. by Derrydale Bks) Outlet Bk Co.
Gruenbaum, Hannah. Come, Count with Me. Forst, Sigmund, illus. (ps-1). 1.50 (*0-685-86207-0*) Feldheim.
Gruenberg, Hannah C., jt. auth. see Bancroft, Catherine.
Gruenberg, Linda. Hummer. 192p. (gr. 5-9). 1990. 13.45 (*0-395-51080-5*) HM.
Grumbine, Robert W. Discover Weather. (Illus.). 48p. (gr. 3-6). 1992. PLB 14.95 (*1-56674-032-0*, HTS Bks) Forest Hse.
Grumet, Robert S. The Lenapes. (Illus.). 112p. (gr. 5 up). 1990. 17.95 (*1-55546-712-1*); pap. 9.95 (*0-7910-0385-X*) Chelsea Hse.
Grummer, Arnold E. The Great Balloon Game Book & More Balloon Activities. Wenger-Marsh, Beth, illus. 112p. (gr. 2 up). 1987. 12.95 (*0-938251-00-7*) G Markim.
—Paper by Kids. rev. ed. LC 79-22904. (Illus.). 116p. (gr. 5 up). 1990. RSBE 12.95 (*0-87518-191-0*, Dillon) Macmillan Child Grp.

—Tin Can Papermaking: Recycle for Earth & Art. Grummer, Arnold & Rotzel, Spencer, illus. 80p. (Orig.). (gr. 1 up). 1992. pap. 7.95 (*0-938251-01-5*) G Markim.

This book describes how to gather everything you need to make paper right from your own kitchen. Featuring chapters on art & decorative techniques, recycling, paper history, what paper is made of & more, this 80 page book (complete with over 60 photos) is also a small encyclopedia of paper art & science. Written by Arnold Grummer, former curator of the Dard Hunter Paper Museum housed in the Institute of Paper Chemistry, the language in this book is so simple a grade school student would have no trouble using it, yet the science discussed in the book has compelled many adults. The book also gives step-by-step instructions for making invitations, envelopes, round stationery, flower embedments, & much more using a set of tin cans & other common kitchen items. An excellent resource material or home craft guide. "... beginners will be able to create something genuinely beautiful in a short period of time..environmental information about paper & recycling is presented without preaching."-- Bloomsbury Review.
Publisher Provided Annotation.

Grummond, Lena De see De Grummond, Lena & Delaune, Lynn.
Grund, Diane F., ed. see Verne, Jules.
Grundtvig, Sven. Danish Fairy Tales. Cramer, J. Grant, tr. from DAN. Van Heusen, Drew, illus. vii, 115p. (gr. k-5). 1972. pap. 4.95 (*0-486-22891-6*) Dover.
Grundy, Lynn A., illus. A Is for Apple. 28p. (ps). 1992. 3.50 (*0-7214-1508-3*) Ladybird Bks.
—Let's Count. 28p. (ps). 1992. 3.50 (*0-7214-1509-1*) Ladybird Bks.
Grundy, Lynn N. A Is for Apple. (ps-k). 1989. pap. text ed. 3.95 cased (*0-7214-5052-0*) Ladybird Bks.
Grunsell, Angela. Bullying. LC 89-28332. (ps-3). 1990. PLB 11.40 (*0-531-17213-9*) Watts.
—Hablemos del Rascismo. Mlawer, Teresa, tr. (Illus.). 32p. (gr. 4-6). 1993. 12.95 (*1-880507-09-9*) Lectorum Pubns.
—Racism. LC 90-43994. (Illus.). 32p. (gr. k-3). 1991. PLB 11.40 (*0-531-17279-1*, Gloucester Pr) Watts.
—Stepfamilies. (Illus.). 32p. (gr. 2-5). 1990. PLB 11.40 (*0-531-17244-9*, Gloucester Pr) Watts.
Grunze, R., ed. see Fehlauer, Adolph.
Grunze, R., ed. see Groth, Lynn.
Grunze, Richard. Searching in God's Word-New Testament. Most, Richard, illus. 142p. (gr. 5-6). 1986. 4.95 (*0-938272-41-1*) WELS Board.

—Searching in God's Word-Old Testament. Most, Richard, illus. 140p. (gr. k up). 1986. 4.95 (0-938272-40-3) WELS Board.
Grunze, Richard, ed. see Fehlauer, Adolph.
Grunze, Richard, ed. see Groth, Lynn.
Gruver, Kate E., ed. see MacDougall, Mary-Katherine.
Gryski, Camilla. Friendship Bracelets. LC 92-31097. (Illus.). 48p. (gr. 5 up). 1993. 14.00 (0-688-12435-6); PLB 13.93 (0-688-12436-4) Morrow Jr Bks.
—Friendship Bracelets. LC 92-31097. (Illus.). (gr. 5 up). 1993. pap. 6.95 (0-688-12437-2, Pub. by Beech Tree Bks) Morrow.
—Hands On, Thumbs Up: Secret Handshakes, Fingerprints, Sign Languages, & More Handy Ways to Have Fun with Hands. 112p. 1991. pap. 8.61 (0-201-56756-3) Addison-Wesley.
—Lanyard: Having Fun with Plastic Lace. Hendry, Linda, illus. LC 93-35992. 1994. Repr. of 1993 ed. write for info. (0-688-13324-X) Morrow Jr Bks.
Gryspeerdt, Rebecca. Colleen & the Hairy Beast. (Illus.). 32p. (gr. 1-4). 1992. 16.95 (1-85681-101-8, Pub. by J MacRae UK) Trafalgar.
—Counting Friends. (Illus.). 24p. (ps-1). 1993. 13.95 (1-85681-092-5, Pub. by J MacRae UK) Trafalgar.
Gryte, Marilyn. No New Baby. Borum, Shari, illus. 24p. 1988. pap. 3.25 (1-56123-041-3) Centering Corp.
Guanzhong, Luo, jt. auth. see Nai'an, Shi.
Guard, David. Deirdre: A Celtic Legend. Guard, Gretchen, illus. 120p. (gr. 4-9). 1993. pap. 8.95 (1-883672-05-8) Tricycle Pr.
—Hale-mano: A Legend of Hawai'i. Sumile, Caridad, illus. & intro. by. 92p. 1993. page. 9.95 (1-883672-04-X) Tricycle Pr.
Guard, Jean & Williamson, Ray A. They Dance in the Sky. Stewart, Edgar, illus. (gr. 6 up). 1987. 14.45 (0-395-39970-X) HM.
Guardia-Heikkila, Alba. Drugs: The Big, Bad Monster. (Illus.). 40p. (gr. 2-4). 1991. wkbk. 4.95 (0-9631390-0-2) A Guardia-Heikkila.
Guareschi. Don Camillo. (gr. 7-12). 1972. pap. 5.95 (0-88436-121-7, 55255) EMC.
Guarino, Deborah. Is Your Mama a Llama? LC 87-32315. (ps-2). 1989. 12.95 (0-590-41387-2, Scholastic Hardcover) Scholastic Inc.
—Is Your Mama a Llama? Kellogg, Steven, illus. 1991. pap. 3.95 (0-590-44725-4, Blue Ribbon Bks) Scholastic Inc.
Guarnaschelli, Maria D., ed. see Gruber, Gary R.
Guastella, jt. auth. see Strong.
Guback, Georgia. The Carolers. LC 90-41756. (Illus.). 32p. 1992. 14.00 (0-688-09772-3); PLB 13.93 (0-688-09773-1) Greenwillow.
—Luka's Quilt. LC 93-12241. (Illus.). 32p. (ps up). 1994. write for info. (0-688-12154-3); PLB write for info. (0-688-12155-1) Greenwillow.
Guccione, Leslie D. Nobody Listens to Me. 176p. (gr. 3-7). 1991. pap. 2.75 (0-590-43106-4, Apple Paperbacks) Scholastic Inc.
—Tell Me How the Wind Sounds. 1992. pap. 3.25 (0-590-41714-2, Point) Scholastic Inc.
Gudeman, Janice. Creative Encounters with Creative People. Beebe, Mark & Filkins, Vanessa, illus. 144p. (gr. 4 up). 1984. wkbk. 11.95 (0-86653-258-7, GA 623) Good Apple.
—Learning from the Lives of Amazing People. 144p. (gr. 4 up). 1988. wkbk. 11.95 (0-86653-446-6, GA1055) Good Apple.
Guderjahn, Ernie L. A Children's Trilogy: Ali's Flying Rug, the Shadow Workers, & the Magic Cricket. (Orig.). (gr. 3 up). 1984. pap. 6.00 play script (0-88734-504-2) Players Pr.
Guengerich, Galen, jt. auth. see Barrett, Linda.
Guenter, H. Jugendlexikon Wirtschaft. (GER.). 192p. 1976. 12.95 (0-8288-5715-6, M7492, Pub. by Rowohlt) Fr & Eur.
Guentert, Kenneth. The Young Server's Book of the Mass. LC 86-60894. 88p. (gr. 6-8). 1987. pap. 4.95 (0-89390-078-8) Resource Pubns.
Guenther, Luisa, tr. see D'Andrea, Deborah B.
Guenther, Luisa, tr. see D'Andrea, Joseph C.
Guerette, Doris J. Penny Pinching Activities. Goldfluss, Karen J., et al, eds. (Illus.). 80p. (ps-3). 1993. wkbk. 7.95 (1-55734-150-8) Tchr Create Mat.
Guerney, Bernard G., tr. see Babel, Issac.
Guerney, Bernard G., tr. see Turgenev, Ivan S.
Guernsey, JoAnn B. Animal Rights. LC 90-33664. (Illus.). 48p. (gr. 5-6). 1990. RSBE 12.95 (0-89686-534-7, Crestwood Hse) Macmillan Child Grp.
—Hillary Rodham Clinton, a New Kind of First Lady. LC 93-21856. 1993. PLB 13.50 (0-8225-2875-4); pap. 6.95 (0-8225-9650-4) Lerner Pubns.
—Rape. LC 90-33666. (Illus.). 48p. (gr. 5-6). 1990. RSBE 12.95 (0-89686-533-9, Crestwood Hse) Macmillan Child Grp.
—Should We Have Capital Punishment? (Illus.). 96p. (gr. 6 up). 1992. PLB 17.50 (0-8225-2602-6) Lerner Pubns.
—Teen Pregnancy. LC 89-1384. (Illus.). 48p. (gr. 4 up). 1989. RSBE 12.95 (0-89686-435-9, Crestwood Hse) Macmillan Child Grp.
—Tipper Gore. LC 93-8165. 1993. PLB 17.50 (0-8225-2876-2); pap. 6.95 (0-8225-9651-2) Lerner Pubns.
Guernsey, JoAnn B., ed. see Brandenburg, Jim.

Guernsey, Paul. Noah & the Ark. Lohstoeter, Lori, illus. 40p. (gr. k up). 1993. incl. cass. 19.95 (0-88708-293-9, Rabbit Ears); 14.95 (0-88708-292-0, Rabbit Ears) Picture Bk Studio.
Guerrero Rea, Jesus, jt. auth. see Rohmer, Harriet.
Guerrero Rea, Jesus, tr. see Garcia, Richard.
Guerrier, Charlie. A Collage of Crafts. Schwartz, Marc, photos by. Colomb, Etienne, contrib. by. LC 93-24968. (Illus.). Date not set. 13.95 (0-395-68377-7) Ticknor & Fields.
Guerry, Jack. Silvio Scionti: Remembering a Master Pianist & Teacher. LC 91-10498. (Illus.). 240p. 1991. 25.00 (0-929398-27-0) UNTX Pr.
Guertin, Carolyn W., jt. auth. see Blank, Florence W.
Guest, Dean. The Other Side of Sex: An Open Letter to My Grandchildren. 50p. (Orig.). (gr. 5-10). 1991. pap. 2.50 (1-879667-00-2) Dove Pr TX.
Guest, Elissa H. The Handsome Man. 160p. (gr. 7 up). 1981. pap. 1.95 (0-440-93437-0, LFL) Dell.
—Over the Moon. LC 85-28505. 160p. (gr. 7 up). 1986. 12.95 (0-688-04148-5) Morrow Jr Bks.
Guglielmino, Terese. The Red Tag Mystery. Weinberger, Jane, ed. 160p. (gr. 4-8). 1993. pap. 9.95 (0-932433-14-6) Windswept Hse.
Guhm, Karl, jt. auth. see Guhm, Susan.
Guhm, Susan & Guhm, Karl. The Great Bodie Activity Book. (Illus.). 1991. write for info. (0-9627621-1-3) Froggy Bywater.
Guiberson & Lloyd. Winter Wheat. 1993. 14.95 (0-8050-1582-5) H Holt & Co.
Guiberson, Brenda. Into the Sea. 1994. 15.95 (0-8050-2263-5) H Holt & Co.
Guiberson, Brenda Z. Cactus Hotel. Lloyd, Megan, illus. LC 90-41748. 32p. (ps-2). 1991. 15.95 (0-8050-1333-4, Bks Young Read) H Holt & Co.
—Cactus Hotel. Lloyd, Megan, illus. LC 90-41748. 32p. (ps-3). 1993. pap. 4.95 (0-8050-2960-5, Bks Young Read) H Holt & Co.
—Instant Soup. LC 90-20415. 128p. (gr. 3-7). 1991. SBE 12.95 (0-689-31688-7, Atheneum Child Bk) Macmillan Child Grp.
—Lighthouses. 1995. write for info. (0-8050-3170-7) H Holt & Co.
—Lobster Boat. Lloyd, Megan, illus. LC 92-4055. 32p. (ps-3). 1993. PLB 14.95 (0-8050-1756-9, Bks Young Read) H Holt & Co.
—Salmon Story. Guiberson, Brenda, illus. LC 93-1360. 64p. (gr. 2-4). 1993. PLB 14.95 (0-8050-2754-8, Bks Young Read) H Holt & Co.
—Spoonbill Swamp. Lloyd, Megan, illus. LC 91-8555. 32p. (ps-3). 1992. 14.95 (0-8050-1583-3, Bks Young Read) H Holt & Co.
—Spotted Owl. 1995. write for info. (0-8050-3171-5) H Holt & Co.
—Turtle People. LC 90-388. 112p. (gr. 3-6). 1990. SBE 12.95 (0-689-31647-X, Atheneum Child Bk) Macmillan Child Grp.
Guibert, Rita, tr. see Berenstain, Stan & Berenstain, Jan.
Guibert, Rita, tr. see Wetzel, Rick & Swanson, Maggie.

Guida, Frank J. Shakespeare for Children: Romeo & Juliet - with a Happy Ending, Vol. 1. rev. ed. Guida, Frank J., illus. 20p. 1991. lib. bdg. write for info. (1-878476-00-9) Rockmasters Intl.
This children's adaptation of William Shakespeare's classic "ROMEO & JULIET" is intended to cultivate at an early age some of the most dramatic writing in literature. Wait till you hear your youngster reading, understanding & quoting The Bard! "What a wonderful treasure you have added to the shelves of children's literature in your adaptation of Romeo & Juliet. I thank & applaud you as future generations are certain to do like-wise." --Constance F. Zimmerman, Chairperson, Norfolk Reading Council. "The presentation is superb; the art work attractive; & the text very interesting."--James Cullinan, Finnbar Books, Kent, England. "I like your story Mr. Guida because it's with a happy ending. If they're sad, I start to cry & I have bad dreams. But I wonder where you got that name wink milch?"--Crystal (Drew School, 8 years old, Washington, D.C.). "My favorite part is when the two families become friends again & nobody got killed!"--Brett (Drew School, 9 years old). "In a unique adaptation, Frank Guida has forged a new method of bringing great literary works to young minds."--(Julie Cimino, Educator, Wash., D.C.). "Guida's adaptation incorporates portions of the original in all capital letters, such as Juliet's famous balcony scene."--Philip Walzer (Virginian-Pilot, Norfolk, Va.).** Publisher Provided Annotation.*

Guidoux, Valerie. Worried Little Lamb. Jensen, Patricia, adapted by. Pio, illus. LC 93-27048. 1994. write for info. (0-89577-563-8, Readers Digest Kids) RD Assn.
Guild, Anne V. Mickey Mouse in Let's Go...on a Beach Picnic. Scholefield, Ron, et al, illus. 26p. (ps up). 1987. pap. 14.95 (1-55578-800-9) Worlds Wonder.
—Mickey Mouse in Let's Go...on a Camping Caper. Scholefield, Ron, et al, illus. 26p. (ps up). 1987. pap. 14.95 (1-55578-803-3) Worlds Wonder.
—Mickey Mouse in Let's Go...to Disneyland. Scholefield, Ron, et al, illus. 26p. (ps up). 1988. pap. 14.95 (1-55578-801-7) Worlds Wonder.
—Mickey Mouse in Let's Go...to the Zoo! Scholefield, Ron, et al, illus. 26p. (ps up). 1987. pap. 14.95 (1-55578-802-5) Worlds Wonder.
Guild, I., jt. auth. see Potter, T.
Guild, Pat, jt. auth. see Ulrich, Cindy.
Guild, Robert W., Jr., jt. auth. see Rundquist, Thomas J.
Guiley, Rosemary E. Career Opportunities for Writers. rev. ed. 232p. (gr. 9-12). 1992. pap. 14.95 (0-8160-2462-6) Facts on File.
Guiliani, Alfred, illus. The Little Engine That Could: Busy Book. 48p. (ps-2). 1992. pap. 0.42 (0-448-40378-1, Platt & Munk Pubs) Putnam Pub Group.
Guillen, Nicholas. Tengo. Carr, Richard, tr. (gr. 12 up). 1974. 7.25 (0-910296-28-6); pap. 4.25 (0-685-00871-1) Broadside Pr.
Guillermo, Edenia, jt. auth. see Hernandez, Juana A.
Guillot, Rene. Sirga. Kiddell-Monroe, Joan, illus. LC 59-12198. (gr. 6-9). 1959. 21.95 (0-87599-046-0) S G Phillips.
—The Three Hundred Ninety-Seventh White Elephant. Leatham, Moyra, illus. (gr. 3-7). 1957. 20.95 (0-87599-043-6) S G Phillips.
—Wind of Chance. Dale, Norman, tr. Collot, Pierre, illus. (gr. 6-9). 1958. 21.95 (0-87599-048-7) S G Phillips.
Guin, Ursala K. Le see Le Guin, Ursala K.
Guin, Ursula K. Le see Le Guin, Ursula K.
Guin, Ursula K. le see Le Guin, Ursula K.
Guin, Ursula K. Le see Le Guin, Ursula K.
Guin, Ursula Le see Le Guin, Ursula K.
Guinness, Gerald, tr. from SPA. see Gonzales, Jose L.
Guittard, Charles. The Romans: Life in the Empire. LaRose, Mary K., tr. from FRE. Martin, Annie-Claude, illus. LC 92-9467. 64p. (gr. 4-6). 1992. PLB 14.90 (1-56294-200-X) Millbrook Pr.
Guitterez, Ruben, tr. see Woolley, Merle E.
Gulik, Van see Van Gulik.
Gullander, Elizabeth. Oswald Hoot: The Owl Who Was Scared of the Dark. Youra, Dan, illus. 64p. (ps-6). 1982. PLB 7.95 (0-940828-06-5); pap. 4.95 (0-940828-05-7) Olympic Pub.
Gullette, Margaret M. The Lost Bellybutton. Udry, Leslie, illus. LC 76-26377. 32p. (Orig.). (ps-2). 1976. pap. 4.95 (0-914996-11-8) Lollipop Power.
Gulley, Greg & Watts, David. Greatest Star of All. LC 92-73629. 30p. 1993. 10.99 (1-56384-017-0) Huntington Hse.
Gulley, Judie. Rodeo Summer. LC 84-9129. 192p. (gr. 5-9). 1984. 11.95 (0-395-36174-5) HM.
Gullic, Bob, ed. see Coltharpe, Barbara A.
Gullo, Catherine A. Gearing up for College: Guidelines for High School Students & Parents. 20p. (gr. 9-12). 1992. pap. 10.00 spiral bdg. (1-883374-00-6) Scholar Cnslt.
—A Simple Guide to Applying & Preparing for the College of Your Choice. 19p. (gr. 11-12). 1992. pap. 10.00 spiral bdg. (1-883374-01-4) Scholar Cnslt.
Gump, Patricia L., ed. see Wallower, Lucille.
Gunby, Lise. Early Farm Life. (Illus.). 80p. (gr. 3-4). 1983. 15.95 (0-86505-027-9); pap. 7.95 (0-86505-026-0) Crabtree Pub Co.
Gundersen, Ben. Memory Verse Bulletin Boards. 96p. (ps-7). 1988. 10.95 (0-86653-426-1, SS1827, Shining Star Pubns) Good Apple.
Gundersheimer, Karen. Colors to Know. Gundersheimer, Karen, illus. LC 85-45390. 32p. (ps-1). 1986. HarpC Child Bks.
Gunderson, Sandy, jt. auth. see Mehl, Ron, Jr.
Gunderson, Vivian D. The Enemy Guest. (gr. k-8). 1964. pap. 2.50 (0-915374-11-0, 11-0) Rapids Christian.
—Island Prisoner. (gr. k-8). 1974. pap. 2.50 (0-915374-12-9, 12-9) Rapids Christian.
—Over the Cliff. (gr. k-8). 1974. pap. 2.50 (0-915374-13-7, 13-7) Rapids Christian.
—Saved on Monday. (gr. k-8). 1964. pap. 2.50 (0-915374-14-5, 14-5) Rapids Christian.
—The Wrong Road. (gr. k-8). 1964. pap. 2.50 (0-915374-15-3, 15-3) Rapids Christian.
Gunn, Jeffrey. Pen Pals Series, No. 1. Wolfe, Debra, illus. (Orig.). (gr. 1). 1991. pap. write for info. (1-879146-00-2) Knowldg Pub.
—Pen Pals, Vol. 1: The Beginning. Doughty, Virgina, illus. (Orig.). (gr. 3). 1990. pap. write for info. (1-879146-01-0) Knowldg Pub.

—Pen Pals, Vol. 10: Facts about Nicotine. Wolfe, Debra, illus. (Orig.). (gr. 3). 1990. pap. write for info. (*1-879146-10-X*) Knowldg Pub.
—Pen Pals, Vol. 11: Facts about Alcohol. Wolfe, Debra, illus. (Orig.). (gr. 3). 1990. pap. write for info. (*1-879146-11-8*) Knowldg Pub.
—Pen Pals, Vol. 2: Facts about Cocaine. Wolfe, Debra, illus. (Orig.). (gr. 3). 1990. pap. write for info. (*1-879146-02-9*) Knowldg Pub.
—Pen Pals, Vol. 3: Facts about Heroin. Wolfe, Debra, illus. (Orig.). (gr. 3). 1990. pap. write for info. (*1-879146-03-7*) Knowldg Pub.
—Pen Pals, Vol. 4: Facts about Pot. Wolfe, Debra, illus. (Orig.). (gr. 3). 1990. pap. write for info. (*1-879146-04-5*) Knowldg Pub.
—Pen Pals, Vol. 5: Facts about Dust. Doughty, Virgina, illus. (Orig.). (gr. 3). 1990. pap. write for info. (*1-879146-05-3*) Knowldg Pub.
—Pen Pals, Vol. 6: Facts about Speed. Wolfe, Debra, illus. (Orig.). (gr. 3). 1990. pap. write for info. (*1-879146-06-1*) Knowldg Pub.
—Pen Pals, Vol. 7: Facts about Downers. Wolfe, Debra, illus. (Orig.). (gr. 3). 1990. pap. write for info. (*1-879146-07-X*) Knowldg Pub.
—Pen Pals, Vol. 8: Facts about Acid. Wolfe, Debra, illus. (Orig.). (gr. 3). 1990. pap. write for info. (*1-879146-08-8*) Knowldg Pub.
—Pen Pals, Vol. 9: Facts about Crack. Wolfe, Debra, illus. (Orig.). (gr. 3). 1990. pap. write for info. (*1-879146-09-6*) Knowldg Pub.
Gunn, Robin J. Mountains, Meadows, & More: A Book about Places God Has Made. Lauck, Dawn, illus. LC 93-9990. 1994. write for info. (*0-7814-0101-1*, Chariot Bks) Cook.
—Mrs. Rosey-Posey & the Chocolate Cherry Treat. Duca, Bill, illus. 32p. (ps-2). 1991. pap. 4.49 (*1-55513-370-3*, 33704, Chariot Bks) Cook.
—Mrs. Rosey Posey & the Empty Nest. LC 92-12955. (gr. k-3). 1993. write for info. (*0-7814-0329-4*, Chariot Bks) Cook.
—Mrs. Rosey-Posey & the Treasure Hunt. Duca, Bill, illus. 32p. (ps-2). 1991. pap. 4.49 (*1-55513-372-X*, 33720, Chariot Bks) Cook.
—Seventeen Wishes. LC 93-11278. 1993. write for info. (*1-56179-169-5*) Focus Family.
—Summer Promise. 171p. (Orig.). (gr. 7-11). 1989. pap. 4.99 (*0-929608-13-5*) Focus Family.
—Surprise Endings. 160p. (Orig.). (gr. 7-11). 1991. pap. 4.99 (*1-56179-024-9*) Focus Family.
—When I Celebrate His Birthday. Acquistapace, David & Gary, N. C., illus. (ps). 1988. bds. 4.99 (*1-55513-567-6*, Chariot Bks) Cook.
—When I Go to the Park. Acquistapace, David & Gary, N. C., illus. (ps). 1988. bds. 4.99 (*1-55513-589-7*, Chariot Bks) Cook.
—When I Have a Babysitter. Acquistapace, David & Gary, N. C., illus. (ps). 1988. bds. 4.99 (*1-55513-573-0*, Chariot Bks) Cook.
—When I Help My Mommy. Acquistapace, David & Gary, N. C., illus. (ps). 1988. 4.99 (*1-55513-566-8*, Chariot Bks) Cook.
—A Whisper & a Wish. 176p. (Orig.). (gr. 7-11). 1989. pap. 4.99 (*0-929608-29-1*) Focus Family.
—Yours Forever. 160p. (Orig.). (gr. 7-11). 1990. pap. 4.99 (*0-929608-90-9*) Focus Family.
Gunning, Monica. Not a Copper Penny in Me House: Poems from the Caribbean. Lessac, Frane, illus. 32p. 1993. 14.95 (*1-56397-050-3*, Wordsong) Boyds Mills Pr.
Gunning, Peter. Alas in Blunderland. Henderson, Catherine, illus. 32p. (Orig.). (gr. 5-7). 1991. pap. 10.95 (*0-86278-271-6*, Pub. by OBrien Pr IE) Dufour.
Gunning, Thomas G. Dream Cars. LC 88-37438. 72p. (gr. 3 up). 1989. RSBE 14.95 (*0-87518-419-7*, Dillon) Macmillan Child Grp.
—Dream Planes. LC 92-8397. (Illus.). 72p. (gr. 3 up). 1992. RSBE 14.95 (*0-87518-556-8*, Dillon) Macmillan Child Grp.
—Dream Trains. LC 92-9802. (Illus.). 72p. (gr. 3 up). 1992. RSBE 14.95 (*0-87518-584-3*, Dillon) Macmillan Child Grp.
—Strange Mysteries. 96p. (gr. 4-7). 1992. pap. 2.95 (*0-8167-1371-5*) Troll Assocs.
Gunsher, Cheryl. Danny the Dizzy Draydl. Webb, Sandra, ed. Gunsher, Cheryl, illus. 24p. (ps). 1992. 6.00 (*1-881602-00-1*) Prism NJ.

—**Lev the Lucky Lulav.** (Illus.). 24p. (ps-k). 1993. 10.00 (*1-881602-01-X*) Prism NJ.
Lev is a lucky Lulav, but what is a lulav? This charming story about Lev & his good friend Ettie the Etrog not only answers this question but provides young children with an adorable introduction to the Jewish holiday of Succot. LEV THE LUCKY LULAV is the second in a new series of books about Jewish themes written for the nursery school & kindergarten set. Each book in this series utilizes the various symbols associated with Jewish tradition to familiarize children with the customs of their heritage. Lev is indeed lucky! He is lucky because he has a best friend named Ettie. A friend who cares about him & with whom he can celebrate the holiday of Succot. He learns that together with someone else we can accomplish things that we may not be able to do alone. Children can learn about the value of friendship while enjoying this engaging tale. By combining traditional Jewish values with the important issues of growing up, LEV THE LUCKY LULAV provides parents & educators with an important addition to their libraries of Jewish juvenile literature. Distributed by Prism Press (908) 572-6586. *Publisher Provided Annotation.*

Gunter, Annetta, illus. Kitchen Cosmetics: Using Herbs, Fruits & Eatables in Natural Cosmetics. 2nd, rev. ed. 131p. (gr. 8 up). 1988. pap. 9.95 (*0-9620838-0-1*) Herb Studies.
Gunzi, Christiane. Cave Life. Greenaway, Frank, photos by. LC 92-53490. (Illus.). 32p. (gr. 2-5). 1993. 9.95 (*1-56458-212-4*) Dorling Kindersley.
—Tide Pool. Greenaway, Frank, photos by. LC 92-52823. (Illus.). 32p. (gr. 2-5). 1992. 9.95 (*1-56458-131-4*) Dorling Kindersley.
Gupta, Mallika C., jt. auth. see Ray, Irene R.
Gupta, Mallika C. see Ramakrishna, Swami.
Gupta, Rupa. Tales from Indian Classics. Basu, R. K., illus. 136p. (gr. 1-9). 1981. 7.50 (*0-89744-233-4*, Pub. by Hemkunt India) Auromere.
—Tales from Indian Mythology. (Illus.). 96p. (gr. 2-8). 1982. text ed. 7.50 (*0-89744-058-7*, Pub. by Hemkunt Indig) Auromere.
Guralnik, David B., ed. Webster's New World Dictionary of the American Language: Second College Edition, 24 vols. large type ed. (Illus.). (gr. 10 up). Set. 1201.66 (*0-317-01962-7*, 4-27260-00) Am Printing Hse.
Gurasich, Marj. Benito & the White Dove: A Story of Jose Antonio Navarro, Hero of Early Texas. (Illus.). 112p. (gr. 6-8). 1989. 10.95 (*0-89015-693-X*) Eakin-Sunbelt.
—Did You Ever Meet a Texas Hero? LC 91-19544. (Illus.). (gr. 3-5). 1992. 12.95 (*0-89015-819-3*) Eakin-Sunbelt.
—A House Divided. LC 93-14189. 1994. pap. write for info. (*0-87565-122-4*) Tex Christian.
—Letters to Oma, a Young German Girl's Account of Her First Year in Texas, 1847. Whitehead, Barbara, illus. LC 88-38747. 162p. (gr. 4-8). 1989. pap. 9.95 (*0-87565-037-6*) Tex Christian.
Gurasich, Marjorie. Red Wagons & White Canvas: Mollie Bailey, Circus Queen of the Southwest. Roberts, Melissa, ed. Hill, Francis, illus. 88p. (gr. 4-7). 1988. 10.95 (*0-89015-646-8*, Pub. by Panda Bks) Eakin-Sunbelt.
Gurau, Peter K. & Lieberthal, Edwin M. Fingermath. Gafney, Leo, ed. 192p. (gr. 3-8). 1980. text ed. 6.56 (*0-07-025223-8*) McGraw.
—Fingermath, Bk. 2. Gafney, Leo, ed. (Illus.). (gr. 2-6). 1980. text ed. 6.56 (*0-07-025222-X*) McGraw.
Gurko, Miriam. Theodor Herzl: The Road to Israel. Weihs, Erika, illus. 96p. (gr. 3-7). 1988. 14.95 (*0-8276-0312-6*) JPS Phila.
Gurley, Heather & Larson, Bob. Sunlight Works: Educational Activities for Children. (Illus.). 31p. (gr. 3-7). 1993. wkbk. 10.00 (*0-9634694-2-8*) Sun Light Wks.
Gurney, Eric, jt. auth. see Gurney, Nancy.
Gurney, John S., illus. Over the River & Through the Woods. 1992. pap. 2.50 (*0-590-45258-4*, Cartwheel) Scholastic Inc.
Gurney, Nancy & Gurney, Eric. King, the Mice & the Cheese. Vallier, Jean, illus. LC 89-8463. 72p. (gr. k-3). 1965. 6.95 (*0-394-80039-7*); lib. bdg. 7.99 (*0-394-90039-1*) Random Bks Yng Read.
Gustafson, Anita. The Case of the Purloined Pork. Gordon, Melinda, illus. 72p. (gr. 2-3). 1985. 7.95 (*0-88700-004-5*) Natl Live Stock.
Gustafson, Helen. Dinner's Ready, Mom. LC 86-11802. 96p. (Orig.). (gr. k-3). 1986. pap. 8.95 (*0-89087-470-0*) Celestial Arts.
Gustafson, John. Planets, Moons, & Meteors. (gr. 4-7). 1992. lib. bdg. 12.98 (*0-671-72534-3*, J Messner); pap. 6.95 (*0-671-72535-1*, J Messner) S&S Trade.
—Stars, Clusters, & Galaxies. LC 92-11228. (gr. 3-7). 1993. lib. bdg. 12.98 (*0-671-72536-X*, J Messner); pap. 6.95 (*0-671-72537-8*, J Messner) S&S Trade.
Gustafson, Ronald, jt. auth. see Dibner, Ellen J.
Gustafson, Sarah. Eye on Nature: The Snake Dictionary. Nienhaus, Laura L., illus. 48p. 1993. pap. 5.95 (*1-56565-070-0*) Lowell Hse.
Gustason, Gerilee & Zawolkow, Esther. Signing Exact English. LC 93-86649. (Illus.). 472p. (gr. k-12). 1993. text ed. 39.95 (*0-916708-22-5*); pap. text ed. 29.95 (*0-916708-23-3*) Modern Signs.
Gustason, Gerilee, jt. auth. see Wojcio, Michael D.
Gustavson, Carl G. Preface to History. (gr. 9-12). 1955. pap. text ed. 5.95 (*0-07-025279-3*) McGraw.

Gustavson, Cynthia B. Scents of Place: Season of the St. Croix Valley. Pennie, Dawn, illus. (Orig.). (gr. 9-12). 1987. pap. 8.95 (*0-317-91094-9*) Country Messenger Inc.
Gutelle, Andrew. All-Time Great World Series. Forbes, Bart, illus. LC 93-35668. 1994. write for info. (*0-448-40471-0*, G&D) Putnam Pub Group.
—Baseball's Best: Five True Stories. Spohn, Cliff, illus. LC 89-35413. 48p. (Orig.). (gr. 2-4). 1990. lib. bdg. 7.99 (*0-394-90983-6*); 3.50 (*0-394-80983-1*) Random Bks Yng Read.
Gutelle, Andrew, jt. auth. see Jones, Brian.
Guten, Mimi, jt. auth. see Mazzola, Toni.
Gutfreund, Geraldine M. Animals Have Cousins Too: Five Surprising Relatives of Animals You Know. LC 90-31027. (Illus.). 64p. (gr. 5-8). 1990. PLB 12.90 (*0-531-10861-9*) Watts.
—Vanishing Animal Neighbors. LC 92-25530. (Illus.). 64p. (gr. 5-8). 1993. PLB 12.90 (*0-531-20060-4*) Watts.
—Vanishing Animal Neighbors. (Illus.). 64p. (gr. 5-8). 1993. pap. 5.95 (*0-531-15674-5*) Watts.
Guth, A. Richard & Cohen, Stan B. Red Skies of Eighty-Eight: The 1988 Forest Fire Season in the Northern Rockies, the Northern Great Plains & the Greater Yellowstone Area. LC 89-50399. (Illus.). 136p. (Orig.). 1989. pap. text ed. 12.95 (*0-929521-17-X*) Pictorial Hist.
Guth, Phyllis & Goff, Georgeanna. Sewing with Scraps. (Illus.). (gr. 10 up). 1977. pap. 6.95 (*0-8306-6878-0*, 878) TAB Bks.
Guthridge, Sue. Thomas A. Edison: Young Inventor. Wook, Wallace, illus. LC 86-10862. 192p. (gr. 2-6). 1986. pap. 3.95 (*0-02-041850-7*, Aladdin) Macmillan Child Grp.
Guthrie, Alfred B., Jr. The Big Sky. LC 85-4717. 384p. (gr. 6 up). 1984. pap. 4.95 (*0-553-26683-7*) Bantam.
Guthrie, Donna. Frankie Murphy's Kiss List. LC 93-16172. (gr. 6). 1993. pap. 14.00 (*0-671-75624-9*, S&S BFYR) S&S Trade.
—I Can't Believe It's History! Amsteen, Katy, illus. 32p. (gr. 4-7). 1993. pap. 3.99 (*0-8431-3621-9*) Price Stern.
—Mrs. Gigglebelly is Coming For Tea. 1990. pap. 6.95 (*0-671-67937-6*, S&S BFYR) S&S Trade.
—Mrs. Gigglebelly Is Coming to Tea. Arnsteen, Katy K., illus. 32p. (ps-2). 1993. pap. 2.50 (*0-671-79605-4*, Little Simon) S&S Trade.
—Nobiah's Well: A Modern African Folk Tale. Roth, Robert, illus. LC 93-586. 32p. (ps-2). 1993. 15.00 (*0-8249-8631-8*, Ideals Child); 14.95 (*0-8249-8622-9*) Hambleton-Hill.
—Not for Babies. Arnsteen, Katy K., illus. 24p. (ps-1). 1993. pap. 2.50 (*0-685-63280-6*, Little Simon) S&S Trade.
—A Rose for Abby. Hockerman, Dennis, illus. LC 88-10577. (gr. 2 up). 1988. 11.95 (*0-687-36586-4*) Abingdon.
—The Witch Has an Itch. Arnsteen, Katy K., illus. 24p. (ps-1). 1990. pap. 2.50 (*0-671-70346-3*, Little Simon) S&S Trade.
—The Witch Who Lives down the Hall. Schwartz, Amy, illus. LC 85-887. 32p. (gr. k-3). 1985. 12.95 (*0-15-298610-3*, HB Juv Bks) HarBrace.
—Witch Who Lives Down the Hall. 32p. (gr. k-3). 1991. pap. 4.95 (*0-15-298611-1*, HB Juv Bks) HarBrace.
Guthrie, Donna, et al. The Young Author's Do-It-Yourself Book: How to Write, Illustrate, & Produce Your Own Book. Arnsteen, Katy K., illus. LC 93-9736. 64p. (gr. 2-4). 1994. PLB 14.90 (*1-56294-350-2*) Millbrook Pr.
Guthrie, Donna W. Grandpa Doesn't Know It's Me: A Family Adjusts to Alzheimer's Disease. Arnsteen, Katy, illus. Aronson, Miriam, intro. by. (Illus.). (ps-5). 1986. 14.95 (*0-89885-302-8*); pap. 9.95 (*0-89885-308-7*) Human Sci Pr.
Guthrie, Feliz, tr. see Barbosa, Rogerio A.
Guthrie, Kari H. National Anthems, Bk. 1. Nichols, Brooke & Guthrie, Kari H., illus. Guthrie, Kari H., intro. by. 36p. (Illus.). (gr. 2-8). 1992. pap. 6.95 (*0-9631333-0-6*) Hi I Que Pub.

—**National Anthems: Western & Middle Europe, 4 bks.** (Illus.). 163p. (Orig.). (gr. 4-9). 1993. Set. pap. 24.95 (*0-9631333-4-9*) Hi I Que Pub.
NATIONAL ANTHEMS - WESTERN & MIDDLE EUROPE is an integrated learning book series. Each anthem includes a map of the individual country & surrounding countries, form of government, language spoken, capital, currency, national holiday. The cover displays the flags of the included countries in vibrant color. Also included are words in original language & English translations. Music is in piano score, arranged for easy to intermediate abilities. This book is suitable for all ages, but is specifically formatted to appeal to grades 4-9. These books

provide a wonderful aspect of cultural, historical & heritage information. Ideal reference for schools, teachers, & libraries; also as gifts to young students of history or music. Since these anthems are not easily accesible it is important to note that college age students studying culture, history, music or language may be interested in this series. NATIONAL ANTHEMS (WESTERN & MIDDLE EUROPE) is a series of 4 books. Book 1 (0-9631333-0-6) includes France, Iceland, Ireland, Portugal, Spain. Book 2 (0-9631333-1-4), Andorra, Belgium, Denmark, Germany, Lichtenstein, Luxembourg, Monaco, Netherlands, Norway, Switzerland. Book 3 (0-9631333-2-2), Albania, Austria, Czechoslovakia (1918-1993), Hungary, Italy, Malta, San Marino, Sweden. Book 4 (0-9631333-0-0), Bulgaria, Finland, Greece, Poland, Romania, the former U.S.S.R., Yugoslavia. Each book also available separately at $6.95 each. Order directly from: Hi. I. Que Publishing, P.O. Box 508, Claremont, CA 91711-0508. (909) 622-7501, or your local distributor. *Publisher Provided Annotation.*

Guthrie, Robert. Freestyle Skiing & Snowboarding. (Illus.). 48p. (gr. 3-6). 1992. PLB 12.95 (*1-56065-052-4*) Capstone Pr.
Guthrie, Woody. Woody's Twenty Grow Big Songs. Guthrie, Woody, illus. LC 91-753710. 48p. (ps up). 1992. 16.00 (*0-06-020282-3*); incl. cassette 24.95 (*0-06-021033-8*); PLB 15.89 (*0-06-020283-1*) HarpC Child Bks.
Gutierrez, Douglas. The Night of the Stars. Dearden, Carmen D., tr. from SPA. Oliver, Maria F., illus. 24p. (ps-1). 1988. 9.95 (*0-916291-17-0*) Kane-Miller Bk.
Gutierrez, Marda L. Beginning Reading & Writing in French: A Children's French Grammar Workbook. Guiterrez, Marda L., illus. 64p. (Orig.). (gr. k-4). 1986. 8.95 (*0-938733-03-6*) Avantage Pub.
Gutkind, Lee. The Veterinarians. 1996. write for info. (*0-8050-3321-1*) H Holt & Co.
Gutkoska, Joseph P. Developing Comprehension Skills Through the Use of Analogies. (Orig.). (gr. 5-12). 1985. pap. 6.95 (*0-930723-00-7*) Nutshell Enterprises.
Gutman, Bessie P., illus. I Love You: Verses & Sweet Sayings. Gutman, Bessie P., illus. 1994. 4.95 (*0-448-40258-0*, G&D) Putnam Pub Group.
Gutman, Bill. Across the Wild River. (gr. 4-7). 1993. pap. 3.50 (*0-06-106159-X*, Harp PBks) HarpC.
—Barry Sanders: Football's Rushing Champ. LC 92-18165. (Illus.). 48p. (gr. 3-6). 1993. PLB 12.90 (*1-56294-227-1*) Millbrook Pr.
—Baseball. LC 89-7377. (Illus.). 64p. (gr. 3-8). 1990. PLB 14.95 (*0-942545-84-2*) Marshall Cavendish.
—Basketball. LC 89-7606. (Illus.). 64p. (gr. 3-8). 1990. PLB 14.95 (*0-942545-92-3*) Marshall Cavendish.
—Blazing Bladers. 1992. pap. 6.99 (*0-8125-1939-6*) Tor Bks.
—David Robinson, NBA Super Center. LC 92-18164. (Illus.). 48p. (gr. 3-6). 1993. PLB 12.90 (*1-56294-228-X*) Millbrook Pr.
—Field Hockey. LC 89-7587. (Illus.). 64p. (gr. 3-8). 1990. PLB 14.95 (*0-942545-93-1*) Marshall Cavendish.
—Football. LC 89-7585. (Illus.). 64p. (gr. 3-8). 1990. PLB 14.95 (*0-942545-85-0*) Marshall Cavendish.
—Football Super Teams. (Illus.). 160p. (gr. 5 up). 1991. pap. 2.95 (*0-671-74098-9*, Archway) PB.
—Gamebreakers of the NFL. (Illus.). 144p. (gr. 5 up). 1973. lib. bdg. 3.69 (*0-394-92501-7*) Random Bks Yng Read.
—Go for It Sports Library Series, 12 vols. (gr. 3-8). 1990. Set. PLB 179.40 (*0-942545-98-2*) Marshall Cavendish.
—Great Moments in Baseball. Clancy, Lisa, ed. (Illus.). 128p. (gr. 5 up). 1989. pap. 2.99 (*0-671-67914-7*, Archway) PB.
—Great Quarterbacks of the N. F. L. Clancy, Lisa, ed. (Illus.). 144p. (Orig.). (gr. 5 up). 1993. pap. 2.99 (*0-671-79244-X*, Archway) PB.
—Ice Hockey. LC 89-9714. (Illus.). 64p. (gr. 3-8). 1990. PLB 14.95 (*0-942545-86-9*) Marshall Cavendish.
—Jennifer Capriati, Teenage Tennis Star. LC 92-18163. (Illus.). 48p. (gr. 3-6). 1993. PLB 12.90 (*1-56294-225-5*) Millbrook Pr.
—Jim Abbott: Star Pitcher. LC 92-7540. (Illus.). 48p. (gr. 3-6). 1992. PLB 12.90 (*1-56294-083-X*) Millbrook Pr.
—Jim Abbott: Star Pitcher. (gr. 4-7). 1992. pap. 4.95 (*0-395-64543-3*) HM.
—Ken Griffey, Sr. & Ken Griffey, Jr. Father & Son Teammates. LC 92-18162. (Illus.). 48p. (gr. 3-6). 1993. PLB 12.90 (*1-56294-226-3*) Millbrook Pr.

—The Kids' World Almanac of Football. 1994. 14.95 (*0-88687-765-2*, World Almanac); pap. 7.95 (*0-88687-764-4*, World Almanac) F&W Inc NJ.
—Magic Johnson: Hero or Off Court. LC 92-5002. (Illus.). 48p. (gr. 3-6). 1992. PLB 12.90 (*1-56294-287-5*) Millbrook Pr.
—Magic Johnson: Hero or Off Court. (gr. 4-7). 1992. pap. 4.95 (*0-395-64546-8*) HM.
—Mario Lemieux: Wizard with a Puck. LC 92-5003. (Illus.). 48p. (gr. 3-6). 1992. PLB 12.90 (*1-56294-084-8*) Millbrook Pr.
—Mario Lemieux: Wizard with a Puck. (gr. 4-7). 1992. pap. 4.95 (*0-395-64544-1*) HM.
—Michael Jordan: Basketball Camp. LC 92-7541. (Illus.). 48p. (gr. 3-6). 1992. PLB 12.90 (*1-56294-085-6*) Millbrook Pr.
—Michael Jordan: Basketball Champ. (gr. 4-7). 1992. pap. 4.95 (*0-395-64545-X*) HM.
—Over the Rugged Mountain. (gr. 4-7). 1994. pap. 3.50 (*0-06-106171-9*, Harp PBks) HarpC.
—Pro Football Record Breakers. (Illus.). 128p. (gr. 5 up). 1989. pap. 2.99 (*0-671-68623-2*, Archway) PB.
—Pro Sports Champions. (Illus.). 144p. (Orig.). (gr. 5 up). 1990. pap. 2.75 (*0-671-69334-4*, Archway) PB.
—Rookie Summer. (gr. 7-12). 1988. PLB 2.95 (*0-89872-300-0*) Turman Pub.
—Skateboarding. 128p. 1992. pap. 6.99 (*0-8125-1938-8*) Tor Bks.
—Smitty. (gr. 7-12). 1988. PLB 2.95 (*0-89872-301-9*) Turman Pub.
—Soccer. LC 89-7379. (Illus.). 64p. (gr. 3-8). 1990. PLB 14.95 (*0-942545-90-7*) Marshall Cavendish.
—Softball. LC 89-7608. (Illus.). 64p. (gr. 3-8). 1990. PLB 14.95 (*0-942545-91-5*) Marshall Cavendish.
—Sports Illustrated: Great Moments in Pro Football. Clancy, Lisa, ed. 128p. (gr. 5 up). 1990. pap. 2.95 (*0-671-70969-0*, Archway) PB.
—Sports Illustrated Strange & Amazing Baseball Stories. 128p. (gr. 5 up). 1990. pap. 2.99 (*0-671-70120-7*, Archway) PB.
—Sports Illustrated Strange & Amazing Football Stories. Clancy, Lisa, ed. 128p. (gr. 5 up). 1989. pap. 2.99 (*0-671-70716-7*, Archway) PB.
—Swimming. LC 89-7380. (Illus.). 64p. (gr. 3-8). 1990. PLB 14.95 (*0-942545-89-3*) Marshall Cavendish.
—Tennis. LC 89-7607. (Illus.). 64p. (gr. 3-8). 1990. PLB 14.95 (*0-942545-88-5*) Marshall Cavendish.
—Track & Field. LC 89-7378. (Illus.). 64p. (gr. 3-8). 1990. PLB 14.95 (*0-942545-87-7*) Marshall Cavendish.
—Volleyball. LC 89-7584. (Illus.). 64p. (gr. 3-8). 1990. PLB 14.95 (*0-942545-95-8*) Marshall Cavendish.
—World Series Classics. (gr. 5 up). 1973. lib. bdg. 3.69 (*0-394-92467-3*) Random Bks Yng Read.
—Wrestling. LC 89-7596. (Illus.). 64p. (gr. 3-8). 1990. PLB 14.95 (*0-942545-94-X*) Marshall Cavendish.
Gutman, Dan. Baseball's Greatest Games. LC 93-31504. (Illus.). 160p. (gr. 4-7). 1994. 14.99 (*0-670-84604-X*) Viking Child Bks.
Gutman, William. Andrew Jackson & the New Populism. (Illus.). 144p. (gr. 3-6). 1987. pap. 4.95 (*0-8120-3917-3*) Barron.
Gutmann, Bessie P. Nursery Poems & Prayers. (Illus.). 32p. 1990. 9.95 (*0-448-23458-0*, G&D) Putnam Pub Group.
—Nursery Poems & Prayers. 32p. 1992. mini ed. 3.95 (*0-448-40259-9*, G&D) Putnam Pub Group.
—Nursery Songs & Lullabies. (Illus.). 32p. 1990. 9.95x (*0-448-23457-2*, G&D) Putnam Pub Group.
—Nursery Songs & Lullabies. 32p. 1992. mini ed. 3.95 (*0-448-40260-2*, G&D) Putnam Pub Group.
Gutmann, John W. Robot Hobby: The Complete Manual for Individuals & Clubs. (Illus.). 320p. (Orig.). (gr. 5-12). 1992. text ed. 36.95 (*0-9634272-5-3*); pap. 29.95 (*0-9634272-4-5*) Machine Pr.
Gutnik, Martin. Genetics Projects for Young Scientists. 1989. pap. 6.95 (*0-531-15131-X*) Watts.
Gutnik, Martin A. Ecology Projects for Young Scientists. 1989. pap. 5.95 (*0-531-15128-X*) Watts.
Gutnik, Martin J. The Challenge of Clean Air. LC 89-39422. (Illus.). 64p. (gr. 6 up). 1990. lib. bdg. 15.95 (*0-89490-272-5*) Enslow Pubs.
—The Energy Question: Thinking about Tomorrow. LC 92-31315. (Illus.). 104p. (gr. 6 up). 1993. lib. bdg. 17.95 (*0-685-63563-5*) Enslow Pubs.
—Experiments That Explore Acid Rain. LC 91-19958. (Illus.). 72p. (gr. 5-8). 1992. PLB 13.90 (*1-56294-115-1*) Millbrook Pr.
—Experiments That Explore Oil Spills. (Illus.). 72p. (gr. 5-8). 1991. PLB 13.90 (*1-56294-013-9*) Millbrook Pr.
—Experiments That Explore Recycling. LC 91-26147. (Illus.). 72p. (gr. 5-8). 1992. PLB 13.90 (*1-56294-116-X*) Millbrook Pr.
—Experiments That Explore the Greenhouse Effect. (Illus.). 72p. (gr. 5-8). 1991. PLB 13.90 (*1-56294-012-0*) Millbrook Pr.
—How to Do a Science Project & Report. (gr. 7 up). 1980. PLB 11.90 (*0-531-04129-8*) Watts.
—Michael Faraday: Creative Scientist. LC 86-11702. (Illus.). 112p. (gr. 4 up). 1986. PLB 18.60 (*0-516-03224-0*) Childrens.
—Recycling: Learning the Four R's: Reduce, Reuse, Recycle, Recover. LC 92-24330. (Illus.). 104p. (gr. 6 up). 1993. lib. bdg. 17.95 (*0-89490-399-3*) Enslow Pubs.
Gutnik, Martin J. & Browne-Gutnik, Natalie. Projects That Explore Energy. LC 93-7787. (Illus.). 72p. (gr. 5-8). 1994. PLB 13.90 (*1-56294-334-0*) Millbrook Pr.

Gutsch, William A., Jr. The Search for Extraterrestrial Life. (Illus.). 144p. (gr. 5-9). 1991. 14.00 (*0-517-57818-2*) Crown Bks Yng Read.
Guttmacher, Peter. Jeep. LC 93-10476. (Illus.). 48p. (gr. 5-6). 1994. RSBE 13.95 (*0-89686-830-3*, Crestwood Hse) Macmillan Child Grp.
Guttmacher, Peter, jt. auth. see Brownstein, Robin.
Guttormson, Lorraine, jt. auth. see Roberts, Gail C.
Gutwein, Kenneth C. Multiple Choice Questions in Preparation for the AP European History Examination. 2nd ed. 121p. (gr. 11-12). 1991. wkbk. 15.95 (*1-878621-08-4*); tchr's. manual, 67p. avail. (*1-878621-09-2*) D & S Mktg Syst.
Guy, Ginger F. Black Crow, Black Crow. Parker, Nancy W., illus. LC 89-34619. 24p. (ps up). 1991. 13.95 (*0-688-08956-9*); PLB 13.88 (*0-688-08957-7*) Greenwillow.
Guy, Lucien. Scatterbrain Sam. (Illus.). 32p. (gr. 3-5). 1991. 18.50 (*0-89565-754-6*); 12.95s.p. (*0-685-55092-3*) Childs World.
Guy, Richard K. Fair Game: How to Play Impartial Combinatorial Games. Malkevitch, Joseph, ed. Joliffe, Dale, illus. 113p. (Orig.). (gr. 9-12). 1989. pap. text ed. 12.95 (*0-912843-16-0*) COMAP Inc.
Guy, Rosa. And I Heard a Bird Sing. LC 86-19907. 240p. (gr. 7 up). 1987. pap. 14.95 (*0-385-29563-4*) Delacorte.
—Billy the Great. Binch, Caroline, illus. LC 92-34704. 32p. (gr. k-3). 1992. 15.00 (*0-385-30666-0*) Delacorte.
—Billy the Great. (ps-3). 1994. pap. 4.99 (*0-440-40920-9*) Dell.
—The Disappearance. LC 79-50672. 224p. 1979. pap. 9.95 (*0-385-28129-3*) Delacorte.
—The Disappearance. 256p. (gr. 7 up). 1992. pap. 3.50 (*0-440-92064-7*, LFL) Dell.
—Edith Jackson. (gr. 7 up). 1992. pap. 3.50 (*0-440-21137-9*) Dell.
—The Friends. LC 72-11068. 208p. (gr. 4-6). 1973. 13.95 (*0-8050-1742-9*, Bks Young Read) H Holt & Co.
—The Friends. (gr. 7-12). 1983. pap. 2.95 (*0-553-26519-9*) Bantam.
—The Friends. 1981. pap. 3.99 (*0-553-27326-4*) Bantam.
—Mirror of Her Own. LC 80-69448. 192p. (gr. 7 up). 1981. 8.95 (*0-385-28636-8*) Delacorte.
—Mother Crocodile: An Uncle Amadou Tale from Senegal. Steptoe, John, illus. LC 80-393. 32p. (ps-3). 1982. 8.89 (*0-385-28455-1*); pap. 8.95 (*0-385-28454-3*) Delacorte.
—The Music of Summer. (gr. 7 up). 1991. 14.00 (*0-685-52466-3*) Delacorte.
—The Music of Summer. 1992. pap. 15.00 (*0-385-30599-0*) Doubleday.
—New Guys Around the Block. LC 82-72818. 192p. (gr. 7 up). 1983. pap. 11.95 (*0-385-29247-3*) Delacorte.
—New Guys Around the Block. (gr. k-12). 1992. pap. 3.50 (*0-440-95888-1*, LFL) Dell.
—New Guys Around the Block. (gr. 7 up). 1992. pap. 3.50 (*0-685-57133-5*, LFL) Dell.
—Paris, Pee Wee & Big Dog. Binch, Caroline, illus. LC 85-1654. 112p. (gr. 4-6). 1985. 13.95 (*0-385-29407-7*) Delacorte.
—Paris, Pee Wee, & Big Dog. 112p. (gr. 3 up). 1988. pap. 3.25 (*0-440-40072-4*) Dell.
—Ruby. 1992. pap. 3.50 (*0-440-21130-1*) Dell.
—The Ups & Downs of Carl Davis III. (gr. 5 up). 1989. 13.95 (*0-385-29724-6*) Delacorte.
—Ups & Downs of Carl Davis the Third. (gr. 4-7). 1993. pap. 3.50 (*0-440-40744-3*) Dell.
Guyatt, John. The American Revolution. Yapp, Malcolm, et al, eds. (Illus.). 32p. (gr. 6-11). 1980. pap. text ed. 3.45 (*0-89908-110-X*) Greenhaven.
—Ancient America. Killingray, Margaret, et al, eds. (Illus.). 32p. (gr. 6-11). 1980. pap. text ed. 3.45 (*0-89908-008-1*) Greenhaven.
—Bolivar. Yapp, Malcolm, et al, eds. (Illus.). 32p. (gr. 6-11). 1980. pap. text ed. 3.45 (*0-89908-020-0*) Greenhaven.
Guyette, Elise. Vermont: A Cultural Patchwork. (Illus.). 144p. (Orig.). (gr. 4-8). 1986. pap. text ed. 9.85 (*0-9607638-5-6*) Cobblestone Pub.
Guymon, Maurine B. The Adventures of Micki Microbe. Zagone, Arlene T., illus. 88p. (gr. 2-5). 1987. 15.00 (*0-9618650-0-8*) ModEl Pubs.
Guyon, Madeline H. American Crafts: Easy-to-Make Projects from Traditional Folk Crafts. LC 92-4789. (Illus.). 56p. (ps-3). 1992. 18.95 (*0-8478-1579-X*) Rizzoli Intl.
Guzzetti, Paula. A Family Called Bronte. LC 93-8101. (Illus.). 128p. (gr. 5). 1994. RSBE 13.95 (*0-87518-592-4*, Dillon) Macmillan Child Grp.
Guzzo, Sandra E. Miguel & the Santero. Sandoval, Richard C., illus. 32p. (Orig.). (gr. k-5). 1993. pap. text ed. 6.95 (*0-937206-30-X*) New Mexico Mag.
Gwin, Paul, ed. see Bradley, Melvin.
Gwynne, Fred. A Chocolate Moose for Dinner. Gwynne, Fred, illus. LC 88-14150. (gr. 1-6). 1988. pap. 13.00 jacketed (*0-671-66685-1*, S&S BFYR); pap. 5.95 (*0-671-66741-6*, S&S BFYR) S&S Trade.
—Easy to See Why. LC 92-27705. 1993. pap. 14.00 (*0-671-79776-X*, S&S BFYR) S&S Trade.
—The King Who Rained. (gr. 1-5). 11.95 (*0-317-62057-6*); pap. 5.95 (*0-317-62058-4*) P-H.
—The King Who Rained. Gwynne, Fred, illus. LC 80-12939. 40p. (gr. 4 up). 1987. P-H.
—The King Who Rained. Gwynne, Fred, illus. LC 80-12939. (gr. 1-6). 1988. pap. 14.00 jacketed (*0-671-66363-1*, S&S BFYR); pap. 5.95 (*0-671-66744-0*, S&S BFYR) S&S Trade.

—A Little Pigeon Toad. 1988. pap. 12.95 jacketed (*0-671-66659-2*, S&S BFYR) S&S Trade.
—Little Pigeon Toad. (ps-3). 1990. pap. 5.95 (*0-671-69444-8*, S&S BFYR) S&S Trade.
—Pondlarker. LC 90-9524. (Illus.). 40p. (gr. k-4). 1992. pap. 13.95 jacketed (*0-671-70846-5*, S&S BFYR); pap. 4.95 (*0-671-77818-8*, S&S BFYR) S&S Trade.
—The Sixteen-Hand Horse. Gwynne, Fred, illus. LC 79-13284. (gr. 1-5). 1987. P-H Gen Ref & Trav.
—The Sixteen Hand Horse. Gwynne, Fred, illus. LC 79-13284. (gr. 1-6). 1987. pap. 11.95 (*0-671-66291-0*, S&S BFYR); pap. 5.95 (*0-671-66968-0*, S&S BFYR) S&S Trade.
Gybin, Sasha, tr. see **Mahoney, Judy.**
Gygax, Gary. The Necropolis: And the Land of Egypt. Smith, Lester, ed. 208p. (Orig.). 1992. pap. 18.00 (*1-55878-143-9*) Game Designers.
Gygax, Gary & Smith, Lester. Mythus Magick. 384p. (Orig.). 1992. pap. 24.00 (*1-55878-133-1*) Game Designers.
Gyldendal, tr. see **Berliner, Franz.**

H

Haaland, Lynn. Acadia Seacoast: A Guidebook for Appreciation. Mills, Louise & Johnson, Mercy, eds. Swensson, Dale I. & Welles, T., illus. 32p. (Orig.). (gr. k up). 1984. pap. 3.00 (*0-915189-01-1*) Oceanus.
Haalman, Perry. Mordechai. McBride, Shawn, illus. 36p. (gr. 4 up). 1990. pap. 8.00 (*0-9624155-2-9*) Cottage Wordsmiths.
Haan, Sheri D. The First Woman: Bible Stories in Rhythm & Rhyme. Hochstatter, Dan, illus. 80p. (ps-3). 1992. 6.99 (*0-8010-4368-9*) Baker Bk.
—Precious Moments Stories from the Bible. Butcher, Samuel, illus. LC 78-97507. 288p. (gr. 1-6). 1987. 14. 99 (*0-8010-4311-5*) Baker Bk.
—The Time the World Drowned: Bible Stories in Rhythm & Rhyme. Hochstatter, Dan, illus. 80p. 1992. 6.99 (*0-8010-4369-7*) Baker Bk.
Haaren, John H., et al. Famous Men of Greece. 146p. (gr. 4-8). 1989. pap. 15.95 (*1-882514-01-7*) Greenleaf TN.
—Famous Men of Rome. 154p. (gr. 4-8). 1989. pap. 15. 95 (*1-882514-03-3*) Greenleaf TN.
—Famous Men of the Middle Ages. 159p. (gr. 4-8). 1992. pap. 15.95 (*1-882514-05-X*) Greenleaf TN.
Haarhoff, Dorian. Desert December. Vermeulen, Leon, illus. 32p. (ps-3). 1992. 13.95 (*0-395-61300-0*, Clarion Bks) HM.
Haas, Carol. Engle vs. Vitale: Separation of Church & State. LC 93-26381. 1994. write for info. (*0-89490-461-2*) Enslow Pubs.
Haas, Carolyn, jt. auth. see **Cole, Ann.**
Haas, Carolyn B. Big Book of Fun: Creative Learning Activities for Home & School. Phillips, Jane B., illus. LC 87-20325. 288p. (Orig.). (ps-7). 1987. pap. 9.95 (*1-55652-020-4*) Chicago Review.
—Look at Me: Creative Learning Activities for Babies & Toddlers. Phillips, Jane B., illus. LC 87-20288. 230p. (Orig.). 1987. pap. 9.95 (*1-55652-021-2*) Chicago Review.
Haas, Dorothy. The Baby Hugs Bear & Baby Tugs Bear Counting Book. Cooke, Tom, illus. 40p. (ps). 1984. 5.95 (*0-910313-71-7*) Parker Bros.
—Burton & the Giggle Machine. Bobak, Cathy, illus. LC 91-25411. 160p. (gr. 5-8). 1992. SBE 13.95 (*0-02-738203-6*, Bradbury Pr) Macmillan Child Grp.
—Burton's Zoom Zoom Va-room Machine. MacDonald, Pat, ed. 144p. (gr. 4-7). 1993. pap. 2.99 (*0-671-74702-9*, Minstrel Bks) PB.
—Burton's Zoom Zoom Va-room Machine. Bobak, Cathy, illus. LC 89-77426. 144p. (gr. 5-8). 1990. SBE 13.95 (*0-02-738201-X*, Bradbury Pr) Macmillan Child Grp.
—The Hugs & Tugs Counting Book. Cooke, Tom, illus. (ps). 5.95 (*0-317-13462-0*) Parker Bros.
—The Secret Life of Dilly McBean. LC 86-8255. 224p. (gr. 5-7). 1986. SBE 14.95 (*0-02-738200-1*, Bradbury Pr) Macmillan Child Grp.
—Trouble at Alcott School. 1989. pap. 2.50 (*0-590-41509-3*) Scholastic Inc.
—Two Friends Too Many. (gr. 4-7). 1990. pap. 2.50 (*0-590-43557-4*) Scholastic Inc.
Haas, Irene. The Maggie B. Haas, Irene, illus. LC 74-18183. 32p. (ps-2). 1975. SBE 14.95 (*0-689-50021-1*, M K McElderry) Macmillan Child Grp.
—The Maggie B. LC 74-18183. (Illus.). 32p. (ps-3). 1984. pap. 4.95 (*0-689-70764-9*, Aladdin) Macmillan Child Grp.
Haas, Irene, jt. auth. see **De Regniers, Beatrice S.**
Haas, James. Charles Caterpillar. Kendzia, Mary C., ed. Uzanus, Phil, illus. 32p. (Orig.). 1992. pap. 4.95 (*0-89622-530-5*) Twenty-Third.
—Paco Pumpkin. Kendzia, Mary C., ed. Meyer, Mary A., illus. 32p. (Orig.). 1992. pap. 4.95 (*0-89622-529-1*) Twenty-Third.
Haas, Jessie. Beware the Mare. Haas, Martha, illus. LC 92-14505. 64p. (gr. 2 up). 1993. 13.00 (*0-688-11762-7*) Greenwillow.
—Busybody Brandy. Abolafia, Yossi, illus. LC 93-29569. 1994. write for info. (*0-688-12792-4*); lib. bdg. write for info. (*0-688-12793-2*) Greenwillow.

—Chipmunk! Smith, Joseph A., illus. LC 92-30080. 24p. (ps up). 1993. 14.00 (*0-688-11874-7*); PLB 13.93 (*0-688-11875-5*) Greenwillow.
—A Horse Like Barney. LC 92-34386. 176p. (gr. 5 up). 1993. 13.00 (*0-688-12415-1*) Greenwillow.
—Keeping Barney. LC 81-7029. 160p. (gr. 5-9). 1982. reinforced bdg. 11.75 (*0-688-00859-3*) Greenwillow.
—Mowing. Smith, Joseph A., illus. LC 93-12240. 32p. (ps up). 1994. write for info. Greenwillow.
—Mowing. Smith, Joseph A., photos by. LC 93-12240. 1994. write for info. (*0-688-11680-9*); lib. bdg. write for info. (*0-688-11681-7*) Greenwillow.
—The Sixth Sense & Other Stories. LC 88-45226. 192p. (gr. 1-5). 1988. 11.95 (*0-688-08129-0*) Greenwillow.
—Skipping School. LC 91-37642. (gr. 6-12). 1992. 14.00 (*0-688-10179-8*) Greenwillow.
—Uncle Daney's Way. LC 93-22192. (gr. 4 up). 1994. write for info. (*0-688-12794-0*) Greenwillow.
—Working Trot. LC 83-1696. 160p. (gr. 5-9). 1983. reinforced 10.25 (*0-688-02384-3*) Greenwillow.
Haas, Lois J. Tell Me about God: 12 Lessons, Vol. 1. (ps). 1966. complete kit 14.95 (*0-86508-011-9*); text only 3.45 (*0-86508-012-7*); color & action book 1.75 (*0-86508-013-5*) BCM Pubn.
—Tell Me about Jesus: 16 Lessons, Vol. 2. (ps). 1967. complete kit 14.95 (*0-86508-014-3*); text only 3.45 (*0-86508-015-1*); color & action book 1.75 (*0-86508-016-X*) BCM Pubn.
—Tell Me How to Please God: 16 Lessons, Vol. 4. (ps). 1974. complete kit 14.95 (*0-86508-020-8*); text only 3.45 (*0-86508-021-6*); color & action book 1.75 (*0-86508-022-4*) BCM Pubn.
—Tell Me How to Trust God: 16 Lessons, Vol. 3. (ps). 1970. complete kit 14.95 (*0-86508-017-8*); text only 3.45 (*0-86508-018-6*); color & action book 1.75 (*0-86508-019-4*) BCM Pubn.
—Tiny Steps of Faith Series. 1985. pap. text ed. 3.45 (*0-86508-010-0*) BCM Pubn.
Haas, Merle, tr. see **De Brunhoff, Jean.**
Haas, Rudi & Blohm, Hans. The Egg-Carton Zoo, No. 1. Suzuki, David, intro. by. (Illus.). 64p. 1987. pap. 11.95 (*0-19-540513-7*) OUP.
Haas, Shelly O., jt. auth. see **Aroner, Miriam.**
Haas, William P. The Constitutional Convention of Seventeen Eighty-Seven: The Evolution of the Constitution of the U. S. 64p. (Orig.). (gr. 7-12). 1987. pap. 2.00 (*0-940527-08-1*) Savant Pub.
Haasl, Beth & Marrocha, Jean. Bereavement Support Group Program for Children: Participant Workbook. 39p. (Orig.). (ps-8). 1990. 6.95 (*1-55959-012-2*) Accel Devel.
Haban, Rita D. How Proudly They Wave: Flags of the Fifty States. LC 89-2302. (Illus.). 111p. (gr. 5 up). 1989. 23.95 (*0-8225-1799-X*) Lerner Pubns.
Habegger, Christa, ed. see **Watkins, Dawn L.**
Haber, Jon Z. see **Rojany, Lisa & Strong, Stacie.**
Haber, Louis. Black Pioneers of Science & Invention. LC 77-109090. (Illus.). 181p. (gr. 5 up). 1970. 17.95 (*0-15-208565-3*, HB Juv Bks) HarBrace.
—Black Pioneers of Science & Invention. (gr. 5 up). 1992. pap. 5.95 (*0-15-208129-1*, HB Juv Bks) HarBrace.
Hablallah, Jeanette. Color a Story: Nuh. 32p. (ps). 1989. pap. 3.50 (*1-56744-251-X*) Kazi Pubns.
Hable, Mary P., jt. auth. see **Wortman, Alexandra.**
Hacker, Jeffrey. Franklin D. Roosevelt. LC 90-48973. (Illus.). 176p. (gr. 6-10). 1991. PLB 13.95 (*1-55905-096-9*) Marshall Cavendish.
Hacker, Michael & Barden, Robert. Living with Technology. 2nd ed. 1991. text ed. 26.60 (*0-8273-4907-6*) Delmar.
Hacker, Randi & Kaufman, Jackie. Habitats: Where the Wild Things Live. (Illus.). 48p. (Orig.). (gr. 3 up). Date not set. pap. 9.95 (*1-56261-060-0*) John Muir.
Hackett, Christine. Little House in the Classroom. Filkins, Vanessa, illus. 112p. (gr. 3-5). 1989. wkbk. 9.95 (*0-86653-444-X*, GA1052) Good Apple.
Hackney, Ann. The Epic Adventure...Texas. 2nd ed. Hodges, Carol, illus. Johnson, Lady Bird, intro. by. LC 85-24854. (Illus.). 64p. (gr. 4-7). 1985. text ed. 19.95 includes tape (*0-935077-11-1*); pap. 12.95 includes tape (*0-935077-12-X*); pap. 5.95 (*0-935077-07-3*); tchr's guide 16.95 (*0-935077-10-3*); cassette 7.95 (*0-935077-08-1*) Hist Jefferson Found.
Hackwell, W. John. Desert of Ice: Life & Work in Antarctica. LC 89-35002. (Illus.). 48p. (gr. 5 up). 1991. SBE 14.95 (*0-684-19085-0*, Scribners Young Read) Macmillan Child Grp.
—Digging to the Past: Excavations in Ancient Lands. LC 86-13115. (Illus.). 64p. (gr. 3-7). 1986. SBE 14.95 (*0-684-18692-6*, Scribners Young Read) Macmillan Child Grp.
—Diving to the Past: Recovering Ancient Wrecks. Hackwell, W. John, illus. LC 87-233529. 64p. (gr. 3-7). 1988. RSBE 14.95 (*0-684-18918-6*, Scribners Young Read) Macmillan Child Grp.
—Signs, Letters, Words: Archaeology Discovers Writing. Hackwell, W. John, illus. LC 86-26237. 72p. (gr. 7 up). 1987. SBE 14.95 (*0-684-18807-4*, Scribners Young Read) Macmillan Child Grp.
Hadary, Rivka. Israel. (Illus.). 32p. (gr. 4-6). 1991. 17.95 (*0-237-60190-7*, Pub. by Evans Bros Ltd) Trafalgar.
Hadas, Moses, ed. see **Tacitus.**
Hadden, Mary, jt. auth. see **Philips, Martha.**
Hadden, Sue. Insects. LC 91-15625. (Illus.). 32p. (gr. 2-6). 1993. 14.95g (*1-56847-009-6*) Thomson Lrning.
Haddock, Eric W. New Orleans. 64p. (Orig.). 1991. pap. 10.00 (*1-55878-080-7*) Game Designers.

Haddock, Patricia. Careers in Banking & Finance. Rosen, Ruth, ed. (gr. 7-12). 1989. PLB 13.95 (*0-8239-0962-X*) Rosen Group.
—Lee Iacocca: Standing up for America: A Biography of Lee Iacocca. LC 86-32965. (Illus.). 128p. (gr. 6 up). 1987. RSBE 13.95 (*0-87518-362-X*, Dillon) Macmillan Child Grp.
—Mysteries of the Moon: Opposing Viewpoints. (Illus.). 112p. (gr. 5-8). 1992. PLB 14.95 (*0-89908-094-4*) Greenhaven.
—San Francisco. LC 88-20200. (Illus.). 60p. (gr. 3 up). 1988. RSBE 13.95 (*0-87518-383-2*, Dillon) Macmillan Child Grp.
Haddock, Peter. Fairy Tale Shape Board Book: Cinderella. 1988. 2.49 (*0-671-09409-2*) S&S Trade.
—Hansel & Gretel. 1988. 2.49 (*0-671-09408-4*) S&S Trade.
Haddon, Mark. Toni & the Tomato Soup. Haddon, Mark, illus. 21p. (ps-1). 1989. 12.95 (*0-15-200610-9*, Gulliver Bks) HarBrace.
Hader, Berta & Hader, Elmer. The Big Snow. 2nd ed. Hader, Berta & Hader, Elmer, illus. LC 87-38488. 48p. (gr. k-4). 1988. pap. 4.95 (*0-689-71260-X*, Aladdin) Macmillan Child Grp.
—The Big Snow. 2nd ed. Hader, Berta & Hader, Elmer, illus. LC 92-46365. 48p. (gr. k-4). 1994. pap. 4.95 (*0-689-71757-1*, Aladdin) Macmillan Child Grp.
Hader, Berta, jt. auth. see **Hader, Elmer.**
Hader, Berta & Hader, Elmer, illus. Chicken Little and Little Half Chick. LC 93-38611. 1994. pap. write for info. (*0-486-27979-0*) Dover.
—Humpty Dumpty and Other Mother Goose Rhymes. LC 93-38612. 1994. pap. write for info. (*0-486-27488-8*) Dover.
—The Little Red Hen. LC 93-33702. (gr. 2 up). 1994. pap. write for info. (*0-486-27977-4*) Dover.
Hader, Elmer & Hader, Berta. The Big Snow. LC 48-10240. (Illus.). 48p. (gr. 1-3). 1972. RSBE 14.95 (*0-02-737910-8*, Macmillan Child Bk); pap. 4.95 (*0-02-043300-X*) Macmillan Child Grp.
Hader, Elmer, jt. auth. see **Hader, Berta.**
Hadingham, Evan & Hadingham, Janet. Garbage! Where It Comes from, Where It Goes. (Illus.). 48p. (gr. 5 up). 1990. pap. 14.95 jacketed (*0-671-69424-3*, Little Simon); pap. 5.95 (*0-671-69426-X*, Little Simon) S&S Trade.
Hadingham, Janet, jt. auth. see **Hadingham, Evan.**
Hadithi, Mwenye. Baby Baboon. Kennaway, Adrienne, illus. LC 92-56397. 1993. 15.95 (*0-316-33729-3*) Little.
—Crafty Chameleon. Kennaway, Adrienne, illus. 32p. (ps-3). 1987. 15.95 (*0-316-33723-4*) Little.
—Greedy Zebra. 1984 ed. Kennaway, Adrienne, illus. (ps-3). 1984. 15.95 (*0-316-33721-8*) Little.
—Hot Hippo. Kennaway, Adrienne, illus. (ps-3). 1986. lib. bdg. 14.95 (*0-316-33722-6*) Little.
—Lazy Lion. (ps-4). 1990. 15.95 (*0-316-33725-0*) Little.
—Tricky Tortoise. Kennaway, Adrienne, illus. (ps-3). 1988. 15.95 (*0-316-33724-2*) Little.
Hadithi, Mwenye. Tricky Tortoise. (ps-3). 1992. pap. 4.95 (*0-316-33727-7*) Little.
Hadland, Beverly J. Hang on to Your Hormones: Straight Talk on Sex, Love & Dating. Paterson, Jim, illus. 192p. (Orig.). 1992. pap. 4.95x (*0-919225-38-1*) Life Cycle Bks.
Hadley, Dee W. Up-Date. LC 81-65308. 112p. (gr. 9 up). 1988. pap. 3.95 (*0-87747-847-3*) Deseret Bk.
Hadley, Eric & Hadley, Tessa. Legends of Earth, Air, Fire & Water. (Illus.). 32p. 1985. 13.95 (*0-521-26311-5*) Cambridge U Pr.
—Legends of the Sun & Moon. LC 82-17720. (Illus.). 32p. (gr. 3-7). 1989. 13.95 (*0-521-25227-X*); pap. 9.95 (*0-521-37912-1*) Cambridge U Pr.
Hadley, Roberta, jt. auth. see **Horton, Edna C.**
Hadley, Tessa, jt. auth. see **Hadley, Eric.**
Hadlow, Ruth, et al. Children's Books Too Good to Miss. 8th ed. (gr. 1-6). 1992. write for info. (*0-9616276-0-3*) Lucas Comns.
Haefli, Tom. The Prince of Westmont. Shauck, Chuck, illus. 36p. 1993. write for info. saddle stitched (*1-56167-124-X*) Am Literary Pr.
Haener, Donald R. & Fry, Janice. The Times of Our Constitution. 2nd ed. Baruffa, Joan, et al, illus. Ridge, Tom, intro. by. 24p. (gr. 2-6). 1987. pap. 3.00 (*0-942661-03-6*) Discovry Enterp.
Haener, Donald R. & Fry, Janice K. The Era & Our Constitution. rev. ed. Baruffa, Joanne & Tunis, Edwin, illus. (gr. 6 up). 1987. pap. text ed. 5.00 (*0-942661-02-8*) Discovry Enterp.
Haensel, Phyllis C. Certain Choices. Hoff, Marshall G. & Bock, Glenn H., eds. Belding, Pam, illus. 32p. (Orig.). (gr. 7-9). 1984. pap. text ed. write for info. (*0-940210-01-0*) Minn Med Found.
Hafen, Lyman. Over the Joshua Slope: A Novel. LC 93-30712. 160p. (gr. 4-8). 1994. SBE 14.95 (*0-02-741100-1*, Bradbury Pr) Macmillan Child Grp.
Hafer, Jan & Wilson, Robert. Come Sign with Us: Sign Language Activities for Children. LC 90-3478. (Illus.). 157p. (gr. 2-6). 1990. pap. text ed. 19.95 (*0-930323-72-6*, Clerc Bks) Gallaudet Univ Pr.
Haff, Gerry, jt. auth. see **Campbell, Alexander.**
Haffey, Richard. H. R. Cornelius Learns about Love: A Commandments Book for Children. (Illus.). 20p. (Orig.). (gr. 2-5). 1985. pap. 2.95 (*0-89622-235-7*) Twenty-Third.
Hafford, Jeanette N. Tiny's Self Help Books for Children. (Illus.). 18p. (Orig.). (gr. k-5). 1986. pap. 4.22 (*0-685-14506-9*) Tinys Self Help Bks.

Hafford, Jeannette N. Boys & Girls & Doctors & Dentists. 24p. (Orig.). 1986. pap. 7.22 (0-9616549-0-2) Tinys Self Help Bks.
—Help Mates for Your Playmates. (Illus.). 18p. (ps-7). 1986. pap. 4.22 (0-9616549-1-0) Tinys Self Help Bks.
—Run Children Run: Tiny Warns Children about the Dangers of Drugs. (Illus.). (ps-8). 1989. pap. text ed. write for info. (0-9616549-2-9) Tinys Self Help Bks.
—Tiny Goes to the Doctor. 48p. (Orig.). (gr. 3-8). 1990. pap. write for info. Tinys Self Help Bks.
Hafner, Everett. Sports Riddles. Hafner, Marylin, illus. 48p. (gr. 1-4). 1991. pap. 3.95 (0-14-032497-6, Puffin) Puffin Bks.
Hageman, Marybeth. I Want to Be Like Jesus. LC 89-80615. 32p. (Orig.). 1989. pap. 5.99 (0-8066-2419-1, 9-2419) Augsburg Fortress.
—Thank You, God, for Me. (Illus.). (ps). 1987. pap. 2.50 (0-570-09114-4, 56-1589) Concordia.
Hagen. Hiawatha. 1992. 15.95 (0-8050-1832-8) H Holt & Co.
Hagerman, Paul. It's a Weird World. LC 90-37643. (Illus.). 128p. (Orig.). (gr. 10 up). 1990. pap. 5.95 (0-8069-7412-5) Sterling.
Haggard, H. Rider. Allan Quartermain. (Illus.). 288p. (gr. 5 up). 1991. pap. 2.95 (0-14-035117-5, Puffin) Puffin Bks.
—King Solomon's Mines. Gemme, F. R., intro. by. (gr. 8 up). 1967. pap. 1.95 (0-8049-0140-6, CL-140) Airmont.
—King Solomon's Mines. 256p. (gr. 3-7). 1983. pap. 2.95 (0-14-035014-4, Puffin) Puffin Bks.
—She. Wollheim, D., intro. by. (gr. 8 up). 1967. pap. 1.95 (0-8049-0146-5, CL-146) Airmont.
Haggblade, Berle, jt. auth. see Marshall, Grace L.
Haggerty, Mary E. A Crack in the Wall. De Anda, Ruben, illus. LC 92-59952. 32p. (gr. k-3). 1993. 14.95 (1-880000-03-2) Lee & Low Bks.
Haggott, Mikko, tr. see Brewster, Dorothy P.
Hagler, Elizabeth, jt. auth. see Beers, Gil.
Hagman, Harlan L. A Seasonal Present & Other Stories. LC 88-34712. (Illus.). xiv, 341p. (gr. 9 up). 1989. 19.95 (0-931600-08-1) Green Oak Pr.
Hagman, Ruth. The Crow. LC 90-37679. (Illus.). 48p. (gr. k-4). 1990. PLB 15.27 (0-516-01103-0); pap. 4.95 (0-516-41103-9) Childrens.
Hagstrom, Amy. Strong & Free. Hagstrom, Amy, illus. LC 87-3942. 24p. (gr. 1 up). 1987. PLB 14.95 (0-933849-15-X) Landmark Edns.
Hague & Burgess. Old Mother West Wind. (gr. 4 up). 1991. 18.95 (0-8050-1426-8) H Holt & Co.
Hague & Grahame. Wind in the Willows. 1991. 19.95 (0-8050-1422-5) H Holt & Co.
Hague, Kathleen. Alphabears. Hague, Michael, illus. (ps-2). 1985. PLB incl. cassette 19.95 (0-941078-99-X) Live Oak Media.
—Alphabears: An ABC Book. Hague, Michael, illus. LC 83-26476. 32p. (ps-2). 1984. 12.95 (0-8050-0841-1, Bks Young Read) H Holt & Co.
—Alphabears: An ABC Book. Hague, Michael, illus. LC 83-26476. 32p. (ps-2). 1991. pap. 4.95 (0-8050-1637-6, Bks Young Read) H Holt & Co.
—Bear Hugs. Hague, Michael, illus. LC 88-28458. 32p. (ps-2). 1989. 9.95 (0-8050-0512-9, Bks Young Read) H Holt & Co.
—Bear Hugs. Hague, Michael, illus. LC 88-28458. 64p. (ps-2). 1992. pap. 4.95 (0-8050-2344-5, Bks Young Read) H Holt & Co.
—The Legend of the Veery Bird. Hague, Michael, illus. LC 84-19732. 32p. (ps up). 1985. 13.95 (0-15-243824-6, HB Juv Bks) HarBrace.
—The Man Who Kept House. Hague, Michael, illus. LC 80-26258. 32p. (ps-3). 1988. pap. 3.95 (0-15-251699-9, Voyager Bks) HarBrace.
—Numbears: A Counting Book. Hague, Michael, illus. LC 85-27006. 32p. (ps-2). 1986. 12.95 (0-8050-0309-6, Bks Young Read) H Holt & Co.
—Numbears: Alphabears. Hague, Michael, illus. LC 85-27006. 32p. (ps-2). 1991. pap. 4.95 (0-8050-1679-1, Bks Young Read) H Holt & Co.
—Out of the Nursery, into the Night. Hague, Michael, illus. LC 86-14270. 32p. (ps-2). 1986. 13.95 (0-8050-0088-7, Bks Young Read) H Holt & Co.
Hague, Kathleen & Hague, Michael. East of the Sun & West of the Moon. Hague, Michael, illus. LC 80-13499. (Illus.). 32p. (gr. 3 up). 1989. pap. 4.95 (0-15-224703-3, Voyager Bks) HarBrace.
—The Man Who Kept House. Hague, Michael, illus. LC 80-26258. 32p. (ps-3). 1981. 12.95 (0-15-251698-0, HB Juv Bks) HarBrace.
Hague, M., jt. auth. see Norton, M.
Hague, M., ed. see Michener, J. A.
Hague, Michael. Aesop's Fables. LC 84-19166. 32p. (gr. 2-4). 1985. 14.95 (0-8050-0210-3, Bks Young Read) H Holt & Co.
—A Child's Book of Prayers. LC 85-8380. (Illus.). 32p. (ps-2). 1985. 13.95 (0-8050-0211-1, Bks Young Read) H Holt & Co.
—Jingle Bells. Hague, Michael, illus. LC 90-32066. 32p. (ps up). 1990. 4.95 (0-8050-1413-6, Bks Young Read) H Holt & Co.
—Michael Hague, No. 10. 1994. write for info. (0-8050-1011-4) H Holt & Co.
—My Secret Garden Diary. 1990. 14.95 (1-55970-070-X) Arcade Pub Inc.
Hague, Michael, jt. auth. see Hague, Kathleen.
Hague, Michael, compiled by. & illus. Sleep, Baby, Sleep: Lullabies & Night Poems. LC 93-27119. 1994. PLB write for info. (0-688-10877-6) Morrow Jr Bks.

Hague, Michael, illus. Deck the Halls. LC 90-25628. 32p. (ps up). 1991. 4.95 (0-8050-1007-6, Bks Young Read) H Holt & Co.
—The Fairy Tales of Oscar Wilde. LC 92-14305. 192p. 1993. 19.95 (0-8050-1009-2, Bks Young Read) H Holt & Co.
—Magic Moments: A Book of Days. 96p. 1990. 14.95 (1-55970-069-6) Arcade Pub Inc.
—Mother Goose: A Collection of Classic Nursery Rhymes. LC 83-22559. 80p. (ps-2). 1984. 15.95 (0-8050-0214-6, Bks Young Read) H Holt & Co.
—O Christmas Tree. LC 90-25527. 32p. (ps up). 1991. 4.95 (0-8050-1538-8, Bks Young Read) H Holt & Co.
—Teddy Bear, Teddy Bear: A Classic Action Rhyme. LC 92-17997. 32p. (ps up). 1993. 14.00 (0-688-10671-4); PLB 13.93 (0-688-12085-7) Morrow Jr Bks.
—A Unicorn Journal. 64p. 1990. 12.95 (1-55970-068-8) Arcade Pub Inc.
—We Wish You a Merry Christmas. LC 90-32067. 32p. (gr. k up). 1990. 4.95 (0-8050-1006-8, Bks Young Read) H Holt & Co.
Hahn, Deborah, retold by. & illu see Andersen, Hans Christian.
Hahn, Elizabeth. Inuit. (Illus.). 32p. (gr. 5-8). 1990. lib. bdg. 15.74 (0-86625-386-6); lib. bdg. 11.95s.p. (0-685-46459-8) Rourke Corp.
Hahn, Mary D. Daphne's Book. LC 83-20933. 192p. (gr. 4-8). 1983. 14.45 (0-89919-183-5, Clarion Bks) HM.
—Daphne's Book. 192p. 1985. pap. 2.50 (0-553-15360-9, Skylark) Bantam.
—The Dead Man in Indian Creek. 144p. (gr. 4-5). 1991. pap. 3.50 (0-380-71362-4, Camelot) Avon.
—December Stillness. LC 88-2572. 192p. (gr. 5-9). 1988. 13.95 (0-89919-758-2, Clarion Bks) HM.
—Doll in the Garden. 144p. 1990. pap. 3.50 (0-380-70865-5, Camelot) Avon.
—The Doll in the Garden: A Ghost Story. 160p. (gr. 4-6). 1989. 13.45 (0-89919-848-1, Pub. by Clarion) HM.
—Following the Mystery Man. LC 87-17896. 192p. (gr. 4-8). 1988. 13.45 (0-89919-680-2, Clarion Bks) HM.
—Following the Mystery Man. 192p. (gr. 4 up). 1989. pap. 3.50 (0-380-70677-6, Camelot) Avon.
—The Jellyfish Season. 176p. (gr. 5). 1992. pap. 3.50 (0-380-71635-6, Camelot) Avon.
—The Sara Summer. 160p. (gr. 5 up). 1985. pap. 2.75 (0-553-15481-8) Bantam.
—The Sara Summer. 1985. pap. 2.99 (0-553-15600-4) Bantam.
—The Spanish Kidnapping Disaster. Giblin, James, ed. 144p. (gr. 4-7). 1991. 13.95 (0-395-55696-1, Clarion Bks) HM.
—The Spanish Kidnapping Disaster. 144p. 1993. pap. 3.50 (0-380-71712-3, Camelot) Avon.
—Stepping on the Cracks. 240p. (gr. 4-7). 1991. 14.45 (0-395-58507-4, Clarion Bks) HM.
—Stepping on the Cracks. 224p. 1992. pap. 3.99 (0-380-71900-2, Camelot) Avon.
—Tallahassee Higgins. LC 86-17513. 192p. (gr. 5-7). 1987. 13.95 (0-89919-495-8, Clarion Bks) HM.
—Tallahassee Higgins. 1988. pap. 3.50 (0-380-70500-1, Camelot) Avon.
—Time for Andrew: A Ghost Story. LC 93-2877. 1994. write for info. (0-395-66556-6, Clarion Bks) HM.
—The Time of the Witch. (gr. 4-8). 1982. 13.45 (0-89919-115-0, Clarion Bks) HM.
—The Time of the Witch. 176p. 1991. pap. 3.50 (0-380-71116-8, Camelot) Avon.
—Wait Till Helen Comes: A Ghost Story. LC 86-2648. 192p. (gr. 4-7). 1986. 14.45 (0-89919-453-2, Clarion Bks) HM.
—Wait till Helen Comes: Ghost Story. (gr. 3-7). 1987. pap. 3.50 (0-380-70442-0, Camelot) Avon.
—The Wind Blows Backward. LC 92-12245. 272p. (gr. 9 up). 1993. 13.95 (0-395-62975-6, Clarion Bks) HM.
—The Wind Blows Backwards. large type ed. LC 93-31870. (gr. 9-12). 1993. 15.95 (0-7862-0064-2) Thorndike Pr.
Hahn, Mary Downing. The Dead Man in Indian Creek. 160p. (gr. 4-8). 1990. 14.95 (0-395-52397-4) HM.
Haidle, David & Haidle, Helen. He Is My Shepherd: The Twenty-Third Psalm for Children. Davis, Deena, ed. Haidle, David & Haidle, Helen, illus. LC 89-31428. 27p. (gr. 3-8). 1989. 8.99 (0-88070-278-8, Gold & Honey) Questar Pubs.
Haidle, Elizabeth. Elmer the Grump. Thatch, Nancy R., ed. Haidle, Elizabeth, illus. Melton, David, intro. by. LC 89-31872. (Illus.). 26p. (gr. k-5). 1989. PLB 14.95 (0-933849-20-6) Landmark Edns.
Haidle, Helen, jt. auth. see Haidle, David.
Haiduck, Robert. Ten Tiny Tales, Bk. 1. 87p. (gr. 1-8). 1990. write for info. (0-9627661-0-0) Ten Tiny Tales.
Haigh, Rosemary & Pulver, Carol. C'est Ton Tour. (FRE., Illus.). 160p. (Orig.). (gr. 7-9). 1990. wkbk. 14.94 (1-879279-02-9, TX 3-018-187) Proficiency Pr.
Haigh, Sheila. The Little Gymnast. 144p. (Orig.). (gr. 3-7). 1987. pap. 2.95 (0-590-43015-7) Scholastic Inc.
Haight, G. S., ed. see Eliot, George.
Haigis, Debbie, ed. see Wilkinson, Jack & Tubbs, Orrin.
Haign, Rosemary, et al. The Foreign Language Teacher's Handbook: Aiming for Proficiency in French. (FRE., Illus.). 240p. (Orig.). (gr. 8). 1989. tchr's ed. 28.95 (1-879279-00-2, TX 2-787-775) Proficiency Pr.
Hail, Patricia. Saga of the Spotted Cow. (Illus.). 32p. (gr. k-3). 1992. 9.95 (1-879894-00-9) Laffing Cow.
Haines. Ferrari: The Legend. 1991. 12.50s.p. (0-86593-146-1); lib. bdg. 16.67 (0-685-66098-2) Rourke Corp.

—Lamborghini: The Fastest. 1991. 12.50s.p. (0-86593-145-3); lib. bdg. 16.67 (0-685-59195-6) Rourke Corp.
—Mercedes: The First & the Best. 1991. 12.50s.p. (0-86593-142-9); lib. bdg. 16.67 (0-685-59196-4) Rourke Corp.
—Porsche: Fast & Beautiful. 1991. 12.50s.p. (0-86593-143-7); lib. bdg. 16.67 (0-685-59197-2) Rourke Corp.
Haines, Gail B. The Challenge of Supplying Energy. LC 89-28498. (Illus.). 64p. (gr. 6 up). 1991. lib. bdg. 15.95 (0-89490-269-5) Enslow Pubs.
Haines, Gail K. Sugar Is Sweet...& So Are Lots of Other Things. LC 91-10606. (Illus.). 32p. (gr. 2-5). 1992. SBE 13.95 (0-689-31723-9, Atheneum Child Bk) Macmillan Child Grp.
Haines, Harry, jt. auth. see Haines, Shirley.
Haines, Joan. A Banana for Rosie. Barker, Melissa & Logan, Ann, illus. 16p. (Orig.). (ps-1). 1985. pap. 2.65 (0-936652-03-9, Pub. by Ed Concern Pubns) Two Ems.
—Meet Rosie Posie. Barker, Melissa & Logan, Ann, illus. 16p. (Orig.). (ps-1). 1985. pap. 2.65 (0-936652-00-4, Pub. by Ed Concern Pubns) Two Ems.
—Rosie Posie Has a Bath. Barker, Melissa & Logan, Ann, illus. 16p. (ps-1). 1985. pap. 2.65 (0-936652-02-0, Pub. by Ed Concern Pubns) Two Ems.
—Rosie Posie Makes Friends. Berker, Melissa & Logan, Ann, illus. 16p. (Orig.). (ps-1). 1985. pap. 2.65 (0-936652-01-2, Pub. by Ed Concern Pubns) Two Ems.
Haines, Rashelle. Jimmy's Last Wish: A Story about Forever. Alvarado, Carol, illus. 32p. 1992. 22.95 (0-944963-23-4); PLB 20.95 (0-944963-32-3); audio tape 9.95 (0-944963-20-X) Glastonbury Pr.
Haines, Shirley & Haines, Harry. BMW: Performance with Luxury. LC 92-43260. 1993. 17.26 (0-86593-251-4); 12.95s.p. (0-685-66288-8) Rourke Corp.
—Cadillac: Standard of the World. LC 92-42305. 1993. 17.26 (0-86593-252-2); 12.95s.p. (0-685-66358-2) Rourke Corp.
—Corvette: The American Sports Car. LC 93-18066. 1993. 17.26 (0-86593-253-0); 12.95s.p. (0-685-66578-X) Rourke Corp.
Hains, Harriet. My Baby Brother. LC 91-58199. (Illus.). 24p. (ps-3). 1992. 9.95 (1-879431-76-9) Dorling Kindersley.
—My New Puppy. LC 91-58200. (Illus.). 24p. (ps-3). 1992. 9.95 (1-879431-77-7) Dorling Kindersley.
—My New School. LC 92-52812. (Illus.). 24p. (ps-1). 1993. 9.95 (1-56458-116-0) Dorling Kindersley.
—Our New Kitten. LC 92-52813. (Illus.). 24p. (ps-1). 1993. 9.95 (1-56458-117-9) Dorling Kindersley.
Hair, Johnny. Who's Hot -- Red Hot Chili Peppers. (gr. 4-7). 1993. pap. 1.49 (0-440-21595-1) Dell.
Hairston, Earnestine. Let's Tour the Roanoke Valley: A Story Coloring Book. Hicks, Celeste H., illus. 52p. (ps-4). 1987. pap. 3.95 (0-944890-00-8) Hairston & Hicks.
Haislip, Barbara. Stars, Spells, Secrets & Sorcery. 288p. (gr. 9 up). 1978. pap. 1.75 (0-440-98454-8, LFL) Dell.
Haith, Betty. Bonnie's Thirteenth Summer. 52p. 1992. pap. 4.95 (1-882185-01-3) Crnrstone Pub.
Haker, Loren F. The Li'l Rascals: Tale of a Fish. Haker, Loren F., illus. 66p. (gr. 1-8). 1984. 7.95 (0-9609964-2-7); pap. 4.95 (0-9609964-3-5) Haker Books.
—The Li'l Rascals: Timmy & the Bees. (Illus.). 56p. (gr. 1-8). 1984. 7.95 (0-9609964-0-0); pap. 4.95 (0-9609964-1-9) Haker Books.
Hakim, Joy. The First Americans. LC 92-50114. 1993. PLB 19.95 (0-19-507745-8); pap. 9.95 (0-19-507746-6) OUP.
—A History of the United States: An Age of Extremes, Vol. 8. (Illus.). 160p. 1993. PLB 19.95 (0-19-507759-8); pap. 9.95 (0-19-507760-1) OUP.
—A History of the United States: From Colonies to Country, Vol. 3. (Illus.). 160p. 1993. PLB 19.95 (0-19-507749-0); pap. 9.95 (0-19-507750-4) OUP.
—A History of the United States: Liberty for All, Vol. 5. (Illus.). 160p. 1993. PLB 19.95 (0-19-507753-9); pap. 9.95 (0-19-507754-7) OUP.
—A History of the United States: Making Thirteen Colonies, Vol. 2. (Illus.). 160p. 1993. PLB 19.95 (0-19-507747-4); pap. 9.95 (0-19-507748-2) OUP.
—A History of the United States: Reconstruction & Reform, Vol. 7. (Illus.). 160p. 1993. PLB 19.95 (0-19-507757-1); pap. 9.95 (0-19-507758-X) OUP.
—A History of the United States: The New Nation, Vol. 4. (Illus.). 160p. 1993. PLB 19.95 (0-19-507751-2); pap. 9.95 (0-19-507752-0) OUP.
—A History of the United States: War, Terrible War, Vol. 6. (Illus.). 160p. 1993. PLB 19.95 (0-19-507755-5); pap. 9.95 (0-19-507756-3) OUP.
—A History of US, 10 vols. (Illus.). 1600p. 1994. PLB 199.50 (0-19-507765-2); pap. 99.50 (0-19-507766-0) OUP.
—War, Peace, & All That Jazz. LC 93-28768. (Illus.). 160p. 1994. PLB 19.95 (0-19-507761-X); pap. 9.95 (0-19-507762-8) OUP.
Hakim, Rita. Martin Luther King, Jr. And the March Toward Freedom. (Illus.). 32p. (gr. 2-4). 1991. PLB 12.40 (1-878841-13-0) Millbrook Pr.
Hakkinen. Summer Legs. 1993. 15.95 (0-8050-2262-7) H Holt & Co.

Hakowski, Maryann. Vine & Branches, Vol. 1. Stamschror, Robert P., ed. St. George, Carolyn, illus. 168p. (gr. 7-12). 1992. spiral bdg. 22.95 (0-88489-255-7) St Marys.
—Vine & Branches, Vol. 2. Stamschror, Robert P., ed. St. George, Carolyn, illus. 168p. (gr. 7-12). 1992. spiral bdg. 22.95 (0-88489-278-6) St Marys.

Halak, Glenn. A Grandmother's Story. LC 91-18058. (Illus.). 48p. (ps). 1992. 14.00 (0-671-74953-6, Green Tiger) S&S Trade.

Halam, Ann. King Death's Garden. large type ed. (gr. 1-8). 1991. 13.95 (0-7451-0657-9, Galaxy Child Lrg Print) Chivers N Amer.

Halasa, Malu. Elijah Muhammad. King, Coretta Scott, intro. by. (Illus.). (gr. 5 up). 1990. 17.95 (1-55546-602-8) Chelsea Hse.
—Mary McLeod Bethune. King, Coretta Scott. (Illus.). 112p. (gr. 5 up). 1989. lib. bdg. 17.95x (1-55546-549-9) Chelsea Hse.
—Mary McLeod Bethune. (gr. 4-7). 1993. pap. 7.95 (0-7910-0225-X) Chelsea Hse.

Halasi-kun, George, jt. auth. see Erdogan, Haydar.

Halasz, Robert. The U. S. Marines. LC 92-36811. (Illus.). 64p. (gr. 3-6). 1993. PLB 14.90 (1-56294-251-4) Millbrook Pr.

Halbur, Donna K. Accountants Visit School. Kearney, Paul, illus. 24p. (gr. 3-5). 1979. pap. 3.00 (0-686-25249-7) Halbur.

Haldane, Suzanne. Helping Hands: How Monkeys Assist People Who Are Disabled. Haldane, Suzanne, photos by. LC 90-27382. (Illus.). 48p. (gr. 3-7). 1991. 14.95 (0-525-44723-7, DCB) Dutton Child Bks.
—Painting Faces. LC 88-3706. (Illus.). 32p. (gr. 3 up). 1988. 13.95 (0-525-44408-4, DCB) Dutton Child Bks.

Hale, Anita. My Room at Church. LC 85-24344. (Illus.). (ps). 1986. 4.95 (0-8054-4168-9) Broadman.

Hale, Anna. Mystery on Mackinac Island. McLane, Lois, illus. LC 89-35484. 184p. (Orig.). (gr. 3-5). 1989. pap. 9.95 (0-943173-34-5) Harbinger AZ.

Hale, Beverly M. A Rainbow Book of Song: Key of "C" 2nd ed. Hale, Beverly M., illus. 57p. (ps up). 1993. Blue spine bdg. pap. text ed. 13.95 (0-9634305-1-3) E-Z Keys Method.

Hale, Bruce. The Legend of the Laughing Gecko: A Hawaiian Fantasy. Hale, Bruce, illus. Brown, Susana, concept by. (Illus.). 32p. (Orig.). (ps-3). 1989. pap. write for info. Geckostufs.
—Surf Gecko to the Rescue! Hale, Bruce, illus. 32p. (ps-4). 1991. write for info. (0-9621280-1-5) Geckostufs.

Hale, Duane & Gibson, Arrell M. The Chickasaw. (Illus.). 112p. (gr. 5 up). 1991. 17.95 (1-55546-697-4); pap. 9.95 (0-7910-0372-8) Chelsea Hse.

Hale, Edward E. Man Without a Country & Other Stories. (gr. 5 up). 1968. pap. 1.95 (0-8049-0185-6, CL-185) Airmont.

Hale, Hanna. Zelda Orangutan. Hale, Hanna, illus. 64p. (gr. 4-6). 1994. Perfect bdg. pap. 12.95 (0-9638724-0-0) Cando Pubng.
Zelda, an orphaned baby orangutan is adopted by an actress. Cathy takes her to Hollywood, where together they star in a movie. The picture is a great success, but Zelda is lonely until she makes friends with Laddie, a collie & Kat, a kitten. Together they experience amusing as well as dangerous adventures. The animals foil a kidnapping attempt. Zelda protects two children who are being bullied by older classmates. She assists a forest ranger in an effort for the preservation of a California condor egg. Because of her great strength & climbing ability, the orangutan is able to help her friends frequently. As Zelda matures, she misses her orangutan family. Cathy understands her needs & returns Zelda to Sumatra & a free life in the jungle protectorate. Ordering information: Paperback--Perfect binding--64 pages-- (c) Hanna Hale 1994--Printed in U.S. A.--All rights reserved--Price: US $12. 95/Can. $18.95. Order from: CANDO PUBLISHING CORP. 1299 Springside Drive, Ft. Lauderdale, FL 33326-2748. *Publisher Provided Annotation.*

Hale, Irina. Boxman. Hale, Irina, illus. 32p. (ps-1). 1992. 12.00 (0-670-84287-7) Viking Child Bks.
—How I Found a Friend. Hale, Irina, illus. 32p. (ps-1). 1992. PLB 12.50 (0-670-84286-9) Viking Child Bks.
—The Naughty Crow. Hale, Irina, illus. LC 91-39929. 32p. (gr. k-4). 1992. SBE 14.95 (0-689-50546-9, M K McElderry) Macmillan Child Grp.
—Small Big Bad Boy. (ps-3). 1991. 11.95 (0-670-83818-7) Viking Child Bks.

Hale, Janet. April Monthly Activities. Apodaca, Blanqui, illus. 80p. (gr. 1-5). 1990. wkbk. 7.95 (1-55734-158-3) Tchr Create Mat.
—August Monthly Activities. Apodaca, Blanqui, et al, illus. 80p. (gr. 1-5). 1990. wkbk. 7.95 (1-55734-166-4) Tchr Create Mat.
—The Conners of Conner Prairie. Baxter, Nancy N., ed. Day, Richard, illus. LC 89-80212. 120p. (gr. 4-6). 1989. 13.95 (0-9617367-5-5) Guild Pr IN.
—Fall Think & Do Shape Books. Hale, Janet, illus. 48p. (gr. k-2). 1989. wkbk. 5.95 (1-55734-127-3) Tchr Create Mat.
—February Monthly Activities. Apodaca, Blanqui & Spence, Paula, illus. 80p. (gr. 1-5). 1989. wkbk. 7.95 (1-55734-156-7) Tchr Create Mat.
—January Monthly Activities. Apodaca, Blanqui & Spence, Paula, illus. 80p. (gr. 1-5). 1989. wkbk. 7.95 (1-55734-155-9) Tchr Create Mat.
—July Monthly Activities. Apodaca, Blanqui, et al, illus. 80p. (gr. 1-5). 1990. wkbk. 7.95 (1-55734-165-6) Tchr Create Mat.
—June Monthly Activities. Apodaca, Blanqui & Spence, Paula, illus. 80p. (gr. 1-5). 1990. wkbk. 7.95 (1-55734-164-8) Tchr Create Mat.
—March Monthly Activities. Apodaca, Blanqui, et al, illus. 80p. (gr. 1-5). 1990. wkbk. 7.95 (1-55734-157-5) Tchr Create Mat.
—May Monthly Activities. Apodaca, Blanqui, et al, illus. 80p. (gr. 1-5). 1990. wkbk. 7.95 (1-55734-159-1) Tchr Create Mat.
—Spring & Summer Think & Do Shape Books. Hale, Janet, illus. 48p. (gr. k-2). 1989. wkbk. 5.95 (1-55734-129-X) Tchr Create Mat.

Hale, Janet C. The Owl's Song. 144p. (gr. 7 up). 1976. pap. 2.50 (0-380-00605-7, 60212-1, Flare) Avon.
—The Owl's Song. (gr. 5 up). 1991. pap. 2.95 (0-553-28829-6, Starfire) Bantam.

Hale, Kathleen. Orlando's Evening Out. Hale, Kathleen, illus. 32p. (ps-3). 1992. 15.95 (0-7232-3652-6) Warne.
—Orlando's Home Life. (Illus.). 32p. (ps-3). 1992. 16.00 (0-7232-3653-4) Warne.

Hale, Lucretia. The Lady Who Put Salt in Her Coffee. Schwartz, Amy, adapted by. & illus. 28p. (ps-3). 1989. 13.95 (0-15-243475-5) HarBrace.

Hale, Sarah J. Mary Had a Little Lamb. De Paola, Tomie, illus. LC 83-22369. 32p. (ps-3). 1984. reinforced bdg 14.95 (0-8234-0509-5); pap. 5.95 (0-8234-0519-2) Holiday.
—Mary Had a Little Lamb. De Paola, Tomie, illus. (ps-2). 1989. bk. & cassette 19.95 (0-87499-125-0); pap. 12.95 bk. & cassette (0-87499-124-2); pap. 27.95 4 cassettes & guide (0-87499-126-9) Live Oak Media.
—Mary Had a Little Lamb. 32p. (ps-1). 1990. 12.95 (0-590-43773-9) Scholastic Inc.
—Mary Had a Little Lamb. 1992. 3.95 (0-590-43774-7, 045, Blue Ribbon Bks) Scholastic Inc.

Halecroft, David. Benched! 128p. (gr. 3-7). 1992. pap. 2.99 (0-14-036038-7) Puffin Bks.
—Blindside Blitz. (gr. 4-7). 1991. pap. 2.95 (0-14-034906-5, Puffin) Puffin Bks.
—Breaking Loose. (gr. 4 up). 1990. pap. 2.95 (0-14-034546-9, Puffin) Puffin Bks.
—Breaking Loose. LC 92-12084. 128p. (gr. 3-7). 1992. 13.00 (0-670-84697-X) Viking Child Bks.
—Championshp Summer. 128p. (gr. 5-7). 1991. pap. 2.95 (0-14-034808-5, Puffin) Puffin Bks.
—Hotshot on Ice. (gr. 4-7). 1991. pap. 2.95 (0-14-034907-3, Puffin) Puffin Bks.
—Power Play. (gr. 4 up). 1990. pap. 2.95 (0-14-034549-3, Puffin) Puffin Bks.
—Power Play. LC 92-12605. 128p. (gr. 3-7). 1992. 13.00 (0-670-84698-8) Viking Child Bks.
—Setting the Pace. (Illus.). 128p. (gr. 3-7). 1991. pap. 2.95 (0-14-034547-7, Puffin) Puffin Bks.
—Wild Pitch. (Illus.). 128p. (gr. 3-7). 1991. pap. 2.95 (0-14-034548-5, Puffin) Puffin Bks.

Hales, Dianne. Depression. LC 88-34176. (Illus.). 104p. (gr. 6-12). 1989. 18.95 (0-7910-0046-X) Chelsea Hse.
—The Family. (Illus.). 120p. (gr. 6-12). 1988. lib. bdg. 18. 95 (0-7910-0038-9) Chelsea Hse.
—Pregnancy & Birth. (Illus.). 112p. (gr. 6-12). 1989. 18. 95 (0-7910-0040-0) Chelsea Hse.

Haley, Beverly A. Focus on School: A Reference Handbook. 217p. 1990. lib. bdg. 39.00 (0-87436-099-4) ABC-CLIO.

Haley, Gail. Sea Tale. Haley, Gale E., illus. LC 89-34453. 32p. (ps-2). 1990. 13.95 (0-525-44567-6, DCB) Dutton Child Bks.

Haley, Gail E. Dream Peddler. Haley, Gail E., illus. LC 92-42074. 32p. (ps-3). 1993. 14.99 (0-525-45153-6, DCB) Dutton Child Bks.
—Marguerite. Haley, Gail E., illus. (ps-3). 1993. pap. 16. 95 (0-87460-262-9) Lion Bks.
—A Story, a Story. Haley, Gail E., illus. LC 69-18961. 36p. (ps-3). 1970. SBE 15.95 (0-689-20511-2, Atheneum Child Bk) Macmillan Child Grp.
—A Story, a Story. Haley, Gail E., illus. LC 87-17412. 36p. (ps-3). 1988. pap. 4.95 (0-689-71201-4, Aladdin) Macmillan Child Grp.

Haley, Gail E., retold by. & illus. Jack & the Fire Dragon. 40p. (gr. k-4). 1988. PLB 14.95 (0-517-56814-4) Crown Bks Yng Read.

—Puss in Boots. LC 90-20629. 32p. (ps-3). 1991. 13.95 (0-525-44740-7, DCB) Dutton Child Bks.

Haley, Gail E., illus. Jack & the Bean Tree. 48p. (gr. k-3). 1986. 13.95 (0-517-55717-7) Crown Bks Yng Read.
—Mountain Jack Tales. 144p. (gr. 3-8). 1992. 15.99 (0-525-44974-4, DCB) Dutton Child Bks.

Haley, Irene. see Fischer, Maureen.

Haley, Neale. Birds for Pets & Pleasure. Carroll, Pamela, illus. LC 80-68740. 224p. (gr. 7 up). 1981. PLB 8.95 (0-385-28053-X); pap. 4.95 (0-440-00475-6) Delacorte.

Haley, Patrick. The Little Person. Kool, Jonna, illus. LC 81-65114. 64p. (gr. 2-3). 1981. PLB 9.00 (0-9605738-0-1) East Eagle.
—Wildflower & the Big Voice in the Sky. Kool, Jonna, illus. LC 82-82990. 44p. (gr. 3-4). 1982. 9.00 (0-9605738-1-X) East Eagle.
—The Woodpecker & the Oak Tree. Kool, Jonna, illus. LC 82-82991. 64p. (gr. 3-4). 1982. 9.00 (0-9605738-2-8) East Eagle.

Haley, Patrick, ed. see Fischer, Maureen.

Halioua, Jean-Pierre, et al. Aventures En Ville. LC 79-63579. (gr. 9-12). 1980. pap. 14.64 (0-395-27833-3) HM.

Halkin, Hillel, tr. see Bergman, Tamar.

Halkin, Hillel, tr. see Orlev, Uri.

Halkin, Hillel, tr. see Semel, Nava.

Halkin, John. Fangs of the Werewolf. 160p. (gr. 6 up). 1988. pap. 2.95 (0-8120-4071-6) Barron.

Hall. The Easter Story. 1992. write for info. (0-7814-0020-1, Chariot Bks) Cook.
—Loaves & Fishes. 1992. write for info. (Chariot Bks) Cook.

Hall, Alice. Dairy Goats: Selecting, Fitting, Showing. Holleran, Betsy. Jackson, Robert A., frwd. by. LC 77-153203. (Illus.). (gr. 7 up). 1975. pap. 4.00x (0-932218-02-6) Hall Pr.

Hall, Andy & Hall, Maggie. The Romans Pop-Up. (Illus.). 32p. (Orig.). (gr. 3 up). 1985. pap. 7.95 (0-906212-29-4, Pub. by Tarquin UK) Parkwest Pubns.

Hall, Avery & Korty, John. Twice upon a Time. (Illus.). 48p. 1983. 6.95 (0-671-45633-4) S&S Trade.

Hall, Barbara. Dixie Storms. 197p. (gr. 7 up). 1990. 15. 95 (0-15-223825-5) HarBrace.
—Dixie Storms. 1992. pap. 3.50 (0-553-29047-9) Bantam.
—Fool's Hill. 1992. 16.00 (0-553-08993-5) Bantam.

Hall, Betty L. Michigan Survival. rev. ed. 160p. (gr. 10-12). 1986. pap. text ed. 5.84 (0-936159-02-2) Westwood Pr.
—Ohio Survival. rev. ed. 160p. (gr. 10-12). 1986. pap. text ed. 5.84 (0-936159-00-6) Westwood Pr.
—Wisconsin Survival. rev. ed. 160p. (gr. 10-12). 1986. pap. text ed. 5.84 (0-936159-01-4) Westwood Pr.

Hall, Betty L. & Burchfield, Ellen. Alabama Survival. 160p. (Orig.). (gr. 10-12). 1979. pap. text ed. 5.84 (0-03-055461-6) Westwood Pr.

Hall, Brenny, illus. Old MacDonald. (ps-3). 1981. 3.50 (0-913545-04-X) Moonlight FL.

Hall, Brian. The Performer's Guide to Theater Songs, Vol. 1: The Best Solo Songs for Study, Auditions & Revues. Lazarus, Joan, frwd. by. 201p. (gr. 5-12). 1991. write for info. plasticoil bdg. (0-9627847-0-2) Rovey Res Per Arts.

Hall, Candace C. Shelley's Day: The Day of a Legally Blind Child. Hall, Candace C., illus. 24p. (Orig.). (gr. k-4). 1980. pap. 2.95 (0-9603840-0-6) Andrew Mtn Pr.

Hall, Clyde R., compiled by. Handbook for Youth Discipleship. LC 87-30903. 240p. (Orig.). (gr. 7-12). 1991. pap. 7.95 (0-8054-6003-9) Broadman.

Hall, David E. Living with a Learning Disability: A Guide for Students. LC 92-46600. 1993. 15.95 (0-8225-0036-1) Lerner Pubns.

Hall, Derek. Baby Animals: Five Stories of Endangered Species. Butler, John, illus. LC 91-71861. 64p. (ps up). 1992. 14.95 (1-56402-004-5) Candlewick Pr.

Hall, Donald. I Am the Dog, I Am the Cat. Moser, Barry, illus. LC 93-28060. 1994. write for info. (0-8037-1504-8); PLB write for info. (0-8037-1505-6) Dial Bks Young.
—Lucy's Cristmas. McMurdy, Michael, illus. LC 92-46292. (gr. 1 up). 1994. write for info. (0-15-276870-X, Browndeer Pr) HarBrace.
—Lucy's Summer. McCurdy, Michael, illus. LC 93-17130. 1995. write for info. (0-15-276873-4, HB Juv Bks) HarBrace.
—The Man Who Lived Alone. Azarian, Mary, illus. LC 84-47655. 36p. (gr. 2 up). 1984. 12.50 (0-87923-538-1) Godine.
—Ox-Cart Man. Cooney, Barbara, illus. LC 79-14466. (gr. k-3). 1979. 15.00 (0-670-53328-9) Viking Child Bks.
—Ox-Cart Man. Cooney, Barbara, illus. 40p. (ps-3). 1983. pap. 4.99 (0-14-050441-9, Puffin) Puffin Bks.
—Oxcart Man. Cooney, Barbara, tr. (gr. 1-5). 1984. incl. cassette 19.95 (0-941078-41-8); pap. 12.95 incl. cassette (0-941078-40-X); pap. 27.95 4 bks, cassette & guide (0-941078-42-6) Live Oak Media.
—Summer of 1944. Moser, Barry, illus. LC 92-38613. 32p. 1994. 13.99 (0-8037-1501-3); PLB 13.89 (0-8037-1502-1) Dial Bks Young.

Hall, Donald, ed. The Oxford Book of Children's Verse in America. 368p. (gr. 3 up). 1990. pap. 9.95 (0-19-506761-4) OUP.

Hall, Douglas. Douglas Hall's Nursery Rhymes. 1989. 4.98 (0-671-07573-X) S&S Trade.

Hall, Duane L., jt. auth. see Watry, Charles A.

Hall, Ed Y., jt. auth. see Davis, Anita P.
Hall, Elizabeth, jt. auth. see O'Dell, Scott.
Hall, Elvajean. Margaret Pumphrey's Pilgrim Stories. 128p. 1991. pap. 2.95 (0-590-45202-9, Apple Paperbacks) Scholastic Inc.
Hall, George. Hot Wings, A Photo-Fact Book. (Illus.). 24p. (Orig.). 1988. pap. 1.95 (0-942025-48-2) Kidsbks.
—Hot Wings, A Photo-Fact Book, Vol. 2. (Illus.). 24p. (Orig.). 1988. pap. 1.95 (0-942025-95-4) Kidsbks.
—Hot Wings of Desert Storm. (Illus.). 32p. 1991. pap. 2.50 (1-56156-025-1) Kidsbks.
—Hot Wings of the World. (Illus.). 24p. (Orig.). 1990. pap. 2.50 (0-942025-86-5) Kidsbks.
Hall, Godfrey. Mind Twisters. Oxford Illustrators Staff, et al, illus. LC 91-27688. 96p. (Orig.). (gr. 3-7). 1992. PLB 13.99 (Orig.). (gr. 3-7). 1992. (0-679-82038-8) Random Bks Yng Read.
Hall, Howard. A Charm of Dolphins. rev. ed. Leon, Vicki, ed. LC 93-9752. (Illus.). 48p. (Orig.). (gr. 5 up). 1993. perfect bdg. 9.95 (0-918303-33-8) Blake Pub.
—The Kelp Forest. Leon, Vicki, ed. (Illus.). 40p. (Orig.). (gr. 5 up). 1990. pap. 7.95 (0-918303-21-4) Blake Pub.
—Sharks: The Perfect Predators. rev. ed. LC 93-27061. (gr. 5 up). 1993. pap. 9.95 (0-918303-36-2) Blake Pub.
—Sharks: The Perfect Predators. rev. ed. Leon, Vicki, ed. LC 93-27061. (Illus.). 48p. (gr. 5 up). 1993. pap. 9.95 Blake Pub.
Hall, James N. see Gravel, Fern, pseud.
Hall, James N., jt. auth. see Nordhoff, Charles.
Hall, Jan. Maggie & Jumper. LC 92-61595. (Illus.). 44p. (ps-3). 1993. 6.95 (1-55523-566-2) Winston-Derek.
Hall, John. Maze Craze Three. (Illus.). 40p. (gr. 1-12). 1974. pap. 3.50 (0-8431-1734-6) Price Stern.
—Maze Craze Two. (Illus.). 40p. (gr. 1-12). 1973. pap. 3.50 (0-8431-1733-8) Price Stern.
Hall, Judy A. Don't Just Say No! Safety Workbook for Children. 2nd ed. Edwards, Juanita, ed. Hall, Judy A., illus. 40p. (Orig.). (gr. k-5). 1991. pap. text ed. write for info. saddlestitch (0-9629597-1-5) Personal Prods.
—What Every Child Should Know & Do...for Surviving in the 90's: A Small Picture Book. Edwards, Juanita, ed. Hall, Judy A., illus. 24p. (Orig.). (gr. k-5). 1992. saddlestitched 9.95 (0-9629597-0-7) Personal Prods.
—What Every Child Should Know & Do...for Surviving in the 90's: Big Book Version. Edwards, Juanita, ed. 24p. (gr. k-5). 1992. 18.95 (0-9629597-3-1) Personal Prods.
Hall, K. Bunny, Bunny. (Illus.). 28p. (ps-2). 1990. 12.33 (0-516-05352-3); pap. 3.95 (0-516-45352-1) Childrens.
—Nursery Rhymes. 1990. 3.50 (0-685-31997-0, G018) Hansen Ed Mus.
Hall, K. & Flaxman, J. Who Says? (Illus.). 28p. (ps-2). 1990. 12.33 (0-516-05362-0); pap. 3.95 (0-516-45362-9) Childrens.
Hall, Kathy. One Hundred One Cat & Dog Jokes. 1990. pap. 1.95 (0-590-43336-9) Scholastic Inc.
Hall, Katy. Grizzly Riddles. LC 86-29275. 1989. 9.95 (0-8037-0376-7); PLB 9.89 (0-8037-0377-5) Dial Bks Young.
—Skeletons! Skeletons! All about Bones. Billin-Frye, Paige, illus. LC 90-82153. 32p. (ps-3). 1991. (G&D); pap. 2.25 (0-448-40108-8, G&D) Putnam Pub Group.
—Snakey Riddles. 1990. 9.95 (0-8037-0669-3); PLB 9.89 (0-8037-0670-7) Dial Bks Young.
Hall, Katy & Eisenberg, Lisa. Baseball Bloopers. Callen, Liz, illus. LC 89-62210. 96p. (Orig.). (gr. 2-6). 1991. pap. 12.95 (0-679-80335-1) Random Bks Yng Read.
—Batty Riddles. Rubel, Nicole, illus. LC 91-20777. 48p. (ps-3). 1993. 11.99 (0-8037-1217-0); lib. bdg. 11.89 (0-8037-1218-9) Dial Bks Young.
—Buggy Riddles. Taback, Simms, illus. LC 85-1450. 48p. (ps-3). 1986. 9.95 (0-8037-0139-X); PLB 9.89 (0-8037-0140-3) Dial Bks Young.
—Buggy Riddles. Taback, Simms, illus. (gr. 2-5). 1989. bk. & cassette 19.95 (0-87499-118-8); bk. & cassette 12.95 (0-87499-119-6); 4 cassettes & guide 27.95 (0-87499-120-X) Live Oak Media.
—Buggy Riddles. Taback, Simms, illus. LC 85-1450. 48p. (ps-3). 1988. pap. 4.95 (0-8037-0554-9) Dial Bks Young.
—Buggy Riddles. Taback, Simms, illus. LC 93-6556. (gr. 1-4). 1993. pap. 3.25 (0-14-036543-5) Puffin Bks.
—Bunny Riddles. Rubel, Nicole, illus. LC 93-13241. (ps-4). 1996. write for info. (0-8037-1519-6); PLB write for info. (0-8037-1521-8) Dial Bks Young.
—Fishy Riddles. LC 82-22135. (Illus.). 48p. (ps-3). 1983. pap. 4.99 (0-8037-2419-5) Dial Bks Young.
—Fishy Riddles. Taback, Simms, illus. (gr. 3-5). 1985. bk. & cassette 19.95 (0-941078-72-8); pap. 12.95 bk. & cassette (0-941078-70-1); cassette, 4 paperbacks & guide 27.95 (0-941078-71-X) Live Oak Media.
—Fishy Riddles. Taback, Simms, illus. LC 93-6551. (gr. 1-4). 1993. pap. 3.25 (0-14-036546-X) Puffin Puffin Bks.
—Grizzly Riddles. Rubel, Nicole, illus. LC 86-29275. 48p. (ps-3). 1992. pap. 3.99 (0-14-036116-2, Dial Easy to Read) Puffin Bks.
—Oddball Baseball. Callen, Liz, illus. LC 89-62206. 96p. (Orig.). (gr. 2-6). 1991. pap. 2.95 (0-679-80336-X) Random Bks Yng Read.
—One Hundred One School Jokes. Orehek, Don, illus. 96p. (gr. 4-7). 1987. pap. 1.95 (0-590-41182-9) Scholastic Inc.
—Sheepish Riddles. Alley, Robert, illus. LC 93-32212. 1995. write for info. (0-8037-1535-8); lib. bdg. write for info. (0-8037-1536-6) Dial Bks Young.
—Snakey Riddles. Taback, Simms, illus. 48p. (ps-3). 1993. pap. 3.99 (0-14-054588-3) Puffin Bks.

—Spacey Riddles. LC 90-42508. (Illus.). 48p. (ps-3). 1992. 11.00 (0-8037-0814-9); PLB 10.89 (0-8037-0815-7) Dial Bks Young.
Hall, Katy, jt. auth. see Eisenberg, Lisa.
Hall, L. The Soul of the Silver Dog. 1992. 16.95 (0-15-277196-4, HB Juv Bks) HarBrace.
Hall, Leo D. B'tween: Messages from Michael. Warnick, Kelly & Hall, Leo D., illus. 180p. (Orig.). (gr. 6-12). 1992. pap. 8.75 (0-914107-03-8) Lion House Pr.
Hall, Leo D. & Daggett, John M. Equal Value: A Prologue. (Illus.). 64p. (Orig.). (gr. 6 up). 1984. pap. 4.95 (0-914107-02-X) Lion House Pr.
Hall, Lindsey & Cohn, Leigh. Dear Kids of Alcoholics. Lingenfelter, Rosemary E., illus. 96p. (gr. 3-10). 1988. pap. 6.95 (0-936077-18-2) Gurze Bks.
Hall, Lynn. Barry: The Bravest Saint Bernard. Castro, Antonio, illus. LC 92-1228. 48p. (Orig.). (gr. 2-4). 1992. PLB 7.99 (0-679-93054-X); pap. 3.50 (0-679-83054-5) Random Bks Yng Read.
—Dagmar Schultz & the Angel Edna. LC 88-36862. 96p. (gr. 5-8). 1989. SBE 12.95 (0-684-19097-4, Scribners Young Read) Macmillan Child Grp.
—Dagmar Schultz & the Angel Edna. LC 91-39608. 96p. (gr. 3-7). 1992. pap. 3.95 (0-689-71615-X, Aladdin) Macmillan Child Grp.
—Dagmar Schultz & the Green-Eyed Monster. LC 90-43524. 80p. (gr. 5-8). 1991. SBE 12.95 (0-684-19254-3, Scribners Young Read) Macmillan Child Grp.
—Dagmar Schultz & the Powers of Darkness. LC 88-30806. 80p. (gr. 5-8). 1989. SBE 12.95 (0-684-19037-0, Scribners Young Read) Macmillan Child Grp.
—Dagmar Schultz & the Powers of Darkness. LC 91-27939. 80p. (gr. 3-7). 1992. pap. 3.95 (0-689-71547-1, Aladdin) Macmillan Child Grp.
—Danger Dog. LC 86-13914. 112p. (gr. 4-7). 1986. SBE 13.95 (0-684-18680-2, Scribners Young Read) Macmillan Child Grp.
—Danza! LC 88-8047. 192p. (gr. 5-7). 1989. pap. 3.95 (0-689-71289-8, Aladdin) Macmillan Child Grp.
—Fair Maiden. LC 90-30629. 128p. (gr. 7 up). 1990. SBE 13.95 (0-684-19213-6, Scribners Young Read) Macmillan Child Grp.
—Flying Changes. D'Andrade, Diane, ed. 148p. (gr. 9 up). 1991. 13.95 (0-15-228790-6) HarBrace.
—Flying Changes. 1992. write for info. HarBrace.
—Flying Changes. LC 90-45516. (gr. 9-12). 1993. pap. 4.95 (0-15-228791-4) HarBrace.
—Halsey's Pride. LC 89-34998. 128p. (gr. 7 up). 1990. SBE 13.95 (0-684-19155-5, Scribners Young Read) Macmillan Child Grp.
—Here Comes Zelda Claus: And Other Holiday Disasters. 149p. (gr. 3-7). 1989. 13.95 (0-15-233790-3) HarBrace.
—If Winter Comes. LC 85-43348. 128p. (gr. 7 up). 1986. SBE 13.95 (0-684-18575-X, Scribners Young Read) Macmillan Child Grp.
—In Trouble Again, Zelda Hammersmith. Cruz, Ray, illus. 138p. (gr. 3-5). 1987. 13.95 (0-15-238780-3) HarBrace.
—In Trouble Again, Zelda Hammersmith? 96p. (gr. 5 up). 1989. pap. 3.25 (0-380-70612-1, Camelot) Avon.
—Just One Friend. LC 88-4293. 128p. (gr. 7 up). 1988. pap. 2.95 (0-02-043311-5, Collier Young Ad) Macmillan Child Grp.
—A Killing Freeze. LC 88-5143. 128p. (gr. 7 up). 1988. 12.95 (0-688-07867-2) Morrow Jr Bks.
—The Leaving. 128p. (gr. 7 up). 1988. pap. 2.95 (0-02-043310-7, Collier Young Ad) Macmillan Child Grp.
—Mrs. Portree's Pony. LC 85-43353. 96p. (gr. 4-7). 1986. SBE 12.95 (0-684-18576-8, Scribners Young Read) Macmillan Child Grp.
—Murder at the Spaniel Show. LC 88-18244. 128p. (gr. 7 up). 1988. SBE 13.95 (0-684-18961-5, Scribners Young Read) Macmillan Child Grp.
—Murder in a Pig's Eye. (gr. 7 up). 1990. 14.95 (0-15-256268-0) HarBrace.
—Murder in a Pig's Eye. (gr. 4-7). 1992. pap. 4.95 (0-15-256269-9) HarBrace.
—The Mystery of Pony Hollow. Sanderson, Ruth, illus. LC 91-29861. 64p. (Orig.). (gr. 2-4). 1992. PLB 6.99 (0-679-93052-3); pap. 2.50 (0-679-83052-9) Random Bks Yng Read.
—The Mystery of the Phantom Pony. Cassels, Jean, illus. 64p. (Orig.). (gr. 2-4). 1993. PLB 6.99 (0-679-94335-8); pap. 2.50 (0-679-84335-3) Random Bks Yng Read.
—Ride a Dark Horse. LC 87-12310. 176p. (gr. 7 up). 1987. 14.95 (0-688-07471-5) Morrow Jr Bks.
—The Secret Life of Dagmar Schultz. LC 87-28499. 96p. (gr. 5-8). 1988. SBE 12.95 (0-684-18915-1, Scribners Young Read) Macmillan Child Grp.
—The Secret Life of Dagmar Schultz. LC 90-24502. 96p. (gr. 3-7). 1991. pap. 3.95 (0-689-71446-7, Aladdin) Macmillan Child Grp.
—The Solitary. 128p. (gr. 7 up). 1989. pap. 2.95 (0-02-043315-8, Collier Young Ad) Macmillan Child Grp.
—The Something-Special Horse. Rabinowitz, Sandy, illus. LC 84-23636. 112p. (gr. 4-7). 1985. SBE 13.95 (0-684-18343-9, Scribners Young Read) Macmillan Child Grp.
—The Tormentors. 319p. (gr. 3-7). 1990. 14.95 (0-15-289470-5) HarBrace.
—Tormentors. LC 90-4805. (gr. 4-7). 1993. pap. 4.95 (0-15-289471-3) HarBrace.

—Where Have All the Tigers Gone? LC 88-28835. 144p. (gr. 7 up). 1989. SBE 13.95 (0-684-19003-6, Scribners Young Read) Macmillan Child Grp.
—Windsong. LC 91-46075. 80p. (gr. 6-8). 1992. SBE 11.95 (0-684-19439-2, Scribners Young Read) Macmillan Child Grp.
—Zelda Strikes Again! 151p. (gr. 3-7). 1988. 13.95 (0-15-299966-3) HarBrace.
Hall, Maggie, jt. auth. see Hall, Andy.
Hall, Mahji. T Is for "Terrific", Mahji's ABC's. Hall, Mahji, illus. LC 88-62371. 32p. (Orig.). (ps-3). 1989. PLB 9.95 (0-940880-21-0); pap. text ed. 4.95 (0-940880-22-9) Open Hand.
Hall, Nancy M. & Snodden, Ruth V. Guided Research Discovery Units: Six Project Books. Incl. Animals! Animals! Animals! 1983. pap. text ed. write for info. 9.95 (0-87628-373-3); It's A Small World! 1983. pap. text ed. 9.95 (0-87628-378-4); Fascinating People (0-87628-376-8); Fun Pac! 1983. pap. text ed. 9.95 (0-87628-377-6); Bookshelf Adventures! 1983. pap. text ed. 9.95 (0-87628-375-X); Blast Off! 1983. pap. text ed. 9.95 (0-87628-374-1). 64p. (gr. 3-9). 1983. pap. 9.95x ea. Ctr Appl Res.
Hall, Patricia, jt. auth. see Hillery, Mable.
Hall, Rachel. Seventeen. 45p. (Orig.). 1989. pap. 5.00 (0-9624855-0-0) R Hall.
Hall, Richard, jt. auth. see Tokuda, Wendy.
Hall, Robin. Three Tales from Japan. (gr. 1-9). 1973. 4.50 (0-87602-209-3) Anchorage.
Hall, Roger. Julie Rescues Big Mack. Antonie, Joy, illus. LC 93-26217. 1994. 4.25 (0-383-03755-7) SRA Schl Grp.
—Putting on a Concert: The Television News. Mancini, Rob, illus. LC 93-24527. (gr. 4 up). 1994. 4.25 (0-383-03770-0) SRA Schl Grp.
—The Tiger & the Millionaire. Newman, Jack, illus. LC 93-38932. 1994. 4.25 (0-383-03786-7) SRA Schl Grp.
Hall, Sara, ed. see Lindsay, Norene.
Hall, Sara, ed. see Ludden, LaVerne.
Hall, Sarabel. Hannah Hummingbird. Lobley, Robert E., illus. LC 88-30357. 16p. (Orig.). (gr. 1-3). 1989. pap. 6.95 (0-86534-131-1) Sunstone Pr.
Hall, Sherry see Davenport, May.
Hall, Steve & Manus, Ron. Scales & Modes for Bass: A Fun & Easy Way to Use Scales & Modes. 33p. (Orig.). 1992. pap. 4.50 (0-88284-546-2, 4434) Alfred Pub.
—Scales & Modes for Guitar: A Fun & Easy Way to Use Scales & Modes. 33p. (Orig.). 1992. pap. 4.50 (0-88284-545-4, 4433) Alfred Pub.
Hall, Steven. Down Came the Sun. Steffan, Leonard, illus. Hall, Mary A. LC 72-176097. (Illus.). 64p. (gr. 3 up). 1972. 8.95 (0-87929-010-2) Barlenmir.
Hall, Susan T. Baby Jesus Is Born: Tickle Giggle Book. (ps). 6.99 (1-55513-772-5) Cook.
—God's Creation. (Illus.). 10p. (ps). 1991. bds. 7.49 (1-55513-482-3, 63230, Chariot Bks) Cook.
—Noah's Ark. Hall, Susan T., illus. 12p. (ps). 1990. pap. text ed. 5.95 (0-927106-03-5) Prod Concept.
—Noah's Ark: Tickle Giggle Book. 6.99 (1-55513-739-3) Cook.
—Perfect Pals. Hall, Susan T., illus. 12p. (ps). 1989. pap. text ed. 5.95 (0-927106-00-0) Prod Concept.
—Perfect Pals God Made for Me. (Illus.). (ps). 1989. 7.49 (1-55513-933-7, Chariot Bks) Cook.
—So Sleepy. Hall, Susan T., illus. 12p. (ps). 1989. pap. text ed. 5.95 (0-927106-01-9) Prod Concept.
—So Sleepy Fuzzy Book. 10p. (ps). 1989. pap. 7.49 (1-55513-280-4, Chariot Bks) Cook.
—Thank You, God, for Peanut Butter & Jelly. (Illus.). 10p. (ps). 1991. bds. 5.99 (1-55513-487-4, 63248, Chariot Bks) Cook.
—Thank You, God, for Watermelon. (Illus.). 10p. (ps). 1991. bds. 5.99 (1-55513-486-6, 63255, Chariot Bks) Cook.
Hall, Tom T. Christmas & the Old House. Seeley, Laura L., illus. 48p. 1989. 13.95 (0-934601-91-7) Peachtree Pubs.
Hall, Tony. Whales. (Illus.). 64p. 1990. 7.99 (0-517-05149-4) Outlet Bk Co.
Hall, Willis. Dragon Days. large type ed. 200p. (gr. 3-7). 1991. 13.95 (0-7451-1294-3, Galaxy Child Lrg Print) Chivers N Amer.
—The Return of the Antelope. large type ed. 256p. (gr. 3-7). 1990. 13.95 (0-7451-1103-3, Galaxy Child Lrg Print) Chivers N Amer.
Hallam, Leslie T. Andy's Headache. 1990. 6.95 (0-533-08821-6) Vantage.
Hallenbeck, Gertrude & Hugo, Adele. Four Children's Dances. 32p. (gr. k-6). 1957. pap. 10.00 (0-932582-63-X) Dance Notation.
Hallenstein, Kathy. I Can Be a TV Camera Operator. LC 84-7665. (Illus.). 32p. (gr. k-3). 1984. PLB 14.60 (0-516-01842-6); pap. 3.95 (0-516-41842-4) Childrens.
Haller, Lynda. Cheerleader U. S. A. - Tryouts to Triumph. 68p. (gr. 1-12). 1989. 10.00 spiral bdg. (0-317-93086-9) Cheertime USA.
—More Cheers & Chants. rev. ed. Whitman, Rick, photos by. (Illus.). 39p. (Orig.). (gr. 3-12). 1988. pap. text ed. 8.00 (0-685-22930-0); cassette 6.00 (0-9614174-5-5) Cheertime USA.
—Pom Pon U. S. A. rev. ed. 98p. (gr. 6-12). 1988. spiral bdg. 10.00 (0-317-93087-7) Cheertime USA.
Haller, Margaret A. Essential Vocabulary for College-Bound Students. 2nd ed. 224p. (gr. 11-12). 1987. pap. 7.95 wkbk. (0-13-289356-8) P-H.

Hallett, Bill & Hallett, Jane. Look up Look down Look All Around Bandelier National Monument. (Illus.). 32p. (Orig.). (gr. 3-8). 1990. pap. 3.95 activity bk. (1-877827-02-9) Look & See.

—Look up Look Down Look All Around Canyon de Chelly National Monument. Yazzie, William P., illus. 32p. (gr. 3-8). 1990. activity bk. 3.95 (1-877827-05-3) Look & See.

—Look up Look Down Look All Around Chaco Culture National Historical Park. Jackson, Lori, illus. 32p. (Orig.). (gr. 3-8). 1989. pap. 3.45 activity bk. (0-685-26277-4) Look & See.

—Look up Look down Look All Around East African Safari. Jackson, Lori, illus. 32p. (Orig.). (gr. 3-8). 1990. pap. 2.95 activity bk. (1-877827-01-0) Look & See.

—Look up Look Down Look All Around El Morro National Monument. Chaffee, Dan, illus. 32p. (Orig.). (gr. 3-8). 1988. pap. 3.45 activity bk. (0-943087-04-X) Look & See.

—Look up Look Down Look All Around Hubbell Trading Post. Yazzie, William P., illus. 16p. (Orig.). (gr. 3-8). 1990. write for info. activity bk. (1-877827-06-1) Look & See.

—Look up, Look down, Look All Around Mesa Verde National Park. Yazzie, William P., illus. 32p. (Orig.). (gr. 3-8). 1990. pap. 3.95 activity bk. (1-877827-04-5) Look & See.

—Look up, Look down, Look All Around Red River, New Mexico. (Illus.). 16p. (Orig.). (gr. 3-8). 1990. pap. 2.50 activity bk. (1-877827-03-7) Look & See.

—National Park Service: Activities & Adventures for Kids. Paltrow, Robert, illus. 32p. (Orig.). (gr. 3-8). 1991. activity bk. (1-877827-07-X) Look & See.

—Pueblo Indians of New Mexico: Activities & Adventures for Kids. Castiano, Robert, illus. (Orig.). (gr. 3-8). 1991. activity bk. 3.95 (1-877827-08-8) Look & See.

Hallett, Jane, jt. auth. see Hallett, Bill.

Halliburton, Warren J. African Industries. LC 92-27325. (Illus.). 48p. (gr. 6). 1993. RSBE 13.95 (0-89686-672-6, Crestwood Hse) Macmillan Child Grp.

—African Landscapes. (Illus.). 48p. (gr. 6). 1993. RSBE 13.95 (0-89686-673-4, Crestwood Hse) Macmillan Child Grp.

—African Wildlife. LC 91-43514. (Illus.). 48p. (gr. 6). 1992. RSBE 13.95 (0-89686-674-2, Crestwood Hse) Macmillan Child Grp.

—Africa's Struggle for Independence. LC 92-3755. (Illus.). 48p. (gr. 6). 1992. RSBE 13.95 (0-89686-679-3, Crestwood Hse) Macmillan Child Grp.

—Africa's Struggle to Survive. LC 92-7501. (Illus.). 48p. (gr. 6). 1993. RSBE 13.95 (0-89686-675-0, Crestwood Hse) Macmillan Child Grp.

—Celebrations of African Heritage. LC 92-7989. (Illus.). 48p. (gr. 6). 1992. RSBE 13.95 (0-89686-676-9, Crestwood Hse) Macmillan Child Grp.

—City & Village Life. (Illus.). 48p. (gr. 6). 1993. RSBE 13.95 (0-89686-677-7, Crestwood Hse) Macmillan Child Grp.

—Clarence Thomas: Supreme Court Justice. LC 92-30951. (Illus.). 104p. (gr. 6 up). 1993. lib. bdg. 17.95 (0-89490-414-0) Enslow Pubs.

—Historic Speeches of African Americans. LC 92-39318. (Illus.). 192p. (gr. 9-12). 1993. PLB 13.90 (0-531-11034-6) Watts.

—Historic Speeches of African Americans. (Illus.). (gr. 7-12). 1993. pap. 6.95 (0-531-15677-X) Watts.

—Nomads of the Sahara. (Illus.). 48p. (gr. 6). 1992. RSBE 13.95 (0-89686-678-5, Crestwood Hse) Macmillan Child Grp.

—The West Indian-American Experience. LC 93-19233. (Illus.). 64p. (gr. 4-6). 1994. lib. bdg. 14.90 (1-56294-340-5) Millbrook Pr.

Halliday, Ian. Saturn. 48p. 1989. 13.95 (0-8160-2049-3) Facts on File.

Hallinan, P. K. Easy Does It. Hallinan, P. K., illus. 32p. 1992. pap. 5.00 (0-89486-673-7) Hazelden.

—For the Love of Our Earth. Hallinan, P. K., illus. 24p. (gr. k-3). 1992. PLB 10.95 (1-878363-73-5) Forest Hse.

—For the Love of Our Earth. (Illus.). 24p. (ps-2). 1992. pap. 3.95 (0-8249-8539-7, Ideals Child) Hambleton-Hill.

—How Do I Love You? (Illus.). 24p. (ps-k). 1990. pap. 3.95 perfect bdg. (0-8249-8505-2, Ideals Child) Hambleton-Hill.

—How Do I Love You. Hallinan, P. K., illus. 24p. (ps-4). 1991. PLB 10.95 (1-878363-27-1) Forest Hse.

—I Know I Belong. Hallinan, P. K., illus. 28p. 1991. pap. 5.00 (0-89486-782-2) Hazelden.

—I Know There's a Power. Hallinan, P. K., illus. 28p. 1991. pap. 5.00 (0-89486-780-6) Hazelden.

—I Know Who I Am. Hallinan, P. K., illus. 28p. 1991. pap. 5.00 (0-89486-781-4) Hazelden.

—I'm Thankful Each Day! Hallinan, P. K., illus. 24p. (gr. k-2). 1989. pap. 3.95 perfect bdg. (0-8249-8535-4, Ideals Child) Hambleton-Hill.

—Just Open a Book. Hallinan, P. K., illus. LC 80-22099. 32p. (ps-3). 1981. pap. 3.95 (0-516-43521-3) Childrens.

—Live & Let Live. Hallinan, P. K., illus. 32p. 1990. pap. 5.00 (0-89486-650-8) Hazelden.

—My First Day of School. Hallinan, P. K., illus. 24p. (gr. k-6). 1987. perfect bdg. 3.95 (0-8249-8533-8, Ideals Child) Hambleton-Hill.

—My Teacher's My Friend. (Illus.). 24p. (ps-3). 1989. pap. 3.95 perfect bdg. (0-8249-8542-7, Ideals Child) Hambleton-Hill.

—My Very Best Rainy Day. (Illus.). 24p. (Orig.). (ps-3). 1991. pap. 3.95 (0-8249-8497-8, Ideals Child) Hambleton-Hill.

—My Very Best Rainy Day. Hallinan, P. K., illus. 24p. (ps-4). 1991. PLB 10.95 (1-878363-28-X) Forest Hse.

—One Day At a Time. Hallinan, P. K., illus. 28p. 1990. pap. 5.00 (0-89486-640-0) Hazelden.

—That's What a Friend Is. Hallinan, P. K., illus. LC 76-27744. 32p. (gr. k-3). 1977. pap. 3.95 (0-516-43628-7) Childrens.

—That's What a Friend Is. Hallinan, P. K., illus. 32p. (gr. k-2). 1985. pap. 3.95 (0-8249-8006-9, Ideals Child) Hambleton-Hill.

—Today Is Christmas. Hallinan, P. K., illus. 24p. (ps-3). 1993. PLB 10.95 (1-878363-93-X) Forest Hse.

—Today Is Christmas! Hallinan, P. K., illus. 24p. (ps-2). 1993. pap. 3.95 (0-8249-8643-1, Ideals Child) Hambleton-Hill.

—Today Is Easter! Hallinan, P. K., illus. 24p. (Orig.). (ps-2). 1993. pap. 3.95 (0-8249-8604-0, Ideals Child) Hambleton-Hill.

—Today Is Easter. Hallinan, P. K., illus. 24p. (ps-3). 1993. PLB 10.95 (1-878363-94-8) Forest Hse.

—Today Is Halloween! Hallinan, P. K., illus. 24p. (ps-2). 1992. pap. text ed. 3.95 (0-8249-8557-5, Ideals Child) Hambleton-Hill.

—Today Is Halloween. Hallinan, P. K., illus. 24p. (ps-3). 1992. PLB 10.95 (1-878363-95-6) Forest Hse.

—Today Is Thanksgiving. Hallinan, P. K., illus. 24p. (ps-3). 1993. PLB 10.95 (1-878363-96-4) Forest Hse.

—Today Is Thanksgiving. Hallinan, P. K., illus. 24p. (ps-2). 1993. pap. 3.95 (0-8249-8637-7, Ideals Child) Hambleton-Hill.

—Today is Your Birthday. (Illus.). 24p. (Orig.). (ps-3). 1991. pap. 3.95 (0-8249-8493-5, Ideals Child) Hambleton-Hill.

—We're Very Good Friends, My Brother & I. Hallinan, P. K., illus. 24p. (ps-2). 1990. 3.95 (0-8249-8469-2, Ideals Child) Hambleton-Hill.

—We're Very Good Friends, My Father & I. Hallinan, P. K., illus. (ps-2). 1990. pap. 3.95 perfect bdg. (0-8249-8520-6, Ideals Child) Hambleton-Hill.

—We're Very Good Friends, My Mother & I. Hallinan, P. K., illus. 24p. (ps-2). 1990. pap. 3.95 perfect bdg. (0-8249-8519-2, Ideals Child) Hambleton-Hill.

—We're Very Good Friends, My Sister & I. Hallinan, P. K., illus. 24p. (ps-2). 1990. 3.95 (0-8249-8470-6, Ideals Child) Hambleton-Hill.

Hallinan, P. K., illus. Today Is Your Birthday. 24p. (ps-4). 1991. PLB 10.95 (1-878363-29-8) Forest Hse.

Hallinan, Patrick. The Small Town Children's Easter. Hallinan, Patrick, illus. 24p. (ps-3). 1989. pap. 2.95 (0-8249-8319-X, Ideals Child) Hambleton-Hill.

—We're Very Good Friends, My Grandma & I. Hallinan, Patrick, illus. 24p. (ps-2). 1989. pap. 3.95 perfect bdg. (0-8249-8548-6, Ideals Child) Hambleton-Hill.

—We're Very Good Friends, My Grandpa & I. Hallinan, Patrick, illus. 24p. (ps-2). 1989. pap. 3.95 perfect bdg. (0-8249-8549-4, Ideals Child) Hambleton-Hill.

Halloran, Phyllis. Cat Purrs. McKissack, Patricia & McKissack, Fredrick, eds. Ching, illus. LC 87-61648. 32p. (Orig.). (gr. 1-3). 1987. text ed. 8.95 (0-88335-723-2); pap. text ed. 4.95 (0-88335-743-7) Milliken Pub Co.

—I'd Like to Hear a Flower Grow. Reynolds, Carol, illus. LC 89-60979. 56p. (gr. k-8). 1989. 12.95 (0-943867-02-9) Reading Inc.

—Oh, Brother! Oh, Sister! McKissack, Patricia & McKissack, Fredrick, eds. Shoemaker, Katheryn, illus. LC 88-60392. 32p. (Orig.). (gr. 1-3). 1988. text ed. 8.95 (0-88335-788-7); pap. text ed. 4.95 (0-88335-767-4) Milliken Pub Co.

—Red Is My Favorite Color. Reynolds, Carol, illus. LC 88-60132. 32p. (gr. k up). 1988. 12.95 (0-943867-01-0) Reading Inc.

Hallowell, Tommy. Duel on the Diamond. 128p. (gr. 3 up). 1990. pap. 3.50 (0-14-032910-2, Puffin) Puffin Bks.

—Duel on the Diamond. 1991. pap. 12.95 (0-670-83729-6) Viking Child Bks.

—Jester in the Backcourt. 128p. (gr. 3 up). 1990. pap. 2.95 (0-14-032911-0, Puffin) Puffin Bks.

—Jester in the Backcourt. (gr. 4-7). 1991. 12.95 (0-670-83732-6) Viking Child Bks.

—Last Chance Quarterback. 112p. (gr. 3 up). 1990. pap. 3.50 (0-14-032909-9, Puffin) Puffin Bks.

—Last Chance Quarterback. (gr. 4-7). 1991. 12.95 (0-670-83731-8) Viking Child Bks.

—Shot from Midfield. 112p. (gr. 3 up). 1990. pap. 3.50 (0-14-032912-9, Puffin) Puffin Bks.

—Shot from Midfield. (gr. 4-7). 1991. 12.95 (0-670-83730-X) Viking Child Bks.

—Varsity Coach. 128p. (Orig.). 1986. pap. 2.50 (0-553-26033-2, Starfire) Bantam.

Halman, Talat. The Turkish Americans. Moynihan, Daniel P., intro. by. (Illus.). 112p. (gr. 5 up). 1990. lib. bdg. 17.95 (1-55546-137-9) Chelsea Hse.

Halper, Roe. Passover Haggadah. Halper, Roe, illus. 40p. (Orig.). 1986. pap. 5.00 (0-916326-03-9) Bayberry Pr.

Halperin, Michael, jt. auth. see Drucker, Malka.

Halperin, Susan, ed. see Hawkins, Colin & Hawkins, Jacqui.

Halpern, C. The Homontash That Ran Away. Halpern, C., illus. (ps-4). 2.95 (0-87306-995-1) Feldheim.

Halpern, Chaiky. The Dink That Stopped the Clock. 24p. (Orig.). (ps-3). 1985. pap. 2.95 (0-87306-379-1) Feldheim.

Halpern, Gina. Where Is Tibet? Jorden, Ngawang, tr. Halpern, Gina, illus. 62p. (gr. k-4). 1991. pap. 12.95 (0-937938-93-9) Snow Lion.

Halpern, Robert R. Green Planet Rescue: Saving the Earth's Endangered Plants. LC 93-10583. (Illus.). 56p. (gr. 5-7). 1993. 15.90 (0-531-15261-8); PLB 15.90 (0-531-11095-8) Watts.

Halpern, Shari. Moving from One to Ten. Halpern, Shari, illus. LC 92-26992. 32p. (ps-1). 1993. RSBE 13.95 (0-02-741981-9, Macmillan Child Bk) Macmillan Child Grp.

—My River. Halpern, Shari, illus. LC 91-33582. 32p. (gr. k-2). 1992. RSBE 13.95 (0-02-741980-0, Macmillan Child Bk) Macmillan Child Grp.

Halpern, Solomon A. Prisoner & Other Tales of Faith: Twenty-Six Heart Warming Stories. (gr. 3-7). 1980. pap. 6.95 (0-87306-243-4) Feldheim.

Halpern-Gold, Julia & Adler, Robin W. Travel Tales: A Mobility Storybook. Binns, Brenda S., illus. LC 88-62588. 107p. (Orig.). (ps-3). 1988. pap. text ed. 20.00 (0-922637-00-8) Most Mobil.

Halpern-Segal, Janice, jt. auth. see Nelson, Jackie.

Halpin, Marlene. At Home with God, Vol. I: A Child's Book of Prayer. 30p. 1992. 3.95 (22000) Tabor Pub.

Halsey, Megan. Jump for Joy: A Book of Months. LC 92-39082. (Illus.). 32p. (ps-1). 1994. SBE 13.95 (0-02-742040-X, Bradbury Pr) Macmillan Child Grp.

—Three Pandas Planting: Counting down to Help the Earth. Halsey, Megan, illus. LC 93-22971. 40p. (ps-2). 1994. RSBE 14.95 (0-02-742035-3, Bradbury Pr) Macmillan Child Grp.

Halstead, Bruce W. & Landa, Bonnie L. Tropical Fish. Sandstrom, George F., illus. 160p. (gr. 7 up). 1975. pap. write for info. (0-307-24361-3, Golden Pr) Western Pub.

Halsted, Henry F. Boating Basics. Seiden, Art, illus. LC 85-9406. 48p. (gr. 4-9). 1985. 10.95 (0-13-078502-4) P-H.

Halton, Cheryl M. Those Amazing Bats. LC 90-3959. (Illus.). 96p. (gr. 4 up). 1991. RSBE 13.95 (0-87518-458-8, Dillon) Macmillan Child Grp.

—Those Amazing Eels. LC 89-25613. (Illus.). 96p. (gr. 4 up). 1990. RSBE 13.95 (0-87518-431-6, Dillon) Macmillan Child Grp.

—Those Amazing Leeches. LC 88-35908. (Illus.). 112p. (gr. 4 up). 1990. RSBE 13.95 (0-87518-408-1, Dillon) Macmillan Child Grp.

Halverson, Delia T. Oak Street Chronicles & the Good News: Everyday Life & Christian Faith. Dotts, M. Franklin, ed. (Illus., Orig.). 1989. pap. 4.75 tchr's. ed. 48p. (0-687-75340-6); student ed., 40p. 3.35 (0-687-75339-2) Abingdon.

Halverson, Lydia, illus. The Animals' Ballgame. LC 92-9416. 24p. (ps-2). 1991. PLB 16.93 (0-685-62659-8); pap. 5.95 (0-516-45139-1) Childrens.

Halverson, Marilyn. Dare. 1992. pap. 3.25 (0-590-43545-0) Scholastic Inc.

Halverson, Patricia A. I Heard the Owl Call My Name - Study Guide. Friedland, Joyce & Kessler, Rikki, eds. (gr. 6-10). Date not set. pap. text ed. 14.95 (0-88122-100-7) Lrn Links.

Halverson, Sandy. Book of Mormon Activity Book: Creative Scripture Learning Experiences for Children 4-12. Halverson, Sandy, illus. 80p. (gr. 3-8). 1982. pap. 5.95 (0-88290-188-5, 4521) Horizon Utah.

—Church History Activity Book: Creative Scripture Learning Experiences about the Restoration for Children 4-12. 36p. (Orig.). (gr. 3-6). 1983. pap. 5.95 (0-88290-213-X) Horizon Utah.

—Preparing for Baptism. 28p. (gr. 1-3). 1983. pap. 5.95 (0-88290-233-4) Horizon-Utah.

Halvorson, Marilyn. Cowboys Don't Cry. (gr. 6 up). 1986. pap. 3.50 (0-440-91303-9, LFL) Dell.

—Hold on, Geronimo. LC 87-25656. 240p. (gr. 7 up). 1988. pap. 14.95 (0-385-29665-7) Delacorte.

—Let It Go. (gr. 5 up). 1988. pap. 2.95 (0-440-20053-9, LFL) Dell.

Ham, Wayne. Paul's First Missionary Journey. (Illus.). 24p. 1989. pap. 4.00 (0-8309-0538-3) Herald Hse.

Hamada, Cheryl, retold by. The Farmer, the Buffalo, & the Tiger: A Folktale from Vietnam. Regan, Rick, illus. LC 93-21725. 32p. (ps-3). 1993. PLB write for info. (0-516-05143-1) Childrens.

—The Fourth Question: A Chinese Folktale. Skivington, Janice, illus. LC 93-18237. 32p. (ps-3). 1993. PLB write for info. (0-516-05144-X) Childrens.

—Kao & the Golden Fish: A Folktale from Thailand. Liu, Monica, illus. LC 93-298. 32p. (ps-3). 1993. PLB write for info. (0-516-05145-8) Childrens.

—The White Hare of Inaba: A Japanese Folktale. Halverson, Lydia, illus. LC 93-6772. 32p. (ps-3). 1993. PLB write for info. (0-516-05147-4) Childrens.

Hamanaka, Sheila. All the Colors of Earth. LC 93-27118. 1994. write for info. (0-688-11131-9); PLB write for info. (0-688-11132-7) Morrow Jr Bks.

—The Journey: Japanese Americans, Racism, & Renewal. LC 89-22877. (Illus.). 40p. (gr. 5 up). 1990. 18.95 (0-531-05849-2); PLB 18.99 (0-531-08449-3) Orchard Bks Watts.

Hamanaka, Sheila, retold by. & illus. Screen of Frogs: An Old Tale. LC 92-24172. 32p. (ps-2). 1993. 15.95 (0-531-05464-0); PLB 15.99 (0-531-08614-3) Orchard Bks Watts.

Hamblen, Priscilla C. The Magic Garden. 1993. 7.95 (0-8062-4596-4) Carlton.

Hambly, Wilfrid D. Talking Animals. Porter, James A., illus. 1990. 7.95 (*0-87498-025-9*) Assoc Pubs DC.

Hamel, Jean-Marie. Heart Tales: A Collection of Stories from a Child's Heart. Hamel, Jean-Marie, illus. 40p. (ps-3). 1990. 12.95g (*0-929684-50-8*) Silver Forest Pub.

Hamel, Joan de see De Hamel, Joan.

Hamer, Sylvia. C. B. & the Pink Pointe Shoes. Hamer, Sylvia, illus. LC 87-70557. 32p. (gr. 3-4). 1987. pap. 9.95 (*0-942479-00-9*) Anderson Pr.

Hamersky, Jean. Vocabulary Maps: Strategies for Developing Word Meanings. LC 92-37290. (gr. 5-12). 1993. 29.00 (*0-930599-81-0*) Thinking Pubns.

Hamerstrom, Frances. Adventure of the Stone Man. (gr. 4-7). 1990. pap. 10.95 (*1-55821-084-9*) Lyons & Burford.

—Walk When the Moon Is Full. Katona, Robert, illus. LC 75-33878. 64p. (gr. 3-8). 1975. 15.95 (*0-912278-69-2*); pap. 6.95 (*0-912278-84-6*) Crossing Pr.

Hames, Karen, ed. see Fifth Period LEAP & Honors English Classes.

Hamid, J. Islamic Activity Book, Nos. I, II & III. 1988. pap. 3.50 ea. (*0-317-43011-4*) No. I (*0-933511-13-2*) No. II (*0-934905-08-8*) No. III (*0-933511-02-7*) Kazi Pubns.

Hamilton, Alan. Prince Philip. (Illus.). 64p. (gr. 5-9). 1991. 11.95 (*0-237-60012-9*, Pub. by Evans Bros Ltd) Trafalgar.

Hamilton, Alfred T., jt. auth. see Hamilton, Jacklyn.

Hamilton, Arthur. Sing a Rainbow Big Book. Izaguirre, Oscar, illus. (ps-2). 1988. pap. text ed. 14.00 (*0-922053-21-9*) N Edge Res.

Hamilton, Carol. The Dawn Seekers. Levine, Abby, ed. LC 86-15820. (Illus.). 144p. (gr. 3-7). 1987. PLB 11.95 (*0-8075-1480-2*) A Whitman.

Hamilton, Dorothy. Amanda Fair. Converse, James, illus. LC 80-25073. 136p. (gr. 5-10). 1981. pap. 3.95 (*0-8361-1943-6*) Herald Pr.

—Anita's Choice. Moon, Ivan, illus. LC 70-131535. 96p. (gr. 4-9). 1971. pap. 3.95 (*0-8361-1741-7*) Herald Pr.

—Bittersweet Days. Graber, Esther R., illus. LC 77-18867. 120p. (gr. 4-8). 1978. pap. 3.95 (*0-8361-1846-4*) Herald Pr.

—The Blue Caboose. Needler, Jerry, illus. LC 72-5474. 135p. (gr. 3-6). 1973. pap. 3.95 (*0-8361-1696-8*) Herald Pr.

—Busboys at Big Bend. Ponter, James, illus. LC 74-8689. 112p. (gr. 8-12). 1974. o. p. 4.95 (*0-8361-1744-1*); pap. 3.95 (*0-8361-1745-X*) Herald Pr.

—Carlie's Pink Room. Graber, Esther Rose, illus. LC 83-26437. 88p. (gr. 7-9). 1984. pap. 3.95 (*0-8361-3354-4*) Herald Pr.

—The Castle. Graber, Esther R., illus. LC 75-15599. 112p. (gr. 4-8). 1975. pap. 3.95 (*0-8361-1776-X*) Herald Pr.

—Christmas for Holly. Graber, Esther R., illus. LC 72-141831. 112p. (gr. 4-9). 1971. pap. 3.95 (*0-8361-1658-5*) Herald Pr.

—Cricket. Van Demark, Paul, illus. LC 74-30421. 80p. (gr. 3-7). 1975. pap. 3.95 (*0-8361-1761-1*) Herald Pr.

—Daniel Forbes: A Pioneer Boy. King, Barbara L., illus. (Orig.). (gr. ps-4). 1980. pap. 3.95 (*0-686-32860-4*) Barnwood Pr.

—Eric's Discovery. Wind, Betty, illus. LC 79-18537. 120p. (gr. 4-9). 1979. pap. 3.95 (*0-8361-1903-7*) Herald Pr.

—The Gift of a Home. LC 73-13989. 120p. (gr. 9-11). 1974. pap. 3.95 (*0-8361-1727-1*) Herald Pr.

—Gina In-Between. Converse, James, illus. LC 81-13387. 128p. (Orig.). (gr. 5 up). 1982. pap. 3.95 (*0-8361-1986-X*) Herald Pr.

—Holly's New Year. Graber, Esther R., illus. LC 81-4098. 112p. (gr. 3-9). 1981. pap. 3.95 (*0-8361-1961-4*) Herald Pr.

—Jason. LC 73-14813. 120p. (gr. 10-12). 1974. pap. 3.95 (*0-8361-1728-X*) Herald Pr.

—Joel's Other Mother. Graber, Esther R., illus. 120p. (gr. 3-7). 1984. pap. 3.95 (*0-8361-3355-2*) Herald Pr.

—Ken's Bright Room. Converse, James L., photos by. LC 82-23351. (Illus.). 88p. (Orig.). (gr. 7-10). 1982. pap. 3.95 (*0-8361-3328-5*) Herald Pr.

—Last One Chosen. Converse, James, illus. LC 82-3150. 112p. (Orig.). (gr. 5-10). 1982. pap. 3.95 (*0-8361-3306-4*) Herald Pr.

—Mari's Mountain. Graber, Esther R., illus. LC 78-10620. 120p. (gr. 7-10). 1978. pap. 3.95 (*0-8361-1869-3*) Herald Pr.

—Rosalie. Unada, illus. LC 76-39961. 128p. (gr. 3-10). 1977. pap. text ed. 3.95 (*0-8361-1807-3*) Herald Pr.

—Winter Caboose. Converse, James, illus. LC 83-10816. 104p. (Orig.). (gr. 4-8). 1983. pap. 3.95 (*0-8361-3341-2*) Herald Pr.

Hamilton, Edith. Mythology. Savage, Steele, illus. (gr. 7 up). 1942. 21.95 (*0-316-34114-2*) Little.

—Mythology. (RL 7). 1953. pap. 5.95 (*0-451-62803-9*, Ment) NAL-Dutton.

Hamilton, Elizabeth L. Remember Pearl Harbor. Kaser, Robert, illus. 29p. (gr. 3). 1981. pap. 2.95 (*0-685-63557-0*) AZ Mem Mus.

Hamilton, Gail. Aunt Hetty's Ordeal. (gr. 4-7). 1993. pap. 3.99 (*0-553-48039-1*) Bantam.

—Family Rivalry. (gr. 4-6). 1993. pap. 3.99 (*0-553-48042-1*) Bantam.

—Felicity's Challenge. (gr. 4-7). 1992. pap. 3.99 (*0-553-48035-9*) Bantam.

—May the Best Man Win. (gr. 4-6). 1993. pap. 3.99 (*0-553-48043-X*) Bantam.

—Nothing Endures But Change. (gr. 4-7). 1993. pap. 3.99 (*0-553-48037-5*) Bantam.

—The Story Girl Earns Her Name, No. 2. (gr. 3-7). 1992. pap. 3.99 (*0-553-48028-6*, Skylark) Bantam.

Hamilton, Harley. Grandfather Moose: Children's Sign Language Book with Rhymes, Games & Chants. 32p. 1989. pap. 8.50 (*0-916708-21-7*) Modern Signs.

Hamilton, Harley & Jones, Nancy K. Sport Signs. Incl. Signs & Printed Words, General Vocabulary. 64p. pap. 6.00 (*0-317-42767-9*); Football. 48p. pap. 5.00 (*0-317-42768-7*); Basketball. 48p. pap. 5.00 (*0-317-42769-5*); Baseball-Softball. 48p. pap. 5.00 (*0-317-42770-9*); Track & Field. 40p. pap. 4.00 (*0-317-42771-7*); Volley Ball. 28p. pap. 3.00 (*0-317-42772-5*). 1985. pap. 17.00 set (*0-317-42766-0*) Modern Signs.

Hamilton, Jacklyn & Hamilton, Alfred T. ABC's of Football. Tank-Richard, James, illus. 320p. (Orig.). 1992. pap. 12.00 (*0-9635876-0-9*) J&A Bks.

Hamilton, Jamar W. Julie's Angel. (gr. 4-7). 1990. pap. 5.95 (*0-925928-06-2*) Tiny Thought.

Hamilton, Jean. Tropical Rainforests. rev. ed. Leon, Vicki, ed. LC 93-12987. (Illus.). 48p. (Orig.). (gr. 5 up). 1993. perfect bdg. 9.95 (*0-918303-35-4*) Blake Pub.

Hamilton, John. ECO-Careers: A Guide to Jobs in the Environental Field. LC 93-7601. 1993. 14.96 (*1-56239-209-3*) Abdo & Dghtrs.

—Eco-Disasters. LC 93-10259. 1993. 14.96 (*1-56239-200-X*) Abdo & Dghtrs.

—ECO-Groups: Joining Together to Protect the Environment. LC 93-7596. 1993. 14.96 (*1-56239-210-7*) Abdo & Dghtrs.

—The Secretary of the Treasury. LC 93-11214. 1993. 13.99 (*1-56239-254-9*) Abdo & Dghtrs.

Hamilton, John, ed. see Hamilton, Sue.

Hamilton, John, ed. see Hamilton, Sue L.

Hamilton, John C., ed. see Hamilton, Sue L.

Hamilton, Kersten. Natalie Jean & Tag-along Tessa. 1991. 2.99 (*0-8423-4621-X*) Tyndale.

—Natalie Jean & the Flying Machine. 1991. 2.99 (*0-8423-4620-1*) Tyndale.

—Natalie Jean & the Haints' Parade. 1991. 2.99 (*0-8423-4622-8*) Tyndale.

—Natalie Jean Goes Hog Wild. 1991. 2.99 (*0-8423-4623-6*) Tyndale.

Hamilton, Leni. Clara Barton. Horner, Matina, intro. by. (Illus.). 112p. (gr. 5 up). 1988. lib. bdg. 17.95 (*1-55546-641-9*) Chelsea Hse.

Hamilton, Leslie. Child's Play Six-Twelve: One Hundred Sixty Instant Activities, Crafts & Science Projects. 1992. 10.00 (*0-517-58354-2*, Crown) Crown Pub Group.

Hamilton, Mary M. Christmas Magic: A Modern Christmas Fable. Miles, Leona & Kelly, Robert T., eds. Babcock, Patricia, illus. 208p. 1989. lib. bdg. 15.95 (*0-317-93677-8*) Havet Pr.

Hamilton, Morse. Effie's House. LC 89-11918. 224p. (gr. 7 up). 1990. 13.95 (*0-688-09307-8*) Greenwillow.

—Little Sister for Sale. Fiammenghi, Gioia, illus. LC 91-8139. 32p. (ps-3). 1992. 13.00 (*0-525-65078-4*, Cobblehill Bks) Dutton Child Bks.

—Yellow Blue Bus Means I Love You. (gr. 6 up). 1994. write for info. (*0-688-12800-9*) Greenwillow.

Hamilton, Morse, retold by see Pogorelsky, Antony.

Hamilton, N., jt. auth. see Stewart, J.

Hamilton, Ron. Alan & the Baron. Deal, Peggy B., illus. 50p. (Orig.). (gr. 3-7). 1983. pap. 2.95x (*0-913072-54-0*) Natl Assn Deaf.

Hamilton, Sally. Spin Your Wheels. 48p. (gr. 4-6). 1982. 5.95 (*0-88160-051-2*, LW 237) Learning Wks.

Hamilton, Sue. Arnold Schwarzenegger. LC 92-16035. 1992. 12.94 (*1-56239-144-5*) Abdo & Dghtrs.

—The Assassination of a President: John F. Kennedy. Hamilton, John, ed. LC 89-84903. (Illus.). 32p. (gr. 4). 1990. PLB 11.96 (*0-939179-55-5*) Abdo & Dghtrs.

—The Assassination of Abraham Lincoln. Hamilton, John, ed. LC 89-84902. (Illus.). 32p. (gr. 4). 1990. PLB 11.96 (*0-939179-54-7*) Abdo & Dghtrs.

—The Death of a Cult Family: Jim Jones. Hamilton, John, ed. LC 89-84906. (Illus.). 32p. (gr. 4). 1989. PLB 11.96 (*0-939179-58-X*) Abdo & Dghtrs.

—Exxon Valdez Oil Spill. Hamilton, John, ed. LC 90-82628. (Illus.). 32p. (gr. 4). 1990. PLB 11.96 (*0-939179-84-9*) Abdo & Dghtrs.

—Hurricane Hugo. Hamilton, John, ed. LC 90-82627. (Illus.). 32p. (gr. 4). 1990. PLB 11.96 (*0-939179-85-7*) Abdo & Dghtrs.

—The Killing of a Candidate: Robert F. Kennedy. Hamilton, John, ed. LC 89-84905. (Illus.). 32p. (gr. 4). 1989. PLB 11.96 (*0-939179-57-1*) Abdo & Dghtrs.

—The Killing of a Leader: Dr. Martin Luther King. Hamilton, John, ed. LC 89-84904. (Illus.). 32p. (gr. 4). 1989. PLB 11.96 (*0-939179-56-3*) Abdo & Dghtrs.

—The Killing of a Rock Star: John Lennon. Hamilton, John, ed. LC 89-84907. (Illus.). 32p. (gr. 4). 1989. PLB 11.96 (*0-939179-59-8*) Abdo & Dghtrs.

—Mount St. Helen's Eruption. Hamilton, John, ed. LC 88-71721. (Illus.). 32p. (gr. 4). 1989. PLB 11.96 (*0-939179-41-5*) Abdo & Dghtrs.

—Public Enemy No. One: Baby Face Nelson. Hamilton, John, ed. LC 89-84922. (Illus.). 32p. (gr. 4). 1989. PLB 11.96 (*0-939179-61-X*) Abdo & Dghtrs.

—Public Enemy No. One: Bonnie & Clyde. Hamilton, John, ed. LC 89-84921. (Illus.). 32p. (gr. 4). 1989. PLB 11.96 (*0-939179-62-8*) Abdo & Dghtrs.

—Public Enemy No. One: John H. Dillinger. Hamilton, John, ed. LC 89-84920. (Illus.). 32p. (gr. 4). 1989. PLB 11.96 (*0-939179-60-1*) Abdo & Dghtrs.

—Public Enemy No. One: Ma Barker. Hamilton, John, ed. LC 89-84925. (Illus.). 32p. (gr. 4). 1989. PLB 11.96 (*0-939179-65-2*) Abdo & Dghtrs.

—Public Enemy No. One: Machine Gun Kelly. Hamilton, John, ed. LC 89-84924. (Illus.). 32p. (gr. 4). 1989. PLB 11.96 (*0-939179-64-4*) Abdo & Dghtrs.

—Public Enemy No. One: Pretty Boy Floyd. Hamilton, John, ed. LC 89-84923. (Illus.). 32p. (gr. 4). 1989. PLB 11.96 (*0-939179-63-6*) Abdo & Dghtrs.

—R. M. S. Titanic's Sinking. Hamilton, John, ed. LC 88-71722. (Illus.). 32p. (gr. 4). 1989. PLB 11.96 (*0-939179-42-3*) Abdo & Dghtrs.

—San Francisco Earthquake. Hamilton, John, ed. LC 88-71723. (Illus.). 32p. (gr. 4). 1989. PLB 11.96 (*0-939179-43-1*) Abdo & Dghtrs.

—Space Shuttle Challenger's Explosion. Hamilton, John, ed. LC 88-71720. (Illus.). 32p. (gr. 4). 1989. PLB 11.96 (*0-939179-40-7*) Abdo & Dghtrs.

Hamilton, Sue L. Chernobyl: Nuclear Power Plant Explosion. Hamilton, John C., ed. LC 91-73040. 1991. 11.96 (*1-56239-060-0*) Abdo & Dghtrs.

—Los Angeles Riots. Hamilton, John, ed. LC 92-28400. 1992. 11.96 (*1-56239-149-6*) Abdo & Dghtrs.

—Pearl Harbor. Hamilton, John C., ed. LC 91-73041. 1991. 11.96 (*1-56239-059-7*) Abdo & Dghtrs.

Hamilton, V. Drylongso. Pinkney, J., illus. 1992. write for info. (*0-15-224241-4*, HB Juv Bks) HarBrace.

Hamilton, Virginia. All Jahdu Storybook. 108p. (gr. 3 up). 1991. 19.95 (*0-15-239498-2*, HB Juv Bks) HarBrace.

—Anthony Burns: The Defeat & Triumph of a Fugitive Slave. LC 87-38063. 192p. (gr. 5 up). 1988. lib. bdg. 12.99 (*0-394-98185-5*); pap. 3.99 (*0-679-83997-6*) Knopf Bks Yng Read.

—Bells of Christmas. 59p. (ps up). 1989. 17.95 (*0-15-206450-8*) HarBrace.

—Cousins. 128p. (gr. 5 up). 1990. 14.95 (*0-399-22164-6*, Philomel Bks) Putnam Pub Group.

—Cousins. (gr. 4-7). 1993. pap. 2.95 (*0-590-45436-6*) Scholastic Inc.

—The Dark Way: Stories from the Spirit World. Davis, Lambert, illus. 154p. (gr. 3 up). 1990. 19.95 (*0-15-222340-1*); Numbered, signed & Ltd. ed. 100.00 (*0-15-222341-X*) HarBrace.

—Dustland. LC 79-19003. 192p. (gr. 7 up). 1980. 13.00 (*0-688-80228-1*); PLB 12.88 (*0-688-84228-3*) Greenwillow.

—Dustland. 224p. (gr. 7 up). 1989. pap. 3.95 (*0-15-224315-1*, Odyssey) HarBrace.

—The Gathering. 214p. (gr. 7 up). 1989. pap. 3.95 (*0-15-230592-0*, Odyssey) HarBrace.

—The House of Dies Drear. reissued ed. Keith, Eros, illus. LC 68-23059. 256p. (gr. 6-9). 1984. SBE 15.95 (*0-02-742500-2*, Macmillan Child Bk); pap. 3.95 (*0-02-043520-7*, Collier) Macmillan Child Grp.

—In the Beginning: Creation Stories from Around the World. Moser, Barry, illus. 161p. (ps up). 1988. 22.95 (*0-15-238740-4*) HarBrace.

—In the Beginning: Creation Stories from Around the World. 161p. (ps up). 1991. pap. 14.95 (*0-15-238742-0*, HB Juv Bks) HarBrace.

—Junius over Far. LC 84-48344. 288p. (gr. 7 up). 1985. PLB 14.89 (*0-06-022195-X*) HarpC Child Bks.

—Justice & Her Brother. 282p. (gr. 7 up). 1989. pap. 3.95 (*0-15-241640-4*, Odyssey) HarBrace.

—Justice & Her Brothers. (gr. 4-7). 1992. 16.50 (*0-8446-6577-0*) Peter Smith.

—M. C. Higgins, the Great. LC 72-92439. 288p. (gr. 7 up). 1974. SBE 15.95 (*0-02-742480-4*, Macmillan Child Bk) Macmillan Child Grp.

—M. C. Higgins, the Great. LC 87-6330. 288p. (gr. 7 up). 1987. pap. 3.95 (*0-02-043490-1*, Collier Young Ad) Macmillan Child Grp.

—M. C. Higgins, the Great. large type ed. 320p. (gr. 3-7). 1988. Repr. of 1974 ed. lib. bdg. 15.95 (*1-55736-075-8*, Crnrstn Bks) BDD LT Grp.

—M. C. Higgins, the Great. 2nd ed. LC 92-27919. 288p. (gr. 3-7). 1993. pap. 3.95 (*0-689-71694-X*, Aladdin) Macmillan Child Grp.

—The Magical Adventures of Pretty Pearl. LC 82-48629. 320p. (gr. 7 up). 1983. PLB 17.89 (*0-06-022187-9*) HarpC Child Bks.

—The Magical Adventures of Pretty Pearl. LC 84-48344. 320p. (gr. 6 up). 1986. pap. 5.95 (*0-06-440178-2*, Trophy) HarpC Child Bks.

—Many Thousand Gone: African-Americans from Slavery to Freedom. Dillon, Leo & Dillon, Diane, illus. LC 89-19988. 160p. (gr. 4-9). 1992. 16.00 (*0-394-82873-9*); PLB 16.99 (*0-394-92873-3*) Knopf Bks Yng Read.

—The Mystery of Drear House. reinforced ed. LC 86-9829. 224p. (gr. 5 up). 1987. 13.95 (*0-688-04026-8*) Greenwillow.

—The Mystery of Drear House: The Conclusion of the Dies Drear Chronicle. LC 88-2887. 224p. (gr. 7 up). 1988. pap. 3.95 (*0-02-043480-4*, Collier Young Ad) Macmillan Child Grp.

—Paul Robeson: The Life & Times of a Free Black Man. LC 72-82892. (Illus.). 240p. (gr. 7 up). 1974. 14.89 (*0-06-022189-5*) HarpC Child Bks.

—The People Could Fly. Dillon, Leo & Dillon, Diane, illus. LC 84-25020. 192p. (ps-12). 1985. 18.00 (*0-394-86925-7*); lib. bdg. 18.99 (*0-394-96925-1*) Knopf Bks Yng Read.

—The People Could Fly: American Black Folktales. Dillon, Leo & Dillon, Diane, illus. LC 85-25020. 192p. 1993. pap. 10.00 (*0-679-84336-1*) Knopf Bks Yng Read.

—The People Could Fly: American Black Folktales. Dillon, Leo & Dillon, Diane, illus. Jones, James E., contrib. by. 192p. 1994. pap. 15.00 incl. cass. (*0-679-85465-7*) Knopf Bks Yng Read.

—The People Could Fly: American Black Tales. Jones, James Earl, contrib. by. (ps up). 1988. 9.95 (*0-394-89301-8*); cassette avail. Knopf Bks Yng Read.

—Plain City. LC 93-19910. 176p. (gr. 3-7). 1993. 13.95 (*0-590-47364-6*) Scholastic Inc.

—Planet of Junior Brown. LC 71-155264. 240p. (gr. 5-9). 1971. SBE 14.95 (*0-02-742510-X*, Macmillan Child Bk) Macmillan Child Grp.

—The Planet of Junior Brown. Pinkney, Jerry, photos by. LC 85-16651. (Illus.). 224p. (gr. 5-9). 1986. pap. 3.95 (*0-02-043540-1*, Collier Young Ad) Macmillan Child Grp.

—Planet of Junior Brown. large type, unabr. ed. 400p. (gr. 5 up). 1988. lib. bdg. 13.95 (*0-8161-4642-X*) G K Hall.

—The Planet of Junior Brown. 2nd ed. LC 92-40350. 224p. (gr. 3-7). 1993. pap. 3.95 (*0-689-71721-0*, Aladdin) Macmillan Child Grp.

—Primos - Cousins. (SPA.). (gr. 5-8). Date not set. pap. write for info. (*84-204-4747-1*) Santillana.

—Sweet Whispers, Brother Rush. 224p. (gr. 7 up). 1982. 15.95 (*0-399-20894-1*, Philomel) Putnam Pub Group.

—A White Romance. 200p. (gr. 8 up). 1987. 14.95 (*0-399-21213-2*, Philomel Bks) Putnam Pub Group.

—White Romance. 233p. (gr. 7 up). 1989. pap. 3.95 (*0-15-295888-6*, Odyssey) HarBrace.

—Willie Bea & the Time the Martians Landed. LC 83-1659. 192p. (gr. 5-9). 1983. reinforced bdg. 15.00 (*0-688-02390-8*) Greenwillow.

—Willie Bea & the Time the Martians Landed. LC 89-6821. 224p. (gr. 4-7). 1989. pap. 3.95 (*0-689-71328-2*, Aladdin) Macmillan Child Grp.

—Zeely. Shimin, Symeon, illus. LC 67-10266. 128p. (gr. 5-7). 1967. SBE 13.95 (*0-02-742470-7*, Macmillan Child Bk) Macmillan Child Grp.

—Zeely. 2nd ed. LC 92-28769. (Illus.). 128p. (gr. 3-7). 1993. pap. 3.95 (*0-689-71695-8*, Aladdin) Macmillan Child Grp.

Hamilton, Wanda W. Peter Pelican's Pouch Problem. Hamilton, Wanda W., illus. 22p. (Orig.). (gr. k-6). 1986. pap. 3.95 (*0-935357-01-7*) CRIC Prod.

Hamilton-MacLaren, Alistair. Houses & Homes. (Illus.). 48p. (gr. 4-8). 1992. PLB 12.90 (*0-531-18424-2*, Pub. by Bookwright Pr) Watts.

—Water Transportation. (Illus.). 48p. (gr. 4-8). 1992. PLB 12.90 (*0-531-18414-5*, Pub. by Bookwright Pr) Watts.

Hamilton-MacLaren, Alistair, jt. auth. see Lambert, Mark.

Hamilton-Merritt, Jane. Our New Baby. Hamilton-Merritt, Jane, illus. 32p. (ps-k). 1982. 4.80 (*0-671-44416-6*) S&S Trade.

Hamilton-Paterson, James. House in the Waves. LC 76-103043. (gr. 8 up). 1970. 21.95 (*0-87599-171-8*) S G Phillips.

Hamilton-Wilkes, Viola, jt. auth. see Wilkes, Donald L.

Hamlett, Christina. Humorous Plays for Teenagers. LC 86-16916. (Orig.). (gr. 7-12). 1987. pap. 12.95 (*0-8238-0276-0*) Plays.

Hamley, Dennis. Hare's Choice. Rutherford, Meg, illus. 96p. (gr. 5 up). 1992. pap. 3.25 (*0-440-40698-6*, YB) Dell.

—Pageants of Despair. LC 74-10841. 180p. (gr. 7-10). 1974. 21.95 (*0-87599-205-6*) S G Phillips.

—Tigger & Friends. Briley, D., ed. Rutherford, Meg, illus. LC 88-8385. (gr. k-3). 1989. 12.95 (*0-688-08606-3*); PLB 12.88 (*0-688-08605-5*) Lothrop.

Hamley, Harold, ed. How to Write & Sell. 4th ed 121p. (Orig.). (gr. 9-12). Repr. of 1989 ed. lib. bdg. 8.95 (*0-9621758-0-3*) Raconteurs.

Hamlin, Griffith A. House by the Water: Twelve Generations in Virginia. LC 93-70018. 139p. (gr. 9 up). 1993. 10.95 (*0-9631511-1-8*) G A Hamlin.

Hamlyn, J. Sheba Learns the Great Outdoors. 65p. (gr. 1-4). 1990. pap. 5.25 (*1-878950-00-2*) Sheba Bks Intl.

Hamm, Anita M. Lisa & the Raindrops. (gr. 1-4). 1977. 3.50 (*0-935513-01-9*) Samara Pubns.

—Lisa in Sugarland, a Child's Book on Nutrition to Be Digested Before Eating. (gr. 1-4). 1978. 3.50x (*0-935513-02-7*) Samara Pubns.

Hamm, Diane J. Bunkhouse Journal. LC 90-8062. 96p. (gr. 7 up). 1990. SBE 12.95 (*0-684-19206-3*, Scribners Young Read) Macmillan Child Grp.

—Grandma Drives a Motor Bed. Tucker, Kathleen, ed. LC 87-2197. (Illus.). 32p. (ps-3). 1987. PLB 11.95 (*0-8075-3025-5*) A Whitman.

—How Many Feet in the Bed. LC 90-35724. (Illus.). 40p. (ps). 1991. pap. 13.95 incl. jacket (*0-671-72638-2*, S&S BFYR) S&S Trade.

—Laney's Lost Momma. Mathews, Judith, ed. Ward, Sally, illus. LC 90-26824. 32p. (ps-1). 1991. 13.95 (*0-8075-4340-3*) A Whitman.

—Rockabye Farm. Brown, Rick, illus. LC 91-19127. 40p. (ps-1). 1992. pap. 14.00 jacketed (*0-671-74773-8*, S&S BFYR) S&S Trade.

—Second Family. LC 91-42968. 128p. (gr. 5-7). 1992. SBE 12.95 (*0-684-19436-8*, Scribners Young Read) Macmillan Child Grp.

Hamm, Diane Johnston. Rockabye Farm. LC 91-109127. (ps-3). 1994. pap. 4.95 (*0-671-88630-4*, Half Moon Bks) S&S Trade.

Hamman, Marc. Hamman Jammin' Music. (Illus.). 18p. (Orig.). (gr. k-6). 1990. pap. 12.95 (*1-56516-062-2*) Houston IN.

Hammar, Asa. Fit for Pigs. Moller, Johanna, illus. 40p. (gr. k-3). 1992. 9.95 (*1-56288-265-1*) Checkerboard.

Hammer, Charles. Me, the Beef, & the Bum. LC 83-25521. 181p. (gr. 5 up). 1984. 15.00 (*0-374-34903-7*) FS&G.

Hammer, Jeff. Dying to Know. 176p. (Orig.). 1991. pap. 3.50 (*0-380-76143-2*, Flare) Avon.

—Field Trip. 160p. (gr. 6). 1991. pap. 2.99 (*0-380-76144-0*, Flare) Avon.

Hammer, Roger A. American Woman: Hidden in History, Forging the Future. 2nd & enl. ed. Hallin, Britta, et al, illus. 80p. (gr. 7 up). 1993. pap. 19.95 (*0-932991-27-0*) Place in the Woods.

—Hidden America: A Collection of Multi-Cultural Stories, 4 bks. rev. ed. Schlosser, Cy, et al, illus. (gr. 6 up). Set. pap. 29.95 (*0-932991-00-9*) Place in the Woods.

—My Own Book! Reading Is Fundamental (RIF) 20th Anniversary. Schlosser, Cy, illus. LC 86-30410. 128p. (gr. 3-12). 1987. pap. 14.95 (*0-932991-50-5*) Place in the Woods.

Hammerslough, Jane. Home Alone Survival Guide. (gr. 4-7). 1993. pap. 3.50 (*0-440-83023-0*) Dell.

Hammerstein, Oscar, II & Rodgers, Richard. Rodgers & Hammerstein's My Favorite Things. Warhola, James, illus. LC 93-26116. 1994. write for info. (*0-671-79457-4*, S&S BFYR) S&S Trade.

Hammerstein, Oscar, II, jt. auth. see Rodgers, Richard.

Hammett, Dashiell. The Maltese Falcon. large type ed. (gr. 10 up). Repr. of 1959 ed. Set. write for info. NAVH.

Hammond. Discovering Maps: A Young Person's World Atlas. 1993. 11.95 (*0-8437-3414-0*) Hammond Inc.

—Ten Little Ducks. 1993. pap. 28.67 (*0-590-73338-9*) Scholastic Inc.

Hammond, Anna & Matunis, Joe. This Home We Have Made: Esta Casa Que Memos Hecho. Mendell, Olga K., tr. LC 92-28954. (ENG & SPA.). 24p. (ps-3). 1993. 14.00 (*0-517-59339-4*, Crown) Crown Bks Yng Read.

Hammond, Arissa, et al. My Friends ABC Book. LC 88-70949. (Illus.). 32p. (gr. 2 up). 1988. 10.00 (*0-9605968-4-4*) Bright Bks.

Hammond, Doreen. Freda the Frog & Other Poems. 48p. (gr. 7-10). 1986. pap. 20.00X (*0-317-52593-X*, Pub. by A H Stockwell Stapl St Mut.

Hammond, Elizabeth. My Rainbow Friends. Taylor, Neil, illus. LC 87-51495. 44p. (ps). 1989. 5.95 (*1-55523-023-7*) Winston-Derek.

—A Pocket Book of Manners for Young People. Oppenheimer, Jennie, illus. LC 90-90325. 96p. (Orig.). (gr. 4-8). 1990. pap. 5.95 (*0-9627061-0-8*) Trotwood Press.

Hammond, Franklin. Ten Little Ducks. Hammond, Frank, illus. 24p. (ps). 1992. pap. 4.95 (*0-88899-153-3*, Pub. by Groundwood-Douglas & McIntyre CN) Firefly Bks Ltd.

Hammond Incorporated Editors. World Atlas for Students. LC 80-81916. 56p. (gr. 8-12). 1993. pap. text ed. 7.00 (*0-8437-7820-2*) Hammond Inc.

Hammond Incorporated Staff. The World Atlas. LC 82-675036. 112p. (gr. 5 up). 1982. lib. bdg. 11.99 (*0-394-94663-4*); pap. 13.00 smyth-sewn (*0-394-84663-X*) Random Bks Yng Read.

Hammond, Janice M. When My Dad Died: A Child's View of Death. Hammond, Janice M., illus. 48p. (Orig.). (gr. k-6). 1981. pap. 6.95 (*0-9604690-3-6*) Cranbrook Pub.

—When My Mommy Died: A Child's View of Death. Hammond, Janice M., illus. 27p. (Orig.). (ps-5). 1980. pap. 6.95 (*0-9604690-0-1*) Cranbrook Pub.

Hammond, Pearle L. The Prize in the Packard. La Mont, Violet, illus. 100p. (Orig.). (gr. 5-8). 1990. pap. 8.95 (*0-9615161-6-X*) Incline Pr.

Hammond, Tim. Sports. King, Dave, photos by. LC 88-1573. (Illus.). 64p. (gr. 5 up). 1988. 15.00 (*0-394-89616-5*); lib. bdg. 15.99 (*0-394-99616-X*) Knopf Bks Yng Read.

Hammond, Vicky L. & Dalby, Judy N. Primary Passages Plus: Favorite Songs & Hymns Arranged for Newcomers to the Piano. Waller, Nancy G., illus. 32p. (Orig.). 1989. pap. 5.95 (*0-9624262-3-7*) Hammond Dalby Music.

Hammond, Vicky L. & Smith, Jerry. Accent on Youth: Piano Solos of Favorite Songs & Hymns. 24p. (Orig.). 1989. pap. 6.95 (*0-9624262-7-X*) Hammond Dalby Music.

Hammontree, Marie. Albert Einstein: Young Thinker. Doremus, Robert, illus. LC 86-10730. 192p. (gr. 2-6). 1986. pap. 3.95 (*0-02-041860-4*, Aladdin) Macmillan Child Grp.

Hamoy, Carol. What's Wrong? What's Wrong? Hamoy, Carol, illus. (gr. k-3). 1965. 8.95 (*0-685-00564-X*) Astor-Honor.

Hample, Stoo. Stoo Hample's Silly Joke Book. LC 78-50431. (Illus.). (gr. 1-6). 1978. pap. 5.47 (*0-440-08142-6*); pap. 2.50 (*0-440-08154-8*) Delacorte.

Hample, Stuart, compiled by. Dear Mr. President. Karas, G. Brian, illus. 96p. (Orig.). 1993. pap. 6.95 (*1-56305-504-X*, 3504) Workman Pub.

Hampton, Bill. Captive. 1989. pap. 2.50 (*0-553-28009-0*) Bantam.

Hampton, Cindy Van Way see Pugh, Ann, et al.

Hampton, J. World Health. (Illus.). 48p. (gr. 5 up). 1988. PLB 18.60 (*0-86592-281-0*); PLB 13.95s.p. (*0-685-58318-X*) Rourke Corp.

Hampton, Janie. Come Home Soon, Baba. Brent, Jenny, illus. 32p. (gr. 4 up). 1993. 12.95 (*0-87226-511-0*, Bedrick Blackie) P Bedrick Bks.

Hamsa, Bobbie. Animal Babies. Dunnington, Tom, illus. LC 84-27459. 32p. (ps-2). 1985. lib. bdg. 11.93 (*0-516-02066-8*); pap. 2.95 (*0-516-42066-6*) Childrens.

—Dirty Larry. LC 83-10079. (Illus.). 32p. (ps-2). 1983. PLB 11.93 (*0-516-02040-4*); pap. 2.95 (*0-516-42040-2*) Childrens.

—Fast Draw Freddie Big Book. 32p. (ps-2). 1990. PLB 30.60 (*0-516-49453-8*) Childrens.

—Fast Draw Freddie (Rookie Readers) LC 83-23931. (Illus.). 32p. (ps-2). 1984. lib. bdg. 11.93 (*0-516-02046-3*); pap. 2.95 (*0-516-42046-1*) Childrens.

—Federico Lapiz Rapido: Fast Draw Freddie. Hayes, Stephen, illus. LC 83-23931. (SPA.). 32p. (ps-2). 1991. PLB 11.93 (*0-516-32046-7*); pap. 2.95 (*0-516-52046-6*) Childrens.

—Lucio el Sucio (Dirty Larry) LC 83-10079. (SPA., Illus.). 32p. (ps-2). 1991. pap. 2.95 (*0-516-52040-7*) Childrens.

—Polly Wants a Cracker. Warshaw, Jerry, illus. LC 85-30000. 32p. (ps-2). 1986. PLB 11.93 (*0-516-02071-4*); pap. 2.95 (*0-516-42071-2*) Childrens.

Hamza, A. Color & Learn the Names of the Prophets. (Orig.). (ps). Date not set. pap. 3.50 (*0-934905-11-8*) Kazi Pubns.

Han, Carolyn, retold by. Why Snails Have Shells: Minority & Han Folktales of China. Han, Jay, tr. Ji, Li, illus. 1993. 14.95 (*0-685-65268-8*, Kolowalu Bk) UH Pr.

Han, Carolyn, ed. Why Snails Have Shells: Minority & Han Folktales of China. Han, Jay, tr. from CHI. Ji, Li, illus. 80p. (gr. 3-8). 1993. 14.95 (*0-8248-1505-X*) UH Pr.

Han, Jay, tr. see Han, Carolyn.

Han, Oki S. & Plunkett, Stephanie H., eds. Kongi & Potgi: A Cinderella Story from Korea. Han, Oki S., illus. LC 93-28426. 1994. write for info. (*0-8037-1571-4*); PLB write for info. (*0-8037-1572-2*) Dial Bks Young.

—Sir Whong & the Golden Pig. Han, Oki S., illus. LC 91-43389. 32p. (ps-3). 1993. 13.99 (*0-8037-1344-4*); PLB 13.89 (*0-8037-1345-2*) Dial Bks Young.

Han, Suzanne C. Let's Color Korea: Traditional Lifestyles. 24p. (gr. k-3). 1989. oversized 7.95x (*0-930878-94-9*) Hollym Intl.

—The Rabbit's Judgment. Heo, Yumi, illus. LC 93-11031. (ENG & KOR.). 1994. write for info. (*0-8050-2674-6*) H Holt & Co.

Hanable, William S., jt. auth. see Antonson, Joan M.

Hanak, Mirko, illus. Animals We Love, Bks. 1 & 2. LC 72-89571. 32p. (gr. k-4). 1973. 9.95 ea. Bk. 1 (*0-87592-005-5*) Bk. 2 (*0-87592-006-3*) Scroll Pr.

Hanauer, Ethel. Biology Experiments for Children. LC 68-9305. (Illus.). 96p. (gr. 5 up). 1969. pap. 2.95 (*0-486-22032-X*) Dover.

Hanavan, Louise, jt. auth. see Relf, Pat.

Hanby, Benjamin. Up on the Housetop. Harrison, Susan, illus. 24p. (Orig.). (ps-2). 1991. pap. 3.95 (*0-8249-8521-4*, Ideals Child) Hambleton-Hill.

Hancock, Lyn. Northwest Territories. (Illus.). 144p. (gr. 4 up). 1992. PLB 26.60 (*0-516-06615-3*) Childrens.

Hancock, Sibyl. Esteban & the Ghost. Zimmer, Dirk, illus. LC 82-22125. 32p. (ps-3). 1983. PLB 10.89 (*0-8037-2411-X*) Dial Bks Young.

—Famous Firsts of Black Americans. Haynes, Jerry, illus. LC 82-612. 128p. (gr. 3-9). 1983. 11.95 (*0-88289-240-1*) Pelican.

—Spindletop. Gholson, Virginia S., illus. (gr. 4-7). 1981. 7.95 (*0-89015-265-9*, Pub. by Panda Bks) Eakin-Sunbelt.

Hand, Desmond, jt. auth. see Robbie, Dorothy.

Hand, Elizabeth. Winterlong. 1990. pap. 4.95 (*0-553-28772-9*, Spectra) Bantam.

Hand, Julia. The Wonderful World of Wigglers: The Mysteries & Magic of the Mighty Earthworm. Peduzzi, Carolyn, illus. 181p. (Orig.). (gr. 1-6). 1993. pap. write for info. (*1-884430-00-7*) Food Works.

Hand, Julia, jt. auth. see DeNee, JoAnne.

Hand, Phyllis. Breaking into Bible Games. McClure, Nancee, illus. 48p. (gr. 3-6). 1984. wkbk. 6.95 (*0-86653-181-5*, SS 819, Shining Star Pubns) Good Apple.

—Celebrate God & Country. Nygaard, Elizabeth, illus. 144p. (gr. k-6). 1987. pap. 11.95 (*0-86653-390-7*, SS 843, Shining Star Pubns) Good Apple.

—Celebrate Special Days. Hierstein, Judy, illus. 144p. (gr. k-6). 1985. wkbk. 11.95 (*0-86653-280-3*, SS 841, Shining Star Pubns) Good Apple.

—Seasonal Bulletin Boards That Teach. Henson, Grace, illus. 48p. (gr. 1-5). 1984. wkbk. 6.95 (*0-86653-203-X*, SS 820, Shining Star Pubns) Good Apple.

Handal, Joan S., jt. auth. see Frisch, Vern A.

Handel, George F. Messiah: The Wordbook for the Oratorio. Hogwood, Christopher, intro. by. LC 91-21661. (Illus.). 48p. (gr. 3 up). 1992. 20.00 (*0-06-021779-0*); ltd. ed. 16.00 (*0-06-021038-9*); incls. cassette 35.00 (*0-06-021148-2*) HarpC Child Bks.

Handelsman, Judith F. Gardens from Garbage: How to Grow Plants from Recycled Kitchen Scraps. LC 92-9146. (Illus.). 48p. (gr. 4-6). 1993. PLB 13.90 (*1-56294-229-8*) Millbrook Pr.

Handford, Martin. Donde Esta Waldo? LC 92-54399. (Illus.). 32p. (ps up). 1993. PLB 14.88 (*1-56402-228-5*); pap. text ed. cancelled (*1-56402-225-0*) Candlewick Pr.
—Donde Esta Waldo Ahora? LC 92-54507. (Illus.). 32p. (ps up). 1993. PLB 14.88 (*1-56402-229-3*); pap. text ed. cancelled (*1-56402-226-9*) Candlewick Pr.
—Find Waldo Now. Handford, Martin, illus. (ps up). 1988. 12.95 (*0-316-34292-0*) Little.
—Fun with Waldo. (ps-3). 1992. 3.95 (*0-316-34380-3*) Little.
—The Great Waldo Search. Handford, Martin, illus. (ps up). 1989. 12.95 (*0-316-34282-3*) Little.
—More Fun with Waldo. (ps-3). 1992. 3.95 (*0-316-34383-8*) Little.
—Waldo y la Gran Busqueda. LC 92-54508. (Illus.). 32p. (ps up). 1993. PLB 14.88 (*1-56402-230-7*); pap. text ed. cancelled (*1-56402-227-7*) Candlewick Pr.
—Where's Waldo? (ps up). 1987. 12.95 (*0-316-34293-9*) Little.
—Where's Waldo? 1993. 5.95 (*0-316-34391-9*) Little.
—Where's Waldo? in Hollywood. Handford, Martin, illus. LC 91-71819. 32p. (ps up). Nov. 1993 14.95, (*1-56402-044-4*); PLB 14.88, Jan. 1994 (*1-56402-294-3*) Candlewick Pr.
—Where's Waldo? The Magnificent Poster Book. (Illus.). 1991. pap. 16.95 (*0-316-34352-8*) Little.
—Where's Waldo? The Ultimate Fun Book. 24p. 1990. 7.95 (*0-316-34344-7*) Little.
Handforth, Thomas. Mei Li. Handforth, Thomas, illus. 48p. (k-3). 1955. PLB 14.95 (*0-385-07401-8*) Doubleday.
Handler, Andrew & Meschel, Susan V. Young People Speak: Surviving the Holocaust in Hungary. (Illus.). 160p. (gr. 9-12). 1993. PLB 13.90 (*0-531-11044-3*) Watts.
Handler, Kalindi. The Boy Behind the Counter. 160p. (Orig.). (gr. 7 up). 1989. pap. 2.50 (*0-380-75646-3*, Flare) Avon.
Handley, Phyllis. First Day Out. (Illus.). 32p. (gr. 2). 1992. 8.95 (*0-8059-3228-3*) Dorrance.
Handville, Elizabeth, ed. OCCU-FACTS: Facts on over 565 Occupations. 624p. (Orig.). (gr. 6 up). 1989. pap. text ed. 38.00 (*0-9623657-0-X*) Careers Inc.
Handwerk, Sandra, jt. auth. see Kolehmainen, Janet.
Handy. My Poppa Loves Old Movies. 1993. pap. 28.67 (*0-590-50152-6*) Scholastic Inc.
Handy, Libby. Boss for a Week. 32p. (gr. k-3). Big Book. 28.67 (*0-590-64641-9*) Scholastic Inc.
Hanen, Joyce. Yellow Bird & Me. LC 85-484. 128p. (gr. 3-7). 1991. pap. 3.80 (*0-395-55388-1*, Clarion Bks) HM.
Hanes, Betsy. Taffy Sinclair & the Romance Machine Disaster. 128p. (Orig.). 1987. pap. 2.75 (*0-553-15644-6*, Skylark) Bantam.
Haney, David. Captain James Cook & the Explorers of the Pacific. Goetzmann, William H.; ed. Collins, Michael, intro. by. (Illus.). 112p. (gr. 5 up). 1992. lib. bdg. 18.95 (*0-7910-1310-3*) Chelsea Hse.
Haney, John. Cesare Borgia. Schlesinger, Henry M., Jr., intro. by. (Illus.). 112p. (gr. 5 up). 1986. lib. bdg. 17.95 (*0-87754-595-2*) Chelsea Hse.
—Clement Attlee. Schlesinger, Arthur M., Jr., intro. by. (Illus.). (gr. 5 up). 1988. lib. bdg. 17.95 (*0-87754-508-1*) Chelsea Hse.
—Vladimir Lenin. Schlesinger, Arthur M., Jr., intro. by. (Illus.). 112p. (gr. 5 up). 1988. lib. bdg. 17.95 (*0-87754-570-7*) Chelsea Hse.
Haney, Joy. Behold the Nazarite Woman. Agnew, Tim, illus. LC 90-30639. 96p. (Orig.). 1990. pap. 5.99 (*0-932581-63-3*) Word Aflame.
—May I Wash Your Feet. Agnew, Tim, illus. LC 91-21855. 100p. (Orig.). 1991. pap. 5.99 (*0-932581-87-0*) Word Aflame.
Hanff, Helene. Movers & Shakers: Young Activists of the Sixties. LC 77-110432. (Illus.). (gr. 10 up). 1970. 27.95 (*0-87599-166-1*) S G Phillips.
Hanft, Philip. Never Fear, Flip the Dip Is Here. Allen, Thomas B., illus. LC 90-3385. 32p. (ps-3). 1991. 12.95 (*0-8037-0897-1*); PLB 12.89 (*0-8037-0899-8*) Dial Bks Young.
Hanft, Robert M. Pine Across the Mountain. LC 71-164462. (Illus.). 224p. (gr. 11). 1990. Repr. of 1971 ed. 44.95 (*0-87046-099-4*, Pub. by Trans-Anglo) Interurban.
Hanhart, Brigitte, adapted by see Tolstoy, Leo.
Hankin, Rebecca. I Can Be a Doctor. LC 84-23304. (Illus.). 32p. (gr. k-3). 1985. PLB 14.60 (*0-516-01846-9*); pap. 3.95 (*0-516-41846-7*) Childrens.
—I Can Be a Fire Fighter. LC 84-29282. (Illus.). 32p. (gr. k-3). 1985. PLB 14.60 (*0-516-01847-7*); pap. 3.95 (*0-516-41847-5*) Childrens.
—I Can Be a Musician. LC 84-12136. (Illus.). 32p. (gr. k-3). 1984. PLB 14.60 (*0-516-01844-2*) Childrens.
—Puedo Ser Bombero: (I Can Be a Firefighter) LC 84-29282. (SPA & ENG.). 32p. (gr. k-3). 1989. PLB 13.93 (*0-516-31847-0*); pap. 3.95 (*0-516-51847-X*) Childrens.
—Puedo Ser Medico (I Can Be a Doctor) LC 84-23304. (SPA., Illus.). 32p. (gr. k-3). 1990. PLB 13.93 (*0-516-31846-2*) Childrens.
Hanks, Jacqueline. Splash! A Little Otter in Big Trouble. (Illus.). 24p. (gr. k-3). 1992. pap. 1.99 (*0-87406-600-X*) Willowisp Pr.
Hanley, Boniface. With Minds of Their Own: Eight Women Who Made a Difference. LC 91-72117. (Illus.). 232p. (Orig.). (gr. 7-12). 1991. pap. 9.95 (*0-87793-454-1*) Ave Maria.

Hanley, Sally. A. Philip Randolph. King, Coretta Scott, intro. by. (Illus.). (gr. 5 up). 1989. 17.95 (*1-55546-607-9*); pap. 9.95 (*0-7910-0222-5*) Chelsea Hse.
Hanmer, Trudy. Uganda. LC 89-31171. (Illus.). 128p. (gr. 6 up). 1989. PLB 13.40 (*0-531-10816-3*) Watts.
Hanmer, Trudy J. Affirmative Action: Opportunity for All? (Illus.). 104p. (gr. 6 up). 1993. lib. bdg. 17.95 (*0-89490-451-5*) Enslow Pubs.
—Leningrad. LC 92-14. (Illus.). 96p. (gr. 6 up). 1992. RSBE 14.95 (*0-02-742615-7*, New Discovery) Macmillan Child Grp.
—Taking a Stand Against Sexism & Sex Discrimination. LC 90-12567. (Illus.). 144p. (gr. 9-12). 1990. PLB 14.40 (*0-531-10962-3*) Watts.
Hanna, J. Steven. The New American Storybook. 1993. 7.95 (*0-533-10553-6*) Vantage.
Hanna, Jack. Petting Zoo. (ps). 1992. 10.00 (*0-385-41694-6*) Doubleday.
Hanna, Ken. My Life & Times: For Whatever They're Worth. LC 88-51575. 128p. (gr. 7-9). 1989. pap. 6.95 (*1-55523-211-6*) Winston-Derek.
Hanna, Nick, jt. auth. see Wells, Sue.
Hannah, Jack, jt. auth. see Barks, Carl.
Hannah, Valerie. Cyril Squirrel & Sheryl: An Ecological Tale. Herrick, George H., ed. Meek, Barbara, illus. 46p. (Orig.). (gr. k-3). 1991. 6.95 (*0-941281-78-7*) V H Pub.
—Little Jollys Find a Home. Herrick, George H., ed. Kokino, Olga, illus. 36p. (Orig.). (gr. k-3). 1991. pap. 5.95 (*0-941281-79-5*) V H Pub.
—Sheryl Visits Cyril: An Ecological Tale. Herrick, George, ed. (Illus.). 1992. pap. 6.95x (*0-941281-87-6*) V H Pub.
Hannam, Charles. A Boy in Your Situation. 216p. (gr. 7-9). 1989. pap. 9.95 (*0-233-98279-5*, Pub. by A Deutsch England) Trafalgar.
Hannan, Peter. The Battle of Sillyville. Hannan, Peter, illus. LC 90-4544. 32p. (ps-2). 1991. pap. 3.95 (*0-679-80286-X*) Knopf Bks Yng Read.
—Escape from Camp Wannabarf. Hannan, Peter, illus. LC 90-33203. 32p. (Orig.). (ps-2). 1991. pap. 3.95 (*0-679-80287-8*) Knopf Bks Yng Read.
—School after Dark. Hannan, Peter, illus. LC 90-33407. 32p. (Orig.). (ps-2). 1991. pap. 3.95 (*0-679-80288-6*) Knopf Bks Yng Read.
—Sillyville or Bust. Hannan, Peter, illus. LC 89-35342. 32p. (Orig.). (ps-2). 1991. pap. 3.95 (*0-679-80285-1*) Knopf Bks Yng Read.
Hannan, R., ed. see Rowe, Jeanine C.
Hannant, Judith S. The Doorknob Collection of Bedtime Rhymes, Vol. 1. Hannant, Judith S., illus. (ps). 1993. 12.95 (*0-316-34366-8*) Little.
Hanneman, Tamara. Election Book: People Pick a President. (gr. 4-7). 1992. pap. 1.95 (*0-590-46414-0*) Scholastic Inc.
Hannon, Robert J. & Slattery, Anastasia S. Marriage & Family: A Complete Course. 172p. (Orig.). (gr. 11 up). 1978. tchrs. ed. 30.00 (*0-9606040-0-6*) Patio Pubns.
Hannon, Ruth. My First Bible. 1982. 5.95 (*0-88271-031-1*) Regina Pr.
Hannum, Dotti. A Visit to the Fire Station. Holmes, Dave & Markson, Sue, illus. LC 84-12155. 32p. (gr. k-3). 1985. PLB 15.00 (*0-516-01491-9*); pap. 3.95 (*0-516-41491-7*) Childrens.
—A Visit to the Police Station. Flanagan, Romie, photos by. LC 84-12700. (Illus.). 32p. (gr. k-3). 1985. PLB 15.00 (*0-516-01493-5*) Childrens.
Hannum, Thomasina, tr. see Comber, Geoffrey, et al.
Hanon & Lindquist, A. Technical Variants. 32p. (Orig.). (gr. k-12). 1929. pap. text ed. 5.95 (*0-87487-657-5*) Summy-Birchard.
Hanrahan, Brendan. My Sisters Love My Clothes. (Illus.). 32p. (gr. 1-4). 1992. 12.95 (*0-9630181-0-8*) Perry Heights.
—NBA Dynamic Duos. (ps-3). 1993. pap. 2.25 (*0-307-12769-9*, Golden Pr) Western Pub.
Hansard, Peter. A Field Full of Horses. Lilly, Kenneth, illus. LC 92-45830. 1994. write for info. (*1-56402-302-8*) Candlewick Pr.
—I Like Monkeys Because. Casey, Patricia, illus. LC 92-54409. 32p. (ps up). 1993. 14.95 (*1-56402-196-3*) Candlewick Pr.
Hansberry, Lorraine. A Raisin in the Sun. (RL 9). 1961. pap. 3.99 (*0-451-16137-8*, Sig) NAL-Dutton.
—To Be Young, Gifted & Black. Baldwin, James, intro. by. 272p. (RL 7). 1970. pap. 5.50 (*0-451-15952-7*, Sig) NAL-Dutton.
Hansel, Bettina. The Exchange Student Survival Kit. Gregory, Bettina, pref. by. LC 93-10449. 122p. 1993. pap. 12.95 (*1-877864-17-X*) Intercult Pr.
Hansel, E. Van see Van Hansel, E.
Hansel, Steven. Dog School. 8p. (gr. 1). 1990. pap. text ed. 2.50 (*1-882225-04-X*) Tott Pubns.
Hansel, Tim. Real Heroes Eat Hamburgers. Harmon, Jeannie & Davis, Cathy, eds. 64p. (gr. 3-7). 1989. pap. 4.99 (*1-55513-334-7*, Chariot Bks) Cook.
—Real Heroes Wear Jeans. Harmon, Jeannie & Davis, Cathy, eds. 64p. (gr. 3-7). 1989. pap. 4.99 (*1-55513-333-9*, Chariot Bks) Cook.
—Through the Wilderness of Loneliness. 128p. 1991. 12.99 (*1-55513-290-1*, 62901) Cook.
Hansen, Carol, et al. Shilpa: Folk Dances, Music, Crafts & Puppetry of India. rev. ed. LC 90-12985. (Illus.). 205p. 1990. tchr. looseleaf 44.95 (*0-930141-38-5*) World Eagle.
Hansen, Cindy. Knowing God's Will. 48p. (Orig.). (gr. 9-12). 1990. pap. 7.99 (*1-55945-205-6*) Group Pub.

Hansen, Ellen, intro. by. The New England Transcendentalists: Life of the Mind & of the Spirit. (Illus.). 64p. (Orig.). (gr. 5-12). 1993. pap. 4.95 (*1-878668-26-6*) Disc Enter Ltd.
—Underground Railroad: Life on the Road to Freedom. (Illus.). 64p. (Orig.). (gr. 5-12). 1993. pap. 4.95 (*1-878668-27-7*) Disc Enter Ltd.
Hansen, Elvig. Guinea Pigs. (ps-3). 1992. 19.95 (*0-87614-687-1*) Carolrhoda Bks.
—Guinea Pigs. (gr. 4-7). 1993. pap. 6.95 (*0-87614-613-2*) Carolrhoda Bks.
Hansen, Harlan S., ed. see Sandell, Elizabeth.
Hansen, Joseph. Living Upstairs. LC 93-2716. 224p. (gr. 5 up). 1993. 20.00 (*0-525-93682-3*, Dutton) NAL-Dutton.
—A Smile in His Lifetime. 304p. (gr. 7 up). 1985. pap. 8.95 (*0-452-26267-4*, Plume) NAL-Dutton.
Hansen, Joyce. Between Two Fires: Black Soldiers in the Civil War. LC 92-37381. (Illus.). 160p. (gr. 9-12). 1993. PLB 13.90 (*0-531-11151-2*) Watts.
—Bewteen Two Fires: Black Soldiers in the Civil War. (Illus.). (gr. 7-12). 1993. pap. 6.95 (*0-531-15676-1*) Watts.
—The Gift-Giver. LC 79-13812. 128p. (gr. 4-8). 1980. 14.45 (*0-395-29433-9*, Clarion Bks) HM.
—The Gift-Giver. (gr. 3-6). 1989. pap. 6.70 (*0-89919-852-X*, Clarion Bks) HM.
—Home Boy. 160p. (gr. 6 up). 1982. 13.95 (*0-89919-114-2*, Clarion Bks) HM.
—Out from This Place. 144p. 1992. pap. 3.50 (*0-380-71409-4*, Camelot) Avon.
—Which Way Freedom? 128p. 1992. pap. 3.50 (*0-380-71408-6*, Camelot) Avon.
—Yellow Bird & Me. LC 85-484. (gr. 3-7). 1986. 12.95 (*0-89919-335-8*, Clarion Bks) HM.
Hansen, Judith. Seashells in My Pocket: A Child's Nature Guide to Exploring the Atlantic Coast. 2nd ed. Sabaka, Donna, illus. LC 92-24397. 160p. (gr. 6 up). 1992. pap. 10.95 (*1-878239-15-5*) AMC Books.
Hansen, Kathleen. A New Sibling. 2nd ed. Silverthorn, Tina, illus. 16p. (ps). 1989. color book 1.95x (*0-685-29408-0*) Time Grow Co.
Hansen, Lee. My Christmas Counting Book. (ps-3). 1993. pap. 4.95 (*0-307-10361-7*, Golden Pr) Western Pub.
Hansen, Michael C. Coal: How It Is Found & Used. LC 89-34452. (Illus.). 64p. (gr. 6 up). 1990. lib. bdg. 15.95 (*0-89490-286-5*) Enslow Pubs.
Hansen, Robin. Sunny's Mittens: Learn to Knit - Lovikka Mittens. Stock, Lois L., illus. LC 90-61410. 48p. (gr. 3-6). 1990. pap. 12.95 wire-o bdg. (*0-89272-290-8*) Down East.
Hansen, Robyn, jt. auth. see Thieme, Jeanne.
Hansen, Ron. The Shadowmaker. Tomes, Margot, illus. LC 85-45272. 80p. (gr. 2-6). 1987. PLB 10.89 (*0-06-022203-4*) HarpC Child Bks.
—The Shadowmaker. Tomes, Margot, illus. LC 85-45272. 80p. (gr. 2-5). 1989. pap. 3.95 (*0-06-440287-8*, Trophy) HarpC Child Bks.
Hansen, Ron, ed. & illus. see Barlass, Gail.
Hansen, Ronnie, ed. & illus. see Henry, Gilson.
Hansen, Rosanna & Bell, Robert. My First Book about Space. (ps-3). 1985. pap. 9.95 (*0-671-60262-4*, S&S BFYR) S&S Trade.
Hansen, Rosanna, adapted by see Lowrey, Janette S.
Hanshaw, Carol A., retold by. Cinderella: The Fairy Tale. 16p. (ps-2). 1993. write for info. (*1-883366-19-4*) YES Ent.
—The Sleeping Beauty. 16p. (ps-2). 1993. write for info. (*1-883366-20-8*) YES Ent.
Hansjurgen Press & Littlewood, Barbara S. The Adventures of the Black Hand Gang. Littlewood, Barbara S., illus. 128p. (gr. 3-7). 1983. pap. 6.95 (*0-13-013938-6*, Pub. by Treehouse); pap. 4.95 (*0-13-014035-X*) P-H.
Hansom, Dick, tr. see Mitchetz, Marc.
Hanson, Amy. The Annual Manual for Girls. 192p. (Orig.). (gr. 3-7). 1993. pap. 4.95 (*1-56565-057-3*) Lowell Hse.
Hanson, Ann R., ed. & illus. see Hanson, Fred E.
Hanson, Don & Helfrich, R. L. Celebrate Halloween with Hog, Dog, & Frog. Helfrich, Nathan, illus. 64p. (Orig.). 1993. pap. 9.95 (*1-56883-018-1*) Colonial Pr AL.
—A Holiday on a Log with Hog, Dog & Frog: Greet the Easter Bunny. Helfrich, Nathan, illus. 64p. 1993. pap. 9.95 (*1-56883-020-3*) Colonial Pr AL.
Hanson, Fred. Down a Magic Stream. Hanson, Ann R., illus. 65p. (Orig.). (gr. 2-5). 1992. pap. 9.95 (*0-9624292-2-8*) Black Willow Pr.
Hanson, Fred E. Norman. Hanson, Ann R., ed. & illus. LC 89-90961. 63p. (Orig.). (gr. 4-6). 1989. pap. 7.95 (*0-685-28895-1*) Black Willow Pr.
—Norman. 2nd ed. Hanson, Ann R., illus. 64p. (gr. 3-5). 1989. pap. 7.95 (*0-9624292-0-1*) Black Willow Pr.
—Simon. Hanson, Ann R., illus. 54p. (gr. 3-5). 1990. pap. 7.95 (*0-9624292-1-X*) Black Willow Pr.
Hansson, Peter, jt. auth. see Gipson, Morrell.
Hantzig, Deborah. A Visit to the Sesame Street Hospital. Mathieu, Joe, illus. LC 84-17852. 32p. (ps-4). 1985. lib. bdg. 5.99 (*0-394-97062-4*); pap. 2.25 (*0-394-87062-X*) Random Bks Yng Read.
Hanus, Karen. One-Eyed Cat: A Study Guide. Friedland, Joyce & Kessler, Rikki, eds. (gr. 5-8). 1991. pap. text ed. 14.95 (*0-88122-580-0*) LRN Links.
Happy, Elizabeth. Bailey's Birthday. Chase, Andra, illus. LC 93-32519. 32p. (gr. 1-4). 1994. 16.95 (*1-55942-059-6*, 7658); video, tchr's. guide & storybook 79.95 (*1-55942-062-6*, 9377) Marshfilm.

Happy House Staff. Hurry up, Santa. 1992. 0.60 (*0-394-82496-2*) Random.
—When Dinosaurs Ruled the Earth-Coloring Book. (ps-3). 1987. 0.49 (*0-394-89206-2*) Random Bks Yng Read.
—When Dinosaurs Ruled the Earth: Dot-to-Dot Coloring Book. (ps-3). 1987. 0.49 (*0-394-89204-6*) Random Bks Yng Read.
—When Dinosaurs Ruled the Earth: Number Fun Coloring Book. (ps-3). 1987. 0.49 (*0-394-89208-9*) Random Bks Yng Read.
—When Dinosaurs Ruled the Earth: Riddles-Coloring Book. (ps-3). 1987. 0.49 (*0-394-89205-4*) Random Bks Yng Read.
—When Dinosaurs Ruled the Earth: Show & Tell Coloring Book. (ps-3). 1987. 0.49 (*0-394-89209-7*) Random Bks Yng Read.
—When Dinosaurs Ruled the Earth: Sports & Games Coloring Book. (ps-3). 1987. 0.49 (*0-394-89207-0*) Random Bks Yng Read.
Happy Jack Feder. Clown Skits for Everyone. Zapel, Arthur, ed. Locke, Lafe, illus. LC 90-29297. 176p. (gr. 9 up). 1990. pap. 9.95 (*0-916260-75-5*, B147) Meriwether Pub.
Haq, M. Fazal, tr. see Sharafuddin, Sadruddin.
Harada, Joyce. It's the A B C Book. (ENG & VIE., Illus.). 32p. (Orig.). (gr. k-2). 1992. pap. 8.95 (*0-89346-344-2*) Heian Intl.
—It's the A B C Book. (ENG & CAM., Illus.). 32p. (Orig.). (gr. k-2). 1992. pap. 8.95 (*0-89346-345-0*) Heian Intl.
—It's the 0-1-2-3 Book. Harada, Joyce, illus. 32p. (ps-3). 1985. pap. 7.95 (*0-89346-252-7*) Heian Intl.
Harada, Joyce, illus. It's the A.B.C. Book. 32p. (ps). 1982. limp 7.95 (*0-89346-157-1*) Heian Intl.
Haragan, Donald R. Blue Northers to Sea Breezes: Texas Weather & Climate. (Illus.). 98p. (gr. 7 up). 1983. pap. 12.95 (*0-937460-10-9*) Hendrick-Long.
—Reproducible Exercises for Blue Northers to Sea Breezes: Texas Weather & Climate. (Illus.). 58p. (gr. 7 up). 1984. pap. 8.95 (*0-937460-16-8*) Hendrick-Long.
Haramilio, Alyce, jt. ed. see Bowser, Milton.
Harben, Peter W., jt. auth. see Harris, Jeanette M.
Harbin, Carey E. Bucky Leaves Home. (Illus.). 26p. (Orig.). (ps-1). 1991. pap. 2.95 (*0-918995-02-7*) Voc-Offers.
—Fay, Jay & Adding Numbers. (Illus.). 29p. (Orig.). (ps-1). 1990. pap. text ed. 2.95 (*0-918995-04-3*) Voc-Offers.
—Fay's New Computer. (Illus.). 30p. (Orig.). (ps-1). 1990. pap. text ed. 2.95 (*0-918995-03-5*) Voc-Offers.
Harbo, Gary. Bad Bart's Revenge: Advanced Reader. Harbo, Gary & Wallace, Shawn, illus. 35p. (gr. 1-4). 1991. text ed. 8.95 (*1-884149-03-0*) Kutie Kari Bks.
—Bart Becomes a Friend: Advanced Reader. Harbo, Gary, illus. 33p. (gr. 1-4). 1992. text ed. 8.95 (*1-884149-05-7*) Kutie Kari Bks.
—My New Friend: Advanced Reader. Harbo, Gary, illus. 33p. (gr. 1-4). 1988. text ed. 8.95 (*1-884149-01-4*) Kutie Kari Bks.
Harbor, B. Arms Trade. (Illus.). 48p. (gr. 5 up). 1988. PLB 18.60 (*0-86592-283-7*); 13.95 (*0-685-58315-5*) Rourke Corp.
Harbor, Bernard. Conflict in Eastern Europe. LC 93-3035. (Illus.). 48p. (gr. 6 up). 1993. RSBE 13.95 (*0-02-742626-2*, New Discovery Bks) Macmillan Child Grp.
—Conflicts: The Breakup of the Soviet Union. LC 92-19917. (Illus.). 48p. (gr. 6 up). 1993. RSBE 13.95 (*0-02-742625-4*, New Discovery) Macmillan Child Grp.
Harbor, Bernard, jt. auth. see Smith, Chris.
Harbour, Jennie, illus. My Book of Favorite Fairy Tales. LC 92-37669. 1993. 8.99 (*0-517-09125-9*, Pub. by Derrydale Bks) Outlet Bk Co.
Harby, Mary L., jt. auth. see McCall, William A.
Hard, Charlotte, illus. Find Mouse in the Yard. LC 93-12825. (gr. 3 up). 1994. write for info. (*1-56402-350-8*) Candlewick Pr.
Hardaway, Billie T. see Signer, Billie T., pseud.
Hardcastle, Michael. Quake. 128p. (gr. 7 up). 1988. 11.95 (*0-317-69550-9*) Faber & Faber.
Hardegrove, Nelle A. Ten Stories for Children. Miller, Dennis, illus. 10p. (Orig.). (gr. 1-5). 1987. pap. text ed. 7.95 (*0-9619227-3-7*) N A Hardegrove.
Hardel, Dick. Jesus' Death & Resurrection. (Illus.). 48p. (gr. 9-12). 1991. pap. 7.99 (*1-55945-211-0*) Group Pub.
—Who Is Jesus? (Illus.). 48p. (gr. 9-12). 1991. pap. 7.99 (*1-55945-219-6*) Group Pub.
Harden, Cleo. How to Preserve Animal & Other Specimens in Clear Plastic. Harden, David G., illus. 64p. (gr. 4 up). 1963. 12.95 (*0-911010-47-5*); pap. 4.95 (*0-911010-46-7*) Naturegraph.
Harden, E., tr. see Collodi, Carlo.
Harder, Eleanor. Goldilocks & the Christmas Bears. 1981. pap. text ed. 3.45 (*0-87129-198-3*, G06) Dramatic Pub.
Harder, Eleanor & Harder, Ray. Good Grief, a Griffin: Musical. 1968. 4.50 (*0-87602-131-3*) Anchorage.
—The Near-Sighted Knight & the Far-Sighted Dragon: Musical. (gr. 1-9). 1977. 4.50 (*0-87602-161-5*) Anchorage.
—Sacramento Fifty Miles: Musical. (gr. 1-7). 1969. 4.50 (*0-87602-198-4*) Anchorage.

Harder, Geraldine & Harder, Milton. Christmas Goose. Shelly, Maynard, ed. Dyck, Lavonne, illus. LC 90-84535. 80p. (Orig.). (gr. k-6). 1990. pap. 5.95 (*0-87303-146-6*) Faith & Life.
Harder, Geraldine G. A Penny & Two Fried Eggs: And Other Stories. Hannon, Holly, illus. LC 91-16999. 144p. (Orig.). (gr. 2-5). 1991. pap. 6.95 (*0-8361-3564-4*) Herald Pr.
Harder, Milton, jt. auth. see Harder, Geraldine.
Harder, Ray, jt. auth. see Harder, Eleanor.
Hardgrove, Nelle. Hurrah for Funny Bunny. Goodman, Joe, ed. (Illus.). 48p. 1987. pap. write for info. (*0-9619227-1-0*) N A Hardegrove.
Hardgrove, Tanya. Alaska in the Days That Were Before. (gr. 2-10). 1985. pap. 2.45 (*0-89992-098-5*) Coun India Ed.
Harding. Alvin's No Horse. 1994. pap. write for info. (*0-8050-3274-6*) H Holt & Co.
Harding, Emma. Cock-a-Doodle-Doo! LC 93-11030. 1994. write for info. (*0-8050-3059-X*) H Holt & Co.
Harding, Jacqueline. Building: First Readers. Trotter, Stuart, illus. 28p. (ps-k). 1992. 3.50 (*0-7214-1491-5*) Ladybird Bks.
—Farm: First Readers. Sliwinska, Sara, illus. 28p. (ps-k-1). 1992. 3.50 (*0-7214-1482-6*, 929-1) Ladybird Bks.
—Wheels: First Readers. Chapman, Gaynor, illus. 28p. (ps-k). 1992. 3.50 (*0-7214-1483-4*) Ladybird Bks.
—Zoo: First Readers. Hallahan, Maureen, illus. 28p. (ps-k). 1992. 3.50 (*0-7214-1490-7*) Ladybird Bks.
Harding, Mary. All Aboard Trains. Courtney, Richard, illus. 32p. (Orig.). 2. 1989. pap. 2.25 (*0-448-19111-3*, Platt & Munk Pubs) Putnam Pub Group.
Harding, Roger, jt. auth. see Symes, R. F.
Harding, Susan. Grow in Wisdom. 24p. (ps-2). 1984. pap. 1.75 (*0-85151-437-5*) Banner of Truth.
—Tell Me about God: Simple Studies in the Doctrine of God for Children. (Illus.). 64p. (ps-4). 1985. pap. 7.95 (*0-85151-510-X*) Banner of Truth.
Harding, William H. Alvin's Famous No-Horse. Chesworth, Michael, illus. LC 92-13834. 64p. (gr. 2-4). 1992. alk. paper 14.95 (*0-8050-2227-9*, Redfeather BYR) H Holt & Co.
Harding, William J. Infant Child. LC 92-56939. (Illus.). 40p. (gr. k-3). 1993. 6.95 (*1-55523-581-6*) Winston-Derek.
Hardinge, Miriam. Long Ago Stories. Wheeler, Gerald, ed. 144p. (Orig.). (ps). 1987. pap. 6.95 (*0-8280-0351-3*) Review & Herald.
Hardt, Elaine. Stories from Beyond the Double Rainbow. (Orig.). (gr. 1-8). 1982. pap. 10.50 (*0-932960-03-0*) Thinking Caps.
—Writing Poetry. Kruck, Gerry, illus. 32p. (Orig.). (gr. 1-9). 1983. pap. 1.95 (*0-940406-09-8*) Perception Pubns.
Hardy, Lois L., jt. auth. see Santa, Beauel M.
Hardy, Myronn E. Jenni & the Talking Tulip. (Illus.). 110p. (ps-3). 1989. pap. 4.95 (*0-9621696-3-3*) Ezra Pub Inc.
Hardy, Robin. The Killer's Club. (gr. 7 up). 1994. pap. 3.50 (*0-553-29829-1*) Bantam.
Hardy, Sally M., illus. The Three Bears. (ps-3). 1982. 3.50 (*0-913545-08-2*) Moonlight FL.
Hardy, Thomas. Far from the Madding Crowd. Gemme, F. R., intro. by. (gr. 11 up). 1967. pap. 2.50 (*0-8049-0136-8*, CL-136) Airmont.
—Jude the Obscure. Teitel, N. R., intro. by. (gr. 11 up). 1966. pap. 1.95 (*0-8049-0108-2*, CL-108) Airmont.
—Jude the Obscure. Howe, Irving, ed. LC 65-5860. (gr. 9 up). 1972. pap. 7.96 (*0-395-05191-6*, RivEd) HM.
—Mayor of Casterbridge. Bigoness, J. W., intro. by. (gr. 11 up). 1965. pap. 1.95 (*0-8049-0063-9*, CL-63) Airmont.
—Mayor of Casterbridge. Heilman, Robert B., ed. LC 62-1552. (gr. 9 up). 1962. pap. 9.16 (*0-395-05158-4*, RivEd) HM.
—Return of the Native. (gr. 10 up). 1964. pap. 2.75 (*0-8049-0038-8*, CL-38) Airmont.
—Return of the Native. Litz, A. Walton, ed. LC 67-5356. (gr. 9 up). 1967. pap. 9.16 (*0-395-05201-7*, RivEd) HM.
—Tess of the D'Urbervilles. Hogan, A. H., intro. by. (gr. 11 up). 1965. pap. 3.50 (*0-8049-0082-5*, CL-82) Airmont.
—Tess of the D'Urbervilles. Buckler, William E., ed. LC 60-707. (gr. 9 up). 1960. pap. 7.96 (*0-395-05144-4*, RivEd) HM.
Hare, Eric B. Pip Pip the Naughty Chicken. 31p. 1989. pap. 6.95 incl. cassette (*0-8163-0806-3*) Pacific Pr Pub Assn.
Hare, Tony. Acid Rain. (Illus.). 32p. (gr. 5-8). 1990. PLB 12.40 (*0-531-17247-3*, Gloucester Pr) Watts.
—Domestic Waste. LC 91-34099. (Illus.). 32p. (gr. 4-8). 1992. PLB 12.40 (*0-531-17347-X*, Gloucester Pr) Watts.
—Greenhouse Effect. (ps-3). 1990. PLB 12.40 (*0-531-17217-1*) Watts.
—Habitat Destruction. LC 91-8402. (Illus.). 32p. (gr. 5-8). 1991. PLB 12.40 (*0-531-17307-0*, Gloucester Pr) Watts.
—Nuclear Waste Disposal. (Illus.). 32p. (gr. 4-8). 1991. PLB 12.40 (*0-531-17291-0*) Watts.
—Ozone Layer. 1990. PLB 12.40 (*0-531-17218-X*, Gloucester Pr) Watts.
—Polluting the Air. (Illus.). 32p. (gr. 4-8). 1992. PLB 12.40 (*0-531-17346-1*, Gloucester Pr) Watts.
—Polluting the Sea. (Illus.). 32p. (gr. 4-8). 1991. PLB 12.40 (*0-531-17290-2*, Gloucester Pr) Watts.

—Rainforest Destruction. (Illus.). 32p. (gr. 5-8). 1990. PLB 12.40 (*0-531-17248-1*, Gloucester Pr) Watts.
—Recycling. (Illus.). 32p. (gr. k-4). 1991. PLB 11.90 (*0-531-17352-6*, Gloucester Pr) Watts.
—Toxic Waste. LC 91-8666. (Illus.). 32p. (gr. 5-8). 1991. PLB 12.40 (*0-531-17308-9*, Gloucester Pr) Watts.
—Vanishing Habitats. (Illus.). 32p. (gr. k-4). 1991. PLB 11.90 (*0-531-17350-X*, Gloucester Pr) Watts.
Harel, Nira. La Escuela de Maria. Writer, C. C. & Nielsen, Lisa C., trs. Eagle, Mike, illus. (SPA.). 24p. (Orig.). (ps). 1992. pap. text ed. 3.00x (*1-56134-153-3*) Dushkin Pub.
—Maria's School. Kriss, David, tr. from HEB. Eagle, Mike, illus. 24p. (Orig.). (ps). 1992. pap. text ed. 3.00x (*1-56134-143-6*) Dushkin Pub.
Hargreaves, Roger. Mr. Greedy. 32p. (ps-k). 1980. 1.75 (*0-8431-0817-7*) Price Stern.
Hargittai, Magdolna. Cooking the Hungarian Way. (Illus.). 48p. (gr. 5 up). 1986. PLB 14.95 (*0-8225-0916-6*) Lerner Pubns.
Hargrave, et al. The Cthulhu Casebook: Adventures & Atmosphere for Call of Cthulhu. Petersen, Sandy, ed. Peterson, Sandy & Monroe, John B., eds. Gibbons, Lee, et al, illus. 130p. (Orig.). (gr. 12 up). 1990. pap. 18.95 (*0-933635-67-2*, 3305) Chaosium.
Hargrave, J. Michael & Gibson, Christine R. The Tator Tales: Cool Spuds Avoid Drugs, a Story & Activity Book on Substance Abuse Prevention. Majewski, Chuck, illus. 96p. (Orig.). (gr. 4-8). 1990. pap. 8.95 (*0-9624285-1-5*) Tator Enterprises.
Hargrave, J. Michael, jt. auth. see Gibson, Christine R.
Hargreaves, Adam, jt. auth. see Rojany, Lisa.
Hargreaves, Connie, jt. auth. see Arrigo, Mary.
Hargreaves, Margaret & Davis, Pat. At Home & School. (Illus.). (gr. 1). 1988. text incl. activity program 259.00 (*0-318-41078-8*) Southwinds Pr.
—Extending My World. (gr. 3). 1988. text incl. activity program 259.00 (*0-318-41080-X*) Southwinds Pr.
—My Neighborhood & Me. (gr. 2). 1988. text incl. activity program 259.00 (*0-318-41081-8*) Southwinds Pr.
Hargreaves, Roger. Little Miss Bossy. Hargreaves, Roger, illus. 32p. (ps-k). 1981. 1.75 (*0-8431-0893-2*) Price Stern.
—Little Miss Chatterbox. 32p. (ps-k). 1984. pap. 1.75 (*0-8431-1479-7*) Price Stern.
—Little Miss Contrary. 32p. (ps-k). 1984. pap. 1.75 (*0-8431-1480-0*) Price Stern.
—Little Miss Dotty. 32p. (ps-k). 1984. pap. 1.75 (*0-8431-1478-9*) Price Stern.
—Little Miss Fickle. 32p. (ps-k). 1984. pap. 1.75 (*0-8431-1481-9*) Price Stern.
—Little Miss Giggles. (ps-k). 1984. pap. 1.75 (*0-8431-1475-4*) Price Stern.
—Little Miss Helpful. Hargreaves, Roger, illus. 32p. (ps-k). 1981. pap. 1.75 (*0-8431-0897-5*) Price Stern.
—Little Miss Late. Hargreaves, Roger, illus. 32p. (ps-k). 1981. pap. 1.75 (*0-8431-0896-7*) Price Stern.
—Little Miss Lucky. 32p. (ps-k). 1984. pap. 1.75 (*0-8431-1476-2*) Price Stern.
—Little Miss Magic. 32p. 1982. pap. 1.75 (*0-8431-1483-5*) Price Stern.
—Little Miss Naughty. Hargreaves, Roger, illus. 32p. (ps-k). 1984. pap. 1.75 (*0-8431-0889-4*) Price Stern.
—Little Miss Neat. Hargreaves, Roger, illus. 32p. (ps-k). 1981. pap. 1.75 (*0-8431-0894-0*) Price Stern.
—Little Miss Plump. Hargreaves, Roger, illus. 32p. (ps-k). 1981. pap. 1.75 (*0-8431-0895-9*) Price Stern.
—Little Miss Scatterbrain. Hargreaves, Roger, illus. 32p. (ps-k). 1981. pap. 1.75 (*0-8431-0891-6*) Price Stern.
—Little Miss Shy. (Illus.). 32p. pap. 1.75 (*0-8431-0898-3*) Price Stern.
—Little Miss Star. 32p. (ps-k). 1984. pap. 1.75 (*0-8431-1482-7*) Price Stern.
—Little Miss Sunshine. Hargreaves, Roger, illus. 32p. (ps-k). 1981. 1.75 (*0-8431-0899-1*) Price Stern.
—Little Miss Tiny. Hargreaves, Roger, illus. 32p. (ps-k). 1981. pap. 1.75 (*0-8431-0892-4*) Price Stern.
—Little Miss Trouble. Hargreaves, Roger, illus. 32p. (ps-k). 1981. pap. 1.75 (*0-8431-0890-8*) Price Stern.
—Little Miss Twins. 32p. (ps-k). 1984. pap. 1.75 (*0-8431-1477-0*) Price Stern.
—Mr. Bounce. (ps-k). 1976. 1.75 (*0-8431-0809-6*) Price Stern.
—Mr. Bounce. 32p. (ps up). 1976. PLB 9.95s.p. (*0-87191-814-5*) Creative Ed.
—Mr. Bump. (ps up). 1971. 1.75 (*0-8431-0814-2*) Price Stern.
—Mr. Bump. 32p. (ps up) 1971. PLB 9.95s.p. (*0-87191-815-3*) Creative Ed.
—Mr. Busy. Hargreaves, Roger, illus. 32p. (ps-k). 1980. pap. 1.75 (*0-8431-0818-5*) Price Stern.
—Mr. Chatterbox. 1p. (ps-k). 1991. 1.75 (*0-8431-0808-8*) Price Stern.
—Mr. Clever. Hargreaves, Roger, illus. 32p. (ps-k). 1982. pap. 1.75 (*0-8431-1131-3*) Price Stern.
—Mr. Clumsy. 32p. (ps up). 1978. PLB 9.95s.p. (*0-87191-817-X*) Creative Ed.
—Mr. Daydream. Hargreaves, Roger, illus. 32p. (ps-k). 1982. pap. 1.75 (*0-8431-1127-5*) Price Stern.
—Mr. Dizzy. Hargreaves, Roger, illus. 32p. (ps-k). 1982. pap. 1.75 (*0-8431-1132-1*) Price Stern.
—Mr. Dizzy. 32p. (ps up). 1976. PLB 9.95s.p. (*0-87191-906-0*) Creative Ed.
—Mr. Forgetful. 32p. (ps-k). 1980. 1.75 (*0-8431-0805-3*) Price Stern.
—Mr. Funny. (Illus.). 32p. (ps-3). 1982. pap. 1.75 (*0-8431-0878-9*) Price Stern.

—Mr. Fussy. 32p. (ps-k). 1980. 1.75 (0-8431-0807-X) Price Stern.
—Mr. Grumpy. 32p. (ps-k). 1980. 1.75 (0-8431-0804-5) Price Stern.
—Mr. Happy. (ps-k). 1980. 1.75 (0-8431-0813-4) Price Stern.
—Mr. Impossible. Hargreaves, Roger, illus. 32p. 1981. pap. 1.75 (0-8431-0819-3) Price Stern.
—Mr. Lazy. 32p. (ps-k). 1980. 1.75 (0-8431-0806-1) Price Stern.
—Mr. Messy. 32p. (ps-k). 1980. 1.75 (0-8431-0812-6) Price Stern.
—Mr. Mischief. 32p. (ps-k). 1980. 1.75 (0-8431-0802-9) Price Stern.
—Mr. Muddle. Hargreaves, Roger, illus. 32p. (ps-k). 1981. pap. 1.75 (0-8431-0820-7) Price Stern.
—Mr. Muddle. 32p. (ps up). 1976. PLB 9.95.s.p. (0-87191-910-9) Creative Ed.
—Mr. Noisy. 32p. (ps-k). 1980. 1.75 (0-8431-0810-X) Price Stern.
—Mr. Nonsense. Hargreaves, Roger, illus. 32p. (ps-k). 1981. pap. 1.75 (0-8431-0821-5) Price Stern.
—Mr. Nonsense. 32p. (ps up). 1978. PLB 9.95.s.p. (0-87191-820-X) Creative Ed.
—Mr. Nosey. 32p. (ps-k). 1980. 1.75 (0-8431-0816-9) Price Stern.
—Mr. Quiet. 32p. (ps-k). 1980. 1.75 (0-8431-0803-7) Price Stern.
—Mr. Rush. (Illus.). 32p. (ps-3). 1982. pap. 1.75 (0-8431-0880-0) Price Stern.
—Mr. Silly. 32p. (ps-k). 1980. 1.75 (0-8431-0811-8) Price Stern.
—Mr. Skinny. 32p. (ps up). 1978. PLB 9.95.s.p. (0-87191-823-4) Creative Ed.
—Mr. Slow. (Illus.). 32p. (ps-3). 1982. pap. 1.75 (0-8431-0881-9) Price Stern.
—Mr. Small. Hargreaves, Roger, illus. 32p. (ps-k). 1981. pap. 1.75 (0-8431-0823-1) Price Stern.
—Mr. Small. 32p. (ps up). 1972. PLB 9.95.s.p. (0-87191-824-2) Creative Ed.
—Mr. Sneeze. Hargreaves, Roger, illus. 32p. (ps-k). 1982. pap. 1.75 (0-8431-1125-9) Price Stern.
—Mr. Snow. Hargreaves, Roger, illus. 32p. (ps-k). 1982. pap. 1.75 (0-8431-1133-X) Price Stern.
—Mr. Snow. 32p. (ps up). 1971. PLB 9.95.s.p. (0-87191-915-X) Creative Ed.
—Mr. Stingy. Hargreaves, Roger, illus. 32p. (ps-k). 1982. pap. 1.75 (0-8431-1130-5) Price Stern.
—Mr. Strong. (Illus.). 32p. (ps-3). 1982. pap. 1.75 (0-8431-0877-0) Price Stern.
—Mr. Strong. 32p. (ps up). 1976. PLB 9.95.s.p. (0-87191-917-6) Creative Ed.
—Mr. Tall. Hargreaves, Roger, illus. 32p. (ps-k). 1982. pap. 1.75 (0-8431-1126-7) Price Stern.
—Mr. Tickle. 32p. (ps-k). 1980. 1.75 (0-8431-0815-0) Price Stern.
—Mr. Tickle. 32p. (ps up). 1971. PLB 9.95.s.p. (0-87191-759-9) Creative Ed.
—Mr. Topsy-Turvy. (Illus.). 32p. 1982. pap. 1.75 (0-8431-1129-1) Price Stern.
—Mr. Uppity. (Illus.). 32p. (ps-3). 1982. pap. 1.75 (0-8431-0882-7) Price Stern.
—Mr. Uppity. 32p. (ps up). 1972. PLB 9.95.s.p. (0-87191-920-6) Creative Ed.
—Mr. Worry. (ps-k). 1980. 1.75 (0-8431-0800-2) Price Stern.
—Mr. Wrong. (Illus.). 32p. (ps-3). 1982. pap. 1.75 (0-8431-0879-7) Price Stern.
Hargrove, J. Nelson Mandela: South Africa's Silent Voice of Protest. (Illus.). (gr. 4 up). 1989. 18.60 (0-516-03266-6); pap. 5.95 (0-516-43266-4) Childrens.
Hargrove, James. Martin Van Buren. LC 87-16023. (Illus.). (gr. 3 up). 1987. PLB 17.27 (0-516-01391-2) Childrens.
Hargrove, Jim. Abraham Lincoln (President's Biographies) (Illus.). 100p. (gr. 4-7). 1988. 17.27 (0-516-01359-9); pap. 6.95 (0-516-41359-7) Childrens.
—Belgium. LC 87-36753. (Illus.). 128p. (gr. 5-9). 1988. PLB 26.60 (0-516-02701-8) Childrens.
—Daniel Boone: Pioneer Trailblazer. LC 85-13309. (Illus.). 124p. (gr. 5-7). 1985. PLB 18.60 (0-516-03215-1) Childrens.
—Diego Rivera: Mexican Muralist. LC 89-25453. (Illus.). 128p. (gr. 4 up). 1990. PLB 18.60 (0-516-03268-2); pap. 5.95 (0-516-43268-0) Childrens.
—Dr. An Wang: Computer Pioneer. LC 92-35061. (Illus.). 152p. (gr. 4 up). 1993. PLB 18.60 (0-516-03290-9); pap. 5.95 (0-516-43290-7) Childrens.
—Dwight D. Eisenhower. LC 86-29918. (Illus.). 100p. (gr. 3 up). 1987. PLB 17.27 (0-516-01389-0) Childrens.
—Ferdinand Magellan: First Around the World. LC 89-15781. (Illus.). 128p. (gr. 3 up). 1990. PLB 26.60 (0-516-03051-5) Childrens.
—Germany. LC 91-22645. 128p. (gr. 5-9). 1991. PLB 26.60 (0-516-02601-1) Childrens.
—Harry S. Truman. (Illus.). 100p. (gr. 3 up). 1987. PLB 17.27 (0-516-01388-2) Childrens.
—Lyndon B. Johnson. LC 87-15890. (Illus.). 100p. (gr. 3 up). 1987. 17.27 (0-516-01396-3) Childrens.
—Mark Twain: The Story of Samuel Clemens. LC 83-23157. (Illus.). 128p. (gr. 4 up). 1984. PLB 18.60 (0-516-03204-6) Childrens.
—Martin Sheen: Actor & Activist. LC 91-7793. (Illus.). 152p. (gr. 4 up). 1991. PLB 18.60 (0-516-03274-7); pap. 5.95 (0-516-43274-5) Childrens.
—Nebraska. LC 88-11746. (Illus.). 144p. (gr. 4 up). 1988. PLB 26.60 (0-516-00473-5) Childrens.

—Nebraska. 177p. 1993. text ed. 15.40 (1-56956-140-0) W A T Braille.
—Pablo Casals: Cellist of Conscience. LC 90-21047. (Illus.). 152p. (gr. 4 up). 1991. PLB 18.60 (0-516-03272-0); pap. 5.95 (0-516-43272-9) Childrens.
—Rene-Robert Cavelier, Sieur De La Salle: Explorer of the Mississippi River. LC 89-25442. (Illus.). 128p. (gr. 3 up). 1990. 26.60 (0-516-03054-X) Childrens.
—Richard M. Nixon: The Thirty-Seventh President. LC 84-27416. (Illus.). 128p. (gr. 4 up). 1985. PLB 18.60 (0-516-03212-7) Childrens.
—Steven Spielberg: Amazing Filmmaker. LC 87-13249. (Illus.). 128p. (gr. 4-8). 1988. PLB 18.60 (0-516-03263-1) Childrens.
—The Story of Jonas Salk & the Discovery of the Polio Vaccine. LC 89-25361. (Illus.). 32p. (gr. 3-6). 1990. PLB 13.27 (0-516-04747-7); pap. 3.95 (0-516-44747-5) Childrens.
—The Story of Presidential Elections. LC 88-1021. (Illus.). 31p. (gr. 2-4). 1988. pap. 3.95 (0-516-44737-8) Childrens.
—The Story of the FBI. LC 87-36815. (Illus.). 32p. (gr. 3-6). 1988. PLB 13.27 (0-516-04733-7); pap. 3.95 (0-516-44733-5) Childrens.
—The Story of the Teapot Dome Scandal. LC 89-33785. 32p. (gr. 3-6). 1989. PLB 13.27 (0-516-04722-1); pap. 3.95 (0-516-44722-X) Childrens.
—The Story of the Unification of Germany. LC 91-12650. (Illus.). 32p. (gr. 3-6). 1991. PLB 13.27 (0-516-04761-2); pap. 3.95 (0-516-44761-0) Childrens.
—The Story of Watergate. LC 88-11881. (Illus.). 32p. (gr. 3-6). 1988. PLB 13.27 (0-516-04741-8); pap. 3.95 (0-516-44741-6) Childrens.
—Thomas Jefferson. LC 86-9658. (Illus.). 100p. (gr. 3 up). 1987. PLB 17.27 (0-516-01385-8); pap. 6.95 (0-516-41385-6) Childrens.
Hargrove, Jim, jt. auth. see Nofsinger, Ray.
Hari Dass, Baba. A Child's Garden of Yoga. Thomas, Steven N., photos by. Ault, Karuna, ed. LC 80-80299. (Illus.). 108p. (ps-7). 1980. pap. 9.95 (0-918100-02-X) Sri Rama.
Harik, Elsa M. The Lebanese in America. (Illus.). 96p. (gr. 5 up). 1987. PLB 15.95 (0-8225-0234-8); pap. 5.95 (0-8225-1032-4) Lerner Pubns.
Haring, Keith. The Keith Haring Coloring Book. Haring, Keith, illus. 20p. (Orig.). (ps-5). 1992. pap. 6.95 (1-881270-51-3) FotoFolio.
—My First Coloring Book. Haring, Keith, illus. 32p. (Orig.). (ps-5). 1993. pap. 4.95 (1-881270-61-0) FotoFolio.
Hariton, Anca. Egg Story. LC 91-34588. (Illus.). 24p. (gr. k-2). 1992. 12.00 (0-525-44861-6, DCB) Dutton Child Bks.
Harjo, Lisa, jt. auth. see Harvey, Karen.
Harker, Jillian. Best Friends: Toddler's. Russell, Chris, illus. 26p. (ps). 1992. 3.50 (0-7214-1504-0) Ladybird Bks.
—First Science: Practice at Home Science Activity. James, Claire, illus. 24p. (gr. k-2). 1992. pap. 2.95 wkbk. (0-7214-3244-1) Ladybird Bks.
—Fun with Science: Practice at Home. Sliwinska, Sara, illus. 24p. (Orig.). 1992. pap. 2.95 wkbk. (0-7214-3239-5, S9115-2) Ladybird Bks.
Harkin, Janet Quin see Quin-Harkin, Janet.
Harkonen, Reijo. The Children of China. Pitkanen, Matti A., illus. 40p. (gr. 3-6). 1990. PLB 19.95 (0-87614-394-X) Carolrhoda Bks.
—The Children of Egypt. Pitkanen, Matti A., photos by. (Illus.). 40p. (gr. 3-6). 1991. PLB 19.95 (0-87614-396-6) Carolrhoda Bks.
—The Children of Nepal. Pitkanen, Matti A., illus. 48p. (gr. 3-6). 1990. PLB 19.95 (0-87614-395-8) Carolrhoda Bks.
—The Grandchildren of the Incas. Pitkanen, Matti A., photos by. (Illus.). 40p. (gr. 3-6). 1991. PLB 19.95 (0-87614-397-4) Carolrhoda Bks.
Harkrider, Jack. Getting Started in Journalism. 2nd ed. 128p. (gr. 7-12). 1993. pap. text ed. 8.95 (0-685-62768-3, C5725-7, Natl Textbk); tchr's guide 4.95 (0-685-66252-7, C5726-5, Natl Textbk) NTC Pub Grp.
Harlan, Judith. Bilingualism in the United States: Conflict & Controversy. (Illus.). 128p. (gr. 9-12). 1991. PLB 12.90 (0-531-13001-0) Watts.
—Rachel Carson: Sounding the Alarm: A Biography of Rachel Carson. LC 88-35909. (Illus.). 128p. (gr. 5 up). 1989. RSBE 13.95 (0-87518-407-3, Dillon) Macmillan Child Grp.
Harley, Rex. Mary's Tiger. Porter, Sue, illus. LC 89-49009. 23p. (ps-2). 1990. 13.95 (0-15-200524-2, Gulliver Bks) HarBrace.
—Troublemaker. 160p. (gr. 5-8). 1990. 17.95 (0-575-04471-3, Pub. by Gollancz UK) Trafalgar.
Harley, Ruth. Captain James Cook. new ed. LC 78-18044. (Illus.). 48p. (gr. 4-7). 1979. PLB 10.59 (0-89375-177-4); pap. 3.50 (0-89375-169-3) Troll Assocs.
—Ferdinand Magellan. new ed. LC 78-18058. (Illus.). 48p. (gr. 4-7). 1979. PLB 10.59 (0-89375-176-6); pap. 3.50 (0-89375-168-5) Troll Assocs.
—Henry Hudson. new ed. LC 78-18053. (Illus.). 48p. (gr. 4-7). 1979. PLB 10.59 (0-89375-171-5); pap. 3.50 (0-89375-163-4) Troll Assocs.
Harlow, Jules, ed. see Prose, Francine.
Harlow, Jules, ed. see Simms, Laura & Kozodoy, Ruth.
Harlow, Rosie & Morgan, Gareth. Cycles & Seasons. Peperell, Liz, illus. LC 91-2567. 40p. (gr. 5-8). 1991. PLB 12.90 (0-531-19123-0, Warwick) Watts.

—Energy & Growth. Kuo Kang Chen & Fitzsimmons, Cecilia, illus. 40p. (gr. 5-8). 1991. PLB 12.90 (0-531-19124-9, Warwick) Watts.
—Observing Minibeasts. Kuo Kang Chen, illus. 40p. (gr. 5-8). 1991. PLB 12.90 (0-531-19125-7, Warwick) Watts.
—One Hundred Seventy-Five Amazing Nature Experiments. Kuo Kang Chen, et al, illus. LC 91-21113. 176p. (Orig.). 1992. pap. 12.00 (0-679-82043-4) Random Bks Yng Read.
—The Random House Book of One Thousand One Questions & Answers about Planet Earth. LC 92-15497. (Illus.). 176p. (gr. 4-7). 1993. PLB cancelled (0-679-93699-8); pap. 13.00 (0-679-83699-3) Random Bks Yng Read.
—Trees & Leaves. Peperell, Liz, illus. 40p. (gr. 5-8). 1991. PLB 12.90 (0-531-19126-5, Warwick) Watts.
Harman, Betty & Meador, Nancy. Paco & the Lion of the North. Roberts, Melissa, ed. 112p. (gr. 4-7). 1987. 10.95 (0-89015-598-4, Pub. by Panda Bks) Eakin-Sunbelt.
Harman, Betty & Meador, Nancy, eds. Seven Ears of Corn. Tieman, Peggy, illus. 149p. (gr. 5-9). 1991. pap. 6.00 (0-9630661-0-2) Harman & Meador.
Harmer, Juliet. Prayers for Children. (ps-3). 1990. 12.95 (0-670-83348-7) Viking Child Bks.
—Prayers for Children. LC 92-10624. (gr. 4 up). 1992. 4.99 (0-14-054523-9) Puffin Bks.
Harmer, Mabel. Circus. LC 81-7709. (Illus.). 48p. (gr. k-4). 1981. PLB 15.27 (0-516-01610-5) Childrens.
Harmey, Barbara E. I Used to Be Older. (ps-k). pap. 4.95 (0-317-62508-X) St Martin.
Harmon. My Jesus Pocket Book of Prayer. 1992. write for info. (1-55513-733-4, Chariot Bks) Cook.
Harmon, ed. Prayertime Bible Stories. 1992. write for info. (0-7814-0045-7, Chariot Bks) Cook.
Harmon, Ed & Jarmin, Marge. Haciendome Cargo de Mi Vida: Opciones, Cambios y Yo. Lerma, Olivia, tr. Feign, Larry, illus. (SPA.). (gr. 5-12). 1993. pap. 9.95 (0-918588-26-X) Barksdale Foun.
—Taking Active Charge of Your Life: Facilitator's Manual. Feign, Larry, illus. 149p. (gr. 5-12). 1987. Repr. of 1984 ed. bk. & video or Filmstrip 175.00 (0-918588-09-X) Barksdale Foun.
—Taking Charge of My Life: Choices, Changes & Me. Feign, Larry, illus. LC 88-988. 184p. (Orig.). (gr. 5-12). 1988. pap. 9.95 (0-918588-10-3) Barksdale Foun.
Harmon, James, Jr. How to Go from Geek to Chic (In Less Than 6 Weeks) Adams, Ben, illus. (Orig.). 1987. pap. 4.95 (0-942379-09-8) Wild Bore Bks.
Harmon, Jeannie, ed. Gerbert Let's Read a Story: Bible Favorites for Girls & Boys. LC 92-14580. 1992. write for info. (0-7814-0934-9, Chariot Bks) Cook.
Harmon, Jeannie, ed. see Hansel, Tim.
Harms, Larry, jt. auth. see Clary, Linda.
Harms, Valerie. Frolic's Dance. Chapin, Tom, narrated by. Buzzanco, Eileen M., illus. LC 88-64155. 32p. (gr. k-4). 1989. 11.95 (0-924483-01-6); incl. audiocassette 16.95 (0-924483-04-0); incl. audiocassette & toy combination 39.95 (0-924483-07-5); incl. audiocassette & small toy combination 25.95 (0-924483-37-7); pap. 5.95 (0-924483-77-6); write for info. (0-924483-10-5) Soundprints.
Harnack, Andrew. Writing Research Papers: A Student Guide for the Use with Opposing Viewpoints. LC 93-4317. 1994. 9.95 (1-56510-099-9) Greenhaven.
Harner, Carol. The Three Sisters Cookbook: Recipes & Remembrances. (Illus.). 164p. (Orig.). (gr. 12). 1989. pap. 9.95 (0-685-26082-8) Harner Pubns.
Harner, David L. Attracting & Feeding Wild Birds in the Prescott Area. (Illus.). 96p. (Orig.). (gr. 12). 1989. pap. 3.95 (0-685-26081-X) Harner Pubns.
—How to Publish a Tabloid Shopper. (Illus.). 248p. (Orig.). (gr. 12). 1989. pap. 22.95 (0-685-26080-1) Harner Pubns.
Harner, Ruth. Rejoicing with Joy. Butcher, Sam, illus. 21p. (gr. k-6). 1988. pap. text ed. 4.25 (1-55976-145-8) CEF Press.
—Send Someone to Tell Me. Smith, Dale, illus. 16p. (gr. k-6). 1988. pap. text ed. 4.25 (1-55976-135-0) CEF Press.
—Ti-Fam: Witch Doctor's Daughter. (Illus.). 40p. (gr. k-6). 1986. pap. text ed. 8.99 (1-55976-051-6) CEF Press.
Harness, Cheryl. The Queen with Bees in Her Hair. Harness, Cheryl, illus. LC 92-14429. 32p. (ps-3). 1993. PLB 14.95 (0-8050-1715-1, Bks Young Read) H Holt & Co.
—Three Young Pilgrims. Harness, Cheryl, illus. LC 91-7289. 40p. (gr. k-5). 1992. RSBE 15.95 (0-02-742643-2, Bradbury Pr) Macmillan Child Grp.
—The Windchild. Harness, Cheryl, illus. LC 90-46372. 32p. (ps-4). 1991. 14.95 (0-8050-0558-7, Bks Young Read) H Holt & Co.
—Young John Quincy. Harness, Cheryl, illus. LC 92-37266. 48p. (gr. k-5). 1994. RSBE 15.95 (0-02-742644-0, Bradbury Pr) Macmillan Child Grp.
Harnett, Cynthia. Cargo of the Madalena. Harnett, Cynthia, illus. LC 83-24874. 240p. (gr. 5 up). 1984. 13.50 (0-8225-0890-7) Lerner Pubns.
—The Great House. Harnett, Cynthia, illus. LC 83-24880. 180p. (gr. 5 up). 1984. 13.50 (0-8225-0893-1) Lerner Pubns.
—The Merchant's Mark. Harnett, Cynthia, illus. LC 83-24879. 192p. (gr. 5 up). 1984. 13.50 (0-8225-0891-5) Lerner Pubns.

—The Sign of the Green Falcon. Harnett, Cynthia, illus. LC 83-24831. 288p. (gr. 5 up). 1984. 13.50 (0-8225-0888-5) Lerner Pubns.
—Stars of Fortune. Harnett, Cynthia, illus. LC 83-24836. 288p. (gr. 5 up). 1984. 13.50 (0-8225-0892-3) Lerner Pubns.
—The Writing on the Hearth. Floyd, Gareth, illus. LC 83-23904. 300p. (gr. 5 up). 1984. PLB 13.50 (0-8225-0889-3) Lerner Pubns.
Harnett, Juli O. & Oxman, Fannie-Rose. Goodbye Hello. (Illus.). 25p. (Orig.). (gr. 2-6). 1988. pap. 6.95 (0-9620137-0-6) Lumanett Pr.
Haron, jt. auth. see Amery.
Harp, Bill, ed. Assessment & Evaluation in Whole Language Programs. 296p. (gr. k-6). 1991. text ed. 32.95 (0-926842-06-4) CG Pubs Inc.
Harp, David. Make Me Musical: Instant Harmonica Education for Kids. 2nd, rev. ed. (Illus.). (ps-4). 1989. pap. 19.95 (0-918321-15-8); cassette & harmonica incl. Musical Idiot.
Harper, et al. Flashpoints, 7 bks, Set I, Reading Level 8. (Illus.). 560p. (gr. 7 up). 1988. PLB 130.20 (0-86592-025-7); 97.65s.p. (0-685-58792-4) Rourke Corp.
Harper, Anita. It's Not Fair. Hellard, Susan, illus. LC 86-4950. 24p. (ps-k). 1986. 10.95 (0-399-21365-1, Philomel) Putnam Pub Group.
Harper, Jo. The Harper's Voices: Caves & Cowboys: Family Song Book. George, R. Jefferson, photos by. Boustany, Robert, illus. (ENG & SPA.). 20p. (Orig.). (gr. 1-5). 1988. pap. 8.95 incl. cassette (0-929932-00-5) JCH Pr.
—Jalapeno Hal. Haris, Jennifer B., illus. LC 92-16921. 40p. (ps-2). 1993. RSBE 14.95 (0-02-742645-9, Four Winds) Macmillan Child Grp.

—Pals, Potions, & Pixies: Family Songbook. George, R. Jefferson, photos by. Boustany, Robert, illus. (SPA & ENG.). 20p. (Orig.). (gr. 1-5). 1988. pap. 8.95 incl. cassette (0-929932-01-3) JCH Pr.
PALS, POTIONS, & PIXIES is a read-along songbook. New, original songs. Bright colors. Lively illustrations for each song. Upbeat, modern rhythms. 50 minutes of music, one side cassette vocals, one side instrumental. Educator approved. Family values. Five children in a family sing about their experiences. Companion volume to CAVES & COWBOYS, FAMILY SONGBOOK. By the author of JALAPENO HAL. *Publisher Provided Annotation.*

Harper, Peter & Peplow, Evelyn. Philippines Handbook. (Illus.). 596p. (Orig.). 1991. pap. 12.95 (0-918373-62-X) Moon Pubns CA.
Harper, Wilhelmina, ed. Gunniwolf. Wiesner, William, illus. LC 67-22387. 32p. (ps-3). 1970. 13.00 (0-525-31139-4, DCB) Dutton Child Bks.
Harper-Deiters, Cyndi. Jonathan Michael & Mother Nature's Fury. Ruggles, Robert & Ruggles, Grace, eds. Bowers, Helen M., illus 36p. (Orig.). (gr. 2-4). 1993. pap. text ed. 4.95x (0-9632513-2-5) Cntry Home.
—Jonathan Michael & the Perilous Flight. Ruggles, Robert & Ruggles, Grace, eds. (Illus.). 34p. (Orig.). (gr. 2-5). 1993. pap. text ed. 4.95x (0-685-66847-9) Cntry Home.
—Jonathan Michael & the Perilous Flight. Ruggles, Robert & Ruggles, Grace, eds. Bowers, Helen M., illus. 34p. (gr. 2-4). Date not set. pap. 4.95 (0-9632513-3-3) Cntry Home.
—Jonathan Michael & the Uninvited Guest. Ruggles, Robert & Ruggles, Grace, eds. Bowers, Helen M., illus. 34p. (Orig.). (gr. 2-4). 1992. pap. text ed. 4.95x (0-9632513-1-7) Cntry Home.

—The Jonathan Michael Series. Ruggles, Robert & Ruggles, Grace, eds. Bowers, Helen M., illus. (Orig.). (gr. 2-5). 1993. pap. text ed. write for info. (0-9632513-4-1) Cntry Home.
This series is designed to encourage 2-5 grade readers to problem-solve without the use of physical violence. The complete set will include ten books, with two books being released annually. The masterful illustrations by HELEN M. BOWERS depict the events of each story as they unfold. Meet JONATHAN MICHAEL & his barnyard friends in the introductory story, JONATHAN MICHAEL THE RESIDENT ROOSTER. Mrs. Skunk

& her babies move in underneath the house porch in the second book, JONATHAN MICHAEL & THE UNINVITED GUEST. Can JONATHAN MICHAEL through advisory problem-solving methods convince her to move before they are discovered & destroyed? JONATHAN MICHAEL & MOTHER NATURE'S FURY, the third book, emphasizes completing a task regardless of the obstacles. Will JONATHAN MICHAEL'S rescue mission for a lost chick in the violent storm come in time? Find out the importance of team work in the FORTHCOMING fourth book, JONATHAN MICHAEL & THE PERILOUS FLIGHT. Will JONATHAN MICHAEL & his barnyard friends find a south-bound flock for Ercella, a young duck, to join before it is too late? Country Home Publishers, 930 N. Osborn, White Cloud, MI 49349. (616) 924-0817. *Publisher Provided Annotation.*

—Jonathan Michael: The Resident Rooster. LC 92-70663. 40p. (gr. 3). 1992. pap. 4.95 (0-9632513-0-9) Cntry Home.
Harpstead, Milo I., et al. Soil Science Simplified. 2nd ed. (Illus.). 204p. (gr. 9-12). 1988. text ed. 21.95 (0-8138-1514-2); wkbk. 8.95 (0-8138-1512-6) Iowa St U Pr.
Harrah, Madge. Honey Girl. 128p. 1990. pap. 2.95 (0-380-75828-8, Camelot) Avon.
—No Escape. 112p. (Orig.). 1993. pap. 3.50 (0-380-76569-1, Camelot) Avon.
Harranth, Wolf. My Old Grandad. Oppermann-Dimow, Christina, illus. Carter, Peter, tr. (Illus.). 30p. (ps-6). 1987. 11.95 (0-19-279787-5) OUP.
Harrar, George. Radical Robots: Can You Be Replaced? (Illus.). 48p. (gr. 5 up). 1990. (S&S BFYR); pap. 5.95 (0-671-69421-9, S&S BFYR) S&S Trade.
Harrar, George & Harrar, Linda. Signs of the Apes, Songs of the Whales. LC 89-30061. (Illus.). (gr. 3 up). 1989. pap. 14.95 (0-671-67748-9, S&S BFYR); pap. 5.95 (0-671-67767-5, S&S BFYR) S&S Trade.
Harrar, Linda, jt. auth. see Harrar, George.
Harrast, Tracy & Craft, Louise. Discover Ancient Egypt: Activity Book. Girdler, Netta & Belcher, Cynthia, illus. 24p. (gr. 2-7). 1990. wkbk. 2.95 (0-911239-28-6) Carnegie Mus.
—Discover Ancient Egypt at the Carnegie. (Illus.). 24p. (gr. 3-7). 1990. wkbk. 2.95 (0-911239-27-8) Carnegie Mus.
Harrell, Irene B. Little History of Star Books. rev. ed. 1990. 0.50 (0-915541-85-8) Star Bks Inc.
Harrell, Janice. Dead Girls Can't Scream. 1993. pap. 3.50 (0-06-106790-3, Harp PBks) HarpC.
—Dusty Brannigan. 160p. (Orig.). 1993. pap. 3.50 (0-380-76113-0, Flare) Avon.
—The Great Egg Bust. Ashby, Ruth, ed. Montgomery, Lucy, illus. 112p. (Orig.). 1993. pap. 2.99 (0-671-72861-X, Minstrel Bks) PB.
—Tiffany, the Disaster. Ashby, Ruth, ed. 112p. (Orig.). (gr. 3-6). 1992. pap. 2.99 (0-671-72860-1, Minstrel Bks) PB.
Harrell, John. Here Comes Maurice: A Musical for One Puppet. (Illus.). 15p. (gr. 6 up). 1987. Incls. cassette. pap. 10.95 (0-9615389-6-1) York Hse.
Harrill, Ronald. Makeda, Queen of Sheba. LC 93-60916. (Illus.). 50p. (gr. 2-8). 1994. pap. 7.95 (1-55523-651-0) Winston-Derek.
Harrill, Suzanne E. Empowering Teens to Build Self-Esteem. Wilkensen, Diane, illus. 80p. (Orig.). (gr. 5-12). 1993. pap. 8.95 (1-883648-00-9) Innerworks Pub.
—I Am a Star. DiaGrammatics Staff, illus. 50p. (Orig.). (gr. 1-6). 1992. pap. write for info. (0-9625996-3-8); business-size cards 8.95 (0-685-52563-5) Innerworks Pub.
—The I Love the Earth Book: A Coloring Book. Harrill, Sarah, illus. 12p. (ps-2). 1992. write for info. (0-9625996-4-6) Innerworks Pub.
Harriman, Edward. Leroy the Lobster & Crabby Crab. (Illus.). (ps-1). 1967. pap. 7.95 (0-89272-000-X) Down East.
Harriman, Marinell & Harriman, Robert. A Myriad of Minstrels. Harriman, Marinell & Harriman, Robert, illus. 32p. (Orig.). (gr. 5-7). pap. 3.50 (0-940920-00-X) Drollery Pr.
Harriman, Robert, jt. auth. see Harriman, Marinell.
Harrington, John P. Indian Tales from Picuris Pueblo. Roberts, Helen H. & Roberts, Helen H.contrib. by. LC 88-72051. (Illus.). 104p. (gr. 3 up). 1989. 22.95 (0-941270-51-3); pap. 10.95 (0-941270-50-5) Ancient City Pr.
Harrington, John P., ed. see Clark, Ann N.
Harrington, Lois G., ed. see Chadwick, Charley G., et al.

Harrington, M. R. The Indians of New Jersey: Dickon Among the Lenapes. LC 63-15519. (Illus.). (gr. 4-6). 1963. pap. 9.95x (0-8135-0425-2) Rutgers U Pr.
—The Iroquois Trail: Dickon among the Onondagas & Senecas. Perceval, Don, illus. 215p. 1991. pap. 9.95 (0-8135-0480-5) Rutgers U Pr.
Harrington, Ty. Maine. LC 88-38399. (Illus.). 144p. (gr. 4 up). 1989. PLB 26.60 (0-516-00465-4) Childrens.
—Maine. 179p. 1993. text ed. 15.40 (1-56956-157-5) W A T Braille.
Harrington, William F. Theories of Muscle Contraction. Head, J. J., ed. LC 77-94953. (Illus.). 32p. (gr. 10 up). 1981. pap. 3.00 (0-89278-314-1, 45-9714) Carolina Biological.
Harriot, Ray. Stories for Around the Campfire. 2nd ed. (Illus.). 224p. (gr. 5-10). 1986. pap. 5.95 (0-317-93072-9) Campfire Pub.
Harris. Communicable Diseases. 1993. write for info. (0-8050-3040-9) H Holt & Co.
—Hereditary Diseases. 1993. write for info. (0-8050-3042-5) H Holt & Co.
—Learning Disorders. 1993. write for info. (0-8050-3043-3) H Holt & Co.
—One Hundred One Wacky Facts about Mummies. 1992. pap. 1.95 (0-590-44889-7) Scholastic Inc.
Harris, Alan, jt. auth. see Weissman, Paul.
Harris, Alan, ed. Birds. LC 92-54484. 1993. 12.95 (1-56458-216-7) Dorling Kindersley.
Harris, Anne, jt. auth. see Waters, Elizabeth.
Harris, Aurand. Androcles & the Lion: Musical. 1964. 4.50 (0-87602-105-4) Anchorage.
—The Arkansaw Bear. (Orig.). (gr. 5 up). 1980. playscript 4.50 (0-87602-226-3) Anchorage.
—The Brave Little Tailor. 1961. 4.50 (0-87602-109-7) Anchorage.
—Buffalo Bill. 1954. 4.50 (0-87602-110-0) Anchorage.
—A Doctor in Spite of Himself. 1968. 4.50 (0-87602-120-8) Anchorage.
—The Flying Prince. (Orig.). (gr. k up). 1985. 4.50 (0-87602-262-X) Anchorage.
—Huck Finn's Story. 42p. 1988. Playscript. 4.50 (0-87602-280-8) Anchorage.
—Just So Stories: Musical. 1971. 4.50 (0-87602-145-3) Anchorage.
—Monkey Magic: Chinese Story Theatre. 58p. (Orig.). (ps-8). 1990. pap. 4.50 playscript (0-87602-290-5) Anchorage.
—No Dogs Allowed (or Junket) 43p. 1959. 4.50 (0-87602-164-X) Anchorage.
—Peck's Bad Boy. (gr. 1-9). 1974. playscript 4.50 (0-87602-170-4) Anchorage.
—The Pinballs. 1992. pap. 4.50 playscript (0-87602-301-4) Anchorage.
—The Plain Princess: Musical. 1955. 4.50 (0-87602-176-3) Anchorage.
—Pocahontas. 1961. 4.50 (0-87602-177-1) Anchorage.
—Punch & Judy: Musical. 47p. (Orig.). 1970. 4.50 (0-87602-183-6) Anchorage.
—Rags to Riches: Musical. 1966. 4.50 (0-87602-185-2) Anchorage.
—Ride a Blue Horse. 44p. (Orig.). (gr. k-3). 1986. pap. 4.50 playscript (0-87602-264-6) Anchorage.
—Star Spangled Salute. (gr. 1-12). 1974. 4.50 (0-87602-205-0) Anchorage.
—Steal Away Home: Musical. (gr. 1-9). 1972. 4.50 (0-87602-206-9) Anchorage.
—A Toby Show. (gr. k up). 1978. 4.50 (0-87602-210-7) Anchorage.
—Treasure Island. (gr. 4 up). 1983. pap. 4.50 (0-87602-253-0) Anchorage.
—Yankee Doodle: Musical. (gr. 1-7). 1975. 4.50 (0-87602-223-9) Anchorage.
Harris, Aurand & Shakespeare, William. Robin Goodfellow. 1977. 4.50 (0-87602-190-9) Anchorage.
Harris, Aurand, jt. auth. see Jennings, Coleman A.
Harris, Aurand, selected by. Short Plays of Theatre Classics. 1991. 30.00 (0-87602-032-5) Anchorage.
Harris, Betsy. Here in My Heart. LC 89-20419. 128p. (gr. 5-9). 1989. pap. text ed. 2.95 (0-8167-1911-X) Troll Assocs.
—Only Friends. LC 89-20371. 128p. (gr. 5-9). 1990. pap. text ed. 2.95 (0-8167-1912-8) Troll Assocs.
Harris, Colin. Protecting the Planet. LC 93-18936. (Illus.). 32p. (gr. 4-6). 1993. 14.95 (1-56847-055-X) Thomson Lrning.
Harris, Deborah. Sweet Clara & the Freedom Quilt. Ransome, James, illus. LC 91-11601. 40p. (gr. k-5). 1993. 15.00 (0-679-82311-5) Knopf Bks Yng Read.
—Sweet Clara & the Freedom Quilt. LC 91-11601. (Illus.). 40p. (gr. k-5). 1993. PLB 15.99 (0-679-92311-X) Knopf Bks Yng Read.
Harris, Denise, illus. The Kitten Pop-up Book. Costello, Linda, contrib. by. LC 90-85726. (Illus.). 12p. (ps-3). 1991. 9.95 (1-878093-04-5) Boyds Mills Pr.
Harris, E. Trees. (Illus.). 64p. (gr. 10 up). 1993. pap. 4.50 (0-7460-1627-1) EDC.
Harris, Edward D. John Charles Fremont & the Great Western Reconnaissance. Goetzmann, William H., ed. Collins, Michael, intro. by. (Illus.). 112p. (gr. 5 up). 1990. lib. bdg. 18.95 (0-7910-1312-X) Chelsea Hse.
Harris, Edward N., compiled by. The Rice Fairy: Karen Stories from Southeast Asia. LC 89-21946. (Illus.). 105p. (gr. 4-6). 1989. Repr. of 1987 ed. lib. bdg. 20.00 (0-929225-33-3) Simplicity Pr.
Harris, Emily. Hilary & Lars. LC 88-50753. 82p. (gr. 5-8). 1988. 6.95 (1-55523-148-9) Winston-Derek.
Harris, Frank. Great Games to Play with Groups. (gr. 1 up). 1989. 9.95 (0-8224-3379-6) Fearon Teach Aids.

Harris, Geraldine. Ancient Egypt. (Illus.). 96p. 1990. 17. 95 *(0-8160-1971-1)* Facts on File.
—The Children of the Wind. (gr. k-12). 1987. pap. 2.50 *(0-440-91210-5,* LFL) Dell.
—The Dead Kingdom. (gr. k-12). 1987. pap. 2.50 *(0-440-91810-3,* LFL) Dell.
—Gods & Pharaohs from Egyptian Mythology. O'Connor, David & Sibbick, John, illus. LC 90-23455. 132p. (gr. 6 up). 1992. 22.50 *(0-87226-907-8)* P Bedrick Bks.
—Gods & Pharaohs from Egyptian Mythology. O'Connor, David & Sibbick, John, illus. 128p. (gr. 6 up). 1993. pap. 14.95 sewn *(0-87226-908-6)* P Bedrick Bks.
—Prince of the Godborn. (gr. k-12). 1987. pap. 2.50 *(0-440-95407-X,* LFL) Dell.
—The Seventh Gate, No. 4. (gr. k-12). 1987. pap. 2.95 *(0-440-97747-9,* LFL) Dell.
Harris, Gregg & Harris, Josh. Uncommon Courtesy for Kids Kit. 56p. 1990. pap. text ed. 13.00 *(0-923463-72-0)* Noble Pub Assocs.
Harris, Gregg, ed. see Purtell, April, et al.
Harris, Hazel. The History of South Carolina in the Building of the Nation. (Illus.). 330p. (gr. 8). 1991. tchr's ed. 15.00 *(0-9628232-1-X)* A G Furman.
Harris, Jack. Batman: The Case of the Sticky Fingers. (ps-3). 1990. pap. write for info. *(0-307-12607-2)* Western Pub.
—The Kentucky Derby. 32p. (gr. 4). 1990. PLB 14.95 s.p. *(0-88682-312-9)* Creative Ed.
—Test Pilots. LC 89-31126. (Illus.). 48p. (gr. 4-5). 1989. RSBE 11.95 *(0-89686-429-4,* Crestwood Hse) Macmillan Child Grp.
—The Winter Olympics. 32p. (gr. 4). 1990. PLB 14.95 s.p. *(0-88682-317-X)* Creative Ed.
Harris, Jack C. Adventure Gaming. LC 91-3885. (Illus.). 48p. (gr. 5 up). 1993. lib. bdg. 12.95 RSBE *(0-89686-621-1,* Crestwood Hse) Macmillan Child Grp.
—Big Boats, Little Boats. (Illus.). 24p. (ps). 1990. pap. write for info. *(0-307-11667-0,* Pub. by Golden Bks) Western Pub.
—Dream Cars. LC 88-1827. (Illus.). 48p. (gr. 5-6). 1988. RSBE 11.95 *(0-89686-376-X,* Crestwood Hse) Macmillan Child Grp.
—The Greenhouse Effect. LC 90-36294. (Illus.). 48p. (gr. 5-6). 1990. RSBE 12.95 *(0-89686-543-6,* Crestwood Hse) Macmillan Child Grp.
—Gun Control. (Illus.). 48p. (gr. 4 up). 1990. 12.95 *(0-89686-493-6,* Crestwood Hse) Macmillan Child Grp.
—Milwaukee Bucks. (Illus.). 32p. (gr. 4 up). 1993. PLB 14.95 *(0-88682-541-5)* Creative Ed.
—My First Book of Fire Trucks. (Illus.). 24p. (ps). 1990. pap. write for info. *(0-307-11666-2,* Pub. by Golden Bks) Western Pub.
—New Jersey Nets. (gr. 5 up). 1993. PLB 14.95 *(0-88682-516-4)* Creative Ed.
—Personal Watercraft. LC 88-18930. (Illus.). 48p. (gr. 5-6). 1988. RSBE 11.95 *(0-89686-377-8,* Crestwood Hse) Macmillan Child Grp.
—Plastic Model Kits. LC 91-25201. (Illus.). 48p. (gr. 5 up). 1993. lib. bdg. 12.95 RSBE *(0-89686-623-8,* Crestwood Hse) Macmillan Child Grp.
—A Step-by-Step Book about Guppies. (Illus.). 64p. (gr. 9-12). 1988. pap. 3.95 *(0-86622-464-5,* SK-035) TFH Pubns.
Harris, Jacqueline L. Communicable Diseases. (Illus.). 64p. (gr. 5-8). 1993. PLB 14.95 *(0-8050-2599-5)* TFC Bks NY.
—Drugs & Disease. (Illus.). 64p. (gr. 5-8). 1993. PLB 14. 95 *(0-8050-2602-9)* TFC Bks NY.
—Environmental Diseases. (Illus.). 64p. (gr. 5-8). 1993. PLB 14.95 *(0-8050-2600-2)* TFC Bks NY.
—Hereditary Diseases. (Illus.). 64p. (gr. 5-8). 1993. PLB 14.95 *(0-8050-2603-7)* TFC Bks NY.
—The History & Achievement of the NAACP. LC 92-8930. (Illus.). 160p. (gr. 9-12). 1992. PLB 13.90 *(0-531-11035-4)* Watts.
—Learning Disorders. (Illus.). 64p. (gr. 5-8). 1993. PLB 14.95 *(0-8050-2604-5)* TFC Bks NY.
—Nutritional Diseases. (Illus.). 64p. (gr. 5-8). 1993. PLB 14.95 *(0-8050-2601-0)* TFC Bks NY.
—Science in Ancient Rome. Rasof, Henry, ed. LC 88-2649. (Illus.). 72p. (gr. 5-8). 1988. PLB 10.90 *(0-531-10595-4)* Watts.
Harris, James B., tr. see Rampo, Edogawa.
Harris, Jeanette M. & Harben, Peter W. Mined It! A Fairy Tale with Mineral Content. 60p. (gr. 1-12). 1992. pap. text ed. 12.98 *(0-9632303-0-1)* Butternut Bks.
Harris, Jennifer. What Was I Like? Childhood Memory Book Series, 6 bks, Set 1. Innes, George C., illus. (ps). 1992. Set. slipcased 49.95 *(1-879956-12-8)* Tintern Abbey.
—What Was I Like? Childhood Memory Book Series, 5 bks, Set 2. Innes, George C., illus. (ps). 1992. Set. slipcased 49.95 *(1-879956-13-6)* Tintern Abbey.
Harris, Jesse. The Vampire's Kiss. LC 92-9019. 1992. 9.99 *(0-679-93669-6)* Knopf.
Harris, Joel C. Brer Rabbit & the Wonderful Tar Baby. Drescher, Henrik, illus. 64p. 1992. Repr. of 1990 ed. Mini-bk. incl. cass. 9.95 *(0-88708-250-5,* Rabbit Ears) Picture Bk Studio.
—Complete Tales of Uncle Remus. Chase, Richard, ed. (Illus.). 832p. (gr. 7 up). 1955. 35.00 *(0-395-06799-5)* HM.

—Favorite Uncle Remus. Van Santvoord, George & Coolidge, Archibald C., eds. Van Santvoord, George & Coolidge, Archibald C., illus. 320p. (gr. 4-8). 1973. 17. 45 *(0-395-06800-2)* HM.
—Jump Again! More Adventures of Brer Rabbit. Moser, Barry, illus. & adapted by. 40p. (ps-3). 1987. 16.95 *(0-15-241352-9,* HB Juv Bks) HarBrace.
—Jump: The Adventures of Brer Rabbit. Parks, Van D. & Jones, Malcolm, eds. Goldberg, Whoopi, read by. LC 86-7654. (Illus.). 40p. (ps-3). 1986. 15.95 *(0-15-241350-2,* HB Juv Bks) HarBrace.
—Little Treasury of Br'er Rabbit, 6 vols. 1988. Set. 5.99 *(0-517-66567-0)* Outlet Bk Co.
—Uncle Remus & Br'er Rabbit. 1986. Repr. lib. bdg. 17. 95x *(0-89966-540-3)* Buccaneer Bks.
—Uncle Remus Stories. (gr. 5-6). 22.95 *(0-89190-311-9,* Pub. by Am Repr) Amereon Ltd.
—Walt Disney's Uncle Remus Stories. Palmer, Marion, ed. Dempster, Al & Justice, Bill, illus. (gr. 3-5). 1964. write for info. *(0-307-15551-X,* Golden Bks) Western Pub.
Harris, Joel C. & Metaxas, Eric, eds. Brer Rabbit & the Wonderful Tar Baby. Drescher, Henrik, illus. LC 90-7166. 32p. (gr. k up). 1991. pap. 14.95 *(0-88708-144-4,* Rabbit Ears) pap. 19.95 incl. cass. *(0-88708-145-2,* Rabbit Ears) Picture Bk Studio.
Harris, John, jt. auth. see Loring, Honey.
Harris, Jonathan. Drugged America. LC 90-47649. 192p. (gr. 7 up). 1991. SBE 14.95 *(0-02-742745-5,* Four Winds) Macmillan Child Grp.
—Drugged Athletes: The Crisis in American Sports. LC 86-29396. 204p. (gr. 5-9). 1987. SBE 14.95 *(0-02-742740-4,* Four Winds) Macmillan Child Grp.
—The Land & People of France. LC 88-19211. (Illus.). 256p. (gr. 6 up). 1989. 18.00 *(0-397-32320-4,* Lipp Jr Bks); PLB 17.89 *(0-397-32321-2,* Lipp Jr Bks) HarpC Child Bks.
—This Drinking Nation. (Illus.). 208p. (gr. 5 up). 1994. SBE 15.95 *(0-02-742744-7,* Four Winds) Macmillan Child Grp.
Harris, Josh, jt. auth. see Harris, Gregg.
Harris, Kathleen K., jt. auth. see Pohl, Constance.
Harris, Kathleen M. The Wonderful Hay Tumble. Gackenbach, Dick, illus. LC 87-12305. 32p. (ps-2). 1988. 12.95 *(0-688-07151-1);* PLB 12.88 *(0-688-07152-X,* Morrow Jr Bks) Morrow Jr Bks.
Harris, Kemp. Snow: A Big Song Kid Book. (Illus.). 32p. (ps-2). 1993. incl. cass. 16.95 *(1-883181-03-8);* cass. only 4.95 *(1-883181-04-6)* Big Song Bk.
Harris, Laurie L., ed. Biography Today: Profiles of People of Interest to Young Readers. 1993. PLB 42.00 annual cumulation *(1-55888-139-5)* Omnigraphics Inc.
Harris, Leon. Night Before Christmas - in Texas, That Is. Wohlberg, Meg, illus. (gr. k-7). 1977. Repr. of 1952 ed. *(0-88289-175-8)* Pelican.
Harris, Linda B. Las Cruces: An Illustrated History. Ireland, Joe, et al, illus. Priestley, Lee, intro. by. LC 93-22913. 144p. 1993. 29.95 *(0-9623682-5-3)* Arroyo Pr.
Harris, Linda K. Kids' Talk. Auth, Tony, illus. LC 93-16169. 96p. 1993. pap. 6.95 *(0-8362-8019-9)* Andrews & McMeel.
Harris, Lisa. Hockey. LC 93-23282. 1993. write for info. *(0-8114-5781-8)* Raintree Steck-V.
Harris, Lois J. Big Mama. (Illus.). 16p. 1994. saddle-stitch 5.95 *(0-8059-3483-9)* Dorrance.
Harris, Lorle K. The Caribou. LC 88-18953. (Illus.). 60p. (gr. 3 up). 1989. RSBE 13.95 *(0-87518-391-3,* Dillon) Macmillan Child Grp.
Harris, Mark. The Doctor Who Technical Manual. Nathan-Turner, John, intro. by. LC 83-42868. (Illus.). 64p. (gr. 5 up). 1983. lib. bdg. 6.99 *(0-394-96214-1)* Random Bks Yng Read.
Harris, Mark J. Come the Morning. LC 88-24213. 176p. (gr. 5-9). 1989. SBE 13.95 *(0-02-742750-1,* Bradbury Pr) Macmillan Child Grp.
—Solay. LC 92-33012. 160p. (gr. 4-7). 1993. SBE 13.95 *(0-02-742655-6,* Bradbury Pr) Macmillan Child Grp.
Harris, Nancy. Little Engine Number 18. (Illus.). (gr. k-3). 1992. pap. 2.95 *(0-936206-36-5)* Mntn Automation.
Harris, Nathan. Pearl Harbor. (Illus.). 64p. (gr. 6-8). 1987. 19.95 *(0-85219-669-5,* Pub. by Batsford UK) Trafalgar.
Harris, Nathanial. Hitler. (Illus.). 64p. (gr. 7-10). 1989. 19.95 *(0-7134-5961-1,* Pub. by Batsford UK) Trafalgar.
Harris, Nathaniel. The Coal Mines. (Illus.). 64p. (gr. 7-12). 1986. 19.95 *(0-7134-5097-5,* Pub. by Batsford UK) Trafalgar.
—Napoleon. (Illus.). 64p. (gr. 6-9). 1989. 19.95 *(0-7134-5730-9,* Pub. by Batsford UK) Trafalgar.
Harris, Neil. Drugs & Crime. LC 89-31685. (Illus.). 62p. (gr. 10-12). 1990. PLB 12.40 *(0-531-10800-7)* Watts.
Harris, Nicholas. Owlbert. Horvat, Karl J., illus. LC 89-4445. 32p. (gr. 2-3). 1989. PLB 18.60 *(0-8368-0110-5)* Gareth Stevens Inc.
Harris, Paul & Walsh, Adrian. You Can Control the Soccer Ball: World Champion Adrian Walsh's Little Book of Secrets. (Illus.). 48p. (gr. 2-6). 1977. pap. 3.95 *(0-916802-05-1)* Soccer for Am.
Harris, Paula. Pisces. 40p. (gr. 4). 1989. PLB 13.95 s.p. *(0-88682-254-8)* Creative Ed.
—Scorpio. 40p. (gr. 4). 1989. PLB 13.95 s.p. *(0-88682-260-2)* Creative Ed.
Harris, Peter, ed. see Hughes, Paul.
Harris, Peter, ed. see Nash, Paul.
Harris, Randolph. The Terrorists. (Orig.). (ps-12). 1988. pap. 2.50 *(0-87067-283-5)* Holloway.

Harris, Raymond. Best-Selling Chapters: Advanced Level. Anthony, Stephen R. & Suvari, Mari-Ann, illus. 496p. (gr. 9 up). 1978. text ed. 17.00 *(0-89061-706-6, 621H);* pap. text ed. 13.25 *(0-89061-702-3,* 621) Jamestown Pubs.
—Best Short Stories: Advanced Level. Burgoyne, Mari-Ann S., illus. 560p. (Orig.). (gr. 9 up). 1980. text ed. 17.00 *(0-89061-705-8,* 620H); pap. text ed. 13.25 *(0-89061-701-5,* 620) Jamestown Pubs.
—Best Short Stories: Middle Level. Lawrence, George, et al, illus. (gr. 6-10). 1983. text ed. 16.50 *(0-89061-322-2,* 793H); pap. text ed. 12.95 *(0-89061-321-4,* 793) Jamestown Pubs.
Harris, Raymond, ed. Best-Selling Chapters: Middle Level. 2nd ed. 460p. (gr. 6-8). 1994. pap. 13.95 *(0-89061-755-4)* Jamestown Pubs.
—Best-Selling Chapters: Middle Level. 2nd ed. 460p. (gr. 6-8). 1994. text ed. 17.00 *(0-89061-756-2)* Jamestown Pubs.
—Best Short Stories Hardcover: Middle Level. 2nd ed. 460p. (gr. 6-8). 1994. text ed. 17.00 *(0-89061-754-6)* Jamestown Pubs.
—Best Short Stories: Middle Level. 2nd ed. 460p. (gr. 6-8). 1994. pap. 13.95 *(0-89061-753-8)* Jamestown Pubs.
Harris, Richard. I Can Read About Basketball. Milligan, John, illus. LC 76-54397. (gr. 2-5). 1977. pap. 1.95 *(0-89375-032-8)* Troll Assocs.
—I Can Read About Football. Milligan, John, illus. LC 76-54398. (gr. 2-5). 1977. pap. 1.95 *(0-89375-033-6)* Troll Assocs.
—I Can Read About Horses. LC 72-96960. (Illus.). (gr. 2-4). 1973. pap. 1.95 *(0-89375-054-9)* Troll Assocs.
—I Can Read About the Sun & Other Stars. Krasnoborski, William, illus. LC 76-54577. (gr. 2-4). 1977. pap. 1.95 *(0-89375-044-1)* Troll Assocs.
Harris, Robbie & Levy, Elizabeth. Before You Were Three: How You Began to Walk, Talk, Explore & Have Feelings. Gordillo, Henry E., photos by. LC 76-5587. 160p. (gr. 1 up). 1981. pap. 7.95 *(0-440-00471-3)* Delacorte.
Harris, Robert A., jt. auth. see Lasky, Michael S.
Harris, Rosemary. The Bright & Morning Star: The Egyptian Trilogy. 224p. (gr. 3-7). 1991. pap. 4.95 *(0-571-14291-5)* Faber & Faber.
—Child in the Bamboo Grove. Le Cain, Errol, illus. LC 72-4064. (gr. 1-3). 1972. 21.95 *(0-87599-194-7)* S G Phillips.
—The Lotus & the Grail: Legends from East to East. Le Cain, Erro, illus. 272p. (gr. 7 up). 1985. 7.95 *(0-571-13536-6)* Faber & Faber.
—The Moon in the Cloud. (gr. 3-6). 19.75 *(0-8446-6429-4)* Peter Smith.
—Moon in the Cloud. 176p. (gr. 3-6). 1990. pap. 4.95 *(0-571-15338-0)* Faber & Faber.
—The Shadow on the Sun. 192p. (gr. 2-6). 1991. pap. 4.95 *(0-571-14185-4)* Faber & Faber.
—Summers of the Wild Rose. 188p. 1988. 11.95 *(0-571-14702-X)* Faber & Faber.
—Zed. 185p. (gr. 7 up). 1990. pap. 4.95 *(0-571-12922-6)* Faber & Faber.
Harris, Sarah. Finding Out about Life in Britain in the 1950's. (Illus.). 48p. (gr. 7-12). 1985. 19.95 *(0-7134-4424-X,* Pub. by Batsford UK) Trafalgar.
—Finding out About: Women in Twentieth Century Britain, Finding Out About Ser. (Illus.). 48p. (gr. 7-10). 1989. 19.95 *(0-7134-5661-2,* Pub. by Batsford UK) Trafalgar.
—How & Why: The Second World War. (Illus.). 64p. (gr. 7-10). 1989. 19.95 *(0-85219-805-1,* Pub. by Batsford UK) Trafalgar.
—Sharpeville. (gr. 7 up). 1989. 19.95 *(0-85219-767-5,* Pub. by Batsford UK) Trafalgar.
—Timeline: South Africa. (Illus.). 64p. (gr. 7-9). 1988. 19. 95 *(0-85219-724-1,* Pub. by Batsford UK) Trafalgar.
Harris, Stephen, ed. see Martin, Michael.
Harris, Steve, ed. Electronic Gaming - Fall Preview. 84p. 1990. pap. 3.95 *(1-878667-01-7)* Amer Dist Serv.
Harris, Steven M. This Is My Trunk. Welliver, Norma, illus. LC 85-74621. 32p. (ps-4). 1985. SBE 13.95 *(0-689-31128-1,* Atheneum Child Bk) Macmillan Child Grp.
Harris, Susan Y., jt. auth. see Gerstein, Mordicai.
Harris, Tina, et al. Worldwide Wonders. (Illus.). 32p. (gr. 3 up). 1986. incl. hand held Decoder 5.95 *(0-88679-461-7)* Educ Insights.
—Inventions & Discoveries. (Illus.). 32p. (gr. 3 up). 1989. incl. hand held Decoder 5.95 *(0-88679-458-7)* Educ Insights.
Harris, Violet J., ed. Teaching Multicultural Literature in Grades K-8. 296p. (gr. k-8). 1992. text ed. 24.95 *(0-926842-13-7)* CG Pubs Inc.
—Teaching Multicultural Literature in Grades K-8. 296p. (gr. k-8). 1993. pap. 19.95 *(0-926842-30-7)* CG Pubs Inc.
Harriso, Alferdteen. A History of the Most Worshipful Stringer Grand Lodge. 1990. 15.95 *(0-87498-090-9)* Assoc Pubs DC.
Harrison, Ann S. & Spuler, Frances B. Hot Tips for Teachers. (gr. k-8). 1983. pap. 10.95 *(0-8224-3700-7)* Fearon Teach Aids.
Harrison, Barbara & Terris, Daniel. A Twilight Struggle: The Life of John Fitzgerald Kennedy. LC 91-1492. (Illus.). 224p. (gr. 5 up). 1992. 17.00 *(0-688-08830-9)* Lothrop.
Harrison, Brenda M., ed. see Bittinger, Gayle.

Harrison, D. James. Saturn Storm's Broccoli Adventure. LC 89-51459. (Illus.). 44p. (gr. k-3). 1989. 5.95 (*1-55523-278-7*) Winston-Derek.

Harrison, David. Somebody Catch My Homework. 32p. (gr. 4-7). 1993. 13.95 (*1-878093-87-8*) Boyds Mills Pr.

—Wake up! Sun! Wilhelm, Hans, illus. LC 85-30053. 32p. (ps-1). 1986. lib. bdg. 7.99 (*0-394-98256-8*); 3.50 (*0-394-88256-3*) Random Bks Yng Read.

Harrison, David L. When Cows Come Home. Demarest, Chris L., illus. 32p. (ps-3). 1994. 14.95 (*1-56397-143-7*) Boyds Mills Pr.

Harrison, Grant Von see Von Harrison, Grant.

Harrison, Hank, ed. see Joyce, P. W.

Harrison, Henry. Play the Game: Tenpin Bowling. (Illus.). 80p. (gr. 10-12). 1991. pap. 6.95 (*0-7063-6659-X*, Pub. by Ward Lock UK) Sterling.

Harrison House Staff. Confessions for Kids. Titolo, Nancy, illus. 29p. (Orig.). (gr. 1-3). 1984. pap. 0.98 (*0-89274-322-0*) Harrison Hse.

—Prayers That Avail Much, for Children, Bk. 2. 32p. (Orig.). (gr. 1-6). 1990. pap. 3.98 (*0-89274-806-0*, HH806) Harrison Hse.

Harrison, James. The Young People's Atlas of the United States. LC 92-53116. (Illus.). (gr. 3 up). 1992. 17.95 (*1-85697-804-4*) Kingfisher Bks.

Harrison, John, et al. Akbar & the Mughal Empire. Yapp, Malcolm & Killingray, Margaret, eds. (Illus.). 32p. (gr. 6-11). 1980. pap. text ed. 3.45 (*0-89908-006-5*) Greenhaven.

Harrison, Kathryn & Kohn, Valerie. Easy-to-Make Costumes. (Illus.). 80p. (gr. 4 up). 1993. pap. 9.95 (*1-895669-10-9*, Pub. by Tamos Bks CN) Sterling.

Harrison, Maggie. Angels on Roller Skates. (Illus.). 112p. (gr. k-3). 1992. 14.95 (*1-56402-003-7*) Candlewick Pr.

—Lizzie's List. Matthews, Bethan, illus. LC 92-54580. (gr. 3-6). 1993. 14.95 (*1-56402-197-1*) Candlewick Pr.

Harrison, Mark & Tuttle, Lisa. Dreamlands. (Illus.). 128p. (Orig.). (gr. 5 up). 1991. pap. 19.95 (*1-85028-132-7*, PTB UK) Avery Pub.

Harrison, Maureen & Gilbert, Steve. Landmark Decisions of the United States Supreme Court, No. II. LC 90-84578. 237p. 1991. 15.95 (*0-685-57136-X*) Excellent Bks.

Harrison, Michael. The Curse of the Ring. (gr. 5-8). 1987. 18.95 (*0-19-274131-4*) OUP.

—Doom of the Gods. Humphries, Tudor, illus. 80p. (gr. 3 up). 1987. 18.95 (*0-19-274128-4*) OUP.

—Scolding Tongues: The Persecution of Witches. 52p. (gr. 1 up). 1987. pap. 7.95 (*0-85950-543-X*, Pub. by S Thornes UK) Dufour.

Harrison, Michael & Stuart-Clark, Christopher. The Oxford Book of Story Poems. (Illus.). 176p. (gr. 3 up). 1990. jacketed 17.95 (*0-19-276087-4*) OUP.

Harrison, Michael, compiled by. Splinters: A Book of Very Short Poems. Heap, Sue, illus. 128p. (gr. 5 up). 1989. jacketed 10.95 (*0-19-276072-6*) OUP.

Harrison, Michael & Stuart-Clark, Christopher, eds. The Oxford Book of Animal Poems. (Illus.). 160p. 1992. 19.00 (*0-19-276105-6*) OUP.

—The Oxford Book of Christmas Poems. (Illus.). 160p. (gr. 3 up). 1988. 16.95 (*0-19-276051-3*); pap. 10.95 (*0-19-276080-7*) OUP.

—The Oxford Treasury of Children's Poems. (Illus.). 174p. (gr. k up). 1988. 17.95 (*0-19-276055-6*) OUP.

—A Year Full of Poems. (Illus.). 142p. (gr. 3 up). 1991. jacketed 19.95 (*0-19-276097-1*) OUP.

Harrison, Nick. While Yet We Live. 224p. 1991. pap. 6.95 (*0-940652-08-0*) Sunrise Bks.

Harrison, Pat. Jeanne Kirkpatrick. Horner, Matina, intro. by. (Illus.). 112p. (gr. 5 up). 1991. lib. bdg. 17.95 (*1-55546-663-X*) Chelsea Hse.

Harrison, Patricia, jt. auth. see Harrison, Steve.

Harrison, Sidney. The Young Person's Guide to Playing the Piano. 2nd ed. (Illus.). 104p. (Orig.). (gr. 4 up). 1982. pap. 7.95 (*0-571-11864-X*) Faber & Faber.

Harrison, Steve & Harrison, Patricia. Egypt. (Illus.). 48p. (gr. 7-9). 1992. 13.95 (*0-563-34754-6*, BBC-Parkwest); pap. 6.95 (*0-563-34589-6*, BBC-Parkwest) Parkwest Pubns.

Harrison, Supenn & Monroe, Judy. Cooking the Thai Way. (Illus.). 48p. (gr. 5 up). 1986. PLB 14.95 (*0-8225-0917-2*) Lerner Pubns.

Harrison, Susan. AlphaZoo Christmas. Harrison, Susan, illus. LC 93-20351. 40p. (ps-2). 1993. 13.95 (*0-8249-8623-7*, Ideals Child); PLB 14.00 (*0-8249-8632-6*) Hambleton-Hill.

—Twelve Days of Christmas. Harrison, Susan, illus. 24p. (ps-3). 1990. pap. 2.95 (*0-8249-8391-2*, Ideals Child) Hambleton-Hill.

Harrison, Susan, illus. My First Book of Christmas Carols. 24p. 1992. pap. 3.95 (*0-8249-8568-0*, Ideals Child) Hambleton-Hill.

Harrison, Susan J. Christmas with the Bears. Harrison, Susan J., illus. (Illus.). (gr. up). 1987. PLB 9.95 (*0-525-44329-0*, 0966-290, DCB) Dutton Child Bks.

Harrison, Ted. Children of the Yukon. LC 77-79543. (Illus.). (gr. 1-4). 1977. pap. 6.95 (*0-88776-163-1*) Tundra Bks.

—A Northern Alphabet. Harrison, Ted, illus. LC 82-50244. 32p. (ps-1). 1989. 14.95 (*0-88776-209-3*); pap. 6.95 (*0-88776-233-6*) Tundra Bks.

—O Canada. LC 92-39800. 1993. 14.45 (*0-395-66075-0*) Ticknor & Fields.

Harrison, Troon. The Long Weekend. Foreman, Michael, illus. LC 93-307. (gr. k). 1994. write for info. (*0-15-248842-1*) HarBrace.

Harrison, Virginia. How Mountain Gorillas Live. Nichols, Michael, illus. LC 91-2022. 32p. (gr. 2-3). 1991. PLB 15.93 (*0-8368-0446-5*) Gareth Stevens Inc.

—Mountain Gorillas & Their Young. Nichols, Michael, illus. LC 91-7600. 32p. (gr. 2-3). 1991. PLB 15.93 (*0-8368-0445-7*) Gareth Stevens Inc.

—The World of a Falcon. Oxford Scientific Films Staff, photos by. LC 87-42611. (Illus.). 32p. (gr. 2-3). 1988. PLB 15.93 (*1-55532-308-1*) Gareth Stevens Inc.

—The World of Dragonflies. Oxford Scientific Films Staff, illus. LC 87-42610. 32p. (gr. 2-3). 1988. PLB 15. 93 (*1-55532-310-3*) Gareth Stevens Inc.

—The World of Elephants. Oxford Scientific Films Staff, photos by. LC 89-11547. (Illus.). 32p. (gr. 2-3). 1989. PLB 15.93 (*0-8368-0141-5*) Gareth Stevens Inc.

—The World of Honeybees. Oxford Scientific Films Staff, photos by. LC 89-33936. (Illus.). 32p. (gr. 2-3). 1989. PLB 15.93 (*0-8368-0142-3*) Gareth Stevens Inc.

—The World of Hummingbirds. Oxford Scientific Films Staff, photos by. LC 89-31913. (Illus.). 32p. (gr. 2-3). 1989. PLB 15.93 (*0-8368-0140-7*) Gareth Stevens Inc.

—The World of Lizards. Oxford Scientific Films Staff, photos by. LC 87-42608. (Illus.). 32p. (gr. 2-3). 1988. PLB 15.93 (*1-55532-307-3*) Gareth Stevens Inc.

—The World of Mice. Oxford Scientific Films Staff, photos by. LC 87-42609. (Illus.). 32p. (gr. 2-3). 1988. PLB 15.93 (*1-55532-309-X*) Gareth Stevens Inc.

—The World of Snakes. Oxford Scientific Films Staff, photos by. LC 89-4634. (Illus.). 32p. (gr. 2-3). 1989. PLB 15.93 (*0-8368-0143-1*) Gareth Stevens Inc.

Harrison, Virginia & Banks, Martin. The World of Polar Bears. LC 89-4470. (Illus.). 32p. (gr. 2-3). 1989. PLB 15.93 (*0-8368-0139-3*) Gareth Stevens Inc.

Harrison, Virginia & Losito, Linda. The World of Ants. LC 89-4466. (Illus.). 32p. (gr. 2-3). 1989. PLB 15.93 (*0-8368-0136-9*) Gareth Stevens Inc.

Harrison, Virginia & Pollack, Steve. The World of Animals. LC 89-11357. (Illus.). 64p. (gr. 2-3). 1989. PLB 19.93 (*0-8368-0028-1*) Gareth Stevens Inc.

Harrison, Virginia & Riley, Helen. The World of Bats. LC 89-4471. (Illus.). 32p. (gr. 2-3). 1989. PLB 15.93 (*0-8368-0137-7*) Gareth Stevens Inc.

Harrison, Virginia & Rowland-Entwistle, Theodore. The Prehistoric World. LC 89-11276. (Illus.). 64p. (gr. 2-3). 1990. PLB 19.93 (*0-8368-0031-1*) Gareth Stevens Inc.

Harrison, Virginia & Scott, Jim. The World of Eagles. Shahild, Wendy & Rosinski, Bob, photos by. LC 89-4459. (Illus.). 32p. (gr. 2-3). 1989. PLB 15.93 (*0-8368-0138-5*) Gareth Stevens Inc.

Harrison, William F. & Welker, Dorothy W. Spanish Memory Book: A New Approach to Vocabulary Building. Nelson, Anita, illus. LC 93-12717. 96p. (Orig.). (gr. 7-12). 1993. text ed. 22.50x (*0-292-73079-9*); pap. 8.95 (*0-292-73081-0*) U of Tex Pr.

Harriss, Susan C. Jamie's Way: Stories for Worship & Family Devotion. Read, David H., intro. by. LC 90-23649. 217p. (ps-9). 1991. pap. 9.95 (*1-56101-031-6*) Cowley Pubns.

—Moral Dilemmas for Young School Children. 61p. (gr. k-5). 1990. pap. 16.50 (*1-881678-02-4*) CRIS.

Harrop, Beatrice, compiled by. Sing Hey Diddle Diddle. Harris, Frank & Cheese, Bernard, illus. 96p. (ps-3). 1991. pap. 14.95 (*0-317-04680-2*, Pub. by A&C Black UK) Talman.

Harrow, Harriett, ed. see Kaczorek, Keith.

Harryman, Diana L., ed. see Dean, Wayne.

Harshman, Marc. Little Excitement. LC 88-32660. (Illus.). 1989. 13.95 (*0-525-65001-6*, Cobblehill Bks) Dutton Child Bks.

—Only One. Garrison, Barbara, illus. LC 92-11349. 32p. (ps-3). 1993. 12.99 (*0-525-65116-0*, Cobblehill Bks) Dutton Child Bks.

—Snow Company. LC 89-23941. (Illus.). (ps-3). 1990. 12. 95 (*0-525-65029-6*, Cobblehill Bks) Dutton Child Bks.

—Uncle James. Dooling, Michael, illus. 32p. (gr. 1-4). 1993. reinforced bdg. 13.99 (*0-525-65110-1*, Cobblehill Bks) Dutton Child Bks.

Harshman, Marc & Collins, Bonnie. Rocks in My Pocket. 32p. (ps-3). 1991. 13.95 (*0-525-65055-5*, Cobblehill Bks) Dutton Child Bks.

Harshman, Terry W. Porcupine's Pajama Party. Cushman, Doug, illus. LC 87-45681. 64p. (gr. k-3). 1988. PLB 13.89 (*0-06-022249-2*) HarpC Child Bks.

—Porcupine's Pajama Party. Cushman, Doug, illus. LC 87-45681. 64p. (gr. k-3). 1990. pap. 3.50 (*0-06-444140-7*, Trophy) HarpC Child Bks.

Harst, Linda N. & Wiederhold, Margaret S. Building Language Power I: Lessons to Provide Experience, Study, & Observation for Skillful Use of the English Language. 96p. (gr. 4-9). 1992. pap. text ed. 12.95 (*0-944459-51-X*) ECS Lrn Systs.

—Building Language Power II: Lessons to Provide Experience, Study, & Observation for Skillful Use of the English Language. 96p. (gr. 4-9). 1992. pap. text ed. 12.95 (*0-944459-52-8*) ECS Lrn Systs.

Hart, Avery & Mantell, Paul. Kids & Weekends! Creative Ways to Make Special Days. Weathers, Marcy, contrib. by. Braren, Loretta T., illus. LC 91-25314. 176p. (Orig.). (gr. k-7). 1992. pap. 12.95 (*0-913589-47-0*) Williamson Pub Co.

—Kids Make Music! Clapping & Tapping from Bach to Rock. Trezzo-Braren Studio Staff, illus. 160p. (Orig.). (ps-4). 1993. pap. 12.95 (*0-913589-69-1*) Williamson Pub Co.

—Ninth Grade Outcast. LC 91-2492. 128p. (gr. 6-9). 1992. lib. bdg. 9.89 (*0-8167-2392-3*); pap. text ed. 2.95 (*0-8167-2393-1*) Troll Assocs.

Hart, Bruce & Hart, Carole. Breaking up Is Hard to Do. LC 86-90994. 256p. (gr. 7 up). 1987. pap. 3.50 (*0-380-89970-1*, Flare) Avon.

—Cross Your Heart. 256p. (Orig.). (gr. 6 up). 1988. pap. 3.50 (*0-380-89971-X*, Flare) Avon.

—Waiting Games. 320p. (gr. 7 up). 1981. pap. 3.50 (*0-380-79012-2*, Flare) Avon.

Hart, Carole, jt. auth. see Hart, Bruce.

Hart, Carole, ed. see Thomas, Marlo.

Hart, Corinne. Damos Gracias: Libro de la Eucaristia para Ninos. Silva, P. Fidencio & Di Raimondo, P. Domenico, trs. from ENG. Benner, Patti, illus. (SPA.). 32p. (ps-2). 1991. pap. 1.90 (*1-55944-006-6*) Franciscan Comns.

—We Say Thanks: A Young Child's Book for Eucharist. rev. ed. Benner, Patti, illus. 32p. (ps-2). 1991. pap. 1.90 (*1-55944-004-X*) Franciscan Comns.

Hart, Corinne & Shannon, Ellen. We Ask Forgiveness: A Young Child's Book for Reconciliation. rev. ed. Benner, Patti, illus. 32p. (ps-2). 1991. pap. 1.90 (*1-55944-005-8*) Franciscan Comns.

Hart, Corinne, jt. auth. see Shannon, Ellen.

Hart, George. Ancient Egypt. Biesty, Stephen, illus. LC 88-30065. 64p. (gr. 3-7). 1989. 14.95 (*0-15-200449-1*) HarBrace.

Hart, Jan S. Hanna, the Immigrant. Roberts, Melissa, ed. Shaw, Charles, illus. 114p. (gr. 6-8). 1991. 12.95 (*0-89015-805-3*) Eakin-Sunbelt.

—The Many Adventures of Minnie. Wilson, Kay, illus. LC 92-17740. 96p. (gr. 4-7). 1992. 12.95 (*0-89015-859-2*) Eakin-Sunbelt.

Hart, Jane, ed. Singing Bee! A Collection of Favorite Children's Songs. Lobel, Anita, illus. LC 82-15296. 160p. 1989. Repr. of 1982 ed. 17.95 (*0-688-41975-5*) Lothrop.

—Singing Bee! A Collection of Favorite Children's Songs. Lobel, Anita, illus. LC 82-15296. 160p. 1991. pap. 12. 00 (*0-688-09113-X*, Mulberry) Morrow.

Hart, Kingsley, tr. see Jansson, Tove.

Hart, Marj. Big Black Dot. (ps-2). 1990. pap. 8.95 (*0-8224-0680-2*) Fearon Teach Aids.

—Discovery Units for Young Children. (gr. k-3). 1991. pap. 11.95 (*0-8224-2323-5*) Fearon Teach Aids.

—Fold-&-Cut Stories & Fingerplays. (gr. k-3). 1987. pap. 9.95 (*0-8224-3150-5*) Fearon Teach Aids.

Hart, Marj & Shelly, Walt. Pom-Pom Puppets, Stories, & Stages. (gr. 5-8). 1989. pap. 13.95 (*0-8224-5596-X*) Fearon Teach Aids.

Hart, Philip S. Flying Free: America's First Black Aviators. Lindbergh, Reeve, frwd. by. (Illus.). 72p. (gr. 5 up). 1992. 19.95 (*0-8225-1598-9*) Lerner Pubns.

Hart, Rhonda M. You Can Carve Fantastic Jack-O-Lanterns. Foster, Kim, ed. Noyes, Leslie, illus. LC 90-55042. 112p. 1990. pap. 6.95 (*0-88266-580-4*) Storey Comm Inc.

Hart, Rosana. Living with Llamas: Tales from Juniper Ridge. rev. ed. (Illus.). 192p. 1991. pap. 11.95 (*0-916289-13-3*) Juniper Ridge.

Hart, Tom. Fairies & Friends. Pearson-Cooper, Michelle, illus. 120p. 1981. 8.95 (*0-685-01043-0*, Pub. by Quartet England) Charles River Bks.

Hart, Tony. Animals & Figures. (Illus.). 32p. (gr. 1-4). 1984. 5.95 (*0-7182-2950-9*, Pub. by W Heinemann Ltd) Trafalgar.

—Leonardo Da Vinci. Hellard, Susan, illus. LC 93-2385. 24p. (ps-3). 1994. pap. 5.95 (*0-8120-1828-1*) Barron.

—Michaelangelo. Hellard, Susan, illus. LC 93-2384. 24p. (ps-3). 1994. pap. 5.95 (*0-8120-1827-3*) Barron.

—Picasso. Hellard, Susan, illus. LC 93-8750. 24p. (ps-3). 1994. pap. 5.95 (*0-8120-1826-5*) Barron.

—Toulouse-Lautrec. Hellard, Susan, illus. LC 93-22146. 24p. (ps-3). 1994. pap. 5.95 (*0-8120-1825-7*) Barron.

Hart, Trish. Antarctic Diary. Hart, Trish, illus. LC 93-110. 1994. nap. write for info. (*0-383-03675-5*) SRA Schl Grp.

—There Are No Polar Bears down There. Hart, Trish, illus. LC 92-31949. 1993. 3.75 (*0-383-03597-X*) SRA Schl Grp.

Hart-Davis, Adam. Scientific Eye: Exploring the Marvels of Science. LC 88-31333. (Illus.). 96p. 1990. pap. 7.95 (*0-8069-5758-1*) Sterling.

Harte, Bret. The Outcasts of Poker Flat. Nuemeier, Marty, illus. 48p. (gr. k up). 1980. PLB 13.95s.p. (*0-87191-768-8*) Creative Ed.

—Outcasts of Poker Flat & Other Stories. (gr. 8 up). 1964. pap. 1.95 (*0-8049-0051-5*, CL51) Airmont.

Harte, Cheryl. Jingle Bear. Harte, Cheryl, illus. 1991. sponge-filled 5.95 (*0-679-80750-0*) Random Bks Yng Read.

Harte, Cheryl, illus. Bunny Rattle. 12p. (ps). 1989. sponge-filled cloth 4.95 (*0-394-89956-3*) Random Bks Yng Read.

—Ducky Squeak. 12p. (ps). 1989. sponge-filled cloth 5.99 (*0-394-89955-5*) Random Bks Yng Read.

—My Chalkboard Book: Green Ladder Books for Kids Through 6 Years. 14p. (ps-1). 1988. bds. 6.95 (*0-394-89401-4*) Random Bks Yng Read.

—Push-a-Lamb. 14p. (ps). 1989. bds. 5.95 with plastic wheels (*0-394-82986-7*) Random Bks Yng Read.

Harte, J. P. & Dunbar, C. Skills in Geography. LC 93-27487. 1993. write for info. (*0-521-44635-X*) Cambridge U Pr.

Harte, Kathleen M. There's Lots That I Can Do. Harte, Kathleen M., illus. LC 92-43904. 32p. (ps-k). 1993. pap. 2.25 (*0-679-84798-7*) Random Bks Yng Read.

Hartelius, Margaret. Hide & Ghost Seek. Hartelius, Margaret A., illus. 32p. (ps-3). 1992. pap. 2.95 (*0-448-40475-3*, G&D) Putnam Pub Group.
Hartelius, Margaret A. The Great Egg Mystery. Hartelius, Margaret A., illus. 16p. (Orig.). (ps-2). 1994. pap. 2.95 (*0-590-33427-1*, Cartwheel) Scholastic Inc.
—Knot Again! The Complete Lanyard Kit! Hartelius, Margaret A., illus. 24p. (gr. 1-7). 1993. pap. 7.95 (*0-448-40456-7*, G&D) Putnam Pub Group.
—Knot Now! The Complete Friendship Bracelet Kit. (Illus.). 24p. (gr. 1-6). 1992. pap. 6.95 (*0-448-40598-9*, G&D) Putnam Pub Group.
—ZOOM! The Complete Paper Airplane Kit. Hartelius, Margaret A., illus. LC 90-84671. 32p. (ps-3). 1991. 6.95 (*0-448-40138-X*, G&D) Putnam Pub Group.
Hartelius, Margaret A., illus. Over in the Meadow. 1987. pap. 6.99 incl. audiocassette (*0-553-45900-7*) Bantam.
Hartelius, Marge. Halloween Puzzle Bag. 32p. 1991. pap. 1.95 (*0-590-44581-2*) Scholastic Inc.
Harter, Walter. The Phantom Hand. Totten, Robert, illus. 128p. (gr. 4 up). 1976. pap. 5.96 (*0-13-661843-X*, Pub. by Treehouse) P-H.
Hartley, Al. Family Fun. Hartley, Al, illus. (gr. 1). 1988. pap. text ed. 1.29 (*1-55748-004-4*) Barbour & Co.
—Flying Colors. Hartley, Al, illus. 32p. (gr. 1). 1988. pap. text ed. 1.29 (*1-55748-000-1*) Barbour & Co.
—Fun in the Car. Hartley, Al, illus. 32p. (gr. 1). 1988. pap. text ed. 1.29 (*1-55748-001-X*) Barbour & Co.
—Fun with Friends. Hartley, Al, illus. (gr. 1). 1988. pap. text ed. 1.29 (*1-55748-002-8*) Barbour & Co.
—Happy Home. Hartley, Al, illus. (gr. 1). 1988. pap. text ed. 1.29 (*1-55748-005-2*) Barbour & Co.
—School Fun. Hartley, Al, illus. (gr. 1). 1988. pap. text ed. 1.29 (*1-55748-003-6*) Barbour & Co.
Hartley, David. Wacky Fill-Ins, No. 2. (gr. 5-7). 1990. pap. 1.95 (*0-590-42563-3*) Scholastic Inc.
Hartley, David, ed. Freaky Fillins, No. 3. 48p. (Orig.). (gr. 3-5). 1980. pap. 1.50 (*0-937518-02-6*) Hartley Hse.
Hartley, Deborah. Up North in Winter. Dabcovich, Lydia, illus. 32p. (ps-3). 1986. 11.95 (*0-525-44268-5*, DCB) Dutton Child Bks.
—Up North in Winter. Dabcovich, Lydia, illus. 32p. (ps-3). 1993. pap. 4.99 (*0-14-054943-9*, Puffin Unicorn) Puffin Bks.
Hartley, Desmond, tr. see De Amicis, Edmondo.
Hartley, Eugene L. Hopi Shields & the Best Defense. 32p. (gr. 3-8). 1991. pap. 4.95 (*0-89992-127-2*) Coun India Ed.
Hartley, Fred. Dare to Be Different: Dealing with Peer Pressure. 128p. (Orig.). 1980. pap. 7.99 (*0-8007-5041-1*) Revell.
—Flops: Turn Your Wipeouts into Winners. 160p. (Orig.). 1985. pap. 6.99 (*0-8007-5191-4*) Revell.
—Growing Pains: First Aid for Teenagers. 160p. (Orig.). (gr. 7-12). 1981. pap. 6.99 (*0-8007-5067-5*) Revell.
—Teenage Book of Manners Please. 1991. pap. 9.95 (*1-55748-246-2*) Barbour & Co.
—The Teenage Book of Manners...Please! 14.95 (*1-55748-245-4*) Barbour & Co.
Hartley, Linda, ed. see Bornthal, Mark.
Hartley, Linda, ed. see Dowdy, Linda.
Hartley, Linda, ed. see Dudko, Mary A. & Larsen, Margie.
Hartley, Linda, ed. see Kearns, Kimberly & O'Brien, Marie.
Hartley, Linda, ed. see White, Stephen.
Hartley, Mary M. Mariposa: A Tough Texan in a Time Capsule. 64p. (gr. 4-7). 1986. 10.95 (*0-89015-544-5*, Pub. by Panda Bks) Eakin-Sunbelt.
Hartley, Melissa, ed. Freaky Fillins, No. 4. 48p. (Orig.). (gr. 3-5). 1980. pap. 1.50 (*0-937518-03-4*) Hartley Hse.
Hartling, Peter. Ben Loves Anna. Auerbach, J. H., tr. from GER. (gr. 4-7). 1990. 12.95 (*0-87951-401-9*) Overlook Pr.
—Crutches. Crawford, Elizabeth D., tr. from GER. LC 88-80400. 160p. (gr. 5 up). 1988. 12.95 (*0-688-07991-1*) Lothrop.
—Old John. Crawford, Elizabeth D., tr. from GER. LC 89-12976. 128p. (gr. 4-9). 1990. 11.95 (*0-688-08734-5*) Lothrop.
Hartman, Alan G., ed. see Bowman, Crystal.
Hartman, Bob. Angels, Angels All Around. Rayevsky, Robert, illus. 96p. (gr. 1-5). 1993. 15.95 (*0-7459-2623-1*) Lion USA.
—The Birthday of a King. Mcguire, Michael, illus. 24p. (ps-2). 1993. 7.99 (*1-56476-043-X*, Victor Books) SP Pubns.
—Birthday of a King: Jesus' Birthday. (ps-3). 1993. 7.99 (*1-56476-144-4*, Victor Books) SP Pubns.
—The Edge of the River. McGuire, Michael, illus. 24p. (ps-2). 1993. 7.99 (*1-56476-041-3*, Victor Books) SP Pubns.
—Johnny Thumbs. Kolding, Max, illus. 48p. (Orig.). (gr. 1-3). 1993. pap. 3.99 (*0-7847-0093-1*, 24-03943) Standard Pub.
—Lobster for Lunch. Stammen, JoEllen M., illus. LC 91-77611. 32p. (gr. k-3). 1992. 14.95 (*0-89272-302-5*) Down East.
—The Middle of the Night. McGuire, Michael, illus. 24p. (ps-2). 1993. 7.99 (*1-56476-042-1*, Victor Books) SP Pubns.
—The Morning of the World. McGuire, Michael, illus. 24p. (ps-2). 1993. 7.99 (*1-56476-040-5*, Victor Books) SP Pubns.

—The One & Only Delgado Cheese: A Tale of Talent, Fame, & Friendship. Nelson, Donna K., illus. LC 92-29059. 40p. (gr. k-3). 1993. 13.95 (*0-7459-2405-0*) Lion USA.
Hartman, Gail. As the Crow Flies: A First Book of Maps. Stevenson, Harvey, illus. LC 90-33982. 32p. (ps-1). 1991. RSBE 12.95 (*0-02-743005-7*, Bradbury Pr) Macmillan Child Grp.
—As the Crow Flies: A First Book of Maps. Stevenson, Harvey, illus. LC 93-22101. 32p. (ps-1). 1993. pap. 4.95 (*0-689-71762-8*, Aladdin) Macmillan Child Grp.
—For Sand Castles or Seashells. Weiss, Ellen, illus. LC 89-35994. 32p. (ps-1). 1990. RSBE 13.95 (*0-02-743091-X*, Bradbury Pr) Macmillan Child Grp.
Hartman, Karen L. Dream Catcher: The Legend & the Lady. 56p. (gr. 6 up). 1993. 17.95 (*0-9635204-0-7*) Weeping Heart.
Hartman, Mary E., jt. auth. see Dehnbostel, Nancy L.
Hartman, Victoria. The Silliest Joke Book Ever. Alley, R. W., photos by. LC 92-22161. (Illus.). 1993. write for info. (*0-688-10109-7*); pap. write for info. (*0-688-10110-0*) Lothrop.
—Westward Ho, Ho, Ho. Karas, G. Brian, illus. 48p. (gr. 2-6). 1994. pap. 3.99 (*0-14-036851-5*) Puffin Bks.
—Westward Ho Ho! Jokes from the Wild West. Karas, G. Brian, illus. 48p. (gr. 2-6). 1992. PLB 11.00 (*0-670-84040-8*) Viking Child Bks.
Hartman, Victoria G. The Silly Joke Book. Orehek, Don, illus. 96p. (gr. 4-6). 1987. pap. 1.95 (*0-590-33846-3*) Scholastic Inc.
Hartmann, Wendy. All the Magic in the World. Daly, Niki, illus. LC 92-38289. 32p. (gr. k-3). 1993. 12.99 (*0-525-45092-0*, DCB) Dutton Child Bks.
Hartophilis, Georgene, illus. How to Draw Dinosaurs. 32p. (Orig.). 1990. pap. 2.95 (*0-942025-74-1*) Kidsbks.
—How to Draw Dinosaurs. 32p. 1991. 3.98 (*1-56156-022-7*) Kidsbks.
—How to Draw Endangered Animals. 32p. 1991. 3.98 (*1-56156-018-9*) Kidsbks.
—How to Draw Endangered Animals. 32p. 1991. pap. 2.95 (*1-56156-027-8*) Kidsbks.
Hartsell, Lynn. Pitch in & Play Fair. Ewers, Joe & Sustendal, Pat, illus. 40p. (ps-3). write for info (*0-910313-75-X*) Parker Bros.
Hartstrom, Noelle, ed. see Ross, Elena & Champlin, Allen R., Sr.
Hartwig, Judy. Celebrate Winter. Filkins, Vanessa, illus. 144p. (gr. k-3). 1985. wkbk. 11.95 (*0-86653-266-8*, SS 839, Shining Star Pubns) Good Apple.
—Easter Bulletin Boards. (Illus.). 96p. (ps-8). 1989. 10.95 (*0-86653-480-6*, SS1829, Shining Star Pubns) Good Apple.
Harty, Annelle & Harty, Robert. Made to Grow. 32p. (gr. 1-3). 1973. 6.95 (*0-8054-4222-7*) Broadman.
Harty, Robert, jt. auth. see Harty, Annelle.
Hartzler, Arlene & Gaeddert, John, eds. Children's Hymnary. LC 67-24327. (gr. k-7). 1967. 5.95 (*0-87303-095-8*) Faith & Life.
Harvey & McGuire. So, There Are Laws about Sex! Answers on Legal Sex for Canadian Children & Youth. 48p. 1989. pap. 8.95 (*0-409-88936-9*) Butterworth Legal Pubs.
Harvey & Watson-Russell. So, You Have to Go to Court! A Child's Guide to Testifying As a Witness in Child Abuse Cases. 3rd ed. 48p. 1991. pap. 8.95 (*0-409-90611-5*) Butterworth Legal Pubs.
Harvey, jt. auth. see Watson-Russell.
Harvey, Amanda. The Iron Needle. LC 93-32679. 1994. write for info. (*0-688-13192-1*) Lothrop.
—Stormy Weather. Pearson, Susan, ed. LC 91-13950. (Illus.). 32p. (gr. k up). 1992. 14.00 (*0-688-10607-2*); PLB 13.93 (*0-688-10608-0*) Lothrop.
Harvey, Anne. Shades of Green. Lawrence, John, illus. LC 91-15234. 192p. 1992. 18.00 (*0-688-10890-3*) Greenwillow.
Harvey, Anthony. The World of the Dinosaurs. LC 79-5065. (Illus.). 36p. (gr. 3-6). 1980. PLB 13.50 (*0-8225-1187-8*, First Ave Edns); pap. 4.95 (*0-8225-9511-7*, First Ave Edns) Lerner Pubns.
Harvey, Bob & Harvey, Diane K. A Journey of Hope: Una Jornada de Esperanza. Johnson, Carol, illus. LC 91-4556. (ENG & SPA.). 48p. (gr. k-6). 1991. 12.95 (*0-89802-603-2*) Beautiful Am.
—Melody's Mystery: El Misterio de Melodia. LC 91-4557. (ENG & SPA.). 48p. (gr. k-6). 1991. 12.95 (*0-89802-604-0*) Beautiful Am.
Harvey, Bob & Harvey, Diane K., photos by. Fishing with Peter: Pescando Con Pedro. Harvey, Bob, text by. (ENG & SPA., Illus.). 48p. (gr. k-6). 1992. 12.95 (*0-89802-592-3*) Beautiful Am.
Harvey, Bonnie C., jt. ed. see Phillips, Cheryl.
Harvey, Bonnie C., jt. ed. see Phillips, Cheryl M.
Harvey, Bonnie C., ed. see Stirrup Associates, Inc. Staff.
Harvey, Brett. Cassie's Journey: Going West in the 1860s. Ray, Deborah K., illus. LC 87-23599. 40p. (gr. 1-4). 1988. reinforced bdg. 13.95 (*0-8234-0684-9*) Holiday.
—Farmers & Ranchers. 1994. PLB write for info. (*0-8050-2999-0*) H Holt & Co.
—Immigrant Girl: Becky of Eldridge Street. Ray, Deborah K., illus. LC 86-15038. 40p. (gr. 1-4). 1987. reinforced bdg. 13.95 (*0-8234-0638-5*) Holiday.
—My Prairie Christmas. Ray, Deborah K., illus. LC 90-55104. 32p. (ps-3). 1990. reinforced 14.95 (*0-8234-0827-2*) Holiday.
—My Prairie Christmas. Ray, Deborah K., illus. 1993. pap. 5.95 (*0-8243-1064-0*) Holiday.

—My Prairie Year. Ray, Deborah K., illus. (ps-3). 1993. pap. 4.95 (*0-8234-1028-5*) Holiday.
—My Prairie Year: Based on the Diary of Elenore Plaisted. Ray, Deborah K., illus. LC 85-27177. 40p. (gr. 1-4). 1986. reinforced bdg. 13.95 (*0-8234-0604-0*) Holiday.
Harvey, Catherine, tr. see Chetin, Helen.
Harvey, Dean. The Secret Elephant of Harlan Kooter. Richardson, Mark, illus. LC 91-45955. 160p. (gr. 2-5). 1992. 13.95 (*0-395-62523-8*) HM.
Harvey, Diane K., jt. auth. see Harvey, Bob.
Harvey, Gail. Prayers, Graces, & Hymns for Children. LC 92-39152. (Illus.). (gr. 2 up). 1993. 8.99 (*0-517-09276-X*) Outlet Bk Co.
—Read to Me, Grandpa. 1993. pap. 8.99 (*0-517-09349-9*) Outlet Bk Co.
Harvey, Jane. Marvin & Max Big Word Book. (Illus.). 64p. (ps-1). 1991. 6.99 (*0-517-05391-8*) Outlet Bk Co.
—Marvin the Mouse Look & Find Book. (Illus.). 64p. (ps-1). 1991. 6.99 (*0-517-05389-6*) Outlet Bk Co.
—Marvin the Mouse Opposites Book. (Illus.). 64p. (ps-1). 1991. 6.99 (*0-517-05390-X*) Outlet Bk Co.
Harvey, Jayne. Great-Uncle Dracula. Carter, Abby, illus. LC 91-31460. 80p. (Orig.). (gr. 2-4). 1992. PLB 6.99 (*0-679-92448-5*); pap. 2.50 (*0-679-82448-0*) Random Bks Yng Read.
—Great-Uncle Dracula & the Dirty Rat. Carter, Abby, illus. LC 92-93018. 64p. (gr. 2-4). 1993. PLB 6.99 (*0-679-93457-X*); pap. 2.50 (*0-679-83457-5*) Random Bks Yng Read.
Harvey, Karen & Harjo, Lisa. Indian Country: A History of Native People in America. (Illus.). 400p. (gr. 6-12). 1993. 27.95x (*1-55591-911-1*, North Amer Pr) Fulcrum Pub.
Harvey, Miles. Barry Bonds: Baseball's Most Complete Player. LC 93-41053. 1994. write for info. (*0-516-04381-1*) Childrens.
Harvey, Paul H. & Heseltine, Janet E., eds. Oxford Companion to French Literature. 771p. (gr. 9 up). 1959. 55.00x (*0-19-866104-5*) OUP.
Harvey, T. Railroads. LC 79-5062. (Illus.). 36p. (gr. 3-6). 1980. PLB 13.50 (*0-8225-1184-3*, First Ave Edns); pap. 4.95 (*0-8225-9539-7*, First Ave Edns) Lerner Pubns.
Harvey, Thomas. Harvey's Elementary Grammar & Composition. (Illus.). (gr. 4-6). 1986. 10.95 (*0-88062-041-2*) Mott Media.
—Harvey's Revised English Grammar. (Illus.). (gr. 7-11). 1986. 13.95 (*0-88062-042-0*) Mott Media.
Harvey, Virginia. Split-Ply Twining. LC 75-4651. (Illus.). 44p. (gr. 7 up). 1976. pap. 7.95 (*0-916658-32-5*) Shuttle Craft.
Harwayne. Writers Shelf: Literature Through. Date not set. Pt. I. 174.05 (*0-06-027097-7*, Festival); Pt. II. PLB 154.55 (*0-06-027098-5*, Festival) HarpC Child Bks.
Harwell, Christine C. & Harwell, Mark A. Nuclear Famine. LC 87-70224. (Illus.). 16p. (Orig.). (gr. 10 up). 1990. pap. text ed. 2.75 (*0-89278-185-8*, 45-9785) Carolina Biological.
Harwell, Helen B. Candy the Zoo Truck. Dollar, Diane, illus. 32p. 1987. 3.95 (*0-938991-37-X*) Colonial Pr AL.
Harwell, Ivy E. The Servant. Ellison, Chris, illus. 180p. (Orig.). (gr. 9 up). 1993. pap. 7.98 (*1-882671-09-0*) Wrds of Life.
Harwell, Mark A., jt. auth. see Harwell, Christine C.
Harwich, Mary B. & Hay, John W. Shell of Wonder. (Illus.). 1991. 11.95 (*0-88138-149-7*, Green Tiger) S&S Trade.
Harwood, Lynne. Honeybees at Home. Harwood, Lynne, illus. LC 93-33552. 40p. (gr. 3-8). 1994. 16.95 (*0-88448-119-0*) Tilbury Hse.
Harwood, William N. Writing & Editing School News. 3rd, rev. ed. 364p. (gr. 11-12). 1990. pap. text ed. 17.33 (*0-931054-21-4*) Clark Pub.
Hasan, Khurshid. Manzur Goes to the Airport. (Illus.). 25p. (gr. 2-4). 1991. 15.95 (*0-237-60159-1*, Pub. by Evans Bros Ltd) Trafalgar.
Hasan, Khurshid & Warner, Rachel. Rumana's New Clothes. (Illus.). 25p. (gr. 2-4). 1991. 15.95 (*0-237-60160-5*, Pub. by Evans Bros Ltd) Trafalgar.
Hasegawa, Yo. The Cricket. Pohl, Kathy, ed. LC 85-28201. (Illus.). 32p. (gr. 3-7). 1986. text ed. 17.96 (*0-8172-2532-3*) Raintree Steck-V.
—The Grasshopper. Pohl, Kathy, ed. LC 85-28228. (Illus.). 32p. (gr. 3-7). 1986. text ed. 17.96 (*0-8172-2536-6*) Raintree Steck-V.
Haseley, Dennis. The Cave of Snores. Beddows, Eric, illus. LC 85-48845. 40p. (gr. k-4). 1987. HarpC Child Bks.
—Ghost Catcher. Bloom, Lloyd, illus. LC 91-4426. 40p. (gr. 1-5). 1991. PLB 15.89 (*0-06-022247-6*) HarpC Child Bks.
—Horses with Wings. Curlee, Lynn, illus. LC 92-29869. 32p. (gr. k-4). 1993. 16.00 (*0-06-022885-7*); PLB 15.89 (*0-06-022886-5*) HarpC Child Bks.
—Kite Flier. Wiesner, David, illus. LC 92-22721. 32p. (ps-3). 1993. pap. 4.95 (*0-689-71668-0*, Aladdin) Macmillan Child Grp.
—The Old Banjo. Gammell, Stephen, illus. LC 89-36796. 32p. (gr. 1-5). 1990. pap. 3.95 (*0-689-71380-0*, Aladdin) Macmillan Child Grp.
—The Pirate Who Tried to Capture the Moon. new ed. Truesdell, Sue, illus. LC 82-47734. 64p. (gr. k-4). 1992. pap. 3.95 (*0-06-440420-X*, Trophy) HarpC Child Bks.
—Shadows. Bowman, Leslie, illus. 80p. (gr. 2-6). 1991. 12.95 (*0-374-36761-2*) FS&G.

—Shadows. (gr. 4-7). 1993. pap. 3.95 (*0-374-46611-4*, Sunburst) FS&G.
Haselton, Scott E. Cactus & Succulents & How to Grow Them. (gr. 6-12). 1983. 1.25 (*0-9605656-1-2*) Desert Botanical.
Hasenau, F. A. Benjamin Visits the Jungle. LC 82-81827. (Illus.). (gr. k-2). 1982. 6.00 (*0-913042-14-5*) Holland Hse Pr.
Hasenau, James. Fuzzy Bear. LC 82-81828. (Illus.). (gr. k-4). 1985. 6.00 (*0-913042-15-3*) Holland Hse Pr.
Hasenav, Florence A. Pinkey. (Illus.). (gr. 1-6). 1975. 6.00 (*0-913042-02-1*) Holland Hse Pr.
Hashim, A. S. Al-Khulafe al-Rashidoon. pap. 5.95 (*0-935782-29-X*) Kazi Pubns.
—Eleven Surahs Explained. pap. 5.95 (*0-935782-90-7*) Kazi Pubns.
—Ibadat. pap. 5.95 (*1-56744-047-9*) Kazi Pubns.
—Iman, Basic Beliefs. pap. 5.95 (*1-56744-055-X*) Kazi Pubns.
—Islamic Arabic. pap. 5.95 (*1-56744-089-4*) Kazi Pubns.
—Islamic Ethics. pap. 5.95 (*1-56744-095-9*) Kazi Pubns.
—Life of Prophet Muhammad-I. pap. 7.50 (*1-56744-125-4*) Kazi Pubns.
—Life of Prophet Muhammad-II. pap. 6.50 (*1-56744-126-2*) Kazi Pubns.
—Stories of Some of the Prophets, Vol. I. pap. 5.95 (*0-933511-61-2*) Kazi Pubns.
—Stories of Some of the Prophets, Vol II. pap. 5.95 (*0-933511-64-7*) Kazi Pubns.
Hashimoto, Yasuko & Edades, Jean. Tales of a Japanese Grandmother, 5 Vols. Kubota, Kenji, illus. (Orig.). (gr. k-3). 1982. Set. pap. 12.50 (*0-686-37564-5*, Pub. by New Day Pub PI) Cellar.
Hasija, Nipla, retold by. Legends from Northern India. Bose, R. K., illus. (gr. 5-10). 1981. 7.25 (*0-89744-241-5*, Pub. by Hemkunt India) Auromere.
Haskelevich, B., ed. & tr. from ENG & HEB. My First Siddur: A Selection of Prayers for Jewish Boys & Girls. LC 90-82127. (RUS., Illus.). 32p. (Orig.). (gr. k-8). 1990. pap. 1.50 (*1-878860-01-1*) Noviysvet.

Haskell, Bess C. The Hunky Dory. Poole, Ann, illus. 48p. (Orig.). (gr. 3-8). 1992. pap. 10.95 (*0-9626857-2-0*) Coastwise Pr.
THE HUNKY DORY is the second in the six-volume WIND, WAVES & AWAY! SERIES written by Bess C. Haskell of Tenants Harbor, Maine. Bess, who was born September 9, 1896, wrote these books in the early '20s to read to her own children. Bess & her husband, Henry Haskell, both taught school for many years & co-founded the first interracial summer camp for children in Maine in the '40s. In 1936, while teaching in a private school, Henry read the books to his students, who loved them. Each of the six books centers around the adventures of two children & a different water craft. The children, Dan & Margaret Currier, learn the proper handling of each boat-- raft, dory, sailboat, canoe, motorboat & schooner--through a series of misadventures. Their pet dog & cat always join, & sometimes, cause the fun. From their parents, the children also learn the essential family values prevalent at the turn of the century. After 1936, these stories were lost for many years. When they resurfaced in the early '80s, Bess revised them for publication. The first book, THE RAFT, was published in 1988. Every page of THE HUNKY DORY is beautifully illustrated with line drawings.
Publisher Provided Annotation.

—The Raft. Fetz, Ingrid, illus. (gr. 5 up). 1988. write for info. (*0-933858-26-4*) Kennebec River.
The safe handling of watercraft is the first lesson children need to learn to enjoy life on the seashore, & this series provides the lessons needed, each within a story built around the characters of Dan & Muffin & their dog & cat. Handling a raft involves safety rules, just as handling a dory, or

motorboat or any other craft. Author Bess Haskell trained as a teacher at the Bank Street School in New York City before moving to Tenants Harbor, Maine. THE RAFT is the first in a planned six volume series. The stories were written in the Twenties.
Publisher Provided Annotation.

—Sailing to Pint Pot. Poole, Ann M., illus. 72p. (Orig.). (gr. 4 up). 1993. pap. 10.95 (*0-9626857-4-7*) Coastwise Pr.
SAILING TO PINT POT takes the Currier family sailing to a Maine island. After a fun-filled day of picnicking & discovering natural wonders, they encounter danger when they go off course on the way home. PINT POT is the third book in the six-part WIND, WAVES & AWAY! series written by Bess C. Haskell of Tenants Harbor, Maine. Each book in the series illustrates proper handling of a different water craft through the adventures of Margaret & Dan Currier, their mom & dad, & sometimes their pet cat & dog. The old-fashioned but universal tales engage & delight all young children while teaching valuable but non-preachy lessons. All books in the series are beautifully illustrated with line drawings that capture the rocky, spruce-dotted coast of Maine.
Publisher Provided Annotation.

Haskell, John F., ed. see Cavalier, Richard.
Haskett, M. R., ed. see Haskett, William P.
Haskett, William P. Grandpa Haskett Presents: Original New Christmas Stories for the Young & Young-at-Heart. Haskett, M. R., ed. Haskett, Merelaine, illus. Haskett, M. R., intro. by. (Illus.). 20p. (Orig.). (ps-2). 1982. pap. 3.00g (*0-9609724-0-4*) Haskett Spec.
Haskin, Dorothy. The One Who Was Different. Butcher, Sam, illus. 16p. (gr. k-6). 1983. pap. text ed. 4.25 (*1-55976-130-X*) CEF Press.
Haskins. Black Gray & Blue. Date not set. 15.00 (*0-06-023403-2*, Festival); PLB 14.89 (*0-06-023404-0*, Festival) HarpC Child Bks.
—The Negro Leagues. 1993. 16.95 (*0-8050-2207-4*) H Holt & Co.
Haskins, Charles, jt. auth. see Gravelle, Karen.
Haskins, Francine. I Remember "121" LC 91-16647. (Illus.). 32p. (gr. k-5). 1991. 13.95 (*0-89239-100-6*) Childrens Book Pr.
—Things I Like about Grandma. Haskins, Francine, illus. 32p. (gr. 3-4). 1992. PLB 21.34 (*0-89239-107-3*) Childrens Book Pr.
Haskins, James. Black Dance in America: A History Through Its People. LC 89-35529. (Illus.). 240p. (gr. 7 up). 1990. 15.00 (*0-690-04657-X*, Crowell Jr Bks); PLB 14.89 (*0-690-04659-6*, Crowell Jr Bks) HarpC Child Bks.
—Black Dance in America: A History Through Its People. LC 89-35529. (Illus.). 240p. (gr. 7 up). 1992. pap. 6.95 (*0-06-446121-1*, Trophy) HarpC Child Bks.
—Black Music in America: A History Through Its People. LC 85-47885. (Illus.). 224p. (gr. 7 up). 1987. 16.00 (*0-690-04460-7*, Crowell Jr Bks); PLB 15.89 (*0-690-04462-3*, Crowell Jr Bks) HarpC Child Bks.
—Black Music in America: A History Through Its People. LC 86-47885. (Illus.). 208p. (gr. 7 up). 1993. pap. 6.95 (*0-06-446136-X*, Trophy) HarpC Child Bks.
—Black Theater in America. LC 81-43874. (Illus.). 160p. (gr. 7 up). 1991. PLB 14.89 (*0-690-04319-2*, Crowell Jr Bks) HarpC Child Bks.
—Colin Powell: A Biography. 112p. 1992. pap. 2.95 (*0-590-45243-6*) Scholastic Inc.
—Corazon Aquino: Leader of the Philippines. LC 87-24440. (Illus.). 128p. (gr. 6 up). 1988. lib. bdg. 17.95 (*0-89490-152-4*) Enslow Pubs.
—The Headless Haunt & Other African-American Ghost Stories. Otera, Ben, illus. LC 93-26223. 1994. write for info. (*0-06-022994-2*); PLB write for info. (*0-06-022997-7*) HarpC Child Bks.
—I Am Somebody! A Biography of Jesse Jackson. LC 91-34079. (Illus.). 112p. (gr. 6 up). 1992. lib. bdg. 17.95 (*0-89490-240-7*) Enslow Pubs.
—India under Indira & Rajiv Gandhi. LC 88-21209. (Illus.). 104p. (gr. 6 up). 1989. lib. bdg. 17.95 (*0-89490-146-X*) Enslow Pubs.
—The Life & Death of Martin Luther King, Jr. LC 77-3157. (Illus.). (gr. 5 up). 1977. PLB 13.88 (*0-688-51802-8*) Lothrop.

—The Life & Death of Martin Luther King, Jr. ALC Staff, ed. LC 77-3157. (Illus.). 176p. (gr. 6-12). 1992. pap. 3.95 (*0-688-11690-6*, Pub. by Beech Tree Bks) Morrow.
—The March on Washington. LC 92-13626. (Illus.). 128p. (gr. 5 up). 1993. 15.00 (*0-06-021289-6*); PLB 14.89 (*0-06-021290-X*) HarpC Child Bks.
—The Scottsboro Boys. 160p. (gr. 8 up). 1993. PLB 15.95 (*0-8050-2206-6*, Bks Young Read) H Holt & Co.
—Sports Great Magic Johnson. rev. & expanded ed. LC 92-9188. (Illus.). 80p. (gr. 4-10). 1992. lib. bdg. 15.95 (*0-89490-348-9*) Enslow Pubs.
—Street Gangs: Yesterday & Today. (Illus.). (gr. 6 up). 1977. pap. 4.95 (*0-8038-2662-1*) Hastings.
—Sugar Ray Leonard. LC 82-15227. (Illus.). 160p. (gr. 4 up). 1982. 14.95 (*0-688-01436-4*) Lothrop.
—Thurgood Marshall: A Life for Justice. 172p. (gr. 7 up). 1992. 14.95 (*0-8050-2095-0*, Bks Young Read) H Holt & Co.
Haskins, James & Benson, Kathleen. The Sixties Reader. LC 85-40886. (Illus.). 256p. (gr. 7 up). 1988. pap. 13.95 (*0-670-80674-9*) Viking Child Bks.
—Space Challenger: The Story of Guion Bluford. LC 84-4251. (Illus.). 64p. (gr. 3-6). 1984. PLB 17.50 (*0-87614-259-5*) Carolrhoda Bks.
Haskins, James S. Diana Ross: Star Supreme. Spence, Jim, photos by. LC 84-21897. (Illus.). 64p. (gr. 2-6). 1985. pap. 10.95 (*0-670-80549-1*) Viking Child Bks.
—Diana Ross: Star Supreme. Spence, Jim, illus. 64p. (gr. 2-6). 1986. pap. 3.95 (*0-14-032096-2*, Puffin) Puffin Bks.
—I'm Gonna Make You Love Me: The Story of Diana Ross. 176p. (gr. 7 up). 1982. pap. 2.25 (*0-440-94172-5*, LFL) Dell.
—Shirley Temple Black: Actress to Ambassador. Ruff, Donna, illus. 64p. (gr. 2-5). 1989. pap. 3.95 (*0-14-032491-7*, Puffin) Puffin Bks.
Haskins, James S. & Stifle, J. M. Donna Summer: An Unauthorized Biography. (Illus.). 144p. (gr. 7 up). 1983. 14.95 (*0-316-35003-6*, Joy St Bks) Little.
Haskins, Jim. Against All Opposition: Black Explorers in America. 128p. 1992. 13.95 (*0-8027-8137-3*); PLB 14.85 (*0-8027-8138-1*) Walker & Co.
—Amazing Grace: The Story Behind the Song. LC 91-20999. (Illus.). 48p. (gr. 3-5). 1992. PLB 13.90 (*1-56294-117-8*) Millbrook Pr.
—Bill Cosby: America's Most Famous Father. 128p. (gr. 7-9). 1988. 13.95 (*0-8027-6785-0*); PLB 14.85 (*0-8027-6786-9*) Walker & Co.
—Christopher Columbus: Admiral of the Ocean Sea. Lasker, Joe, illus. 64p. (gr. 2-5). 1991. pap. 2.95 (*0-590-42396-7*) Scholastic Inc.
—Count Your Way Through Africa. Knutson, Barbara, illus. 24p. (gr. 1-4). 1989. 17.50 (*0-87614-347-8*); pap. 5.95 (*0-87614-514-4*) Carolrhoda Bks.
—Count Your Way Through Canada. Michaels, Steve, illus. 24p. (gr. 1-4). 1989. 17.50 (*0-87614-350-8*); pap. 5.95 (*0-87614-515-2*) Carolrhoda Bks.
—Count Your Way Through China. (Illus.). 24p. (gr. 1-4). 1987. lib. bdg. 17.50 (*0-87614-302-8*) Carolrhoda Bks.
—Count Your Way Through China. Skoro, Martin, illus. 24p. (gr. 1-4). 1988. pap. 5.95 (*0-87614-486-5*, First Ave Edns) Lerner Pubns.
—Count Your Way Through Germany. Byers, Helen, illus. 24p. (gr. 1-4). 1990. PLB 17.50 (*0-87614-407-5*) Carolrhoda Bks.
—Count Your Way Through Germany. LC 89-22232. (ps-3). 1991. pap. 5.95 (*0-87614-532-2*) Carolrhoda Bks.
—Count Your Way Through India. Dodson, Liz B., illus. 24p. (gr. 1-4). 1990. PLB 17.50 (*0-87614-414-8*) Carolrhoda Bks.
—Count Your Way Through India. (ps-3). 1992. pap. 5.95 (*0-87614-577-2*) Carolrhoda Bks.
—Count Your Way Through Israel. Hanson, Rick, illus. 24p. (gr. 1-4). 1990. PLB 17.50 (*0-87614-415-6*) Carolrhoda Bks.
—Count Your Way Through Israel. (ps-3). 1992. pap. 5.95 (*0-87614-558-6*) Carolrhoda Bks.
—Count Your Way Through Italy. Wright, Beth, illus. 24p. (gr. 1-4). 1990. PLB 17.50 (*0-87614-406-7*) Carolrhoda Bks.
—Count Your Way Through Italy. LC 89-37455. (ps-3). 1991. pap. 5.95 (*0-87614-533-0*) Carolrhoda Bks.
—Count Your Way Through Japan. (Illus.). 24p. (gr. 1-4). 1987. lib. bdg. 17.50 (*0-87614-301-X*); pap. 4.95 (*0-87614-485-7*) Carolrhoda Bks.
—Count Your Way Through Korea. Hockerman, Dennis, illus. 24p. (gr. 1-4). 1989. 17.50 (*0-87614-348-6*); pap. 5.95 (*0-87614-516-0*) Carolrhoda Bks.
—Count Your Way Through Mexico. Byers, Helen, illus. 24p. (gr. 1-4). 1989. 17.50 (*0-87614-349-4*); pap. 5.95 (*0-87614-517-9*) Carolrhoda Bks.
—Count Your Way Through Russia. (Illus.). 24p. (gr. 1-4). 1987. lib. bdg. 17.50 (*0-87614-303-6*); pap. 5.95 (*0-87614-488-1*) Carolrhoda Bks.
—Count Your Way Through the Arab World. (Illus.). 24p. (gr. 1-4). 1987. lib. bdg. 17.50 (*0-87614-304-4*); pap. 5.95 (*0-685-13264-1*) Carolrhoda Bks.
—Count Your Way Through World. Skoro, Martin, illus. 24p. (gr. 1-4). 1988. pap. 5.95 (*0-87614-487-3*, First Ave Edns) Lerner Pubns.
—The Day Martin Luther King, Jr. Was Shot: A Photo History of the Civil Rights Movement. (gr. 4-7). 1992. pap. 5.95 (*0-590-43661-9*) Scholastic Inc.

—Get On Board: The Story of the Underground Railroad. LC 92-13247. 160p. (gr. 4-7). 1993. 13.95 (0-590-45418-8) Scholastic Inc.
—I Have a Dream: The Life & Words of Martin Luther King, Jr. LC 91-42528. (Illus.). 112p. (gr. 5 up). 1992. PLB 19.90 (1-56294-087-2) Millbrook Pr.
—I Have a Dream: The Life & Words of Martin Luther King, Jr. 1992. pap. 8.70 (0-395-64549-2) HM.
—One More River to Cross: The Story of Twelve Black Americans. (gr. 8-12). 1994. pap. 3.50 (0-590-42897-7) Scholastic Inc.
—One More River to Cross: Twelve Black Americans. 160p. 1992. 13.95 (0-590-42896-9, Scholastic Hardcover) Scholastic Inc.
—Outward Dreams: Black Inventors & Their Inventions. 128p. (gr. 7). 1991. 13.95 (0-8027-6993-4); PLB 14.85 (0-8027-6994-2) Walker & Co.
—Outward Dreams: Black Inventors & Their Inventions. (gr. 7 up). 1992. pap. 3.50 (0-553-29480-6, Starfire) Bantam.
—The Statue of Liberty: America's Proud Lady. LC 85-18061. (Illus.). 48p. (gr. 4-8). 1986. lib. bdg. 14.95 (0-8225-1706-X) Lerner Pubns.
Haslam, Andrew, jt. auth. see Baker, Wendy.
Hasler, Eveline. En Suenos Puedo Volar: In His Dreams He Could Fly. Krohn, Hildegard M., tr. from GER. Bhend, Kathi, illus. (SPA). 26p. (gr-ps-5). 1990. 13.95 (968-6465-05-7) Hispanic Bk Dist.
—Winter Magic. Lemieux, Michele, illus. LC 85-2944. 32p. (ps-3). 1985. lib. bdg. 12.88 (0-688-05258-4) Morrow Jr Bks.
Hass, E. A. BookBrain. (Illus.). 100p. (gr. 1-3). 1989. Incl. 3 1/2" or 5 1/4" disks & protective case. pap. 195.00 manual (0-685-48997-3) Apple II version (0-89774-412-8) IBM version (0-89774-618-X) Oryx Pr.
—BookBrain (Version 2.0). (Illus.). 100p. (gr. 7-9). 1990. Incl. 3 1/2" or 5 1/4" disks & protective case. pap. 195.00 manual (0-685-48999-X) Apple II version (0-89774-621-X) IBM version (0-89774-619-8) Oryx Pr.
—Incognito Mosquito, Private Insective. Hass, E. A., illus. LC 82-205. 96p. (gr. 2-5). 1982. PLB 13.88 (0-688-01434-8) Lothrop.
Hass, Marv E. Women's Perspectives on the Vietnam War. Starr, Jerold M., ed. (Illus.). 32p. (Orig.). 1991. pap. text ea. 3.00 ea., 10 or more (0-945919-14-X) Ctr Social Studies.
Hassal, P., jt. auth. see Hassal, S.
Hassal, S. & Hassal, P. Brunei. (Illus.). 96p. (gr. 5 up). 1988. 14.95 (0-7910-0158-X) Chelsea Hse.
Hassall, Neil. Heavenly Horse. LC 91-2549. (ps-3). 1992. 15.00 (0-671-75434-3, Green Tiger) S&S Trade.
Hassall, P. J., jt. auth. see Hassall, S.
Hassall, S. Bahrain. (Illus.). 96p. (gr. 5 up). 1988. 14.95 (0-222-01093-2) Chelsea Hse.
Hassall, S. & Hassall, P. J. Seychelles. (Illus.). 96p. (gr. 5 up). 1988. 14.95 (0-7910-0104-0) Chelsea Hse.
Hassall, William C., et al. The Coloring Book of Valley Forge. 44p. (gr. 1-6). 1991. coloring book 3.95 (0-9629564-0-6) PH-Enterp.
Hassett, Ann & Hassett, John. Moose on the Loose. Hassett, John, illus. 48p. (Orig.). (ps-4). 1987. pap. 7.95 (0-89272-245-2) Down East.
Hassett, Ann, jt. auth. see Hassett, John.
Hassett, John & Hassett, Ann. Junior - A Little Loon Tale. Hassett, John, illus. 32p. (gr. 2-5). 1993. 14.95 (0-89272-324-6) Down East.
—We Got My Brother at the Zoo. LC 92-1681. 1993. 14. 95 (0-395-62429-0) HM.
Hassett, John, jt. auth. see Hassett, Ann.
Hassig, Susan M. Iraq. LC 92-12178. 1992. Set. write for info. (1-85435-529-5); 21.95 (1-85435-533-3) Marshall Cavendish.
Hassler, Jon. Jemmy. (gr. 5 up). 1988. pap. 3.95 (0-449-70302-9, Juniper) Fawcett.
Hastings. Rufus & Christopher & the Box of Laughter. LC 77-190270. (Illus.). 32p. (gr. 2-4). 1972. PLB 9.95 (0-87783-060-6); pap. 3.94 deluxe ed. (0-87783-106-8); cassette 7.94x (0-87783-196-3) Oddo.
—Rufus & Christopher & the Magic Bubble. LC 73-87799. (Illus.). 32p. (gr. 2-4). 1974. PLB 9.95 (0-87783-127-0); pap. 3.94 deluxe ed. (0-87783-128-9); cassette 7.94x (0-87783-197-1) Oddo.
—Rufus & Christopher in the Land of Lies. LC 70-190271. (Illus.). 32p. (gr. 2-4). 1972. PLB 9.95 (0-87783-061-4); pap. 3.94 deluxe ed. (0-87783-107-6); cassette 7.94x (0-87783-198-X) Oddo.
—Rufus & Christopher Series, 3 vols. (Illus.). (gr. 2-4). Set. PLB 29.95 (0-87783-168-8); Set. pap. 11.82 deluxe edition (0-87783-169-6); cassettes 23.82x (0-87783-234-X) Oddo.
Hastings, Beverly. Home Before Dark. 224p. (Orig.). 1993. pap. 3.99 (0-425-14011-3) Berkley Pub.
—Watcher in the Dark. 160p. 1986. pap. 3.99 (0-425-10131-2, Berkley-Pacer) Berkley Pub.
Hastings, Catt. Romance on the Run. 1993. pap. 3.50 (0-553-29987-5) Bantam.
Hastings, Jill M. & Typpo, Marion H. Elephant in the Living Room: The Children's Book. Noland, Mimi, illus. LC 84-70189. 88p. (Orig.). (gr. 3-8). 1984. wkbk. 9.95 (0-89638-071-8) CompCare.

Hastings, Scott E., Jr. Miss Mary Mac All Dressed in Black: Tongue Twisters, Jump-Rope Rhymes, & Other Children's Lore from New England. 128p. (Orig.). 1990. pap. 8.95 (0-87483-156-3) August Hse.
Hastings, Selina. The Firebird. Cartwright, Reg, illus. LC 92-52997. 40p. (gr. 1-8). 1993. 15.95 (1-56402-096-7) Candlewick Pr.
—Peter & the Wolf. Cartwright, Reg, illus. LC 86-27004. 32p. (ps-2). 1990. 5.95 (0-8050-1362-8, Bks Young Read) H Holt & Co.
—Sir Gawain & the Green Knight. Wijngaard, Juan, illus. LC 80-85379. 32p. (gr. 3-7). 1981. 12.95 (0-688-00592-6) Lothrop.
Hastings, Selina, retold by. The Children's Illustrated Bible. Thomas, Eric, illus. LC 93-30814. 1994. write for info. (1-56458-472-0) Dorling Kindersley.
—Reynard the Fox. Percy, Graham, illus. LC 90-11105. 80p. (gr. 1-8). 1991. 16.95 (0-688-09949-1, Tambourine Bks); PLB 16.88 (0-688-10156-9, Tambourine Bks) Morrow.
—Sir Gawain & the Loathly Lady. Wijngaard, Juan, illus. LC 85-63. 32p. (ps-3). 1987. pap. 4.95 (0-688-07046-9, Mulberry) Morrow.
Hasty, Kathy N. Murphy Wants to Be Famous. Newcomer, Carolyn, illus. 27p. (Orig.). (ps-2). 1991. pap. 3.99 (0-9631480-0-1) Story Time Pubns.
Hatay, Nona. Charlie's ABC. Hatay, Nona, illus. LC 92-72030. 32p. (ps-k). 1993. 10.95 (1-56282-352-3); PLB 10.89 (1-56282-353-1) Hyprn Child.
Hatcher, John. Conversations. Marcus, Audrey F., illus. 208p. (gr. 8-10). 1988. 0.00; pap. 12.95 (0-85398-275-9) G Ronald Pub.
Hatchett, Clint. The Glow-in-the-Dark Night Sky Book. Marchesi, Stephen, illus. LC 87-61531. 24p. (gr. 3-7). 1988. 12.00 (0-394-89113-9) Random Bks Yng Read.
Hatchett, Eve B., jt. auth. see Cowden, Frances B.
Hatchigan, Jessica. Count Dracula, Me & Norma D. (gr. 3-7). 1987. pap. 2.95 (0-380-75414-2, Camelot) Avon.
—Dinosaurs Aren't Forever. 112p. (Orig.). 1991. pap. 2.95 (0-380-76137-8, Camelot) Avon.
Hately, David. Dinosaurs. 1987. Series S808-13. text ed. 3.95 cased (0-7214-9543-5) Ladybird Bks.
Hathaway, Joe & Hathaway, Nancy. How John Was Unique. 12p. (Orig.). (gr. k-3). 1984. pap. text ed. 3.95 (0-918335-01-9) Natl Marfan Foun.
Hathaway, Nancy, jt. auth. see Hathaway, Joe.
Hatherly, Janelle & Nicholls, Delia. Dolphins & Porpoises. 32p. 1990. 17.95 (0-8160-2272-0) Facts on File.
Hatheway, Flora. Chief Plenty Coups: Life of the Crow Indian Chief. (gr. 4). 1971. 1.95 (0-89992-005-5) Coun India Ed.
Hathon, Elizabeth. We Go to School. LC 92-80390. (Illus.). 14p. (ps). 1992. bds. 2.99 (0-679-83377-3) Random Bks Yng Read.
—We Go to the Zoo. LC 92-80391. (Illus.). 14p. (ps) 1992. bds. 2.99 (0-679-83376-5) Random Bks Yng Read.
Hathon, Elizabeth, illus. My Fuzzy Friends. 18p. (ps). 1993. bds. 2.95 (0-448-40523-7, G&D) Putnam Pub Group.
—Sleepy Time. 18p. (ps). 1993. bds. 2.95 (0-448-40524-5, G&D) Putnam Pub Group.
Hathon, Elizabeth, photos by. Let's Get Together. LC 91-62668. (Illus.). 14p. (ps). 1992. bds. 2.99 (0-679-82225-9) Random Bks Yng Read.
—Sharing & Caring. LC 91-62663. (Illus.). 14p. (ps). 1992. bds. 2.99 (0-679-82226-7) Random Bks Yng Read.
Hathorn, Elizabeth. The Tram to Bondi Beach. Vivas, Julie, illus. 32p. (gr. 4-8). 1989. 12.95 (0-916291-20-0) Kane-Miller Bk.
Hathorn, Libby. Freya's Fantastic Surprise. Thompson, Sharon, illus. 32p. (ps-3). 1989. 12.95 (0-590-42442-4, Scholastic Hardcover) Scholastic Inc.
—Looking for Felix. Culio, Ned, illus. LC 92-34259. 1993. 4.25 (0-383-03638-0) SRA Schl Grp.
—The Surprise Box. Cutter, Priscilla, illus. LC 93-28957. 1994. 4.25 (0-383-03778-6) SRA Schl Grp.
—There & Back. LC 92-27236. 1993. 4.25 (0-383-03659-3) SRA Schl Grp.
—Thunderwith. 1991. 15.95 (0-316-35034-6) Little.
Hatonn & L-L Research Staff. What Is Love? A Coloring Book for Kids. (Illus.). 34p. (ps-2). 1984. pap. 6.95 (0-945007-05-1) L-L Resrch.
Hatter, Mari, tr. see Segal, Bertha E.
Hattery-Beyer, Lynn, tr. see Kordon, Klaus.
Haubrich-Casperson, Jane & Van Nispen, Doug. Coping with Teen Gambling. LC 92-41549. 1993. 13.95 (0-8239-1512-3) Rosen Group.
Haug, Arden, tr. see Nordqvist, Sven.
Haugaard, Erik. The Death of Mr. Angel. 167p. (gr. 9-12). 1992. 13.95 (1-879373-26-2) R Rinehart.
Haugaard, Erik & Haugaard, Masako. The Story of Yuriwaka. (Illus.). 42p. (gr. 3-6). 1991. 12.95 (1-879373-02-5) R Rinehart.
Haugaard, Erik C. The Boy & the Samurai. LC 90-47535. 256p. (gr. 5-9). 1991. 14.45 (0-395-56398-4) HM.
—A Boy's Will. (gr. 4-7). 1990. pap. 4.95 (0-395-54962-0) HM.
—Cromwell's Boy. (gr. 4-7). 1990. pap. 5.95 (0-395-54975-2) HM.
—Prince Boghole. Downing, Julie, illus. LC 86-61. 32p. (gr. k-3). 1988. 14.95 (0-02-743440-0, Macmillan Child Bk) Macmillan Child Grp.
—Princess Horrid. Hearne, Diane D., illus. LC 89-8227. 48p. (gr. k-4). 1990. RSBE 14.95 (0-02-743445-1, Macmillan Child Bk) Macmillan Child Grp.

—The Samurai's Tale. 256p. (gr. 7 up). 1984. 14.45 (0-395-34559-6, 5-87439) HM.
—Samurai's Tale. 1990. pap. 4.95 (0-395-54970-1) HM.
—Under the Black Flag. LC 93-85476. 150p. (gr. 6 up). 1993. pap. 8.95 (1-879373-63-7) R Rinehart.
Haugaard, Erik C., tr. see Andersen, Hans Christian.
Haugaard, Masako, jt. auth. see Haugaard, Erik.
Hauge, Veronica, tr. see Basu, Romen.
Haugen, Tormod. The Night Birds. La Farge, Sheila, tr. from NOR. LC 82-70311. 160p. (gr. 4-6). 1982. 11.95 (0-385-28735-6, Sey Lawr); pap. 9.89 (0-385-28736-4) Delacorte.
—Zeppelin. Diamond, Donna, illus. Jacobs, David R., tr. from NOR. LC 92-8319. (Illus.). 128p. (gr. 4-7). 1992. 15.00 (0-06-020881-3); PLB 14.89 (0-06-020882-1) HarpC Child Bks. Postponed.
Haught, James A. Science in a Nanosecond: Illustrated Answers to 100 Basic Science Questions. (Illus.). 110p. (Orig.). (gr. 4 up). 1991. pap. 13.95 (0-87975-637-3) Prometheus Bks.
Haugo, John E. Introduction to Microcomputers: Apple Set. (Illus.). 40p. (gr. 4-6). 1982. Set. 71.92 (0-07-079115-5) McGraw.
—Introduction to Microcomputers: TRS-80 Model III. (Illus.). 40p. (gr. 4-6). 1982. 71.92 (0-07-079221-6) McGraw.
—Math Regrouping Games: Apple Set. 32p. (gr. 4-6). 1982. Set. 71.92 (0-07-079118-X) McGraw.
—Math Regrouping Games: TRS-80 Model III Set. (Illus.). 32p. (gr. 4-6). 1982. Set. 71.92 (0-07-079224-0) McGraw.
—Math Skill Games: Apple Set. (Illus.). 40p. (gr. 4-6). 1982. Set. 71.92 (0-07-079116-3) McGraw.
—Math Skill Games: TRS-80 Model III Set. Kovaleik, Terry, illus. 40p. (gr. 4-6). 1982. Set. 71.92 (0-07-079222-4) McGraw.
Haun, Eugene. Cardinal Points & Other Poems. LC 81-82658. 85p. (gr. 9-12). 1981. pap. 5.00 perfect bd. (0-916418-32-4) Lotus.
Haundsfield, Hunter see Landau, Elaine.
Hauptly, Denis J. A Convention of Delegates: The Creation of the Constitution. LC 86-17260. (Illus.). 160p. (gr. 3-7). 1987. SBE 13.95 (0-689-31148-6, Atheneum Child Bk) Macmillan Child Grp.
—In Vietnam. LC 85-7464. (Illus.). 224p. (gr. 5 up). 1985. SBE 13.95 (0-689-31079-X, Atheneum Child Bk) Macmillan Child Grp.
—Puerto Rico: An Unfinished Story. LC 90-37953. (Illus.). 160p. (gr. 5 up). 1991. SBE 13.95 (0-689-31431-0, Atheneum Child Bk) Macmillan Child Grp.
Haury, Emil W., jt. auth. see Udall, Stewart L.
Haus, Felice. Big Bird Flies Alone. Fritz, Ron, illus. LC 88-62523. 32p. (Orig.). (ps-3). 1989. pap. 1.50 (0-394-83932-3) Random Bks Yng Read.
—Happy Birthday, Cookie Monster! A Step One Book. Nicklaus, Carol, illus. LC 85-25639. 32p. (ps-1). 1986. lib. bdg. 7.99 (0-394-98182-0); pap. 3.50 (0-394-88182-6) Random Bks Yng Read.
Hausberger, Petra, ed. see St. Onge, Susan, et al.
Hauser, Pierre. The Illegal Aliens. Moynihan, Daniel P., intro. by. (Illus.). 112p. (gr. 5 up). 1990. 17.95x (0-87754-889-7) Chelsea Hse.
Hauserr, Rosmarie. Children & the AIDS Virus: A Book for Children, Parents, & Teachers. Hausherr, Rosmarie, illus. (gr. up). 1989. 15.45 (0-89919-834-1, Clarion Bks); pap. 5.95 (0-395-51167-4, Clarion Bks) HM.
—The City Girl Who Went to Sea. Hausherr, Rosmarie, illus. LC 89-27236. 80p. (gr. 3-6). 1990. SBE 14.95 (0-02-743421-4, Four Winds) Macmillan Child Grp.
—My First Kitten. Hausherr, Rosmarie, illus. LC 85-42804. 48p. (gr. 1-4). 1985. RSBE 13.95 (0-02-743420-6, Four Winds) Macmillan Child Grp.
—My First Puppy. Hausherr, Rosmarie, illus. LC 86-14979. 64p. (gr. 1-4). 1986. RSBE 14.95 (0-02-743410-9, Four Winds) Macmillan Child Grp.
—The One-Room School at Squabble Hollow. LC 87-17774. (Illus.). 80p. (gr. 4-6). 1988. SBE 14.95 (0-02-743250-5, Pub. by Four Winds Pr) Macmillan Child Grp.
—What Food is This? LC 93-17328. (Illus.). 40p. (ps-3). 1994. 14.95 (0-590-46583-X) Scholastic Inc.
—What Instrument Is This? 1992. 14.95 (0-590-44644-4, Scholastic Hardcover) Scholastic Inc.
Hausman, Gerald. Beth: The Little Girl of Pine Knoll. Totten, Bob, illus. LC 74-822228. 32p. (gr. 6 up). 1974. 15.00 (0-912846-08-9) Bookstore Pr.
—Ghost Walk: Native American Tales of the Spirit. Hausman, Sid, illus. 32p. (Orig.). (gr. 3). 1991. pap. 9.95 (0-933553-07-2) Mariposa Print Pub.
—Turtle Island ABC: A Gathering of Native American Symbols. Moser, Barry & Moser, Cara, illus. LC 92-14982. 32p. (ps-2). Date not set. 15.00 (0-06-021307-8); PLB 14.89 (0-06-021308-6) HarpC Child Bks. Postponed.
Hausman, Gerald, compiled by. Coyote Walks on Two Legs. Cooper, Floyd, illus. LC 92-25115. 1993. write for info. (0-399-22018-6, Philomel Bks) Putnam Pub Group.
Hausman, Gerald & Hausman, Gerald, eds. How Chipmunk Got Tiny Feet: Native American Animal Origin Stories. Hague, Michael, illus. LC 92-44186. (ps-6). 1995. 15.00 (0-06-022906-3, HarpT); PLB 14.89 (0-06-022907-1) HarpC.
Hausman, Karen. My Uncle Mike. 1994. 7.95 (0-8062-4849-1) Carlton.

Hausman, Suzanne, illus. Yes, Virginia. 6.95 (0-685-86235-6) Pubns Devl Co TX.

Hauswald, Carol & Maskowski, Alice. Body Art: Holidays. (Illus.). 79p. (gr. k-1). 1992. pap. 8.95 (1-878279-41-6) Monday Morning Bks.

—Body Art: Nature. (Illus.). 80p. (ps-1). 1992. pap. 8.95 (1-878279-40-8) Monday Morning Bks.

—Body Art: People. (Illus.). 80p. (gr. k-1). 1992. pap. 8.95 (1-878279-42-4) Monday Morning Bks.

Hautzig, David. At the Supermarket. LC 93-26976. (Illus.). 32p. (gr. k-3). 1994. 14.95 (0-531-06832-3); lib. bdg. 14.99 RLB (0-531-08682-8) Orchard Bks Watts.

—DJs, Ratings, & Hook Tapes: Pop Music Broadcasting. Hautzig, David, illus. LC 91-33588. 48p. (gr. 3-7). 1993. SBE 15.95 (0-02-743471-0, Macmillan Child Bk) Macmillan Child Grp.

Hautzig, Deborah. Aladdin & the Magic Lamp. Mitchell, Kathy, illus. LC 92-1608. 48p. (Orig.). (gr. 2-3). 1993. PLB 7.99 (0-679-93241-0); pap. 3.50 (0-679-83241-6) Random Bks Yng Read.

—Big Bird at the Beach. Nicklaus, Carol, illus. LC 89-61613. 32p. (Orig.). (ps-3). 1990. pap. 1.50 (0-679-80159-6) Random Bks Yng Read.

—Big Bird Plays the Violin. Mathieu, Joe, illus. LC 90-8967. 40p. (ps-3). 1991. 4.95 (0-679-81675-5); PLB 6.99 (0-679-91675-X) Random Bks Yng Read.

—Ernie & Bert's New Kitten. Mathieu, Joe, illus. LC 89-10583. 40p. (ps-3). 1990. 4.95 (0-679-80420-X); PLB 6.99 (0-679-90420-4) Random Bks Yng Read.

—Ernie & Bert's New Kitten. Mathieu, Joe, illus. LC 89-10583. 40p. (ps-3). 1993. 2.99 (0-679-83954-2) Random Bks Yng Read.

—Get Well, Granny Bird. Mathieu, Joe, illus. LC 88-18446. 40p. (ps-3). 1989. PLB 6.99 (0-394-92247-6) Random Bks Yng Read.

—Grover's Bad Dream. Mathieu, Joe, illus. LC 90-32085. 40p. (ps-3). 1990. 4.95 (0-679-80898-1); lib. bdg. 6.99 (0-679-90898-6) Random Bks Yng Read.

—Grover's Lucky Jacket. Chartier, Normand, illus. LC 89-30102. 40p. (ps-3). 1989. PLB 6.99 (0-679-90077-2); pap. 4.95 (0-679-80077-8) Random Bks Yng Read.

—Happy Birthday Little Witch. Brown, Marc, illus. 1985. pap. 2.95 (0-394-87365-3) Random Bks Yng Read.

—Happy Mother's Day. Chartier, Normand, illus. LC 88-14002. 32p. (Orig.). (ps-1). 1989. PLB 7.99 (0-394-92204-2); pap. 2.95 (0-394-82204-8) Random Bks Yng Read.

—Hey, Dollface. LC 78-54685. 160p. (gr. 7-9). 1978. PLB 11.88 (0-688-84170-8) Greenwillow.

—It's a Secret! Leigh, Tom, illus. LC 87-20542. 40p. (ps-3). 1988. 4.95 (0-394-89672-6); lib. bdg. 6.99 (0-394-99672-0) Random Bks Yng Read.

—It's Easy! Mathieu, Joe, illus. LC 88-6441. 40p. (ps-3). 1988. 4.95 (0-394-81376-6) Random Bks Yng Read.

—It's Not Fair. Leigh, Tom, illus. LC 85-30154. 40p. (ps-3). 1986. 4.95 (0-394-88151-6) Random Bks Yng Read.

—It's Not Fair! Leigh, Tom, illus. LC 85-30154. 40p. (ps-3). 1993. pap. 2.99 (0-679-83951-8) Random Bks Yng Read.

—Little Witch's Big Night. Brown, Marc, illus. LC 84-3309. 48p. (ps-2). 1984. PLB 7.99 (0-394-96587-6); pap. 2.95 (0-394-86587-1) Random Bks Yng Read.

—Little Witch's Book of Magic Spells. Brown, Marc, illus. LC 87-63196. 24p. (ps-1). 1993. 2.99 (0-679-84769-3) Random Bks Yng Read.

—The Story of the Nutcracker Ballet. Goode, Diane, illus. 32p. (ps-1). 1986. pap. 5.95 (0-394-88296-2) Random Bks Yng Read.

—The Story of the Nutcracker Ballet. Goode, Diane, illus. LC 85-30149. 32p. (ps-1). 1993. 2.25 (0-394-88178-8) Random Bks Yng Read.

—A Visit to the Sesame Street Library. Mathieu, Joe, illus. LC 85-18312. 32p. (ps-1). 1986. 2.25 (0-394-87744-6); lib. bdg. 5.99 (0-394-97744-0) Random Bks Yng Read.

—Una Visita a la Biblioteca De Sesame Street. Saunders, Paola B., tr. Mathieu, Joe, illus. LC 92-16609. (SPA.). 32p. (ps-3). 1993. pap. 2.25 (0-679-83943-7) Random Bks Yng Read.

—Una Visita Al Hospital De Sesame Street. Saunders, Paola B., tr. Mathieu, Joe, illus. LC 92-16610. (SPA.). 32p. (ps-3). 1993. pap. 2.25 (0-679-83944-5) Random Bks Yng Read.

—Why Are You So Mean to Me? Cooke, Tom, illus. LC 85-18434. 40p. (ps-3). 1992. pap. 2.99 (0-679-82402-2) Random Bks Yng Read.

Hautzig, Deborah, adapted by. Big Bird Visits the Dodos. Mathieu, Joe, illus. LC 84-43051. 32p. (ps-3). 1985. lib. bdg. 5.99 (0-394-97373-9) Random Bks Yng Read.

Hautzig, Deborah, ed. The Christmas Story: Based on the Gospels According to St. Matthew & St. Luke. Beckett, Sheila, illus. LC 83-60411. 24p. (ps-2). 1983. 2.95 (0-394-86124-8) Random Bks Yng Read.

Hautzig, Deborah, adapted by. Follow That Bird. LC 84-43052. (Illus.). (gr. 1-4). 1985. lib. bdg. 7.99 (0-394-97225-2) Random Bks Yng Read.

Hautzig, Deborah, retold by. The Nutcracker Ballet. Ewing, Carolyn, illus. LC 92-3320. 48p. (Orig.). (gr. 1-3). 1992. PLB 7.99 (0-679-92385-3); pap. 3.50 (0-679-82385-9) Random Bks Yng Read.

—The Pied Piper of Hamelin: A Step 2 Book. Schindler, S. D., illus. LC 89-3968. 48p. (Orig.). (gr. 1-3). 1989. lib. bdg. 7.99 (0-394-96579-5); pap. 3.50 (0-394-86579-0) Random Bks Yng Read.

Hautzig, Deborah, adapted by see Andersen, Hans Christian.

Hautzig, Esther. The Endless Steppe. LC 68-13582. 256p. (gr. 7 up). 1987. pap. 3.95 (0-06-447027-X, Trophy) HarpC Child Bks.

—Endless Steppe: Growing up in Siberia. LC 68-13582. 256p. (gr. 7 up). 1992. 15.00 (0-690-26371-6, Crowell Jr Bks); PLB 14.89 (0-690-04919-6, Crowell Jr Bks) HarpC Child Bks.

—A Gift for Mama. Diamond, Donna, illus. 64p. (gr. 3-7). 1987. pap. 3.95 (0-14-032384-8, Puffin) Puffin Bks.

—A Gift for Mama. (gr. 1-4). 1992. 16.50 (0-8446-6570-3) Peter Smith.

—Holiday Treats. Yaroslava, illus. LC 83-9347. 96p. (gr. 3 up). 1983. SBE 13.95 (0-02-743350-1, Macmillan Child Bk) Macmillan Child Grp.

—Make It Special: Cards, Decorations, & Party Favors for Holiday & Other Celebrations. Weston, Martha, illus. LC 86-8616. 96p. (gr. 3-7). 1986. SBE 13.95 (0-02-743370-6, Macmillan Child Bk) Macmillan Child Grp.

—On the Air: Behind the Scenes at a TV Newscast. Hautzig, David, photos by. LC 91-6407. (Illus.). 48p. (gr. 1-4). 1991. RSBE 15.95 (0-02-743361-7, Macmillan Child Bk) Macmillan Child Grp.

—Riches. Diamond, Donna, illus. LC 89-26904. 32p. (gr. 3 up). 1992. 14.00 (0-06-022259-X); PLB 13.89 (0-06-022260-3) HarpC Child Bks.

Hautzig, Esther, tr. from YID. The Seven Good Years & Other Stories of I. L. Peretz. Kogan, Deborah, illus. 96p. (gr. 3-6). 1984. 10.95 (0-8276-0244-8) JPS Phila.

Havel, Jennifer. The Wacky Rulebook. Ewers, Joe, illus. 40p. (ps-3). write for info (0-910313-77-6) Parker Bros.

Haven, Susan. Is It Them or Is It Me? 176p. 1990. 14.95 (0-399-21916-1, Putnam) Putnam Pub Group.

—Maybe I'll Move to the Lost & Found. 160p. (gr. 5 up). 1988. 14.95 (0-399-21509-3, Putnam) Putnam Pub Group.

Haven, Tom de see De Haven, Tom.

Havens, Ami. Now You're Talking. Richey, Donald, illus. LC 90-10764. 128p. (gr. 5-9). 1991. lib. bdg. 10.89 (0-8167-2142-4); pap. text ed. 2.95 (0-8167-2143-2) Troll Assocs.

Havens, Betty. In Search of the Golden Teardrop. (Illus.). 53p. (gr. k up). 1972. pap. 10.00 director's script (0-88680-092-7); bk. 2.00 (0-88680-091-9); royalty on application 20.00 (0-685-57898-4) I E Clark.

Haverson, Susan, jt. auth. see Haverson, Wayne W.

Haverson, Wayne W. & Haverson, Susan. Celebration! Festivities for Reading. ESL ed. Munch, Helen, ed. Sardar, Zahid, illus. 340p. (gr. 3-12). 1987. pap. text ed. 9.00 (0-88084-241-5); Om ex. sheets & binder 79.95 (0-13-122086-1); poster set 102.60 (0-88084-240-7) Alemany Pr.

Haverstock, Nathan A. Brazil in Pictures. rev. ed. (Illus.). 64p. (gr. 5 up). 1987. PLB 17.50 (0-8225-1802-3) Lerner Pubns.

—Cuba in Pictures. (Illus.). 64p. (gr. 5 up). 1987. PLB 17.50 (0-8225-1811-2) Lerner Pubns.

—The Dominican Republic in Pictures. (Illus.). 64p. (gr. 5 up). 1988. PLB 17.50 (0-8225-1812-0) Lerner Pubns.

—El Salvador in Pictures. (Illus.). 64p. (gr. 5 up). 1987. PLB 17.50 (0-8225-1806-6) Lerner Pubns.

—Nicaragua in Pictures. (Illus.). 64p. (gr. 5 up). 1987. PLB 17.50 (0-8225-1817-1) Lerner Pubns.

—Paraguay in Pictures. (Illus.). 64p. (gr. 5 up). 1987. PLB 17.50 (0-8225-1819-8) Lerner Pubns.

—Uruguay in Pictures. (Illus.). 64p. (gr. 5 up). 1987. PLB 17.50 (0-8225-1823-6) Lerner Pubns.

Haviland, Virginia. The Talking Pot, Vol. 1: A Danish Folktale. (ps-4). 1990. 14.95 (0-316-35060-5, Joy St Bks) Little.

Haviland, Virginia, selected by. Favorite Fairy Tales Told Around the World. Schindler, S. D., illus. (ps-6). 1985. 24.95 (0-316-35044-3) Little.

Haviland, Virginia, compiled by. Favorite Fairy Tales Told in England. Chambliss, Maxie, illus. LC 93-29707. 1994. write for info. (0-688-12595-6, Pub. by Beech Tree Bks) Morrow.

—Favorite Fairy Tales Told in France. Ambrus, Victor, illus. LC 93-29665. 1994. write for info. (0-688-12596-4, Pub. by Beech Tree Bks) Morrow.

Haviland, Virginia, ed. see Briggs, Raymond.

Havill, Juanita. It Always Happens to Leona. McCully, Emily, illus. (gr 2 up). 1989. 12.95 (0-517-57227-3) Crown Bks Yng Read.

—Jamaica & Brianna. O'Brien, Anne S., illus. LC 92-36508. 1993. 13.95 (0-395-64489-5) HM.

—Jamaica Tag-Along. O'Brien, Anne S., illus. (ps-3). 1989. 13.45 (0-395-49602-0) HM.

—Jamaica Tag-Along. O'Brien, Anne S., illus. 1990. pap. 4.80 (0-395-54949-3) HM.

—Jamaica's Find. O'Brien, Anne S., illus. (ps-3). 1986. 13.45 (0-395-39376-0) HM.

—Jamaica's Find. O'Brien, Anne S., illus. LC 85-14542. 32p. (gr. 4-8). 1987. pap. 4.80 (0-395-45357-7) HM.

—Jennier, Too. (Illus.). 56p. (gr. 2-5). 1994. 11.95 (1-56282-618-2); PLB 11.89 (1-56282-619-0) Hyprn Child.

—Kentucky Troll. LC 90-27850. (ps-3). 1993. 13.00 (0-688-10457-6); PLB 12.93 (0-688-10458-4) Lothrop.

—Leona & Ike. McCully, Emily, illus. LC 90-40411. 128p. (gr. 2-6). 1991. 13.95 (0-517-57687-2); PLB 14.99 (0-517-57688-0) Crown Bks Yng Read.

—Magic Fort. Shute, Linda, illus. LC 90-42012. 32p. (gr. k-3). 1991. 13.45 (0-395-50067-2) HM.

—Sato & the Elephants. LC 91-26096. (ps-3). 1993. 15.00 (0-688-11155-6); PLB 14.93 (0-688-11156-4) Lothrop.

—Treasure Nap. Savadier, Elivia, illus. 32p. (gr. k-3). 1992. 13.95 (0-395-57817-5) HM.

Havlik, Rich. Life Long League Digest. 138p. (Orig.). (gr. 7 up). 1993. pap. 12.95 (0-9638188-3-X) R Havlik.

Haworth, L., jt. auth. see Tyler, J.

Hawcock, David. Archaepteryx. 1994. write for info. (0-8050-3194-4) H Holt & Co.

—Mini Dinos: Brontosaurus. (Illus.). 10p. (ps-2). 1993. bds. 5.95 (0-8050-2361-5) H Holt & Co.

—Mini Dinos: Stegosaurus. (Illus.). 10p. (ps-2). 1993. bds. 5.95 (0-8050-2362-3) H Holt & Co.

—Mini Dinos: Triceratops. (Illus.). 10p. (ps-2). 1993. bds. 5.95 (0-8050-2364-X) H Holt & Co.

—Mini Dinos: Tyrannosaurus. (Illus.). 10p. (ps-2). 1993. bds. 5.95 (0-8050-2363-1) H Holt & Co.

—Plesiosaur-Minibeast. 1994. write for info. (0-8050-3196-0) H Holt & Co.

—Sabre Toothed Tiger. 1994. write for info. (0-8050-3193-6) H Holt & Co.

—Shipwrecks: A Three-Dimensional Exploration. Walton, Garry, illus. 24p. (gr. k-2). 1993. 15.95 (0-694-00452-9, Festival) HarpC Child Bks.

—Wooly Mammoth. 1994. write for info. (0-8050-3195-2) H Holt & Co.

Hawes, Charles B. The Dark Frigate. rev. ed. Chappell, Warren, illus. (gr. 7 up). 1971. 18.95 (0-316-35096-6, Joy St Bks) Little.

Hawes, Judith. Fireflies in the Night. rev. ed. Alexander, Ellen, illus. LC 90-1587. 32p. (ps-1). 1991. PLB 13.89 (0-06-022485-1) HarpC Child Bks.

—Fireflies in the Night. rev. ed. Alexander, Ellen, illus. LC 90-4255. 32p. (ps-1). 1991. pap. 4.50 (0-06-445101-1, Trophy) HarpC Child Bks.

Hawes, Judy. Fireflies in the Night. LC 63-15088. (Illus.). (gr. k-3). 1963. pap. 4.95 (0-690-01259-4, Crowell Jr Bks) HarpC Child Bks.

Hawes, Louise. Nelson Malone Meets the Man from Mush-Nut. (gr. 3-7). 1988. pap. 2.50 (0-380-70508-7, Camelot) Avon.

—Nelson Malone Saves Flight 942. 160p. 1990. pap. 2.95 (0-380-70758-6, Camelot) Avon.

Hawke, Sharryl D., jt. auth. see Davis, James E.

Hawke, Sharryl D., ed. see Davis, James.

Hawke, Sharryl D., ed. see Davis, James E.

Hawke, Sherryl D., jt. auth. see Davis, Jim.

Hawkes, Bob. Playbook: Football, No. 2. (gr. 4-7). 1991. pap. 4.95 (0-316-34349-8, Spts Illus Kids) Little.

Hawkes, Kevin. His Royal Buckliness. Pearson, Susan, ed. LC 91-40347. (Illus.). 32p. (gr. k up). 1992. 15.00 (0-688-11062-2); PLB 14.93 (0-688-11063-0); poster avail. Lothrop.

—Then the Troll Heard the Squeak. (ps-3). 1991. PLB 13.88 (0-688-09758-8) Lothrop.

—Then the Troll Heard the Squeak. (ps-3). 1991. 13.95 (0-688-09757-X) Lothrop.

—Then the Troll Heard the Squeak. LC 92-12528. (gr. 4 up). 1992. 4.50 (0-14-054469-0) Puffin Bks.

Hawkes, N. International Drug Trade. (Illus.). 48p. (gr. 5 up). 1988. PLB 18.60 (0-86592-280-2); 13.95 (0-685-58317-1) Rourke Corp.

Hawkes, Nigel. Genetic Engineering. (Illus.). 32p. (gr. 5-8). 1991. PLB 12.40 (0-531-17273-2, Gloucester Pr) Watts.

—Glasnost & Perestroika. (Illus.). 48p. (gr. 5 up). 1990. lib. bdg. 18.60 (0-86592-149-0); lib. bdg. 13.95.p. (0-685-36378-3) Rourke Corp.

—Into Space. LC 93-13468. (Illus.). 32p. (gr. 5-8). 1993. PLB 12.40 (0-531-17416-6, Gloucester Pr) Watts.

—Nuclear Power. (Illus.). 48p. (gr. 5 up). 1990. lib. bdg. 18.60 (0-86592-098-2); lib. bdg. 13.95.p. (0-685-36380-5) Rourke Corp.

—Safety in the Sky. 1990. PLB 12.40 (0-531-17207-4) Watts.

—Toxic Waste & Recycling. (Illus.). 32p. (gr. 5-8). 1991. PLB 12.40 (0-531-17359-3, Gloucester Pr) Watts.

Hawkes, Richard R., et al. Mastermind for the Primary Grades. (Illus.). 120p. (Orig.). (gr. k up). 1992. pap. 9.95 (0-673-36018-0) GdYrBks.

Hawkes, Robert. Play Book, No. 3: Football. (Illus.). (gr. 3-7). 1999. pap. 4.95 (0-316-34353-6, Spts Illus Kids) Little.

Hawkes, Sharlene W., jt. auth. see Jones, Barbara B.

Hawkey, Dick. Play the Game: Squash. (Illus.). 80p. (gr. 10-12). 1991. pap. 6.95 (0-7063-6662-X, Pub. by Ward Lock UK) Sterling.

Hawkins. Audio & Radio. 32p. (gr. 5-9). 1982. (Usborne-Hayes); PLB 13.96 (0-88110-001-3) EDC.

Hawkins, Colin. Monsters. (gr. 4-7). 1993. pap. 7.00 (0-00-664020-6) HarpC Child Bks.

—Old McDonald Had a Farm. (ps-3). 1991. 9.95 (0-8431-2884-4) Price Stern.

—Witches. (gr. 4-7). 1993. pap. 7.00 (0-00-662574-6) HarpC Child Bks.

Hawkins, Colin & Hawkins, Jacqui. Come for a Ride on the Ghost Train. Halperin, Susan, ed. Hawkins, Colin & Hawkins, Jacqui, illus. 40p. (gr. up). 1993. 12.95 (1-56402-236-6) Candlewick Pr.

—Crocodile Creek. 1989. 9.95 (0-385-24979-9); PLB 10.99 (0-385-24980-2) Doubleday.

—Hey Diddle Diddle. LC 91-71848. (Illus.). 8p. (ps). 1992. 5.95 (1-56402-014-2) Candlewick Pr.

—Humpty Dumpty. LC 91-71847. (Illus.). 8p. (ps). 1992. 5.95 (1-56402-015-0) Candlewick Pr.

—Knock! Knock! Hawkins, Colin & Hawkins, Jacqui, illus. LC 91-17313. 28p. 1991. POB 14.95 (0-689-71475-0, Aladdin) Macmillan Child Grp.
—Max & the Magic Word. (Illus.). 32p. (ps-3). 1988. pap. 3.50 (0-14-050568-7, Puffin) Puffin Bks.
—The Numberlies: Number Eight. (Illus.). 32p. (ps-k). 1993. 8.95 (0-370-31513-8, Pub. by Bodley Head UK) Trafalgar.
—The Numberlies: Number Five. (Illus.). 32p. (ps-2). 1992. 8.95 (0-370-31510-3, Pub. by Bodley Head UK) Trafalgar.
—The Numberlies: Number Four. (Illus.). 32p. (ps-2). 1992. 8.95 (0-370-31509-X, Pub. by Bodley Head UK) Trafalgar.
—The Numberlies: Number Nine. (Illus.). 32p. (ps-k). 1993. 8.95 (0-370-31514-6, Pub. by Bodley Head UK) Trafalgar.
—The Numberlies: Number One. (Illus.). 32p. (ps-1). 1992. 8.95 (0-370-31506-5, Pub. by Bodley Head UK) Trafalgar.
—The Numberlies: Number Seven. (Illus.). 32p. (ps-k). 1993. 8.95 (0-370-31512-X, Pub. by Bodley Head UK) Trafalgar.
—The Numberlies: Number Six. (Illus.). 32p. (ps-k). 1993. 8.95 (0-370-31511-1, Pub. by Bodley Head UK) Trafalgar.
—The Numberlies: Number Three. (Illus.). 32p. (ps-2). 1992. 8.95 (0-370-31508-1, Pub. by Bodley Head UK) Trafalgar.
—The Numberlies: Number Two. (Illus.). 32p. (ps-2). 1992. 8.95 (0-370-31507-3, Pub. by Bodley Head UK) Trafalgar.
—The Numberlies: Zero. (Illus.). 32p. (ps-k). 1993. 8.95 (0-370-31640-1, Pub. by Bodley Head UK) Trafalgar.
—Pat the Cat. LC 82-18104. (Illus.). (ps-1). 1986. 9.95 (0-399-20957-3, Putnam) Putnam Pub Group.
—Terrible, Terrible Tiger. Hawkins, Colin & Hawkins, Jacqui, illus. LC 87-40675. 32p. (ps-3). 1988. bds. 5.95 (1-55782-043-0, Pub. by Warner Juvenile Bks) Little.
Hawkins, Colin & Hawkins, Jacqui, eds. I Know an Old Lady Who Swallowed a Fly. Hawkins, Colin & Hawkins, Jacqui, illus. 24p. (ps-1). 1987. 12.95 (0-399-21484-4, Putnam) Putnam Pub Group.
Hawkins, Jacqui, jt. auth. see Hawkins, Colin.
Hawkins, Jacqui, jt. ed. see Hawkins, Colin.
Hawkins, Jim W. Baton Twirling Is for Me. Bible, William, illus. LC 82-245. 48p. (gr. 2-5). 1982. PLB 13.50 (0-8225-1134-7) Lerner Pubns.
—Cheerleading Is for Me. Moral, Jean D., illus. LC 81-3719. (gr. 2-5). 1981. PLB 13.50 (0-8225-1127-4, AACRZ) Lerner Pubns.
Hawkins, Laura. The Cat That Could Spell Mississippi. LC 92-8025. 160p. (gr. 3-5). 1992. 13.95 (0-395-61627-1) HM.
—Figment, Your Dog, Speaking. (gr. 3-5). 1991. 160p. 13.45 (0-395-57032-8, Sandpiper); pap. 4.80 (0-395-60473-7, Sandpiper) HM.
—Valentine to a Flying Mouse. (ps-7). 1993. 13.95 (0-395-61628-X) HM.
Hawkins, Leslie V. Art Metal & Enameling. 234p. (gr. 9-12). 1974. text ed. 17.60 (0-02-662240-8) Bennett IL.
Hawkins, Mary E. & ed. see Foster, Cass.
Hawkins, Mary E., ed. see Latterman, Terry.
Hawkins, Tommy. The Voice Underneath the Pillow. LC 91-41233. (Illus.). 80p. (ps-3). 1992. 12.00g (1-880691-17-5) Blackbird MI.
Hawkinson, Annie. Living in France. Fantini, Alvino E., ed. 42p. (Orig.). 1986. pap. 2.50 (0-936141-12-3) Experiment Pr.
Hawkins-Walsh, Elizabeth. Katie's Premature Brother. Johnson, Joy, ed. Borum, Shari, illus. 24p. (Orig.). (ps). 1990. pap. 2.65 (1-56123-005-7) Centering Corp.
Hawks, Robert. Hall Pass. 160p. (Orig.). 1993. pap. 3.50 (0-380-76951-4, Flare) Avon.
—The Richest Kid in the World. 144p. (Orig.). 1992. pap. 2.99 (0-380-76241-2, Camelot) Avon.
—The Richest Kid in the World: The Sixty Billion Dollar Fugitive. 160p. (Orig.). (gr. 5). 1992. pap. 3.50 (0-380-76242-0, Camelot) Avon.
—This Stranger, My Father. LC 87-26245. 228p. (gr. 5-9). 1988. 13.45 (0-395-44089-0) HM.
—This Stranger, My Father. 240p. (gr. 4). 1990. pap. 2.95 (0-380-70739-X, Flare) Avon.
—The Twenty-Six Minutes. 190p. (Orig.). (gr. 8-12). 1988. pap. 4.95 (0-938961-03-9, Stamp Out Sheep Press) Sq One Pubs.
Hawksley, Gerald. At Home. Hawksley, Gerald, illus. 10p. (ps). 1990. bds. 4.95 (1-878624-18-0) McClanahan Bk.
—Building Wheels. (Illus.). 8p. 1992. bds. 3.95 (0-681-41557-6) Longmeadow Pr.
—Farm. Hawksley, Gerald, illus. 10p. (ps). 1990. bds. 4.95 (1-878624-16-4) McClanahan Bk.
—Farm Wheels. 8p. 1992. bds. 3.95 (0-681-41556-8) Longmeadow Pr.
—Farm Window. (Illus.). 10p. (ps). 1988. 3.95 (0-681-40467-1) Longmeadow Pr.
—Racing Wheels. (Illus.). 8p. 1992. bds. 3.95 (0-681-41558-4) Longmeadow Pr.
—Rescue Wheels. (Illus.). 8p. 1992. bds. 3.95 (0-681-41559-2) Longmeadow Pr.
—Trucks. Hawksley, Gerald, illus. 10p. (ps). 1990. bds. 4.95 (1-878624-17-2) McClanahan Bk.
—Trucks Window. (Illus.). 10p. (ps). 1988. 3.95 (0-681-40469-8) Longmeadow Pr.
—Zoo. Hawksley, Gerald, illus. 10p. (ps). 1990. bds. 4.95 (1-878624-19-9) McClanahan Bk.

—Zoo Window. (Illus.). 10p. (ps). 1988. 3.95 (0-681-40468-X) Longmeadow Pr.
Hawksley, Jane. Teen Guide to Pregnancy, Drugs & Smoking. LC 89-31845. (Illus.). 62p. (gr. 6-9). 1989. PLB 13.40 (0-531-10835-X) Watts.
—Teen Guide to Pregnancy, Drugs, & Smoking. (Illus.). 64p. (gr. 7 up). 1990. pap. 4.95 (0-531-15210-3) Watts.
Hawley, Frances, ed. The Children's Pages of Metro Denver - Fall Edition, 1988: A Directory of Products & Services for Children of All Ages & Their Parents. (gr. 7 up). 1988. pap. write for info. (0-932439-08-X) Denver Busn Media.
Hawley, Richard. Drugs & Society. rev. ed. 160p. (gr. 7 up). 1992. PLB 15.85 (0-8027-8114-4); pap. 9.95 (0-8027-7366-4) Walker & Co.
—Shining Still. (Illus.). 192p. 1989. 12.95 (0-374-36811-2) FS&G.
Hawley, Richard A. Think about Drugs & Society: Responding to an Epidemic. LC 87-21681. 157p. 1988. 14.85 (0-8027-6749-4); pap. 5.95 (0-8027-6750-8) Walker & Co.
Hawthorn, P. Animal Jokes. (Illus.). 32p. (gr. 2-5). 1992. PLB 12.96 (0-88110-533-3, Usborne); pap. 4.95 (0-7460-0665-9, Usborne) EDC.
—Easy Piano Classics. (Illus.). 64p.(gr. 2-6). 1991. PLB 14.96 (0-88110-424-8, Usborne); pap. 8.95 (0-7460-0643-8, Usborne) EDC.
—First Book of the Recorder. (Illus.). 64p. (gr. 2-6). 1987. pap. 8.95 (0-7460-0069-3) EDC.
—Jokes. (Illus.). 64p. (gr. 2-5). 1992. pap. 7.95 (0-7460-0724-8, Usborne) EDC.
—Silly Jokes. (Illus.). 32p. (gr. 2-5). 1991. PLB 12.96 (0-88110-532-5, Usborne); pap. 4.95 (0-7460-0612-8, Usborne) EDC.
—Two Hundred Easy Recorder Tunes. (gr. 4-7). 1993. pap. 17.95 (0-7460-1397-3, Usborne) EDC.
Hawthorn, P. & Armstrong, S. Easy Piano Tunes. (Illus.). 64p. (gr. 2-6). 1989. PLB 14.96 (0-88110-410-8, Usborne); pap. 8.95 (0-7460-0459-1, Usborne) EDC.
Hawthorn, P. & Roberts, S. Easy Recorder Tunes. (Illus.). 64p. (gr. 2-6). 1990. PLB 14.96 (0-88110-414-0, Usborne); pap. 8.95 (0-7460-0457-5, Usborne) EDC.
Hawthorn, Philip. Bedtime Stories. Cartwright, Stephen, illus. (ps-4). 1992. 10.95 (0-7460-0538-5, Usborne) EDC.
Hawthorne, Dorothy. Chocolate Wildcat. Washington, Bill, illus. LC 87-72602. (gr. 4-6). 1988. pap. 5.95 (0-931722-65-9) Corona Pub.
Hawthorne, Grace & Mayfield, Larry. Christmas Fever. Date not set. 4.50 (0-685-68515-2, BCMC-42); cassette 9.98 (0-685-68516-0, BCTA-9022C) Lillenas.
Hawthorne, Margaret, jt. auth. see Buzhardt, Gail.
Hawthorne, Nathaniel. Dr. Heidegger's Experiment. 1991. PLB 13.95s.p. (0-88682-465-6) Creative Ed.
—House of the Seven Gables. (gr. 9 up). 1964. pap. 2.95 (0-8049-0016-7, CL-16) Airmont.
—House of the Seven Gables. 288p. (RL 8). 1961. pap. 2.50 (0-451-52309-1, Sig Classics) NAL-Dutton.
—The House of the Seven Gables. abr. ed. Farr, Naunerle, ed. Trinidad, Angel & Guitierez, Domy, illus. (gr. 4-12). 1977. pap. text ed. 2.95 (0-88301-265-0) Pendulum Pr.
—Marble Faun. Fisher, N. H., intro. by. (gr. 11 up). 1966. pap. 1.95 (0-8049-0104-X, CL-104) Airmont.
—Scarlet Letter. (gr. 9 up). 1964. pap. 2.95 (0-8049-0007-8, CL-7) Airmont.
—Scarlet Letter. Levin, Harry, ed. LC 60-2662. (gr. 9 up). 1960. pap. 7.96 (0-395-05142-8, RivEd) HM.
—The Scarlet Letter. Thomson, Hugh, illus. 312p. 1991. 9.99 (0-517-64302-2) Outlet Bk Co.
—Tanglewood Tales. (Illus.). (gr. 7 up). 1968. pap. 2.50 (0-8049-0175-9, CL-175) Airmont.
—Tanglewood Tales for Girls & Boys. 1992. Repr. of 1853 ed. lib. bdg. 75.00 (0-7812-3046-2) Rprt Serv.
—Three Golden Apples. (gr. 5 up). 1992. PLB 29.95 (0-88682-517-2) Creative Ed.
—True Stories from History & Biography. Charvat, William, et al, eds. LC 73-150220. 380p. (gr. 5 up). 1972. 45.00 (0-8142-0157-1) Ohio St U Pr.
—Twice Told Tales. Gemme, F. R., intro. by. (gr. 9 up). 1965. pap. 2.50 (0-8049-0066-3, CL-66) Airmont.
—Wonder Book. Hogan, A. H., intro. by. (gr. 5 up). 1966. pap. 2.25 (0-8049-0118-X, CL-118) Airmont.
—A Wonder Book & Tanglewood Tales. Charvat, William, et al, eds. LC 77-150221. (Illus.). 476p. (gr. 5 up). 1972. 50.00 (0-8142-0158-X) Ohio St U Pr.
—A Wonder Book for Girls & Boys. LC 87-50436. 362p. (gr. 3-7). 1987. pap. 12.95 (0-940561-07-7) White Rose Pr.
—A Wonder Book for Girls & Boys. 1992. Repr. of 1852 ed. lib. bdg. 75.00 (0-7812-3045-4) Rprt Serv.
—Young Goodman Brown. (gr. 5 up). 1992. PLB 13.95 (0-88682-498-2) Creative Ed.
Hawthorne, Nathaniel & Andersen, Hans Christian. King Midas & The Emperor's New Clothes. (Illus.). 48p. (ps-3). 1985. 5.95 (0-88110-253-9) EDC.
Hawthorne, Sadie H. Racky. (Illus.). 60p. (gr. k-7). 1992. 10.00 (0-931647-03-7) S & B Pubs.
Hawthorne, Terri B. & Brown, Diane B. GAIA Celebration for Children: A Workshop & Activities Book. Brown, Diane B., illus. 32p. 1990. pap. 5.99 (0-929404-02-5) Tara Educ Servs.
—Winter Solstice Celebrations Through the Ages: A Coloring Book for All Ages. Brown, Diane B., illus. 32p. 1990. pap. 5.99 (0-929404-01-7) Tara Educ Servs.

Hawtin, Jeff. Secret Messages: A Collection of Puzzles Using Codes & Ciphers. 48p. 1991. 6.95 (0-906212-78-2, Pub. by Tarquin UK) Parkwest Pubns.
Hawxhurst, Joan C. Antonia Novello, U. S. Surgeon General. LC 92-19564. (Illus.). 32p. (gr. 2-4). 1993. PLB 12.40 (1-56294-299-9) Millbrook Pr.
—Mother Jones. LC 92-22191. (Illus.). 128p. (gr. 7-10). 1992. PLB 22.80 (0-8114-2327-1) Raintree Steck-V.
Hay, Henry. The Amateur Magician's Handbook. 432p. (RL 7). 1983. pap. 5.99 (0-451-15502-5, AE2256, Sig) NAL-Dutton.
Hay, John. Mama, Were You Ever Young? (Illus.). 32p. (gr. k-4). 1991. 13.95 (0-88138-134-9, Green Tiger) S&S Trade.
—Rover & Coo Coo. Solliday, Tim, illus. 32p. (gr. 3-6). 1991. 12.95 (0-88138-078-4, Green Tiger) S&S Trade.
Hay, John W., jt. auth. see Harwich, Mary B.
Hay, Maureen E. & Kuntz, Margy. Digging into Literature. (gr. 5-8). 1987. pap. 6.95 (0-8224-1917-3) Fearon Teach Aids.
Hay, Melba P., intro. by. see Clark, Thomas D.
Hayashi, Nancy. Cosmic Cousin. Hayashi, Nancy, illus. (gr. 2-5). 1990. pap. 2.95 (0-553-15841-4, Skylark) Bantam.
—The Fantastic Stay-Home-from-School Day. Hayashi, Nancy, illus. LC 91-21095. 105p. (gr. 2-5). 1992. 12. 00 (0-525-44864-0, DCB) Dutton Child Bks.
Haycock, Kate. Gymnastics. LC 91-16118. (Illus.). 48p. (gr. 5-6). 1991. RSBE 13.95 (0-89686-666-1, Crestwood Hse) Macmillan Child Grp.
—Pasta. (Illus.). 32p. (gr. 1-4). 1991. PLB 13.50 (0-87614-656-6) Carolrhoda Bks.
—Plays. Stefoff, Rebecca, ed. LC 90-13937. (Illus.). 32p. (gr. 4-8). 1991. PLB 17.26 (0-944483-98-4) Garrett Ed Corp.
—Science Fiction Films. LC 91-31672. (Illus.). 48p. (gr. 5-6). 1992. RSBE 12.95 (0-89686-716-1, Crestwood Hse) Macmillan Child Grp.
—Skiing. LC 91-670. (Illus.). 48p. (gr. 5-6). 1991. RSBE 13.95 (0-89686-669-6, Crestwood Hse) Macmillan Child Grp.
Hayden, Jan & Kistler, Mary. Has Anyone Seen Allie? LC 90-14027. 144p. (gr. 5 up). 1991. 13.95 (0-525-65057-1, Cobblehill Bks) Dutton Child Bks.
Hayden, Melissa, retold by. The Nutcracker Ballet. Johnson, Stephen T., illus. LC 92-20654. 32p. 1992. 14.95 (0-8362-4501-6) Andrews & McMeel.
Hayden, Robert. Nine African-American Inventors. rev. ed. (Illus.). 171p. (gr. 5-8). 1992. Repr. of 1972 ed. PLB 14.95 (0-8050-2133-7) TFC Bks NY.
—Seven African-American Scientists. rev. ed. (Illus.). 173p. (gr. 5-8). 1992. Repr. of 1970 ed. PLB 14.95 (0-8050-2134-5) TFC Bks NY.
Hayden, Robert C. Eleven African-American Doctors. rev. ed. (Illus.). 208p. (gr. 5-8). 1992. Repr. of 1976 ed. PLB 14.95 (0-8050-2135-3) TFC Bks NY.
Haye, Caroline, ed. see Cook, John M.
Hayes. Brain Twisters. (Illus.). 32p. (gr. 2-6). 1988. pap. 2.95 (0-88625-149-4) Durkin Hayes Pub.
—Number Mysteries. (Illus.). 32p. (gr. 2-6). 1988. pap. 2.95 (0-88625-145-1) Durkin Hayes Pub.
—Picture Puzzles. (Illus.). 32p. (gr. 2-6). 1988. pap. 2.95 (0-88625-147-8) Durkin Hayes Pub.
—Word Teasers. (Illus.). 32p. (gr. 2-6). 1988. pap. 2.95 (0-88625-148-6) Durkin Hayes Pub.
Hayes & Hook. Meu Livro de Historias Biblicas. (POR.). (gr. k-6). 1979. 3.00 (0-8297-0758-1) Life Pubs Intl.
Hayes, Ann. Meet the Orchestra. D'Andrade, Diane, ed. Thompson, Karmen, illus. 32p. (ps-3). 1991. 13.95 (0-15-200526-9, Gulliver Bks) HarBrace.
Hayes, Bert. Nineteen Seventy-Eight: The Human Race Begins. Courington, D., as told to. (Illus.). 64p. (Orig.). 1989. pap. 4.95 (0-318-41429-5) M C Cook.
Hayes, D. W. Shorty Gordy. LC 91-65922. (Illus.). (gr. k-3). 1992. 7.95 (1-55523-449-6) Winston-Derek.
Hayes, Dan, illus. The Easter Activity Book. 24p. (Orig.). (ps-3). 1991. pap. 4.95 (0-8249-8499-4, Ideals Child) Hambleton-Hill.
—The Thanksgiving Activity Book. 24p. (ps-3). 1992. pap. 4.95 (0-8249-8550-8, Ideals Child) Hambleton-Hill.
Hayes, Daniel. Eye of the Beholder. (Illus.). 192p. (gr. 6 up). 1992. 14.95 (0-87923-881-X) Godine.
—The Trouble with Lemons. LC 89-46192. 128p. (gr. 6 up). 1991. 16.95 (0-87923-825-9) Godine.
—The Trouble with Lemons. 1992. pap. 3.99 (0-449-70416-5, Juniper) Fawcett.
Hayes, Dympna. Fun with Rhymes. Davis, Annelies, illus. 32p. (gr. 1). 1987. PLB 14.97 (0-88625-165-6); pap. 2.95 (0-88625-144-3) Durkin Hayes Pub.
Hayes, Dympna & Lehman, Melanie. Fun with Nature. Kelly, Teri, ed. Davis, Annelies, illus. 32p. (gr. 2). 1987. PLB 14.97 (0-88625-154-0); pap. 2.95 (0-685-30766-2) Durkin Hayes Pub.
—Fun with Things Around the House. Seeman, Tina, illus. 32p. (gr. 2). 1987. PLB 14.97 (0-88625-166-4); pap. 2.95 (0-88625-155-9) Durkin Hayes Pub.
Hayes, Dympna, jt. auth. see Goodwin, Bob.
Hayes, Dympna, ed. see Roberts, Alison J.
Hayes, Edward J. & Hayes, Paul J. Catholicism & Life. 264p. (gr. 8-12). 1981. pap. 7.95 (0-913382-28-0, 103-18); tchr's. manual, 128p. 3.50 (0-913382-29-9, 103-19) Prow Bks-Franciscan.
Hayes, Edward J., et al. Catholicism & Reason. 256p. (gr. 8-12). 1981. pap. 7.95 (0-913382-23-X, 103-14); tchr's. manual 3.50 (0-913382-25-6, 103-15) Prow Bks-Franciscan.

—Catholicism & Society. 223p. (gr. 8-12). 1982. pap. 7.95 (*0-913382-26-4*, 103-16); tchr's. manual 3.50 (*0-913382-27-2*, 103-17) Prow Bks-Franciscan.

Hayes, Frederick & Hayes, Jean. The Adventures of Pinto Bean & Chapulin. Kiefer, Jill, illus. 20p. (Orig.). (gr. 1-8). 1988. pap. text ed. 6.95 (*0-317-93098-2*) Pinto Pub.

—The Chile Pot. 1988. 6.95 (*0-925605-00-X*) Pinto Pub.

Hayes, Geoffrey. The Curse of the Cobweb Queen. LC 92-37272. 1994. 7.99 (*0-679-93878-8*); pap. 3.50 (*0-679-83878-3*) Random Bks Yng Read.

—The Mystery of the Pirate Ghost: An Otto & Uncle Tooth Adventure. Hayes, Geoffrey, illus. LC 84-18228. 48p. (gr. 2-3). 1985. 3.50 (*0-394-87220-7*) Random Bks Yng Read.

—Patrick & Ted Ride the Train: (Just Right for 4's & 5's) Hayes, Geoffrey, illus. LC 88-3084. 32p. (Orig.). (ps-k). 1988. 4.95 (*0-394-89872-9*) Random Bks Yng Read.

—Patrick Goes to Bed. Hayes, Geoffrey, illus. LC 84-6099. 40p. (ps-1). 1985. 4.95 (*0-394-87264-9*) Knopf Bks Yng Read.

—The Secret of Foghorn Island. Hayes, Geoffrey, illus. LC 87-16095. 48p. (Orig.). (gr. 2-3). 1988. lib. bdg. 7.99 (*0-394-99614-3*); pap. 2.95 (*0-394-89614-9*) Random Bks Yng Read.

—The Treasure of the Lost Lagoon: A Step Three Book. Hayes, Geoffrey, illus. LC 90-40118. 48p. (Orig.). (gr. 2-3). 1991. pap. 2.95 (*0-679-81484-1*); lib. bdg. 7.99 (*0-679-91484-6*) Random Bks Yng Read.

Hayes, Jean, jt. auth. see Hayes, Frederick.

Hayes, Joe. Everyone Knows Gato Pinto: More Tales from Spanish New Mexico. Mowrey, Joe, ed. Jelinek, Lucy, illus. 80p. (Orig.). (gr. 2-12). 1993. pap. 9.95 (*0-933553-09-9*) Mariposa Print Pub.

—La Llorona. Treog-Hill, Vicki, illus. 32p. (Orig.). (gr. 1-9). 1986. pap. 4.95 (*0-938317-02-4*) Cinco Puntos.

—Mariposa, Mariposa. Jelinek, Lucy, illus. (SPA & ENG.). 32p. (Orig.). (gr. k-5). 1988. pap. 3.95 (*0-939729-08-3*); Bk. & cass. pkg. 7.95 (*0-939729-09-1*) Trails West Pub.

—Monday, Tuesday, Wednesday, Oh! Lunes, Martes, Miercoles, O! Jelinek, Lucy, illus. 32p. (Orig.). (gr. 2-5). 1987. pap. 3.95 (*0-939729-04-0*); bk. & cassette 7.95, (*0-939729-05-9*) Trails West Pub.

—No Way, Jose! De Ninguna Manera, Jose! Jelinek, Lucy, illus. 32p. (Orig.). (ps-3). 1986. pap. 3.95 (*0-939729-00-8*); cassette & bk. pkg. 7.95 (*0-939729-01-6*) Trails West Pub.

—Soft Child. Sather, Kay, illus. LC 93-1641. 32p. (Orig.). (ps-3). 1993. pap. 8.95 (*0-943173-89-2*) Harbinger AZ.

—The Terrible Tragadabas: El Terrible Tragadabas. Jelinek, Lucy, illus. 32p. (Orig.). (ps-4). 1987. pap. 3.95 (*0-939729-02-4*); bk. & cassette 7.95, (*0-939729-03-2*) Trails West Pub.

—That's Not Fair! Earth Friendly Tales. (Illus.). 32p. (Orig.). (gr. k-6). 1991. pap. 5.95 (*0-939729-21-0*) Trails West Pub.

—The Wise Little Burro. Jelinek, Lucy, illus. 48p. (Orig.). (gr. k-6). 1991. pap. 5.95 (*0-939729-20-2*) Trails West Pub.

Hayes, John & Finck, Lila. Jawaharlal Nehru. Schlesinger, Arthur M., Jr., intro. by. (Illus.). 112p. (gr. 5 up). 1987. lib. bdg. 17.95 (*0-87754-543-X*) Chelsea Hse.

Hayes, John P., jt. auth. see Matusky, Gregory.

Hayes, John P., Jr., jt. auth. see Matusky, Gregory.

Hayes, K. H. Stories of Great Muslims. 5.95 (*0-933511-63-9*) Kazi Pubns.

Hayes, Kenn. I Know Rhino. (ps). 1993. 14.95 (*1-56729-024-8*) Newport Pubs.

—Let's Go Hippo. (ps). 1993. 14.95 (*1-56729-025-6*) Newport Pubs.

Hayes, Marilyn. Basic Skills Health Workbook: Grade 4. 32p. (gr. 4). 1982. tchr's. ed. 1.98 (*0-8209-0414-7*, HW-E) ESP.

—Basic Skills Health Workbook: Grade 5. 32p. (gr. 5). 1982. tchr's. ed. 1.98 (*0-8209-0415-5*, HW-F) ESP.

—Basic Skills Words We Use Workbook. 32p. (gr. k-1). 1983. 1.98 (*0-8209-0577-1*, EEW-7) ESP.

—Jumbo Health Yearbook: Grade 3. 96p. (gr. 3). 1978. 18.00 (*0-8209-0063-X*, JHY 3) ESP.

—Jumbo Health Yearbook: Grade 4. 96p. (gr. 4). 1979. 18.00 (*0-8209-0064-8*, JHY 4) ESP.

Hayes, Paul J., jt. auth. see Hayes, Edward J.

Hayes, Sarah. Blancanieves y los Siete Enanitos (Snow White & the Seven Dwarfs) Puncel, Maria, tr. from ENG. Anestey, Caroline, illus. (SPA.). 32p. (gr. 2-4). 1990. Incl. cass. 11.95 (*84-372-8053-2*) Santillana. Beautifully illustrated version of the traditional story in Spanish. A cassette with original music & dramatic narrations presented by Alma Flor Ada & Suni Paz accompanies the storybook. Two other stories are also included in the collection: UNA MUJERCITA CON SURTE (Lucky Woman) & TRES CHIVOS TESTARUDOS (Three Billy Goats

---

Gruff). To order: Santillana, 901 West Walnut, Compton, CA 90220. Telephone 1-310-763-0455. *Publisher Provided Annotation.*

—The Cats of Tiffany Street. Hayes, Sarah, illus. LC 91-58720. 32p. (ps up). 1992. 13.95 (*1-56402-094-0*) Candlewick Pr.

—Cenicienta (Cinderella) Puncel, Maria, tr. from ENG. Tomblin, Gill, illus. (SPA.). 32p. (gr. 2-4). 1990. Incl. cass. 11.95 (*84-372-8055-9*) Santillana. Beautifully illustrated version of the traditional story in Spanish. A cassette with original music & dramatic narrations presented by Alma Flor Ada & Suni Paz accompanies the storybook. Two other stories are also included in the collection: JUAN EL VAGO (Lazy Jack) & LA REINA DE LAS ABEJAS (Queen Bee). To order: Santillana, 901 W. Walnut, Compton, CA 90220. Telephone: 1-310-763-0455. *Publisher Provided Annotation.*

—Clap Your Hands: Finger Rhymes. Goffe, Toni, illus. LC 87-16958. (ps-1). 1988. 13.00 (*0-688-07692-0*); lib. bdg. 12.88 (*0-688-07693-9*) Lothrop.

—Crumbling Castle. Craig, Helen & Craig, Helen, illus. LC 91-58723. 80p. (gr. 3-6). 1992. 13.95 (*1-56402-108-4*) Candlewick Pr.

—Crumbling Castle. LC 91-58723. (gr. 4-7). 1994. pap. 3.99 (*1-56402-274-9*) Candlewick Pr.

—Eat up, Gemma. Ormerod, Jan, illus. LC 87-36205. 32p. (ps-1). 1988. 13.00 (*0-688-08149-5*) Lothrop.

—The Grumpalump. Firth, Barbara, illus. 32p. (ps-2). 1991. 15.45 (*0-89919-871-6*, Clarion Bks) HM.

—Happy Christmas, Gemma. Ormerod, Jan, illus. LC 85-23674. 32p. (ps-1). 1986. 13.95 (*0-688-06508-2*) Lothrop.

—Happy Christmas, Gemma. ALC Staff, ed. Ormerod, Jan, illus. LC 85-23674. 32p. (ps up). 1992. pap. 4.95 (*0-688-11702-3*, Mulberry) Morrow.

—Mary Mary. Craig, Helen, illus. LC 90-5964. 32p. (gr. k-3). 1990. SBE 13.95 (*0-689-50514-0*, M K McElderry) Macmillan Child Grp.

—Nine Ducks Nine. 1990. 12.95 (*0-688-09534-8*); PLB 12.88 (*0-688-09535-6*) Lothrop.

—Stamp Your Feet. Ormerod, Jan, illus. LC 87-29779. 32p. (ps-1). 1988. 13.00 (*0-688-07694-7*); PLB 12.88 (*0-688-07695-5*) Lothrop.

—This Is the Bear. Craig, Helen, illus. LC 92-53421. 32p. (ps). 1993. 12.95 (*1-56402-189-0*) Candlewick Pr.

—This Is the Bear. LC 92-53421. (ps). 1994. pap. 3.99 (*1-56402-270-6*) Candlewick Pr.

—This Is the Bear & the Picnic Lunch. Craig, Helen, illus. 32p. (ps-1). 1989. 12.95 (*0-316-35248-9*, Joy St Bks) Little.

—This Is the Bear & the Scary Night. Craig, Helen, illus. (ps-1). 1992. 13.95 (*0-316-35250-0*, Joy St Bks) Little.

Hayes, Sarah & Craig, Helen. This Is the Bear. LC 92-53421. (Illus.). 32p. (ps up). 1993. 4.95 (*1-56402-253-6*) Candlewick Pr.

Hayes, Sarah, ed. The Candlewick Book of Fairy Tales. Lynch, P. J., illus. LC 92-54961. 96p. (ps up). 1993. 16.95 (*1-56402-260-9*) Candlewick Pr.

Hayes, Theresa. Celebrate the Birth of Jesus. Chase, Andra, illus. 16p. (gr. 3-6). 1992. wkbk. 7.99 (*0-87403-930-4*, 14-03502) Standard Pub.

Hayes, Theresa, ed. see Downey, Melissa C. & Lingo, Susan L.

Hayes, Theresa, ed. see Uhrich, Ethel.

Hayes, Wanda. Jesus Makes Me Happy. Hook, Frances, illus. (gr. k-2). 1990. pasted 2.50 (*0-87403-705-0*, 24-03905) Standard Pub.

—Saying Thank You Makes Me Happy. Hook, Frances, illus. 32p. (gr. k-2). 1990. pasted 2.50 (*0-87403-708-5*, 24-03908) Standard Pub.

Hayford, James. Gridley Firing. Azarian, Mary, illus. LC 87-61473. 160p. (Orig.). (gr. 4 up). 1987. pap. 9.95 (*0-933050-49-6*) New Eng Pr VT.

Hayhurst, L. W. The Christian Boy, 4 vols. 1964. pap. 2.35 ea. Vol. 1 (CB100) Vol. 2 (CB200) Vol. 3 (CB300) Vol. 4 (CB400) Quality Pubns.

Hayhurst, Mamie W. The Christian Girl, 4 vols. 1964. pap. 2.35 ea. Vol. 1 (CG100) Vol. 2 (CG200) Vol. 3 (CG300) Vol. 4 (CG400) Quality Pubns.

Hayles, Karen, jt. auth. see Fuge, Charles.

Hayman, Leroy. Assassinations of John & Robert Kennedy. (gr. 4-7). 1993. pap. 2.95 (*0-590-46539-2*) Scholastic Inc.

—The Death of Lincoln: A Picture History of the Assassination. 128p. (gr. 4 up). 1989. pap. 2.95 (*0-590-44570-7*) Scholastic Inc.

Haynes, Betsy. Against Sinclair. 1984. pap. 2.75 (*0-553-15712-4*) Bantam.

—The Against Taffy Sinclair Club. 112p. (gr. 3-6). 1984. pap. 2.50 (*0-553-15413-3*) Bantam.

—The Boys Only Club. (gr. 4 up). 1990. pap. 2.95 (*0-553-15809-0*) Bantam.

—The Bragging War. 120p. (gr. 5-7). 1989. pap. 2.75 (*0-553-15651-9*) Bantam.

—Breaking Up. (gr. 4-7). 1991. pap. 2.99 (*0-553-15871-6*) Bantam.

—Breaking Up. (gr. 4-7). 1991. pap. 2.99 (*0-553-15873-2*) Bantam.

—Celebrity Auction. (gr. 4 up). 1990. pap. 2.75 (*0-553-15784-1*) Bantam.

—Class Trip Calamity. (gr. 4-7). 1992. pap. 2.99 (*0-553-15969-0*) Bantam.

—Fabulous Five Minus One. (gr. 4-7). 1991. pap. 2.99 (*0-553-15867-8*) Bantam.

—Fabulous Five, No. 21. (gr. 4-7). 1990. pap. 2.75 (*0-553-15840-6*) Bantam.

—The Fabulous Five, No. 30. 1992. pap. 2.99 (*0-553-15875-9*) Bantam.

—Fabulous Five Parent Game. (ps-1). 1989. pap. 2.75 (*0-553-15670-5*, #06) Bantam.

—Fabulous Five Super, No. 3: Missing You. 192p. 1991. pap. 2.99 (*0-553-15876-7*) Bantam.

—Grade Me. (gr. 7). 1989. pap. 2.75 (*0-685-33584-4*) Bantam.

—The Great Boyfriend Trap. 160p. (gr. 4-7). 1987. pap. 2.75 (*0-553-15530-X*, Skylark) Bantam.

—Great Mom Swap. 160p. (Orig.). 1986. pap. 2.50 (*0-553-15398-6*, Skylark) Bantam.

—The Great Mom Swap. 1986. pap. 2.95 (*0-553-15675-6*) Bantam.

—The Great TV Turnoff. (gr. 4-7). 1991. pap. 2.95 (*0-553-15861-9*) Bantam.

—In Trouble. (gr. 3-6). 1990. pap. 2.95 (*0-553-15814-7*) Bantam.

—Mall Mania. (gr. 4-7). 1991. pap. 2.95 (*0-553-15852-X*) Bantam.

—Melanie Edwards. 1992. pap. 2.99 (*0-553-15874-0*) Bantam.

—Melanie's Valentine. (gr. 4-7). 1991. pap. 2.95 (*0-553-15845-7*) Bantam.

—Nobody Likes Taffy Sinclair. (gr. 4-7). 1991. pap. 2.99 (*0-553-15877-5*) Bantam.

—The Popularity Trap: The Fabulous Five, No. 3. (gr. 4-7). 1988. pap. 2.95 (*0-553-15634-9*, Skylark) Bantam.

—The Power. (Orig.). (gr. 5 up). 1982. pap. 1.95 (*0-440-97164-0*, LFL) Dell.

—Scapegoat. (gr. 4-7). 1991. pap. 2.99 (*0-553-15872-4*) Bantam.

—Seventh-Grade Menace. (gr. 4 up). 1989. pap. 2.75 (*0-553-15763-9*) Bantam.

—Seventh-Grade Rumors: The Fabulous Five, No. 1. (gr. 4-7). 1988. pap. 2.95 (*0-553-15625-X*, Skylark) Bantam.

—Taffy Sinclair & the Melanie Makeover. (gr. 2-6). 1988. pap. 2.75 (*0-553-15604-7*, Skylark) Bantam.

—Taffy Sinclair & the Secret Admirer Epidemic. (gr. 2-6). 1988. pap. 2.50 (*0-553-15582-2*, Skylark) Bantam.

—Taffy Sinclair, Baby Ashley, & Me. 128p. (gr. 4-7). 1988. pap. 2.50 (*0-553-15557-1*, Skylark) Bantam.

—Taffy Sinclair Goes to Hollywood. (gr. 4 up). 1990. pap. 2.95 (*0-553-15819-8*) Bantam.

—Taffy Sinclair, Queen of the Soaps. (ps-7). 1988. pap. 3.25 (*0-553-15647-0*, Skylark) Bantam.

—Taffy Sinclair Strikes Again. 128p. (gr. 4-6). 1991. pap. 2.99 (*0-553-15645-4*, Skylark) Bantam.

—Taffy Sinclair's Romance. 1992. pap. 3.25 (*0-553-15494-X*) Bantam.

—Teen Taxi. (gr. 4-7). 1990. pap. 2.75 (*0-553-15794-9*) Bantam.

—The Trouble with Flirting. (gr. 4-7). 1988. pap. 2.95 (*0-553-15633-0*, Skylark) Bantam.

—The Witches of Wakeman. (gr. 4-7). 1990. pap. 2.75 (*0-553-15830-9*) Bantam.

—Yearbook Memories. 1992. pap. 3.50 (*0-553-15975-5*) Bantam.

Haynes, Betty B., ed. see White, Kathy.

Haynes, Dorothy K. The Gay Goshawk. LC 85-32531. 32p. (gr. 4 up). 1986. PLB 10.95 s.p. (*0-88682-073-1*) Creative Ed.

Haynes, Glenda, ed. see Martin, Bill.

Haynes, Harold J. I Just Wanna Tell Somebody. (Illus.). 48p. (Orig.). (gr. 7 up). 1987. pap. 3.50 (*0-88680-285-7*); piano-vocal score 10.00 (*0-88680-286-5*); royalty on application 60.00 (*0-685-58887-4*) I E Clark.

—Isolation. (Illus.). 26p. (Orig.). (gr. 7-12). 1993. pap. 3.00 (*0-88680-395-0*) I E Clark.

Haynes, James. Voices in the Dark. (gr. 5 up). 1982. pap. 1.95 (*0-440-99317-2*, LFL) Dell.

Haynes, Mary. The Great Pretenders. LC 90-32162. 128p. (gr. 4-7). 1990. SBE 13.95 (*0-02-743452-4*, Bradbury Pr) Macmillan Child Grp.

Haynes, Max. Dinosaur Island. LC 90-48148. (Illus.). 32p. (ps up). 1991. 13.95 (*0-688-10329-4*); PLB 13.88 (*0-688-10330-8*) Lothrop.

—Sparky's Rainbow Repair. LC 91-1687. (ps-3). 1992. 15.00 (*0-688-11193-9*); PLB 14.93 (*0-688-11194-7*) Lothrop.

Haynes, Richard. The Wright Brothers. (Illus.). 144p. (gr. 5-9). 1992. PLB 13.98 (*0-382-24168-1*); pap. 7.95 (*0-382-24175-4*) Silver Burdett Pr.

Haynes, Richard M. Ida B. Wells. LC 92-22192. (Illus.). 128p. (gr. 7-10). 1992. PLB 22.80 (*0-8114-2325-5*) Raintree Steck-V.

Haynes, Richard T. The Thong Tree. Haynes, Richard T., illus. LC 90-70508. 64p. (gr. 3-7). 1990. 11.95 (*0-929146-02-6*) Voyageur Pub.

Haynes, Sarah, retold by. Robin Hood. Benson, Patrick, illus. LC 89-33419. 80p. (gr. 4-6). 1989. 12.95 (0-8050-1206-0, Bks Young Read) H Holt & Co.

Hays, Marion P. In the Land Where Time Began. 124p. (Orig.). 1993. pap. 9.95 (0-685-67842-3) Smyth & Helwys.

Hays, Scott. Capital Punishment. (Illus.). 64p. (gr. 7 up). 1990. lib. bdg. 17.27 (0-86593-074-0); lib. bdg. 12. 95s.p. (0-685-36322-8) Rourke Corp.
—Landsailing. (Illus.). 48p. (gr. 3-6). 1992. PLB 12.95 (1-56065-057-5) Capstone Pr.
—Surfing. LC 93-32164. 1993. write for info. (0-86593-349-9) Rourke Corp.

Hays, Scott, et al. Troubled Society, 6 bks. (Illus.). 384p. (gr. 7 up). 1990. Set. lib. bdg. 103.62 (0-86593-068-6); Set. lib. bdg. 77.70s.p. (0-685-36321-X) Rourke Corp.

Hays, Scott R. Hall of Famers. LC 92-5638. 1992. PLB 17.26 (0-86593-155-0); 12.95s.p. (0-685-59287-1) Rourke Corp.

Hayward, Charles. Cabinet Making for Beginners. rev. ed. LC 78-24432. (Illus.). 218p. (gr. 10-12). 1983. pap. 9.95 (0-8069-8184-9) Sterling.

Hayward, Charles H. Making Toys in Wood. rev. & updated ed. Bridgewater, Alan & Bridgewater, Gill, eds. LC 92-44019. (Illus.). 160p. (gr. 10-12). 1993. pap. 12.95 (0-8069-8720-0) Sterling.

Hayward, Linda. All Stuck Up. Chartier, Normand, illus. LC 89-34675. 32p. (Orig.). (ps-1). 1990. PLB 7.99 (0-679-90216-3); pap. 2.95 (0-679-80216-9) Random Bks Yng Read.
—Baby Moses. (Illus.). 32p. (Orig.). (ps-1). 1989. PLB 7.99 (0-394-99410-8); pap. 2.95 (0-394-89410-3) Random Bks Yng Read.
—The Biggest Cookie in the World. Ewers, Joe, illus. LC 88-36247. 24p. (Orig.). (ps-1). 1989. pap. 2.25 (0-394-84049-6) Random Bks Yng Read.
—Elmo Goes to Day Camp. Nicklaus, Carol, illus. LC 89-61614. 32p. (Orig.). 1990. pap. 1.25 (0-679-80158-8) Random Bks Yng Read.
—Ernie & Bert's Summer Project. Nicklaus, Carol, illus. LC 90-60821. 32p. (Orig.). (ps-3). 1991. pap. 1.50 (0-679-81051-X) Random Bks Yng Read.
—The First Thanksgiving. reissue ed. Watling, James, illus. 48p. (gr. k-4). 1992. pap. 6.99 incl. cass. (0-679-83058-8) Random Bks Yng Read.
—The First Thanksgiving: A Step 2 Book - Grades 1-3. Watling, James, illus. LC 90-52517. 48p. (Orig.). (gr. k-3). 1990. lib. bdg. 7.99 (0-679-90218-X); pap. 2.95 (0-679-80218-5) Random Bks Yng Read.
—Grover's Summer Vacation. Fritz, Ron, illus. LC 88-62524. 32p. (Orig.). (ps-3). 1989. pap. 1.50 (0-394-83969-2) Random Bks Yng Read.
—Hello, House! Munsinger, Lynn, illus. LC 86-22080. 32p. (Orig.). (ps-1). 1988. lib. bdg. 6.99 (0-394-98864-7); pap. 3.50 (0-394-88864-2) Random Bks Yng Read.
—I Spy. Cooke, Tom, illus. 32p. (Orig.). (ps-1). 1993. PLB 7.99 (0-679-94979-8); pap. 3.50 (0-679-84979-3) Random Bks Yng Read.
—Mine! A Sesame Street Book about Sharing: (Just Right for 2's & 3's) Gorbaty, Norman, illus. LC 87-42810. 24p. (ps). 1988. 6.00 (0-394-89599-1) Random Bks Yng Read.
—Noah's Ark. Wright, Freire, illus. LC 86-17790. 32p. (ps-1). 1987. lib. bdg. 6.99 (0-394-98716-0); pap. 3.50 (0-394-88716-6) Random Bks Yng Read.
—Noah's Ark. Flynn, Amy, illus. LC 92-64138. 22p. (ps). 1993. 3.25 (0-679-83600-4) Random Bks Yng Read.

Hayward, Linda, jt. auth. see Sesame Street Staff.

Hayward, Ruth A. & Warner, Margaret B. What's Cooking? Favorite Recipes from Around the World. (gr. 4 up). 1981. 16.95 (0-316-35252-7) Little.

Hayward, Stan. The Shutterbug. Godfrey, Bob, illus. (ps-5). 1987. pap. 2.25 (0-671-63776-2) S&S Trade.

Haywood, Carolyn. B Is for Betsy. Haywood, Carolyn, illus. LC 85-16381. 159p. (gr. 1-5). 1939. 12.95 (0-15-204975-4, HB Juv Bks) HarBrace.
—B Is for Betsy. Yakovetic, Joe, contrib. by. 120p. (gr. 2-5). 1990. pap. 3.95 (0-15-204977-0, Odyssey) HarBrace.
—Back to School with Betsy. Haywood, Carolyn, illus. LC 85-16380. 176p. (gr. 1-5). 1943. 12.95 (0-15-205512-6, HB Juv Bks) HarBrace.
—Back to School with Betsy. Yakovetic, Joe, contrib. by. 135p. (gr. 2-5). 1990. pap. 3.95 (0-15-205515-0, Odyssey) HarBrace.
—Betsy & Billy. Haywood, Carolyn, illus. LC 41-51926. 119p. (gr. 1-5). 1941. 12.95 (0-15-206765-5, HB Juv Bks) HarBrace.
—Betsy & Billy. Yakovetic, Joe, contrib. by. 119p. (gr. 2-5). 1990. pap. 3.95 (0-15-206768-X) HarBrace.
—Betsy & Mr. Killpatrick. (gr. k-6). 1989. pap. 3.25 (0-440-40204-2, YB) Dell.
—Betsy & the Boys. LC 45-35133. 140p. (gr. 1-5). 1945. 12.95 (0-15-206944-5, HB Juv Bks) HarBrace.
—Betsy & the Boys. Yakovetic, Joe, contrib. by. 140p. (gr. 2-5). 1990. pap. 3.95 (0-15-206947-X) HarBrace.
—Betsy's Busy Summer. Haywood, Carolyn, illus. LC 56-7894. 32p. (gr. 3-7). 1956. PLB 13.88 (0-688-31087-7) Morrow Jr Bks.
—Betsy's Busy Summer. (gr. k-6). 1989. pap. 3.25 (0-440-40171-2, YB) Dell.
—Betsy's Little Star. 160p. (gr. 3-6). 1989. pap. 3.25 (0-440-40172-0, YB) Dell.
—Betsy's Play School. (gr. k-6). 1989. pap. 3.25 (0-440-40213-1, YB) Dell.

—Betsy's Winterhouse. Haywood, Carolyn, illus. LC 55-8453. 192p. (gr. 3-7). 1958. PLB 13.88 (0-688-31090-7) Morrow Jr Bks.
—Betsy's Winterhouse. (gr. k-6). 1989. pap. 3.25 (0-440-40227-1, YB) Dell.
—Eddie & His Big Deals. 190p. (gr. 3-7). 1990. Repr. of 1955 ed. 3.95 (0-688-10075-9, Pub. by Beech Tree Bks) Morrow.
—Eddie & the Fire Engine. Haywood, Carolyn, illus. LC 49-9873. 192p. (gr. 1-5). 1949. PLB 12.88 (0-688-31252-7) Morrow Jr Bks.
—Eddie & the Fire Engine. ALC Staff, ed. Lewin, Betsy, illus. 192p. (gr. 2-8). 1992. pap. 4.95 (0-688-11498-9, Pub. by Beech Tree Bks) Morrow.
—Eddie's Friend Boodles. Stock, Catherine, illus. LC 91-3212. (gr. 1 up). 1991. 12.95 (0-688-09028-1) Morrow Jr Bks.
—Eddie's Menagerie. Fetz, Ingrid, illus. LC 78-6519. (gr. 4-6). 1978. PLB 12.88 (0-688-32158-5) Morrow Jr Bks.
—Eddie's Menagerie. 192p. (gr. 2-4). 1987. pap. 2.95 (0-8167-1042-2) Troll Assocs.
—Eddie's Valuable Property. Haywood, Carolyn, illus. LC 74-17499. 192p. (gr. 3-7). 1975. PLB 12.88 (0-688-32014-7) Morrow Jr Bks.
—Halloween Treats. De Larrea, Victoria, illus. LC 81-3959. 176p. (gr. 4-6). 1981. lib. bdg. 12.88 (0-688-00709-0) Morrow Jr Bks.
—Halloween Treats. (gr. 2-4). 1987. pap. 2.95 (0-8167-1039-2) Troll Assocs.
—Happy Birthday from Carolyn Haywood. (gr. 2-4). 1987. pap. 2.95 (0-8167-1040-6) Troll Assocs.
—Hello, Star. 64p. (gr. 2-4). 1992. pap. 2.50 (0-8167-1310-3) Troll Assocs.
—Here's a Penny. Rev. ed. Haywood, Carolyn & Yakovetic, Joe, illus. LC 44-7329. 150p. (gr. 1-5). 1986. pap. 4.95 (0-15-640062-6, Voyager Bks) HarBrace.
—How the Reindeer Saved Santa. Ambrus, Victor G., illus. LC 85-28456. 32p. (ps-3). 1986. 12.95 (0-688-05903-1); lib. bdg. 12.88 (0-688-05904-X) Morrow Jr Bks.
—How the Reindeer Saved Santa. Ambrus, Victor G., illus. LC 85-28456. 64p. (ps-3). 1991. pap. 4.95 (0-688-11073-8, Mulberry) Morrow.
—Little Eddie. 160p. (gr. 3-7). 1990. Repr. of 1947 ed. 3.95 (0-688-10074-0, Pub. by Beech Tree Bks) Morrow.
—Merry Christmas from Betsy. (gr. k-6). 1989. pap. 3.25 (0-440-40187-9, YB) Dell.
—Merry Christmas from Eddie. Durrell, Julie, illus. LC 86-2466. 112p. (gr. 1-4). 1986. 12.95 (0-688-05828-0) Morrow Jr Bks.
—Merry Christmas from Eddie. (gr. 2-4). 1987. pap. 2.95 (0-8167-1041-4) Troll Assocs.
—Penny & Peter. rev. ed. Haywood, Carolyn & Yakovetic, Joe, illus. LC 46-21128. 160p. (gr. 1-5). 1986. pap. 4.95 (0-15-260467-7, Voyager Bks) HarBrace.
—Primrose Day. Haywood, Carolyn, illus. LC 86-4620. 200p. (gr. k-3). 1986. pap. 4.95 (0-15-263510-6, Voyager Bks) HarBrace.
—Santa Claus Forever! Ambrus, Victor G., illus. LC 83-1017. 32p. (gr. k-3). 1983. 11.95 (0-688-10098-5); lib. bdg. 11.88 (0-688-02345-2) Morrow Jr Bks.
—Snowbound with Betsy. (gr. k-6). 1992. 16.25 (0-8446-6597-5) Peter Smith.
—Summer Fun. Durrell, Julie, illus. LC 85-25864. 128p. (gr. 1-4). 1986. 11.95 (0-688-04958-3) Morrow Jr Bks.
—Summer Fun. (gr. 2-4). 1987. pap. 2.95 (0-8167-1037-6) Troll Assocs.
—Two & Two Are Four. Haywood, Carolyn, illus. LC 86-4619. 171p. (gr. k-3). 1986. pap. 4.95 (0-15-291771-3, Voyager Bks) HarBrace.
—A Valentine Fantasy. Ambrus, Victor G. & Ambrus, Victor G., illus. LC 75-23083. 32p. (gr. k-3). 1976. PLB 14.88 (0-688-32055-4) Morrow Jr Bks.

Hazard, David. A Place Behind the World. 192p. (Orig.). (gr. 9-12). 1991. text ed. 7.99 (1-55661-168-4) Bethany Hse.

Hazard, David, ed. see Theresa of Avila.

Hazard, James. Look Both Ways. 55p. (Orig.). (gr. 4-6). 1987. pap. 4.25 (0-935399-03-8) Main St Pub.

Hazbry, Nancy. How to Get Rid of Bad Dreams. (ps-3). 1990. pap. 3.95 (0-590-43474-8) Scholastic Inc.

Hazeltine, Alice I., compiled by. The Year Around: Poems for Children. Hazeltine, Smith, compiled by. LC 72-11921. (gr. 7 up). 1973. Repr. of 1956 ed. 15.00 (0-8369-6403-9) Ayer.

Hazen, Barbara. Hello Gnu, How Do You Do? (ps-3). 1990. 14.95 (0-385-26449-6) Doubleday.

Hazen, Barbara S. Alone at Home. Trivas, Irene, illus. LC 91-15878. 64p. (gr. 2-4). 1992. SBE 13.95 (0-689-31691-7, Atheneum Child Bk) Macmillan Child Grp.
—Even If I Did Something Awful? Kincade, Nancy, illus. LC 81-1907. 32p. (ps-2). 1981. SBE 13.95 (0-689-30843-4, Atheneum Child Bk) Macmillan Child Grp.
—Even If I Did Something Awful? Kincade, Nancy, illus. LC 91-23143. 32p. (ps-2). 1992. pap. 3.95 (0-689-71600-1, Aladdin) Macmillan Child Grp.
—Fang. Morrill, Leslie, illus. LC 86-28697. 32p. (ps-2). 1987. SBE 13.95 (0-689-31307-1, Atheneum Child Bk) Macmillan Child Grp.
—Fang. Morrill, Leslie H., illus. LC 91-1966. 32p. (gr. k-2). 1991. pap. 4.95 (0-689-71501-3, Aladdin) Macmillan Child Grp.

—The Gorilla Did It. Cruz, Ray, illus. LC 73-84828. 32p. (ps-1). 1974. RSBE 13.95 (0-689-30138-3, Atheneum Child Bk) Macmillan Child Grp.
—The Gorilla Did It. LC 87-23589. (Illus.). 32p. (ps-1). 1988. pap. 3.95 (0-689-71214-6, Aladdin) Macmillan Child Grp.
—How Can I Help? rev. ed. Sweat, Lynn, illus. 32p. (gr. 2-4). 1990. Repr. of 1988 ed. PLB 9.95 (1-878363-13-1) Forest Hse.
—If It Weren't for Benjamin: (I'd Always Get to Lick the Icing Spoon) Hartman, Laura, illus. LC 78-26403. 32p. (ps-3). 1979. 16.95 (0-87705-384-7); pap. 9.95 (0-89885-172-6) Human Sci Pr.
—It's a Shame about the Rain: The Bright Side of Disappointment. Simmons, Bernadette, illus. LC 81-13163. 32p. (ps-3). 1982. 16.95 (0-89885-050-9) Human Sci Pr.
—The Knight Who Was Afraid of the Dark. Ross, Tony, illus. LC 88-18149. 32p. (ps-3). 1989. 12.95 (0-8037-0667-7); PLB 12.89 (0-8037-0668-5) Dial Bks Young.
—The Knight Who Was Afraid of the Dark. Ross, Tony, illus. LC 88-18149. 32p. (ps-3). 1994. pap. 3.99 (0-14-054545-X, Puffin Pied Piper) Puffin Bks.
—Last, First, Middle & Nick: All About Names. Weissman, Sam Q., illus. (gr. 1-4). 1979. 7.95 (0-13-523944-3) P-H.
—The Magic Stick. 16p. (ps-2). 1992. pap. 14.95 (1-56784-053-1) Newbridge Comms.
—Mommy's Office. Soman, David, illus. LC 91-25013. 32p. (ps-1). 1992. SBE 13.95 (0-689-31601-1, Atheneum Child Bk) Macmillan Child Grp.
—Rudolph the Red-Nosed Reindeer. Scarry, Richard, illus. 24p. (ps-1). 1985. Repr. of 1958 ed. write for info. (0-307-10203-3, Pub. by Golden Bks) Western Pub.
—Stay, Fang. LC 89-32359. (Illus.). 32p. (gr. k-3). 1990. SBE 13.95 (0-689-31599-6, Atheneum Child Bk) Macmillan Child Grp.
—The Story of Santa Claus. (Illus.). 32p. (ps up). 1989. write for info. (0-307-12097-X, Pub. by Golden Bks) Western Pub.
—Tight Times. Hyman, Trina S., illus. LC 78-31867. (gr. k-3). 1979. pap. 12.95 (0-670-71287-6) Viking Child Bks.
—Tight Times. Hyman, Trina S., illus. 32p. (ps-3). 1983. pap. 3.99 (0-14-050442-7, Puffin) Puffin Bks.
—To Be Me. Hook, Frances, illus. LC 75-12960. (ps-2). 1975. PLB 21.35 (0-913778-09-5); PLB 14.95s.p. (0-685-55554-2) Childs World.
—Turkey in the Straw. Sneed, Brad, illus. LC 92-27516. 32p. (ps-3). 1993. 13.99 (0-8037-1298-7); PLB 13.89 (0-8037-1299-5) Dial Bks Young.
—Two Homes to Live In: A Child's-Eye View of Divorce. Luks, Peggy, illus. LC 77-21849. 32p. (ps-3). 1978. 16.95 (0-87705-313-8); pap. 9.95 (0-89885-173-4) Human Sci Pr.
—Very Shy. Chan, Bonnie, illus. LC 81-6809. 32p. (ps-3). 1983. 16.95 (0-89885-067-3) Human Sci Pr.
—What Are Feelings? rev. ed. Sweat, Lynn, illus. 32p. (gr. 2-4). 1990. Repr. of 1988 ed. PLB 9.95 (1-878363-16-6) Forest Hse.
—Who Lost a Shoe? 16p. (ps-2). 1992. pap. 14.95 (1-56784-050-7) Newbridge Comms.
—World, World, What Can I Do? LC 90-43764. 32p. (ps-3). 1991. 8.95 (0-8192-1537-6) Morehouse Pub.

Hazen, Barbara Shook. The Knight Who Was Afraid to Fight. Goffe, Toni, photos by. LC 93-4608. 1994. write for info. (0-8037-1591-9); lib. bdg. write for info. (0-8037-1592-7) Dial Bks Young.

Hazen, Nancy. Grownups Cry Too: Los Adultos Tambien Lloran-English-Spanish Text. 2nd ed. Cotera, Martha P., tr. LC 78-71542. (Illus.). 25p. (ps-1). 1978. pap. 5.00 (0-914996-19-3) Lollipop Power.

Hazen, Shook. Tiempos Duros: Tight Times. Hyman, Trina S., illus. 32p. (ps-3). 1993. PLB 12.99 (0-670-84841-7) Viking Child Bks.

Hazlett, Richard W. Haleakala Discovery. rev. ed. Hazlett, Richard W., illus. 52p. (gr. 3-7). 1988. pap. 3.00 activity-color book (0-940295-08-3) HI Natural Hist.

Hazouri, Sandra P. & Smith, Miriam F. Peer Listing in the Middle School: Training Activities for Students. Brown, Christine M., illus. LC 91-75586. 134p. (Orig.). (gr. 6-8). 1991. pap. text ed. 8.95x (0-932796-34-6) Ed Media Corp.

Hazzan, Anne-Francoise. Let's Learn English Coloring Book. (Illus.). 64p. 1988. pap. 3.95 (0-8442-5451-7, Passport Bks) NTC Pub Grp.
—Let's Learn French Coloring Book. (Illus.). 64p. (gr. 4 up). 1988. pap. 3.95 (0-8442-1389-6, Passport Bks) NTC Pub Grp.
—Let's Learn German Coloring Book. (Illus.). 64p. (gr. 4 up). 1988. pap. 3.95 (0-8442-2164-3, Passport Bks) NTC Pub Grp.
—Let's Learn Italian Coloring Book. (Illus.). 64p. (gr. 4 up). 1988. pap. 3.95 (0-8442-8060-7, Passport Bks) NTC Pub Grp.
—Let's Learn Spanish Coloring Book. (Illus.). 64p. (gr. 4 up). 1988. pap. 3.95 (0-8442-7549-2, Passport Bks) NTC Pub Grp.

Heacox, Diane. Up from Underachievement: How Teachers, Students, & Parents Can Work Together to Promote Student Success. Espeland, Pamela, ed. LC 91-19069. 144p. (Orig.). 1991. pap. 14.95 (0-915793-35-0) Free Spirit Pub.

Head, Ann. Mr. & Mrs. Bo Jo Jones. 192p. (RL 9). 1968. pap. 2.75 (0-451-15734-6, Sig) NAL-Dutton.

—Mr. & Mrs. Bo Jo Jones. (Illus.). 192p. (gr. 9-12). 1968. pap. 3.99 (0-451-16319-2, Sig) NAL-Dutton.

Head, Bessie. When Rain Clouds Gather. 188p. (Orig.). 1987. pap. 8.95 (0-435-90726-3, 90726) Heinemann.

Head, Constance. Isaiah: The Prophet Prince. 384p. (Orig.). (gr-s6). 1988. pap. 4.50 (0-8423-1751-1) Tyndale.

—Jeremiah & the Fall of Jerusalem. (Illus.). 24p. (gr. k-4). 1986. pap. 1.89 saddlestitched (0-570-06201-2, 59-1424) Concordia.

—The Man Who Carried the Cross for Jesus. (Illus.). (gr. k-4). 1979. 1.89 (0-570-06124-5, 59-1242) Concordia.

—The Story of Deborah. (Illus.). (gr. k-3). 1978. 1.89 (0-570-06116-4, 59-1234) Concordia.

Head, J. J., ed. see Alexander, R. McNeill.

Head, J. J., ed. see Blythe, William B.

Head, J. J., ed. see Breslow, Ronald.

Head, J. J., ed. see Day, M. H.

Head, J. J., ed. see Dees, Susan C.

Head, J. J., ed. see Edwards, R. G.

Head, J. J., ed. see Erdogan, Haydar & Halasi-kun, George.

Head, J. J., ed. see Felman, Yehudi M.

Head, J. J., ed. see Fingert, Howard J.

Head, J. J., ed. see Flint, S. Jane.

Head, J. J., ed. see Fox, Cecil H.

Head, J. J., ed. see Gerbi, Susan A.

Head, J. J., ed. see Harrington, William F.

Head, J. J., ed. see Hinde, R. A. & Hinde, J. S.

Head, J. J., ed. see Hobson, J. Allan.

Head, J. J., ed. see Legge, Gordon E. & Campbell, Fergus W.

Head, J. J., ed. see Lo Pinto, Richard W.

Head, J. J., ed. see Mallick, Joan.

Head, J. J., ed. see Miller, Kenneth.

Head, J. J., ed. see Moner, John G.

Head, J. J., ed. see Montagna, William.

Head, J. J., ed. see Nakatani, Herbert Y.

Head, J. J., ed. see North, A. C. & Attwood, Teresa K.

Head, J. J., ed. see Ostrom, John.

Head, J. J., ed. see Palmer, J. D.

Head, J. J., ed. see Pardee, Arthur B. & Veer Reddy, G. P.

Head, J. J., ed. see Poirier-Brode, Karen.

Head, J. J., ed. see Ralston, Diane D. & Ralston, Henry J., III.

Head, J. J., ed. see Rambaut, Paul.

Head, J. J., ed. see Smith, Robert E.

Head, J. J., ed. see Tarling, D. H.

Head, J. J., ed. see Terborgh, John.

Head, J. J., ed. see Tulchinsky, Dan.

Head, J. J., ed. see Upton, Arthur C.

Head, J. J., ed. see Villee, Claude A., Jr.

Head, J. J., ed. see Wittwer, Sylvan H.

Head, John J., ed. see Goodenough, J. E.

Head, W. S. The California Chaparral: An Elfin Forest. LC 75-24239. 96p. (gr. 4 up). 1972. 15.95 (0-87961-003-4); pap. 7.95 (0-87961-002-6) Naturegraph.

Headapohl, Bette. Lessons in Love. 1993. pap. 2.99 (0-553-29982-4) Bantam.

Headington, Christopher. Sweet Sleep: A Collection of Lullabies & Cradle Songs. LC 88-26898. (Illus.). 96p. 1990. (Clarkson Potter) Crown Pub Group.

Headlam, Catherine, ed. The Kingfisher Science Encyclopedia. 808p. (gr. 3 up). 1993. 39.95 (1-85697-842-7) Kingfisher Bks.

Headstrom, Richard. Adventures with Freshwater Animals. (Illus.). 217p. (gr. 5 up). 1983. pap. 5.95 (0-486-24453-9) Dover.

Heady, Eleanor B. Sage Smoke: Tales of the Shoshoni-Bannock Indians. Stewart, Arvis, illus. LC 92-46731. 94p. (gr. 4-6). 1993. PLB 12.98 (0-382-24361-7); 10. 98 (0-382-24370-6) Silver Burdett Pr.

Heafford, Philip. Great Book of Math Puzzles. LC 93-25890. (Illus.). 96p. (gr. 10-12). 1993. pap. 4.95 (0-8069-8814-2) Sterling.

Healey, Tim. My Wonderful Word Box. (ps-3). 1993. 16. 00 (0-89577-528-X, Readers Digest Kids) RD Assn.

—The Nineteen Seventies. FS-Ltd Staff, ed. (Illus.). 48p. (gr. 4-9). 1989. PLB 13.40 (0-531-10552-0) Watts.

—The Nineteen Sixties. FS-Ltd Staff, ed. (Illus.). 48p. (gr. 4-9). 1989. PLB 13.40 (0-531-10551-2) Watts.

—The Story of the Wheel. Hewetson, Nicholas, illus. LC 91-40417. 32p. (gr. 1-4). 1993. PLB 11.89 (0-8167-2713-9); pap. text ed. 3.95 (0-8167-2714-7) Troll Assocs. Postponed.

Healock, William, et al. Harry Northwood: The Wheeling Years, 1901-1925. (Illus.). 207p. (Orig.). 1991. 42.95 (0-915410-75-3, 3091); pap. 34.95 (0-915410-74-5, 3090) Antique Pubns.

Healton, Sarah H. & Whiteside, Kay H. Baskets, Beads, & Black Walnut Owls: Creative Crafts for Ages 9-12. Hartzog, Sherri, illus. LC 41247. (gr. 4-7). 1993. pap. 9.95 (0-8306-4040-1) TAB Bks.

Healton, Sarah H. & Whiteside, Kay H., eds. Look What I Made! Creative Crafts for Ages 6-8. (Illus.). 112p. (gr. 1-3). 1992. 16.95 (0-8306-4037-1, 4181); pap. 9.95 (0-8306-4038-X, 4181) TAB Bks.

Healy, Christopher C. Build-a-Book Geometry. 239p. (gr. 9-12). 1993. pap. 6.95 (1-55935-066-0) Key Curr Pr.

—Build-a-Book Geometry. 239p. (gr. 9-12). 1993. pap. 9.95 (1-55953-066-9) Key Curr Pr.

Healy, Therese. A to Z with Quincy. Martin, Joan S., illus. 50p. (Orig.). (ps-1). 1986. pap. text ed. 8.95 spiral bdg. (0-9617581-0-4) T Healy.

Heam, Emily. Woosh! I Heard a Sound. Cooper, Heather, illus. 24p. (ps-1). 1987. pap. 0.99 (0-920303-21-8, Pub. by Annick CN) Firefly Bks Ltd.

Heaney, Liz, ed. see Littleton, Mark.

Heaney, Liz, ed. see Littleton, Mark R.

Heaney, Liz, ed. see Sanford, Doris.

Heaney, Seamus & Hughes, Ted, eds. The Rattle Bag: An Anthology of Poetry. 498p. (gr. 3 up). 1985. pap. 15. 95 (0-571-11976-X) Faber & Faber.

Heap, Jonathon. Joha & the Three Merchants. 1991. 7. 95x (0-86685-569-6) Intl Bk Ctr.

Heap, Sue. Fraser's Grump. (Illus.). 32p. (ps-k). 1994. 17. 99 (1-85681-015-1, Pub. by J MacRae UK) Trafalgar.

Heard, Georgia. Creatures of Earth, Sea, & Sky. Dewey, Jennifer O., illus. LC 91-65978. 32p. (gr. 1-4). 1992. 15.95 (1-56397-013-9, Wordsong) Boyds Mills Pr.

Heard, Regie & Langenhahn, Bonnie. Regie's Love: A Daughter of Former Slaves Recalls. 2nd, rev. ed. Glueck, illus. Bonjean, Marilyn, frwd. by. LC 87-61795. (Illus.). 168p. (gr. 8 up). 1989. pap. 9.95 (0-9618212-1-3) McCormick & Schilling.

Hearn, Diana D. Who Lives in the Field? (ps). 1992. 4.95 (0-87483-244-6) August Hse.

—Who Lives in the Forest? (ps). 1992. 4.95 (0-87483-245-4) August Hse.

—Who Lives in the Garden? (ps). 1992. 4.95 (0-87483-246-2) August Hse.

—Who Lives in the Lake? (ps). 1992. 4.95 (0-87483-247-0) August Hse.

Hearn, Diane D. Dad's Dinosaur Day. LC 92-22549. (Illus.). 32p. (gr. k-3). 1993. RSBE 14.95 (0-02-743485-0, Macmillan Child Bk) Macmillan Child Grp.

Hearne, Betsy. Love Lines: Poetry in Person. LC 87-1737. 72p. (gr. 9 up). 1987. SBE 12.95 (0-689-50437-3, M K McElderry) Macmillan Child Grp.

—Polaroid: And Other Poems of View. LC 90-45577. (Illus.). 80p. (gr. 7 up). 1991. SBE 12.95 (0-689-50530-2, M K McElderry) Macmillan Child Grp.

Hearne, Betsy G. Eli's Ghost. Himler, Ronald, illus. LC 86-21096. 112p. (gr. 3-7). 1987. SBE 13.95 (0-689-50420-9, M K McElderry) Macmillan Child Grp.

Hearne, T. Gerbils. (Illus.). 32p. (gr. 2-5). 1989. lib. bdg. 15.94 (0-86625-186-3); 11.95s.p. (0-685-58608-1) Rourke Corp.

—Parakeets. (Illus.). 32p. (gr. 2-5). 1989. lib. bdg. 15.94 (0-86625-182-0); 11.95 (0-685-58611-1) Rourke Corp.

—Rabbits. (Illus.). 32p. (gr. 2-5). 1989. lib. bdg. 15.94 (0-86625-187-1); 11.95s.p. (0-685-58609-X) Rourke Corp.

Hearne, Tina, jt. auth. see Jameson, Pam.

Heartland, Amanda. Prodigy Quick Reference Guide. Berkemeyer, Kathy, ed. (Illus.). 140p. (gr. 9-12). 1993. spiral bdg. 8.95 (1-56243-106-4, P-18) DDC Pub.

Heater, Derek. The Cold War. LC 88-7546. (Illus.). 63p. (gr. 7 up). 1989. PLB 13.40 (0-531-18275-4, Pub. by Bookwright Pr) Watts.

Heater, Derek & Owen, Gwyneth. Health & Wealth. Yapp, Malcolm & Killingray, Margaret, eds. (Illus.). (gr. 6-11). 1980. pap. text ed. 3.45 (0-89908-117-7) Greenhaven.

Heater, Derek, jt. auth. see Middleton, Hayden.

Heath, Amy. Sofie's Role. Hamanaka, Sheila, illus. LC 91-33488. 40p. (gr. k-2). 1992. RSBE 14.95 (0-02-743505-9, Four Winds) Macmillan Child Grp.

Heath, Dixie. My Alphabet Animals Draw Along Book: Alphabet Animals Drawing Book. Wexler, Terry, ed. Heath, Dixie, illus. 70p. (gr. k-5). 1993. 14.95 (0-9637484-0-8) Knight Pub WA. MY ALPHABET ANIMALS DRAW ALONG BOOK is unique because of the variety of things it does for children. This book teaches children our alphabet via big, beautiful & colorful illustrations. Writing the letters & then drawing them into animals helps you to visually remember the letters. The reading of the basic sentence also stimulates the memory of the alphabet in young minds. For example: A-Airedale-Amanda's Airedale Abode. B-Bunny-Blue Bonnie Bunny Bites, etc. The children also have draw along friends to help them through the book. Anni Alphadraw, Pencil Dude & Paper Pals Pad take them on a learning & drawing safari. This helps the children feel it's a personal book, with friends helping which is more fun & adventurous. From beginning to end the children are involved with each step. MY ALPHABET ANIMALS DRAW ALONG BOOK also teaches

---

awareness of our endangered animal friends. Seventeen of the animals in this book are endangered--either their lives or their habitat. There's also a glossary of words new to young minds & their meaning. I have taught this book in three different schools & the teachers & children love it - even the 6th graders. The expressions on the illustrations will leave a lasting impression for young & old to keep them coming back for more. *Publisher Provided Annotation.*

Heath, Lou. Daniel: Faithful Captive. Myers, William, illus. (gr. 1-6). 1977. bds. 5.95 (0-8054-4231-6, 4242-31) Broadman.

—Ed Taylor: Father of Migrant Missions. LC 81-70911. (gr. k-3). 1982. 5.95 (0-8054-4278-2, 4242-78) Broadman.

Heath, Lou & Taylor, Beth. Reading My Bible in Fall. LC 85-30947. (Orig.). (gr. 1-6). 1986. pap. 4.50 (0-8054-4322-3) Broadman.

—Reading My Bible in Spring. (Orig.). (gr. 3-6). 1987. pap. 4.50 (0-8054-4320-7) Broadman.

—Reading My Bible in Summer. (Orig.). (gr. 3-6). 1987. pap. 4.50 (0-8054-4321-5) Broadman.

—Reading My Bible in Winter. LC 85-30940. (Orig.). (gr. 1-6). 1986. pap. 4.50 (0-8054-4323-1) Broadman.

Heath, Royal V. Mathemagic: Magic, Puzzles & Games with Numbers. (Illus.). 128p. (gr. 2 up). pap. 3.95 (0-486-20110-4) Dover.

Heathcote, Nick, et al. The New Discovery Book of Space. (Illus.). 96p. (gr. 6 up). 1994. PLB 15.95 RSBE (0-02-743506-7, New Discovery Bks) Macmillan Child Grp.

Hebblethwaite, Margaret. My Secret Life: A Friendship with God. LC 90-21550. 32p. (gr. 3-7). 1991. 11.95 (0-8192-1538-4) Morehouse Pub.

Hebert, Marie-F. A Witch in My Soup. (Illus.). 54p. (Orig.). 1993. pap. 5.95 (0-929005-52-X, Pub. by Second Story Pr CN) InBook.

Hebert, Marie-Francine. A Ghost in My Mirror. (Illus.). 54p. (Orig.). 1992. pap. 5.95 (0-929005-31-7, Pub. by Second Story Pr CN) InBook.

Hechler, Ellen. Mental Math, Series I: Two Complete Games Using Mental Math Brain Skills. (Orig.). (gr. 5-10). 1991. pap. 7.00 (0-9638483-2-1) Midmath.

—Mental Math, Series II: Two Complete Games Using Mental Math Brain Skills. (Orig.). (gr. 6-10). 1992. pap. 7.00 (0-9638483-7-2) Midmath.

—**Simulated Real Life Experiences Using Classified Ads in the Classroom.** (Illus.). 54p. (Orig.). (gr. 6-10). 1991. pap. 10.00 (0-9638483-3-X) Midmath. SIMULATED REAL-LIFE EXPERIENCES USING CLASSIFIED ADS IN THE CLASSROOM is a tool to be used as a supplemental unit. The unit applies a variety of middle school concepts to real life situations & motivates students to develop their mathematical & estimation skills. The book contains many open-ended lessons focusing on specific problems, such as using the classified ads to find a job, finance a car, & looking for an apartment. Budgeting & estimation skills are used throughout this unit. Each lesson provides a guided dialogue for first time use. Then the creativity of the individual teacher takes over. There are many different ways to conduct the activities within the framework of class discussion. The book's strongest feature is its discovery-learning method - letting the students find practical life applications in the use of newspaper advertisements rather than creating artificial textbook examples. After students have worked through the initial lessons, they might expand & include checking & charge accounts, or stocks & bonds in the financial section. The possibilities are endless. The book includes student worksheets using open-ended type questions for figuring out budgeting, transportation, apartment cost, expenses, & groceries. There are different forms of evaluations included. To order contact: Midmath, P.O. Box 2892, Farmington Hills, MI 48333; telephone (313) 855-2895. *Publisher Provided Annotation.*

Hecht, Jeff. Optics: Light for a New Age. LC 87-23398. (Illus.). 44p. (gr. 5-9). 1988. SBE 15.95 (*0-684-18879-1*, Scribners Young Read) Macmillan Child Grp.
—Shifting Shores: Rising Seas, Retreating Coastlines. LC 89-37812. (Illus.). 160p. (gr. 7 up). 1990. SBE 14.95 (*0-684-19087-7*, Scribners Young Read) Macmillan Child Grp.
—Vanishing Life: The Mystery of Mass Extinctions. LC 92-41713. (Illus.). 176p. (gr. 7 up). 1993. SBE 15.95 (*0-684-19331-0*, Scribners Young Read) Macmillan Child Grp.
Hecht, Joan B. Best Things about Dolls. Hecht, Muriel, illus. 16p. (ps-3). 1987. pap. 4.95 (*0-931271-08-8*) Hi Plains Pr.
Hecht, Johanna, notes by. The Nativity. Svensson, Borje, illus. LC 81-65400. (ps-3). 1981. pop-up bk. 9.95 (*0-385-28713-5*) Delacorte.
Hecht, Joyce C., jt. auth. see Hines, Sharon R.

Heck, Bessie H. Danger on the Homestead. rev. ed. Anderson, Peggy P., illus. LC 93-71892. 160p. (gr. 3-6). 1993. Repr. of 1991 ed. 14.95 (*0-9637259-0-4*) Dinosaur Pr. What Others Say About DANGERS ON THE HOMESTEAD: "Todd, 9, accompanies his father on the expedition to find & legally register a new home. While the father goes to file on the claim, Todd stays on it overnight & is compelled to defend it against Blackjack Bice, an outlaw who tries to steal it while Todd's father is gone. This is an excellent story about the 1889 run into the Unassigned Lands of what is today central Oklahoma. The author's rich research of this aspect of the run lends a delightful authenticity to this historical novel for boys & girls."--Harold Keith, Two-Time Winner of the Newbery Award. "I love Peggy Anderson's lively drawings. I expect to see more good things from this talented young illustrator."--Gail Haley, Winner of the Caldecott & Kate Greenaway Medals. "It has a strong story line, well-developed characters, it is well researched, accurate in frontier detail; a real good book."--Ken Jackson, Editor, World of Books, Sunday Tulsa World. "It is very exciting...I'm promoting it for a class "reader" in the whole language program."--Sybil Connolly, Library Media Specialist, Windsor Hills Elementary, Oklahoma City, OK. "My fourth grade class learned more about that run from DANGER ON THE HOMESTEAD than from their text books.--Barbara Marks, Barnes Elementary, Owasso, OK. Send orders to: Dinosaur Press, P.O. Box 50414, Tulsa, OK 74150-0414. *Publisher Provided Annotation.*

Heck, H. J., ed. see Schuster, Ignatius.
Heck, Joseph. Dinosaur Riddles. Barish, Wendy, ed. Hoffman, Sandy, illus. 128p. (gr. 3-7). 1982. 9.29 (*0-685-05613-9*, Little Simon) S&S Trade.
Heckart, Barbara H. Edmond Halley: The Man & His Comet. LC 83-24000. (Illus.). 112p. (gr. 4 up). 1984. PLB 18.60 (*0-516-03202-X*) Childrens.
Heckert, Connie. Dribbles. Sayles, Elizabeth, illus. LC 92-24846. 1993. 14.45 (*0-395-62336-7*, Clarion Bks) HM.
Heckert, Connie K., jt. auth. see Becker, Kayla M.

Heckman, Philip. The Magic of Holography. LC 85-27489. (Illus.). 256p. (gr. 7 up). 1986. SBE 19.95 (*0-689-31168-0*, Atheneum Child Bk) Macmillan Child Grp.
—The Moon Is Following Me. Young, Mary O., illus. LC 89-14921. 32p. (ps-1). 1991. SBE 13.95 (*0-689-31565-1*, Atheneum Child Bk) Macmillan Child Grp.
Hedayat, Sadegh & Batmanglij, N. The Patient Stone. Batmanglij, M. & Batmanglij, N., trs. from PER. Franta, illus. LC 86-33301. 32p. (gr. 4 up). 1987. Bilingual. 18.50 (*0-934211-02-7*); English. 18.50 (*0-934211-07-8*) Mage Pubs Inc.
Hedderwick, Mairi. Katie Morag & the Two Grandmothers. Hedderwick, Mairi, illus. 32p. (gr. k-3). 1986. picture bk. 10.95 (*0-316-35400-7*) Little.
Heddle, R. Science & Your Body. (Illus.). 24p. (gr. 1-4). 1993. PLB 12.96 (*0-88110-632-1*); pap. 4.50 (*0-7460-1425-2*) EDC.
Heddle, R. & Keable-Elliott, I. Book of Magic Tricks. (Illus.). 64p. (gr. 4-12). 1992. PLB 13.96 (*0-88110-509-3*, Usborne); pap. 7.95 (*0-7460-0653-5*, Usborne) EDC.
Heddle, Rebecca & Shipton, Paul. Science Activities, Vol. III. (Illus.). 72p. (gr. k-5). 1993. pap. 9.95 (*0-7460-1427-9*, Usborne) EDC.
—Science with Weather. (Illus.). 24p. (gr. k-5). 1993. PLB 12.96 (*0-88110-654-2*, Usborne); pap. 4.50 (*0-7460-1421-X*, Usborne) EDC.
Hedge-Cheney, Jacquelyn & Cheney, Roland J. The Little Daisy Girl & Other Poems. Hedge-Cheney, Jacquelyn & Cheny, Roland J., illus. 48p. (Orig.). (gr. 6 up). 1989. pap. write for info (*0-9621283-0-9*) Lil Daisy Bks.
Hedgpeth, Joel. Common Seashore Life of Southern California. Hinton, Sam, illus. 64p. (gr. 4 up). 1961. 14.95 (*0-911010-63-7*); pap. 6.95 (*0-911010-62-9*) Naturegraph.
Hedlund, Irene. Mighty Mountain & the Three Strong Women. LC 89-28052. (Illus.). 32p. (gr. 2-5). 1990. 14.95 (*0-912078-86-3*) Volcano Pr.

Hedren, Tippi & Taylor, Theodore. The Cats of Shambala. rev. ed. Dow, Bill, photos by. (Illus.). 300p. (gr. 6 up). 1992. pap. 14.95 (*0-9631549-0-7*) Tiger Isld Pr. Here is the riveting, lavishly illustrated saga of how actress Tippi Hedren, in the process of making a feature film as a plea to save wildlife, came to share her home & hearth with its "stars" - some hundred lions, tigers, leopards, cheetahs, & cougars - on a 180 acre preserve in California. Over a hundred photos bring the big cats, & the humans who worked, lived, raised them from cubs & sometimes slept with them, vividly to life. "An exciting read.. ."--Library Journal. "An intriguing tale of obsession..."--Kirkus Review. "This is a rare & captivating book... fascinating, unusual & engrossing"--John Barkham Reviews. "Animal lovers will have difficulty putting Hedren's book down..."--Charleston Evening Post. *Publisher Provided Annotation.*

Hedrick, Basil & Savage, Susan. Steamboats on the Chena: The Founding & Development of Fairbanks, Alaska. (Orig.). (gr. 9-12). 1988. pap. 9.95 (*0-945397-00-3*) Epicenter Pr.
Heegaard, Marge. When a Family Gets Diabetes. (Illus.). 50p. (Orig.). (gr. 1-9). 1990. pap. 6.95 (*0-937721-75-1*) Chronimed.
—When a Family Is in Trouble: Children Can Cope with Grief from Drug & Alcohol Addictions. (gr. 4-7). 1993. pap. 6.95 (*0-9620502-7-X*) Woodland Pr.
—When a Parent Marries Again. (ps-3). 1993. pap. 6.95 (*0-9620502-6-1*) Woodland Pr.
—When Someone Has a Very Serious Illness: Children Learn to Cope with Loss & Change Workbook. (gr. 4-7). 1992. pap. 6.95 (*0-9620502-4-5*) Woodland Pr.
Heegaard, Marge E. Coping with Death & Grief. (Illus.). 64p. (gr. 3-6). 1990. PLB 15.95 (*0-8225-0043-4*) Lerner Pubns.
—When Mom & Dad Separate: Children Can Learn to Cope with Grief from Divorce. (Illus.). 35p. (Orig.). (gr. k-6). 1990. pap. 5.95 wkbk. (*0-9620502-2-9*) Woodland Pr.
—When Someone Very Special Dies: Children Can Learn to Cope with Grief. (Illus.). 32p. (gr. 1-6). 1988. wkbk. 4.95 (*0-9620502-0-2*) Woodland Pr.
—When Something Terrible Happens: Children Can Learn to Cope with Grief Workbook. (gr. 4-7). 1992. pap. 6.95 (*0-9620502-3-7*) Woodland Pr.
Heerboth, Sharon, jt. auth. see Hitzeroth, Deborah.

Heerey, Frances. My First Prayer Book. 1986. pap. 3.95 (*0-88271-131-8*) Regina Pr.
Heerey, Frances C. First Holy Communion. 1988. pap. 3.95 (*0-88271-057-5*) Regina Pr.
Heesakkers, Wim. My Little Rooster Woodbook. (ps). 1985. 9.95 (*0-8120-5628-0*) Barron.
Heese. Jugendhandbuch Naturwissen: Saeugetiere, Vol. 3. (GER.). 144p. 1976. pap. 5.95 (*0-686-56619-X*, M-7488, Pub. by Rowohlt) Fr & Eur.
—Jugendhandbuch Naturwissen, Vol. 4: Erde und Weltall. (GER.). 128p. 1976. pap. 5.95 (*0-7859-0412-3*, M7489) Fr & Eur.
—Jugendhandbuch Naturwissen, Vol. 5: Energie. (GER.). 128p. 1976. pap. 5.95 (*0-7859-0413-1*, M7490) Fr & Eur.
—Jugendhandbuch Naturwissen, Vol. 6: Elektrizitaet und Elektronic. (GER.). 144p. 1976. pap. 5.95 (*0-7859-0414-X*, M7491) Fr & Eur.
Hefley, Lynn C. Purple Mountain Majesty. Brummett, Nancy P., ed. Harness, Cheryl, illus. LC 93-84708. 24p. (Orig.). (gr. 3-6). 1993. pap. text ed. write for info. (*0-944943-42-X*) Current Inc.
Hefter, Richard. ABC Coloring Book. 1978. pap. 2.50 (*0-486-22969-6*) Dover.
—Babysitter Bears. Hefter, Richard, illus. LC 83-8205. (gr. 3-6). 1983. 5.95 (*0-911787-08-9*) Optimum Res Inc.
—Bears at Work. Hefter, Richard, illus. LC 83-2192. 32p. (ps-1). 1983. 5.95 (*0-911787-00-3*) Optimum Res Inc.
—Bears Away from Home. Hefter, Richard, illus. LC 83-4149. (gr. 3-6). 1983. 5.95 (*0-911787-05-4*) Optimum Res Inc.
—Fast Food. Hefter, Richard, illus. LC 83-6734. (gr. 3-6). 1983. 5.95 (*0-911787-09-7*) Optimum Res Inc.
—Jobs for Bears. Hefter, Richard, illus. LC 83-2197. 32p. (ps-1). 1983. 5.95 (*0-911787-02-X*) Optimum Res Inc.
—Lots of Little Bears. Hefter, Richard, illus. LC 83-2184. 32p. (ps-1). 1983. 5.95 (*0-911787-04-6*) Optimum Res Inc.
—Neat Feet. Hefter, Richard, illus. LC 83-8035. (gr. 3-6). 1983. 5.95 (*0-911787-07-0*) Optimum Res Inc.
—The Stickybear Book of Weather. Hefter, Richard, illus. LC 83-2191. 32p. (ps-1). 1983. 5.95 (*0-911787-01-1*) Optimum Res Inc.
—The Stickybear's Scary Night. (Illus.). 29p. (ps-1). 1984. 1.95 (*0-911787-41-0*) Optimum Res Inc.
—Watch Out! Hefter, Richard, illus. LC 83-2190. 32p. (ps-1). 1983. 5.95 (*0-911787-03-8*) Optimum Res Inc.
—Where Is the Bear? Hefter, Richard, illus. LC 83-6296. 32p. (gr. 3-6). 1983. 5.95 (*0-911787-06-2*) Optimum Res Inc.
Hegarty, Sue & Geoghegan, Judy. Carousel Coloring Book. Hennigh, Susan, illus. 32p. (Orig.). (gr. k-8). 1989. pap. 4.50 (*0-9622526-1-1*) Freels Fndtn.
Hegeman, Kathryn T. The Animal Kingdom. Hegeman, Mark, et al, illus. (gr. k-3). 1982. tchr's manual 10.00 (*0-89824-031-X*); wkbk. 4.99 (*0-89824-030-1*) Trillium Pr.
—Our Community. Hegeman, Mark, et al, illus. (Orig.). (gr. k-3). 1982. tchr's manual 10.00 (*0-89824-034-4*); wkbk. 4.99 (*0-89824-035-2*) Trillium Pr.
—What to Do? Creative Problem-Solving Level A. (gr. 1-2). 1984. pap. 15.00 tchr's cards (*0-89824-045-X*); PLB 4.99 wkbk. (*0-89824-043-3*) Trillium Pr.
—What to Do? Creative Problem-Solving Level B. (gr. 3-4). 1985. pap. 15.00 tchr's cards (*0-89824-088-3*); PLB 4.99 wkbk. (*0-89824-089-1*) Trillium Pr.
Hegeman, Kathryn T., ed. Aesop's Fables, 4 vols. (gr. 1-4). 1984. Set. 16.00 (*0-89824-050-6*); Vol. I. 5.00 (*0-89824-051-4*); Vol. II. 5.00 (*0-89824-052-2*); Vol. III. 5.00 (*0-89824-053-0*); Vol. IV. 5.00 (*0-89824-054-9*) Trillium Pr.
Hegene, Barbara M. Wood Homestead. (Illus.). 10p. (gr. 9-12). 1990. pap. write for info. (*0-9623847-5-5*) B Hegne.
Hegg, Tom. A Cup of Christmas Tea. Hanson, Warren, illus. 46p. (gr. 4 up). 1991. 10.95 (*0-931674-08-5*) Waldman Hse Pr.
—The Mark of the Maker. Hanson, Warren, illus. 46p. (gr. 4 up). 1991. 10.95 (*0-931674-18-2*) Waldman Hse Pr.
Hegler, Jodi, jt. auth. see Hegler, Michele.
Hegler, Michele & Hegler, Jodi. Faces of the World. Cuthbert, Peter, illus. 79p. (gr. 9-12). 1989. pap. 7.95 (*0-945362-02-1*) Best Sllrs TX.
Hehner, B. E. Blue Planet. 1992. write for info. (*0-15-200423-8*, Gulliver Bks) HarBrace.
Hehner, Barbara, jt. auth. see Suzuki, David.
Heide, F. God & Me. (Illus.). 32p. (ps). 1987. pap. 3.99 (*0-570-07792-3*, 56-1316) Concordia.
Heide, Florence P. The Adventures of Treehorn. Gorey, Edward, illus. LC 83-2072. (gr. k-3). 1983. pap. 1.95 (*0-440-40045-7*, YB) Dell.
—Banana Blitz. 128p. (gr. 3-7). 1984. pap. 2.50 (*0-553-15258-0*, Skylark) Bantam.
—The Bigness Contest. Chess, Victoria, illus. LC 92-12663. 1993. 14.95 (*0-316-35444-9*, Joy St Bks) Little.
—The Day of Ahmed's Secret. 32p. 1990. 13.95 (*0-688-08984-5*); PLB 13.88 (*0-688-08895-3*) Lothrop.
—Grim & Ghastly Goings-On. Pearson, Susan, ed. Chess, Victoria, illus. LC 89-8071. 24p. (gr. k up). 1992. 14.00 (*0-688-08319-6*); PLB 13.93 (*0-688-08322-6*) Lothrop.
—The Problem with Pulcifier. Glasser, Judy, illus. LC 81-48606. 64p. (gr. 2 up). 1992. pap. 3.95 (*0-688-11507-5*, Mulberry) Morrow.
—The Shrinking of Treehorn. (gr. k-3). 1979. pap. 0.95 (*0-440-47684-4*, YB) Dell.

—The Shrinking of Treehorn. Gorey, Edward, illus. LC 78-151753. 64p. (gr. 3-6). 1971. reinforced bdg. 13.95 (0-8234-0189-8); pap. 4.95 (0-8234-0975-9) Holiday.
—Tales for the Perfect Child. Chess, Victoria, illus. 80p. (gr. 3-6). 1985. 14.95 (0-688-03892-1); PLB 14.88 (0-688-03893-X) Lothrop.
—Tales for the Perfect Child. (gr. 4-7). 1991. pap. 2.99 (0-440-40463-0) Dell.
—Time Flies! Hafner, Marylin, illus. LC 84-47833. 112p. (gr. 3-7). 1984. 13.95 (0-8234-0542-7) Holiday.
—Time Flies! 112p. 1985. pap. 2.50 (0-553-15370-6, Skylark) Bantam.
—Time's Up. large type ed. 148p. (gr. 4-6). 1988. Repr. of 1982 ed. 38.20 (0-317-01949-X, 4-25830-00) Am Printing Hse.
—Timothy Twinge. LC 91-39013. (ps-3). 1993. 14.00 (0-688-10762-1); PLB 13.93 (0-688-10763-X) Lothrop.
—Treehorn Times Three. (gr. 4-7). 1992. pap. 3.50 (0-440-40553-X) Dell.
—Treehorn's Treasure. Gorey, Edward, illus. LC 81-4043. 64p. (gr. 3-6). 1981. reinforced bdg. 13.95 (0-8234-0425-0) Holiday.
—Treehorn's Wish. Gorey, Edward, illus. LC 83-6240. 64p. (gr. 3-6). 1984. reinforced bdg 8.95 (0-8234-0493-5) Holiday.
Heide, Florence P. & Gilliland, Judith H. Sami & the Time of the Troubles. Lewin, Ted, illus. 32p. (gr. k-4). 1992. 13.45 (0-395-55964-2, Clarion Bks) HM.
Heide, John von der see Von der Heide, John.
Heiderscheit, Sara M. The Bandalars. Froiland, Gary, illus. 12p. (Orig.). (ps-4). 1988. pap. 3.50 (0-9620385-0-4) S Heiderscheit.
Heidinger, James V., II, et al, eds. see Case, Riley B. & Keysor, Charles W.
Heiferling, Mindy. A Taste of Spring. LC 92-14705. 1993. 16.00 (0-517-59016-6, Clarkson Potter) Crown Pub Group.
Heifetz, Jeanne. Colorful Names. 1994. write for info. (0-8050-3178-2) H Holt & Co.
Heifner, Fred. Isaiah: Messenger for God. Johnston, Cliff, illus. (gr. 1-6). 1978. 5.95 (0-8054-4243-X, 4242-43) Broadman.
Heiges, Shawn, illus. Jamestown Children's Activity Book. 40p. (gr. 1-6). 1992. pap. 2.00 (0-939631-53-9) Thomas Publications.
Heikkinen, Henry & Atkinson, Gordon. Reactions & Reason: An Introductory Chemistry Module. Gardner, Marjorie, intro. by. (Illus.). 106p. (Orig.). (gr. 9-12). 1991. pap. text ed. 8.20 (1-879827-00-X) Vistas.
Heilbroner, Joan. Robert the Rose Horse. LC 62-9218. (Illus.). 72p. (gr. 1-2). 1962. 6.95 (0-394-80025-7); lib. bdg. 7.99 (0-394-90025-1) Beginner.
—This Is the House Where Jack Lives. Aliki, illus. LC 62-7311. 64p. (gr. k-3). 1962. PLB 13.89 (0-06-022286-7) HarpC Child Bks.
—Tom the TV Cat: A Step Two Book. Murdocca, Sal, illus. LC 83-24600. 48p. (ps-2). 1984. lib. bdg. 7.99 (0-394-96708-9); pap. 2.95 (0-394-86708-4) Random Bks Yng Read.
Heiligman. Its a Butterfly. Date not set. 14.00 (0-06-024264-7, Festival); PLB 13.89 (0-06-024268-X, Festival) HarpC Child Bks.
Heilman, Joan R. Bluebird Rescue: A Harrowsmith Country Life Nature Guide. rev. ed. LC 91-40618. (Illus.). 48p. (gr. 10 up). 1992. lib. bdg. 16.95 (0-944475-27-2); pap. 6.95 (0-944475-24-8) Camden Hse Pub.
—Tons of Trash: Why You Should Recycle & What Happens When You Do. 80p. (gr. 2-4). 1992. pap. 3.50 (0-380-76379-6, Camelot) Avon.
Heilman, Robert B., ed. see Hardy, Thomas.
Heim, Michael, tr. see Uspenski, Eduard.
Heimann, Rolf. Amazing Mazes. (gr. 4-7). 1990. pap. 3.95 (0-8167-2201-3) Troll Assocs.
—Bizarre Brain Benders. (Illus.). 32p. (gr. 4-7). 1993. pap. 3.95 (0-8167-3035-0, Pub. by Watermill Pr) Troll Assocs.
—For Eagle Eyes Only. (gr. 4-7). 1990. pap. 3.95 (0-8167-2202-1) Troll Assocs.
Heine, Helme. Friends. Heine, Helme, illus. LC 82-49350. 32p. (ps-2). 1982. SBE 14.95 (0-689-50256-7, M K McElderry) Macmillan Child Grp.
—Friends. Heine, Helme, illus. LC 86-3379. 32p. (ps-3). 1986. pap. 3.95 (0-689-71083-6, Aladdin) Macmillan Child Grp.
—The Marvelous Journey Through the Night. Manheim, Ralph, tr. (Illus.). 26p. (gr. 4-8). 1990. 15.00 (0-374-38478-9) FS&G.
—The Marvelous Journey Through the Night. Manheim, Ralph, tr. (Illus.). 26p. (ps-3). 1992. pap. 5.95 (0-374-44741-1, Sunburst) FS&G.
—Mollywoop. Manheim, Ralph, tr. (Illus.). 32p. (ps-3). 1991. bds. 14.95 bds. (0-374-35001-9) FS&G.
—The Most Wonderful Egg in the World. Heine, Helme, illus. LC 82-49350. 32p. (gr. k-3). 1983. SBE 14.95 (0-689-50280-X, M K McElderry) Macmillan Child Grp.
—The Most Wonderful Egg in the World. Heine, Helme, illus. LC 82-22251. 32p. (gr. k-3). 1987. pap. 4.95 (0-689-71117-4, Aladdin) Macmillan Child Grp.
—One Day in Paradise. Heine, Helme, illus. LC 85-72492. 32p. (ps-4). 1986. SBE 14.95 (0-689-50394-6, M K McElderry) Macmillan Child Grp.
—The Pearl. Heine, Helme, illus. LC 84-72404. 32p. (gr. k-4). 1985. SBE 14.95 (0-689-50321-0, M K McElderry) Macmillan Child Grp.

—The Pearl. Heine, Helme, illus. LC 88-3220. 32p. (gr. k-4). 1988. pap. 3.95 (0-689-71262-6, Aladdin) Macmillan Child Grp.
—The Pigs' Wedding. reissue ed. Heine, Helme, illus. LC 78-57691. 32p. (ps-3). 1986. SBE 14.95 (0-689-50409-8, M K McElderry) Macmillan Child Grp.
—The Pigs' Wedding. Heine, Helme, illus. LC 90-40996. 32p. (gr. k-3). 1991. pap. 4.95 (0-689-71478-5, Aladdin) Macmillan Child Grp.
—Seven Wild Pigs. LC 87-3448. (Illus.). 120p. (gr. k up). 1988. SBE 18.95 (0-689-50439-X, M K McElderry) Macmillan Child Grp.
Heinlein, Robert A. Citizen of the Galaxy. LC 86-26172. 312p. (gr. 7 up). 1987. SBE 15.95 (0-684-18818-X, Scribners Young Read) Macmillan Child Grp.
—Door into Summer. (RL 7). pap. 2.50 (0-451-13777-9, AE2363, Sig) NAL-Dutton.
—Time for the Stars. LC 90-33408. 256p. (gr. 7 up). 1990. SBE 15.95 (0-684-19211-X, Scribners Young Read) Macmillan Child Grp.
—Tunnel in the Sky. reissued ed. LC 55-10142. 288p. (gr. 7 up). 1988. SBE 15.95 (0-684-18916-X, Scribners Young Read) Macmillan Child Grp.
Heinrich, Annette. Not a Hollywood Family: Realistic Devotions for Teens. 110p. (Orig.). (gr. 7 up). 1989. pap. 5.99 (0-87788-584-2) Shaw Pubs.
—One in a Zillion: Realistic Devotions for Teens. 112p. (Orig.). (gr. 9-12). 1990. pap. 5.99 (0-87788-621-0) Shaw Pubs.
Heinrich, Bernd. Owl in the House. Heinrich, Bernd, illus. Calaprice, Alice, adapted by. (gr. 5-9). 1990. 14. 95 (0-316-35456-2, Joy St Bks) Little.
Heinrichs, Ann. Alaska. LC 90-33847. (Illus.). 144p. (gr. 4 up). 1990. PLB 26.60 (0-516-00448-4) Childrens.
—Alaska. 201p. 1993. text ed. 15.40 (1-56956-127-3) W A T Braille.
—Arizona. LC 90-21118. (Illus.). 144p. (gr. 5-8). 1991. PLB 26.60 (0-516-00449-2) Childrens.
—Arizona. 200p. 1993. text ed. 15.40 (1-56956-150-8) W A T Braille.
—Arkansas. LC 88-38529. (Illus.). 144p. (gr. 4 up). 1989. PLB 26.60 (0-516-00450-6) Childrens.
—Arkansas. 186p. 1993. text ed. 15.40 (1-56956-155-9) W A T Braille.
—Montana. LC 90-21035. (Illus.). 144p. (gr. 5-8). 1991. PLB 26.60 (0-516-00472-7) Childrens.
—Montana. 199p. 1993. text ed. 15.40 (1-56956-135-4) W A T Braille.
—Oklahoma. LC 88-11743. (Illus.). 144p. (gr. 4 up). 1988. PLB 26.60 (0-516-00482-4) Childrens.
—Rhode Island. LC 89-25284. (Illus.). 144p. (gr. 4 up). 1990. PLB 26.60 (0-516-00485-9) Childrens.
—Rhode Island. 195p. 1993. text ed. 15.40 (1-56956-165-6) W A T Braille.
—Wyoming. LC 91-544. 144p. (gr. 4 up). 1991. PLB 26. 60 (0-516-00496-4) Childrens.
—Wyoming. 215p. 1993. text ed. 15.40 (1-56956-148-6) W A T Braille.
Heinrichs, Ann A. Oklahoma. 196p. 1993. text ed. 15.40 (1-56956-131-1) W A T Braille.
Heinrichs, Susan. The Atlantic Ocean. LC 86-9578. (Illus.). 48p. (gr. k-4). 1986. PLB 15.27 (0-516-01289-4) Childrens.
—The Indian Ocean. LC 86-9579. (Illus.). 48p. (gr. k-4). 1986. PLB 15.27 (0-516-01293-2) Childrens.
—The Pacific Ocean. LC 86-9653. (Illus.). 48p. (gr. k-4). 1986. PLB 15.27 (0-516-01295-9); pap. 4.95 (0-516-41295-7) Childrens.
Heins, Paul, tr. see Grimm, Jacob & Grimm, Wilhelm K.
Heinsohn, Beth & Cohen, Andrew. The Department of Defense. (Illus.). 120p. (gr. 5 up). 1990. 14.95 (0-87754-837-4) Chelsea Hse.
Heinst, Marie. My First Number Book. LC 91-58193. (Illus.). 48p. (ps-3). 1992. 12.95 (1-879431-73-4); PLB 13.99 (1-879431-74-2) Dorling Kindersley.
Heintze, Ty. Valley of the Eels: A Science Fiction Mystery. Heintze, Ty, illus. LC 93-2906. 1993. 14.95 (0-89015-904-1) Eakin-Sunbelt.
Heinz, Brian J. Alley Cat. (gr. 4 up). 1993. 14.95 (0-385-31042-0) Doubleday.
—Beachcrafts Too. LC 87-35232. (Illus.). 112p. (Orig.). 1988. pap. 9.95 (0-936335-01-7) Ballyhoo Bks.
Heinzerling, Doris M. The Barefoot Ballerina. Nelson, Jane E., illus. 24p. (gr. k-1). 1993. write for info. (1-879094-40-1) Avonstoke Pr.
Heisch, Elisabeth, jt. auth. see Heisch, Glan.
Heisch, Glan & Heisch, Elisabeth. The Cinnamon Bear: The Missing Star. Bishop, Kathryn, ed. Jackson, Jett & Arnoff, Julie, illus. Bishop, Kathryn, intro. by. 32p. 1992. PLB 13.95 (1-880623-01-3); pap. 8.95 (1-880623-02-1) Stiles-Bishop.

Heise, Robert F. Twas the Night Before Jesus. Wade, John, illus. 28p. (gr. 3-6). 1990. smyth-sewn 12.95 (0-9627049-0-3) Dogwood NC. This new family-oriented book promises to be a fast & steady seller with wide appeal for both Christian & general audiences. Based loosely on the time-honored Christmas classic, "The Night Before Christmas," Bud Heise has created a Christmas tale that will

delight both children & their parents, as the story of the Christ Child's birth is retold in rhyme & striking full color illustrations. 'TWAS THE NIGHT BEFORE JESUS is a 8 1/2" X 11" hardcover book, beautifully bound in a durable, washable cloth which will make reading aloud with a child or grandchild on one knee a family strengthening pleasure for the Holidays. Christian parents especially will appreciate the instructive value as well as the aesthetic appeal of this unique book. 'TWAS THE NIGHT BEFORE JESUS returns to the true meaning of Christmas. It promises to become a classic in years to come. Order now in time for the Christmas season.
Publisher Provided Annotation.

Heisel, Sharon E. A Little Magic. LC 90-46341. 144p. (gr. 3-7). 1991. 13.45 (0-395-55722-4) HM.
—Wrapped in a Riddle. LC 92-26954. 1993. 13.95 (0-395-65026-7) HM.
Heitler, Susan M. David Decides about Thumbsucking: A Motivating Story for Children & an Informative Guide for Parents. Singer, Paula, illus. LC 85-61019. 52p. (ps-3). 1985. PLB 17.95 (0-9614780-1-2); pap. 9.95 (0-9614780-0-4) Reading Matters.
Heitz, True. Mommy Moon & the Rainbow Children. Mattos, D., illus. 13p. (Orig.). (ps-2). 1982. pap. 3.00 (0-686-37664-1) True Heitz.
Hejl, Pauline, tr. see Esterl, Arnica.
Hejtmanek, Debra M. Mr. Marble's Moose. 48p. (ps-2). 1993. 9.99 (0-8499-0969-4) Word Inc.
Helakisa, Kaarina. The Journey of Pietari & His Wolf. Rollerson, Michael, tr. from SWE. Tikka, Saara, illus. LC 84-80571. 72p. (gr. 7-12). 1991. pap. 12.95 (0-88138-043-1, Green Tiger) S&S Trade.
Helberg, Bob, ed. see Prather, Hugh E., Jr.
Helen, Mary. Wait for Me: The Life of Junipero Serra. Thien, Denis, illus. LC 88-13103. 100p. (gr. 4-8). 1988. 3.00 (0-8198-8232-1) St Paul Bks.
Helfer, Andrew. Batman: Mask of the Phantasm: M-TV. (gr. 4-7). 1993. pap. 3.99 (0-553-48174-6, Skylark) Bantam.
—Batman Returns. (Illus.). 80p. 1992. pap. 2.95 (0-316-17757-1) Little.
—Batman: The House of Horrors. (ps-3). 1993. pap. 3.50 (0-307-11471-6, Golden Pr) Western Pub.
—Batman: The Purrfect Crime. (Illus.). (ps-3). 1991. pap. write for info. (0-307-12621-8, Golden Pr) Western Pub.
Helfer, Andrew, ed. see Pratt, George.
Helfer, Judith. Aleph Bet for You. Helfer, Judith, illus. LC 70-88355. (ps-2). 1969. pap. 4.00 (0-88400-024-9) Shengold.
Helfman, Elizabeth. On Being Sarah. Mathews, Judith, ed. Saffioti, Lino, illus. 144p. (gr. 5-9). 1992. 11.95g (0-8075-6068-5) A Whitman.
Helfrich, R. L., jt. auth. see Hanson, Don.
Helgadottir, Gudrun. Flumbra: An Icelandic Folktale. Sanders, Christopher, tr. from ICE. Pilkington, Brian, illus. LC 86-6173. 32p. (gr. 1-6). 1986. lib. bdg. 18.95 (0-87614-243-9) Carolrhoda Bks.
Helgesen, M., et al. New English Firsthand: Developing Communicative Language Skills. (Illus.). 1993. pap. text ed. 14.95 (0-582-06851-7); tchr's. ed. 16.95 (0-582-06852-5); cass. 23.95 (0-582-06853-3) Addison-Wesley.
—New English Firsthand Plus: Expanding Communicative Language Skills. (Illus.). 1993. pap. text ed. 14.95 (0-582-06854-1); tchr's. ed. 16.95 (0-582-06855-X); cass. 23.95 (0-582-06856-8) Longman.
Helgeson, M., et al. English Firsthand Plus: Expanding Communicative Language Skills. 136p. 1988. pap. text ed. 14.95 (0-934457-11-5, 78383); tchr's. ed. 16.95 (0-934457-12-3, 78382); cassette 23.95 (0-934457-13-1, 78381) Longman.
—English Firsthand: A Communicative Approach to Developing Language Skills. 123p. 1986. pap. text ed. 14.95 (0-8013-0523-3, 78369); tchr's. ed. 16.95 (0-8013-0524-1, 78370); cassette 23.95 (0-8013-0525-X, 78371) Longman.
Helgoe, Cathy, ed. see Barrowman, Tom, et al.
Hellard, Susan. Eleanor & the Babysitter. (ps-3). 1991. 13.95 (0-316-35459-7) Little.
Hellbroner, Joan. Meet George Washington. Marchesi, Stephen, illus. LC 88-19067. 72p. (gr. 2-4). 1989. PLB 6.99 (0-394-91965-3); pap. 2.99 (0-394-81965-9) Random Bks Yng Read.
Hellden, Daniel. Hi! Said the Blackbird: And Twelve Other American Folk Songs to Sing & Play. 24p. (gr. 1-4). 1981. pap. 6.00 (0-918812-17-8) MMB Music.
Helldorfer, M. C. Cabbage Rose. Downing, Julie, illus. LC 91-9833. 32p. (ps-3). 1993. RSBE 14.95 (0-02-743513-X, Bradbury Pr) Macmillan Child Grp.

—Daniel's Gift. Downing, Julie, illus. LC 87-5160. 32p. (ps-3). 1987. RSBE 13.95 (0-02-743511-3, Bradbury Pr) Macmillan Child Grp.
—Daniel's Gift. Downing, Julie, illus. LC 90-186. 32p. (gr. k-3). 1990. pap. 4.95 (0-689-71440-8, Aladdin) Macmillan Child Grp.
—The Darling Boys. Halsey, Megan, illus. LC 91-44708. 32p. (gr. k-3). 1992. RSBE 14.95 (0-02-743516-4, Bradbury Pr) Macmillan Child Grp.
—The Mapmaker's Daughter. Hunt, Jonathan, illus. LC 89-39330. 40p. (ps-3). 1991. RSBE 15.95 (0-02-743515-6, Bradbury Pr) Macmillan Child Grp.
—Moon Trouble. Hunt, Jonathan, illus. LC 92-22233. 32p. (gr. k-4). 1994. RSBE 16.95 (0-02-743517-2, Bradbury Pr) Macmillan Child Grp.
—Spook House. LC 88-30026. 160p. (gr. 4 up). 1989. SBE 13.95 (0-02-743514-8, Bradbury Pr) Macmillan Child Grp.
Helldorfer, Mary C. Clap Clap! Speidel, Sandra, illus. 32p. (ps-2). 1993. reinforced bdg. 13.99 (0-670-85155-8) Viking Child Bks.
—Sailing into the Sea. Krupinski, Loretta, illus. R. (ps-3). 1991. 13.95 (0-670-83520-X) Viking Child Bks.
—Sailing into the Sea. Krupinski, Loretta, illus. R. (ps-3). 1993. pap. 4.99 (0-14-054317-1, Puffin) Puffin Bks.
Hellen, Nancy. Animals of the Jungle. Hellen, Nancy, illus. 16p. (ps). 1991. 6.95 (0-87226-458-0, Bedrick Blackie) P Bedrick Bks.
—The Bus Stop. LC 88-504. (Illus.). 18p. (ps-1). 1988. 11.95 (0-531-05765-8) Orchard Bks Watts.
—Creatures of the Ocean. Hellen, Nancy, illus. 16p. (ps). 1991. 6.95 (0-87226-457-2, Bedrick Blackie) P Bedrick Bks.
—Old MacDonald Had a Farm. LC 89-25587. (Illus.). 18p. (ps-1). 1990. 13.95 (0-531-05872-7) Orchard Bks Watts.
—On the Farm: Match It Up. 1989. 3.99 (0-517-68250-8) Outlet Bk Co.
—A Visit to the Farm. Hellen, Nancy, illus. 16p. (ps). 1991. 6.95 (0-87226-432-7, Bedrick Blackie) P Bedrick Bks.
—A Visit to the Zoo. Hellen, Nancy, illus. 16p. (ps). 1990. 6.95 (0-87226-431-9, Bedrick Blackie) P Bedrick Bks.
Heller, David. Dear God, What Religion Were the Dinosaurs? More Children's Letters to God. 1990. 14.95 (0-385-26127-6) Doubleday.
Heller, Elaine. Half & Half Design & Color, Bks. 1 & 2. (gr. 4-6). 1981. Bk. 1. 9.00 (0-87879-832-3, Ann Arbor Div); instr. manual 1.00 (0-87879-834-X); manual 1.50 (0-685-57832-1) Acad Therapy.
Heller, Jeffrey. Joan Baez: Singer with a Cause. LC 90-21046. (Illus.). 152p. (gr. 4 up). 1991. PLB 18.60 (0-516-03271-2); pap. 5.95 (0-516-43271-0) Childrens.
Heller, Linda. The Castle on Hester Street. Heller, Linda, illus. 32p. (gr. k-3). 1990. pap. 6.95t (0-8276-0323-1) JPS Phila.
Heller, Nicholas. An Adventure at Sea. LC 87-25525. (Illus.). 24p. (ps-3). 1988. 11.95 (0-688-07846-X); PLB 11.88 (0-688-07847-8) Greenwillow.
—Fish Stories. Heller, Nicholas, illus. LC 86-14906. 24p. (gr. k-3). 1987. 11.75 (0-688-06931-2); PLB 11.88 (0-688-06932-0) Greenwillow.
—The Front Hall Carpet. LC 89-38360. (Illus.). 24p. (ps up). 1990. 12.95 (0-688-05272-X); PLB 12.88 (0-688-05273-8) Greenwillow.
—Happy Birthday, Moe Dog. LC 87-14851. (Illus.). 24p. (gr. k up). 1988. 11.95 (0-688-07670-X); lib. bdg. 11.88 (0-688-07671-8) Greenwillow.
—Mathilda the Dream Bear. LC 88-3830. (Illus.). 32p. (ps up). 1989. 12.95 (0-688-08238-6); PLB 12.88 (0-688-08239-4) Greenwillow.
—The Monster in the Cave. Heller, Nicholas, illus. LC 86-29598. (Illus.). 32p. (ps-3). 1987. 11.75 (0-688-07313-1); lib. bdg. 11.88 (0-688-07314-X) Greenwillow.
—Peas. LC 92-29740. 24p. 1993. 14.00 (0-688-12406-2); PLB 13.93 (0-688-12407-0) Greenwillow.
—Ten Old Pails. Abolafia, Yossi, illus. LC 92-31511. 24p. (ps up). 1994. write for info. (0-688-12419-4); PLB write for info. (0-688-12420-8) Greenwillow.
—The Tooth Tree. LC 90-39791. (Illus.). 24p. (ps up). 1991. 13.95 (0-688-09392-2); PLB 13.88 (0-688-09393-0) Greenwillow.
—A Troll Story. LC 88-34906. (Illus.). 24p. (ps up) 1990. 12.95 (0-688-08970-4); PLB 14.88 (0-688-08971-2) Greenwillow.
—Up the Wall. LC 91-14783. 24p. 1992. 14.00 (0-688-10633-1); PLB 13.93 (0-688-10634-X) Greenwillow.
—Woody. (Illus.). 24p. (ps up). 1994. write for info. (0-688-12804-1); PLB write for info. (0-688-12805-X) Greenwillow.
Heller, Pete. Peppy Learns to Play Baseball. Kinsey, Thomas D., ed. Schaeffer, Bob, illus. 32p. (gr. k-5). pap. 3.95 (0-932423-00-0) Summa Bks.
Heller, Rachael F., jt. auth. see Heller, Richard F.
Heller, Richard F. & Heller, Rachael F. AP Exam in Biology. 2nd ed. 288p. (gr. 9-12). 1990. pap. 12.95 (0-13-038704-5, Arco Test) P-H Gen Ref & Trav.
Heller, Robert, et al. Earth Science. 2nd ed. (Illus.). 1978. text ed. 32.24 (0-07-028037-1) McGraw.
Heller, Ruth. Animals Born Alive & Well. Heller, Ruth, illus. LC 82-80872. 48p. (gr. k-2). 1982. 10.95 (0-448-01822-5, G&D) Putnam Pub Group.
—Animals Born Alive & Well. (Illus.). 48p. (ps-3). 1993. pap. 6.95 (0-448-40453-2, G&D) Putnam Pub Group.

—A Cache of Jewels & Other Collective Nouns. (ps-3). 1989. 13.95 (0-448-19211-X, G&D) Putnam Pub Group.
—A Cache of Jewels & Other Collective Nouns. (Illus.). 48p. 1991. pap. 5.95 (0-448-40075-8, G&D) Putnam Pub Group.
—Chickens Aren't the Only Ones. Heller, Ruth, illus. LC 80-85257. 48p. (ps-1). 1981. 10.95 (0-448-01872-1, G&D) Putnam Pub Group.
—Chickens Aren't the Only Ones. (Illus.). 48p. (ps-3). 1993. pap. 6.95 (0-448-40454-0, G&D) Putnam Pub Group.
—Designs for Coloring Optical Art. (Illus.). 64p. 1992. pap. 3.95 (0-448-03143-4, G&D) Putnam Pub Group.
—Designs for Coloring Seashells. (Illus.). 64p. 1992. pap. 3.95 (0-448-03144-2, G&D) Putnam Pub Group.
—How to Hide a Butterfly. Heller, Ruth, illus. LC 85-70287. 32p. (ps-2). 1986. 5.95 (0-448-10478-4, G&D) Putnam Pub Group.
—How to Hide a Butterfly: And Other Insects. Heller, Ruth, illus. 32p. (ps-3). 1992. pap. 2.25 (0-448-40477-X, Platt & Munk Pubs) Putnam Pub Group.
—How to Hide a Crocodile. Heller, Ruth, illus. 32p. (ps-2). 1986. 5.95 (0-448-19028-1, G&D) Putnam Pub Group.
—How to Hide a Gray Tree Frog. Heller, Ruth, illus. 32p. (ps-2). 1986. 4.95 (0-448-19026-5, G&D) Putnam Pub Group.
—How to Hide a Polar Bear. Heller, Ruth, illus. LC 85-70286. 32p. (ps-2). 1986. 5.95 (0-448-10477-6, G&D) Putnam Pub Group.
—How to Hide a Whippoorwill. Heller, Ruth, illus. 32p. (ps-2). 1986. 4.95 (0-448-19027-3, G&D) Putnam Pub Group.
—How to Hide an Octopus. Heller, Ruth, illus. LC 85-70288. 32p. (ps-2). 1986. 5.95 (0-448-10476-8, G&D) Putnam Pub Group.
—How to Hide an Octopus: And Other Sea Creatures. Heller, Ruth, illus. 32p. (ps-3). 1992. pap. 2.25 (0-448-40478-8, Platt & Munk Pubs) Putnam Pub Group.
—Kites Sail High: A Book about Verbs. LC 87-82718. (Illus.). 48p. (ps-3). 1988. PLB 13.95 (0-448-10480-6, G&D) Putnam Pub Group.
—Kites Sail High: A Book about Verbs. (Illus.). 48p. (ps-3). 1991. pap. 5.95 (0-448-40074-X, G&D) Putnam Pub Group.
—Many Luscious Lollipops. (Illus.). 48p. (ps-3). 1992. pap. 6.95 (0-448-40316-1, G&D) Putnam Pub Group.
—Many Luscious Lollipops: A Book about Adjectives. Heller, Ruth, illus. (ps-3). 1989. 13.95 (0-448-03151-5, G&D) Putnam Pub Group.
—Maze Craze. (Illus.). 40p. (gr. 1-12). 1971. pap. 3.50 (0-8431-1732-X) Price Stern.
—Merry Go-Round. (Illus.). 48p. (ps-3). 1992. pap. 6.95 (0-448-40315-3, G&D) Putnam Pub Group.
—Merry-Go-Round: A Book about Nouns. (Illus.). 48p. (gr. 1 up). 1990. 13.95 (0-448-40085-5, G&D) Putnam Pub Group.
—Plants That Never Ever Bloom. Heller, Ruth, illus. 48p. (ps-2). 1984. 9.95 (0-448-18964-X, G&D) Putnam Pub Group.
—Plants That Never Ever Bloom. Heller, Ruth, illus. 48p. (ps-3). 1992. pap. 5.95 (0-448-41092-3, Sandcastle Bks) Putnam Pub Group.
—The Reason for a Flower. Heller, Ruth, illus. (ps-2). 1983. 9.95 (0-448-14495-6, G&D) Putnam Pub Group.
—The Reason for a Flower. Heller, Ruth, illus. 48p. (ps-3). 1992. pap. 5.95 (0-448-41091-5, Sandcastle Bks) Putnam Pub Group.
—Up, Up & Away: A Book about Adverbs. Heller, Ruth, illus. 48p. (gr. 1 up). 1991. 13.95 (0-448-40249-1, G&D) Putnam Pub Group.
—Up, up & Away: A Book about Adverbs. Heller, Ruth, illus. 48p. (gr. 1 up). 1993. pap. 6.95 (0-448-40159-2, G&D) Putnam Pub Group.
Heller, Wendy. My Name Is Nabil. (Illus.). 48p. (gr. 3-6). 1981. 11.95 (0-933770-17-0) Kalimat.
Heller, Wendy M., jt. auth. see Nida, Patricia C.
Hellings, Colette. Too Little, Too Big: Trop Petite, Trop Grande. Maes, Dominique, illus. 40p. (ps-3). 1993. 10.95 (0-8118-0530-1) Chronicle Bks.
Hellman, Hal. Computer Basics. Tvaryanas, Alphonse, illus. LC 82-21483. 48p. (gr. 3-7). 1983. 9.95 (0-13-164574-9) P-H.
—Computer Basics. Seiden, Art, illus. 48p. (Orig.). (gr. 3-7). 1986. pap. 5.95 (0-13-165697-X) P-H.
Hellman, Lillian. Pentimento (Julia) movie ed. (Illus.). 256p. (RL 10). 1977. pap. 3.95 (0-451-14089-3, AE1543, Sig) NAL-Dutton.
Hellman, Nina & Brouwer, Norman. A Mariner's Fancy: The Whaleman's Art of Scrimshaw. (Illus.). 96p. 1992. pap. 22.50 (0-295-97212-2) U of Wash Pr.
—A Mariner's Fancy: The Whaleman's Art of Scrimshaw. Aron, Jack R. & Neill, Peterpref. by. (Illus.). 96p. (Orig.). 1992. pap. 22.50 (0-917439-14-7) Balsam Pr.
Hellman-Hurpoil, Odile. Prince Oliver Doesn't Want to Take a Bath. (Illus.). (gr. 1-8). 1992. PLB 8.95 (0-89565-887-9); Resale. 12.75 (0-685-60986-3) Childs World.
Hellsing, Lennart. Cantankerous Crow. Stroyer, Paul, illus. (gr. k-3). 1962. 9.95 (0-8392-3002-8) Astor-Honor.
Hellstern, Dorothy. Seven Steps to Bible Skills: An Easy Step by Step Guide for Learning to Use Your Bible. (Illus.). 168p. 1991. wkbk. 10.95 (1-56322-029-6) V W Hensley.

Hellweg, Paul. The Facts on File Student's Thesaurus. 304p. 1991. 24.95 (0-8160-1634-8) Facts on File.
—Macmillan Children's Thesaurus. LC 93-21773. (gr. 1-8). 1994. write for info. (0-02-743525-3) Macmillan Child Grp.
Helm, Harvey E. Making Wood Banks. LC 83-474. (Illus.). 128p. (Orig.). (gr. 10-12). 1983. pap. 9.95 (0-8069-7714-0) Sterling.
Helmer, Diana S. Belles of the Ballpark. LC 92-12683. (Illus.). 112p. (gr. 7 up). 1993. PLB 14.90 (1-56294-230-1) Millbrook Pr.
Helmrath, M. O. & Bartlett, J. L. Bobby Bear & the Bees. LC 68-56806. (Illus.). 32p. (ps-1). 1968. PLB 12.35 prebound (0-87783-003-7); cassette 7.94x (0-87783-177-7) Oddo.
—Bobby Bear Finds Maple Sugar. LC 68-56805. (Illus.). 32p. (ps-1). 1968. PLB 12.35 prebound (0-87783-005-3) cassette 7.94x (0-87783-178-5) Oddo.
—Bobby Bear Goes Fishing. LC 68-56807. (Illus.). 32p. (ps-1). 1968. pap. 12.35 prebound (0-87783-006-1); cassette 7.94x (0-87783-179-3) Oddo.
—Bobby Bear in the Spring. LC 68-56810. (Illus.). 32p. (ps-1). 1968. PLB 12.35 prebound (0-87783-007-X); cassette 7.94x (0-87783-180-7) Oddo.
—Bobby Bear Series, 18 bks. (Illus.). (ps-1). Set. PLB 189.60 set (0-87783-163-7) 8 cassettes 63.52x (0-87783-181-5) Oddo.
—Bobby Bear's Halloween. LC 68-56808. (Illus.). 32p. (ps-1). 1968. PLB 9.95 (0-87783-004-5); cassette 7.94x (0-87783-183-1) Oddo.
—Bobby Bear's Rocket Ride. LC 68-56809. (Illus.). 32p. (ps-1). 1968. PLB 12.35 prebound (0-87783-008-8); cassette 7.94x (0-87783-186-6) Oddo.
Helprin, Mark. Swan Lake. Van Allsburg, Chris, illus. 112p. (gr. 4-7). 1992. pap. 12.95 (0-395-64647-2) HM.
Helprin, Mark, as told by. Swan Lake. Van Allsburg, Chris, illus. (gr. 1-8). 1989. 19.45 (0-395-49858-9) HM.
Helstrom, David C. My Tacoma Dome. Hamer, Bonnie, illus. 24p. (Orig.). (gr. 1-4). 1983. pap. 2.75 (0-933992-29-7) Coffee Break.
—Visiting Mt. Rainier. Harder, Arvid & Hamer, Bonnie, illus. 28p. (Orig.). (gr. 1-4). 1984. pap. 2.75 (0-933992-37-8) Coffee Break.
Helton, Sonia F. Classroom Bulletin Board Activities Kit: One Hundred Seventy-Eight Interactive Displays for Grades k-6. 288p. (gr. k-6). 1987. pap. text ed. 24.95 (0-87628-231-1) Ctr Appl Res.
Helweg, Hans. Farm Animals. LC 79-27483. (Illus.). 32p. (ps-3). 1980. pap. 2.25 (0-394-83733-9) Random Bks Yng Read.
Helwig, Barbara & Stewart, Susan. Math Mysteries. (Illus.). 40p. (gr. 2-5). 1991. spiral bound 4.95 (1-881285-00-6) Arbus Pub.
—Math Mysteries. rev. ed. (Illus.). 90p. (gr. 2-6). 1992. spiral bdg. 4.95 (1-881285-03-0) Arbus Pub.
—Shape Alert. (Illus.). 90p. (gr. 2-6). 1992. spiral bdg. 4.95 (1-881285-04-9) Arbus Pub.
—Travel Treats: Fun for Kids on the Move, 3 bks. (Illus.). 90p. (gr. 2-6). 1993. Set. spiral bdg. 19.95 (1-881285-07-3) Arbus Pub.
—Tree Spree. (Illus.). 56p. (gr. 2-5). 1991. spiral bound 4.95 (1-881285-01-4) Arbus Pub.
—Tree Spree. rev. ed. (Illus.). 90p. (gr. 2-6). 1992. spiral bdg. 4.95 (1-881285-05-7) Arbus Pub.
—Wishful Thinking. (Illus.). 44p. (gr. 2-5). 1991. spiral bound 4.95 (1-881285-02-2) Arbus Pub.
—Wishful Thinking. rev. ed. (Illus.). 90p. (gr. 2-6). 1992. spiral bdg. 4.95 (1-881285-06-5) Arbus Pub.
Hemalata, jt. auth. see Dutta, S.
Hembree, Mike, et al. Journey Home. Todd, Sharon, ed. (Illus.). 208p. (gr. 8 up). 1988. text ed. 22.95 (0-685-22594-1) GNP Pub.
Hemingway, Ernest. A Clean, Well-Lighted Place. (gr. 4-9). Date not set. 13.95 (0-88682-345-5, 97212-098) Creative Ed.
Heminway, Annie, jt. auth. see Wilkes, Angela.
Heminway, Annie, tr. see Wilkes, Angela.
Hemming, Judith. Why Do People Take Drugs? FS-Aladdin Staff, ed. LC 88-50515. (Illus.). 32p. (gr. 1-3). 1988. PLB 11.40 (0-531-17113-2, Gloucester Pr) Watts.
Hemon, Louis. Maria Chapdelaine. Brown, Alan, tr. from FRE. Tibo, Gilles, illus. Carrier, Roch, intro. by. LC 89-50775. (Illus.). 96p. (gr. 6 up). 1989. Repr. of 1914 ed. 29.95 (0-88776-236-0) Tundra Bks.
—Maria Chapdelaine. Tibo, Gilles, illus. LC 89-50775. 192p. 1991. pap. 9.95 (0-88776-242-5) Tundra Bks.
Hemp, Kevin. Just Hogweed. Hemp, Kevin, illus. 128p. (Orig.). (gr. 9-12). 1988. pap. 4.95 (0-9622059-0-7, VA-U-105-990) Wise Guys Pub.
Hemphill, John A. West Pointers & Early Washington. Cumbow, Robert C., ed. 235p. (gr. 4-9). 1992. 29.95 (0-9635925-0-5) W Pt Soc Puget.
Hemsley, William. Feeding to Digestion: Projects with Biology. LC 91-34410. (Illus.). 32p. (gr. 5-9). 1992. PLB 12.40 (0-531-17327-5, Gloucester Pr) Watts.
—Fins to Wings: Projects with Biology. LC 91-34410. (Illus.). 32p. (gr. 5-9). 1992. PLB 12.40 (0-531-17271-6, Gloucester Pr) Watts.
—Jellyfish to Insects: Projects with Biology. LC 90-45657. (Illus.). 32p. (gr. 5-9). 1991. PLB 12.40 (0-531-17291-0, Gloucester Pr) Watts.
Henbest, N. The Night Sky. (Illus.). 64p. (gr. 10 up). 1993. pap. 4.50 (0-86020-284-4) EDC.
Henbest, N., jt. auth. see Couper, H.

Henckel, Mark. Battle of the Little Bighorn. Potter, John, illus. 32p. (Orig.). (gr. 3-7). 1992. pap. 5.95 (*1-56044-042-2*) Falcon Pr MT.
—Outdoors Just for Kids. Potter, John, illus. 128p. (Orig.). (gr. 1-8). 1992. pap. 8.95 spiral bdg. (*0-9627618-3-4*) Billings Gazette.
Hendee, Stephanie & Bodourian, Marilyn. More TALK: Teaching Activities for Language Knowledge. (gr. k-3). 1988. tchr's. ed. 18.95 (*0-944584-10-1*) Sopris.
Hendershot, Jack G. You Gotta Wanna: A Physician's Autobiography. LC 91-90994. (Illus.). 416p. (gr. 10). 1993. text ed. 21.95 (*0-9629567-3-2*) Von Hayderschatte.
Hendershot, Judith. In Coal Country. Foster, Frances, ed. Rosenthal, Eileen, designed by. LC 86-15311. (Illus.). 48p. (ps-1). 1987. 16.00 (*0-394-88190-7*) Knopf Bks Yng Read.
Hendershot, Judy. Up the Tracks to Grandma's. Allen, Thomas B., illus. LC 91-2749. 40p. (ps-2). 1993. 15.00 (*0-679-81964-9*); PLB 15.99 (*0-679-91964-3*) Knopf Bks Yng Read.
Henderson, Angela. JoJo Meets Scrappy. (Illus.). (ps-3). 1992. write for info. (*1-882185-07-2*) Crnrstone Pub.
Henderson, Ann, jt. auth. see Katzen, Mollie.
Henderson, Douglas. Dinosaur Tree. LC 93-34204. 1994. write for info. (*0-02-743547-4*, Bradbury Pr) Macmillan Child Grp.
Henderson, Felicity. My Little Box of Bible Friends. (ps-1). 1991. 10.95 (*0-7459-2012-8*) Lion USA.
—My Little Box of Prayers, 4 bks. Goffe, Toni, illus. 32p. (ps-1). 1988. Set. casebound 10.95 (*0-7459-1250-8*) Lion USA.
Henderson, Florence, jt. auth. see Lewis, Shari.
Henderson, Harold V. Haiku in English. LC 67-16413. (Illus.). 75p. (gr. 9 up). 1967. pap. 7.95 (*0-8048-0228-9*) C E Tuttle.
Henderson, Kathy. The Baby's Book of Babies. Sieveking, Anthea, photos by. LC 88-20428. (Illus.). 24p. (ps-k). 1989. 9.95 (*0-8037-0634-0*) Dial Bks Young.
—The Baby's Book of Babies. Sieveking, Anthea, photos by. (Illus.). 24p. (ps-k). 1993. pap. 4.50 (*0-14-054882-3*, Puffin Pied Piper) Puffin Bks.
—Bounce, Bounce, Bounce. Thompson, Carol, illus. LC 93-3556. 1994. write for info. (*1-564023-11-7*) Candlewick Pr.
—Bumpety Bump. Thompson, Carol, illus. LC 93-3541. (ps). 1994. write for info. (*1-56402-312-5*) Candlewick Pr.
—Christmas Trees. LC 89-859. (Illus.). 48p. (gr. k-4). 1989. PLB 15.27 (*0-516-01162-6*); pap. 4.95 (*0-516-41162-4*) Childrens.
—Dairy Cows. LC 88-11123. 48p. (gr. k-4). 1988. PLB 15.27 (*0-516-01152-9*); pap. 4.95 (*0-516-41152-7*) Childrens.
—The Great Lakes. LC 88-34670. (Illus.). 48p. (gr. k-4). 1989. PLB 15.27 (*0-516-01163-4*); pap. 4.95 (*0-516-41163-2*) Childrens.
—I Can Be a Basketball Player. LC 90-21648. 32p. (gr. k-3). 1991. PLB 14.60 (*0-516-01963-5*); pap. 3.95 (*0-516-41963-3*) Childrens.
—I Can Be a Farmer. LC 88-37716. (Illus.). 32p. (gr. k-3). 1989. PLB 14.60 (*0-516-01923-6*); pap. 3.95 (*0-516-41923-4*) Childrens.
—I Can Be a Horse Trainer. LC 89-29203. (Illus.). 32p. (gr. k-3). 1990. PLB 14.60 (*0-516-01960-0*); pap. 3.95 (*0-516-41960-9*) Childrens.
—I Can Be a Rancher. LC 90-37678. (Illus.). 32p. (gr. k-3). 1990. PLB 14.60 (*0-516-01962-7*); pap. 3.95 (*0-516-41962-5*) Childrens.
—In the Middle of the Night. Eachus, Jennifer, illus. LC 91-29982. 32p. (ps-1). 1992. 13.95 (*0-02-743545-8*, Macmillan Child Bk) Macmillan Child Grp.
—Market Guide for Young Artists & Photographers. LC 90-39084. (Illus.). 176p. (Orig.). (gr. 3 up). 1990. pap. 12.95 (*1-55870-176-1*) Shoe Tree Pr.
—Market Guide for Young Writers. 3rd ed. LC 90-38770. (Illus.). 192p. (gr. 3 up). 1990. pap. 12.95 (*1-55870-175-3*) Shoe Tree Pr.
—What Would We Do Without You? A Guide to Volunteer Activities for Kids. LC 89-29938. (Illus.). 160p. (Orig.). 1990. pap. 6.95 (*1-55870-152-4*) Shoe Tree Pr.
Henderson, Kathy, selected by. The Bedtime Book. Ives, Penny, illus. LC 92-9413. (ps-3). 1992. 14.95 (*0-8120-6295-7*) Barron.
Henderson, Richard. First Sail. Wharton, Jennifer H., illus. 42p. (gr. 3-8). 1993. bds. 15.95 (*0-87033-442-5*) Tidewater.
Henderson, Shelia & George, Bonnie S. The Littlest Aggie. Darr, S. C., ed. La Rue, Doug, et al, illus. Williams, Clayton, Jr., frwd. by. 56p. 1990. 18.95 (*0-9623171-2-8*); coloring bk. 4.95 (*0-9623171-3-6*) LBCo Pub.
Hendrickson, James M. Spanish Grammar Flipper: A Guide to Correct Spanish Usage. 49p. (gr. 5 up). 1988. trade edition 5.95 (*1-878383-11-6*) C Lee Pubns.
Hendrick, Mary J. If Anything Ever Goes Wrong at the Zoo. LC 91-25566. (ps-3). 1993. 13.95 (*0-15-238007-8*) HarBrace.
Hendricks, Elrod, jt. auth. see Newberger, Joe.
Hendricks, Janie, ed. see Scherer, Bonnie L.
Hendricks, Meg, jt. auth. see Enk, Jean.
Hendrickson, Helen T. The Shy Princess. 1993. 6.95 (*0-8062-4412-7*) Carlton.

Hendrickson, Karen. Baby & I Can Play & Fun with Toddlers. rev. ed. Steelsmith, Shari, ed. LC 89-64200. (Illus.). 56p. (ps-3). 1990. lib. bdg. 17.95 (*0-943990-57-2*); pap. 6.95 (*0-943990-56-4*) Parenting Pr.
Hendrie, Alison. Kid Heroes. (gr. 4 up). 1993. pap. 3.50 (*0-440-84816-4*) Dell.
—Rescue Nine One One Kid Heroes. (gr. 4-7). 1993. pap. 3.50 (*0-440-83074-5*) Dell.
Hendry, Diana. Camel Called April. (ps-3). 1991. 12.95 (*0-688-10193-3*) Lothrop.
—The Carey Street Cat. Wickstrom, Thor, illus. LC 91-52852. 48p. (gr. 1 up). 1991. text ed. 10.95 (*0-688-10289-1*) Lothrop.
—Christmas on Exeter Street. Lawrence, John, illus. LC 89-45256. 32p. (gr. k-3). 1989. PLB 13.99 (*0-679-90134-5*) Knopf Bks Yng Read.
—Double Vision. LC 92-52996. 272p. (gr. 8 up). 1993. 14.95 (*1-56402-125-4*) Candlewick Pr.
—Not Anywhere House. (ps-3). 1991. 12.95 (*0-688-10194-1*) Lothrop.
—The Rainbow Watchers. Wickstrom, Thor, illus. LC 91-52853. 48p. (gr. 1 up). 1991. text ed. 10.95 (*0-688-10305-7*) Lothrop.
Hendry, Frances M. Quest for a Maid. 240p. (gr. 5 up). 1992. pap. 4.95 (*0-374-46155-4*, Sunburst) FS&G.
Hendryx, Brian, illus. One Hundred One Wacky Facts about Bugs & Spiders. 96p. 1992. pap. 1.95 (*0-590-44892-7*) Scholastic Inc.
—One Hundred One Wacky Facts about Kids. 96p. 1992. pap. 1.95 (*0-590-44890-0*) Scholastic Inc.
Heneghan, James. Torn Away. (Illus.). 192p. (gr. 7 up). 1994. 14.99 (*0-670-85180-9*) Viking Child Bks.
Henkel, Arlene. Phonics Review. Hoffman, Joan, ed. Cook, Chris, illus. 32p. (gr. 2-3). 1980. wkbk. 1.99 (*0-938256-08-4*) Sch Zone Pub Co.
Henken, Heidi. Cobb's Cave. Kratoville, Betty L., ed. (Illus.). 64p. (gr. 3-9). 1989. PLB 4.95 (*0-87879-655-X*) High Noon Bks.
Henkes, Kevin. Bailey Goes Camping. Henkes, Kevin, illus. LC 84-29027. 24p. (ps-1). 1985. 14.00 (*0-688-05701-2*); lib. bdg. 13.93 (*0-688-05702-0*) Greenwillow.
—Bailey Goes Camping. (Illus.). 24p. (ps-1). 1989. pap. 3.95 (*0-14-050979-8*, Puffin) Puffin Bks.
—Chester's Way. Henkes, Kevin, illus. 32p. (ps-3). 1988. 13.95 (*0-688-07607-6*); lib. bdg. 13.88 (*0-688-07608-4*) Greenwillow.
—Chester's Way. Henkes, Kevin, illus. 32p. (ps-3). 1989. pap. 3.99 (*0-14-054053-9*, Puffin) Puffin Bks.
—Chrysanthemum. LC 90-39803. (Illus.). 32p. (ps up). 1991. 13.95 (*0-688-09699-9*); PLB 13.88 (*0-688-09700-6*) Greenwillow.
—Clean Enough. Henkes, Kevin, illus. LC 81-6386. 24p. (gr. k-3). 1982. PLB 10.88 (*0-688-00829-1*) Greenwillow.
—Grandpa & Bo. Henkes, Kevin, illus. LC 85-14869. 32p. (ps-3). 1986. 14.88 (*0-688-04956-7*); PLB 14.95 (*0-688-04957-5*) Greenwillow.
—Jessica. LC 87-38087. (Illus.). 24p. (gr. k up). 1989. 14.00 (*0-688-07829-X*); PLB 13.93 (*0-688-07830-3*) Greenwillow.
—Jessica. (Illus.). 32p. (ps-3). 1990. pap. 4.99 (*0-14-054194-2*, Puffin) Puffin Bks.
—Julius, the Baby of the World. LC 88-34904. (Illus.). 32p. (ps up). 1990. 15.00 (*0-688-08943-7*); PLB 14.93 (*0-688-08944-5*) Greenwillow.
—Once Around the Block. Chess, Victoria, illus. LC 85-24901. 24p. (gr. k-3). 1987. 11.75 (*0-688-04954-0*); PLB 11.88 (*0-688-04955-9*) Greenwillow.
—Sheila Rae, the Brave. Henkes, Kevin, illus. LC 86-25761. 32p. (gr. 1 up). 1987. 13.95 (*0-688-07155-4*); PLB 13.88 (*0-688-07156-2*) Greenwillow.
—Sheila Rae, the Brave. (ps-3). 1990. pap. 3.95 (*0-14-050835-X*, Puffin) Puffin Bks.
—Sheila Rae, the Brave. LC 87-62370. (ps-3). 1988. pap. 4.99 (*0-14-050897-X*, Puffin) Puffin Bks.
—Shhhh. LC 88-18771. (Illus.). 24p. (ps up) 1989. 11.95 (*0-688-07985-7*); PLB 11.88 (*0-688-07986-5*) Greenwillow.
—Two under Par. Henkes, Kevin, illus. LC 86-7556. 128p. (gr. 2-6). 1987. 10.25 (*0-688-06708-5*) Greenwillow.
—A Weekend with Wendell. Henkes, Kevin, illus. LC 85-24822. 32p. (ps-3). 1986. 13.95 (*0-688-06325-X*); PLB 13.88 (*0-688-06326-8*) Greenwillow.
—A Weekend with Wendell. (ps-3). 1987. pap. 3.99 (*0-14-050728-0*, Puffin) Puffin Bks.
—Words of Stone. LC 91-28543. (gr. 5-12). 1992. 13.00 (*0-688-11356-7*) Greenwillow.
—Words of Stone. LC 93-7488. 160p. (gr. 4-7). 1993. pap. 3.99 (*0-14-036601-6*, Puffin) Puffin Bks.
—The Zebra Wall. LC 87-18454. 160p. (gr. 3 up) 1988. 10.95 (*0-688-07568-1*) Greenwillow.
—The Zebra Wall. (Illus.). 32p. (gr. 3-7). 1989. pap. 3.95 (*0-14-032969-2*, Puffin) Puffin Bks.
Henley, Claire. At the Zoo. Henley, Claire, illus. LC 91-25906. 32p. (ps-2). 1992. 11.95 (*1-56282-151-2*); PLB 11.89 (*1-56282-152-0*) Hyprn Child.
—In the Ocean. Henley, Claire, illus. LC 91-25905. 32p. (ps). 1992. 11.95 (*1-56282-153-9*); PLB 11.89 (*1-56282-154-7*) Hyprn Child.
—Joe's Pool. LC 92-33946. (Illus.). 32p. (ps-1). 1994. 12.95 (*1-56282-431-7*); PLB 12.89 (*1-56282-432-5*) Hyprn Child.
—Stormy Day. Henley, Claire, illus. LC 92-72025. 32p. (ps). 1993. 11.95 (*1-56282-342-6*); PLB 11.89 (*1-56282-343-4*) Hyprn Child.

—Sunny Day. Henley, Claire, illus. LC 92-72024. 32p. (ps). 1993. 11.95 (*1-56282-340-X*); PLB 11.89 (*1-56282-341-8*) Hyprn Child.
Henley, Claire, illus. The Baby in the Manger. 10p. (ps-1). 1992. bds. 6.99 (*0-7459-2181-7*) Lion USA.

Henley, Karyn. The Beginner's Bible: Timeless Children's Stories. Davis, Dennas, illus. 528p. (ps-8). 1989. 16.99 (*0-945564-31-7*, Gold & Honey) Questar Pubs. STILL NUMBER ONE on the children's bestseller list in BOOKSTORE JOURNAL (ever since March 1990), this one has sold more than 1,000,000 copies! Ideal for ages two through eight, THE BEGINNER'S BIBLE includes ninety-five Bible stories told chronologically from Genesis to Revelation. Children will love the more than five hundred pages of Bible stories - with a full-sized, full-color picture on every page! There's also a thorough index to "Favorite Characters, Topics, & Stories," & each story is tagged with a reference line indicating the story's Scripture source. With its clear, young-hearted writing style & charming illustrations, this book is a proven winner! Order from Questar Publishers, P.O. Box 1720, Sisters, OR 97759, 503-549-1144. *Publisher Provided Annotation.*

—My First Hymnal: Seventy-Five Favorite Bible Songs & What They Mean. Davis, Dennas, illus. 160p. 1994. incl. cass. 14.95 (*0-917143-35-3*) Sparrow TN.
Hennech, Michael C., intro. by. Texas History According to Us. (Illus.). 116p. (Orig.). (gr. 7). 1991. pap. text ed. 7.95 (*1-881301-01-X*) Ale Pub.
Hennedy, Hugh. Halcyon Time. Chu, Charles, illus. 160p. (Orig.). 1993. pap. 12.95 (*1-552291-54-5*) Oyster River Pr.
Hennessy, B. G. A, B, C, D, Tummy, Toes, Hands, Knees. Watson, Wendy, illus. 32p. (ps-1). 1989. pap. 13.95 (*0-670-81703-1*) Viking Child Bks.
—A, B, C, D, Tummy, Toes, Hands, Knees. Watson, Wendy, illus. 32p. (ps-1). 1991. pap. 4.50 (*0-14-050739-6*, Puffin) Puffin Bks.
—The Dinosaur Who Lived in My Backyard. Davis, Susan, illus. LC 87-19867. 32p. (ps-1). 1988. pap. 12.95 (*0-670-81685-X*) Viking Child Bks.
—The Dinosaur Who Lived in My Backyard. Davis, Susan, illus. 32p. (ps-3). 1990. pap. 3.99 (*0-14-050736-1*, Puffin) Puffin Bks.
—Eeney Meeney Miney Mo. LC 90-31535. (ps-3). 1990. 13.95 (*0-670-82864-5*) Viking Child Bks.
—Eeney, Meeney, Miney, Mo. Galli, Letizia, photos by. LC 92-23527. (Illus.). 1993. 3.99 (*0-14-054090-3*) Puffin Bks.
—The First Night. Johnson, Steve & Fancher, Lou, illus. LC 93-9659. 32p. (ps-3). 1993. 13.99 (*0-670-83026-7*) Viking Child Bks.
—Jake Baked the Cake. Morgan, Mary, illus. 32p. (ps-3). 1990. pap. 12.95 (*0-670-82237-X*) Viking Child Bks.
—Jake Baked the Cake. Morgan, Mary, illus. 32p. (ps-3). 1992. pap. 3.99 (*0-14-050882-1*) Puffin Bks.
—The Missing Tarts. Pearson, Tracey C., illus. 32p. (ps-3). 1989. pap. 12.95 (*0-670-82039-3*) Viking Child Bks.
—The Missing Tarts. Pearson, Tracey C., illus. 32p. (ps-3). 1991. pap. 3.95 (*0-14-050815-5*, Puffin) Puffin Bks.
—School Days. (ps-3). 1990. 13.95 (*0-670-83025-9*) Viking Child Bks.
—School Days. Pearson, Tracey C., illus. LC 92-12008. (gr. 4 up). 1992. pap. 3.99 (*0-14-054179-9*, Puffin) Puffin Bks.
—Sleep Tight. Carnabuci, Anthony, illus. 32p. (ps-1). 1992. RB 14.00 (*0-670-83567-6*) Viking Child Bks.
—When You Were Just a Little Girl. (ps-3). 1991. 12.95 (*0-670-82998-6*) Viking Child Bks.
—When You Were Just a Little Girl. Arnold, Jeanne, illus. 32p. (ps-3). 1994. pap. 4.99 (*0-14-054172-1*) Puffin Bks.
Hennessy, B. G. see Freeman, Don.
Henney, Carolee W. Calbert & His Adventures. Macneil, Melanie F., illus. LC 90-83140. 104p. (Orig.). (gr. 2-5). 1990. collector's first ed., numbered, signed by author, with dust jacket, sim. gold imprint title-author on spine 24.95 (*0-9626580-1-4*); pap. 9.95 (*0-9626580-0-6*) Aton Pr.
Hennig, Anna, jt. auth. see Peak, Jan.
Henning, Ann. The Connemara Stallion. 224p. (Orig.). (gr. 7-10). 1991. pap. 9.95 (*1-85371-158-6*, Pub. by Poolbeg Pr ER) Dufour.
—The Connemara Whirlwind. 201p. (Orig.). (gr. 10-12). 1990. pap. 8.95 (*1-85371-079-2*, Pub. by Poolbeg Pr ER) Dufour.

Henning, Jean M. Six Days to Swim-Jeff Farrell: A Story of Olympic Courage. Daland, P., intro. by. LC 71-103031. (Illus.). (gr. 6-12). 1970. 3.50 (0-911822-02-X) Swimming.

Henningfield, Jack E. & Atar, Nancy A. Barbiturates: Sleeping Potion or Intoxicant. (Illus.). 32p. (gr. 5 up). 1991. pap. 4.49 (0-7910-0004-4) Chelsea Hse.

Hennings, Jennifer. The Penny Doll. LC 93-34496. 1994. write for info. (0-8114-4461-9) Raintree Steck-V.

Henno, Robert. Animal Bandits. Winants, Jean-Marie, illus. LC 93-31750. 1993. 14.95 (0-88106-672-9) Charlesbridge Pub.

Henri, Adrian. The Postman's Palace. Henwood, Simon, illus. LC 90-30568. 32p. (ps-2). 1990. SBE 13.95 (0-689-31667-4, Atheneum Child Bk) Macmillan Child Grp.

Henrich, Jean, jt. auth. see Henrich, Stephen.

Henrich, Soren, illus. With Hope We Can All Find Ogo Pogo: For the Child Within Us All! 100p. 1991. 5.95 (0-9693583-1-8, Green Tiger) S&S Trade.

Henrich, Stephen & Henrich, Jean. Adventure Math, No. 1: Addition & Subtraction. (Illus.). 80p. (Orig.). 1988. pap. write for info. wkbk. (HE 600) Henrich Enter.

—Adventure Math, No. 2: Multiplication & Division. Henrich, Jean, illus. 80p. (Orig.). (gr. 4-12). 1988. pap. write for info. (HE 700) Henrich Enter.

—Story Starters on Colonial-Revolutionary America. rev. ed. (Illus.). 80p. (gr. 4-12). 1988. write for info. wkbk. (HE 200) Henrich Enter.

—Story Starters on Present Day. rev. ed. Henrich, Jean, illus. 80p. (gr. 4-12). 1989. write for info. wkbk. (HE 400) Henrich Enter.

—Story Starters on the Civil War - Old West. rev. ed. Henrich, Jean, illus. 80p. (gr. 4-12). 1988. write for info. wkbk. (HE 300) Henrich Enter.

—Story Starters on the Future. rev. ed. Henrich, Jean, illus. 80p. (gr. 4-12). 1989. write for info. wkbk. (HE 500) Henrich Enter.

Henricksson, John. Rachel Carson: The Environmental Movement. (Illus.). 96p. (gr. 7 up). 1991. PLB 14.90 (1-878841-16-5) Millbrook Pr.

Henrietta. A Mouse in the House. LC 91-60514. (Illus.). 32p. (ps-3). 1991. 13.95 (1-879431-11-4); PLB 14.99 (1-879431-26-2) Dorling Kindersley.

—Un Raton en Casa - A Mouse in the House. Puncel, Maria & Vasquez, Juan J., eds. Puncel, Maria, tr. (SPA., Illus.). 29p. (gr. k-1). 1992. write for info. (84-372-6619-X) Santillana.

Henriod, Lorraine. Grandma's Wheelchair. Tucker, Kathy, ed. LC 81-12918. (Illus.). 32p. (ps-1). 1982. PLB 13.95 (0-8075-3035-2) A Whitman.

Henriques, Pegotty. Dressage for the Young Rider. (Illus.). 160p. (gr. 6 up). 1990. 26.95 (0-901366-99-4, Pub. by Threshold Bks Uk) Half Halt Pr.

Henry, Boyd. Experiments with Patterns in Mathematics. (Illus., Orig.). (gr. 7 up). 1987. pap. text ed. 10.95 (0-86651-346-9, DS01720) Seymour Pubns.

Henry, Carol A. George Mason, Father of the Bill of Rights. Henry, Crystal A., illus. 44p. (Orig.). (gr. k-5). 1991. pap. 9.95 (0-9633634-3-3) C A Henry. GEORGE MASON, FATHER OF THE BILL OF RIGHTS is a children's biography which contains 16 black & white full page pictures opposite each written page with easy-to-read large print. Children can learn about George Mason growing up in the Virginia & Maryland areas; how he was devoted to his family, county, state, & country; & finally why he is called "The Father of the Bill of Rights". Included are a glossary of terms; a worksheet; an answer sheet; & a copy of the Bill of Rights & The Virginia Declaration of Rights. The worksheet can be copied by teachers so students can draw lines matching parts in the Virginia Declaration of Rights, which was drafted by George Mason, to parts in the Constitution with the Bill of Rights. The illustrations are beautifully done & capture the children's interest as they read. The author is an elementary teacher who wrote the book upon requests from her students when an easy-to-read book could not be found in print. Now children can read or be "read to" & learn about this famous American who is called "The Father of the Bill of Rights." *Publisher Provided Annotation.*

Henry, Chantal. Most Marvelous Machine, Your Body. (ps-3). 1994. 4.95 (0-944589-45-6) Young Discovery Lib.

Henry, Charles L., et al. French Study-Aid. 1974. pap. 2.75 (0-87738-032-5) Youth Ed.

Henry, Gilson. Animal Squares: An Animal Picture & Rhyme Book for Imaginative Children. Hansen, Ronnie, ed. & illus. LC 87-62123. 24p. (ps-4). 1987. pap. 3.95 (0-943925-01-0) Purple Turtle Bks.

—How the Tooth Fairy Got Her Job. Eide, Joyce, illus. LC 87-62126. 24p. (ps-5). 1987. pap. 3.95 (0-943925-03-7) Purple Turtle Bks.

—Purple Turtles Say No, No to Drugs. Hansen, Ronnie, ed. & illus. LC 87-62124. 24p. (ps-4). 1987. pap. 3.95 (0-943925-00-2) Purple Turtle Bks.

Henry, Joanne L. A Clearing in the Forest: A Story about a Real Settler Boy. Robinson, Charles, illus. LC 91-18554. 64p. (gr. 3-6). 1992. RSBE 14.95 (0-02-743671-3, Four Winds) Macmillan Child Grp.

—Log Cabin in the Woods: A True Story about a Pioneer Boy. LC 87-21138. (Illus.). 64p. (gr. 2-5). 1988. RSBE 14.95 (0-02-743670-5, Four Winds) Macmillan Child Grp.

Henry, Kay V. Jesus Was a Helper. LC 86-17540. (ps). 1987. pap. 5.95 (0-8054-4176-X) Broadman.

Henry, Lucia K. Nature Study Mini-Units: Ducks, Otters, Whales, Rabbits, Pandas. (Illus.). 48p. (gr. k-2). 1987. wkbk. 5.95 (1-55734-219-9) Tchr Create Mat.

—Science & Ourselves. (gr. 1-3). 1989. pap. 6.95 (0-8224-6456-X) Fearon Teach Aids.

—Science in Special Places. (gr. 1-3). 1989. pap. 6.95 (0-8224-6457-8) Fearon Teach Aids.

—Science Through the Seasons. (gr. 1-3). 1989. pap. 6.95 (0-8224-6304-0) Fearon Teach Aids.

Henry, Maeve. A Gift for a Gift. 1992. 14.00 (0-385-30562-1) Doubleday.

Henry, Marcia K. Words. (gr. 3-9). 1990. write for info. (1-878653-00-8) Lex Pr.

Henry, Marguerite. Album of Horses. Dennis, Wesley, illus. LC 92-33009. 112p. (gr. 2-5). 1993. pap. 9.95 (0-689-71709-1, Aladdin) Macmillan Child Grp.

—Black Gold. 2nd ed. LC 91-4907. (Illus.). 176p. (gr. 3-7). 1992. pap. 3.95 (0-689-71562-5, Aladdin) Macmillan Child Grp.

—Born to Trot. 2nd ed. LC 92-24139. (Illus.). 224p. (gr. 3-6). 1993. pap. 3.95 (0-689-71692-3, Aladdin) Macmillan Child Grp.

—Brighty: Of the Grand Canyon. reissued ed. Dennis, Wesley, illus. LC 53-7233. 224p. (gr. 3-7). 1991. SBE 13.95 (0-02-743664-0, Macmillan Child Bk) Macmillan Child Grp.

—Brighty: Of the Grand Canyon. Dennis, Wesley, illus. LC 90-28636. 224p. (gr. 3-7). 1991. pap. 3.95 (0-689-71485-8, Aladdin) Macmillan Child Grp.

—Justin Morgan Had a Horse. 2nd ed. Dennis, Wesley, illus. LC 91-13973. 176p. (gr. 3-7). 1991. pap. 3.95 (0-689-71534-X, Aladdin) Macmillan Child Grp.

—King of the Wind: The Story of the Godolphin Arabian. 2nd ed. Dennis, Wesley, illus. LC 48-8773. 176p. (gr. 3-7). 1990. SBE 13.95 (0-02-743629-2, Macmillan Child Bk) Macmillan Child Grp.

—King of the Wind: The Story of the Godolphin Arabian. Dennis, Wesley, illus. 176p. (gr. 3-7). 1991. pap. 3.95 (0-689-71486-6, Aladdin) Macmillan Child Grp.

—Marguerite Henry's Horseshoe Library: Stormy, Misty's Foal; Sea Star, Orphan of Chincoteague; Misty of Chincoteague, 3 bks. (Illus.). (gr. 3-7). 1992. Set. pap. 11.85 (0-689-71624-9, Aladdin) Macmillan Child Grp.

—Misty of Chincoteague. reissued ed. Dennis, Wesley, illus. LC 47-11404. 176p. (gr. 3-7). 1990. SBE 13.95 (0-02-743622-5, Macmillan Child Bk); pap. 3.95 (0-02-688759-2) Macmillan Child Grp.

—Misty of Chincoteague. Dennis, Wesley, illus. LC 90-27237. 176p. (gr. 3-7). 1991. pap. 3.95 (0-689-71492-0, Aladdin) Macmillan Child Grp.

—Misty's Twilight. Pre, Karen G., illus. LC 91-42582. 144p. (gr. 3-7). 1992. SBE 13.95 (0-02-743623-3, Macmillan Child Bk) Macmillan Child Grp.

—Mustang, Wild Spirit of the West. Lougheed, Robert, illus. LC 91-25187. 224p. (gr. 3-7). 1992. pap. 3.95 (0-689-71601-X, Aladdin) Macmillan Child Grp.

—San Domingo: The Medicine Hat Stallion. Lougheed, Robert, illus. LC 91-46020. 240p. (gr. 3-7). 1992. pap. 3.95 (0-689-71631-1, Aladdin) Macmillan Child Grp.

—Sea Star: Orphan of Chincoteague. LC 49-11474. (Illus.). 176p. (gr. 3-7). 1991. SBE 13.95 (0-02-743627-6); pap. 3.95 (0-689-71530-7, Aladdin) Macmillan Child Grp.

—Stormy, Misty's Foal. Dennis, Wesley, illus. LC 90-27306. 224p. (gr. 3-7). 1991. pap. 3.95 (0-689-71487-4, Aladdin) Macmillan Child Grp.

—The White Stallion of Lipizza. Dennis, Wesley, illus. LC 93-86024. 112p. (gr. 3-7). 1994. Repr. of 1964 ed. SBE 15.95 (0-02-743628-4, Macmillan Child Bk) Macmillan Child Grp.

—White Stallion of Lipizza. Dennis, Wesley, illus. 112p. 1994. 9.95 (0-689-71824-1, Aladdin) Macmillan Child Grp.

Henry, Marguerite & Tucker, Ezra, illus. Marguerite Henry's Album of Horses: A Pop-up Book. 12p. (gr. k-3). 1993. bds. 14.95 (0-689-71685-0, Aladdin) Macmillan Child Grp.

Henry, Marie. Hannah Whitall Smith. (Orig.). 1993. pap. 8.99 (1-55661-316-4) Bethany Hse.

Henry, Peggy. The Great Seed Mystery. Balkovek, Jim, illus. Copeland, Alan & Shapiro, Barry, photos by. LC 92-20193. (Illus.). 1993. 7.95 (1-880281-11-2) NK Lawn & Garden.

Henry, Robert. Universal Monsters: Frankenstein. Easley, Jeff, illus. 48p. (gr. 2-4). 1992. pap. write for info. (0-307-11467-8, 11467, Golden Pr) Western Pub.

Henry, Sondra & Taitz, Emily. Betty Friedan: Fighter for Women's Rights. LC 89-23582. (Illus.). 128p. (gr. 6 up). 1990. lib. bdg. 17.95 (0-89490-292-X) Enslow Pubs.

—Coretta Scott King: Keeper of the Dream. LC 91-31082. (Illus.). 128p. (gr. 6 up). 1992. lib. bdg. 17.95 (0-89490-334-9) Enslow Pubs.

—Gloria Steinem: One Woman's Power: A Biography of Gloria Steinem. Steinem, Gloria, afterword by. LC 86-11631. (Illus.). 128p. (gr. 6 up). 1987. RSBE 13.95 (0-87518-346-8, Dillon) Macmillan Child Grp.

—Levi Strauss: Everyone Wears His Name. LC 87-32455. (Illus.). 112p. (gr. 5 up). 1990. RSBE 13.95 (0-87518-375-1, Dillon) Macmillan Child Grp.

Henry, Sondra, jt. auth. see Taitz, Emily.

Henry, Susan V., jt. auth. see Dixon, Debra S.

Henry, Terry H. The Witch Who Couldn't. O'Toole, Tom, illus. 96p. (gr. 5). 1988. 10.95 (0-947962-39-5, Pub. by Anvil Bks Ltd Ireland) Irish Bks Media.

Henry-Biabaud, Chantal. Living in South America. Bogard, Vicki, tr. from FRE. Dagan, Bernard, illus. LC 90-50773. 38p. (gr. k-5). 1991. 4.95 (0-944589-28-6, 286) Young Discovery Lib.

—Living in the Heart of Africa. Bogard, Vicki, tr. from FRE. Poissenot, Jean-Marie, illus. LC 90-50774. 38p. (gr. k-5). 1991. 4.95 (0-944589-29-4, 294) Young Discovery Lib.

Henry Tall Bull & Weist, Tom. Cheyenne Legends of Creation. (gr. 4-9). 1972. 1.25 (0-89992-025-X) Coun India Ed.

—Cheyenne Warriors. (gr. 4-12). 1976. pap. 1.25 (0-89992-015-2) Coun India Ed.

—Grandfather & the Popping Machine. (gr. 2-12). 1970. 4.95 (0-89992-004-7) Coun India Ed.

—The Rolling Head: Cheyenne Tales. (gr. 3-9). 1971. 1.50 (0-89992-013-6) Coun India Ed.

—The Spotted Horse. (gr. 2-10). 1970. 4.95 (0-89992-002-0) Coun India Ed.

—The Winter Hunt. 32p. (gr. 3-9). 1971. 4.95 (0-89992-006-3) Coun India Ed.

Hensel, Lila. Who Is My Neighbor? A Primer for Group Discussion. 32p. (Orig.). 1989. pap. 3.95 (0-932727-29-8) Hope Pub Hse.

Henshall, Barbara E. Empty Masks. Williams, Maya, illus. 32p. (gr. 3-6). 1986. pap. 3.50 (0-936983-00-0) Safari Museum Pr.

Hensley, Dana & Prentice, Diana. Mastering Competitive Debate. 3rd ed. 190p. (gr. 10-12). 1987. pap. text ed. 14.00 (0-931054-17-6) Clark Pub.

Henson, Jim. Sesame Street Musical Storybook: Big Bird's Tea Party. 1989. 12.99 (0-88704-096-9) Sight & Sound.

Hentoff, Nat. American Heroes: In & Out of School. LC 86-29140. 192p. (gr. 7 up). 1987. pap. 14.95 (0-385-29565-0) Delacorte.

—The Day They Came to Arrest the Book. 160p. (gr. 7 up). 1983. pap. 3.50 (0-440-91814-6, LFL) Dell.

—Does This School Have Capital Punishment? 160p. (gr. 7-11). 1983. pap. 3.50 (0-440-92070-1, LFL) Dell.

—The First Freedom: The Tumultuous History of Free Speech in America. LC 78-72860. (gr. 7 up). 1980. 11.95 (0-440-03850-2) Delacorte.

—Jazz Country. 144p. (gr. 7 up). 1986. pap. 2.25 (0-440-94203-9, LFL) Dell.

Hentoff, Nat, jt. ed. see Shapiro, Nat.

Henwood, Chris. The Handbook of Rodents in Captivity. (Illus.). 124p. (Orig.). 1991. pap. 12.95 (0-86025-898-X, Pub. by Ian Henry Pubns UK) Empire Pub Srvs.

Henwood, Simon. The Hidden Jungle. (Illus.). 32p. (ps-3). 1992. 15.00 (0-374-33070-0) FS&G.

—The Troubled Village. (Illus.). 26p. (ps-3). 1991. 13.95 (0-374-37780-4) FS&G.

Hepburn, Lawrence R. State Government in Georgia. 3rd ed. 200p. (gr. 8-12). 1991. text ed. 12.25 (0-89854-176-X) U of GA Inst Govt.

Hepburn, Mary A. Local Government in Georgia. 2nd ed. 240p. (gr. 8-12). 1991. text ed. 13.75 (0-89854-148-4) U of GA Inst Govt.

Hepler, Donald E. & Wallach, Paul I. Architecture: Drafting & Design. 3rd ed. (gr. 9-12). 1976. text ed. 36.32 (0-07-028291-9) McGraw.

Hepler, Donald E., et al. Architecture: Drafting & Design. 4th ed. (Illus.). 608p. (gr. 10-12). 1982. text ed. 34.24 (0-07-028301-X) McGraw.

Hepworth, Cathi. Antics! An Alphabetical Anthology. Hepworth, Cathi, illus. 32p. (ps-6). 1992. PLB 14.95 (0-399-21862-9, Putnam) Putnam Pub Group.

Herald, Jacqueline. The Nineteen Seventies. Cumming, Valerie & Feldman, Elane, eds. (Illus.). (gr. 7-12). 1992. bds. 16.95x (0-8160-2470-7) Facts on File.

—The Nineteen Twenties. Cumming, Valerie & Feldman, Elane, eds. (Illus.). 64p. (gr. 7-12). 1991. 16.95x (0-8160-2465-0) Facts on File.

Herber, Keith & Morrison, Mark. Mansions of Madness: Mythos Mysteries in the Abodes of Man. Willis, Lynn, ed. Gibbons, Lee & Aulisio, Janet, illus. 130p. (Orig.). (gr. 12 up). 1990. pap. 17.95 (0-933635-63-X, 2327) Chaosium.

Herber, Keith, ed. see Isynwill, L. N. & Keith, Herbert.

Herberman, Ethan. The City Kid's Field Guide. (gr. 3 up). 1989. pap. 14.95 jacketed (*0-671-67749-7*, S&S BFYR); pap. 5.95 (*0-671-67746-2*, S&S BFYR) S&S Trade.
—The Great Butterfly Hunt: The Mystery of the Migrating Monarchs. (Illus.). (gr. 5 up). 1990. pap. 14. 95 jacketed (*0-671-69427-8*, Little Simon); pap. 5.95 (*0-671-69428-6*, Little Simon) S&S Trade.
Herbert, Don. Mr. Wizard's Experiments for Young Scientists. 1990. pap. 10.00 (*0-385-26585-9*) Doubleday.
—Mr. Wizard's Supermarket Science. McKie, Roy, illus. LC 79-27217. 96p. (gr. 4-7). 1980. lib. bdg. 9.99 (*0-394-93800-J*); pap. 9.00 (*0-394-83800-9*) Random Bks Yng Read.
Herbert, Henry W. Fish & Fishing: Fish & Fishing of the United States & British Provinces of North America. (Illus.). 438p. (gr. 10 up). 1993. Repr. of 1855 ed. 42. 90 (*1-56416-114-5*) Derrydale Pr.
Herbert, Janet. Hurray for Birthdays. (ps-1). 1986. comb bdg. 3.95 (*1-55513-040-2*, Chariot Bks) Cook.
—Love Is Kind. Herbert, Janet, illus. 1985. plastic comb bdg. 3.95 (*0-89191-928-7*, 59287, Chariot Bks) Cook.
Herbert, Laurence. Leona Devours Books. (Illus.). 32p. (gr. k-2). 1991. 18.50 (*0-89565-755-4*); 12.95s.p. (*0-685-55075-3*) Childs World.
Herbert, Michael. Michael Jordan: The Bull's Air Power. rev. ed. LC 87-20868. 48p. (gr. 2 up). 1987. PLB 13. 27 (*0-516-04362-5*); pap. 3.95 (*0-516-44362-3*) Childrens.
Herbert, S. Latisha. The Visit. (Illus.). 20p. 1991. 12.95 (*0-87868-477-8*, 4778) Child Welfare.
Herbert, Solomon & Hill, George. Bill Cosby. (Illus.). 104p. (gr. 5 up). 1992. lib. bdg. 17.95 (*0-7910-1121-6*) Chelsea Hse.
Herbert, Stefon. I Miss My Foster Parents. (Illus.). 36p. 1991. 12.95 (*0-87868-476-X*, 4760) Child Welfare.
Herbert, Stephanie. Being Adopted. (Illus.). 24p. 1991. 12.95 (*0-87868-478-4*, 4786) Child Welfare.
Herbert, Victor. Babes in Toyland: Musical. Holamon, Ken, adapted by. (Orig.). (ps up) 1987. playscript 5.50 (*0-87602-275-1*) Anchorage.
Herbrechtsmeier, Keith, ed. see Watkins, Tracy D.
Herbst, Eric, ed. see Kelley, Shirley.
Herbst, Helen. God's Children Share Their Faith with You. Connor, Genevieve, illus. 48p. (gr. 1-4). 1988. coloring bk. 2.50 (*0-913382-55-8*, 103-20) Prow Bks-Franciscan.
Herbst, Judith. Animal Amazing. LC 90-62. 192p. (gr. 5 up). 1991. SBE 14.95 (*0-689-31556-2*, Atheneum Child Bk) Macmillan Child Grp.
—The Golden Book of Stars & Planets. LaPadula, Tom, illus. 48p. (gr. 3-7). 1988. write for info. (*0-307-15572-2*) Western Pub.
—Star Crossing: How to Get Around in the Universe. LC 92-8475. (Illus.). 224p. (gr. 5-9). 1993. SBE 16.95 (*0-689-31523-6*, Atheneum Child Bk) Macmillan Child Grp.
Herda, D. J. Afghan Rebels. LC 89-22603. (ps-3). 1990. PLB 13.90 (*0-531-10897-X*) Watts.
—Cancer. Green, Anne C., illus. LC 89-34131. 112p. (gr. 7-10). 1989. PLB 12.90 (*0-531-10803-1*) Watts.
—Environmental America: The North Central States. (Illus.). 64p. (gr. 5-8). 1991. PLB 14.90 (*1-878841-08-4*) Millbrook Pr.
—Environmental America: The Northeastern States. LC 91-29899. (Illus.). 64p. (gr. 5-8). 1991. PLB 14.90 (*1-878841-06-8*) Millbrook Pr.
—Environmental America: The Northwestern States. (Illus.). 64p. (gr. 5-8). 1991. PLB 14.90 (*1-878841-10-6*) Millbrook Pr.
—Environmental America: The South Central States. (Illus.). 64p. (gr. 5-8). 1991. PLB 14.90 (*1-878841-09-2*) Millbrook Pr.
—Environmental America: The Southeastern States. (Illus.). 64p. (gr. 5-8). 1991. PLB 14.90 (*1-878841-07-6*) Millbrook Pr.
—Environmental America: The Southwestern States. LC 91-29901. (Illus.). 64p. (gr. 5-8). 1991. PLB 14.90 (*1-878841-11-4*) Millbrook Pr.
—Ethnic America: The North Central States. (Illus.). 64p. (gr. 5-8). 1991. PLB 14.90 (*1-56294-016-3*) Millbrook Pr.
—Ethnic America: The Northeastern States. (Illus.). 64p. (gr. 5-8). 1991. PLB 14.90 (*1-56294-014-7*) Millbrook Pr.
—Ethnic America: The Northwestern States. (Illus.). 64p. (gr. 5-8). 1991. PLB 14.90 (*1-56294-018-X*) Millbrook Pr.
—Ethnic America: The South Central States. (Illus.). 64p. (gr. 5-8). 1991. PLB 14.90 (*1-56294-017-1*) Millbrook Pr.
—Ethnic America: The Southeastern States. (Illus.). 64p. (gr. 5-8). 1991. PLB 14.90 (*1-56294-015-5*) Millbrook Pr.
—Ethnic America: The Southwestern States. (Illus.). 64p. (gr. 5-8). 1991. PLB 14.90 (*1-56294-019-8*) Millbrook Pr.
—Historical America: The North Central States. LC 92-16311. (Illus.). 64p. (gr. 5-8). 1993. PLB 14.90 (*1-56294-120-8*) Millbrook Pr.
—Historical America: The Northeastern States. LC 92-14162. (Illus.). 64p. (gr. 5-8). 1993. PLB 14.90 (*1-56294-118-6*) Millbrook Pr.
—Historical America: The Northwestern States. LC 92-16312. (Illus.). 64p. (gr. 5-8). 1993. PLB 14.90 (*1-56294-122-4*) Millbrook Pr.
—Historical America: The Southeastern States. LC 92-16315. (Illus.). 64p. (gr. 5-8). 1993. PLB 14.90 (*1-56294-119-4*) Millbrook Pr.
—Historical America: The Southwestern States. LC 92-28206. (Illus.). 64p. (gr. 5-8). 1993. PLB 14.90 (*1-56294-123-2*) Millbrook Pr.
—New York Times vs. United States: National Security & Censorship. LC 93-32156. 1994. write for info. (*0-89490-490-6*) Enslow Pubs.
—Operation Rescue: Satellite Maintenance & Repair. LC 90-12369. (Illus.). 64p. (gr. 5-8). 1990. PLB 12.90 (*0-531-10873-2*) Watts.
Herda, D. J. & Madden, Margaret L. Energy Resources: Towards a Renewable Future. LC 91-3034. (Illus.). 144p. (gr. 9-12). 1991. PLB 13.90 (*0-531-11005-2*) Watts.
—Land Use & Abuse. LC 90-37573. (Illus.). 144p. (gr. 9-12). 1990. PLB 13.90 (*0-531-10953-4*) Watts.
Herds, D. J. Historical America: The South Central States. LC 92-10746. (Illus.). 64p. (gr. 5-8). 1993. PLB 14.90 (*1-56294-121-6*) Millbrook Pr.
Herford, Oliver. The Most Timid in the Land: A Bunny Romance. Long, Sylvia, illus. (ps-1). 1992. 12.95 (*0-87701-862-6*) Chronicle Bks.
Herge. Affaire Tournesol. (FRE., Illus.). (gr. 7-9). lib. bdg. 19.95 looseleaf bdg. (*0-8288-6087-4*, F6867) Fr & Eur.
—Der Arumbaya-Fetisch. (GER., Illus.). 62p. pap. 19.95 (*0-8288-5008-9*) Fr & Eur.
—El Asunto Tornasol. (SPA., Illus.). 62p. 19.95 (*0-8288-5009-7*) Fr & Eur.
—Aterrizaje en la Luna. (SPA., Illus.). 62p. 19.95 (*0-8288-5010-0*) Fr & Eur.
—Bijoux de la Castafiore. (FRE., Illus.). 62p. (gr. 7-9). looseleaf bdg. 19.95 (*0-8288-5011-9*) Fr & Eur.
—The Black Island. (Illus.). 62p. 19.95 (*0-8288-5012-7*) Fr & Eur.
—The Black Island. LC 74-21624. (gr. k up). 1975. pap. 7.95 (*0-316-35835-5*, Joy St Bks) Little.
—Der Blaue Lotos. (GER., Illus.). 62p. pap. 19.95 (*0-8288-5013-5*) Fr & Eur.
—Blue Lotus. (ENG., Illus.). 19.95 (*0-8288-5480-7*) Fr & Eur.
—The Blue Lotus. (Illus.). 64p. 1992. 12.95 (*0-316-35891-6*, Joy St Bks) Little.
—The Calculus Affair. (Illus.). 62p. 19.95 (*0-8288-5014-3*) Fr & Eur.
—El Cangrejo Pinzas Oro. (SPA., Illus.). 62p. 19.95 (*0-8288-5015-1*) Fr & Eur.
—The Castafiore Emerald. (Illus.). 62p. (Also avail. in FR. & Span.). (*0-8288-5016-X*) Fr & Eur.
—The Castafiore Emerald. (gr. k up). 1975. pap. 7.95 (*0-316-35842-8*, Joy St Bks) Little.
—El Cetro de Ottokar. (SPA., Illus.). 62p. 19.95 (*0-8288-5017-8*) Fr & Eur.
—Les Cigares du Pharaon. (FRE.). (gr. 7-9). looseleaf bdg. 19.95 (*0-8288-5018-6*) Fr & Eur.
—Los Cigarros del Faraon. (SPA., Illus.). 62p. 19.95 (*0-8288-5019-4*) Fr & Eur.
—Les Cigars du Pharon. (FRE., Illus.). 62p. 19.95 (*0-8288-5020-8*) Fr & Eur.
—Cigars of the Pharaoh. (Illus.). 62p. 19.95 (*0-8288-5021-6*) Fr & Eur.
—Cigars of the Pharaoh. LC 74-21620. (gr. k up). 1975. pap. 7.95 (*0-316-35836-3*, Joy St Bks) Little.
—Coke En Stock. (FRE., Illus.). (gr. 7-9). looseleaf bdg. 19.95 (*0-8288-5022-4*) Fr & Eur.
—The Crab with the Golden Claws. (Illus.). 62p. (gr. 3-8). 19.95 (*0-8288-5023-2*) Fr & Eur.
—The Crab with the Golden Claws. LC 73-21249. (Illus.). 64p. (Orig.). (gr. k up). 1974. pap. 7.95 (*0-316-35833-9*, Joy St Bks) Little.
—Crabe aux Pinces d'or. (FRE., Illus.). 62p. 19.95 (*0-8288-5024-0*) Fr & Eur.
—Crabe aux Pinces d'or. (FRE., Illus.). (gr. 7-9). looseleaf bdg. 19.95 (*0-8288-5025-9*) Fr & Eur.
—Destination Moon. (gr. 3-8). looseleaf bdg. 19.95 (*0-8288-5026-7*) Fr & Eur.
—Destination Moon. (Illus.). 62p. 19.95 (*0-8288-5027-5*) Fr & Eur.
—Il Drago Blu. (ITA., Illus.). 62p. pap. 19.95 (*0-8288-5028-3*) Fr & Eur.
—La Estrella Misteriosa. (SPA., Illus.). 62p. 19.95 (*0-8288-5029-1*) Fr & Eur.
—Etoile Mysterieuse. (FRE., Illus.). (gr. 7-9). looseleaf bdg. 19.95 (*0-8288-5030-5*) Fr & Eur.
—Explorers of the Moon. (Illus.). 62p. 19.95 (*0-8288-5031-3*) Fr & Eur.
—Explorers on the Moon. (gr. k up). 1976. pap. 7.95 (*0-316-35846-0*, Joy St Bks) Little.
—Explorers on the Moon: The Adventures of Tintin. Herge, illus. 24p. (ps-3). 1992. 16.95 (*0-316-35860-6*, Joy St Bks) Little.
—Der Fall Bienlein. (GER., Illus.). 62p. pap. 19.95 (*0-8288-5033-X*) Fr & Eur.
—Flight Seven-Fourteen. (Illus.). 62p. 19.95 (*0-8288-5034-8*) Fr & Eur.
—Flight Seven-Fourteen. LC 74-21623. (gr. k up). 1975. pap. 7.95 (*0-316-35837-1*, Joy St Bks) Little.
—Flug 714 nach Sydney. (GER., Illus.). 62p. pap. 19.95 (*0-8288-5035-6*) Fr & Eur.
—Das Geheimnis der "Einhorn" (GER., Illus.). 62p. pap. 19.95 (*0-8288-5036-4*) Fr & Eur.
—Der Geheimnisvolle Stern. (GER., Illus.). 62p. pap. 19. 95 (*0-8288-5037-2*) Fr & Eur.
—Il Granchio d'Oro. (ITA., Illus.). 62p. pap. 19.95 (*0-8288-5038-0*) Fr & Eur.
—Ile Noire. (FRE., Illus.). (gr. 7-9). looseleaf bdg. 19.95 (*0-8288-5039-9*) Fr & Eur.
—Im Reiche des Schwarzen Goldes. (GER., Illus.). 62p. pap. 19.95 (*0-8288-5040-2*) Fr & Eur.
—La Isla Negra. (SPA., Illus.). 62p. 19.95 (*0-8288-5041-0*) Fr & Eur.
—Las Joyas de la Castafiore. (SPA., Illus.). 62p. 19.95 (*0-8288-5042-9*) Fr & Eur.
—Die Juwelen der Sangerin. (GER., Illus.). 62p. pap. 19. 95 (*0-8288-5043-7*) Fr & Eur.
—King Ottokar's Sceptre. (Illus.). 62p. 19.95 (*0-8288-5044-5*) Fr & Eur.
—King Ottokar's Sceptre. (Illus., Orig.). (gr. k up). 1974. pap. 7.95 (*0-316-35831-2*, Joy St Bks) Little.
—Kohle an Bord. (GER., Illus.). 62p. pap. 19.95 (*0-8288-5045-3*) Fr & Eur.
—Konig Ottokars Zepter. (GER., Illus.). 62p. pap. 19.95 (*0-8288-5046-1*) Fr & Eur.
—Die Krabbe mit den Goldenen Scheren. (GER., Illus.). 62p. pap. 19.95 (*0-8288-5047-X*) Fr & Eur.
—Land of Black Gold. (Illus.). 62p. 19.95 (*0-8288-5048-8*) Fr & Eur.
—El Loto Azul. (SPA., Illus.). 62p. 19.95 (*0-8288-5049-6*) Fr & Eur.
—Le Lotus Bleu. (FRE.). (gr. 2-9). 19.95 (*0-8288-5050-X*) Fr & Eur.
—Objectif Lune. (FRE., Illus.). (gr. 7-9). looseleaf bdg. 19.95 (*0-8288-5051-8*) Fr & Eur.
—Objetivo: la Luna. (SPA., Illus.). 62p. 19.95 (*0-8288-5052-6*) Fr & Eur.
—On a Marche Sur la Lune. (FRE., Illus.). (gr. 7-9). looseleaf bdg. 19.95 (*0-8288-5053-4*) Fr & Eur.
—L' Oreille Cassee. (FRE., Illus.). 62p. 19.95 (*0-8288-5054-2*) Fr & Eur.
—La Oreja Rota. (SPA., Illus.). 62p. 19.95 (*0-8288-5055-0*) Fr & Eur.
—Prisoners of the Sun. (Illus.). 62p. 19.95 (*0-8288-5056-9*) Fr & Eur.
—Red Rackham's Treasure. (Illus.). 62p. 19.95 (*0-8288-5057-7*) Fr & Eur.
—Red Rackham's Treasure. LC 73-21253. (Illus.). 64p. (Orig.). (gr. k up). 1974. pap. 7.95 (*0-316-35834-7*, Joy St Bks) Little.
—Red Rackham's Treasure. (Illus.). 64p. 1992. 12.95 (*0-316-35893-2*, Joy St Bks) Little.
—The Red Sea Sharks. (Illus., J). (gr. 3-8). 19.95 (*0-8288-5058-5*) Fr & Eur.
—The Red Sea Sharks. (gr. k up). 1976. pap. 7.95 (*0-316-35848-7*, Joy St Bks) Little.
—Reiseziel Mond. (GER., Illus.). 62p. pap. 19.95 (*0-8288-5059-3*) Fr & Eur.
—Sceptre D'ottokar. (FRE., Illus.). (gr. 7-9). looseleaf bdg. 19.95 (*0-8288-5060-7*) Fr & Eur.
—Lo Scettro di Ottokar. (ITA., Illus.). 62p. pap. 19.95 (*0-8288-5061-5*) Fr & Eur.
—Der Schatz Rackhams des Roten. (GER., Illus.). 62p. pap. 19.95 (*0-8288-5062-3*) Fr & Eur.
—Schritte auf dem Mond. (GER., Illus.). 62p. pap. 19.95 (*0-8288-5063-1*) Fr & Eur.
—Die Schwarze Insel. (GER., Illus.). 62p. pap. 19.95 (*0-8288-5064-X*) Fr & Eur.
—Secret de la Licorne. (FRE., Illus.). (gr. 7-9). 19.95 (*0-8288-5065-8*) Fr & Eur.
—The Secret of the Unicorn. (Illus.). 62p. 19.95 (*0-8288-5066-6*) Fr & Eur.
—The Secret of the Unicorn. LC 73-21250. (Illus.). 64p. (Orig.). (gr. k up). 1974. pap. 7.95 (*0-316-35832-0*, Joy St Bks) Little.
—The Secret of the Unicorn. (Illus.). 64p. 1992. 12.95 (*0-316-35902-5*, Joy St Bks) Little.
—El Secreto del Unicornio. (SPA., Illus.). 62p. 19.95 (*0-8288-5067-4*) Fr & Eur.
—Il Segreto del Liocorno. (ITA., Illus.). 62p. pap. 19.95 (*0-8288-5068-2*) Fr & Eur.
—Sept Boules de Cristal. (FRE., Illus.). (gr. 7-9). 19.95 (*0-8288-5069-0*) Fr & Eur.
—Le Sette Sfere di Cristallo. (ITA., Illus.). 62p. pap. 19. 95 (*0-8288-5070-4*) Fr & Eur.
—The Seven Crystal Balls. (Illus.). 62p. (gr. 3-8). 19.95 (*0-8288-5071-2*) Fr & Eur.
—Shooting Star. (Illus.). (gr. 3-8). looseleaf bdg. 19.95 (*0-8288-5073-9*) Fr & Eur.
—Die Sieben Kristallkugeln. (GER., Illus.). 62p. pap. 19. 95 (*0-8288-5074-7*) Fr & Eur.
—Las Siete Bolas de Cristal. (SPA., Illus.). 62p. 19.95 (*0-8288-5075-5*) Fr & Eur.
—I Sigari del Faraone. (ITA., Illus.). 62p. pap. 19.95 (*0-8288-5075-5*) Fr & Eur.
—Der Sonnentempel. (GER., Illus.). 62p. pap. 19.95 (*0-8288-5076-3*) Fr & Eur.
—Stock de Coque. (SPA., Illus.). 62p. 19.95 (*0-8288-5077-1*) Fr & Eur.
—Temple du Soleil. (FRE., Illus.). (gr. 7-9). 19.95 (*0-8288-5078-X*) Fr & Eur.
—El Templo del Sol. (SPA., Illus.). 62p. 19.95 (*0-8288-5079-8*) Fr & Eur.
—Il Templo del Sol. (ITA., Illus.). 62p. pap. 19.95 (*0-8288-5080-1*) Fr & Eur.
—El Tesoro de Rackham. (SPA., Illus.). 62p. 19.95 (*0-8288-5081-X*) Fr & Eur.
—Il Tesoro di Rakam. (ITA., Illus.). 62p. pap. 19.95 (*0-8288-5082-8*) Fr & Eur.
—Tim in Tibet. (GER., Illus.). 62p. pap. 19.95 (*0-8288-5083-6*) Fr & Eur.
—Tim und der Haifchsee. (GER., Illus.). 62p. pap. 19.95 (*0-8288-5084-4*) Fr & Eur.
—Tim und die Picaros. (GER., Illus.). 62p. pap. 19.95 (*0-8288-5085-2*) Fr & Eur.

—The Tintin Adventure Series. (Illus.). 1991. pap. 222.60 (*0-316-35859-2*) Little.
—Tintin & the Broken Ear. (Illus.). 62p. 19.95 (*0-8288-5086-0*) Fr & Eur.
—Tintin & the Golden Fleece. (gr. 3-8). 19.95 (*0-8288-5087-9*) Fr & Eur.
—Tintin & the Lake of Sharks. (Illus.). 62p. 19.95 (*0-416-78950-1*) Fr & Eur.
—Tintin & the Picaros. (Illus.). 62p. 19.95 (*0-8288-5089-5*) Fr & Eur.
—Tintin au Congo. (FRE., Illus.). (gr. 7-9). 19.95 (*0-8288-5090-9*) Fr & Eur.
—Tintin au Pays de L'or Noir. (FRE.). (gr. 7-9). 19.95 (*0-8288-5091-7*) Fr & Eur.
—Tintin Au Tibet. (gr. 7-9). looseleaf bdg. 19.95 (*0-8288-5092-5*) Fr & Eur.
—Tintin en America. (SPA., Illus.). 62p. 19.95 (*0-8288-5094-1*) Fr & Eur.
—Tintin en Amerique. (FRE., Illus.). 62p. 19.95 (*0-8288-5093-3*) Fr & Eur.
—Tintin en el Congo. (SPA., Illus.). 62p. 19.95 (*0-8288-5095-X*) Fr & Eur.
—Tintin en el Pais del Oro Negro. (SPA., Illus.). 62p. 19. 95 (*0-8288-4995-1*) Fr & Eur.
—Tintin en el Tibet. (SPA., Illus.). 62p. 19.95 (*0-8288-4996-X*) Fr & Eur.
—Tintin et les Picaros. (FRE., Illus.). 62p. 19.95 (*0-8288-4997-8*) Fr & Eur.
—Tintin Games Book, Vol. 1. 1990. pap. 6.95 (*0-316-35858-4*) Little.
—Tintin im Amerika. (GER., Illus.). 62p. pap. 19.95 (*0-8288-4999-4*) Fr & Eur.
—Tintin im Kongo. (GER., Illus.). 62p. pap. 19.95 (*0-8288-4998-6*) Fr & Eur.
—Tintin in America. (Illus.). 62p. 19.95 (*0-8288-5000-3*) Fr & Eur.
—Tintin in Tibet. (Illus.). 62p. 19.95 (*0-8288-5001-1*) Fr & Eur.
—Tintin in Tibet. LC 74-21621. (gr. k up). 1975. pap. 7.95 (*0-316-35839-8*, Joy St Bks) Little.
—Tintin in Tibet. (Illus.). 64p. 1992. 12.95 (*0-316-35863-0*, Joy St Bks) Little.
—Tintin y los Picaros. (SPA., Illus.). 62p. 19.95 (*0-8288-5002-X*) Fr & Eur.
—Tresor De Rackham le Rouge. (FRE., Illus.). 62p. (gr. 7-9). 19.95 (*0-8288-5003-8*) Fr & Eur.
—Vuelo 714 para Sidney. (SPA., Illus.). 62p. 19.95 (*0-8288-5004-6*) Fr & Eur.
—Y las Naranjas Azules. (SPA., Illus.). 62p. 19.95 (*0-8288-5005-4*) Fr & Eur.
—Die Zigarren des Pharaos. (GER., Illus.). 62p. pap. 19. 95 (*0-8288-5006-2*) Fr & Eur.
Herguth, Margaret S. North Dakota. LC 89-25283. (Illus.). 144p. (gr. 4 up). 1990. PLB 26.60 (*0-516-00480-8*) Childrens.
—North Dakota. 205p. 1993. text ed. 15.40 (*1-56956-142-7*) W A T Braille.
Herigstad, Joni. I Was So Mad: Storybook for Young Children in Sign Language. Herigstad, Joni, illus. 50p. (Orig.). 1986. pap. 4.95 (*0-916708-16-0*) Modern Signs.
Herlihy, Dirlie. Ludie's Song. LC 87-30305. 224p. (gr. 5 up). 1988. 14.95 (*0-8037-0533-6*) Dial Bks Young.
—Ludie's Song. 224p. (gr. 4 up). 1990. pap. 4.95 (*0-14-034245-1*, Puffin) Puffin Bks.
Herman. Max Malone Million. 1992. 13.95 (*0-8050-2332-1*) H Holt & Co.
Herman, Barry, jt. auth. see Criscuolo, Nicholas P.
Herman, Charlotte. House on Walenska Street. (gr. 4-7). 1991. pap. 3.95 (*0-14-034405-5*, Puffin) Puffin Bks.
—Max Malone Makes a Million. Smith, Cat B., illus. LC 90-46373. 80p. (gr. 2-4). 1991. 13.95 (*0-8050-1374-1*, Redfeather BYR) H Holt & Co.
—Max Malone Makes a Million. Smith, Cat B., illus. LC 90-46373. 64p. (gr. 2-4). 1992. pap. 4.95 (*0-8050-2328-3*, Redfeather BYR) H Holt & Co.
—Max Malone, Superstar. Smith, Cat B., illus. LC 91-25191. 64p. (gr. 2-4). 1992. 14.95 (*0-8050-1375-X*, Redfeather BYR) H Holt & Co.
—Max Malone the Magnificent. Smith, Cat B., illus. LC 92-14123. 64p. (gr. 2-4). 1993. PLB 14.95 (*0-8050-2282-1*, Bks Young Read) H Holt & Co.
—Millie Cooper, Take a Chance. Cogancherry, Helen, illus. LC 88-11881. 112p. (gr. 3 up). 1989. 11.95 (*0-525-44442-4*, DCB) Dutton Child Bks.
—Millie Cooper, Take a Chance. Cogancherry, Helen, illus. 112p. (gr. 3 up). 1990. pap. 3.95 (*0-14-034119-6*, Puffin) Puffin Bks.
—Millie Cooper, 3B. Cogancherry, Helen, illus. 80p. (gr. 3-7). 1986. pap. 3.95 (*0-14-032072-5*, Puffin) Puffin Bks.
—Millie Cooper, 3B. Cogancherry, Helen, illus. LC 84-25951. 112p. (gr. 2-6). 1985. 11.95 (*0-525-44157-3*, DCB) Dutton Child Bks.
—Summer on Thirteenth Street. LC 91-21156. 188p. (gr. 3-7). 1991. 13.95 (*0-525-44642-7*, DCB) Dutton Child Bks.
Herman, Charlotte & Smith, Charlotte B. Max Malone & the Great Cereal Rip-Off. Smith, Catherine, illus. LC 89-26920. 64p. (gr. 2-4). 1991. 12.95 (*0-8050-1069-6*, Redfeather BYR); pap. 4.95 (*0-8050-1843-3*, Redfeather BYR) H Holt & Co.
Herman, Emily. Hubknuckles. Ray, Deborah K., illus. LC 84-21355. 32p. (gr. 1-4). 1985. 9.95 (*0-517-55646-4*) Crown Bks Yng Read.
Herman, Emmi. Christmas KidDoodles, No. 5. Radtke, Becky, illus. 64p. (ps-2). 1992. pap. 0.99 (*1-56293-270-5*) McClanahan Bk.

—Christmas KidDoodles, No. 6. Loh, Carolyn, illus. 64p. (ps-2). 1992. pap. 0.99 (*1-56293-271-3*) McClanahan Bk.
—Christmas KidDoodles, No. 7. Radtke, Becky, illus. 64p. (ps-2). 1992. pap. 0.99 (*1-56293-269-1*) McClanahan Bk.
—Christmas KidDoodles, No. 8. Loh, Carolyn, illus. 64p. (ps-2). 1992. pap. 0.99 (*1-56293-272-1*) McClanahan Bk.
Herman, Emmi S. Christmas KidDoodles, Bk. 1. Sims, Deborah, illus. 64p. (Orig.). (ps-2). 1991. pap. 0.99 activity pad (*1-56293-153-9*) McClanahan Bk.
—The Dress-up Parade. Learner, Vickie, illus. 24p. (ps-2). 1992. pap. 0.99 (*1-56293-112-1*) McClanahan Bk.
—KidDoodles, Bk. 1. Boyd, Patti, illus. 64p. (ps-2). 1991. pap. 0.99 activity pad (*1-878624-50-4*) McClanahan Bk.
—KidDoodles, Bk. 3. Colrus, Bill, illus. 64p. (Orig.). (ps-2). 1991. pap. 0.99 activity pad (*1-878624-52-0*) McClanahan Bk.
—My First Day at School. Flanigan, Ruth J., illus. 24p. (ps-2). 1992. pap. 0.99 (*1-56293-106-7*) McClanahan Bk.
Herman, Ethel & Everett, Karen H. Grammar for Teens. (gr. 5-12). 1989. spiral wkbk. 27.95 (*1-55999-042-2*) LinguiSystems.
—Grammar-Semantics for Teens. (gr. 7-12). 1989. spiral wkbk. 27.95 (*1-55999-043-0*) LinguiSystems.
—Semantics for Teens. (gr. 5-12). 1989. spiral wkbk. 27. 95 (*1-55999-070-8*) LinguiSystems.
Herman, Gail. Babar the Boy King. Prebenna, David, illus. LC 88-63343. 32p. (Orig.). (ps-3). 1989. pap. text ed. 1.50 (*0-394-84533-1*) Random Bks Yng Read.
—Big Bird Visits Granny Bird. Nicklaus, Carol, illus. LC 90-60822. 32p. (Orig.). (ps-3). 1991. pap. 1.50 (*0-679-81050-1*) Random Bks Yng Read.
—Count the Days of Hanukkah. Kalish, Lionel, illus. LC 92-82914. 16p. (ps-3). 1993. 3.95 (*0-590-47081-7*, Cartwheel) Scholastic Inc.
—Doll Party. Flynn, Amy, illus. LC 93-12685. (ps-1). 1994. pap. write for info. (*0-448-40182-7*, G&D) Putnam Pub Group.
—Double-Header. Smath, Jerry, illus. LC 92-34175. 32p. (ps-1). 1993. pap. 3.50 (*0-448-40157-6*, G&D) Putnam Pub Group.
—Fievel to the Rescue. Nicklaus, Carol, illus. LC 91-70106. 24p. (ps-2). 1991. pap. 2.25 (*0-448-40207-6*, G&D) Putnam Pub Group.
—Fievel's Big Showdown. Lazor-Bahr, Beverly, illus. Kirschner, David, created by. (Illus.). 32p. (ps-3). 1992. pap. 3.50 (*0-448-40392-7*, G&D) Putnam Pub Group.
—Fievel's Big Showdown: An American Tail. (ps-3). 1992. 9.95 (*0-448-40379-X*, G&D) Putnam Pub Group.
—Fievel's Journey. LC 91-70105. (Illus.). 24p. (ps-2). 1991. pap. 2.25 (*0-448-40204-1*, G&D) Putnam Pub Group.
—The Fire-Engine Book & Puzzle Set. (Illus.). 18p. (ps-6). 1991. incl. 26-piece puzzle 2.99 (*0-517-05124-9*) Outlet Bk Co.
—The Haunted House: Book & Puzzle Set. Nicklaus, Carol, illus. 24p. (ps-1). 1989. 5.95 (*0-394-82717-1*) Random Bks Yng Read.
—Make Way for Trucks: Big Machines on Wheels. Santoro, Christopher, illus. LC 89-34458. 32p. (ps-2). 1990. lib. bdg. 10.99 (*0-679-90110-8*) Random Bks Yng Read.
—The Puppy Who Went to School. Ogden, Betina, illus. 32p. (ps-3). 1992. pap. 2.25 (*0-448-40481-8*, G&D) Putnam Pub Group.
—Time for School, Little Dinosaur. Gorbaty, Norman, illus. LC 89-70331. 24p. (Orig.). (ps-2). 1990. pap. 2.25 (*0-679-80789-6*) Random Bks Yng Read.
—What a Hungry Puppy! Gorbaty, Norman, illus. LC 92-24468. 32p. (ps-1). 1993. lib. bdg. 7.99 (*0-448-40537-7*, G&D); pap. 3.50 (*0-448-40536-9*, G&D) Putnam Pub Group.
—Wizard of Oz. (ps-3). 1993. pap. 2.95 (*0-590-46994-0*) Scholastic Inc.
Herman, Gail, retold by see Kent, Jack.
Herman, Jon, jt. auth. see Fraser, Judith.
Hermes, Jules. The Children of Micronesia. LC 93-31268. 1994. 14.95 (*0-87614-819-4*) Carolrhoda Bks.
Hermes, Jules M. The Children of India. LC 92-35103. 1993. 19.95 (*0-87614-759-7*) Carolrhoda Bks.
Hermes, Patricia. Be Still My Heart. 160p. (gr. 5-9). 1990. 14.95 (*0-399-21917-X*, Putnam) Putnam Pub Group.
—Be Still My Heart. MacDonald, Patricia, ed. 160p. 1991. pap. 2.99 (*0-671-70645-4*) PB.
—Friends Are Like That. LC 83-18407. 128p. (gr. 3-7). 1984. 14.95 (*0-15-229722-7*, HB Juv Bks) HarBrace.
—Heads, I Win. Newsome, Carol, illus. LC 87-19249. 132p. (gr. 3-7). 1988. 12.95 (*0-15-233659-1*, HB Juv Bks) HarBrace.
—Heads, I Win. (gr. 3-6). 1989. pap. 2.99 (*0-671-67408-0*, Minstrel Bks) PB.
—I Hate Being Gifted. 144p. 1990. 14.95 (*0-399-21687-1*, Putnam) Putnam Pub Group.
—Kevin Corbett Eats Flies. Newsom, Carol, illus. LC 85-27086. 160p. (gr. 3-7). 1986. 13.95 (*0-15-242290-0*, HB Juv Bks) HarBrace.
—Mama, Let's Dance. (gr. 5 up). 1991. 14.95 (*0-316-35861-4*) Little.
—Mama, Let's Dance. (gr. 4-7). 1993. pap. 2.95 (*0-590-46633-X*) Scholastic Inc.

—Nobody's Fault. 112p. (gr. 5 up). 1983. pap. 2.75 (*0-440-46523-0*, YB) Dell.
—Nothing but Trouble, Trouble, Trouble. LC 93-13968. 160p. (gr. 3-7). 1994. 13.95 (*0-590-43499-3*) Scholastic Inc.
—A Place for Jeremy. LC 86-31793. (Illus.). 160p. (gr. 3-7). 1987. 13.95 (*0-15-262350-7*) HarBrace.
—Someone to Count On. LC 93-13502. (ps-6). 1993. 14. 95 (*0-316-35925-4*) Little.
—Take Care of My Girl: A Novel. LC 92-9819. 1992. 14. 95 (*0-316-35913-0*) Little.
—A Time to Listen: Preventing Youth Suicide. 132p. (gr. 5 up). 1987. 13.95 (*0-15-288196-4*, HB Juv Bks) HarBrace.
—What If They Knew? 128p. (gr. k-6). 1989. pap. 2.95 (*0-440-49515-6*, YB) Dell.
—Who Will Take Care of Me? LC 82-48757. 128p. (gr. 3-7). 1983. 11.95 (*0-15-296265-4*, HB Juv Bks) HarBrace.
—You Shouldn't Have to Say Good-Bye. LC 82-47933. 117p. (gr. 3-7). 1982. 11.95 (*0-15-299944-2*, HB Juv Bks) HarBrace.
—You Shouldn't Have to Say Good-Bye. 128p. (gr. 3-7). 1989. pap. 2.75 (*0-590-43174-9*) Scholastic Inc.
Hermoso, Elizabeth S. The Chair. Hermoso, Elizabeth S., illus. 15p. (Orig.). (gr. k-2). 1991. pap. 3.00x (*971-10-0442-9*, Pub. by New Day Pub PI) Cellar.
—Fireworks in the Sky. Hermoso, Elizabeth S., illus. 18p. (Orig.). (gr. k-2). 1991. pap. 3.00x (*971-10-0444-5*, Pub. by New Day Pub PI) Cellar.
—The Smartians. Hermoso, Elizabeth S., illus. 15p. 1991. pap. 3.00x (*971-10-0443-7*, Pub. by New Day Pub PI) Cellar.
Hernandez, Betsy & Monk, Donny. Silent Night: A Mouse Tale. Boddy, Joe, illus. 48p. (ps-5). 1992. write for info. (*0-917143-17-5*) Sparrow TN.
—The Story of Silent Night: A Mouse Tale. (Illus.). 48p. (ps-5). 1992. 12.95 (*0-917143-10-8*) Sparrow TN.
Hernandez, Betsy, jt. auth. see Hernandez, Frank.
Hernandez, Betsy, et al. The Boy Who Wanted the Moon. Hilliard, Cindy & French, Marty, illus. 26p. (ps up). 1986. Book & Cassette. 7.95 (*1-55578-100-4*); cass. incl. Worlds Wonder.
Hernandez, Frank & Hernandez, Betsy. Hide em in Your Heart: Activity Book. Dugan, Terry & Slonim, David, illus. 40p. (Orig.). (ps-6). 1991. pap. 7.95 (*0-917143-06-X*) Sparrow TN.
Hernandez, Irene B. Heartbeat - Drumbeat. LC 91-48246. 200p. (Orig.). (gr. 6-12). 1992. pap. text ed. 9.50 (*1-55885-052-X*) Arte Publico.
Hernandez, Juana A. & Guillermo, Edenia. Cuentos Contemporaneos Espanoles: Advanced Intermediate Through Advanced. (SPA.). 176p. 1993. pap. 14.95 (*0-685-62803-5*, F7313-9, Natl Textbk) NTC Pub Grp.
Hernandez, Maria. Cocina de Abuela. (SPA.). 176p. (Orig.). 1989. pap. 2.95 (*0-929281-03-9*) Best Pubs Inc.
Hernandez, Xavier. San Rafael: A Central American City Through the Ages. Ballonga, Jordi & Escofet, Josep, illus. LC 91-39906. 64p. (gr. 4-7). 1992. 17.45 (*0-395-60645-4*) HM.
Hernandez, Xavier & Ballonga, Jordi. Lebek: A City of Northern Europe Through the Ages. Leverich, Kathleen, tr. Corni, Francesco, illus. 64p. 1991. 16.45 (*0-395-57442-0*, Sandpiper) HM.
Hernandez, Xavier, jt. auth. see Comes, Pilar.
Herndon, Ernest. Double-Crossed in Gator Country. 144p. 1994. pap. 4.99 (*0-310-38261-0*) Zondervan.
—Night of the Jungle Cat. (gr. 5 up). 1994. pap. 4.99 (*0-310-38271-8*) Zondervan.
—The Secret of Lizard Island. LC 93-5011. 144p. 1994. pap. 4.99 (*0-310-38251-3*) Zondervan.
—Smugglers on Grizzly Mountain. 144p. 1994. pap. 4.99 (*0-310-38281-5*) Zondervan.
Herndon, Jerry A., & intro. by see Stuart, Jesse.
Herndon, Jerry A. see Stuart, Jesse.
Herndon, Jerry A., ed. see Stuart, Jesse.
Herndon, Jerry A., et al, eds. see Stuart, Jesse.
Herold, Ann B. Aaron's Dark Secret. (gr. 3 up). 1985. pap. 3.99 (*0-934998-21-3*) Bethel Pub.
—The Butterfly Birthday. McCully, Emily A., illus. LC 90-6628. 48p. (gr. 1-5). 1991. RSBE 12.95 (*0-02-743691-8*, Macmillan Child Bk) Macmillan Child Grp.
—The Hard Life of Seymour E. Newton. 96p. (Orig.). (gr. 2-5). 1990. pap. 5.95 (*0-8361-3532-6*) Herald Pr.
—The Mysterious Passover Visitors. (Illus.). 112p. (Orig.). (gr. 8-12). 1989. pap. 4.95 (*0-8361-3494-X*) Herald Pr.
Herold, Meri G., ed. see Reed, Kevin J.
Heron, Ann & Maran, Meredith. How Would You Feel If Your Dad Was Gay? Martins, George, illus. 32p. (gr. 1-5). 1991. text ed. 9.95 (*1-55583-188-5*) Alyson Pubns.
—How Would You Feel If Your Dad Was Gay? Kovick, Kris, illus. 48p. (gr. 1-5). 1994. pap. 6.95 (*1-55583-243-1*) Alyson Pubns.
Heron, Ann, ed. One Teenager in Ten: Writings by Gay & Lesbian Youth. 120p. (gr. 7-12). 1983. pap. 4.95 (*0-932870-26-0*) Alyson Pubns.
—Two Teenagers in Twenty: Writings by Lesbian & Gay Youth. 200p. (gr. 8-12). 1994. 17.95 (*1-55583-229-6*) Alyson Pubns.
Heron, Helen H. College Countdown: A Planning Guide for High School Students. 155p. (gr. 9-12). 1992. pap. 14.95 (*1-880639-24-6*) Heron Pub CA.

Heron, Jackie. Careers in Health & Fitness. rev. ed. Rosen, Ruth, ed. (Illus.). 160p. (gr. 7 up). 1990. 13.95 (*0-8239-1162-4*) Rosen Group.
—Exploring Careers in Nursing. rev. ed. 144p. (gr. 7-12). 1990. 13.95 (*0-8239-1136-5*) Rosen Group.
Heron, Jean O. Voyage d'Alice ou Comment Sont Nes les Droits de l'Enfant. Dumas, Philippe, illus. (FRE.). 151p. (gr. 3-7). 1990. pap. 11.95 (*0-685-60281-8*) Schoenhof.
Herr, Amy, ed. Bible Nuture & Reader Series. rev. ed. (gr. 1-4). 1986. write for info. Rod & Staff.
Herr, Selma & Piequet, Miriam. Manners Matter. Anyone Can Read Staff, ed. 150p. (Orig.). (gr. 3-7). 1987. pap. 10.50 (*0-914275-12-7*) Anyone Can Read Bks.
Herr, Selma E. Read for Understanding, Bk. I. new ed. Anyone Can Read Press Staff, ed. Herr, Selma E., illus. 225p. (gr. 6-12). 1987. pap. 6.95 (*0-914275-04-6*) Anyone Can Read Bks.
Herr, Ted & Johnson, Ken. Problem Solving Strategies: Crossing the River with Dogs. (gr. 9-12). 1993. write for info. (*1-55953-068-5*) Key Curr Pr.
—Problem Solving Strategies: Crossing the River with Dogs - Teacher's Resource Book & Answer Key. (gr. 9-12). 1993. write for info. (*1-55953-069-3*) Key Curr Pr.
Herren, Janet M., jt. auth. see Morss, Willard N.
Herrick, Amy. Kimbo's Marble. Gazsi, Edward, illus. LC 91-18988. 48p. (gr. 1-5). 1993. 16.00 (*0-06-020373-0*); PLB 15.89 (*0-06-020374-9*) HarpC Child Bks.
Herrick, Ann. The Perfect Guy. (gr. 5 up). 1989. pap. 2.95 (*0-553-27927-0*) Bantam.
Herrick, George, ed. see Hannah, Valerie.
Herrick, George H., ed. see Hannah, Valerie.
Herrick, George H., intro. by see Weisberg, Valerie H.
Herridge, Douglas & Hughes, Susan. The Environmental Detective Kit. LC 90-48247. (Illus.). 80p. (gr. 3 up). 1991. pap. 4.00 (*0-06-107408-X*) HarpC Child Bks.
Herriman, George. The Komplete Kolor Krazy Kat, Vol. I: 1935-1936. Marschall, Richard, intros. by. Watterson, Bill. (Illus.). 96p. (gr. 6 up). 1990. 34.95 (*0-924359-06-4*) Remco WrldServ Bks.
Herriot, James. All Creatures Great & Small. (gr. 6 up). 1985. pap. 5.99 (*0-553-26812-0*) Bantam.
—Blossom Comes Home. Brown, Ruth, illus. 1988. 13.00 (*0-312-02169-0*) St Martin.
—Blossom Comes Home. Brown, Ruth, illus. (gr. 1-8). 1993. pap. 6.95 (*0-312-09131-1*) St Martin.
—Bonny's Big Day. Brown, Ruth, illus. 32p. (gr. k up). 1987. 13.00 (*0-312-01000-1*) St Martin.
—Bonny's Big Day. Brown, Ruth, illus. 32p. 1991. pap. 6.95 (*0-312-06571-X*) St Martin.
—Christmas Day Kitten. Brown, Ruth, illus. LC 86-13890. (ps up). 1986. 12.95 (*0-312-13407-X*) St Martin.
—The Christmas Day Kitten. (Illus.). 32p. (gr. 3 up). 1993. pap. 6.95 (*0-312-09767-0*) St Martin.
—James Herriot's Treasury for Children. 260p. 1992. 18. 95 (*0-312-08512-5*) St Martin.
—The Market Square Dog. Brown, Ruth, illus. 32p. 1989. 13.00 (*0-312-03397-4*) St Martin.
—The Market Square Dog. Brown, Ruth, illus. 32p. 1991. pap. 6.95 (*0-312-06567-1*) St Martin.
—Moses the Kitten. Barrett, Peter, illus. LC 84-50930. 32p. (ps up). 1984. 13.00 (*0-312-54905-9*) St Martin.
—Moses the Kitten. Barrett, Peter, illus. 1991. pap. 6.95 (*0-312-06419-5*) St Martin.
—Only One Woof. Barrett, Peter, illus. 32p. (ps up). 1985. 13.00 (*0-312-58583-7*) St Martin.
—Only One Woof. Barrett, Peter, illus. 32p. (gr. 1-8). 1993. pap. 6.95 (*0-312-09129-X*) St Martin.
—Oscar, Cat-about-Town. Brown, Ruth, illus. 32p. (gr. 1-3). 1993. pap. 6.95 (*0-312-09130-3*) St Martin.
—Smudge, the Little Lost Lamb. Brown, Ruth, illus. 32p. 1991. 12.95 (*0-312-06404-7*) St Martin.
Herrmann, Dagmar, tr. see Skutina, Vladimir.
Herron, John. The Land of Numm. Hallock, Michelle, illus. 14p. 1992. pap. 9.95 (*1-881617-07-6*) Teapot Tales.
Hersh, Iffy. Mommy Is an Histologist. (Illus., Orig.). (gr. k-2). pap. 10.00 (*0-936735-04-X*) Grove Educ Tech.
Hershberger, Carol, jt. auth. see Kelley, Gail.
Hershberger, Priscilla. Make Costumes! for Creative Play. (Illus.). 48p. (gr. 4-7). 1992. 11.95 (*0-89134-450-0*) North Light Bks.
Hershenburgh, Anne. Animal Designs. (ps-3). 1991. pap. 2.95 (*0-8431-1931-4*) Price Stern.
Hershey, Katerine. The Message of a Star. Bates, Stephen & Williamson, Kevin, illus. 9p. (gr. k-6). 1982. pap. 4.25 (*1-55976-133-4*) CEF Press.
Hershey, Katherine. Beginnings. (Illus.). 51p. (gr. k-6). 1979. pap. text ed. 9.45 (*1-55976-004-4*) CEF Press.
—The Christian Soldier. Biel, Bill, et al, illus. 10p. (gr. k-6). 1981. pap. text ed. 4.25 (*1-55976-138-5*) CEF Press.
—Daniel, Strong in the Lord. (Illus.). (gr. k-6). 1992. pap. text ed. 9.45 (*1-55976-035-4*) CEF Press.
—David, Vol. I. Butcher, Sam, illus. 52p. (gr. k-6). 1972. pap. text ed. 9.45 (*1-55976-020-6*) CEF Press.
—David, Vol. II. Butcher, Sam, illus. 55p. (gr. k-6). 1973. pap. text ed. 9.45 (*1-55976-021-4*) CEF Press.
—Joseph. (Illus.). 40p. (gr. k-6). 1979. pap. text ed. 9.45 (*1-55976-006-0*) CEF Press.
—Life of Christ, Vol. I. Banse, Charles & Chappell, David, illus. 54p. (gr. k-6). 1987. pap. text ed. 9.45 (*1-55976-000-1*) CEF Press.
—Life of Christ, Vol. III. Banse, Charles, illus. 51p. (gr. k-6). 1978. pap. text ed. 9.45 (*1-55976-002-8*) CEF Press.
—Life of Christ, Vol. IV. Banse, Charles, illus. 49p. (gr. k-6). 1978. pap. text ed. 9.45 (*1-55976-003-6*) CEF Press.
—Life of Christ, Vol. II. (Illus.). 55p. (gr. k-6). 1987. pap. 9.45 (*1-55976-001-X*) CEF Press.
—Patriarchs. (Illus.). 51p. (gr. k-6). 1979. pap. text ed. 9.45 (*1-55976-005-2*) CEF Press.
—A Shepherd for You. (Illus.). 22p. (gr. k-6). 1988. pap. text ed. 4.25 (*1-55976-149-0*) CEF Press.
—A Very Special Day. Seals, Thelma, et al, illus. 21p. (gr. k-6). 1980. 4.25 (*1-55976-131-8*) CEF Press.
Hershey, Kathleen. Cotton Mill Town. Winter, Jeanette, illus. LC 92-7379. (ps-2). 1993. 12.99 (*0-525-44966-3*, DCB) Dutton Child Bks.
Hershey, Robert L. How to Think with Numbers. 142p. (gr. 7 up). 1987. pap. 7.95 (*0-939765-14-4*, GK108) Janson Pubns.
Hershoff, Evelyn G. It's Fun to Make Things from Scrap Materials. (Illus.). (gr. 4 up). 1944. pap. 6.95 (*0-486-21251-3*) Dover.
Hersom, Kathleen. The Half Child. LC 90-24079. 176p. (gr. 5-9). 1991. pap. 13.95 jacketed, 3-pc. bdg. (*0-671-74225-6*, S&S BFYR) S&S Trade.
—The Half Child. LC 91-30352. 104p. (gr. 5 up). 1993. pap. 4.95 (*0-671-86696-6*, Half Moon Bks) S&S Trade.
Hertz, Grete J. Yellow House. Clante, Iben, tr. (Illus.). (gr. 2-7). 1991. 12.95 (*0-920236-15-4*, Pub. by Annick CN) Firefly Bks Ltd.
Herweck, Dona. Literature Unit: The Witch of Blackbird Pond. Spence, Paula, illus. 48p. (Orig.). (gr. 5-8). 1992. pap. 5.95 wkbk. (*1-55734-404-3*) Tchr Create Mat.
Herz, Roger J. Claude Humphrey Dwickens: The Old Man with the Mustache. Aldworth, Susan, illus. 32p. (Orig.). (ps-6). 1988. pap. text ed. 3.95 (*0-9619560-0-3*) TGNW Pr.
—The Old Man of the Mountain. Aldworth, Susan, illus. 1989. pap. text ed. 3.95 (*0-9619560-1-1*) TGNW Pr.
Herzel, Catherine B. She Made Many Rich: Sister Emma Francis of the Virgin Islands. Youngblood, Paul, illus. (Illus.). 24p. (gr. 6 up). 1990. pap. 4.50 (*0-935357-06-8*) CRIC Prod.
Herzfeld, Gerald & Powell, Robin. Coping for Kids: A Complete Stress-Control Program for Students Ages 8-18. 202p. (gr. 3-12). 1985. pap. 47.95x (*0-87628-234-6*); wkbk. 6.95x (*0-317-43482-9*) Ctr Appl Res.
Herzig, Alison. Mystery on October Road. (gr. 4-7). 1991. 11.95 (*0-670-83635-4*) Viking Child Bks.
Herzig, Alison C. The Big Deal. Gladden, Scott, illus. 80p. (gr. 3-7). 1992. 13.50 (*0-670-84251-6*) Viking Child Bks.
—Boonsville Bombers. (gr. 4-7). 1991. 11.95 (*0-670-83595-1*) Viking Child Bks.
—The Boonsville Bombers. Andreasen, Dan, illus. 96p. (gr. 3-7). 1993. pap. 3.99 (*0-14-034578-7*, Puffin) Puffin Bks.
Herzig, Alison C. & Mali, Jane L. Mystery on October Road. LC 93-7487. 64p. (gr. 3-7). 1993. pap. 3.99 (*0-14-034614-7*, Puffin) Puffin Bks.
—Sam & the Moon Queen. 176p. (gr. 4-8). 1990. 13.45 (*0-395-53342-2*, Clarion Bks) HM.
—Sam & the Moon Queen. 176p. (gr. 3-7). 1992. pap. 3.99 (*0-14-034979-0*, Puffin) Puffin Bks.
—Ten-Speed Babysitter. 144p. (gr. 2-9). 1988. pap. 2.95 (*0-8167-1368-5*) Troll Assocs.
Herzog, B. G., abridged by see Castillo, Bernal D. de.
Herzog, George, jt. auth. see Courlander, Harold.
Hesburgh, Theodore see Kaczorek, Keith.
Heseltine, Janet E., jt. ed. see Harvey, Paul H.
Hesh, Joseph M. Is My Family Crazy or Is It Me? Jr. High Discussion Guide. 64p. (Orig.). (gr. 7-9). 1990. pap. 4.00 (*0-89109-343-5*) NavPress.
—Swimming for Shore in a Sea of Sharks: Jr. High Discussion Guide. 64p. (Orig.). (gr. 7-9). 1990. pap. 4.00 (*0-89109-342-7*) NavPress.
—Under the Influence: Jr. High Discussion Guide. 64p. (Orig.). (gr. 7-9). 1990. pap. 4.00 (*0-89109-344-3*) NavPress.
—What's the Big Idea? Jr. High Discussion Guide. 64p. (Orig.). (gr. 7-9). 1990. pap. 4.00 (*0-89109-341-9*) NavPress.
Heshiki, Kazumi, tr. see Roebuck, Susan H.
Heslewood, Juliet. Earth, Air, Fire & Water. Lydbury, Jane, et al, illus. 182p. (gr. 4-8). 1989. jacketed 15.95 (*0-19-278107-3*) OUP.
—Introducing Picasso: Painter, Sculptor. LC 92-29653. 1993. 15.95 (*0-316-35917-3*) Little.
Hess, Debra. Alien Alert! Newsom, Carol, illus. LC 93-528. 128p. (gr. 3-6). 1993. pap. 3.50 (*1-56282-567-4*) Hyprn Ppbks.
—Escape from Earth. Newsom, Carol, illus. 1994. write for info. (*1-56282-682-4*) Hyprn Child.
—Spies Incorporated, Vol. 4: The Spy from Outer Space. Newsom, Carol, illus. 1994. pap. write for info. (*1-56282-683-2*) Hyprn Child.
—Three Little Witches, No. 1. (gr. 4-7). 1991. pap. 2.99 (*0-06-106056-9*, Harp PBks) HarpC.
—Three Little Witches & the Blue-Eyed Frog. (gr. 1-6). 1991. pap. 2.99 (*0-06-106114-X*, Harp PBks) HarpC.
—Three Little Witches & the Christmas Ghost. (gr. 1-6). 1991. pap. 2.99 (*0-06-106116-6*, Harp PBks) HarpC.
—Three Little Witches & the Fortune-Teller's Curse. (gr. 4-7). 1992. pap. 2.99 (*0-06-106117-4*, Harp PBks) HarpC.
—Three Little Witches & the Shrinking House. (gr. 1-6). 1991. pap. 2.99 (*0-06-106057-7*, Harp PBks) HarpC.
—Three Little Witches & the Two-Day Spell. (gr. 1-6). 1991. pap. 2.99 (*0-06-106115-8*, Harp PBks) HarpC.
—Thurgood Marshall: The Fight for Equal Justice. Gallin, Richard, ed. Young, Andrew, intro. by. (Illus.). 128p. (gr. 5 up). 1990. lib. bdg. 16.98 (*0-382-09921-4*); pap. 7.95 (*0-382-24058-8*) Silver Burdett Pr.
—Too Many Spies. Newsom, Carol, illus. 128p. (gr. 3-6). 1993. pap. 3.50 (*1-56282-569-0*) Hyprn Ppbks.
—Wilson Sat Alone. Greenseid, Diane, illus. LC 93-17616. 1994. pap. 15.00 (*0-671-87046-7*, S&S BFYR) S&S Trade.
Hess, Donna. In Search of Honor. 153p. (Orig.). (gr. 9 up). 1991. pap. 4.95 (*0-89084-595-6*) Bob Jones Univ Pr.
Hess, Donna L. A Father's Promise. (Illus.). 268p. (Orig.). (gr. 6). 1987. pap. 6.94 (*0-89084-379-1*) Bob Jones Univ Pr.
Hess, Jeffrey A. Three Immigrant Stories. (Illus.). 32p. (gr. 3 up). 1991. pap. 1.75 (*0-685-54662-4*, E-14/B) Minn Hist.
Hess, Joan. Red Rover, Red Rover. (gr. 6 up). 1988. pap. 2.25 (*0-373-98016-7*) S&S Trade.
Hess, Karl. Capitalism for Kids: Growing Up to be Your Own Boss. (gr. 5 up). 1992. 12.95 (*0-942103-03-3*, 5615-34, Enter-Dearbrn); pap. 8.95 (*0-942103-06-8*, 5615-35, Enter-Dearbrn) Dearborn Finan.
Hess, Lilo. That Snake in the Grass. Hess, Lilo, photos by. LC 86-24826. (Illus.). 48p. (gr. 3-6). 1987. SBE 13. 95 (*0-684-18591-1*, Scribners Young Read) Macmillan Child Grp.
Hesse, Bonnie, ed. see Sheperd, Scott.
Hesse, Hermann. Siddhartha. (gr. 10-12). 1982. pap. 3.99 (*0-553-20884-5*) Bantam.
Hesse, Karen. Lavender. Glass, Andrew, illus. 64p. (gr. 2-4). 1993. PLB 14.95 (*0-8050-2528-6*, Bks Young Read) H Holt & Co.
—Lester's Dog. Carpenter, Nancy, illus. LC 92-27674. 32p. (ps-2). 1993. 13.00 (*0-517-58357-7*); PLB 13.99 (*0-517-58358-5*) Crown Bks Yng Read.
—Letters from Rifka. 192p. (gr. 4-7). 1992. 14.95 (*0-8050-1964-2*, Bks Young Read) H Holt & Co.
—Letters from Rifka. LC 93-7486. 160p. (gr. 3-7). 1993. pap. 3.99 (*0-14-036391-2*, Puffin) Puffin Bks.
—Phoenix Rising. 1994. write for info. (*0-8050-3108-1*) H Holt & Co.
—Poppy's Chair. Life, Kay, illus. LC 91-47708. 32p. (gr. k-3). 1993. RSBE 14.95 (*0-02-743705-1*, Macmillan Child Bk) Macmillan Child Grp.
—Sable. 1994. write for info. (*0-8050-2416-6*) H Holt & Co.
—Wish on a Unicorn. LC 90-5320. 128p. (gr. 4-6). 1991. 13.95 (*0-8050-1572-8*, Bks Young Read) H Holt & Co.
—Wish on a Unicorn. LC 92-26792. 112p. (gr. 3-7). 1993. pap. 3.99 (*0-14-034935-9*) Puffin Bks.
Hessell, Jenny. Clouds. Ogden, Betina, illus. LC 92-27099. 1993. 3.75 (*0-383-03561-9*) SRA Schl Grp.
—Staying at Sam's. Williams, Jenny, illus. LC 89-14561. 32p. (ps-3). 1990. (Lipp Jr Bks); (Lipp Jr Bks) HarpC Child Bks.
—Troublesome Snout. Axelsen, Stephen, illus. 32p. (gr. 92-34274. 1993. 14.00 (*0-383-03662-3*) SRA Schl Grp.
Hessler, Edward W. & Stubbs, Harriett. Acid Rain Science Projects. 20p. (Orig.). (gr. 5-12). 1987. pap. 9.95 (*0-935577-09-2*) Acid Rain Found.
Hest, Amy. Best-Ever Good-Bye Party. DiSalvo-Ryan, DyAnne, illus. LC 88-13208. 32p. (gr. k up). 1989. 13. 95 (*0-688-07325-5*); PLB 13.88 (*0-688-07326-3*, Morrow Jr Bks) Morrow Jr Bks.
—The Crack of Dawn Walkers. Schwartz, Amy, illus. LC 83-19597. 32p. (ps-3). 1984. RSBE 12.95 (*0-02-743710-8*, Macmillan Child Bk) Macmillan Child Grp.
—The Crack-of-Dawn Walkers. Schwartz, Amy, illus. 32p. (Orig.). (ps-3). 1988. pap. 3.99 (*0-14-050829-5*, Puffin) Puffin Bks.
—Fancy Aunt Jess. LC 88-34370. (ps-3). 1990. 12.95 (*0-688-08096-0*) Morrow Jr Bks.
—Getting Rid of Krista. Rogers, Jacqueline, illus. LC 87-23981. 80p. (gr. 2-5). 1988. 11.95 (*0-688-07149-X*) Morrow Jr Bks.
—Getting Rid of Krista. 80p. (gr. 4-7). 1992. pap. 2.95 (*0-8167-1841-5*) Troll Assocs.
—The Go-Between. DiSalvo-Ryan, DyAnne, illus. LC 90-24561. 32p. (gr. k-3). 1992. RSBE 14.95 (*0-02-743632-2*, Four Winds) Macmillan Child Grp.
—Love You, Soldier. LC 90-25161. 48p. (gr. 2-5). 1991. SBE 11.95 (*0-02-743635-7*, Four Winds) Macmillan Child Grp.
—Love You, Soldier. 48p. (gr. 2-6). 1993. pap. 3.99 (*0-14-036174-X*) Puffin Bks.
—Maybe Next Year. LC 93-9627. (gr. 5 up). 1994. pap. 3.95 (*0-688-12491-7*, Pub. by Beech Tree Bks) Morrow.
—The Midnight Eaters. Gundersheimer, Karen, illus. LC 88-24381. 32p. (gr. k-3). 1989. RSBE 13.95 (*0-02-743630-6*, Four Winds) Macmillan Child Grp.
—The Mommy Exchange. DiSalvo-Ryan, DyAnne, illus. LC 87-7539. 32p. (ps-2). 1988. RSBE 13.95 (*0-02-743650-0*, Pub. by Four Winds Pr) Macmillan Child Grp.
—The Mommy Exchange. DiSalvo-Ryan, Dyanne, illus. LC 90-40596. 32p. (ps-2). 1991. pap. 3.95 (*0-689-71450-5*, Aladdin) Macmillan Child Grp.

—Nana's Birthday Party. Schwartz, Amy, illus. LC 92-10260. 32p. (gr. k up). 1993. 15.00 (0-688-07497-9); PLB 14.93 (0-688-07498-7) Morrow Jr Bks.
—Nannies for Hire. Triva, Irene, illus. LC 93-7040. 1994. write for info. (0-688-12527-1); PLB write for info. (0-688-12528-X) Morrow Jr Bks.
—Pajama Party. Trivas, Irene, illus. LC 91-13676. 48p. (gr. 2 up). 1992. 14.00 (0-688-07866-4); PLB 13.93 (0-688-07870-2) Morrow Jr Bks.
—Pajama Party. Trivas, Irene, illus. 48p. (gr. 3 up). 1994. pap. 4.95 (0-688-12949-8, Pub. by Beech Tree Bks) Morrow.
—Pete & Lily. LC 85-13992. 120p. (gr. 4-7). 1986. 11.95 (0-89919-354-4, Clarion Bks) HM.
—Pete & Lily. (gr. k-6). 1989. pap. 2.75 (0-440-40145-3, YB) Dell.
—Pete & Lily. LC 92-42319. 128p. (gr. 6 up). 1993. pap. 4.95 (0-688-12490-9, Pub. by Beech Tree Bks) Morrow.
—The Purple Coat. Schwartz, Amy, illus. LC 85-29186. 32p. (gr. k-3). 1986. RSBE 13.95 (0-02-743640-3, Four Winds) Macmillan Child Grp.
—The Purple Coat. Schwartz, Amy, illus. LC 91-38499. 32p. (gr. k-3). 1992. pap. 4.95 (0-689-71634-6, Aladdin) Macmillan Child Grp.
—Rosie's Fishing Expedition. Howard, Paul, illus. LC 93-28543. 1994. write for info. (1-56402-296-X) Candlewick Pr.
—Ruby's Storm. Cote, Nancy, illus. LC 92-31242. 32p. (ps-2). 1994. RSBE 14.95 (0-02-743160-6, Four Winds) Macmillan Child Grp.
—A Sort-of Sailor. Rockwell, Lizzie, illus. LC 89-38252. 32p. (gr. k-3). 1990. RSBE 13.95 (0-02-743641-1, Four Winds) Macmillan Child Grp.
—Travel Tips from Harry: A Guide to Family Vacations in the Sun. Truesdell, Sue, illus. LC 88-39887. 64p. (gr. 2 up). 1989. 11.95 (0-688-07972-5); PLB 11.88 (0-688-09291-8, Morrow Jr Bks) Morrow Jr Bks.
—Weekend Girl. Stevenson, Harvey, illus. LC 92-9193. 32p. (gr. k up). 1993. 15.00 (0-688-09689-1); PLB 14.93 (0-688-09690-5) Morrow Jr Bks.
—Where in the World Is the Perfect Family? LC 88-20391. 112p. (gr. 4-7). 1989. 12.70 (0-89919-659-4, Clarion Bks) HM.
—Where in the World Is the Perfect Family? 96p. (gr. 3-7). 1991. pap. 3.95 (0-14-034584-1, Puffin) Puffin Bks.

Hester & Vincent. Philosophy for Young Thinkers Program. Incl. Series Foundation Volume. 15.00 (0-89824-075-1); About Me: Kindergarten. (gr. k). 21 cards 25.00 (0-89824-651-2); Living Together: First Grade Student Book. 7.99 (0-89824-652-0); My Expanding World: Second Grade Student Book. 7.99 (0-89824-653-9); But, I'm Different: Third Grade Student Book. 7.99 (0-89824-654-7); Human Community: Fourth Grade Student Book. 7.99 (0-89824-656-3); Great Experiment: Fifth Grade Student Book. 7.99 (0-89824-657-1); Global Village: Sixth Grade Student Book. 7.99 (0-89824-658-X); Teachers Manual. (gr. k-3). 10.00 (0-89824-650-4); Teachers Manual. (gr. 4-6). 10.00 (0-89824-655-5); Human Configurations: Seventh Grade. (gr. 7). 9.99 (0-89824-660-1); Beat Him If He Sneezes: Eighth Grade. (gr. 8). 9.99 (0-89824-661-X); Not Think - Not Think: Ninth Grade. (gr. 9). 9.99 (0-89824-662-8); Teachers Manual. (gr. 7-8). 10.00 (0-89824-659-8). (gr. k-12). 1989. write for info. Trillium Pr.

Hester, Nigel. The Living House. (Illus.). 32p. (gr. 5-8). 1991. PLB 12.40 (0-531-14120-9) Watts.
—The Living Pond. (Illus.). 32p. (gr. 5-8). 1990. PLB 12.40 (0-531-14006-7) Watts.
—The Living River. (Illus.). 32p. (gr. 5-8). 1991. PLB 12.40 (0-531-14121-7) Watts.
—The Living Seashore. (Illus.). 32p. (gr. 5-8). 1992. PLB 12.40 (0-531-14190-X) Watts.
—The Living Town. (Illus.). 32p. (gr. 5-8). 1992. PLB 12.40 (0-531-14202-7) Watts.
—The Living Tree. (Illus.). 32p. (gr. 5-8). 1990. PLB 12.40 (0-531-14007-5) Watts.

Heuck, Sigrid. The Cloud's Journey. Koch, Sis, illus. 28p. (ps-2). 1991. pap. 9.95 smythe sewn reinforced bdg. (1-56182-021-0) Atomium Bks.
—Pony & Bear Are Friends. Heuck, Sigrid, illus. LC 89-77711. 32p. (ps-1). 1990. PLB 10.99 (0-394-92311-1) Knopf Bks Yng Read.

Heuer, Elaine E. I Want to Paint a Zebra, but I Don't Know How: Creating Art in the Classroom, a Daily Experience. (Illus.). 32p. (gr. k-3). 1987. tchr's ed. 14.95 (0-942221-00-1) Small Busn Pr.

Heun, Joseph H. Graduate High School - A Formula for Success. LC 91-71723. (Illus.). 150p. (gr. 10). 1991. pap. 19.95 (0-9629317-0-5) Ace Pub Prodns.

Heuninck, Ronald. A New Day. (Illus.). (ps). 1988. bds. 5.50 (0-685-25277-9, 20233) Gryphon Hse.
—Playtime. Heuninck, Ronald, illus. 14p. (ps). 1991. Repr. bds. 5.50 (0-86315-124-8) Gryphon Hse.
—Rain or Shine. (Illus.). 12p. (ps). 1990. bds. 5.95 (0-86315-089-6, 1361, Pub. by Floris Bks UK) Anthroposophic.

Heupel, DuWayne. Kitten in the Country. Craig, Michael, illus. 32p. (gr. 1-2). 1993. text ed. 10.95 (1-882841-05-0) Educare CO.

Heus, John & Robinson, Tom. The Tale of Humphrey the Humpback Whale. Brost, Victoria, illus. 32p. (Orig.). (ps-3). 1985. pap. 6.95 (0-9616109-0-5) Brost Heus.

Heuvel, Karen. The Magic Crystal. (Illus.). 32p. (ps-8). 1990. pap. 5.95 (0-317-93237-3) Blue Water Pub.

Hevly, Nancy. Teachers & Preachers. 1994. PLB write for info. (0-8050-2996-6) H Holt & Co.
Hewavisenti, Latshmi. Counting. LC 91-9189. (Illus.). 32p. (gr. k-4). 1991. PLB 11.90 (0-531-17266-X, Gloucester Pr) Watts.
—Measuring. LC 91-10767. (Illus.). 32p. (gr. k-4). 1991. PLB 11.90 (0-531-17319-4, Gloucester Pr) Watts.
—Problem Solving. (Illus.). 32p. (gr. k-4). 1991. PLB 11.90 (0-531-17318-6, Gloucester Pr) Watts.
—Shapes & Solids. LC 91-9170. (Illus.). 32p. (gr. k-4). 1991. PLB 11.90 (0-531-17320-8, Gloucester Pr) Watts.

Hewett, Joan. Camera. (gr. 4-7). 1990. pap. 5.70 (0-395-54788-1, Clarion Bks) HM.
—Getting Elected: The Diary of a Campaign. Hewett, Richard, photos by. LC 88-11109. (Illus.). 48p. (gr. 4-7). 1989. 13.95 (0-525-67259-1, Lodestar Bks) Dutton Child Bks.
—Hector Lives in the United States Now: The Story of a Mexican-American Child. Hewett, Richard R., illus. LC 89-36572. 48p. (gr. 2-5). 1990. (Lipp Jr Bks); PLB 13.89 (0-397-32278-X, Lipp Jr Bks) HarpC Child Bks.
—Laura Loves Horses. Hewett, Richard, photos by. (Illus.). 48p. (gr. 2-5). 1990. 14.45 (0-89919-844-9) HM.
—Motorcycle on Patrol. LC 86-2689. (gr. 4-7). 1990. pap. 5.95 (0-395-54789-X, Clarion Bks) HM.
—Public Defender: Lawyer for the People. Hewett, Richard, photos by. (Illus.). 48p. (gr. 4-8). 1991. 14.95 (0-525-67340-7, Lodestar Bks) Dutton Child Bks.
—Rosalie. Carrick, Donald, illus. LC 86-7333. 32p. (ps-2). 1987. 13.95 (0-688-06228-8); PLB 13.88 (0-688-06229-6) Lothrop.
—Tiger, Tiger, Growing Up. Hewett, Richard, photos by. LC 92-9741. (Illus.). 32p. (ps-2). 1993. 13.95 (0-395-61583-6, Clarion Bks) HM.

Hewish, Mark. Jets. (gr. 5-9). 1976. pap. 6.95 (0-86020-051-5, Usborne-Hayes) EDC.

Hewitson, Tom, et al. Power Tunes. LC 83-91427. (gr. k-7). PLB write for info. (0-938762-13-3) Eagle Mktg Corp.

Hewitt, David, jt. auth. see Parker, Donald.
Hewitt, Joseph W., jt. auth. see Mather, Maurice W.
Hewitt, Kathryn. King Midas & the Golden Touch. Hewitt, Kathryn, illus. LC 86-7681. 29p. (ps-3). 1987. 12.95 (0-15-242800-3) HarBrace.
—Two by Two: The Untold Story. Hewitt, Kathryn, illus. LC 84-4579. 32p. (ps-3). 1984. 12.95 (0-15-291801-9, HB Juv Bks) HarBrace.
—Two by Two: The Untold Story. Hewitt, Kathryn, illus. 32p. (ps-1). 1989. pap. 3.95 (0-15-291802-7, Voyager Bks) HarBrace.

Hewitt, Sally. Busy Little Artist. 1990. 5.99 (0-517-03604-5) Outlet Bk Co.

Heyde, Christiane. The Happy Girl. Hawkins, Linda, illus. LC 89-85861. 40p. 1990. 11.95 (0-87516-618-0) DeVorss.

Heyer, Carol. The Christmas Story. Heyer, Carol, illus. LC 91-9101. 32p. (ps-1). 1991. 11.95 (0-8249-8512-5, Ideals Child) Hambleton-Hill.
—The Easter Story. Heyer, Carol, illus. 32p. (ps-1). 1990. 10.95 (0-8249-8439-0, Ideals Child) Hambleton-Hill.
—Excalibur. Heyer, Carol, illus. 32p. (gr. k-4). 1991. 14.95 (0-8249-8487-0, Ideals Child) Hambleton-Hill.
Heyer, Carol, retold by. & illus. Beauty & the Beast. 32p. (ps-3). 1989. 13.95 (0-8249-8359-9, Ideals Child) Hambleton-Hill.
Heyer, Carol, adapted by. & illus. Excalibur. 32p. (ps-3). 1993. pap. 4.95 (0-8249-8638-5, Ideals Child) Hambleton-Hill.
Heyer, Carol, retold by. & illus. Robin Hood. LC 93-18591. 32p. (ps-3). 1993. 14.95 (0-8249-8634-2, Ideals Child); PLB 15.00 (0-8249-8648-2) Hambleton-Hill.
Heyer, Carol, illus. Beauty & the Beast. 32p. (gr. k-3). 1992. pap. 4.95 (0-8249-8579-6, Ideals Child) Hambleton-Hill.

Heyer, Georgette. Sylvester (Or the Wicked Uncle) 1991. pap. 3.99 (0-06-100257-7, Harp PBks) HarpC.

Heyer, Marilee. The Forbidden Door. 32p. (ps-3). 1988. pap. 14.95 (0-670-81740-6) Viking Child Bks.
—The Forbidden Door. (Illus.). 32p. (ps-3). 1992. pap. 4.99 (0-14-050752-3, Puffin) Puffin Bks.
—The Weaving of a Dream. Heyer, Marilee, illus. 32p. (ps-3). 1989. pap. 4.99 (0-14-050528-8, Puffin) Puffin Bks.
—The Weaving of a Dream: A Chinese Folktale. Heyer, Marilee, illus. LC 85-20187. 32p. (gr. k-6). 1986. pap. 15.99 (0-670-80555-6) Viking Child Bks.

Heyer, Sandra. More True Stories in the News: A Beginning Reader. (Illus.). 1989. pap. text ed. 11.95 (0-8013-0223-4, 75881) Longman.

Heyes, Eileen. Adolf Hitler. LC 93-31269. 1994. PLB write for info. (1-56294-343-X) Millbrook Pr.
—Children of the Swastika: The Hitler Youth. LC 92-13204. (Illus.). 96p. (gr. 7 up). 1993. PLB 14.90 (1-56294-237-9) Millbrook Pr.
—Where the Wind Goes. Christensen, Carrie, illus. 32p. (ps-2). Date not set. 11.95 (1-56065-148-2) Capstone Pr. Postponed.

Heyman, Eva. The Diary of Eva Heyman: Child of the Holocaust. (Illus.). 124p. (gr. 7-12). 1988. 14.95 (0-933503-64-4); pap. 7.95 (0-933503-89-X) Shapolsky Pubs.

Heymann, Georgianne. Weevils. (Illus.). 32p. (gr. 3-7). 1986. PLB 17.96 (0-8172-2713-X) Raintree Steck-V.
Heymann, Georgianne, adapted by. Aphids. (Illus.). 32p. (gr. 3-7). 1986. PLB 17.96 (0-8172-2717-2) Raintree Steck-V.

Heymans, Annemie & Heymans, Margriet. The Princess in the Kitchen Garden. (Illus.). 48p. (ps-3). 1993. bds. 16.00 (0-374-36122-3) FS&G.
Heymans, Margriet, jt. auth. see Heymans, Annemie.
Heymsfeld, Carla. Coaching Ms. Parker. O'Connor, Jane, illus. LC 91-28484. 96p. (gr. 3-5). 1992. SBE 12.95 (0-02-743715-9, Bradbury Pr) Macmillan Child Grp.
—Digging into Language. (gr. 5-8). 1987. pap. 8.95 (0-8224-1916-5) Fearon Teach Aids.
—Where Was George Washington? Koury, Jennifer, illus. LC 92-17341. 1992. 14.95 (0-931917-20-4); pap. write for info. (0-931917-21-2) Mt Vernon Ladies.
Heymsfield, Carla & Lewis, Joan. Writer's Triangle: A Literature-Based Writing Program. (gr. 5 up). 1989. pap. 15.95 (0-8224-7496-4) Fearon Teach Aids.

Heyward, Du Bose. The Country Bunny & the Little Gold Shoes. Flack, Marjorie, illus. 48p. (gr. k-3). 1974. reinforced bdg. 13.45 (0-395-15990-3, Sandpiper); pap. 4.80 (0-395-18557-2, Sandpiper) HM.
Heyward, DuBose. The Country Bunny & the Little Gold Shoes. Flack, Marjorie, illus. (ps-3). 1989. pap. 7.70 incl. cassette (0-395-52140-8) HM.
Heyward Du, Bose see Heyward, Du Bose.

Hezlep, William. Cayman Duppy. (gr. 5 up). 1984. pap. 5.00 play script (0-88734-403-8) Players Pr.
—Ghost Town. LC 91-51080. (Orig.). (gr. 3-12). 1985. pap. 5.00 play script (0-88734-402-X) Players Pr.
—Nessie. (gr. 3-12). 1980. pap. 5.00 play script (0-88734-401-1) Players Pr.
—Pharaoh's Dagger. LC 92-53871. 70p. (Orig.). (gr. 3-12). 1992. pap. 5.00 play script (0-88734-404-6) Players Pr.

Hibbard, Ann. Rough Roads & Rainbows. Nielsen, Ann, illus. 32p. (gr. k-4). 1990. text ed. 6.99 (0-929608-71-2) Focus Family.
—Shadows & Shining Lights. Neilsen, Ann, illus. 32p. (gr. k-4). 1990. text ed. 6.99 (0-929608-20-8) Focus Family.
—Tree Forts & Trumpets. Neilsen, Ann, illus. 32p. (gr. k-4). 1990. text ed. 6.99 (0-929608-21-6) Focus Family.

Hibschman, Barbara. A Heart for Imbabura. (Illus.). 30p. (gr. 5 up). 1992. pap. 3.99 (0-87509-487-2) Chr Pubns.
—I Want to Be a Missionary. Wulf, Barbara L., illus. 24p. (Orig.). (gr. 1-6). 1990. pap. 3.99 (0-87509-436-8) Chr Pubns.
—No Sacrifice Too Great. (Illus., Orig.). (gr. k-3). 1993. pap. 4.99 (0-87509-515-1) Chr Pubns.
—One Shall Chase a Thousand. 30p. (gr. k-3). 1993. pap. 3.99 (0-87509-516-X) Chr Pubns.

Hickey. Mother Goose & More: Classic Nursery Rhymes with Added Lines. Moss, Marissa, illus. 48p. (ps-3). 1990. 7.77 (0-9623940-0-9); lib. bdg. 7.00 (0-685-45370-7); text ed. 12.95 (0-685-45371-5); tchr's. ed. 9.00 (0-685-45372-3) Additions Pr.

Hickey, Tony. Joe in the Middle. 205p. 1988. pap. 5.95 (1-85371-021-0, Pub. by Poolbeg Press Ltd Eire) Dufour.
—Spike & the Professor. Ballagh, Robert, illus. LC 89-51005. 160p. (Orig.). (gr. 4-7). 1989. pap. 5.95 (1-85371-039-3, Pub. by Poolbeg Press Ltd Eire) Dufour.

Hickle, Victoria. A Big Day for Brum. Mones, Isidre, illus. LC 92-45105. 32p. (ps-1). 1993. pap. 2.25 (0-679-84494-5) Random Bks Yng Read.
—Out & about with Brum. Mones, Isidre, illus. 14p. (ps-k). 1993. 4.99 (0-679-84470-8) Random Bks Yng Read.
—Tire Trouble for Brum. Mones, Isidre, illus. 24p. (Orig.). (ps-k). 1993. pap. 1.50 (0-679-84495-3) Random Bks Yng Read.

Hickman, C. N., et al, eds. Archery the Technical Side. St. Charles, Glenn, frwd. by. (Illus.). 281p. (gr. 10 up). 1992. Repr. of 1947 ed. 39.95 (1-56416-091-2) Derrydale Pr.

Hickman, Janet. Jericho. LC 93-37309. 1994. write for info. (0-688-13398-3) Greenwillow.
Hickman, Janet & Cullinan, Bernice E., eds. Children's Literature in the Classroom: Weaving Charlotte's Web. (Illus.). 296p. (gr. k-8). 1989. text ed. 19.95 (0-926842-00-5) CG Pubs Inc.

Hickman, Lori. ArticuMAZEment: A Pathfinding Game for Articulation & Language Practice, 4 bklts. (gr. 5-10). 1990. Set. incl. gameboard 34.95 (1-55999-101-1) LinguiSystems.

Hickman, Martha W. And God Created Squash: How the World Began. Levine, Abby, ed. Ferri, Giuliano, illus. LC 92-22654. 32p. (ps-3). 1993. PLB 14.95 (0-8075-0340-1) A Whitman.
—When Andy's Father Went to Prison. rev. ed. Levine, Abby, ed. Raymond, Larry, illus. LC 89-77318. 40p. (gr. 2-5). 1990. PLB 11.95 (0-8075-8874-1) A Whitman.

Hickman, Pamela M. Bugwise. 1991. pap. 8.95 (0-201-57074-2) Addison-Wesley.
—Habitats. English, Sarah J., illus. LC 93-12683. 1993. write for info. (0-201-62651-9); pap. 9.57 (0-201-62618-7) Addison-Wesley.

Hicks, Donna E. The Most Fascinating Places on Earth. Hicks, Mark A., illus. LC 92-41777. 128p. 14.95 (0-8069-8692-1) Sterling.

Hicks, Grace R. The Critters of Gazink. Hicks, Bruce & Ashcraft, Karen H., illus. 64p. (gr. 4-7). 1992. 11.95 (0-89015-816-9) Eakin-Sunbelt.
—The Most Mannerly Cow & the Rude Cowbird. (Illus.). 1992. 11.95 (0-89015-882-7) Eakin-Sunbelt.

Hicks, Joe B. Making Classic Cars in Wood. LC 89-26175. (Illus.). 128p. (Orig.). (gr. 10-12). 1990. pap. 10.95 (0-8069-6988-1) Sterling.

Hicks, Nancy. The Honorable Shirley Chisholm: Congresswoman from Brooklyn. (gr. 7 up). PLB 12.95 (0-87460-259-9) Lion Bks.

Hicks, Peter. The Aztecs. LC 92-44377. 32p. (gr. 4-6). 1993. 14.95 (1-56847-058-4) Thomson Lrning.

—The Romans. LC 93-11653. (Illus.). 32p. (gr. 4-6). 1994. 14.95 (1-56847-063-0) Thomson Lrning.

Hicks, Roger. Successful Black & White Photography: A Practical Handbook. (Illus.). 192p. (gr. 10-12). 1992. 27.95 (0-7153-9825-3, Pub. by David & Charles Pub UK) Sterling.

Hicyilmaz, Gaye. Against the Storm. 176p. (gr. 7 up). 1992. 14.95 (0-316-36078-3, Joy St Bks) Little.

—Against the Storm. 1993. pap. 3.50 (0-440-40892-X) Dell.

Hidaka, Masako. Girl from the Snow Country. Stinchecum, Amanda M., tr. from JPN. LC 86-10584. (Illus.). 32p. (ps-4). 1986. 13.95 (0-916291-06-5, Cranky Nell Bk) Kane-Miller Bk.

Hieatt, Constance B., ed. Beowulf & Other Old English Poems. 2nd, rev. & enl. ed. Hieatt, A. Kent, intro. by. 192p. (gr. 9-12). 1988. pap. 2.95 (0-553-21347-4) Bantam.

Hieronymis, Elve F. De see De Hieronymis, Elve F.

Hierstein, Judy, jt. auth. see Daniel, Rebecca.

Hierstein-Morris, Jill. Christmas: Facts & Fun. Hierstein-Morris, Jill, illus. 72p. (Orig.). (gr. 1 up). 1990. pap. 9.95 (1-877588-02-4) Creatively Yours.

—Halloween: Facts & Fun. Hierstein-Morris, Jill, illus. 72p. (gr. 1 up). 1988. pap. 9.95 (1-877588-00-8) Creatively Yours.

Higa, Mandy. The Moongift. Weinberger, Jane, ed. Whitaker, Kate, illus. 40p. (ps-4). 1994. pap. 9.95 (0-932433-69-3) Windswept Hse.

Higa, Tomiko. The Girl with the White Flag. Britton, Dorothy, tr. (Illus.). 144p. (gr. 5 up). 1992. pap. 3.50 (0-440-40720-6, YB) Dell.

Higa, Tomiko & Yorimitsu. The Girl with the White Fang. Britton, Dorothy, tr. from JPN. (Illus.). 180p. 1991. write for info. (4-7700-1537-2) Kodansha.

Higbee, Brenda, jt. auth. see Kingore, Bertie.

Higbie, William F. Circle of Power. Knight, Denise E., ed. LC 90-82883. (Illus.). 96p. (gr. 3 up). 1990. 13.95 (0-943604-29-X); pap. 7.95 perfect bdg. (0-943604-27-3) Eagles View.

Higby, Roy C. A Man from the Past. 2nd ed. Lux, Don, illus. McLoughlin, William G., intro. by. (Illus.). (gr. 5-12). pap. 8.00 (0-914692-02-X) Big Moose.

Higgins, Ardis O. Portraits of Courageous Women. (Illus.). (gr. 5-8). 1978. pap. text ed. 4.00x (0-912256-12-5) Halls of Ivy.

Higgins, Betty. The Knight Riders. Sun Star Publications Staff, ed. (Illus.). 32p. (gr. 3-8). 1986. pap. 2.95 (0-937787-17-5) Sun Star Pubns.

—Passing Through. Sun Star Publications Staff, ed. (Illus.). 26p. (gr. 3-8). 1986. pap. 2.95 (0-937787-03-5) Sun Star Pubns.

—Witch Watch. Sun Star Publications Staff, ed. Yazzie, Johnson, illus. August, Clara & Schatt, Paulintro. by. (Illus.). 24p. (Orig.). (gr. 3-8). 1986. pap. 2.95 (0-937787-05-1) Sun Star Pubns.

Higgins, Bill. God's Faithful Goose: John Hus. (gr. 3-6). 1994. pap. 8.95 (1-883405-02-5) Grey Pilgrim.

Higgins, Jane H. Discovering Genetics. West, James A., illus. 48p. (Orig.). (gr. 4-12). 1983. pap. text ed. 9.95 tchr's. enrichment bk. (0-88047-033-X, 8315) DOK Pubs.

Higgins, John. Meet God! A Young Christian's Handbook for Knowing God. LC 88-80294. (Illus.). 128p. (gr. 4-6). 1988. 6.50 (0-88243-488-8, 02-0488) Gospel Pub.

Higgins, Susan O. The Bunny Book. 3rd ed. Wexner, V. I., ed. Higgins, Susan O., illus. 76p. (ps-3). 1985. pap. 3.95 (0-939973-03-0) Pumpkin Pr Pub Hse.

—The Pumpkin Book. 4th ed. Wexner, V. I., ed. Higgins, Susan O., illus. 66p. (gr. k-3). 1983. pap. 3.95 (0-939973-00-6) Pumpkin Pr Pub Hse.

—The Thanksgiving Book. 3rd ed. Wexner, V. I., ed. Higgins, Susan O., illus. 74p. (ps-3). 1984. pap. 3.95 (0-939973-01-4) Pumpkin Pr Pub Hse.

Higgins, Susan O. & Co-Op Kids. Stories & Poems by the Co-Op Kids. Co-Op Kids, illus. 70p. (Orig.). (ps-3). 1987. pap. 4.00 (0-939973-04-9) Pumpkin Pr Pub Hse.

Higginsen, Vy & Bolden, Tonya. Mama, I Want to Sing. 1992. 13.95 (0-590-44201-5, Scholastic Hardcover) Scholastic Inc.

Higginson, Thomas W. Young Folks History of the United States. 1992. Repr. of 1875 ed. lib. bdg. 75.00 (0-7812-3113-2) Rprt Serv.

Higginson, William J., ed. Wind in the Long Grass: A Collection of Haiku. Speidel, Sandra, illus. LC 89-21804. 48p. (gr. 2-5). 1991. pap. 13.95 jacketed (0-671-67978-3, S&S BFYR) S&S Trade.

—Wind in the Long Grass: A Collection of Haiku. (gr. 4). 1992. pap. write for info. (0-663-56239-2) Silver Burdett Pr.

High, Jackie L. The Rise & Fall of Ilsa: (The Female Lady Giant) Hillen, Rodolfo, ed. Campbell, Dwayne, illus. 26p. (ps-3). 1991. laminated 8.95x (1-880605-00-7) J Laverne Mus.

Higham, Jon. Nursery Cats. (Illus.). 32p. (ps-1). 1991. 15.95 (0-575-04773-9, Pub. by Gollancz UK) Trafalgar.

Highland, Jean. The Federal Communications Commission. (gr. 5 up). 1992. 14.95 (1-55546-108-5) Chelsea Hse.

Highlights Editors. Hidden Pictures & Other Challengers. (Illus.). 32p. (Orig.). (gr. 1-6). 1981. pap. 2.95 (0-87534-227-2) Highlights.

—Hidden Pictures & Other Fun. (Illus.). 32p. (Orig.). (gr. 1-6). 1981. pap. 2.95 (0-87534-178-0) Highlights.

—Hidden Pictures & Other Puzzlers. (Illus.). 32p. (Orig.). (gr. 1-6). 1981. pap. 2.95 (0-87534-180-2) Highlights.

—Hidden Pictures Plus Brain Benders. (Illus.). 32p. (Orig.). (gr. 1-6). 1986. pap. 2.95 (0-87534-104-7) Highlights.

—Hidden Pictures Plus Brain Stretchers. (Illus.). 32p. (Orig.). (gr. 1-6). 1986. pap. 2.95 (0-87534-103-9) Highlights.

—Hidden Pictures Plus Brain Teasers. (Illus.). 32p. (Orig.). (gr. 1-6). 1986. pap. 2.95 (0-87534-102-0) Highlights.

—Hidden Pictures Plus Fun for Masterminds. 32p. (Orig.). (gr. 1-6). 1986. pap. 2.95 (0-87534-101-2) Highlights.

—Highlights Best Board Games from Around the World. Dugan, Robert, ed. (Illus.). 40p. (gr. 1-7). 1993. spiral bound 19.95 (1-56397-244-1) Boyds Mills Pr.

—One Hundred Thirty-Two Gift Crafts Kids Can Make. (Illus.). 48p. (Orig.). (gr. 1-6). 1981. pap. 2.95 (0-87534-308-2) Highlights.

—One Hundred Twenty-Eight Holiday Crafts Kids Can Make. (Illus.). 48p. (Orig.). (gr. 1-6). 1981. pap. 2.95 (0-87534-309-0) Highlights.

—One Hundred Twenty-Seven Anytime Crafts Kids Can Make. (Illus.). 48p. (Orig.). (gr. 1-6). 1981. pap. 2.95 (0-87534-307-4) Highlights.

—Party Ideas with Crafts Kids Can Make. (Illus.). 48p. (Orig.). (gr. 1-6). 1981. pap. 2.95 (0-87534-310-4) Highlights.

Highlights for Children Editors. Eagles. (Illus.). 32p. (gr. 2-5). 1994. pap. 3.95 (1-56397-290-5) Boyds Mills Pr.

—Elephants. (Illus.). 32p. (gr. 2-5). 1994. pap. 3.95 (1-56397-289-1) Boyds Mills Pr.

—Gift from the Storm: And Other Stories of Children Around the World. 96p. (Orig.). (gr. 3 up). 1994. pap. 2.95 (1-56397-268-9) Boyds Mills Pr.

—Jack's Best Boots: And Other Stories of Long Ago. 96p. 1994. pap. 2.95 (1-56397-266-2) Boyds Mills Pr.

—Let's Make Games: Puzzles, Board Games, Games for Groups. (Illus.). 48p. (Orig.). (ps-3). 1993. pap. 5.95 (1-56397-061-9) Boyds Mills Pr.

—Let's Pretend: Costumes, Props, Projects. (Illus.). 48p. (Orig.). (ps-5). 1993. pap. 5.95 (1-56397-060-0) Boyds Mills Pr.

—Pandas. 322p. (Orig.). (gr. 2-5). 1993. pap. 3.95 (1-56397-285-9) Boyds Mills Pr.

—Rebus Treasury: Forty-Four Stories Kids Can Read by Following the Pictures. LC 90-85899. (Illus.). 48p. (ps-2). 1991. 9.95 (1-878093-23-1) Boyds Mills Pr.

—Rebus Treasury 2: Forty-Four Stories Kids Can Read by Following the Pictures. (Illus.). 48p. (Orig.). (ps-2). 1993. pap. 4.95 (1-56397-063-5) Boyds Mills Pr.

—Rupert & the Royal Hiccups: And Other Silly Stories. 96p. (Orig.). 1994. pap. 2.95 (1-56397-267-0) Boyds Mills Pr.

—Seals. (Illus.). 32p. (Orig.). (gr. 2-5). 1993. pap. 3.95 (1-56397-286-7) Boyds Mills Pr.

—Second Jumbo Book of Hidden Pictures. 96p. (ps-3). 1993. pap. 4.95 (1-56397-185-2) Boyds Mills Pr.

—Tigers. (Illus.). 32p. (Orig.). (gr. 2-5). 1993. pap. 3.95 (1-56397-287-5) Boyds Mills Pr.

—Tis the Season: Holiday Stories from Highlights. (Illus.). 96p. (Orig.). (gr. 2-5). 1993. pap. 2.95 (1-56397-279-4) Boyds Mills Pr.

Highlights for Children Editors, compiled by. The Jumbo Book of Hidden Pictures. LC 91-72975. (Illus.). 96p. (ps-5). 1992. pap. 4.95 (1-56397-021-X) Boyds Mills Pr.

Highlights for Children Staff. Action Book of Sports. Highlights for Children Staff, illus. 32p. (gr. 3-8). 1988. pap. 2.95 (0-87534-229-9) Highlights.

—Activity Books. Highlights for Children Staff, illus. 32p. (gr. 1-6). 1989. pap. 2.95 (0-87534-381-3) Highlights.

—Activity Books. Highlights for Children Staff, illus. 32p. (gr. 1-6). 1989. pap. 2.95 (0-87534-382-1) Highlights.

—Activity Books. Highlights for Children Staff, illus. 32p. (gr. 1-6). 1989. pap. 2.95 (0-87534-383-X) Highlights.

—Activity Books. Highlights for Children Staff, illus. 32p. (gr. 1-6). 1989. pap. 2.95 (0-87534-384-8) Highlights.

—Activity Books. Highlights for Children Staff, illus. 32p. (gr. 1-6). 1989. pap. 2.95 (0-87534-385-6) Highlights.

—Activity Books. Highlights for Children Staff, illus. 32p. (gr. 1-6). 1989. pap. 2.95 (0-87534-386-4) Highlights.

—Activity Books. Highlights for Children Staff, illus. 32p. (gr. 1-6). 1989. pap. 2.95 (0-87534-387-2) Highlights.

—Activity Books. Highlights for Children Staff, illus. 32p. (gr. 1-6). 1989. pap. 2.95 (0-87534-388-0) Highlights.

—Activity Books. Highlights for Children Staff, illus. 32p. (gr. 1-6). 1989. pap. 2.95 (0-87534-389-9) Highlights.

—Activity Books. Highlights for Children Staff, illus. 32p. (gr. 1-6). 1989. pap. 2.95 (0-87534-390-2) Highlights.

—Activity Books. (Illus.). 32p. (gr. 1-6). 1991. pap. 2.95 (0-87534-328-7) Highlights.

—Baby Di Changes Color. (Illus.). (ps-2). 1991. pap. 2.95 (0-87534-332-5) Highlights.

—Basketball. Highlights for Children Staff, illus. 48p. (gr. 3-7). 1990. pap. 2.95 (0-87534-353-8) Highlights.

—The Bears' Blitz: And Other Sports Stories. LC 90-85908. (Illus.). 96p. (gr. 3-7). 1992. pap. 2.95 (1-878093-29-0); Set of 6 bks. pap. 17.70 (1-56397-075-9) Boyds Mills Pr.

—Best Board Games from Around the World. (Illus.). (gr. 2-9). 1991. text ed. 14.95 (0-87534-377-5) Highlights.

—Dinosaurs: A Closer Look. Highlights for Children Staff, illus. 32p. (gr. 3-10). 1992. pap. 3.50 (0-87534-316-3) Highlights.

—Dinosaurs: All Shapes & Sizes. Highlights for Children Staff, illus. 32p. (gr. 3-10). 1992. pap. 3.50 (0-87534-315-5) Highlights.

—Dinosaurs: Giants of the Earth. Highlights for Children Staff, illus. 32p. (gr. 3-10). 1992. pap. 3.50 (0-87534-313-9) Highlights.

—Dinosaurs: the Fossil Hunters. Highlights for Children Staff, illus. 32p. (gr. 3-10). 1992. pap. 3.50 (0-87534-317-1) Highlights.

—Dinosaurs: The Real Monsters. Highlights for Children Staff, illus. 32p. (gr. 3-10). 1992. pap. 3.50 (0-87534-314-7) Highlights.

—The Ghostly Bell Ringer: And Other Mysteries. LC 90-85912. (Illus.). 96p. (gr. 3-7). 1992. pap. 2.95 (1-878093-39-8); Set of 6 bks. pap. 17.70 (1-56397-073-2) Boyds Mills Pr.

—Hidden Pictures & Brain Bogglers. Highlights for Children Staff, illus. 32p. (gr. 1-5). 1992. pap. 2.95 (0-87534-094-6) Highlights.

—Hidden Pictures & Brain Twisters. Highlights for Children Staff, illus. 32p. (gr. 1-5). 1992. pap. 2.95 (0-87534-092-X) Highlights.

—Hidden Pictures & Mind Boosters. Highlights for Children Staff, illus. 32p. (gr. 1-5). 1992. pap. 2.95 (0-87534-098-9) Highlights.

—Hidden Pictures & More Fun. Highlights for Children Staff, illus. 32p. (gr. 1-5). 1992. pap. 2.95 (0-87534-095-4) Highlights.

—Hidden Pictures & Thinking Games. Highlights for Children Staff, illus. 32p. (gr. 1-5). 1992. pap. 2.95 (0-87534-097-0) Highlights.

—Hidden Pictures & Tricky Teasers. Highlights for Children Staff, illus. 32p. (gr. 1-5). 1992. pap. 2.95 (0-87534-090-3) Highlights.

—Hidden Pictures Plus Brain Bafflers. Highlights for Children Staff, illus. 32p. (gr. 1-5). 1992. pap. 2.95 (0-87534-089-X) Highlights.

—Hidden Pictures Plus Mind Stretchers. Highlights for Children Staff, illus. 32p. (gr. 1-5). 1992. pap. 2.95 (0-87534-093-8) Highlights.

—Hidden Pictures Plus Mind Tanglers. Highlights for Children Staff, illus. 32p. (gr. 1-5). 1992. pap. 2.95 (0-87534-091-1) Highlights.

—Hidden Pictures Plus Other Stumpers. Highlights for Children Staff, illus. 32p. (gr. 1-5). 1992. pap. 2.95 (0-87534-096-2) Highlights.

—In the Shadow of an Eagle: And Other Adventure Stories. LC 91-77001. (Illus.). 96p. (gr. 3-7). 1992. pap. 2.95 (1-56397-078-3); Set of 6 bks. pap. 17.70 (1-56397-079-1) Boyds Mills Pr.

—Jack Koala is Back. (Illus.). (ps-2). 1991. pap. 2.95 (0-87534-336-8) Highlights.

—The Joinables. (Illus.). (ps-2). 1991. pap. 2.95 (0-87534-339-2) Highlights.

—Ketchup Goes to Town. (Illus.). (ps-2). 1991. pap. 2.95 (0-87534-338-4) Highlights.

—Marvin Composes a Tea: And Other Humorous Stories. LC 90-85916. (Illus.). 96p. (gr. 3-7). 1992. pap. 2.95 (1-878093-40-1); Set of 6 bks. pap. 17.70 (1-56397-072-4) Boyds Mills Pr.

—Ms. Grace Gives a Party. (Illus.). (ps-2). 1991. pap. 2.95 (0-87534-331-7) Highlights.

—No Pets Allowed! And Other Animal Stories. LC 91-77000. (Illus.). 96p. (gr. 3-7). 1992. pap. 2.95 (1-56397-102-X); Set of 6 bks. pap. 17.70 (0-685-59148-4) Boyds Mills Pr.

—One Hundred Eighteen Recyclable Crafts Kids Can Make. Highlights for Children Staff, illus. 40p. (gr. 1-5). 1993. pap. 2.95 (0-87534-106-3) Highlights.

—One Hundred Nineteen Any Time Crafts Kids Can Make. Highlights for Children Staff, illus. 40p. (gr. 1-5). 1993. pap. 2.95 (0-87534-108-X) Highlights.

—One Hundred Thirty-Six Party Ideas & Crafts Kids Can Make. Highlights for Children Staff, illus. 40p. (gr. 1-5). 1993. pap. 2.95 (0-87534-110-1) Highlights.

—One Hundred Twenty-One Holiday Crafts Kids Can Make. Highlights for Children Staff, illus. 40p. (gr. 1-5). 1993. pap. 2.95 (0-87534-109-8) Highlights.

—One Hundred Twenty-Three Gift Crafts Kids Can Make. Highlights for Children Staff, illus. 40p. (gr. 1-5). 1993. pap. 2.95 (0-87534-107-1) Highlights.

—Preschool Headwork. Highlights for Children Staff, illus. 32p. (ps-2). 1968. pap. 2.95 (0-87534-220-5) Highlights.

—Puzzlemania. Highlights for Children Staff, illus. (gr. 3-7). 1989. pap. 2.98 48p. (0-87534-701-0); pap. 2.98 32p. (0-87534-801-7) Highlights.

—Puzzlemania. Highlights for Children Staff, illus. (gr. 3-7). 1989. pap. 2.98 48p. (0-87534-702-9); pap. 2.98 32p. (0-87534-802-5) Highlights.

—Puzzlemania. Highlights for Children Staff, illus. (gr. 3-7). 1989. pap. 2.98 48p. (0-87534-703-7); pap. 2.98 32p. (0-87534-803-3) Highlights.

—Puzzlemania. Highlights for Children Staff, illus. (gr. 3-7). 1989. pap. 2.98 48p. (0-87534-704-5); pap. 2.98 32p. (0-87534-804-1) Highlights.

—Puzzlemania. Highlights for Children Staff, illus. (gr. 3-7). 1989. pap. 2.98 48p. (0-87534-705-3); pap. 2.98 32p. (0-87534-805-X) Highlights.

—Puzzlemania. Highlights for Children Staff, illus. (gr. 3-7). 1989. pap. 2.98 48p. (0-87534-706-1); pap. 2.98 32p. (0-87534-806-8) Highlights.
—Puzzlemania. Highlights for Children Staff, illus. (gr. 3-7). 1989. pap. 2.98 48p. (0-87534-707-X); pap. 2.98 32p. (0-87534-807-6) Highlights.
—Puzzlemania. Highlights for Children Staff, illus. (gr. 3-7). 1989. pap. 2.98 48p. (0-87534-708-8); pap. 2.98 32p. (0-87534-808-4) Highlights.
—Puzzlemania. Highlights for Children Staff, illus. (gr. 3-7). 1989. pap. 2.98 48p. (0-87534-709-6); pap. 2.98 32p. (0-87534-809-2) Highlights.
—Puzzlemania. Highlights for Children Staff, illus. (gr. 3-7). 1989. pap. 2.98 48p. (0-87534-710-X); pap. 2.98 32p. (0-87534-810-6) Highlights.
—Puzzlemania. Highlights for Children Staff, illus. 48p. (gr. 3-7). 1990. pap. 2.98 (0-87534-711-8) Highlights.
—Puzzlemania. Highlights for Children Staff, illus. 48p. (gr. 3-7). 1990. pap. 2.98 (0-87534-712-6) Highlights.
—Puzzlemania. Highlights for Children Staff, illus. 48p. (gr. 3-7). 1990. pap. 2.98 (0-87534-713-4) Highlights.
—Puzzlemania. Highlights for Children Staff, illus. 48p. (gr. 3-7). 1990. pap. 2.98 (0-87534-714-2) Highlights.
—Puzzlemania. Highlights for Children Staff, illus. 48p. (gr. 3-7). 1990. pap. 2.98 (0-87534-715-0) Highlights.
—Puzzlemania. Highlights for Children Staff, illus. 48p. (gr. 3-7). 1990. pap. 2.98 (0-87534-716-9) Highlights.
—Puzzlemania. Highlights for Children Staff, illus. 48p. (gr. 3-7). 1990. pap. 2.98 (0-87534-717-7) Highlights.
—Puzzlemania. Highlights for Children Staff, illus. 48p. (gr. 3-7). 1990. pap. 2.98 (0-87534-718-5) Highlights.
—Puzzlemania. Highlights for Children Staff, illus. 48p. (gr. 3-7). 1990. pap. 2.98 (0-87534-719-3) Highlights.
—Puzzlemania. Highlights for Children Staff, illus. 48p. (gr. 3-7). 1990. pap. 2.98 (0-87534-720-7) Highlights.
—Puzzlemania. Highlights for Children Staff, illus. 48p. (gr. 3-7). 1990. pap. 2.98 (0-87534-721-5) Highlights.
—Puzzlemania. Highlights for Children Staff, illus. 48p. (gr. 3-7). 1990. pap. 2.98 (0-87534-722-3) Highlights.
—Puzzlemania. Highlights for Children Staff, illus. 48p. (gr. 3-7). 1991. pap. 2.98 (0-87534-723-1) Highlights.
—Puzzlemania. Highlights for Children Staff, illus. 48p. (gr. 3-7). 1991. pap. 2.98 (0-87534-724-X) Highlights.
—Puzzlemania. Highlights for Children Staff, illus. 48p. (gr. 3-7). 1991. pap. 2.98 (0-87534-725-8) Highlights.
—Puzzlemania. Highlights for Children Staff, illus. 48p. (gr. 3-7). 1991. pap. 2.98 (0-87534-726-6) Highlights.
—Puzzlemania. Highlights for Children Staff, illus. 48p. (gr. 3-7). 1991. pap. 2.98 (0-87534-727-4) Highlights.
—Puzzlemania. Highlights for Children Staff, illus. 48p. (gr. 3-7). 1991. pap. 2.98 (0-87534-728-2) Highlights.
—Puzzlemania. (Illus.). 48p. (gr. 3-7). 1991. pap. 2.98 (0-87534-729-0) Highlights.
—Puzzlemania. (Illus.). 48p. (gr. 3-7). 1991. pap. 2.98 (0-87534-730-4) Highlights.
—Puzzlemania. (Illus.). 48p. (gr. 3-7). 1991. pap. 2.98 (0-87534-731-2) Highlights.
—Puzzlemania. (Illus.). 48p. (gr. 3-7). 1991. pap. 2.98 (0-87534-732-0) Highlights.
—Puzzlemania. (Illus.). 48p. (gr. 3-7). 1991. pap. 2.98 (0-87534-733-9) Highlights.
—Puzzlemania. (Illus.). 48p. (gr. 3-7). 1991. pap. 2.98 (0-87534-734-7) Highlights.
—Puzzlemania. (Illus.). 48p. (gr. 3-7). 1991. pap. 2.98 (0-87534-735-5) Highlights.
—Puzzlemania. (Illus.). 48p. (gr. 3-7). 1991. pap. 2.98 (0-87534-736-3) Highlights.
—Puzzlemania. (Illus.). 48p. (gr. 3-7). 1991. pap. 2.98 (0-87534-737-1) Highlights.
—Puzzlemania. (Illus.). 48p. (gr. 3-7). 1991. pap. 2.98 (0-87534-738-X) Highlights.
—Puzzlemania. (Illus.). 48p. (gr. 3-7). 1991. pap. 2.98 (0-87534-739-8) Highlights.
—Puzzlemania. (Illus.). 48p. (gr. 3-7). 1991. pap. 2.98 (0-87534-740-7) Highlights.
—Sir Good is on His Way. (Illus.). (ps-2). 1991. pap. 2.95 (0-87534-334-1) Highlights.
—Skills Fun: Critters. Highlights for Children Staff, illus. (ps-3). 1991. pap. text ed. 2.95 (0-87534-192-6) Highlights.
—Skills Fun: Free Time. Highlights for Children Staff, illus. (ps-3). 1991. pap. text ed. 2.95 (0-87534-193-4) Highlights.
—Skills Fun: Mystery. Highlights for Children Staff, illus. (ps-3). 1991. pap. text ed. 2.95 (0-87534-194-2) Highlights.
—Skills Fun: Outdoors. Highlights for Children Staff, illus. (ps-3). 1991. pap. text ed. 2.95 (0-87534-198-5) Highlights.
—Skills Fun: Space. Highlights for Children Staff, illus. (ps-3). 1991. pap. text ed. 2.95 (0-87534-199-3) Highlights.
—Skills Fun: Trips. Highlights for Children Staff, illus. (ps-3). 1991. pap. text ed. 2.95 (0-87534-200-0) Highlights.
—Storm's Fury: And Other Horse Stories. LC 90-85910. (Illus.). 96p. (gr. 3-7). 1992. pap. 2.95 (1-878093-31-2); Set of 6 bks. pap. 17.70 (1-56397-071-6) Boyds Mills Pr.
—Summer Games. Highlights for Children Staff, illus. 48p. (gr. 3-7). 1990. pap. 2.95 (0-87534-352-X) Highlights.
—What's Wrong & Other Mixed-up Fun. Highlights for Children Staff, illus. 32p. (gr. k-6). 1990. pap. 2.95 (0-87534-464-X) Highlights.
—What's Wrong & Other Mixed-up Fun. Highlights for Children Staff, illus. 32p. (gr. k-6). 1990. pap. 2.95 (0-87534-444-5) Highlights.

—What's Wrong & Other Mixed-up Fun. Highlights for Children Staff, illus. 32p. (gr. k-6). 1990. pap. 2.95 (0-87534-449-6) Highlights.
—What's Wrong & Other Mixed-up Fun. Highlights for Children Staff, illus. 32p. (gr. k-6). 1990. pap. 2.95 (0-87534-455-0) Highlights.
—What's Wrong & Other Mixed-up Fun. Highlights for Children Staff, illus. 32p. (gr. k-6). 1990. pap. 2.95 (0-87534-463-1) Highlights.
—What's Wrong & Other Mixed-up Fun. Highlights for Children Staff, illus. 32p. (gr. k-6). 1990. pap. 2.95 (0-87534-466-6) Highlights.
—What's Wrong & Other Mixed-up Fun. (Illus.). 32p. (gr. k-6). 1991. pap. 2.95 (0-87534-468-2) Highlights.
—Winter Sports. Highlights for Children Staff, illus. 48p. (gr. 3-7). 1990. pap. 2.95 (0-87534-351-1) Highlights.

Hightower, Robert see Rasmussen, Lore.
Highwater, Jamake. ANPAO: An American Indian Odyssey. Scholder, Fritz, illus. LC 77-9264. 256p. (gr. 7 up). 1992. pap. 6.95 (0-06-440437-4, Trophy) HarpC Child Bks.
—Anpao: An American Indian Odyssey. Scholder, Fritz, illus. LC 77-9264. 256p. (gr. 7 up). 1993. PLB 14.89 (0-06-022878-4) HarpC Child Bks.
—The Ceremony of Innocence. LC 84-48334. 192p. (gr. 7 up). 1985. HarpC Child Bks.
—Eyes of Darkness. LC 82-187. 192p. (gr. 6 up). 1985. 13.00 (0-688-41993-3) Lothrop.
—I Wear the Morning Star. LC 85-45258. 160p. (gr. 7 up). 1986. PLB 12.89 (0-06-022356-1) HarpC Child Bks.
—Moonsong Lullaby. Keegan, Marcia, illus. LC 81-1909. 32p. (ps-3). 1981. 14.95 (0-688-00427-X) Lothrop.
—Songs for the Seasons. Speidel, Sandra, illus. LC 93-8094. 1994. write for info. (0-688-10658-7); PLB write for info. (0-688-10659-5) Lothrop.
Higman, Anita. Willing to Grow. Cuthbert, Peter, illus. 45p. (gr. 9-12). 1988. pap. 4.95 (0-945362-01-3) Best Sllrs TX.
Higton, Bernard, ed. see Andersen, Hans Christian.
Higton, Bernard, jt. ed. see Ash, Russell.
Hijazi, N. Color & Learn the Names of Animals. (Orig.). (ps). Date not set. pap. 3.50 (0-934905-12-6) Kazi Pubns.
Hilbert, Vi, as told by. Loon & Deer Were Traveling: A Story of the Upper Skagit. Nelson, Anita, illus. LC 92-5450. 24p. (ps-3). 1992. PLB 16.93 (0-516-05140-7); pap. 5.95 (0-516-45140-5) Childrens.
Hildebrand, Eckart, jt. auth. see Hildebrand, Sigrid S.
Hildebrand, Janice. Sheboygan County: One Hundred Fifty Years of Progress: An Illustrated History. (Illus.). 208p. (gr. 7 up). 1988. 29.95 (0-89781-252-2) Windsor Pubns Inc.
Hildebrand, June. A Book of Flowers. (Illus.). 72p. (Orig.). 1982. write for info. Claremount Pr.
Hildebrand, Sigrid S. & Hildebrand, Eckart. Gehen. Rohrer, Josef, ed. Baker, Syd, illus. Winitz, Harris, intro. by. (GER., Illus.). 85p. (gr. 7 up). 1990. Incls. cass. tape. pap. 22.00 (0-939990-64-4) Intl Linguistics.
—Stellen, Legen und Setzen. Rohrer, Josef, ed. Baker, Syd, illus. Winitz, Harris, intro. by. (GER., Illus.). 80p. (Orig.). (gr. 7 up). 1990. Incls. cass. tape. pap. text ed. 22.00 (0-939990-65-2) Intl Linguistics.
Hildebrandt, Greg. A Christmas Treasury. (Illus.). 72p. 1984. 11.95 (0-88101-107-X) Unicorn Pub.
Hildebrandt, Greg, illus. Aladdin & the Magic Lamp. 48p. (ps-2). 1992. 5.95 (0-88101-266-1) Unicorn Pub.
—Alice in Wonderland. 48p. (gr. 2-5). 1991. 6.95 (0-88101-109-6) Unicorn Pub.
—Favorite Fairy Tales. 160p. (ps-7). 1985. 14.95 (0-88101-268-8) Unicorn Pub.
—Peter Pan. 48p. (gr. 2-5). 1991. 6.95 (0-88101-111-8) Unicorn Pub.
—Pinocchio. 48p. (gr. 2-5). 1992. 6.95 (0-88101-267-X) Unicorn Pub.
—Robin Hood. 48p. (gr. 2-5). 1991. 6.95 (0-88101-110-X) Unicorn Pub.
—Twas the Night Before Christmas: Includes Christmas Carols & The Nativity. 48p. 1985. 6.95 (0-88101-181-9) Unicorn Pub.
—Wizard of Oz. 48p. (gr. 2-5). 1992. 6.95 (0-88101-217-3) Unicorn Pub.
Hildebrandt, Greg & Hildebrandt, Greg, illus. Twas the Night Before Christmas: And Other Holiday Favorites. LC 90-10976. 48p. (gr. k-2). 1990. 4.95 (0-88101-103-7) Unicorn Pub.
Hildebrandt, Mary, illus. I'm a Little Teapot. 48p. (ps). 1993. 5.95 (0-88101-281-5) Unicorn Pub.
—Story of the Easter Bunny. 48p. (ps). 1993. 5.95 (0-88101-275-0) Unicorn Pub.
Hildebrandt, Tim & Laurence, Jim, eds. Shoemaker & the Christmas Elves. Hildebrandt, Tim, illus. 1993. 6.99 (0-517-08488-0) Outlet Bk Co.
Hilderbrand, Karen & Thompson, Kim. Addition. (Illus.). 49p. (gr. 3). 1991. wkbk. 6.99 (0-9632249-2-1) Twin Sisters.
—Division. (Illus.). 49p. (gr. 3). 1991. wkbk. 6.99 (0-9632249-4-8) Twin Sisters.
—Multiplication. (Illus.). 49p. (gr. 3). 1991. wkbk. 6.99 (0-9632249-1-3) Twin Sisters.
—Subtraction. (Illus.). 49p. (gr. 3). 1991. wkbk. 6.99 (0-9632249-3-X) Twin Sisters.
Hilderbrand, Karen M. & Thompson, Kim M. Rhythm, Rhyme & Read: Phonics. 64p. (gr. 3). 1992. wkbk. 6.99 (0-9632249-0-5) Twin Sisters.

Hilderbrand, Karen M., jt. auth. see Thompson, Kim M.
Hildick, E. W. The Case of the Desperate Drummer: A McGurk Mystery. LC 92-22726. 160p. (gr. 3-7). 1993. SBE 13.95 (0-02-743961-5, Macmillan Child Bk) Macmillan Child Grp.
—The Case of the Dragon in Distress: A McGurk Fantasy. LC 90-13538. 160p. (gr. 3-7). 1991. SBE 13.95 (0-02-743931-3) Macmillan Child Grp.
—The Case of the Fantastic Footprints: A McGurk Mystery. 144p. (gr. 3-7). 1994. SBE 13.95 (0-02-743967-4, Macmillan Child Bk) Macmillan Child Grp.
—The Case of the Muttering Mummy: A McGurk Mystery. LC 85-23747. (Illus.). 144p. (gr. 3-6). 1986. SBE 13.95 (0-02-743960-7, Macmillan Child Bk) Macmillan Child Grp.
—The Case of the Nervous Newsboy. Lane, John, illus. 112p. (gr. 3-6). 1991. pap. 2.95 (0-88741-807-4, 01304) Sundance Pubs.
—The Case of the Purloined Parrot: A McGurk Mystery. LC 89-37924. 144p. (gr. 3-7). 1990. SBE 13.95 (0-02-743965-8, Macmillan Child Bk) Macmillan Child Grp.
—Case of the Wandering Weathervanes. 160p. (gr. 4-7). 1992. pap. 2.95 (0-8167-1790-7) Troll Assocs.
—The Case of the Wandering Weathervanes: A McGurk Mystery. Brunkus, Denise, illus. LC 87-13171. 160p. (gr. 3-7). 1988. SBE 13.95 (0-02-743970-4, Macmillan Child Bk) Macmillan Child Grp.
—The Case of the Weeping Witch: A McGurk Fantasy. LC 91-38231. 160p. (gr. 3-7). 1992. SBE 13.95 (0-02-743785-X, Macmillan Child Bk) Macmillan Child Grp.
—The Ghost Squad & the Halloween Conspiracy. 176p. 1986. pap. 1.95 (0-8125-6852-4) Tor Bks.
—The Ghost Squad Breaks Through. LC 84-3985. 144p. (gr. 5-9). 1984. 12.95 (0-525-44097-6, 01063-320, DCB) Dutton Child Bks.
Hildreth, Dolly, et al. The Money God. (gr. 6). 1972. 1.95 (0-89992-031-4) Coun India Ed.
Hilgartner, Beth. The Feast of the Trickster. 240p. (gr. 5-9). 1991. 14.45 (0-395-55008-4, Sandpiper) HM.
—A Murder for Her Majesty. 256p. (gr. 5 up). 1986. 13.45 (0-395-41451-2) HM.
—Murder for Her Majesty. (gr. 4-7). 1992. pap. 4.80 (0-395-61619-0) HM.
Hilgers, Laura. Great Skates. (Illus.). (gr. 3-7). 1991. pap. 14.95 (0-316-36240-9, Spts Illus Kids) Little.
Hill. Dog & Puppies. Goaman, Karen, ed. Kennan, Elaine & Ward, Fredrick, illus. (gr. 2-5). 1983. pap. 4.50 (0-86020-646-7); lib. bdg. 11.96 (0-88110-086-2) EDC.
—Small Pets. Cork, Barbara, ed. Jackson, Ian & Shields, Chris, illus. (gr. 3-6). pap. 4.50 (0-86020-648-3, 15122); lib. bdg. 11.96 (0-88110-087-0) EDC.
Hill, Barbara. Cooking the English Way. LC 82-257. (Illus.). 48p. (gr. 5 up). 1982. PLB 14.95 (0-8225-0903-2) Lerner Pubns.
Hill, Betty, ed. see Woofenden, Louise.
Hill, Charlotte, ed. see Hill, Fred D.
Hill, Charlotte M. Poetry for Wee Folks. Hill, Fred D., ed. Young, Elaine, et al, illus. LC 88-70281. 31p. (gr. k-3). 1988. 11.95 (0-9620182-0-1); pap. 6.95 (0-9620182-2-8) Charill Pubs.
—Wee Folks Inching On: A Phonetic Approach to Beginning Reading. Shortridge, Cleona, frwd. by. Jefferson, Sharon, illus. LC 90-832256. 95p. (gr. k-3). 1991. pap. text ed. 7.95 (0-9620182-4-4) Charill Pubs.
—Wee Folks Learn to Read: A Phonetic Approach to Beginning Reading. Young, Elaine, et al, eds. Fields, Theodore & Jefferson, Sharon, illus. LC 90-83256. (Orig.). (gr. k-3). 1991. pap. text ed. 7.95 (0-9620182-3-6) Charill Pubs.
—Wee Folks Moving Up: A Phonetic Approach to Beginning Reading. Shortridge, Cleona, intro. by. Jefferson, Sharon & Fields, Theodore, illus. LC 91-70303. (Orig.). (gr. k-3). 1991. pap. text ed. 7.95 (0-9620182-5-2) Charill Pubs.

—**Wee Folks Readers: A Phonetic Approach to Beginning Reading, 5 vols.** Shortridge, Cleona, ed. Fields, Theodore, et al, illus. LC 90-832256. 70p. (Orig.). (gr. k-5). 1992. Set. pap. write for info. (0-9620182-9-5) Charill Pubs.
This five volume reading series is an eclectic approach to beginning reading. Phonics is introduced in story form, lending itself to building comprehension, skills & simultaneously, sight words to build vocabulary as well. Each sound is introduced with illustrations that represent that sound. Books One through Four teach the vowel sounds & this teaching of sounds in context allows for the immediate application of phonetic skills learned. This approach follows the principle of use & reinforcement. Book Five, "Wee Folks

on Top" (Adventures in Reading), **contains stories, fables & poetry with follow-up questions to improve comprehension. A bookstore owner & mother of a six year old daughter who lives in San Antonio, Texas, wrote, "My daughter was reading the first hour after I started her in Book I. I called relatives all over the country to tell them that she was reading." A director of a Prep School in Seattle, Washington, writes, "Your reading series is excellent. I am an experienced teacher & have always believed that a phonics based reading program is the best way to teach reading."** *Publisher Provided Annotation.*

—Wee Folks Soaring High: A Phonetic Approach to Beginning Reading. Shortridge, Cleona, ed. LC 91-73581. (Illus.). 101p. (Orig.). (gr. k-3). 1992. pap. text ed. 7.95 (0-9620182-6-0) Charill Pubs.

Hill, Charlotte M. & Hill, Fred D. Wee Folks on Top: Adventures in Reading. Shortridge, Cleona, ed. Fields, Theodore, illus. LC 92-90056. 66p. (Orig.). (gr. 3-5). 1992. pap. 8.95 (0-9620182-7-9) Charill Pubs.

Hill, Charlotte M., jt. auth. see Hill, Fred.

Hill, Chip. Black Lizard's Startling Encounter. Hill, Darlene, illus. LC 91-16081. (gr. 4-9). 1991. 4.00 (0-915541-75-0) Star Bks Inc.

Hill, Dave. Most Wonderful King. Wind, B., illus. (gr. 3-4). 1968. laminated bdg. 1.89 (0-570-06032-X, 59-1145) Concordia.

Hill, Donald, jt. auth. see Blacke, Terry L.

Hill, Douglas. The Caves of Klydor. 144p. 1986. pap. 2.75 (0-553-25929-6, Spectra) Bantam.

—Day of the Starwind. (Orig.). (gr. k-12). 1987. pap. 2.50 (0-440-91762-X, LFL) Dell.

—Deathwing over Veynaa. (Orig.). (gr. k-12). 1987. pap. 2.50 (0-440-91743-3, LFL) Dell.

—Galactic Warlord. (Orig.). (gr. k-12). 1987. pap. 2.50 (0-440-92787-0, LFL) Dell.

—Goblin Party. Demeyer, Paul, illus. 44p. (gr. 3-5). 1990. 13.95 (0-575-04338-5, Pub. by Gollancz England) Trafalgar.

—The Moon Monster. Ford, Jeremy, illus. 42p. (gr. 2-4). 1989. 3.95 (0-8120-6138-1) Barron.

—Penelope's Pendant. (gr. 5-7). 1991. 12.95 (0-385-41641-5) Doubleday.

—Planet of the Warlord. (gr. 7 up). 1987. pap. 2.50 (0-440-97126-8) Dell.

—Young Legionary. (gr. k-12). 1987. pap. 2.50 (0-440-99910-3, LFL) Dell.

Hill, Elizabeth S. The Banjo Player. 160p. (gr. 5-9). 1993. 14.99 (0-670-84967-7) Viking Child Bks.

—Broadway Chances. 160p. (gr. 3-7). 1992. RB 14.00 (0-670-84197-8) Viking Child Bks.

—Evan's Corner. (ps-3). 1991. 13.00 (0-670-82830-0) Viking Child Bks.

—Evan's Corner. Speidel, Sandra, illus. LC 92-25334. 1993. pap. 4.99 (0-14-054406-2) Puffin Bks.

—The Street Dancers. 192p. (gr. 3-7). 1991. 13.95 (0-670-83435-1) Viking Child Bks.

—The Street Dancers. 176p. (gr. 3-7). 1993. pap. 3.99 (0-14-034491-8, Puffin) Puffin Bks.

—When Christmas Comes. (gr. 4-6). 1991. pap. 3.95 (0-14-032682-0, Puffin) Puffin Bks.

Hill, Eric. Animals. (Illus.). 8p. (ps). 1993. 4.95 (0-399-22524-2, Putnam) Putnam Pub Group.

—Ayna Boby. (ARA., Illus.). 24p. (ps-2). 1988. 10.95 (0-940793-01-6, Pub. by Crocodile Bks.) Interlink Pub.

—Boby Yath'hab Ilal Madrasa. (ARA., Illus.). 24p. (ps-2). 1988. 10.95 (0-940793-03-2, Pub. by Crocodile Bks) Interlink Pub.

—Book of Colors. (ps). 6.95 (0-317-13663-1) Determined Prods.

—Book of Shapes. (ps). 6.95 (0-317-13666-6) Determined Prods.

—Clothes. (Illus.). 8p. (ps). 1993. 4.95 (0-399-22521-8, Putnam) Putnam Pub Group.

—Donde Esta Spot? (Where's Spot?) Hill, Eric, illus. (SPA.). 22p. (ps-2). 1983. 12.95 (0-399-21018-0, Putnam) Putnam Pub Group.

—Fairy Tales. 24p. (Orig.). (ps-k). 1985. 4.95 (0-8431-0919-X) Price Stern.

—La Hermanita de Spot. (SPA., Illus.). 22p. (ps-k). 1990. 12.95 (0-399-21828-9, Putnam) Putnam Pub Group.

—Home. (Illus.). 8p. (ps). 1993. 4.95 (0-399-22522-6, Putnam) Putnam Pub Group.

—Khatawat Boby Al- Oula. (ARA., Illus.). 22p. (ps-2). 1988. 10.95 (0-940793-02-4, Pub. by Crocodile Bks.) Interlink Pub.

—More Opposites. 20p. (Orig.). (ps-k). 1985. 4.95 (0-8431-0921-1) Price Stern.

—My Very Own Spot Book: A Special Book to Fill in & Keep. Hill, Eric, illus. 28p. (ps). 1993. 9.95 (0-399-22601-X, Putnam) Putnam Pub Group.

—Play. (Illus.). 8p. (ps). 1993. 4.95 (0-399-22523-4, Putnam) Putnam Pub Group.

—La Primera Navidad de Spot. Hill, Eric, illus. (SPA.). (ps-2). 1983. 12.95 (0-399-21024-5, Putnam) Putnam Pub Group.

—S. S. Happiness Crew Book of Numbers. (Illus.). 11p. (ps). (0-915696-65-7) Determined Prods.

—Spot at Home. (Illus.). 14p. (ps-k). 1991. bds. 3.95 (0-399-21774-6, Putnam) Putnam Pub Group.

—Spot at Play. Hill, Eric, illus. LC 84-17848. 14p. (ps-1). 1985. bds. 3.95 (0-399-21228-0, Putnam) Putnam Pub Group.

—Spot at the Fair. Hill, Eric, illus. LC 84-17849. 14p. (ps-1). 1985. bds. 3.75 (0-399-21229-9, Putnam) Putnam Pub Group.

—Spot Counts from One to Ten. Hill, Eric, illus. 14p. (ps-k). 1989. 3.95 (0-399-21672-3, Putnam) Putnam Pub Group.

—Spot Goes Splash! Hill, Eric, illus. 8p. (gr. k-1). 1984. vinyl foam-filled 3.95 (0-399-21068-7, Putnam) Putnam Pub Group.

—Spot Goes to a Party. (Illus.). 22p. (ps). 1992. 11.95 (0-399-22409-2, Putnam) Putnam Pub Group.

—Spot Goes to School. Hill, Eric, illus. LC 84-42695. 22p. (ps-2). 1984. 11.95 (0-399-21073-3, Putnam) Putnam Pub Group.

—Spot Goes to School. (ARA & ENG., Illus.). 24p. (ps-2). 1988. 10.95 (0-940793-06-7, Pub. by Crocodile Bks.) Interlink Pub.

—Spot Goes to the Beach. LC 84-18291. (Illus.). 22p. (gr. k). 1985. 11.95 (0-399-21247-7, Putnam) Putnam Pub Group.

—Spot Goes to the Circus. Hill, Eric, illus. LC 85-24471. 22p. (ps). 1986. 11.95 (0-399-21317-1, Putnam) Putnam Pub Group.

—Spot Goes to the Farm. (Illus.). 22p. (ps-1). 1987. 11.95 (0-399-21434-8, Putnam) Putnam Pub Group.

—Spot Goes to the Park. Hill, Eric, illus. 22p. 1991. 11.95 (0-399-21833-5, Putnam) Putnam Pub Group.

—Spot in the Garden. (Illus.). 14p. (ps-k). 1991. bds. 3.95 (0-399-21772-X, Putnam) Putnam Pub Group.

—Spot Learns to Count. Hill, Eric, illus. (ps-2). 1983. 1.95 (0-399-20985-9, Putnam) Putnam Pub Group.

—Spot Looks at Colors. Hill, Eric, illus. 14p. (ps-k). 1986. 3.95 (0-399-21349-X, Putnam) Putnam Pub Group.

—Spot Looks at Opposites. Hill, Eric, illus. 14p. (ps-k). 1989. bds. 3.75 (0-399-21681-2, Putnam) Putnam Pub Group.

—Spot Looks at Shapes. Hill, Eric, illus. 14p. (ps-1). 1986. 3.95 (0-399-21350-3, Putnam) Putnam Pub Group.

—Spot Looks at the Weather. Hill, Eric, illus. 14p. (ps-k). 1989. bds. 3.75 (0-399-21673-1, Putnam) Putnam Pub Group.

—Spot on the Farm. Hill, Eric, illus. LC 84-17850. 14p. (ps-1). 1985. bds. 3.95 (0-399-21230-2, Putnam) Putnam Pub Group.

—Spot Sleeps Over. (Illus.). 22p. (ps-k). 1990. 11.95 (0-399-21815-7, Putnam) Putnam Pub Group.

—Spot Sleeps Over: (Se Pasa la Noche) (SPA., Illus.). 22p. (ps-k). 1991. 12.95 (0-399-21835-1, Putnam) Putnam Pub Group.

—Spot Va a lo Circo (Spot Goes to the Circus) Hill, Eric, illus. (SPA.). 22p. (ps). 1986. 11.95 (0-399-21318-X, Putnam) Putnam Pub Group.

—Spot Va a la Granja. (SPA., Illus.). 22p. (ps-1). 1987. 12.95 (0-399-21463-1, Putnam) Putnam Pub Group.

—Spot Va Al Parque. (SPA., Illus.). 22p. (ps-k). 1993. 12.95 (0-399-22345-2, Putnam) Putnam Pub Group.

—Spot's Alphabet. Hill, Eric, illus. (ps-2). 1983. pap. 1.95 (0-399-20984-0, Putnam) Putnam Pub Group.

—Spot's Baby Sister: A Lift-the-Flap Book. Hill, Eric, illus. 22p. (ps-k). 1989. 11.95 (0-399-21640-5, Putnam) Putnam Pub Group.

—Spot's Big Book of Words. (gr. 2 up). 1988. 10.95 (0-399-21563-8, Putnam) Putnam Pub Group.

—Spot's Big Book of Words - El Libro Grande de las Palabras de Spot. Hill, Eric, illus. (SPA & ENG.). 32p. (ps-1). 1989. 11.95 (0-399-21689-8, Putnam) Putnam Pub Group.

—Spot's Birthday Party. (Illus.). (ps-k). 1982. 11.95 (0-399-20903-4, Putnam) Putnam Pub Group.

—Spot's Birthday Party. (Illus.). 1991. mini ed. 4.95 (0-399-21770-3, Putnam) Putnam Pub Group.

—Spot's Busy Year. Hill, Eric, illus. (ps-2). 1993. pap. 1.95 (0-399-20987-5, Putnam) Putnam Pub Group.

—Spot's First Christmas. Hill, Eric, illus. LC 82-23073. (ps-2). 1983. 11.95 (0-399-20963-8, Putnam) Putnam Pub Group.

—Spot's First Christmas: Mini Edition. (Illus.). 22p. (ps). 1992. 4.95 (0-399-22410-6, Putnam) Putnam Pub Group.

—Spot's First Easter. (Illus.). 22p. (ps-1). 1988. 11.95 (0-399-21435-6, Putnam) Putnam Pub Group.

—Spot's First Easter: A Lift-the-Flap Book. (Illus.). 22p. (ps-k). 1993. 4.95 (0-399-22424-6, Putnam) Putnam Pub Group.

—Spot's First Walk. Hill, Eric, illus. 22p. (ps). 1981. 11.95 (0-399-20838-0, Putnam) Putnam Pub Group.

—Spot's First Walk. (ARA & ENG., Illus.). 24p. (ps-2). 1988. 11.95 (0-940793-05-9, Pub. by Crocodile Bks) Interlink Pub.

—Spot's First Walk. (Illus.). 16p. (ps-1). 1994. pap. 5.99 (0-14-050725-6) Puffin Bks.

—Spot's First Words. Hill, Eric, illus. 14p. 1986. 3.95 (0-399-21348-1, Putnam) Putnam Pub Group.

—Spot's Friends. Hill, Eric, illus. 8p. (gr. k-1). 1984. vinyl foam-filled 3.95 (0-399-21066-0, Putnam) Putnam Pub Group.

—Spot's Toy Box. Hill, Eric, illus. (ps-k). 1991. bds. 3.95 (0-399-21773-8) Putnam Pub Group.

—Spot's Toys. Hill, Eric, illus. 8p. (gr. k-1). 1984. 3.95 (0-399-21067-9, Putnam) Putnam Pub Group.

—Spot's Walk in the Woods. Hill, Eric, illus. 14p. (ps). 1993. 12.95 (0-399-22528-5, Philomel) Putnam Pub Group.

—Sweet Dreams, Spot! Hill, Eric, illus. 8p. (gr. k-1). 1984. 3.95 (0-399-21069-5, Putnam) Putnam Pub Group.

—Where's Spot? (ENG & ARA., Illus.). 24p. (ps-2). 1988. 11.95 (0-940793-04-0, Pub. by Crocodile Bks) Interlink Pub.

—Where's Spot? (Illus.). 22p. (ps-1). 1980. 11.95 (0-399-20758-9, Putnam) Putnam Pub Group.

—Where's Spot? (Illus.). 16p. (ps-1). 1994. pap. 5.99 (0-14-050740-X) Puffin Bks.

—Where's Spot? A Lift-the-Flap Book Miniature Edition. Hill, Eric, illus. 22p. (ps-k). 1990. 4.95 (0-399-21822-X, Putnam) Putnam Pub Group.

—Who Does What? 20p. (ps-k). 1982. 4.95 (0-8431-0909-2) Price Stern.

Hill, Faith, jt. auth. see Crowder, Jack L.

Hill, Fred & Hill, Charlotte M. Treasure Chest: Practice Exercises for "Wee Folks Readers" Young, Elaine A., ed. Fields, Theodore, illus. LC 93-71070. 90p. (Orig.). (gr. 1-3). 1993. wkbk. 6.95 (0-9620182-8-7) Charill Pubs.

Hill, Fred D. Christopher & Cumulus Cloud. Young, Elaine A. & Hill, Charlotte, eds. Rhiney, Sharon, illus. LC 90-80285. 31p. (Orig.). (gr. k-4). 1990. pap. 5.95 (0-9620182-1-X) Charill Pubs.

Hill, Fred D., jt. auth. see Hill, Charlotte M.

Hill, Fred D., ed. see Hill, Charlotte M.

Hill, G. L. The Best Birthday: A Christmas Entertainment for Children. (gr. 5-6). 12.95 (0-89190-404-2, Pub. by Am Repr) Amereon Ltd.

Hill, George, jt. auth. see Herbert, Solomon.

Hill, Gerald N. The Year of the Indians. Hill, Gerald, Jr., illus. 54p. (Orig.). (gr. 4-7). 1985. pap. 4.95 (0-912133-06-6) Hilltop Pub Co.

Hill, Grace L. Marcia Schuyler. 1992. 9.95 (1-55748-261-6) Barbour & Co.

—Phoebe Deane. 1992. 9.95 (1-55748-262-4) Barbour & Co.

Hill, Howard. Hunting the Hard Way. Naylor, Raymon, illus. St. Charles, Glenn, frwd. by. (Illus.). 318p. (gr. 10 up). 1993. Repr. of 1953 ed. 39.95 (1-56416-095-5) Derrydale Pr.

Hill, Jan C., jt. auth. see Hill, William E.

Hill, Janis, jt. auth. see Patrick, Jane.

Hill, John. Exploring Information Technology. Hill, John, illus. LC 92-28172. 48p. (gr. 4-8). 1992. PLB 19.92 (0-8114-2605-X) Raintree Steck-V.

Hill, Kirkpatrick. Toughboy & Sister. LC 90-31297. 128p. (gr. 3-7). 1990. SBE 13.95 (0-689-50506-X, M K McElderry) Macmillan Child Grp.

—Toughboy & Sister. 128p. (gr. 3-7). 1992. pap. 3.99 (0-14-034866-2) Puffin Bks.

—Winter Camp. LC 92-41200. (Illus.). 192p. (gr. 3-7). 1993. SBE 14.95 (0-689-50588-4, M K McElderry) Macmillan Child Grp.

Hill, Laura, jt. auth. see Jacobson, Michael.

Hill, Laurence D. A Season of Dreams. LC 90-37674. 320p. 1990. 19.95 (0-8397-7591-1) Eriksson.

Hill, Lee. Wally, the Scholarly Walrus. 1990. 6.95 (0-533-08401-6) Vantage.

Hill, Margaret. Coping with Family Expectations. Rosen, Ruth, ed. (gr. 7-12). 1990. PLB 13.95 (0-8239-1159-4) Rosen Group.

Hill, Marie, jt. auth. see Collier, Jaunell.

Hill, Michael & Kahan, B., eds. Justice League of America Archives, Vol. 1. Gambaccini, Paul, intro. by. (Illus.). 256p. 1992. text ed. 39.95 (1-56389-043-7) DC Comics.

Hill, Michael, ed. see Barr, Mike, et al.

Hill, Michael C., ed. All Star Comics Archives, Vol. 1. Thompson, Don, intro. by. (Illus.). 272p. 1992. text ed. 49.95 (1-56389-019-4) DC Comics.

—The Legion of Super-Heroes Archives, Vol. 1. Gold, Mike, intro. by. (Illus.). 256p. 1991. text ed. 39.95 (1-56389-020-8) DC Comics.

Hill, R. Pets & Pet Care. 24p. (gr. 1-4). 1983. 10.95 (0-86020-650-5) EDC.

Hill, Stanford, et al. Integrated Science, Bks. 1 & 2. (Illus.). 528p. (gr. 7-8). 1990. text ed. 22.00 ea. Bk. 1, 496p (0-89089-358-6) Bk. 2, 520p (0-89089-360-8) Carolina Acad Pr.

Hill, Stephanie. Donald's Wild Adventure. Disney Studios Staff, illus. 24p. (Orig.). (ps-7). 1992. pap. 8.98 incl. cassette (0-943351-55-3, XD 1002) Astor Bks.

—Mickey's Marching Band. Disney Studios Staff, illus. 24p. (Orig.). (ps-7). 1992. pap. 8.95 incl. cassette (0-943351-54-5, XD 1001) Astor Bks.

—Special Delivery Symphony. Warner Bros. Studios Staff, illus. 24p. 1993. pap. 7.98 incl. 20 min. cassette (0-943351-58-8, XL1001) Astor Bks.

—What's Opera Doc? Warner Bros. Studios Staff, illus. 24p. 1993. pap. 7.95 (0-943351-59-6, XL1002) Astor Bks.

Hill, Susan. Beware, Beware. Barrett, Angela, illus. LC 92-54960. 32p. (ps up). 1993. 14.95 (1-56402-245-5) Candlewick Pr.

—Glass Angels. Littlewood, Valerie & Littlewood, Valerie, illus. LC 91-58731. 96p. (gr. 3-6). 1992. 16.95 (1-56402-111-4) Candlewick Pr.

—Go Away, Bad Dreams. Julian-Ottie, Vanessa, illus. Lerner, Sharon, ed. LC 84-17759. (Illus.). 32p. (ps-2). 1985. pap. 2.25 (0-394-87222-3) Random Bks Yng Read.

—King of Kings. Lawrence, John, illus. LC 92-54624. 32p. (ps up). 1993. 14.95 (*1-56402-210-2*) Candlewick Pr.
Hill, Susan, ed. The Random House Book of Ghost Stories. Barrett, Angela, illus. 224p. (gr. 3-7). 1991. 18.95 (*0-679-81234-2*); lib. bdg. 19.99 (*0-679-91234-7*) Random Bks Yng Read.
Hill, Tom & Friedman, Donna. Pat the Stimpy: A Nitty Gritty Touchy Smelly Book. Reccardi, Chris, illus. 14p. (gr. 3 up). 1993. 9.95 (*0-448-40199-1*, G&D) Putnam Pub Group.

Hill, William E. & Hill, Jan C. Heading Southwest: Along the Santa Fe Trail. (Illus.). 32p. (Orig.). (gr. k-4). 1993. pap. 3.95 (*0-9636071-1-1*) HillHouse Pub.

HEADING SOUTHWEST: ALONG THE SANTA FE TRAIL is an educational activity book for young children in grades k-4. It presents the history of the Santa Fe Trail through an entertaining & educationally sound approach. Written in the same style as Jan & Bill's successful HEADING WEST (about the Oregon-California trails), this new book also provides youngsters with a variety of activities all of which are appropriate for their age. Basic coloring, dot to dots, map work, puzzles, figure-ground, word search, classification, art projects, a song & recipes can all be found. Children will learn while doing. All the activities are tied into the history of the Santa Fe Trail. Perfect for young children, elementary school teachers, or grandparents looking for a gift. Thirty-two pages of history come alive for children! To order contact HillHouse, 91 Wood Road, Centereach, NY 11720. 516-585-2592.

Publisher Provided Annotation.

—Heading West: An Activity Book for Children. Hill, William E. & Hill, Jan C., illus. 32p. (Orig.). (gr. k-4). 1992. pap. 3.95 (*0-9636071-0-3*) HillHouse Pub.
Hillam, Corbin. Bible Story Clip & Copy Patterns. (Illus.). 96p. (ps-3). 1992. 10.95 (*0-86653-693-0*, SS2823, Shining Star Pubns) Good Apple.
—The Big Bible Story Coloring Book. (Illus.). 240p. (ps-3). 1992. 8.95 (*0-86653-700-7*, SS2830, Shining Star Pubns) Good Apple.
—Christian Clip & Copy Time-Savers. 96p. (ps up). 1990. 10.95 (*0-86653-553-5*, SS1822, Shining Star Pubns) Good Apple.
—Jennifer of the City. Hillam, Corbin, illus. 32p. (ps-2). 1990. text ed. 5.00 (*0-570-04183-X*) Concordia.
—Jennifer of the Jungle. Hillam, Corbin, illus. 32p. (ps-2). 1990. text ed. 5.00 (*0-685-45916-0*) Concordia.
Hillbrand, Percie V. The Norwegians in America. rev. ed. LC 67-15683. (Illus.). 80p. (gr. 5 up). PLB 15.95 (*0-8225-0243-7*); pap. 5.95 (*0-8225-1041-3*) Lerner Pubns.
Hilleary, Jane K. Fletcher & the Great Big Dog. Brown, Richard, illus. 32p. (gr. k-3). 1988. 13.45 (*0-395-46761-6*) HM.
—Fletcher & the Great Big Dog. Brown, Richard, illus. 32p. (gr. k-3). 1992. pap. 4.80 (*0-395-62982-9*, Sandpiper) HM.
Hillebrand, Linda L. & Riekehof, Lottie L. The Joy of Signing Puzzle Book: Have Fun Learning to Sign. (Illus.). 57p. (Orig.). 1989. pap. 2.95 (*0-88243-676-7*, 02-0676) Gospel Pub.
Hillen, J., ed. see Hoover, Evalyn, et al.
Hillen, Judith, ed. see Hoover, Evalyn, et al.
Hillen, Judith A. Piezas y Disenos, un Mosaico de Matematicas y Ciencias. (SPA & ENG). 160p. (gr. 5-9). 1992. pap. text ed. 16.95 (*1-881431-31-2*) AIMS Educ Fnd.
Hillen, Rodolfo, ed. see High, Jackie L.
Hiller, Annie, ed. see Grimes, Rich.
Hiller, B. B. Bingo Digest. 132p. 1991. pap. 2.75 (*0-590-45276-2*) Scholastic Inc.
—Horse Crazy, No. 1. 144p. (Orig.). 1988. pap. 3.25 (*0-553-15594-6*, Skylark) Bantam.
—M-TV. (gr. 4-7). 1991. pap. 3.50 (*0-440-40451-7*) Dell.
—Rent a Third Grader. 192p. (gr. 2-4). 1988. pap. 2.75 (*0-590-40966-2*) Scholastic Inc.
—The Sacred Scroll of Death. (gr. 4-7). 1993. pap. 3.99 (*0-440-40800-8*) Dell.
—The Saddle Club, Bk. 2. 144p. (Orig.). 1988. pap. 3.25 (*0-553-15611-X*, Skylark) Bantam.
—Teenage Mutant Ninja Turtles. 1990. pap. 2.95 (*0-440-40322-7*) Dell.
—Teenage Mutant Ninja Turtles. 94p. (gr. 3-6). 1990. 7.52 (*0-685-63791-3*, BR8238) W A T Braille.

—Teenage Mutant Ninja Turtles. 94p. 1991. text ed. 7.52 (*1-56956-320-9*) W A T Braille.
Hiller, B. B., adapted by. Honey, I Blew up the Kid. LC 91-73816. (Illus.). 80p. (Orig.). (gr. 2-6). 1992. pap. 2.95 (*1-56282-139-3*) Disney Pr.
Hiller, Ilo. Introducing Birds to Young Naturalists: From Texas Parks & Wildlife Magazine. LC 89-4398. (Illus.). (gr. 6). 1989. 21.50x (*0-89096-412-2*); pap. 12.95 (*0-89096-410-6*) Tex A&M Univ Pr.
—Introducing Mammals to Young Naturalists. LC 89-35523. (Illus.). 112p. (gr. 6). 1990. 21.50x (*0-89096-427-0*); pap. 12.95 (*0-89096-428-9*) Tex A&M Univ Pr.
—Young Naturalist: From Texas Parks & Wildlife Magazine. LC 83-45107. (Illus.). 176p. (gr. 2-8). 1983. 15.95 (*0-89096-163-8*) Tex A&M Univ Pr.
Hiller, Laurie L. Visions of Wonder. Hiller, Laurie L., illus. 52p. (Orig.). (gr. 5-12). 1993. pap. text ed. 4.95 (*0-9632332-0-3*) Precision Pr.
Hillerich, Robert L. The American Heritage Picture Dictionary. Swanson, Maggie, illus. 144p. (gr. k-1). 1986. 9.70 (*0-395-42531-X*) HM.
Hillerman, Anne. Children's Guide to Santa Fe. LC 84-8782. (Illus.). 48p. (Orig.). (gr. 3 up). 1984. pap. 4.95 (*0-86534-030-7*) Sunstone Pr.
—Done in the Sun: Solar Projects for Children. Yamashita, Mina, illus. LC 83-638. 48p. (Orig.). (gr. 3-5). 1983. pap. 6.95 (*0-86534-018-8*) Sunstone Pr.
Hillerman, Tony. The Boy Who Made Dragonfly: A Zuni Myth. Grado, Janet, illus. LC 86-6996. 85p. (gr. 5 up). 1986. pap. 8.95 (*0-8263-0910-0*) U of NM Pr.
—The Fly on the Wall. 224p. (gr. 7 up). 1979. pap. 3.95 (*0-380-44156-X*) Avon.
—Listening Woman. (gr. 7 up). 1979. pap. 3.95 (*0-380-43554-3*) Avon.
Hillert, Margaret. Away Go the Boats. (Illus.). (ps-k). 1981. PLB 6.95 (*0-8136-5073-9*, TK2270); pap. 3.50 (*0-8136-5573-8*, TK2271) Modern Curr.
—The Baby Bunny. (Illus.). (ps-k). 1981. PLB 6.95 (*0-8136-5064-X*, TK2272); pap. 3.50 (*0-8136-5564-1*, TK2273) Modern Curr.
—The Ball Book. (Illus.). (ps-k). 1981. PLB 6.95 (*0-8136-5106-9*, TK2158); pap. 3.50 (*0-8136-5606-0*, TK2159) Modern Curr.
—The Birthday Car. (Illus.). (ps-k). 1966. PLB 6.95 (*0-8136-5031-3*, TK2278); pap. 3.50 (*0-8136-5531-5*, TK2279) Modern Curr.
—The Boy & the Goats. (Illus.). (ps-k). 1982. PLB 6.95 (*0-8136-5092-5*, TK2160); pap. 3.50 (*0-8136-5592-7*, TK2161) Modern Curr.
—Cinderella at the Ball. (Illus.). (ps-k). 1970. PLB 6.95 (*0-8136-5032-1*, TK2282); pap. 3.50 (*0-8136-5532-3*, TK2283) Modern Curr.
—Circus Fun. (Illus.). (ps-k). 1969. PLB 6.95 (*0-8136-5011-9*, TK2284); pap. 3.50 (*0-8136-5511-0*, TK2285) Modern Curr.
—City Fun. (Illus.). (ps-k). 1981. PLB 6.95 (*0-8136-5071-2*, TK2286); pap. 3.50 (*0-8136-5571-4*, TK2287) Modern Curr.
—Come Play with Me. (Illus.). (ps-k). 1975. PLB 6.95 (*0-8136-5036-4*, TK2292); pap. 3.50 (*0-8136-5536-6*, TK2293) Modern Curr.
—Come to School, Dear Dragon. (Illus.). (ps-k). 1985. PLB 6.95 (*0-8136-5133-6*, TK2966); pap. 3.50 (*0-8136-5633-8*) Modern Curr.
—Cookie House. (Illus.). (ps-k). 1978. PLB 6.95 (*0-8136-5012-7*, TK2290); pap. 3.50 (*0-8136-5512-9*, TK2291) Modern Curr.
—The Cow That Got Her Wish. (Illus.). (ps-2). 1981. PLB 6.95 (*0-8136-5121-2*, TK2608); pap. 3.50 (*0-8136-5621-4*, TK2607) Modern Curr.
—Four Good Friends. (Illus.). (ps-k). 1981. PLB 6.95 (*0-8136-5061-5*, TK2298); pap. 3.50 (*0-8136-5561-7*, TK2299) Modern Curr.
—Friend for Dear Dragon. (Illus.). (ps-k). 1985. PLB 6.95 (*0-8136-5136-0*, TK2972); pap. 3.50 (*0-8136-5636-2*, TK2973) Modern Curr.
—Fun Days. (Illus.). (ps-k). 1982. PLB 6.95 (*0-8136-5093-3*, TK2162); pap. 3.50 (*0-8136-5593-5*, TK2163) Modern Curr.
—Funny Baby. (Illus.). (ps-k). 1963. PLB 6.95 (*0-8136-5016-X*, K2300); pap. 3.50 (*0-685-50733-5*, TK2301) Modern Curr.
—Funny Ride. (Illus.). (ps-k). 1982. PLB 6.95 (*0-8136-5101-8*, TK2164); pap. 3.50 (*0-8136-5601-X*, TK2165) Modern Curr.
—Go to Sleep Dear Dragon. (Illus.). (ps-k). 1985. PLB 6.95 (*0-8136-5135-2*, TK2970); pap. 3.50 (*0-8136-5635-4*, TK2971) Modern Curr.
—God's Big Book. Hohag, Linda, illus. 24p. (gr. k-1). 1988. 4.99 (*0-87403-457-4*, 24-03696) Standard Pub.
—The Golden Goose. (Illus.). (ps-k). 1978. PLB 6.95 (*0-8136-5051-8*, TK2306); pap. 3.50 (*0-8136-5551-X*, TK2307) Modern Curr.
—Guess, Guess. O'Connell, Ruth, illus. 24p. (gr. k-1). 1988. 4.99 (*0-87403-456-6*, 24-03695) Standard Pub.
—Happy Birthday, Dear Dragon. (Illus.). (ps-k). 1977. PLB 6.95 (*0-8136-5021-6*, TK2308); pap. 3.50 (*0-8136-5521-8*, TK2309) Modern Curr.
—Happy Easter, Dear Dragon. (Illus.). (ps-k). 1981. PLB 6.95 (*0-8136-5022-4*, TK2310); pap. 3.50 (*0-8136-5522-6*, TK2311) Modern Curr.
—Help for Dear Dragon. (Illus.). (ps-k). 1981. PLB 6.95 (*0-8136-5131-X*, TK2962); pap. 3.50 (*0-8136-5631-1*, TK2963) Modern Curr.
—House for Little Red. (Illus.). (ps-k). 1970. PLB 6.95 (*0-8136-5013-5*, TK2312); pap. 3.50 (*0-8136-5513-7*, TK2313) Modern Curr.

—I Like Things. (Illus.). (ps-k). 1982. PLB 6.95 (*0-8136-5102-6*, TK2166); pap. 3.50 (*0-8136-5602-8*, TK2167) Modern Curr.
—I Love You, Dear Dragon. (Illus.). (ps-k). 1981. PLB 6.95 (*0-8136-5023-2*); pap. 3.50 (*0-8136-5523-4*) Modern Curr.
—I Need You, Dear Dragon. (Illus.). (ps-k). 1985. PLB 6.95 (*0-8136-5134-4*, TK2968); pap. 3.50 (*0-8136-5634-6*, TK2969) Modern Curr.
—It's Circus Time, Dear Dragon. (Illus.). (ps-k). 1985. PLB 6.95 (*0-8136-5132-8*, TK2964); pap. 3.50 (*0-8136-5632-X*, TK2965) Modern Curr.
—It's Halloween Time, Dear Dragon. (Illus.). (ps-k). 1981. PLB 6.95 (*0-8136-5024-0*, TK2318); pap. 3.50 (*0-8136-5524-2*, TK2319) Modern Curr.
—Jesus Grows Up. Endres, Helen, illus. 24p. (gr. k-1). 1988. 4.99 (*0-87403-459-0*, 24-03698) Standard Pub.
—Let's Go Dear Dragon. (Illus.). (ps-k). 1981. PLB 6.95 (*0-8136-5025-9*, TK2322); pap. 3.50 (*0-8136-5525-0*, TK2323) Modern Curr.
—Let's Have a Play. (Illus.). (ps-k). 1981. PLB 6.95 (*0-8136-5094-1*, TK2168); pap. 3.50 (*0-8136-5594-3*, TK2169) Modern Curr.
—The Little Cookie. (Illus.). (ps-k). 1981. PLB 6.95 (*0-8136-5062-3*, TK2324); pap. 3.50 (*0-8136-5562-5*, TK2325) Modern Curr.
—Little Cowboy & Big... (Illus.). (ps-k). 1981. PLB 6.95 (*0-8136-5076-3*, TK2326); pap. 3.50 (*0-8136-5576-5*, TK2327) Modern Curr.
—Little Puff. (Illus.). (ps-2). 1973. PLB 6.95 (*0-8136-5014-3*, TK2328); pap. 3.50 (*0-8136-5514-5*, TK2329) Modern Curr.
—Little Quack. (Illus.). (ps-k). 1961. PLB 6.95 (*0-8136-5044-5*, TK2330); pap. 3.50 (*0-8136-5544-7*, TK2331) Modern Curr.
—Little Red Riding Hood. (Illus.). (ps-k). 1982. PLB 6.95 (*0-8136-5095-X*, TK2170); pap. 3.50 (*0-8136-5595-1*, TK2171) Modern Curr.
—Little Runaway. (Illus.). (ps-k). 1966. PLB 6.95 (*0-8136-5052-6*, TK2334); pap. 3.50 (*0-8136-5552-8*, TK2335) Modern Curr.
—Mabel the Whale. (Illus.). (ps-2). 1958. PLB 6.95 (*0-8136-5046-1*, TK2336); pap. 3.50 (*0-8136-5546-3*, TK2337) Modern Curr.
—Magic Beans. (Illus.). (ps-k). 1966. PLB 6.95 (*0-8136-5053-4*, TK2338); pap. 3.50 (*0-8136-5553-6*, TK2339) Modern Curr.
—The Magic Nutcracker. (Illus.). (ps-k). 1981. PLB 6.95 (*0-8136-5074-7*, TK2340); pap. 3.50 (*0-8136-5574-9*, TK2341) Modern Curr.
—Merry Christmas, Dear Dragon. (Illus.). (ps-k). 1981. PLB 6.95 (*0-8136-5026-7*, TK2344); pap. 3.50 (*0-8136-5526-9*, TK2345) Modern Curr.
—Not I, Not I. (Illus.). (ps-k). 1981. PLB 6.95 (*0-8136-5063-1*, TK2350); pap. 3.50 (*0-8136-5563-3*, TK2351) Modern Curr.
—Pinocchio. (Illus.). (ps-k). 1981. PLB 6.95 (*0-8136-5103-4*, TK2172); pap. 3.50 (*0-8136-5603-6*, TK2173) Modern Curr.
—Play Ball. (Illus.). (ps-2). 1978. PLB 6.95 (*0-8136-5034-8*, TK2355); pap. 3.50 (*0-8136-5534-X*, TK2356) Modern Curr.
—Purple Pussycat. (Illus.). (ps-k). 1981. PLB 6.95 (*0-8136-5072-0*, TK2357); pap. 3.50 (*0-8136-5572-2*, TK2358) Modern Curr.
—Run to the Rainbow. (Illus.). (ps-k). 1981. PLB 6.95 (*0-8136-5065-8*, TK2361); pap. 3.50 (*0-8136-5565-X*, TK2362) Modern Curr.
—The Snow Baby. (Illus.). (ps-k). 1969. PLB 6.95 (*0-8136-5055-0*, TK2363); pap. 3.50 (*0-8136-5555-2*, TK2364) Modern Curr.
—Take a Walk, Johnny. (Illus.). (ps-2). 1981. PLB 6.95 (*0-8136-5111-5*, TK2256); pap. 3.50 (*0-8136-5611-7*, TK2257) Modern Curr.
—Three Bears. (Illus.). (ps-k). 1963. PLB 6.95 (*0-8136-5015-1*, TK2366); pap. 3.50 (*0-8136-5515-3*, TK2367) Modern Curr.
—Three Goats. (Illus.). (ps-k). 1963. PLB 6.95 (*0-8136-5054-2*, TK2368); pap. 3.50 (*0-8136-5554-4*, TK2369) Modern Curr.
—Three Little Pigs. (Illus.). (ps-k). 1963. PLB 6.95 (*0-8136-5035-6*, TK2370); pap. 3.50 (*0-8136-5535-8*, TK2371) Modern Curr.
—Tom Thumb. (Illus.). (ps-k). 1982. PLB 6.95 (*0-8136-5091-7*, TK2174); pap. 3.50 (*0-8136-5591-9*, TK2175) Modern Curr.
—Up, up & Away. (Illus.). (ps-2). 1982. PLB 6.95 (*0-8136-5096-8*, TK2176); pap. 3.50 (*0-8136-5596-X*, TK2177) Modern Curr.
—What Am I? (Illus.). (ps-k). 1981. PLB 6.95 (*0-8136-5066-6*, TK2376); pap. 3.50 (*0-8136-5566-8*, TK2377) Modern Curr.
—What Is It? (Illus.). (ps-2). 1978. PLB 6.95 (*0-8136-5056-9*, TK2378); pap. 3.50 (*0-8136-5556-0*, TK2379) Modern Curr.
—Who Goes to School? (Illus.). (ps-k). 1981. pap. 3.50 (*0-685-38662-7*, TK2383) Modern Curr.
—Who Goes to School? (Illus.). (ps-k). 1981. PLB 6.95 (*0-8136-5075-5*, TK2382); pap. 3.50 (*0-685-50736-X*, TK2383) Modern Curr.
—Why We Have Thanksgiving. (Illus.). (ps-k). 1962. PLB 6.95 (*0-8136-5104-2*, TK2384); pap. 3.50 (*0-8136-5604-4*, TK2385) Modern Curr.
—The Witch Who Went... (Illus.). (ps-k). 1981. PLB 6.95 (*0-8136-5105-0*, TK2386); pap. 3.50 (*0-8136-5605-2*, TK2387) Modern Curr.

—Yellow Boat. (Illus.). (ps-k). 1966. PLB 6.95 (0-8136-5033-X, TK2388); pap. 3.50 (0-8136-5533-1, TK2389) Modern Curr.

Hillery, Mable & Hall, Patricia. A Guide to the Use of Street-Folk-Musical Games in the Classroom: Chanting Games. rev. ed. Kendrick, John & May, Warren, illus. Freeman, Harold, Jr., intro. by. 77p. (ps-6). 1982. pap. 12.00 (0-939632-05-5) ILM.

Hillery, Mable & Simmons, Patricia M. Guide to the Use of Street-Folk-Musical Games in the Classroom: Song Games. Kendrick, John, illus. 71p. (ps-6). 1974. pap. 12.00 (0-939632-01-2) ILM.

Hilliard, Beverly Valenti see Hilliard, Dick & Valenti-Hilliard, Beverly.

Hilliard, Dick & Valenti-Hilliard, Beverly. Happenings! Collopy, George F., illus. LC 81-52715. 60p. (gr. 1 up). 1981. pap. text ed. 4.95 (0-89390-033-8) Resource Pubns.

—Surprises! Collopy, George F., illus. LC 81-52714. 64p. (Orig.). (gr. 1 up). 1981. pap. text ed. 4.95 (0-89390-031-1) Resource Pubns.

—Wonders! Collopy, George F., illus. LC 81-52713. 64p. (Orig.). (gr. 1 up). 1981. pap. text ed. 4.95 (0-89390-032-X) Resource Pubns.

Hillig, Chuck. The Magic King. Hesik, Blue, illus. LC 84-50928. 32p. (ps-2). 1984. 12.95 (0-913299-07-3, Dist. by PGW) Stillpoint.

Hillila, Bernhard, tr. from FIN. see Kaukola, Olavi.

Hillings, Phyllis. A Web of Good Manners: Grown-up Manners for Young People. Tegtmeyer, John, illus. LC 92-85125. 96p. (gr. 3 up). 1993. 14.95 (0-9634642-1-3) Manhattan Pr.

Hillis, Don. Heaven Is Out of This World. (Illus.). 47p. 1982. pap. 1.00 (0-89323-032-4) Bible Memory.

Hillis, Don W. Stories of Love that Lasts. 80p. (gr. 9-12). 1980. pap. 1.00 (0-89323-015-4) Bible Memory.

Hillman, Carole D. It's Different Now...a New Beginning. Hillman, Carole D., illus. 10p. (Orig.). 1990. pap. text ed. write for info. (0-9624257-1-0) Early Childhood.

Hillman, E. Min-Yo & the Moon Dragon. Wallner, J., illus. 1992. 14.95 (0-15-254230-2, HB Juv Bks) HarBrace.

Hillman, Priscilla. Merry Mouse Christmas ABC. Hillman, Priscilla, illus. LC 79-6586. 32p. (ps-1). 1980. pap. 4.95 (0-385-15596-4) Doubleday.

Hillman, Susan, et al. Future World. Smith, Guy, et al, illus. LC 89-42981. 48p. (gr. 4-5). 1989. PLB 17.27 (0-8368-0135-0) Gareth Stevens Inc.

Hillmann, W. Children's Bible. 95p. (ps-8). 1959. pap. 3.95 (0-8146-0120-0) Liturgical Pr.

Hills, C. A. The Second World War. (Illus.). 72p. (gr. 7-12). 1985. 19.95 (0-7134-4531-9, Pub. by Batsford UK) Trafalgar.

Hills, Gavin. Skate Boarding. LC 92-8433. (gr. 4 up). 1993. 17.50 (0-8225-2483-X) Lerner Pubns.

Hills, J. S. Magical Piece of Sand. Fitting, Devin & Fitting, Brian, illus. 32p. (ps-2). 1989. pap. 6.95 (0-923889-27-2) Inquisitors Pub.

Hills, Ken. Arab-Israeli Wars. (Illus.). 32p. (gr. 3-9). 1991. PLB 10.95 (1-85435-261-X) Marshall Cavendish.

—Crusades. (Illus.). 32p. (gr. 3-9). 1991. PLB 10.95 (1-85435-260-1) Marshall Cavendish.

—French Revolution. (Illus.). 32p. (gr. 3-9). 1988. PLB 10.95 (0-86307-934-2) Marshall Cavendish.

—Nineteen Forties. (Illus.). 47p. (gr. 6-7). 1992. PLB 22.80 (0-8114-3077-4) Raintree Steck-V.

—Nineteen Sixties. (Illus.). 47p. (gr. 6-7). 1992. PLB 22.80 (0-8114-3079-0) Raintree Steck-V.

—Nineteen Thirties. LC 91-42164. (Illus.). 47p. (gr. 6-7). 1992. PLB 22.80 (0-8114-3076-6) Raintree Steck-V.

—Vietnam. (Illus.). 32p. (gr. 3-9). 1991. PLB 10.95 (1-85435-259-8) Marshall Cavendish.

—The Voyages of Columbus. Wright, Paul, et al, illus. LC 91-7580. 32p. (gr. 3-7). 1991. 9.00 (0-679-82185-6); lib. bdg. 12.99 (0-679-92185-0) Random Bks Yng Read.

—World History. LC 93-20105. (Illus.). 96p. (Orig.). (gr. 5 up). 1993. 15.95 (1-85697-854-0); pap. 9.95 (1-85697-853-2) Kingfisher Bks.

—World War One. (Illus.). 32p. (gr. 3-9). 1988. PLB 10.95 (0-86307-931-8) Marshall Cavendish.

—World War Two. (Illus.). 32p. (gr. 3-9). 1988. PLB 10.95 (0-86307-932-6) Marshall Cavendish.

Hills, Peter B. Inspector Hare & the Black Pearls. Hills, Stephen, illus. LC 93-28977. 1994. 4.25 (0-383-03751-4) SRA Schl Grp.

—Inspector Hare & the Locked Room. Hills, Stephen, illus. LC 93-11734. 1994. 4.25 (0-383-03752-2) SRA Schl Grp.

Hills, Ron, ed. High Fives & High Hopes: Favorite Talks Especially for Youth. LC 90-81267. 150p. (Orig.). (gr. 9-12). 1990. write for info. 5.95 (0-87579-356-8) Deseret Bk.

Hillyard, Paul. Insects & Spiders. LC 93-19074. (Illus.). 1993. 12.95 (1-56458-385-6) Dorling Kindersley.

Hilston, Christine R., jt. auth. see Hilston, Paul.

Hilston, Paul & Hilston, Christine R. A Field Guide to Planet Earth: Projects for Reading Rocks, Rivers, Mountains, & the Forces That Shape Them. LC 93-8740. (Illus.). 288p. (gr. 6 up). 1993. pap. 14.95 (1-55652-198-7) Chicago Review.

Hilton, James. Good-Bye, Mr. Chips. (Illus.). (gr. 7 up). 1962. 14.95 (0-316-36420-7, Pub. by Atlantic Monthly Pr) Little.

—Goodbye, Mr. Chips. (gr. 7 up). 1969. pap. 2.95 (0-553-25613-0) Bantam.

Hilton, Kathlyn G. Come, Walk in the Woods with Me. Presutto, Josephine, illus. LC 92-72704. 32p. (gr. 7-9). 1993. 12.95 (1-880851-04-0) Greene Bark Pr.

Hilton, Nette. Andrew Jessup. Wilcox, Cathy, illus. LC 92-39799. 1993. 13.45 (0-395-66900-6) Ticknor & Fields.

—Dirty Dave. Harvey, Roland, illus. LC 89-35402. 32p. (ps-1). 1990. 12.95 (0-531-05861-1); PLB 12.99 (0-531-08461-2) Orchard Bks Watts.

—The Long Red Scarf. Margaret, illus. 32p. (ps-3). 1990. PLB 18.95 (0-87614-399-0) Carolrhoda Bks.

—Long Red Scarf. (ps-3). 1992. pap. 5.95 (0-87614-561-6) Carolrhoda Bks.

—Prince Lachlan. James, Ann, illus. LC 89-22846. 32p. (ps-1). 1990. 13.95 (0-531-05863-8); PLB 13.99 (0-531-08463-9) Orchard Bks Watts.

—A Proper Little Lady. Wilcox, Cathy, illus. LC 89-35399. 32p. (ps-1). 1990. 12.95 (0-531-05860-3); PLB 12.99 (0-531-08460-4) Orchard Bks Watts.

Hilton, Suzanne. A Capital Capital City, 1790-1814. LC 91-31340. (Illus.). 160p. (gr. 4 up). 1992. SBE 14.95 (0-689-31641-0, Atheneum Child Bk) Macmillan Child Grp.

—Miners, Merchants, & Maids. 1994. PLB write for info. (0-8050-2998-2) Walker & Co.

—The World of Young Andrew Jackson. Lynn, Patricia, illus. (gr. 5-8). 1988. 12.95 (0-8027-6814-8); PLB 13.85 (0-8027-6815-6) Walker & Co.

—The World of Young George Washington. Bock, William S., illus. LC 86-13296. 112p. (gr. 5-9). 1987. 12.95 (0-8027-6657-9); PLB 12.85 (0-8027-6658-7) Walker & Co.

—The World of Young Herbert Hoover. Steins, Deborah, illus. (gr. 5-8). 1987. 12.95 (0-8027-6708-7); PLB 13.85 (0-8027-6709-5) Walker & Co.

—The World of Young Tom Jefferson. Bock, William S., illus. 96p. (gr. 3-6). 1986. 12.95 (0-8027-6621-8); lib. bdg. 12.85 (0-8027-6622-6) Walker & Co.

Hilts, Len. Quanah Parker: Warrior for Freedom, Ambassador for Peace. LC 87-8488. 148p. (gr. 3-7). 1987. 12.95 (0-15-200565-X, Gulliver Bks) HarBrace.

—Quanah Parker: Warrior for Freedom, Ambassador for Peace. (gr. 4-7). 1992. pap. 4.95 (0-15-264447-4) HarBrace.

—Timmy O-Dowd & the Big Ditch: A Story of the Glory Days on the Old Erie Canal. 91p. (gr. 3-7). 1988. 13.95 (0-15-200606-0, Gulliver Bks) HarBrace.

Hilty, Hiram H. By Land & by Sea: Quakers Confront Slavery & Its Aftermath in North Carolina. LC 92-82623. (Illus.). 156p. (Orig.). (gr. 9-12). 1993. pap. 13.00 (0-942727-22-3) NC Yrly Pubns Bd.

Hilvosky, Judy, ed. see Hughes, R. K.

Himeda, Clark K. The Official Martian-English Handbook: Be an Expert in "Martian" Without Studying. 37p. (Orig.). (gr. 1-6). 1991. pap. 3.50 (0-9621721-0-3) C K Himeda.

Himmelman, John. Amanda & the Witch Switch. (ps-3). 1987. pap. 4.99 (0-14-050635-7, Puffin) Puffin Bks.

—The Clover County Carrot Contest. Himmelman, John, illus. 48p. (ps-3). 1991. PLB 8.98 (0-671-69637-8); pap. 3.95 (0-671-69641-6) Silver Pr.

—The Day-Off Machine. Brook, Bonnie, ed. Himmelman, John, illus. 48p. (ps-3). 1990. PLB 8.98 (0-671-69635-1); pap. 3.95 (0-671-69639-4) Silver Pr.

—Fix-It Family Series, 4 vols. Himmelman, John, illus. 192p. (ps-3). 1991. Set. PLB 35.92 (0-671-31232-4); Set. PLB 26.94s.p. (0-685-46993-X); Set. pap. 15.80 (0-671-31233-2) Silver Pr.

—The Great Leaf Blast-Off. Brook, Bonnie, ed. Himmelman, John, illus. 48p. (ps-3). 1990. PLB 8.98 (0-671-69636-3); pap. 3.95 (0-671-69638-6) Silver Pr.

—A Guest Is a Guest. Himmelman, John, illus. LC 90-43020. 32p. (ps-2). 1991. 13.95 (0-525-44720-2, DCB) Dutton Child Bks.

—Ibis: A True Whale Story. 1990. 12.95 (0-590-42848-9) Scholastic Inc.

—Montigue on the High Seas. (Illus.). 32p. (ps-3). 1990. pap. 3.95 (0-14-050789-2, Puffin) Puffin Bks.

—Simpson Snail Sings. (Illus.). 48p. (gr. k-2). 1992. 11.00 (0-525-44978-7, DCB) Dutton Child Bks.

—The Super Camper Caper. Himmelman, John, illus. 48p. (ps-3). 1991. PLB 8.98 (0-671-69636-X); pap. 3.95 (0-671-69640-8) Silver Pr.

—The Ups & Downs of Simpson Snail. Himmelman, John, illus. LC 89-30547. 48p. (ps-3). 1989. 9.95 (0-525-44542-0, DCB) Dutton Child Bks.

—Wanted: Perfect Parents. LC 93-22201. (Illus.). 32p. (ps-3). 1993. PLB 13.95 (0-8167-3028-8); pap. write for info. (0-8167-3029-6) BridgeWater.

Hincks, J. The Rourke Dinosaur Dictionary. (Illus.). 96p. (gr. k-8). 1987. PLB 26.60 (0-86592-049-4) Rourke Corp.

Hinde, J. S., jt. auth. see Hinde, R. A.

Hinde, R. A. & Hinde, J. S. Instinct & Intelligence. 3rd ed. Head, J. J., ed. LC 87-70404. (Illus.). 16p. (gr. 10 up). 1987. pap. 2.75 (0-89278-063-0, 45-9663) Carolina Biological.

Hinden, Stan, jt. auth. see Wyatt, Elaine.

Hinding, Andrea, ed. Feminism: Opposing Viewpoints. LC 86-3096. (Illus.). 32p. (gr. 9 up). 1986. PLB 17.95 (0-89908-388-9); pap. 9.95 (0-89908-363-3) Greenhaven.

Hindley. Counting Book. (gr. k-2). 1979. 6.95 (0-86020-361-1, Usborne-Hayes); PLB 11.96 (0-88110-066-8) EDC.

—Knights & Castles. (gr. 4-6). 1976. (Usborne-Hayes); PLB 13.96 (0-88110-100-1); pap. 6.95 (0-86020-068-X) EDC.

Hindley & Rawson. How Your Body Works. (gr. 2-5). 1975. (Usborne-Hayes); PLB 13.96 (0-88110-113-3); pap. 6.95 (0-86020-198-8) EDC.

Hindley & Rumbelow. Detection. (gr. 4-6). 1981. pap. 5.95 (0-86020-124-4, Usborne-Hayes) EDC.

Hindley, J., jt. auth. see Curtis, A.

Hindley, J., jt. auth. see Travis, F.

Hindley, J., et al. Time Traveller's Omnibus. (Illus.). 32p. 1977. text ed. 17.95 (0-86020-222-4) EDC.

Hindley, Judy. Funny Walks. Ayliffe, Alex, illus. LC 93-28446. 32p. (ps-2). 1993. PLB 13.95 (0-8167-3313-9); pap. 3.95t (0-8167-3314-7) Troll Assocs.

—How Many Twos? (ps). 1992. 14.00 (0-385-30661-X) Doubleday.

—Into the Jungle. Epps, Melanie, illus. 1994. write for info. (1-56402-423-7) Candlewick Pr.

—Maybe It's a Pirate. Young, Selina, illus. LC 92-7261. 32p. (ps-3). 1992. 14.95 (1-56566-016-1) Thomasson-Grant.

—Mrs. Mary Malarky's Seven Cats. Teasdale, Denise, illus. LC 88-25873. 32p. (ps-2). 1990. 12.95 (0-531-05822-0); PLB 12.99 (0-531-08422-1) Orchard Bks Watts.

—A Piece of String Is a Wonderful Thing. Chamberlain, Margaret, illus. LC 92-53137. 32p. (gr. k-3). 1993. 14.95 (1-56402-147-5) Candlewick Pr.

—The Sleepy Book: A Lullaby. Aggs, Patrice, illus. LC 91-15787. 32p. (ps-1). 1992. 12.95 (0-531-05971-5); lib. bdg. 12.99 (0-531-08571-6) Orchard Bks Watts.

—Soft & Noisy. Aggs, Patrice, illus. LC 91-39110. 32p. (ps). 1992. 13.95 (1-56282-224-1); PLB 13.89 (1-56282-225-X) Hyprn Child.

—The Tree. Wisenfeld, Alison, illus. LC 89-16105. 32p. (gr. k-3). 1990. 13.95 (0-517-57630-9, Crown); PLB 14.99 (0-517-57669-4) Crown Pub Group.

—Uncle Harold & the Green Hat. Utton, Peter, illus. 26p. (ps-3). 1991. bds. 13.95 (0-374-38030-9) FS&G.

—Zoom on a Broom: Six Fun-Filled Stories. Goffe, Toni, illus. LC 92-53100. 72p. (gr. k-3). 1992. 10.95 (1-85697-826-5) Kingfisher Bks.

Hindley, Judy & Reyes, Gregg. Once There Was a Knight & You Can Be One too! Bartelt, Robert, illus. LC 87-20485. 32p. (ps-2). 1988. lib. bdg. 5.99 (0-394-99007-2) Random Bks Yng Read.

Hindman, Darwin A. Eighteen Hundred Riddles, Enigmas & Conundrums. 159p. (Orig.). (gr. 4 up). 1963. pap. 3.50 (0-486-21059-6) Dover.

Hindman, Sandra. Sealed in Parchment: Rereadings of Knighthood in the Illuminated Manuscripts of Chretien de Troyes. LC 93-5300. (Illus.). 1994. write for info. (0-226-34155-0); pap. write for info. (0-226-34156-9) U Ch Pr.

Hinds, Bill. Buzz Beamer's Out of This World Series. (Illus.). (gr. 3-7). 1991. pap. 3.95 (0-316-36451-7, Spts Illus Kids) Little.

—Buzz Beamer's Radical Olympics. Hinds, Bill, illus. 32p. (gr. 3-7). 1992. pap. 4.95 (0-316-36452-5, Spts Illus Kids) Little.

—Buzz Beamer's Radical Sports. (gr. 4-7). 1990. pap. 3.95 (0-316-36448-7, Spts Illus Kids) Little.

Hinds, P. Mignon. Baby Calf. (ps-1). 1990. write for info. (0-307-12605-6) Western Pub.

—Baby Pig. (ps-1). 1990. write for info. (0-307-12606-4) Western Pub.

Hine, Darlene C. From the Scottsboro Case to the Breaking of Baseball's Color Barrier, 1931-1947. LC 93-16016. (Illus.). 112p. (gr. 9 up). 1994. 18.95 (0-7910-2251-X, Am Art Analog); pap. 7.95 (0-7910-2677-9, Am Art Analog) Chelsea Hse.

Hines, Anna. Boys Are Yucko! (gr. 4-7). 1990. pap. 2.95 (0-590-43109-9) Scholastic Inc.

Hines, Anna C. Maybe a Band-Aid Will Help. Hines, Anna C., illus. LC 84-1533. 24p. (ps-1). 1984. 8.95 (0-525-44115-8, 0869-260, DCB) Dutton Child Bks.

Hines, Anna G. Big Like Me. LC 88-18772. (Illus.). 32p. (ps up). 1989. 15.00 (0-688-08354-4); PLB 13.93 (0-688-08355-2) Greenwillow.

—Come to the Meadow. Hines, Anna G., illus. LC 83-14408. 32p. (ps-3). 1984. 12.95 (0-89919-227-0, Clarion Bks) Hm.

—Daddy Makes the Best Spaghetti. Hines, Anna G., illus. LC 85-13993. (ps-1). 1986. 13.45 (0-89919-388-9, Clarion Bks) HM.

—Daddy Makes the Best Spaghetti. Hines, Anna G., illus. LC 85-13993. 32p. (ps-1). 1988. pap. 4.95 (0-89919-794-9, Clarion Bks) HM.

—Gramma's Walk. LC 92-30085. 32p. (ps up). 1993. 14.00 (0-688-11480-6); PLB 13.93 (0-688-11481-4) Greenwillow.

—Grandma Gets Grumpy. Hines, Anna G., illus. LC 87-17874. (ps-1). 1988. 13.95 (0-89919-529-6, Clarion Bks) HM.

—Grandma Gets Grumpy. Hines, Anna G., illus. LC 87-17874. 32p. (ps-1). 1990. pap. 4.80 (0-395-52595-0) HM.

—The Greatest Picnic in the World. Giblin, James, ed. Hines, Anna G., illus. 32p. 1991. 13.45 (0-395-55266-4, Clarion Bks) HM.

—I'll Tell You What They Say. Hines, Anna G., illus. LC 86-4743. 24p. (ps-1). 1987. 10.75 (0-688-06486-8); PLB 11.88 (0-688-06487-6) Greenwillow.

—It's Just Me, Emily. Hines, Anna G., illus. (ps-1). 1987. 12.95 (0-89919-487-7, Clarion Bks) HM.

—It's Just Me, Emily. 1989. pap. 4.95 (0-89919-853-8, Clarion Bks) HM.

—Jackie's Lunch Box. LC 90-39715. (Illus.). 24p. (ps up).
1991. 13.95 (0-688-09693-X); PLB 13.88
(0-688-09694-8) Greenwillow.
—Maybe a Band-Aid Will Help. LC 84-1533. (Illus.).
24p. (ps-1). 1990. pap. 3.95 (0-525-44561-7, DCB)
Dutton Child Bks.
—Moompa, Toby, & Bomp. Hines, Anna G., illus. LC 92-
5667. 32p. (ps-1). 1993. 14.95 (0-395-61301-9, Clarion
Bks) HM.
—Moon's Wish. Hines, Anna G., illus. 32p. (ps-1). 1992.
14.45 (0-395-58114-1, Clarion Bks) HM.
—Remember the Butterflies. Hines, Anna G., illus. LC
90-3536. 32p. (ps-2). 1991. 12.95 (0-525-44679-6,
DCB) Dutton Child Bks.
—Rumble Thumble Boom! LC 91-31808. (Illus.). 24p.
(ps-4). 1992. 14.00 (0-688-10911-X); PLB 13.93
(0-688-10912-8) Greenwillow.
—The Secret Keeper. LC 89-34618. (Illus.). 24p. (ps up)
1990. 12.95 (0-688-08945-3); PLB 12.88
(0-688-08946-1) Greenwillow.
—Tell Me Your Best Thing. Ritz, Karen, illus. LC 91-
7833. 124p. (gr. 2-4). 1991. 13.95 (0-525-44734-2,
DCB) Dutton Child Bks.
—Tell Me Your Best Thing. Ritz, Karen, illus. 128p. (gr.
2-5). 1994. pap. 3.99 (0-14-036447-1) Puffin Bks.
—They Really Like Me! LC 87-24211. (Illus.). 24p. (ps
up). 1989. 11.95 (0-688-07733-1); PLB 11.88
(0-688-07734-X) Greenwillow.
Hines, Donald M. The Forgotten Tribes: Oral Tales of
the Teninos & Adjacent Mid-Columbia River Indian
Nations. 142p. 1991. pap. 10.95 (0-9629539-0-3)
Great Eagle Pub.
Hines, Gary. The Day of the High Climber. Hines, Anna
G., illus. LC 93-12254. 32p. (ps-up). 1993. write for
info. (0-688-11494-6); PLB write for info.
(0-688-11495-4) Greenwillow.
—Flying Firefighters. Hines, Anna G., illus. LC 92-
35500. 1993. 14.95 (0-395-61197-0, Clarion Bks) HM.
—A Ride in the Crummy. Hines, Anna G., illus. LC 90-
30848. 24p. (ps-1). 1991. 13.95 (0-688-09691-3);
PLB 13.88 (0-688-09692-1) Greenwillow.
Hines, Jane B. Kentucky Boy. Graves, Helen, ed. Taylor,
Neil, illus. LC 86-40281. 155p. (Orig.). (gr. 4-8). 1986.
pap. 7.95 (1-55523-033-4) Winston-Derek.
Hines, Sharon R. & Hecht, Joyce C. Food for Wet
Fingers. Reyes, Eric S., illus. 28p. (Orig.). (gr. 7-12).
1981. pap. 3.00 (0-941904-02-4) Hot Water Pubs.
Hinke, George, illus. Christmas Memories: A Journal &
Photographic Record Book. 48p. 1993. 17.95
(0-8249-8567-2, Ideals Child) Hambleton-Hill.
Hinkle, Don, ed. see Douglas-Wiggins, Kate.
Hinkle, Don, ed. see Ollivant, Alfred.
Hinkle, Don, ed. see Pyle, Howard.
Hinshaw, Mary E. Quaker Adventures: Three Hundred
Years in Carolina. (Illus.). 74p. (Orig.). (gr. 5-7). 1971.
pap. 1.50x (0-942727-01-0) NC Yrly Pubns Bd.
Hinshaw, Seth B. Carolina Quakers. (Illus.). 74p. (Orig.).
(gr. 5-7). 1971. pap. 1.50x (0-942727-15-0) NC Yrly
Pubns Bd.
Hinsley, Sandra. Brain Gym Surfer. Corvey, Linda, illus.
6.00 (0-685-64789-7, 5) Edu-Kinesthetics.
Hinton, S. E. The Outsiders. 160p. (gr. k up). 1968. pap.
3.99 (0-440-96769-4, LFL) Dell.
—The Outsiders. (gr. 7 up). 16.75 (0-8446-6372-7) Peter
Smith.
—Rumble Fish. LC 75-8004. 112p. (gr. 7 up). 1975. pap.
13.95 (0-385-28675-9) Delacorte.
—Taming the Star Runner. LC 88-7065. 144p. (gr. 7 up).
1988. pap. 14.95 (0-440-50058-3) Delacorte.
—Taming the Star Runner. (gr. 7 up) 1989. pap. 3.99
(0-440-20479-8, LFL) Dell.
—Tex. 192p. (gr. k up). 1989. pap. 3.99 (0-440-97850-5,
LFL) Dell.
—That Was Then, This Is Now. 224p. (gr. k up). 1989.
pap. 3.99 (0-440-98652-4, LFL) Dell.
Hinton, Susie E. Outsiders. (gr. 7 up). 1967. 13.00
(0-670-53257-6) Viking Child Bks.
—That Was Then, This Is Now. Siegel, Hal, illus. (gr. 7
up). 1971. 13.95 (0-670-69798-2) Viking Child Bks.
—That Was Then, This Is Now. (gr. 7 up). 1989. 18.00
(0-8446-6371-9) Peter Smith.
Hinton, Wayne K. Utah: Unusual Beginning to Unique
Present. (Illus.). 192p. (gr. 7 up). 1988. 29.95
(0-89781-247-6) Windsor Pubns Inc.
Hintz, Martin. Argentina. LC 85-2638. (Illus.). 127p. (gr.
4-6). 1985. PLB 26.60 (0-516-02752-2) Childrens.
—Chile. LC 84-23104. (Illus.). 128p. (gr. 5-9). 1985. PLB
26.60 (0-516-02755-7) Childrens.
—Denmark. LC 93-35487. 1994. write for info.
(0-516-02620-8) Childrens.
—Finland. LC 82-17856. (Illus.). 128p. (gr. 5-9). 1983.
PLB 26.60 (0-516-02764-6) Childrens.
—Ghana. LC 86-29935. (Illus.). 128p. (gr. 5-9). 1987.
PLB 26.60 (0-516-02773-5) Childrens.
—Hungary. LC 88-10899. (Illus.). 128p. (gr. 5-9). 1988.
PLB 26.60 (0-516-02707-7) Childrens.
—Morocco. LC 84-23269. (Illus.). 128p. (gr. 5-9). 1985.
PLB 26.60 (0-516-02774-3) Childrens.
—Norway. LC 82-9400. (Illus.). 128p. (gr. 5-9). 1982. PLB 26.
60 (0-516-02780-8) Childrens.
—Switzerland. LC 86-9581. (Illus.). 128p. (gr. 5-9). 1986.
PLB 26.60 (0-516-02790-5) Childrens.
—West Germany. LC 82-17882. (Illus.). 128p. (gr. 5-9).
1983. PLB 26.60 (0-516-02793-X) Childrens.
Hintze, Barbara. Mary: Mother of Jesus. Padgett, James
R., illus. (gr. 1-6). 1977. bds. 5.95 (0-8054-4232-4,
4242-32) Broadman.

Hinz, Martin. Sweden. LC 85-2643. 128p. (gr. 5-9).
1985. PLB 26.60 (0-516-02788-3) Childrens.
Hipp, Earl. Feed Your Head: Some Excellent Stuff on
Being Yourself. Hanson, L. K., illus. 137p. (gr. 6-12).
1991. pap. 10.00 perfect bdg. (0-89486-755-5, T5034)
Hazelden.
—Fighting Invisible Tigers: A Stress Management Guide
for Teens. Galbraith, Judy, intro. by. LC 85-80632.
(Illus.). 120p. (Orig.). (gr. 6-12). 1985. pap. 9.95
(0-915793-04-0) Free Spirit Pub.
—The First Step - Humility. Yencho, Mike, illus. 30p.
(gr. 9-12). 1992. pap. 2.50 (0-89486-624-9) Hazelden.
—The Second Step - Hope. Yencho, Mike, illus. 28p. (gr.
9-12). 1992. pap. 2.50 (0-89486-642-7) Hazelden.
—The Third Step - POWER. Yencho, Mike, illus. 35p.
(gr. 9-12). 1992. pap. 2.50 (0-89486-643-5) Hazelden.
Hippely, Hilary H. The Crimson Ribbon. McAllister-
Stammen, Joellen, illus. LC 93-35214. 1994. write for
info. (0-399-22542-0, Putnam) Putnam Pub Group.
—September Song. Baker, Leslie, illus. LC 93-32625. (gr.
5 up). 1995. write for info. (0-399-22646-X, Putnam)
Putnam Pub Group.
Hirabayashi, Liane. Japanese Americans Struggle for
Equality. LC 92-14633. 1992. 22.60 (0-86593-183-6);
16.95s.p. (0-685-59713-X) Rourke Corp.
Hirano, Cathy, tr. see Kaizuki, Kiyonori.
Hirashima, Jean, illus. Wee Mouse's Peekaboo House.
LC 89-64279. 14p. (ps). 1991. bds. 3.99
(0-679-80786-1) Random Bks Yng Read.
Hirate, Susan H. & Kawaura, Noriko. Nihongo Daisuki!
Japanese Language Activities for Children. LC 89-
81822. (JPN & ENG., Illus.). 208p. (gr. k-6). 1990.
tchr's ed. 19.95 (0-935848-82-7) Bess Pr.
Hird, Nancy E. Marty's Monster. Damon, Valerie, illus.
48p. (Orig.). (gr. 1-3). 1993. pap. 3.99 (0-7847-0098-2,
24-03948) Standard Pub.
Hirokawa, Ryuichi. Children of the World: Greece. LC
87-42581. (Illus.). 64p. (gr. 5-6). 1987. PLB 19.93
(1-55532-269-7) Gareth Stevens Inc.
Hirokazu Miyazaki. Croc & the Baby Tree. Clements,
Andrew, adapted by. Hirokazu Miyazaki, illus. LC 91-
41719. 28p. (gr. k up). 1993. Repr. of 1990 ed. 14.95
(0-88708-224-6) Picture Bk Studio.
Hirsch, Charles. Taxation. LC 92-5198. (Illus.). 48p. (gr.
5-6). 1992. PLB 21.34 (0-8114-7356-2) Raintree
Steck-V.
Hirsch, Christian, jt. ed. see Maletsky, Evan.
Hirsch, Hope, jt. auth. see Hirsch, Phil.
Hirsch, Karen. Becky. Egenberger, Carl, illus. LC 80-
27619. 40p. (gr. 1-4). 1981. PLB 13.50
(0-87614-144-0) Carolrhoda Bks.
—Ellen Anders on Her Own. LC 93-13350. (Illus.). 96p.
(gr. 3-7). 1994. SBE 13.95 (0-02-743975-5, Macmillan
Child Bk) Macmillan Child Grp.
Hirsch, Linda. You're Going Out There a Kid, but You're
Coming Back a Star. Wallner, John, illus. 128p.
(Orig.). (gr. 3-7). 1984. pap. 2.25 (0-553-15272-6,
Skylark) Bantam.
Hirsch, Lynn. Do You Know Where I Am? Hirsch, Lynn
A., illus. LC 92-11189. 1992. 4.99 (0-517-07394-3,
Pub. by Derrydale Bks) Outlet Bk Co.
Hirsch, Lynn A., illus. Count With Me: One, Two,
Three. 32p. (ps-k). 1992. 4.99 (0-517-07395-1, Pub. by
Derrydale Bks) Outlet Bk Co.
—Have You Met the Alphabet? 32p. (ps-k). 1992. 4.99
(0-517-07393-5, Pub. by Derrydale Bks) Outlet Bk Co.
Hirsch, Phil. One Hundred & One Hamburger Jokes.
96p. (gr. 4-7). 1986. pap. 1.95 (0-590-40374-5)
Scholastic Inc.
—One Hundred One Dinosaur Jokes. (Illus.). 96p. (gr. 3
up). 1989. pap. 1.95 (0-590-41691-X) Scholastic Inc.
Hirsch, Phil & Hirsch, Hope. One Hundred & One Pet
Jokes. Eaton, Tom, illus. 96p. (Orig.). (gr. 3-7). 1981.
pap. 1.95 (0-590-30380-5, Schol Pap) Scholastic Inc.
Hirsch, Virginia R. Heart Country Destiny: Twenty
Poems by the Heart Country Lady. 28p. (Orig.). 1990.
pap. 4.00 (0-9616334-4-1) Heart Ctry Pubns.
—Heart Country Tennessee: A Tribute to the Tennessee
Songmaker. rev. ed. LC 85-82468. 80p. (gr. 5 up).
1986. pap. 5.00 (0-9616334-0-9) Heart Ctry Pubns.
Hirschfelder, Arlene. Happily May I Walk: American
Indians & Alaska Natives Today. LC 85-43349. 160p.
(gr. 5 up). 1986. SBE 14.95 (0-684-18624-1, Scribners
Young Read) Macmillan Child Grp.
Hirschfelder, Arlene & Singer, Beverly R. Rising Voices:
Writings of Young Native Americans. LC 92-12). 1993.
pap. 3.99 (0-8041-1167-7) Ivy Books.
Hirschfelder, Arlene B. & Singer, Beverly R., eds. Rising
Voices: Writings of Young Native Americans. LC 91-
32083. 128p. (gr. 7 up). 1992. SBE 12.95
(0-684-19207-1, Scribners Young Read) Macmillan
Child Grp.
Hirschi & Bauer. Save Our Forests. 1993. pap. 9.95
(0-385-31127-3) Dell.
—Save Our Oceans & Coasts. (gr. 4 up). 1993. pap. 9.95
(0-385-31126-5) Dell.
Hirschi & Burrell. Who Lives in the Mountains? (gr.
5-8). 1989. 9.95 (0-399-21900-5, Putnam) Putnam Pub
Group.
—Who Lives on the Prairie? (gr. 5-8). 1989. 9.95
(0-399-21901-3, Putnam) Putnam Pub Group.
Hirschi, E. & Bauer, P. Save Our Forests. 1993. 17.95
(0-385-31077-3) Delacorte.
Hirschi, Ron. Desert. 1992. 13.00 (0-553-08012-1, Little
Rooster); pap. 4.99 (0-553-35497-3, Little Rooster)
Bantam.

—Fall. Mangelsen, Thomas D., photos by. LC 90-19595.
(Illus.). 32p. (ps-3). 1991. 14.00 (0-525-65053-9,
Cobblehill Bks) Dutton Child Bks.
—Forest. (ps-3). 1991. 12.00 (0-553-07469-5); pap. 4.99
(0-553-35213-X) Bantam.
—Harvest Song. Haeffele, Deborah, illus. LC 90-27009.
32p. (ps-3). 1991. 13.95 (0-525-65067-9, Cobblehill
Bks) Dutton Child Bks.
—Loon Lake. Cox, Daniel J., photos by. LC 90-34396.
(Illus.). 32p. (ps-3). 1991. 13.95 (0-525-65046-6,
Cobblehill Bks) Dutton Child Bks.
—Mountain. 1992. 13.00 (0-553-07998-0, Little Rooster);
pap. 4.99 (0-553-35495-7, Little Rooster) Bantam.
—The Mountain Bluebird. LC 88-32663. (Illus.). (gr. 5
up). 1989. 14.95 (0-525-65010-5, Cobblehill Bks)
Dutton Child Bks.
—Ocean. (ps-3). 1991. 12.00 (0-553-07470-9); pap. 4.99
(0-553-35214-8) Bantam.
—Save Our Forests. Bauer, Erwin & Bauer, Peggy, photos
by. LC 92-37385. (Illus.). 1992. write for info.
(0-553-09521-8); pap. write for info. (0-553-37239-4)
Bantam.
—Save Our Forests. (gr. 4-7). 1993. 17.95
(0-385-31076-5) Delacorte.
—Save Our Oceans & Coasts. Bauer, Erwin A. & Bauer,
Peggy, photos by. LC 92-37384. (gr. 5 up). 1993. write
for info. (0-553-09520-X) Bantam.
—Save Our Prairies & Grasslands. Bauer, Erwin & Bauer,
Peggy, photos by. LC 93-4985. (Illus.). 1994. 17.95
(0-385-31149-4); pap. 9.95 (0-385-31199-0) Delacorte.
—Save Our Wetlands. Bauer, Erwin & Bauer, Peggy,
photos by. LC 93-4984. (Illus.). 1994. 17.95
(0-385-31152-4); pap. 9.95 (0-385-31197-4) Delacorte.
—Seya's Song. Bergum, Constance R., illus. LC 92-5029.
32p. (ps up). 1992. text ed. 14.95 (0-912365-62-5)
Sasquatch Bks.
—Seya's Song. Bergum, Connie, illus. 32p. (gr. 1 up).
1993. pap. 7.95 (0-912365-91-9) Sasquatch Bks.
—Spring. LC 89-49039. (Illus.). (ps-3). 1990. 13.95
(0-525-65042-8, Cobblehill Bks) Dutton Child Bks.
—Summer. Mangelsen, Thomas D., photos by. LC 90-
19596. (Illus.). 32p. (ps-3). 1991. 13.95
(0-525-65054-7, Cobblehill Bks) Dutton Child Bks.
—A Time for Babies. Mangelsen, Thomas D., photos by.
LC 92-21409. (Illus.). 32p. (ps-3). 1993. 13.99
(0-525-65095-4, Cobblehill Bks) Dutton Child Bks.
—A Time for Sleeping. Mangelsen, Thomas D., photos
by. LC 92-21408. (Illus.). 32p. (ps-3). 1993. 13.99
(0-525-65128-4, Cobblehill Bks) Dutton Child Bks.
—What Is a Bird? Walker, Galen B., photos by. (Illus.).
(ps-4). 1987. 10.95 (0-8027-6720-6); PLB 11.85
(0-8027-6721-4) Walker & Co.
—What Is a Cat? Younker, Linda Q., illus. 32p. (gr. 1-3).
1991. 13.95 (0-8027-8122-5); PLB 14.85
(0-8027-8123-3) Walker & Co.
—What Is a Horse? Younker, Linda Q., photos by.
(Illus.). 32p. (ps-4). 1989. 11.95 (0-8027-6876-8); PLB
12.85 (0-8027-6877-6) Walker & Co.
—Where Are My Bears? (ps-3). 1992. 16.00
(0-553-07805-4); pap. 8.00 (0-553-35473-6) Bantam.
—Where Are My Prairie Dogs & Black-Footed Ferrets?
(ps-3). 1992. pap. 8.00 (0-553-35471-X) Bantam.
—Where Are My Puffins, Whales & Seals? (ps-3). 1992.
16.00 (0-553-07803-8); pap. 8.00 (0-553-35472-8)
Bantam.
—Where Are My Swans, Whooping Cranes & Singing
Loons? (ps-3). 1992. pap. 8.00 (0-553-35470-1)
Bantam.
—Where Do Birds Live? Walker, Galen B., photos by.
(Illus.). (ps-4). 1987. 10.95 (0-8027-6722-2); PLB 11.
85 (0-8027-6723-0) Walker & Co.
—Where Do Cats Live? Younker, Linda Q., illus. 32p.
(gr. 1-3). 1991. 13.95 (0-8027-8109-8); PLB 14.85
(0-8027-8110-1) Walker & Co.
—Where Do Horses Live? 1989. 11.95 (0-8027-6878-4);
lib. bdg. 12.85 (0-8027-6879-2) Walker & Co.
—Winter. LC 89-23935. (Illus.). (ps-3). 1990. 14.00
(0-525-65026-1, Cobblehill Bks) Dutton Child Bks.
Hirschland, Roger. How Animals Care for Their Babies.
Crump, Donald J., ed. (Illus.). 32p. (ps-3). 1987. Set.
13.95 (0-87044-678-9); Set. lib. bdg. 16.55
(0-87044-683-5) Natl Geog.
Hirschler, Gertrude, tr. see Lehmann, Asher.
Hirsh, Marilyn. I Love Hanukkah. Hirsh, Marilyn, illus.
LC 84-497. 32p. (ps-3). 1984. reinforced bdg. 13.95
(0-8234-0525-7); pap. 5.95 (0-8234-0622-9) Holiday.
—I Love Hanukkah. Hirsh, Marilyn, illus. (gr. k-3). 1989.
incl. cass. 19.95 (0-87499-131-5); pap. 12.95 incl. cass.
(0-87499-130-7); Set; incl. 4 bks., cass., & guide. pap.
27.95 (0-87499-132-3) Live Oak Media.
—Joseph Who Loved the Sabbath. Grebu, Devis, illus.
32p. (ps-3). 1988. pap. 3.95 (0-14-050670-5, Puffin)
Puffin Bks.
—Potato Pancakes All Around: A Hanukkah Tale.
(Illus.). 34p. (gr. k-3). 1982. pap. 6.95 (0-8276-0217-0)
JPS Phila.
Hirsh, Phil. One Hundred One Fast Funny Food Jokes.
Orehek, Don, illus. 96p. (Orig.). (gr. 4-6). 1987. pap.
1.95 (0-590-32421-7) Scholastic Inc.
Hirst, Robin & Hirst, Sally. My Place in Space. Harvey,
Roland & Levine, Joe, illus. LC 89-37893. 40p. (ps-2).
1990. 13.95 (0-531-05859-X); PLB 13.99
(0-531-08459-0) Orchard Bks Watts.
—My Place in Space. Harvey, Roland & Levine, Joe,
illus. LC 89-37893. 40p. (ps-2). 1992. pap. 5.95
(0-531-07030-1) Orchard Bks Watts.
Hirst, Sally, jt. auth. see Hirst, Robin.
Hirt-Manheimer, Judith, jt. auth. see Techner, David.

Hisa, Kunihiko & Johnson, Sylvia A. The Dinosaur Family Tree. (Illus.). 64p. (gr. 4 up). 1990. PLB 17.50 (0-8225-2203-9) Lerner Pubns.
—How Did Dinosaurs Live? (Illus.). 64p. (gr. 4 up). 1990. PLB 17.50 (0-8225-2202-0) Lerner Pubns.
—What Were Dinosaurs? (Illus.). 64p. (gr. 4 up). 1990. PLB 17.50 (0-8225-2201-2) Lerner Pubns.
Hisako Aoki. Santa's Favorite Story. Gantschev, Ivan, illus. 64p. 1991. pap. 4.95 (0-590-44454-9, Blue Ribbon Bks) Scholastic Inc.
Hiscock, Bruce. The Big Rock. Hiscock, Bruce, illus. LC 87-31834. 32p. (gr. 1-5). 1988. RSBE 13.95 (0-689-31402-7, Atheneum Child Bk) Macmillan Child Grp.
—The Big Storm. Hiscock, Bruce, illus. LC 92-13973. 32p. (gr. 1-5). 1993. SBE 14.95 (0-689-31770-0, Atheneum Child Bk) Macmillan Child Grp.
—The Big Tree. Hiscock, Bruce, illus. LC 89-18286. 32p. (gr. 1-5). 1991. RSBE 13.95 (0-689-31598-8, Atheneum Child Bk) Macmillan Child Grp.
—The Big Tree. Hiscock, Bruce, illus. LC 93-25564. 32p. (gr. 1-5). 1994. pap. 4.95 (0-689-71803-9, Aladdin) Macmillan Child Grp.
—Tundra: The Arctic Land. Hiscock, Bruce, illus. LC 85-28769. 144p. (gr. 3 up). 1986. SBE 13.95 (0-689-31219-9, Atheneum Child Bk) Macmillan Child Grp.
Hiser, Constance. Critter Sitters. Smith, Cat B., illus. LC 91-23002. 96p. (gr. 3-7). 1992. 13.95 (0-8234-0928-7) Holiday.
—Critter Sitters. MacDonald, Patricia, ed. 96p. 1993. pap. 2.99 (0-671-86521-8, Minstrel Bks) PB.
—Dog on Third Base. Ewing, Carolyn, illus. LC 90-29062. 64p. (gr. 2-6). 1991. 13.95 (0-8234-0898-1) Holiday.
—Dog on Third Base. MacDonald, Pat, ed. Ewing, Carolyn S., illus. 80p. (gr. 2-4). 1993. pap. 2.99 (0-671-78962-7, Minstrel Bks) PB.
—Ghosts in Fourth Grade. Smith, Cat B., illus. LC 90-47564. 80p. (gr. 2-5). 1991. 13.95 (0-8234-0865-5) Holiday.
—Ghosts in the Fourth Grade. MacDonald, Pat, ed. Smith, Cat B., illus. 80p. 1992. pap. 2.99 (0-671-75880-2, Minstrel Bks) PB.
—The Missing Doll. Ramsey, Marcy, illus. (gr. 4-7). 1993. 13.95 (0-8234-1046-3) Holiday.
—Night of the Werepoodle. Fisher, Cynthia, illus. LC 93-25732. 128p. (gr. 7-11). 1994. 14.95 (0-8234-1116-8) Holiday.
—No Bean Sprouts, Please! Ewing, Carolyn, illus. LC 89-1817. 64p. (gr. 2-5). 1989. 13.95 (0-8234-0760-8) Holiday.
—No Bean Sprouts, Please! MacDonald, Patricia, ed. Ewing, Carolyn S., illus. 64p. 1991. pap. 2.99 (0-671-72325-1, Minstrel Bks) PB.
—Scoop Snoops. Smith, Cat B., illus. LC 92-25922. 112p. (gr. 3-7). 1993. 13.95 (0-8234-1011-0) Holiday.
—Sixth-Grade Star. LC 92-52856. 96p. (gr. 3-7). 1992. 13.95 (0-8234-0967-8) Holiday.
Hiskey, Iris. Cassandra Who? (ps-3). 1992. pap. 14.00 (0-671-70574-1, S&S BFYR) S&S Trade.
—Hannah the Hippo's No Mud Day. LC 90-37071. (Illus.). 40p. (ps). 1991. pap. 13.95 incl. jacket (0-671-69194-5, Little Simon) S&S Trade.
Hislop, Julia. Coping with Rejection. LC 90-29123. 107p. (gr. 7-12). 1991. PLB 13.95 (0-8239-1183-7) Rosen Group.
Hissey, Jane. Best Friends: More Old Bear Tales. Hissey, Jane, illus. 80p. (ps-3). 1989. 16.95 (0-399-21674-X, Philomel Bks) Putnam Pub Group.
—The Jane Hissey Collection, 3 bks. (Illus.). 96p. 1991. Set. slipcase 14.95 (0-399-21758-4, Philomel Bks) Putnam Pub Group.
—Jane Hissey Little Bear & Book Set. Hissey, Jane, illus. 12p. (ps). 1993. bds. 16.00 (0-679-84762-6) Random Bks Yng Read.
—Jolly Snow: An Old Bear Story. (Illus.). (ps-1). 1991. 14.95 (0-399-22131-X, Philomel Bks) Putnam Pub Group.
—Jolly Tall. (Illus.). 32p. (ps-3). 1990. 14.95 (0-399-21827-0, Philomel Bks) Putnam Pub Group.
—Little Bear Lost. Hissey, Jane. 32p. (ps-1). 1989. 14.95 (0-399-21743-6, Philomel Bks) Putnam Pub Group.
—Little Bear Lost. (Illus.). 32p. (ps-3). 1992. PLB 4.95 (0-399-21760-6, Philomel Bks) Putnam Pub Group.
—Little Bear's Bedtime. Hissey, Jane, illus. LC 92-64019. 12p. (ps). 1993. bds. 3.99 (0-679-84176-8) Random Bks Yng Read.
—Little Bear's Day. Hissey, Jane, illus. LC 92-64017. 12p. (ps). 1993. bds. 3.99 (0-679-84175-X) Random Bks Yng Read.
—Little Bear's Trousers. (ps-2). 1987. 15.95 (0-399-21493-3, Philomel Bks) Putnam Pub Group.
—Little Bear's Trousers. (Illus.). 32p. (ps-3). 1992. PLB 5.95 (0-399-21761-4, Philomel Bks) Putnam Pub Group.
—Little Bear's Trousers: An Old Bear Story. (Illus.). 32p. (ps-3). 1990. pap. 5.95 (0-399-22016-X, Sandcastle Bks) Putnam Pub Group.
—Old Bear. (Illus.). 32p. (ps-2). 1986. 14.95 (0-399-21401-1, Philomel Bks) Putnam Pub Group.
—Old Bear. Hissey, Jane, illus. 32p. (ps-3). 1989. pap. 5.95 (0-399-22015-1, Sandcastle Bks, Sandcastle Bks) Putnam Pub Group.
—Old Bear Birthday Book. 128p. (gr. 1 up). 1990. 9.95 (0-8120-6154-3) Barron.
—Old Bear: Miniature Edition. (ps-3). 1992. 4.95 (0-399-21764-9, Philomel Bks) Putnam Pub Group.
—Old Bear Tales. Hissey, Jane, illus. LC 88-14155. 80p. 1988. 16.95 (0-399-21642-1, Philomel Bks) Putnam Pub Group.
Historic Santa Fe Association Staff, ed. We're So Lucky to Live in Santa Fe: An Activities Book in Historical Preservation. (Illus.). 26p. (gr. 4 up). pap. 4.95 (0-89013-196-1) Museum NM Pr.
Hitchcock, Alfred. Alfred Hitchcock's Spellbinders in Suspense. Isen, Harold, illus. (gr. 7-11). 1982. 4.99 (0-394-84900-0) Random Bks Yng Read.
Hitchcock, Alfred, ed. Alfred Hitchcock Presents: The Master's Choice. 1979. 12.95 (0-394-50419-4) Random Bks Yng Read.
—Alfred Hitchcock's Daring Detectives. Shilstone, Arthur, illus. LC 76-79077. (gr. 5 up). 1982. pap. 4.99 (0-394-84902-7) Random Bks Yng Read.
—Alfred Hitchcock's Ghostly Gallery. LC 62-14298. (Illus.). 272p. (gr. 5 up). 1984. pap. 4.99 (0-394-86762-9) Random Bks Yng Read.
—Alfred Hitchcock's Haunted Houseful. LC 84-15949. (Illus.). 272p. (gr. 4-9). 1985. pap. 4.99 (0-394-87041-7, Random Juv) Random Bks Yng Read.
—Alfred Hitchcock's Monster Museum. LC 81-13883. (Illus.). 224p. (gr. 5 up). 1982. pap. 4.99 (0-394-84899-3) Random Bks Yng Read.
—Alfred Hitchcock's Solve-Them-Yourself Mysteries. LC 63-7818. (Illus.). 256p. (gr. 6-9). 1986. (Random Juv); pap. 3.95 (0-394-88240-7, Random Juv) Random Bks Yng Read.
—Alfred Hitchcock's Supernatural Tales of Terror & Suspense. (Illus.). (gr. 5 up). 1983. pap. 4.99 (0-394-85622-8) Random Bks Yng Read.
Hitchcock, Alfred, ed. see Arden, William.
Hitchcock, Alfred, ed. see Arthur, Robert.
Hitchcock, Alfred, ed. see Carey, Mary V.
Hitchcock, Ruth. Tim's Dad: A Story about a Boy Whose Father Dies. Borum, Shari, illus. 24p. (gr. 4-6). 1988. pap. 2.65 (1-56123-045-6) Centering Corp.
Hitchcox, Linda. Refugees. (Illus.). 32p. (gr. 5-8). 1990. PLB 12.40 (0-531-17242-2, Gloucester Pr) Watts.
Hitchner, Earle, adapted by see Carroll, Lewis.
Hitchner, Earle, adapted by see Irving, Washington.
Hitchner, Earle, ed. see London, Jack.
Hitchner, Earle, adapted by see Pyle, Howard.
Hitchner, Earle, ed. see Stevenson, Robert Louis.
Hite, Nancy. A Pocket Book of Puzzles. 200p. (ps up). 1979. 6.95 (0-916456-47-1, GA98) Good Apple.
Hite, Sid. Dither Farm. LC 91-31323. 224p. (gr. 7 up). 1992. 15.95 (0-8050-1871-9, Bks Young Read) H Holt & Co.
Hitzeroth, Deborah. Guns: Tools of Destructive Force. LC 93-19130. 1994. 15.95 (1-56006-228-2) Lucent Bks.
—Radar: The Silent Detector. LC 90-35500. (Illus.). 96p. (gr. 5-8). 1990. PLB 15.95 (1-56006-201-0) Lucent Bks.
—Telescopes: Searching the Heavens. LC 91-16711. (Illus.). 96p. (gr. 5-8). 1991. PLB 15.95 (1-56006-209-6) Lucent Bks.
Hitzeroth, Deborah & Heerboth, Sharon. Galileo Galilei. LC 92-25957. (Illus.). 112p. (gr. 5-8). 1992. PLB 14.95 (1-56006-027-1) Lucent Bks.
—Movies: The World on Film. LC 91-16712. (Illus.). 96p. (gr. 5-8). 1991. PLB 15.95 (1-56006-210-X) Lucent Bks.
Hjelm, J. Thaddeus Jones & the Dragon. LC 68-56830. (Illus.). 64p. (gr. 2-5). 1968. PLB 10.95 (0-87783-039-8); pap. 3.94 deluxe ed. (0-87783-110-6) Oddo.
Hjelmeland, Andy. Drinking & Driving. LC 89-25406. (Illus.). 48p. (gr. 4 up). 1990. RSBE 12.95 (0-89686-496-0, Crestwood Hse) Macmillan Child Grp.
—Kids in Jail. Wolf, Dennis, photos by. (Illus.). 40p. (gr. 4-8). 1992. PLB 17.50 (0-8225-2552-6) Lerner Pubns.
Ho, Jane. ABC Alphabet Book, No. 1. 29p. (ps). Date not set. 20.00 (0-9619126-0-X) J H Childs Bks.
Ho, Minfong. Brother Rabbit. Ras, Saphan, tr. from CAM. LC 92-38206. 1994. write for info. (0-688-12552-2); lib. bdg. write for info. (0-688-12553-0) Lothrop.
—The Clay Marble. 160p. (gr. 7 up). 1991. 13.95 (0-374-31340-7) FS&G.
—Clay Marble. (gr. 4-7). 1993. pap. 3.95 (0-374-41229-4) FS&G.
—Rice without Rain. LC 86-33745. 236p. (gr. 7 up). 1990. 12.95 (0-688-06355-1) Lothrop.
Hoare, Robert. Travel by Sea. Unstead, R. J., ed. (gr. 7 up). 1975. 14.95 (0-7136-0119-1) Dufour.
Hoare, Stephen. The Assassination of John F. Kennedy. (gr. 7 up). 1989. 19.95 (0-85219-766-7, Pub. by Batsford UK) Trafalgar.
Hoare, Stephen & Dyson, Sue. The Modern World. LC 92-2405. (Illus.). 80p. (gr. 2-6). 1993. 17.95x (0-8160-2792-7) Facts on File.
Hoban, Gordon. Handy Andrews: A Novel. LC 91-90475. 176p. (Orig.). 1991. pap. 14.95 (0-944204-11-2) Omniun.
—High Jinks: A Play. LC 91-90470. 160p. (Orig.). 1991. pap. 14.95 (0-944204-13-9) Omniun.
Hoban, Julia. Amy Loves the Rain. Hoban, Lillian, illus. LC 88-45851. 32p. (ps). 1989. PLB 9.89 (0-06-022358-8) HarpC Child Bks.
—Amy Loves the Rain. Hoban, Lillian, illus. LC 87-45851. 24p. (ps). 1993. pap. 3.95 (0-06-443293-9, Trophy) HarpC Child Bks.
—Amy Loves the Snow. Hoban, Lillian, illus. LC 76-45852. 24p. (ps). 1989. PLB 10.89 (0-06-022395-2) HarpC Child Bks.
—Amy Loves the Snow. Hoban, Lillian, illus. LC 87-45852. 24p. (ps). 1993. pap. 3.95 (0-06-443294-7, Trophy) HarpC Child Bks.
—Amy Loves the Wind. Hoban, Lillian, illus. LC 87-45986. 24p. (ps). 1988. PLB 9.89 (0-06-022403-7) HarpC Child Bks.
—Buzby. Himmelman, John, illus. LC 89-29408. 64p. (gr. k-3). 1990. PLB 11.89 (0-06-022398-7) HarpC Child Bks.
—Buzby. Himmelman, John, illus. LC 89-29408. 64p. (gr. k-3). 1992. pap. 3.50 (0-06-444152-0, Trophy) HarpC Child Bks.
—Buzby to the Rescue. Himmelman, John, illus. LC 91-46085. 64p. (gr. k-3). 1993. 14.00 (0-06-021025-7); PLB 13.89 (0-06-021024-9) HarpC Child Bks.
—Quick Chick. Hoban, Lillian, illus. LC 88-30894. 32p. (ps-2). 1989. 9.95 (0-525-44490-4, DCB) Dutton Child Bks.
Hoban, Lillian. Arthur's Camp-Out. Hoban, Lillian, illus. LC 91-27528. 64p. (gr. k-3). 1993. 13.00 (0-06-020525-3); PLB 13.89 (0-06-020526-1) HarpC Child Bks.
—Arthur's Christmas Cookies. LC 72-76496. (Illus.). 64p. (gr. k-3). 1972. PLB 13.89 (0-06-022368-5) HarpC Child Bks.
—Arthur's Christmas Cookies. Hoban, Lillian, illus. LC 72-76596. 64p. (gr. k-3). 1986. incl. cassette 5.98 (0-694-00160-0, Trophy); pap. 3.50 (0-06-444055-9, Trophy) HarpC Child Bks.
—Arthur's Christmas Cookies. unabr. ed. (Illus.). (ps-3). 1990. 6.95 incl. cassette (1-55994-217-7, Caedmon) HarperAudio.
—Arthur's Funny Money. Hoban, Lillian, illus. LC 80-7903. 64p. (gr. k-3). 1981. PLB 13.89 (0-06-022344-8) HarpC Child Bks.
—Arthur's Funny Money. Hoban, Lillian, illus. LC 80-7903. 64p. (gr. k-3). 1987. incl. cassette 5.98 (0-694-00173-2, Trophy); pap. 3.50 (0-06-444048-6, Trophy) HarpC Child Bks.
—Arthur's Funny Money. unabr. ed. (Illus.). (ps-3). 1990. pap. 6.95 incl. cassette (1-55994-218-5, Caedmon) HarperAudio.
—Arthur's Great Big Valentine. Hoban, Lillian, illus. LC 88-21202. 64p. (gr. k-3). 1989. PLB 13.89 (0-06-022407-X) HarpC Child Bks.
—Arthur's Great Big Valentine. Hoban, Lillian, illus. LC 88-21202. 64p. (gr. k-3). 1991. pap. 3.50 (0-06-444149-0, Trophy) HarpC Child Bks.
—Arthur's Halloween Costume. LC 83-49465. (Illus.). 64p. (gr. k-3). 1984. PLB 13.89 (0-06-022391-X) HarpC Child Bks.
—Arthur's Halloween Costume. LC 83-49465. (Illus.). 64p. (gr. k-3). 1986. pap. 3.50 (0-06-444101-6, Trophy) HarpC Child Bks.
—Arthur's Honey Bear. Hoban, Lillian, illus. LC 73-14325. 64p. (gr. k-3). 1974. 14.00 (0-06-022369-3); PLB 13.89 (0-06-022370-7) HarpC Child Bks.
—Arthur's Honey Bear. Hoban, Lillian, illus. LC 73-14324. 64p. (gr. k-3). 1986. incl. cassette 5.98 (0-694-00116-3, Trophy); pap. 3.50 (0-06-444033-8, Trophy) HarpC Child Bks.
—Arthur's Honey Bear. unabr. ed. (Illus.). (ps-3). 1990. pap. 6.95 incl. cassette (1-55994-219-3, Caedmon) HarperAudio.
—Arthur's Loose Tooth. Hoban, Lillian, illus. LC 85-42611. 64p. (ps-3). 1985. PLB 13.89 (0-06-022354-5) HarpC Child Bks.
—Arthur's Loose Tooth. Hoban, Lillian, illus. LC 85-42611. 64p. (gr. k-3). 1987. pap. 3.50 (0-06-444093-1, Trophy) HarpC Child Bks.
—Arthur's Pen Pal. Hoban, Lillian, illus. LC 75-6289. 64p. (gr. k-3). 1976. PLB 13.89 (0-06-022372-3) HarpC Child Bks.
—Arthur's Pen Pal. LC 75-6289. (Illus.). 64p. (gr. k-3). 1982. pap. 3.50 (0-06-444032-X, Trophy) HarpC Child Bks.
—Arthur's Pen Pal. Hoban, Lillian, illus. 32p. (ps-2). 1990. pap. 6.95 (0-00-004236-6, Caedmon) HarperAudio.
—Arthur's Pen Pal. unabr. ed. (Illus.). (ps-3). 1990. pap. 6.95 incl. cassette (1-55994-238-X, Caedmon) HarperAudio.
—Arthur's Prize Reader. Hoban, Lillian, illus. LC 77-25637. 64p. (ps-3). 1978. PLB 13.89 (0-06-022380-4) HarpC Child Bks.
—Arthur's Prize Reader. LC 77-25637. (Illus.). 64p. (ps-3). 1985. incl. cassette 5.98 (0-694-00016-7, Trophy); pap. 3.50 (0-06-444049-4, Trophy) HarpC Child Bks.
—Arthur's Prize Reader. unabr. ed. (Illus.). (ps-3). 1990. pap. 6.95 incl. cassette (1-55994-220-7, Caedmon) HarperAudio.
—The Case of the Two Masked Robbers. LC 85-45819. (Illus.). 64p. (gr. k-3). 1986. PLB 13.89 (0-06-022299-9) HarpC Child Bks.
—The Case of the Two Masked Robbers. Hoban, Lillian, illus. LC 85-45819. 64p. (gr. k-3). 1988. pap. 3.50 (0-06-444121-0, Trophy) HarpC Child Bks.
—Mr. Pig & Sonny Too. LC 76-58731. (Illus.). 64p. (gr. k-3). 1977. PLB 13.89 (0-06-022341-3) HarpC Child Bks.

—Silly Tilly & the Easter Bunny. Hoban, Lillian, illus. LC 86-7682. 32p. (ps-3). 1987. 13.00 (0-06-022392-8); PLB 13.89 (0-06-022393-6) HarpC Child Bks.
—Silly Tilly & the Easter Bunny. Hoban, Lillian, illus. LC 86-7682. 32p. (ps-2). 1989. pap. 3.50 (0-06-444127-X, Trophy) HarpC Child Bks.
—Silly Tilly's Thanksgiving Dinner. Hoban, Lillian, illus. LC 89-29287. 64p. (gr. k-3). 1990. 14.00 (0-06-022422-3); PLB 13.89 (0-06-022423-1) HarpC Child Bks.
—Silly Tilly's Thanksgiving Dinner. Hoban, Lillian, illus. LC 89-29287. 64p. (gr. k-3). 1991. pap. 3.50 (0-06-444154-7, Trophy) HarpC Child Bks.
—Stick-in-the-Mud-Turtle. (ps-3). 1992. pap. 2.99 (0-440-40622-6) Dell.
—Turtle Spring. (ps-3). 1992. pap. 2.99 (0-440-40606-4) Dell.
Hoban, Lillian & Hoban, Phoebe. The Laziest Robot in Zone One. Hoban, Lillian, illus. LC 82-48613. 64p. (gr. k-3). 1983. PLB 12.89 (0-06-022352-9) HarpC Child Bks.
—The Laziest Robot in Zone One. Hoban, Lillian, illus. LC 82-48613. 64p. (gr. k-3). 1985. pap. 3.50 (0-06-444089-3, Trophy) HarpC Child Bks.
—Ready...Set...Robot! LC 81-47731. (Illus.). 64p. (gr. k-3). 1982. PLB 13.89 (0-06-022346-4) HarpC Child Bks.
Hoban, Lillian, jt. auth. see Hoban, Russell.
Hoban, Phoebe, jt. auth. see Hoban, Lillian.
Hoban, Russell. Arthur's New Power. Barton, Byron, illus. LC 77-11550. (gr. 1-5). 1978. PLB 12.89 (0-690-01371-X, Crowell Jr Bks) HarpC Child Bks.
—Baby Sister for Frances. newly illust. ed. Hoban, Lillian, illus. LC 92-32603. 32p. (ps-3). 1964. 15.00 (0-06-022335-9); PLB 14.89 (0-06-022336-7) HarpC Child Bks.
—A Baby Sister for Frances. newly illustrated ed. Hoban, Lillian, illus. LC 92-32603. 32p. (ps-3). 1976. pap. 4.95 (0-06-443006-5, Trophy) HarpC Child Bks.
—Bargain for Frances. newly illus. ed. Hoban, Lillian, illus. LC 91-12265. 64p. (gr. k-3). 1970. 13.00 (0-06-022329-4); PLB 12.89 (0-06-022330-8) HarpC Child Bks.
—A Bargain for Frances. newly illus. ed. Hoban, Lillian, illus. LC 91-12267. 64p. (gr. k-3). 1978. pap. 3.50 (0-06-444001-X, Trophy) HarpC Child Bks.
—Bedtime for Frances. Williams, Garth, illus. LC 60-8347. 32p. (gr. k-3). 1960. 14.00 (0-06-022350-2); PLB 13.89 (0-06-022351-0) HarpC Child Bks.
—Bedtime for Frances. Williams, Garth, illus. LC 60-8347. (ps-2). 1976. pap. 4.95 (0-06-443005-7, Trophy) HarpC Child Bks.
—Best Friends for Frances. Hoban, Lillian, illus. LC 71-77935. 32p. (ps-3). 1969. 14.00 (0-06-022327-8); PLB 13.89 (0-06-022328-6) HarpC Child Bks.
—Best Friends for Frances. Hoban, Lillian, illus. LC 71-77935. (ps-2). 1976. pap. 4.95 (0-06-443008-1, Trophy) HarpC Child Bks.
—Birthday for Frances. Hoban, Lillian, illus. LC 68-24321. 32p. (gr. k-3). 1968. 14.00 (0-06-022338-3); PLB 13.89 (0-06-022339-1) HarpC Child Bks.
—A Birthday for Frances. Hoban, Lillian, illus. LC 68-24321. (ps-2). 1976. pap. 4.95 (0-06-443007-3, Trophy) HarpC Child Bks.
—Bread & Jam for Frances. newly illus. ed. Hoban, Lillian, illus. LC 92-13622. 32p. (ps-3). 1965. 15.00 (0-06-022335-6); PLB 14.89 (0-06-022360-X) HarpC Child Bks.
—Bread & Jam for Frances. newly illustrated ed. Hoban, Lillian, illus. LC 92-13622. 32p. (ps-3). 1986. pap. 4.95 (0-06-443096-0, Trophy) HarpC Child Bks.
—Bread & Jam for Frances: Big Book. Hoban, Lillian, illus. LC 92-13622. 32p. (ps-3). 1993. pap. 19.95 (0-06-443336-6, Trophy) HarpC Child Bks.
—Dinner at Alberta's. Marshall, James, illus. 48p. (gr. k-6). 1980. pap. 2.95 (0-440-41864-X, YB) Dell.
—Dinner at Alberta's. Marshall, James, illus. LC 73-94796. 40p. (gr. 1-3). 1975. PLB 12.89 (0-690-23993-9, Crowell Jr Bks) HarpC Child Bks.
—Egg Thoughts & Other Frances Songs. Hoban, Lillian, illus. LC 70-183162. 32p. (ps-3). 1972. 12.95 (0-06-022331-6); PLB 12.89 (0-06-022332-4) HarpC Child Bks.
—Emmet Otter's Jug Band Christmas. (Illus.). 42p. 1992. Repr. PLB 11.95x (0-89966-951-4) Buccaneer Bks.
—Jim Hedgehog & the Lonesome Tower. Lewin, Betsy, illus. 48p. (gr. 1-4). 1992. 12.95 (0-395-59760-9, Clarion Bks) HM.
—Jim Hedgehog's Supernatural Christmas. Lewin, Betsy, illus. 48p. (gr. 2-5). 1992. 12.70 (0-395-56240-6, Clarion Bks) HM.
—The Marzipan Pig. Blake, Quentin, illus. LC 86-24253. 40p. (gr. 1-4). 1987. 13.00 (0-374-34859-6) FS&G.
—The Marzipan Pig. Blake, Quentin, illus. 40p. (gr. 1 up). 1989. pap. 3.50 (0-374-44750-0) FS&G.
—Monsters. Blake, Quentin, illus. 1990. 13.95 (0-590-43422-5) Scholastic Inc.
—Monsters. Blake, Quentin, illus. 32p. (ps-2). 1993. pap. 4.95 (0-590-43421-7) Scholastic Inc.
—Mouse & His Child. Hoban, Lillian, illus. LC 67-19624. (gr. 1-5). 1967. PLB 13.89 (0-06-022378-2) HarpC Child Bks.
—The Mouse & His Child. (gr. k-6). 1990. pap. 3.50 (0-440-40293-X, YB) Dell.
—The Mouse & His Child. large type ed. 312p. (gr. 3-7). 1990. 13.95 (0-7451-1104-1, Galaxy Child Lrg Print) Chivers N Amer.

—The Rain Door. Blake, Quentin, illus. LC 86-47719. 32p. (ps-3). 1987. (Crowell Jr Bks) HarpC Child Bks.
—Tom & the Two Handles. Hoban, Lillian, illus. LC 65-11459. 64p. (gr. k-3). 1965. PLB 13.89 (0-06-022431-2) HarpC Child Bks.
Hoban, Russell & Hoban, Lillian. The Stone Doll of Sister Brute. (Illus.). (gr. 1-4). 1992. pap. 2.99 (0-440-40681-1, YB) Dell.
Hoban, Tana. A, B, See! LC 81-6890. (Illus.). 32p. (gr. k-3). 1982. PLB 14.93 (0-688-00833-X) Greenwillow.
—All about Where. LC 90-30849. (Illus.). 32p. (ps up). 1991. 13.95 (0-688-09697-2); PLB 13.88 (0-688-09698-0) Greenwillow.
—Black on White. LC 92-18897. (Illus.). 12p. (ps up). 1993. bds. 4.95 (0-688-11918-2) Greenwillow.
—A Children's Zoo. Hoban, Tana, illus. LC 84-25318. 24p. (ps-1). 1985. 15.00 (0-688-05202-9); lib. bdg. 14.93 (0-688-05204-5) Greenwillow.
—A Children's Zoo. LC 84-25318. (Illus.). (ps-3). 1987. pap. text ed. 4.95 (0-688-07044-2, Mulberry) Morrow.
—Circles, Triangles & Squares. Hoban, Tana, illus. LC 72-93305. 32p. (ps-2). 1974. RSBE 13.95 (0-02-744830-4, Macmillan Child Bk) Macmillan Child Grp.
—Colors. LC 93-24847. (gr. 3 up). 1994. pap. write for info. (0-688-12762-2); PLB write for info. Greenwillow.
—Count & See. Hoban, Tana, illus. LC 72-175597. 40p. (ps-2). 1972. RSBE 13.95 (0-02-744800-2, Macmillan Child Bk) Macmillan Child Grp.
—Dig, Drill, Dump, Fill. LC 75-11987. (Illus.). 32p. (ps-3). 1975. 13.88 (0-688-84016-7) Greenwillow.
—Dig, Drill, Dump, Fill. LC 75-11987. (Illus.). 32p. (ps up). 1992. pap. 3.95 (0-688-11703-1, Mulberry) Morrow.
—Dots, Spots, Speckles, & Stripes. (ps-3). 1987. 11.75 (0-688-06862-6); PLB 11.88 (0-688-06863-4) Greenwillow.
—Exactly the Opposite. LC 89-27227. (Illus.). 32p. (ps up). 1990. 12.95 (0-688-08861-9); PLB 12.88 (0-688-08862-7) Greenwillow.
—I Read Signs. Hoban, Tana, illus. LC 83-1482. 32p. (ps-1). 1983. 15.00 (0-688-02317-7); PLB 14.93 (0-688-02318-5) Greenwillow.
—I Read Signs. LC 83-1482. (ps-1). 1987. pap. 4.95 (0-688-07331-X, Mulberry) Morrow.
—I Read Symbols. Hoban, Tana, illus. LC 83-1481. 32p. (ps-1). 1983. 14.95 (0-688-02331-2); PLB 14.88 (0-688-02332-0) Greenwillow.
—I Walk & Read. Hoban, Tana, illus. LC 83-14215. 32p. (ps-1). 1984. 14.95 (0-688-02575-7); PLB 14.88 (0-688-02576-5) Greenwillow.
—Is It Larger? Is It Smaller? LC 84-13719. (Illus.). 32p. (ps-1). 1985. 14.95 (0-688-04027-6); PLB 14.88 (0-688-04028-4) Greenwillow.
—Is It Red? Is It Yellow? Is It Blue? LC 78-2549. (Illus.). 32p. (gr. k-3). 1978. 16.00 (0-688-80171-4); PLB 15.93 (0-688-84171-6) Greenwillow.
—Is It Red? Is It Yellow? Is It Blue? LC 78-2549. (Illus.). 32p. (ps-3). 1987. pap. 4.95 (0-688-07034-5, Mulberry) Morrow.
—Is It Rough? Is It Smooth? Is It Shiny? Hoban, Tana, illus. LC 83-25460. 32p. (ps-1). 1984. 15.95 (0-688-03823-9); PLB 15.88 (0-688-03824-7) Greenwillow.
—Look Again! LC 72-127469. (Illus.). 40p. (ps-1). 1971. SBE 13.95 (0-02-744050-8, Macmillan Child Bk) Macmillan Child Grp.
—Look! Look! Look! Hoban, Tana, illus. LC 87-25655. 40p. (ps-1). 1988. 12.95 (0-688-07239-9); lib. bdg. 12.88 (0-688-07240-2) Greenwillow.
—Look up, Look Down. LC 91-12613. 32p. (ps up). 1992. 14.00 (0-688-10577-7); lib. bdg. 13.93 (0-688-10578-5) Greenwillow.
—Of Colors & Things. LC 92-43785. (Illus.). 24p. (ps-12). 1989. 15.00 (0-688-07534-7); PLB 14.93 (0-688-07535-5) Greenwillow.
—One Little Kitten. LC 78-31862. (Illus.). 24p. (gr. k-3). 1979. PLB 14.88 (0-688-84222-4) Greenwillow.
—One Little Kitten. LC 78-31862. (Illus.). 24p. (ps up). 1992. pap. 3.95 (0-688-11506-3, Mulberry) Morrow.
—One, Two, Three. Hoban, Tana, illus. LC 84-10306. 12p. (ps). 1985. bds. 4.95 (0-688-02579-X) Greenwillow.
—Over, Under & Through. Hoban, Tana, illus. LC 86-20675. 32p. (ps-3). 1987. pap. 3.95 (0-689-71111-5, Aladdin) Macmillan Child Grp.
—Over, Under & Through & Other Special Concepts. Hoban, Tana, photos by. LC 72-81055. (Illus.). 32p. (ps-2). 1973. RSBE 13.95 (0-02-744820-7, Macmillan Child Bk) Macmillan Child Grp.
—Panda, Panda. Hoban, Tana, illus. LC 86-3088. 12p. (ps). 1986. pap. 3.95 (0-688-06564-3) Greenwillow.
—Push, Pull, Empty, Full: A Book of Opposites. LC 72-90410. (Illus.). 32p. (ps-2). 1972. RSBE 13.95 (0-02-744810-X, Macmillan Child Bk) Macmillan Child Grp.
—Red, Blue, Yellow Shoe. Hoban, Tana, illus. LC 86-3095. 12p. (ps). 1986. bds. 4.95 (0-688-06563-5) Greenwillow.
—Round & Round & Round. Hoban, Tana, illus. LC 82-11984. 32p. (gr. k-3). 1983. 14.95 (0-688-01813-0); PLB 14.88 (0-688-01814-9) Greenwillow.
—Shadows & Reflections. LC 89-30461. (Illus.). 32p. (ps up). 1990. 12.95 (0-688-07089-2); lib. bdg. 12.88 (0-688-07090-6) Greenwillow.

—Shapes, Shapes, Shapes. Hoban, Tana, photos by. LC 85-17569. (Illus.). 32p. (ps-3). 1986. 14.95 (0-688-05832-9); PLB 14.88 (0-688-05833-7) Greenwillow.
—Spirals, Curves, Fanshapes, & Lines. LC 91-30159. (Illus.). 32p. (ps-4). 1992. 14.00 (0-688-11228-5); PLB 13.93 (0-688-11229-3) Greenwill ow.
—Take Another Look. LC 80-21342. (Illus.). 32p. (ps-3). 1981. PLB 15.93 (0-688-84249-4) Greenwillow.
—Twenty-Six Letters & Ninety-Nine Cents. LC 86-11993. (Illus.). 32p. (ps-3). 1987. 15.00 (0-688-06361-6); PLB 14.93 (0-688-06362-4) Greenwillow.
—What Is It? Hoban, Tana, illus. LC 84-13483. 12p. (ps). 1985. bds. 4.95 (0-688-02577-3) Greenwillow.
—Where Is It? LC 73-8573. (Illus.). 32p. (ps-1). 1974. RSBE 13.95 (0-02-744070-2, Macmillan Child Bk) Macmillan Child Grp.
—White on Black. LC 92-20092. (Illus.). 12p. (ps up). 1993. bds. 4.95 (0-688-11919-0) Greenwillow.
Hoban, Tana, illus. Shapes & Things. LC 70-102965. 32p. (ps-2). 1970. 13.95 (0-02-744060-3, Macmillan Child Bk) Macmillan Child Grp.
Hobart, Ann. Morganfield Mouse. 48p. (gr. 2-5). 1985. pap. 7.95 (0-930096-72-X) G Gannett.
Hobbis, Charles I. Pencil Drawing for the Architect. (gr. 10-12). 1954. 9.95 (0-85458-100-6); pap. 7.95 (0-85458-101-4) Transatl Arts.
Hobbs, Anne S. & Noble, Mary, eds. A Victorian Naturalist: Beatrix Potter's Drawings from the Armitt Collection. (Illus.). 192p. 1992. 40.00 (0-7232-3990-8) Warne.
Hobbs, Clara M. Begin-Again Land. 1993. 10.95 (0-533-10386-X) Vantage.
Hobbs, Jack & Salome, Richard. The Visual Experience. (Illus.). 1990. text ed. 36.95 (0-87192-226-6, 226-6) Davis Mass.
Hobbs, Richard R., rev. by see Sundt, Wilbur A.
Hobbs, Will. Beardance. LC 92-44874. 208p. (gr. 5-9). 1993. SBE 14.95 (0-689-31867-7, Atheneum Child Bk) Macmillan Child Grp.
—Bearstone. LC 89-6641. 144p. (gr. 6-5). 1989. SBE 13.95 (0-689-31496-5, Atheneum Child Bk) Macmillan Child Grp.
—Bearstone. 160p. (gr. 5). 1991. pap. 3.50 (0-380-71249-0, Camelot) Avon.
—The Big Wander. LC 92-825. 192p. (gr. 5-9). 1992. SBE 14.95 (0-689-31767-0, Atheneum Child Bk) Macmillan Child Grp.
—Changes in Latitudes. LC 87-17462. 176p. (gr. 7 up). 1988. SBE 13.95 (0-689-31385-3, Atheneum Child Bk) Macmillan Child Grp.
—Changes in Latitudes. 176p. 1993. pap. 3.50 (0-380-71619-4, Flare) Avon.
—Downriver. LC 90-1044. 208p. (gr. 7 up). 1991. SBE 14.95 (0-689-31690-9, Atheneum Child Bk) Macmillan Child Grp.
—Downriver. (gr. 7 up). 1992. pap. 3.50 (0-553-29717-1, Starfire) Bantam.
Hober, David. Kobi the Elf, Magic & Adventure in Hawaii. Pickett, Timothy & Okaze, Kunio, eds. Nagaoki, Kobun, tr. Fontilis, Glen, illus. (ENG & JPN.). 32p. (Orig.). (gr. 1 up). 1990. pap. 4.95 (0-9623215-0-8) Moonbeam Magic Pub.
Hoberman, Mary A. The Cozy Book. Fraser, Betty, illus. LC 93-10826. 1995. write for info. (0-15-276620-0, Browndeer Pr) HarBrace.
—Fathers, Mothers, Sisters, Brothers: A Collection of Family Poems. Hafner, Marylin, illus. (ps-3). 1991. 14.95 (0-316-36736-2) Little.
—Fathers, Mothers, Sisters, Brothers: A Collection of Family Poems. Hafner, Marylin, illus. LC 92-26587. 1993. pap. 4.99 (0-14-054849-1, Puffin) Puffin Bks.
—A House Is a House for Me. Fraser, Betty, illus. 1993. pap. 6.99 incl. cassette (0-14-095116-4, Puffin) Puffin Bks.
Hoberman, Mary Ann. A Fine Fat Pig: And Other Animal Poems. Zeldis, Malcah, illus. LC 90-37403. 32p. (ps-2). 1991. PLB 14.89 (0-06-022426-6) HarpC Child Bks.
—A House Is a House for Me. Fraser, Betty, illus. LC 77-15518. (gr. k-3). 1978. pap. 14.00 (0-670-38016-4) Viking Child Bks.
—A House Is a House for Me. Fraser, Betty, illus. (gr. k-3). 1984. incl. cassette 19.95 (0-941078-33-7); pap. 12.95 incl. cassette (0-941078-31-0); incl. 4 bks., cassette, & guide 27.95 (0-317-07117-3) Live Oak Media.
—A House Is a House for Me. Fraser, Betty, illus. 48p. (ps-3). 1982. pap. 3.99 (0-14-050394-3, Puffin) Puffin Bks.
—Mr. & Mrs. Muddle. Hoberman, Mary Ann, illus. LC 87-27320. 32p. (gr. k-4). 1988. 13.95 (0-316-36735-4, Joy St Bks) Little.
Hobson, Burton H. Coin Collecting As a Hobby. rev. ed. Obojski, Robert, ed. LC 67-27759. (Illus.). 192p. (gr. 4-10). 1986. 9.95 (0-8069-4748-9) Sterling.
Hobson, J. Allan. Sleep & Dreams. Head, J. J., ed. Whittington, Julianne S., illus. 16p. (Orig.). (gr. 10 up). 1992. pap. text ed. 2.75 (0-89278-117-3, 45-9617) Carolina Biological.
Hoch, Dean & Hoch, Nancy. The Sex Education Dictionary for Today's Teens & Preteens. Severe, Camille H., illus. LC 89-63577. 128p. (Orig.). (gr. 5-12). 1990. pap. 12.95 (0-9624209-0-5) Landmark ID.
Hoch, Nancy, jt. auth. see Hoch, Dean.

Hochman, Doris Z. Kid Koala's Fun Book. Hochman, Doris Z., illus. 44p. (gr. 2-5). 1991. wkbk. 6.95 (*1-878070-00-2*) Three Elves Pr.

Hochman, Eleanor, rev. by. & t see Dumas, Alexandre.

Hochstatter, Daniel J., illus. Sammy's Excellent Real-Life Adventures. LC 92-40532. (gr. 5 up). 1993. 9.99 (*0-8407-9675-7*) Nelson.

—Sammy's Fabulous Holy Land Travels. LC 93-34525. 1994. write for info. (*0-89528-281-X*) Oliver-Nelson.

—Sammy's Incredible Travels with Jesus & His Friends: A New Testament Adventure. LC 92-18748. 1992. 9.99 (*0-8407-9162-3*) Oliver-Nelson.

—Sammy's Tree-Mendous Christmas Adventure. LC 93-22314. 1993. 9.99 (*0-8407-9234-4*) Oliver-Nelson.

Hockenberry, Debra. The Craftmaker's Handbook. (Illus.). 60p. (Orig.). (gr. 12). 1990. pap. 8.00 (*1-878056-06-9*) D Hockenberry.

Hockerman, Dennis. Baby Moses in the Basket. LC 87-70410. (ps). 1987. 3.99 (*1-55513-783-0*, Chariot Bks) Cook.

—The Little Children Visit Jesus. LC 87-70411. (ps). 1987. 3.99 (*1-55513-779-2*, Chariot Bks) Cook.

—A Young Girl Helps Naaman. LC 87-70409. (ps). 1987. 3.99 (*1-55513-089-5*, Chariot Bks) Cook.

Hockerman, Dennis, jt. auth. see Davoll, Barbara.

Hockett, Betty M. Down a Winding Road. (Illus.). 80p. (gr. 3-8). 1985. pap. 3.50 (*0-943701-11-2*) George Fox Pr.

—Eight of a Kind & More Than Empty Dreams. Loewen, Janelle, illus. (Orig.). (gr. 3-8). 1988. Set. pap. 13.95 (*0-913342-66-1*) Barclay Pr.

—From Here to There & Back Again. Cammack, Phyllis, illus. LC 84-81034. 80p. (Orig.). (gr. 3-8). 1984. pap. 3.50 (*0-943701-09-0*) George Fox Pr.

—Happiness under the Indian Trees. LC 86-81349. (Illus.). 80p. (gr. 3-8). 1986. pap. 3.50 (*0-943701-12-0*) George Fox Pr.

—Keeping Them All in Stitches: The Life-Story of Geraldine Custer. Loewen, Janelle, illus. 80p. (Orig.). (gr. 3-6). 1990. pap. 3.50 (*0-943701-18-X*) George Fox Pr.

—More Than Empty Dreams. Loewen, Janelle, illus. LC 88-71327. 140p. (Orig.). (gr. 3-8). 1988. pap. 7.50 (*0-913342-65-3*) Barclay Pr.

—Mud on Their Wheels: The Life-Story of Vern & Lois Ellis. Loewen, Janelle, illus. LC 88-81703. 80p. (Orig.). (gr. 3-6). 1988. pap. 3.50 (*0-943701-14-7*) George Fox Pr.

—No Time Out: The Life-Story of George & Dorothy Thomas. Loewen, Janelle, illus. 80p. (Orig.). (gr. 3-6). 1991. pap. 3.95 (*0-943701-19-8*) George Fox Pr.

—Outside Doctor on Call: The Life-Story of Dr. Ezra & Frances DeVol. Loewen, Janelle, illus. 80p. (Orig.). (gr. 3-6). 1992. pap. 4.95 (*0-943701-20-1*) George Fox Pr.

—What Will Tomorrow Bring? LC 85-70504. (Illus.). 80p. (gr. 3-8). 1985. pap. 3.50 (*0-943701-10-4*) George Fox Pr.

—Whistling Bombs & Bumpy Trains: The Life-Story of Anna Nixon. Loewen, Janelle, illus. LC 89-84572. 80p. (Orig.). (gr. 3-6). 1989. pap. 3.50 (*0-943701-15-5*) George Fox Pr.

Hocking, Colin, et al. Acid Rain. Bergman, Lincoln & Fairwell, Kay, eds. Bavilacqua, Carol & Craig, Rose, illus. Hoyt, Richard & Bergman, Lincoln, photos by. 168p. (gr. 6-10). 1990. pap. 12.00 (*0-912511-74-5*) Lawrence Science.

—Global Warming & the Greenhouse Effect. Bergman, Lincoln & Fairwell, Kay, eds. Klofkorn, Lisa & Craig, Rose, illus. Hoyt, Richard, photos by. 168p. (gr. 7-10). 1990. pap. 12.00 (*0-912511-75-3*) Lawrence Science.

Hodes, Aubrey, tr. see Shamir, Moshe.

Hodgdon, Linda Q. Things to Do in the Car. Knoop, Gayle, illus. 52p. (Orig.). pap. write for info. (*0-9616786-0-7*) Young Ideas.

Hodge, Anthony. Cartooning. Kline, Marjory, ed. Hodge, Anthony, illus. LC 91-34409. 32p. (gr. 5-9). 1992. PLB 12.40 (*0-531-17322-4*, Gloucester Pr) Watts.

—Collage. Kline, Marjory, ed. Hodge, Anthony, illus. LC 91-34408. 32p. (gr. 5-9). 1992. PLB 12.40 (*0-531-17323-2*, Gloucester Pr) Watts.

—Drawing. Hayward, Ron, illus. Kline, M., ed. (Illus.). 32p. (gr. 5-9). 1991. PLB 12.40 (*0-531-17300-3*, Gloucester Pr) Watts.

—Painting. Hodge, Anthony, illus. Kline, M., ed. 32p. (gr. 5-9). 1991. PLB 12.40 (*0-531-17299-6*, Gloucester Pr) Watts.

Hodge, Ellen, ed. see Thomas, Mary A.

Hodge, Lois L. A Season of Change. LC 87-18945. 112p. (gr. 7-12). 1987. pap. 2.95 (*0-930323-27-0*, Kendall Green Pubns) Gallaudet Univ Pr.

Hodge, Merle. For the Life of Laetitia. 1993. 15.00 (*0-374-32447-6*) FS&G.

Hodge, Peter. Roman House. (Illus.). 64p. (Orig.). (gr. 7-12). 1971. pap. text ed. 9.00 (*0-582-20300-7*, 70709) Longman.

Hodgeman, Ann. My Babysitter Has Fangs. Ashby, Ruth, ed. Pierard, John, illus. 128p. (Orig.). 1992. pap. 2.99 (*0-671-75868-3*, Minstrel Bks) PB.

Hodges. Moses & the Ten Plagues. 24p. (Orig.). (gr. k-4). 1985. pap. 1.89 (*0-570-06190-3*, 59-1291) Concordia.

—Stephen, the First Martyr. 24p. (Orig.). (gr. k-4). 1985. pap. 1.89 (*0-570-06194-6*, 59-1295) Concordia.

Hodges, et al. Basic Studies: Reading & Word Skills. rev. ed. 271p. (gr. 4-8). 1988. pap. text ed. 17.00 (*0-913310-19-0*) Irwin.

—Basic Studies: Understanding Mathematics. rev. ed. 165p. (gr. 4-8). 1988. pap. text ed. 15.00 (*0-913310-30-1*) Irwin.

—Basic Studies: Writing, Speaking & Listening. rev. ed. 155p. (gr. 4-8). 1988. pap. text ed. 15.00 (*0-913310-34-4*) Irwin.

Hodges, Jean. Smocking Design. 1989. pap. 10.95 (*0-486-26036-4*) Dover.

Hodges, M. Constance. Alice in Danceland. Hodges, Del & Mavity, Dennis, photos by. Troxel, Rose, illus. (Orig.). (gr. 3-8). 1979. PLB 5.95 (*0-934856-00-1*) Delcon.

Hodges, Margaret. The Arrow & the Lamp: The Story of Psyche. Diamond, Donna, illus. LC 86-2728. (gr. 4-8). 1989. 14.95 (*0-316-36790-7*) Little.

—Brother Francis & the Friendly Beasts. Lewin, Ted, illus. LC 90-33206. 32p. (gr. 1-3). 1991. SBE 13.95 (*0-684-19173-3*, Scribners Young Read) Macmillan Child Grp.

—Buried Moon, Vol. 1. (ps-3). 1990. 14.95 (*0-316-36793-1*) Little.

—Hero of Bremen. (ps-3). 1993. 15.95 (*0-8234-0934-1*) Holiday.

—The Kitchen Knight: A Tale of King Arthur. Hyman, Schart, illus. 1993. pap. 5.95 (*0-8234-1063-3*) Holiday.

—The Little Humpbacked Horse. Conover, Chris, illus. 32p. (ps up). 1987. pap. 3.95 (*0-374-44495-1*) FS&G.

—Making a Difference: The Story of an American Family. LC 88-31131. (Illus.). 208p. (gr. 7 up). 1989. SBE 14.95 (*0-684-18979-8*, Scribners Young Read) Macmillan Child Grp.

—Making a Difference: The Story of an American Family. ALC Staff, ed. LC 88-31131. (Illus.). (gr. 8-12). 1992. pap. 4.95 (*0-688-11780-5*, Pub. by Beech Tree Bks) Morrow.

—Saint George & the Dragon. (ps-4). 1990. pap. 6.95 (*0-316-36795-8*) Little.

—Saint Patrick & the Peddler. Johnson, Paul B., illus. LC 92-44522. 40p. (gr. k-3). 1993. 15.95 (*0-531-05489-6*); PLB 15.99 (*0-531-08639-9*) Orchard Bks Watts.

—Wave. Lent, Blair, illus. (gr. k-3). 1964. 3.50 (*0-395-06817-7*) HM.

Hodges, Margaret & Evernden, Margery. Of Swords & Sorcerers: The Adventures of King Arthur & His Knights. Frampton, David, illus. LC 91-40811. 112p. (gr. 5-7). 1993. SBE 14.95 (*0-684-19437-6*, Scribners Young Read) Macmillan Child Grp.

Hodges, Margaret, adapted by. Don Quixote & Sancho Panza. Marchesi, Stephen, illus. LC 90-24098. 80p. (gr. 6 up). 1992. SBE 16.95 (*0-684-19235-7*, Scribners Young Read) Macmillan Child Grp.

Hodges, Margaret, retold by. The Golden Deer. San Souci, Daniel, illus. LC 90-42873. 32p. (gr. 1-3). 1992. SBE 14.95 (*0-684-19218-7*, Scribners Young Read) Macmillan Child Grp.

—Hauntings: Ghosts & Ghouls from Around the World. Wenzel, David, illus. (gr. 3-7). 1991. 16.95 (*0-316-36796-6*) Little.

—Hidden in Sand. LC 92-41746. (Illus.). 32p. (ps-2). 1994. SBE 14.95 (*0-684-19559-3*, Scribners Young Read) Macmillan Child Grp.

—The Kitchen Knight. Hyman, Trina S., illus. LC 89-11215. 32p. (gr. 1-4). 1990. reinforced bdg. 15.95 (*0-8234-0787-X*) Holiday.

Hodges, Margaret, adapted by. St. George & the Dragon. Hyman, Trina S., illus. LC 83-19980. (gr. 6-8). 1984. 15.95 (*0-316-36789-3*) Little.

Hodges, Margaret, retold by. St. Jerome & the Lion. Moser, Barry, illus. LC 90-22142. 32p. (ps-2). 1991. 14.95 (*0-531-05938-3*); RLB 14.99 (*0-531-08538-4*) Orchard Bks Watts.

Hodges, Michael. Britain in the 1970's. (Illus.). 72p. (gr. 7-10). 1989. 19.95 (*0-7134-5913-1*, Pub. by Batsford UK) Trafalgar.

Hodges-Caballero, Jane. Air & Space Activities. rev. ed. LC 85-81658. 152p. (ps-3). 1993. pap. text ed. 17.95 (*0-685-65254-8*) Humanics Ltd.

Hodge-Wright, Toni, et al, eds. The Handbook of Historically Black Colleges & Universities, Premier Edition 1992-94: Comprehensive Profiles & Photos of Black Colleges & Universities. Evans, Christine, et al, illus. LC 92-71364. 248p. (gr. 10 up). 1992. 19.95 (*0-9632669-0-X*) Jireh & Assocs.

Hodgman, Ann. Dark Dreams. LC 93-15039. 224p. (gr. 7 up). 1993. pap. 3.50 (*0-14-036374-2*, Puffin) Puffin Bks.

—Dark Music, No. 2. 224p. (gr. 7 up). 1994. pap. 3.50 (*0-14-036375-0*) Puffin Bks.

—A Day in the Life of a Fashion Designer. Jann, Gayle, illus. LC 87-13394. 32p. (gr. 4-8). 1988. PLB 11.79 (*0-8167-1119-4*); pap. text ed. 2.95 (*0-8167-1120-8*) Troll Assocs.

—A Day in the Life of a Theater Set Designer. Jann, Gayle, illus. LC 87-10951. 32p. (gr. 4-8). 1988. PLB 11.79 (*0-8167-1127-5*); pap. text ed. 2.95 (*0-8167-1128-3*) Troll Assocs.

—Galaxy High School. 96p. (gr. 2-6). 1987. pap. 2.50 (*0-553-15545-8*, Skylark) Bantam.

—The Missing Mermaid. 128p. (Orig.). 1987. pap. 2.25 (*0-553-26471-0*) Bantam.

—My Babysitter Bites Again. Ashby, Ruth, ed. Pierard, John, illus. 144p. (gr. 3-6). 1993. pap. 2.99 (*0-671-79378-0*, Minstrel Bks) PB.

—My Babysitter Is a Vampire. Ashby, Ruth, ed. Pierard, John, illus. (Orig.). 1991. pap. 2.99 (*0-671-64751-2*, Minstrel Bks) PB.

—Stinky Stanley. MacDonald, Pat, ed. Cymerman, John E., illus. 128p. (Orig.). (gr. 3-6). 1993. pap. 2.99 (*0-671-78548-6*, Minstrel Bks) PB.

—Stinky Stanley Stinks Again. MacDonald, Pat, ed. Cymerman, John E., illus. 128p. (Orig.). 1993. pap. 2.99 (*0-671-78560-5*, Minstrel Bks) PB.

—There's a Bat Wing in My Lunchbox. Pierard, John, illus. 96p. 1988. pap. 2.95 (*0-380-75426-6*, Camelot) Avon.

Hodgson, Harriet. Artworks. Savage, Beth, illus. 64p. (gr. k-3). 1986. 6.95 (*0-912107-42-1*, Dist. by Good Apple) Monday Morning Bks.

—Gameworks. 64p. (gr. k-3). 1986. 6.95 (*0-912107-41-3*) Monday Morning Bks.

Hodgson, Harriet W. My First Fourth of July Book. Hohag, Linda, illus. LC 86-30987. 32p. (ps-2). 1987. pap. 3.95 (*0-516-42907-8*) Childrens.

Hodgson, Joan. Hullo Sun. Ripper, Peter, illus. (ps-3). 1972. 6.95 (*0-85487-019-9*) DeVorss.

—Our Father. Ripper, Peter, illus. (ps-3). 1977. pap. 2.95 (*0-85487-040-7*) DeVorss.

Hodgson, Karen. Boop! Boop! I'm Better. Davis, Wesley, ed. (Illus.). 24p. 1993. pap. 1.25 (*1-56794-046-3*, C2316) Star Bible.

Hodgson-Burnett, Frances. The Land of the Blue Flower. Griffith, Judith A., illus. LC 93-77029. 48p. (ps-5). 1993. Repr. of 1938 ed. 15.95 (*0-915811-46-4*) H J Kramer Inc.

Back in print for the first time since 1938. In the finest fairy-tale tradition, THE LAND OF THE BLUE FLOWER tells of the transformation of the hateful kingdom of King Mordreth into the idyllic Land of the Blue Flower. Raised in isolation by a seer known only as the Ancient One, the infant King Amor is taught by him to respect & learn from the beauty & mysteries of nature. In this process, he becomes a wise ruler who is able to restore harmony, unity & compassion to his kingdom. Using the theme of learning from & living in harmony with nature, THE LAND OF THE BLUE FLOWER tells a spectacular tale demonstrating the healing power of love. Because of the social & ecological concerns that are central to the story, as well as the spiritual values, woven throughout, the book has significance & meaning for us in the 1990s. In addition to the many exquisite full-page, full-color illustrations by artist Judith Ann Griffith, beautifully rendered blue flower borders frame each page, lending an illuminated manuscript look to the book. *Publisher Provided Annotation.*

Hodrick, Robert J. The Empirical Evidence on the Efficiency of Forward & Futures Foreign Exchange Markets. 184p. (gr. 7 up). 1987. pap. text ed. 37.00 (*3-7186-0415-9*, Pub. by Harwood Acad Pubs) Gordon & Breach.

Hoeft, Pam. Holiday Art a la Carte. 112p. (gr. 4-8). 1982. 9.95 (*0-88160-049-0*, LW 235) Learning Wks.

Hoehn, Richard A., jt. ed. see Cohen, Marc J.

Hoehn, Robert. Science Starters! Over One Thousand Ready-to-Use Attention-Grabbers That Make Science Fun. 288p. (gr. 6-12). 1993. pap. 27.95x (*0-87628-860-3*) Ctr Appl Res.

Hoehne, Marcia. A Place of My Own. LC 92-44336. 128p. (Orig.). (gr. 4-7). 1993. pap. 4.99 (*0-89107-718-9*, Crossway Bks) Good News.

Hoellwarth, Cathryn. The Underbed. LC 89-28884. 32p. (ps-3). 1990. 12.95 (*0-934672-79-2*) Good Bks PA.

Hoelscher, Gwen. Prince Skippy's Quest. (Illus.). 64p. (Orig.). (gr. 6 up). 1986. pap. 7.95 (*0-9617597-0-4*) Wright Monday Pr.

Hoenack, Peg. Let's Sing & Play: Easy-to-Learn Letter Notation Method for Recorder, "Flutes," Keyboard. 4th ed. Morris, Alix & Hayden, Marilyn, illus. 64p. (gr. 2-7). 1991. student easel book, wire binding 5.50 (*0-913500-43-7*, L-1); Set 1, for teaching 32 songs. transparencies for overhead projector 64.00 (*0-913500-40-2*, L-8) Peg Hoenack MusicWorks.

Hoenack, Peg & Jones, Kay. Let's Sing & Play Carols & Holiday Songs: Thanksgiving, Hanukkah, Christmas, New Year's: Easy-to-Read Letter Notation for Recorder, "Flutes," Piano, any Melody Instrument. 2nd ed. Morris, Alix & Hayden, Marilyn, illus. 48p. (gr. 2-7). 1978. pap. text ed. 4.95 (*0-913500-18-6*, L-3) Peg Hoenack MusicWorks.

—Let's Sing & Play While Learning Rhythm Notation, Bk. 2-R: Easy Transition from Letter Notes to Rhythm Symbols. 2nd ed. Morris, Alix & Hayden, Marilyn, illus. 32p. (gr. 2-7). 1992. A-frame easel book with wire binding 5.50 (0-913500-44-5, L-2R) Peg Hoenack MusicWorks.

Hoenack, Peg, et al. Let's Sing & Play an Opera: Hansel & Gretel, Humperdinck Arr. 2nd ed. Hoenack, Frank & Morris, Alix, illus. 16p. (gr. 2-6). 1972. Student's Book in Peg Hoenack Letter Notation, with Words for Singing. pap. 4.50 (0-913500-19-4, L-4); Piano Accompaniment. tchr's. ed. 4.50 (0-913500-07-0, L-5) Peg Hoenack MusicWorks.

—Songs I Can Play: Easy-to-Learn Numeral Notation Method for 8-Bar Xylophone, Resonator Bells, Piano. 5th ed. Morris, Alix & Hayden, Marilyn, illus. 40p. (ps-2). 1983. Repr. of 1972 ed. Little Book - Child's Size. A-frame easel, wirebound 4.75 (0-913500-21-6, S-1); write for info. braille; Big Book - Classroom Size. wirebound, standup covers 46.00 (0-913500-17-8, S-3) Peg Hoenack MusicWorks.

Hoest, Bunny. Howard Huge Comes to Stay. Reiner, John, illus. LC 91-23629. 32p. (Orig.). (ps-1). 1992. pap. 2.25 (0-679-82033-7) Random Bks Yng Read.

Hoestlandt, Jo. Back to School with Mom. (Illus.). 48p. (gr. k-4). 1990. 12.75 (0-89565-815-1); 8.95s.p. (0-685-55096-6) Childs World.

Hofer, Angelika. The Lion Family Book. Ziesler, Gunter, illus. LC 88-15139. 52p. (gr. k up) 1991. pap. 15.95 (0-88708-070-7) Picture Bk Studio.

Hofer, Grace & Day, Rachel. Oyen Ninos, Listen Children. Day, Rachel, tr. Moncus, Stephen, illus. 96p. (gr. 4-7). 1993. 12.95 (0-89015-865-7) Eakin-Sunbelt.

Hoff, B. J. An Emerald Ballad 1-3 Giftset. 1992. 29.99 (1-55661-771-2) Bethany Hse.

—Song of the Silent Harp. 400p. (Orig.). (gr. 9-12). 1991. 9.99 (1-55661-110-2) Bethany Hse.

Hoff, Benjamin. The Te of Piglet. (Illus.). 224p. 1992. 16.00 (0-525-93496-0, Dutton) NAL-Dutton.

Hoff, Bernard. Duncan the Dancing Duck. LC 93-13058. (Illus.). 32p. (ps-3). 1994. 13.95 (0-395-67400-X, Clarion Bks) HM.

Hoff, Carol. Johnny Texas. Myers, Bob, illus. 150p. (gr. 4 up). 1992. lib. bdg. 15.95 (0-937460-80-X); pap. 9.95 (0-937460-81-8) Hendrick-Long.

—Johnny Texas on the San Antonio Road. (Illus.). 191p. (gr. 4 up). 1984. Repr. of 1953 ed. 13.95 (0-937460-15-X) Hendrick-Long.

—Wilderness Pioneer: Stephen F. Austin of Texas. Todd, Robert, illus. LC 55-7501. 192p. (gr. 4-8). 1987. Repr. of 1955 ed. PLB 13.95 (0-937460-25-7) Hendrick-Long.

Hoff, Mark. Gloria Steinem: The Women's Movement. (Illus.). 96p. (gr. 7 up). 1991. PLB 14.90 (1-878841-19-X) Millbrook Pr.

—Gloria Steinem: The Women's Movement. 1992. pap. 5.95 (0-395-63567-5) HM.

Hoff, Marshall G., jt. ed. see Bock, Glenn N.
Hoff, Marshall G., ed. see Haensel, Phyllis C.
Hoff, Mary. Oceans: Our Endangered Planet. (gr. 4-7). 1993. pap. 8.95 (0-8225-9628-8) Lerner Pubns.

Hoff, Mary & Roders, Mary M. Our Endangered Planet: Tropical Rain Forests. (Illus.). 64p. (gr. 4-6). 1991. PLB 21.50 (0-8225-2503-8) Lerner Pubns.

Hoff, Mary & Rodgers, Mary M. Life on Land. (Illus.). 72p. (gr. 4-6). 1992. PLB 21.50 (0-8225-2507-0) Lerner Pubns.

—Our Endangered Planet: Groundwater. (Illus.). 64p. (gr. 4-6). 1991. PLB 21.50 (0-8225-2500-3) Lerner Pubns.

—Our Endangered Planet: Population Growth. (Illus.). 64p. 1991. PLB 21.50 (0-8225-2502-X) Lerner Pubns.

—Our Endangered Planet: Rivers & Lakes. (Illus.). 64p. (gr. 4-6). 1991. PLB 21.50 (0-8225-2501-1) Lerner Pubns.

Hoff, Mary, jt. auth. see Rodgers, Mary M.
Hoff, Syd. Albert the Albatross. Hoff, Syd, illus. LC 61-5767. 32p. (gr. k-3). 1961. PLB 13.89 (0-06-022446-0) HarpC Child Bks.

—Barkley. Hoff, Syd, illus. LC 75-6290. 32p. (gr. k-3). 1975. PLB 13.89 (0-06-022448-7) HarpC Child Bks.

—Barney's Horse. Hoff, Syd, illus. LC 87-66. 32p. (ps-3). 1987. PLB 13.89 (0-06-022450-9) HarpC Child Bks.

—Barney's Horse. Hoff, Syd, illus. LC 87-66. 32p. (ps-2). 1990. pap. 3.50 (0-06-444142-3, Trophy) HarpC Child Bks.

—Bernard on His Own. Hoff, Syd, illus. LC 92-21770. 32p. (gr. k-3). 1993. 14.95 (0-395-65226-X, Clarion Bks) HM.

—Captain Cat. Hoff, Syd, illus. LC 91-27518. 48p. (ps-2). 1993. 14.00 (0-06-020527-X); PLB 13.89 (0-06-020528-8) HarpC Child Bks.

—Chester. Hoff, Syd, illus. LC 61-5768. 64p. (gr. k-3). 1961. PLB 13.89 (0-06-022456-8) HarpC Child Bks.

—Chester. Hoff, Syd, illus. LC 61-5768. 64p. (gr. k-3). 1986. pap. 3.50 (0-06-444095-8, Trophy) HarpC Child Bks.

—Danielito y el Dinosauria. Mlawer, Teresa, tr. from ENG. Hoff, Syd, illus. 64p. (gr. 5-7). 1991. PLB 11.95 (0-9625162-2-8) Lectorum Pubns.

—Danny & the Dinosaur. newly illus. ed. Hoff, Syd, illus. LC 92-13609. 64p. (gr. k-3). 1958. 14.00 (0-06-022465-7); PLB 13.89 (0-06-022466-5) HarpC Child Bks.

—Danny & the Dinosaur. newly illustrated ed. Hoff, Syd, illus. LC 58-7754. 64p. (gr. k-3). 1985. incl. cassette 5.98 (0-694-00017-5, Trophy); pap. 3.50 (0-06-444002-8, Trophy) HarpC Child Bks.

—Grizzwold. Hoff, Syd, illus. LC 64-14366. 64p. (gr. k-3). 1963. PLB 13.89 (0-06-022481-9) HarpC Child Bks.

—Grizzwold. LC 63-14366. (Illus.). 64p. (gr. k-3). 1984. pap. 3.50 (0-06-444057-5, Trophy) HarpC Child Bks.

—Horse in Harry's Room. Hoff, Syd, illus. LC 71-104753. 32p. (gr. k-3). 1970. PLB 13.89 (0-06-022483-5) HarpC Child Bks.

—The Horse in Harry's Room. Hoff, Syd, illus. LC 71-104753. 32p. (ps-2). 1985. pap. 3.50 (0-06-444073-7, Trophy) HarpC Child Bks.

—How to Draw Cartoons. (Illus.). 32p. (Orig.). (gr. k-3). 1991. pap. 1.95 (0-590-40689-2) Scholastic Inc.

—Julius. Hoff, Syd, illus. LC 59-8971. 64p. (gr. k-3). 1959. PLB 13.89 (0-06-022491-6) HarpC Child Bks.

—The Lighthouse Children. LC 92-41172. (Illus.). 32p. (ps-2). 1994. 14.00 (0-06-022958-6); PLB 13.89 (0-06-022959-4) HarpC Child Bks.

—Little Chief. Hoff, Syd, illus. LC 61-12098. 64p. (gr. k-3). 1961. PLB 13.89 (0-06-022501-7) HarpC Child Bks.

—Little Chief. Hoff, Syd, illus. LC 61-12098. 64p. (gr. k-3). 1990. pap. 3.50 (0-06-444135-0, Trophy) HarpC Child Bks.

—Mrs. Brice's Mice. Hoff, Syd, illus. LC 87-45680. 32p. (ps-2). 1988. PLB 13.89 (0-06-022452-5) HarpC Child Bks.

—Mrs. Brice's Mice. Hoff, Syd, illus. LC 87-45680. 32p. (ps-2). 1991. pap. 3.50 (0-06-444145-8, Trophy) HarpC Child Bks.

—Oliver. Hoff, Syd, illus. LC 60-5779. 64p. (gr. k-3). 1960. PLB 13.89 (0-06-022516-5) HarpC Child Bks.

—Oliver. Hoff, Syd, illus. LC 60-5779. 64p. (gr. k-3). 1986. pap. 3.50 (0-06-444097-4, Trophy) HarpC Child Bks.

—Sammy the Seal. Hoff, Syd, illus. LC 59-5316. 64p. (gr. k-3). 1959. PLB 13.89 (0-06-022526-2) HarpC Child Bks.

—Sammy the Seal. Hoff, Syd, illus. LC 59-5316. 64p. (gr. k-3). 1980. pap. 3.50 (0-06-444028-1, Trophy) HarpC Child Bks.

—Stanley. newly illus. ed. Hoff, Syd, illus. LC 91-15034. 64p. (gr. k-3). 1962. 13.00 (0-06-022535-1); PLB 12.89 (0-06-022536-X) HarpC Child Bks.

—Stanley. newly illus. ed. Hoff, Syd, illus. LC 91-12266. 64p. (gr. k-3). 1978. pap. 3.50 (0-06-444010-9, Trophy) HarpC Child Bks.

—Syd Hoff's Animal Jokes. Hoff, Syd, illus. LC 84-48353. 48p. (gr. k-3). 1986. (Lipp Jr Bks) HarpC Child Bks.

—Thunderhoof. Hoff, Syd, illus. LC 75-129855. (gr. k-3). 1971. PLB 13.89 (0-685-02069-X) HarpC Child Bks.

—When Will It Snow? Chalmers, Mary, illus. LC 64-16657. 32p. (gr. k-3). 1971. HarpC Child Bks.

—Who Will Be My Friends? Hoff, Syd, illus. 32p. (gr. k-2). 1960. PLB 13.89 (0-06-022556-4) HarpC Child Bks.

—Who Will Be My Friends? Hoff, Syd, illus. LC 60-14096. 32p. (ps-2). 1985. pap. 3.50 (0-06-444072-9, Trophy) HarpC Child Bks.

—The Young Cartoonist. LC 82-5980. (Illus.). 192p. (gr. 6-9). 1983. 19.95 (0-87396-094-7) Stravon.

Hoffa, Darlene. Creation Crafts. (Illus.). 64p. (Orig.). 1993. pap. 5.99 (0-570-04758-7) Concordia.

Hoffecker, Carol E. Delaware, the First State. (Illus.). 256p. (Orig.). 1987. pap. 9.95 (0-912608-47-1) Mid Atlantic.

Hoffecker, Felicity. Betsy Bigmouth. Bates, Virginia, illus. LC 89-13254. 28p. (gr. 2-5). 1990. 7.95 (0-8192-1519-8) Morehouse Pub.

Hoffius, Stephen. Winners & Losers. LC 92-42394. (gr. 6 up). 1993. pap. 15.00 (0-671-79194-X, S&S BFYR) S&S Trade.

Hoffman, Beverly. Skipper & Jade: A Love Story. LC 90-71859. 44p. 1991. pap. 6.95 (1-55523-411-9) Winston-Derek.

Hoffman, Beverly & Fiorilla, Sal J. A Flower for Iggey. Hoffman, Beverly & Robinson, Michael D., illus. LC 92-85530. 150p. (Orig.). (gr. 3-6). 1993. 12.95 (0-9634122-1-3); cass. musical tape avail. Feather Fables.

Hoffman, Beverly, et al, eds. see Lesterson, David.
Hoffman, Christine. Learning to Sew. Barton, Harriett, illus. LC 92-9516. 32p. (gr. 2-5). 1994. 11.00 (0-06-021146-6); PLB 10.89 (0-06-021147-4) HarpC Child Bks. Postponed.

Hoffman, Dustin, narrated by see Dr. Seuss.
Hoffman, E. T. The Nutcracker. Angus, Fay, adapted by. Welply, Michael, illus. (gr. 2 up). 1989. pap. 16.95 casebound, pop-up (0-671-68617-8, Little Simon) S&S Trade.

—Nutcracker. Black, Fiona, retold by. Gustafson, Scott, illus. 40p. 1991. 6.95 (0-8362-4934-8) Andrews & McMeel.

—The Nutcracker: Xmas Treasury Pop-Up. 1993. pap. 4.99 (0-517-08788-X) Outlet Bk Co.

Hoffman, Elizabeth, ed. Lectionary for Masses with Children: Sundays - Year A. American Bible Society Staff, tr. Erspamer, Steve, illus. Gregory, Wilton, intro. by. (Illus.). (gr. 1-8). Date not set. text ed. 42.00 (0-929650-71-9); pap. text ed. 10.00 (1-56854-000-0) Liturgy Tr Pubns.

—Lectionary for Masses with Children: Sundays - Year B. American Bible Society Staff, tr. Erspamer, Steve, illus. Gregory, Wilton, intro. by. (Illus.). 291p. (gr. 1-8). 1993. 42.00 (0-929650-73-5); pap. 10.00 (1-56854-002-7) Liturgy Tr Pubns.

—Lectionary for Masses with Children: Sundays - Year C. American Bible Society Staff, tr. Erspamer, Steve, illus. Gregory, Wilton, intro. by. (Illus.). (gr. 1-8). 1994. 42.00 (0-929650-74-3); pap. 10.00 (1-56854-003-5) Liturgy Tr Pubns.

—Lectionary for Masses with Children: Weekdays. American Bible Society Staff, tr. Erspamer, Steve, illus. Gregory, Wilton, intro. by. (Illus.). 503p. (gr. 1-8). 1993. 49.00 (0-929650-72-7); pap. 10.00 (1-56854-001-9) Liturgy Tr Pubns.

Hoffman, Elizabeth, ed. see Jeep, Elizabeth M.
Hoffman, James. Reading Stories, Grades 3-4. Hoffman, Joan, ed. Thrall, Mary, illus. 32p. (gr. 3-4). 1979. wkbk. 1.99 (0-938256-13-0) Sch Zone Pub Co.

Hoffman, Jane. Backyard Scientist, Series Four. Ostroff, Lanny, illus. 54p. (ps-7). 1992. pap. text ed. 8.50 (0-9618663-4-9) Backyard Scientist. **THE BACKYARD SCIENTIST SERIES provides the young scientist with excitement & fun to do hands-on science experiments & projects covering chemistry, physics & the life sciences (biology, entomology, physiology) & more. Experiments use materials usually found in most homes. Each experiment carries a sprightly illustration, & has a list of supplies needed for the experiment, step-by-step instructions & questions that lead the children through the observation process. The questions are designed to improve critical thinking skills. An explanation of the experiment & the scientific principles at work are given after each experiment. Experiments are meant to develop the young scientist's curiosity to do further exploration of the scientific concepts, thus further developing conceptual thought processes. The format makes the book easy to use for teachers, parents & students. Little advance preparation is required & with tight budgets, the inexpensive supplies required by the experiments allow for more science instruction. While all this learning takes place, the author has not forgotten to make the learning experience fun for student & teacher or parent. Author Jane Hoffman has appeared at prestigious museums throughout the country. Jane also lectures & conducts workshops for educators & parent groups throughout the nation.** *Publisher Provided Annotation.*

—Backyard Scientist: Series One. Ostroff, Lanny, illus. 52p. (Orig.). (gr. k-6). 1987. pap. text ed. 8.50 (0-9618663-0-6) Backyard Scientist.

—Backyard Scientist: Series Two. (Illus.). (gr. 4-9). 1989. pap. 8.50 (0-9618663-2-2) Backyard Scientist.

—Backyard Scientist, Series 3: Experiments in the Life Sciences. (Illus.). 52p. (gr. k-7). 1990. text ed. 8.50 (0-9618663-3-0) Backyard Scientist.

—The Original Backyard Scientist. Ostroff, Lanny, illus. 58p. (Orig.). (gr. k-6). 1987. text ed. 8.50 (0-9618663-1-4) Backyard Scientist.

Hoffman, Janet T. The Pattersons: Missionary Publishers. LC 83-71836. (gr. 4-6). 1984. 5.95 (0-8054-4288-X, 4242-88) Broadman.

Hoffman, Jeanne & Prizzi, Elaine. Big Fearon Dictionary & Library Skills Kit. (gr. 4-8). 1989. pap. 20.95 (0-8224-3055-X) Fearon Teach Aids.

—Re: Thinking. (gr. 5 up). 1989. pap. 11.95 (0-8224-5789-X) Fearon Teach Aids.

Hoffman, Jeanne, jt. auth. see Prizzi, Elaine.
Hoffman, Jennifer. Art Starts. Gregorich, Barbara, ed. (Illus.). 32p. (gr. 3 up). 1992. pap. 1.99 (0-88743-261-1, 02901) Sch Zone Pub Co.

—More Art Starts. Gregorich, Barbara, ed. (Illus.). 32p. (gr. 3 up). 1992. pap. 1.99 wkbk. (0-88743-262-X, 02902) Sch Zone Pub Co.

Hoffman, Jim. Fabulous Principal Pie. Hoffman, Joan, ed. (Illus.). 32p. (gr. k-2). 1992. pap. 3.95 (0-88743-427-4, 06079) Sch Zone Pub Co.

—Fabulous Principal Pie. Hoffman, Joan, ed. (Illus.). 16p. (gr. k-2). 1992. pap. 2.25 (0-88743-266-2, 06033) Sch Zone Pub Co.

Hoffman, Joan. Alphabet. rev. ed. Cook, Chris, illus. 32p.
(ps-1). 1987. wkbk. 1.99 (*0-938256-03-3*) Sch Zone
Pub Co.
—Cursive Writing. Cook, Chris, illus. 32p. (gr. 3-4). 1981.
wkbk. 1.99 (*0-938256-02-5*) Sch Zone Pub Co.
—The Last Game. (Illus.). 32p. (gr. k-2). 1992. pap. 3.95
(*0-88743-429-0*, 06081) Sch Zone Pub Co.
—The Last Game. (Illus.). 16p. (gr. k-2). 1992. pap. 2.25
(*0-88743-268-9*, 06035) Sch Zone Pub Co.
—Manuscript Writing. (Illus.). 32p. (gr. k-2). 1981. wkbk.
1.99 (*0-938256-01-7*) Sch Zone Pub Co.
—Mouse & Owl. Gregorich, Barbara, ed. Sanford, John,
illus. 32p. (gr. k-2). 1987. wkbk. 1.99 (*0-88743-102-X*,
02602) Sch Zone Pub Co.
—Numbers One to Twelve. rev. ed. Cook, Chris, illus.
32p. (ps-1). 1987. wkbk. 1.99 (*0-938256-26-2*) Sch
Zone Pub Co.
—Peter's Dream. (Illus.). 32p. (gr. k-2). 1992. pap. 3.95
(*0-88743-425-8*, 06077) Sch Zone Pub Co.
—Peter's Dream. (Illus.). 16p. (gr. k-2). 1992. pap. 2.25
(*0-88743-264-6*, 06031) Sch Zone Pub Co.
—Reading Readiness, Bk. 1. Cook, Chris, illus. 32p.
(ps-1). 1980. wkbk. 1.99 (*0-938256-04-1*) Sch Zone
Pub Co.
—Reading Readiness, Bk. 2. Cook, Chris, illus. 32p.
(ps-1). 1980. wkbk. 1.99 (*0-938256-05-X*) Sch Zone
Pub Co.
Hoffman, Joan, ed. see Bannister, Roberta.
Hoffman, Joan, ed. see DeYoung, Lorie.
Hoffman, Joan, ed. see Gregorich, Barbara.
Hoffman, Joan, ed. see Henkel, Arlene.
Hoffman, Joan, ed. see Hoffman, James.
Hoffman, Joan, ed. see Hoffman, Jim.
Hoffman, Joan, ed. see Lane, Shirley.
Hoffman, Joan, ed. see Palmer, Martha.
Hoffman, Joan, ed. see Schwaller, Catherine.
Hoffman, Joan, ed. see Syswerda, Jean.
Hoffman, Joan, ed. see Vinje, Marie.
Hoffman, Joan, ed. see Witty, Bruce.
**Hoffman, Joan, ed. see Witty, Bruce & Gregorich,
Barbara.**
Hoffman, John, ed. see Spacone, Carl.
Hoffman, Judy, jt. auth. see Frankel, Max.
Hoffman, Mary. Amazing Grace. (ps-3). 1991. 14.00
(*0-8037-1040-2*) Dial Bks Young.
—Antelope. LC 86-17715. (Illus.). 24p. (gr. k-5). 1987.
PLB 14.64 (*0-8172-2703-2*); pap. 3.95 (*0-8114-6870-4*)
Raintree Steck-V.
—Babies' Hotel. Willow, illus. 32p. (ps-1). 1993. pap. 8.95
(*0-460-88091-8*, Pub. by J M Dent & Sons) Trafalgar.
—Bear. LC 86-6775. (Illus.). 24p. (gr. k-5). 1986. PLB 14.
64 (*0-8172-2396-7*); pap. 3.95 (*0-8114-6871-2*)
Raintree Steck-V.
—Bird of Prey. LC 86-17832. (Illus.). 24p. (gr. k-5). 1987.
PLB 14.64 (*0-8172-2701-6*); pap. 3.95 (*0-8114-6872-0*)
Raintree Steck-V.
—Dracula's Daughter. Riddell, Chris, illus. 42p. (gr. 2-4).
1989. 3.95 (*0-8120-6135-7*) Barron.
—Elephant. LC 84-15119. (Illus.). 24p. (gr. k-5). 1985.
PLB 14.64 (*0-8172-2408-4*); pap. 3.95 (*0-8114-6874-7*)
Raintree Steck-V.
—The Four-Legged Ghosts. Seeley, Laura L., illus. 96p.
(gr. 2-6). 1993. 13.99 (*0-8037-1466-1*); lib. bdg. 13.89
(*0-8037-1645-1*) Dial Bks Young.
—Giraffe. LC 86-6770. (Illus.). 24p. (gr. k-5). 1986. PLB
14.64 (*0-8172-2397-5*); pap. 3.95 (*0-8114-6875-5*)
Raintree Steck-V.
—Gorilla. LC 84-24906. (Illus.). 24p. (gr. k-5). 1985. PLB
14.64 (*0-8172-2413-0*); pap. 3.95 (*0-8114-6876-3*)
Raintree Steck-V.
—Henry's Baby. Winter, Susan, illus. LC 92-53485. 32p.
(gr. 1-4). 1993. 13.95 (*1-56458-196-9*) Dorling
Kindersley.
—Hippo. LC 84-24792. (Illus.). 24p. (gr. k-5). 1985. PLB
14.64 (*0-8172-2412-2*); pap. 3.95 (*0-8114-6877-1*)
Raintree Steck-V.
—Leon's Lucky Lunch-Break. Noakes, Polly, illus. 32p.
(ps-k). 1993. 14.95 (*0-460-88021-7*, Pub. by J M Dent
& Sons) Trafalgar.
—Lion. LC 84-24794. (Illus.). 24p. (gr. k-5). 1985. PLB
14.64 (*0-8172-2411-4*); pap. 3.95 (*0-8114-6881-X*)
Raintree Steck-V.
—Monkey. LC 84-15117. (Illus.). 24p. (gr. k-5). 1985.
PLB 14.64 (*0-8172-2406-8*); pap. 3.95 (*0-8114-6883-6*)
Raintree Steck-V.
—My Grandma Has Black Hair. Burroughes, Joanna,
illus. LC 87-24654. 32p. (ps-3). 1988. 9.95
(*0-8037-0510-7*) Dial Bks Young.
—Nancy No-Size. Northway, Jennifer, illus. 32p. (gr.
k-3). 1987. 9.95 (*0-19-520596-0*) OUP.
—Panda. LC 84-15882. (Illus.). 24p. (gr. k-5). 1985. PLB
14.64 (*0-8172-2407-6*); pap. 3.95 (*0-8114-6884-4*)
Raintree Steck-V.
—Seal. LC 86-17806. (Illus.). 24p. (gr. k-5). 1987. PLB
14.64 (*0-8172-2702-4*); pap. 3.95 (*0-8114-6887-9*)
Raintree Steck-V.
—Snake. LC 86-6774. (Illus.). 24p. (gr. k-5). 1986. PLB
14.64 (*0-8172-2398-3*); pap. 3.95 (*0-8114-6889-5*)
Raintree Steck-V.
—Tiger. LC 84-15120. (Illus.). 24p. (gr. k-5). 1984. PLB
14.64 (*0-8172-2405-X*); pap. 3.95 (*0-8114-6890-9*)
Raintree Steck-V.
—Wild Cat. LC 86-10007. (Illus.). 24p. (gr. k-5). 1986.
PLB 14.64 (*0-8172-2399-1*); pap. 3.95 (*0-8114-6893-3*)
Raintree Steck-V.
—Zebra. LC 84-24795. (Illus.). 24p. (gr. k-5). 1985. PLB
14.64 (*0-8172-2414-9*); pap. 3.95 (*0-8114-6895-X*)
Raintree Steck-V.

Hoffman, Nina K., jt. auth. see Williams, Tad.
Hoffman, Richard L., jt. ed. see Baker, Nancy.

Hoffman, Robert B., Jr. Christmas Trees.
Birdsall, Josh, illus. 62p. (Orig.). (gr. 3
up). 1991. pap. 9.95 (*0-9633156-0-9*) R
B Hoffman.
A Christmas storybook & diary for all
ages. If you like Christmas &
Christmas trees -- you will enjoy these
five stories that tell the spirit of giving,
receiving, sharing, love & fellowship
during the Christmas season. You will
never look at a Christmas tree again
without thinking about these stories.
According to the Alaska News Agency,
these stories out-sell other Christmas
books in Alaska bookstores 6 to 1.
LITTLE TREE: A little Christmas tree
doesn't "think" it will be picked for
Christmas because of its small size.
THE MOST BEAUTIFUL
CHRISTMAS TREE EVER: A little
boy decides a tree you can see from his
home will be his own special Christmas
tree. THE PAINTED TREE: An old
Indian "spirit" woman helps the
members of a lost wagon train find
their way to safe haven. THE
TREASURE TREE: A young boy's
father plants a tree & years later its
treasure is discovered. THE LAST
CHRISTMAS TREE: A broken down
tree is left on a tree lot the night
before Christmas with a "free" tag on
it. To order: write or call -- Robert B.
Hoffman, Jr., 7761 Ingram Street,
Anchorage, AK 99502. (907) 243-0626.
Publisher Provided Annotation.

Hoffman, Virginia. Lucy Learns to Weave: Gathering
Plants. Denetsosie, Hoke, illus. LC 74-4894. 46p. (gr.
1-4). 1974. pap. 7.00 (*0-89019-009-7*) Rough Rock Pr.
Hoffman, Yair & Shamir, Ilana. The World of the Bible
for Young Readers. (Illus.). 96p. (gr. 7 up). 1989. pap.
15.95 (*0-670-81739-2*) Viking Child Bks.
Hoffmann, E. T. Best Tales of Hoffmann. Bleiler, E. F.,
ed. (Illus., Orig.). (gr. 9-12). 1963. pap. 8.95
(*0-486-21793-0*) Dover.
—The Nutcracker. Bell, Anthea, adapted by. Zwerger,
Lisbeth, illus. LC 87-15249. (gr. 1 up). 1991. pap. 14.
95 (*0-88708-051-0*) Picture Bk Studio.
—Nutcracker. Madden, Andrea C., tr. Goodrich, Carter,
illus. LC 86-45271. 104p. 1987. 14.95 (*0-394-55384-5*)
Knopf Bks Yng Read.
—The Nutcracker. Chorao, Kay, illus. Schulman, Janet,
adapted by. LC 79-11223. (Illus.). 64p. (gr. 3-7). 1988.
pap. 2.95 (*0-394-82018-5*) Knopf Bks Yng Read.
—The Nutcracker. 2nd, abr. ed. Bell, Anthea, tr.
Zwerger, Lisbeth, illus. LC 87-15249. 28p. (gr. k up).
1991. pap. 4.95 (*0-88708-156-8*) Picture Bk Studio.
—The Nutcracker. Delamare, David, illus. LC 91-2167.
48p. (gr. 1-5). 1991. 9.95 (*0-88101-115-0*) Unicorn
Pub.
—The Nutcracker. Manheim, Ralph, tr. Sendak, Maurice,
illus. 120p. 1991. pap. 16.00 (*0-517-58659-2*, Crown)
Crown Pub Group.
—Nutcracker. Black, Fiona, retold by. Gustafson, Scott,
illus. LC 92-24140. 32p. 1992. 4.95 (*0-8362-3026-4*)
Andrews & McMeel.
—The Strange Child. Zweger, Lisbeth, illus. LC 84-8404.
28p. (gr. 3 up). 1991. pap. 16.95 (*0-907234-60-7*)
Picture Bk Studio.
Hoffmann, Henry. Slovenly Peter: or Cheerful Stories &
Funny Pictures for Good Little Folks. (Illus.). 88p.
1991. Repr. PLB 25.95x (*0-89966-765-1*) Buccaneer
Bks.
Hoffmann, Jeanne, jt. auth. see Prizzi, Elaine.
Hoffmann, Peggy, jt. auth. see Hunter, Gerald R.
Hofman, Ginnie. The Runaway Teddy Bear. Hofman,
Ginnie, illus. LC 84-23740. 32p. (ps-3). 1986. pap.
2.25 (*0-394-86286-4*) Random Bks Yng Read.
Hofman, Joan, ed. see Gregorich, Barbara.
Hofmann, Ginnie. The Bear Next Door: Story & Pictures.
LC 93-616. (ps-3). 1994. write for info.
(*0-679-83957-7*); write for info. (*0-679-93957-1*)
Random Bks Yng Read.
—One Teddy Bear Is Enough! Hofmann, Ginnie, illus.
LC 88-18166. 32p. (Orig.). (ps-3). 1991. lib. bdg. 5.99
(*0-394-99582-1*); pap. 2.25 (*0-394-89582-7*) Random
Bks Yng Read.
—Who Wants an Old Teddy Bear? Hofmann, Ginnie,
illus. LC 80-10445. 32p. (ps-3). 1980. lib. bdg. 5.99
(*0-394-93925-5*); pap. 2.25 (*0-394-83925-0*) Random
Bks Yng Read.

Hofsepian, Sylvia A. Why Not? Henstra, Friso, illus. LC
89-39333. 32p. (gr. k-3). 1991. RSBE 13.95
(*0-02-743980-1*, Four Winds) Macmillan Child Grp.
Hofsinde, Robert. Indian Costumes. Hofsinde, Robert,
illus. LC 68-11895. (gr. 3-7). 1968. PLB 12.88
(*0-688-31614-X*) Morrow Jr Bks.
—Indian Sign Language. Hofsinde, Robert, illus. LC 56-
5178. (gr. 5 up). 1956. PLB 13.88 (*0-688-31610-7*)
Morrow Jr Bks.
—Indian Warriors & Their Weapons. Hofsinde, Robert,
illus. LC 65-11041. (gr. 4-7). 1965. PLB 11.88
(*0-688-31613-1*) Morrow Jr Bks.
Hofstrand, Mary. By the Sea. (Illus.). 32p. (ps-3). 1990.
pap. 3.95 (*0-14-054208-6*, Puffin) Puffin Bks.
Hogan, Jan. Gladdys Makes Peace. Wine, Jeanine M.,
illus. 22p. (gr. 1-5). 1985. 9.95 (*0-87178-313-4*)
Brethren.
Hogan, Kirk, jt. auth. see Hogan, Paula Z.
Hogan, Paula. The Compass. LC 82-70439. (Illus.). 64p.
(gr. 4-6). 1982. PLB 8.85 (*0-8027-6453-3*) Walker &
Co.
—Dying Oceans. LC 91-10216. (Illus.). 32p. (gr. 3-4).
1991. PLB 17.27 (*0-8368-0476-7*) Gareth Stevens Inc.
—Expanding Deserts. LC 90-27799. (Illus.). 32p. (gr.
3-4). 1991. PLB 17.27 (*0-8368-0474-0*) Gareth
Stevens Inc.
—Fragile Mountains. LC 91-2019. (Illus.). 32p. (gr. 3-4).
1991. PLB 17.27 (*0-8368-0475-9*) Gareth Stevens Inc.
—Vanishing Rain Forests. (Illus.). 32p. (gr. 3-4). 1991.
PLB 17.27 (*0-8368-0477-5*) Gareth Stevens Inc.
Hogan, Paula & Seidenberg, Steven. Ecology: Our Living
Planet. LC 89-11282. (Illus.). 64p. (gr. 2-3). 1990.
PLB 19.93 (*0-8368-0030-3*) Gareth Stevens Inc.
Hogan, Paula Z. The Beaver. Miyake, Yoshi, illus. LC
79-13305. 32p. (gr. 1-4). 1979. PLB 17.96
(*0-8172-1502-6*) Raintree Steck-V.
—The Beaver. LC 79-13305. (Illus.). 32p. (gr. 1-4). 1981.
PLB 29.28 incl. cassette (*0-8172-1848-3*) Raintree
Steck-V.
—The Black Swan. Hockerman, Dennis, illus. LC 78-
27416. 32p. (gr. 1-4). 1979. PLB 17.96
(*0-8172-1254-X*) Raintree Steck-V.
—The Black Swan. LC 78-27416. (Illus.). 32p. (gr. 1-4).
1984. PLB 29.28 incl. cassette (*0-8172-2225-1*)
Raintree Steck-V.
—The Butterfly. LC 78-26827. (Illus.). 32p. (gr. 1-4).
1979. PLB 17.96 (*0-8172-1252-3*); pap. 4.95
(*0-8114-8176-X*); pap. 9.95 incl. cassette
(*0-8114-8184-0*) Raintree Steck-V.
—The Butterfly. LC 78-26827. (Illus.). 32p. (gr. k-3).
1984. PLB 29.28 incl. cassette (*0-8172-2226-X*)
Raintree Steck-V.
—The Crocodile. Nachreiner, Tom, illus. LC 79-13699.
32p. (gr. 1-4). 1979. PLB 17.96 (*0-8172-1503-4*)
Raintree Steck-V.
—The Crocodile. LC 79-13699. (Illus.). 32p. (gr. 1-4).
1981. PLB 29.28 incl. cassette (*0-8172-1842-4*)
Raintree Steck-V.
—The Dandelion. LC 78-21155. (Illus.). 32p. (gr. 1-4).
1979. PLB 17.96 (*0-8172-1250-7*); pap. 4.95
(*0-8114-8182-4*); pap. 9.95 incl. cassette
(*0-8114-8190-5*) Raintree Steck-V.
—The Dandelion. LC 78-21155. (Illus.). 32p. (gr. 1-4).
1984. PLB 29.28 incl. cassette (*0-8172-2227-8*)
Raintree Steck-V.
—The Elephant. Craft, Kinuko Y., illus. LC 79-13307.
(gr. 1-4). 1979. PLB 29.28 incl. cassette
(*0-8172-1844-0*); PLB 17.96 (*0-8172-1505-0*); pap.
4.95 (*0-8114-8177-8*); pap. 9.95 incl. cassette
(*0-8114-8185-9*) Raintree Steck-V.
—The Frog. Strigenz, Geri K., illus. LC 78-21240. 32p.
(gr. 1-4). 1979. PLB 17.96 (*0-8172-1253-1*); pap. 4.95
(*0-8114-8175-1*); pap. 9.95 incl. cassette
(*0-8114-8183-2*) Raintree Steck-V.
—The Frog. LC 78-21240. (Illus.). 32p. (gr. 1-4). 1984.
PLB 29.28 incl. cassette (*0-8172-2228-6*) Raintree
Steck-V.
—The Gorilla. LC 79-13602. (Illus.). 32p. (gr. 1-4). 1979.
PLB 17.96 (*0-8172-1501-8*) Raintree Steck-V.
—The Gorilla. LC 79-13602. (Illus.). 32p. (gr. 1-4). 1981.
PLB 29.28 incl cassette (*0-8172-1845-9*) Raintree
Steck-V.
—The Honeybee. Strigenz, Geri K., illus. LC 78-21165.
32p. (gr. 1-4). 1979. PLB 17.96 (*0-8172-1256-6*); pap.
4.95 (*0-8114-8179-4*); pap. 9.95 incl. cassette
(*0-8114-8187-5*) Raintree Steck-V.
—The Honeybee. LC 78-21165. (Illus.). 32p. (gr. 1-4).
1984. PLB 29.28 incl. cassette (*0-8172-2229-4*)
Raintree Steck-V.
—Hospital Scares Me. (ps-3). 1993. pap. 3.95
(*0-8114-7153-5*) Raintree Steck-V.
—I Hate Boys-I Hate Girls. Hockerman, Dennis, illus.
McDonald, Paula & McDonald, Dickintro. by. LC 79-
24056. (Illus.). 32p. (gr. k-6). 1980. PLB 17.96
(*0-8172-1358-9*) Raintree Steck-V.
—The Kangaroo. Mayo, Gretchen, illus. LC 79-13660.
(gr. 1-4). 1979. PLB 17.96 (*0-8172-1504-2*); pap. 4.95
(*0-8114-8181-6*); pap. 9.95 incl. cassette
(*0-8114-8189-1*) Raintree Steck-V.
—The Kangaroo. LC 79-13660. (Illus.). 32p. (gr. 1-4).
1981. PLB 29.28 incl. cassette (*0-8172-1843-2*)
Raintree Steck-V.
—The Oak Tree. LC 78-21183. (Illus.). 32p. (gr. 1-4).
1979. PLB 17.96 (*0-8172-1251-5*) Raintree Steck-V.
—The Oak Tree. LC 78-21183. (Illus.). 32p. (gr. 1-4).
1984. PLB 29.28 incl. cassette (*0-8172-2230-8*)
Raintree Steck-V.

—The Penguin. Strizenz, Geri K., illus. LC 78-21225. 32p. (gr. 1-4). 1979. PLB 17.96 (0-8172-1257-4) Raintree Steck-V.
—The Penguin. LC 78-21225. (Illus.). 32p. (gr. 1-4). 1984. PLB 29.28 incl. cassette (0-8172-2231-6) Raintree Steck-V.
—The Salmon. Hockerman, Dennis, illus. LC 78-21178. 32p. (gr. 1-4). 1979. PLB 17.96 (0-8172-1255-8); pap. 4.95 (0-8114-8178-6); pap. 9.95 incl. cassette (0-8114-8186-7) Raintree Steck-V.
—The Salmon. LC 78-21178. (Illus.). 32p. (gr. 1-4). 1984. PLB 29.28 incl. cassette (0-8172-2232-4) Raintree Steck-V.
—Sometimes I Don't Like School. Ford, Pam, illus. Smith, David L., intro. by. LC 79-24055. (Illus.). 32p. (gr. k-6). 1980. PLB 17.96 (0-8172-1357-0) Raintree Steck-V.
—Sometimes I Don't Like School. (ps-3). 1993. pap. 3.95 (0-8114-7155-1) Raintree Steck-V.
—Sometimes I Get So Mad. Shapiro, Karen, illus. Silverman, Manuel S., intro. by. LC 79-24057. (Illus.). 32p. (gr. k-6). 1980. PLB 17.96 (0-8172-1359-7) Raintree Steck-V.
—Sometimes I Get So Mad. (ps-3). 1993. pap. 3.95 (0-8114-5207-7) Raintree Steck-V.
—The Tiger. Nachreiner, Tom, illus. LC 79-13604. (gr. 1-4). 1979. PLB 17.96 (0-8172-1506-9) Raintree Steck-V.
—The Tiger. LC 79-13604. (Illus.). 32p. (gr. 1-4). 1981. PLB 29.28 incl. cassette (0-8172-1841-6) Raintree Steck-V.
—The Whale. Ruth, Rod, illus. LC 79-13379. 32p. (gr. 1-4). 1979. PLB 17.96 (0-8172-1500-X); pap. 4.95 (0-8114-8180-8); pap. 9.95 incl. cassette (0-8114-8188-3) Raintree Steck-V.
—The Whale. LC 79-13379. (Illus.). 32p. (gr. 1-4). 1981. PLB 29.28 incl. cassette (0-8172-1847-5) Raintree Steck-V.
—Will Dad Ever Move Back Home? Leder, Dora, illus. Muir, Martha F., intro. by. LC 79-24058. (Illus.). 32p. (gr. k-6). 1980. PLB 17.96 (0-8172-1356-2) Raintree Steck-V.
—Will Dad Ever Move Back Home? (ps-3). 1993. pap. 3.95 (0-8114-7160-8) Raintree Steck-V.
—The Wolf. Maxwell, Barbara, illus. LC 79-13309. 32p. (gr. 1-4). 1979. PLB 17.96 (0-8172-1507-7) Raintree Steck-V.
—The Wolf. LC 79-13309. (Illus.). 32p. (gr. 1-4). 1981. PLB 29.28 incl. cassette (0-8172-1846-7) Raintree Steck-V.
Hogan, Paula Z. & Hogan, Kirk. The Hospital Scares Me. Thelen, Mary, illus. Wilson, Jerrian M., intro. by. LC 79-23886. (Illus.). 32p. (gr. k-6). 1980. PLB 17.96 (0-8172-1351-1) Raintree Steck-V.
Hogan, Ryan. Double Scoop in a Day at the Babysitters. Hogan, Ryan, illus. 18p. (ps-5). 1993. 12.95 (0-9635529-0-2) Cult Exchange.
Hogan, Stephen. Johnny Lynch. Nivens, Chuck, illus. 165p. (gr. 5-6). 1991. PLB 13.00x (0-945253-07-9) Thornsbury Bailey Brown.
Hogg, Elizabeth. Gorgonzola Summer. 88p. (gr. 6-8). 1989. 16.95 (0-09-173653-6, Pub. by Hutchinson UK) Trafalgar.
Hogg, Gary. Friendship in the Forest. Anderson, Gary, illus. (gr. k-6). 1991. 11.95 (0-89868-204-5); pap. 4.95 (0-89868-205-3) ARO Pub.
—The Half-Hearted Hare. Anderson, Gary, illus. (gr. k-6). 1991. 11.95 (0-89868-206-1); pap. 4.95 (0-89868-207-X) ARO Pub.
—Happy Hawk Series, 6 bks. Anderson, Gary, illus. (gr. k-6). 1991. Set. 71.70 (0-89868-243-6); Set. pap. 29.70 (0-89868-242-8) ARO Pub.
—I Heard of a Nerd Bird. Anderson, Gary, illus. (gr. k-6). 1991. 11.95 (0-89868-200-2); pap. 4.95 (0-89868-201-0) ARO Pub.
—The Lion Who Couldn't Roar. Anderson, Gary, illus. (gr. k-6). 1991. 11.95 (0-89868-210-X); pap. 4.95 (0-89868-211-8) ARO Pub.
—Lizzie Learns About Lying. Anderson, Gary, illus. (gr. k-6). 1991. 11.95 (0-89868-202-9); pap. 4.95 (0-89868-203-7) ARO Pub.
—Sir William the Worm. Anderson, Gary, illus. (gr. k-6). 1991. 11.95 (0-89868-208-8); pap. 4.95 (0-89868-209-6) ARO Pub.
Hogg, Ian V. Tanks. Sarson, Peter & Bryan, Tony, illus. LC 84-9650. 48p. (gr. 5 up). 1985. PLB 14.95 (0-8225-1378-1, First Ave Edns); pap. 4.95 (0-8225-9507-9, First Ave Edns) Lerner Pubns.
Hogner, Franz. From Blueprint to House. Lerner, Mark, tr. from GER. (Illus.). 24p. (ps-3). 1986. lib. bdg. 10.95 (0-87614-295-1) Carolrhoda Bks.
Hogrogian, Nonny. The Cat Who Loved to Sing. LC 86-27358. (Illus.). 40p. (ps-2). 1988. lib. bdg. 13.99 (0-394-99004-8) Knopf Bks Yng Read.
—The Contest. LC 76-40389. (Illus.). 32p. (gr. k-3). 1976. PLB 12.88 (0-688-84042-6) Greenwillow.
—Handmade Secret Hiding Places. LC 75-4379. (Illus.). 48p. (ps-5). 1990. pap. 7.95 (0-87951-033-1); deluxe ed. 4.95 (0-87951-376-4) Overlook Pr.
—One Fine Day. Hogrogian, Nonny, illus. LC 75-119834. 32p. (gr. k-3). 1974. pap. 3.95 (0-02-043620-3, Aladdin) Macmillan Child Grp.
—One Fine Day. LC 75-119834. (Illus.). 32p. (gr. k-3). 1971. RSBE 13.95 (0-02-744000-1, Macmillan Child Bk) Macmillan Child Grp.
Hoguet, Susan, jt. auth. see Lindbergh, Anne M.

Hoguet, Susan R. I Unpacked My Grandmother's Trunk. Houget, Susan R., illus. LC 83-1701. 58p. (ps-3). 1983. 13.95 (0-525-44069-0, DCB) Dutton Child Bks.
—Solomon Grundy. Hoguet, Susan R., illus. LC 85-20453. 32p. (ps-3). 1986. 13.95 (0-525-44239-1, DCB) Dutton Child Bks.
Hoh. The Wish. 1993. pap. 3.50 (0-590-46013-7) Scholastic Inc.
Hoh, Diane. The Accident. 1991. pap. 3.25 (0-590-44330-5) Scholastic Inc.
—Deadly Attraction. (gr. 9-12). 1993. pap. 3.50 (0-590-46015-3) Scholastic Inc.
—The Fever. 176p. 1992. pap. 3.25 (0-590-45401-3, Point) Scholastic Inc.
—Funhouse. 1990. pap. 3.25 (0-590-43050-5) Scholastic Inc.
—Guilty. (gr. 12 up). 1993. pap. 3.50 (0-590-49452-X) Scholastic Inc.
—The Invitation. 1991. 3.25 (0-590-44904-4, Point) Scholastic Inc.
—The Roommate. (gr. 9-12). 1993. pap. 3.50 (0-590-47136-8) Scholastic Inc.
—The Scream Team. 1993. pap. 3.50 (0-590-47137-6) Scholastic Inc.
—The Silent Scream. (gr. 9-12). 1993. pap. 3.50 (0-590-46014-5) Scholastic Inc.
—The Train. 1992. 3.25 (0-590-45640-7, 068, Point) Scholastic Inc.
Hoig, Stan. Capital for the Nation. LC 90-2783. (Illus.). (gr. 4-7). 1990. 15.95 (0-525-65034-2, Cobblehill Bks) Dutton Child Bks.
—The Cheyenne. Porter, Frank W., III, intro. by. (Illus.). 112p. (gr. 5 up). 1989. 17.95 (1-55546-696-6); pap. 9.95 (0-7910-0358-2) Chelsea Hse.
—People of the Sacred Arrow. (Illus.). 144p. (gr. 6 up). 1992. 15.00 (0-525-65088-1, Cobblehill Bks) Dutton Child Bks.
Hokett, Norene. Main Street Was Two Blocks Long. 192p. (gr. 9 up). 1993. 16.95 (1-55853-263-3) Rutledge Hill Pr.
Hol, Coby. Bela, Etoile du Cirque. Hol, Coby, illus. (FRE.). 32p. (gr. k-3). 1992. 14.95 (3-314-20724-7) North-South Bks NYC.
—Bela Wird Zirkuspony. Hol, Coby, illus. (GER.). 32p. (gr. k-3). 1992. 14.95 (3-314-00533-4) North-South Bks NYC.
—La Ferme Des Tournesols. Hol, Coby, illus. (FRE.). 32p. (gr. k-3). 1992. 13.95 (3-85539-660-4) North-South Bks NYC.
—Henrietta Saves the Show. Hol, Coby, illus. Graves, Helen, tr. from GER. LC 90-47063. (Illus.). 32p. (ps-k). 1991. 14.95 (1-55858-102-2) North-South Bks NYC.
—Lisa & the Snowman. Hol, Coby, illus. LC 89-42614. 32p. (ps-k). 1989. 13.95 (1-55858-022-0) North-South Bks NYC.
—Niki's Little Donkey. James, J. Alison, tr. from GER. Hol, Coby, illus. LC 92-31332. 32p. (gr. k-3). 1993. 14.95 (1-55858-183-9); PLB 14.88 (1-55858-184-7) North-South Bks NYC.
—Der Sonnenhof. Hol, Coby, illus. (GER.). 32p. (gr. k-3). 1992. 13.95 (3-85825-315-4) North-South Bks NYC.
—Tippy Bear & Little Sam. Hol, Coby, illus. LC 91-29672. 32p. (ps-k). 1992. 11.95 (1-55858-138-3); lib. bdg. 11.88 (1-55858-149-9) North-South Bks NYC.
—Tippy Bear Goes to a Party. Hol, Coby, illus. LC 91-8167. 32p. (ps-k). 1991. 11.95 (1-55858-129-4) North-South Bks NYC.
—Tippy Bear Hunts for Honey. Hol, Coby, illus. LC 91-10477. 32p. (ps-k). 1991. 11.95 (1-55858-128-6) North-South Bks NYC.
—Tippy Bear's Christmas. LC 91-45679. (Illus.). 32p. (ps-k). 1992. 11.95 (1-55858-156-1); PLB 11.88 (1-55858-157-X) North-South Bks NYC.
—A Visit to the Farm. Hol, Coby, illus. LC 88-25366. 32p. (gr. k-3). 1989. 13.95 (1-55858-000-X) North-South Bks NYC.
Holabird, Katharine. Alexander & the Dragon. Craig, Helen, illus. 24p. (ps-2). 1988. 13.00 (0-517-56996-5, Clarkson Potter) Crown Bks Yng Read.
—Alexander & the Magic Boat. Craig, Helen, illus. 24p. (ps-2). 1990. 11.95 (0-517-58142-6); PLB 12.99 (0-517-58149-3) Crown Bks Yng Read.
—Angelina & Alice. Craig, Helen, illus. (ps-2). 1988. 14.00 (0-517-56074-7, Clarkson Potter) Crown Bks Yng Read.
—Angelina at the Fair. Craig, Helen, illus. LC 84-28931. 24p. (ps-2). 1988. 13.00 (0-517-55744-4, Clarkson Potter) Crown Bks Yng Read.
—Angelina Ballerina. Craig, Helen, illus. LC 83-8233. (ps-2). 1988. 13.00 (0-517-55083-0, Clarkson Potter) Crown Bks Yng Read.
—Angelina Ballerina. miniature ed. Craig, Helen, illus. 24p. (ps-2). 1990. 4.99 (0-517-57668-6, Clarkson Potter) Crown Bks Yng Read.
—Angelina Book & Doll Package. Craig, Helen, illus. LC 83-8233. 32p. (ps-2). 1989. book & doll 20.00 (0-517-57089-0, Clarkson Potter) Crown Bks Yng Read.
—Angelina Dances. Craig, Helen, illus. LC 92-80524. 6p. (ps-k). 1992. bds. 5.99 (0-679-83484-2) Random Bks Yng Read.
—Angelina Ice Skates. Craig, Helen, illus. 32p. (ps-2). 1993. 15.00 (0-517-59619-9) Crown Bks Yng Read.
—Angelina on Stage. Craig, Helen, illus. 24p. (ps-2). 1988. 14.00 (0-517-56073-9, Clarkson Potter) Crown Bks Yng Read.

—Angelina's Baby Sister. (ps-2). 1991. 13.00 (0-517-58600-2, Clarkson Potter) Crown Bks Yng Read.
—Angelina's Birthday Surprise. Craig, Helen, illus. LC 89-3513. 32p. (ps-2). 1989. 14.00 (0-517-57325-3, Clarkson Potter) Crown Bks Yng Read.
—Angelina's Christmas. Craig, Helen, illus. LC 85-12389. 32p. (gr. 1 up). 1986. 13.00 (0-517-55823-8, Clarkson Potter); pap. 4.95 (0-685-22929-7, C N Potter Bks) Crown Bks Yng Read.
—Christmas with Angelina. Craig, Helen, illus. LC 92-80523. 6p. (ps-k). 1992. bds. 5.99 (0-679-83485-0) Random Bks Yng Read.
Holbrook, Janet M. Little Red Hiding Wolf. McNutt, Mary M., illus. 35p. (gr. k-12). 1992. pap. 8.95 (0-9636203-0-4) Holbrook Dogwds.
Holbrook, Mike. Snorkeling. LC 92-45219. (Illus.). 48p. (gr. 5-6). 1994. RSBE 13.95 (0-89686-823-0, Crestwood Hse) Macmillan Child Grp.
Holbrook, Sara. The Dog Ate My Homework. 44p. (gr. 4-8). 1990. pap. 6.95 (1-881786-00-5) Kid Poems.
—Feelings Make Me Real. 46p. (gr. 4-8). 1990. pap. 6.95 (1-881786-02-1) Kid Poems.
—I Never Said I Wasn't Difficult. (Orig.). (gr. 4-8). Date not set. pap. 6.95 (1-881786-05-6) Kid Poems.

—Kid Poems for the Not-So-Bad, 4 vols. (gr. 4-8). 1992. pap. 24.95 (1-881786-06-4) Kid Poems.
Are you not-so-bad? Are you maybe not the brightest or the best, not the richest or the fastest, but overall, not-so-bad? KID POEMS FOR THE NOT-SO-BAD are for the silly, the wondering, the sometimes hopeless & helpless & misunderstood. Kids who hate their bodies, hate to say they're wrong, & think their self conscious should keep quiet! Kids who maybe say gross things at the dinner table, secretly stick out their tongues, & who feel embarrassment is worse than death. KID POEMS are also for adults who once promised themselves when they were grown-up they would remember how it was. The four book set of KID POEMS FOR THE NOT-SO-BAD includes: The Dog Ate My Homework (poems about school), Feelings Make Me Real (40 poems about about different feelings), Some Families: I Want To Move Across The Street (over 40 poems that tell us family's where we find it) & I Never Said I Wasn't Difficult (poems about individuality, rebellion & relationships). Order by contacting KID POEMS, P.O. Box 40084, Bay Village, OH 44140, FAX (216) 899-0192.
Publisher Provided Annotation.

—Some Families: I Want to Move Across the Street. 51p. (gr. 4-8). 1990. pap. 6.95 (1-881786-01-3) Kid Poems.
Holcomb, Ann, ed. see Hooker, Dennis.
Holcomb, J. Paul & Holcomb, Sue A. Tex R Masaur: The Beginning. Holcomb, Sue A., illus. 32p. (Orig.). (gr. k-3). 1993. pap. 3.95 (0-9636122-1-2) Post Oak Hill.
Holcomb, Nan. Andy Finds a Turtle. Yoder, Dot, illus. 32p. (Orig.). (ps-2). 1988. pap. 6.95 (0-944727-02-6) Jason & Nordic Pubs.
—Andy Finds a Turtle. Yoder, Dot, illus. 32p. (ps-2). 1992. Repr. of 1988 ed. 13.95 (0-944727-13-1) Jason & Nordic Pubs.
—Andy Opens Wide. Yoder, Dot, illus. 32p. (ps-2). 1990. pap. 6.95 (0-944727-06-9) Jason & Nordic Pubs.
—Andy Opens Wide. Yoder, Dot, illus. 32p. (ps-2). 1992. Repr. of 1990 ed. 13.95 (0-944727-17-4) Jason & Nordic Pubs.
—Danny & the Merry-Go-Round. Lucia, Virginia, illus. 32p. (Orig.). 1988. pap. 6.95 (0-944727-00-X) Jason & Nordic Pubs.
—Danny & the Merry-Go-Round. Lucia, Virginia, illus. 32p. (ps-2). 1992. Repr. of 1988 ed. 13.95 (0-944727-11-5) Jason & Nordic Pubs.
—Fair & Square. Yoder, Dot, illus. 32p. (ps-2). 1992. pap. 6.95 (0-944727-09-3) Jason & Nordic Pubs.
—Fair & Square. Yoder, Dot, illus. 32p. (ps-2). 1992. 13.95 (0-944727-10-7) Jason & Nordic Pubs.
—How About A Hug. Taggart, Tricia, illus. 32p. (Orig.). (ps). 1988. pap. 6.95 (0-944727-01-8) Jason & Nordic Pubs.
—How about a Hug. Taggart, Tricia, illus. 32p. (ps-2). 1992. Repr. of 1988 ed. 13.95 (0-944727-12-3) Jason & Nordic Pubs.

—Patrick & Emma Lou. Yoder, Dot, illus. 32p. (ps-2). 1989. pap. 6.95 (0-944727-03-4) Jason & Nordic Pubs.

—Patrick & Emma Lou. Yoder, Dot, illus. 32p. (ps-3). 1992. Repr. of 1989 ed. 13.95 (0-944727-14-X) Jason & Nordic Pubs.

—Sarah's Surprise. Yoder, Dot, illus. 32p. (ps-2). 1990. pap. 6.95 (0-944727-07-7) Jason & Nordic Pubs.

—Sarah's Surprise. Yoder, Dot, illus. 32p. (ps-3). 1992. Repr. of 1990 ed. 13.95 (0-944727-18-2) Jason & Nordic Pubs.

—A Smile from Andy. Yoder, Dot, illus. 32p. (ps-2). 1989. pap. 6.95 (0-944727-04-2) Jason & Nordic Pubs.

—A Smile from Andy. Yoder, Dot, illus. 32p. (ps-3). 1992. Repr. of 1989 ed. 13.95 (0-944727-15-8) Jason & Nordic Pubs.

Holcomb, Sue A. Tex R Masur: Down in the Dump. Holcomb, J. Paul & Holcomb, Sue A., illus. 32p. (Orig.). Date not set. pap. 3.95 (gr. k-3). (0-9636122-2-0) Post Oak Hill.

Holcomb, Sue A., jt. auth. see Holcomb, J. Paul.

Holden, George P. Ildy of the Split Bamboo. Van Dyke, Henry, intro. by. (Illus.). 278p. (gr. 10 up). 1993. Repr. of 1920 ed. 42.90 (1-56416-113-7) Derrydale Pr.

Holden, L. Dwight. Gran-Gran's Best Trick: A Story for Children Who Have Lost Someone They Love. Chesworth, Michael, illus. LC 89-8336. 48p. 1989. 16.95 (0-945354-19-3); pap. 6.95 (0-945354-16-9) Magination Pr.

Holden, Lorraine & Malcarne, Vanessa. Animal Places & Faces: A Drawing Book for Kids Who Care. Arnstrong, Beverly, illus. 30p. 1983. 3.50 (0-317-60991-2) NAHEE.

Holden, Phil. Wind & Surf. (Illus.). 48p. (gr. 4-12). 1992. PLB 17.50 (0-8225-2477-5) Lerner Pubns.

Holden, Queen. Best Friends-Paper Dolls in Full Color. 1985. pap. 3.50 (0-486-24973-5) Dover.

Holden, Sue. My Daddy Died & It's All God's Fault. (Illus.). (gr. 4-7). 1991. 8.99 (0-8499-0879-5) Word Inc.

Holder, et al. Original People, 5 bks, Set I, Reading Level 5. (Illus.). 288p. (gr. 4-8). 1987. Set. PLB 83.35 (0-86625-256-8); 62.50s.p. (0-685-58808-4) Rourke Corp.

Holder, Glenn, ed. Last of the Mohicans - Robin Hood. Pyle, Howard, illus. 384p. 1993. Repr. of 1952 ed. 29.95 (1-877767-82-4) Regal Pubns.

Holder, Heidi. Carmine the Crow. (ps-3). 1992. 16.00 (0-374-31119-6) FS&G.

Holder, Heidi, jt. auth. see Aesop.

Holder, Heidi, illus. Aesop's Fables. 32p. (ps-3). 1993. pap. 4.99 (0-14-054872-6) Puffin Bks.

—Crows: An Old Rhyme. LC 87-45364. 32p. (ps up). 1987. 14.95 (0-374-31660-0) FS&G.

Holder, Meir. History of the Jewish People, Vol. II: From Yavneh to Pumbedisa. Goldwurm, Hersh, ed. (Illus.). 332p. (gr. 7-8). 1993. 18.95 (0-89906-499-X); pap. 15.95 (0-89906-475-2) Mesorah Pubns.

Holder, Meir, jt. auth. see Goldwurm, Hersh.

Holder, William G. Monster 4-Wheelers. LC 87-15733. (Illus.). 48p. (gr. 5-6). 1987. RSBE 11.95 (0-89686-353-0, Crestwood Hse) Macmillan Child Grp.

Holderness-Roddam, Jane. First Aid. Vincer, Carole, illus. 24p. (Orig.). (gr. 3 up). 1989. pap. 10.00 (0-901366-98-6, Pub. by Threshold Bks) Half Halt Pr.

—Preparing for a Show. Vincer, Carole, illus. 24p. (gr. 3 up). 1989. pap. 10.00 (0-901366-09-9, Pub. by Threshold Bks) Half Halt Pr.

Holdgate, Charles. Net Making. LC 72-84056. (Illus.). (gr. 7 up). 1972. 12.95 (0-87523-180-2) Emerson.

Holdridge, Barbara, ed. see Shakespeare, William.

Hole, Dorothy. The Air Force & You. LC 92-9774. (Illus.). 48p. (gr. 4 up). 1993. RSBE 12.95 (0-89686-764-1, Crestwood Hse) Macmillan Child Grp.

—The Army & You. LC 92-2214. (Illus.). 48p. (gr. 4-6). 1993. RSBE 12.95 (0-89686-765-X, Crestwood Hse) Macmillan Child Grp.

—The Coast Guard & You. LC 92-9775. (Illus.). 48p. (gr. 4 up). 1993. RSBE 12.95 (0-89686-766-8, Crestwood Hse) Macmillan Child Grp.

—Margaret Thatcher: Britain's Prime Minister. LC 89-16996. (Illus.). 128p. (gr. 6 up). 1990. lib. bdg. 17.95 (0-89490-246-6) Enslow Pubs.

—The Marines & You. LC 92-9771. (Illus.). 48p. (gr. 4 up). 1993. RSBE 12.95 (0-89686-768-4, Crestwood Hse) Macmillan Child Grp.

—The Navy & You. LC 92-9055. (Illus.). 48p. (gr. 4-6). 1993. RSBE 12.95 (0-89686-767-6, Crestwood Hse) Macmillan Child Grp.

Holecek, Marie K., tr. from CZE. see Jirasek, Alois.

Holelson, Doug, jt. auth. see Krogman, Dane.

Holen, Anne M., ed. see Holen, Susan D.

Holen, Anne M., ed. see Roebuck, Susan H.

Holen, Susan D. Alaska Wildlife: A Coloring Book. Holen, Anne M., ed. Holen, Betsy L., illus. 48p. (gr. 3-8). 1988. pap. 4.95 (0-922127-00-X) Paisley Pub.

—Alaska's Wild Activity Book. Arehart, Betsy L. & Holen, Susan D., illus. 48p. (gr. 3-8). 1994. pap. 4.95 (0-922127-03-4) Paisley Pub.

—Alaska's Wild Coast. Holen, Anne M., ed. Holen, Betsy L., illus. 48p. (gr. 3-8). 1994. pap. 4.95 (0-922127-02-6) Paisley Pub.

Holen-Roebuck, Susan D. Arctic Animal Babies. Arehart, Betsy L., illus. 40p. (Orig.). (ps-3). 1993. pap. 4.95

(0-922127-04-2) Paisley Pub. This high-quality, educational coloring book features 40 simple, beautiful, accurate pictures of baby animals of the Arctic in their natural habitat. Illustrated by Alaskan artist Betsy L. Arehart. The cover printed on coated cover stock, is colorful & brilliant, the inside pages are high quality 70# recycled vellum. Children age 3 & up will love using paints, crayons, or markers to color pictures of playful polar bear cubs leaving their den for the first time in spring, a caribou calf kicking up his heels while his mother grazes in the background, a walrus pup & his watchful mother "hauled out" on an ice floe, a beluga whale calf swimming beneath the sea ice with a pod of other belugas, a family of river otters sliding down a snowy river bank. A line or two of descriptive text accompanies each drawing. Each drawing includes a border & the name of the animal in inch-high "open" lettering, that can be colored in. Paisley Publishing also Publishes ALASKAN WILDLIFE (ISBN 0-922127-00-X) an educational coloring book for children age 8 & up featuring 20 of Alaska's animals with a full page of text accompanying each picture. To order: Paisley Publishing, P.O. Box 201853, Anchorage, AK 99520; or call (907) 272-6604.
Publisher Provided Annotation.

Holing, Dwight. Coral Reefs. Leon, Vicki, ed. (Illus.). 40p. (Orig.). (gr. 5 up). 1990. pap. 7.95 (0-918303-22-2) Blake Pub.

—EarthTrips: A Guide to Nature Travel on a Fragile Planet. (Illus.). 224p. (Orig.). 1991. pap. 12.95 (1-879326-05-1) Living Planet Pr.

Holkner, Jean. The Wind. Greenstein, Susan, illus. LC 92-21450. 1993. 3.75 (0-383-03668-2) SRA Schl Grp.

Holl, Adelaide. My Weekly Reader Picture Word Book. Perry, Alfred, illus. 128p. (ps-k). 1981. pap. LC 65-22026 (0-671-42542-0) S&S Trade.

—Rain Puddle. Duvoisin, Roger, illus. LC 65-22026. 32p. (gr. k-3). 1965. PLB 14.88 (0-688-51096-5) Lothrop.

Holl, Kristi. Danger at Hanging Rock. (gr. 7-9). 1989. pap. 3.99 (1-55513-067-4, Chariot Bks) Cook.

—Rose Beyond the Wall. 160p. (gr. 2-9). 1988. pap. 2.95 (0-8167-1309-X) Troll Assocs.

Holl, Kristi D. First Things First. (gr. k-6). 1989. pap. 2.95 (0-440-40147-X, YB) Dell.

—Footprints up My Back. (gr. 3-6). 1986. pap. 2.95 (0-440-42649-9, YB) Dell.

—Just Like a Real Family. LC 82-16239. 132p. (gr. 4-6). 1983. SBE 13.95 (0-689-30970-8, Atheneum Child Bk) Macmillan Child Grp.

—No Strings Attached. LC 87-22688. 128p. (gr. 3-7). 1988. SBE 12.95 (0-689-31399-3, Atheneum Child Bk) Macmillan Child Grp.

—Perfect or Not, Here I Come. 160p. (gr. 4-8). 1987. pap. 2.95 (0-8167-1048-1) Troll Assocs.

Holland, Alex N. Alice's Amazing Butterfly. Holland, Alex N., illus. 15p. (gr. 1-3). 1992. pap. 11.95 (1-56606-001-X) Bradley Mann.

—Child Art: A Book of Drawings. Holland, Alex N., illus. Lewis, Glenn A., intro. by. (Illus.). 56p. (gr. 1-12). 1991. pap. text ed. 23.95 (0-9627882-2-8) Bradley Mann.

—The Children's Big Airplane. Holland, Alex N., illus. 12p. (gr. 1-4). 1992. pap. 10.95 (1-56606-000-1) Bradley Mann.

—Harvey Learns to Drive. Holland, Alex N., illus. 17p. (gr. k-3). 1992. pap. 10.95 (1-895583-52-7) MAYA Pubs.

—Skip. Holland, Alex N., illus. 12p. (gr. 1-3). 1992. pap. 6.95 (1-895583-02-0) MAYA Pubs.

—Time to Learn Our ABC's. Holland, Alex N., illus. 10p. (gr. k-3). 1992. pap. 8.95 (1-895583-14-4) MAYA Pubs.

—Time to Sing Songs. Holland, Alex N., illus. 13p. (gr. k-3). 1992. pap. 12.95 (1-895583-10-1) MAYA Pubs.

—What It Means to Be a Bad Boy. Holland, Alex N., illus. 13p. (gr. k-3). 1992. pap. 4.95 (1-895583-51-9) MAYA Pubs.

Holland, Audrey E. How Many More to Go, Mom? Holland, Audrey E., illus. 15p. (gr. k-3). 1992. pap. 13.95 (1-895583-13-6) MAYA Pubs.

—When Is It My Turn. Holland, Audrey E., illus. 15p. (gr. k-3). 1992. pap. 15.95 (1-895583-11-X) MAYA Pubs.

—When We Start Having Fun. Holland, Audrey E., illus. 13p. (gr. k-3). 1992. pap. 10.95 (1-895583-12-8) MAYA Pubs.

Holland, Barbara. The Pony Problem. 128p. (gr. 3-7). 1993. pap. 3.99 (0-14-036339-4) Puffin Bks.

Holland, Gini. Poland. LC 89-43181. (Illus.). 64p. (gr. 5-6). 1992. PLB 19.93 (0-8368-0233-0) Gareth Stevens Inc.

Holland, Gini, adapted by. Cuba Is My Home. Lopez, Mercedes, photos by. LC 92-17725. (Illus.). 1992. PLB 18.60 (0-8368-0848-7) Gareth Stevens Inc.

Holland, I. I., jt. ed. see Anderson, David.

Holland, Isabelle. After the First Love. (gr. 7 up). 1983. pap. 2.25 (0-449-70064-X, Juniper) Fawcett.

—Behind the Lines. LC 93-2576. (Illus.). 240p. (gr. 7 up). 1994. 13.95 (0-590-45113-8, Scholastic Hardcover) Scholastic Inc.

—Dinah & the Green Fat Kingdom. 192p. (gr. 5 up). 1986. pap. 1.75 (0-440-91918-5, LE) Dell.

—Henry & Grudge. Guida, Liisa C., illus. 64p. (gr. 3-6). 1986. 10.95 (0-8027-6611-0); lib. bdg. 10.85 (0-8027-6612-9) Walker & Co.

—House in the Woods. 1991. 15.95 (0-316-37178-5) Little.

—The Island. 240p. (gr. 6 up). 1984. 14.95 (0-316-36993-4) Little.

—Journey Home. (gr. 4-7). 1990. 13.95 (0-590-43110-2) Scholastic Inc.

—The Journey Home. 224p. (gr. 3-7). 1993. pap. 2.95 (0-590-43111-0, Apple Paperbacks) Scholastic Inc.

—The Man Without a Face. Reissue ed. LC 71-37736. 144p. (gr. 7 up). 1988. Repr. of 1972 ed. (Lipp Jr Bks); PLB 12.89 (0-397-32264-X, Lipp Jr Bks) HarpC Child Bks.

—The Man Without a Face. LC 71-37736. 144p. (gr. 7 up). 1987. pap. 3.95 (0-06-447028-8, Trophy) HarpC Child Bks.

—Now Is Not Too Late. LC 79-22610. (gr. 5-8). 1980. 12.95 (0-688-41937-2) Lothrop.

—Now Is Not Too Late. 160p. (gr. 4 up). 1985. pap. 2.75 (0-553-15548-2) Bantam.

—Now Is Not Too Late. LC 79-22610. 160p. (gr. 4-7). 1991. pap. 3.95 (0-688-10497-5, Pub. by Beech Tree Bks) Morrow.

—Search. 1991. pap. 3.95 (0-449-70342-8) Fawcett.

—Thief. (gr. 4 up). 1988. pap. 3.95 (0-449-70269-3, Juniper) Fawcett.

—Toby the Splendid. LC 86-24681. 160p. (gr. 5 up). 1987. 13.95 (0-8027-6674-9); PLB 14.85 (0-8027-6675-7) Walker & Co.

—The Unfrightened Dark. LC 89-31570. 128p. (gr. 6-8). 1990. 13.95 (0-316-37173-4) Little.

Holland, Jeffrey. Chessie, the Sea Monster That Ate Annapolis. Ramsey, Marcy D., illus. 32p. (gr. k-4). 1990. 8.95 (0-9618461-0-0) BaySailor Bks.

Holland, Kenneth J. & McFarland, Ken. The Carpenter: A Personal Look at Jesus. Tank, Darrel, illus. 54p. (Orig.). (gr. 10). 1992. saddlestitch 3.95 (0-945460-15-5) Upward Way.

Holland, Lynda. The Snicker-Snees. LC 90-71710. 44p. 1991. 5.95 (1-55523-403-8) Winston-Derek.

Holland, Margaret. Abraham Lincoln. (Illus.). 48p. (Orig.). (gr. 3-8). 1990. pap. text ed. 2.99 (0-87406-563-1) Willowisp Pr.

—Christopher Columbus. (Illus.). 48p. (gr. 3-5). 1992. pap. 2.99 (0-87406-584-4) Willowisp Pr.

—Mother Teresa. (Illus.). 48p. (gr. 3-5). 1992. pap. 2.99 (0-87406-585-2) Willowisp Pr.

—Willowisp Christmas Songbook. (Illus.). 24p. (gr. k-8). 1987. incl. cassette 3.50 (0-87406-253-5) Willowisp Pr.

Holland, Marion. Big Ball of String. 2nd ed. Mickie, Roy, illus. LC 92-16355. 72p. (gr. 1-2). 1993. 6.95 (0-394-80005-2); PLB 7.99 (0-394-90005-7) Random Bks Yng Read.

Holland, Penny & Kubota, Carole. Puzzles & Thinking Games. (Illus.). 32p. (gr. 3 up). 1986. incl. hand held Decoder 5.95 (0-88679-459-5) Educ Insights.

Holland, Royce Q. Old Lop-Ear Wolf. Gilliland, Hap, ed. Jeffery, Megan E., illus. (gr. 4-10). 1991. pap. 6.95 (0-89992-129-9) Coun India Ed.

Holland, Royce Q., et al. Search for Identity: Five American Indian Stories. Reyhner, Jon & Schaffer, Rachel, eds. (gr. 4-9). 1991. pap. 6.95 (0-89992-432-8) Coun India Ed.

Holland, Shirley. Grandma Holland's Three Tiny Bedtime Stories. Hansen, Heidi, illus. LC 91-70485. 48p. (ps-5). 1991. 12.95 (0-89802-574-5) Beautiful Am.

Hollander, Cass. The Littlest Christmas Tree. Verstraete, Elaine, illus. 24p. (Orig.). (gr. k-1). 1990. pap. 0.99 (1-878624-44-X) McClanahan Bk.

—My Phonics Word Book. Morgado, Richard, illus. 64p. 1993. pap. 5.95 (1-56293-321-3) McClanahan Bk.

—A New Friend for Me. Ulrich, George, illus. 24p. (ps-2). 1992. pap. 0.99 (1-56293-108-3) McClanahan Bk.

—The Night the Toys Came Alive. Pollard, Nan, illus. 24p. (Orig.). (gr. k-1). 1990. pap. 0.99 (1-878624-42-3) McClanahan Bk.

—Teddy Bear Bedtime Stories. Bates, Louise, illus. 24p. (ps-2). 1992. pap. 0.99 (1-56293-115-6) McClanahan Bk.

Hollander, P. Scott. Herne's Promise. Hollander, P. Scott, illus. (gr. k-4). 1992. pap. write for info. (0-9630657-2-6) Godolphin Hse.

Hollander, Phyllis & Hollander, Zander. Amazing but True Sports Stories. (Illus.). 128p. (Orig.). (gr. 3 up). 1986. pap. 2.50 (0-590-43736-4) Scholastic Inc.

—More Sports Bloopers. (Illus.). 64p. (gr. 3-7). 1991.
2.95 (0-590-43873-5) Scholastic Inc.
Hollander, Zander. The Complete Handbook of Pro
Football, 1993. 19th ed. 368p. (Orig.). 1993. pap. 5.99
(0-451-17765-7, Sig) NAL-Dutton.
Hollander, Zander, jt. auth. see Hollander, Phyllis.
Hollander, Zander, ed. The Baseball Book. rev. ed. LC
90-38060. (Illus.). 192p. (gr. 5 up). 1991. PLB 13.99
(0-679-91055-7); pap. 9.95 (0-679-81055-2) Random
Bks Yng Read.
Hollands, Judith. An Elf for Christmas. MacDonald,
Patricia, ed. De Rosa, Dee, illus. 80p. (Orig.). (gr.
2-5). 1990. pap. 2.99 (0-671-70170-3, Minstrel Bks)
PB.
—The Secret of the Haunted Doghouse. DeRosa, Dee,
illus. 80p. (Orig.). (gr. 2-5). 1990. pap. 2.99
(0-671-66812-9, Minstrel) PB.
Hollands, Judith W., et al. Non-Stop Stories. 45p. (gr. 3-
10). 1986. pap. 6.00x (0-8290-1227-3) Irvington.
Hollaway, Lee. David: Shepherd, Musician, & King.
Karch, Paul, illus. (gr. 1-6). 1977. bds. 5.95
(0-8054-4230-8, 4242-30) Broadman.
—The Donald Orrs: Missionary Duet. LC 82-732666. (gr.
4-6). 1983. 5.95 (0-8054-4283-9, 4242-83) Broadman.
—Los Orr: Duo Misionero. 64p. 1987. pap. 2.75
(0-311-01073-3) Casa Bautista.
Hollenbeck, Beatrice. Esther. (Illus.). 53p. (gr. k-6).
1964. pap. text ed. 9.45 (1-55976-014-1) CEF Press.
—God's Word & Me, Vol. 1. (Illus.). 82p. (gr. k-6). 1971.
pap. text ed. 12.99 (1-55976-018-4) CEF Press.
—God's Word & Me, Vol. 2. (Illus.). 70p. (gr. k-6). 1971.
pap. text ed. 12.99 (1-55976-019-2) CEF Press.
Hollenbeck, Joan W. Sea Scapes: In Kairos Time. Banks,
Doris, ed. Rinek, Susan, illus. 96p. (gr. 10 up). 1993.
pap. 14.95x (0-936822-01-5) Peppertree.
Hollenbeck, K. Around the Community: Activity Book.
90p. (gr. 3). 1993. 4.95 (0-87746-376-X) Graphic
Learning.
—Around the Community: Copy Masters File. 90p. (gr.
3). 1993. 85.00 (0-87746-377-8) Graphic Learning.
—Around the Community: Teacher's Guide. 300p. (gr. 3).
1993. 60.00 (0-87746-375-1) Graphic Learning.
—At Home & at School: Activity Book. 40p. (gr. 1).
1993. 3.25 (0-87746-368-9) Graphic Learning.
—At Home & at School: Copy Masters File. 40p. (gr. 1).
1993. 60.00 (0-87746-369-7) Graphic Learning.
—At Home & at School: Resource Book. 48p. (gr. 1).
1993. 5.75 (0-87746-370-0) Graphic Learning.
—At Home & at School: Teacher's Guide. 236p. (gr. 1).
1993. 60.00 (0-87746-367-0) Graphic Learning.
—In the Neighborhood: Activity Book. 44p. (gr. 2). 1993.
3.60 (0-87746-372-7) Graphic Learning.
—In the Neighborhood: Copy Masters File. 44p. (gr. 2).
1993. 70.00 (0-87746-373-5) Graphic Learning.
—In the Neighborhood: Resource Book. 48p. (gr. 2).
1993. 5.75 (0-87746-374-3) Graphic Learning.
—In the Neighborhood: Teacher's Guide. 288p. (gr. 2).
1993. 60.00 (0-87746-371-9) Graphic Learning.
Hollenbeck, K., retold by. Ananse & the Stories: West
African Story Pak. (ENG & SPA., Illus.). (gr. k-3).
1992. incl. story cards 39.00 (0-87746-261-5) Graphic
Learning.
—The Ant & the Cricket: Story Pak. (ENG & SPA.,
Illus.). (gr. k-3). 1992. incl. story cards 39.00
(0-87746-237-2) Graphic Learning.
—City Mouse, Country Mouse: Story Pak. (ENG &
SPA., Illus.). (gr. k-3). 1992. incl. story cards 39.00
(0-87746-239-9) Graphic Learning.
—The Enormous Turnip: Story Pak. (ENG & SPA.,
Illus.). (gr. k-3). 1992. incl. story cards 39.00
(0-87746-225-9) Graphic Learning.
—The Great Wave: Japanese Story Pak. (ENG & SPA.,
Illus.). (gr. k-3). 1992. incl. story cards 39.00
(0-87746-263-1) Graphic Learning.
—The House That Jack Built: Story Pak. (ENG & SPA.,
Illus.). (gr. k-3). 1992. incl. story cards 39.00
(0-87746-227-5) Graphic Learning.
—King Midas: Story Pak. (ENG & SPA., Illus.). (gr. k-3).
1992. incl. story cards 39.00 (0-87746-241-0) Graphic
Learning.
—The Little Goat: Story Pak. (ENG & SPA., Illus.). (gr.
k-3). 1992. incl. story cards 39.00 (0-87746-243-7)
Graphic Learning.
—Lucky Hans: Story Pak. (ENG & SPA., Illus.). (gr.
k-3). 1992. incl. story cards 39.00 (0-87746-229-1)
Graphic Learning.
—The Mighty Cat: Russian Story Pak. (ENG & SPA.,
Illus.). (gr. k-3). 1992. incl. story cards 39.00
(0-87746-265-8) Graphic Learning.
—The Mouse, the Rooster & the Cat: Story Pak. (ENG
& SPA., Illus.). (gr. k-3). 1992. incl. story cards 39.00
(0-87746-245-3) Graphic Learning.
—Paul Bunyan: American Story Pak. (ENG & SPA.,
Illus.). (gr. k-3). 1992. incl. story cards 39.00
(0-87746-267-4) Graphic Learning.
—Peter Rabbit: Story Pak. (ENG & SPA., Illus.). (gr.
k-3). 1992. incl. story cards 39.00 (0-87746-231-3)
Graphic Learning.
—The Princess & the Frog: Story Pak. (ENG & SPA.,
Illus.). (gr. k-3). 1992. incl. story cards 39.00
(0-87746-233-X) Graphic Learning.
—The Star & the Lily: Native American Story Pak.
(ENG & SPA., Illus.). (gr. k-3). 1992. 39.00
(0-87746-269-0) Graphic Learning.
—The Three Wishes: Puerto Rican Story Pak. (ENG &
SPA., Illus.). (gr. k-3). 1992. 39.00 (0-87746-271-2)
Graphic Learning.

—Thumbelina: Story Pak. (ENG & SPA., Illus.). (gr. k-3).
1992. incl. story cards 39.00 (0-87746-235-6) Graphic
Learning.
—The Tortoise & the Hare: Story Pak. (ENG & SPA.,
Illus.). (gr. k-3). 1992. incl. story cards 39.00
(0-87746-247-X) Graphic Learning.
Hollenbeck, K., jt. ed. see Johnson, L.
Hollender, Betty R. Bible Stories for Little Children, Bk.
1. rev. ed. Bearson, Lee, illus. 80p. (Orig.). (gr. 1-3).
1985. pap. text ed. 6.00 (0-8074-0309-1, 103100)
UAHC.
—Bible Stories for Little Children, Vol. 2. rev. ed. (Illus.).
80p. (gr. 1-3). 1987. pap. text ed. 6.00 (0-8074-0324-5,
103101) UAHC.
—Bible Stories for Little Children, Vol. 3. rev. ed. (Illus.).
80p. (gr. 1-3). 1988. pap. text ed. 6.00 (0-8074-0416-0,
103102) UAHC.
—Bible Stories for Little Children, Vol. 4. rev. ed. (Illus.).
80p. (gr. 1-3). 1989. pap. text ed. 6.00 (0-8074-0418-7,
103103) UAHC.
Holler, Anne. Chief Powhatan & Pocahontas. (Illus.).
112p. (gr. 5 up). 1993. PLB 17.95 (0-7910-1705-2)
Chelsea Hse.
—Pocahontas. (gr. 4-7). 1992. pap. 7.95 (0-7910-1952-7)
Chelsea Hse.
Holley, Charles. The Chihuahua That Roared. 32p. 1993.
pap. 8.95 (0-9636754-0-0) Sequitur Systs.
Holley, Cindy, jt. auth. see Connelly, Tony.
Holley, Cynthia & Walkup, Jane. First Time, Circle
Time. (ps). 1993. pap. 18.95 (0-86653-993-X) Fearon
Teach Aids.
Holley, Cynthia, jt. auth. see Burditt, Faraday.
Holley, Dennis. Animals Alive! An Ecological Guide to
Animal Activities. Payne, Brian, illus. 300p. (gr. 5-12).
1993. pap. text ed. 24.95 (1-879373-58-0) R Rinehart.
Holleyman, Sonia. Mona the Brilliant. LC 92-23332.
1993. pap. 13.95 (0-385-30907-4) Doubleday.
Hollier, Jo. Charlie Churchmouse Finds a Home.
Kichejian, Janet, ed. Pullig, Louis, illus. 16p. 1989. 14.
95 (0-685-29440-4) Silver Pubns.
Holliman, Linda. Monkeys, Mice, Monsters. (Illus.). 48p.
(gr. 1-3). 1991. pap. 5.95 (1-55799-216-9) Evan-Moor
Corp.
Holliman, Mary C., ed. see Bloom, Edgar B.
Hollindale, Peter, intro. by see Barrie, J. M.
Hollindale, Peter, ed. see Sewell, Anna.
Holling, Holling C. Minn of the Mississippi. (Illus.). (gr.
4-6). 1992. 16.95 (0-395-17578-X) HM.
—Minn of the Mississippi. Holling, Holling C., illus. (gr.
4-6). 1978. pap. 7.70 (0-395-27399-4) HM.
—Paddle-to-the-Sea. (Illus.). (gr. 4-6). 1980. 17.45
(0-395-15082-5); pap. 7.95 (0-395-29203-4) HM.
—Pagoo. Holling, Holling C., W., illus. (gr. 3-9). 1957. 16.45
(0-395-06826-6) HM.
—Pagoo. Holling, Lucille W., illus. 96p. (gr. 4-6). 1990.
pap. 7.70 (0-395-53964-1) HM.
—Seabird. (Illus.). (gr. 4-6). 1973. 17.95 (0-395-18230-1)
HM.
—Seabird. Holling, Holling C., illus. (gr. 4-6). 1978. pap.
7.70 (0-395-26681-5) HM.
—Tree in the Trail. (Illus.). (gr. 4-6). 16.45
(0-395-18228-X) HM.
—Tree in the Trail. Holling, Holling C., illus. 64p. (gr.
4-6). 1990. pap. 7.70 (0-395-54534-X) HM.
Hollingsworth, Mary. Captain, the Countess & Cobbie
the Swabby. (ps-3). 1992. pap. 8.95 (0-7814-0967-5)
Cook.
—Charlie & the Gold Mine. (Illus.). (ps-3). 1989. 5.99
(0-915720-28-0) Brownlow Pub Co.
—Charlie & the Jinglemouse. (Illus.). (ps-3). 1989. 5.99
(0-915720-25-6) Brownlow Pub Co.
—Charlie & the Missing Music. (Illus.). (ps-3). 1989. 5.99
(0-915720-27-2) Brownlow Pub Co.
—Charlie & the Shabby Tabby. (Illus.). (ps-3). 1989. 5.99
(0-915720-26-4) Brownlow Pub Co.
—Christmas in Happy Forest. (Illus.). (ps-2). 1990. 6.99
(1-877719-05-6) Brownlow Pub Co.
—Journey to Jesus: A Four-in-One Story. Eubank, Mary
G., illus. 32p. 1993. 13.99 (0-8010-4371-9) Baker Bk.
—Kids Life Bible Storybook. 1993. 15.99 (0-7814-0126-7)
Cook.
—My Very First Book of Bible Heroes. Incrocci, Rick,
illus. LC 93-7292. 1993. 4.99 (0-8407-9230-1) Nelson.
—My Very First Book of Bible Lessons. LC 93-9641.
1993. pap. 4.99 (0-8407-9227-1) Nelson.
—My Very First Book of Bible Words. LC 93-21843.
1993. 4.99 (0-8407-9226-3) Oliver-Nelson.
—My Very First Book of Prayers. Incrocci, Rick, illus.
LC 93-7291. 1993. 4.99 (0-8407-9229-8) Nelson.
—Parrots, Pirates & Walking the Plank. (ps-3). 1992. pap.
8.95 (0-7814-0668-4) Cook.
—Polka Dots, Stripes, Humps 'n Hatracks: How God
Created Happy Forest. (Illus.). (ps-2). 1990. 6.99
(1-877719-00-5) Brownlow Pub Co.
—Twizzler, the Unlikely Hero. (Illus.). (ps-2). 1990. 6.99
(1-877719-01-3) Brownlow Pub Co.
Hollingsworth, Mary, jt. auth. see Eubank, Mary G.
Hollingsworth, Patricia & Hollingsworth, Stephen.
Smart Art: Learning to Classify & Critique Art.
(Illus.). 112p. (Orig.). (gr. 3-8). 1989. pap. text ed. 15.
95 (0-913705-31-4) Zephyr Pr AZ.
**Hollingsworth, Stephen, jt. auth. see Hollingsworth,
Patricia.**
Hollingsworth, T. R. Ezra of Galilee. 80p. (Orig.). (gr.
3-6). 1987. pap. text ed. 6.95 (0-9617668-0-8)
Hollybridge Pubns.

Hollis, Barbara. Birds: A Thematic Unit. Goldfluss,
Karen, ed. Vasconcelles, Keith, illus. 80p. (Orig.). (gr.
1-3). 1992. pap. 7.95 wkbk. (1-55734-256-3) Tchr
Create Mat.
**Hollis, Myrlys, ed. see Turner, Peggy & Brewer, Linda
S.**
Hollman, Fred. How to Profit from Baseball Card
Collecting: A Basic Guide for the New Collector-
Investor. Scherer, D. J., ed. 24p. (ps-12). 1991. 4.95
(0-918734-36-3) Reymont.
Hollow, Fern. All in a Day. (Illus.). (ps-1). 1985. 2.98
(0-517-48288-6) Outlet Bk Co.
Holloway, Cheryl W., jt. auth. see Maxwell, Arthur S.
Holly, Brian. Bugs & Critters. Gruettner, Diane & Black,
Diane, illus. 32p. (gr. 3-7). 1985. pap. 3.50
(0-88625-118-4) Durkin Hayes Pub.
—Plants & Flowers. McGee, Martin, illus. 32p. (gr. 3-7).
1985. pap. 3.50 (0-88625-114-1) Durkin Hayes Pub.
Holm, Anne. North to Freedom. (gr. 5-9). 1984. 17.00
(0-8446-6156-2) Peter Smith.
—North to Freedom. 239p. (gr. 3-7). 1990. pap. 3.95
(0-15-257553-7, Odyssey) HarBrace.
Holm, Astrid. Brum. Mones, Isidre, illus. LC 92-61952.
22p. (ps). 1993. 3.25 (0-679-84493-7) Random Bks
Yng Read.
—Teenage Mutant Ninja Turtles: School Daze. Mateu,
Franc, illus. LC 90-61185. 32p. (Orig.). (ps-3). 1991.
pap. 1.50 (0-679-81169-9) Random Bks Yng Read.
—Teenage Mutant Ninja Turtles: The Final Lesson.
Daste, Larry, illus. 32p. (Orig.). (ps-3). 1990. pap. 1.25
(0-679-80669-5) Random Bks Yng Read.
Holm, Astrid, adapted by. Teenage Mutant Ninja
Turtles: A Visit to Stump Asteroid. Herbert, S. I.,
illus. LC 90-61217. 48p. (Orig.). (ps-3). 1991. pap.
1.50 (0-679-81170-2) Random Bks Yng Read.
Holm, Carlton, jt. auth. see Baker, Tanya.
Holman, David. Whale. 46p. (gr. 6-10). 1990. pap. 7.95
(0-413-63090-0, A0470, Pub. by Methuen UK)
Heinemann.
Holman, Dianne K. Plenty to Do at MSU. (Illus.). 32p.
(Orig.). 1989. pap. 5.95 (0-9626188-0-2) Cupery Pr.
Holman, Felice. Secret City, U. S. A. LC 89-39841.
208p. (gr. 5-9). 1990. SBE 14.95 (0-684-19168-7,
Scribners Young Read) Macmillan Child Grp.
—Secret City, U. S. A. LC 92-44798. 208p. (gr. 4-7).
1993. pap. 3.95 (0-689-71755-5, Aladdin) Macmillan
Child Grp.
—Slake's Limbo. LC 74-11675. 126p. (gr. 4-8). 1974.
RSBE 13.95 (0-684-13926-X, Scribners Young Read)
Macmillan Child Grp.
—Slake's Limbo. LC 85-26795. 128p. (gr. 6 up). 1986.
pap. 3.95 (0-689-71066-6, Aladdin) Macmillan Child
Grp.
—The Wild Children. LC 85-3541. 152p. (gr. 5-9). 1985.
pap. 4.99 (0-14-031930-1, Puffin) Puffin Bks.
Holman, Patsy S. At the Ranch with Taylor. (Illus.). 16p.
(ps-3). 1992. PLB 12.99 (0-9630729-8-6); pap. 6.99
(0-9630729-9-4) KAP Pubns.
Holmas, Stig. Son-of-Thunder. Born, Anne, tr. from
NOR. Hurford, John, illus. LC 93-4211. 128p. (gr. 7
up). 1993. 16.95 (0-943173-88-4); pap. 10.95
(0-943173-87-6) Harbinger AZ.
Holmes, Alice C., jt. auth. see Carl, Angela R.
Holmes, Andy. Away in a Manger. (ps-3). 1992. 5.99
(0-929216-49-0) HSH Edu Media Co.
—Fairest Lord Jesus. (ps). 1992. 5.99 (0-929216-58-X)
HSH Edu Media Co.
—Gerberts Goodnight Prayer. (ps). 1992. 12.99
(0-929216-75-X) HSH Edu Media Co.
—Jesus Is All the World to Me. (ps-3). 1992. 5.99
(0-929216-54-7) HSH Edu Media Co.
—Jesus Loves Me. (ps-3). 1992. 5.99 (0-929216-55-5)
HSH Edu Media Co.
—Jesus Loves the Little Children. (ps). 1992. 5.99
(0-929216-56-3) HSH Edu Media Co.
—O' How I Love Jesus. (ps). 1992. 5.99 (0-929216-57-1)
HSH Edu Media Co.
—O' Little Town of Bethlehem. (ps-3). 1992. 5.99
(0-929216-51-2) HSH Edu Media Co.
—Silent Night. (ps-3). 1992. 5.99 (0-929216-50-4) HSH
Edu Media Co.
—Tell Me the Stories of Jesus. (ps-3). 1992. 5.99
(0-929216-59-8) HSH Edu Media Co.
Holmes, Anita. Flowers for You: Blooms for Every
Month. Wright-Frierson, Virginia, illus. LC 91-9482.
48p. (gr. 2-5). 1993. SBE 16.95 (0-02-744280-2,
Bradbury Pr) Macmillan Child Grp.
—I Can Save the Earth: A Kid's Handbook for Keeping
Earth Healthy & Green. Neuhaus, David, illus. LC 91-
30611. 96p. (gr. 2-5). 1993. lib. bdg. 13.98
(0-671-74544-1, J Messner); bib. bdg. 7.95
(0-671-74545-X, J Messner) S&S Trade.
Holmes, B., ed. see Weinberg, Ben.
Holmes, Barbara W. Charlotte Shakespeare & Annie the
Great. Himmelman, John, illus. LC 89-2037. 160p.
(gr. 4-6). 1989. PLB 13.89 (0-06-022615-3) HarpC
Child Bks.
—Charlotte Shakespeare & Annie the Great.
Himmelman, John, illus. LC 89-2037. 160p. (gr. 4-6).
1991. pap. 3.95 (0-06-440385-8, Trophy) HarpC Child
Bks.
Holmes, Burnham. Cesar Chavez. LC 92-18225. 1992.
write for info. (0-8114-2331-X) Raintree Steck-V.
—Cesar Chavez. LC 92-18225. (Illus.). 128p. (gr. 7-10).
1992. PLB 22.80 (0-8114-2326-3) Raintree Steck-V.
—George Eastman. (Illus.). 144p. (gr. 5-9). 1992. lib. bdg.
13.98 (0-382-24170-3); pap. 7.95 (0-382-24176-2)
Silver Burdett Pr.

—Nefertiti: The Mystery Queen. LC 77-10445. (Illus.). 48p. (gr. 4-5). 1983. PLB 18.64 (0-8172-1056-3) Raintree Steck-V.

Holmes, Darryl, ed. see Keel-Williams, Mildred.

Holmes, Efner T. Amy's Goose. reissued ed. Tudor, Tasha, illus. LC 85-45391. 32p. (ps-3). 1986. pap. 5.95 (0-06-443091-X, Trophy) HarpC Child Bks.

—Christmas Cat. Tudor, Tasha, illus. LC 80-8432. 32p. (ps-3). 1989. pap. 4.95 (0-06-443208-4, Trophy) HarpC Child Bks.

—Deer in the Hollow. DeChristoper, Marlowe, illus. 32p. (ps-3). 1993. 15.95 (0-399-21735-5, Philomel) Putnam Pub Group.

—My Sadie. (Illus.). 128p. (gr. 3-6). 1993. pap. 3.50 (1-56288-350-X) Checkerboard.

Holmes, Frank, Jr. & Montgomery, K. C. Crystal's Vision. 28p. (gr. 1-4). 1992. 16.95 (1-883005-00-0) Holmes & Mont.

Holmes, Jean E. Norah's Ark. Woolsey, Raymond H., ed. 128p. 1989. pap. 4.95 (0-8280-0417-X) Review & Herald.

Holmes, Jimmy. Backpacking. (Illus.). 48p. (gr. 4-12). 1992. PLB 17.50 (0-8225-2479-1) Lerner Pubns.

Holmes, Marjorie. Saturday Night. 224p. (gr. 7 up). 1982. pap. 1.95 (0-440-97645-6, LFL) Dell.

Holmes, Martha. Deadly Animals! Vaughan, Mike, illus. LC 90-26903. 32p. (gr. k-3). 1991. SBE 13.95 (0-689-31737-9, Atheneum Child Bk) Macmillan Child Grp.

—Time to Rhyme. (Illus.). 52p. (gr. k-1). 1990. lib. bdg. 17.95 (0-89796-042-4) New Dimens Educ.

Holmes, Mary Z. Cross of Gold. Strigenz, Geri, illus. LC 91-37280. 48p. (gr. 4-5). 1992. PLB 20.70 (0-8114-3507-5); pap. write for info. (0-8114-6432-6) Raintree Steck-V.

—Dear Dad. Strigenz, Geri, illus. LC 91-37774. 48p. (gr. 4-5). 1992. PLB 20.70 (0-8114-3503-2); pap. write for info. (0-8114-6428-8) Raintree Steck-V.

—Dust of Life. Stringenz, Geri, illus. LC 91-34805. 48p. (gr. 4-5). 1992. PLB 20.70 (0-8114-3504-0); pap. write for info. (0-8114-6429-6) Raintree Steck-V.

—For Bread. Strigenz, Geri, illus. LC 91-37279. 48p. (gr. 4-5). 1992. PLB 20.70 (0-8114-3501-6); pap. write for info. (0-8114-6426-1) Raintree Steck-V.

—See You in Heaven. Whipple, Rick, illus. LC 91-37283. 48p. (gr. 4-5). 1992. PLB 20.70 (0-8114-3502-4); pap. write for info. (0-8114-6427-X) Raintree Steck-V.

—Thunder Foot. Strigenz, Geri, illus. LC 91-37548. 48p. (gr. 4-5). 1992. PLB 20.70 (0-8114-3500-8); pap. write for info. (0-8114-6425-3) Raintree Steck-V.

—Two Chimneys. Strigenz, Geri, illus. LC 91-35817. 48p. (gr. 4-5). 1992. PLB 20.70 (0-8114-3506-7); pap. write for info. (0-8114-6431-8) Raintree Steck-V.

—Year of the Ghosts. Strigenz, Geri, illus. LC 91-33190. 48p. (gr. 4-5). 1992. PLB 20.70 (0-8114-3505-9); pap. write for info. (0-8114-6430-X) Raintree Steck-V.

Holmes, Oliver W. Autocrat of the Breakfast-Table. Andrews, C. A., intro. by. (gr. 11 up). 1968. pap. 1.95 (0-8049-0159-7, CL-159) Airmont.

Holmes, Olivia, tr. see Piumini, Roberto.

Holmes, Olivia, tr. see Plumini, Roberto.

Holmes, Pamela. Alcohol. LC 91-30344. (Illus.). 64p.(gr. 6-12). 1991. PLB 19.92 (0-8114-3203-3); pap. text ed. write for info. (0-8114-3206-8) Raintree Steck-V.

Holmes, Sally, illus. The Complete Fairy Tales of Charles Perrault. Philip, Neil & Simborowski, Nicoletta, trs. Philip, Neil & Philip, Neilintro. by. LC 92-17781. (Illus.). 1993. 18.45 (0-395-57002-6, Clarion Bks) HM.

Holmes, Sharon, ed. see Smith, Nancy J. & Milligan, Lynda.

Holmes, Sharon, ed. see Smith, Nancy & Milligan, Lynda.

Holmes, Stephen. Hidden Numbers. LC 89-78486. (Illus.). 20p. (ps-2). 1990. 13.95 (0-15-200469-6, Gulliver Bks) HarBrace.

Holmes, Tracey, ed. see Tufts, Lorraine S.

Holmes, Tracey I., ed. see Tufts, Lorraine S.

Holmgren, Virginia. The Pheasant. LC 82-23672. (Illus.). 48p. (gr. 4 up). 1983. RSBE 12.95 (0-89686-222-4, Crestwood Hse) Macmillan Child Grp.

Holmgren, Virginia C. Raccoons: In Folklore, History & Today's Backyards. LC 89-48704. (Illus.). 174p. (Orig.). 1990. pap. 10.95 (0-88496-312-8) Capra Pr.

Holroyd, Angela. The Big Book of Animal Masks. Anstey, David, illus. 32p. (gr. k-4). 1990. pap. 8.95 heavy card (0-671-72580-7, Little Simon) S&S Trade.

—The Big Book of Monster Masks. Anstey, David, illus. 32p. (gr. k-4). 1990. pap. 8.95 heavy card (0-671-72579-3, Little Simon) S&S Trade.

—Pumpkin Pie. 1991. 4.98 (0-8317-7161-5) Smithmark.

Holsinger, Donald C., et al. Master Guide to the World History Slide Collection. rev. ed. 312p. (gr. 7 up). 1989. pap. text ed. 40.00 (0-923805-07-9) Instruc Resc MD.

—The World History Slide Collection: Non-European History. (gr. 7 up). 1988. incl. 2100 slides 995.00 (0-923805-08-7) Instruc Resc MD.

Holsinger, Rosemary. Karuk Tales. Piemme, P. I., illus. 70p. (gr. 4-8). 1992. pap. 7.95 (1-880922-00-2) Bell Bks CA.

Holstead, Christy & Linder, Pamela. Learn about Growing Friendships with Little Bud. rev. ed. Arlt, Bob, illus. (ps-3). 1992. activity bk. 3.98 (1-881037-00-2) McGreen Wisdom.

Holstine, Craig. Forgotten Corner: A HIstory of the Colville National Forest, Washington. 1st ed. (Illus.). 144p. (Orig.). (gr. 7-12). 1987. pap. 14.95 (0-940151-03-0) Statesman Exam.

Holt. Holt Little Class Special. (gr. 3 up). 1993. write for info. (0-8050-3107-3) H Holt & Co.

Holt, Janice M. Do I Like Myself? Coy, Venture, illus. LC 82-82332. 119p. (gr. 3-9). 1983. pap. 39.95 (0-9608812-1-2) Greenlf Pubns.

Holt, Michael. Inventions. (Illus.). 64p. (gr. 4-6). 1990. PLB 19.93 (0-8368-0010-9) Gareth Stevens Inc.

Holt, Roy D. Children Indian Captives. (gr. 4-7). 1980. 9.95 (0-89015-245-4, Pub. by Panda Bks) Eakin-Sunbelt.

Holt, S. Marie. Mike Goes to the North Pole. Holt, Shirley, illus. 28p. (gr. k-5). 1993. 21.95x (0-9613476-6-X) Shirlee.

—Mike Moves to the City. Holt, Shirley, illus. 28p. (gr. k-5). 1992. 21.95x (0-9613476-5-1) Shirlee.

Holt, Shirley. Mother Goose Nursery Rhymes, Vol. II. Holt, Shirley, illus. 28p. (gr. k-3). 1990. 19.95x (0-9613476-3-5) Shirlee.

Holt, Shirley, jt. ed. see Richardson, Lee.

Holt, Shirley, illus. Mother Goose Nursery Rhymes, Vol. II. (gr. k-3). 1991. 19.95x (0-9613476-4-3) Shirlee.

Holt, Virginia. A, My Name Is Alice: A Sesame Street Alphabet Book. Mathieu, Joe, illus. LC 88-18520. 32p. (Orig.). (ps). 1989. lib. bdg. 5.99 (0-394-92241-7); pap. 2.25 (0-394-82241-2) Random Bks Yng Read.

Holt-Fortin, Cher. The Ayyam-i Ha Camel. Irvine, Rex J., illus. 48p. (Orig.). (gr. 2-6). 1989. 9.95 (0-933770-73-1) Kalimat.

Holthaus, Mary. The Hunter & the Ravens. 32p. (gr. 1-6). 1976. 2.00 (0-89992-049-7) Coun India Ed.

Holtze, Sally H. Presenting Norma Fox Mazer. (gr. k-12). 1989. pap. 3.95 (0-440-20486-0, LE) Dell.

Holyer, Erna M. Reservoir Road Adventure. (Orig.). (gr. 5-8). 1982. pap. 3.99 (0-8010-4261-5) Baker Bk.

Holz, Laurie, ed. Words of Love. Blake, Michael, intro. by. 144p. (gr. 8 up). 1992. lib. bdg. 15.00 (1-56508-001-7) Seven Wolves.

Holzenthaler, Jean. My Hands Can. Tafuri, Nancy, illus. (ps-k). 1978. 12.95 (0-525-35490-5, DCB) Dutton Child Bks.

Holzer, Hans. In Quest of Ghosts. (gr. 4-7). 1993. pap. 2.95 (0-590-47346-8) Scholastic Inc.

Holzwarth, Werner & Erlbruch, Wolf. The Story of the Little Mole who Went in Search of Whodunit. LC 93-17676. (ENG). (gr. 3 up). 1993. 12.95 (1-55670-348-1) Stewart Tabori & Chang.

Homer. Iliad. Lang, Andrew, tr. Budgey, N. F., intro. by. (gr. 9 up). 1966. pap. 2.95 (0-8049-0115-5, CL-115) Airmont.

—Iliad. Rieu, Emil V., tr. (Orig.). (gr. 9 up). 1950. pap. 5.95 (0-14-044014-3) Viking Child Bks.

—The Iliad. Shaw, Charlie, illus. Stewart, Diana, adapted By. LC 80-15669. (Illus.). 48p. (gr. 4 up). 1983. PLB 18.64 (0-8172-1663-4) Raintree Steck-V.

—Odysseus & the Cyclops. Richardson, I. M., adapted by. Frenck, Hal, illus. LC 83-14236. 32p. (gr. 4-8). 1984. lib. bdg. 11.79 (0-8167-0007-9); pap. text ed. 2.95 (0-8167-0008-7) Troll Assocs.

—Odysseus & the Giants. Richardson, I. M., adapted by. Frenck, Hal, illus. LC 83-14233. 32p. (gr. 4-8). 1984. PLB 11.79 (0-8167-0009-5); pap. text ed. 2.95 (0-8167-0010-9) Troll Assocs.

—Odysseus & the Great Challenge. Richardson, I. M., adapted by. Frenck, Hal, illus. LC 83-14232. 32p. (gr. 4-8). 1984. lib. bdg. 11.79 (0-8167-0013-3); pap. text ed. 2.95 (0-8167-0014-1) Troll Assocs.

—Odysseus & the Magic of Circe. Richardson, I. M., adapted by. Frenck, Hal, illus. LC 83-14237. 32p. (gr. 4-8). 1984. lib. bdg. 11.79 (0-8167-0011-7); pap. text ed. 2.95 (0-8167-0012-5) Troll Assocs.

—Odyssey. (gr. 9 up). 1965. pap. 2.95 (0-8049-0057-4, CL-57) Airmont.

—Odyssey. Rouse, William H., tr. (gr. 7 up). 1946. pap. 3.99 (0-451-62805-5, Sig Classics) NAL-Dutton.

—Odyssey. Rieu, Emil V., tr. (Orig.). (gr. 9 up). 1950. pap. 4.95 (0-14-044001-1, Penguin Classics) Viking Penguin.

—The Odyssey. Hack, Konrad, illus. Stewart, Diana, adapted by. LC 79-24480. (Illus.). 48p. (gr. 4 up). 1983. PLB 18.64 (0-8172-1654-5) Raintree Steck-V.

—The Return of Odysseus. Richardson, I. M., adapted by. Frenck, Hal, illus. LC 83-14234. 32p. (gr. 4-8). 1984. lib. bdg. 11.79 (0-8167-0015-X); pap. text ed. 2.95 (0-8167-0016-8) Troll Assocs.

—The Voyage of Odysseus. Richardson, I. M., adapted by. Frenck, Hal, illus. LC 83-14235. 32p. (gr. 4-8). 1984. lib. bdg. 11.79 (0-8167-0005-2); pap. text ed. 2.95 (0-8167-0006-0) Troll Assocs.

—The Wooden Horse. Richardson, I. M., adapted by. Frenck, Hal, illus. LC 83-18061. 32p. (gr. 4-8). 1984. PLB 11.79 (0-8167-0057-5); pap. text ed. 2.95 (0-8167-0058-3) Troll Assocs.

Homer, Larona. Blackbeard the Pirate & Other Stories of the Pine Barrens. Bock, William S., illus. 96p. (gr. 3-5). 1987. pap. 8.95 (0-912608-04-8) Mid Atlantic.

—The Shore Ghosts & Other Stories of New Jersey. Bock, William S., illus. 154p. (gr. 4-8). 1986. 8.95 (0-912608-14-5) Mid Atlantic.

Homes, A. M. Jack. LC 89-31061. 208p. (gr. 7 up). 1989. SBE 14.95 (0-02-744831-2, Macmillan Child Bk) Macmillan Child Grp.

Homes, Patricia. Muffin's Book, Bk. II. Morehead, Arlene, illus. 40p. Date not set. pap. 8.95 (0-9618379-6-9) Parkside Pubns.

Honda, Maasaki. Shinichi Suzuki: Man of Love. Selden, Kyoko, tr. from JPN. 72p. (Orig.). (gr. 7-12). 1984. pap. text ed. 7.95 (0-87487-199-9, Suzuki Method) Summy-Birchard.

Honda, Noriko, tr. see Cohen, Donald.

Honda, Tetsuya. Wild Horse Winter. (Illus.). 32p. (ps-3). 1992. 12.95 (0-8118-0251-5) Chronicle Bks.

Hone, Elizabeth, ed. see Jorgensen, Eric, et al.

Honey, Michael. Milestone Documents in the National Archives: Records of Impeachment. LC 86-16307. (Illus.). 20p. (Orig.). 1987. pap. text ed. 3.50x (0-911333-49-5, 200109) Natl Archives & Records.

Honeycutt, Natalie. The All New Jonah Twist. LC 85-28048. 128p. (gr. 3-5). 1986. SBE 12.95 (0-02-744840-1, Bradbury Pr) Macmillan Child Grp.

—The All New Jonah Twist. 128p. (gr. 3-5). 1987. pap. 2.95 (0-380-70317-3, Camelot) Avon.

—Ask Me Something Easy. LC 90-7765. 160p. (gr. 6-9). 1991. 13.95 (0-531-05894-8); PLB 13.99 (0-531-08494-9) Orchard Bks Watts.

—Ask Me Something Easy. 160p. 1993. pap. 3.50 (0-380-71723-9, Flare) Avon.

—The Best-Laid Plans of Jonah Twist. LC 88-7288. 128p. (gr. 3-5). 1988. SBE 13.95 (0-02-744850-9, Bradbury Pr) Macmillan Child Grp.

—The Best-Laid Plans of Jonah Twist. 128p. (gr. 2). 1990. pap. 2.95 (0-380-70762-4, Camelot) Avon.

—Invisible Lissa. Rutherford, Jenny, illus. LC 84-20466. 192p. (gr. 4-6). 1985. SBE 13.95 (0-02-744360-4, Bradbury Pr) Macmillan Child Grp.

—Invisible Lissa. 128p. (gr. 3-7). 1986. pap. 2.75 (0-380-70120-0, Camelot) Avon.

—Josie's Beau. 128p. 1988. pap. 2.95 (0-380-70524-9, Camelot) Avon.

—Juliet Fisher & the Foolproof Plan. LC 91-28119. 144p. (gr. 2-6). 1992. SBE 13.95 (0-02-744845-2, Bradbury Pr) Macmillan Child Grp.

—Lydia Jane Bly & the Baby-Sitter Exchange. LC 92-46363. 128p. (gr. 2-6). 1993. SBE 13.95 (0-02-744362-0, Bradbury Pr) Macmillan Child Grp.

—Whistle Home. Cannon, Annie, illus. LC 92-47052. 32p. (ps-1). 1993. 14.95 (0-531-05490-X); PLB 14.99 (0-531-08640-2) Orchard Bks Watts.

Hong, Jane C., jt. auth. see Ward, James M.

Hong, Lily T. How the Ox Star Fell from Heaven. Fay, Ann, ed. Hong, Lily T., illus. LC 90-38978. 32p. (gr. k-3). 1991. 14.95 (0-8075-3428-5) A Whitman.

Hongo, Florence M., ed. see Japanese American Curriculum Project, Inc. Staff.

Hoobler, Dorothy & Hoobler, Thomas. African Portraits. Gampert, John, illus. LC 92-17284. 96p. (gr. 7-8). 1992. PLB 22.80 (0-8114-6378-8) Raintree Steck-V.

—Aloha Means Come Back: The Story of a World War II Girl. Bleck, Cathie, illus. 64p. (gr. 4-6). 1992. 11.95 (0-382-24156-8); PLB 13.98 (0-382-24148-7); pap. 7.95 (0-382-24349-8) Silver Burdett Pr.

—And Now a Word from Our Sponsor. Leer, Rebecca, illus. 64p. (gr. 4-6). 1992. 11.95 (0-382-24153-3); PLB 13.98 (0-382-24146-0); pap. 7.95 (0-382-24350-1) Silver Burdett Pr.

—Chinese Portraits. Bruck, Victoria, illus. LC 92-13617. 96p. (gr. 7-8). 1992. PLB 22.80 (0-8114-6375-3) Raintree Steck-V.

—Cleopatra. (Illus.). 112p. (gr. 5 up). 1987. lib. bdg. 17.95x (0-87754-589-8) Chelsea Hse.

—Drugs & Crime. Mendelson, Jack H. & Mello, Nancyintro. by. (Illus.). 128p. 1988. lib. bdg. 19.95 (1-55546-228-6) Chelsea Hse.

—George Washington. Brook, Bonnie, ed. Himler, Ronald, illus. 32p. (gr. k-2). 1990. 6.95 (0-671-69114-7); PLB 10.98 (0-671-69108-2) Silver Pr.

—Her Story Series. Hewitson, Jennifer, illus. (gr. 4-6). 1992. 95.60 (0-382-24149-5); PLB 111.84 (0-382-24142-8); pap. 63.60 (0-382-24355-2) Silver Burdett Pr.

—Italian Portraits. Fujiwara, Kim, illus. LC 92-13641. 96p. (gr. 7-8). 1992. PLB 22.80 (0-8114-6377-X) Raintree Steck-V.

—Mandela: The Man, the Struggle, the Triumph. Roxas, Reni, ed. (Illus.). 144p. (gr. 9-12). 1992. 14.45 (0-531-15245-6); PLB 14.40 (0-531-11141-5) Watts.

—Mexican Portraits. Kuester, Robert, illus. LC 92-13642. 96p. (gr. 7-8). 1992. PLB 22.80 (0-8114-6376-1) Raintree Steck-V.

—Next Stop, Freedom: The Story of a Slave Girl. Hanna, Cheryl, illus. 64p. (gr. 4-6). 1991. 11.95 (0-382-24152-5); PLB 13.98 (0-382-24145-2); pap. 7.95 (0-382-24347-1) Silver Burdett Pr.

—A Promise at the Alamo. Hewitson, Jennifer, illus. 64p. (gr. 4-6). 1992. 13.98 (0-382-24154-1); lib. bdg. 13.98 (0-382-24147-9); pap. 7.95 (0-382-24352-8) Silver Burdett Pr.

—Showa: The Age of Hirohito. 228p. (gr. 7 up). 1990. 15.95 (0-8027-6966-7); lib. bdg. 16.85 (0-8027-6967-5) Walker & Co.

—The Sign Painter's Secret: The Story of a Revolutionary Girl. Ayers, Donna, illus. 64p. (gr. 4-6). 1991. 11.95 (0-382-24150-9); PLB 13.98 (0-382-24143-6); pap. 7.95 (0-382-24345-5) Silver Burdett Pr.

—Toussaint L'Ouverture. (Illus.). 112p. (gr. 5 up). 1990. 17.95 (1-55546-818-7) Chelsea Hse.

—Treasure in the Stream: The Story of a Gold Rush Girl. Carpenter, Nancy, illus. 64p. (gr. 4-6). 1991. 11.95 (0-382-24151-7); PLB 13.98 (0-382-24144-4); pap. 7.95 (0-382-24346-3) Silver Burdett Pr.

—Vietnam: An Illustrated History. LC 89-71645. (Illus.). 208p. (gr. 5 up). 1990. 17.95 (*0-394-81943-8*) Knopf Bks Yng Read.
—Zhou Enlai. Schlesinger, Arthur M., Jr., intro. by. (Illus.). 112p. (gr. 5 up). 1986. 17.95 (*0-87754-516-2*) Chelsea Hse.
Hoobler, Dorothy & Hoobler, Tom. The Fact or Fiction Files: Lost Civilizations. 160p. (gr. 7-10). 1992. 14.95 (*0-8027-8152-7*); lib. bdg. 15.85 (*0-8027-8153-5*) Walker & Co.
—Vanished. 144p. (gr. 7 up). 1992. 16.95 (*0-8027-8148-9*); PLB 17.85 (*0-8027-8149-7*) Walker & Co.
Hoobler, Dorothy, jt. auth. see Hoobler, Thomas.
Hoobler, Thomas. The Revenge of Ho-Tai. 208p. (gr. 7 up). 1989. 15.95 (*0-8027-6870-9*) Walker & Co.
Hoobler, Thomas & Hoobler, Dorothy. Joseph Stalin. (Illus.). 112p. (gr. 5 up). 1985. lib. bdg. 17.95 (*0-87754-576-6*) Chelsea Hse.
Hoobler, Thomas, jt. auth. see Hoobler, Dorothy.
Hoobler, Tom, jt. auth. see Hoobler, Dorothy.
Hood, Fran. Cow Cat. 1991. 5.95 (*0-533-08028-2*) Vantage.
Hood, Thomas. Before I Go to Sleep. Begin-Callanan, Maryjane, illus. 32p. (ps-3). 1990. 14.95 (*0-399-21638-3*, Putnam) Putnam Pub Group.
—Before I Go to Sleep. Begin-Callanan, Maryjane, illus. 32p. (ps-1). 1992. pap. 4.95 (*0-399-22440-8*, Putnam) Putnam Pub Group.
Hoofnagle, Keith L. Hawaii Volcanoes Coloring Book. Hoofnagle, Keith L., illus. 32p. (ps-3). 1979. pap. 1.50 coloring book (*0-940295-07-5*) HI Natural Hist.
Hooge, Selma. More Than a Number Book. Dirksen, Helen, illus. 32p. (ps-k). 1990. pap. 7.95 (*0-919797-95-4*) Kindred Pr.
Hook, jt. auth. see Hayes.
Hook, Beverly Van see Van Hook, Beverly.
Hook, Donald D. Gun Control: The Continuing Debate. LC 92-28902. 1992. pap. 9.95 (*0-936783-09-5*) Merril Pr.
Hook, Frances, illus. Frances Hook Picture Book. Hayes, Wanda. (Illus.). (gr. k-2). 1989. 10.99 (*0-87239-243-0*, 3548) Standard Pub.
Hook, Francis. How Do You Tell? (Illus.). 32p. (ps-2). 1979. PLB 21.35 (*0-913778-01-X*); PLB 14.95s.p. (*0-685-62605-9*) Childs World.
Hook, Jason. Twenty Names in Aviation. LC 89-23912. (Illus.). 48p. (gr. 3-8). 1990. PLB 12.95 (*1-85435-253-9*) Marshall Cavendish.
—The Vikings. LC 93-13990. (Illus.). 32p. (gr. 4-6). 1993. 14.95 (*1-56847-060-6*) Thomson Lrning.
—The Voyages of Captain Cook. LC 89-78512. (Illus.). 32p. (gr. 5-8). 1990. PLB 11.90 (*0-531-18349-1*, Pub. by Bookwright Pr) Watts.
Hook, Richard, jt. auth. see Humble, Richard.
Hook, Richard, jt. auth. see Windrow, Martin.
Hooker, Dennis. I Am (Already) Successful: Getting Motivated, Being Me. Holcomb, Ann, ed. Kreffel, Mike, illus. 156p. (gr. 7-12). 1990. pap. 6.95 (*0-942784-41-3*, AM); instr's. manual, 32p. 12.95 (*0-942784-42-1*, AMIG) JIST Works.
Hooker, Irene H. & Brindle, Susan A. The Caterpillar That Came to Church - la Oruga Que Fue a Misa: A Story of the Eucharist - Un Cuento de la Eucaristia. Lademan, Miriam A., ed. Houtman, Jane F. & De Martinez, Luz M., trs. Hooker, Irene H. & Brindle, Susan A., illus. LC 92-63219. (ENG & SPA.). 64p. (Orig.). 1993. 9.95 (*0-87973-874-X*, 874); pap. 6.95 (*0-87973-875-8*, 875) Our Sunday Visitor.
Hooker, Merrilee. Hurricanes. LC 92-42920. 1993. 12.67 (*0-86593-243-3*); 9.50s.p. (*0-685-67762-1*) Rourke Corp.
—Tornadoes. LC 92-41101. 1993. 12.67 (*0-86593-248-4*); 9.50s.p. (*0-685-66349-3*) Rourke Corp.
—Volcanoes. LC 92-43121. 1993. 12.67 (*0-86593-244-1*); 9.50s.p. (*0-685-66351-5*) Rourke Corp.
Hooker, Russel. Tales of Dunsworth P. Dragon: The Dragon Who Eats Marshmallows. Hooker, Russel, illus. 64p. (ps-3). Date not set. pap. 9.95 (*1-56883-005-X*) Colonial Pr AL.
Hooker, Ruth. Matthew the Cowboy. Tucker, Kathy, ed. Smith, Cat B., illus. LC 89-21456. 32p. (ps-2). 1990. PLB 13.95 (*0-8075-4999-1*) A Whitman.
Hooks, Benjamin L. see Cryan-Hicks, Kathryn.
Hooks, Margaret Anne. God Cares for Timothy. (ps-3). 1982. 7.15 (*0-686-36253-5*) Rod & Staff.
Hooks, William A. Gruff Brothers. 1990. 9.99 (*0-553-05855-X*) Bantam.
Hooks, William A., et al. Let's Get Dressed! Bank Street College Media Group, ed. Schick, Joel, illus. 32p. (Orig.). (ps). 1986. write for info. (*0-9617460-0-9*) Levi Strauss.
Hooks, William H. The Ballad of Belle Dorcas. Pinkney, Brian, illus. LC 89-2715. 48p. (gr. 2-7). 1990. 13.95 (*0-394-84645-1*); lib. bdg. 14.99 (*0-394-94645-6*) Knopf Bks Yng Read.
—Circle of Fire. LC 82-3982. 144p. (gr. 5-9). 1982. SBE 13.95 (*0-689-50241-9*, M K McElderry) Macmillan Child Grp.
—Dirty Dozen Dizzy Dogs-Bank Street. (ps-3). 1990. PLB 9.99 (*0-553-05892-4*, Little Rooster); pap. 3.50 (*0-553-34923-6*) Bantam.
—Freedom's Fruit. Ransome, James, illus. LC 93-235. 1995. 15.00 (*0-679-82438-3*); lib. bdg. 15.95 (*0-679-92438-8*) Knopf.

—The Legend of the White Doe. Nolan, Denis, illus. LC 87-11176. 48p. (gr. 3 up). 1988. RSBE 13.95 (*0-02-744350-7*, Macmillan Child Bk) Macmillan Child Grp.
—Lo-Jack & the Pirates. (ps-3). 1991. 9.99 (*0-553-07092-4*); pap. 3.50 (*0-553-35210-5*) Bantam.
—Mean Jake & the Devils. Zimmer, Dirk, illus. LC 81-65846. 64p. (gr. 3-6). 1981. Dial Bks Young.
—The Mighty Santa Fe. Thomas, Angela T., illus. LC 92-17026. 32p. (gr. k-3). 1993. RSBE 14.95 (*0-02-744432-5*, Macmillan Child Bk) Macmillan Child Grp.
—Mr. Baseball. (ps-3). 1991. 9.99 (*0-553-07315-X*); pap. 3.50 (*0-553-35303-9*) Bantam.
—Mr. Bubble Gum: Level 3. Meisel, Paul, illus. 1989. 9.99 (*0-553-05834-7*) Bantam.
—Mr. Bubblegum-Bank Street. (ps-3). 1989. pap. 3.50 (*0-553-34694-6*) Bantam.
—Mr. Dinosaur. Meisel, Paul, illus. LC 92-33476. 1994. 10.95 (*0-553-09042-9*, Little Rooster); pap. 3.50 (*0-553-37234-3*, Little Rooster) Bantam.
—Mr. Monster, Level 3. Meisel, Paul, illus. 1990. PLB 9.99 (*0-553-05897-5*, Little Rooster); pap. 3.50 (*0-553-34927-9*, Little Rooster) Bantam.
—Monster from the Sea. (ps-3). 1992. 9.99 (*0-553-08951-X*); pap. 3.50 (*0-553-37024-3*) Bantam.
—Moss Gown. Carrick, Donald, illus. (gr. k-4). 1987. 13.95 (*0-89919-460-5*, Clarion Bks) HM.
—Moss Gown. Carrick, Donald, illus. (ps-3). 1990. pap. 5.70 (*0-395-54793-8*, Clarion Bks) HM.
—Peach Boy. (ps-3). 1992. 9.99 (*0-553-07621-3*) Bantam.
—Peach Boy. Otani, June, illus. (ps-3). 1992. pap. 3.50 (*0-553-35429-9*, Little Rooster) Bantam.
—Rainbow Ribbon. 1991. 11.95 (*0-670-82866-1*) Viking Child Bks.
—Rough Tough Rowdy. Munsinger, Lynn, illus. 32p. (ps-3). 1992. PLB 12.50 (*0-670-82868-8*) Viking Child Bks.
—Snowbear Whittington. Lisi, Victoria, illus. LC 93-8691. 1994. write for info. (*0-02-744355-8*) Macmillan.
—The Three Little Pigs & the Fox. Schindler, S. D., illus. LC 88-29296. 32p. (gr. k-3). 1989. RSBE 13.95 (*0-02-744431-7*, Macmillan Child Bk) Macmillan Child Grp.
Hooks, William H. & Boegehold, Betty. The Rainbow Ribbon. Munsinger, Lynn, illus. LC 93-27706. 1994. write for info. (*0-14-054092-X*) Puffin Bks.
Hooks, William H. & Brenner, Barbara. Lion & Lamb, Level 3. Degen, Bruce, illus. (ps-3). 1989. pap. 3.50 (*0-553-34692-X*) Bantam.
Hooks, William H. & Brenner, Barbara A. Lion & Lamb: Level 3. Degen, Bruce, illus. (ps-3). 1989. 9.99 (*0-553-05829-0*) Bantam.
Hooks, William J. Pioneer Cat. Robinson, Charles, illus. LC 88-4708. 64p. (Orig.). (gr. 2-4). 1988. lib. bdg. 6.99 (*0-394-92038-4*); 2.50 (*0-394-82038-X*) Knopf Bks Yng Read.
Hooper, Anne, ed. see Albertson, Jon.
Hooper, Mary. Follow That Dream. (Orig.). (gr. 6 up). 1986. pap. 2.50 (*0-440-92644-0*, LFL) Dell.
—Friends & Rivals. (Orig.). (gr. 6 up). 1986. pap. 2.50 (*0-440-92660-2*, LFL) Dell.
Hooper, Maureen B. The Violin Man. LC 90-70417. 80p. (gr. 3-7). 1991. 12.95 (*1-878093-79-7*) Boyds Mills Pr.
Hooper, Meredith. Seven Eggs. reissued ed. McKenna, Terry, illus. 24p. (ps-1). 1986. 5.95 (*0-694-00144-9*, Festival) HarpC Child Bks.
Hooper, N. John, ed. see Albertson, Jon.
Hooper, Patrica. A Bundle of Beasts. Steele, Mark, illus. LC 86-34413. 64p. (gr. 3-7). 1987. 12.70 (*0-395-44259-1*) HM.
Hooper, Patricia. Bundle of Beasts. (gr. 4-7). 1992. pap. 3.80 (*0-395-61620-4*) HM.
Hooper, Rosanne. Living in Towns. LC 93-12514. (gr. 4 up). 1994. write for info. (*0-531-14266-3*) Watts.
Hooper, Tony. Electricity. LC 93-17023. (Illus.). 48p. (gr. 5-8). 1993. PLB 22.80 (*0-8114-2334-4*) Raintree Steck-V.
—Genetics. LC 93-12060. (Illus.). 48p. (gr. 5-8). 1993. PLB 22.80 (*0-8114-2332-8*) Raintree Steck-V.
—Surgery. LC 93-19708. (Illus.). 48p. (gr. 5-8). 1993. PLB 22.80 (*0-8114-2335-2*) Raintree Steck-V.
Hooper-Trout, Lawana. The Maya. (Illus.). 128p. (gr. 5 up). 1991. 17.95 (*1-55546-714-8*); pap. 9.95 (*0-7910-0387-6*) Chelsea Hse.
Hoopes, Lyn L. Wing-a-Ding, Vol. 1. (ps-4). 1990. 14.95 (*0-316-37237-4*, Joy St Bks) Little.
Hoopes, Ned E. & Peck, Richard, eds. Edge of Awareness: Twenty-Five Contemporary Essays. 240p. (gr. 7 up). 1990. pap. 3.95 (*0-440-92218-6*, LE) Dell.
Hoopes, Roy, jt. auth. see Fry, William R.
Hoose, Phillip. It's Our World, Too! (gr. 4-7). 1993. pap. 12.95 (*0-316-37245-5*) Little.
—It's Our World, Too! Young People Who Are Making a Difference (& How They're Doing It) LC 92-24873. 1993. 19.95 (*0-316-37241-2*, Joy St Bks) Little.
Hoover, Evalyn & Mercier, Sheryl. Primariamente Plantas. (SPA & ENG.). 149p. (gr. k-3). 1992. pap. text ed. 16.95 (*1-881431-32-0*) AIMS Educ Fnd.
Hoover, Evalyn, et al. The Budding Botanist: Investigations with Plants. Winkleman, Gretchen & Hillen, Judith, eds. Mercier, Sheryl, illus. 109p. (Orig.). (gr. 3-6). 1993. pap. text ed. 14.95 (*1-881431-40-1*, 1213) AIMS Educ Fnd.
—Primariamente Fisica. Hillen, J., ed. Sands, Iso, tr. (SPA & ENG., Illus.). 155p. (Orig.). (gr. k-3). 1992. pap. 16.95 (*1-881431-34-7*, 1404) AIMS Educ Fnd.

Hoover, F. L. Art Activities for the Very Young. LC 61-11263. (Illus.). (gr. k-3). 1961. nap. 7.95 (*0-87192-000-X*) Davis Mass.
Hoover, H. M. Away Is a Strange Place to Be. LC 89-34455. 192p. (gr. 4-7). 1990. 14.95 (*0-525-44505-6*, DCB) Dutton Child Bks.
—Only Child. LC 91-33037. 128p. (gr. 4-7). 1992. 13.00 (*0-525-44865-9*, DCB) Dutton Child Bks.
—Orvis. 192p. (gr. 4 up). 1990. pap. 3.95 (*0-14-032113-6*, Puffin) Puffin Bks.
Hoover, Herbert T. The Yankton Sioux. Porter, Frank, intro. by. (Illus.). 112p. (gr. 5 up). 1988. lib. bdg. 17.95 (*1-55546-736-9*); pap. 9.95 (*0-7910-0369-8*) Chelsea Hse.
Hoover, Rosalie & Murphy, Barbara. Learning about Our Five Senses. 64p. (gr. k-3). 1981. 7.95 (*0-86653-013-4*, GA 241) Good Apple.
Hope, Anthony. Prisoner of Zenda. Teitel, N. R., intro. by. (Illus.). (gr. 8 up). 1967. pap. 1.25 (*0-8049-0139-2*, CL-139) Airmont.
—Prisoner of Zenda. 176p. (gr. 4-6). 1984. pap. 2.95 (*0-14-035032-2*, Puffin) Puffin Bks.
Hope, Cathy. Who's He & Who's Out. Kelly, Geoff, illus. LC 92-21396. 1993. 4.25 (*0-383-03607-0*) SRA Schl Grp.
Hope, Irene. Ai-Chan's Secret. 1989. pap. 2.95 (*9971-972-85-9*) OMF Bks.
Hope, Laura L. Bobbsey Twins' Adventure in Washington. rev. ed. (gr. 1-4). 1963. 4.50 (*0-448-40118-5*, G&D) Putnam Pub Group.
—Bobbsey Twins' Big Adventure at Home. 120p. (gr. 1-4). 1990. 4.50 (*0-448-09134-8*, G&D) Putnam Pub Group.
—The Bobbsey Twins of Lakeport. Gonzalez, Pepe, illus. 120p. (gr. 2-5). 1989. 4.50 (*0-448-09071-6*, G&D) Putnam Pub Group.
—The Bobbsey Twins on a Houseboat. Gonzalez, Pepe, illus. 120p. 1990. 4.50 (*0-448-09099-6*, G&D) Putnam Pub Group.
—The Bobbsey Twins on Blueberry Island. Harden, Laurie, illus. 1991. 4.50 (*0-448-40110-X*, G&D) Putnam Pub Group.
—Bobbsey Twins: The Missing Pony Mystery. Sanderson, Ruth, illus. 112p. (gr. 2-5). 1981. 7.95 (*0-671-42295-2*) S&S Trade.
—The Bobbsey Twins: The Music Box Mystery. Barish, Wendy, ed. Speirs, John, illus. 128p. (gr. 2-5). 1983. 8.95 (*0-671-43588-4*) S&S Trade.
—The Case of the Close Encounter. Jennis, Paul, illus. 96p. (gr. 2-3). 1988. pap. 2.95 (*0-671-62656-6*, Minstrel Bks) PB.
—The Case of the Goofy Game Show. Greenberg, Anne, ed. Barrett, Randy, illus. 96p. (Orig.). 1991. pap. 2.95 (*0-671-69296-8*, Minstrel Bks) PB.
—The Case of the Runaway Money. (gr. 2-4). 1987. pap. 2.95 (*0-671-62652-3*, Minstrel Bks) PB.
—The Case of the Tricky Trickster. Greenberg, Anne, ed. Henderson, David F., illus. 96p. (Orig.). 1992. pap. 2.99 (*0-671-73041-X*) PB.
—The Case of the Vanishing Video. Greenberg, Ann, ed. Henderson, David F., illus. 96p. (Orig.). 1992. pap. 2.99 (*0-671-73040-1*) PB.
—The Clue at Casper Creek. Greenberg, Anne, ed. Henderson, David F., illus. 96p. (Orig.). 1991. pap. 2.99 (*0-671-73038-X*, Minstrel Bks) PB.
—The Clue That Flew Away. Tsui, George, illus. (gr. 2-4). 1987. pap. 2.95 (*0-671-62653-1*, Minstrel Bks) PB.
—The Monster Mouse Mystery. Greenberg, Ann, ed. Barrett, Randy, illus. 96p. (Orig.). 1991. pap. 2.95 (*0-671-69295-X*, Minstrel Bks) PB.
—Mystery at Meadowbrook. Gonzalez, Pepe, illus. 120p. 1990. 4.50 (*0-448-09100-3*, G&D) Putnam Pub Group.
—Mystery at School. Gonzalez, Pepe, illus. 120p. (gr. 2-5). 1989. 5.95 (*0-448-09074-0*, G&D) Putnam Pub Group.
—Mystery on the Deep Blue Sea. Harden, Laurie, illus. 1991. 4.50 (*0-448-40113-4*, G&D) Putnam Pub Group.
—Mystery on the Mississippi. Jennis, Paul, illus. 96p. (Orig.). (gr. 2-4). 1988. pap. 2.95 (*0-671-62657-4*, Minstrel Bks) PB.
—The Secret at the Seashore. Gonzalez, Pepe, illus. 120p. (gr. 2-5). 1989. 5.95 (*0-448-09073-2*, G&D) Putnam Pub Group.
—The Secret of Jungle Park. Tsui, George, illus. (gr. 2-4). 1987. pap. 2.95 (*0-671-62651-5*, Minstrel Bks) PB.
—Visit to the Great West. Harden, Laurie, illus. 1991. 4.50 (*0-448-40112-6*, G&D) Putnam Pub Group.
Hope, Laura Lee. Bobbsey Twins, 4 vols. (gr. 4-7). 1990. pap. 11.80 boxed (*0-671-96364-3*) S&S Trade.
Hopf, Alice L. Spiders. Moreton, Ann, illus. LC 89-9716. 64p. (gr. 5 up). 1990. 13.95 (*0-525-65017-2*, Cobblehill Bks) Dutton Child Bks.
Hopke, Bill, jt. auth. see Parramore, Barbara.
Hopke, William E., jt. auth. see Parramore, Barbara.
Hopkins, Andrea. Harald the Ruthless. 1994. write for info. (*0-8050-3176-6*) H Holt & Co.
Hopkins, Del & Hopkins, Margaret. Careers As a Rock Musician. Rosen, Ruth, ed. (gr. 7-12). 1993. PLB 13.95 (*0-8239-1518-2*); pap. 9.95 (*0-8239-1725-8*) Rosen Group.
Hopkins, Joan, jt. auth. see Kelly, Karen.
Hopkins, Judy, et al. Rotary Roundup. La Framboise, Karin, illus. LC 93-27838. 96p. (Orig.). 1994. pap. write for info. (*1-56477-028-1*, B164) That Patchwork.
Hopkins, L. B. Ring Out, Wild Bells. Baumann, K., ed. 1992. 17.95 (*0-15-267100-5*, HB Juv Bks) HarBrace.

—Voyages. Mikolaycak, C., ed. 1992. pap. 8.95 (0-15-294496-6, HB Juv Bks) HarBrace.
Hopkins, Lee B. Animals from Mother Goose. 11p. (ps-k). 1989. 6.95 (0-15-200406-8) HarBrace.
—Dinosaurs. Tinkleman, Murray, illus. 47p. (ps-3). 1987. 12.95 (0-15-223495-0) HarBrace.
—Dinosaurs. 1990. pap. 4.95 (0-15-223496-9, Voyager Bks) HarBrace.
—Easter Buds Are Springing. (ps-3). 1993. 9.95 (1-878093-58-4) Boyds Mills Pr.
—Good Morning to You, Valentine. 32p. (ps-3). 1991. 9.95 (1-878093-59-2) Boyds Mills Pr.
—Happy Birthday. Knight, Hilary, illus. LC 90-10086. 40p. (ps-2). 1991. pap. 5.95 (0-671-79851-0, S&S BYR) S&S Trade.
—Let Them Be Themselves. 3rd ed. LC 91-19119. 224p. 1992. pap. 10.95 (0-06-446126-2, Trophy) HarpC Child Bks.
—Mama. 112p. (gr. 4-6). 1978. pap. 1.25 (0-440-96174-2, LFL) Dell.
—Mama. Marchesi, Stephen, illus. LC 91-24712. 112p. (gr. 2-8). 1992. 13.00 jacketed, 3-pc. bdg. (0-671-74985-4, S&S BFYR) S&S Trade.
—Mama & Her Boys. Marchesi, Stephen, illus. LC 91-23399. 176p. (gr. 5 up). 1993. pap. 13.00 JRT (0-671-74986-2, S&S BFYR) S&S Trade.
—Merrily Comes Our Harvest In: Poems for Thanksgiving. Shecter, Ben, illus. 32p. (gr. 2 up). 1993. 9.95 (1-878093-57-6, Wordsong) Boyds Mills Pr.
—More Surprises. LC 86-45335. (Illus.). 64p. (gr. k-3). 1989. pap. 3.50 (0-06-444131-8, Trophy) HarpC Child Bks.
—On the Farm: Poems. Molk, Laurel, illus. (ps-3). 1991. 14.95 (0-316-37274-9) Little.
—People from Mother Goose. 18p. (ps-k). 1989. 6.95 (0-15-200558-7) HarBrace.
—Ragged Shadows: Poems of Halloween Night. (ps-3). 1993. 15.95 (0-316-37276-5) Little.
—The Sea Is Calling Me. Gaffney-Kessell, W., illus. LC 85-16412. 32p. (gr. 3-7). 1986. 14.95 (0-15-271155-4, HB Juv Bks) HarBrace.
—The Sky Is Full of Song. Zimmer, Dirk, illus. LC 82-48263. 48p. (gr. k-3). 1987. pap. 4.95 (0-06-446064-9, Trophy) HarpC Child Bks.
—Surprises. Lloyd, Megan, illus. LC 83-47712. 64p. (gr. k-3). 1986. pap. 3.50 (0-06-444105-9, Trophy) HarpC Child Bks.
—Through Our Eyes: Poems & Pictures about Growing Up. (ps-3). 1992. 15.95 (0-316-19654-1) Little.
Hopkins, Lee B., compiled by. April, Bubbles, Chocolate. Root, Barrett, illus. LC 92-17100. 1994. pap. 15.00 (0-671-75911-6, S&S BFYR) S&S Trade.
Hopkins, Lee B., selected by. Beat the Drum: Independence Day Has Come. De Paola, Tomie, illus. LC 92-85033. 32p. (gr. 1-4). 1993. reinforced 9.95 (1-878093-60-6, Wordsong) Boyds Mills Pr.
Hopkins, Lee B., ed. Best Friends. Watts, James, illus. LC 85-45257. 48p. (gr. k-4). 1986. PLB 14.89 (0-06-022562-9) HarpC Child Bks.
Hopkins, Lee B., ed. Blast Off! Poems about Space. Sweet, Melissa, illus. LC 93-24536. 1995. 14.00 (0-06-024260-4); PLB 13.89 (0-06-024261-2) HarpC Child Bks.
Hopkins, Lee B., ed. Click, Rumble, Roar: Poems about Machines. Audette, Anna H., illus. LC 86-47746. 48p. (gr. 2-6). 1987. (Crowell Jr Bks); PLB 13.89 (0-690-04589-1, Crowell Jr Bks) HarpC Child Bks.
—Creatures. Ormai, Stella, illus. LC 84-15698. 32p. (ps-3). 1985. 14.95 (0-15-220875-5, HB Juv Bks) HarBrace.
—Creatures: Poems. (Illus.). 32p. (ps-3). 1990. pap. 3.95 (0-15-220876-3, Voyager Bks) HarBrace.
Hopkins, Lee B., selected by. Extra Innings: Baseball Poems. Medlock, Scott, illus. LC 92-13013. (gr. 4 up). 1993. write for info. (0-15-226833-2) HarBrace.
Hopkins, Lee B., compiled by. Flit, Flutter, Fly! Poems about Bugs & Other Crawly Creatures. Palagonia, Peter, illus. LC 91-12441. 32p. (gr. k-4). 1992. pap. 14.00 (0-385-41468-4) Doubleday.
Hopkins, Lee B., ed. Good Books, Good Times. Stevenson, Harvey, illus. LC 89-49108. 32p. (gr. k-3). 1990. 14.00 (0-06-022527-0); PLB 13.89 (0-06-022528-9) HarpC Child Bks.
Hopkins, Lee B., selected by. Happy Birthday. Knight, Hilary, illus. 40p. (ps-2). 1991. pap. 11.95 jacketed (0-671-70973-9, S&S BFYR) S&S Trade.
Hopkins, Lee B., ed. Hey-How for Halloween! McGaffrey, Janet, illus. LC 74-5601. 32p. (gr. 1-5). 1974. 12.95 (0-15-233900-0, HB Juv Bks) HarBrace.
Hopkins, Lee B., compiled by. It's about Time. Novak, Matt, illus. LC 92-12128. (ps-3). 1993. pap. 14.00 JRT (0-671-78512-5, S&S BFYR) S&S Trade.
Hopkins, Lee B., ed. More Surprises. Lloyd, Megan, illus. LC 86-45335. 64p. (gr. k-3). 1987. PLB 13.89 (0-06-022605-9) HarpC Child Bks.
—Munching: Poems about Eating. Davis, Nelle, illus. 48p. (gr. 3-6). 1985. 14.95 (0-316-37269-2) Little.
Hopkins, Lee B., compiled by. My Country, 'tis of Thee. Fiore, Peter, illus. LC 92-24230. 1994. pap. 16.00 (0-671-73315-X, S&S BFYR) S&S Trade.
Hopkins, Lee B., selected by. Questions. Croll, Carolyn, illus. LC 90-21745. 64p. (gr. k-3). 1992. 13.00 (0-06-022412-6); PLB 12.89 (0-06-022413-4) HarpC Child Bks.

Hopkins, Lee B., ed. Rainbows Are Made: Poems by Carl Sandburg. Eichenberg, Fritz, illus. LC 82-47934. 82p. (gr. k up). 1982. 17.95 (0-15-265480-1, HB Juv Bks) HarBrace.
—Side by Side: Poems to Read Together. Knight, Hilary, illus. LC 87-33025. 96p. (gr. 1 up). 1988. pap. 14.95 (0-671-63579-4, S&S BFYR) S&S Trade.
—Side by Side: Poems to Read Together. (gr. 1 up). 1991. pap. 7.95 (0-671-73622-1, S&S BFYR) S&S Trade.
—The Sky Is Full of Song. Zimmer, Dirk, illus. LC 82-48263. 48p. (gr. 3-7). 1983. PLB 13.89 (0-06-022583-1) HarpC Child Bks.
Hopkins, Lee B., selected by. Still As a Star: A Book of Nighttime Poems. Milone, Karen, illus. 32p. (ps-3). 1989. 14.95 (0-316-37272-2) Little.
Hopkins, Lee B., ed. Surprises. LC 83-47712. (Illus.). 64p. (gr. k-3). 1984. PLB 13.89 (0-06-022585-8) HarpC Child Bks.
Hopkins, Lee B., compiled by. To the Zoo: Animal Poems. Wallner, John, illus. LC 89-12559. 32p. (ps-3). 1992. 14.95 (0-06-021462-7) HarpC Child Bks.
—Weather. Hall, Melanie, photos by. LC 92-14913. (Illus.). 64p. (gr. k-3). 1994. 14.00 (0-06-021463-5); PLB 13.89 (0-06-021462-7) HarpC Child Bks.
Hopkins, Lila. Talking Turkey. 128p. (gr. 7-9). 1990. 13.90 (0-531-10797-3) Watts.
Hopkins, Margaret. Bible Stories from the New Testament. Coville, Katherine D., illus. 96p. (ps-3). 1989. 12.95 (0-448-19184-9, G&D) Putnam Pub Group.
—Sleepytime for Baby Mouse. Schmidt, Karen L., illus. 12p. (ps-3). 1985. 3.95 (0-448-40875-9, G&D) Putnam Pub Group.
Hopkins, Margaret, jt. auth. see Hopkins, Del.
Hopkins, Margo. Honey Rabbit. Szekeres, Cyndy, illus. 14p. (ps). 1982. write for info. (0-307-12268-9, Golden Bks) Western Pub.
Hopkinson, Deborah. Pearl Harbor. LC 91-22472. (Illus.). 64p. (gr-6). 1991. RSBE 13.95 (0-87518-475-8, Dillon) Macmillan Child Grp.
Hoppe, Joanne. Dream Spinner. 240p. (gr. 7 up). 1992. 14.00 (0-688-08559-8) Morrow Jr Bks.
—Pretty Penny Farm. LC 86-1516. 224p. (gr. 7 up). 1987. 12.95 (0-688-07201-1) Morrow Jr Bks.
—Pretty Penny Farm. 224p. (gr. 7 up). 1989. pap. 2.50 (0-8167-1326-X) Troll Assocs.
Hoppe, Matthias. Mouse & Elephant. (ps-3). 1991. 14.95 (0-316-37284-6) Little.
Hopper, Hilary L. Around the World Program Series. (gr. 4 up). 1993. Smyth sewn casebound. 17.95 (0-939923-28-9); Perfect bdg. 7.95 (0-939923-27-0); Family ed. 48.00 (0-939923-26-2) M & W Pub Co.
Hopper, Nancy. The Queen of Put-Down. LC 90-22604. 144p. (gr. 4-7). 1991. RSBE 12.95 (0-02-744411-2, Four Winds) Macmillan Child Grp.
Hopper, Nancy J. Carrie's Games. 128p. (gr. 7 up). 1989. pap. 2.50 (0-380-70538-9, Flare) Avon.
—Hang on, Harvey! 96p. (gr. 5-9). 1984. pap. 2.25 (0-440-43371-1, YB) Dell.
—I Was a Fifth-Grade Zebra. LC 92-30731. (gr. 3-6). 1993. 13.99 (0-8037-1420-3); PLB 13.89 (0-8037-1595-1) Dial Bks Young.
—The Interrupted Education of Huey B. 192p. (gr. 7 up). 1991. 14.95 (0-525-67336-9, Lodestar Bks) Dutton Child Bks.
—The Queen of Put-Down. LC 92-19559. 112p. (gr. 4-6). 1993. pap. 3.95 (0-689-71670-2, Aladdin) Macmillan Child Grp.
—The Seven & One-Half Sins of Stacey Kendall. (gr. 5-9). 1983. pap. 2.75 (0-440-47736-0, YB) Dell.
—The Truth or Dare Trap. (gr. 7 up). 1988. pap. 2.50 (0-380-70269-X, Flare) Avon.
Hopping, Lorraine J. Wild Weather: Tornadoes! Wheeler, Jody, illus. LC 92-27947. 48p. (gr. k-3). 1994. pap. 3.50 (0-590-46338-1) Scholastic Inc.
Hopson, Glover E. The Veteran's Administration. Schlesinger, Arthur M., Jr., intro. by. (Illus.). 96p. (gr. 5 up). 1988. lib. bdg. 14.95 (1-55546-131-X) Chelsea Hse.
Hopton, Marilyn, jt. auth. see Ruse, Christina.
Hopwood, Clive. Dinosaur Fun File. Green, Barry, illus. (gr. 3-6). 1992. pap. 4.95 (1-56680-508-2) Mad Hatter Pub.
Hora, Bayard, ed. Trees & Forests of the World, 2 vols. LC 90-36009. (Illus.). 290p. 1990. PLB 79.95 (1-85435-330-6) Marshall Cavendish.
Horejs, Vit. Pig & Bear. Henstra, Friso, illus. LC 88-21304. 48p. (gr. 2-4). 1989. RSBE 12.95 (0-02-744421-X, Four Winds) Macmillan Child Grp.
—Twelve Iron Sandals: And other Czechoslovak Tales. Spanfeller, Jim, illus. LC 84-22272. 128p. (gr. 4-6). 1985. 11.95 (0-13-934159-5) P-H.
Horemis, Spyros. Geometrical Design-Color Book. 1976. pap. 2.95 (0-486-20180-5) Dover.
Horenstein, Henry. How Is a Bicycle Made? LC 92-2375. 1993. pap. 9.95 (0-671-77749-1, S&S BFYR) S&S Trade.
—How Is a Sneaker Made? LC 92-23811. 1993. pap. 9.95 (0-671-77747-5, S&S BFYR) S&S Trade.
—My Mom's a Vet. LC 93-24964. (gr. 3 up). 1994. write for info. (1-56402-234-X) Candlewick Pr.
—Sam Goes Trucking. Horenstein, Henry, illus. (ps-3). 1989. 14.45 (0-395-44313-X) HM.
—Sam Goes Trucking. (ps-3). 1990. pap. 5.70 (0-395-54950-7) HM.
—Sams Goes Trucking. (Illus.). 32p. (gr. k-3). 1990. pap. 4.95 (0-685-45556-4) HM.

Horenstein, Henry, photos by. Mike Goes Trucking. 1988. write for info. HM.
Horenstein, Sidney. Rocks Tell Stories. LC 92-16562. (Illus.). 72p. (gr. 4-6). 1993. PLB 14.90 (1-56294-238-7) Millbrook Pr.
Horgan, Dorothy. Then the Zeppelins Came. 112p. (gr. 6 up). 1990. jacketed 14.95 (0-19-271598-4) OUP.
Horibuchi, Seiji. ed. see Asamiya, Kia.
Horibuchi, Seiji. ed. see Koike, Kazuo.
Horie, Hildegard, jt. auth. see Horie, Michiaki.
Horie, Michiaki & Horie, Hildegard. Lost Identity. Huff, Dawn, tr. from GER. 96p. (Orig.). (gr. 7 up). 1987. pap. 5.95 (0-939925-09-5) R C Law & Co.
—Steps to Inner Freedom. Huff, Dawn, tr. from GER. Paff, Mike, illus. 120p. (Orig.). (gr. 7 up). 1987. pap. 5.95 (0-939925-06-0) R C Law & Co.
Horii, Jane, jt. auth. see Araki, Nancy K.
Horio, Seishi. The Monkey & the Crab. Ooka, D. T., tr. from JPN. Murakami, Tsutomu, illus. 32p. 1985. 11.95 (0-89346-246-2) Heian Intl.
Horn, Brian Van see Van Horn, Brian & Van Horn, Chris.
Horn, Chris Van see Van Horn, Brian & Van Horn, Chris.
Horn, Donna. Party & Holiday Decorations: A Handbook of Wafer Fun. Horn, Donna, illus. LC 87-50697. 88p. (Orig.). (gr. 4-12). 1988. pap. 14.95 (0-935009-97-3) Wafer Mache.
Horn, Gabriel. The Crane. LC 88-12031. (Illus.). 48p. (gr. 5-6). 1988. RSBE 12.95 (0-89686-393-X, Crestwood Hse) Macmillan Child Grp.
—Steller's Sea Cow. LC 89-7702. (Illus.). 48p. (gr. 5-6). 1989. 12.95 (0-89686-460-X, Crestwood Hse) Macmillan Child Grp.
Horn, Geoffrey & Cavanaugh, Arthur. Bible Stories for Children. Stewart, Arvis, illus. LC 79-27811. 336p. (gr. 1-5). 1980. SBE 13.95 (0-02-554060-2, Macmillan Child Bk) Macmillan Child Grp.
Horn, George F., jt. auth. see Brommer, Gerald F.
Horn, Marilyn, jt. auth. see Chernus-Mansfield, Nancy.
Horn, Myrna. Krista's Magic Hat. LC 90-71359. (Illus.). 44p. (gr. k-3). 1991. 5.95 (1-55523-397-X) Winston-Derek.
Horn, Pierre. Louis XIV. (Illus.). 112p. (gr. 5 up). 1986. lib. 17.95 (0-87754-591-X) Chelsea Hse.
—Marquis de Lafayette. Schlesinger, Arthur M. (Illus.). 112p. (gr. 5 up). 1989. 17.95 (1-55546-813-6) Chelsea Hse.
Horn, Tryntje. Nana's Adoption Farm: The Story of Little Rachell. Lacroix, Dana, illus. 40p. (gr. k-6). 1992. 16.95 (0-9617426-8-2) J N Townsend.
Hornbeck-Tanner, Helen. The Ojibwa. (Illus.). 120p. (gr. 5 up). 1992. 17.95 (1-55546-721-0) Chelsea Hse.
Hornblow, Arthur, jt. auth. see Hornblow, Leonora.
Hornblow, Leonora & Hornblow, Arthur. Animals Do the Strangest Things. Kohler, Keith, illus. LC 88-37710. 64p. (gr. 2-4). 1990. lib. bdg. 6.99 (0-394-94308-2); pap. 3.95 (0-394-84308-8) Random Bks Yng Read.
—Birds Do the Strangest Things. (Illus.). 32p. (gr. 2-6). 1965. 6.95 (0-394-80061-3) Random Bks Yng Read.
—Birds Do the Strangest Things. Singer, Alan D., illus. LC 90-8583. 64p. (gr. 2-4). 1991. pap. 3.95 (0-679-81159-1) Random Bks Yng Read.
—Fish Do the Strangest Things. Eggert, John F., illus. LC 88-30202. 64p. (gr. 2-4). 1990. Repr. lib. bdg. 6.99 (0-394-94309-0); 4.99 (0-394-84309-6) Random Bks Yng Read.
—Insects Do the Strangest Things. Barlowe, Dorothy, illus. LC 88-30201. 64p. (gr. 2-4). 1990. lib. bdg. 6.99 (0-394-94306-6); pap. 3.95 (0-394-84306-1) Random Bks Yng Read.
—Prehistoric Monsters Did the Strangest Things. abr. ed. Barlowe, Sy, illus. LC 88-30212. 64p. (gr. 2-4). 1990. Repr. lib. bdg. 6.99 (0-394-94307-4); 4.99 (0-394-84307-X) Random Bks Yng Read.
—Reptiles Do the Strangest Things. Frith, Michael K., illus. LC 70-106500. (gr. 2-4). 1970. 6.95 (0-394-80074-5); lib. bdg. 8.99 (0-394-90074-X, 90074) Random Bks Yng Read.
—Reptiles Do the Strangest Things. reissued ed. Graber, Jack, illus. LC 90-8598. 64p. (gr. 2-4). 1991. PLB 6.99 (0-679-91158-8); pap. 3.95 (0-679-81158-3) Random Bks Yng Read.
Hornbostel, Lois. The Classroom Dulcimer. Heath, Sarah, illus. 64p. (gr. 5-8). 1991. pap. text ed. 12.95 (0-9614939-6-8) Backyard Music.
Horne, Carmon Van see Van Horne, Carmon.
Horne, Lee. Pyramid Explorer's Kit. (Illus.). 64p. (gr. 3 up). 1991. 16.95 (1-56138-031-8) Running Pr.
Horneck, Heribert. Tracks in the Snow. Young, Richard G., ed. Mangold, Paul, illus. LC 89-11890. 24p. (gr. 1-3). 1989. PLB 14.60 (0-944483-53-4) Garrett Ed Corp.
Horner, Althea J. Little Big Girl. Rosamilia, Patricia, illus. 32p. (ps-3). 1982. 14.95 (0-89885-098-3); pap. 9.95 (0-89885-287-0) Human Sci Pr.
Horner, Jack & Lessem, Don. Digging up Tyrannosaurus Rex. LC 92-2204. (Illus.). 36p. (gr. 2-6). 1992. 14.00 (0-517-58783-1); PLB 14.99 (0-517-58784-X) Crown Bks Yng Read.
Horner, Jill. TestMaster ACT. 175p. (gr. 10-12). 1993. tchr's. ed. 99.00 (1-883859-08-5); incl. video 79.00 (1-883859-07-7) Resource Netwrk.
Horner, Jill, jt. auth. see Whyte, Margaret.
Horner, Jill, ed. see Whyte, Margaret.

Horner, John & Gorman, James. Maia: A Dinosaur Grows Up. Henderson, Doug, illus. LC 88-43384. 46p. (gr. 2 up). 1989. pap. 5.95 (0-89471-691-3) Running Pr.

Hornidge, Marilis. Christmas Tales. Weinberger, Jane, ed. DeVito, Pamela, illus. LC 88-51378. 72p. (gr. 1-6). 1988. pap. 7.95 (0-932433-50-2) Windswept Hse.

Horning, Robert, illus. My Pop-up Photo Book. Costello, Linda, contrib. by. LC 90-85727. (Illus.). 8p. (ps-1). 1991. 10.95 (1-878093-05-3) Boyds Mills Pr.

Hornock, Marcia. Preschool ABC Bible Heroes. (Illus.). 96p. (ps-1). 1992. 10.95 (0-86653-697-3, SS2827, Shining Star Pubns) Good Apple.

Hornsby, Sarah. At the Name of Jesus. Hornsby, Sarah, illus. 256p. 1986. 12.99 (0-8007-9078-2) Chosen Bks.
—Getting to Know Jesus from A to Z. 1989. 9.99 (0-8007-1624-8) Revell.

Horosko, Marian, retold by. Sleeping Beauty: The Ballet Story. Doney, Todd L., illus. LC 93-14399. 1994. text ed. 15.95 (0-689-31885-5, Atheneum) Macmillan.

Horowitz, Anthony, retold by. Myths & Legends. LC 93-11878. 1994. 6.95 (1-85697-975-X) Kingfisher Bks.

Horowitz, H. Working with Wood. large type ed. 116p. (gr. 7-12). 1983. Repr. of 1970 ed. 20.75 (0-317-01971-6, 4-27860-00) Am Printing Hse.

Horowitz, Janet & Faggella, Kathy. My Dad. Jenkins, Steve, illus. 48p. 1991. 9.95 (1-55670-174-8) Stewart Tabori & Chang.
—My Mom. Jenkins, Steve, illus. 48p. 1991. 9.95 (1-55670-173-X) Stewart Tabori & Chang.
—My Pet: A Photolog Book. Jenkins, Steve, illus. 48p. 1992. bds. 9.95 (1-55670-268-X) Stewart Tabori & Chang.
—My School. Jenkins, Steve, illus. 48p. 1991. 9.95 (1-55670-176-4) Stewart Tabori & Chang.
—My Town. Jenkins, Steve, illus. 48p. 1991. 9.95 (1-55670-175-6) Stewart Tabori & Chang.
—My Trip to Walt Disney World Resort: A Photolog Book. Disney Staff, illus. 48p. 1991. 9.95 (1-55670-141-7) Stewart Tabori & Chang.

Horowitz, Jordan. Aladdin & the Magic Lamp. (ps-3). 1993. pap. 2.50 (0-590-46417-5) Scholastic Inc.
—Behind the Scenes of Home Alone 2: Lost in New York. 1992. 3.95 (0-590-45720-9) Scholastic Inc.
—Dennis the Menace. (Illus.). (gr. 4-7). 1993. pap. 3.25 (0-590-47350-6) Scholastic Inc.
—Dennis the Menace. (Illus.). (gr. k-2). 1993. pap. 2.95 (0-590-47349-2) Scholastic Inc.
—Dennis the Menace. (ps-3). 1993. pap. 2.95 (0-590-47399-9) Scholastic Inc.
—Free Willy. (gr. 9-12). 1993. pap. 3.25 (0-590-46755-7) Scholastic Inc.
—Home Alone Two: Lost in New York Picture Book Adaptation. (Illus.). 1992. 2.95 (0-590-45719-5) Scholastic Inc.
—Three's a Crowd. Ong, Cristina, illus. 32p. (ps-3). 1992. pap. 2.50 (0-590-45459-5) Scholastic Inc.
—Tom & Jerry: The Movie. (ps-3). 1993. pap. 2.95 (0-590-47116-3) Scholastic Inc.
—Working Hard with the Busy Fire Truck. (ps-3). 1993. pap. 2.50 (0-590-46602-X) Scholastic Inc.

Horowitz, Lynn R. The Good Bad Wolf. Urbahn, Clara, illus. LC 89-63141. 26p. (Orig.). (ps-1). 1989. pap. 7.95 spiral bdg. (0-938678-12-4) New Seed.

Horowitz, Ruth. Bat Time. Avishai, Susan, illus. LC 90-35772. 32p. (ps-2). 1991. RSBE 13.95 (0-02-744541-0, Four Winds) Macmillan Child Grp.
—Mommy's Lap. (ps-3). 1993. 13.00 (0-688-07235-6); PLB 12.93 (0-688-07236-4) Lothrop.

Horowitz, Shelly, tr. see Mahoney, Judy.

Horrigan, Joe. The Official Pro Football Hall of Fame Answer Book. (Illus.). 96p. (gr. 3 up). 1990. (S&S BFYR); pap. 11.95 reinforced trade (0-671-71001-X, S&S BFYR) S&S Trade.

Horstman, Lisa. Fast Friends: A Tail & Tongue Tale. Horstman, Lisa, illus. LC 93-28630. 1994. 13.00 (0-679-85404-X); PLB 13.99 (0-679-95404-X) Knopf Bks Yng Read.

Hort, Lenny. The Boy Who Held Back the Sea. Locker, Thomas, illus. LC 86-32893. 1987. 15.00 (0-8037-0406-2); PLB 14.89 (0-8037-0407-0) Dial Bks Young.
—Goathed & the Shepherdess. Bloom, Lloyd, illus. LC 93-18178. 1994. 14.99 (0-8037-1352-5); PLB 14.89 (0-8037-1353-3) Dial Bks Young.
—How Many Stars in the Sky. Ransome, James, illus. LC 90-36044. 32p. (ps-3). 1991. 13.95 (0-688-10103-8, Tambourine Bks); PLB 13.88 (0-688-10104-6, Tambourine Bks) Morrow.

Hort, Lenny, retold by see Afanasyev, Alexander.

Hort, Lenny, tr. see Damjan, Mischa.

Horton, et al. Amazing Fact Book of Animals. (Illus.). 32p. 1987. PLB 14.95s.p. (0-87191-840-4) Creative Ed.
—Amazing Fact Book of Birds. (Illus.). 32p. 1987. PLB 14.95s.p. (0-87191-842-0) Creative Ed.
—Amazing Fact Book of Fish. (Illus.). 32p. 1987. PLB 14.95s.p. (0-87191-844-7) Creative Ed.
—Amazing Fact Book of Insects. (Illus.). 32p. 1987. PLB 14.95s.p. (0-87191-845-5) Creative Ed.
—Amazing Fact Book of Machines. (Illus.). 32p. 1987. PLB 14.95s.p. (0-87191-846-3) Creative Ed.
—Amazing Fact Book of Monsters. (Illus.). 32p. 1987. PLB 14.95s.p. (0-87191-847-1) Creative Ed.
—Amazing Fact Book of Spiders. (Illus.). 32p. 1987. PLB 14.95s.p. (0-87191-850-1) Creative Ed.
—Amazing Fact Book of Weapons. (Illus.). 32p. 1987. PLB 14.95s.p. (0-88682-170-3) Creative Ed.

Horton, Barbara S. What Comes in Spring? Young, Ed, illus. LC 89-39695. 40p. (ps-1). 1992. 14.00 (0-679-80268-1); PLB 14.99 (0-679-90268-6) Knopf Bks Yng Read.

Horton, Casey. Ancient Greeks. (Illus.). 40p. (gr. 3-7). 1992. 13.95 (0-237-60163-X, Pub. by Evans Bros Ltd) Trafalgar.

Horton, Edna C. & Hadley, Roberta. El Cuidado de Dios. Villasenor, Emma Z., tr. (Illus.). (gr. 1-3). 1989. pap. 1.40 (0-311-38555-9) Casa Bautista.

Horton, Madelyn. The Lockerbie Airline Crash. LC 91-25741. (Illus.). 96p. (gr. 5-8). 1991. PLB 11.95 (1-56006-017-4) Lucent Bks.

Horton, Marion. Springboards for English: Thirty-Three Creative & Cooperative Lessons for Grades 6-12. 96p. (gr. 6-12). 1992. pap. text ed. 11.95 (0-944459-49-8) ECS Lrn Systs.

Horton, Randy. Fraud, Fame, Alien Life Forms. Parker, Liz, ed. Taylor, Marjorie, illus. 45p. (Orig.). (gr. 6-12). 1992. pap. text ed. 2.95 (1-56254-053-X) Saddleback Pubns.

Horton, Stanley M. The Book of Acts: A Radiant Commentary on the New Testament. LC 80-65892. 304p. (Orig.). (gr. 12). 1981. 8.95 (0-88243-317-2, 02-0317) Gospel Pub.
—What the Bible Says about the Holy Spirit. Zimmerman, Thomas F., frwd. by. LC 75-43154. 316p. (gr. 12). 1976. pap. 8.95 (0-88243-647-3, 02-0647) Gospel Pub.

Horton, Tom. Swanfall: Journey of the Tundra Swans. Harp, Dave, photos by. (Illus.). 48p. (gr. 1-3). 1991. 15.95 (0-8027-8106-3); PLB 16.85 (0-8027-8107-1) Walker & Co.

Horvat, Dilwyn. Assault on Omega Four. 128p. (Orig.). (gr. 6 up). 1989. pap. text ed. 4.99 (0-7459-1730-5) Lion USA.
—Operation Titan. 128p. (Orig.). (gr. 6 up). 1989. pap. text ed. 4.99 (0-7459-1731-3) Lion USA.

Horvath, Polly. No More Cornflakes. (gr. 4-7). 1993. pap. 4.50 (0-374-45516-3, Sunburst) FS&G.
—An Occasional Cow. (Illus.). 112p. (gr. 3-7). 1989. 13.95 (0-374-35559-2) FS&G.
—An Occasional Cow. (Illus.). 112p. (gr. 3-7). 1991. pap. 3.95 (0-374-44573-2, Sunburst) FS&G.

Horvatic, Anne. Simple Machines. Bruner, Stephen, photos by. LC 88-29997. (Illus.). 32p. (gr. 1-4). 1989. 13.95 (0-525-44492-0, DCB) Dutton Child Bks.

Horwitz, Janet, ed. see Wagner, Donald R.

Horwitz, Joshua. Night Markets: Bringing Food to a City. Horwitz, Joshua, illus. LC 85-45401. 96p. (gr. 2-6). 1986. pap. 6.95 (0-06-446046-0, Trophy) HarpC Child Bks.
—Night Markets: Bringing Food to the City. LC 83-45242. (Illus.). 96p. (gr. 3-7). 1984. (Crowell Jr Bks); PLB 13.89 (0-690-04379-1, Crowell Jr Bks) HarpC Child Bks.

Horwitz, Lynn. Lulu Turns Four. Urbahn, Clara, illus. 32p. (ps-k). 1993. 13.95 (0-9625620-5-X) DOT Garnet. A little chimp named Lulu is about to celebrate her fourth birthday, & like every small person in the process of getting bigger, she wonders if she'll master the challenges: standing by herself all the time; going to the doctor without feeling afraid; sharing happily with her little sister; eating bugs & green leaves like the grownups. Release from her fears comes in the form of a birthday present from her mother, a helpless kitten who needs Lulu to help her grow up, in this charming book about the pleasures--& the pleasures--of birthdays. LYNN HOROWITZ, a Yale graduate with a Masters in education, is the author of two previous books for young readers, THE GOOD BAD WOLF & MANOS A LA OBRA. She lives in Berkeley, California. CLARA URBAHN, an artist & illustrator of children's books, lives in Nantucket, Massachusetts. To order: Talman Company, 131 Spring St., New York, NY 10012. (212) 431-7175; FAX (212) 431-7215. *Publisher Provided Annotation.*

Hosea Hilker, Cathryn. A Cheetah Named Angel. LC 92-14623. (Illus.). 32p. (gr. k-4). 1992. 15.95 (0-531-15252-9); PLB 15.90 (0-531-11055-9) Watts.

Hosie, Bounar. Life Belts. LC 92-43048. 1993. 14.95 (0-385-31074-9) Delacorte.

Hoskins, Thurman. Cannibals. (Orig.). (ps-12). 1988. pap. 2.95 (0-87067-350-5) Holloway.

Hossack, Sylvie A. Flying Chickens of Paradise Lane. LC 92-14527. 144p. (gr. 3-7). 1992. RSBE 13.95 (0-02-744565-8, Four Winds) Macmillan Child Grp.

Hostetler, Bob, jt. auth. see McDowell, John.

Hostetler, Bob, jt. auth. see McDowell, Josh.

Hostetler, Jacob. My Backyard Giant. adpt. ed. Sawicki, Mary, adapted by. LC 93-29762. (Illus.). 32p. (ps-2). 1994. 10.95 (0-8120-6399-6); pap. 4.95 (0-8120-1736-6) Barron.

Hostetler, Marian. Mystery at the Mall. Stamm, Gwen, illus. LC 85-13951. 88p. (Orig.). (gr. 5-6). 1985. pap. 3.95 (0-8361-3401-X) Herald Pr.
—We Knew Jesus. 160p. (Orig.). (gr. 4-8). 1994. pap. 5.95 (0-8361-3653-5) Herald Pr.
—We Knew Paul. 128p. (Orig.). (gr. 4-8). 1992. pap. 4.95 (0-8361-3589-X) Herald Pr.

Hostetler, Paul. A Wing & a Prayer. Pierce, Glen, ed. Phipps, Weston & Deyhle, Karen, illus. LC 92-75502. 159p. (Orig.). 1993. pap. 7.95 (0-916035-58-1) Evangel Indiana.

Hostvedt, Jan. Loving Somebody. 32p. (ps-1). 1986. comb bdg. 3.95 (0-89191-270-3, Chariot Bks) Cook.

Hoth, Iva. The Picture Bible. (gr. 3-7). 1981. 12.99 (0-89191-501-X, Chariot Bks) Cook.

Hotshots, illus. Cabbage Patch Kids Adventure. 24p. (gr. 1-5). 1984. 5.95 (0-910313-31-8) Parker Bros.

Hott, Michael, jt. auth. see Brown, Julie.

Hotze, Sollace. Acquainted with the Night. 256p. (gr. 7 up). 1992. 13.95 (0-395-61576-3, Clarion Bks) HM.
—A Circle Unbroken. LC 88-2569. 224p. (gr. 7 up). 1988. 13.95 (0-89919-733-7, Clarion Bks) HM.
—A Circle Unbroken. 244p. (gr. 6 up). 1991. pap. 4.95 (0-395-59702-1, Clarion Bks) HM.
—Summer Endings. Giblin, James, ed. 176p. (gr. 4-7). 1991. 13.45 (0-395-56197-3, Clarion Bks) HM.

Houbre, Gilbert, illus. Carotte. (FRE.). (ps-1). 1989. 14.95 (2-07-035711-2) Schoenhof.

Houck, Eric L., Jr. Rabbit Surprise. Catalano, Dominic, illus. LC 92-1318. 32p. (ps-2). 1993. 14.00 (0-517-58777-7); PLB 14.99 (0-517-58778-5) Crown Bks Yng Read.

Hough, B. L. Help! for Primary Teachers. 64p. (gr. k-3). 1981. 5.95 (0-86653-008-8, GA 236) Good Apple.

Hough, Belva L. Help! For Primary Art. (gr. k-3). 1986. pap. 6.95 (0-8224-3615-9) Fearon Teach Aids.

Hough, Judith. Mary Mack - A Paper Doll Circa 1895: Color Decorate Authentic Fashions & Ethnic Costumes. Hough, Judith, illus. 26p. (gr. 2-6). 1992. pap. 7.95 (0-9633769-1-8) Touch The Sky.

Hough, Judith M. My School Days Memories: Grades K-6. Hough, Judith, illus. 40p. (gr. k-6). 1992. pap. 7.95 (0-9633769-0-X) Touch The Sky.

Houghton, Cleo, jt. ed. see Olson, Kenfield.

Houghton, Eric. The Backwards Watch. Abel, Simone, illus. LC 91-16951. 32p. (ps-2). 1992. 13.95 (0-531-05968-5); PLB 13.99 (0-531-08568-6) Orchard Bks Watts.
—Walter's Magic Wand. Teasdale, Denise, illus. LC 89-35400. 32p. (ps-1). 1990. 13.95 (0-531-05851-4); PLB 13.99 (0-531-08451-5) Orchard Bks Watts.

Houghton, Graham & Rickard, Graham. Alternative Energy, 5 vols. (Illus.). 32p. (gr. 4-6). 1991. Set. PLB 86.35 (0-8368-0712-X) Gareth Stevens Inc.

Houghton Mifflin Company Staff, ed. The American Heritage Children's Dictionary. Webber, Howard, contrib. by. LC 86-7349. (Illus.). 864p. (gr. 3-6). 1986. 14.95 (0-395-42529-8) HM.

Houghton Mifflin Company Staff, ed. & contrib. by. The American Heritage Student's Dictionary. rev. ed. LC 86-7337. (Illus.). 1024p. (gr. 6-9). 1986. 12.70 (0-395-40417-7) HM.

Houghton Mifflin Company Staff, ed. Children's Dictionary. Rev. ed. LC 78-27760. (Illus.). 864p. (gr. 3-6). 1979. 12.70 (0-395-27512-1) HM.
—First Dictionary. Ulrich, George, illus. LC 78-27760. 864p. (gr. 3-6). 1979. text ed. 11.95 (0-685-07955-4) HM.

Houghton, Norris, ed. Romeo & Juliet & West Side Story. 256p. (gr. 7 up). 1965. pap. 3.99 (0-440-97483-6, LFL) Dell.

Houghton, Patricia, ed. The Cassell Book of Proverbs. LC 92-12608. (Illus.). 160p. (gr. 10-12). 1992. 14.95 (0-304-34165-7, Pub. by Cassell UK) Sterling.

Houghton, Sue. Dolphin. Camm, Martin, illus. LC 91-44819. 32p. (gr. 4-6). 1993. lib. bdg. 11.59 (0-8167-2767-8); pap. text ed. 3.95 (0-8167-2768-6) Troll Assocs. Postponed.

Houk, Margaret. Soy Joven! Soy Importante! - That Very Special Person - Me! La Autoestima En la Adolescencia - Self-Esteem for Teens. Morales, Edgar O., tr. from ENG. (SPA.). 144p. (gr. 8 up). 1993. pap. 5.00 (0-311-46134-4) Casa Bautista.
—That Very Special Person - Me. 136p. (Orig.). 1990. pap. 6.95 (0-8361-3514-8) Herald Pr.

Houk, Randy. Bentley & Blueberry. Houk, Randy, illus. 32p. (gr. k-3). 1993. 14.95 (1-882728-00-9); read-along cass. 7.95 (1-882728-03-3) Benefactory.
—Jasmine. Houk, Randy, illus. 32p. (gr. k-3). 1993. 14.95 (1-882728-01-7); read-along cass. 7.95 (1-882728-04-1) Benefactory.
—Ruffle, Coo & Hoo Doo. Houk, Randy, illus. 32p. (gr. k-3). 1993. 14.95 (1-882728-02-5); read-along cass. 7.95 (1-882728-05-X) Benefactory.

Houk, Rose. Black Canyon of the Gunnison National Monument. Priehs, T. J. & Jorgen, Randolph, eds. Collier, Michael, photos by. LC 91-60464. 16p. (Orig.). 1991. pap. 2.95 (0-911408-93-2) SW Pks Mnmts.
—Curecanti National Recreation Area. Priehs, T. J. & Jorgen, Randolph, eds. LC 91-60465. 16p. (Orig.). 1991. pap. 2.95 (0-911408-92-4) SW Pks Mnmts.

Houldsworth, Jim. And So You Want to Go Cross-Country Skiing? (Illus.). 46p. (Orig.). (gr. 5 up). 1981. pap. 3.95 (*0-936198-06-0*) Hollow Spring Pr.

Houlton, Betsy. Tad & Me: How I Found Out about Fetal Alcohol Syndrome. Hanson, Eric, illus. 24p. (gr. 6-12). 1991. pap. 1.75 (*0-89486-739-3*) Hazelden.

Houlton, Betsy, jt. auth. see Mann, Peggy.

House, Charles L. Van see Van House, Charles L., Sr. & Swoszowski, Sarah M.

House, James & Steffens, Bradley. The San Francisco Earthquake. LC 89-33558. (Illus.). 64p. (gr. 5-8). 1989. PLB 11.95 (*1-56006-003-4*) Lucent Bks.

Household, Geoffrey. The Exploits of Xenophon. Fisher, Leonard E., illus. LC 89-12396. lx, 180p. (gr. 5-12). 1989. Repr. of 1955 ed. lib. bdg. 18.00 (*0-208-02224-4*, Linnet) Shoe String.

Houselander, Caryll. Petook: An Easter Story. De Paola, Tomie, illus. LC 87-21228. 32p. (ps-3). 1988. reinforced bdg. 15.95 (*0-8234-0681-4*) Holiday.

Housman, Laurence. Rocking - Horse Land. Rodanas, Kristina, illus. LC 89-45902. 32p. (gr. k-3). 1990. 13. 95 (*0-688-09014-1*); lib. bdg. 13.88 (*0-688-09015-X*) Lothrop.

Houston, Dick. Safari Adventure. Houston, Dick, photos by. LC 91-8038. (Illus.). 160p. (gr. 6 up). 1991. 15.95 (*0-525-65051-2*, Cobblehill Bks) Dutton Child Bks.

Houston, Gloria. But No Candy. Bloom, Lloyd, illus. 32p. (ps-3). 1992. PLB 14.95 (*0-399-22142-5*, Philomel Bks) Putnam Pub Group.

—Littlejim. Allen, Thomas, illus. 176p. 1990. 14.95 (*0-399-22220-0*, Philomel Bks) Putnam Pub Group.

—Littlejim. Allen, Thomas B., illus. LC 92-43775. 176p. (gr. 5 up). 1993. pap. 4.95 (*0-688-12112-8*, Pub. by Beech Tree Bks) Morrow.

—Mountain Valor. LC 92-26218. 1993. write for info. (*0-399-22519-6*, Philomel Bks) Putnam Pub Group.

—My Great-Aunt Arizona. Lamb, Susan C., illus. LC 90-44112. 32p. (gr. 1-4). 1992. 15.00 (*0-06-022606-4*); PLB 14.89 (*0-06-022607-2*) HarpC Child Bks.

Houston, Gloria M. The Year of the Perfect Christmas Tree: An Appalachian Story. Cooney, Barbara, illus. LC 87-245515. 32p. (ps-3). 1988. 14.95 (*0-8037-0299-X*); PLB 14.89 (*0-8037-0300-7*) Dial Bks Young.

Houston, Jack. Basic Skills Health Workbook: Grade 9. 32p. (gr. 9). 1982. tchr's. ed. 1.98 (*0-685-06462-X*, HW-J) ESP.

—Jumbo Health Yearbook: Grade 5. 96p. (gr. 5). 1979. 18.00 (*0-8209-0065-6*, JHY 5) ESP.

—Jumbo Health Yearbook: Grade 6. 96p. (gr. 6). 1979. 18.00 (*0-8209-0066-4*, JHY 6) ESP.

—Jumbo Health Yearbook: Grade 7. 96p. (gr. 7). 1979. 18.00 (*0-8209-0067-2*, JHY 7) ESP.

—Jumbo Health Yearbook: Grade 8. 96p. (gr. 8). 1979. 18.00 (*0-8209-0068-0*, JHY 8) ESP.

Houston, James. Akavak. 80p. (gr. 4 up). 1990. pap. 8.95 (*0-15-201731-3*) HarBrace.

—Drifting Snow: An Arctic Search. Houston, James, illus. LC 91-42674. 160p. (gr. 5 up). 1992. SBE 13.95 (*0-689-50563-9*, M K McElderry) Macmillan Child Grp.

—Drifting Snow: An Arctic Search. 160p. 1994. pap. 3.99 (*0-14-036530-3*) Puffin Bks.

—The Falcon Bow: An Arctic Legend. (Illus.). 96p. (gr. 5 up). 1992. pap. 3.99 (*0-14-036078-6*, Puffin) Puffin Bks.

—Frozen Fire: A Tale of Courage. Houston, James, illus. LC 77-6366. 160p. (gr. 7 up). 1977. SBE 13.95 (*0-689-50083-1*, M K McElderry) Macmillan Child Grp.

—Frozen Fire: A Tale of Courage. 2nd ed. Houston, James, illus. LC 91-46062. 160p. (gr. 3-7). 1992. pap. 4.95 (*0-689-71612-5*, Aladdin) Macmillan Child Grp.

—Long Claws: An Arctic Adventure. (Illus.). 32p. (ps-3). 1992. pap. 4.99 (*0-14-054522-0*, Puffin) Puffin Bks.

—River Runners: A Tale of Hardship & Bravery. 160p. (gr. 5 up). 1992. pap. 4.50 (*0-14-036093-X*, Puffin) Puffin Bks.

—The White Archer: An Eskimo Legend. LC 79-14458. (Illus.). 95p. (gr. 5 up). 1990. pap. 8.95 (*0-15-696224-1*, Voyager Bks) HarBrace.

Houston, James R. Tikta'liktak. 63p. (gr. 5 up). 1990. pap. 8.95 (*0-15-287748-7*) HarBrace.

Houtman, Jane F., tr. see Hooker, Irene H. & Brindle, Susan A.

Houts, Amy. An A-B-C Christmas. Munger, Nancy, illus. 28p. (ps-k). 1993. 4.99 (*0-7847-0063-X*, 24-03843) Standard Pub.

Houts, Marshall. Cousin Charlie, the Crow. Ryan, Donna, illus. 84p. (Orig.). (gr. 2-8). 1992. pap. 10.95 (*1-880812-00-2*) S Ink WA.

Hovanec. Double Clued Crossword Puzzles. 1992. pap. 1.95 (*0-590-44726-2*) Scholastic Inc.

Hovanec, Helene. Crazy Crosswords. 48p. (gr. 1-6). 1993. pap. 2.95 (*0-8431-3492-5*) Price Stern.

—Doubletalk: Codes, Signs & Symbols. Wimmer, Chuck, illus. (gr. 7-10). 1993. pap. 1.25 (*0-553-37218-1*) Bantam.

—Numbzzles. 48p. (gr. 1-6). 1993. pap. 2.95 (*0-8431-3493-3*) Price Stern.

—Think Fast: Nickelodeon's Brain-Bending Games & Puzzles. Zimmerman, Jerry, illus. LC 90-86410. 96p. (Orig.). (gr. 2-6). 1992. pap. 2.95 (*0-448-40200-9*, G&D) Putnam Pub Group.

Hovde, Jane. Jane Addams. 144p. (gr. 5 up). 1989. 16.95 (*0-8160-1547-3*) Facts on File.

Hovde, Jeanne. A Horse for Cassie. LC 88-7355. 132p. (gr. 3-7). 1988. pap. 4.49 (*1-55513-587-0*, Chariot Bks) Cook.

Hover, Herman. How Many Three-Cent Stamps in a Dozen? or How Logical Are You? 1976. pap. 2.95 (*0-8431-0408-2*) Price Stern.

Hover, M. Here Comes Santa Claus. Santoro, Christopher, illus. 14p. (ps). 1982. write for info. (*0-307-12267-0*, Golden Bks.) Western Pub.

Hovey, Tamara. Paris Underground. LC 90-7980. (Illus.). 96p. (gr. 5 up). 1991. 14.95 (*0-531-05931-6*); PLB 14. 99 (*0-531-08531-7*) Orchard Bks Watts.

Hoving, Walter. Tiffany's Table Manners for Teenagers. Eula, Joe, illus. LC 88-23964. 96p. (gr. 5 up). 1989. Repr. of 1962 ed. 13.00 (*0-394-82877-1*) Random Bks Yng Read.

Howard, Barbara. Journey of Joy. 157p. (gr. 5 up). 1990. pap. text ed. 11.00 (*0-8309-0562-6*) Herald Hse.

Howard, Brett. Memphis Blues. (Orig.). (ps-12). 1984. pap. 3.50 (*0-87067-356-4*, BH356) Holloway.

Howard, David. Missions Alive: Experiential Games for Youth. Nelson, Becky, ed. 46p. (Orig.). (gr. 7-12). 1993. pap. 5.95 (*1-56309-071-6*) Womans Mission Union.

Howard, Deane H. Student Survival: Succeeding in School: A Quick Guide & Reference of Study Skills & Procedures. 250p. (gr. 6 up). 1991. pap. 24.95 (*0-9629207-0-3*) Ed Res Pub Co.

Howard, Diane W. Jeremy Firefly: Oh to Glow. Kight, Joshua, illus. 48p. (Orig.). (gr. k-3). 1991. PLB 13.95 (*0-9623524-2-X*) Hunt Hse Pub.

—Swimming Upstream: A Complete Guide to the College Application Process for the Learning Disabled Student. Lord, J. R., intro. by. (Illus.). 140p. (Orig.). (gr. 8-12). 1989. pap. write for info. wkbk. Hunt Hse Pub.

Howard, Dumont. Lady Dither's Ghost. (Illus.). 36p. (Orig.). (gr. k up). 1986. pap. 3.50 (*0-88680-263-6*); piano-vocal score 15.00 (*0-88680-264-4*); royalty on application 60.00 (*0-685-67534-3*) I E Clark.

—Talking Leaves. (Illus.). 25p. (Orig.). (gr. 2 up). 1989. Piano/Vocal Score 15.00 (*0-88680-305-5*); pap. 3.00 (*0-88680-304-7*); royalty on application 60.00 (*0-685-67716-8*) I E Clark.

Howard, Elizabeth F. Aunt Flossie's Hats (& Crab Cakes Later) Ransome, James, illus. 32p. (ps-1). 1991. 14.95 (*0-395-54682-6*, Clarion Bks) HM.

—Chita's Christmas Tree. Cooper, Floyd, illus. LC 88-26250. 32p. (ps-2). 1989. RSBE 14.95 (*0-02-744621-2*, Bradbury Pr) Macmillan Child Grp.

—Chita's Christmas Tree. Cooper, Floyd, illus. LC 92-44482. 32p. (gr. k-2). 1993. pap. 4.95 (*0-689-71739-3*, Aladdin) Macmillan Child Grp.

—Mac & Marie & the Train Toss Surprise. Carter, Gail G., illus. LC 92-17918. 32p. (ps-2). 1993. RSBE 14.95 (*0-02-744640-9*, Four Winds) Macmillan Child Grp.

—Papa Tells Chita a Story. Cooper, Floyd, illus. LC 93-1252. 1994. write for info. (*0-02-744623-9*, Four Winds) Macmillan Child Grp.

—The Train to Lulu's. Casilla, Robert, illus. LC 86-33429. 32p. (ps-2). 1988. RSBE 14.95 (*0-02-744620-4*, Bradbury Pr) Macmillan Child Grp.

—The Train to Lulu's. Castille, Robert, illus. LC 93-255565. 32p. 1994. pap. 4.95 (*0-689-71797-0*, Aladdin) Macmillan Child Grp.

Howard, Ellen. Big Seed. (ps-6). 1993. pap. 14.00 (*0-671-73956-5*, S&S BFYR) S&S Trade.

—The Cellar. Mulvihill, Patricia, illus. LC 90-23190. 64p. (gr. 2-4). 1992. SBE 11.95 (*0-689-31724-7*, Atheneum Child Bk) Macmillan Child Grp.

—The Chickenhouse House. LC 90-38007. (Illus.). 64p. (gr. 2-5). 1991. SBE 12.95 (*0-689-31695-X*, Atheneum Child Bk) Macmillan Child Grp.

—Circle of Giving. LC 83-15631. 112p. (gr. 4-6). 1984. SBE 13.95 (*0-689-31027-7*, Atheneum Child Bk) Macmillan Child Grp.

—Edith Herself. Hinter, Ronald, illus. LC 86-10826. 144p. (gr. 3-7). 1987. SBE 13.95 (*0-689-31314-4*, Atheneum Child Bk) Macmillan Child Grp.

—Edith Herself. LC 93-28061. 144p. (gr. 3-7). 1994. 3.95 (*0-689-71795-4*, Aladdin) Macmillan Child Grp.

—Gillyflower. LC 86-3584. 128p. (gr. 4-8). 1986. SBE 12.95 (*0-689-31274-1*, Atheneum Child Bk) Macmillan Child Grp.

—Gilly's Secret. LC 92-44896. 128p. (gr. 3-7). 1993. pap. 3.95 (*0-689-71746-6*, Aladdin) Macmillan Child Grp.

—Her Own Song. LC 88-3393. 176p. (gr. 4-7). 1988. SBE 13.95 (*0-689-31444-2*, Atheneum Child Bk) Macmillan Child Grp.

—Murphy & Kate. Graham, Mark, illus. LC 93-26002. 1994. write for info. (*0-671-79775-1*, S&S BFYR) S&S Trade.

—Sister. LC 90-196. 160p. (gr. 3-7). 1990. SBE 13.95 (*0-689-31653-4*, Atheneum Child Bk) Macmillan Child Grp.

—The Tower Room. LC 92-39240. 160p. (gr. 3-7). 1993. SBE 13.95 (*0-689-31856-1*, Atheneum Child Bk) Macmillan Child Grp.

—When Daylight Comes. LC 85-7963. 192p. (gr. 5-9). 1985. SBE 14.95 (*0-689-31133-8*, Atheneum Child Bk) Macmillan Child Grp.

Howard, Esther & Faulk, Diane. KinderUnits. (gr. k). 1990. pap. 11.95 (*0-8224-4101-2*) Fearon Teach Aids.

Howard, Goldena, jt. auth. see Howard, Oliver.

Howard, Jane. When I'm Hungry. (Illus.). 24p. (ps-k). 1992. 12.50 (*0-525-44983-3*, DCB) Dutton Child Bks.

Howard, Jane R. When I'm Sleepy. Cherry, Lynne, illus. LC 84-25895. 24p. (ps-3). 1985. 12.95 (*0-525-44204-9*, DCB) Dutton Child Bks.

Howard, Jean G. Bound by the Sea: A Summer Diary. LC 86-50255. (Illus.). 96p. (gr. k-2). 1986. text ed. 15.00 (*0-930954-25-4*); pap. 10.00 (*0-930954-26-2*) Tidal Pr.

—Half a Cage. Howard, Jean G., illus. LC 78-62962. 319p. (gr. 4-12). 1978. 5.50 (*0-930954-07-6*) Tidal Pr.

—Of Mice & Mice. limited ed. Howard, Jean G., illus. LC 78-50486. (gr. k-4). 1978. 5.50 (*0-930954-03-3*); deluxe ed. 35.00 deluxe ed. (*0-930954-04-1*) Tidal Pr.

Howard, John. Backyard Mystery. (Illus.). (gr. 2-3). 1972. pap. 1.95 (*0-89375-046-8*) Troll Assocs.

—I Can Read About Dinosaurs. (Illus.). (gr. 2-4). 1972. pap. 1.95 (*0-89375-051-4*) Troll Assocs.

—I Can Read About Fossils. Nodel, Norman, illus. LC 76-54446. (gr. 2-5). 1977. pap. 1.95 (*0-89375-038-7*) Troll Assocs.

—Mexico. (Illus.). 48p. (gr. 5 up). 1992. PLB 16.98 (*0-382-24247-5*) Silver Burdett Pr.

Howard, Julie. Walk on the Water. 24p. (Orig.). 1990. pap. 5.95 (*0-8146-2011-6*) Liturgical Pr.

Howard, Katherine. Do You Know Colors? Miller, J. P., illus. LC 78-1133. (ps-1). 1979. lib. bdg. 5.99 (*0-394-93957-3*); 2.25 (*0-394-83957-9*) Random Bks Yng Read.

—I Can Count to One Hundred...Can You? Smollin, Michael J., illus. LC 78-62700. (ps). 1979. pap. 2.25 (*0-394-84090-9*) Random Bks Yng Read.

—Little Bunny Follows His Nose. Miller, J. P., illus. 32p. (ps-2). 1971. write for info. (*0-307-13536-5*, Golden Bks.) Western Pub.

Howard, Kim. In Wintertime. LC 93-10979. 1994. write for info. (*0-688-11378-8*); lib. bdg. write for info. (*0-688-11379-6*) Lothrop.

Howard, Lati, et al. Learning English Book: A TV-Video Standard Program. McLaughlin, Michael & Schneider, Amy, eds. Murphy, Marty, illus. 240p. (Orig.). 1992. pap. text ed. 10.95 (*0-937354-76-7*) Delta Systems.

Howard, Lori A. What to Do With a Squirt of Glue: And Paper, Paint & Scissors, Too! (Illus.). 96p. (gr. k-6). 1987. pap. text ed. 8.95 (*0-86530-086-0*, IP 86-0) Incentive Pubns.

Howard, Marie, jt. auth. see Lena, Dan.

Howard, Marie, jt. auth. see Lena, Daniel S.

Howard, Mildred T. These Are My People. (Illus.). 152p. (Orig.). (gr. 3). 1984. pap. 6.94 (*0-89084-242-6*) Bob Jones Univ Pr.

Howard, Milly. Brave the Wild Trail. (Illus.). 96p. (Orig.). (gr. 4-6). 1987. pap. 4.95 (*0-89084-384-8*) Bob Jones Univ Pr.

—The Mystery of Pelican Cove. LC 93-25966. 1993. write for info. (*0-89084-711-8*) Bob Jones Univ Pr.

—On Yonder Mountain. (Illus.). 127p. (Orig.). (gr. 1-6). 1989. pap. 5.50 (*0-89084-462-3*) Bob Jones Univ Pr.

—The Runaway Princess. (Illus.). 126p. (Orig.). 1988. pap. 4.95 (*0-89084-465-8*) Bob Jones Univ Pr.

—The Treasure of Pelican Cove. (Illus.). 112p. (Orig.). 1988. pap. 4.95 (*0-89084-464-X*) Bob Jones Univ Pr.

Howard, Neva. Tommy & James Cell. 32p. 1989. write for info. N Howard.

Howard, Nina. Barber, Barber, Shave a Pig. Rayl, Eleanor, illus. 16p. (ps-k). 1981. tchr's ed. 4.95 (*0-917206-13-4*) Children Learn Ctr.

—Classroom Chefs. Rayl, Eleanor, illus. 96p. (gr. 2). 1981. 7.95 (*0-917206-14-2*) Children Learning Ctr.

Howard, Oliver & Howard, Goldena. The Mark Twain Book. LC 84-61875. (Illus.). 147p. (gr. 5 up). 1985. 14.95 (*9-9962889-3-5*) Ralls Cnty Bk.

Howard, Richard, tr. see De Brunhoff, Laurent.

Howard, Richard, tr. see Leprince de Beaumont's, Marie.

Howard, Susie, jt. auth. see Carpenter, Karen.

Howard, Tom. The Cat Chronicles. (Illus.). 128p. (gr. 7 up). 1993. 15.95 (*1-56138-291-4*) Running Pr.

—The Love of Cats. (Illus.). 96p. 1992. Repr. 12.98 (*0-8317-1203-1*) Smithmark.

Howard, Tom, jt. auth. see Adamoli, Vida.

Howard, Tom, jt. auth. see Clayton, Michael.

Howard, Velma S., tr. see Lagerlof, Selma.

Howard, Wayne. The Friendly Forest. Perle, Ruth L., ed. Howard, Wayne, illus. (gr. k-1). 1977. pap. text ed. 0.60 (*0-89796-855-7*) New Dimens Educ.

—Heat Wave. Perle, Ruth L., ed. Howard, Wayne, illus. (gr. k-1). 1977. pap. text ed. 0.60 (*0-89796-856-5*) New Dimens Educ.

—The Well. Perle, Ruth L., ed. Howard, Wayne, illus. (gr. k-1). 1977. pap. text ed. 0.60 (*0-89796-859-X*) New Dimens Educ.

Howard-Moineau, Henrietta. Twiggy: The Abandoned, Diabetic Dog. (Illus.). 73p. (Orig.). (gr. 4 up). 1982. pap. 5.00 (*0-318-01113-1*) Hampshire Pr.

Howarth, Sarah. Medieval People. (Illus.). 48p. (gr. 4-6). 1992. PLB 13.90 (*1-56294-153-4*) Millbrook Pr.

—Medieval Places. (Illus.). 48p. (gr. 4-6). 1992. PLB 13. 90 (*1-56294-152-6*) Millbrook Pr.

—The Middle Ages. (Illus.). 48p. (gr. 3-7). 1993. 14.99 (*0-670-85098-5*) Viking Child Bks.

—Renaissance People. (Illus.). 48p. (gr. 4-6). 1992. PLB 13.90 (*1-56294-088-0*) Millbrook Pr.

—Renaissance Places. (Illus.). 48p. (gr. 4-6). 1992. PLB 13.90 (*1-56294-089-9*) Millbrook Pr.

Howe, D. H. American Start with English. (Orig.). (gr. 7-11). 1983. pap. write for info. OUP.

Howe, Deborah & Howe, James. Bunnicula: A Rabbit Tale of Mystery. Daniel, Alan, illus. LC 78-11472. 112p. (gr. 4-6). 1979. SBE 12.95 (0-689-30700-4, Atheneum Child Bk) Macmillan Child Grp.
—Bunnicula: A Rabbit-Tale of Mystery. Daniel, Alan, illus. 100p. (gr. 3-7). 1980. pap. 3.99 (0-380-51094-4, Camelot) Avon.
—Teddy Bear's Scrapbook. Rose, David S., illus. LC 87-1096. 80p. (gr. 2-6). 1988. pap. 3.50 (0-689-71168-9, Aladdin) Macmillan Child Grp.
—Teddy Bear's Scrapbook. 2nd ed. Rose, David S., illus. 80p. (gr. 3-7). 1994. pap. 3.95 (0-689-71812-8, Aladdin) Macmillan Child Grp.
Howe, E. W. The Moonlight Boy. 1988. Repr. of 1886 ed. lib. bdg. 59.00x (0-7812-1288-X) Rprt Serv.
Howe, G. E., jt. auth. see Canon.
Howe, Imogen. Vicious Circle. (gr. 5-9). 1983. pap. 1.95 (0-440-99318-0, LFL) Dell.
Howe, Irving & Greenberg, Eliezer, eds. Favorite Yiddish Stories. 128p. 1992. Repr. 5.99 (0-517-06656-4, Pub. by Wings Bks) Outlet Bk Co.
Howe, Irving, ed. see Hardy, Thomas.
Howe, James. Babes in Toyland. Atkinson, Allen, illus. 79p. (gr. 3-7). 1988. pap. 9.95 (0-15-200410-6) HarBrace.
—The Bunnicula Fun Book. Daniel, Alan, illus. LC 92-34561. 176p. 1993. pap. 9.95 (0-688-11952-2) Morrow Jr Bks.
—The Case of the Missing Mother. Cleaver, William, illus. LC 82-13287. 32p. (gr. 1-6). 1983. pap. 1.95 (0-394-85729-1) Random Bks Yng Read.
—The Celery Stalks at Midnight. Morrill, Leslie, illus. LC 83-2665. 128p. (gr. 4-6). 1983. SBE 12.95 (0-689-30987-2, Atheneum Child Bk) Macmillan Child Grp.
—The Celery Stalks at Midnight. Morrill, Leslie H., illus. 128p. (gr. 3-7). 1984. pap. 3.99 (0-380-69054-3, Camelot) Avon.
—Creepy-Crawly Birthday. Morrill, Leslie, illus. LC 90-35370. 48p. (gr. k up). 1991. 13.95 (0-688-09687-5); PLB 13.88 (0-688-09688-3) Morrow Jr Bks.
—Creepy-Crawly Birthday. 48p. 1992. pap. 5.99 (0-380-75984-5, Camelot) Avon.
—The Day the Teacher Went Bananas. Hoban, Lillian, illus. LC 84-1536. 32p. (ps-2). 1984. 12.95 (0-525-44107-7, DCB); pap. 3.95 (0-525-44321-5, DCB) Dutton Child Bks.
—Dew Drop Dead. 128p. 1991. pap. 3.99 (0-380-71301-2, Camelot) Avon.
—Dew Drop Dead: A Sebastian Barth Mystery. LC 89-34697. 160p. (gr. 3-7). 1990. SBE 13.95 (0-689-31425-6, Atheneum Child Bk) Macmillan Child Grp.
—Eat Your Poison, Dear. LC 86-3582. 144p. (gr. 4-7). 1986. SBE 13.95 (0-689-31206-7, Atheneum Child Bk) Macmillan Child Grp.
—Eat Your Poison, Dear. 144p. (gr. 4-7). 1991. pap. 3.50 (0-380-71332-2, Camelot) Avon.
—The Fright Before Christmas. Morrill, Leslie, illus. LC 87-26280. 48p. (gr. k-3). 1988. 13.95 (0-688-07664-5); PLB 13.88 (0-688-07665-3, Morrow Jr Bks) Morrow Jr Bks.
—The Fright Before Christmas. Morrill, Leslie H., illus. 48p. 1989. pap. 5.95 (0-380-70445-5, Camelot) Avon.
—The Hospital Book. Warshaw, Mal, photos by. LC 93-15701. (gr. 1-8). 1994. write for info. (0-688-12731-2); pap. write for info. (0-688-12734-7) Morrow Jr Bks.
—Hot Fudge. Morrill, Leslie, illus. LC 89-13468. 48p. (gr. k up). 1990. 13.95 (0-688-08237-8); PLB 13.88 (0-688-09701-4, Morrow Jr Bks) Morrow Jr Bks.
—Hot Fudge. 48p. 1991. pap. 3.99 (0-380-70610-5, Camelot) Avon.
—How the Ewoks Saved the Trees: An Old Ewok Legend. Velez, Walter, illus. LC 83-13708. 48p. (gr. k-3). 1984. lib. bdg. 6.99 (0-394-96129-3) Random Bks Yng Read.
—Howliday Inn. Munsinger, Lynn, illus. LC 81-10886. 208p. (gr. 4-6). 1982. SBE 13.95 (0-689-30846-9, Atheneum Child Bk) Macmillan Child Grp.
—Howliday Inn. Munsinger, Lynn, illus. 200p. 1983. pap. 3.99 (0-380-64543-2, Camelot) Avon.
—I Wish I Were a Butterfly. Young, Ed, illus. LC 86-33635. 28p. (ps-3). 1987. 15.95 (0-15-200470-X, Gulliver Bks) HarBrace.
—Morgan's Zoo. Morrill, Leslie, illus. LC 84-6325. 192p. (gr. 3-6). 1984. SBE 13.95 (0-689-31046-3, Atheneum Child Bk) Macmillan Child Grp.
—Morgan's Zoo. (Illus.). 192p. (gr. 3-7). 1986. pap. 3.99 (0-380-69994-X, Camelot) Avon.
—The Muppet Guide to Magnificent Manners. Elwell, Peter, illus. LC 83-25063. 64p. (gr. 3-7). 1984. lib. bdg. 5.99 (0-394-96351-2); pap. 4.95 (0-394-86351-8) Random Bks Yng Read.
—A Night Without Stars. LC 82-16278. 192p. (gr. 4-7). 1983. SBE 13.95 (0-689-30957-0, Atheneum Child Bk) Macmillan Child Grp.
—A Night Without Stars. 192p. (gr. 7 up) 1985. pap. 2.95 (0-380-69877-3, Flare) Avon.
—A Night Without Stars. 192p. 1993. pap. 3.50 (0-380-71867-7, Camelot) Avon.
—Nighty-Nightmare. Morrill, Leslie, illus. LC 86-22334. 128p. (gr. 3-7). 1987. SBE 12.95 (0-689-31207-5, Atheneum Child Bk) Macmillan Child Grp.
—Nighty-Nightmare. 128p. (gr. 3-7). 1988. pap. 3.99 (0-380-70490-0, Camelot) Avon.
—Pinky & Rex. Sweet, Melissa, illus. 48p. (gr. 2). 1991. pap. 3.50 (0-380-71190-7, Pub. by Young Camelot) Avon.
—Pinky & Rex. LC 89-30786. (Illus.). 48p. (gr. k-3). 1990. SBE 12.95 (0-689-31454-X, Atheneum Child Bk) Macmillan Child Grp.
—Pinky & Rex & the Mean Old Witch. Sweet, Melissa, illus. LC 89-78204. 48p. (gr. k-3). 1991. SBE 11.95 (0-689-31617-8, Atheneum Child Bk) Macmillan Child Grp.
—Pinky & Rex & the Mean Old Witch. 48p. 1992. pap. 3.50 (0-380-71644-5, Camelot Young) Avon.
—Pinky & Rex & the New Baby. Sweet, Melissa, illus. LC 91-39801. 48p. (gr. k-3). 1993. SBE 12.95 (0-689-31717-4, Atheneum Child Bk) Macmillan Child Grp.
—Pinky & Rex & the Spelling Bee. Sweet, Melissa, illus. LC 89-78305. 48p. (gr. k-3). 1991. SBE 11.95 (0-689-31618-6, Atheneum Child Bk) Macmillan Child Grp.
—Pinky & Rex & the Spelling Bee. 48p. 1992. pap. 3.50 (0-380-71643-7, Camelot Young) Avon.
—Pinky & Rex Get Married. Sweet, Melissa, illus. LC 89-406. 48p. (gr. k-3). 1990. SBE 11.95 (0-685-58512-3, Atheneum Child Bk); 11.95 (0-689-31453-1, Atheneum Childrens Bks) Macmillan Child Grp.
—Pinky & Rex Go to Camp. Sweet, Melissa, illus. LC 91-16123. 48p. (ps-3). 1992. SBE 11.95 (0-689-31718-2, Atheneum Child Bk) Macmillan Child Grp.
—Pinky & Rex Go to Camp. 48p. (gr. 2-8). 1993. pap. 3.99 (0-380-72082-5, Camelot Young) Avon.
—Rabbit Cadabra! Daniel, Alan, illus. LC 91-34656. 48p. (gr. k up). 1993. 15.00 (0-688-10402-9); PLB 14.93 (0-688-10403-7) Morrow Jr Bks.
—Rabbit-Cadabra! 48p. 1994. pap. 5.99 (0-380-71336-5, Camelot Young) Avon.
—Return to Howliday Inn. Daniels, Alan, illus. LC 91-29505. 176p. (gr. 3-7). 1992. SBE 13.95 (0-689-31661-5, Atheneum Child Bk) Macmillan Child Grp.
—Return to Howliday Inn. 128p. 1993. pap. 3.99 (0-380-71972-X, Camelot) Avon.
—Scared Silly. 48p. 1990. pap. 4.95 (0-380-70446-3, Camelot) Avon.
—Scared Silly: A Halloween Treat. Morrill, Leslie, illus. LC 88-7837. 48p. (gr. k up). 1989. 13.95 (0-688-07666-1); PLB 13.88 (0-688-07667-X, Morrow Jr Bks) Morrow Jr Bks.
—Stage Fright. 144p. 1991. pap. 3.50 (0-380-71331-4, Camelot) Avon.
—Stage Fright. 1987. pap. 2.95 (0-380-70173-1, Flare) Avon.
—Stage Fright: A Sebastian Barth Mystery. 160p. (gr. 3-7). 1986. 12.95 (0-689-31160-5, Atheneum Child Bk) Macmillan Child Grp.
—Stage Fright: A Sebastian Barth Mystery. 2nd ed. LC 85-20025. 160p. (gr. 3-7). 1986. SBE 11.95 (0-689-31701-8, Atheneum Child Bk) Macmillan Child Grp.
—There's a Dragon in My Sleeping Bag. Rose, David S., illus. LC 93-26572. 1994. 14.95 (0-689-31873-1, Atheneum Child Bk) Macmillan Child Grp.
—There's a Monster under My Bed. Rose, David S., illus. LC 85-20026. 32p. (ps-2). 1986. SBE 13.95 (0-689-31178-8, Atheneum Child Bk) Macmillan Child Grp.
—There's a Monster under My Bed. Rose, David, illus. LC 89-18664. 32p. (gr. k-3). 1990. pap. 3.95 (0-689-71409-2, Aladdin) Macmillan Child Grp.
—What Eric Knew: A Sebastian Barth Mystery. LC 85-7418. 156p. (gr. 4-6). 1985. SBE 13.95 (0-689-31702-6, Atheneum Child Bk) Macmillan Child Grp.
Howe, James & Sweet, Melissa. Pinky & Rex Get Married. (Illus.). 48p. (gr. 2). 1991. pap. 3.50 (0-380-71191-5, Pub. by Young Camelot) Avon.
Howe, James, jt. auth. see Howe, Deborah.
Howe, James, adapted by. Dances with Wolves Storybook: A Story for Children. LC 91-20283. (Illus.). 64p. (ps-2). 1991. bds. 14.95 (1-55704-104-0) Newmarket.
Howe, James, adapted by see Burnett, Frances H.
Howe, John. Jack & the Beanstalk, Vol. 1. 1989. 15.95 (0-316-37579-9) Little.
Howe, John, retold by. & illus. The Knight with the Lion: The Story of Yvain. LC 92-25940. 1993. 14.95 (0-316-37583-7) Little.
Howe, John, retold by. & illu see Irving, Washington.
Howe, Norma. In With the Out Crowd. 208p. (gr. 7 up). 1986. 12.95 (0-395-40490-8) HM.
—Shoot for the Moon. LC 91-24585. 224p. (gr. 5-9). 1992. 15.00 (0-517-58150-7); PLB 15.99 (0-517-58151-5) Crown Bks Yng Read.
Howe, Quincy. Streetsmart. LC 93-1397. (gr. 9-12). 1993. write for info. (0-932765-42-4) Close Up.
Howe, Robert T. Ohio: Our State. (Illus.). 408p. (gr. 7). 1992. text ed. 24.00 (0-9631313-0-3); tchr's. hdbk. 12.00 (0-9631313-1-1) Roblen Pub.
Howell, Ann C. Communication: A Salute to Black Inventors. rev. ed. Ivery, Evelyn L., ed. Chandler, Alton, et al, illus. Chandler, Alton, intro. by. 24p. (gr. 3-7). 1992. pap. text ed. 1.50 (1-877804-05-3) Chandler White.
—Conscious Choices of African-Americans During the American Revolution. Ivery, Evelyn L., ed. Still, Wayne A. & Chandler, Alton, illus. Barboza, Maurice A., intro. by. 32p. (Orig.). (gr. 3-7). 1991. pap. text ed. 2.50 (1-877804-09-6) Chandler White.
—Food: A Salute to Black Inventors. rev. ed. Ivery, Evelyn L., ed. Venable, James, et al, illus. Chndler, Alton, intro. by. 24p. (gr. 3-7). 1992. pap. text ed. 1.50 (1-877804-01-0) Chandler White.
—Old West: A Salute to Black Inventors. rev. ed. Ivery, Evelyn L., ed. Chandler, Alton, et al, illus. Chandler, Alton, pref. by. 24p. (gr. 3-7). 1992. pap. text ed. 1.50 (1-877804-03-7); tchr's. guide 1.75 (1-877804-07-X) Chandler White.
—Safety: A Salute to Black Inventors. rev. ed. Ivery, Evelyn L., ed. Chandler, Alton, et al, illus. Chandler, Alton H., intro. by. 24p. (gr. 3-7). 1992. pap. text ed. 1.50 (1-877804-02-9) Chandler White.
—Transportation - Food - Safety - Old West - Working Easier - Communication - Black Women: A Salute to Black Inventors. rev. ed. Ivery, Evelyn L., ed. Chandler, Alton, et al, illus. 24p. (gr. 3-7). 1992. pap. text ed. 10.50 (1-877804-10-X) Chandler White.
—Transportation: A Salute to Black Inventors. rev. ed. Ivery, Evelyn L., ed. Venable, James, et al, illus. Chandler, Alton, intro. by. 24p. (gr. 3-7). 1992. pap. text ed. 1.50 (1-877804-00-2) Chandler White.
—Working Easier: A Salute to Black Inventors. rev. ed. Ivery, Evelyn L., ed. Chandler, Alton, et al, illus. Chandler, Alton, intro. by. 24p. (gr. 3-7). 1992. pap. text ed. 1.50 (1-877804-04-5) Chandler White.
Howell, Ann C. & Massey, Grace C. Black Science Communications: Coloring - Learning Activities. Ivery, Evelyn, ed. Venable, James, et al, illus. Chandler, Alton, intro. by. (Orig.). (gr. 1-6). 1987. pap. text ed. 1.50 (0-685-26060-7) Chandler White.
—Black Science Food: Coloring - Learning Activities. Ivery, Evelyn L., ed. Venable, James, et al, illus. Chandler, Alton H., intro. by. (Orig.). (gr. 1-6). 1987. pap. text ed. 1.50 (0-685-26061-5) Chandler White.
—Black Science Oldwest: Coloring - Learning Activities. Ivery, Evelyn L., ed. Venable, James, et al, illus. Chandler, Alton H., intro. by. (Orig.). (gr. 1-6). 1987. pap. text ed. 1.50 (0-685-26062-3) Chandler White.
—Black Science Safety: Coloring - Learning Activities. Ivery, Evelyn L., ed. Venable, James, et al, illus. Chandler, Alton H., intro. by. (Orig.). (gr. 1-6). 1987. pap. text ed. 1.50 (0-685-26059-3) Chandler White.
—Black Science Transportation: Coloring - Learning Activities. Ivery, Evelyn L., ed. Venable, James, et al, illus. Chandler, Alton H., intro. by. (Orig.). (gr. 1-6). 1987. pap. text ed. 1.50 (0-685-26063-1) Chandler White.
—Black Science Working Easier: Coloring - Learning Activities. Ivery, Evelyn L., ed. Chandler, Alton H., et al, illus. Chandler, Alton, intro. by. (Orig.). (gr. 1-6). 1987. pap. text ed. 1.50 (0-685-26058-5) Chandler White.
Howell, Catherine H. Reptiles & Amphibians. (gr. 1-3). 1993. write for info. (0-87044-891-9) Natl Geog.
Howell, Dean. The Story of Chinaman's Hat. Howell, Dean, illus. 36p. (ps-4). 1990. 7.95 (0-89610-149-5) Island Heritage.
Howell, Judd, intro. by. Wildlife California. (Illus.). 64p. (ps-7). 1990. text ed. 9.95 (0-87701-886-3) Chronicle Bks.
Howell, Melissa. Back Home in Japan: An Activity Book. Hackney, Rick, illus. 64p. (gr. 1-4). 1991. tchr's. ed. 1.95 (981-3009-02-0); wkbk. 3.95 (981-3009-24-1) OMF Bks.
Howell, Sherry. Willy on Wheels. (Illus.). 63p. (Orig.). (gr. k-4). 1986. pap. 2.95 (0-931563-05-4) Wishing Rm.
Howell, Troy, retold by. & illu see Andersen, Hans Christian.
Howell, War Cry. Gramma Curlychief's Pawnee Indian Stories. 3rd ed. Burns, Kathy, illus. LC 82-71948. 88p. (Orig.). (gr. 5-12). 1991. pap. 4.95x (0-943864-22-4) Davenport.
Howell, Will C. Basic Scribbling: How to Draw from Scratch. (ps-3). 1992. pap. 2.99 incl. chipboard (0-8431-3414-3) Price Stern.
—Grid & Bear It. (gr. 1-3). 1987. pap. 6.95 (0-8224-3510-1) Fearon Teach Aids.
—Grid & Graph It. (gr. 4-6). 1987. pap. 6.95 (0-8224-3511-X) Fearon Teach Aids.
—Marc Brown Connection. (gr. 1-6). 1991. 10.95 (0-8224-4378-3) Fearon Teach Aids.
—Robert McCloskey Connection. (gr. 1-3). 1990. pap. 10.95 (0-8224-5829-2) Fearon Teach Aids.
—Steven Kellog Connection. (gr. 1-6). 1990. pap. 10.95 (0-8224-6452-7) Fearon Teach Aids.
—Susan Jeffers Connection. (gr. 1-6). 1991. pap. 10.95 (0-86653-980-8) Fearon Teach Aids.
Howells, William Dean. Editha. LC 92-44053. 1994. write for info. (0-88682-585-7) Creative Ed.
—Modern Instance. Gibson, W., ed. LC 57-13839. (gr. 9 up). 1957. pap. 9.16 (0-395-05119-3, RivEd) HM.
—Rise of Silas Lapham. Hillerich, R. L., intro. by. (gr. 11 up). 1968. pap. 2.95 (0-8049-0165-1, CL-165) Airmont.
—Rise of Silas Lapham. Cady, Edwin H., ed. LC 57-14612. (gr. 9 up). 1957. pap. 9.16 (0-395-05126-6, RivEd) HM.
—Rise of Silas Lapham. (RL 9). 1963. pap. 4.95 (0-451-52496-9, CE1850, Sig Classics) NAL-Dutton.
Howes, Janice. A Classroom Presents the Constitution of the United States: A Story for Elementary School Children. Howes, Janice, illus. LC 87-50078. 35p. (Orig.). (gr. k-5). 1987. pap. 7.00 (0-942431-00-6) Teachers Pub Hse.

Howes, Joan. That's How Love Is. Shaw, Charles, illus. LC 91-316. 32p. (gr. k-4). 1991. 12.95 (*0-938349-62-7*); pap. 6.95 (*0-938349-63-5*) State House Pr.

Howes, Kathi. Nez Perce. (Illus.). 32p. (gr. 5-8). 1990. lib. bdg. 15.94 (*0-86625-379-3*); lib. bdg. 11.95s.p. (*0-685-36389-9*) Rourke Corp.

Howker, Janni. Isaac Campion. LC 86-9843. 128p. (gr. 5 up). 1987. 10.25 (*0-688-06658-5*) Greenwillow.
—Isaac Campion. (gr. k-6). 1990. pap. 2.95 (*0-440-40280-8*, YB) Dell.
—The Nature of the Beast. LC 84-25328. 137p. (gr. 7-9). 1985. reinforced bdg. 10.25 (*0-688-04233-3*) Greenwillow.

Howland, Joe, ed. see Thompson, Denisse & Van Loy, Merrie.

Howland, Naomi. ABCDrive! A Car Trip Alphabet. LC 93-11530. 1994. write for info. (*0-395-66414-4*, Clarion Bks) HM.

Howlett, Bud. I'm New Here. LC 92-7478. 1993. 14.95 (*0-395-64049-0*) HM.

Howlett, Charles F., jt. auth. see Perrin, Janet.

Howse, Cathy. Ultra Black Hair Growth: Six Inches Longer One Year from Now. (Illus.). 92p. (Orig.). (gr. 8 up). 1990. pap. text ed. 10.95 (*0-9628330-0-2*) UBH Pubns.

Howton, Louise, ed. see Eliot, T. S.

Hoxie, Frederick E. The Crow. (Illus.). 128p. (gr. 5 up). 1989. 17.95 (*1-55546-704-0*); pap. 9.95 (*0-7910-0379-5*) Chelsea Hse.

Hoy, Ken. Frightful Winged Creatures. Felts, Shirley, illus. 5p. (ps-3). 1993. 12.95 (*0-8249-8618-0*, Ideals Child) Hambleton-Hill.
—Gruesome Land Creatures. Bowring, Isabel, illus. 5p. (ps-3). 1993. 12.95 (*0-8249-8617-2*, Ideals Child) Hambleton-Hill.
—Land Life. (Illus.). 12p. (gr. k-4). 1990. 11.95 (*0-8249-8472-2*, Ideals Child) Hambleton-Hill.
—Water Life. (Illus.). 12p. (gr. k-4). 1990. 11.95 (*0-8249-8473-0*, Ideals Child) Hambleton-Hill.

Hoy, Linda. Emmeline Pankhurst. (Illus.). 64p. (gr. 5-9). 1991. 11.95 (*0-237-60019-6*, Pub. by Evans Bros Ltd) Trafalgar.

Hoyal, Dawna T. Pat & the Leprechaun. 1992. 7.95 (*0-533-10158-1*) Vantage.

Hoye, Regena. Giggle Pie. LC 93-78442. 20p. (Orig.). Date not set. pap. write for info. (*0-9636906-1-2*) Ishnuvu Pub.

Hoyt. A Gentleman of Broadway, 3 vols. large type ed. (gr. 10 up). Repr. of 1964 ed. Set. write for info. NAVH.

Hoyt, Doris, jt. auth. see Hoyt, George.

Hoyt, Eric. Meeting the Whales: The Equinox Guide to Giants of the Deep. Folkens, Pieter, illus. 72p. (gr. 5 up). 1991. lib. bdg. 17.95 (*0-921820-25-9*, Pub. by Camden Hse CN); pap. 9.95 (*0-921820-23-2*, Pub. by Camden Hse CN) Firefly Bks Ltd.

Hoyt, Erich. Extinction A-Z. LC 90-23701. 128p. (gr. 6 up). 1991. lib. bdg. 17.95 (*0-89490-325-X*) Enslow Pubs.
—Riding with the Dolphins: The Equinox Guide to Dolphins & Porpoises. Folkens, Pieter, illus. 64p. (gr. 5 up). 1992. PLB 17.95 (*0-921820-55-0*, Pub. by Camden Hse CN); pap. 9.95 (*0-921820-57-7*, Pub. by Camden Hse CN) Firefly Bks Ltd.

Hoyt, George & Hoyt, Doris. A Bird's-Eye View of California. Atkinson, Mary, illus. 48p. (Orig.). (gr. k-4). 1989. pap. 4.95 (*0-9622364-4-6*) Adona Pub.

Hoyt, Marie A. Kitchen Chemistry & Front Porch Physics. Finkler, C. Etana, illus. 60p. (Orig.). (gr. 3-8). 1983. pap. 5.00 (*0-914911-00-7*) Educ Serv Pr.

KITCHEN CHEMISTRY & FRONT PORCH PHYSICS for children ages 7-14 has instructions on how to make a **SHOEBOX CHEMISTRY SET** to be used in performing the 32 science experiments which demystify physics & chemistry. Its use of common materials & everyday household chemicals make the teaching of science fun, safe & in-depth. The simple understandable reading level enables students to discover science concepts by "Hands On" experience. Additionally, the glossary teacher-parent guide along with the Future Scientists of America awards make this book a science treasure to teachers, children, science group leaders & parents of both mainstream & minorities alike. *Publisher Provided Annotation.*

—Magnet Magic Etc. (Illus.). 12p. (gr. 2-8). 1983. pap. text ed. 2.50 (*0-914911-01-5*) Educ Serv Pr.

—Work-Game Sheets for Magnet Magic Etc. Bye, C. J., et al, illus. 28p. (Orig.). (gr. 2-8). 1984. pap. text ed. 2.50 (*0-914911-03-1*) Educ Serv Pr.
—Workbook Game Sheets for Kitchen Chemistry & Front Porch Physics. Green, Victor D. & Loor, Robin, illus. 44p. (Orig.). (gr. 3-8). 1983. pap. text ed. 4.00 (*0-914911-02-3*) Educ Serv Pr.

Hoyt-Goldsmith, Diane. Arctic Hunter. Migdale, Lawrence, illus. LC 92-2563. 32p. (gr. 3-7). 1992. reinforced bdg. 15.95 (*0-8234-0972-4*) Holiday.
—Celebrating Kwanzaa. Migale, Lawrence, photos by. LC 93-16799. (Illus.). (gr. 3-7). 1993. reinforced bdg. 15.95 (*0-8234-1048-X*) Holiday.
—Cherokee Summer. Migdale, Lawrence, illus. LC 92-54416. (Illus.). 32p. (gr. 3-7). 1993. reinforced bdg. 15.95 (*0-8234-0995-3*) Holiday.
—Hoang Anh: A Vietnamese-American Boy. Migdale, Lawrence, photos by. LC 91-28880. (Illus.). 32p. (gr. 3-7). 1992. reinforced bdg. 14.95 (*0-8234-0948-1*) Holiday.
—Pueblo Storyteller. Migdale, Lawrence, illus. LC 90-46405. 32p. (gr. 3-7). 1991. reinforced bdg. 15.95 (*0-8234-0864-7*) Holiday.
—Totem Pole. Migdale, Lawrence, illus. LC 89-26720. 32p. (gr. 3-7). 1990. reinforced bdg. 15.95 (*0-8234-0809-4*) Holiday.

Hrebic, Herbert J., jt. auth. see Cahill, Robert B.

Hrebic, Herbert J., ed. see Knight, Tanis & Lewin, Larry.

HRM the Empress of Japan, tr. see Mado, Michio.

Hronas, G. H. The Illustrated Life of the Theotokos for Children. 1990. pap. 5.95 (*0-937032-73-5*) Light&Life Pub Co MN.

Hru, Dakari. Joshua's Masai Mask. Rich, Anna, illus. LC 92-73219. 32p. (gr. k-4). 1993. 14.95 (*1-880000-02-4*) Lee & Low Bks.

Hrynko, Tamara. It's Not Alexander's Fault. Geurts, Kelly, illus. LC 91-67916. 96p. 1993. pap. 8.00 (*1-56002-177-2*, Univ Edtns) Aegina Pr.

Hsiung, S. I. Lady Precious Stream. Taylor, C. W., retold by. (Illus.). (gr. k-6). 1971. pap. text ed. 3.95x (*0-19-638235-1*) OUP.

Huang, Benrei, illus. Boo! Guess Who? LC 89-61374. 14p. (ps). 1990. bds. 3.99 (*0-679-80278-9*) Random Bks Yng Read.
—Pop-up Merry Christmas. 14p. (ps-1). 1992. 3.95 (*0-448-40253-X*, G&D) Putnam Pub Group.
—Pop-up Monster Party. 14p. (ps-1). 1992. 3.95 (*0-448-40255-6*, G&D) Putnam Pub Group.
—Pop-up Santa's Workshop. 14p. (ps-1). 1992. 3.95 (*0-448-40252-1*, G&D) Putnam Pub Group.
—Pop-up Spooky Night. 14p. (ps-1). 1992. 3.95 (*0-448-40254-8*, G&D) Putnam Pub Group.
—The Teeny Tiny Woman. 18p. (ps). 1993. bds. 3.95 (*0-448-40176-2*, G&D) Putnam Pub Group.

Hubalek, Linda K. see Dunlea, Nancy.

Hubbard, Freeman, jt. auth. see Knapke, William F.

Hubbard, Inez. Danny. Edgell, Kyle, illus. LC 84-62082. 48p. (Orig.). (gr. k-3). 1984. pap. 3.95 (*0-931571-00-6*) Lifetime Pr.

Hubbard, Kate & Berlin, Evelyn. Help Yourself to Safety: A Guide to Avoiding Dangerous Situations with Strangers & Friends. Meyer, Linda D., ed. Megale, Marina, illus. Walsh, John & Walsh, Whiteintro. by. Lyons, Carole, ed. LC 84-82541. (Illus.). 48p. (Orig.). (gr. 4-6). 1985. lib. bdg. 9.00 (*0-932091-00-8*); pap. 3.95 (*0-932091-01-6*) Franklin Pr WA.

Hubbard, L. Ron, concept by. Grammar & Communication for Children. 468p. (gr. 3-7). 1992. 49.99 (*0-88404-746-6*) Bridge Pubns Inc.
—How to Use a Dictionary Picture Book for Children. 260p. (gr. 3-7). 1992. 34.99 (*0-88404-747-4*) Bridge Pubns Inc.
—Learning How to Learn. 190p. (gr. 3-7). 1992. 34.99 (*0-88404-771-7*) Bridge Pubns Inc.
—Study Skills for Life. 128p. (gr. 7-10). 1992. 34.99 (*0-88404-744-X*) Bridge Pubns Inc.

Hubbard, Woodleigh. C Is for Curious: An ABC of Feelings. Hubbard, Woodleigh, illus. 40p. (ps-1). 1990. 12.95 (*0-87701-679-8*) Chronicle Bks.
—Two Is for Dancing: A One, Two, Three of Actions. Hubbard, Woodleigh, illus. 32p. (ps-1). 1991. 13.95 (*0-87701-895-2*) Chronicle Bks.

Hubbard-Brown, Janet. Comanche Indians: Great Plains. (gr. 4-7). 1993. pap. 6.95 (*0-7910-1957-8*) Chelsea Hse.
—A History Mystery: The Curse of the Hope Diamond. 96p. (Orig.). (gr. 6). 1991. pap. 2.99 (*0-380-76222-6*, Camelot) Avon.
—A History Mystery: The Disappearance of the Anasazi. Saffioti, Lino, illus. 96p. (Orig.). 1992. pap. 3.50 (*0-380-76643-6*, Camelot) Avon.
—A History Mystery: The Secret of Roanoke Island. 96p. (Orig.). 1991. pap. 3.50 (*0-380-76223-4*, Camelot) Avon.
—The Mohawk Indians. LC 93-18247. 1993. write for info. (*0-7910-1667-6*); pap. write for info. (*0-7910-1991-8*) Chelsea Hse.

Hubbell, Andra. Supercat. Dally, Tim, illus. LC 88-63735. 16p. (ps-3). 1989. PLB 16.95 (*0-9621759-1-9*); PLB 11.95 (*0-317-93727-8*) Rochester Pub Lib Dist.

Hubbell, Patricia. A Grass Green Gallop. Himler, Ronald, illus. LC 89-36354. 48p. (gr. 4-8). 1990. SBE 14.95 (*0-689-31604-6*, Atheneum Child Bk) Macmillan Child Grp.

Hubble, Edwin. Realm of the Nebulae. 1991. pap. 6.95 (*0-486-66762-6*) Dover.

Hubbs, Carl L. & Lagler, Karl F. Fishes of the Great Lakes Region. LC 58-7693. (Illus.). (gr. 9 up). 1964. 27.50 (*0-472-08465-8*) U of Mich Pr.

Huber, Carey. Gymnastics: A Step-By-Step Guide. LC 89-27394. (Illus.). 64p. (gr. 4-8). 1990. PLB 9.79 (*0-8167-1939-X*); pap. text ed. 2.95 (*0-8167-1940-3*) Troll Assocs.

Huber, Cary. Nature Explorer: A Step-By-Step Guide. LC 89-27391. (Illus.). 64p. (gr. 4-8). 1990. PLB 9.79 (*0-8167-1953-5*); pap. text ed. 2.95 (*0-8167-1954-3*) Troll Assocs.

Huber, Joanna & Claudius, Christel. Easy & Fun Paper Folding. LC 90-9829. (Illus.). 128p. (gr. 2-8). 1990. 12.95 (*0-8069-7444-3*) Sterling.

Huber, Johanna & Claudius, Christel. Easy & Fun Paper Folding. (Illus.). 128p. (gr. 4-11). 1991. pap. 4.95 (*0-8069-7445-1*) Sterling.

Huber, Judy. Gardening & Cooking with Children. 60p. (gr. 1-8). 1987. plastic comb. 4.95 (*0-944793-00-2*); pap. 2.95 (*0-944793-01-0*) Prairie Family Pubs.

Huber, Maureen. Cherry Cobbler. 1976. 7.15 (*0-686-15735-4*) Rod & Staff.

Huber, Miriam B., et al, eds. The Poetry Book: Vol. 4. Hartwell, Marjorie, illus. LC 79-51968. (gr. 4). 1980. Repr. of 1926 ed. 18.00x (*0-89609-183-X*) Roth Pub Inc.

Huber, Peter. Sandra Day O'Connor. (Illus.). 112p. (gr. 5 up). 1990. 17.95 (*1-55546-672-9*) Chelsea Hse.
—Sandra Day O'Connor: American Women of Achievement. (gr. 4-7). 1992. pap. 7.95 (*0-7910-0448-1*) Chelsea Hse.

Huberman, Caryn & Wetzel, JoAnne. Onstage Backstage. Huberman, Caryn & Wetzel, JoAnne, photos by. (Illus.). 56p. (gr. 2-5). 1987. PLB 21.50 (*0-87614-307-9*) Carolrhoda Bks.

Huberman, Leo. Man's Worldly Goods. 352p. (gr. 9-12). 1952. pap. 10.00 (*0-85345-070-6*) Monthly Rev.

Huberman, Leo & Sweezy, Paul M. Cuba: Anatomy of a Revolution. rev. ed. LC 60-14686. (Illus.). 208p. (gr. 9-12). 1961. pap. 8.00 (*0-85345-006-4*) Monthly Rev.
—Introduction to Socialism. Einstein, A., intro. by. LC 68-24055. (gr. 9 up). 1968. pap. 7.50 (*0-85345-067-6*) Monthly Rev.

Hubert, Amelia. Sweet Dreams for Sally. Cooke, Tom, illus. 40p. (ps-3). 1983. 5.95 (*0-910313-01-6*, 7002) Parker Bros.

Hubley, Faith & Towe, Kenneth M. Enter Life. Hubley, Faith, illus. LC 82-71680. 32p. (gr. 4 up). 1983. pap. 9.95 (*0-440-02357-2*, E Friede) Delacorte.

Hubley, John & Hubley, Penny. A Family in Italy. (Illus.). 32p. (gr. 2-5). 1987. PLB 13.50 (*0-8225-1673-X*) Lerner Pubns.
—A Family in Jamaica. LC 85-6887. (Illus.). 32p. (gr. 2-5). 1985. PLB 13.50 (*0-8225-1657-8*) Lerner Pubns.

Hubley, Penny, jt. auth. see Hubley, John.

Hubner, Carol K. The Haunted Shul. Kramer, Devorah, illus. (gr. 3-8). 1979. 6.95 (*0-910818-14-2*) Judaica Pr.
—Silent Shofar. Forst, Sigmund, illus. (gr. 3 up). 6.95 (*0-910818-53-3*); pap. 5.95 (*0-910818-54-1*) Judaica Pr.
—The Tattered Tallis. Kramer, Devorah, illus. 128p. (gr. 3-8). 1979. 6.95 (*0-910818-19-3*) Judaica Pr.
—The Whispering Mezuzah. Kramer, Devorah, illus. (gr. 3-9). 1979. 6.95 (*0-910818-18-5*) Judaica Pr.

Huck, Charlotte. Princess Furball. Lobel, Anita, illus. LC 88-18780. 40p. (ps up). 1989. 13.95 (*0-688-07837-0*); PLB 13.88 (*0-688-07838-9*) Greenwillow.
—Princess Furball. Lobel, Anita, illus. 40p. (ps up). 1994. pap. 4.95 (*0-688-13107-7*, Mulberry) Morrow.

Huck, Charlotte, selected by. Secret Places: Poems. George, Lindsay B., illus. LC 92-29014. 32p. (ps up). 1993. 15.00 (*0-688-11669-8*); PLB 14.93 (*0-688-11670-1*) Greenwillow.

Hucklesly, Hope. In My Head. Forss, Ian, illus. LC 92-34267. 1993. 2.50 (*0-383-03634-8*) SRA Schl Grp.

Huddleston, Steve. What Is God's Purpose for Me? (Illus.). 48p. (gr. 6-8). 1992. pap. 7.99 (*1-55945-132-7*) Group Pub.

Huddy, Delia. Puffin Ashore. Heap, Sue, illus. 32p. (ps-1). 1993. 13.95 (*1-85681-171-9*, Pub. by J MacRae UK) Trafalgar.
—Puffin at Sea. Heap, Sue, illus. 32p. (ps-1). 1993. 13.95 (*1-85681-161-1*, Pub. by J MacRae UK) Trafalgar.
—Snowman's Christmas. 1990. 13.95 (*0-385-30173-1*) Delacorte.

Hudson & Weaver. On the Job. large type ed. 76p. (gr. 7-12). 1983. Repr. of 1965 ed. 15.21 (*0-317-01916-3*, 4-20450-00) Am Printing Hse.
—Reading, Writing, & Speaking Here & Now, Bk. 1: A Framework for Fundamental Communication, 2 vols. large type ed. 300p. (gr. 7-12). 1983. Repr. of 1980 ed. 55.19 (*0-317-01925-2*, 4-22440-00) Am Printing Hse.

Hudson, Angus. Two Ears for Hearing. (Illus.). 8p. (ps). 1993. bds. 2.49 (*1-56476-179-7*, Victor Books) SP Pubns.
—Two Eyes for Seeing. (Illus.). 8p. (ps). 1993. bds. 2.49 (*1-56476-180-0*, Victor Books) SP Pubns.
—Two Feet for Walking. (Illus.). 8p. (ps). 1993. bds. 2.49 (*1-56476-177-0*, Victor Books) SP Pubns.
—Two Hands for Helping. (Illus.). 8p. (ps). 1993. bds. 2.49 (*1-56476-178-9*, Victor Books) SP Pubns.

Hudson, Anne & Daniels, Neil. Ozzie: An Odyssey of Love. Daniels, Neil, illus. LC 83-81305. 72p. (Orig.). (gr. 1-6). 1983. pap. 3.95 (*0-940258-10-2*) Kripalu Pubns.

Hudson, Cheryl W. Afro-Bets A B C Book. Hudson, Cheryl W., illus. LC 87-81580. 24p. (ps-3). 1987. pap. 3.95 (*0-940975-00-9*) Just Us Bks.

—Afro-Bets 1 2 3 Book. Hudson, Cheryl W., illus. LC 87-82952. 24p. (ps-3). 1988. pap. 3.95 (0-940975-01-7) Just Us Bks.
—Good Morning Baby. (Illus.). 1992. bds. 5.95 (0-590-45760-8, Cartwheel) Scholastic Inc.
—Good Night Baby. Ford, George, illus. 1992. bds. 5.95 (0-590-45761-6, Cartwheel) Scholastic Inc.
Hudson, Cheryl W. & Ford, Bernette G. Bright Eyes, Brown Skin. Ford, George, illus. LC 90-81648. 24p. (ps-2). 1990. 12.95 (0-940975-10-6); pap. 6.95 (0-940975-23-8) Just Us Bks.
Hudson, Eleanor. Teenage Mutant Ninja Turtles Pizza Party: A Step 1 Book - Preschool-Grade 1. Herbert, S. I., illus. 32p. (Orig.). (ps-1). 1991. PLB 7.99 (0-679-91452-8); pap. 2.95 (0-679-81452-3) Random Bks Yng Read.
Hudson, Jan. Dawn Rider. 192p. (gr. 6 up). 1990. 14.95 (0-399-22178-6, Philomel Bks) Putnam Pub Group.
—Dawn Rider. 176p. 1992. pap. 3.25 (0-590-44987-7, Point) Scholastic Inc.
—Sweetgrass. 160p. (gr. 3-7). 1989. 13.95 (0-399-21721-5, Philomel Bks) Putnam Pub Group.
—Sweetgrass. 1991. pap. 2.95 (0-590-43486-1) Scholastic Inc.
Hudson, Mary C. Christmas Birds. (Illus.). 12p. Date not set. pap. text ed. write for info. M C Hudson.
—Pouorina. (Illus.). 16p. Date not set. pap. text ed. write for info. (0-9627745-0-2) M C Hudson.
Hudson, Randolph. The Methuselah Factor. 237p. 1992. pap. 5.25 (0-9632097-0-1) Rattlesnake.
Hudson, Terry & Peacock, Graham. The Super Science Book of Light. LC 93-6837. 32p. (gr. 4-8). 1993. 14.95 (1-56847-022-3) Thomson Lrning.
Hudson, Terry, jt. auth. see Peacock, Graham.
Hudson, Wade. Afro-Bets Kids: I'm Gonna Be! Blair, Culverson, illus. LC 92-72000. 32p. (Orig.). (ps up) 1992. pap. 6.95 (0-940975-40-8) Just Us Bks.
—I Love My Family. Massey, Cal, illus. 32p. (ps-2). 1993. 10.95 (0-590-45763-2) Scholastic Inc.
Hudson, Wade & Wesley, Valerie W. Afro-Bets Book of Black Heroes from A to Z: An Introduction to Important Black Achievers. LC 87-82951. (Illus.). 64p. (gr. 3-6). 1988. pap. 7.95 (0-940975-02-5) Just Us Bks.
Hudson, Wade, jt. auth. see Chocolate, Debbi.
Hudson, Wade, compiled by. Pass It On: African-American Poetry for Children. Cooper, Floyd, illus. LC 92-16034. 32p. (gr. k-4). 1993. 14.95 (0-590-45770-5) Scholastic Inc.
Hudson, Wade, et al. Jamal's Busy Day. LC 90-81646. (Illus.). 24p. (gr. 1-3). 1991. lib. bdg. 12.95 (0-940975-21-1); pap. 6.95 (0-940975-24-6) Just Us Bks.
Hudson, William H. Green Mansions. Teitel, N. R., intro. by. (gr. 8 up). 1965. pap. 1.95 (0-8049-0087-6, CL-87) Airmont.
Hudson, Wilma J. Dwight D. Eisenhower: Young Military Leader. LC 92-8377. (Illus.). 192p. (gr. 3-7). 1992. pap. 3.95 (0-689-71656-7, Aladdin) Macmillan Child Grp.
—Harry S. Truman: Missouri Farm Boy. Doremus, Robert, illus. LC 92-7513. 192p. (gr. 3-7). 1992. pap. 3.95 (0-689-71658-3, Aladdin) Macmillan Child Grp.
Huebel, Russ. The Big Bad Wolf in Texas. Espinosa, Tony, illus. 48p. (Orig.). 1983. pap. 6.25 (0-9611604-2-X) C Del Grullo.
Huelsberg, Enid L. Alphabet Mastery Manuscript, Level 1: Reusable Edition. 32p. (ps-3). 1977. 5.00 (0-87879-785-8, Ann Arbor Div) Acad Therapy.
—Crossword Puzzle Mastery, Level 1. 32p. (gr. 1-3). 1975. wkbk. 5.00 (0-87879-783-1, Ann Arbor Div) Acad Therapy.
—Crossword Puzzle Mastery: Level 2. 32p. (gr. 4-6). 1975. wkbk. 3.00 (0-87879-784-X, Ann Arbor Div) Acad Therapy.
—Michigan Programmed Spelling Series, Basic Word List Level 1: Reusable Edition. (gr. 1). 1974. wkbk. 8.50 (0-87879-772-6, Ann Arbor Div) Acad Therapy.
—Michigan Programmed Spelling Series, Basic Word List, Level 3: Reusable Edition. (gr. 3). 1974. wkbk. 8.50 (0-87879-774-2, Ann Arbor Div) Acad Therapy.
—Michigan Programmed Spelling Series, Basic Word List, Level 2: Reusable Edition. (gr. 2). 1974. 8.50 (0-87879-773-4, Ann Arbor Div) Acad Therapy.
—Michigan Programmed Spelling Series, Use Frequency Based Words, Level 4: Reusable Edition. (gr. 4). 1975. wkbk. 8.50 (0-87879-778-5, Ann Arbor Div) Acad Therapy.
—Michigan Programmed Spelling Series, Use Frequency Based Words, Level 5: Reusable Edition. (gr. 5). 1975. wkbk. 8.50 (0-87879-779-3, Ann Arbor Div) Acad Therapy.
—Michigan Programmed Spelling Series, Use Frequency Based Words, Level 6: Reusable Edition. (gr. 6). 1975. wkbk. 8.50 (0-87879-780-7, Ann Arbor Div) Acad Therapy.
—Sometimes of Children. (gr. k-2). 1976. pap. 3.00 (0-89039-172-6, Ann Arbor Div) Acad Therapy.
Huff, Archie V., Jr. The History of South Carolina in the Building of the Nation. (Illus.). 528p. (gr. 8). 1991. text ed. 20.99 (0-9628232-0-1) A G Furman.
Huff, Barbara A. Greening the City Streets: The Story of Community Gardens. Ziebel, Peter, photos by. (Illus.). 80p. (gr. 3-7). 1990. 15.45 (0-89919-741-8, Clarion Bks) HM.
—Once Inside the Library, Vol. 1. (ps-4). 1990. 14.95 (0-316-37967-0) Little.

Huff, Brenda. A King Is Born. Fagan, Todd, et al, illus. 20p. Date not set. 15.95 (1-883909-01-5) Wisdom Tree.
Huff, Dawn, tr. see Horie, Michiaki & Horie, Hildegard.
Huff, Gary. Indian Tales That Teach. 80p. (gr. k-4). 1988. saddle stitch 9.50x (0-87322-129-X, 4919, Pub. by YMCA USA) Human Kinetics.
Huff, Ocie B. The How-To's of Baby Sitting: A Baby Sitter's Handbook. 104p. (gr. 6-9). 1993. pap. 12.50 (0-9633799-0-9) Hlth Educ Srvs.
Huffman, Marlys B. A Cave to Share. Faucheux, Wallace, illus. 22p. (Orig.). 1991. pap. 3.95 (0-8198-0733-8) St Paul Bks.
Huggett, Frank. Farming in Great Britain. (Illus.). 64p. (gr. 7 up). 1970. 14.95 (0-7136-1527-3) Dufour.
Hugh, Mitchell. Always Take Time to Pray. (Illus.). (gr. k-6). 1973. visualized song 4.99 (3-90117-014-6) CEF Press.
Hughes, jt. auth. see Drummond, H.
Hughes, Alice. Mickey Mouse & His Boat. Waltz, Dick, illus. LC 87-83494. 40p. (gr. k-2). 1988. write for info. (0-307-11692-1) Western Pub.
Hughes, Alice D. Cajun Columbus. rev. ed. Rice, James, illus. LC 91-16783. 40p. 1991. 12.95 (0-88289-875-2) Pelican.
Hughes, Ann K. Mary, Martha, Lottie & You. Gross, Karen, ed. 32p. (gr. k-6). 1992. pap. text ed. 3.95 (1-56309-045-7) Womans Mission Union.
Hughes, Barb. Spot, the Guinea Pig. Bogan, Rachel, ed. Baskerville, Leana, illus. (Illus.). 32p. (gr. k-3). 1992. pap. 7.95 (1-878036-10-6) Hughes Taylor. Postponed.
Hughes, Barbara & Dwiggins, Gwen. God Loves Children. Dow, Bonnie, illus. (ps-3). 1987. 0.99 (0-8091-6562-7) Paulist Pr.
—God Loves Colors. Dow, Bonnie, illus. (ps-3). 1987. 0.99 (0-8091-6566-X) Paulist Pr.
—God Loves Fun. Dow, Bonnie, illus. (ps-3). 1987. 0.99 (0-8091-6564-3) Paulist Pr.
—God Loves Love. Dow, Bonnie, illus. (ps-3). 1987. 0.99 (0-8091-6565-1) Paulist Pr.
—God Loves Seasons. Dow, Bonnie, illus. (ps-3). 1987. 0.99 (0-8091-6563-5) Paulist Pr.
Hughes, Barbara A., jt. auth. see Mitchel, Sue A.
Hughes, David. Story of the Universe. LC 90-11025. (Illus.). 32p. (gr. 4-6). 1991. PLB 11.89 (0-8167-2128-9); pap. text ed. 3.95 (0-8167-2129-7) Troll Assocs.
Hughes, Dean. Big Base Hit. Lyall, Dennis, illus. LC 89-37875. 96p. (Orig.). (gr. 2-6). 1990. PLB 6.99 (0-679-90427-1); pap. 2.95 (0-679-80427-7) Knopf Bks Yng Read.
—Brothers. LC 85-31208. 105p. (gr. 7-12). 1989. pap. 4.95 (0-87579-232-4) Deseret Bk.
—End of the Race. LC 92-37747. 160p. (gr. 5 up). 1993. SBE 13.95 (0-689-31779-4, Atheneum Child Bk) Macmillan Child Grp.
—Facing the Enemy. LC 82-12810. 143p. (gr. 3-9). 1991. pap. 4.95 (0-87579-498-X) Deseret Bk.
—Family Pose. LC 88-28501. 192p. (gr. 3-7). 1989. SBE 14.95 (0-689-31396-9, Atheneum Child Bk) Macmillan Child Grp.
—Lucky Breaks Loose. LC 90-30850. 136p. (Orig.). (gr. 3-6). 1990. pap. 4.95 (0-87579-194-8) Deseret Bk.
—Lucky Fights Back. LC 91-31416. 150p. (Orig.). (gr. 3-6). 1991. pap. text ed. 4.95 (0-87579-559-5) Deseret Bk.
—Lucky in Love. 161p. (Orig.). (gr. 3-7). 1993. pap. 4.95 (0-87579-805-5) Deseret Bk.
—Lucky, the Detective. LC 92-24537. 149p. (Orig.). (gr. 3-7). 1992. pap. 4.95 (0-87579-654-0) Deseret Bk.
—Lucky's Cool Club. (gr. 3-7). 1993. pap. 4.95 (0-87579-786-5) Deseret Bk.
—Lucky's Crash Landing. LC 90-30991. 160p. (Orig.). (gr. 3-6). 1990. pap. 4.95 (0-87579-193-X) Deseret Bk.
—Lucky's Gold Mine. LC 90-31072. 132p. (Orig.). (gr. 3-6). 1990. pap. 4.95 (0-87579-350-9) Deseret Bk.
—Lucky's Mud Festival. LC 91-34494. 141p. (Orig.). (gr. 3-6). 1991. pap. text ed. 4.95 (0-87579-566-8) Deseret Bk.
—Lucky's Tricks. LC 92-25025. 167p. (Orig.). (gr. 3-7). 1992. pap. 4.95 (0-87579-655-9) Deseret Bk.
—Millie Willenheimer & the Chestnut Corporation. LC 82-13758. 144p. (gr. 3-7). 1983. 10.95 (0-689-30958-9, Atheneum Childrens Bks) Macmillan Child Grp.
—Nutty & the Case of the Mastermind Thief. 128p. 1986. pap. 2.75 (0-553-15414-1, Skylark) Bantam.
—Nutty & the Case of the Ski-Slope Spy. LC 85-7962. 144p. (gr. 4-6). 1985. SBE 13.95 (0-689-31126-5, Atheneum Child Bk) Macmillan Child Grp.
—Nutty & the Case of the Ski-Slope Spy. LC 90-176. 128p. (gr. 3-7). 1990. pap. 3.95 (0-689-71438-6, Aladdin) Macmillan Child Grp.
—Nutty Can't Miss. LC 86-20556. 144p. (gr. 3-7). 1987. SBE 13.95 (0-689-31319-5, Atheneum Child Bk) Macmillan Child Grp.
—Nutty Can't Miss. 144p. (gr. 2-5). 1988. pap. 2.75 (0-553-15584-9, Skylark) Bantam.
—Nutty for President. 128p. 1986. pap. 2.50 (0-553-15376-5, Skylark) Bantam.
—Nutty Knows All. LC 88-886. 160p. (gr. 3-7). 1988. SBE 13.95 (0-689-31410-8, Atheneum Child Bk) Macmillan Child Grp.
—Nutty Knows All. LC 90-40282. 160p. (gr. 3-7). 1991. pap. 3.95 (0-689-71470-X, Aladdin) Macmillan Child Grp.
—Nutty, the Movie Star. LC 88-36614. 144p. (gr. 3-7). 1989. SBE 13.95 (0-689-31509-0, Atheneum Child Bk) Macmillan Child Grp.

—Nutty, the Movie Star. LC 91-15517. 144p. (gr. 3-7). 1991. pap. 3.95 (0-689-71524-2, Aladdin) Macmillan Child Grp.
—Nutty's Ghost. LC 92-8530. 144p. (gr. 3-7). 1993. SBE 13.95 (0-689-31743-3, Atheneum Child Bk) Macmillan Child Grp.
—On the Line. (gr. 4 up). 1993. pap. 7.99 (0-679-93490-1) McKay.
—Quarterback Pass. LC 93-8039. Date not set. 3.50 (0-679-84360-4, Bullseye Bks) Knopf Bks Yng Read.
—Quick Moves. Lyall, Dennis, illus. LC 92-44933. 112p. (Orig.). (gr. 2-6). 1993. pap. 3.50 (0-679-84358-2, Bullseye Bks) Random Bks Yng Read.
—Under the Same Stars. LC 79-10472. 143p. (gr. 4-8). 1988. pap. 4.95 (0-87579-159-X) Deseret Bk.
Hughes, Dean & Hughes, Tom. Baseball Tips. Lyall, Dennis, illus. LC 92-13406. 96p. (gr. 2-6). 1993. RLB 9.99 (0-679-93642-4); pap. 5.99 (0-679-83642-X) Random Bks Yng Read.
Hughes, Deborah L. A Treasure in the Enchanted Forest. Robertson-Boudreaux, Jane, ed. Whitmore, Janice N., illus. 30p. (Orig.). (gr. 2-4). 1991. pap. 6.95g (1-879203-03-0) Metagnosis.
Hughes, Fiona. On the Farm. (Illus.). 16p. 1993. 6.95 (0-87226-504-8, Bedrick Blackie) P Bedrick Bks.
Hughes, Francine. Beethoven's 2nd: The/Movie Storybook. (gr. 5-8). 1993. pap. 6.95 (0-448-40462-1, G&D) Putnam Pub Group.
—A Sheepful of Dollars. Thompson, Dana, illus. LC 93-83722. 32p. (Orig.). 1993. pap. 2.25 (0-679-85111-9) Random Bks Yng Read.
—Thumbelina & the Prince. 24p. (ps-3). 1993. pap. 2.25 (0-448-40506-7, G&D) Putnam Pub Group.
—Thumbelina Finds Her Way. 24p. (ps-3). 1993. pap. 2.25 (0-448-40507-5, G&D) Putnam Pub Group.
—Wetward, Whoa. Thompson, Del, illus. LC 93-83721. 32p. (Orig.). (ps-3). 1993. pap. 2.25 (0-679-85281-6) Random Bks Yng Read.
Hughes, Francine, adapted by. Dinosaurs on Parade. (Illus.). (ps-3). 1993. pap. 2.50 (0-448-40446-X, G&D); pap. 5.95 incl. tape (0-448-40448-6, G&D) Putnam Pub Group.
—The Wildest Show on Earth. (Illus.). (ps-3). 1993. pap. 2.50 (0-448-40447-8, G&D); pap. 5.95 incl. cass. tape (0-448-40449-4, G&D) Putnam Pub Group.
Hughes, Helga. Cooking the Austrian Way. Wolfe, Bob & Wolfe, Diane, photos by. (Illus.). 48p. (gr. 5 up). 1990. PLB 14.95 (0-8225-0924-5) Lerner Pubns.
Hughes, Jan. Noah & the Ark. Hughes, Jan, illus. 28p. (Orig.). (gr. 1 up). 1988. 9.95 (0-914544-97-7); pap. 6.95 (0-914544-98-5) Living Flame Pr.
Hughes, Jeremie. Will My Rabbit Go to Heaven? And Other Questions Children Ask. (Illus.). 128p. 1988. pap. 5.99 (0-7459-1221-4) Lion USA.
Hughes, Jill. Aztecs. (Illus.). 32p. (gr. 4-6). 1991. 13.95 (0-237-60172-9, Pub. by Evans Bros Ltd) Trafalgar.
—Deserts. (Illus.). 32p. (gr. 4-6). 1991. 13.95 (0-237-60175-3, Pub. by Evans Bros Ltd) Trafalgar.
—Eskimos. (Illus.). 40p. (gr. 4-8). 1992. 13.95 (0-237-60177-X, Pub. by Evans Bros Ltd) Trafalgar.
—Imperial Rome. (Illus.). 32p. (gr. 4-6). 1991. 13.95 (0-237-60167-2, Pub. by Evans Bros Ltd) Trafalgar.
—Lions & Tigers. (Illus.). 32p. (gr. 4-6). 1991. 13.95 (0-237-60164-8, Pub. by Evans Bros Ltd) Trafalgar.
Hughes, John, adapted by. Home Alone. (Illus.). 32p. (gr. k-3). 1991. 2.50 (0-590-45207-X) Scholastic Inc.
Hughes, Langston. The Best of Simple. (Illus.). 245p. (gr. 4-6). 1990. pap. 9.95 (0-374-52133-6, Noonday) FS&G.
—Dream Keeper. Sewell, Helen, illus. (gr. 7-11). 1962. PLB 10.99 (0-394-91096-6) Knopf Bks Yng Read.
—The Dream Keeper: And Other Poems. Pinkney, Brian, illus. 96p. 1994. 12.00 (0-679-84421-X); PLB 12.99 (0-679-94421-4) Knopf Bks Yng Read.
—Not Without Laughter. LC 79-81544. 320p. (gr. 8 up). 1986. pap. 6.95 (0-02-052200-2, Collier Young Ad) Macmillan Child Grp.
—Simple Speaks His Mind. (gr. 5-6). Repr. lib. bdg. 19. 95x (0-88411-061-3, Pub. by Aeonian Pr) Amereon Ltd.
—Thank You M'am. 1991. PLB 13.95s.p. (0-88682-478-8) Creative Ed.
Hughes, Langston, jt. auth. see Bontemps, Arna.
Hughes, Libby. From Prison to Prime Minister: A Biography of Benazir Bhutto. (Illus.). 128p. (gr. 5 up). 1990. RSBE 13.95 (0-87518-438-3, Dillon) Macmillan Child Grp.
—Margaret Thatcher: Madam Prime Minister: A Biography of Margaret Thatcher. LC 89-11974. (Illus.). 128p. (gr. 5 up). 1989. RSBE 13.95 (0-87518-410-3, Dillon) Macmillan Child Grp.
—Nelson Mandela: Voice of Freedom. LC 91-31543. (Illus.). 144p. (gr. 5 up). 1992. RSBE 12.95 (0-87518-484-7, Dillon) Macmillan Child Grp.
—Norman Schwartzkopf: Hero with a Heart. LC 92-13598. (Illus.). 144p. (gr. 5 up). 1992. RSBE 13.95 (0-87518-521-5, Dillon) Macmillan Child Grp.
—Valley Forge. LC 92-23391. (Illus.). 72p. (gr. 4 up). 1993. RSBE 14.95 (0-87518-547-9, Dillon) Macmillan Child Grp.
—West Point. LC 92-20641. (Illus.). 72p. (gr. 4 up). 1993. RSBE 14.95 (0-87518-529-0, Dillon) Macmillan Child Grp.
Hughes, Linda. Disney's the Little Mermaid. (ps-3). 1993. pap. 2.25 (0-307-12787-7, Golden Pr) Western Pub.
Hughes, Margaret, jt. auth. see Forsse, Ken.

Hughes, Margaret A. Mother Goose Favorite Lullabies. Hicks, Russell, et al, illus. 26p. (ps). 1987. 9.95 (0-934323-51-8); pre-programmed audio cass. tapes avail. Alchemy Comms.
—The Sleeping Beauty. Forsse, Ken & Becker, Mary, eds. Hicks, Russell, et al, illus. 26p. (ps). 1986. 9.95 (0-934323-27-5) Alchemy Comms.
Hughes, Margaret A. & Forsse, Ken, eds. Peter & the Wolf. Hicks, Russell, et al, illus. 26p. (ps). 1986. packaged with preprogrammed audio cass. tape 9.95 (0-934323-33-X) Alchemy Comms.
Hughes, Monica. The Crystal Drop. LC 92-27706. (gr. 5-9). 1993. pap. 14.00 JR3 (0-671-79195-8, S&S BFYR) S&S Trade.
—Devil on My Back. LC 84-21657. 180p. (gr. 6-9). 1985. SBE 13.95 (0-689-31095-1, Atheneum Child Bk) Macmillan Child Grp.
—Hunter in the Dark. LC 82-13807. 144p. (gr. 5-9). 1982. SBE 13.95 (0-689-30959-7, Atheneum Child Bk) Macmillan Child Grp.
—Hunter in the Dark. 144p. (gr. 7 up). 1984. pap. 2.95 (0-380-67702-4, Flare) Avon.
—Invitation to the Game. LC 90-22832. (Illus.). 192p. (gr. 5-9). 1991. pap. 14.00 jacketed, 3-pc. bdg. (0-671-74236-1, S&S BFYR) S&S Trade.
—Invitation to the Game. LC 90-22832. 208p. (gr. 5-9). 1993. pap. 3.95 (0-671-86692-3, Half Moon Bks) S&S Trade.
—Invitation to the Game. (gr. 8). 1990. pap. write for info. (0-663-56260-0) Silver Burdett Pr.
—The Promise. LC 91-21674. 208p. (gr. 5-9). 1992. pap. 13.00 jacketed, 3-pc. bdg. (0-671-75033-X, S&S BFYR) S&S Trade.
Hughes, Paul. The Days of the Week. Harris, Peter, ed. Burn, Jeffery, illus. LC 89-11758. 62p. (gr. 4-7). 1989. PLB 17.26 (0-944483-32-1) Garrett Ed Corp.
—The Months of the Year. Harris, Peter, ed. Burn, Jeffery, illus. LC 89-11759. 62p. (gr. 4-7). 1989. PLB 17.26 (0-944483-33-X) Garrett Ed Corp.
Hughes, Phyllis. Indian Children Paper Dolls. LC 91-60334. 12p. 1991. pap. 5.95 perforated (1-878610-05-8) Red Crane Bks.
Hughes, R. K. Omicron. Hilvosky, Judy, ed. LC 90-32436. 1990. pap. 18.95 (0-87949-286-4) Ashley Bks.
Hughes, Richard. Bound for Boston. Wheeler, Jill, ed. Lowery, Carol, illus. LC 88-71730. 48p. (gr. 4). 1989. lib. bdg. 10.95 (0-939179-44-X) Abdo & Dghtrs.
—Lost in London. Wheeler, Jill, ed. Lowery, Carol, illus. LC 88-71732. 48p. (gr. 4). 1988. lib. bdg. 10.95 (0-939179-47-4) Abdo & Dghtrs.
Hughes, Robert D. Gabriel's Trumpet. (Orig.). Date not set. pap. 5.99 (0-8054-6059-4) Broadman.
Hughes, Shirley. The Alfie Collection: Alfie's Feet; An Evening at Alfie's; Alfie Gives a Hand; Alfie Gets in First, 4 bks. (Illus.). (ps up). 1993. Set. boxed, shrink-wrapped 16.95 (0-688-12750-9, Tupelo Bks) Morrow.
—Alfie Gets in First. Hughes, Shirley, illus. LC 81-8427. 32p. (ps-1). 1982. 13.95 (0-688-00848-8); PLB 13.88 (0-688-00849-6) Lothrop.
—Alfie Gives a Hand. Hughes, Shirley, illus. LC 83-14883. 32p. (ps-1). 1984. 12.95 (0-688-02386-X); PLB 14.88 (0-688-02387-8) Lothrop.
—Alfie Gives a Hand. LC 83-14883. (Illus.). (ps-3). 1986. 4.95 (0-688-06521-X, Mulberry) Morrow.
—Alfie's Feet. Hughes, Shirley, illus. LC 82-13012. 32p. (ps-1). 1983. 14.95 (0-688-01658-8); PLB 14.88 (0-688-01660-X) Lothrop.
—Alfie's Feet. LC 82-13012. (Illus.). 32p. (ps-3). 1988. pap. 3.95 (0-688-07812-5, Mulberry) Morrow.
—All Shapes & Sizes. LC 86-2734. (Illus.). 24p. (ps). 1986. 4.95 (0-688-04205-8) Lothrop.
—Angel Mae: A Tale of Trotter Street. Hughes, Shirley, illus. LC 89-45288. 32p. (ps-1). 1989. 12.95 (0-688-08538-5); PLB 12.88 (0-688-08539-3) Lothrop.
—Angel Mae: A Tale of Trotter Street. ALC Staff, ed. LC 89-45288. (Illus.). 32p. (ps up). 1992. pap. 4.95 (0-688-11847-X, Mulberry) Morrow.
—Another Helping of Chips. Hughes, Shirley, illus. LC 86-20958. 64p. (gr-2). 1987. 11.95 (0-688-06871-5); PLB 11.88 (0-688-06872-3) Lothrop.
—Bathwater's Hot. LC 84-14389. (Illus.). 24p. (gr. k-1). 1985. 4.95 (0-688-04202-3) Lothrop.
—The Big Alfie & Annie Rose Storybook. Hughes, S., illus. LC 88-11149. 64p. (ps-1). 1989. 15.00 (0-688-07672-6); PLB 14.88 (0-688-07673-4) Lothrop.
—The Big Alfie Out of Doors Storybook. Pearson, Susan, ed. LC 91-28635. (Illus.). 64p. (ps up). 1992. reinforced bdg. 16.00 (0-688-11428-8) Lothrop.
—The Big Concrete Lorry: A Tale of Trotter Street. Hughes, Shirley, illus. LC 89-8051. 32p. (ps-1). 1990. 13.95 (0-688-08534-2); lib. bdg. 13.88 (0-688-08535-0) Lothrop.
—Bouncing. Hughes, Shirley, illus. LC 92-53001. 24p. (ps). 1993. 12.95 (1-56402-128-9) Candlewick Pr.
—Charlie Moon & the Big Bonanza Bust-Up. large type ed. 184p. (gr. 3-7). 1990. 14.95x (0-7451-1151-3, Lythway Large Print) Hall.
—Chatting. LC 93-22747. (gr. 5 up). Date not set. write for info. (1-56402-340-0) Candlewick Pr.
—Colors. LC 86-2732. (Illus.). 24p. (ps). 1986. 4.95 (0-688-04206-6) Lothrop.
—David & Dog. (ps-2). 1981. pap. 3.95 (0-13-198044-0, Pub. by Treehouse) P-H.
—Dogger. Hughes, Shirley, illus. LC 87-33787. 32p. (ps-2). 1988. 11.95 (0-688-07980-6); PLB 11.88 (0-688-07981-4) Lothrop.
—Dogger. LC 92-24602. (Illus.). 32p. (ps). 1993. pap. 4.95 (0-688-11704-X, Mulberry) Morrow.

—An Evening at Alfie's. Hughes, Shirley, illus. LC 84-11297. 32p. (ps-1). 1985. 14.95 (0-688-04122-1); PLB 14.88 (0-688-04123-X) Lothrop.
—An Evening at Alfie's. LC 84-11297. (Illus.). 32p. (ps up). 1992. pap. 3.95 (0-688-11520-9, Mulberry) Morrow.
—Giving. Hughes, Shirley, illus. LC 92-53002. 24p. (ps). 1993. 12.95 (1-56402-129-7) Candlewick Pr.
—Here Comes Charlie Moon. Hughes, Shirley, illus. LC 85-24125. 128p. (gr. 2-5). 1986. Repr. of 1980 ed. 11.95 (0-688-06401-9) Lothrop.
—Here Comes Charlie Moon. large type ed. (gr. 1-8). 1991. 13.95 (0-7451-1067-3, Galaxy Child Lrg Print) Chivers N Amer.
—Lucy & Tom at the Seaside. (Illus.). 32p. (ps-k). 1994. 17.95 (0-575-05227-9, Pub. by Gollancz UK) Trafalgar.
—Lucy & Tom's Christmas. (ps-1). 1987. pap. 4.95 (0-14-050698-5, Puffin) Puffin Bks.
—Lucy & Tom's Day. Hughes, Shirley, illus. 32p. (ps-1). 1986. pap. 3.50 (0-14-050068-5, Puffin) Puffin Bks.
—Moving Molly. Hughes, Shirley, illus. 32p. (ps-2). 1982. pap. 3.95 (0-13-604579-0, Pub. by Treehouse) P-H.
—Moving Molly. Hughes, Shirley, illus. LC 87-34250. 32p. (ps-2). 1988. 11.95 (0-688-07982-2); PLB 11.88 (0-688-07984-9) Lothrop.
—Noisy. LC 84-12632. (Illus.). 24p. (gr. k-1). 1985. 4.95 (0-688-04203-1) Lothrop.
—Out & About. LC 87-17000. (Illus.). 48p. (ps-2). 1988. 14.95 (0-688-07690-4); PLB 14.88 (0-688-07691-2) Lothrop.
—The Snow Lady. 32p. 1990. 13.95 (0-688-09874-6); PLB 13.88 (0-688-09875-4) Lothrop.
—Stories by Firelight. LC 92-38207. 1993. write for info. (0-688-04568-5) Lothrop.
—Two Shoes, New Shoes. LC 86-2733. (Illus.). 24p. (ps). 1986. 4.95 (0-688-04207-4) Lothrop.
—Up & Up. LC 85-24166. (Illus.). 32p. (gr. k-2). 1986. Repr. of 1979 ed. 11.95 (0-688-06261-X) Lothrop.
—Wheels. (ps-3). 1991. 13.95 (0-688-09880-0) Lothrop.
—Wheels. (ps-3). 1991. PLB 13.88 (0-688-09881-9) Lothrop.
—When We Went to the Park. LC 84-12624. (Illus.). 24p. (gr. k-1). 1985. 4.95 (0-688-04204-X) Lothrop.
Hughes, Susan, jt. auth. see Herridge, Douglas.
Hughes, Ted. The Iron Giant: A Story in Five Nights. Zimmer, Dirk, illus. LC 87-45089. 64p. (gr. 3-7). 1988. PLB 11.89 (0-06-022639-0) HarpC Child Bks.
—The Iron Giant: A Story in Five Nights. Zimmer, Dirk, illus. LC 87-45089. 64p. (gr. 3-7). 1988. pap. 4.95 (0-06-440214-2, Trophy) HarpC Child Bks.
—Tales of the Early World. (gr. 4-8). 1991. 13.95 (0-374-37377-9) FS&G.
Hughes, Ted, jt. ed. see Heaney, Seamus.
Hughes, Thomas. Tom Brown's School Days. Andrew, C., intro. by. (gr. 7 up). 1968. pap. 1.95 (0-8049-0174-0, CL-174) Airmont.
—Tom Brown's School Days. 1987. Repr. lib. bdg. 21.95x (0-89966-554-3) Buccaneer Bks.
—Tom Brown's Schooldays. (Illus.). 32p. (gr. 4-6). 1984. pap. 3.50 (0-14-035022-5, Puffin) Puffin Bks.
Hughes, Thomas P. Tom Brown's Schooldays. Sanders, Andrew, ed. (Illus.). 456p. 1989. pap. 3.50 (0-19-282198-9) OUP.
Hughes, Tom, jt. auth. see Hughes, Dean.
Hughes, Tracy. Everything You Need to Know about Teen Pregnancy. rev. ed. Rosen, Roger, ed. Glassman, Richard, photos by. (Illus.). 64p. (gr. 7 up). 1992. PLB 13.95 (0-8239-1460-7) Rosen Group.
Hughes-Calero, Heather. Secrets of Arhirit. Scandia School, illus. 176p. (Orig.). (gr. 5 up). pap. 8.95 (0-932927-04-1) Coastline Pub Co.
Hughey, Pat. Scavengers & Decomposers: The Cleanup Crew. Hiscock, Bruce, illus. LC 83-17474. 64p. (gr. 4-6). 1984. SBE 13.95 (0-689-31032-3, Atheneum Child Bk) Macmillan Child Grp.
Hughs, Monica, as told by. Little Fingerling. Clark, Brenda, illus. 32p. (gr. k-3). 1992. 13.95 (0-8249-8553-2, Ideals Child) Hambleton-Hill.
Hugo, Adele, jt. auth. see Hallenbeck, Gertrude.
Hugo, Victor. Hunchback of Notre Dame. Canon, R. R., intro. by. (gr. 11 up). 1968. pap. 2.25 (0-8049-0162-7, CL-162) Airmont.
—The Hunchback of Notre Dame. Shaw, Charles, illus. Stewart, Diana, adapted by. LC 81-5151. (Illus.). 48p. (gr. 4 up). 1983. PLB 18.64 (0-8172-1671-5) Raintree Steck-V.
Huheey, James. Diversity & Periodicity: An Inorganic Chemistry Module. Gardner, Marjorie, intro. by. (Illus.). 106p. (Orig.). (gr. 9-12). 1991. pap. text ed. 8.20 (1-879827-05-0) Vistas.
Huigin, S. O. Scary Poems for Rotten Kids. (Illus.). 32p. (ps-8). 1988. pap. 4.95 (0-88753-177-6, Pub. by Black Moss Pr) Firefly Bks Ltd.
Huigin, Sean O. Monsters, He Mumbled. Fraser, John & Hughes, Scott, illus. 28p. (ps-7). 1989. pap. 4.95 (0-88753-187-3, Pub. by Black Moss Pr CN) Firefly Bks Ltd.
Huisingh, Rosemary, et al. ACHIEV-Blue (Activities for Children Involving Everyday Vocabulary) (ps-5). 1989. complete pkg. 192.70 (1-55999-002-3) LinguiSystems.
—ACHIEV-Blue Books (Activities for Children Involving Everyday Vocabulary) (ps-5). 1986. spiral manual 49.95 (1-55999-004-X) LinguiSystems.
Hulbert, Elizabeth M. I Love to Ski. Hulbert, Elizabeth M., illus. LC 87-51331. 64p. (Orig.). (gr. 1-3). 1986. pap. 4.95 (0-932433-25-1) Windswept Hse.

—The Memory Quilt. Hulbert, Elizabeth M., illus. LC 87-51331. 64p. (gr. 1-4). 1989. pap. 5.95 (0-932433-42-1) Windswept Hse.
Hulbert, Jay. The Bedtime Beast. (Illus.). 32p. (gr. 1-4). 1989. PLB 15.96 (0-8172-3516-7); pap. 3.95 (0-8114-6712-0) Raintree Steck-V.
—Pete Pig Cleans Up. (Illus.). 32p. (gr. 1-4). 1989. PLB 15.96 (0-8172-3504-3); pap. 3.95 (0-8114-6703-1) Raintree Steck-V.
Hulbert, Jay & Kantor, Sid. Armando Asked "Why?" Hoggan, Pat, illus. 24p. (ps-2). 1990. PLB 14.60 (0-8172-3576-0); pap. 10.95 pkg. of 3 (0-685-58548-4) Raintree Steck-V.
Hulett, Michael. Around the World in Eighty Days. (Illus.). 48p. (Orig.). (gr. 4 up). 1985. pap. 4.00 (0-88680-233-4); royalty on application 50.00 (0-685-58013-X) I E Clark.
Hull, Eddy, ed. see Lehman, Paula D.
Hull, Jeannie. Clay. Fairclough, Chris, photos by. LC 89-9959. (Illus.). 48p. (gr. 3-6). 1989. PLB 12.40 (0-531-10757-4) Watts.
Hull, Mary. Rosa Parks: Civil Rights Leader. LC 93-17699. (Illus.). (gr. 5-8). 1994. PLB 18.95 (0-7910-1881-4, Am Art Analog); write for info. (0-7910-1910-1, Am Art Analog) Chelsea Hse.
Hull, Nancy, ed. & illus. see Krall, Charlotte B. & Jim, Judith M.
Hull, Robert. African Stories. Kettle, Peter, illus. LC 92-40632. 48p. (gr. 5-9). 1993. 15.95 (1-56847-004-5) Thomson Lrning.
—Egyptian Stories. Loftus, Barbara & Bateman, Noel, illus. LC 93-35684. 48p. (gr. 5-9). 1994. 15.95 (1-56847-155-6) Thomson Lrning.
—Greek Stories. Stower, Adam & Robinson, Claire, illus. 48p. (gr. 5-9). 1994. 15.95 (1-56847-106-8) Thomson Lrning.
—Norse Stories. Heap, Johnathan & Stower, Adam, illus. LC 93-30731. 48p. (gr. 5-9). 1993. 15.95 (1-56847-131-9) Thomson Lrning.
—Poems for Spring. LC 90-20592. (Illus.). 48p. (gr. 3-7). 1991. PLB 18.60 (0-8114-7802-5) Raintree Steck-V.
—Poems for Summer. LC 90-20591. (Illus.). 48p. (gr. 3-7). 1991. PLB 18.60 (0-8114-7803-3) Raintree Steck-V.
—Poems for Winter. LC 90-20589. (Illus.). 48p. (gr. 3-7). 1991. PLB 18.60 (0-8114-7801-7) Raintree Steck-V.
—Roman Stories. Smith, Tony, illus. LC 93-29996. 48p. (gr. 5-9). 1993. 15.95 (1-56847-105-X) Thomson Lrning.
Hull, Robert, jt. auth. see Emmerich, Elsbeth.
Hull, Robert, retold by. Native North American Stories. LC 92-39440. 48p. (gr. 5-9). 1993. 15.95 (1-56847-005-3) Thomson Lrning.
Hull, Robert, ed. Poems for Autumn. LC 90-20590. (Illus.). 48p. (gr. 3-7). 1991. PLB 18.60 (0-8114-7800-9) Raintree Steck-V.
Hull, Robert, selected by. A Prose Anthology of the First World War. LC 92-18045. (Illus.). 64p. (gr. 7 up). 1993. PLB 12.90 (1-56294-222-0) Millbrook Pr.
—A Prose Anthology of the Second World War. LC 92-20425. (Illus.). 64p. (gr. 7 up). 1993. PLB 12.90 (1-56294-223-9) Millbrook Pr.
Hull, Shirley, jt. ed. see Wilson, Valerie.
Hullinger, Annette C. Winning Is Virtue. LC 80-85339. (gr. 7-10). PLB write for info. (0-938762-25-7) Eagle Mktg Corp.
Hulme, Joy N. Climbing the Rainbow. LC 92-1109. 186p. (Orig.). (gr. 3-7). 1992. pap. 4.95 (0-87579-584-6) Deseret Bk.
—The Other Side of the Door. LC 90-41020. 168p. (gr. 3-6). 1990. pap. 4.95 (0-87579-412-2) Deseret Bk.
—Sea Squares. Schwartz, Carol, illus. LC 91-71381. 32p. (ps-3). 1991. 13.95 (1-56282-079-6); PLB 13.89 (1-56282-080-X) Hyprn Child.
—Sea Squares. Schwartz, Carol, illus. LC 91-71381. 32p. (ps-3). 1993. pap. 4.95 (1-56282-520-8) Hyprn Ppbks.
—What If? Just Wondering Poems. Gorbachev, Valeri, illus. LC 90-60863. 32p. (ps-1). 1993. 14.95 (1-56397-186-0, Wordsong) Boyds Mills Pr.
Hulser, Andrea. Henry in the Caribbean. Hulser, Andrea, illus. 40p. 1993. pap. 14.95 (0-89825-007-2) Pub Resces Pr.
Hulsizer, Carol, jt. auth. see Charren, Peggy.
Human, Gerrie. An Owl Feather for Emily. Sawyer, Barbara, illus. LC 91-26734. 32p. (Illus.). (ps-2). 1992. pap. 4.95 (0-931093-77-5) Red Hen Pr.
Human, Johnnie. Finlay & Julia Graham: Missionary Partners. LC 86-4148. (gr. 4-6). 1986. 5.95 (0-8054-4327-4) Broadman.
—John the Baptist: Forerunner of Jesus. Padgett, James, illus. (gr. 1-6). 1978. 5.95 (0-8054-4240-5, 4242-40) Broadman.
Humberstone. Things at Home. (gr. 2-5). 1981. (Usborne-Hayes); pap. 4.50 (0-86020-501-0) EDC.
—Things That Go. (gr. 2-5). 1981. 6.95 (0-86020-500-2, Usborne-Hayes); pap. 4.50 (0-86020-493-6) EDC.
Humberstone, Eliot. Things Outdoors. (gr. 2-5). 1981. (Usborne-Hayes); pap. 4.50 (0-86020-464-2) EDC.
Humbert, Jack & Williams, Larry. Petroleum Marketing. (Illus.). (gr. 11-12). 1979. text ed. 12.04 (0-07-031206-0) McGraw.
Humble, Richard. Battle of Leif Eiriksson. Hook, Richard, illus. LC 89-8867. 32p. (gr. 5-8). 1989. PLB 12.40 (0-531-10741-8) Watts.
—The Expeditions of Amundsen. Kline, Marjory, ed. Aloof, Andrew, illus. 32p. (gr. 5-7). 1992. PLB 12.40 (0-531-14200-0) Watts.

—Hitler's Generals. (gr. 7 up). 1981. pap. 2.25 (0-89083-788-0) Zebra.
—Ships. Cornwall, Peter, illus. LC 93-19705. 32p. (gr. 4-6). 1993. PLB 19.97 (0-8114-6158-0) Raintree Steck-V.
—Ships: Sailors & the Sea. (Illus.). 48p. (gr. 5-8). 1991. 13.95 (0-531-15234-0) Watts.
—The Travels of Livingstone. LC 90-32379. (Illus.). 32p. (gr. 5-8). 1991. PLB 12.40 (0-531-14101-2) Watts.
—Travels of Marco Polo. 1990. PLB 12.40 (0-531-14022-9) Watts.
—The Voyages of Columbus. Hook, Richard, illus. 32p. (gr. 5-8). 1991. PLB 12.40 (0-531-14189-6) Watts.
—The Voyages of Jacques Cartier. LC 92-6266. 1993. 12. 40 (0-531-14216-7) Watts.
—A World War Two Submarine. Bergin, Mark, illus. 48p. (gr. 5 up). 1991. 17.95 (0-87226-351-7) P Bedrick Bks.
Humble, Richard & Hook, Richard. The Voyage of Magellan. (Illus.). 32p. (gr. 4-7). 1989. PLB 12.40 (0-531-10638-1) Watts.
Hume, Lotta C. Favorite Children's Stories from China & Tibet. Lo-Koon-Chiu, illus. LC 61-6219. 120p. (gr. 1-4). 1962. pap. 14.95 (0-8048-1605-0) C E Tuttle.
Hume, Pat. Dick Whittington & His Amazing Cat. (Orig.). (gr. k up). 1980. 4.50 (0-87602-230-1) Anchorage.
Hume, Rob. Birdwatching. LC 92-11300. (Illus.). 80p. (gr. 5 up). 1993. 13.00 (0-679-82663-7); PLB 13.99 (0-679-92663-1) Random.
Hummel, Berta. The Hummel. Hummel, Berta, illus. 1972. 17.00 (0-88431-129-5) IBD Ltd.
Hummel, Nancy, jt. auth. see Moser, Cindy.
Hummel, Ruth. Where Do Babies Come From? 32p. (gr. 1-3). 1988. 7.99 (0-570-08482-2, 14-1622) Concordia.
Humphrey, Doris. The Art of Making Dances. (Illus.). 192p. (gr. 9 up). 1987. pap. 9.95 (0-8021-3073-9) Grove-Atltic.
Humphrey, Judy. Genghis Khan. Schlesinger, Arthur M., Jr., intro. by. (Illus.). 112p. (gr. 5 up). 1987. 17.95 (0-87754-527-8) Chelsea Hse.
Humphrey, Kathryn L. Pompeii: Nightmare at Midday. (Illus.). 1990. PLB 12.90 (0-531-10895-3) Watts.
—Shipwrecks: Terror & Treasure. LC 91-16962. (Illus.). 64p. (gr. 5-8). 1991. PLB 12.90 (0-531-20031-0) Watts.
Humphrey, L. Spencer. Aladdin. 32p. 1994. pap. 2.95 (0-8125-2319-9) Tor Bks.
—Heidi. 32p. 1994. pap. 2.95 (0-8125-2323-7) Tor Bks.
Humphrey, Margo. The River That Gave Gifts. LC 78-61980. (Illus.). (gr. 2-9). 1987. 13.95 (0-89239-027-1) Children's Book Pr.
Humphrey, Maude, illus. Nursery Rhymes. LC 92-13790. 1992. 4.99 (0-517-08274-8, Pub. by Derrydale Bks) Outlet Bk Co.
Humphrey, Sally. A Family in Liberia. (Illus.). 32p. (gr. 2-5). 1987. PLB 13.50 (0-8225-1674-8) Lerner Pubns.
Humphrey, Sandra see Davenport, May.
Humphreys, B. J. A Hundred Ways to Save Money on Model Rocket Building. (Illus.). 1977. pap. text ed. 1.50 (0-912468-19-X) CA Rocketry.
Humphreys, Martha. Until Whatever. 176p. (gr. 9 up). 1991. 13.45 (0-395-58022-6, Clarion Bks) HM.
—Until Whatever. 1993. pap. 3.25 (0-590-46616-X) Scholastic Inc.
Humphreys, W. J., jt. auth. see Bentley, W. A.
Humphries, C. Wildflowers. (Illus.). 64p. (gr. 10 up). 1993. pap. 4.50 (0-7460-1628-X) EDC.
Humphries, Tom, et al. A Basic Course in American Sign Language. Paul, F. A., illus. 280p. (gr. 9 up). 1980. pap. text ed. 26.95 spiral bdg. (0-932666-24-8, 013S) T J Pubs.
Hunger, Bill. When Two Saints Meet. Ripley, Jill, ed. Martin, Alice, et al, illus. 100p. (Orig.). (gr. 6-12). pap. 9.95 (0-9625782-0-7) Two Saints Pub.
Hunig, Klaus. Astro-Dome Book: 3-D Map of the Night Sky. Solensten, Lori, ed. Zerner, Amy & Drake, Charles, illus. Himelfarb, Donna, intro. by. 68p. (Orig.). (gr. 4 up). 1983. pap. 9.95 incl. Constellation Handbook (0-913319-00-7) Sunstone Pubns.
Hunka, Alison. Violin & Stringed Instruments: Young Musician Plays. (gr. 4-7). 1993. 17.71 (0-531-17424-7, Gloucester Pr) Watts.
Hunka, Alison & Bunting, Philippa. Violin & Stringed Instruments. (Illus.). 32p. (gr. 4-7). 1993. PLB 12.40 (0-685-65609-8, Gloucester Pr) Watts.
Hunken, Jorie. Birdwatching for All Ages: Activities for Children & Adults. (Illus.). 160p. (Orig.). 1991. pap. 13.95 (0-87106-234-8) Globe Pequot.
Hunkins, Francis P. Teaching Thinking Through Effective Questioning. (Illus.). 296p. (gr. 8-12). 1989. text ed. 27.50 (0-926842-02-1) CG Pubs Intl.
Hunley, Debbie, jt. auth. see Buschman, Janis.
Hunsinger, Ruth A., ed. see Whitfield, Karen & Tackett, Eric.
Hunt, jt. auth. see Pipe, Rhona.
Hunt, jt. auth. see Hunt, Gary.
Hunt, Angela E. The Case of the Counterfeit Cash. (Orig.). (gr. 4-7). 1992. pap. 6.99 (0-8407-4412-9) Nelson.
—The Case of the Haunting of Lowell Lanes. (Orig.). (gr. 4-7). 1992. pap. 6.99 (0-8407-4421-8) Nelson.
—The Case of the Mystery Mark. 128p. (Orig.). (gr. 4-7). 1991. pap. 6.99 (0-8407-4477-3) Nelson.
—The Case of the Phantom Friend. 128p. (Orig.). (gr. 4-7). 1991. pap. 6.99 (0-8407-4294-0) Nelson.
—The Case of the Teenage Terminator. 128p. (Orig.). (gr. 4-7). 1991. pap. 6.99 (0-8407-4437-4) Nelson.

—The Case of the Terrified Track Star. (Orig.). (gr. 4-7). 1992. pap. 6.99 (0-8407-4422-6) Nelson.
—Cassie Perkins: A Dream to Cherish. 176p. (gr. 4-8). 1992. pap. 4.99 (0-8423-1064-9) Tyndale.
—Cassie Perkins: Love Burning Bright. 176p. (gr. 4-8). 1992. pap. text ed. 4.99 (0-8423-1066-5) Tyndale.
—Cassie Perkins: Much Adored Shore. 176p. (gr. 4-8). 1992. pap. 4.99 (0-8423-1065-7) Tyndale.
—Cassie Perkins, No. 1: No More Broken Promises. 1991. PLB 4.99 (0-8423-0461-4) Tyndale.
—Cassie Perkins, No. 2: A Forever Friend. (gr. 4-7). 1991. pap. 4.99 (0-8423-0462-2) Tyndale.
—Cassie Perkins, No. 3: A Basket of Roses. 1991. PLB 4.99 (0-8423-0463-0) Tyndale.
—Cassie Perkins, No. 7: Star Light, Star Bright. LC 92-18796. 1993. 4.99 (0-8423-1117-3) Tyndale.
—The Chance of a Lifetime. LC 92-20635. 1993. pap. 4.99 (0-8423-1118-1) Tyndale.
—Gift for Grandpa. (ps-3). 1992. 12.95 (1-55513-425-4) Cook.
—Howie Hugemouth. Newton-King, Laurie, illus. 28p. (ps-k). 1993. 4.99 (0-7847-0066-4, 24-03846) Standard Pub.
—If God Is Real, Where in the World Is He? LC 90-21285. (Illus.). 188p. (Orig.). (gr. 7-12). 1991. pap. 7.99 (0-8407-4411-0) Nelson.
—The Riddle of Baby Rosalind. LC 93-11173. 1993. pap. write for info. Nelson.
—The Secret of Cravenhill Castle. LC 93-11181. Date not set. pap. write for info. Nelson.
—Singing Shepherd. (Illus.). 32p. (ps-6). 1992. 13.95 (0-7459-2224-4) Lion USA.
—Tale of Three Trees. (Illus.). 32p. (gr. 5-7). 1989. 13.95 (0-7459-1743-7) Lion USA.
Hunt, Angela E. & Calenberg, Laura K. Beauty from the Inside Out: Becoming the Best You Can Be. Herron, Sandra & White, Kim, illus. LC 93-7132. 1993. pap. 12.99 (0-8407-6789-7) Nelson.
Hunt, Arnold, et al. Ethics of World Religions. 2nd, rev. ed. LC 91-21259. (Illus.). 180p. (gr. 10 up). 1991. lib. bdg. 16.95 (0-89008-824-4); pap. 9.95 (0-89008-823-6) Greenhaven.
Hunt, Brian, compiled by. Count Me In. Axworthy, Anni, illus. 64p. (ps-3). 12.95 (0-7136-2622-4, Pub. by A&C Black UK) Talman.
Hunt, Christopher. Holland. (Illus.). 32p. (gr. 4-6). 1991. 17.95 (0-237-60188-5, Pub. by Evans Bros Ltd) Trafalgar.
Hunt, Dave. The Archon Conspiracy. LC 89-31535. 256p. (Orig.). (gr. 9 up). 1989. pap. 8.99 (0-89081-766-9) Harvest Hse.
Hunt, Gary & Hunt, Angela. Now That He's Asked You Out: Straight Talk for Girls. LC 89-30704. 132p. (Orig.). (gr. 7-12). 1989. pap. 7.99 (0-89840-258-1) Nelson.
—Now That You've Asked Her Out: Straight Talk for Guys. LC 89-30703. 132p. (Orig.). (gr. 7-12). 1989. pap. 7.99 (0-8407-4457-9) Nelson.
Hunt, Irene. Across Five Aprils. LC 92-46736. 212p. (gr. 4 up). 1993. PLB 13.98 (0-382-24358-7); 11.98 (0-382-24367-6) Silver Burdett Pr.
—The Everlasting Hills. LC 85-2449. 192p. (gr. 6-8). 1985. SBE 14.95 (0-684-18340-4, Scribners Young Read) Macmillan Child Grp.
—No Promises in the Wind. 100p. 1987. pap. 3.50 (0-425-09969-5, Berkley-Pacer) Berkley Pub.
—Trail of Apple Blossoms. Partridge, Sherri, illus. LC 92-46739. 64p. (gr. 4-6). 1993. PLB 13.98 (0-382-24359-5); 11.98 (0-382-24368-4) Silver Burdett Pr.
—Up a Road Slowly. 100p. 1987. pap. 3.50 (0-425-10003-0, Berkley-Pacer) Berkley Pub.
—Up a Road Slowly. LC 92-47118. 192p. 1993. PLB 13. 98 (0-382-24357-9); 11.98 (0-382-24366-8) Silver Burdett Pr.
Hunt, Jeffrey. The Treasure Hunt Activity Book. (Orig.). 1994. pap. 2.99 (0-8125-9440-1) Tor Bks.
Hunt, Jonathan. Illuminations. Hunt, Jonathan, illus. LC 88-38967. 40p. RSBE 16.95 (0-02-745770-2, Bradbury Pr) Macmillan Child Grp.
—Illuminations. Hunt, Jonathan, illus. LC 92-23542. 40p. (ps-12). 1993. pap. 5.95 (0-689-71700-8, Aladdin) Macmillan Child Grp.
Hunt, Joni P. Bears. Leon, Vicki, ed. LC 93-9568. (Illus.). 48p. (Orig.). (gr. 5 up). 1993. pap. 9.95 perfect bdg. (0-918303-31-1) Blake Pub.
—A Chorus of Frogs. Leon, Vicki, ed. (Illus.). 40p. (Orig.). (gr. 5 up). 1992. pap. 7.95 (0-918303-29-X) Blake Pub.
—The Desert. Leon, Vicki, ed. (Illus.). 40p. (Orig.). (gr. 5 up). 1991. pap. 7.95 (0-918303-28-1) Blake Pub.
—A Shimmer of Butterflies. Leon, Vicki, ed. (Illus.). 40p. (Orig.). (gr. 5 up). 1992. pap. 7.95 (0-918303-30-3) Blake Pub.
Hunt, Joyce. Four of Us & Victoria Chubb. (gr. 4-7). 1990. pap. 2.75 (0-590-42976-0) Scholastic Inc.
Hunt, Joyce, jt. auth. see Selsam, Millicent.
Hunt, Joyce, jt. auth. see Selsam, Millicent E.
Hunt, Joyce, ed. see Selsam, Millicent E.
Hunt, Leslie L. Twenty-Five Kites That Fly. (Illus.). (gr. 5 up). 16.50 (0-8446-0157-9) Peter Smith.
Hunt, Linda & Frase, Marianne. Loaves & Fishes. LC 80-12165. (Illus.). 176p. (gr. 2-5). 1980. pap. 9.95 spiral bdg. (0-8361-1922-3) Herald Pr.
Hunt, Lynn B. An Artist Game Bag. 2nd ed. Hunt, Lynn B., illus. 106p. (gr. 10 up). 1990. Repr. of 1936 ed. 39. 95 (0-381-20045-0) Derrydale Pr.

Hunt, Nan. Families Are Funny. Niland, Deborah, illus. LC 91-15628. 32p. (ps-1). 1992. 13.95 (0-531-05969-3); lib. bdg. 13.99 (0-531-08569-4) Orchard Bks Watts.
Hunt, P. Bible Stories from the Old Testament. (Illus.). (gr. k-5). 4.98 (0-517-43909-3) Outlet Bk Co.
Hunt, Rod. Mole Wins a Prize. Gordon, Mike, illus. 32p. (ps-k). 1987. 6.95 (0-09-167520-0, Pub. by Hutchinson UK) Trafalgar.
Hunt, Roderick. Ghosts, Witches & Things Like That... (Illus.). 144p. (gr. ps-6). 1987. 16.00 (0-19-278108-1) OUP.
—Ghosts, Witches & Things Like That. 144p. 1990. pap. 10.95 (0-19-278130-8) OUP.
Hunt, Tamara & Renfro, Nancy. Celebrate: Holidays, Puppets & Creative Drama. Schwalb, Ann W., ed. Sears, Lori, illus. 208p. (ps-4). 1987. 24.95 (0-931044-09-X); pap. 18.95 (0-317-58474-X) Renfro Studios.
—Pocketful of Puppets: Mother Goose Rhymes. Schwalb, Ann, ed. (Illus.). 80p. (Orig.). (ps-2). 1982. pap. 11.95 (0-931044-06-5) Renfro Studios.
Hunter, Aileen. The Green Gang. 108p. (gr. 3-5). 1994. pap. 6.95 (0-86241-364-8, Pub. by Cnngt UK) Trafalgar.
Hunter, Bob, jt. auth. see Snypp, Wilbur.
Hunter, C. W. The Green Gourd: A North Carolina Folktale. Griego, Tony, illus. 32p. (ps-3). 1992. PLB 14.95 (0-399-22278-2, Whitebird Bks) Putnam Pub Group.
Hunter, Dan. The Magic Blue Giant. LC 90-70450. (Illus.). 80p. (Orig.). (gr. 3-6). 1991. pap. 7.00 (1-56002-107-1) Aegina Pr.
Hunter, Dard. Papermaking in the Classroom. Morris, Henry, intro. by. (Illus.). 88p. 1991. Repr. of 1931 ed. 28.00 (0-938768-24-7) Oak Knoll.
Hunter, David. The Night Is Mine. 224p. (gr. 10 up). 1993. 16.95 (1-55853-259-5) Rutledge Hill Pr.
Hunter, Edith F. Child of the Silent Night: The Story of Laura Bridgman. Holmes, Bea, illus. 128p. (gr. 2-5). 1963. 14.45 (0-395-06835-5) HM.
Hunter, Elrose. A Friend for Zacchaeus. Oakley, John, illus. 10p. (ps). 1993. 5.95 (0-687-47215-6) Abingdon.
—The Good Neighbor. Oakley, John, illus. 10p. (ps). 1993. 5.95 (0-687-15525-8) Abingdon.
—Joseph the Dreamer. Oakley, John, illus. 10p. (ps). 1993. 5.95 (0-687-20544-1) Abingdon.
—Moses the Leader. Oakley, John, illus. 10p. (ps). 1993. 5.95 (0-687-27246-7) Abingdon.
Hunter, Emily. The Bible-Time Nursery Rhyme Book. 96p. 1988. 12.99 (0-89081-404-X) Harvest Hse.
—My Bedtime Nursery Rhyme Book. (Illus.). (ps-1). 1991. 12.99 (0-89081-890-8) Harvest Hse.
Hunter, Erica C. D. First Civilizations. LC 93-41079. (Illus.). 1994. write for info. (0-8160-2976-8) Facts on File.
Hunter, Gerald R. & Hoffmann, Peggy. Bake a Snake: How to Survive by Your Own Cooking. Massingill, Susan, illus. LC 81-10293. 68p. (Orig.). (gr. 1-7). 1981. 9.00 (0-939710-10-2); pap. 4.75 (0-939710-09-9) Meridional Pubns.
Hunter, Higel. Twenty Names in the Movies. LC 89-23912. (Illus.). 48p. (gr. 3-8). 1990. PLB 12.95 (1-85435-254-7) Marshall Cavendish.
Hunter, Holly, jt. ed. see Roberts, Tom.
Hunter, Jane N. Ghost Games. LC 91-32416. (ps-3). 1993. 13.00 (0-385-30701-2) Doubleday.
Hunter, John, ed. see Sizemore, Denver.
Hunter, Latoya. Diary of Latoya Hunter. LC 92-8384. 1992. 16.00 (0-517-58511-1, Crown) Crown Pub Group.
—The Diary of Latoya Hunter: My First Year in Junior High. LC 93-13106. 1993. pap. 8.00 (0-679-74606-4, Vin) Random.
Hunter, Marjorie B. M. E. Beverly Hunter Great Masterpiece: Beverly Entertaining & Interesting Thoughts & Beverly Entertaining Melody. Hunter, Marjorie B. & Williams, Mark, illus. (Orig.). (gr. 5 up). 1986. pap. text ed. 30.00 (0-317-93273-X); tape 10.00 (0-317-93274-8) MH & Pr.
Hunter, Mollie. Gilly Martin the Fox. (Illus.). 40p. (gr. k-4). 1994. write for info. (1-56282-517-8); PLB write for info. (1-56282-518-6) Hyprn Child.
—Knight of the Golden Plain. Simont, Marc, illus. LC 82-48747. 48p. (gr. k-4). 1983. 12.95 (0-06-022685-4) HarpC Child Bks.
—Lothian Run. 221p. (gr. 5-8). 1990. pap. 6.95 (0-86241-069-X, Pub. by Cnngt UK) Trafalgar.
—The Mermaid Summer. LC 87-45984. 160p. (gr. 3-7). 1988. PLB 13.89 (0-06-022628-5) HarpC Child Bks.
—The Mermaid Summer. LC 87-45984. 160p. (gr. 3-7). 1990. pap. 3.95 (0-06-440344-0, Trophy) HarpC Child Bks.
—A Pistol in Greenyards. 192p. (gr. 5-8). 1990. pap. 6.95 (0-86241-175-0, Pub. by Cnngt UK) Trafalgar.
—A Sound of Chariots. LC 72-76523. 256p. (gr. 7 up). 1972. PLB 12.89 (0-06-022669-2) HarpC Child Bks.
—A Sound of Chariots. LC 72-76523. 256p. (gr. 5-8). 1988. pap. 3.95 (0-06-440235-5, Trophy) HarpC Child Bks.
—Spanish Letters. 173p. (gr. 5-8). 1990. pap. 6.95 (0-86241-057-6, Pub. by Cnngt UK) Trafalgar.
—A Stranger Came Ashore. LC 75-10814. 176p. (gr. 5-8). 1975. PLB 13.89 (0-06-022652-8) HarpC Child Bks.
—A Stranger Came Ashore. LC 75-10814. (gr. 4-8). 1977. pap. 3.95 (0-06-440082-4, Trophy) HarpC Child Bks.

—Talent Is Not Enough: Mollie Hunter on Writing for Children. LC 76-3841. 144p. 1990. pap. 9.95 (0-06-446105-X, Trophy) HarpC Child Bks.
—The Three-Day Enchantment. Simont, Marc, illus. LC 84-43350. 64p. (gr. k-4). 1985. PLB 12.89 (0-06-022693-5) HarpC Child Bks.
—The Wicked One: A Story of Suspense. LC 76-41515. 136p. (gr. 5-8). 1980. pap. 1.95 (0-06-440117-0, Trophy) HarpC Child Bks.
Hunter, Molly. The Thirteenth Member. (gr. 6-9). 1988. 19.25 (0-8446-6362-X) Peter Smith.
Hunter, Nigel. The Movies. LC 90-9937. (Illus.). 48p. (gr. 6-12). 1990. PLB 19.92 (0-8114-2363-8) Raintree Steck-V.
Hunter, Norman. The Incredible Adventure of Professor Branestawm. large type ed. 288p. (gr. 3-7). 1991. 13.95 (0-7451-1320-6, Galaxy Child Lrg Print) Chivers N Amer.
Hunter, Tammy. Chuckle Mountain. Williams, Harland, illus. 64p. (Orig.). (gr. 3-6). 1992. pap. 2.95 (0-88625-280-6) Durkin Hayes Pub.
Hunter, Ted, jt. auth. see Scovel, Karen.
Hunting, Constance, ed. see Young, Douglas.
Huntington, Andrew S., jt. auth. see Huntington, Seiko.
Huntington, Lee P. Brothers in Arms. Karpen, Florence B., illus. 72p. (gr. 3-8). 1991. pap. 8.00 (0-88150-214-6) Countryman.
Huntington, Mairi. The Great Game. 173p. 1987. pap. 6.00 (1-57043-063-2) ECKANKAR.
Huntington, Seiko. Japanese "ABCs" Hiragana Learning Cards. Huntington, Seiko, illus. 128p. (Orig.). (gr. 1 up). 1988. pap. 16.95 (0-936845-05-8) Sakura Press.
—Untangling Nihongo III: A Japanese Workbook, Vol. III. (Illus.). 135p. (Orig.). 1986. pap. 14.95 (0-936845-02-3) Sakura Press.
Huntington, Seiko & Huntington, Andrew S. Japanese "ABCs" II: Katakana Learning Cards. (Illus.). 128p. (Orig.). 1990. pap. 16.95 (0-936845-06-6) Sakura Press.
Huntley, Beth. Amazon Adventure. LC 88-42908. (Illus.). 32p. (gr. 4-5). 1989. PLB 15.93 (1-55532-917-9) Gareth Stevens Inc.
Huntley, Chris. The Beast in the Bathroom. Huntley, Chris, illus. 32p. (ps) 1991. write for info. Smythe bdg. (0-9616679-2-3) Aquarelle Pr.
Hunziker, Ray. Your First Snake. (Illus.). 34p. (Orig.). (gr. 1-6). 1991. pap. 1.95 (0-86622-072-0, YF-115) TFH Pubns.
Hupping, Carol, ed. see Curless, Maura R.
Hupping, Carol, ed. see Peterson, Linda.
Hurd, Edith T. Come & Have Fun. Hurd, Clement, illus. LC 62-13324. 32p. (gr. k-3). 1962. PLB 13.89 (0-06-022681-1) HarpC Child Bks.
—Day the Sun Danced. Hurd, Clement, illus. LC 64-16641. 32p. (gr. k-3). 1966. PLB 13.89 (0-06-022692-7) HarpC Child Bks.
—I Dance in My Red Pajamas. McCully, Emily A., illus. LC 81-47721. 32p. (gr. 1-3). 1982. PLB 14.89 (0-06-022700-1) HarpC Child Bks.
—Johnny Lion's Bad Day. LC 78-85035. (Illus.). 64p. (gr. k-3). 1970. PLB 13.89 (0-06-022708-7) HarpC Child Bks.
—Johnny Lion's Book. Hurd, Clement, illus. LC 65-14490. 64p. (gr. k-3). 1965. PLB 13.89 (0-06-022706-0) HarpC Child Bks.
—Johnny Lion's Book. Hurd, Clement, illus. LC 65-14490. 64p. (gr. k-3). 1985. pap. 3.50 (0-06-444074-5, Trophy) HarpC Child Bks.
—Johnny Lion's Rubber Boots. Hurd, Clement, illus. LC 70-183165. 64p. (gr. k-3). 1972. PLB 13.89 (0-06-022710-9) HarpC Child Bks.
—Last One Home Is a Green Pig. Hurd, Clement, illus. LC 59-8972. 64p. (gr. k-3). 1959. PLB 11.89 (0-06-022718-8) HarpC Child Bks.
—Song of the Sea Otter. Dewey, Jennifer, illus. LC 83-4675. 48p. (gr. 2-7). 1983. (Pant Bks Young); PLB 9.95 (0-394-86191-4) Pantheon.
—Song of the Sea Otter. Dewey, Jennifer, illus. 40p. (gr. 2-5). 1989. pap. 5.95 (0-316-38323-6) Sierra.
—Starfish. Bloch, Lucienne, illus. LC 62-7743. 40p. (gr. k-2). 1962. PLB 13.89 (0-690-77069-3, Crowell Jr Bks) HarpC Child Bks.
—Stop Stop. Hurd, Clement, illus. LC 61-12095. 64p. (gr. k-3). 1961. PLB 13.89 (0-06-022746-X) HarpC Child Bks.
Hurd, Inis I. The Magic Lamp. Gesner, Ethel & Irvine, Bonnie, illus. LC 87-30728. 140p. (gr. 4-7). 1989. PLB 14.50 (0-944517-00-5) Christian Center.
Hurd, Thacher. Axle the Freeway Cat. Hurd, Thacher, illus. LC 80-8432. 32p. (ps-3). 1988. pap. 3.95 (0-06-443173-8, Trophy) HarpC Child Bks.
—Little Mouse's Big Valentine. Hurd, Thacher, illus. LC 89-34515. 32p. (ps-1). 1990. 13.00 (0-06-026192-7); PLB 12.89 (0-06-026193-5) HarpC Child Bks.
—Little Mouse's Big Valentine. Hurd, Thacher, illus. LC 89-34515. 32p. (ps-1). 1992. pap. 3.95 (0-06-443281-5, Trophy) HarpC Child Bks.
—Little Mouse's Birthday Cake. Hurd, Thacher, illus. LC 91-11919. 32p. (ps-1). 1992. 15.00 (0-06-020215-7); PLB 14.89 (0-06-020216-5) HarpC Child Bks.
—Little Mouse's Birthday Cake. Hurd, Thacher, illus. LC 91-11919. 32p. (ps-1). 1994. pap. 4.95 (0-06-443353-6, Trophy) HarpC Child Bks.
—Mama Don't Allow. LC 83-47703. (Illus.). 40p. (ps-3). 1984. 16.00 (0-06-022689-7); PLB 15.89 (0-06-022690-0) HarpC Child Bks.

—Mama Don't Allow. Hurd, Thacher, illus. LC 83-47703. 40p. (ps-3). 1985. pap. 4.95 (0-06-443078-2, Trophy) HarpC Child Bks.
—Mystery on the Docks. Hurd, Thacher, illus. LC 82-48261. 32p. (ps-3). 1983. 13.00 (0-06-022701-X); PLB 14.89 (0-06-022702-8) HarpC Child Bks.
—Mystery on the Docks. Hurd, Thacher, illus. LC 82-48261. 32p. (gr. k-3). 1984. pap. 4.95 (0-06-443058-8, Trophy) HarpC Child Bks.
—The Quiet Evening. LC 90-24179. (ps up). 1992. 15.00 (0-688-10526-2) Greenwillow.
—Tomato Soup. Hurd, Thacher, illus. LC 90-21421. 40p. (ps-3). 1992. 15.00 (0-517-58237-6); PLB 15.99 (0-517-58238-4) Crown Bks Yng Read.
Huriet, Genevieve. Beechwood Bunny Tales Series. Jouannigot, Loic, illus. (gr. k-2). 1991. Set. PLB 120.89 (0-8368-0524-0) Gareth Stevens Inc.
—Dandelion's Vanishing Vegetable Garden. Jouannigot, Loic, illus. LC 90-4857. 32p. (gr. k-2). 1991. lib. bdg. 17.27 (0-8368-0526-7) Gareth Stevens Inc.
—Mistletoe & the Baobab Tree. Jouannigot, Loic, illus. LC 90-4856. 32p. (gr. k-2). 1991. PLB 17.27 (0-8368-0527-5) Gareth Stevens Inc.
—Perriwinkle at the Full Moon Ball. Jouannigot, Loic, illus. LC 90-4859. 32p. (gr. k-2). 1991. lib. bdg. 17.27 (0-8368-0525-9) Gareth Stevens Inc.
—Poppy's Dance. Jouannigot, Loic, illus. LC 90-4858. 32p. (gr. k-2). 1991. PLB 17.27 (0-8368-0528-3) Gareth Stevens Inc.
Hurlburt, Virginia E., jt. auth. see Matthews, Billie L.
Hurlbut, Jesse L. The Bedtime Bible Story Book. Sortor, Toni, ed. Arbuckle, Kathy, illus. 1989. text ed. 17.95 (1-55748-096-6); pap. text ed. 9.95 (1-55748-095-8); leather bdg. 24.95 (1-55748-113-X) Barbour & Co.
—The Bedtime Bible Story Book. Sortor, Toni, ed. (Illus.). (gr. k up). 1993. pap. 8.95 (1-55748-264-0) Barbour & Co.
—Hurlbut's Story of the Bible. rev. ed. (Illus.). (gr. k-4). 1967. 24.99 (0-310-26520-7, 6524) Zondervan.
Hurlbut, Phillip R., Jr. Jeraboam & the Amazing Spaghetti Mountain. Renfroe, Dan, illus. LC 79-90933. 123p. (Orig.). (gr. 3 up). 1979. pap. 2.95 (0-936086-00-9) Entertainment Factory.
Hurley, L. ZX-81 TS-1000: Programming for Young Programmers. (Illus.). 96p. (gr. 9up). 1983. pap. text ed. 9.95 (0-07-031449-7, BYTE Bks) McGraw.
Hurmence, Belinda. Dixie in the Big Pasture. LC 93-9983. (gr. 4 up). 1994. write for info. (0-395-52002-9, Clarion) HM.
—A Girl Called Boy. 180p. (gr. 3-6). 1982. 14.45 (0-395-31022-9, Clarion Bks) HM.
—A Girl Called Boy. (gr. 3-6). 1990. pap. 4.80 (0-395-55698-8, Clarion Bks) HM.
—The Nightwalker. LC 88-2827. 114p. (gr. 4-7). 1988. 12.95 (0-89919-732-9, Clarion Bks) HM.
Hurnard, Hannah. Hinds Feet on High Places. Layton, Barry & Layton, Dian, eds. Edington, Jo A., illus. 112p. (gr. 5). 1993. PLB 19.95 (1-56043-111-3) Destiny Image.
Hursh, Heidi & Prevedel, Michael. Activities Using the New State of the World Atlas. rev. ed. (Illus.). 155p. (gr. 7-12). 1991. pap. 29.95 (0-943804-56-6) U of Denver Teach.
Hurst, Brian S., jt. auth. see Newton-John, Olivia.
Hurst, Ida Olivia. My Kaleidoscope of Poetry & Stories. Meyer, Monty Dale, illus. LC 91-92380. 96p. (Orig.). 1992. pap. 11.95 (0-9632521-0-0) Gemstone OR.
Hurst, James. The Scarlet Ibis: A Classic Story of Brotherhood. (Illus.). (gr. 4 up). 1987. PLB 13.95s.p. (0-88682-000-6) Creative Ed.
Hurt, R. Douglas. The Department of Agriculture. Schlesinger, Arthur M., Jr., intro. by. (Illus.). 112p. (gr. 5 up). 1989. lib. bdg. 14.95 (0-87754-833-1) Chelsea Hse.
Hurt, Roger. Exploring Science: Practice at Home Science Activity. Trotter, Stuart, illus. 24p. (Orig.). (gr. 2-5). 1992. pap. 2.95 wkbk. (0-7214-3246-8) Ladybird Bks.
Hurt, Rory, ed. see Breakstone, Steve.
Hurwitz, Ann, jt. auth. see Kitman, Carol.
Hurwitz, Ann R. & Hurwitz, Sue. Hallucinogens. Rosen, Ruth, ed. LC 92-8599. (gr. 7-12). 1992. 14.95 (0-8239-1461-5) Rosen Group.
—Klal Yisrael: Our Jewish Community. Siegel, Adam & Strauss, Ruby G., eds. (Illus.). 95p. (Orig.). (gr. 5-6). 1991. pap. text ed. 5.95 (0-87441-511-X) Behrman.
Hurwitz, Carol, jt. auth. see Kitman, Carol.
Hurwitz, Hilda A. & Wasburn, Hope. Dear Hope-- Love, Grandma. Wasburn, Mara H., ed. LC 93-2213. 1993. 12.95 (1-88128-303-8) Alef Design.
Hurwitz, Jane, jt. auth. see Hurwitz, Sue.
Hurwitz, Johanna. The Adventures of Ali Baba Bernstein. LC 84-27387. (Illus.). 96p. (gr. 2-5). 1985. 12.95 (0-688-04161-2); PLB 12.88 (0-688-04345-3, Morrow Jr Bks) Morrow Jr Bks.
—Aldo Applesauce. Wallner, John, illus. LC 79-16200. 128p. (gr. 4-6). 1979. 12.95 (0-688-22199-8); PLB 12.88 (0-688-32199-2, Morrow Jr Bks) Morrow Jr Bks.
—Aldo Applesauce. Wallner, John, illus. 128p. (gr. 3-5). 1989. pap. 3.99 (0-14-034083-1, Puffin) Puffin Bks.
—Aldo Ice Cream. Wallner, John, illus. LC 80-24371. 128p. (gr. 4-6). 1981. 13.95 (0-688-00375-3); PLB 13.88 (0-688-00374-5, Morrow Jr Bks) Morrow Jr Bks.
—Aldo Ice Cream. Wallner, John, illus. 128p. (gr. 3-7). 1989. pap. 3.99 (0-14-034084-X, Puffin) Puffin Bks.
—Aldo Peanut Butter. De Groat, Diane, illus. LC 90-35366. 128p. (gr. 2 up) 1990. 12.95g (0-688-09751-0) Morrow Jr Bks.

—Aldo Peanut Butter. DeGroat, Diane, illus. 112p. (gr. 3-7). 1992. pap. 3.99 (0-14-036020-4) Puffin Bks.
—Ali Baba Bernstein, Lost & Found. Milone, Karen, illus. LC 92-4774. 96p. (gr. 3-7). 1992. 14.00 (0-688-11454-7); PLB 13.93 (0-688-11455-5) Morrow Jr Bks.
—Anne Frank: A Life in Hiding. Rosenberry, Vera, illus. 64p. (gr. 2-5). 1988. 12.95 (0-8276-0311-8) JPS Phila.
—Anne Frank: Life in Hiding. Rosenberry, Vera, illus. LC 92-29826. 64p. (gr. 4). 1993. pap. 3.95 (0-688-12405-4, Pub. by Beech Tree Bks) Morrow.
—Astrid Lindgren. Dooling, Michael, illus. 64p. (gr. 2-6). 1991. 3.95 (0-14-032692-8) Puffin Bks.
—Astrid Lindgren: Storyteller to the World. Dooling, Michael, illus. 64p. (gr. 2-6). 1989. pap. 10.95 (0-670-82207-8) Viking Child Bks.
—Baseball Fever. Cruz, Ray, illus. LC 81-5633. 128p. (gr. 4-6). 1981. 12.95 (0-688-00710-4); PLB 12.88 (0-688-00711-2, Morrow Jr Bks) Morrow Jr Bks.
—Baseball Fever. 128p. (gr. 4-7). 1983. pap. 2.95 (0-440-40311-1, YB) Dell.
—Baseball Fever. Cruz, Ray, illus. LC 81-5633. 128p. (gr. 3 up). 1991. pap. 3.95 (0-688-10495-9, Pub. by Beech Tree Bks) Morrow.
—Busybody Nora. Jeschke, Susan, illus. 64p. (gr. 1-5). 1982. pap. 1.50 (0-440-41019-3, YB) Dell.
—Busybody Nora. Hoban, Lillian, illus. LC 89-13649. 64p. (ps up). 1990. Repr. of 1976 ed. 12.95 (0-688-09092-3); PLB 12.88 (0-688-09093-1, Morrow Jr Bks) Morrow Jr Bks.
—Busybody Nora. Hoban, Lillian, illus. 64p. (gr. 2-5). 1991. pap. 3.99 (0-14-034592-2, Puffin) Puffin Bks.
—Class Clown. Hamanaka, Sheila, illus. LC 86-23624. 112p. (gr. 1-4). 1987. 12.95 (0-688-06723-9) Morrow Jr Bks.
—Class Clown. Hamanaka, Sheila, illus. 112p. (gr. 2-5). 1988. pap. 2.75 (0-590-41821-1, Little Apple) Scholastic Inc.
—Class President. Hamanaka, Sheila, illus. LC 89-28600. 96p. (gr. 2 up). 1990. 12.95 (0-688-09114-8) Morrow Jr Bks.
—Class President. 96p. (gr. 3-7). 1991. pap. 2.75 (0-590-44064-0, Apple Paperbacks) Scholastic Inc.
—The Cold & Hot Winter. Ewing, Carolyn, illus. LC 88-5144. 144p. (gr. 3-7). 1988. 12.95 (0-688-07839-7) Morrow Jr Bks.
—The Cold & Hot Winter. (gr. 3-7). 1989. pap. 2.95 (0-590-42619-2, Apple Paperbacks) Scholastic Inc.
—DeDe Takes Charge! De Groat, Diane, illus. LC 84-9085. 128p. (gr. 3-7). 1984. 12.95 (0-688-03853-0) Morrow Jr Bks.
—DeDe Takes Charge! De Groat, Diane, illus. LC 84-9085. 144p. (gr. 4 up). 1992. pap. 3.95 (0-688-11499-7, Pub. by Beech Tree Bks) Morrow.
—E is for Elisa. Hoban, Lillian, illus. LC 91-159. 80p. (ps up). 1991. 12.95 (0-688-10439-8); PLB 12.88 (0-688-10440-1) Morrow Jr Bks.
—E Is for Elisa. Hoban, Lillian, illus. LC 92-26796. 96p. (gr. 2-5). 1993. pap. 3.99 (0-14-036033-6) Puffin Bks.
—Hot & Cold Summer. Owen, Gail, illus. LC 83-19336. 176p. (gr. 3-5). 1984. 12.95 (0-688-02746-6) Morrow Jr Bks.
—Hot & Cold Summer. 1985. pap. 2.95 (0-590-42858-6) Scholastic Inc.
—Hurray for Ali Baba Bernstein. Owens, Gail, illus. LC 88-19107. 112p. (gr. 3-7). 1989. 11.95 (0-688-08241-6); PLB 11.88 (0-688-08242-4, Morrow Jr Bks) Morrow Jr Bks.
—Hurray for Ali Baba Bernstein. (gr. 4-7). 1990. pap. 2.75 (0-590-43169-2) Scholastic Inc.
—Hurricane Elaine. De Groat, Diane, illus. LC 86-12409. 112p. (gr. 5-8). 1986. 12.95 (0-688-06461-2) Morrow Jr Bks.
—The Law of Gravity. Fetz, Ingrid, illus. LC 77-13656. 192p. (gr. 3-7). 1991. pap. 3.95 (0-688-10498-3, Pub. by Beech Tree Bks) Morrow.
—Leonard Bernstein: A Passion for Music. Lisker, Sonia O., illus. 80p. (gr. 4 up). 1993. 12.95 (0-8276-0501-3) JPS Phila.
—Make Room for Elisa. Hoban, Lillian, illus. LC 92-45864. 80p. (gr. k up). 1993. lib. bdg. 13.93 (0-688-12429-1, Pub. by Beech Tree Bks) Morrow.
—Make Room for Elisa. Hoban, Lillian, illus. LC 92-45864. 80p. (gr. k up). 1993. 14.00 (0-688-12404-6) Morrow Jr Bks.
—Much Ado about Aldo. Wallner, John, illus. LC 78-5434. 96p. (gr. 4-6). 1978. PLB 13.88 (0-688-32160-7) Morrow Jr Bks.
—Much Ado about Aldo. Wallner, John, illus. 96p. (gr. 3-7). 1989. pap. 3.99 (0-14-034082-3, Puffin) Puffin Bks.
—Much Ado about Aldo. 63p. (gr. 2-4). 1978. pap. 5.04 (0-685-63784-0, BR8561) W A T Braille.
—Much Ado about Aldo. 63p. 1992. Braille. 5.04 (1-56956-287-3) W A T Braille.
—New Neighbors for Nora. Jeschke, Susan, illus. LC 78-12631. 80p. (gr. k-3). 1979. 11.95 (0-688-22173-4) Morrow Jr Bks.
—New Neighbors for Nora. reissued ed. Hoban, Lillian, illus. LC 90-47882. 80p. (ps up). 1991. Repr. of 1979 ed. 12.95 (0-688-09947-5); PLB 12.88 (0-688-09948-3, Morrow Jr Bks) Morrow Jr Bks.
—New Neighbors for Nora. Hoban, Lillian, illus. 80p. (gr. 2-5). 1991. pap. 3.99 (0-14-034594-9, Puffin) Puffin Bks.
—New Shoes for Silvia. Pinkney, Jerry, illus. LC 92-40868. 32p. (ps up). 1993. 15.00 (0-688-05286-X); PLB 14.93 (0-688-05287-8) Morrow Jr Bks.

—Nora & Mrs. Mind-Your-Own-Business. Jeschke, Susan, illus. LC 76-54283. 64p. (gr. k-3). 1982. 11.95 (0-688-22097-5) Morrow Jr Bks.
—Nora & Mrs. Mind-Your-Own Business. reissued ed. Hoban, Lillian, illus. LC 90-47997. 80p. (ps up). 1991. Repr. of 1977 ed. 12.95 (0-688-09945-9); PLB 12.88 (0-688-09946-7, Morrow Jr Bks) Morrow Jr Bks.
—Nora & Mrs. Mind-Your-Own-Business. Hoban, Lillian, illus. 80p. (gr. 2-5). 1991. pap. 3.99 (0-14-034595-7, Puffin) Puffin Bks.
—Once I Was a Plum Tree. Fetz, Ingrid, illus. LC 79-23518. 160p. (gr. 4-6). 1980. PLB 12.88 (0-688-32223-9) Morrow Jr Bks.
—Once I Was a Plum Tree. ALC Staff, ed. Fetz, Ingrid, illus. LC 79-23518. 160p. (gr. 5-12). 1992. pap. 3.95 (0-688-11848-8, Pub. by Beech Tree Bks) Morrow.
—The Rabbi's Girls. Johnson, Pamela, illus. LC 82-2102. 192p. (gr. 4-6). 1982. 11.95 (0-688-01089-X) Morrow Jr Bks.
—The Rabbi's Girls. Johnson, Pamela, illus. 96p. (gr. 3-7). 1989. pap. 3.95 (0-14-032951-X, Puffin) Puffin Bks.
—Rip-Roaring Russell. Hoban, Lillian, illus. LC 83-1019. 96p. (ps-1). 1983. 12.95 (0-688-02347-9); lib. bdg. 12. 88 (0-688-02348-7, Morrow Jr Bks) Morrow Jr Bks.
—Rip-Roarring Russell. Hoban, Lillian, illus. 96p. (gr. 2-5). 1989. pap. 3.99 (0-14-032939-0, Puffin) Puffin Bks.
—Roz & Ozzie. McKeating, Eileen, illus. LC 91-42338. 128p. (gr. 2 up). 1992. 13.00 (0-688-10945-4) Morrow Jr Bks.
—Russell & Elisa. Hoban, Lillian, illus. LC 88-37578. 96p. (gr. k up). 1989. 11.95 (0-688-08792-2); lib. bdg. 11.88 (0-688-08793-0, Morrow Jr Bks) Morrow Jr Bks.
—Russell & Elisa. (gr. 4 up). 1990. pap. 3.99 (0-14-034406-3) Puffin Bks.
—Russell Rides Again. Hoban, Lillian, illus. LC 85-7287. 96p. (ps-2). 1985. 12.95 (0-688-04628-2); lib. bdg. 12. 88 (0-688-04629-0, Morrow Jr Bks) Morrow Jr Bks.
—Russell Rides Again. Hoban, Lillian, illus. 96p. (gr. 2-5). 1989. pap. 3.99 (0-14-032941-2, Puffin) Puffin Bks.
—Russell Sprouts. Hoban, Lillian, illus. LC 87-5494. 80p. (ps-2). 1987. 12.95 (0-688-07165-1); lib. bdg. 12.88 (0-688-07166-X, Morrow Jr Bks) Morrow Jr Bks.
—Russell Sprouts. Hoban, Lillian, illus. 80p. (gr. 2-5). 1989. pap. 3.99 (0-14-032942-0, Puffin) Puffin Bks.
—School's Out. Hamanaka, Sheila, illus. LC 90-13446. 128p. (gr. 2 up) 1991. 12.95 (0-688-09938-6) Morrow Jr Bks.
—School's Out! Hamanaka, Sheila, illus. 96p. 1992. pap. 2.75 (0-590-45053-0, Little Apple) Scholastic Inc.
—Superduper Teddy. Hoban, Lillian, illus. LC 89-13592. 80p. (gr. k-3). 1990. Repr. of 1980 ed. 12.95 (0-688-09094-X); PLB 12.88 (0-688-09095-8, Morrow Jr Bks) Morrow Jr Bks.
—Superduper Teddy. Hoban, Lillian, illus. 80p. (gr. 2-5). 1991. pap. 3.95 (0-14-034593-0, Puffin) Puffin Bks.
—Teacher's Pet. Hamamaka, Sheila, illus. LC 87-24003. 128p. (gr. 2-5). 1988. 12.95 (0-688-07506-1) Morrow Jr Bks.
—Teacher's Pet. (gr. 2-5). 1989. pap. 2.75 (0-590-42031-3, Apple Paperbacks) Scholastic Inc.
—Tough-Luck Karen. Groat, Diane de, illus. LC 82-6443. 160p. (gr. 4-6). 1982. 12.95 (0-688-01485-2) Morrow Jr Bks.
—Tough Luck Karen. LC 82-6443. (Illus.). 160p. (gr. 4-6). 1991. pap. 3.95 (0-688-10974-8, Pub. by Beech Tree Bks) Morrow.
—The Up & Down Spring. Owens, Gail, illus. LC 92-21337. 112p. (gr. 3 up). 1993. 14.00 (0-688-11922-0) Morrow Jr Bks.
—Yellow Blue Jay. Carrick, Donald, illus. LC 85-25868. 128p. (gr. 2-5). 1986. 11.95 (0-688-06078-1) Morrow Jr Bks.
—Yellow Blue Jay. Carrick, Donald, illus. LC 92-24597. 128p. (gr. 3 up). 1993. pap. 3.95 (0-688-12278-7, Pub. by Beech Tree Bks) Morrow.

Hurwitz, Johanna, compiled by. A Word to the Wise: And Other Proverbs. Rayevsky, Robert, illus. LC 93-26836. 1993. write for info. (0-688-12065-2); PLB write for info. (0-688-12066-0) Morrow Jr Bks.

Hurwitz & Hurwitz, Jane. Staying Healthy. Rosen, Ruth, ed. (gr. 7-12). 1993. 12.95 (0-8239-1471-2) Rosen Group.

Hurwitz, Sue, jt. auth. see Hurwitz, Ann R.
Hurwitz, Sue, jt. auth. see Shniderman, Jeffrey.
Hurwitz, Sue, jt. auth. see Shniderman, Nancy.

Hurwood, Bernhardt J. Eerie Tales of Terror & Dread. 1992. 2.95 (0-590-44650-9, Point) Scholastic Inc.

Husain, A. Revolution in Iran. (Illus.). 80p. (gr. 7 up). 1988. PLB 18.60 (0-86592-038-9) Rourke Corp.

Husain, Shahrukh. Mecca. (Illus.). 48p. (gr. 5 up). 1993. lib. bdg. 13.95 RSBE (0-87518-572-X, Dillon) Macmillan Child Grp.

Huskey, Freeda, ed. see Stoner, Laura M.

Hussain, Shahrukh A. India. (Illus.). 32p. (gr. 4-8). 1992. 17.95 (0-237-60185-0, Pub. by Evans Bros Ltd) Trafalgar.

Huston, David A. The Light of the Pentecost: A Unique Historical Account of the New Testament Church. Penton, Ben, illus. (gr. 7 up). 1989. pap. 5.95 (0-932345-03-4) Antioch Publishes.

Huston, Dwayne L., ed. see Linn, James R.

Hutchcraft, Doug & Hutchcraft, Ronald P. Letters from the College Front: Guys' Edition. (Illus.). 80p. (gr. 9-12). 1993. 7.99 (0-8010-4379-4) Baker Bk.

Hutchcraft, Ronald P., jt. auth. see Hutchcraft, Doug.
Hutchcraft, Ronald P., jt. auth. see Whitmer, Lisa H.

Hutchcroft, Vera. Give What You Can. Butcher, Sam, illus. 20p. (gr. 1-4). 1984. 4.99. pap. text ed. 4.25 (1-55976-142-3) CEF Press.

Hutchens, Paul. The Case of the Missing Calf. (gr. 2-7). 1988. pap. text ed. 4.99 (0-8024-4837-2) Moody.
—The Killer Bear. rev. ed. (gr. 2-7). 1989. pap. 4.99 (0-8024-6957-4) Moody.
—Locked in the Attic. 128p. (gr. 2-7). 1973. pap. 4.99 (0-8024-4831-3) Moody.
—The Lost Campers. rev. ed. (gr. 2-7). 1989. pap. 4.99 (0-8024-6959-0) Moody.
—Lost in the Blizzard. (gr. 2-7). 1970. pap. 4.99 (0-8024-4817-8) Moody.
—The Mystery Cave. rev. ed. (gr. 2-7). 1989. pap. 4.99 (0-8024-4807-0) Moody.
—On the Mexican Border. (gr. 2-7). 1968. pap. 4.99 (0-8024-4818-6) Moody.
—The Secret Hideout. rev. ed. 1989. pap. 4.99 (0-8024-6960-4) Moody.
—The Sugar Creek Gang & Blue Cow. (Illus.). 128p. (gr. 3-7). 1971. pap. 4.99 (0-8024-4822-4) Moody.
—Sugar Creek Gang & Screams in the Night. (gr. 3-7). 1967. pap. 4.99 (0-8024-4812-7) Moody.
—Sugar Creek Gang & the Battle of the Bees. 128p. (gr. 3-7). 1972. pap. 4.99 (0-8024-4830-5) Moody.
—Sugar Creek Gang & the Brown Box Mystery. (gr. 3-7). 1970. pap. 4.99 (0-8024-4834-8) Moody.
—The Sugar Creek Gang & the Bull Fighter. (gr. 3-7). pap. 4.99 (0-8024-4820-8) Moody.
—Sugar Creek Gang & the Cemetery Vandals. 128p. (gr. 3-7). 1972. pap. 4.99 (0-8024-4829-1) Moody.
—Sugar Creek Gang & the Chicago Adventure & One Stormy Day. (gr. 3-7). 1968. pap. 6.99 (0-8024-1237-8) Moody.
—Sugar Creek Gang & the Colorado Kidnapping. (gr. 3-7). 1970. pap. 4.99 (0-8024-4827-5) Moody.
—Sugar Creek Gang & the Ghost Dog. (gr. 3-7). 1968. pap. 4.99 (0-8024-4832-1) Moody.
—The Sugar Creek Gang & the Green Tent Mystery. (gr. 3-7). pap. 4.99 (0-8024-4819-4) Moody.
—Sugar Creek Gang & the Haunted House. (gr. 3-7). 1967. pap. 4.99 (0-8024-4816-X) Moody.
—Sugar Creek Gang & the Indian Cemetary. (gr. 3-7). 1970. pap. 4.99 (0-8024-4813-5) Moody.
—The Sugar Creek Gang & the Killer Bear. (gr. 3-7). pap. 4.99 (0-8024-4802-X) Moody.
—Sugar Creek Gang & the Killer Cat. (gr. 3-7). 1966. pap. 4.99 (0-8024-4825-9) Moody.
—Sugar Creek Gang & the Lost Campers. (gr. 3-7). 1968. pap. 4.99 (0-8024-4804-6) Moody.
—The Sugar Creek Gang & the Mystery Thief. (gr. 3-7). pap. 4.99 (0-8024-4809-7) Moody.
—Sugar Creek Gang & the Palm Tree Manhunt. (gr. 3-7). 1969. pap. 4.99 (0-8024-4808-9) Moody.
—Sugar Creek Gang & the Runaway Rescue. 96p. (gr. 3-7). 1973. pap. 4.99 (0-8024-4828-3) Moody.
—Sugar Creek Gang & the Secret Hideout. (gr. 3-7). 1968. pap. 4.99 (0-8024-4806-2) Moody.
—Sugar Creek Gang Series, 36 bks. (gr. 2-7). Set. pap. 142.65 (0-8024-4836-4) Moody.
—The Swamp Robber. (gr. 2-7). 1966. pap. 4.99 (0-8024-4801-1) Moody.
—The Teacher Trouble. (gr. 2-7). 1970. pap. 4.99 (0-8024-4811-9) Moody.
—The Thousand Dollar Fish. (gr. 2-7). 1966. pap. 4.99 (0-8024-4815-1) Moody.
—The Timber Wolf. (gr. 3-7). 1965. pap. 4.99 (0-8024-4823-2) Moody.
—The Trapline Thief. 128p. (gr. 2-7). 1971. pap. 4.99 (0-8024-4821-6) Moody.
—The Treasure Hunt. (gr. 2-7). 1967. pap. 4.99 (0-8024-4814-3) Moody.
—The Tree House Mystery. (gr. 2-7). 1972. pap. 4.99 (0-8024-4835-6) Moody.
—The Watermelon Mystery. (Illus.). 128p. (gr. 2-7). 1971. pap. 4.99 (0-8024-4826-7) Moody.
—The Western Adventure. (gr. 2-7). 1966. pap. 4.99 (0-8024-4824-0) Moody.
—The White Boat Rescue. (gr. 3-7). 1970. pap. 4.99 (0-8024-4833-X) Moody.
—The Winter Rescue. rev. ed. 1989. pap. 0.00 cancelled (0-8024-6958-2) Moody.

Hutchings, Amy & Hutchings, Richard. Firehouse Dog. Hutchings, Richard, photos by. (Illus.). 32p. (ps-2). 1993. pap. 2.50 (0-590-46846-4, Cartwheel) Scholastic Inc.

Hutchings, Margaret. Big Book of Stuffed Toy & Doll Making: Instructions & Full-Size Patterns for 45 Playthings. (Illus.). 256p. (gr. 7 up). 1983. pap. 8.95 (0-486-24266-8) Dover.

Hutchings, Richard, jt. auth. see Hutchings, Amy.

Hutchings, Tony. Little Fluffy Duckling. Hutchings, Tony, illus. 12p. (ps-1). 1990. 4.95 (1-878624-14-8, 1553800014) McClanahan Bk.
—Little Pink Piglet. Hutchings, Tony, illus. 12p. (ps-1). 1990. 4.95 (1-878624-15-6, 1553800015) McClanahan Bk.
—Little Spotted Calf. Hutchings, Tony, illus. 12p. (ps-1). 1990. 4.95 (1-878624-12-1, 1553800012) McClanahan Bk.
—Little Woolly Lamb. Hutchings, Tony, illus. 12p. (ps-1). 1990. 4.95 (1-878624-13-X, 1553800013) McClanahan Bk.

Hutchins, H. Ben's Snow Song. (Illus.). 24p. (ps-8). 1987. 12.95 (0-920303-91-9, Pub. by Annick CN); pap. 4.95 (0-920303-90-0, Pub. by Annick CN) Firefly Bks Ltd.
—Leanna Builds a Genie Trap. (Illus.). 24p. (ps-8). 1987. 12.95 (0-920303-54-4, Pub. by Annick CN); pap. 4.95 (0-920303-55-2, Pub. by Annick CN) Firefly Bks Ltd.
—Norman's Snowball. (Illus.). 24p. (ps-8). 1989. 12.95 (1-55037-053-7, Pub. by Annick CN); pap. 4.95 (1-55037-050-2, Pub. by Annick CN) Firefly Bks Ltd.

Hutchins, Hazel. Anastasia Morningstar. 96p. (gr. 2-5). 1992. pap. 3.99 (0-14-034343-1) Puffin Bks.
—And You Can Be the Cat. Ohi, Ruth, illus. 24p. (ps-3). 1992. PLB 14.95 (1-55037-219-X, Pub. by Annick CN); pap. 4.95 (1-55037-216-5, Pub. by Annick CN) Firefly Bks Ltd.
—Katie's Babbling Brother. Ohi, Ruth, illus. 24p. (gr. k-3). 1991. PLB 14.95 (1-55037-153-3, Pub. by Annick CN); pap. 4.95 (1-55037-156-8, Pub. by Annick CN) Firefly Bks Ltd.
—Nicholas at the Library. Ohi, Ruth, illus. 32p. (ps-2). 1990. 14.95 (1-55037-134-7, Pub. by Annick CN); pap. 5.95 (1-55037-132-0, Pub. by Annick CN) Firefly Bks Ltd.
—The Three & Many Wishes of Jason Reid. Tennent, Julie, illus. 96p. (gr. 1-4). 1990. pap. 3.95 (0-14-032178-0, Puffin) Puffin Bks.

Hutchins, Pat. Changes, Changes. Hutchins, Pat, illus. LC 70-123133. 32p. (ps-k). 1971. RSBE 13.95 (0-02-745870-9, Aladdin) Macmillan Child Grp.
—Changes, Changes. Hutchins, Pat, illus. LC 86-22331. 32p. (ps-1). 1987. pap. 4.95 (0-689-71137-9, Aladdin) Macmillan Child Grp.
—Clocks & More Clocks. Hutchins, Pat, illus. LC 93-11208. 32p. (gr. k-3). 1994. pap. 4.95 (0-689-71769-5, Aladdin) Macmillan Child Grp.
—Clocks & More Clocks. reissued ed. Hutchins, Pat, illus. 32p. (ps-3). 1994. RSBE 13.95 (0-02-745921-7, Macmillan Child Bk) Macmillan Child Grp.
—Don't Forget the Bacon! LC 75-17935. (Illus.). 32p. (gr. k-3). 1976. 13.95 (0-688-06787-5); PLB 14.93 (0-688-06788-3) Greenwillow.
—Don't Forget the Bacon. LC 75-17935. (Illus.). 32p. (ps up). 1989. 4.95 (0-688-08743-4, Mulberry) Morrow.
—Don't Forget the Bacon. (Illus.). 32p. (ps up). 1994. pap. 18.95 (0-688-13102-6, Mulberry) Morrow.
—The Doorbell Rang. Hutchins, Pat, illus. LC 85-12615. 24p. (ps-3). 1986. 15.00 (0-688-05251-7); PLB 14.93 (0-688-05252-5) Greenwillow.
—Doorbell Rang. Hutchins, Pat, illus. LC 85-12615. (ps-3). 1989. pap. 3.95 (0-688-09234-9, Mulberry) Morrow.
—The Doorbell Rang. (Illus.). 24p. (ps up). 1994. pap. 18. 95 (0-688-13101-8, Mulberry) Morrow.
—Follow That Bus! Hutchins, Laurence, illus. LC 76-21822. 112p. (gr. 3-7). 1988. pap. 2.95 (0-394-80792-8) Knopf Bks Yng Read.
—Good-Night, Owl! Hutchins, Pat, illus. LC 72-186355. 32p. (ps-2). 1972. RSBE 13.95 (0-02-745900-4, Macmillan Child Bk) Macmillan Child Grp.
—Good Night, Owl. LC 89-17708. 32p. (ps-3). 1990. pap. 3.95 (0-689-71371-1, Aladdin) Macmillan Child Grp.
—Good-Night, Owl! Hutchins, Pat, illus. LC 91-8172. 36p. (gr. k-3). 1991. pap. 16.95 big book ed. (0-689-71541-2, Aladdin) Macmillan Child Grp.
—Happy Birthday, Sam. LC 78-1295. (Illus.). 32p. (gr. k-3). 1978. PLB 13.88 (0-688-84160-0) Greenwillow.
—Happy Birthday, Sam. LC 78-1295. (Illus.). 32p. (ps-3). 1991. pap. 3.95 (0-688-10482-7, Mulberry) Morrow.
—Happy Birthday, Sam Peter. LC 84-18058. (Illus.). 32p. (ps-1). 1985. pap. 3.50 (0-14-050339-0, Puffin) Puffin Bks.
—The House That Sailed Away. Hutchins, Laurence, illus. LC 74-9823. 192p. (gr. 2-6). 1975. PLB 11.88 (0-688-84013-2) Greenwillow.
—Little Pink Pig. LC 93-18176. (Illus.). (ps up). 1994. write for info. (0-688-12014-8); PLB write for info. (0-688-12015-6) Greenwillow.
—My Best Friend. LC 94-48354. (Illus.). 32p. (ps up). 1993. 14.00 (0-688-11485-7); PLB 14.93 (0-688-11486-5) Greenwillow.
—One-Eyed Jake. Hutchins, Pat, illus. 32p. (ps up). 1994. pap. 3.95 (0-688-13113-1, Mulberry) Morrow.
—One Hunter. Hutchins, Pat, illus. LC 81-6352. 24p. (ps-1). 1982. 15.00 (0-688-00614-0); PLB 14.93 (0-688-00615-9) Greenwillow.
—One Hunter. LC 81-6352. (Illus.). 24p. (ps-3). 1994. 4.95 (0-688-06522-8, Mulberry) Morrow.
—Rats! LC 88-11287. (Illus.). 96p. (gr. 2 up). 1989. 11.95 (0-688-07776-5) Greenwillow.
—Rosie's Walk. Hutchins, Pat, illus. LC 68-12090. 32p. (ps-1). 1968. RSBE 14.95 (0-02-745850-4, Macmillan Child Bk) Macmillan Child Grp.
—Rosie's Walk. Hutchins, Pat, illus. LC 87-17550. 32p. (ps-k). 1971. pap. 3.95 (0-02-043750-1, Aladdin) Macmillan Child Grp.
—Rosie's Walk. (ps-3). 1992. pap. 19.95 (0-590-71809-6) Scholastic Inc.
—Silly Billy! LC 91-32561. (Illus.). 32p. (ps-k). 1992. 14. 00 (0-688-10817-2); PLB 13.93 (0-688-10818-0) Greenwillow.
—The Surprise Party. reissued ed. LC 86-7255. (Illus.). 32p. (ps-3). 1986. RSBE 13.95 (0-02-745930-6, Macmillan Child Bk) Macmillan Child Grp.
—The Surprise Party. Hutchins, Pat, illus. LC 91-10599. 32p. (gr. k-3). 1991. big bk. 16.95 (0-689-71542-0, Aladdin); pap. 3.95 (0-689-71543-9, Aladdin) Macmillan Child Grp.
—The Tale of Thomas Mead. LC 79-6398. (Illus.). 32p. (gr. 1-4). 1980. 14.00 (0-688-82082-6); PLB 13.93 (0-688-84282-8) Greenwillow.

—The Tale of Thomas Mead. LC 79-6398. 1988. pap. 2.95 (*0-688-08422-2*, Mulberry) Morrow.
—Three-Star Billy. LC 93-26517. 1994. write for info. (*0-688-13078-X*); lib. bdg. write for info. (*0-688-13079-8*) Greenwillow.
—Tidy Titch. LC 90-38483. (Illus.). 32p. (ps up). 1991. 15.00 (*0-688-09963-7*); PLB 14.93 (*0-688-09964-5*) Greenwillow.
—Titch. Hutchins, Pat, illus. LC 77-146622. 32p. (ps-1). 1971. RSBE 13.95 (*0-02-745880-6*, Macmillan Child Bk) Macmillan Child Grp.
—Titch. Hutchins, Pat, illus. LC 92-1642. 40p. (ps-1). 1993. pap. 4.95 (*0-689-71688-5*, Aladdin) Macmillan Child Grp.
—The Very Worst Monster. Hutchins, Pat, illus. LC 84-5928. 32p. (gr. k-3). 1985. 11.75 (*0-688-04010-1*); PLB 11.88 (*0-688-04011-X*) Greenwillow.
—The Very Worst Monster. LC 84-5928. (Illus.). 32p. (ps-3). 1988. pap. 3.95 (*0-688-07816-8*, Mulberry) Morrow.
—The Very Worst Monster. LC 84-5928. (Illus.). (gr. 1 up). 1989. pap. 7.95 bk. & cassette (*0-688-09038-9*, Mulberry) Morrow.
—What Game Shall We Play? LC 89-34621. (Illus.). 24p. (ps up). 1990. 12.95 (*0-688-09196-2*); PLB 12.88 (*0-688-09197-0*) Greenwillow.
—Where's The Baby? Hutchins, Pat, illus. LC 86-33566. 32p. (ps-3). 1988. 11.95 (*0-688-05933-3*); lib. bdg. 11.88 (*0-688-05934-1*) Greenwillow.
—Which Witch Is Which? LC 88-18781. (Illus.). 24p. (ps up). 1989. 14.95 (*0-688-06357-8*); PLB 14.88 (*0-688-06358-6*) Greenwillow.
—The Wind Blew. LC 73-11691. (Illus.). 32p. (ps-2). 1974. RSBE 13.95 (*0-02-745910-1*, Macmillan Child Bk) Macmillan Child Grp.
—The Wind Blew. Hutchins, Pat, illus. 32p. (ps-1). 1986. pap. 3.99 (*0-14-050236-X*, Puffin) Puffin Bks.
—The Wind Blew. Hutchins, Pat, illus. LC 92-44903. 32p. (ps-1). 1993. pap. 4.95 (*0-689-71744-X*, Aladdin) Macmillan Child Grp.
—You'll Soon Grow into Them, Titch. Hutchins, Pat, illus. LC 82-11755. 32p. (gr. k-3). 1983. 14.95 (*0-688-01770-3*); PLB 14.88 (*0-688-01771-1*) Greenwillow.
—You'll Soon Grow into Them, Titch. Hutchins, Pat, illus. LC 82-11755. 32p. (ps up). 1992. pap. 4.95 (*0-688-11507-1*, Mulberry) Morrow.
Hutchins, Raymond G. Time Tracker, 1990-1991: The High School Student's Weekly Planner & Study Time Manager. 120p. (gr. 9-12). 1990. pap. 5.95 (*0-13-921826-2*) P-H.
Hutchinson, Duane. Grotto Father: Artist-Priest of the West Bend Grotto. LC 89-39029. (Illus.). 64p. 1989. pap. 4.95 (*0-934988-20-X*) Foun Bks.
—The Gunny Wolf & Other Fairy Tales. LC 92-43623. (Illus.). 96p. (Orig.). (gr. k-6). 1992. pap. 6.95 (*0-934988-29-3*) Foun Bks.
—Storyteller's Ghost Stories. 4th ed. LC 89-23689. 112p. (gr. 4 up). 1989. pap. 6.95 (*0-934988-32-3*) Foun Bks.
—A Storyteller's Ghost Stories, Bk. 2. LC 90-3122. 96p. (gr. 4 up). 1990. pap. 6.95 (*0-934988-18-8*) Foun Bks.
—A Storyteller's Hometown. LC 88-82706. (Illus.). 316p. (Orig.). (gr. 7 up). 1989. pap. 9.95 (*0-934988-19-6*) Foun Bks.
Hutchinson, Emily. Golden Leaf Classics: Hatchet - Study Guide. 48p. (gr. 4-12). 1993. wkbk. 9.95 (*1-56872-001-7*) Incent Lrning.
Hutchinson, Gillian. The Story of Boats. James, John, illus. LC 91-39010. 32p. (gr. 1-4). 1993. PLB 11.89 (*0-8167-2705-8*); pap. text ed. 3.95 (*0-8167-2706-6*) Troll Assocs. Postponed.
Hutchinson, Haji U. The Car Theft Kidnapping. Siddiqui, Zeba, ed. Moore, Abd A., illus. 152p. (gr. 6-12). 1992. pap. 6.00 (*0-89259-123-4*) Am Trust Pubns.
—Invincible Abdullah, Vol. 1: The Deadly Mountain Revenge. Siddiqui, Zeba, ed. Al-Amin, Abd A., illus. 222p. (Orig.). (gr. 6-12). 1992. pap. 6.00 (*0-89259-121-8*) Am Trust Pubns.
—The Mystery of the Missing Pearls. Siddiqui, Zeba, ed. Moore, Abd A., illus. 131p. (gr. 6-12). 1993. pap. 6.00 (*0-89259-124-2*) Am Trust Pubns.
Hutchinson, Hanna. Chuyen Ba Con Gau: The Three Bears. Vu, Christine, tr. from ENG. Nofziger, Edward, illus. (VIE.). 22p. (Orig.). (gr. k-2). 1990. pap. 2.95 (*0-922852-10-3*) AIMS Intl.
—Drei Baren: The Three Bears. Proffitt, Bettina, tr. from ENG. Nofziger, Edward, illus. (GER.). 22p. (Orig.). (gr. k-2). 1990. pap. 2.95 (*0-922852-08-1*) AIMS Intl.
—I Tre Orsi: The Three Bears. Amico, Victoria, tr. from ENG. Nofziger, Edward, illus. (ITA.). 22p. (Orig.). (gr. k-2). 1990. pap. 2.95 (*0-922852-09-X*) AIMS Intl.
—Los Tres Osos: The Three Bears. Nofsiger, Edward, illus. (SPA.). 22p. (gr. k-2). 1990. pap. 2.95 (*0-922852-06-5*) AIMS Intl.
Hutchinson, Joy. Twelve Friends Counting Book about Jesus's Disciples. LC 91-71037. 32p. (gr. 2 up). 1991. pap. 4.99 (*0-8066-2559-7*, 9-2559) Augsburg Fortress.
Hutchinson, Robert & Graham, Andrew. Meteorites. LC 93-15955. (Illus.). 60p. (gr. 7 up). 1993. pap. 10.95 (*0-8069-0489-5*) Sterling.
Hutchinson, Veronia S., ed. Chimney Corner Stories: Tales for Little Children. Lenski, Lois, illus. LC 92-10760. 140p. (ps-3). 1992. lib. bdg. 22.50 (*0-208-02339-9*, Pub. by Linnet); (Pub. by Linnet) Shoe String.
Hutchinson Guest, Ann. Primer for Dance, Bk. I. 24p. (ps). 1958. pap. text ed. 6.95 (*0-932582-64-8*) Dance Notation.

—Primer for Dance, Bk. II. 24p. (ps). 1958. pap. text ed. 6.95 (*0-932582-65-6*) Dance Notation.
Hutchison, Wick. The Adventures of Inquisitive Englebert. Davisson, Vanessa, illus. 64p. (gr. k-3). 1991. pap. 7.95 (*0-929690-11-7*) Herit Pubs AZ.
Huth, Christina, ed. see Robinson, Amelia B.
Huth, Mark W. Introduction to Construction. LC 78-60838. (gr. 9-12). 1980. pap. text ed. 25.95 (*0-8273-1737-9*) Delmar.
Hutnick, R. Georgia Studies: Activity Manual. rev. ed. (Illus.). 170p. (gr. 4). 1992. 95.00 (*0-87746-363-8*) Graphic Learning.
—Georgia Studies: Teacher's Guide. 2nd ed. 30p. 1992. 8.25 (*0-87746-362-X*) Graphic Learning.
Hutson, Joan. Hail Mary. Huston, Joan, illus. 28p. (ps). 1987. 3.95 (*0-8198-3324-X*) St Paul Bks.
—I Think... I Know... a Poster Book about God. Hutson, Joan, illus. 32p. (Orig.). (gr. 2-4). 1979. pap. 1.95 (*0-87793-186-0*) Ave Maria.
—I'm Glad I Am: Christian Affirmations for Children. Hutson, Joan, illus. LC 10627. 48p. (Orig.). (gr. 1-4). 1992. pap. 3.95 (*0-8198-3623-0*) St Paul Bks.
—It's Important. Hutson, Joan, illus. 48p. (ps). 1987. 3.95 (*0-8198-3615-X*) St Paul Bks.
—Legend of the Nine Talents. Hutson, Joan, illus. LC 92-26957. 1992. 4.95 (*0-8198-4468-3*) St Paul Bks.
—My Happy Ones. Hutson, Joan, illus. 32p. (ps). 1987. 3.95 (*0-8198-4723-2*) St Paul Bks.
—Who? Hutson, Joan, illus. LC 92-31811. 32p. (ps-2). 1992. 3.50 (*0-8198-8266-6*) St Paul Bks.
Hutson, Ronald, ed. see Moore, Kathryn C.
Hutson-Nechkash, Peg. Storybuilding: A Guide to Structuring Oral Narratives. 128p. (Orig.). (gr. 3-8). 1990. pap. text ed. 24.00x (*0-930599-63-2*) Thinking Pubns.
Huttenbach, Henry. The Jewish Americans. Moynihan, Daniel P., intro. by. 112p. (Orig.). (gr. 5 up). 1989. 17.95 (*0-87754-887-0*); pap. 9.95 (*0-7910-0270-5*) Chelsea Hse.
Hutterian Brethren Staff, ed. see Clement, Jane T.
Hutton, John. Guale. 201p. (gr. 8). 1993. pap. 4.80 (*1-882534-01-8*) Am Efficiency.
—Gulla Island: An Island Kids' Adventure. LC 92-97148. 160p. (gr. 8). 1992. pap. 4.80 (*1-882534-00-X*) Am Efficiency.
Hutton, Warwick. Adam & Eve: The Bible Story. Hutton, Warwick, illus. LC 86-27690. 32p. 1987. SBE 14.95 (*0-689-50433-0*, M K McElderry) Macmillan Child Grp.
—Beauty & the Beast. Hutton, Warwick, illus. LC 84-48441. 32p. 1985. SBE 14.95 (*0-689-50316-4*, M K McElderry) Macmillan Child Grp.
—Jonah & the Great Fish. LC 83-15477. (Illus.). 32p. 1984. SBE 13.95 (*0-689-50283-4*, M K McElderry) Macmillan Child Grp.
—Moses in the Bulrushes. Hutton, Warwick, illus. LC 85-72261. 32p. 1986. SBE 13.95 (*0-689-50393-8*, M K McElderry) Macmillan Child Grp.
—Persephone. Hutton, Warwick, illus. LC 93-20590. 32p. (gr. 2 up). 1994. SBE 14.95 (*0-689-50600-7*, M K McElderry) Macmillan Child Grp.
—Perseus. Hutton, Warwick, illus. LC 92-7639. 32p. (gr. 2 up). 1993. SBE 14.95 (*0-689-50565-5*, M K McElderry) Macmillan Child Grp.
—Theseus & the Minotaur. Hutton, Warwick, illus. LC 88-26875. 32p. (gr. 1-5). 1989. SBE 14.95 (*0-689-50473-X*, M K McElderry) Macmillan Child Grp.
Hutton, Warwick, retold by. & illus. Moses in the Bulrushes. LC 91-13971. 32p. (gr. k-3). 1992. pap. 4.95 (*0-689-71553-6*, Aladdin) Macmillan Child Grp.
—The Trojan Horse. LC 91-21590. 32p. (gr. 2 up). 1992. SBE 14.95 (*0-689-50542-6*, M K McElderry) Macmillan Child Grp.
Huxley, Aldous. Brave New World. abr. ed. 137p. 1973. pap. text ed. 5.95 (*0-582-53033-4*) Longman.
Huxley, Laura A. Oneadayreason to Be Happy. Stuart, Mimi, illus. 70p. (Orig.). (gr. 2up). 1986. 10.95 (*0-89638-112-9*); pap. 7.95 (*0-89638-111-0*) CompCare.
Huynh Quang Nhuong. The Land I Lost. Vo-Dinh, Mai, illus. LC 80-8437. 128p. (gr. 4-7). 1986. pap. 3.95 (*0-06-440183-9*, Trophy) HarpC Child Bks.
—The Land I Lost. (gr. 4-7). 1992. 16.75 (*0-8446-6586-X*) Peter Smith.
Huyser-Honig, Joan & Huyser-Honig, Steve. The Church Serves. 86p. (Orig.). (gr. 7-8). 1987. pap. text ed. 7.25 (*0-930265-38-6*); tchr's ed. 8.95 (*0-930265-39-4*) CRC Pubns.
Huyser-Honig, Steve, jt. auth. see Huyser-Honig, Joan.
Hwa-I Publishing Co., Staff. Chinese Children's Stories, Vol. 1: Two Bushels of Grain, Forget the Turnips! Ching, Emily, et al, eds. Wonder Kids Publications Staff, tr. from CHI. (Illus.). 28p. (gr. 3-6). 1991. Repr. of 1988 ed. 7.95 (*1-56162-001-7*) Wonder Kids.
—Chinese Children's Stories, Vol. 10: The Money Tree, The Coxcomb. Ching, Emily, et al, eds. Wonder Kids Publications Staff, tr. from CHI. Hwa-I Publishing Co., Staff, illus. LC 90-60792. 28p. (gr. 3-6). 1991. Repr. of 1988 ed. 7.95x (*1-56162-010-6*) Wonder Kids.
—Chinese Children's Stories, Vol. 100: From Rice into Flowers, The Shy Rainbow. Ching, Emily, et al, eds. Wonder Kids Publications Staff, tr. from CHI. Hwa-I Publishing Co., Staff, illus. LC 90-60811. 28p. (gr. 3-6). 1991. Repr. of 1988 ed. 7.95x (*1-56162-100-5*) Wonder Kids.

—Chinese Children's Stories, Vol. 11: Ker-Plunk is Coming!, Baby Chicks' Revenge. Ching, Emily, et al, eds. Wonder Kids Publications Staff, tr. from CHI. (Illus.). 28p. (gr. 3-6). 1991. Repr. of 1988 ed. 7.95 (*1-56162-011-4*) Wonder Kids.
—Chinese Children's Stories, Vol. 12: The Snail & the Ox, Sparrows Can't Walk. Ching, Emily, et al, eds. Wonder Kids Publications Staff, tr. from CHI. Hwa-I Publishing Co., Staff, illus. LC 90-60793. 28p. (gr. 3-6). 1991. Repr. of 1988 ed. 7.95x (*1-56162-012-2*) Wonder Kids.
—Chinese Children's Stories, Vol. 13: Rooster Summons the Sun, The White-Haired Bird. Ching, Emily, et al, eds. Wonder Kids Publications Staff, tr. from CHI. Hwa-I Publishing Co., Staff, illus. LC 90-60793. 28p. (gr. 3-6). 1991. Repr. of 1988 ed. 7.95x (*1-56162-013-0*) Wonder Kids.
—Chinese Children's Stories, Vol. 14: Weasel Steals the Chickens, Why is the Crow Black? Ching, Emily, et al, eds. Wonder Kids Publications Staff, tr. from CHI. Hwa-I Publishing Co., Staff, illus. LC 90-60793. 28p. (gr. 3-6). 1991. Repr. of 1988 ed. 7.95x (*1-56162-014-9*) Wonder Kids.
—Chinese Children's Stories, Vol. 15: Jiggle in the Wind, The Bat Can't See the Sun. Ching, Emily, et al, eds. Wonder Kids Publications Staff, tr. from CHI. Hwa-I Publishing Co., Staff, illus. LC 90-60793. 28p. (gr. 3-6). 1991. Repr. of 1988 ed. 7.95x (*1-56162-015-7*) Wonder Kids.
—Chinese Children's Stories, Vol. 16: How to Build a Nest, Moving the Mountain. Ching, Emily, et al, eds. Wonder Kids Publications Staff, tr. from CHI. (Illus.). 28p. (gr. 3-6). 1991. Repr. of 1988 ed. 7.95 (*1-56162-016-5*) Wonder Kids.
—Chinese Children's Stories, Vol. 17: The Monkey & the Fire, Lazy Wife & the Bread Ring. Ching, Emily, et al, eds. Wonder Kids Publications Staff, tr. from CHI. Hwa-I Publishing Co., Staff, illus. LC 90-60794. 28p. (gr. 3-6). 1991. Repr. of 1988 ed. 7.95x (*1-56162-017-3*) Wonder Kids.
—Chinese Children's Stories, Vol. 18: The Little Bamboo Pole, The Wise Old Man. Ching, Emily, et al, eds. Wonder Kids Publications Staff, tr. from CHI. Hwa-I Publishing Co., Staff, illus. LC 90-60794. 28p. (gr. 3-6). 1991. Repr. of 1988 ed. 7.95x (*1-56162-018-1*) Wonder Kids.
—Chinese Children's Stories, Vol. 19: Crow Moves Away, Baby Lion & Baby Rhino. Ching, Emily, et al, eds. Wonder Kids Publications Staff, tr. from CHI. Hwa-I Publishing Co., Staff, illus. LC 90-60794. 28p. (gr. 3-6). 1991. Repr. of 1988 ed. 7.95x (*1-56162-019-X*) Wonder Kids.
—Chinese Children's Stories, Vol. 2: The Blind Man & the Cripple, Orchard Village. Ching, Emily, et al, eds. Wonder Kids Publications Staff, tr. from CHI. (Illus.). 28p. (gr. 3-6). 1991. Repr. of 1988 ed. 7.95 (*1-56162-002-5*) Wonder Kids.
—Chinese Children's Stories, Vol. 20: Ah-Liu Picks Corn, Cuckoo's Winter. Ching, Emily, et al, eds. Wonder Kids Publications Staff, tr. from CHI. Hwa-I Publishing Co., Staff, illus. LC 90-60794. 28p. (gr. 3-6). 1991. Repr. of 1988 ed. 7.95x (*1-56162-020-3*) Wonder Kids.
—Chinese Children's Stories, Vol. 21: Seamless Clothing, The Big Clam & the Snipe. Ching, Emily, et al, eds. Wonder Kids Publications Staff, tr. from CHI. (Illus.). 28p. (gr. 3-6). 1991. Repr. of 1988 ed. 7.95 (*1-56162-021-1*) Wonder Kids.
—Chinese Children's Stories, Vol. 22: The Steal a Bell, The Dropout. Ching, Emily, et al, eds. Wonder Kids Publications Staff, tr. from CHI. Hwa-I Publishing Co., Staff, illus. LC 90-60796. 28p. (gr. 3-6). 1991. Repr. of 1988 ed. 7.95x (*1-56162-022-X*) Wonder Kids.
—Chinese Children's Stories, Vol. 23: Dummy Afa, The Fox in a Tiger's Suit. Ching, Emily, et al, eds. Wonder Kids Publications Staff, tr. from CHI. Hwa-I Publishing Co., Staff, illus. LC 90-60796. 28p. (gr. 3-6). 1991. Repr. of 1988 ed. 7.95x (*1-56162-023-8*) Wonder Kids.
—Chinese Children's Stories, Vol. 24: Running Fifty vs. One-Hundred Strides, Atu Yanks the Rice Seedlings. Ching, Emily, et al, eds. Wonder Kids Publications Staff, tr. from CHI. Hwa-I Publishing Co., Staff, illus. LC 90-60796. 28p. (gr. 3-6). 1991. Repr. of 1988 ed. 7.95x (*1-56162-024-6*) Wonder Kids.
—Chinese Children's Stories, Vol. 25: The Blindmen & the Elephant, Little Frog in the Well. Ching, Emily, et al, eds. Wonder Kids Publications Staff, tr. from CHI. Hwa-I Publishing Co., Staff, illus. LC 90-60796. 28p. (gr. 3-6). 1991. Repr. of 1988 ed. 7.95x (*1-56162-025-4*) Wonder Kids.
—Chinese Children's Stories, Vol. 26: Celebrating New York, Miss Yuan-Tsau. Ching, Emily, et al, eds. Wonder Kids Publications Staff, tr. from CHI. (Illus.). 28p. (gr. 3-6). 1991. Repr. of 1988 ed. 7.95 (*1-56162-026-2*) Wonder Kids.
—Chinese Children's Stories, Vol. 27: Sky-Mending Festival, Decorative Paper for Graves. Ching, Emily, et al, eds. Wonder Kids Publications Staff, tr. from CHI. Hwa-I Publishing Co., Staff, illus. LC 90-60797. 28p. (gr. 3-6). 1991. Repr. of 1988 ed. 7.95x (*1-56162-027-0*) Wonder Kids.
—Chinese Children's Stories, Vol. 28: Mih-Ro River, The Herder & the Seamstress. Ching, Emily, et al, eds. Wonder Kids Publications Staff, tr. from CHI. Hwa-I Publishing Co., Staff, illus. LC 90-60797. 28p. (gr. 3-6). 1991. Repr. of 1988 ed. 7.95x (*1-56162-028-9*) Wonder Kids.

—Chinese Children's Stories, Vol. 29: Moon Cake, Fei's Adventure. Ching, Emily, et al, eds. Wonder Kids Publications Staff, tr. from CHI. Hwa-I Publishing Co., Staff, illus. LC 90-60797. 28p. (gr. 3-6). 1991. Repr. of 1988 ed. 7.95x (1-56162-029-7) Wonder Kids.

—Chinese Children's Stories, Vol. 3: The Redbud Tree, Lazy Bones & the Magical Bowl. Ching, Emily, et al, eds. Wonder Kids Publications Staff, tr. from CHI. (Illus.). 28p. (gr. 3-6). 1991. Repr. of 1988 ed. 7.95 (1-56162-003-3) Wonder Kids.

—Chinese Children's Stories, Vol. 30: La-Ba Porridge, The Stove God. Ching, Emily, et al, eds. Wonder Kids Publications Staff, tr. from CHI. Hwa-I Publishing Co., Staff, illus. LC 90-60797. 28p. (gr. 3-6). 1991. Repr. of 1988 ed. 7.95x (1-56162-030-0) Wonder Kids.

—Chinese Children's Stories, Vol. 31: The Refugee Empress, Chi Jiguang Cookies. Ching, Emily, et al, eds. Wonder Kids Publications Staff, tr. from CHI. (Illus.). 28p. (gr. 3-6). 1991. Repr. of 1988 ed. 7.95 (1-56162-031-9) Wonder Kids.

—Chinese Children's Stories, Vol. 32: Dumplings, Ham. Ching, Emily, et al, eds. Wonder Kids Publications Staff, tr. from CHI. Hwa-I Publishing Co., Staff, illus. LC 90-60798. 28p. (gr. 3-6). 1991. Repr. of 1988 ed. 7.95x (1-56162-032-7) Wonder Kids.

—Chinese Children's Stories, Vol. 33: Noodles over the Bridge, Steamed Bread. Ching, Emily, et al, eds. Wonder Kids Publications Staff, tr. from CHI. Hwa-I Publishing Co., Staff, illus. LC 90-60798. 28p. (gr. 3-6). 1991. Repr. of 1988 ed. 7.95x (1-56162-033-5) Wonder Kids.

—Chinese Children's Stories, Vol. 34: The Stuffed Steamed Bao, Miss Freckle's Tofu. Ching, Emily, et al, eds. Wonder Kids Publications Staff, tr. from CHI. Hwa-I Publishing Co., Staff, illus. LC 90-60798. 28p. (gr. 3-6). 1991. Repr. of 1988 ed. 7.95x (1-56162-034-3) Wonder Kids.

—Chinese Children's Stories, Vol. 35: Monks' Beef Stew, Yue's Tofu Store. Ching, Emily, et al, eds. Wonder Kids Publications Staff, tr. from CHI. Hwa-I Publishing Co., Staff, illus. LC 90-60799. 28p. (gr. 3-6). 1991. Repr. of 1988 ed. 7.95x (1-56162-035-1) Wonder Kids.

—Chinese Children's Stories, Vol. 36: Lu Ban & Old Sir Lee, Umbrellas. Ching, Emily, et al, eds. Wonder Kids Publications Staff, tr. from CHI. (Illus.). 28p. (gr. 3-6). 1991. Repr. of 1988 ed. 7.95 (1-56162-036-X) Wonder Kids.

—Chinese Children's Stories, Vol. 37: Confucius' Bookkeeping, The Scissors Shop. Ching, Emily, et al, eds. Wonder Kids Publications Staff, tr. from CHI. Hwa-I Publishing Co., Staff, illus. LC 90-60799. 28p. (gr. 3-6). 1991. Repr. of 1988 ed. 7.95x (1-56162-037-8) Wonder Kids.

—Chinese Children's Stories, Vol. 38: The Peace Drum, Comb. Ching, Emily, et al, eds. Wonder Kids Publications Staff, tr. from CHI. Hwa-I Publishing Co., Staff, illus. LC 90-60799. 28p. (gr. 3-6). 1991. Repr. of 1988 ed. 7.95x (1-56162-038-6) Wonder Kids.

—Chinese Children's Stories, Vol. 39: Brush Pen, Duan's Ink-Slab. Ching, Emily, et al, eds. Wonder Kids Publications Staff, tr. from CHI. Hwa-I Publishing Co., Staff, illus. LC 90-6079. 28p. (gr. 3-6). 1991. Repr. of 1988 ed. 7.95x (1-56162-039-4) Wonder Kids.

—Chinese Children's Stories, Vol. 4: Golden Needles, Three Treasures. Ching, Emily, et al, eds. Wonder Kids Publications Staff, tr. from CHI. (Illus.). 28p. (gr. 3-6). 1991. Repr. of 1988 ed. 7.95 (1-56162-004-1) Wonder Kids.

—Chinese Children's Stories, Vol. 40: The Ink-Stick, Shiuan Paper. Ching, Emily, et al, eds. Wonder Kids Publications Staff, tr. from CHI. Hwa-I Publishing Co., Staff, illus. LC 90-60799. 28p. (gr. 3-6). 1991. Repr. of 1988 ed. 7.95x (1-56162-040-8) Wonder Kids.

—Chinese Children's Stories, Vol. 41: Brother Cat & Brother Rat, The Rooster's Antlers. Ching, Emily, et al, eds. Wonder Kids Publications Staff, tr. from CHI. (Illus.). 28p. (gr. 3-6). 1991. Repr. of 1988 ed. 7.95 (1-56162-041-6) Wonder Kids.

—Chinese Children's Stories, Vol. 42: Tiger Seeks a Master, Why Are Cats Afraid of Dogs? Ching, Emily, et al, eds. Wonder Kids Publications Staff, tr. from CHI. Hwa-I Publishing Co., Staff, illus. LC 90-60800. 28p. (gr. 3-6). 1991. Repr. of 1988 ed. 7.95x (1-56162-042-4) Wonder Kids.

—Chinese Children's Stories, Vol. 43: The Bunny's Tail, Fox, Monkey, Rabbit & Horse. Ching, Emily, et al, eds. Wonder Kids Publications Staff, tr. from CHI. Hwa-I Publishing Co., Staff, illus. LC 90-60800. 28p. (gr. 3-6). 1991. Repr. of 1988 ed. 7.95x (1-56162-043-2) Wonder Kids.

—Chinese Children's Stories, Vol. 44: Snake's Lost Drum, Ox & Buffalo Change Clothes. Ching, Emily, et al, eds. Wonder Kids Publications Staff, tr. from CHI. Hwa-I Publishing Co., Staff, illus. LC 90-60800. 28p. (gr. 3-6). 1991. Repr. of 1988 ed. 7.95x (1-56162-044-0) Wonder Kids.

—Chinese Children's Stories, Vol. 45: The Goat & the Camel, The Wolf & the Pig. Ching, Emily, et al, eds. Wonder Kids Publications Staff, tr. from CHI. Hwa-I Publishing Co., Staff, illus. LC 90-60800. 28p. (gr. 3-6). 1991. Repr. of 1988 ed. 7.95x (1-56162-045-9) Wonder Kids.

—Chinese Children's Stories, Vol. 46: Ma-Gu's Cock-a-Doodle-Doo, The Crippled Goat. Ching, Emily, et al, eds. Wonder Kids Publications Staff, tr. from CHI. (Illus.). 28p. (gr. 3-6). 1991. Repr. of 1988 ed. 7.95 (1-56162-046-7) Wonder Kids.

—Chinese Children's Stories, Vol. 47: The Crane-Riding Immortal, Lyu Dungbin & Guanyin. Ching, Emily, et al, eds. Wonder Kids Publications Staff, tr. from CHI. Hwa-I Publishing Co., Staff, illus. LC 90-60801. 28p. (gr. 3-6). 1991. Repr. of 1988 ed. 7.95x (1-56162-047-5) Wonder Kids.

—Chinese Children's Stories, Vol. 48: Sir Thunder & Lady Lightning, The Door Guards. Ching, Emily, et al, eds. Wonder Kids Publications Staff, tr. from CHI. Hwa-I Publishing Co., Staff, illus. LC 90-60801. 28p. (gr. 3-6). 1991. Repr. of 1988 ed. 7.95x (1-56162-048-3) Wonder Kids.

—Chinese Children's Stories, Vol. 49: The Slippery Nose Deity, Under the Moonlight. Ching, Emily, et al, eds. Wonder Kids Publications Staff, tr. from CHI. Hwa-I Publishing Co., Staff, illus. LC 90-60801. 28p. (gr. 3-6). 1991. Repr. of 1988 ed. 7.95x (1-56162-049-1) Wonder Kids.

—Chinese Children's Stories, Vol. 5: Sun Valley, A Stone Carver's Dream. Ching, Emily, et al, eds. Wonder Kids Publications Staff, tr. from CHI. (Illus.). 28p. (gr. 3-6). 1991. Repr. of 1988 ed. 7.95 (0-685-49019-X) Wonder Kids.

—Chinese Children's Stories, Vol. 50: Zung Kuei & the Little Ghost, Earth God & Earth Goddess. Ching, Emily, et al, eds. Wonder Kids Publications Staff, tr. from CHI. Hwa-I Publishing Co., Staff, illus. LC 90-60801. 28p. (gr. 3-6). 1991. Repr. of 1988 ed. 7.95x (1-56162-050-5) Wonder Kids.

—Chinese Children's Stories, Vol. 51: Moginlin Saves His Mother, Hwang Shun & His Father. Ching, Emily, et al, eds. Wonder Kids Publications Staff, tr. from CHI. (Illus.). 28p. (gr. 3-6). 1991. Repr. of 1988 ed. 7.95 (1-56162-051-3) Wonder Kids.

—Chinese Children's Stories, Vol. 52: Joining the Army, Beating up the Tiger. Ching, Emily, et al, eds. Wonder Kids Publications Staff, tr. from CHI. Hwa-I Publishing Co., Staff, illus. LC 90-60802. 28p. (gr. 3-6). 1991. Repr. of 1988 ed. 7.95x (1-56162-052-1) Wonder Kids.

—Chinese Children's Stories, Vol. 53: Meeting an Angel, The Child in the Deer Skin. Ching, Emily, et al, eds. Wonder Kids Publications Staff, tr. from CHI. Hwa-I Publishing Co., Staff, illus. LC 90-60802. 28p. (gr. 3-6). 1991. Repr. of 1988 ed. 7.95x (1-56162-053-X) Wonder Kids.

—Chinese Children's Stories, Vol. 54: The Story of Shun, Village of Filial Piety. Ching, Emily, et al, eds. Wonder Kids Publications Staff, tr. from CHI. Hwa-I Publishing Co., Staff, illus. LC 90-60802. 28p. (gr. 3-6). 1991. Repr. of 1988 ed. 7.95x (1-56162-054-8) Wonder Kids.

—Chinese Children's Stories, Vol. 55: Two Baskets of Mulberries, Trun's Little Daughter. Ching, Emily, et al, eds. Wonder Kids Publications Staff, tr. from CHI. Hwa-I Publishing Co., Staff, illus. LC 90-60802. 28p. (gr. 3-6). 1991. Repr. of 1988 ed. 7.95x (1-56162-055-6) Wonder Kids.

—Chinese Children's Stories, Vol. 56: Catching a Thief, The Plum Tree by the Road. Ching, Emily, et al, eds. Wonder Kids Publications Staff, tr. from CHI. (Illus.). 28p. (gr. 3-6). 1991. Repr. of 1988 ed. 7.95 (1-56162-056-4) Wonder Kids.

—Chinese Children's Stories, Vol. 57: The Little-Boy God, A Rooster's Egg. Ching, Emily, et al, eds. Wonder Kids Publications Staff, tr. from CHI. Hwa-I Publishing Co., Staff, illus. LC 90-60803. 28p. (gr. 3-6). 1991. Repr. of 1988 ed. 7.95x (1-56162-057-2) Wonder Kids.

—Chinese Children's Stories, Vol. 58: Three Princes & the Firewood, Wang's Memory. Ching, Emily, et al, eds. Wonder Kids Publications Staff, tr. from CHI. Hwa-I Publishing Co., Staff, illus. LC 90-60803. 28p. (gr. 3-6). 1991. Repr. of 1988 ed. 7.95x (1-56162-058-0) Wonder Kids.

—Chinese Children's Stories, Vol. 59: A Tankful of Water, The Little Hero. Ching, Emily, et al, eds. Wonder Kids Publications Staff, tr. from CHI. Hwa-I Publishing Co., Staff, illus. LC 90-60803. 28p. (gr. 3-6). 1991. Repr. of 1988 ed. 7.95x (1-56162-059-9) Wonder Kids.

—Chinese Children's Stories, Vol. 6: Miss Gold 'n' Silver, Pearl Rice. Ching, Emily, et al, eds. Wonder Kids Publications Staff, tr. from CHI. (Illus.). 28p. (gr. 3-6). 1991. Repr. of 1988 ed. 7.95 (1-56162-006-8) Wonder Kids.

—Chinese Children's Stories, Vol. 60: Weighing an Elephant, The Distant Homeland. Ching, Emily, et al, eds. Wonder Kids Publications Staff, tr. from CHI. Hwa-I Publishing Co., Staff, illus. LC 90-60803. 28p. (gr. 3-6). 1991. Repr. of 1988 ed. 7.95x (1-56162-060-2) Wonder Kids.

—Chinese Children's Stories, Vol. 61: Pan Koo Creates the World, Λ Hole in the Sky. Ching, Emily, et al, eds. Wonder Kids Publications Staff, tr. from CHI. (Illus.). 28p. (gr. 3-6). 1991. Repr. of 1988 ed. 7.95 (1-56162-061-0) Wonder Kids.

—Chinese Children's Stories, Vol. 62: To Catch the Suns, Two Quarrelsome Brothers. Ching, Emily, et al, eds. Wonder Kids Publications Staff, tr. from CHI. Hwa-I Publishing Co., Staff, illus. LC 90-60804. 28p. (gr. 3-6). 1991. Repr. of 1988 ed. 7.95x (1-56162-062-9) Wonder Kids.

—Chinese Children's Stories, Vol. 63: To Speak or Not, The Dark Village. Ching, Emily, et al, eds. Wonder Kids Publications Staff, tr. from CHI. Hwa-I Publishing Co., Staff, illus. LC 90-60804. 28p. (gr. 3-6). 1991. Repr. of 1988 ed. 7.95x (1-56162-063-7) Wonder Kids.

—Chinese Children's Stories, Vol. 64: Why Is the Sky So High?, Turning into Stone. Ching, Emily, et al, eds. Wonder Kids Publications Staff, tr. from CHI. Hwa-I Publishing Co., Staff, illus. LC 90-60804. 28p. (gr. 3-6). 1991. Repr. of 1988 ed. 7.95x (1-56162-064-5) Wonder Kids.

—Chinese Children's Stories, Vol. 65: Lugging Mountains, What's a Life Span? Ching, Emily, et al, eds. Wonder Kids Publications Staff, tr. from CHI. Hwa-I Publishing Co., Staff, illus. LC 90-60804. 28p. (gr. 3-6). 1991. Repr. of 1988 ed. 7.95x (1-56162-065-3) Wonder Kids.

—Chinese Children's Stories, Vol. 66: The Chiao Sisters, Zhou under the Bed. Ching, Emily, et al, eds. Wonder Kids Publications Staff, tr. from CHI. (Illus.). 28p. (gr. 3-6). 1991. Repr. of 1988 ed. 7.95 (1-56162-066-1) Wonder Kids.

—Chinese Children's Stories, Vol. 67: The After-Meal Bell, Passing the Three Gorges. Ching, Emily, et al, eds. Wonder Kids Publications Staff, tr. from CHI. Hwa-I Publishing Co., Staff, illus. LC 90-60805. 28p. (gr. 3-6). 1991. Repr. of 1988 ed. 7.95x (1-56162-067-X) Wonder Kids.

—Chinese Children's Stories, Vol. 68: The Donkey-Riding Poet, The Backyard Song. Ching, Emily, et al, eds. Wonder Kids Publications Staff, tr. from CHI. Hwa-I Publishing Co., Staff, illus. LC 90-60805. 28p. (gr. 3-6). 1991. Repr. of 1988 ed. 7.95x (1-56162-068-8) Wonder Kids.

—Chinese Children's Stories, Vol. 69: The Young Family, Tsuei's Beautiful Bride. Ching, Emily, et al, eds. Wonder Kids Publications Staff, tr. from CHI. Hwa-I Publishing Co., Staff, illus. LC 90-60805. 28p. (gr. 3-6). 1991. Repr. of 1988 ed. 7.95x (1-56162-069-6) Wonder Kids.

—Chinese Children's Stories, Vol. 7: Dragon Eye & Cassia Circle, The Conceited Barber. Ching, Emily, et al, eds. Wonder Kids Publications Staff, tr. from CHI. Hwa-I Publishing Co., Staff, illus. LC 90-60792. 28p. (gr. 3-6). 1991. Repr. of 1988 ed. 7.95x (1-56162-007-6) Wonder Kids.

—Chinese Children's Stories, Vol. 70: Ji's Jokes, The Scrooge. Ching, Emily, et al, eds. Wonder Kids Publications Staff, tr. from CHI. Hwa-I Publishing Co., Staff, illus. LC 90-60805. 28p. (gr. 3-6). 1991. Repr. of 1988 ed. 7.95x (1-56162-070-X) Wonder Kids.

—Chinese Children's Stories, Vol. 71: The Magic Glass Jar, The Pear Tree. Ching, Emily, et al, eds. Wonder Kids Publications Staff, tr. from CHI. (Illus.). 28p. (gr. 3-6). 1991. Repr. of 1988 ed. 7.95 (1-56162-071-8) Wonder Kids.

—Chinese Children's Stories, Vol. 72: The Lotus Child, The Ghost in the Basin. Ching, Emily, et al, eds. Wonder Kids Publications Staff, tr. from CHI. Hwa-I Publishing Co., Staff, illus. LC 90-60806. 28p. (gr. 3-6). 1991. Repr. of 1988 ed. 7.95x (1-56162-072-6) Wonder Kids.

—Chinese Children's Stories, Vol. 73: Walking through Walls, Who Is the Real Lord Ji? Ching, Emily, et al, eds. Wonder Kids Publications Staff, tr. from CHI. Hwa-I Publishing Co., Staff, illus. LC 90-60806. 28p. (gr. 3-6). 1991. Repr. of 1988 ed. 7.95x (1-56162-073-4) Wonder Kids.

—Chinese Children's Stories, Vol. 74: Chaos in the Heavenly Palace, Eating the Ginseng Fruit. Ching, Emily, et al, eds. Wonder Kids Publications Staff, tr. from CHI. Hwa-I Publishing Co., Staff, illus. LC 90-60806. 28p. (gr. 3-6). 1991. Repr. of 1988 ed. 7.95x (1-56162-074-2) Wonder Kids.

—Chinese Children's Stories, Vol. 75: Tang's Strange Journey, Dwarfs & Giants. Ching, Emily, et al, eds. Wonder Kids Publications Staff, tr. from CHI. Hwa-I Publishing Co., Staff, illus. LC 90-60806. 28p. (gr. 3-6). 1991. Repr. of 1988 ed. 7.95x (1-56162-075-0) Wonder Kids.

—Chinese Children's Stories, Vol. 76: The Stinky Emperor, The Hero Who Crawled. Ching, Emily, et al, eds. Wonder Kids Publications Staff, tr. from CHI. (Illus.). 28p. (gr. 3-6). 1991. Repr. of 1988 ed. 7.95 (1-56162-076-9) Wonder Kids.

—Chinese Children's Stories, Vol. 77: Sir Guan's Big Red Face, Turning Cranes into Words. Ching, Emily, et al, eds. Wonder Kids Publications Staff, tr. from CHI. Hwa-I Publishing Co., Staff, illus. LC 90-60807. 28p. (gr. 3-6). 1991. Repr. of 1988 ed. 7.95x (1-56162-077-7) Wonder Kids.

—Chinese Children's Stories, Vol. 78: Tang Buohu's Drawings, The General & the Water Tank. Ching, Emily, et al, eds. Wonder Kids Publications Staff, tr. from CHI. Hwa-I Publishing Co., Staff, illus. LC 90-60807. 28p. (gr. 3-6). 1991. Repr. of 1988 ed. 7.95x (1-56162-078-5) Wonder Kids.

—Chinese Children's Stories, Vol. 79: Black-Faced Sir Bao, Doctor Hwa-Tuo. Ching, Emily, et al, eds. Wonder Kids Publications Staff, tr. from CHI. Hwa-I Publishing Co., Staff, illus. LC 90-60807. 28p. (gr. 3-6). 1991. Repr. of 1988 ed. 7.95x (1-56162-079-3) Wonder Kids.

Thank you for choosing this vital resource from **Reed Reference Publishing**. We offer a full range of information products and services in a variety of formats—print, online, CD-ROM, fiche, and tape leasing. The postage-paid Product Information Request cards below make it easy for you to learn about everything from Bowker's bibliographic references and Marquis Who's Who biographical resources...to National Register Publishing's corporate data services.

Simply complete the card and drop it in the mail. We'll send your information promptly.

Key Titles Available from the Reed Reference Publishing Companies:

R.R. Bowker
- Books in Print
- Literary Market Place

Martindale-Hubbell
- Martindale-Hubbell Law Directory
- Martindale-Hubbell Bar Register of Preeminent Lawyers

K.G. Saur
- Yearbook of International Organizations
- The Directory of European Business

National Register Publishing
- Standard Directory of Advertisers
- Standard Directory of Advertising Agencies
- Directory of Corporate Affiliations

Bowker-Saur
- Who's Who in European Politics
- Collection Development for Libraries

Marquis Who's Who
- Who's Who in America
- The *Official* ABMS Directory of Board Certified Medical Specialists

D.W. Thorpe
- Australian Books in Print
- Australian and New Zealand Booksellers and Publishers

Congressional Information Service
- American Foreign Policy Index
- U.S. Government Periodicals Index

CBIP3

Please send me information on these Reed Reference Publishing products and services:

- ○ Bibliographic References
- ○ Biographical References
- ○ Business References
- ○ CD-ROM and Online Databases
- ○ Children's and Young Adult References
- ○ Entertainment and Performing Arts References
- ○ Government Publications Indexes
- ○ International References
- ○ Legal References
- ○ Professional Directories

○ *Please send me my copy of Reed Reference Publishing's latest catalog.*

○ *I'd like a Sales Representative to call me as soon as possible. I've provided my telephone number below.*

Name ______________________________

Title ______________________________

Institution __________________________

Address ____________________________

City/State/Zip _______________________

Telephone (_____) ___________________

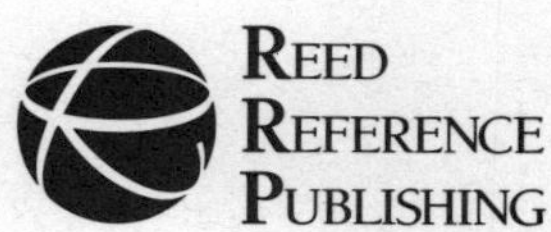

CBIP4

Please send me information on these Reed Reference Publishing products and services:

- ○ Bibliographic References
- ○ Biographical References
- ○ Business References
- ○ CD-ROM and Online Databases
- ○ Children's and Young Adult References
- ○ Entertainment and Performing Arts References
- ○ Government Publications Indexes
- ○ International References
- ○ Legal References
- ○ Professional Directories

○ *Please send me my copy of Reed Reference Publishing's latest catalog.*

○ *I'd like a Sales Representative to call me as soon as possible. I've provided my telephone number below.*

Name ______________________________

Title ______________________________

Institution __________________________

Address ____________________________

City/State/Zip _______________________

Telephone (_____) ___________________

BUSINESS REPLY MAIL

FIRST CLASS MAIL   PERMIT NO 45   NEW PROVIDENCE NJ

POSTAGE WILL BE PAID BY ADDRESSEE

CUSTOMER SERVICE
REED REFERENCE PUBLISHING
PO BOX 31
NEW PROVIDENCE NJ   07974 9904

BUSINESS REPLY MAIL

FIRST CLASS MAIL   PERMIT NO 45   NEW PROVIDENCE NJ

POSTAGE WILL BE PAID BY ADDRESSEE

CUSTOMER SERVICE
REED REFERENCE PUBLISHING
PO BOX 31
NEW PROVIDENCE NJ   07974 9904

—Chinese Children's Stories, Vol. 8: The Millets Won't Go Home, The Immortal Palm. Ching, Emily, et al, eds. Wonder Kids Publications Staff, tr. from CHI. Hwa-I Publishing Co., Staff, illus. LC 90-60792. 28p. (gr. 3-6). 1991. Repr. of 1988 ed. 7.95x (1-56162-008-4) Wonder Kids.
—Chinese Children's Stories, Vol. 80: The Dwarf Minister, The Fabulous Chimera's Gift. Ching, Emily, et al, eds. Wonder Kids Publications Staff, tr. from CHI. Hwa-I Publishing Co., Staff, illus. LC 90-60807. 28p. (gr. 3-6). 1991. Repr. of 1988 ed. 7.95x (1-56162-080-7) Wonder Kids.
—Chinese Children's Stories, Vol. 81: The Emperor vs. the Rebel, The Queen & the Fire. Ching, Emily, et al, eds. Wonder Kids Publications Staff, tr. from CHI. (Illus.). 28p. (gr. 3-6). 1991. Repr. of 1988 ed. 7.95 (1-56162-081-5) Wonder Kids.
—Chinese Children's Stories, Vol. 82: The Fish Minister, The Hidden Sword. Ching, Emily, et al, eds. Wonder Kids Publications Staff, tr. from CHI. Hwa-I Publishing Co., Staff, illus. LC 90-60808. 28p. (gr. 3-6). 1991. Repr. of 1988 ed. 7.95x (1-56162-082-3) Wonder Kids.
—Chinese Children's Stories, Vol. 83: The Revenge of Chao's Orphan, Tien's Wonderful Strategies. Ching, Emily, et al, eds. Wonder Kids Publications Staff, tr. from CHI. Hwa-I Publishing Co., Staff, illus. LC 90-60808. 28p. (gr. 3-6). 1991. Repr. of 1988 ed. 7.95x (1-56162-083-1) Wonder Kids.
—Chinese Children's Stories, Vol. 84: Who Is the Real Liu Bong?, Kong Borrows the East Wind. Ching, Emily, et al, eds. Wonder Kids Publications Staff, tr. from CHI. Hwa-I Publishing Co., Staff, illus. LC 90-60808. 28p. (gr. 3-6). 1991. Repr. of 1988 ed. 7.95x (1-56162-084-X) Wonder Kids.
—Chinese Children's Stories, Vol. 85: The Battle of the Fei River, The Princess' Engagement. Ching, Emily, et al, eds. Wonder Kids Publications Staff, tr. from CHI. Hwa-I Publishing Co., Staff, illus. LC 90-60808. 28p. (gr. 3-6). 1991. Repr. of 1988 ed. 7.95x (1-56162-085-8) Wonder Kids.
—Chinese Children's Stories, Vol. 86: From Crows into Bricks, Two Treasured Swords. Ching, Emily, et al, eds. Wonder Kids Publications Staff, tr. from CHI. (Illus.). 28p. (gr. 3-6). 1991. Repr. of 1988 ed. 7.95 (1-56162-086-6) Wonder Kids.
—Chinese Children's Stories, Vol. 87: Fan Bridge & Escape Alley, The Stream of Flowers. Ching, Emily, et al, eds. Wonder Kids Publications Staff, tr. from CHI. Hwa-I Publishing Co., Staff, illus. LC 90-60809. 28p. (gr. 3-6). 1991. Repr. of 1988 ed. 7.95x (1-56162-087-4) Wonder Kids.
—Chinese Children's Stories, Vol. 88: Five Stone Goats, Six-Foot Street. Ching, Emily, et al, eds. Wonder Kids Publications Staff, tr. from CHI. Hwa-I Publishing Co., Staff, illus. LC 90-60809. 28p. (gr. 3-6). 1991. Repr. of 1988 ed. 7.95x (1-56162-088-2) Wonder Kids.
—Chinese Children's Stories, Vol. 89: Peach Blossom Cave, Mt. Lee. Ching, Emily, et al, eds. Wonder Kids Publications Staff, tr. from CHI. Hwa-I Publishing Co., Staff, illus. LC 90-60809. 28p. (gr. 3-6). 1991. Repr. of 1988 ed. 7.95x (1-56162-089-0) Wonder Kids.
—Chinese Children's Stories, Vol. 9: The Story of Rice, The Cows & the Trumpet. Ching, Emily, et al, eds. Wonder Kids Publications Staff, tr. from CHI. Hwa-I Publishing Co., Staff, illus. LC 90-60792. 28p. (gr. 3-6). 1991. Repr. of 1988 ed. 7.95x (1-56162-009-2) Wonder Kids.
—Chinese Children's Stories, Vol. 90: The Dragon Who Puts out Fires, The Golden Hairpin Well. Ching, Emily, et al, eds. Wonder Kids Publications Staff, tr. from CHI. Hwa-I Publishing Co., Staff, illus. LC 90-60809. 28p. (gr. 3-6). 1991. Repr. of 1988 ed. 7.95x (1-56162-090-4) Wonder Kids.
—Chinese Children's Stories, Vol. 91: A Little City, Beating the Devil. Ching, Emily, et al, eds. Wonder Kids Publications Staff, tr. from CHI. (Illus.). 28p. (gr. 3-6). 1991. Repr. of 1988 ed. 7.95 (1-56162-091-2) Wonder Kids.
—Chinese Children's Stories, Vol. 92: White-Rice Magic Cave, Sun-Moon Lake. Ching, Emily, et al, eds. Wonder Kids Publications Staff, tr. from CHI. Hwa-I Publishing Co., Staff, illus. LC 90-60810. 28p. (gr. 3-6). 1991. Repr. of 1988 ed. 7.95x (1-56162-092-0) Wonder Kids.
—Chinese Children's Stories, Vol. 93: Mt. Anvil & the Sword Well, Two Waters. Ching, Emily, et al, eds. Wonder Kids Publications Staff, tr. from CHI. Hwa-I Publishing Co., Staff, illus. LC 90-60810. 28p. (gr. 3-6). 1991. Repr. of 1988 ed. 7.95x (1-56162-093-9) Wonder Kids.
—Chinese Children's Stories, Vol. 94: Muddy Water Stream, Sister Lakes & Brother Trees. Ching, Emily, et al, eds. Wonder Kids Publications Staff, tr. from CHI. Hwa-I Publishing Co., Staff, illus. LC 90-60810. 28p. (gr. 3-6). 1991. Repr. of 1988 ed. 7.95x (1-56162-094-7) Wonder Kids.
—Chinese Children's Stories, Vol. 95: Half-Shield Mountain, The Adopted Daughter Lake. Ching, Emily, et al, eds. Wonder Kids Publications Staff, tr. from CHI. Hwa-I Publishing Co., Staff, illus. LC 90-60810. 28p. (gr. 3-6). 1991. Repr. of 1988 ed. 7.95x (1-56162-095-5) Wonder Kids.
—Chinese Children's Stories, Vol. 96: Tsi, the Cheat, The Mill in the Sea. Ching, Emily, et al, eds. Wonder Kids Publications Staff, tr. from CHI. (Illus.). 28p. (gr. 3-6). 1991. Repr. of 1988 ed. 7.95 (1-56162-096-3) Wonder Kids.

—Chinese Children's Stories, Vol. 97: Tiger Aunty, Ah-Long & Ah-Hwa. Ching, Emily, et al, eds. Wonder Kids Publications Staff, tr. from CHI. Hwa-I Publishing Co., Staff, illus. LC 90-60811. 28p. (gr. 3-6). 1991. Repr. of 1988 ed. 7.95x (1-56162-097-1) Wonder Kids.
—Chinese Children's Stories, Vol. 98: Ai-Yu Jello, Granny & the Fox. Ching, Emily, et al, eds. Wonder Kids Publications Staff, tr. from CHI. Hwa-I Publishing Co., Staff, illus. LC 90-60811. 28p. (gr. 3-6). 1991. Repr. of 1988 ed. 7.95x (1-56162-098-X) Wonder Kids.
—Chinese Children's Stories, Vol. 99: The Underground People, Half-Street Lai. Ching, Emily, et al, eds. Wonder Kids Publications Staff, tr. from CHI. Hwa-I Publishing Co., Staff, illus. LC 90-60811. 28p. (gr. 3-6). 1991. Repr. of 1988 ed. 7.95x (1-56162-099-8) Wonder Kids.
Hwa-I Publishing Co., Staff, jt. auth. see Wonder Kids Publications Group Staff.
Hwa-I Publishing Co., Staff, jt. auth. see Wonder Kids Publications Group Staff (USA).
Hyamm, Trina S. Award Puzzles: Saint George & the Dragon. 1991. 5.95 (0-938971-68-9) JTG Nashville.
Hyde, Dayton O. The Major, the Poacher, & the Wonderful One-Trout River. LC 84-20442. 168p. (gr. 5 up). 1985. SBE 13.95 (0-689-31107-9, Atheneum Child Bk) Macmillan Child Grp.
Hyde, Lawrence E., jt. auth. see Hyde, Margaret O.
Hyde, Margaret O. AIDS: What Does It Mean to You? rev. ed. 128p. (gr. 7 up). 1987. 12.95 (0-8027-6699-4); lib. bdg. 13.85 (0-8027-6705-2); pap. 6.95 (0-8027-6747-8) Walker & Co.
—Alcohol: Uses & Abuses. LC 87-12161. (Illus.). 96p. (gr. 6 up). 1988. lib. bdg. 16.95 (0-89490-155-9) Enslow Pubs.
—Artificial Intelligence. rev. ed. LC 85-20573. (Illus.). 128p. (gr. 6 up). 1986. lib. bdg. 17.95 (0-89490-124-9) Enslow Pubs.
—Drug Wars. (Illus.). 112p. (gr. 6 up). 1990. 11.95 (0-8027-6900-4); lib. bdg. 12.85 (0-8027-6901-2) Walker & Co.
—The Homeless: Profiling the Problem. LC 88-21195. (Illus.). 96p. (gr. 6 up). 1989. lib. bdg. 16.95 (0-89490-159-1) Enslow Pubs.
—Is This Kid "Crazy"? Understanding Unusual Behavior. LC 83-16916. 96p. (gr. 5-9). 1983. 12.00 (0-664-32707-9, Westminster) Westminster John Knox.
—Know about Abuse. 93p. 1992. 13.95 (0-8027-8176-4); PLB 14.85 (0-8027-8177-2) Walker & Co.
—Know about Drugs. rev. ed. (Illus.). (gr. 3-7). 1990. 12. 95 (0-8027-6922-5); lib. bdg. 13.85 (0-8027-6923-3) Walker & Co.
—Know about Smoking. rev. ed. Kendrick, Dennis, illus. (gr. 3-7). 1990. 12.95 (0-8027-6924-1); lib. bdg. 13.85 (0-8027-6926-8) Walker & Co.
—Peace & Friendship: Russian & American Teens Meet. (Illus.). 96p. (gr. 6 up). 1992. 14.00 (0-525-65107-1, Cobblehill Bks) Dutton Child Bks.
—Sexual Abuse: Let's Talk about It. rev. & enl. ed. Forsyth, Elizabeth H., intro. by. LC 87-133328. 112p. (gr. 5 up). 1987. 10.00 (0-664-32725-7) Westminster John Knox.
—Teen Sex. LC 88-101. 120p. (gr. 7-12). 1988. 10.00 (0-664-32726-5, Westminster) Westminster John Knox.
Hyde, Margaret O. & Forsyth, Elizabeth. AIDS: What Does It Mean to You? 3rd, rev. ed. 124p. (gr. 7 up). 1990. 13.95 (0-8027-6897-0); lib. bdg. 14.85 (0-8027-6898-9) Walker & Co.
—AIDS: What Does It Mean to You? 4th, rev. ed. LC 92-14670. 128p. 1992. 13.95 (0-8027-8202-7); lib. bdg. 14.85 (0-8027-8203-5) Walker & Co.
—Know about AIDS. rev. ed. Weber, Deborah, illus. 102p. (gr. 3-7). 1990. 12.95 (0-8027-6920-9); lib. bdg. 13.85 (0-8027-6921-7) Walker & Co.
Hyde, Margaret O. & Forsyth, Elizabeth H. Know about Gays & Lesbians. LC 92-45854. 128p. (gr. 7 up). 1994. PLB 15.90 (1-56294-298-0) Millbrook Pr.
—Suicide. 3rd, updated ed. LC 90-46872. (Illus.). 144p. (gr. 9-12). 1991. PLB 14.40 (0-531-11003-6) Watts.
—The Violent Mind. LC 91-18566. 144p. (gr. 9-12). 1991. PLB 14.40 (0-531-11060-5) Watts.
Hyde, Margaret O. & Hyde, Lawrence E. Cancer in the Young: A Sense of Hope. LC 84-27126. 96p. (gr. 9 up). 1985. 10.00 (0-664-32722-2, Westminster) Westminster John Knox.
—Meeting Death. 129p. (gr. 5 up). 1989. 14.95 (0-8027-6873-3); PLB 15.85 (0-8027-6874-1) Walker & Co.
Hyde, Mary F. & Shearer, Cynthia A. English for the Thoughtful Child. 119p. (gr. 2-6). 1990. pap. 18.95 (1-882514-07-6) Greenleaf TN.

Hyde, Sharon K. Babies Looking Book: Stimulation for the Newborn to Six Month Old Infant. (Illus.). 36p. 1992. 12.95 (0-9624349-0-6) S K Hyde. Babies tend to orient to faces more than other things around them. Using the technique of preferential looking, preferences have been ordered. For the newborn...color or pattern over grey... high contrast pattern over color...

moderate complexity over high complexity...symmetrical over random. Interest in specific stimuli decreases over time & with the number of exposures. Visual stimulation is more effective when combined with auditory & tactile stimuli. Cognitive skills can be enhanced by appropriate stimulation. Also the nature of the interaction between the parent & the baby is developed. The baby is provided a safe supportive & sensitive environment in which to see & learn. Reading to the baby allows focusing of attention, change of material as often as necessary, develops habit which remains valuable to relationship for years.
Publisher Provided Annotation.

Hyden, Tom & Anderson, Tim. Rock Climbing Is for Me. Wolfe, Bob & Wolfe, Diane, illus. LC 84-2906. 48p. (gr. 2-5). 1984. PLB 13.50 (0-8225-1147-9) Lerner Pubns.
Hyler, Nelson W. Rocks & Minerals. Shannon, Kenyon, illus. (gr. 4-6). pap. 2.95 (0-8431-4274-X) Wonder.
Hylton, Richard M., ed. see Ashworth, Dennis.
Hyman, Jane. Gumby Book of Colors. LC 86-6222. (Illus.). 32p. (ps-3). 1986. 5.95 (0-385-23454-6); PLB 5.95 (0-385-23845-2) Doubleday.
—Gumby Book of Letters. LC 86-6216. (Illus.). 32p. (ps-3). 1986. 5.95 (0-685-38408-X); PLB 5.97 (0-685-38409-8) Doubleday.
—Gumby Book of Numbers. LC 86-6193. (Illus.). 32p. (ps-3). 1986. 5.95 (0-385-23455-4); PLB 5.95 (0-385-23847-9) Doubleday.
—Gumby Book of Shapes. LC 86-6194. (Illus.). 32p. (ps-3). 1986. 5.95 (0-385-23453-8); PLB 5.95 (0-385-23848-7) Doubleday.
Hyman, Jane & Millen-Posner, Barbara. The Fitness Book: The Diet & Exercise Book. Barish, Wendy, ed. (Illus.). 192p. (Orig.). (gr. 5 up). 1984. PLB 9.49 (0-685-09179-1) S&S Trade.
Hyman, Mark. Black Shogun of Japan - Sophonisa: Wife of Two Warring Kings & Other Stories from Antiquity. Massed, Cal, illus. 120p. (Orig.). (gr. 9-12). 1989. pap. 11.00 (0-915515-01-6) The Way Pub.
Hyman, Mark, ed. see Pree, Bernice W.
Hyman, Ramona. Grandma Jackson's Poetry. Omolade, Kip, illus. 32p. 1992. 16.95 (0-685-60764-X); pap. 8.95 (0-685-60765-8) Third World.
Hyman, Trina S. How Six Found Christmas. Hyman, Trina S., illus. LC 91-70462. 32p. (ps-3). 1991. reinforced bdg. 13.95 (0-8234-0914-7) Holiday.
—A Little Alphabet. Hyman, Trina S., illus. LC 92-29692. 40p. 1993. Repr. of 1980 ed. 5.95 (0-688-12034-2); PLB 14.93 (0-688-12035-0) Morrow Jr Bks.
—Self-Portrait: Trina Schart Hyman. Hyman, Trina S., illus. LC 80-26662. 32p. (gr.-4-7). 1989. PLB 14.89 (0-06-022766-4) HarpC Child Bks.
Hyman, Trina S., ed. & illus. The Sleeping Beauty. LC 75-43769. (gr. 1 up). 1983. 15.95 (0-316-38702-9); pap. 6.95 (0-316-38708-8) Little.
Hyman, Trina S., retold by. & illu see Grimm, Jacob & Grimm, Wilhelm K.
Hyndley, Kate. The Voyage of the Beagle. Bull, Peter, illus. LC 88-28695. 32p. (gr. 5-9). 1989. PLB 11.90 (0-531-18272-X, Pub. by Bookwright Pr) Watts.
Hyndman, Donald, ed. see Frye, Keith.
Hyndman, Kathryn. Hidden Picture Fun. 112p. (ps-2). 1991. 9.95 (0-86653-614-0, GA1333) Good Apple.
Hyun, Peter, ed. Korea's Favorite Tales & Lyrics. Park, Dong-Il, illus. 124p. 1986. 12.95 (0-318-32535-7, Pub. by Seoul Intl Tourist SK) C E Tuttle.

I

Iakovina, Theodore. A Special Gift to God. Buchmiller, Therese, illus. 38p. (gr. k-4). 1986. PLB write for info. Amnos Pubns.
Iams, Jim. Competitive Volleyball Drills & Scoring Systems. 63p. (Orig.). (gr. 6-12). Date not set. pap. write for info. (1-56404-024-0) Championship Bks & Vid Prodns.
Ianni, Francis A. World War One Remembered: Paintings by Frank E. Schoonover & Gayle Porter Hoskins. LC 93-73027. 80p. (Orig.). (gr. 7-12). 1993. pap. 5.00 (0-924117-05-2) Delaware HP.
Ianni, Mary D., tr. see Dambrosio, Monica & Barbieri, Roberto.
Ianni, Mary Di see Dambrosio, Monica & Barbieri, Roberto.
Iatlia, Bob. Skiing on the Edge. LC 93-19134. 1993. 13. 99 (1-56239-231-X) Abdo & Dghtrs.
Ibbitson, John. The Wimp. 96p. 1986. pap. text ed. 4.50 (0-8219-0237-7, 35358); wkbk. 1.20 (0-8219-0238-5, 35721) EMC.

Ibbotson, Eve. Not Just a Witch. large type ed. Englander, Alice, illus. 240p. 1992. 13.95 (0-7451-1552-7, Galaxy Child Lrg Print) Chivers N Amer.

Ibsen, Henrik. The Complete Major Prose Plays of Ibsen: The Complete Major Prose Plays. Fjelde, Rolf, tr. 1152p. (gr. 9-12). 1978. pap. 16.95 (0-452-26205-4, Plume) NAL-Dutton.

—Four Major Plays. Grube, J. Incl. A Doll's House; The Wild Duck; Hedda Gabler; The Master Builder. (gr. 11up). 1966. pap. 3.50 (0-8049-0120-1, CL-120) Airmont.

—Four Major Plays, Vol. II. 408p. (gr. 9-12). 1989. pap. 3.50 (0-451-52211-7, Sig Classics) NAL-Dutton.

—Peer Gynt. Canon, R. R., intro. by. (gr. 10 up). 1967. pap. 1.50 (0-8049-0133-3, CL-133) Airmont.

Ichikawa, Satomi. Fickle Barbara. Ichikawa, Satomi, illus. LC 92-23200. 40p. (ps-3). 1993. 14.95 (0-399-22020-8, Philomel Bks) Putnam Pub Group.

—Nora's Castle. Ichikawa, Satomi, illus. LC 85-17293. 32p. (gr. 1-3). 1986. 15.95 (0-399-21302-3, Putnam) Putnam Pub Group.

—Nora's Duck. Ichikawa, Satomi, illus. 40p. (ps-3). 1991. 14.95 (0-399-21805-X, Philomel) Putnam Pub Group.

—Nora's Roses. (Illus.). 32p. (ps up). 1993. PLB 14.95 (0-399-21968-4, Philomel Bks) Putnam Pub Group.

—Nora's Stars. Ichikawa, Satomi, illus. 32p. (ps-3). 1989. 14.95 (0-399-21616-2, Philomel Bks) Putnam Pub Group.

—Nora's Stars. (Illus.). 32p. (ps up). 1992. pap. 5.95 (0-399-21887-4, Philomel Bks) Putnam Pub Group.

—Nora's Surprise. LC 92-39308. 1994. write for info. (0-399-22535-8, Philomel Bks) Putnam Pub Group.

Ichikawa, Satomi & Laird, Elizabeth. Rosy's Garden: A Child's Keepsake of Flowers. (Illus.). 48p. 1990. 16.95 (0-399-21881-5, Philomel Bks) Putnam Pub Group.

Ideals Childrens Book Editors. Funny Faces. (Illus.). 16p. (ps-3). 1989. pap. 2.95 (0-8249-8366-1, Ideals Child) Hambleton-Hill.

—Funny Monsters. (Illus.). 16p. (ps-3). 1989. pap. 2.95 (0-8249-8367-X, Ideals Child) Hambleton-Hill.

Ideals Staff. Jolly Old Santa Claus. Hinke, George, illus. 24p. (gr. k-6). 1985. pap. 2.95 (0-89542-448-7, Ideals Child) Hambleton-Hill.

Idore. Space Needle Journey to Mars. Trebor Eugol, illus. 38p. (gr. k-3). 1991. pap. 4.95 (0-926060-07-4) Anschell Pub Co.

—Space Needle: Journey to Mars. 2nd ed. Eugol, Trebor, illus. 37p. (Orig.). (ps-3). 1991. pap. 4.95 (0-926060-08-2) Anschell Pub Co.

Ife, Elaine & Sutton, Rosalind. Now You Can Read Stories from the Bible. (Illus.). 208p. (gr. 2-4). 1984. 9.99 (0-8407-5396-9) Nelson.

Iglesias, Jose L., jt. auth. see Andujar, Maria D.

Ignatowicz, Nina, tr. see Michels, Tilde.

Ignatowicz, Nina, tr. see Uspenski, Eduard.

Ignoffo, Matthew. Coping with Your Inner Critic. Rosen, Ruth, ed. (gr. 7-12). 1989. PLB 13.95 (0-8239-1001-6) Rosen Group.

Iguchi, Bunshu. The Tiny Sheep. Iguchi, Bunshu, illus. 24p. (ps-3). 1986. 10.00 (0-8170-1108-0) Judson.

Igus, Toyomi. When I Was Little. Bond, Higgins, illus. LC 92-72066. 32p. (Orig.). (gr. 1 up). 1992. 14.95 (0-940975-32-7); pap. 6.95 (0-940975-33-5) Just Us Bks.

Igus, Toyomi, et al. Book of Black Heroes, Vol. 2: Great Women in the Struggle. LC 91-90098. 112p. (gr. 4-8). 1991. lib. bdg. 17.95 (0-940975-27-0); pap. 10.95 (0-940975-26-2) Just Us Bks.

Ikeda, Daisaku. The Cherry Tree. McCaughrean, Geraldine, tr. Wildsmith, Brian, illus. LC 91-22148. 32p. (ps-3). 1992. 15.00 (0-679-82669-6); PLB 15.99 (0-679-92669-0) Knopf Bks Yng Read.

—Over the Deep Blue Sea. McCaughrean, Geraldine, tr. Wildsmith, Brian, illus. LC 92-22557. (Illus.). 32p. (ps-3). 1993. 15.00 (0-679-84184-9); PLB 15.99 (0-679-94184-3) Knopf Bks Yng Read.

—The Princess & the Moon. McCaughrean, Geraldine, tr. from JPN. Wildsmith, Brian, illus. LC 92-148. 32p. (ps-3). 1992. 15.00 (0-679-83620-9); PLB 15.99 (0-679-93620-3) Knopf Bks Yng Read.

—The Snow Country Prince. McCaughrean, Geraldine, tr. Wildsmith, Brian, illus. LC 90-24908. 32p. (ps-3). 1991. 15.00 (0-679-81965-7); lib. bdg. 15.99 (0-679-91965-1) Knopf Bks Yng Read.

Ikemoto, Glenn Y. The Kaua'i Guide to Freshwater Sport Fishing. Boynton, David, photos by. (Illus.). 64p. (Orig.). 1989. pap. 2.50 (0-942255-07-0, G6) Magic Fishes Pr.

Ikhlef, Anne. Busy Little Squirrel. Laffolay, Anne, illus. 10p. (ps). 1991. bds. 4.99 (0-679-81612-7) Random Bks Yng Read.

—Fuzzy Little Bear. Laffolay, Anne, illus. 10p. (ps). 1991. bds. 4.99 (0-679-81613-5) Random Bks Yng Read.

—Happy Little Dolphin. Laffolay, Anne, illus. 10p. (ps). 1991. bds. 4.99 (0-679-81615-1) Random Bks Yng Read.

—Woolly Little Lamb. Laffolay, Anne, illus. 10p. (ps). 1991. bds. 4.99 (0-679-81614-3) Random Bks Yng Read.

Ikuhara, Yoshiyuki. Children of the World: Bolivia. LC 87-42616. (Illus.). (gr. 5-6). 1988. PLB 19.93 (1-55532-321-9) Gareth Stevens Inc.

—Children of the World: Brazil. LC 87-42579. (Illus.). 64p. (gr. 5-6). 1987. PLB 19.93 (1-55532-221-2) Gareth Stevens Inc.

—Children of the World: Mexico. LC 86-42800. (Illus.). 64p. (gr. 5-6). 1987. PLB 19.93 (1-55532-161-5) Gareth Stevens Inc.

IlgenFritz, Elizabeth. Anne Hutchinson. Horner, Matina, intro. by. (Illus.). 112p. (gr. 5 up). 1991. lib. bdg. 17.95 (1-55546-660-5) Chelsea Hse.

Ille, Dorothy B. The Banker's Place. LC 92-63253. 82p. (gr. 6-11). 1993. 7.95 (1-55523-591-3) Winston-Derek.

Illingworth, Lynn, jt. auth. see Vowles, Andrew.

Illsley, Linda. Cheese. (Illus.). 32p. (gr. 1-4). 1991. PLB 14.95 (0-87614-654-X) Carolrhoda Bks.

Ilyon. The Birth of Tangun: The Legend of Korea's First King. Adams, Edward B., tr. from KOR. Yoon, Hak-Jung, illus. 28p. (gr. 5). 1986. 7.50 (0-685-17153-1, Pub. by Seoul Intl Tourist SK) C E Tuttle.

—The Death of Echadon: How Buddhism Came to Silla. Adams, Edward B., tr. Yoon, Hak-Jung, illus. 28p. (gr. 5). 1986. 7.50 (0-685-17155-8, Pub. by Seoul Intl Tourist SK) C E Tuttle.

—King Munmu of Silla: A Korean Ruler Who United His Country. Adams, Edward B., tr. Yoon, Hak-Jung, illus. 28p. (gr. 5). 1986. 7.50 (0-685-17157-4, Pub. by Seoul Intl Tourist SK) C E Tuttle.

—The Three Good Events. Adams, Edward B., tr. from KOR. Yoon, Hak-Jung, illus. 28p. (gr. 5). 1986. 7.50 (0-685-17156-6, Pub. by Seoul Intl Tourist SK) C E Tuttle.

Imershein, Betsy. Animal Doctor. Imershein, Betsy, illus. LC 87-20266. 32p. (gr. 1-5). 1988. (J Messner); lib. bdg. 4.95 (0-671-65862-X) S&S Trade.

—Farmer. Steltenpohl, Jane, ed. (Illus.). 32p. (gr. k-3). 1990. lib. bdg. 9.98 (0-671-68185-0, J Messner) S&S Trade.

—Finding Red Finding Yellow. Imershein, Betsy, photos by. LC 88-35808. (Illus.). 32p. (ps). 1989. 10.95 (0-15-200453-X, Gulliver Bks) HarBrace.

—The Work People Do, 3 bks. (Illus.). 1990. Set, 32p. ea. lib. bdg. 29.94 (0-671-94097-X, J Messner) Set, 32p. ea. pap. 14.85 (0-671-94098-8) S&S Trade.

Immel, Mary B. No Longer Sings the Brown Thrush. 208p. (Orig.). (gr. 4-8). 1988. pap. 7.99 (0-8272-2509-1) Chalice Pr.

Impey, Rose. The Ankle Grabber. (ps-3). 1991. pap. 3.25 (0-440-40503-3) Dell.

—Creepies Jumble Joan. (ps-3). 1991. pap. 3.25 (0-440-40510-6, YB) Dell.

—Creepies Scare Yourself to Sleep. (ps-3). 1991. pap. 3.25 (0-440-40509-2, YB) Dell.

—Desperate for a Dog. Knox, Jolyne, illus. 64p. (gr. 2-5). 1991. pap. 3.50 (0-14-034798-4, Puffin) Puffin Bks.

—The Flat Man. (ps-3). 1991. pap. 3.25 (0-440-40504-1) Dell.

—Joe's Cafe. (ps-3). 1991. 14.95 (0-316-41777-7) Little.

—Letter to Santa Claus. (ps-3). 1991. pap. 3.99 (0-440-40544-0, YB) Dell.

—No-Name Dog. LC 90-30143. (Illus.). 64p. (gr. 2-5). 1990. 10.95 (0-525-44592-7, DCB) Dutton Child Bks.

—No-Name Dog. Knox, Jolyne, illus. LC 92-18957. 64p. (gr. 2-5). 1992. pap. 3.99 (0-14-036164-2) Puffin Bks.

—Who's a Bright Girl? Amstutz, Andre, illus. 42p. (gr. 2-4). 1989. 3.95 (0-8120-6144-6) Barron.

Impey, Rose, as told by. Read Me a Fairy Tale: A Child's Book of Classic Fairy Tales. Beck, Ian, illus. LC 92-41949. (gr. k up). 1993. 14.95 (0-590-49431-7) Scholastic Inc.

Inaba, Darryl S. & Cohen, William E. Uppers, Downers & All Arounders. (Illus.). 260p. 1989. 28.95 (0-926544-00-4) CNS Prods.

Inada, Lawson F., jt. auth. see Zaslow, David B.

Inchaustegui, Sixto, tr. see Kuzmier, Kerrie & McCann, Jennifer.

Information Please Staff. Information Please Student Almanac, 1993: Fast Facts for Students. 96p. (gr. 9-12). 1992. pap. 2.80 (0-395-56006-3) HM.

Ingber, Bonnie V., ed. see Adoff, Arnold.

Ingber, Bonnie V., ed. see Berry, James.

Ingber, Bonnie V., intro. by see Buffett, Jimmy & Buffett, Savannah J.

Ingber, Bonnie V., ed. see Yolen, Jane.

Ingerson, Martha, jt. auth. see Warren, Betsy.

Ingle, Annie. The Bunnies' Ball. Bratun, Katy, illus. 32p. (ps-1). 1993. pap. 2.50 (0-685-68188-2) Random Bks Yng Read.

—The Bunnies' Ball. Bratun, Katy, illus. LC 93-8536. 1994. write for info.; PLB write for info. Random Bks Yng Read.

—Don't Wake the Animals. Barrett, Peter, illus. LC 91-67720. 14p. (ps-k). 1992. bds. 3.99 (0-679-83433-8) Random Bks Yng Read.

—Ernie's Little Toolbox: A Sesame Street Book. Cooke, Tom, illus. LC 90-61312. 22p. (ps). 1991. bds. 2.95 (0-679-80905-8) Random Bks Yng Read.

—Glow-in-the-Dark Dinosaur Skeletons. Barrett, Peter, illus. LC 92-18176. 16p. (ps-1). 1993. pap. 4.99 (0-679-84366-3) Random Bks Yng Read.

—The Glow-in-the-Dark Planetarium Book. Enik, Ted, illus. LC 92-29932. 16p. (Orig.). (ps-1). 1993. pap. 4.99 (0-679-84367-1) Random Bks Yng Read.

—The Monster That Glowed in the Dark. Petach, Heidi, illus. LC 92-30144. 16p. (ps-1). 1993. pap. 4.99 (0-679-84194-6) Random Bks Yng Read.

—The Smallest Elf. Smath, Jerry, illus. LC 90-30388. 32p. (Orig.). (ps-1). 1990. pap. 2.25 (0-679-80846-9) Random Bks Yng Read.

—The Smallest Elf's Big Surprise. Smath, Jerry, illus. LC 91-67670. 22p. (ps). 1992. bds. 2.95 (0-679-83380-3) Random Bks Yng Read.

—Zoo Animals. LC 91-66561. (Illus.). 28p. (ps). 1992. 2.95 (0-679-83070-7) Random Bks Yng Read.

Ingle, Annie, jt. auth. see Walley, Dean.

Ingle, Annie, adapted by. Robin Hood. reissued ed. D'Andrea, Domenick, illus. LC 90-23078. 96p. (Orig.). (gr. 2-6). 1993. pap. 2.99 (0-679-81045-5) Random Bks Yng Read.

Ingle, Lester, jt. auth. see Zim, Herbert S.

Ingle, Valorie L. The Powers of Patrick: The Power of Alone. (Illus.). (gr. 1-4). 1994. write for info. (1-883863-02-3) Legend Prods.

—The Powers of Patrick: The Power of Forgiving. (gr. 1-4). 1994. write for info. (1-883863-04-X) Legend Prods.

—The Powers of Patrick: The Power of Giving. (gr. 1-4). 1993. PLB write for info. (1-883863-01-5) Legend Prods.

—The Powers of Patrick: The Power of Helping. (Illus.). (gr. 1-4). 1994. write for info. (1-883863-10-4) Legend Prods.

—The Powers of Patrick: The Power of Honesty. (gr. 1-4). 1993. pap. write for info. (1-883863-00-7) Legend Prods.

—The Powers of Patrick: The Power of Hope. (Illus.). (gr. 1-4). 1994. write for info. (1-883863-05-8) Legend Prods.

—The Powers of Patrick: The Power of Imagination. (Illus.). (gr. 1-4). 1994. write for info. (1-883863-09-0) Legend Prods.

—The Powers of Patrick: The Power of Joy. (Illus.). (gr. 1-4). 1994. write for info. (1-883863-07-4) Legend Prods.

—The Powers of Patrick: The Power of Love. (Illus.). (gr. 1-4). 1994. write for info. (1-883863-11-2) Legend Prods.

—The Powers of Patrick: The Power of Patience & Understanding. (Illus.). (gr. 1-4). 1994. write for info. (1-883863-08-2) Legend Prods.

—The Powers of Patrick: The Power of Sharing. (Illus.). (gr. 1-4). 1994. write for info. (1-883863-06-6) Legend Prods.

—The Powers of Patrick: The Power of Sympathy. (Illus.). (gr. 1-4). 1994. write for info. (1-883863-03-1) Legend Prods.

Inglehart, Donna W. Breaking the Ring. (gr. 4-7). 1991. 13.95 (0-316-41867-6) Little.

Inglis, Jane. Protein. LC 92-26759. 1993. PLB 14.95 (0-87614-780-5); pap. 5.95 (0-87614-607-8) Carolrhoda Bks.

Inglis, L., jt. auth. see Gee, R.

Inglis, L., jt. auth. see Watts, L.

Ingoglia, Gina. Airplanes & Things That Fly. (Illus.). 24p. (ps-k). 1989. pap. write for info. (0-307-11807-X, Pub. by Golden Bks) Western Pub.

—Art Class. LC 91-58786. (Illus.). 48p. (gr. k-3). 1992. 9.95 (1-56282-047-8); PLB 9.89 (1-56282-227-6) Disney Pr.

—Awesome Animals. MacCombie, Turi, illus. 48p. (gr. 2-4). 1992. pap. write for info. (0-307-11472-4, 11472, Golden Pr) Western Pub.

—The Big Book of Real Airplanes. Guzzi, George, illus. (gr. 1-4). 1987. 7.95 (0-448-19179-2, G&D) Putnam Pub Group.

—The Friendly Duck. (Illus.). 24p. (ps-k). 1989. pap. write for info. (0-307-10069-3, Pub. by Golden Bks) Western Pub.

—Johnny Appleseed & the Planting of the West. LC 92-52978. (Illus.). 80p. (gr. 1-4). 1992. PLB 12.89 (1-56282-259-4); pap. 2.95 (1-56282-258-6) Disney Pr.

—Let's Look at Dinosaurs. (Illus.). 16p. (ps-1). 1991. bds. 11.95 (0-448-40086-3, G&D) Putnam Pub Group.

—Look Inside the Earth. (Illus.). 16p. (ps-1). 1991. bds. 11.95 (0-448-40087-1, G&D) Putnam Pub Group.

—Nature Babies. (Illus.). 24p. (ps-k). 1989. pap. write for info. (0-307-11716-2, Pub. by Golden Bks) Western Pub.

—Sacajawea & the Journey to the Pacific. LC 92-52977. (Illus.). 80p. (gr. 1-4). 1992. PLB 12.89 (1-56282-263-2); pap. 2.95 (1-56282-262-4) Disney Pr.

—Sylvester & Tweety: What a Mess. (ps-3). 1990. write for info. (0-307-11595-X) Western Pub.

—Tecumseh: One Nation for His People. Shaw, Charlie & Bill Smith Studios Staff, illus. LC 92-56162. 80p. (Orig.). (gr. 1-4). 1993. PLB 12.89 (1-56282-490-2); pap. 2.95 (1-56282-489-9) Disney Pr.

—Those Mysterious Dinosaurs. (Illus.). 24p. (ps-k). 1989. pap. write for info. (0-307-11747-2, Pub. by Golden Bks) Western Pub.

—Three Bears. (ps-3). 1990. write for info. (0-307-11594-1) Western Pub.

—Tweety & Sylvester. (ps-3). 1990. write for info. (0-307-10034-0) Western Pub.

—Walt Disney's Pinocchio & the Whale. Ortiz, Phil & Wakeman, Diana, illus. 16p. (gr. 2-6). 1992. write for info. (0-307-11583-6, 11583, Golden Pr) Western Pub.

—Walt Disney's Pinocchio & the Whale. Ortiz, Phil & Wakeman, Diana, illus. 32p. (ps-1). 1993. pap. 3.25 (0-307-15975-2, 15975, Golden Pr) Western Pub.

Ingoglia, Gina & Patrick, Denice. Look Inside a Tree - Learning Book. LC 88-82991. (Illus.). (ps-1). 1989. 11.95 (0-448-21032-0, Platt & Munk Pubs) Putnam Pub Group.

Ingoglia, Gina, adapted by. Walt Disney's Pinocchio. LC 91-73974. (Illus.). 64p. (Orig.). (gr. 2-6). 1992. pap. 2.95 (0-307-15626-5) Disney Pr.

Ingpen, Robert. The Age of Acorns. Ingpen, Robert, illus. LC 90-433. 28p. (gr. k-3). 1990. PLB 14.95 (0-87226-436-X, Bedrick Blackie) P Bedrick Bks.

—The Idle Bear. Ingpen, Robert, illus. LC 87-1187. 32p. (gr. k-3). 1987. PLB 12.95 (0-87226-159-X, Bedrick Blackie) P Bedrick Bks.
—The Miniature Idle Bear. LC 87-1187. (Illus.). 28p. (gr. k-3). 1989. 4.95 (0-87226-418-1, Bedrick Blackie) P Bedrick Bks.
Ingraham, Erick, adapted by. & illu see MacDonald, George.
Ingram, Anne & O'Donnell, Peggy. Family Car Book. Graham, Bob, illus. 48p. (gr. 4 up). 1992. pap. 6.95 (0-920775-43-8, Pub. by Greey dePencier CN) Firefly Bks Ltd.
—Rainy Day Book. Peters, Shirley, illus. 48p. (gr. 3 up). 1992. pap. 6.95 (0-920775-44-6, Pub. by Greey dePencier CN) Firefly Bks Ltd.
Ingram, Cecil B. Ulsterheart: An Ancient Irish Habitation. LC 88-72366. (Illus.). 350p. (gr. 12). 1988. 60.00x (0-9621544-0-7) All Ireland Inc.
Ingram, Jay. Amazing Investigations: Twins. Chan, Harvey, illus. 48p. (gr. 3 up). 1989. pap. 12.95 (0-671-66263-5) S&S Trade.
—Real Live Science: Top Scientists Present Amazing Activities Any Kid Can Do. Ingram, Jay, illus. 48p. (gr. 4 up). 1992. text ed. 16.95 (1-895688-00-0, Pub. by Greey de Pencier CN); pap. 8.95 (0-920775-87-X, Pub. by Greey de Pencier CN) Firefly Bks Ltd.
Ingram, Margaret L. Junior Capers. Hamilton, Sharon L., illus. 28p. (Orig.). (gr. 1-6). 1990. pap. text ed. 5.95 (0-9624721-0-7) Imagery Pubns.
Ingram, Robert D. Who Taught Frogs to Hop? A Child's Book about God. Goldsborough, June, illus. LC 89-82552. 32p. (ps). 1990. pap. 5.99 (0-8066-2457-4, 9-2457) Augsburg Fortress.
Ingram, William R., ed. see Graham, Billy, et al.
Ingrid, Charles. Lasertown Blues. (gr. 9-12). 1988. pap. 3.50 (0-88677-260-5) DAW Bks.
—Solar Kill. (gr. 9-12). 1987. pap. 3.50 (0-88677-209-5) DAW Bks.
Inkiow, Dimiter. Me & Clara & Casimir the Cat. Reiner, Walter & Reiner, Traudl, illus. LC 78-31316. (gr. 1-4). 1979. 2.95 (0-394-84124-7) Pantheon.
Inkpen, M. Kipper's Toybox. 1992. write for info. (0-15-200501-3, Gulliver Bks) HarBrace.
Inkpen, Mich, jt. auth. see Butterworth, Nick.
Inkpen, Mick. Anything Cuddly Will Do! (Illus.). 12p. (gr. 4-7). 1993. 4.99 (1-878685-71-6, Bedrock Press) Turner Pub GA.
—Billy's Beetle. (ps-3). 1992. 13.95 (0-15-200427-0, HB Juv Bks) HarBrace.
—The Blue Balloon. (Illus.). (ps-3). 1990. 12.95 (0-316-41886-2) Little.
—Crocodile! (Illus.). (gr. 4-7). 1993. 4.99 (1-878685-73-2, Bedrock Press) Turner Pub GA.
—Gumboot's Chocolatey Day. 1991. pap. 11.95 (0-385-41489-7) Doubleday.
—If I Had a Pig. Inkpen, Mick, illus. (ps). 1988. 7.95 (0-316-41887-0) Little.
—If I Had a Pig. (ps). 1992. pap. 3.99 (0-440-40609-9, Pub. by Yearling Classics) Dell.
—If I Had a Sheep. Inkpen, Mick, illus. (ps). 1988. 7.95 (0-316-41888-9) Little.
—If I Had a Sheep. (ps). 1992. pap. 3.99 (0-440-40612-9, Pub. by Yearling Classics) Dell.
—Kipper. (ps-3). 1992. 14.95 (0-316-41883-8) Little.
—Kipper's Birthday. LC 92-28202. 1993. PLB write for info. (0-15-200503-X) HarBrace.
—Penguin Small. (ps-3). 1993. pap. 14.95 (0-15-200567-6) HarBrace.
—This Troll That Troll. (Illus.). (gr. 4-7). 1993. 4.99 (1-878685-70-8, Bedrock Press) Turner Pub GA.
—Threadbear. (Illus.). (ps-3). 1991. 14.95 (0-316-41884-6) Little.
—The Very Good Dinosaur. (Illus.). 12p. (gr. 4-7). 1993. 4.99 (1-878685-72-4, Bedrock Press) Turner Pub GA.
Inkpen, Mick, jt. auth. see Butterworth, Nick.
Innes, Dick. I Hate Witnessing. 150p. 1991. 5.99 (0-8307-1005-1, S181319); leader's guide 14.99 (0-8307-1544-4, SH135) Regal.
Innis, Pauline. Ernestine or the Pig in the Potting Shed. Weinberger, Jane, ed. Evans, Timothy, illus. 128p. 1992. pap. 9.95 (0-932433-97-9) Windswept Hse.
Innocenti, Roberto. Rose Blanche. LC 90-49981. (Illus.). 32p. 1991. 15.95 (1-55670-207-8) Stewart Tabori & Chang.
Inoue, Keiko. Hello in Japanese, Vol. 1: Workbook. (Illus.). 122p. (Orig.). (gr. 9-12). 1990. pap. 13.50 (0-89346-341-8) Heian Intl.
—Hello in Japanese, Vol. 2: Workbook. (Illus.). 106p. (Orig.). (gr. 9-12). 1991. pap. 13.50 (0-89346-348-5) Heian Intl.
Insel, Eunice & Edson, Ann. Developing Critical Thinking, Bk. 1. (gr. 3-4). 1983. wkbk. 4.25 (1-55737-651-4) Ed Activities.
—Developing Critical Thinking, Bk. 2. (gr. 5-6). 1983. wkbk. 4.25 (1-55737-652-2) Ed Activities.
—Ready-Go-Begin-To-Learn. (Illus.). (ps-1). 1980. wkbk. 4.25 (0-89525-098-5) Ed Activities.
Insel, Eunice, jt. auth. see Edson, Ann.
Insley, Jane, jt. auth. see Cooper, Chris.
Institute for Women's Policy Research, The Young Women's Project Staff. The Young Women's Handbook: Beyond Surviving in the 90s. Moritz, Nadia, intro. by. 675p. (Orig.). (gr. 10 up). 1991. pap. 30.00 (1-878428-05-5) Inst Womens Policy Rsch.
Institute of Public Affairs Staff, ed. see Carter, Brian.
Institute of Texan Cultures Staff, ed. see Martinello, Marian L. & Nesmith, Samuel P.

International Bible Society Staff, intro. by. The Holy Bible: New International Version. (gr. 7 up). 1990. pap. write for info. (1-56320-001-5) Intl Bible Soc.
Intervisional Communications Staff. Viking Circus Block Books: Circus Parade Zoo-A Book in-a-Box with a Performing Picture, 3 vols. LC 83-80225. (Illus.). (gr. 1-5). 1983. Set. 10.95 (0-685-42583-5) Viking Child Bks.
Intervisual Staff. Golf-o-Rama. (Illus.). 8p. 1994. 17.95 (1-56282-635-2) Hyprn Child.
Intia, Perla S. The Magic Seed. Enriquez, Jesse B., illus. 20p. (Orig.). (gr. k-2). 1989. pap. 3.50x (971-10-0327-9, Pub. by New Day Pub PI) Cellar.
Ionesco, Eugene. Conte..., 1: Contes Numero 1 (Pour Enfants de Moins de Trois Ans) (FRE., Illus.). 26p. 1976. 11.95 (0-8288-9826-X, F105951) Fr & Eur.
—Conte..., 2: Contes Numero 2 (Pour Enfants de Moins de Trois Ans) (FRE., Illus.). 18p. 1976. 11.95 (0-8288-9823-5, F105910) Fr & Eur.
—Conte..., 3: Contes Numero 3 (Pour Enfants de Moins de Trois Ans) (FRE., Illus.). 30p. 1976. 11.95 (0-8288-9827-8, F105960) Fr & Eur.
—Conte..., 4: Contes Numero 4 (Pour Enfants de Moins de Trois Ans) (FRE., Illus.). 24p. 1976. 11.95 (0-8288-9829-4, F105990) Fr & Eur.
Iosa, Ann, jt. auth. see Park, Margaret.
Iozzi, Louis A. Space Encounters. rev. ed. (gr. 6-9). 1991. tchr's. ed. 45.00 (0-944584-30-6) Sopris.
Iozzi, Louis A. & Bastardo, Peter J. Decisions for Today & Tomorrow. (gr. 9-12). 1990. tchr's. ed. 60.00 (0-944584-22-5) Sopris.
Ipcar, Dahlov. The Lobsterman. (Illus.). (ps-1). 1977. pap. 7.95 (0-89272-032-8) Down East.
—My Wonderful Christmas Tree. 32p. (gr. 2-5). 1985. pap. 6.95 (0-930096-85-1) G Gannett.
Ippolito, Donna, ed. see Dowd, Tom & Kubasik, Chris.
Ippolito, Donna, ed. see Findley, Nigel D.
Ippolito, Donna, ed. see McGregor, Philip.
Ippolito, Donna, ed. see Nystul, Mike & Smith, Lester.
Ippolito, Donna, ed. see Rice, Peter L.
Ippolito, Donna, ed. see Sargent, Carl.
Ipsen, D. C. Archimedes: Greatest Scientist of the Ancient World. LC 88-31006. (Illus.). 64p. (gr. 6 up). 1988. lib. bdg. 15.95 (0-89490-161-3) Enslow Pubs.
Iqbal, Muhammad. Guiding Crescent. Aziz, Tariq, tr. 50p. (Orig.). (gr. 6-12). 1985. pap. 3.00 (1-56744-285-4) Kazi Pubns.
—Way of the Muslim. (gr. 3-7). 1983. pap. 7.95 (0-7175-0632-0) Dufour.
Irani, Meheru. Nursery Rhymes in Meher's Time. White, Susan, illus. (gr. 3 up). 1977. pap. text ed. 5.95 (0-913078-29-8) Sheriar Pr.
Irbinskas, Heather. How the Jackrabbit Got His Very Long Ears. Spengler, Ken, illus. 32p. (gr. k up). 1994. 14.95 (0-87358-566-6) Northland AZ.
Irby, Beverly J., jt. auth. see Mathes, Patricia G.
Ireland, Karin. Albert Einstein. (Illus.). 144p. (gr. 5-9). 1989. PLB 13.98 (0-382-09523-5) Silver Burdett Pr.
Ireland, Shep. Merry Christmas. Ireland, Shep, illus. 1992. 4.75 (0-8378-3799-5) Gibson.
—Wesley & Wendell: At Home. Ireland, Shep, illus. 40p. (gr. 1). 1991. lib. bdg. 4.75 (0-8378-0330-6) Gibson.
—Wesley & Wendell: Happy Birthday. Ireland, Shep, illus. 40p. (gr. 1). 1991. lib. bdg. 4.75 (0-8378-0333-0) Gibson.
—Wesley & Wendell: In the Garden. Ireland, Shep, illus. 40p. (gr. 1). 1991. lib. bdg. 4.75 (0-8378-0331-4) Gibson.
—Wesley & Wendell: Vacation. Ireland, Shep, illus. 40p. (gr. 1). 1991. lib. bdg. 4.75 (0-8378-0332-2) Gibson.
Ireland, Vicky. The Town Mouse & the Country Mouse. 38p. (Orig.). (gr. k-3). 1987. pap. 4.50 playscript (0-87602-266-2) Anchorage.
Irland, Nancy B. Very Strange Story of Blaze the Cat. (gr. 4-7). 1991. pap. 7.95 (0-8163-1046-7) Pacific Pr Pub Assn.
Iroaganachi, John, jt. auth. see Achebe, Chinua.
IRosoff, ed. see Corwin, Judith H.
Irsch, Ed. As It Was Told: A Play for Christmas. 16p. (Orig.). (gr. k-4). 1980. pap. text ed. 3.95 (0-89536-439-5, 0146) CSS OH.
Irvin, Nathanial, Jr., ed. see Young, Tommy S.
Irvine, Georgeanne. Let's Visit a Super Zoo. Fuller, Tim W., illus. LC 89-34370. 32p. (gr. 2-4). 1990. lib. bdg. 10.79 (0-8167-1745-1); pap. text ed. 2.95 (0-8167-1746-X) Troll Assocs.
—Protecting Endangered Species. (ps-6). 1993. pap. 5.95 (0-671-79616-X, S&S BFYR) S&S Trade.
—Protecting Endangered Species at the San Diego Zoo. (Illus.). 48p. (gr. 3-7). 1990. pap. 14.95 jacketed (0-671-68776-X, S&S BFYR) S&S Trade.
—Raising Gordy the Gorilla. (ps-6). 1993. pap. 5.95 (0-671-79615-1, S&S BFYR) S&S Trade.
Irvine, Georgeanne, jt. auth. see McKeever, Michael.
Irvine, Joan. Build It with Boxes. Hendry, Linda, illus. LC 91-45589. 96p. (gr. 3 up). 1993. 14.00 (0-688-12081-4); PLB 13.93 (0-688-11524-1) Morrow Jr Bks.
—Build It with Boxes. LC 91-45589. 1993. pap. 6.95 (0-688-11525-X, Pub. by Beech Tree Bks) Morrow.
—How to Make Super Pop-ups. Hendry, Linda, illus. LC 92-26137. 96p. (gr. 3 up). 1992. 14.00 (0-688-10690-0) Morrow Jr Bks.
—How to Make Super Pop-Ups. (ps-3). 1992. pap. 6.95 (0-688-11521-7, Pub. by Beech Tree Bks) Morrow.
—How to Make Super Pop-Ups. (ps-3). 1992. 13.93 (0-688-10691-9) Morrow Jr Bks.

Irvine, John. Treasury of Irish Saints. (gr. 1 up). 1984. 9.95 (0-85105-902-3, Pub. by Colin Smythe Ltd Britain) Dufour.
Irving, David. The Trail of the Fox. (gr. 7 up). 1978. pap. 5.95 (0-380-40022-7) Avon.
Irving, Lynn. Pocketful of Puppets: Poems for Church School. Keller, Merily H., ed. Renfro, Nancy, illus. 48p. (Orig.). (ps-3). 1982. pap. 9.95 (0-931044-05-7) Renfro Studios.
Irving, N. The Biggest. (Illus.). 24p. (ps-2). 1988. 3.95 (0-7460-0159-2) EDC.
—Fastest, The. (Illus.). 24p. (gr. 1-3). 1988. 3.95 (0-7460-0161-4) EDC.
—Learn French. (Illus.). 64p. (gr. 5 up). 1992. PLB 13.96 (0-88110-596-1); pap. 7.95 (0-7460-0532-6) EDC.
—Learn French Language Pack. (Illus.). 64p. (gr. 7 up). 1993. pap. 16.95 incl. tape (0-7460-1439-2, Usborne) EDC.
—Learn German. (Illus.). 64p. (gr. 5 up). 1992. PLB 13.96 (0-88110-597-X); pap. 7.95 (0-7460-0534-2) EDC.
—Learn German Language Pack. (Illus.). 64p. (gr. 7 up). 1993. pap. 16.95 incl. tape (0-7460-1440-6, Usborne) EDC.
—Learn Spanish. (Illus.). 64p. (gr. 6 up). 1993. PLB 13.96 (0-88110-598-8); pap. 7.95 (0-7460-0536-9) EDC.
Irving, N., jt. auth. see Colvin, L.
Irving, Pierre, ed. see Irving, Washington.
Irving, Washington. The Legend of Sleepy Hollow. Van Nutt, Robert, adapted by. & illus. LC 88-33375. 32p. (ps up). 1991. PLB pap. 14.95 (0-88708-088-X, Rabbit Ears); incl. cassette 19.95 (0-88708-089-8, Rabbit Ears) Picture Bk Studio.
—Legend of Sleepy Hollow. Hitchner, Earle, adapted by. Van Buuren, John, illus. SR 89-33942. 48p. (gr. 3-6). 1990. PLB 12.89 (0-8167-1869-5); pap. text ed. 3.95 (0-8167-1870-9) Troll Assocs.
—The Legend of Sleepy Hollow. facsimile ed. Rackham, Arthur, illus. Glassman, Peter, afterword by. LC 90-591. (Illus.). 112p. (ps up). 1990. Repr. of 1928 ed. 16.95 (0-688-05276-2) Morrow Jr Bks.
—Legend of Sleepy Hollow. 1991. pap. 2.50 (0-8125-0475-5) Tor Bks.
—The Legend of Sleepy Hollow. 1991. pap. 7.00 (0-385-41929-5) Doubleday.
—The Legend of Sleepy Hollow. Flint, Russ, illus. LC 91-72020. 32p. (gr. k-3). 1991. 12.95 (0-8249-8162-6, Ideals Child) (0-685-48861-6) Hambleton-Hill.
—The Legend of Sleepy Hollow. Garland, Michael, illus. 64p. 1992. PLB 15.95 (1-56397-027-9) Boyds Mills Pr.
—The Legend of Sleepy Hollow. Flint, Russ, illus. 32p. (gr. k-4). 1992. pap. 4.95 (0-8249-8574-5, Ideals Child) Hambleton-Hill.
—The Legend of Sleepy Hollow. Close, Glenn, read by. Van Nutt, Robert, illus. Story, Tim, contrib. by. (Illus.). 32p. (ps up). 1992. pap. write for info. slipcase pkg., incl. cassette (0-307-14326-0, 14326, Golden Pr) Western Pub.
—The Legend of Sleepy Hollow. 69p. 1992. text ed. 5.25 (1-56956-119-2) W A T Braille.
—The Legend of Sleepy Hollow. Moses, Will, as told by. LC 93-21910. (Illus.). Date not set. write for info. (0-399-22687-7, Philomel Bks) Putnam Pub Group.
—The Legend of Sleepy Hollow. Kelley, Gary, illus. (gr. 4-12). Date not set. lib. bdg. 19.95 RLB smythe-sewn (0-88682-328-5, 97206-098) Creative Ed.
—Legend of Sleepy Hollow & Other Stories. (gr. 6 up). 1964. pap. 2.95 (0-8049-0050-7, CL-50) Airmont.
—The Legend of Sleepy Hollow: Minibook Edition. Van Nutt, Robert, illus. LC 93-12153. 1993. incl. cass. 9.95 (0-88708-321-8, Rabbit Ears) Picture Bk Studio.
—Rip Van Winkle. 1987. pap. 2.99 (0-14-035051-9, Puffin Bks.) Puffin Bks.
—Rip Van Winkle. Wyeth, N. C., illus. Glassman, Peter, afterword by. LC 87-60720. (Illus.). 110p. (ps up). 1987. 15.00 (0-688-07459-6) Morrow Jr Bks.
—Rip Van Winkle. Howe, John, retold by. & illus. (ps-3). 1988. 14.95 (0-316-37578-0) Little.
—Rip Van Winkle. Howe, John, retold by. & illus. (ps-3). 1991. pap. 5.95 (0-316-37584-5) Little.
—Rip Van Winkle. Rackham, Arthur, illus. LC 92-9843. 128p. (gr. 1 up). 1992. 19.00 (0-8037-1264-2) Dial Bks Young.
—Rip Van Winkle. Kelley, Gary, illus. LC 93-17093. 1993. PLB 21.95s.p. (0-88682-631-4) Creative Ed.
—Rip Van Winkle. Kelley, Gary, illus. 64p. Apr. 1993. 21.95 (1-56846-082-1) Creat Editions.
—Rip Van Winkle: The Mountain Top Edition. rev. ed. Oakes, Donald T., ed. Wyeth, N. C. & Murtagh, Mark, illus. Hommel, Justine L., contrib. by. LC 89-62869. 92p. (gr. 9). 1989. pap. write for info. (0-9624216-0-X) MTH Soc Inc.
—Sketch Book. 389p. (RL 5). 1961. pap. 5.50 (0-451-52495-0, CE1614, Sig Classics) NAL-Dutton.
—Spanish Papers. Irving, Pierre, ed. LC 78-74516. (gr. 7 up). 1979. Repr. of 1868 ed. 42.50x (0-8486-0219-6) Roth Pub Inc.
—Washington Irving's Tales of the Supernatural. Wagenknecht, Edward, ed. Alley, R. W., illus. LC 80-29313. 288p. (gr. 6 up). 1982. 17.95 (0-916144-64-X) Stemmer Hse.
Irving, Washington see York, Carol B.
Irvings, H. T. Furello, the Unicorn. 64p. (gr. 1-4). 1992. 15.95 (1-881547-13-2) Pioneer Pubns.
Irwin, Colin, ed. see Moore, Clement C.
Irwin, Hadley. Abby, My Love. LC 84-24571. 168p. (gr. 7 up). 1985. SBE 13.95 (0-689-50323-7, M K McElderry) Macmillan Child Grp.

—Can't Hear You Listening. LC 90-32675. 208p. (gr. 7 up). 1990. SBE 14.95 (*0-689-50513-2*, M K McElderry) Macmillan Child Grp.
—Jim-Dandy. LC 93-22611. (Illus.). 144p. (gr. 5-9). 1994. SBE 14.95 (*0-689-50594-9*, M K McElderry) Macmillan Child Grp.
—Kim-Kimi. LC 86-21416. 208p. (gr. 7 up). 1987. SBE 14.95 (*0-689-50428-4*, M K McElderry) Macmillan Child Grp.
—Kim-Kimi. 1988. pap. 3.99 (*0-14-032593-X*, Puffin) Puffin Bks.
—The Lilith Summer. LC 78-24379. 128p. (gr. 4-8). 1979. 8.95 (*0-912670-52-5*) Feminist Pr.
—The Original Freddie Ackerman. Hosten, James, illus. LC 91-43145. 192p. (gr. 5 up). 1992. SBE 14.95 (*0-689-50562-0*, M K McElderry) Macmillan Child Grp.
—So Long at the Fair. LC 88-12813. 208p. (gr. 9 up). 1988. SBE 14.95 (*0-689-50454-3*, M K McElderry) Macmillan Child Grp.
—We Are Mesquakie, We Are One. LC 80-19000. 128p. (gr. 5 up). 1980. 10.95 (*0-912670-85-1*) Feminist Pr.
—What about Grandma? 176p. 1991. pap. 2.99 (*0-380-71138-9*, Flare) Avon.
Irwin, Susan, jt. auth. see Bluestone, Carol.
Isaacman, Clara & Grossman, Joan A. Clara's Story. LC 84-14339. 180p. (gr. 3-7). 1984. 11.95 (*0-8276-0243-X*); pap. 9.95 (*0-8276-0506-4*) JPS Phila.
Isaacs, Gwynne L. While You Are Asleep. Hepworth, Cathi, illus. 32p. (gr. 4-8). 1991. 12.95 (*0-8027-6985-3*); lib. bdg. 13.85 (*0-8027-6986-1*) Walker & Co.
Isaacs, Judith A. Secondary School Journalism. 227p. (gr. 7-12). 1991. pap. text ed. 15.95 (*0-9629645-0-6*); tchr's. resource guide 85.00 (*0-9629645-1-4*) Butterfly Bear.
Isaacson, Philip M. A Short Walk Around the Pyramids & Through the World of Art. LC 91-8854. (Illus.). 112p. (gr. 3-7). 1993. 20.00 (*0-679-81523-6*); PLB 20.99 (*0-679-91523-0*) Knopf Bks Yng Read.
Isaacson, Phillip M. Round Buildings, Square Buildings & Buildings That Wiggle Like a Fish. Isaacson, Phillip M., illus. LC 87-16967. 128p. (gr. 5 up). 1990. 14.95 (*0-394-89382-4*); lib. bdg. 16.99 (*0-394-99382-9*); pap. 10.95 (*0-679-80649-0*) Knopf Bks Yng Read.
Isaak, Betty. Classifying Cat. Armstrong, Bev, illus. 24p. (ps). 1982. wkbk. 2.95 (*0-88160-087-3*, LW 123) Learning Wks.
—Garbage Games. 112p. (gr. 1-4). 1980. 9.95 (*0-88160-012-1*, LW 115) Learning Wks.
—Perception Panda. Armstrong, Bev, illus. 24p. (ps). 1982. wkbk. 2.95 (*0-88160-088-1*, LW 122) Learning Wks.
—Sequencing Seal. Armstrong, Bev, illus. 24p. (ps). 1982. wkbk. 2.95 (*0-88160-090-3*, LW 124) Learning Wks.
Isaaman. Computer Battlegames. (gr. 5-9). 1983. 10.96 (*0-88110-132-X*, 24052); pap. 3.95 (*0-86020-685-8*) EDC.
—Computer Spacegames. 48p. (gr. 5-9). 1983. pap. 3.95 (*0-86020-683-1*, 24062); lib. bdg. 10.96 (*0-88110-133-8*) EDC.
Isack, Hussein A. People of the North: Boran. (Illus.). 42p. (gr. 6-9). 1991. pap. 4.95 (*0-237-50724-2*, Pub. by Evans Bros Ltd) Trafalgar.
Isadora, Rachel. At the Crossroads. LC 90-30751. (Illus.). 32p. (ps up). 1991. 15.00 (*0-688-05270-3*); PLB 14.93 (*0-688-05271-1*) Greenwillow.
—At the Crossroads. Isadora, Rachel, illus. 32p. (ps up) Date not set. pap. 4.95 (*0-688-13103-4*, Mulberry) Morrow.
—Babies. LC 88-18782. (Illus.). (ps up). 1990. 13.95 (*0-688-08031-6*); PLB 13.88 (*0-688-08032-4*) Greenwillow.
—Ben's Trumpet. Isadora, Rachel, illus. LC 78-12885. 32p. (gr. k-3). 1979. 14.00 (*0-688-80194-3*) Greenwillow.
—Ben's Trumpet. Isadora, Rachel, illus. LC 79-12885. (Illus.). 32p. (gr. ps-3). 1991. pap. 4.95 (*0-688-10988-8*, Mulberry) Morrow.
—City Seen from A to Z. Isadora, Rachel, illus. LC 82-11966. 32p. (gr. k-3). 1983. PLB 11.88 (*0-688-01803-3*) Greenwillow.
—City Seen from A to Z. ALC Staff, ed. LC 82-11966. (Illus.). 32p. (gr. k up). 1992. pap. 3.95 (*0-688-12032-6*, Mulberry) Morrow.
—Friends. LC 88-11753. (Illus.). (ps up). 1990. 13.95 (*0-688-08264-5*); PLB 13.88 (*0-688-08265-3*) Greenwillow.
—I Hear. Isadora, Rachel, illus. LC 84-6103. 32p. (ps). 1985. 15.00 (*0-688-04061-6*); PLB 14.93 (*0-688-04062-4*) Greenwillow.
—I See. Isadora, Rachel, illus. LC 84-6104. 32p. (ps). 1985. 15.00 (*0-688-04059-4*); PLB 14.93 (*0-688-04060-8*) Greenwillow.
—I See. LC 90-48254. (Illus.). 24p. (ps up) 1991. bds. 6.95 (*0-688-10523-8*) Greenwillow.
—I Touch. Isadora, Rachel, illus. LC 84-13673. 32p. (ps). 1985. 15.00 (*0-688-04255-4*); lib. bdg. 14.93 (*0-688-04256-2*) Greenwillow.
—I Touch. LC 90-48260. (Illus.). 24p. (ps up) 1991. bds. 6.95 (*0-688-10524-6*) Greenwillow.
—Lili at Ballet. Isadora, Rachel, illus. LC 92-8429. 32p. (ps-3). 1993. PLB 14.95 (*0-399-22423-8*, Putnam) Putnam Pub Group.
—Max. Isadora, Rachel, illus. LC 76-9088. 32p. (gr. k-3). 1976. RSBE 13.95 (*0-02-747450-X*, Macmillan Child Bk) Macmillan Child Grp.
—Max. LC 84-7649. (Illus.). 32p. (gr. k-3). 1984. pap. 3.95 (*0-02-043800-1*, Aladdin) Macmillan Child Grp.

—My Ballet Class. LC 79-16297. (Illus.). 32p. (gr. k-3). 1980. 15.00 (*0-688-80253-2*) Greenwillow.
—Over the Green Hills. LC 91-12761. 32p. (ps up). 1992. 14.00 (*0-688-10509-2*); PLB 13.93 (*0-688-10510-6*) Greenwillow.
—The Pirates of Bedford Street. LC 84-25904. (Illus.). 32p. (ps-3). 1988. 11.95 (*0-688-05206-1*); lib. bdg. 11.88 (*0-688-05208-8*) Greenwillow.
—The Princess & the Frog. LC 88-61. (Illus.). 32p. (ps up). 1989. 12.95 (*0-688-06373-X*); PLB 12.88 (*0-688-06374-8*) Greenwillow.
—Swan Lake. LC 88-29843. (Illus.). 32p. 1991. 14.95 (*0-399-21730-4*, Putnam) Putnam Pub Group.
Isaksen, Lisa A., ed. see Bozanich, Tony L.
Isami, Ikuyo. The Fox's Egg. Isami, Ikuyo, illus. 40p. (ps-2). 1989. 18.95 (*0-87614-339-7*) Carolrhoda Bks.
Isberg, Emily. Peak Performance. (gr. 3 up). 1989. pap. 14.95 jacketed (*0-671-67750-0*, S&S BFYR); pap. 5.95 (*0-671-67745-4*, S&S BFYR) S&S Trade.
Iscaro, Nancy L., ed. Pier Pleasure I. Figueroa, Mariano, et al, illus. 80p. (gr. 9-12). 1989. pap. text ed. write for info. West Side Pubns.
Iscaro, Nancy L., frwd. by see Beane, Kelly D.
Iscaro, Nancy L., ed. see Fernandez, Brenda.
Iscaro, Nancy L., ed. see Garay, Julio.
Iscaro, Nancy L., ed. see Ortiz, Elizabeth.
Iscaro, Nancy L., ed. see Warwick, Catherine A.
Isdell, Wendy. A Gebra Named Al. LC 93-15294. 128p. (Orig.). (gr. 5 up). 1993. pap. 4.95 (*0-915793-58-X*) Free Spirit Pub.
Isenbart, Hans-Heinrich. Birth of a Foal. David, Thomas, illus. LC 85-17406. 48p. (gr. 2-5). 1986. lib. bdg. 19.95 (*0-87614-239-0*) Carolrhoda Bks.
Isenberg, Barbara & Jaffe, Marjorie. Albert the Running Bear's Exercise Book. De Groat, Diane, illus. LC 84-7064. 64p. (Orig.). (ps-4). 1984. (Clarion Bks) HM.
Isenberg, Barbara & Wolf, Susan. The Adventures of Albert, the Running Bear. Gackenbach, Dick, illus. (gr. k-3). 1985. pap. 12.95 incl. cassette (*0-941078-88-4*); pap. 27.95 incl. cassette, 4 paperbacks guide (*0-941078-89-2*); PLB incl. cassette 19.95 (*0-941078-90-6*) Live Oak Media.
—The Adventures of Albert the Running Bear. Gackenbach, Dick, illus. LC 82-1311. 32p. (ps-3). 1982. (Clarion Bks); pap. 6.70 (*0-89919-125-8*, Clarion Bks) HM.
—Albert the Running Bear Gets the Jitters. De Groat, Diane, illus. 40p. (gr. k-4). 1987. 13.95 (*0-89919-517-2*, Clarion Bks); (Clarion Bks) HM.
Isern, Thomas D. & Wilson, Raymond. Kansas Land. (Illus.). 237p. (gr. 7). 1987. 22.00 (*0-685-24529-2*, Peregrine Smith) Gibbs Smith Pub.
Isham, Joy & Annis, Scott E. Color in Nebraska Coloring Album. Annis, Scott E., illus. 32p. (Orig.). (gr. 1-5). 1985. pap. 3.95 (*0-9615584-1-5*) Little Gnome.
Isherwood, Millicent. The Guitar. 48p. (gr. 4-7). 1986. pap. 9.95 (*0-19-321334-6*) OUP.
Isherwood, Shirley. A Surprise for Mrs. Pinkerton-Trunks. (Illus.). 96p. (gr. k-2). 1986. 12.95 (*0-09-160380-3*, Pub. by Hutchinson UK) Trafalgar.
Ishii, Momoko. Tongue-Cut Sparrow. Paterson, Katherine, tr. Akaba, Suekichi, illus. LC 86-29314. 40p. (ps-3). 1987. 13.95 (*0-525-67199-4*, Lodestar Bks) Dutton Child Bks.
Ishikawa, Eiko, illus. Mother Goose. 16p. (ps). 1992. pap. 4.95 (*0-671-77012-8*, Little Simon) S&S Trade.
—What's Inside? 16p. (ps). 1992. pap. 4.95 (*0-671-77017-9*, Little Simon) S&S Trade.
—Where Is Kitty? 16p. (ps). 1992. pap. 4.95 (*0-671-77018-7*, Little Simon) S&S Trade.
—Who Lives Here? 16p. (ps). 1992. pap. 4.95 (*0-671-77023-3*, Little Simon) S&S Trade.
Ishinabe, Fusako, jt. auth. see Barnes, Jill.
Ish-Kishor, Sulamith. Our Eddie. reissued ed. LC 92-7719. 192p. (gr. 5-). 1992. 15.00 (*0-394-81455-X*) Knopf Bks Yng Read.
Island, John. World of the Heart. Redford, Jim L., illus. 48p. (ps-6). Date not set. text ed. 14.95 (*0-9637712-0-5*) Island Flowers.
Ismaeel, Saeed. The Difference Between the Shiites & the Majority of Muslim Scholars. 35p. 1988. pap. write for info. Wamy Intl.
Ismail, Latifa, ed. see Kaahena, Yuhaayaa L.
Ison, Colleen. Skits That Teach Children: Including "Goliath's Last Stand" & Fifteen Other Short Dramas. rev. ed. Fittro, Pat, ed. 112p. (ps-7). 1993. pap. 5.99 (*0-87403-947-9*, 14-03347) Standard Pub.
—Skits That Teach Teens: Including "Three Ways to Mess up a Relationship" & Nine Other Short Dramas. Fittro, Pat, ed. 112p. (Orig.). 1993. pap. 5.99 (*0-7847-0108-3*, 14-03348) Standard Pub.
Isphording, Julie. Food Fun For Kids: A Recipe Coloring Book. Wolterman, Jan, ed. (Illus.). 48p. (gr. 1-6). 1991. pap. 6.95 spiral bdg. (*0-9629589-0-5*) Kids Kitchen.
Israel, Fred L. The Amish. Moynihan, Daniel P., intro. by. (Illus.). 112p. 1986. lib. bdg. 17.95 (*0-87754-853-6*) Chelsea Hse.
—The Federal Bureau of Investigation. Schlesinger, Arthur M., Jr., intro. by. (Illus.). 96p. (gr. 5 up). 1986. lib. bdg. 14.95 (*0-87754-821-8*) Chelsea Hse.
—Franklin D. Roosevelt. (Illus.). 112p. (gr. 5 up). 1985. lib. bdg. 17.95x (*0-87754-573-1*); pap. 9.95 (*0-7910-0599-2*) Chelsea Hse.
Issaroff, Penina. Kindergarten Carousel. (ps). 1993. 12.95 (*0-943706-12-2*) Yllw Brick Rd.

Isserman, Maurice. The Korean War: America at War. Bowman, John, ed. LC 92-10201. (Illus.). 128p. 1992. PLB 16.95 (*0-8160-2688-2*) Facts on File.
—World War II. 192p. (gr. 7-12). 1991. 17.95x (*0-8160-2374-3*) Facts on File.
Isynwill, L. N. & Keith, Herbert. At Your Door: A Modern-Day Campaign. Willis, Lynn & Herber, Keith, eds. Gibbons, Lee, illus. 162p. (Orig.). (gr. 12 up). 1990. pap. 17.95 (*0-933635-64-8*, 2326) Chaosium.
Italia, Bob. Adolf Hitler. Wallner, Rosemary, ed. LC 90-82613. (Illus.). 32p. (gr. 4). 1990. PLB 11.96 (*0-939179-79-2*) Abdo & Dghtrs.
—After the Storm. Wallner, Rosemary, ed. LC 92-17392. (gr. 4 up). 1992. PLB 13.99 (*1-56239-147-X*) Abdo & Dghtrs.
—Al Gore: Vice President of the United States. LC 93-26099. (gr. 5 up). 1993. lib. bdg. 13.99 (*1-56239-253-0*) Abdo & Dghtrs.
—Amy Grant. Wallner, Rosemary, ed. LC 92-16692. 1992. PLB 12.94 (*1-56239-161-5*) Abdo & Dghtrs.
—Andie MacDowell. LC 92-13690. 1992. PLB 12.94 (*1-56239-111-9*) Abdo & Dghtrs.
—Anita Hill. LC 93-4615. 40p. 1993. 12.94 (*1-56239-259-X*) Abdo & Dghtrs.
—Anthony Kennedy. Deegan, Paul, ed. LC 92-13710. 40p. 1992. PLB 13.99 (*1-56239-094-5*) Abdo & Dghtrs.
—Antonin Scalia. Deegan, Paul, ed. LC 92-13712. 40p. 1992. PLB 13.99 (*1-56239-093-7*) Abdo & Dghtrs.
—Baseball's Greatest Players. LC 93-13085. 1993. write for info. (*1-56239-241-7*) Abdo & Dghtrs.
—Benito Mussolini. Walner, Rosemary, ed. LC 90-82618. (Illus.). 32p. (gr. 4). 1990. PLB 11.96 (*0-939179-81-4*) Abdo & Dghtrs.
—Bill Clinton: The 42nd President of the United States. LC 93-24849. 1993. 13.99 (*1-56239-249-2*) Abdo & Dghtrs.
—Brooke Shields. LC 92-13689. 1992. PLB 12.94 (*1-56239-110-0*) Abdo & Dghtrs.
—Bungee Jumping. LC 93-15331. (gr. 6 up). 1993. 13.99 (*1-56239-230-1*) Abdo & Dghtrs.
—Byron White. Deegan, Paul, ed. LC 92-13714. 1992. 13.95 (*1-56239-095-3*) Abdo & Dghtrs.
—Cheryl Tiegs. LC 92-13688. 1992. PLB 12.94 (*1-56239-107-0*) Abdo & Dghtrs.
—Chief Justice William Rehnquist. Deegan, Paul, ed. LC 92-13709. 1992. PLB 13.95 (*1-56239-096-1*) Abdo & Dghtrs.
—Chris Burke. LC 92-16037. 1992. 12.94 (*1-56239-143-7*) Abdo & Dghtrs.
—Christie Brinkley. LC 92-13693. 1992. PLB 12.94 (*1-56239-108-9*) Abdo & Dghtrs.
—Christopher Columbus. Walner, Rosemary, ed. LC 90-82621. (Illus.). 32p. (gr. 4). 1990. PLB 11.96 (*0-939179-94-6*) Abdo & Dghtrs.
—Cindy Crawford. LC 92-13692. 1992. PLB 12.94 (*1-56239-106-2*) Abdo & Dghtrs.
—Clara Hale: Mother to Those Who Needed One. Wallner, Rosie, ed. LC 93-15261. 1993. 12.94 (*1-56239-235-2*) Abdo & Dghtrs.
—The Dallas Cowboys: Nineteen Ninety-Three Super Bowl Champions. LC 93-15260. 1993. 14.96 (*1-56239-238-7*) Abdo & Dghtrs.
—David Souter. Deegan, Paul, ed. LC 92-13708. 1992. 13.99 (*1-56239-092-9*) Abdo & Dghtrs.
—Earth Words: Target Earth Ser. LC 93-19062. 1993. 14.96 (*1-56239-212-3*) Abdo & Dghtrs.
—Elle McPherson. LC 92-13691. 1992. PLB 12.94 (*1-56239-109-7*) Abdo & Dghtrs.
—Emperor Hirohito. Walner, Rosemary, ed. LC 90-82620. (Illus.). 32p. (gr. 4). 1990. PLB 11.96 (*0-939179-80-6*) Abdo & Dghtrs.
—Football's Finest. LC 93-2285. 1993. 14.96 (*1-56239-242-5*) Abdo & Dghtrs.
—Franklin D. Roosevelt. Walner, Rosemary, ed. LC 90-82619. (Illus.). 32p. (gr. 4). 1990. PLB 11.96 (*0-939179-82-2*) Abdo & Dghtrs.
—Free Style Water Skiing. LC 93-19135. 1993. 13.99 (*1-56239-232-8*) Abdo & Dghtrs.
—General H. Norman Schwarzkopf. Wallner, Rosemary, ed. LC 92-17393. (gr. 4 up). 1992. PLB 13.99 (*1-56239-148-8*) Abdo & Dghtrs.
—H. Ross Perot: The Man Who Woke up America. LC 93-3682. 1993. 12.94 (*1-56239-236-0*) Abdo & Dghtrs.
—Harry Blackmun. Deegan, Paul, ed. LC 92-13711. 1992. PLB 13.99 (*1-56239-090-2*) Abdo & Dghtrs.
—Hockey's Heroes. LC 93-21230. 1993. 14.96 (*1-56239-244-1*) Abdo & Dghtrs.
—Joe Montana. Wallner, Rosemary, ed. LC 92-19753. 1992. PLB 12.94 (*1-56239-123-2*) Abdo & Dghtrs.
—Joseph Stalin. Walner, Rosemary, ed. LC 90-82614. (Illus.). 32p. (gr. 4). 1990. PLB 13.99 (*0-939179-83-0*) Abdo & Dghtrs.
—Kirby Puckett. Wallner, Rosemary, ed. LC 92-19752. 1992. PLB 12.94 (*1-56239-125-9*) Abdo & Dghtrs.
—Larry Bird. Wallner, Rosemary, ed. LC 92-20131. 1992. PLB 12.94 (*1-56239-122-4*) Abdo & Dghtrs.
—Magic Johnson. Wallner, Rosemary, ed. LC 92-19754. 1992. 12.94 (*1-56239-120-8*) Abdo & Dghtrs.
—Marco Polo. Walner, Rosemary, ed. LC 90-82626. (Illus.). 32p. (gr. 4). 1990. PLB 11.96 (*0-939179-92-X*) Abdo & Dghtrs.
—Mario Lemieux. Wallner, Rosemary, ed. LC 92-19751. 1992. PLB 12.94 (*1-56239-124-0*) Abdo & Dghtrs.
—Michael Jordan. Wallner, Rosemary, ed. LC 92-20132. 1992. PLB 12.94 (*1-56239-121-6*) Abdo & Dghtrs.

—The Montreal Canadiens: Nineteen Ninety Three Stanley Cup Champions. LC 93-30672. 1993. 14.96 (*1-56239-240-9*) Abdo & Dghtrs.
—Motocross. LC 93-19140. 1993. 13.99 (*1-56239-233-6*) Abdo & Dghtrs.
—Robert Ballard. Walner, Rosemary, ed. LC 90-82623. (Illus.). 32p. (gr. 4). 1990. PLB 11.96 (*0-939179-95-4*) Abdo & Dghtrs.
—The Toronto Blue Jays: World Champion of Baseball. LC 93-13084. 1993. 14.96 (*1-56239-239-5*) Abdo & Dghtrs.
—The Vikings. Walner, Rosemary, ed. LC 90-82625. (Illus.). 32p. (gr. 4). 1990. PLB 11.96 (*0-939179-93-8*) Abdo & Dghtrs.
—Voyagers One & Two. Walner, Rosemary, ed. LC 90-82622. (Illus.). 32p. (gr. 4). 1990. PLB 11.96 (*0-939179-96-2*) Abdo & Dghtrs.
—Will Steger. Walner, Rosemary, ed. LC 90-82624. (Illus.). 32p. (gr. 4). 1990. PLB 11.96 (*0-939179-97-0*) Abdo & Dghtrs.
—Winston Churchill. Walner, Rosemary, ed. LC 90-82615. (Illus.). 32p. (gr. 4). 1990. PLB 11.96 (*0-939179-78-4*) Abdo & Dghtrs.
Italia, Bob & Deegan, Paul. John Paul Stevens. LC 92-13713. 1992. PLB 13.99 (*1-56239-091-0*) Abdo & Dghtrs.
Italia, Bob, ed. see Deegan, Paul.
Italia, Bob, ed. see Kallen, Stuart.
Italia, Bob, ed. see Owen, Oliver S.
Italia, Bob, ed. see Zingg, Eduard.
Italia, Robert. Armed Forces. Walner, Rosemary, ed. LC 91-73075. 202p. (gr. 4 up). 1991. 13.99 (*1-56239-026-0*) Abdo & Dghtrs.
—Great Auto Makers & Their Cars. LC 92-43464. (Illus.). 160p. (gr. 5-12). 1993. PLB 14.95 (*1-881508-08-0*) Oliver Pr MN.
—In-Line Skating. Walner, Rosemary, ed. LC 91-73021. 1991. PLB 13.99 (*1-56239-076-7*) Abdo & Dghtrs.
—Jet Skiing. Walner, Rosemary, ed. LC 91-73022. 1991. PLB 13.99 (*1-56239-075-9*) Abdo & Dghtrs.
—Maya Lin: Honoring Our Forgotten Heroes. LC 93-10257. 1993. 12.94 (*1-56239-234-4*) Abdo & Dghtrs.
—Mickey Mouse. Walner, Rosemary, ed. LC 91-73048. 202p. 1991. 13.95 (*1-56239-053-8*) Abdo & Dghtrs.
—Mountain Biking. Walner, Rosemary, ed. LC 91-73023. 202p. 1991. PLB 13.99 (*1-56239-074-0*) Abdo & Dghtrs.
—The Muppets. Wallner, Rosemary, ed. LC 91-73049. 202p. 1991. 13.95 (*1-56239-052-X*) Abdo & Dghtrs.
—Roseanne Barr. Wallner, Rosemary, ed. LC 91-73035. 1991. 12.94 (*1-56239-058-9*) Abdo & Dghtrs.
—Sailboarding. Wallner, Rosemary, ed. LC 91-73019. 1991. PLB 13.99 (*1-56239-078-3*) Abdo & Dghtrs.
—The Simpsons. Wallner, Rosemary, ed. LC 91-73050. 1991. 13.95 (*1-56239-051-1*) Abdo & Dghtrs.
—Skateboarding. Wallner, Rosemary, ed. LC 91-73020. 1991. PLB 13.99 (*1-56239-077-5*) Abdo & Dghtrs.
—Snowboarding. Wallner, Rosemary, ed. LC 91-73024. 1991. PLB 13.99 (*1-56239-073-2*) Abdo & Dghtrs.
—Teenage Mutant Ninja Turtles. Wallner, Rosemary, ed. LC 91-73051. 1991. 13.95 (*1-56239-050-3*) Abdo & Dghtrs.
—Weapons of War. LC 91-73074. (gr. 4 up). 1991. 13.99 (*1-56239-027-9*) Abdo & Dghtrs.
Itoh, Motoshige & Negishi, Takashi. Disequilibrium Trade Theories. 110p. (gr. 7 up). 1987. pap. text ed. 29.00 (*3-7186-0412-4*, Pub. by Harwood Acad Pubs) Gordon & Breach.
Ivanovsky, Elisabeth. Little Treasury of Pierre Bear, 6 bks. 1992. Set. 5.99 (*0-517-08293-4*) Outlet Bk Co.
—Things in My House. (Illus.). (ps). 1985. bds. 3.98 (*0-517-47341-0*) Outlet Bk Co.
—What Color Is It. (Illus.). (ps) 1985. bds. 3.98 (*0-517-47342-9*) Outlet Bk Co.
—What Time Is It? (Illus.). (ps) 1985. bds. 3.98 (*0-517-47343-7*) Outlet Bk Co.
Ivemey, John W. Three Blind Mice. Mark, Steve, illus. LC 92-41175. (gr. 2 up). Date not set. write for info. (*1-56766-090-8*) Childs World. Postponed.
Iverson, Carol. Fish Sleep with Their Eyes Open: And Other Facts & Curiosities. (gr. 4-7). 1991. pap. 3.95 (*0-8225-9607-5*) Lerner Pubns.
—Hummingbirds Can Fly Backwards: And Other Facts & Curiosities. (gr. 4-7). 1991. pap. 3.95 (*0-8225-9606-7*) Lerner Pubns.
—I Bet You Didn't Know That Fish Sleep with Their Eyes Open & Other Facts & Curiosities. Lindstrom, Jack, illus. 32p. (gr. 3-6). 1990. PLB 10.95 (*0-8225-2277-2*) Lerner Pubns.
—I Bet You Didn't Know That Hummingbirds Can Fly Backwards & Other Facts & Curiosities. Lindstrom, Jack, illus. 32p. (gr. 3-6). 1990. PLB 10.95 (*0-8225-2276-4*) Lerner Pubns.
—I Bet You Didn't Know That There Are Golf Balls on the Moon & Other Facts & Curiosities. Lindstrom, Jack, illus. 32p. (gr. 3-6). 1990. PLB 10.95 (*0-8225-2275-6*) Lerner Pubns.
—I Bet You Didn't Know That You Can't Sink in the Dead Sea & Other Facts & Curiosities. Lindstrom, Jack, illus. 32p. (gr. 3-6). 1990. PLB 10.95 (*0-8225-2278-0*) Lerner Pubns.
—There Are Golf Balls on the Moon: And Other Facts & Curiosities. (gr. 4-7). 1991. pap. 3.95 (*0-8225-9609-1*) Lerner Pubns.
—You Can't Sink in the Dead Sea: And Other Facts & Curiosities. (gr. 4-7). 1991. pap. 3.95 (*0-8225-9608-3*) Lerner Pubns.

Iverson, Diane. I Celebrate Nature. 32p. (ps). 1993. 13.95 (*1-883220-01-7*); pap. 5.95 (*1-883220-00-9*) Dawn CA.
—I Celebrate the World. (Illus.). 32p. (Orig.). 1989. pap. 5.95 (*0-9623349-0-1*) MS Pub.
—Where Are the Babies? Iverson, Diane, illus. 48p. (Orig.). (ps). 1992. 14.95 (*0-9623349-1-X*); pap. 8.95 (*0-9623349-2-8*) MS Pub.
Iverson, Peter. Carlos Montezuma. Viola, Herman, intro. by. Fujiwara, Kim, illus. 32p. (gr. 3-6). 1990. 17.96 (*0-8172-3408-X*); pap. 4.95 (*0-8114-4092-3*) Raintree Steck-V.
—The Navajos. (Illus.). 112p. (gr. 5 up). 1990. 17.95 (*1-55546-719-9*); pap. 9.95 (*0-7910-0390-6*) Chelsea Hse.
Ivery, Evelyn, ed. see Howell, Ann C. & Massey, Grace C.
Ivery, Evelyn L., ed. see Chandler, Ann.
Ivery, Evelyn L., ed. see Howell, Ann C.
Ivery, Evelyn L., ed. see Howell, Ann C. & Massey, Grace C.
Ivery, Evelyn L., ed. see Massey, Grace C.
Ives, Penny. Mrs. Santa Claus. 1993. pap. 3.99 (*0-440-40877-6*) Dell.
—My Nursery Book. (Illus.). 64p. 1991. 6.99 (*0-517-05399-3*) Outlet Bk Co.
Ives, Penny, illus. Goldilocks & the Three Bears: A Peek-Through-the-Window Book. 24p. (ps-1). 1992. 14.95 (*0-399-22121-2*, Putnam) Putnam Pub Group.
Ives, Sally B., et al. The Divorce Workbook: A Guide for Kids & Families. (Illus.). 160p. (Orig.), (ps-7). 1985. plastic comb bdg. 14.95 (*0-914525-04-2*); pap. 12.95 (*0-914525-05-0*) Waterfront Bks.
Ivimey, John W. The Complete Story of the Three Blind Mice. LC 87-689. (gr. k-3). 1987. 13.95 (*0-89919-481-8*, Clarion Bks) HM.
—The Complete Story of the Three Blind Mice. Galdone, Paul, illus. LC 87-689. 32p. (ps). 1989. pap. 4.80 (*0-395-51585-8*, Clarion Bks) HM.
Ivory, Lesley A. Cats in the Sun. Ivory, Lesley A., illus. LC 90-43068. 32p. (ps up). 1991. 14.95 (*0-8037-0955-2*) Dial Bks Young.
—Cats in the Sun. LC 90-43068. (Illus.). 32p. 1992. miniature ed. 5.95 (*0-8037-1242-1*) Dial Bks Young.
—Meet My Cats. (gr. 2 up). 1989. 13.95 (*0-8037-0602-2*) Dial Bks Young.
—Meet My Cats. LC 89-1526. (Illus.). 32p. 1992. miniature ed. 5.95 (*0-8037-1241-3*) Dial Bks Young.
Ivory, Lesley A., jt. auth. see Van der Meer, Ron.
Ivory, Leslie A. The Birthday Cat. Ivory, Leslie A., illus. LC 93-129. 32p. (ps-3). 1993. 15.00 (*0-8037-1622-2*) Dial Bks Young.
Ivy, Elizabeth. Gymnast Commandos. (gr. 4-7). 1991. pap. 2.75 (*0-590-43835-2*) Scholastic Inc.
Ivy, Richard. The Whooptie Whooptie Whatie Whatiee Bird. 28p. (ps-6). 1993. pap. 8.50 (*1-884095-00-3*) Ivy Hill Pubs.
Iwamura, Kazuo. The Fourteen Forest Mice & the Harvest Moon Watch. Knowlton, Mary L., tr. from JPN. Iwamura, Kazuo, illus. LC 90-50706. 32p. (gr. k-3). 1991. PLB 17.27 (*0-8368-0497-X*) Gareth Stevens Inc.
—The Fourteen Forest Mice & the Spring Meadow Picnic. Knowlton, Mary L., tr. from JPN. Iwamura, Kazuo, illus. LC 90-50704. 32p. (gr. k-3). 1991. PLB 17.27 (*0-8368-0498-8*) Gareth Stevens Inc.
—The Fourteen Forest Mice & the Summer Laundry Day. Knowlton, Mary L., tr. from JPN. Iwamura, Kazuo, illus. LC 90-50705. 32p. (gr. k-3). 1991. PLB 17.27 (*0-8368-0576-3*) Gareth Stevens Inc.
—The Fourteen Forest Mice & the Winter Sledding Day. Knowlton, Mary L., tr. from JPN. Iwamura, Kazuo, illus. LC 90-50707. 32p. (gr. k-3). 1991. PLB 17.27 (*0-8368-0499-6*) Gareth Stevens Inc.
Izawa, Tadasu & Hijkata, Shigemi, illus. What Time Is It? 18p. (gr. k-2). 1981. (G&D); PLB 3.95 (*0-448-03701-7*, G&D) Putnam Pub Group.
Izcoa, Carmen R., jt. auth. see Pico, Fernando.
Izen, Marshal & West, Jim. Why the Willow Weeps: A Story Told with Hands. LC 91-47077. 32p. (gr. k-3). 1992. pap. 14.00 (*0-385-30683-0*) Doubleday.

J

J. Sainsbury's Pure Tea Staff. Cinderella: Full Color Picture Book. (Illus.). 12p. (Orig.). 1993. pap. text ed. 1.00t (*0-486-27797-2*) Dover.
—Goldilocks & the Three Bears: Full-Color Picture Book. LC 92-38398. 1993. write for info. (*0-486-27503-5*) Dover.
—Jack & the Beanstalk: Full-Color Picture Book. LC 92-35299. 1993. pap. 1.00 (*0-486-27504-3*) Dover.
—Puss-in-Boots. (Illus.). 12p. (Orig.). 1993. pap. text ed. 1.00t (*0-486-27800-X*) Dover.
Jabar, Cynthia. Alice Ann Gets Ready for School, Vol. 1. 1989. 13.95 (*0-316-43457-4*) Little.
—Bored Blue? Think What You Can Do. (ps-3). 1991. 14.95 (*0-316-43458-2*) Little.
—Party Day! Jabar, Cynthia, illus. (ps-1). 1987. 11.95 (*0-316-43456-6*, Joy St Bks) Little.
Jabar, Cynthia, compiled by. & illus. Shimmy Shake Earthquake: Don't Forget to Dance Poems. 32p. (ps-3). 1992. 14.95 (*0-316-43459-0*, Joy St Bks) Little.
Jabbari, Ahmad, ed. see Bahar, Mehrdad.
Jabbari, Ahmad, ed. & tr. see Farjam, Farideh.

Jabbari, Ahmad, ed. & tr. see Farjam, Farideh & Azaad, Meyer.
Jablonsky, Alice. Descubre La Vida En el Oceano. University of Mexico City Staff, tr. from SPA. O'Neill, Pablo M. & Robare, Lorie, illus. 48p. (gr. 3-8). 1993. PLB 16.95 (*1-56674-050-9*, HTS Bks) Forest Hse.
—Discover Ocean Life. (Illus.). 48p. (gr. 3-6). 1992. PLB 14.95 (*1-878363-69-7*, HTS Bks) Forest Hse.
—One Hundred One Questions: Desert Life. Foreman, Ronald J., et al, eds. LC 93-84874. (Illus.). 48p. (Orig.). Date not set. pap. write for info. (*1-877856-32-0*) SW Pks Mnmts.
Jack, Susan, ed. see Ferriss, Lloyd.
Jack, Susan, ed. see Snow, John.
Jack, Susan, ed. see Swenson, Peter J.
Jacka, Martin. Waiting for Billy. LC 90-7957. (Illus.). 32p. (ps-3). 1991. 13.95 (*0-531-05933-2*); PLB 13.99 (*0-531-08533-3*) Orchard Bks Watts.
Jackman, Wayne. Gas. LC 93-7256. 32p. (gr. 3-6). 1993. 13.95 (*1-56847-049-5*) Thomson Lrning.
—Plastics. LC 92-45669. 32p. (gr. 3-6). 1993. 13.95 (*1-56847-040-1*) Thomson Lrning.
Jackson, jt. auth. see Vaughan, Genevieve.
Jackson, Al & Tardy, Gene. Drag Boat Racing: The National Championships. (Illus.). 48p. (gr. 3-7). 1973. PLB 6.89x (*0-914844-05-9*); pap. 3.95 (*0-914844-06-7*) J Alden.
Jackson, Al, jt. auth. see Tardy, Gene.
Jackson, Alison. Blowing Bubbles with the Enemy. LC 93-2888. 120p. (gr. 3-7). 1993. 13.99 (*0-525-45056-4*, DCB) Dutton Child Bks.
—Crane's Rebound. Hearn, Diane D., illus. LC 90-20648. 128p. (gr. 3-7). 1991. 12.95 (*0-525-44722-9*, DCB) Dutton Child Bks.
—My Brother, the Star. LC 89-34480. 112p. (gr. 3-7). 1990. 12.95 (*0-525-44512-9*, DCB) Dutton Child Bks.
Jackson, Bobby. Pops, Chops & Crops. LC 89-51297. 44p. (gr. k-3). 1990. 5.95 (*1-55523-259-0*) Winston-Derek.
—Pops, Chops, & Crops. (gr. k-4). 1990. 9.95 (*0-9634932-4-8*); pap. 5.95 (*0-9634932-5-6*) Multicult Pubns.
Jackson, Bobby L. Boon the Raccoon & Easel the Weasel: A Fable by Bobby L. Jackson. King, Kevin, illus. Reuter, Janet R., frwd. by. LC 92-62211. (Illus.). 32p. (ps-4). 1993. 9.95 (*0-9634932-0-5*, Dist. by Baker & Taylor Bks.); pap. 5.95 (*0-9634932-1-3*) Multicult Pubns.
—The Magic Moments of a Poet. 2nd ed. LC 83-50265. (Orig.). (gr. 10 up). 1994. pap. 7.95 (*0-9634932-7-2*) Multicult Pubns.
—Makimba's Animal World. Gordon, April, ed. Jones, Julienne, illus. LC 93-79595. 32p. (Orig.). (gr. k-4). 1994. 12.95 (*0-9634932-9-9*); pap. 7.95 (*0-9634932-8-0*) Multicult Pubns.
Jackson, Bobby L. & Carter, Michael C. Martin "The Hero" Merriweather. Fultz, Jim, illus. Reuter, Janet R., frwd. by. LC 93-77056. (Illus.). 48p. (Orig.). (gr. 4-8). 1993. 12.95g (*0-9634932-2-1*); pap. 7.95g (*0-9634932-3-X*) Multicult Pubns.
Jackson, Byron M., jt. auth. see Kruschke, Earl R.
Jackson, C. Paul. How to Play Better Soccer. Madden, Don, illus. LC 76-51450. (gr. 3-7). 1978. 8.95 (*0-690-01363-9*, Crowell Jr Bks); (Crowell Jr Bks) HarpC Child Bks.
Jackson, Carol. Jesus & Me. Plunkett, Mark W., ed. Steele, Martha, illus. 29p. (gr. 1-2). 1993. pap. 24.99 (*0-87403-850-2*, 13-42031) Standard Pub.
Jackson, Cherry R. Agate Eyes. Morbiim, illus. (Orig.). 1978. pap. text ed. 4.00 (*0-9605208-1-3*) Sea Urchin.
Jackson, Daniel & Summers-Dawes, Kate. Monsters You've Never Heard of & Never Will Unless You Read This Book. (gr. 1-5). 1991. pap. 5.95 (*1-880722-00-3*) S L Jackson.

Jackson, Darcy. Another Fuzz Bugg Adventure. Sheppard, Scott O., illus. 40p. (gr. k-5). 1993. 15.95 (*1-883016-00-2*) Moonglow Pubns. Imagine through the eyes of a child... Everywhere you look, there are Fuzz Buggs, Bojacks, pink porpoises & more. Travel to an island that is south of the border in your imagination. THE FUZZ BUGGS OF CABBAGE KEY are responsible for the antics of a lovable, but mischievous Captain Terry. Escape into the first of a delightful series of books illustrated & written for children of all ages. Created not only to entertain children, the Fuzz Buggs & their friends will exercise the imagination of adults as well. Scott O. Sheppard, award-winning commercial artist, illustrator, graphic designer & on a good day, all of the above, coupled with the writing talent of Darcy, form a dazzling team. Since both think on a level paralleled only by the brilliant imagination of a child, they are certain

to entertain everyone. You will delight in Captain Terry's search for the very best shell. Please join us in the adventure.
Publisher Provided Annotation.

Jackson, Dave. Listen for the Whippoorwill. (gr. 4-7). 1993. pap. 4.99 (*1-55661-272-9*) Bethany Hse.
—Shanghaied to China. (gr. 4-7). 1993. pap. 4.99 (*1-55661-271-0*) Bethany Hse.
Jackson, Dave & Jackson, Neta. The Bandit of Ashley Downs. 128p. (Orig.). 1993. pap. 4.99 (*1-55661-270-2*) Bethany Hse.
—The Chimney Sweep's Ransom. 128p. (Orig.). 1992. pap. 4.99 (*1-55661-268-0*) Bethany Hse.
—Escape from the Slave Traders. LC 92-11170. 128p. (Orig.). (gr. 3-7). 1992. pap. 4.99 (*1-55661-263-X*) Bethany Hse.
—The Hidden Jewel. 128p. (Orig.). (gr. 3-7). 1992. pap. 4.99 (*1-55661-245-1*) Bethany Hse.
—Imprisoned in the Golden City. 128p. (Orig.). 1993. pap. 4.99 (*1-55661-269-9*) Bethany Hse.
—Kidnapped by River Rats. Jackson, Julian, illus. 144p. (Orig.). (gr. 3-7). 1991. pap. 4.99 (*1-55661-220-6*) Bethany Hse.
—The Queen's Smuggler. Jackson, Julian, illus. 144p. (Orig.). (gr. 3-7). 1991. pap. 4.99 (*1-55661-221-4*) Bethany Hse.
—Spy for the Night Riders. 128p. (gr. 3-7). 1992. pap. 4.99 (*1-55661-237-0*) Bethany Hse.
Jackson, Denise. Dreading Locks. 16p. (gr. 1-3). 1992. pap. 5.50 (*1-879721-09-0*) Libthelit.
—The Fall with the Ball. 20p. (gr. 1-3). 1992. pap. 5.50 (*1-879721-07-4*) Libthelit.
—Firecracker Time. 15p. (gr. 1-3). 1992. pap. 5.50 (*1-879721-05-8*) Libthelit.
—Gobley Goop. 20p. (gr. 1-3). 1992. pap. 5.50 (*1-879721-03-1*) Libthelit.
—The Panthers & the Balloons. 25p. (gr. 1-3). 1992. pap. 5.50 (*1-879721-01-5*) Libthelit.
Jackson, Donald, jt. auth. see Perry, Shauneille.
Jackson, Edgar N. Green Mountain Hero. 192p. (gr. 6 up). 1988. pap. 9.95 (*0-933050-61-5*) New Eng Pr VT.
Jackson, Edwin L., et al. The Georgia Studies Book. (Illus.). 464p. (gr. 8). 1991. text ed. 19.85 (*0-89854-149-2*) U of GA Inst Govt.
Jackson, Ellen. Ants Can't Dance. Remkiewicz, Frank, illus. LC 90-5942. 32p. (gr. k-3). 1991. RSBE 12.95 (*0-02-747661-8*, Macmillan Child Bk) Macmillan Child Grp.
—Boris the Boring Boar. Chartier, Normand, illus. LC 91-48670. 32p. (gr. k-3). 1992. RSBE 14.95 (*0-02-747662-6*, Macmillan Child Bk) Macmillan Child Grp.
—Cinder Edna. O'Malley, Kevin, illus. LC 92-44160. (gr. 3 up). 1994. write for info. (*0-688-12322-8*); lib. bdg. write for info. (*0-688-12323-6*) Lothrop.
—The Tree of Life: The Wonders of Evolution. Winter, Judeanne, illus. 40p. (gr. k-3). 1993. 14.95 (*0-87975-819-8*) Prometheus Bks.
—The Winter Solstice. Ellis, Jan D., illus. LC 92-45065. 32p. (gr. 2-4). 1994. PLB 14.90 (*1-56294-400-2*) Millbrook Pr.
Jackson, Garnet N. Benjamin Banneker, Scientist. Pate, Rodney, illus. LC 92-28799. 1992. write for info. (*0-8136-5228-6*); pap. write for info. (*0-8136-5701-6*) Modern Curr.
—Elijah McCoy, Inventor. Thomas, Gary, illus. LC 92-28797. 1992. 56.50 (*0-8136-5230-8*); pap. 28.50 (*0-8136-5703-2*) Modern Curr.
—Frederick Douglass, Freedom Fighter. Holliday, Keaf, illus. LC 92-28777. 1992. 56.40 (*0-8136-5229-4*); pap. 28.50 (*0-8136-5702-4*) Modern Curr.
—Garrett Morgan, Inventor. Hudson, Thomas, illus. LC 92-28801. 1992. write for info. (*0-8136-5231-6*); pap. write for info. (*0-8136-5704-0*) Modern Curr.
—Phillis Wheatley, Poet. Hanna, Cheryl, illus. LC 92-28778. 1992. 56.40 (*0-8136-5233-2*); pap. 28.50 (*0-8136-5706-7*) Modern Curr.
—Rosa Parks: Hero of Our Time. Wade, Tony, illus. LC 92-28583. 1992. write for info. (*0-8136-5232-4*); pap. write for info. (*0-8136-5705-9*) Modern Curr.
Jackson, Jack. Comanche Moon. Fehrenbach, T. R., intro. by. 128p. pap. 5.95 (*0-89620-079-5*) Rip Off.
Jackson, Jack & Jackson, Jack. Long Shadows: Indian Leaders Standing in the Path of Manifest Destiny, 1600-1900. Newcomb, W. W., Jr., frwd. by. (Illus.). 128p. (gr. 6 up). 1985. hardbound pictorial cover 17.95 (*0-942376-07-2*) Paramount TX.
Jackson, James W. A Steward-ship Adventure: Christianomics for Kids. (Illus.). 24p. (Orig.). (gr. 3-6). 1988. wkbk. 2.95 (*1-55513-840-3*, 68403) Cook.
Jackson, John F. Genetics & You. (Illus.). 64p. (Orig.). (gr. 12). 1991. pap. 3.95 (*0-9628981-0-4*) Fenwick Pr.
Jackson, Julia A. Gemstones: Treasures from the Earth's Crust. LC 88-1380. (Illus.). 104p. (gr. 6 up). 1989. lib. bdg. 17.95 (*0-89490-201-6*) Enslow Pubs.
Jackson, Kathryn. Golden Book of Three Hundred Sixty-Five Stories. Scarry, Richard, illus. 1955. write for info. (*0-307-15557-9*, Golden Bks) Western Pub.
Jackson, Kim. First Day of School. Goodman, John, illus. LC 84-8631. 32p. (gr. k-2). 1985. PLB 11.59 (*0-8167-0359-0*); pap. text ed. 2.95 (*0-8167-0439-2*) Troll Assocs.
—The Planets. Watling, James, illus. LC 84-16451. 32p. (gr. k-2). 1985. lib. bdg. 11.59 (*0-8167-0450-3*); pap. text ed. 2.95 (*0-8167-0451-1*) Troll Assocs.
Jackson, Mark. Ready Set Grow! A Faith & Practice Primer for Regular Baptists. LC 89-38819. (Illus.). 112p. (Orig.). 1989. pap. text ed. 3.95 (*0-87227-138-2*) Reg Baptist.
Jackson, Michael. Making Music: Shake, Rattle & Roll with Instruments You Make Yourself. (gr. 4-7). 1993. pap. 3.95 (*0-207-17175-0*, Pub. by Angus & Robertson AT) HarpC.
—Moonwalk Coloring Book. (Illus.). 1989. pap. 2.95 (*0-385-26155-1*) Doubleday.
Jackson, Neta. Loving One Another. Gavitt, Anne, illus. 192p. (ps-2). 1993. 10.99 (*0-945564-66-X*, Gold & Honey) Questar Pubs.
Jackson, Neta, jt. auth. see Jackson, Dave.
Jackson, Paul. Tricks & Games with Paper. (gr. 4-7). 1992. pap. 3.95 (*0-207-15038-9*, Pub. by Angus & Robertson AT) HarpC.
—Tricks & Games with Paper. (gr. 4-7). 1992. pap. 3.95 (*0-207-17721-X*, Pub. by Angus & Robertson AT) HarpC.
Jackson, R. Eugene. Babes in Toyland: Stage Magic Plays for Children's Theatre. Alette, Carl, adapted by. (Illus.). 48p. (Orig.). (ps up). 1987. pap. 4.50 (*0-88680-267-9*); piano-vocal score 15.00 (*0-88680-268-7*); royalty on application 90.00 (*0-685-58886-6*) I E Clark.
—Christmas with the Three Bears. Alette, Carl, contrib. by. (Illus.). 48p. (Orig.). (gr. 1-10). 1990. pap. 4.00 (*0-88680-326-8*); piano-vocal score 10.00 (*0-88680-327-6*); royalty on application 50.00 (*0-685-58893-9*) I E Clark.
—Coffey Pott Meets the Wolf Man. 64p. (gr. 3 up). 1982. pap. 2.50 (*0-88680-031-5*); royalty on application 25.00 (*0-317-03575-4*) I E Clark.
—Pinocchio. Ellis, David, contrib. by. (Illus.). 36p. (Orig.). (gr. k-12). 1985. pap. 3.50 (*0-88680-245-8*); piano & vocal score 10.00 (*0-88680-246-6*); royalty on application 60.00 (*0-685-58021-0*) I E Clark.
—The Princess & the Goblin: A Two-Act Play for Children's Theatre. 48p. (gr. 3 up). 1983. pap. 3.00 (*0-88680-207-5*); royalty on application 35.00 (*0-685-57857-7*) I E Clark.
—Rock 'n Roll Santa. Alette, Carl, contrib. by. (Illus.). 55p. (Orig.). (gr. 1 up). 1991. pap. 4.25 (*0-88680-346-2*); piano/vocal score 15.00 (*0-88680-347-0*); royalty on application 60.00 (*0-685-59131-X*) I E Clark.
—Rumpelstiltskin Is My Name. 52p. (gr. k up). 1978. pap. 3.00 (*0-88680-166-4*); royalty on application 35.00 (*0-317-03617-3*) I E Clark.
—Unidentified Flying Reject. 56p. (gr. 4 up). 1982. pap. 2.50 (*0-88680-201-6*); royalty on application 25.00 (*0-317-03576-2*) I E Clark.
—Who Can Fix the Dragon's Wagon? 52p. (ps up). 1966. pap. 3.00 (*0-88680-202-4*); Director's Production Script. pap. 10.00 (*0-88680-203-2*); royalty 35.00 (*0-317-03603-3*) I E Clark.
Jackson, R. Eugene, jt. auth. see Osterberg, Susan S.
Jackson, R. Eugene, adapted by. The Song of Hiawatha. Ellis, David, contrib. by. (Illus.). 44p. (Orig.). (gr. 2 up). 1988. pap. 3.00 (*0-88680-302-0*); piano-vocal score 15.00 (*0-88680-303-9*); royalty on application 75.00 (*0-685-58412-7*) I E Clark.
Jackson, R. Eugene, ed. see Carroll, Lewis.
Jackson, Ralph, et al. The Romans. (Illus.). (gr. 2-6). pap. 3.95 (*0-7141-1282-8*, Pub. by Brit Mus UK) Parkwest Pubns.
Jackson, Robert B. The Remarkable Ride of the Abernathy Boys. rev. ed. Griffis, Molly L., ed. LC 88-82956. (Illus.). 69p. (gr. 4 up). 1988. PLB 12.00 (*0-927562-07-3*); pap. 6.00 (*0-9618634-6-3*) Levite Apache.
Jackson, Sarah & Patterson, Mary Ann. A Child's History of Texas. Jackson, Sarah & Patterson, Mary Ann, illus. (gr. 1-6). 1972. 5.95 (*0-89015-056-7*, Pub. by Panda Bks) Eakin-Sunbelt.
Jackson, Shirley. Charles. 1991. PLB 13.95s.p. (*0-88682-470-2*) Creative Ed.
—The Lottery. LC 83-71789. 32p. (gr. 6 up). 1983. PLB 13.95s.p. (*0-87191-964-8*) Creative Ed.
—Witchcraft of Salem Village. (Illus.). (gr. 4-6). 1963. lib. bdg. 9.99 (*0-394-90369-2*) Random Bks Yng Read.
Jackson, Sonia. Eeeeaaassy Party Planning. Negrini, Wendy, illus. 80p. 1988. pap. 6.95 (*0-9619056-0-3*) Entrtnmnt Enter.
Jackson, Steve & Livingstone, Ian. Appointment with F.E.A.R. (Orig.). (gr. 5 up). 1986. pap. 2.50 (*0-440-90258-4*, LFL) Dell.
—Demons of the Deep. (Orig.). (gr. k-12). 1987. pap. 2.50 (*0-440-91843-X*, LFL) Dell.
—Rebel Planet. (Orig.). (gr. 5 up). 1986. pap. 2.50 (*0-440-97360-0*, LFL) Dell.
—The Rings of Kether. (Orig.). (gr. 6-12). 1986. pap. 2.50 (*0-440-97407-0*, LFL) Dell.
—Seas of Blood. (Orig.). (gr. 5 up). 1986. pap. 2.50 (*0-440-97708-8*, LFL) Dell.
—Sword of the Samurai. (Orig.). (gr. k-12). 1987. pap. 2.50 (*0-440-97795-9*, LFL) Dell.
—The Warlock of Firetop Mountain. (gr. 5 up). 1983. pap. 1.95 (*0-440-99381-4*, LFL) Dell.
Jackson, Steve, jt. auth. see Livingstone, Ian.
Jackson, Thomas C. Hammers, Nails, Planks & Paint. Chewning, Randy, illus. 32p. (ps-3). 1994. pap. 2.50 (*0-590-44642-8*, Cartwheel) Scholastic Inc.
Jackson, Tim. AIDS: Just the Facts Jack. Jackson, Tim, illus. (Orig.). (gr. 5 up). 1988. pap. 1.95 (*0-942675-06-1*, 6) Creative License.
—The Case of: The Great Graffiti. Jackson, Tim, illus. 19p. (Orig.). (gr. 5-8). 1987. pap. 1.95 (*0-942675-04-5*) Creative License.
—Friends & Choices. Jackson, Tim, illus. & intro. by. 24p. (Orig.). (gr. 6-12). 1987. pap. 1.95 (*0-942675-05-3*) Creative License.
—Friends Are For, Being Different. Jackson, Tim, illus. & intro. by. 18p. (gr. 5-9). 1985. pap. 1.95 (*0-942675-01-0*) Creative License.
—Just Like a Happy Family. Jackson, Tim, illus. 17p. (gr. 4 up). 1985. pap. 1.95 (*0-942675-00-2*) Creative License.
—That's All They're Good For. Jackson, Tim, illus. & intro. by. 20p. (gr. 5-9). 1986. pap. 1.95 (*0-942675-02-9*) Creative License.
—What Are Friends For? HIV Safe Coloring Book. Jackson, Tim, illus. 32p. (Orig.). (gr. 3-6). 1990. pap. write for info. (*0-942675-08-8*, 0942675088) Creative License.
Jackson, W. A., ed. Soviet Union. rev. ed. LC 87-83270. (Illus.). 96p. (gr. 6 up). 1988. text ed. 16.95 (*0-934291-34-9*); tchr's guide 9.95 (*0-934291-35-7*); mastery test packet 5.95 (*0-934291-40-3*) Gateway Pr MI.
Jacob, Ellen. Great Skaters Learn-by-Coloring Book: Famous Figures of the Sport & Their Inspiring Stories. (Illus.). 48p. (ps-7). 1991. pap. 4.95 (*0-937180-07-6*) Variety Arts.
—Nutcracker Learn-by-Coloring Book: Scenes from the Best Loved Ballet of All Times. (Illus.). 48p. (Orig.). (ps-7). 1991. pap. 4.95 (*0-937180-09-2*) Variety Arts.
—Stars of the Ballet. (Illus.). 48p. (ps-7). 1991. pap. 4.95 (*0-937180-06-8*) Variety Arts.
—Story of Gymnastics. (Illus.). 48p. (ps-7). 1991. pap. 4.95 (*0-937180-08-4*) Variety Arts.
Jacob, Suzanne, ed. Children's Living French. (Illus.). 1987. pap. 4.95 manual (*0-517-56331-2*, Crown); pap. 4.95 dictionary (*0-517-56332-0*); cassettes 18.95 (*0-517-56329-0*) Crown Pub Group.
Jacobs. Just Around the Corner. 1993. write for info. (*0-8050-3024-7*) H Holt & Co.
Jacobs, Alan, ed. see Cornell, Pat.
Jacobs, Anita. Where Has Deedie Wooster Been All These Years? LC 81-65493. 224p. (gr. 7 up). 1981. pap. 9.95 (*0-385-29133-7*) Delacorte.
—Where Has Deedie Wooster Been All These Years? 240p. (gr. 7 up). 1983. pap. 2.25 (*0-440-98955-8*, LFL) Dell.
Jacobs, Arthur. New Dictionary of Music. (Orig.). (gr. 9 up). 1958. pap. 8.95 (*0-14-051012-5*, Penguin Bks) Viking Penguin.
Jacobs, Barbara. Stolen Kisses. (Orig.). (gr. 6 up). 1986. pap. 2.50 (*0-440-97734-7*, LFL) Dell.
Jacobs, Chana R. Elimelech Wakes Up. Frank, Connie, illus. 32p. (ps-3). 1993. 8.95 (*0-922613-54-0*); pap. 6.95 (*0-922613-55-9*) Hachai Pubns.
—Take Care of Me. Rosenfeld, Dina, ed. Zelcer, Amir, illus. 32p. (ps-1). 1989. 8.95 (*0-922613-06-0*); pap. 6.95 (*0-922613-07-9*) Hachai Pubns.
Jacobs, Daniel. What Does It Do? Inventions Then & Now. (Illus.). 24p. (ps-2). 1990. PLB 14.60 (*0-8172-3586-8*); PLB 10.95 pkg. of 3 (*0-685-58554-9*) Raintree Steck-V.
Jacobs, David R., tr. see Haugen, Tormod.
Jacobs, Dee. Laura's Gift. Karlsson, Kris, illus. 64p. (Orig.). (gr. 6-12). 1980. PLB 15.95 (*0-938628-00-3*); pap. 9.95 (*0-938628-01-1*) Oriel Pr.
Jacobs, Don. Happy Exercise: An Adventure into a Fit World. Speidel, Sandy, illus. LC 80-23547. 48p. (Orig.). (ps-5). 1980. pap. 4.95 (*0-89037-170-9*) Anderson World.
Jacobs, Edgar P. The Time Trap. Surbeck, Jean-Jacques, tr. from FRE. Jacobs, Edgar P., illus. 49p. (Orig.). (gr. 12 up). 1989. pap. 8.95 (*0-87416-066-9*, Comcat Comics) Catalan Communs.
Jacobs, Flora G. The Doll House Mystery. (Illus.). 96p. 1958. 5.95 (*0-686-31594-4*) Wash Dolls Hse.
—The Toy Shop Mystery. (Illus.). 96p. 1960. 5.95 (*0-686-31595-2*) Wash Dolls Hse.
Jacobs, Francine. Cosmic Countdown: What Astronomers Have Learned about the Life of the Universe. Jastrow, Robert, frwd. by. LC 83-5535. (Illus.). 160p. (gr. 7 up). 1983. 9.95 (*0-87131-404-5*) M Evans.
—A Passion for Danger: Nansen's Arctic Adventures. LC 93-5674. 1994. write for info. (*0-399-22674-5*) Putnam Pub Group.
—Sam the Sea Cow. 32p. (gr. 1-3). 1992. lib. bdg. 14.85 (*0-8027-8147-0*); pap. 7.95 (*0-8027-7373-7*) Walker & Co.
—The Tainos: The People Who Welcomed Columbus. Collins, Patrick, illus. 112p. (gr. 5-9). 1992. 15.95 (*0-399-22116-6*, Putnam) Putnam Pub Group.
Jacobs, George W., jt. auth. see Kerrins, Joseph.
Jacobs, Gregory Van see Van Jacobs, Gregory.
Jacobs, Howard, ed. see Trosclair.
Jacobs, Joseph. Adventures of Tom Thumb. Cutts, David, adapted by. Fuka, illus. LC 87-10980. 32p. (gr. k-3). 1988. PLB 9.79 (*0-8167-1071-6*); pap. text ed. 1.95 (*0-8167-1072-4*) Troll Assocs.
—Celtic Fairy Tales. Batten, John D., illus. 18.25 (*0-8446-2302-4*) Peter Smith.
—Indian Fairy Tales. (Illus.). (gr. 4-12). 18.75 (*0-8446-0723-1*) Peter Smith.

—King of the Cats. Galdone, Paul, illus. LC 79-16659. 32p. (ps-3). 1980. 14.45 (0-395-29030-9, Clarion Bks) HM.

Jacobs, Joseph, ed. Celtic Fairy Tales. Batten, John D., illus. LC 67-24223. xvi, 267p. (ps-6). 1968. pap. 5.95 (0-486-21826-0) Dover.
—English Fairy Tales. Batten, John D., illus. LC 67-19703. xv, 261p. (gr. 3-6). 1898. pap. 5.95 (0-486-21818-X) Dover.
—English Fairy Tales. 1993. 13.95 (0-679-42809-7, Everymans Lib) Knopf.
—The Fables of Aesop. LC 66-29408. (Illus.). (gr. k up). 1966. pap. 8.95 (0-8052-0138-6) Schocken.
—Indian Fairy Tales. Batten, John D., illus. xvi, 255p. (ps-4). 1969. pap. 6.95 (0-486-21828-7) Dover.
—More Celtic Fairy Tales. Batten, John D., illus. LC 67-24224. x, 234p. (ps-6). 1968. pap. 5.95 (0-486-21827-9) Dover.
Jacobs, Judy. Indonesia: A Nation of Islands. (Illus.). 128p. (gr. 5 up). 1990. RSBE 14.95 (0-87518-423-5, Dillon) Macmillan Child Grp.
Jacobs, Leland. Alphabet of Girls. rev. ed. Ohlsson, Ib, illus. LC 93-8328. 1994. write for info. (0-8050-3018-2) H Holt & Co.
Jacobs, Leland B. Is Somewhere Always Far Away? Poems about Places. Kaufman, Jeff, illus. 32p. (gr. k-3). 1993. PLB 14.95 (0-8050-2677-0, Bks Young Read) H Holt & Co.
—Just Around the Corner: Poems about the Seasons. Kaufman, Jeff, illus. LC 93-18342. 32p. (gr. k-3). 1993. PLB 14.95 (0-8050-2676-2, Bks Young Read) H Holt & Co.
Jacobs, Linda. Letting off Steam: The Story of Geothermal Energy. (Illus.). 48p. (gr. 3-6). 1989. lib. bdg. 19.95 (0-87614-300-1); pap. 6.95 (0-87614-510-1) Carolrhoda Bks.
Jacobs, Louis. The Book of Jewish Practice. (gr. 9 up). 8.95 (0-317-70168-1) Behrman.
—Hasidic Thought. (gr. 8-10). 8.95 (0-317-70162-2) Behrman.
—Jewish Personal & Social Ethics. 156p. (Orig.). (gr. 9). 1990. pap. text ed. 12.50 (0-87441-510-1) Behrman.
Jacobs, Mildred Spires. Come unto Me. (Illus.). 56p. (Orig.). (gr. 5-6). 1982. pap. 2.95 (0-9609612-0-8) Enrich Enter.
Jacobs, Paul S. Sleepers, Wake. (ps-3). 1991. 13.95 (0-590-42397-5) Scholastic Inc.
Jacobs, Russell, ed. see Wright, Patricia.
Jacobs, Russell F. Algebra by Design. 48p. (gr. 8-10). 1990. wkbk. 11.95 (0-918272-17-3) Jacobs.
—Problem Solving with the Calculator. 3rd ed. (Illus.). 168p. (gr. 6-12). 1990. pap. text ed. 8.95 (0-918272-18-1); tchr's. guide-answer key 2.50 (0-918272-19-X) Jacobs.
Jacobs, Russell F., ed. see McCully, Ron.
Jacobs, Shannon K. Boy Who Loved Morning. (ps-3). 1993. 15.95 (0-316-45556-3) Little.
—Song of the Giraffe. Johnson, Pamela, illus. (gr. 2-4). 1991. 11.95 (0-316-45555-5) Little.
Jacobs, W. W. The Monkey's Paw. Richardson, I. M., adapted by. Lawn, John, illus. LC 81-19824. 32p. (gr. 5-10). 1982. PLB 10.79 (0-89375-628-8); pap. text ed. 2.95 (0-89375-629-6) Troll Assocs.
—The Monkey's Paw. LC 86-2329. 48p. (gr. 6 up). 1986. PLB 13.95s.p. (0-88682-060-X) Creative Ed.
—The Monkey's Paw. LC 89-13709. 48p. (gr. 9-12). 1989. Repr. of 1905 ed. multi-media kit 35.00 (0-685-31128-7) Balance Pub.
Jacobs, William J. Champlain: A Life of Courage. LC 93-31176. 1994. write for info. (0-531-20112-0) Watts.
—Coronado: Dreamer in Golden Armor. LC 93-31174. 1994. write for info. (0-531-20140-6) Watts.
—Cortes, Conqueror of Mexico. LC 93-31177. 1994. write for info. (0-531-20138-4) Watts.
—Eleanor Roosevelt: A Life of Happiness & Tears. LC 90-48974. (Illus.). 128p. (gr. 6-10). 1991. PLB 13.95 (1-55905-095-0) Marshall Cavendish.
—Ellis Island: New Hope in a New Land. LC 89-38075. (Illus.). 40p. (gr. 2-5). 1990. RSBE 13.95 (0-684-19171-7, Scribners Young Read) Macmillan Child Grp.
—Great Lives: Human Rights. LC 89-37211. (Illus.). 288p. (gr. 4-6). 1990. SBE 22.95 (0-684-19036-2, Scribners Young Read) Macmillan Child Grp.
—Great Lives: World Government. LC 91-42368. (Illus.). 320p. (gr. 4-6). 1992. SBE 22.95 (0-684-19285-3, Scribners Young Read) Macmillan Child Grp.
—Lincoln. LC 90-8815. (Illus.). 48p. (gr. 4-6). 1991. SBE 13.95 (0-684-19274-8, Scribners Young Read) Macmillan Child Grp.
—Magellan: Voyager with a Dream. LC 93-29698. 1994. write for info. (0-531-20139-2) Watts.
—Mother Teresa: Helping the Poor. (Illus.). 48p. (gr. 2-4). 1991. PLB 12.40 (1-56294-020-1) Millbrook Pr.
—Pizarro, Conqueror of Peru. LC 93-31158. 1994. write for info. (0-531-20107-4) Watts.
—Search for Peace: The Story of the United Nations. LC 93-27149. (Illus.). 144p. (gr. 5-8). 1994. SBE 14.95 (0-684-19652-2, Scribners Young Read) Macmillan Child Grp.
—War with Mexico. LC 92-46115. (Illus.). 64p. (gr. 4-6). 1993. PLB 14.90 (1-56294-366-9) Millbrook Pr.
—Washington. LC 90-8844. (Illus.). 48p. (gr. 4-6). 1991. SBE 13.95 (0-684-19275-6, Scribners Young Read) Macmillan Child Grp.
Jacobsen, Alice, jt. auth. see Richter, Betts.
Jacobsen, Judith, ed. see Jacobsen, Mark & Kozlovski, Jane.

Jacobsen, Karen. Argentina. LC 90-36526. (Illus.). 48p. (gr. k-4). 1990. PLB 15.27 (0-516-01101-4); pap. 4.95 (0-516-41101-2) Childrens.
—Bolivia. LC 91-8889. 48p. (gr. k-4). 1991. PLB 15.27 (0-516-01122-7); pap. 4.95 (0-516-41122-5) Childrens.
—Brazil. LC 89-10042. 48p. (gr. k-4). 1989. PLB 15.27 (0-516-01171-5); pap. 4.95 (0-516-41171-3) Childrens.
—Chile. LC 90-20818. (Illus.). 48p. (gr. k-4). 1991. PLB 15.27 (0-516-01111-1); pap. 4.95 (0-516-41111-X) Childrens.
—China. LC 90-2200. (Illus.). 48p. (gr. k-4). 1990. PLB 15.27 (0-516-01102-2); pap. 4.95 (0-516-41102-0) Childrens.
—The Commonwealth of Independent States. LC 92-12946. (Illus.). 48p. (gr. k-4). 1992. PLB 15.27 (0-516-02194-X) Childrens.
—Commonwealth of Independent States. LC 92-12946. (Illus.). 48p. (gr. k-4). 1993. pap. 4.95 (0-516-42194-8) Childrens.
—Cuba. LC 89-25426. (Illus.). 48p. (gr. k-4). 1990. PLB 15.27 (0-516-01183-9); pap. 4.95 (0-516-41183-7) Childrens.
—Egypt. LC 89-25347. (Illus.). 48p. (gr. k-4). 1990. PLB 15.27 (0-516-01184-7); pap. 4.95 (0-516-41184-5) Childrens.
—Farm Animals. LC 81-7686. (Illus.). 48p. (gr. k-4). 1981. PLB 15.27 (0-516-01619-9); pap. 4.95 (0-516-41619-7) Childrens.
—Ghana. LC 91-35273. (Illus.). 48p. (gr. k-4). 1992. PLB 15.27 (0-516-01135-9); pap. 4.95 (0-516-41135-7) Childrens.
—Greece. LC 89-25343. (Illus.). 48p. (gr. k-4). 1990. PLB 15.27 (0-516-01185-5); pap. 4.95 (0-516-41185-3) Childrens.
—Japan. LC 82-4445. (Illus.). (gr. k-4). 1982. PLB 15.27 (0-516-01630-X); pap. 4.95 (0-516-41630-8) Childrens.
—Kenya. LC 90-20009. (Illus.). 48p. (gr. k-4). 1991. PLB 15.27 (0-516-01112-X); pap. 4.95 (0-516-41112-8) Childrens.
—Korea. LC 89-10043. 48p. (gr. k-4). 1989. PLB 15.27 (0-516-01174-X); pap. 4.95 (0-516-41174-8) Childrens.
—Laos. LC 90-21034. (Illus.). 48p. (gr. k-4). 1991. PLB 15.27 (0-516-01113-8); pap. 4.95 (0-516-41113-6) Childrens.
—Mexico. Kratky, Lada, tr. from ENG. LC 82-4437. (SPA., Illus.). 48p. (gr. k-4). 1984. PLB 15.27 (0-516-31632-X); pap. 4.95 (0-516-51632-9) Childrens.
—The Netherlands. LC 91-37974. (Illus.). 48p. (gr. k-4). 1992. PLB 15.27 (0-516-01137-5); pap. 4.95 (0-516-41137-3) Childrens.
—Russia. LC 93-36996. (gr. 5 up). 1994. write for info. (0-516-01060-3) Childrens.
—South Africa. LC 89-10044. 48p. (gr. k-4). 1989. PLB 15.27 (0-516-01176-6); pap. 4.95 (0-516-41176-4) Childrens.
—The Soviet Union. LC 90-2177. (Illus.). 48p. (gr. k-4). 1990. PLB 15.27 (0-516-01109-X); pap. 4.95 (0-516-41109-8) Childrens.
—Stamps. LC 83-7591. 48p. (gr. k-4). 1983. PLB 15.27 (0-516-01709-8) Childrens.
—Thailand. LC 89-34413. 48p. (gr. k-4). 1989. PLB 15.27 (0-516-01179-0); pap. 4.95 (0-516-41179-9) Childrens.
—Vietnam. LC 91-35272. (Illus.). 48p. (gr. k-4). 1992. PLB 15.27 (0-516-01147-2); pap. 4.95 (0-516-41147-0) Childrens.
—Zimbabwe. LC 90-2202. (Illus.). 48p. (gr. k-4). 1990. PLB 15.27 (0-516-01110-3); pap. 4.95 (0-516-41110-1) Childrens.

Jacobsen, Mark & Kozlovski, Jane. Baby's Book. Jacobsen, Judith, ed. La Belle, Susan, illus. 1989. 24.95 (0-9623800-0-8) Me Two Pubns.
—Baby's First Year. Jacobsen, Judith, ed. La Belle, Susan, illus. 1989. pap. 19.95 (0-9623800-1-6) Me Two Pubns.
Jacobson, Claire, tr. see Leroi-Gourhan, Andre.
Jacobson, Gloria. Two for America: The True Story of a Swiss Immigrant. Cliff, Don, illus. 36p. (gr. 4). 1989. pap. 8.50 (0-9618399-1-0) G Jacobson.
Jacobson, Jane. City, Sing, for Me: A Country Child Moves to the City. Rowen, Amy, illus. LC 77-11130. 32p. (gr. 1-5). 1978. 16.95 (0-87705-358-8) Human Sci Pr.
Jacobson, Karen. Mexico. LC 82-4437. (Illus.). (gr. k-4). 1982. PLB 15.27 (0-516-01632-6); pap. 4.95 (0-516-41632-4) Childrens.
—Television. LC 82-4456. (Illus.). (gr. k-4). 1982. pap. 4.95 (0-516-41659-6) Childrens.
—Zoos. LC 82-9545. (Illus.). (gr. k-4). 1982. PLB 15.27 (0-516-01664-4); pap. 4.95 (0-516-41664-2) Childrens.
Jacobson, Mark I. Antero Aquamarines: Minerals from the Mount Antero-White Mountain Region, Chaffee County, Colorado. (Illus.). 160p. 1993. 34.95 (0-928693-08-2); pap. 19.95 (0-928693-07-4) L R Ream.
Jacobson, Michael & Hill, Laura. Kitchen Fun for Kids: Healthy Recipes & Nutrition Facts for 7-12 Year Old Cooks. 128p. (gr. 2-7). 1991. 14.95 (0-8050-1609-0, Bks Young Read) H Holt & Co.
Jacobson, Michael F., et al. Safe Food: Eating Wisely in a Risky World. (Illus.). 252p. (Orig.). 1991. pap. 9.95 (1-879326-01-9) Living Planet Pr.
Jacobson, Sheldon A. Fleet Surgeon to Pharaoh. LC 71-126923. 306p. (gr. 9 up). 1971. 14.95 (0-685-45134-8); PLB 12.95 (0-87071-316-7) Educare Pr.
—The Man Who Moved the World. LC 80-83024. 300p. (gr. 4-10). 1980. 14.95 (0-685-45133-X) Educare Pr.

—The Valiant Captains: Epics of the Gallant Ships That Challenged the English Channel. O'Mahony, Kieran, ed. LC 90-80517. 250p. (Orig.). (gr. 9-12). 1990. 19.95 (0-944638-03-1); pap. 12.95 (0-944638-01-5) Educare Pr.
Jacoby, Alice. My Mother's Boyfriend & Me. (gr. 9 up). 1988. pap. 2.95 (0-449-70311-8, Juniper) Fawcett.
Jacome, Felipe, jt. auth. see Jacome, Karen.
Jacome, Karen & Jacome, Felipe. Trivial Pursuit - Science (Intermediate) (Illus.). 64p. (gr. 4-6). 1992. 12.95 (0-86653-649-3, GA1386) Good Apple.
Jacoubek, Robert E. The Assassination of Abraham Lincoln. LC 92-10900. (Illus.). 64p. (gr. 4-6). 1993. PLB 14.40 (1-56294-239-5) Millbrook Pr.
Jacques, Brian. Mariel of Redwall. 400p. (gr. 5-9). 1992. 17.95 (0-399-22144-1, Philomel Bks) Putnam Pub Group.
—Martin the Warrior. LC 93-26434. 1994. write for info. (0-03-992267-7, Philomel Bks) Putnam Pub Group.
—Mattimeo. 1990. 16.95 (0-399-21741-X, Philomel Bks) Putnam Pub Group.
—Mossflower. Chalk, Gary, illus. LC 88-17921. 432p. (gr. 5 up). 1988. 16.95 (0-399-21549-2, Philomel Bks) Putnam Pub Group.
—Redwall. LC 86-25467. (gr. k up). 1987. 16.95 (0-399-21424-0, Philomel Bks) Putnam Pub Group.
—Salamandastron: A Tale from Red Wall. Chalk, Gary, illus. 400p. (gr. 5 up). 1993. 17.95 (0-399-21992-7, Philomel Bks) Putnam Pub Group.
—Seven Strange & Ghostly Tales. (gr. 3 up). 1991. 14.95 (0-399-22103-4, Philomel Bks) Putnam Pub Group.
—Seven Strange & Ghostly Tales. 144p. 1993. pap. 3.50 (0-380-71906-1, Camelot) Avon.
Jacques, Ethel M., jt. auth. see Muller, Carrel.
Jacques, Geoffrey. The African-American Movement Today. LC 92-17086. (Illus.). 144p. (gr. 9-12). 1992. PLB 13.90 (0-531-11033-8) Watts.
Jacques, Reginald & Willcocks, David. Carols for Choirs: Fifty Christmas Carols, Bk. 1. (gr. 9 up). 1961. pap. 11.95 (0-19-353222-0) OUP.
Jacques, Reginald, ed. Oxford S-A-B Song Book, 2 vols. (gr. 7-9). 1951. Vol. 1. 6.95 (0-19-330511-9); Vol. 2. 6.95 (0-19-330513-5) OUP.
Jaeger, Gerard. Vespucci. 1992. PLB 14.95s.p. (0-88682-485-0) Creative Ed.
Jafa, Manorama. The Donkey on the Bridge. Bhusan, Rboti, illus. 24p. (Orig.). (gr. k-3). 1980. pap. 2.50 (0-89744-209-1, Pub. by Childrens Bk Trust IA) Auromere.
Jaffe, David. The New College Financial Aid System: Making It Work for You. 141p. (gr. 11-12). 1993. pap. 14.95 (0-933031-82-3) Coun Oak Bks.
Jaffe, Marjorie, jt. auth. see Isenberg, Barbara.
Jaffe, Nina. In the Month of Kislev: A Story for Hanukkah. August, Louise, illus. 32p. (ps-3). 1992. 15.00 (0-670-82863-7) Viking Child Bks.
—Patakin: World Drums. 1994. write for info. (0-8050-3005-0) H Holt & Co.
—The Three Riddles: A Jewish Folktale. Waldman, Bryna, illus. (ps-3). 1989. incl. cassette 7.95 (0-553-45910-4) Bantam.
—The Three Riddles: A Jewish Folktale. Waldman, Bryna, illus. (ps-3). 1989. pap. 3.95 (0-553-34649-0) Bantam.
—The Uninvited Guest & Other Jewish Holiday Tales. Savadier, Elivia, illus. LC 92-36308. 1993. write for info. (0-590-44653-3) Scholastic Inc.
Jaffe, Nina & Zeitlin, Steve. While Standing on One Foot: Puzzle Stories & Wisdom Tales from the Jewish Tradition. Segal, John, illus. 128p. (gr. 3-7). 1993. PLB 14.95 (0-8050-2594-4, Bks Young Read) H Holt & Co.
Jaffe, Nina, adapted by. & tr. The Golden Flower: A Taino Myth from Puerto Rico. Moiles, Holly B., illus. LC 92-42364. 32p. (ps-3). 1994. RSBE 15.95 (0-02-747585-9, Macmillan Child Bk) Macmillan Child Grp.
Jaffe, Steve. Who Were Fathers? 1994. write for info. (0-8050-3102-2) H Holt & Co.
Jaffke, Freya. Toymaking with Children. 1988. pap. 10.95 (0-86315-069-1, 20244) Gryphon Hse.
Jaffrey, Madhur. Seasons of Splendor. Foreman, Michael, illus. (ps up). pap. 7.95 (0-317-62172-6, Puffin) Puffin Bks.
—Seasons of Splendour: Tales, Myths & Legends of India. Foreman, Michael, illus. 128p. (gr. 4 up). 1992. pap. 16.95 (1-85145-933-2, Pub. by Pavilion UK) Trafalgar.
Jafolla, Mary-Alice. The Simple Truth. LC 81-69084. 109p. 1993. pap. 9.95 (0-87159-199-5) Unity Bks.
Jagen, Edward J. A Good Knight Story: The Quest for the Missing Children. Gregory, G., et al, eds. Blank, Diane, et al, illus. McCarthy, Dennis, intro. by. 64p. (Orig.). (gr. k-7). 1990. pap. 14.95x (0-9625641-0-9); wkbk. 4.95 (0-9625641-2-5) White Feather & Co.
—The Good Knights' Quest to Rescue the Flower Faeries. Blank, Diane, illus. 44p. (gr. k-6). 1991. pap. text ed. 14.95 (0-9625641-3-3) White Feather & Co.
—The Quest of the Junior Blue Knights. Blank, Diane, illus. Jagen, E. J., intro. by. (Illus.). 32p. (gr. k-7). 1990. wkbk. 4.95 (0-9625641-1-7) White Feather & Co.
Jagger, Alice, et al. Power of the Nation States - AppleWorks Version. 81p. (gr. 9-12). 1988. Classroom license. incl. pub. 2 dbl. sided data disks 59.95 (0-924667-42-7); School site license. incl. 2 dbl. sided data disks 95.00 (0-685-24470-9) Intl Society Tech Educ.

—Power of the Nation States - Microsoft Works Version. 106p. (gr. 9-12). 1989. Classroom license. tchr's. guide incl. 1 dbl-sided data disks 59.95 (*0-924667-43-5*); School site license. incl. 2 dbl-sided data disks 94.50 (*0-685-24471-7*) Intl Society Tech Educ.

Jahsmann, Allan H. & Simon, Martin P. Little Visits with God. (gr. k-3). 1957. 12.99 (*0-570-03016-1*, 6-1055); pap. 9.99 (*0-570-03032-3*, 6-1158) Concordia.

Jahsmann, Allan H., jt. auth. see Gross, Arthur W.

Jai. Coe the Good Dragon at the Center of the World. 6th ed. LC 85-71009. (FRE & ENG., Illus.). (ps up). 1985. 8.95 (*0-934003-00-9*); French ed. pap. 5.00 (*0-934003-01-7*) Bluebird Pr CA.

Jain, Ash. Don't Steal My Blocks! The Children's Storybook of Operation Desert Storm. Cavallotti, Carolina, illus. 12p. (Orig.). (ps-3). 1991. pap. 2.95 (*0-9629992-1-0*) Arlington Pr.

Jakes, John. Susanna of the Alamo. (Illus.). 32p. (gr. 1-5). 1990. pap. 4.95 (*0-15-200595-1*, Voyager Bks) HarBrace.

—Susanna of the Alamo: A True Story. Bacon, Paul, illus. LC 85-27143. 32p. (gr. 1-5). 1986. 13.95 (*0-15-200592-7*, Gulliver Bks) HarBrace.

Jakmayan, Diana. The Velvet Ribbon. 1991. 6.95 (*0-533-09306-6*) Vantage.

Jakob, Donna. My Bike. (Illus.). 32p. (ps-2). 1994. 13.95 (*1-56282-454-6*); PLB 13.89 (*1-56282-455-4*) Hyprn Child.

Jakobsen, Kathy. My New York. 1993. 15.95 (*0-316-45653-5*) Little.

Jakobson, Cathryn. Teenage Pregnancy. rev. ed. 160p. (gr. 7 up). 1992. PLB 15.85 (*0-8027-8128-4*); pap. 9.95 (*0-8027-7372-9*) Walker & Co.

—Think About: The Environment. 160p. (gr. 7 up). 1992. PLB 15.85 (*0-8027-8105-5*); pap. 9.95 (*0-8027-7357-5*) Walker & Co.

Jakoubek, Robert. Adam Clayton Powell, Jr. King, Coretta Scott, intro. by. (Illus.). 112p. 1988. lib. bdg. 17.95x (*1-55546-606-0*); pap. 9.95 (*0-7910-0213-6*) Chelsea Hse.

—The Colonial Mosaic: American Women, 1600-1760. (Illus.). 144p. 1994. PLB 20.00 (*0-19-508015-7*) OUP.

—Edward R. Murrow. (Illus.). (gr. 5 up). 1992. lib. bdg. 17.95 (*0-7910-1639-0*) Chelsea Hse.

—Harriet Beecher Stowe. Horner, Matina S., intro. by. (Illus.). 112p. (gr. 5 up). 1989. 17.95 (*1-55546-680-X*) Chelsea Hse.

—Jack Johnson. King, Coretta Scott, intro. by. (Illus.). 112p. (gr. 5 up). 1990. PLB 17.95 (*0-7910-1113-5*) Chelsea Hse.

—Jesse Jackson. King, Coretta Scott, intro. by. (Illus.). 112p. (gr. 5 up). 1991. PLB 17.95 (*0-7910-1130-5*) Chelsea Hse.

—Martin Luther King, Jr. King, Coretta Scott, intro. by. (Illus.). (gr. 5 up). 1990. 17.95 (*1-55546-597-8*) Chelsea Hse.

—Martin Luther King, Jr. (gr. 5 up). 1990. pap. 9.95 (*0-7910-0243-8*) Chelsea Hse.

Jakoubek, Robert E. James Farmer & the Freedom Rides. (Illus.). 32p. (gr. 2-4). 1994. 12.40 (*1-56294-381-2*) Millbrook Pr.

—Walter White & the Power of Organized Protest. (Illus.). 32p. (gr. 2-4). 1994. 12.40 (*1-56294-378-2*) Millbrook Pr.

Jakubowsky, Frank. Frank on a Farm. 60p. (Orig.). 1988. pap. 4.95 (*0-932588-11-5*) Jesus Bks.

—Lake Merritt. 60p. (Orig.). 1988. pap. 4.95 (*0-932588-10-7*) Jesus Bks.

Jam, Teddy. Dr. Kiss Says Yes. Fitzgerald, Joanne, illus. 32p. (ps-1). 1992. 12.95 (*0-88899-141-X*, Pub. by Groundwood-Douglas & McIntyre CN) Firefly Bks Ltd.

—The Year of Fire. Wallace, Ian, illus. LC 92-2882. 48p. (gr. 1-5). 1993. SBE 14.95 (*0-689-50566-3*, M K McElderry) Macmillan Child Grp.

James. Lapps - Reindeer Herders of Lapland, Reading Level 5. (Illus.). 48p. (gr. 4-8). 1989. PLB 16.67 (*0-86625-263-0*); pap. 12.50s.p. (*0-685-58811-4*) Rourke Corp.

—Shoebag. 1992. pap. 2.95 (*0-590-43030-0*, Apple Paperbacks) Scholastic Inc.

James, Alan. Castles & Mansions. (Illus.). 32p. (gr. 2-5). 1989. 13.50 (*0-8225-2128-8*) Lerner Pubns.

—Homes in Cold Places. (Illus.). 32p. (gr. 2-5). 1989. 13.50 (*0-8225-2131-8*) Lerner Pubns.

—Homes in Hot Places. (Illus.). 32p. (gr. 2-5). 1989. 13.50 (*0-8225-2132-6*) Lerner Pubns.

—Homes on Water. (Illus.). 32p. (gr. 2-5). 1989. 13.50 (*0-8225-2127-X*) Lerner Pubns.

James, Alison, tr. see Ostheeren, Ingrid.

James, Barbara. Conserving the Polar Regions. LC 90-46064. (Illus.). 48p. (gr. 4-9). 1990. PLB 19.92 (*0-8114-2393-X*); pap. 5.95 (*0-8114-3458-3*) Raintree Steck-V.

—Easter Basket Book - Easter Egg Hunt. 10p. (ps-3). 1991. pap. 2.95 (*0-8167-2226-9*) Troll Assocs.

—Easter Basket Book - Easter Surprises. 10p. (ps-3). 1991. pap. 2.95 (*0-8167-2079-7*) Troll Assocs.

—Easter Basket Book - Teddy's Easter Basket. 10p. (ps-3). 1991. pap. 2.95 (*0-8167-2072-X*) Troll Assocs.

—Easter Basket Book: Bunny's Beans. 10p. (ps-3). 1991. pap. 2.95 (*0-8167-2073-8*) Troll Assocs.

—Use of Land. LC 93-8529. (Illus.). 32p. (gr. 4-6). 1993. 14.95 (*1-56847-119-X*) Thomson Lrning.

—Waste & Recycling. LC 89-26274. (Illus.). 48p. (gr. 4-9). 1990. PLB 19.92 (*0-8114-2386-7*); pap. 5.95 (*0-8114-3457-5*) Raintree Steck-V.

James, Betsy. Blow Away Soon. Vojtech, Anna, illus. LC 93-27135. 1995. write for info. (*0-399-22648-6*, Putnam) Putnam Pub Group.

—Dark Heart. LC 91-45319. 180p. (gr. 7 up). 1992. 14.00 (*0-525-44951-5*, DCB) Dutton Child Bks.

—The Dream Stair. Watson, Richard J., illus. LC 89-36420. 32p. (gr. k-2). 1990. PLB 13.89 (*0-06-022788-5*) HarpC Child Bks.

—He Wakes Me. David, Helen K., illus. LC 90-28920. 32p. (ps-1). 1991. 14.95 (*0-531-05954-5*); RLB 14.99 (*0-531-08554-6*) Orchard Bks Watts.

—Long Night Dance. LC 88-38837. 176p. (gr. 7 up). 1989. 13.95 (*0-525-44485-8*, DCB) Dutton Child Bks.

—Mary Ann. James, Betsy, illus. LC 93-13364. 32p. (ps-3). 1994. 13.99 (*0-525-45077-7*) Dutton Child Bks.

—The Mud Family. Morin, Paul, illus. LC 92-43537. 1994. write for info. (*0-399-22549-8*, Putnam) Putnam Pub Group.

James, Carollyn. Digging up the Past: The Story of an Archaeological Adventure. Schindler, S. D., illus. 64p. (gr. 5-8). 1990. PLB 11.90 (*0-531-10878-3*) Watts.

James, Cary. Julia Morgan. Horner, Matina S., intro. by. (Illus.). 112p. (gr. 5 up). 1990. 17.95 (*1-55546-669-9*) Chelsea Hse.

James, Christopher. Bump & the Bucket. (Illus.). 24p. (ps-3). 1990. 6.95 (*0-88625-279-2*) Durkin Hayes Pub.

—Bump & the Trees. (Illus.). 24p. (ps-3). 1990. 6.95 (*0-88625-276-8*) Durkin Hayes Pub.

—Bump the Builder. (Illus.). 24p. (ps-3). 1990. pap. 6.95 (*0-88625-277-6*) Durkin Hayes Pub.

—Bump's Umbrella. (Illus.). 24p. (ps-3). 1990. 6.95 (*0-88625-277-6*) Durkin Hayes Pub.

James, D. H. Sheba Consumes Whatever She Can. 98p. 1990. 19.95 (*1-878950-01-0*) Sheba Bks Intl.

James, Darcy. Let's Make a Jesse Tree. 32p. (gr. k-3). 1988. pap. 5.95 (*0-687-21439-4*) Abingdon.

James, Dean. Melrose Place - Keeping the Faith. (gr. 4-7). 1993. pap. 3.99 (*0-06-106789-X*, Harp PBks) HarpC.

—Three's a Crowd. 1993. pap. 3.99 (*0-06-106205-7*, Harp PBks) HarpC.

James, Diane. Design. Maudsley, Toby & Johnson, James, photos by. Bulloch, Ivan, designed by. LC 93-35626. (Illus.). 48p. (gr. 3-7). 1994. 16.95 (*1-56847-148-3*) Thomson Lrning.

—The Dressing-up Book. Baker, Wendy, illus. LC 93-36430. 48p. (gr. 4-8). 1994. 16.95 (*1-56847-136-X*) Thomson Lrning.

—Fashion. Baker, Wendy, illus. LC 93-21215. 48p. (gr. 3-7). 1994. 16.95 (*1-56847-145-9*) Thomson Lrning.

—The Party Book. Tofts, Hannah, illus. LC 93-21219. 48p. (gr. 4-8). 1994. 16.95 (*1-56847-135-1*) Thomson Lrning.

—Playing with Paint. Lynn, Sara, photos by. (Illus.). 24p. (ps-1). 1992. pap. 3.95 (*0-590-45739-X*, Cartwheel) Scholastic Inc.

—Playing with Paper. Lynn, Sara, photos by. (Illus.). 24p. (ps-1). 1992. pap. 3.95 (*0-590-45738-1*, Cartwheel) Scholastic Inc.

James, Diane, jt. auth. see James, Sara L.

James, Diane, jt. auth. see Lynn, Sara.

James, Elizabeth & Barkin, Carol. How to Be School Smart: Secrets of Successful Schoolwork. Doty, Roy, photos by. Greenlaw, M. Jean, intro. by. LC 87-2899. (Illus.). (gr. 4-7). 1988. lib. bdg. 12.88 (*0-688-06799-9*) Lothrop.

—How to Be School Smart: Secrets of Successful Schoolwork. Doty, Roy, illus. LC 87-2899. 96p. (gr. 4-7). 1988. pap. 6.95 (*0-688-06798-0*, Pub. by Beech Tree Bks) Morrow.

—How to Write a Great School Report. Greenlaw, M. Jean, intro. by. LC 83-764. (Illus.). 167p. (gr. 3-5). 1983. PLB 11.88 (*0-688-02283-9*) Lothrop.

—How to Write a Great School Report. Greenlaw, M. Jean, intro. by. LC 83-764. (Illus.). 80p. (gr. 3-5). 1988. pap. 6.95 (*0-688-02278-2*, Pub. by Beech Tree Bks) Morrow.

—How to Write a Term Paper. Jacobs, Leland B., intro. by. LC 80-13734. 96p. (gr. 7 up). 1980. 11.88 (*0-685-03103-9*) Lothrop.

—How to Write a Term Paper. Jacobs, Leland B., intro. by. LC 80-13734. (Illus.). 96p. (gr. 7 up). 1980. pap. 3.95 (*0-688-41951-8*, Pub. by Beech Tree Bks) Morrow.

—How to Write Your Best Book Report. Doty, Roy, illus. LC 86-8597. 80p. (gr. 3-7). 1986. 11.88 (*0-688-05744-6*) Lothrop.

—How to Write Your Best Book Report. Doty, Roy, illus. LC 86-8597. 80p. (gr. 3-7). 1986. pap. 6.00 (*0-688-05743-8*, Pub. by Beech Tree Bks) Morrow.

—A Place of Your Own. Jacobs, Lou, Jr., illus. 96p. (gr. 9 up). 1981. (Dutton). pap. o.p. (*0-525-37099-4*) NAL-Dutton.

—Sincerely Yours: How to Write Great Letters. 192p. (gr. 4-8). 1993. 14.95 (*0-395-58831-6*, Clarion Bks); pap. 6.95 (*0-395-58832-4*, Clarion Bks) HM.

James, Elizabeth, jt. auth. see Barkin, Carol.

James, Emily. Hillside Live! 128p. (Orig.). (gr. 3-9). 1993. pap. 2.95 (*0-448-40495-8*, G&D) Putnam Pub Group.

—Santa's Surprise. (ps). 1992. 3.99 (*0-553-37117-7*) Bantam.

James, George. Let's Sing about Animals. Hoggan, Pat, illus. LC 91-763080. 32p. (gr. k-2). 1992. lib. bdg. 11.89 (*0-8167-2980-8*); pap. text ed. 2.95 (*0-8167-2981-6*) Troll Assocs.

James, Henry. Ambassadors. Edel, Leon, ed. LC 85-7211. (gr. 9 up). 1972. pap. 9.16 (*0-395-05137-1*, RivEd) HM.

—American. Bruccoli, M. J. & Pearce, R. H., eds. LC 62-4689. (gr. 9 up). 1962. pap. 7.96 (*0-395-05163-0*, RivEd) HM.

—Daisy Miller & Other Stories. LC 84-29480. (gr. 9 up). 1968. pap. 1.75 (*0-8049-0178-3*, CL-178) Airmont.

—Portrait of a Lady. Fisher, N. H., intro. by. (gr. 11 up). 1966. pap. 2.50 (*0-8049-0098-1*, CL-98) Airmont.

—Portrait of a Lady. Edel, Leon, ed. LC 56-13883. (gr. 9 up). 1972. pap. 9.16 (*0-395-05106-1*, RivEd) HM.

—Turn of the Screw. Andrews, C. A., intro. by. (gr. 9 up). 1967. pap. 1.75 (*0-8049-0155-4*, CL-155) Airmont.

—The Turn of the Screw. Shaw, Charles, illus. Stewart, Diana, adapted by. LC 81-5217. (Illus.). 48p. (gr. 4 up). 1983. PLB 18.64 (*0-8172-1672-3*) Raintree Steck-V.

—The Turn of the Screw. 160p. 1993. pap. 2.50 (*0-8125-3341-0*) Tor Bks.

—Washington Square. Tate, E., intro. by. (gr. 10 up). 1969. pap. 1.50 (*0-8049-0210-0*, CL-210) Airmont.

James, Henry, tr. see Daniells, Trenna.

James, Henry G. Limericks, Fables & Poems. (Orig.). (gr. 12). 1987. 12.00 (*0-942951-00-X*); PLB 12.00 (*0-942951-01-8*); pap. 12.00 (*0-942951-02-6*) Universal Res LA.

James, Ian. Australia. (Illus.). 32p. (gr. k-6). 1989. PLB 11.90 (*0-531-10759-0*) Watts.

—China. LC 89-8928. (Illus.). 32p. (gr. 3-4). 1989. PLB 11.90 (*0-531-10833-3*) Watts.

—France. Fairclough, Chris, photos by. LC 88-50362. (Illus.). 32p. (gr. 3-6). 1989. PLB 11.90 (*0-531-10640-3*) Watts.

—Japan. (Illus.). 32p. (gr. k-6). 1989. PLB 11.90 (*0-531-10760-4*) Watts.

—Mexico. (Illus.). 32p. (gr. k-6). 1989. PLB 11.90 (*0-531-10761-2*) Watts.

—The Netherlands. (Illus.). 32p. (gr. 5-8). 1990. PLB 11.90 (*0-531-14044-X*) Watts.

—Soviet Union. (Illus.). 32p. (gr. k-6). 1989. PLB 11.90 (*0-531-10762-0*) Watts.

—Spain. (Illus.). 32p. (gr. k-6). 1989. PLB 11.90 (*0-531-10834-1*) Watts.

—United States. 1990. PLB 11.90 (*0-531-14029-6*) Watts.

James, J. Alison. Sing for a Gentle Rain. LC 90-639. 224p. (gr. 7 up). 1990. SBE 14.95 (*0-689-31561-9*, Atheneum Child Bk) Macmillan Child Grp.

James, J. Alison, tr. see Hol, Coby.

James, J. Alison, tr. see Ostheeren, Ingrid.

James, J. Alison, tr. see Pfister, Marcus.

James, J. Alison, tr. see Scheffler, Ursel.

James, J. Alison, tr. see Scheidl, Gerda M.

James, J. Alison, tr. see Vainio, Pirkko.

James, J. Allison. Runa. LC 92-13936. 160p. (gr. 5-9). 1993. SBE 13.95 (*0-689-31708-5*, Atheneum Child Bk) Macmillan Child Grp.

James, Janet C. Jeremy Gates & the Magic Key. 101p. (gr. 9-12). 1986. 7.95 (*0-920806-32-5*, Pub. by Penumbra Pr CN) U of Toronto Pr.

—My Name Is Louis. 96p. (gr. 9-12). 1988. 9.95 (*0-921254-06-7*, Pub. by Penumbra Pr CN) U of Toronto Pr.

James, Jody, ed. see Boulais, Sue.

James, Jody, ed. see Leder, Jane M.

James, Jody, ed. see Snodgrass, M. E.

James, John, jt. auth. see Morley, Jacqueline.

James L. & Collier, Christopher. War Comes to Willy Freeman. (gr. k-6). 1987. pap. 3.99 (*0-440-49504-0*, YB) Dell.

James, Lillie, illus. What is Easter? 16p. (ps). 1994. 5.95 (*0-694-00480-4*, Festival) HarpC Child Bks.

James, Mark. The Mound People: An Earth Parable. ltd. ed. Lambert, Cindy & Kozar, Elaine, eds. Peterson, Sherry, et al, illus. 80p. (Orig.). (gr. 5-12). 1985. pap. 6.95 (*0-943806-03-8*) Neahtawanta Pr.

James, Marquis. The Raven: A Biography of Sam Houston. (Illus.). 527p. (gr. 10-12). 1988. pap. 12.95 (*0-292-77040-5*) U of Tex Pr.

James, Mary. Shoebag. (gr. 5-7). 1990. pap. 12.95 (*0-590-45029-7*) Scholastic Inc.

—The Shuteyes. LC 92-16170. 176p. (gr. 3-7). 1993. 13.95 (*0-590-45069-7*) Scholastic Inc.

James, R. S. Mozambique. (Illus.). 104p. (gr. 5 up). 1988. lib. bdg. 14.95 (*1-55546-194-8*) Chelsea Hse.

James, Raymond, ed. see Swift, Jonathan.

James, Raymond, ed. see Twain, Mark.

James, Raymond, ed. see Verne, Jules.

James, Raymond, adapted by see Verne, Jules.

James, Raymond, ed. see Wells, H. G.

James, Raymond, ed. see Wyss, Johann.

James, Richard. Move One! A Chess Course for Beginners. (Illus.). 144p. (Orig.). (gr. 1-4). 1991. pap. 13.95 (*0-571-14063-7*) Faber & Faber.

James, Robert. Twenty Names in Theater. LC 89-23949. (Illus.). 48p. (gr. 3-8). 1990. PLB 12.95 (*1-85435-257-1*) Marshall Cavendish.

James, Robert, jt. auth. see Sussman, Susan.

James, Robin. Butterwings. James, Robin, illus. 32p. (gr. 1-6). 1993. pap. 2.95 (*0-8431-3494-1*) Price Stern.

—Maynard's Mermaid. James, Robin, illus. 32p. (gr. 1-6). 1993. pap. 2.95 (*0-8431-3495-X*) Price Stern.

—Morgan's Magical Island Coloring Book. (ps-3). 1992. pap. 4.25 (*0-8431-1406-1*) Price Stern.

—Napolean's Rainbow. James, Robin, illus. 32p. (Orig.). (gr. 4-6). 1993. pap. 2.95 (*0-8431-3610-3*) Price Stern.

—Sadie. James, Robin, illus. 32p. (gr. 4-6). 1994. pap. 2.95 (*0-8431-3611-1*) Price Stern.

James, Robin, jt. auth. see Cosgrove, Stephen.

James, Robin, illus. Creole's Clever Collection of Puzzles. 48p. (gr. 2-6). 1983. Repr. wkbk. 2.95 (*0-8431-1403-7*) Price Stern.

—Maui Maui's Mindbogglers. 48p. (gr. 2-6). 1983. Repr. wkbk. 2.95 (*0-8431-1402-9*) Price Stern.

—Raz Ma Taz' Dazzling Dot-to-Dot. (gr. 2-6). 1983. wkbk. 2.95 (*0-8431-1404-5*) Price Stern.

James, Sara. Boots & the Spooky House. Barcita, Pamela, illus. 24p. 1993. PLB 3.98 (*1-56156-133-9*) Kidsbks.

—Boots Goes to School. Barcita, Pamela, illus. 24p. 1993. 3.98 (*1-56156-132-0*) Kidsbks.

—Boots Loses a Tooth. Barcita, Pamela, illus. 7p. 1993. 4.98 (*1-56156-126-6*) Kidsbks.

—Boots Loses a Tooth. Barcita, Pamela, illus. 14p. 1993. 4.98 (*0-8317-0608-2*) Smithmark.

—Boots Plays Hide & Seek. Barcita, Pamela, illus. 7p. 1993. 4.98 (*1-56156-127-4*) Kidsbks.

—Boots Plays Hide & Seek. Barcita, Pamela, illus. 14p. (ps-k). 1993. 4.98 (*0-8317-0607-4*) Smithmark.

—Boots Sleeps Over. Barcita, Pamela, illus. 24p. 1993. 3.98 (*1-56156-135-5*) Kidsbks.

—Boots Sleeps Over. Barcita, Pamela, illus. 24p. (ps-k). 1993. 3.98 (*0-8317-0604-X*) Smithmark.

—Boots Visits Grandma. Barcita, Pamela, illus. 24p. 1993. PLB 3.98 (*1-56156-134-7*) Kidsbks.

—Boots Visits Grandma. Barcita, Pamela, illus. 24p. (ps-k). 1993. 3.98 (*0-8317-0603-1*) Smithmark.

—Bootsflat: Boots & the Spooky House. (Illus.). 24p. (ps). 1993. 3.98 (*0-8317-0605-8*) Smithmark.

—Bootsflat: Boots Goes to School. (Illus.). 24p. (ps). 1993. 3.98 (*0-8317-0606-6*) Smithmark.

—Gals & Guys from Beverly Hills 90210. (Illus.). 64p. 1992. pap. 2.95 (*1-56156-137-1*) Kidsbks.

—Littlest Dinosaur Finds a Friend. Digregorio, Elizabeth, illus. 24p. (Orig.). 1992. pap. 2.50 (*1-56156-110-X*) Kidsbks.

—Superstars of Beverly Hills 90210. (Illus.). 64p. 1992. pap. 2.95 (*1-56156-166-5*) Kidsbks.

—What Does Boots Hear? Barcita, Pamela, illus. 6p. 1993. 2.98 (*1-56156-129-0*) Kidsbks.

—What Does Boots Hear? Barcita, Pamela, illus. 12p. (ps). 1993. 2.98 (*0-8317-9606-5*) Smithmark.

—What Does Boots See? Barcita, Pamela, illus. 6p. 1993. 2.98 (*1-56156-128-2*) Kidsbks.

—What Does Boots See? Barcita, Pamela, illus. 12p. (ps). 1993. 2.98 (*0-8317-9605-7*) Smithmark.

—What Does Boots Smell? Barcita, Pamela, illus. 6p. 1993. PLB 2.98 (*1-56156-130-4*) Kidsbks.

—What Does Boots Smell? Barcita, Pamela, illus. 12p. (ps). 1993. 2.98 (*0-8317-9607-3*) Smithmark.

—What Does Boots Touch? Barcita, Pamela, illus. 6p. 1993. PLB 2.98 (*1-56156-131-2*) Kidsbks.

—What Does Boots Touch? Barcita, Pamela, illus. 12p. (ps). 1993. 2.98 (*0-8317-9608-1*) Smithmark.

James, Sara L. & James, Diane. What We Eat. Wright, Joe, illus. LC 93-55627. 32p. (gr. k-2). 1994. 15.95 (*1-56847-141-6*) Thomson Lrning.

James, Shirley K. Going to a Horse Farm. (Illus.). 32p. (ps-8). 1992. 15.95 (*0-88106-477-7*) Charlesbridge Pub.

James, Shirley M., jt. auth. see Lutgendorf, Philip.

James, Simon. Ancient Rome. (Illus.). 48p. (gr. 3-7). 1992. 15.00 (*0-670-84493-4*) Viking Child Bks.

—The Day Jake Vacuumed. (ps-3). 1989. pap. 7.95 (*0-553-05840-1*) Bantam.

—Dear Mr. Blueberry. James, Simon, illus. LC 90-50815. 32p. (ps-2). 1991. SBE 13.95 (*0-689-50529-9*, M K McElderry) Macmillan Child Grp.

—My Friend Whale. (ps-3). 1991. 12.95 (*0-553-07065-7*) Bantam.

—Sally & the Limpet. James, Simon, illus. LC 90-40088. 32p. (ps-3). 1991. SBE 13.95 (*0-689-50528-0*, M K McElderry) Macmillan Child Grp.

—The Wild Woods. James, Simon, illus. LC 92-54582. 32p. (ps up). 1993. 13.95 (*1-56402-219-6*) Candlewick Pr.

James, Thomas. Harry Helps Out. (Illus.). (gr. 1-2). 1972. pap. 1.95 (*0-89375-048-4*) Troll Assocs.

James, Will. Smoky the Cow Horse. 2nd ed. James, Will, illus. LC 92-28753. 324p. (gr. 3-7). 1993. pap. 3.95 (*0-689-71682-6*, Aladdin) Macmillan Child Grp.

James, William. Intelligence & Cryptanalytic Activities of the British Navy in World War I. rev. ed. 230p. (gr. 7). 1984. lib. bdg. 30.80 (*0-89412-107-3*); pap. text ed. 20.80 (*0-89412-065-4*) Aegean Park Pr.

Jameson, J. Franklin. American Revolution Considered As a Social Movement. Tolles, Frederick B., intro. by. (gr. 9-12). 1940. pap. 9.95x (*0-691-00550-8*) Princeton U Pr.

Jameson, P. Cats. (Illus.). 32p. (gr. 2-5). 1989. lib. bdg. 15.94 (*0-86625-183-9*) Rourke Corp.

—Dogs. (Illus.). 32p. (gr. 2-5). 1989. lib. bdg. 15.94 (*0-86625-184-7*); 11.95s.p. (*0-685-58610-3*) Rourke Corp.

—Tropical Fish. (Illus.). 32p. (gr. 2-5). 1989. lib. bdg. 15. 94 (*0-86625-185-5*); lib. bdg. 11.95s.p. (*0-685-58612-X*) Rourke Corp.

Jameson, Pam & Hearne, Tina. Responsible Pet Care, 6 bks, Reading Level 3. (Illus.). 192p. (gr. 2-5). 1989. Set. PLB 95.64 (*0-86625-188-X*); 71.70s.p. (*0-685-58765-7*) Rourke Corp.

Jameson, W. C. Buried Treasures of the American South. (Illus.). 224p. (gr. 6 up). 1992. pap. 9.95 (*0-87483-286-1*) August Hse.

Jamestown Editorial Group Staff. Calamities. 158p. (gr. 6-8). 1994. pap. 8.75 (*0-89061-748-1*) Jamestown Pubs.

Jamieson, Rita. Felt Fun, Flannel Board Stories. Jamieson, Myles, illus. (ps-8). 1990. pap. text ed. 5.00 (*0-9622329-1-2*) R Jamieson.

Jamiolkowski, Raymond M. Coping in a Dysfunctional Family. LC 93-13665. 1993. write for info. (*0-8239-1660-X*) Rosen Group.

Jance, Judy. Dial Zero for Help: A Story of Parental Kidnapping. Meyer, Linda D. & Lyons, Carole, eds. Megale, Marina, illus. 30p. (Orig.). (gr. k-4). 1985. lib. bdg. 9.00 (*0-932091-06-7*); pap. 3.95 (*0-932091-07-5*) Franklin Pr WA.

—It's Not Your Fault. Meyer, Linda D. & Lyons, Carole R., eds. Megale, Mauna, illus. LC 85-70434. 32p. (gr. k-4). 1985. lib. bdg. 9.00 (*0-932091-03-2*) Franklin Pr Wa.

Jander, Martha. Philip & the Ethiopian. (Illus.). 24p. (gr. k-4). 1990. pap. 1.89 (*0-570-09024-5*, 59-1447) Concordia.

—The Tower of Babel. Swisher, Elizabeth, illus. 24p. (Orig.). (gr. k-4). 1991. pap. 1.89 (*0-570-09026-1*) Concordia.

Jane, Pamela. Just Plain Penny. 160p. (gr. 3-7). 1990. 13. 45 (*0-395-52807-0*) HM.

—Noelle of the Nutcracker. Brett, Jan, illus. 64p. (gr. 2-5). 1986. 13.95 (*0-395-39969-6*) HM.

Janeczko, Paul. Poetspeak: In Their Work, About Their Work: A Special Kind of Poetry Anthology. LC 91-15532. 256p. (gr. 7 up). 1991. pap. 9.95 (*0-02-043850-8*, Collier Young Ad) Macmillan Child Grp.

Janeczko, Paul B. Brickyard Summer. Rush, Ken, illus. LC 89-42542. 64p. (gr. 7 up). 1989. 13.95 (*0-531-05846-8*); PLB 13.99 (*0-531-08446-9*) Orchard Bks Watts.

—Going over to Your Place: Poems for Each Other. LC 86-26439. 176p. (gr. 7 up). 1987. SBE 14.95 (*0-02-747670-7*, Bradbury Pr) Macmillan Child Grp.

—Loads of Codes & Secret Ciphers. LC 84-5791. (Illus.). 144p. (gr. 5-9). 1984. SBE 13.95 (*0-02-747810-6*, Macmillan Child Bk) Macmillan Child Grp.

—The Place My Words Are Looking For: What Poets Say about & Through Their Work. LC 89-39331. 128p. (gr. 4-8). 1990. SBE 13.95 (*0-02-747671-5*, Bradbury Pr) Macmillan Child Grp.

—Stardust Otel. Leech, Dorothy, illus. LC 92-44514. 64p. (gr. 7 up). 1993. 14.95 (*0-531-05498-5*); lib. bdg. 14.99 (*0-531-08648-8*) Orchard Bks Watts.

—Strings: A Gathering of Family Poems. LC 83-19033. 144p. (gr. 7 up). 1984. SBE 13.95 (*0-02-747790-8*, Bradbury Pr) Macmillan Child Grp.

Janeczko, Paul B., selected by. Looking for Your Name: A Collection of Contemporary Poems. LC 92-25648. 160p. (gr. 7-12). 1993. 14.95 (*0-531-05475-6*); PLB 14.99 (*0-531-08625-9*) Orchard Bks Watts.

—The Music of What Happens: Poems That Tell Stories. LC 87-30791. 208p. (gr. 7 up). 1988. 15.95 (*0-531-05757-7*); PLB 15.99 (*0-531-08357-8*) Orchard Bks Watts.

Janeczko, Paul B., ed. Pocket Poems. LC 84-21537. 160p. (gr. 7 up). 1985. SBE 12.95 (*0-02-747820-3*, Bradbury Pr) Macmillan Child Grp.

—Poetspeak: In Their Work, About Their Work. LC 83-2715. 256p. (gr. 7 up). 1983. SBE 15.95 (*0-02-747770-3*, Bradbury Pr) Macmillan Child Grp.

Janeczko, Paul B., selected by. Preposterous: Poems of Youth. LC 90-39644. 144p. (gr. 7 up). 1991. 14.95 (*0-531-05901-4*); PLB 14.99 (*0-531-08501-5*) Orchard Bks Watts.

Janeczko, Paul B., compiled by. This Delicious Day: Sixty-Five Poems. LC 87-7717. 96p. (gr. 4-6). 1987. 11.95 (*0-531-05724-0*); PLB 11.99 (*0-531-08324-1*) Orchard Bks Watts.

Janeway, Elizabeth. The Vikings. LC 81-867. (Illus.). 160p. (gr. 5-9). 1981. pap. 3.95 (*0-394-84885-3*) Random Bks Yng Read.

—Vikings. (Illus.). (gr. 7-9). 1964. lib. bdg. 8.99 (*0-394-90312-9*) Random Bks Yng Read.

Janger, Kathie, ed. Rainbow Collection, 1987: Stories & Poetry by Young People. Ishikawa, Yoko, illus. Johnson, Rafer, intro. by. (Illus.). 160p. (gr. 1-8). 1987. pap. text ed. 6.00 (*0-929889-02-9*) Young Writers Contest Found.

—Rainbow Collection, 1988: Stories & Poetry by Young People. Turtiainen, Tuomas, illus. Valenti, Jack, intro. by. (Illus.). 160p. (gr. 1-8). 1988. pap. 6.00 (*0-929889-03-7*) Young Writers Contest Found.

—Rainbow Collection, 1989: Stories & Poetry by Young People. Viorst, Judith, frwd. by. Sarecky, Melody, illus. 176p. (gr. 1-8). 1989. pap. 6.00 (*0-929889-04-5*) Young Writers Contest Found.

—Rainbow Collection, 1990: Stories & Poetry by Young People. Sarecky, Melody, illus. Bush, Barbara, frwd. by. (Illus.). 176p. 1990. pap. 6.00 (*0-929889-06-1*) Young Writers Contest Found.

—Rainbow Collection, 1990-91: Stories & Poetry by Young People. Sarecky, Melody, illus. DeVito, Danny, intro. by. (Illus.). 160p. (Orig.). (gr. 1-8). 1991. pap. 6.00 (*0-929889-07-X*) Young Writers Contest Found.

Janger, Kathie & Korenblit, Joan, eds. Rainbow Collection, 1985: Stories & Poetry by Young People. Allen, Steve, frwd. by. 160p. (gr. 1-8). 1985. pap. 6.00 (*0-929889-00-2*) Young Writers Contest Found.

—Rainbow Collection, 1986: Stories & Poetry by Young People. Scott, Willard, frwd. by. 160p. (gr. 1-8). 1986. pap. 6.00 (*0-929889-01-0*) Young Writers Contest Found.

Jangl, Alda M. & Jangl, James F. Ancient Legends of the Twelve Birthflowers. Jangl, Alda M., illus. 40p. (gr. 9-12). 1987. pap. 3.95 (*0-942647-01-7*) Prisma Pr.

Jangl, James F. Birthstone Coloring Book: Birthstone Legends & Other Gem Folklore. Jangl, Alda M. & Jangl, James F., illus. 32p. (gr. k up). 1987. pap. 3.50 (*0-942647-03-3*) Prisma Pr.

Jangl, James F., jt. auth. see Jangl, Alda M.

Janice. Little Bear Marches in the Saint Patrick's Day Parade. Mariana, illus. LC 67-15712. 40p. (gr. k-3). PLB 11.88 (*0-688-51075-2*) Lothrop.

—Little Bear's Christmas. Mariana, illus. LC 64-21191. (gr. k-3). 1964. PLB 12.88 (*0-688-51076-0*) Lothrop.

—Little Bear's Thanksgiving. Mariana, illus. LC 67-22593. 32p. (gr. k-3). 1967. PLB 12.88 (*0-688-51078-7*) Lothrop.

Janin, Hunt. Saudi Arabia. LC 92-13448. 1992. 21.95 (*1-85435-532-5*) Marshall Cavendish.

Janisch, Heinz. Till Eulenspiegel's Merry Pranks. Bell, Anthea, tr. from GER. Zwerger, Lisbeth, illus. LC 90-7168. 32p. (gr. 3 up). 1991. pap. 15.95 (*0-88708-150-9*) Picture Bk Studio.

Jann, Gayle. A Day in the Life of a Construction Foreman. Jann, Gayle, illus. LC 87-13761. 32p. (gr. 4-8). 1988. PLB 11.79 (*0-8167-1121-6*); pap. text ed. 2.95 (*0-8167-1122-4*) Troll Assocs.

—A Day in the Life of a Photographer. Jann, Gayle, illus. LC 87-13751. 32p. (gr. 4-8). 1988. PLB 11.79 (*0-8167-1123-2*); pap. text ed. 2.95 (*0-8167-1124-0*) Troll Assocs.

Janney, Rebecca P. The Cryptic Clue. 1993. pap. 3.99 (*0-8499-3834-1*) Word Inc.

—The Eerie Echo. (gr. 5-9). 1993. pap. 4.99 (*0-8499-3400-1*) Word Inc.

—Model Mystery. (gr. 4-7). 1993. pap. 4.99 (*0-8499-3835-X*) Word Inc.

—The Toxic Secret. (gr. 5-9). 1993. pap. 4.99 (*0-8499-3401-X*) Word Inc.

Jannson, Tove. The Fillyjonk Who Believed in Disasters. 32p. (gr. 6). 1990. PLB 13.95s.p. (*0-88682-299-8*) Creative Ed.

Janosch. The Cricket & the Mole. Janosch, illus. Bell, Anthea, tr. (Illus.). 70p. (ps-1). 1987. 8.95 (*0-86264-043-1*, Pub. by Anderson Pr UK) Trafalgar.

—I'll Make You Well, Tiger, Said the Bear. Janosch, illus. LC 86-11274. 48p. (ps up). 1987. 9.95 (*0-915361-42-6*) Modan-Adama Bks.

Janover, Caroline. Josh: A Boy with Dyslexia. LC 88-10661. (Illus.). 100p. (gr. 3-6). 1988. pap. 7.95 (*0-914525-10-7*); 11.95 (*0-914525-18-2*) Waterfront Bks.

Janovitz, Marilyn, adapted by. & illus. Baa Baa Black Sheep. LC 91-71384. 32p. (ps-2). 1991. 6.95 (*1-56282-085-0*); PLB 6.89 (*1-56282-086-9*) Hyprn Child.

—Hey Diddle Diddle. LC 91-26483. 32p. (ps-k). 1992. 6.95 (*1-56282-168-7*); PLB 6.89 (*1-56282-169-5*) Hyprn Child.

—Hickory Dickory Dock. LC 91-71378. 32p. (ps-k). 1991. 6.95 (*1-56282-083-4*); PLB 6.89 (*1-56282-084-2*) Hyprn Child.

—Pat-a-Cake. Janovitz, Marilyn, adapted by. LC 91-26950. 32p. (ps-k). 1992. 6.95 (*1-56282-170-9*); PLB 6.89 (*1-56282-171-7*) Hyprn Child.

Jansen, Curt, et al. Badger & Her Babies. (Orig.). (gr. k-4). pap. write for info. (*0-9614904-2-X*) Adventure Prods.

—Bobcat & Her Babies. (Orig.). (gr. k-4). pap. write for info. (*0-9614904-3-8*) Adventure Prods.

—Cougar & Her Babies. (Orig.). (gr. k-4). write for info.; pap. write for info. Adventure Prods.

Jansen, Rick. Incredible NIV Bible Crosswords. 96p. 1992. pap. 3.99 (*0-310-60611-X*, Youth Bks) Zondervan.

Janson, Anthony F., jt. auth. see Janson, H. W.

Janson, H. W. & Janson, Anthony F. History of Art for Young People. 4th ed. (Illus.). 528p. 1992. 35.00 (*0-8109-3405-1*) Abrams.

Janssen, James S. The Elves of Bellaire Drive. Dietrich, Helen R., ed. Hunn, Diane, illus. Roniger, Mary S., frwd. by. (Illus.). 66p. (Orig.). 1989. pap. 5.95 (*0-944784-02-X*) Habersham.

—Further Adventures of the Elves of Bellaire Drive. Hunn, Diane, illus. Roiniger, Mary Sue, intro. by. (Illus.). (ps-5). 1991. pap. 5.95 (*0-9619160-1-X*) W S Nelson & Co.

—**More Fun with the Elves of Bellaire Drive.** Hunn, Diane, illus. Roniger, Mary S., intro. by. (Illus.). 66p. (gr. 2-10). 1992. pap. text ed. 5.95 (*0-9619160-2-8*) W S Nelson & Co. This is the third book of short stories about the three elves, Ajax, Brice, & Calvin, who live in the big hollow oak tree in the backyard of the Little White Cottage on Bellaire Drive. The first book, THE ELVES OF BELLAIRE DRIVE, appeared in 1989. Since it was well received, the author,

James S. Janssen, wrote a second volume, FURTHER ADVENTURES OF THE ELVES OF BELLAIRE DRIVE, which was published in 1991. It also went well, so it was decided to write & publish a third book, MORE FUN WITH THE ELVES OF BELLAIRE DRIVE. The elves continue to maintain pleasant & amicable relations with the children of the neighborhood. Although these children never get to see the elves, they do visit the hollow tree, knock on the little red door, sing to the elves & speak aloud to them, hoping that their voices & messages are being heard by their unseen wee friends. In the silence of the night, the elves perform kind deeds for the neighborhood, especially for the children, the animals & even for the fairies who occasionally visit the area. They set many good examples for the children. This book, as the previous two, is illustrated with drawings by Diane Hunn, a local artist. *Publisher Provided Annotation.*

Janssen, Lawrence H. Earth Care a Mandate: Nature Study Guide Keyed to the Black Hills. Janssen, Lawrence H., illus. LC 85-73644. 80p. (Orig.). (gr. 7-12). 1985. pap. 3.95 (*0-917575-03-2*) Cedars WI.
—Green Lake Tales & Trails. Janssen, Beverly B., illus. LC 84-71073. 96p. (ps-6). 1984. pap. 4.95 (*0-917575-00-8*) Cedars WI.
—Horsethief Lake Old Baldy Trail Guides. Janssen, Lawrence H., illus. (Orig.). (gr. 7-12). 1986. pap. 1.00 (*0-917575-04-0*) Cedars WI.
Janssen, Martha. Secret Shame. LC 91-4398. 112p. (gr. 4 up). 1991. pap. 5.99 (*0-8066-2542-2, 9-2542*) Augsburg Fortress.
Jansson, Tove. Comet in Moominland. Portch, Elizabeth, tr. (Illus.). 192p. (gr. 2-5). 1990. 13.95 (*0-374-31526-4*) FS&G.
—Comet in Moominland. Portch, Elizabeth, tr. (Illus.). 192p. (gr. 2-5). 1991. pap. 3.95 (*0-374-41331-2*, Sunburst) FS&G.
—Moominland Midwinter. (gr. 4-7). 1992. 14.00 (*0-374-35041-8*) FS&G.
—Moominland Midwinter. (gr. 4-7). 1992. 4.50 (*0-374-45303-9*) FS&G.
—Moominpappa at Sea. Hart, Kingsley, tr. from FIN. LC 93-1434. 1993. 15.00 (*0-374-35044-2*); pap. 4.50 (*0-374-45306-3*) FS&G.
—Moominsummer Madness. (gr. 4-7). 1991. 13.95 (*0-374-35039-6*) FS&G.
—Moominsummer Madness. Warburton, Thomas, tr. (Illus.). 144p. (gr. 2-5). 1992. pap. 4.50 (*0-374-45310-1*, Sunburst) FS&G.
Jantzen, Steven L. Hooray for Peace, Hurrah for War: The United States During World War I. (Illus.). 192p. 1990. 17.95x (*0-8160-2453-7*) Facts on File.
Japan Foreign Rights Centre Staff, tr. see Barnes, Jill & Asuka, Ken.
Japan Foreign Rights Centre Staff, tr. see Barnes, Jill & Ishinabe, Fusako.
Japan Foreign Rights Centre Staff, tr. see Barnes, Jill & Kanabe, Junkichi.
Japan Foreign Rights Centre Staff, tr. see Barnes, Jill & Sato, Wakiko.
Japan Foreign Rights Centre Staff, tr. see Barnes, Jill & Sueyoshi, Akiko.
Japan Foreign Rights Centre Staff, tr. see Barnes, Jill & Teramura, Terua.
Japan Foreign Rights Centre Staff, tr. see Barnes, Jill & Tsurmi, Masao.
Japanese American Curriculum Project, Inc. Staff. Japanese American Journey: The Story of a People. Hongo, Florence M. & Burton, Miyo, eds. LC 85-80521. (Illus.). 181p. (Orig.). (gr. 5-8). 1985. 22.50x (*0-934609-00-4*); pap. 12.95x (*0-934609-01-2*) JACP Inc.
Jaqua, Ida, jt. auth. see McClenahan, Pat.
Jarka, Jeff, illus. The Very Busy Baker. 12p. (ps-k). 1993. bds. 2.50 (*1-56293-308-6*) McClanahan Bk.
—The Very Busy Farmer. 12p. (ps-k). 1993. bds. 2.50 (*1-56293-305-1*) McClanahan Bk.
—The Very Busy Toymaker. 12p. (ps-k). 1993. bds. 2.50 (*1-56293-306-X*) McClanahan Bk.
—The Very Busy Zookeeper. 12p. (ps-k). 1993. bds. 2.50 (*1-56293-307-8*) McClanahan Bk.
Jarmin, Marge, jt. auth. see Harmon, Ed.
Jarnow, Jill. Lifeguard Summer, No. 142. 192p. (Orig.). (gr. 7-9). 1988. pap. 2.50 (*0-553-27124-5*, Sweet Dreams) Bantam.
Jarrell, Mary. The Knee-Baby. Shimin, Symeon, illus. 32p. (ps up) 1988. pap. 4.95 (*0-374-44244-4*) FS&G.
Jarrell, Randall. The Animal Family. facsimile ed. Sendak, Maurice, illus. LC 65-20659. 200p. (gr. 1 up). 1985. 16.95 (*0-394-81043-0*) Knopf Bks Yng Read.

—Animal Family. facsimile ed. LC 65-20659. (Illus.). 192p. (gr. 1 up). 1987. pap. 5.95 (*0-394-88964-9*) Knopf Bks Yng Read.
—The Animal Family. 93p. 1992. text ed. 7.44 (*1-56956-107-9*) W A T Braille.
—The Animal Family: (Familia Animal) (SPA.). 6.95 (*84-204-4105-8*) Santillana.
—Bat-Poet. Sendak, Maurice, illus. LC 64-16812. 44p. (gr. 3-6). 1964. RSBE 13.95 (*0-02-747640-5*, Macmillan Child Bk) Macmillan Child Grp.
—Fly by Night. Sendak, Maurice, illus. LC 76-27313. 40p. (ps up). 1985. 14.00 (*0-374-32348-8*); pap. 2.95, 1986 (*0-374-42350-4*) FS&G.
Jarrell, Randall, tr. see Grimm, Jacob & Grimm, Wilhelm K.
Jarrell, Steve. Working Out with Weights. LC 77-1919. (gr. 8 up). 1984. pap. 8.95 (*0-668-04221-4*) P-H.
Jarrett, William. Timetables of Sports History: Baseball. (Illus.). 96p. (gr. 6 up). 1989. 17.95 (*0-8160-1918-5*) Facts on File.
—TimeTables of Sports History: Basketball. (Illus.). 96p. 1990. 17.95x (*0-8160-1920-7*) Facts on File.
—Timetables of Sports History: Football. (Illus.). 96p. (gr. 6 up). 1989. 17.95 (*0-8160-1919-3*) Facts on File.
—Timetables of Sports History: The Olympic Games. (Illus.). 96p. 1990. 17.95x (*0-8160-1921-5*) Facts on File.
Jarrow, Gail. The Two-ton Secret. 144p. (gr. 5). 1989. pap. 2.95 (*0-380-75904-7*, Camelot) Avon.
Jarvis, Bruce & Mazzocchi, Paul. Form & Function: An Organic Chemistry Module. Gardner, Marjorie, intro. by. (Illus.). 136p. (Orig.). (gr. 9-12). 1991. pap. text ed. 8.20 (*1-879827-01-8*) Vistas.
Jarvis, Mary B. The Leaning Tower of Pisa. 48p. (gr. 3-4). 1991. PLB 11.95 (*1-56065-031-1*) Capstone Pr.
Jarvis, Tina. Children & Primary Science. (Illus.). 241p. 1991. pap. 34.95 (*0-89397-413-7*) Nichols Pub.
Jarvis McGraw, Eloise & McGraw, Lauren. Merry Go Round in Oz. Martin, Dick, illus. 303p. (gr. 3-6). 1989. 24.95 (*0-929605-06-3*) Books Wonder.
Jarvis-Sladky, Kay. Un Grabado de Goya: Reader 3. Bakke, Eric, illus. LC 81-7783. (SPA.). 40p. (Orig.). (gr. 7-12). 1982. pap. 2.75 (*0-88436-860-2*, 70261) EMC.
—La Guitarra Misteriosa: Reader 1. Bakke, Eric, illus. LC 81-7785. (SPA.). 40p. (Orig.). (gr. 7-12). 1982. pap. 2.95 (*0-88436-858-0*, 70259) EMC.
—El Penitente Elusivo: Reader 4. Bakke, Eric, illus. LC 81-7842. (SPA., Orig.). (gr. 7-12). 1982. pap. 2.95 (*0-88436-861-0*, 70262) EMC.
—Secretos de Famalia: Reader 2. Bakke, Eric, illus. LC 81-7780. (SPA.). 40p. (Orig.). (gr. 7-12). 1982. pap. 2.95 (*0-88436-859-9*, 70260) EMC.
Jasmine, Cairo. Our Brother Has Down's Syndrome. (Illus.). 24p. (ps-8). 1985. PLB 14.95 (*0-920303-30-7*, Pub. by Annick CN); pap. 4.95 (*0-920303-31-5*, Pub. by Annick CN) Firefly Bks Ltd.
Jasper, James M. & Morgan, Edith. Developing Speaking Skills. Filkins, Vanessa, illus. 64p. (gr. k-6). 1985. 7.95 (*0-86653-268-4*, GA 633) Good Apple.
Jaspersohn, Bill, jt. auth. see Ettinger, Tom.
Jaspersohn, W. Senator: A Profile of Bill Bradley in the U. S. Senate. 1992. 19.95 (*0-15-272880-5*) HarBrace.
Jaspersohn, William. Cookies. Jaspersohn, William, illus. LC 91-45023. 48p. (gr. 3-6). 1993. RSBE 14.95 (*0-02-747822-X*, Macmillan Child Bk) Macmillan Child Grp.
—Cranberries. LC 90-41989. (Illus.). 32p. (gr. 2-6). 1991. 14.45 (*0-395-52098-3*) HM.
—A Day in the Life of a Marine Biologist. (Illus.). 96p. (gr. 5 up). 1982. 15.95 (*0-316-45814-7*) Little.
—How the Forest Grew. Eckart, Chuck, illus. LC 79-16286. 56p. (gr. 1 up). 1989. Repr. of 1980 ed. 13.95 (*0-688-80232-X*) Greenwillow.
—How the Forest Grew. Eckart, Chuck, illus. LC 79-16286. 56p. (gr. k up). 1992. pap. 4.95 (*0-688-11508-X*, Mulberry) Morrow.
—Ice Cream. LC 87-38331. (Illus.). 48p. (gr. 3-7). 1988. RSBE 14.95 (*0-02-747821-1*, Macmillan Child Bk) Macmillan Child Grp.
—My Hometown Library. LC 92-17372. 1993. write for info. (*0-395-55723-2*) HM.
—A Week in the Life of an Airline Pilot. (gr. 4-7). 1991. 14.95 (*0-316-45822-8*) Little.
Jassem, Kate. Chief Joseph, Leader of Destiny. new ed. LC 78-18048. (Illus.). 48p. (gr. 4-6). 1979. PLB 10.59 (*0-89375-155-3*); pap. 3.50 (*0-89375-145-6*) Troll Assocs.
—Pocahontas, Girl of Jamestown. LC 78-18045. (Illus.). 48p. (gr. 4-6). 1979. PLB 10.59 (*0-89375-152-9*); pap. 3.50 (*0-89375-142-1*) Troll Assocs.
—Sacajawea, Wilderness Guide. new ed. LC 78-60118. (Illus.). 48p. (gr. 4-6). 1979. PLB 10.59 (*0-89375-160-X*); pap. 3.50 (*0-89375-150-2*) Troll Assocs.
—Squanto, the Pilgrim Adventure. new ed. LC 78-18042. (Illus.). 48p. (gr. 4-6). 1979. PLB 10.59 (*0-89375-161-8*); pap. 3.50 (*0-89375-151-0*) Troll Assocs.
Jauck, Andrea & Points, Larry. Assateague: Island of the Wild Ponies. LC 92-5908. (Illus.). 32p. (gr. 1-5). 1993. RSBE 14.95 (*0-02-774695-X*, Macmillan Child Bk) Macmillan Child Grp.
Javernick, Ellen. Celebrate Me Made in God's Image. 144p. (gr. 1-6). 1988. 11.95 (*0-86653-452-0*, SS846, Shining Star Pubns) Good Apple.

—Celebrate the Christian Family. Mohler, Sarah, illus. 144p. (gr. k-6). 1987. pap. 11.95 (*0-86653-391-5*, SS 844, Shining Star Pubns) Good Apple.
—Christmas Bulletin Boards, Walls, Windows, Doors & More. Grossmann, Dan, illus. 96p. (gr. k-8). 1986. wkbk. 10.95 (*0-86653-371-0*, SS 1824, Shining Star Pubns) Good Apple.
—What If Everybody Did That? Hackney, Richard, illus. LC 89-28625. 32p. (ps-3). 1990. PLB 15.00 (*0-516-03669-6*); pap. 3.95 (*0-516-43669-4*) Childrens.
—Where's Brooke? Hackney, Richard, illus. LC 92-11097. 32p. (ps-2). 1992. PLB 11.93 (*0-516-02012-9*) Childrens.
—Where's Brooke? Hackney, Richard, illus. LC 92-11097. 32p. (ps-2). 1993. pap. 2.95 (*0-516-42012-7*) Childrens.
Javna, John. Fifty Simple Things Kids Can Do to Save the Earth. 156p. (gr. 1-12). 1990. pap. 6.95 (*0-8362-2301-2*) Andrews & McMeel.
Jaworski, Jo, ed. see Elbek, Gail.
Jay, Ruth J. Learning from God's Animals. Ratzlaff, Lynette, illus. 36p. (Orig.). (ps-k). 1981. pap. 2.99 (*0-934998-04-3*) Bethel Pub.
—Learning from God's Birds. Ratzlaff, Lynette, illus. 34p. (Orig.). (ps-k). 1981. pap. 2.99 (*0-934998-05-1*) Bethel Pub.
Jay, Stephen, jt. auth. see Darazs, Arpad.
Jayant, Amber. Silas & the Mad-Sad People. LC 80-83882. (Illus.). (gr. 1-5). 1981. 6.95 (*0-938678-08-6*) New Seed.
Jayne, Caroline F. String Figures & How to Make Them. (Illus.). 407p. (gr. 7 up). 1906. pap. 5.95 (*0-486-20152-X*) Dover.
Jaynes, Ruth. Yo-Ho & Kim. 58p. (gr. 1-6). 1965. 2.50 (*0-89986-386-8*) Oriental Bk Store.
—Yo-Ho & Kim at Sea. 58p. (gr. 1-6). 1965. 2.50 (*0-89986-387-6*) Oriental Bk Store.
Jean, G., jt. auth. see Charpentreau, J.
Jean, Georges. Plaisir des Mots: Dictionnaire Poetique Illustre. 352p. (gr. 4-9). 1982. 29.95 (*2-07-039499-9*) Schoenhof.
Jean, Priscilla. Pattie Round & Wally Square. Jean, Priscilla, illus. (gr. k-3). 1965. 8.95 (*0-8392-3048-6*) Astor-Honor.
Jean de, La Fontaine see De la Fontaine, Jean.
Jean-Jacques, Tony. Pour Mieux t'Aimer. Jean-Jacques, Tony, illus. (FRE & CRP.). 128p. (gr. 6-12). 1993. text ed. 10.00x (*0-938534-01-7*) Soup Nuts Pr.
Jedrosz, Aleksander. Eyes. Farmer, Andrew & Green, Robina, illus. LC 90-42177. 32p. (gr. 4-6). 1992. lib. bdg. 11.89 (*0-8167-2094-0*); pap. text ed. 3.95 (*0-8167-2095-9*) Troll Assocs.
Jeep, Elizabeth M. Children's Daily Prayer: For the School Year 1993-1994. Hoffman, Elizabeth, ed. (Illus.). 352p. (Orig.). (gr. k-8). 1993. pap. 15.00 (*0-929650-58-1*, CDP94) Liturgy Tr Pubns.
Jeffares, Jeanne. An Around-the-World Alphabet. Jeffares, Jeanne, illus. LC 89-32135. 36p. 1989. 14.95 (*0-87226-324-X*) P Bedrick Bks.
Jefferies, David. The Human Body: A Thematic Unit. Bruce, Kathy, illus. 80p. (gr. 3-5). 1993. wkbk. 7.95 (*1-55734-235-0*) Tchr Create Mat.
Jefferies, Lawrence. Air, Air, Air. Johnson, Lewis, illus. LC 82-15808. 32p. (gr. 3-6). 1983. PLB 10.59 (*0-89375-880-9*); pap. text ed. 2.95 (*0-89375-881-7*) Troll Assocs.
—All about Stars. Veno, Joseph, illus. LC 82-20027. 32p. (gr. 3-6). 1983. PLB 10.59 (*0-89375-888-4*); pap. text ed. 2.95 (*0-89375-889-2*) Troll Assocs.
—Amazing World of Animals. D'Adamo, Anthony, illus. LC 82-20061. 32p. (gr. 3-6). 1983. PLB 10.59 (*0-89375-898-1*); pap. text ed. 2.95 (*0-89375-899-X*) Troll Assocs.
Jefferies, Richard. Bevis. 384p. (gr. 4-6). 1984. pap. 2.25 (*0-14-035026-8*, Puffin) Puffin Bks.
—Wood Magic. LC 74-82725. 1974. 20.00 (*0-89388-177-5*) Okpaku Communications.
Jefferis, David. Battle Kings: The History of Tanks. LC 90-46259. (Illus.). 32p. (gr. 5-8). 1991. PLB 12.40 (*0-531-14193-4*) Watts.
—Helicopters. (ps-3). 1990. PLB 11.40 (*0-531-19069-2*) Watts.
—Making Kites. LC 92-42913. (Illus.). 40p. (gr. 3-7). 1993. 10.05 (*1-85697-923-7*); pap. 5.95 (*1-85697-922-9*) Kingfisher Bks.
—Submarines. (Illus.). 32p. (gr. k-4). 1990. PLB 11.40 (*0-531-19101-X*) Watts.
—Trail Bikes & Motocross. 1990. PLB 12.90 (*0-531-19076-5*, Warwick) Watts.
—Trains: The History of Railroads. (Illus.). 32p. (gr. 5-8). 1991. PLB 12.40 (*0-531-14192-6*) Watts.
Jefferis, David & Lafferty, Peter. Checkered Flag! The History of the Racing Car. LC 90-32128. (Illus.). 32p. (gr. 5-8). 1991. PLB 12.40 (*0-531-14122-5*) Watts.
—Giants of the Road: The History of the Truck. LC 90-31659. (Illus.). 32p. (gr. 5-8). 1991. PLB 12.40 (*0-531-14123-3*) Watts.
Jefferis, David, jt. auth. see Lafferty, Peter.
Jeffers, Lance. Grandsire. LC 78-61607. 55p. (gr. 7-12). 1979. pap. 3.00x perf. bound (*0-916418-17-0*) Lotus.
—O Africa, Where I Baked My Bread. LC 77-75581. (Illus.). 77p. (gr. 9-12). 1977. pap. 3.50x (*0-916418-11-1*) Lotus.
Jeffers, Susan. If Wishes Were Horses. LC 79-9986. (Illus.). 32p. (ps-3). 1987. pap. 3.95 (*0-525-44325-8*, 0383-120, DCB) Dutton Child Bks.

—If Wishes Were Horses: Mother Goose Rhymes. Jeffers, Susan, illus. LC 79-9986. 32p. (ps-3). 1979. 13.95 (0-525-32531-X, DCB) Dutton Child Bks.
—Silent Night. (Illus.). 1992. pap. 4.99 (0-525-44431-9, DCB) Dutton Child Bks.
—The Three Jovial Huntsmen. Jeffers, Susan, illus. LC 88-32708. 32p. (ps-2). 1989. pap. 3.95 (0-689-71309-6, Aladdin) Macmillan Child Grp.
—Wild Robin. Jeffers, Susan, illus. LC 76-21343. 40p. (ps-3). 1986. pap. 4.95 (0-525-44244-8, DCB) Dutton Child Bks.
Jeffers, Susan, jt. auth. see Wells, Rosemary.
Jeffers, Susan, illus. Brother Eagle, Sister Sky: A Message from Chief Seattle. LC 90-27713. 32p. 1991. 16.00 (0-8037-0969-2); PLB 14.89 (0-8037-0963-3) Dial Bks Young.
Jefferson, Margo & Skinner, Elliott P. Roots of Time: A Portrait of African Life & Culture. LC 90-80149. 1990. pap. 7.95 (0-86543-169-8) Africa World.
Jeffery, Lisa E., ed. see Thompson-Peters, Flossie E.
Jeffredo-Warden, Louise V. Ishi. Fujiwara, Kim, illus. LC 92-8602. 32p. (gr. 4-5). 1992. PLB 17.96 (0-8114-6578-0); pap. 4.95 (0-8114-4096-6) Raintree Steck-V.
Jeffrey, David. Geronimo. Viola, Herman, intro. by. (Illus.). 32p. (gr. 3-6). 1990. PLB 17.96 (0-8172-3404-7); pap. 4.95 (0-8114-4090-7) Raintree Steck-V.
Jeffrey, Graham. The Little Man. (Illus.). 32p. (ps-k). 1993. 14.95 (0-460-88068-3, Pub. by J M Dent & Sons) Trafalgar.
Jeffries, David. Multicultural Folk Tales: A Thematic Unit. Fullam, Sue & Vasconcelles, Keith, illus. 80p. (gr. 3-5). 1992. wkbk. 7.95 (1-55734-230-X) Tchr Create Mat.
Jeffs, Stephanie. The Little Christmas Tree. Barker, Chris, illus. 16p. (ps-8). 1991. 12.95 (0-7459-2118-3) Lion USA.
Jelks, Peggie A. Much Ado about Math: Ideas & Activities for Math. LC 81-65610. (Illus.). 250p. 1981. perfect bdg. 16.95 (0-88247-596-7) R & E Pubs.
Jelliff, Theodore. North Dakota: A Living Legacy. Hetland, David J., illus. 400p. (gr. 8 up). 1983. 19.50 (0-9612140-0-7) K K Pub Co.
Jelliff, Theodore B., jt. auth. see Tweton, D. Jerome.
Jenison, Norma J. & Benjamin, Starr J. The Eyes of the Storm: Belmond, Iowa Recalls the 1966 Homecoming Day Tornado. LC 89-84423. (Illus.). 256p. (Orig.). 1989. pap. 8.95 (0-9623288-0-4) T Lydia Pr.
Jenkin-Pearce, Susie. Seashell Song. LC 91-772960. (ps-3). 1993. 15.00 (0-688-11725-2); PLB 14.93 (0-688-11726-0) Lothrop.
—When I Was a Little Girl. (Illus.). 32p. (gr. k-2). 1993. 17.95 (0-09-176359-2, Pub. by Hutchinson UK) Trafalgar.
Jenkins. Nest Full of Eggs. Date not set. 15.00 (0-06-023441-5, Festival); PLB 14.89 (0-06-023442-3, Festival) HarpC Child Bks.
—Toxic Waste. 1991. 12.95s.p. (0-86593-111-9) Rourke Corp.
Jenkins, Betty. Vowel Fun. Brown, Virginia, illus. 96p. (gr. 1-3). 1983. wkbk. 9.95 (0-86653-107-6, GA 465) Good Apple.
Jenkins, Catherine. Monday Came. Thomas, Meredith, illus. LC 93-28982. 1994. 4.25 (0-383-03762-X) SRA Schl Grp.
Jenkins, Christine L. Loving Our Neighbor the Earth: Creation Spirituality Activities for 9-11 Year Olds. LC 91-10968. (Illus.). 120p. (Orig.). (gr. 4-6). 1991. pap. 14.95 wkbk. (0-89390-204-7) Resource Pubns.
Jenkins, Ella. This Is Rhythm. Manning, Garrian, illus. 1993. pap. 14.95 (1-881322-02-5) Sing Out Corp.
Jenkins, George. Constitution. (Illus.). 96p. (gr. 7 up). 1990. lib. bdg. 18.60 (0-86593-085-6); lib. bdg. 13.95s.p. (0-685-46456-3) Rourke Corp.
—Cycling. LC 93-36545. 1993. write for info. (0-86593-350-2) Rourke Corp.
Jenkins, Gerald & Bear, Magdalen. The Compound of the Five Cubes. (Illus.). 24p. (Orig.). (gr. 5-9). 1986. pap. 4.95 (0-906212-47-2, Pub. by Tarquin UK) Parkwest Pubns.
—The Final Stellation of the Icosahedron. (Illus.). 24p. (Orig.). (gr. 5-9). 1986. pap. 4.95 (0-906212-48-0, Pub. by Tarquin UK) Parkwest Pubns.
—The Sixth Stellation of the Icosahedron. 24p. (Orig.). (gr. 5-9). 1986. pap. 4.95 (0-906212-46-4, Pub. by Tarquin UK) Parkwest Pubns.
Jenkins, Gerald & Wild, Anne. Make Shapes One. (Illus.). 24p. (Orig.). (gr. 4 up). 1985. pap. 4.95 (0-906212-00-6, Pub. by Tarquin UK) Parkwest Pubns.
—Make Shapes Three. 24p. (Orig.). (gr. 4 up). 1985. pap. 4.95 (0-906212-02-2, Pub. by Tarquin UK) Parkwest Pubns.
—Make Shapes Two. 24p. (Orig.). (gr. 4 up). 1985. pap. 4.95 (0-906212-01-4, Pub. by Tarquin UK) Parkwest Pubns.
—Mathematical Curiosities Three. (Illus.). 60p. (gr. 5-9). 1986. pap. 5.95 (0-906212-25-1, Pub. by Tarquin UK) Parkwest Pubns.
Jenkins, Jerry. The Angry Gymnast. (Orig.). (gr. 7-12). 1986. pap. text ed. 4.99 (0-8024-8235-X) Moody.
—The Bizarre Hockey Tournament. (Orig.). (gr. 7-12). 1986. pap. text ed. 4.99 (0-8024-8236-8) Moody.
—The Mysterious Football Team. (Orig.). (gr. 7-12). 1986. pap. text ed. 4.99 (0-8024-8234-1) Moody.
—The Scary Basketball Player. (Orig.). (gr. 7-12). 1986. pap. text ed. 4.99 (0-8024-8233-3) Moody.

—The Secret Baseball Challenge. (Orig.). (gr. 7-12). 1986. pap. text ed. 4.99 (0-8024-8232-5) Moody.
—The Silent Track Star. (Orig.). (gr. 7-12). 1986. pap. text ed. 4.99 (0-8024-8239-2) Moody.
—The Strange Swimming Coach. (Orig.). (gr. 7-12). 1986. pap. text ed. 4.99 (0-8024-8238-4) Moody.
—The Weird Soccer Match. (Orig.). (gr. 7-12). 1986. pap. text ed. 4.99 (0-8024-8237-6) Moody.
Jenkins, Jerry B. Dallas O'Neil & the Baker Street Sports Club Series, 8 bks. (gr. 2-7). Set. pap. 39.92 (0-8024-2164-4) Moody.
—Dallas O'Neil Mysteries Ser, 8 bks. (gr. 2-7). Set. pap. 39.92 (0-8024-8389-5) Moody.
—Mystery of the Golden Palomino. (Orig.). 1989. pap. 4.99 (0-8024-8386-0) Moody.
—Mystery of the Kidnapped Kid. (gr. 2-7). 1988. pap. 4.99 (0-8024-8376-3) Moody.
—Mystery of the Missing Sister. (gr. 2-7). 1988. pap. 4.99 (0-8024-8378-X) Moody.
—Mystery of the Mixed-Up Teacher. (Orig.). (gr. 2-7). 1988. pap. 4.99 (0-8024-8377-1) Moody.
—Mystery of the Phony Murder. 1989. pap. 4.99 (0-8024-8388-7) Moody.
—Mystery of the Scorpion Threat. (gr. 9-12). 1988. pap. 4.99 (0-8024-8379-8) Moody.
—Mystery of the Skinny Sophomore. (Orig.). 1989. pap. 4.99 (0-8024-8387-9) Moody.
—Mystery on the Midway. (Orig.). 1989. pap. 4.99 (0-8024-8385-2) Moody.
Jenkins, Jessica. Thinking about Colors. LC 91-33460. (Illus.). 32p. (gr. k-5). 1992. 14.00 (0-525-44908-6, DCB) Dutton Child Bks.
Jenkins, Lee. The Balance Book. (Illus., Orig.). (gr. 2-8). 1974. pap. 7.95 (0-918932-02-5) Activity Resources.
—Coin Stamp Mathematics. Merrick, Paul, illus. (Orig.). (gr. k-4). 1977. pap. 7.95 (0-918932-05-X) Activity Resources.
—Daniel: A Melodrama. Jenkins, Todd, illus. Greeno, Ron, frwd. by. (Illus.). 32p. (Orig.). (ps-3). 1993. pap. 6.95 (1-883952-02-6) Hse of Steno.
—Time & Time Again. Laycock, Mary, ed. Gittings, Elisa, illus. 72p. (Orig.). (gr. 1-6). 1985. pap. text ed. 7.95 (0-918932-85-8) Activity Resources.
—Zacchaeus. Chansler, Jim, illus. Greeno, Ron, frwd. by. (Illus.). 32p. (Orig.). (ps-3). 1993. pap. 6.95 (1-883952-03-4) Hse of Steno.
Jenkins, Lee & McLean, Peggy. Fraction Tile Program. (Illus., Orig.). (gr. 2-9). 1972. pap. 5.50 student's bk. (0-918932-17-3); tchr's. bk. 4.95 (0-918932-18-1); manipulative bk. 6.50 (0-918932-19-X); acrylic tiles 35.95 (0-686-67783-8); entire program 50.95 (0-685-00119-9) Activity Resources.
—It's a Tangram World. rev. ed. Laycock, Mary, ed. 48p. (gr. 3-6). 1981. pap. 7.95 (0-918932-70-X) Activity Resources.
Jenkins, Lee & Nordberg, Marion. Place Value & Regrouping Games. (Illus., Orig.). (gr. 1-4). 1976. pap. 7.95 (0-918932-39-4) Activity Resources.
Jenkins, Lee, et al. Geoblocks & Geojackets. (gr. 3-10). 1976. 9.50 (0-918932-22-X) Activity Resources.
Jenkins, Lyll B. de see De Jenkins, Lyll B.
Jenkins, Lyll Becerra De see Becerra de Jenkins, Lyll.
Jenkins, Patrick. Animation. (gr. 2-7). 1991. pap. 8.61 (0-201-56757-1) Addison-Wesley.
Jenkins, Sarah & Foote, Margaret. Adventures with Art. (Illus.). 112p. (Orig.). (gr. 1-6). 1993. pap. 9.95 (0-673-46415-6) GdYrBks.
Jenkins, Sheila. Polka Dotted Pals, Pt. 2. Goodwin, Irene & Silvers, Rath, eds. LC 80-84112. (Orig.). (gr. k). 1980. pap. 8.95 (0-932970-20-6) Prinit Pr.
Jenkins, Sheila, et al. Polka Dotted Pals, Pt. 1. 100p. (gr. k-1). 1980. pap. 8.95 (0-932970-13-3) Prinit Pr.
Jenkins, Tony. Nicaragua & the United States: Years of Conflict. LC 89-5758. (Illus.). 187p. (gr. 9 up). 1989. PLB 15.40 (0-531-10795-7) Watts.
Jenkinson, Denis. Racing Driver: The Theory & Practice of Fast Driving. LC 59-3790. (Illus.). 1959. 14.95 (0-8376-0200-9) Bentley.
Jenkins-Pearce, Susie. Rosie & the Pavement Bears. (Illus.). 32p. (ps-1). 1993. 15.95 (0-09-174164-5, Pub. by Hutchinson UK) Trafalgar.
Jenks, Graham. Here a Mom, There a Mom. Burris, Priscilla, illus. 1994. write for info. (0-7852-8215-7) Nelson.
Jenner, Caryn. Clashing Hearts. 1992. pap. 2.99 (0-553-29458-X) Bantam.
Jenness, Aylette. Come Home with Me: A Multicultural Treasure Hunt. (gr. 4-7). 1993. 16.95 (1-56584-064-X) New Press NY.
—Come Home with Me: Multicultural Treasure Hunt. LC 92-50699. (gr. 4 up). 1993. write for info. (1-56584-053-4) New Press.
—Families: A Celebration of Diversity, Commitment & Love. (Illus.). 48p. (gr. 3-5). 1990. 13.45 (0-395-47038-2) HM.
—Families: A Celebration of Diversity, Commitment, & Love. (gr. 4-7). 1993. pap. 4.95 (0-395-66952-9) HM.
—Ven a Mi Casa. (gr. 4-7). 1993. 16.95 (1-56584-118-2) New Press NY.
Jenness, Aylette & Rivers, Alice. In Two Worlds: A Yup'ik Eskimo Family. Jenness, Aylette, illus. (gr 6 up). 1989. 13.45 (0-395-42797-5) HM.
Jennet, Judith. Snorkeling for Kids. 2nd ed. Nakanishi, Nadine, illus. 56p. (ps-9). 1992. pap. text ed. 5.95 (0-916974-50-2, 212) NAUI.
Jennings, A., jt. auth. see Wangerin, W., Jr.

Jennings, Coleman A. & Harris, Aurand. Plays Children Love, Vol. II. Channing, Carol, frwd. by. 512p. 1988. 19.95x (0-312-01490-2) St Martin.
Jennings, Coleman A. & Berghammer, Gretta, eds. Theatre for Youth: Twelve Plays with Mature Themes. Davis, Jed H., frwd. by. LC 85-26515. 524p. (gr. 8 up). 1986. 30.00 (0-292-78081-8); pap. 17.95 (0-292-78085-0) U of Tex Pr.
Jennings, Donna A. Baby Brendon's Busy Day: A Sexuality Primer. Hall, Bruce, illus. Wilson, Pamela M., intro. by. (Illus.). 32p. (ps). 1994. 15.95 (0-9638079-0-0) Goose Pond.
Jennings, Elizabeth. Secret Brother & Other Poems. Stevens, Meg, illus. LC 69-14765. (gr. 1-5). 1966. 13.95 (0-8023-1194-6) Dufour.
Jennings, Gordon. Minibikes! Coker, Paul, Jr., illus. (gr. 5 up). 1974. P-H.
Jennings, Jay. Comebacks. (Illus.). 64p. (gr. 5-7). 1991. PLB 14.98 (0-382-24109-6); PLB 11.24s.p. (0-685-47013-X); pap. 8.95 (0-382-24115-0); pap. 6.71s.p. (0-685-47014-8) Silver Burdett Pr.
—Long Shots. 64p. (gr. 5-7). 1991. PLB 14.98 (0-382-24105-3); pap. 8.95 (0-382-24112-6) Silver Burdett Pr.
—Moments of Courage. (Illus.). 64p. (gr. 5-7). 1991. PLB 14.98 (0-382-24108-8); PLB 11.24s.p. (0-685-47015-6); pap. 8.95 (0-382-24114-2); pap. 6.71s.p. (0-685-47016-4) Silver Burdett Pr.
—Sports Triumphs Series, 4 vols. (Illus.). 256p. (gr. 5-7). 1991. Set. PLB 44.94s.p. (0-685-47011-3); Set. pap. 26.85s.p. (0-685-47012-1) Silver Burdett Pr.
—Teamwork. 64p. (gr. 5-7). 1991. PLB 14.98 (0-382-24106-1); pap. 8.95 (0-382-24113-4) Silver Burdett Pr.
Jennings, Linda. The Dog Who Found Christmas. Walters, Catherine, illus. 40p. (ps-2). 1993. 11.99 (0-525-45155-2, DCB) Dutton Child Bks.
—My Christmas Book of Stories & Carols. 1991. 5.99 (0-517-05189-3) Outlet Bk Co.
Jennings, Linda, compiled by. A Treasury of Stories from Around the World. Ambrus, Victor, illus. LC 92-43153. 160p. (gr. k-4). 1993. write for info. (1-85697-932-6) Kingfisher Bks.
Jennings, Paul. Uncanny! (gr. 5-7). 1991. 13.95 (0-670-84174-9) Viking Child Bks.
—Uncanny! Even More Surprising Stories. 144p. (gr. 5 up). 1993. pap. 3.99 (0-14-034909-X, Puffin) Puffin Bks.
—Unmentionable! More Amazing Stories. LC 92-25930. 112p. (gr. 5 up). 1993. 14.99 (0-670-84734-8) Viking Child Bks.
—Unreal! (gr. 4-7). 1991. 14.00 (0-670-84175-7) Viking Child Bks.
—Unreal! Eight Surprising Stories. 112p. (gr. 5 up). 1993. pap. 3.99 (0-14-034910-3, Puffin) Puffin Bks.
Jennings, Sharon. Jeremiah & Mrs. Ming. Levert, Mireille, illus. 24p. (ps). 1990. PLB 15.95 (1-55037-079-0, Pub. by Annick CN); pap. 5.95 (1-55037-078-2, Pub. by Annick CN) Firefly Bks Ltd.
—Jeremiah & Mrs. Ming Big Book. (Illus.). 24p. (ps). 1990. 21.95 (1-55037-124-X, Pub. by Annick CN) Firefly Bks Ltd.
—Une Journee avec Jeremie et Mme. Ming: When Jeremiah Found Mrs. Ming. Levert, Mireille, illus. (FRE.). 24p. (ps). 1992. PLB 15.95 (1-55037-247-5, Pub. by Annick Pr); pap. 6.95 (1-55037-248-3, Pub. by Annick Pr) Firefly Bks Ltd.
—When Jeremiah Found Mrs. Ming. Levert, Mireille, illus. 24p. (ps). 1992. PLB 15.95 (1-55037-237-8, Pub. by Annick Pr); pap. 5.95 (1-55037-234-3, Pub. by Annick Pr) Firefly Bks Ltd.
Jennings, Terry. Air. LC 89-453. (Illus.). 32p. (gr. 3-6). 1989. pap. 4.95 (0-516-48435-4) Childrens.
—Balancing. Anstey, David, illus. LC 88-83615. 28p. (gr. k-4). 1989. PLB 10.90 (0-531-17175-2, Gloucester Pr) Watts.
—Birds. LC 89-455. (Illus.). 32p. (gr. 3-6). 1989. pap. 4.95 (0-516-48436-2) Childrens.
—Bouncing & Rolling. Franklin Watts Ltd., ed. Anstey, David, illus. LC 87-82971. 24p. (gr. k-3). 1988. PLB 10.90 (0-531-17085-3, Gloucester Pr) Watts.
—Colors. Anstey, David, illus. LC 88-93098. 24p. (ps-2). 1989. PLB 10.90 (0-531-17129-9, Gloucester Pr) Watts.
—Cranes, Dump Trucks, Bulldozers & Other Building Machines. LC 92-23370. 1993. RLB 10.95 (1-85697-866-4); pap. 5.95 (1-85697-865-6) Kingfisher Bks.
—Electricity & Magnetism. LC 88-36215. (Illus.). 32p. (gr. 3-6). 1989. PLB 15.00 (0-516-08437-2); pap. 4.95 (0-516-48437-0) Childrens.
—Energy. LC 88-36214. (Illus.). 32p. (gr. 3-6). 1989. PLB 15.00 (0-516-08438-0); pap. 4.95 (0-516-48438-9) Childrens.
—Everyday Chemicals. LC 88-22888. (Illus.). 32p. (gr. 3-6). 1989. PLB 15.00 (0-516-08401-1); pap. 4.95 (0-516-48401-X) Childrens.
—Flowers. LC 88-37553. (Illus.). 32p. (gr. 3-6). 1989. pap. 4.95 (0-516-48439-7) Childrens.
—Food. LC 88-22866. (Illus.). 32p. (gr. 3-6). 1989. pap. 4.95 (0-516-48402-8) Childrens.
—Heat. LC 88-22866. (Illus.). 32p. (gr. 3-6). 1989. pap. 4.95 (0-516-48403-6) Childrens.
—Hot & Cold. Anstey, David, illus. LC 88-83099. 24p. (ps-2). 1989. PLB 10.90 (0-531-17127-2, Gloucester Pr) Watts.
—The Human Body. LC 88-22859. (Illus.). 32p. (gr. 3-6). 1989. pap. 4.95 (0-516-48404-4) Childrens.

—Insects. Anstey, David, illus. LC 90-44675. 24p. (gr. 1-3). 1991. PLB 10.90 (0-531-17275-9, Gloucester Pr) Watts.
—Light & Color. LC 88-36220. (Illus.). 32p. (gr. 3-6). 1989. PLB 15.00 (0-516-08440-2); pap. 4.95 (0-516-48440-0) Childrens.
—Light & Dark. Anstey, David, illus. LC 90-44678. 24p. (gr. 1-3). 1991. PLB 10.90 (0-531-17277-5, Gloucester Pr) Watts.
—Making Sounds. (Illus.). 24p. (gr. k-4). 1990. PLB 10. 90 (0-531-17212-0, Gloucester Pr) Watts.
—Materials. LC 88-22884. (Illus.). 32p. (gr. 3-6). 1989. PLB 15.00 (0-516-08405-4); pap. 4.95 (0-516-48405-2) Childrens.
—Planes, Gliders, Helicopters, & Other Flying Machines. LC 92-28422. (Illus.). 40p. (gr. 3-8). 1993. 10.95 (1-85697-870-2); pap. 5.95 (1-85697-869-9) Kingfisher Bks.
—Pond Life. LC 88-22880. (Illus.). 32p. (gr. 3-6). 1989. pap. 4.95 (0-516-48406-0) Childrens.
—Rocks & Soil. LC 88-22889. (Illus.). 32p. (gr. 3-6). 1989. pap. 4.95 (0-516-48407-9) Childrens.
—Sea & Seashore. LC 89-454. (Illus.). 32p. (gr. 3-6). 1989. pap. 4.95 (0-516-48441-9) Childrens.
—Seeds. Franklin Watts Ltd., ed. Anstey, David, illus. 24p. (gr. k-3). 1988. PLB 10.90 (0-531-17087-X, Gloucester Pr) Watts.
—Seeds & Seedlings. LC 88-22890. (Illus.). 32p. (gr. 3-6). 1989. PLB 15.00 (0-516-08408-9); pap. 4.95 (0-516-48408-7) Childrens.
—Slugs & Snails. Anstey, David, illus. LC 88-83101. 24p. (ps-2). 1989. PLB 10.90 (0-531-17128-0, Gloucester Pr) Watts.
—Small Garden Animals. LC 88-36216. (Illus.). 32p. (gr. 3-6). 1989. PLB 15.00 (0-516-08442-9); pap. 4.95 (0-516-48442-7) Childrens.
—Sounds. LC 88-36213. (Illus.). 32p. (gr. 3-6). 1989. pap. 4.95 (0-516-48443-5) Childrens.
—Spiders. Anstey, David, illus. LC 88-83614. 24p. (gr. 1-3). 1989. PLB 10.40 (0-531-17176-0) Denison.
—Structures. LC 88-22879. (Illus.). 32p. (gr. 3-6). 1989. PLB 15.00 (0-516-08409-7); pap. 4.95 (0-516-48409-5) Childrens.
—Trees. LC 88-37552. (Illus.). 32p. (gr. 3-6). 1989. PLB 15.00 (0-516-08444-5); pap. 4.95 (0-516-48444-3) Childrens.
—Trees. Kline, M., ed. Anstey, David, illus. 24p. (gr. 1-3). 1991. PLB 10.90 (0-531-17276-7, Gloucester Pr) Watts.
—Water. LC 88-22871. (Illus.). 32p. (gr. 3-6). 1989. PLB 15.00 (0-516-08410-0); pap. 4.95 (0-516-48410-9) Childrens.
Jennings, Terry & Anstey, David. Sliding & Rolling. LC 88-83100. (Illus.). 24p. (ps-2). 1989. PLB 10.90 (0-531-17130-2, Gloucester Pr) Watts.
Jennings, Terry J. Rocks. Stefoff, Rebecca, ed. Barber, Ed, photos by. LC 91-18190. (Illus.). 32p. (gr. 3-5). 1991. PLB 15.93 (1-56074-000-0) Garrett Ed Corp.
—Wood. Stefoff, Rebecca, ed. Barber, Ed, photos by. LC 91-18187. (Illus.). 32p. (gr. 3-5). 1991. PLB 15.93 (1-56074-002-7) Garrett Ed Corp.
Jenny, Gerri. Birthday Parties for Children. (Illus.). 128p. (ps-4). PLB 16.95 (1-878363-63-8) Forest Hse.
—Birthday Parties for Children: Activities, Games, Cakes & Fun for Children from 4-10. Macdonald, Roland B. & Gray, Dan, illus. 128p. (gr. k-5). 1991. pap. 9.95 (1-878767-15-1) Murdoch Bks.
—Outdoor Projects for Children. 1992. pap. 10.95 (1-878767-55-0) Murdoch Bks.

Jensen, Ann D. The World Turned Upside Down: Children of 1776. Travis-Keene, Gayle, illus. 32p. (Orig.). (gr. 4-5). 1993. pap. 5.95 (0-9638113-0-4) Sands Hse. THE WORLD TURNED UPSIDE DOWN opens in Annapolis, Maryland on the eve of the American Revolution. Young readers meet the Sands family: parents John & Ann, & their 5 children; Will, 18; Nan, 15; Johnny, 12; Sarah, 7; & Joseph, 6. They were a real family & their home still stands in Annapolis. In reading about this family children learn what it was like to live during the Revolutionary War, & how the world of families like the Sands really was turned upside down. A section of thumbnail sketches of the day-to-day life of the story's main characters help youngsters to further understand how children lived during this critical time in American history. Here is a real life story of the Revolutionary War & of people, neither rich nor famous, who gave their lives & contributed in other significant ways to the cause of liberty. The book includes an extensive glossary, as well as a map & brief description of Maryland's capital city as it was in 1776. *Publisher Provided Annotation.*

Jensen, Anne F. India: Its Culture & People. LC 90-23051. (Illus.). 272p. (Orig.). (gr. 1-8). 1991. pap. text ed. 18.32 (0-8013-0343-5) Longman.
Jensen, Antony & Bolt, Stephen. Undersea Mission. LC 88-42907. (Illus.). 32p. (gr. 4-5). 1989. PLB 15.93 (1-55532-918-7) Gareth Stevens Inc.
Jensen, Delwin A. Fort Pierre-Deadwood Trail: Route to the Gold Fields of the Black Hills. (Illus.). 60p. (Orig.). (gr. 8-12). 1989. pap. text ed. 4.00 (0-9624413-0-9) D A Jensen.
Jensen, Dorothea. Riddle of Penncroft Farm. (gr. 3-7). 1989. 14.95 (0-15-200574-9) HarBrace.
—Riddle of Penncroft Farm. 242p. (gr. 3-7). 1991. pap. 4.95 (0-15-266908-6, Odyssey) HarBrace.
Jensen, Jeffry. Hispanic American Struggle for Equality. LC 92-7471. 1992. 22.60 (0-86593-180-1); 16.95s.p. (0-685-59289-8) Rourke Corp.
Jensen, Karen. Goldilocks & the Three Bears. Rigg, Lucy, illus 32p. (ps up) 1987. 9.95 (0-910079-05-6) Lucy & Co.
Jensen, Kathryn. Pocket Change. LC 88-13450. 176p. (gr. 7 up). 1989. SBE 13.95 (0-02-747731-2, Macmillan Child Bk) Macmillan Child Grp.
—Pocket Change. (gr. 7 up). 1991. pap. 2.95 (0-590-43419-5, Point) Scholastic Inc.
Jensen, Kent W. Slippers & Wraparound Wraps. Traba, Henry & Faigin, Cecilia, illus. 41p. (ps-2). 1988. pap. 7.95 (0-9621024-0-7) K Jensen.
Jensen, Kiersten. Possum in the House. Sherwood, Rhoda, ed. Olliver, Tony, illus. LC 88-42910. 32p. (gr. 1-2). 1988. PLB 18.60 (1-55532-933-0) Gareth Stevens Inc.
Jensen, Lillian. Mother Goose in the Space Age. Larson, Leonard, illus. (gr. 5-9). 1985. 7.95 (0-933494-28-9) Earthwise Pubns.
Jensen, Marilyn. Phillis Wheatley: Negro Slave. 242p. (gr. 5-9). 1987. 18.95 (0-87460-326-9) Lion Bks.
Jensen, P. The Mess. (Illus.). 28p. (ps-2). 1990. 12.33 (0-516-05357-4); pap. 3.95 (0-516-45357-2) Childrens.
—My House. (Illus.). 28p. (ps-2). 1990. 12.33 (0-516-05359-0); pap. 3.95 (0-516-45359-9) Childrens.
Jensen, Patricia. Barbie: Show Time! Duarte, Pamela, illus. 24p. (ps-3). 1992. pap. write for info. (0-307-12691-9, 12691, Golden Pr) Western Pub.
—A Funny Man. Becker, Wayne, illus. LC 92-36007. 1993. 3.95 (0-590-46190-7) Scholastic Inc.
—Go to Sleep, Little Groundhog. (Illus.). (ps-3). 1993. 6.99 (0-89577-487-9, Readers Digest Kids) RD Assn.
—Little Puppy Saves the Day. (Illus.). (ps-3). 1993. 6.99 (0-89577-473-9, Readers Digest Kids) RD Assn.
Jensen, Patricia, adapted by see Chottin, Ariane.
Jensen, Patricia, adapted by see Clement, Claude.
Jensen, Patricia, adapted by see Guidoux, Valerie.
Jensen, Patricia A. John Henry & His Mighty Hammer. Litzinger, Roseanne, illus. LC 93-4810. 32p. (gr. k-2). 1993. PLB 11.59 (0-8167-3156-X); pap. text ed. 2.95 (0-8167-3157-8) Troll Assocs.
—Johnny Appleseed goes a 'Planting. Hogan, Patricia M., illus. LC 93-4811. 32p. (gr. k-2). 1993. PLB 11.59 (0-8167-3159-4); pap. text ed. 2.95 (0-8167-3160-8) Troll Assocs.
—The Legend of Sleepy Hollow. Barnes-Murphy, Rowan S., illus. LC 93-24803. (gr. k-3). 1993. PLB 9.89 (0-8167-3168-3); pap. text ed. 2.95 (0-8167-3169-1) Troll Assocs.
—Paul Bunyan & His Blue Ox. Pidgeon, Jean L., illus. LC 93-24802. 32p. (gr. k-2). 1993. PLB 11.59 (0-8167-3162-4); pap. text ed. 2.95 (0-8167-3163-2) Troll Assocs.
—Pecos Bill, the Roughest, Toughest Best. Mahan, Benton, illus. LC 93-2217. 32p. (gr. k-2). 1993. PLB 11.59 (0-8167-3165-9); pap. text ed. 2.95 (0-8167-3166-7) Troll Assocs.
Jensen, Rosemary D., ed. see Leahy, Barbara H.
Jensen, Steve. Great Alphabet Fight. (ps-3). 1993. 12.99 (0-88070-612-0, Gold & Honey) Questar Pubs.
Jensen, Steve, jt. auth. see Tada, Joni E.
Jensen, Steven & Tada, Joni E. The Great Alphabet Fight. Tada, Joni E., illus. (ps-3). 1993. 12.99 (0-88070-572-8, Gold & Honey) Questar Pubs.
Jepson, Maud. Illustrated Biology, 2 pts. (Illus.). (gr. 8-12). Animals, Pt. 2. 6.95x (0-7195-0734-0) Transatl Arts.
Jerald, Michael, jt. auth. see Clark, Raymond C.
Jeram, Anita. Bill's Belly Button. (ps-3). 1991. 14.95 (0-316-46114-8) Little.
—It Was Jake. (ps-3). 1991. 14.95 (0-316-46120-2) Little.
Jernigan, Gisela. Agave Blooms Just Once. Jernigan, E. Wesley, illus. LC 89-35428. 32p. (Orig.). (ps-1). 1989. pap. 8.95 (0-943173-44-2) Harbinger AZ.
—One Green Mesquite Tree. 2nd ed. Jernigan, E. Wesley, illus. LC 88-2294. 24p. (Orig.). (ps-1). 1989. 12.95 (0-943173-35-3); pap. 8.95 (0-943173-39-6) Harbinger AZ.
—Sonoran Seasons: A Year in the Desert. Jernigan, E. Wesley, illus. 32p. (Orig.). (ps-2). 1994. pap. 8.95 (0-943173-91-4) Harbinger AZ.
Jerome, Jerome K. After Supper Ghost Stories: And Other Tales. 176p. (gr. 6-9). 1990. pap. 8.00 (0-86299-762-3) A Sutton Pub.

—Diary of a Pilgrimage. (Illus.). 176p. (gr. 6-9). 1990. pap. 8.00 (0-86299-010-6) A Sutton Pub.
—Novel Notes. 240p. (gr. 7-8). 1991. pap. 8.00 (0-86299-923-5) A Sutton Pub.
—On the Stage - & Off: The Brief Career of a Would-Be Actor. (Illus.). 192p. (gr. 6-9). 1991. text ed. 30.00 (0-86299-886-7) A Sutton Pub.
—Sense & Nonsense. 208p. (gr. 7-8). 1991. pap. 8.00 (0-86299-922-7) A Sutton Pub.
—Three Men in a Boat. Carpenter, Humphrey, intro. by. (Illus.). 224p. (gr. 6-9). 1989. 22.00 (0-86299-569-8); pap. 8.00 (0-86299-028-9); pap. 18.00 Commerative Ed. (0-7509-0062-8) A Sutton Pub.
—Three Men on the Bummel. (Illus.). 240p. (gr. 6-9). 1991. pap. 8.00 (0-86299-029-7) A Sutton Pub.
Jerome, Leah. Dian Fossey. (gr. 4-7). 1991. pap. 3.50 (0-553-15929-1) Bantam.
—Pink Parrots, No. 6: No-Hitter. Ellis, Lucy, created by. (gr. 3-7). 1991. pap. 3.95 (0-316-47427-4, Spts Illus Kids) Little.
—Schwarzenegger. (Illus.). 48p. 1992. 1.49 (0-440-21430-0) Dell.
—Tevin Campbell. (Illus.). 48p. 1992. 1.49 (0-440-21431-9) Dell.
Jerrard, Jane, adapted by. Beauty & the Beast. Nilles, Burgandy & Thiewes, Sam, illus. 24p. 1993. PLB 10. 95 (1-56674-061-4, HTS Bks) Forest Hse.
—Cinderella. Spellman, Susan & Thiewes, Sam, illus. 24p. (gr. k-4). 1993. PLB 10.95 (1-56674-062-2, HTS Bks) Forest Hse.
—Goldilocks & the Three Bears. Nilles, Burgandy & Thiewes, Sam, illus. 24p. (gr. k-4). 1993. PLB 10.95 (1-56674-063-0, HTS Bks) Forest Hse.
—Jack & the Beanstalk. Spellman, Susan & Thiewes, Sam, illus. 24p. (gr. k-4). 1993. PLB 10.95 (1-56674-064-9, HTS Bks) Forest Hse.
—Little Red Riding Hood. Spellman, Susan & Thiewes, Sam, illus. 24p. (gr. k-4). 1993. PLB 10.95 (1-56674-065-7, HTS Bks) Forest Hse.
—The Ugly Duckling. Spellman, Susan & Thiewes, Sam, illus. 24p. (gr. k-4). 1993. PLB 10.95 (1-56674-066-5, HTS Bks) Forest Hse.
Jerris, Tony. The Littlest Piggy. Lyness, Katy, illus. 20p. (Orig.). (ps up). 1992. pap. 9.95 (0-9630107-2-7) Little Spruce.
—The Littlest Spruce. Weinberger, Tanya, illus. 20p. (Orig.). (ps up). 1991. pap. 9.95 (0-9630107-1-9) Little Spruce.
Jerrold, Walter, ed. Mother Goose's Nursery Rhymes. LC 93-22604. 1993. Repr. of 1903 ed. 13.95 (0-679-42815-1, Everymans Lib) Knopf.
Jerry S, jt. auth. see Friends in Recovery.
Jervis, Alastair. Camera Technology. (Illus.). 48p. (gr. 5-8). 1991. PLB 12.90 (0-531-18385-8, Pub. by Bookwright Pr) Watts.
Jeschke, Susan. Perfect the Pig. Jeschke, Susan, illus. LC 80-39998. 48p. (ps-2). 1981. 14.95 (0-8050-0704-0, Bks Young Read) H Holt & Co.
—Perfect the Pig. Jeschke, Susan, illus. 40p. (gr. k-3). 1985. pap. 3.50 (0-590-43710-0) Scholastic Inc.
Jesep, Paul P. A December Gift from the Shoals. Bowdren, John, illus. 16p. (Orig.). (gr. 4). 1993. pap. 5.95 (0-9634360-1-5) Seacoast Pubns New Eng.
—Lady-Ghost of the Isles of Shoals. LC 91-68204. 13p. (gr. 4). 1992. pap. 5.95 (0-9634360-0-7) Seacoast Pubns New Eng.
—The Witch & the Sunflower Garden. Bowdren, John, illus. LC 92-63205. 20p. (Orig.). (gr. 4-5). 1993. pap. 9.95 (0-9634360-3-1) Seacoast Pubns New Eng.
Jespersen, James & Fitz-Randolph, Jane. From Quarks to Quasars: A Tour of the Universe. Hiscock, Bruce, illus. LC 86-17276. 224p. (gr. 7 up). 1987. SBE 16.95 (0-689-31270-9, Atheneum Child Bk) Macmillan Child Grp.
—Looking at the Invisible Universe. Hiscock, Bruce, illus. LC 89-14998. 160p. (gr. 7 up). 1990. SBE 13.95 (0-689-31457-4, Atheneum Child Bk) Macmillan Child Grp.
Jesseau, Patricia. The Story of an Arabian Foal. Lightwood, Jeannette, illus. 32p. (ps-8). 1985. 6.95 (0-920806-70-8, Pub. by Penumbra Pr CN) U of Toronto Pr.
Jessel, Camilla. The Kitten Book. Jessel, Camilla, illus. LC 91-71841. 32p. (ps up). 1992. 14.95 (1-56402-020-7) Candlewick Pr.
—Kitten Book. LC 91-71841. (ps-3). 1994. pap. 4.99 (1-56402-278-1) Candlewick Pr.
—Life at the Royal Ballet School. Jessel, Camilla, illus. LC 79-12162. 143p. (gr. 4 up). 1979. 15.95 (0-416-30191-6, NO. 0137) Routledge Chapman & Hall.
—The Puppy Book. Jessel, Camilla, illus. LC 91-71825. 32p. (ps up). 1992. 14.95 (1-56402-021-5) Candlewick Pr.
—Puppy Book. LC 91-71825. (ps-3). 1994. pap. 4.99 (1-56402-279-X) Candlewick Pr.
Jessen, Grace D. Royal Rewards: A Tribute to Fathers. (Illus.). 28p. 1986. pap. 1.50 (0-88290-019-6) Horizon Utah.
Jessie. Please Tell. Jessie, illus. 33p. 1991. pap. 8.00 (0-89486-776-8) Hazelden.
—Por Favor, Di! Un Cuento Para Ninos Sobre el Abuso Sexual. (ps-3). 1993. pap. 8.00 (0-89486-943-4) Hazelden.
Jessie, Willcox Smith see Willcox Smith, Jessie.
Jessop, Joanne. Planet Earth. Wood, Gerald, illus. LC 93-28339. 1994. write for info. (0-8114-9244-3) Raintree Steck-V.

—The X-Ray Picture Book of Buildings of the Ancient World. Salariya, David, created by. LC 93-36704. (gr. 3 up). 1994. write for info. (0-531-14286-8); write for info. (0-531-15709-1) Watts.

Jessops, Joanne. Crusaders. (ps-3). 1990. PLB 10.90 (0-531-18324-6, Pub. by Bookwright Pr) Watts.

Jester, Harold D. Pulling Together: Crisis Prevention for Teens & Their Parents. LC 91-41371. 155p. (Orig.). 1992. pap. 9.95 (0-938179-30-6) Mills Sanderson.

Jetsmark, Torben. Peter the Postman. 37p. 1988. Playscript. 4.50 (0-87602-279-4) Anchorage.

Jeunesse, Gallimard, created by. Boats. Broutin, Christian, illus. LC 92-41414. 1993. 11.95 (0-590-47131-7) Scholastic Inc.

Jeunesse, Gallimard & Bour, Laura, eds. The River. Bour, Laura, illus. LC 92-41415. 1993. 11.95 (0-590-47128-7) Scholastic Inc.

Jeunesse, Gallimard, et al, eds. The Camera: Snapshots, Movies, Videos, & Cartoons. Valat, Pierre-Marie, illus. LC 92-41412. 1993. 11.95 (0-590-47129-5) Scholastic Inc.

Jewell. Two Silly Trolls. Date not set. 14.00 (0-06-024292-2, Festival); PLB 13.89 (0-06-024293-0, Festival) HarpC Child Bks.

Jewell, Nancy. The Family under the Moon. Kessler, Leonard, illus. LC 76-2344. (ps-3). 1976. PLB 14.89i (0-06-022827-X) HarpC Child Bks.
—Two Silly Trolls. Thiesing, Lisa, illus. LC 90-4387. 64p. (gr. k-3). 1992. 14.00 (0-06-022829-6); PLB 13.89 (0-06-022830-X) HarpC Child Bks.
—Two Silly Trolls. Thiesing, Lisa, illus. LC 90-4387. 64p. (ps-3). 1994. pap. 3.50 (0-06-444173-3, Trophy) HarpC Child Bks.

Jewett, Sarah O. A White Heron. LC 83-71791. 40p. (gr. 6 up). 1983. PLB 13.95s.p. (0-87191-966-4) Creative Ed.

Jezek, Alisandra. Miloli's Orchids. (Illus.). 32p. (gr. 2-4). 1990. 29.28 clipper (0-8172-2789-X); PLB 17.96 (0-8172-2784-9) Raintree Steck-V.
—Miloli's Orchids. (ps-3). 1993. pap. 3.95 (0-8114-5209-3) Raintree Steck-V.

Jezer, Marty. Rachel Carson. Horner, Matina, intro. by. (Illus.). 112p. (gr. 5 up). 1988. lib. bdg. 17.95 (1-55546-646-X) Chelsea Hse.

Jiang, Cheng A., jt. auth. see Jiang, Wei.

Jiang, Wei & Jiang, Cheng A. The Legend of Mulan - A Heroine of Ancient China: (Hu Mulan de Gushi - Zhong Guo Gudai Nu Yingxiong) (CHI & ENG., Illus.). 32p. (gr. 1 up). 1992. 13.95 (1-878217-00-3) Victory Press.
—The Legend of Mulan - A Heroine of Ancient China: (Hoa Moc Lan - Truyen Ve Nu Anh Hung Co Dai Trung Quoc) (VIE & ENG., Illus.). 32p. (gr. 1 up). 1992. 13.95 (1-878217-02-X) Victory Press.
—The Legend of Mulan - A Heroine of Ancient China: (La Heroina Hua Mulan - Una Leyenda de la Antigua China) (SPA & ENG., Illus.). 32p. (gr. 1 up). 1992. 13.95 (1-878217-01-1) Victory Press.
—The Legend of Mulan - A Heroine of Ancient China: (La Legende de Mulan, Heroine de la Chine Antique) (FRE & ENG., Illus.). 32p. (gr. 1 up). 1992. 13.95 (1-878217-04-6) Victory Press.
—The Legend of Mulan - A Heroine of Ancient China. (CAM & ENG., Illus.). 32p. (gr. 1 up). 1992. 13.95 (1-878217-03-8) Victory Press.

Jill, Jodi. Childrens Money Making Jobs. 32p. 1993. pap. 6.95 (1-883438-04-7) J J Features.
On the playground & around the house, children scout for mall mad money. Spending on their toys means making money first. From walking dogs to recycling in their neighborhood, children find unique easy jobs with CHILDRENS MONEY MAKING JOBS by Jodi Jill. In the current society it is harder for children to find safe & responsible jobs to do in their neighborhood, their community or even at their house without their parents worrying. CHILDRENS MONEY MAKING JOBS is packed with simple, safe, & exciting jobs done by kids living all across America. The jobs provide opportunities for mad money as well as showing responsibility without worried parents. Also included are helpful hints, sales techniques, price schedules, & cool illustrations that make children want to get started right away. CHILDRENS MONEY MAKING JOBS is an excellent resource for libraries, schools, classrooms, & at the home. To order call: (303) 575-1319. Mail Orders: J.J. Features, 1705 14th Street, Suite 321,

Boulder, CO 80302.
Publisher Provided Annotation.

—Kids' Money Making Environmental Jobs. 34p. 1993. pap. 5.95 (1-883438-03-9) J J Features.

Jillette, Penn & Teller. Penn & Teller's How to Play with Your Food. LC 92-50150. 1992. pap. 20.00 (0-679-74311-1, Villard Bks) Random.

Jim, Judith M., jt. auth. see Krall, Charlotte B.

Jimenez, Juan R., compiled by. Platero. Livingston, Myra C. & Dominguez, Joseph F., trs. Frasconi, Antonio, illus. LC 92-11634. (ENG & SPA.). 1993. write for info. (0-395-62365-0, Clarion Bks) HM.

Jin, Sarunna. My First American Friend. (Illus.). 32p. (gr. 2-4). 1990. 16.67 (0-8172-2785-7); pap. 3.95 (0-8114-4310-8) Raintree Steck-V.

Jin, Yu, et al. Chinese Myths. Axing, Xi, illus. 96p. (gr. 2). 1987. pap. 6.95 (0-8351-1795-2) China Bks.

Jirasek, Alois. Old Czech Legends. Holecek, Marie K., tr. from CZE. & pref. by. 199p. (Orig.). 1992. pap. 25.00 (1-85610-020-0, Pub. by Forest Bks UK) Dufour.

JIST Staff, ed. see U. S. Department of Labor Staff.

Joachim, Ann, jt. ed. see Greenman, Joseph.

Joachim, Mary J. Captain & Joey & the Tumbled down Cabin. Decker, Tim, illus. LC 89-81198. 47p. (Orig.). 1990. pap. 4.95 (0-916383-99-7) Aegina Pr.

Joan & Gene. Dog. Abell, ed. & illus. 50p. Date not set. 25.00 (1-56611-048-3); pap. 15.00 (1-56611-049-1) Jones.

Joan, et al. The Rain Duck: A First Poem for Preschoolers & Kindergarten. Abell, ed. & illus. 50p. (ps). Date not set. 25.00 (1-56611-050-5); pap. 15.00 (1-56611-051-3) Jones.

Job, Kenneth. Indians in New York State. Whitman, Bernard, ed. Whitman, Shirley, illus. 48p. (Orig.). (gr. 4-7). 1989. pap. text ed. 5.00 (0-918433-01-0) In Educ.

Jobb, Jamie. The Night Sky Book. (gr. 5 up). 1977. pap. 9.95 (0-316-46552-6) Little.

Jobin, Claire. All about Wool. Matthews, Sarah, tr. from FRE. Felix, Monique, illus. LC 87-31751. 38p. (gr. k-5). 1988. 4.95 (0-944589-18-9, 189) Young Discovery Lib.

Jobson, Joy. The Kaua'i Guide to Kaua'i Products & Speciality Shopping. Stanger, Susan E., illus. 64p. (Orig.). 1988. pap. 2.50 (0-942255-03-8, G2) Magic Fishes Pr.

Joe, Jeanne. Ying-Ying: Pieces of a Childhood. Caigoy, Faustino, illus. 112p. (Orig.). (gr. 4 up). 1982. pap. 4.95 (0-934788-02-2) E-W Pub Co.

Johanning, Jolynn. God Made All of Me: Activities for Young Children. (Illus.). 120p. 1992. pap. text ed. 11.95 (0-89390-210-1) Resource Pubns.

Johannson, Anna T. The Great ABC Search. Lowe, Dave, illus. 48p. (ps-k). 1993. pap. 5.95 (1-56565-059-X) Lowell Hse.
—The Great One Two Three Search. Lowe, Dave, illus. 48p. Date not set. pap. text ed. 5.95 (1-56565-066-2) Lowell Hse.

Johansen, Carol, jt. auth. see Cotter, Paulette.

Johansen, Hanna. Duck & the Owl. Bhend, Kathi, illus. LC 91-33011. 64p. (gr. 2-5). 1992. 12.95 (0-525-44828-4, DCB) Dutton Child Bks.
—A Tomcat's Tale. No 4-39067. (Illus.). 144p. (gr. 5 up). 1991. 13.95 (0-525-44583-8, DCB) Dutton Child Bks.

Johanson, Chris-Ellyn. Cocaine: A New Epidemic. (Illus.). 32p. (gr. 5 up). 1991. pap. 4.49 (1-55546-998-1) Chelsea Hse.

John, Anthony. School Fun Activity Book. (Illus.). 64p. (Orig.). 1991. pap. 1.95 (1-56156-036-7) Kidsbks.

John, Charlotte St. see St. John, Charlotte.

John, Da Free. I Am Happiness: A Rendering for Children of the Spiritual Adventure of Master Da Free John. Bodha, Daji & Closser, Lynne, eds. (Illus., Orig.). (gr. 2 up). 1982. pap. 8.95 (0-913922-68-4) Dawn Horse Pr.

John, Maddie St. see St. John, Maddie, et al.

John, Marie De see Stevenson, Robert Louis.

John, Mary. A Shilling for the Gate. 68p. 1991. pap. 23.00x (0-86383-763-8, Pub. by Gomer Pr UK) St Mut.

John, Nicholas. Opera. 48p. (gr. 4-7). 1986. pap. 9.95 (0-19-321335-4) OUP.

John, Patricia St. see St. John, Patricia.

Johns, Helen & Leadley, Robert. Choices: A Stewardship Study for Teens. Pierce, Glen A., ed. (Orig.). 1989. tchr's. ed. 5.95 (0-916035-34-4); wkbk. 4.95 (0-916035-35-2) Evangel Indiana.

Johns, Helen, ed. see Buckwalter, Leoda.

Johnsen, Karen. The Trouble with Secrets. Forssell, Linda, illus. LC 85-51803. 32p. (Orig.). (ps-3). 1986. lib. bdg. 15.95 (0-943990-23-8); pap. 4.95 (0-943990-22-X) Parenting Pr.

Johnson. How to Be a Receptionist. (gr. 7-12). pap. 1.45x (0-87783-077-0) Oddo.
—Photocabulary. (Illus.). (gr. 3-9). pap. 2.79x (0-87783-075-4) Oddo.

Johnson, jt. auth. see Bargar.

Johnson, jt. auth. see Barger.

Johnson, Allen, Jr. The Christmas Tree Express. Keetle, Lisbeth, illus. (gr. 4-8). Date not set. 12.95 (1-878561-21-9) Seacoast AL.
Twin school bullies threaten to disrupt

the peaceful, rural Vermont world of teen T.J. Flint at the beginning of Allen Johnson, Jr.'s new novel for intermediate readers, THE CHRISTMAS TREE EXPRESS. This tension sets the stage for a summer of adventure for T.J. & his best friend Sally. From their rescue of sled-dog Silver to a train ride with T.J.'s grandfather, a retired train engineer, to the rescue of the bullies themselves in a real cliff-hanger, to working alongside Dad on a real Christmas tree farm, T.J. & Sally's experiences define the depth of their rural life. Neither rich or privileged materially, T.J.'s prevailing thought on Christmas Eve is to count his blessings. At a glance, this book is a fun adventure story that offers a view of rural New England life. More importantly, at its depth, THE CHRISTMAS TREE EXPRESS is an invitation--to a place where family & community values not only still exist, but are shown to provide happiness, success & meaning to the lives of ALL of the characters. To order THE CHRISTMAS TREE EXPRESS, contact Southern Publishers Group by calling 1-800-628-0903.
Publisher Provided Annotation.

—**Picker McClikker. Hanson, Stephen, illus. (gr. k-3). 1993. 16.95 (1-878561-20-0) Seacoast AL.**
Through the eyes of a small child, the world is a mighty big place often dominated by big characters, big heroes, & big events. Not so with PICKER McCLIKKER, a delightful story in which the hero is a pint-sized four year-old! Author Allen Johnson, Jr., shares the discovery of the magical talents of Joe McClikker, the youngest of six children in a sharecropper's family from Evergreen, Alabama. The youngster earns the name "Picker" due to his extraordinary speed in picking-- picking anything that comes his way, beginning with the burrs on his hound dog Bone to the family's cotton harvest. Picker saves the day! In addition to its young hero, PICKER McCLIKKER features wonderfully detailed & colorful illustrations by Stephen Hanson who includes many favorite images of small children--farm animals, trains, & foreign lands. PICKER McCLIKKER, for children ages 3-8, is both fun & ennobling for the young reader. In fact, PICKER McCLIKKER just received special recognition from the Alabama Literacy Council, which will use the book in some of its programs. To order PICKER McCLIKKER, contact Southern Publishers Group by calling 1-800-628-0903.
Publisher Provided Annotation.

Johnson, Angela. Do Like Kyla. Ransome, James, illus. LC 89-16229. 32p. (ps-2). 1990. 14.95 (0-531-05852-2); PLB 14.99 (0-531-08452-3) Orchard Bks Watts.
—Do Like Kyla. Ransome, James E., illus. LC 89-16229. 32p. (ps-2). 1993. pap. 5.95 (0-531-07040-9) Orchard Bks Watts.
—The Girl Who Wore Snakes. Ransome, James E., illus. LC 92-44521. 32p. (ps-2). 1993. 14.95 (0-531-05491-8); PLB 14.99 (0-531-08641-0) Orchard Bks Watts.

—Julius. Pilkey, Dav, photos by. LC 92-24175. (Illus.). 32p. (ps-1). 1993. 14.95 (0-531-05465-9); PLB 14.99 (0-531-08615-1) Orchard Bks Watts.
—The Leaving Morning. Soman, David, illus. LC 91-21123. 32p. (ps-2). 1992. 14.95 (0-531-05992-8); PLB 14.99 (0-531-08592-9) Orchard Bks Watts.
—One of Three. Soman, David, illus. LC 90-29316. 32p. (ps-1). 1991. 14.95 (0-531-05955-3); RLB 14.99 (0-531-08555-4) Orchard Bks Watts.
—Shoes Like Miss Alice's. Page, Ken, illus. LC 93-4872. 1994. write for info. (0-531-06814-5); PLB write for info. (0-531-08664-X) Orchard Bks Watts.
—Tell Me a Story, Mama. Soman, David, illus. LC 88-17917. 32p. (ps-1). 1989. 14.95 (0-531-05794-1); PLB 14.99 (0-531-08394-2) Orchard Bks Watts.
—Tell Me a Story, Mama. Soman, David, illus. LC 88-17917. 32p. (ps-1). 1992. pap. 4.95 (0-531-07032-8) Orchard Bks Watts.
—Toning the Sweep: A Novel. LC 92-34062. 112p. (gr. 6 up). 1993. 13.95 (0-531-05476-4); PLB 13.99 (0-531-08626-7) Orchard Bks Watts.
—When I Am Old with You. Soman, David, illus. LC 89-70928. 32p. (ps-2). 1992. 14.95 (0-531-05884-0); PLB 14.99 (0-531-08484-1) Orchard Bks Watts.
—When I Am Old with You. Soman, David, illus. LC 89-70928. 32p. (ps-2). 1993. pap. 4.95 (0-531-07035-2) Orchard Bks Watts.
Johnson, Annabel. I Am Leaper. (gr. 4-7). 1990. 11.95 (0-590-43400-4) Scholastic Inc.
—I Am Leaper. 112p. 1992. pap. 2.75 (0-590-43399-7, Apple Paperbacks) Scholastic Inc.
Johnson, Annabel & Johnson, Edgar. The Danger Quotient. LC 83-48439. 224p. (gr. 7 up). 1987. pap. 2.95 (0-06-447029-6, Trophy) HarpC Child Bks.
—Gamebuster. Marchesi, Stephen, illus. LC 90-1330. 192p. (gr. 7 up). 1990. 14.95 (0-525-65033-4, Cobblehill Bks) Dutton Child Bks.
—The Grizzly. Riswold, Gilbert, illus. LC 64-11831. 194p. (gr. 5-9). 1973. pap. 3.95 (0-06-440036-0, Trophy) HarpC Child Bks.
Johnson, Anne A. & Stoneking, Robin. Braids & Bows: A Book of Instruction. (Illus.). 80p. 1992. wire-o bound, incl. 1 pony-tail ornament, 5 ribbons, 6 barrettes & 5 elastic bands in acrylic box 17.95 (1-878257-17-X) Klutz Pr.
Johnson, Audean. Fuzzy As a Puppy. Johnson, Audean, illus. LC 92-80353. 14p. (ps). 1993. 8.00 (0-679-83239-4) Random Bks Yng Read.
Johnson, Audean, illus. A to Z: Look & See. 32p. (Orig.). 1989. pap. 2.25 (0-394-86127-2) Random Bks Yng Read.
—Soft as a Kitten. 14p. (ps). 1982. bds. 8.00 (0-394-85517-5) Random Bks Yng Read.
Johnson, B. J. Baa Baa Book. (Illus.). 12p. (ps). 1993. pap. 3.50 (0-671-86530-7, Little Simon) S&S Trade.
—Baby Bubbles. (ps). 1994. pap. 3.50 (0-671-88606-1, Little Simon) S&S Trade.
—Baby Giggles. (ps). 1994. pap. 3.50 (0-671-88605-3, Little Simon) S&S Trade.
—Beddy Bye. (Illus.). 12p. (ps). 1993. pap. 3.50 (0-671-86533-1, Little Simon) S&S Trade.
—I Twirl. (Illus.). 12p. (ps). 1993. pap. 3.50 (0-671-86531-5, Little Simon) S&S Trade.
—On a Blossom. (Illus.). 12p. (ps). 1993. pap. 3.50 (0-671-86532-3, Little Simon) S&S Trade.
—Teeney Poppers: Baby Hugs. (ps). 1994. pap. 3.50 (0-671-88604-5, Little Simon) S&S Trade.
—Teeney Poppers: Baby Joys. (ps). 1994. pap. 3.50 (0-671-88603-7, Little Simon) S&S Trade.
Johnson, Barbara. Cup Cooking: Individual Child-Portion Picture Recipes. 12th ed. (Illus.). (ps up). 1990. pap. 2.95 (0-317-99815-3) Early Educators.
Johnson, Barbara L. Careers in Beauty Culture. Rosen, Ruth, ed. (gr. 7-12). 1989. PLB 13.95 (0-8239-1002-4) Rosen Group.
Johnson, Barry L. The Visit of the Tomten. 46p. 1990. pap. 7.95 (0-8358-0439-9) Upper Room.
Johnson, Betty. Gifts & Rewards. Butcher, Sam, illus. 13p. (gr. k-6). 1981. pap. text ed. 4.25 (1-55976-137-7) CEF Press.
—Teach Me Now, Vol. I. (Illus.). 80p. (ps). 1981. pap. text ed. 24.99 kit (1-55976-108-3) CEF Press.
—Teach Me Now, Vol. II. (Illus.). 90p. (ps). 1982. pap. text ed. 24.99 kit (1-55976-110-5) CEF Press.
—Teach Me Now, Vol. III. (Illus.). 80p. (ps). 1983. pap. text ed. 24.99 kit (1-55976-111-3) CEF Press.
—Teach Me Now, Vol. IV. (Illus.). 87p. (ps). 1984. pap. text ed. 24.99 kit (1-55976-111-3) CEF Press.
Johnson, Bruce, jt. auth. see Johnson, Odette.
Johnson, Bruce H., jt. auth. see Johnson, Odette.
Johnson, C. Merle, jt. auth. see Bradley-Johnson, Sharon.
Johnson, Cathleen. People You Should Know: Famous Black Americans. 86p. (gr. 4). 1991. write for info. wkbk. (0-9631180-0-5) Perspect NC.
Johnson, Charles. Pieces of Eight. Nelson, Jennie A., illus. 110p. (gr. 3-6). 1989. 9.95 (0-944770-00-2) Discovery GA.
Johnson, Charles & Chernow, Ron. In Search of a Voice. LC 91-36518. 36p. 1991. pap. 1.00 (0-685-53462-6) Lib Congress.
Johnson, Connie. Skeletons, Word Problems & Dinosaurs. new ed. Roes, Ruth, ed. & illus. (gr. 9-12). 1978. pap. text ed. 7.95 (0-918932-53-X) Activity Resources.
Johnson, Connie, jt. auth. see Bureloff, Morris.

Johnson, Crockett. Frowning Prince. Johnson, Crockett, illus. (gr. 1-4). 1974. Repr. 15.00 (0-912846-09-7) Bookstore Pr.
—Harold & the Purple Crayon. Johnson, Crockett, illus. LC 55-7683. (gr. k-3). 1958. 12.00 (0-06-022935-7); PLB 11.89 (0-06-022936-5) HarpC Child Bks.
—Harold & the Purple Crayon. Johnson, Crockett, illus. LC 55-7683. 64p. (gr. k-3). 1981. pap. 3.95 (0-06-443022-7, Trophy) HarpC Child Bks.
—Harold's ABC. Johnson, Crockett, illus. LC 63-14444. 64p. (ps-3). 1981. pap. 3.95 (0-06-443023-5, Trophy) HarpC Child Bks.
—Harold's Circus. LC 59-5318. (ps-3). 1959. PLB 11.89 (0-06-022966-7) HarpC Child Bks.
—Harold's Circus. Johnson, Crockett, illus. LC 59-5318. 64p. (ps-3). 1981. pap. 3.95 (0-06-443024-3, Trophy) HarpC Child Bks.
—Harold's Fairy Tale. Johnson, Crockett, illus. LC 56-8147. 64p. (ps up). 1994. 12.89 (0-06-022975-6) HarpC Child Bks.
—Harold's Fairy Tale. Johnson, Crockett, illus. LC 56-8147. 64p. (ps-1). 1994. pap. 4.95 (0-06-443347-1, Trophy) HarpC Child Bks.
—Harold's Trip to the Sky. Johnson, Crockett, illus. LC 57-9262. (gr. k-3). 1957. PLB 11.89 (0-06-022986-1) HarpC Child Bks.
—Harold's Trip to the Sky. Johnson, Crockett, illus. LC 57-9262. 64p. (ps-3). 1981. pap. 3.95 (0-06-443025-1, Trophy) HarpC Child Bks.
—Picture for Harold's Room. Johnson, Crockett, illus. LC 60-6372. (gr. k-3). 1960. PLB 13.89 (0-06-023006-1) HarpC Child Bks.
—A Picture for Harold's Room. Johnson, Crockett, illus. LC 60-6372. 64p. (ps-3). 1985. pap. 3.50 (0-06-444085-0, Trophy) HarpC Child Bks.
—Who's Upside Down? LC 89-28059. (Illus.). 32p. (ps-3). 1990. Repr. of 1952 ed. bdg. 15.00 (0-208-02276-7, Pub. by Linnet) Shoe String.
—Will Spring Be Early or Will Spring Be Late? Johnson, Crockett, illus. LC 59-9424. 48p. (gr. k-3). 1961. PLB 13.89 (0-690-89423-6, Crowell Jr Bks) HarpC Child Bks.
—Will Spring Be Early? or Will Spring Be Late? Johnson, Crockett, illus. LC 59-9424. 48p. (gr. k-3). 1990. pap. 3.95 (0-06-443224-6, Trophy) HarpC Child Bks.
Johnson, Daniel S. Creative Rebellion: Positive Options for Teens in the 90s. LC 91-61346. 160p. (gr. 6-12). 1991. pap. 11.95 (0-922848-11-4) Mystic Garden.
Johnson, David. The Boy Who Drew Cats. Johnson, David, illus. 40p. (gr. k up). 1991. pap. 14.95 (0-88708-194-0, Rabbit Ears); incls. cassette 19.95 (0-88708-195-9, Rabbit Ears) Picture Bk Studio.
—The Perfect Cartoon. 1992. 9.95 (0-533-09529-8) Vantage.
Johnson, Debbie, ed. see Dombrower, Jan.
Johnson, Diane, jt. auth. see Penland, Violet.
Johnson, Dolores. The Best Bug to Be. Johnson, Dolores, illus. LC 90-22231. 32p. (gr. k-3). 1992. RSBE 13.95 (0-02-747842-4, Macmillan Child Bk) Macmillan Child Grp.
—Now Let Me Fly: The Story of a Slave Family. Johnson, Dolores, illus. LC 92-33683. 32p. (gr. k-10). 1993. RSBE 14.95 (0-02-747699-5, Macmillan Bk) Macmillan Child Grp.
—Papa's Stories. Johnson, Dolores, illus. LC 93-17534. 32p. (gr. k-3). 1994. RSBE 14.95 (0-02-747847-5, Macmillan Child Bk) Macmillan Child Grp.
—What Kind of Baby-Sitter Is This? LC 90-42860. (Illus.). 32p. (gr. k-3). 1991. RSBE 13.95 (0-02-747846-7, Macmillan Child Bk) Macmillan Child Grp.
—What Will Mommy Do When I'm at School? Johnson, Dolores, illus. LC 90-5559. 32p. (ps-1). 1990. RSBE 13.95 (0-02-747845-9, Macmillan Child Bk) Macmillan Child Grp.
—Your Dad Was Just Like You. Johnson, Dolores, illus. LC 92-6347. 32p. (gr. k-3). 1993. RSBE 13.95 (0-02-747838-6, Macmillan Child Bk) Macmillan Child Grp.
Johnson, Donald E. Jamie: A Novel. (Illus.). 104p. (Orig.). (gr. 6-8). 1993. pap. 8.95 (1-56474-052-8) Fithian Pr.
Johnson, Donovan A. Mathmagic with Flexagons. Kaz, Diane, ed. (Orig.). (gr. 4-12). 1974. pap. 7.95 (0-918932-30-0) Activity Resources.
Johnson, Doug. Never Babysit the Hippopotamuses! Carter, Abby, illus. LC 93-18341. 32p. (ps-2). 1993. PLB 14.95 (0-8050-1873-5, Bks Young Read) H Holt & Co.
—Never Ride Elephants. 1994. write for info. (0-8050-2880-3) H Holt & Co.
Johnson, Edgar, jt. auth. see Johnson, Annabel.
Johnson, Eileen, ed. An Ancient Watering Hole: The Lubbock Lake Landmark Story. Dean, David & Cokendolpher, Jean, illus. LC 90-90258. 32p. (Orig.). (gr. 1-2). 1990. pap. 3.00 (0-89672-218-X) Tex Tech Univ Pr.
Johnson, Eileen R. Gregory Matoose: The Christmas Wish. 16p. (gr. k-6). 1991. text ed. 9.95 (1-881617-00-9) Teapot Tales.
Johnson, Elden. The Prehistoric Peoples of Minnesota. rev. ed. LC 87-32663. (Illus.). 35p. (gr. 9-12). 1988. pap. 3.95 (0-87351-223-5) Minn Hist.
Johnson, Eleanor. Pirate, the Lighthouse Cat. (gr. 2-5). 1986. pap. 6.95 (0-930096-77-0) G Gannett.

Johnson, Emily R. A House Full of Strangers. 160p. (gr. 5 up). 1992. 14.00 (0-525-65091-1, Cobblehill Bks) Dutton Child Bks.
Johnson, Eric. You Are the Editor: Sixty-One Editing Lessons That Improve Writing Skills. (gr. 5 up). 1981. pap. 12.95 (0-8224-7696-7); wkbk. o.p. 4.95 (0-8224-7697-5) Fearon Teach Aids.
Johnson, Eric W. How to Live with Parents & Teachers. LC 86-9273. 156p. (gr. 5-10). 1986. 15.00 (0-664-21273-5, Westminster) Westminster John Knox.
—Improve Your Own Spelling. (gr. 6-9). 1977. pap. text ed. 4.95 (0-88334-093-3) Longman.
—Love & Sex & Growing Up. (gr. 3-7). 1990. pap. 3.99 (0-553-15800-7, Skylark) Bantam.
—People, Love, Sex & Families. Wool, David, illus. 144p. (gr. 4 up). 1985. PLB 14.85 (0-8027-6605-6) Walker & Co.
Johnson, Esther G. Cats in My Life from Granny to Ginger. Johnson, Dagny, illus. 103p. (gr. 9-12). 1990. pap. 7.95 (0-9629143-0-4) Skyehill Pubns.
Johnson, Evelyne & Santoro, Christopher. A First Cookbook for Children: With Illustrations to Color. (Illus.). 48p. (Orig.). (gr. 4 up). 1983. pap. 2.95 (0-486-24275-7) Dover.
Johnson, Evelyne, retold by. The Cow in the Kitchen. Rao, Anthony, illus. LC 90-85905. 24p. (ps-2). 1991. Repr. 8.95 (1-878093-45-2) Boyds Mills Pr.
Johnson, Florence. Santa's ABC. (Illus.). 1993. pap. 4.95 (0-307-10360-9, Golden Pr) Western Pub.
Johnson, Frances. Coyote Tales: How the Sandbur Came to West Texas. Zweiger, Jackie, illus. 32p. (gr. 1-3). 1992. 11.95 (0-89015-866-5) Eakin-Sunbelt.
Johnson, Frances R. Share with a Friend Love Above All. LC 92-61594. (Illus.). 44p. (gr. k-3). 1993. pap. 5.95 (1-55523-564-6) Winston-Derek.
Johnson, Gail E. Phantom Horse of Collister's Fields. (gr. 4-12). 1994. 1.50 (0-89992-062-4) Coun India Ed.
Johnson, Gaylord & Bleifeld, Maurice. Hunting with the Microscope. rev. ed. Beller, Joe L., rev. by. LC 79-10271. (Illus.). (gr. 7 up). 1985. lib. bdg. 8.95 (0-668-04973-1, Arco Test) P-H Gen Ref & Trav.
Johnson, George, et al. The Story of the Church. LC 80-51329. 521p. (gr. 9). 1980. pap. 16.50 (0-89555-156-X) Tan Bks Pubs.
Johnson, George C., illus. Baby's First Words. 20p. (ps-1). 1986. bds. 4.95 (0-448-03093-4, G&D) Putnam Pub Group.
Johnson, George F. Poems & Things, Vol. 1. 98p. (Orig.). (gr. 9-12). 1989. write for info. G F Johnson.
Johnson, Georgia A. Towpath to Freedom. 144p. (Orig.). (gr. 9-12). 1988. pap. 7.95 (0-9626450-0-1) G A Johnson Pub.
Johnson, Gillian. Sahara-Sara: Saranohair. Johnson, Gillian, illus. (FRE.). 56p. 1992. 12.95 (1-55037-258-0, Pub. by Annick Pr) Firefly Bks Ltd.
Johnson, Gillian K. Saranohair. Johnson, Gillian K., illus. 56p. 1992. 12.95 (1-55037-211-4, Pub. by Annick Pr) Firefly Bks Ltd.
Johnson, Gordon G. Our Church: There's More to It Than You Think. Putman, Bob, adapted by. Ferris, Ron, illus. LC 83-82990. 92p. (gr. 5-6). 1993. wkbk. 5.99 (0-935797-33-5) Harvest IL.
Johnson, Greg & Shellenberger, Susie. Getting Ready for the Guy-Girl Thing: Two Ex-Teenagers Reveal the Shocking Truth about God's Plan for Success with the Opposite Sex! Duncan, Kyle, ed. Fisher, Barbara L., illus. LC 91-14818. 200p. (gr. 5-9). 1991. pap. 8.99 (0-8307-1485-5, 5422705) Regal.
—Keeping Your Cool While Sharing Your Faith. LC 93-7532. (Illus.). 1993. 7.99 (0-8423-7036-6) Tyndale.
Johnson, Gwen, jt. auth. see Rawls, Bea O.
Johnson, Gyneth. How the Donkeys Came to Haiti & Other Folk Tales. Di Benedetto, Angelo, illus. 124p. (gr. 4-9). 12.95 (0-8159-5706-8) Devin.
Johnson, Harriet. Honolulu Zoo Riddles. Thompson, Judi, illus. (ps-5). 1974. pap. 1.25 (0-914916-07-6) Topgallant.
Johnson, Helen M. How Do I Love Me? 2nd ed. 105p. (gr. 10 up). 1986. pap. text ed. 9.95 (0-88133-224-0) Sheffield WI.
Johnson, Herschel. A Visit to the Country. Bearden, Romare, illus. LC 87-25083. 32p. (ps-3). 1989. PLB 13.89 (0-06-022854-7) HarpC Child Bks.
Johnson, Hilda S. A Child's Diary - the 1930's. Johnson, Hilda S., illus. LC 88-51304. 64p. (Orig.). (gr. 3-8). 1988. pap. 3.95 (0-931563-02-X) Wishing Rm.
Johnson, Jacqueline. Stokely Carmichael: The Story of Black Power. Gallin, Richard, ed. Young, Andrew, intro. by. (Illus.). 128p. (gr. 5 up). 1990. lib. bdg. 16.98 (0-382-09920-6); pap. 7.95 (0-382-24056-1) Silver Burdett Pr.
Johnson, James E. The Scots & Scotch-Irish in America. LC 66-10151. (Illus.). 88p. (gr. 5 up). 1991. PLB 15.95 (0-8225-0242-9) Lerner Pubns.
—Scots & Scotch-Irish in America. 1992. pap. 5.95 (0-8225-1038-3) Lerner Pubns.
Johnson, James E. & Kavanagh, Jack. Irish in America. LC 93-25991. 1994. lib. bdg. 15.95 (0-8225-1954-2); pap. 5.95 (0-8225-1975-5) Lerner Pubns.
Johnson, James H., Jr. They Walked the Earth. Johnson, James H., Jr., illus. 112p. (Orig.). (gr. 1-6). 1992. 12.95 (0-9632717-0-9) P Q Pubns.
Johnson, James Weldon. The Creation. Ransome, James, illus. LC 93-3207. 32p. (gr. 4-8). 1994. 15.95 (0-8234-0973-1) Holiday.
—The Creation: A Poem. Golembe, Carla, photos by. LC 92-24304. (Illus.). 1993. 15.95 (0-316-46744-8) Little.

—Lift Every Voice & Sing. Catlett, Elizabeth, illus. 36p. 1993. 14.95 (*0-8027-8250-7*); PLB 15.85 (*0-8027-8251-5*) Walker & Co.

Johnson, Janice. Rosamund. Haeffele, Deobrah, illus. LC 92-44115. (gr. 5 up). 1994. pap. 14.00 (*0-671-79329-2*, S&S BFYR) S&S Trade.

Johnson, Jay. What's Inside the Magic Box? Using Personal Computers in the 21st Century. (gr. 4 up). 1991. 14.00 (*0-910609-24-1*) Gifted Educ Pr.

Johnson, Jean. Firefighters: A to Z. Johnson, Jean, photos by. LC 85-5348. (Illus.). 39p. (gr. 1-3). 1985. 11.95 (*0-8027-6589-0*); PLB 11.85 (*0-8027-6590-4*) Walker & Co.

—Librarians A to Z. Johnson, Jean, photos by & illus. 48p. (gr. 1-3). 1989. 11.95 (*0-8027-6841-5*); lib. bdg. 12.85 (*0-8027-6842-3*) Walker & Co.

—Police Officers: A to Z. (Illus.). 48p. (gr. k-3). 1986. 11. 95 (*0-8027-6614-5*); lib. bdg. 12.85 (*0-8027-6615-3*) Walker & Co.

—Postal Workers: A to Z. (Illus.). 48p. (gr. 1-3). 1987. 11.95 (*0-8027-6663-3*); PLB 12.85 (*0-8027-6664-1*) Walker & Co.

—Sanitation Workers: A to Z. (Illus.). (gr. k-3). 1988. 11. 95 (*0-8027-6772-9*); PLB 12.85 (*0-8027-6773-7*) Walker & Co.

—Teachers: A to Z. (Illus.). (gr. 1-3). 1987. 11.95 (*0-8027-6676-5*); PLB 12.85 (*0-8027-6677-3*) Walker & Co.

Johnson, Jinny. Desert Wildlife. (gr. 4-7). 1993. 9.95 (*0-685-65845-7*, Readers Digest Kids) RD Assn.

—Ocean Wildlife. (gr. 4-7). 1993. 9.95 (*0-89577-536-0*, Readers Digest Kids) RD Assn.

—Poles & Tundra Wildlife. (gr. 4-7). 1993. 9.95 (*0-89577-538-7*, Readers Digest Kids) RD Assn.

—Rain Forest Wildlife. (gr. 4-7). 1993. 9.95 (*0-89577-537-9*, Readers Digest Kids) RD Assn.

Johnson, Joan J. America's War on Drugs. (Illus.). 160p. (gr. 9-12). 1990. 13.95 (*0-531-15179-4*); PLB 14.40 (*0-531-10954-2*) Watts.

—Kids Without Homes. (Illus.). 192p. (gr. 9-12). 1991. 14.45 (*0-531-15228-6*); PLB 14.40 (*0-531-11064-8*) Watts.

—Teen Prostitution. LC 92-15231. (Illus.). 192p. (gr. 9-12). 1992. 14.45 (*0-531-15256-1*); PLB 14.40 (*0-531-11099-0*) Watts.

Johnson, Joanne C. Aunt Joanne's Collection of Skits, Vol. 1. LC 88-51620. (Illus.). 88p. (Orig.). 1988. pap. 9.95 (*0-945383-05-3*, 945-5801); pap. 10.95 spiral comb bdg. (*0-945383-06-1*, 945-5804) Teach Servs.

Johnson, John E. The Me Book. Johnson, John E., illus. LC 79-62042. (ps). 1979. 3.50 (*0-394-84243-X*) Random Bks Yng Read.

Johnson, John E., illus. Here Comes the Bus. 14p. (gr. 2-5). 1985. 3.99 (*0-394-87544-3*) Random Bks Yng Read.

—Here Comes the Circus. 14p. (gr. 2-5). 1985. 3.99 (*0-394-87543-5*) Random Bks Yng Read.

—Here Comes the Farmer. 14p. (gr. ps-3). 1985. 3.99 (*0-394-87552-4*) Random Bks Yng Read.

—Here Comes the Train. 14p. (gr. 2-5). 1985. 3.99 (*0-394-87551-6*) Random Bks Yng Read.

—My First Book of Things. LC 78-64609. (ps). 1979. 3.95 (*0-394-84128-X*) Random Bks Yng Read.

Johnson, Joy & Johnson, Marvin. Hurting Yourself: For Teens Who Have Attempted Suicide. Borum, Shari, illus. 24p. (Orig.). (gr. 9-12). 1986. pap. 2.65 (*1-56123-038-3*) Centering Corp.

—New Baby: A Coloring Book for Big Sisters & Brothers. Borum, Shari, illus. 24p. (Orig.). (ps). 1981. pap. 1.00 (*1-56123-018-9*) Centering Corp.

—Tell Me, Papa: A Family Book for Children's Questions about Death & Funerals. Borum, Shari, illus. 24p. (Orig.). (gr. 2-7). 1978. pap. 3.25 (*1-56123-011-1*) Centering Corp.

Johnson, Joy, ed. see Blackburn, Lynn B.

Johnson, Joy, ed. see Hawkins-Walsh, Elizabeth.

Johnson, Julia. United Arab Emirates. (Illus.). 96p. (gr. 5 up). 1988. 14.95 (*1-55546-178-6*) Chelsea Hse.

Johnson, Julie. Understanding Mental Illness: For Teens Who Care about Someone with Mental Illness. 72p. (gr. 6 up). 1989. 15.95 (*0-8225-0042-6*) Lerner Pubns.

Johnson, Julie T. Celebrate You: Building Your Self-Esteem. 72p. (gr. 4 up). 1990. PLB 15.95 (*0-8225-0046-9*) Lerner Pubns.

—Understanding Mental Illness: For Teens Who Care about Someone with Mental Illness. 70p. (gr. 6 up). Repr. of 1989 ed. 4.95g (*0-8225-9574-5*) Lerner Pubns.

Johnson, Katharine, jt. auth. see Bruce, Preston.

Johnson, Kathryn T. & Balczon, Mary-Lynne J. The Sexual Dictionary: Terms & Expressions for Teens & Parents. St. John, Charlotte, ed. (Illus.). 176p. 1993. pap. 12.95 (*0-89896-400-8*) Larksdale.

Johnson, Ken, jt. auth. see Herr, Ted.

Johnson, Ken, jt. auth. see Myers, Bill.

Johnson, Kendall. Turning Yourself Around: Self-Help Strategies for Troubled Teens. 224p. (gr. 7-12). 1992. 9.95 (*0-89793-092-4*) Hunter Hse.

Johnson, Kendall, jt. auth. see Deaton, Wendy.

Johnson, Kevin. Can I Be a Christian Without Being Weird? LC 92-15804. 1992. pap. 6.99 (*1-55661-281-8*) Bethany Hse.

—Who Should I Listen To?: Readings for Early Teens on Identifying Truth from Lies. 1993. pap. 6.99 (*1-55661-283-4*) Bethany Hse.

—Why Is God Looking for Friends? 128p. (Orig.). (gr. 6-9). 1993. pap. 6.99 (*1-55661-282-6*) Bethany Hse.

Johnson, Kipchak. A Worm's Eye View: Make Your Own Wildlife Refuge. (Illus.). 40p. (gr. 2-6). 1991. PLB 12.90 (*1-878841-30-0*) Millbrook Pr.

Johnson, Kristopher K. A Day Without Cartoons: Poetry for Gifted Students. Kester, Ellen S., ed. (Illus.). 50p. (Orig.). (gr. 3-8). 1989. pap. 6.95 (*0-685-26282-0*) Pickwick Pubs.

Johnson, L. Biographies Literature Set, 6 stories. (ENG & SPA., Illus.). (gr. k-3). 1992. incl. story cards 225.00 (*0-87746-310-7*) Graphic Learning.

—Booker T. Washington: Story Pak. (ENG & SPA., Illus.). (gr. k-3). 1992. incl. story cards 39.00 (*0-87746-259-3*) Graphic Learning.

—Elizabeth Cady Stanton: Story Pak. (ENG & SPA., Illus.). (gr. k-3). 1992. incl. story cards 39.00 (*0-87746-257-7*) Graphic Learning.

—Jane Addams: Story Pak. (ENG & SPA., Illus.). (gr. k-3). 1992. incl. story cards 39.00 (*0-87746-249-6*) Graphic Learning.

—Johnny Appleseed: Story Pak. (ENG & SPA., Illus.). (gr. k-3). 1992. incl. story cards 39.00 (*0-87746-251-8*) Graphic Learning.

—Junipero Serra: Story Pak. (ENG & SPA., Illus.). (gr. k-3). 1992. incl. story cards 39.00 (*0-87746-255-0*) Graphic Learning.

—Sequoyah: Story Pak. (ENG & SPA., Illus.). (gr. k-3). 1992. incl. story cards 39.00 (*0-87746-253-4*) Graphic Learning.

Johnson, L., ed. Around the Community: Literature Set, 6 stories. (ENG & SPA., Illus.). (gr. 3). 1993. incl. story cards 225.00 (*0-87746-321-2*) Graphic Learning.

—At Home & at School: Literature Set, 6 stories. (ENG & SPA., Illus.). (gr. 1). 1993. incl. story cards 225.00 (*0-87746-319-0*) Graphic Learning.

—In the Neighborhood: Literature Set, 6 stories. (ENG & SPA., Illus.). (gr. 2). 1993. incl. story cards 225.00 (*0-87746-320-4*) Graphic Learning.

—Me & My World: Literature Set, 6 stories. (ENG & SPA., Illus.). (gr. k). 1993. incl. story cards 225.00 (*0-87746-318-2*) Graphic Learning.

Johnson, L. & Hollenbeck, K., eds. Classic Tales Literature Set, 6 stories. (ENG & SPA., Illus.). (gr. k-3). 1992. incl. story cards 225.00 (*0-87746-302-6*) Graphic Learning.

—Fables Literature Set, 6 stories. (ENG & SPA., Illus.). (gr. k-3). 1992. incl. story cards 225.00 (*0-87746-306-9*) Graphic Learning.

—Folktales Literature Set, 6 stories. (Illus.). (gr. k-3). 1992. 225.00 (*0-87746-314-X*) Graphic Learning.

Johnson, Larry. Road Kill. Tabb, Doug, ed. (Illus.). 32p. (Orig.). (gr. 12). 1991. pap. 7.00 (*1-55806-117-7*, 415) Iron Crown Ent Inc.

Johnson, Larry D. & Mills, Jane L. Arnie the Astronaut. Hebert, Kim T., illus. LC 86-60353. 22p. (Orig.). (ps-1). 1986. pap. 4.50 (*0-938155-02-4*); pap. 12.00 set of 3 bks. (*0-685-13517-9*) Read A Bol.

—Arnie the Detective. Hebert, Kim T., illus. LC 86-60364. 24p. (ps). 1986. pap. 4.50 (*0-938155-06-7*); pap. 12.00 set of 3 bks. (*0-685-13514-4*) Read A Bol.

Johnson, Larry D., jt. auth. see Mills, Jane L.

Johnson, Laura R. The Teddy Bear ABC. Sanford, Margaret L., illus. 64p. (gr. ps-2). 1991. pap. 7.95 (*0-914676-86-5*, Green Tiger) S&S Trade.

—The Teddy Bear ABC. Sanford, Margaret L., illus. LC 91-18207. 64p. (ps-2). 1992. 12.00 (*0-671-74979-X*, Green Tiger); pap. 7.95 (*0-671-75949-3*, Green Tiger) S&S Trade.

Johnson, LaVerne C. Bessie Coleman: Writer. Perry, Craig R., illus. LC 92-35255. 1992. 3.95 (*0-922162-95-6*) Empak Pub.

—George Washington Carver: Writer. Perry, Craig R., illus. LC 92-35254. (gr. 6-9). 1992. pap. 3.95 (*0-922162-91-3*) Empak Pub.

—Harriet Tubman: Writer. Perry, Craig R., illus. LC 92-35251. 1992. 3.95 (*0-922162-92-1*) Empak Pub.

—Heritage Kids Volume Set: George Washington Carver: Bessie Coleman: Harriet Tubman: Jean Baptiste DuSable. Perry, Craig P., illus. LC 92-35256. 1992. 3.95 (*0-922162-90-5*); Set. write for info. (*0-922162-99-9*) Empak Pub.

—Jean Baptiste DuSable: Writer. Perry, Craig R., illus. LC 92-35252. 1992. 3.95 (*0-922162-93-X*) Empak Pub.

Johnson, Lee & Johnson, Sue K. If I Ran the Family. Espeland, Pamela, ed. Collier-Morales, Roberta, illus. LC 92-948. 32p. (ps-3). 1992. 13.95 (*0-915793-41-5*) Free Spirit Pub.

Johnson, Liliane & Dufton, Jo S. Children's Chillers & Thrillers. Bruhn, Joan, illus. 136p. (Orig.). Date not set. pap. 10.00 (*0-930069-04-8*) Jasmine Pr.

Johnson, Linda, jt. auth. see Bargar, Sherie.

Johnson, Linda C. Barbara Jordan: Congresswoman. (Illus.). 64p. (gr. 3-7). PLB 14.95 (*1-56711-031-2*) Blackbirch.

—Barbara Jordan: Congresswomen. (Illus.). 64p. (gr. 3-7). 1993. pap. 7.95 (*1-56711-050-9*) Blackbirch.

—Mother Teresa: Protector of the Sick. (Illus.). 64p. (gr. 3-7). PLB 14.95 (*1-56711-034-7*) Blackbirch.

—Our Constitution. LC 91-43232. (Illus.). 48p. (gr. 2-4). 1992. PLB 12.90 (*1-56294-090-2*) Millbrook Pr.

—Our National Symbols. LC 91-38893. (Illus.). 48p. (gr. 2-4). 1992. PLB 12.90 (*1-56294-108-9*) Millbrook Pr.

—Patriotism. (Illus.). 64p. (gr. 7-12,RL 4-6). 1990. PLB 13.95 (*0-8239-1507-7*) Rosen Group.

—Responsibility. (Illus.). 64p. (gr. 7-12,RL 4-6). 1990. PLB 13.95 (*0-8239-1107-1*) Rosen Group.

Johnson, Lindsay L. & Kowitt, Holly. A Week with Zeke & Zach. (Illus.). 64p. (gr. 2-5). 1993. 11.99 (*0-525-45097-1*, DCB) Dutton Child Bks.

Johnson, Lois. Just a Minute, Lord: Prayers for Girls. LC 73-78265. (Illus.). 96p. (Orig.). (gr. 3-8). 1973. pap. 5.99 (*0-8066-1329-7*, 10-3605, Augsburg) Augsburg Fortress.

Johnson, Lois W. The Creeping Shadows. 144p. (Orig.). (gr. 2-8). 1990. pap. 5.99 (*1-55661-102-1*) Bethany Hse.

—The Disappearing Stranger. 144p. (Orig.). (gr. 3-5). 1990. pap. 5.99 (*1-55661-100-5*) Bethany Hse.

—Grandpa's Stolen Treasure. LC 92-30093. 144p. (Orig.). (gr. 3-8). 1992. pap. 5.99 (*1-55661-239-7*) Bethany Hse.

—The Hidden Message. LC 89-78390. 144p. (Orig.). (gr. 3-8). 1990. pap. 5.99 (*1-55661-101-3*) Bethany Hse.

—Mysterious Hideaway: Adventures of the Northwoods. (gr. 4-7). 1992. pap. 5.99 (*1-55661-238-9*) Bethany Hse.

—The Runaway Clown. 144p. (Orig.). 1993. pap. 5.99 (*1-55661-240-0*) Bethany Hse.

—Secrets of the Best Choice. Peck, Virginia, illus. LC 88-60475. 192p. (Orig.). 1988. pap. 7.00 (*0-89109-232-3*) NavPress.

—Thanks for Being My Friend. Peck, Virginia, illus. LC 88-60473. 180p. (Orig.). 1988. pap. 7.00 (*0-89109-234-X*) NavPress.

—Trouble at Wild River. 144p. (Orig.). (gr. 3-8). 1991. pap. 5.99 (*1-55661-144-7*) Bethany Hse.

—Vanishing Footprints. 144p. (Orig.). (ps-8). 1991. pap. 5.99 (*1-55661-103-X*) Bethany Hse.

—You Are Wonderfully Made! Peck, Virginia, illus. LC 88-60474. 192p. (Orig.). 1988. pap. 7.00 (*0-89109-235-8*) NavPress.

—You're My Best Friend, Lord. LC 76-3866. 112p. (Orig.). (gr. 4-7). 1976. pap. 5.99 (*0-8066-1541-9*, 10-7490, Augsburg) Augsburg Fortress.

—You're Worth More Than You Think! Peck, Virginia, illus. LC 88-60476. 180p. (Orig.). 1988. pap. 7.00 (*0-89109-233-1*) NavPress.

Johnson, M., et al. Science Fun. (Illus.). 192p. (gr. 4 up). 1993. pap. 8.95 (*0-7460-0361-7*) EDC.

Johnson, Mabel. Escape from Scrooby. (gr. 7 up). 1975. pap. 4.50 (*0-9600838-2-0*) M Johnson.

—One Land - One Nation. (Illus.). 64p. (gr. 7 up). 1987. pap. 3.95 (*0-9600838-6-3*) M Johnson.

Johnson, Marjorie. Book of Mormon Stories for Little Children. LC 76-3991. (Illus.). 96p. (Orig.). (gr. ps-7). 1976. pap. 7.95 (*0-88290-063-3*) Horizon Utah.

Johnson, Mark. Campfire Favorites: A Songbook for Balance-Control Karaoke. Johnson, Mark, illus. 24p. (Orig.). (gr. k-12). Date not set. pap. 2.49 (*1-883988-08-X*); pap. 8.99 incl. cassette (*1-883988-02-0*) RSV Prods.

—The Complete Bugler: Practice & Performance Aid for the Young Bugler. Johnson, Mark, illus. 24p. (Orig.). (gr. 4-12). 1993. pap. 2.95 (*1-883988-10-1*); pap. 8.95 incl. cassette (*1-883988-04-7*) RSV Prods.

—Cowboy Classics: A Songbook for Balance-Control Karaoke. Johnson, Mark, illus. 24p. (Orig.). (gr. k-12). 1993. pap. 2.49 (*1-883988-06-3*); pap. 8.99 incl. cassette (*1-883988-00-4*) RSV Prods.

—Fun-to-Sing: A Songbook for Balance-Control Karaoke. Johnson, Mark, illus. 24p. (Orig.). (gr. k-12). 1993. pap. 2.49 (*1-883988-07-1*); pap. 8.99 incl. cassette (*1-883988-01-2*) RSV Prods.

—Good 'n Gross: A Songbook for Balance-Control Karaoke. Johnson, Mark, illus. 24p. (Orig.). (gr. k-12). 1993. pap. 2.49 (*1-883988-09-8*); pap. 8.99 incl. cassette (*1-883988-03-9*) RSV Prods.

—Sing-Along Fun: Cowboy Classics, Fun-to-Sing, Campfire Favorites & Good 'n Gross, 4 vols. (Illus.). 24p. (Orig.). (gr. k-12). 1993. Set, incl. 4 audio cass. pap. 31.99 (*1-883988-05-5*) RSV Prods. SING-ALONG FUN (SERIES), These four songbook & cassette packages, originally developed for boys in scouting, cover all the bases with songs that everyone loves to sing. The songbooks present complete lyrics along with diagrammed guitar chords & tips on playing. The tapes are recorded with a versatile & easy-to-use balance-control karaoke option that allows the user to select as much or as little of the recorded vocals as desired. COWBOY CLASSICS is a collection of sing-along greats for the old West, with all the popular verses & arrangements, plus some little-known lyric gems that bring new enjoyment to old favorites like "Home on the Range" & "Red River Valley." FUN-TO-SING features foot-stompers, knee-slappers & tongue-twisters including "Coming 'Round the Mountain" & "On Top of

Spaghetti" for sing your head off fun! CAMPFIRE FAVORITES presents songs from the heart of America's musical heritage & a mood that runs from robust to mellow with the likes of "Working on the Railroad" & "Kumbayah." GOOD 'N GROSS is an hilarious & exquisitely disgusting batch of songs to provoke enthusiastic singalongs from you-know-who; with "Greasy Grimy Gopher Guts", "Found a Peanut" & many more. Each package also sold separately. To order: RSVProducts, Box 26, Hopkins, MN 55343. Tel. (612) 936-0400. *Publisher Provided Annotation.*

Johnson, Marvin, jt. auth. see Johnson, Joy.
Johnson, Mary A. One Way Ticket: The True Story of Herta Taussig Freitag. Freitag, Herta, illus. 150p. (Orig.). (gr. 5 up). 1988. pap. 15.95 (0-9621465-0-1) Mary Ann Johnson.
Johnson, Mary O. The President. (Illus.). (gr. 5-6). 1992. PLB 21.34 (0-8114-7352-X) Raintree Steck-V.
Johnson, May. Chemistry Experiments. King, Colin, illus. 64p. (gr. 3-6). 1983. lib. bdg. 11.96 (0-88110-161-3); pap. 4.95 (0-86020-527-4) EDC.
Johnson, Mercy, ed. see Haaland, Lynn.
Johnson, Mercy, ed. see Welles, Ted.
Johnson, Meredith, illus. The Children's Macbeth. (gr. 5-9). 1993. pap. 3.95 (0-88388-186-1) Bellerophon Bks.
Johnson, Mildred. Wait, Skates! Dunnington, Tom, illus. LC 82-22228. 32p. (ps-2). 1983. PLB 11.93 (0-516-02039-0); pap. 2.95 (0-516-42039-9) Childrens.
Johnson, Nancy, intro. by see Lagerlof, Selma.
Johnson, Nancy, ed. see Lagerlof, Selma.
Johnson, Nancy L. The Best Teacher "Stuff" from Nancy L. Johnson. (Illus.). (gr. k-8). 1993. pap. write for info. (1-880505-06-1) Pieces of Lrning.
—Questioning Makes the Difference. (Illus.). 80p. (Orig.). (gr. k-12). 1990. pap. 8.95 (0-9623835-3-8) Pieces of Lrning.
—Thinking Is the Key: Questioning Makes the Difference. (Illus.). 96p. (gr. k-12). 1992. pap. 9.95 (1-880505-01-0) Pieces of Lrning.
Johnson, Neil. All in a Day's Work: Twelve Americans Talk About Their Jobs, Vol. 1. 1994. 14.95 (0-316-46957-2, Joy St Bks) Little.
—Batter Up. 1990. pap. 12.95 (0-590-42729-6) Scholastic Inc.
—Batter UP! 32p. 1992. pap. 3.95 (0-590-42730-X) Scholastic Inc.
—The Battle of Gettysburg. Johnson, Neil, illus. LC 88-30414. 64p. (gr. 5 up). 1989. SBE 14.95 (0-02-747831-9, Four Winds) Macmillan Child Grp.
—The Battle of Lexington & Concord. Johnson, Neil, photos by. LC 91-22790. (Illus.). 40p. (gr. 4 up). 1992. RSBE 15.95 (0-02-747841-6, Four Winds) Macmillan Child Grp.
—Born to Run. (ps-4). 1989. pap. 3.95 (0-590-42836-5) Scholastic Inc.
—Fire & Silk: Flying in a Hot Air Balloon. (ps-3). 1991. 15.95 (0-316-46959-9) Little.
—Jack Creek Cowboy. Johnson, Neil, photos by. LC 92-921. (Illus.). 32p. (gr. 2-5). 1993. 14.99 (0-8037-1228-6); PLB 14.89 (0-8037-1229-4) Dial Bks Young.
—Step into China. Johnson, Neil, illus. LC 87-20266. 32p. (gr. 3-6). 1988. lib. bdg. 9.98 (0-671-64338-X, J Messner); pap. 5.95 (0-671-65852-2) S&S Trade.
Johnson, Norma. Bats on the Bedstead. LC 86-27823. 128p. (gr. 3-7). 1987. 13.95 (0-395-43022-4) HM.
Johnson, Norma T. Bats on the Bedstead. 128p. 1988. pap. 2.95 (0-380-70540-0, Camelot) Avon.
—The Witch House. 144p. (Orig.). 1990. pap. 2.95 (0-380-75789-3, Camelot) Avon.
Johnson, Odette & Johnson, Bruce. One Prickly Porcupine. (Illus.). 32p. (ps up) 1992. laminated boards 13.95 (0-19-540834-9) OUP.
Johnson, Odette & Johnson, Bruce H. Apples, Alligators, & Also Alphabets. (Illus.). 32p. (ps-1). 1991. 13.95 (0-19-540757-1) OUP.
Johnson, Pamela. How to Draw the Circus. LC 86-50467. (Illus.). 32p. (gr. 2-6). 1987. PLB 10.65 (0-8167-0856-8, Pub. by Watermill Pr); pap. text ed. 1.95 (0-8167-0857-6, Pub. by Watermill Pr) Troll Assocs.
—Let's Celebrate St. Patricks's Day: A Book of Drawing Fun. LC 87-61374. (Illus.). (gr. 2-6). 1988. PLB 10.65 (0-8167-1135-6); pap. 1.95 (0-8167-1136-4) Troll Assocs.
—A Mouse's Tale. D'Andrade, Diane, ed. (Illus.). 32p. (ps-3). 1991. 11.95 (0-15-256032-7) HarBrace.
Johnson, Pamela, illus. The Story of the First Christmas. LC 90-23154. 24p. (ps up). 1991. 2.95 (0-694-00364-6) HarpC Child Bks.
Johnson, Patricia. Mistletoe. 1992. 7.95 (0-533-09706-1) Vantage.
Johnson, Patricia G. Confederate Woman of New River Border Country. (Illus.). 80p. (Orig.). 1993. pap. 12.00 (1-878188-03-8) Walpa Pub.

—The New River Early Settlement. LC 83-81157. (Illus.). 232p. (gr. 6 up). 1991. Repr. of 1983 ed. 20.00 (0-9614765-3-2) Walpa Pub. Regional History New River in N.C., Va./W.Va. The United States Army Invades the New River Valley, May 1864, rep. 1986 ed. Crook's Army Raids New River Railroads. ISBN 0-9614765-7-5, 137 pages, soft. $12.00. Techman of the Twenties, ISBN 0-9614765-9-1, hardcover, illus. 117 pages. Student life, Virginia Polytechnic, Blacksburg, 1920s. $15.00. James Patton & Appalachian Colonists. Biography, region history, New & Holston Valley - Colonists 1738-1755. hardcover, illus. 246p. 1980 rep. 1973 ed. $15.00. ISBN 0-9614765-4-0. William Preston & Allegheny Patriots. American Revolution on New & Holston river. Tories, patriots, Indian conflict. 318 p. ISBN 0-9614765-5-9 $20.00. Irish Burks of Colonial Va. & New River. Burks-1640s Ireland Rebellion Refugees to Virginia mountains - Genealogy, regional history. 300p. illus. hard. ISBN 1-878188-02-X. $20.00. Christianburg in Allegheny Mountains. Town-county story, county seat, Montgomery Co., Va. ISBN 0-9614765-1-6. $15.00. Andrew Lewis of Roanoke & Greenbrier. French & Indian War officer & Revolutionary Western Virginia General-Colonizer. ISBN 0-9614765-6-7. 259 p. soft. illus. $15.00. Confederate Women of New River Border Country. 83p. soft. illus. maps. ISBN 1-878188-03-8. $12.00. Mountain Lakes Resort 1751-1900. History. Virginia's Famed Resort. ISBN 0-9614765-8-3. 90p. illus. hard. $15.00. Springfield Saga. Fort Thompson on New River. 1750s French/Indian War Fort-New River Plantation, Pulaski, Co., Va. Thompson genealogy. ISBN 0-9614765-0-8. 70 p. illus. soft. $15.00. Walpa Publishing, 4201 Prices Fork Rd. Blacksburg, Va. 24060. *Publisher Provided Annotation.*

Johnson, Patricia P. & Williams, Donna R. Morgan's Baby Sister: A Read-Aloud Book for Families Who Have Experienced the Death of a Newborn. Schaffhausen, Suzanne, illus. 64p. (Orig.). (ps-2). 1993. pap. 10.95 (0-89390-257-8) Resource Pubns.
Johnson, Paul, illus. Christmas Prayers. 16p. (ps). 1993. bds. 2.98 (0-8317-4277-1) Smithmark.
—Family Prayers. 16p. (ps). 1993. bds. 2.98 (0-8317-4278-X) Smithmark.
Johnson, Paul B. The Cow Who Wouldn't Come Down. LC 92-27592. (Illus.). 32p. (ps-1). 1993. 14.95 (0-531-05481-0); PLB 14.99 (0-531-08631-3) Orchard Bks Watts.
Johnson, Paul H. Samurai in Valhalla - Past the Future. 367p. (Orig.). (gr. 9 up). 1993. pap. 5.95 (0-9636833-1-4) Piros Pr.
Johnson, Paul T., ed. see Johnson, Ralph E.
Johnson, Pauline, ed. see Johnson, William R.
Johnson, Pauline D., ed. see Johnson, William R.
Johnson, Pete. Catch You on the Flip Side. 135p. (gr. 7-9). 1989. pap. 9.95 (0-233-98074-1, Pub. by A Deutsch England) Trafalgar.
Johnson, Peter D., intro. by. Clay Modelling for Everyone: Sculpture, Pottery & Jewellery Without a Wheel. De la Bedoyere, C., tr. (Illus.). 112p. (Orig.). (gr. 7 up). 1988. pap. 14.95 (0-85532-564-X, Pub. by Search Pr UK) Pathway Bk Serv.
Johnson, Philip E. Celebrating the Seasons with Children (Year B) LC 84-14791. 112p. (Orig.). (ps-3). 1984. pap. 8.95 (0-8298-0723-3) Pilgrim OH.
Johnson, Philip R. Chase of the Sorceress. LC 89-50958. 152p. (gr. 7-12). 1989. pap. 8.25x (0-943864-58-5) Davenport.
Johnson, Phyllis. The Boy Toy. Shiffman, Lena, illus. 32p. (gr. k-3). 1988. pap. 5.95 (0-914996-26-6) Lollipop Power.

Johnson, Ralph E. Children's Stories Two: Coloring Nature's Harmony. Johnson, Paul T., ed. Clark, Melissa & Johnson, Gloria, illus. Johnson, Paul. 100p. (Orig.). (gr. k-12). 1989. pap. write for info. (0-9621929-0-2) J-p Press.
Johnson, Rebecca L. Diving into Darkness: A Submersible Explores the Sea. (Illus.). 64p. (gr. 5 up). 1989. 22.95 (0-8225-1587-3) Lerner Pubns.
—The Great Barrier Reef: A Living Laboratory. (Illus.). 64p. (gr. 5 up). 1991. PLB 21.50 (0-8225-1596-2) Lerner Pubns.
—The Greenhouse Effect: Life on a Warmer Planet. (Illus.). 112p. (gr. 5 up). 1990. PLB 23.95 (0-8225-1591-1) Lerner Pubns.
—The Greenhouse Effect: Life on a Warmer Planet. LC 93-17178. 1993. PLB 23.95 (0-8225-1572-5); pap. 9.95 (0-8225-9652-0) Lerner Pubns.
—Investigating the Ozone Hole. LC 93-15225. 1993. 23.95 (0-8225-1574-1) Lerner Pubns.
—The Secret Language: Pheromones in the Animal World. (Illus.). 64p. (gr. 5 up). 1989. 21.50 (0-8225-1586-5) Lerner Pubns.
Johnson, Renae, jt. auth. see Johnson, Stephen.
Johnson, Richard. Look at Me in a Funny Hat! Chatterton, Martin, illus. LC 93-32379. 1994. 4.99 (1-56402-414-8) Candlewick Pr.
—Look at Me in Funny Clothes! Chatterton, Martin, illus. LC 93-32380. 1994. 4.99 (1-56402-415-6) Candlewick Pr.
Johnson, Rick L. Bo Jackson: Baseball-Football Superstar. LC 91-17910. (Illus.). 64p. (gr. 4-6). 1991. RSBE 13.95 (0-87518-489-8, Dillon) Macmillan Child Grp.
—Jim Abbott: Beating the Odds. (Illus.). 64p. (gr. 3 up). 1991. RSBE 13.95 (0-87518-459-6, Dillon) Macmillan Child Grp.
—Magic Johnson: Basketball's Smiling Superstar. LC 92-3175. (Illus.). 64p. (gr. 3 up). 1992. RSBE 13.95 (0-87518-553-3, Dillon) Macmillan Child Grp.
Johnson, Robin. Horse Stories. (Illus.). 96p. (Orig.). (gr. 5-9). 1988. pap. 1.95 (0-942025-18-0) Ishbks.
Johnson, Rolf E. & Piggins, Carol A. Dinosaur Hunt! LC 91-50336. (Illus.). 32p. (gr. 2-8). 1993. PLB 15.93 (0-8368-0740-5); PLB 15.93 s.p. (0-685-61502-2) Gareth Stevens Inc.
Johnson, Russell. Trouble at Christmas. Watts, Bernadette, illus. LC 90-28988. 32p. (gr. k-3). 1991. 14.95 (1-55858-116-2) North-South Bks NYC.
Johnson, Ruth I. Devotions for Early Teens. (gr. 7-12). 1960-74. Vol. 1. pap. 4.50 (0-8024-2181-4) Moody.
Johnson, Ryerson. Kenji & the Magic Geese. LC 91-3644. (ps-3). 1992. pap. 15.00 (0-671-75974-4, S&S BFYR) S&S Trade.
—Why Is Baby Crying? Tucker, Kathy, ed. DiSalvo-Ryan, DyAnne, illus. LC 89-5380. 32p. (ps-2). 1989. PLB 13.95 (0-8075-9084-3) A Whitman.
Johnson, S. F., ed. see Shakespeare, William.
Johnson, Samuel & Boswell, James. A Journey to the Western Islands of Scotland. Wendt, Allan, ed. Bd. with The Journal of a Tour to the Hebrides. LC 66-175. (gr. 9 up). 1965. pap. 9.16 (0-395-05181-9, RivEd) HM.
Johnson, Sandra. The Other Louvre. 1992. 8.95 (0-533-09499-2) Vantage.
Johnson, Scott. One of the Boys. LC 91-19262. 256p. (gr. 7 up). 1992. SBE 15.95 (0-689-31520-1, Atheneum Child Bk) Macmillan Child Grp.
—Overnight Sensation. LC 93-23084. 176p. (gr. 7 up). 1994. SBE 15.95 (0-689-31831-6, Atheneum Child Bk) Macmillan Child Grp.
Johnson, Seddon. Alien, Go Home. 1990. pap. 3.25 (0-553-28482-7) Bantam.
—South Pole Sabotage. 1989. pap. 2.50 (0-553-27770-7) Bantam.
Johnson, Sharon S. I Want to Be a Clown. Gregorich, Barbara, ed. (Illus.). 16p. (Orig.). (gr. k-2). 1985. pap. 2.25 (0-88743-014-7, 06014) Sch Zone Pub Co.
—I Want to be a Clown. Gregorich, Barbara, ed. (Illus.). 32p. (gr. k-2). 1992. pap. 3.95 (0-88743-412-6, 06064) Sch Zone Pub Co.
Johnson, Sherrie. The Broken Bow. 1994. pap. 4.95 (0-87579-253-7) Deseret Bk.
Johnson, Sherry M., ed. see Schenk, Julie W.
Johnson, Stacie. The Party. 1992. pap. 3.50 (0-553-29720-1) Bantam.
—The Prince. 1992. pap. 3.50 (0-553-29721-X) Bantam.
—Sky Man. 1993. pap. 3.50 (0-553-29723-6) Bantam.
—Sort of Sisters. 1992. pap. 3.50 (0-553-29719-8) Bantam.
Johnson, Stacy. Cindy's Baby. 1993. pap. 3.50 (0-553-56312-2) Bantam.
—Kwame's Girl. 1994. pap. 3.50 (0-553-56313-0) Bantam.
Johnson, Stephanie. Confused Quarterbacks, Jumpy Gymnasts, & Other Sports Jokes. (Orig.). 1994. pap. 3.99 (0-8125-2052-1) Tor Bks.
—Hoppin' Magic: My First Card & Coin Magic Tricks. Manwaring, Kerry, illus. 32p. 1993. pap. 5.95 (1-56565-089-1) Lowell Hse.
—My First Kitchen Kaper Magic Tricks. 1992. 3.98 (0-8317-6240-3) Smithmark.
—My First Strings & Knots Magic Tricks. 1992. 3.98 (0-8317-6241-1) Smithmark.
Johnson, Stephen & Johnson, Renae. Around the World with Jesus. (Illus.). 144p. (gr. 1-6). 1989. 24.95 (1-55513-872-1, 68726) Cook.

Johnson, Sue. At Grandma's House: Story Book for Young Children in Sign Language. Herigstad, Joni, illus. 28p. 1985. pap. 4.50 (0-916708-14-4) Modern Signs.
—The Little Green Monsters. Herigstad, Joni, illus. 36p. (ps-6). 1985. pap. 4.75 (0-916708-15-2) Modern Signs.
—Popsicles Are Cold: Storybook for Young Children in Sign Languages. Herigstad, Joni, illus. 30p. (Orig.). (ps-3). 1984. pap. 4.75 (0-916708-12-8) Modern Signs.
Johnson, Sue K., jt. auth. see Johnson, Lee.
Johnson, Susan. Erte Fashion Paper Dolls of the Twenties. 1979. pap. 3.95 (0-486-23627-7) Dover.
Johnson, Sylvia. Mosses. Izawa, Masana, photos by. (Illus.). 48p. (gr. 4 up). pap. 5.95g (0-8225-9563-X) Lerner Pubns.
Johnson, Sylvia A. Albatrosses of Midway Island. Lanting, Frans, illus. 48p. (gr. 2-5). 1990. PLB 19.95 (0-87614-391-5) Carolrhoda Bks.
—Apple Trees. Koike, Hiro, illus. LC 83-16230. 48p. (gr. 4 up). 1983. PLB 19.95 (0-8225-1479-6) Lerner Pubns.
—Bats. Masuda, Modoki, illus. LC 85-15999. 48p. (gr. 4 up). 1985. PLB 19.95 (0-8225-1461-3, First Ave Edns); pap. 5.95 (0-8225-9500-1, First Ave Edns) Lerner Pubns.
—A Beekeeper's Year. Von Ohlen, Nick, photos by. LC 93-10199. (Illus.). Date not set. 14.95 (0-316-46745-6) Little.
—Beetles. Kishida, Isao, illus. LC 82-7230. 48p. (gr. 4 up). 1982. lib. bdg. 19.95 (0-8225-1476-1) Lerner Pubns.
—Chirping Insects. Sato, Yuko, illus. LC 86-15380. 48p. (gr. 4 up). 1986. PLB 19.95 (0-8225-1486-9) Lerner Pubns.
—Chirping Insects. 1990. pap. 5.95 (0-8225-9562-1) Lerner Pubns.
—Coral Reefs. Shirai, Shohei, illus. LC 84-816. 48p. (gr. 4 up). 1984. PLB 19.95 (0-8225-1451-6); pap. 5.95 (0-8225-9545-1) Lerner Pubns.
—Crabs. Sakurai, Atsushi, illus. LC 82-10056. 48p. (gr. 4 up). 1982. PLB 19.95 (0-8225-1471-0) Lerner Pubns.
—Elephant Seals. Lanting, Frans, photos by. LC 88-12924. (Illus.). 48p. (gr. 4 up). 1989. PLB 19.95 (0-8225-1487-7) Lerner Pubns.
—Fireflies. Kuribayashi, Satoshi, illus. 48p. (gr. 4 up). 1986. PLB 19.95 (0-8225-1485-0) Lerner Pubns.
—Hermit Crabs. Kawashima, Kazunari, illus. 48p. (gr. 4 up). 1989. PLB 19.95 (0-8225-1488-5) Lerner Pubns.
—Hermit Crabs. LC 89-8221. (Illus.). (gr. 4-7). 1991. pap. 5.95 (0-8225-9577-X) Lerner Pubns.
—How Leaves Change. Sato, Yuko, illus. 48p. (gr. 4 up). 1986. PLB 19.95 (0-8225-1483-4, First Ave Edns); pap. 5.95 (0-8225-9513-3, First Ave Edns) Lerner Pubns.
—Inside an Egg. LC 81-17235. (Illus.). 48p. (gr. 4 up). 1982. PLB 19.95 (0-8225-1472-9); pap. 5.95 (0-8225-9522-2) Lerner Pubns.
—Ladybugs. Sato, Yuko, illus. LC 83-18777. 48p. (gr. 4 up). 1983. PLB 19.95 (0-8225-1481-8) Lerner Pubns.
—Morning Glories. Sato, Yuko, illus. 48p. (gr. 4-10). 1985. PLB 19.95 (0-8225-1462-1) Lerner Pubns.
—Mosses. Izawa, Masana, illus. LC 83-17488. 48p. (gr. 4 up). 1983. PLB 19.95 (0-8225-1482-6) Lerner Pubns.
—Mushrooms. Izawa, Masana, illus. LC 82-212. 48p. (gr. 4 up). 1982. PLB 19.95 (0-8225-1473-7) Lerner Pubns.
—Penguins. LC 80-28180. (Illus.). 48p. (gr. 4 up). 1981. PLB 19.95 (0-8225-1453-2) Lerner Pubns.
—Potatoes. Suzuki, Masaharu, illus. 48p. (gr. 4 up). 1984. lib. bdg. 19.95 (0-8225-1459-1) Lerner Pubns.
—Rice. Moriya, Noboru, illus. 48p. (gr. 4 up). 1985. PLB 19.95 (0-8225-1466-4) Lerner Pubns.
—Roses Red, Violets Blue: Why Flowers Have Colors. (Illus.). 64p. (gr. 5 up). 1991. PLB 19.95 (0-8225-1594-6) Lerner Pubns.
—Silkworms. Kishida, Isao, illus. LC 82-250. 48p. (gr. 4 up). 1982. PLB 19.95 (0-8225-1478-8, First Ave Edns); pap. 5.95 (0-8225-9557-5, First Ave Edns) Lerner Pubns.
—Snails. Masuda, Modoki, illus. LC 82-10086. 48p. (gr. 4 up). 1982. PLB 19.95 (0-8225-1475-3, First Ave Edns); pap. 5.95 (0-8225-9544-3, First Ave Edns) Lerner Pubns.
—Snakes. Masuda, Modoki, photos by. LC 87-7162. (Illus.). 48p. (gr. 4 up). 1986. PLB 19.95 (0-8225-1484-2, First Ave Edns); pap. 5.95 (0-8225-9503-6, First Ave Edns) Lerner Pubns.
—Tree Frogs. Masuda, Modoki, illus. LC 84-2721. 48p. (gr. 4 up). 1986. PLB 19.95 (0-8225-1467-2) Lerner Pubns.
—Wasps. Ogawa, Hiroshi, illus. LC 83-23847. 48p. (gr. 4 up). 1984. PLB 19.95 (0-8225-1460-5) Lerner Pubns.
—Water Insects. Masuda, Modoki, illus. 48p. (gr. 4 up). 1989. PLB 19.95 (0-8225-1489-3) Lerner Pubns.
—Wheat. Suzuki, Masaharu, illus. 48p. (gr. 4 up). 1990. PLB 19.95 (0-8225-1490-7) Lerner Pubns.
Johnson, Sylvia A. & Aamodt, Alice. Wolf Pack: Tracking Wolves in the Wild. (Illus.). 96p. (gr. 5 up). 1985. PLB 22.95 (0-8225-1577-6) Lerner Pubns.
—Wolf Pack: Tracking Wolves in the Wild. (Illus.). 96p. (gr. 5 up). 1987. pap. 6.95 (0-8225-9526-5, First Ave Edns) Lerner Pubns.
Johnson, Sylvia A., jt. auth. see Casagrande, Louis B.
Johnson, Sylvia A., jt. auth. see Dallinger, Jane.
Johnson, Sylvia A., jt. auth. see Hisa, Kunihiko.
Johnson, Tara. Huckleberry Fun. LC 89-51090. 44p. (gr. k-3). 1990. 5.95 (1-55523-248-5) Winston-Derek.

Johnson, Thomas H. Oxford Companion to American History. 912p. (gr. 9 up). 1966. 49.95x (0-19-500597-X) OUP.
Johnson, Tom. Heaven Is an Action, Not a Place. 32p. (Orig.). 1990. pap. 3.50 (0-941992-22-5) Los Arboles Pub.
—What Religious Science Is. 18p. (gr. 7-12). 1989. Repr. of 1977 ed. 2.00 (0-941992-19-5) Los Arboles Pub.
Johnson, Vargie. Charles Darwin, the Adventurer. 1992. 10.00 (0-533-10092-5) Vantage.
Johnson, W. Cameron. Boy on a Bus. Johnson, W. Cameron, illus. McKay, Dermot, contrib. by. (Illus.). (gr. 3-7). 1991. pap. 3.50 (1-85239-009-3) Grosvenor USA.
Johnson, Ward. Ben's New Buddy. Cooke, Tom, illus. 40p. (ps-3). 1984. 5.95 (0-910313-16-4) Parker Bros.
—Caring Is What Counts. Cooke, Tom, illus. 40p. (ps-3). 1983. 5.95 (0-685-06604-5, 7004) Parker Bros.
—A Koosa for the Kids. Yealdhall, Gary, illus. (ps-3). 1985. pap. 0.99 (0-87372-007-5) Parker Bros.
Johnson, William. Dinosaur Fun Book. (Illus.). 48p. (gr. k-12). 1979. pap. 3.50 (0-8431-1704-4) Price Stern.
Johnson, William R. Color Monkeys. Johnson, Pauline, ed. (Illus.). 48p. (ps-2). 1989. write for info. (0-936917-05-9, B608) Blip Prods.
—Dinosaurs & Other Prehistorics. Johnson, Pauline D., ed. Johnson, William R., illus. 48p. (gr. k-6). 1986. pap. 4.95 (0-936917-02-4, B606) Blip Prods.
—Kids of the World: Cursive. Johnson, Pauline D., ed. Johnson, William R., illus. 48p. (gr. 3-6). 1986. pap. 4.95 (0-936917-01-6, B604) Blip Prods.
—Kids of the World: Manuscript. Johnson, Pauline D., ed. Johnson, William R., illus. 48p. (Orig.). (ps-2). 1986. pap. 4.95 (0-936917-00-8, B603) Blip Prods.
—Monthly Calendars. Johnson, Pauline, ed. (Illus.). 48p. (gr. k-4). 1989. write for info. (0-936917-04-0, B607) Blip Prods.
—Numbers One to Twenty: The Circus & the Bees. Johnson, Pauline D., ed. Johnson, William R., illus. 48p. (ps-2). 1986. pap. 4.95 (0-936917-03-2, B605) Blip Prods.
Johnson, Zenobia M. Afro-American Copy Color Fun. (Illus.). 32p. (Orig.). (ps-1). 1979. wkbk. 3.00 (0-9617411-2-0) Z M Johnson.
—Black Footprints. (Illus.). 32p. (Orig.). (gr. 4-7). 1979. wkbk. 3.00 (0-9617411-1-2) Z M Johnson.
Johnson, Zenobia M. & Broussard, Lucretia-del J. Louisiana Reading Adventures. (Illus.). 32p. (Orig.). (gr. 4-7). 1984. 3.50 (0-9617411-0-4) Z M Johnson.
Johnson-Calvo, Sarita. A Beach Party with Alexis. (Illus.). 32p. (Orig.). (gr. k-3). 1993. saddle-stitched wkbk. 2.95 (1-55583-230-X) Alyson Pubns.
Johnson-Feelings, Dianne. The Painter Man. Granderson, Eddie, illus. LC 93-4063. 1993. write for info. (0-89334-220-3) Humanics Ltd.
Johnston, Abigail, jt. auth. see Johnston, Johanna.
Johnston, Agnes N. Beyond the Moongate. LC 86-45961. (Illus.). 102p. (Orig.). (gr. 7-12). 1987. pap. 7.00 perfect bdg. (0-916418-64-2) Lotus.
Johnston, Allyn, ed. see Enright, Elizabeth.
Johnston, Allyn, ed. see Frasier, Debra.
Johnston, Allyn, ed. see Martin, Bill, Jr.
Johnston, Annie F. Joel: A Boy of Galilee. Coven, Peggy, illus. Slater, Rosalie J., intro. by. LC 92-75820. (Illus.). 254p. (gr. 4-8). 1992. pap. 12.00 (0-912498-11-0) F A C E.
—The Little Colonel at Boarding School. (gr. 5 up). 13.95 (0-89201-032-0) Zenger Pub.
—The Little Colonel in Arizona. (gr. 5 up). 13.95 (0-89201-033-9) Zenger Pub.
—The Little Colonel: Maid of Honor. (gr. 5 up). 13.95 (0-89201-034-7) Zenger Pub.
—The Little Colonel Stories: First Series. (gr. 5 up). 13. 95 (0-89201-070-3) Zenger Pub.
—The Little Colonel Stories: Second Series. (gr. 5 up). 15.95 (0-89201-071-1) Zenger Pub.
—The Little Colonel's Christmas Vacation. (gr. 5 up). 13. 95 (0-89201-035-5) Zenger Pub.
—The Little Colonel's Chum: Mary Ware. (gr. 5 up). 13. 95 (0-89201-036-3) Zenger Pub.
—The Little Colonel's Hero. (gr. 5 up). 13.95 (0-89201-037-1) Zenger Pub.
—The Little Colonel's Holidays. (gr. 5 up). 13.95 (0-89201-038-X) Zenger Pub.
—The Little Colonel's House Party. (gr. 5 up). 13.95 (0-89201-039-8) Zenger Pub.
—The Little Colonel's Knight Comes Riding. (gr. 5 up). 13.95 (0-89201-072-X) Zenger Pub.
Johnston, Brenda A. & Pruitt, Pamela. Struggle for Freedom & Henry Box Brown. McCluskey, John A., ed. Murchison, Leon & Howard, Cecelia, illus. 22p. (gr. 2-4). 1987. pap. 4.00 incl. audiocassette (0-913678-16-3) New Day Pr.
Johnston, Brenda A., et al. Stories from Black History Series II, 3 bks. 2nd ed. McCluskey, John A., ed. (Illus.). (gr. 4-7). 1993. Set. pap. 8.00 (0-913678-24-4) New Day Pr.
Johnston, Catherine D. I Hear the Day. Mark, Joseph, illus. (gr. 2-3). 1977. 9.00 (0-914562-04-5); wkbk 3.00 (0-914562-05-3) Merriam-Eddy.
Johnston, Charles H. Famous Frontiersmen & Heroes of the Border. facsimile ed. LC 72-152178. (gr. 7 up). Repr. of 1913 ed. 23.00 (0-8369-2231-X) Ayer.
Johnston, D. John & the Little Horse. 1993. 7.95 (0-533-10264-2) Vantage.
Johnston, Deanna. What Dreams Are Made Of. 1993. 7.95 (0-533-09736-3) Vantage.

Johnston, Deborah. Mathew Michael's Beastly Day. LC 91-3084. (ps-3). 1992. write for info. (0-15-200521-8, HB Juv Bks) HarBrace.
Johnston, Dorothy G. & Abbas, Kathleen. Church Time for Children. LC 80-67855. 120p. (Orig.). (gr. 1-6). 1981. 10.95 (0-89636-056-3, Chariot Bks) Cook.
Johnston, Edith. Regional Dances of the Mexico. (Illus.). 64p. (gr. 3 up). 1983. pap. 7.95 (0-8442-7509-3, Passport Bks) NTC Pub Grp.
Johnston, Frances M. Wordless Book Song. (gr. k-6). 1976. visualized song 2.99 (3-90117-016-2) CEF Press.
Johnston, Ginny & Cutchins, Judy. Andy Bear: A Polar Cub Grows Up at the Zoo. Noble, Constance, illus. LC 85-3095. 64p. (gr. 2-5). 1985. 13.00 (0-688-05627-X); lib. bdg. 12.88 (0-688-05628-8, Morrow Jr Bks) Morrow Jr Bks.
—Scaly Babies: Reptiles Growing Up. LC 87-18599. (Illus.). 48p. (gr. 2-5). 1988. 13.95 (0-688-07305-0); PLB 13.88 (0-688-07306-9, Morrow Jr Bks) Morrow Jr Bks.
—Scaly Babies: Reptiles Growing Up. LC 87-18599. (Illus.). 48p. (gr. 2 up). 1990. pap. 4.95g (0-688-09998-X, Pub. by Beech Tree Bks) Morrow.
—Slippery Babies: Young Frogs, Toads, & Salamanders. LC 90-49665. (Illus.). 48p. (gr. 2 up). 1991. 13.95 (0-688-09605-0); PLB 13.88 (0-688-09606-9) Morrow Jr Bks.
—Windows on Wildlife. LC 89-34487. (Illus.). 48p. (gr. 2 up). 1990. 13.95 (0-688-07872-9); PLB 13.88 (0-688-07873-7, Morrow Jr Bks) Morrow Jr Bks.
Johnston, Ginny, jt. auth. see Cutchins, Judy.
Johnston, Helen & Elvidge, Vivian, eds. Eastside Historic Coloring Book. Lippie, Joel & Lippie, Jane, illus. McClelland, John M., Jr. 32p. (Orig.). (gr. 1-4). 1985. pap. 2.00 (0-685-28865-X) Marymoor Mus.
Johnston, Janet. Ellie Brader Hates Mr. G. 144p. (gr. 3-6). 1991. 13.45 (0-395-58195-8, Clarion Bks) HM.
Johnston, Joan. Feast of Famine: A Physician's Personal Struggle to Overcome Anorexia Nervosa. LC 93-10620. 384p. (Orig.). (gr. 12 up). 1993. pap. 13.95 (0-941405-26-5) Recovery CA.
Johnston, Johanna. A Birthday for General Washington. Burgeson, Marjorie, illus. LC 75-38545. 32p. (gr. k-4). 1976. PLB 15.93 (0-516-08881-5, Golden Gate) Childrens.
—They Led the Way: Fourteen American Women. 1987. 2.95 (0-590-44431-X) Scholastic Inc.
Johnston, Johanna & Johnston, Abigail. Great Gravity the Cat. rev. ed. Mathis, Melissa B., illus. LC 88-13351. 64p. (gr. 3-7). 1989. lib. bdg. 15.00 (0-208-02223-6, Linnet) Shoe String.
Johnston, Joyce. Alaska. LC 93-25401. (gr. 5 up). 1994. lib. bdg. write for info. (0-8225-2735-9) Lerner Pubns.
—Maryland. 72p. (gr. 3-6). 1991. PLB 17.50 (0-8225-2713-8) Lerner Pubns.
—Puerto Rico. LC 93-36950. 1994. write for info. (0-8225-2752-9) Lerner Pubns.
—Washington, D. C. LC 92-44848. 1993. PLB 17.50 (0-8225-2751-0) Lerner Pubns.
Johnston, Julie. Adam & Eve & Pinch-Me. LC 93-21023. 1994. 14.95 (0-316-46990-4) Little.
—Hero of Lesser Causes. LC 92-37268. 1993. 14.95 (0-316-46988-2, Joy St Bks) Little.
Johnston, Lucile. Celebrations of a Nation: Early American Holidays. 3rd ed. (Illus.). 174p. (gr. 8-12). 1989. 10.95 (0-9620343-0-4); pap. 6.95 (0-9620343-1-2) Johnston Bicent Found.
Johnston, Lynn. Is This "One of Those Days," Daddy? Johnston, Lynn, illus. LC 82-72417. 128p. (gr. 5 up). 1982. pap. 8.95 (0-8362-1197-9) Andrews & McMeel.
Johnston, Mary. To Have & to Hold. Gemme, F. R., intro. by. (gr. 8 up). 1968. pap. 1.95 (0-8049-0160-0, CL-160) Airmont.
Johnston, Mary G. Paper Sculpture. rev. & enl. ed. LC 64-24721. (Illus.). (gr. 4-12). 1965. 9.95 (0-87192-019-0) Davis Mass.
Johnston, Norma. Carlisles All. 192p. (Orig.). 1986. pap. 2.50 (0-553-26139-8, Starfire) Bantam.
—The Carlisle's Hope. 192p. (Orig.). (gr. 7-12). 1986. pap. 2.50 (0-553-25467-7, Starfire) Bantam.
—The Delphic Choice. LC 88-24570. 208p. (gr. 7 up). 1989. SBE 14.95 (0-02-747711-8, Four Winds) Macmillan Child Grp.
—The Dragon's Eye. LC 90-34388. 176p. (gr. 7 up). 1990. SBE 13.95 (0-02-747701-0, Four Winds) Macmillan Child Grp.
—Glory in the Flower. 200p. (gr. 4 up). 1990. pap. 3.95 (0-14-034292-3, Puffin) Puffin Bks.
—Harriet: The Life & World of Harriet Beecher Stowe. (Illus.). 192p. 1994. SBE 15.95 (0-02-747714-2, Four Winds) Macmillan Child Grp.
—The Keeping Days. 240p. (gr. 4 up). 1990. pap. 3.95 (0-14-034291-5, Puffin) Puffin Bks.
—Louisa May: The World & Works of Louisa May Alcott. LC 91-7896. (Illus.). 224p. (gr. 6 up). 1991. SBE 15.95 (0-02-747705-3, Four Winds) Macmillan Child Grp.
—The Potter's Wheel. LC 87-24697. 256p. (gr. 7 up). 1988. 12.95 (0-688-06463-9) Morrow Jr Bks.
—Return to Morocco. LC 88-6880. 176p. (gr. 7 up). 1988. SBE 13.95 (0-02-747712-6, Four Winds) Macmillan Child Grp.
—The Time of the Cranes. LC 89-39818. 208p. (gr. 7 up). 1990. SBE 13.95 (0-02-747713-4, Four Winds) Macmillan Child Grp.

—To Jess with Love & Memories, No. 2. 176p. (Orig.). (gr. 6-10). 1986. pap. 2.50 (*0-553-25882-6*, Starfire) Bantam.

—The Watcher in the Mist. 208p. 1986. pap. 2.95 (*0-553-26032-4*, Starfire) Bantam.

—Whisper of the Cat. 192p. (Orig.). 1988. pap. 2.95 (*0-553-26947-X*, Starfire) Bantam.

Johnston, Ollie & Thomas, Frank. The Disney Villain. (Illus.). 224p. (gr. 5 up). 1993. 45.00 (*1-56282-792-8*) Disney Pr.

Johnston, Rhoda O. Iyabo of Nigeria. Samuel, A. Nupo, illus. (gr. 5-12). 1973. pap. 5.00x (*0-914522-01-9*, 163808) Alpha Iota.

Johnston, Richard, jt. auth. see Johnston, Helen.

Johnston, S. Paper Doll-Godey Fashion. 1979. pap. 3.95 (*0-486-23511-4*) Dover.

Johnston, Sammie. The Dream Builders. 192p. (Orig.). (gr. 7-12). 1989. pap. text ed. 4.95 (*0-936625-64-3*, New Hope AL) Womans Mission Union.

Johnston, Scott. Monster Truck Racing. 48p. (gr. 3-10). 1994. PLB 17.27 (*1-56065-204-7*) Capstone Pr.

—The Original Monster Truck: Bigfoot. 48p. (gr. 3-10). 1994. PLB 17.27 (*1-56065-200-4*) Capstone Pr.

Johnston, T. Lorenzo the Naughty Parrot. Politi, L., illus. 1992. write for info. (*0-15-249350-6*, HB Juv Bks) HarBrace.

—Slither McCreep & His Brother, Joe. Chess, V., illus. 1992. 13.95 (*0-15-276100-4*, HB Juv Bks) HarBrace.

Johnston, Tom. Air, Air Everywhere. Pooley, Sarah, illus. LC 87-42752. 32p. (gr. 4-6). 1988. PLB 15.93 (*1-55532-406-1*) Gareth Stevens Inc.

—Electricity Turns the World On! Pooley, Sarah, illus. LC 87-42655. 32p. (gr. 4-6). 1987. PLB 15.93 (*1-55532-410-X*) Gareth Stevens Inc.

—Energy: Making It Work. Pooley, Sarah, illus. LC 87-42751. 32p. (gr. 4-6). 1987. PLB 15.93 (*1-55532-405-3*) Gareth Stevens Inc.

—The Forces with You! Pooley, Sarah, illus. LC 87-42753. 32p. (gr. 4-6). 1987. PLB 15.93 (*1-55532-408-8*) Gareth Stevens Inc.

—Light! Color! Action! Pooley, Sarah, illus. LC 87-42754. 32p. (gr. 4-6). 1988. PLB 15.93 (*1-55532-409-6*) Gareth Stevens Inc.

—Science in Action, 6 vols. Pooley, Sarah, illus. 32p. (gr. 4-6). 1987. Set. PLB 95.58 (*1-55532-412-6*) Gareth Stevens Inc.

—Water, Water! Pooley, Sarah, illus. LC 87-42750. 32p. (gr. 4-6). 1988. PLB 15.93 (*1-55532-407-X*) Gareth Stevens Inc.

Johnston, Tony. The Adventures of Mole & Troll. (gr. k-6). 1989. pap. 2.95 (*0-440-40218-2*, YB) Dell.

—Amber on the Mountain. Duncan, Robert, illus. LC 93-16292. (ps-6). 1994. write for info. (*0-8037-1219-7*); pap. write for info. (*0-8037-1220-0*) Dial Bks Young.

—The Badger & the Magic Fan: A Japanese Folktale. De Paola, Tomie, illus. 32p. (ps-3). 1990. 13.95 (*0-399-21945-5*, Putnam) Putnam Pub Group.

—The Cowboy & the Blackeyed Pea. Ludwig, Warren, illus. 32p. (ps-3). 1992. 14.95 (*0-399-22330-4*, Putnam) Putnam Pub Group.

—Four Scary Stories. LC 77-13027. (Illus.). 32p. (ps-3). 1980. pap. 5.95 (*0-399-20727-9*, Putnam) Putnam Pub Group.

—Goblin Walk. Degen, Bruce, illus. LC 90-22985. 32p. (gr. 3-6). 1991. 14.95 (*0-399-22238-3*, Putnam) Putnam Pub Group.

—Grandpa's Song. Sneed, Brad, illus. LC 90-43836. 32p. (ps-3). 1991. 12.95 (*0-8037-0801-7*); lib. bdg. 12.89 (*0-8037-0802-5*) Dial Bks Young.

—Happy Birthday Mole & Troll. (gr. k-6). 1989. pap. 2.95 (*0-440-40217-4*, YB) Dell.

—I'm Gonna Tell Mama I Want an Iguana. Hoban, Lillian, illus. 32p. (ps-3). 1990. 14.95 (*0-399-21934-X*, Putnam) Putnam Pub Group.

—The Last Snow of Winter. Henstra, Friso, illus. LC 92-33862. 32p. (ps up). 1993. 14.00 (*0-688-10749-4*, Tambourine Bks); PLB 13.93 (*0-688-10750-8*, Tambourine Bks) Morrow.

—Little Bear Sleeping. (Illus.). 32p. 1991. 13.95 (*0-399-22157-3*, Putnam) Putnam Pub Group.

—Little Rabbit Goes to Sleep. Stevenson, Harvey, illus. LC 92-8543. 32p. (ps-k). 1994. 15.00 (*0-06-021239-X*); PLB 14.89 (*0-06-021241-1*) HarpC Child Bks.

—My Friend Bear. 1989. cased 3.95 (*0-7214-5224-8*) Ladybird Bks.

—Night Noises & Other Mole & Troll Stories. (gr. k-6). 1989. pap. 2.95 (*0-440-40232-8*, YB) Dell.

—Pages of Music. De Paola, Tomie, illus. 32p. (gr. k-3). 1988. PLB 13.95 (*0-399-21436-4*, Putnam) Putnam Pub Group.

—The Quilt Story. De Paola, Tomie, illus. LC 84-18212. 32p. (gr. k-2). 1992. 14.95 (*0-399-21009-1*, Putnam); pap. 5.95 (*0-399-22403-3*, Putnam) Putnam Pub Group.

—Soup Bone. (Illus.). 32p. (ps-3). 1990. 12.95 (*0-15-277255-3*) HarBrace.

—Soup Bone. LC 89-1990. (ps-3). 1992. pap. 4.95 (*0-15-277256-1*, HB Juv Bks) HarBrace.

—The Tale of Rabbit & Coyote. De Paola, Tomie, illus. LC 92-43652. 1994. write for info. (*0-399-22258-8*, Putnam) Putnam Pub Group.

—The Vanishing Pumpkin. De Paola, Tomie, illus. 32p. (ps-2). 1990. (Putnam). pap. 5.95 (*0-399-20992-1*, Putnam) Putnam Pub Group.

—Whale Song. Young, Ed, illus. 32p. (ps-3). 1987. 14.95 (*0-399-21402-X*, Putnam) Putnam Pub Group.

—Whale Song. Young, Ed, illus. 32p. (ps-3). 1992. pap. 5.95 (*0-399-22408-4*, Putnam) Putnam Pub Group.

—Witch's Hat. (ps-3). 1991. pap. 4.99 (*0-553-35354-3*) Bantam.

—Yonder. Bloom, Lloyd, illus. LC 86-11549. 32p. (ps-3). 1988. 12.95 (*0-8037-0277-9*); PLB 12.89 (*0-8037-0278-7*) Dial Bks Young.

—Yonder. Bloom, Lloyd, illus. LC 86-11549. 32p. (ps-3). 1991. pap. 4.95 (*0-8037-0907-0*, Dial Pied Piper) Puffin Bks.

Johnstone, Jill. You Can Change the World. 128p. (gr. 3-7). 1993. Printed caseside. 19.99 (*0-310-40041-4*, Pub. by Youth Spec) Zondervan.

Johnstone, Michael. Family Matters: Children's Party Games. (Illus.). 96p. (gr. 2-10). 1991. pap. 4.95 (*0-7063-6611-5*, Pub. by Ward Lock UK) Sterling.

—One Thousand What's What Jokes for Kids. (gr. k up). 1987. pap. 3.95 (*0-345-34654-8*) Ballantine.

Johsnton, Helen & Johnston, Richard. Willowmoor: The Story of Marymoor Park. (Illus.). 48p. (Orig.). (gr. 9-12). 1976. pap. 2.50 (*0-685-28867-6*) Marymoor Mus.

Joiner, Lee M., ed. see Jones, Ralph E.

Jolliffe, Susan D. & McVeigh, Amy. Mackinac Island for Kids-on-the-Go. Zimmerman, Paul & Dearth, D. L., illus. 32p. (Orig.). (ps-7). 1993. pap. 5.00 (*0-9623213-2-X*) Mackinac Pub.

Jolly, Christopher. The Animal Jiglets. Stephen, Lib, illus. (ps-1). 1994. 11.95 (*1-870946-33-2*, Pub. by Jolly Lrning UK) Am Intl Dist.

—The Stencilets. Stephen, Lib, illus. (ps-1). 1994. 14.95 (*1-870946-35-9*, Pub. by Jolly Lrning UK) Am Intl Dist.

—The Vehicle Jiglets. Stephen, Lib, illus. (ps-1). 1994. 11.95 (*1-870946-34-0*, Pub. by Jolly Lrning UK) Am Intl Dist.

Joly, Dominique. Grains of Salt. Perols, Sylvaine, illus. LC 87-34534. 38p. (gr. k-5). 1988. 4.95 (*0-944589-20-0*, 200) Young Discovery Lib.

Jon, jt. auth. see Tab, Joan.

Jonas, Ann. Aardvarks, Disembark! LC 89-27225. (Illus.). 40p. (ps up). 1990. 14.95 (*0-688-07206-2*); PLB 14.88 (*0-688-07207-0*) Greenwillow.

—Color Dance. LC 88-5446. (Illus.). 32p. 1989. 14.00 (*0-688-05990-2*); PLB 13.93 (*0-688-05991-0*) Greenwillow.

—Holes & Peeks. Jonas, Ann, illus. LC 83-14128. 24p. (ps-1). 1984. 15.95 (*0-688-02537-4*); PLB 15.88 (*0-688-02538-2*) Greenwillow.

—Now We Can Go. Jonas, Ann, illus. LC 85-12614. 24p. (ps-1). 1986. 11.75 (*0-688-04802-1*); PLB 11.88 (*0-688-04803-X*) Greenwillow.

—The Quilt. Jonas, Ann, illus. LC 83-25385. 32p. (ps-1). 1984. 16.00 (*0-688-03825-5*); PLB 15.93 (*0-688-03826-3*) Greenwillow.

—Reflections. LC 86-33545. (Illus.). 24p. (gr. k-3). 1987. 15.00 (*0-688-06140-0*); lib. bdg. 14.93 (*0-688-06141-9*) Greenwillow.

—Round Trip. Jonas, Ann, illus. LC 82-12026. 32p. (gr. k-3). 1983. 16.00 (*0-688-01772-X*); PLB 15.93 (*0-688-01781-9*) Greenwillow.

—Round Trip. LC 82-12026. (Illus.). 32p. (ps-2). 1990. pap. 3.95 (*0-688-09986-6*, Mulberry) Morrow.

—The Thirteenth Clue. LC 91-34586. (Illus.). 32p. (ps-6). 1992. 14.00 (*0-688-09742-1*); PLB 13.93 (*0-688-09743-X*) Greenwillow.

—The Thirteenth Clue. 1993. pap. 4.99 (*0-440-40887-3*) Dell.

—El Trayecto: The Trek. Mlawer, Teresa, tr. from ENG. (Illus.). 32p. (ps-7). 1991. PLB 13.95 (*0-9625162-3-6*) Lectorum Pubns.

—The Trek. Jonas, Ann, illus. LC 84-25962. 32p. (gr. k-3). 1985. 14.95 (*0-688-04799-8*); lib. bdg. 14.88 (*0-688-04800-5*) Greenwillow.

—The Trek. LC 84-25962. (ps up) 1989. 3.95 (*0-688-08742-6*, Mulberry) Morrow.

—Two Bear Cubs. Jonas, Ann, illus. LC 82-2860. 24p. (gr. k-3). 1982. PLB 14.88 (*0-688-01408-9*) Greenwillow.

—When You Were a Baby. Jonas, Ann, illus. LC 81-12800. 24p. (ps-1). 1982. 15.00 (*0-688-00863-1*); PLB 14.93 (*0-688-00864-X*) Greenwillow.

—When You Were a Baby. LC 90-47799. (Illus.). 24p. (ps up). 1991. bds. 6.95 (*0-688-10525-4*) Greenwillow.

—Where Can It Be? Jonas, Ann, illus. LC 86-304. 32p. (ps-1). 1986. 14.95 (*0-688-05169-3*); PLB 14.88 (*0-688-05246-0*) Greenwillow.

Jonasson, Dianne, tr. see Boholm-Olsson, Eva.

Jones. Creative Quickies. (Illus.). 100p. (gr. k-8). 1982. pap. 7.50 (*0-685-55702-2*) Arts Pubns.

—Pygmies of Central Africa, Reading Level 5. (Illus.). 48p. (gr. 4-8). 1989. PLB 16.67 (*0-86625-268-1*); 12. 50s.p. (*0-685-55813-0*) Rourke Corp.

Jones & Gorney. Creative Quickies, 2 bks. 100p. 1992. 7.95 ea. (*0-9607458-0-7*) No. I. No. II (*1-878079-06-9*) Arts Pubns.

Jones, jt. auth. see Dadey.

Jones, Adrienne. Long Time Passing. LC 90-4046. 256p. (gr. 7 up). 1993. pap. 3.95 (*0-06-447070-9*, Trophy) HarpC Child Bks.

Jones, Allan, ed. see Christensen, Kathryn.

Jones, Alonzo T. The Consecrated Way: The Consecrated Way to Christian Perfection. 96p. (gr. 9-12). 1988. pap. 3.95 (*0-945460-02-3*) Upward Way.

Jones, Amy. Abracadabra. Thatch, Nancy R., ed. Jones, Amy, illus. Melton, David, intro. by. LC 93-13421. (Illus.). 29p. (gr. 3-5). 1993. PLB 14.95 (*0-933849-46-X*) Landmark Edns.

Jones, B. J. Let's Color Korea: Everyday Life in Traditional. 24p. (gr. k-3). 1990. oversized 7.50x (*0-930878-98-1*) Hollym Intl.

Jones, Barbara, jt. auth. see Baron, Jane.

Jones, Barbara B. & Hawkes, Sharlene W. The Inside-Outside Beauty Book. LC 89-37561. (Illus.). 100p. (Orig.). (gr. 9 up). 1989. pap. 5.95 (*0-87579-271-5*) Deseret Bk.

Jones, Beau F., et al. Insights: Reading As Thinking. (gr. k-8). 1989. pap. write for info. Charlesbridge Pub.

—Strategies for Reading Series. (Orig.). (gr. 1-6). 1989. student wkbk. 5.00 (*0-88106-087-9*, 7130) Charlesbridge Pub.

Jones, Bill. No Problem! 176p. 1992. pap. 4.99 (*0-89693-613-9*) SP Pubns.

Jones, Bill, jt. auth. see St. Clair, Barry.

Jones, Brian. Space: A Three-Dimensional Journey. Clifton-Dey, Richard, illus. 14p. (gr. k-4). 1991. 15.95 (*0-8037-0759-2*) Dial Bks Young.

—Space Exploration. LC 89-11359. (Illus.). 64p. (gr. 4-6). 1989. PLB 19.93 (*0-8368-0004-4*) Gareth Stevens Inc.

Jones, Brian, jt. auth. see Brown, Robert.

Jones, C. Sue. Rudy. 1992. 6.95 (*0-8062-4311-2*) Carlton.

Jones, Candy & McGee, Lea. Playkits. Barr, Marilynn G., illus. 64p. (ps-2). 1991. pap. 7.95 (*1-878279-26-2*) Monday Morning Bks.

—Story Kits. Barr, Marilynn G., illus. 64p. (ps-2). 1991. pap. 7.95 (*1-878279-28-9*) Monday Morning Bks.

Jones, Candy & McGee, Lee. Showkits. (Illus.). 64p. (ps-2). 1991. pap. 7.95 (*1-878279-27-0*) Monday Morning Bks.

Jones, Carol. This Old Man. Jones, Carol, illus. 48p. (gr. k-3). 1990. 13.45 (*0-395-54699-0*) HM.

Jones, Carol, illus. The Cat Sat on the Mat. LC 93-14341. 1994. write for info (*0-395-68392-0*) HM.

—Hickory Dickory Dock. 48p. (gr. k-3). 1992. 10.70 (*0-395-60834-1*) HM.

—Old MacDonald Had a Farm. (ps-3). 1989. 12.70 (*0-395-49212-2*) HM.

Jones, Carolyn E. Lottie Moon Storybook. Ellis, Debbie, illus. 20p. (gr. k-4). 1984. pap. 2.50 (*0-9616996-0-4*) Honor Pub.

Jones, Ceri, jt. auth. see Adams, Pam.

Jones, Charla. Literature Activities for Primary Social Studies. Dillon, Paul, illus. 128p. (Orig.). (gr. 1-4). 1993. pap. 12.95 (*1-879287-24-2*) Bk Lures.

—Poetry Patterns. 2nd, expanded ed. (Illus.). 48p. (gr. 3-6). 1992. pap. 5.95 (*1-879287-11-0*) Bk Lures.

Jones, Charles. Monkey, Monkey. 25p. (Orig.). (gr. k-3). 1986. pap. 4.50 playscript (*0-87602-265-4*) Anchorage.

Jones, Charlotte F. Mistakes That Worked. (gr. 4-7). 1991. 15.95 (*0-385-26246-9*) Doubleday.

Jones, Chris. Lord, I Want to Tell You Something: Prayers for Boys. LC 73-78266. (Illus.). 96p. (Orig.). (gr. 5-8). 1973. pap. 5.99 (*0-8066-1330-0*, 10-4100, Augsburg) Augsburg Fortress.

—What Do I Do Now Lord? LC 76-3860. 112p. (Orig.). (gr. 4-7). 1976. pap. 5.99 (*0-8066-1539-7*, 10-7044, Augsburg) Augsburg Fortress.

Jones, Claire. Sailboat Racing. LC 80-12846. (Illus.). 48p. (gr. 4-9). 1981. PLB 14.95 (*0-8225-0434-0*) Lerner Pubns.

Jones, Cody L. Twinkle Toes. 1991. 7.95 (*0-533-09261-2*) Vantage.

Jones, Constance. Karen Horney. Horner, Matina S., intro. by. (Illus.). 112p. (gr. 5 up). 1989. 17.95 (*1-55546-659-1*) Chelsea Hse.

—A Short History of Africa, 1500-1900. LC 92-22677. 144p. (gr. 6-9). 1993. 17.95x (*0-8160-2774-9*) Facts on File.

Jones, Cordelia. Cat Called Camouflage. LC 79-166339. (Illus.). (gr. 7 up). 1971. 21.95 (*0-87599-189-0*) S G Phillips.

Jones, David. Your Book of Money. (gr. 7 up). 1971. 7.95 (*0-571-09341-8*) Transatl Arts.

Jones, Davy & Green, Alan. Monkees, Memories & Media Madness. Kirshner, Don, frwd. by. (Illus.). 176p. (gr. 9 up). 1992. 39.95 (*0-9631235-1-3*); pap. 29.95 (*0-9631235-0-5*) Click Pub.

Jones, Diana W. Archer's Goon. LC 83-17199. 256p. (gr. 7 up). 1984. reinforced 10.25 (*0-688-02582-X*) Greenwillow.

—Aunt Maria. LC 90-24742. (Illus.). (gr. 7 up). 1991. 13.95 (*0-688-10611-0*) Greenwillow.

—Castle in the Air. LC 90-30266. (Illus.). 208p. (gr. 6 up). 1991. 13.95 (*0-688-09686-7*) Greenwillow.

—Dogsbody. LC 76-28715. 256p. (gr. 5-9). 1988. 11.95 (*0-688-08191-6*) Greenwillow.

—Dogsbody. LC 76-28714. 256p. (gr. 4-9). 1990. pap. 3.50 (*0-394-82031-2*) Random Bks Yng Read.

—Eight Days of Luke. LC 88-220. 166p. (gr. 7 up). 1988. Repr. of 1975 ed. 11.95 (*0-688-08006-5*) Greenwillow.

—Fire & Hemlock. LC 84-4084. 352p. (gr. 7 up). 1984. reinforced bdg. 13.00 (*0-688-03942-1*) Greenwillow.

—Hexwood. LC 93-18172. (gr. 6 up). 1994. write for info. (*0-688-12488-1*) Greenwillow.

—Hidden Turnings. LC 89-11742. (gr. 7 up). 1990. 12.95 (*0-688-09163-6*) Greenwillow.

—The Homeward Bounders. LC 81-1905. 224p. (gr. 5 up). 1981. 11.75 (*0-688-00678-7*) Greenwillow.

—Howl's Moving Castle. LC 85-21981. 224p. (gr. 7 up). 1986. reinforced bdg. 13.00 (*0-688-06233-4*) Greenwillow.

—The Lives of Christopher Chant. LC 87-24540. (gr. 7 up). 1988. 11.95 (*0-688-07806-0*) Greenwillow.

—The Lives of Christopher Chant. LC 87-24540. 240p. (gr. 4-7). 1990. pap. 3.50 (*0-394-82205-6*) Random Bks Yng Read.
—The Ogre Downstairs. LC 89-11741. 192p. (gr. 5 up). 1990. 12.95 (*0-688-09195-4*) Greenwillow.
—Stopping for a Spell. LC 92-12196. 160p. (gr. 3 up). 1993. 14.00 (*0-688-11367-2*) Greenwillow.
—A Tale of Time City. LC 86-33304. (Illus.). 288p. (gr. 7 up). 1987. 11.75 (*0-688-07315-8*) Greenwillow.
—A Tale of Time City. LC 86-33304. 288p. (gr. 5-9). 1989. pap. 3.95 (*0-394-82030-4*) Knopf Bks Yng Read.
—Wild Robert. large type ed. Clark, Emma C., illus. 120p. 1992. 13.95 (*0-7451-1471-7*, Galaxy Child Lrg Print) Chivers N Amer.
—Witch Week. LC 82-6074. 256p. (gr. 3-7). 1988. pap. 2.95 (*0-394-80600-X*) Knopf Bks Yng Read.
—Witch Week. reissued ed. LC 82-6074. 224p. (gr. 7 up). 1993. PLB 14.00 (*0-688-12374-0*) Greenwillow.
—Yes, Dear. Pinkard, Graham, illus. LC 91-17733. 32p. (ps-6). 1992. 14.00 (*0-688-11195-5*) Greenwillow.
Jones, Diane W. Witch Week. LC 82-6074. 224p. (gr. 7 up). 1982. reinforced bdg. 11.75 (*0-688-01534-4*) Greenwillow.
Jones, Dianne. Old Russia 1400-1917. 47p. (gr. k-8). 1989. 19.95 (*0-913705-46-2*) Zephyr Pr AZ.
Jones, Donna J. Barnabas Bear. Grove, Jason, illus. 32p. (gr. k-5). 1987. pap. 3.50 (*0-9617382-1-9*) Glacier Pub.
—Oolik: The Owl Who Couldn't Whoo. Grove, Jason, illus. 29p. (Orig.). (gr. k-5). 1987. pap. 3.50 (*0-9617382-0-0*) Glacier Pub.
Jones, Earl, Sr. Map Rap: A Fun Way to Learn Geography Through Rap. Smallwood, James, illus. Coleman, Booker T., intro. by. LC 90-84037. (Illus.). 60p. (Orig.). (gr. 2-12). 1990. pap. 12.75 (*0-935132-18-X*) C H Fairfax.
Jones, Elizabeth. Award Puzzles: Prayer for a Child. 1991. 5.95 (*0-938971-64-6*) JTG Nashville.
Jones, Ernest, jt. auth. see Scott, Victoria.
Jones, Eugene P. Which Was, Which Is, Which Is to Come. (Illus.). 105p. (Orig.). 1989. pap. 24.95 (*0-925039-00-4*) River-Light Pub.
Jones, Evelyn. World's Wackiest Riddle Book. 1991. 3.99 (*0-517-07353-6*) Outlet Bk Co.
Jones, Frances. Nature's Deadly Creatures: A Pop-up Exploration. (Illus.). 16p. (gr. 1-5). 1992. 15.00 (*0-8037-1342-8*) Dial Bks Young.
Jones, Gerard, jt. auth. see Giffen, Keith.
Jones, Graham. How They Lived in Bible Times. Deverell, Richard & Deverell, Christine, illus. LC 91-30420. 48p. (gr. 1-8). 1992. 12.99 (*0-8307-1574-6*, 5112125) Regal.
Jones, Gwyn, retold by. Scandinavian Legends & Folk-Tales. Kiddell-Monroe, Joan, illus. 192p. (gr. 4 up). 1992. pap. 10.95 (*0-19-274150-0*) OUP.
Jones, Harold. Tales to Tell: Six Traditional Stories. LC 84-4121. 48p. 1985. 12.95 (*0-688-03999-5*) Morrow Jr Bks.
Jones, Helen H. Israel. LC 85-5740. (Illus.). 128p. (gr. 5-9). 1986. PLB 26.60 (*0-516-02766-2*) Childrens.
—Over the Mormon Trail. Rogers, Carol, illus. LC 63-9706. 128p. (gr. 3-10). 1980. PLB 15.00 (*0-516-03354-9*) Childrens.
Jones, Hettie. The Trees Stand Shining: Poetry of the North American Indians. reissue ed. Parker, Robert A., illus. LC 79-142452. 32p. (gr. k up). 1993. 13.99 (*0-8037-9083-X*); PLB 13.89 (*0-8037-9084-8*) Dial Bks Young.

Jones, J. David. The Adventures of Little Red. Krull, Kathleen, ed. Sieck, Judythe, illus. 64p. 1993. write for info. (*1-883088-01-1*) Source CA. THE ADVENTURES OF LITTLE RED is about an eight year old boy living out his fantasy of flying & adventure with his secret friend, a pilot named Buzz. Together they dive out of the sky over the coast of Malibu for a close-up look at a school of dolphin; fly so close to the Hollywood sign they can almost touch it; fly through the metropolitan downtown Los Angeles; cruise over the international airport as commercial airliners take off & land below them; fly in formation with the Good Year blimp over the Rose Bowl during a football game; discover a sinking boat & lead a Coast Guard helicopter to the scene for a dramatic rescue. Although Little Red assumes that his adventure has all been a fantastic dream, he soon learns that any dream can come true, as long as he believes in it & is willing to work hard to make it happen. These are just a few scenes from THE ADVENTURES OF LITTLE RED, illustrated with spectacular four-color ground & aerial photographs, directed by J. David Jones who has been stunt pilot & director in the motion picture industry for almost 30 years. Book store owners & librarians agree that this is a one of a kind book & a must! Available from Source Productions, 800-538-0603 or 818-990-6724. *Publisher Provided Annotation.*

Jones, James. Why Do People Suffer? The Scandal of Pain in God's World. LC 92-36019. (Illus.). 128p. (gr. 10 up). 1993. 9.99 (*0-7459-2419-0*) Lion USA.
Jones, James A., III. Conversations with Children. Cook, Debbie, illus. LC 85-40201. 96p. (gr. 4-8). 1985. 8.95 (*0-938232-72-X*) Winston-Derek.
Jones, Jane A. The Arts - Frida Kahlo. LC 92-44758. 1993. 19.93 (*0-86625-485-4*); 14.95s.p. (*0-685-66535-6*) Rourke Pubns.
Jones, Jay S. Rosalia, Be Proud. Jones, MariaElena G., illus. 41p. (gr. k-6). 1992. 14.95 (*0-9632040-0-9*); PLB 14.95 (*0-9632040-1-7*) Integrity Inst.
Jones, Jayne C. The American Indian in America, Vol. II. LC 73-13378. (Illus.). 96p. (gr. 5 up). 1973. PLB 11.95 (*0-8225-0227-5*); pap. 5.95 (*0-8225-1002-2*) Lerner Pubns.
—American Indian in America, Vol. 2. 1991. pap. 5.95 (*0-8225-1037-5*) Lerner Pubns.
—The Greeks in America. rev. ed. LC 68-31504. (Illus.). 80p. (gr. 5 up). PLB 15.95 (*0-8225-0215-1*); pap. 5.95 (*0-8225-1010-3*) Lerner Pubns.
Jones, Jo. Amanda's Tree. Kuse, James A., illus. (gr. 3-6). 1979. pap. 2.95 (*0-89542-514-9*) Jo-Jo Pubns.
—Amanda's Tree. Vansant, Jo, illus. (gr. 3-6). 1977. pap. 3.50 (*0-9602266-0-5*) Jo-Jo Pubns.
—That Hardhead Cinnamon. Vansant, Jo, illus. LC 89-92753. 36p. (Orig.). (gr. 2-5). 1989. pap. 6.95 (*0-9602266-1-3*) Jo-Jo Pubns.
Jones, Joan. Projects for Autumn & Holiday Activities. Young, Richard G., ed. Wheele, Stephen, illus. LC 89-17008. 32p. (gr. 3-5). 1989. PLB 15.93 (*0-944483-42-9*) Garrett Ed Corp.
Jones, Joseph C., Jr. I Told You So or Wish I Had: A Father's Perspective on Things to Do for Living an Enjoyable, Productive, Successful & Meaningful Life. LC 92-83882. 46p. (Orig.). 1993. pap. 4.95 (*0-9607572-2-8*) Jobeco Bks.
Jones, Judy, jt. auth. see Zeplin, Zeno.
Jones, K. Maurice. Say It Loud! The Story of Rap Music. LC 93-1939. (Illus.). 160p. (gr. 7 up). 1994. PLB 17.90 (*1-56294-386-3*) Millbrook Pr.
Jones, Kathleen I. I Am This & More, Bk. 1. Jones, Kert, illus. 12p. (ps-5). 1989. write for info. (*0-9624790-0-4*) Kindle Bks.
Jones, Kathryn. Happy Birthday Dr. King. (gr. 4-7). 1994. pap. 4.95 (*0-671-87523-X*, Half Moon Bks) S&S Trade.
Jones, Kathryn D., jt. auth. see Burden-Patmon, Denise.
Jones, Kathy. Acting for God. Henson, Grace, illus. 48p. (gr. 4-8). 1984. wkbk. 6.95 (*0-86653-236-6*, SS 818, Shining Star Pubns) Good Apple.
—Celebrate Christmas. Filkins, Vanessa, illus. 144p. (gr. k-6). 1985. wkbk. 11.95 (*0-86653-279-X*, SS 840, Shining Star Pubns) Good Apple.
—I Am This & More, Bk. 2. Jones, Kert, illus. 12p. (ps-5). 1990. write for info. (*0-9624790-1-2*) Kindle Bks.
—Noah's ABC Ark. 48p. (ps-1). 1988. 6.95 (*0-86653-455-5*, SS1805, Shining Star Pubns) Good Apple.
Jones, Kathy, jt. auth. see Daniel, Rebecca.
Jones, Kay, jt. auth. see Hoenack, Peg.
Jones, Lewis. Great Britain. (Illus.). 32p. (gr. 4-6). 1991. 17.95 (*0-237-60182-6*, Pub. by Evans Bros Ltd) Trafalgar.
Jones, Lewis P. South Carolina: One of the Fifty States. LC 85-1882. (Illus.). 720p. (gr. 8). 1985. text ed. 30.95 (*0-87844-062-3*); tchr's. manual avail. (*0-87844-063-1*) Sandlapper Pub Co.
Jones, Lily. Baby Kermit's Playtime ABC. Prebenna, David, illus. 24p. (ps-k). 1992. pap. 1.79 laminated covers (*0-307-10024-3*, 10024, Golden Pr) Western Pub.
—Whooo's There? 16p. (ps-3). 1992. 9.95 (*0-89577-439-9*) RD Assn.
Jones, Linda K. Fear Strikes at Midnight. 128p. 1990. pap. 5.95 (*0-8361-3507-5*) Herald Pr.
Jones, Lorraine H. & Tsumura, Ted K. Health & Safety for You. 7th ed. 480p. 1987. text ed. 29.96 (*0-07-065386-0*) McGraw.
Jones, Lorraine H., jt. auth. see Tsumura, Ted K.
Jones, Louis C. Spooks of the Valley: Ghost Stories for Boys & Girls. Austin, Erwin H., illus. 111p. pap. 11.95 (*0-910746-10-9*, SOT01) Hope Farm.
Jones, Lucile. Hop, Skip, & Jump. Van Dolson, Bobbie J., ed. (gr. k up). 1981. pap. 3.95 (*0-8280-0038-7*) Review & Herald.
—Tony's Tummy. Van Dolson, Bobbie J., ed. 32p. (gr. k up). 1981. pap. 3.95 (*0-8280-0039-5*) Review & Herald.
Jones, M. L., ed. see Buchheit, Paul.
Jones, M. L., ed. see Lester, Will.
Jones, M. L., ed. see Morris, A. Earl.
Jones, M. L., ed. see Overson, David.
Jones, M. L., ed. see Price, Joyce.

Jones, Madeline. Finding Out about Industrial Britain. (Illus.). 64p. (gr. 7-12). 1984. 19.95 (*0-7134-4353-7*, Pub. by Batsford UK) Trafalgar.
—Knights & Castles. (Illus.). 72p. (gr. 7-11). 1991. 19.95 (*0-7134-6352-X*, Pub. by Batsford UK) Trafalgar.
Jones, Malcolm. Jump! An HBJ Book & Musical Cassette. Goldberg, Whoopi, narrated by. Parks, Van Dyke, contrib. by. (Illus.). 32p. (gr. 1-5). 1990. 19.95 (*0-15-241351-0*) HarBrace.
Jones, Malcolm, ed. see Harris, Joel C.
Jones, Marcia, jt. auth. see Dadey, Debbie.
Jones, Marcia, jt. auth. see Dadey, Debra.
Jones, Margaret. Martin Luther King, Jr. Scott, R., illus. LC 68-9483. 36p. (gr. 2-4). 1968. PLB 14.60 (*0-516-03524-X*); pap. 3.95 (*0-516-43524-8*) Childrens.
Jones, Margaret W. The Christmas Invitation: A Child's Christmas in the South. Easson, Roger R., ed. Robinson, Susan, illus. LC 85-2035. 48p. (gr. 5 up). 1985. 9.95 (*0-918518-42-3*) St Lukes Pr.
Jones, Martha R. Willow Finds a Friend. (Illus.). 32p. (gr. 2-4). 1993. pap. 6.95 (*0-8059-3315-8*) Dorrance.
Jones, Martha T. The Ghost at the Old Stone Fort. LaFreniere, Annette, ed. Loughran, Donna, illus. LC 90-4087. 104p. (gr. 4 up). 1990. lib. bdg. 11.95 (*0-937460-61-3*); pap. 6.95 (*0-937460-87-7*) Hendrick-Long.
—The Great Texas Scare: A Story of the Runaway Scrape. La Freniere, Annette, ed. LC 88-767. (Illus.). 96p. (gr. 3-7). 1988. lib. bdg. 10.95 (*0-937460-31-1*) Hendrick-Long.
—The Mystery of Y'Barbo's Tunnel. LaFreniere, Annette, ed. Loughran, Donna, illus. LC 91-2980. 112p. (gr. 3-7). 1991. 14.95 (*0-937460-68-0*) Hendrick-Long.
Jones, Mary E., ed. Christopher Columbus & His Legacy: Opposing Viewpoints. LC 92-18160. (Illus.). 240p. (gr. 10 up). 1992. PLB 17.95 (*0-89908-196-7*); pap. text ed. 9.95 (*0-89908-171-1*) Greenhaven.
Jones, Mary L. Woody Watches the Masters, Bk. 2: Four Artists in France. 1986. 4.95 (*0-533-06699-9*) Vantage.
—Woody Watches the Masters, Bk. 3: Early Western Civilization. 1991. 5.95 (*0-533-07901-2*) Vantage.
—Woody Watches the Masters, Bk. 4: American Artists. 1991. 5.95 (*0-533-07900-4*) Vantage.
—Woody Watches the Masters: Four Great Artists, Bk. 1. (Illus.). 36p. (gr. 3-7). 1985. 4.95 (*0-533-05814-7*) Vantage.
Jones, Maurice. I'm Going on a Dragon Hunt. Firmin, Charlotte, illus. LC 86-19399. 32p. (gr. k-3). 1987. SBE 13.95 (*0-02-748000-3*, Four Winds) Macmillan Child Grp.
Jones, Maxine D. & McCarthy, Kevin. African-Americans in Florida: An Illustrated History. (Illus.). pap. 4.95. 1993. PLB 24.95 (*1-56164-030-1*); pap. 17.95 (*1-56164-031-X*) Pineapple Pr.
Jones, Michael P. Halloween Bats. (Illus.). 24p. 1984. write for info. (*0-89904-065-9*) Crumb Elbow Pub.
—Halloween Ghosts. (Illus.). 24p. (ps-4). 1983. write for info. (*0-89904-064-0*); pap. text ed. write for info. (*0-89904-063-2*) Crumb Elbow Pub.
—Halloween Pumpkins. (Illus.). 24p. (ps-4). 1984. write for info. (*0-89904-067-5*); pap. text ed. write for info. (*0-89904-066-3*) Crumb Elbow Pub.
—Halloween Witches. (Illus.). 24p. (ps-4). 1983. write for info. (*0-89904-061-6*); pap. text ed. write for info. (*0-89904-062-4*) Crumb Elbow Pub.
—Land of the Animal Spirits: A One Act Play. Willis, Kathy & Boldt, Jeanine frwd. by. (Illus.). 132p. (Orig.). 1985. text ed. 15.00 (*0-89904-113-2*); pap. text ed. 9.99 (*0-89904-114-0*) Crumb Elbow Pub.
—Works in Progress, Vol. 1. (Illus.). 16p. 1984. pap. text ed. 1.60 (*0-89904-075-6*) Crumb Elbow Pub.
Jones, Michael P., ed. Andorff the Energy Ant's Coloring Book. abr. ed. (Illus.). 34p. 1984. text ed. 11.00 (*0-89904-071-3*); pap. text ed. 6.00 (*0-89904-072-1*) Crumb Elbow Pub.
—Oregon River Watch: A Contemporary History of Oregon's Waterways, Vol. 1. Bachmann, Mark, et al, illus. 48p. (Orig.). 1985. text ed. 9.95 (*0-89904-143-4*); pap. text ed. 5.00 (*0-89904-144-2*); composition 8.00 (*0-89904-145-0*) Crumb Elbow Pub.
—Oregon River Watch: A Contemporary History of Oregon's Waterways, Vol. 2. Bachmann, Mark, et al, illus. 50p. (Orig.). 1985. text ed. 9.95 (*0-89904-146-9*); pap. text ed. 5.00 (*0-89904-147-7*); composition 8.00 (*0-89904-148-5*) Crumb Elbow Pub.
—What Getting Drunk Doesn't Make You. (Illus.). 20p. 1984. text ed. 5.00 (*0-89904-027-6*); pap. text ed. 2.00 (*0-89904-197-3*) Crumb Elbow Pub.
—Writing Works Catalogue: Wholesale Edition Vol. 1. (Illus.). 202p. 1984. pap. 5.00 (*0-89904-059-4*); composition 6.00 (*0-89904-058-6*) Crumb Elbow Pub.
Jones, Michael P. & Boldt, Jeanine, eds. The Mountaineer, Vol. 1, No. 1. (Illus.). 42p. 1984. pap. text ed. 4.00 (*0-89904-017-9*) Crumb Elbow Pub.
Jones, Mother. Autobiography of Mother Jones: Pittston Strike Commemorative Edition. Parton, Mary F., ed. Darrow, Clarence & LeSueur, Merideli intro. by. (Illus.). 240p. (Orig.). (gr. 6-12). 1990. 25.95 (*0-88286-167-0*); pap. 12.95 (*0-88286-166-2*) C H Kerr.
Jones, Nancy K., jt. auth. see Hamilton, Harley.
Jones, Norma, et al, eds. Energy: Is There Enough? 76p. 1992. pap. text ed. 12.95 (*1-878623-35-4*) Info Plus TX.
—Food: What Do We Eat & Where Does It Come From? 52p. (gr. 6-9). 1992. pap. text ed. 11.95 (*1-878623-43-5*) Info Plus TX.

—Social Welfare: A Helping Hand? 44p. 1992. pap. text ed. 11.95 (*1-878623-34-6*) Info Plus TX.
Jones, Norma H., et al. Endangered Animals: Quickly Disappearing. (Illus.). 48p. (Orig.). (gr. 6-9). 1993. pap. text ed. 11.95 (*1-878623-51-6*) Info Plus TX.
—Recreation: What Do We Do to Have Fun? (Illus.). 64p. (gr. 6-9). 1993. pap. text ed. 12.95 (*1-878623-53-2*) Info Plus TX.
Jones, Norma H., et al, eds. Women - New Roles in Society. 68p. (gr. 6-9). 1992. pap. 11.95 (*1-878623-45-1*) Info Plus TX.
Jones, O. Garfield. Parliamentary Procedure at a Glance. (gr. 9 up). 1971. pap. 4.95 (*0-8015-5766-6*, 0481-140, Dutton) NAL-Dutton.
Jones, Penny. The Brown Bottle. 40p. (gr. 4 up). 1983. text ed. 4.00 (*0-89486-170-0*) Hazelden.
Jones, Ralph E. Straight Talk: Answers to Questions Young People Ask about Alcohol. Joiner, Lee M., ed. 64p. (Orig.). (gr. 10 up). 1988. pap. 4.95 (*0-943519-08-X*, B1908) Sulzburger & Graham Pub.
—Straight Talk: Answers to Questions Young People Ask about Alcohol. 1989. No. 70005. pap. 4.95 (*0-8306-9005-0*) TAB Bks.
Jones, Rebecca. The Biggest (& Best) Flag That Ever Flew. Geer, Charles, illus. LC 87-40609. 32p. (gr. k-4). 1988. 8.95 (*0-87033-381-X*) Tidewater.
—Germy Blew It. 112p. (gr. 2-9). 1988. pap. 2.95 (*0-8167-1314-6*) Troll Assocs.
Jones, Rebecca C. The Believers. 144p. (gr. 6 up). 1989. 13.95 (*1-55970-035-1*) Arcade Pub Inc.
—Down at the Bottom of the Deep Dark Sea. Wright-Frierson, Virginia, illus. LC 90-33981. 40p. (ps-k). 1991. RSBE 14.95 (*0-02-747901-3*, Bradbury Pr) Macmillan Child Grp.
—Germy Blew It. LC 86-19950. 112p. (gr. 3-7). 1987. 12.95 (*0-525-44294-4*, DCB) Dutton Child Bks.
—Germy Blew It Again. LC 88-22696. 124p. (gr. 2-4). 1988. 13.95 (*0-8050-0905-1*, Bks Young Read) H Holt & Co.
—Germy Blew the Bugle. 128p. (gr. 2-5). 1990. 14.95 (*1-55970-088-2*) Arcade Pub Inc.
—Germy in Charge. LC 92-42076. 128p. (gr. 4-7). 1993. 13.95 (*0-525-45093-9*, DCB) Dutton Child Bks.
—I Am Not Afraid. (Illus.). (ps). 1987. pap. 2.50 (*0-570-09113-6*, 56-1588) Concordia.
—Matthew & Tilly. Peck, Beth, illus. LC 90-3730. 32p. (ps-3). 1991. 13.95 (*0-525-44684-2*, DCB) Dutton Child Bks.
Jones, Renata. The Little White Ladybug. De Tuerk, Lif, illus. LC 90-70475. 54p. (ps-3). 1990. 8.95 (*0-932433-67-7*) Windswept Hse.
Jones, Rhodri. Different Friends. 122p. (gr. 6-9). 1990. pap. 9.95 (*0-233-98096-2*, Pub. by A Deutsch England) Trafalgar.
—Slaves & Captains. 121p. (gr. 6-9). 1990. pap. 9.95 (*0-233-98356-2*, Pub. by A Deutsch England) Trafalgar.
Jones, Richard C., jt. auth. see Ledbetter, Cynthia E.
Jones, Rick. Escalera al Infierno: La Bien Planificada Destruccion de la Juventud. (SPA., Illus.). 206p. (gr. 7-12). 1991. 7.95 (*0-937958-39-5*) Chick Pubns.
—Stairway to Hell: The Well-Planned Destruction of Teens. LC 88-72362. (Illus.). 206p. (Orig.). (gr. 7-12). 1988. pap. 7.95 (*0-937958-30-1*) Chick Pubns.
Jones, Robert F. Jake: A Labrador Puppy at Work & Play. (gr. 4-7). 1992. 15.00 (*0-374-33655-5*) FS&G.
Jones, Robert W. Boston & Maine: Three Colorful Decades of New England Railroading. Drury, George, frwd. by. LC 91-2112. (Illus.). 208p. (gr. 11). 1991. 79.95 (*0-87046-101-X*, Pub. by Trans-Anglo) Interurban.
Jones, Robin D. The Beginning of Unbelief. LC 92-22907. 160p. (gr. 7 up). 1993. SBE 13.95 (*0-689-31781-6*, Atheneum Child Bk) Macmillan Child Grp.
Jones, Ron. The Acorn People. 1990. pap. 3.50 (*0-553-27385-X*) Bantam.
—B-Ball: The Team That Never Lost a Game. (gr. 5 up). 1990. 14.95 (*0-553-05867-3*) Bantam.
—B-Ball: The Team That Never Lost a Game. 1991. pap. 3.50 (*0-553-29404-0*) Bantam.
Jones, S. Preprimer Cooking: Or, Cooking Techniques for the Blind, 2 vols. rev., large type ed. 304p. (gr. 9 up). 1973. Set. 80.00 (*0-317-01923-6*, J-21820-00) Am Printing Hse.
—Sewing Techniques for the Blind Girl. rev., large type ed. 40p. (gr. 9 up). 1973. 10.00 (*0-317-01934-1*, J-23520-00) Am Printing Hse.
Jones, Sally L. Friends of God. Pistone, Nancy, illus. 10p. (ps-3). 1993. text ed. 10.99 (*0-7847-0047-8*, 24-03657) Standard Pub.
—The Hippo's Adventure. Weissman, Bari, illus. 8p. (ps). 1993. vinyl 8.49 (*0-7847-0049-4*, 24-03687) Standard Pub.
—In the Beginning. Pistone, Nancy, illus. 10p. (ps-3). 1993. text ed. 10.99 (*0-7847-0046-X*, 24-03656) Standard Pub.
—Three Special Journeys, 3 bks. Weissman, Bari, illus. (ps). 1993. Set. 9.99 (*0-7847-0075-3*, 24-03645) Standard Pub.
—The Whale's Tale. Weissman, Bari, illus. 8p. (ps). 1993. vinyl 8.49 (*0-7847-0048-6*, 24-03686) Standard Pub.
Jones, Sally L., jt. auth. see Wilson, Etta.
Jones, Sandy. Love on Wheels. 1993. pap. 2.99 (*0-553-29981-6*) Bantam.
Jones, Sheila B. Country Spunky Gets Lost. Lewis, Cynthia V., illus. LC 92-56938. 40p. (gr. k-3). 1993. 6.95 (*1-55523-582-4*) Winston-Derek.

Jones, Shelagh. Save the Unicorns. Myler, Terry, illus. 140p. (gr. 4-7). 1989. 11.95 (*0-947962-48-4*, Pub. by Childrens Pr) Irish Bks Media.
Jones, Shelley D. When Laughing Isn't Funny. (Illus.). 1990. 6.95 (*0-533-08541-1*) Vantage.
Jones, Susan L. Llamas: Woolly, Winsome & Wonderful. LC 87-29279. (Illus.). 68p. (Orig.). 1987. pap. text ed. 12.95 (*0-942280-47-4*) Pub Horizons.
Jones, T. Llew. One Moonlit Night. Clarke, Gillian, tr. 108p. 1991. 65.00x (*0-86383-627-5*, Pub. by Gomer Pr UK) St Mut.
Jones, Taffy. Who Is Uncle Sam? Martin, Sandy, illus. LC 91-52615. 64p. (Orig.). 1991. pap. 6.95 (*0-917882-32-6*) MD Hist Pr.
Jones, Teri C. Birds. (Illus.). 64p. (gr. k-4). 1992. PLB 12.95 (*1-878363-81-6*, HTS Bks) Forest Hse.
—Dogs. (Illus.). 64p. (gr. k-4). 1992. PLB 12.95 (*1-878363-83-2*, HTS Bks) Forest Hse.
—Little Book of Questions & Answers: Animals. Marsh, T. F., illus. 32p. (gr. k-3). 1992. PLB 10.95 (*1-56674-012-6*, HTS Bks) Forest Hse.
—Little Book of Questions & Answers: My Home. Marsh, T. F., illus. 32p. (gr. k-3). 1992. PLB 10.95 (*1-56674-013-4*, HTS Bks) Forest Hse.
—Little Book of Questions & Answers: Nature. Marsh, T. F., illus. 32p. (gr. k-3). 1992. PLB 10.95 (*1-56674-014-2*, HTS Bks) Forest Hse.
—Little Book of Questions & Answers: Things That Go. Marsh, T. F., illus. 32p. (gr. k-3). 1992. PLB 10.95 (*1-56674-015-0*, HTS Bks) Forest Hse.
Jones, Terry. Fantastic Stories. large type ed. Foreman, Michael, illus. 1993. 15.95 (*0-7451-1908-5*, Galaxy Child Lrg Print) Chivers N Amer.
—Nicobobinus. Foreman, Michael, illus. LC 85-28630. 176p. (gr. k-6). 1986. 16.95 (*0-87226-065-8*) P Bedrick Bks.
—Nicobobinus. large type ed. 224p. (gr. 3-7). 1991. lib. bdg. 17.95x (*0-7451-1319-2*, Lythway Large Print) Hall.
—The Saga of Eric the Viking. large type ed. 248p. (gr. 3 up). 1990. lib. bdg. 16.95x (*0-7451-1152-1*, Lythway Large Print) Hall.
—Saga of Erik the Viking. Foreman, Michael, illus. 144p. (ps up). 1986. pap. 9.95 (*0-14-031713-9*, Puffin) Puffin Bks.
—The Saga of Erik the Viking. Foreman, Michael, illus. 192p. (gr. 3-7). 1993. pap. 3.99 (*0-14-032261-2*, Puffin) Puffin Bks.
—Terry Jones' Fairy Tales. Foreman, Michael, illus. 128p. (ps up). 1986. pap. 8.95 (*0-14-031642-6*, Puffin) Puffin Bks.
—Terry Jones Fairy Tales. Foreman, Michael, illus. 160p. (gr. 3-7). 1993. pap. 3.99 (*0-14-032262-0*, Puffin) Puffin Bks.
—Terry Jones' Fantastic Stories. Foreman, Michael, illus. 128p. 1993. 16.99 (*0-670-84899-9*) Viking Child Bks.
Jones, Tim & Butterworth, Jim. Another Way of Putting It: Twenty Short Plays with a Point. 128p. (gr. 7-12). 1991. pap. 7.99 (*0-87403-854-5*, 14-03354) Standard Pub.
Jones, Tim, photos by. Wild Critters. Walker, Tom, text by. Sturgis, Kent, ed. Newman, Leslie, illus. LC 91-7308. 48p. (Orig.). 1992. 15.95x (*0-945397-10-0*); pap. 7.95, Feb. 1993 (*0-945397-25-9*) Epicenter Pr.
Jones, Vada L. Kids Can Make Money Too! How Young People Can Succeed Financially...Over 200 Ways to Earn Money & How to Make It Grow. LC 87-71607. (Illus., Orig.). (gr. 3-12). 1988. pap. 9.95 (*0-944104-00-2*) Calico Paws.
Jones, William E. & Goldberg, Minerva J. Going to School. LC 68-56811. (Illus.). 32p. (ps-1). 1968. PLB 9.95 (*0-87783-015-0*) Oddo.
Jonge, Joanne De see De Jonge, Joanne.
Jons, John A. Studies of the French Dog Sports "Championship of France" (1982-1988) & the Belgian Shepherd Dog Breeds (Malinois, Tereuren Groenendael, Laenenois) in Schutzhund Competition in the U. S. A. (1979-1988) 1989. pap. text ed. 12.50 (*0-685-29411-0*) J Jons LA.
Jonsen, George. Favorite Tales of Monsters & Trolls. O'Brien, John, illus. Lerner, Sharon, ed. LC 76-24182. (Illus.). (ps-2). 1977. lib. bdg. 5.99 (*0-394-93477-6*) Random Bks Yng Read.
Jonson, Ben see Bald, Robert C.
Jonson, Liz & Silliman, Emery. Beginning Math. Nayer, Judith E., ed. Cocca, Maryann, illus. 32p. (gr. k-1). 1991. wkbk. 1.95 (*1-878624-59-8*) McClanahan Bk.
—Beginning to Add. Nayer, Judith E., ed. Appleby, Ellen, illus. 32p. (gr. k-1). 1991. wkbk. 1.95 (*1-878624-55-5*) McClanahan Bk.
—Counting. Nayer, Judith E., ed. Tomonari, Itsuko, illus. 32p. (gr. k-1). 1991. wkbk. 1.95 (*1-878624-54-7*) McClanahan Bk.
Jonson, Liz, jt. auth. see Silliman, Emery.
Jonsson, Phillip R. see Williams, C. Fred.
Joos, Francoise. The Golden Snowflake. Joos, Frederic, illus. (ps-3). 1991. 14.95 (*0-316-47328-6*) Little.
Joos, Francoise & Joos, Frederic. Sarah & the Stone Man. (Illus.). 32p. (gr. k-2). 1989. 13.95 (*0-86264-202-7*, Pub. by Anderson Pr UK) Trafalgar.
Joos, Francoise, jt. auth. see Joos, Frederic.
Joos, Frederic & Joos, Francoise. Puss in Palace. (Illus.). 32p. (gr. k-2). 1990. 13.95 (*0-86264-235-3*, Pub. by Anderson Pr UK) Trafalgar.
Joos, Frederic, jt. auth. see Joos, Francoise.
Joos, Louis, illus. Oregon's Journey. LC 93-11796. 40p. (gr. k-4). 1993. PLB 15.95 (*0-8167-3305-8*); pap. text ed. 3.95 (*0-8167-3306-6*) Troll Assocs.

Joosse, Barbara. Wild Willie & King Kyle Detectives. Truesdell, Sue, illus. LC 92-9816. 80p. (gr. 2-5). 1993. 12.95 (*0-395-64338-4*, Clarion Bks) HM.
Joosse, Barbara M. Anna & the Cat Lady. Mayo, Gretchen W., illus. LC 91-12510. 176p. (gr. 3-7). 1992. 14.00 (*0-06-020242-4*); PLB 13.89 (*0-06-020243-2*) HarpC Child Bks.
—Anna, the One & Only. Mayo, Gretchen W., illus. LC 88-890. 144p. (gr. 3-7). 1988. (Lipp Jr Bks); PLB 11.89 (*0-397-32323-9*, Lipp Jr Bks) HarpC Child Bks.
—Anna, the One & Only. Mayo, Gretchen W., illus. LC 88-890. 144p. (gr. 2-6). 1990. pap. 3.50 (*0-06-440345-9*, Trophy) HarpC Child Bks.
—Dinah's Mad, Bad Wishes. McCully, Emily A., illus. LC 88-884. 32p. (gr. k-3). 1989. PLB 12.89 (*0-06-023099-1*) HarpC Child Bks.
—Fourth of July. McCully, Emily A., illus. LC 82-17301. 48p. (ps-2). 1985. PLB 11.99 (*0-394-95195-6*) Knopf Bks Yng Read.
—Jam Day. McCully, Emily A., illus. LC 86-46117. 32p. (gr. k-3). 1987. HarpC Child Bks.
—The Losers Fight Back. Truesdell, Sue, illus. LC 92-40783. 1994. write for info. (*0-395-62335-9*, Clarion Bks) HM.
—Mama, Do You Love Me? Lavallee, Barbara, illus. 32p. (ps-1). 1991. 13.95 (*0-87701-759-X*) Chronicle Bks.
—The Morning Chair. Sewall, Marcia, illus. LC 93-4870. Date not set. write for info. (*0-395-62337-5*, Clarion Bks) HM.
—Nobody's Cat. Sewall, Marcia, illus. LC 91-37619. 32p. (gr. k-3). 1992. 15.00 (*0-06-020834-1*); PLB 14.89 (*0-06-020835-X*) HarpC Child Bks.
—Pieces of the Picture. LC 88-28150. 144p. (gr. 5-7). 1991. pap. 3.50 (*0-06-440310-6*, Trophy) HarpC Child Bks.
—The Pitiful Life of Simon Schultz. LC 90-22352. 192p. (gr. 5-9). 1991. 13.95 (*0-06-022486-X*); PLB 13.89 (*0-06-022487-8*) HarpC Child Bks.
Jordan, Alton, ed. see Smith, Glenna C.
Jordan, Bernice C. Acts: 14 Lessons, Vol. 1. (gr. 3-9). 1954. pap. text ed. 3.25 (*0-86508-039-9*); figure text 11.95 (*0-86508-040-2*) BCM Pubn.
—Acts: 15 Lessons, Vol. 2. (gr. 3-9). 1954. pap. text ed. 3.25 (*0-86508-041-0*); figure text 11.95 (*0-86508-042-9*) BCM Pubn.
—Fighting Giants: Joshua-Solomon 14 Lessons, Vol. 3. (gr. 3-9). 1957. pap. text ed. 3.25 (*0-86508-031-3*); figures text 12.95 (*0-86508-032-1*) BCM Pubn.
—Footsteps to God: Six Basic Bible Truth Lessons. (Illus.). (gr. 3-9). 1970. pap. text ed. 6.50 (*0-86508-025-9*) BCM Pubn.
—Genesis: Fifteen Lessons, Vol. 1. (gr. 3-9). 1960. pap. text ed. 3.25 (*0-86508-027-5*); figures text 12.95 (*0-86508-028-3*) BCM Pubn.
—God's Storehouse: Exodus 16 Lessons, Vol. 2. (Illus.). (gr. 3-9). 1961. pap. text ed. 3.25 (*0-86508-029-1*); 12.95 (*0-86508-030-5*) BCM Pubn.
—Gospels: Fourteen Lessons, Vol. 1. (gr. 3-9). 1955. pap. text ed. 3.25 (*0-86508-035-6*); figures text 12.95 (*0-86508-036-4*) BCM Pubn.
—Gospels: Fourteen Lessons, Vol. 2. (gr. 3-9). 1956. pap. text ed. 3.25 (*0-86508-037-2*); figures text 12.95 (*0-86508-038-0*) BCM Pubn.
Jordan, Cathleen & Manson, Cynthia, eds. Tales from Alfred Hitchcock's Mystery Magazine. Jordan, Cathleen, intro. by. LC 88-9013. 320p. (gr. 7 up). 1988. 12.95 (*0-688-08176-2*) Morrow Jr Bks.
Jordan, Helene J. How a Seed Grows. Low, Joseph, illus. LC 60-11541. 33p. (gr. k-3). 1972. pap. 4.95 (*0-690-40646-0*, Crowell Jr Bks) HarpC Child Bks.
—How a Seed Grows. rev. ed. Krupinski, Loretta, illus. LC 91-10166. 32p. (ps-1). 1992. 14.00 (*0-06-020104-5*); PLB 13.89 (*0-06-020185-1*) HarpC Child Bks.
—How a Seed Grows. rev. ed. Krupinski, Loretta, illus. LC 91-10165. 32p. (ps-1). 1992. pap. 4.50 (*0-06-445107-0*, Trophy) HarpC Child Bks.
Jordan, Hope D. Haunted Summer. LC 67-15713. (gr. 5 up). 1967. 11.95 (*0-688-41638-1*) Lothrop.
Jordan, James L. Ricky's Last Chance. 104p. (gr. 4-6). 1991. pap. 3.95 (*0-9630534-0-X*) Living Water.
Jordan, June. Kimako's Story. Burford, Kay, illus. 42p. (gr. k-3). 1991. pap. 3.80 (*0-395-60338-2*, Sandpiper) HM.
Jordan, Loraine, jt. auth. see Jordan, Stanley.
Jordan, Louise & Ramsay, Jo. Capital Games: An Activity Book about Raleigh, North Carolina. 32p. (gr. 3-5). 1984. pap. 2.50 (*0-9631710-2-X*) Jr League Raleigh.
Jordan, Martin, jt. auth. see Jordan, Tanis.
Jordan, MaryKate. Losing Uncle Tim. Levine, Abby, ed. Wennekes, Ron, illus. LC 89-5280. 32p. (gr. 2-6). 1989. PLB 13.95 (*0-8075-4756-5*); pap. 5.95 (*0-8075-4758-1*) A Whitman.
Jordan, Michael. Michael Jordan. (Illus.). (gr. 4-7). 1990. pap. 4.95 (*0-316-09229-0*, Spts Illus Kids) Little.
Jordan, Myra J. & Grant, Roy E. Floppy Rabbit: An Easter Musical. (Illus.). 30p. (Orig.). (ps-1). 1980. pap. 5.00 (*0-914562-09-6*) Merriam-Eddy.
—Santa's Problem. (Illus.). 30p. (Orig.). (ps-1). 1980. pap. 5.00 (*0-914562-08-8*) Merriam-Eddy.
Jordan, P. D. Cooper Street. 147p. (Orig.). (gr. 5-12). 1989. pap. 4.25 (*0-929885-21-X*) Haypenny Pr.
Jordan, Polly, illus. In the Jungle. 24p. (ps-2). 1993. pap. text ed. 2.95 (*1-56293-320-5*) McClanahan Bk.
—In the Ocean. 24p. (ps-2). 1993. pap. text ed. 2.95 (*1-56293-319-1*) McClanahan Bk.

—One Hundred Birds & Ten Bugs. 10p. (ps-1). 1992. bds. 2.95 (1-56293-253-5) McClanahan Bk.
—One Hundred Cats & Ten Mice. 10p. (ps-1). 1992. bds. 2.95 (1-56293-251-9) McClanahan Bk.
—One Hundred Fish & Ten Worms. 10p. (ps-1). 1992. bds. 2.95 (1-56293-254-3) McClanahan Bk.
—One Hundred Frogs & Ten Flies. 10p. (ps-1). 1992. bds. 2.95 (1-56293-252-7) McClanahan Bk.
Jordan, Sandra. Christmas Tree Farm. LC 93-20142. (Illus.). 32p. (ps-2). 1993. 14.95 (0-531-05499-3); PLB 14.99 (0-531-08649-6) Orchard Bks Watts.
Jordan, Sandra, jt. auth. see Greenberg, Jan.
Jordan, Sherryl. Juniper Game. 1991. 13.95 (0-590-44728-9, Scholastic Hardcover) Scholastic Inc.
—Time of Darkness. (gr. 9-12). 1990. 13.95 (0-590-43363-6) Scholastic Inc.
—Time of Darkness. 1992. pap. 3.25 (0-590-43362-8, Point) Scholastic Inc.
—Wednesday Wizard. (gr. 4-7). 1993. pap. 2.95 (0-590-46759-X) Scholastic Inc.
—Winter of Fire. LC 92-2587. 336p. (gr. 7 up). 1993. 13. 95 (0-590-45288-6) Scholastic Inc.
Jordan, Stanley & Jordan, Loraine. The Fru-Vee Vision. 16p. 1993. text ed. 4.95 saddlestitch (0-8059-3409-X) Dorrance.
Jordan, Tanis. Journey of the Red-Eyed Tree Frog. Jordan, Martin, illus. LC 91-29526. 40p. (ps-3). 1992. 16.00 (0-671-76903-0, Green Tiger) S&S Trade.
Jordan, Tanis & Jordan, Martin. Jungle Days, Jungle Nights. LC 92-40366. (Illus.). 40p. (gr. k-4). 1993. 14. 95 (1-8569-7885-0) Kingfisher Bks.
Jordan, Tina. A Visit to the Eagles' Nest. Jordan, Debra, illus. 20p. (gr. 3-5). 1980. PLB 2.25 (0-938574-00-0) Cherubim.
Jorden, Ngawang, tr. see Halpern, Gina.
Jorgen, Randolph, ed. see Houk, Rose.
Jorgen, Randolph, ed. see Parent, Laurence E.
Jorgen, Randolph, ed. see Udall, Stewart L. & Haury, Emil W.
Jorgen, Randolph, ed. see Utley, Robert.
Jorgensen, Dan. Andrea's Best Shot. LC 87-33760. 1988. pap. 4.49 (1-55513-860-8, Chariot Bks) Cook.
—Dawn's Diamond Choice. LC 87-11735. 1988. pap. 4.49 (1-55513-062-3, Chariot Bks) Cook.
—Kelli's Choice. 144p. (gr. 7 up). 1991. pap. 4.49 (1-55513-773-3, 37739) Cook.
Jorgensen, Eric, et al. Manure, Meadows & Milkshakes. Hone, Elizabeth, ed. Hendrick, Andrea, illus. 132p. (Orig.). (ps-8). 1986. pap. text ed. 9.95 tchrs. ed. (0-318-20228-X) Trust Hidden Villa.
Jorgensen, Gail. Crocodile Beat. Mullins, Patricia, illus. LC 89-578. 32p. (ps-1). 1989. RSBE 14.95 (0-02-748010-0, Bradbury Pr) Macmillan Child Grp.
Jorgensen, Karen L. & Venable, James W. History Workshop: Reconstructing the Past with Elementary Children. LC 92-42158. (gr. 1-5). 1993. pap. text ed. 16.00 (0-435-08900-5, 08900) Heinemann.
Jorgensen, Kermit. Ten-Boy. 64p. (Orig.). (gr. 7 up). 1988. pap. 5.95 (0-9621221-0-6) Jordane Pub.
Jorgenson, Lisa. Grand Trees of America: Champion Trees of the Fifty States. (Illus.). 96p. (gr. 2-8). 1992. pap. 8.95 (1-879373-15-7) R Rinehart.
Jose, Christine San see Dixon, Debra S. & Henry, Susan V.
Jose, Eduard, adapted by. Aladdin's Lamp: A Classic Tale. Suire, Diane D., tr. from SPA. Lavarello, Jose M., illus. LC 88-35312. 32p. (gr. 1-4). 1988. PLB 19. 95 (0-89565-481-4); PLB 13.95s.p. (0-685-56030-9) Childs World.
—Ali Baba & the Forty Thieves: A Classic Tale. Riehecky, Janet, tr. from SPA. Rovira, Francesc, illus. LC 88-36871. 32p. (gr. 1-4). 1988. PLB 19.95 (0-89565-485-7); PLB 13.95s.p. (0-685-56049-X) Childs World.
—Fearless John: A Classic Tale. Moncure, Jane B., tr. Lavarello, Jose M., illus. LC 88-35215. 32p. (gr. 1-4). 1988. PLB 19.95 (0-89565-470-9); PLB 13.95s.p. (0-685-56038-4) Childs World.
—Goldilocks & the Three Bears: A Classic Tale. McDonnell, Janet, tr. Lavarello, Jose M., illus. LC 88-36870. 32p. (gr. 1-4). 1988. PLB 19.95 (0-89565-465-2); PLB 13.95s.p. (0-685-56047-3) Childs World.
—The Old Sandman: A Classic Tale. Riehecky, Janet, tr. Asensio, Augusti, illus. LC 88-36793. 32p. (gr. 1-4). 1988. PLB 19.95 (0-89565-461-X); PLB 13.95s.p. (0-685-56042-2) Childs World.
—Sinbad the Sailor: A Classic Tale. Riehecky, Janet, tr. from SPA. Rovira, Francesc, illus. LC 88-36872. 32p. (gr. 1-4). 1988. PLB 19.95 (0-89565-472-5); PLB 13. 95s.p. (0-685-56048-1) Childs World.
—Snow White & the Seven Dwarfs: A Classic Tale. McDonnell, Janet, tr. Asensio, Augusti. LC 88-35210. 32p. (gr. 1-4). 1988. PLB 19.95 (0-89565-479-2); PLB 13.95s.p. (0-685-56035-X) Childs World.
—The Three Little Pigs: A Classic Tale. McDonnell, Janet, tr. Asensio, Augusti, illus. LC 88-35314. 32p. (gr. 1-4). 1988. PLB 19.95 (0-89565-459-8); PLB 13. 95s.p. (0-685-58429-1) Childs World.
—Till Eulenspiegel's Merry Pranks: A Classic Tale. Riehecky, Janet, tr. Rovira, Francesc, illus. LC 88-36794. 32p. (gr. 1-4). 1988. PLB 19.95 (0-89565-475-X); PLB 13.95s.p. (0-685-56043-0) Childs World.

—The Vain Little Mouse: A Classic Tale. Riehecky, Janet, tr. Asensio, Augusti, illus. LC 88-35214. 32p. (gr. 1-4). 1988. PLB 19.95 (0-89565-464-4); PLB 13. 95s.p. (0-685-56021-X) Childs World.
Jose, Eduard, adapted by see Andersen, Hans Christian.
Jose, Eduard, adapted by see Browning, Robert.
Jose, Eduard, adapted by see Carroll, Lewis.
Jose, Eduard, adapted by see Collodi, Carlo.
Jose, Eduard, adapted by see Grimm, Jacob & Grimm, Wilhelm K.
Jose, Eduard, ed. see Perrault, Charles.
Jose, Eduard, adapted by see Perrault, Charles.
Josef, Marion. God Loves Us. Mayfield, Ana M., illus. 32p. (Orig.). (ps-1). 1993. pap. 3.95 (0-8198-3037-2) St Paul Bks.
—We Thank God. Mayfield, Ana M., illus. 28p. (Orig.). (gr. k-4). 1993. pap. 0.95 (0-8198-8267-4) St Paul Bks.
Josefowitz, Natasha. A Hundred Scoops of Ice Cream. 60p. 1989. pap. 3.95 (0-88166-157-0) Prestwick Pub.
—A Hundred Scoops of Ice Cream: Tiny Tales. Mietzelfeld, Mary, illus. 64p. (gr. 1 up). 1988. bds. 7. 95x (0-312-01444-9) St Martin.
Joseph, Andre. The Psycho-Mathematical Basic Skills Learning Workbooklet. 67p. (gr. 6-7). 1980. 8.00 (0-936240-00-4); write for info. (0-936264-01-2) Andres & Co.
Joseph, Catherine D. Blue Ridge Parkway: Four Seasons of Splendor. 56p. (Illus.). (gr. ps-12). 1987. pap. text ed. 5.25 (0-936672-74-9) Aerial Photo.
Joseph, Daniel M. Dressed up & Nowhere to Go. (ps-3). 1993. 14.95 (0-89686-607-9) HM.
Joseph, James, et al. Tuna & Billfish: Fish Without a Country. 2nd ed. Mattson, George, illus. Revelle, Roger, intro. by. LC 80-81889. (Illus.). 53p. (Orig.). (gr. 7-12). 1980. pap. 7.95 (0-9603078-1-8) Inter-Am Tropical.
Joseph, Joan, jt. auth. see Levy, Robert.
Joseph, Joel. The Magic Word. Moyer, Barry, illus. 12p. (Orig.). (ps-2). 1986. pap. 9.95 (0-915765-31-4) Natl Pr Bks.
Joseph, Lorraine F. My Island: A Picture Storybook. Washington, Helen, illus. 23p. (Orig.). (gr. k-3). 1985. pap. 2.95 (0-935357-00-9) Cric Prod.
Joseph, Lynn. Coconut Kind of Day. 32p. 1990. 13.95 (0-688-09119-9); PLB 13.88 (0-688-09120-2) Lothrop.
—Coconut Kind of Day: Island Poems. 1992. pap. 4.99 (0-14-054867-X, Puffin) Puffin Bks.
—Coconut Kind of Day: Island Poems. (gr. 4 up). 1992. pap. 4.99 (0-14-054527-1) Puffin Bks.
—An Island Christmas. Stock, Catherine, illus. 32p. (ps-3). 1992. 14.45 (0-395-58761-1, Clarion Bks) HM.
—The Mermaid's Twin Sister: More Stories from Trinidad. Perrone, Donna, illus. LC 93-28436. 1994. write for info. (0-395-64365-1, Clarion Bks) HM.
—Wave in Her Pocket: Stories from Trinidad. Stevenson, Dinah, ed. Pinkney, Brian, illus. 64p. (gr. 3-7). 1991. 13.95 (0-395-54432-7, Clarion Bks) HM.
Joseph, Samuel. The Madrikhim Handbook. Grishaver, Joel L., intro. by. 96p. (gr. 10-12). 1990. pap. text ed. 4.95 (0-933873-52-2) Torah Aura.
Josephs, Anna C. Mountain Boy. LC 85-12238. (Illus.). 32p. (gr. 2-4). 1985. PLB 17.96 (0-940742-51-9) Raintree Steck-V.
Josephson, Judith, jt. auth. see Fine, Edith.
Josephson, Judith P. The Loon. LC 88-9599. (Illus.). 48p. (gr. 5-6). 1988. RSBE 12.95 (0-89686-390-5, Crestwood Hse) Macmillan Child Grp.
—The Monarch Butterfly. LC 88-10871. (Illus.). 48p. (gr. 5-6). 1988. RSBE 12.95 (0-89686-389-1, Crestwood Hse) Macmillan Child Grp.
Josephy, Alvin M., Jr. Alvin Josephy's History of the Native Americans Series, 6 bks. (Illus.). 864p. (gr. 5-7). 1989. Set. PLB 77.88 (0-382-09808-0); Set. pap. 47.70 (0-382-09809-9) Silver Burdett Pr.
Joshi, Jagadish, jt. auth. see Davidar, E. R.
Joshi, Uma. Stories from Bapu's Life. Patel, Mickey, illus. (gr. 1-9). 1979. pap. 2.50 (0-89744-180-X) Auromere.
Joslin, Margaret. See What I Can Do Today: A Year's Worth of Fascinating Fun for Your Pre-Schooler. 366p. (Orig.). (ps). 1992. pap. 8.50 (1-882835-07-7) STA-Kris.
Joslin, Sesyle. What Do You Do, Dear? Sendak, Maurice, illus. LC 84-43139. 48p. (ps-3). 1986. pap. 4.95 (0-06-443113-4, Trophy) HarpC Child Bks.
—What Do You Do, Dear? Sendak, Maurice, illus. LC 84-43139. 48p. 1958. 13.95 (0-201-09387-1); PLB 13. 89 (0-06-023075-4) HarpC Child Bks.
—What Do You Say, Dear? Sendak, Maurice, illus. LC 84-43140. 48p. (ps-3). 1986. pap. 4.95 (0-06-443112-6, Trophy) HarpC Child Bks.
—What Do You Say, Dear? Sendak, Maurice, illus. LC 84-43140. 48p. 1958. 14.00 (0-201-09391-X); PLB 13. 89 (0-06-023074-6) HarpC Child Bks.
Joubert, Jean. White Owl & Blue Mouse. Levertov, Denise, tr. from FRE. Gay, Michel, illus. LC 90-70710. 64p. (gr. 1-3). 1990. 13.95 (0-944072-13-5) Zoland Bks.
Joval, Nomi. El Color de la Luz. Kubinyi, Laszlo, illus. (SPA). 16p. (ps-4). 1993. PLB 13.95 (1-879567-20-2, Valeria Bks) Wonder Well.
—Color of Light. Kubinyi, Laszlo, illus. 16p. (ps-4). 1993. PLB 13.95 (1-879567-19-9, Valeria Bks) Wonder Well.
—La Lupa Maravillosa. Kubinyi, Laszlo, illus. (SPA). 24p. (ps-4). 1993. PLB 13.95 (1-879567-22-9, Valeria Bks) Wonder Well.
—Power of Glass. Kubinyi, Laszlo, illus. 16p. (ps-4). 1993. PLB 13.95 (1-879567-21-0, Valeria Bks) Wonder Well.

—Room of Mirrors. Kubinyi, Laszlo, illus. 16p. (gr. k-4). 1991. PLB 13.95 (1-879567-06-7, Valeria Bks) Wonder Well.
—Salon de Espejos. Kubinyi, Laszlo, illus. (SPA). 16p. (gr. k-4). 1992. PLB 13.95 (1-879567-07-5, Valeria Bks) Wonder Well.
Jowett, Benjamin, tr. see Plato.
Joy, Flora. Creative Writing. (Illus.). 64p. (gr. 1-6). 1992. wkbk. 7.95 (0-86653-679-5, 1413) Good Apple.
—Creative Writing Booklets. 64p. (gr. k-6). 1985. 7.95 (0-86653-274-9, GA626) Good Apple.
—Creative Writing Booklets, No. 2. 64p. (gr. k-6). 1985. 7.95 (0-86653-284-6, GA629) Good Apple.
—Shortcuts for Teaching Writing. 144p. (gr. 3-6). 1991. 11.95 (0-86653-590-X, GA1303) Good Apple.
—Whole Language Celebrations. (Illus.). 176p. (gr. k-4). 1992. wkbk. 12.95 (0-86653-690-6, 1424) Good Apple.
—Whole Language for the Holidays. (Illus.). 144p. (gr. k-4). 1992. wkbk. 12.95 (0-86653-689-2, 1423) Good Apple.
—Word Wizardry, Level II. Harroll, Pat, illus. 112p. (gr. 4-12). 1987. pap. 11.95 (0-86653-404-0, GA 1017) Good Apple.
—Word Wizardry, Level I. Harroll, Pat, illus. 112p. (gr. 2-8). 1987. pap. 11.95 (0-86653-403-2, GA 1016) Good Apple.
Joyce, James. The Boarding House. (Illus.). 1982. PLB 13.95s.p. (0-87191-895-1) Creative Ed.
—The Encounter. 32p. (gr. 6 up). 1982. PLB 13.95s.p. (0-87191-896-X) Creative Ed.
—Eveline. 32p. (gr. 6). 1990. PLB 13.95s.p. (0-88682-308-0) Creative Ed.
Joyce, Mary R. Friends: For Teens. (Illus.). 144p. (Orig.). (gr. 10-12). 1990. pap. text ed. 10.95 (0-9615722-1-3) LifeCom.
Joyce, P. W. A Child's History of Ireland. Harrison, Hank, ed. (Illus.). 225p. (gr. 8-12). 14.95 (0-918501-24-5); pap. write for info. (0-918501-26-1) Archives Pr.
Joyce, Susan. Naro, the Ancient Spider. DuBosque, D. C., illus. (gr. 4). 1990. 12.00 (0-939217-04-X) Peel Prod.
—Peel, el Elefant Extraordinario. Sampson, Jennifer, tr. from ENG. DuBosque, D. C., illus. (SPA). 48p. (ps-7). 1990. lib. bdg. 13.95x (0-939217-02-3); pap. 7.95 (0-939217-03-1) Peel Prod.
—Peel, the Extraordinary Elephant. DuBosque, D. C., illus. LC 86-61990. 48p. (ps up). 1988. pap. 7.95 sewn bdg. (0-939217-01-5) Peel Prod.
—Pilon, el Extraordinario Elefanton. Marcuse, Aida, tr. from ENG. DuBosque, D. C., illus. LC 92-35437. (SPA). 48p. (Orig.). (gr. 1-6). 1993. pap. 8.95 (0-939217-05-8) Peel Prod.
Joyce, Susan, ed. see Wees, Marty.
Joyce, William. Bently & Egg. Joyce, William, illus. LC 91-55499. 32p. (ps-3). 1992. 15.00 (0-06-020385-4); PLB 14.89 (0-06-020386-2) HarpC Child Bks.
—A Day with Wilbur Robibson. Joyce, William, illus. LC 90-4066. 32p. (ps-3). 1993. pap. 5.95 (0-06-443339-0, Trophy) HarpC Child Bks.
—A Day with Wilbur Robinson. Joyce, William, illus. LC 90-4066. 32p. (ps-3). 1990. 13.95 (0-06-022967-5); PLB 14.89 (0-06-022968-3) HarpC Child Bks.
—Dinosaur Bob: And His Adventures with the Family Lazardo. Joyce, William, illus. LC 87-30796. 32p. (ps-3). 1988. 15.00 (0-06-023047-9); PLB 14.89 (0-06-023048-7) HarpC Child Bks.
—George Shrinks. Joyce, William, illus. LC 83-47697. 32p. (ps-2). 1985. 14.00 (0-06-023070-3); PLB 13.89 (0-06-023071-1) HarpC Child Bks.
—George Shrinks. Joyce, William, illus. LC 83-47697. 32p. (ps-2). 1987. 3.95 (0-06-443129-0, Trophy) HarpC Child Bks.
—George Shrinks. miniature ed. Joyce, William, illus. LC 90-46285. 32p. (ps-2). 1991. 3.95 (0-06-023299-4) HarpC Child Bks.
—Santa Calls. Joyce, William, illus. LC 92-52691. 40p. (ps up). 1993. 18.00 (0-06-021133-4); PLB 17.89 (0-06-021134-2); ltd. ed. 125.00 (0-06-023355-9) HarpC Child Bks.
Joyer, Mike & Roberts, Zack. One Hundred Excuses for Kids. Black, Cynthia, ed. Kerr, Kathleen, illus. 96p. (Orig.). 1990. pap. 4.95 (0-941831-48-5) Beyond Words Pub.
Joyner, Jerry, jt. auth. see Charlip, Remy.
Judd, Dick & Linse, Barbara. Fiesta! Mexico & Central America for Children in Grades 2-5. (gr. 2-5). 1993. pap. 25.95 (0-8224-4232-9) Fearon Teach Aids.
Judge, Joseph W., jt. auth. see DeOld, Alan R.
Judge, Matt, ed. see Poelker, Kathy.
Judson, Bay, et al. Art Ventures: A Guide for Families to Ten Works of Art in the Carnegie Museum of Art. Koren, Edward, illus. LC 87-858. 24p. (Orig.). (gr. 4-6). 1987. pap. text ed. 5.95 (0-88039-014-X) Mus Art Carnegie.
Judson, Harry P. Caesar's Army: A Study of the Military Art of the Romans in the Last Days of the Republic. LC 61-12877. (Illus.). 127p. (gr. 7 up). 1888. 24.00 (0-8196-0113-6) Biblo.
Judson, Thomas, illus. Color Me Cleveland: A Cleveland Coloring Book. Johnston, Christopher, text by. (Illus.). 32p. 1993. pap. 4.95 (0-9631738-2-0) Gray & Co Pubs.
Judy. The Artificial Grandma. Delton, Alan T., illus. 1990. pap. 2.95 (0-440-40315-4, YB) Dell.

Juengst, Sara C. Silver Ships-Green Fields. Pace, Anne, illus. 52p. (Orig.). (gr. 1-6). 1986. pap. 5.95 (0-377-00161-9) Friendship Pr.
Jukes, Mavis. Blackberries in the Dark. Allen, Thomas B., illus. LC 85-4259. 48p. (gr. 2-6). 1993. 14.00 (0-394-87599-0) Knopf Bks Yng Read.
—Blackberries in the Dark. (gr. k-6). 1987. pap. 2.99 (0-440-40647-1, YB) Dell.
—Getting Even. LC 87-25053. 160p. (gr. 4-7). 1988. PLB 12.99 (0-394-99594-5) Knopf Bks Yng Read.
—Getting Even. LC 87-25053. 176p. (gr. 4-7). 1989. pap. 2.95 (0-394-82593-4) Knopf Bks Yng Read.
—I'll See You in My Dreams. Schuett, Stacey, illus. LC 91-47605. 40p. (gr. k-5). 1993. 15.00 (0-679-82690-4); PLB 15.99 (0-679-92690-9) Knopf Bks Yng Read.
—Like Jake & Me. Bloom, Lloyd, illus. LC 83-8380. 32p. (gr. k up). 1984. PLB 13.99 (0-394-95608-7) Knopf Bks Yng Read.
—Like Jake & Me. Bloom, Lloyd, illus. LC 83-8380. 32p. (gr. 1-5). 1987. pap. 6.00 (0-394-89263-1) Knopf Bks Yng Read.
—Wild Iris Bloom. LC 90-24315. 192p. (gr. 5-9). 1992. 14.00 (0-679-81891-X); PLB 14.99 (0-679-91891-4) Knopf Bks Yng Read.
Julian, Faye. A Magic Christmas: A Play for Children in One Act. (Illus.). 28p. (gr. k-12). 1983. pap. 2.00 (0-88680-121-4); royalty on application 15.00 (0-685-57861-5) I E Clark.
Julien, Ophelia. Dead of Summer. LC 90-55256. 78p. (Orig.). (gr. 4 up). 1991. pap. 7.00 (1-56002-065-2) Aegina Pr.
Julivert, M. Angels. The Life of Plants. (Illus.). 1994. 13.95 (0-7910-2129-7, Am Art Analog) Chelsea Hse.
Julivert, Maria A. El Fascinante Mundo: Las Serpientes, The Fascinating World of Snakes. Marcel Socias Studio Staff, ed. Arridondo, F., illus. 32p. (gr. 3-7). Date not set. pap. 7.95 (0-8120-1799-4) Barron.
—El Fascinante Mundo, The Fascinating World: Las Ranas y Los Sapos, Of Frogs & Toads. Marcel Socias Studio Staff, ed. Arridondo, F., illus. 32p. (gr. 3-7). Date not set. pap. 7.95 (0-8120-1795-1) Barron.
—The Fascinating World of Ants. Marcel Socias Studio Staff & Arridondo, F., illus. 32p. (gr. 3-7). 1991. 11.95 (0-8120-6281-7) Barron.
—Fascinating World of Birds. Arrendondo, Francisco, illus. LC 92-5684. (gr. 4-7). 1992. pap. 7.95 (0-8120-1378-6) Barron.
—The Fascinating World of Butterflies & Moths. Marcel Socias Studio Staff & Arridondo, F., illus. 32p. (gr. 3-7). 11.95 (0-8120-6282-5) Barron.
—The Fascinating World of Frogs & Toads. Marcel Socias Studio Staff & Arridondo, F., illus. 32p. (gr. 3-7). 1993. 11.95 (0-8120-6345-7); pap. 7.95 (0-8120-1565-7) Barron.
—The Fascinating World of Snakes. Marcel Socias Studio Staff & Arridondo, F., illus. 32p. (gr. 3-7). 1993. 11.95 (0-8120-6346-5); pap. 7.95 (0-8120-1564-9) Barron.
—Fascinating World of Spiders. (gr. 4-7). 1992. pap. 6.95 (0-8120-1377-8) Barron.
Jumper, Moses & Sonder, Ben. Osceola, Patriot & Warrior. Soper, Patrick, illus. LC 92-25209. 76p. (gr. 2-5). 1992. PLB 21.34 (0-8114-7225-6) Raintree Steck-V.
Juneau, Barbara F. Sad, but O.K. - My Daddy Died Today: A Child's View of Death. LC 88-155937. (Illus.). 112p. (Orig.). (gr. 5 up). 1988. pap. 9.95 (0-931892-19-8) Borgo Pr.
—Sad, but O.K. - My Daddy Died Today: A Child's View of Death. LC 89-7174. 112p. 1989. Repr. of 1988 ed. lib. bdg. 25.00x (0-8095-6557-9) Borgo Pr.
Jung, Minna. William's Ninth Life. Rosenberry, Vera, illus. LC 92-44520. 32p. (ps-2). 1993. 14.95 (0-531-05492-6); PLB 14.99 (0-531-08642-9) Orchard Bks Watts.
Jungman, Ann. When the People Are Away. Birch, Linda, illus. (ps-3). 1993. 12.95 (1-56397-202-6) Boyds Mills Pr.
Jungreis, Abigail. Know Your Hometown History: Projects & Activities. LC 92-15407. (Illus.). 64p. (gr. 5-8). 1992. PLB 12.90 (0-531-11124-5) Watts.
Junior League of San Francisco Staff & Brown, Tricia. The City by the Bay: A Magical Journey Around San Francisco. Kleven, Elisa, illus. LC 92-32104. 1993. 12.95 (0-8118-0233-7) Chronicle Bks.
Junior Publishers of San Francisco Bay Area Book Council Staff, ed. Window to Our World: An International Collection of Kids' Art. Caduto, Michael J., intro. by. (Illus.). 82p. (Orig.). 1992. pap. 5.99 (0-935701-03-6) Foghorn Pr.
Juntune, Joyce E. Developing Creative Thinking. Dougherty, Edie, illus. 30p. (gr. k-4). 1984. pap. 5.00 (0-912773-09-X) One Hund Twenty Creat.
—Developing Creative Thinking: Fun Book, No. 2. Dougherty, Edie, illus. (gr. k-4). 1984. pap. 5.00 (0-912773-08-1) One Hund Twenty Creat.
—Developing Creative Thinking: Fun Book, No. 3. Dougherty, Edie, illus. (ps-5). 1985. pap. 6.00 (0-912773-10-3) One Hund Twenty Creat.
Jupp, Michael. Ipostas' - Poems: Chetvertaia Kniga Stikhotvorenii, 1968-1988. Pronin, Anatolii, illus. LC 88-6090. (RUS.). 164p. (gr. 9-12). 1991. 30.00 (0-911971-30-0) Effect Pub.
Jurcic, Dana. By the Itching of My Nose Something Wicked This Way Goes. 1991. 7.95 (0-533-09489-5) Vantage.

Jurie, Jeri. Bizzy Bubbles: Santa's Littlest Elf. Fahs, Anita, illus. LC 77-82535. (gr. k-6). 1977. 10.95x (0-686-01311-5); pap. 6.95x (0-686-01312-3) Al Fresco.
Jurmain, Suzanne. One upon a Horse: A History of Horses--& How They Shaped Our History. LC 88-17522. (Illus.). 176p. (gr. 4 up). 1989. 15.95 (0-688-05550-8) Lothrop.
Jurovskii, A., ed. see Sesemann, Dimitri.
Jussim, Daniel. Drug Tests & Polygraphs: Essential Tools or Violations of Privacy? LC 87-11192. (Illus.). 128p. (gr. 7 up). 1988. lib. bdg. 12.98 (0-671-64438-6, J Messner); lib. bdg. 5.95 (0-671-65977-4) S&S Trade.
—Euthanasia: The "Right to Die" Issue. LC 92-42147. (Illus.). 112p. (gr. 6 up). 1993. lib. bdg. 17.95 (0-89490-429-9) Enslow Pubs.
—Medical Ethics. (Illus.). 144p. (gr. 7 up). 1990. lib. bdg. 13.98 (0-671-70015-4, J Messner) S&S Trade.
Just Us Books Editors. Black History Month Activity & Enrichment Handbook. LC 90-60068. 24p. (gr. 3-12). 1990. 8.95 (0-940975-25-4); pap. 6.50 (0-940975-14-9) Just Us Bks.
Juster, Norman. Otter Nonsense. Witte, Michael, illus. LC 93-22041. (gr. 3 up). 1994. write for info. (0-688-12282-5); PLB write for info. (0-688-12283-3) Morrow Jr Bks.
Juster, Norton. Aberic the Wise. Baskin, Leonard, illus. LC 92-7807. 28p. (gr. 1 up). 1992. 16.95 (0-88708-243-2) Picture Bk Studio.
—As: A Surfeit of Similes. Small, David, illus. LC 88-8449. 80p. 1989. 9.95 (0-688-08139-8); PLB 9.89 (0-688-08140-1, Morrow Jr Bks) Morrow Jr Bks.
—The Phantom Tollbooth. (gr. 5 up). 1972. 16.95 (0-394-81500-9) Knopf Bks Yng Read.
—The Phantom Tollbooth. Feiffer, Jules, illus. LC 61-13202. 256p. (gr. 3-7). 1993. Repr. of 1961 ed. 3.95 (0-394-82037-1) Knopf Bks Yng Read.
—The Phantom Tollbooth. large type ed. 320p. (gr. 3-7). 1989. lib. bdg. 14.95 (0-8161-4801-5, Large Print Bks) Hall.
Justus. Jumping Jack. LC 73-87803. (Illus.). 32p. (gr. k-3). 1974. PLB 9.95 (0-87783-123-8); pap. 3.94 deluxe ed. (0-87783-124-6); cassette o.s.i. 7.94x (0-87783-189-0) Oddo.
Justus, Fred. Jumbo Math Yearbook: Grade 1. 96p. (gr. 1). 1980. 18.00 (0-8209-0030-3, JMY 1) ESP.
JV-Warwick Press Staff, ed. see Royston, Angela.
Jwing-Ming, Yang. How to Defend Yourself: Effective & Practical Martial Arts Techniques. Dougall, Alan, ed. Painter, John, frwd. by. (Illus.). 120p. (Orig.). 1992. pap. text ed. 12.95 (0-940871-27-0) Yangs Martial Arts.
Jwing-Ming Yang. The Fox Borrows the Tiger's Awe. Dougall, Alan, ed. Xieu-Lin, Li, illus. 54p. (gr. 4 up). 1990. 4.95 (0-940871-12-2) Yangs Martial Arts.

K

K, King. Rainbow Chase. 1992. 10.95 (0-533-10031-3) Vantage.
K, Lisa. The Adventures of Frenchy & Joe. 1993. 12.95 (0-533-10415-7) Vantage.
Kaahena, Yuhaayaa L. Children Style Quran: Stories for Children from Quran. Ismail, Latifa, ed. 22p. (Orig.). (gr. k-5). 1991. pap. 5.00 (1-883781-04-3) Yuhaaya.
Kaaki, Lisa. The Awakening. Zhou, Hoda D., illus. 30p. (Orig.). (gr. 1-4). 1991. pap. 3.50 (0-89259-118-8) Am Trust Pubns.
Kabell, Margaret. Prophet of the Pacific. (gr. 5-9). 1979. pap. 3.95 (0-87508-619-5) Chr Lit.
Kabes, Todd, jt. auth. see McGee, William.
Kabeto, Rita T. The Bradburys. 70p. (gr. 3-7). 1993. pap. write for info. (0-9635416-0-9) Buchonia Pub.
Kabisch, Cecilia D. Welcome to Success in E. S. L. Apple Pie (Personalized Instruction in English) (Illus.). (gr. k-6). 1982. text ed. write for info. (0-911149-00-7); write for info. tchrs' guide (0-911149-07-4); Set. 85.00 (0-911149-08-2); write for info. wkbk. 1 (0-911149-01-5); write for info. wkbk. 2 (0-911149-02-3); write for info. wkbk. 3 (0-911149-03-1); write for info. wkbk. 4 (0-911149-04-X) Apple Pie Pub Co.
Kachaturoff, Grace. Michigan! (Illus.). 298p. (gr. 4). 1987. 23.00 (0-685-24531-4, Peregrine Smith) Gibbs Smith Pub.
Kachel, Limana. Homer Littlebird's Rabbit: Cheyenne Indian Story for Children. 32p. (ps-2). 1983. pap. 2.45 (0-89992-084-5) Coun India Ed.
Kachenmeister, Cherryl. On Monday When It Rained. Berthiaume, Tom, photos by. (Illus.). 40p. (gr. k-3). 1989. 11.95 (0-395-51940-3) HM.
Kaczmarek, Constant S. This Is Living. (Illus.). 325p. 1990. text ed. 75.00 (0-9626041-0-0) C Kaczmarek.
Kaczorek, Keith. The Spirit & Vision of Notre Dame: The First 150 Years. Harrow, Harriett, ed. Griffin, David, et al, illus. Hesburgh, Theodore & Roberson, Kenneth, frwd. by. 96p. 1992. 28.00 (0-9623171-4-4); pap. 18.50 (0-9623171-5-2); pap. text ed. 8.50 black & white ed. (0-9623171-6-0); write for info. coloring bk. (0-9623171-7-9) LBCo Pub.
Kadesch, M., et al. Insights into Academic Writing: Strategies for Advanced Students. 176p. (gr. 9 up). 1991. pap. text ed. 19.95 (0-8013-0364-8, 78139) Longman.

Kadlec, Robert F., ed. They "Knew" Billy the Kid Interviews with Old-Time New Mexicans. Dykes, Jeff, afterword by. LC 87-70295. (Illus.). 136p. (Orig.). (gr. 9-12). 1987. pap. 10.95 (0-941270-36-X) Ancient City Pr.
Kadra, Sheila & Smith, Patricia. Painting with Words. 1987. pap. text ed. 12.90 (0-88334-195-6, 76160) Longman.
Kaetler, Sarah. More Stories from Grandpa's Rocking Chair. Kaetler, Sarah, illus. 73p. (gr. 3-6). 1991. pap. 4.95 (0-919797-75-X) Kindred Pr.
—Stories from Grandpa's Rocking Chair. Klassen, Neil, illus. 64p. (Orig.). (gr. 1-5). 1984. pap. 3.95 (0-919797-11-3) Kindred Pr.
Kaffa. The Best Ever Costume Party. 1993. pap. 6.95 (0-590-46958-4) Scholastic Inc.
Kagan, Myrna. Vision in the Sky: New Haven's Early Years, 1638-1783. LC 89-2762. (Illus.). xiv, 161p. (gr. 4-8). 1989. lib. bdg. 17.50 (0-208-02246-5, Linnet Shoe String.
Kagan, Neil, ed. see Time Life Book Editors.
Kagan, Neil, ed. see Time-Life Books Editors.
Kagan, Neil, ed. see Time Life Inc. Editors.
Kagan, Neil, ed. see Time Life Inc. Editors.
Kagan, Neil, ed. see Time Life Inc. Editors.
Kagan, Neil, ed. see Time Life Inc., Staff.
Kageler, Len. Short Stops with the Lord. 104p. (gr. 9-12). 1984. 8.99 (0-87509-348-5) Chr Pubns.
Kageyama, Akiko. Journey to Bethlehem. 26p. (ps-3). 1983. 10.00 (0-8170-1012-2) Judson.
Kaghan, Joan. The Billy Goat Show. 32p. 1993. 14.00 (0-374-30711-3) FS&G.
Kahalewai, Marilyn. Maui Mouse's Supper. LC 87-92276. (Illus.). 16p. (ps-3). 1989. 7.95 (0-935848-57-6); pap. 5.95 (1-880188-68-6) Bess Pr.
—Whose Slippers Are Those? Kahalewai, Marilyn, illus. LC 87-92272. 16p. (ps-6). 1988. 7.95 (0-935848-58-4) Bess Pr.
Kahalewai, Marilyn & Poepoe, Karen. Too Many Curls. Kahalewai, Marilyn & Poepoe, Karen, illus. LC 89-82131. 16p. (ps-2). 1992. 12.95 (0-935848-83-5); pap. 5.95 (1-880188-20-1) Bess Pr.
Kahan, B., jt. ed. see Hill, Michael.
Kahan, Bob, ed. The Death of Superman. (Illus.). 168p. (Orig.). 1992. pap. 4.95 (1-56389-097-6) DC Comics.
—World Without a Superman. 240p. (Orig.). 1993. pap. 7.50 (1-56389-118-2) DC Comics.
Kahan, Bob, ed. see Friedman, Michael J.
Kahan, Bob, ed. see Gibbons, Dave.
Kahaner, Ellen. Courage. (Illus.). 64p. (gr. 7-12, RL 4-6). 1990. PLB 13.95 (0-8239-1112-8) Rosen Group.
—Fourth Grade Loser. Henderson, David F., illus. LC 90-26791. 96p. (gr. 3-5). 1992. lib. bdg. 9.89 (0-8167-2384-2); pap. text ed. 2.95 (0-8167-2385-0) Troll Assocs.
—Motorcycles. 48p. (gr. 3-4). 1991. PLB 11.95 (1-56065-070-2) Capstone Pr.
—What's So Great about Fourth Grade? Henry, Paul, illus. LC 89-20602. 96p. (gr. 3-5). 1990. PLB 9.89 (0-8167-1702-8); pap. text ed. 2.95 (0-8167-1703-6) Troll Assocs.
Kahkonen, Sharon. Honey Bees. 32p. (gr. 1-4). 1989. PLB 15.96 (0-8172-3508-6); pap. 3.95 (0-8114-6707-4) Raintree Steck-V.
Kahl. Duchess Bakes a Cake. 1985. 2.95 (0-684-16007-2, Scribner) Macmillan.
Kahl, Jonathan. Weatherwise: Learning about the Weather. (Illus.). 64p. (gr. 4-12). 1992. PLB 19.95 (0-8225-2525-9) Lerner Pubns.
—Wet Weather: Rain Showers & Snowfall. (Illus.). 64p. (gr. 4-12). 1992. PLB 19.95 (0-8225-2526-7) Lerner Pubns.
Kahl, Jonathan D. Storm Warning: The Power of Tornadoes & Hurricanes. LC 92-13627. 1993. 19.95 (0-8225-2527-5) Lerner Pubns.
—Thunderbolt: Learning about Lightning. LC 92-45177. 1993. 19.95 (0-8225-2528-3) Lerner Pubns.
Kahla, Robert. Mr. X from Planet X: And Other Animules. Kahla, Robert, illus. 64p. Date not set. pap. 8.95 (1-882820-00-2) Cracked Egg.
Kahn, et al. Pacemaker Practical Arithmetic Series. large type ed. Incl. Using Dollars & Sense, 2 vols. 260p. 1963. Set. 65.00 (0-317-02425-6, J-27090-00). (gr. 4-12). Repr (J-27090-00) Am Printing Hse.
Kahn, Betsey, ed. see Kirsten, Suzanne.
Kahn, Elithe A. Lani Goose Sings...for Hawaii's Children. Ruble, Allison, illus. (Orig.). 1988. pap. 14.95 incl. audio cassette (0-944264-03-4) Lani Goose Pubns.
Kahn, Elithe M. Legends of Maui As Told by Lani Goose. Shiu, Tom, illus. 20p. (gr. k-6). 1989. pap. 8.95 incl. audiocassette (0-944264-04-2) Lani Goose Pubns.
Kahn, Joan. Ready or Not: Here Come Fourteen Frightening Stories! LC 86-31875. (Illus.). 176p. (gr. 7 up). 1987. 11.75 (0-688-07167-8) Greenwillow.
Kahn, Jonathan. Patulous: The Prairie Rattlesnake. Thatch, Nancy R., ed. Kahn, Jonathan, illus. Melton, David, intro. by. LC 91-13652. (Illus.). 26p. (gr. k-4). 1991. PLB 14.95 (0-933849-36-2) Landmark Edns.
Kahn, Katherine, illus. The Shofar Calls to Us. LC 91-60592. 12p. (ps). 1991. bds. 4.95 (0-929371-61-5) Kar Ben.
Kahn, Katherine J. Alef Is One: A Hebrew Alphabet & Counting Book. Kahn, Katherine J., illus. LC 89-24428. 48p. (ps-4). 1989. 12.95 (0-929371-05-4); pap. 7.95 (0-929371-04-6) Kar Ben.

—Passover Fun: For Little Hands. Kahn, Katherine J., illus. 32p. (ps-2). 1991. wkbk. 3.95 (0-929371-56-9) Kar Ben.

Kahn, Michel. My Everyday Spanish Word Book. (Illus.). 46p. (gr. 3-9). 1982. 10.95 (0-8120-5429-6) Barron.

Kahn, Michele. Mi Libro de Palabras Usadas Cada Dia En Ingles. (gr. k-6). 1982. pap. 11.95 (0-8120-5431-8) Barron.

—My Everyday French Word Book. LC 79-89631. 44p. (gr. 1-6). 1981. 10.95 (0-8120-5344-3) Barron.

Kahn, Peggy. The Care Bears & the Whale Tale. Fritz, Ron, illus. LC 91-53214. 32p. (Orig.). (ps-1). 1992. pap. 2.25 (0-679-82764-1) Random Bks Yng Read.

—The Care Bears' Book of ABC's. Bracken, Carolyn, illus. LC 82-18538. 40p. (ps-2). 1983. lib. bdg. 4.99 (0-394-95808-X) Random Bks Yng Read.

—The Care Bears' Circus of Shapes. Bracken, Carolyn, illus. LC 83-51590. 14p. (ps-1). 1984. bds. 3.95 (0-394-86726-2) Random Bks Yng Read.

—The Care Bears Help Santa. Fleming, Denise, illus. LC 84-3385. 40p. (ps-3). 1984. lib. bdg. 4.99 (0-394-96807-7, BYR) Random Bks Yng Read.

—The Care Bears: Try, Try Again! Fahrion, Michael, illus. LC 85-2152. 40p. (ps-3). 1985. lib. bdg. 4.99 (0-394-97503-0) Random Bks Yng Read.

—Christmastime at Santa's Workshop. Paris, Pat, illus. 14p. (ps-3). 1992. 7.99 (0-679-82451-0) Random Bks Yng Read.

—The Handy Girls Can Fix It! Jensen, Enola, illus. LC 83-21086. 32p. (ps-5). 1984. pap. 1.95 (0-394-86252-X) Random Bks Yng Read.

—Popple Opposites. Ewers, Joe, illus. LC 85-63459. 28p. (ps). 1986. 2.95 (0-394-88266-0) Random Bks Yng Read.

Kahn, Peggy & Beylon, Cathy. When Do You Snuzzle a Wuzzle? LC 84-62808. (Illus.). 14p. (gr. 2-5). 1985. 1.95 (0-394-87433-1) Random Bks Yng Read.

Kahn, Roger. Good Enough to Dream. 352p. (gr. 9-12). 1986. pap. 4.50 (0-451-15280-8, Sig) NAL-Dutton.

Kahn, Rosemary. Grandma's Hat. (ps-3). 1991. 13.95 (0-670-84023-8) Viking Child Bks.

Kahney, Regina. The Glow-in-the Dark Book of Animal Skeletons. Santoro, Christopher, illus. LC 91-3810. 24p. (gr. 2-5). 1992. 14.00 (0-679-81080-3) Random Bks Yng Read.

Kahng, David & Kahng, Kim, eds. The Loathsome Dragon. (Illus.). (gr. k-4). 1987. lib. 14.95 (0-399-21407-0, Putnam) Putnam Pub Group.

Kahng, Kim, jt. ed. see Kahng, David.

Kahrimanis, Leola. Blue Hills Robbery. Roberts, M., ed. (Illus.). 128p. (gr. 6-8). 1991. 10.95 (0-89015-753-7) Eakin-Sunbelt.

Kai, Nubia. Solos. LC 88-83010. 121p. (gr. 9-12). 1988. pap. 8.50 perf. bdg. (0-916418-71-5) Lotus.

—The Sweetest Berry on the Bush. Cochran, Marie, illus. LC 92-63010. 121p. (Orig.). 1993. pap. 8.00 (0-88378-059-3) Third World.

Kain, Carolyn. The Story of Money. Wood, Gerry, illus. LC 91-38898. 32p. (gr. 3-6). 1993. PLB 11.89 (0-8167-2711-2); pap. text ed. 3.95 (0-8167-2712-0) Troll Assocs. Postponed.

Kaisei-sha, tr. see Akiko Sueyoshi.

Kaisei-sha, tr. see Asuka, Ken.

Kaisei - Sha, tr. see Fusako Ishinabe.

Kaisei-sha, tr. see Gomi, Taro.

Kaiser, Eldor. Your Journey into the Future. 108p. (Orig.). (gr. 9-12). 1990. pap. 6.99 (0-931529-97-2) Group Pub.

Kaiser, Judith B. Quick-Line Stories for Young Children. 1975. spiral bdg. 3.95 (0-916406-12-1) Accent CO.

Kaiser Syndicated Features Staff. Four Seasons Activity Book. (Illus.). 190p. (gr. k-5). 1992. pap. 3.75 (0-9634746-0-X) Kaiser Syndicated.

Kaiulani, jt. auth. see Roes, Carol.

Kaizuki, Kiyonori. A Calf Is Born. Hirano, Cathy, tr. Kaizuki, Kiyonori, illus. LC 89-23091. (JPN.). 40p. (ps-2). 1990. LC (0-531-05862-X); PLB 13.99 (0-531-08462-0) Orchard Bks Watts.

Kajpust, Melissa. A Dozen Silk Diapers. Tomova, Veselina, illus. LC 92-41937. 32p. (ps-2). 1993. 13.95 (1-56282-456-2); PLB 13.89 (1-56282-457-0) Hyprn Child.

Kakutani, Akiko. Japanese for Today: Beginning Japanese Language Workbook. (Illus.). 229p. (Orig.). 1989. wkbk. 5.00 (0-9619977-3-7) Earlham College Pr.

Kalakaua, David. The Legends & Myths of Hawaii: The Fables & Folk-Lore of a Strange People. Daggett, R. M., ed & illus. LC 72-77519. 530p. (gr. 9 up). 1972. pap. 12.95 (0-8048-1032-X) C E Tuttle.

Kalan, Robert. Blue Sea. Crews, Donald, illus. LC 78-18396. 24p. (gr. k-3). 1979. 14.95 (0-688-80184-6); PLB 14.88 (0-688-84184-8) Greenwillow.

—Blue Sea. Crews, Donald, illus. LC 78-18396. 24p. (ps up). 1992. pap. 3.95 (0-688-11509-8, Mulberry) Morrow.

—Rain. Crews, Donald, illus. LC 77-25312. 24p. (gr. k-3). 1978. PLB 13.93 (0-688-84139-2) Greenwillow.

—Rain. LC 77-25312. 32p. (ps-3). 1991. pap. 3.95 (0-688-10479-7, Mulberry) Morrow.

—Stop, Thief! Abolafia, Yossi, illus. LC 92-30081. 24p. (ps up). 1993. 14.00 (0-688-11876-3); PLB 13.93 (0-688-11877-1) Greenwillow.

Kalas, Klaus, jt. auth. see Kalas, Sybille.

Kalas, Sybille. The Goose Family Book. Crampton, Patricia, tr. LC 85-30986. (Illus.). 53p. (gr. 1 up). 1991. pap. 15.95 (0-88708-019-7) Picture Bk Studio.

—Polar Bear Family Book. (ps-3). 1991. pap. 15.95 (0-88708-157-6) Picture Bk Studio.

—The Wild Horse Family Book. Crampton, Patricia, tr. Kalas, Sybille, illus. LC 89-3929. (ps up). 1991. pap. 15.95 (0-88708-110-X) Picture Bk Studio.

Kalas, Sybille & Kalas, Klaus. The Beaver Family Book. Crampton, Patricia, tr. LC 87-13914. (Illus.). (gr. k up). 1991. pap. 15.95 (0-88708-050-2) Picture Bk Studio.

Kalas, Sybille, jt. auth. see Somme, Lauritz.

Kalashnikoff, Nicholas. The Defender. Louden, Claire & Louden, George, Jr., illus. LC 92-33560. 144p. (gr. 3-7). 1993. pap. 6.95 (0-8027-7397-4) Walker & Co.

Kalb, Jonah. The Easy Baseball Book. Kossin, Sandy, illus. LC 75-44085. 64p. (gr. 2-5). 1976. 14.45 (0-395-24385-8) HM.

—The Easy Hockey Book. Morrison, Bill, illus. 64p. (gr. 2-5). 1977. 13.95 (0-395-25842-1) HM.

Kalb, Jonah & Viscott, David. What Every Kid Should Know. LC 75-44123. (Illus.). 128p. (gr. 5-9). 1976. 14.45 (0-395-24386-6) HM.

—What Every Kid Should Know. Kuchera, John & Margolis, Al, illus. 128p. (gr. 4-7). 1992. pap. 4.80 (0-395-62983-7, Sandpiper) HM.

Kalbacken, Joan. The Menominee Nation. 1994. write for info. (0-516-01054-9) Childrens.

—White-Tailed Deer. LC 91-35277. (Illus.). 48p. (gr. k-4). 1992. PLB 15.27 (0-516-01138-3); pap. 4.95 (0-516-41138-1) Childrens.

Kalbacken, Joan, jt. auth. see Lepthien, Emilie U.

Kaldhol, Marit. Goodbye Rune. Crosby-Jones, Michael, tr. from NOR. Yen, Wenche, illus. (NOR.). 32p. (ps-5). 1987. 13.95 (0-916291-11-1) Kane-Miller Bk.

Kalin, Robert. Jump, Frog, Jump! Barton, Byron, illus. 32p. (gr. k-3). Big Book. 19.95 (0-590-71722-7); pap. 2.95 (0-590-71723-5) Scholastic Inc.

Kalish, Lionel, jt. auth. see Kalish, Muriel.

Kalish, Muriel & Kalish, Lionel. Bears on Stairs: A Beginner's Book of Rhymes. LC 92-10144. (Illus.). 12p. (ps-1). 1993. 7.95 (0-590-44918-4) Scholastic Inc.

—Who Says Moo? A Beginner's Book of Rhymes. LC 92-10145. (Illus.). 12p. (ps-1). 1993. 7.95 (0-590-44917-6) Scholastic Inc.

Kalkstein, Paul, et al. English Competence Handbook. 3rd ed. 1981. pap. text ed. 12.60 (0-88334-143-3, 76111) Longman.

Kallas, John L. BASIC. 252p. (Orig.). (gr. 8-12). 1985. pap. text ed. 14.99 (0-89824-145-6); 14.99 (0-89824-167-7) Trillium Pr.

Kallen, Stuart. Life in the Thirteen Colonies 1650-1750. Wallner, Rosemary, ed. LC 90-82617. (Illus.). 64p. (gr. 4). 1990. PLB 12.94 (0-939179-87-3) Abdo & Dghtrs.

—A Modern Nation. Wallner, Rosemary, ed. LC 90-82629. (Illus.). 32p. (gr. 4). 1990. PLB 12.94 (0-939179-91-1) Abdo & Dghtrs.

—A Nation Divided Eighteen Fifty to Nineteen Hundred. Walner, Rosemary, ed. LC 90-82612. (Illus.). 64p. (gr. 4). 1990. PLB 12.95 (0-939179-90-3) Abdo & Dghtrs.

—A Nation United 1780-1850. Wallner, Rosemary, ed. LC 90-82610. (Illus.). 64p. (gr. 4). 1990. lib. bdg. 12.95 (0-939179-89-X) Abdo & Dghtrs.

—New Comers to America, Fourteen Hundred to Sixteen Fifty. Walner, Rosemary, ed. LC 90-82616. (Illus.). 64p. (gr. 4). 1990. PLB 12.95 (0-939179-86-5) Abdo & Dghtrs.

—Renaissance of Rock: British Invasion - The Sixties. Italia, Bob, ed. LC 89-84917. (Illus.). 48p. (gr. 4). 1989. PLB 12.94 (0-939179-75-X) Abdo & Dghtrs.

—Renaissance of Rock: Sounds of America - The Sixties. Italia, Bob, ed. LC 89-84916. (Illus.). 48p. (gr. 4). 1989. PLB 12.94 (0-939179-74-1) Abdo & Dghtrs.

—Retrospect of Rock: The Eighties. Italia, Bob, ed. LC 89-84919. (Illus.). 48p. (gr. 4). 1989. PLB 12.94 (0-939179-77-6) Abdo & Dghtrs.

—Revolution of Rock: The Seventies. Italia, Bob, ed. LC 89-84918. (Illus.). 48p. (gr. 4). 1989. PLB 12.94 (0-939179-76-8) Abdo & Dghtrs.

—Road to Freedom, Seventeen Fifty to Seventeen Eighty-Three. Wallner, Rosemary, ed. LC 90-82611. (Illus.). 64p. (gr. 4). 1990. PLB 12.94 (0-939179-88-1) Abdo & Dghtrs.

—Roots of Rock, Vol. 2: The Fifties. Italia, Bob, ed. LC 89-84414. (Illus.). 48p. (gr. 4). 1989. PLB 12.94 (0-939179-73-3) Abdo & Dghtrs.

Kallen, Stuart, ed. see Wheeler, Jill.

Kallen, Stuart A. Amazing Animal Records. Wallner, Rosemary, ed. LC 91-73055. 1991. 12.94 (1-56239-046-5) Abdo & Dghtrs.

—Amazing Human Feats. Wallner, Rosemary, ed. LC 91-73052. 1991. 12.94 (1-56239-049-X) Abdo & Dghtrs.

—Awesome Entertainment Records. LC 91-73054. 32p. 1991. 12.94 (1-56239-047-3) Abdo & Dghtrs.

—Before the Communist Revolution. Wallner, Rosemary, ed. LC 92-13472. 1992. PLB 13.99 (1-56239-100-3) Abdo & Dghtrs.

—Brain Teasers. LC 92-14774. 1992. 12.94 (1-56239-130-5) Abdo & Dghtrs.

—The Brezhnev Era. Wallner, Rosemary, ed. LC 92-13475. 1992. PLB 13.99 (1-56239-104-6) Abdo & Dghtrs.

—Earth Keepers. LC 93-15329. (gr. 4 up). 1993. 14.96 (1-56239-211-5) Abdo & Dghtrs.

—Eco-Arts & Crafts. LC 93-19059. (gr. 3 up). 1993. 14.96 (1-56239-208-5) Abdo & Dghtrs.

—Eco-Fairs & Carnivals. LC 93-4156. 1993. 14.96 (1-56239-205-0) Abdo & Dghtrs.

—Eco-Games. LC 93-7750. 1993. 14.96 (1-56239-201-8) Abdo & Dghtrs.

—Funny Answers to Foolish Questions. LC 92-14771. 1992. 12.94 (1-56239-131-3) Abdo & Dghtrs.

—Ghosts of the Seven Seas. LC 91-73060. 1991. 12.94 (1-56239-041-4) Abdo & Dghtrs.

—Gorbachev-Yeltsin: The Fall of Communism. Wallner, Rosemary, ed. LC 92-13477. 1992. PLB 13.99 (1-56239-105-4) Abdo & Dghtrs.

—Haunted Hangouts of the Undead. LC 91-73065. 1991. 12.94 (1-56239-036-8) Abdo & Dghtrs.

—How to Catch a Ghost. Wallner, Rosemary, ed. LC 91-73063. 1991. 12.94 (1-56239-038-4) Abdo & Dghtrs.

—Human Oddities. LC 91-73057. 202p. 1991. 12.94 (1-56239-044-9) Abdo & Dghtrs.

—If Animals Could Talk. Berg, Julie, ed. LC 93-18958. 1993. 14.96 (1-56239-187-9) Abdo & Dghtrs.

—If the Sky Could Talk. LC 93-10177. 1993. 14.96 (1-56239-185-2) Abdo & Dghtrs.

—If the Trees Could Talk. LC 93-18891. (gr. 4 up). 1993. 14.96 (1-56239-184-4) Abdo & Dghtrs.

—The Khrushchev Era. Wallner, Rosemary, ed. LC 92-13476. 1992. PLB 13.99 (1-56239-103-8) Abdo & Dghtrs.

—The Lenin Era. Wallner, Rosemary, ed. LC 92-13473. 1992. PLB 13.99 (1-56239-101-1) Abdo & Dghtrs.

—Mad Science Experiments. LC 92-14776. 1992. 12.94 (1-56239-128-3) Abdo & Dghtrs.

—Martin Luther King: A Man & His Dream. LC 93-2296. (gr. 7 up). 1993. 14.96 (1-56239-256-5) Abdo & Dghtrs.

—Mathmagical Fun. LC 92-14777. 1992. 12.94 (1-56239-129-1) Abdo & Dghtrs.

—Monsters, Dinosaurs & Beasts. LC 91-73061. 202p. 1991. 12.94 (1-56239-040-6) Abdo & Dghtrs.

—Only the Funniest Joke Book. LC 92-14778. 1992. 12.94 (1-56239-133-X) Abdo & Dghtrs.

—Phantoms of the Rich & Famous. LC 91-73064. 1991. 12.94 (1-56239-037-6) Abdo & Dghtrs.

—Precious Creatures A-Z. Berg, Julie, ed. LC 93-19060. 1993. 14.96 (1-56239-202-6) Abdo & Dghtrs.

—Ridiculous Riddles. LC 92-14772. 1992. 12.94 (1-56239-126-7) Abdo & Dghtrs.

—Silly Stories. LC 92-14773. 1992. 12.94 (1-56239-132-1) Abdo & Dghtrs.

—Spectacular Sports Records. Wallner, Rosemary, ed. LC 91-73056. 1991. PLB 12.94 (1-56239-045-7) Abdo & Dghtrs.

—The Stalin Era. Wallner, Rosemary, ed. LC 92-13474. 1992. PLB 13.99 (1-56239-102-X) Abdo & Dghtrs.

—Super Structures of the World. Wallner, Rosemary, ed. LC 91-73053. 202p. 1991. 12.94 (1-56239-048-1) Abdo & Dghtrs.

—Tricky Tricks. LC 92-14775. 1992. 12.94 (1-56239-127-5) Abdo & Dghtrs.

—Vampires, Werewolves, & Zombies. LC 91-73062. 1991. 12.94 (1-56239-039-2) Abdo & Dghtrs.

—Witches, Magic & Spells. Wallner, Rosemary, ed. LC 91-73058. 1991. 12.94 (1-56239-043-0) Abdo & Dghtrs.

—World of the Bizarre. LC 91-73059. 202p. 1991. 12.94 (1-56239-042-2) Abdo & Dghtrs.

Kallen, Stuart A. & Berg, Julie. If the Waters Could Talk. LC 93-18953. 1993. lib. bdg. 14.96 (1-56239-186-0) Abdo & Dghtrs.

Kallen, Stuart A., ed. see Wheeler, Jill C.

Kallevig, Christine P. Bible Folding Stories: Old Testament Stories & Paperfolding Together As One. LC 93-85089. (Illus.). 80p. (gr. k-8). 1993. pap. write for info. (0-9628769-4-1) Storytime Ink.

—Folding Stories: Storytelling & Origami Together As One. LC 91-90852. (Illus.). 96p. (Orig.). (gr. k-8). 1991. pap. text ed. 11.50 (0-9628769-0-9, 1001); pre-folded origami models 9.50 (0-9628769-2-5) Storytime Ink.

—Holiday Folding Stories: Storytelling & Origami Together for Holiday Fun. LC 91-68161. (Illus.). 96p. (Orig.). 1992. pap. 11.50 (0-9628769-1-7) Storytime Ink.

Kallstrom, Theresa. Lyndy. York, Sherri, ed. Iarsen, Barbara, illus. LC 87-50259. 44p. (Orig.). (gr. 3 up). 1987. pap. 3.95 (1-55523-081-4) Winston-Derek.

Kalman, Bobbie. All about Me Activity Guide. (Illus.). 96p. (gr. k-2). 1985. pap. 15.95 (0-86505-066-X) Crabtree Pub Co.

—Animal Babies. (Illus.). 56p. (gr. 3-4). 1987. 15.95 (0-86505-166-6); pap. 7.95 (0-86505-186-0) Crabtree Pub Co.

—Animal Worlds. (Illus.). 32p. (gr. 2-3). 1986. 15.95 (0-86505-071-6); pap. 7.95 (0-86505-093-7) Crabtree Pub Co.

—Arctic Animals. (Illus.). 56p. (gr. 3-4). 1988. 15.95 (0-86505-145-3); pap. 7.95 (0-86505-155-0) Crabtree Pub Co.

—The Arctic Land. (Illus.). 56p. (gr. 3-4). 1988. 15.95 (0-86505-144-5); pap. 7.95 (0-86505-154-2) Crabtree Pub Co.

—Arctic Whales & Whaling. (Illus.). 56p. (gr. 3-4). 1988. 15.95 (0-86505-146-1); pap. 7.95 (0-86505-156-9) Crabtree Pub Co.

—Birds at My Feeder. (Illus.). 56p. (gr. 3-4). 1987. 15.95 (0-86505-167-4); pap. 7.95 (0-86505-187-9) Crabtree Pub Co.

—Buried in Garbage. 32p. (gr. 3-4). 1991. PLB 15.95 (0-86505-424-X); pap. 7.95 (0-86505-454-1) Crabtree Pub Co.

—Canada Celebrates Multiculturalism. (Illus.). 32p. (Orig.). (gr. 3-6). 1993. PLB 15.95 (0-86505-220-4); pap. 7.95 (0-86505-300-6) Crabtree Pub Co.

—China - the Culture. (Illus.). 32p. (gr. 4-5). 1989. PLB 15.95 (*0-86505-209-3*); pap. 7.95 (*0-86505-289-1*) Crabtree Pub Co.
—China - The Land. (Illus.). 32p. (gr. 4-5). 1989. PLB 15.95 (*0-86505-207-7*); pap. 7.95 (*0-86505-287-5*) Crabtree Pub Co.
—China - The People. (Illus.). 32p. (gr. 4-5). 1989. PLB 15.95 (*0-86505-208-5*); pap. 7.95 (*0-86505-288-3*) Crabtree Pub Co.
—Colonial Crafts. (Illus.). 32p. (gr. k-9). 1992. PLB 15.95 (*0-86505-490-8*); pap. 7.95 (*0-86505-510-6*) Crabtree Pub CO.
—Colonial Life. (Illus.). 32p. (gr. k-9). 1992. PLB 15.95 (*0-86505-491-6*); pap. 7.95 (*0-86505-511-4*) Crabtree Pub Co.
—A Colonial Town: Williamsburg. (Illus.). 32p. (gr. k-9). 1992. PLB 15.95 (*0-86505-489-4*); pap. 7.95 (*0-86505-509-2*) Crabtree Pub Co.
—The Colors of Nature. (Illus.). 32p. (Orig.). (gr. 3-6). 1993. PLB 15.95 (*0-86505-557-2*); pap. 7.95 (*0-86505-583-1*) Crabtree Pub Co.
—Come to My Place. (Illus.). 32p. (gr. k-2). 1985. 15.95 (*0-86505-062-7*); pap. 7.95 (*0-86505-086-4*) Crabtree Pub Co.
—Early Artisans. (Illus.). 64p. (gr. 4-5). 1983. 15.95 (*0-86505-023-6*); pap. 7.95 (*0-86505-022-8*) Crabtree Pub Co.
—Early Christmas. (Illus.). 64p. (gr. 4-5). 1981. 15.95 (*0-86505-001-5*); pap. 7.95 (*0-86505-003-1*) Crabtree Pub Co.
—Early City Life. (Illus.). 64p. (gr. 4-5). 1983. 15.95 (*0-86505-029-5*); pap. 7.95 (*0-86505-028-7*) Crabtree Pub Co.
—The Early Family Home. (Illus.). 64p. (gr. 4-5). 1982. 15.95 (*0-86505-017-1*); pap. 7.95 (*0-86505-016-3*) Crabtree Pub Co.
—Early Health & Medicine. (Illus.). 64p. (gr. 4-5). 1983. 15.95 (*0-86505-031-7*); pap. 7.95 (*0-86505-030-9*) Crabtree Pub Co.
—Early Pleasures & Pastimes. (Illus.). 96p. (gr. 4-5). 1983. 15.95 (*0-86505-025-2*); pap. 8.95 (*0-86505-024-4*) Crabtree Pub Co.
—Early Schools. (Illus.). 64p. (gr. 4-5). 1982. 15.95 (*0-86505-015-5*); pap. 7.95 (*0-86505-014-7*) Crabtree Pub Co.
—Early Settler Children. (Illus.). 64p. (gr. 4-5). 1982. 15.95 (*0-86505-019-8*); pap. 7.95 (*0-86505-018-X*) Crabtree Pub Co.
—Early Settler Storybook. (Illus.). 64p. (gr. 4-5). 1982. 15.95 (*0-86505-021-X*); pap. 7.95 (*0-86505-020-1*) Crabtree Pub Co.
—Early Stores & Markets. (Illus.). 64p. (gr. 4-5). 1981. 15.95 (*0-86505-002-3*); pap. 7.95 (*0-86505-004-X*) Crabtree Pub Co.
—Early Travel. (Illus.). 64p. (gr. 4-5). 1981. 15.95 (*0-86505-007-4*); pap. 7.95 (*0-86505-008-2*) Crabtree Pub Co.
—Early Village Life. (Illus.). 64p. (gr. 4-5). 1981. 15.95 (*0-86505-009-0*); pap. 7.95 (*0-86505-010-4*) Crabtree Pub Co.
—Eighteenth Century Clothing. DeBiasi, Antoinette, illus. 32p. (Orig.). (gr. 3-6). 1993. PLB 15.95 (*0-86505-492-4*); pap. 7.95 (*0-86505-512-2*) Crabtree Pub Co.
—Food for the Settler. (Illus.). 96p. (gr. 4-5). 1982. 15.95 (*0-86505-013-9*); pap. 8.95 (*0-86505-012-0*) Crabtree Pub Co.
—The Food We Eat. (Illus.). 32p. (gr. 2-3). 1986. 15.95 (*0-86505-073-2*); pap. 7.95 (*0-86505-095-3*) Crabtree Pub Co.
—Forest Mammals. Loates, Glen, illus. 56p. (gr. 3-4). 1987. 15.95 (*0-86505-165-8*); pap. 7.95 (*0-86505-185-2*) Crabtree Pub Co.
—Fun with My Friends. (Illus.). 32p. (gr. k-2). 1985. 15.95 (*0-86505-063-5*); pap. 7.95 (*0-86505-087-2*) Crabtree Pub Co.
—The Gristmill. (Illus.). 32p. (gr. 3-4). 1991. PLB 15.95 (*0-86505-486-X*); pap. 7.95 (*0-86505-506-8*) Crabtree Pub Co.
—Happy to Be Me. (Illus.). 32p. (gr. k-2). 1985. 15.95 (*0-86505-060-0*); pap. 7.95 (*0-86505-084-8*) Crabtree Pub Co.
—Home Crafts. (Illus.). 32p. (gr. 3-4). 1990. PLB 15.95 (*0-86505-485-1*); pap. 7.95 (*0-86505-505-X*) Crabtree Pub Co.
—How We Communicate. (Illus.). 32p. (gr. 2-3). 1986. 15.95 (*0-86505-074-0*) Crabtree Pub Co.
—How We Travel. (Illus.). 32p. (gr. 2-3). 1986. 15.95 (*0-86505-076-7*) Crabtree Pub Co.
—I Like School. (Illus.). 32p. (gr. k-2). 1985. 15.95 (*0-86505-064-3*); pap. 7.95 (*0-86505-088-0*) Crabtree Pub Co.
—I Live in a City. (Illus.). 32p. (gr. 2-3). 1986. 15.95 (*0-86505-070-8*); pap. 7.95 (*0-86505-092-9*) Crabtree Pub Co.
—India: The Culture. (Illus.). 32p. (gr. 4-5). 1990. PLB 15.95 (*0-86505-212-3*); pap. 7.95 (*0-86505-292-1*) Crabtree Pub Co.
—India: The Land. (Illus.). 32p. (gr. 4-5). 1990. PLB 15.95 (*0-86505-210-7*); pap. 7.95 (*0-86505-290-5*) Crabtree Pub Co.
—India: The People. (Illus.). 32p. (gr. 4-5). 1990. PLB 15.95 (*0-86505-211-5*); pap. 7.95 (*0-86505-291-3*) Crabtree Pub Co.
—Japan: The Culture. (Illus.). 32p. (gr. 4-5). 1989. PLB 15.95 (*0-86505-206-9*); pap. 7.95 (*0-86505-286-7*) Crabtree Pub Co.

—Japan: The Land. (Illus.). 32p. (gr. 4-5). 1989. PLB 15.95 (*0-86505-204-2*); pap. 7.95 (*0-86505-284-0*) Crabtree Pub Co.
—Japan: The People. (Illus.). 32p. (gr. 4-5). 1989. PLB 15.95 (*0-86505-205-0*); pap. 7.95 (*0-86505-285-9*) Crabtree Pub Co.
—The Kitchen. (Illus.). 32p. (gr. 3-4). 1990. PLB 15.95 (*0-86505-484-3*); pap. 7.95 (*0-86505-504-1*) Crabtree Pub Co.
—Life Through the Ages. (Illus.). 32p. (gr. 2-3). 1986. 15.95 (*0-86505-075-9*) Crabtree Pub Co.
—Mexico - the Culture. (Illus.). 32p. (Orig.). (gr. 3-6). 1993. PLB 15.95 (*0-86505-216-6*); pap. 7.95 (*0-86505-296-4*) Crabtree Pub Co.
—Mexico - the Land. (Illus.). 32p. (Orig.). (gr. 3-6). 1993. PLB 15.95 (*0-86505-214-X*); pap. 7.95 (*0-86505-294-8*) Crabtree Pub Co.

—Mexico - The People. (Illus.). 32p. (Orig.). (gr. 3-6). 1993. PLB 15.95 (*0-86505-215-8*); pap. 7.95 (*0-86505-295-6*) Crabtree Pub Co. MEXICO: THE PEOPLE--Mexico is an old land with a very young population. More than 50% of its people are under the age of twenty & nearly 75% are under thirty. Mexico's population is increasing much faster than that of the United States or Canada. In this colorful volume, young readers will see the lives of Mexicans at home, at school, & at work. They will get a glimpse of the difficult lives many children must lead because of poverty. The values & traditions of these people will be explored, as well as how life differs in urban & rural settings. Readers will also be shown the problems facing the people of Mexico, & why many are forced to leave their homeland. For children who want to understand our world today, MEXICO: THE PEOPLE is essential reading. Topics in MEXICO: THE PEOPLE include: The many faces of Mexico; Family life; Clothes & costumes; Religions & beliefs; The working world; Language & education; Mexican heroes; Mexico's future & many more. MEXICO: THE PEOPLE is one of three books about Mexico in Crabtree's LANDS, PEOPLES, & CULTURES SERIES. Also included are MEXICO: THE LAND & MEXICO: THE CULTURE. *Publisher Provided Annotation.*

—My Busy Body. (Illus.). 32p. (gr. k-2). 1985. 15.95 (*0-86505-065-1*); pap. 7.95 (*0-86505-089-9*) Crabtree Pub Co.
—Natural Resources. (Illus.). 32p. (gr. 2-3). 1987. 15.95 (*0-86505-077-5*); pap. 7.95 (*0-86505-099-6*) Crabtree Pub Co.
—Nineteenth Century Clothing. DeBiasi, Antoinette, illus. 32p. (Orig.). (gr. 3-6). 1993. PLB 15.95 (*0-86505-493-2*); pap. 7.95 (*0-86505-513-0*) Crabtree Pub Co.
—Our Earth. (Illus.). 32p. (gr. 2-3). 1987. 15.95 (*0-86505-078-3*); pap. 7.95 (*0-86505-100-3*) Crabtree Pub Co.
—Owls. Loates, Glen, illus. 56p. (gr. 3-4). 1987. 15.95 (*0-86505-164-X*); pap. 7.95 (*0-86505-184-4*) Crabtree Pub Co.
—People & Places. (Illus.). 32p. (gr. 2-3). 1987. 15.95 (*0-86505-079-1*); pap. 7.95 (*0-86505-101-1*) Crabtree Pub Co.
—People at Play. (Illus.). 32p. (gr. 2-3). 1986. 15.95 (*0-86505-069-4*); pap. 7.95 (*0-86505-091-0*) Crabtree Pub Co.
—People at Work. (Illus.). 32p. (gr. 2-3). 1986. 15.95 (*0-86505-068-6*); pap. 7.95 (*0-86505-090-2*) Crabtree Pub Co.
—People in My Family. (Illus.). 32p. (gr. k-2). 1985. 15.95 (*0-86505-061-9*); pap. 7.95 (*0-86505-085-6*) Crabtree Pub Co.
—The Primary Ecology Series, 6 vols. (Illus.). 32p. (gr. k-8). 1992. Set. PLB 95.70 (*0-86505-576-9*); Set. pap. 47.70 (*0-86505-602-1*) Crabtree Pub Co.
—Reducing, Reusing, & Recycling. (Illus.). 32p. (gr. 3-4). 1991. PLB 15.95 (*0-86505-426-6*); pap. text ed. 7.95 (*0-86505-456-8*) Crabtree Pub Co.
—Tibet. (Illus.). 32p. (gr. 4-5). 1990. PLB 15.95 (*0-86505-213-1*); pap. 7.95 (*0-86505-293-X*) Crabtree Pub Co.

—Time & the Seasons. (Illus.). 32p. (gr. 2-3). 1986. 15.95 (*0-86505-072-4*); pap. 7.95 (*0-86505-094-5*) Crabtree Pub Co.
—Tools & Gadgets. (Illus.). 32p. (gr. k-9). 1992. PLB 15.95 (*0-86505-488-6*); pap. 7.95 (*0-86505-508-4*) Crabtree Pub CO.
—Visiting a Village. (Illus.). 32p. (gr. 3-4). 1990. PLB 15.95 (*0-86505-487-8*); pap. 7.95 (*0-86505-507-6*) Crabtree Pub Co.
—We Celebrate Christmas. (Illus.). 56p. (gr. 3-4). 1985. 15.95 (*0-86505-040-6*); pap. 7.95 (*0-86505-050-3*) Crabtree Pub Co.
—We Celebrate Easter. (Illus.). 56p. (gr. 3-4). 1985. 15.95 (*0-86505-042-2*); pap. 7.95 (*0-86505-052-X*) Crabtree Pub Co.
—We Celebrate Family Days. (Illus.). 56p. (gr. 3-4). 1986. 15.95 (*0-86505-048-1*); pap. 7.95 (*0-86505-058-9*) Crabtree Pub Co.
—We Celebrate Halloween. (Illus.). 56p. (gr. 3-4). 1985. 15.95 (*0-86505-039-2*); pap. 7.95 (*0-86505-049-X*) Crabtree Pub Co.
—We Celebrate Hanukkah. (Illus.). 56p. (gr. 3-4). 1986. 15.95 (*0-86505-045-7*); pap. 7.95 (*0-86505-055-4*) Crabtree Pub Co.
—We Celebrate Harvest. (Illus.). 56p. (gr. 3-4). 1986. 15.95 (*0-86505-044-9*); pap. 7.95 (*0-86505-054-6*) Crabtree Pub Co.
—We Celebrate New Year. (Illus.). 56p. (gr. 3-4). 1985. 15.95 (*0-86505-041-4*); pap. 7.95 (*0-86505-051-1*) Crabtree Pub Co.
—We Celebrate Spring. (Illus.). 56p. (gr. 3-4). 1985. 15.95 (*0-86505-043-0*); pap. 7.95 (*0-86505-053-8*) Crabtree Pub Co.
—We Celebrate Valentine's Day. (Illus.). 56p. (gr. 3-4). 1986. 15.95 (*0-86505-047-3*); pap. 7.95 (*0-86505-057-0*) Crabtree Pub Co.
—We Celebrate Winter. (Illus.). 56p. (gr. 3-4). 1986. 15.95 (*0-86505-046-5*); pap. 7.95 (*0-86505-056-2*) Crabtree Pub Co.
Kalman, Bobbie & Belsey, William. An Arctic Community. (Illus.). 56p. (gr. 3-4). 1988. 15.95 (*0-86505-147-X*); pap. 7.95 (*0-86505-157-7*) Crabtree Pub Co.
Kalman, Bobbie & Everts, Tammy. Customs & Traditions. LC 93-39882. 1994. PLB 15.95 (*0-86505-495-9*); pap. 7.95 (*0-86505-515-7*) Crabtree Pub Co.
Kalman, Bobbie & Schaub, Janine. The Air I Breathe. DeBiasi, Antoinette, illus. 32p. (Orig.). (gr. k-8). 1993. PLB 15.95 (*0-86505-556-4*); pap. 7.95 (*0-86505-582-3*) Crabtree Pub Co.
—Canada - the Culture. (Illus.). 32p. (Orig.). (gr. 3-6). 1993. PLB 15.95 (*0-86505-219-0*); pap. 7.95 (*0-86505-299-9*) Crabtree Pub Co.

—Canada - the Land. (Illus.). 32p. (Orig.). (gr. 3-6). 1993. PLB 15.95 (*0-86505-217-4*); pap. 7.95 (*0-86505-297-2*) Crabtree Pub Co. CANADA: THE LAND--Canada: the name brings to mind images of wilderness & wide-open spaces. It suggests snow-capped mountains, prairie grasslands, rugged coastlines, & thousands of freshwater lakes. Canada offers a great store of natural resources--timber, minerals, & wheat are just a few. From its southern border with the United States, Canada rises to meet the far north--the Land of the Midnight Sun. Between the Atlantic & Pacific oceans, an endless variety of landscapes forever change with each season. Huge cosmopolitan cities, bustling with life draw immigrants & visitors from all over the world. Exciting color photographs capture the natural wonder of this vast, beautiful land. Topics in CANADA: THE LAND including: Canada's six regions; industry & business; agriculture; Canadian cities; transportation--trains, boats, & snowmobiles; national parks & wildlife; across the provinces & territories, & many, many others. CANADA: THE LAND is one of four books about Canada in Crabtree's LANDS, PEOPLES, & CULTURES SERIES. Others include CANADA: THE PEOPLE; CANADA: THE CULTURE; & CANADA CELEBRATES

MULTICULTURALISM.
Publisher Provided Annotation.

—Canada - the People. (Illus.). 32p. (Orig.). (gr. 3-6). 1993. PLB 15.95 (*0-86505-218-2*); pap. 7.95 (*0-86505-298-0*) Crabtree Pub Co.
—How Trees Help Me. (Illus.). 32p. (gr. k-8). 1992. PLB 15.95 (*0-86505-554-8*); pap. 7.95 (*0-86505-580-7*) Crabtree Pub Co.
—I Am a Part of Nature. (Illus.). 32p. (gr. k-8). 1992. PLB 15.95 (*0-86505-552-1*); pap. 7.95 (*0-86505-578-5*) Crabtree Pub Co.
—Squirmy Wormy Composters. (Illus.). 32p. (gr. k-8). 1992. PLB 15.95 (*0-86505-555-6*); pap. 7.95 (*0-86505-581-5*) Crabtree Pub Co.
—Wonderful Water. (Illus.). 32p. (gr. k-8). 1992. PLB 15.95 (*0-86505-553-X*); pap. 7.95 (*0-86505-579-3*) Crabtree Pub Co.
Kalman, Bobbie, ed. see Taylor, Dave.
Kalman, Maira. Chicken Soup, Boots. Kalman, Maira, illus. 40p. 1993. reinforced bdg. 14.99 (*0-670-85201-5*) Viking Child Bks.
—Hey Willy, See the Pyramids. (ps-3). 1988. pap. 14.95 (*0-670-82163-2*) Viking Child Bks.
—Hey Willy, See the Pyramids. (ps-3). 1990. pap. 4.95 (*0-14-050840-6*, Puffin) Puffin Bks.
—Max in Hollywood, Baby. Kalman, Maira, illus. 32p. 1992. 15.00 (*0-670-84479-9*) Viking Child Bks.
—Max Makes a Million. 1990. 15.00 (*0-670-83545-5*) Viking Child Bks.
—Ooh la la (Max in Love) 1991. 15.00 (*0-670-84163-3*) Viking Child Bks.
—Roarr! Calder's Circus. (ps-3). 1993. pap. 16.95 (*0-385-30916-3*) Doubleday.
—Sayonara, Mrs. Kackleman. Kalman, Maira, illus. 40p. (ps-5). 1989. pap. 14.95 (*0-670-82945-5*) Viking Child Bks.
—Sayonara, Mrs. Kackleman. 32p. 1991. 4.95 (*0-14-054159-4*, Puffin) Puffin Bks.
Kalmenoff, Matthew. Dinosaur Dioramas to Cut & Assemble. 1983. pap. 4.95 (*0-486-24541-1*) Dover.
Kalnay, Francis. Chucaro: Wild Pony of the Pampa. De Miskey, Julian, illus. 115p. 1993. pap. 6.95 (*0-8027-7387-7*) Walker & Co.
Kalnoky, Julius, tr. see Erben, Karel J.
Kamatsu, Yoshio. Children of the World: Bhutan. LC 88-21051. (Illus.). 64p. (gr. 5-6). 1988. PLB 19.93 (*1-55532-867-9*) Gareth Stevens Inc.
Kamba, Polo. Why Do Africans Hate Cats. Scalist, Paula, ed. (Illus.). 98p. 1990. pap. 7.95x (*0-685-28131-0*) Backwards & Backwards.
Kamen, Betty. The Chromium Diet, Supplement & Exercise Strategy: An Easy to Follow Routine for Everyone. Rosenbaum, Michael E., intro. by. (Illus.). 216p. (Orig.). 1990. pap. 9.95 (*0-944501-03-6*) Nutrition Encounter.
—New Facts about Fiber: Health Builder Disease Fighter Vital Nutrient. (Illus.). 152p. (Orig.). 1991. pap. 8.95 (*0-944501-04-4*) Nutrition Encounter.
Kamen, Gloria. Charlie Chaplin. Kamen, Gloria, illus. LC 82-1674. 96p. (gr. 2-6). 1982. SBE 13.95 (*0-689-30925-2*, Atheneum Child Bk) Macmillan Child Grp.
—Edward Lear: King of Nonsense. Lear, Edward, illus. LC 89-28023. 80p. (gr. 2-7). 1990. SBE 13.95 (*0-689-31419-1*, Atheneum Child Bk) Macmillan Child Grp.
—Kipling: Storyteller of East & West. LC 85-7945. (Illus.). 80p. (gr. 3 up). 1985. SBE 13.95 (*0-689-31195-8*, Atheneum Child Bk) Macmillan Child Grp.
—Paddle, Said the Swan. Kamen, Gloria, illus. LC 88-16749. 32p. (ps-1). 1989. SBE 13.95 (*0-689-31330-6*, Atheneum Child Bk) Macmillan Child Grp.
—The Ringdoves: From the Fables of Bidpai. Kamen, Gloria, illus. LC 87-17404. 32p. (gr. k-3). 1988. SBE 13.95 (*0-689-31312-8*, Atheneum Child Bk) Macmillan Child Grp.
—Second-Hand Cat. Kamen, Gloria, illus. LC 91-250. 32p. (gr. k-3). 1992. SBE 13.95 (*0-689-31631-3*, Atheneum Child Bk) Macmillan Child Grp.
Kamenetz. The Pool of Nectar. (gr. 4 up). 1993. 22.50 (*0-8050-2226-0*) H Holt & Co.
Kamerman, Sylvia E. Plays of Great Achievers. 366p. (Orig.). 1992. pap. 16.95 (*0-8238-0297-3*) Plays.
Kamerman, Sylvia E., ed. The Big Book of Christmas Plays. LC 88-15691. (gr. 4-12). 1988. 18.95 (*0-8238-0288-4*) Plays.
—The Big Book of Comedies. 1989. 18.95 (*0-8238-0289-2*) Plays.
—The Big Book of Dramatized Classics: 25 Adaptations of Favorite Novels, Stories, & Plays for Stage & Round-the-Table Reading. LC 93-3387. 400p. (gr. 1-8). 1993. 18.95 (*0-8238-0299-X*) Plays.
—The Big Book of Folktale Plays. 336p. (gr. 3-7). 1991. 18.95 (*0-8238-0294-9*) Plays.
—The Big Book of Holiday Plays. LC 90-7615. 335p. 1990. 18.95 (*0-8238-0291-4*) Plays.
—Children's Plays from Favorite Stories. 583p. (gr. 1-6). 1990. pap. 16.95 (*0-8238-0270-1*) Plays.
—Christmas Play Favorites for Young People. (Orig.). (gr. 4-12). 1982. pap. 12.00 (*0-8238-0257-4*) Plays.
—Patriotic & Historical Plays for Young People. rev. ed. LC 87-15413. 200p. (gr. 3-9). 1987. pap. 13.95 (*0-8238-0285-X*) Plays.
—Plays from Favorite Folk Tales. LC 87-12960. (Orig.). (gr. 2 up). 1987. pap. 13.95 (*0-8238-0280-9*) Plays.

—Plays of Black Americans. LC 87-12207. (Orig.). (gr. 2-9). 1987. pap. 13.95 (*0-8238-0279-5*) Plays.
Kamhi, Ralph. Hi Fives. (Illus.). 8p. (gr. 4-5). 1990. write for info. wkbk. (*0-9627292-1-3*) Extra NY.
—The Times of Your Life. 8p. (gr. 6-12). 1989. write for info. (*0-9627292-0-5*) Extra NY.
Kamins, Tamar. The B. Y. Times Kid Sisters: The "I-Can't-Cope-Club, No. 1. 1992. pap. 5.95 (*0-944070-84-1*) Targum Pr.
—The B. Y. Times Kid Sisters: The Treehouse Kids, No. 2. 1992. pap. 5.95 (*0-944070-92-2*) Targum Pr.
Kaminski, Gerald. Good Questions. Cooper, Ryan M., illus. 32p. (Orig.). (gr. k-3). 1980. pap. 5.95 (*0-931896-00-2*) Cove View.
Kamm, Anthony. The Story of Islam. Galvani, Maureen, illus. 32p. (gr. 4-8). 1987. pap. 3.95 (*0-317-59499-0*) Cambridge U Pr.
Kamm, Karlyn & Chastain, Gerald, Jr. Central Thought. (gr. 5). Date not set. incl. software 95.00 (*0-912899-14-X*) Lrning Multi-Systs.
—Central Thought. (gr. 3). Date not set. incl. software 70.00 (*0-912899-10-7*) Lrning Multi-Systs.
—Paraphrase. (gr. 5). Date not set. incl. software 95.00 (*0-912899-16-6*) Lrning Multi-Systs.
—Paraphrase. (gr. 3). Date not set. incl. software 70.00 (*0-912899-12-3*) Lrning Multi-Systs.
—Relationships - Conclusions. (gr. 3). Date not set. incl. software 70.00 (*0-912899-13-1*) Lrning Multi-Systs.
—Sequence. (gr. 5). Date not set. incl. software 95.00 (*0-912899-15-8*) Lrning Multi-Systs.
—Sequence. (gr. 3). Date not set. incl. software 70.00 (*0-912899-11-5*) Lrning Multi-Systs.
—SolarTrack. (gr. 5). Date not set. incl. software 95.00 (*0-912899-17-4*) Lrning Multi-Systs.
Kanabe, Junkichi, jt. auth. see Barnes, Jill.
Kanagy, Ruth A., tr. see Takeshita, Fumiko.
Kanao, Keiko. Kitten up a Tree. Spinner, Stephanie, ed. Greenstein, Mina, designed by. LC 86-21075. (Illus.). 24p. (ps-1). 1987. 7.95 (*0-394-88817-0*) Knopf Bks Yng Read.
Kandoian, Ellen. Maybe She Forgot. LC 89-25271. (Illus.). (ps). 1990. 12.95 (*0-525-65031-8*, Cobblehill Bks) Dutton Child Bks.
—Molly's Seasons. Kandoian, Ellen, illus. LC 91-8039. 32p. (ps-3). 1992. 13.00 (*0-525-65076-8*, Cobblehill Bks) Dutton Child Bks.
Kane, Andrea L. & Martorana, Barbara. Writing Competency Practice. (gr. 7-12). 1980. wkbk. 5.75 (*0-89525-134-5*) Ed Activities.
Kane, Bob, et al. Batman Archives, Vol. 2. Gold, Mike, ed. Robinson, Jerry, et al, illus. Marschall, Rick, intro. by. 288p. 1991. text ed. 39.95 (*1-56389-000-3*) DC Comics.
Kane, George. What's the Next Move? LC 74-12618. (Illus.). (gr. 4-6). 1974. 1.79 (*0-684-15841-8*, Scribner) Macmillan.
Kane, Harnett T. Young Mark Twain & the Mississippi. Bjorklund, L., illus. LC 87-4531. 176p. (gr. 5-9). 1987. lib. bdg. 8.99 (*0-394-90413-3*); pap. 4.99 (*0-394-89182-1*) Random Bks Yng Read.
Kane, June K. Coping with Diet Fads. Rosen, Ruth, ed. (gr. 7-12). 1990. PLB 13.95 (*0-8239-1005-9*) Rosen Group.
Kane, Penny. A Hidden Treasure. LC 89-50049. 87p. (gr. 8-11). 1989. pap. 5.95 (*1-55523-226-4*) Winston-Derek.
Kane, Sandy, ed. see Vrooman, Christine W.
Kane, Thomas. Tales of the Loremasters. Amthor, Terry K. & Ruemmler, John D., eds. Roberts, Tony & Jaquays, Paul, illus. 32p. (Orig.). (gr. 12). 1989. pap. 6.00 (*1-55806-073-1*, 6004) Iron Crown Ent Inc.
Kane, Tom. Tales of the Loremasters, Book 2. Ruemmler, John D., ed. Martin, David & Jaquays, Paul, illus. 32p. (Orig.). (gr. 12). 1989. pap. 6.00 (*1-55806-034-0*, 6008) Iron Crown Ent Inc.
Kaner, Etta. Balloon Science. (gr. 4-7). 1990. pap. 9.95 (*0-201-52378-7*) Addison-Wesley.
—Balloon Science. (gr. 4-7). 1993. pap. 9.95 (*0-201-62640-3*) Addison-Wesley.
Kaner, Steve. I Am Not Jenny. Beinicke, Steve, illus. 32p. (ps-2). 1991. 13.95 (*0-88899-142-8*, Pub. by Groundwood-Douglas & McIntyre CN) Firefly Bks Ltd.
Kanetzke, Howard W. Airplanes & Balloons. rev. ed. LC 87-23230. (Illus.). 48p. (gr. 2-6). 1987. PLB 18.64 (*0-8172-3251-6*) Raintree Steck-V.
—The Story of Cars. rev. ed. LC 87-23231. (Illus.). 48p. (gr. 2-6). 1987. PLB 18.64 (*0-8172-3261-3*); pap. 4.49 (*0-8114-8217-0*) Raintree Steck-V.
—Trains & Railroads. rev. ed. LC 87-20813. (Illus.). 48p. (gr. 2-6). 1987. PLB 18.64 (*0-8172-3263-X*); pap. 4.49 (*0-8114-8222-7*) Raintree Steck-V.
Kangas, Juli. Fluffy Bunny's Friend. Kangas, Juli, illus. LC 90-84676. 12p. (ps). 1992. 2.95 (*0-448-40140-1*, G&D) Putnam Pub Group.
—Ginger Kitten's Surprise. Kangas, Juli, illus. LC 90-84675. 12p. (ps). 1992. 2.95 (*0-448-40139-8*, G&D) Putnam Pub Group.
—Hello, Honey Bear. Kangas, Juli, illus. LC 90-84672. 12p. (ps). 1992. 2.95 (*0-448-40141-X*, G&D) Putnam Pub Group.
Kanitkar, Helen & Kanitkar, Hemant. Asoka & Indian Civilization. Yapp, Malcolm, et al, eds. (Illus.). 32p. (gr. 6-11). 1980. pap. text ed. 3.45 (*0-89908-010-3*) Greenhaven.
Kanitkar, Hemant, jt. auth. see Kanitkar, Helen.
Kanner, Catherine, illus. Fun with Ballet. 1992. incl. cass. 16.95 (*0-8362-4214-9*) Andrews & McMeel.

Kanno, Wendy. Bags the Lamb. Reese, Bob, illus. (gr. k-2). 1984. 7.95 (*0-89868-165-0*); pap. 2.95 (*0-89868-166-9*) ARO Pub.
—Elmo Pig. Reese, Bob, illus. (gr. k-2). 1984. 7.95 (*0-89868-161-8*); pap. 2.95 (*0-89868-162-6*) ARO Pub.
—Elmo Pig. Reese, Bob, illus. (gr. k-3). 1984. pap. 20.00 (*0-685-50870-6*) ARO Pub.
—The Funny Farm House. Reese, Bob, illus. (gr. k-2). 1984. 7.95 (*0-89868-155-3*); pap. 2.95 (*0-89868-156-1*) ARO Pub.
—Holy Moley Cow. Reese, Bob, illus. (gr. k-2). 1984. 7.95 (*0-89868-159-6*); pap. 2.95 (*0-89868-160-X*) ARO Pub.
—Sampson Horse. Reese, Bob, illus. (gr. k-2). 1984. 7.95 (*0-89868-163-4*); pap. 2.95 (*0-89868-164-2*) ARO Pub.
—Twenty Word Funny Farm Series, 6 bks. Reese, Bob, illus. (gr. k-2). 1984. Set. 47.70 (*0-685-50866-8*); Set. pap. 29.50 (*0-89868-154-5*) ARO Pub.
—Waldo Duck. Reese, Bob, illus. (gr. k-2). 1984. 7.95 (*0-89868-157-X*); pap. 2.95 (*0-89868-158-8*) ARO Pub.
Kanome, Kayoko. Little Mop Lost. (ps-3). 1992. 18.95 (*0-87614-738-4*) Carolrhoda Bks.
Kansas City Barbeque Inner Circle Staff. Absolute Barbeque. Venable, Bill, et al, eds. Westman, David, illus. 176p. (Orig.). 1993. pap. 9.95 (*1-882907-04-3*) Old Market.
Kantenwein, Louise. Billy, Kitty & Mousey. 1992. 6.95 (*0-8062-4353-8*) Carlton.
—Danny Boy. 1992. 7.95 (*0-533-10175-1*) Vantage.
—Tiny Tina, Messy Maggie, & Perfect Pal. 1992. 7.95 (*0-533-10174-3*) Vantage.
Kantor, MacKinlay. Gettysburg. LC 87-4576. (Illus.). (gr. 5-9). 1963. pap. 3.95 (*0-394-89181-3*) Random Bks Yng Read.
Kantor, Sid, jt. auth. see Hulbert, Jay.
Kantrowitz, Mildred. Willy Bear. Parker, Nancy W., illus. LC 89-31868. 32p. (ps-1). 1989. pap. 3.95 (*0-689-71345-2*, Aladdin) Macmillan Child Grp.

Kaopuiki, Stacey. Peter Panini's Children's Guide to the Hawaiian Islands, 4 bks. (Illus.). (ps-5). 1991. Set. write for info. (*1-878498-01-0*) Hawaiian Isl Concepts.
Children's educational Hawaiiana series (4 books) (ISBN 1-878498-01-0) Hawaiian Island Concepts, publishers of creative excellence, presents a dynamic series of contemporary children's books designed to teach children about Hawaii. (June 1990/ June 1991). Each title is available separately. The PETER PANINI KEIKI READER ADVENTURE SERIES: BRING ME WHAT I ASK, Kaopuiki, $12.95, 32p., color illus., (gr. pre-2) Entertaining Hawaiian story that will teach children numbers & how to say them in English, Hawaiian & Sign language. Bold & colorful illus. (ISBN 1-878498-03-7); SECRET OF THE HAWAIIAN RAINBOW, Kaopuiki/Wagstaff, $12.95, 32p., color illus., (gr. pre-2) Delightful tale about the making of the Hawaiian rainbow. Chldren will learn about colors & how to say them in English, Hawaiian & Sign language. Exciting beautiful artwork. (ISBN 1-878498-02-9); PETER PANINI'S CHILDREN'S GUIDE TO THE HAWAIIAN ISLANDS, Kaopuiki, $12.95, 52 p., color illus., (gr. 1-5) Informative & magical tour of the special places in Hawaii. Educational & enjoyable reading. A classic in children's Hawaiiana. (ISBN 1-878498-01-0); PETER PANINI & THE SEARCH FOR THE MENEHUNE, Kaopuiki, $10.95, 44p., color illus., (gr. 1-4) A charming story about a search for the elusive & mysterious "MENEHUNE" (Little People). Children will enjoy looking for the hidden Menehune throughout the book. (ISBN 1-878498-00-2).
Publisher Provided Annotation.

Kaopuiki, Stacey S. Bring Me What I Ask: A Hawaiian Story about Numbers. Despins, Cindy R., ed. Wagstaff Advertising Design Staff & Kaopuiki, Stacey S., illus. 32p. (ps-3). 1991. 10.95 (*1-878498-03-7*) Hawaiian Isl Concepts.

—The Secret of the Hawaiian Rainbow: A Hawaiian Story about Colors. Despins, Cindy R., ed. Wagstaff Advertising Design Staff & Wagstaff, Bob, illus. 32p. (ps-3). 1991. 10.95 (*1-878498-02-9*) Hawaiian Isl Concepts.

Kapelman, Helen H. Nini's Way, Bk. 1. Kapelman, Helen H., illus. (gr. k-2). 1988. 4.95 (*0-9621807-0-X*) H H Kapelman.

Kaplan, Andrew. Careers for Artistic Types. (Illus.). 64p. (gr. 7 up). 1991. PLB 13.90 (*1-878841-20-3*) Millbrook Pr.

—Careers for Computer Buffs. (Illus.). 64p. (gr. 7 up). 1991. PLB 13.90 (*1-56294-021-X*) Millbrook Pr.

—Careers for Computer Buffs. 1992. pap. 4.95 (*0-395-63560-8*) HM.

—Careers for Number Lovers. (Illus.). 64p. (gr. 7 up). 1991. PLB 13.90 (*1-878841-21-1*) Millbrook Pr.

—Careers for Outdoor Types. (Illus.). 64p. (gr. 7 up). 1991. PLB 13.90 (*1-56294-022-8*) Millbrook Pr.

—Careers for Outdoor Types. 1992. pap. 4.95 (*0-395-63561-6*) HM.

—Careers for Sports Fans. (Illus.). 64p. (gr. 7 up). 1991. PLB 13.90 (*1-56294-023-6*) Millbrook Pr.

—Careers for Sports Fans. 1992. pap. 4.95 (*0-395-63562-4*) HM.

—Careers for Wordsmiths. (Illus.). 64p. (gr. 7 up). 1991. PLB 13.90 (*1-56294-024-4*) Millbrook Pr.

—Careers for Wordsmiths. 1992. pap. 4.95 (*0-395-63563-2*) HM.

Kaplan, Carol & Becker, Sandi. Three Nanny Goats Gruff. Mitter, Kathy, illus. 33p. (ps). 1989. tchr's. ed. 16.95 (*0-88734-409-7*) Players Pr.

Kaplan, Carol & Lyss, Ester. We're Moving. Gellman, Sim, illus. 32p. (gr. 1-4). 1993. pap. 3.99 (*0-8431-3498-4*) Price Stern.

Kaplan, Carol & Lyss, Esther. Don't Flip, It's Only a Trip. Gellman, Sim, illus. 32p. (gr. 1-4). 1993. pap. 3.99 (*0-8431-3497-6*) Price Stern.

Kaplan, Carol B. Animal Tales Big Book Package, 6 bks. Bolinske, Janet L., ed. Quenell, Midge, illus. 144p. (ps-k). 1988. Set of 6 bks., 24 pgs. ea. bk. 100.00 (*0-88335-759-3*) Milliken Pub Co.

—The Brown Bear Who Wasn't. Bolinske, Janet L., ed. Quenell, Midge, illus. LC 87-63000. (ps-k). 1988. 17.95 (*0-88335-753-4*); pap. 4.95 (*0-88335-076-9*) Milliken Pub Co.

—The Haunted Picnic. Bolinske, Janet L., ed. Quenell, Midge, illus. LC 87-62999. 24p. (Orig.). (ps-k). 1988. 17.95 (*0-88335-754-2*); pap. write for info. (*0-88335-077-7*) Milliken Pub Co.

—Holiday Plays. Mitter, Kathy, illus. 37p. (ps). 1989. tchr's. ed. 16.95 (*0-88734-410-0*) Players Pr.

—The Not-So-Fast Rabbit. Bolinske, Janet L., ed. Quenell, Midge, illus. LC 87-62997. 24p. (Orig.). (ps-k). 1988. 17.95 (*0-88335-755-0*); pap. 4.95 (*0-88335-079-3*) Milliken Pub Co.

—The Picky Pig. Bolinske, Janet L., ed. Quenell, Midge, illus. LC 87-62998. 24p. (Orig.). (ps-k). 1988. spiral bdg. 17.95 (*0-88335-756-9*); pap. 4.95 (*0-88335-078-5*) Milliken Pub Co.

—Tikki Tikki Tembo. Mitter, Kathy, illus. 32p. (ps). 1989. 16.95 (*0-88734-406-2*) Players Pr.

—The Underground Tea Party. Bolinske, Janet L., ed. Quenell, Midge, illus. LC 87-62996. 24p. (Orig.). (ps-k). 1988. spiral-bound Big Book 17.95 (*0-88335-758-5*); pap. 4.95 (*0-88335-080-7*) Milliken Pub Co.

—Wicker's Wishes. Bolinske, Janet L., ed. Quenell, Midge, illus. LC 87-63001. 24p. (Orig.). (ps-k). 1988. 17.95 (*0-88335-757-7*); pap. 4.95 (*0-88335-075-0*) Milliken Pub Co.

Kaplan, David E., jt. auth. see Kaplan, Marcia P.

Kaplan, Don. See with Your Ears: The Creative Music Book. Hoburg, Maryanne R., illus. LC 82-81463. 128p. (Orig.). (gr. 1-7). 1982. pap. 6.95 (*0-938530-09-7*, 09-7); tchr's guide cancelled 2.00 (*0-938530-20-8*, 20-8) Lexikos.

Kaplan, Gisela, jt. auth. see Rajendra, Vijeya.

Kaplan, Jim. The Official Baseball Hall of Fame Book of Super Stars. (gr. 3 up). 1989. pap. 4.95 (*0-671-67379-3*, Little Simon) S&S Trade.

Kaplan, Lawrence. Oliver Cromwell. (Illus.). 112p. (gr. 5 up). 1987. lib. bdg. 17.95 (*0-87754-580-4*) Chelsea Hse.

Kaplan, Lee. Four Eyes. LC 90-71708. 44p. (gr. 1-3). 1991. 5.95 (*1-55523-402-X*) Winston-Derek.

Kaplan, Leslie S. Coping with Stepfamilies. rev. ed. (gr. 7-12). 1991. PLB 13.95 (*0-8239-1371-6*) Rosen Group.

Kaplan, Lisa. Once upon a Cook Book. Kinne, Kathy, illus. 80p. (Orig.). (gr. k-3). pap. 4.00 (*0-937730-01-7*) Good Sign.

Kaplan, Marcia P. & Kaplan, David E. Happiness. Mendez, Phil, et al, illus. 96p. (Orig.). (gr. 1 up). 1986. 5.95 (*0-9617744-3-6*) Cheers.

Kaplan, Marjorie. Henry & the Boy Who Thought Numbers Were Fleas. Chang, Heidi, illus. LC 90-43852. 80p. (gr. 2-4). 1991. SBE 12.95 (*0-02-749351-2*, Four Winds) Macmillan Child Grp.

Kaplan, Shelley. Chameleon. Warshaw, Johanna, illus. LC 92-70212. 24p. 1992. 15.00 (*0-9631833-0-3*) Kaplan IL.

Kaplan, Zoe. Eleanor of Aquitaine. Schlesinger, Arthur M., Jr., intro. by. (Illus.). 112p. (gr. 5 up). 1987. lib. bdg. 17.95 (*0-87754-522-7*) Chelsea Hse.

Kaplow, Robert. Alessandra in Between. LC 91-45343. 208p. (gr. 7 up). 1992. 14.00 (*0-06-023297-8*); PLB 13.89 (*0-06-023298-6*) HarpC Child Bks.

—Alessandra in Love. LC 87-45883. 160p. (gr. 7 up). 1991. pap. 3.50 (*0-06-447053-9*, Trophy) HarpC Child Bks.

Kapoor. Sikh Festivals, Reading Level 4. (Illus.). 48p. (gr. 3-8). 1989. PLB 15.94 (*0-86592-984-X*); 11.95 (*0-685-58774-6*) Rourke Corp.

Kapp, jt. auth. see Larson.

Kappeler, Markus. Big Cats. (Illus.). 32p. (gr. 4-6). 1991. PLB 17.27 (*0-8368-0685-9*) Gareth Stevens Inc.

—Dogs Wild & Domestic. LC 91-2682. (Illus.). 32p. (gr. 4-6). 1991. PLB 17.27 (*0-8368-0686-7*) Gareth Stevens Inc.

—Owls. (Illus.). 32p. (gr. 4-6). 1991. PLB 17.27 (*0-8368-0687-5*) Gareth Stevens Inc.

—Small Cats. LC 92-10655. 1992. PLB 17.27 (*0-8368-0843-6*) Gareth Stevens Inc.

Karabatsos, Lewis T., ed. Bricks & Brackets: A Lowell Activity Book. 19p. (Orig.). (gr. 1-6). 1981. pap. 0.95 (*0-942472-04-7*) Lowell Museum.

Karadzic, Vuk, compiled by. Nine Magic Pea-Hens & Other Serbian Folk-Tales. Adlard, John, tr. 112p. (gr. 3-4). 1990. pap. 10.95 (*0-86315-068-3*, 1310, Pub. by Floris Bks UK) Anthroposophic.

Karas, G. Brian. I Know an Old Lady. LC 93-30420. 1994. 14.95 (*0-590-46575-9*) Scholastic Inc.

Karas, Jacqueline. The Dollhouse. Riches, Judith, illus. LC 92-32262. 32p. (ps up). 1993. 15.00 (*0-688-12480-1*, Tambourine Bks); PLB 14.93 (*0-688-12481-X*, Tambourine Bks) Morrow.

Karasov, Corliss, jt. auth. see Field, Nancy.

Karch, Cheri, ed. see Westfall, Tanja & Miles, Patrick.

Karch, Cheri, ed. see Westfall, Tanja & Miles, Patrick.

Karcher, Pamela, ed. see MacLaurin, Diane.

Karchmer, Sylvan. A Fistful of Alamo Heroes. LC 92-44501. 1994. write for info. (*0-88682-590-3*) Creative Ed.

Karim, F. Heroes of Islam. Incl. Bk. 1. Muhammad; Bk. 2. Abu Bakr; Bk. 3. Umar; Bk. 4. Othman; Bk. 5. Ali; Bk. 6. Khalid Bin Walid; Bk. 7. Mohammad Bin Qasim; Bk. 8. Mahmood of Ghazni; Bk. 9. Mohyuddin; Bk. 10. Sultan Tipu; Bk. 11. Aisha the Truthful; Bk. 12. Hussain the Martyr; Bk. 13. Some Companions of the Prophet-I; Bk. 14. Some Companions of the Prophet-II; Bk. 15. Some Companions of the Prophet-III. Set. pap. 45.00 (*1-56744-036-3*); pap. 3.00 ea. Kazi Pubns.

Karim, Sharon L. The Unicorn Without a Name. 32p. (ps-3). 1994. 12.95 (*1-883703-00-X*) Big Heart Pub.

Karin, Nurit. Ten Little Bunnies. Wilhelm, Hans, illus. LC 93-13450. 1994. pap. 14.00 (*0-671-88026-8*, S&S BFYR) S&S Trade.

Karkowsky, Nancy. Grandma's Soup. Haas, Shelly O., illus. LC 89-30875. 32p. (gr. k-5). 1989. 10.95 (*0-930494-98-9*) Kar Ben.

—The Ten Commandments: Text & Activity Book. (gr. 3-4). 5.95 (*0-317-70145-2*) Behrman.

Karl, Herb. Toom County Mud Race. 1992. pap. 15.00 (*0-385-30540-0*) Doubleday.

Karl, Jean. America Alive. Schoenherr, Ian, illus. LC 92-40539. 1994. write for info. (*0-399-22013-5*, Philomel Bks) Putnam Pub Group.

—Search For the Ten-Winged Dragon. (ps-3). 1990. PLB 14.95 (*0-385-26493-3*) Doubleday.

—Strange Tomorrow. (gr. 7 up). 1988. pap. 2.95 (*0-440-20052-0*, LFL) Dell.

Karl, Jean E. Strange Tomorrow. LC 84-28609. 144p. (gr. 4-7). 1985. 12.95 (*0-525-44162-X*, DCB) Dutton Child Bks.

Karl, Linda & Siegel, Seth M. Daisy Bunny's Teatime. Guell, Fernando & Beelaerts, Marie, illus. 12p. (ps-k). 1994. 3.99 (*0-679-84001-X*) Random Bks Yng Read.

—Rose Bunny's Teatime. Guell, Fernando & Beelaerts, Marie, illus. 12p. (ps-k). 1994. 3.99 (*0-679-84002-8*) Random Bks Yng Read.

—Tulip Bunny's Teatime. Guell, Fernando & Beelaerts, Marie, illus. 12p. (ps-k). 1994. 3.99 (*0-679-84003-6*) Random Bks Yng Read.

—Violet Bunny's Teatime. Guell, Fernando & Beelaerts, Marie, illus. 12p. (ps-k). 1994. 3.99 (*0-679-84004-4*) Random Bks Yng Read.

Karl, Nancy. Activities with Myths. 2nd, expanded ed. (Illus.). 48p. (gr. 4-8). 1991. pap. 5.95 (*1-879287-00-5*) Bk Lures.

Karlenstein, Tzira. Reb Aryeh: A Portrait of the Jerusalem Tzaddik Reb Aryeh Levin. (Illus.). (gr. 4-7). 1989. 11.95 (*0-87306-490-9*) Feldheim.

Karlin, Barbara, retold by. Cinderella. Marshall, James, illus. 32p. (ps-3). 1992. pap. 4.95 (*0-316-48303-6*) Little.

Karlin, Bernie. Meow. 32p. (gr. k-3). 1991. pap. 12.95 jacketed (*0-671-72639-0*, S&S BFYR) S&S Trade.

—Meow! (Illus.). 32p. (ps-3). 1993. pap. 2.50 (*0-671-79603-8*, Little Simon) S&S Trade.

—Shapes: Circle - Square - Triangle, 3 bks. (Illus., 12 pgs. ea. bk.). (ps). 1992. Set. pap. 6.95 (*0-671-74625-1*, Little Simon) S&S Trade.

Karlin, Bernie & Karlin, Mati. Night Ride. Karlin, Bernie, illus. (ps-2). 1988. pap. 12.95 jacketed (*0-671-66733-5*, S&S BFYR) S&S Trade.

Karlin, Mati, jt. auth. see Karlin, Bernie.

Karlin, Nurit. Little Big Mouse. Karlin, Nurit, illus. LC 90-36192. 32p. (ps-1). 1991. PLB 13.89 (*0-06-021608-5*) HarpC Child Bks.

—Ten Little Bunnies. (ps-3). 1994. pap. 4.95 (*0-671-88601-0*, Little Simon) S&S Trade.

—The Tooth Witch. Karlin, Nurit, illus. LC 84-62553. 32p. (ps-2). 1985. pap. 4.95 (*0-06-443079-0*, Trophy) HarpC Child Bks.

Karlins, Mark. A Christmas Fable. Hyde, Maureen, illus. LC 89-29321. 32p. (gr. 1-5). 1990. SBE 13.95 (*0-689-31480-9*, Atheneum Child Bk) Macmillan Child Grp.

—Salmon Moon. Poppel, Hans, illus. LC 92-15702. 1993. pap. 14.00 (*0-671-73624-8*, S&S BFYR) S&S Trade.

Karlinsky, Isaiah & Karlinsky, Ruth. My First Book of Mitzvos. (Illus.). (gr. k-3). 1986. 8.95 (*0-87306-388-0*) Feldheim.

Karlinsky, Ruth, jt. auth. see Karlinsky, Isaiah.

Karlsberg, Elizabeth. How to Make & Keep Friends. Magnuson, Diana, illus. LC 90-48252. 128p. (gr. 5-9). 1991. lib. bdg. 10.89 (*0-8167-2295-1*); pap. text ed. 2.95 (*0-8167-2296-X*) Troll Assocs.

Karnes, Frances A. & Bean, Suzanne M. Girls & Young Women Leading the Way: Twenty True Stories about Leadership. Wallner, Rosemary, ed. LC 93-25874. 168p. (gr. 5 up). 1993. pap. 11.95 (*0-915793-52-0*) Free Spirit Pub.

Karnofsky, Florence & Weiss, Trudy. How to Improve Your Child's Language & Thinking Skills. (ps-5). 1993. pap. 7.95 (*0-86653-931-X*) Fearon Teach Aids.

—How to Make Your Child a Better Listener. (ps-5). 1993. pap. 7.95 (*0-86653-933-6*) Fearon Teach Aids.

—How to Prepare Your Child for Kindergarten. (ps). 1993. pap. 7.95 (*0-86653-932-8*) Fearon Teach Aids.

Karolyi, Otto. Introducing Music. (Orig.). (gr. 11 up). 1965. pap. 5.95 (*0-14-020659-0*, Penguin Bks) Viking Penguin.

Karp, Deborah. Heroes of American Jew History. (Illus.). (gr. 6-7). 1966. pap. 7.95x (*0-87068-539-2*) Ktav.

Karpfinger, Beth, adapted by. The Wonder of Black Bears. Rogers, Lynn, photos by. LC 92-16944. (Illus.). 1992. PLB 18.60 (*0-8368-0855-X*) Gareth Stevens Inc.

Karpin, Florence B. Tree Spirits: The Story of a Boy Who Loved Trees. Karpin, Florence B., illus. 32p. (Orig.). (ps-3). 1992. PLB 14.00 (*0-88150-248-0*) Countryman.

Karr, Kathleen. Gideon & the Mummy Professor. 1993. 16.00 (*0-374-32563-4*) FS&G.

—It Ain't Always Easy. (Illus.). 236p. (gr. 5 up). 1990. 14.95 (*0-374-33645-8*) FS&G.

—Oh, Those Harper Girls! 176p. (gr. 7 up). 1992. 16.00 (*0-374-35609-2*) FS&G.

Karshner, Roger. Monologues for Teenagers. 64p. (gr. 7-12). 1986. pap. 6.95 (*0-9611792-8-7*) Dramaline Pubns.

—Teenage Mouth. 64p. (Orig.). (gr. 8-12). 1991. pap. 7.95 (*0-940669-17-X*) Dramaline Pubns.

Karwatka, Dennis, et al. Introductory Auto Mechanics. 608p. (gr. 9-12). 1986. text ed. 22.95 (*0-8219-0182-6*, 80452); wkbk. 6.95 (*0-8219-0183-4*, 80652); tchr's. guide 28.00 (*0-8219-0184-2*, 80902); transparency masters 89.00 (*0-8219-0489-2*, 80980) EMC.

Kary, Stanley K. Raising Kids: It Ain't Easy, But It Can Be Fun. 1992. 12.95 (*0-533-09576-X*) Vantage.

Kasahara, Kunihiko. Creative Origami. LC 67-87040. (Illus.). 1977. pap. 15.95 (*0-87040-411-3*) Japan Pubns USA.

Kasakov. Goluboe i Zelenoe. (gr. 7-12). 1972. pap. 5.95 (*0-88436-053-9*, 65253) EMC.

Kasakove, David P. & Olitzky, Kerry M. Hebrew, Holidays, & Heroes: The Jewish Fun Book. Lerer, Mark, illus. (gr. 4-6). 1992. pap. 7.00 (*0-8074-0478-0*, 123937) UAHC.

Kasdon, Lawrence, jt. auth. see Potter, Norris.

Kase, Judith B. The Emperor's New Clothes. (gr. k up). 1978. 4.50 (*0-87602-125-9*) Anchorage.

Kase-Baker, Judith. Snow White & the Seven Dwarfs. (ps-6). 1984. pap. 4.50 (*0-87602-256-5*) Anchorage.

Kash, Conrad, adapted by. The Addams Family in "Sir Pugsley" (Illus.). 24p. (ps-4). 1993. 20.00 (*0-307-74031-5*, 64031, Golden Pr) Western Pub.

Kaslow, Florence R. The Puzzled Pumpkin. Phillips, Jennifer, illus. LC 91-60798. 24p. (Orig.). (gr. k-4). 1991. pap. 4.95 (*0-9628321-0-3*) Pumpkin Patch Pubs.

—T-Bend Bagelmaker. Leigh, Avra, ed. 24p. (Orig.). (gr. k-5). 1993. pap. 4.95 (*0-9628321-1-1*) Pumpkin Patch Pubs.

Kaspar, Maria H., jt. auth. see Annable, Toni.

Kaspar, Maria H., jt. auth. see Annable, Toni.

Kasperitis, Brian G. Grandad's Old Tuba. (gr. 4 up). 1993. 7.95 (*0-8062-4726-6*) Carlton.

Kass, Kimberly, retold by. The Velveteen Rabbit. abr. ed. Carpenter, Nancy, illus. LC 92-6036. 22p. (ps). 1993. 3.25 (*0-679-83617-9*) Random Bks Yng Read.

Kassel, April. Slow Joe. Block, Lori, illus. Sargent, Dave, intro. by. (Illus.). 36p. (Orig.). (gr. k-8). 1993. text ed. 12.95 (*1-56763-067-7*); pap. text ed. 5.95 (*1-56763-068-5*) Ozark Pub.

Kassem, Lou. A Haunting in Williamsburg: A Ghost Story. 112p. (gr. 5-6). 1990. pap. 3.50 (*0-380-75892-X*, Camelot) Avon.

—Listen for Rachel. 176p. (gr. 5). 1992. pap. 3.50 (*0-380-71231-8*, Flare) Avon.

—Middle School Blues. 192p. (gr. 3-7). 1987. pap. 3.50 (*0-380-70363-7*, Camelot) Avon.

—Middle School Blues. (gr. 4-7). 1986. 13.45 (*0-395-39499-6*) HM.

—Secret Wishes. 144p. (gr. 3-7). 1989. pap. 2.95 (0-380-75544-0, Camelot) Avon.
—A Summer for Secrets. 112p. 1989. pap. 2.95 (0-380-75759-1, Camelot) Avon.
—The Treasures of Witch Hat Mountain. 112p. (Orig.). 1992. pap. 2.99 (0-380-76519-5, Camelot) Avon.
Kassier, Sue, retold by see Grimm, Jacob & Grimm, Wilhelm K.
Kassirer, Sue. The Gingerbread Boy. Williams, Jennie, illus. 24p. (Orig.). (ps-k). 1993. pap. 1.50 (0-679-84795-2) Random Bks Yng Read.
—The Three Billy Goats Gruff. Fritz, Ron, illus. 24p. (Orig.). (ps-k). pap. 1.50 (0-679-84796-0) Random Bks Yng Read.
Kassirer, Sue, adapted by see Collodi, Carlo.
Kastner. Drei Manner Im Schnee. (gr. 7-12). pap. 5.95 (0-88436-038-5, 45271) EMC.
—Mein Onkel Franz. (gr. 7-12). pap. 4.95 (0-88436-037-7, 45259) EMC.
Kastner, Erich. Lisa & Lottie. Books, Cyrus, tr. De Larrea, Victoria, illus. 136p. (gr. 3-7). 1982. pap. 2.95 (0-380-57117-X, Camelot) Avon.
Kastner, Jill. Snake Hunt. Kastner, Jill, illus. LC 92-32601. 32p. (ps-2). 1993. RSBE 14.95 (0-02-749395-4, Four Winds) Macmillan Child Grp.
Kastner, Joseph. John James Audubon. (Illus.). 92p. 1992. 19.95 (0-8109-1918-4) Abrams.
Kasza, Keiko. A Mother for Choco. Kasza, Keiko, illus. 32p. (ps-1). PLB 14.95 (0-399-21841-6, Putnam) Putnam Pub Group.
—The Pigs' Picnic. Kasza, Keiko, illus. 32p. (ps-1). 1988. PLB 13.95 (0-399-21543-3, Putnam) Putnam Pub Group.
—The Pigs' Picnic. Kasza, Keiko, illus. 32p. (ps-3). 1992. pap. 5.95 (0-399-21883-1, Sandcastle Bks) Putnam Pub Group.
—The Rat & the Tiger. (Illus.). 32p. (ps-3). 1993. PLB 14.95 (0-399-22404-1, Putnam) Putnam Pub Group.
—When the Elephant Walks. Kasza, Keiko, illus. 32p. (ps-1). 1990. 13.95 (0-399-21755-X, Putnam) Putnam Pub Group.
—The Wolf's Chicken Stew. Kasza, Keiko, illus. (gr. k-3). 1987. 13.95 (0-399-21400-3, Putnam) Putnam Pub Group.
—Wolf's Chicken Stew. (ps-3). 1989. (Sandcastle Bks); pap. 5.95 (0-399-22000-3, Sandcastle Bks) Putnam Pub Group.
Katan, Norma J. & Mintz, Barbara. Hieroglyphs: The Writing of Ancient Egypt. Katan, Norma J., illus. LC 80-13576. 96p. (gr. 4-7). 1981. SBE 13.95 (0-689-50176-5, M K McElderry) Macmillan Child Grp.
Katchen, Carole. Your Friend Annie. 1989. pap. 2.75 (0-590-42732-6) Scholastic Inc.
Kates, Bobbi J. We're Different, We're the Same. Mathieu, Joe, illus. LC 91-38545. 32p. (Orig.). (ps-3). 1992. pap. 2.25 (0-679-83227-0) Random Bks Yng Read.

Katherine, Sharon. Sugar Princess. Wood, Paul, ed. Tolley, Lynn & Olds, Tom, illus. 31p. 1989. pap. 8.95 (0-685-68779-1) Jungle Pr.
On a lush tropical island, a lonely voice cries out. Here in this one spot, the land has become parched, cracked & barren. The forces of nature gather around -- the wind, the water, the plants & animals -- & they listen to the lonely voice calling. She cannot come out & play, for she has no "Self." In sympathy, all natural elements work together, each contributing a gift to the lonely voice. The flowers give their colors, the mountain its strength, the moon its brilliance, & so on. In the end, the little voice steps forth in her true condition, a beautiful Sugar Princess! This brilliantly illustrated read-aloud story, which includes a color-it-yourself poster, is the first in a series of "Sharon Katherine" books by author Sharon Morneau. (Jungle Press, P.O. Box 1058, Makawao, HI 96768. (808) 572-3453. FAX: (808) 572-4886.) In this simple tale of transformation, children see the forces of nature working together to create beauty. They learn about cooperation & respect for the environment. By means of the book's glossary, they also learn a few Hawaiian words & the names of various tropical plants & animals. *Publisher Provided Annotation.*

Kato, Horoshi & Takada, Noriko. Just Listen 'n Learn Japanese: Beginning Through Intermediate. (JPN.). 1993. 10.95 (0-685-62854-X, F8387-8, Natl Textbk); pkg. incl. 3 60-min. audiocassettes 29.95 (0-685-62855-8, F8386-X, Natl Textbk) NTC Pub Grp.
Kato, Yoshiko. Animal Foot Prints. 2nd ed. (Illus.). 49p. 1993. Repr. of 1989 ed. 12.95 (0-89346-428-7) Heian Intl.
Kattan-Ibarra, Juan. Conversando: Early Intermediate Through Advanced. 140p. 1993. pap. 14.95 (0-685-62794-2, F7150-0, Natl Textbk); tchr's. manual 7.95 (0-685-62795-0, F7151-9, Natl Textbk); audiocassette tape 15.00 (0-685-62796-9, F7153-5, Natl Textbk) NTC Pub Grp.
Katz, Adrienne. Naturewatch. Lewer, Bridget, illus. (ps up). 1986. pap. 8.61 (0-201-10457-1) Addison-Wesley.
Katz, Avner. Tortoise Solves a Problem. Katz, Avner, illus. LC 91-32503. 40p. (gr. k-3). 1993. 13.00 (0-06-020798-1); PLB 12.89 (0-06-020799-X) HarpC Child Bks.
Katz, Bobbi. The Care Bears & the Big Clean-Up. Kolding, Richard, illus. LC 91-52705. 40p. (ps-4). 1991. 4.99 (0-679-82367-0) Random Bks Yng Read.
—The Family Book of Jewish Holidays. Herzfeld, Caryl, illus. LC 93-27375. 1993. 10.00 (0-679-85820-2) Random Bks Yng Read.
—A Family Hanukkah. Herzfeld, Caryl, illus. LC 91-51093. 40p. (ps-3). 1992. 7.99 (0-679-83240-8); PLB 8.99 (0-679-93240-2) Random Bks Yng Read.
—A Family Hanukkah. Herzfeld, Caryl, illus. 32p. (ps-3). 1993. incl. cass. 7.99 (0-679-85010-4) Random Bks Yng Read.
—Ghosts & Goose Bumps: Poems to Chill Your Bones. Ray, Deborah K., illus. LC 89-37134. 32p. (Orig.). (ps-3). 1991. lib. bdg. 5.99 (0-679-90372-0); pap. 2.25 (0-679-80372-6) Random Bks Yng Read.
—Teenage Mutant Ninja Turtles Don't Do Drugs! A Rap Song. Mones, Isidre, illus. LC 90-53244. 32p. (Orig.). (ps-3). 1991. PLB 5.99 (0-679-91485-4); pap. 2.25 (0-679-81485-X) Random Bks Yng Read.
—Ten Little Care Bears Counting Book. Barto, Bobbi, illus. LC 83-60084. 14p. (ps-k). 1983. 4.95 (0-394-86088-8) Random Bks Yng Read.
—Tick Tock, Let's Beat the Clock: Green Ladder Books for Kids Through 6 Years. Nicklaus, Carol, illus. 16p. (ps-1). 1988. incl. clock 7.99 (0-394-89399-9) Random Bks Yng Read.
—Upside Down & Inside Out: Poems for All Your Pockets. Watson, Wendy, illus. 48p. (ps-3). 1992. PLB 14.95 (1-56397-122-4) Boyds Mills Pr.
Katz, Bobbi & Moseley, Keith. The Fox in the Farmyard. Wilson, Ann, illus. 14p. (ps-3). 1986. 5.95 (0-394-87425-5) Random Bks Yng Read.
Katz, Bobbi, ed. Ghosts & Goose Bumps: Poems to Chill Your Bones. Ray, Deborah K., illus. 32p. (ps-1). 1993. incl. cass. 5.95 (0-679-84799-5) Random Bks Yng Read.
—Puddle Wonderful: Poems to Welcome Spring. Morgan, Mary, illus. LC 91-8066. 32p. (Orig.). (ps-1). 1992. PLB 5.99 (0-679-91493-5); pap. 2.25 (0-679-81493-0) Random Bks Yng Read.
Katz, David. You Can Be a Winner Today: Reading Rap. 40p. (Orig.). (gr. k-4). 1991. pap. 6.00 (1-880599-00-7) Cascade Pass.
Katz, David, jt. auth. see Allison, Linda.
Katz, Ellie. The Conception Connection: The Journey into Creation. rev. ed. Neyndorff, Mark, illus. 100p. (gr. k-12). 1991. pap. 12.95 (1-880806-00-2) Playology Hlth.
Katz, Illana. Joey & Sam: Autism. (ps-3). 1993. pap. 9.95 (1-882388-06-2) Real Life Strybks.
—Sarah: Sexual Abuse. (ps-3). 1993. 16.95 (1-882388-07-0); pap. 9.95 (1-882388-08-9) Real Life Strybks.
—Uncle Jimmy. Schwartz, Stanley, epilogue by Borowitz, Franz, illus. 40p. (gr. k-6). 1993. Smythe Sewn 16.95 (1-882388-03-8) Real Life Strybks.
—Uncle Jimmy: AIDS. (ps-3). 1993. pap. 9.95 (1-882388-09-7) Real Life Strybks.
Katz, Illana & Ritvo, Edward. Joey & Sam: A Heartwarming Storybook about Autism, a Family, & a Brother's Love. Borowitz, Franz, illus. LC 92-38812. 40p. (gr. k-6). 1993. smythe sewn 16.95 (1-882388-00-3) Real Life Strybks.
Katz, Illana & Rosenthal, Alan. Show Me Where It Hurts! Chiropractic Care. (ps-3). 1993. pap. 9.95 (1-882388-10-0) Real Life Strybks.
Katz, Illana & Rosenthal, Alan D. Show Me Where It Hurts. Borowitz, Franz, illus. 40p. (gr. k-6). 1993. smythe sewn 16.95 (1-882388-01-1) Real Life Strybks.
Katz, Marjorie P & Arbeiter, Jean S., eds. Pegs to Hang Ideas on: A Book of Quotations. LC 76-187739. 320p. (gr. 6 up). 1976. 12.95 (0-87131-085-6) M Evans.
Katz, Phyllis. Exploring Science Through Art. (Illus.). (ps-3). 1990. PLB 12.90 (0-531-10890-2) Watts.
Katz, Phyllis & Frekko, Janet. Great Science Fair Projects. Cohn, Tom, ed. (Illus.). 80p. (gr. 3-6). 1992. PLB 12.40 (0-531-11015-X) Watts.
—Great Science Fair Projects. (Illus.). 80p. (gr. 5-8). 1992. pap. 6.95 (0-531-15628-1) Watts.
Katz, Welwyn W. Come Like Shadows. (Illus.). 304p. (gr. 7 up). 1993. 13.99 (0-670-84861-1) Viking Child Bks.
—False Face. LC 88-12847. 176p. (gr. 5-9). 1988. SBE 14.95 (0-689-50456-X, M K McElderry) Macmillan Child Grp.

—Whalesinger. LC 90-34091. 212p. (gr. 7 up). 1991. SBE 14.95 (0-689-50511-6, M K McElderry) Macmillan Child Grp.
—Whalesinger. 1993. pap. 3.50 (0-440-21419-X) Dell.
—Witchery Hill. (gr. k up). 1990. pap. 3.50 (0-440-20637-5, LFL) Dell.
Katz, William. Black Indians: A Hidden Heritage. LC 85-28770. (Illus.). 208p. (gr. 5 up). 1986. SBE 15.95 (0-689-31196-6, Atheneum Child Bk) Macmillan Child Grp.
Katz, William L. The Black West. rev. ed. LC 87-28067. (Illus.). 352p. (gr. 8-12). 1987. 29.95 (0-940880-17-2); pap. 15.95 (0-940880-18-0) Open Hand.
—Breaking the Chains: African-American Slave Resistance. LC 89-36355. (Illus.). 208p. (gr. 5 up). 1990. SBE 15.95 (0-689-31493-0, Atheneum Child Bk) Macmillan Child Grp.
—The Civil War to the Last Frontier, 1850-1880. LC 92-17924. (Illus.). 96p. (gr. 7-8). 1992. PLB 22.80 (0-8114-6277-3) Raintree Steck-V.
—From Exploration to the War of 1812, 1492-1814. LC 92-17363. (Illus.). 96p. (gr. 7-8). 1992. PLB 22.80 (0-8114-6275-7) Raintree Steck-V.
—From World War Two to the New Frontier, 1940-1963. LC 92-42801. (Illus.). 96p. (gr. 7-8). 1993. PLB 22.80 (0-8114-6280-3) Raintree Steck-V.
—The Great Migrations, 1880-1912. LC 92-22426. (Illus.). 96p. (gr. 7-8). 1992. PLB 22.80 (0-8114-6278-1) Raintree Steck-V.
—The Great Society to the Reagan Era, 1964-1993. LC 92-43709. (Illus.). 96p. (gr. 7-8). 1993. PLB 22.80 (0-8114-6282-X) Raintree Steck-V.
—Minorities Today. LC 92-47438. (Illus.). 96p. (gr. 7-8). 1992. PLB 22.80 (0-8114-6281-1) Raintree Steck-V.
—The New Freedom to the New Deal, 1913-1939. LC 92-39948. (Illus.). 96p. (gr. 7-8). 1993. PLB 22.80 (0-8114-6279-X) Raintree Steck-V.
—The Westward Movement & Abolitionism, 1815-1850. LC 92-14965. (Illus.). 96p. (gr. 7-8). 1992. PLB 22.80 (0-8114-6276-5) Raintree Steck-V.
Katz, William L. & Crawford, Marc. The Lincoln Brigade: A Picture History. LC 88-27522. (Illus.). 96p. (gr. 5 up). 1989. SBE 14.95 (0-689-31406-X, Atheneum Child Bk) Macmillan Child Grp.
Katz, William L. & Franklin, Paula A. Proudly Red & Black: Stories of Native & African Americans. LC 92-36119. (Illus.). 96p. (gr. 4-7). 1993. SBE 13.95 (0-689-31801-4, Atheneum Child Bk) Macmillan Child Grp.
—Proudly Red & Black: Tales of Native & African Americans. LC 92-36119. 1993. 13.95 (0-684-31801-6, Atheneum Child Bk) Macmillan Child Grp.
Katz, Wilton W. The Third Magic. LC 88-8387. 208p. (gr. 7 up). 1989. SBE 14.95 (0-689-50480-2, M K McElderry) Macmillan Child Grp.
Katzen, Mollie & Henderson, Ann. Pretend Soup: And Other Real Recipes. Katzen, Mollie, illus. 96p. (ps). 1993. 14.95 (1-883672-06-6) Tricycle Pr.
Kauffman, M. K. The Right Moves. (gr. 7 up). pap. 2.25 (0-317-62895-X) X&S Trade.
Kauffman, Suzanne. God Comforts His People: Activity Book. Converse, James, illus. 84p. (Orig.). (gr. k-6). 1986. pap. 3.00 (0-8361-3411-7) Herald Pr.
—God's Suffering Servant Activity Book. 64p. 1988. pap. 3.00 (0-8361-3450-8) Herald Pr.
Kaufman, Allan. Exploring Solar Energy: Principles & Projects. LC 86-60262. (Illus.). 98p. (gr. 7-12). 1989. pap. 8.95 (0-911168-60-5) Prakken.
Kaufman, Cheryl. Cooking the Caribbean Way. (Illus.). 48p. (gr. 5 up). 1988. PLB 14.95 (0-8225-0920-2) Lerner Pubns.
Kaufman, Curt & Kaufman, Gita. Hotel Boy. Curt, Kaufman, illus. LC 86-25925. 40p. (gr. k-3). 1987. SBE 12.95 (0-689-31287-3, Atheneum Child Bk) Macmillan Child Grp.
Kaufman, Gershen. Journey to a Magic Castle. Jeffery, Megan E., illus. LC 91-78278. 30p. (gr. 5-8). 1993. pap. write for info. incl. worksheets (0-916634-14-0) Double M Pr.
Kaufman, Gershen & Raphael, Lev. Stick up for Yourself! Every Kid's Guide to Personal Power & Positive Self-Esteem. LC 89-28642. (Illus.). 96p. (gr. 2-7). 1990. pap. 8.95 (0-915793-17-2) Free Spirit Pub.
Kaufman, Gita, jt. auth. see Kaufman, Curt.
Kaufman, Jackie, jt. auth. see Hacker, Randi.
Kaufman, John. Milk Rock. 1994. write for info. (0-8050-2814-5) H Holt & Co.
Kaufman, Les & NEA Staff. Alligators to Zooplankton: A Dictionary of Water Babies. (Illus.). 64p. (gr. 5-7). 1991. 15.95 (0-531-15215-4); PLB 15.90 (0-531-10995-X) Watts.
Kaufman, Les, jt. auth. see New England Aquarium Staff.
Kaufman, Mervyn D. Thomas Alva Edison: Miracle Maker. (Illus.). 80p. (gr. 2-6). 1993. Repr. of 1962 ed. lib. bdg. 12.95 (0-7910-1426-6) Chelsea Hse.
—The Wright Brothers: Kings of the Air. (Illus.). 80p. (gr. 2-6). 1993. Repr. of 1964 ed. lib. bdg. 12.95 (0-7910-1428-2) Chelsea Hse.
Kaufman, Tanya & Wishny, Judith. School Events. Piltch, Benjamin, ed. Bartick, Robert, illus. 64p. (gr. 2-5). 1983. 4.00 (0-934618-04-6) Learning Well.
Kaufman, Wallace, tr. see Montejo, Victor.
Kaufmann, Herbert. Adventure in the Desert. Karlin, Eugene, illus. (gr. 7 up). 1961. 10.95 (0-8392-3000-1) Astor-Honor.
—Lost Freedom. (Illus.). (gr. 7 up). 1969. 12.95 (0-8392-3083-4) Astor-Honor.

—Lost Sahara Trail. (gr. 7 up). 1962. 10.95 (0-8392-3022-2) Astor-Honor.
Kaukola, Olavi. About Time to Pray. Hillila, Bernhard, tr. from FIN. & intro. by. 123p. (Orig.). 1991. pap. 7.95 (0-9622985-1-4) Polaris AZ.
—The Riches of Prayer. Hillila, Bernhard, tr. from FIN. & pref. by. 80p. 1991. pap. 7.95 (0-8006-1861-0) Polaris AZ.
Kaur, Sharon. Food in India. LC 88-31294. (Illus.). 32p. (gr. 3-6). 1989. lib. bdg. 15.94 (0-86625-339-4); 11. 95s.p. (0-685-58500-X) Rourke Corp.
Kavanagh, Jack. Dizzy Dean. Murray, Jim, intro. by. (Illus.). 64p. (gr. 3 up). 1991. PLB 14.95 (0-7910-1173-9) Chelsea Hse.
—Honus Wagner. (Illus.). 1994. 14.95 (0-7910-1193-3, Am Art Analog) Chelsea Hse.
—Rogers Hornsby. Murray, Jim, intro. by. (Illus.). 64p. (gr. 3 up). 1991. lib. bdg. 14.95 (0-7910-1178-X) Chelsea Hse.
—Sports Great Joe Montana. LC 91-41527. (Illus.). 64p. (gr. 4-10). 1992. lib. bdg. 15.95 (0-89490-371-3) Enslow Pubs.
—Sports Great Larry Bird. LC 91-41525. (Illus.). 64p. (gr. 4-10). 1992. lib. bdg. 15.95 (0-89490-369-1) Enslow Pubs.
—Sports Great Patrick Ewing. LC 91-41531. (Illus.). 64p. (gr. 4-10). 1992. lib. bdg. 15.95 (0-89490-369-1) Enslow Pubs.
—Walter Johnson. (Illus.). 64p. (gr. 3 up). 1992. lib. bdg. 14.95 (0-7910-1179-8) Chelsea Hse.
Kavanagh, Jack, jt. auth. see Johnson, James E.
Kavanagh, Katie. Home Is Where Your Family Is. Fitzhugh, Greg, illus. 1994. write for info. (0-8114-4462-7) Raintree Steck-V.
Kavanaugh, James. The Crooked Angel. 2nd ed. Havelock, Elaine, illus. LC 90-62058. 64p. (ps-3). 1990. pap. 9.95 (1-878995-02-2) S J Nash Pub.
—A Village Called Harmony - A Fable. 2nd ed. Biamonte, Daniel, illus. LC 90-62063. 70p. 1990. pap. 7.95 (1-878995-06-5) S J Nash Pub.
Kavanaugh, Peter, jt. auth. see Christie, Sally.
Kawai'ae'a, Keiki C. Let's Learn to Count in Hawaiian. Tanaka, Cliff, illus. 24p. (ps-k). 1988. 7.95 (0-89610-076-6) Island Heritage.
—Let's Learn to Count in Hawaiian. Tanaka, Cliff, illus. 24p. (ps-k). 1988. incl. cassette 11.95 (0-89610-080-4) Island Heritage.
Kawami, David. Cut & Assemble Paper Dragons That Fly. 1989. pap. 3.50 (0-486-25325-2) Dover.
Kawaura, Noriko, jt. auth. see Hirate, Susan H.
Kay, Alan N. Jamestown Journey. Van Bergen, Jamie, illus. 56p. (gr. 4-7). 1992. pap. 4.95 (0-939631-52-0) Thomas Publications.
Kay, Gene. Speedy O'Hare's Sun Valley Race. Kay, Gene, illus. 36p. (ps-7). 1987. pap. 8.95 (0-945222-24-6) Gazelle Prodns.
Kay, Helen. The First Teddy Bear. Detwiler, Susan, illus. LC 85-2706. 40p. (gr. 1 up). 1985. 12.95 (0-88045-042-8) Stemmer Hse.
Kay, James T. De see De Kay, James T.
Kay, James T. De see De Kay, James T.
Kay, Jerry. Living in Space. Allison, Linda & Wells, William S., illus. 22p. (Orig.). (gr. 3-7). 1988. 9.95 (0-929201-06-X) Kay Productions.
Kaye. Life of Daniel H. Williams. 1993. write for info. (0-8050-3045-X) H Holt & Co.
Kaye, B. L. Word Tracking: High Frequency Words - Blackline Masters. 64p. (ps-2). 1989. tchr's. ed. 7.50 (0-87879-870-6, 870-6, Ann Arbor Div) Acad Therapy.
Kaye, Catherine B. Word Works: Why the Alphabet Is a Kid's Best Friend. Weston, Martha, illus. 128p. (gr. 4 up). 1985. 14.95 (0-316-48376-1); pap. 7.95 (0-316-48375-3) Little.
Kaye, Geraldine. A Breath of Fresh Air. 164p. (gr. 7-9). 1989. pap. 9.95 (0-233-98163-2, Pub. by A Deutsch England) Trafalgar.
—Great Comfort. 178p. (gr. 6-9). 1990. pap. 9.95 (0-233-98300-7, Pub. by A Deutsch England) Trafalgar.
—Someone Else's Baby. LC 91-73834. 144p. (gr. 7 up). 1992. 13.95 (1-56282-149-0); PLB 13.89 (1-56282-150-4) Hyprn Child.
Kaye, Judith. The Life of Alexander Fleming. (Illus.). 80p. (gr. 4-7). 1993. PLB 13.95 (0-8050-2300-3) TFC Bks NY.
—The Life of Benjamin Spock. (Illus.). 80p. (gr. 4-7). 1993. PLB 13.95 (0-8050-2301-1) TFC Bks NY.
—The Life of Daniel Hale Williams. (Illus.). 80p. (gr. 4-8). 1993. PLB 13.95 (0-8050-2302-X) TFC Bks NY.
—The Life of Florence Sabin. (Illus.). 80p. (gr. 4-7). 1993. PLB 13.95 (0-8050-2299-6) TFC Bks NY.
Kaye, M. M. Ordinary Princess. 1993. pap. 3.50 (0-440-40880-6) Dell.
Kaye, Marilyn. The Atonement of Mindy Wise. Van Doren, Liz, ed. 160p. (gr. 7 up). 1991. 15.95 (0-15-200402-5, Gulliver Bks) HarBrace.
—Cabin Six Plays Cupid. 128p. (Orig.). (ps-8). 1989. pap. 2.95 (0-380-75701-X, Camelot) Avon.
—Camp Sunnyside Back to School Special: School Daze. 128p. (Orig.). 1992. pap. 3.50 (0-380-76920-4, Camelot) Avon.
—Camp Sunnyside Friends: Balancing Act, No. 18. 128p. (Orig.). (gr. 5-12). 1992. pap. 3.50 (0-380-76918-2, Camelot) Avon.
—Camp Sunnyside Friends Christmas Special: The Spirit of Sunnyside. 128p. (Orig.). 1992. pap. 3.50 (0-380-76921-2, Camelot) Avon.

—Camp Sunnyside Friends, No. 11: The Problem with Parents. 128p. 1991. pap. 2.95 (0-380-76183-1, Camelot) Avon.
—Camp Sunnyside Friends, No. 13: Big Sister Blues. 128p. (Orig.). 1991. pap. 2.95 (0-380-76551-9, Camelot) Avon.
—Camp Sunnyside Friends, No. 14: Megan's Ghost. 128p. (Orig.). (gr. 5). 1991. pap. 2.99 (0-380-76552-7, Camelot) Avon.
—Camp Sunnyside Friends, No. 15: Christmas Break. 128p. (Orig.). 1991. pap. 2.99 (0-380-76553-5, Camelot) Avon.
—Camp Sunnyside Friends, No. 16: Happily Ever After. 128p. (Orig.). 1992. pap. 3.50 (0-380-76555-1, Camelot) Avon.
—Camp Sunnyside Friends, No. 17: Camp Spaghetti. 128p. (Orig.). (gr. 4). 1992. pap. 3.50 (0-380-76556-X, Camelot) Avon.
—Camp Sunnyside Friends: The Tennis Trap, No. 12. 128p. (Orig.). (gr. 5). 1991. pap. 2.95 (0-380-76184-X, Camelot) Avon.
—Cassie. LC 87-11944. 134p. (gr. 3-7). 1987. 13.95 (0-15-200421-1, Gulliver Bks); pap. 4.95 (0-15-200422-X, Gulliver Bks) HarBrace.
—Choose Me. 1992. pap. 3.50 (0-06-106714-8, Harp PBks) HarpC.
—Color War! 128p. (Orig.). (gr. 3 up). 1989. pap. 3.50 (0-380-75702-8, Camelot) Avon.
—Daphne. LC 86-29420. (Illus.). 160p. (gr. 3-7). 1987. 13.95 (0-15-200434-3, Gulliver Bks); pap. 4.95 (0-15-200433-5) HarBrace.
—A Friend Like Phoebe, No. 5. 132p. (gr. 3-7). 1989. 13. 95 (0-15-200450-5, Gulliver Bks) HarBrace.
—Home's a Nice Place to Visit, But I Wouldn't Want to Live There. (gr. 4-7). 1990. pap. 3.50 (0-06-106023-2, PL) HarpC.
—Katie Steals the Show. 128p. 1990. pap. 2.95 (0-380-75910-1, Camelot) Avon.
—Looking for Trouble. 128p. (gr. 4). 1990. pap. 2.95 (0-380-75909-8, Camelot) Avon.
—Lydia. LC 87-12763. 129p. (gr. 3-7). 1987. 13.95 (0-15-200510-2, Gulliver Bks); pap. 4.95 (0-15-200511-0, Gulliver Bks) HarBrace.
—Mindy Wise. 144p. (gr. 5). 1993. pap. 3.50 (0-380-71879-0, Camelot) Avon.
—The New & Improved Sarah. 144p. (Orig.). 1990. pap. 2.95 (0-380-76180-7, Camelot) Avon.
—New Girl in Cabin Six. 128p. (Orig.). 1989. pap. 2.95 (0-380-75703-6, Camelot) Avon.
—No Boys Allowed. 128p. (Orig.). (ps-8). 1989. pap. 2.95 (0-380-75700-1, Camelot) Avon.
—One Hundred & One Ways to Win Homecoming Queen. (gr. 4-7). 1991. pap. 3.50 (0-06-106060-7, Harp PBks) HarpC.
—Phoebe. 146p. (gr. 3-7). 1987. 13.95 (0-15-200430-0); pap. 4.95 (0-15-200431-9) HarBrace.
—Real Heroes. 11th ed. (gr. 4-7). 1993. 13.95 (0-15-200563-3) HarBrace.
—Real Tooth Fairy. Cogancherry, Helen, illus. 32p. (ps-3). 1990. 12.95 (0-15-265780-0) HarBrace.
—Reflections of Arsulu. LC 92-53935. (Illus.). 1992. pap. 2.95 (1-56282-248-9) Disney Pr.
—Runaway. (gr. 7 up). 1992. pap. 3.50 (0-06-106782-2, Harp PBks) HarpC.
—The Same Old Song. LC 92-53936. (Illus.). 1992. pap. 2.95 (1-56282-249-7) Disney Pr.
—Three of a Kind, No. 1: With Friends Like These, Who Needs Enemies. (gr. 4-7). 1990. pap. 3.50 (0-06-106001-1, Harp PBks) HarpC.
—Three of a Kind, No. 4: Two's Company, Four's a Crowd. (gr. 4-7). 1991. pap. 3.50 (0-06-106058-5, Harp PBks) HarpC.
—Three of a Kind, No. 5: Cat Morgan, Working Girl. (gr. 4-7). 1991. pap. 3.50 (0-06-106059-3, Harp PBks) HarpC.
—Too Many Counselors. 128p. 1990. pap. 2.95 (0-380-75913-6, Camelot) Avon.
—What a Teddy Bear Needs. 1989. cased 3.95 (0-7214-5225-6) Ladybird Bks.
—What a Teddy Bear Needs. Wheeler, Jody, illus. 26p. 1993. 2.95 (0-7214-3510-6) Ladybird Bks.
—Will the Real Becka Morgan Please Stand Up? (gr. 4-7). 1991. pap. 3.50 (0-06-106041-0, PL) HarpC.
—A Witch in Cabin Six. 128p. (gr. 3-4). 1990. pap. 2.95 (0-380-75912-8, Camelot) Avon.
Kaye, Sally, ed. see Knudsen, Eric A.
Kaye, Tony. Lech Walesa. (Illus.). 112p. (gr. 5 up). 1989. 17.95 (1-55546-856-X); pap. 9.95 (0-7910-0689-1) Chelsea Hse.
—Lyndon B. Johnson. Schlesinger, Arthur M., Jr., intro. by. (Illus.). 112p. (gr. 5 up). 1988. lib. bdg. 17.95 (0-87754-536-7) Chelsea Hse.
Kaylor, Mike. Where to Find the Best of Huntsville. 2nd ed. Sayers, Fred, illus. Easterling, Bill, intro. by. (Illus.). 150p. (Orig.). (gr. 9-12). 1985. pap. text ed. 4.95 (0-916039-01-3) Kaylor Christ Co.
Kayton, JoAnn & Levorsen, Sally. Discover Washington. (Illus., Orig.). (gr. 1-6). 1988. pap. 3.00 (0-317-94116-X) Assist Lea Bellingham.
Kaywell, Joan F., ed. Adolescent Literature As a Complement to the Classics. (Illus.). (Orig.). (gr. 7-12). 1992. pap. text ed. 19.95 (0-926842-23-4) CG Pubs Inc.
Kaz, Diane, ed. see Johnson, Donovan A.
Kazin, Alfred, ed. see Melville, Herman.
Keable-Elliott, I., jt. auth. see Evans, C.
Keable-Elliott, I., jt. auth. see Heddle, R.

Keagy, Denita. Minicomputer to the Rescue! Sistare, Betty L., illus. LC 87-62051. 36p. (gr. k-5). 1987. PLB 10.95 (0-944027-01-6) New Memories.
Keane, Bil. Look Who's Here. 1987. pap. 3.99 (0-449-13276-5, GM) Fawcett.
—Wanna Be Smiled At? (Illus.). 128p. (gr. 4 up). 1985. pap. 3.50 (0-449-12816-4, GM) Fawcett.
Keane, Glen. Adam Raccoon & the Circusmaster. LC 86-26889. (ps-2). 1989. 7.99 (1-55513-090-9, Chariot Bks) Cook.
—Adam Raccoon & the Flying Machine. LC 88-17006. (Illus.). 48p. (ps-2). 1989. 7.99 (1-55513-287-1, Chariot Bks) Cook.
—Adam Raccoon & the King's Big Dinner. (ps-3). 1992. 7.99 (1-55513-362-2) Cook.
—Adam Raccoon at Forever Falls. (ps-2). 1987. 7.99 (1-55513-087-9, Chariot Bks) Cook.
—Adam Raccoon in Lost Woods. (ps-2). 1987. 7.99 (1-55513-088-7, Chariot Bks) Cook.
Keaney, Leonie, jt. auth. see Brennan, John.
Kear, Dennis, jt. auth. see Carroll, Jeri.
Kearns, Kimberly & O'Brien, Marie. Baby Bop's Toys. Hartley, Linda, ed. 24p. (ps). 1993. 3.95 (0-7829-0369-X) Barney Pub.
—Barney's Farm Animals. Hartley, Linda, ed. Malzeke-McDonald, Karen, illus. 24p. (ps). 1993. 3.95 (0-7829-0370-3) Barney Pub.
Keast, Winifred. What Happened to Duchess's Pups? (Illus.). 92p. (Orig.). (gr. 7 up). 1984. pap. 10.00 (0-9613847-0-0); PLB 5.00 (0-9613847-1-9) W Keast.
Keathley, Jean. Pennies, Nickels, & Dreams. Graves, Helen, ed. LC 88-50117. 44p. (gr. k-3). 1988. 7.95 (1-55523-137-3) Winston-Derek.
Keating, August. Uncle Wooley. LC 87-82084. 55p. (Orig.). (gr. 9 up). 1988. pap. 5.00 (0-916383-47-4) Aegina Pr.
Keating, Maurice, jt. auth. see Gibbons, Maurice.
Keatley, Lu. Automobiles. LC 76-50372. (Illus.). (gr. 4-7). 1977. pap. text ed. 4.91 (0-89445-010-7) Specialty Bks Intl.
Keaton, Phyllis H. Buggies. LC 88-5951. (Illus.). 48p. (gr. 5-6). 1988. RSBE 11.95 (0-89686-375-1, Crestwood Hse) Macmillan Child Grp.
Keats. Over in the Meadow. (gr. 5 up). pap. 19.95 (0-590-72809-1) Scholastic Inc.
—Song about Myself. 1993. 14.95 (0-8050-1746-1) H Holt & Co.
Keats, Ezra. The Trip. Keats, Ezra, illus. LC 77-24907. 32p. (gr. k-3). 1978. PLB 15.93 (0-688-84123-6) Greenwillow.
Keats, Ezra J. Apartment Three. LC 85-26791. (Illus.). 32p. (gr. 1-5). 1986. pap. 3.95 (0-689-71059-3, Aladdin) Macmillan Child Grp.
—Un Dia de Nieve. (SPA.). (ps). 1991. 12.95 (0-670-83747-4) Viking Child Bks.
—Un Dia de Nieve. (SPA., Illus.). 32p. (ps-1). 1991. pap. 4.50 (0-14-054363-5, Puffin) Puffin Bks.
—Dreams. 2nd ed. LC 91-25572. (Illus.). 32p. (gr. 1-3). 1992. pap. 4.95 (0-689-71599-4, Aladdin) Macmillan Child Grp.
—Dreams. reissued ed. Keats, Ezra J., illus. LC 73-15857. 32p. (gr. 1-3). 1992. RSBE 14.95 (0-02-749611-2, Macmillan Child Bk) Macmillan Child Grp.
—Goggles! Keats, Ezra J., illus. LC 86-28718. 40p. (gr. k-3). 1987. pap. 4.95 (0-689-71157-3, Aladdin) Macmillan Child Grp.
—Hi, Cat! 2nd ed. Keats, Ezra J., illus. LC 87-37433. 40p. (gr. k-4). 1988. pap. 4.95 (0-689-71258-8, Aladdin) Macmillan Child Grp.
—Hi, Cat! (gr. k-3). 1990. incl. cass. 19.95 (0-87499-180-3); pap. 12.95 incl. cass. (0-87499-179-X); Set; incl. 4 bks., cass., & guide. pap. 27.95 (0-685-38540-X) Live Oak Media.
—Jennie's Hat. Keats, Ezra J., illus. LC 66-15683. 32p. (gr. k-3). 1966. 15.00i (0-06-023113-0); PLB 14.89 (0-06-023114-9) HarpC Child Bks.
—Jennie's Hat. Keats, Ezra J., illus. LC 66-15683. 32p. (ps-3). 1985. pap. 5.95 (0-06-443072-3, Trophy) HarpC Child Bks.
—John Henry: An American Legend. Schwartz, Anne, ed. LC 65-11444. (Illus.). 32p. (ps-3). 1987. lib. bdg. 12.99 (0-394-99052-8); pap. 5.00 (0-394-89052-3) Knopf Bks Yng Read.
—Kitten for a Day. Keats, Ezra J., illus. LC 81-69518. 32p. (ps-3). 1984. RSBE 14.95 (0-02-749630-9, Four Winds) Macmillan Child Grp.
—Kitten for a Day. Keats, Ezra J., illus. LC 92-40563. 32p. (ps-1). 1993. pap. 4.95 (0-689-71737-7, Aladdin) Macmillan Child Grp.
—Letter to Amy. Keats, Ezra J., illus. LC 68-24329. (gr. k-3). 1968. 15.00 (0-06-023108-4); PLB 14.89 (0-06-023109-2) HarpC Child Bks.
—A Letter to Amy. LC 68-24329. (Illus.). 32p. (gr. k-3). 1984. pap. 5.95 (0-06-443063-4, Trophy) HarpC Child Bks.
—The Little Drummer Boy. Keats, Ezra J., illus. LC 68-25714. 32p. (gr. k-3). 1987. pap. 3.95 (0-689-71158-1, Aladdin) Macmillan Child Grp.
—Louie. Keats, Ezra J., illus. LC 75-6766. 32p. (gr. k-3). 1983. PLB 14.88 (0-688-02383-5) Greenwillow.
—Louie's Search. Keats, Ezra J., illus. LC 80-10176. 40p. (gr. k-3). 1980. RSBE 13.95 (0-02-749700-3, Four Winds) Macmillan Child Grp.
—Louie's Search. Keats, Ezra J., illus. LC 89-15128. 32p. (gr. k-3). 1989. pap. 4.95 (0-689-71354-1, Aladdin) Macmillan Child Grp.

—Maggie & the Pirate. Keats, Ezra J., illus. LC 85-29347. 32p. (gr. k-3). 1987. Repr. of 1979 ed. RSBE 13.95 (0-02-749710-0, Four Winds) Macmillan Child Grp.
—Maggie & the Pirate. (ps-3). 1992. pap. 3.95 (0-590-44852-8, Blue Ribbon Bks) Scholastic Inc.
—Pet Show! LC 73-156843. (Illus.). 40p. (gr. k-3). 1972. RSBE 14.95 (0-02-749620-1) Macmillan Child Grp.
—Pet Show! Keats, Ezra J., illus. LC 86-17225. 40p. (gr. k-3). 1987. pap. 4.95 (0-689-71159-X, Aladdin) Macmillan Child Grp.
—Peter's Chair. Keats, Ezra J., illus. LC 67-4816. (gr. k-3). 1967. 15.00i (0-06-023111-4); PLB 14.89 (0-06-023112-2) HarpC Child Bks.
—Peter's Chair. LC 67-4816. (Illus.). 32p. (ps-3). 1983. pap. 4.95 (0-06-443040-5, Trophy) HarpC Child Bks.
—Peter's Chair Big Book. Keats, Ezra J., illus. LC 67-4816. 32p. (ps-3). 1993. pap. 19.95 (0-06-443325-0, Trophy) HarpC Child Bks.
—Regards to the Man in the Moon. Keats, Ezra J., illus. LC 86-28774. 32p. (gr. k-3). 1987. pap. 3.95 (0-689-71160-3, Aladdin Bks) Macmillan Child Grp.
—Silba por Willie: (Whistle for Willie) (SPA., Illus.). 40p. (ps-1). 1992. 14.00 (0-670-84395-4) Viking Child Bks.
—The Snowy Day. (Illus.). (ps-k). 1976. pap. 4.99 (0-14-050182-7, Puffin) Puffin Bks.
—The Snowy Day. Keats, Ezra J., illus. LC 62-15441. 40p. (ps-1). 1962. pap. 13.00 (0-670-65400-0) Viking Child Bks.
—Snowy Day. (SPA.). (ps-3). 1993. pap. 19.95 (0-590-72632-3) Scholastic Inc.
—Snowy Day. (ps-3). 1993. pap. 19.95 (0-590-73323-0) Scholastic Inc.
—The Trip. LC 77-24907. (ps-3). 1987. pap. 4.95 (0-688-07328-X, Mulberry) Morrow.
—Whistle for Willie. Keats, Ezra J., illus. LC 64-13595. (ps-1). 1977. pap. 4.50 (0-14-050202-5, Puffin) Puffin Bks.
—Whistle for Willie. Keats, Ezra J., illus. (ps-1). 1964. pap. 14.00 (0-670-76240-7) Viking Child Bks.
Keats, John. Selected Poems & Letters. Bush, Douglas, ed. LC 59-3635. (gr. 9 up). 1959. pap. 7.96 (0-395-05140-1, RivEd) HM.
Keats, Robin. Why Frogs Go to School & Other Weird Facts You Never Learned. Erkmann, Chris, illus. 96p. (Orig.). 1992. pap. 3.50 (0-380-76718-X, Camelot) Avon.
Keavney, Pamela. The Promise. LC 89-26896. (Illus.). 32p. (ps-3). 1992. 15.00 (0-06-023019-3); PLB 14.89 (0-06-023020-7) HarpC Child Bks.
Keboyan, V. Alex. Partner's for Change: A Peer Helping Manual & Guide for Training & Prevention Programs. 464p. (gr. k-12). 1992. spiral bdg. 49.95 (0-915190-87-7, JP9087-7); pap. 44.95 (0-915190-69-9, JP9069-9) Jalmar Pr.
Keck, Saundria. God Made Me. LC 86-17572. (ps). 1987. 5.95 (0-8054-4173-5) Broadman.
Keckeis, M. B. The Black Rose. Steiner, Frank, et al, trs. Cassidy, Christoph, illus. (ENG, SPA, FRE & GER.). 256p. (gr. 3-9). 1991. 23.50 (1-879870-54-1) Pro Lingua Pr.
Keckeis, M. B. & Beaubeau, Anne. The White Dove. Steiner, Frank, tr. Cassidy, Christophe, illus. (ENG, SPA, FRE & GER.). 256p. (gr. 6-10). 1993. 23.50 (1-879870-56-8) Pro Lingua Pr.
Keckeis, M. B., et al. The Black Rose. 2nd ed. Steiner, Frank & Mercer, Denis, trs. Cassidy, Christophe, illus. (ENG, SPA, FRE & GER.). 256p. (gr. 6-10). 1993. Repr. of 1991 ed. 23.50 (1-879870-55-X) Pro Lingua Pr.
Kedron, Jane, tr. see Seidler, Babara.
Keefauver, John. The Three-Day Traffic Jam. LC 91-30583. 80p. (gr. 4-8). 1992. pap. 13.00 jacketed, 3-pc. bdg. (0-671-75599-4, S&S BFYR) S&S Trade.
Keefauver, Larry. Who Is the Holy Spirit? (Illus.). 48p. (gr. 9-12). 1992. pap. 7.99 (1-55945-217-X) Group Pub.
Keefauver, Larry, jt. auth. see Stone, J. David.
Keefe, Betty. Fingerpuppet ABC. Champlin, John, ed. Keefe, Betty, illus. 100p. (ps-2). 1988. pap. 17.95 (0-938594-10-9) Spec Lit Pr.
—Fingerpuppet Tales: Making & Using Puppets with Folk & Fairytales. (Illus.). 148p. (ps-3). 1986. spiral bdg. 17.95 (0-938594-08-7) Spec Lit Pr.
—Fingerpuppets, Fingerplays & Holidays. (Illus.). 136p. (ps-3). 1984. spiral bdg. 17.95 (0-938594-05-2) Spec Lit Pr.
Keefer, Mikal. I Like Sunday School! Stites, Joe, illus. 28p. (ps-k). 1993. 4.99 (0-7847-0040-0, 24-03830) Standard Pub.
—Ready for Something New. Yacoba, illus. 48p. (Orig.). (gr. 1-3). 1993. pap. text ed. 3.99 (0-7847-0097-4, 24-03947) Standard Pub.
Keegan, Marcia. Pueblo Boy: Growing up in Two Worlds. Keegan, Marcia, photos by. LC 90-45187. (Illus.). 48p. (gr. 2-6). 1991. 15.00 (0-525-65060-1, Cobblehill Bks) Dutton Child Bks.
Keegan, Shannon. Haunted Tacos: Culinary Verse with a Curse. (gr. 4-7). 1992. pap. 2.50 (0-590-45815-9) Scholastic Inc.
Keehn, Sally. I Am Regina. 192p. 1991. 15.95 (0-399-21797-5, Philomel Pub Group.
Keehn, Sally M. I Am Regina. (gr. 4-7). 1993. pap. 3.50 (0-440-40754-0) Dell.
Keeler, Barbara. Energy Alternatives. LC 90-40172. (Illus.). 96p. (gr. 5-8). 1990. PLB 14.95 (1-56006-118-9) Lucent Bks.
Keeler, Patricia, jt. auth. see Fleisher, Paul.

Keeler, Ronald F. Games for Children: For Indoors & Outdoors. 64p. (Orig.). (ps-2). 1982. pap. 3.99 (0-8010-5478-8) Baker Bk.
Keeling, Jan, ed. see LaMorte, Kathy & Lewis, Sharen.
Keeling, Jan, ed. see Meissel, Chris.
Keeling, Jan, ed. see Pelphrey, Jo Ann.
Keel-Williams, Mildred. Legacies of a Shopping Bag Lady: Poems of Life. Holmes, Darryl, ed. George, Anthony & Washington, Ruby, photos by. Harewood, Lasana K., frwd. by. LC 84-62520. (Illus.). 72p. (Orig.). (gr. 7 up). 1984. pap. 6.00 (0-9614084-1-3) Mus Fed Ink.
Keen, G. Daniel, jt. auth. see Bonnet, Robert L.
Keen, Martin L. Prehistoric Mammals. Hull, John, illus. (gr. 4-6). pap. 2.95 (0-8431-4255-3) Wonder.
Keene, Ann T. Earthkeepers: Observers & Protectors of Nature. (Illus.). 224p. 1993. 30.00 (0-19-507867-5) OUP.
Keene, Carolyn. Bad Medicine. (Orig.). (gr. 7 up). 1989. pap. 2.95 (0-671-64702-4, Archway) PB.
—Best of Enemies. Greenberg, Ann, ed. 224p. (Orig.). 1991. pap. 3.99 (0-671-67465-X, Archway) PB.
—The Bluebeard Room. 1988. pap. 3.50 (0-671-66857-9, Minstrel Bks) PB.
—Broken Anchor. 1991. pap. 3.50 (0-671-74228-0) PB.
—Buried In Time. Greenberg, Ann, ed. 224p. (gr. 7 up). 1990. pap. 3.99 (0-671-67463-3, Archway) PB.
—Buried Secrets. (gr. 7 up). 1991. pap. 3.50 (0-671-73664-7, Archway) PB.
—Buried Secrets: The Nancy Drew Files, Case 10. large type ed. 151p. (gr. 7-10). 1988. Repr. of 1987 ed. 9.50 (0-942545-41-9); PLB 10.50 (0-942545-36-2, Dist. by Grolier) Grey Castle.
—The Case of the Artful Crime. Winkler, Ellen, ed. 160p. (Orig.). 1992. pap. 3.99 (0-671-73052-5) PB.
—The Case of the Disappearing Deejay. (Orig.). (gr. 7 up). 1989. pap. 3.50 (0-671-66314-3, Minstrel Bks) PB.
—The Case of the Disappearing Diamonds. (gr. 3-6). 1987. pap. 3.99 (0-671-64896-9, Minstrel Bks) PB.
—The Case of the Photo Finish. Greenberg, Ann, ed. 160p. (Orig.). (gr. 3-6). 1990. pap. 3.99 (0-671-69281-X, Minstrel Bks) PB.
—The Case of the Twin Teddy Bears. Winkler, Ellen, ed. 160p. (Orig.). 1993. pap. 3.99 (0-671-79302-0, Minstrel Bks) PB.
—The Case of the Vanishing Veil. reissued ed. Greenberg, Anne, ed. 160p. (Orig.). (gr. 3-6). 1988. pap. 3.99 (0-671-63413-5, Minstrel Bks) PB.
—Choosing Sides. Greenberg, Anne, ed. 160p. (Orig.). 1993. pap. 3.99 (0-671-73088-6, Archway) PB.
—The Clue in the Antique Trunk. Greenberg, Ann, ed. 160p. (Orig.). 1992. pap. 3.99 (0-671-73051-7) PB.
—The Clue in the Camera. Greenberg, Ann, ed. 160p. (gr. 3-6). 1988. pap. 3.99 (0-671-64962-0, Minstrel Bks) PB.
—Cold As Ice. Greenberg, Ann, ed. 160p. (Orig.). (gr. 7 up). 1990. pap. 3.75 (0-671-70031-6, Archway) PB.
—A Crime for Christmas. (gr. 7 up). 1991. pap. 3.99 (0-671-74617-0, Archway) PB.
—Crosscurrents. Greenberg, Ann, ed. 160p. (Orig.). 1992. pap. 3.75 (0-671-73072-X) PB.
—Cutting Edge. Greenberg, Anne, ed. 160p. (Orig.). 1992. pap. 3.75 (0-671-73074-6) PB.
—Danger on Parade. Greenberg, Anne, ed. 160p. (Orig.). (gr. 7 up). 1992. pap. 3.75 (0-671-73081-9, Archway) PB.
—Deadly Doubles. (gr. 7 up). 1991. pap. 3.50 (0-671-73662-0, Archway) PB.
—Deadly Doubles: The Nancy Drew Files, Case 7. large type ed. 147p. (gr. 5-10). 1988. Repr. of 1987 ed. 9.50 (0-942545-38-9); PLB 10.50 (0-942545-33-8, Dist. by Grolier) Grey Castle.
—Deadly Intent. 155p. (gr. 5-8). 1991. pap. 3.75 (0-671-74611-1, Archway) PB.
—Deadly Intent. large type ed. (gr. 5-10). 1988. 9.50 (0-942545-23-0); PLB 10.50 (0-942545-28-1, Dist. by Grolier) Grey Castle.
—Deep Secrets. Greenberg, Ann, ed. 160p. (gr. 7 up). 1991. pap. 3.50 (0-671-74525-5, Archway) PB.
—Designs in Crime. Greenberg, Anne, ed. 160p. (Orig.). 1993. pap. 3.99 (0-671-79481-7, Archway) PB.
—Diamond Deceit. Greenberg, Ann, ed. 160p. (Orig.). 1993. pap. 3.99 (0-671-73087-8, Archway) PB.
—Don't Look Twice. Greenberg, Ann, ed. 160p. (Orig.). 1991. pap. 3.75 (0-671-70032-4, Archway) PB.
—Double Crossing. 224p. (Orig.). (gr. 7 up). 1991. pap. 3.99 (0-671-74616-2, Archway) PB.
—The Double Horror of Fenley Place. Greenberg, Ann, ed. (gr. 3-6). 1987. pap. 3.99 (0-671-64387-8, Minstrel Bks) PB.
—Easy Marks. Greenberg, Anne, ed. 160p. (Orig.). 1991. pap. 3.50 (0-671-73066-5, Archway) PB.
—The Emerald Eyed Cat Mystery. 1987. pap. 3.50 (0-671-64282-0) PB.
—Enemy Match. 192p. (gr. 3-6). 1987. pap. 3.50 (0-671-64283-9, Minstrel Bks) PB.
—Eskimo Secret. 1991. pap. 3.50 (0-671-73003-7) PB.
—Evil in Amsterdam. Greenberg, Ann, ed. 224p. (Orig.). 1993. pap. 3.99 (0-671-78173-1, Archway) PB.
—False Impressions. 160p. 1991. pap. 3.50 (0-671-74392-9, Archway) PB.
—False Moves. (gr. 7 up). 1989. pap. 3.75 (0-671-70493-1, Archway) PB.
—Final Notes. Greenberg, Anne, ed. 160p. (Orig.). 1991. pap. 3.75 (0-671-73069-X, Archway) PB.

—The Ghost of Craven Cove. Greenberg, Anne, ed. 160p. 1989. pap. 3.99 (0-671-66317-8, Minstrel Bks) PB.
—The Girl Who Couldn't Remember. Greenberg, Ann, ed. 160p. (Orig.). 1989. pap. 3.99 (0-671-66316-X, Minstrel Bks) PB.
—Going Too Far. 160p. 1990. pap. 2.95 (0-671-67761-6, Archway) PB.
—Greek Odyssey. Greenberg, Anne, ed. 160p. (Orig.). 1992. pap. 3.75 (0-671-73078-9, Archway) PB.
—The Greek Symbol Mystery. (gr. 2-7). 1984. 8.50 (0-685-09397-2) S&S Trade.
—Guilty Secrets. 160p. (gr. 6 up). 1989. pap. 2.95 (0-671-67760-8, Archway) PB.
—Hard to Handle. 160p. (Orig.). 1991. pap. 2.95 (0-671-73116-5, Archway) PB.
—The Haunted Carousel. 192p. (gr. 7). 1988. pap. 3.50 (0-671-66227-9, Minstrel Bks) PB.
—The Haunting of Horse Island. Greenberg, Ann, ed. 160p. (Orig.). (gr. 3-6). 1990. pap. 3.99 (0-671-69284-4, Minstrel Bks) PB.
—Heart of Danger. (gr. 7 up). 1991. pap. 3.50 (0-671-73665-5, Archway) PB.
—High Marks for Malice. (gr. 7 up). 1989. pap. 3.50 (0-671-64699-0, Archway) PB.
—High Risk. Greenberg, Anne, ed. 160p. (Orig.). 1991. pap. 3.50 (0-671-70036-7, Archway) PB.
—High Survival. Greenberg, Ann, ed. 224p. (Orig.). 1991. pap. 3.99 (0-671-67466-8, Archway) PB.
—Hit & Run Holiday. large type ed. (gr. 5-10). 1989. 9.50 (0-942545-25-7); lib. bdg. 10.50 (0-942545-31-1, Dist. by Grolier) Grey Castle.
—Hits & Misses. Greenberg, Ann, ed. 224p. (Orig.). 1993. pap. 3.99 (0-671-78169-3, Archway) PB.
—Hot Pursuit. Greenberg, Anne, ed. 160p. (Orig.). 1991. pap. 3.50 (0-671-70035-9, Archway) PB.
—Hot Tracks. Greenberg, Anne, ed. 160p. (Orig.). 1992. pap. 3.75 (0-671-73075-4) PB.
—Illusions of Evil. 1994. pap. 3.99 (0-671-79486-8, Archway) PB.
—The Joker's Revenge. Greenberg, Ann, ed. 1988. pap. 3.99 (0-671-63414-3, Minstrel Bks) PB.
—The Joker's Revenge. (Orig.). (gr. 7 up). 1988. pap. 3.50 (0-671-63426-7, Minstrel Bks) PB.
—Junior Class Trip. Greenberg, Ann, ed. 224p. (Orig.). 1991. pap. 2.95 (0-671-73124-6, Archway) PB.
—The Kachina Doll Mystery. (gr. 3-7). 1988. pap. 3.99 (0-671-67220-7, Minstrel Bks) PB.
—Last Dance. (Orig.). (gr. 7 up). 1991. pap. 3.50 (0-671-74657-X, Archway) PB.
—The Last Resort: A Nancy Drew & Hardy Boys Supermystery. 224p. (gr. 7 up). 1990. pap. 3.99 (0-671-67461-7, Archway) PB.
—The Legend of Miner's Creek. Greenberg, Anne, ed. 160p. (Orig.). 1992. pap. 3.99 (0-671-73053-3, Minstrel Bks) PB.
—Let's Talk Terror. 160p. (Orig.). 1993. pap. 3.99 (0-671-79478-7, Archway) PB.
—Love & Games. Greenberg, Anne, ed. 160p. (Orig.). 1992. pap. 2.99 (0-671-73118-1, Archway) PB.
—Love Times Three. (Orig.). (gr. 9-12). 1991. pap. 3.50 (0-671-96703-7, Archway) PB.
—Making Waves. Greenberg, Ann, ed. 160p. (Orig.). (gr. 6 up). 1993. pap. 3.99 (0-671-73085-1, Archway) PB.
—The Mardi Gras Mystery. Greenberg, Ann, ed. 160p. (gr. 3-6). 1988. pap. 3.99 (0-671-64961-2, Minstrel Bks) PB.
—A Mind of Her Own. Greenberg, Ann, ed. 160p. (Orig.). 1991. pap. 2.99 (0-671-73117-3, Archway) PB.
—Mixed Signals. Greenberg, Ann, ed. 160p. (Orig.). 1991. pap. 3.50 (0-671-73067-3, Archway) PB.
—A Model Crime. Greenberg, Ann, ed. 160p. (Orig.). (gr. 7 up). 1990. pap. 3.75 (0-671-70028-6, Archway) PB.
—Moving Target. Greenberg, Anne, ed. 160p. (Orig.). (gr. 6 up). 1993. pap. 3.99 (0-671-79479-5, Archway) PB.
—Murder on Ice. (gr. 7 up). 1989. pap. 3.50 (0-671-68729-8, Archway) PB.
—Murder on Ice. large type ed. (gr. 5-10). 1988. 9.50 (0-942545-24-9); PLB 10.50 (0-942545-29-X, Dist. by Grolier) Grey Castle.
—The Mystery at Magnolia Mansion. Greenberg, Ann, ed. 160p. (gr. 3-6). 1990. pap. 3.99 (0-671-69282-8, Minstrel Bks) PB.
—The Mystery of Misty Canyon. (gr. 3-7). 1988. pap. 3.99 (0-671-63417-8, Minstrel Bks) PB.
—The Mystery of the Jade Tiger. Greenberg, Anne, ed. 160p. (Orig.). 1991. pap. 3.99 (0-671-73050-9, Minstrel Bks) PB.
—The Mystery of the Masked Rider. Winkler, Ellen, ed. 160p. (Orig.). 1992. pap. 3.99 (0-671-73055-X, Minstrel Bks) PB.
—The Mystery of the Missing Millionairess. Greenberg, Anne, ed. 160p. (Orig.). 1991. pap. 3.99 (0-671-69287-9, Minstrel Bks) PB.
—Mystery of the Winged Lion. (gr. 7 up). 1989. pap. 3.50 (0-318-41224-1, Minstrel Bks) PB.
—Mystery Train. Greenberg, Ann, ed. 224p. (Orig.). (gr. 7 up). 1990. pap. 3.99 (0-671-67464-1, Archway) PB.
—Nancy Drew & the Flying Saucer Mystery, No. 58. (gr. 4-7). 1990. pap. 3.50 (0-671-72320-0) S&S Trade.
—Nancy Drew Digest. 1987. Boxed. pap. 14.00 (0-671-91515-0, Minstrel Bks) PB.
—Nancy Drew Files, 5 vols. 1991. Set. pap. 17.50 (0-671-96785-1) PB.
—The Nancy Drew Files, No. 6: White Water Terror. 1991. pap. 3.50 (0-671-73661-2) PB.

—The Nancy Drew Files, No. 88: False Pretenses. 160p. (Orig.). (gr. 6 up). 1993. pap. 3.99 (0-671-79480-9, Archway) PB.
—Nancy Drew Files, No.1: Ghost Stories. 1983. pap. 3.50 (0-671-46468-X) S&S Trade.
—The Nancy Drew Ghost Stories. Schneider, Meg, ed. Frame, Paul, illus. (gr. 3-7). 1983. 8.95 (0-685-06733-5); pap. 3.50 (0-685-42561-4) S&S Trade.
—Nancy Drew Ghost Stories. Frame, Paul, illus. 160p. 1983. 8.50 (0-685-06755-6); pap. 2.85 (0-685-06756-4) S&S Trade.
—Nancy Drew Ghost Stories. Greenberg, Ann, ed. 160p. (gr. 3-7). 1989. pap. 3.50 (0-671-69132-5, Minstrel Bks) PB.
—Nancy Drew Gift Set, 3 vols. Boxed Set. pap. 8.55 (0-317-12425-0) S&S Trade.
—Nancy Drew Mystery Stories: Back-to-Back Edition. (gr. 3-7). 1987. 7.95 (0-448-09570-X, G&D) Putnam Pub Group.
—Nancy Drew, No. 114: The Suspect in Smoke. 160p. (Orig.). (gr. 3-7). 1993. pap. 3.99 (0-671-79301-2, Minstrel Bks) PB.
—Nancy Drew, No. 2: The Hidden Staircase. LC 91-46734. 1991. 12.95 (1-55709-156-0) Applewood.
—Nancy Drew, No. 3: The Bungalow Mystery. LC 91-46732. 1991. 12.95 (1-55709-157-9) Applewood.
—Nancy Drew: The Bluebeard Room. Barish, Wendy & LeVert, Suzanne, eds. 160p. (Orig.). (gr. 3-7). 1985. write for info. S&S Trade.
—Nancy Drew: The Ghost in the Gondola. Barish, Wendy & LeVert, Suzanne, eds. 160p. (Orig.). (gr. 3-7). 1985. write for info. S&S Trade.
—Nancy Drew: The Kachina Doll Mystery. (Illus.). 192p. (gr. 3-7). 1981. 3.50 (0-671-42347-9) S&S Trade.
—Nancy Drew: The Sinister Omen. Frame, Paul, illus. 192p. (gr. 3-7). 1991. (Little Simon); pap. 3.50 (0-671-73938-7) S&S Trade.
—Nancy Drew: The Swami's Ring. (Illus.). 192p. (gr. 3-7). 1981. S&S Trade.
—Nancy Drew: The Twin Dilemma. (Illus.). 192p. (gr. 3-7). 1981. pap. 2.95 (0-671-42359-2) S&S Trade.
—Nancy Hardy Desperate Measurs. 1994. 3.99 (0-671-78174-X, Archway) PB.
—Nancy's Mysterious Letter. (gr. 4-7). 1963. 4.95 (0-448-09508-4, G&D) Putnam Pub Group.
—Never Say Die. (gr. 7 up). 1991. pap. 3.50 (0-671-73666-3, Archway) PB.
—New Year's Evil. Greenberg, Anne, ed. 224p. (Orig.). 1991. pap. 3.99 (0-671-67467-6, Archway) PB.
—No Laughing Matter. Greenberg, Anne, ed. 160p. (Orig.). 1993. pap. 3.75 (0-671-73083-5, Archway) PB.
—The Nutcracker Ballet Mystery. Winkler, Ellen, ed. 160p. (Orig.). (gr. 3-6). 1992. pap. 3.99 (0-671-73056-8, Minstrel Bks) PB.
—Out of Bounds. 160p. 1991. pap. 3.50 (0-671-73911-5, Archway) PB.
—Over the Edge. (Orig.). (gr. 7 up). 1991. pap. 3.50 (0-671-74656-1, Archway) PB.
—The Paris Connection: A Nancy Drew & Hardy Boys Supermystery. 224p. 1991. pap. 3.99 (0-671-74675-8, Archway) PB.
—The Perfect Plot. Greenberg, Anne, ed. 160p. (Orig.). 1992. pap. 3.75 (0-671-73080-0, Archway) PB.
—The Phantom of Venice. 1991. pap. 3.50 (0-671-73422-9) PB.
—Poison Pen. Greenberg, Ann, ed. 160p. (Orig.). 1991. pap. 3.50 (0-671-70037-5, Archway) PB.
—Portrait in Crime. Greenberg, Ann, ed. 160p. (Orig.). 1991. pap. 3.50 (0-671-73996-4, Archway) PB.
—Power of Suggestion. Greenberg, Anne, ed. 160p. (Orig.). 1993. pap. 3.75 (0-671-73084-3, Archway) PB.
—The Puzzle at Pineview School. Greenberg, Ann, ed. (Orig.). (gr. 7 up). 1989. pap. 3.99 (0-671-66315-1, Minstrel Bks) PB.
—Rendezvous in Rome. Greenberg, Anne, ed. 160p. (Orig.). 1992. pap. 3.75 (0-671-73077-0, Archway) PB.
—Sea of Suspicion. Greenberg, Ann, ed. 160p. (Orig.). 1993. pap. 3.99 (0-671-79477-9, Archway) PB.
—The Search for Cindy Austin. (Orig.). (gr. 3-7). 1989. pap. 3.50 (0-671-66313-5, Minstrel Bks) PB.
—The Search for the Silver Persian. 160p. (Orig.). (gr. 3-7). 1993. pap. 3.99 (0-671-79300-4, Minstrel Bks) PB.
—A Secret in Time. Greenberg, Anne, ed. 160p. (Orig.). 1991. pap. 3.99 (0-671-69286-0, Minstrel Bks) PB.
—The Secret of Shady Glen. Greenberg, Ann, ed. 160p. (gr. 5 up). 1988. pap. 3.99 (0-671-63416-X, Minstrel Bks) PB.
—Secret of the Tibetan Treasure. Winkler, Ellen, ed. 160p. (Orig.). 1992. pap. 3.99 (0-671-73054-1, Minstrel Bks) PB.
—Secrets Can Kill. large type ed. (gr. 5-10). 1988. 9.50 (0-942545-22-2); PLB 10.50 (0-942545-27-3, Dist. by Grolier) Grey Castle.
—Shock Waves. (gr. 7 up). 1991. pap. 3.99 (0-671-74393-7, Archway) PB.
—The Silver Cobweb. Schneider, Meg, ed. Frame, Paul, illus. 192p. (Orig.). (gr. 3-7). 1983. 9.95 (0-685-06731-9) S&S Trade.
—The Silver Cobweb. Frame, Paul, illus. 192p. 1983. 8.95 (0-685-06757-2); pap. 3.50 (0-685-42563-0) S&S Trade.
—Sisters in Crime. 160p. (Orig.). (gr. 7 up). 1988. pap. 3.75 (0-671-67957-0, Archway) PB.
—Smile & Say Murder. (gr. 7 up). 1991. pap. 3.75 (0-671-73659-0, Archway) PB.

—Smile & Say Murder. large type ed. (gr. 5-10). 1988. 9.50 (0-942545-26-5); PLB 10.50 (0-942545-30-3, Dist. by Grolier) Grey Castle.
—Something to Hide. 160p. 1991. pap. 3.50 (0-671-74659-6, Archway) PB.
—Spies & Lies. Greenberg, Anne, ed. 224p. 1992. pap. 3.99 (0-671-73125-4, Archway) PB.
—Stage Fright. Greenberg, Anne, ed. 160p. (Orig.). 1993. pap. 3.99 (0-671-79482-5, Archway) PB.
—Stay Tuned for Danger. 160p. (Orig.). (gr. 7 up). 1991. pap. 3.50 (0-671-73667-1, Archway) PB.
—Stolen Kisses. 160p. 1990. pap. 2.95 (0-671-67762-4, Archway) PB.
—The Stranger in the Shadows. Greenberg, Anne, ed. 160p. (Orig.). 1991. pap. 3.99 (0-671-73049-5, Minstrel Bks) PB.
—The Suspect Next Door. (Orig.). (gr. 7 up). 1991. pap. 3.50 (0-671-74612-X, Archway) PB.
—Sweet Revenge. Greenberg, Ann, ed. 160p. (Orig.). 1991. pap. 3.50 (0-671-73065-7, Archway) PB.
—Swiss Secrets. Greenberg, Anne, ed. 160p. 1992. pap. 3.75 (0-671-73076-2, Archway) PB.
—A Talent for Murder. Greenberg, Anne, ed. 160p. (Orig.). 1992. pap. 3.75 (0-671-73079-7, Archway) PB.
—Tall, Dark & Deadly. Greenberg, Ann, ed. 160p. (Orig.). 1991. pap. 3.50 (0-671-73070-3, Archway) PB.
—Till Death Do Us Part. 1988. pap. 2.95 (0-318-35168-4) PB.
—Tour of Danger. Greenberg, Anne, ed. 224p. (Orig.). 1992. pap. 3.99 (0-671-67468-4) PB.
—Trail of Lies. Greenberg, Ann, ed. 160p. (Orig.). (gr. 7 up). 1990. pap. 3.75 (0-671-70030-8, Archway) PB.
—The Triple Hoax. (gr. 2-7). 1984. 8.85 (0-685-09396-4) S&S Trade.
—Tropic of Fear. Greenberg, Anne, ed. 224p. (Orig.). (gr. 7 up). 1992. pap. 3.99 (0-671-73126-2, Archway) PB.
—Trouble at Tahoe. 1994. pap. 3.99 (0-671-79304-7, Minstrel Bks) PB.
—The Twin Dilemma. (gr. 3-7). 1988. pap. 3.99 (0-671-67301-7, Minstrel Bks) PB.
—Two Points to Murder. (gr. 7 up). 1991. pap. 3.50 (0-671-73663-9, Archway) PB.
—Two Points to Murder: The Nancy Drew Files, Case 8. large type ed. 151p. (gr. 5-10). 1988. Repr. of 1987 ed. 9.50 (0-942545-39-7); PLB 10.50 (0-942545-34-6, Dist. by Grolier) Grey Castle.
—Update on Crime. Greenberg, Anne, ed. 160p. (Orig.). (gr. 7 up). 1992. pap. 3.75 (0-671-73082-7, Archway) PB.
—White Water Terror: The Nancy Drew Files, Case 6. large type ed. 169p. (gr. 5-10). 1988. Repr. of 1986 ed. 9.50 (0-942545-37-0); PLB 10.50 (0-942545-32-X, Dist. by Grolier) Grey Castle.
—Win, Place or Die. 160p. 1990. pap. 3.50 (0-671-67498-6, Archway) PB.
—The Wrong Track. Greenberg, Anne, ed. 160p. (Orig.). 1991. pap. 3.50 (0-671-73068-1, Archway) PB.
Keene, Carolyn & Dixon, Franklin W. Nancy Drew & the Hardy Boys. Barish, Wendy, ed. Frame, Paul, illus. 192p. (Orig.). (gr. 3 up). 1984. pap. 2.95 (0-685-09176-7) S&S Trade.
—Nancy Drew & the Hardy Boys Be a Detective Mystery Stories: Ticket to Intrigue. Arico, Diane, ed. Frame, Paul, illus. 128p. (Orig.). (gr. 3-7). 1985. pap. 2.95 (0-671-55735-1) S&S Trade.
—Nancy Drew & the Hardy Boys: Jungle of Evil. Arico, Diane, ed. Frame, Paul, illus. 128p. (Orig.). (gr. 3-7). 1985. pap. 2.95 (0-671-55734-3) S&S Trade.
—The Nancy Drew & the Hardy Boys Super Sleuths: Seven New Mysteries. (Illus.). 192p. (Orig.). (gr. 3-7). 1982. (Little Simon) S&S Trade.
—Super Sleuths, No. 2. Frame, Paul, illus. (gr. 2-7). 1984. 3.50 (0-685-09395-6) S&S Trade.
Keene, Dennis, tr. see Maruya, Saiichi.
Keene, Michael & Wood, Angela. Being a Jew. (Illus.). 64p. (gr. 7-12). 1987. 19.95 (0-7134-4668-4, Pub. by Batsford UK) Trafalgar.
Keene, Raymond. The Simon & Schuster Pocket Book of Chess. LC 88-30555. (gr. 4 up). 1989. pap. 12.95 (0-671-67923-6, S&S BFYR); pap. 7.95 (0-671-67924-4, S&S BFYR) S&S Trade.
Keener, Joseph. Music Series. (gr. 1-7). 1982. pap. write for info. (0-686-37780-X) Rod & Staff.
Keens-Douglas, Richardo. El Misterio De la Isla De las Especies: The Nutmeg Princess. Galouchko, Annoushka, illus. (SPA.). 32p. (ps-2). 1992. pap. 6.95 (1-55037-260-2, Pub. by Annick Pr) Firefly Bks Ltd.
—Le Mystere de l'Iles aux Epices: The Nutmeg Princess. Galouchko, Annouchka, illus. (FRE.). 32p. (ps-2). 1992. PLB 15.95 (1-55037-249-1, Pub. by Annick Pr); pap. 6.95 (1-55037-250-5, Pub. by Annick Pr) Firefly Bks Ltd.
—The Nutmeg Princess. Galouchko, Annoushka, illus. 32p. (ps-2). 1992. PLB 15.95 (1-55037-239-4, Pub. by Annick Pr); pap. 5.95 (1-55037-236-X, Pub. by Annick Pr) Firefly Bks Ltd.
Keep, Robert P., tr. see Autenrieth, Georg.
Keeper, Berry. The Old Ones Told Me: American Indian Stories for Children. (Illus.). 36p. (Orig.). 1989. pap. 4.95 (0-8323-0473-5) Binford Mort.
Keesing UK Ltd. Staff, ed. Travel Crosswords for Kids. 96p. (Orig.). 1993. pap. 9.95x (0-572-01786-3, Pub. by W Foulsham UK) Trans-Atl Phila.
Keffer, Christine & Long, Carolyn. Semantic Fitness. (gr. 8 up). 1986. spiral reproducible wkbk. 31.95 (1-55999-069-4) LinguiSystems.

Keffer, Lois. Getting along with Your Family. (Illus.). 48p. (gr. 9-12). 1992. pap. 7.99 (1-55945-233-1) Group Pub.
Kehl, Richard. Further Departures. 1991. pap. 5.95 (0-88138-138-1, Green Tiger) S&S Trade.
Kehle, Mary. In the Middle: What to Do When Your Parents Divorce. LC 86-31319. 96p. (Orig.). (gr. 4-8). 1987. pap. 5.99 (0-87788-375-0) Shaw Pubs.
Kehoe, Michael. A Book Takes Root: The Making of a Picture Book. LC 92-32534. 1993. 19.95 (0-87614-756-2) Carolrhoda Bks.
Kehoe, Patricia. Something Happened & I'm Scared to Tell: A Book for Young Children Victims of Abuse. Deach, Carol, illus. LC 86-62032. 32p. (Orig.). (ps-1). 1987. PLB 15.95 (0-943990-29-7); pap. 4.95 (0-943990-28-9) Parenting Pr.
Kehret, Peg. Acting Natural: Monologs, Dialogs, & Playlets for Teens. Zapel, Arthur L., ed. Panowski, James A., frwd. by. LC 91-43552. (Orig.). (gr. 9-12). 1992. pap. text ed. 10.95 (0-916260-84-4, B133) Meriwether Pub.
—Cages. LC 90-21230. 160p. (gr. 5 up). 1991. 14.99 (0-525-65062-8, Cobblehill Bks) Dutton Child Bks.
—Cages. MacDonald, Pat, ed. 160p. 1993. pap. 3.50 (0-671-75879-9, Minstrel Bks) PB.
—Deadly Stranger. 176p. (gr. 2-9). 1988. pap. 2.95 (0-8167-1308-1) Troll Assocs.
—Horror at the Haunted House. 160p. (gr. 4 up). 1992. 14.00 (0-525-65106-3, Cobblehill Bks) Dutton Child Bks.
—Night of Fear. LC 93-24051. 144p. (gr. 5 up). 1994. 13.99 (0-525-65136-5, Cobblehill Bks) Dutton Child Bks.
—Nightmare Mountain. Mckeating, Eileen, illus. LC 89-1535. 176p. (gr. 5 up). 1989. 13.95 (0-525-65008-3, Cobblehill Bks) Dutton Child Bks.
—Nightmare Mountain. MacDonald, Patricia, ed. 176p. (Orig.). 1991. pap. 2.99 (0-671-72864-4, Minstrel Bks) PB.
—Sisters, Long Ago. Kelly, Kathleen M., illus. LC 89-38677. 160p. (gr. 5 up). 1990. 14.95 (0-525-65021-0, Cobblehill Bks) Dutton Child Bks.
—Terror at the Zoo. 160p. (gr. 5 up). 1992. 14.00 (0-525-65083-0, Cobblehill Bks) Dutton Child Bks.
—Terror at the Zoo. 144p. (gr. 4-7). 1993. pap. 3.50 (0-671-79394-2, Minstrel Bks) PB.
—Wally Amos Presents Chip & Cookie: The First Adventure. (gr. 4-7). 1991. 14.95 (0-87491-988-6) Acropolis.
—The Winner. (gr. 7-12). 1988. PLB 2.95 (0-89872-302-7) Turman Pub.
—Winning Monologs for Young Actors. Zapel, Arthur & Pijanowski, Kathy, eds. LC 86-61109. 160p. (Orig.). (gr. 6-12). 1986. pap. text ed. 9.95 (0-916260-38-0, B-127) Meriwether Pub.
Keightley, Moy. Investigating Art: A Practical Guide for Young People. (Illus.). 160p. (gr. 7 up). 17.95x (0-87196-973-4) Facts on File.
Keim, Will S. The Education of Character: Lesson for Beginners. Prosser, Donna, illus. Pittman, Bruce, intro. by. (Illus.). 96p. 1992. 14.95 (0-9631834-0-0) Viaticum Pr.
Kein, Sybil. Delta Dancer. LC 84-48327. 89p. (gr. 9-12). 1984. pap. 9.00 perf. bdg. (0-916418-57-X) Lotus.
Keirns, Johanna L. The Cone Connection: A Guide to Cone-Bearing Trees in California's Mountains. 30p. (gr. 3-7). 1992. pap. 5.95 (1-882346-00-9) Virgilio Integrat.
—The Cone Connection: The Young Traveler's Guide to Cone-Bearing Trees in California's Mountains. 30p. (gr. 3-7). 1992. pap. 5.95 (1-882346-01-7) Virgilio Integrat.
Keiser, Gayle, et al. My Peanut Butter Pond Think-Along Funbook. Ducey, Elizabeth P., illus. Britt, Stephanie M., contrib. by. (Illus.). 100p. (ps-4). 1991. wkbk., spiral bdg. 3.95 (1-55999-156-9) LinguiSystems.
Keith, Evan. Amy Grant: Who's Hot! 48p. (gr. 4-7). 1992. 1.49 (0-440-21377-0) Dell.
—The Girls of Beverly Hills, 90210. (Illus.). 48p. 1993. 1.49 (0-440-21426-2) Dell.
—Luke Perry: Who's Hot! 48p. (gr. 4-7). 1992. pap. 1.49 (0-440-21375-4) Dell.
—Who's Hot ~ Cindy Crawford. (gr. 4-7). 1993. pap. 1.49 (0-440-21592-7) Dell.
—Who's Hot! Denzel Washington. (gr. 4-7). 1993. pap. 1.49 (0-440-21476-9) Dell.
—Winona Ryder. (Illus.). 48p. 1992. 1.49 (0-440-21432-7) Dell.
Keith, Gretchen L. The Life to Come: Stories for Children about the Spiritual World. Cook, Richard J., illus. 89p. (Orig.). (gr. 3-7). 1990. pap. 5.00 (0-945003-03-X) General Church.
Keith, Harold. Komantcia. 2nd ed. LC 91-60777. 299p. (gr. 5 up). 1991. 17.00x (0-927562-03-0) Levite Apache.
—The Obstinate Land: Cherokee Strip Run of 1893. 2nd ed. LC 77-1826. 214p. (gr. 4 up). pap. 12.95 (0-927562-15-4) Levite Apache.
—Rifles for Watie. LC 57-10280. 322p. (gr. 7 up). 1957. 14.95 (0-690-70181-0, Crowell Jr Bks) HarpC Child Bks.
—Rifles for Watie. LC 57-10280. 352p. (gr. 7 up). 1987. pap. 3.95 (0-06-447030-X, Trophy) HarpC Child Bks.
—Rifles for Watie. reissued ed. LC 57-10280. 332p. (gr. 7 up). 1991. PLB 14.89 (0-690-04907-2, Crowell Jr Bks) HarpC Child Bks.

—The Sound of Strings: Sequel to Komantcia. LC 91-62777. 175p. (Orig.). (gr. 5 up). 1992. 17.00 (0-927562-10-3) Levite Apache.
—Will Rogers, a Boy's Life: An Indian Territory Childhood. rev. ed. LC 91-62354. 271p. (gr. 3 up). 1992. 17.00 (0-927562-08-1); pap. 11.00 (0-927562-09-X) Levite Apache.
Keith, Herbert, jt. auth. see Isynwill, L. N.
Keith, Ian & Van Loan, Derek. Sailing with Ham Radio. (Illus.). 132p. (Orig.). (gr. 5-9). 1987. pap. 9.95 (0-939837-17-X) Paradise Cay Pubns.
Keith, Margaret. Patrick & the Actors. 206p. (gr. 9-12). 1981. 15.95 (0-920806-31-7, Pub. by Penumbra Pr CN); pap. 10.95 (0-920806-34-1, Pub. by Penumbra Pr CN) U of Toronto Pr.
Kelch, Joseph W. Millions of Miles to Mars. Byrne, Connell, illus. LC 93-33798. (gr. 3 up). 1994. write for info. (0-671-88249-X, J Messner); pap. write for info. (0-671-88250-3, J Messner) S&S Trade.
—Small Worlds: Sixty Moons of Our Solar System. Steltenpohl, Jane, ed. (Illus.). 128p. (gr. 6-8). 1990. 13.95 (0-671-70014-6, J Messner); lib. bdg. 16.98 (0-671-70013-8) S&S Trade.
Kelemen, Julie. Advent Is for Children. 64p. (Orig.). (gr. 3 up). 1988. pap. 2.95 (0-89243-292-6) Liguori Pubns.
—Lent Is for Children: Stories, Activities, Prayers. 64p. (Orig.). (gr. 4-8). 1987. pap. 2.95 (0-89243-280-2) Liguori Pubns.
—Lent Is for Children: Stories, Activities, Prayers. rev. ed. (Illus.). 80p. 1993. map. text ed. 2.95 (0-89243-532-1) Liguori Pubns.
—Prayer Is for Children: Stories, Prayers, Activities. LC 91-66154. 80p. (gr. 4-6). 1992. pap. 2.95 (0-89243-413-9) Liguori Pubns.
Kelinson, Roberta, jt. auth. see McGreevey, Carla.
Kelinson, Roberta M., jt. auth. see McGreevey, Carla.
Kelleher, D. V. Defenders of the Universe. Brown, Jane C., illus. LC 92-1617. 128p. (gr. 3-5). 1993. 13.45 (0-395-60515-6) HM.
Kelleher, Victor. Brother Night. LC 90-19743. 160p. (gr. 7 up). 1991. 16.95 (0-8027-8100-4) Walker & Co.
—Del-Del. (gr. 7-10). 1992. 17.95 (0-8027-8154-3) Walker & Co.
—Master of the Grove. (gr. 5-9). 1988. pap. 3.95 (0-317-69634-3, Puffin) Puffin Bks.
—Rescue! LC 91-30490. 224p. (gr. 5 up). 1992. 15.00 (0-8037-0900-5) Dial Bks Young.
Keller, Beverly. Camp Trouble. (gr. 4-7). 1993. pap. 2.95 (0-590-43728-3) Scholastic Inc.
—Desdemona Moves On. LC 92-7127. 176p. (gr. 3-7). 1992. SBE 13.95 (0-02-749751-8, Bradbury Pr) Macmillan Child Grp.
—Desdemona: Twelve Going on Desperate. LC 86-10655. 160p. (gr. 3-7). 1986. 12.95 (0-688-06076-5) Lothrop.
—Desdemona: Twelve Going on Desperate. LC 87-45287. 160p. (gr. 3-7). 1988. pap. 3.95 (0-06-440226-6, Trophy) HarpC Child Bks.
—Fowl Play, Desdemona. LC 88-9481. 176p. (gr. 4-7). 1989. 11.95 (0-688-06920-7) Lothrop.
—Fowl Play, Desdemona. 192p. (gr. 3-7). 1991. pap. 3.95 (0-06-440393-9, Trophy) HarpC Child Bks.
—A Garden of Love to Share. Paris, Pat & Posey, Pam, illus 40p. (ps-3). 1984. 5.95 (0-910313-49-0) Parker Bros.
—A Small, Elderly Dragon. Malone, Nola L., illus. LC 83-13632. 144p. (gr. 5 up). 1984. 12.95 (0-688-02553-6) Lothrop.
Keller, Charles. Alexander the Grape: Fruit & Vegetable Jokes. Filling, Gregory, illus. 48p. (gr. 2-6). 1985. 10.95 (0-13-021410-8); pap. 4.95 (0-13-020918-X) P-H.
—Astronauts: Space Jokes & Riddles. (gr. 4-7). 1991. pap. 2.95 (0-671-73984-0, Little Simon) S&S Trade.
—Ballpoint Bananas & Other Jokes for Kids. Barrios, David, illus. LC 72-7338. 96p. (gr. 3-7). 1976. pap. 5.95 (0-671-66965-6, S&S BFYR) S&S Trade.
—Belly Laughs! Food Jokes & Riddles. Fritz, Ron, illus. LC 89-28201. 32p. (gr. k-3). 1990. pap. 13.95 jacketed (0-671-70068-5, S&S BFYR); pap. 5.95 (0-671-70069-3, S&S BFYR) S&S Trade.
—Colossal Fossils: Dinosaur Riddles. 64p. (gr. 4-7). 1991. pap. 2.95 (0-671-73985-9, Little Simon) S&S Trade.
—Count Draculations! Monster Riddles. Frascino, Edward, illus. 64p. (gr. 3-7). 1986. 10.95 (0-13-183641-2) P-H.
—Count Draculations: Monster Riddles. 64p. (gr. 4-7). 1991. pap. 2.95 (0-671-73983-2, Little Simon) S&S Trade.
—Driving Me Crazy: Fun on Wheels Jokes. Lorenz, Lee, illus. 40p. (gr. 2-5). 1989. 13.95 (0-945912-05-6) Pippin Pr.
—Giggle Puss: Pet Jokes for Kids. Coker, Paul, Jr., illus. LC 76-44837. (gr. 3-7). 1977. (Pub. by Treehouse); pap. 3.95 (0-13-356303-0) P-H.
—Grime Doesn't Pay: Law & Order Jokes. Kent, Jack, illus. 64p. 1984. 9.95 (0-13-365503-2) P-H.
—It's Raining Cats & Dogs: Cat & Dog Jokes. Quackenbush, Robert, illus. 40p. (gr. 2-6). 1988. 13.95 (0-945912-01-3) Pippin Pr.
—King Henry the Ape: Animal Jokes. Frascino, Edward, illus. 40p. (gr. 2-5). 1990. PLB 13.95 (0-945912-08-0) Pippin Pr.
—Little Witch Presents a Monster Joke Book. Glovach, Linda, illus. 40p. (ps-4). 1983. pap. 4.95 (0-13-537811-7, Pub. by Treehouse) P-H.
—Norma Lee I Don't Knock on Doors: Knock Knock Jokes. Galdone, Paul, illus. LC 82-21549. 44p. (gr. 3-7). 1983. 9.95 (0-13-623587-5) P-H.

—Oh, Brother: And Other Family Jokes. Frascino, Edward, illus. 48p. (gr. 2-6). 1982. 8.95 (0-13-633305-2) P-H.
—Ohm on the Range. Cummings, Art, illus. 48p. (gr. 3-7). 1985. pap. 4.95 (0-13-633546-2) P-H.
—Ohm on the Range: Robot & Computer Jokes. Cumings, Art, illus. 48p. (gr. 3-7). 1982. 8.95 (0-13-633552-7) P-H.
—Planet of the Grapes: Show Biz Jokes & Riddles. Richter, Mischa, illus. 40p. (gr. 3-7). 1992. 13.95 (0-945912-17-X) Pippin Pr.
—Remember the Ala Mode: Riddles & Puns. Lorenz, Lee, illus. Keller, Charles, compiled by. 64p. (gr. 3-7). 1986. pap. 5.95 (0-13-773342-9) P-H.
—School Daze. Weissman, Sam Q., illus. (gr. 2-5). 1981. pap. 3.95 (0-13-793612-5, Pub. by Treehouse) P-H.
—Smokey the Shark: And Other Fishy Stories. Lorenz, Lee, illus. (gr. 2-6). 1981. 8.95 (0-13-814707-8) P-H.
—Take Me to Your Liter: Science & Math Jokes. Filling, Gregory, illus. 40p. (gr. 2-5). 1991. PLB 13.95 (0-945912-13-7) Pippin Pr.
—Tongue Twisters. Fritz, Ron, illus. LC 88-26448. (ps-4). 1989. map. 13.95 (0-671-67123-5, S&S BFYR); pap. 5.95 (0-671-67975-9, S&S BFYR) S&S Trade.
—Waiter, There's a Fly in My Soup. Lorenz, Lee, illus. LC 86-12222. 64p. (gr. 3-7). 1986. 10.95 (0-13-944182-4) P-H.
—Waiter, There's a Fly in My Soup. (gr. 4-7). 1991. pap. 2.95 (0-671-73982-4, S&S BFYR) S&S Trade.
—What's up, Doc? Doctor & Dentist Jokes. Kessler, Leonard, illus. LC 84-6821. 64p. (gr. 3-7). 1984. 9.95 (0-13-954967-6) P-H.
Keller, Charles, compiled by. Going Bananas: Jokes for Kids. Wilson, Roger B., illus. (gr. 2-5). 1977. 8.95 (0-13-357772-4, Pub. by Treehouse); pap. 3.95 (0-13-357780-5) P-H.
—Lend Me Your Ears: Telephone Jokes. Kessler, Leonard, illus. 40p. (gr. 2-5). 1993. PLB 13.95 (0-945912-23-4) Pippin Pr.
—More Ballpoint Bananas. Shortall, Leonard, illus. LC 77-5356. (gr. 1-3). 1980. 7.95 (0-13-600767-8, Pub. by Treehouse) P-H.
Keller, Charles, ed. Remember the a la Mode! Riddles & Puns. Lorenz, Lee, illus. LC 83-13832. 64p. (gr. 3-5). 1983. 10.95 (0-13-773358-5) P-H.
Keller, Charles & Baker, Richard, eds. Star-Spangled Banana: And Other Revolutionary Riddles. De Paola, Tomie. (Illus.). 62p. (gr. 2 up). 1974. 3.95 (0-13-842971-5, Pub. by Treehouse) P-H.
Keller, Charles, compiled by. Daffynitions. Fitzgerald, F. A., illus. LC 75-34280. (gr. 3 up). 1978. (Pub. by Treehouse); pap. 3.95 (0-13-196576-X) P-H.
—Growing up Laughing: Humorists Look at American Youth. (Illus.). (gr. 5 up). 1981. 10.95 (0-13-367870-9) P-H.
Keller, David. Great Disasters. 112p. 1990. pap. 2.95 (0-380-76043-6, Camelot) Avon.
Keller, Emily. Margaret Bourke-White: A Photographer's Life. LC 92-44382. (gr. 4-9). 1993. 21.50 (0-8225-4916-6) Lerner Pubns.
Keller, Gunter. A Step-by-Step Book about Discus. (Illus.). 64p. (gr. 9-12). 1988. pap. 3.95 (0-86622-465-3, SK-008) TFH Pubns.
Keller, Helen. Story of My Life. Barnett, M. R., intro. by. (gr. 8 up). 1965. pap. 2.95 (0-8049-0070-1, CL-70) Airmont.
—Story of My Life. LC 54-11951. (Illus.). (gr. 7 up). 1954. 15.95 (0-385-04453-4) Doubleday.
—Story of My Life. (gr. 7 up). 1991. pap. 2.95 (0-590-44353-4) Scholastic Inc.
Keller, Holly. A Bear for Christmas. Keller, Holly, illus. LC 85-12645. 32p. (ps-3). 1986. 11.75 (0-688-05988-0); PLB 11.88 (0-688-05989-9) Greenwillow.
—The Best Present. LC 87-38086. (Illus.). 32p. (gr. k up). 1989. 11.95 (0-688-07319-0); PLB 11.88 (0-688-07320-4) Greenwillow.
—Cromwell's Glasses. Keller, Holly, illus. LC 81-6644. 32p. (gr. k-3). 1982. 14.95 (0-688-00834-8) Greenwillow.
—Furry. LC 90-24645. (Illus.). 24p. 1992. 14.00 (0-688-10519-X); PLB 13.93 (0-688-10520-3) Greenwillow.
—Geraldine's Baby Brother. (gr. 3 up). 1994. write for info. (0-688-12005-9); PLB write for info. (0-688-12006-7) Greenwillow.
—Geraldine's Big Snow. LC 87-14936. (Illus.). 24p. (ps-3). 1988. 11.95 (0-688-07513-4); lib. bdg. 11.88 (0-688-07514-2) Greenwillow.
—Geraldine's Blanket. Keller, Holly, illus. LC 83-14062. 32p. (ps-1). 1984. 13.95 (0-688-02539-0); PLB 13.88 (0-688-02540-4) Greenwillow.
—Geraldine's Blanket. LC 83-14062. (Illus.). 32p. (ps-3). 1988. pap. 3.95 (0-688-07810-9, Mulberry) Morrow.
—Goodbye, Max. Keller, Holly, illus. LC 86-4680. 32p. (ps-3). 1987. 12.95 (0-688-06561-9); PLB 12.88 (0-688-06562-7) Greenwillow.
—Grandfather's Dream. LC 93-18186. (Illus.). 32p. (ps up). 1994. write for info. (0-688-12339-2); PLB write for info. (0-688-12340-6) Greenwillow.
—Harry & Tuck. LC 91-45674. (Illus.). 24p. (ps up). 1993. 14.00 (0-688-11462-8); PLB 13.93 (0-688-11463-6) Greenwillow.
—Henry's Fourth of July. LC 84-13707. (Illus.). 32p. (ps-1). 1985. PLB 10.88 (0-688-04013-6) Greenwillow.
—Henry's Happy Birthday. LC 89-23324. (Illus.). 32p. (ps up). 1990. 12.95 (0-688-09450-3); PLB 12.88 (0-688-09451-1) Greenwillow.

—Horace. LC 90-30750. (Illus.). 32p. (ps up). 1991. 15.00 (0-688-09831-2); PLB 14.93 (0-688-09832-0) Greenwillow.
—Island Baby. LC 91-32491. (Illus.). 32p. (ps-8). 1992. 14.00 (0-688-10579-3); PLB 13.93 (0-688-10580-7) Greenwillow.
—Lizzie's Invitation. LC 86-19380. (ps-3). 1987. 11.75 (0-688-06124-9); PLB 11.88 (0-688-06125-7) Greenwillow.
—Maxine in the Middle. LC 88-18783. (Illus.). 32p. (ps up). 1989. 12.95 (0-688-08150-9); PLB 12.88 (0-688-08151-7) Greenwillow.
—The New Boy. LC 90-41757. (Illus.). 24p. (ps up). 1991. 13.95 (0-688-09827-4); PLB 13.88 (0-688-09828-2) Greenwillow.
—Ten Sleepy Sheep. Keller, Holly, illus. LC 83-1477. 32p. (gr. k-3). 1983. 10.25 (0-688-02306-1); PLB 13.93 (0-688-02307-X) Greenwillow.
—What Alvin Wanted. LC 88-34917. (Illus.). 32p. (ps up). 1990. 12.95 (0-688-08933-X); lib. bdg. 12.88 (0-688-08934-8) Greenwillow.
Keller, Irene. The Thingumajig Book of Manners. Keller, Dick, illus. 32p. (ps-3). 1989. pap. 3.95 (0-8249-8346-7, Ideals Child) Hambleton-Hill.
Keller, Jack. Tom Edison's Bright Idea. (Illus.). 32p. (gr. 1-4). 1989. PLB 15.96 (0-8172-3532-9); pap. 3.95 (0-8114-6733-3) Raintree Steck-V.
Keller, Merily H., ed. see Irving, Lynn.
Keller, Merily H., ed. see Winer, Yvonne.
Keller, Paul F. Studies in Lutheran Doctrine. LC 60-15574. (gr. 7-8). 1959. pap. 6.00 (0-570-03517-1, 14-1265); correction & profile chart 0.40 (0-570-03526-0, 14-1267); tests 0.60 (0-570-03525-2, 14-1266) Concordia.
Keller, Rosanne. Stormy Night Stories: Reading Level 3-4, 10 bks. Kempster, Teddy, illus. 160p. (gr. 8-12). 1993. Boxed Set. incl. tchr's. guide 14.95 (0-88336-992-3); tchr's guide 1.65 (0-88336-991-5) New Readers.
Keller, Stella. Ice Cream. (Illus.). 32p. (gr. 1-4). 1989. PLB 15.96 (0-8172-3523-X); pap. 3.95 (0-8114-6720-1) Raintree Steck-V.
Keller, W. Phillip. A Child's Look at the Twenty-Third Psalm. Jarrett, Lauren, illus. LC 84-13718. 96p. (gr. 3 up). 1985. pap. 7.95 (0-385-15457-7, Galilee) Doubleday.
Keller, Wallace E. The Wrong Side of the Bed. (Illus.). 32p. (ps-1). 1993. 14.95 (0-87663-799-3) Universe.
Kelley, Barbara. Harpo's Horrible Secret. Block, Lori, illus. Sargent, Dave, intro. by. (Illus.). 120p. (Orig.). (gr. k-8). 1993. text ed. 16.95 (1-56763-058-8); pap. text ed. 8.95 (1-56763-059-6) Ozark Pub.
Kelley, Colleen. Kids' Stuff: Simple Science & Nature Projects for Children. Kelley, Colleen, illus. 96p. (gr. k-6). 1989. pap. text ed. 4.95 (0-9618052-2-6) Daily Hampshire.
Kelley, Emily. April Fool's Day. Nobens, Cheryl A., illus. LC 82-23559. 48p. (gr. k-4). 1983. PLB 14.95 (0-87614-218-8); pap. 3.95 (0-87614-481-4) Carolrhoda Bks.
—Christmas around the World. Kiedrowski, Priscilla, illus 48p. (gr. k-4). 1986. lib. bdg. 14.95 (0-87614-249-8) Carolrhoda Bks.
—Christmas Around the World. Kiedrowski, Priscilla, illus. 48p. (ps-4). 1986. pap. 5.95 (0-87614-453-9, First Ave Edns) Lerner Pubns.
—Happy New Year. Kiedrowski, Priscilla, illus. 48p. (gr. k-4). 1984. PLB 14.95 (0-87614-269-2) Carolrhoda Bks.
—Happy New Year. Kiedrowski, Priscilla, illus. (gr. k-4). 1987. pap. 3.95 (0-87614-469-5, First Ave Edns) Lerner Pubns.
Kelley, Gail & Hershberger, Carol. Come Mime with Me: A Guide to Preparing Scriptural Dramas for Children. LC 86-62621. (Illus.). 104p. (gr. 1 up). 1987. 10.95 (0-89390-089-3) Resource Pubns.

Kelley, Robert P. Make These Paper Snow Flakes, Vol. 1. (Illus.). 64p. (Orig.). 1993. wkbk. 4.95 (0-9636818-6-9) Just Write CO. With this delightful workbook you can make your own artist-quality paper snowflakes fashioned from real ice crystals. By following the easy directions you can make hexagonal plates, broad branch crystals, stellar stars as well as "art crystal" such as a snow blossom, valentine doily & crystal crest. The author has worked in the public school system testing & refining these designs &, as intricate as these designs may seem, with a little help getting started, the average third-grader can do most of them (older children, adults & even senior citizens enjoy making paper snowflakes as well). Repeating symmetrical patterns cut from paper is a folk art more than two thousand years old & present in

nearly every culture in history. This unique & inexpensive book makes a great gift...Christmas, Valentine's Day, birthday parties, etc. You may want to buy several! So try your hand; unfolding one of these snowflakes is like opening a present. Make your own snow storm of winter wonderland fun! Order from Just Write Publishing Co. 2577 Butte Circle, Sedalia, CO 80135; 303-688-5825.
Publisher Provided Annotation.

Kelley, Rosemary S. Seavy Seagull & the Friendship Sloop Race. 2nd ed. Kelley, Rosemary S., illus. 39p. (ps-k). 1985. pap. 5.95 (*0-9616905-0-X*) R S Kelley.
Kelley, Shirley. The Good, the Bad & the Two Cookie Kid: The Two Cookie Kid. Herbst, Eric & Genee, Gloria, eds. Claridy, Jimmy, illus. Cash, Johnny, intro. by. (Illus.). 32p. (ps-4). 1993. 9.95 (*1-882436-02-4*) Better Pl Pub.
—Little Settlers of Vermont. 1987. 7.95 (*0-685-43894-5*) Equity Pub NH.
—The Rainy Day Blues. Herbst, Eric & Genee, Gloria, eds. Claridy, Jimmy, illus. King, B. B., intro. by. (Illus.). 32p. (ps-4). 1993. 9.95 (*1-882436-01-6*) Better Pl Pub.
Kelley, Steven. Airplanes & Other Things That Fly. (Illus.). 48p. (ps-2). 1990. write for info. (*0-307-17867-6*, Pub. by Golden Bks) Western Pub.
Kelley, True. Buggly Bear's Hiccup Cure. LC 81-16903. (Illus.). 48p. (ps-3). 1982. 5.95 (*0-8193-1081-6*); PLB 5.95 (*0-8193-1082-4*) Parents.
—Hammers, Mops, Pens, & Pots. LC 93-25294. 1994. 12.00 (*0-517-59626-1*, Crown) Crown Pub Group.
—I've Got Chicken Pox. Kelley, True, illus. LC 93-11685. 1994. write for info. (*0-525-45185-4*) Dutton Child Bks.
—Let's Eat. Kelley, True, illus. LC 88-25699. 32p. (ps-1). 1989. 11.95 (*0-525-44482-3*, DCB) Dutton Child Bks.
—Look Baby! Listen Baby! Do Baby! Kelley, True, illus. LC 87-6800. 32p. (ps). 1987. 9.95 (*0-525-44320-7*, DCB) Dutton Child Bks.
—A Valentine for Fuzzboom. Kelley, True, illus. LC 80-24284. 24p. (gr. k-3). 1982. HM.
Kelley, True, jt. auth. see Kleitsch, Christel.
Kelling, Furn F. Prayer Is... (Illus.). (gr. k-3). 1979. 6.95 (*0-8054-4256-1*, 4242-56) Broadman.
Kellman, A., ed. see Zakutinsky, Ruth.
Kellman, Jerold L. & Kellman, Nancy L. Birthday Bonanza: Celebrating People Who Made Our World. (gr. 4-8). 1986. pap. 8.95 (*0-673-18347-5*) Scott F.
Kellman, Nancy L., jt. auth. see Kellman, Jerold L.
Kellner, Douglas. Ernesto "Che" Guevara. Schlesinger, Arthur M., intro. by. (Illus.). 112p. (gr. 5 up). 1989. 17.95 (*1-55546-835-7*) Chelsea Hse.
Kellog, Steven. Chicken Little. LC 84-25519. (Illus.). (gr. 1 up). 1989. pap. 7.95 bk. & cassette (*0-688-09041-9*, Mulberry) Morrow.
Kellogg, Cynthia. Corn: What It Is, What It Does. LC 88-18784. (Illus.). 48p. 1989. 11.95 (*0-688-08024-3*); PLB 11.88 (*0-688-08026-X*) Greenwillow.
Kellogg, Marjorie. Like the Lion's Tooth. 1992. pap. 3.95 (*0-374-44477-3*) FS&G.
—Tell Me That You Love Me, Junie Moon. Fox, Paula, intro. by. LC 68-24600. 216p. (gr. 9 up). 1984. pap. 6.95 (*0-374-51825-4*) FS&G.
—Tell Me That You Love Me, Junie Moon. 224p. 1993. pap. 3.95 (*0-374-47510-5*) FS&G.
Kellogg, Mary G. Doing Things & Happenings. Rytter, Peggy, illus. LC 80-80271. 90p. (gr. 1-6). 1979. 6.95 (*0-9603972-0-5*); pap. 4.95 (*0-9603972-1-3*) Bks by Kellogg.
Kellogg, Nancy R. AIDS: Elementary-Intermediate Curriculum. (gr. 5-7). 1990. tchr's. ed. 8.95 (*0-944584-11-X*) Sopris.
Kellogg, Steven. Aster Aardvark's Alphabet Adventures. Kellogg, Steven, illus. LC 87-5715. 40p. (gr. k up). 1987. 13.95 (*0-688-07256-9*); lib. bdg. 13.88 (*0-688-07257-7*, Morrow Jr Bks) Morrow Jr Bks.
—Aster Aardvark's Alphabet Adventures. LC 87-5715. (Illus.). 40p. (gr. 1 up). 1992. pap. 3.95 (*0-688-11571-3*, Mulberry) Morrow.
—Best Friends. Kellogg, Steven, illus. LC 85-15971. 32p. (ps-3). 1986. 13.95 (*0-8037-0099-7*); PLB 13.89 (*0-8037-0101-2*) Dial Bks Young.
—Best Friends. Fogelman, Phyllis J., ed. Kellogg, Steven, illus. LC 85-15971. 32p. (ps-3). 1990. pap. 4.99 (*0-8037-0829-7*) Dial Bks Young.
—Can I Keep Him? Kellogg, Steven, illus. LC 72-142453. (ps-3). 1971. 13.99 (*0-8037-0988-9*); PLB 12.89 (*0-8037-0989-7*) Dial Bks Young.
—The Christmas Witch. Kellogg, Steven, illus. LC 91-32688. 40p. (gr. k-3). 1992. 15.00 (*0-8037-1268-5*); PLB 14.89 (*0-8037-1269-3*) Dial Bks Young.
—The Island of the Skog. LC 73-6019. (Illus.). (gr. k-3). 1976. pap. 4.95 (*0-8037-4122-7*) Dial Bks Young.
—The Island of the Skog. Kellogg, Steven, illus. LC 73-6019. 32p. (ps-3). 1973. 15.00 (*0-8037-3842-0*); PLB 13.89 (*0-8037-3840-4*) Dial Bks Young.
—Island of the Skog. (ps-3). 1993. pap. 4.99 (*0-14-054649-9*, Puffin) Puffin Bks.

—Johnny Appleseed. Kellogg, Steven, illus. LC 87-27317. 48p. (gr. 2 up). 1988. 14.95 (*0-688-06417-5*); PLB 14.88 (*0-688-06418-3*, Morrow Jr Bks) Morrow Jr Bks.
—Much Bigger Than Martin. Kellogg, Steven, illus. LC 75-2799. 32p. (ps-3). 1976. 12.95 (*0-8037-5809-X*); PLB 11.89 (*0-8037-5810-3*) Dial Bks Young.
—Much Bigger Than Martin. Kellogg, Steven, illus. LC 75-27599. (ps-3). 1976. pap. 3.95 (*0-8037-5811-1*) Dial Bks Young.
—The Mysterious Tadpole. LC 77-71517. (Illus.). (ps-3). 1987. 14.99 (*0-8037-6245-3*); PLB 13.89 (*0-8037-6246-1*) Dial Bks Young.
—The Mysterious Tadpole. Kellogg, Steven, illus. LC 77-71517. 32p. (ps-3). 1979. pap. 4.95 (*0-8037-6244-5*) Dial Bks Young.
—The Mysterious Tadpole. giant ed. (Illus.). 32p. (ps-3). 1992. pap. 17.99 (*0-14-054569-7*, Puffin Pied Piper) Puffin Bks.
—The Mystery of the Flying Orange Pumpkin. Kellogg, Steven, illus. LC 80-11748. 32p. (ps-2). 1983. pap. 3.50 (*0-8037-0019-9*) Dial Bks Young.
—The Mystery of the Missing Red Mitten. LC 73-15439. (Illus.). (gr. k-2). 1979. pap. 3.50 (*0-8037-5749-2*) Dial Bks Young.
—The Mystery of the Stolen Blue Paint. Kellogg, Steven, illus. LC 81-15314. 32p. (ps-2). 1982. PLB 8.89 (*0-8037-5659-3*) Dial Bks Young.
—Mystery of the Stolen Blue Paint. Kellogg, Steven, illus. LC 81-15314. 32p. (ps-2). 1986. pap. 3.95 (*0-8037-0285-X*) Dial Bks Young.
—Paul Bunyan. enl. ed. Kellogg, Steven, illus. 48p. (ps up). 1993. pap. 18.95 (*0-688-12610-3*, Mulberry) Morrow.
—Paul Bunyan. Marcuse, Aida, tr. from ENG. Kellogg, Steven, illus. (SPA.). 48p. (gr. k up). 1994. pap. 5.95 (*0-688-13202-2*, Mulberry) Morrow.
—Pecos Bill. Kellogg, Steven, illus. LC 86-784. 32p. (ps up). 1986. 15.95 (*0-688-05871-X*); lib. bdg. 15.88 (*0-688-05872-8*, Morrow Jr Bks) Morrow Jr Bks.
—Pecos Bill. ALC Staff, ed. LC 86-784. (Illus.). 48p. (gr. k up). 1992. pap. 4.95 (*0-688-09924-6*, Mulberry) Morrow.
—Pinkerton, Behave! Kellogg, Steven, illus. LC 78-31794. (ps-2). 1979. 13.95 (*0-8037-6573-8*); PLB 13.89 (*0-8037-6575-4*) Dial Bks Young.
—Pinkerton, Behave! Kellogg, Steven, illus. 32p. (gr. k-3). 1982. pap. 4.95 (*0-8037-7250-5*) Dial Bks Young.
—Pinkerton, Behave. giant ed. (ps-3). 1990. 17.99 (*0-8037-0841-6*) Dial Bks Young.
—Prehistoric Pinkerton. Kellogg, Steven, illus. LC 86-2201. 32p. (ps-3). 1987. 12.95 (*0-8037-0322-8*); PLB 12.89 (*0-8037-0323-6*) Dial Bks Young.
—Prehistoric Pinkerton. (ps-3). 1991. pap. 4.95 (*0-8037-1053-4*, Dial Pied Piper) Puffin Bks.
—Ralph's Secret Weapon. Kellogg, Steven, illus. LC 82-22115. (ps-3). 1983. 13.95 (*0-8037-7086-3*); PLB 13.89 (*0-8037-7087-1*); pap. 3.95 (*0-8037-0307-4*) Dial Bks Young.
—Ralph's Secret Weapon. Kellogg, Steven, illus. LC 82-22115. 32p. (ps-3). 1986. pap. 4.95 (*0-8037-0024-5*) Dial Bks Young.
—A Rose for Pinkerton. Kellogg, Steven, illus. LC 81-65848. 32p. (ps-3). 1981. 14.00 (*0-8037-7502-4*); PLB 12.89 (*0-8037-7503-2*) Dial Bks Young.
—Tallyho, Pinkerton! Kellogg, Steven, illus. LC 82-70198. 32p. (ps-3). 1983. 14.95 (*0-8037-8731-6*) Dial Bks Young.
—Tallyho, Pinkerton! Kellogg, Steven, illus. LC 82-2341. 32p. (ps-3). 1985. 4.95 (*0-8037-0166-7*) Dial Bks Young.
—Tallyho Pinkerton. (gr. 4-7). 1993. pap. 4.99 (*0-14-054710-X*, Puffin) Puffin Bks.
—Won't Somebody Play with Me? LC 72-708. (Illus.). (gr. k-3). 1976. pap. 4.95 (*0-8037-9612-9*) Dial Bks Young.
Kellogg, Steven, retold by. & illus. Jack & the Beanstalk. LC 90-45990. 48p. 1991. 14.95 (*0-688-10250-6*); PLB 14.88 (*0-688-10251-4*) Morrow Jr Bks.
—Mike Fink. LC 91-46014. 48p. 1992. 15.00 (*0-688-07003-5*); PLB 14.93 (*0-688-07004-3*) Morrow Jr Bks.
Kellogg, Steven, retold by. There Was an Old Woman. reissued ed. LC 80-15293. (Illus.). 48p. (ps-3). 1984. SBE 13.95 (*0-02-749780-1*, Four Winds) Macmillan Child Grp.

Kells, Elizabeth C. Taking Notes in the Classroom: A Guide to Higher Grades, Preparation for Exams, Reduced Study Time, Less Stress. (Orig.). (gr. 10-12). 1993. pap. text ed. 7.95 (*0-9634458-7-1*) Pubs Northeast.
TAKING NOTES IN THE CLASSROOM: A GUIDE TO HIGHER GRADES, PREPARATION FOR EXAMS, REDUCED STUDY TIME, LESS STRESS, develops note-taking & study skills in students grades ten through graduate school. It explains & demonstrates how to set up note-taking paper, how to take notes, how, when &

where to write down summarized notes, how & when to review notes & how & when to study for exams. It is concise, easy to read & to follow. The emphasis is on scheduled review periods for comprehension, class & exam preparation. It includes how to work with a classroom buddy when either student is absent from class, suggestions on scheduling time, sample note-taking paper, 83 shorthand aids & a page to record 22 grades. It is designed to fit into the inside pocket of a three ring binder cover & be readily available as a reference. E.C. Kells holds a B.A. from Boston University & an Ed.M. from Harvard. To order: Tel. 206-768-0104 or $7.95 plus $2.05 shipping to Publishers Northeast, Attn: C.G., 6702 16th SW, Seattle, WA 98250.
Publisher Provided Annotation.

Kelly, Andrew. Australia. LC 90-38123. (Illus.). 32p. (gr. k-3). 1991. PLB 12.40 (*0-531-18381-5*, Pub. by Bookwright Pr) Watts.
Kelly, Desmond. Breaking the Circle. 192p. (gr. 7 up). 1993. pap. 9.95 (*0-86327-348-3*, Pub. by Wolfhound Pr EIRE) Dufour.
Kelly, Doug, jt. auth. see Nelson, Ray, Jr.
Kelly, Eamon. Bridge of Feathers. LC 89-82490. 128p. (gr. 4-8). 1990. pap. 6.95 (*1-85371-054-7*, Pub. by Poolbeg Pr ER) Dufour.
Kelly, Emery. Kites on the Wind: Easy-to-Make Kites that Fly Without Sticks. Hagerman, Jennifer, illus. 64p. (gr. 4 up). 1991. PLB 22.95 (*0-8225-2400-7*) Lerner Pubns.
Kelly, Eric P. The Trumpeter of Krakow. Domanska, Janina, illus. LC 66-16712. 224p. (gr. 7 up). 1966. 14.95 (*0-02-750140-X*, Collier Young Ad); (Aladdin) Macmillan Child Grp.
—The Trumpeter of Krakow. Domanska, Janina, illus. LC 91-26879. 224p. (gr. 3-7). 1992. pap. 3.95 (*0-689-71571-4*, Aladdin) Macmillan Child Grp.
Kelly, Francis D., pref. by. Choose Life! Unborn Children & the Right to Life. (Illus.). 72p. (Orig.). (gr. 11-12). 1991. pap. 12.95 (*1-55833-106-9*) Natl Cath Educ.
Kelly, Gary F. Sex & Sense: A Contemporary Guide for Teenagers. 240p. 1993. pap. 7.95 (*0-8120-1446-4*) Barron.
Kelly, Jeffrey. The Basement Baseball Club. LC 86-27545. 160p. (gr. 3-5). 1987. 13.45 (*0-395-40774-5*) HM.
Kelly, Karen & Hopkins, Joan. Tilda's Treat: A New Way to Eat. Smith, Richard, illus. LC 74-15232. 128p. (gr. 6-12). 1975. pap. 2.95 (*0-87983-091-3*) Keats.
Kelly, Karla, et al. The Adventure of the Wandering Wolves in Vulcan's Vent. Crosby, Harriet, ed. Chan, Peter, illus. 40p. (Orig.). (gr. 1-6). 1993. pap. 6.95 (*1-883871-01-8*) Nature Co.
—Tales of Terratopia: The Secret of the Dragonfly & the Daring Dino Rescue. (Illus.). 36p. (gr. 1-6). 1993. 6.95 (*1-883871-00-X*) Nature Co.
Kelly, Kathryn, jt. auth. see Walters, Julie.
Kelly, Lawrence C. Federal Indian Policy. (Illus.). 112p. (gr. 5 up). 1990. 17.95 (*1-55546-706-7*) Chelsea Hse.
Kelly, Leslie A., jt. auth. see Anderson, William.
Kelly, M. A. A Child's Book of Wildflowers. Powzyk, Joyce, illus. LC 91-30368. 32p. (gr. k-4). 1992. RSBE 15.95 (*0-02-750142-6*, Four Winds) Macmillan Child Grp.
Kelly, Michael. Your First Lovebird. (Illus.). 34p. (Orig.). 1991. pap. 1.95 (*0-86622-069-0*, YF-112) TFH Pubns.
Kelly, Orly, ed. see Koff, Richard M.
Kelly, Paul. Deciphering Jesus' Parables. (Illus.). 48p. (gr. 9-12). 1992. pap. 7.99 (*1-55945-237-4*) Group Pub.
—First & Second Corinthians: Christian Discipleship. (Illus.). 48p. (gr. 9-12). 1992. pap. 7.99 (*1-55945-230-7*) Group Pub.
—Forgiveness. (Illus.). 48p. (gr. 9-12). 1992. pap. 7.99 (*1-55945-223-4*) Group Pub.
Kelly, Regina Z. Henry Clay. Walker, C., illus. (gr. 4-6). 1960. (Piper); pap. 2.44 (*0-395-01717-3*) HM.
—James Madison: Statesman & President. LC 90-49166. (Illus.). (gr. 6-10). 1991. PLB 13.95 (*1-55905-091-8*) Marshall Cavendish.
Kelly, Robert. How Do I Make up My Mind, Lord? LC 82-70948. 112p. (Orig.). (gr. 3-7). 1982. pap. 5.99 (*0-8066-1923-6*, 10-3168, Augsburg) Augsburg Fortress.
Kelly, Robert T., ed. see Hamilton, Mary M.
Kelly, Rosemary & Kelly, Tony. City at War: Oxford 1642-46. 52p. (gr. 11 up). 1987. pap. 7.95 (*0-85950-540-5*, Pub. by S Thornes UK) Dufour.
Kelly, Sean. Becky Makes a Wish. Kispert, Bill, adapted by. Allcroft, Britt, created by. 40p. (ps-3). 1993. pap. 5.95 (*1-884336-03-5*) Qual Family.

Kelly, Susan & Kelly, Thomas. Fishes of Hawaii Coloring Book. Kelly, Susan & Kelly, Thomas, illus. 32p. (ps-2). 1992. pap. 3.95 (*1-880188-32-5*) Bess Pr.

Kelly, Teri, ed. see Goodwin, Bob & Hayes, Dympna.

Kelly, Teri, ed. see Hayes, Dympna & Lehman, Melanie.

Kelly, Terry, et al. Daring Deeds. Gagne, Dennis, illus. 48p. (gr. 5-9). 1985. pap. 5.95 (*0-88625-092-7*) Durkin Hayes Pub.

Kelly, Thomas, jt. auth. see Kelly, Susan.

Kelly, Tim. The Adventure of the Speckled Band. 52p. (gr. 4 up). 1981. pap. 3.50 (*0-88680-000-5*); royalty on application 50.00 (*0-685-57877-1*) I E Clark.

—Dracula: The Vampire Play. 56p. (gr. 4 up). 1978. pap. 4.00 (*0-88680-043-9*); royalty on application 50.00 (*0-317-03593-2*) I E Clark.

—The Lalapalooza Bird. (Illus.). 24p. (Orig.). (gr. 5-12). 1981. pap. 2.00 (*0-88680-105-2*); royalty on application 20.00 (*0-685-59257-X*) I E Clark.

—Tom Sawyer: A Comedy in Two Acts. 56p. (gr. 2 up). 1983. pap. 3.50 (*0-88680-191-5*); royalty on application 40.00 (*0-685-57863-1*) I E Clark.

Kelly, Tony. Children in Tudor England. 52p. (gr. 6-9). 1987. pap. 7.95 (*0-85950-545-6*, Pub. by S Thornes UK) Dufour.

Kelly, Tony, jt. auth. see Kelly, Rosemary.

Kelly, Walt. Pogo: Romances Recaptured. (Illus.). 320p. 1975. pap. 9.95 incl. MS-DOS computer pro (*0-671-22184-1*, Fireside) S&S Trade.

Kelner, Lenore. The Creative Classroom: A Guide for Using Drama in the Classroom. (Illus.). 174p. (gr. 1-6). 1993. 17.50 (*0-435-08628-6*, 08628) Heinemann.

Kelsch, Gregg B. A World of Dinosaurs Series. Kelsch, Gregg B., illus. 1993. write for info. (*1-883736-01-3*) Acorn Pub UT.
What did Dinosaurs look like? What did they eat? Gregg B. Kelsch has been intrigued with Dinosaurs & has asked these same questions too. He then set out to study Dinosaurs & what scientists have discovered about them, & found that ideas vary greatly. His interest in Dinosaurs & his love of drawing came together as Gregg expressed his own ideas of what Dinosaurs were like. Being an artist, Gregg knows the importance of imagination & creativity; so he decided to make a coloring book for Dinosaur lovers everywhere to use their skill & imagination in coloring these magnificent animals. Four volumes are available in A WORLD OF DINOSAURS: Volume 1 is on a pre-school level, Volume 2 is for lower elementary school ages, Volume 3 is for upper-elementary & junior high school ages, & Volume 4 is upper level young adult to adult. Volumes 1 through 3 are created in a cartoon effect with Volume 4 being more intricate in design & true to life. Available from Acorn Publishing at 250 West 2855 South, Salt Lake City, UT 84115. You may also phone us at (801) 485-2424 or FAX us at (801) 484-6961 for volume pricing information. *Publisher Provided Annotation.*

Kelso, Mary J. Abducted! Kelso, Mary J., illus. 144p. (Orig.). (gr. 6 up). 1987. pap. 6.95 (*0-9621406-0-0*) MarKel Pr.

—Goodbye, Bodie. Kelso, Mary J., illus. 120p. (Orig.). (gr. 6 up). 1989. pap. 6.95 (*0-9621406-1-9*) MarKel Pr.

—Sierra Summer. Kelso, Mary J., illus. 120p. (Orig.). (gr. 6 up). 1992. pap. 6.95 (*0-9621406-3-5*) MarKel Pr.

—A Virginia City Mystery. (Illus.). 120p. (Orig.). (gr. 6 up). 1992. pap. 9.95 (*0-9621406-2-7*) MarKel Pr.

Kelso, Richard. Building a Dream: Mary Bethune's School. Heller, Debbie, illus. LC 92-18069. 46p. (gr. 2-5). 1992. PLB 21.34 (*0-8114-7217-5*) Raintree Steck-V.

—Days of Courage: The Little Rock Story. Williges, Mel, illus. LC 92-12805. 88p. (gr. 2-5). 1992. PLB 21.34 (*0-8114-7230-2*) Raintree Steck-V.

—Walking for Freedom: The Montgomery Bus Boycott. Newton, Michael, illus. LC 92-18080. 52p. (gr. 2-5). 1992. PLB 21.34 (*0-8114-7218-3*) Raintree Steck-V.

Keltner, Nancy, compiled by. If You Print This, Please Don't Use My Name: Questions from Teens & Their Parents about Things That Matter. Coffman, Gina, illus. Keltner, Nancy, intro. by. LC 91-36306. (Illus.). 256p. (Orig.). (gr. 7-12). 1992. pap. 8.95 (*0-944176-03-8*) Terra Nova.

Kelty, Jean M. If You Have a Duck... rev. ed. Ford, Elizabeth, illus. LC 82-51120. 104p. (gr. 1-9). 1982. pap. 9.95 (*0-910781-00-1*) G Whittell Mem.

Kemer, Eric, jt. auth. see Gardner, Robert.

Kemnitz, T. M. & Mass, Lynne. Kids Working with Computers: Acorn BASIC. (gr. 2-6). 1984. 4.99 (*0-89824-086-7*) Trillium Pr.

—Kids Working with Computers: Commodore LOGO. (gr. 2-6). 1985. 4.99 (*0-89824-093-X*) Trillium Pr.

—Kids Working with Computers: IBM LOGO. (gr. 2-6). 1985. 4.99 (*0-89824-094-8*) Trillium Pr.

Kemnitz, Thomas M. & Mass, Lynne. Kids Working with Computers: An Apple LOGO Manual. Schlendorf, Lori, illus. 58p. (gr. 4-7). 1983. pap. 4.99 (*0-89824-073-5*) Trillium Pr.

—Kids Working with Computers: The Apple BASIC Manual. Schlendorf, Lori, illus. 42p. (gr. 4-7). 1983. pap. 4.99 (*0-89824-092-1*) Trillium Pr.

—Kids Working with Computers: The Atari BASIC Manual. Schlendorf, Lori, illus. 48p. (gr. 4-7). 1983. pap. 4.99 (*0-89824-062-X*) Trillium Pr.

—Kids Working with Computers: The Commodore BASIC Manual. Schlendorf, Lori, illus. 48p. (gr. 4-7). 1983. pap. 4.99 (*0-89824-060-3*) Trillium Pr.

—Kids Working with Computers: The IBM BASIC Manual. Schlendorf, Lori, illus. 48p. (gr. 4-7). 1983. pap. 4.99 (*0-89824-063-8*) Trillium Pr.

—Kids Working with Computers: The Texas Instruments BASIC Manual. Schlendorf, Lori, illus. 48p. (gr. 4-7). 1983. pap. 4.99 (*0-89824-059-X*) Trillium Pr.

—Kids Working with Computers: The Timex-Sinclair BASIC Manual. Schlendorf, Lori, illus. 48p. (gr. 4-7). 1983. pap. 4.99 (*0-89824-058-1*) Trillium Pr.

—Kids Working with Computers: TRS-80 BASIC Manual. Schlendorf, Lori, illus. 44p. (gr. 4-7). 1983. pap. 4.99 (*0-89824-055-7*) Trillium Pr.

Kemnitz, Thomas M. & Romanowich, Barbara. Buckfang's Primary LOGO Activity Cards: Apple & IBM LOGO. 32p. (gr. k-3). 1985. pap. text ed. 12.99 (*0-89824-117-0*) Trillium Pr.

—Buckfang's Primary LOGO Activity Cards: Commodore & Apple Terrapin. 32p. (gr. k-3). 1985. pap. text ed. 12.99 (*0-89824-118-9*) Trillium Pr.

Kemntz, T. M. & Mass, Lynne. Kids Working with Computers: TRS-80 Color LOGO. 1984. 4.95 (*0-89824-078-6*) Trillium Pr.

Kemp, Franklin. One Sane & the Crazy Nine. 1993. 10.95 (*0-8062-4770-3*) Carlton.

Kemp, Gene. Just Ferret. large type ed. (gr. 1-8). 1991. 13.95 (*0-7451-1427-X*, Galaxy Child Lrg Print) Chivers N Amer.

—Matty's Midnight Monster. Timms, Diann, illus. 32p. (ps up). 1991. bds. 14.95 (*0-571-14336-9*) Faber & Faber.

—The Mink War. Davidson, Andrew, illus. 48p. (Orig.). (gr. 5 up). 1992. pap. 8.95 (*0-571-16312-2*) Faber & Faber.

—The Room with No Windows. 114p. (gr. 3-6). 1989. pap. 4.95 (*0-571-16117-0*) Faber & Faber.

Kemp, Jan. The Other Hemisphere. (Orig.). (gr. 10 up). 1991. pap. 10.00x (*0-89410-717-8*) Three Continents.

Kemp, Moira, jt. auth. see Morgan, Michaela.

Kemp, Moira, illus. Baa, Baa, Black Sheep. 10p. (ps). 1991. bds. 4.95 (*0-525-67331-8*, Lodestar Bks) Dutton Child Bks.

—Baa, Baa, Black Sheep. LC 93-18703. 12p. (ps). 1994. 2.99 (*0-525-67443-8*, Lodestar Bks) Dutton Child Bks.

—Hey Diddle Diddle. 10p. (ps). 1991. bds. 4.95 (*0-525-67329-6*, Lodestar Bks) Dutton Child Bks.

—Hey Diddle Diddle. LC 93-18702. 12p. (ps). 1994. 2.99 (*0-525-67445-4*, Lodestar Bks) Dutton Child Bks.

—Hickory, Dickory, Dock. 10p. (ps). 1991. bds. 4.95 (*0-525-67328-8*, Lodestar Bks) Dutton Child Bks.

—Hickory, Dickory, Dock. LC 93-18704. 12p. (ps). 1994. 2.99 (*0-525-67444-6*, Lodestar Bks) Dutton Child Bks.

—I'm a Little Teapot. 12p. (ps). 1992. bds. 2.50 (*0-525-67394-6*, Lodestar Bks) Dutton Child Bks.

—Knock at the Door. 12p. (ps). 1992. bds. 2.50 (*0-525-67396-2*, Lodestar Bks) Dutton Child Bks.

—Pat-a-Cake. 12p. (ps). 1992. bds. 2.50 (*0-525-67393-8*, Lodestar Bks) Dutton Child Bks.

—Round & Round the Garden. 12p. (ps). 1992. bds. 2.50 (*0-525-67395-4*, Lodestar Bks) Dutton Child Bks.

—This Little Piggy. 10p. (ps). 1991. bds. 4.95 (*0-525-67326-1*, Lodestar Bks) Dutton Child Bks.

—This Little Piggy. LC 93-18683. 12p. (ps). 1994. 2.99 (*0-525-67446-2*, Lodestar Bks) Dutton Child Bks.

Kemper, jt. auth. see Sebranek.

Kemper, Kristen. Co-Workers in Creation: First Steps in Ecology. 68p. (Orig.). (gr. 1-6). 1991. pap. 9.95 (*1-877871-19-2*) Ed Ministries.

Kempf, Michael J. Love Violated. Luquire, Jerry, ed. 136p. 1991. pap. 7.95 (*0-9637662-0-1*) From Blues to Bless.

Kempher, Ruth M. Mother Goose on Wheels. Hogan, Wayne, illus. 30p. (Orig.). 1992. pap. 4.95 (*0-934536-51-1*) Rose Shell Pr.

Kempler, Susan, et al. A Man Can Be... Dian, Russell, photos by. (Illus.). (ps-3). 1984. 16.95 (*0-89885-046-0*); pap. 9.95 (*0-89885-208-0*) Human Sci Pr.

Kempster, Teddy, ed. see Keller, Rosanne.

Kemvichanuvat, Cherdchai. The Poor Lizard. Rodriguez, Gloria F., ed. Chang, Phillip, illus. Pinta, Thanom, tr. (Illus.). (gr. k-3). 1979. pap. 3.50 (*0-686-26621-8*, Pub. by New Day Pub PI) Cellar.

Kenah, Katharine. Eggs over Easy. Chambliss, Maxie, illus. 96p. (gr. 2-5). 1993. 13.99 (*0-525-45071-8*, DCB) Dutton Child Bks.

Kenan, Randall. James Baldwin. (Illus.). 1994. 19.95 (*0-7910-2301-X*, Am Art Analog) Chelsea Hse.

Kenda, Margaret. Science Wizardry for Kids. (gr. 4-7). 1992. pap. 13.95 (*0-8120-4766-4*) Barron.

Kenda, Margaret & Williams, Phyllis S. Cooking Wizardry for Kids. (gr. 4-7). 1990. pap. 13.95 (*0-8120-4409-6*); pap. 19.95 incl. chef's apron & hat (*0-8120-7703-2*) Barron.

Kendall, Benjamin. Alien Invasions. Thatch, Nancy R., ed. Kendall, Benjamin, illus. Melton, David, intro. by. LC 93-13423. (Illus.). 29p. (gr. 2-4). 1993. PLB 14.95 (*0-933849-42-7*) Landmark Edns.

Kendall, Carol. The Gammage Cup. Garcia, Manuel, contrib. by. 283p. (gr. 4-7). 1990. pap. 3.95 (*0-15-230575-0*, Odyssey) HarBrace.

—The Gammage Cup. (gr. 3 up). 1992. 17.00 (*0-8446-6564-9*) Peter Smith.

—Sweet & Sour: Tales from China. (gr. 4-7). 1990. pap. 5.70 (*0-395-54798-9*, Clarion Bks) HM.

—The Wedding of the Ra* Family. Watts, James, illus. LC 88-2197. 32p. (gr. 2-5). 1988. SBE 13.95 (*0-689-50450-0*, M K McElderry) Macmillan Child Grp.

—Whisper of Glocken. Gobbato, Imero & Garcia, Manuel, illus. LC 85-17634. 256p. (Orig.). (gr. 3-7). 1986. pap. 4.95 (*0-15-295699-9*, Voyager Bks) HarBrace.

—The Whisper of Glocken. (gr. 3 up). 1992. 17.00 (*0-8446-6574-6*) Peter Smith.

Kendall, Carol, retold by. Haunting Tales from Japan. LC 85-50684. (Illus.). 40p. (Orig.). (gr. 6-9). 1985. pap. 6.00 (*0-913689-22-X*) Spencer Muse Art.

Kendall, Catherine W. More Stories of Composers for Young Musicians. (Illus.). 340p. (Orig.). (gr. 1-10). 1985. pap. 12.95 (*0-9610878-1-1*) Toadwood Pubs.

—Stories of Women Composers for Young Musicians. large type ed. LC 83-103936. (Illus.). 192p. (Orig.). (gr. 1-10). 1981. pap. 12.95 (*0-9610878-0-3*) Toadwood Pubs.
Composers, well-known & some not-so-well known, come alive as real & believable people for children ages 6-16. Based on extensive research & study of the composers' lives & their milieu but without use of excessive dates, pedantic factual material or musicological jargon, each story sets the emotional tone of the life of each musician, beginning with early childhood. The books are set in large type & wide margins, with portraits of composers, a birthday calendar, & recorded sources of composers' works. --"delightful & charming introduction to the world of music composition & performance" --"gives a feel for some of the exciting common threads that run through the lives of extraordinarily gifted musicians" --"communicates the essence of a composer's life in a warmly, perceptive, quiet way" --"Vividly fleshed out each life" --"careful research has been done."--Susan Grille, music educator, SAA Journal. "Composers are introduced as children, who, like the young readers, take music lessons, have brothers & sisters, & get excited over special events. It eavesdrops on conversations between the composer as a child & his parents & draws the reader into the setting, the lifestyle, & the attitudes of the day."-- Phyllis Young, Professor of Cello, American String Teachers Journal. Also available "More Stories of Composers for Young Musicians," 1985, ISBN 0-9610878-1-1. To order contact: Shar Inc., P.O. Box 1411, Ann Arbor, MI 48106. 1-800-248-7427. *Publisher Provided Annotation.*

Kendall, Cindy. Bats. Bennish, Gracia, illus. Dudley, Dick, created by. LC 93-3114. (ps). 1994. 4.99 (*0-8037-1272-3*) Dial Bks Young.

—Butterflies. Bennish, Gracia, illus. Dudley, Dick. LC 93-3117. (ps). 1994. pap. 3.95 (*0-8037-1275-8*) Dial Bks Young.

Kendall, Jane. Miranda & the Movies. Kendall, Jane, illus. LC 89-1515. 224p. (gr. 6 up). 1989. PLB 14.99 (*0-517-57357-1*) Crown Bks Yng Read.
Kendall, Joan. The Story of Samuel. (gr. k-4). 1984. 1.59 (*0-87162-271-8*, D8500) Warner Pr.
Kendall, Jonathan. My Name Is Rachamim. (Illus.). (gr. 2-3). 1987. 7.95 (*0-8074-0321-0*, 123925) UAHC.
Kendall, Katherine W. Stories of Women Composers for Young Musicians. large type ed. (Illus.). 212p. (Orig.). (gr. 1-12). 1993. pap. 12.95 (*0-9610878-2-X*) Toadwood Pubs.
Kendall, Martha E. Elizabeth Cady Stanton. Knight, Anne R., illus. LC 88-81556. 72p. (gr. 3-5). 1987. text ed. 10.95 (*0-945783-03-5*); pap. 5.95 (*0-945783-02-7*) Highland Pub Group.
—John James Audubon: Artist of the Wild. LC 92-11423. (Illus.). 48p. (gr. 2-4). 1993. PLB 12.40 (*1-56294-297-2*) Millbrook Pr.
—Nellie Bly: Reporter for the World. LC 91-37643. (Illus.). 48p. (gr. 2-4). 1992. PLB 12.40 (*1-56294-061-9*) Millbrook Pr.
—Nellie Bly: Reporter for the World. (gr. 4-7). 1992. pap. 4.95 (*0-395-64538-7*) HM.
—Pinata Party. (Illus.). 24p. (gr. k-3). 1993. pap. 2.50 (*0-87406-654-9*) Willowisp Pr.
Kendall, Russ. Russian Girl: Life in an Old Russian Town. LC 93-13198. (Illus.). 40p. (ps-4). 1994. 14.95 (*0-590-45789-6*) Scholastic Inc.
Kendall, Russell. Eskimo Boy. 32p. 1992. 13.95 (*0-590-43695-3*, Scholastic Hardcover) Scholastic Inc.
Kendall, Sarita. The Bell Reef. Hudson, Mark, illus. 144p. (gr. 5-9). 1990. 13.45 (*0-395-53354-6*) HM.
—Cocaine. LC 90-87578. (Illus.). 64p. (gr. 6-12). 1991. PLB 19.92 (*0-8114-3200-9*) Raintree Steck-V.
—The Incas. LC 91-513. (Illus.). 64p. (gr. 6 up). 1992. RSBE 14.95 (*0-02-750160-4*, New Discovery) Macmillan Child Grp.
—Ransom for a River Dolphin. LC 93-19929. 1993. 18.95 (*0-8225-0735-8*) Lerner Pubns.
Kendra, Judith. Tibetans. LC 93-36356. (Illus.). 48p. (gr. 6-10). 1994. 16.95 (*1-56847-152-1*) Thomson Lrning.
Kendrick, Rosalyn. In the Steps of Jesus. 158p. (gr. 8-10). 1985. pap. 10.95 (*0-7175-1309-2*) Dufour.
Kendris, Christopher. How to Prepare for SAT II: French. 6th, rev. ed. LC 93-2558. 1994. pap. 16.95 incl. 60 min. cass. (*0-8120-1766-8*) Barron.
—How to Prepare for SAT II: Spanish. 7th ed. LC 93-20714. 1994. pap. 16.95 incl. 60-min. cass. (*0-8120-1764-1*) Barron.
Kendzia, Mary C., ed. see Costello, Gwen.
Kendzia, Mary C., ed. see Haas, James.
Kenji, Miyazawa. Night of the Milky Way Railway. Strong, Sarah M., tr. Barnard, Bryn, illus. Strong, Sarah M., intro. by. LC 91-6608. 192p. (gr. 7 up). 1991. 22.50 (*0-87332-820-5*) M E Sharpe.
Kenkes, Kevin. Owen. LC 92-30084. 24p. (ps up). 1993. 14.00 (*0-688-11449-0*); lib. bdg. 13.93 (*0-688-11450-4*) Greenwillow.
Kennaley, Lucinda H. My Mom Is Pregnant! Kennaley, Lucinda H., illus. 60p. (Orig.). (ps). 1990. pap. text ed. 9.95 (*0-9628067-0-6*) Thoth MO.
—Only Soldiers Go to War. Curtis, Charmaine, illus. LC 91-65288. 42p. (ps-4). 1991. 14.95 (*0-9628067-1-4*) Thoth MO.
Kennaway, Adrienne. Bushbaby. (Illus.). (ps-3). 1991. 15.95 (*0-316-48890-9*) Little.
—Little Elephant's Walk. Kennaway, Adrienne, illus. LC 91-19727. 32p. (ps-2). 1992. 13.95 (*0-06-020377-3*); PLB 13.89 (*0-06-020378-1*) HarpC Child Bks.
Kennaway, Adrienne, jt. auth. see Kennaway, Mwalimu.
Kennaway, James. Tunes of Glory. 192p. 1989. pap. 9.95 (*0-86241-223-4*, Pub. by Cnngt Pub Ltd) Trafalgar.
Kennaway, Mwalimu & Kennaway, Adrienne. Awful Aardvark. Kennaway, Mwalimu & Kennaway, Adrienne, illus. LC 89-80028. (ps-2). 1989. 14.95 (*0-316-59218-8*) Little.
Kennedy, Alice, jt. auth. see Barrier, Jean.
Kennedy, Alice see Barrier, Jean & Kennedy, Alice.
Kennedy, Anne, illus. Colors & Shapes. 6p. (ps). 1992. bds. 3.95 (*1-56293-185-7*) McClanahan Bk.
Kennedy, Barbara. The Boy Who Loved Alligators. LC 93-15982. 144p. (gr. 3-7). 1994. SBE 14.95 (*0-689-31876-6*, Atheneum Child Bk) Macmillan Child Grp.
Kennedy, Christine & Smith, Mark. The Pathfinder's Adventure Kit. Kimber, William, illus. LC 92-34711. 56p. (Orig.). (gr. 4-7). 1993. pap. 15.00 (*0-679-83491-5*) Random Bks Yng Read.
Kennedy, Don. Exploring Careers on Cruise Ships. LC 93-20293. (gr. 7 up). 1993. 13.95 (*0-8239-1665-0*); 9.95 (*0-8239-1714-2*) Rosen Group.
Kennedy, Dora, et al. Exploring Languages: Upper Elementary Through First Year High School. (SPA.). 304p. 1993. pap. 10.95 (*0-685-62797-7*, F9360-1, Natl Textbk); tchr's. manual, 96p. 7.95 (*0-685-62798-5*, F9362-8, Natl Textbk) NTC Pub Grp.
Kennedy, Doris F., jt. ed. see Pearl, Lauren.
Kennedy, Dorothy M., jt. auth. see Kennedy, X. J.
Kennedy, Dorothy M., jt. ed. see Kennedy, X. J.
Kennedy, Dorothy M., et al, eds. I Thought I'd Take My Rat to School: Poems for September to June. Soto, Gary & Kuskin, Karla. Carter, Abby, illus. LC 92-12775. 1993. 15.95 (*0-316-48893-3*) Little.
Kennedy, Fiona. Time for Bed. Endersby, Frank, illus. 26p. (ps-k). 1992. pap. 5.95 (*0-8120-4996-9*) Barron.
Kennedy, Fiona & Noakes, Polly. The Last Little Duckling. LC 92-21695. (Illus.). 28p. (ps-1). 1993. 12.95 (*0-8120-6326-0*); pap. 4.95 (*0-8120-1355-7*) Barron.

Kennedy, Gregory P. Apollo to the Moon. (Illus.). 112p. (gr. 5 up). 1992. lib. bdg. 18.95 (*0-7910-1322-7*) Chelsea Hse.
—The First Men in Space. Goetzmann, William H., ed. Collins, Michael, intro. by. (Illus.). 112p. (gr. 5 up). 1991. PLB 18.95 (*0-7910-1324-3*) Chelsea Hse.
Kennedy, Jimmy. The Miniature Teddy Bear's Picnic. Theobalds, Prue, illus. LC 86-32111. 32p. (gr. k-3). 1989. 5.95 (*0-87226-417-3*, Bedrick Blackie) P Bedrick Bks.
—The Teddy Bears' Picnic. Day, Alexandra, illus. LC 91-24944. 40p. (ps-2). 1991. 13.00 (*0-671-75589-7*, Green Tiger); incl. cass. tape 19.95 (*0-671-74902-1*); incl. record 15.95 (*0-671-74903-X*) S&S Trade.
—The Teddy Bears' Picnic. Theobalds, Prue, illus. LC 86-32111. 32p. (ps-2). 1987. PLB 14.95 (*0-87226-153-0*, Bedrick Blackie); pap. 6.95 (*0-685-67547-5*) P Bedrick Bks.
—The Teddy Bears' Picnic. Theobalds, Prue, illus. LC 86-32111. 32p. 1990. pap. 6.95 (*0-87226-424-6*, Bedrick Blackie) P Bedrick Bks.
—The Teddy Bears' Picnic. Hague, Michael, illus. LC 91-27709. 32p. (ps-2). 1992. 16.95 (*0-8050-1008-4*, Bks Young Read); poster avail. H Holt & Co.
Kennedy, John G. The Tarahumara. (Illus.). 112p. (gr. 5 up). 1990. 17.95 (*1-55546-730-X*) Chelsea Hse.
Kennedy, Joy. Jellybean Dreams. Shaw, Charles, illus. LC 92-46429. 12p. (gr. 6-12). 1993. 14.95 (*0-89015-864-9*) Eakin-Sunbelt.
Kennedy, Kathy. Den Four Meets the Jinx. (gr. 4-7). 1991. pap. 3.25 (*0-440-40505-X*) Dell.
Kennedy, Moorhead, jt. auth. see Arnold, Terrell E.
Kennedy, Pam, ed. see Dickens, Charles.
Kennedy, Pamela. A, B, C, Bunny. Chartier, Normand, illus. 12p. (ps-k). 1990. bds. 4.99 (*0-929608-69-0*) Focus Family.
—All Mine, Bunny. Chartier, Normand, illus. 12p. (ps-k). 1990. bds. 4.99 (*0-929608-65-8*) Focus Family.
—An Easter Celebration: Traditions & Customs from Around the World. Bachleda, F. Lynn, illus. 32p. (gr. 1-5). 1991. 10.95 (*0-8249-8506-0*, Ideals Child) Hambleton-Hill.
—Night, Night, Bunny. Chartier, Normand, illus. 12p. (ps-k). 1990. bds. 4.99 (*0-929608-70-4*) Focus Family.
—Oh, Oh, Bunny. Chartier, Normand, illus. 12p. (ps-k). 1990. bds. 4.99 (*0-929608-67-4*) Focus Family.
—One, Two, Three, Bunny. Chartier, Normand, illus. 12p. (ps-k). 1990. bds. 4.99 (*0-929608-68-2*) Focus Family.
—Prayers at Christmastime. Britt, Stephanie M., illus. 24p. (ps-k). 1990. 3.95 (*0-8249-8480-3*, Ideals Child) Hambleton-Hill.
—Prayers at Eastertime. Britt, Stephanie, illus. 24p. (ps-k). 1990. pap. 3.95 (*0-8249-8422-6*, Ideals Child) Hambleton-Hill.
—Red, Yellow, Blue, Bunny. Chartier, Normand, illus. 12p. (ps-k). 1990. bds. 4.99 (*0-929608-66-6*) Focus Family.
Kennedy, Pamela, compiled by. Nursery Songs & Lap Games. Covell, Joan, illus. 32p. 1990. 13.95 (*0-8249-8486-2*, Ideals Child); incl. 50-min. cassette 17.95 (*0-8249-7399-2*) Hambleton-Hill.
Kennedy, Pamela, adapted by see Van Dyke, Henry.

Kennedy, Philip R. Get a Move on, Neuron! Kennedy, Philip R., illus. LC 92-97171. 42p. (Orig.). (gr. 5-8). 1992. pap. text ed. 10.00 (*0-9635701-0-2*); Tchr's. ed. 12.00 (*0-9635701-1-0*) Your Chlds Neuro.
This fun book succeeds in stimulating the child's imagination about how the brain works. It takes the child on a walk through the special places in the brain as he or she performs a familiar routine. Each place is described along with its connections to other places, its function, & lack of function after an injury. Each chapter ends with an activity that the child can do with parents or teachers. A revision quiz follows each chapter. (ISBN 0-9635701-0-2, $10.00 plus $2.00 s/h). Praise from fellow neuroscientists, who write: "This is terrific. From the homey, accurate description to the philosophical aside at the end. Good work!" "My wife is a third grade teacher & has been in search of materials such as your book for a long time!" "Wonderful!" "Excellent place to start." The teacher's manual (0-9635701-1-0, $12.00 plus $2.00 s/h) is an expanded book with extra activities. The fun play (0-9635701-2-9) is based on the book & adds an interactive learning program for over 20 pupils.

Kennedy, Richard. Amy's Eyes. Egielski, Richard, illus. LC 82-48841. 448p. (ps up). 1985. 15.00 (*0-06-023219-6*) HarpC Child Bks.
—Amy's Eyes. Egielski, Richard, illus. LC 82-48841. 448p. (gr. 5 up). 1988. pap. 10.95 (*0-06-440220-7*, Trophy) HarpC Child Bks.
—Little Love Song. Mathers, Petra, illus. LC 91-2053. 32p. 1992. 8.00 (*0-679-81177-X*) Knopf Bks Yng Read.
Kennedy, Rosemary G. Bach to Rock: An Introduction to Famous Composers & Their Music. 6th, rev. ed. Ronniger, Mary S., illus. 161p. (gr. 4-9). 1989. pap. 14.95 (*0-685-45404-5*); audio cassette 16.95 (*0-685-45405-3*) Rosemary Corp.
Kennedy, S. A. Hey, Didi Darling. (gr. 5 up). 1989. pap. 2.75 (*0-553-15708-6*, Skylark) Bantam.
Kennedy, Sandra. Introduction to Computing, Bk. 1. Schroeder, Bonnie, ed. Knapp, William & Kennedy, Kara, illus. (gr. 2). 1989. wkbk. 5.95 (*1-56177-101-5*, 491-1) CES Compu-Tech.
Kennedy, Sandra & MacDonald, James. Adventures in SeeLogo: Course Code 192-2. Schroeder, Bonnie, ed. Anastasia, Karyn & Knapp, William, illus. (gr. 4). 1989. wkbk. 6.95 (*0-917531-44-2*) CES Compu-Tech.
Kennedy, Suzanne, ed. see Sommers, Maxine S.
Kennedy, Teresa. Bringing Back the Animals. Williams, Sue, illus. 32p. (gr. 3 up). 1991. lib. bdg. 15.95 incl. dust jacket (*0-944256-06-6*) Amethyst Bks.
Kennedy, Trish & Schodorf, Timothy. Baseball Card Crazy. LC 92-14597. 80p. (gr. 4-6). 1993. SBE 11.95 (*0-684-19536-4*, Scribner Young Read) Macmillan Child Grp.
Kennedy, William. Charlie Malarkey & the Belly Button Machine. (ps-3). 1990. pap. 4.95 (*0-14-054239-6*, Puffin) Puffin Bks.
Kennedy, X. J. The Beasts of Bethlehem. McCurdy, Michael, illus. LC 91-38417. 48p. (gr. 1 up). 1992. SBE 13.95 (*0-689-50561-2*, M K McElderry) Macmillan Child Grp.
—Brats. Watts, James, illus. LC 85-20018. 48p. (gr. 3 up). 1986. SBE 12.95 (*0-689-50392-X*, M K McElderry) Macmillan Child Grp.
—Drat These Brats! Watts, James, illus. LC 92-33686. 48p. (gr. 3 up). 1993. SBE 12.95 (*0-689-50589-2*, M K McElderry) Macmillan Child Grp.
—The Forgetful Wishing Well: Poems for Young People. Incisa, Monica, illus. LC 84-45977. 96p. (gr. 4 up). 1985. SBE 12.95 (*0-689-50317-2*, M K McElderry) Macmillan Child Grp.
—Fresh Brats. Watts, James, illus. LC 89-38031. 48p. (gr. 3-5). 1990. SBE 12.95 (*0-689-50499-3*, M K McElderry) Macmillan Child Grp.
—Ghastlies, Goops & Pincushions: Nonsense Verse. Barrett, Ron, illus. LC 88-28663. 64p. (gr. 3 up). 1989. SBE 13.95 (*0-689-50477-2*, M K McElderry) Macmillan Child Grp.
—The Kite That Braved Old Orchard Beach: Year-Round Poems for Young People. LC 90-20100. (Illus.). 96p. (gr. 4 up). 1991. SBE 13.95 (*0-689-50507-8*, M K McElderry) Macmillan Child Grp.
—The Owlstone Crown. 224p. 1985. pap. 2.50 (*0-553-15349-8*, Skylark) Bantam.
Kennedy, X. J. & Kennedy, Dorothy M. Knock at a Star: A Child's Introduction to Poetry. Weinhaus, Karen A., illus. 160p. (gr. 2-6). 1985. pap. 8.95 (*0-316-48854-2*) Little.
Kennedy, X. J. & Kennedy, Dorothy M., eds. Talking Like the Rain: A First Book of Poems. Dyer, Jane, illus. (ps up). 1992. 18.95 (*0-316-48889-5*) Little.
Kennemuth, Caroline. Kate Gleeson's What Shall I Do Today? (ps-3). 1993. pap. 1.95 (*0-307-10551-2*, Golden Pr) Western Pub.
—Kate Gleeson's Wonderful You. (ps-3). 1993. pap. 1.95 (*0-307-10550-4*, Golden Pr) Western Pub.
Kennet, Frances. Looking at Painting. LC 89-7156. (Illus.). 48p. (gr. 4-8). 1990. 13.95 (*1-85435-102-8*) Marshall Cavendish.
Kenneway, Eric, tr. see Nakano, Dokuihtei.
Kenneway, Eric, tr. see Nakano, Dokuohtei.
Kennon, Donald R. & Strincer, Richard. Washington Past & Present: A Guide to the Nation's Capital. rev. ed. Schwengel, Fred & Burger, Warren E.frwd. by. (Illus.). 144p. (gr. 7-12). 1993. pap. 5.95t (*0-685-64855-9*) US Capitol Hist.
Kenny, Kevin. Sometimes My Mom Drinks Too Much. (ps-3). 1993. pap. 3.95 (*0-8114-7159-4*) Raintree Steck-V.
Kenny, Kevin & Krull, Helen. Sometimes My Mom Drinks Too Much. Cogancherry, Helen, illus. Neidengard, Ted, intro. by. LC 80-14515. (Illus.). 32p. (gr. k-6). 1980. PLB 17.96 (*0-8172-1366-X*) Raintree Steck-V.
Kenslea, Timothy, jt. auth. see Caffrey, Stephanie.
Kenslea, Timothy, jt. ed. see Caffrey, Stephanie.
Kent. Benjamin Franklin: Extraordinary Patriot. 1993. pap. 2.95 (*0-590-46012-9*) Scholastic Inc.
Kent, Charlotte. Barbara McClintock. Horner, Matina, intro. by. (Illus.). 112p. (gr. 5 up). 1991. lib. bdg. 17.95 (*1-55546-666-4*) Chelsea Hse.

Kent, Deborah. Colorado. LC 88-11745. (Illus.). 144p. (gr. 4 up). 1988. PLB 26.60 (0-516-00452-2) Childrens.
—Colorado. 187p. 1993. text ed. 15.40 (1-56956-138-9) W A T Braille.
—Connecticut. LC 89-17297. 144p. (gr. 4 up). 1989. PLB 26.60 (0-516-00453-0) Childrens.
—Connecticut. 184p. 1993. text ed. 15.40 (1-56956-132-X) W A T Braille.
—Delaware. LC 90-21116. (Illus.). 144p. (gr. 5-8). 1991. PLB 26.60 (0-516-00454-9) Childrens.
—Delaware. 174p. 1993. text ed. 15.40 (1-56956-137-0) W A T Braille.
—The Freedom Riders. LC 92-33424. (Illus.). 32p. (gr. 3-6). 1993. PLB 15.27 (0-516-06662-5); pap. 3.95 (0-516-46662-3) Childrens.
—Iowa. LC 90-21276. (Illus.). 144p. (gr. 5-8). 1991. PLB 26.60 (0-516-00461-1) Childrens.
—Iowa. 179p. 1993. text ed. 15.40 (1-56956-149-4) W A T Braille.
—Jane Addams & Hull House. LC 91-37882. (Illus.). 32p. (gr. 3-6). PLB 15.27, Apr. 1992 (0-516-04852-X); pap. 3.95, Jul. 1992 (0-516-44852-8) Childrens.
—Louisiana. LC 87-9403. (Illus.). 144p. (gr. 4 up). 1988. PLB 26.60 (0-516-00464-6) Childrens.
—Louisiana. 196p. 1993. text ed. 15.40 (1-56956-166-4) W A T Braille.
—Maryland. LC 89-25282. (Illus.). 144p. (gr. 4 up). 1990. PLB 26.60 (0-516-00466-2) Childrens.
—Maryland. 184p. 1993. text ed. 15.40 (1-56956-136-2) W A T Braille.
—Massachusetts. LC 87-9402. (Illus.). 144p. (gr. 4 up). 1987. PLB 26.60 (0-516-00467-0) Childrens.
—Massachusetts. 212p. 1993. text ed. 15.40 (1-56956-134-6) W A T Braille.
—New Jersey. LC 87-9401. (Illus.). 144p. (gr. 4 up). 1987. PLB 26.60 (0-516-00476-X) Childrens.
—New Jersey. 191p. 1993. text ed. 15.40 (1-56956-126-5) W A T Braille.
—Ohio. LC 88-38401. (Illus.). 144p. (gr. 4 up). 1989. PLB 26.60 (0-516-00481-6) Childrens.
—Ohio. 196p. 1993. text ed. 15.40 (1-56956-164-8) W A T Braille.
—Pennsylvania. LC 87-36754. (Illus.). 144p. (gr. 4 up). 1988. PLB 26.60 (0-516-00484-0) Childrens.
—Pennsylvania. 201p. 1993. text ed. 15.40 (1-56956-141-9) W A T Braille.
—Puerto Rico. LC 91-543. 144p. (gr. 4 up). 1991. PLB 26.60 (0-516-00498-0) Childrens.
—Puerto Rico. 190p. 1993. text ed. 15.40 (1-56956-154-0) W A T Braille.
—South Carolina. LC 89-858. 144p. (gr. 4 up). 1989. PLB 26.60 (0-516-00486-7) Childrens.
—South Carolina. 188p. 1993. text ed. 15.40 (1-56956-172-9) W A T Braille.
—Talk to Me, My Love. (Orig.). (gr. k-12). 1987. pap. 2.75 (0-440-97810-6, LFL) Dell.
—The Titanic. LC 93-12688. (Illus.). 32p. (gr. 3-6). 1993. PLB 15.93 (0-516-06672-2) Childrens.
—Washington, D. C. LC 90-35386. (Illus.). 144p. (gr. 4 up). 1990. PLB 26.60 (0-516-00497-2) Childrens.
—Washington, D. C. 200p. 1993. text ed. 15.40 (1-56956-152-4) W A T Braille.
—Why Me? (gr. 4-7). 1992. pap. 2.95 (0-590-44179-5) Scholastic Inc.
Kent, Gordon. All Day Suckers. LC 92-12843. (gr. 2). 1992. 13.99 (1-56239-156-9) Abdo & Dghtrs.
Kent, J. Racing Bikes. (Illus.). 48p. (gr. 6-10). 1990. (Usborne); pap. 5.95 (0-7460-0518-0) EDC.
Kent, Jack. The Biggest Shadow in the Zoo. Kent, Jack, illus. LC 80-25517. 48p. (ps-3). 1981. 5.95 (0-8193-1047-6); PLB 5.95 (0-8193-1048-4) Parents.
—The Caterpillar & the Polliwog. LC 82-7533. (Illus.). 32p. (gr. k-4). 1985. pap. 14.00 jacketed (0-671-66280-5, S&S BFYR); pap. 5.95 (0-671-66281-3, S&S BFYR) S&S Trade.
—Ice Cream Soup. Herman, Gail, retold by. Alley, R. W., illus. LC 89-43680. 24p. (Orig.). (ps-2). 1990. pap. 2.25 (0-679-80790-X) Random Bks Yng Read.
—Jack Kent's Valentine Sticker Book. 40p. (ps-3). 1987. pap. 2.50 (0-590-32400-4) Scholastic Inc.
—Joey. LC 84-4694. (Illus.). 32p. (gr. k-4). 1987. jacketed 11.95 (0-671-66459-X, S&S BFYR); pap. 5.95 (0-671-66460-3, S&S BFYR) S&S Trade.
—Joey Runs Away. LC 85-3673. (Illus.). 32p. (gr. k-4). 1989. (S&S BFYR); pap. 5.95 (0-671-67936-8, S&S BFYR) S&S Trade.
—Little Peep. Kent, Jack, illus. 32p. (gr. 3-6). 1989. pap. 12.95 jacketed (0-671-67051-4, S&S BFYR); pap. 5.95 (0-671-67052-2, S&S BFYR) S&S Trade.
—Mrs. Mooley. (ps-3). 1993. 12.95 (0-307-17550-2, Artsts Writrs) Western Pub.
—Round Robin. Kent, Jack, illus. (ps up) 1989. pap. 12. 95 jacketed (0-671-66698-3, S&S BFYR); pap. 5.95 (0-671-66969-9, S&S BFYR) S&S Trade.
—Silly Goose. Kent, Jack, illus. LC 82-21441. 32p. (ps-3). 1986. 10.95 (0-13-809947-2); pap. 5.95 (0-13-810177-9) P-H.
—Silly Goose. LC 82-21441. (Illus.). 32p. (gr. k-4). 1982. PLB 10.95 (0-671-66676-2, S&S BFYR); pap. 5.95 (0-671-66677-0, S&S BFYR) S&S Trade.
—Socks for Supper. Kent, Jack, illus. LC 78-6224. 40p. (ps-3). 1978. 5.95 (0-8193-0964-8); PLB 5.95 (0-8193-0965-6) Parents.
—Socks for Supper. 33p. LC 93-7771. 1993. PLB 13.27 (0-8368-0975-0) Gareth Stevens Inc.
—Supermarket Magic. LC 78-55908. (ps-2). 1978. 3.95 (0-394-83921-8) Random Bks Yng Read.

—The Wizard. rev. ed. Kent, Jack, illus. 32p. (gr. k-3). 1989. pap. 5.95 (0-927370-00-X) WW Pr.
Kent, Lisa. Love Is Always There. Machlin, Mikki, illus. LC 93-20412. 32p. 1993. pap. 4.95 (0-8091-6611-9) Paulist Pr.
Kent, Renee. Kelli's Discovery. (Illus.). 64p. (Orig.). (gr. 4-6). 1989. pap. text ed. 3.50 (0-936625-71-6, New Hope AL) Womans Mission Union.
—Yes, You Can Kelli! McClain, Cindy, ed. 109p. (Orig.). (gr. 1-6). 1991. pap. text ed. 3.50 (1-56309-012-0, New Hope AL) Womans Mission Union.
—You Can Be a Musician & a Missionary, Too. McClain, Cindy, ed. Sealy, Kathy, illus. 64p. (Orig.). (gr. 4-6). 1988. pap. 3.95 (0-936625-37-6, PZ7.K419Y) Womans Mission Union.
Kent, Richard. Play On! 2nd ed. LC 85-50588. 124p. (gr. 9-12). 1989. 5.95 (0-932433-04-9) Windswept Hse.
Kent, Robert. Graveyard Jokes: That Everyone & Their Dead Ancestors Think Are Funny! LC 93-24478. 1993. pap. 3.95 (1-56565-101-4) Lowell Hse.
Kent, Zachary. Andrew Johnson. LC 88-39115. (Illus.). 100p. (gr. 3 up). 1989. PLB 17.27 (0-516-01363-7) Childrens.
—The Battle of Antietam. LC 92-12097. (Illus.). 32p. (gr. 3-6). 1992. PLB 15.27 (0-516-06657-9) Childrens.
—The Battle of Antietam. LC 92-12097. (Illus.). 32p. (gr. 3-6). 1993. pap. 3.95 (0-516-46657-7) Childrens.
—Bill Clinton. (Illus.). 100p. (gr. 3 up). 1993. PLB 17.27 (0-516-01350-5) Childrens.
—Calvin Coolidge. LC 88-10880. (Illus.). 100p. (gr. 3 up). 1988. PLB 17.27 (0-516-01362-9) Childrens.
—Christopher Columbus: Expeditions to the New World. LC 91-13863. 128p. (gr. 3 up). 1991. PLB 26.60 (0-516-03064-7); pap. 9.95 (0-516-43064-5) Childrens.
—The Civil War: A House Divided. LC 93-33622. (gr. 6 up). 1994. write for info. (0-89490-522-8) Enslow Pubs.
—George Bush. LC 89-33744. 100p. (gr. 3 up). 1989. PLB 17.27 (0-516-01374-2); pap. 6.95 (0-516-41374-0) Childrens.
—George Washington. LC 86-12896. (Illus.). 100p. (gr. 3 up). 1986. PLB 17.27 (0-516-01381-5); pap. 6.95 (0-516-41381-3) Childrens.
—Georgia. LC 87-35455. (Illus.). 144p. (gr. 4 up). 1988. PLB 26.60 (0-516-00456-5) Childrens.
—Grover Cleveland. LC 88-10885. (Illus.). 100p. (gr. 3 up). 1988. PLB 17.27 (0-516-01360-2) Childrens.
—Idaho. LC 89-25280. (Illus.). 144p. (gr. 4 up). 1990. PLB 26.60 (0-516-00458-1) Childrens.
—Idaho. 192p. 1993. text ed. 15.40 (1-56956-133-8) W A T Braille.
—Jacques Marquette & Louis Jolliet. LC 92-36888. 128p. (gr. 3 up). 1993. 26.60 (0-516-03072-8) Childrens.
—James Cook: Pacific Voyager. LC 91-12571. 128p. (gr. 3 up). 1991. PLB 26.60 (0-516-03066-3) Childrens.
—Jefferson Davis. LC 92-36894. (Illus.). 32p. (gr. 3-6). 1993. PLB 15.27 (0-516-06664-1); pap. 3.95 (0-516-46664-X) Childrens.
—John F. Kennedy. (Illus.). (gr. 3 up). 1987. PLB 17.27 (0-516-01390-4); pap. 6.95 (0-516-41390-2) Childrens.
—John Quincy Adams. LC 86-31022. (Illus.). 100p. (gr. 3 up). 1987. PLB 17.27 (0-516-01386-6); pap. 6.95 (0-516-41386-4) Childrens.
—Kansas. LC 90-35385. (Illus.). 144p. (gr. 4 up). 1990. PLB 26.60 (0-516-00462-X) Childrens.
—Kansas. 203p. 1993. text ed. 15.40 (1-56956-145-1) W A T Braille.
—Marco Polo: Traveler to Central & Eastern Asia. LC 91-34521. (Illus.). 128p. (gr. 3 up). PLB 26.60 (0-516-03070-1); pap. 9.95, Jul. 1992 (0-516-43070-X) Childrens.
—Ronald Reagan. LC 89-33746. 100p. (gr. 3 up). 1989. PLB 17.27 (0-516-01373-4); pap. 6.95 (0-516-41373-2) Childrens.
—Rutherford B. Hayes. LC 88-8679. (Illus.). 100p. (gr. 3 up). 1989. PLB 17.27 (0-516-01365-3) Childrens.
—The Story of Admiral Peary at the North Pole. LC 88-11824. (Illus.). 32p. (gr. 3-6). 1988. pap. 3.95 (0-516-44738-6) Childrens.
—The Story of Ford's Theatre & the Death of Lincoln. LC 87-17662. (Illus.). 32p. (gr. 3-6). 1987. PLB 13.27 (0-516-04729-9); pap. 3.95 (0-516-44729-7) Childrens.
—The Story of Geronimo. LC 88-37005. (Illus.). 32p. (gr. 3-6). 1989. PLB 13.27 (0-516-04743-4); pap. 3.95 (0-516-44743-2) Childrens.
—The Story of Henry Ford & the Automobile. LC 90-2163. (Illus.). 32p. (gr. 3-6). 1990. PLB 13.27 (0-516-04751-5); pap. 3.95 (0-516-44751-3) Childrens.
—The Story of John Brown's Raid on Harpers Ferry. LC 87-35714. (Illus.). 32p. (gr. 3-6). 1988. PLB 13.27 (0-516-04734-5); pap. 3.95 (0-516-44734-3) Childrens.
—The Story of Sherman's March to the Sea. Canaday, Ralph, illus. LC 86-31054. 32p. (gr. 3-6). 1987. PLB 13.27 (0-516-04728-0); pap. 3.95 (0-516-44728-9) Childrens.
—The Story of the Battle of Bull Run. Catrow, David J., III, illus. LC 86-9642. 32p. (gr. 3-6). 1986. PLB 13.27 (0-516-04703-5); pap. 3.95 (0-516-44703-3) Childrens.
—The Story of the Battle of Shiloh. LC 90-21646. (Illus.). 32p. (gr. 3-6). 1991. PLB 13.27 (0-516-04754-X); pap. 3.95 (0-516-44754-8) Childrens.
—The Story of the Brooklyn Bridge. LC 88-16220. (Illus.). 32p. (gr. 3-6). 1988. pap. 3.95 (0-516-44739-4) Childrens.
—The Story of the Challenger Disaster. LC 86-6822. (Illus.). 32p. (gr. 3-6). 1986. PLB 13.27 (0-516-04673-X) Childrens.

—The Story of the Election of Abraham Lincoln. Canaday, Ralph, illus. LC 85-23277. 32p. (gr. 3-6). 1986. pap. 3.95 (0-516-44669-X) Childrens.
—The Story of the New York Stock Exchange. LC 89-25374. (Illus.). 32p. (gr. 3-6). 1990. PLB 13.27 (0-516-04748-5); pap. 3.95 (0-516-44748-3) Childrens.
—The Story of the Peace Corps. LC 90-2113. (Illus.). 32p. (gr. 3-6). 1990. pap. 3.95 (0-516-44752-1) Childrens.
—The Story of the Rough Riders. LC 90-22444. (Illus.). 32p. (gr. 3-6). 1991. PLB 13.27 (0-516-04756-6); pap. 3.95 (0-516-44756-4) Childrens.
—The Story of the Saigon Airlift. LC 91-15847. (Illus.). 32p. (gr. 3-6). 1991. PLB 13.27 (0-516-04760-4); pap. 3.95 (0-516-44760-2) Childrens.
—The Story of the Salem Witch Trials. Canaday, Ralph, illus. LC 86-9632. 32p. (gr. 3-6). 1986. pap. 3.95 (0-516-44704-1) Childrens.
—The Story of the Sinking of the Battleship Maine. LC 87-35465. (Illus.). 30p. (gr. 3-6). 1988. pap. 3.95 (0-516-44736-X) Childrens.
—The Story of the Surrender at Appomattox Court House. LC 87-22468. (Illus.). 32p. (gr. 3-6). 1987. pap. 3.95 (0-516-44732-7) Childrens.
—The Story of the Surrender at Yorktown. LC 89-33784. 32p. (gr. 3-6). 1989. PLB 13.27 (0-516-04723-X); pap. 3.95 (0-516-44723-8) Childrens.
—The Story of the Triangle Factory Fire. LC 88-36223. (Illus.). 32p. (gr. 3-6). 1989. pap. 3.95 (0-516-44742-4) Childrens.
—Tecumseh. LC 92-8217. 32p. (gr. 3-6). 1992. PLB 15. 27 (0-516-06660-9) Childrens.
—Tecumseh. LC 92-8217. (Illus.). 32p. (gr. 3-6). 1993. pap. 3.95 (0-516-46660-7) Childrens.
—Theodore Roosevelt. LC 87-35184. (Illus.). 100p. (gr. 3 up). 1988. PLB 17.27 (0-516-01354-8); pap. 6.95 (0-516-41354-6) Childrens.
—Ulysses S. Grant. LC 88-38056. (Illus.). 100p. (gr. 3 up). 1989. PLB 17.27 (0-516-01364-5); pap. 6.95 (0-516-41364-3) Childrens.
—U. S. Olympians. LC 92-4812. 32p. (gr. 3-6). 1992. PLB 15.27 (0-516-06659-5) Childrens.
—William McKinley. LC 88-10881. (Illus.). 100p. (gr. 3 up). 1988. PLB 17.27 (0-516-01361-0) Childrens.
—Williamsburg. LC 91-35055. (Illus.). 32p. (gr. 3-6). PLB 15.27, Apr. 1992 (0-516-04854-6); pap. 3.95, Jul. 1992 (0-516-44854-4) Childrens.
—Zachary Taylor. LC 87-35774. (Illus.). 100p. (gr. 3 up). 1988. PLB 17.27 (0-516-01352-1) Childrens.
Kent, Zachary A. Georgia. 204p. 1993. text ed. 15.40 (1-56956-130-3) W A T Braille.
Kentley, Eric. Boat. Stevenson, Jim, photos by. LC 91-53136. (Illus.). 64p. (gr. 5 up). 1992. 15.00 (0-679-81678-X); PLB 15.99 (0-679-91678-4) Knopf Bks Yng Read.
Kenton, Nathaniel, ed. see Altsheler, Joseph A.
Kenvin, Helene. This Land of Liberty: A History of America's Jews. 216p. (gr. 7-9). 1986. pap. text ed. 8. 95x (0-87441-421-0) Behrman.
Keown, Elizabeth. Emily's Snowball: The World's Biggest. Trivas, Irene, illus. LC 90-1181. 32p. (ps-3). 1992. SBE 13.95 (0-689-31518-X, Atheneum Child Bk) Macmillan Child Grp.
Kepes, Juliet. Cock-A-Doodle-Doo. Kepes, Juliet, illus. LC 76-44433. (ps-2). 1978. 6.95 (0-394-83867-X) Pantheon.
—Frogs Merry. Kepes, Juliet, illus. (ps-2). 1963. lib. bdg. 6.99 (0-394-91176-8) Pantheon.
Keran, Shirley. Underwater Specialists. LC 88-14890. (Illus.). 48p. (gr. 5-6). 1988. RSBE 11.95 (0-89686-400-6, Crestwood Hse) Macmillan Child Grp.
Kerber, Karen M. Walking Is Wild, Weird & Wacky. rev. ed. Thatch, Nan, ed. Melton, David, intro. by. LC 89-13547. (Illus.). 32p. (ps-2). 1989. PLB 14.95 (0-933849-29-X) Landmark Edns.
Kerbo, Ronal C. Caves. LC 81-4514. (Illus.). 48p. (gr. 3 up). 1981. pap. 4.95 (0-516-47638-6) Childrens.
Kerby, Mona. Amelia Earhart: Courage in the Sky. (gr. 4-7). 1990. pap. 10.95 (0-670-83024-0) Viking Child Bks.
—Amelia Earhart: Courage in the Sky. McKeating, Eileen, illus. LC 92-19520. 64p. (gr. 3-5). 1992. pap. 3.99 (0-14-034263-X) Puffin Bks.
—Asthma. LC 89-8905. (Illus.). 128p. (gr. 7-12). 1989. PLB 12.90 (0-531-10697-7) Watts.
—Cockroaches. LC 88-37857. (Illus.). 64p. (gr. 3 up). 1989. PLB 12.90 (0-531-10689-6) Watts.
—Samuel Morse. LC 90-13109. 72p. (gr. 3-5). 1991. PLB 12.90 (0-531-20023-X) Watts.
—Thirty-Eight Weeks Till Summer Vacation. Rosales, Melodye, illus. 128p. (gr. 3-7). 1989. 12.00 (0-670-82887-4) Viking Child Bks.
—Thirty-Eight Weeks Till Summer Vacation. 1991. pap. 3.95 (0-14-034205-2, Puffin) Puffin Bks.
Kerby, Rob, ed. see Trammell, Larry.
Keremis, Constance A. Hootenanny Night. LC 91-32505. (Illus.). (gr. k-4). 1992. 12.95 (0-938349-79-1); pap. 6.95 (0-938349-80-5) State House Pr.
Kerensky, Elaine. Far Away Gramma. Tremblay, Ruth, illus. 24p. (Orig.). (gr. k-3). 1990. pap. text ed. write for info. (0-9627228-0-4) Far Away Fam Playhse.
Kergueno, Jacqueline & Seignolle, Claude. The Man with Seven Wolves. (Illus.). (gr. 1-8). 1992. PLB 8.95 (0-89565-895-X); Resale. 12.75 (0-685-60993-6) Childs World.

Kerina, Jane. African Crafts. Feelings, Tom, illus. LC 69-18916. (gr. 2-6). 1970. PLB 13.95 (*0-87460-084-7*) Lion Bks.

Kerins, Anthony. Tat Rabbit's Treasure. Kerins, Anthony, illus. LC 92-32600. 32p. (ps-1). 1993. SBE 14.95 (*0-689-50553-1*, M K McElderry) Macmillan Child Grp.

Kerl, Mary A. Where Are You, Lord? LC 82-70949. 112p. (Orig.). (gr. 3-6). 1982. pap. 5.99 (*0-8066-1924-4*, 10-7069, Augsburg) Augsburg Fortress.

Kerley, Joy. Guys vs. Gals: (World War III) (Illus.). pap. text ed. 8.00 (*0-9614268-1-0*) Teen Round Up.

Kermode, Frank. Sense of an Ending: Studies in the Theory of Fiction. (gr. 10 up). 1967. pap. 8.95 (*0-19-500770-0*) OUP.

Kermond, Carolyn. Little Ways to Heaven. LC 83-18850. (Illus.). (gr. 3 up). 1988. 5.00 (*0-8198-4434-9*, CH0336); pap. 6.00 (*0-8198-4435-7*) St Paul Bks.

Kern, Phil, jt. auth. see Kern, Susan.

Kern, Phil, et al. When the Hippos Crashed the Dance. (Illus.). 125p. (gr. 1-6). 1991. pap. 69.95 (*1-56516-008-8*) Houston IN.

Kern, Phyllis F. Bumble Cat: How She Came to Be. Kern, Phyllis F., illus. 32p. (gr. k-3). 1985. HM.

Kern, Roger G., jt. auth. see Abresch, Richard T.

Kern, Susan & Kern, Phil. Anything Toy. (Illus.). 125p. (gr. 1-6). 1991. pap. 69.95 (*1-56516-009-6*) Houston IN.

—Concerto in A Minor Dispute. (Illus.). 125p. (gr. 2-6). 1991. pap. 79.95 (*1-56516-011-8*) Houston IN.

Kernaghan, Pamela. The Crusades: Cultures in Conflict. LC 93-27297. 1993. pap. 8.95 (*0-521-42846-7*) Cambridge U Pr.

Kerner Rettino, Debbie, jt. auth. see Retino, Ernie.

Kerner Rettino, Debbie, jt. auth. see Rettino, Ernie.

Kerr. The Alamo Cat. (Illus.). 64p. (gr. 4-6). 1988. 10.95 (*0-89015-639-5*, Pub. by Panda Bks) Eakin-Sunbelt.

Kerr, George. Judo. (Illus.). 32p. (gr. 2-5). 1992. PLB 11.90 (*0-531-18465-X*, Pub. by Bookwright Pr) Watts.

Kerr, James. Egyptian Farmers. (Illus.). 24p. (gr. 2-5). 1991. PLB 10.90 (*0-531-18374-2*, Pub. by Bookwright Pr) Watts.

Kerr, Jessica. Shakespeare's Flowers. Dowden, Anne O., illus. LC 68-13585. 96p. (gr. 7 up). 1982. (Crowell Jr Bks); (Crowell Jr Bks) HarpC Child Bks.

—Shakespeare's Flowers. Dowden, Anne O., illus. 86p. (gr. 7 up). 1992. PLB 16.89 (*0-06-022877-6*) HarpC Child Bks.

Kerr, Judith. Look Out, Mog! Kerr, Judith, illus. LC 90-62202. 24p. (ps-1). 1991. 7.95 (*0-679-81067-6*) Random Bks Yng Read.

—Mog & Bunny. Kerr, Judith, illus. LC 88-16899. 40p. (ps-1). 1989. 8.95 (*0-394-82249-8*) Knopf Bks Yng Read.

—When Hitler Stole Pink Rabbit. (gr. 3 up). 1987. pap. 3.50 (*0-440-49017-0*, YB) Dell.

Kerr, M. E. Dinky Hocker Shoots Smack! LC 72-80366. 204p. (gr. 7 up). 1972. PLB 15.89 (*0-06-023151-3*) HarpC Child Bks.

—Dinky Hocker Shoots Smack. LC 72-80366. 208p. (gr. 7 up). 1989. pap. 2.95 (*0-06-447006-7*, Trophy) HarpC Child Bks.

—Fell. LC 86-45776. 160p. (gr. 7 up). 1987. PLB 12.89 (*0-06-023268-4*) HarpC Child Bks.

—Fell. LC 86-45776. 176p. (gr. 7 up). 1988. pap. 3.95 (*0-06-447031-8*, Trophy) HarpC Child Bks.

—Fell Back. LC 88-35762. 192p. (gr. 7 up). 1989. 12.00 (*0-06-023292-7*); PLB 11.89 (*0-06-023293-5*) HarpC Child Bks.

—Fell Back. LC 88-35762. 192p. (gr. 7 up). 1991. pap. 3.95 (*0-06-447057-1*, Trophy) HarpC Child Bks.

—Fell Down. LC 90-49921. 208p. (gr. 7 up). 1991. 10.95 (*0-06-021763-4*); PLB 14.89 (*0-06-021764-2*) HarpC Child Bks.

—Fell Down. LC 90-49921. 208p. (gr. 7 up). 1993. pap. 3.95 (*0-06-447086-5*, Trophy) HarpC Child Bks.

—Gentlehands. LC 77-11860. (gr. 7-9). 1978. PLB 16.89 (*0-06-023177-7*) HarpC Child Bks.

—Gentlehands. LC 77-11860. 192p. (gr. 7 up). 1990. pap. 3.95 (*0-06-447067-9*, Trophy) HarpC Child Bks.

—Him She Loves? LC 83-48818. 224p. (gr. 7 up). 1984. PLB 12.89 (*0-06-023239-0*) HarpC Child Bks.

—I Stay Near You. LC 84-48342. 192p. (gr. 7 up). 1985. PLB 12.89 (*0-06-023105-X*) HarpC Child Bks.

—If I Love You, Am I Trapped Forever? 192p. (gr. 7 up). 1974. pap. 2.25 (*0-440-94320-5*, LFL) Dell.

—If I Love You, Am I Trapped Forever? LC 72-9860. 176p. (gr. 7 up). 1973. PLB 12.89 (*0-06-023149-1*) HarpC Child Bks.

—If I Love You, Am I Trapped Forever? LC 72-9860. 192p. (gr. 7 up). 1988. pap. 3.95 (*0-06-447032-6*, Trophy) HarpC Child Bks.

—I'll Love You When You're More Like Me. 176p. (gr. 7 up). 1979. pap. 2.25 (*0-440-94405-8*, LE) Dell.

—I'll Love You When You're More Like Me. LC 76-58709. 192p. (gr. 7 up). 1989. pap. 3.50 (*0-06-447004-0*, Trophy) HarpC Child Bks.

—Is That You, Miss Blue? LC 74-2627. 176p. (gr. 7 up). 1987. pap. 2.95 (*0-06-447033-4*, Trophy) HarpC Child Bks.

—Linger. LC 92-30988. 224p. (gr. 7 up). 1993. 15.00 (*0-06-022879-2*); PLB 14.89 (*0-06-022882-2*) HarpC Child Bks.

—Little Little. LC 80-8454. 160p. (gr. 7 up). 1981. PLB 14.89 (*0-06-023185-8*) HarpC Child Bks.

—Little Little. LC 80-8454. 192p. (gr. 7 up). 1991. pap. 3.50 (*0-06-447061-X*, Trophy) HarpC Child Bks.

—Me Me Me Me Me: Not a Novel. LC 82-48521. 224p. (gr. 7 up). 1983. PLB 16.89 (*0-06-023193-9*) HarpC Child Bks.

—Night Kites. LC 85-45386. 192p. (gr. 7 up). 1986. PLB 14.89 (*0-06-023254-4*) HarpC Child Bks.

—Night Kites. LC 85-45386. 224p. (gr. 7 up). 1987. pap. 3.95 (*0-06-447035-0*, Trophy) HarpC Child Bks.

—The Son of Someone Famous. LC 73-14338. 240p. (gr. 7 up). 1991. pap. 3.95 (*0-06-447069-5*, Trophy) HarpC Child Bks.

—What I Really Think of You. LC 81-47735. 224p. (gr. 7 up). 1982. 13.00 (*0-06-023188-2*) HarpC Child Bks.

—What I Really Think of You. LC 81-47735. 224p. (gr. 7 up). 1991. pap. 3.50 (*0-06-447062-8*, Trophy) HarpC Child Bks.

Kerr, Rita. Christopher & Pony Boy. Kerr, Rita, illus. 96p. (gr. 4-7). 1991. 10.95 (*0-89015-843-6*) Eakin-Sunbelt.

—The Ghost of Panna Maria. Eakin, Ed, ed. Kerr, Rita, illus. 96p. (gr. 2-4). 1990. 10.95 (*0-89015-791-X*); pap. 3.95 (*0-89015-803-7*) Eakin-Sunbelt.

—The Haunted House. LC 92-18783. 96p. (gr. 4-7). 1992. 10.95 (*0-89015-858-4*) Eakin-Sunbelt.

—The Immortal Thirty-Two. 64p. (gr. 4-7). 1986. 10.95 (*0-89015-538-0*, Pub. by Panda Bks) Eakin-Sunbelt.

—Juan Seguin: Hero of the Texas Revolution. Roberts, M., ed. 64p. (gr. 5-8). 1985. 10.95 (*0-89015-502-X*) Eakin-Sunbelt.

—Texas Cavalier: The Story of James Butler Bonham. Roberts, Melissa, ed. Kerr, Rita, illus. 64p. (gr. 4-7). 1989. 10.95 (*0-89015-714-6*, Pub. by Panda Bks) Eakin-Sunbelt.

—Texas Footprints. (gr. 3-7). 1988. 10.95 (*0-89015-676-X*, Pub. by Panda Bks) Eakin-Sunbelt.

—Texas Marvel. Roberts, Melissa, ed. 120p. (gr. 4-7). 1987. 10.95 (*0-89015-597-6*, Pub. by Panda Bks) Eakin-Sunbelt.

—Texas Rebel. Eakin, Edwin M., ed. Kerr, Rita, illus. 80p. (gr. 4-6). 1989. 10.95 (*0-89015-695-6*) Eakin-Sunbelt.

—Texas Rebel. Roberts, M., ed. Kerr, Rita, illus. 80p. (gr. 5-7). 1989. 10.95 (*0-685-50916-8*) Eakin-Sunbelt.

—A Wee Bit of Texas. Kerr, Rita, illus. 80p. (gr. 1-4). 1991. 10.95 (*0-89015-809-6*) Eakin-Sunbelt.

Kerr, Sandra, compiled by. Sing for Your Life. Samapatti, illus. 80p. (gr. 3 up). 12.95 (*0-7136-5546-1*, Pub. by A&C Black UK) Talman.

Kerrins, Joseph & Jacobs, George W. The AIDS File. 2nd ed. Doohan, Julie, ed. (Illus.). 160p. (gr. 8 up). 1989. cloth 14.95 (*0-9618059-2-7*) Cromlech Bks.

Kerrod, Robin. Air in Action. LC 89-997. (Illus.). 32p. (gr. 3-8). 1990. PLB 9.95 (*1-85435-152-4*) Marshall Cavendish.

—Amazing Flying Machines. Dunning, Mike, photos by. LC 91-53137. (Illus.). 32p. (Orig.). (gr. 1-5). 1992. PLB 9.99 (*0-679-92765-4*); pap. 6.95 (*0-679-82765-X*) Knopf Bks Yng Read.

—Birds: Water Birds. Bailey, Jill, contrib. by. (Illus.). 1989. 17.95x (*0-8160-1962-2*) Facts on File.

—The Challenge of Space. LC 79-64385. (Illus.). 36p. (gr. 3-6). 1980. PLB 13.50 (*0-8225-1177-0*) Lerner Pubns.

—The Children's Space Atlas. LC 91-30148. (Illus.). 96p. (gr. 2-6). 1992. 18.95 (*1-56294-100-3*); PLB 18.90 (*1-56294-164-X*) Millbrook Pr.

—Children's Space Atlas. LC 92-30418. (gr. 4-7). 1993. pap. 10.95 (*1-56294-717-6*) Millbrook Pr.

—Communications. Evans, Ted, illus. LC 93-1913. 1993. write for info. (*1-85435-624-0*) Marshall Cavendish.

—Energy Resources. LC 93-34611. (Illus.). 32p. (gr. 4-7). 1994. 14.95 (*1-56847-107-6*) Thomson Lrning.

—The Environment. (Illus.). 64p. (gr. 5 up). 1993. PLB 15.95g (*1-85435-625-9*) Marshall Cavendish.
Each title in this series introduces scientific concepts through situations & observations familiar to the young reader. The students are encouraged to pursue their inquiries through investigations that require a hands-on approach to learning. Each volume contains, in addition to a central text & plentiful color illustrations, the following features: MILESTONES-featuring key discoveries, theories, & inventions; QUIZ QUESTIONS to test the readers' knowledge; (answers are provided); IT'S AMAZING-features to add interest by drawing attention to surprising & exciting scientific information. Each title also includes an index, glossary, answers section, & guide to further readings. The combination of engaging writing style & vibrant color illustrations makes this a very attractive & practical reference work for young readers. Each volume features a library binding; 64 pages; 8 X 10 size. This series is being published in two groups of five titles each. Group 1 is available as of November, 1993. The titles are: The Solar System, Animal Life, Force & Motion, Communications, The Environment. Group 2 will be available in February, 1994. The titles in the second group are: Electricity & Magnetism, Plant Life, Geology & Natural Resources, Transportation, Weather.
Publisher Provided Annotation.

—Fire & Water. LC 89-917. (Illus.). 32p. (gr. 3-8). 1990. PLB 9.95 (*1-85435-153-2*) Marshall Cavendish.

—Food Resources. LC 93-34612. (Illus.). 32p. (gr. 4-7). 1994. 14.95 (*1-56847-108-4*) Thomson Lrning.

—Force & Motion. Evans, Ted, illus. LC 93-4550. 1993. Set. write for info.; pap. 15.95 (*1-85435-622-4*) Marshall Cavendish.

—How Things Work. LC 89-918. (Illus.). 32p. (gr. 3-8). 1990. PLB 9.95 (*1-85435-154-0*) Marshall Cavendish.

—Is It Magic. LC 89-919. (Illus.). 32p. (gr. 3-8). 1990. PLB 9.95 (*1-85435-155-9*) Marshall Cavendish.

—Let's Investigate Science. (Illus.). (gr. 5 up). 1994. Group 1, The Solar System, Animal Life, Force & Motion, Communications, The Environment. PLB write for info.; Group 2, Electricity & Magnetism, Plant Life, Geology & Natural Resources, Transportation, Weather. PLB write for info. (*1-85435-688-7*) Marshall Cavendish.
Each title in this series introduces scientific concepts through situations & observations familiar to the young reader. The students are encouraged to pursue their inquiries through investigations that require a hands-on approach to learning, Each volume contains, in addition to a central text & plentiful color illustrations, the following features: MILESTONES-featuring key discoveries, theories & inventions; QUIZ QUESTIONS to test the readers' knowledge; (answers are provided); IT'S AMAZING-features to add interest by drawing attention to surprising & exciting scientific information. Each title also includes an index, glossary, answers section & guide to further readings. The combination of engaging writing style & vibrant color illustrations makes this a very attractive & practical reference work for young readers. Each volume features a library binding; 64 pages; 8 X 10 size. The series is being published in two groups of five titles each. Group 1, (*1-85435-620-8*) is available as of November 1993. The titles are: The Solar System, (*1-85435-621-6*); Animal Life, (*1-85435-623-2*); Force & Motion, (*1-85435-622-4*); Communications, (*1-85435-624-0*); The Environment, (*1-85435-625-9*). Group 2 will be available in February, 1994. The titles in this second group are: Electricity & Magnetism, Plant Life, Geology & Natural Resources, Transportation, Weather.
Publisher Provided Annotation.

—Light Fantastic. LC 89-998. (Illus.). 32p. (gr. 3-8). 1990. PLB 9.95 (*1-85435-156-7*) Marshall Cavendish.

—Mission Outer Space. LC 79-64388. (Illus.). 36p. (gr. 3-6). 1980. PLB 13.50 (*0-8225-1180-0*) Lerner Pubns.

—Plants in Action. LC 89-996. (Illus.). 32p. (gr. 3-8). 1990. PLB 9.95 (*1-85435-157-5*) Marshall Cavendish.

—Primates, Insect Eaters & Baleen Whales. (Illus.). 96p. 1988. 17.95x (*0-8160-1961-4*) Facts on File.

—Race for the Moon. LC 79-2347. (Illus.). 36p. (gr. 3-6). 1980. PLB 13.50 (0-8225-1183-5) Lerner Pubns.
—S&S Young Reader's Book of Science. 1991. pap. 12.95 (0-671-73128-9, S&S BFYR); pap. 7.95 (0-671-73240-4, S&S BFYR) S&S Trade.
—Secrets of Science Series, 6 vols. (Illus.). (gr. 3-8). 1990. PLB 65.70 (1-85435-151-6) Marshall Cavendish.
—Secrets of Science Series: Group Two, 4 vols. (Illus.). (gr. 3-8). 1991. Set. PLB 39.80 (1-85435-268-7) Marshall Cavendish.
—The Solar System. Evans, Ted, illus. LC 93-4339. 1993. Set. write for info. (1-85435-620-8); pap. 15.95 (1-85435-621-6) Marshall Cavendish.
—Sounds & Music. LC 90-25543. (Illus.). 32p. (gr. 3-8). 1991. PLB 9.95 (1-85435-270-9) Marshall Cavendish.
—Space Sticker Book. (Illus.). 1988. pap. 5.99 (0-517-64549-1) Outlet Bk Co.
—Spacecraft. Full, Roger, et al, illus. LC 88-17655. 24p. (Orig.). (gr. 2-5). 1989. PLB 5.99 (0-394-99989-4) Random Bks Yng Read.
—Weights & Measures. LC 90-25570. (Illus.). 32p. (gr. 3-8). 1991. PLB 9.95 (1-85435-269-5) Marshall Cavendish.
Kersell, Jim. The Little Kitten's Very Scary Day. (Illus.). 24p. (gr. k-3). 1992. pap. 1.99 (0-87406-641-7) Willowisp Pr.
Kershaw, F. M. Heaven's Above. 1993. 13.95 (0-533-10231-6) Vantage.
Kershen, L. Michael. Why Buffalo Roam. Hansen, Monica, illus. Kershen, Drew L., intro. by. (Illus.). 32p. (gr. k-4). 1992. PLB 15.00 (0-88045-043-6) Stemmer Hse.
Kerson, Adrian. Terror in the Towers: Amazing Stories from the World Trade Center Disaster. 80p. (Orig.). (gr. 2-5). 1993. PLB 9.99 (0-679-95332-9); pap. 2.99 (0-679-85332-4) Random Bks Yng Read.
Kerswell, James. Horses. (Illus.). 64p. 1991. 4.99 (0-517-05154-0) Outlet Bk Co.
Kerven, Rosalind. Earth Magic, Sky Magic: North American Indian Tales. (Illus.). 96p. 1991. 14.95 (0-521-36235-0); pap. 8.50 (0-521-36806-5) Cambridge U Pr.
—Equal Rights for Animals. LC 92-6262. 1993. 11.90 (0-531-14227-2) Watts.
—King Leopard's Gift: And Other Legends of the Animal World. Waldman, Bryna, illus. 32p. 1990. 14.95 (0-521-36180-X) Cambridge U Pr.
—Legends of the Animal World. (Illus.). 32p. (gr. 3-7). 1986. 13.95 (0-521-30576-4) Cambridge U Pr.
—Saving Planet Earth. (Illus.). 32p. (gr. 5-8). 1992. PLB 11.90 (0-531-14199-3) Watts.
—The Tree in the Moon & Other Legends of Plants & Trees. (Illus.). 1989. 15.95 (0-521-34269-4) Cambridge U Pr.
Kerven, Rosalind, retold by. The Woman Who Went to Fairyland: A Welsh Folk Tale. De Lacey, Honey, illus. LC 91-40382. 32p. (gr. k-3). 1992. PLB 14.95 (0-87226-466-1, Bedrick Blackie) P Bedrick Bks.
Kesey, Ken. Little Tricker the Squirrel Meets Big Double the Bear. Moser, Barry, illus. 1990. 14.95 (0-670-81136-X) Viking Child Bks.
—The Little Trickler, The Squirrel. 1988. write for info. Viking Child Bks.
—Little Trickster the Squirrel Meets Big Double the Bear. Moser, Barry, illus. LC 92-10605. (gr. 4 up). 1992. 4.99 (0-14-050623-3) Puffin Bks.
—The Sea Lion. Waldman, Neil, illus. 48p. (ps up). 1991. 14.95 (0-670-83916-7) Viking Child Bks.
Kesler, Jay & Stafford, Tim. Making Life Make Sense: Answers to Hard Questions about God & You. 176p. 1991. pap. 7.99 (0-310-71191-6, Campus Life) Zondervan.
Kessel. Le Lion. (gr. 7-12). pap. 5.95 (0-88346-112-8, 40277) EMC.
Kessel, Joyce K. Halloween. Carlson, Nancy L., illus. LC 80-15890. 48p. (gr. k-4). 1980. PLB 14.95 (0-87614-132-7) Carolrhoda Bks.
—Halloween. Carlson, Nancy, illus. 48p. (gr. k-4). 1987. pap. 3.95 (0-87614-475-X, First Ave Edns) Lerner Pubns.
—St. Patrick's Day. Gilchrist, Cathy, illus. LC 82-1254. 48p. (gr. k-4). 1982. lib. bdg. 14.95 (0-87614-193-9); pap. 3.95 (0-87614-482-2) Carolrhoda Bks.
—Squanto & the First Thanksgiving. Donze, Lisa, illus. LC 82-10313. 48p. (gr. k-4). 1983. PLB 14.95 (0-87614-199-8); pap. 5.95 (0-87614-452-0) Carolrhoda Bks.
—Valentine's Day. Ritz, Karen, illus. LC 81-3842. 48p. (gr. k-4). 1981. PLB 14.95 (0-87614-166-1) Carolrhoda Bks.
—Valentine's Day. Ritz, Karen, illus. 48p. (gr. k-4). 1988. pap. 5.95 (0-87614-502-0, First Ave Edns) Lerner Pubns.
Kesselman, Wendy. Becca: (Musical) 61p. 1988. playscript 5.50 (0-87602-277-8) Anchorage.
—Emma. 1993. pap. 4.99 (0-440-40847-4) Dell.
Kesselman-Turkel, Judi & Peterson, Franklynn. Study Smarts: How to Learn More in Less Time. 64p. 1981. pap. 6.95 (0-8092-5852-8) Contemp Bks.
Kessler, Brad. Brer Rabbit & Boss Lion. Mayer, Bill, illus. 40p. (gr. k up). 1993. incl. cass. 19.95 (0-88708-274-2, Rabbit Ears); 14.95 (0-88708-273-4, Rabbit Ears) Picture Bk Studio.
Kessler, Deirdre. Prince Edward Island. (Illus.). 144p. (gr. 4 up). 1992. PLB 26.60 (0-516-06616-1) Childrens.

Kessler, Ethel. IS There a Gorilla in the Band? (ps). 1994. pap. 4.95 (0-671-88303-8, Little Simon) S&S Trade.
—Is There a Penguin at Your Party? (ps). 1994. pap. 4.95 (0-671-88302-X, Little Simon) S&S Trade.
Kessler, Ethel & Kessler, Leonard. Are There Hippos on the Farm? (Illus.). 32p. (ps-k). 1986. casebound, padded cover 4.95 (0-671-62066-5, Little Simon) S&S Trade.
—Are There Seals in the Sandbox? Kessler, Leonard, illus. 24p. (ps). 1990. pap. 4.95 casebound, padded cover (0-671-70539-3, Little Simon) S&S Trade.
—Is There a Horse in Your House? Kessler, Leonard, illus. 22p. (ps). 1990. casebound with padded cov 4.95 (0-671-70540-7, Little Simon) S&S Trade.
—Is There an Elephant in Your Kitchen? (Illus.). 32p. (ps-k). 1986. 4.95 (0-671-62065-7, Little Simon) S&S Trade.
—Stan the Hot Dog Man. Kessler, Leonard, illus. LC 89-34474. 64p. (gr. k-3). 1990. PLB 13.89 (0-06-023280-3) HarpC Child Bks.
Kessler, Jascha, tr. see Olujic, Grozdana.
Kessler, Leonard. The Big Mile Race. Kessler, Leonard, illus. LC 82-9274. 48p. (gr. 1-3). 1983. 9.00 (0-688-01420-8) Greenwillow.
—Big Mile Race. (gr. 4-7). 1991. pap. 2.95 (0-440-40413-4) Dell.
—Here Comes the Strikeout. newly illus. ed. Kessler, Leonard, illus. LC 91-14717. 64p. (gr. k-3). 1965. 13.00 (0-06-023155-6); PLB 12.89 (0-06-023156-4) HarpC Child Bks.
—Here Comes the Strikeout. newly illus. ed. Kessler, Leonard, illus. LC 91-14720. 64p. (gr. k-3). 1978. pap. 3.50 (0-06-444011-7, Trophy) HarpC Child Bks.
—Here Comes the Strikeout. Kessler, Leonard, illus. LC 65-10728. 64p. (gr. k-3). 1987. incl. cassette 5.98 (0-694-00174-0, Trophy) HarpC Child Bks.
—Kick, Pass, & Run. Kessler, Leonard, illus. LC 66-18656. 64p. (ps-3). 1966. PLB 13.89 (0-06-023160-2) HarpC Child Bks.
—Kick, Pass & Run. Kessler, Leonard, illus. LC 66-18656. (gr. k-3). 1978. pap. 3.50 (0-06-444012-5, Trophy) HarpC Child Bks.
—Last One in Is a Rotten Egg. Kessler, Leonard, illus. LC 69-10209. 64p. (gr. k-3). 1969. PLB 13.89 (0-06-023158-0) HarpC Child Bks.
—Last One in Is a Rotten Egg. Kessler, Leonard, illus. LC 69-10209. 64p. (gr. k-3). 1989. pap. 3.50 (0-06-444118-0, Trophy) HarpC Child Bks.
—Old Turtle's Baseball Stories. Kessler, Leonard, illus. LC 81-6390. 56p. (gr. 1-3). 1982. 13.95 (0-688-00723-6); PLB 13.88 (0-688-00724-4) Greenwillow.
—Old Turtle's Ninety Knock-Knocks, Jokes, & Riddles. LC 89-77505. (Illus.). 48p. (gr. k up). 1991. 13.95 (0-688-09585-2); PLB 13.88 (0-688-09586-0) Greenwillow.
—Old Turtle's Ninety Knock-Knocks, Jokes, & Riddles. (Illus.). 48p. (gr. 1 up). 1993. pap. 4.95 (0-688-04586-3, Mulberry) Morrow.
—Old Turtle's Riddle & Joke Book. Kessler, Leonard, illus. LC 85-12565. 48p. (gr. 1-4). 1986. 12.95 (0-688-05953-8); PLB 12.88 (0-688-05954-6) Greenwillow.
—Old Turtle's Riddle & Joke Book. (gr. k-6). 1990. pap. 2.95 (0-440-40268-9, YB) Dell.
—Old Turtle's Soccer Team. LC 87-14870. (Illus.). 48p. (gr. k-3). 1988. 11.95 (0-688-07157-0); lib. bdg. 11.88 (0-688-07158-9) Greenwillow.
—Old Turtle's Soccer Team. 1990. pap. 2.95 (0-440-40285-9) Dell.
—Old Turtle's Winter Games. (gr. k-6). 1990. pap. 2.95 (0-440-40261-1, YB) Dell.
—Super Bowl. LC 80-10171. (Illus.). 56p. (gr. 1-4). 1980. PLB 12.88 (0-688-84270-4) Greenwillow.
—Super Bowl. (gr. k-6). 1991. pap. 2.95 (0-440-40403-7, Pub. by Yearling Classics) Dell.
—The Worst Team Ever. Kessler, Leonard, illus. LC 84-25883. 47p. (gr. 1-3). 1985. 10.25 (0-688-04234-1); lib. bdg. 10.88 (0-688-04235-X) Greenwillow.
—Worst Team Ever. (ps-3). 1991. pap. 2.95 (0-440-40428-2) Dell.
Kessler, Leonard, jt. auth. see Kessler, Ethel.
Kessler, R., ed. see Christopher, Garrett.
Kessler, R., ed. see Diamond, Laurie.
Kessler, R., ed. see Golden, Michael.
Kessler, R., ed. see Spencer, Anne.
Kessler, Rikki, jt. auth. see Friedland, Joyce.
Kessler, Rikki, ed. see Albert, Toni.
Kessler, Rikki, ed. see Bachelder, Marvin.
Kessler, Rikki, ed. see Christopher, Garrett.
Kessler, Rikki, ed. see Claydon, Dina.
Kessler, Rikki, ed. see Croil, Marianne.
Kessler, Rikki, ed. see Danielson, Kathy.
Kessler, Rikki, ed. see Diamond, Laurie.
Kessler, Rikki, ed. see Dobrow, Vicki.
Kessler, Rikki, ed. see Fischer, Elyse.
Kessler, Rikki, ed. see Forsten, Charlene.
Kessler, Rikki, ed. see Gluzband, Cheryl.
Kessler, Rikki, ed. see Golden, Michael.
Kessler, Rikki, ed. see Goldish, Meish.
Kessler, Rikki, ed. see Halverson, Patricia A.
Kessler, Rikki, ed. see Hanus, Karen.
Kessler, Rikki, ed. see Klitzner, Carol.
Kessler, Rikki, ed. see Levine, Gloria.
Kessler, Rikki, ed. see Levine, Gloria & Fischer, Kathleen M.
Kessler, Rikki, ed. see McGee, Brenda.

Kessler, Rikki, ed. see McGee, Brenda H.
Kessler, Rikki, ed. see Marsh, Norma.
Kessler, Rikki, ed. see Medland, Mary.
Kessler, Rikki, ed. see Murphy, Michael.
Kessler, Rikki, ed. see Norris, Crystal.
Kessler, Rikki, ed. see Peitz, Mary.
Kessler, Rikki, ed. see Pilar, Arlene.
Kessler, Rikki, ed. see Reeves, Barbara.
Kessler, Rikki, ed. see Snodgrass, Mary E.
Kessler, Rikki, ed. see Sussman, Linda.
Kessler, Rikki, ed. see Tretler, Marcia.
Kessler, Rikki, ed. see Villanella, Rosemary.
Kessler, Rikki, ed. see Witt, Sandi & Petrovich, Janice.
Kester, Ellen S. Word Magic: Shakespeare's Rhetoric for Gifted Students: Elementary & Secondary Shakespearian Excerpts. 2nd ed. Turner, Joseph R., III, illus. 194p. 1989. pap. text ed. 35.00 (0-685-26279-0) Pickwick Pubs.
Kester, Ellen S. see Johnson, Kristopher K.
Kester, Ellen S., ed. see Schuyler, Royce.
Keston, Louise, ed. Math Skills by Objectives. 240p. (gr. 7-9). 1985. pap. text ed. 5.25 (0-317-46527-9) Cambridge Bk.
Ketcham, Hank. Dennis the Menace: Everybody's Little Helper. (Illus.). 128p. 1984. pap. 1.95 (0-449-12732-X, GM) Fawcett.
—Dennis the Menace: Little Man in a Big Hurry. (Illus.). 128p. 1984. pap. 1.95 (0-449-12778-8, Gm) Fawcett.
—Dennis the Menace: Make-Believe Angel. (Illus.). 1981. pap. 1.95 (0-449-13902-6, GM) Fawcett.
—Dennis the Menace: Prayers & Graces. Graham, Ruth, intros. by. LC 92-17186. (Illus.). 64p. (Orig.). 1993. 10.00 (0-664-21993-4); pap. 5.99 (0-664-25252-4) Westminster John Knox.
—Dennis the Menace: Teacher's Threat. (Illus.). 1981. pap. 1.50 (0-449-13643-4, GM) Fawcett.
—Dennis the Menace: The Short Swinger. (Illus.). 1981. pap. 1.50 (0-449-13641-8, GM) Fawcett.
—Dennis the Menace: Voted Most Likely. (Illus.). (gr. 7 up). 1982. pap. 1.75 (0-449-13747-3, GM) Fawcett.
—Dennis the Menace: Where the Action Is. (Illus.). 128p. 1981. pap. 1.50 (0-449-13669-8, GM) Fawcett.
—Dennis the Menace: Your Friendly Neighborhood Kid. (Illus.). 1979. pap. 1.25 (0-449-13778-3, GM) Fawcett.
Ketcham, Ruth. The Tale of Alex Trueblood. 32p. (ps-3). 1991. 5.95 (1-56322-032-6) V W Hensley.
Ketchum, Lynne, jt. auth. see Beaudry, Jo.
Ketchum, Mary. The Clapper Rail. 1994. write for info. (0-8050-2359-3) H Holt & Co.
Ketner, Mary G. Ganzy Remembers. Sparks, Barbara, illus. LC 89-78261. 32p. (gr. k-3). 1991. SBE 13.95 (0-689-31610-0, Atheneum Child Bk) Macmillan Child Grp.
Kettelkamp, Larry. Bill Cosby: Family Funny Man. LC 86-23809. 128p. (gr. 3 up). 1987. lib. bdg. 12.98 (0-671-62382-6, J Messner); pap. 3.95 (0-671-64029-1) S&S Trade.
—Computer Graphics: How it Works, What it Does. LC 88-38924. (Illus.). 144p. (gr. 7 up). 1989. 12.95 (0-688-07504-5) Morrow Jr Bks.
—Electronic Musical Instruments: What They Do, How They Work. Deutsch, Herbert, frwd. by. LC 83-23819. (Illus.). 128p. (gr. 7up). 1984. 11.95 (0-688-02781-4) Morrow Jr Bks.
—High Tech for the Handicapped: New Ways to Hear, See, Talk, & Walk. LC 90-37527. (Illus.). 128p. (gr. 6 up). 1991. lib. bdg. 17.95 (0-89490-202-4) Enslow Pubs.
—Living in Space. LC 92-35118. (Illus.). 128p. (gr. 3 up). 1993. 14.00 (0-688-10018-X) Morrow Jr Bks.
—Magic Made Easy. rev. ed. Eutemey, Loring, illus. Klotzbeacher, Donovan, photos by. LC 80-22947. (Illus.). 96p. (gr. 3-7). 1981. 13.95 (0-688-00458-X); PLB 13.88 (0-688-00377-X, Morrow Jr Bks) Morrow Jr Bks.
—The Magic of Sound. Rev. ed. Kramer, Anthony, illus. LC 82-6510. 96p. (gr. 4-6). 1982. lib. bdg. 12.88 (0-688-01493-3) Morrow Jr Bks.
—Modern Sports Science. LC 86-8754. (Illus.). 160p. (gr. 7 up). 1986. 12.95 (0-688-05494-3) Morrow Jr Bks.
—A Partnership of Mind & Body: Biofeedback. LC 76-24818. (Illus.). (gr. 5-9). 1976. PLB 12.88 (0-688-32088-0) Morrow Jr Bks.
Ketteman, Helen. Not Yet, Yvette. Mathews, Judith, ed. Trivas, Irene, illus. LC 91-19608. 24p. (ps-2). 1992. PLB 11.95 (0-8075-5771-4) A Whitman.
—One Baby Boy. Flynn-Stanton, Maggie, illus. LC 93-23044. 1994. pap. 15.00 (0-671-87278-8, S&S BFYR) S&S Trade.
—The Year of No More Corn. Parker, Robert A., illus. LC 90-29092. 32p. (ps-2). 1993. 14.95 (0-531-05950-2); PLB 14.99 (0-531-08550-3) Orchard Bks Watts.
Ketteman, Hellen. Aunt Hilarity's Bustle. LC 91-2198. (ps-3). 1992. pap. 14.00 (0-671-77861-7, S&S BFYR) S&S Trade.
Kettler, Edward. South Atlantic War. 136p. (Orig.). 1991. pap. 12.00 (1-55878-064-5) Game Designers.
Kettner, Christine. An Ordinary Cat. Kettner, Christine, illus. LC 90-19441. 32p. (ps-3). 1991. PLB 13.89 (0-06-023173-4) HarpC Child Bks.
Kett-O'Connor, Pamela. The Arts - Julia Morgan. LC 92-46285. 1993. 19.93 (0-86625-489-7); 14.95s.p. (0-685-66538-0) Rourke Pubns.
Key, Alexander. Escape to Witch Mountain. 1979. pap. 1.75 (0-671-56044-1) S&S Trade.
—The Forgotten Door. 144p. (gr. 3-7). 1986. pap. 2.95 (0-590-43130-7) Scholastic Inc.

Keydel, D. F., jt. ed. see Beyer, W. F.
Keyes see Sohn, David A.
Keyes, Daniel. Flowers for Algernon. (gr. 8 up). 1970. pap. 3.50 (0-553-25665-3) Bantam.
—Flowers for Algernon: A Classic Story of Struggle. (Illus.). (gr. 4 up). 1987. PLB 13.95s.p. (0-88682-007-3) Creative Ed.
Keyes, Fenton. Opportunities in Psychiatry. LC 76-42885. (Illus.). (gr. 9 up). 1982. 13.95 (0-8442-6367-2, VGM Career Bks); pap. 10.95 (0-8442-6368-0, VGM Career Bks) NTC Pub Grp.
Keyes, Joan R. Now You're Talking. (Illus.). (gr. 4-9). 1988. wkbk. 5.95 (1-55737-067-2) Ed Activities.
Keyishian, Elizabeth. Everything You Need to Know about Smoking. rev. ed. Rosen, Ruth, ed. (gr. 7-12). 1993. PLB 13.95 (0-8239-1615-4) Rosen Group.
Keysor, Charles W., jt. auth. see Case, Riley B.
Keyworth, C. L. California Indians. (Illus.). (gr. 5-8). 1990. 18.95x (0-8160-2386-7) Facts on File.
Keyworth, Valerie. New Zealand: Land of the Long White Cloud. LC 89-11716. (Illus.). 128p. (gr. 5 up). 1990. RSBE 14.95 (0-87518-414-6, Dillon) Macmillan Child Grp.
Kezer, Claude D. Principles of Stage Combat. (Illus.). 62p. 1983. pap. 12.50 (0-88680-156-7) I E Clark.
Kezzeiz, Ediba. Fatima's Surprise. Arostu, Salma, illus. 21p. (Orig.). (ps-1). 1991. pap. 3.50 (0-89259-114-5) Am Trust Pubns.
—Grandma's Garden. Hubbi, Mona, illus. 21p. (Orig.). (ps-4). 1991. pap. 3.50 (0-89259-113-7) Am Trust Pubns.
—Inside & Under the World of Wonder. Mir, Anjum, illus. 38p. (Orig.). (ps). 1992. pap. text ed. 4.00 (0-89259-112-9) Am Trust Pubns.
—Ramadan Adventures of Fasfoose Mouse. Shishani, Ami, illus. 36p. (Orig.). (gr. 1-6). 1991. pap. write for info. (0-89259-117-X) Am Trust Pubns.
—When I Grow up. Shishani, Ami, illus. 17p. (Orig.). (ps-1). 1991. pap. write for info. (0-89259-116-1) Am Trust Pubns.
Kgositsile, Aneb. Blood River. (gr. 12 up). 1983. pap. 5.00 (0-685-18304-1) Broadside Pr.
Khalsa, Dayal K. Cowboy Dreams. Khalsa, Dayal K., illus. LC 89-22782. 32p. (gr. k-4). 1990. 16.00 (0-517-57490-X, Clarkson Potter); PLB 16.99 (0-517-57491-8, Clarkson Potter) Crown Bks Yng Read.
—How Pizza Came to Our Town. Khalsa, Dayal K., illus. 32p. (gr. k-8). 1989. 14.95 (0-88776-231-X) Tundra Bks.
—How Pizza Came to Queens. Khalsa, Dayal K., illus. (gr. 1 up). 1989. PLB 13.95 (0-517-57126-9, Clarkson Potter) Crown Bks Yng Read.
—I Want a Dog. (Illus.). 24p. (ps up). 1988. 13.95 (0-517-56532-3, 557452, C N Potter Bks) Crown Bks Yng Read.
—Julian. Khalsa, Dayal K., illus. 24p. (gr. k-8). 1989. 17. 95 (0-88776-237-9) Tundra Bks.
—My Family Vacation. Khalsa, Dayal K., illus. (gr. 1-3). 1988. PLB 13.95 (0-517-56697-4, Clarkson Potter) Crown Bks Yng Read.
—My Family Vacation. Khalsa, Dayal K., illus. 24p. (gr. k-8). 1988. 14.95 (0-88776-226-3) Tundra Bks.
—Sleepers. (Illus.). 24p. (ps-1). 1988. PLB 7.95 (0-517-56917-5, Clarkson Potter) Crown Bks Yng Read.
—The Snow Cat. Khalsa, Dayal K., illus. LC 92-8988. 32p. (ps-2). 1992. 14.00 (0-517-59183-9, Clarkson Potter) Crown Bks Yng Read.
—Tales of a Gambling Grandma. (Illus.). 32p. (gr. 1 up). 1991. 14.95 (0-88776-179-8) Tundra Bks.
Khalsa, Tej K., ed. see Bhajan, Yogi.
Khan, Christa. First Two Hundred Words in German. Sleight, Katy, illus. LC 93-29559. 1994. 3.95 (1-85697-955-5) Kingfisher Bks.
Khanduri, K. Polar Wildlife. (Illus.). 32p. (gr. 3-7). 1993. PLB 13.96 (0-88110-601-1); pap. 6.95 (0-7460-0938-0) EDC.
Khanna & Ridley. RoleMaster Companion II. Velez, Walter, illus. 112p. (Orig.). (gr. 10-12). 1987. pap. 12. 00 (0-915795-97-3, 1600) Iron Crown Ent Inc.
Khanna, K. As They Saw India. Khanna, Krishna, illus. (gr. 1-9). 1979. pap. 2.50 (0-89744-172-9) Auromere.
Kharik, Nina. The Fish's Tail. LC 93-60416. (Illus.). 44p. (gr. k-3). 1994. pap. 5.95 (1-55523-629-4) Winston-Derek.
Kharms, Daniil. The Story of a Boy Named Will, Who Went Sledding Down the Hill. Radunsky, Vladimir, illus. Gambrell, Jamey, tr. from RUS. (Illus.). 32p. (gr. k-3). 1993. 14.95 (1-55858-214-2); lib. bdg. 14.88 (1-55858-215-0) North-South Bks NYC.
Khayyam, Omar. Rubaiyat of Omar Khayyam. Fitzgerald, Edward, tr. (Illus.). (gr. 9 up). 1969. pap. 1.50 (0-8049-0204-6, CL-204) Airmont.
Khdir, Kate & Nash, Sue. Little Ghost. Church, Caroline, illus. 32p. (ps-2). 1991. incl. dust jacket 12.95 (0-8120-6203-5); pap. 5.95 (0-8120-4779-6) Barron's.
Kherdian, David. Asking the River. Hogrogian, Nonny, illus. LC 92-34912. 112p. (gr. 5 up). 1993. 14.95 (0-531-05483-7, Orchard Bks); PLB 14.99 (0-531-08633-X, Orchard Bks) Watts.
—Beat Poetry. 1994. write for info. (0-8050-3315-7) H Holt & Co.
—Bridger: The Story of Mountain Man. LC 86-7558. 160p. (gr. 7 up). 1987. 11.75 (0-688-06510-4) Greenwillow.

—By Myself. Hogrogian, Nonny, illus. LC 92-44366. 32p. (ps-2). 1993. PLB 14.95 (0-8050-2386-0, Bks Young Read) H Holt & Co.
—Feathers & Tails. Hogrogian, Nonny, illus. 96p. (gr. 1 up). 1992. PLB 19.95 (0-399-21876-9, Philomel Bks) Putnam Pub Group.
—The Great Fishing Contest. (Illus.). 48p. (ps-3). 1991. 14.95 (0-399-22263-4, Philomel Bks) Putnam Pub Group.
—Juna's Journey. Hogrogian, Nonny, illus. LC 92-12333. 48p. (gr. 3 up). 1993. PLB 15.95 (0-399-22010-0, Philomel Bks) Putnam Pub Group.
—Lullaby for Emily. 1994. write for info. (0-8050-2957-5) H Holt & Co.
—The Mystery of the Diamond in the Wood. Geiger, Paul, illus. LC 83-272. 128p. (gr. 3 up). 1983. lib. bdg. 9.99 (0-394-95603-6) Knopf Bks Yng Read.
—Road from Home. (gr. 7 up). 1988. pap. 5.99 (0-14-032524-7, Puffin) Puffin Bks.
—Road from Home: The Story of an Armenian Girl. LC 78-72511. 256p. (gr. 7 up). 1979. 13.95 (0-688-80205-2); PLB 13.93 (0-688-84205-4) Greenwillow.
—A Song for Uncle Harry. Hogrogian, Nonny, illus. 80p. (gr. 3-7). 1989. 13.95 (0-399-21895-5, Philomel Bks) Putnam Pub Group.
—Toad & the Green Princess. Hogrogian, Nonny, illus. LC 92-39314. 1994. write for info. (0-399-22539-0, Philomel Bks) Putnam Pub Group.
Khosho, Francis K. The Eagle Who Thought He Was a Chicken. Hardy, Suzanne, illus. 24p. (Orig.). (gr. 7 up). 1993. pap. 8.00 (0-9619310-2-7) Khosho.
Khotianovsky, Olga, ed. see Kogan, Mark.
Khurelblat, B. & Narain, Aditya. Folk Tales of Mongolia. 85p. 1992. pap. 5.95 (81-207-1341-9, Pub. by Sterling Pubs IA) Apt Bks.
Kiaie, Catherine C. Workbook - Math 1: Basic Skills, Grade 1-2. (ps-3). 1984. pap. 2.50 (0-307-23541-6, Golden Pr) Western Pub.
Kiang, John. The Early One World Movement. LC 91-68335. 360p. (Orig.). 1992. pap. 14.95 (0-916301-03-6) One World Pub.
Kibbe, Pat. Mrs. Kiddy & the Moonbooms. Rutherford, Jenny, illus. LC 90-24406. 112p. (gr. 1-4). 1991. pap. 2.95 (0-689-71469-6, Aladdin) Macmillan Child Grp.
Kibbey, Marsha. The Helping Place. Hagerman, Jennifer, illus. 40p. (gr. 1-4). 1991. PLB 13.50 (0-87614-680-9) Carolrhoda Bks.
—Helping Place. (ps-3). 1992. pap. 4.95 (0-87614-557-8) Carolrhoda Bks.
—My Grammy. Ritz, Karen, illus. 32p. (gr. 1-4). 1988. PLB 13.50 (0-87614-328-1) Carolrhoda Bks.
—My Grammy: A Book about Alzheimer's Disease. (ps-3). 1991. pap. 4.95 (0-87614-544-6) Carolrhoda Bks.
Kichejian, Janet, ed. see Hollier, Jo.
Kidd, Diana. Onion Tears. Montgomery, Lucy, illus. LC 90-43011. 72p. (gr. 2-5). 1991. 12.95 (0-531-05870-0); PLB 12.99 (0-531-08470-1) Orchard Bks Watts.
—Onion Tears. Montgomery, Lucy, illus. LC 92-46601. 80p. (gr. 5 up). 1993. pap. 3.95 (0-688-11862-3, Pub. by Beech Tree Bks) Morrow.
Kidd, Jane. Horses & Ponies. (Illus.). 64p. 1989. 7.99 (0-517-69206-6) Outlet Bk Co.
Kidd, Jane, ed. A First Guide to Horse & Pony Care: What Every Young Rider Must Know about Feeding, Grooming & Handling. (Illus.). 208p. (gr. 3-7). 1991. 24.95 (0-87605-833-0) Howell Bk.
—Learning to Ride. (Illus.). 208p. (gr. 4-9). 1993. 30.00 (0-87605-961-2) Howell Bk.
Kidd, Leonice T. They All Sat Down: Pianists in Profile. (Illus.). viii, 133p. (Orig.). (gr. 8-12). 1986. pap. 9.95 (0-9619974-0-0) Chrlstn SC.
—They All Sat Down: Pianists in Profile. 2nd ed. (Illus.). 151p. (Orig.). (gr. 8 up). 1989. pap. write for info. (0-9619974-1-9) Chrlstn SC.
Kidd, Nina. Draw Science - Dinosaurs. 64p. (ps-3). 1992. pap. 4.95 (0-929923-89-8) Lowell Hse.
—Draw Science - Wild Animals. 64p. (ps-3). 1992. pap. 4.95 (0-929923-90-1) Lowell Hse.
—June Mountain Secret. Kidd, Nina, illus. LC 90-31574. 32p. (gr. k-3). 1991. 15.00 (0-06-023167-X); PLB 14. 89 (0-06-023168-8) HarpC Child Grp.
Kidd, Ron. The Nutcracker. Reinert, Rick, illus. 48p. (gr. k-6). 1985. 6.95 (0-8249-8095-6, Ideals Child) Hambleton-Hill.
Kidd, Ronald. Danny Dorfman's Dream Band, No. 3: The Case of the Missing Case. Jones, Bob, illus. LC 92-17208. 80p. (gr. 2-6). 1992. pap. 2.99 (0-14-034988-X) Puffin Bks.
—Danny Dorfman's Dream Band, No. 4: Rapunzel, Sort Of. Jones, Bob, illus. LC 92-16495. 80p. (gr. 2-6). 1992. pap. 3.50 (0-14-034987-1) Puffin Bks.
—Dunker. 176p. (gr. 5 up). pap. 2.50 (0-553-26431-1) Bantam.
—A Legend in His Own Mind. Jones, Bob, illus. 80p. (gr. 3-6). 1992. pap. 2.99 (0-14-034986-3, Puffin) Puffin Bks.
—Meet Maximum Clyde. 80p. (gr. 3-6). 1992. pap. 2.99 (0-14-034989-8, Puffin) Puffin Bks.
—On Top of Old Smoky: A Collection of Songs & Stories from Appalachia. Anderson, Linda, illus. LC 92-14437. 40p. 1992. 13.95 (0-8249-8569-9, Ideals Child); PLB 14.00 (0-8249-8586-9); incl. 60-min. cassette 17.95 (0-8249-7513-8) Hambleton-Hill.
—Sammy Carducci's Guide to Women. 112p. (gr. 3-7). 1991. 14.95 (0-525-67363-6, Lodestar Bks) Dutton Child Bks.

—Sammy Carducci's Guide to Women. 112p. (gr. 3-7). 1994. pap. 3.99 (0-14-036481-1) Puffin Bks.
—Second Fiddle. 176p. (gr. 4-7). 1992. pap. 2.95 (0-8167-1823-7) Troll Assocs.
—Sizzle & Splat. (gr. 5-8). 1986. pap. 2.95 (0-440-47970-3, YB) Dell.
—Winnie the Pooh & Tigger Too! 24p. (gr. up). 1992. write for info. (0-307-14019-9, 64019) Western Pub.
Kidd, Ronald, adapted by. Disney's Aladdin. Mateu, illus. 24p. (ps-4). 1992. 20.00 (0-307-74026-9, 64026, Golden Pr) Western Pub.
—Goldilocks & the Three Bears. (Illus.). 24p. (ps up) 1992. write for info. (0-307-74803-0, 64803, Golden Pr) Western Pub.
—Jack & the Beanstalk. 20p. (ps up). 1992. write for info. (0-307-74701-8, 64701) Western Pub.
—The Jungle Book. Kurtz, John, illus. 24p. (ps-4). 1993. 20.00 (0-307-74028-5, 64028, Golden Pr) Western Pub.
—Robin Hood. 20p. (ps up). 1992. write for info. (0-307-74703-4, 64703) Western Pub.
—Snow White & the Seven Dwarfs. Mateu, illus. 24p. (ps up). 1991. write for info. (0-307-74018-8, 64018) Western Pub.
Kidder, Harvey. The Kids' Book of Chess & Chess Set. LC 89-40787. (Illus.). 96p. (Orig.). (gr. 3-7). 1990. pap. 14.95 (0-89480-767-6, 1767) Workman Pub.
Kidman-Cox, R., et al. First Book of Nature. (Illus.). 168p. (gr. k-6). 1993. pap. 14.95 (0-7460-0563-6, Usborne) EDC.
Kidner, Maria C. ABC Come See Wyoming. Campbell, Loreen, illus. 56p. (Orig.). (gr. k-3). 1990. pap. 4.95 (0-9625920-0-5) Rainbow Rhapsody.
—ABC Come See Wyoming. Rev. ed. Campbell, Lorene, illus. 56p. (gr. k-3). 1990. pap. 4.95 (0-9625920-1-3) Rainbow Rhapsody.
Kidney, Dorothy. The Mystery of the Old Clock Shop. 112p. (Orig.). (gr. 4-6). 1981. pap. 4.95 (0-8341-0728-7) Beacon Hill.
Kids at Heart, Inc. Staff. It's the Little Friggles That Really Count! (Illus.). 20p. 1992. Personalized. text ed. 12.95 (1-883842-01-8); text ed. 7.95 (1-883842-00-X) Kids at Heart.
Kidsbooks, Inc. Staff. Dial-a-Dinosaur. (Illus.). 16p. (gr. 1-4). 1988. pap. 4.95 (0-8431-2289-7) Price Stern.
Kidship Associates Staff. Lluvia de Palabras. Kidship Associates Staff, illus. (SPA.). 109p. (gr. 1-3). 1988. pap. text ed. 2.00 (1-878742-00-0) Kidship Assoc.
Kiebanow, Barbara & Fischer, Sara. American Holidays: Exploring Traditions, Customs, & Backgrounds. (Illus.). 128p. (gr. 5 up). 1986. 9.50x (0-86647-018-2) Pro Lingua.
Kiefer, Irene. Poisoned Land: The Problems of Hazardous Waste. LC 80-22120. (Illus.). 96p. (gr. 6-9). 1981. SBE 13.95 (0-689-30837-X, Atheneum Child Bk) Macmillan Child Grp.
Kiefer, James. Hudson Taylor. Beerhorst, Adrian, illus. 53p. (gr. k-6). 1973. pap. text ed. 8.99 (1-55976-054-0) CEF Press.
Kiemel Anderson, Ann. God's Little Dreamer. Lane, Sandy, illus. LC 90-33475. 32p. (ps-8). 1990. 10.99 (0-89081-785-5) Harvest Hse.
Kienlen, Helen & Sandercock, Lois. Big Boss Charger. Bower, J. R., illus. 16p. (gr. k-4). 1989. pap. text ed. 4.00 (0-9626864-1-7) Holistic Learning.
—Llamas. Bower, J. R., illus. 16p. (Orig.). (gr. k-4). 1989. pap. text ed. 4.00 (0-9626864-0-9) Holistic Learning.
Kiesel, Stanley. Skinny Malinky Leads the War for Kidness. 176p. (gr. 7 up). 1985. pap. 2.50 (0-380-69875-7, Flare) Avon.
—The War Between the Pitiful Teachers & the Splendid Kids. 208p. (gr. 7 up). 1982. pap. 3.50 (0-380-57802-6, Flare) Avon.
Kieveach, Marshal. Counting on Cold Friends. (ps-3). 1992. 3.99 (0-8431-3426-7) Price Stern.
—Going Wild. (ps-3). 1992. 3.99 (0-8431-3427-5) Price Stern.
—Nature Colors. (ps-3). 1992. 3.99 (0-8431-3428-3) Price Stern.
—Ocean of Opposites. (ps). 1992. 5.75 (0-8431-3429-1) Price Stern.
Kightley, Lynn, et al. One Two Three. (Illus.). 32p. (ps-1). 1986. pap. 6.95 (0-316-54004-8) Little.
—Opposites. (Illus.). 32p. (ps-1). 1986. pap. 6.95 (0-316-49931-5) Little.
Kightley, Rosalinda. The Farmer. Kightley, Rosalinda, illus. LC 88-19431. 32p. (ps-2). 1989. pap. 3.95 (0-689-71222-7, Aladdin) Macmillan Child Grp.
Kightley, Rosalinda, et al. My First Book: Words & Pictures for the Very Young. Kightly, Rosalinda, et al, illus. LC 91-71831. 64p. (ps). 1992. 14.95 (1-56402-034-7) Candlewick Pr.
Kiki. Maya & the Town That Loved a Tree. (ps-3). 1992. 14.95 (0-8478-1563-3) Rizzoli Intl.
Kikukawa, Cecily H. Ka Mea Ho'ala, the Awakener: The Story of Henry Obookiah. Burningham, Robin, illus. LC 82-70246. 100p. (Orig.). (gr. 7-10). 1982. pap. 6.95 (0-935848-10-X) Bess Pr.
Kilborne, Sarah S. Peach & Blue. Fancher, Lou & Johnson, Steve, illus. LC 93-26562. 1994. write for info. (0-679-83929-1); PLB write for info. (0-679-93929-6) Knopf Bks Yng Read.
Kilburn, Greta, tr. see Tornqvist, Rita.
Kilduff, Lee. Blossom. (Illus.). 64p. 1992. pap. 2.95 (1-56156-167-3) Kidsbks.

Kile, Joan. God's Mustard Seed, Vol. 1. Ragland, Teresa, illus. 32p. (ps-5).

1993. PLB 15.00 (*0-9636314-0-3*)
Musty the Mustard.
**GOD'S MUSTARD SEED is the first
in a series of Musty the Mustard Seed
Books. Geared to children 3-10 yrs. of
age, it is a book that encourages
children to pray, read the Bible & love
Jesus. Musty the Mustard Seed, the
little character, inspires children to
have faith as a grain of mustard seed.
Musty leads the reader through the
pages of the Bible. Books are written
from scripts of the Mustard Seed
Gospel Radio Program, narrated by
Joan Kile. Many children who
participated in the radio programs drew
picture ideas for the illustrations of
Musty the Mustard Seed Books. The
colorful illustrations came from the
hearts of children. The MMSB have
been used with great success during
Joan Kile's 21 years of teaching. The
children have enthusiastically
responded to GOD'S MUSTARD
SEED by saying, "Read it again!"
Order from SPRING ARBOR,
BAKER & TAYLOR or Musty the
MustardSeed Books, 104 Stable Court,
Franklin, TN 37064, 615-790-1996.**
Publisher Provided Annotation.

Kile, Marilyn & Baird, Kristin. My Body Belongs to Me. (gr. k-2). 1986. text ed. 17.50 (*0-88671-173-8*, 7202) Am Guidance.
—What Would You Do If...? 1986. pap. text ed. 17.25 (*0-88671-172-X*, 7205) Am Guidance.
Kilgarriff, Michael. Oh No! Not Another One Thousand Jokes for Kids. (gr. k up). 1987. pap. 3.95 (*0-345-34035-3*) Ballantine.
—One Thousand Jokes for Kids of All Ages. (gr. k up). 1986. pap. 4.99 (*0-345-33480-9*) Ballantine.
—One Thousand More Jokes for Kids. (gr. k up). 1987. pap. 4.99 (*0-345-34034-5*) Ballantine.
Kilgore, James C. African Violet: Poem for a Black Woman. 76p. (gr. 7-12). 1982. pap. 5.00 perfect bd. (*0-916418-46-4*) Lotus.
Kilian, Crawford. Wonders, Inc. Larrecq, John M., illus. (gr. 1 up). 1968. 6.95 (*0-87466-058-0*, Pub. by Parnassus) HM.
Kilian, Pamela. What Was Watergate. 1990. 16.95 (*0-312-04446-1*) St Martin.
Kille, Jullien, jt. auth. see Peaslee, Ann.
Killeen, Leah R. At the Park. Killeen, Leah R., illus. 32p. (ps-2). Date not set. 11.95 (*1-56065-154-7*) Capstone Pr. Postponed.
—Rainbow Fruit Salad. Killeen, Leah R., illus. 32p. (ps-2). Date not set. 11.95 (*1-56065-155-5*) Capstone Pr. Postponed.
Killen, Barbara. Economics & the Consumer. (Illus.). 88p. (gr. 5 up). 1989. 21.50 (*0-8225-1775-2*) Lerner Pubns.
Killen, M. Barbara. Introduction to Economic Reasoning. (Illus.). 88p. (gr. 5 up). 1991. PLB 21.50 (*0-8225-1784-1*) Lerner Pubns.
Killen, M. Barbara, jt. auth. see Walz, Michael K.
Killien, Christi. All of the Above. LC 86-27872. (gr. 5-9). 1987. 13.95 (*0-395-43023-2*) HM.
—All of the Above. (gr. k up). 1989. pap. 2.95 (*0-440-20316-3*, LFL) Dell.
—Artie's Brief: The Whole Truth & Nothing But. (gr. 3 up). 1989. 13.45 (*0-395-49697-7*) HM.
—Artie's Brief: The Whole Truth & Nothing But. 112p. 1990. pap. 2.95 (*0-380-71108-7*, Camelot) Avon.
—The Daffodils. 144p. 1992. 13.95 (*0-590-44241-4*, Scholastic Hardcover) Scholastic Inc.
—Daffodils. (gr. 4-7). 1993. pap. 2.95 (*0-590-44242-2*) Scholastic Inc.
—Putting on an Act. (gr. 4-9). 1988. pap. 2.95 (*0-440-20186-1*, LFL) Dell.
—Rusty Fertlanger, Lady's Man. LC 87-31001. 144p. (gr. 5-9). 1988. 13.95 (*0-395-46762-4*) HM.
Killilea, Marie. Newf. Schoenherr, Ian, illus. 32p. (ps up). 1992. PLB 14.95 (*0-399-21875-0*, Philomel Bks) Putnam Pub Group.
—Wren. Riger, Robert, illus. (gr. 3-7). 1981. pap. 0.95 (*0-440-49704-3*, YB) Dell.
Killinger, Margaret, ed. see Painter, Desmond & Shepard, John.
Killingray, David. The American Frontier. Yapp, Malcolm, et al, eds. (Illus.). 32p. (gr. 6-11). 1980. pap. text ed. 3.45 (*0-89908-206-8*) Greenhaven.
—The Atom Bomb. Yapp, Malcolm, et al, eds. (Illus.). 32p. (gr. 6-11). 1980. pap. text ed. 3.45 (*0-89908-210-6*) Greenhaven.
—Henry Ford. Yapp, Malcolm, et al, eds. (Illus.). 32p. (gr. 6-11). 1980. pap. text ed. 3.45 (*0-89908-024-3*) Greenhaven.

—The Mexican Revolution. Yapp, Malcolm, et al, eds. (Illus.). 32p. (gr. 6-11). 1980. pap. text ed. 3.45 (*0-89908-112-6*) Greenhaven.
—The Neolithic Revolution. Yapp, Malcolm, et al, eds. (Illus.). 32p. (gr. 6-11). 1980. pap. text ed. 3.45 (*0-89908-105-3*) Greenhaven.
—Nyerere & Nkrumah. Yapp, Malcolm & Killingray, Margaret, eds. (Illus.). 32p. (gr. 6-11). 1980. pap. text ed. 3.45 (*0-89908-104-5*) Greenhaven.
—Population. O'Connor, Edmund, ed. (Illus.). 32p. (gr. 6-11). 1980. pap. text ed. 3.45 (*0-89908-116-9*) Greenhaven.
—The Russian Revolution. Yapp, Malcolm, et al, eds. (Illus.). (gr. 6-11). 1980. pap. text ed. 3.45 (*0-89908-113-4*) Greenhaven.
—The Slave Trade. Yapp, Malcolm & Killingray, Margaret, eds. (Illus.). (gr. 6-11). 1980. pap. text ed. 3.45 (*0-89908-124-X*) Greenhaven.
—The Two World Wars. Yapp, Malcolm & Killlingray, Margaret, eds. (Illus.). 32p. (gr. 6-11). 1980. pap. text ed. 3.45 (*0-89908-209-2*) Greenhaven.
—A World Economy. Yapp, Malcolm, et al, eds. (Illus.). 32p. (gr. 6-11). 1980. pap. text ed. 3.45 (*0-89908-118-5*) Greenhaven.
Killingray, David & Yapp, Malcolm. The Enlightenment. (Illus.). 32p. (gr. 6-11). 1980. pap. text ed. 3.45 (*0-89908-200-9*) Greenhaven.
—Hollywood. (Illus.). 32p. (gr. 6-11). 1980. pap. text ed. 3.45 (*0-89908-213-0*) Greenhaven.
Killingray, David, et al. Stalin. Yapp, Malcolm, et al, eds. (Illus.). 32p. (gr. 6-11). 1980. pap. text ed. 3.45 (*0-89908-101-0*) Greenhaven.
Killingray, Margaret. The Agricultural Revolution. Yapp, Malcolm & O'Connor, Edmund, eds. (Illus.). 32p. (gr. 6-11). 1980. pap. text ed. 3.45 (*0-89908-106-1*) Greenhaven.
—Ancient Greece. Yapp, Malcolm & O'Connor, Edmund, eds. (Illus.). 32p. (gr. 6-11). 1980. pap. text ed. 3.45 (*0-89908-001-4*) Greenhaven.
—Constantine. Yapp, Malcolm, et al, eds. (Illus.). 32p. (gr. 6-11). 1980. pap. text ed. 3.45 (*0-89908-015-4*) Greenhaven.
Killingray, Margaret, ed. see Addison, John, et al.
Killingray, Margaret, ed. see Booth, Martin, et al.
Killingray, Margaret, ed. see Doncaster, Islay.
Killingray, Margaret, ed. see Duckworth, John, et al.
Killingray, Margaret, ed. see Harrison, John, et al.
Killingray, Margaret, ed. see Heater, Derek & Owen, Gwyneth.
Killingray, Margaret, ed. see Killingray, David.
Killingray, Margaret, ed. see O'Connor, Edmund.
Killingray, Margaret, ed. see Painter, Desmond.
Killingray, Margaret, ed. see Pearson, Eileen.
Killingray, Margaret, ed. see Read, James & Yapp, Malcolm.
Killingray, Margaret, ed. see Tames, Richard.
Killingray, Margaret, ed. see Yapp, Malcolm.
Killingray, Margaret, et al, eds. see Guyatt, John.
Killingray, Margaret, et al, eds. see Tames, Richard.
Killingray, Margaret, et al, eds. see Townson, Duncan.
Killingray, Margaret, et al, eds. see Yapp, Malcolm.
Killingray, Marget, ed. see O'Connor, Edmund.
Killingsworth, Monte. Circle Within a Circle. LC 93-17244. 176p. (gr. 7 up). 1994. SBE 15.95 (*0-689-50598-1*, M K McElderry) Macmillan Child Grp.
—Eli's Songs. LC 91-6452. 144p. (gr. 5 up). 1991. SBE 13.95 (*0-689-50527-2*, M K McElderry) Macmillan Child Grp.
Killion, Bette. The Apartment House Tree. Szilagyi, Mary, illus. LC 88-35700. 32p. (ps-2). 1989. PLB 14.89 (*0-06-023274-9*) HarpC Child Bks.
—The Same Wind. LC 92-7786. (Illus.). 32p. (ps-3). 1992. 15.00 (*0-06-021050-8*); PLB 14.89 (*0-06-021051-6*) HarpC Child Bks.
—Think of It. Saldutti, Denise, illus. LC 89-26878. 32p. (ps-1). 1993. 12.00 (*0-06-023257-9*); PLB 11.89 (*0-06-023258-7*) HarpC Child Bks.
Killlingray, Margaret, ed. see Killingray, David.
Killoran, James, et al. The Key to Understanding Global Studies: A Regents-RCT Review Book. Zimmer, Ronald, illus. LC 89-92425. 362p. (Orig.). (gr. 9-10). 1990. pap. text ed. 5.95 (*0-9624723-0-1*) Jarrett Pub.
Kilpatrick. Creepy Crawlies. (gr. 2-5). 1982. (Usborne-Hayes); PLB 11.96 (*0-88110-076-5*); pap. 3.95 (*0-86020-630-0*) EDC.
Kilpatrick, jt. auth. see Civardi.
Kilroy, Sally. Noah & the Rabbits. (Illus.). 20p. (ps-1). 1991. pap. 4.99 (*0-14-054346-5*, Puffin) Puffin Bks.
Kim, Joy. Come on Up. Harvey, Paul, illus. LC 81-2356. 32p. (gr. k-2). 1981. PLB 11.59 (*0-89375-511-7*); pap. text ed. 2.95 (*0-89375-512-5*) Troll Assocs.
—Rainbows & Frogs: A Story about Colors. Harvey, Paul, illus. LC 81-4685. 32p. (gr. k-2). 1981. PLB 11.59 (*0-89375-505-2*); pap. text ed. 2.95 (*0-89375-506-0*) Troll Assocs.
—You Look Funny! Boyd, Patti, illus. LC 86-30839. 32p. (gr. k-2). 1988. PLB 7.89 (*0-8167-0976-9*); pap. text ed. 1.95 (*0-8167-0977-7*) Troll Assocs.
Kim, Melissa. The Blue Whale. Strugnell, Ann, illus. 32p. (gr. 1-5). 1993. PLB 12.00 (*0-8249-8614-8*, Ideals Child); pap. 4.95 (*0-8249-8628-8*) Hambleton-Hill.
—The Mountain Gorilla. Strugnell, Ann, illus. 32p. (gr. 1-5). 1993. PLB 12.00 (*0-8249-8629-6*, Ideals Child); pap. 4.95 (*0-8249-8615-6*) Hambleton-Hill.
Kim, Richard E. Lost Names: Scenes from a Boyhood in Japanese-Occupied Korea. 224p. 1988. 14.95 (*0-87663-678-4*) Universe.

Kim, Yong-Kol. Brave Hong Kil-Dong: The Man Who Bought the Shade of a Tree. Kang, Mi-Sun & Kim, Yong-Kyong, illus. 46p. (gr. 2-5). 1990. PLB 9.95x (*0-930878-91-4*) Hollym Intl.
Kimball, Don. Who's Gonna Love Me? 160p. (Orig.). (gr. 9-12). 1988. pap. 5.95 (*0-89505-769-7*, 22027) Tabor Pub.
Kimball, Kathleen M. Big Foot, Little Foot. LoBue, Elisa M., illus. LC 78-68822. (ps). 1979. 6.95 (*0-933308-00-0*) West Village.

Kimball, Richard S. A Christmas Wrinkle. LC 88-16310. (Illus.). 48p. (Orig.). (gr. 3 up). 1988. pap. 4.95 (*0-944443-01-X*) Green Timber.
**A different holiday story...for ages
eight to adult. Yes, there is a Santa
Claus. He lives in each of us who will
give him room. That's the message in
this Christmas coming-of-age story.
Dan, aged 10, is troubled during the
holiday season by the contrast between
Christmas glitter & the human
suffering he discovers not just from the
news but in his own backyard, visited
daily by a bag lady searching the
family garbage cans. Prospects for a
pleasant Christmas become dimmer still
when Dan's younger sister begins to
doubt the magic of Santa Claus. In the
cold & dark of earliest Christmas
morning, Dan turns from worry to
action, rekindles the warmth of
Christmas, & sees its meaning by new
light. Charcoal drawings throughout
the text add warmth & depth of feeling
to the story. Full color cover.
Paperback, $4.95.**
Publisher Provided Annotation.

—A Funny Feeling. Reid, William K., Jr., illus. LC 87-32155. 64p. (Orig.). (gr. 3 up). 1988. pap. 7.95 (*0-944443-00-1*) Green Timber.
**This collection of 41 cleverly
illustrated poems explores common
feelings & sayings about them for
entertainment & enlightenment of
youngsters aged eight & above. Eight-
year olds will identify with Reginald
Botts who was "tied up in knots &
couldn't get his thoughts undone." Ten-
year olds will enjoy the image of
Louise being made small by the weight
of the grudge she carries. Twelve-year
olds will sympathize with Annie who
has reached the age "when staying in
means being left out" & "going out
means being in." Everybody will be
delighted by "tongue tied" Sid & by the
many other characters & poems. With
humor, this book allows readers &
listeners to think about their own
funny feelings & can open the way for
discussion with parents, teachers,
counselors, church groups, & friends.
Paperback, $7.95.**
Publisher Provided Annotation.

Kimball, Virginia. A Day for Doughnuts: April 19, 1775. (Illus.). (gr. 9-12). pap. 2.00 (*0-917250-02-8*) Parable Pr.
Kimber, Julianne S. I Love America, Pt. 1: Teacher's Resource Kit. Kimber, Julianne S., illus. 313p. (gr. k-2). 1986. wkbk. 14.95 (*0-88080-018-6*) Natl Ctr Constitutional.
Kimberling, Bryce, illus. One Elephant Went Out to Play Big Book. (ps-2). 1988. pap. text ed. 14.00 (*0-922053-16-2*) N Edge Res.
Kimeldorf, Martin. Exciting Writing, Successful Speaking: Activities to Make Language Come Alive. Espeland, Pamela, ed. LC 93-30613. 272p. (Orig.). (gr. 5 up). 1994. pap. 14.95 (*0-915793-65-2*) Free Spirit Pub.
Kimelman, Paul M. & Wolfson, David. Life in the Fat Lane. Selvan, Amos, intro. by. (Illus.). 273p. (Orig.). (gr. 6 up). 1991. pap. 6.25 (*0-9624540-0-1*) Fat Lane.

Kimmel, Eric A. Anansi & the Moss-Covered Rock. Stevens, Janet, illus. LC 87-31766. (ps-3). 1988. reinforced bdg. 15.95 (*0-8234-0689-X*); pap. 5.95 (*0-8234-0798-5*) Holiday.
—Asher & the Capmakers: A Hanukkah Story. Hillenbrand, Will, illus. LC 92-37978. 32p. (ps-3). 1993. reinforced bdg. 15.95 (*0-8234-1031-5*) Holiday.
—Baba Yaga: A Russian Folktale. Lloyd, Megan, illus. Date not set. pap. 5.95 (*0-8234-1060-9*) Holiday.
—The Chanukkah Guest. Carmi, Giora, illus. LC 89-20073. 32p. (ps-3). 1990. reinforced bdg. 14.95 (*0-8234-0788-8*); pap. 5.95 (*0-8234-0978-3*) Holiday.
—The Chanukkah Tree. Carmi, Giora, illus. LC 88-4510. 32p. (ps-3). 1988. reinforced bdg. 14.95 (*0-8234-0705-5*) Holiday.
—Charlie Drives the Stage. Rounds, Glen, illus. LC 88-24558. 32p. (ps-3). 1989. reinforced bdg. 13.95 (*0-8234-0738-1*) Holiday.
—Days of Awe: Stories for Rosh Hashanah & Yom Kippur. (gr. 4-7). 1991. 13.95 (*0-670-82772-X*) Viking Child Bks.
—Days of Awe: Stories for Rosh Hashanah & Yom Kippur. Weihs, Erika, illus. LC 93-583. 48p. (gr. 3-7). pap. 4.99 (*0-14-050271-8*, Puffin) Puffin Bks.
—Four Dollars & Fifty Cents. Rounds, Glen, illus. LC 89-77515. 32p. (ps-3). 1990. reinforced 14.95 (*0-8234-0817-5*) Holiday.
—Four Dollars & Fifty Cents. Rounds, Glen, illus. (ps-3). 1993. pap. 5.95 (*0-8234-1024-2*) Holiday.
—Hershel & the Hanukkah Goblins. Hyman, Trina S., illus. LC 89-1954. 32p. (ps-3). 1989. reinforced bdg. 15.95 (*0-8234-0769-1*) Holiday.
—I Took My Frog to the Library. Sims, Blanche, illus. 32p. (ps-3). 1990. pap. 13.00 (*0-670-82418-6*) Viking Child Bks.
—I Took My Frog to the Library. Sims, Blanche, illus. 32p. (ps-3). 1992. pap. 3.99 (*0-14-050916-X*) Puffin Bks.
—Nanny Goat & the Seven Little Kids. Stevens, Janet, illus. LC 89-20058. 32p. (ps-3). 1990. reinforced bdg. 15.95 (*0-8234-0789-6*); pap. 5.95 (*0-8234-0953-8*) Holiday.
—Valiant Red Rooster. 1994. write for info. (*0-8050-2781-5*) H Holt & Co.
—The Witch's Face: A Mexican Tale. Vanden Broeck, Fabricio, illus. LC 92-44380. 32p. (ps-3). 1993. reinforced bdg. 15.95 (*0-8234-1038-2*) Holiday.
Kimmel, Eric A., retold by. Anansi Goes Fishing. Stevens, Janet, illus. LC 91-17813. 32p. (ps-3). 1992. reinforced bdg. 15.95 (*0-8234-0918-X*) Holiday.
—Anansi Goes Fishing. Stevens, Janet, illus. (ps-3). 1993. pap. 5.95 (*0-8234-1022-6*) Holiday.
—Baba Yaga: A Russian Folktale. Lloyd, Megan, illus. LC 90-39215. 32p. (ps-3). 1991. reinforced bdg. 14.95 (*0-8234-0854-X*) Holiday.
Kimmel, Eric A., adapted by. Bearhead: A Russian Folktale. Mikolaycak, Charles, illus. LC 91-55026. 32p. (ps-3). 1991. reinforced 15.95 (*0-8234-0902-3*) Holiday.
Kimmel, Eric A., retold by. Boots & His Brothers: A Tale from Norway. Root, Kimberly B., illus. LC 90-23659. 32p. (ps-3). 1992. reinforced bdg. 14.95 (*0-8234-0886-8*) Holiday.
Kimmel, Eric A., ed. The Four Gallant Sisters. Yuditskaya, Tatyana, illus. LC 91-28231. 32p. (gr. 1-4). 1992. 15.95 (*0-8050-1901-4*, Bks Young Read) H Holt & Co.
Kimmel, Eric A., retold by. The Gingerbread Man. Lloyd, Megan, illus. 32p. (ps-3). 1993. reinforced bdg. 14.95 (*0-8234-0824-8*) Holiday.
—The Goose Girl: A Story from the Brothers Grimm. Sauber, Robert, illus. LC 93-13138. 1994. write for info. (*0-8234-1074-9*) Holiday.
—The Greatest of All: A Japanese Folktale. Carmi, Giora, illus. LC 90-23658. 32p. (ps-3). 1991. reinforced 14.95 (*0-8234-0885-X*) Holiday.
Kimmel, Eric A., adapted by. I-Know-Not-What, I-Know-Not-Where: A Russian Tale. Sauber, Robert, illus. LC 92-32692. 64p. (gr. 6-10). 1994. 16.95 (*0-8234-1020-X*) Holiday.
—The Old Woman & Her Pig. Carmi, Giora, illus. LC 91-44185. 32p. (ps-3). 1992. reinforced bdg. 14.95 (*0-8234-0970-8*) Holiday.
Kimmel, Eric A., retold by. The Spotted Pony: A Collection of Hanukkah Stories. Fisher, Leonard E., illus. LC 91-24214. 72p. (gr. 2-6). 1992. 14.95 (*0-8234-0936-8*) Holiday.
—The Three Princes: A Middle Eastern Tale. Fisher, Leonard E., illus. LC 93-25862. 32p. (gr. 4-8). 1994. 15.95 (*0-8234-1115-X*) Holiday.
Kimmel, Eric A., adapted by. Three Sacks of Truth: A Story from France. Rayevsky, Robert, illus. 32p. (ps-3). 1993. reinforced bdg. 15.95 (*0-8234-0921-X*) Holiday.
Kimmel, Eric A., retold by see Arabian Nights Staff.
Kimmel, Joan G., jt. auth. see Shroyer, Susan P.
Kimmel, Larry. Letter City & the Alphabet Winds. Hukill, Marilyn, illus. LC 91-65466. 32p. (ps-2). 1991. text ed. 12.95 (*0-9628129-4-3*) Sagebrush Bks.
Kimmel, Margaret M. Magic in the Mist. Hyman, Trina S., illus. LC 74-18186. 32p. (gr. k-4). 1975. SBE 13.95 (*0-689-50026-2*, M K McElderry) Macmillan Child Grp.
Kimmel, Margaret M. & Segal, Elizabeth. For Reading Out Loud! A Guide to Sharing Books with Children. LC 82-70436. 224p. 1982. pap. 12.95 (*0-385-28304-0*) Delacorte.
Kimmel, Tim, jt. auth. see McAllister, Dawson.

Kimmel, Tim, jt. auth. see MacAllister, Dawson.
Kimmelman, Leslie. Frannie's Fruits. Mathers, Petra, illus. LC 91-17637. 32p. (ps-3). 1989. PLB 13.89 (*0-06-023164-5*) HarpC Child Bks.
—Hanukkah Lights, Hanukkah Nights. Himmelman, John, illus. LC 91-15633. 32p. (ps-k). 1992. 12.00 (*0-06-020368-4*); PLB 11.89 (*0-06-020369-2*) HarpC Child Bks.
Kimura, Hideo M. How to Pick & Strum the Ukulele, Bk. II. rev. ed. Kimura, Hideo M., illus. 44p. (gr. 7 up). 1988. pap. text ed. write for info. (*0-917822-18-8*) Heedays.
—Sing, Pick & Strum Nineteen Christmas Carols with Your Ukulele. (Illus.). 74p. (Orig.). 1992. pap. 12.95 (*0-917822-27-7*) Heedays.
Kinard, Lee. Harriet Tubman's Famous Christmas Eve Raid. LC 93-60260. (Illus.). 44p. (gr. k-3). 1993. 10.95 (*1-55523-612-X*) Winston-Derek.
Kincaid, Jamaica see Endore, Guy.
Kincaid, James R. see Carroll, Lewis.
Kincher, Jonni. Dreams Can Help: A Journal Guide to Understanding Your Dreams & Making Them Work for You. Morse, Mary & Espeland, Pamela, eds. Staeck, Roy, illus. LC 88-7630. 96p. (Orig.). (gr. 3-9). 1988. pap. 9.95 (*0-915793-15-6*) Free Spirit Pub.
—The First Honest Book about Lies. Espeland, Pamela, ed. LC 92-13403. (Illus.). 176p. (Orig.). (gr. 7 up). 1992. pap. 12.95 (*0-915793-43-1*) Free Spirit Pub.
—Psychology for Kids: Forty Fun Tests That Help You Learn about Yourself. Bach, Julie, ed. Maclean & Tuminell, illus. Elliott, Thomas, frwd. by. LC 90-47742. 160p. (Orig.). (gr. 4 up). 1990. pap. 11.95 (*0-915793-23-7*) Free Spirit Pub.
Kindell, Roy. Night Sky Star Lore. (Illus.). 52p. (Orig.). (gr. 7 up). 1989. pap. 5.95 (*0-9625388-0-9*) Ursa Major Corp.
Kindergarten, Henry O. The Farmer's Huge Carrot. (Illus.). 24p. (Orig.). (gr. k-3). 1990. pap. text ed. 2.95 (*0-87406-437-6*) Willowisp Pr.
Kindergarteners of Paul Mort Elementary. Looking for a Rainbow. (Illus.). 24p. (gr. k-3). 1987. 3.50 (*0-87406-227-6*) Willowisp Pr.
Kindersley, Dorling. Baby Animals. LC 91-27723. (Illus.). 24p. (ps-k). 1992. POB 7.95 (*0-689-71563-3*, Aladdin) Macmillan Child Grp.
—Birds. Kindersley, Dorling, illus. LC 92-8601. 24p. (ps-k). 1992. POB 7.95 (*0-689-71644-3*, Aladdin) Macmillan Child Grp.
—Farm Animals. LC 90-48332. (Illus.). 24p. (ps-k). 1991. POB 6.95 (*0-689-71403-3*, Aladdin) Macmillan Child Grp.
—Sea Animals. LC 91-27724. (Illus.). 24p. (ps-k). 1992. POB 7.95 (*0-689-71565-X*, Aladdin) Macmillan Child Grp.
—Ships & Boats. LC 91-25687. (Illus.). 24p. (ps-k). 1992. POB 7.95 (*0-689-71566-8*, Aladdin) Macmillan Child Grp.
—Trains. LC 92-12351. (Illus.). 24p. (ps-k). 1992. POB 7.95 (*0-689-71647-8*, Aladdin) Macmillan Child Grp.
—Trucks. LC 90-49260. (Illus.). 24p. (ps-k). 1991. POB 6.95 (*0-689-71405-X*, Aladdin) Macmillan Child Grp.
—Zoo Animals. LC 90-48751. (Illus.). 24p. (ps-k). 1991. POB 6.95 (*0-689-71406-8*, Aladdin) Macmillan Child Grp.
Kindl, Patrice. Owl in Love. LC 92-26952. 1993. 13.95 (*0-395-66162-5*) HM.
Kindle, Pat & Finney, Susan. Russia to the Revolution. McKay, Ardis, illus. 64p. (gr. 4-8). 1987. pap. 7.95 (*0-86653-398-2*, GA 1020) Good Apple.
Kindle, Patricia & Finney, Susan. American Indians. McKay, Ardis, illus. 64p. (gr. 4-8). 1985. wkbk. 7.95 (*0-86653-290-0*, GA 673) Good Apple.
—Fantasy & Fairy Tales. McKay, Ardis, illus. 64p. (gr. 4-8). 1985. wkbk. 7.95 (*0-86653-317-6*, GA 669) Good Apple.
Kindle, Patricia, jt. auth. see Finney, Susan.
Kinens, Janis J. The Old Woodcutter. Kinens, Janis J., illus. LC 88-81904. 32p. (gr. k-12). 1988. PLB 12.95 (*0-9620999-0-2*); 12.95 (*0-9620999-1-0*) Guzzy Pr.
King & Emery. Word Detective in English. (gr. k-3). 1982. 8.95 (*0-7460-0398-6*, Usborne-Hayes) EDC.
King, Bob. Sitting on the Farm. Slavin, Bill, illus. LC 91-17253. 32p. (ps-1). 1992. 13.95 (*0-531-05985-5*); lib. bdg. 13.99 (*0-531-08585-6*) Orchard Bks Watts.
King, Buzz. Silicon Songs. 1990. 14.95 (*0-385-30087-5*) Doubleday.
—Silicon Songs. 1992. pap. 3.25 (*0-440-21164-6*) Dell.
King, Celia. Seven Ancient Wonders: A Pop-up Book. (Illus.). 7p. 1990. text ed. 8.95 (*0-87701-707-7*) Chronicle Bks.
—Seven Modern Wonders of the World: A Pop-up Book. King, Celia, illus. 7p. (gr. 3 up). 1992. 9.95 (*0-8118-0159-4*) Chronicle Bks.
—Seven Mysterious Wonders: A Pop-up Book. LC 93-8179. 1993. 9.95 (*0-8118-0361-9*) Chronicle Bks.
—The Seven Natural Wonders of the World: A Pop-up Book. King, Celia, illus. 7p. (ps up). 1991. 8.95 (*0-8118-0001-6*) Chronicle Bks.
King, Charles S., Jr. Dreams, Things & I Remember When. King, Charles S., Jr., illus. 64p. (Orig.). 1989. 9.95 (*0-685-25964-1*) Swan Sea Music.
King, Charlyce, ed. see King, Gary.
King, Christopher. The Case of the Missing Links. 11p. 1990. pap. 17.95 incls. puzzle (*0-922242-15-1*) Lombard Mktg.

King, Christopher L. The Vegetables Go to Bed. GrandPre, Mary, illus. LC 92-27650. 1994. write for info. (*0-517-59125-1*); PLB write for info. (*0-517-59126-X*) Crown Bks Yng Read.
King, Clive, ed. Adventure Stories. Walker, Brian, illus. LC 92-26452. 1993. pap. 6.95 (*1-85697-882-6*) Kingfisher Bks.
King, Colin. Amazing Book of Jokes. 32p. 1990. 3.50 (*0-517-69192-2*) Outlet Bk Co.
—Amazing Book of Puzzles & Tricks. 32p. 1990. 3.50 (*0-517-69194-9*) Outlet Bk Co.
King, Coretta S. My Life with Martin Luther King, Jr. rev. ed. King, Bernice, et al. (Illus.). 368p. (gr. 7 up). 1994. pap. 4.99 (*0-14-036805-1*) Puffin Bks.
King, Coretta Scott. My Life with Martin Luther King, Jr. rev. ed. 256p. (gr. 6 up). 1993. 17.95 (*0-8050-2445-X*, Bks Young Read) H Holt & Co.
King, Coretta Scott, intro. by. Black Americans of Achievement Series, 25 vols, No. 2. (Illus.). 1991. Set. lib. bdg. 448.75 (*0-7910-1112-7*) Chelsea Hse.
—Duke Ellington: Bandleader & Composer. (Illus.). 112p. (gr. 7-12). PLB 16.95 (*0-685-21875-9*, 200417) Know Unltd.
King, Deanna, jt. auth. see Thiesen, Charles.
King, Deborah. Custer: The Story of a Horse. King, Deborah, illus. 32p. (ps-3). 1992. PLB 14.95 (*0-399-22147-6*, Philomel Bks) Putnam Pub Group.
King, Ed. All-American Dinosaur Family: Meet the Hoadleys. (Illus.). 24p. (gr. k-12). 1993. 3.95 (*1-56288-387-9*) Checkerboard.
—All-American Dinosaur Family: The Hoadleys in Town. (Illus.). 24p. (ps-12). 1993. 3.95 (*1-56288-390-9*) Checkerboard.
—All-American Dinosaur Family: The Hoadleys on Vacation. (Illus.). 24p. (ps-12). 1993. 3.95 (*1-56288-388-7*) Checkerboard.
—All-American Dinosaur Family: The Hoadleys Travel in Time. (Illus.). 24p. (ps-12). 1993. 3.95 (*1-56288-389-5*) Checkerboard.
King, Ed, illus. Gus Is Gone. LC 90-28634. 24p. (ps up). 1991. pap. 3.95 (*1-56288-008-X*) Checkerboard.
—Lucy is Lost. LC 90-27675. 24p. 1991. pap. 3.95 (*1-56288-009-8*) Checkerboard.
—William Wanders Off. LC 90-27677. 24p. 1991. pap. 3.95 (*1-56288-011-X*) Checkerboard.
King, Elizabeth. Backyard Sunflower. King, Elizabeth, photos by. LC 92-31002. (Illus.). (ps-3). 1993. 13.99 (*0-525-45082-3*, DCB) Dutton Child Bks.
—Pumpkin Patch. LC 89-25938. (Illus.). 40p. (ps-3). 1990. 14.00 (*0-525-44640-0*, DCB) Dutton Child Bks.
King, Elmont. Classical Data. (gr. 11-12). 1992. pap. 8.95 (*0-913412-59-7*) Brandon Hse.
King, Fred M. Palmer Method Cursive, Consumable. Pace Studios, illus. (gr. 5). 1979. wkbk. 3.96 (*0-914268-66-X*, 79-5C); tchr's. ed. 5.60 (*0-914268-67-8*, 79-5CTE) A N Palmer.
—Palmer Method Cursive, Non-Consumable. Pace Studios, illus. (gr. 6). 1979. wkbk. 4.24 (*0-914268-82-1*, N79-6C); tchr's. ed. 5.60 (*0-914268-83-X*, N79-6CTE) A N Palmer.
—Palmer Method Cursive, Non-Consumable. Pace Studios, illus. (ps-8). 1979. tchr's. ed. 5.60 (*0-914268-81-3*, N79-5CTE); wkbk. 4.24 (*0-914268-80-5*, N79-5C) A N Palmer.
—Palmer Method Cursive, Non-Consumable. (gr. 4). 1979. wkbk. 4.24 (*0-914268-78-3*, N79-4C); tchr's. ed. 5.60 (*0-914268-79-1*, N79-4CTE) A N Palmer.
King, Gary. An Autumn Remembered: Reflections of College Football's Greatest Team. King, Charlyce, ed. LC 87-73386. 300p. (Orig.). (gr. 9 up). 1988. pap. 12. 95 (*0-9619712-0-7*) Red Earth OK.
King, Helen. Soul of Christmas. Anderson, Fred, illus. 32p. (gr. k-4). 1972. 4.50 (*0-87485-057-6*) Johnson Chi.
King, Helen B. Sandy. King, Helen B., illus. 18p. (ps-3). 1985. pap. 4.95 (*0-9615366-4-0*) King ME.
—Stokey: The Story of a Playful Pig. (Illus.). (gr. 4-8). 1989. pap. 4.95 plastic cover (*0-9615366-1-6*) King ME.
King, Jeanne. Tide Pools & Coral Reefs. Sima, Patricia M., ed. Buhler, Cheryl, illus. 80p. (gr. 1-3). 1993. wkbk. 7.95 (*1-55734-249-0*) Tchr Create Mat.
King, Jesse J., Sr. You Can Say No to Drugs. King, Linda L., ed. King, Jesse J., Sr., illus. 24p. (Orig.). (gr. k-5). 1989. pap. text ed. 1.25 (*0-685-25956-0*) J Lynn Pub.
—You Can Say No to Drugs: For Fifth Grade. King, Linda L., ed. King, Jesse J., Sr., illus. 24p. (Orig.). (gr. 5). 1990. pap. text ed. 1.25 (*0-685-25962-5*) J Lynn Pub.
—You Can Say No to Drugs: For First Grade. King, Linda L., ed. King, Jesse J., Sr., illus. 24p. (Orig.). (gr. 1). 1989. pap. text ed. 1.25 (*0-685-25958-7*) J Lynn Pub.
—You Can Say No to Drugs: For Fourth Grade. King, Linda L., ed. King, Jesse J., Sr., illus. 24p. (Orig.). (gr. 4). 1990. pap. text ed. 1.25 (*0-685-25961-7*) J Lynn Pub.
—You Can Say No to Drugs: For Kindergarten. King, Linda L., ed. King, Jesse J., Sr., illus. 24p. (Orig.). (gr. k). 1989. pap. text ed. 1.25 (*0-685-25957-9*) J Lynn Pub.
—You Can Say No to Drugs: For Second Grade. King, Linda L., ed. King, Jesse J., Sr., illus. 24p. (Orig.). (gr. 2). 1989. pap. text ed. 1.25 (*0-685-25959-5*) J Lynn Pub.

—You Can Say No to Drugs: For Third Grade. King, Linda L., ed. King, Jesse J., Sr., illus. 24p. (Orig.). (gr. 3). 1990. pap. text ed. 1.25 (0-685-25960-9) J Lynn Pub.
King, Jill. Penelope the Fairy. 1993. 7.95 (0-533-10362-2) Vantage.
King, John. Bedouin. LC 92-16506. (Illus.). 48p. (gr. 5-6). 1992. PLB 22.80 (0-8114-2304-2) Raintree Steck-V.
—Conflict in the Middle East. LC 93-346. (Illus.). 48p. (gr. 6 up). 1993. RSBE 13.95 (0-02-785955-X, New Discovery Bks) Macmillan Child Grp.
—The Gulf War. LC 91-25744. (Illus.). 48p. (gr. 4-6). 1991. RSBE 13.95 (0-87518-514-2, Dillon) Macmillan Child Grp.
—Kurds. LC 93-35568. (Illus.). 48p. (gr. 6-10). 1994. 16.95 (1-56847-149-1) Thomson Lrning.
King, Larry L. Because of Lozo Brown. Schwartz, Amy, illus. LC 88-3952. (ps-3). 1988. 11.95 (0-670-81031-2) Viking Child Bks.
—Because of Lozo Brown. (ps-3). 1990. pap. 3.95 (0-14-050593-8, Puffin) Puffin Bks.
King, Laurie. Hear My Voice: A Multicultural Anthology of Literature from the United States. 1993. Bibliography. pap. 11.20 (0-201-81841-8); Student ed. pap. 17.45 (0-201-81839-6); tchr's. guide 16.20 (0-201-81840-X) Addison-Wesley.
King, Lincoln, jt. auth. see Sitton, Thad.
King, Linda L., ed. see King, Jesse J., Sr.
King, Lise, jt. auth. see Greinke, Pamylle.
King, Loretta M. The Purple Sea Horse & Other Stories. LC 79-56712. (Illus., Orig.). (gr. k-3). 1979. pap. 4.95 (0-934104-02-6) Woodland.
King, Martha B. A Christmas Carol. 1941. 4.50 (0-87602-114-3) Anchorage.
—Riddle Me Ree. 1977. 4.50 (0-87602-188-7) Anchorage.
King, Nadia. Inside Truths about the Stock Brokerage Business. Kriks, Bill, ed. 75p. (Orig.). 1989. pap. text ed. 5.00 (0-685-29786-1) Kings Inc.
King, Neil, ed. see Shakespeare, William.
King, P. E. Down on the Funny Farm: A Step Two Book. Graham, Alastair, illus. LC 85-11893. 48p. (gr. 1-3). 1986. PLB 7.99 (0-394-97460-3); pap. 3.50 (0-394-87460-9) Random Bks Yng Read.
King, Paul, jt. auth. see Coccola, Raymond de.
King, Perry. Jefferson Davis. (Illus.). 112p. (gr. 5 up). 1990. 17.95 (1-55546-806-3) Chelsea Hse.
—Pericles. Schlesinger, Arthur M., Jr., intro. by. (Illus.). 112p. (gr. 5 up). 1988. lib. bdg. 17.95 (0-87754-547-2) Chelsea Hse.
King, Ron. Rad Boards: Skateboarding, Snowboarding, Bodyboarding. (gr. 4-7). 1991. pap. 9.95 (0-316-49355-4, Spts Illus Kids) Little.
King, Sandra. Shannon: An Ojibway Dancer. Whipple, Catherine, photos by. Dorris, Michael, frwd. by. LC 92-27261. (Illus.). 1993. PLB 19.95 (0-8225-2652-2) Lerner Pubns.
—Shannon: An Ojibway Dancer. (gr. 4-7). 1993. pap. 6.95 (0-8225-9643-1) Lerner Pubns.
King, Sarah E. Maya Angelou: Greeting the Morning. LC 93-4572. (Illus.). 48p. (gr. 2-4). 1994. PLB 12.40 (1-56294-431-2) Millbrook Pr.
King, Stephen. The Eyes of the Dragon. Palladini, David, illus. 336p. 1987. pap. 21.95 (0-670-81458-X) Viking Child Bks.
—Night Shift: Excursions into Horror. 352p. (RL 4). 1991. pap. 5.95 (0-451-16045-2, Sig) NAL-Dutton.
King, Tony, tr. see Rayner, Claire.
King, Virginia. The Band. Reynolds, Pat, illus. LC 92-21390. 1993. 2.50 (0-383-03553-8) SRA Schl Grp.
—Breakfast. Fleming, Leanne, illus. LC 92-21391. 1993. 2.50 (0-383-03556-2) SRA Schl Grp.
—Hello, Puppet. Mancini, Rob, illus. LC 92-21392. 1993. 2.50 (0-383-03572-4) SRA Schl Grp.
—Sand. Quinn, Annie, illus. LC 92-31959. 1993. 2.50 (0-383-03591-0) SRA Schl Grp.
King, Vivienne, et al. Let's Go on Safari. O'Halloran, Tim, illus. 32p. (ps-3). 1985. pap. 3.95 (0-88625-107-9) Durkin Hayes Pub.
King-Dickman, Kathy. Dinosaurs: Games That Teach: Children's Literature Through Whole Language - A Board Game. (Illus.). 20p. (gr. 1-6). 1990. pap. text ed. 15.95 tchr's. guide, incl. gameboard (0-927867-06-0) SkippingStone Pr.
King-Dickman, Kathy & Kulp, Katherine. Friendship: Games That Teach: Children's Literature Through Whole Language - A Board Game. (Illus.). 34p. (gr. 1-6). 1990. pap. text ed. 15.00 tchr's. guide, incl. gameboard (0-927867-08-7) SkippingStone Pr.
—Games That Teach: Humor: Children's Literature Through Whole Language - A Board Game. (Illus.). 20p. (gr. 1-6). 1990. pap. text ed. 10.00 incl. gameboard (0-927867-07-9) SkippingStone Pr.
Kingett, Robert P. P. W. Liveaboard Cat. (Illus.). 48p. (Orig.). 1988. pap. write for info. Catalina Creations.
Kinghorn, Harriet & Morberg, Mary. Research Shapes: Animals. (Illus.). 64p. (gr. 2-5). 1989. 6.95 (1-878279-02-5, MM1919) Monday Morning Bks.
—Research Shapes: Inventions. (Illus.). 64p. (gr. 2-5). 1989. 6.95 (1-878279-01-7, MM1918) Monday Morning Bks.
—Research Shapes: Transportation. (Illus.). 64p. (gr. 2-5). 1989. 6.95 (1-878279-03-3, MM1920) Monday Morning Bks.
Kingman, Lee. The Best Christmas. Cooney, Barbara, illus. (gr. 2-5). 1984. 16.50 (0-8446-6160-0) Peter Smith.

—The Best Christmas. Cooney, Barbara, illus. LC 92-21152. 96p. (gr. 5 up). 1993. pap. 3.95 (0-688-11838-0, Pub. by Beech Tree Bks) Morrow.
—Break a Leg, Betsy, Maybe. 192p. (gr. 7 up). 1979. pap. 1.50 (0-440-90794-2, LFL) Dell.
—Break a Leg, Betsy Maybe. LC 92-26975. 256p. (gr. 7 up). 1993. pap. 4.95 (0-688-11789-9, Pub. by Beech Tree Bks) Morrow.
—Catch the Baby! (ps). 1990. 12.95 (0-670-81751-1) Viking Child Bks.
—Catch the Baby! Natti, Susanna, photos by. LC 92-26588. (Illus.). 1993. pap. 4.99 (0-14-050762-0) Puffin Bks.
—Head over Wheels. 224p. (gr. 7 up). 1981. pap. 1.75 (0-440-93129-0, LE) Dell.
—Luck of the Miss L. (gr. 4-6). 1986. 12.95 (0-685-11813-4) HM.
—The Luck of the Miss L. LC 92-24600. 160p. (gr. 5 up). 1993. pap. 4.95 (0-688-11779-1, Pub. by Beech Tree Bks) Morrow.
Kingore, Bertie & Higbee, Brenda. We Care for Summer. (Illus.). 224p. (Orig.). (ps-k). 1992. pap. 13.95 (0-673-36017-2) GdYrBks.
Kingsbury, Kenneth, jt. auth. see Buchanan-Hedman, Pat.
Kingshead Corporation Staff. Cut, Color & Create: Make Your Own: Alphabet Blocks. Kingshead Corporation Staff, illus. 24p. (ps-3). 1987. pap. 2.97 (1-55941-005-1) Kingshead Corp.
—Cut, Color & Create: Make Your Own: Alphabet Friends. Kingshead Corporation Staff, illus. 24p. (ps-3). 1987. pap. 2.97 (1-55941-003-5) Kingshead Corp.
—Cut, Color & Create: Make Your Own: Beach. Kingshead Corporation Staff, illus. 24p. (ps-4). 1987. pap. 2.97 (1-55941-011-6) Kingshead Corp.
—Cut-Color-&-Create: Make Your Own: Box Magic. Kingshead Corporation Staff, illus. 24p. (ps-1). 1989. pap. 2.97 (1-55941-039-6) Kingshead Corp.
—Cut-Color-&-Create: Make Your Own: Box Magic. Kingshead Corporation Staff, illus. 24p. (ps-1). 1989. pap. 2.97 (1-55941-038-8) Kingshead Corp.
—Cut, Color & Create: Make Your Own: Christmas Cards. Kingshead Corporation Staff, illus. 24p. (gr. k-4). 1987. pap. 2.97 (1-55941-021-3) Kingshead Corp.
—Cut, Color & Create: Make Your Own: Christmas Garland. Kingshead Corporation Staff, illus. 24p. (ps-2). 1987. pap. 2.97 (1-55941-020-5) Kingshead Corp.
—Cut, Color & Create: Make Your Own: Circus. Kingshead Corporation Staff, illus. 24p. (ps-4). 1987. pap. 2.97 (1-55941-008-6) Kingshead Corp.
—Cut, Color & Create: Make Your Own: Christmas Ornaments. Kingshead Corporation Staff, illus. 24p. (gr. 2 up). 1987. pap. 2.97 (1-55941-018-3) Kingshead Corp.
—Cut, Color & Create: Make Your Own: Christmas Snowflakes. Kingshead Corporation Staff, illus. 24p. (gr. k-3). 1987. pap. 2.97 (1-55941-017-5) Kingshead Corp.
—Cut, Color & Create: Make Your Own: Christmas Snowflakes. Kingshead Corporation Staff, illus. 24p. (gr. 3 up). 1987. pap. 2.97 (1-55941-019-1) Kingshead Corp.
—Cut, Color & Create: Make Your Own: Doll's Christmas. Kingshead Corporation Staff, illus. 24p. 1987. pap. 2.97 (1-55941-013-2) Kingshead Corp.
—Cut-Color & Create: Make Your Own: Dinosaur Playmates. (Illus.). 24p. (ps-8). 1989. pap. write for info. (1-55941-041-8) Kingshead Corp.
—Cut-Color-&-Create: Make Your Own: Easter Fun. Kingshead Corporation Staff, illus. 24p. (ps-1). 1989. pap. 2.97 (1-55941-022-1) Kingshead Corp.
—Cut-Color-&-Create: Make Your Own: Easter Fun. Kingshead Corporation Staff, illus. 24p. (ps-1). 1989. pap. 2.97 (1-55941-023-X) Kingshead Corp.
—Cut-Color-&-Create: Make Your Own: Easter Fun. Kingshead Corporation Staff, illus. 24p. (ps-1). 1989. pap. 2.97 (1-55941-024-8) Kingshead Corp.
—Cut, Color & Create: Make Your Own: Easy Christmas Ornaments. Kingshead Corporation Staff, illus. 24p. (ps-2). 1987. pap. 2.97 (1-55941-016-7) Kingshead Corp.
—Cut, Color & Create: Make Your Own: Farm. Kingshead Corporation Staff, illus. 24p. (ps-4). 1987. pap. 2.97 (1-55941-007-8) Kingshead Corp.
—Cut-Color & Create: Make Your Own: Fashions of the Ages. (Illus.). 24p. (ps-8). 1989. pap. write for info. (1-55941-028-0) Kingshead Corp.
—Cut-Color & Create: Make Your Own: Land of the Dinosaurs. (Illus.). 24p. (ps-8). 1989. pap. write for info. (1-55941-040-X) Kingshead Corp.
—Cut, Color & Create: Make Your Own: Masks. Kingshead Corporation Staff, illus. 24p. (ps-4). 1988. pap. 2.97 (0-685-22520-8) Kingshead Corp.
—Cut, Color & Create: Make Your Own: Number People. Kingshead Corporation Staff, illus. 24p. (ps-3). 1987. pap. 2.97 (1-55941-004-3) Kingshead Corp.
—Cut, Color & Create: Make Your Own: Number Blocks. Kingshead Corporation Staff, illus. 24p. (ps-3). 1987. pap. 2.97 (1-55941-006-X) Kingshead Corp.
—Cut, Color & Create: Make Your Own: Places to Go. Kingshead Corporation Staff, illus. 24p. (ps-4). 1987. pap. 2.97 (1-55941-012-4) Kingshead Corp.

—Cut, Color & Create: Make Your Own: Paperplate Puppets. Kingshead Corporation Staff, illus. 24p. (ps-3). 1987. pap. 2.97 (1-55941-002-7) Kingshead Corp.
—Cut, Color & Create: Make Your Own: Paperbag Puppets. Kingshead Corporation Staff, illus. 24p. (ps-3). 1987. pap. 2.97 (1-55941-001-9) Kingshead Corp.
—Cut-Color-&-Create: Make Your Own: Pumpkin Magic. Kingshead Corporation Staff, illus. 24p. (ps-1). 1988. pap. 2.97 (1-55941-037-X) Kingshead Corp.
—Cut, Color & Create: Make Your Own: Safari. Kingshead Corporation Staff, illus. 24p. (ps-4). 1987. pap. 2.97 (1-55941-010-8) Kingshead Corp.
—Cut-Color & Create: Make Your Own: Space Settlers. (Illus.). 24p. (ps-8). 1989. pap. write for info. (1-55941-042-6) Kingshead Corp.
—Cut, Color & Create: Make Your Own: Valentine Fun. Kingshead Corporation Staff, illus. 24p. (gr. k-3). 1987. pap. 2.97 (1-55941-015-9) Kingshead Corp.
—Cut, Color & Create: Make Your Own: Valentines. Kingshead Corporation Staff, illus. 24p. (gr. k-3). 1987. pap. 2.97 (1-55941-014-0) Kingshead Corp.
—Cut, Color & Create: Make Your Own: Zoo. Kingshead Corporation Staff, illus. 24p. (ps-4). 1987. pap. 2.97 (1-55941-009-4) Kingshead Corp.
Kingsland, L. W., tr. see Andersen, Hans Christian.
Kingsland, Robin. Bus Stop Bop. Ayliffe, Alex, illus. 32p. (ps-3). 1991. 14.95 (0-670-83919-1) Viking Child Bks.
Kingsley, Charles. The Water Babies. 192p. (gr. 5 up). 1986. pap. 2.95 (0-14-035035-7, Puffin) Puffin Bks.
—The Water Babies. Smith, Jessie W., illus. 256p. (gr. k-6). 1986. 10.99 (0-517-61817-6) Outlet Bk Co.
—Water Babies. Adam, G. Mercer, ed. Childers, Norman, illus. (gr. k-4). Repr. of 1905 ed. 12.95 (0-940561-09-3) White Rose Pr.
—The Water-Babies. (Illus.). 256p. 1987. Repr. PLB 22.95x (0-89966-579-9) Buccaneer Bks.
—Westward Ho. (gr. 8 up). 1968. pap. 1.25 (0-8049-0184-8, CL-184) Airmont.
—Westward Ho! reissue ed. Wyeth, N. C., illus. LC 20-18930. 432p. (gr. 7 up). 1992. deluxe, limited ed. 75.00 (0-684-19443-0, Scribners Young Read); SBE 26.95 (0-684-19444-9, Scribners Young Read) Macmillan Child Grp.
Kingsley, Emily P. A Baby Sister for Herry. Walz, Richard, illus. LC 83-83280. 24p. (ps). 1984. write for info. (0-307-12011-2, 12011, Golden Bks) Western Pub.
—Sesame Street Big Bird & Little Bird's Book of Big & Little. Delaney, A., illus. 24p. (ps-k). 1977. pap. write for info (0-307-10073-1, Pub. by Golden Bks) Western Pub.
Kingsley, Emily P., et al. Sesame Street One, Two, Three Story Book: Stories About the Numbers from One to Ten. (Illus.). (ps-4). 1973. 6.95 (0-394-82694-9); lib. bdg. 6.99 (0-394-92694-3) Random Bks Yng Read.
Kingsley, Henry. Henry Kingsley. Mellick, J. S., ed. LC 81-19990. 603p. 1982. (Pub. by Univ. Queensland Pr AT); pap. 17.95 (0-7022-1760-3) Intl Spec Bk.
Kingsley, Stuart. My Name Is Jesus. (Illus.). 44p. (gr. 3 up). 1988. 6.95 (1-55523-127-6) Winston-Derek.
King-Smith, David. Cuckoobush Farm. Kazuko, illus. LC 87-14871. 32p. (ps-1). 1988. 11.95 (0-688-07680-7); lib. bdg. 11.88 (0-688-07681-5) Greenwillow.
King-Smith, Deborah. Ace: The Very Important Pig. 112p. 1990. text ed. 8.96 (0-685-66865-7) W A T Braille.
—Ace: The Very Important Pig. 112p. 1990. text ed. 8.96 (1-56956-178-8) W A T Braille.
King-Smith, Dick. Ace: The Very Important Pig. Hemmant, Lynette, illus. LC 90-1447. 144p. (gr. 2-7). 1990. 13.00 (0-517-57832-8); PLB 13.99 (0-517-57833-6) Crown Bks Yng Read.
—Ace: The Very Important Pig. 112p. (gr. 4-7). 1990. 8.96 (0-685-63778-6, BR8565) W A T Braille.
—All Pigs Are Beautiful. Jeram, Anita, illus. LC 92-53136. 32p. (ps-3). 1993. 14.95 (1-56402-148-3) Candlewick Pr.
—Alphabeasts. Blake, Quentin, illus. LC 91-38435. 64p. (gr. 1 up). 1992. SBE 14.95 (0-02-750720-3, Macmillan Child Bk) Macmillan Child Grp.
—The Animal Parade. Wild, Jocelyn, illus. LC 91-30332. 96p. (gr. 1-8). 1992. 16.00 (0-688-11375-3, Tambourine Bks) Morrow.
—Babe: The Gallant Pig. reissued ed. Rayner, Mary, illus. LC 84-11429. 176p. (gr. 3-6). 1993. 13.00 (0-517-55556-5) Crown Bks Yng Read.
—Babe the Gallant Pig: The Gallant Pig. (gr. k-6). 1987. pap. 3.25 (0-440-40420-7, YB) Dell.
—The Cuckoo Child. Bowman, Leslie, illus. LC 92-72029. 128p. (gr. 3-6). 1993. 13.95 (1-56282-350-7); PLB 13.89 (1-56282-351-5) Hyprn Child.
—Daggie Dogfoot. large type ed. 192p. (gr. 1-7). 1990. 14.95 (0-7451-1229-3) G K Hall.
—Dodos Are Forever. large type ed. Parkins, David, illus. 112p. 1993. 13.95 (0-7451-1682-5, Galaxy Child Lrg Print) Chivers N Amer.
—Find the White Horse. large type ed. Wilkes, Larry, illus. 1993. 15.95 (0-7451-1804-6, Galaxy Child Lrg Print) Chivers N Amer.
—The Fox Busters. Miller, Jon, illus. LC 87-37409. 128p. (gr. 4-7). 1988. 13.95 (0-440-50064-8) Delacorte.
—Harry's Mad. (gr. 3-6). 1988. 11.95 (0-517-56254-5) Crown Bks Yng Read.
—Harry's Mad. (gr. k-6). 1988. pap. 3.25 (0-440-40112-7, YB) Dell.

—Harry's Mad. large type ed. 136p. (gr. 2-7). 1990. lib. bdg. 15.95x (*0-7451-1101-7*, Lythway Large Print) Hall.
—The Invisible Dog. Roth, Roger, illus. LC 92-26978. 80p. (gr. 2-5). 1993. 14.00 (*0-517-59424-2*); PLB 14.99 (*0-517-59425-0*) Crown Bks Yng Read.
—Lady Daisy. Smith, Joseph A., illus. LC 92-21834. 1993. 14.00 (*0-385-30891-4*) Delacorte.
—Martin's Mice. Alborough, Jez, illus. LC 88-20359. 128p. (gr. 3 up). 1988. 13.00 (*0-517-57113-7*) Crown Bks Yng Read.
—Martin's Mice. large print ed. (gr. 4-7). 1989. lib. bdg. 16.50 (*0-7451-0956-X*, Lythway Large Print) Hall.
—Martin's Mice. 1990. pap. 3.25 (*0-440-40380-4*, Pub. by Yearling Classics) Dell.
—The Mouse Butcher. Smith, Wendy, illus. 144p. (gr. 3-7). 1992. pap. 3.99 (*0-14-031457-1*) Puffin Bks.
—The Mouse Butcher. large type ed. Smith, Wendy, illus. 144p. (gr. 3-7). 1992. 13.95 (*0-7451-1498-9*, Galaxy Child Lrg Print) Chivers N Amer.
—Paddy's Pot of Gold. Parkins, David, illus. LC 91-24586. 128p. (gr. 2-7). 1992. 14.00 (*0-517-58136-1*); PLB 14.99 (*0-517-58137-X*) Crown Bks Yng Read.
—Pigs Might Fly. (gr. 4 up). 1990. pap. 3.95 (*0-14-034537-X*, Puffin) Puffin Bks.
—Pretty Polly. Peck, Marshall, illus. LC 91-42449. 128p. (gr. 2-7). 1992. 14.00 (*0-517-58606-1*); PLB 14.99 (*0-517-58607-X*) Crown Bks Yng Read.
—Sophie Hits Six. 1st U.S. ed. Parkins, David, illus. LC 92-54692. (gr. k-4). 1993. 14.95 (*1-56402-216-1*) Candlewick Pr.
—Sophie in the Saddle. Parkins, David, illus. LC 93-26723. 1994. write for info. (*1-56402-329-X*) Candlewick Pr.
—Sophie's Tom. Parkins, David & Parkins, David, illus. LC 91-58756. 112p. (gr. k-4). 1992. 14.95 (*1-56402-107-6*) Candlewick Pr.
—The Swoose. (Illus.). (gr. 3-7). 1994. 13.95 (*1-56282-658-1*); PLB 13.89 (*1-56282-659-X*) Hyprn Child.
—The Toby Man. Hemmant, Lynette, illus. LC 90-28443. 128p. (gr. 2-7). 1991. 14.00 (*0-517-58134-5*); lib. bdg. 14.99 (*0-517-58135-3*) Crown Bks Yng Read.
—The Water Horse. large type ed. Parkins, David, illus. 124p. 1992. PLB 13.95 (*0-7451-1610-8*, Lythway Large Print) Hall.
Kingsriter, Debbie & Kingsriter, Doug. Clipper's Crazy Race. Iosa, Ann, illus. LC 92-12327. 32p. 1992. 7.99 (*0-8499-0921-X*) Word Pub.
—Finny's Big Break. Iosa, Ann, illus. LC 92-12325. 32p. (ps-2). 1992. 7.99 (*0-8499-0920-1*) Word Pub.
—Gilroy's Goof. Iosa, Ann, illus. LC 92-12580. 32p. (ps-2). 1992. 7.99 (*0-8499-0922-8*) Word Pub.
Kingsriter, Doug, jt. auth. see Kingsriter, Debbie.
Kingston, Arlene. The Bagels Are Coming. Kingston, Arlene, illus. 40p. (ps up). 1988. pap. 5.95 (*0-929934-00-8*) Child Time Pubs.
—I'm Small That's All. (Illus.). (ps up). 1989. pap. write for info. (*0-929934-02-X*) Child Time Pubs.
Kingston, Laura. Happy Birthday, Hector! Hearne, Diane D., illus. 24p. (ps-k). 1992. write for info. (*0-307-11522-4*, 11522) Western Pub.
Kingston, Peter. My First Book of Mazes: Super Activities for Juniors. (gr. 4-7). 1992. pap. 2.95 (*0-8431-3457-7*) Price Stern.
Kinin, Claudia. My Christmas Book of Numbers. (ps-3). 1993. 6.95 (*0-307-13721-X*, Golden Pr) Western Pub.
Kinkoph, Sherry. Alpha-Bytes Count with Computers. (ps up). 1993. pap. 16.95 incl. disk (*1-56761-031-5*) Alpha Bks IN.
—Alpha-Bytes Draw with Computers. (ps up). 1993. 16.95 (*1-56761-032-3*) Alpha Bks IN.
—Alpha-Bytes Fun with Computers. (ps up). 1992. pap. 16.95 incl. disk (*0-672-30238-1*) Alpha Bks IN.
Kinnealy, Janice. How to Draw Flowers. LC 86-50468. (Illus.). 32p. (gr. 2-6). 1987. PLB 10.65 (*0-8167-0846-0*, Pub. by Watermill Pr); pap. text ed. 1.95 (*0-8167-0847-9*, Pub. by Watermill Pr) Troll Assocs.
—Let's Celebrate Thanksgiving: A Book of Drawing Fun. Kinnealy, Janice, illus. LC 87-61373. 32p. (gr. 2-6). 1988. PLB 10.65 (*0-8167-1131-3*); pap. text ed. 1.95 (*0-8167-1132-1*) Troll Assocs.
Kinnell, Galway. How the Alligator Missed Breakfast. Munsinger, Lynn, illus. 32p. (gr. k-3). 1982. 8.95 (*0-395-32436-X*) HM.
Kinney, Karin, ed. Geography. LC 93-28237. (Illus.). 88p. (gr. k-3). 1994. write for info. (*0-8094-9462-0*); PLB write for info. (*0-8094-9463-9*) Time-Life.
—Inventions. LC 93-24417. (Illus.). 88p. (gr. k-3). 1994. write for info. (*0-8094-9454-X*); PLB write for info. (*0-8094-9455-8*) Time-Life.
Kino Learning Center Staff & Sanders, Corinne. My Choices & Decisions. Mirocha, Kay, illus. 64p. (gr. 5-9). 1987. pap. 7.95 (*0-86653-421-0*, GA1031) Good Apple.
Kino Learning Center Staff, et al. My Changing Body. Mirocha, Kay, illus. 64p. (gr. 5-9). 1987. pap. 7.95 (*0-86653-420-2*, GA1030) Good Apple.
—My Journal of Personal Growth. Mirocha, Kay, illus. 64p. (gr. 5-9). 1987. pap. 7.95 (*0-86653-418-0*, GA 1028) Good Apple.
—My Relationships with Others. Mirocha, Kay, illus. 64p. (gr. 5-9). 1987. pap. 7.95 (*0-86653-419-9*, GA 1029) Good Apple.
Kinsey, Helen, jt. auth. see Kinsey-Warnock, Natalie.
Kinsey, Thomas D., ed. see Heller, Pete.

Kinsey-Warnock, Natalie. The Canada Geese Quilt. Bowman, Leslie W., illus. LC 88-32661. 64p. (gr. 4 up). 1989. 13.00 (*0-525-65004-0*, Cobblehill Bks) Dutton Child Bks.
—The Canada Geese Quilt. Bowman, Leslie, illus. 60p. (gr. 5 up). 1992. pap. 3.50 (*0-440-40719-2*, YB) Dell.
—The Fiddler of the Northern Lights. Bowman, Leslie W., illus. LC 92-36703. 1994. write for info. (*0-525-65143-8*, Cobblehill Bks) Dutton Child Bks.
—The Night the Bells Rang. Bowman, Leslie W., illus. LC 91-3053. 80p. (gr. 4 up). 1991. 12.95 (*0-525-65074-1*, Cobblehill Bks) Dutton Child Bks.
—On a Starry Night. McPhail, David, illus. LC 93-4878. 1994. write for info. (*0-531-06820-X*); PLB write for info. (*0-531-08670-4*) Orchard Bks Watts.
—When Spring Comes. Schuett, Stacey, illus. LC 92-14066. (ps-3). 1993. 14.99 (*0-525-45008-4*, DCB) Dutton Child Bks.
—Wild Horses of Sweetbriar. LC 89-32280. (Illus.). (ps-3). 1990. 13.95 (*0-525-65015-6*, Cobblehill Bks) Dutton Child Bks.
—Wilderness Cat. Graham, Mark, illus. LC 90-24250. 32p. (ps-3). 1992. 14.00 (*0-525-65068-7*, Cobblehill Bks) Dutton Child Bks.
Kinsey-Warnock, Natalie & Kinsey, Helen. The Bear That Heard Crying. Rand, Ted, illus. 32p. (ps-3). 1993. reinforced bdg. 13.99 (*0-525-65103-9*, Cobblehill Bks) Dutton Child Bks.
Kinzey, Bert. F-15 Eagle in Detail & Scale. (Illus.). 72p. (Orig.). (gr. 5 up). 1984. pap. 8.95 (*0-8168-5028-3*, 25028, TAB-Aero) TAB Bks.
Kinzie, Juliette. Wau-Bun: The Early Day in the Northwest. (Illus.). xxii, 395p. (gr. 9-12). 1987. pap. 20.00 (*1-55613-054-6*) Heritage Bk.
Kipkorir, Benjamin. People of the Rift Valley: Kalenjin. (Illus.). 43p. (gr. 6-9). 1991. pap. 4.95 (*0-237-50892-3*, Pub. by Evans Bros Ltd) Trafalgar.
Kipling, Rudyard. The Beginning of the Armadillos. Cauley, Lorinda B., illus. LC 85-5444. 43p. (ps-3). 1985. 14.95 (*0-15-206380-3*, Pub. by HJ) HarBrace.
—Beginning of the Armadillos. 48p. (ps-3). 1990. pap. 3.95 (*0-15-206381-1*, Voyager Bks) HarBrace.
—Captains Courageous. (gr. 6 up). 1964. pap. 1.75 (*0-8049-0027-2*, CL-27) Airmont.
—Captains Courageous. 176p. (gr. 6). 1964. pap. 2.50 (*0-451-52381-4*, CJ1751, Sig Classics) NAL-Dutton.
—Captains Courageous. new & abr. ed. Fago, John N., ed. Bercasio, E., illus. (gr. 4-12). 1977. pap. text ed. 2.95 (*0-88301-262-6*) Pendulum Pr.
—Cat That Walked by Himself. LC 90-34357. 1989. 11.95 (*0-85953-276-3*) Childs Play.
—The Cat Who Walked by Himself. LC 90-34357. 1990. pap. 5.95 (*0-85953-309-3*) Childs Play.
—The Elephant's Child. Cauley, Lorinda B., illus. LC 85-9098. 48p. (ps-3). 1988. pap. 4.95 (*0-15-225386-6*, HB Juv Bks) HarBrace.
—The Elephant's Child. Frascino, Edward, illus. 32p. (gr. k-3). 1986. 13.95 (*0-13-273640-3*) P-H.
—The Elephant's Child. Raglin, Tim, illus. LC 86-377. 48p. (gr. k up). 1986. incl. cassette 14.95 (*0-394-88300-4*) Knopf Bks Yng Read.
—The Elephant's Child. Cauley, Lorinda B., illus. 44p. (ps-3). 1983. 14.95 (*0-15-225385-8*, Voyager Bks) HarBrace.
—The Elephant's Child. Mogensen, Jan, illus. LC 89-7787. 48p. 1989. 13.95 (*0-940793-41-5*, Pub. by Crocodile Bks) Interlink Pub.
—Elephants Child. LC 90-46609. 1989. 14.95 (*0-85953-275-5*) Childs Play.
—The Elephant's Child. (ps-2). 1988. 4.95 (*0-7232-3449-3*) Warne.
—The Elephant's Child. Mogensen, Jan, illus. LC 89-7787. 48p. 1991. pap. 6.95 (*0-940793-77-6*, Crocodile Bks) Interlink Pub.
—The Elephant's Child. Bolam, Emily, illus. LC 91-19378. 24p. (gr. k). 1992. 13.95 (*0-525-44862-4*, DCB) Dutton Child Bks.
—The Elephant's Child & Other Just So Stories. (Illus.). 96p. 1993. pap. text ed. 1.00t (*0-486-27821-2*) Dover.
—Gunga Din. Parker, Robert A., illus. LC 86-19388. 28p. (gr. 1 up). 1987. 12.95 (*0-15-200456-4*, Gulliver Bks) HarBrace.
—El Hijo del Elefante: The Elephant's Child. Martinez, Lourdes, tr. from GER. Mogensen, Jan, illus. (SPA.). 42p. (gr. k-4). 1990. 13.95 (*87-14-18825-2*) Hispanic Bk Dist.
—How the Camel Got His Hump. Raglin, Tim, illus. LC 88-33366. 32p. (ps up). 1991. pap. 14.95 (*0-88708-096-0*, Rabbit Ears); incl. cassette 19.95 (*0-88708-097-9*, Rabbit Ears) Picture Bk Studio.
—How the Leopard Got His Spots. Loestoeter, Lori, illus. LC 89-31374. (ps up). 1991. pap. 14.95 (*0-88708-111-8*, Rabbit Ears); book & cassette package 19.95 (*0-88708-112-6*, Rabbit Ears) Picture Bk Studio.
—How the Leopard Got His Spots. Glover, Danny, read by. Lohstoeter, Lori, illus. (Illus.). 32p. (ps up). 1992. pap. write for info. slipcase pkg., incl. cassette (*0-307-14330-9*, 14330, Golden Pr) Western Pub.
—How the Leopard Got His Spots. Lohstoeter, Lori, illus. 64p. 1993. Repr. of 1989 ed. incl. cass. 9.95 (*0-88708-301-3*, Rabbit Ears) Picture Bk Studio.
—How the Leopard Got His Spots & Other Just So Stories. Kliros, Thea, illus. LC 92-20780. 96p. 1992. pap. text ed. 1.00 (*0-486-27297-4*) Dover.
—How the Leopard Got Its Spots: And Other Just So Stories. Kipling, Rudyard & Gleeson, Joseph, illus. LC 93-540. 184p. 1993. 6.00 (*1-56957-902-4*) Shambhala Pubns.

—How the Rhinoceros Got His Skin. Raglin, Tim, illus. LC 88-11439. 28p. (ps up). 1991. pap. 14.95 (*0-88708-078-2*, Rabbit Ears); bk. & cass. pkg. 19.95 (*0-88708-083-9*, Rabbit Ears) Picture Bk Studio.
—How the Rhinoceros Got His Skin. Raglin, Tim, illus. LC 92-22119. 64p. 1992. Repr. of 1988 ed. 5.95 (*0-88708-255-6*, Rabbit Ears); Mini-bk. incl. cass. 9.95 (*0-88708-254-8*, Rabbit Ears) Picture Bk Studio.
—The Jungle Book. 336p. (RL 4). pap. 3.95 (*0-451-51716-4*, CE1716, Sig Classics) NAL-Dutton.
—The Jungle Book. (gr. 5 up). pap. 2.25 (*0-317-62281-1*, Puffin) Puffin Bks.
—The Jungle Book. 1987. pap. 2.95 (*0-14-035074-8*, Puffin) Puffin Bks.
—The Jungle Book. Detmold, Maurice, et al illus. 320p. 1989. 12.99 (*0-517-67902-7*) Outlet Bk Co.
—The Jungle Book. Foreman, Michael, illus. (gr. 5-9). 1987. 19.99 (*0-670-80241-7*) Viking Child Bks.
—The Jungle Book. Bergh, Jerald E. & Donovan, Michael, eds. LC 90-64201. (gr. 3-4). 1991. pap. 5.95 incls. cassette (*1-879551-51-9*); cassette 2.95 (*1-879551-52-7*) Saban Pub.
—The Jungle Book. Alexander, Gregory, illus. 120p. (gr. 1 up). 1991. 17.95 (*1-55970-127-7*) Arcade Pub Inc.
—The Jungle Book. (Illus.). 1991. pap. text ed. 4.87 (*0-582-03587-2*) Longman.
—The Jungle Book. Robson, W. W., intro. by. 432p. 1992. pap. 4.95 (*0-19-282901-7*) OUP.
—Jungle Book. 240p. 1992. 9.49 (*0-8167-2552-7*); pap. 2.95 (*0-8167-2553-5*) Troll Assocs.
—The Jungle Book. Ashachik, Diane M., ed. Hannon, Holly, illus. LC 92-5806. 48p. (gr. k-6). 1992. PLB 12.89 (*0-8167-2868-2*); pap. text ed. 3.95 (*0-8167-2869-0*) Troll Assocs.
—The Jungle Book: Based on the Mowgli Tales from "The Jungle Book" by Rudyard Kipling. Oliver, Tony, ed. Animation Cottage Staff, illus. LC 90-64201. 36p. (Orig.). (gr. 3-4). 1990. pap. 2.95 (*1-879551-50-0*) Saban Pub.
—Jungle Books. (gr. 5 up). 1966. pap. 1.95 (*0-8049-0109-0*, CL-109) Airmont.
—The Jungle Books. 336p. 1961. pap. 3.95 (*0-451-52340-7*, Sig Classics) NAL-Dutton.
—Just So Stories. (gr. 3 up). 1966. pap. 1.75 (*0-8049-0123-6*, CL-123) Airmont.
—Just So Stories. 158p. (RL 4). 1974. pap. 3.50 (*0-451-52433-0*, Sig Classics); (Sig Classics) NAL-Dutton.
—Just So Stories. (Illus.). 224p. (gr. 2-9). 1979. 5.99 (*0-517-26655-5*) Outlet Bk Co.
—Just So Stories. Gleeson, Joseph M. & Kipling, Rudyard, illus. 244p. (gr. 2-9). 1988. 12.99 (*0-517-63177-6*) Outlet Bk Co.
—Just So Stories. (gr. 5 up). pap. 2.25 (*0-317-62284-6*, Puffin) Puffin Bks.
—Just So Stories. Salter, Safaya, illus. LC 86-46271. 96p. (gr. 2-4). 1987. 16.95 (*0-8050-0439-4*, Bks Young Read) H Holt & Co.
—Just So Stories. 1987. pap. 2.95 (*0-14-035075-6*, Puffin) Puffin Bks.
—Just So Stories. Foreman, Michael, illus. (ps up). 1987. 15.00 (*0-670-80242-5*) Viking Child Bks.
—Just So Stories. Frampton, David, illus. LC 90-19429. 128p. (gr. 3-7). 1991. 19.95 (*0-06-023294-3*); PLB 19.89 (*0-06-023296-X*) HarpC Child Bks.
—Just So Stories. Kipling, Rudyard, illus. LC 92-53177. 192p. 1992. 12.95 (*0-679-41797-4*, Evrymans Lib Childs Class) Knopf.
—Just So Stories. Brent, Isabelle, illus. Philip, Neil, frwd. by. (Illus.). 160p. 1993. 19.99 (*0-670-85196-5*) Viking Child Bks.
—Kim. (gr. 8 up). 1965. pap. 1.95 (*0-8049-0075-2*) Airmont.
—Kim. Said, Edward, ed. & intro. by. LC 87-50331. 320p. (gr. 5 up). 1987. pap. 2.99 (*0-14-035076-4*, Puffin) Puffin Bks.
—Kim. 384p. (gr. 5 up). 1992. pap. 3.50 (*0-440-40695-1*, Pub. by Yearling Classics) Dell.
—Kim. large type ed. 519p. 1992. Repr. lib. bdg. 22.00 (*0-939495-39-2*) North Bks.
—Light That Failed. (gr. 8 up). 1969. pap. 1.50 (*0-8049-0199-6*, CL-199) Airmont.
—Livre de la Jungle. Pilorget, Bruno, illus. (FRE.). 254p. (gr. 5-10). 1987. pap. 9.95 (*2-07-033456-2*) Schoenhof.
—The Maltese Cat. 1991. PLB 13.95s.p. (*0-88682-475-3*) Creative Ed.
—The Miracle of Purun Bhagat. LC 85-26956. 40p. (gr. 6 up). 1986. PLB 13.95s.p. (*0-88682-052-9*) Creative Ed.
—Mowgli's Brothers. Wormell, Christopher, illus. (gr. 5 up). 1992. PLB 19.95 (*0-88682-488-5*) Creative Ed.
—New Illustrated Just So Stories. Nicholas, illus. (gr. 1-7). 1952. PLB o.p. (*0-385-02180-1*) Doubleday.
—Puck of Pook's Hill. Wintle, Sarah H., ed. LC 87-50328. 224p. (gr. 5 up). 1987. pap. 3.95 (*0-14-043284-1*) Viking Child Bks.
—Puck of Pook's Hill. 1987. pap. 2.25 (*0-14-035077-2*, Puffin) Puffin Bks.
—Puck of Pook's Hill: And Rewards & Fairies. Mackenzie, Donald, ed. LC 92-14450. (gr. 4 up). 1993. pap. 7.95 (*0-19-282575-5*) OUP.
—Reader's Digest Best Loved Books for Young Readers: The Jungle Books. Ogburn, Jackie, ed. Jouve, Paul, illus. 160p. (gr. 4-12). 1989. 3.99 (*0-945260-26-1*) Choice Pub NY.
—Rewards & Fairies. 1988. pap. 2.25 (*0-14-035081-0*, Puffin) Puffin Bks.
—Rikki-Tikki-Tavi. 1992. 16.95 (*0-15-267015-7*, HB Juv Bks) HarBrace.

—Rudyard Kipling's Verse. LC 40-29931. 1940. 19.95 (*0-385-04407-0*) Doubleday.
—The Second Jungle Book. (gr. 5 up). pap. 2.25 (*0-317-62282-X*, Puffin) Puffin Bks.
—The Second Jungle Book. 1987. pap. 2.95 (*0-14-035079-9*, Puffin) Puffin Bks.
—The Sing-Song of Old Man Kangaroo. Rowe, John A., illus. LC 90-7382. 32p. (gr. k up). 1991. pap. 14.95 (*0-88708-152-5*) Picture Bk Studio.
—Stalky & Co. (gr. 4-7). 1991. pap. 3.50 (*0-440-40519-X*, Pub. by Yearling Classics) Dell.
—Stalky & Company. (gr. 5 up). 1988. pap. 2.25 (*0-317-69643-2*, Puffin) Puffin Bks.
—Tales from the Jungle Book. McKinley, Robin, adapted by. Smith, J. A., illus. LC 84-11724. 64p. (gr. k-3). 1985. lib. bdg. 8.99 (*0-394-96940-5*) Random Bks Yng Read.
Kipling, Rudyard, jt. auth. see Perrault, Charles.
Kipnis, Nahum. Rediscovering Optics. xii, 259p. (gr. 10-12). 1992. pap. 24.95 (*0-9636784-0-X*) BENA Pr.
Kipper, Lenore & Bogot, Howard. Alef-Bet of Jewish Values: Code Words of Jewish Life. Paiss, Jana, illus. 64p. (gr. 4-6). 1985. pap. text ed. 6.00 (*0-8074-0267-2*, 101087) UAHC.
Kira, Gene S. Understanding Soccer: Rules & Procedures for Players, Parents & Coaches. (Illus.). 80p. (Orig.). (gr. 5 up). 1993. pap. 9.95 (*0-929637-02-X*) Apples & Oranges Inc.
Kiraithe, Jackie. Magic Links: Manual. Gonzales, Linda, ed. 200p. Date not set. 48.00 (*0-942787-95-1*) Binet Intl.
Kiraithe, Jackie & Gonzales, Linda. Magic Links Big Book. (Illus.). 36p. 1992. 48.00 (*0-942787-94-3*) Binet Intl.
Kirberger, R. M. Equine Art for Fun & Profit. 60p. 1991. wkbk. 19.95 (*1-880495-00-7*) Rhenaria.
Kirby, David, jt. auth. see Woodman, Allen.
Kirby, Jackie M. Chris Has An Accident. McCormack, Nancy, ed. McCoig, Rich, photos by. (Illus.). 52p. (Orig.). (gr. 3-4). 1987. pap. 5.95 (*0-942459-00-8*) McCormack Co.
Kirby, Mansfield. The Secret of Thut-Mouse III: or Basil Beaudesert's Revenge. Post, Mance, illus. LC 85-47588. 64p. (ps up). 1985. 14.00 (*0-374-36677-2*) FS&G.
Kirby, Philippa. Glorious Days, Dreadful Days: The Battle of Bunker Hill. Edens, John, illus. LC 92-18084. 88p. (gr. 2-5). 1992. PLB 21.34 (*0-8114-7226-4*) Raintree Steck-V.
Kirby, Susan. Partners in Love. 1993. pap. 2.99 (*0-553-29460-1*) Bantam.
—Too Good to Be True. 1991. pap. 2.99 (*0-553-29213-7*) Bantam.
Kirby, Susan E. Shadow Boy. LC 90-7687. 160p. (gr. 7 up). 1991. 13.95 (*0-531-05869-7*); PLB 13.99 (*0-531-08469-8*) Orchard Bks Watts.
Kirchner, Audrey B. Basic Beginnings: A Handbook of Learning Games & Activities for Young Children. LC 79-597. (Illus.). (ps-2). 1985. pap. 12.95 (*0-87491-229-6*) Acropolis.
Kirchoff, Mary L. Kendermore. LC 88-51719. (Illus.). 352p. (Orig.). 1989. pap. 4.95 (*0-88038-754-8*) TSR Inc.
Kiri, Te Kanawa. Land of the Long White Cloud: Maori Myths, Tales, & Legends. Foreman, Michael, illus. (gr. 3 up). 1990. 16.95 (*1-55970-046-7*) Arcade Pub Inc.
Kirilenko, Katrina, jt. auth. see Amery, Heather.
Kirk, Barbara D. van see Van Kirk, Barbara D.
Kirk, Daniel. Skateboard Monsters. (Illus.). 32p. (ps-1). 1993. 12.95 (*0-685-66619-0*) Universe.
Kirk, David. Miss Spider's Tea Party. LC 93-15710. (Illus.). 32p. 1994. 15.95 (*0-590-47724-2*) Scholastic Inc.
Kirk, Jim. Environmental Geometry. (Illus.). (gr. 3-8). 1975. 5.50 (*0-918932-61-0*) Activity Resources.
Kirk, Pat & Brown, Alice. Bear Buddies: A Child Learns to Make Friends. (Illus.). (ps-2). 1986. 4.99 (*0-915720-55-8*) Brownlow Pub Co.
—Bear Up: A Child Learns to Handle Ups & Downs. (Illus.). 1986. 4.99 (*0-915720-51-5*) Brownlow Pub Co.
—Bearing Burdens: A Child Learns to Help. (Illus.). (ps-2). 1986. 4.99 (*0-915720-54-X*) Brownlow Pub Co.
—Bearing Fruit: A Child Learns about the Fruit of the Spirit. (Illus.). (ps-2). 1987. 4.99 (*0-915720-62-0*) Brownlow Pub Co.
—I Can Bearly Wait: A Child Learns Patience. (Illus.). (ps-2). 1987. 4.99 (*0-915720-63-9*) Brownlow Pub Co.
—Love Bears All Things: A Child Learns to Love. (Illus.). (ps-2). 1986. 4.99 (*0-915720-50-7*) Brownlow Pub Co.
Kirkbride, John. Thank You for Your Application. 160p. (gr. 6-9). 1990. pap. 7.95 (*0-233-98446-1*, Pub. by A Deutsch England) Trafalgar.
Kirkland, Dianna C. Last Year I Failed...but. Orlowski, Dennis, illus. 32p. (Orig.). (ps-5). 1981. pap. 6.50 (*0-940370-04-2*); counseling activity guide-failure 6.50 (*0-940370-07-7*) Aid-U Pub.
Kirkland, Dianna K. I Have a Stepfamily but... Orlowski, Dennis, illus. 40p. (Orig.). (ps-5). 1981. pap. 6.50 (*0-685-00148-2*); counseling activity guide-stepfamilies 6.50 (*0-686-96649-X*) Aid-U Pub.
Kirkland, Gelsey & Lawrence, Greg. Side Saddle Ballerina. Rogers, Jacqueline, illus. LC 93-20355. 1993. pap. 14.95 (*0-385-46978-0*) Doubleday.
Kirkman, Will. Nature Crafts Workshop. LC 80-84186. (gr. 3-8). 1981. pap. 10.95 (*0-8224-9781-6*) Fearon Teach Aids.

Kirkpatrick, Patricia. Plowie. Kirkpatrick, Joey, illus. LC 93-13712. Date not set. write for info. (*0-15-262802-9*) HarBrace.
Kirkpatrick, Rena K. Look at Flowers. rev. ed. Milne, Annabel & Stebbing, Peter, illus. LC 84-26227. 32p. (gr. 2-4). 1985. PLB 17.28 (*0-8172-2352-5*); pap. 4.95 (*0-8114-6898-4*) Raintree Steck-V.
—Look at Insects. rev. ed. Farmer, Andrew, illus. LC 84-26228. 32p. (gr. 2-4). 1985. PLB 17.28 (*0-8172-2351-7*); pap. 4.95 (*0-8114-6897-6*) Raintree Steck-V.
—Look at Leaves. rev. ed. Milne, Annabel & Stebbing, Peter, illus. LC 84-26360. 32p. (gr. 2-4). 1985. PLB 17.28 (*0-8172-2353-3*); pap. 4.95 (*0-8114-6899-2*) Raintree Steck-V.
—Look at Magnets. rev. ed. Knight, Ann, illus. LC 84-26252. 32p. (gr. 2-4). 1985. PLB 17.28 (*0-8172-2354-1*); pap. 4.95 (*0-8114-6900-X*) Raintree Steck-V.
—Look at Pond Life. rev. ed. Milne, Annabel & Stebbing, Peter, illus. LC 84-26249. 32p. (gr. 2-4). 1985. PLB 17.28 (*0-8172-2355-X*); pap. 4.95 (*0-8114-6901-8*) Raintree Steck-V.
—Look at Rainbow Colors. rev. ed. Barnard, Anna, illus. LC 84-26250. 32p. (gr. 2-4). 1985. PLB 17.28 (*0-8172-2356-8*); pap. 4.95 (*0-8114-6902-6*) Raintree Steck-V.
—Look at Seeds & Weeds. rev. ed. King, Debbie, illus. LC 84-26226. 32p. (gr. 2-4). 1985. PLB 17.28 (*0-8172-2357-6*); pap. 4.95 (*0-8114-6903-4*) Raintree Steck-V.
—Look at Shore Life. rev. ed. Milne, Annabel & Stebbing, Peter, illus. LC 84-26249. 32p. (gr. 2-4). 1985. PLB 17.28 (*0-8172-2358-4*); pap. 4.95 (*0-8114-6904-2*) Raintree Steck-V.
—Look at Trees. rev. ed. Worth, Jo & Knight, Ann, illus. LC 84-26225. 32p. (gr. 2-4). 1985. PLB 17.28 (*0-8172-2359-2*); pap. 4.95 (*0-8114-6905-0*) Raintree Steck-V.
—Look at Weather. rev. ed. Lewin, Janetta, illus. LC 84-26251. 32p. (gr. 2-4). 1985. PLB 17.28 (*0-8172-2360-6*); pap. 4.95 (*0-8114-6906-9*) Raintree Steck-V.
Kirksmith, Tommie. Ride Western Style: A Guide for Young Riders. (Illus.). 192p. (gr. 3-7). 1991. 16.95 (*0-87605-895-0*) Howell Bk.
—Western Performance: A Guide for Young Riders. Burt, Don, frwd. by. (Illus.). 224p. 1993. 20.00 (*0-87605-844-6*) Howell Bk.
Kirkwood, James. There Must Be a Pony. 1989. pap. 4.50 (*0-440-20238-8*) Dell.
Kirkwood, Tim. The Flight Attendant Career Guide. Gibbons Plummer, Jeanne, ed. (Illus.). 96p. (Orig.). (gr. 9-12). 1993. pap. 14.95 (*0-9637301-4-2*) T K Enterprises.
Kirn, Elaine, adapted by see Melville, Herman.
Kirn, Mille. Pocketwatch. 140p. (gr. 12 up). 1992. wkbk. 18.00 (*0-9632915-1-3*) Ellim & Ange.
Kirsch, George B. Multiple Choice Questions in Preparation for the AP United States History Examination. 2nd ed. 122p. (gr. 11-12). 1991. wkbk. 15.95 (*1-878621-06-8*); tchr's. manual, 68p. avail. (*1-878621-07-6*) D & S Mktg Syst.
Kirschner, David. The Pagemaster. Tiritilli, Jerry, illus. 128p. (gr. 4 up). 1993. 19.95 (*1-878685-43-0*) Turner Pub GA.
Kirschner, Frances & Sorrentino, Joanna. Nosey Notes. Kirschner, Robert, illus. 60p. (gr. 3-9). 1983. pap. 3.00 (*0-9612696-0-X*) Frantasy Wkshp.
Kirschstein, Carolyn. Hooray for Oklahoma Eighteen Eighty-Nine. (Illus.). 72p. (gr. k-4). 1989. 9.95 (*0-926521-00-4*) B C Pub Inc.
Kirschstein, Carolyn V. Hooray for Oklahoma (1889) Merrell, David, illus. 48p. (gr. k-4). 1989. write for info. B C Pub Inc.
Kirstein, Lincoln, retold by. Puss in Boots. Vaes, Alain, illus. 32p. (ps-3). 1992. 15.95 (*0-316-89506-7*) Little.
Kirsten, Suzanne. Begin with Phonics. Kahn, Betsey, ed. LC 81-85695. (Illus.). 80p. (Orig.). (gr. 1-4). 1982. pap. 4.95 (*0-89709-033-0*) Liberty Pub.
Kirwan-Vogel, Anna. The Jewel of Life. Yolen, Jane, ed. 118p. (gr. 5-9). 1991. 15.95 (*0-15-200750-4*, J Yolen Bks) HarBrace.
Kiser, Kevin. Sherman the Sheep. Barnes-Murphy, Rowan, illus. LC 92-22745. 32p. (gr. k-3). 1994. RSBE 14.95 (*0-02-750825-0*, Macmillan Child Bk) Macmillan Child Grp.
Kiser, Kevin, jt. auth. see Kiser, SuAnn.
Kiser, SuAnn. The Catspring Somersault Flying One-Handed Flip-Flop. Catalanotto, Peter, illus. LC 92-44519. 32p. (ps-2). 1993. 14.95 (*0-531-05493-4*); PLB 14.99 (*0-531-08643-7*) Orchard Bks Watts.
—Hazel Saves the Day. Day, Betsy, illus. LC 92-34782. 1994. write for info. (*0-8037-1488-2*); PLB write for info. (*0-8037-1489-0*) Dial Bks Young.
Kiser, SuAnn & Kiser, Kevin. The Birthday Thing. Abolafia, Yossi, illus. LC 87-38085. 24p. (gr. k up). 1989. 11.95 (*0-688-07772-2*); PLB 11.88 (*0-688-07773-0*) Greenwillow.
Kishta, Leila. ABC Rhymes for Young Muslims. Quinlan, Hamid, ed. Ali, Abdullah, illus. LC 83-70183. 32p. (gr. 1-6). 1983. pap. 3.00 (*0-89259-044-0*) Am Trust Pubns.
Kiskalt, Isolde. Dough Crafts. (Illus.). 144p. (gr. 8 up). 1992. pap. 14.95 (*0-8069-5843-X*) Sterling.
Kisling, Lee. The Fools' War. LC 91-47695. 176p. (gr. 5 up). 1992. 14.00 (*0-06-020836-8*); PLB 13.89 (*0-06-020837-6*) HarpC Child Bks.

Kismaric, Carole, adapted by. A Gift from Saint Nicholas. Mikolaycak, Charles, illus. LC 87-8797. 32p. (ps-3). 1988. reinforced bdg. 15.95 (*0-8234-0674-1*) Holiday.
—The Rumor of Pavel & Paali: A Ukrainian Folktale. Mikolaycak, Charles, illus. LC 87-19958. 32p. (gr. 1-3). 1988. HarpC Child Bks.
Kisner, R. & Knowles, B. Warm-up Exercises: Calisthenics for the Brain, Bk. III. 107p. (gr. 5-12). pap. 15.00 (*0-930599-77-2*) Thinking Pubns.
Kisner, Rita & Knowles, Brooke. Warm-Up Exercises, Bk. I. 100p. (gr. 5-12). 1984. spiral-wire bdg. 15.00x (*0-9610370-8-3*) Thinking Pubns.
—Warm-up Exercises, Bk. II. 100p. (gr. 5-12). 1985. wire spiral bdg. 15.00x (*0-9610370-9-1*) Thinking Pubns.
Kispert, Bill. Who's At Shining Time Station. Allcroft, Britt, created by. (Illus.). 22p. (ps-2). 1993. bds. 4.95 (*1-884336-02-7*) Qual Family.
—The Wonderful Stop. Allcroft, Britt, created by. (Illus.). 40p. (ps-3). 1994. pap. 5.95 (*1-884336-04-3*) Qual Family.
Kispert, Bill, adapted by see Kelly, Sean.
Kissinger, Rosemary. Quanah Parker: Comanche Chief. LC 90-23036. (Illus.). 96p. (gr. 5). 1991. 12.95 (*0-88289-785-3*) Pelican.
Kisslinger, Jerome. The Serbian Americans. Moynihan, Daniel P., intro. by. (Illus.). 112p. (gr. 5 up). 1990. lib. bdg. 17.95 (*1-55546-133-6*) Chelsea Hse.
Kistler, Darci. Ballerina: My Story. Ashby, Ruth, ed. 128p. (Orig.). 1993. pap. 3.50 (*0-671-64437-8*, Minstrel Bks) PB.
Kistler, Mary, jt. auth. see Hayden, Jan.
Kitamura, Keiji. Origami Treasure Chest. (Illus.). 80p. (Orig.). 1991. pap. 16.95 (*0-87040-868-2*) Japan Pubns USA.
Kitamura, Satoshi. From Acorn to Zoo & Everything in Between in Alphabetical Order. (Illus.). 32p. (ps-3). 1992. bds. 15.00 (*0-374-32470-0*) FS&G.
—Lily Takes a Walk. LC 87-8894. (Illus.). 32p. (ps-1). 1991. pap. 3.95 (*0-525-44699-0*, Puffin) Puffin Bks.
—UFO Diary. (ps up). 1989. 14.00 (*0-374-38026-0*) FS&G.
—UFO Diary. (ps up). 1991. pap. 4.95 (*0-374-48041-9*) FS&G.
—What's Inside? Kitamura, Satoshi, illus. 32p. (ps up). 1987. pap. 4.95 (*0-374-48324-8*) FS&G.
—What's Inside: The Alphabet Book. Kitamura, Satoshi, illus. LC 84-73117. 32p. (ps up). 1985. 14.00 (*0-374-38306-5*) FS&G.
—When Sheep Cannot Sleep. LC 86-45000. (Illus.). 32p. (ps up). 1986. 13.00 (*0-374-38311-1*) FS&G.
—When Sheep Cannot Sleep. (ps up). 1988. pap. 3.95 (*0-374-48359-0*) FS&G.
—When Sheep Can't Sleep: (Cuando los Borregos no Pueden Dormir) (SPA). (gr. 1-6). 19.95 (*84-372-6605-X*) Santillana.
Kitamura, Satoshi, illus. My Friend Mr. Morris. LC 87-542. (gr. k-2). 1988. pap. 2.50 (*0-317-69489-8*) Delacorte.
Kitano, Harry. The Japanese Americans. Moynihan, Daniel P., intro. by. (Illus.). 112p. (gr. 5 up). 1987. lib. bdg. 17.95 (*0-87754-856-0*) Chelsea Hse.
—Japanese Americans. (gr. 4-7). 1993. pap. 8.95 (*0-7910-0269-1*) Chelsea Hse.
Kitchen, Bert. And So They Build. Kitchen, Bert, illus. LC 92-54403. 32p. (ps up). 1993. 15.95 (*1-56402-217-X*) Candlewick Pr.
—Animal Alphabet. Kitchen, Bert, illus. LC 83-23929. 32p. (ps up). 1984. 13.95 (*0-8037-0117-9*) Dial Bks Young.
—Animal Alphabet. Kitchen, Bert, illus. LC 83-23929. 32p. (Orig.). (ps up). 1988. pap. 4.95 (*0-8037-0431-3*, Dial Pied Piper) Puffin Bks.
—Animal Alphabet. 06/1992 ed. 1992. pap. 5.99 (*0-14-054601-4*) Viking Child Bks.
—Animal Numbers. LC 87-5365. (Illus.). 24p. (ps up). 1987. 12.95 (*0-8037-0459-3*) Dial Bks Young.
—Animal Numbers. LC 87-5365. (Illus.). 24p. (gr. k up). 1991. pap. 4.95 (*0-8037-0910-2*, Dial Pied Piper) Puffin Bks.
—Gorilla-Chinchilla: And Other Animal Rhymes. Fogelman, Phyllis J., ed. Kitchen, Bert, illus. LC 89-16851. 32p. (ps up). 1990. 13.95 (*0-8037-0770-3*); PLB 13.89 (*0-8037-0771-1*) Dial Bks Young.
—Pig in a Barrow. Kitchen, Bert, illus. LC 90-43413. 32p. (ps-3). 1991. 13.95 (*0-8037-0943-9*) Dial Bks Young.
—Somewhere Today. Kitchen, Bert, illus. LC 91-58754. 32p. (ps up). 1992. 15.95 (*1-56402-074-6*) Candlewick Pr.
—Tenrec's Twigs. Kitchen, Bert, illus. 32p. (gr. k-4). 1989. 14.95 (*0-399-21720-7*, Philomel Bks) Putnam Pub Group.
—When Hunger Calls. LC 93-32360. 1994. write for info. (*1-56402-316-8*) Candlewick Pr.
Kitchen, Dennis, ed. see Finger, Bill & Schwartz, Alvin.
Kite, Patricia. Down in the Sea: The Crab. LC 93-21494. 1994. write for info. (*0-8075-1709-7*) A Whitman.
—Down in the Sea: The Jellyfish. Levine, Abby, ed. LC 92-12834. (Illus.). 24p. (ps-3). 1993. 13.95 (*0-8075-1712-7*) A Whitman.
—Down in the Sea: The Octopus. Levine, Abby, ed. LC 92-12284. (Illus.). 24p. 1993. 13.95g (*0-8075-1715-1*) A Whitman.
—Down in the Sea: The Sea Slug. LC 93-3765. 1994. write for info. (*0-8075-1717-8*) A Whitman.
—Noah's Ark: Opposing Viewpoints. LC 89-11635. (Illus.). 112p. (gr. 5-8). 1989. PLB 14.95 (*0-89908-073-1*) Greenhaven.

Kite, Virginia G. Three Hundred Sixty-Five Kids' Confessions: Making God's Word Personal in Little Lives. (Illus.). 224p. (gr. k-7). 1990. 12.95 (0-942847-02-4) Nugget Truth Minist.
Kitman, Carol & Hurwitz, Ann. One Mezuzah: A Jewish Counting Book. (gr. k). 6.95 (0-317-70144-4) Behrman.
Kitman, Carol & Hurwitz, Carol. One Mezuzah: A Jewish Counting Book. (Illus.). 48p. (ps-k). 1984. pap. 6.95 (0-940646-54-4) Rossel Bks.
Kittelson, Pat & Connor, Brooke. Cedar Breaks for Kids. (Illus.). (gr. k-4). 1979. pap. 1.00 (0-915630-14-1) Zion.
Kitto, Humphrey D. Greeks. (Orig.). (gr. 9 up). 1950. pap. 5.95 (0-14-020220-X) Viking Child Bks.
Kittredge, Elaine. Twelve. Riley, Cyd, illus. 84p. 1989. pap. 9.95 (0-9611266-1-2); audiotape, 80 mins. 9.95 (0-9611266-2-0) Optext.
Kittredge, Mary. The Common Cold. (Illus.). 104p. (gr. 6-12). 1990. 18.95 (0-7910-0060-5) Chelsea Hse.
—Emergency Medicine. 112p. (gr. 6-12). 1991. lib. bdg. 18.95 (0-7910-0063-X) Chelsea Hse.
—Frederick the Great. Schlesinger, Arthur M., Jr., intro. by. (Illus.). 112p. (gr. 5 up). 1988. lib. bdg. 17.95 (0-87754-525-1) Chelsea Hse.
—Headaches. (Illus.). 104p. (gr. 6-12). 1989. 18.95 (0-7910-0064-8) Chelsea Hse.
—Helen Hayes. Horner, Martina, intro. by. (Illus.). 112p. (gr. 5 up). 1990. lib. bdg. 17.95 (1-55546-656-7) Chelsea Hse.
—The Human Body: An Overview. (Illus.). 144p. (gr. 6-12). 1990. 18.95 (0-7910-0019-2) Chelsea Hse.
—Jane Addams. Horner, Matina, intro. by. (Illus.). 112p. (gr. 5 up). 1988. lib. bdg. 17.95 (1-55546-636-2) Chelsea Hse.
—Marc Antony. Schlesinger, Arthur M., Jr., intro. by. (Illus.). 112p. (gr. 5 up). 1988. lib. bdg. 17.95 (0-87754-505-7) Chelsea Hse.
—Organ Transplants. (Illus.). 112p. (gr. 6-12). 1989. lib. bdg. 18.95 (0-7910-0071-0) Chelsea Hse.
—Pain. (Illus.). 112p. (gr. 6-12). 1992. 18.95 (0-7910-0072-9) Chelsea Hse.
—Prescription & OTC Drugs. (Illus.). 112p. (gr. 6-12). 1989. 18.95 (0-7910-0062-1) Chelsea Hse.
—The Respiratory System. Koop, C. Everett, intro. by. (Illus.). 112p. (gr. 6-12). 1989. 18.95 (0-7910-0026-5) Chelsea Hse.
—Teens with AIDS Speak Out. (gr. 7 up). 1992. lib. bdg. 8.95 (0-671-74543-3, J Messner); lib. bdg. 13.98 (0-671-74542-5, J Messner) S&S Trade.
—Teens with AIDS Speak Out. large type ed. Garell, Dale C., intro. by. LC 93-6878. 161p. 1993. Alk. paper. lib. bdg. 15.95 (1-56054-691-3) Thorndike Pr.
Kittredge, Sonya. Chickadee Rescue. Weinberger, Jane, ed. Kittredge, Sonya, photos by. (Illus.). 32p. (Orig.). (ps-3). 1993. pap. 7.95 (0-932433-78-2) Windswept Hse.
Kittredge, William & Krauser, Steven M. The Great American Detectives. (Orig.). (RL 6). 1978. pap. 4.95 (0-451-62462-9, Ment) NAL-Dutton.
Kitzinger, Sheila. Being Born. Nilsson, Lennart, illus. 64p. (gr. 2-5). 1986. 17.95 (0-448-18990-9, G&D) Putnam Pub Group.
—Being Born. Nilsson, Lennart, illus. (ps-1). 1992. pap. 11.95 (0-399-22225-1, Putnam) Putnam Pub Group.
Kizer, Kathryn. God Made... Sealy, Kathy, illus. (Orig.). (ps). 1988. pap. 3.50 (0-936625-43-0, New Hope AL) Womans Mission Union.
—Tell Me about Prayer. Gross, Karen, ed. 64p. (Orig.). (gr. 1-3). 1993. pap. 4.95 (1-56309-067-8, New Hope AL) Womans Mission Union.
—Two Hundred Plus Games & Fun Activities for Teaching Preschoolers. (Illus.). 72p. (Orig.). (ps). 1989. pap. text ed. 4.95 (0-936625-70-8, New Hope AL) Womans Mission Union.
Kizer, Kathryn W. The Harley Shields: Alaskan Missionaries. LC 84-5821. (gr. k-3). 1984. 5.95 (0-8054-4285-5, 4242-85) Broadman.
Kjelgaard, Jim. Big Red. 224p. (gr. 4-7). 1992. pap. 3.99 (0-553-15434-6, Skylark) Bantam.
—Big Red. Kuhn, Bob, illus. 254p. (gr. 6 up). 1956. 15.95 (0-8234-0007-7) Holiday.
—Desert Dog. LC 56-14250. (gr. 5 up). 1975. pap. 2.75 (0-553-15491-5) Bantam.
—Haunt Fox. 160p. 1981. pap. 2.50 (0-553-15547-4) Bantam.
—Haunt Fox. 1981. pap. 3.99 (0-553-15743-4) Bantam.
—Haunt Fox. (gr. 4-7). 1992. 16.00 (0-8446-6593-2) Peter Smith.
—Irish Red: Son of Big Red. large type ed. (gr. 4-8). 1984. pap. 3.50 (0-553-15546-6) Bantam.
—Lion Hound. (gr. 4-8). 1983. pap. 2.95 (0-553-15427-3) Bantam.
—A Nose for Trouble. 1984. pap. 3.50 (0-553-15578-4) Bantam.
—Outlaw Red. (gr. 4-8). 1977. pap. 2.75 (0-553-15535-0) Bantam.
—Outlaw Red. 230p. (gr. 6 up). 1953. 15.95 (0-8234-0084-0) Holiday.
—Outlaw Red. 1988. pap. 3.50 (0-553-15686-1) Bantam.
—Snow Dog. 160p. 1980. pap. 2.95 (0-553-15365-X) Bantam.
—Snow Dog. 1983. pap. 3.50 (0-553-15560-1) Bantam.
—Snow Dog. (gr. 4-7). 1992. 16.50 (0-8446-6595-9) Peter Smith.
—Stormy. 160p. (gr. 4-8). 1983. pap. 3.99 (0-553-15468-0, Skylark) Bantam.

—Wild Trek. 272p. 1981. pap. 2.75 (0-553-15466-4) Bantam.
—Wild Trek. 1984. pap. 3.99 (0-553-15687-X) Bantam.
—Wild Trek. (gr. 4-7). 1992. 16.50 (0-8446-6594-0) Peter Smith.
Kjellander, Mike. Power Slalom - Twenty-Eight Breakthrough Concepts for Mastering the Sport. Robertson, Jo, ed. (Illus.). 100p. (Orig.). 1989. pap. 14.95 (0-944406-06-8) World Pub FL.
Klabacken, Joan, jt. auth. see Lepthien, Emilie U.
Klar, Elizabeth. TAAS Quick Review Mathematics: Grade 3. (Illus.). 128p. (gr. 3). 1991. pap. text ed. 15.95 (0-944459-31-5) ECS Lrn Systs.
Klar, Elizabeth & Cunningham, Beverly. TAAS Quick Review Mathematics: Grade 5. (Illus.). 112p. (gr. 5). 1992. pap. text ed. 14.95 (0-944459-32-3) ECS Lrn Systs.
Klar, Elizabeth, jt. auth. see Cunningham, Beverly.
Klare, Judy. Manners. (Illus.). 32p. (gr. 5 up). 1990. PLB 15.94 (0-86625-419-6); PLB 11.95s.p. (0-685-36384-8) Rourke Corp.
Klarich, Tony. Hot Dog Slalom Skiing: An Illustrated Guide to over Thirty Amazing Maneuvers. Robertson, Jo, ed. (Illus.). 128p. (Orig.). (gr. 7 up). 1988. pap. 11.95 (0-944406-02-5) World Pub FL.
Klas, Nell. McDurfee: Billy's Special Pal. Picha, Amy, illus. 20p. (Orig.). (gr. k-3). 1991. pap. 4.00 (0-9628560-0-2) N Klas.
Klass, David. California Blue. LC 93-13705. 224p. (gr. 7 up). 1994. 13.95 (0-590-46688-7) Scholastic Inc.
—A Different Season. LC 87-19969. 208p. (gr. 7 up). 1988. 14.95 (0-525-67237-0, Lodestar Bks) Dutton Child Bks.
—Wrestling with Honor. LC 88-16147. 208p. (gr. 7 up). 1989. 14.95 (0-525-67268-0, Lodestar Bks) Dutton Child Bks.
—Wrestling with Honor. 208p. (gr. 8-12). 1990. pap. 2.95 (0-590-43187-0) Scholastic Inc.
Klass, Sheila S. The Bennington Stitch. 144p. (gr. 7-12). 1986. pap. 2.50 (0-553-26049-9) Bantam.
—Credit-Card Carole. 144p. 1989. pap. 2.95 (0-553-27355-8, Starfire) Bantam.
—Kool Ada. (gr. 4-7). 1991. 13.95 (0-590-43902-2, Scholastic Hardcover) Scholastic Inc.
—Kool Ada. 04/1993 ed. (gr. 4-7). pap. 2.95 (0-590-43903-0) Scholastic Inc.
—Page Four. 176p. 1988. pap. 2.95 (0-553-26901-1, Starfire) Bantam.
Klassen, Julie. The Adventures of Heart Longing. LC 86-82881. 128p. (gr. 1-6). 1987. pap. 2.95 (0-88243-557-4, 02-0557) Gospel Pub.
Klatt, Mary J., jt. ed. see Brazouski, Antoinette.
Klaus, Sandra. Chris Finds the Answer. Bates, Stephen, illus. 20p. (gr. k-6). 1988. pap. text ed. 4.25 (1-55976-127-X) CEF Press.
—Life Is Valuable. Hilterbrand, Greg, illus. (gr. k-6). 1987. pap. 4.25 (1-55976-152-0) CEF Press.
—Mustapha's Secret. (Illus.). 42p. (gr. k-6). 1988. 8.99 (1-55976-075-3) CEF Press.
—Mustapha's Secret: A Muslim Boy's Search to Know God. Espe, Marvin, illus. 42p. (gr. 2-7). 1988. pressboard cover, plastic bdg. 9.95 (0-9617490-1-6) Gospel Missionary.
—Pythons & Book Reports. Bates, Steve, illus. 51p. (gr. k-6). 1987. pap. text ed. 6.99 (1-55976-178-4) CEF Press.
—Surrounded by Headhunters. (Illus.). 32p. (gr. k-6). 1986. 8.99 (1-55976-076-1) CEF Press.
—Surrounded by Headhunters. Espe, Marvin, illus. 32p. (gr. 2-7). 1986. pressboard cover, plastic bdg. 9.95 (0-9617490-0-8) Gospel Missionary.
Klaus, Tom. If Your Parent Drinks Too Much. 96p. (Orig.). (gr. 7-12). 1990. pap. 7.99 (1-55945-006-1) Group Pub.
Klause, Annette C. Alien Secrets. LC 92-31326. 1993. 14.95 (0-385-30928-7) Delacorte.
—The Silver Kiss. (gr. 9 up). 1990. 14.95 (0-385-30160-X) Delacorte.
—The Silver Kiss. 208p. (gr. 7 up). 1992. pap. 3.50 (0-440-21346-0, LFL) Dell.
Klausmeier, Robert, ed. see Greene, Carol.
Klausner, Janet. Sequoyah's Gift: A Portrait of the Cherokee Leader. King, Duane, afterword by. LC 92-24939. (Illus.). 128p. (gr. 4 up). 1993. 15.00 (0-06-021235-7); PLB 14.89 (0-06-021236-5) HarpC Child Bks.
—Talk about English: How Words Travel & Change. Doniger, Nancy, illus. LC 89-49116. 208p. (gr. 5 up). 1990. 14.95 (0-690-04831-9, Crowell Jr Bks) (Crowell Jr Bks) HarpC Child Bks.
—The White Elephant: Modern Expressions & the Ancient Stories Behind Them. Wawiorka, Matthew, illus. LC 93-4373. 1994. 16.00 (0-06-023564-0); PLB 15.89 (0-06-023565-9) HarpC Child Bks.
Klaveness, Jan O. Beyond the Cellar Door. (gr. 4-7). 1993. pap. 2.95 (0-590-43022-X) Scholastic Inc.
—Ghost Island. (gr. k-12). 1987. pap. 2.95 (0-440-93097-9, LFL) Dell.
—The Griffin Legacy. (gr. 4-6). 1985. pap. 3.25 (0-440-43165-4, YB) Dell.
—Keeper of the Light. LC 90-38530. 224p. (gr. 7 up). 1990. 12.95g (0-688-06996-7) Morrow Jr Bks.
Klawitter, P. Bookworks. 64p. (gr. 4-8). 1993. 8.95 (0-88160-212-4, LW204) Learning Wks.
—Mapworks. LC 92-81914. 48p. (gr. 4-8). 1992. 5.95 (0-88160-206-X, LW254) Learning Wks.
—Poetry Parade. (gr. 4-6). 1987. 5.95 (0-88160-156-X, LW 274) Learning Wks.

—Wordwise. (gr. 7-12). 1989. 5.95 (0-88160-193-4, LW1009) Learning Wks.
Klawitter, Pamela A. Book Report Bandstand. 48p. (gr. 4-6). 1987. 5.95 (0-88160-149-7, LW262) Learning Wks.
—Book Report Beagle. 48p. (gr. 1-4). 1987. 5.95 (0-88160-148-9, LW143) Learning Wks.
Kleckner. Humor, Reading Level 2. (Illus.). 32p. (gr. 1-4). 1989. PLB 15.74 (0-86592-399-X); lib. bdg. 11.95 (0-685-58783-5) Rourke Corp.
Kleeberg, Irene C. Fund Raising. Rakos, Jennie, ed. LC 88-5655. (Illus.). 72p. (gr. 4-9). 1988. 10.90 (0-531-10583-0) Watts.
Kleef Douthit, Gretchen Van see Van Kleef Douthit, Gretchen.
Kleg, Milton, jt. auth. see Totten, Samuel.
Klein, Alan. Carousel Horses. 1991. 6.95 (0-533-09160-8) Vantage.
Klein, Dave. Stars of the Major Leagues. LC 73-18739. (Illus.). 160p. (gr. 7-12). 1974. lib. bdg. 3.69 (0-394-92762-1) Random Bks Yng Read.
Klein, David. To See or Not to See. (Illus.). 32p. (gr. 1-6). 1986. incl. audiocassette 29.28 (0-8172-2472-6) Raintree Steck-V.
Klein, David J. Irwin the Sock. LC 87-16535. (Illus.). 32p. (gr. 2-4). 1987. PLB 17.96 (0-8172-3157-9) Raintree Steck-V.
—Irwin the Sock. (Illus.). 32p. (gr. 2-4). 1987. incl. audiocassette 29.28 (0-8172-2473-4) Raintree Steck-V.
—Irwin the Sock. (ps-3). 1993. pap. 3.95 (0-8114-5211-5) Raintree Steck-V.
Klein, Gerda W. Peregrinations: Adventures with the Green Parrot. Chabela, Elizabeth H., illus. LC 86-80966. 48p. (gr. 3-4). 1986. 12.95 (0-9616699-0-X); pap. 5.95 (0-9616699-1-8) CHB Goodyear Comm.
Klein, H. Arthur, ed. see Busch, Wilhelm.
Klein, Hannah E. Brief Adventures of Agnes, a Camel, & Her Good Friend Shopworth. 1991. 6.95 (0-533-09153-5) Vantage.
Klein, John F. & Gaskin, Carol. A Day in the Life of a Commercial Fisherman. Klein, John F., illus. LC 87-10949. 32p. (gr. 4-8). 1988. PLB 11.79 (0-8167-1109-7); pap. text ed. 2.95 (0-8167-1110-0) Troll Assocs.
Klein, Leab. Nechama on Strike. 144p. (Orig.). (gr. 4-9). 1993. pap. 7.95 (1-56871-029-1) Targum Pr.
Klein, Leah. The B. Y. Times: Here We Go Again, No. 9. 1992. pap. 7.95 (0-944070-90-6) Targum Pr.
—B. Y. Times, No. 1: Shani's Scoop. 1993. pap. 7.95 (0-685-65290-4) Feldheim.
—B. Y. Times, No. 10: The New Kids. 1993. pap. 7.95 (0-685-65299-8) Feldheim.
—B. Y. Times, No. 11: Dollars & Sense. 1993. pap. 7.95 (1-56871-005-4) Feldheim.
—B. Y. Times, No. 12: Talking It Over. 1993. pap. 7.95 (1-56871-010-0) Feldheim.
—B. Y. Times, No. 2: Batya's Search. 1993. pap. 7.95 (0-685-65291-2) Feldheim.
—B. Y. Times, No. 3: Twins in Trouble. 1993. pap. 7.95 (0-685-65292-0) Feldheim.
—B. Y. Times, No. 4: War! 1993. pap. 7.95 (0-685-65293-9) Feldheim.
—B. Y. Times, No. 5: Spring Fever. 1993. pap. 7.95 (0-685-65294-7) Feldheim.
—B. Y. Times, No. 6: Party Time. 1993. pap. 7.95 (0-685-65295-5) Feldheim.
—B. Y. Times, No. 7: Changing Times. 1993. pap. 9.95 (0-685-65296-3) Feldheim.
—B. Y. Times, No. 8: Summer Daze. 1993. pap. 7.95 (0-685-65297-1) Feldheim.
—B. Y. Times, No. 9: Here We Go Again. 1993. pap. 7.95 (0-685-65298-X) Feldheim.
—The B. Y. Times: Summer Daze, No. 8. 7.95 (0-944070-83-3) Targum Pr.
—The B. Y. Times: The New Kids, No. 10. 1992. pap. 7.95 (0-944070-91-4) Targum Pr.
—Flying High. 200p. (gr. 6-9). 1993. pap. 9.95 (1-56871-019-4) Targum Pr.
—Kid Sisters, No. 1: The I-Can't-Cope Club. 1993. pap. 5.95 (0-685-65300-5) Feldheim.
—Kid Sisters, No. 2: The Treehouse Kids. 1993. pap. 5.95 (0-685-65301-3) Feldheim.
—Kid Sisters, No. 3: Ricky's Great Idea. 1993. pap. 5.95 (1-56871-004-6) Feldheim.
—Kid Sisters, No. 4: Sarah's Room. 1993. pap. 5.95 (1-56871-008-9) Feldheim.
Klein, Norma. The Cheerleader. LC 85-224. (Illus.). 144p. (gr. 7-12). 1985. lib. bdg. 11.99 (0-394-97574-4); pap. 11.95 (0-394-87577-X) Knopf Bks Yng Read.
—Girls Can Be Anything. Doty, Roy, illus. LC 72-85258. 32p. (ps-1). 1975. 11.95 (0-525-30662-5, DCB) pap. 3.95 (0-525-45029-7, DCB) Dutton Child Bks.
—Going Backwards. 92p. (gr. 7 up). 1986. pap. 12.95 (0-590-40328-1) Scholastic Inc.
—Just Friends. LC 89-11148. 192p. (gr. 7 up). 1990. PLB 13.99 (0-679-90213-9) Knopf Bks Yng Read.
—Just Friends. 160p. 1991. pap. 3.95 (0-449-70352-5, Juniper) Fawcett.
—Learning How to Fall. 1989. 14.95 (0-553-05809-6, Starfire) Bantam.
—No More Saturday Nights. LC 88-678. 288p. (gr. 7 up). 1988. 12.95 (0-394-81944-6); lib. bdg. 13.99 (0-394-91944-0) Knopf Bks Yng Read.
—Now That I Know. LC 87-32080. 160p. (gr. 7 up). 1988. 13.95 (0-553-05472-4) Bantam.
—Older Men. 192p. 1988. pap. 2.95 (0-449-70261-8, Juniper) Fawcett.

—Visiting Pamela. Chorao, Kay, illus. LC 78-72203. (ps-3). 1979. Dial Bks Young.
Klein, Patricia, ed. Growing up Born Again. (Illus.). 160p. (gr. 10 up). 1987. pap. 7.99 (0-8007-5259-7) Revell.
Klein, Robin. All in the Blue Unclouded Weather. (gr. 3-7). 1992. 11.95 (0-670-83909-4) Viking Child Bks.
—Boris & Borsch. Wilcox, Cathy, illus. 32p. (Orig.). (gr. k-4). 1993. 16.95 (0-04-442266-0) Pub. by Allen & Unwin Aust Pty AT); pap. 6.95 (1-86373-048-6, Pub. by Allen & Unwin Aust Pty AT) IPG Chicago.
—Boss of the Pool. 96p. (gr. 3-7). 1992. pap. 3.99 (0-14-036037-9) Puffin Bks.
—Came Back to Show You I Could Fly. 196p. (gr. 4 up). 1990. pap. 11.95 (0-670-82901-3) Viking Child Bks.
—Dresses of Red & Gold. 184p. (gr. 5-9). 1993. 12.50 (0-670-84733-X) Viking Child Bks.
—Enemies. (gr. 4-7). 1991. pap. 2.50 (0-590-43689-9) Scholastic Inc.
—Penny Pollard in Print. James, Ann, illus. 64p. (gr. 4 up). 1988. bds. 10.95 (0-19-554638-5) OUP.
—Penny Pollard's Diary. James, Ann, illus. 56p. (ps-6). 1987. pap. 7.00 (0-19-554649-0) OUP.
—Penny Pollard's Letters. James, Ann, illus. 64p. (ps-6). 1987. 10.95 (0-19-554575-3) OUP.
—Penny Pollard's Passport. James, Ann, illus. 74p. (gr. 6 up). 1990. bds. 10.95 (0-19-554868-X) OUP.
—Seeing Things. 200p. (gr. 7 up). 1994. 12.50 (0-670-85282-1) Viking Child Bks.
—Tearaways: Stories to Make You Think Twice. 144p. (gr. 5-9). 1991. 12.95 (0-670-83212-X) Viking Child Bks.
Klein, Tom. Loon Magic for Kids. 48p. 1990. 14.95 (1-55971-047-0); pap. 6.95 (1-55971-121-3) NorthWord.
—Loon Magic for Kids. LC 90-9860. (Illus.). 48p. (gr. 3-4). 1990. PLB 18.60 (0-8368-0402-3) Gareth Stevens Inc.
Klein, Tom & Wolpert, Tom. Animal Magic for Kids Series, 6 vols. (Illus.). 1991. Set. PLB 111.60 (0-8368-0659-X) Gareth Stevens Inc.
Klein, William J. Learning under the Sun. (Illus.). 392p. (gr. 7-12). 1988. pap. 24.95 (0-8138-1038-1); tchrs. manual 7.00 (0-8138-1041-8) Iowa St U Pr.
Klein, Zanvel, ed. see Skutina, Vladimir.
Kleinbard, Gitel. Oh, Zalmy! Or, Tales of Two Esthers, Bk. 3. Vorhand, Rachel, illus. (gr. 1-4). 1979. pap. 3.95 (0-917274-05-9) Mah Tov Pubns.
—Oh, Zalmy! Or, the Tale of the Porcelain Pony, Bk. 1. (Illus.). (gr. k-3). 1976. 5.95 (0-917274-04-0); pap. 3.95 (0-917274-01-6) Mah Tov Pubns.
—Oh, Zalmy! or, the Tale of the Tooth: Book 2. Kunda, Shmuel, illus. (gr. k-3). 1977. 5.95 (0-917274-02-4); pap. 3.95 (0-917274-03-2) Mah Tov Pubns.
Klein-Ehlich, Tzvia. A Children's Treasure of Sephardic Tales. Galitzer, Channa, illus. 64p. (gr. 4-10). 1985. 11.95 (0-89906-787-5); pap. 8.95 (0-89906-788-3) Mesorah Pubns.
Kleinman, Estelle, ed. see Papagapitos, Karen.
Kleitsch, Christel. Cousin Markie & Other Disasters. LC 91-34641. (Illus.). 96p. (gr. 2-4). 1992. 13.00 (0-525-44891-8, DCB) Dutton Child Bks.
Kleitsch, Christel & Kelley, True. It Happened at Pickle Lake. (Illus.). 64p. (gr. 2-5). 1993. 11.99 (0-525-45058-0, DCB) Dutton Child Bks.
Kleman, James & Kleman, MaryLouise. Stateside. (gr. 4up). 1982. 14.00 (0-938464-06-X) JML Enter MD.
Kleman, James, jt. auth. see Kleman, Mary L.
Kleman, James A. Short Shots..A Drill a Day: The Easy Way to Language Literacy. 2nd ed. 44p. (gr. 4-8). 1982. manual 5.00 (0-938464-09-4) JML Enter MD.
Kleman, Mary L. & Kleman, James. Listening Comprehension Training Program: Manuals A-E. 40p. (gr. 4-8). 1982. manual 5.00 (0-938464-01-9) JML Enter MD.
Kleman, MaryLouise, jt. auth. see Kleman, James.
Klemin, Diana. How Do You Wrap a Horse? Demarest, Chris L., illus. 32p. (ps-3). 1993. 14.95 (1-56397-187-9) Boyds Mills Pr.
Klettenheimer, Ingrid. Great Paper Craft Projects. LC 91-43519. (Illus.). 64p. (gr. 8-12). 1992. 14.95 (0-8069-8556-9) Sterling.
—Great Paper Folding Projects. LC 91-46524. (Illus.). 64p. (gr. 8-12). 1992. 14.95 (0-8069-8554-2) Sterling.
Kletter, Lenore. Santabear's High Flying Adventure. (Illus.). 32p. (gr. 1-3). 1987. 12.99 (0-9619204-0-8) Santabear Bks.
Klevan, Miriam. West Indian Americans. Moynihan, Daniel P., intro. by. (Illus.). 112p. (gr. 5 up). 1990. lib. bdg. 17.95 (1-55546-140-9) Chelsea Hse.
Kleven, Elisa. Ernst. Kleven, Elisa, illus. LC 89-1634. 32p. (ps-3). 1989. 11.95 (0-525-44515-3, DCB) Dutton Child Bks.
—Ernst. (Illus.). 32p. (ps-3). 1993. pap. 4.50 (0-14-054944-7, Puffin Unicorn) Puffin Bks.
—The Lion & the Little Red Bird. LC 91-36691. (Illus.). 32p. (ps-2). 1992. 13.50 (0-525-44898-5, DCB) Dutton Child Bks.
—The Paper Princess. LC 93-32612. (Illus.). 1994. write for info. (0-525-45231-1, DCB) Dutton Child Bks.
Klevin, Jill R. The Turtle Street Trading Co. Edwards, Linda S., illus. LC 82-70312. 144p. (gr. 4-6). 1982. 11.95 (0-385-29043-8); PLB 11.95 (0-685-05625-2) Delacorte.
—Turtles Together Forever! Edwards, Linda S., illus. LC 82-70313. 160p. (gr. 4-6). 1982. pap. 9.95 (0-385-29045-4); pap. 9.89 (0-385-29046-2) Delacorte.

Kliment, Bud. Billie Holiday. King, Coretta Scott, intro. by. (Illus.). 112p. (gr. 5 up). 1990. lib. bdg. 17.95 (1-55546-592-7) Chelsea Hse.
—Billie Holiday: Black Americans of Achievement. (gr. 4-7). 1992. pap. 7.95 (0-7910-0241-1) Chelsea Hse.
—Count Basie. King, Coretta Scott, intro. by. (Illus.). 112p. (gr. 5 up). 1992. lib. bdg. 17.95 (0-7910-1118-6) Chelsea Hse.
—Ella Fitzgerald. King, Coretta Scott, intro. by. (Illus.). 112p. (Orig.). (gr. 5 up). 1989. 17.95 (1-55546-586-2); pap. 9.95 (0-7910-0220-9) Chelsea Hse.
Klimo, Joan F. What Can I Do Today? A Treasury of Crafts for Children. Klimo, Joan F., illus. LC 73-15110. 64p. (gr. k-3). 1974. pap. 2.95 (0-394-82809-7) Pantheon.
Klimo, Kate, ed. see Boynton, Sandra.
Klimo, Kate, ed. see Durrell, Julie.
Klimo, Kate, ed. see Miller, Suzanne S.
Klimo, Kate, ed. see Moskowitz, Stewart.
Klimo, Kate, ed. see Schongut, Emanuel.
Klimo, Kate, ed. see Tallarico, Tony.
Klimo, Kate, ed. see Williams, Margery.
Klimo, Kate, ed. see Zokeisha.
Kline, M., ed. see Bright, Michael.
Kline, M., ed. see Carter, Alden R.
Kline, M., ed. see Gay, Kathlyn.
Kline, M., ed. see Graham, Ian.
Kline, M., ed. see Hodge, Anthony.
Kline, M., ed. see Jennings, Terry.
Kline, M., ed. see Kosof, Anna.
Kline, M., ed. see Lampton, Christopher.
Kline, M., ed. see McGowen, Tom.
Kline, M., ed. see Mills, Judie.
Kline, M., ed. see Nourse, Alan E.
Kline, M., ed. see Petty, Kate.
Kline, M., ed. see Stwertka, Eve.
Kline, M., ed. see Tauber, Gerald E.
Kline, Marjory, ed. see Bailey, Donna.
Kline, Marjory, ed. see Bellew, Bob.
Kline, Marjory, ed. see Caldecott, Barrie.
Kline, Marjory, ed. see Davies, Eryl.
Kline, Marjory, ed. see Devonshire, Hilary.
Kline, Marjory, ed. see Ganeri, Anita.
Kline, Marjory, ed. see Hodge, Anthony.
Kline, Marjory, ed. see Humble, Richard.
Kline, Marjory, ed. see Lambert, David & Wright, Rachel.
Kline, Marjory, ed. see Maxwell, Colin.
Kline, Marjory, ed. see Parker, Steve.
Kline, Marjory, ed. see Steele, Philip.
Kline, Marjory, ed. see Turvey, Peter.
Kline, Marjory, ed. see Watts, Barrie.
Kline, Marjory, ed. see Wright, Rachel.
Kline, Paula. Tu Cuerpo: El Aprendizaje A Traves el Cuerpo y los Sentidos. 160p. (ps-3). 1993. tchr's. guide incl. audio cass. 24.00 (0-9637958-0-5) Inst Promo Educ.
Kline, Rufus. Watch Out for These Weirdos. Carlson, Nancy, illus. 32p. (ps-3). 1990. pap. 12.95 (0-670-82376-7) Viking Child Bks.
—Watch Out for These Weirdos! Carlson, Nancy, illus. 32p. (ps-3). 1992. pap. 3.99 (0-14-050907-0, Puffin) Puffin Bks.
Kline, Susan. Horrible Harry & the Green Slime. Remkiewicz, Frank, illus. 64p. (gr. 2-5). 1989. pap. 10. 95 (0-670-82468-2) Viking Child Bks.
Kline, Suzy. Don't Touch! Tucker, Kathleen, ed. Leder, Dora, illus. LC 85-612. 32p. (ps-1). 1985. 13.95 (0-8075-1707-0) A Whitman.
—Don't Touch! Leder, Dora, illus. 32p. (gr. 2-6). 1988. pap. 3.95 (0-14-050861-9, Puffin) Puffin Bks.
—Herbie Jones. Williams, Richard, illus. LC 84-24915. 96p. (gr. 2-6). 1985. 13.95 (0-399-21183-7, Putnam) Putnam Pub Group.
—Herbie Jones. Williams, Richard, illus. 96p. (gr. 3-7). 1986. pap. 3.95 (0-14-032071-7, Puffin) Puffin Bks.
—Herbie Jones & Hamburger Head. Williams, Richard, illus. 112p. (gr. 2-6). 1989. 13.95 (0-399-21748-7, Putnam) Putnam Pub Group.
—Herbie Jones & Hamburger Head. (gr. 4-7). 1991. pap. 3.95 (0-14-034583-3, Puffin) Puffin Bks.
—Herbie Jones & the Birthday Showdown. 96p. (gr. 2-6). 1993. 14.95 (0-399-22600-1, Putnam) Putnam Pub Group.
—Herbie Jones & the Class Gift. Williams, Richard, illus. 96p. (gr. 2-6). 1987. 12.95 (0-399-21452-6, Putnam) Putnam Pub Group.
—Herbie Jones & the Class Gift. Williams, Richard, illus. 96p. (gr. 3-7). 1989. pap. 3.99 (0-14-032723-1, Puffin) Puffin Bks.
—Herbie Jones & the Dark Attic. Williams, Richard, illus. 112p. (gr. 2-6). 1992. 14.95 (0-399-21838-6, Putnam) Putnam Pub Group.
—Herbie Jones & the Monster Ball. Williams, Richard, illus. 112p. (gr. 2-6). 1988. 12.95 (0-399-21569-7, Putnam) Putnam Pub Group.
—Herbie Jones & the Monster Ball. Williams, Richard, illus. 128p. (gr. 3 up). 1990. pap. 3.99 (0-14-034170-6, Puffin) Puffin Bks.
—The Herbie Jones Reader's Theater. Williams, Richard, illus. 160p. (gr. 2-6). 1992. pap. 8.95 (0-399-22120-4, Putnam) Putnam Pub Group.
—The Hole Book. Newton, Laurie, illus. 24p. (ps-k). 1989. 9.95 (0-399-21719-3, Putnam) Putnam Pub Group.
—Horrible Harry & the Ant Invasion. Remkiewicz, Frank, illus. 64p. (gr. 2-5). 1989. pap. 11.00 (0-670-82469-0) Viking Child Bks.

—Horrible Harry & the Ant Invasion. Remkiewicz, Frank, illus. 64p. (gr. 2-5). 1991. 2.95 (0-14-032914-5) Puffin Bks.
—Horrible Harry & the Christmas Surprise. Remkiewecz, Frank, illus. 64p. (gr. 2-5). 1991. 10.95 (0-670-83357-6) Viking Child Bks.
—Horrible Harry & the Christmas Surprise. Remkiewicz, Frank, illus. LC 93-15137. 64p. (gr. 2-5). 1993. pap. 2.99 (0-14-034452-7, Puffin) Puffin Bks.
—Horrible Harry & the Green Slime. Remkiewecz, Frank, illus. 64p. (gr. 2-5). 1991. pap. 2.99 (0-14-032913-7, Puffin) Puffin Bks.
—Horrible Harry & the Kickball Wedding. Remkiewicz, Frank, illus. LC 92-5827. 64p. (gr. 2-5). 1992. 11.00 (0-670-83358-4) Viking Child Bks.
—Horrible Harry in Room Two B. 31p. 1992. text ed. 2.48 (1-56956-113-3) W A T Braille.
—Horrible Harry in Room 2B. Remkiewicz, Frank, illus. (gr. 2-5). 1988. pap. 10.95 (0-670-82176-4) Viking Child Bks.
—Horrible Harry in Room 2B. Remkiewicz, Frank, illus. 64p. (gr. 2-5). 1990. pap. 2.99 (0-14-032825-4, Puffin) Puffin Bks.
—Horrible Harry's Secret. LC 90-32482. (gr. 4-7). 1990. 11.00 (0-670-82470-4) Viking Child Bks.
—Horrible Harry's Secret. Remkiewicz, Frank, illus. 64p. (gr. 2-5). 1992. pap. 2.99 (0-14-032915-3) Puffin Bks.
—Mary Marony & the Snake. Sims, Blanche, illus. LC 90-31071. 64p. (gr. 2-6). 1992. 12.95 (0-399-22044-5, Putnam) Putnam Pub Group.
—Mary Marony Hides Out. Sims, Blanche, illus. LC 92-16064. 80p. (gr. 1-4). 1993. 13.95 (0-399-22433-5, Putnam) Putnam Pub Group.
—Mary Marony, Mummy Girl. Sims, Blanche, illus. LC 93-14348. 1994. write for info. (0-399-22609-5, Putnam) Putnam Pub Group.
—Ooops! Fay, Ann, ed. Leder, Dora, illus. LC 87-25429. 32p. (ps-2). 1988. PLB 13.95 (0-8075-6122-3) A Whitman.
—Ooops! Leder, Dora, illus. 32p. (ps). 1989. pap. 3.95 (0-14-050986-0, Puffin) Puffin Bks.
—Orp. 96p. (gr. 3-7). 1989. 13.95 (0-399-21639-1, Putnam) Putnam Pub Group.
—Orp. 96p. 1990. pap. 3.50 (0-380-71038-2, Camelot) Avon.
—Orp & the Chop Suey Burgers. (Illus.). 112p. (gr. 4-8). 1990. 13.95 (0-399-22185-9, Putnam) Putnam Pub Group.
—Orp & the Chop Suey Burgers. (gr. 4). 1992. pap. 3.50 (0-380-71359-4, Camelot) Avon.
—Orp Goes to the Hoop. 96p. 1991. 13.95 (0-399-21834-3, Putnam) Putnam Pub Group.
—Orp Goes to the Hoop. 96p. (gr. 4). 1993. pap. 3.50 (0-380-71829-4, Camelot) Avon.
—Song Lee in Room Two B. Remkiewicz, Frank, illus. 64p. (gr. 2-5). 1993. RB 10.99 (0-670-84772-0) Viking Child Bks.
—What's the Matter with Herbie Jones? Williams, Richard, illus. (gr. 3-7). pap. 3.95 (0-317-62246-3, Puffin) Puffin Bks.
—Who's Orp's Girlfriend? 112p. (gr. 3-6). 1993. 13.95 (0-399-22431-9, Putnam) Putnam Pub Group.
Kline, Suzy W. SHHHH! Fay, Ann, ed. LC 83-26032. (Illus.). (ps-1). 1984. PLB 11.95 (0-8075-7321-3) A Whitman.

Kling, Imogene. The Tree Frog Sings. Gibbs, Jeanne, ed. Kling, Fred, illus. 32p. (gr. k-2). 1993. PLB 14.95X (0-932762-19-0) Ctr Source Pubns. This is a delightful book for children, ages 4 to 8, but with a symbolic message for readers of any age. Four-color illustrations express the magical beauty of the fine garden in which Buffy, the tree frog lives. The story tells us that... Buffy is a one inch long tree frog who is tired of having three cats, many birds, large toads & bigger frogs frighten him away from the beautiful garden. More than anything he longs for his own quiet time beside the fountain. One day he decides he will not hide anymore, but will do something different. He climbs the garden wall, & to everyone's surprise finds an exciting magical way to sound bigger than he ever has been before. The whimsical story will appeal to anyone who has ever felt too small or insignificant in the midst of larger noisy creatures...& who also may have longed for the space to sing his or her own song in a quiet garden at sunset. Volume discounts available from Publisher: Center Source Publications, 805 Tesconi Circle, Santa Rosa, CA

95401, Phone: 707-577-8233.
Publisher Provided Annotation.

Klingel, Cindy. Women of America: Dolly Madison. (gr. 2-4). 1987. PLB 14.95s.p. (*0-88682-167-3*) Creative Ed.
—Women of America: Elizabeth Blackwell. rev. ed. (gr. 2-4). 1987. PLB 14.95s.p. (*0-88682-169-X*) Creative Ed.
—Women of America: Harriet Tubman. (gr. 2-4). 1987. PLB 14.95s.p. (*0-88682-166-5*) Creative Ed.
Klingel, Cynthia. Bicycle Safety. (Illus.). 32p. (ps-3). 1986. PLB 12.95s.p. (*0-88682-085-5*) Creative Ed.
—Safety First: Fire. LC 86-72672. (ps up). 1986. PLB 12.95s.p. (*0-88682-080-4*) Creative Ed.
Klingel, Cynthia & Zadra, Dan. Clara Barton. (Illus.). 32p. 1987. PLB 14.95s.p. (*0-88682-168-1*) Creative Ed.
—Jane Addams. (Illus.). 32p. 1987. PLB 14.95s.p. (*0-88682-165-7*) Creative Ed.
—Susan B. Anthony. (Illus.). 32p. 1987. PLB 14.95s.p. (*0-88682-164-9*) Creative Ed.
Klingel, Cynthia F. Safety First - School. LC 86-72593. (ps up). 1986. PLB 12.95s.p. (*0-88682-084-7*) Creative Ed.
—Safety First - Water. LC 86-72673. (ps up). 1986. PLB 12.95s.p. (*0-88682-083-9*) Creative Ed.
Klingel, Fitterer. Home Safety. (Illus.). 32p. (ps up). 1986. PLB 12.95s.p. (*0-88682-081-2*) Creative Ed.
—Outdoor Safety. (Illus.). 32p. (ps up). 1986. PLB 12.95s.p. (*0-88682-082-0*) Creative Ed.
Klingsheim, Arild. Julius. (gr. 4-7). 1991. pap. 4.95 (*0-440-40431-2*) Dell.
Klinker, Philip A., et al. The American Heritage History of the Bill of Rights, 10 vols. Burger, Warren E. (Illus.). (gr. 7 up). 1991. Set, 128-184p. ea. PLB 299.00 (*0-382-24190-8*) Silver Burdett Pr.
Klipper, Ilse. Magic Journey. Osborne, Gretchen, illus. 83p. (Orig.). (gr. k-5). 1983. pap. 5.95 (*0-9605022-1-1*) Pathwys Pr CA.
—My Magic Garden. Green, Maureen, et al, illus. 91p. (Orig.). (gr. 2-6). 1980. pap. 5.95 (*0-9605022-0-3*) Pathwys Pr CA.
Kliros, Thea, adapted by see Burgess, Thornton W.
Klischer, Beth, ed. see Dickens, Charles.
Klitzner, Carol. Reading Books for Science: A Study Guide. Friedland, Joyce & Kessler, Rikki, eds. (gr. 1-3). 1991. pap. text ed. 19.95 (*0-88122-691-2*) LRN Links.
Kllair, Bevan. Elferina & the Christmas Cha Cha. LC 79-91132. (ps-6). 1979. pap. 3.00 (*0-935712-00-3*) B A Scott.
—The Ziggle Dance at the Zoo. LC 79-91133. (ps-6). 1979. pap. 3.00 (*0-935712-01-1*) B A Scott.
Klobas, John. Life Cycle of the Pacific Gray Whale. Rovetta, Ane, illus. 32p. (gr. 6-9). 1993. 12.95 (*0-89346-532-1*) Heian Intl.
Klopsteg, Paul E. & Reichart, Natalie. Turkish Archery; &, Modern Methods in Archery, 2 vols. in 1. St. Charles, Glenn, frwd. by. (Illus.). (gr. 10 up). 1993. Repr. 39.95 (*1-56416-093-9*) Derrydale Pr.
Klose, Hyacinthe. Celebrated Method for the Clarinet: Complete Edition. Bellison, Simeon, ed. 293p. (Orig.). 1946. pap. 18.95 (*0-8258-0051-X*, 0304) Fischer Inc NY.
Klots, Steve. Ida Wells-Barnett, Civil Rights Leader. LC 93-14250. (gr. 5 up). 1994. write for info. (*0-7910-1885-7*); pap. write for info. (*0-7910-1914-4*) Chelsea Hse.
—Richard Allen. KIng, Coretta Scott, intro. by. (Illus.). 112p. (gr. 5 up). 1991. lib. bdg. 17.95 (*1-55546-570-6*) Chelsea Hse.
Klotter, James C. Our Kentucky; a Study of the Bluegrass State. LC 91-48220. 360p. 1992. 29.00 (*0-8131-1783-6*, F451) U Pr of Ky.
Klug, Lyn, jt. auth. see Klug, Ron.
Klug, Lyn, jt. ed. see Klug, Ron.
Klug, Ron. You Promised, Lord: Prayers for Boys. LC 83-70502. 80p. (Orig.). (gr. 3-7). 1983. pap. 5.99 (*0-8066-2008-0*, 10-7417, Augsburg) Augsburg Fortress.
Klug, Ron & Klug, Lyn. Jesus Comes: the Story of Jesus' Birth for Children. Konsterile, Paul, illus. LC 86-81808. 32p. (Orig.). (gr. 3-8). 1986. pap. 5.99 saddlestitch (*0-8066-2234-2*, 10-3497, Augsburg) Augsburg Fortress.
—Jesus Lives. LC 82-72848. 32p. (Orig.). (ps). 1982. pap. 5.99 (*0-8066-1952-X*, 10-3527, Augsburg) Augsburg Fortress.
—Jesus Loves: Stories about Jesus for Children. Konsterile, Paul, illus. LC 86-81807. 32p. (Orig.). (gr. 3-8). 1986. saddlestitch 5.99 (*0-8066-2235-0*, 10-3526, Augsburg) Augsburg Fortress.
Klug, Ron & Klug, Lyn, eds. The Christian Family Christmas Book. LC 87-1391. (Illus.). 128p. (ps-7). 1987. text ed. 14.99 (*0-8066-2270-9*, 10-1113, Augsburg) Augsburg Fortress.
Klugman, Miriam. Captain David. 100p. 1991. 9.95 (*1-56062-095-1*) CIS Comm.
Klusmeyer, Joann. Shelly from Rockytop Farm. Taylor, Neil, illus. 65p. (gr. 3-6). 1986. 5.95 (*1-55523-014-8*) Winston-Derek.
—The Us 4 Ever Club. (Illus.). 96p. (gr. 4-7). 1987. pap. 3.99 (*0-570-03644-5*, 39-1128) Concordia.
—What about Me? (Illus.). (gr. 4-7). 1987. 3.99 (*0-570-03641-0*, 39-1125) Concordia.

Klutz Press Editors. KidsShenanigans: Great Things to Do That Mom & Dad Will Just Barely Approve Of. 1992. 13.95 (*1-878257-41-2*) Klutz Pr.
Klutz Press Staff. The Klutz Book of Jacks. (Illus.). 30p. (Orig.). 1989. pap. 7.95 incl. jacks, ball & pouch (*0-932592-21-X*) Klutz Pr.
—The Klutz Book of Marbles. (Illus.). 30p. (Orig.). 1989. pap. 7.95 incl. marbles, shooter & pouch (*0-932592-22-8*) Klutz Pr.
Klyce, Katherine P., jt. auth. see McLean, Virginia O.
Knack, John W., Sr., jt. auth. see Grimes, Harriette H.
Knapik, Jane A. Sarah's Flag for Texas. Wilson, Jo K., illus. LC 93-16171. (gr. 3-6). 1993. 12.95 (*0-89015-900-9*) Eakin-Sunbelt.
Knapke, William F. & Hubbard, Freeman. Railroad Caboose. LC 67-28316. (Illus.). (gr. 10 up). 1968. 29.95 (*0-87095-011-8*) Gldn West Bks.
Knapp, Brian. Drought. LC 89-19730. (Illus.). 48p. (gr. 5-9). 1990. PLB 19.92 (*0-8114-2376-X*) Raintree Steck-V.
—Earthquake. LC 89-21574. (Illus.). 48p. (gr. 5-9). 1990. PLB 19.92 (*0-8114-2375-1*) Raintree Steck-V.
—Fire. LC 89-11423. (Illus.). 48p. (gr. 5-9). 1990. PLB 19.92 (*0-8114-2377-8*) Raintree Steck-V.
—Flood. LC 89-11437. (Illus.). 48p. (gr. 5-9). 1990. PLB 19.92 (*0-8114-2374-3*) Raintree Steck-V.
—Storm. LC 89-11536. (Illus.). 48p. (gr. 5-9). 1990. PLB 19.92 (*0-8114-2372-7*) Raintree Steck-V.
—Volcano. LC 89-11584. (Illus.). 48p. (gr. 5-9). 1990. PLB 19.92 (*0-8114-2373-5*) Raintree Steck-V.
—What Do We Know about Rainforests? LC 92-5187. (Illus.). 40p. (gr. 4-6). PLB 15.95 (*0-87226-358-4*) P Bedrick Bks.
—What Do We Know about the Grasslands? LC 92-7888. (Illus.). 40p. (gr. 4-6). 1992. PLB 15.95 (*0-87226-359-2*) P Bedrick Bks.
Knapp, Elsie M. & Faithful, Denise. Numbers Mean More Than You Think. 51p. (gr. 6 up). 1974. pap. 3.00 (*0-686-05514-4*) Sandollar Pr.
Knapp, John, II. My Book of Bible Rhymes. Deckert, Dianne T., illus. LC 87. 1987. 13.95 (*1-55513-161-1*, 51615, Chariot Bks) Cook.
Knapp, Paul E. False Positive. LC 89-51296. 167p. 1990. 7.95 (*1-55523-260-4*) Winston-Derek.
Knapp, Ron. Sports Great Barry Sanders. LC 92-38432. (Illus.). 64p. (gr. 4-10). 1993. lib. bdg. 15.95 (*0-89490-418-3*) Enslow Pubs.
—Sports Great Bo Jackson. LC 89-29059. (Illus.). 64p. (gr. 4-10). 1990. lib. bdg. 15.95 (*0-89490-281-4*) Enslow Pubs.
—Sports Great Bobby Bonilla. LC 92-38431. (Illus.). 64p. (gr. 4-10). 1993. lib. bdg. 15.95 (*0-89490-417-5*) Enslow Pubs.
—Sports Great Hakeem Olajuwon. LC 91-41526. (Illus.). 64p. (gr. 4-10). 1992. lib. bdg. 15.95 (*0-89490-372-1*) Enslow Pubs.
—Sports Great Isiah Thomas. LC 91-41528. (Illus.). 64p. (gr. 4-10). 1992. lib. bdg. 15.95 (*0-89490-374-8*) Enslow Pubs.
—Sports Great Orel Hershiser. LC 92-11329. (Illus.). 64p. (gr. 4-10). 1993. lib. bdg. 15.95 (*0-89490-389-6*) Enslow Pubs.
—Sports Great Will Clark. LC 92-521. (Illus.). 64p. (gr. 4-10). 1993. lib. bdg. 15.95 (*0-89490-390-X*) Enslow Pubs.
Knapp, Toni, ed. The Gossamer Tree: A Christmas Fable. Brown, Craig M., illus. LC 88-90759. 32p. (Orig.). (gr. 2 up). 1988. 14.95 (*1-882092-00-7*); pap. 8.95 (*1-882092-02-3*) Travis Ilse.
—The Six Bridges of Humphrey the Whale. Brown, Craig M., illus. LC 89-8417. 48p. (gr. 8 up). 1989. 15.95 (*1-882092-01-5*) Travis Ilse.
Knappert, Jan. Kings, Gods & Spirits from African Mythology. Pelizzoli, Francesca, illus. LC 93-12903. 88p. (gr. 6 up). 1993. 22.50 (*0-87226-916-7*); pap. 12.95 sewn (*0-87226-917-5*) P Bedrick Bks.
Knecht, F. J. Child's Bible History. Schumacher, Philip, tr. (Illus.). (gr. 5). 1973. pap. 4.00 (*0-89555-005-9*) TAN Bks Pubs.
Knecker, Don, illus. The First Christmas According to Luke. 32p. (ps-4). 1993. incl. dust jacket 15.99 (*0-570-04753-6*) Concordia.
Kneeland, Linda. Cookie. Fargo, Todd, illus. 32p. (ps-3). 1992. Repr. of 1989 ed. 13.95 (*0-944727-16-6*) Jason & Nordic Pubs.
Kneeland, Linda C. Cookie. Fargo, Todd, illus. 32p. (ps-2). 1989. pap. 6.95 (*0-944727-05-0*) Jason & Nordic Pubs.
Kneen. Twelve Days of Christmas: A Revolving Picture Book. (Illus.). 12p. (ps-6). 1992. 13.95 (*0-525-44654-0*, DCB) Dutton Child Bks.
Kneen, Maggie. Too Many Cooks: And Other Proverbs. LC 91-4455. (ps-3). 1992. 13.00 (*0-671-78120-0*, Green Tiger) S&S Trade.
—Who's Getting Ready for Christmas? Kneen, Maggie, illus. LC 93-11061. (gr. 4-7). 1993. 13.95 (*0-8118-0470-4*) Chronicle Bks.
Kneidel, Sally S. Creepy Crawlies & the Scientific Method: Over 100 Hands-on Science Experiments for Children. LC 92-53033. (Illus.). 224p. (Orig.). 1993. pap. 15.95 (*1-55591-118-8*) Fulcrum Pub.
Kneissler, Irmgard. Origami for Children. Jonas, Dieter, illus. LC 92-453. 64p. (ps up). 1992. PLB 19.93 (*0-516-09261-8*) Childrens.
—Origami for Children. Jonas, Dieter, illus. LC 92-453. 64p. (ps up). 1993. pap. 8.95 (*0-516-49261-6*) Childrens.

Knief, William. The Golden Monster. Weber, Susan M., illus. 30p. (Orig.). 1971. pap. 1.00 staple bound (*0-685-30030-7*) Cottonwood KS.
Kniffen, Fred. Indians of Louisiana. LC 91-8499. (Illus.). 108p. (gr. 6-12). 1976. 13.95 (*0-911116-97-4*) Pelican.
Knight, Arthur. The Liveliest Art: A Panoramic History of the Movies. rev. ed. (Illus.). 384p. (gr. 9-12). 1979. pap. 5.99 (*0-451-62652-4*, Ment) NAL-Dutton.
Knight, Christopher, photos by. Monarchs. Lasky, Kathryn, text by. LC 92-33972. (Illus.). 1993. 16.95 (*0-15-255296-0*); pap. 8.95 (*0-15-255297-9*) HarBrace.
Knight, Christopher G., illus. & photos by see Lasky, Kathryn.
Knight, David. Best True Ghost Stories of the 20th Century. 1987. pap. 5.95 (*0-671-66557-X*) S&S Trade.
—I Can Read About Alligators & Crocodiles. LC 78-73733. (Illus.). (gr. 2-4). 1979. pap. 1.95 (*0-89375-200-2*) Troll Assocs.
—I Can Read About Christopher Columbus. LC 78-73774. (Illus.). (gr. 2-5). 1979. pap. 1.95 (*0-89375-206-1*) Troll Assocs.
—Vasco Da Gama. LC 78-18057. (Illus.). 48p. (gr. 4-7). 1979. PLB 10.59 (*0-89375-175-8*); pap. 3.50 (*0-89375-167-7*) Troll Assocs.
Knight, David C. All about Sound. Johnson, Lewis, illus. LC 82-17387. 32p. (gr. 3-6). 1983. PLB 10.59 (*0-89375-878-7*); pap. text ed. 2.95 (*0-89375-879-5*) Troll Assocs.
—The Battle of the Dinosaurs. Ames, Lee J., illus. 96p. (gr. 3-7). 1982. (Pub. by Treehouse); pap. 5.95 (*0-13-069518-1*) P-H.
—Best True Ghost Stories of the Twentieth Century. Waldman, Neil, illus. LC 83-23075. 64p. (gr. 3-7). 1984. pap. 11.95 jacketed (*0-671-66556-1*) S&S Trade.
Knight, Denise E., ed. see Berry, Lori S.
Knight, Denise E. ed. see Higbie, William F.
Knight, Eric. Lassie Come Home. (gr. 4-7). 1992. pap. 3.50 (*0-440-40750-8*) Dell.
—Lassie Come Home. 1992. pap. 3.50 (*0-440-40760-5*) Dell.
Knight, Eric M. Lassie Come Home. 234p. 1981. Repr. PLB 16.95x (*0-89966-346-X*) Buccaneer Bks.
—Lassie Come Home. (gr. k-6). 1989. pap. 4.95 (*0-440-40136-4*, YB) Dell.
—Lassie Come Home. 224p. 1981. Repr. PLB 12.95x (*0-89967-020-2*) Harmony Raine.
—Lassie Come Home. Kirmse, Marguerite, illus. LC 78-3570. 265p. (gr. 4-6). 1978. 16.95 (*0-8050-0721-0*, Bks Young Read) H Holt & Co.
Knight, Etheridge. Belly Song & Other Poems. LC 72-90098. 50p. (Orig.). (gr. 12 up). 1973. pap. 5.00 (*0-910296-88-X*) Broadside Pr.
—Poems from Prison. LC 68-22139. (gr. 12 up). 1968. pap. 4.00 (*0-685-00870-3*); tape o.p. 5.00 (*0-685-07550-8*) Broadside Pr.
Knight, George, ed. see Laster, Jim.
Knight, Ginny. Jessie Helps a Wish. Knight, Ginny, illus. 1991. 3.00 (*0-940248-82-4*) Guild Pr.
Knight, Ginny, et al. A Sampler of Women. LC 83-82097. 60p. (Orig.). (gr. 9-12). 1984. pap. text ed. 6.50 (*0-940248-18-2*) Guild Pr.
Knight, Hilary. Christmas Nutshell Library, 4 bks. Knight, Hilary, illus. Incl. Angels & Berries & Candy Canes; Christmas Stocking Story (*0-06-023205-6*); Firefly in a Fir Tree (*0-06-023190-4*); The Night Before Christmas. LC 63-18904. (Illus.). (gr. 1 up). 1963. Set. 11.00 (*0-06-023165-3*) HarpC Child Bks.
—Cinderella. Knight, Hilary, illus. LC 80-18660. 32p. (ps-2). 1982. lib. bdg. 5.99 (*0-394-93759-7*) Random Bks Yng Read.
—Hilary Knight's the Owl & the Pussycat. LC 89-31667. (Illus.). 32p. (ps-3). 1989. pap. 3.95 (*0-689-71331-2*, Aladdin) Macmillan Child Grp.
—Hilary Knight's the Twelve Days of Christmas. Knight, Hilary, illus. LC 87-1137. 34p. (ps up). 1987. pap. 4.95 (*0-689-71150-6*, Aladdin) Macmillan Child Grp.
—Where's Wallace? Knight, Hilary, illus. LC 64-19717. (ps-3). 1964. 15.00 (*0-06-023170-X*); PLB 14.89 (*0-06-023171-8*) HarpC Child Bks.
—Where's Wallace? Knight, Hilary, illus. LC 64-19717. 48p. (ps-3). 1986. pap. 5.95 (*0-06-443094-4*, Trophy) HarpC Child Bks.
Knight, James E. Blue Feather's Vision, the Dawn of Colonial America. Guzzi, George, illus. LC 81-23082. 32p. (gr. 5-9). 1982. PLB 11.59 (*0-89375-722-5*); pap. text ed. 2.95 (*0-89375-723-3*) Troll Assocs.
—Boston Tea Party, Rebellion in the Colonies. Wenzel, David, illus. LC 81-23077. 32p. (gr. 5-9). 1982. PLB 11.59 (*0-89375-734-9*); pap. text ed. 2.95 (*0-89375-735-7*) Troll Assocs.
—The Farm, Life in Colonial Pennsylvania. Milone, Karen, illus. LC 81-23083. 32p. (gr. 5-9). 1982. PLB 11.59 (*0-89375-730-6*); pap. text ed. 2.95 (*0-89375-731-4*) Troll Assocs.
—Jamestown, New World Adventure. Wenzel, David, illus. LC 81-23086. 32p. (gr. 5-9). 1982. PLB 11.59 (*0-89375-724-1*); pap. text ed. 2.95 (*0-89375-725-X*) Troll Assocs.
—Journey to Monticello, Traveling in Colonial Times. Guzzi, George, illus. LC 81-23156. 32p. (gr. 5-9). 1982. PLB 11.59 (*0-89375-736-5*); pap. text ed. 2.95 (*0-89375-737-3*) Troll Assocs.
—Sailing to America, Colonists at Sea. Guzzi, George, illus. LC 81-23161. 32p. (gr. 5-9). 1982. PLB 11.59 (*0-89375-726-8*); pap. text ed. 2.95 (*0-89375-727-6*) Troll Assocs.

—Salem Days, Life in a Colonial Seaport. Wenzel, David, illus. LC 81-23076. 32p. (gr. 5-9). 1982. PLB 11.59 (0-89375-732-2); pap. text ed. 2.95 (0-89375-733-0) Troll Assocs.
—Seventh & Walnut, Life in Colonial Philadelphia. Guzzi, George, illus. LC 81-24036. 32p. (gr. 5-9). 1982. PLB 11.59 (0-89375-740-3); pap. text ed. 2.95 (0-89375-741-1) Troll Assocs.
—The Village, Life in Colonial Times. Palmer, Jan, illus. LC 81-23084. 32p. (gr. 5-9). 1982. PLB 11.59 (0-89375-728-4); pap. text ed. 2.95 (0-89375-729-2); cassette avail. Troll Assocs.
—The Winter at Valley Forge, Survival & Victory. Guzzi, George, illus. LC 81-23151. 32p. (gr. 5-9). 1982. PLB 11.59 (0-89375-738-1); pap. text ed. 2.95 (0-89375-739-X) Troll Assocs.
Knight, Joan. The Baby Who Would Not Come Down. Santini, Debrah, illus. LC 89-3987. 28p. (ps up). 1991. pap. 14.95 (0-88708-107-X) Picture Bk Studio.
—Bon Appetit, Bertie! Winter, Susan, illus. LC 92-54319. 32p. (ps-1). 1993. 13.95 (1-56458-195-0) Dorling Kindersley.
—Opal in the Closet. Estrada, Pau, illus. LC 91-659. 28p. (gr. k up). 1992. pap. 14.95 (0-88708-174-6) Picture Bk Studio.
Knight, Margy B. Talking Walls. O'Brien, Anne S., illus. LC 91-67867. 40p. (gr. k-8). 1992. 17.95 (0-88448-102-6) Tilbury Hse.
—Who Belongs Here? An American Story. O'Brien, Anne S., illus. 40p. (gr. 3-8). 1993. 16.95 (0-88448-110-7) Tilbury Hse.
Knight, Marilyn, jt. auth. see Links, Marty.
Knight, Marilyn, jt. auth. see Linse, Barbara.
Knight, Meribah, jt. auth. see Lasky, Kathryn.
Knight, Sarah K. The Journal of Madam Knight. LC 91-46984. 88p. 1992. pap. 7.95 (1-55709-115-3) Applewood.
Knight, Tanis & Lewin, Larry. Open the Deck. Carmichael, Stanrod, intros. by. Cahill, Bob. (gr. 6-9). 1982. text ed. 9.10 (0-933282-09-5); pap. 6.00 (0-933282-07-9) Stack the Deck.
—Tap the Deck. Hrebic, Herbert J., ed. Boehm, Terrie W., illus. (Orig.). (gr. 5-6). 1985. text ed. 9.10 (0-933282-18-4); pap. text ed. 6.00 (0-933282-17-6) Stack the Deck.
Knight, Theodore. The Olympic Games. LC 91-15562. (Illus.). 112p. (gr. 5-8). 1991. PLB 14.95 (1-56006-119-7) Lucent Bks.
Knill, Harry. American Revolution. (gr. 1-9). 1992. pap. 3.95 (0-88388-021-0) Bellerophon Bks.
—Ancient Africa, Vol. II. (gr. 1-9). 1993. pap. 2.50 (0-88388-174-8) Bellerophon Bks.
—The Black Cowboy. (gr. 1-9). 1993. pap. 2.50 (0-88388-176-4) Bellerophon Bks.
—Cleopatra. (gr. 1-9). 1993. pap. 2.50 (0-88388-175-6) Bellerophon Bks.
—Great American Inventors. (gr. 1-9). 1992. pap. 3.95 (0-88388-183-7) Bellerophon Bks.
—The Iliad. (gr. 1-9). Date not set. pap. 3.95 (0-88388-179-9) Bellerophon Bks.
—Japan. (gr. 1-9). 1992. pap. 3.95 (0-88388-006-7) Bellerophon Bks.
—Magnificient Helmets. (gr. 1-9). 1992. pap. 6.95 (0-88388-167-5) Bellerophon Bks.
—Old Cars. (gr. 1-9). Date not set. pap. 3.95 (0-88388-145-4) Bellerophon Bks.
—Our Fighting Men & Women. (gr. 1-9). 1992. pap. 2.50 (0-88388-172-1) Bellerophon Bks.
—Rosie & the Bear. (gr. 1-9). 1992. pap. 3.95 (0-88388-055-5) Bellerophon Bks.
—Southern Soldiers of American Revolution. (gr. 1-9). 1992. pap. 3.95 (0-88388-164-0) Bellerophon Bks.
—The Story of Early California to 1849, Vol. 1. Archambault, Alan, illus. 48p. (Orig.). (gr. 4 up). 1988. pap. 3.95 (0-88388-129-2) Bellerophon Bks.
—The Thirteen Colonies. (gr. 1-9). 1992. pap. 3.95 (0-88388-103-9) Bellerophon Bks.
Knill, Harry, jt. auth. see Nunis.
Knill, Harry, ed. see Vallejo, Mariano, et al.
Knill, Henry, jt. auth. see Tomb, Eric.
Knobbe, Czeslaw, ed. & tr. see Sikirycki, Igor.
Knobbe, Jeff C. The Train. 16p. (gr. 4 up). 1993. pap. 3.95 (0-9630328-0-1); 7.95 (0-9630328-5-2) SDPI.
Knobloch, Madge. Havasupai Years. (gr. 9 up). 1988. pap. 8.95 (0-89992-117-5, NO. 117-5) Coun India Ed.
Knoedler, Michael. Callie's Way Home. 160p. (gr. 6-12). 1991. pap. 3.95 perfect bdg. (0-89486-729-6, T5116) Hazelden.
Knoepfel, Marilyn & Farber, Betty. Look, I'm Growing Up. Hutton, Kathryn, illus. 32p. (gr. k-2). 1991. pasted 2.50 (0-87403-819-7, 24-03919) Standard Pub.
Knoles, David. Spooky Magic Tricks. Knoles, David, illus. LC 93-1642. 128p. (gr. 3-10). 1993. 12.95 (0-8069-0418-6) Sterling.
Knopf, Jerry E. The Zebra with No Stripes. 1993. 7.95 (0-533-10365-7) Vantage.
Knot, Madonna. Sex for Straights: A Call for Critical Thinking by Teenagers Who Oppose Sexual Perversion. Rachner, Mary J., intro. by. Turner, William, illus. 34p. (gr. 7-12). 1993. PLB 49.95 (0-9623133-5-1) Oxner Inst.
Knowledge Unlimited Staff. Afghanistan: The Long Fight for Freedom. (Illus.). 22p. (gr. 4-12). 1983. incl. filmstrip, cass., guide 28.00 (0-915291-00-2) Know Unltd.
—The Earth Exhales: The Story of Volcanoes. (Illus.). 28p. (gr. 7 up). 1983. incl. filmstrip, cass., guide 25.00 (0-915291-02-9) Know Unltd.

—Energy: Conserving a Vital Resource. (Illus.). 19p. (Orig.). (gr. 4-12). 1984. tchr's guide 13.00 (0-915291-22-3) Know Unltd.
Knowledge Unlimited Staff, ed. What Is Money: From Barter to Banking. (Illus.). 21p. (gr. 4-12). incl. 2 filmstrips, 2 cass., 2 guides 66.00 (0-915291-34-7) Know Unltd.
—What Is Money: The Ups & Downs of the Money Supply. (Illus.). 27p. (gr. 4-12). 1984. incl. 2 filmstrips, 2 cass., 2 guides 66.00 (0-915291-27-4) Know Unltd.
Knowles, Andrew. The Crossroad Children's Bible. (Illus.). 448p. (gr. 4-8). 1982. pap. 9.95 (0-8245-0473-9) Crossroad NY.
—Discovering Prayer. LC 92-44876. (Illus.). 128p. (gr. 10 up). 1993. 9.99 (0-7459-2644-4) Lion USA.
Knowles, Anne. Under the Shadow. LC 82-48857. 128p. (gr. 5 up). 1983. HarpC Child Bks.
Knowles, B., jt. auth. see Kisner, R.
Knowles, Brooke, jt. auth. see Kisner, Rita.
Knowles, James, compiled by. King Arthur & His Knights. Rhead, Louis & Wheelwright, Rowland, illus. 416p. 1986. 12.99 (0-517-61885-0) Outlet Bk Co.
Knowles, John. Separate Peace. (gr. 7 up). 1985. pap. 3.95 (0-553-28041-4) Bantam.
Knowles, Sheena. Edward the Emu. (ps-3). 1992. pap. 7.00 (0-207-17051-7, Pub. by Angus & Robertson AT) HarpC.
Knowlton, Jack. Books & Libraries. Barton, Harriett, illus. LC 89-70804. 48p. (gr. 2-5). 1991. PLB 14.89 (0-06-021610-7) HarpC Child Bks.
—Books & Libraries. Barton, Harriett, illus. LC 89-70804. 48p. (gr. 2-5). 1993. pap. 5.95 (0-06-446153-X, Trophy) HarpC Child Bks.
—Deserts of the World. Barton, Harriett, illus. LC 92-19169. 48p. (gr. 2-5). 1995. 15.00 (0-06-021309-4); PLB 14.89 (0-06-021310-8) HarpC Child Bks.
—Geography from A to Z: A Picture Glossary. Barton, Harriett, illus. LC 86-4594. 48p. (gr. 2-5). 1988. 14.00 (0-690-04616-2, Crowell Jr Bks); PLB 13.89 (0-690-04618-9) HarpC Child Bks.
—Maps & Globes. Barton, Harriett, illus. LC 85-47537. 48p. (gr. 2-5). 1985. 15.00 (0-690-04457-7, Crowell Jr Bks); PLB 14.89 (0-690-04459-3) HarpC Child Bks.
—Maps & Globes. Barton, Harriett, illus. LC 85-47537. 48p. (gr. 2-5). 1986. pap. 4.95 (0-06-446049-5, Trophy) HarpC Child Bks.
Knowlton, Mary L., tr. see Iwamura, Kazuo.
Knox, Diana. The Industrial Revolution. Yapp, Malcolm, et al, eds. (Illus.). (gr. 6-11). 1980. pap. text ed. 3.45 (0-89908-108-8) Greenhaven.
Knox, Jean. Death & Dying. Koop, C. Everett, intro. by. (Illus.). 112p. (gr. 6-12). 1989. 18.95 (0-7910-0037-0) Chelsea Hse.
—Learning Disabilities. (Illus.). (gr. 6-12). 1989. 18.95 (0-7910-0049-4); pap. 9.95 (0-7910-0529-1) Chelsea Hse.
Knox, Jean M. Drinking, Driving & Drugs. Mendelson, Jack H. & Mello, Nancyintro. by. (Illus.). 112p. (gr. 5 up). 1988. lib. bdg. 19.95x (1-55546-231-6); pap. 9.95 (0-7910-0783-9) Chelsea Hse.
—Drinking, Driving & Drugs. (Illus.). 32p. (gr. 5 up). 1991. pap. 4.49 (1-55546-997-3) Chelsea Hse.
—Drugs Through the Ages. Mendelson, Jack H. & Mello, Nancyintro. by. (Illus.). 112p. (gr. 5 up). 1987. lib. bdg. 19.95x (1-55546-221-9) Chelsea Hse.
Knox, Jeri A. Introducing Nikki & Kiana. 82p. (Orig.). (gr. 6-10). Date not set. pap. text ed. 7.00 (1-880679-03-5) Mtn MD.
Knox, Montye S. My Day in the Country. 1991. 6.95 (0-533-09308-2) Vantage.
Knudsen, Eric A. Spooky Stuffs: Hawaiian Ghost Stories. Kaye, Sally, ed. Buffet, Guy, illus. LC 74-80510. 64p. 1987. pap. 7.95 (0-89610-047-2) Island Heritage.
Knudson, R. R. Babe Didrikson: Athlete of the Century. Lewin, Ted, illus. 64p. (gr. 2-6). 1986. pap. 3.95 (0-14-032095-4, Puffin) Puffin Bks.
—Fox Running. 128p. (gr. 7 up). 1977. pap. 2.50 (0-380-00930-7, 60286-5, Flare) Avon.
—Just Another Love Story. (gr. 7 up). 1984. pap. 2.50 (0-380-65532-2, 60172-9, Flare) Avon.
—Martina Navratilova: Tennis Power. Angelini, George, illus. LC 85-40832. 64p. (gr. 2-6). 1986. pap. 10.95 (0-670-80665-X) Viking Child Bks.
—Rinehart Lifts. 88p. (gr. 4-7). 1982. pap. 1.95 (0-380-57059-9, 57059-9, Camelot) Avon.
—Rinehart Shouts. LC 86-29540. 115p. (gr. 4 up) 1987. 13.00 (0-374-36296-3) FS&G.
—Sanboomer. 192p. (gr. 6 up) 1980. pap. 1.95 (0-440-99908-1, LFL) Dell.
—The Wonderful Pen of May Swenson. LC 93-637. (Illus.). 128p. (gr. 3-9). 1993. SBE 13.95 (0-02-750915-X, Macmillan Child Bk) Macmillan Child Grp.
—You Are the Rain. LC 73-15397. 160p. (gr. 7 up). 1974. pap. 5.95 (0-440-08759-7) Delacorte.
Knudson, R. R. & Swenson, May, eds. American Sports Poems. LC 87-24384. 240p. (gr. 6 up). 1988. 15.95 (0-531-05753-4); PLB 15.99 (0-531-08353-5) Orchard Bks Watts.
Knudson, Richard L. Rallying. LC 80-17863. (Illus.). 48p. (gr. 4-9). 1981. PLB 14.95 (0-8225-0445-6) Lerner Pubns.
Knuppel, Helga. The Adventures of Christabel Crocodile. LC 90-21029. (Illus.). 32p. (ps-5). 1991. 13.95 (0-940793-74-1, Crocodile Bks) Interlink Pub.
—Christabel Crocodile's Birthday Egg. Knuppel, Helga, illus. LC 92-24360. 32p. (ps-3). 1993. 13.95 (1-56656-113-2, Crocodile Bks) Interlink Pub.

Knutson, Barbara. How the Guinea Fowl Got Her Spots. (ps-3). 1991. pap. 6.95 (0-87614-537-3) Carolrhoda Bks.
—How the Guinea Fowl Got Her Spots: A Swahili Tale of Friendship. Knutson, Barbara, illus. 24p. (ps-4). 1990. PLB 18.95 (0-87614-416-4) Carolrhoda Bks.
—Why the Crab Has No Head: An African Folktale. (Illus.). 24p. (ps-3). 1987. lib. bdg. 15.95 (0-87614-322-2); pap. 4.95 (0-87614-489-X) Carolrhoda Bks.
Knutson, Barbara, retold by. & illus. Sungura & Leopard: A Swahili TricksterTale. LC 92-31905. 1993. 15.95 (0-316-50010-0) Little.
Knutson, C. M. North Dakota. 24p. (Orig.). (gr. k-6). 1986. pap. 1.00 (0-938451-01-4) Selena Pr.
Knutson, Kimberley. Muddigush. LC 91-15393. (Illus.). 32p. (ps-1). 1992. RSBE 13.95 (0-02-750843-9, Macmillan Child Bk) Macmillan Child Grp.
Knutson, Kimberly. Ska-Tat! Knutson, Kimberley, illus. LC 92-38072. 32p. (ps-1). 1993. RSBE 14.95 (0-02-750846-3, Macmillan Child Bk) Macmillan Child Grp.
Ko, Tonya, tr. see La Fonatine, Jean de.
Kobaine, Chayale. A House Full of Guests. (gr. 4-5). 1991. 16.95 (1-56062-103-6); pap. 8.95 (1-56062-104-4) CIS Comm.
Kobayashi, Kiyoshi & Sharp, Harold E. Sport of Judo: As Practiced in Japan. LC 57-75. (Illus.). 104p. (gr. 9 up). 1957. pap. 9.95 (0-8048-0542-3) C E Tuttle.
Kobayashi, Robert. Maria Mazaretti Loves Spaghetti. Kobayashi, Robert, illus. LC 90-20015. 40p. (ps-2). 1991. 14.00 (0-679-81659-3); lib. bdg. 14.99 (0-679-91659-8) Knopf Bks Yng Read.
Kobayashi, Yuji. Miss Josephine's Secret Walk. (Illus.). 32p. (ps-2). 1991. 12.95 (0-88138-096-2, Green Tiger) S&S Trade.
Kobeh, Ana G., jt. auth. see Kurtycz, Marcos.
Kobre, Faige. A Sense of Shabbat. LC 89-40361. (Illus.). 32p. 1990. 11.95 (0-933873-44-1) Torah Aura.
Koch, Carl, ed. Dreams Alive: Prayers by Teenagers. St. George, Carolyn, illus. 88p. (Orig.). (gr. 9-12). 1991. pap. 4.95 (0-88489-262-X) St Marys.
Koch, Frances K. Mariculture: Farming the Fruits of the Sea. Roxas, Reni, ed. (Illus.). 56p. (gr. 5-8). 1992. 15.95 (0-531-15239-1); PLB 15.90 (0-531-11116-4) Watts.
Koch, Janice. Our Baby: A Birth & Adoption Story. Goldberg, Pat, illus. LC 85-6392. 27p. (ps-2). 1985. 10.95 (0-9609504-3-5) Perspect Indiana.
Koch, Karl-Heinz. Pencil & Paper Games. LC 90-24245. (Illus.). 128p. (gr. 7-12). 1992. pap. 4.95 (0-8069-8263-2) Sterling.
Koch, Kenneth & Farrell, Kate. Talking to the Sun: An Illustrated Anthology of Poems for Young People. LC 85-15428. 112p. (ps up). 1985. 22.95 (0-8050-0144-1, Bks Young Read) H Holt & Co.
Koch, Michelle. By the Sea. LC 89-23344. (Illus.). 24p. (ps up). 1991. 13.95 (0-688-09549-6); PLB 13.88 (0-688-09550-X) Greenwillow.
—Hoot, Howl, Hiss. LC 90-38484. (Illus.). 24p. (ps up). 1991. 13.95 (0-688-09651-4); PLB 13.88 (0-688-09652-2) Greenwillow.
—Just One More. LC 88-17736. (Illus.). 32p. (ps up). 1989. 11.95 (0-688-08127-4); PLB 11.88 (0-688-08128-2) Greenwillow.
—World Water Watch. LC 91-48371. (Illus.). 32p. (ps up). 1993. 14.00 (0-688-11464-4); PLB 13.93 (0-688-11465-2) Greenwillow.
Koch, Susan C. Colormore Travels - Austin, Texas: The Travel Guide for Kids. Koch, Susan C., illus. 32p. (Orig.). (gr. k-4). 1988. pap. 4.50 (0-945600-00-3) Colormore Inc.
—Colormore Travels - Ft. Worth, Texas: The Travel Guide for Kids. Koch, Susan C., illus. (Orig.). (gr. k-4). 1989. pap. 4.50 (0-945600-02-X) Colormore Inc.
—Colormore Travels - San Antonio, Texas: The Travel Guide for Kids. Koch, Susan C., illus. (Orig.). (gr. k-4). 1990. pap. 4.50 (0-945600-05-4) Colormore Inc.
Kochevitsky, George. Art of Piano Playing: A Scientific Approach. (Illus.). 80p. (gr. 9 up). 1967. pap. text ed. 11.95 (0-87487-068-2) Summy-Birchard.
Koci, Marta. Katie's Kitten. LC 82-60893. (Illus.). 28p. (ps-2). 1991. pap. 14.95 (0-907234-21-6) Picture Bk Studio.
—Katie's Kitten. (gr. k up). 1991. pap. 4.95 (0-88708-181-9) Picture Bk Studio.
—Sarah's Bear. LC 86-30241. (Illus.). 28p. (ps). 1991. pap. 14.95 (0-88708-038-3) Picture Bk Studio.
Koda-Callan, Elizabeth. The Cat Next Door. (Illus.). 40p. (ps-3). 1993. 12.95 (1-56305-502-3, 3502) Workman Pub.
—Good Luck Pony. LC 90-50366. 40p. (ps-3). 1990. 12.95 (0-89480-859-1, 1859) Workman Pub.
—The Magic Locket. Koda-Callan, Elizabeth, illus. LC 88-5508. 40p. (ps-3). 1988. 12.95 (0-89480-602-5, 1602) Workman Pub.
—Shiny Skates. LC 92-50293. (ps-3). 1992. 12.95 (1-56305-309-8, 3309) Workman Pub.
—The Silver Slippers. Koda-Callan, Elizabeth, illus. LC 89-40370. 40p. (ps-3). 1989. 12.95 (0-89480-618-1, 1618) Workman Pub.
—The Tiny Angel. LC 91-50386. (Illus.). 40p. (ps-3). 1991. 12.95 (1-56305-120-6, 3120) Workman Pub.
Koebner, Linda. For Kids Who Love Animals. 160p. (Orig.). 1993. pap. 4.50 (0-425-13632-9) Berkley Pub.
—For Kids Who Love Animals: A Guide to Sharing the Planet. (Illus.). 150p. (Orig.). (gr. 2-7). 1991. pap. 6.95 (1-879326-03-5) Living Planet Pr.

—Zoo Book. 128p. 1994. 13.95 (*0-312-85322-X*) Forge NYC.
Koechlin, Lionel. Apartment for Rent. (Illus.). 32p. (gr. k-2). 1991. 18.50 (*0-89565-742-2*); 12.95s.p. (*0-685-55070-2*) Childs World.
—The Love Affair of Mr. Ding & Mrs. Dong. (Illus.). 32p. (gr. k-2). 1991. 18.50 (*0-89565-817-8*); 12.95s.p. (*0-685-55076-1*) Childs World.
—Lulu & the Artist. (Illus.). 32p. (gr. k-2). 1991. 18.50 (*0-89565-741-4*); 12.95s.p. (*0-685-55077-X*) Childs World.
Koehler, Ed, jt. auth. see Logan, Anna.
Koehler, Michael & Wilson, Judy. School's Cool. (gr. 3-5). 1989. incl. 6 cass., 6 posters, guide 49.95 (*0-89290-800-9*) Soc for Visual.
Koehler, Phoebe. The Day We Met You. LC 89-35344. 32p. (ps-k). 1990. SBE 13.95 (*0-02-750901-X*, Bradbury Pr) Macmillan Child Grp.
—Making Room. Koehler, Phoebe, illus. LC 91-41356. 48p. (ps-3). 1993. SBE 14.95 (*0-02-750875-7*, Bradbury Pr) Macmillan Child Grp.
Koehler-Pentacoff, Elizabeth. Curtain Call. (Illus.). 80p. (gr. k-6). 1989. pap. text ed. 7.95 (*0-86530-065-8*, IP 166-4) Incentive Pubns.
Koehn, Ilse. Mischling, Second Degree: My Childhood in Nazi Germany. LC 77-6189. 240p. (gr. 7 up). 1977. PLB 14.93 (*0-688-84110-4*) Greenwillow.
—Mischling, Second Degree: My Childhood in Nazi Germany. 240p. (gr. 6 up). 1990. pap. 4.95 (*0-14-034290-7*, Puffin) Puffin Bks.
Koeleman, Paul. Dr. Paul's Amazing Eyewear. (ps-3). 1993. 12.95 (*0-8478-5707-7*) Rizzoli Intl.
—Dr. Paul's Amazing Eyewear. 10p. (Orig.). (ps-3). 1993. pap. 12.95 (*1-55550-883-9*) Universe.
Koenig, Andrea. Thumbelina: The Journal of a Young Girl. LC 93-30652. 1994. 15.00 (*0-06-023338-9*, Festival); PLB 14.89 (*0-06-023339-7*, Festival) HarpC Child Bks.
Koenig, Herbert G., et al. RCT Science Review. 6th ed. Gamsey, Wayne H., ed. Fairbanks, Eugene B., illus. 288p. (gr. 7-12). 1992. pap. text ed. 5.17 (*0-935487-09-3*) N & N Pub Co.
—Earth Science: A Concise Competency Review. rev. ed. Gamsey, Wayne, ed. Fairbanks, Eugene B., illus. 96p. (gr. 7-12). 1991. pap. text ed. 4.11 (*0-935487-44-1*) N & N Pub Co.
—Life Science: A Concise Competency Review. rev. ed. Gamsey, Wayne, ed. Fairbanks, Eugene B., illus. 96p. (gr. 7-12). 1991. pap. text ed. 4.11 (*0-935487-42-5*) N & N Pub Co.
—Physical Science: A Concise Competency Review. rev. ed. Gamsey, Wayne, ed. Fairbanks, Eugene B., illus. 96p. (gr. 7-12). 1991. pap. text ed. 4.11 (*0-935487-46-8*) N & N Pub Co.
Koenig, John. Narrow Bartholomew. (ps up). 1988. pap. 2.50 (*0-8198-5104-3*, CH0404) St Paul Bks.
Koenig, Norma E. The Runaway Heart. (Orig.). (gr. 4-6). 1981. pap. 4.95 (*0-377-00112-0*) Friendship Pr.
Koenig, Teresa & Bell, Rivian. Eddie Murphy. (Illus.). 48p. (gr. 4-9). 1985. PLB 13.50 (*0-8225-1602-0*) Lerner Pubns.
Koenig, Viviane. The Ancient Egyptians: Life in the Nile Valley. LaRose, Mary K., tr. from FRE. Ageorges, Veronique, illus. LC 91-25772. 64p. (gr. 4-6). 1992. PLB 14.90 (*1-56294-161-5*) Millbrook Pr.
Koertge, Ron. The Arizona Kid. (gr. 9 up). 1988. 14.95 (*0-316-50101-8*, Joy Street Bks) Little.
—The Arizona Kid. 224p. (gr. 7 up). 1989. pap. 3.50 (*0-380-70776-4*, Flare) Avon.
—The Boy in the Moon. 176p. 1992. pap. 3.99 (*0-380-71474-4*, Flare) Avon.
—Boy in the Moon, Vol. 1. (gr. 4-7). 1990. 15.95 (*0-316-50102-6*, Joy St Bks) Little.
—Harmony Arms. 1992. 15.95 (*0-316-50104-2*, Joy St Bks) Little.
—Mariposa Blues. 1991. 15.95 (*0-316-50103-4*) Little.
—Mariposa Blues. 176p. 1993. pap. 3.50 (*0-380-71761-1*, Flare) Avon.
—Tiger, Tiger, Burning Bright. 160p. (gr. 5 up). 1994. 14.95 (*0-531-06840-4*); lib. bdg. 14.99 RLB (*0-531-08690-9*) Orchard Bks Watts.
—Where the Kissing Never Stops. LC 86-10947. 224p. (gr. 7 up). 1986. 14.95 (*0-316-50096-8*) Little.
—Where the Kissing Never Stops. (gr. k-12). 1988. pap. 2.95 (*0-440-20167-5*) Dell.
—Where the Kissing Never Stops. 224p. 1993. pap. 3.50 (*0-380-71796-4*, Flare) Avon.
Koester, Pat. Careers in Fashion Retailing. Rosen, Ruth, ed. (gr. 7-12). 1990. PLB 13.95 (*0-8239-1007-5*) Rosen Group.
Koff, Richard M. Christopher. Kelly, Orly, ed. Reinertson, Barbara, illus. LC 81-65885. 128p. (gr. 7 up). 1981. 8.95 (*0-89742-050-0*) Celestial Arts.
—Christopher. 160p. 1985. pap. text ed. 2.25 (*0-553-15363-3*) Bantam.
Koftan, Jenelle & Koftan, Kenneth. Long-Distance Grandparenting. (Illus.). 96p. (Orig.). (ps-k). 1988. pap. 12.95 (*0-945184-00-X*) Spring Creek Pubns.
—Long-Distance Grandparenting. (Illus.). 96p. (gr. k-2). 1988. pap. 12.95 (*0-945184-01-8*) Spring Creek Pubns.
—Long-Distance Grandparenting. (Illus.). 112p. (Orig.). (gr. 3-5). 1988. pap. 12.95 (*0-945184-02-6*) Spring Creek Pubns.
Koftan, Kenneth, jt. auth. see Koftan, Jenelle.
Kogan, Mark. Archivist, Vol. 1. Khotianovsky, Olga, ed. (RUS., Illus.). 300p. (Orig.). (gr. 9-12). 1990. pap. text ed. write for info. (*0-9624922-0-5*) Hazar NY.

—Mother, Father, Big Sopha & Me. Chotianovsky, Olga, ed. Kogan, Mark, illus. 104p. (Orig.). 1991. pap. text ed. 6.00 (*0-9624922-2-1*) Hazar NY.
—Zabavi Nasmeshlivoi Zvezdi. Chotianovsky, Olga, ed. Kogan, Mark, illus. 129p. (Orig.). 1991. pap. text ed. 9.00 (*0-9624922-3-X*) Hazar NY.
Kogawa, Joy. Naomi's Road. Gould, Matt, illus. 82p. (Orig.). (gr. 3 up). 1988. pap. 7.50 (*0-19-540547-1*) OUP.
Koger, Dorothy P. DPK Inspirations: Little Hearts - Little Minds. 50p. 1994. pap. 5.00 (*1-882821-04-1*) DPK Pubns.
—DPK Inspirations: Little Minds - Little Hearts. 56p. (gr. 6-8). 1994. pap. 5.00 (*1-882821-03-3*) DPK Pubns.
Koh, Frances M. Korean Holidays & Festivals. Dodson, Liz B., illus. 32p. (gr. 2-5). 1990. PLB 14.95 (*0-9606090-5-9*) EastWest Pr.
Koh, Frances M., ed. English-Korean Picture Dictionary. Vignes, Denise S., illus. LC 87-83309. 49p. (Orig.). (ps up). 1987. pap. 7.95 (*0-9606090-3-2*) EastWest Pr.
Kohaine, Chayele. Operation C. H. E. S. E. D. & other Stories. Scheinberg, Shepsil, illus. 139p. (gr. 2-5). 1989. 10.95 (*0-935063-81-1*); pap. text ed. 7.95 (*0-935063-82-X*) CIS Comm.

Kohen, Clarita. El Agua y Tu. Barath, Judith, illus. (SPA.). 16p. (gr. k-5). 1993. PLB 7.50x (*1-56492-101-8*) Laredo.
A creative way of educating children about the importance of water conservation. An historical link with the past & present towards the future. Fully illustrated in color with simple, repetitive text. In Spanish.
Publisher Provided Annotation.

—**El Conejo y el Coyote.** Menicucci, Gina, illus. (SPA.). 16p. (Orig.). (gr. k-5). 1993. PLB 7.50x (*1-56492-100-X*) Laredo.
A humorous rhyme adaptation of a traditional Mexican tale of the rabbit & the coyote. When the coyote wants to trick the rabbit, the rabbit surprises him & proves to be more clever. Vividly illustrated with simple text for early readers. In Spanish.
Publisher Provided Annotation.

—Pajaritos. Torrecilla, Pablo, illus. 24p. (Orig.). (gr. k-3). 1993. pap. 7.50x (*1-56492-104-2*) Laredo.
—El Rabo de Gato. Sanchez, Jose R., illus. (SPA.). 16p. (gr. k-3). 1993. pap. 7.50x (*1-56492-102-6*) Laredo.
Kohen, Gabriela. The Circus. Sanchez, Jose R., illus. 24p. (Orig.). (gr. 2-6). 1992. pap. 9.95x (*1-56492-023-2*) Laredo.
—The Circus: Big Book. Sanchez, Jose R., illus. 24p. (gr. 2-6). 1992. pap. 19.95x (*1-56492-024-0*) Laredo.
—The Theatre. Sanchez, Jose R., illus. 24p. (Orig.). (gr. 2-6). 1992. pap. 9.95x (*1-56492-012-7*) Laredo.
—The Theatre: Big Book. Sanchez, Jose R., illus. 24p. (Orig.). (gr. 2-6). 1992. pap. 19.95x (*1-56492-013-5*) Laredo.
Kohen, Gabriela, tr. see Bell, Clarisa.
Kohen, Gabriele. Circus Animals. Sanchez, Jose R., illus. 24p. (Orig.). (gr. k-5). 1993. pap. 9.95x (*1-56492-026-7*) Laredo.
Kohl, Candice. The String on a Roast Won't Catch Fire in the Oven: An A-Z Encyclopedia of Common Sense for the Newly Independent Young Adult. LC 93-3961. (Illus.). 188p. 1993. pap. 12.95 (*1-880197-07-3*) Gylantic Pub.
Kohl, Herbert, jt. auth. see Kohl, Judith.
Kohl, Judith & Kohl, Herbert. Pack, Band & Colony: The World of Social Animals. La Farge, Margaret, illus. LC 82-20951. 114p. (gr. 6 up). 1983. 13.95 (*0-374-35694-7*) FS&G.
Kohl, Marguerite, jt. auth. see Young, Frederica.
Kohl, MaryAnn & Potter, Jean. ScienceArts: Discovering Science Through Art Experiences. Macleod, Andi, illus. 144p. (Orig.). (ps-4). Date not set. pap. text ed. 15.95 (*0-935607-04-8*) Bright Ring.
Kohl, MaryAnn F. Mudworks: Creative Clay, Dough, & Modeling Experiences. LC 88-92897. (Illus.). 152p. (Orig.). (ps-6). 1989. pap. 14.95 (*0-935607-02-1*) Bright Ring.
—Scribble Cookies & Other Independent Creative Art Experiences for Children. McCoy, Judy, illus. LC 85-72820. 144p. (ps-6). 1985. pap. 12.95 (*0-935607-10-2*) Bright Ring.
Kohl, MaryAnn F. & Gainer, Cindy. Good Earth Art: Environmental Art for Kids. Gainer, Cindy, illus. 224p. (Orig.). (ps-8). 1991. pap. 16.95 (*0-935607-01-3*) Bright Ring.
Kohlenbert, Sherry. Sammy's Mommy Has Cancer. Crow, Lauri, ed. LC 93-22773. (Illus.). (gr. 4 up). 1993. 16.95 (*0-945354-56-8*); pap. 8.95 (*0-945354-55-X*) Magination Pr.

Kohler, Jan. Piggy-T Goes to Town. Van Treese, James B., ed. 28p. 1992. 9.95 (*1-880416-30-1*) NW Pub.
Kohler, Pierre. Earth & the Conquest of Space. (gr. 6 up). 1988. 4.95 (*0-8120-3831-2*) Barron.
—Weather. (gr. 6 up). 1988. 4.95 (*0-8120-3833-9*) Barron.
Kohls, Tom. Gathering Fruit. 31p. 1987. pap. 3.25 (*0-8163-0701-6*) Pacific Pr Pub Assn.
—Green Cord. 31p. 1987. pap. 3.25 (*0-8163-0705-9*) Pacific Pr Pub Assn.
—The Missing Hair Net. 31p. 1987. pap. 3.25 (*0-8163-0713-X*) Pacific Pr Pub Assn.
—A Trip to Heaven. 31p. 1987. pap. 3.25 (*0-8163-0708-3*) Pacific Pr Pub Assn.
Kohn, Bernice. One Sad Day. Isaac, Barbara K., illus. LC 78-169153. 48p. 1972. 11.95 (*0-89388-026-4*) Okpaku Communications.
Kohn, Eugene. Photography: A Manual for Shutterbugs. Plasencia, Peter P., illus. Noa, Pedro A., photos by. (Illus.). (gr. 3-7). 1965. pap. 1.25 (*0-685-03891-2*) P-H.
Kohn, Valerie, jt. auth. see Harrison, Kathryn.
Kohr, Louise. In the Bag Stories: Object Talks for Children. 48p. 1990. pap. 3.50 (*0-87403-758-1*, 14-02862) Standard Pub.
Koide, Tan. May We Sleep Here Tonight? Koide, Yasuko, illus. LC 82-72247. 32p. (ps-3). 1983. SBE 12.95 (*0-689-50261-3*, M K McElderry) Macmillan Child Grp.
Koike, Kay, jt. auth. see Rehm, Karl.
Koike, Kazuo. Crying Freeman, Vol. 1. Horibuchi, Seiji, ed. Fujii, Satoru, et al, trs. from JPN. Ikegami, Ryoichi, illus. 64p. (Orig.). (gr. 12 up). 1989. pap. text ed. 3.50 (*0-929279-50-6*) Viz Commns Inc.
—Crying Freeman, Vol. 2. Horibuchi, Seiji, ed. Fujii, Satoru, et al, trs. from JPN. Ikegami, Ryoichi, illus. 64p. (Orig.). (gr. 12 up). 1989. pap. text ed. 3.50 (*0-929279-51-4*) Viz Commns Inc.
—Crying Freeman, Vol. 3. Horibuchi, Seiji, ed. Fujii, Satoru, et al, trs. from JPN. Ikegami, Ryoichi, illus. 64p. (Orig.). (gr. 12 up). 1989. pap. text ed. 3.50 (*0-929279-52-2*) Viz Commns Inc.
—Crying Freeman, Vol. 4. Horibuchi, Seiji, ed. Fujii, Satoru, et al, trs. from JPN. Ikegami, Ryoichi, illus. 64p. (Orig.). (gr. 12 up). 1990. pap. text ed. 3.50 (*0-929279-53-0*) Viz Commns Inc.
—Crying Freeman, Vol. 5. Horibuchi, Seiji, ed. Fujii, Satoru, et al, trs. from JPN. Ikegami, Ryoichi, illus. 64p. (Orig.). (gr. 12 up). 1990. pap. text ed. 3.50 (*0-929279-54-9*) Viz Commns Inc.
—Crying Freeman, Vol. 6. Horibuchi, Seiji, ed. Fujii, Satoru, et al, trs. from JPN. Ikegami, Ryoichi, illus. 64p. (Orig.). (gr. 12 up). 1990. pap. text ed. 3.50 (*0-929279-55-7*) Viz Commns Inc.
—Crying Freeman, Vol. 7. Horibuchi, Seiji, ed. Fujii, Satoru, et al, trs. from JPN. Ikegami, Ryoichi, illus. 64p. (Orig.). (gr. 12 up). 1990. pap. text ed. 3.50 (*0-929279-56-5*) Viz Commns Inc.
—Crying Freeman, Vol. 8. Horibuchi, Seiji, ed. Fugii, Satoru, et al, trs. from JPN. Ikegami, Ryoichi, illus. 64p. (Orig.). (gr. 12 up). 1990. pap. text ed. 3.50 (*0-929279-57-3*) Viz Commns Inc.
—Crying Freeman, Pt. II, Vol. 9. Horibuchi, Seiji, ed. Fujii, Satoru, et al, trs. from JPN. Ikegami, Ryoichi, illus. 72p. (Orig.). (gr. 12 up). 1991. pap. text ed. 3.75 (*0-929279-37-9*) Viz Commns Inc.
—Shades of Death, Pt. 1: Crying Freeman Graphic Novel. Horibuchi, Seiji, ed. Fujii, Satoru, tr. from JPN. Ikegami, Ryoichi, illus. 212p. (Orig.). (gr. 12 up). 1991. pap. 14.95 (*0-929279-75-1*) Viz Commns Inc.
—Shades of Death, Pt. 2: Crying Freeman Graphic Novel. Horibuchi, Seiji, ed. Fujii, Satoru, tr. from JPN. Ikegami, Ryoichi, illus. 212p. (Orig.). (gr. 12 up). 1992. pap. 14.95 (*0-929279-76-X*) Viz Commns Inc.
—Shades of Death, Pt. 3: Crying Freeman Graphic Novel. Horibuchi, Seiji, ed. Fujii, Satoru, tr. from JPN. Ikegami, Ryoichi, illus. 212p. (gr. 12 up). 1992. pap. 14.95 (*0-929279-77-8*) Viz Commns Inc.
Kojima, Takashi. Japanese Abacus: Its Use & Theory. LC 55-3550. (Illus.). 102p. (gr. 7 up). 1955. pap. 6.95 (*0-8048-0278-5*) C E Tuttle.
Koken, Tom, et al. AAA Travel Activity Book: The Official AAA Fun Book for Kids. Koken, Tom, et al, illus. 144p. 1990. pap. 4.95 (*1-56288-071-3*) Checkerboard.
Kolanovic, Dubravka. A Special Day. Thatch, Nancy R., ed. Kolanovic, Dubravka, illus. Melton, David, intro. by. LC 93-13419. (Illus.). 29p. (gr. k-2). 1993. PLB 14.95 (*0-933849-45-1*) Landmark Edns.
Kolatch, A. J. The Jewish Child's First Book of Why. LC 91-25352. 32p. 1992. 14.95 (*0-8246-0354-0*) Jonathan David.
Kolatch, Alfred J. Classic Bible Stories for Jewish Children. Araten, Harry, illus. LC 93-10165. 72p. (gr. 3 up). 1993. 14.95 (*0-8246-0362-1*) Jonathan David.
Kolb, Doris K., jt. auth. see Kolb, Kenneth E.
Kolb, James A. Hands on Puget Sound: An Interactive Workbook for the Young & Curious. Boardman, Diane, illus. 80p. (Orig.). (gr. 3-7). 1994. pap. text ed. 5.95 (*1-57061-000-2*) Sasquatch Bks.
Kolb, Kenneth E. & Kolb, Doris K. Glass: Its Many Facets. LC 86-32785. (Illus.). 64p. (gr. 6 up). 1988. lib. bdg. 15.95 (*0-89490-150-8*) Enslow Pubs.
Kolbisen, Irene M. Froggie Kicks & Duck Dives: A Child's Primer for Beginning Swimming. Reiter, John, ed. Zmolek, Sandy D., illus. Graves, Steve, intro. by. (Illus.). (ps). 1990. 12.95 (*1-877863-02-5*); pap. 8.95 (*0-685-26751-2*) I Think I Can.

—Starfish Floats & Motorboats: A Child's Primer for Beginning Swimming. Reiter, John, ed. Zmolek, Sandy D., illus. Graves, Steve, intro. by. (Illus.). 20p. (ps). 1990. 12.95g (*1-877863-01-7*); pap. 8.95g (*0-685-26750-4*) I Think I Can.

—Wiggle-Butts & Up-Faces: A Child's Primer for Beginning Swimming. Reiter, John, ed. Zmolek, Sandy D., illus. Graves, Steve, intro. by. (Illus.). 32p. (ps). 1989. PLB 14.95 (*1-877863-00-9*) I Think I Can.

Kolbrek, Loyal. The Day God Made It Rain. (gr. k-2). 1977. pap. 1.89 (*0-570-06108-3*, 59-1226) Concordia.

—Paul Believes in Jesus. (Illus.). 24p. (gr. k-4). 1987. pap. 1.89 (*0-570-09008-3*, 59-1436) Concordia.

Kolbrek, Loyal & Larsen, Chris. Samson's Secret. (Orig.). (ps-4). 1970. pap. 1.89 (*0-570-06052-4*, 59-1168) Concordia.

Kolehmainen, Janet & Handwerk, Sandra. Teen Suicide: A Book for Friends, Family, & Classmates. 72p. (gr. 7 up). 1986. PLB 15.95 (*0-8225-0037-X*, First Ave Edns); pap. 4.95 (*0-8225-9514-1*, First Ave Edns) Lerner Pubns.

Kolf, June C. Teenagers Talk about Grief. 64p. (Orig.). 1990. pap. 4.99 (*0-8010-5292-0*) Baker Bk.

Kolia, Christina, ed. see Amini, Majid.

Koliai, Christina, ed. see Amini, Majid.

Kolkmeyer, Alexandra. The Clear Red Stone: A Myth & the Meaning of Menstruation. Goldstein, Lynn, ed. Kirby, Thomas, illus. LC 82-2956. 64p. (gr. 3-12). 1982. text ed. 9.50 (*0-942524-01-2*) In Sight Pr NM.

Kollay, Jocelyne. French Holiday Activity Workbook. (FRE & ENG., Illus.). 100p (Orig.). (gr. 9-12). 1988. wkbk. 16.95 (*0-9617764-1-2*) PS Enterprises.

Koller, Jackie F. A Dragon in the Family. Mitchell, Judith, illus. LC 93-7028. 1993. 12.95 (*0-316-50151-4*) Little.

—Dragonling. LC 89-27145. (ps-4). 1990. 10.95 (*0-316-50148-4*) Little.

—Fish Fry Tonight. O'Neill, Catharine, illus. LC 89-49369. 32p. (ps-3). 1992. 13.00 (*0-517-57814-X*); PLB 13.99 (*0-517-57815-8*) Crown Bks Yng Read.

—If I Had One Wish. (gr. 3-7). 1991. 14.95 (*0-316-50150-6*) Little.

—If I Had One Wish. (gr. 4-7). 1993. pap. 3.50 (*0-440-40807-5*) Dell.

—Impy for Always. Newsom, Carol, illus. 64p. (gr. 2-4). 1989. 9.95 (*0-316-50147-6*) Little.

—Impy for Always. (ps-3). 1991. pap. 3.95 (*0-316-50149-2*) Little.

—The Last Voyage of the Misty Day. LC 91-17482. 160p. (gr. 4-8). 1992. SBE 13.95 (*0-689-31731-X*, Atheneum Child Bk) Macmillan Child Grp.

—Mole & Shrew. Ormai, Stella, illus. LC 90-609. 32p. (ps-3). 1991. SBE 12.95 (*0-689-31611-9*, Atheneum Child Bk) Macmillan Child Grp.

—Mole & Shrew Step Out. Ormai, Stella, illus. LC 91-20531. 32p. (ps-3). 1992. SBE 13.95 (*0-689-31713-1*, Atheneum Child Bk) Macmillan Child Grp.

—Nothing to Fear. Grove, Karen, ed. 279p. (gr. 5 up). 1991. 14.95 (*0-15-200544-7*, Gulliver Bks) HarBrace.

—Nothing to Fear. LC 90-39444. 1993. pap. 4.95 (*0-15-257582-0*, HB Juv Bks) HarBrace.

—The Primrose Way. 1992. write for info. (*0-15-256745-3*, Gulliver Bks) HarBrace.

Kollock, John, jt. auth. see Williams, G. Walton.

Kolodny, Nancy J. When Food's a Foe: How to Confront & Conquer Eating Disorders. (Illus.). 224p. (gr. 7 up). 1987. 14.95 (*0-316-50167-0*) Little.

—When Food's a Foe: How to Confront & Conquer Eating Disorders. rev. ed. 192p. (gr. 7 up). 1992. pap. 7.95 (*0-316-50181-6*) Little.

Kolodny, Nancy J., et al. Smart Choices. (Illus.). 352p. (gr. 7 up). 1986. 17.95 (*0-316-50163-8*) Little.

Kolosick, Helga, jt. auth. see Kolosick, Timothy.

Kolosick, Timothy & Kolosick, Helga. The Canons Austrian Children Sing. (Illus.). 32p. (Orig.). (gr. k-8). 1987. pap. text ed. 15.00 (*0-943121-00-0*) AZU Music Pr.

Koltz, Tony. Terror Island. 128p. (gr. 4). 1986. pap. 2.25 (*0-553-25885-0*) Bantam.

—Vampire Express. 128p. (Orig.). (gr. 4-7). 1984. pap. text ed. 2.25 (*0-553-26185-1*) Bantam.

—Vampire Express, No. 31. 1984. pap. 2.99 (*0-553-27053-2*) Bantam.

Komacek, et al. Exploring Construction Systems. (Illus.). 451p. 1990. text ed. 38.34 (*0-87192-234-7*) Delmar.

Komaiko, Leah. Annie Bananie. Cornell, Laura, illus. LC 86-45767. 32p. (ps-3). 1987. 15.00 (*0-06-023259-5*) HarpC Child Bks.

—Annie Bananie. Cornell, Laura, illus. LC 86-45767. 32p. (gr. k-3). 1989. pap. 4.95 (*0-06-443198-3*, Trophy) HarpC Child Bks.

—Aunt Elaine Does the Dance from Spain. Mathers, Petra, illus. LC 91-45474. 32p. (ps-3). 1992. 15.00 (*0-385-30674-1*) Doubleday.

—Broadway Banjo Bill. LC 91-29382. (ps-3). 1993. 15.00 (*0-385-30524-9*) Doubleday.

—Earl's Too Cool for Me. Cornell, Laura, illus. LC 87-30803. 40p. (gr. k-3). 1988. 14.00 (*0-06-023281-1*) HarpC Child Bks.

—Earl's Too Cool for Me. Cornell, Laura, illus. LC 87-30803. 40p. (gr. k-3). 1990. pap. 5.95 (*0-06-443245-9*, Trophy) HarpC Child Bks.

—Fritzi Fox Flew in from Florida. Hurd, Thacher, illus. LC 93-4754. 1994. 16.00 (*0-06-021506-2*); PLB 14.89 (*0-06-021507-0*) HarpC Child Bks.

—Great Aunt Ida & Her Great Dane, Doc. Schindler, Steve, illus. LC 92-34196. 1994. 14.95 (*0-385-30682-2*) Doubleday.

—I Like the Music. Westman, Barbara, illus. LC 87-170. 32p. (ps-3). 1987. HarpC Child Bks.

—I Like the Music. Westman, Barbara, illus. LC 87-170. 32p. (ps-3). 1989. pap. 5.95 (*0-06-443189-4*, Trophy) HarpC Child Bks.

—Leonora O'Grady. Cornell, Laura, illus. LC 91-23208. 32p. (gr. k-3). 1992. 15.00 (*0-06-021766-9*); PLB 14.89 (*0-06-021767-7*) HarpC Child Bks.

—My Perfect Neighborhood. Westman, Barbara, illus. LC 89-37871. 32p. (ps-3). 1990. PLB 13.89 (*0-06-023288-9*) HarpC Child Bks.

—Shoe Shine Shirley. Spohn, Franz, illus. LC 92-25816. 1993. 14.95 (*0-385-30526-5*) Doubleday.

Komarc, Marilyn & Clay, Gwen. Exploring with Polydrons, Vol. 1. 48p. (gr. 3-9). 1991. pap. 7.95 (*0-938587-20-X*) Cuisenaire.

—Exploring with Polydrons, Vol. 2. 48p. (gr. 3-9). 1991. pap. 7.95 (*0-938587-21-8*) Cuisenaire.

Komicar, Alexi, narrated by see Rogers, Bettye.

Komisar, Alexi, narrated by see Boyle, Doe.

Komlos, Katalin, et al. One Hundred & Fifty American Folk Songs to Sing, Read & Play. LC 74-76415. 117p. (gr. k-6). 1974. pap. text ed. 10.95 (*0-913932-04-3*) Boosey & Hawkes.

Komoda, Beverly. The Winter Day. Komoda, Beverly, illus. LC 91-104. 32p. (ps-1). 1991. PLB 13.89 (*0-06-023302-8*) HarpC Child Bks.

Komoto, Sachiko. Chessie, the Long Island Squirrel. Komoto, Sachiko, illus. LC 90-46860. 64p. (gr. 1-3). 1993. PLB 19.93 (*0-8368-0198-9*); PLB 19.93 s.p. (*0-685-58720-7*) Gareth Stevens Inc.

Komroff, Manuel. Thomas Jefferson. LC 90-49177. (Illus.). 160p. (gr. 6-10). 1991. PLB 13.95 (*1-55905-083-7*) Marshall Cavendish.

Konczal, Dee & Pesetski, Loretta. We All Come in Different Packages. 88p. (gr. 3-6). 1983. 8.95 (*0-88160-099-7*, LW 243) Learning Wks.

Kondakov, Georgi I. The Island of Dread. 1991. 30.00 (*0-86299-941-3*) A Sutton Pub.

Kondeatis, Christos. Bible Stories of the Old Testament. (ps-6). 1993. pap. 18.00 (*0-671-87573-6*, S&S BFYR) S&S Trade.

Kong, Emilie, jt. auth. see Dudley, Don.

Kong, Emilie, illus. A Hug Is for Happiness. 12p. (ps). 1985. 2.65 (*0-317-18485-7*) Parker Bros.

—One-Two-Three Hug. 12p. (ps). 1985. 2.65 (*0-910313-93-8*) Parker Bros.

Konig, Hans-Jost. Geheime Mission. LC 75-2362. (gr. 7-12). 1975. pap. 7.50 (*0-88436-181-0*, 45253) EMC.

Konigsburg, E. L. About the B'nai Bagels. Konigsburg, E. L., illus. LC 69-13529. 176p. (gr. 4-6). 1971. SBE 14. 95 (*0-689-20631-3*, Atheneum Child Bk) Macmillan Child Grp.

—About the B'nai Bagels. Konigsburg, E. L., illus. 176p. (gr. 4-7). 1985. pap. 3.50 (*0-440-40034-1*, YB) Dell.

—Altogether, One at a Time. Haley, Gail E., et al, illus. LC 70-134814. 88p. (gr. 4-7). 1971. 14.95 (*0-689-20638-0*, Atheneum Child Bk) Macmillan Child Grp.

—Altogether, One at a Time. 2nd ed. Mayer, Mercer, et al, illus. 96p. (gr. 3-7). 1989. pap. 2.95 (*0-689-71290-1*, Aladdin) Macmillan Child Grp.

—Amy Elizabeth Explores Bloomingdale's. Konigsburg, E. L., illus. LC 91-40132. 32p. (ps-3). 1992. SBE 14. 95 (*0-689-31766-2*, Atheneum Child Bk) Macmillan Child Grp.

—The Dragon in the Ghetto Caper. 128p. (gr. 5-6). 1985. pap. 2.75 (*0-440-42148-9*, YB) Dell.

—Father's Arcane Daughter. LC 76-5495. 128p. (gr. 4-8). 1976. SBE 13.95 (*0-689-30524-9*, Atheneum Child Bk) Macmillan Child Grp.

—Father's Arcane Daughter. (gr. 5-8). 1986. pap. 3.50 (*0-440-42496-8*, YB) Dell.

—From the Mixed-Up Files of Mrs. Basil E. Frankweiler. Konigsburg, E. L., illus. LC 67-18988. 168p. (gr. 3-7). 1970. SBE 13.95 (*0-689-20586-4*, Atheneum Child Bk) Macmillan Child Grp.

—From the Mixed-Up Files of Mrs. Basil E. Frankweiler. 160p. (gr. 5 up). 1977. pap. 3.99 (*0-440-43180-8*, YB) Dell.

—From the Mixed-Up Files of Mrs. Basil E. Frankweiler. 208p. (gr. 5 up). 1973. pap. 3.99 (*0-440-93180-0*, LFL) Dell.

—From the Mixed-Up Files of Mrs. Basil E. Frankweiler. LC 86-25903. (Illus.). 176p. (gr. 4-7). 1987. pap. 3.95 (*0-689-71181-6*, Aladdin) Macmillan Child Grp.

—From the Mixed-up Files of Mrs. Basil E. Frankweiler. large type ed. 260p. (gr. 3-8). 1988. Repr. of 1968 ed. lib. bdg. 15.95 (*1-55736-036-7*, Crnrstn Bks) BDD LT Grp.

—From the Mixed-Up Files of Mrs. Basil E. Frankweiler. (Illus.). 168p. 1992. Repr. PLB 16.95x (*0-89966-942-5*) Buccaneer Bks.

—George. 160p. (gr. k-6). 1985. pap. 3.50 (*0-440-42847-5*, YB) Dell.

—Jennifer, Hecate, Macbeth, William McKinley & Me, Elizabeth. Konigsburg, E. L., illus. LC 67-10458. 128p. (gr. 3-5). 1971. SBE 12.95 (*0-689-30007-7*, Atheneum Child Bk) Macmillan Child Grp.

—Jennifer, Hecate, Macbeth, William McKinley & Me, Elizabeth. 128p. (gr. 3-6). 1985. pap. 3.50 (*0-440-44162-5*, YB) Dell.

—Jennifer, Hecate, Macbeth, William McKinley, & Me, Elizabeth. large type ed. (gr. 3-7). 1989. Repr. of 1967 ed. lib. bdg. 15.95 (*1-55736-143-6*, Crnrstn Bks) BDD LT Grp.

—Journey to an Eight Hundred Number. 114p. (gr. 5-8). 1985. pap. 3.50 (*0-440-44264-8*, YB) Dell.

—Journey to an 800 Number. LC 81-10829. 144p. (gr. 5-9). 1982. SBE 13.95 (*0-689-30901-5*, Atheneum Child Bk) Macmillan Child Grp.

—A Proud Taste for Scarlet & Miniver. Konigsburg, E. L., illus. LC 73-76320. 208p. (gr. 5-9). 1973. SBE 14. 95 (*0-689-30111-1*, Atheneum Child Bk) Macmillan Child Grp.

—A Proud Taste for Scarlet & Miniver. 208p. (gr. 5-8). 1985. pap. 3.50 (*0-440-47201-6*, YB) Dell.

—Samuel Todd's Book of Great Colors. Konigsburg, E. L., illus. LC 89-6640. 32p. (ps-k). 1990. SBE 13.95 (*0-689-31593-7*, Atheneum Child Bk) Macmillan Child Grp.

—Samuel Todd's Book of Great Inventions. Konigsburg, E. L., illus. LC 90-23688. 32p. (ps-2). 1991. SBE 13. 95 (*0-689-31680-1*, Atheneum Child Bk) Macmillan Child Grp.

—The Second Mrs. Giaconda. LC 75-6946. (Illus.). 144p. (gr. 5-9). 1978. pap. 4.95 (*0-689-70450-X*, Aladdin) Macmillan Child Grp.

—T-Backs, T-Shirts, Coat, & Suit. 160p. (gr. 4-8). 1993. SBE 13.95 (*0-689-31855-3*, Atheneum Child Bk) Macmillan Child Grp.

—Throwing Shadows. 168p. (gr. 7 up). 1988. pap. 3.95 (*0-02-044140-1*, Collier Young Ad) Macmillan Child Grp.

—Up from Jericho Tel. LC 85-20061. 192p. (gr. 5 up). 1986. SBE 14.95 (*0-689-31194-X*, Atheneum Child Bk) Macmillan Child Grp.

Konigsburg, E. L., et al. In My Own Words Series, 4 vols. (Illus.). 512p. (gr. 5-7). 1990. s.p. 33.71 (*0-685-58837-8*, J Messner); (J Messner); (J Messner) S&S Trade.

Konigslow, A. Wayne von see Von Konigslow, A. Wayne.

Konigslow, Andrea Von see Von Konigslow, Andrea & Granfield, Linda.

Konigslow, Andrea W. von see Von Konigslow, Andrea W.

Kono, Juliet S. & Song, Cathy, eds. Sister Stew, Fiction & Poetry by Women. 330p. (gr. 9-12). 1991. pap. 10. 00 (*0-910043-22-1*); cass. avail. (*0-910043-25-6*) Bamboo Ridge Pr.

Konopka, Gisela. Courage & Love. (Orig.). (gr. 7 up). 1988. pap. 10.95 (*0-9621328-0-2*) G Konopka.

Kontoyiannaki, Elizabeth. The Adventures of Millie. Kontoyiannaki, Elizabeth, illus. 15p. (gr. 1-3). 1992. pap. 10.95 (*1-56606-012-5*) Bradley Mann.

—Bozo Is a Dog. Kontoyiannaki, Elizabeth, illus. 17p. (gr. k-3). 1992. pap. 8.95 (*1-895583-44-6*) MAYA Pubs.

—Dad, Play Chess with Me. Kontoyiannaki, Elizabeth, illus. 13p. (gr. k-3). 1993. pap. 12.95 (*1-56606-015-X*) Bradley Mann.

—I Can Count. Kontoyiannaki, Elizabeth, illus. 16p. (gr. k-3). 1992. pap. 12.95 (*1-895583-41-1*) MAYA Pubs.

—An Island Called Samos. Kontoyiannaki, Elizabeth, illus. 14p. (gr. k-3). 1992. pap. 9.95 (*1-895583-42-X*) MAYA Pubs.

—Leo & His Friends. Kontoyiannaki, Elizabeth, illus. 12p. (gr. 1-4). 1992. pap. 12.95 (*1-56606-011-7*) Bradley Mann.

—Plants Grow in Gardens. Kontoyiannaki, Elizabeth, illus. 18p. (gr. k-3). 1992. pap. 10.95 (*1-895583-43-8*) MAYA Pubs.

—Run, Don't Walk. Kontoyiannaki, Elizabeth, illus. (gr. k-3). Date not set. pap. 13.95 (*1-56606-016-8*) Bradley Mann.

—Where Does the World End? Kontoyiannaki, Elizabeth, illus. 14p. (gr. k-3). 1992. pap. 12.95 (*1-895583-45-4*) MAYA Pubs.

Kontoyiannaki, Kosta. Agean Fun. Kontoyiannaki, Kosta, illus. 16p. (gr. k-3). 1992. pap. 12.95 (*1-895583-23-3*) MAYA Pubs.

—Can You Find Greece on the Map? Kontoyiannaki, Kosta, illus. 14p. (gr. k-3). 1992. pap. 14.95 (*1-895583-20-9*) MAYA Pubs.

—Frankie Bear's Birthday Cake. Kontoyiannaki, Kosta, illus. 14p. (gr. 1-6). 1992. pap. 13.95 (*1-56606-004-4*) Bradley Mann.

—Horse Rides for Homer. Kontoyiannaki, Kosta, illus. 15p. (gr. k-3). 1992. pap. 12.95 (*1-895583-21-7*) MAYA Pubs.

—Ralph Takes a Train Ride. Kontoyiannaki, Kosta, illus. 18p. (gr. k-3). 1992. pap. 13.95 (*1-895583-24-1*) MAYA Pubs.

—Time. Kontoyiannaki, Kosta, illus. 12p. (gr. k-3). 1992. pap. 10.95 (*1-895583-22-5*) MAYA Pubs.

Kontoyiannaki, Kosta & Smith, Kaitlin M. Art Ideas. Lewis, Glenn, intro. by. (Illus.). 55p. (gr. 1-12). 1991. pap. text ed. 15.95 (*0-9627882-4-4*) Bradley Mann.

Konwicki, Tadeusz. Anthropos-Specter-Beast. Korwin-Rodziszewski, George & Korwin-Rodziszewski, Audrey, trs. from POL. LC 77-13500. 320p. (gr. 9 up). 1977. 21.95 (*0-87599-218-8*) S G Phillips.

Koontz, Phyllis, ed. see Farrell, Don A.

Koontz, Robin M. Chicago & the Cat. Koontz, Robin M., illus. LC 91-34863. 32p. (gr. k-3). 1993. 12.00 (*0-525-65097-0*, Cobblehill Bks) Dutton Child Bks.

—Chicago & the Cat: The Camping Trip. Koontz, Robin M., illus. LC 92-46685. 32p. (gr. k-3). 1994. 12.99 (*0-525-65137-3*, Cobblehill Bks) Dutton Child Bks.

—Chicago & the Cat: The Halloween Party. Koontz, Robin M., illus. LC 93-27043. 1994. write for info. (*0-525-65138-1*, Cobblehill Bks) Dutton Child Bks.

—I See Something You Don't See: A Riddle-Me Picture Book. Koontz, Robin M., illus. LC 91-8025. 32p. (ps-3). 1992. 13.00 (*0-525-65077-6*, Cobblehill Bks) Dutton Child Bks.

Koop, C. Everett. Safe Sex in the Age of AIDS. 1992. pap. 3.99 (*0-8129-2063-5*, Times Bks) Random.

Koopman, Anne. Charles P. Lazarus: The Titan of Toys R Us. Young, Richard G., ed. LC 91-32054. (Illus.). 64p. (gr. 4-8). 1992. PLB 17.26 (*1-56074-022-1*) Garrett Ed Corp.

Koopmans, Loek. The Woodcutter's Mitten: An Old Tale. Koopmans, Loek, illus. LC 90-2545. 32p. (ps-2). 1990. 13.95 (*0-940793-67-9*, Crocodile Bks) Interlink Pub.

Koosak, Tara. Boy Girl Daze Craze. Koosak, Tara, illus. LC 91-91469. 60p. (Orig.). (gr. 4-8). 1992. pap. 3.50 (*0-934426-44-9*) NAPSAC Reprods.

—School Biz Is..., Bk. 1. rev. ed. LC 90-70016. (Illus.). 52p. (gr. 1-8). 1991. pap. 3.50 (*0-934426-33-3*) NAPSAC Reprods.

Koosman, Jerry. Jerry Koosman's Guide for Young Pitchers. Meyers, Susan, ed. Oster, Don, et al. (Illus., Orig.). (gr. 2-6). 1989. pap. 5.95 (*0-9618437-0-5*) Young Creations.

Kopald, Suanne K. Serina's First Flight: A Tooth Fairy's Tale. Kopald, Suanne K., illus. LC 91-12783. 32p. (gr. k-3). 1992. 13.95 (*0-934738-88-2*) Thomasson-Grant.

Kopelman, Yvonne A. I Am a Gift! Auld-Lonie, Margaret, ed. Hiner, Stewart, illus. (Orig.). (ps-k). 1993. pap. 7.95 (*1-883976-00-6*) I Am The Power.

—I Am Feeling! Auld-Lonie, Margaret, ed. Hiner, Stuart, illus. (Orig.). (gr. 1-5). 1993. pap. 7.95 (*1-883976-26-X*) I Am The Power.

—I Am Who I Am & I Love It! Auld-Lonie, Margaret, ed. Hiner, Stuart, illus. (Orig.). (gr. 5-8). 1993. pap. 7.95 (*1-883976-50-2*) I Am The Power.

—I Have the Power of Choice! Auld-Lonie, Margaret, ed. Hiner, Stewart, illus. (gr. 9-12). 1993. pap. 7.95 (*1-883976-75-8*) I Am The Power.

Kopen, Dan F., jt. auth. see Kopen, Pamela A.

Kopen, Pamela A. Grandpa's Magic Drawer. Kopen, Pamela A., illus. Kopen, Dan F., intro. by. LC 91-91475. (Illus.). 32p. (ps-3). 1992. 14.95 (*0-9628914-1-X*) Padakami Pr.

—Read to Me - Just One More Book. Kopen, Dan F., intro. by. LC 91-60425. (Illus.). 32p. (gr. k-3). 1991. 14.95 (*0-9628914-0-1*) Padakami Pr.

Kopen, Pamela A. & Kopen, Dan F. The Trillium Trail. Kopen, Pamela A., illus. LC 93-28228. 32p. (ps-12). 1993. pap. 9.95 (*0-9628914-3-6*) Padakami Pr.

Koplow, Lesley. Tanya & the Tobo Man: A Story for Children Entering Therapy. LC 91-85. (SPA & ENG., Illus.). 32p. (ps-4). 1991. 16.95 (*0-945354-34-7*); pap. 6.95 (*0-945354-33-9*) Magination Pr.

—Tanya & the Tobo Man: A Story for Children Entering Therapy. Velasquez, Eric, illus. LC 92-56875. 1993. PLB 17.26 (*0-8368-0936-X*) Gareth Stevens Inc.

Kopp, Jaine. Frog Math. Bergman, Lincoln & Fairwell, Kay, eds. (Illus.). 106p. (gr. k-3). 1992. pap. 12.00 (*0-912511-79-6*) Lawrence Science.

Kopper, Lisa. Daisy Thinks She's a Baby. LC 92-44539. (gr. 1-8). 1994. 12.99 (*0-679-94723-X*); 12.00 (*0-679-84723-5*) Knopf Bks Yng Read.

Kopper, Lisa, illus. Happy Birthday! 18p. (ps). 1992. bds. 4.95 (*0-448-41088-5*, G&D) Putnam Pub Group.

—Hush-a-Bye Baby. 18p. (ps). 1992. bds. 4.95 (*0-448-40266-1*, G&D) Putnam Pub Group.

—Peek-a-Boo Baby. 12p. (ps). 1993. bds. 3.95 (*0-448-40197-5*, G&D) Putnam Pub Group.

—Peek-a-Boo Kitty. 12p. (ps). 1993. bds. 3.95 (*0-448-40196-7*, G&D) Putnam Pub Group.

—Peek-a-Boo Teddy. 12p. (ps). 1993. bds. 3.95 (*0-448-40195-9*, G&D) Putnam Pub Group.

—Ten Little Babies. LC 89-49478. 24p. (ps). 1990. 9.95 (*0-525-44643-5*, DCB) Dutton Child Bks.

Koral, April. An Album of the Great Wave of Immigration. LC 92-15009. (Illus.). 64p. (gr. 5-8). 1992. PLB 13.90 (*0-531-11123-7*) Watts.

—An Album of War Refugees. LC 89-30948. (Illus.). 96p. (gr. 6-9). 1989. PLB 13.90 (*0-531-10765-5*) Watts.

—Florence Griffith Joyner: Track & Field Star. Mathews, V., ed. LC 91-32827. (Illus.). 64p. (gr. 3-6). 1992. PLB 12.90 (*0-531-20061-2*) Watts.

—Our Global Greenhouse. (Illus.). 64p. (gr. 3 up). 1991. pap. 5.95 (*0-531-15601-X*) Watts.

Koralek, Jenny. The Cobweb Curtain: A Christmas Story. Baynes, Pauline, illus. LC 88-27035. 32p. (ps-2). 1989. 13.95 (*0-8050-1051-3*, Bks Young Read) H Holt & Co.

—Hanukkah: The Festival of Lights. Wijngaard, Juan, illus. LC 89-8064. 32p. (gr. k-4). 1990. 13.95 (*0-688-09329-9*); lib. bdg. 13.88 (*0-688-09330-2*) Lothrop.

Koram, Gamal. When Lions Could Fly. (Illus.). 42p. (gr. 4-12). 1989. pap. 5.00 (*1-877610-01-1*) Sea Island.

Korch, Rick. The Official Pro Football Hall of Fame Playbook. (Illus.). 64p. (gr. 3 up). 1990. pap. 11.95 (*0-671-71002-8*) S&S Trade.

Kordon, Klaus. The Big Fish. Hattery-Beyer, Lynn, tr. from GER. Tjong Khing, illus. LC 91-28467. 32p. (ps-3). 1992. 13.95 (*0-02-750945-1*, Macmillan Child Bk) Macmillan Child Grp.

—Brothers Like Friends. Crawford, Elizabeth D., tr. from GER. 192p. (gr. 5 up). 1992. 14.95 (*0-399-22137-9*, Philomel Bks) Putnam Pub Group.

Korenblit, Joan, jt. ed. see Janger, Kathie.

Korman. A Semester in the Life of a Garbage Bag. 1993. pap. 3.25 (*0-590-44429-8*) Scholastic Inc.

Korman, Bernice, jt. auth. see Korman, Gordon.

Korman, Gordon. Beware the Fish. (Illus., Orig.). (gr. 4-7). 1991. pap. 2.95 (*0-590-44205-8*, Apple Paperbacks) Scholastic Inc.

—Don't Care High. 256p. (gr. 7 up). 1986. pap. 2.50 (*0-590-40251-X*, Point) Scholastic Inc.

—Don't Care High. 1986. pap. 3.25 (*0-590-43129-3*) Scholastic Inc.

—Go Jump in the Pool! 192p. (gr. 4-6). 1991. pap. 2.95 (*0-590-44209-0*, Apple Paperbacks) Scholastic Inc.

—I Want to Go Home! 192p. (Orig.). (gr. 3-7). 1991. pap. 3.25 (*0-590-44210-4*) Scholastic Inc.

—Losing Joe's Place. 240p. 1991. pap. 3.25 (*0-590-42769-5*, Point) Scholastic Inc.

—Macdonald Hall Goes Hollywood. 176p. (gr. 3-7). 1991. 12.95 (*0-590-43940-5*, Scholastic Hardcover) Scholastic Inc.

—No Coins, Please. 192p. (Orig.). (gr. 3-7). 1991. pap. 2.95 (*0-590-44208-2*, Apple Paperbacks) Scholastic Inc.

—Radio Fifth Grade. (gr. 4-7). 1989. pap. 11.95 (*0-590-41928-5*) Scholastic Inc.

—Radio Fifth Grade. 192p. (gr. 4-7). 1991. pap. 2.95 (*0-590-41927-7*, Apple Paperbacks) Scholastic Inc.

—This Can't Be Happening at MacDonald Hall. 128p. 1990. pap. 2.95 (*0-590-44213-9*) Scholastic Inc.

—The Toilet Paper Tigers. LC 92-27277. 1993. 13.95 (*0-590-46230-X*) Scholastic Inc.

—The Twinkie Squad. 1992. 13.95 (*0-590-45249-5*, Scholastic Hardcover) Scholastic Inc.

—The War with Mr. Wizzle. 192p. (gr. 3-7). 1990. pap. 3.25 (*0-590-44206-6*) Scholastic Inc.

—Who Is Bugs Potter? 1991. pap. 2.95 (*0-590-44207-4*) Scholastic Inc.

—The Zucchini Warriors. 208p. (gr. 4-7). 1988. pap. 10.95 (*0-590-41335-X*, Pub. by Scholastic Hardcover) Scholastic Inc.

—The Zucchini Warriors. 208p. 1991. pap. 3.25 (*0-590-44174-4*, Apple Paperbacks) Scholastic Inc.

Korman, Gordon & Korman, Bernice. The D-Poems of Jeremy Bloom. 1992. pap. 2.95 (*0-590-44819-6*, 059, Apple Paperbacks) Scholastic Inc.

Korman, Justine. Big Bird's New Nest & Other Good-Night Stories. Cooke, Tom, illus. (ps-1). 1989. write for info. (*0-307-12060-0*, 12060) Western Pub.

—Davy Crockett & the Creek Indians. Wepplo, Mike, illus. LC 91-71357. 80p. (gr. 1-4). 1991. PLB 12.89 (*1-56282-004-4*); pap. 2.95 (*1-56282-005-2*) Disney Pr.

—Davy Crockett at the Alamo. Wepplo, Mike, illus. LC 91-71350. 80p. (gr. 1-4). 1991. PLB 12.89 (*1-56282-008-7*); pap. 2.95 (*1-56282-009-5*) Disney Pr.

—The Little Mermaid. Ong, Cristina, illus. 32p. (ps-1). 1993. pap. 2.50 (*0-590-46448-5*, Cartwheel) Scholastic Inc.

—Thumbelina: The Novelization. (Illus.). 64p. (gr. 4-7). 1993. pap. 2.95 (*0-448-40508-3*, G&D) Putnam Pub Group.

—We're Back! The Illustrated Story. Lazor-Bahr, Beverly, illus. 48p. (ps-3). 1993. 9.95 (*0-448-40444-3*, G&D) Putnam Pub Group.

—Working Hard with the Mighty Dump Truck. (ps-3). 1993. pap. 2.50 (*0-590-46481-7*) Scholastic Inc.

—Working Hard with the Mighty Mixer. (ps-3). 1993. pap. 2.50 (*0-590-47308-5*) Scholastic Inc.

Korman, Justine & Fontes, Ron. Batman Returns: The Movie Storybook. (Illus.). 48p. (ps-3). 1992. write for info. (*0-307-15954-X*, 15954, Golden Pr) Western Pub.

—Universal Monsters: The Wolf Man. Ruiz, Art, illus. 96p. (gr. 3-7). 1992. pap. 2.95 (*0-307-22336-1*, 22336, Golden Pr) Western Pub.

Korman, Justine, jt. auth. see Fontes, Ron.

Korman, Justine H. The Monster in Room 202. Chesworth, Michael D., illus. LC 93-2215. 32p. (gr. 2-4). 1993. pap. text ed. 2.95 (*0-8167-3182-9*); pap. 2.95 (*0-8167-3183-7*) Troll Assocs.

—The Teacher from Outer Space. Matthews, Bonnie J., illus. LC 93-24846. 32p. (gr. 1-4). 1993. PLB 9.59 (*0-8167-3180-2*); pap. text ed. 2.95 (*0-8167-3181-0*) Troll Assocs.

Kornblatt, Marc. Eli & the Dimplemeyers. Ziegler, Jack, illus. LC 92-36793. 32p. (gr. k-3). 1994. RSBE 14.95 (*0-02-750947-8*, Macmillan Child Bk) Macmillan Child Grp.

—Flame of the Inquisition, No. 15. 144p. 1986. pap. 2.50 (*0-553-26160-6*) Bantam.

—Search for Sidney's Smile. Gurney, John, illus. LC 92-12824. 1993. pap. 13.00 JRT (*0-671-76912-X*, S&S BFYR); pap. 2.50 (*0-671-79362-4*, Little Simon) S&S Trade.

Kornblatt, Marc, jt. auth. see Nanus, Susan.

Kornblith, Regina L., tr. see Bomans, Godfried.

Kornbluth, Adina F. Kaleidoscope. Nodel, Norman, illus. 160p. (gr. 6-10). 1992. 10.95 (*0-922613-31-1*); pap. 8.95 (*0-922613-32-X*) Hachai Pubns.

Korner, David. Come out & Play. Korner, David, illus. LC 86-2811. 56p. (gr. 1-5). 1987. pap. 9.95 (*0-939827-00-X*) Korn Kompany.

Kornfield, Elizabeth. Dreams Come True. Kornfield, Lee, ed. (Illus.). 32p. (gr. 3-6). 1986. pap. 5.95 (*0-940611-00-7*) Rocky Mntn Child.

Kornfield, Lee, ed. see Kornfield, Elizabeth.

Kornhauser, Barry. This Is Not a Pipe Dream. (Orig.). 1992. pap. 4.50 playscript (*0-87602-316-2*) Anchorage.

Korschunow, Irina. The Foundling Fox. Skofield, James, tr. from GER. Michl, Reinhard, illus. LC 84-47631. 48p. (gr. k-3). 1984. HarpC Child Bks.

—Piebald Pup. Oberlander, Gerhard, illus. (gr. k-3). 1959. 9.95 (*0-8392-3026-5*) Astor-Honor.

—Small Fur. Skofield, James, tr. from GER. Michl, Reinhard, illus. LC 87-45289. 80p. (gr. 1-4). 1988. HarpC Child Bks.

Kort, Michael. Marxism in Power: The Rise & Fall of a Doctrine. LC 92-15697. (Illus.). 176p. (gr. 7 up). 1993. PLB 16.90 (*1-56294-241-7*) Millbrook Pr.

—The Rise & Fall of the Soviet Union. (Illus.). 128p. (gr. 9-12). 1992. PLB 13.90 (*0-531-11040-0*) Watts.

Kort, Michael G. The Cold War. LC 93-1934. (Illus.). 160p. (gr. 7 up). 1994. PLB 16.90 (*1-56294-353-7*) Millbrook Pr.

Korte, Gene J. Green Pickle Pie. Caroland, Mary, ed. LC 90-71141. (Illus.). 44p. 1991. 6.95 (*1-55523-369-4*) Winston-Derek.

Korth, Bob, ed. see Matthews, Velda & Beard, Ray.

Korth-Sander, Irmtraut. Will You Be My Friend? Korth-Sander, Irmtraut, illus. Lanning, Rosemary, tr. from GER. LC 86-60485. (Illus.). 32p. (gr. k-2). 1986. 14.95 (*1-55858-071-9*) North-South Bks NYC.

Kortum, Jeanie. Ghost Vision. Stermer, Dugald, illus. LC 83-4706. 160p. (gr. 5-9). 1983. 10.95 (*0-394-86190-6*, Pant Bks Young) Pantheon.

Kortum, Jeanie & Stermer, Dugald. Ghost Vision. LC 82-19410. (Illus.). 144p. (gr. 5-9). o.s.i 10.99 (*0-685-42976-8*); PLB 10.99 (*0-685-42977-6*) Sierra.

Korty, Carol. Writing Your Own Plays: Creating, Adapting, Improvising. LC 86-21969. 112p. (gr. 6 up). 1986. SBE 13.95 (*0-684-18470-2*, Scribners Young Read) Macmillan Child Grp.

Korty, John, jt. auth. see Hall, Avery.

Korwin-Rodziszewski, Audrey, tr. see Konwicki, Tadeusz.

Korwin-Rodziszewski, George, tr. see Konwicki, Tadeusz.

Koscielniak, Bruce. Bear & Bunny Grow Tomatoes. Koscielniak, Bruce, illus. LC 92-10065. 40p. (ps-2). 1993. 8.99 (*0-679-83687-X*); PLB 9.99 (*0-679-93687-4*) Knopf Bks Yng Read.

—Hector & Prudence. Koscielniak, Bruce, illus. LC 88-31359. 40p. (ps-2). 1990. 12.95 (*0-394-84514-5*); lib. bdg. 14.99 (*0-394-94514-X*) Knopf Bks Yng Read.

—Hector & Prudence - All Aboard! Koscielniak, Bruce, illus. LC 89-2008. 40p. (ps-2). 1990. PLB 13.99 (*0-679-90486-7*) Knopf Bks Yng Read.

Koshinski, Sondra. The Plum Blossom. LC 93-77177. (gr. 1-3). 1993. spiral bdg. 8.95 (*1-883251-00-1*) Hgh Desert Pr.

Koski, Mary. The Stowaway Fairy in Hawaii. (Illus.). 36p. (gr. k-5). 1991. 9.95 (*0-89610-225-4*) Island Heritage.

Koslow, Philip. El Cid: Spanish Military Leader. LC 92-33377. (Illus.). 1993. PLB 18.95 (*0-7910-1239-5*, Am Art Analog); pap. write for info. (*0-7910-1266-2*, Am Art Analog) Chelsea Hse.

—The Securities & Exchange Commission. (Illus.). 112p. (gr. 5 up). 1990. 14.95 (*1-55546-119-0*) Chelsea Hse.

—The Seminole Indians. LC 93-35441. (Illus.). 80p. (gr. 2-5). 1994. PLB 13.95 (*0-7910-1672-2*, Am Art Analog); pap. write for info. (*0-7910-2486-5*, Am Art Analog) Chelsea Hse.

Kosman, Miriam. Family for a While. LC 93-72272. 176p. (gr. 6-10). 1993. write for info. (*1-56062-202-4*); pap. write for info. (*1-56062-203-2*) CIS Comm.

Kosof, Anna. The Civil Rights Movement & Its Legacy. LC 89-9166. (Illus.). 112p. (gr. 7-12). 1989. PLB 13.40 (*0-531-10791-4*) Watts.

—Homeless in America. Kline, M., ed. LC 87-26230. (Illus.). 96p. (gr. 7-12). 1988. PLB 13.40 (*0-531-10519-9*) Watts.

—Jesse Jackson. LC 87-10500. (Illus.). 128p. (gr. 7-12). 1987. PLB 13.40 (*0-531-10413-3*) Watts.

Kosowsky, Cindy. Wordless Counting Book. (Illus.). 24p. (ps-k). 1992. 10.95 (*1-880851-00-8*) Greene Bark Pr.

Koss, Amy. City Critters Around the World. (ps-3). 1991. 9.95 (*0-8431-2794-5*) Price Stern.

Koss, Amy G. Curious Creatures in Peculiar Places. (Illus.). 32p. (gr. 6-10). 1990. 8.95 (*0-8431-2732-5*) Price Stern.

—Where Fish Go in Winter: And Answers to Other Great Mysteries. (Illus.). 32p. (ps-2). 1988. 9.95 (*0-8431-2218-8*) Price Stern.

Koss, Larry. Could UFOs Be Real? (Illus.). 48p. (gr. 3-6). 1991. 11.95 (*1-56065-093-1*) Capstone Pr.

Kossmann, Walter, ed. see Parker, Steve.

Koste, Virginia G. The Medicine Show. (gr. 4-12). 1975. 4.50 (*0-87602-258-1*) Anchorage.

—The Trial of Tom Sawyer. (gr. 4 up). 1978. 4.50 (*0-87602-213-1*) Anchorage.

Koster, Hans-Curt, jt. auth. see Lindwall, Bo.

Kostic, Diane. The Biography of Me. (Illus.). 160p. (gr. 5-9). 1992. wkbk. 12.95 (*0-86653-687-6*, 1421) Good Apple.

Kostich, Beverly E. Stepping into the Bible. LC 87-34169. (ps-6). 1988. pap. 2.95 (*0-687-40060-0*) Abingdon.

Kostick, Anne. My First Camera Book. LC 88-40560. 64p. (ps-3). 1989. pap. 9.95 (*0-89480-381-6*, 1381) Workman Pub.

Kostyal, Karen. Raccoons. Crump, Donald J., ed. (Illus.). 32p. (ps-3). 1987. Set. 13.95 (*0-87044-677-0*); Set. lib. bdg. 16.95 (*0-87044-682-7*) Natl Geog.

Koteff, Ellen, ed. see Tufts, Lorraine S.

Kotes, F. F. A Kitty to Love: A Child's Guide to Cat Care. 40p. (Orig.). (gr. 3-8). 1993. pap. 9.95 (*1-878500-02-3*, Valley Hse Bk) Martin Mgmt.

—A Puppy to Love: A Child's Guide to Dog Care. LC 91-67328. 40p. (Orig.). (gr. 3-8). 1991. pap. 9.95 (*1-878500-00-7*, Valley Hse Bk) Martin Mgmt.

Kotter, Deborah. Arnold Always Answers. Conteh-Morgan, Jane, illus. LC 92-18578. 1993. 14.95 (*0-385-30905-8*, Zephyr-BFYR) Doubleday.

Kotzwinkle, William. The Empty Notebook. Servello, Joe, illus. LC 89-46198. 96p. (gr. 4). 1990. 13.95 (0-87923-826-7) Godine.
—The Million Dollar Bear. Catrow, David, illus. LC 93-6262. 1994. write for info. (0-679-85295-6); PLB write for info. (0-679-95295-0) Knopf Bks Yng Read.
—Trouble in Bugland: A Collection of Inspector Mantis Mysteries. Servello, Joe, illus. LC 82-49338. 160p. (gr. 5 up). 1986. pap. 12.95 (0-87923-555-1) Godine.
Kouhi, Elizabeth. North Country Spring. Rickels, Robert E., illus. 54p. (ps-8). 1980. 6.95 (0-920806-10-4, Pub. by Penumbra Pr CN) U of Toronto Pr.
Kouhoupt, Rudy & Marti, Donald B., Jr. How on Earth Do We Recycle Metal? Seiden, Art, illus. LC 91-28953. 64p. (gr. 4-6). 1992. PLB 12.90 (1-56294-142-9) Millbrook Pr.
Koulomzin, Sophie. Sbornik Detskij, Tysacha Let (988-1988) (RUS.). (gr. 2-4). 1985. write for info. RBR.
Kovach, Tom, jt. auth. see Gilliland, Hap.
Kovacs, Deborah. Brewster's Courage. Mathieu, Joe, illus. LC 91-21481. 112p. (gr. 2-6). 1992. pap. 14.00 jacketed, 3-pc. bdg. (0-671-74016-4, S&S BFYR) S&S Trade.
—A Day Under Water. (Illus.). 32p. (gr. k-3). 1987. pap. 2.50 (0-590-40746-5) Scholastic Inc.
—Moonlight on the River. Shattuck, William, illus. LC 92-28377. 1993. 13.99 (0-670-84463-2) Viking Child Bks.
—The Tooth Fairy Book. Lydecker, Laura, illus. LC 92-53679. 32p. 1992. 9.95 (1-56138-147-0) Running Pr.
—Woody's First Dictionary. Rose, Eve, illus. 24p. (ps-2). 1988. 3.95 (0-448-09287-5, G&D) Putnam Pub Group.
Kovalski, Maryann. Jingle Bells. Kovalski, Maryann, illus. 32p. (ps-2). 1988. 12.95 (0-316-50258-8) Little.
—Jingle Bells. (Illus.). (ps-3). 1991. pap. 4.95 (0-316-50261-8) Little.
—Pizza for Breakfast. Kovalski, Maryann, illus. LC 90-46078. 32p. (gr. k up). 1991. Repr. of 1990 ed. 13.95 (0-688-10409-6); PLB 13.88 (0-688-10410-X, Morrow Jr Bks) Morrow Jr Bks.
—Take Me Out to the Ballgame. LC 92-10155. (Illus.). (gr. k-3). 1993. 14.95 (0-590-45638-5) Scholastic Inc.
—The Wheels on the Bus. Kovalski, Maryann, illus. 32p. (ps-k). 1987. 14.95 (0-316-50256-1, Joy St Bks) Little.
Kovitch, Lisa G. I Want to Decorate, Too! (Illus.). 34p. (Orig.). 1992. pap. 3.50 (0-9635108-1-9) Fragments Lghts.
Kowalczyk, Carolyn. El Morado es Parte del Arco Iris-Libro Grande: Purple Is Part of a Rainbow-Big Book. 32p. (ps-2). 1988. PLB 30.60 (0-516-59513-X) Childrens.
—El Morado Es Parte del Arco Iris (Purple Is Part of a Rainbow) Sharp, Gene, illus. LC 85-11693. (SPA.). 32p. (ps-2). 1988. PLB 11.93 (0-516-32068-8); pap. 2.95 (0-516-52068-7) Childrens.
—Purple Is Part of a Rainbow Big Book. 32p. (ps-2). 1988. PLB 30.60 (0-516-49513-5) Childrens.
—Purple Is Part of the Rainbow. Sharp, Gene, illus. LC 85-11693. 32p. (ps-2). 1985. PLB 11.93 (0-516-02068-4); pap. 2.95 (0-516-42068-2) Childrens.
Kowitt, Holly. The Fenderbenders Get Lost in America. 1991. pap. 2.95 (0-590-44845-5, Blue Ribbon Bks) Scholastic Inc.
—The Fenderbenders Get Lost in America...Again. (Illus.). 1992. 2.95 (0-590-45891-4, 048) Scholastic Inc.
Kowitt, Holly, jt. auth. see Johnson, Lindsay L.
Kownslar, Allan O. & Smart, Terry L. Civics: Citizens & Society. 2nd ed. (Illus.). 576p. (gr. 7-8). 1983. text ed. 31.88 (0-07-035433-2) McGraw.
Kowtaluk. Discovering Food. (gr. 7-9). 1982. 14.00 (0-02-663350-7) Bennett IL.
Kozar, Elaine, ed. see James, Mark.
Koziakin, Vladimir. Sports Mazes. 64p. (gr. 3-7). 1991. 1.95 (0-590-43537-X) Scholastic Inc.
Kozielski, Dolores, jt. auth. see Wolff, Ferida.
Kozikowski, Renate. Teddy Bears' Picnic. (Illus.). 32p. (ps-2). 1990. POB 10.95 (0-689-71362-2, Aladdin) Macmillan Child Grp.
Kozlovski, Jane, jt. auth. see Jacobsen, Mark.
Kozodoy, Neil, ed. see Rossel, Seymour.
Kozodoy, Ruth. The Book of Jewish Holidays. Rossel, Seymour, ed. Suba, Suzanne, illus. 192p. (Orig.). (gr. 4-5). 1981. pap. text ed. 7.95x (0-87441-334-6); tchr's. guide with duplicating masters by Moshe Ben-Aharon 12.50x (0-87441-367-2); By Morris J. Sugarman. student's activity bk. 4.25 (0-87441-338-9) Behrman.
—Isadora Duncan. Horner, Matina, intro. by. (Illus.). 112p. (gr. 5 up). 1988. lib. bdg. 17.95x (1-55546-650-8) Chelsea Hse.
Kozodoy, Ruth, jt. auth. see Simms, Laura.
Kozuki, Russell. Junior Karate. LC 71-167665. (Illus.). 128p. (gr. 11 up). 1971. 12.95 (0-8069-4446-3) Sterling.
Kracht, Susan. The Sloppy Monster. Corns, Marvin A., illus. LC 92-60289. 44p. (ps-3). 1992. 5.95 (1-55523-527-1) Winston-Derek.
Kraehenbuehl, David see Clark, Frances.
Kraehenbuehl, David, et al. Supplementary Solos: Level 1. Clark, Frances & Goss, Louise, eds. 32p. (gr. k-12). 1979. pap. text ed. 5.95 (0-87487-105-0) Summy-Birchard.
—Supplementary Solos: Level 2. Clark, Frances & Goss, Louise, eds. 32p. (gr. k-12). 1980. pap. text ed. 5.95 (0-87487-106-9) Summy-Birchard.
Kraehenbuehl, David, jt. auth. see George, Jon.

Krafft, Maurice. Volcano! Bogard, Vicki, tr. from FRE. Favreau, Luc, illus. LC 92-968. 38p. (gr. k-5). 1992. 4.95 (0-944589-41-3) Young Discovery Lib.
—Volcano! Favreau, Luc, illus. 40p. (gr. k-5). 1993. PLB 9.95 (1-56674-074-6, HTS Bks) Forest Hse.
Kraft, Jim. Garfield Goes Camping. (Illus.). 24p. 1991. 10.95 (0-448-19287-X, G&D) Putnam Pub Group.
Kraft, Jim & Fentz, Mike. Garfield's Ghost Stories. Davis, Jim, illus. 32p. 1992. 10.95 (0-448-40577-6, G&D) Putnam Pub Group.
Kraft, Victoreen. Are You Afraid. Chappell, David & Bates, Steve, illus. 20p. (gr. k-6). 1983. pap. text ed. 4.25 (1-55976-139-3) CEF Press.
Kraft, Wolfgang S. Deutsch: Aktuell 1. LC 78-11445. (gr. 7-12). 1979. 15.95 (0-88436-539-5, 45450) EMC.
Krahn, Fernando. Amanda & the Mysterious Carpet. Krahn, Fernando, illus. LC 84-14201. 32p. (ps-3). 1985. 13.45 (0-89919-258-0, Clarion Bks) HM.
—How Santa Had a Long & Difficult Journey Delivering His Presents. (gr. k-6). 1988. pap. 3.95 (0-440-40118-6, YB) Dell.
Krajnc, Anton C., jt. auth. see Nobisso, Josephine.
Krakauer, Hoong Y. Rabbit Mooncakes. LC 92-23409. 1994. 14.95 (0-316-50327-4, Joy St Bks) Little.
Krakoff, S. B. The Magick Cave. 175p. (Orig.). (gr. 6-7). 1989. pap. write for info. Charcoal St Pr.
Kral, Brian. Apologies. 42p. (Orig.). (gr. 9-12). 1988. playscript 5.00 (0-87602-278-6) Anchorage.
—East of the Sun, West of the Moon. 56p. (Orig.). (ps up). 1987. playscript 5.50 (0-87602-273-5) Anchorage.
—One to Grow On. (Orig.). 1993. pap. 4.50 playscript (0-87602-320-0) Anchorage.
—Ransom of Red Chief. (Orig.). (gr. 3 up). 1980. playscript 4.50 (0-87602-227-1) Anchorage.
—Troubled Waters. (Orig.). 1991. Playscript. pap. 4.50 (0-87602-300-6) Anchorage.
Krall, Charlotte B. & Jim, Judith M. Fat Dog's First Visit: A Child's View of the Hospital. Hull, Nancy, ed. & illus. LC 87-2745. 28p. (Orig.). (ps-3). 1987. pap. text ed. 4.00 (0-939838-23-0) Pritchett & Hull.
Kramer, Alan. How to Make a Chemical Volcano. 1989. 12.95 (0-531-15120-4); PLB 12.90 (0-531-10771-X) Watts.
—How to Make a Chemical Volcano & Other Mysterious Experiments. Harvey, Paul, illus. 112p. (gr. 5 up). 1991. pap. 6.95 (0-531-15610-9) Watts.
Kramer, Anthony, jt. auth. see Giff, Patricia R.
Kramer, Clifford J. Picture Book Companion, No. I. 96p. (gr. k-3). 1992. pap. text ed. 12.95 (0-944459-58-7) ECS Lrn Systs.
—Picture Book Companion, No. II. 96p. (gr. k-3). 1992. pap. text ed. 12.95 (0-944459-59-5) ECS Lrn Systs.
—Picture Book Companion, Bk. III. 96p. (gr. k-3). 1993. pap. text ed. 12.95 (0-944459-64-1) ECS Lrn Systs.
Kramer, Estelle & Waller, Victoria. Traveling with Children by Plane. (Illus.). 64p. (ps-3). 1992. 19.95 (1-56282-117-2) Disney Pr.
Kramer, Estelle R. & Waller, Victoria E. Traveling with Children by Car. (Illus.). 64p. (ps-3). 1992. 19.95 (1-56282-116-4) Disney Pr.
Kramer, Janice & Mathews. Good Samaritan. LC 63-23369. (Illus.). (ps-k). 1964. laminated bdg. 1.89 (0-570-06000-1, 59-1102) Concordia.
Kramer, Linda, ed. see Loomans, Diane, et al.
Kramer, Linda, ed. see Pandell, Karen.
Kramer, Lyneve W. & Cole, Carole O. The Winning Young Woman. (Illus.). 92p. (Orig.). (gr. 7 up). 1988. pap. 5.95 (0-945767-00-5) Write Place.
Kramer, Michael. Funny Facts about Animals. 1991. 4.99 (0-517-05663-1) Outlet Bk Co.
Kramer, Patricia. Discovering Personal Goals. (gr. 7-12). 1991. PLB 14.95 (0-8239-1277-9) Rosen Group.
—Discovering Self-Confidence. (gr. 7-12). 1991. PLB 14.95 (0-8239-1275-2) Rosen Group.
—Discovering Self-Expression & Communication. (gr. 7-12). 1991. PLB 14.95 (0-8239-1276-0) Rosen Group.
—Discovering the Real You. (gr. 7-12). 1991. PLB 14.95 (0-8239-1274-4) Rosen Group.
—The Dynamics of Relationships. rev. ed. (Illus.). 430p. (Orig.). (gr. 8-12). 1990. pap. text ed. 34.95 tchr's. manual (0-317-90984-3) Equal Partners.
—The Dynamics of Relationships: A Guide to Developing Self-Esteem & Social Skills for Teens & Young Adults, Bk. 1. rev. ed. (Illus.). 331p. (Orig.). (gr. 8-12). 1990. pap. text ed. 16.95 student manual (0-317-90983-5) Equal Partners.
—The Dynamics of Relationships: A Guide to Developing Self-Esteem & Social Skills for Teens & Young Adults, Bk. 2. rev. ed. (Illus.). 49p. (gr. 8-12). 1990. pap. text ed. 8.95 student manual (sexuality) (0-317-90981-9) Equal Partners.
Kramer, Patricia & Frazer, Linda. The Dynamics of Relationships. rev. ed. (Illus.). 125p. (gr. 4-7). 1990. pap. text ed. 13.95 student manual (0-317-90982-7) Equal Partners.
—The Dynamics of Relationships: A Guide for Developing Self-Esteem & Social Skills for Preteens & Young Children. rev. ed. (Illus.). (gr. 9 up). 1990. pap. text ed. 17.95 tchr's. manual (0-929577-03-5) Equal Partners.
Kramer, Paula M. The Kyla Trilogy. 60p. (ps-3). 1993. pap. 4.95 (1-883412-03-X) Woodrose Pr.
Kramer, Remi. Legend of LoneStar Bear, Bk. III: The Mystery of the Walking Cactus. (Illus.). 80p. (gr. 1-6). 1990. 14.95 (0-945887-03-5) Northwind Pr.
—The Legend of LoneStar Bear, Bk. One: How LoneStar Got His Name. Kramer, Remi, illus. 64p. 1988. PLB 12.95 (0-945887-01-9) Northwind Pr.

—The Legend of LoneStar Bear, Bk. Two: Soaring with Eagles. Kramer, Remi, illus. 72p. 1989. 14.95 (0-945887-02-7) Northwind Pr.
—Legend of LoveStar Bear, Bk. 1: How LoveStar Got His Name. rev. ed. (Illus.). 60p. 1989. pap. 12.95 (0-945887-08-6) Northwind Pr.
Kramer, S. A. Adventure in Alaska. 80p. (Orig.). (gr. 2-7). 1993. PLB 9.99 (0-679-94511-3); pap. 2.99 (0-679-84511-9) Random Bks Yng Read.
—Baseball's Greatest Pitchers. Campbell, Jim, illus. LC 91-27892. 48p. (Orig.). (gr. 2-4). 1992. PLB 7.99 (0-679-92149-4); pap. 3.50 (0-679-82149-X) Random Bks Yng Read.
—To the Top! Climbing the World's Highest Mountain. La Padula, Thomas, illus. LC 92-22164. 48p. (Orig.). (gr. 2-4). 1993. PLB 7.99 (0-679-93885-0); pap. 3.50 (0-679-83885-6) Random Bks Yng Read.
Kramer, Stephen. Avalanche. Cone, Patrick, photos by. (Illus.). 48p. (gr. 1-4). 1991. PLB 17.50 (0-87614-422-9) Carolrhoda Bks.
—Lightning. Cone, Patrick, photos by. (Illus.). 48p. (gr. 1-4). 1991. PLB 17.50 (0-87614-659-0) Carolrhoda Bks.
—Lightning. (ps-3). 1993. pap. 7.95 (0-87614-617-5) Carolrhoda Bks.
—Tornado. (ps-3). 1992. 17.50 (0-87614-660-4) Carolrhoda Bks.
Kramer, Stephen P. How to Think Like a Scientist: Answering Questions by the Scientific Method. Bond, Felicia, illus. LC 85-43604. 48p. (gr. 3-7). 1987. 14.00 (0-690-04563-8, Crowell Jr Bks); PLB 13.89 (0-690-04565-4, Crowell Jr Bks) HarpC Child Bks.
Kramer, Sydelle, jt. auth. see Donnelly, Judy.
Kramer, William A. Teenagers Pray. LC 55-12193. (gr. 8-12). 1956. 5.99 (0-570-03018-8, 6-1054) Concordia.
Kramer-Lampher, A. H. Baby Born in a Stable. LC 65-15145. (gr. k-4). 1965. pap. 1.89 (0-570-06013-3, 59-1118) Concordia.
Kramkowski, Bernice C. Syllabic Reading. LC 83-90226. (Illus.). 118p. (Orig.). (gr. 1-5). 1983. comb bdg. 9.95 (0-912145-00-5) MMI Pr.
Krampe, Leesa. My Number Book. Curlee, Jane, illus. 126p. (ps-1). 1986. pap. text ed. 3.95 (0-932957-99-4) Natl School.
—My Number Word Book. Ehrlich, Doris, ed. O'Rourke, Dawn, illus. 100p. (Orig.). (ps-1). 1987. pap. text ed. 3.95 (0-932957-94-3) Natl School.
Kranepool, Harry A. New Investigations in Modern Chemistry. Plass, Richard M., ed. (Illus.). 1989. lab manual & wkbk., 270p. 9.95 (0-685-29318-1); 5.95 ea. Lab manual, 116p. Lab reports, 154p. Amer Scholastic.
Kranhold, jt. auth. see Burke.
Kranich, Roger E. & Corcoran, Eileen L. Our United States. (Illus.). 256p. (gr. 4-5). 1989. Incl. tchr's. key, 314. pap. text ed. 7.95 (0-88323-247-2, 311) Pendergrass Pub.
Kranz, Rachel, jt. auth. see Dentemaro, Christine.
Kranz, Rachel, jt. auth. see Maloney, Michael.
Kranz, Rachel, jt. auth. see Mufson, Susan.
Kranz, Rachel, jt. auth. see Rendon, Marion B.
Kranzberg, Melvin & Pursell, Carroll W., Jr., eds. Technology in Western Civilization, 2 vols. Incl. Vol. 1. The Emergence of Modern Industrial Society: Earliest Times to 1900; Vol. 2. Technology in the Twentieth Century. (gr. 9up). 1967. OUP.
Kranzler, Gershon. Golden Shoes: And Other Stories. (Illus.). (gr. 4-9). 8.95 (0-87306-123-3); pap. 6.95 (0-685-01628-5) Feldheim.
—Yoshko the Dumbbell. (gr. 4-9). pap. 6.95 (0-87306-246-9) Feldheim.
Krasilovsky, Phyllis. Cow Who Fell in the Canal. Spier, Peter, illus. LC 56-8236. 38p. (gr. k-1). 1985. pap. 11.95 (0-385-07585-5) Doubleday.
—Cow Who Fell in the Canal. (ps-3). 1993. 4.99 (0-440-40825-3) Dell.
—The Man Who Was Too Lazy to Fix Things. Cymerman, John E., illus. LC 91-435. 32p. (ps-3). 1992. 15.00 (0-688-10394-4, Tambourine Bks); PLB 14.93 (0-688-10395-2, Tambourine Bks) Morrow.
—The Very Little Boy. (Illus.). (ps). 1992. pap. 4.95 (0-590-44762-9, 030, Cartwheel) Scholastic Inc.
—The Very Little Girl. (Illus.). (ps). 1992. pap. 4.95 (0-590-44761-0, 029, Cartwheel) Scholastic Inc.
—The Woman Who Saved Things. Cymerman, John E., illus. LC 92-5126. 32p. (gr. k up). 1993. 14.00 (0-688-11162-9, Tambourine Bks); PLB 13.93 (0-688-11163-7, Tambourine Bks) Morrow.
Kraske, Robert. Harry Houdini: Master of Magic. (gr. 2-6). 1989. pap. 2.50 (0-590-42402-5) Scholastic Inc.
Krasnewich, Diane, jt. auth. see Trainor, Timothy N.
Krass, Peter. Sojourner Truth. King, Coretta Scott, intro. by. (Illus.). 112p. (gr. 5 up). 1988. 17.95 (1-55546-611-7); pap. 9.95 (0-7910-0215-2) Chelsea Hse.
Kratavil, Helen S. Parables of Christ. Butcher, Sam, illus. 64p. (gr. k-6). 1974. pap. text ed. 11.50 (1-55976-015-X) CEF Press.
Kratky, Lada, tr. see Behrens, June.
Kratky, Lada, tr. see Broekel, Ray.
Kratky, Lada, tr. see Charles, Donald.
Kratky, Lada, tr. see Chlad, Dorothy.
Kratky, Lada, tr. see Clark, Mary.
Kratky, Lada, tr. see Downing, Joan.
Kratky, Lada, tr. see Friskey, Margaret.
Kratky, Lada, tr. see Greene, Carol.
Kratky, Lada, tr. see Jacobsen, Karen.
Kratky, Lada, tr. see Lewellen, John.

Kratky, Lada, tr. see Reece, Colleen L.
Kratky, Lada, tr. see Webster, Vera.
Kratky, Lada, tr. see Wylie, Joanne.
Kratky, Lada J. Los Animales y Sus Crias. (SPA., Illus.). 24p. (Orig.). (gr. 1-3). 1991. pap. text ed. 29.95 big bk. (*1-56334-020-8*); pap. text ed. 6.00 small bk. (*1-56334-034-8*) Hampton-Brown.
—Animals & Their Young. (Illus.). 24p. (Orig.). (gr. 1-3). 1991. pap. text ed. 29.95 big.bk. (*1-56334-048-8*); pap. text ed. 6.00 small bk. (*1-56334-054-2*) Hampton-Brown.
—Chirrinchinchina Que Hay en la Tina? Kalthoff, Sandra C., illus. (SPA.). 24p. (Orig.). (gr. k-3). 1989. pap. text ed. 29.95 big bk. (*0-917837-11-8*) Hampton-Brown.
—Chirrinchinchina Que Hay en la Tina? Kalthoff, Sandra C., illus. (SPA.). 24p. (Orig.). (gr. k-3). 1989. pap. text ed. 6.00 small bk. (*0-917837-13-4*) Hampton-Brown.
—Chirrinchinchina Que Hay en la Tina? Kalthoff, Sandra C., illus. (SPA.). 24p. (Orig.). (gr. k-3). 1989. Six-Pack Set. pap. text ed. 36.00 (*0-917837-44-4*) Hampton-Brown.
—El Chivo en la Huerta (Big Book) Remkiewicz, Frank, illus. (SPA.). 16p. (Orig.). (gr. k-3). 1988. pap. text ed. 29.95 (*0-917837-04-5*) Hampton-Brown.
—El Chivo en la Huerta (Small Book) Remkiewicz, Frank, illus. (SPA.). 16p. (Orig.). (gr. k-3). 1992. pap. text ed. 6.00 (*1-56334-080-1*) Hampton-Brown.
—La Familia Villarreal. Lovell, Craig, photos by. (SPA., Illus.). 24p. (Orig.). (gr. 1-3). 1991. pap. text ed. 29.95 big.bk. (*1-56334-022-4*); pap. text ed. 4.15 small bk. (*1-56334-036-4*) Hampton-Brown.
—La Gallinita, el Gallo y el Frijol (Big Book) Yerkes, Lane, illus. (SPA.). 24p. (Orig.). (gr. k-3). 1988. pap. text ed. 29.95 (*0-917837-05-3*) Hampton-Brown.
—La Gallinita, el Gallo y el Frijol (Small Book) Yerkes, Lane, illus. (SPA.). 24p. (Orig.). (gr. k-3). 1992. pap. text ed. 6.00 (*1-56334-081-X*) Hampton-Brown.
—Meet the Villarreals. Lovell, Craig, photos by. (Illus.). 24p. (Orig.). (gr. 1-3). 1991. pap. text ed. 29.95 big bk. (*1-56334-050-X*); pap. text ed. 4.15 small bk. (*1-56334-056-9*) Hampton-Brown.
—Pequeno Coala Busca Casa. Kalthoff, Sandra C., illus. (SPA.). 24p. (Orig.). (gr. k-3). 1989. pap. text ed. 6.00 (*0-917837-14-2*) Hampton-Brown.
—Pequeno Coala Busca Casa. Kalthoff, Sandra C., illus. (SPA.). 24p. (Orig.). (gr. k-3). 1989. Six-Pack Set. pap. text ed. 36.00 (*0-917837-45-2*) Hampton-Brown.
—Pequeno Coala Busca Casa (Big Book) Kalthoff, Sandra C., illus. (SPA.). 24p. (Orig.). (gr. k-3). 1989. pap. text ed. 29.95 (*0-917837-12-6*) Hampton-Brown.
—Pinta, Pinta, Gregorita (Big Book) Hockerman, Dennis, illus. (SPA.). 16p. (Orig.). (gr. k-3). 1990. pap. text ed. 29.95 (*0-917837-53-3*) Hampton-Brown.
—Pinta, Pinta, Gregorita (Small Book) Hockerman, Dennis, illus. (SPA.). 16p. (Orig.). (gr. k-3). 1992. pap. text ed. 6.00 (*1-56334-084-4*) Hampton-Brown.
—Veo, Veo, Que Veo? (Big Book) Yerkes, Lane, illus. (SPA.). 16p. (Orig.). (gr. k-3). 1990. pap. text ed. 29.95 (*0-917837-57-6*) Hampton-Brown.
—Veo, Veo, Que Veo? (Small Book) Yerkes, Lane, illus. (SPA.). 16p. (Orig.). (gr. k-3). 1992. pap. text ed. 6.00 (*1-56334-082-8*) Hampton-Brown.
Kratoville, B. L., ed. see Boga, Steve.
Kratoville, B. L., ed. see Mullin.
Kratoville, B. L., ed. see Mullin, Penn.
Kratoville, B. L., ed. see Wilson, Kay W.
Kratoville, Betty L., ed. see Cunningham, Marilyn.
Kratoville, Betty L., ed. see Henken, Heidi.
Kratoville, Betty L., ed. see Lipman, Michel & Furniss, Cathy.
Kratoville, Betty L., ed. see Miller, W. Wesley.
Kratoville, Betty L., ed. see Mullin, Penn.
Kratoville, Betty L., ed. see Nelson, Ginger K.
Kratoville, Betty L., ed. see Pageler, Elaine.
Kratoville, Betty L., ed. see Scariano, Margaret.
Kratoville, Betty L., ed. see Spremich, Andrew.
Krauel, Mary E., ed. see Estes, James L.
Kraul, Edward G. & Beatty, Judith. Little Herman Meets la Llorona at the Santa Fe Fiestas: A Story-Color Book in English & Spanish. Gomez, Jose, illus. (ENG & SPA.). 24p. (gr. 3-6). 1989. story-color book 2.95 (*0-945937-03-2*) Word Process.
Kraul, Walter. Earth, Water, Fire & Air: Playful Explorations in the Four Elements. (Illus.). 120p. (gr. 4-8). pap. 12.95 (*0-86315-090-X*, Pub. by Floris Bks UK) Gryphon Hse.
Kraus International Publications. How to Get to the College of Your Choice: By Road, Plane or Train: A Practical Guide to Campus Visits, Central States. (Illus.). 440p. (Orig.). (gr. 9-12). 1993. pap. 17.95 (*0-527-42650-4*) Kraus Intl.
Kraus International Publications Staff, ed. How to Get to the College of Your Choice by Road, Plane or Train: A Practical Guide to Campus Visits. LC 92-16704. (Illus.). 427p. (Orig.). (gr. 11-12). 1992. pap. 17.95x (*0-527-52864-1*) Kraus Intl.
—How to Get to the College of Your Choice by Road, Plane or Train: A Practical Guide to Campus Visits (Western States), 1993. (Illus.). (Orig.). (gr. 11-12). 1993. pap. 17.95 (*0-527-42648-2*) Kraus Intl.
Kraus, Joanna. The Dragon Hammer & the Tale of Oniroku. LC 77-83857. (Illus.). 64p. (gr. 3-5). 1977. pap. 4.95 (*0-932720-17-X*); 7.95 (*0-932720-18-8*) New Plays Inc.
Kraus, Joanna H. The Shaggy Dog Murder Trial. (Orig.). (gr. 4-7). 1988. playscript 4.50 (*0-87602-274-3*) Anchorage.

—Tall Boy's Journey. (gr. 4-7). 1992. 17.50 (*0-87614-746-5*) Carolrhoda Bks.
—Tall Boy's Journey. (gr. 4-7). 1993. pap. 5.95 (*0-87614-616-7*) Carolrhoda Bks.
Kraus, Pam, ed. see Kraus, Robert, et al.
Kraus, Robert. The Adventures of Wise Old Owl. Kraus, Robert, illus. LC 92-20436. 32p. (ps-3). 1992. PLB 10.89 (*0-8167-2943-3*); pap. text ed. 2.95 (*0-8167-2944-1*) Troll Assocs.
—Another Mouse to Feed. Aruego, Jose & Dewey, Ariane, illus. LC 78-21259. 32p. (gr. 4 up). 1987. P-H.
—Another Mouse to Feed. Aruego, Jose & Dewey, Ariane, illus. 32p. (ps-1). 1988. pap. 6.95 bk. & cassette (*0-671-67146-4*, S&S BFYR) S&S Trade.
—Another Mouse to Feed. Aruego, Jose & Dewey, Ariane, illus. LC 78-21259. (ps). 1987. pap. 13.95 jacketed (*0-671-66522-7*, S&S BFYR); pap. 5.95 (*0-671-66688-6*, S&S BFYR) S&S Trade.
—Boris Bad Enough. Aruego, Jose & Dewey, Ariane, illus. 32p. (ps-3). 1988. pap. 12.95 jacketed (*0-671-66894-3*, S&S BFYR); pap. 5.95 (*0-671-66895-1*, S&S BFYR) S&S Trade.
—Buggy Bear Cleans Up. Brook, Bonnie, ed. Kraus, Robert, illus. 48p. (ps-3). 1989. PLB 8.98 (*0-671-68608-9*); pap. 3.95 (*0-671-68612-7*) Silver Pr.
—Bunny's Nutshell Library, 4 bks. Kraus, Robert, illus. Incl. The First Robin (*0-06-023285-4*); Juniper (*0-06-023295-1*); The Silver Dandelion (*0-06-023300-1*); Springfellow's Parade. LC 65-11450. (gr. 1 up). 1965. Set. 10.95 (*0-06-023225-0*) HarpC Child Bks.
—Bunya the Witch. 1989. pap. 3.95 (*0-671-68422-1*, Little Simon) S&S Trade.
—Daddy Long Ears. Kraus, Robert, illus. (ps-1). 1989. 4.95 (*0-671-67415-3*, Little Simon) S&S Trade.
—Daddy Long Ears Christmas Surprise. 1989. 4.95 (*0-671-68150-8*, Little Simon) S&S Trade.
—Daddy Long Ears' Halloween. (Illus.). 40p. (ps-1). 1990. 4.95 (*0-671-70352-8*, Little Simon) S&S Trade.
—Dance, Spider, Dance! (Illus.). 32p. (gr. k-2). 1993. 4.50 (*0-307-11566-6*, 11566, Golden Pr) Western Pub.
—Dance, Spider, Dance! A Golden Easy Reader, Level 2. (ps-3). 1993. pap. 3.50 (*0-307-15970-1*, Golden Pr) Western Pub.
—Dr. Mouse, Bungle Jungle Doctor. (Illus.). 40p. (ps-2). 1992. write for info. (*0-307-11550-X*, 11550) Western Pub.
—Dr. Mouse, Bungle Jungle Doctor. (Illus.). 32p. (ps-2). 1992. pap. write for info. (*0-307-15964-7*, 15964) Western Pub.
—Ella the Bad Speller. Brook, Bonnie, ed. Kraus, Robert, illus. 48p. (ps-3). 1989. PLB 8.98 (*0-671-68606-2*); pap. 3.95 (*0-671-68610-0*) Silver Pr.
—Good Morning, Miss Gator. Brook, Bonnie, ed. Kraus, Robert, illus. 48p. (ps-3). 1989. PLB 8.98 (*0-671-68605-4*); pap. 3.95 (*0-671-68609-3*) Silver Pr.
—Here Comes Tardy Toad. Brook, Bonnie, ed. Kraus, Robert, illus. 48p. (ps-3). 1989. PLB 8.98 (*0-671-68607-0*); pap. 3.95 (*0-671-68611-9*) Silver Pr.
—Herman the Helper. Aruego, Jose & Dewey, Ariane, illus. LC 73-9319. (ps). 1987. pap. 12.95 jacketed (*0-671-66887-0*, S&S BFYR); pap. 5.95 (*0-671-66270-8*, S&S BFYR) S&S Trade.
—Herman the Helper, Vol. 1. 1986. 10.95 (*0-13-387127-4*); pap. text ed. 33.95 (*0-13-389321-9*) P-H.
—How Spider Saved Easter. (Illus.). 32p. (ps-2). 1988. pap. 2.50 (*0-590-41092-X*) Scholastic Inc.
—How Spider Saved Easter. Kraus, Robert, illus. 32p. (ps-2). 1991. 12.95 (*0-8038-9331-0*) Hastings.
—How Spider Saved Halloween. Kraus, Robert, illus. 32p. (ps-3). 1988. pap. 2.25 (*0-671-66689-7*, Little Simon) S&S Trade.
—How Spider Saved Halloween. (Illus.). 32p. (Orig.). (ps-2). 1988. pap. 2.50 (*0-590-42117-4*) Scholastic Inc.
—How Spider Saved Santa Bug. (ps-3). 1990. pap. 2.50 (*0-590-42444-0*) Scholastic Inc.
—How Spider Saved Thanksgiving. 32p. 1991. pap. 2.50 (*0-590-44411-5*) Scholastic Inc.
—How Spider Saved the Flea Circus. (ps-3). 1991. pap. 2.50 (*0-590-42459-9*) Scholastic Inc.
—How Spider Saved Valentine's Day. Kraus, Robert, illus. 32p. (ps-1). 1986. pap. 2.50 (*0-590-42514-5*) Scholastic Inc.
—How Spider Stopped Litterbugs. (ps-3). 1991. pap. 2.50 (*0-590-44462-X*) Scholastic Inc.
—Jack Galaxy, Space Cop. (ps-3). 1990. pap. 2.75 (*0-553-15777-9*, Skylark) Bantam.
—Jack O'Lantern's Scary Halloween. (ps-3). 1993. pap. 2.25 (*0-307-10016-2*, Golden Pr) Western Pub.
—Klunky Monkey, New Kid in Class. Brook, Bonnie, ed. Kraus, Robert, illus. 48p. (ps-3). 1990. lib. bdg. 8.98 (*0-671-70853-8*); pap. 3.95 (*0-671-70854-6*) Silver Pr.
—Leo the Late Bloomer. Reissue. ed. Aruego, Jose, illus. LC 70-159154. 32p. (gr. k-3). 1971. 15.00 (*0-87807-042-7*, Crowell Jr Bks); PLB 14.89 (*0-87807-043-5*) HarpC Child Bks.
—Leo the Late Bloomer. Aruego, Jose, illus. LC 70-159154. 32p. (gr. k-3). 1994. pap. 4.95 (*0-06-443348-X*, Trophy) HarpC Child Bks.
—Mert the Blurt. Aruego, Jose & Dewey, Ariane, illus. LC 80-1458. 32p. (gr. 4 up). 1987. 10.95 (*0-13-577164-1*) P-H.
—Miss Gator's School House, 6 bks. Kraus, Robert, illus. (gr. k-3). 1989. Set, 48p. ea. lib. bdg. 53.88 (*0-671-94105-4*, J Messner); Set, 48p. ea. pap. 21.00 (*0-671-94106-2*) S&S Trade.

—Musical Max. Aruego, Jose & Dewey, Ariane, illus. LC 89-77079. 40p. 1990. pap. 13.95 jacketed (*0-671-68681-X*, Little Simon) S&S Trade.
—Musical Max. LC 89-77707. (ps-3). 1992. pap. 5.95 (*0-671-79250-4*, S&S BFYR) S&S Trade.
—Noel the Coward. Aruego, Jose & Dewey, Ariane, illus. 32p. (ps-3). 1988. pap. 12.95 jacketed (*0-671-66845-5*, S&S BFYR); pap. 5.95 (*0-671-66846-3*, S&S BFYR) S&S Trade.
—Owliver. Aruego, Jose & Dewey, Ariane, illus. LC 80-13664. (ps). 1987. pap. 13.95 jacketed (*0-671-66523-5*, S&S BFYR) S&S Trade.
—Phil the Ventriloquist. LC 88-11. (Illus.). 32p. (ps up). 1989. 11.95 (*0-688-07987-3*); PLB 11.88 (*0-688-07988-1*) Greenwillow.
—Spider's Baby-Sitting Job. 1990. pap. 2.50 (*0-590-42445-9*) Scholastic Inc.
—Squeaky. (Illus.). 10p. (ps). 1982. vinyl cover 3.50 (*0-671-44861-7*) S&S Trade.
—Three Friends. Arvego, Jose & Dewey, Ariane, illus. (gr. k-3). 1975. (Dutton); pap. 2.95 (*0-525-62346-9*) NAL-Dutton.
—Where Are You Going, Little Mouse? Aruego, Jose & Dewey, Ariane, illus. LC 84-25868. 32p. (ps-1). 1986. 15.00 (*0-688-04294-5*); PLB 14.93 (*0-688-04295-3*) Greenwillow.
—Where Are You Going, Little Mouse? Dewey, Jose & Aruego, Ariane, illus. LC 84-25868. (ps up). 1989. 4.95 (*0-688-08747-7*, Mulberry) Morrow.
—Whose Mouse Are You? Aruego, Jose, illus. LC 70-89931. 32p. (ps-k). 1986. pap. 4.95 (*0-689-71142-5*, Aladdin) Macmillan Child Grp.
—Whose Mouse Are You? Aruego, Jose, illus. LC 70-89931. 32p. (ps-k). 1970. RSBE 13.95 (*0-02-751190-1*, Macmillan Child Bk) Macmillan Child Grp.
—Wise Old Owl's Christmas Adventure. LC 93-25544. (Illus.). 32p. (ps-3). 1993. PLB 11.89 (*0-8167-2945-X*); pap. text ed. 2.95 (*0-8167-2946-8*) Troll Assocs.
—Wise Old Owl's Halloween Adventure. LC 92-18686. (Illus.). 32p. (gr. k-3). 1993. PLB 11.89 (*0-8167-2949-2*); pap. text ed. 2.95 (*0-8167-2950-6*) Troll Assocs.
Kraus, Robert & Brook, Bonnie. Squirmy's Big Secret. Kraus, Robert, illus. 48p. (ps-3). 1990. lib. bdg. 8.98 (*0-671-70851-1*); pap. 3.95 (*0-671-70852-X*) Silver Pr.
Kraus, Robert see Tubby, I. M., pseud.
Kraus, Robert, ed. & illus. Wise Old Owl's Canoe Trip Adventure. LC 91-39014. 32p. (ps-3). 1993. text ed. 10.89 (*0-8167-2947-6*); 2.95 (*0-8167-2948-4*) Troll Assocs.
Kraus, Robert, ed. see Tubby, I. M.
Kraus, Robert, et al. The Old-Fashioned Raggedy Ann & Andy ABC Book. Kraus, Pam, ed. Gruelle, Johnny, illus. 32p. (ps-2). 1980. 5.95 (*0-671-42552-8*) S&S Trade.
Kraus, Scott & Mallory, Ken. The Search for the Right Whale. LC 92-18091. (Illus.). 36p. (gr. 2-6). 1993. 14.00 (*0-517-57844-1*); PLB 14.99 (*0-517-57845-X*) Crown Bks Yng Read.
Kraus, Theresa. The Department of the Navy. (Illus.). 112p. (gr. 5 up). 1990. 14.95 (*0-87754-845-5*) Chelsea Hse.
Krause, Elaine. For Pete's Sake, Tell! Sullivan, Linda, illus. 54p. (Orig.). (gr. k-3). 1983. pap. text ed. 3.95 (*0-930359-02-X*) Krause Hse.
—Speak up, Say No! 3rd ed. Sullivan, Linda, illus. 40p. (ps-3). 1989. pap. text ed. 3.95 (*0-930359-01-1*) Krause Hse.
Krause, Marina C. Multicultural Mathematics Materials. LC 83-10613. (Illus.). 80p. (gr. 1-8). 1983. pap. 8.00 (*0-87353-206-6*) NCTM.
Krause, Ute. Nora & the Great Bear. (Illus.). 32p. (ps-3). 1992. pap. 3.99 (*0-14-054565-4*, Puffin Pied Piper) Puffin Bks.
—Pig Surprise. Krause, Ute, illus. LC 88-31108. 32p. (ps-3). 1989. 11.95 (*0-8037-0714-2*) Dial Bks Young.
—Pig Surprise. (Illus.). 32p. (ps-3). 1993. pap. 4.50 (*0-14-054592-1*) Puffin Bks.
Krauser, Steven M., jt. auth. see Kittredge, William.
Krauss. Bears. 1993. pap. 28.67 (*0-590-71703-0*) Scholastic Inc.
—Carrot Seed. 1993. pap. 28.67 (*0-590-73301-X*) Scholastic Inc.
—La Semilla de Zanahoria. (SPA.). 1993. pap. 2.95 (*0-590-45092-1*) Scholastic Inc.
Krauss, Robert. Leo the Late Bloomer. Aruego, Jose, illus. LC 80-12511. (ps). 1987. pap. 5.95 (*0-671-66271-6*, S&S BFYR) S&S Trade.
—Mert the Blurt. Aruego, Jose & Dewey, Ariane, illus. LC 80-14508. (ps). 1987. pap. 10.95 jacketed (*0-671-66537-5*, S&S BFYR); (S&S BFYR) S&S Trade.
—Milton the Early Riser. Aruego, Jose & Dewey, Ariane, illus. LC 81-9460. (ps). 1987. pap. 13.95 jacketed (*0-671-66272-4*, S&S BFYR); pap. 5.95 (*0-671-66911-7*, S&S BFYR) S&S Trade.
Krauss, Ruth. Birthday Party. Sendak, Maurice, illus. (gr. k-3). 1978. PLB 11.89 (*0-06-023330-3*) HarpC Child Bks.
—Carrot Seed. Johnson, Crockett, illus. LC 45-4530. 24p. (gr. k-3). 1945. 13.00 (*0-06-023350-8*); PLB 12.89 (*0-06-023351-6*) HarpC Child Bks.
—The Carrot Seed. Johnson, Crockett, illus. LC 45-4530. 32p. (ps-1). 1989. pap. 3.95 (*0-06-443210-6*, Trophy) HarpC Child Bks.

—The Carrot Seed. Johnson, Crockett, illus. (ps-3). 1990. incl. cass. 19.95 *(0-87499-177-3)*; pap. 12.95 incl. cass. *(0-87499-176-5)*; Set; incl. 4 bks., guide, & cass. pap. 27.95 *(0-685-38538-8)* Live Oak Media.
—Carrot Seed Board Book. Johnson, Crockett, illus. LC 45-4530. 24p. (ps-2). 1993. 4.95 *(0-694-00492-8,* Festival) HarpC Child Bks.
—Charlotte & the White Horse. LC 55-8819. (Illus.). 24p. (gr. k-3). 1969. PLB 11.89 *(0-06-023361-3)* HarpC Child Bks.
—Growing Story. Rowand, Phyllis, illus. LC 47-30688. (gr. k-3). 1947. 11.95i *(0-06-023380-X)* HarpC Child Bks.
—The Happy Day. Simont, Marc, illus. LC 49-10568. 30p. (ps-3). 1949. PLB 14.89 *(0-06-023396-6)* HarpC Child Bks.
—The Happy Day. Simont, Marc, illus. LC 49-10568. 36p. (gr. k-3). 1989. pap. 4.95 *(0-06-443191-6,* Trophy) HarpC Child Bks.
—A Hole Is to Dig. Sendak, Maurice, illus. (gr. k-3). 1990. incl. cass. 19.95 *(0-87499-174-9)*; pap. 12.95 incl. cass. *(0-87499-173-0)*; Set; incl. 4 bks., cass., & guide. pap. 27.95 *(0-87499-175-7)* Live Oak Media.
—A Hole Is to Dig: A First Book of Definitions. Sendak, Maurice, illus. LC 52-7731. 48p. (ps up). 1989. pap. 3.95 *(0-06-443205-X,* Trophy) HarpC Child Bks.
—Hole Is to Dig: A First Book of First Definitions. Sendak, Maurice, illus. LC 52-7731. (ps-1). 1952. 14.00 *(0-06-023405-9)*; PLB 13.89 *(0-06-023406-7)* HarpC Child Bks.
—I Can Fly. reissued ed. Blair, Mary, illus. 24p. (ps-k). 1992. write for info. *(0-307-00146-6,* 312-12, Golden Pr) Western Pub.
—I'll Be You & You Be Me. Sendak, Maurice, illus. LC 54-9214. (gr. k-3). 1954. PLB 12.89 *(0-06-023431-8)* HarpC Child Bks.
—I'll Be You-You Be Me. Sendak, Maurice, illus. (gr. k-5). 1973. pap. 8.00 *(0-912846-14-3)* Bookstore Pr.
—Monkey Day. Rowand, Phyllis, illus. 23p. (gr. k-5). 1973. pap. 8.00 *(0-912846-05-4)* Bookstore Pr.
—Open House for Butterflies. reissued ed. Sendak, Maurice, illus. LC 60-5782. 48p. (ps-3). 1990. 11.00 *(0-06-023445-8)*; PLB 10.89 *(0-06-023446-6)* HarpC Child Bks.
—Somebody Else's Nut Tree & Other Tales from Children. Sendak, Maurice, illus. LC 89-28056. 43p. (ps-5). 1990. Repr. of 1958 ed. lib. bdg. 14.00 *(0-208-02264-3,* Linnet) Shoe String.
—This Breast Gothic. Krauss, Ruth, illus. 48p. (gr. 7 up). 1973. pap. 8.00 *(0-912846-02-X)* Bookstore Pr.
—Very Special House. Sendak, Maurice, illus. LC 53-7115. (ps-1). 1953. PLB 15.89 *(0-06-023456-3)* HarpC Child Bks.
—A Very Special House. Sendak, Maurice, illus. LC 53-7115. 32p. (ps-1). 1990. pap. 4.95 *(0-06-443228-9,* Trophy) HarpC Child Bks.
Krautwurst, Terry, jt. auth. see Diehn, Gwen.
Kraven, Mae, ed. see McBurney, Jim.
Kravitz, Alvin & Dramer, Dan. Skillbooster Series Level C. Incl. Building Wordpower. 1978. pap. text ed. 3.04 *(0-8136-1203-9)*; Increasing Comprehension. 1978. pap. text ed. 3.04 *(0-8136-1210-1)*; Organizing Information. 1978. pap. text ed. 3.04 *(0-8136-1224-1)*; Using References. 1978. pap. text ed. 3.04 *(0-8136-1231-4)*; Working with Facts & Details. 1978. pap. text ed. 1.92 *(0-87895-343-4)*. 48p. (gr. 3) Modern Curr.
Krayer, Christina, ed. Crossroads, 84 titles. (Illus.). (gr. 9-12). Date not set. Set. pap. 299.00 *(1-882869-00-1)* Read Advent.
—Drug Awareness, 13 titles. (Illus.). (gr. k-6). Date not set. PLB 199.00 *(1-882869-01-X)* Read Advent.
—It's a Hit, 86 titles. (Illus.). (gr. 3-8). Date not set. Set. pap. 299.00 *(1-882869-06-0)* Read Advent.
—Laugh Track, 96 titles. (Illus.). (gr. 3-8). Date not set. Set. pap. 299.00 *(1-882869-04-4)* Read Advent.
—Mystery Express, 88 titles. (Illus.). (gr. 6-10). Date not set. Set. pap. 379.00 *(1-882869-07-9)* Read Advent.
—Simply Romance, 95 titles. (Illus.). (gr. 6-10). Date not set. Set. pap. 329.00 *(1-882869-02-8)* Read Advent.
—Spine Tinglers, 96 titles. (Illus.). (gr. 3-8). Date not set. Set. pap. 299.00 *(1-882869-03-6)* Read Advent.
Kreeft, Peter. Prayer: The Great Conversation. LC 91-75444. 178p. 1991. pap. 9.95 *(0-89870-357-3)* Ignatius Pr.
Kreeft, Peter J. Letters to Jesus (Answered) LC 88-83743. 294p. (Orig.). 1989. 17.95 *(0-89870-243-7)*; pap. 10.95 *(0-89870-233-X)* Ignatius Pr.
Kreeger, Charlene. The Alaska ABC Book. (Illus.). 36p. (Orig.). (gr. k-1). 1978. pap. 8.95 *(0-933914-01-6)* Paws Four Pub.
—The Loop Train. Cartwright, Shannon, illus. 48p. 1991. pap. 11.95 *(0-933914-02-4)* Lone Raven.
Kreider, Karen. Disney's Aladdin. Baker, Darrell, illus. 24p. (ps-3). 1992. write for info. *(0-307-12348-0,* 12348, Golden Pr) Western Pub.
—Disney's Aladdin: The Genie's Tale. Marderosian, Mark & Kurtz, John, illus. 24p. (ps). 1993. pap. 1.95 *(0-307-10019-7,* 10019, Golden Pr) Western Pub.
Kreikemeier, Gregory S. Come with Me to Africa. (gr. 4-7). 1993. 11.95 *(0-307-15660-5,* Golden Pr) Western Pub.
Krein, Linda. Bible Crossword Fun. 48p. (gr. 3 up). 1990. 6.95 *(0-86653-547-0,* SS892, Shining Star Pubns) Good Apple.
—Bible Crosswords. Hyndman, Kathryn, illus. 48p. (gr. 3 up). 1986. wkbk. 6.95 *(0-86653-366-4,* SS 881, Shining Star Pubns) Good Apple.

Kreisberg, Darlene, jt. auth. see Euretig, Mary.
Kreischer, Elsie. Navaho Magic of Hunting. 32p. (gr. 4-10). 1988. pap. 4.95 *(0-89992-099-3)* Coun India Ed.
Kreisler, Ken, jt. auth. see Rotner, Shelley.
Kreiswirth, Kinny, jt. auth. see Bodily, Jolene.
Krell-Oishi, Mary. Scenes That Happen: Dramatized Snapshots about the Real Life of Highschoolers. Zapel, Theodore O., ed. Glore, John, intro. by. LC 91-26778. 176p. (Orig.). (gr. 9-12). 1991. pap. 10.95 *(0-916260-79-8,* B156) Meriwether Pub.
Kreloff, Elliot, illus. Kitten. (ps-k). 1993. Set, lg. bk. 12p., small bk. 6p. bds. 4.95 *(1-56293-360-4)* McClanahan Bk.
—Puppy. (ps-k). 1993. Set, lg. bk. 12p., small bk. 6p. bds. 4.95 *(1-56293-359-0)* McClanahan Bk.
—Train. (ps-k). 1993. Set, lg. bk. 12p., small bk. 6p. bds. 4.95 *(1-56293-357-4)* McClanahan Bk.
—Truck. (ps-k). 1993. Set, lg. bk. 12p., small bk. 6p. bds. 4.95 *(1-56293-358-2)* McClanahan Bk.
Krementz, Jill. How It Feels to Fight for Your Life. Krementz, Jill, illus. 1989. 15.95 *(0-316-50364-9,* Joy St Bks) Little.
—How It Feels to Live with a Physical Disability. (Illus.). 136p. (gr. 5-9). 1992. 18.00 *(0-671-72371-5)* S&S Trade.
—Jack Goes to the Beach. Krementz, Jill, photos by. LC 85-62038. (Illus.). 14p. (ps). 1986. bds. 3.95 *(0-394-88001-3)* Random Bks Yng Read.
—A Very Young Circus Flyer. (gr. k-6). 1987. pap. 6.95 *(0-440-49216-5,* YB) Dell.
—A Very Young Dancer. (gr. 3-6). 1986. pap. 7.95 *(0-440-49212-2,* YB) Dell.
—A Very Young Gardener. Krementz, Jill, photos by. LC 90-2766. (Illus.). 40p. (ps-3). 1991. 13.95 *(0-8037-0874-2)* Dial Bks Young.
—A Very Young Musician. Krementz, Jill, photos by. (Illus.). 48p. (gr. 3-7). 1991. pap. 14.95 jacketed *(0-671-72687-0,* S&S BFYR) S&S Trade.
—Very Young Musician. LC 90-1001. 48p. (gr. 4-7). 1992. pap. 5.95 *(0-671-79251-2,* S&S BFYR) S&S Trade.
—A Very Young Rider. (gr. k-6). 1987. pap. 6.95 *(0-440-49215-7,* YB) Dell.
—A Very Young Skier. LC 89-28760. (Illus.). 48p. (gr. k up). 1992. pap. 5.99 *(0-8037-1141-7,* Dial Pied Piper) Puffin Bks.
Krensky. Four Against the Odds: The Struggle to Save Our Environment. 1992. pap. 2.95 *(0-590-44743-2)* Scholastic Inc.
Krensky, Stephen. All about Magnets. (ps-3). 1993. pap. 4.95 *(0-590-45567-2)* Scholastic Inc.
—Big Time Bears. Cocca-Leffler, Maryann, illus. LC 88-30793. (ps-k). 1989. 14.95 *(0-316-50375-4)* Little.
—Children of the Earth & Sky: Five Stories about Native American Children. (ps-3). 1992. pap. 3.95 *(0-590-42853-5)* Scholastic Inc.
—Christopher Columbus: A Step Two Book. Green, Norma, illus. LC 89-62507. 48p. (Orig.). (gr. 1-3). 1991. lib. bdg. 7.99 *(0-679-90369-0)*; pap. 3.50 *(0-679-80369-6)* Random Bks Yng Read.
—The Dragon Circle. 128p. (gr. 7 up). 1990. pap. 3.95 *(0-689-71365-7,* Aladdin) Macmillan Child Grp.
—Fraidy Cats. Lewin, Betsy, illus. LC 92-35360. (gr. 3 up). 1993. 2.95 *(0-590-46438-8)* Scholastic Inc.
—George Washington: The Man Who Would Not Be King. 1991. pap. 2.95 *(0-590-43730-5)* Scholastic Inc.
—Ghostly Business. LC 89-29584. 160p. (gr. 4-7). 1990. pap. 3.95 *(0-689-71364-9,* Aladdin) Macmillan Child Grp.
—Los Hios de la Tierra y el Cielo: Children of the Earth & Sky. (ps-3). 1993. pap. 4.95 *(0-590-46861-8)* Scholastic Inc.
—The Iron Dragon Never Sleeps. Fulweiler, Frank, illus. LC 93-31167. 1994. write for info. *(0-385-31171-0)* Delacorte.
—Lionel & Louise. LC 91-16992. (Illus.). 48p. (ps-3). 1992. 11.00 *(0-8037-1055-0)*; PLB 10.89 *(0-8037-1056-9)* Dial Bks Young.
—Lionel at Large. Natti, Susanna, illus. LC 85-1450. 56p. (ps-3). 1986. 9.95 *(0-8037-0240-X)* Dial Bks Young.
—Lionel at Large. Natti, Susanna, illus. LC 85-15930. 56p. (ps-3). 1988. pap. 4.95 *(0-8037-0556-5)* Dial Bks Young.
—Lionel at Large. Natti, Susanna, illus. (gr. 1-4). 1993. pap. 3.25 *(0-14-036542-7,* Puffin) Puffin Bks.
—Lionel in the Fall. Natti, Susanna, illus. LC 86-32876. 48p. (ps-3). 1987. 9.95 *(0-8037-0384-8)*; PLB 9.89 *(0-8037-0385-6)* Dial Bks Young.
—Lionel in the Fall. 1989. pap. 4.95 *(0-8037-0683-9,* Dial) Doubleday.
—Lionel in the Fall. Natti, Susanna, illus. (gr. 1-4). 1993. pap. 3.25 *(0-14-036545-1,* Puffin) Puffin Bks.
—Lionel in the Spring. LC 88-30885. 1990. 9.95 *(0-8037-0630-8)*; PLB 9.89 *(0-8037-0631-6)* Dial Bks Young.
—Lionel in the Spring. Natti, Susanna, illus. LC 88-30885. 48p. (ps-3). 1992. pap. 3.99 *(0-14-036117-0,* Dial Easy to Read) Puffin Bks.
—Lionel in Winter. Natti, Susanna, illus. LC 92-36121. 1994. write for info. *(0-8037-1333-9)*; PLB write for info. *(0-8037-1334-7)* Dial Bks Young.
—Missing Mother Goose: Original Stories from Favorite Rhymes. (ps-3). 1991. 15.00 *(0-385-26273-6)* Doubleday.
—The Pizza Book. (Illus.). 1992. pap. 2.50 *(0-590-44844-7,* 042, Cartwheel) Scholastic Inc.

—Who Really Discovered America? Sullivan, Steve, illus. 64p. (Orig.). (gr. 4-6). 1987. pap. 2.50 *(0-590-40854-2)* Scholastic Inc.
—Who Really Discovered America? Donnelly, Judy, ed. Sullivan, Steve, illus. 64p. (gr. 3-7). 1991. Repr. of 1987 ed. 12.95 *(0-8038-9306-X)* Hastings.
—Witch Hunt: It Happened in Salem Village. Watling, James, illus. LC 88-42865. 48p. (Orig.). (gr. 2-4). 1989. PLB 7.99 *(0-394-91923-8)*; pap. 2.95 *(0-394-81923-3)* Random Bks Yng Read.
—Witching Hour. 144p. (gr. 4-6). 1990. pap. 3.95 *(0-689-71366-5,* Aladdin) Macmillan Child Grp.
Krensky, Stephen, jt. auth. see Brown, Marc.
Krensky, Stephen, ed. The American Heritage First Dictionary. Ulrich, George, illus. LC 86-7363. (Illus.). (gr. 1-2). 1986. 12.70 *(0-395-42530-1)* HM.
Krenz, Nancy, jt. auth. see Byrnes, Patricia.
Krenzer, Rolf & Schmid, Eleonore. To Bethlehem with the Shepherds. 100p. (gr. 1-7). 1989. 35.00x *(0-85439-300-5,* Pub. by St Paul Pubns UK) St Mut.
Krescholleck, Marg. Goof-Proof Microwave Cookbook for Kids. 1992. pap. 9.50 *(0-553-35255-5)* Bantam.
Kresh, Paul. Isaac Bashevis Singer: The Story of a Storyteller. Scofield, Penrod, illus. LC 84-10271. 192p. (gr. 5 up). 1984. 13.95 *(0-525-67156-0,* Lodestar Bks) Dutton Child Bks.
Kreuger, Cynthia M. & Kreuger, Kirsten M. Adventure to Orbital. LC 92-61367. 45p. (gr. k-4). 1993. pap. 5.95 *(1-55523-558-1)* Winston-Derek.
Kreuger, David. What Is a Feeling? Whitney, Jean, illus. 32p. (ps-3). 1993. lib. bdg. 16.95 *(0-943990-76-9)*; pap. 5.95 *(0-943990-75-0)* Parenting Pr.
Kreuger, Kirsten M., jt. auth. see Kreuger, Cynthia M.
Kreutzer, Rudolph. Forty-Two Studies for Violin. Singer, Edmund, ed. 73p. pap. 8.00 *(0-8258-0025-0)* Fischer Inc NY.
Kreye, Walter. The Giant from the Little Island. Bogacki, Tomek, illus. LC 89-43726. 32p. (ps-3). 1990. 13.95 *(1-55858-085-9)* North-South Bks NYC.
Kreysa, Francis J. The Year Christmas Almost Stopped. 1st. ed. Woodard, Chris, illus. 106p. (gr. 4-7). 1982. pap. 3.00 *(0-9611398-0-3)* Kreysa.
Kricher, John & Morrison, Gordon. A Field Guide to Tropical Forests Coloring Book. Kricher, John & Morrison, Gordon, illus. 64p. 1991. pap. 4.80 *(0-395-57321-1)* HM.
Kricher, John C. Peterson First Guide to Dinosaurs. Morrison, Gordon, illus. Peterson, Roger T., frwd. by. (Illus.). 128p. 1990. pap. 4.80 *(0-395-52440-7)* HM.
Kricher, John C. & Morrison, Gordon. Peterson First Guide to Seashores. Kricher, John C. & Morrison, Gordon, illus. 128p. (gr. 5 up). 1992. pap. 4.80 *(0-395-61901-7)* HM.
Krichevsky, David J. What Price Revolution. LC 76-18448. 175p. (gr. 9-12). 1976. 8.95 *(0-87881-052-8)* Mojave Bks.
Krickenberger, Jt. auth. see Welchons.
Krieg, Fred J. Group Leadership Training & Supervision Manual. 3rd ed. LC 88-70010. 260p. (gr. 7 up). 1988. pap. text ed. 20.95 *(0-915202-80-8)* Accel Devel.
Krieger, Melanie J. How to Excel in Science Competitions. LC 91-17790. (Illus.). 144p. (gr. 9-12). 1991. PLB 13.90 *(0-531-11004-4)* Watts.

Krieger, Michael T. Melvin Howard's Fireside Chats. Mills, Tiffany, illus. 149p. (Orig.). (gr. 7 up). 1992. pap. 9.00 *(0-9634329-0-7)* M T Krieger.
Day-dreaming Martin Hovrick, a shy, under-confident teenager, is having trouble growing up. He has many questions about life, girls, friendship, & the future. But, all of his burdens start to become surprisingly easier to carry after his accidental introduction to Melvin Howard, a grandfatherly man, who provides young Martin with guidance & friendship at a critical time in both characters' lives. Set in Northwest Ohio, the book exemplifies finding adventure & worthwhile living in common "everyday" life. As well as being a reflection of the people akin to this area of the Midwest, MELVIN HOWARD'S FIRESIDE CHATS also takes readers, through Melvin's memories, to many places, like a photo safari in the Congo & a deep sea fishing trip just off the Bahamas. But, mostly this novel is a nostalgic journey through time that takes readers back to a simpler, yet more vulnerable period. Melvin Howard's memories, as they are told to Martin, touch many emotions, & supply wise advice to curing traditional woes that have plagued the young throughout time. Each tale that

Melvin weaves subtly conveys a poignant life lesson. Since the stories are pulled from all points in Melvin's past, the emphasis indicates that growing up never really stops. Martin listens to Melvin's stories intently at first as entertainment, but then later he realizes the bigger picture: life is a non-stop growing experience. Martin finds that everyone occasionally lacks self-confidence, & knowing that he is not alone in this effort is a comfort that helps Martin begin to grow within himself, for himself. To order copies, call 419-666-1380.
Publisher Provided Annotation.

Kriegman, Mitchell. The Adventures of Puppycat. Barrett, Deborah, illus. (ps-3). 1990. PLB 8.95 (*0-553-05888-6*, Little Rooster) Bantam.
—Clarissa's All-in-One. (Illus.). 96p. 1993. pap. 2.95 (*0-448-40098-7*, G&D) Putnam Pub Group.
Kriegsman, Kay H., et al. Taking Charge: Teenagers Talk about Life & Physical Disabilities. (Illus.). 186p. (gr. 7-12). 1992. pap. 14.95 (*0-933149-46-8*) Woodbine House.
Kriks, Bill, ed. see King, Nadia.
Krill, Richard M. Forty Fabulous Fables of Aesop. Grant, Peggy, illus. 90p. (gr. 3-6). 1982. 7.95 (*0-942624-00-9*) Promethean Arts.
Krings, Antoon. Oliver's Bicycle. Krings, Antoon, illus. LC 91-25030. 32p. (ps-k). 1992. 6.95 (*1-56282-164-4*); PLB 6.89 (*1-56282-165-2*) Hyprn Child.
—Oliver's Pool. Krings, Antoon, illus. LC 91-24589. 32p. (ps-k). 1992. 6.95 (*1-56282-160-1*); PLB 6.89 (*1-56282-161-X*) Hyprn Child.
—Oliver's Strawberry Patch. Krings, Antoon, illus. LC 91-27022. 32p. (ps-k). 1992. 6.95 (*1-56282-162-8*); PLB 6.89 (*1-56282-163-6*) Hyprn Child.
Kripke, Dorothy K. & Levin, Meyer. God & the Story of Judaism. LC 62-17078. (gr. 4-6). 1962. By Toby K. Kurzband. 6.95x (*0-87441-000-2*) Behrman.
Krishef, Robert, jt. auth. see Lake, Bonnie.
Krishef, Robert K. Dolly Parton. LC 79-28247. (Illus.). 72p. (gr. 5 up). 1980. PLB 10.95 (*0-8225-1411-7*) Lerner Pubns.
—Grand Ole Opry. LC 77-90151. (Illus.). 72p. (gr. 5 up). 1978. PLB 10.95 (*0-8225-1405-2*) Lerner Pubns.
—Jimmie Rodgers. LC 77-90156. (Illus.). 64p. (gr. 5 up). 1978. PLB 10.95 (*0-8225-1404-4*) Lerner Pubns.
Krisher, Trudy. Kathy's Hats: A Story of Hope. Levine, Abby, ed. Westcott, Nadine B., illus. LC 92-2659. 32p. (gr. 1-5). 1992. 13.95g (*0-8075-4116-8*) A Whitman.
Kriss, David, tr. see Amir, Tami.
Kriss, David, tr. see Assaf, Yael.
Kriss, David, tr. see Bar, Amos.
Kriss, David, tr. see Baram, Bella.
Kriss, David, tr. see Burla, Oded.
Kriss, David, tr. see Eitan, Ora.
Kriss, David, tr. see Fleisher, Gila M.
Kriss, David, tr. see Gelbart, Ofra.
Kriss, David, tr. see Gelbert, Ofra.
Kriss, David, tr. see Harel, Nira.
Kriss, David, tr. see Ofek, Uriel.
Kriss, David, tr. see Shinhav, Chaya.
Kroeber, Theodora. Green Christmas. Larrecq, John M., illus. LC 67-26304. (gr. k-2). 1967. 6.95 (*0-87466-047-5*, Pub. by Parnassus) HM.
—The Inland Whale: Nine Stories Retold from California Indian Legends. (Illus.). (gr. 8 up). 1959. pap. 12.00 (*0-520-00676-3*) U CA Pr.
—Ishi: Last of His Tribe. Robbins, Ruth, illus. 208p. 1964. PLB 14.45 (*0-395-27644-6*) HM.
Kroecker, Beth. Bible ABC: Primer Pages. 30p. (gr. 1-6). 1987. lib. bdg. 10.95 (*0-88946-040-X*) E Mellen.
Krogman, Dane & Holelson, Doug. Skeleton Boy: The Nuclear Hero. (Illus.). 80p. (gr. 6-12). 1982. 8.95 (*0-910519-00-5*) Daneco Pubns.
Krohn, Hildegard M., tr. see Brodmann, Aliana.
Krohn, Hildegard M., tr. see Hasler, Eveline.
Krohn, Katherine E. Elvis Presley: The King. LC 93-23905. (gr. 4 up). 1993. 29.95 (*0-8225-2877-0*) Lerner Pubns.
—Lucille Ball: Pioneer of Comedy. (Illus.). 64p. (gr. 4-7). 1992. PLB 13.50 (*0-8225-0543-6*); pap. 4.95 (*0-8225-9603-2*) Lerner Pubns.
—Roseanne Arnold: Comedy's Queen Bee. LC 92-42653. 1993. 13.50 (*0-8225-0520-7*) Lerner Pubns.
—Roseanne Arnold: Comedy's Queen Bee. (gr. 4-7). 1993. pap. 4.95 (*0-8225-9644-X*) Lerner Pubns.
Kroll, Carol. The Hobbit: A Study Guide. 1983. tchr's. ed. & wkbk. 14.95 (*0-88122-036-1*) LRN Links.
Kroll, Stephen. The Big Bunny & the Easter Eggs. (Illus.). 1992. pap. 2.95 (*0-685-54832-5*) Scholastic Inc.
Kroll, Steven. Amanda & the Giggling Ghost. Gackenbach, Dick, illus. LC 79-28379. 40p. (ps-3). 1980. reinforced bdg. 14.95 (*0-8234-0408-0*) Holiday.
—Andrew Wants a Dog. Delaney, Molly, illus. LC 91-25637. 64p. (gr. 2-6). 1992. 11.95 (*1-56282-118-0*); PLB 11.89 (*1-56282-119-9*) Hyprn Child.

—Andrew Wants a Dog. Delany, Molly, illus. LC 91-25637. 64p. (gr. 2-4). 1993. pap. 2.95 (*1-56282-521-6*) Hyprn Ppbks.
—Annabelle's Un-Birthday. Owens, Gail, illus. LC 90-24316. 40p. (gr. 1-5). 1991. RSBE 13.95 (*0-02-751171-5*, Macmillan Child Bk) Macmillan Child Grp.
—Annie's Four Grannies. Christelow, Eileen, illus. LC 85-27193. 32p. (ps-3). 1986. reinforced bdg. 12.95 (*0-8234-0605-9*) Holiday.
—Big Bunny & the Easter Egg. Stevens, Janet, illus. 32p. (gr. k-3). 1988. pap. 2.95 (*0-590-41660-X*) Scholastic Inc.
—The Big Bunny & the Easter Eggs. LC 81-11613. (Illus.). 32p. (ps-3). 1982. reinforced bdg. 14.95 (*0-8234-0436-6*) Holiday.
—The Big Bunny & the Magic Show. Stevens, Janet, illus. LC 85-14147. 32p. (ps-3). 1986. reinforced bdg. 14.95 (*0-8234-0589-3*) Holiday.
—The Big Bunny & the Magic Show. Stevens, Janet, illus. 32p. (ps-2). 1987. pap. 3.95 (*0-590-44633-9*) Scholastic Inc.
—Big Jeremy. Carrick, Donald, illus. LC 88-35812. 32p. (ps-3). 1989. reinforced bdg. 14.95 (*0-8234-0759-4*) Holiday.
—The Biggest Pumpkin Ever. Bassett, Jeni, illus. LC 83-18492. 32p. (ps-3). 1984. reinforced bdg. 14.95 (*0-8234-0505-2*) Holiday.
—The Biggest Pumpkin Ever. Bassett, Jeni, illus. 32p. (gr. k-3). 1985. pap. 2.50 (*0-590-41113-6*) Scholastic Inc.
—The Biggest Pumpkin Ever. Bassett, Jeni, illus. 32p. (ps-1). 1993. pap. 2.50 (*0-590-46463-9*, Cartwheel) Scholastic Inc.
—Branigan's Cat & the Halloween Ghost. Ewing, Carolyn, illus. LC 89-77509. 32p. (ps-3). 1990. reinforced 14.95 (*0-8234-0822-1*) Holiday.
—By the Dawn's Early Light: The Story of the Star Spangled Banner. Andreasen, Dan, illus. LC 92-27101. 40p. (ps-5). 1994. 14.95 (*0-590-45054-9*) Scholastic Inc.
—The Candy Witch. Hafner, Marylin, illus. LC 79-10141. 32p. (ps-3). 1979. reinforced bdg. 14.95 (*0-8234-0359-0*) Holiday.
—Candy Witch. Hafner, Marilyn, illus. (ps up). 1988. pap. 2.50 (*0-590-44509-X*) Scholastic Inc.
—Doctor on an Elephant. 1994. write for info. (*0-8050-2876-5*) H Holt & Co.
—The Goat Parade. Kirk, Tim, illus. LC 82-10604. 48p. (ps-3). 1983. 5.50 (*0-8193-1099-9*); PLB 5.95 (*0-8193-1100-6*) Parents.
—Gone Fishing. Stevenson, Harvey, illus. LC 89-22241. 48p. (ps-2). 1990. PLB 13.99 (*0-517-57590-6*) Crown Bks Yng Read.
—The Hand-Me-Down Doll. Ness, Evaline, illus. LC 83-4394. 32p. (ps-3). 1983. reinforced bdg. 12.95 (*0-8234-0495-1*) Holiday.
—Happy Father's Day. Hafner, Marylin, illus. LC 87-7559. 32p. (ps-3). 1988. reinforced bdg. 14.95 (*0-8234-0671-7*) Holiday.
—Happy Mother's Day. Hafner, Marilyn, illus. LC 83-18498. 32p. (ps-3). 1985. reinforced bdg. 14.95 (*0-8234-0504-4*) Holiday.
—Happy Mother's Day. Hafner, Marilyn, illus. LC 86-25461. 32p. (ps-3). 1987. pap. 3.99 (*0-14-050730-2*, Puffin) Puffin Bks.
—The Hit & Run Gang, No. 3: The Slump. 80p. (Orig.). (gr. 2). 1992. pap. 3.50 (*0-380-76408-3*, Camelot Young) Avon.
—The Hit & Run Gang, No. 5: Pitching Trouble. 96p. 1994. 3.50 (*0-380-77366-X*, Camelot Young) Avon.
—The Hit & Run Gang, No. 6: You're Out! 96p. 1994. pap. 3.50 (*0-380-77367-8*, Camelot Young) Avon.
—The Hit & Run Gang: The Streak, No. 4. 80p. (Orig.). (gr. 2). 1992. pap. 2.99 (*0-380-76410-5*, Camelot Young) Avon.
—The Hokey-Pokey Man. Ray, Deborah K., illus. LC 88-17012. 32p. (ps-3). 1989. reinforced bdg. 14.95 (*0-8234-0728-4*) Holiday.
—I Love Spring. Shoemaker, Kathryn E., illus. LC 86-14844. 32p. (ps-3). 1987. reinforced bdg. 12.95 (*0-8234-0634-2*) Holiday.
—I'd Like to Be. Appleby, Ellen, illus. LC 86-25215. 48p. (ps-3). 1987. 5.95 (*0-8193-1141-3*) Parents.
—I'm George Washington & You're Not. (Illus.). 64p. (gr. 3-7). 1994. 11.95 (*1-56282-579-8*); PLB 11.89 (*1-56282-580-1*) Hyprn Child.
—It's April Fools' Day! Bassett, Jeni, illus. LC 88-28434. 32p. (ps-3). 1990. reinforced bdg. 14.95 (*0-8234-0747-0*) Holiday.
—It's April Fools' Day! Bassett, Jeni, illus. 32p. (ps-3). 1991. pap. 2.50 (*0-590-44348-8*) Scholastic Inc.
—It's Groundhog Day! Bassett, Jeni, illus. LC 86-22924. 32p. (ps-3). 1987. reinforced bdg. 14.95 (*0-8234-0643-1*) Holiday.
—It's Groundhog Day. (ps-3). 1991. pap. 2.50 (*0-590-44669-X*) Scholastic Inc.
—Lewis & Clark: Explorers of the Far West. Williams, Richard, illus. LC 92-40427. (gr. 3-7). 1994. write for info. (*0-8234-1034-X*) Holiday.
—Looking for Daniela: A Romantic Adventure. Lobel, Anita, illus. LC 87-29071. 32p. (ps-3). 1988. reinforced bdg. 14.95 (*0-8234-0695-4*) Holiday.
—Loose Tooth. (Illus.). 1992. 3.95 (*0-590-45713-6*) Scholastic Inc.
—The Magic Rocket. Hillenbrand, Will, illus. LC 91-10114. 32p. (ps-3). 1992. reinforced bdg. 14.95 (*0-8234-0916-3*) Holiday.

—Mary McLean & the St. Patrick's Day Parade. Dooling, Michael, illus. 32p. (ps-3). 1991. 13.95 (*0-590-43701-1*, Scholastic Hardcover) Scholastic Inc.
—Mary McLean & the St. Patrick's Day Parade. (gr. 4-7). 1990. 3.95 (*0-590-43702-X*) Scholastic Inc.
—Mrs. Claus's Crazy Christmas. Wallner, John, illus. LC 84-25218. 32p. (ps-3). 1985. reinforced bdg. 14.95 (*0-8234-0563-X*) Holiday.
—New Kid in Town. (ps-3). 1992. pap. 3.50 (*0-380-76407-5*, Camelot) Avon.
—Newsman Ned & the Broken Rules. Brunkus, Denise, illus. 32p. (Orig.). (ps-1). 1989. pap. 2.95 (*0-590-41368-6*) Scholastic Inc.
—Oh, What a Thanksgiving! Schindler, S. D., illus. LC 88-1973. (gr. k-3). 1988. pap. 12.95 (*0-590-40613-2*, Scholastic Hardcover) Scholastic Inc.
—Oh, What a Thanksgiving! (Illus.). 32p. 1991. pap. 3.95 (*0-590-44874-9*, Blue Ribbon Bks) Scholastic Inc.
—One Tough Turkey. Wallner, John, illus. LC 82-2925. 32p. (ps-3). 1982. reinforced bdg. 14.95 (*0-8234-0457-9*) Holiday.
—Otto. Delaney, Ned, illus. LC 82-19024. 48p. (ps-3). 1983. 5.95 (*0-8193-1105-7*); PLB 5.95 (*0-8193-1106-5*) Parents.
—Patrick's Tree House. Wilson, Roberta, illus. LC 93-4571. 64p. (gr. 2-5). 1994. RSBE 13.95 (*0-02-751005-0*, Macmillan Child Bk) Macmillan Child Grp.
—The Pigrates Clean Up. Bassett, Jeni, illus. LC 92-21823. 32p. (ps-k). 1993. PLB 14.95 (*0-8050-2368-2*, Bks Young Read) H Holt & Co.
—Pigs in the House. Kirk, Tim, illus. LC 83-13310. 48p. (ps-3). 1983. 5.95 (*0-8193-1111-1*) Parents.
—Playing Favorites. (gr. 4-7). 1992. pap. 3.50 (*0-380-76409-1*, Camelot) Avon.
—Princess Abigail & the Wonderful Hat. Brewster, Patience, illus. LC 90-39213. 32p. (ps-3). 1991. reinforced 14.95 (*0-8234-0853-1*) Holiday.
—Queen of the May. Brewster, Patience, illus. LC 92-16393. 32p. (ps-3). 1993. reinforced bdg. 15.95 (*0-8234-1004-8*) Holiday.
—Santa's Crash-Bang Christmas. De Paola, Tomie, illus. LC 77-3025. 32p. (ps-3). 1977. reinforced bdg. 14.95 (*0-8234-0302-5*); pap. 5.95 (*0-8234-0621-0*) Holiday.
—The Squirrels' Thanksgiving. Bassett, Jeni, illus. LC 89-77513. 32p. (ps-3). 1991. reinforced 14.95 (*0-8234-0823-X*) Holiday.
—The Tyrannosaurus Game. De Paola, Tomie, illus. LC 75-37078. 40p. (ps-3). 1976. reinforced bdg. 14.95 (*0-8234-0275-4*); pap. 5.95 (*0-8234-0620-2*) Holiday.
—The Tyrannosaurus Game. De Paola, Tomie, illus. 1988. bk. & cassette 19.95 (*0-87499-096-3*); bk. & cassette 12.95 (*0-87499-095-5*); 4 cassettes & guide 27.95 (*0-87499-097-1*) Live Oak Media.
—Will You Be My Valentine? Hoban, Lillian, illus. 32p. (ps-3). 1993. reinforced bdg. 14.95 (*0-8234-0925-2*) Holiday.
Kroll, Steven & Appleby, Ellen. I'd Like to Be. (Illus.). (ps-3). 1990. pap. 2.95 (*0-448-04332-7*, G&D) Putnam Pub Group.
Kroll, Virginia. Africa Brothers & Sisters. French, Vanessa & French, Vanessa, illus. LC 91-20346. 32p. (ps-2). 1993. RSBE 14.95 (*0-02-751166-9*, Four Winds) Macmillan Child Grp.
—Jaha & Jamil Went down the Hill: An African Mother Goose. (Illus.). 32p. (ps-4). 1994. 14.95 (*0-88106-866-7*); PLB 15.00 (*0-88106-867-5*); pap. 6.95 (*0-88106-865-9*) Charlesbridge Pub.
—Masai & I. Carpenter, Nancy, illus. LC 91-24561. 32p. (gr. k-2). 1992. RSBE 13.95 (*0-02-751165-0*, Four Winds) Macmillan Child Grp.
—My Sister, Then & Now. (ps-3). 1992. 13.50 (*0-87614-718-X*) Carolrhoda Bks.
—My Sister, Then & Now. (ps-3). 1992. pap. 4.95 (*0-87614-584-5*) Carolrhoda Bks.
—The Seasons & Someone. Kiuchi, Tatsuro, illus. LC 93-11123. Date not set. write for info. (*0-15-271233-X*) HarBrace.
—Sweet Magnolia. Jacques, Laura, illus. LC 93-11966. 32p. (ps-4). 1994. 14.95 (*0-88106-415-7*); PLB 15.00 (*0-88106-416-5*); pap. 6.95 (*0-88106-414-9*) Charlesbridge Pub.
—Wood-Hoopoe Willie. (Illus.). 32p. (ps-4). 1993. 14.95 (*0-88106-409-2*); PLB 15.00 (*0-88106-410-6*) Charlesbridge Pub.
Kroll, Virginia L. Beginnings: How Families Came to Be. Schuett, Stacey, illus. LC 93-29594. 1994. write for info. (*0-8075-0602-8*) A Whitman.
—A Carp for Kimiko. Roundtree, Katherine, illus. LC 93-6940. 32p. 1993. 14.95 (*0-88106-412-2*); PLB 15.00 (*0-88106-413-0*) Charlesbridge Pub.
—Helen the Fish. Mathews, Judith, ed. Weidner, Teri, illus. LC 91-17230. 32p. (gr. k-3). 1992. PLB 13.95 (*0-8075-3194-4*) A Whitman.
—I Wanted to Know All about God. Jenkins, Debra R., illus. LC 93-37382. 1993. write for info. (*0-8028-5078-2*) Eerdmans.
—Naomi Knows It's Springtime. Kastner, Jill, illus. LC 92-71267. 32p. (ps-3). 1993. reinforced 14.95 (*1-56397-006-6*) Boyds Mills Pr.
Kroll, William, ed. see Provost, C. Antonio.
Krone, Chester. United States of America. LC 89-26177. (Illus.). 96p. (gr. 6-12). 1990. PLB 19.92 (*0-8114-2434-0*) Raintree Steck-V.
Kronenwetter, Michael. Covert Action. LC 90-46209. (Illus.). (gr. 9-12). 1991. PLB 13.40 (*0-531-13018-5*) Watts.

—Drugs in America. (Illus.). 144p. (gr. 7 up). 1990. lib. bdg. 13.98 (0-671-70557-1, J Messner) S&S Trade.
—London. LC 91-30306. (Illus.). 96p. (gr. 6 up). 1992. RSBE 13.95 (0-02-751050-6, New Discovery) Macmillan Child Grp.
—Managing Toxic Wastes. Steltenpohl, Jane, ed. (Illus.). 126p. (gr. 7-10). 1989. lib. bdg. 13.98 (0-671-69051-5, J Messner) S&S Trade.
—The New Eastern Europe. LC 91-18512. (Illus.). 192p. (gr. 9-12). 1991. PLB 14.40 (0-531-11066-4) Watts.
—Northern Ireland. LC 90-33571. (Illus.). 160p. (gr. 9-12). 1990. PLB 14.40 (0-531-10942-9) Watts.
—The Peace Commandos: Nonviolent Heroes in the Struggle Against War & Injustice. LC 93-31204. (Illus.). 176p. (gr. 6 up). 1994. RSBE 14.95 (0-02-751051-4, New Discovery Bks) Macmillan Child Grp.
—Prejudice in America: Causes & Cures. (Illus.). 144p. (gr. 7-12). 1993. PLB 13.40 (0-531-11163-6) Watts.
—Taking a Stand Against Human Rights Abuses. LC 89-70450. 1990. PLB 14.40 (0-531-10921-6) Watts.
—Under Eighteen: Knowing Your Rights. LC 93-6605. (Illus.). 112p. (gr. 6 up). 1993. lib. bdg. 17.95 (0-89490-434-5) Enslow Pubs.
—United They Hate: White Supremacists in America. 133p. 1992. 14.95 (0-8027-8162-4); lib. bdg. 15.85 (0-8027-8163-2) Walker & Co.
—The War Against Terrorism. Steltenpohl, Jane, ed. (Illus.). 138p. (gr. 7-10). 1989. lib. bdg. 13.98 (0-671-69050-7, J Messner) S&S Trade.
—Welfare State America: Safety Net or Social Contract? LC 92-35880. 144p. (gr. 9-12). 1993. PLB 13.90 (0-531-13010-X) Watts.
Kronstadt, Janet. Florence Sabin. Horner, Matina S., intro. by. (Illus.). 112p. (gr. 5 up). 1990. 17.95 (1-55546-676-1) Chelsea Hse.
Kronzek, Allan Z. A Book of Magic for Young Magicians: The Secrets of Alkazar. (Illus.). 128p. 1992. pap. 6.95t (0-486-27134-X) Dover.
Kropa, Susan. A Nose Is a Nose. 144p. (gr. 4-6). 1988. wkbk. 11.95 (0-86653-449-0, GA1058) Good Apple.
—Sky Blue, Grass Green. Kropa, Susan, illus. 128p. (gr. 1-3). 1986. wkbk. 11.95 (0-86653-355-9, GA 698) Good Apple.
Kropa, Susie. Faces, Legs, & Belly Buttons. Kropa, Susie, illus. 80p. (ps). 1984. wkbk. 8.95 (0-86653-239-0, GA 564) Good Apple.
Kropp, Paul. Dope Deal. Macpherson, Elaine, illus. LC 81-9766. 96p. (gr. 7-12). 1982. pap. 4.50 (0-88436-818-1, 35272); wkbk. 1.20 (0-88436-927-7, 35685); read-along cassette 10.00 (0-88436-951-X, 35106) EMC.
—Getting Even. 192p 1986. pap. 3.50 (0-7704-2112-1) Bantam.
—Moonkid & Liberty. (gr. 3-6). 1990. 13.95 (0-316-50485-8, Joy St Bks) Little.
Krosnick, Teresa A. Scales & Arpeggios in Letter Format: One Octave, Bk. 1. 32p. (Orig.). 1992. pap. text ed. 10.00 GVC bdg. (1-882176-00-6) Theory Aids Keybd.
Kroupa, Melanie. see Richmond, Sandra.
Krudop, Walter L. Blue Claws. Krudop, Walter, illus. LC 92-9922. 36p. (gr. 1-3). 1993. SBE 14.95 (0-689-31787-5, Atheneum Child Bk) Macmillan Child Grp.
Krueger, Caryl W. One Thousand One Things to Do with Your Kids. LC 87-30794. 320p. (gr. 9-12). 1988. pap. 14.95 (0-687-29192-5) Abingdon.
Krueger, Martin T. Two Speeches of the Mayor: Martin T. Krueger. Rinehart, Betty M., intro. by. 44p. (Orig.). (gr. 8 up). 1989. pap. text ed. 2.00 (0-935549-13-7) MI City Hist.
Krueger, Ron, jt. auth. see Weber, Ane.
Krueger, Ron, et al. Bearly There at All. French, Marty, illus. 26p. (ps). 1986. Incl. cass. 7.95 (1-55578-106-3) Worlds Wonder.
—Bearly There at All. French, Marty, illus. 26p. (ps). 1988. incl. cassette 7.95 (1-55578-912-9) Worlds Wonder.
Kruetzer, Peter. Little League's Official How-to-Play Baseball Book. 1990. pap. 12.95 (0-385-41278-9) Doubleday.
—Little League's Official How-to-Play Baseball Handbook. 1990. pap. 9.95 (0-385-24700-1) Doubleday.
Kruger, Herbert O., et al. American History Study Aid. 1975. pap. 1.95 (0-87738-043-0) Youth Ed.
—World Geography Study Aid. 1986. pap. 1.95 (0-87738-044-9) Youth Ed.
Kruglak, Fredlyn. Blue Ribbon Winner's Bakebook. Radtke, Bruce, illus. 320p. (Orig.). (gr. 6-12). 1980. pap. 7.95 (0-9606686-0-8) Bakebks & Cookbks.
Krulik. All about the Fifty States: A Picture Puzzle Book. 1992. pap. 1.95 (0-590-45223-1) Scholastic Inc.
—Ballerina Trolls on Their Toes. 1993. pap. 2.50 (0-590-46893-6) Scholastic Inc.
Krulik, Nancy. Jesse's Full House Snapshot Album. (gr. 4-7). 1993. pap. 4.95 (0-590-46622-4) Scholastic Inc.
—Little Duck's Easter Surprise. (ps-3). 1993. pap. 4.95 (0-590-46261-X) Scholastic Inc.
—On the Road with New Kids on the Block. 1990. pap. 2.50 (0-590-44301-1) Scholastic Inc.
Krulik, Nancy E. The Fifty States Activity Book. 64p. (gr. 2-4). 1991. 1.95 (0-590-43908-1) Scholastic Inc.
—Free Willy. (ps-3). 1993. pap. 2.95 (0-590-46757-3) Scholastic Inc.
—Home Alone Two: Lost in New York, Kevin's Christmas Vacation Scrapbook. 1992. 2.95 (0-590-46187-7) Scholastic Inc.

—M. C. Hammer & Vanilla Ice. 1991. pap. 2.95 (0-590-44980-X) Scholastic Inc.
—My Picture Book of the Planets. (ps-3). 1991. pap. 2.50 (0-590-43907-3) Scholastic Inc.
—Penny & the Four Questions. Young, Marian, illus. 32p. (gr. 1-3). 1993. pap. 2.50 (0-590-46339-X) Scholastic Inc.
—Ralph Troll's New Bicycle. (Illus.). 1992. 2.50 (0-590-45924-4, 047) Scholastic Inc.
Krull, Helen, jt. auth. see Kenny, Kevin.
Krull, Kathleen. Alex Fitzgerald, TV Star. (ps-3). 1991. 10.95 (0-316-50479-3) Little.
—Alex Fitzgerald's Cure for Night, Vol. 1. (gr. 4-7). 1990. 10.95 (0-316-50478-5, Joy St Bks) Little.
—City Within a City: How Kids Live in New York's Chinatown. Hautzig, David, photos by. LC 93-15846. 1994. write for info. (0-525-67437-3, Lodestar Bks) Dutton Child Bks.
—It's My Earth Too: How I Can Help the Earth Stay Alive. Greenberg, Melanie H., illus. (ps-2). 1992. 13.50 (0-385-42088-9) Doubleday.
—The Other Side: How Kids Live in a California Latino Neighborhood. Hautzig, David, photos by. LC 93-15845. (Illus.). (ps-6). 1994. write for info. (0-525-67438-1, Lodestar Bks) Dutton Child Bks.
—Songs of Praise. LC 87-751091. 1993. pap. 5.95 (0-15-277109-3) HarBrace.
Krull, Kathleen, jt. auth. see Allington, Richard L.
Krull, Kathleen see Allington, Richard L.
Krull, Kathleen, selected by. Gonna Sing My Head Off! Garns, Allen, illus. Guthrie, Arlo, intro. by. LC 89-49562. (Illus.). 160p. 1992. 20.00 (0-394-81991-8) Knopf Bks Yng Read.
—Songs of Praise. De Paola, Tomie, illus. 32p. (ps up). 1989. 15.95 (0-15-277108-5) HarBrace.
Krull, Kathleen, ed. see Jones, J. David.
Krumgold, Joseph. And Now Miguel. Charlot, Jean, illus. LC 53-8415. 245p. (gr. 5 up). 1987. 15.00 (0-690-09118-4, Crowell Jr Bks); PLB 14.89 (0-690-04696-0, Crowell Jr Bks) HarpC Child Bks.
—And Now Miguel. Charlot, Jean, illus. LC 53-8415. 245p. (gr. 5 up). 1984. pap. 3.95 (0-06-440143-X, Trophy) HarpC Child Bks.
—Onion John. Shimin, Symeon, illus. LC 59-11395. 248p. (gr. 5 up). 1987. (Crowell Jr Bks); PLB 14.89 (0-690-04698-7, Crowell Jr Bks) HarpC Child Bks.
—Onion John. Shimin, Symeon, illus. LC 59-11395. 248p. (gr. 5 up). 1984. pap. 3.95 (0-06-440144-8, Trophy) HarpC Child Bks.
Krumgold, Joseph, et al. Newbery Award Library II:... And Now Miguel - Bridge to Terabithia - Sarah, Plain & Tall - The Wheel on the School, 4 bks. Charlot, Jean, et al, illus. (gr. 4-6). 1988. Set. pap. 11.95 (0-06-440277-0, Trophy) HarpC Child Bks.
Krupinski. Tea Party Book. Date not set. 15.00 (0-06-023436-9, Festival); PLB 14.89 (0-06-023437-7, Festival) HarpC Child Bks.
Krupinski, Loretta. New England Scrapbook: A Journey through Poems, Prose, & Pictures. LC 92-37705. (gr. 5 up). 1994. 15.00 (0-06-022950-0); PLB 14.89 (0-06-022951-9) HarpC Child Bks.
Krupinski, Loretta, adapted by. & illu see Bacheller, Irving.
Krupinsky, Jacquelyn S. Henry, the Hesitant Heron. Cutri, Anne C. & Cutri, Anne, illus. 32p. (Orig.). (gr. k-3). 1987. pap. 6.95 (0-912123-02-8) Woodbury Pr.
—Look Out for Loons. Krupinsky, Lisa A., ed. Arbuckle, Jane & Krupinsky, Lisa, illus. 28p. (gr. k-3). 1983. pap. 5.95 (0-912123-01-X) Woodbury Pr.
Krupinsky, Lisa A., ed. see Krupinsky, Jacquelyn S.
Krupp, E. C. Big Dipper & You. Krupp, Robin R., illus. LC 88-1501. 48p. (gr. 2 up). 1989. 13.95 (0-688-07191-0); PLB 13.88 (0-688-07192-9, Morrow Jr Bks) Morrow Jr Bks.
—The Moon & You. Krupp, Robin R., illus. LC 92-16231. 48p. (gr. k-4). 1993. RSBE 13.95 (0-02-751142-1, Macmillan Child Bk) Macmillan Child Grp.
Krupp, Edwin C. The Comet & You. Krupp, Robin R., illus. LC 84-20152. 48p. (gr. 1-4). 1985. RSBE 13.95 (0-02-751250-9, Macmillan Child Bk) Macmillan Child Grp.
Krupp, Robin R. Get Set to Wreck! Krupp, Robin R., illus. LC 86-19956. 32p. (gr. 1-3). 1988. RSBE 14.95 (0-02-751140-5, Pub. by Four Winds Pr) Macmillan Child Grp.
—Let's Go Traveling. Krupp, Robin R., illus. LC 91-21845. 40p. (gr. 2 up). 1992. 15.00 (0-688-08989-5); PLB 14.93 (0-688-08990-9) Morrow Jr Bks.
Kruschke, Earl R. & Jackson, Byron M. Nuclear Energy Policy: A Reference Handbook. 250p. 1989. lib. bdg. 39.50 (0-87436-238-5) ABC-CLIO.
Kruss, James & Lewis, Naomi. Johnny Longnose. Eidrigevicius, Stasys, illus. LC 89-42612. 32p. (gr. k-3). 1990. 13.95 (1-55858-023-9) North-South Bks NYC.
Kualter, Anne, jt. auth. see Quinn, John.
Kubasch, Heike. Bree & the Barrow-Downs. (Illus.). 40p. (gr. 10-12). 1984. pap. 7.00 (0-915795-16-7, 8010) Iron Crown Ent Inc.
Kubasik, Chris, jt. auth. see Dowd, Tom.
Kubat, Frank J., Jr., ed. see Lang, W. Harold.
Kubersky, Rachel. Everything You Need to Know about Eating Disorders. (gr. 7-12). 1992. PLB 13.95 (0-8239-1321-X) Rosen Group.
Kubick, Dana. Pop-Up Ballerina Bear. Kubick, Dana, illus. 16p. (ps up). 1993. Incl. 4 1/2" doll. 12.95 (0-590-46753-0, Cartwheel) Scholastic Inc.

Kubler, Annie. Albert Moves In. LC 90-1977. 1989. 11.95 (0-85953-240-2) Childs Play.
—Annie's Body Paint Academy. (ps-3). 1993. pap. 13.95 (0-85953-527-4) Childs Play.
—The Champion. LC 90-24246. (gr. 4 up). 1991. 3.95 (0-85953-531-2) Childs Play.
—Counting Kids. LC 90-1978. 1989. 11.95 (0-85953-241-0) Childs Play.
—Daphne Dragon. 1985. 4.95 (0-85953-260-7) Childs Play.
—I Know a Secret. LC 90-46183. 1989. 11.95 (0-85953-315-8) Childs Play.
—Noah's Ark. 1985. 4.95 (0-85953-255-0) Childs Play.
—Panic Farm. 1985. 4.95 (0-85953-258-5) Childs Play.
—Rolling Along. 1991. 5.95 (0-85953-448-0) Childs Play.
—The Street Cleaner. LC 90-25105. 1991. 3.95 (0-85953-530-4) Childs Play.
—When I Grow Up. LC 91-27125. 1992. 5.95 (0-85953-505-3) Childs Play.
—Where Do We Live? 1985. 4.95 (0-85953-256-9) Childs Play.
Kubler-Ross, Elisabeth. Remember the Secret. Preston, Heather, illus. LC 81-68454. 32p. (ps up). 1988. pap. 9.95 (0-89087-524-3) Celestial Arts.
Kublin, Hyman. India: Regional Study. rev. ed. (Illus.). 228p. (gr. 9-12). 1973. pap. 20.56 (0-395-13928-7) HM.
—The Middle East: Regional Study. rev. ed. LC 72-6696. (Illus.). 258p. (gr. 9-12). 1973. pap. 20.56 (0-395-13931-7) HM.
Kubota, Carole, jt. auth. see Holland, Penny.
Kubota, Makota. Children of the World: South Korea. LC 86-42804. (Illus.). 64p. (gr. 5-6). 1987. PLB 19.93 (1-55532-168-2) Gareth Stevens Inc.
Kuchalla, Susan. All about Seeds. McBee, Jane, illus. LC 81-11480. 32p. (gr. k-2). 1982. lib. bdg. 10.89 (0-89375-658-X); pap. 2.95 (0-89375-659-8) Troll Assocs.
—Baby Animals. Snyder, Joel, illus. LC 81-11434. 32p. (gr. k-2). 1982. lib. bdg. 11.59 (0-89375-666-0); pap. 2.95 (0-89375-667-9) Troll Assocs.
—Bears. Kelleher, Kathie, illus. LC 81-11368. 32p. (gr. k-2). 1982. PLB 11.59 (0-89375-674-1); pap. 2.95 (0-89375-675-X) Troll Assocs.
—Birds. Britt, Gary, illus. LC 81-11412. 32p. (gr. k-2). 1982. lib. bdg. 11.59 (0-89375-656-3); pap. 2.95 (0-89375-657-1) Troll Assocs.
—What Is a Reptile? Harvey, Paul, illus. LC 81-11364. 32p. (gr. k-2). 1982. PLB 11.59 (0-89375-672-5); pap. 2.95 (0-89375-673-3) Troll Assocs.
Kuchler, Lena. My Hundred Children. (Orig.). (gr. k-12). 1987. pap. 3.50 (0-440-95263-8, LFL) Dell.
Kuchn, Nora A. Thunder, the Maverick Mustang. 96p. 1991. pap. 6.95 (0-8163-0932-9) Pacific Pr Pub Assn.
Kuckreja, Madhari. Prince Norodom Sihanouk. (Illus.). 112p. (gr. 5 up). 1990. 17.95 (1-55546-851-9) Chelsea Hse.
Kudalis, Eric. Dracula & Other Vampire Stories. 48p. (gr. 3-10). 1994. PLB 17.27 (1-56065-212-8) Capstone Pr.
—Frankenstein & Other Stories of Man-Made Monsters. 48p. (gr. 3-10). 1994. PLB 17.27 (1-56065-213-6) Capstone Pr.
—Stories of Mummies & the Living Dead. 48p. (gr. 3-10). 1994. PLB 17.27 (1-56065-214-4) Capstone Pr.
—Werewolves & Stories about Them. 48p. (gr. 3-10). 1994. PLB 17.27 (1-56065-215-2) Capstone Pr.
Kudla, Pamela, jt. auth. see Lewis, Marguerite.
Kudlinski, Kathleen V. Animal Tracks & Traces. Morgan, Mary, illus. 32p. (gr. 1 up). 1991. 12.95 (0-531-15185-9); PLB 12.90 (0-531-10742-6) Watts.
—Earthquake! A Story of Old San Francisco. Himler, Ronald, illus. 64p. (gr. 2-6). 1993. RB 12.99 (0-670-84874-3) Viking Child Bks.
—Helen Keller. Diamond, Donna, illus. 64p. (gr. 2-6). 1991. 3.95 (0-14-032902-1) Puffin Bks.
—Helen Keller: A Light for the Blind. Diamond, Donna, illus. 64p. (gr. 2-6). 1989. pap. 10.95 (0-670-82460-7) Viking Child Bks.
—Hero over Here. Dodson, Bert, illus. 64p. (gr. 2-6). 1990. pap. 13.00 (0-670-83050-X) Viking Child Bks.
—Hero over Here: A Story of World War I. Dodson, Bert, illus. 64p. (gr. 2-6). 1992. pap. 3.99 (0-14-034286-9, Puffin) Puffin Bks.
—Juliette Gordon Low: America's First Girl Scout. Hamanaka, Sheila, illus. 64p. (gr. 2-6). 1988. pap. 10.95 (0-670-82208-6) Viking Child Bks.
—Lone Star: A Story of the Texas Rangers. Himler, Ronald, illus. 64p. (gr. 2-6). 1994. PLB 12.99 (0-670-85179-5) Viking Child Bks.
—Night Bird: A Story of the Seminole Indians. Watling, James, illus. 64p. (gr. 2-6). 1990. PLB 12.99 (0-670-83157-3) Viking Child Bks.
—Pearl Harbor is Burning: A Story of World War II. (gr. 4-7). 1991. 11.95 (0-670-83475-0) Viking Child Bks.
—Pearl Harbor is Burning! A Story of World War II. Himler, Ronald, illus. 64p. (gr. 2-6). 1993. pap. 3.99 (0-14-034509-4, Puffin) Puffin Bks.
—Rachel Carson: Pioneer of Ecology. Lewin, Ted, illus. 64p. (gr. 2-6). 1988. pap. 10.95 (0-670-81488-1) Viking Child Bks.
—Rachel Carson: Pioneer of Ecology. Lewin, Ted, illus. 64p. (gr. 2-6). 1989. pap. 3.99 (0-14-032242-6, Puffin) Puffin Bks.
Kudlovich, David. Why Me? 1992. 7.95 (0-533-09652-9) Vantage.
Kudrna, C. Imbior. To Bathe a Boa. Kudrna, C. Imbiore., illus. 32p. (ps-4). 1986. PLB 18.50 (0-87614-306-0); pap. 5.95 (0-87614-490-3) Carolrhoda Bks.

Kuebler, Sharon. Noon to Night. Kirkeeide, Deborah, illus. 32p. (ps-2). Date not set. 11.95 (*1-56065-161-X*) Capstone Pr. Postponed.
Kuehne, Tom, jt. auth. see Barnes, F. A.
Kugler, Lisa. A New Baby for Us: Sibling Preparation & Activity Book for Big Brothers & Sisters. Kugler, Lisa, illus. 32p. (Orig.). (ps-1). 1990. pap. 5.95 (*0-944782-03-5*) Glover Pr.
Kuhn, Dwight. More Than Just a Flower Garden. Brook, Bonnie, ed. (Illus.). 40p. (gr. 2 up). 1990. 13.95 (*0-671-69644-0*); PLB 15.98 (*0-671-69642-4*) Silver Pr.
—More Than Just a Vegetable Garden. Brook, Bonnie, ed. (Illus.). 40p. (gr. 2 up). 1990. 13.95 (*0-671-69645-9*); PLB 15.98 (*0-671-69643-2*) Silver Pr.
—More Than Just a...Series, 2 vols. Kuhn, Dwight, photos by. (Illus.). 80p. (gr. 2 up). 1990. Set. 27.90 (*0-671-94439-8*); Set. PLB 31.96 (*0-671-94438-X*) Silver Pr.
Kuhn, Dwight, photos by. The Hidden Life of the Forest. Schwartz, David M., text by. (Illus.). 40p. (gr. 1 up). 1988. PLB 15.00 (*0-517-57058-0*) Crown Bks Yng Read.
—The Hidden Life of the Meadow. Schwartz, David M., text by. (Illus.). 40p. (gr. 1 up). 1988. PLB 12.95 (*0-517-57059-9*) Crown Bks Yng Read.
—The Hidden Life of the Pond. Schwartz, David M., text by. (Illus.). 40p. (gr. 1 up). 1988. PLB 15.00 (*0-517-57060-2*) Crown Bks Yng Read.
—Hungry Little Frog. Hirschi, Ron, text by. (Illus.). 32p. (ps-2). 1992. 9.95 (*0-525-65109-8*, Cobblehill Bks) Dutton Child Bks.
Kuhn, Dwight R. My First Book of Nature. LC 92-14329. 64p. 1993. 11.95 (*0-590-45502-8*) Scholastic Inc.
Kuhn, Ferdinand. Commodore Perry & the Opening of Japan. (Illus.). (gr. 4-6). 1955. 2.95 (*0-394-80356-6*) Random Bks Yng Read.
Kujoko. Pig Tales: The Adventures of Arnold the Chinese Potbelly Miniature Pig. Clifford, Sandy, illus. 21p. (Orig.). (ps-8). 1988. pap. 4.95 (*0-9623210-0-1*) Kiyoko & Co.
Kukkonen, Walter J. Off Broadway. 32p. (Orig.). 1990. pap. text ed. 1.00 (*0-685-49153-6*) Polaris AZ.
Kuklin, Susan. A Doll Named Autumn. (Illus.). 32p. (gr. k-4). 1994. write for info. (*1-56282-666-2*); PLB write for info. (*1-56282-667-0*) Hyprn Child.
—Fighting Back: What Some People Are Doing about AIDS. (Illus.). 144p. (gr. 8 up). 1989. 14.95 (*0-399-21621-9*, Putnam) Putnam Pub Group.
—Fighting Fires. LC 92-38678. (Illus.). 32p. (ps-2). 1993. RSBE 14.95 (*0-02-751238-X*, Bradbury Pr) Macmillan Child Grp.
—Going to My Ballet Class. Kuklin, Susan, illus. LC 88-37556. 32p. (ps-2). 1989. RSBE 13.95 (*0-02-751225-5*, Bradbury Pr) Macmillan Child Grp.
—Going to My Gymnastics Class. Kuklin, Susan, illus. LC 90-20206. 40p. (ps-1). 1991. RSBE 13.95 (*0-02-751236-3*, Bradbury Pr) Macmillan Child Grp.
—Going to My Nursery School. Kuklin, Susan, illus. LC 89-37077. 40p. (ps-k). 1990. RSBE 13.95 (*0-02-751237-1*, Bradbury Pr) Macmillan Child Grp.
—How My Family Lives in America. Kuklin, Susan, illus. LC 91-22949. 40p. (ps-3). 1992. RSBE 13.95 (*0-02-751239-8*, Bradbury Pr) Macmillan Child Grp.
—Reaching for Dreams: A Ballet from Rehearsal to Opening Night. Kuklin, Susan, illus. LC 86-15356. (gr. 4-9). 1987. 12.95 (*0-688-06316-0*) Lothrop.
—Speaking out. 192p. (gr. 6 up). 1993. 15.95 (*0-399-22343-6*, Putnam); pap. 8.95 (*0-399-22532-3*) Putnam Pub Group.
—Surviving Suicide: Conversations about Living. LC 93-33141. 1994. write for info. (*0-399-22605-2*, Putnam) Putnam Pub Group.
—Taking My Cat to the Vet. Kuklin, Susan, illus. LC 88-5052. 32p. (ps-k). 1988. RSBE 13.95 (*0-02-751233-9*, Bradbury Pr) Macmillan Child Grp.
—Taking My Dog to the Vet. Kuklin, Susan, illus. LC 88-5047. 32p. (ps-k). 1988. RSBE 13.95 (*0-02-751234-7*, Bradbury Pr) Macmillan Child Grp.
—Thinking Big: The Story of a Young Dwarf. LC 85-10425. (Illus.). 48p. (ps-1). 1986. 12.95 (*0-688-05826-4*); PLB 12.88 (*0-688-05827-2*) Lothrop.
—What Do I Do Now? (Illus.). 1991. 15.95 (*0-399-21843-2*, Putnam); pap. 7.95 (*0-399-22043-7*, Putnam) Putnam Pub Group.
—When I See My Dentist. LC 87-25695. (Illus.). 32p. (ps-k). 1988. RSBE 13.95 (*0-02-751231-2*, Bradbury Pr) Macmillan Child Grp.
—When I See My Doctor. LC 87-25621. (Illus.). 32p. (ps-k). 1988. RSBE 13.95 (*0-02-751232-0*, Bradbury Pr) Macmillan Child Grp.
Kukoff, Lydia, jt. auth. see Einstein, Stephen J.
Kulkarni, Shyamkant. The Sun Dance & Other Poems. Andrews, Duane, illus. LC 91-90016. iv, 32p. (Orig.). (gr. 5 up). 1991. pap. 5.50 (*0-9627083-1-3*) S Kulkarni.
Kuller, Alison M. An Outward Bound School. Stewart, Thomas R. & Kuller, Alison M., illus. LC 89-5169. 32p. (gr. 3-6). 1990. PLB 10.79 (*0-8167-1731-1*); pap. text ed. 2.95 (*0-8167-1732-X*) Troll Assocs.
Kulling, Monica. I Hate You, Marmalade. Ayliffe, Alex, illus. 32p. (ps-3). 1992. 14.00 (*0-670-84480-2*) Viking Child Bks.
—Waiting for Amos. Lowe, Vicky, illus. LC 92-19550. 32p. (ps-2). 1993. SBE 13.95 (*0-02-751245-2*, Bradbury Pr) Macmillan Child Grp.
Kulling, Monica, adapted by see Alcott, Louisa May.

Kulman, Andrew. Red Light Stop, Green Light Go. Kulman, Andrew, illus. LC 92-14228. (ps). 1993. pap. 15.00 JRT (*0-671-79493-0*, S&S BFYR) S&S Trade.
Kulp, Katherine, jt. auth. see King-Dickman, Kathy.
Kulper, Eileen. The Boston Marathon. (gr. 5 up). 1992. PLB 14.95 (*0-88682-536-9*) Creative Ed.
—Rollerskating. 48p. (gr. 3-4). 1991. PLB 11.95 (*1-56065-050-8*) Capstone Pr.
Kumalo, Alf. Mandela Echoes of Era. Es'Kia Mphahlele & Sisulu, Waltertext by. 176p. (ps-3). 1990. pap. 16.95 (*0-14-014316-5*) Viking Child Bks.
Kumbaraci, Turkan & Gardenier, George H. Branching Trees: Statistical Methods: Games & Songs. Gardenier, Turhan K., illus. LC 89-90944. 27p. (gr. 1-8). 1989. 30.00x (*0-685-29039-5*, 0003) Teka Trends.
—Computer Models: Statistical Methods: Games & Songs. Gardenier, Turhan K., illus. LC 89-90944. 19p. (gr. 1-8). 1989. Incl. manipulatives. 20.00 (*0-685-29040-9*, 0004) Teka Trends.
—Fun with Numbers: Statistical Methods: Games & Song. Gardenier, Turhan K., illus. LC 89-90944. 15p. (gr. 1-8). 1989. 20.00x (*0-685-29038-7*, 0002) Teka Trends.
—Time: Statistical Methods: Games & Songs. Gardenier, Turhan K., illus. LC 89-90944. 19p. (gr. 1-8). 1989. 20.00 (*0-685-29041-7*, 0005) Teka Trends.
—Two-by-Two: Statistical Methods: Games & Songs. Gardenier, Turhan K., illus. LC 89-90944. 19p. (gr. 1-8). 1989. 20.00 (*0-685-29042-5*, 0006) Teka Trends.
Kumin, Maxine. The Microscope. Lobel, Arnold, illus. LC 82-47728. 32p. (ps-3). 1984. PLB 12.89 (*0-06-023524-1*) HarpC Child Bks.
Kung, Edward, ed. see Advance Cal-Tech Inc.
Kunhardt, Dorothy. Pat the Bunny. Kunhardt, Dorothy, illus. (ps). 1942. write for info. (*0-307-12000-7*, Golden Bks) Western Pub.
—Pat the Bunny. Kunhardt, Dorothy, illus. (ps). 1988. Includes Touch & Feel Book with Plush Doll. pap. write for info. (*0-307-14000-8*, Pub. by Golden Bks) Western Pub.
—Pat the Puppy. (ps). 1993. 6.95 (*0-307-12004-X*, Golden Pr) Western Pub.
—Pudding Is Nice. Kunhardt, Dorothy, illus. LC 75-19948. 64p. (gr. 1 up). 1975. 15.00 (*0-912846-18-6*); pap. 8.00 (*0-912846-12-7*) Bookstore Pr.
Kunhardt, Edith. The Airplane Book. Bracken, Carolyn, illus. 24p. (ps-k). 1987. pap. write for info. (*0-307-10083-9*, Pub. by Golden Bks) Western Pub.
—Danny's Christmas Star. LC 88-18785. (Illus.). 24p. (ps up). 1989. 12.95 (*0-688-07905-9*); PLB 12.88 (*0-688-07906-7*) Greenwillow.
—Danny's Mystery Valentine. (Illus.). 24p. (ps-1). 1987. 11.75 (*0-688-06853-7*); PLB 11.88 (*0-688-06854-5*) Greenwillow.
—Pat the Cat. Kunhardt, Edith, illus. LC 83-83106. (ps-3). 1984. write for info. comb. bdg. (*0-307-12001-5*, 12001, Golden Bks) Western Pub.
—Pompeii... Buried Alive! Eagle, Michael, illus. LC 87-4512. 48p. (gr. 2-3). 1987. lib. bdg. 6.99 (*0-394-98866-3*); 3.50 (*0-394-88866-9*) Random Bks Yng Read.
—Red Day, Green Day. Hafner, Marylin, illus. LC 90-38490. 32p. (ps up). 1992. 14.00 (*0-688-09399-X*); PLB 13.93 (*0-688-09400-7*) Greenwillow.
—Trick or Treat, Danny! LC 87-14963. (Illus.). 24p. (ps-1). 1988. 11.95 (*0-688-07310-7*); lib. bdg. 11.88 (*0-688-07311-5*) Greenwillow.
—Where's Peter? LC 86-27061. (Illus.). 24p. (ps-3). 1988. 11.95 (*0-688-07204-6*); lib. bdg. 11.88 (*0-688-07205-4*) Greenwillow.
—Which One Would You Choose? LC 87-37200. (Illus.). 24p. (ps up). 1989. 11.95 (*0-688-07907-5*); PLB 11.88 (*0-688-07908-3*) Greenwillow.
—Which Pig Would You Choose? LC 88-35588. (Illus.). (ps up). 1990. 12.95 (*0-688-08981-X*); lib. bdg. 12.88 (*0-688-08982-8*) Greenwillow.
Kunhardt, Edith I. Danny & the Easter Egg. LC 88-1164. (Illus.). 24p. (ps up). 1989. 11.95 (*0-688-08035-9*); PLB 11.88 (*0-688-08036-7*) Greenwillow.
Kunic, Debbie. Cats & Kittens Coloring Album. Warner, Rita, illus. 32p. 1977. pap. 4.50 (*0-8431-1720-6*, 80-9) Price Stern.
Kunin, Claudia. My Christmas Alphabet. (ps-3). 1993. 6.95 (*0-307-13720-1*, Golden Pr) Western Pub.
—My Hanukkah Alphabet. (ps-3). 1993. 6.95 (*0-307-13719-8*, Golden Pr) Western Pub.
—My Hanukkah Book of Numbers. (ps-3). 1993. 6.95 (*0-307-13718-X*, Golden Pr) Western Pub.
Kunjufu, Jawanza. Lessons from History: A Celebration in Blackness. 108p. (gr. 1-5). 1987. 12.95 (*0-913543-05-5*); pap. 6.95 (*0-913543-04-7*) African Am Imag.
—Lessons from History: A Celebration in Blackness. 116p. (gr. 6-12). 1987. 13.95 (*0-913543-07-1*); pap. 7.95 (*0-913543-06-3*) African Am Imag.
Kunsch de Sokoluk, M. Cristina. Cartas de Ester. (SPA.). 110p. (gr. 10 up). 1988. pap. 3.75 (*0-311-37027-6*) Casa Bautista.
Kunstadter, Maria. Women Working A-Z. (Illus.). 32p. (ps-3). 1993. PLB 15.00 (*0-917846-25-7*, 95564) Highsmith Pr.
Kunstler, James H. Annie Oakley. Warter, Fred, illus. LC 93-19246. 1993. 14.95 (*0-88708-338-2*, Rabbit Ears); pap. 19.95 incl. cassette (*0-88708-337-4*, Rabbit Ears) Picture Bk Studio.

Kuntz, J. L. Tennessee Tiger. LC 93-60259. (Illus.). 57p. (ps-3). 1994. 7.95 (*1-55523-611-1*) Winston-Derek.
Kuntz, Margy. Adventures in Life Science. (gr. 4-6). 1987. pap. 6.95 (*0-8224-2317-0*) Fearon Teach Aids.
—Adventures in Physical Science. (gr. 4-6). 1987. pap. 6.95 (*0-8224-2319-7*) Fearon Teach Aids.
—Kermit Learns How Computers Work. 48p. (Orig.). (gr. 4 up). 1993. pap. 9.95 (*1-55958-367-3*) Prima Pub.
—Kermit Learns How Computers Work. LC 93-13339. 1993. 9.95 (*1-55958-368-1*) Prima Pub.
Kuntz, Margy, jt. auth. see Hay, Maureen E.
Kuntz, Margy, et al. Big Fearon Book of Doing Science. (gr. 1-6). 1989. pap. 25.95 (*0-8224-2737-0*) Fearon Teach Aids.
Kunz, Virginia B. The French in America. LC 66-10146. (Illus.). 96p. (gr. 5 up). PLB 15.95 (*0-8225-0204-6*); pap. 5.95 (*0-8225-1008-1*) Lerner Pubns.
Kurelek, William. Lumberjack. (Illus.). 48p. (gr. 5 up). text ed. 17.95 (*0-88776-052-X*, Dist. by U of Toronto Pr) Tundra Bks.
—A Northern Nativity. Kurelek, William, illus. (gr. 4 up). 1976. 14.95 (*0-88776-099-6*); pap. 7.95 (*0-685-04960-4*) Tundra Bks.
—A Prairie Boy's Summer. Kurelek, William, illus. 48p. (gr. 5 up). 1975. 14.95 (*0-88776-058-9*); pap. 6.95 (*0-88776-116-X*) Tundra Bks.
—A Prairie Boy's Winter. Kurelek, William, illus. LC 73-8913. 48p. (gr. k-3). 1984. 14.45 (*0-395-17708-1*); pap. 6.70 (*0-395-36609-7*) HM.
Kurelek, William & Engelhart, Margaret S. They Sought a New World: The Story of European Immigration to North America. (Illus.). 48p. (gr. 4 up). 1985. 14.95 (*0-88776-172-0*, Dist. by U of Toronto Pr); pap. 7.95 (*0-88776-213-1*) Tundra Bks.
Kuribayashi, Pam. A Summer Madness. 79p. (Orig.). (gr. 10-12). 1988. pap. 5.95 (*0-685-22514-3*) Prairie Shark Pr.
Kurjian, Judi. In My Own Backyard. Wagner, David, illus. LC 93-18472. 32p. (ps-8). 1993. 14.95 (*0-88106-442-4*); PLB 15.00 (*0-88106-443-2*) Charlesbridge Pub.
Kurkowski, David C., ed. Curren: Leaders of Nations. LC 89-81456. (Illus.). 180p. (gr. 9-12). 1990. 3-ring binder 95.00 (*0-9624900-0-8*) Current Leaders Pub.
Kurkul, Edward. Tiger in the Lake. Petie, Haris, illus. LC 68-11183. (gr. 1-3). 1968. write for info. (*0-8313-0076-0*); PLB 7.19 (*0-685-42237-2*) Lantern.
Kurland, Adrienne. Coping with Being Pregnant. Rosen, Ruth, ed. LC 88-18433. (gr. 7 up). 1988. PLB 13.95 (*0-8239-0791-0*) Rosen Group.
Kurland, Alexandra. Sara's Story: The Bear Nobody Wanted. (Illus.). 64p. (gr. k-4). 1988. 12.95 (*0-938209-34-5*) Bear Hollow Pr.
—Teddies to the Rescue. Kenyon, Mark, illus. 56p. (gr. k-4). 1986. 11.95 (*0-938209-27-2*) Bear Hollow Pr.
Kurland, Gerald. Alexander Hamilton: Architect of American Nationalism. Rahmas, D. Steve, ed. LC 73-190245. 32p. (gr. 7-12). 1972. lib. bdg. 4.95 incl. catalog cards (*0-87157-527-2*) SamHar Pr.
—Andrew Carnegie: Philanthropist & Early Tycoon of the Steel Industry. Rahmas, D. Steve, ed. LC 72-81901. 32p. (gr. 7-12). 1972. lib. bdg. 4.95 incl. catalog cards (*0-87157-553-1*) SamHar Pr.
—The Arab-Israeli Conflict. Rahmas, D. Steve, ed. LC 72-89221. 32p. (Orig.). (gr. 7-12). 1973. lib. bdg. 4.95 incl. catalog cards (*0-87157-802-6*) SamHar Pr.
—Benjamin Franklin: America's Universal Man. Rahmas, D. Steve, ed. LC 72-190250. 32p. (Orig.). (gr. 7-12). 1972. lib. bdg. 4.95 incl. catalog cards (*0-87157-533-7*) SamHar Pr.
—Clarence Darrow: Attorney for the Damned. Rahmas, D. Steve, ed. LC 75-190240. 32p. (gr. 7-12). 1972. lib. bdg. 4.95 incl. catalog cards (*0-87157-522-1*) SamHar Pr.
—Communism & the Red Scare. Rahmas, Sigurd C., ed. 32p. (Orig.). (gr. 7-12). 1982. 4.95 (*0-87157-819-0*) SamHar Pr.
—The Czechoslovakian Crisis of 1968. 32p. (gr. 7-12). lib. bdg. 4.95 incl. catalog cards (*0-87157-716-X*) SamHar Pr.
—Fidel Castro: Communist Dictator of Cuba. Rahmas, D. Steve, ed. 32p. (Orig.). (gr. 7-12). 1972. lib. bdg. 4.95 incl. catalog cards (*0-87157-536-1*) SamHar Pr.
—Fiorello LaGuardia: The People's Mayor of New York. Rahmas, D. Steve, ed. LC 77-190238. 32p. (Orig.). (gr. 7-12). 1972. lib. bdg. 4.95 incl. catalog cards (*0-87157-520-5*) SamHar Pr.
—George Wallace: Southern Governor & Presidential Candidate. Rahmas, D. Steve, ed. 32p. (Orig.). (gr. 7-12). 1972. lib. bdg. 4.95 incl. catalog cards (*0-87157-529-9*) SamHar Pr.
—The Gulf of Tonkin Incidents. new ed. Rahmas, D. Steve, ed. 32p. (gr. 7-12). 1975. lib. bdg. 4.95 incl. catalog cards (*0-87157-722-4*) SamHar Pr.
—The Hungarian Rebellion of 1956. 32p. (Orig.). (gr. 7-12). 1974. lib. bdg. 4.95 incl. catalog cards (*0-87157-718-6*) SamHar Pr.
—James Hoffa: Convicted Leader of the American Teamsters Union. Rahmas, D. Steve, ed. LC 72-89208. 32p. (Orig.). (gr. 7-12). 1972. lib. bdg. 4.95 incl. catalog cards (*0-87157-540-X*) SamHar Pr.
—John D. Rockefeller: Nineteenth Century Industrialist & Oil Baron. Rahmas, D. Steve, ed. 32p. (gr. 7-12). 1972. lib. bdg. 4.95 incl. catalog cards (*0-87157-535-3*) SamHar Pr.

—Lucretia Mott: Early Leader of the Women's Liberation Movement. Rahmas, D. Steve, ed. LC 72-81902. 32p. (gr. 7-12). 1972. lib. bdg. 4.95 incl. catalog cards (*0-87157-549-3*) SamHar Pr.
—Lyndon Baines Johnson: President Caught in an Ordeal of Power. Rahmas, D. Steve, ed. LC 76-190243. 32p. (Orig.). (gr. 7-12). 1972. lib. bdg. 4.95 incl. catalog cards (*0-87157-525-6*) SamHar Pr.
—Mao Tse-Tung: Founder of Communist China. Rahmas, D. Steve, ed. LC 75-190232. 32p. (Orig.). (gr. 7-12). 1972. lib. bdg. 4.95 incl. catalog cards (*0-87157-514-0*) SamHar Pr.
—The My Lai Massacre. Rahmas, D. Steve, ed. 32p. (gr. 7-12). 1973. lib. bdg. 4.95 incl. catalog cards (*0-87157-708-9*) SamHar Pr.
—Richard Daley: The Strong Willed Mayor of Chicago. Rahmas, D. Steve, ed. LC 70-190236. 32p. (Orig.). (gr. 7-12). lib. bdg. 4.95 incl. catalog cards (*0-87157-518-3*) SamHar Pr.
—Samuel Gompers: Founder of the American Labor Movement. Rahmas, D. Steve, ed. LC 72-190242. 32p. (Orig.). (gr. 7-12). 1972. lib. bdg. 4.95 incl. catalog cards (*0-87157-524-8*) SamHar Pr.
—Spiro Agnew: Controversial Vice-President of the Nixon Administration. Rahmas, D. Steve, ed. LC 72-190234. 32p. (Orig.). (gr. 7-12). 1972. PLB 4.95 incl. catalog cards (*0-87157-516-7*) SamHar Pr.
—Suez Crisis, Nineteen Fifty-Six. Rahmas, D. Steve, ed. LC 73-78400. 32p. (gr. 7-12). 1973. lib. bdg. 4.95 incl. catalog cards (*0-87157-711-9*) SamHar Pr.
Kurland, Gerald, jt. auth. see Fredman, Lionel E.
Kurland, Gerald, ed. see Mushkat, Jerome.
Kurland, Morton L. Coping with AIDS: Facts & Fears. rev. & updated ed. (gr. 7-12). 1990. PLB 13.95 (*0-8239-1148-9*) Rosen Group.
—Coping with Family Violence. rev. ed. Rosen, R., ed. 141p. (gr. 7-12). 1990. PLB 13.95 (*0-8239-1050-4*) Rosen Group.
—Our Sacred Honor. Rosen, R., ed. 196p. (gr. 7-12). 1987. PLB 12.95 (*0-8239-0692-2*) Rosen Group.
Kurokawa, Mitsuhiro. Dinosaur Valley. Kurokawa, Mitsuhiro, illus. LC 92-10788. 48p. (gr. 1-5). 1992. 14. 95 (*0-8118-0257-4*) Chronicle Bks.
—The Great Big Book of Dinosaurs. Kurokawa, Mitsuhiro, illus. Obata, Ikuo, contrib. LC 88-24779. (Illus.). 32p. (gr. 4-5). 1989. PLB 21.26 (*0-8368-0000-1*) Gareth Stevens Inc.
—The Great Dinosaur Timescape. Strigens, Jerry, illus. (gr. 4-5). 1989. PLB 22.60 (*0-8368-0001-X*) Gareth Stevens Inc.
Kurosaki, Tamiko, tr. see Mori, Hana.
Kurtycz, Marcos & Kobeh, Ana G. Tigers & Opossums: Animal Legends. Kurtycz, Marcos & Kobeh, Ana G., illus. LC 82-17949. (gr. k-3). 1984. 12.95 (*0-316-50718-0*) Little.
Kurtz, Henry I. The U. S. Army. LC 92-12660. (Illus.). 64p. (gr. 3-6). 1993. PLB 14.90 (*1-56294-242-5*) Millbrook Pr.
Kurtz, Jane. Ethiopia: The Roof of Africa. LC 91-18660. (Illus.). 128p. (gr. 4-6). 1991. RSBE 14.95 (*0-87518-483-9*, Dillon) Macmillan Child Grp.
—Pulling the Lion's Tail. Cooper, Floyd, illus. LC 93-22836. 1994. pap. 14.00 (*0-671-88183-3*, S&S BFYR) S&S Trade.
Kurtz, Shirley. Applesauce. Benner, Cheryl, illus. LC 92-32017. 32p. (Orig.). (ps-5). 1992. pap. 6.95 (*1-56148-065-7*) Good Bks PA.
—The Boy & the Quilt. Benner, Cheryl A., illus. 32p. (ps-5). 1991. pap. 6.95 (*1-56148-009-6*) Good Bks PA.
Kurtzman, Harvey. My Life As a Cartoonist. (Illus.). 1988. pap. 2.75 (*0-671-63453-4*, Minstrel Bks) PB.
Kurz, Ann. Cranberries from A to Z: An Educational Picture Book. Kurz, Ann, illus. LC 89-61059. 32p. (gr. k-8). 1989. PLB 13.95 (*0-9622784-0-8*) Cranberry Origs.
Kurzband, Toby, jt. auth. see Levin, Meyer.
Kurzweg, Carol. A Kid's Cookbook: Educational & Edible Delights. (Illus.). 120p. (Orig.). (ps-6). 1993. pap. 13. 95 (*0-673-36065-2*) GdYrBks.
Kuse, James A., ed. see Jones, Jo.
Kusel, George. The Martial Musician's Mentor: A Complete Course of Instruction for the Fife, Pt. 1. rev., 2nd ed. (Illus.). 52p. (gr. 6 up). 1979. pap. 4.95 (*0-9604476-1-X*) Kusel.
Kushner, Arlene. Falasha No More: An Ethiopian Jewish Child Comes Home. Kalina, Amy, illus. 58p. (gr. 1-5). 1986. 9.95 (*0-933503-43-1*) Shapolsky Pubs.
Kushner, Donn. The Violin-Maker's Gift. large type ed. Panton, Doug, illus. 88p. (gr. 5-6). Repr. of 1981 ed. 17.16 (*0-317-01960-0*, 4-27120-00) Am Printing Hse.
Kushner, Ellen. The Camelot Caper. 176p. (Orig.). (gr. 4 up). 1988. pap. 2.50 (*0-553-27595-X*) Bantam.
—Enchanted Kindom. (ps-7). 1986. pap. 2.25 (*0-553-25861-3*) Bantam.
—The Knights of the Round Table. 128p. (gr. 4). 1988. pap. 2.50 (*0-318-37113-8*) Bantam.
—Mystery of the Secret Room. (gr. 5-12). 1987. pap. 2.25 (*0-553-26270-X*) Bantam.
—Outlaws of Sherwood Forest. 128p. (Orig.). (gr. 5 up). 1985. pap. 2.25 (*0-553-26388-9*) Bantam.
—Statue of Liberty Adventure. (ps-7). 1986. pap. 2.25 (*0-553-25813-3*) Bantam.
—Statue of Liberty Adventure. 1986. pap. 2.75 (*0-553-28176-3*) Bantam.
Kushner, Lawrence. The Book of Miracles: A Young Person's Guide to Jewish Spirituality. (Illus.). 96p. (Orig.). (gr. 4-6). 1987. pap. text ed. 7.95 (*0-8074-0323-7*, 123926) UAHC.

Kushner, Maureen. Great All-Time Excuse Book. Hoffman, Sanford, illus. LC 89-49403. 96p. (gr. 2-8). 1991. pap. 3.95 (*0-8069-6965-2*) Sterling.
Kusinitz, Marc. Celebrity Drug Use. (Illus.). 32p. (gr. 5 up). 1991. pap. 4.49 (*1-55546-995-7*) Chelsea Hse.
—Poisons & Toxins. (Illus.). (gr. 6-12). 1992. 18.95 (*0-7910-0074-5*) Chelsea Hse.
—Tropical Medicine. (Illus.). 112p. (gr. 6-12). 1990. 18. 95 (*0-7910-0079-6*) Chelsea Hse.
Kusinitz, Mark. Folk Medicine. (Illus.). 112p. (gr. 6-12). 1992. 18.95 (*0-7910-0083-4*) Chelsea Hse.
Kuska, George, jt. ed. see Linse, Barbara B.
Kuske, David P. Luther's Catechism. Wolters, Ronald & Weaver, Duane, illus. 383p. (gr. 7-8). 1982. text ed. 7.50 (*0-938272-11-X*); pap. 2.50 catechism aid bklet. (*0-938272-13-6*) WELS Board.
Kuskin, Karla. Any Me I Want to Be. Kuskin, Karla, illus. LC 77-105485. 64p. (gr. 1-4). 1972. PLB 11.89 (*0-06-023616-7*) HarpC Child Bks.
—City Dog. LC 93-8252. 1994. write for info. (*0-395-66138-2*, Clarion Bks) HM.
—The Dallas Titans Get Ready for Bed. Simont, Marc, illus. LC 83-49470. 48p. (gr. k-3). 1986. 12.00 (*0-06-023562-4*); PLB 11.89 (*0-06-023563-2*) HarpC Child Bks.
—The Dallas Titans Get Ready for Bed. Simont, Marc, illus. LC 83-49470. 48p. (ps-3). 1988. pap. 3.95 (*0-06-443180-0*, Trophy) HarpC Child Bks.
—Dogs & Dragons, Trees & Dreams. Kuskin, Karla, illus. LC 79-2814. 96p. (gr. k-3). 1992. pap. 4.95 (*0-06-446122-X*, Trophy) HarpC Child Bks.
—Dogs & Dragons, Trees & Dreams: A Collection of Poems. Kuskin, Karla, illus. LC 79-2814. 96p. (gr. 1-6). 1980. PLB 13.89 (*0-06-023544-6*) HarpC Child Bks.
—A Great Miracle Happened There: A Chanukah Story. Parker, Robert A., illus. LC 92-17909. 32p. (gr. k-3). 1993. 15.00 (*0-06-023617-5*); PLB 14.89 (*0-06-023618-3*) HarpC Child Bks.
—Jerusalem, Shining Still. Frampton, David, illus. LC 86-25841. 32p. (ps up). 1987. 13.95 (*0-06-023548-9*); PLB 13.89 (*0-06-023549-7*) HarpC Child Bks.
—Jerusalem, Shining Still. Frampton, David, illus. LC 86-25841. 32p. (gr. 1 up). 1990. pap. 5.50 (*0-06-443243-2*, Trophy) HarpC Child Bks.
—Just Like Everyone Else. LC 59-5320. (Illus.). 32p. (ps-3). 1982. pap. 4.95 (*0-06-443032-4*, Trophy) HarpC Child Bks.
—Near the Window Tree: Poems & Notes. Kuskin, Karla, illus. LC 74-20394. 64p. (gr. 2-6). 1975. PLB 13.89 (*0-06-023540-3*) HarpC Child Bks.
—Patchwork Island. Mathers, Petra, illus. LC 92-10344. 1994. 14.00 (*0-06-021242-X*, HarpT); PLB 13.89 (*0-06-021284-5*, HarpT) HarpC.
—Paul. Avery, Milton, illus. 48p. (gr. k-3). 1994. 16.95 (*0-06-023568-3*); PLB 16.89 (*0-06-023573-X*) HarpC Child Bks.
—The Philharmonic Gets Dressed. LC 81-48658. (Illus.). 48p. (gr. k-3). 1982. 14.00 (*0-06-023622-1*); PLB 13. 89 (*0-06-023623-X*) HarpC Child Bks.
—The Philharmonic Gets Dressed. Simont, Marc, illus. LC 81-48658. 48p. (ps-3). 1986. pap. 4.95 (*0-06-443124-X*, Trophy) HarpC Child Bks.
—Roar & More. LC 56-8138. (Illus.). 32p. (ps-3). 1977. pap. 1.95 (*0-06-443019-7*, Trophy) HarpC Child Bks.
—Roar & More. rev. ed. Kuskin, Karla, illus. LC 89-15650. 48p. (ps-1). 1990. PLB 13.89 (*0-06-023619-1*) HarpC Child Bks.
—Roar & More. rev. ed. Kuskin, Karla, illus. LC 89-15650. 48p. (ps-1). 1990. pap. 4.95 (*0-06-443244-0*, Trophy) HarpC Child Bks.
—Soap Soup: And Other Verses. Kuskin, Karla, illus. LC 91-22947. 64p. (gr. k-3). 1992. 14.00 (*0-06-023571-3*); PLB 13.89 (*0-06-023572-1*) HarpC Child Bks.
—Soap Soup: and Other Verses. Kuskin, Karla, illus. LC 90-27357. 32p. (gr. k-4). 1994. pap. 3.50 (*0-06-444174-1*, Trophy) HarpC Child Bks.
—Something Sleeping in the Hall. Kuskin, Karla, illus. LC 82-47721. 64p. (gr. k-3). 1985. PLB 13.89 (*0-06-023634-5*) HarpC Child Bks.
—Which Horse Is William? LC 90-24619. 24p. 1992. 14. 00 (*0-688-10637-4*); lib. bdg. 13.93 (*0-688-10638-2*) Greenwillow.
Kuskin, Karla see Kennedy, Dorothy M., et al.
Kuslan, Louis I. & Kuslan, Richard D. Ham Radio. (gr. 7 up). 1981. 10.95 (*0-13-372334-8*) P-H.
Kuslan, Richard D., jt. auth. see Kuslan, Louis I.
Kuss, Daniele. Incas. LC 91-17741. (Illus.). 48p. (gr. 4-8). 1991. PLB 13.95 (*1-85435-267-9*) Marshall Cavendish.
Kusugak, M., jt. auth. see Munsch, Robert.
Kusugak, Michael. Baseball Bats for Christmas. (JPN., Illus.). 24p. 1993. pap. 5.95 (*1-55037-314-5*, Pub. by Annick CN) Firefly Bks Ltd.
—Hide-&-Sneak. Krykorka, Vladyana, illus. 32p. (ps-3). 1992. PLB 14.95 (*1-55037-229-7*, Pub. by Annick CN); pap. 4.95 (*1-55037-228-9*, Pub. by Annick CN) Firefly Bks Ltd.
Kusugak, Michael A. Baseball Bats for Christmas. Krykorka, Vladyana, illus. 24p. (gr. k-3). 1990. 15.95 (*1-55037-145-2*, Pub. by Annick CN); pap. 5.95 (*1-55037-144-4*, Pub. by Annick CN) Firefly Bks Ltd.
Kuttner, Paul, tr. see Bauzen, Peter & Bauzen, Susanne.
Kuttner, Paul, tr. see Paraquin, Charles.
Kuttner, Paul, tr. see Paraquin, Charles H.
Kuttner, Paul, tr. see Pfluger, A.
Kuttner, Paul, tr. see Zechlin, Katharina.

Kutz, Eleanor, et al. The Discovery of Competence: Teaching & Learning with Diverse Student Writers. LC 93-16574. 1993. pap. 20.00 (*0-86709-323-4*, 0323) Boynton Cook Pubs.
Kuyper, Vicki J. I'm the Greatest Me There Could Ever Be! Gress, Jonna, ed. LC 92-72843. (Illus.). 14p. (ps-1). 1992. pap. text ed. 11.60 (*0-944943-12-8*) Current Inc.
—I'm the Greatest Me There Could Ever Be! Gress, Jonna, ed. Regan, Dana, illus. LC 92-72843. 14p. (Orig.). (ps-3). 1993. pap. 5.40 (*0-944943-30-6*, CODE 21175-5*) Current Inc.
Kuzmier, Kerrie & McCann, Jennifer. Manatees & Dugongs: A Coloring Book in English & Spanish. Inchaustegui, Sixto, tr. Beath, Mary, illus. (ENG & SPA.). 28p. (Orig.). (gr. 3-6). 1991. pap. text ed. 4.00 (*0-685-39509-X*) Ctr Marine Cnsrv.
Kvasnicka, Robert M. Hole-in-the-Day. Viola, Herman, intro. by. Whipple, Rick, illus. 32p. (gr. 3-6). 1990. PLB 17.96 (*0-8172-3405-5*); pap. 4.95 (*0-8114-4091-5*) Raintree Steck-V.
Kveton, Steven. The Legend of Fredbird. Koehler, Ed, illus. 16p. (Orig.). (ps up). 1986. pap. text ed. 2.95 (*0-9616799-0-5*) Water St Missouri.
Kveton, Steven P. If I Could Fly. 14p. (Orig.). (ps-6). 1987. pap. text ed. 0.75 (*0-9616799-1-3*) Water St Missouri.
Kwatera, Michael. The Ministry of Servers. Stuckenschneider, Placid, illus. 48p. (Orig.). (gr. 6-8). 1982. pap. 1.95 (*0-8146-1300-4*) Liturgical Pr.
Kwitz, Mary D. Gumshoe Goose, Private Eye. Ernst, Lisa C., illus. LC 86-29331. 48p. (ps-3). 1988. 9.95 (*0-8037-0423-2*); PLB 9.89 (*0-8037-0424-0*) Dial Bks Young.
—Gumshoe Goose, Private Eye. (ps-3). 1991. pap. 3.95 (*0-8037-0923-4*, Dial Easy to Read) Puffin Bks.
—Little Chick's Friend Duckling. Degen, Bruce, illus. LC 90-5027. 32p. (ps-2). 1992. 13.00 (*0-06-023638-8*); PLB 12.89 (*0-06-023639-6*) HarpC Child Bks.
Kwon, Holly H., retold by. The Moles & the Mireuk: A Korean Folktale. Hubbard, Woodleigh, illus. LC 92-437. 32p. (gr. k-3). 1993. 14.95 (*0-395-64347-3*) HM.
Kyle, Jamie. Great Hair for Girls. (Illus.). 32p. (gr. 3 up). 1993. 17.95 (*1-56288-414-X*) Checkerboard.
—Great Nails for Girls. (Illus.). 32p. (gr. 3 up). 1993. 17. 95 (*1-56288-413-1*) Checkerboard.
Kyle, Louisa V. My Virginia Childhood. (Illus.). 45p. (gr. 3). 1976. write for info. Four Oclock Farms.
—Ram Lam. Grandy, Chamie O., illus. 76p. (gr. 3). 1985. 5.95 (*0-927044-02-1*) Four Oclock Farms.
—The Witch of Pungo. Dool, Jan, illus. 87p. (gr. 3). 1973. 12.95 (*0-927044-00-5*) Four Oclock Farms.
Kyte, Cwolde. Sensen-Ti Thef Black Dragon C'Hi Kung: Chi King Kofamitic Afrikan Beginnings. (Illus.). 155p. (Orig.). (gr. 9 up). 1985. pap. 14.90x (*0-936901-01-2*) Ctr Sacred Healing.
Kyte, Dennis. Mattie - Cataragus. 1988. pap. 13.95 (*0-385-24403-7*) Doubleday.
—Zackary Raffles. 1989. pap. 13.95 (*0-385-24652-8*) Doubleday.
Kyte, Kathy S. The Kids' Complete Guide to Money. Brown, Richard, illus. LC 84-3962. 96p. (gr. 5 up). 1984. lib. bdg. 10.99 (*0-394-96672-4*) Knopf Bks Yng Read.

L

L-L Research Staff, jt. auth. see Hatonn.
Laan, Nancy van see Van Laan, Nancy.
Laan, Nancy Van see Van Laan, Nancy.
LaBarre, Alice, et al. Sexual Abuse! What Is It? An Informational Book for the Hearing Impaired. Nelson, Mary F., illus. LC 92-80161. 80p. (gr. 1-6). 1992. pap. 9.00 (*0-9629302-1-0*) Liberty.
LaBastida, Aurora. Nine Days to Christmas. (ps-3). 1991. 14.95 (*0-670-84165-X*) Viking Child Bks.
Labastida, Aurora, jt. auth. see Ets, Marie H.
LaBelle, Susan. Flopsy, Mopsy & Cottontail: A Little Book of Paper Dolls in Full Color. (Illus.). 48p. (gr. 1 up). 1983. pap. 2.95 (*0-486-24376-1*) Dover.
LaBelle, Susan W. Little Peter Rabbit Paper Dolls in Full Color. (gr. 3 up). 1985. pap. 2.95 (*0-486-24813-5*) Dover.
LaBonte, Gail. The Arctic Fox. LC 88-18967. (Illus.). 60p. (gr. 3 up). 1988. RSBE 13.95 (*0-87518-390-5*, Dillon) Macmillan Child Grp.
—Leeches, Lampreys, & Other Cold-Blooded Bloodsuckers. LC 91-12620. (Illus.). 64p. (gr. 5-8). 1991. PLB 12.90 (*0-531-20027-2*) Watts.
—The Llama. LC 88-16407. (Illus.). 60p. (gr. 3 up). 1988. RSBE 13.95 (*0-87518-393-X*, Dillon) Macmillan Child Grp.
—The Miniature Horse. LC 89-26046. (Illus.). 60p. (gr. 3 up). 1990. RSBE 13.95 (*0-87518-424-3*, Dillon) Macmillan Child Grp.
—The Tarantula. (Illus.). 60p. (gr. 3 up). 1991. RSBE 13. 95 (*0-87518-452-9*, Dillon) Macmillan Child Grp.
LaBranche, Bud. Woodcarving the Female Head. (Illus.). 60p. (gr. 8 up). 1986. pap. 8.95 (*0-88625-137-0*) Durkin Hayes Pub.
Labrosse, Darcia. Greg's My Egg! (Illus.). 32p. (ps-1). 1994. 15.95 (*0-86264-411-9*, Pub. by Andersen Pr UK) Trafalgar.

Lacapa, Michael. Antelope Woman: An Apache Folktale. Lacapa, Michael, illus. LC 92-4198. 48p. (gr. 3 up). 1992. 14.95 (0-87358-543-7) Northland AZ.
—The Flute Player: An Apache Folktale. Lacapa, Michael, illus. LC 89-63749. 48p. (gr. 1-3). 1990. 14.95 (0-87358-500-3) Northland AZ.
Lace, William W. Michelangelo. (Illus.). 111p. (gr. 5-8). 1993. PLB 14.95 (1-56006-038-7) Lucent Bks.
—Sports Great Nolan Ryan. (Illus.). 64p. (gr. 4-10). 1993. lib. bdg. 15.95 (0-89490-394-2) Enslow Pubs.
Lacey, Elizabeth A. The Complete Frog: A Guide for the Very Young Naturalist. Santoro, Christopher, illus. LC 88-9343. 72p. (gr. k-4). 1989. 12.95 (0-688-08017-0); PLB 12.88 (0-688-08018-9) Lothrop.
—What's the Difference? A Guide to Some Familiar Animal Look-Alikes. Shetterly, Robert, illus. 80p. (gr. 4-7). 1993. 14.95 (0-395-56182-5, Clarion Bks) HM.
Lacoe, Addie. Just Not the Same. Estrada, Pau, illus. LC 91-44041. 32p. (ps-3). 1992. 14.45 (0-395-59347-6) HM.
Lacome, Julie. Funny Business. Lacome, Julie, illus. LC 90-36258. (ps up). 1991. 11.95 (0-688-10159-3, Tambourine Bks) Morrow.
—Hocus Pocus. Lacome, Julie, illus. LC 90-36257. (ps up). 1991. 11.95 (0-688-10158-5, Tambourine Bks) Morrow.
—I'm a Jolly Farmer. LC 92-47374. 1994. write for info. (1-56402-318-4) Candlewick Pr.
—Walking Through the Jungle. Lacome, Julie, illus. LC 92-53018. 32p. (ps). 1993. 13.95 (1-56402-137-8) Candlewick Pr.
Lacosta, Francisco C., ed. see **Poncela, Enrique J.**
Lacret-Subirat, Fabian. Lacret: Algebra One. (Illus.). 488p. (gr. 9-12). 1982. text ed. 15.00 (0-943144-03-5); text ed. 8.00 school price (0-685-05744-5) Lacret Pub.
—Lacret Mathematics Basic Skills. (Illus.). 467p. (gr. 7-12). 1986. text ed. 15.00 softcover (0-943144-17-5) Lacret Pub.
—Lacret Plane Geometry. (Illus.). 510p. (gr. 7-12). 1983. 15.00 (0-943144-05-1) Lacret Pub.
—Mastering HSPT-Math Skills. (Illus.). 250p. (gr. 7-12). 1986. pap. 15.00 (0-943144-19-1); answer key school use only avail. Lacret Pub.
—Mastering Math Basic Skills Workbook. (Illus.). 251p. (gr. 7). 1987. pap. 8.48 (0-943144-21-3) Lacret Pub.
La Croix, Alice de see **De La Croix, Alice.**
LaCroix, John W. Troggs & Doogles in Thistledom. 1992. 7.95 (0-533-10129-8) Vantage.
Lacroix, Pat, jt. auth. see **Fernandes, Kim.**
LaCure, Jeffrey R. Adopted Like Me. 24p. (ps-2). 1993. pap. 9.95 (0-9635717-0-2) Adoption Advocate.
Ladd, James D. Amphibious Techniques. Sarson, Peter & Bryan, Tony, illus. LC 84-10003. 48p. (gr. 5 up). 1985. PLB 13.50 (0-8225-1379-X, First Ave Edns); pap. 4.95 (0-8225-9505-2, First Ave Edns) Lerner Pubns.
—Military Helicopters. Gibbons, Tony, et al, illus. 48p. (gr. 5 up). 1987. PLB 14.95 (0-8225-1382-X) Lerner Pubns.
Ladd, Louise. The Double Fudge Dare. (gr. 3-7). 1989. pap. 2.95 (0-553-15684-5) Bantam.
LaDell, Leo. The Durandrium Find. Amthor, Terry K., ed. Velez, Waller & Martin, Ellisa, illus. 32p. (Orig.). (gr. 12). 1989. pap. 6.00 (1-55806-021-9, 9105) Iron Crown Ent Inc.
—Legacy of the Ancients. Amthor, Terry K., ed. Ridge, Jeff & Waltrip, Jason, illus. 32p. (Orig.). (gr. 12). 1989. pap. 6.00 (1-55806-035-9, 9106) Iron Crown Ent Inc.
LaDell, Leo, ed. see **Crowdis, John.**
LaDell, Leo, ed. see **Foley, Tod.**
Lademan, Miriam A., ed. see **Hooker, Irene H. & Brindle, Susan A.**
Ladizinsky, Eric, jt. auth. see **Amato, Carol.**
Ladizinsky, Eric, jt. auth. see **Melton, Lisa.**
Lado, Robert. The Big Bad Wolf: Level 2. (Illus.). 24p. (ps). 1985. pap. 3.95 (1-879580-53-5); card pack 1.95 (1-879580-52-7) Lado Intl Pr.
—My First Thirty-Two Words: Level 1. (Illus.). 34p. (ps). 1985. card pack 9.95 (1-879580-51-9) Lado Intl Pr.
Ladoux, Cathryn. Yani: Stories for Childhood. (Illus.). 150p. (Orig.). (gr. 4-7). 1993. pap. 19.95 (0-943861-18-7) Lone Tree.
LaDoux, Rita C. Georgia. (Illus.). 72p. (gr. 3-6). 1991. PLB 17.50 (0-8225-2703-0) Lerner Pubns.
—Iowa. Lerner Geography Department Staff, ed. (Illus.). 72p. (gr. 3-6). 1992. PLB 17.50 (0-8225-2724-3) Lerner Pubns.
—Louisiana. LC 92-13365. 1993. PLB 17.50 (0-8225-2740-5) Lerner Pubns.
—Missouri. 72p. (gr. 3-6). 1991. PLB 17.50 (0-8225-2710-3) Lerner Pubns.
—Montana. Lerner Geography Department Staff, ed. (Illus.). 72p. (gr. 4-7). 1992. 17.50 (0-8225-2714-6) Lerner Pubns.
—Oklahoma. Lerner Geography Department Staff, ed. (Illus.). 72p. (gr. 3-6). 1992. PLB 17.50 (0-8225-2717-0) Lerner Pubns.

Ladson, Etta M. Strange Land Songs. (Illus.). 146p. (gr. 7-12). 1992. text ed. 14.95 (0-9630574-0-5) Jewelgate.
A collection of 71 classroom sonnets written by a former Chairperson of English. The poems celebrate the genius of the African transplanted & the glory of emerging woman. An incredible little volume of multicultural poetry, the first 41 sonnets support the characterization of Americans of African descent as a "masterpiece" epic-in-progress, while the final 30 sonnets affirm woman as the fairest of them all in the mirror of the new millennium. The poems reveal an astonishing command of language, powerful use of metaphor & unrivaled originality. An accompanying set of reading tests is sold separately. *Publisher Provided Annotation.*

Laemmlen, Ann & Owen, Jackie. The Articles of Faith Learning Book. 171p. (gr. 3-6). 1990. pap. 7.95 wkbk. (0-87579-400-9) Deseret Bk.
La Farge, Ann. Gertrude Stein. Horner, Matina, intro. by. (Illus.). 112p. (gr. 5 up). 1988. lib. bdg. 17.95 (1-55546-678-8) Chelsea Hse.
LaFarge, Ann. Pearl Buck. Horner, Matina, intro. by. (Illus.). 112p. (gr. 5 up). 1988. lib. bdg. 17.95 (1-55546-645-1) Chelsea Hse.
LaFarge, Oliver. Laughing Boy. 245p. 1981. Repr. PLB 24.95 (0-89966-367-2) Buccaneer Bks.
La Farge, Oliver. Laughing Boy. 259p. 1981. Repr. PLB 21.95 (0-89967-041-5) Harmony Raine.
LaFarge, Oliver. Laughing Boy. 192p. (RL 10). 1971. pap. 3.50 (0-451-52244-3, Sig Classics) NAL-Dutton.
—The Mother Ditch. Ortego, Pedro R., tr. Larsson, Karl, illus. LC 82-10712. (ENG & SPA.). 64p. (gr. 1-12). 1983. pap. 8.95 (0-86534-009-9) Sunstone Pr.
La Farge, Sheila, tr. see **Haugen, Tormod.**
Lafferty, Jerry. Learning Power: A Student's Guide to Success. Moore, Melissa, ed. Foss, Debbie, illus. LC 92-72769. 138p. (Orig.). (gr. 7-12). 1993. Incl. six audio cass. pap. 34.95 (1-881843-29-7) Alpha Educ Inst.
Lafferty, Peter. Albert Einstein. (Illus.). 48p. (gr. 5-9). 1992. PLB 12.40 (0-531-18458-7, Pub. by Bookwright Pr) Watts.
—Archimedes. (Illus.). 48p. (gr. 5-8). 1991. RLB 12.40 (0-531-18403-X, Pub. by Bookwright Pr) Watts.
—Burning & Melting: Projects with Heat. (Illus.). 32p. (gr. 5-8). 1990. PLB 12.40 (0-531-17235-X, Gloucester Pr) Watts.
—Energy & Light. (Illus.). 40p. (gr. 7-9). 1990. 12.40 (0-531-17144-2, Gloucester Pr) Watts.
—Magnets to Generators: Projects with Magnetism. (Illus.). 32p. (gr. 5-6). 1989. PLB 12.40 (0-531-17165-5) Watts.
Lafferty, Peter & Jefferis, David. Pedal Power: The History of Bicycles. (Illus.). 32p. (gr. 5-8). 1990. PLB 12.40 (0-531-14084-9) Watts.
—Superbikes: The History of Motorcycles. (Illus.). 32p. (gr. 5-8). 1990. PLB 12.40 (0-531-14039-3) Watts.
—To the Rescue: The History of Emergency Vehicles. (Illus.). 32p. (gr. 5-8). 1990. PLB 12.40 (0-531-14085-7) Watts.
—Top Gear: The History of Automobiles. (Illus.). 32p. (gr. 5-8). 1990. PLB 12.40 (0-531-14038-5) Watts.
Lafferty, Peter & Rowe, Julian. The Inventor Through History. Smith, Tony & Wheele, Steve, illus. 48p. 1993. 15.95 (1-56847-013-4) Thomson Lrning.
Lafferty, Peter, jt. auth. see **Jefferis, David.**
Laffin, John. British Butchers & Bunglers of World War I. LC 92-18632. (Illus.). 224p. (gr. 9-12). 1992. pap. text ed. 16.00 (0-7509-0179-9) A Sutton Pub.
LaFleur, Tom & Brennan, Gale. Bingo the Bear. Kritchman-Knuteson, Joan, illus. 16p. (Orig.). (gr. k-6). 1981. pap. 1.25 (0-685-02454-7) Brennan Bks.
—Henry the Hound. Flint, Russ, illus. 16p. (Orig.). (gr. k-6). 1982. pap. 1.25 (0-685-05556-6) Brennan Bks.
—Isadore the Dinosaur. Berghauer, Meri H., illus. 16p. (Orig.). (gr. k-6). 1981. pap. 1.25 (0-685-02456-3) Brennan Bks.
—Spunky the Monkey. Murtagh, Betty, illus. 16p. (Orig.). (gr. k-6). 1981. pap. 1.25 (0-685-02457-1) Brennan Bks.
—Tuffy the Tiger. Murtagh, Betty, illus. 16p. (gr. k-6). 1982. pap. 1.25 (0-685-05557-4) Brennan Bks.
—Woolly the Wolf. Bond, Bruce, illus. 16p. (Orig.). (gr. k-6). 1981. pap. 1.25 (0-685-02459-8) Brennan Bks.
La Fonatine, Jean de. Dona Zorra y Dona Ciguena - Mrs. Fox & Mrs. Stork. 2nd ed. Elgorriaga, Jose A., adapted by. Nofziger, Edward, illus. (SPA.). 19p. (gr. k-12). 1993. pap. 2.95 (0-922852-19-7) AIMS Intl.
—Mrs. Fox & Mrs. Stork. Ko, Tonya, tr. from ENG. Nofziger, Edward, illus. (KOR.). 19p. (Orig.). (gr. k-12). 1993. pap. 2.95 (0-922852-24-3) AIMS Intl.
—Mrs. Fox & Mrs. Stork. Suwa, Naomi, tr. from ENG. Nofziger, Edward, illus. (JPN.). 19p. (Orig.). (gr. k-12). 1993. pap. 2.95 (0-922852-23-5) AIMS Intl.
—Mrs. Fox & Mrs. Stork. Nofziger, Edward, illus. 19p. (Orig.). (gr. k-12). 1993. pap. 2.95 (0-922852-21-9) AIMS Intl.
—Mrs. Fox & Mrs. Stork. Do, Le, tr. from ENG. Nofziger, Edward, illus. (VIE.). 19p. (Orig.). (gr. k-12). 1993. pap. 2.95 (0-922852-25-1) AIMS Intl.
—Mrs. Fox & Mrs. Stork. Wang, May S., tr. from ENG. Nofziger, Edward, illus. (CHI.). 19p. (Orig.). (gr. k-12). 1993. pap. 2.95 (0-922852-22-7) AIMS Intl.

La Fontaine. The Hare & the Tortoise. Wildsmith, Brian, illus. 32p. 1987. 16.00 (0-19-279625-9); pap. 7.50 (0-19-272126-7) OUP.
—The Lion & the Rat. Wildsmith, Brian, illus. 32p. 1987. 16.00 (0-19-279607-0); pap. 7.50 (0-19-272167-4) OUP.
—The North Wind & the Sun. Wildsmith, Brian, illus. 32p. 1987. 16.00 (0-19-279610-0); pap. 7.50 (0-19-272168-2) OUP.
La Fontaine, Jean de. A Hundred Fables of La Fontaine. Billinghurst, P. J., illus. 208p. (gr. 2-6). 2.98 (0-517-40206-8) Outlet Bk Co.
LaFontaine, Jean de, jt. auth. see **Wildsmith, Brian.**
LaFortune, Claude. Greeting Jesus: Let's Make the Nativity Scene. (Illus.). 24p. (Orig.). 1988. wkbk. 5.95 (0-89622-384-1) Twenty-Third.
La Freniere, Annette, ed. see **Jones, Martha T.**
LaFreniere, Annette, ed. see **Jones, Martha T.**
LaFreniere, Annette, intro. by see **Neeley, Gwen C.**
La Freniere, Annette, ed. see **Seib, Philip.**
La Freniere, Annette, ed. see **Warren, Betsy.**
Lager, Claude. A Tale of Two Rats. Rutten, Nicole, illus. 32p. (gr. k-3). 1991. 13.95 (1-55670-228-0) Stewart Tabori & Chang.
Lagercrantz, Rose & Lagercrantz, Samuel. Is It Magic? Norlen, Paul, tr. from SWE. Eriksson, Eva, illus. LC 89-63054. (gr. k-3). 1990. 13.95 (91-29-59182-1, Pub. by R & S Bks) FS&G.
Lagercrantz, Samuel, jt. auth. see **Lagercrantz, Rose.**
Lagerlof, Selma. The Changeling. Stevens, Susanna, tr. from SWE. Winter, Jeanette, illus. LC 90-45277. 48p. (gr. k-5). 1992. 15.00 (0-679-81035-8); PLB 15.99 (0-679-91035-2) Knopf Bks Yng Read.
—The Further Adventures of Nils. rev. ed. Johnson, Nancy, ed. Howard, Velma S., tr. from SWE. Pantheon Books Staff, illus. 250p. (gr. 2 up). 1992. pap. 12.95x (0-9615394-4-5) Skandisk.
—The Legend of the Christmas Rose. Mikolaycak, Charles, illus. Greene, Ellin, retold by. LC 89-77511. (Illus.). 32p. (ps up). 1990. reinforced 15.95 (0-8234-0821-3) Holiday.
—The Wonderful Adventures of Nils, Bk. 1. Johnson, Nancy, intro. by. Howard, Velma S., tr. from SWE. Pantheon Books Staff, illus. 250p. (gr. 2 up). 1991. pap. 12.95 (0-9615394-3-7) Skandisk.
Lagerquist, Syble. Philip Johnston & the Navajo Code Talkers. (gr. 4-12). 1975. 4.95 (0-89992-038-1) Coun India Ed.
Lagler, Karl F., jt. auth. see **Hubbs, Carl L.**
Lagos, Deloris K. The Sun Shall Shine. 1993. 7.95 (0-8062-4786-X) Carlton.
LaGrange, Lynn M. Joey, the Little Reindeer & the Land of Forgotten Children. Hall, Kenneth L., illus. 40p. (ps-6). 1990. lib. bdg. 10.95 (1-878790-02-1) Fables CO.
—Joey, the Little Reindeer & the Land of Forgotten Children. Hall, Kenneth L., illus. 40p. (ps-6). 1990. pap. 6.95 (1-878790-05-6) Fables CO.
—Paul, the Shepherd Boy & the Birthday Sandals. Sanchez, Larry M., illus. 36p. (ps-6). 1990. lib. bdg. 10.95 (1-878790-00-5) Fables CO.
—Paul, the Shepherd Boy & the Birthday Sandals. Sanchez, Larry M., illus. 36p. (ps-6). 1990. pap. 6.95 (1-878790-03-X) Fables CO.
—Polly & the Frog. Hall, Kenneth L., illus. 36p. (ps-5). 1991. 10.95 (1-878790-08-0); pap. 6.95 (1-878790-09-9) Fables Co.
—Sir Cedrick Peabody: The Royal Little Snail. Hall, Kenneth L., illus. 32p. (ps-5). 1991. PLB 10.95 (1-878790-06-4) Fables Co.
—Sir Cedrick Peabody: The Royal Little Snail. Hall, Kenneth L., illus. 32p. (ps-5). 1991. pap. 6.95 (1-878790-07-2) Fables Co.
—Winnie, the Humpback Whale. (Illus.). 32p. 1989. PLB 10.95 (0-915765-64-0) Fables Co.
—Winnie, the Humpback Whale & Her Second Tale. Wilcox, Kelly K., illus. 40p. (ps-3). 1990. lib. bdg. 10.95 (1-878790-01-3) Fables CO.
—Winnie, the Humpback Whale & Her Second Tale. Wilcox, Kelly K., illus. 38p. (ps-3). 1990. pap. 6.95 (1-878790-04-8) Fables CO.
LaGrone, Oliver. Dawnfire & Other Poems. LC 88-83008. (Illus.). 133p. (gr. 9-12). 1989. pap. 9.00 perf. bdg. (0-916418-72-3) Lotus.
Laha, R. G., jt. auth. see **Lukacs, E.**
Lahey, David. Athletic Scholarships: Making Your Sports Pay. 200p. 1992. pap. 12.95 (1-895629-06-3, Pub. by Warwick Pub CN) Firefly Bks Ltd.
Lahey, Nicholas, tr. see **Vandersteen, Willy.**
Lahey, Nicholas J., tr. see **Vandersteen, Willy.**
Lahey, Richard. Quiz Bowl I. Sellers, Marci, illus. 56p. (Orig.). (gr. 4-12). 1982. tchr's. manual 7.50 (0-88047-012-7, 8216) DOK Pubs.
—Quiz Bowl II. Sellers, Marci, illus. 56p. (Orig.). (gr. 4-12). 1984. 7.50 (0-88047-037-2, 8408) DOK Pubs.
Laidman, Hugh. Animals: How to Draw Them. LC 75-11930. (Illus.). 160p. (gr. 7 up). 1979. pap. 12.95 (0-685-46950-6, Dutton) NAL-Dutton.
Laik, Judy. Under Whose Influence? Strecker, Rebekah, illus. LC 93-86233. 64p. 1994. lib. bdg. 16.95 (0-943990-98-X); pap. 5.95 (0-943990-97-1) Parenting Pr.
Laing, David & Lampiris, Nicholas. Aspen High Country: The Geology, a Pictorial Guide to Roads & Trails. Laing, Jennifer, illus. 144p. (Orig.). (gr. 9-12). 1980. pap. write for info. (0-9604274-0-6) Thunder River.
Laing, John. One Cool Cat. 43p. 1988. pap. 5.95 (0-413-54220-3, A0197) Heinemann.

Laing, Martha. Grandma Moses: The Grand Old Lady of American Art. Rahmas, D. Steve, ed. LC 71-190231. 32p. (Orig.). 1972. lib. bdg. 4.95 incl. catalog cards (0-87157-513-2) SamHar Pr.

Laird. The Alphabet Zoo. LC 74-190264. (Illus.). 32p. (ps-2). 1972. PLB 9.95 (0-87783-053-3); pap. 3.94 deluxe ed. o.s.i (0-87783-079-7) Oddo.

Laird, Charlton. Webster's New World Thesaurus. 854p. (gr. 9-12). 1987. pap. 10.95 (0-13-948126-5) P-H.

Laird, Christa. Shadow of the Wall. LC 89-34469. (gr. 7 up). 1990. 12.95 (0-688-09336-1) Greenwillow.

Laird, Donivee. The Three Little Hawaiian Pigs & the Magic Shark. Jossem, Carol, illus. LC 81-67047. 40p. (ps-3). 1981. 7.95x (0-940350-19-X) Barnaby Bks.

Laird, Donivee M. Fantastic Hawaiian Energy Adventure. (Illus.). 32p. (gr. 3-5). 1989. write for info. (0-940350-16-5) Barnaby Bks.
—Keaka & the Liliko'i Vine. Jossem, Carol, illus. LC 82-72452. 42p. (gr. k-3). 1982. 7.95x (0-940350-10-6) Barnaby Bks.
—Ula Li'i & the Magic Shark. LC 86-3390. (Illus.). 42p. (gr. k-3). 1985. 7.95x (0-940350-12-2) Barnaby Bks.
—Will Wai Kula & the Three Mongooses. Jossem, Carol, illus. LC 83-8805. 44p. (gr. k-3). 1983. 7.95x (0-940350-13-0) Barnaby Bks.

Laird, Elizabeth. American Homes. (Illus.). 31p. 1989. pap. text ed. 5.25 (0-582-01716-5, 78664) Longman.
—Americans on the Move. (Illus.). 31p. (Orig.). 1989. pap. text ed. 5.25 (0-582-01715-7, 78663) Longman.
—Children's Treasury of Graces, Hymns & Prayers, 3 vols. (Illus.). 1991. 7.99 (0-517-05384-5) Outlet Bk Co.
—The Day Patch Stood Guard. Reeder, Colin, illus. LC 90-11153. 32p. (gr. k up). 1991. 11.95 (0-688-10239-5, Tambourine Bks); PLB 11.88 (0-688-10240-9, Tambourine Bks) Morrow.
—The Day Sidney Ran Off. Reeder, Colin, illus. LC 90-11154. 32p. (gr. k up). 1991. 11.95 (0-688-10241-7, Tambourine Bks); PLB 11.88 (0-688-10242-5, Tambourine Bks) Morrow.
—The Day the Ducks Went Skating. Reeder, Colin, illus. LC 90-25899. 32p. (gr. k up). 1991. 11.95 (0-688-10246-8, Tambourine Bks); PLB 11.88 (0-688-10247-6, Tambourine Bks) Morrow.
—The Day Veronica Was Nosy. Reeder, Colin, illus. LC 90-24063. 32p. (gr. k up). 1991. 11.95 (0-688-10248-4, Tambourine Bks); PLB 11.88 (0-688-10249-2, Tambourine Bks) Morrow.
—Faces of the U. S. A. 1987. pap. text ed. 12.95 (0-582-74923-9, 78237); cassette 24.95 (0-582-01896-X, 78271) Longman.
—Kiss the Dust. LC 91-43517. 284p. (gr. 5 up). 1992. 15.00 (0-525-44893-4, DCB) Dutton Child Bks.
—Kiss the Dust. 288p. (gr. 5 up). 1994. pap. 4.50 (0-14-036855-8) Puffin Bks.
—Loving Ben. (gr. 5 up). 1989. 14.95 (0-385-29810-2) Delacorte.

Laird, Elizabeth, jt. auth. see Ichikawa, Satomi.

Laird, Peter, jt. auth. see Eastman, Kevin.

Laird, Rebecca. Robinson Rabbit, What Do You Hear? Boddy, Joe, illus. LC 89-82550. 32p. (ps-k). 1990. pap. 5.99 (0-8066-2463-9, 9-2463) Augsburg Fortress.

Laitin, Ken & Laitin, Steve. Playing Soccer. Laitin, Lindy, illus. LC 79-63980. (gr. 2-7). 1979. pap. 9.95 (0-916802-22-1) Soccer for Am.

Laitin, Steve, jt. auth. see Laitin, Ken.

Lake, A. L. Gold Fever. (Illus.). 32p. (gr. 3-8). 1990. PLB 18.00 (0-86625-374-2); PLB 13.50s.p. (0-685-34710-9) Rourke Corp.
—Pony Express. (Illus.). 32p. (gr. 3-8). 1990. PLB 18.00 (0-86625-368-8); 13.50s.p. (0-685-58648-0) Rourke Corp.
—Women of the West. (Illus.). 32p. (gr. 3-8). 1990. PLB 18.00 (0-86625-373-4); PLB 13.50s.p. (0-685-58656-1) Rourke Corp.

Lake, Bonnie & Krishef, Robert. Western Stars of Country Music. LC 77-90149. (Illus.). 72p. (gr. 5 up). 1978. PLB 7.95 (0-8225-1407-9) Lerner Pubns.

Lake, Charles. Swine Lake. Filling, Gregory, illus. 48p. (gr. 3-7). 1985. 9.95 (0-13-879743-9) P-H.

Lake, Simon. Death Cycle. 1993. pap. 3.50 (0-553-56102-2) Bantam.
—He Told Me To. 1993. pap. 3.50 (0-553-56168-5) Bantam.
—Something's Watching. 1993. pap. 3.50 (0-553-29791-0) Bantam.

Lakin, Patricia. The Birthday Mystery. (Illus.). 13p. (gr. 3-6). 1991. incls. puzzle 12.95 (0-922242-21-6) Lombard Mktg.
—The Case of the Missing Ribbons. (Illus.). 14p. (gr. 3-6). 1991. incls. puzzle 12.95 (0-922242-20-8) Lombard Mktg.
—The Case of the Stolen Jewels: Puzzling Pen Pal Mysteries Ser. (Illus.). 24p. (gr. 3-4). 1992. bklt., incl. puzzle & pouch 12.95 (0-922242-33-X) Lombard Mktg.
—Don't Forget. Rand, Ted, illus. LC 93-20341. 32p. 1994. 14.00 (0-688-12075-X, Tambourine Bks); PLB 13.93 (0-688-12076-8, Tambourine Bks) Morrow.
—Don't Touch My Room. Brewster, Patience, illus. 32p. (ps-3). 1988. 12.95 (0-316-51230-3); pap. 5.95 (0-316-51228-1) Little.
—Jennifer Capriati. LC 93-18131. 1993. 15.93 (0-86592-090-7); 11.95s.p. (0-685-66545-3) Rourke Enter.
—Jet Black Pickup Truck. Hoffman, Rosekrans, illus. LC 89-71010. 32p. (ps-1). 1990. 14.95 (0-531-05885-9); PLB 14.99 (0-531-08485-X) Orchard Bks Watts.

—Just Like Me, Vol. 1. 1989. 14.95 (0-316-51233-8) Little.
—The Palace of Stars. Root, Kimberly B., illus. LC 92-36796. 32p. (ps up). 1993. 14.00 (0-688-11176-9, Tambourine Bks); PLB 13.93 (0-688-11177-7, Tambourine Bks) Morrow.

Lakin, Patty. Menace or Tennis: A Tennis Twins Mystery. (Illus.). 24p. (gr. 4-8). 1992. bklt., incl. puzzle & pouch 12.95 (0-922242-35-6) Lombard Mktg.

Lakritz, Esther. Developing Library Skills. 112p. (gr. 4-8). 1989. 9.95 (0-86653-481-4, GA1081) Good Apple.

Lalli, Judy. Feelings Alphabet: An Album of Emotions from A to Z. (Illus.). 72p. (ps-4). 1991. pap. 7.95 (0-915190-82-6, JP-9082-6) Jalmar Pr.

Lally, Dick. Boston Red Sox. 1991. pap. 2.99 (0-517-05790-5) Outlet Bk Co.
—The Chicago Cubs. 1991. pap. 2.99 (0-517-05791-3) Outlet Bk Co.

Lam, Roger. The Cuckoo Clock Adventure. Gibb, George, ed. Sweetman, Daniel, illus. LC 82-99848. (Orig.). (gr. 5-12). 1983. pap. 2.25 (0-943310-01-6) Six Pr.

LaMac, Liz. The Story of Dummyland: Little King Joe & the Witch's Maze. LaMac, Liz, illus. 130p. (gr. 4-5). 1990. 9.95 (0-927278-03-0) L LaMac Productions.

Lamancusa, Jim. Dynamite Crafts for Special Occasions. (gr. 4-7). 1993. pap. 12.95 (0-8306-4272-2) TAB Bks.

Lamancusa, Joe. Kid Cash: Creative Money-Making Ideas. (gr. 4-7). 1993. pap. 9.95 (0-8306-4265-X) TAB Bks.

La Mann, Angela. Mom Is Going to Stop It. 27p. (gr. k). 1992. pap. text ed. 23.00 big bk. (1-56843-014-0); pap. text ed. 4.50 (1-56843-064-7) BGR Pub.

LaMarche, Bob. Tennis Basics. Gow, Bill, illus. LC 82-21542. 48p. (gr. 3-7). 1983. 9.95 (0-13-903237-1) P-H.

La Mare, Walter de see De la Mare, Walter.

Lamb, Cecile, jt. auth. see Stagg, Mildred A.

Lamb, Charles. Roast Pig & Other Essays. large type ed. (gr. 10 up). Repr. write for info. NAVH.

Lamb, Charles & Lamb, Mary. Tales from Shakespeare. (gr. k-6). 1986. 8.98 (0-685-16860-3, 621568) Outlet Bk Co.
—Tales from Shakespeare. (gr. 5 up). 1988. pap. 3.99 (0-14-035088-8, Puffin) Puffin Bks.

Lamb, Harold. Genghis Khan & the Mongol Horde. Fax, Elton, illus. LC 90-6328. viii, 182p. (gr. 5 up). 1990. Repr. of 1954 ed. lib. bdg. 16.50 (0-208-02287-2, Linnet) Shoe String.

Lamb, Jane C., tr. see Coblence, Jean-Michel.

Lamb, Jane M. Sharing with Thumpy: My Story of Love & Grief. Dodge, Nancy C., illus. 48p. (gr. k-12). 1985. pap. 8.95 workbook (0-918533-10-4) Prairie Lark.

Lamb, Mary, jt. auth. see Lamb, Charles.

Lamb, Nancy. The Great Mosquito, Bull, & Coffin Caper. Pearson, Susan, ed. Remkiewicz, Frank, illus. LC 91-31125. 160p. (gr. 3 up). 1992. reinforced bdg. 12.00 (0-688-10933-0) Lothrop.
—The Great Mosquito, Bull, & Coffin Caper. Remkiewicz, Frank, illus. 128p. (gr. 5 up). 1994. pap. 3.95 (0-688-12944-7, Pub. by Beech Tree Bks) Morrow.

Lamb, Nancy & Singer, Muff. The World's Greatest Toe Show. Sims, Blanche, illus. LC 93-28440. 64p. (gr. 2-5). 1993. PLB 13.95 (0-8167-3322-8); pap. 3.95 (0-8167-3323-6) Troll Assocs.

Lamb, Patricia C. All Men by Nature. 56p. (Orig.). 1993. pap. 6.95 (0-9615145-2-3) Harbottle Pr.

Lamb, Ruth S. Latin America: Sites & Insights. (gr. 9-12). 1963. pap. 4.00 (0-912434-02-3) Ocelot Pr.

Lamb, Sandra & Bellows, Dena. Parties for Home & School: A Piece of Cake. Hyndman, Kathryn, illus. 144p. (gr. 4-7). 1985. wkbk. 11.95 (0-86653-328-1, GA 647) Good Apple.

Lamb, Susan. Montezuma Castle National Monument. Foreman, Ronald J. & Priehs, T. J., eds. 16p. (Orig.). 1992. pap. 2.95 (1-877856-19-3) SW Pks Mnmts.
—Petroglyph National Monument. Foreman, Ronald J. & Priehs, T. J., eds. 16p. (Orig.). 1993. pap. 2.95 (1-877856-22-3) SW Pks Mnmts.

Lamb, Wendy. Hey Little Walter & Other Prize-Winning Plays. 1991. pap. 3.99 (0-440-21025-9) Dell.

Lamb, Wendy, ed. Meeting the Winter Bike Rider & Other Winning Plays. (Orig.). (gr. 5 up). 1986. pap. 3.50 (0-440-95548-3, LFL) Dell.
—Ten Out of Ten: Ten Winning Plays Selected from the Young Playwrights Festival 1982-1991. Quinn, Nancy & Wasserstein, Wendyintro. by. LC 92-7944. 320p. (gr. 7 up). 1992. 18.00 (0-385-30811-6) Delacorte.

Lamberg, Lynn. Skin Disorders. (Illus.). 112p. (gr. 6-12). 1990. 18.95 (0-7910-0076-1) Chelsea Hse.

Lambert, Alan & Scott-Hughes, Brian. Junior Drama Workshop. (Illus.). 96p. (Orig.). 1990. pap. 14.95 (0-333-43459-5, McMillan Ed UK) Players Pr.

Lambert, Cindy, ed. see James, Mark.

Lambert, David. The Children's Animal Atlas. LC 91-30147. (Illus.). 96p. (gr. 2-6). 1992. 18.95 (1-56294-101-1); PLB 18.90 (1-56294-167-4) Millbrook Pr.
—Children's Animal Atlas. LC 92-30147. (gr. 4-7). 1993. pap. 10.95 (1-56294-716-8) Millbrook Pr.
—Dinosaurs. LC 89-22542. (ps-3). 1990. PLB 11.40 (0-531-19070-6) Watts.
—Fires & Floods. LC 92-8687. (Illus.). 48p. (gr. 6 up). 1992. RSBE 13.95 (0-02-751350-5, New Discovery) Macmillan Child Grp.

—Forests. Camm, Martin, et al, illus. LC 89-20311. 32p. (gr. 4-6). 1990. PLB 11.59 (0-8167-1971-3); pap. text ed. 3.95 (0-8167-1972-1) Troll Assocs.
—The Golden Concise Encyclopedia of Mammals. (Illus.). 96p. (gr. 1-6). 1992. 10.95 (0-307-16559-0, 16559, Golden Pr) Western Pub.
—Grasslands. Furstinger, Nancy, ed. (Illus.). 48p. (gr. 5-8). 1989. PLB 16.98 (0-382-09789-0) Silver Burdett Pr.
—Planet Earth 2000. (Illus.). 64p. (gr. 7 up). 1986. 14.95x (0-8160-1153-2) Facts on File.
—Polar Regions. (Illus.). 48p. (gr. 5-8). 1987. PLB 16.98 (0-382-09502-2) Silver Burdett Pr.
—Seas & Oceans. (Illus.). 48p. (gr. 5-8). 1987. PLB 16.98 (0-382-09503-0) Silver Burdett Pr.
—Seas & Oceans. Salariya, David, created by. Scrace, Carolyn & Bergin, Mark, illus. LC 93-6352. 1994. write for info. (0-8114-9245-1) Raintree Steck-V.
—Stars & Planets. Donohoe, Bill & Townsend, Tony, illus. LC 93-28282. 1994. write for info. (0-8114-9246-X) Raintree Steck-V.
—Weather. Camm, Martin, illus. LC 89-20304. 32p. (gr. 4-6). 1990. PLB 11.59 (0-8167-1979-9); pap. text ed. 3.95 (0-8167-1980-2) Troll Assocs.
—The World's Population. LC 93-716. (Illus.). 32p. (gr. 4-6). 1993. 14.95 (1-56847-050-9) Thomson Lrning.

Lambert, David & Current, Andrew. The World Before Man. (Illus.). 64p. (gr. 7 up). 15.95x (0-8160-1067-6) Facts on File.

Lambert, David & McConnell, Anita. Seas & Oceans. LC 84-1654. (Illus.). 64p. (gr. 7 up). 1985. 15.95x (0-8160-1064-1) Facts on File.

Lambert, David & Wright, Rachel. Dinosaurs. Kline, Marjory, ed. LC 91-21118. (Illus.). 32p. (gr. k-4). 1992. PLB 11.90 (0-531-14159-4) Watts.

Lambert, David, jt. auth. see Davis, Ken.

Lambert, David, jt. auth. see Diagram Group.

Lambert, David, jt. auth. see Diagram Group Staff.

Lambert, Jonathan. Giant Jungle Pop-up Book: Animals of the Endangered Rain Forest. Lambert, Jonathan, illus. (ps-3). 1992. 28.00 (1-56021-183-0) W J Fantasy.
—Twelve Days of Christmas. (ps-3). 1992. pap. 12.00 (0-671-78396-3, S&S BFYR) S&S Trade.

Lambert, Jonathan, illus. Colors. 18p. (ps-1). 1992. bds. 1.95 (0-681-41562-2) Longmeadow Pr.
—Numbers. 18p. (ps-1). 1992. bds. 1.95 (0-681-41563-0) Longmeadow Pr.
—Opposites. 18p. (ps-1). 1992. bds. 1.95 (0-681-41565-7) Longmeadow Pr.
—Shapes. 18p. (ps-1). 1992. bds. 1.95 (0-681-41564-9) Longmeadow Pr.

Lambert, Kathy. Martin Luther King, Jr. (Illus.). 80p. (gr. 3-5). 1993. PLB 12.95 (0-7910-1759-1) Chelsea Hse.

Lambert, Kathy K. Martin Luther King, Jr. Junior World Biographies. (gr. 4-7). 1992. pap. 4.95 (0-7910-1954-3) Chelsea Hse.

Lambert, Lee. Basic Library of the World's Greatest Music. (Illus.). 155p. (gr. 7 up). 1988. pap. text ed. 39.00 (0-9621630-1-5) L Lambert.

Lambert, Lisa A. The Leakeys. LC 92-46046. 1993. 19.93 (0-86625-492-7); 14.95s.p. (0-685-66536-4) Rourke Pubns.

Lambert, M. Copper. (Illus.). 48p. (gr. 5 up). 1985. PLB 17.27 (0-86592-270-5); lib. bdg. 12.95s.p. (0-685-58324-4) Rourke Corp.
—Iron & Steel. (Illus.). 48p. (gr. 5 up). 1985. PLB 17.27 (0-86592-268-3); 12.95 (0-685-58325-2) Rourke Corp.
—Plastics. (Illus.). 48p. (gr. 5 up). 1985. PLB 17.27 (0-86592-269-1); 12.95s.p. (0-685-58326-0) Rourke Corp.

Lambert, Mark. Building Technology. (Illus.). 48p. (gr. 5-8). 1991. 12.90 (0-531-18399-8, Pub. by Bookwright Pr) Watts.
—Energy Technology. LC 89-9709. (Illus.). 48p. (gr. 5-8). 1991. 12.90 (0-531-18457-9, Pub. by Bookwright Pr) Watts.
—Farming & the Environment. LC 90-45614. (Illus.). 48p. (gr. 4-9). 1990. PLB 19.92 (0-8114-2392-1); pap. 5.95 (0-685-58851-3) Raintree Steck-V.
—Farming Technology. (Illus.). 48p. (gr. 5-8). 1990. PLB 12.90 (0-531-18350-5) Watts.
—Food Technology. (Illus.). 48p. (gr. 5-9). 1992. PLB 12.90 (0-531-18400-5, Pub. by Bookwright Pr) Watts.
—Homes in the Future. (Illus.). 32p. (gr. 2-5). 1989. 13.50 (0-8225-2126-1) Lerner Pubns.
—Information Technology. (Illus.). 48p. (gr. 5-8). 1991. PLB 12.90 (0-531-18386-6, Pub. by Bookwright Pr) Watts.
—Ship Technology. (Illus.). 48p. (gr. 5-8). 1990. PLB 12.90 (0-531-18339-4, Pub. by Bookwright Pr) Watts.
—Transportation. LC 93-24990. (Illus.). 32p. (gr. 4-6). 1993. 14.95 (1-56847-118-1) Thomson Lrning.
—TV & Video Technology. 1990. PLB 12.90 (0-531-18327-0) Watts.

Lambert, Mark & Hamilton-MacLaren, Alistair. Machines. (Illus.). 48p. (gr. 5-8). 1991. 12.90 (0-531-18413-7, Pub. by Bookwright Pr) Watts.

Lambert, Matthew. My First Spring Day. Beckes, Shirley, illus. 1994. write for info. (0-8114-4459-1) Raintree Steck-V.

Lambert, Stephen. The Snowmaiden. Riordan, James, retold by. (Illus.). 32p. (gr. 1-3). 1992. 15.95 (0-09-173861-X, Pub. by Hutchinson UK) Trafalgar.

Lambord, Creede & Lambord, Sharleen. Heart of Darkness. 64p. (Orig.). 1991. pap. 10.00 (0-685-61116-7) Game Designers.

Lambord, Sharleen, jt. auth. see Lambord, Creede.

Lamborn, Florence, tr. see Lindgren, Astrid.

Lambourne, Mike. Down the Hatch! Find Out about
Your Food. LC 91-22686. (Illus.). 40p. (gr. 2-6). 1992.
PLB 12.90 (*1-56294-150-X*) Millbrook Pr.
—Inside Story: The Latest News about Your Body. LC
91-22960. (Illus.). 40p. (gr. 2-6). 1992. PLB 12.90
(*1-56294-148-8*) Millbrook Pr.
Lambroza, Shlomo. World Leaders - Boris Yeltsin. LC
92-46479. 1993. 19.93 (*0-86625-482-X*); 14.95s.p.
(*0-685-66417-1*) Rourke Pubns.
Lamerisse, Albert. The Red Balloon. 32p. (gr. 6). 1990.
PLB 13.95s.p. (*0-88682-304-8*) Creative Ed.
Lamm, C. Drew. Anniranni & Mollymishi the Wild-
Haired Doll. Ohi, Ruth, illus. 24p. (ps-2). 1990. 14.95
(*1-55037-105-3*, Pub. by Annick CN); pap. 5.95
(*1-55037-106-1*, Pub. by Annick CN) Firefly Bks Ltd.
Lammert, John M. Microbes. LC 92-9123. 1992. 12.67
(*0-86625-430-7*); 12.50s.p. (*0-685-59398-3*) Rourke
Pubns.
Lamont, Priscilla. Our Mammoth Goes to School.
Lamont, Pricilla, illus. LC 86-26939. 32p. (ps-3). 1988.
11.95 (*0-15-258837-X*, HB Juv Bks) HarBrace.
—Ring-a-Round-a Rosy: Nursery Rhymes, Action
Rhymes & Lullabies. Lamont, Priscilla, illus. (ps).
1990. 15.95 (*0-316-51292-3*, Joy St Bks) Little.
Lamont-Clarke, Ginette & Stevens, Florence. Et Si Papa
se Perd au Zoo? Langevin, Isabelle, illus. LC 91-
65364. (FRE.). 24p. (ps-2). 1991. 12.95
(*0-88776-266-2*); pap. 6.95 (*0-88776-273-5*) Tundra
Bks.
Lamont-Clarke, Ginette, jt. auth. see Stevens, Florence.
LaMore, Gregory S. Now I Understand. Ensing-Keelean,
Jan, illus. LC 85-20639. 56p. (gr. 3-6). 1986. 8.95
(*0-930323-13-0*, Kendall Green Pubns) Gallaudet Univ
Pr.
Lamorisse, Albert. Red Balloon. Lamorisse, Albert,
photos by. LC 57-9229. (Illus.). 45p. (gr. 3-7). 1967.
13.95 (*0-685-01494-0*) Doubleday.
—The Red Balloon. LC 57-9229. (Illus.). 45p. (ps-3).
1978. 15.95 (*0-385-00343-9*, Zephyr-BFYR); pap. 7.95
(*0-385-14297-8*, Zephyr-BFYR) Doubleday.
LaMorte, Kathy & Lewis, Sharen. Ecology Green Pages
for Students & Teachers. Keeling, Jan, ed. LaMorte,
Kathy, illus. 64p. (Orig.). 1993. pap. text ed. 7.95
(*0-86530-269-3*) Incentive Pubns.
—U. S. Social Studies Yellow Pages for Students &
Teachers. Keeling, Jan, ed. LaMorte, Kathy, illus. 64p.
(Orig.). 1993. pap. text ed. 7.95 (*0-86530-267-7*)
Incentive Pubns.
—World Social Studies Yellow Pages for Students &
Teachers. Newton, Rebecca, ed. LaMorte, Kathy, illus.
64p. (Orig.). 1993. pap. text ed. 7.95 (*0-86530-268-5*)
Incentive Pubns.
L'Amour, Louis. How the West Was Won. (gr. 7-12).
1984. pap. 4.50 (*0-553-26913-5*) Bantam.
Lamp Light Press Staff. Noah's Ark: A Story Rhyme.
(Illus.). 23p. (ps-6). 1992. pap. text ed. 6.95
(*0-917593-11-1*, Lamp Light Pr) Prosperity & Profits.
Lampert, Diane, jt. auth. see Farrow, Peter.
Lampert, Emily. A Little Touch of Monster. Kroupa,
Melanie, illus. LC 85-26847. 32p. (ps-3). 1986. lib.
bdg. 12.95 (*0-316-51287-7*, 512877, Joy St Bks) Little.
Lampi, Kathlyn. Lighten Up, Jennifer. (gr. 6 up). 1988.
write for info. (*0-373-98015-9*) S&S Trade.
Lamping, Ed. The Awareness Book. (Illus.). 40p. (gr.
3-6). 1982. 5.00 (*0-940444-15-1*) Kabyn.
Lampiris, Nicholas, jt. auth. see Laing, David.
Lampl, C., ed. Walt Disney's Snow White & the Seven
Dwarfs. Mateo, Franc, illus. LC 92-53432. 12p. (ps-k).
1993. 11.95 (*1-56282-365-5*) Disney Pr.
Lampl, Cathy, ed. Aladdin: The Magic Carpet Ride.
Vaccaro, Garparo, illus. LC 92-54878. 10p. (ps-k).
1993. 4.95 (*1-56282-396-5*) Disney Pr.
—Pinocchio: Geppetto's Surprise. Marvin, Fred, illus. LC
92-54877. 10p. (ps-k). 1993. 4.95 (*1-56282-397-3*)
Disney Pr.
Lampman, Evelyn S. Treasure Mountain. (Illus.). 207p.
(gr. 4). 1990. pap. 6.95 (*0-87595-231-3*) Oregon Hist.
Lamport, Joan & Perle, Ruth L. Taking Tests & Relaxing
Activity Book. Hefter, Richard, illus. (gr. 2-3). 1976.
0.95 (*0-89796-847-6*, XTW 07) New Dimens Educ.
Lamport, Joan, et al. Story Builders Activity Book.
Hefter, Richard, illus. (gr. 2-3). 0.95 (*0-89796-844-1*,
XTW 03) New Dimens Educ.
—The WordShop Activity Book. Hefter, Richard, illus.
(gr. 2-3). 1976. 0.95 (*0-89796-845-X*, XTW 05) New
Dimens Educ.
Lamprey, Louise. Children of Ancient Gaul. LC 60-
16708. (Illus.). (gr. 7-11). 1968. 20.00 (*0-8196-0109-8*)
Biblo.
—Children of Ancient Rome. LC 61-12876. (Illus.). (gr.
7-11). 1967. 18.00 (*0-8196-0114-4*) Biblo.
Lampton, Christopher. Bathtubs, Slides, Roller Coaster
Rails: Simple Machines That Are Really Inclined
Planes. Nicklaus, Carol, illus. 32p. (gr. 2-4). 1991.
PLB 12.40 (*1-878841-23-8*) Millbrook Pr.
—Blizzard. (Illus.). 64p. (gr. 4-6). 1991. PLB 13.40
(*1-56294-029-5*) Millbrook Pr.
—Blizzard: A Disaster Book. (gr. 4-7). 1992. pap. 5.95
(*0-395-63641-8*) HM.
—Chemical Accident. (Illus.). 48p. (gr. 4-6). 1994. 13.40
(*1-56294-316-2*) Millbrook Pr.
—Coral Reefs in Danger. LC 91-41441. (Illus.). 64p. (gr.
4-8). 1992. PLB 14.90 (*1-56294-091-0*) Millbrook Pr.
—DNA Fingerprinting. (Illus.). 112p. (gr. 9-12). 1991.
PLB 13.40 (*0-531-13003-7*) Watts.
—Drought. LC 91-18053. (Illus.). 64p. (gr. 4-6). 1992.
PLB 13.40 (*1-56294-125-9*) Millbrook Pr.

—Drought: A Disaster Book. (gr. 4-7). 1992. pap. 5.95
(*0-395-62465-7*) HM.
—Earthquake. (Illus.). 64p. (gr. 4-6). 1991. PLB 13.40
(*1-56294-031-7*) Millbrook Pr.
—Earthquake: A Disaster Book. (gr. 4-7). 1992. pap. 5.95
(*0-395-62466-5*) HM.
—Endangered Species. Kline, M., ed. LC 87-25161.
(Illus.). 128p. (gr. 7-12). 1988. PLB 13.40
(*0-531-10510-5*) Watts.
—Epidemic. LC 91-21413. (Illus.). 64p. (gr. 4-6). 1992.
PLB 13.40 (*1-56294-126-7*) Millbrook Pr.
—Epidemic: A Disaster Book. (gr. 4-7). 1992. pap. 5.95
(*0-395-62466-5*) HM.
—Famine. LC 93-9428. (Illus.). 48p. (gr. 4-6). 1994. PLB
13.40 (*1-56294-317-0*) Millbrook Pr.
—Forest Fire. (Illus.). 64p. (gr. 4-6). 1991. PLB 13.40
(*1-56294-030-9*) Millbrook Pr.
—Forest Fire: A Disaster Book. (gr. 4-7). 1992. pap. 5.95
(*0-395-63646-9*) HM.
—Gene Technology: Confronting the Issues. LC 90-
37572. (Illus.). 144p. (gr. 9-12). 1990. PLB 13.90
(*0-531-10951-8*) Watts.
—Hurricane. (Illus.). 64p. (gr. 4-6). 1991. PLB 13.40
(*1-56294-030-9*) Millbrook Pr.
—Hurricane: A Disaster Book. (gr. 4-7). 1992. pap. 5.95
(*0-395-63643-4*) HM.
—Insect Attack. LC 91-26155. (Illus.). 64p. (gr. 4-6).
1992. PLB 13.40 (*1-56294-127-5*) Millbrook Pr.
—Insect Attack: A Disaster Book. (gr. 4-7). 1992. pap.
5.95 (*0-395-62467-3*) HM.
—Jupiter. LC 93-31094. 1994. write for info.
(*0-89686-756-0*, Crestwood Hse) Macmillan Child
Grp.
—Marbles, Roller Skates, Doorknobs: Simple Machines
That Are Really Wheels. Nicklaus, Carol, illus. LC 92-
34332. 32p. (gr. 2-4). 1991. PLB 12.40
(*1-878841-24-6*) Millbrook Pr.
—Mars. LC 93-30152. 1994. write for info.
(*0-89686-757-9*, Crestwood Hse) Macmillan Child
Grp.
—Mercury. LC 93-31290. 1994. write for info.
(*0-89686-758-7*, Crestwood Hse) Macmillan Child
Grp.
—Neptune. LC 93-31093. 1994. write for info.
(*0-89686-759-5*, Crestwood Hse) Macmillan Child
Grp.
—New Theories on the Birth of the Universe. (Illus.).
176p. (gr. 7-12). 1989. PLB 13.90 (*0-531-10782-5*)
Watts.
—New Theories on the Dinosaurs. LC 89-31829. (Illus.).
144p. (gr. 7-12). 1989. PLB 14.40 (*0-531-10781-7*)
Watts.
—New Theories on the Origin of the Human Race. LC
89-9169. (Illus.). 160p. (gr. 7-12). 1989. PLB 14.40
(*0-531-10783-3*) Watts.
—Nintendo Action Games. (Illus.). 72p. (gr. 4-6). 1991.
PLB 14.90 (*1-878841-26-2*) Millbrook Pr.
—Nintendo Role-Playing Games. (Illus.). 72p. (gr. 4-6).
1991. PLB 14.90 (*1-878841-25-4*) Millbrook Pr.
—Nuclear Accident. LC 91-43564. (Illus.). 48p. (gr. 4-6).
1992. PLB 13.40 (*1-56294-073-2*) Millbrook Pr.
—Oil Spill. LC 91-43565. (Illus.). 48p. (gr. 4-6). 1992.
PLB 13.40 (*1-56294-071-6*) Millbrook Pr.
—Pluto. LC 93-30151. 1994. write for info.
(*0-89686-760-9*, Crestwood Hse) Macmillan Child
Grp.
—Predicting AIDS & Other Epidemics. LC 89-8972.
(Illus.). 144p. (gr. 9-12). 1989. PLB 13.90
(*0-531-10785-X*) Watts.
—Predicting Nuclear & Other Technological Disasters.
LC 89-9160. (Illus.). 144p. (gr. 9-12). 1989. PLB 13.90
(*0-531-10784-1*) Watts.
—Rocketry: From Goddard to Space Travel. Kline, M.,
ed. LC 87-21558. (Illus.). 96p. (gr. 7-9). 1988. PLB 10.
90 (*0-531-10483-4*) Watts.
—Sailboats, Flag Poles, Cranes: Using Pulleys as Simple
Machines. (Illus.). 32p. (gr. 2-4). 1991. PLB 12.40
(*1-56294-026-0*) Millbrook Pr.
—Saturn. LC 93-30150. 1994. write for info.
(*0-89686-761-7*, Crestwood Hse) Macmillan Child
Grp.
—Science of Chaos: Complexity in the Natural World.
Cohn, Tom, ed. LC 91-40896. (Illus.). 128p. (gr. 7-12).
1992. PLB 13.40 (*0-531-12513-0*) Watts.
—Seesaws, Nutcrackers, Brooms: Simple Machines That
Are Really Levers. Nicklaus, Carol, illus. 32p. (gr.
2-4). 1991. PLB 12.40 (*1-878841-22-X*) Millbrook Pr.
—Telecommunications: From Telegraphs to Modems. LC
90-48230. (Illus.). 96p. (gr. 7-9). 1991. PLB 12.90
(*0-531-12527-0*) Watts.
—Thomas Alva Edison. LC 90-49178. (Illus.). 88p. (gr. 6-
10). 1991. PLB 13.95 (*1-55905-079-9*) Marshall
Cavendish.
—Tidal Wave. LC 91-21518. (Illus.). 64p. (gr. 4-6). 1992.
PLB 13.40 (*1-56294-124-0*) Millbrook Pr.
—Tidal Wave: A Disaster Book. (gr. 4-7). 1992. pap. 5.95
(*0-395-62464-9*) HM.
—Tornado. (Illus.). 64p. (gr. 4-6). 1991. PLB 13.40
(*1-56294-032-5*) Millbrook Pr.
—Tornado: A Disaster Book. (gr. 4-7). 1992. pap. 5.95
(*0-395-63644-2*) HM.
—Uranus. LC 93-31291. 1994. write for info.
(*0-89686-762-5*, Crestwood Hse) Macmillan Child
Grp.
—Venus. LC 93-31289. 1994. write for info.
(*0-89686-763-3*, Crestwood Hse) Macmillan Child
Grp.

—Volcano. (Illus.). 64p. (gr. 4-6). 1991. PLB 13.40
(*1-56294-028-7*) Millbrook Pr.
—Volcano: A Disaster Book. (gr. 4-7). 1992. pap. 5.95
(*0-395-63645-0*) HM.
Lampton, Christopher F. Particle Physics: The New View
of the Universe. LC 90-48049. (Illus.). 64p. (gr. 6 up).
1991. lib. bdg. 15.95 (*0-89490-328-4*) Enslow Pubs.
—Sound: More Than What You Hear. LC 91-22331.
(Illus.). 96p. (gr. 6 up). 1992. lib. bdg. 16.95
(*0-89490-327-6*) Enslow Pubs.
—Superconductors. LC 88-31562. (Illus.). 96p. (gr. 6 up).
1989. lib. bdg. 16.95 (*0-89490-203-2*) Enslow Pubs.
Lanagan, Margo. Tankermen. 1993. pap. 6.95
(*1-86373-253-5*, Pub. by Allen & Unwin Aust Pty AT)
IPG Chicago.
—Wildgame. 160p. (Orig.). (gr. 4-8). 1993. pap. 7.95
(*1-86373-069-9*, Pub. by Allen & Unwin Aust Pty AT)
IPG Chicago.
Lancaster, Beverly, jt. auth. see Woods, Elsa.
Lancaster, Derek. Picture America: States & Capitals.
Lancaster, Derek, illus. Anderson, Stevens, ed. (Illus.).
136p. (gr. 5). 1991. pap. 4.95 (*1-880184-02-8*)
Compact Classics.
Lancaster, Francine. Favorite Animal Songs. (gr. k up).
1985. Boxed Set incl. cassette. 16.95 (*0-930647-01-7*)
Lancaster Prodns.
—Mother Goose & Other Nursery Songs: From the
Collection of the Museum of Fine Arts, Boston. (ps
up). 1987. incl. cassette 16.95 (*0-930647-03-3*)
Lancaster Prodns.
—Nursery Songs & Lullabies. (gr. k up). 1984. 16.95
(*0-930647-00-9*); cassette incl. Lancaster Prodns.
Lancaster, John. Art with Found Materials. LC 91-2875.
(Illus.). 48p. (gr. 5-8). 1991. PLB 12.40
(*0-531-14204-3*) Watts.
—Decorated Lettering. (Illus.). 48p. (gr. 5-8). 1990. PLB
12.90 (*0-531-14074-1*) Watts.
—Fabric Art. LC 90-12281. (Illus.). 48p. (gr. 5-8). 1991.
PLB 12.40 (*0-531-14102-0*) Watts.
Lancaster-Brown, Peter. Skywatch: Eyes-on Activities
for Getting to Know the Stars, Planets & Galaxies. LC
92-40580. (Illus.). 128p. 1993. 14.95 (*0-8069-8627-1*)
Sterling.
Lance, Janice. First Literature Experiences. Dillon, Paul,
illus. 48p. (gr. k-3). 1991. pap. 5.95 (*1-879287-01-3*)
Bk Lures.
Lance, Kathryn. Going to See Grassy Ella. LC 92-16237.
1993. write for info. (*0-688-12163-2*) Lothrop.
Land, Leslie. The New England Epicure: Reading
Between the Recipes. 1988. pap. 9.95 (*0-440-50078-8*,
Dell Trade Pbks) Dell.
Landa, Bonnie L., jt. auth. see Halstead, Bruce W.
Landa, Norbert. How Does It Feel? Littlewood, Karin,
illus. LC 92-39238. 26p. 1993. 14.95 (*1-56566-032-3*)
Thomasson-Grant.
—Rabbit & Chicken Count Eggs. Turk, Hanne, illus. LC
90-33436. (ps). 1992. bds. 4.95 (*0-688-09971-8*,
Tambourine Bks) Morrow.
—Rabbit & Chicken Find a Box. Turk, Hanne, illus. LC
90-33379. (ps). 1992. bds. 4.95 (*0-688-09968-8*,
Tambourine Bks) Morrow.
—Rabbit & Chicken Play Hide & Seek. Turk, Hanne,
illus. LC 90-33484. (ps). 1992. bds. 4.95
(*0-688-09970-X*, Tambourine Bks) Morrow.
—Rabbit & Chicken Play with Colors. Turk, Hanne, illus.
LC 90-33485. (ps). 1992. bds. 4.95 (*0-688-09969-6*,
Tambourine Bks) Morrow.
Landau, Elaine. Allergies. 1994. PLB write for info.
(*0-8050-2989-3*) H Holt & Co.
—Armed America. (Illus.). 128p. (gr. 6 up). 1990. lib.
bdg. 12.98 (*0-671-72386-3*, J Messner); lib. bdg. 5.95
(*0-671-72387-1*) S&S Trade.
—The Beauty Trap. LC 93-29641. (Illus.). 128p. (gr. 6
up). 1994. RSBE 13.95 (*0-02-751389-0*, New
Discovery Bks) Macmillan Child Grp.
—Big Brother Is Watching. 1992. 14.95 (*0-8027-8160-8*);
lib. bdg. 15.85 (*0-8027-8161-6*) Walker & Co.
—Bill Clinton. rev. ed. LC 92-39174. (Illus.). (gr. 5-8).
1993. PLB 12.40 (*0-531-11143-1*); pap. 5.95
(*0-531-15670-2*) Watts.
—Blindness. 1994. PLB write for info. (*0-8050-2992-3*) H
Holt & Co.
—Cancer. 1994. PLB write for info. (*0-8050-2990-7*) H
Holt & Co.
—Chemical & Biological Warfare. 128p. (gr. 5-9). 1991.
14.95 (*0-525-67364-4*, Lodestar Bks) Dutton Child
Bks.
—The Cherokees. Rosoff, Iris, ed. LC 91-30262. (Illus.).
64p. (gr. 3-5). 1992. PLB 12.90 (*0-531-20066-3*)
Watts.
—The Cherokees. (Illus.). 64p. (gr. 5-8). 1992. pap. 5.95
(*0-531-15635-4*) Watts.
—Child Abuse: An American Epidemic. rev. ed. 128p.
(gr. 7 up). 1990. lib. bdg. 12.98 (*0-671-68874-X*, J
Messner); lib. bdg. 5.95 (*0-671-68875-8*) S&S Trade.
—Child Abuse: An American Epidemic. LC 84-996.
(Illus.). 128p. (gr. 7 up). 1984. lib. bdg. 11.29
(*0-671-47988-1*, J Messner) S&S Trade.
—The Chilulas. LC 93-31423. 1994. write for info.
(*0-531-20132-5*); pap. write for info. (*0-531-15685-0*)
Watts.
—Colin Powell: Four Star General. LC 91-12860. (Illus.).
64p. (gr. 5-8). 1991. PLB 12.90 (*0-531-20143-0*)
Watts.
—Cowboys. (Illus.). 64p. (gr. 5-8). 1990. PLB 12.90
(*0-531-10866-X*) Watts.
—Deafness. 1994. PLB write for info. (*0-8050-2993-1*) H
Holt & Co.

—Diabetes. 1994. PLB write for info. (*0-8050-2988-5*) H Holt & Co.
—Different Drummer: Homosexuality in America. (gr. 7 up). 1986. lib. bdg. write for info. (*0-671-54997-9*, J Messner) S&S Trade.
—Dyslexia. (Illus.). 64p. (gr. 5-8). 1991. PLB 12.90 (*0-531-20030-2*) Watts.
—Endangered Plants. Rosoff, Iris, ed. LC 91-34926. (Illus.). 64p. (gr. 3-5). 1992. PLB 12.90 (*0-531-20134-1*) Watts.
—Endangered Plants. (Illus.). 64p. (gr. 5-8). 1992. pap. 5.95 (*0-531-15645-1*) Watts.
—Environmental Groups: The Earth Savers. LC 92-23679. (Illus.). 112p. (gr. 6 up). 1993. lib. bdg. 17.95 (*0-89490-396-9*) Enslow Pubs.
—Epilepsy. 1994. PLB write for info. (*0-8050-2991-5*) H Holt & Co.
—The Homeless. 128p. (gr. 6-9). 1987. lib. bdg. 13.98 (*0-671-53492-0*, J Messner); PLB 9.74s.p. (*0-685-47105-5*) S&S Trade.
—The Hopi. LC 93-31964. 1994. write for info. (*0-531-20098-1*); pap. write for info. (*0-531-15684-2*) Watts.
—Interesting Invertebrates: A Look at Some Animals Without Backbones. (Illus.). 64p. (gr. 5-8). 1991. PLB 12.90 (*0-531-20036-1*) Watts.
—Interracial Dating. LC 92-44814. (gr. 7 up). 1993. lib. bdg. 13.98 (*0-671-75258-8*, J Messner); lib. bdg. 7.95 (*0-671-75261-8*) S&S Trade.
—Jupiter. LC 90-13099. (Illus.). 64p. (gr. 3-5). 1991. PLB 12.90 (*0-531-20015-9*) Watts.
—The Loch Ness Monster. LC 92-35145. (Illus.). 48p. (gr. 3-6). 1993. PLB 13.90 (*1-56294-347-2*) Millbrook Pr.
—Lyme Disease. LC 89-70514. (Illus.). 1990. PLB 12.90 (*0-531-10931-3*) Watts.
—Mars. LC 90-13097. (Illus.). 64p. (gr. 3-5). 1991. PLB 12.90 (*0-531-20012-4*) Watts.
—Nazi War Criminals. (Illus.). 128p. (gr. 9-12). 1990. 12.95 (*0-531-15181-6*); PLB 13.40 (*0-531-10957-7*) Watts.
—Neptune. LC 90-13098. (Illus.). 64p. (gr. 3-5). 1991. PLB 12.90 (*0-531-20014-0*) Watts.
—On the Streets: The Lives of Adolescent Prostitutes. LC 86-21825. 112p. (gr. 9 up). 1987. lib. bdg. 12.98 (*0-671-62135-1*, J Messner) S&S Trade.
—Rabies. LC 92-26117. 64p. (gr. 2-5). 1993. 14.99 (*0-525-67403-9*, Lodestar Bks) Dutton Child Bks.
—The Right to Die. (Illus.). 208p. (gr. 7-12). 1993. PLB 13.40 (*0-531-13015-0*) Watts.
—Robert Fulton. LC 90-47865. (Illus.). 64p. (gr. 3-5). 1991. PLB 12.90 (*0-531-20016-7*) Watts.
—Sasquatch, Wild Man of the Woods. LC 92-35144. (Illus.). 48p. (gr. 3-6). 1993. PLB 13.90 (*1-56294-348-0*) Millbrook Pr.
—Saturn. (Illus.). 64p. (gr. 3-5). 1991. PLB 12.90 (*0-531-20013-2*) Watts.
—Sexual Harassment. LC 92-43748. 128p. (gr. 5 up). 1993. 14.95 (*0-8027-8265-5*); PLB 15.85 (*0-8027-8266-3*) Walker & Co.
—Sexually Transmitted Diseases. Heimlich, Hermelie, illus. Armstrong, Donald & Haundsfield, Hunterfrwd. by. LC 85-4349. (Illus.). 96p. (gr. 6 up). 1986. lib. bdg. 16.95 (*0-89490-115-X*) Enslow Pubs.
—Sibling Rivalry: Brothers & Sisters at Odds. (Illus.). 64p. (gr. 4-6). 1994. 14.90 (*1-56294-328-6*) Millbrook Pr.
—The Sioux. LC 89-5654. (Illus.). 64p. (gr. 4-7). 1989. PLB 12.90 (*0-531-10754-X*) Watts.
—The Sioux. (Illus.). 64p. (gr. 3 up). 1991. pap. 5.95 (*0-531-15606-0*) Watts.
—State Birds: Including the Commonwealth of Puerto Rico. LC 92-8949. (Illus.). 64p. 1992. PLB 13.90 (*0-531-20058-2*); pap. 6.95 (*0-531-15629-X*) Watts.
—State Flowers: Including the Commonwealth of Puerto Rico. LC 92-8950. 1992. 13.90 (*0-531-20059-0*) Watts.
—State Flowers: Including the Commonwealth of Puerto Rico. (gr. 4-7). 1992. pap. 6.95 (*0-531-15631-1*) Watts.
—Surrogate Mothers. Rosoff, Iris, ed. LC 88-5551. (Illus.). 144p. (gr. 7 up). 1988. PLB 13.40 (*0-531-10603-9*) Watts.
—Teenage Violence. Steltenpohl, Jane, ed. (Illus.). 128p. (gr. 7 up). 1990. lib. bdg. 12.98 (*0-671-70153-3*, J Messner); lib. bdg. 5.95 (*0-671-70154-1*) S&S Trade.
—Teenagers Talk about School. Steltenpohl, Jane, ed. LC 88-23065. 120p. (gr. 7 up). 1989. lib. bdg. 5.95 (*0-671-68148-6*, J Messner); lib. bdg. 12.98 (*0-671-64568-4*) S&S Trade.
—Teens & the Death Penalty. LC 91-23351. 112p. (gr. 6 up). 1992. lib. bdg. 17.95 (*0-89490-297-0*) Enslow Pubs.
—Terrorism: America's Growing Threat. 128p. (gr. 5-9). 1992. 15.00 (*0-525-67382-2*, Lodestar Bks) Dutton Child Bks.
—Tropical Rain Forests Around the World. LC 89-24810. (gr. 3-5). 1990. PLB 12.90 (*0-531-10896-1*) Watts.
—Tropical Rain Forests Around the World. (Illus.). 64p. (gr. 3 up). 1991. pap. 5.95 (*0-531-15600-1*) Watts.
—The Warsaw Ghetto Uprising. LC 92-15851. (Illus.). 144p. (gr. 6 up). 1992. RSBE 14.95 (*0-02-751392-0*, New Discovery) Macmillan Child Grp.
—We Have AIDS. 1990. 13.95 (*0-531-15152-2*) Watts.
—We Have AIDS. LC 89-24801. 126p. (gr. 7 up). 1990. PLB 13.40 (*0-531-10898-8*) Watts.

—We Survived the Holocaust. LC 91-16982. (Illus.). 144p. (gr. 9-12). 1991. 14.45 (*0-531-15229-4*); PLB 14.40 (*0-531-11115-6*) Watts.
—Weight: A Teenage Concern. 160p. (gr. 7 up). 1991. 15.00 (*0-525-67335-0*, Lodestar Bks) Dutton Child Bks.
—The White Power Movement: America's Racist Hate Groups. LC 92-40920. (Illus.). 96p. (gr. 7 up). 1993. PLB 14.90 (*1-56294-327-8*) Millbrook Pr.
—Why Are They Starving Themselves? Understanding Anorexia Nervosa & Bulimia. Schor, Ellen, intro. by. LC 82-24913. 160p. (gr. 7 up). 1983. lib. bdg. 13.98 (*0-671-45582-6*, J Messner); lib. bdg. 5.95 (*0-671-49492-9*) S&S Trade.
—Wildflowers Around the World. LC 90-13090. (Illus.). 64p. (gr. 3-5). 1991. PLB 12.90 (*0-531-20005-1*) Watts.
—Wildflowers Around the World. 64p. (gr. 5-8). 1992. pap. 5.95 (*0-531-15649-4*) Watts.
—Yeti, Abominable Snowman of the Himalayas. LC 92-35147. (Illus.). 48p. (gr. 3-6). 1993. PLB 13.90 (*1-56294-349-9*) Millbrook Pr.
Landaw, Jonathan. The Story of Buddha. Basu, R. K., illus. (gr. 3-10). 1979. 7.95 (*0-89744-140-0*) Auromere.
Landaw, Jonathan & Brooke, Janet. Prince Siddhartha. rev. ed. (Illus.). 144p. (gr. 1-8). 1984. 15.95 (*0-86171-016-9*) Wisdom MA.
Landeck, Michael. International Trade: Regional & Global Issues. LC 93-14617. (gr. 6 up). 1993. write for info. (*0-312-10257-7*) St Martin.
Lander, Kerstin, tr. see Cuthburth, Ronald W.
Lander, Michael. Teenage Mutant Ninja Turtle Trivia Quiz Book. (gr. 4-7). 1991. pap. 3.50 (*0-440-40543-2*) Dell.
Lander, Patricia, jt. auth. see Charbonneau, Claudette.
Lander, Patricia S. & Charbonneau, Claudette. The Land & People of Finland. LC 88-27144. (Illus.). 224p. (gr. 6 up). 1990. 18.00 (*0-397-32357-3*, Lipp Jr Bks); PLB 17.89 (*0-397-32358-1*, Lipp Jr Bks) HarpC Child Bks.
Landers, Andy. Women's Basketball Drills - Defensive Drills. (Orig.). (gr. 7 up). 1989. pap. 6.95 (*0-932741-56-8*) Championship Bks & Vid Prodns.
Landers-Henry, Joanne. Robert Fulton: Steamboat Builder. Mawicke, Tran, illus. 80p. (gr. 2-6). 1991. Repr. of 1975 ed. lib. bdg. 12.95 (*0-7910-1411-8*) Chelsea Hse.
Landes, William-Alan. Aladdin n' His Magic Lamp. rev. ed. LC 89-43679. 52p. (gr. 3-12). 1985. pap. 6.00 play script (*0-88734-102-0*); dir. guide 30.00 (*0-88734-003-2*) Players Pr.
—Aladdin n' His Magic Lamp: Music & Lyrics. rev. ed. (gr. 3-12). 1985. pap. text ed. 15.00 (*0-88734-002-4*) Players Pr.
—Alice n' Wonderland. LC 89-63870. (Orig.). (gr. 3 up). 1984. pap. 6.00 play script (*0-88734-112-8*) Players Pr.
—Jack 'n the Beanstalk. rev. ed. LC 89-43681. (gr. 3-12). 1985. pap. 6.00 play script (*0-88734-101-2*); tchr's. ed. 30.00 (*0-88734-001-6*) Players Pr.
—Jack 'n the Beanstalk: Music & Lyrics. rev. ed. (gr. 3-12). 1985. pap. text ed. 15.00 (*0-88734-000-8*) Players Pr.
—Peter N' the Wolf. rev. ed. LC 89-69871. (gr. 3-12). 1988. pap. 6.00 play script (*0-88734-106-3*); tchr's. ed. 30.00 (*0-88734-013-X*) Players Pr.
—Pyramus & Thisbe. rev. ed. LC 90-53083. (gr. 3 up). 1984. pap. 5.00 play script (*0-88734-103-9*) Players Pr.
—Rapunzel 'N the Witch. rev. ed. LC 89-43682. (gr. 3-12). 1985. pap. 6.00 play script (*0-88734-107-1*); tchr's. ed. 30.00 (*0-88734-007-5*) Players Pr.
—Rapunzel 'N the Witch: Music & Lyrics. rev. ed. (gr. 3-12). 1985. pap. 15.00 play script (*0-88734-006-7*) Players Pr.
—Rhyme Tyme. rev. ed. LC 89-63869. (gr. 3-12). 1985. pap. 6.00 play script (*0-88734-108-X*) Players Pr.
—Rumpelstiltskin. rev. ed. LC 89-43683. 52p. (gr. 3-12). 1985. pap. 6.00 play script (*0-88734-104-7*); tchr's. ed. 30.00 (*0-88734-005-9*) Players Pr.
Landes, William-Alan & Lasky, Mark A. Grandpa's Bedtime Story. rev. ed. LC 89-63868. (gr. 3-12). 1985. pap. 6.00 play script (*0-88734-505-0*) Players Pr.
Landes, William-Alan & Rizzo, Jeff. Rhyme Tyme: Music & Lyrics. rev. ed. (gr. 3-12). 1985. pap. text ed. 15.00 (*0-88734-008-3*) Players Pr.
—Rumpelstiltskin: Music & Lyrics. rev. ed. (gr. 3-12). 1985. pap. text ed. 15.00 (*0-88734-004-0*) Players Pr.
Landes, William-Alan & Standish, Marilyn. The Wizard of Oz. rev. ed. LC 89-63872. (gr. 3-12). 1985. pap. 6.00 play script (*0-88734-105-5*); tchr's. ed. 30.00 (*0-88734-011-3*) Players Pr.
—The Wizard of Oz: Music & Lyrics. rev. ed. (gr. 3-12). 1985. pap. text ed. 15.00 (*0-88734-010-5*) Players Pr.
Landgren, Le. Old Mother Bear's Book of Hug Rhymes. Cannon, Christy, illus. LC 88-38973. 40p. (Orig.). (ps-9). 1989. pap. 6.95 (*0-943867-02-6*) Princess Pub.
Landgren, Le see Le Landgren.
Landin, Les & Gardner, Mary. Homework Sweet Homework. 1990. pap. 6.95 (*0-8224-3603-5*) Fearon Teach Aids.
Landin, Les & Thibault, Frank. Creative Chalkboard Activities. (gr. 1-6). 1986. pap. 5.95 (*0-8224-1636-0*) Fearon Teach Aids.
Landin, Leslie & Meredith, Paul. One Hundred Activities for Gifted Children. (gr. 1-6). 1957. pap. 5.95 (*0-8224-5050-X*) Fearon Teach Aids.
Landis, Frederick, illus. The Emperors New Clothes. (LAT.). 52p. (gr. 9-12). 3.55 (*0-939507-04-8*, B710) Amer Classical.

Landis, J. D. The Band Never Dances. LC 88-28401. 288p. (gr. 7 up). 1989. PLB 13.89 (*0-06-023722-8*) HarpC Child Bks.
—The Band Never Dances. LC 88-28401. 288p. (gr. 7 up). 1993. pap. 3.95 (*0-06-447075-X*, Trophy) HarpC Child Bks.
—Looks Aren't Everything. (gr. 7 up). 1990. 13.95 (*0-553-05847-9*, Starfire) Bantam.
—Looks Aren't Everything. 1991. pap. 3.50 (*0-553-28860-1*) Bantam.
Landis, James D. Joey & the Girls. 192p. (Orig.). (gr. 7-12). 1987. pap. 2.95 (*0-553-26415-X*, Starfire) Bantam.
—The Sisters Impossible. 160p. 1981. pap. 2.50 (*0-553-26013-8*) Bantam.
Landis, Mary. Anthony Gets Ready for Church. 1990. pap. 2.15 (*0-317-02906-1*) Rod & Staff.
—God's Wonderful Trees. 1990. pap. 2.15 (*0-317-02907-X*) Rod & Staff.
—God's Wonderful Water. 1990. pap. 2.15 (*0-317-02908-8*) Rod & Staff.
—My Thank You Book. 1990. pap. 2.15 (*0-317-02909-6*) Rod & Staff.
Landis, Mary M. The Coon Tree Summer: Merry Brook Farm Story. (gr. 5 up). 1978. 9.05 (*0-686-22987-8*) Rod & Staff.
—Health for the Glory of God. (gr. 4-5). 1976. write for info. (*0-686-15484-3*); tchr's. ed. avail. (*0-686-15485-1*) Rod & Staff.
—Ice Slide Winter: Merry Brook Farm Story. (gr. 5 up). 1981. 8.50 (*0-686-30772-0*) Rod & Staff.
—The Missing Popcorn & Other Stories. (gr. 3-6). 1976. 6.55 (*0-686-15480-0*) Rod & Staff.
—Trouble at Windy Acres. (gr. 5-10). 1976. 7.15 (*0-686-15486-X*) Rod & Staff.
Landis, Paul H. Your Marriage & Family Living. 4th ed. (Illus.). (gr. 10-12). 1976. text ed. 32.00 (*0-07-036187-8*) McGraw.
Lando, Miriam. Funny Friday. 176p. 1992. write for info. CIS Comm.
Landon, Joseph W. Music Lab. (Illus.). 182p. (Orig.). (gr. 3-8). 1982. pap. 10.95x packet & guide (*0-943988-00-4*) Music Educ Pubns.
Landon, Linda L. Earth Angel Child: You May Be One. Landon, Linda L., illus. (Orig.). (gr. 3 up). 1992. pap. 8.80 (*0-9633759-0-3*) Harmony Hill.
Landon, Lucinda. Meg MacKintosh & the Case of the Curious Whale Watch. Landon, Lucinda, illus. 48p. (gr. 2-5). 1987. 13.95 (*0-316-51362-8*, Joy St Bks) Little.
—Meg MacKintosh & the Case of the Missing Babe Ruth Baseball: A Solve-It-Yourself Mystery. Landon, Lucinda, illus. LC 85-20055. 48p. (gr. 2-5). 1986. 13.95 (*0-316-51318-0*, 513180, Joy St Bks) Little.
—Meg MacKintosh & the Mystery at C. (gr. 4-7). 1990. 13.95 (*0-316-51367-9*, Joy St Bks) Little.
—Meg MacKintosh & the Mystery at the Medieval Castle. Landon, Lucinda, illus. 64p. (gr. 2-5). 1989. 13.95 (*0-316-51363-6*, Joy St Bks) Little.
—Meg Mackintosh & the Mystery at the Medieval Castle. (ps-3). 1993. pap. 4.95 (*0-316-51376-8*) Little.
—Meg MacKintosh & the Mystery in the Locked Library: A Solve-It-Yourself Mystery. LC 92-19948. 1993. 13.95 (*0-316-51374-1*, Joy St Bks) Little.
Landon, Margaret. Anna & the King of Siam. Ayer, M., illus. 1944. 16.95 (*0-381-98135-5*, A05201); 16.45 (*0-685-02093-2*) HarpC Child Bks.
Landry, Sarah. Field Guide to Fishes Coloring Book. 1987. pap. 4.80 (*0-395-44095-5*) HM.
Landry, Tom. The Ballad of Tont Lala. (Illus.). 32p. (gr. k-8). leather 6.00 (*0-931108-11-X*) Little Cajun Bks.
Landsman, Sandra G. I'm Special: An Experiential Workbook for the Child in Us All. Landman, Rodney G., illus. (gr. k up). 1986. pap. 6.95 (*0-935571-02-7*) Treehouse.
Landsman, Susan. A History Mystery: What Happened to Amelia Earhart? 96p. (Orig.). 1991. pap. 3.50 (*0-380-76221-8*, Camelot) Avon.
—A History Mystery: Who Shot JFK? 96p. (Orig.). 1992. pap. 3.50 (*0-380-77063-6*, Camelot) Avon.
—Survival! In the Desert. 112p. (Orig.). 1993. pap. 3.50 (*0-380-76601-9*, Camelot) Avon.
—Survival! In the Jungle. 112p. (Orig.). 1993. pap. 3.50 (*0-380-76605-1*, Camelot) Avon.
Landstrom, Lena, jt. auth. see Landstrom, Olof.
Landstrom, Olof & Landstrom, Lena. Will Gets a Haircut. LC 93-660. (Illus.). 1993. Repr. 13.00 (*91-29-62075-9*, Pub. by R & S Bks) FS&G.
—Will's New Cap. Fisher, Richard E., tr. 32p. (ps-2). 1992. 13.00 (*91-29-62062-7*, Pub. by R & S Bks) FS&G.
Landy, Joanne. Ready to Use Physical Education Activities. (gr. 5-9). 1993. pap. 27.95 (*0-685-63549-X*) P-H.
Landy, Maxwell. Ready-To-Use Physical Education Activities for Grades 3-4, Vol. 2. (gr. 3-4). 1993. pap. 27.95 (*0-13-673088-4*) P-H.
Lane, Barry, ed. see Barrows, Clifford, et al.
Lane, Ben, ed. see Fogle, Jeanne S.
Lane, Christopher. King Leonard's Great Grape Harvest. Dahl, Sharon, illus. 32p. 1991. text ed. 7.99 (*0-89693-268-0*, Victor Books) SP Pubns.
—Mrs. Beaver & the Wolf at the Door. Dahl, Sharon, illus. 32p. 1991. text ed. 7.99 (*0-89693-269-9*, Victor Books) SP Pubns.
Lane, Daniel. Billy's Choice. 1993. 7.95 (*0-8062-4620-0*) Carlton.
Lane, Helen, tr. see Merino, Jose M.

Lane, Julie. The Life & Adventures of Santa Claus. (Illus.). 144p. 1987. 12.95 (*0-685-19459-0*) Equity Pub NH.
—The Life & Legends of Santa Claus. Hokie, illus. Zinnott, Nicholas H., intro. by. LC 84-2741. (Illus.). 160p. (gr. 3-6). 1983. 10.95 (*0-917057-00-7*) Tonnis.
Lane, Kristi. Feelings Are Real: Intermediate Workbook. 48p. (gr. 4-6). 1991. 6.95 (*1-55959-016-5*) Accel Devel.
—Feelings Are Real: Primary Workbook. 40p. (gr. 2-3). 1991. 6.95 (*1-55959-015-7*) Accel Devel.
Lane, Linda. Focus on Pronunciation: Principles & Practice for Effective Communication. LC 92-33239. 1993. pap. text ed. 21.95 (*0-8013-0806-2*); tchr's. ed. 14.95 (*0-8013-1098-9*); 4 cassettes 66.00 (*0-8013-0807-0*) Longman.
Lane, Margaret. The Beaver. Nockels, David, illus. LC 81-67074. 32p. (gr. k-4). 1993. 13.99 (*0-8037-0624-3*) Dial Bks Young.
—The Beaver. Nockels, David, illus. 32p. (gr. k-4). 1993. pap. 4.99 (*0-14-054925-0*, Puffin Pied Piper) Puffin Bks.
—The Fish: The Story of the Stickleback. Butler, John, illus. 32p. (gr. k-4). 1994. pap. 4.99 (*0-14-055276-6*, Puffin Pied Piper) Puffin Bks.
—The Spider. Firth, Barbara, illus. LC 82-71354. 32p. (ps-4). 1983. 9.95 (*0-8037-8303-5*, 0339-110) Dial Bks Young.
—The Spider. Firth, Barbara, illus. 32p. (gr. k-4). 1994. pap. 4.99 (*0-14-055277-4*, Puffin Pied Piper) Puffin Bks.
—The Squirrel. Lilly, Kenneth, illus. LC 81-1229. 32p. (gr. k-4). 1993. 13.99 (*0-8037-8230-6*) Dial Bks Young.
—The Squirrel. Lilly, Kenneth, illus. 32p. (gr. k-4). 1993. pap. 4.99 (*0-14-054926-9*, Puffin Pied Piper) Puffin Bks.
—Tale of Beatrix Potter: A Biography. rev ed. 192p. 1985. Warne.
Lane, Martha S. Malawi. LC 89-25433. (Illus.). 128p. (gr. 5-9). 1990. PLB 26.60 (*0-516-02720-4*) Childrens.
Lane, Megan H. Something to Crow About. (ps-2). 1990. 10.95 (*0-8037-0697-9*); PLB 10.89 (*0-8037-0698-7*) Dial Bks Young.
Lane, Rose W. Let the Hurricane Roar. LC 85-42742. 128p. (gr. 5-9). 1985. pap. 3.50 (*0-06-440158-8*, Trophy) HarpC Child Bks.
Lane, Rose W., ed. see Wilder, Laura I.
Lane, Sarah & Turkovich, Marilyn. Days of the Dead (Los Dias de los Muertos) 39p. (gr. 6-12). 1991. pap. 10.95 (*0-930141-42-3*) World Eagle.
Lane, Sarah, et al. Batz'i K'op: True Speech. 93p. (gr. 6-12). 1988. pap. 11.95 (*0-941379-03-5*, 5115) World Eagle.
—The Cora: People of the Sierra Madre. 51p. (gr. 6-12). 1989. pap. 9.95 (*0-941379-06-X*, 5114) World Eagle.
Lane, Shirley. Reading Sentences, Grade 2. Hoffman, Joan, ed. Cook, Chris, illus. 32p. (gr. 2). 1979. wkbk. 1.99 (*0-938256-09-2*) Sch Zone Pub Co.
—Reading Stories, Grade 2. Hoffman, Joan, ed. Cook, Chris, illus. 32p. (gr. 2). 1979. wkbk. 1.99 (*0-938256-10-6*) Sch Zone Pub Co.
Lane, W. Ben, ed. see Fogle, Jeanne S.
Lanes, Selma, jt. auth. see Gish, Lillian.
Lang, et al. Action Library Three Program. large type ed. Incl. Cop's Son. 100p. 25.00 (*0-317-02056-0*, J-00040-00); Rodeo Road. 100p. 25.00 (*0-317-02059-7*, J-00050-00); Sky-Jacked. 25.00 (*0-317-02058-7*, J-00060-00); Wade's Place. 100p. 18.98 (*0-317-02059-5*, 4-00070-00); Witches Get Everything. 100p. 18.98 (*0-317-02060-9*, 4-00080-00); Teacher's Guide. 16p. (gr. 7-12). 1981. Am Printing Hse.
Lang, Alan R. Alcohol: Teenage Drinking. updated ed. (Illus.). (gr. 5 up). 1992. lib. bdg. 19.95 (*0-685-52236-9*) Chelsea Hse.
Lang, Andrew. Aladdin. Le Cain, Errol, illus. 32p. (gr. k-3). 1983. pap. 4.95 (*0-14-050389-7*, Puffin) Puffin Bks.
—The Blue Fairy Book. 18.75 (*0-8446-5495-7*) Peter Smith.
—The Brown Fairy Book. 18.75 (*0-8446-5496-5*) Peter Smith.
—The Crimson Fairy Book. Ford, H. J., illus. LC 67-17988. (gr. 4-8). 18.75 (*0-8446-0753-3*) Peter Smith.
—Green Fairy Book. LC 34-28314. (Illus.). (gr. 4 up). 1969. pap. 2.95 (*0-8049-0197-X*, CL-197) Airmont.
—The Lilac Fairy Book. (Illus.). (gr. 4-12). 18.75 (*0-8446-2425-X*) Peter Smith.
—The Olive Fairy Book. Ford, H. J., illus. (gr. 2 up). 17.00 (*0-8446-0754-1*) Peter Smith.
—The Orange Fairy Book. Ford, illus. (gr. 4-12). 18.75 (*0-8446-4770-5*) Peter Smith.
—Pink Fairy Book. Ford, Henry J., illus. 360p. (gr. 4-6). 1966. pap. 6.95 (*0-486-21792-2*) Dover.
—The Pink Fairy Book. Ford, H. J., illus. (gr. 2 up). 18.75 (*0-8446-0755-X*) Peter Smith.
—The Rainbow Fairy Book. Hague, Michael, illus. Glassman, Peter, intro. by. LC 92-31439. (Illus.). 288p. 1993. 20.00 (*0-688-10878-4*) Morrow Jr Bks.
—The Red Fairy Book. Ford, H. J. & Speed, illus. (gr. 2 up). 18.75 (*0-8446-0756-8*) Peter Smith.
—The Violet Fairy Book. Ford, H. J., illus. (gr. 2 up). 18.75 (*0-8446-0757-6*) Peter Smith.
—The Yellow Fairy Book. Ford, H. J., illus. (gr. 2 up). 18.75 (*0-8446-0758-4*) Peter Smith.
—Yellow Fairy Book. (gr. 5 up). 1988. pap. 2.25 (*0-14-035089-6*, Puffin) Puffin Bks.

Lang, Andrew, ed. Arabian Nights Entertainments. Ford, H. J., illus. LC 69-17098. xv, 424p. (gr. k-6). 1969. pap. 6.95 (*0-486-22289-6*) Dover.
—Blue Fairy Book. LC 34-28315. (Illus.). (gr. 4 up). 1969. pap. 2.95 (*0-8049-0196-1*, CL-196) Airmont.
—Blue Fairy Book. Ford, Henry J. & Hood, G. P., illus. LC 34-28315. 390p. (gr. 1-6). 1965. pap. 6.95 (*0-486-21437-0*) Dover.
—Brown Fairy Book. Ford, Henry J., illus. (gr. 1-6). pap. 6.95 (*0-486-21438-9*) Dover.
—Crimson Fairy Book. Ford, Henry J., illus. LC 67-17988. 371p. (gr. 4-6). 1966. pap. 6.95 (*0-486-21799-X*) Dover.
—Green Fairy Book. Ford, Henry J., illus. LC 34-28314. 366p. (gr. 4-6). 1965. pap. 6.95 (*0-486-21439-7*) Dover.
—The Green Fairy Book. Ford, H. J., illus. (gr. 4 up). 18.75 (*0-8446-5056-0*) Peter Smith.
—Grey Fairy Book. Ford, Henry J., illus. LC 67-17983. 387p. (gr. 4-6). 1900. pap. 6.95 (*0-486-21791-4*) Dover.
—Grey Fairy Book. (Illus.). (gr. 4 up). 18.75 (*0-8446-2424-1*) Peter Smith.
—Lilac Fairy Book. Ford, H. J., illus. 367p. (ps-4). 1968. pap. 6.95 (*0-486-21907-0*) Dover.
—Olive Fairy Book. Ford, H. J., illus. 330p. (gr. 4-6). 1966. pap. 5.95 (*0-486-21908-9*) Dover.
—Orange Fairy Book. Ford, H. J., illus. 358p. (gr. 1-6). 1968. pap. 6.95 (*0-486-21909-7*) Dover.
—Red Fairy Book. Ford, Henry J. & Speed, Lancelot, illus. 367p. (gr. 4-6). pap. 6.95 (*0-486-21673-X*) Dover.
—Violet Fairy Book. Ford, Henry J. & Lang, H. J., illus. (gr. 4-6). pap. 6.95 (*0-486-21675-6*) Dover.
Lang, Andrew, compiled by. A World of Fairy Tales. Ford, Henry J., illus. Philip, Neil, intro. by. LC 92-46245. 256p. 1993. 20.00 (*0-8037-1250-2*) Dial Bks Young.
Lang, Andrew, ed. Yellow Fairy Book. Ford, Henry J., illus. 321p. (gr. 4-6). pap. 6.95 (*0-486-21674-8*) Dover.
Lang, Andrew, tr. see Homer.
Lang, Aubrey. Eagles. (gr. 3-6). 1990. 15.95 (*0-316-51387-3*) Little.
—Rudy Visits the North. Hope, Muriel, illus. LC 91-75423. 40p. (ps-2). 1992. 14.95 (*1-56282-182-2*); PLB 14.89 (*1-56282-208-X*) Hyprn Child.
Lang, Denise V. But Everyone Else Looks So Sure of Themselves: A Guide to Surviving the Teen Years. LC 90-39087. 160p. (Orig.). (gr. 7 up). 1991. pap. 7.95 (*1-55870-177-X*) Shoe Tree Pr.
Lang, Jenny, adapted by. The Tortoise & the Hare. Baker, Darrell, illus. 24p. (ps-k). 1993. 9.00 (*0-307-74814-6*, 64814, Golden Pr) Western Pub.
Lang, Margaret A. Gramma's Stories & Rhymes for Little Christians. Smith, Linda G., illus. 104p. (ps-5). 1982. 9.95 (*0-685-42235-6*) Lang Pubns.
Lang, Paul, jt. auth. see Lang, Susan S.
Lang, Stephen J. The Illustrated Book of Bible Trivia. (Illus.). 1991. PLB 12.99 (*0-8423-1613-2*) Tyndale.
Lang, Susan S. Extremist Groups in America. LC 89-38533. 1990. PLB 14.40 (*0-531-10901-1*) Watts.
—Invisible Bugs & Other Creepy Creatures That Live with You. Lindstrom, Eric C., illus. LC 91-43712. 96p. 1992. 12.95 (*0-8069-8208-X*) Sterling.
—Invisible Bugs & Other Creepy Creatures That Live with You. Lindstrom, Eric C., illus. 96p. (gr. 4-10). 1993. pap. 4.95 (*0-8069-8209-8*) Sterling.
—Teen Violence. (Illus.). 176p. (gr. 9-12). 1991. PLB 14.40 (*0-531-11057-5*) Watts.
Lang, Susan S. & Lang, Paul. Censorship. (Illus.). 96p. (gr. 9-12). 1993. PLB 13.40 (*0-531-10999-2*) Watts.
Lang, W. Harold. Islands of the Pacific. Kubat, Frank J., Jr., ed. LC 87-83228. (Illus.). 168p. 1988. 44.95 (*0-945201-00-1*) Gannam-Kubat.
Langcaon, Jeff. Where's Kimo? Langcaon, Jeff, illus. 24p. (gr. k-2). 1993. pap. 5.95 (*1-880188-65-1*) Bess Pr.
Lange, Suzanne. The Year. LC 78-120787. (gr. 8 up). 1970. 21.95 (*0-87599-173-4*) S G Phillips.
Langenhahn, Bonnie, jt. auth. see Heard, Regie.
Langenscheidt Staff. Langenscheidt Picture Dictionary. (gr. 4-7). 1993. 19.95 ea. English (*0-88729-850-8*) FRE-ENG (*0-88729-851-6*) GER-ENG (*0-88729-852-4*) ITA-ENG (*0-88729-853-2*) SPA-ENG (*0-88729-854-0*) JPN-ENG. 24.95 (*0-88729-855-9*) GRE-ENG (*0-88729-862-1*) HEB-ENG (*0-88729-863-X*) Langenscheidt.
—Langenscheidt Picture Dictionary. (gr. 4-7). 1993. pap. 14.95 ea. ENG (*0-88729-856-7*) FRE-ENG (*0-88729-857-5*) GER-ENG (*0-88729-858-3*) ITA-ENG (*0-88729-859-1*) SPA-ENG (*0-88729-860-5*) JPN-ENG. pap. 17.95 (*0-88729-861-3*) Langenscheidt.
—Langenscheidt Picture Dictionary. (gr. 4-7). 1993. 19.95 ea. POL-ENG (*0-88729-864-8*) POR-ENG (*0-88729-865-6*) RUS-ENG (*0-88729-866-4*) CHI-ENG (*0-88729-867-2*) Langenscheidt.
Langenus, Ron. Mission West: Journey of Mystery & Adventure to the Edge of the World. Dunne, Jeanette, illus. 128p. (Orig.). 1990. pap. 8.95 (*0-86327-239-8*, Pub. by Wolfhound Pr EIRE) Dufour.
Langer, Shirley, tr. see Morgan, Allen.
Langer, Shirley, tr. see Munsch, Robert.
Langerman, Jean. No Carrots for Harry! Remkiewicz, Frank, illus. LC 89-3373. (ps-3). 1989. 5.95 (*0-8193-1190-1*) Parents.
—No Carrots for Harry! Remkiewicz, Frank, illus. 48p. (ps-2). 1992. pap. 2.95 (*0-448-40320-X*, G&D) Putnam Pub Group.

—No Carrots for Harry. (Illus.). 42p. (ps-3). 1992. PLB 13.26 (*0-8368-0876-2*); PLB 13.26 s.p. (*0-685-61506-5*) Gareth Stevens Inc.
Langford, Anne. Meditation for Little People. Bethards, David, illus. LC 75-46191. 40p. (gr. k-4). 1976. pap. 6.95 (*0-87516-211-8*) DeVorss.
Langford, Michael. Starting Photography. 2nd ed. LC 93-17759. (gr. 7 up). 1993. write for info. (*0-240-51348-7*) Focal Pr.
Langham, Tony, jt. auth. see Breese, Gillian.
Langill, Ellen. Pompey Poems... Celebrating a Cat. Davenport, May, illus. LC 86-91603. 64p. (Orig.). (gr. 7-12). 1986. 10.25x (*0-943864-28-3*); pap. 3.50x (*0-943864-26-7*) Davenport.
Langley, Andrew. Dinosaurs. rev. ed. Franklin Watts Ltd., ed. (Illus.). 32p. (gr. 2-4). 1985. PLB 10.90 (*0-531-10449-4*) Watts.
—Grasslands. LC 93-77348. (gr. 4-7). 1993. 14.00 (*0-89577-515-8*, Readers Digest Kids) RD Assn.
—Let's Look at Monster Machines. (Illus.). 32p. (gr. k-4). 1990. PLB 11.40 (*0-531-18341-6*, Pub. by Bookwright Pr) Watts.
—Let's Look at Racing Cars. (Illus.). 32p. (gr. k-4). 1990. PLB 11.40 (*0-531-18330-0*, Pub. by Bookwright Pr) Watts.
—Nature Search: Wetlands: A Hands-On Guide for Nature Sleuths. (gr. 4-7). 1993. 14.00 (*0-89577-482-8*, Readers Digest Kids) RD Assn.
—Paper. LC 93-6818. (Illus.). 32p. (gr. 3-5). 1993. 13.95 (*1-56847-047-9*) Thomson Lrning.
—Passport to Great Britain. LC 93-21187. 1994. write for info. (*0-531-14297-3*) Watts.
—Sports & Politics. (Illus.). 48p. (gr. 5 up). 1990. lib. bdg. 18.60 (*0-86592-117-2*); lib. bdg. 13.95 s.p. (*0-685-46458-X*) Rourke Corp.
—Steel. LC 93-6834. 32p. (gr. 3-6). 1993. 13.95 (*1-56847-044-4*) Thomson Lrning.
—Travel Games for Kids. rev. ed. LC 90-84702. (Illus.). 112p. (gr. k-8). 1992. pap. 10.95 (*0-936399-09-0*) Berkshire Hse.
—Twenty Explorers. LC 89-23852. (Illus.). 48p. (gr. 3-8). 1990. PLB 12.95 (*1-85435-252-0*) Marshall Cavendish.
Langley, Andrew & Butterfield, Maira. People. Young, Norman, illus. LC 89-42986. 48p. (gr. 5-6). 1989. PLB 17.27 (*0-8368-0132-6*) Gareth Stevens Inc.
Langley, Andy. The Hungry Mice. (Illus.). 8p. 1992. bds. 3.95 (*0-681-41517-7*) Longmeadow Pr.
—The Naughty Mice. (Illus.). 8p. 1992. bds. 3.95 (*0-681-41516-9*) Longmeadow Pr.
Langley, Bill & Dias, Ron, illus. Walt Disney's One Hundred One Dalmatians. (ps-2). 1991. write for info. (*0-307-12346-4*, Golden Pr) Western Pub.
Langley, Bob. Autumn Tiger. 256p. 1988. pap. 3.50 (*0-685-19806-5*) Bantam.
Langley, Glynis. The Age of Dinosaurs. Atkinson, Mike, illus. 64p. (gr. k-5). 1992. pap. 6.95 (*0-8249-8537-0*, Ideals Child) Hambleton-Hill.
Langley, James. The New Bike Book: How to Get the Most Out of Your New Bicycle. LC 89-81204. (Illus.). 128p. (Orig.). 1990. pap. 4.95 (*0-933201-28-1*) Bicycle Books.
Langley, Jonathan. Goldilocks & the Three Bears. Langley, Jonathan, illus. LC 91-33155. 32p. (gr. k-3). 1993. 11.00 (*0-06-020814-7*); PLB 10.89 (*0-06-020815-5*) HarpC Child Bks.
—The Three Billy Goats Gruff. Langley, Jonathan, illus. LC 92-4842. 32p. (ps-3). 1994. 15.00 (*0-06-021224-1*); PLB 14.89 (*0-06-021474-0*) HarpC Child Bks.
Langley, Jonathan, retold by. & illus. Rumpelstiltskin. LC 91-11133. 32p. (ps-3). 1992. 14.95 (*0-06-020198-3*); PLB 14.89 (*0-06-020199-1*) HarpC Child Bks.
Langley, Jonathan, illus. Rain, Rain, Go Away! A Book of Nursery Rhymes. LC 89-34594. 96p. (ps-1). 1991. 12.95 (*0-8037-0762-2*) Dial Bks Young.
Langley, Virginia. Thar She Blows. (gr. 2-5). 1986. pap. 6.95 (*0-930096-87-8*) G Gannett.
Langone, John. Dead End: A Book about Suicide. LC 85-25620. (gr. 6 up). 1986. 14.95 (*0-316-51432-2*) Little.
—Growing Older. (gr. 9-12). 1991. 15.95 (*0-316-51459-4*) Little.
—In the Shogun's Shadow: Understanding a Changing Japan. Parton, Steve, illus. LC 93-23999. 1994. 15.95 (*0-316-51409-8*) Little.
—Our Endangered Earth: Our Fragile Environment & What We Can Do to Save It. (gr. 6 up). 1992. 16.95 (*0-316-51415-2*) Little.
—Spreading Poison: A Book about Racism & Prejudice. LC 92-17847. 1993. 15.95 (*0-316-51410-1*) Little.
Langoulant, Allan. Everybody's Different. Langoulant, Allan, illus. LC 90-36811. 32p. (gr. 2-3). 1990. PLB 18.60 (*0-8368-0435-X*) Gareth Stevens Inc.
—A Prize for Percival. Sherwood, Rhoda, ed. Langoulant, Allan, illus. LC 88-42912. 32p. (gr. 2-3). 1988. PLB 18.60 (*1-55532-931-4*) Gareth Stevens Inc.
Langronet, Michel. Enciclopedia Juvenil Larousse: Childrens Larousse Encyclopedia, 8 vols. 4th ed. (SPA.). 1552p. 1978. Set. 495.00 (*0-8288-5226-X*, S50479) Fr & Eur.
Langstaff, John. Oh, A-Hunting We Will Go. Parker, Nancy W., illus. LC 74-76274. 32p. (ps-3). 1974. SBE 14.95 (*0-689-50007-6*, M K McElderry) Macmillan Child Grp.
—Oh, A-Hunting We Will Go. Parker, Nancy W., illus. LC 91-1987. 32p. (gr. k-3). 1991. pap. 4.95 (*0-689-71503-X*, Aladdin) Macmillan Child Grp.
—Over in the Meadow. Rojankovsky, Feodor, illus. (ps-1). 1992. pap. 19.95 (*0-15-258853-1*) HarBrace.

—What a Morning! The Christmas Story in Black Spirituals. Bryan, Ashley, illus. LC 87-750130. 32p. 1987. SBE 14.95 (*0-689-50422-5*, M K McElderry) Macmillan Child Grp.

Langstaff, John & Bryan, Ashley. Climbing Jacob's Ladder: Heroes of the Bible in African-American Spirituals. LC 90-27297. (Illus.). 32p. 1991. SBE 13.95 (*0-689-50494-2*, M K McElderry) Macmillan Child Grp.

Langstaff, John & Langstaff, Nancy. The Christmas Revels Songbook. (Illus.). 160p. 1985. pap. 14.95 (*0-87923-927-1*) Godine.

Langstaff, John & Rojankovsky, Feodor. Frog Went A-Courtin' Rojankovsky, Feodor, illus. LC 55-5237. (ps-3). 1983. 14.95 (*0-15-230214-X*, HB Juv Bks) HarBrace.

—Frog Went A-Courtin' Rojankovsky, Feodor, illus. LC 55-5237. 32p. (ps-3). 1972. pap. 4.95 (*0-15-633900-5*, Voyager Bks) HarBrace.

—Over in the Meadow. Rojankovsky, Feodor, illus. LC 57-8587. (ps-3). 1957. 14.95 (*0-15-258854-X*, HB Juv Bks) HarBrace.

—Over in the Meadow. Rojankovsky, Feodor, illus. LC 57-8587. 32p. (ps-3). 1973. pap. 3.95 (*0-15-670500-1*, Voyager Bks) HarBrace.

Langstaff, John, jt. auth. see Langstaff, Nancy.

Langstaff, Nancy & Langstaff, John. Sally Go Round the Moon & Other Revels Songs & Singing Games for Young Children. Pienkowski, Jan, illus. LC 86-90535. 127p. (ps-1). 1986. pap. 12.95 (*0-9618334-0-8*) Revels Pubns.

Langstaff, Nancy, jt. auth. see Langstaff, John.

Langton, Jane. The Diamond in the Window. Blegvad, Erik, illus. LC 62-7312. 256p. (gr. 5 up). 1973. pap. 3.95 (*0-06-440042-5*, Trophy) HarpC Child Bks.

—The Diamond in the Window. (gr. 5 up). 17.50 (*0-8446-6414-6*) Peter Smith.

—Fledgling. LC 79-2008. 192p. (gr. 3-7). 1980. PLB 13.89 (*0-06-023679-5*) HarpC Child Bks.

—The Fledgling. LC 79-2008. 192p. (gr. 3-7). 1981. pap. 3.95 (*0-06-440121-9*, Trophy) HarpC Child Bks.

—The Fragile Flag. Blegvaad, Erik, illus. LC 83-49471. 224p. (gr. 3-7). 1984. PLB 14.89 (*0-06-023699-X*) HarpC Child Bks.

—Fragile Flag. LC 83-49471. 288p. (gr. 5 up). 1989. pap. 4.95 (*0-06-440311-4*, Trophy) HarpC Child Bks.

Langton, Jane, retold by. Salt: A Russian Folktale. Plume, Alice, tr. from RUS. Plume, Ilse, illus. LC 91-74007. 48p. (gr. k-3). 1992. 14.95 (*1-56282-178-4*); PLB 14.89 (*1-56282-179-2*) Hyprn Child.

Lanham, Url N. Origins of Modern Biology. LC 68-24478. 273p. (gr. 11-12). 1971. text ed. 46.50x (*0-231-02872-5*); pap. text ed. 18.00x (*0-231-08660-1*) Col U Pr.

Lanhei Kim Park. The Heavenly Pomegranate. 76p. (gr. 5-7). 1973. pap. text ed. 3.00 (*0-686-05501-2*) Simpson Pub.

Lanier, Henry W. A. B. Frost: American Sportsman's Artist. 2nd ed. Frost, A. B., illus. 170p. (gr. 10 up). 1990. Repr. 39.95 (*1-56416-003-3*) Derrydale Pr.

Lanier, Sidney. The Boy's King Arthur. reissued ed. Wyeth, N. C., illus. LC 73-13451. 336p. 1989. SBE 24.95 (*0-684-19111-3*, Scribners Young Read); deluxe ed. 75.00 (*0-684-19118-0*, Scribner) Macmillan Child Grp.

Lanier, Sidney, ed. see Mallory, Thomas.

Lankford, Mary D. Christmas Around the World. Dugan, Karen, illus. LC 93-38566. 1994. write for info. (*0-688-12166-7*, Tambourine Bks); PLB write for info. (*0-688-12167-5*, Tambourine Bks) Morrow.

—Hopscotch Around the World. Milone, Karen, illus. LC 91-17152. 48p. (gr. 4 up). 1992. 15.00 (*0-688-08419-2*); PLB 14.93 (*0-688-08420-6*) Morrow Jr Bks.

—Is It Dark? Is It Light? Schuett, Stacey, illus. LC 90-21492. 32p. (ps-2). 1991. 13.00 (*0-679-81579-1*); lib. bdg. 13.99 (*0-679-91579-6*) Knopf Bks Yng Read.

—Quinceanera: A Latina's Journey to Womanhood. Herrera, Jesse, photos by. (Illus.). 48p. (gr. 6-9). 1994. 13.90 (*1-56294-363-4*) Millbrook Pr.

Lankford, Robert D. Dream Weaver in the Face of Fear, Vol. 1, No. 3. (Illus.). 48p. (gr. 11 up). 1991. pap. 2.75 (*0-9621811-2-9*) Lankford Comics.

—Dream Weaver: Survive until Dawn, Vol. 1, Issue 1. Lankford, Robert D., illus. 24p. (gr. 11 up). 1987. pap. 1.95 (*0-9621811-0-2*) Lankford Comics.

—Dreamweaver, Vol. 1. 2nd ed. (Illus.). 24p. (gr. 10 up). 1988. pap. 1.95 (*0-685-44540-2*) Lankford Comics.

—Dreamweaver, Vol. 1. 4th ed. (Illus.). 24p. (gr. 10 up). 1989. pap. 1.95 (*0-317-93324-8*) Lankford Comics.

Lankton, Stephen R. The Blammo-Surprise! Book: A Story to Help Children Overcome Fears. LC 88-13566. (Illus.). 48p. (gr. 1 up). 1988. PLB 16.95 (*0-945354-11-8*); pap. 6.95 (*0-945354-10-X*) Magination Pr.

Lannert. Mexican Americans. 1991. 13.95s.p. (*0-86593-139-9*); PLB 18.60 (*0-685-59187-5*) Rourke Corp.

Lanni, Deborah. What's a Duck Like You Doing in a Place Like This? (Illus.). iv, 23p. (gr. 3-6). 1984. pap. 2.00 (*0-942788-12-5*) Marginal Med.

Lanning, Rosemary, tr. see Korth-Sander, Irmtraut.
Lanning, Rosemary, tr. see Moers, Hermann.
Lanning, Rosemary, tr. see Ostheeren, Ingrid.
Lanning, Rosemary, tr. see Pfister, Marcus.
Lanning, Rosemary, tr. see Scheidl, Gerda M.
Lanning, Rosemary, tr. see Siegenthaler, Kathrin & Pfister, Marcus.

Lanning, Rosemary, tr. see Velthuijs, Max.
Lanning, Rosemary, tr. see Waas, Uli.
Lanning, Rosemary, tr. see Wilkon, Jozef & Moers, Hermann.
Lanning, Rosemary, tr. see Wilkon, Piotr & Wilkon, Jozef.
Lano-Nellist, Cassandra see Nellist, Cassandra L.

Lansdown, Andrew. Beyond the Open Door. (gr. 4-7). 1993. pap. 2.95 (*0-590-47160-0*) Scholastic Inc.

Lansing, Karen E. Time to Be a Friend. LC 92-13010. 96p. (gr. 4-8). 1993. pap. 4.95 (*0-8361-3614-4*) Herald Pr.

—Time to Fly. LC 91-14393. 104p. (Orig.). (gr. 4-8). 1991. pap. 5.95 (*0-8361-3560-1*) Herald Pr.

Lansky. Microwave Cooking for Kids. 1992. 6.95 (*0-590-44203-1*) Scholastic Inc.

Lansky, Bruce. New Adventures of Mother Goose: Gentle Rhymes for Happy Times. Carpenter, Stephen, illus. LC 93-11129. 32p. 1993. 15.00 (*0-88166-201-1*) Meadowbrook.

—The New Adventures of Mother Goose: Gentle Rhymes for Happy Times. Carpenter, Stephen, illus. LC 93-11129. 1993. 15.00 (*0-671-87288-5*) S&S Trade.

Lansky, Bruce, compiled by. Kids Pick the Funniest Poems. LC 91-31072. (Illus.). 120p. 1991. 14.00 (*0-88166-149-X*) Meadowbrook.

Lansky, Vicki. Dear Babysitter Handbook. 60p. (gr. 7 up). 1990. pap. 3.95 (*0-916773-16-7*) Book Peddlers.

—Koko Bear's Big Earache: Preparing for Ear Tube Surgery. 32p. (Orig.). (ps). 1990. pap. 4.95 (*0-916773-26-4*) Book Peddlers.

—Koko Bear's New Babysitter. 32p. (Orig.). (ps). 1989. pap. 3.95 (*0-916773-24-8*) Book Peddlers.

—Koko Bear's New Potty, No. 1. Prince, Jane L., illus. 32p. 1986. pap. 3.50 (*0-553-34243-6*) Bantam.

—Koko Bear's Potty. 1986. pap. 3.99 (*0-553-34444-7*) Bantam.

—A New Baby at Koko Bear's House. reissued ed. Prince, Jane, illus. 32p. (Orig.). 1991. pap. 4.95 (*0-916773-22-1*) Book Peddlers.

—Vicki Lansky's Sing Along as You Ride Along Travel Songs. (ps-1). 1988. pap. 5.95 (*0-590-63233-7*) Scholastic Inc.

—Vicki Lansky's Sing along Birthday Fun Book & Cassette. 48p. (ps-1). 1989. pap. 5.95 incl. cassette (*0-590-63234-5*) Scholastic Inc.

Lantier, Patricia, adapted by see Bentley, James.
Lantier, Patricia, adapted by see Birch, Beverley.
Lantier, Patricia, adapted by see Wimer, David.

Lantier-Sampon, Patricia. Airplanes. (I!lus.). 24p. (ps-2). 1991. PLB 17.27 (*0-8368-0539-9*) Gareth Stevens Inc. Postponed.

—Birds. LC 91-50345. (Illus.). 24p. (ps-2). 1991. PLB 17.27 (*0-8368-0541-0*) Gareth Stevens Inc. Postponed.

—Flying Animals. (Illus.). 24p. (ps-2). 1991. PLB 17.27 (*0-8368-0540-2*) Gareth Stevens Inc. Postponed.

—Flying Insects. (Illus.). 34p. (ps-2). 1991. PLB 17.27 (*0-8368-0542-9*) Gareth Stevens Inc. Postponed.

—Wings, 8 vols. (Illus.). 24p. (ps-2). 1991. Set. PLB 138.16 (*0-8368-0538-0*) Gareth Stevens Inc. Postponed.

Lantier-Sampon, Patricia, adapted by. The Wonder of Loons. LC 92-16945. 1992. PLB 18.60 (*0-8368-0856-8*) Gareth Stevens Inc.

—The Wonder of Whitetails. Cox, Daniel J., photos by. LC 92-16947. (Illus.). 1992. PLB 18.60 (*0-8368-0858-4*) Gareth Stevens Inc.

—The Wonder of Wolves. Baldwin, Bob, et al, photos by. LC 92-16948. (Illus.). 1992. PLB 18.60 (*0-8368-0859-2*) Gareth Stevens Inc.

Lanton, Sandy. Baby's Dinner. Clark, Linda F., illus. 32p. (ps-2). Date not set. 11.95 (*1-56065-145-8*) Capstone Pr. Postponed.

—Bedtime. Sagasti, Miriam, illus. 32p. (ps-2). Date not set. 11.95 (*1-56065-141-5*) Capstone Pr. Postponed.

—Daddy's Chair. Haas, Shelly O., illus. LC 90-44908. 32p. (gr. k-4). 1991. 12.95 (*0-929371-51-8*) Kar Ben.

—The Girl Who Wouldn't See. Noll, Cheryl K., illus. 32p. (ps-2). Date not set. 11.95 (*1-56065-140-7*) Capstone Pr. Postponed.

—Is That Our Car? Drum, Stacy, illus. 32p. (ps-2). Date not set. 11.95 (*1-56065-143-1*) Capstone Pr. Postponed.

—That's Not the Way Mommy Does It. Noll, Cheryl K., illus. 32p. (ps-2). Date not set. 11.95 (*1-56065-142-3*) Capstone Pr. Postponed.

Lantz, Fran. Making It on Our Own. (gr. 6-12). 1986. pap. 2.75 (*0-440-95202-6*, LFL) Dell.

—Rock, Rap, & Rad: How to Be a Rock Or Rap Star. 224p. (Orig.). 1992. pap. 3.99 (*0-380-76793-7*, Flare) Avon.

Lantz, Frances. Mom, There's a Pig in My Bed! 144p. (Orig.). (gr. 4). 1992. pap. 3.50 (*0-380-76112-2*, Camelot) Avon.

Lantz, Francess. Dear Celeste, My Life Is a Mess. (gr. 4-7). 1992. pap. 3.25 (*0-553-15961-5*) Bantam.

—Truth about Making Out. (gr. 4 up). 1990. pap. 3.50 (*0-553-15813-9*) Bantam.

Lanza, Barbara. First Christmas Pop-up Book. (ps-3). 1993. 6.95 (*0-307-12464-9*, Golden Pr) Western Pub.

Lanza, Janet, jt. auth. see Nelson, Tina.

La Paz, Myrna De see De La Paz, Myrna J.

La Pierre, Keith C. That Strange Little Man, Bk. 1. (Illus.). 32p. (gr. 2 up). 1991. lib. bdg. 14.95 (*0-9631513-0-4*) Lee Pub NY.

—The Wanna Beezzz. La Pierre, Keith C., illus. LC 93-78057. 34p. (ps-3).

1993. 8.95 (*0-9631513-1-2*); PLB write for info. (*0-9631513-2-0*) Lee Pub NY. THE WANNA BEEZZZ is a comically illustrated picture book in which an imaginative swarm of bees try desperately to educate a bewildered bear cub in the ways of make-believe. The story begins when the bear cub finds a bee hive in an old tree, but what he finds is not honey. What he does find is five whimsical bees. Each bee tries in vain to teach the cub how to play make-believe, to use his imagination. The story comes alive as the author uses rhyme & verse to guide the young reader through the make believe world of the Wanna Beezzz. Keith La Pierre's writing style adds excitement & energy to an already spirited plot. Teachers & librarians alike will find this title to be a welcome edition to their Children's book collection. ISBN: 0-9631513-1-2, 34 pages, $8.95. Lee Publishing, P.O. Box 726, Glenwood Landing, NY 11547. Tel. 516-358-0785. *Publisher Provided Annotation.*

Lapine, Jennifer & Lapine, Susan. My First Hebrew Alphabet Book. (Illus.). 48p. (ps-1). 1977. pap. 3.95 (*0-8197-0399-0*) Bloch.

Lapine, Susan, jt. auth. see Lapine, Jennifer.

Lapka, Fay S. Dark Is a Color. 264p. (Orig.). (gr. 9-12). 1990. pap. 6.99 (*0-87788-163-4*) Shaw Pubs.

—Hoverlight. (Orig.). 1991. pap. 6.99 (*0-87788-352-1*) Shaw Pubs.

—The Sea, the Song & the Trumpetfish. 160p. (Orig.). (gr. 7-12). 1991. pap. 6.99 (*0-87788-754-3*) Shaw Pubs.

LaPlaca, Annette. Are We Almost There? The Kids' Book of Travel Fun. Bryer, Debbie, illus. 45p. (Orig.). (gr. 1-5). 1992. pap. 4.99 wkbk. (*0-87788-051-4*) Shaw Pubs.

—How Long 'til Christmas? The Kid's Book of Holiday Fun. Bryer, Debbie, illus. 48p. (Orig.). (gr. ·3-6). 1993. pap. 4.99 saddle-stitch (*0-87788-369-6*) Shaw Pubs.

Laplaca, Michael. Easter Decorations: Make & Color Your Own. (ps-3). 1989. pap. 1.95 (*0-89375-647-4*) Troll Assocs.

—How to Draw Boats, Trains, & Planes. Laplaca, Michael, illus. LC 81-52123. 32p. (gr. 2-6). 1982. PLB 10.65 (*0-89375-682-2*); pap. text ed. 1.95 (*0-89375-497-8*) Troll Assocs.

—How to Draw Cars & Trucks. LaPlaca, Michael, illus. LC 81-52122. 32p. (gr. 2-6). 1982. PLB 10.65 (*0-89375-681-4*); pap. text ed. 1.95 (*0-89375-498-6*) Troll Assocs.

—How to Draw Dinosaurs. LaPlaca, Michael, illus. LC 81-52118. 32p. (gr. 2-6). 1982. PLB 10.65 (*0-89375-683-0*); pap. text ed. 1.95 (*0-89375-496-X*) Troll Assocs.

Lappin, Peter. Dominic Savio Teenage Saint. rev. ed. LC 81-67928. 145p. (gr. 4-10). 1981. pap. 2.95 (*0-89944-055-X*, Patron) Don Bosco Multimedia.

—Dominic Savio: Teenage Saint. 2nd ed. LC 54-11044. 155p. (gr. 5-10). 1989. 1.95 (*0-685-30656-9*); pap. write for info. Don Bosco Multimedia.

—The Falcon & the Dove: The Story of Laura Vicuna. (Illus.). 180p. (gr. 9-12). 1985. pap. 4.95 (*0-89944-067-3*) Don Bosco Multimedia.

—General Mickey. 167p. (Orig.). (gr. 5-10). 1977. pap. 2.95 (*0-89944-029-0*) Don Bosco Multimedia.

—Stories of Don Bosco. 2nd ed. LC 78-72525. (Illus.). 272p. (gr. 5-12). 1979. pap. 2.95 (*0-89944-036-3*) Don Bosco Multimedia.

Larcada, Luis I. Tierra del Sur. Arnal, Encarna, illus. (SPA.). 48p. 1993. lib. bdg. 7.00 (*0-937509-09-4*) Edit Arcos.

Larche, Douglas W. see Father Gander, pseud.

Larcombe, Jennifer R. The Angels' Christmas Story. (Illus.). 32p. 1991. 10.00 (*0-8007-7127-3*) Revell.

—Through-the-Bible Storybook. 1992. 19.99 (*0-310-56380-1*, Youth Bks) Zondervan.

Lardner, Kym. Arnold the Prickly Teddy. Lardner, Kym, illus. LC 92-31919. 1993. 14.00 (*0-383-03552-X*) SRA Schl Grp.

Lardner, Ring. Haircut. (gr. 5 up). 1992. PLB 13.95 (*0-88682-499-0*) Creative Ed.

Larimer, Tamela. Buck. LC 86-90774. 176p. (Orig.). (gr. 7 up). 1986. pap. 2.50 (*0-380-75172-0*, Flare) Avon.

Larios, Julie. On the Stairs. Hofstrand, Mary, illus. LC 93-20588. Date not set. write for info. (*0-689-31643-7*, Atheneum) Macmillan Child Grp.

Larios, Richard, jt. auth. see De Ruiz, Dana C.

Larke, Joe. The Bullfrog & the Grasshopper & Other "Tails". Larke, Karol, illus. 72p. (gr. k-6). 1987. 10.00 (*0-9620112-0-7*) Grin A Bit.

—Can't Reach the Itch. Larke, Karol, illus. 72p. (gr. 1-6). 1988. 10.00x (0-9620112-1-5) Grin A Bit.
—Dopie Dope Goes to the Fair. Larke, Karol, illus. 49p. (gr. k-5). 1992. 13.95 (0-9620112-7-4) Grin A Bit.
—Dopie Dope Grin A Bit Poetry Series. Larke, Karol, illus. (gr. k-6). 1992. write for info. (0-9620112-9-0) Grin A Bit.
—Two Pigs in Wigs. (ps-3). 1991. 11.95 (0-9620112-2-3) Grin A Bit.
Larkin, Howard. Nature Puzzle & Color Book. 32p. (ps). 1983. pap. 0.99 (0-317-00058-6) Pacific Pr Pub Assn.
Larkin, Judy, jt. auth. see McFarland, Kathleen.
La Rochelle, David. A Christmas Guest. Skoro, Martin, illus. 32p. (ps-3). 1988. PLB 18.95 (0-87614-325-7); pap. 5.95 (0-87614-506-3) Carolrhoda Bks.
LaRochelle, David. A Christmas Guest. Skoro, Martin, illus. 32p. (ps-3). 1989. pap. 5.95 (0-685-25636-7, First Ave Edns) Lerner Pubns.
—The Evening King. Stock, Catherine, illus. LC 91-1970. 32p. (ps-3). 1993. SBE 14.95 (0-689-31640-2, Atheneum Child Bk) Macmillan Child Grp.
Larocque, Jean-Paul. Numbers Time. Larocque, Jean-Paul, illus. 17p. (gr. k-3). 1993. pap. 11.95 (1-895583-62-4) MAYA Pubs.
—What Is Two Plus Two. Larocque, Jean-Paul, illus. 12p. (gr. k-3). 1993. pap. 10.95 (1-895583-63-2) MAYA Pubs.
—Wille Wacka Land. Larocque, Jean-Paul, illus. 12p. (gr. 1-3). 1992. pap. 6.95 (1-895583-04-7) MAYA Pubs.
Laron, Carl. Computer Software Basics. Seiden, Art, illus. LC 84-22292. 48p. (gr. 4-9). 1985. 9.95 (0-13-163858-0) P-H.
LaRose, Mary K., tr. see Descamps-Lequime, Sophie & Vernerey, Denise.
LaRose, Mary K., tr. see Guittard, Charles.
LaRose, Mary K., tr. see Koenig, Viviane.
LaRose, Mary K., tr. see Moktefi, Mokhtar.
LaRose-Weaver, Diane & Cusick, Dawn. Fireside Christmas: Celebrate the Holidays with More Than 120 Festive Projects to Make. LC 92-37316. (Illus.). 160p. (gr. 8 up). 1992. 26.95 (0-8069-8378-7, Pub. by Lark Bks) Sterling.

Larrabee, Lisa. Grandmother Five Baskets. Sawyer, Lori, illus. LC 93-10451. 64p. (gr. 3-7). 1993. 14.95 (0-943173-86-8); pap. 9.95 (0-943173-90-6) Harbinger AZ. Multi-cultural, Native American themes are the focus of three children's titles by Harbinger House of Tucson. These well-researched & sensitive presentations highlight family values, coming-of-age lessons, & respect for all. For beginning, middle & young adult readers, as noted. 1) GRANDMOTHER FIVE BASKETS. ISBN 0-943173-86-8 (hc), $14.95, ISBN 0-943173-90-6 (pb), $9.95. ages 8-12, by Lisa Larrabee, fully illustrated by Lori Sawyer. Authentic, multi-generational story of a contemporary American Indian woman who teaches the young girls of her tribe to make baskets in the traditional way. Interwoven are gentle lessons about life, love & the value of family. 2) SOFT CHILD: HOW RATTLESNAKE GOT ITS FANGS. ISBN 0-943173-89-2, $8.95, ages 4-8, retold by Joe Hayes, illustrated by Kay Sather. Soft Child, a poor gentle snake, is defenseless in his desert environment until Sky God provides Soft Child with fangs. Adapted from Tohono O'odham (Papago) folklore. 3) SON-OF-THUNDER. ISBN 0-943173-88-4 (hc), $16.95, ISBN 0-943173-87-6, $10.95 (pb), by Stig Holmas, illustrated by John Hurford. The coming-of-age of a young Apache warrior. A straightforward, well-researched novel set in the time & homeland of Cochise & Geronimo, with new insights--from the Apache point of view--to balance conventional history. Order from Harbinger House, Inc., Books of Integrity or from your local distributor.
Publisher Provided Annotation.

Larramendi, Alberto Ruiz De see Ruiz de Larramendi, Alberto.
Larramendi Ruiz, Alberto de see De Larramendi Ruis, Alberto.
Larranaga, Robert D. The King's Shadow. Greenwald, Joe, illus. 32p. (gr. k-3). 1991. PLB 18.95 (0-87614-688-4) Carolrhoda Bks.
Larrick, Nancy. Bring Me All of Your Dreams. LC 79-26892. 128p. (gr. 10 up). 1988. pap. 6.95 (0-87131-550-5) M Evans.
—Crazy to Be Alive in Such a Strange World: Poems about People. Crosby, Alexander L., photos by. LC 76-49667. (Illus.). 192p. (gr. 5 up). 1989. pap. 6.95 (0-87131-566-1) M Evans.
—Let's Do a Poem. 1991. 15.95 (0-385-30292-4) Delacorte.
—To Ride a Butterfly: Original Pictures, Stories, Poems, & Songs for Children. (ps-3). 1991. 17.00 (0-440-50402-3) Dell.
—When the Dark Comes Dancing: A Bedtime Poetry Book. Wallner, John, illus. LC 81-428. (ps-2). 1983. 17.95 (0-399-20807-0, Philomel) Putnam Pub Group.
Larrick, Nancy, compiled by. Cats Are Cats. Young, Ed, illus. 80p. (gr. 1 up). 1988. 17.95 (0-399-21517-4, Philomel Bks) Putnam Pub Group.
—The Merry-Go-Round Poetry Book. Gundersheimer, Karen, illus. 1989. 14.95 (0-385-29814-5) Delacorte.
Larrick, Nancy, ed. Mice Are Nice. Young, Ed, illus. 48p. (gr. 1990. 15.95 (0-399-21495-X, Philomel Bks) Putnam Pub Group.
—Night of the Whippoorwill. Ray, David, illus. 72p. (ps up). 1992. 19.95 (0-399-21874-2, Philomel Bks) Putnam Pub Group.
—Piping Down the Valleys Wild. 247p. (gr. 10 up). 1982. pap. 3.99 (0-440-46952-X, YB) Dell.
Larrick, Nancy, intro. by. Piping Down the Valleys Wild. Raskin, Ellen, illus. LC 68-27742. 256p. (ps-3). 1985. 14.95 (0-385-29429-8) Delacorte.
Larrick, Nancy, selected by. Room for Me & a Mountain Lion: Poetry of Open Spaces. LC 73-87710. (Illus.). 192p. (gr. 5 up). 1989. pap. 6.95 (0-87131-569-6) M Evans.
Larrison, Roxann. A Garden of Bitter Herbs. (Orig.). 1993. pap. 3.95 (0-87067-389-0) Holloway.
Larrivee-Cohen, Donna, jt. ed. see Baird, Mary.
Larry, Charles. Peboan & Seegun. (ps-3). 1993. 16.00 (0-374-35773-0) FS&G.
Larsen, Anita. Amelia Earhart: Missing, Declared Dead. LC 91-19246. (Illus.). 48p. (gr. 5 up). 1992. RSBE 11.95 (0-89686-613-0, Crestwood Hse) Macmillan Child Grp.
—Lost & Never Found. (gr. 4-7). 1991. pap. 2.75 (0-590-44447-6) Scholastic Inc.
—Lost & Never Found Two. (gr. 4-7). 1991. pap. 2.75 (0-590-43878-6) Scholastic Inc.
—Montezuma's Missing Treasure. LC 91-19259. (Illus.). 48p. (gr. 5 up). 1992. RSBE 11.95 (0-89686-615-7, Crestwood Hse) Macmillan Child Grp.
—Raoul Wallenberg: Missing Diplomat. LC 91-19937. (Illus.). 48p. (gr. 5 up). 1992. RSBE 11.95 (0-89686-616-5, Crestwood Hse) Macmillan Child Grp.
—The Roanoke Missing Persons Case. Watling, James, illus. LC 91-19524. 48p. (gr. 5 up). 1992. RSBE 11.95 (0-89686-619-X, Crestwood Hse) Macmillan Child Grp.
—The Rosenbergs. Ramsey, Mercy, illus. LC 91-22311. 48p. (gr. 5 up). 1992. RSBE 11.95 (0-89686-612-2, Crestwood Hse) Macmillan Child Grp.
—True Crimes & How They Were Solved. (gr. 4-7). 1993. pap. 2.95 (0-590-46856-1) Scholastic Inc.
Larsen, Chris, jt. auth. see Kolbrek, Loyal.
Larsen, Dale & Larsen, Sandy. Discovering Myself: Who Am I Anyway? (Illus.). 32p. (Orig.). (gr. 7-10). 1987. Camper Ed. saddle-stitched 1.50 (0-87788-178-2); Counselor Ed. saddle-stitched 3.50 (0-87788-179-0) Shaw Pubs.
—Got a License, but Where Do I Go? Devotions for Teens on the Move. LC 87-36576. 112p. (Orig.). (gr. 8-12). 1988. pap. 5.99 (0-87788-295-9) Shaw Pubs.
—It's Up to Me: Choosing God's Way. (Illus.). 32p. (gr. 4-6). 1989. saddle-stitched camper ed. 1.50 (0-87788-404-8); saddle-stitched counselor ed. 3.50 (0-87788-405-6) Shaw Pubs.
—Joseph: From Pit to Pyramid. (Illus.). 32p. (gr. 4-6). 1989. saddle-stitched camper ed. 1.50 (0-87788-435-8); saddle-stitched counselor ed. 3.50 (0-87788-436-6) Shaw Pubs.
Larsen, Dale, jt. auth. see Larsen, Sandy.
Larsen, Dan. David Livingstone. (gr. 3 up). 1992. pap. 2.50 perfect bdg. (1-55748-259-4) Barbour & Co.
—Jesus. Bohl, Al, illus. 224p. (gr. 4-8). 1989. pap. text ed. 2.50 (1-55748-100-8) Barbour & Co.
—Jesus. (gr. 3 up). 1992. 9.95 (1-55748-274-8) Barbour & Co.
Larsen, Dan, ed. see Bunyan, John.
Larsen, Dan, adapted by see Bunyan, John.
Larsen, Dan, adapted by see Defoe, Daniel.
Larsen, Dan, adapted by see Sheldon, Charles.
Larsen, Gloria P. Korea Coloring Book. 32p. (gr. k-6). 1992. 4.95 (0-9636374-0-1) Shared Wrld.
Larsen, Margie, jt. auth. see Dudko, Mary A.
Larsen, Rayola C. Alphabet Talk: Gospel Rhymes for Each Letter of the Alphabet. Perry, Lucille R., illus. LC 89-83429. 32p. (Orig.). (gr. k-3). 1989. pap. 4.95 (0-88290-147-8) Horizon Utah.

Larsen, Rebecca. Franklin D. Roosevelt: Man of Destiny. (Illus.). 224p. (gr. 9-12). 1991. 15.45 (0-531-15231-6); PLB 15.40 (0-531-11068-0) Watts.
—Oppenheimer & the Atomic Bomb. FS Staff, ed. LC 88-16981. (Illus.). 192p. (gr. 6-12). 1988. PLB 14.40 (0-531-10607-1) Watts.
—Paul Robeson: Hero Before His Time. LC 89-8880. (Illus.). 158p. (gr. 6-9). 1989. 13.95 (0-531-15117-4); PLB 14.40 (0-531-10779-5) Watts.
—Richard Nixon: The Rise & Fall of a President. (Illus.). 192p. (gr. 9-12). 1991. PLB 15.40 (0-531-10997-6) Watts.
Larsen, Ronald J. The Puerto Ricans in America. (Illus.). 80p. (gr. 5 up). 1989. PLB 15.95 (0-8225-0238-0); pap. 5.95 (0-8225-1036-7) Lerner Pubns.
Larsen, Sandy. Choosing: Which Way Do I Go? (Illus.). 32p. (gr. 7-10). 1985. saddle-stitched camper ed. 1.50 (0-87788-115-4); saddle-stitched counselor ed. 3.50 (0-87788-116-2) Shaw Pubs.
—Eye-Opening Bible Studies. 32p. (gr. 6-10). 1986. saddle-stitched 1.99 (0-87788-247-9) Shaw Pubs.
—For Real People Only. 96p. (gr. 7-9). 1986. pap. 2.99 student bk. (0-89693-516-7, Victor Books); tchr's. ed. 12.99 (0-89693-513-2) SP Pubns.
—Forgiving: Lightening Your Load. (Illus.). 32p. (gr. 6-8). 1985. saddle-stitched campers ed. 1.50 (0-87788-279-7); saddle-stitched counselor ed. 3.50 (0-87788-280-0) Shaw Pubs.
—Running the Race: Keeping the Faith. (Illus.). 64p. (Orig.). (gr. 6-12). 1986. saddle-stitched student ed. 3.99 (0-87788-740-3) Shaw Pubs.
Larsen, Sandy & Larsen, Dale. Celebrating Creation: Exploring God's World. 32p. (gr. 7-10). 1988. Camper. saddle-stitched 1.50 (0-87788-109-X); Counselor. saddle-stitched 3.50 (0-87788-110-3) Shaw Pubs.
Larsen, Sandy, jt. auth. see Larsen, Dale.
Larson & Kapp. I Am a Child of God. pap. 5.95 (0-88494-224-4) Bookcraft Inc.
—My Gift from Jesus. pap. 5.95 (0-88494-244-9) Bookcraft Inc.
Larson, Bob, jt. auth. see Gurley, Heather.
Larson, Charles R., ed. see Thurman, Wallace.
Larson, Dan, ed. see Wallace, Lew.
Larson, Dorothy W. Bright Shadows. Larson, Dorothy W., illus. LC 92-81679. 96p. (gr. 4-6). 1992. 14.95 (0-9621779-0-3) Sandstone Pub.
Larson, Eric M. Variations of the Smooth Bore H & R Handy-Gun: A Pocket Guide to Their Identification. LC 93-91518. (Illus.). 64p. (Orig.). (gr. 12). 1993. pap. 10.00 (0-9636465-0-8) E M Larson.
Larson, Greg. The Magic Garden & Other Stories. Muir, Michael, illus. LC 88-16879. 95p. (gr. 3-6). 1988. 7.95 (0-87579-141-7) Deseret Bk.
Larson, Heidi. Wedding Time. (Illus.). 25p. (gr. 2-4). 1991. 12.95 (0-237-60146-X, Pub. by Evans Bros Ltd) Trafalgar.
Larson, Jennifer, jt. auth. see Goldstein, Margaret J.
Larson, Kirby. Second Grade Pig Pals. Poydar, Nancy, illus. LC 93-16061. (gr. 1-5). 1994. write for info. (0-8234-1107-9) Holiday.
Larson, Mark, jt. auth. see Amberg, Jay.
Larson, Priscilla. Stranger Danger. 1991. 2.99 (0-8423-6599-0) Tyndale.
Larson, Russell J. Africa by Four: Coloring Book. (Illus.). 14p. (Orig.). (gr. k-6). 1992. pap. text ed. 1.85 (1-881087-01-8) Storm Moutain.
—USA Coloring Book. (Illus.). 50p. (Orig.). (gr. k-6). 1992. pap. text ed. 4.95 (1-881087-00-X) Storm Mountain.
Larson, Vicki L. & McKinley, Nancy L. Communication Assessment & Intervention Strategies for Adolescents. Vetter, Dolores, frwd. by. LC 86-51418. 387p. (gr. 5-12). 1987. text ed. 37.00 (0-930599-07-1) Thinking Pubns.
Larson, Wanda Z. Our Flag: Born Through Valor. (Illus.). 48p. (gr. 1 up). 1992. text ed. 60.00 (0-9628584-1-2) Blue Uncrn.
Larson, Wendy. Puppy Love. (gr. 4-8). 1993. pap. 2.50 (0-448-40463-X, G&D) Putnam Pub Group.

Larungu, Rute. African-American Cultures: Myths & Legends from Ghana for Children. Turechek, Lou, illus. LC 92-81116. 96p. (gr. 3 up). 1992. lib. bdg. 14.95 (1-878893-21-1); pap. 8.95 (1-878893-20-3) Telcraft Bks. KIRKUS REVIEWS: "'A story, a story, let it go, let it come.' Three Hausa & five Ashanti tales...one can almost hear the teller's voice." BOOKLIST: "In an insightful, interactive manner, this collection provides a range of fast-paced tales... these stories should be read aloud, perhaps even dramatized, to be fully appreciated." SCHOOL LIBRARY JOURNAL: "...free verse...a fuller background to West African folklore than single-story books." To order: Quality Books, Inc. (libraries); Baker

& Taylor (all).
Publisher Provided Annotation.

Larungu, Rute, as told by. Betty Elizabeth Brown: A Keepsake Book. Ross, Connie, illus. 32p. (ps up). 1992. pap. 2.75 (*1-878893-26-2*) Telcraft Bks.
—Dearie Dot: A Keepsake Book. Ross, Connie, illus. 32p. (ps up). 1992. pap. 2.75 (*1-878893-25-4*) Telcraft Bks.

Lasagna, Michele, jt. auth. see Faber, Gail.

Las Casas, Bartholomew. The Log of Christopher Columbus' First Voyage to America: In the Year 1492, As Copied Out in Brief by Bartholomew Las Casas. LC 88-32567. (Illus.). 84p. (gr. 3 up). 1989. Repr. of 1938 ed. lib. bdg. 17.00 (*0-208-02247-3*, Pub. by Linnet) Shoe String.

Lasell, Vicki. The Complete Book on Taming & Training Your Guinea Pig. (Illus.). 32p. (Orig.). (gr. 5-12). 1987. pap. 3.95 (*0-916005-06-2*) Silver Sea.

Lash, Jamie S. Righteous Rhymes, Vol. 1. Jackson, Jeff, illus. 24p. (gr. 2-7). 1983. pap. 2.95 (*0-915775-00-X*, Dist. by Stardust) Love Song Mess Assn.

Lash, Jamie S., ed. Righteous Rhymes, Vol. 2. Jackson, Jeff, illus. 24p. (Orig.). 1987. pap. 2.95 (*0-915775-01-8*) Love Song Mess Assn.

Lash, John D. Cowboy Stories from East Texas. LC 90-28880. (Illus.). 80p. (gr. 4-7). 1991. Repr. lib. bdg. 14.95 (*0-937460-66-4*) Hendrick-Long.

Lash, Joseph P. Eleanor & Franklin. Schlesinger, Arthur M., Jr. & Roosevelt, Franklin D., Jr.frwd. by. 1024p. (RL 10). 1973. pap. 5.95 (*0-451-14076-1*, AE1231, Sig) NAL-Dutton.

Lash, Michele, et al. My Kind of Family: A Book for Kids in Single-Parent Homes. LC 90-31471. (Illus.). 208p. (ps-6). 1990. plastic comb spiral bdg. 16.95 (*0-914525-13-1*); pap. 16.95 plastic comb spiral (*0-914525-12-3*) Waterfront Bks.

Lashbrook, Marilyn. The Best Day Ever: The Story of Jesus. Sharp, Chris, illus. LC 90-63764. (gr. k-3). 1991. 5.95 (*0-86606-444-3*, 875) Roper Pr.
—Digging for Buried Treasure. Bates, Steve, illus. 12p. (gr. k-6). 1984. pap. text ed. 4.25 (*1-55976-141-5*) CEF Press.
—Don't Rock the Boat: The Story of the Miraculous Catch. Britt, Stephanie M., illus. LC 88-63779. 32p. (ps). 1989. 5.95 (*0-86606-435-4*, 867) Roper Pr.
—Get Lost, Little Brother: The Story of Joseph. Britt, Stephanie M., illus. LC 87-62503. 32p. (ps). 1988. 5.95 (*0-86606-432-X*, 863) Roper Pr.
—God, Please Send Fire: Elijah & the Prophets of Baal. Sharp, Chris, illus. LC 90-60458. 32p. (gr. k-3). 1990. 5.95 (*0-86606-440-0*, 871) Roper Pr.
—God Speaks to Me. Bates, Stephen, illus. 52p. (gr. k-6). 1985. pap. text ed. 8.99 (*1-55976-030-3*) CEF Press.
—The Great Shake-Up: Miracles at Philippi. Sharp, Chris, illus. LC 90-63768. 32p. (gr. k-3). 1991. 5.95 (*0-86606-445-1*, 876) Roper Pr.
—I Don't Want to: The Story of Jonah. Britt, Stephanie M., illus. LC 87-60264. 32p. (ps). 1987. 5.95 (*0-86606-428-1*, 844) Roper Pr.
—I May be Little: The Story of David's Growth. Britt, Stephanie M., illus. LC 87-60262. 32p. (ps). 1987. 5.95 (*0-86606-429-X*, 843) Roper Pr.
—I'll Pray Anyway: The Story of Daniel. LC 87-63502. (Illus.). 32p. (ps). 1988. 5.95 (*0-86606-430-3*, 861) Roper Pr.
—It's Not My Fault: Man's Big Mistake. Sharp, Chris, illus. LC 90-60459. 32p. (gr. k-3). 1990. 5.95 (*0-86606-439-7*, 870) Roper Pr.
—No Tree for Christmas: The Story of Jesus' Birth. Britt, Stephanie M., illus. LC 88-62025. 32p. (ps). 1989. 5.95 (*0-86606-434-6*, 866) Roper Pr.
—Nothing to Fear: Jesus Walks on Water. Sharp, Chris, illus. LC 90-61060. 32p. (gr. k-3). 1991. 5.95 (*0-86606-443-5*, 874) Roper Pr.
—Now I See: The Story of the Man Born Blind. Britt, Stephanie M., illus. LC 88-62520. 32p. (ps). 1989. 5.95 (*0-86606-437-0*, 869) Roper Pr.
—Out on a Limb: The Story of Zacchaeus. LC 88-63782. (Illus.). 32p. (ps). 1989. 5.95 (*0-86606-436-2*, 868) Roper Pr.
—Someone to Love: The Story of Creation. Britt, Stephanie M., illus. LC 87-60261. 32p. (ps). 1987. 5.95 (*0-86606-426-5*, 841) Roper Pr.
—Too Bad, Ahab! Naboth's Vineyard. Sharp, Chris, illus. LC 90-60457. 32p. (gr. k-3). 1990. 5.95 (*0-86606-441-9*, 872) Roper Pr.
—Two by Two: The Story of Noah's Faith. Britt, Stephanie M., illus. LC 87-60263. 32p. (ps). 1987. 5.95 (*0-86606-427-3*, 842) Roper Pr.
—Two Lads & a Dad: The Prodigal Son. Sharp, Chris, illus. LC 90-63769. (gr. k-3). 1991. 5.95 (*0-86606-446-X*, 877) Roper Pr.
—The Wall That Did Not Fall: The Story of Rahab's Faith. Britt, Stephanie M., illus. LC 87-63420. 32p. (ps). 1988. 5.95 (*0-86606-433-8*, 864) Roper Pr.
—The Weak Strongman: Samson. Sharp, Chris, illus. LC 90-60456. 32p. (gr. k-3). 1990. 5.95 (*0-86606-442-7*, 873) Roper Pr.
—Who Needs a Boat? The Story of Moses. Britt, Stephanie M., illus. LC 87-83295. 32p. (ps). 1988. 5.95 (*0-86606-431-1*, 862) Roper Pr.

Lasker, Emanuel. Lasker's Manual of Chess. (gr. 7-12). pap. 6.95 (*0-486-20640-8*) Dover.

Lasker, Joe. The Great Alexander the Great. (ps-3). 1990. pap. 3.95 (*0-14-054318-X*, Puffin) Puffin Bks.

—He's My Brother. Lasker, Joe, illus. LC 73-7318. 40p. (gr. 1-3). 1974. PLB 13.95 (*0-8075-3218-5*) A Whitman.
—Merry Ever After. Lasker, Joe, illus. (gr. 1-3). 1978. pap. 4.95 (*0-14-050280-7*, Puffin) Puffin Bks.
—Mothers Can Do Anything. Lasker, Joe, illus. LC 72-83684. 40p. (gr. k-2). 1972. PLB 13.95 (*0-8075-5287-9*) A Whitman.
—Nick Joins In. Tucker, Kathleen, ed. Lasker, Joe, illus. LC 79-29637. 32p. (gr. 1-3). 1980. PLB 13.95 (*0-8075-5612-2*) A Whitman.
—Tournament of Knights. Lasker, Joe, illus. LC 85-48075. 32p. (gr. 3 up). 1986. (Crowell Jr Bks); PLB 13.89 (*0-690-04542-5*, Crowell Jr Bks) HarpC Child Bks.
—A Tournament of Knights. Lasker, Joe, illus. LC 85-48075. 32p. (gr. 3 up). 1989. pap. 5.95 (*0-06-443192-4*, Trophy) HarpC Child Bks.

Laskin. Spasibo za Vnimanie. (gr. 7-12). pap. 5.95 (*0-88436-052-0*, 65251) EMC.

Laskin, Pamela L. Music from the Heart. 1990. pap. 2.75 (*0-553-28551-3*) Bantam.

Laskin, Pamela L. & Moskowitz, Addie A. Wish upon a Star: A Story for Children with a Parent Who Is Mentally Ill. LC 91-211. (Illus.). 32p. (ps-2). 1991. 16.95 (*0-945354-30-4*); pap. 6.95 (*0-945354-29-0*) Magination Pr.

Lasky, Kathryn. A Baby for Max. Knight, Christopher G., illus. LC 86-22131. 48p. (ps-2). 1987. pap. 4.95 (*0-689-71118-2*, Aladdin) Macmillan Child Grp.
—Beyond the Divide. LC 82-22867. 264p. (gr. 7 up). 1983. SBE 14.95 (*0-02-751670-9*, Macmillan Child Bk) Macmillan Child Grp.
—Beyond the Divide. (gr. 7 up). 1986. pap. 3.25 (*0-440-91021-8*, LFL) Dell.
—The Bone Wars. LC 88-13426. 378p. (gr. 7 up). 1988. 12.95 (*0-688-07433-2*) Morrow Jr Bks.
—The Bone Wars. (gr. 5-9). 1989. pap. 5.99 (*0-14-034168-4*, Puffin) Puffin Bks.
—Dinosaur Dig. Knight, Christopher G., photos by. LC 89-13212. (Illus.). 64p. (gr. 3 up). 1990. 13.95 (*0-688-08574-1*); PLB 13.88 (*0-688-08575-X*, Morrow Jr Bks) Morrow Jr Bks.
—Double Trouble Squared. (gr. 3 up). 1991. 14.95 (*0-15-224126-4*, HB Juv Bks) HarBrace.
—Double Trouble Squared. (gr. 4-7). 1991. pap. 5.95 (*0-15-224127-2*) HarBrace.
—Fourth of July Bear. Cogancherry, Helen, illus. LC 90-37422. 40p. (gr. k up). 1991. 13.95 (*0-688-08287-4*); PLB 13.88 (*0-688-08288-2*, Morrow Jr Bks) Morrow Jr Bks.
—Home Free. (gr. 7 up). 1988. pap. 2.95 (*0-440-20038-5*, LFL) Dell.
—I Have an Aunt on Marlborough Street. Guevara, Susan, illus. LC 91-279. 32p. (gr. k-3). 1992. RSBE 13.95 (*0-02-751701-2*, Macmillan Child Bk) Macmillan Child Grp.
—The Librarian Who Measured the Earth. Hawkes, Kevin, illus. LC 92-42656. (gr. 4 up). 1994. 15.95 (*0-316-51526-4*, Joy St Bks) Little.
—Lunch Bunnies. Hafner, Marylin, illus. LC 92-31554. 1993. 13.95 (*0-316-51525-6*, Joy St Bks) Little.
—Memoirs of a Book Bat. (gr. 4 up). 1994. 10.95 (*0-15-215727-1*) HarBrace.
—My Island Grandma. Schwartz, Amy, illus. LC 91-31000. 32p. (ps up). 1993. 15.00 (*0-688-07946-6*); PLB 14.93 (*0-688-07948-2*) Morrow Jr Bks.
—The Night Journey. Hyman, Trina S., illus. 152p. (gr. 5-9). 1986. pap. 4.99 (*0-14-032048-2*, Puffin) Puffin Bks.
—Pageant. LC 86-12087. 240p. (gr. 7 up). 1986. SBE 14.95 (*0-02-751720-9*, Four Winds) Macmillan Child Grp.
—Pageant. (gr. k-12). 1988. pap. 3.95 (*0-440-20161-6*, LFL) Dell.
—Prank. (gr. 6 up). 1986. pap. 2.75 (*0-440-97144-6*, LFL) Dell.
—Sea Swan. Stock, Catherine, illus. LC 88-1444. 32p. (gr. k-3). 1988. RSBE 14.95 (*0-02-751700-4*, Macmillan Child Bk) Macmillan Child Grp.
—Shadows in the Water: A Starbuck Family Adventure. LC 92-8139. 1992. 16.95 (*0-15-273533-X*, HB Juv Bks); pap. write for info. (*0-15-273534-8*) HarBrace.
—The Solo. McCarthy, Bobette, illus. LC 92-44456. 32p. (ps-2). 1994. RSBE 14.95 (*0-02-751664-4*, Macmillan Child Bk) Macmillan Child Grp.
—Sugaring Time. Knight, Christopher G., illus. & photos by. LC 82-23928. 64p. (gr. 3-7). 1983. RSBE 13.95 (*0-02-751680-6*, Macmillan Child Bk) Macmillan Child Grp.
—Sugaring Time. Knight, Christopher G., photos by. LC 86-3468. (Illus.). 64p. (gr. 3-7). 1986. pap. 4.95 (*0-689-71081-X*, Aladdin) Macmillan Child Grp.
—Surtsey: The Newest Place on Earth. Knight, Christopher, illus. LC 92-52990. 64p. (gr. 3-7). 1992. 15.95 (*1-56282-300-0*); PLB 15.89 (*1-56282-301-9*) Hyprn Child.
—The Tantrum. McCarthy, Bobette, illus. LC 92-3701. 32p. (ps-1). 1993. RSBE 13.95 (*0-02-751661-X*, Macmillan Child Bk) Macmillan Child Grp.
—Think Like an Eagle: At Work with a Wildlife Photographer. Knight, Christopher G. & Swedberg, Jack, photos by. (Illus.). 48p. (gr. 3 up). 1992. 15.95 (*0-316-51519-1*, Joy St Bks) Little.
—Traces of Life: The Origins of Humankind. Powell, Whitney, illus. LC 89-12092. 144p. (gr. 5 up). 1990. 16.95 (*0-688-07237-2*) Morrow Jr Bks.

—Voice in the Wind: A Starbuck Family Adventure. (gr. 4-7). 1993. 16.95 (*0-15-294102-9*, HB Juv Bks); pap. 6.95 (*0-15-294103-7*) HarBrace.

Lasky, Kathryn & Knight, Meribah. Searching for Laura Ingalls: A Reader's Journey. Knight, Christopher G., photos by. LC 92-26188. (Illus.). 48p. (gr. 2-6). 1993. RSBE 15.95 (*0-02-751666-0*, Macmillan Child Bk) Macmillan Child Grp.

Lasky, Mark A., jt. auth. see Landes, William-Alan.

Lasky, Michael S. & Harris, Robert A. The Films of Alfred Hitchcock. (Illus.). 256p. (gr. 9 up). 1976. 14.00 (*0-8065-0509-5*, Pub. by Citadel Pr) Carol Pub Group.

Lasley, Mary. A Day at the Beach. 4p. (ps-2). 1990. incl. 24 puzzle pieces 10.95 (*0-88679-843-4*) Educ Insights.
—A Day at the Park. 4p. (ps-2). 1990. incl. 24 puzzle pieces 10.95 (*0-685-38496-9*) Educ Insights.
—Do-It-Yourself Story Puzzle Book. Brown, Amy L., illus. 2p. (ps). 1988. 9.95 (*0-9622406-0-5*) MOL Bks.

Laslo, Cynthia. The Rosen Photo Guide to a Career in the Circus. (Illus.). (gr. 7-12). 1988. lib. bdg. 12.95 (*0-8239-0819-4*) Rosen Group.

La Sota, Ann de see De la Sota, Ann.

Lassik, Grace E. The Raccoon Connection. rev. ed. Carolock, G. M. & Brown, B. Holborrk, eds. (Illus.). 15p. (ps-2). 1992. pap. 9.95 (*1-880926-00-8*) Four Star SC.

Laster, Jim. The Birthday Gift That Beeped. Knight, George, ed. Erwin, Julie, illus. LC 83-176266. 56p. (gr. k-4). 1983. 10.95 (*0-9612780-0-5*) J Laster Pub Co.

Latella, Lisa. A Song for the Prince. Latella, Lisa, illus. 36p. (Orig.). (gr. k up). 1984. pap. write for info. (*0-9608592-1-7*) Gallery Arts.

Latham, Bill, jt. auth. see Lea, Thomas D.

Latham, Caroline. Katherine Hepburn. Horner, Matina, intro. by. (Illus.). 112p. (gr. 5 up). 1988. 17.95 (*1-55546-658-3*); pap. 9.95 (*0-7910-0416-3*) Chelsea Hse.

Latham, Hugh, tr. see Sehlin, Gunhild.

Latham, Jean L. Carry on, Mr. Bowditch. Cosgrove, John O., illus. LC 55-5219. 256p. (gr. 6 up). 1973. pap. 5.70 (*0-395-13713-6*, Sandpiper) HM.
—Carry on, Mr. Bowditch. Cosgrove, John O., illus. (gr. 6 up). 1955. 14.95 (*0-395-06881-9*) HM.
—David Glasgow Farragut: Our First Admiral. Frame, Paul, illus. 80p. (gr. 2-6). 1991. Repr. of 1967 ed. lib. bdg. 12.95 (*0-7910-1438-X*) Chelsea Hse.
—Eli Whitney: Great Inventor. Cary, illus. 80p. (gr. 2-6). 1991. Repr. of 1963 ed. lib. bdg. 12.95 (*0-7910-1453-3*) Chelsea Hse.
—Elizabeth Blackwell: Pioneer Woman Doctor. Gold, Ethel, illus. 80p. (gr. 2-6). 1991. Repr. of 1975 ed. lib. bdg. 12.95 (*0-7910-1406-1*) Chelsea Hse.
—George W. Goethals: Panama Canal Engineer. Green, Hamilton, illus. 80p. (gr. 2-6). 1991. Repr. of 1965 ed. lib. bdg. 12.95 (*0-7910-1440-1*) Chelsea Hse.
—Rachel Carson: Who Loved the Sea. (Illus.). 80p. (gr. 2-6). 1991. Repr. of 1973 ed. PLB 12.95 (*0-7910-1408-8*) Chelsea Hse.
—Sam Houston: Hero of Texas. (Illus.). 80p. (gr. 2-6). 1991. Repr. of 1965 ed. lib. bdg. 12.95 (*0-7910-1441-X*) Chelsea Hse.
—Samuel F. B. Morse. (Illus.). 80p. (gr. 2-6). 1991. Repr. of 1961 ed. lib. bdg. 12.95 (*0-7910-1447-9*) Chelsea Hse.

Latham, Joy, jt. auth. see Edwards, Mildred.

Latham, Judy. Women in the Bible: Helpful Friends. Karch, Paul, illus. (gr. 1-6). 1979. 5.95 (*0-8054-4248-0*, 4242-48) Broadman.

Lathrop, Dorothy B. Animals of the Bible. Fish, Helen D., selected by. Lathrop, Dorothy, illus. LC 86-46118. 68p. (ps up). 1937. 16.00 (*0-397-31536-8*, Lipp Jr Bks); PLB 15.89 (*0-397-30047-6*) HarpC Child Bks.

Latimer, Heather. Curse of the Painted Cats: A Romantic Suspense Novel. 250p. 1989. 18.95 (*0-943698-03-0*); pap. 4.95 (*0-943698-04-9*); talking bk. with 2 audio cassettes, 3 hrs. 15.95 (*0-943698-06-5*) Papyrus Pubs.

Latimer, Jim. Fox under First Base. McCue, Lisa, illus. LC 89-27576. 32p. (gr. k-2). 1991. SBE 13.95 (*0-684-19053-2*, Scribners Young Read) Macmillan Child Grp.
—Going the Moose Way Home. Carrick, Donald, illus. LC 87-9762. 32p. (gr. 1-3). 1988. SBE 13.95 (*0-684-18890-2*, Scribners Young Read) Macmillan Child Grp.
—The Irish Piper. O'Brien, John, illus. LC 90-34550. 32p. (gr. 1-3). 1991. SBE 13.95 (*0-684-19130-X*, Scribners Young Read) Macmillan Child Grp.
—James Bear & the Goose Gathering. Franco-Feeney, Betsy, illus. LC 92-26190. 32p. (gr. k-2). 1994. SBE 14.95 (*0-684-19526-7*, Scribners Young Read) Macmillan Child Grp.
—James Bear's Pie. Franco-Feeney, Betsy, illus. LC 90-36193. 32p. (ps-2). 1992. SBE 13.95 (*0-684-19226-8*, Scribners Young Read) Macmillan Child Grp.
—Moose & Friends. Ewing, Carolyn, illus. LC 91-14047. 32p. (ps-3). 1993. SBE 14.95 (*0-684-19335-3*, Scribners Young Read) Macmillan Child Grp.
—When Moose Was Young. Carrick, Donald, illus. LC 89-10059. 32p. (gr. 1-3). 1990. SBE 13.95 (*0-684-18932-1*, Scribners Young Read) Macmillan Child Grp.

Latrobe, Kathy H., ed. Exploring the Great Lakes States Through Literature. LC 93-2486. 168p. 1993. pap. 24.95t (*0-89774-731-3*) Oryx Pr.

Latta, Rich. Dinosaur Mazes. 48p. 1990. pap. 2.95 (*0-8431-2822-4*) Price Stern.
—Monster Truck Maze Book. (gr. 4 up). 1992. pap. 2.99 (*0-8431-3419-4*) Price Stern.
—More Dinosaur Mazes. (gr. 4 up). 1992. pap. 2.99 (*0-8431-3420-8*) Price Stern.
—State the Facts. 56p. 1990. pap. 2.95 (*0-8431-2821-6*) Price Stern.
Latta, Richard. Bible Easter Puzzles. 48p. (gr. 3 up). 1988. 6.95 (*0-86653-427-X*, SS885, Shining Star Pubns) Good Apple.
—This Little Pig Had a Riddle. Fay, Anne, ed. Munsinger, Lynn, illus. LC 83-26112. 32p. (gr. 1-5). 1984. PLB 8.95 (*0-8075-7893-2*) A Whitman.
Latterman, Terry. Little Joe, a Hopi Indian Boy, Learns a Hopi Indian Secret. Hawkins, Mary E., ed. Latterman, Terry, illus. LC 85-61836. 32p. (gr. 4-12). 1985. 12.95 (*0-934739-01-3*) Pussywillow Pub.
—The Watermelon Treat. Hawkins, Mary E., ed. Lattermen, Terry, illus. LC 85-63266. 48p. (gr. 1-4). 1987. 8.95 (*0-934739-03-X*); pap. 5.95 (*0-934739-04-8*) Pussywillow Pub.
Lattimore, Deborah. Digging into the Past. (Illus.). 32p. (gr. 3 up). 1986. incl. hand held Decoder 5.95 (*0-88679-460-9*) Educ Insights.
Lattimore, Deborah N. The Dragon's Robe. Lattimore, Deborah N., illus. LC 89-34512. 32p. (gr. 1-5). 1990. 15.00 (*0-06-023719-8*); PLB 14.89 (*0-06-023723-6*) HarpC Child Bks.
—Dragon's Robe. Lattimore, Deborah L., illus. LC 89-34512. 32p. (gr. 1-5). 1993. pap. 4.95 (*0-06-443321-8*, Trophy) HarpC Child Bks.
—The Flame of Peace: A Tale of the Aztecs. Lattimore, Deborah N., illus. LC 86-26934. 48p. (gr. k-3). 1987. PLB 12.89 (*0-06-023709-0*) HarpC Child Bks.
—The Flame of Peace: A Tale of the Aztecs. Lattimore, Deborah N., illus. LC 86-26934. 48p. (ps-3). 1991. pap. 5.95 (*0-06-443272-6*, Trophy) HarpC Child Bks.
—Frida Maria: A Story of the Old Southwest. LC 93-17250. 1994. write for info. (*0-15-276636-7*, Browndeer Pr) HarBrace.
—Lady with the Ship on Her Head. 28p. (ps-3). 1990. 14.95 (*0-15-243525-5*) HarBrace.
—Lady with the Ship on Her Head. (ps-3). 1992. pap. 4.95 (*0-15-243526-3*) HarBrace.
—The Prince & the Golden Ax: A Minoan Tale. Lattimore, Deborah N., illus. LC 87-21193. 40p. (gr. k-3). 1988. PLB 12.89 (*0-06-023716-3*) HarpC Child Bks.
—Punga, Goddess of Ugly. LC 92-23191. 1993. 14.95 (*0-15-292862-6*) HarBrace.
—The Sailor Who Captured the Sea. Lattimore, Deborah N., illus. LC 89-26937. 40p. (gr. 2-5). 1993. pap. 5.95 (*0-06-443342-0*, Trophy) HarpC Child Bks.
—The Sailor Who Captured the Sea: A Story of the Book of Kells. Lattimore, Deborah N., illus. LC 89-26937. 40p. (gr. 2-5). 1991. 16.00 (*0-06-023710-4*); PLB 15.89 (*0-06-023711-2*) HarpC Child Bks.
—Why There Is No Arguing in Heaven: A Mayan Myth. Lattimore, Deborah N., illus. LC 87-35045. 40p. (gr. 1-5). 1989. PLB 13.89 (*0-06-023718-X*) HarpC Child Bks.
—The Winged Cat: A Tale of Ancient Egypt. Lattimore, Deborah N., illus. LC 90-38441. 40p. (gr. 2-5). 1992. 15.00 (*0-06-023635-3*); PLB 14.89 (*0-06-023636-1*) HarpC Child Bks.
Lattimore, Eleanor. Little Pear. D'Andrade, Diane, ed. (Illus.). 106p. (Orig.). (gr. 2-5). 1991. pap. 4.95 (*0-15-246685-1*, HB Juv Bks) HarBrace.
—Little Pear & His Friends. (Illus.). 129p. (Orig.). (gr. 2-5). 1991. pap. 4.95 (*0-15-246863-3*, HB Juv Bks) HarBrace.
Lattimore, Eleanor F. Little Pear. Lattimore, Eleanor F., illus. LC 31-22069. (gr. 2-5). 1968. pap. 3.95 (*0-15-652799-5*, Voyager Bks) HarBrace.
—Little Pear. (Illus.). 1992. Repr. PLB 14.95x (*0-89966-917-4*) Buccaneer Bks.
—Little Pear. (gr. 1-4). 1992. 17.25 (*0-8446-6576-2*) Peter Smith.
—Little Pear & His Friends. (gr. 1-4). 1992. 17.00 (*0-8446-6575-4*) Peter Smith.
Lauber, Pat. Dinosaurs Walked Here & Other Stories Fossils Tell. LC 91-40739. (Illus.). 64p. (gr. 2-5). 1992. pap. 5.95 (*0-689-71603-6*, Aladdin) Macmillan Child Grp.
Lauber, Patricia. Alligators: A Success Story. Silva, Lou, illus. LC 93-3302. 64p. (gr. 2-4). 1993. PLB 14.95 (*0-8050-1909-X*, Bks Young Read) H Holt & Co.
—Be a Friend to Trees. Keller, Holly, illus. LC 92-24082. 32p. (gr. k-4). 1994. 15.00 (*0-06-021528-3*); PLB 14.89 (*0-06-021529-1*) HarpC Child Bks.
—Be a Friend to Trees. Keller, Holly, illus. LC 92-24082. 32p. (gr. k-4). 1994. pap. 4.95 (*0-06-445120-8*, Trophy) HarpC Child Bks.
—Dinosaurs Walked Here & Other Stories Fossils Tell. LC 86-8239. (Illus.). 64p. (gr. 2-4). 1987. SBE 16.95 (*0-02-754510-5*, Bradbury Pr) Macmillan Child Grp.
—From Flower to Flower: Animals & Pollination. Wexler, Jerome, photos by. (gr. 3-6). 1987. 13.95 (*0-517-55539-5*) Crown Bks Yng Read.
—Get Ready for Robots. Kelley, True, illus. LC 85-48255. 32p. (ps-3). 1987. PLB 13.89i (*0-690-04578-6*, Crowell Jr Bks) HarpC Child Bks.
—Great Whales: The Gentle Giants. Folkens, Pieter, illus. 64p. (gr. 2-4). 1991. 14.95 (*0-8050-1717-8*, Redfeather BYR) H Holt & Co.

—Great Whales: The Gentle Giants. Folkens, Pieter, illus. LC 91-692. 64p. (gr. 2-4). 1993. pap. 4.95 (*0-8050-2894-3*, Bks Young Read) H Holt & Co.
—How We Learned the Earth Is Round. Lloyd, Megan, illus. LC 89-49650. 32p. (gr. k-4). 1990. 14.00 (*0-690-04860-2*, Crowell Jr Bks); PLB 13.89 (*0-690-04862-9*, Crowell Jr Bks) HarpC Child Bks.
—How We Learned the Earth Is Round. Lloyd, Megan, illus. LC 89-49650. 32p. (gr. k-4). 1992. pap. 4.50 (*0-06-445109-7*, Trophy) HarpC Child Bks.
—Journey to the Planets. 2nd, rev. ed. NASA Staff, illus. LC 90-33102. 1990. PLB 16.99 (*0-517-58125-6*) Crown Bks Yng Read.
—Journey to the Planets. 4th ed. LC 92-16094. 96p. (gr. 4-9). 1993. 20.00 (*0-517-59029-8*) Crown Bks Yng Read.
—Living with Dinosaurs. Henderson, Doug, illus. LC 90-43265. 48p. (gr. 1-5). 1991. SBE 16.95 (*0-02-754521-0*, Bradbury Pr) Macmillan Child Grp.
—Lost Star: The Story of Amelia Earhart. (gr. 4-7). 1990. pap. 2.75 (*0-590-41159-4*) Scholastic Inc.
—The News about Dinosaurs. reissued ed. Gurche, John, et al, illus. LC 88-24140. 48p. (gr. 1-5). 1989. RSBE 15.95 (*0-02-754520-2*, Bradbury Pr) Macmillan Child Grp.
—An Octopus Is Amazing. Keller, Holly, illus. LC 89-29300. 32p. (ps-1). 1990. 14.00 (*0-690-04801-7*, Crowell Jr Bks); PLB 13.89 (*0-690-04803-3*, Crowell Jr Bks) HarpC Child Bks.
—Seeds: Pop Stick Glide. Wexler, Jerome, photos by. LC 80-14553. (Illus.). 64p. (gr. 2-4). 1988. 12.95 (*0-517-54165-3*) Crown Bks Yng Read.
—Seeds: Pop Stick Glide. Wexler, Jerome, photos by. LC 80-14553. (Illus.). 64p. (gr. 2-4). 1991. lib. bdg. 14.99 (*0-517-58554-5*) Crown Bks Yng Read.
—Seeing Earth from Space. LC 89-77523. (Illus.). 80p. (gr. 5 up). 1990. 19.95 (*0-531-05902-2*); PLB 19.99 (*0-531-08502-3*) Orchard Bks Watts.
—Snakes Are Hunters. Keller, Holly, illus. LC 87-47695. 32p. (ps-3). 1988. (Crowell Jr Bks); PLB 13.89 (*0-690-04630-8*, Crowell Jr Bks) HarpC Child Bks.
—Snakes Are Hunters. LC 87-47695. (Illus.). 32p. (ps-4). 1989. pap. 4.95 (*0-06-445091-0*, Trophy) HarpC Child Bks.
—Summer of Fire: Yellowstone 1988. LC 90-23032. (Illus.). 64p. (gr. 4 up). 1991. 17.95 (*0-531-05943-X*); RLB 17.99 (*0-531-08543-0*) Orchard Bks Watts.
—Tales Mummies Tell. LC 83-46172. (Illus.). 128p. (gr. 5-9). 1985. (Crowell Jr Bks); PLB 15.89 (*0-690-04389-9*, Crowell Jr Bks) HarpC Child Bks.
—Volcano: The Eruption & Healing of Mount St. Helens. LC 85-22442. (Illus.). 64p. (gr. 3-5). 1986. SBE 16.95 (*0-02-754500-8*, Bradbury Pr) Macmillan Child Grp.
—Volcano: The Eruption & Healing of Mount St. Helens. LC 92-23791. (Illus.). 64p. (gr. 2-5). 1993. pap. 6.95 (*0-689-71679-6*, Aladdin) Macmillan Child Grp.
—Voyagers from Space: Meteors & Meteorites. Eagle, Mike, illus. LC 86-47745. 80p. (gr. 5 up). 1989. (Crowell Jr Bks); PLB 15.89 (*0-690-04634-0*, Crowell Jr Bks) HarpC Child Bks.
—What Big Teeth You Have! Weston, Martha, illus. LC 85-47902. 64p. (gr. 2-6). 1986. (Crowell Jr Bks); PLB 13.89 (*0-690-04507-7*, Crowell Jr Bks) HarpC Child Bks.
—What Do You See? Wexler, Jerome, photos by. LC 93-2388. (Illus.). 1994. 15.00 (*0-517-59390-4*); PLB 15.99 (*0-517-59391-2*) Crown Bks Yng Read.
—What's Hatching Out of That Egg? LC 79-12054. (Illus.). 64p. (gr. 2-4). 1991. lib. bdg. 14.99 (*0-517-58553-7*) Crown Bks Yng Read.
—Who Discovered America? Mysteries & Puzzles of the New World. new ed. Eagle, Mike, illus. LC 90-43604. 80p. (gr. 2-6). 1992. 16.00 (*0-06-023728-7*); PLB 15.89 (*0-06-023729-5*) HarpC Child Bks.
—Who Eats What. Keller, Holly, illus. LC 93-10609. (ps-6). 1995. 15.00 (*0-06-022981-0*); PLB 14.89 (*0-06-022982-9*) HarpC Child Bks.
—Your Body & How It Works. (Illus.). (gr. 3-5). 1966. PLB 12.99 (*0-394-90125-8*) Random Bks Yng Read.
Lauer, Alphonse, ed. see Uhing, Mary J.
Laufenberg, Frank. Rock & Pop: Day by Day. (Illus.). 320p. (gr. 10-12). 1992. pap. 16.95 (*0-7137-2319-X*, Pub. by Blandford Pr UK) Sterling.
Laufer, Diana. Hide & Seek. Laufer, Diana, illus. 12p. (gr. 1-4). 1994. lift-a-flap 9.95 (*0-8431-3591-3*) Price Stern.
—Peek-a-Boo Family: My First Photo Album. (Illus.). 12p. (ps-2). 1992. 9.95 (*0-8431-3386-4*) Price Stern.
Laufer, Judy E. Where Did Papa Go: Looking at Death from a Young Child's Perspective. Wingfield, Ken, Jr., illus. 32p. (Orig.). (ps-2). 1991. pap. 9.95 (*1-881669-00-9*) Little Egg Pub.
Lauffer, Butch & Davie, Sandy. Soccer Coach's Guide to Practices, Drills & Skill Training. LC 92-44087. (Illus.). 160p. (gr. 10-12). 1993. pap. 12.95 (*0-8069-8219-5*) Sterling.
Laughlin, Charlotte. Where's Baby Jesus? 1992. 9.99 (*0-8499-0902-3*) Word Inc.
—Where's the Lost Sheep? 1992. 9.99 (*0-8499-0919-8*) Word Inc.
Laughlin, Florence. The Little Leftover Witch. 2nd ed. Greenwald, Sheila, illus. LC 88-10551. 96p. (gr. 2-6). 1988. pap. 3.50 (*0-689-71273-1*, Aladdin) Macmillan Child Grp.
—The Little Leftover Witch. 3rd ed. Greenwald, Sheila, illus. LC 92-41166. 96p. (gr. 1-4). 1996. pap. 3.95 (*0-689-71742-3*, Aladdin) Macmillan Child Grp.

Laughlin, Rosemary M. Trouble on the Shoshone. LC 88-50762. 94p. (gr. 5-8). 1989. pap. 5.95 (*1-55523-154-3*) Winston-Derek.
Laughton, Charles, tr. see Brecht, Bertolt.
Launchbury, Jane. In Nursery Rhyme Land. 1988. 2.98 (*0-671-09597-8*) S&S Trade.
—Monster Stories. 1991. 3.99 (*0-517-06525-8*) Outlet Bk Co.
Laundrie, Amy C. Whinny of the Wild Horses. Helmer, Jean C., illus. LC 88-21460. 128p. (gr. 3-6). 1990. SBE 13.95 (*0-02-754542-3*, Four Winds Press) Macmillan Child Grp.
Laure, Jason. Angola. LC 90-2143. (Illus.). 128p. (gr. 5-9). 1990. PLB 26.60 (*0-516-02721-2*) Childrens.
—Bangladesh. LC 92-8891. (Illus.). 128p. (gr. 5-9). 1992. PLB 26.60 (*0-516-02609-7*) Childrens.
—Botswana. LC 93-753. (Illus.). 128p. (gr. 5-9). 1993. PLB 26.60 (*0-516-02616-X*) Childrens.
—Namibia. LC 92-39137. (Illus.). 128p. (gr. 5-9). 1993. PLB 26.60 (*0-516-02615-1*) Childrens.
—Zambia. LC 89-34281. 128p. (gr. 5-9). 1989. PLB 26.60 (*0-516-02716-6*) Childrens.
—Zimbabwe. LC 87-35426. (Illus.). 127p. (gr. 4-8). 1988. PLB 26.60 (*0-516-02704-2*) Childrens.
Laure, Jason, jt. auth. see Blauer, Ettagale.
Laurence, Jim, jt. ed. see Hildebrandt, Tim.
Laurencin, Genevieve. Music! Bogard, Vicki, tr. from FRE. Millet, Claude & Millet, Denise, illus. LC 89-8892. (gr. k-5). 1989. 4.95 (*0-944589-25-1*, 025) Young Discovery Lib.
Laurgaard, Rachel K. Patty Reed's Doll: The Story of the Donner Party. Michaels, Elizabeth, illus. 144p. (gr. 3-6). 1989. pap. 7.95 (*0-9617357-2-4*) Tomato Enter.
Laurie, Greg. God's Design for Christian Dating. 2nd ed. LC 82-83836. 96p. (gr. 10-12). 1983. pap. 2.99 (*0-89081-373-6*) Harvest Hse.
Laurie, Lucy. A Day in the Country. 1990. 29.00x (*0-85439-374-9*, Pub. by St Paul Pubns UK) St Mut.
Laurin, Anne. Perfect Crane. Mikolaycak, Charles, illus. LC 80-7912. 32p. (gr. 1-4). 1981. PLB 13.89 (*0-06-023744-9*) HarpC Child Bks.
—Perfect Crane. Mikolaycak, Charles, illus. LC 80-7912. 32p. (gr. 1-4). 1987. pap. 4.95 (*0-06-443154-1*, Trophy) HarpC Child Bks.
Laurita, Raymond E. Building Word Power Through Spelling Mastery: Questions & Answers about Words & Their Origins. 64p. (Orig.). (gr. 6-12). 1991. pap. text ed. 9.50 (*0-914051-25-3*) Leonardo Pr.
—The Spelling Doctor Says..., Pt. 1: (Roots 1-10) 87p. (Orig.). 1991. pap. text ed. 11.00 (*0-914051-20-2*) Leonardo Pr.
—Spelling Keys to One Thousand One Words from Ten Greek Based Roots. 80p. (Orig.). (gr. 8-12). 1991. pap. text ed. 11.50 (*0-914051-26-1*) Leonardo Pr.
—The Vowel Category Individual Spelling Set, Pt. 1. 112p. (Orig.). (gr. 1-6). 1980. Incl. vowel category resource lists (30 vowel groups), student lesson bks. of 30 vowel groups, 2 tchr's manuals. pap. 26.95 (*0-914051-08-3*) Leonardo Pr.
—The Vowel Category Individual Spelling Set, Pt. 2. 305p. (Orig.). (gr. 6 up). 1982. Incl. vowel category resource lists for 30 vowel groups, 2 student lesson bks. for the 30 vowel groups & 2 tchr's manuals. pap. 31.95 (*0-914051-09-1*) Leonardo Pr.
—The Vowel Category Resource Lists, Pt. II. 305p. (Orig.). (gr. 6 up). 1989. pap. 16.95 (*0-914051-06-7*); manual, incl. student test lesson, 43p. 7.95 ea. Stages 1-15 (*0-914051-07-5*) Stages 16-30 (*0-914051-17-2*) Leonardo Pr.
—The Vowel Category Resource Lists, Pt. 1. 112p. (Orig.). (ps-8). 1980. pap. 12.95 (*0-914051-04-0*); student test lesson with manual 7.95 ea. Stages 1-15 (*0-914051-05-9*) Stages 16-30 (*0-914051-14-8*) Leonardo Pr.
Lauritzen, Cyndi. Create & Write. 48p. (gr. 4-6). 1982. 5.95 (*0-88160-052-0*, LW 238) Learning Wks.
Laury, Jean R. No Dragons On My Quilt. (gr. k up). 1990. 12.95 (*0-89145-967-7*) Collector Bks.
Lautenschlaeger, Susan J. Olsav see Olsav Lautenschlaeger, Susan J.
Lauture, Denize. Father & Son. Green, Jonathan, illus. 32p. (ps-3). 1993. 14.95 (*0-399-21867-X*, Philomel Bks) Putnam Pub Group.
Laux, Dorothy. John: Beloved Apostle. McPheeters, William, illus. (gr. 1-6). 1977. bds. 5.95 (*0-8054-4234-0*, 4242-34) Broadman.
Lauzen, Elizabeth, ed. see Madison, Kathy.
LaValle, Maria T., tr. see Robertson, Jenny.
LaValle, Teresa, tr. see Ralph, Margaret.
Lavaroni, Charles. California: Roots. 144p. (gr. 4-6). 1984. pap. text ed. 11.45 (*0-911981-04-7*) Cloud Pub.
Lavash, Donald R. A Journey Through New Mexico History. rev. ed. Agogino, George A., frwd. by. LC 92-27191. 1993. 24.95 (*0-86534-194-X*) Sunstone Pr.
Lavelle, Sheila. The Disappearing Granny. Kopper, Lisa, illus. 42p. (gr. 2-4). 1989. 3.95 (*0-8120-6134-9*) Barron.
LaVelle, Steven. Just Passing Through. (Illus.). 32p. (Orig.). (gr. k-3). 1980. pap. 4.95 (*0-87516-402-1*) DeVorss.
Lavender, Cheryl. Moans, Groans & Skeleton Boans: Fun Songs & Activities for Kids. (Illus.). 32p. (Orig.). 1993. pap. text ed. 12.95 incl. CD (*0-7935-2371-0*, HL00330604*) H Leonard Pub Corp.
—Moans, Groans & Skeleton Bones 7SUBTITL<: Fun Songs & Activities for Kids. (Illus.). 32p. (Orig.). 1993. pap. text ed. 9.95 incl. cass. (*0-7935-2372-9*, HL00330605*) H Leonard Pub Corp.

Lavender, David. The Trail to Santa Fe. rev. ed.
Eggenhoffer, Nicholas, illus. LC 58-9634. 112p. (gr.
4-8). 1988. pap. 8.95 (0-939729-15-6) Trails West Pub.

Laverty, Bernard Mac see Mac Laverty, Bernard.

Lavery, Vincent J., ed. see Dewazien, Karl.

Lavetta, Gary. The Lily Trail. 144p. (gr. 7-12). 1990. pap.
4.95 (0-9618951-2-8) Memory Ln Bks.

Lavie, Arlette. The Dinosaur's Cold. (Illus.). 32p. (gr.
k-2). 1988. 15.95 (0-340-39946-5, Pub. by Hodder &
Stoughton UK) Trafalgar.

—Half a World Away. LC 90-49096. (ps-3). 1990. 7.95
(0-85953-335-2); pap. 3.95 (0-85953-334-4) Childs
Play.

—Tower. (ps-3). 1990. 11.95 (0-85953-392-1); pap. 5.95
(0-85953-393-X) Childs Play.

Lavies, Bianca. The Atlantic Salmon. Lavies, Bianca,
photos by. LC 91-27990. (Illus.). 32p. (gr. 2-5). 1992.
14.50 (0-525-44860-8, DCB) Dutton Child Bks.

—Backyard Hunter: The Praying Mantis. LC 89-37485.
(Illus.). 32p. (gr. 2-5). 1990. 13.95 (0-525-44547-1,
DCB) Dutton Child Bks.

—Compost Critters. Lavies, Bianca, illus. LC 92-35651.
32p. (gr. 2-6). 1993. 14.99 (0-525-44763-6, DCB)
Dutton Child Bks.

—A Gathering of Garter Snakes. Lavies, Bianca, photos
by. (Illus.). 32p. (gr. 3 up). 1993. reinforced bdg. 14.99
(0-525-45099-8, DCB) Dutton Child Bks.

—It's an Armadillo! LC 89-31821. (Illus.). 32p. (ps-2).
1989. 13.95 (0-525-44523-4, DCB) Dutton Child Bks.

—It's an Armadillo! (Illus.). 32p. (ps-2). 1994. pap. 4.99
(0-14-050312-9, Puffin Unicorn) Puffin Bks.

—Lily Pad Pond. Lavies, Bianca, photos by. LC 88-
31697. (Illus.). 32p. (ps-2). 1989. 14.00
(0-525-44483-1, DCB) Dutton Child Bks.

—Lily Pad Pond. (Illus.). 32p. (ps-2). 1993. pap. 4.99
(0-14-054836-X) Puffin Bks.

—Mangrove Wilderness: Nature's Nursery. Lavies,
Bianca, photos by. (Illus.). 32p. (gr. 4 up). 1994. 15.99
(0-525-45186-2, DCB) Dutton Child Bks.

—Monarch Butterflies, Mysterious Travelers. (Illus.). 32p.
(gr. 3-6). 1993. 14.99 (0-525-44905-1, DCB) Dutton
Child Bks.

—Secretive Timber Rattlesnake. LC 90-31964. (Illus.).
32p. (gr. 3-6). 1990. 13.95 (0-525-44572-2, DCB)
Dutton Child Bks.

—Tree Trunk Traffic. Lavies, Bianca, photos by. LC 88-
30001. (Illus.). 32p. (ps-2). 1989. 14.95
(0-525-44495-5, DCB) Dutton Child Bks.

—Tree Trunk Traffic. (Illus.). 32p. (ps-2). 1993. pap. 4.99
(0-14-054837-8) Puffin Bks.

—Wasps at Home. Lavies, Bianca, photos by. LC 90-
27338. (Illus.). 32p. (gr. 2-5). 1991. 13.95
(0-525-44704-0, DCB) Dutton Child Bks.

Lavin, Mary. The Story of the Widow's Son. (gr. 5 up).
1992. PLB 13.95 (0-88682-500-8) Creative Ed.

Lavitt, Edward & McDowell, Robert. In the Beginning
Creation Stories. new ed. 156p. (gr. 6-12). 1973. 18.95
(0-89388-096-5) Okpaku Communications.

Lavitt, Edward, jt. ed. see McDowell, Robert E.

LaVoie, Roland. Greenberg's Model Railroading with
Lionel Trains, Vol. I. 144p. (Orig.). (gr. 9-12). 1989.
pap. 19.95 (0-89778-054-X, 10-6745); pap. text ed. 28.
95 (0-685-67522-X, 10-6745LE) Greenberg Bks.

Lavrakas, Paul. The Princess & the Pea. (Orig.). 1993.
pap. 4.50 playscript (0-87602-321-9) Anchorage.

Lavranos, Destini & Ritchie, Sheri. The Magical Tree.
Elston, Dino, illus. 2p. (ps-k). 1993. 14.95
(0-9638393-0-6) Bedtime Bks.

Lavranos, Destini, jt. auth. see Ritchie, Sheri.

Law, Felicia. Doubleday Children's Picture Dictionary.
Holmes, Carol, illus. LC 86-16216. 192p. (gr. k-6).
1987. pap. 16.00 (0-385-23711-1) Doubleday.

Law, Katheryn. Salish Folk Tales. (gr. 2-8). 1972. 1.50
(0-89992-028-4) Coun India Ed.

Law, Kevin J. Canada. (Illus.). (gr. 5 up). 1988. 14.95
(0-222-00912-8) Chelsea Hse.

—Canada. 128p. (gr. 5 up). 1990. lib. bdg. 14.95
(0-7910-1101-1) Chelsea Hse.

—The Environmental Protection Agency. Schlesinger,
Arthur M., Jr., intro. by. (Illus.). 96p. (gr. 5 up). 1988.
lib. bdg. 14.95 (1-55546-105-0) Chelsea Hse.

—Millard Fillmore: Thirteenth President of the United
States. Young, Richard G., ed. LC 89-25651. (Illus.).
128p. (gr. 5-9). 1990. PLB 17.26 (0-944483-61-5)
Garrett Ed Corp.

Lawall, Gilbert. Carmina Catulli I-XI. (gr. 10-12). 1983.
pap. 5.95 (0-88334-166-2) Longman.

Lawhead, Stephen R. In the Hall of the Dragon King.
(gr. 7-12). 1990. pap. 9.95 (0-89107-563-1) Good
News.

—Riverbank Stories: The Tale of Jeremy Vole. 112p. (gr.
4). 1993. pap. 3.50 (0-380-72198-8, Camelot) Avon.

—Riverbank Stories: The Tale of Timothy Mallard. 112p.
(gr. 4). 1993. pap. 3.50 (0-380-72199-6, Camelot)
Avon.

—Sword & the Flame, Bk. 3. (gr. 7-12). 1990. pap. 9.99
(0-89107-565-8) Good News.

—The Tale of Anabelle Hedgehog. (Illus.). 128p. (gr.
4-8). 1990. 9.99 (0-7459-1924-3) Lion USA.

—The Tale of Anabelle Hedgehog. 112p. 1994. pap. 3.50
(0-380-72200-3, Camelot) Avon.

—Tale of Jeremy Vole. (Illus.). 128p. (ps-3). 1990. 9.99
(0-7459-1653-8) Lion USA.

—Tale of Timothy Mallard. (Illus.). 128p. (gr. 4-8). 1990.
9.99 (0-7459-1836-0) Lion USA.

—Warlords of Nin, Bk. 2. (Illus.). (gr. 7-12). 1990. 9.99
(0-89107-564-X) Good News.

Lawhead, Steve. Howard Had a Hot Air Balloon.
Lawhead, Steve, illus. 32p. (gr. k-3). 1988. 7.99
(0-7459-1268-0) Lion USA.

—Howard Had a Shrinking Machine. Lawhead, Steve,
illus. 32p. (gr. k-3). 1988. 7.99 (0-7459-1316-4) Lion
USA.

—Howard Had a Spaceship. (Illus.). 32p. (gr. k-3). 1986.
7.99 (0-7459-1101-3) Lion USA.

—Howard Had a Submarine. (Illus.). 32p. (gr. 1 up).
1987. pap. 7.99 (0-7459-1179-X) Lion USA.

**Lawick-Goodall, Hugo van see Goodall, Jane & Van
Lawick-Goodall, Hugo.**

Lawler, Howard E. Discover Deserts. (Illus.). 48p. (gr.
3-6). 1992. PLB 14.95 (1-56674-029-0, HTS Bks)
Forest Hse.

Lawler, Lillian B. Latin Club. 12th ed. 73p. (gr. 9-12).
3.55 (0-939507-08-0, B905) Amer Classical.

Lawler, Mary. Marcus Garvey. King, Coretta Scott,
intro. by. (Illus.). 112p. (Orig.). (gr. 5 up). 1988. 17.95
(1-55546-587-0); pap. 9.95 (0-7910-0203-9) Chelsea
Hse.

Lawler, T. Sewing & Knitting. (Illus.). 64p. (gr. 5 up).
1979. pap. 2.95 (0-86020-311-5, Usborne) EDC.

Lawless, Joann A. Mysteries of the Mind. LC 77-10726.
(Illus.). 48p. (gr. 4 up). 1983. PLB 18.64
(0-8172-1066-0) Raintree Steck-V.

—Strange Stories of Life. LC 77-10866. (Illus.). 48p. (gr.
4 up). 1983. PLB 18.64 (0-8172-1062-8) Raintree
Steck-V.

Lawless, Richard. The Middle East since 1945. (Illus.).
72p. (gr. 7-10). 1989. 19.95 (0-7134-5991-3, Pub. by
Batsford UK) Trafalgar.

Lawless, Richard & Bleaney, C. H. The First Day of the
Six Day War. (Illus.). 64p. (gr. 7-11). 1990. 19.95
(0-85219-820-5, Pub. by Batsford UK) Trafalgar.

Lawlor, Dorothy. Troubles & Other Poems. 1993. 8.95
(0-533-10522-6) Vantage.

Lawlor, Elizabeth P. Discover Nature at the Seashore:
Things to Know & Things to Do. Archer, Pat, illus.
LC 91-17260. 224p. 1992. pap. 12.95 (0-8117-3079-4)
Stackpole.

Lawlor, Laurie. Addie Across the Prairie. LC 85-15548.
(Illus.). 128p. (gr. 3-6). 1986. 11.95 (0-8075-0165-4) A
Whitman.

—Addie Across the Prairie. MacDonald, Patricia, ed.
Owens, Gail, illus. 128p. 1991. pap. 2.99
(0-671-70147-9, Minstrel Bks) PB.

—Addie Across the Prairie. (gr. 5). 1991. pap. write for
info. (0-663-56244-9) Silver Burdett Pr.

—Addie's Dakota Winter. Tucker, Kathy, ed. Gowing,
Toby, tr. LC 89-5564. (Illus.). 160p. (gr. 2-6). 1989.
PLB 11.95 (0-8075-0171-9) A Whitman.

—Addie's Dakota Winter. MacDonald, Patricia, ed.
Gowing, Toby, illus. 160p. 1991. pap. 2.99
(0-671-70148-7, Minstrel Bks) PB.

—Addie's Long Summer. Tucker, Kathleen, ed. Gowing,
Toby, illus. LC 91-34877. 176p. (gr. 3-6). 1992. PLB
11.95 (0-8075-0167-0) A Whitman.

—Daniel Boone. Tucker, Kathleen, ed. LC 87-27373.
(Illus.). 160p. (gr. 4-8). 1989. PLB 12.95
(0-8075-1462-4) A Whitman.

—George on His Own. Tucker, Kathleen, ed. Gowing,
Toby, illus. 144p. (gr. 3-7). 1993. 11.95g
(0-8075-2823-4) A Whitman.

—How To Survive Third Grade. Levine, Abby, ed. LC
87-25430. (Illus.). 72p. (gr. 2-5). 1988. PLB 9.95
(0-8075-3433-1) A Whitman.

—How to Survive Third Grade. Zarins, Joyce A., illus.
(gr. 2-4). 1991. pap. 2.99 (0-671-67713-6, Minstrel
Bks) PB.

—Second-Grade Dog. Levine, Abby, ed. Fiammenghi,
Gioia, illus. LC 84-22700. 40p. (gr. k-3). 1990. 13.95
(0-8075-7280-2) A Whitman.

Lawrence & Penny, ed. see Effinger, Marta.

Lawrence, Ann. Merlin the Wizard. Hunter, Susan, illus.
32p. (gr. 2-5). 1986. PLB 17.96 (0-8172-2628-1)
Raintree Steck-V.

Lawrence, Ann, tr. see Perrault, Charles.

Lawrence, D. H. Love among the Haystacks. (gr. 5-6).
Repr. lib. bdg. 17.95 (0-88411-676-X, Pub. by
Aeonian Pr) Amereon Ltd.

—The Prussian Officer. 64p. (gr. 6 up). 1982. PLB 13.
95s.p. (0-87191-892-7) Creative Ed.

—The Rocking Horse Winner. 40p. (gr. 6 up). 1982. PLB
13.95s.p. (0-87191-893-5) Creative Ed.

—You Touched Me. 48p. (gr. 6 up). 1982. PLB 13.95s.p.
(0-87191-894-3) Creative Ed.

Lawrence, David. Ex-Mutants Graphic Novel: The Saga
Begins, Vol. 1. Lim, Ron, illus. 88p. 1988. pap. 6.95
(0-944735-03-7) Malibu Graphics.

—Ex-Mutants Graphic Novel, Vol. 2: Gods or Men. Lim,
Ron, illus. 100p. 1988. pap. 7.95 (0-944735-05-3)
Malibu Graphics.

Lawrence, Edgar D. Sign Language Made Simple.
Johnson, Mike, illus. LC 79-10417. 240p. (gr. k up).
1975. text ed. 13.95 (0-88243-604-X, 02-0604); Video
tape. 49.95 (0-685-57733-3); Set, incl. video tape. 58.
90 (0-685-57734-1) Gospel Pub.

Lawrence, Edith. The Wayfaring Princes: A Tale of
Questing & Adventure. Keltz, Martha, illus. 136p.
(Orig.). (gr. 4-7). 1987. pap. 8.00 (0-936132-86-8)
Merc Pr NY.

Lawrence, Elizabeth H. Miss Muffin. 1993. 7.95
(0-8062-4616-2) Carlton.

Lawrence, George, jt. auth. see Brown, Vinson.

Lawrence, Greg, jt. auth. see Kirkland, Gelsey.

Lawrence, H. S. Addition & Subtraction: No Regrouping.
Kifer, Kathy & Solar, Dahna, illus. (ENG & SPA).
30p. (Orig.). (gr. 1-6). 1992. pap. 3.95 wkbk.
(0-931993-51-2, GP-051) Garlic Pr OR.

—Addition: No Regrouping. Kifer, Kathy & Solar,
Dahna, illus. (ENG & SPA). 30p. (Orig.). (gr. 1-6).
1992. pap. 3.95 wkbk. (0-931993-49-0, GP-049) Garlic
Pr OR.

—Multiplication: Factors 1-12. Kifer, Kathy & Solar,
Dahna, illus. (ENG & SPA). 30p. (Orig.). (gr. 3-6).
1992. pap. 3.95 wkbk. (0-931993-52-0, GP-052) Garlic
Pr OR.

—Subtraction: No Regrouping. Kifer, Kathy & Solar,
Dahna, illus. (ENG & SPA). 30p. (Orig.). (gr. 1-6).
1992. pap. 3.95 wkbk. (0-931993-50-4, GP-050) Garlic
Pr OR.

Lawrence, Jacob. The Great Migration: An American
Story. LC 93-16788. (Illus.). 48p. (gr. 3-7). 1993. 22.
50 (0-06-023037-1); PLB 22.89 (0-06-023038-X); ltd.
ed. 125.00 (0-06-023453-9) HarpC Child Bks.

—The Great Migration: An American Story. (Illus.). 48p.
(gr. 3-7). 1993. 22.00 (0-943044-20-0); pap. write for
info. (0-943044-21-9) Phillips Coll.

—Harriet & the Promised Land. LC 92-33740. 1993. pap.
15.00 (0-671-86673-7, S&S BFYR) S&S Trade.

Lawrence, James. Binky Brothers, Detectives. Kessler,
Leonard, illus. LC 68-10374. (gr. k-3). 1978. pap. 3.50
(0-06-444003-6, Trophy) HarpC Child Bks.

—Binky Brothers, Detectives. Kessler, Leonard, illus. LC
68-10374. 64p. (ps-3). 1985. incl. cassette 5.98
(0-694-00018-3, Trophy) HarpC Child Bks.

Lawrence, Jerome & Lee, Robert E. The Night Thoreau
Spent in Jail. 128p. (gr. 8-12). 1983. pap. 4.50
(0-553-27838-X) Bantam.

Lawrence, John. Good Babies, Bad Babies: A Primer for
Expectant Parents. (ps). 1990. 10.95 (0-87923-823-2)
Godine.

Lawrence, Louise. Andra. LC 90-38595. 240p. (gr. 7 up).
1991. 14.95 (0-06-023685-X); PLB 14.89
(0-06-023705-8) HarpC Child Bks.

—Calling B for Butterfly. LC 81-48648. 224p. (gr. 7 up).
1988. pap. 3.95 (0-06-447036-9, Trophy) HarpC Child
Bks.

—Extinction Is Forever & Other Stories. LC 92-35464.
1993. 15.00 (0-06-022913-6, HarpT); PLB 14.89
(0-06-022914-4, HarpT) HarpC.

—Keeper of the Universe. LC 92-2452. 240p. (gr. 7 up).
1993. 13.95 (0-395-64340-6, Clarion Bks) HM.

—Moonwind. LC 85-45507. 192p. (gr. 7 up). 1987. pap.
2.95 (0-06-447037-7, Trophy) HarpC Child Bks.

—The Warriors of Taan. LC 87-45291. 224p. (gr. 7 up).
1988. HarpC Child Bks.

Lawrence, Marcia. How to Take the SAT. 336p. (gr. 9-
12). 1979. pap. 10.00 (0-452-26296-8, Plume) NAL-
Dutton.

Lawrence, R. D. Wolves. (gr. 3-6). 1990. 15.95
(0-316-51676-7) Little.

Lawrence, Rick. Evil & the Occult. 48p. (Orig.). (gr. 6-8).
1990. pap. 7.99 (1-55945-102-5) Group Pub.

Lawrence, V. J. Nine Plays for African American Youth:
Children's Window to Africa. 45p. (gr. 1-12). 1993.
pap. 8.95 (0-929917-06-5) Magnolia PA.

Lawrence, Valerie. What's Yr Hair Like after U Wash It?
Natural Poems by Valerie Lawrence. LC 90-6188.
100p. (gr. 6 up). 1990. 10.95 (0-929917-01-4)
Magnolia PA.

Lawson, A. Star Baby. Apple, M., illus. 1992. 15.95
(0-15-200905-1, HB Juv Bks) HarBrace.

Lawson, Amy. The Talking Bird & the Story Pouch.
Brown, Craig M., illus. LC 86-45493. 96p. (gr. 5up).
1987. HarpC Child Bks.

Lawson, Don. The Abraham Lincoln Brigade: Americans
Fighting Fascism in the Spanish Civil War. LC 88-
20263. (Illus.). 176p. (gr. 7 up). 1989. (Crowell Jr
Bks); PLB 11.89 (0-690-04699-5, Crowell Jr Bks)
HarpC Child Bks.

—America Held Hostage: From the Teheran Embassy
Takeover to the Iran-Contra Affair. (Illus.). 144p. (gr.
9-12). 1991. PLB 12.90 (0-531-11009-5) Watts.

—The Eagle & the Dragon: The History of U. S.-China
Relations. LC 85-47531. (Illus.). 192p. (gr. 7 up).
1985. (Crowell Jr Bks); (Crowell Jr Bks) HarpC Child
Bks.

—Landmark Supreme Court Cases. LC 86-19735. (Illus.).
128p. (gr. 6 up). 1987. lib. bdg. 17.95 (0-89490-132-X)
Enslow Pubs.

—The United States in the Vietnam War. LC 80-2460.
(Illus.). 160p. (gr. 7 up). 1981. (Crowell Jr Bks); PLB
12.89 (0-690-04105-5) HarpC Child Bks.

Lawson, Don & Barish, Wendy. The French Resistance.
192p. (gr. 3-7). 1984. PLB 8.79 (0-685-07808-6) S&S
Trade.

Lawson, Jack. Andro, This Is Crazy. 96p. (Orig.). 1991.
pap. 2.95 (0-380-76234-X, Camelot) Avon.

Lawson, James R., ed. The Pool Player's National Pocket
Billiards Directory. 1991. pap. 19.95 (0-945071-50-7)
Lawco.

Lawson, Jim, jt. auth. see Clarrain, Dean.

Lawson, John. If Pigs Could Fly. 144p. (gr. 5-9). 1989.
13.45 (0-395-50928-9) HM.

Lawson, Julie. The Dragon's Pearl. Morin, Paul, illus.
32p. (gr. k-3). 1993. 15.45 (0-395-63623-X, Clarion
Bks) HM.

Lawson, Michael & Skipp, David. Sexo y Mas: Guia Para
la Juventud. (SPA., Illus.). 110p. (Orig.). (gr. 10-12).
1988. pap. 2.95 (0-945792-02-6) Editorial Unilit.

Lawson, Polly, tr. see Berger, Thomas.

Lawson, Polly, tr. see Leeuwen, M. & Moeskops, J.

Lawson, Polly, tr. see **Lesch, Christiane.**
Lawson, Robert. Ben & Me. (gr. 3-6). 1973. pap. 2.75 (0-440-42038-5, YB) Dell.
—Ben & Me. Lawson, Robert, illus. 1939p. (gr. 7-10). 1988. 15.95 (0-316-51732-1); pap. 5.95 (0-316-51730-5) Little.
—Captain Kidd's Cat. (Illus.). (gr. 2-4). 1984. pap. 7.95 (0-316-51735-6) Little.
—The Fabulous Flight. (Illus.). 152p. (gr. 4-8). 1984. pap. 5.95 (0-316-51731-3) Little.
—The Great Wheel. Lawson, Robert, illus. 180p. 1993. pap. 7.95 (0-8027-7392-3) Walker & Co.
—I Discover Columbus. (Illus.). (gr. 3-6). 1991. pap. 4.95 (0-316-51760-7) Little.
—Mr. Revere & I. (gr. 3-6). 1973. pap. 2.95 (0-440-45897-8, YB) Dell.
—Mr. Revere & I. Lawson, Robert, illus. (gr. 7-10). 1953. 16.95 (0-316-51739-9) Little.
—Mr. Revere & I. Lawson, Robert, illus. 152p. (gr. 3-6). 1988. pap. 5.95 (0-316-51729-1) Little.
—Rabbit Hill. (Illus.). (gr. 1-3). 1977. pap. 3.99 (0-14-031010-X, Puffin) Puffin Bks.
—Rabbit Hill. Lawson, Robert, illus. (gr. 4-6). 1944. pap. 14.00 (0-670-58675-7) Viking Child Bks.
—Robbut: A Tale of Tails. Lawson, Robert, illus. LC 89-32367. 94p. (gr. 2-6). 1989. Repr. of 1948 ed. lib. bdg. 16.00 (0-208-02236-8, Linnet) Shoe String.
—They Were Strong & Good. Lawson, Robert, illus. (gr. 4-6). 1940. pap. 14.00 (0-670-69949-7) Viking Child Bks.
—The Tough Winter. Lawson, Robert, illus. (gr. 3-7). 1979. pap. 3.95 (0-14-031215-3, Puffin) Puffin Bks.
—The Tough Winter. (gr. 2-6). 1992. 16.75 (0-8446-6565-7) Peter Smith.
Lawton, Florrie A. God Loves Me. LC 85-24342. (Illus.). (ps). 1986. 4.95 (0-8054-4163-8) Broadman.
Lawton, Helen. Moggy the Mouser. McAllan, Marina, illus. LC 93-6571. 1994. write for info. (0-383-03702-6) SRA Schl Grp.
Lay, Artie K. & Runnels, Gayle S. Amigo, the Friendly Gray Whale. LC 91-65227. (Illus.). 140p. (gr. 2-6). 1991. incl. audiocassette 24.95 (0-9628626-0-6) Blubber Budd.
Laycock, Mary. Base Ten Mathematics. Jung, Tom, photos by. Moray, Joe, intro. by. (gr. 1-9). 1976. pap. 7.95 (0-918932-03-3) Activity Resources.
—Bucky for Beginners. Kyzer, Martha, illus. 64p. (Orig.). (gr. 4-12). 1984. pap. text ed. 7.95 (0-918932-82-3) Activity Resources.
Laycock, Mary & Dominques, Manuel. Discover It! 32p. (Orig.). (gr. 5-10). 1986. pap. 7.50 (0-918932-87-4) Activity Resources.
Laycock, Mary & Schadler, Reuben. Algebra in Concrete. (gr. 6-10). 1973. pap. 7.95 (0-918932-00-9) Activity Resources.
Laycock, Mary & Smart, Margaret. Solid Sense of Mathematics, 3 vols. (Illus.). 64p. (Orig.). (gr. 4-9). 1981. pap. text ed. 7.95 (0-918932-74-2) Activity Resources.
Laycock, Mary, jt. auth. see **Smart, Margaret A.**
Laycock, Mary, ed. see **Brandes, Louis G.**
Laycock, Mary, ed. see **Bureloff, Morris, et al.**
Laycock, Mary, ed. see **Bureloff, Morris.**
Laycock, Mary, ed. see **Jenkins, Lee.**
Laycock, Mary, ed. see **Jenkins, Lee & McLean, Peggy.**
Laycock, Mary, ed. see **Lund, Charles.**
Laycock, Mary, ed. see **Smart, Margaret.**
Laycock, Mary, ed. see **Stonerod, David.**
Laycock, Mary, et al. Geoblocks & Geojackets: Metric Version. rev., 2nd ed. Laycock, Mary, et al, illus. 96p. (Orig.). (gr. 3-10). 1988. pap. 8.95 (0-918932-91-2) Activity Resources.
—Skateboard Practice: Addition & Subtraction. new ed. Kyzer, Martha, illus. (gr. 1-2). 1978. pap. text ed. 7.95 (0-918932-55-6) Activity Resources.
Layfield, Eleanor N., jt. auth. see **Newman, Gerald.**
Layton, Barry, ed. see **Hurnard, Hannah.**
Layton, Dian, ed. see **Hurnard, Hannah.**
Layton, Karen & Layton, Ron. Bible Word Fun. Hyndman, Kathryn, illus. 48p. (gr. 3 up). 1986. wkbk. 6.95 (0-86653-367-2, SS 882, Shining Star Pubns) Good Apple.
—Bible Word Play. (Illus.). 48p. (gr. 3 up). 1989. 6.95 (0-86653-472-5, SS888, Shining Star Pubns) Good Apple.
Layton, Lesley. Singapore. LC 89-25465. (Illus.). 128p. (gr. 5-9). 1991. PLB 21.95 (1-85435-295-4) Marshall Cavendish.
Layton, Ron, jt. auth. see **Layton, Karen.**
Lazarus, Alan, jt. auth. see **Funes, Marilyn.**
Lazenby, Roland. Georgetown, the Championships & Thompson. Blatty, William P., intro. by. (Illus.). 128p. (gr. 4-12). 1985. 19.95 (0-913767-08-5) Full Court VA.
Lazewnik, Libby. Baker's Dozen, No. 1: On Our Own. 1993. pap. 7.95 (0-685-65302-1) Feldheim.
—Baker's Dozen, No. 5: The Inside Story. 1993. pap. 7.95 (0-685-65306-4) Feldheim.
—Baker's Dozen: The Inside Story, No. 5. 1992. pap. 7.95 (0-944070-93-0) Targum Pr.
—Shira's New Start. (gr. 6-9). 1988. 12.95 (0-87306-471-2); pap. 9.95 (0-685-21963-1) Feldheim.
—Shira's Summer. (gr. 6-9). 1988. 12.95 (0-87306-467-4); pap. 9.95 (0-87306-468-2) Feldheim.
Lazewnik, Libby, et al. Baker's Dozen, No. 6: Trapped. 1993. pap. 7.95 (0-685-65307-2) Feldheim.

Lazicki, Ted. Where Does God Live? Fifty Eight More "Something for the Kids" Children's Sermons for Worship. Zapel, Arthur L. & Wray, Rhonda, eds. Gallardo, Michelle Z., illus. LC 91-8734. 144p. (Orig.). (ps-5). 1991. pap. 8.95 (0-916260-77-1, B189) Meriwether Pub.
Lazier, Christine. Seashore Life. Bogard, Vicki, tr. from FRE. Underhill, Graham, illus. LC 90-50781. 38p. (gr. k-5). 1991. 4.95 (0-944589-39-1, 391) Young Discovery Lib.
Lazo, Caroline. Eleanor Roosevelt. LC 93-6610. (Illus.). 64p. (gr. 4 up). 1993. RSBE 13.95 (0-87518-594-0, Dillon) Macmillan Child Grp.
—Mahatma Gandhi. LC 92-14314. (Illus.). 64p. (gr. 4 up). 1993. RSBE 13.95 (0-87518-526-6, Dillon) Macmillan Child Grp.
—Martin Luther King, Jr. LC 93-9069. (Illus.). 64p. (gr. 4). 1994. RSBE 13.95 (0-87518-618-1, Dillon) Macmillan Child Grp.
—Mother Teresa. LC 92-23765. (Illus.). 64p. (gr. 4 up). 1993. RSBE 13.95 (0-87518-559-2, Dillon) Macmillan Child Grp.
—Rigoberta Menchu. LC 93-8381. (Illus.). 64p. (gr. 4). 1994. RSBE 13.95 (0-87518-619-X, Dillon) Macmillan Child Grp.
—The Terra Cotta Army of Emperor Qin. LC 92-26189. (Illus.). 80p. (gr. 6 up). 1993. RSBE 14.95 (0-02-754631-4, New Discovery) Macmillan Child Grp.
Lazo, Caroline E. Divorce. LC 89-2156. (Illus.). 48p. (gr. 4 up). 1989. RSBE 12.95 (0-89686-436-7, Crestwood Hse) Macmillan Child Grp.
—Endangered Species. LC 90-35494. (Illus.). 48p. (gr. 5-6). 1990. RSBE 12.95 (0-89686-545-2, Crestwood Hse) Macmillan Child Grp.
—Lech Walesa. LC 92-39959. (Illus.). 64p. (gr. 4 up). 1993. RSBE 13.95 (0-87518-525-8, Dillon) Macmillan Child Grp.
—Missing Treasure. (Illus.). 48p. (gr. 5 up). 1990. RSBE 11.95 (0-89686-510-X, Crestwood Hse) Macmillan Child Grp.
Lazor-Bahr, Beverly, illus. Fievel Saves the Day. LC 90-85174. 14p. (ps). 1991. 5.95 (0-448-41075-3, G&D) Putnam Pub Group.
—Fievel the Hero. LC 90-85299. 14p. (ps). 1991. 4.95 (0-448-41080-X, G&D) Putnam Pub Group.
—Westward, Ho! LC 90-85298. 14p. (ps). 1991. 4.95 (0-448-41081-8, G&D) Putnam Pub Group.
Lazorthes, Jean, tr. see **Yvart, Jacques.**
Lea, Thomas D. & Latham, Bill. Sigueme 3. Martinez, Mario, tr. from ENG. (SPA.). 128p. (Orig.). (gr. 5 up). 1989. pap. 3.75 (0-311-13847-0) Casa Bautista.
Leach, Bernard. Potter's Book. 1946. pap. 14.00 (0-693-01157-2) Transatl Arts.
Leach, Douglas E. Flintlock & Tomahawk: New England in King Philip's War. Morison, Samuel E., intro. by. LC 58-5467. 320p. 1992. pap. 12.50t (0-940160-55-2) Parnassus Imprints.
Leach, Maria. The Thing at the Foot of the Bed. 112p. (gr. 4-5). 1981. pap. 3.25 (0-440-48773-0, YB) Dell.
—Thing at the Foot of the Bed. Werth, Kurt, illus. LC 59-6658. 128p. (gr. 3-5). 1987. PLB 12.95 (0-399-21496-8, Philomel) Putnam Pub Group.
—Whistle in the Graveyard: Folktales to Chill Your Bones. Rinciari, Ken, illus. (gr. 3-7). 1982. pap. 4.95 (0-14-031529-2, Puffin) Puffin Bks.
Leach, Norman. My Wicked Stepmother. Browne, Jane, illus. LC 92-19674. 32p. (ps-3). 1993. SBE 13.95 (0-02-754700-0, Macmillan Child Bk) Macmillan Child Grp.
Leach, Rosemary, read by see **Potter, Beatrix.**
Leach, William. Edith Wharton. Horner, Matina, intro. by. (Illus.). 112p. (gr. 5 up). 1987. lib. bdg. 17.95 (1-55546-682-6) Chelsea Hse.
Leach, William R., ed. see **Baum, L. Frank.**
Leachman, Clara G. A Boy Learns to Write: Beginning Writing (Boy's Version) Winn, Leslie, illus. 28p. (gr. k-1). 1990. pap. text ed. write for info. (0-9618517-2-4) C Leachman.
—A Girl Learns to Write: Beginning Writing (Girl's Version) Winn, Leslie, illus. 28p. (gr. k-1). 1990. pap. text ed. write for info. (0-9618517-1-6) C Leachman.
—Julie Learns to Write. Winn, Leslie, illus. 22p. (gr. k-1). 1987. pap. 5.50 (0-9618517-0-8) C Leachman.
Leader, R. L. Faithful Soldiers. (gr. 7 up). 1989. 12.95 (0-944070-12-4) Targum Pr.
Leadley, Robert, jt. auth. see **Johns, Helen.**
Leaf, Hayim, jt. auth. see **Ben-Asher, Naomi.**
Leaf, Margaret. Eyes of the Dragon. Young, Ed, illus. LC 85-11670. 32p. (ps-2). 1987. 14.95 (0-688-06155-9); PLB 14.88 (0-688-06156-7) Lothrop.
Leaf, Munro. El Cuento de Ferdinando. Belpre, Pura, tr. Lawson, Robert, illus. (SPA.). 72p. (ps-3). 1962. pap. 13.00 (0-670-25065-1) Viking Child Bks.
—El Cuento de Ferdinando: The Story of Ferdinand. Lawson, Robert, illus. Belpre, Pura, tr. (SPA., Illus.). 72p. (ps-3). 1990. pap. 4.50 (0-14-054253-1, Puffin) Puffin Bks.
—El Cuento de Ferdinando: (The Story of Ferdinand) Belpre, Pura, tr. Lawson, Robert, illus. (SPA.). (gr. k-3). 1990. Set; incl. 4 bks., guide, & cass. incl. cass. 19.95 (0-87499-189-7); pap. 12.95 incl. cass. (0-87499-188-9); pap. 27.95 (0-87499-191-9) Live Oak Media.
—Four-&-Twenty Watchbirds. LC 89-49742. (Illus.). 32p. (ps-3). 1990. lib. bdg. 15.00 (0-208-02208-2, Pub. by Linnet) Shoe String.

—Gordon the Goat. LC 87-26106. (Illus.). 48p. (ps-3). 1988. Repr. of 1944 ed. 14.50 (0-208-02196-5, Linnet) Shoe String.
—Manners Can Be Fun. 2nd, rev. ed. Leaf, Munro, illus. LC 84-48459. 48p. (gr. k-3). 1985. pap. 4.95 (0-06-443053-7, Trophy) HarpC Child Bks.
—Robert Francis Weatherbee. LC 87-26046. (Illus.). 75p. (ps-3). 1988. Repr. of 1935 ed. PLB 14.50 (0-208-02211-2, Linnet) Shoe String.
—The Story of Ferdinand. Lawson, Robert, illus. LC 36-19452. (gr. k-3). 1936. pap. 13.00 (0-670-67424-9) Viking Child Bks.
—The Story of Ferdinand. Lawson, Robert, illus. (ps-3). 1988. pap. 9.95 (0-14-095075-3, Puffin); bk. & t-shirt 9.95 (0-318-37105-7, Puffin); bk. & cassette 6.95 (0-318-37106-5, Puffin) Puffin Bks.
—The Story of Ferdinand. Lawson, Robert, illus. 1993. pap. 6.99 incl. cassette (0-14-095115-6, Puffin) Puffin Bks.
—The Story of Simpson & Sampson. Lawson, Robert, illus. LC 88-39014. 64p. (gr. 1-3). 1989. Repr. of 1941 ed. lib. bdg. 16.50 (0-208-02244-9, Pub. by Linnet) Shoe String.
Leagjeld, Ted. Voyageur the Moose. Tepley, Marilyn M., illus. (Orig.). (gr. 4-8). Date not set. pap. write for info. (0-9616127-0-3) T Leagjeld.
League of Women Voters of Cleveland Educational Fund, Inc. Staff. From Ordinance to Constitution: Government of & by the People. 73p. (gr. 9-12). 1987. pap. text ed. 10.00 (1-880746-05-0) LOWV Cleve Educ.
—New Voter's Guide to Practical Politics. 61p. (gr. 7-12). 1982. pap. 2.00 (1-880746-02-6) LOWV Cleve Educ.
—Ohio: From Territory to Statehood - From Ordinance to Constitution. 99p. (gr. 7-8). 1987. pap. text ed. 10.00 (1-880746-04-2) LOWV Cleve Educ.
—Ohio: From Wilderness to Territory - The Law of the Land. (gr. 3-6). 1987. pap. text ed. 10.00 (1-880746-03-4) LOWV Cleve Educ.
League of Women Voters Staff. The State We're In: Washington: A Citizen's Guide to Washington State Government. 3rd ed. Bakke, Jean, ed. Haas, Wanda, intro. by. (Illus.). (gr. 9-12). 1990. pap. 6.95 (1-878170-00-7); pap. text ed. 5.50 (0-685-47519-0) LWV WA.
Leah, Devora. Lost Erev Shabbos in the Zoo. rev. ed. Forst, Siegmund, illus. 30p. (gr. k-3). 1986. 8.95 (0-685-18123-5); pap. 6.95 (0-685-18124-3) Judaica Pr.

Leah Komaiko & Kids. A Million Moms & Mine. (Illus.). 28p. 1992. 11.95 (0-9634893-0-5); pap. 5.95 (0-9634893-1-3) L Claiborne.
"Mommy, could you...um...take a few years off work?" The question is a familiar one to moms who work outside the home. It is also one of the aspects of having a working mom that 20 children examine in this rhyming tale. The children's words & heartfelt drawings do not dismiss real concerns, such as needing more time with parents, but also reflect pride in their moms. Published as part of Liz Claiborne's Women's Work, a series of community-based art projects designed to raise awareness & encourage positive social change on issues important to women. Proceeds from sales are donated to Reading is Fundamental. "The sweet genius of Leah Komaiko's A MILLION MOMS & MINE is in the knowledge that all mothers are working mothers, & all working mothers are precious." -- Maya Angelou. "A MILLION MOMS & MINE does one of the most important things a book can do, it opens dialogue between children & their parents." --Joan Lunden. Should be read with parent. Hardcover, $11.95. Paperback, $5.95. Shipping $1.05 per book. NY/NJ add sales tax. Send check or money order to Liz Claiborne Women's Work, PO Box 726, Dept. C, Radio City Station, New York, NY 10101. Quantity orders, Call 212-505-9332.
Publisher Provided Annotation.

Leahy, Barbara H. Marijuana: A Dangerous "High" Way. rev. ed. Farrell, Lee & Jensen, Rosemary D., eds. Moles, Danna, illus. LC 82-62440. 173p. (Orig.). (gr. 4-9). 1983. pap. 6.95 (0-9610312-1-2) B Leahy.

Leahy, Philippa. Spain. LC 93-2663. (Illus.). 32p. (gr. 4 up). 1993. RSBE 13.95 (0-89686-772-2, Crestwood Hse) Macmillan Child Grp.

Leale, Judy. Three-Minute Bible Stories. Beckett, Sheilah, illus. 32p. 1992. 9.95 (1-56156-152-5) Kidsbks.
—Three-Minute Bible Stories. Beckett, Sheila, illus. 24p. (ps-k). 1993. 5.98 (0-8317-8298-6) Smithmark.

Leaman, Christine, ed. see Yates, Elizabeth.

Leamy, Edmund. Fairy Minstrel of Glenmalure & Other Stories for Children. Casseau, Vera, illus. LC 76-9901. (gr. 4-6). 1976. Repr. of 1913 ed. 15.00x (0-8486-0210-2) Roth Pub Inc.
—Golden Spears & Other Fairy Tales. Turner, Corinne, illus. LC 76-9902. (gr. 4-6). 1976. Repr. of 1928 ed. 15.00x (0-8486-0211-0) Roth Pub Inc.
—Irish Fairy Stories for Children. (Illus.). 86p. (gr. 2 up). 1992. resp. 9.95 (1-85635-008-8, Pub. by Mercier Pr Eire) Dufour.

Leanza, Frank. How to Get Started with the Baritone Horn. (Illus.). 32p. 1993. pap. 3.95 (0-934687-15-3) Crystal Pubs.
—How to Get Started with the Bassoon. (Illus.). 24p. 1993. pap. 3.95 (0-934687-10-2) Crystal Pubs.
—How to Get Started with the Cello. (Illus.). 24p. 1993. pap. 3.95 (0-934687-21-8) Crystal Pubs.
—How to Get Started with the Clarinet. (Illus.). 24p. 1993. pap. 3.95 (0-934687-09-9) Crystal Pubs.
—How to Get Started with the Drums. (Illus.). 28p. 1993. pap. 3.95 (0-934687-18-8) Crystal Pubs.
—How to Get Started with the Flute. (Illus.). 24p. 1993. pap. 3.95 (0-934687-07-2) Crystal Pubs.
—How to Get Started with the French Horn. (Illus.). 36p. 1993. pap. 3.95 (0-934687-14-5) Crystal Pubs.
—How to Get Started with the Guitar. (Illus.). 34p. 1993. pap. 3.95 (0-934687-17-X) Crystal Pubs.
—How to Get Started with the Oboe. (Illus.). 1993. pap. 3.95 (0-934687-08-0) Crystal Pubs.
—How to Get Started with the Piano. (Illus.). 24p. 1993. pap. 3.95 (0-934687-23-4) Crystal Pubs.
—How to Get Started with the Saxophone. (Illus.). 24p. 1993. pap. 3.95 (0-934687-11-0) Crystal Pubs.
—How to Get Started with the String Bass. (Illus.). 24p. 1993. pap. 3.95 (0-934687-16-1) Crystal Pubs.
—How to Get Started with the Trombone. (Illus.). 28p. 1993. pap. 3.95 (0-934687-13-7) Crystal Pubs.
—How to Get Started with the Trumpet. (Illus.). 32p. 1993. pap. 3.95 (0-934687-12-9) Crystal Pubs.
—How to Get Started with the Tuba. (Illus.). 28p. 1993. pap. 3.95 (0-934687-16-1) Crystal Pubs.
—How to Get Started with the Viola. (Illus.). 24p. 1993. pap. 3.95 (0-934687-20-X) Crystal Pubs.
—How to Get Started with the Violin. (Illus.). 24p. 1993. pap. 3.95 (0-934687-19-6) Crystal Pubs.
—Music Book for Kids of Any Age, Bk. 1. rev. ed. (Illus.). 32p. (gr. 1-4). 1988. pap. 3.45 (0-934687-02-1) Crystal Pubs.
—Music Book for Kids of Any Age, Vol. 2. rev. ed. (Illus.). 60p. (gr. 1-4). 1988. pap. 3.45 (0-934687-03-X) Crystal Pubs.

Lear, Edward. A Was Once an Apple Pie. Lacome, Julie & Lacome, Julie, illus. LC 91-71865. 32p. (ps). 1992. 13.95 (1-56402-000-2) Candlewick Pr.
—A Book of Nonsense. Lear, Edward, illus. LC 92-53176. 240p. 1992. 12.95 (0-679-41798-2, Evrymans Lib Childs Class) Knopf.
—The Complete Nonsense of Edward Lear. Lear, Edward, illus. Jackson, H., intro. by. (Illus.). xxix, 287p. (gr. 4-6). pap. 5.95 (0-486-20167-8) Dover.
—Daffy Down Dillies: Silly Limericks. O'Brien, John, illus. LC 91-72986. 32p. 1992. 14.95 (1-56397-007-4) Boyds Mills Pr.
—An Edward Lear Alphabet. Newsom, Carol, illus. LC 82-10037. 32p. (gr. k-3). 1983. PLB 11.88 (0-688-00965-4) Lothrop.
—An Edward Lear Alphabet. Newsom, Carol, illus. LC 82-10037. (ps-3). 1986. 4.95 (0-688-06523-6, Mulberry) Morrow.
—How Pleasant to Know Mr. Lear! LC 82-80822. (Illus.). 136p. (gr. 4-6). 1982. 14.95 (0-8234-0462-5) Holiday.
—How Pleasant to Know Mr. Lear. Butenko, Bohdan, illus. 64p. (gr. k-4). Date not set. 14.95 (0-88045-126-2) Stemmer Hse. Postponed.
—Lear's Nonsense ABCs. LC 90-53464. (Illus.). 120p. (ps-8). 1991. 4.95 (0-89471-985-8) Running Pr.
—Nonsense Poems of Edward Lear. Brooke, Leonard L., illus. 128p. 1991. 18.45 (0-395-57001-8, Clarion Bks) HM.
—The Owl & the Pussy-Cat. Voce, Louise, illus. LC 90-39673. 32p. (ps up). 1991. 13.95 (0-688-09536-4); PLB 13.88 (0-688-09537-2) Lothrop.
—The Owl & the Pussy Cat. Todd, Justin, illus. 32p. 1992. 15.95 (0-575-04709-7, Pub. by Gollancz UK) Trafalgar.
—The Owl & the Pussycat. rev. ed. Stevens, Janet, illus. LC 82-12092. 32p. (ps-3). 1983. reinforced bdg. 14.95 (0-8234-0474-9) Holiday.
—The Owl & the Pussycat. Littlejohn, Clare, illus. LC 86-46115. 14p. (ps-3). 1987. 6.95 (0-694-00193-7) HarpC Child Bks.
—The Owl & the Pussycat. (ps-1). 1989. 13.95 (0-89919-505-9, Clarion Bks); pap. 4.95 (0-89919-854-6, Clarion Bks) HM.
—Owl & the Pussycat. (ps-3). 1991. 3.95 (0-8037-1044-5) Dial Bks Young.
—The Owl & the Pussycat. Falconer, Elizabeth, illus. 16p. (ps-3). 1993. pop-up bk. 12.95 (0-8249-8571-0, Ideals Child) Hambleton-Hill.
—The Quangle Wangle's Hat. Stevens, Janet, illus. 32p. (ps-3). 1988. 12.95 (0-15-264450-4) HarBrace.
—The Table & the Chair. Powers, Tom, illus. LC 91-45538. 32p. (ps-3). 1993. 15.00 (0-06-020804-X); PLB 14.89 (0-06-020805-8) HarpC Child Bks.

Lear, Edward & Allen, Jonathan. Nonsense Songs. (Illus.). 176p. (gr. 4-8). 1993. PLB 14.95 (0-8050-2774-2, Bks Young Read) H Holt & Co.

Lear, Edward & Carroll, Lewis. Owls & Pussycats: Nonsense Verse. Palin, Nicki, illus. LC 93-2714. 64p. (gr. 3 up). 1993. 16.95 (0-87226-366-5) P Bedrick Bks.

Lear, Edward & De Paola, Tomie. Bonjour, Mister Satie. (Illus.). (ps-3). 1991. 15.95 (0-399-21782-7, Putnam) Putnam Pub Group.

Lear, Edward & Nash, Ogden. Scroobious Pip. Burkert, Nancy E., illus. LC 68-10373. (gr. 3 up). 1968. HarpC Child Bks.

Lear, Edward, jt. auth. see Brett, Jan.

Lear, Peter. Computer Play. Migliore, Ron, illus. 48p. (gr. 1-5). 1985. pap. 4.95 (0-88625-087-0) Durkin Hayes Pub.
—Computers. (Illus.). 32p. (gr. 1-5). 1985. pap. 4.95 (0-88625-083-8) Durkin Hayes Pub.

Learner, Vickie M., illus. Willoughby Wallaby. 1987. pap. 6.99 incl. audiocassette (0-553-45903-1) Bantam.

Learngis. Amazing Ben Franklin. 80p. (Orig.). 1987. pap. 2.50 (0-553-15504-0) Bantam.

Learning Exchange Staff. Free & Inexpensive Teaching Tools to Make & Use. Murray, Peggy, illus. 112p. (gr. 2-6). 1986. wkbk. 9.95 (0-86653-388-5, GA 1004) Good Apple.
—Seasonal Learning Activities. 112p. (gr. 2-6). 1988. wkbk. 9.95 (0-86653-435-0, GA1045) Good Apple.

Learning Forum Staff. Communications & Motivation Personal Growth Set. (gr. 8-12). 1988. 45.00 (0-945525-14-1) Supercamp.
—Study Skills Set. (gr. 8-12). 1989. 130.00 (0-945525-13-3) Supercamp.
—Success Through Math Mastery. (gr. 8-12). 1989. 24.95 (0-945525-11-7) Supercamp.

Learning Works Staff. Solution Sleuth. (gr. 4-8). 1989. 7.95 (0-88160-170-5, LW 278) Learning Wks.
—Travel Pack, No. 1: Doodle One. (gr. k-6). 1989. 8.95 (0-88160-175-6, LW 290) Learning Wks.
—Travel Pack, No. 2: Doodle Two. (gr. k-6). 1989. 8.95 (0-88160-176-4, LW 291) Learning Wks.
—Travel Pack, No. 3: Games. (gr. k-6). 1989. 14.95 (0-88160-177-2, LW 292) Learning Wks.
—Travel Pack, No. 4: Dinosaurs. (gr. k-6). 1989. 8.95 (0-88160-178-0, LW 293) Learning Wks.

Learsi, Rufus. Prince of Judah & Other Stories of a Great Journey. 1962 ed. LC 62-21985. (Illus.). (gr. 6-10). 11.95 (0-88400-031-1) Shengold.

Leary, Lory B. An Alaskan Child's Garden of Verse. Leary, Lory B., illus. 40p. (Orig.). (gr. 6 up). 1989. pap. 6.95x (0-924663-02-2) Alaskan Viewpoint.

Leary, Mary B., jt. ed. see Ellis, John S.

Leas, Allan. Abolition of the Slave Trade. (Illus.). 72p. (gr. 7-10). 1989. 19.95 (0-7134-5668-X, Pub. by Batsford UK) Trafalgar.
—South Africa. (Illus.). 72p. (gr. 7-12). 1992. 22.95 (0-7134-6499-2, Pub. by Batsford UK) Trafalgar.

Leasure, Paula, ed. see Siembieda, Kevin.

Leatherbury, Leven C., ed. see Dean, Wayne.

Leathers, Noel L. The Japanese in America. LC 67-15684. (Illus.). 72p. (gr. 5 up). 1991. PLB 15.95 (0-8225-0241-0); pap. 5.95 (0-8225-1014-6) Lerner Pubns.
—Japanese in America. 1991. pap. 5.95 (0-8225-1042-1) Lerner Pubns.

Leatherwood, Stephen & Reeves, Randall. The Sea World Book of Dolphins. LC 86-46212. 111p. (gr. 4-7). 1987. pap. 9.95 (0-15-271957-1, Voyager Bks) HarBrace.

Leavell, Perry. Harry S. Truman. (Illus.). 112p. (gr. 5 up). 1988. lib. bdg. 17.95 (0-87754-558-8) Chelsea Hse.
—James Madison. Schlesinger, Arthur M., intro. by. (Illus.). 112p. (gr. 5 up). 1988. 17.95 (1-55546-815-2) Chelsea Hse.
—Woodrow Wilson. (Illus.). 112p. (gr. 5 up). 1987. lib. bdg. 17.95x (0-87754-557-X) Chelsea Hse.

Leavitt, Jerome E. Easy Carpentry Projects for Children. 96p. (gr. 2 up). 1986. pap. 3.95 (0-486-25057-1) Dover.

Leavitt, Joy. Adventures of Huckleberry Finn: A Study Guide. (gr. 10-12). 1983. tchr's ed. & wkbk. 14.95 (0-88122-020-5) LRN Links.
—Adventures of Tom Sawyer: A Study Guide. (gr. 7-12). 1984. tchr's ed. & wkbk. 14.95 (0-88122-103-1) LRN Links.
—All Quiet on the Western Front: A Study Guide. 1983. tchr's ed. & wkbk. 14.95 (0-88122-035-3) LRN Links.
—Death of a Salesman: A Study Guide. (gr. 10-12). 1984. tchr's ed. & wkbk. 14.95 (0-88122-113-9) LRN Links.

Leavitt, Nancy, jt. auth. see Feldman, Annette.

LeBaron, John & Miller, Philip. Portable Video: A Production Guide for Young People. (Illus.). 160p. (Orig.). (gr. 5 up). 1982. (Pub. by Treehouse); pap. 13.95 (0-13-686519-4) P-H.

Lebentritt, Julia & Ploetz, Richard. The Kooken. Oubrerie, Clement, illus. LC 91-26826. 32p. (gr. 1-3). 1992. 14.95 (0-8050-1749-6, Bks Young Read) H Holt & Co.

Lebet, Philip E. & Perry, David J. Vocabula Et Sermones - Basic Vocabulary & Sample Conversations. (LAT.). 25p. (gr. 6-12). 1991. spiral 1.70 (0-939507-19-6, B4) Amer Classical.

Lebitritt, jt. auth. see Ploetz.

Le Blanc, L. Little Frog Learns to Sing. Le Blanc, L., illus. LC 68-16394. 32p. (ps-2). 1967. PLB 9.95 (0-87783-022-3) cassette 7.94x (0-87783-191-2) Oddo.

Lebowitz, Clara. Tuvia & the Tiny Teacher. (Illus.). 100p. (gr. 3-4). 1991. 8.95 (1-56062-105-2) CIS Comm.

Lebowitz, Marcia L. I Think Divorce Stinks. Borguald, Pamela M., illus. 16p. (Orig.). (gr. 7-10). 1989. pap. 4.95 (0-935769-05-6) CDC Pr.

Lebrun, Claude. Little Brown Bear Is Ill. Bour, Daniele, illus. 14p. (gr. k-3). 1982. 4.95 (0-8120-5499-7) Barron.

Le Cain, E., jt. auth. see Price, M.

LeCain, Errol. Thorn Rose. (Illus.). (ps-3). 1978. pap. 3.95 (0-14-050222-X, Puffin) Puffin Bks.
—Twelve Dancing Princesses. 32p. (ps-k). 1981. pap. 3.95 (0-14-050322-6, Puffin) Puffin Bks.

Le Carre, John. The Spy Who Came in from the Cold, 2 vols. large type ed. (gr. 10-12). Repr. of 1965 ed. Set. write for info. (0-89064-058-0) NAVH.

Lecher, Doris. Angelita's Magic Yarn. (Illus.). 32p. (ps-3). 1992. 14.00 (0-374-30332-0) FS&G.

Lechner, Doris E., ed. see Williams, Bill.

Lechner, Susan, jt. auth. see Altman, Susan.

Le Clezio, J. M. Celui Qui N'Avait Jamais vu la Mer. Lemoine, Georges, illus. (FRE.). 107p. (gr. 5-10). 1988. pap. 6.95 (2-07-033492-9) Schoenhof.
—Lullaby. Lemoine, Georges, illus. (FRE.). (gr. 5-10). 1995. pap. 6.95 (2-07-033448-1) Schoenhof.
—Villa Aurore. Lemoine, Georges, illus. (FRE.). 112p. (gr. 5-10). 1990. pap. 6.95 (2-07-033603-4) Schoenhof.
—Voyage au Pays des Arbres. Galero, Henri, illus. (FRE.). 48p. (gr. 3-7). 1990. pap. 7.95 (2-07-031187-2) Schoenhof.

Lecomte, Eva. Paula, the Waldensian. Strong, W. M., tr. (gr. 3-7). 1942. pap. 5.99 (0-87213-511-X) Loizeaux.

Lecourt, Nancy. Abracadabra to Zigzag. (ps-3). 1991. 13.95 (0-688-09481-3) Lothrop.
—Abracadabra to Zigzag. (ps-3). 1991. PLB 13.88 (0-688-09482-1) Lothrop.
—Abracadabra to Zigzag: An Alphabet Book. Lehman, Barbara, illus. LC 92-12503. 32p. (ps-3). 1992. pap. 4.99 (0-14-054470-4) Puffin Bks.
—Rainbow. 32p. (gr. 2). 1980. pap. 1.95 (0-8127-0290-5) Review & Herald.

Lecourt, Nancy H. Teddy the Better-Than-New Bear. 32p. 1993. pap. 5.95 (0-8163-1116-1) Pacific Pr Pub Assn.

Ledbetter, Cynthia E. & Jones, Richard C. John Muir. LC 92-46763. 1993. 19.93 (0-86625-494-3); 14.95s.p. (0-685-67774-5) Rourke Pubns.

Ledbetter, Frances M., jt. auth. see Melton, Dana D.

Ledbetter, Irene & Lomax, John A. Buenas Noches, Irene. Pike, Raffi & Pike, D., eds. Zamora-Pearson, Marissa, tr. from ENG. Ferguson, Kay, illus. (SPA.). (ps-2). 1993. pap. text ed. 15.00 (0-922053-27-8) N Edge Res.
—Goodnight Irene Big Book. Pike, Raffi & Pike, D., eds. Ferguson, Kay, illus. (ps-2). 1988. pap. text ed. 14.00 (0-922053-08-1) N Edge Res.

Leder, Dora, illus. Let's Peek in Santa's Pack. LC 89-61375. 14p. (ps). 1990. bds. 2.95 (0-679-80277-0) Random Bks Yng Read.

Leder, Jane. Amelia Earhart: Opposing Viewpoints. LC 89-12028. (Illus.). 112p. (gr. 5-8). 1989. PLB 14.95 (0-89908-070-7) Greenhaven.

Leder, Jane M. Dead Serious: A Book for Teenagers about Teenage Suicide. LC 86-25880. 160p. (gr. 7 up). 1987. SBE 13.95 (0-689-31262-8, Atheneum Child Bk) Macmillan Child Grp.
—Dead Serious: A Book for Teenagers about Teenage Suicide. 160p. (gr. 7 up). 1989. pap. 3.50 (0-380-70661-X, Flare) Avon.
—Exotic Cars. LC 87-15572. (Illus.). 48p. (gr. 5-6). 1987. RSBE 11.95 (0-89686-351-4, Crestwood Hse) Macmillan Child Grp.
—Learning How: Gymnastics. James, Jody, ed. Concept of Design Staff, illus. 48p. (gr. 4-7). 1992. lib. bdg. 14.95 (0-944280-35-8); pap. 5.95 (0-944280-40-4) Bancroft-Sage.
—Learning How: Karate. James, Jody, ed. Concept of Design Staff, illus. 48p. (gr. 4-7). 1992. lib. bdg. 14.95 (0-944280-34-X); pap. 5.95 (0-944280-39-0) Bancroft-Sage.
—Learning How: Skateboarding. James, Jody, ed. Concept of Design Staff, illus. 48p. (gr. 4-7). 1992. lib. bdg. 14.95 (0-944280-33-1); pap. 5.95 (0-944280-42-0) Bancroft-Sage.
—Learning How: Soccer. James, Jody, ed. Concept of Design Staff, illus. 48p. (gr. 4-7). 1992. lib. bdg. 14.95 (0-944280-32-3); pap. 5.95 (0-944280-38-2) Bancroft-Sage.
—Marcus Allen. LC 84-11375. (Illus.). 48p. (gr. 5-6). 1985. RSBE 11.95 (0-89686-251-8, Crestwood Hse) Macmillan Child Grp.
—Martina Navratilova. LC 89-99550. (Illus.). 48p. (gr. 5-6). 1988. RSBE 10.95 (0-89686-252-6, Crestwood Hse) Macmillan Child Grp.
—Stunt Dogs. LC 85-19469. (Illus.). 48p. (gr. 5-6). 1985. RSBE 10.95 (0-89686-289-5, Crestwood Hse) Macmillan Child Grp.
—Walter Payton. LC 86-16526. (Illus.). 48p. (gr. 5-6). 1986. RSBE 11.95 (0-89686-318-2, Crestwood Hse) Macmillan Child Grp.

—Wayne Gretzky. LC 84-14980. (Illus.). 48p. (gr. 5-6). 1985. RSBE 11.95 (0-89686-255-0, Crestwood Hse) Macmillan Child Grp.

Lederman, David. Multiple Choice Questions in Preparation for the AP Calculus (AB) Examination. 5th ed. 127p. (gr. 11-12). 1991. wkbk. 15.95 (1-878621-00-9); student's solution manual, 90p. 15.95 (1-878621-01-7) D & S Mktg Syst.

—Multiple Choice Questions in Preparation for the AP Calculus (BC) Examination. 4th ed. 121p. (gr. 11-12). 1991. wkbk. 15.95 (1-878621-02-5); student's solutions manual, 90p. 15.95 (1-878621-03-3) D & S Mktg Syst.

Lederman, Diana, illus. Make-Me-a-Match. 1992. spiral bdg. 4.95 (965-229-025-4, Pub. by Gefen Pub Hse IS) Gefen Bks.

Lederman, Raizel, jt. auth. see Teitelbaum, Chaya S.

Leditschke, Anna. Tiny Timothy Turtle. McLean-Carr, Carol, illus. 32p. (ps-2). 1991. PLB 17.27 (0-8368-0667-0) Gareth Stevens Inc.

Ledney, Douglas. My Hero! 1994. 7.95 (0-8062-4865-3) Carlton.

Ledyard, Gleason H., tr. Precious Moments Children's Bible: Easy-to-Read, New Life Version. Butcher, Samuel J., illus. LC 90-36671. 1424p. 1991. 24.99 (0-8010-5664-0) Baker Bk.

Lee. Animal Rights. 1991. 12.95s.p. (0-86593-112-7) Rourke Corp.

—Discrimination. 1991. 12.95s.p. (0-86593-113-5) Rourke Corp.

Lee, A. Laney. Island Eyes: The Adventures of a Shell. Dowd, Ken, illus. LC 85-8972. 112p. (gr. 2-5). 1987. 12.95 (0-688-06094-3) Lothrop.

Lee, Andrew. Lincoln. (Illus.). 64p. (gr. 6-9). 1989. 19.95 (0-7134-5662-0, Pub. by Batsford UK) Trafalgar.

—Workshop of the World. (Illus.). 48p. (gr. 7-10). Date not set. 19.95 (0-7134-6353-8, Pub. by Batsford UK) Trafalgar.

Lee, Anna. Modeling & You! Lee, Tommy, illus. 117p. (Orig.). (gr. 6-12). 1991. pap. 12.95 (0-9629647-0-0) CUE Pubns.

Lee, Anthony A. The Cornerstone: A Story About 'Abdu'l-Baha in America. Irvine, Rex J., illus. 24p. (Orig.). (gr. k-5). 1979. pap. 3.00 (0-933770-01-4) Kalimat.

—The Scottish Visitors: A Story about 'Abdu'l-Baha in Britain. Irving, Rex J., illus. 24p. (Orig.). (gr. k-5). 1981. pap. 3.00 (0-933770-04-9) Kalimat.

—The Unfriendly Governor. Irvine, Rex John, illus. 24p. (gr. k-5). 1980. pap. 3.00 (0-933770-02-2) Kalimat.

Lee, Betsy. Judy Blume's Story. LC 81-12494. (Illus.). 112p. (gr. 5 up). 1981. RSBE 10.95 (0-87518-209-7, Dillon) Macmillan Child Grp.

Lee, Beverly. The Secret of Van Rink's Cellar. LC 79-52909. 180p. (gr. 4 up). 1979. 17.50 (0-8225-0763-3) Lerner Pubns.

Lee, Billie W. Rainshine & Sundrops: Language Fun for Young Children. Andreko, John A., illus. Lee, Billie W., intro. by. (Illus.). 40p. (Orig.). 1987. 6.95 (0-9619675-0-1) P&M Bear Pubns.

Lee, Bob, jt. auth. see Arnold, Henri.

Lee, Chas. Totally Trusting. Ritner, Wanda, illus. 222p. (gr. 4-10). 1992. 19.95 (1-878044-09-5) Mayhaven Pub.

Lee, Dennis. The Ice Cream Store. (Illus.). (ps). 1992. 14.95 (0-590-45861-2, 002, Scholastic Hardcover) Scholastic Inc.

Lee, Don L. Think Black. 3rd ed. LC 70-882333. (gr. 12 up). 1969. pap. 3.00 (0-910296-03-0) Broadside Pr.

—We Walk the Way of the New World. LC 70-121885. (gr. 12 up). 1970. 6.00 (0-910296-26-X) Broadside Pr.

Lee, Essie E. Breaking the Connection: How Young People Achieve Drug-Free Lives. LC 87-18586. (Illus.). 160p. (gr. 7 up). 1988. (J Messner); lib. bdg. 5.95 (0-671-67059-X) S&S Trade.

Lee, Frank. My Bedtime Book of the Saints. rev. ed. Matz, Terry, rev. by. (Illus.). 64p. 1993. pap. 3.95 (0-89243-585-2) Liguori Pubns.

Lee, George L. Worldwide Interesting People: One Hundred Sixty-Two History Makers of African Descent. LC 91-50939. (Illus.). 144p. 1992. lib. bdg. 19.95 (0-89950-670-4) McFarland & Co.

Lee, Greg. Jim Abbott, Pitcher. LC 92-43251. 1993. 14.60 (0-86593-258-1); 10.95s.p. (0-685-66274-8) Rourke Corp.

—Money. LC 92-44074. 1993. 12.67 (0-86593-268-9); 9.50s.p. (0-685-66360-4) Rourke Corp.

—School. LC 92-44073. (gr. 3 up). 1993. 12.67 (0-86593-269-7); 9.50s.p. (0-685-66359-0) Rourke Corp.

—Vacation. LC 92-45692. 1993. 12.67 (0-86593-270-0); 9.50s.p. (0-685-66420-1) Rourke Corp.

Lee, Greg, compiled by. Food: Wacky Words. LC 92-41730. (gr. 3 up). 1993. 12.67 (0-86593-265-4); 9.50s.p. (0-685-66289-6) Rourke Corp.

—Outer Space: Wacky Words. LC 92-43965. (gr. 3 up). 1993. 12.67 (0-86593-267-0); 9.50s.p. (0-685-66292-6) Rourke Corp.

—Pets: Wacky Words. LC 92-43964. (gr. 3 up). 1993. 12.67 (0-86593-266-2); 9.50s.p. (0-685-66291-8) Rourke Corp.

Lee, Gregory. Chris Burke: He Overcame Down Syndrome. LC 93-18213. 1993. 14.60 (0-86593-263-8); 10.95s.p. (0-685-66611-5) Rourke Corp.

Lee, H. D., tr. see Plato.

Lee, Huy-Voun. At the Beach. LC 93-25462. (Illus.). 1994. write for info. (0-8050-2768-8) H Holt & Co.

Lee, James W., ed. Nineteen Forty-One: Texas Goes to War. LC 91-36090. (Illus.). 244p. 1991. pap. 19.95 (0-929398-29-7) UNTX Pr.

Lee, Jasper S. Working in Agricultural Industry. (Illus.). (gr. 9-10). 1978. text ed. 17.96 (0-07-000831-0) McGraw.

Lee, Jeanne. Silent Lotus. (Illus.). 32p. (gr. k-3). 1991. 14.95 (0-374-36911-9) FS&G.

Lee, Jeanne M. Ba-Nam. Lee, Jeanne M., illus. LC 86-27127. 32p. (ps-2). 1987. 4th ed. 13.95 (0-8050-0169-7, Bks Young Read) H Holt & Co.

—Legend of the Li River: An Ancient Chinese Tale. Lee, Jeanne M., illus. LC 83-79. 32p. (ps-2). 1983. 11.95 (0-03-063523-3, Bks Young Read) H Holt & Co.

—Legend of the Milky Way. Lee, Jeanne M., illus. LC 81-6906. 32p. (ps-2). 1990. pap. 5.95 (0-8050-1361-X, Owlet BYR) H Holt & Co.

Lee, Jeanne M., retold by. & illus. The Legend of the Milky Way. LC 81-6906. 32p. (ps-2). 1982. 14.95 (0-8050-0217-0, Bks Young Read) H Holt & Co.

—Toad Is the Uncle of Heaven. LC 85-5639. 32p. (ps-2). 1985. 13.95 (0-8050-1146-3, Bks Young Read) H Holt & Co.

—Toad Is the Uncle of Heaven: A Vietnamese Folk Tale. LC 85-5639. 32p. (ps-2). 1989. pap. 5.95 (0-8050-1147-1, Owlet BYR) H Holt & Co.

Lee, Joanna. I Want to Keep My Baby! 176p. (Orig.). (gr. 9-12). 1977. pap. 3.50 (0-451-15733-8, Sig) NAL-Dutton.

Lee, Joanna & Cook, T. S. Mary Jane Harper Cried Last Night. (Illus., Orig.). (RL 5). 1978. pap. 2.95 (0-451-13980-1, E9692, Sig) NAL-Dutton.

Lee, Kathleen. American Origins: Tracing Our Chinese Roots. LC 93-35616. 1994. 12.95 (1-56261-159-3) John Muir.

—Tracing Our Italian Roots. Butler, Nate & Evans, Beth, illus. 48p. (gr. 4-7). 1993. text ed. 12.95 (1-56261-149-6) John Muir.

Lee, Kristina, et al. Songs of the Season. (Illus.). 80p. (Orig.). 1991. pap. 7.95 (0-89084-555-7) Bob Jones Univ Pr.

Lee, Marie G. Finding My Voice. LC 92-2947. 176p. (gr. 6 up). 1992. 13.95 (0-395-62134-8) HM.

—If It Hadn't Been for Yoon Jun. LC 92-9557. 144p. (gr. 3-7). 1993. 13.95 (0-395-62941-1) HM.

—Saying Goodbye. LC 93-26092. 1994. write for info. (0-395-67066-7) HM.

Lee, Martin. The Seminoles. LC 89-8900. (Illus.). 64p. (gr. 4-7). 1989. PLB 12.90 (0-531-10752-3) Watts.

—The Seminoles. (Illus.). 64p. (gr. 3 up). 1991. pap. 5.95 (0-531-15604-4) Watts.

Lee, Mary P. Coping with Money. Rosen, Ruth, ed. (gr. 7 up). 1988. PLB 13.95 (0-8239-0783-X) Rosen Group.

Lee, Mary P. & Lee, Richard. Careers in the Restaurant Industry. rev. ed. Rosen, R., ed. (Illus.). 160p. (gr. 7-12). 1990. 13.95 (0-8239-1142-X) Rosen Group.

Lee, Mary P. & Lee, Richard S. Careers in Firefighting. Rosen, Ruth, ed. (gr. 7-12). 1993. PLB 13.95 (0-8239-1515-8); pap. 9.95 (0-8239-1724-X) Rosen Group.

—Last Names First..& Some First Names too. Weber, Debora, illus. LC 84-20860. 119p. (gr. 5-9). 1985. 12.00 (0-664-32719-2, Westminster) Westminster John Knox.

Lee, Mary P., jt. auth. see Lee, Richard S.

Lee, Michelle. Estes Park Souvenir Coloring Book. 48p. (ps-8). 1993. 4.50 (0-9637687-0-0) Vacation Color.

Lee, Nancy & Oldham, Linda. Tacos, Tempura & Teem Gok. LC 78-75120. 80p. (ps-8). 1979. 3.95 (0-931178-02-9) Hands On Pubns.

Lee, Patrick. Little Buddy Meets Bobo. LC 92-17406. (ps). 1993. 10.95 (0-670-84803-4) Viking Child Bks.

Lee, Paul A. Florence the Goose: A True Story for Children of All Ages. Smith, Page, illus. 47p. 1992. 14.95 (0-937011-51-7) Platonic Acad Pr.

Lee, Rebecca L. Kori & the Island of Enchantment. LC 89-49376. 80p. (Orig.). (gr. 8 up). 1990. pap. 6.95 (0-931832-46-2) Fithian Pr.

Lee, Richard, jt. auth. see Lee, Mary P.

Lee, Richard S. & Lee, Mary P. Careers for Women in Politics. Rosen, Ruth, ed. (gr. 7-12). 1989. PLB 13.95 (0-8239-0966-2) Rosen Group.

—Drugs & the Media. LC 93-21099. 1993. write for info. (0-8239-1537-9) Rosen Group.

Lee, Richard S., jt. auth. see Lee, Mary P.

Lee, Robert C. Summer of the Green Star. LC 80-27427. 128p. (gr. 5-9). 1981. 11.00 (0-664-32681-1, Westminster) Westminster John Knox.

Lee, Robert E., jt. auth. see Lawrence, Jerome.

Lee, Ronny. Learn to Sing Step by Step. 144p. 1984. pap. 12.95 (0-934401-00-4) Sunrise Pub NY.

Lee, Sally. Donor Banks: Saving Lives with Organ & Tissue Transplants. Solomon, Maury, ed. LC 87-27304. (Illus.). 96p. (gr. 5 up). 1988. PLB 10.90 (0-531-10475-3) Watts.

—Hurricanes. LC 92-27367. (Illus.). 64p. (gr. 5-8). 1993. PLB 12.90 (0-531-20152-X); pap. 5.95 (0-531-15665-6) Watts.

—New Theories on Diet & Nutrition. LC 89-39357. 1990. PLB 14.40 (0-531-10930-5) Watts.

—Pesticides. LC 90-46839. (Illus.). 144p. (gr. 9-12). 1991. PLB 13.90 (0-531-13017-7) Watts.

—Predicting Violent Storms. LC 89-9152. (Illus.). 144p. (gr. 7-12). 1989. PLB 13.90 (0-531-10787-6) Watts.

—San Antonio. LC 91-34303. (Illus.). 60p. (gr. 4 up). 1992. RSBE 12.95 (0-87518-510-X, Dillon) Macmillan Child Grp.

—The Throwaway Society. LC 90-33027. (Illus.). 128p. (gr. 9-12). 1990. PLB 13.40 (0-531-10947-X) Watts.

Lee, Samantha, retold by. Dr. Jekyll & Mr. Hyde. 160p. (gr. 6 up). 1988. pap. 2.95 (0-8120-4072-4) Barron.

Lee, Sandra. Bald Eagles. 32p. 1991. 22.75 (0-89565-706-6); 15.95s.p. (0-685-55046-X) Childs World.

—Giant Pandas. LC 92-35066. 1993. write for info. (1-56766-009-6) Childs World.

—Koalas. LC 92-38807. (gr. k-3). 1993. write for info. (1-56766-013-4) Childs World.

—Lions. 32p. 1991. 22.75 (0-89565-707-4); 15.95s.p. (0-685-55057-5) Childs World.

—Rattlesnakes. (gr. 1-8). 1992. PLB 15.95 (0-89565-842-9); Resale. 22.75 (0-685-61011-X) Childs World.

Lee, Sharon. Jack & the Beanstalk. Williams, Jennie, illus. 24p. (Orig.). (ps-k). 1993. pap. 1.50 (0-679-84794-4) Random Bks Yng Read.

Lee, Sylvia, ed. The Holy Spirit in Christian Education. LC 88-80549. 144p. (Orig.). (gr. k up). 1988. pap. 2.95 tchr's. bk. (0-88243-854-9, 02-0854) Gospel Pub.

Lee, Tanith. Black Unicorn. Cooper, Heather, illus. LC 91-15646. 144p. (gr. 7 up). 1991. SBE 14.95 (0-689-31575-9, Atheneum Child Bk) Macmillan Child Grp.

Lee, Tere. Guidebook to the Tokaido. LC 80-54305. (Illus.). 40p. (Orig.). (gr. 7-10). 1980. pap. 2.00 (0-913689-08-4) Spencer Muse Art.

Lee, Valerie. Dysfunctional Families. (Illus.). 64p. (gr. 7 up). 1990. lib. bdg. 15.93 (0-86593-077-5); lib. bdg. 12.95s.p. (0-685-36296-5) Rourke Corp.

Leeb, Olli. Von Frueh an Fit Mit Nico's Kinderkueche. 2nd ed. (GER., Illus.). 77p. 1990. 17.25x (3-921799-87-2, Pub. by Olli Leeb GW) Lubrecht & Cramer.

Leech, Bryan J. John Jeremy Colton. (Illus.). 32p. (ps-3). 1994. 14.95 (1-56282-650-6); PLB 14.89 (1-56282-651-4) Hyprn Child.

Leeds, Barbara. Fairy Tale Rap: "Jack & the Beanstalk" & Other Stories. Hamilton, Craig, illus. 32p. (Orig.). (gr. k-8). 1990. pap. 5.95 (0-9624932-0-1); pap. 12.95 incl. cass. (0-9624932-2-8); cassette 8.95 (0-9624932-1-X) Miramonte Pr.

—Fairy Tale Rap, No. 2: The Fisherman & His Wife & Other Stories. Hamilton, Craig, illus. 40p. (Orig.). (ps-6). 1992. pap. 6.95 (0-9624932-4-4); pap. 13.95 incl. audiocassette (0-9624932-6-0); audiocassette 8.95 (0-9624932-5-2) Miramonte Pr.

Leeds, Chris. Peace & War: A First Sourcebook. (Illus.). 212p. 1987. pap. 17.95 (0-85950-526-X, Pub. by S Thornes UK) Dufour.

Leedy, Loreen. Big, Small, Short, Tall. Leedy, Loreen, illus. LC 86-46203. 32p. (ps-3). 1987. reinforced bdg. 12.95 (0-8234-0645-8) Holiday.

—Blast off to Earth! A Look at Geography. Leedy, Loreen, illus. LC 92-2567. 32p. (ps-3). 1992. reinforced bdg. 14.95 (0-8234-0973-2) Holiday.

—The Bunny Play. Leedy, Loreen, illus. LC 87-17793. 32p. (ps-3). 1988. reinforced bdg. 12.95 (0-8234-0679-2) Holiday.

—The Dragon ABC Hunt. Leedy, Loreen, illus. LC 85-21907. 36p. (ps-1). 1986. reinforced bdg. 14.95 (0-8234-0596-6) Holiday.

—A Dragon Christmas: Things to Make & Do. Leedy, Loreen, illus. LC 88-4635. 32p. (ps-3). 1988. reinforced bdg. 13.95 (0-8234-0716-0) Holiday.

—The Dragon Halloween Party. Leedy, Loreen, illus. LC 86-286. 32p. (ps-3). 1986. reinforced bdg. 14.95 (0-8234-0611-3); pap. 5.95 (0-8234-0765-9) Holiday.

—The Dragon Thanksgiving Feast: Things to Make & Do. Leedy, Loreen, illus. LC 90-55110. 32p. (ps-3). 1990. reinforced 14.95 (0-8234-0828-0) Holiday.

—Fraction Action. Leedy, Loreen, illus. LC 93-22800. 32p. (gr. 4-8). 1994. 15.95 (0-8234-1109-5) Holiday.

—The Furry News - How to Create a Newspaper: A Reading Rainbow Feature Book. Leedy, Loreen, illus. (ps-3). 1993. pap. 5.95 (0-8234-1026-9) Holiday.

—The Furry News: How to Make a Newspaper. Leedy, Loreen, illus. LC 89-20094. 32p. (ps-3). 1990. reinforced bdg. 13.95 (0-8234-0793-4) Holiday.

—The Great Trash Bash. Leedy, Loreen, illus. LC 90-46554. 32p. (ps-3). 1991. reinforced 14.95 (0-8234-0869-8) Holiday.

—Messages in the Mailbox: How to Write a Letter. Leedy, Loreen, illus. LC 91-8718. 32p. (ps-3). 1991. reinforced 14.95 (0-8234-0889-2) Holiday.

—The Monster Money Book. Leedy, Loreen, illus. LC 91-18168. 32p. (ps-3). 1992. reinforced bdg. 14.95 (0-8234-0922-8) Holiday.

—A Number of Dragons. Leedy, Loreen, illus. LC 85-730. 32p. (ps-1). 1985. reinforced bdg. 14.95 (0-8234-0568-0) Holiday.

—Pingo the Plaid Panda. Leedy, Loreen, illus. LC 88-17005. 32p. (ps-3). 1989. reinforced bdg. 13.95 (0-8234-0727-6) Holiday.

—Postcards from Pluto: A Tour of the Solar System. LC 92-32658. (Illus.). 32p. (ps-3). 1993. reinforced bdg. 15.95 (0-8234-1000-5) Holiday.

—The Potato Party & Other Troll Tales. Leedy, Loreen, illus. LC 89-1746. 32p. (ps-3). 1989. reinforced 14.95 (0-8234-0761-6) Holiday.

—Tracks in the Sand. LC 92-3405. (ps-3). 1993. 15.00 (0-385-30658-X) Doubleday.

Leefeldt, Christine, jt. auth. see Callenbach, Ernest.

Leeka, M. C. The Doll's Tea Party. County Studio Staff, illus. 24p. (ps-2). 1993. pap. text ed. 0.99 (1-56293-343-4) McClanahan Bk.

—Just Like Mommy, Just Like Daddy. Borgo, Deborah, illus. 24p. (ps-2). 1993. pap. text ed. 0.99 (*1-56293-345-0*) McClanahan Bk.
Leeka, Melinda. Andy Goes to the Zoo. LC 89-51092. 44p. (gr. k-3). 1990. 5.95 (*1-55523-247-7*) Winston-Derek.
Leeming, Joseph. Fun with String. (Illus.). (gr. 4-9). 17.25 (*0-8446-5058-7*) Peter Smith.
Leemis, Ralph. Mister Momboo's Hat. Bassett, Jeni, illus. LC 90-34397. 24p. (ps-k). 1991. 11.95 (*0-525-65045-8*, Cobblehill Bks) Dutton Child Bks.
—Smart Dog. 32p. (ps-3). 1993. 14.95 (*1-56397-109-7*) Boyds Mills Pr.
Leeper, Fran. Journey of the Sparrows. (gr. 4-7). 1993. pap. 3.50 (*0-440-40785-0*) Dell.
Lees, Gene. The Modern Rhyming Dictionary. 364p. (Orig.). (gr. 8 up). 1986. 19.95 (*0-89524-129-3*, 8649); pap. 14.95 (*0-89524-317-2*) Cherry Lane.
Leeson, Muriel. The Bedford Adventure. Ponter, James, illus. LC 87-11943. 136p. (Orig.). (gr. 4-9). 1987. pap. 4.50 (*0-8361-3448-6*) Herald Pr.
—Journey to Freedom. Eaton, Lewis, illus. 128p. (Orig.). (gr. 4-8). 1989. pap. 4.95 (*0-8361-3498-2*) Herald Pr.
Leet, Frank R. When Santa Was Late. Winfrey, Buford A., illus. 32p. (ps-4). 1990. 3.95 (*0-8249-8483-8*, Ideals Child) Hambleton-Hill.
Leeuw, Hendrik de see De Leeuw, Hendrik, et al.
Leeuwen, Jean Van. The Great Christmas Kidnapping Caper. (gr. 3-7). 1976. pap. 2.50 (*0-440-43220-0*, YB) Dell.
Leeuwen, Jean van see Van Leeuwen, Jean.
Leeuwen, Jean Van see Van Leeuwen, Jean.
Leeuwen, Jean Van see Van Leeuwen, Jean.
Leeuwen, Jean Van see Van Leeuwen, Jean.
Leeuwen, Jean Van see Van Leeuwen, Jean.
Leeuwen, Jean Van see Van Leeuwen, Jean.
Leeuwen, Jean Van see Van Leeuwen, Jean.
Leeuwen, M. & Moeskops, J. The Nature Corner: Celebrating the Year's Cycle with a Seasonal Tableau. Lawson, Polly, tr. (DUT., Illus.). 88p. (ps-3). 1990. pap. 12.95 (*0-86315-111-6*, Pub. by Floris Bks UK) Gryphon Hse.
Lefer, Diane. Emma Lazarus. Horner, Matina, intro. by. (Illus.). 112p. (gr. 5 up). 1988. lib. bdg. 17.95 (*1-55546-664-8*) Chelsea Hse.
LeFever, Marlene. God's Special Creation--Me! (Illus.). 48p. (Orig.). (gr. 4-6). 1987. Camper Ed. pap. 1.50 (*0-87788-313-0*); Counselor Ed. pap. 3.50 (*0-87788-314-9*) Shaw Pubs.
—Survival Kit for Growing Christians. 32p. (gr. 4-6). 1988. saddle-stitched camper 1.50 (*0-87788-796-9*); saddle-stitched counselor 3.50 (*0-87788-797-7*) Shaw Pubs.
Leffler, Maryann C. My A B C's at Home. (Illus.). 24p. (ps). 1990. bds. 2.50 (*0-448-02257-5*, G&D) Putnam Pub Group.
Lefkon, Wendy, jt. ed. see Birnbaum, Steve.
Lefton, Phillip, jt. auth. see Midgley, David A.
Le Gallienne, Eva, retold by see Andersen, Hans Christian.
Le Gallienne, Eva, tr. see Andersen, Hans Christian.
Legg, Gerald. Amazing Tropical Birds. Young, Jerry, photos by. LC 91-6515. (Illus.). 32p. (Orig.). (gr. 1-5). 1991. lib. bdg. 9.99 (*0-679-91520-6*); pap. 6.95 (*0-679-81520-1*) Knopf Bks Yng Read.
Leggat, Bonnie-Alise. Punt, Pass & Point! Thatch, Nancy R., ed. Leggat, Bonnie-Alise, illus. Melton, David, intro. by. LC 92-17598. (Illus.). 26p. (gr. 3-5). 1992. PLB 14.95 (*0-933849-39-7*) Landmark Edns.
Legge, Gordon E. & Campbell, Fergus W. Vision of Color & Pattern. Head, J. J., ed. Steffen, Ann T., illus. LC 84-45835. 16p. (Orig.). (gr. 10 up). 1987. pap. text ed. 2.75 (*0-89278-365-6*, 45-9765) Carolina Biological.
Leggett, Dennis. People Trap. LC 90-46400. (Illus.). 48p. (gr. 5-9). 1991. PLB 12.95 (*1-85435-378-0*) Marshall Cavendish.
—Troubled Waters. LC 90-46572. (Illus.). 48p. (gr. 5-9). 1991. PLB 12.95 (*1-85435-275-X*) Marshall Cavendish.
Leggett, Dennis, jt. auth. see Leggett, Jeremy.
Leggett, Jeremy. Air Scare. LC 90-46420. (Illus.). 48p. (gr. 5-9). 1991. PLB 12.95 (*1-85435-274-1*) Marshall Cavendish.
—Dying Forests. LC 90-46574. (Illus.). 48p. (gr. 5-9). 1991. PLB 12.95 (*1-85435-276-8*) Marshall Cavendish.
—Energy Gap. LC 90-46431. (Illus.). 48p. (gr. 5-9). 1991. PLB 12.95 (*1-85435-377-2*) Marshall Cavendish.
—Waste War. LC 90-46573. (Illus.). 48p. (gr. 5-9). 1991. PLB 12.95 (*1-85435-277-6*) Marshall Cavendish.
Leggett, Jeremy & Leggett, Dennis. Operation Earth Series, 6 vols. (Illus.). (gr. 5-9). 1991. PLB 77.70 (*1-85435-273-3*) Marshall Cavendish.
Leggett, Linda R. & Andrews, Linda G. The Rose-Colored Glasses: Melanie Adjusts to Poor Vision. Hartman, Laura, illus. LC 79-12501. 32p. (gr. 3 up). 1979. 16.95 (*0-87705-408-8*) Human Sci Pr.
Legrand, Virginia. Miss Molly, Our Librarian. 1994. 7.95 (*0-486-04857-2*) Carlton.
LeGros, Lucy C. Activities & Games. rev. ed. (Illus.). 75p. (Orig.). (gr. k-2). 1989. pap. 7.95 (*0-318-41419-8*) Creat Res NC.
—Instant Centers - Colors. (Illus.). 40p. (Orig.). (gr. k-2). 1984. pap. 5.95 (*0-937306-03-7*) Creat Res NC.
—Instant Centers - Holidays. (Illus.). 45p. (Orig.). (gr. k-2). 1985. 5.95 (*0-937306-06-1*) Creat Res NC.
—Instant Centers - Holidays. rev. ed. Legros, Ivor L., illus. 51p. (gr. k-2). 1988. tchr's ed. 5.95 (*0-317-65724-0*) Creat Res NC.
—Instant Centers - Letters. (Illus.). 46p. (Orig.). (gr. k-2). 1984. pap. 5.95 (*0-937306-04-5*) Creat Res NC.
—Instant Centers - Numbers 10-20. LeGros, Ivor L., illus. 33p. (gr. k-2). 1988. tchr's ed. 5.95 (*0-937306-07-X*) Creat Res NC.
—Instant Centers: Numbers. (Illus.). 48p. (Orig.). (gr. k-2). 1984. pap. 5.95 (*0-937306-05-3*) Creat Res NC.
—Reading Success for School & Home. rev. ed. (Illus.). 230p. (Orig.). 1989. pap. 10.95 (*0-318-41420-1*) Creat Res NC.
—Square One. 41p. (gr. k-2). 1988. tchr's ed. 4.95 (*0-937306-08-8*); 16.95 (*0-937306-09-6*) Creat Res NC.
Le Guin, Ursula K. Catwings. Schindler, S. D., illus. LC 87-33104. 48p. (gr. 2-5). 1988. 11.95 (*0-531-05759-3*); PLB 11.99 (*0-531-08359-4*) Orchard Bks Watts.
—Catwings. Schindler, S. D., illus. 64p. (gr. 2-5). 1992. pap. 2.95 (*0-590-46072-2*) Scholastic Inc.
Le Guin, Ursula K. Catwings Return. Schindler, S. D., illus. LC 88-17902. 56p. (gr. 2-5). 1989. 11.95 (*0-531-05803-4*); PLB 11.99 (*0-531-08403-5*) Orchard Bks Watts.
—Catwing's Return. (ps-3). 1991. pap. 2.95 (*0-590-42832-2*) Scholastic Inc.
—Catwings Return. Schindler, S. D., illus. 64p. (gr. 2-5). 1992. pap. 2.95 (*0-590-46074-9*) Scholastic Inc.
Le Guin, Ursula K. The Farthest Shore. rev. ed. Garraty, Gail, illus. LC 72-75273. 240p. (gr. 6 up). 1990. SBE 16.95 (*0-689-31683-6*, Atheneum Child Bk) Macmillan Child Grp.
—Fire & Stone. LC 88-16799. (Illus.). 32p. (gr. 1-3). 1989. SBE 13.95 (*0-689-31408-6*, Atheneum Child Bk) Macmillan Child Grp.
—Fish Soup. Wynne, Patrick, illus. LC 91-29740. 40p. (gr. 2-4). 1992. SBE 13.95 (*0-689-31733-6*, Atheneum Child Bk) Macmillan Child Grp.
—The Ones Who Walk Away from Omelas. (gr. 5 up). 1992. PLB 13.95 (*0-88682-501-6*) Creative Ed.
—A Ride on the Red Mare's Back. Downing, Julie, illus. LC 91-21677. 48p. (gr. 1-4). 1992. 15.95 (*0-531-05991-X*); PLB 15.99 (*0-531-08591-0*) Orchard Bks Watts.
—Solomon Leviathan's Nine Hundred Thirty-First Trip Around the World. Austin, Alicia, illus. 40p. (gr. 7 up). 1983. 70.00 (*0-941826-03-1*) Cheap St.
—The Tombs of Atuan. Garraty, Gail, illus. LC 70-154753. 176p. (gr. 6-9). 1971. SBE 16.95 (*0-689-31684-4*, Atheneum Child Bk) Macmillan Child Grp.
—Very Far Away from Anywhere Else. LC 76-4472. 96p. (gr. 5-9). 1976. SBE 13.95 (*0-689-30525-7*, Atheneum Child Bk) Macmillan Child Grp.
—Very Far Away from Anywhere Else. (gr. 9-12). 1982. pap. 2.50 (*0-553-25396-4*) Bantam.
Leguin, Ursula K. The Visionary, 2 vols. in 1. Bd. with Wonders Hidden. Sanders, Scott R. 7.50 (*0-685-10479-6*) McGraw.
Le Guin, Ursula K. A Visit from Dr. Katz. Barrow, Ann, illus. LC 87-1783. 32p. (gr. k-3). 1988. SBE 12.95 (*0-689-31332-2*, Atheneum Child Bk) Macmillan Child Grp.
Lehan, Daniel. Crocodile Snaps - Kangaroo Jumps. LC 92-50842. (Illus.). 32p. (ps-k). 1993. 13.95 (*0-531-05484-5*) Orchard Bks Watts.
—This Is Not a Book about Dodos. Lehan, Daniel, illus. LC 91-794. 32p. (gr. k-3). 1992. 14.00 (*0-525-44878-0*, DCB) Dutton Child Bks.
—Wipe Your Feet! Lehan, Daniel, illus. LC 91-44145. 32p. (gr. k-3). 1993. 14.00 (*0-525-44992-2*, DCB) Dutton Child Bks.
Lehen, Judith L. When the Ragman Sings. LC 93-20346. 128p. (gr. 3-7). 1993. 14.00 (*0-06-023316-8*); PLB 13.89 (*0-06-023317-6*) HarpC Child Bks.
Lehman, Bob & Lehman, Elaine. Petey the Peacock Breaks a Leg. LC 93-60914. (Illus.). 44p. (gr. k-3). 1994. 7.95 (*1-55523-649-9*) Winston-Derek.
Lehman, Celia, jt. auth. see Shepard, Eva.
Lehman, Elaine, jt. auth. see Lehman, Bob.
Lehman, Elsie E. God Sends His Son Activity Book. 80p. (Orig.). (gr. 3-9). 1987. pap. 3.00 (*0-8361-3429-X*) Herald Pr.
—God's Wisdom & Power Activity Book. 80p. (ps-1). 1985. pap. 3.00 (*0-8361-3391-9*) Herald Pr.
Lehman, Emil. Israel: Idea & Reality. (Illus.). (gr. 8 up). 3.95x (*0-8381-0205-0*, 10-205) United Syn Bk.
Lehman, James. Invendex, Inventors Index, Sparks the Flash of Genius. (Orig.). (gr. 8 up). 1993. pap. 7.95 (*0-9637633-0-X*) WLC Pub.
Lehman, James H. The Owl & the Tuba. Raschka, Christopher, illus. LC 91-73880. 32p. 1991. 13.95 (*1-878925-02-4*) Brotherstone Pubs.
—The Saga of Shakespeare Pintlewood & the Great Silver Fountain Pen. Raschka, Christopher, illus. LC 90-82303. 32p. (gr. k-3). 1990. PLB 13.95 (*1-878925-00-8*) Brotherstone Pubs.
Lehman, Melanie, jt. auth. see Hayes, Dympna.
Lehman, Patricia J. & Padzik, Alicja, eds. At Babci's Knee. Zurawiecka, Aska, tr. Knowlton, Barbara W., illus. LC 85-51371. (ENG & POL.). 165p. (Orig.). (ps). 1989. pap. 25.00 (*0-935003-01-0*); cassette incl. (*0-935003-00-2*) Talent Ed.
Lehman, Paula D. Journey with Justice. Hull, Eddy & Shelly, Maynard, eds. Dirks, Ray, illus. LC 90-81509. 100p. (Orig.). 1990. pap. 7.95 (*0-87303-139-3*) Faith & Life.
Lehman, Yvette K. Know & Tell: A Work Book for Parents & Children. Myles, Glenn, ed. 50p. (ps-3). 1991. pap. write for info. Artmans Pr.
—Know & Tell: A Workbook for Parents & Children on How to Prevent Child Abuse. 2nd ed. 46p. (ps-4). 1992. wkbk. 9.95 (*0-9638555-0-6*) Y K Lehman.
—Know & Tell: A Workbook for Parents & Children on How to Prevent Child Abuse. 2nd ed. Naeb, Yuli, tr. from CHI. Colloms, Alisa, illus. 46p. (ps-4). 1993. write for info. (*0-9638555-2-2*) Y K Lehman.
—Saber y Decir: El Manual Para Padres e Hijos Sobre Como Prevenir el Abuso a los Ninos. 2nd ed. Chavez, Vivian & Costas, Gloria, trs. from ENG. Colloms, Alisa, illus. 46p. (ps-4). 1993. wkbk. 9.00 (*0-9638555-1-4*) Y K Lehman.
Lehmann, Asher. Young Moses, Crown Prince of Egypt. Goldman, Bonnie & Goldstein-Alpern, Neva, eds. Hirschler, Gertrude, tr. Forst, Siegmund, illus. 150p. (gr. 9-12). 1987. 8.95 (*0-910818-64-9*); pap. 7.95 (*0-685-18059-X*) Judaica Pr.
Lehmann, G. D. The Curse of the Amulet. 164p. (gr. 4-8). 1992. pap. 4.95 (*0-87508-443-5*) Chr Lit.
—Saved by Fire. (Illus.). 125p. (gr. 4-8). 1992. pap. 4.95 (*0-87508-441-9*) Chr Lit.
Lehmann, Marcus. Family y Aguilar. Breuer, Jacob, adapted by. (gr. 7 up). 8.95 (*0-87306-122-5*) Feldheim.
Lehmann, Terry & Nobisso, Joi. How to Fill an Empty Lap. Greenberg, Melanie, illus. 32p. (Orig.). (ps). 1980. pap. text ed. 3.00 (*0-940112-00-0*) Little Feat.
Lehn, Cornelia. God Keeps His Promise: A Bible Story Book for Young Children. Darwin, Beatrice, illus. LC 76-90377. (gr. k-4). 1970. 12.95 (*0-87303-291-8*) Faith & Life.
—I Heard Good News Today. Schlegel, Ralph A., illus. Oyer, Lora S., intro. by. LC 83-80401. (Illus.). 148p. (gr. 1-6). 1983. 12.95 (*0-87303-073-7*) Faith & Life.
—Peace Be with You. Neely, Keith R., illus. Regier, Harold R. & Schwartzentruber, Hubertintro. by. LC 80-70190. (Illus.). 126p. (gr. k-5). 1981. 12.95 (*0-87303-061-3*) Faith & Life.
—The Sun & the Wind. Regier, Robert, illus. 32p. (gr. k-5). 1983. 7.95 (*0-87303-072-9*) Faith & Life.
—The Sun & the Wind. Regier, Robert W., illus. LC 32-+010. 32p. 1987. 7.95 (*0-8361-3466-4*) Herald Pr.
Lehne, Judith L. The Never-Be-Bored Book: Quick Things to Make When There's Nothing to Do. Lipstein, Morissa G., illus. LC 92-16529. 128p. 1992. 17.95 (*0-8069-1254-5*) Sterling.
Lehner, Devony. Tinker's Journey Home. Maloney, P. Dennis, ed. Adamson, Charlotte, illus. 34p. (ps-6). 12. 95 (*0-940305-00-3*) P D Maloney.
Lehr, Norma. The Shimmering Ghost of Riversend. 160p. (gr. 3-6). 1991. PLB 17.50 (*0-8225-0732-3*) Lerner Pubns.
—Shimmering Ghost of Riversend. (gr. 4-7). 1991. pap. 3.95 (*0-8225-9589-3*) Lerner Pubns.
Lehrer, Brian. The Korean Americans. Moynihan, Daniel P., intro. by. (Illus.). 112p. (gr. 5 up). 1988. lib. bdg. 17.95 (*0-87754-888-9*) Chelsea Hse.
Lehrman, Fredric. Loving the Earth. (Illus.). 48p. (gr. 6-12). 1990. 14.95 (*0-89087-603-7*) Celestial Arts.
Lehrman, Robert. Separations. LC 92-26782. 224p. (gr. 5-9). 1993. pap. 3.99 (*0-14-032322-8*) Puffin Bks.
—The Store That Mama Built. LC 91-39983. 128p. (gr. 3-7). 1992. SBE 12.95 (*0-02-754632-2*, Macmillan Child Bk) Macmillan Child Grp.
Lehtinen, Ritva. Grandchildren of the Incas. (gr. 4-7). 1992. pap. 6.95 (*0-87614-566-7*) Carolrhoda Bks.
Leibold, Jay. The Antimatter Formula. 128p. (Orig.). (gr. 4). 1986. pap. 2.25 (*0-553-25741-2*) Bantam.
—Beyond the Great Wall. (gr. 5 up). 1987. pap. 2.50 (*0-553-26725-6*) Bantam.
—Fight for Freedom. 1990. pap. 3.25 (*0-553-28766-4*) Bantam.
—Grand Canyon Odyssey. 128p. (Orig.). (gr. 5). 1985. pap. 2.25 (*0-553-26522-9*) Bantam.
—The Lost Ninja. 1991. pap. 3.25 (*0-553-28960-8*) Bantam.
—Return of the Ninja. 1989. pap. 3.25 (*0-553-27968-8*) Bantam.
—Revenge of the Russian Ghost. 1990. pap. 2.75 (*0-553-28381-2*) Bantam.
—The Search for Aladdin's Lamp. 1991. pap. 3.25 (*0-553-29185-8*) Bantam.
—Spy for George Washington. 128p. (gr. 4). 1985. pap. 2.25 (*0-553-25497-9*) Bantam.
—Surf Monkeys. (gr. 4-7). 1993. pap. 3.25 (*0-553-29301-X*) Bantam.
Leibowitz, Jeff, jt. auth. see Park, Y. H.
Leichner, Jeannine T. Called to His Supper. (Illus.). 64p. (Orig.). (gr. 1-3). 1990. pap. 3.95 (*0-87973-138-9*, 138) Our Sunday Visitor.
—Joy Joy, the Mass: Our Family Celebration. (Illus.). (gr. k-3). 1978. pap. 2.95 (*0-87973-350-0*); Spanish Edition. 2.95 (*0-87973-348-9*, 348) Our Sunday Visitor.
—Making Things Right: The Sacrament of Reconciliation. (Illus.). 62p. (Orig.). (gr. 2-4). 1980. pap. 3.50 (*0-87973-351-9*, 351); Spanish Edition. 3.50 (*0-87973-349-7*, 349) Our Sunday Visitor.
Leigh, Avra, ed. see Kaslow, Florence R.
Leigh, Nila K. Learning to Swim in Swaziland: A Child's Eye-View of a Southern African Country. Leigh, Nila K., illus. LC 92-13223. 48p. (gr. k-3). 1993. 15.95 (*0-590-45938-4*) Scholastic Inc.
Leigh, Oretta. Aloysius Sebastian Mozart Mouse. DeLacre, Lulu, illus. 32p. (gr. k-2). 1984. 6.95 (*0-685-09671-8*, J Messner) S&S Trade.

Leigh, S. The Haunted Tower. (Illus.). 48p. 1989. PLB 11.96 (*0-88110-367-5*, Usborne) EDC.
—Journey to the Lost Temple. (Illus.). 48p. 1989. PLB 11.96 (*0-88110-406-X*); pap. 4.95 (*0-7460-0308-0*) EDC.
—Puzzle Castle. (Illus.). 32p. (ps up). 1993. PLB 13.96 (*0-88110-624-0*); pap. 5.95 (*0-7460-1284-5*) EDC.
—Puzzle Farm. (Illus.). 32p. (ps up). 1992. PLB 13.96 (*0-88110-555-4*, Usborne); pap. 5.95 (*0-7460-0712-4*, Usborne) EDC.
—Puzzle Island. (Illus.). 32p. (ps up). 1991. lib. bdg. 13.96 (*0-7460-0596-2*, Usborne); pap. 5.95 (*0-7460-0554-6*, Usborne) EDC.
—Puzzle Town. (Illus.). 32p. (ps up). 1991. PLB 13.96 (*0-88110-554-6*, Usborne); pap. 5.95 (*0-7460-0681-0*, Usborne) EDC.
—Puzzle World (B - U) (Illus.). 96p. (ps up). 1992. 13.95 (*0-7460-0732-9*) EDC.
Leigh, Susannah. Puzzle Planet. (Illus.). 32p. (gr. k-5). 1993. lib. bdg. 13.96 (*0-88110-646-1*, Usborne); pap. 5.95 (*0-7460-1286-1*, Usborne) EDC.
Leigh, Tom, illus. The Sesame Street Word Book. 72p. (ps). 1983. write for info. (*0-307-15549-8*, 15818, Golden Bks) Western Pub.
Leighton, Maxinne R. An Ellis Island Christmas. Nolan, Dennis, illus. 32p. (gr. 1-4). 1992. 15.00 (*0-670-83182-4*) Viking Child Bks.
Leih, Janet, ed. see Forelle, Helen.
Leiman, Sondra. America: The Jewish Experience. Sarna, Jonathan, ed. (Illus., Orig.). (gr. 4-6). 1994. pap. text ed. 12.00x (*0-8074-0500-0*, 123938); tchr's. guide 10.00 (*0-8074-0501-9*, 208034) UAHC.
Leiner, Katherine. Halloween. LC 92-39343. (Illus.). 48p. (gr. 2-6). 1992. SBE 15.95 (*0-689-31769-7*, Atheneum Child Bk) Macmillan Child Grp.
Leinwand, Gerald. Do We Need a New Constitution? LC 93-31847. 1994. write for info. (*0-531-11127-X*) Watts.
—The Environment. 128p. (gr. 7-12). 1990. 16.95x (*0-8160-2099-X*) Facts on File.
—Public Education. 128p. (gr. 7-12). 1992. lib. bdg. 16.95 (*0-8160-2100-7*) Facts on File.
—Transplants: Today's Medical Miracles. rev. ed. LC 92-17087. (Illus.). (gr. 9-12). 1992. PLB 13.40 (*0-531-13026-6*) Watts.
Leinwand, Gerald, ed. see LeVert, Marianne.
Leiper, Esther M., ed. see Lindow, Sandra.
Leiper, Esther M., ed. see Moore, Eugenia.
Leister, Mary. Wee Green Witch. Arnold, Elaine, illus. LC 78-12380. 44p. (ps up). 1978. 9.95 (*0-916144-30-5*) Stemmer Hse.
Leitch, Gordon, Jr. The Monetary Errors & Deceptions of the Supreme Court. LC 78-57901. 166p. (gr. 9-12). 1978. pap. 5.00 (*0-9605734-0-2*) Bicent Era.
Leithauser, Gladys, jt. auth. see Breitmeyer, Lois.
Leitner, Irving, jt. auth. see Leitner, Isabella.
Leitner, Isabella & Leitner, Irving. The Big Lie: A True Story. 1992. 13.95 (*0-590-45569-9*, 025, Scholastic Hardcover) Scholastic Inc.
Leitz, Pierr M., jt. auth. see Edge, Nellie.
Leiva, Miriam A., ed. see Burton, Grace, et al.
Leivis, Edith M. Haiku Is... a Feeling. King, James B., illus. Leivis, Edith M., intro. by. LC 89-64144. (Illus.). 64p. (Orig.). (gr. 1-3). 1990. pap. 5.95 (*0-9624993-0-7*) Pippin Bks.
LeJeune, Shonda. God Is. LeJeune, Shonda, illus. 32p. (Orig.). (gr. 3-8). 1993. pap. 8.95 (*0-87516-659-8*) DeVorss.
Lekic, Maria D. Ogonyok: Advanced. (RUS.). 160p. 1993. pap. 17.95 (*0-685-62843-4*, F4275-6, Natl Textbk); tchr's. manual 7.95 (*0-685-62844-2*, F4276-4, Natl Textbk) NTC Pub Grp.
Le Landgren. A Touch of Magic: A Fantasy Adventure. LC 90-8183. (Orig.). (gr. 2-7). 1990. pap. 7.95 (*0-943367-03-4*) Princess Pub.
Lelchuk, Alan. On Home Ground. Nacht, Merle, illus. LC 87-8496. 72p. (gr. 5 up). 1987. 9.95 (*0-15-200560-9*, Gulliver Bks) HarBrace.
Lellie, Herman & Bateson, Margaret. A Victorian Dollhouse. (Illus.). 4p. 1991. bds. 19.95 (*0-312-06228-1*) St Martin.
LeLoeuff, Jean. La Aventura de la Vida (The Adventure of Life) Puebla, Luis M., tr. Veronique, illus. (SPA.). 96p. (gr. 4 up). 1992. PLB 15.90 (*1-56294-177-1*) Millbrook Pr.
Leloup, Roger. Vulcan's Forge. Surbeck, Jean-Jacques, tr. from FRE. Leloup, Roger, illus. 49p. (Orig.). (gr. 12 up). 1994. pap. 6.95 (*0-87416-065-0*, Comcat Comics) Catalan Communs.
Lely, James A. Aquarius. 40p. (gr. 4). 1989. PLB 13.95s.p. (*0-88682-258-0*) Creative Ed.
—Libra. 40p. (gr. 4). 1989. PLB 13.95s.p. (*0-88682-262-9*) Creative Ed.
—Virgo. 40p. (gr. 4). 1989. PLB 13.95s.p. (*0-88682-259-9*) Creative Ed.
Le Mair, Henriette W. Mother's Little Rhyme Book. 24p. (ps-3). 1992. 6.95 (*0-399-22140-9*, Philomel Bks) Putnam Pub Group.
LeMair, Henriette W., illus. Baby's Diary. 112p. (ps up). 1987. 12.95 (*0-399-21454-2*, Philomel Bks) Putnam Pub Group.
Lemaitre, Pascal. Emily the Giraffe. Lemaitre, Pascal, illus. LC 92-85508. 32p. (ps-2). 1993. 13.95 (*1-56282-403-1*); PLB 13.89 (*1-56282-404-X*) Hyprn Child.
—Zelda's Secret. Lemaitre, Pascal, illus. LC 93-28448. (ps-3). 1993. PLB 13.95 (*0-8167-3309-0*); pap. 3.95t (*0-8167-3310-4*) Troll Assocs.

Leman, Jill. Sleepy Kittens. Leman, Martin, illus. LC 93-24232. 32p. 1994. 14.00 (*0-688-13288-X*, Tambourine Bks); PLB 13.93 (*0-688-13289-8*, Tambourine Bks) Morrow.
Leman, Martin. The Little Cats ABC Book. LC 93-26272. 1994. write for info. (*0-671-88612-6*) S&S Trade.
Lemans, Martin. Curiouser & Curiouser Cats. (Illus.). 32p. (ps-2). 1993. 16.95 (*0-575-04707-0*, Pub. by Gollancz UK) Trafalgar.
LeMaster, Leslie J. Bacteria & Viruses. LC 84-27414. (Illus.). 48p. (gr. k-4). 1985. PLB 15.27 (*0-516-01937-6*) Childrens.
—Cells & Tissues. LC 85-6695. (Illus.). 45p. (gr. k-3). 1985. PLB 15.27 (*0-516-01266-5*) Childrens.
—Nutrition. LC 85-7728. (Illus.). 45p. (gr. k-3). 1985. PLB 15.27 (*0-516-01271-1*) Childrens.
—Your Brain & Nervous System. LC 84-7635. (Illus.). 48p. (gr. k-4). 1984. PLB 15.27 (*0-516-01931-7*); pap. 4.95 (*0-516-41931-5*) Childrens.
—Your Heart & Blood. LC 84-7604. (Illus.). 48p. (gr. k-4). 1984. PLB 15.27 (*0-516-01933-3*); pap. 4.95 (*0-516-41933-1*) Childrens.
Lemay, Nita K., jt. auth. see Newman, Matt.
Lemberg, Alexis, jt. auth. see Lemberg, Ray.
Lemberg, Ray & Lemberg, Alexis. Daddy, Me & the Adventures of Growing Up. Evers, Melissa, illus. 32p. (Orig.). (gr. k-4). 1988. pap. 6.45 (*0-9619208-5-8*) Small Hands Pr.
Lembo, Diana L., jt. auth. see Gillespie, John T.
Lemelman, Martin. Chanukah Is... (Illus.). 10p. (ps-k). 1988. bds. 4.95 (*0-8074-0424-1*) UAHC.
—My Jewish Home. Lemelman, Martin, illus. 10p. (ps-k). 1988. pap. 3.95 boardbk. (*0-8074-0415-2*, 102002) UAHC.
—My Jewish Home: Simchah Ba'ambatyah - Fun in the Bathtub. (Illus.). 10p. (ps). 1987. polyvinyl 3.95 (*0-8074-0327-X*, 102001) UAHC.
Lemelman, Martin, illus. Jewish Holiday Book. 10p. 1989. bds. 4.95 (*0-8074-0431-4*, 102004) UAHC.
Lemerise, Bruce. Sheldon's Lunch. Lemerise, Bruce, illus. LC 80-10449. (ps-3). 1980. 5.95 (*0-8193-1025-5*) Parents.
LeMieux, A. C. Fruit Flies. DeGroat, Diane, illus. LC 93-29606. 1994. write for info. (*0-688-13299-5*, Tambourine Bks) Morrow.
—The T V Guidance Counselor. LC 92-33664. 240p. (gr. 7 up). 1993. 13.00 (*0-688-12402-X*, Tambourine Bks) Morrow.
Lemieux, Margo. Full Worm Moon. Parker, Robert A., illus. LC 93-14728. 32p. 1994. 15.00 (*0-688-12105-5*, Tambourine Bks); PLB 14.93 (*0-688-12106-3*, Tambourine Bks) Morrow.
Lemieux, Michele. The Pied Piper of Hamelin. Lemieux, Michele, illus. LC 92-21338. 32p. 1993. 15.00 (*0-688-09848-7*); PLB 14.93 (*0-688-09849-5*) Morrow Jr Bks.
—What's That Noise? Lemieux, Michele, illus. LC 84-16631. 32p. (ps-1). 1985. 11.95 (*0-688-04139-6*); PLB 11.88 (*0-688-04140-X*, Morrow Jr Bks) Morrow Jr Bks.
Lemke, Horst, illus. Places & Faces. LC 78-160446. 32p. (ps-k). 1985. 8.95 (*0-87592-041-1*) Scroll Pr.
Lemke, Stefan & Pricken, Marie-Luise L. Making Toys & Gifts. LC 91-3880. (Illus.). 64p. 1991. PLB 19.93 (*0-516-09259-6*); pap. 8.95 (*0-516-49259-4*) Childrens.
Lemley, Jo, jt. auth. see Lemley, Virg.
Lemley, Virg & Lemley, Jo. Children's Cookery, Naturally. (Illus.). 57p. (gr. 1-10). 1980. pap. 3.75 (*0-931798-05-1*) Wilderness Hse.
Lemmon, Tess. Apes. Butler, John, illus. LC 92-37692. (gr. 3 up). 1993. 15.45 (*0-395-66901-4*) Ticknor & Fields.
—Monkeys. (Illus.). 32p. (gr. 2-5). 1992. PLB 12.40 (*0-531-18454-4*, Pub. by Bookwright Pr) Watts.
Lemmons, Cherilynn. Randolph's Wonderful Adventure. (Illus.). 48p. (gr. 1-6). 1992. 6.95 (*0-8059-3289-5*) Dorrance.
Lemoine, Charles A. Louisiana's Cypress Bayou Elves: Pontain the Trapper. Lemoine, Charles A., illus. 40p. (Orig.). (gr. 1-12). 1986. pap. 5.00 (*0-941327-01-9*) Charles A Lemoine.
—Santa Clawfish. Lemoine, Charles A., illus. 32p. (Orig.). 1986. pap. 3.20 (*0-941327-00-0*) Charles A Lemoine.
Lemoine, Georges, illus. The Christmas Story According to St. Luke. 32p. 1978. PLB 13.95s.p. (*0-87191-957-5*) Creative Ed.
—Pied. (FRE.). (ps-1). 1989. 14.95 (*2-07-035701-5*) Schoenhof.
Lemoine, H. Etudes Enfantines for Piano, Op. 37. 52p. 1904. pap. 7.00 (*0-8258-0106-0*, L 323) Fischer Inc NY.
Lemu, Bridget. The Ideal Muslim Husband. 22p. (Orig.). 1993. pap. 1.75 (*1-881963-03-9*) Al-Saadawi Pubns.
—Islam & Alcohol. 18p. (Orig.). 1993. pap. 1.75 (*1-881963-02-0*) Al-Saadawi Pubns.
Lena, Dan & Howard, Marie. Sexual Assault: How to Defend Yourself. (gr. 10 up). 1990. pap. 6.95 (*0-8119-0677-9*) Lifetime.
Lena, Dan & Lena, Marie. My Power Book. (Illus.). 60p. 1991. wkbk. 10.00 (*0-9617032-0-2*) D & M Lena.
Lena, Daniel S. & Howard, Marie. Hands off... I'm Special! How to Tell Your Boyfriend No. Bartimole, John, ed. (Illus.). 96p. (Orig.). (gr. 7 up). 1988. pap. 6.95 (*0-936320-30-3*) Compact Bks.
Lena, Marie, jt. auth. see Lena, Dan.

Lenard, Alexander, notes by. Winnie Ille Pu. (LAT.). 148p. (gr. 9-12). 9.60 (*0-939507-14-5*, B702) Amer Classical.
Lenchner, George. Mathematical Olympiad Contest Problems for Children (Also for Teachers, Parents, & Other Adults) Lenchner, George, illus. LC 90-83825. 176p. (Orig.). (gr. 3-8). 1990. pap. 18.95 (*0-9626662-0-3*) Glenwood Pubns.
Lenett, Robin, et al. Sometimes It's O. K. to Tell Secrets! 128p. (Orig.). 1986. pap. 3.95 (*0-8125-9454-1*) Tor Bks.
Lenga. Amazing Fact Book of Planes. (Illus.). 32p. (gr. 4-8). 1987. PLB 14.95s.p. (*0-87191-848-X*) Creative Ed.
L'Engle, Madeleine. An Acceptable Time. (gr. 7 up). 1989. 16.00 (*0-374-30027-5*) FS&G.
—And Both Were Young. (Orig.). (gr. 7 up). 1983. pap. 3.99 (*0-440-90229-0*, LFL) Dell.
—And Both Were Young. LC 82-72751. 240p. (gr. 7 up). 1983. 14.95 (*0-385-29237-6*) Delacorte.
—The Arm of the Starfish. 240p. (gr. 7 up). 1980. pap. 3.99 (*0-440-90183-9*, LFL) Dell.
—The Arm of the Starfish. LC 65-10919. 256p. (gr. 7 up). 1965. 17.00 (*0-374-30396-7*) FS&G.
—Camila. Barbadillo, Pedro, tr. (SPA.). 197p. (gr. 9-12). 1992. pap. write for info. (*84-204-4555-X*) Santillana.
—Camilla. 288p. (gr. 7 up). 1982. pap. 3.50 (*0-440-91171-0*, LFL) Dell.
—Dance in the Desert. Shimin, Symeon, illus. LC 68-29465. 64p. (ps up). 1969. 14.95 (*0-374-31684-8*) FS&G.
—Dance in the Desert. Shimin, Symeon, illus. 56p. (ps up). 1988. pap. 4.95 (*0-374-41684-2*) FS&G.
—Dragons in the Waters. 288p. (gr. 7 up). 1982. pap. 3.99 (*0-440-91719-0*, LFL) Dell.
—Dragons in the Waters. LC 76-2477. 304p. (gr. 7 up). 1976. 17.00 (*0-374-31868-9*) FS&G.
—The Glorious Impossible. Giotto, illus. 64p. (gr. 3 up). 1990. pap. 19.95 jacketed (*0-671-68690-9*, Little Simon) S&S Trade.
—A House Like a Lotus. LC 84-48471. 307p. (gr. 7 up). 1984. 17.00 (*0-374-33385-8*) FS&G.
—A House Like a Lotus. (gr. 6-12). 1985. pap. 3.99 (*0-440-93685-3*, LFL) Dell.
—The Journey with Jonah. (ps up). 1991. pap. 5.95 (*0-374-43858-7*) FS&G.
—Madeleine L'Engle's Time Quartet, 4 vols. (gr. 4 up). 1987. pap. 14.00 (*0-440-95208-5*) Dell.
—Madeleine L'Engle's Time Trilogy, 3 bks. Incl. A Wrinkle in Time; A Wind in the Door; A Swiftly Tilting Planet. 1986. pap. 9.30 boxed set (*0-440-95207-7*, LE) Dell.
—Many Waters. LC 86-14911. 310p. (gr. 4 up). 1986. 17.00 (*0-374-34796-4*); ltd. ed. o.s.i. 50.00 (*0-374-34797-2*) FS&G.
—Many Waters. (gr. k-12). 1987. pap. 3.50 (*0-440-95252-2*, LFL) Dell.
—Many Waters. (gr. 4-7). 1987. pap. 3.99 (*0-440-40548-3*) Dell.
—Meet the Austins. 192p. (gr. 5-9). 1981. pap. 3.50 (*0-440-95777-X*, LE) Dell.
—The Moon by Night. 256p. (gr. 6 up). 1981. pap. 3.50 (*0-440-95776-1*, LE) Dell.
—The Moon by Night. LC 63-9072. 224p. (gr. 7 up). 1963. 16.00 (*0-374-35049-3*) FS&G.
—A Ring of Endless Light. 336p. (gr. 9 up). 1981. pap. 3.99 (*0-440-97232-9*, LE) Dell.
—The Small Rain: A Novel. LC 84-47839. 371p. (gr. 7 up). 1984. 14.95 (*0-374-26637-9*) FS&G.
—Small Rain: A Novel. LC 84-47839. 371p. (gr. 7 up). 1985. pap. 10.00 (*0-374-51912-9*) FS&G.
—A Swiftly Tilting Planet. (gr. 7 up). 1979. pap. 3.99 (*0-440-90158-8*, LFL) Dell.
—A Swiftly Tilting Planet. LC 78-9648. 288p. (gr. 5 up). 1978. 15.95 (*0-374-37362-0*) FS&G.
—Swiftly Tilting Planet. (gr. 4-7). 1981. pap. 3.99 (*0-440-40158-5*) Dell.
—A Swiftly Tilting Planet. large type ed. LC 93-21812. 1993. Alk. paper. lib. bdg. 15.95 (*1-56054-710-3*) Thorndike Pr.
—The Time Trilogy: A Wrinkle in Time; A Wind in the Door; A Swiftly Tilting Planet, 3 vols. (gr. 5 up). 1979. Boxed Set. 47.85 (*0-374-37592-5*) FS&G.
—Trailing Clouds of Glory: Spiritual Values in Children's Books. Brooke, Avery, contrib. by. LC 84-29081. 144p. (gr. 5-9). 1985. 13.00 (*0-664-32721-4*, Westminster) Westminster John Knox.
—The Twenty-Four Days Before Christmas. (gr. k-6). 1987. pap. 3.50 (*0-440-40105-4*, YB) Dell.
—A Wind in the Door. 224p. (gr. 5-9). 1976. pap. 3.99 (*0-440-98761-X*, LFL) Dell.
—A Wind in the Door. 224p. (gr. 5-9). 1974. pap. 3.99 (*0-440-48761-7*, YB) Dell.
—A Wind in the Door. LC 73-75176. 224p. (gr. 7 up). 1973. 15.95 (*0-374-38443-6*) FS&G.
—A Wind in the Door. large type ed. 270p. 1993. Repr. lib. bdg. 15.95 (*1-56054-615-8*) Thorndike Pr.
—A Wrinkle in Time. 224p. (gr. 5-9). 1976. pap. 3.99 (*0-440-99805-0*, LFL) Dell.
—A Wrinkle in Time. 224p. (gr. 5-9). 1973. pap. 3.99 (*0-440-49805-8*, YB) Dell.
—A Wrinkle in Time. LC 62-7203. 224p. (gr. 7 up). 1962. 17.00 (*0-374-38613-7*) FS&G.
—A Wrinkle in Time: (Una Arruga en el Tiempo) (gr. 1-6). 15.95 (*84-204-4074-4*) Santillana.
—The Young Unicorns. 224p. (gr. 8 up). 1989. pap. 3.99 (*0-440-99919-7*, LFL) Dell.

—The Young Unicorns. LC 68-13682. 256p. (gr. 7 up). 1968. 16.95 (*0-374-38778-8*) FS&G.

Lenihan, Edmund. Stories of Old Ireland for Children. 1990. pap. 9.95 (*0-85342-777-1*) Dufour.

—Strange Irish Tales for Children. Gervin, Joseph, illus. 128p. pap. (*Illus.*). 1992. pap. 9.95 (*0-85342-833-6*, Pub. by Mercier Pr Eire) Dufour.

Lennon, John & McCartney, Paul. Yellow Submarine. Chojnacki, Cathy, illus. 24p. 1993. 12.95 (*0-7935-1859-8*, 00183013) H Leonard Pub Corp.

Lennon, Patricia & Moore, Douglas. Te Toca a Ti. (SPA., Illus.). 160p. (Orig.). (gr. 7-9). 1990. wkbk. 14. 95 (*1-879279-04-5*, TX 3-018-188) Proficiency Pr.

Lennon, Patricia, et al. The Foreign Language Teacher's Handbook: Aiming for Proficiency in Spanish. (SPA., Illus.). 200p. (Orig.). (gr. 8). 1989. tchr's ed. 28.95 (*1-879279-01-0*, TX 2-670-457) Proficiency Pr.

Lennon, Rebecca D. Keyboard Capers: Music Theory for Children. 143p. 1993. pap. text ed. 18.95 (*1-884098-01-0*) Elijah Co.

Lennox, E. R. The Wizard's Dressing-Gown. (Illus.). 32p. (gr. 2-4). 1991. 14.95 (*0-237-51100-2*, Pub. by Evans Bros Ltd) Trafalgar.

Lens, Sidney. Vietnam: A War on Two Fronts. (Illus.). 144p. (gr. 7 up). 1990. 15.95 (*0-525-67320-2*, Lodestar Bks) Dutton Child Bks.

Lenski, Lois. Big Book of Mr. Small. (Illus.). (ps-3). 1980. pap. 9.95 (*0-8098-6026-0*) McKay.

—Cowboy Small. LC 60-12094. (Illus.). (gr. k-3). 1980. 5.25 (*0-8098-1021-2*) McKay.

—Little Airplane. Lenski, Lois, illus. LC 59-12487. (gr. k-3). 1980. 5.25 (*0-8098-1004-2*) McKay.

—Little Auto. Lenski, Lois, illus. LC 58-14239. (gr. k-3). 1980. 5.25 (*0-8098-1001-8*) McKay.

—Little Farm. Lenski, Lois, illus. LC 58-12902. (gr. k-3). 1980. 5.25 (*0-8098-1009-3*) McKay.

—Lois Lenski's Big Big Book of Mr. Small. (Illus.). 300p. (ps-1). 1985. 5.98 (*0-517-46307-5*) Outlet Bk Co.

—Mr. & Mrs. Noah. LC 48-5989. (Illus.). 48p. (ps-1). 1962. PLB 12.89 (*0-690-54562-2*, Crowell Jr Bks) HarpC Child Bks.

—More Mr. Small. (ps-3). 1980. 9.95 (*0-8098-6300-6*, Walk) McKay.

—Sing a Song of People. Laroche, Giles, photos by. (ps-3). 1987. pap. 15.95 (*0-316-52074-8*) Little.

—Sing for Peace. 16p. (ps-2). 1985. pap. 1.50 (*0-8361-3396-X*) Herald Pr.

—Strawberry Girl. Lenski, Lois, illus. 208p. (gr. k-6). 1987. pap. 3.50 (*0-440-48347-6*, YB) Dell.

—Strawberry Girl. Lenski, Lois, illus. LC 45-7609. 192p. (gr. 4-6). 1945. 16.00 (*0-397-30109-X*, Lipp Jr Bks); PLB 15.89 (*0-397-30110-3*, Lipp Jr Bks) HarpC Child Bks.

Lenssen, Ann. A Rainbow Balloon: A Book of Concepts. LC 91-31830. (Illus.). 32p. (ps-3). 1992. 13.50 (*0-525-65093-8*, Cobblehill Bks) Dutton Child Bks.

Lent, Blair. Bayberry Bluff. (ps-3). 1987. 13.45 (*0-395-35384-X*) HM.

—Bayberry Bluff. Lent, Blair, illus. 32p. (gr. k-3). 1992. pap. 4.80 (*0-395-62984-5*, Sandpiper) HM.

—Molasses Flood. Lent, Blair, illus. LC 92-1125. 32p. (ps-3). 1992. 14.45 (*0-395-45314-3*) HM.

Lent, Blair, jt. auth. see Small, Ernest.

Lent, Penny. Young Writer's Manuscript Manual: A Students Guide on How to Submit Their Work for Publication. LC 93-78340. 64p. (Orig.). 1993. pap. 7.95 (*1-877882-07-0*, Kldoscope Pr) SCW Pubns.

—Young Writer's Market Manual: A Students Guide on Where to Send Their Work for Publication. LC 93-78343. (Orig.). 1993. pap. 7.95 (*1-877882-08-9*, Kldoscope Pr) SCW Pubns.

Lenters, William R. The Church Cares. 77p. (Orig.). (gr. 7-8). 1987. pap. text ed. 7.25 (*0-930265-32-7*); tchr's. ed 8.95 (*0-930265-33-5*) CRC Pubns.

Lentz, Pam. My Camera. (ps). 1993. 5.95 (*0-307-15903-5*, Golden Pr) Western Pub.

—My Flightbag. (ps). 1993. 5.95 (*0-307-15902-7*, Golden Pr) Western Pub.

—My Purse. (ps). 1993. 5.95 (*0-307-15901-9*, Golden Pr) Western Pub.

—My Schoolbag. (ps). 1993. 5.95 (*0-307-15900-0*, Golden Pr) Western Pub.

Lenz. Lotte Soll Nicht Sterben. (gr. 7-12). pap. 4.95 (*0-88436-039-3*, 45260) EMC.

Leo, Kathleen R., et al, eds. Waiting for the Apples. LC 82-62746. (Illus.). 100p. (Orig.). (gr. k up). 1983. pap. 6.50 (*0-9606678-2-2*) Sylvan Pubns.

Leo, Punana. Pai Ka Leo. (Illus.). 40p. (Orig.). (ps-6). 1989. pap. 4.95 (*0-935848-63-0*) Bess Pr.

Leodhas, Sorche Nic see Nic Leodhas, Sorche.

Leokum, Arkady. Tell Me Why. rev. ed. (Illus.). 208p. (gr. 2-9). 1986. No. 1. 9.95 ea. (*0-448-22501-8*, G&D) No. 2 (*0-448-22502-6*) No. 3 (*0-448-22503-4*) No. 4 (*0-448-22504-2*) Putnam Pub Group.

—Tell Me Why, No. 5. (Illus.). 176p. (gr. 2-9). 1988. 9.95 (*0-448-19069-9*, G&D) Putnam Pub Group.

Leon, George D. Electronics Projects for Young Scientists. LC 91-17823. (Illus.). 128p. (gr. 9-12). 1991. PLB 13.90 (*0-531-11071-0*) Watts.

—Explorers of the Americas Before Columbus. (Illus.). 64p. (gr. 7-9). 1990. 12.90 (*0-531-10667-5*) Watts.

Leon, Margaret. Barnaby Bear. Leon, Linda, illus. 32p. (ps-8). 1983. 7.95 (*0-920806-42-2*, Pub. by Penumbra Pr CN) U of Toronto Pr.

Leon, Vicki. Parrots, Macaws & Cockatoos. (Illus.). 40p. (Orig.). (gr. 5 up). 1989. pap. text ed. 7.95 (*0-918303-20-6*) Blake Pub.

—A Pod of Killer Whales. Foott, Jeff, photos by. (Illus.). 40p. (gr. 5 up). 1988. pap. 7.95 (*0-918303-16-8*) Blake Pub.

—A Raft of Sea Otters. rev. ed. LC 93-15418. (Illus.). 48p. (Orig.). (gr. 5 up). 1993. perfect bdg. 9.95 (*0-918303-34-6*) Blake Pub.

—Seals & Sea Lions. (Illus.). 40p. (Orig.). (gr. 5 up). 1988. pap. 7.95 (*0-918303-15-X*) Blake Pub.

Leon, Vicki, jt. auth. see Barnhart, Diana.

Leon, Vicki, ed. see Berger, Bruce.

Leon, Vicki, ed. see Brody, Jean.

Leon, Vicki, ed. see Fourie, Denise K.

Leon, Vicki, ed. see Gohier, Francois.

Leon, Vicki, ed. see Hall, Howard.

Leon, Vicki, ed. see Hamilton, Jean.

Leon, Vicki, ed. see Holing, Dwight.

Leon, Vicki, ed. see Hunt, Joni P.

Leon, Vicki, ed. see Wilson, Barbara.

Leonard, Alain. Barnaby & the Big Gorilla. LC 91-25414. (Illus.). 32p. 1992. 15.00 (*0-688-11291-9*, Tambourine Bks); PLB 14.93 (*0-688-11292-7*, Tambourine Bks) Morrow.

—Theodore's Superheroes. Tambourine Books Staff, tr. from FRE. Leonard, Alain, illus. LC 92-82140. 32p. (ps up). 1993. 15.00 (*0-688-12766-5*, Tambourine Bks); PLB 14.93 (*0-688-12767-3*, Tambourine Bks) Morrow.

Leonard, Alison. Tina's Chance. 160p. (gr. 6 up). 1992. pap. 3.99 (*0-14-032882-3*) Puffin Bks.

Leonard, Calista V. Guess Who. 36p. (ps-6). 1992. PLB write for info. (*0-9634165-0-2*) Vistoso Bks.

Leonard, Camille, ed. see Flowers, Sandra H.

Leonard, Hal. Disney Children's Favorites Songbook. (Illus.). 112p. 1991. pap. 12.95 (*0-7935-0090-7*, 00490496) H Leonard Pub Corp.

—Disney Family Fun Activity Book. (Illus.). 80p. 1991. pap. 12.95 (*0-7935-0755-3*, 00290344) H Leonard Pub Corp.

Leonard, Kay. Paper Kaleidoscopes. (Illus.). 40p. (gr. k-12). 1989. pap. 5.95 (*0-685-26430-0*) Pelona Pr.

Leonard, Larry. Far Walker. Gustavson, Susan, illus. LC 88-12290. 92p. (gr. 1 up). 1988. 12.95 (*0-932576-60-5*) Breitenbush Bks.

Leonard, Laura. Finding Papa. LC 90-23742. 192p. (gr. 3-7). 1991. SBE 14.95 (*0-689-31526-0*, Atheneum Child Bk) Macmillan Child Grp.

—Saving Damaris. LC 89-6717. 192p. (gr. 3-7). 1989. SBE 14.95 (*0-689-31553-8*, Atheneum Child Bk) Macmillan Child Grp.

Leonard, Marcia. Alphabet Bandits: An ABC Book. Cocca-Leffler, Maryann, illus. LC 89-4933. 24p. (gr. k-2). 1990. PLB 9.59 (*0-8167-1718-4*); pap. text ed. 1.95 (*0-8167-1719-2*) Troll Assocs.

—Angry. 1988. pap. 3.95 (*0-553-05482-1*) Bantam.

—Bear's Busy Year: A Book about Seasons. LC 89-4946. (Illus.). 24p. (gr. k-2). 1990. PLB 9.59 (*0-8167-1720-6*); pap. text ed. 1.95 (*0-8167-1721-4*) Troll Assocs.

—Best Snowman Ever. 10p. (ps). 1989. Bk. & ornament. pap. 2.95 (*0-8167-1488-6*) Troll Assocs.

—Birthday in a Bathtub. Brook, Bonnie, ed. Wallner, John, illus. 24p. (ps-1). 1989. 5.95 (*0-671-68592-9*); PLB 9.98 (*0-671-68588-0*) Silver Pr.

—Catch a Mouse. 1988. 4.95 (*0-553-05425-2*, Little Rooster) Bantam.

—Chase That Pig. Palmisciano, Diane, illus. 24p. (ps up). 1988. pap. write for info. (*0-553-05476-7*) Bantam.

—Counting Kangaroos, A Book about Numbers. Palmisciano, Diane, illus. LC 89-4960. 24p. (gr. k-2). 1990. PLB 9.59 (*0-8167-1722-2*); pap. text ed. 1.95 (*0-8167-1723-0*) Troll Assocs.

—Eating. 1988. 3.95 (*0-685-18947-3*) Bantam.

—The Elves & the Shoemaker. Brook, Bonnie, ed. Banek, Yvette & Cushman, Doug, illus. 24p. (ps-1). 1990. 5.95 (*0-671-69351-4*); PLB 9.98 (*0-671-69347-6*) Silver Pr.

—Follow Me. 1988. pap. 4.95 (*0-553-05477-5*, Little Rooster) Bantam.

—Getting Dressed. 1988. pap. 3.95 (*0-553-05467-8*) Bantam.

—The Giant Baby & Other Giant Tales. Alley, R. W., illus. LC 93-6225. 1994. pap. 2.95 (*0-590-46892-8*) Scholastic Inc.

—Going to Bed. 1988. 3.95 (*0-553-05468-6*) Bantam.

—Goldilocks & the Three Bears. Brook, Bonnie, ed. Banek, Yvette & Cushman, Doug, illus. 24p. (ps-1). 1990. 5.95 (*0-671-69350-6*); PLB 9.98 (*0-671-69346-8*) Silver Pr.

—Gregory & Mr. Grump. Brook, Bonnie, ed. Chambliss, Maxie & Iosa, Ann W., illus. 24p. (ps-1). 1990. 5.95 (*0-671-70406-0*); lib. bdg. 9.98 (*0-671-70402-8*) Silver Pr.

—Hannah the Hamster Hunter. Brook, Bonnie, ed. Chambliss, Maxie & Iosa, Ann W., illus. 24p. (ps-1). 1990. 5.95 (*0-671-70404-4*); lib. bdg. 9.98 (*0-671-70399-4*) Silver Pr.

—Happy. 1988. pap. 3.95 (*0-553-05483-X*) Bantam.

—Haunted House. 1989. bds. 2.95 (*0-8167-1889-X*) Troll Assocs.

—How Did That Happen? Series, 4 vols. Chambliss, Maxie & Iosa, Ann W., illus. 96p. (ps-1). 1990. Set. 23.80 (*0-671-31233-9*); Set. 14.85s.p. (*0-685-37312-6*); Set. PLB 39.92 (*0-671-31234-0*); Set. PLB 29.94s.p. (*0-685-37313-4*) Silver Pr.

—It's Christmas, Baby-Boo. Regan, Dana, illus. 1992. bds. 3.25 (*0-8378-3798-7*) Gibson.

—Jeffrey Lee, Future Fireman. Brook, Bonnie, ed. Chambliss, Maxie & Iosa, Ann W., illus. LC 90-31299. 24p. (ps-1). 1990. 5.95 (*0-671-70407-9*); lib. bdg. 9.98 (*0-671-70403-6*) Silver Pr.

—King Lionheart's Castle. Wallner, Alexandra, illus. 24p. (ps-1). 1992. 5.95 (*0-382-72974-9*); PLB 9.98 (*0-382-72973-0*) Silver.

—The Kitten Twins: A Book about Opposites. Cocca-Leffler, Maryann, illus. LC 89-4945. 24p. (gr. k-2). 1990. PLB 9.59 (*0-8167-1724-9*); pap. text ed. 1.95 (*0-8167-1725-7*) Troll Assocs.

—Laura Jean the Yard Sale Queen. Brook, Bonnie, ed. Iosa, Ann W., illus. LC 89-70304. 24p. (ps-1). 1990. 5.95 (*0-671-70405-2*); PLB 9.98 (*0-671-70401-X*) Silver Pr.

—Little Duck Finds a Friend. 32p. (ps). 1984. pap. 2.50 (*0-553-15275-0*) Bantam.

—Little Owl Leaves the Nest. Newson, Carol, illus. 32p. 1984. pap. 2.75 (*0-553-15460-5*) Bantam.

—Little Pig's Birthday. Hockerman, Dennis, illus. 32p. 1984. pap. 2.50 (*0-553-15267-X*) Bantam.

—Little Rabbit's Baby Sister. 32p. (Orig.). (ps). 1984. pap. 2.50 (*0-553-15274-2*) Bantam.

—Midnight Cat. 1989. bds. 2.95 (*0-8167-1887-3*) Troll Assocs.

—Noisy Neighbors: A Book about Animal Sounds. Weissman, Bari, illus. LC 89-4959. 24p. (gr. k-2). 1990. PLB 9.59 (*0-8167-1726-5*); pap. text ed. 1.95 (*0-8167-1727-3*) Troll Assocs.

—Paintbox Penguins, A Book about Colors. Palmisciano, Diane, illus. LC 89-4979. 24p. (gr. k-2). 1990. lib. bdg. 9.59 (*0-8167-1716-8*); pap. text ed. 1.95 (*0-8167-1717-6*) Troll Assocs.

—Pumpkin Magic. 1989. bds. 2.95 (*0-8167-1888-1*) Troll Assocs.

—Rainboots for Breakfast. Brook, Bonnie, ed. Himmelman, John, illus. 24p. (ps-1). 1989. 5.95 (*0-671-68591-0*); PLB 9.98 (*0-671-68587-2*) Silver Pr.

—Rumplestilskin. Brook, Bonnie, ed. Banek, Yvette & Cushman, Doug, illus. 24p. (ps-1). 1990. 5.95 (*0-671-69352-2*); PLB 9.98 (*0-671-69348-4*) Silver Pr.

—Scared. 1988. pap. 3.95 (*0-553-05484-8*) Bantam.

—Secret Summer. (gr. 3-7). 1990. 12.95 (*0-943021-04-9*) Funchess Jones.

—Shopping for Snowflakes. Brook, Bonnie, ed. Himmelman, John, illus. 24p. (ps-1). 1989. 5.95 (*0-671-68594-5*); PLB 9.98 (*0-671-68590-2*) Silver Pr.

—Silly. 1988. pap. 3.95 (*0-553-05485-6*) Bantam.

—Swimming in the Sand. Brook, Bonnie, ed. Wallner, John, illus. 24p. (ps-1). 1989. 5.95 (*0-671-68593-7*); PLB 9.98 (*0-671-68589-9*) Silver Pr.

—The Three Little Pigs. Brook, Bonnie, ed. Banek, Yvette & Cushman, Doug, illus. 24p. (ps-1). 1990. 5.95 (*0-671-69349-2*); PLB 9.98 (*0-671-69345-X*) Silver Pr.

—Violet & the Pirates. Wallner, John, illus. 24p. (ps-1). 1992. 5.95 (*0-671-72976-4*); lib. bdg. 9.98 (*0-671-72975-6*) Silver Pr.

—What Next, 4 bks. Himmelman, John & Wallner, John, illus. (ps-1). 1990. Set, 24p. ea. 19.80 (*0-671-94102-X*, J Messner); Set, 24p. ea. lib. bdg. 39.92 (*0-671-94101-1*) S&S Trade.

—What's Missing? Ser, 4 vols. Cushman, Doug & Banek, Yvette, illus. 96p. (ps-1). 1990. Set. 23.80 (*0-671-94433-9*); Set. 14.85s.p. (*0-685-46991-3*); Set. PLB 39.92 (*0-671-94432-0*); Set. PLB 29.94s.p. (*0-685-46992-1*) Silver Pr.

—Your First Adventure: Little Goat's Big Brother, No. 12. Santoro, Chris, illus. 24p. (Orig.). 1987. pap. 2.50 (*0-553-15503-2*) Bantam.

Leonard, Marcia & DeRosa. Little Raccoon Goes to the Beach. (ps-7). 1987. pap. 2.50 (*0-553-15326-9*) Bantam.

Leonard, Marcia & Duell. Little Kangaroo's Bad Day. (ps-7). 1987. pap. 2.75 (*0-553-15461-3*) Bantam.

Leonard, Marcia & Schmidt, Karen. Little Mouse Makes a Mess. 32p. (Orig.). (gr. 1). 1985. pap. 2.50 (*0-553-15301-3*) Bantam.

—Little Panda Gets Lost. 32p. (Orig.). (gr. 1). 1985. pap. 2.50 (*0-553-15302-1*) Bantam.

Leonard, Marcia, adapted by. Your First Adventure: Little Kitten Sleeps Over, No. 9. Schmidt, Karen, illus. 32p. (Orig.). 1987. pap. 2.50 (*0-553-15472-9*) Bantam.

Leonard, Mary K. Art for the Classroom Teacher. Cooper, William H., ed. LC 82-73585. (Illus.). 100p. (Orig.). (gr. k-6). 1982. pap. text ed. 11.93 (*0-914127-00-4*) Univ Class.

Leonard, Michael. Learning BASIC: Answers & Notes. 38p. (gr. 4-8). 1988. pap. text ed. 2.95 (*0-913684-14-7*) Key Curr Pr.

—Learning BASIC, Bk. 1: PRINT & GOTO. 44p. (gr. 4-8). 1988. pap. text ed. 2.30 (*0-913684-10-4*) Key Curr Pr.

—Learning BASIC, Bk. 2: INPUT & IF-THEN. 44p. (gr. 4-8). 1988. pap. text ed. 2.30 (*0-913684-11-2*) Key Curr Pr.

—Learning BASIC, Bk. 3: LET & FOR-NEXT. 52p. (gr. 4-8). 1988. pap. text ed. 2.30 (*0-913684-12-0*) Key Curr Pr.

Leonard, Paul H., jt. auth. see Boone, J. Allen.

Leonard, Robert J. Stupid Stories: Nonstop Nonsense for Children of All Ages. Green, Herb, illus. 108p. (Orig.). (gr. 5-10). 1989. pap. 5.95 (*0-930753-05-4*, Pub. by Spectacle Ln Pr) Spect Ln Pr.

Leonardo, Bianca, ed. see Boone, J. Allen & Leonard, Paul H.

Leonardo, Bianca, ed. see Conwell, Russell H.

Leone, Bruno, ed. Capitalism: Opposing Viewpoints. 2nd, rev. ed. LC 86-3079. (Illus.). 150p. (Orig.). (gr. 9-12). 1986. lib. bdg. 17.95 (*0-89908-384-6*); pap. text ed. 9.95 (*0-89908-359-5*) Greenhaven.
—Communism: Opposing Viewpoints. 2nd rev. ed. LC 86-338. (Illus.). 210p. (Orig.). (gr. 9-12). 1986. lib. bdg. 17.95 (*0-89908-385-4*); pap. text ed. 9.95 (*0-89908-360-9*) Greenhaven.
—Internationalism: Opposing Viewpoints. 2nd rev. ed. LC 86-339. (Illus.). 150p. (gr. 9-12). 1986. 17.95 (*0-89908-383-8*); pap. text ed. 9.95 (*0-89908-358-7*) Greenhaven.
—Nationalism. 2nd rev. ed. LC 86-324. (Illus.). 150p. (gr. 9-12). 1986. lib. bdg. 17.95 (*0-89908-387-0*); pap. text ed. 9.95 (*0-89908-362-5*) Greenhaven.
—Racism: Opposing Viewpoints. 2nd, rev. ed. LC 86-360. (Illus.). 150p. (Orig.). (gr. 9-12). 1986. PLB 17.95 (*0-89908-382-X*); pap. 9.95 (*0-89908-357-9*) Greenhaven.
—Socialism: Opposing Viewpoints. 2nd rev. ed. LC 86-335. (Illus.). 150p. (Orig.). 1986. lib. bdg. 17.95 (*0-89908-386-2*); pap. text ed. 9.95 (*0-89908-361-7*) Greenhaven.
Leone, Dee. Christmas A-Z. 96p. (gr. 2-7). 1989. 10.95 (*0-86653-499-7*, SS1892, Shining Star Pubns) Good Apple.
—The Miracles of Jesus. 48p. (ps-1). 1990. 6.95 (*0-86653-554-3*, SS1874, Shining Star Pubns) Good Apple.
—The Stories of Noah & Joseph. (Illus.). 48p. (ps-1). 1992. 6.95 (*0-86653-645-0*, SS2811, Shining Star Pubns) Good Apple.
—Vacation Bible School Activities. 96p. (gr. 2-7). 1990. 10.95 (*0-86653-525-X*, SS1818, Shining Star Pubns) Good Apple.
—The World God Made. 48p. (ps-1). 1991. 6.95 (*0-86653-636-1*, SS1894, Shining Star Pubns) Good Apple.
Leopold, Nikia C. Sandcastle Seahorses. LC 87-35978. 45p. (Orig.). 1988. pap. 5.95 (*0-913123-17-X*) Galileo.
LePoff, Arlene, jt. auth. see Prager, Janice.
Lepon, Shoshana. Hanukkah Carousel. (ps-1). 1993. 12.95 (*0-943706-11-4*) Yllw Brick Rd.
—Hillel Builds a House. Barr, Marilyn, illus. LC 92-39383. 1993. cancelled (*0-929371-41-0*); pap. 5.95 (*0-929371-42-9*) Kar Ben.
—Noah & the Rainbow. Friedman, Aaron, illus. LC 92-26431. 1993. write for info. (*1-880582-04-X*); pap. write for info. (*1-880582-05-8*) Judaica Pr.
—The Ten Plagues of Egypt. Goldstein-Alpern, Neva, ed. Forst, Siegmund, illus. 32p. (gr. 4-8). 1988. 8.95 (*0-910818-77-0*); pap. 6.95 (*0-910818-76-2*) Judaica Pr.
—The Ten Tests of Abraham. Forst, Siegmund, illus. 32p. (Orig.). (gr. k-4). 1986. 7.95 (*0-317-52412-7*); pap. 5.95 (*0-910818-67-3*) Judaica Pr.
Lepon, Shoshona. Joseph the Dreamer. 32p. (gr. k-4). 1991. 11.95 (*0-910818-92-4*); pap. 8.95 (*0-910818-93-2*) Judaica Pr.
Lepore, Charles S., Jr. A Day at the North Pole. 1993. 7.95 (*0-8062-4688-X*) Carlton.
Leppard, Lois G. Mandie & the Abandoned Mine, Bk. 8. LC 87-70883. 144p. (Orig.). (gr. 5-8). 1987. pap. 3.99 (*0-87123-932-9*) Bethany Hse.
—Mandie & the Angel's Secret. (gr. 4-7). 1993. pap. 3.99 (*1-55661-370-9*) Bethany Hse.
—Mandie & the Charleston Phantom, Bk. 7. LC 86-7098. 128p. (Orig.). (gr. 4-7). 1986. pap. 3.99 (*0-87123-650-8*) Bethany Hse.
—Mandie & the Cherokee Legend, Bk. 2. LC 83-70894. 144p. (Orig.). (gr. 4-7). 1983. pap. 3.99 (*0-87123-321-5*) Bethany Hse.
—Mandie & the Fiery Rescue. 160p. (Orig.). (gr. 3-7). 1993. pap. 3.99 (*1-55661-289-3*) Bethany Hse.
—Mandie & the Forbidden Attic, Bk. 4. LC 84-72710. 144p. (Orig.). (gr. 4-7). 1985. pap. 3.99 (*0-87123-822-5*) Bethany Hse.
—Mandie & the Foreign Spies. 160p. (Orig.). (gr. 3-8). 1990. pap. 3.99 (*1-55661-147-1*) Bethany Hse.
—Mandie & the Ghost Bandits, Bk. 3. LC 84-71151. 128p. (Orig.). (gr. 5-7). 1984. pap. 3.99 (*0-87123-442-4*) Bethany Hse.
—Mandie & the Hidden Treasure, Bk. 9. LC 87-71606. 144p. (Orig.). (gr. 5-8). 1987. pap. 3.99 (*0-87123-977-9*) Bethany Hse.
—Mandie & the Holiday Surprise, Bk. 11. LC 88-71502. 160p. (gr. 3-6). 1988. pap. 3.99 (*1-55661-036-X*) Bethany Hse.
—Mandie & the Jumping Juniper. 160p. (Orig.). (gr. 3-7). 1991. 3.99 (*1-55661-200-1*) Bethany Hse.
—Mandie & the Medicine Man, Bk. 6. LC 85-73426. 150p. (Orig.). (gr. 4-8). 1986. pap. 3.99 (*0-87123-891-8*) Bethany Hse.
—Mandie & the Midnight Journey. 160p. (Orig.). (gr. 1-6). 1989. pap. 3.99 (*1-55661-084-X*) Bethany Hse.
—Mandie & the Mysterious Bells, Bk. 10. LC 87-72792. 160p. (Orig.). (gr. 4-8). 1988. pap. 3.99 (*1-55661-000-9*) Bethany Hse.
—Mandie & the Mysterious Fisherman. (gr. 4-7). 1992. pap. 3.99 (*1-55661-235-4*) Bethany Hse.
—Mandie & the Secret Tunnel, Bk. 1. LC 82-74053. 144p. (Orig.). (gr. 4-7). 1983. pap. 3.99 (*0-87123-320-7*) Bethany Hse.
—Mandie & the Shipboard Mystery, Bk. 14. 160p. (Orig.). (gr. 3-8). 1990. 3.99 (*1-55661-120-X*) Bethany Hse.
—Mandie & the Silent Catacombs. 160p. (gr. 3-8). 1990. 3.99 (*1-55661-148-X*) Bethany Hse.

—Mandie & the Singing Chalet. 160p. (Orig.). (ps-8). 1991. pap. 3.99 (*1-55661-198-6*) Bethany Hse.
—Mandie & the Trunk's Secret, Bk. 5. LC 85-71474. 144p. (Orig.). (gr. 3-7). 1985. pap. 3.99 (*0-87123-839-X*) Bethany Hse.
—Mandie & the Washington Nightmare, Bk. 12. LC 88-63464. 160p. (Orig.). (gr. 4-8). 1989. pap. 3.99 (*1-55661-065-3*) Bethany Hse.
—Mandie & the Windmill's Message. 160p. (Orig.). (gr. 3-7). 1992. pap. 3.99 (*1-55661-288-5*) Bethany Hse.
—Mandie Books 16-20 Giftset. (Orig.). 1992. 19.99 (*1-55661-769-0*) Bethany Hse.
—Mandie's Cookbook. 80p. (Orig.). (gr. 3-7). 1991. spiral bdg. 9.99 (*1-55661-224-9*) Bethany Hse.
Leprince De Beaumont, de see De Leprince de Beaumont.
Leprince de Beaumont's, Marie. Beauty & the Beast. Howard, Richard, tr. Knight, Hilary, illus. Cocteau, Jean. (Illus.). 48p. (gr. 1-5). 1990. pap. 14.95 jacketed (*0-671-70720-5*, S&S BFYR) S&S Trade.
Lepscky, Ibi. Albert Einstein. Cardoni, Paolo, illus. 24p. (gr. k-3). 1992. pap. 4.95 (*0-8120-1452-9*) Barron.
—Amadeus Mozart. Cardoni, Paolo, illus. 24p. (gr. k-3). 1992. pap. 4.95 (*0-8120-1493-6*) Barron.
—Leonardo da Vinci. Cardoni, Paolo, illus. 24p. (gr. k-3). 1992. pap. 4.95 (*0-8120-1451-0*) Barron.
—Marie Curie. Cardoni, Paolo, illus. 24p. (gr. k-3). 1993. 9.95 (*0-8120-6340-6*); pap. 4.95 (*0-8120-1558-4*) Barron.
—Pablo Picasso. Cardoni, Paolo, illus. 24p. (gr. k-3). pap. 4.95 (*0-8120-1450-2*) Barron.
—William Shakespeare. Cardoni, Paolo, illus. 28p. (gr. k-3). 1989. 7.95 (*0-8120-6106-3*) Barron.
Lepthien, Emilie U. Australia. LC 82-4541. (Illus.). (gr. 5-9). 1982. PLB 26.60 (*0-516-02751-4*) Childrens.
—Bald Eagles. LC 88-38055. (Illus.). 45p. (gr. k-2). 1989. PLB 15.27 (*0-516-01160-X*); pap. 4.95 (*0-516-41160-8*) Childrens.
—Beavers. LC 92-14909. (Illus.). 48p. (gr. k-4). 1992. PLB 15.27 (*0-516-01131-6*) Childrens.
—Beavers. (Illus.). 48p. (gr. k-4). 1993. pap. 4.95 (*0-516-41131-4*) Childrens.
—Buffalo. LC 89-457. (Illus.). 48p. (gr. k-4). 1989. PLB 15.27 (*0-516-01161-8*); pap. 4.95 (*0-516-41161-6*) Childrens.
—The Cherokee. LC 84-27476. (Illus.). 48p. (gr. k-4). 1985. PLB 15.27 (*0-516-01938-4*); pap. 4.95 (*0-516-41938-2*) Childrens.
—The Choctaw. LC 87-14583. (Illus.). 48p. (gr. k-4). 1987. PLB 15.27 (*0-516-01240-1*); pap. 4.95 (*0-516-41240-X*) Childrens.
—The Chumash. 1994. write for info. (*0-516-01052-2*) Childrens.
—Corazon Aquino: President of the Philippines. LC 87-14030. (Illus.). 32p. (gr. 2-5). 1987. PLB 14.60 (*0-516-04170-3*) Childrens.
—Coyotes. LC 92-35050. (Illus.). 48p. (gr. k-4). 1993. PLB 15.27 (*0-516-01331-9*); pap. 4.95 (*0-516-41331-7*) Childrens.
—Ecuador. LC 85-26967. (Illus.). 128p. (gr. 5-9). 1986. PLB 26.60 (*0-516-02720-4*) Childrens.
—Greenland. LC 88-37374. (Illus.). 128p. (gr. 5-9). 1989. PLB 26.60 (*0-516-02710-7*) Childrens.
—Iceland. LC 86-29966. (Illus.). 128p. (gr. 5-9). 1987. PLB 26.60 (*0-516-02775-1*) Childrens.
—Koalas. LC 90-2219. (Illus.). 48p. (gr. k-4). 1990. PLB 15.27 (*0-516-01108-1*); pap. 4.95 (*0-516-41108-X*) Childrens.
—Luxembourg. LC 89-34664. 128p. (gr. 5-9). 1989. PLB 26.60 (*0-516-02714-X*) Childrens.
—Manatees. LC 90-21138. (Illus.). 48p. (gr. k-4). 1991. PLB 15.27 (*0-516-01114-6*); pap. 4.95 (*0-516-41114-4*) Childrens.
—The Mandans. LC 89-22235. 48p. (gr. k-4). 1989. PLB 15.27 (*0-516-01180-4*); pap. 4.95 (*0-516-41180-2*) Childrens.
—Monarch Butterflies. LC 89-456. (Illus.). 48p. (gr. k-4). 1989. PLB 15.27 (*0-516-01165-0*); pap. 4.95 (*0-516-41165-9*) Childrens.
—Opossums. LC 93-33516. 1994. write for info. (*0-516-01055-7*) Childrens.
—Ostriches. LC 93-3407. (Illus.). 48p. (gr. k-4). 1993. PLB 16.60 (*0-516-01193-6*) Childrens.
—Otters. LC 93-33515. (gr. 3 up). 1994. write for info. (*0-516-01056-5*) Childrens.
—Penguins. LC 82-17911. (Illus.). 48p. (gr. k-4). 1983. PLB 15.27 (*0-516-01683-0*); pap. 4.95 (*0-516-41683-9*) Childrens.
—Peru. LC 92-4813. (Illus.). 128p. (gr. 5-9). 1992. PLB 26.60 (*0-516-02610-0*) Childrens.
—The Philippines. LC 83-23152. (Illus.). 128p. (gr. 5-9). 1986. PLB 26.60 (*0-516-02782-4*) Childrens.
—The Philippines. LC 93-15017. (Illus.). 48p. (gr. k-4). 1993. PLB 16.60 (*0-516-01195-2*) Childrens.
—Polar Bears. LC 91-8892. 48p. (gr. k-4). 1991. PLB 15.27 (*0-516-01127-8*); pap. 4.95 (*0-516-41127-6*) Childrens.
—Rabbits & Hare. LC 93-33514. 1994. write for info. (*0-516-01058-1*) Childrens.
—Reindeer. LC 93-33513. 1994. write for info. (*0-516-01059-X*) Childrens.
—The Seminole. LC 84-23141. (Illus.). 45p. (gr. 2-4). 1985. PLB 15.27 (*0-516-01941-4*); pap. 4.95 (*0-516-41941-2*) Childrens.
—Skunks. LC 93-3410. (Illus.). 48p. (gr. k-4). 1993. PLB 16.60 (*0-516-01197-9*) Childrens.
—South Dakota. LC 90-211137. 144p. (gr. 4 up). 1991. PLB 26.60 (*0-516-00487-5*) Childrens.

—South Dakota. 195p. 1993. text ed. 15.40 (*1-56956-143-5*) W A T Braille.
—Squirrels. LC 92-9207. (Illus.). 48p. (gr. k-4). 1992. PLB 15.27 (*0-516-01947-3*) Childrens.
—Squirrels. LC 92-9207. (Illus.). 48p. (gr. k-4). 1993. pap. 4.95 (*0-516-41947-1*) Childrens.
—Tropical Rainforests. LC 93-3408. (Illus.). 48p. (gr. k-4). 1993. PLB 16.60 (*0-516-01198-7*) Childrens.
—Wolves. LC 91-3035. 48p. (gr. k-4). 1991. PLB 15.27 (*0-516-01129-4*); pap. 4.95 (*0-516-41129-2*) Childrens.
—Woodchucks. LC 91-35276. (Illus.). 48p. (gr. k-4). 1992. PLB 15.27 (*0-516-01140-5*); pap. 4.95 (*0-516-41140-3*) Childrens.
Lepthien, Emilie U. & Kalbacken, Joan. Foxes. LC 93-3409. (Illus.). 48p. (gr. k-4). 1993. PLB 16.60 (*0-516-01191-X*) Childrens.
—Recycling. LC 90-21275. (Illus.). 48p. (gr. k-4). 1991. PLB 15.27 (*0-516-01118-9*); pap. 4.95 (*0-516-41118-7*) Childrens.
—Wetlands. LC 92-35051. (Illus.). 48p. (gr. k-4). 1993. PLB 15.27 (*0-516-01334-3*); pap. 4.95 (*0-516-41334-1*) Childrens.
Lerangis, Peter. Bingo, Movie Tie In. 144p. 1991. pap. 2.95 (*0-590-45277-0*, Point) Scholastic Inc.
—Foul Play. LC 89-39459. 144p. (Orig.). (gr. 5 up). 1990. pap. 2.95 (*0-679-80090-5*) Knopf Bks Yng Read.
—The Sultan's Secret. (gr. 8 up). 1988. pap. 2.95 (*0-345-35099-5*) Ballantine.
Lerangis, Peter, adapted by. Safari Sleuth. LC 91-53168. (Illus.). 136p. (Orig.). (gr. 4-8). 1992. PLB cancelled (*0-679-92776-X*); pap. 3.50 (*0-679-82776-5*) Random Bks Yng Read.
Lerin, S. D., tr. see Stowell, Gordon.
Lerin, S. D. de, tr. see Stowell, Gordon.
Lerma, Olivia, tr. see Harmon, Ed & Jarmin, Marge.
Lerner, Alan J. My Fair Lady. 128p. (RL 9). 1978. pap. 2.95 (*0-451-13890-2*, AE1900, Sig) NAL-Dutton.
Lerner, Andy. Halloween KidDoodles, No. 4. Silver, Pattie, illus. 64p. (ps-2). 1992. pap. 0.99 (*1-56293-262-4*) McClanahan Bk.
Lerner, Carol. Cactus. Lerner, Carol, illus. LC 91-35678. 32p. 1992. 15.00 (*0-688-09636-0*); PLB 14.93 (*0-688-09637-9*) Morrow Jr Bks.
—A Desert Year. Lerner, Carol, illus. LC 90-44643. 48p. 1991. 13.95 (*0-688-09382-5*); PLB 13.88 (*0-688-09383-3*) Morrow Jr Bks.
—Dumb Cane & Daffodils: Poisonous Plants in the House & Garden. Lerner, Carol, illus. LC 89-33622. 32p. 1990. 13.95 (*0-688-08791-4*); PLB 13.88 (*0-688-08796-5*, Morrow Jr Bks) Morrow Jr Bks.
—A Forest Year. Lerner, Carol, illus. LC 86-9741. 48p. (ps up). 1987. 12.95 (*0-688-06413-2*); lib. bdg. 12.88 (*0-688-06414-0*, Morrow Jr Bks) Morrow Jr Bks.
—Moonseed & Mistletoe: A Book of Poisonous Wild Plants. LC 87-13989. (Illus.). 32p. (ps up). 1988. 12.95 (*0-688-07307-7*); PLB 12.88 (*0-688-07308-5*, Morrow Jr Bks) Morrow Jr Bks.
—Plant Families. Lerner, Carol, illus. LC 88-26653. 32p. (gr. 4 up). 1989. 12.95 (*0-688-07881-8*); PLB 12.88 (*0-688-07882-6*, Morrow Jr Bks) Morrow Jr Bks.
—Plants That Make You Sniffle & Sneeze. Lerner, Carol, illus. LC 92-21561. 32p. 1993. 15.00 (*0-688-11489-X*); PLB 14.93 (*0-688-11490-3*) Morrow Jr Bks.
Lerner, Ethan A. Comprendiendo el SIDA. Wilken, Mark, illus. (SPA.). 64p. (gr. 3-6). 1988. 15.95 (*0-8225-2000-1*) Lerner Pubns.
Lerner Geography Department Staff, ed. Algeria in Pictures. (Illus.). 64p. (gr. 5-12). 1992. PLB 17.50 (*0-8225-1901-1*) Lerner Pubns.
—Armenia. (Illus.). 64p. (gr. 5-12). 1993. PLB 19.95 (*0-8225-2806-1*) Lerner Pubns.
—Azerbaijan. (Illus.). 64p. (gr. 5-12). 1993. PLB 19.95 (*0-8225-2810-X*) Lerner Pubns.
—Belarus. (Illus.). 64p. (gr. 5-12). 1993. PLB 19.95 (*0-8225-2811-8*) Lerner Pubns.
—Cyprus in Pictures. (Illus.). 64p. (gr. 5-12). 1992. PLB 17.50 (*0-8225-1910-0*) Lerner Pubns.
—Estonia. (Illus.). 64p. (gr. 5-12). 1992. PLB 19.95 (*0-8225-2803-7*) Lerner Pubns.
—Georgia. (Illus.). 64p. (gr. 5-12). 1993. PLB 19.95 (*0-8225-2807-X*) Lerner Pubns.
—Greece in Pictures. (Illus.). 64p. (gr. 5-12). 1991. PLB 17.50 (*0-8225-1882-1*) Lerner Pubns.
—Kazakhstan. (Illus.). 64p. (gr. 5-12). 1993. PLB 19.95 (*0-8225-2815-0*) Lerner Pubns.
—Kirghyzstan. (Illus.). 64p. (gr. 5-12). 1993. PLB 19.95 (*0-8225-2814-2*) Lerner Pubns.
—Latvia. LC 92-7260. (Illus.). 64p. (gr. 5-12). 1992. PLB 19.95 (*0-8225-2802-9*) Lerner Pubns.
—Lithuania. LC 92-9698. (Illus.). 64p. (gr. 5-12). 1992. PLB 19.95 (*0-8225-2804-5*) Lerner Pubns.
—Moldova. (Illus.). 64p. (gr. 5-12). 1993. PLB 19.95 (*0-8225-2809-6*) Lerner Pubns.
—Russia. (Illus.). 64p. (gr. 5-12). 1992. PLB 19.95 (*0-8225-2805-3*) Lerner Pubns.
—Tadzhikistan. (Illus.). 64p. (gr. 5-12). 1993. PLB 19.95 (*0-8225-2816-9*) Lerner Pubns.
—Turkmenistan. (Illus.). 64p. (gr. 5-12). 1993. PLB 19.95 (*0-8225-2813-4*) Lerner Pubns.
—Uzbekistan. (Illus.). 64p. (gr. 5-12). 1993. PLB 19.95 (*0-8225-2812-6*) Lerner Pubns.
—Zaire in Pictures. (Illus.). 64p. (gr. 5-12). 1992. PLB 17.50 (*0-8225-1899-6*) Lerner Pubns.
Lerner Geography Department Staff, ed. see Barysh, Ann, et al.
Lerner Geography Department Staff, ed. see Brown, Dottie.

Lerner Geography Department Staff, ed. see Fredeen, Charles.
Lerner Geography Department Staff, ed. see Gelman, Amy.
Lerner Geography Department Staff, ed. see LaDoux, Rita C.
Lerner Geography Department Staff, ed. see Porter, A. P.
Lerner Geography Department Staff, ed. see Sitvaitis, Karen.
Lerner Geography Department Staff, ed. see Swain, Gwenyth.
Lerner Geography Department Staff, ed. see Verba, Joan M.
Lerner Geography Dept. Staff, ed. Denmark in Pictures. (Illus.). 64p. (gr. 5 up). 1991. Repr. PLB 17.50 (0-8225-1880-5) Lerner Pubns.
—Finland in Pictures. (Illus.). 64p. (gr. 5 up). 1991. Repr. PLB 17.50 (0-8225-1881-3) Lerner Pubns.
—Iceland in Pictures. (Illus.). 64p. (gr. 5 up). 1991. Repr. PLB 17.50 (0-8225-1892-9) Lerner Pubns.
—Northern Ireland in Pictures. (Illus.). 64p. (gr. 5 up). 1991. Repr. PLB 17.50 (0-8225-1898-8) Lerner Pubns.
—Portugal in Pictures. (Illus.). 64p. 1991. Repr. PLB 17.50 (0-8225-1886-4) Lerner Pubns.
Lerner, Mark. Bowling Is for Me. Wolfe, Robert L., illus. LC 81-12433. 48p. (gr. 2-5). 1981. PLB 13.50 (0-8225-1099-5) Lerner Pubns.
—Racquetball Is for Me. Wolfe, Robert L., illus. LC 83-13611. 48p. (gr. 2-5). 1983. PLB 13.50 (0-8225-1144-4) Lerner Pubns.
Lerner, Mark, tr. see Hogner, Franz.
Lerner, Mark, tr. see Mitgutsch, Ali.
Lerner Publications Company, Geography Department Staff. Romania: In Pictures. LC 92-32861. 1993. PLB 17.50 (0-8225-1894-5) Lerner Pubns.
Lerner Publications Company Geography Department Staff, compiled by. Ukraine. LC 92-10284. (Illus.). 64p. (gr. 5 up). 1993. PLB 19.95 (0-8225-2808-8) Lerner Pubns.
Lerner Publications, Department of Geography Staff, ed. Afghanistan in Pictures. (Illus.). 64p. (gr. 5 up). 1989. 17.50 (0-8225-1849-X) Lerner Pubns.
—Argentina in Pictures. (Illus.). 64p. (gr. 5 up). 1988. PLB 17.50 (0-8225-1807-4) Lerner Pubns.
—Australia in Pictures. (Illus.). 64p. (gr. 5 up). 1990. PLB 17.50 (0-8225-1855-4) Lerner Pubns.
—Bolivia in Pictures. (Illus.). 64p. (gr. 5 up). 1987. PLB 17.50 (0-8225-1808-2) Lerner Pubns.
Lerner Publications, Department of Geography Staff. Botswana in Pictures. (Illus.). 64p. (gr. 5 up). 1990. PLB 17.50 (0-8225-1856-2) Lerner Pubns.
Lerner Publications, Department of Geography Staff, ed. Cameroon in Pictures. (Illus.). 64p. (gr. 5 up). 1989. PLB 17.50 (0-8225-1857-0) Lerner Pubns.
Lerner Publications, Department of Geography Staff. Canada in Pictures. (Illus.). 64p. (gr. 5 up). 1989. PLB 17.50 (0-8225-1870-8) Lerner Pubns.
Lerner Publications, Department of Geography Staff, ed. Central African Republic in Pictures. (Illus.). 64p. (gr. 5 up). 1989. 17.50 (0-8225-1858-9) Lerner Pubns.
—Chile in Pictures. (Illus.). 64p. (gr. 5 up). 1988. PLB 17.50 (0-8225-1809-0) Lerner Pubns.
—China in Pictures. (Illus.). 64p. (gr. 5 up). 1989. 17.50 (0-8225-1859-7) Lerner Pubns.
—Colombia in Pictures. (Illus.). 64p. (gr. 5 up). 1987. PLB 17.50 (0-8225-1810-4) Lerner Pubns.
Lerner Publications, Department of Geography Staff. Costa Rica in Pictures. (Illus.). 64p. (gr. 5 up). 1987. PLB 17.50 (0-8225-1805-8) Lerner Pubns.
—Ecuador in Pictures. (Illus.). 64p. (gr. 5 up). 1987. PLB 17.50 (0-8225-1813-9) Lerner Pubns.
Lerner Publications, Department of Geography Staff, ed. England in Pictures. (Illus.). 64p. (gr. 5 up). 1990. PLB 17.50 (0-8225-1874-0) Lerner Pubns.
Lerner Publications, Department of Geography Staff. Ghana in Pictures. (Illus.). 64p. (gr. 5 up). 1988. 17.95 (0-8225-1829-5) Lerner Pubns.
—Guatemala in Pictures. (Illus.). 64p. (gr. 5 up). 1987. PLB 17.50 (0-8225-1803-1) Lerner Pubns.
—Guyana in Pictures. (Illus.). 64p. (gr. 5 up). 1988. PLB 17.50 (0-8225-1815-5) Lerner Pubns.
—Haiti in Pictures. (Illus.). 64p. (gr. 5 up). 1987. PLB 17.50 (0-8225-1816-3) Lerner Pubns.
—Honduras in Pictures. (Illus.). 64p. (gr. 5 up). 1987. PLB 17.50 (0-8225-1804-X) Lerner Pubns.
Lerner Publications, Department of Geography Staff, ed. India in Pictures. (Illus.). 64p. (gr. 5 up). 1989. 17.50 (0-8225-1852-X) Lerner Pubns.
—Indonesia in Pictures. (Illus.). 64p. (gr. 5 up). 1990. PLB 17.50 (0-8225-1860-0) Lerner Pubns.
—Iran in Pictures. (Illus.). 64p. (gr. 5 up). 1989. 17.50 (0-8225-1848-1) Lerner Pubns.
Lerner Publications, Department of Geography Staff. Iraq in Pictures. (Illus.). 64p. (gr. 5 up). 1990. PLB 17.50 (0-8225-1847-3) Lerner Pubns.
Lerner Publications, Department of Geography Staff, ed. Ireland in Pictures. (Illus.). 64p. (gr. 5 up). 1990. PLB 17.50 (0-8225-1878-3) Lerner Pubns.
Lerner Publications, Department of Geography Staff. Jamaica in Pictures. (Illus.). 64p. (gr. 5 up). 1987. PLB 17.50 (0-8225-1814-7) Lerner Pubns.
—Japan in Pictures. (Illus.). 64p. (gr. 5 up). 1989. 17.50 (0-8225-1861-9) Lerner Pubns.
—Kenya in Pictures. (Illus.). 64p. (gr. 5 up). 1988. 17.50 (0-8225-1830-9) Lerner Pubns.

Lerner Publications, Department of Geography Staff, ed. Kuwait in Pictures. (Illus.). 64p. (gr. 5 up). 1989. 17.50 (0-8225-1846-5) Lerner Pubns.
—Lebanon in Pictures. (Illus.). 64p. (gr. 5 up). 1988. 17.50 (0-8225-1832-5) Lerner Pubns.
—Malaysia in Pictures. (Illus.). 64p. (gr. 5 up). 1989. 17.50 (0-8225-1854-6) Lerner Pubns.
—Mali in Pictures. (Illus.). 64p. (gr. 5 up). 1990. PLB 17.50 (0-8225-1869-4) Lerner Pubns.
—Morocco in Pictures. (Illus.). 64p. (gr. 5 up). 1988. 17.50 (0-8225-1843-0) Lerner Pubns.
—Nepal in Pictures. (Illus.). 64p. (gr. 5 up). 1989. 17.50 (0-8225-1851-1) Lerner Pubns.
Lerner Publications, Department of Geography Staff. New Zealand in Pictures. (Illus.). 64p. (gr. 5 up). 1990. PLB 17.50 (0-8225-1862-7) Lerner Pubns.
Lerner Publications, Department of Geography Staff, ed. Norway in Pictures. (Illus.). 64p. (gr. 5 up). 1990. PLB 17.50 (0-8225-1871-6) Lerner Pubns.
—Pakistan in Pictures. (Illus.). 64p. (gr. 5 up). 1989. 17.50 (0-8225-1850-3) Lerner Pubns.
Lerner Publications, Department of Geography Staff. Panama in Pictures. (Illus.). 64p. (gr. 5 up). 1987. PLB 17.50 (0-8225-1818-X) Lerner Pubns.
—Peru in Pictures. (Illus.). 64p. (gr. 5 up). 1987. PLB 17.50 (0-8225-1820-1) Lerner Pubns.
Lerner Publications, Department of Geography Staff, ed. Phillipines in Pictures. (Illus.). 64p. (gr. 5 up). 1989. PLB 17.50 (0-8225-1863-5) Lerner Pubns.
Lerner Publications, Department of Geography Staff. Puerto Rico in Pictures. (Illus.). 64p. (gr. 5 up). 1987. PLB 17.50 (0-8225-1821-X) Lerner Pubns.
Lerner Publications, Department of Geography Staff, ed. Saudi Arabia in Pictures. (Illus.). 64p. (gr. 5 up). 1989. 17.50 (0-8225-1845-7) Lerner Pubns.
—Scotland in Pictures. (Illus.). 64p. (gr. 5 up). 1991. PLB 17.50 (0-8225-1875-9) Lerner Pubns.
—South Korea in Pictures. (Illus.). 64p. (gr. 5 up). 1989. PLB 17.50 (0-8225-1868-6) Lerner Pubns.
—Soviet Union in Pictures. (Illus.). 64p. (gr. 5 up). 1989. PLB 17.50 (0-8225-1864-3) Lerner Pubns.
—Sri Lanka in Pictures. (Illus.). 64p. (gr. 5 up). 1988. 17.50 (0-8225-1853-8) Lerner Pubns.
—Sweden in Pictures. (Illus.). 64p. (gr. 5 up). 1990. PLB 17.50 (0-8225-1872-4) Lerner Pubns.
Lerner Publications, Department of Geography Staff. Syria in Pictures. (Illus.). 64p. (gr. 5 up). 1990. lib. bdg. 17.50 (0-8225-1867-8) Lerner Pubns.
Lerner Publications, Department of Geography Staff, ed. Taiwan in Pictures. (Illus.). 64p. (gr. 5 up). 1989. PLB 17.50 (0-8225-1865-1) Lerner Pubns.
—Thailand in Pictures. (Illus.). 64p. (gr. 5 up). 1989. PLB 17.50 (0-8225-1866-X) Lerner Pubns.
—Tunisia in Pictures. (Illus.). 64p. (gr. 5 up). 1989. 17.50 (0-8225-1844-9) Lerner Pubns.
Lerner Publications, Department of Geography Staff. Venezuela in Pictures. (Illus.). 64p. (gr. 5 up). 1987. PLB 17.50 (0-8225-1824-4) Lerner Pubns.
Lerner Publications, Department of Geography Staff, ed. Wales in Pictures. (Illus.). 64p. (gr. 5 up). 1990. PLB 17.50 (0-8225-1877-5) Lerner Pubns.
Lerner, Sharon. Big Bird's Copycat Day: A Step 1 Book. Jacquet, Jean-Pierre & Mathieu, Joe, illus. LC 84-6869. 32p. (ps-2). 1984. lib. bdg. 7.99 (0-394-96912-X); pap. 3.50 (0-394-86912-5) Random Bks Yng Read.
—Follow the Monsters. Cooke, Tom, illus. LC 84-18031. 32p. (ps-1). 1985. pap. 2.95 (0-394-87126-X) Random Bks Yng Read.
Lerner, Sharon, ed. see Berenstain, Stan & Berenstain, Janice.
Lerner, Sharon, ed. see Hill, Susan.
Lerner, Sharon, ed. see Jonsen, George.
Lerner, Sharon, ed. see Lorimer, Lawrence T.
Leroe, Ellen. Ghost Dog. Basso, Bill, illus. LC 92-72020. 64p. (gr. 2-5). 1993. 12.95 (1-56282-268-3); PLB 12.89 (1-56282-269-1) Hyprn Child.
—H. O. W. L. High Goes Bats. MacDonald, Patricia, ed. 144p. (Orig.). 1993. pap. 2.99 (0-671-79838-3, Minstrel Bks) PB.
—Have a Heart, Cupid Delaney. 160p. (gr. 5 up). 1988. pap. 2.95 (0-553-27002-8, Starfire) Bantam.
—Heebie Jeebies at H.O.W.L. High. MacDonald, Patricia, ed. 144p. (gr. 3-6). 1992. pap. 2.99 (0-671-75415-7, Minstrel Bks) PB.
—H.O.W.L. High, No. 1. MacDonald, Patricia, ed. 144p. (gr. 4-7). 1991. pap. 2.95 (0-671-68568-6, Minstrel Bks) PB.
—Leap Frog Friday. DeRosa, Dee, illus. LC 92-8284. 48p. (gr. 2-5). 1992. 12.00 (0-525-67370-9, Lodestar Bks) Dutton Child Bks.
—Meet Your Match, Cupid Delaney. 160p. (gr. 7 up). 1990. 13.95 (0-525-67309-1, Lodestar Bks) Dutton Child Bks.
—Personal Business. 144p. (gr. 6 up). 1987. pap. 2.95 (0-553-26652-7, Starfire) Bantam.
Leroi-Gourhan, Andre. The Hunters of Prehistory. Jacobson, Claire, tr. from FRE. LC 88-8121. (Illus.). 160p. (gr. 6 up). 1989. SBE 13.95 (0-689-31293-8, Atheneum Child Bk) Macmillan Child Grp.
LeRoque, Ellen E. A Tale of a Teddy Bear. Arcaris, Mary, illus. 28p. (Orig.). 1985. pap. 3.95 (0-932967-03-5) Pacific Shoreline.
Leroux, Gaston. The Phantom of the Opera. McMullan, Kate, adapted by. Jennis, Paul, illus. LC 88-34079. 96p. (Orig.). (gr. 3-7). 1993. lib. bdg. 5.99 (0-394-93847-X); pap. 2.99 (0-394-83847-5) Random Bks Yng Read.

—Phantom of the Opera. Hildebrandt, Greg, illus. (gr. 4 up). 1988. 14.95 (0-88101-082-0) Unicorn Pub.
—Phantom of the Opera. Hildebrandt, Greg, illus. 208p. (gr. 7 up). 1988. 9.95 (0-88101-121-5) Unicorn Pub.
LeRoy, Gen. Cold Feet. 192p. (gr. 7 up). 1986. pap. 1.75 (0-440-91336-5, LE) Dell.
—Taxi Cat & Huey. Ritz, Karen, illus. LC 90-27383. 144p. (gr. 3-7). 1992. 14.00 (0-06-021768-5); PLB 13.89 (0-06-021769-3) HarpC Child Bks.
Le Saux, Alain. Daddy Scratches. (Illus.). 28p. (ps). 1992. 6.95 (0-8050-2195-7, Bks Young Read) H Holt & Co.
—Daddy Shaves. Le Saux, Alain, illus. 28p. (ps). 1992. 6.95 (0-8050-2194-9, Bks Young Read) H Holt & Co.
—Daddy Sleeps. (Illus.). 28p. (ps). 1992. 6.95 (0-8050-2196-5, Bks Young Read) H Holt & Co.
—King Daddy. Le Saux, Alain, illus. 28p. (ps). 1992. 6.95 (0-8050-2193-0, Bks Young Read) H Holt & Co.
Lesch, Christiane. A Farmyard Morning. Lawson, Polly, tr. from GER. (Illus.). 24p. (ps-k). 1990. Repr. lib. bdg. 12.95 (0-86315-117-5) Gryphon Hse.
—In Bethlehem Long Ago. Lawson, Polly, tr. from GER. Lesch, Christiane, illus. 28p. (ps-2). Repr. of 1988 ed. 14.95 (0-86315-076-4, Pub. by Floris Bks UK) Gryphon Hse.
LeShan, Eda. Grandparents: A Special Kind of Love. Taggart, Tricia, illus. LC 84-5673. 112p. (gr. 3-7). 1984. SBE 13.95 (0-02-756380-4, Macmillan Child Bk) Macmillan Child Grp.
—Learning to Say Good-bye: When a Parent Dies. Giovanopoulous, Paul, illus. LC 76-15155. 96p. (gr. 3 up). 1976. SBE 13.95 (0-02-756360-X, Macmillan Child Bk) Macmillan Child Grp.
—What Makes Me Feel This Way? Growing up with Human Emotions. Weil, Lisl, illus. LC 71-165573. 128p. (gr. 3-6). 1972. SBE 13.95 (0-02-757320-6, Macmillan Child Bk); pap. 3.95 (0-02-044340-4, Aladdin) Macmillan Child Grp.
—What Makes You So Special? LC 91-16925. 160p. (gr. 3-7). 1992. 15.00 (0-8037-1155-7) Dial Bks Young.
—What's Going to Happen to Me? When Parents Separate or Divorce. reissued ed. Cuffari, Richard, illus. LC 78-4340. 144p. (gr. 3-7). 1984. 13.95 (0-02-759230-8, Four Winds) Macmillan Child Grp.
—What's Going to Happen to Me? When Parents Separate or Divorce. rev. ed. Cuffari, Richard, illus. LC 86-10769. 144p. (gr. 3-7). 1986. pap. 3.95 (0-689-71093-3, Aladdin) Macmillan Child Grp.
—When Grownups Drive You Crazy. LC 87-22005. 128p. (gr. 3-7). 1988. SBE 13.95 (0-02-756340-5, Macmillan Child Bk) Macmillan Child Grp.
—When Kids Drive Kids Crazy: How to Get Along with Your Friends & Enemies. (gr. 5 up). 1990. 12.95 (0-8037-0866-1) Dial Bks Young.
LeSieg, Theo. I Can Write! A Book by Me, Myself. McKie, Roy, illus. 32p. (ps-1). 1993. pap. 2.99 (0-679-84700-6) Random Bks Yng Read.
—I Wish That I Had Duck Feet. McKie, Roy, illus. 64p. (ps-1). 1988. bk. & cassette pkg. 6.95 (0-394-89777-3) Random Bks Yng Read.
—I Wish That I Had Duck Feet. LC 65-21211. (Illus.). 64p. (ps-2). 1965. 6.95 (0-394-80040-0); PLB 7.99 (0-394-90040-5) Random Bks Yng Read.
—The Pop-up Mice of Mr. Brice. McKie, Roy, illus. LC 89-60507. 20p. (ps-3). 1989. 10.00 (0-679-80132-4) Random Bks Yng Read.
LeSieg, Theo see LeSieg, Theo.
Le Sieg, Theodore. Come Over to My House. Erdoes, R., illus. LC 66-10686. 72p. (gr. k-3). 1966. lib. bdg. 7.99 (0-394-90044-8) Beginner.
—Eye Book. McKie, Roy, illus. (ps-1). 1968. 6.95 (0-394-81094-5, BE2); lib. bdg. 7.99 (0-394-91094-X, BE2) Random Bks Yng Read.
—In a People House. (Illus.). (ps-1). 1972. 6.95 (0-394-82395-8); lib. bdg. 7.99 (0-394-92395-2) Random Bks Yng Read.
—Maybe You Should Fly a Jet! Maybe You Should Be a Vet. Smollin, Michael J., illus. LC 80-5084. 48p. (ps-3). 1980. lib. bdg. 9.99 (0-394-94448-8) Beginner.
—Please Try to Remember the First of Octember. Cumings, Arthur, illus. LC 77-4504. 48p. (gr. 1-4). 1977. lib. bdg. 7.99 (0-394-93563-2) Beginner.
—Ten Apples up on Top. LC 61-7068. (Illus.). 72p. (gr. 1-2). 1961. 6.95 (0-394-80019-2); lib. bdg. 7.99 (0-394-90019-7) Beginner.
—The Tooth Book. McKie, Roy, illus. LC 80-28320. 48p. (ps-1). 1981. 6.95 (0-394-84825-X, XBYR); lib. bdg. 7.99 (0-394-94825-4) Random Bks Yng Read.
—Wacky Wednesday. Booth, George, illus. LC 74-5520. 48p. (gr. k-4). 1974. 6.95 (0-394-82912-3); lib. bdg. 7.99 (0-394-92912-8) Beginner.
Leske, Steven. Sir Richard & the Dragon. 14p. (gr. k-6). 1992. pap. text ed. 5.99 (1-881617-01-7) Teapot Tales.
—A Two Headed Tale. 16p. (gr. k-6). 1992. pap. text ed. 5.99 (1-881617-02-5) Teapot Tales.
Lesko, Marian, ed. see Arnold, Marti.
Lesley, Salley M. Cookbook Index Plus. 96p. 1979. pap. 5.95 (0-918544-33-5) Wimmer Bks.
Leslie, Amanda. Play Kitten Play: Ten Animal Fingerwiggles. Leslie, Amanda, illus. LC 91-58752. 10p. (ps up). 1992. 6.95 (1-56402-088-6) Candlewick Pr.
—Play Puppy Play: Ten Animal Fingerwiggles. Leslie, Amanda, illus. LC 91-58753. 10p. (ps up). 1992. 6.95 (1-56402-087-8) Candlewick Pr.
Leslie, Clare W. Nature All Year Long. LC 90-47866. (Illus.). 56p. (gr. 2 up). 1991. 16.95 (0-688-09183-0) Greenwillow.

Leslie, Elsie. Is Satan Real? Bates, Stephen, illus. (gr. k-6). 1987. pap. 4.25 (*1-55976-153-9*) CEF Press.

Leslie, Herman & Bateson, Margaret. A Victorian Farm House. 1993. 19.95 (*0-312-08931-7*) St Martin.

Leslie, Louis A. Twenty Thousand Words. 7th, large type ed. 300p. (gr. 7 up). 1981. Repr. of 1977 ed. 75.00 (*0-317-01950-3*, J-26190-00) Am Printing Hse.

Leslie, Melville B. Elephant Have Right of Way: Life with the Wild Animals of Africa. (Illus.). (gr. 4-7). 1992. 15.00 (*0-385-30622-9*) Doubleday.

Leslie-Melville, Betsy. Daisy Rothschild: The Giraffe That Lives with Me. (gr. 2-6). 1992. 4.99 (*0-440-40671-4*, YB) Dell.

—Walter Warthog: The Warthog Who Moved In. (gr. 2-6). 1992. 4.99 (*0-685-57132-7*, YB) Dell.

—Walter Warthog: The Warthog That Moved In. (Illus.). 48p. (ps-3). 1989. 12.95 (*0-385-26378-3*, Zephyr-BFYR); (Zephyr-BFYR) Doubleday.

—Walter Warthog: The Warthog That Moved In. (gr. 4-7). 1992. pap. 4.99 (*0-440-40672-2*) Dell.

Lessac, Frane. Caribbean Alphabet. Lessac, Frane, illus. LC 93-15833. 32p. 1994. 15.00 (*0-688-12952-8*, Tambourine Bks); PLB 14.93 (*0-688-12953-6*, Tambourine Bks) Morrow.

—My Little Island. Lessac, Frane, illus. LC 84-48355. 48p. (gr. 1-4). 1985. 14.00 (*0-397-32114-7*, Lipp Jr Bks); PLB 13.89 (*0-397-32115-5*) HarpC Child Bks.

—My Little Island. Lessac, Frane, illus. LC 84-48355. 48p. (ps-3). 1987. pap. 4.95 (*0-06-443146-0*, Trophy) HarpC Child Bks.

Lessard, Richard L. The Circus. 32p. 1993. pap. 4.95 (*1-883656-00-1*) Earth Bound.

Lessem, Don. The Iceman. LC 93-31534. 1994. write for info. (*0-517-59596-6*); lib. bdg. write for info. (*0-517-59597-4*) Crown Bks Yng Read.

—Ornithomimids, the Fastest Dinosaur. Franczak, Brian, illus. LC 93-10264. 1993. 19.95 (*0-87614-813-5*) Carolrhoda Bks.

—Troodon, the Smartest Dinosaur. Franczak, Brian, illus. LC 92-44689. 1993. 19.95 (*0-87614-798-8*) Carolrhoda Bks.

Lessem, Don, jt. auth. see Horner, Jack.

Lesser, Carolyn. Flamingo Knees. 3rd ed. 52p. (gr. 5 up). 1991. pap. 10.00 (*0-9630604-0-6*) Oakwood MO.

—The Goodnight Circle. Cauley, Lorinda B., illus. LC 84-4501. 30p. (ps-3). 1984. 14.95 (*0-15-232158-6*, HB Juv Bks) HarBrace.

—The Goodnight Circle. 30p. (ps-3). 1991. pap. 4.95 (*0-15-232159-4*, HB Juv Bks) HarBrace.

—The Knees Knock Again. 2nd ed. 56p. 1991. pap. 10.00 (*0-9630604-1-4*) Oakwood MO.

—What a Wonderful Day to Be a Cow. Mathis, Melissa B., illus. LC 93-13211. 1995. 15.00 (*0-679-82430-8*); PLB 15.99 (*0-679-92430-2*) Knopf.

Lesser, Rika, retold by. Hansel & Gretel. Zelinsky, Paul O., illus. 48p. (ps-3). 1989. pap. 6.95 (*0-399-21725-8*, Sandcastle Bks) Putnam Pub Group.

Lesser, Rika, ed. see Grimm, Wilhelm K.

Lesser, Rika, tr. see Dahlback, Helena.

Lesser, Rika, tr. see Schami, Rafik.

Lessing, Doris. Through the Tunnel. (gr. 4-12). Date not set. 13.95 (*0-88682-346-3*, 97224-098) Creative Ed.

Lester, Alison. Bibs & Boots. (Illus.). 16p. (ps-k). 1989. 3.50 (*0-670-81988-3*) Viking Child Bks.

—Bumping & Bouncing. (Illus.). 16p. (ps-k). 1989. pap. 3.50 (*0-670-81991-3*) Viking Child Bks.

—Clive Eats Alligators. LC 85-17213. (ps-3). 1986. 13.95 (*0-395-40775-3*) HM.

—Clive Eats Alligators. (ps). 1991. pap. 4.80 (*0-395-58408-6*) HM.

—Crashing & Splashing. (Illus.). 16p. (ps-k). 1989. pap. 3.50 (*0-670-81989-1*) Viking Child Bks.

—Happy & Sad. (Illus.). 16p. (ps-k). 1989. pap. 3.50 (*0-670-81990-5*) Viking Child Bks.

—I'm Green & I'm Grumpy. 16p. (ps-1). 1993. pap. 4.99 (*0-14-054478-X*, Puffin) Puffin Bks.

—Imagine. Lester, Alison, illus. 32p. (gr. k-3). 1990. 13. 45 (*0-395-53753-3*) HM.

—Imagine. 1993. pap. 6.95 (*0-395-66953-7*) HM.

—Isabella's Bed. Lester, Alison, illus. LC 92-22935. 32p. (gr. k-3). 1993. Repr. of 1991 ed. 14.95 (*0-395-65565-X*) HM.

—The Journey Home. Lester, Alison, illus. LC 89-28355. 32p. (gr. k-3). 1991. 13.45 (*0-395-53355-4*) HM.

—Magic Beach. Lester, Alison, illus. 32p. (ps-3). 1992. 13.95 (*0-316-52177-9*, Joy St Bks) Little.

—Monsters Are Knocking. 16p. (ps-1). 1999. pap. 4.99 (*0-14-054967-6*, Puffin) Puffin Bks.

—My Farm. LC 93-30894. 1994. write for info. (*0-395-68193-6*) HM.

—Rosie Sips Spiders. Lester, Alison, illus. 32p. (ps-k). 1989. 13.45 (*0-395-51526-2*) HM.

—Tessa Snaps Snakes. Lester, Alison, illus. 32p. (ps-k). 1991. 13.45 (*0-395-59505-3*) HM.

—Tessa Snaps Snakes. Lester, Alison, illus. LC 91-2665. 32p. (ps-k). 1991. pap. 13.95 (*0-685-52551-1*, Sandpiper) HM.

Lester, Andrew D. Sex Is More Than a Word. 80p. (gr. 10-12). 1973. pap. 5.95 (*0-8054-5313-X*) Broadman.

Lester, Helen. It Wasn't My Fault. Munsinger, Lynn, illus. LC 84-19212. 32p. (gr. k-3). 1985. 14.45 (*0-395-35629-6*) HM.

—It Wasn't My Fault. Munsinger, Lynn, illus. (ps-3). 1989. pap. 5.70 (*0-395-51007-4*, Sandpiper) HM.

—Me First. Munsinger, Lynn, illus. LC 91-45808. 32p. (ps up). 1992. 13.45 (*0-395-58706-9*) HM.

—Pookins Gets Her Way. Munsinger, Lynn, illus. (ps-3). 1987. 13.95 (*0-395-42636-7*); pap. 4.80 (*0-395-53965-X*) HM.

—A Porcupine Named Fluffy. LC 85-24820. 32p. (ps-3). 1989. 14.95 (*0-395-36895-2*); pap. 5.95 (*0-395-52018-5*) HM.

—The Revenge of the Magic Chicken. Munsinger, Lynn, illus. 32p. (gr. k-3). 1990. 13.45 (*0-395-50929-7*) HM.

—Tacky the Penguin. Munsinger, Lynn, illus. LC 87-30684. 32p. (ps-3). 1988. 13.45 (*0-395-45536-7*) HM.

—Tacky the Penguin. Munsinger, Lynn, illus. 32p. (gr. k-3). 1990. pap. 4.80 (*0-395-56233-3*) HM.

—Three Cheers for Tacky. Munsinger, Lynn, illus. LC 93-14342. 1994. write for info. (*0-395-66841-7*) HM.

—The Wizard, the Fairy, & the Magic Chicken. Munsinger, Lynn, illus. LC 82-21302. 32p. (gr. k-3). 1988. pap. 5.70 (*0-395-47945-2*) HM.

—The Wizard, the Fairy, & the Magic Chicken. (ps-3). 1983. 10.95 (*0-395-33885-9*) HM.

Lester, James D., Sr. & Lester, James D., Jr. Writing: Style & Grammar. 300p. (gr. 6-10). 1994. pap. 8.95 (*0-673-36093-8*) GdYrBks.

—Writing: Style & Grammar. 300p. (Orig.). (gr. 6-10). 1993. pap. 14.95 spiralbound (*0-673-36128-4*) GdYrBks.

Lester, Julius. How Many Spots Does a Leopard Have? & Other Tales. Shannon, David, illus. (gr. 2-6). 1989. pap. 14.95 (*0-590-41973-0*) Scholastic Inc.

—The Knee-High Man & Other Tales. Pinto, Ralph, illus. LC 72-181785. 32p. (ps-3). 1985. 12.95 (*0-8037-4593-1*) Dial Bks Young.

—The Knee-High Man & Other Tales. Pinto, Ralph, illus. LC 72-181785. 32p. (ps-3). 1985. pap. 3.95 (*0-8037-0234-5*, 0383-120, Dial Pied Piper) Puffin Bks.

—Long Journey Home: Stories from Black History. LC 75-181791. 160p. (gr. 6 up). 1993. 13.99 (*0-8037-4953-8*) Dial Bks Young.

—The Tales of Uncle Remus: The Adventures of Brer Rabbit, Vol. I. Pinckney, Jerry, illus. LC 85-20449. (ps up). 1987. 16.95 (*0-8037-0271-X*); PLB 16.89 (*0-8037-0272-8*) Dial Bks Young.

—This Strange New Feeling. 164p. (gr. 7 up). 1985. pap. 2.75 (*0-590-44047-0*) Scholastic Inc.

—To Be a Slave: Feelings, Tom, illus. LC 68-28738. (gr. 7-12). 1968. 14.95 (*0-8037-8955-6*) Dial Bks Young.

—To Be a Slave. 1986. pap. 3.25 (*0-590-42460-2*) Scholastic Inc.

Lester, Julius, as told by. The Last Tales of Uncle Remus. Pinkney, Jerry, illus. LC 93-7531. (ps-4). 1994. 16.99 (*0-8037-1303-7*); PLB 16.89 (*0-8037-1304-5*) Dial Bks Young.

—More Tales of Uncle Remus: Further Adventures of Brer Rabbit, His Friends, Enemies & Others. Pinkney, Jerry, illus. LC 86-32890. 160p. (ps up). 1988. 15.95 (*0-8037-0419-4*); PLB 15.89 (*0-8037-0420-8*) Dial Bks Young.

Lester, Julius & Fogelman, Phyllis J., eds. Further Tales of Uncle Remus: The Misadventures of Brer Rabbit, Brer Fox, Brer Wolf, the Doodang, & All the Other Creatures. Pinkney, Jerry, illus. LC 88-20223. 160p. (ps up). 1990. 15.00 (*0-8037-0610-3*); PLB 14.89 (*0-8037-0611-1*) Dial Bks Young.

Lester, Vivian. Wee-Dolph, the Tiniest Reindeer. (gr. 1-3). 1990. pap. text ed. 4.95 (*1-881079-00-7*) Antex Corp.

Lester, Will. Are You up There, Mister Jesus? Jones, M. L., ed. 134p. (Orig.). 1992. pap. 5.95 (*1-882270-00-2*) Old Rugged Cross.

Lesterson, David. The Regal Beagle. Hoffman, Beverly, et al, eds. Graham, Jennifer, illus. LC 93-70504. 29p. (gr. 3). Date not set. write for info. (*0-9634122-3-X*) Feather Fables.

L'Estrange, Roger, tr. see Aesop.

Le Sueur, Meridel. Little Brother of the Wilderness: The Story of Johnny Appleseed. LC 87-80574. (Illus.). 68p. (gr. 5 up). 1987. Repr. of 1947 ed. 9.95 (*0-930100-21-2*) Holy Cow.

—Sparrow Hawk. DesJarlait, Robert, illus. LC 87-80573. 176p. (gr. 7 up). 1987. Repr. of 1950 ed. 13.95 (*0-930100-22-0*) Holy Cow.

LeSueur, Meridel see Jones, Mother.

Letch, Rachael. Special People. LC 90-48944. (gr. 4 up). 1990. 7.95 (*0-85953-360-3*); pap. 3.95 (*0-85953-350-6*) Childs Play.

Letley, Emma, ed. see Stevenson, Robert Louis.

Le Tord, Bijou. The Deep Blue Sea. Le Tord, Bijou, illus. LC 89-16314. 32p. 1990. 13.95 (*0-531-05853-0*); PLB 13.99 (*0-531-08453-1*) Orchard Bks Watts.

—Elephant Moon. LC 92-28234. 1993. 14.95 (*0-385-30623-7*) Doubleday.

—Joseph & Nellie. LC 85-26662. (Illus.). 32p. (ps-2). 1986. RSBE 12.95 (*0-02-756450-9*, Bradbury Pr) Macmillan Child Grp.

—Little Shepherd: The Twenty-Third Psalm. 1991. 13.00 (*0-385-30417-X*) Delacorte.

—My Grandma Leonie. LC 86-32656. (Illus.). 32p. (ps-2). 1987. 12.95 (*0-02-756490-8*, Bradbury Pr) Macmillan Child Grp.

—Peace on Earth: A Book of Prayers from Around the World. LC 91-39913. (Illus.). 80p. 1992. 18.00 (*0-385-30692-X*) Doubleday.

—Rabbit Seeds. (ps-3). 1993. pap. 3.99 (*0-440-40767-2*) Dell.

—The River & the Rain: The Lord's Prayer. LC 93-20730. 1994. write for info. (*0-385-32034-5*) Doubleday.

Leuck, Laura. Night Is Calling. Eitan, Ora, illus. LC 93-22837. 1994. pap. 14.00 (*0-671-86940-X*, S&S BFYR) S&S Trade.

Leuning, Kevin. Archie Givens Sr. Collection Curriculum Guide. x, 30p. (ps-12). 1988. pap. text ed. write for info. (*0-9632976-0-0*) A Givens Sr Collect.

Lev, M. The Day the Sky Split. Levin, Debra K., illus. LC 91-71188. 32p. (gr. 1-3). 1991. 12.95 (*1-877-65607-0*) Antroll Pub.

—The Magic Faucet. Kahn, Katherine J., illus. LC 90-85473. 32p. (gr. 1-3). 1991. 12.95 (*1-877-65604-6*) Antroll Pub.

LeValley, Norma. A Tree for Me. Darcy, Tom, illus. LC 87-70974. 50p. (ps-2). 1987. pap. 5.95 (*0-9618740-0-7*) Caring Tree.

Levchuk, Helen. The Dingles. Bianchi, John, illus. 24p. (ps-2). 1991. pap. 4.95 (*0-88899-044-8*, Pub. by Groundwood-Douglas & McIntyre CN) Firefly Bks Ltd.

Levene. The Fastest Car in the County. 1992. write for info. (*1-55513-395-9*, Chariot Bks) Cook.

—The Pet That Never Was. 1992. write for info. (*1-55513-394-0*, Chariot Bks) Cook.

Levene, Bruce, jt. auth. see Collins, William.

Levene, Nancy. Cherry Cola Champions. LC 88-12294. (Illus.). 120p. (gr. 3-7). 1988. pap. 4.49 (*1-55513-519-6*, Chariot Bks) Cook.

—French Fry Forgiveness. (gr. 4-7). 1989. pap. 4.49 (*1-55513-302-9*) Cook.

—Hot Chocolate Friendship. (gr. 4-7). 1989. pap. 4.49 (*1-55513-304-5*) Cook.

—Peach Pit Popularity. (gr. 4-7). 1989. pap. 4.49 (*1-55513-529-3*) Cook.

—Peanut Butter & Jelly Secrets. (gr. 4-7). 1989. pap. 4.49 (*1-55513-303-7*) Cook.

—Salty Scarecrow Solution. (gr. 4-7). 1989. pap. 4.49 (*1-55513-523-4*) Cook.

—Shoelaces & Brussel Sprouts. (gr. 4-7). 1989. pap. 4.49 (*1-55513-301-0*) Cook.

—T-Bone Trouble. (gr. 4-7). pap. 4.49 (*1-55513-765-2*) Cook.

Levene, Nancy S. Chocolate Chips, Trumpet Tricks, & Other Devotions with Alex. LC 93-36195. 1994. write for info. (*0-7814-0103-8*, Chariot Bks) Cook.

—Crocodile Meatloaf. LC 92-32615. (ps-6). 1993. write for info. (*0-7814-0000-7*, Chariot Bks) Cook.

—Mint Cookie Miracles. LC 88-11902. 120p. (gr. 3-7). 1988. pap. 4.49 (*1-55513-514-5*, Chariot Bks) Cook.

Levens, Ann, jt. auth. see Renshaw, Polly.

Leventhal, Debra. What Is Your Language? Wellington, Monica, illus. LC 93-10156. 32p. (ps-1). 1994. 12.99 (*0-525-45133-1*, DCB) Dutton Child Bks.

Leverich, Kathleen. Best Enemies. Lamb, Susan C., illus. LC 88-19150. (gr. 1 up). 1989. 10.95 (*0-688-08316-1*) Greenwillow.

—Best Enemies. Lamb, Susan C., illus. LC 88-19150. 80p. (gr. 1-4). 1990. pap. 2.95 (*0-679-80156-1*) Knopf Bks Yng Read.

—Best Enemies Again. Lorraine, Walter, illus. LC 90-30303. 96p. (gr. 2 up). 1991. 12.95 (*0-688-09440-6*) Greenwillow.

—Hilary & the Troublemakers. Lorraine, Walter, illus. LC 91-15234. 1992. 13.00 (*0-688-10857-1*) Greenwillow.

—Hilary & the Troublemakers. Lorraine, Walter, illus. LC 91-13762. 144p. (Orig.). (gr. 3-7). 1993. pap. 3.99 (*0-679-84716-2*) Random Bks Yng Read.

—The Hungry Fox & the Foxy Duck. Galdone, Paul, illus. LC 78-11215. 48p. (ps-3). 1979. 5.95 (*0-8193-0987-7*); PLB 5.95 (*0-8193-0988-5*) Parents.

—The Hungry Fox & the Foxy Duck. (Illus.). 48p. (ps-2). 1991. pap. 2.95 (*0-448-40102-9*, G&D) Putnam Pub Group.

Leverich, Kathleen, tr. see Hernandez, Xavier & Ballonga, Jordi.

LeVert, John. The Flight of the Cassowary. 304p. (Orig.). 1988. pap. 2.95 (*0-553-27389-2*, Starfire) Bantam.

LeVert, Marianne. Crime in America. Leinwand, Gerald, ed. 160p. (gr. 9-12). 1991. 16.95x (*0-8160-2102-3*) Facts on File.

LeVert, Suzanne. AIDS: In Search of a Killer. LC 86-33218. (Illus.). 128p. (gr. 6 up). 1987. lib. bdg. 12.98 (*0-671-62840-2*, J Messner); lib. bdg. 5.95 (*0-671-65662-7*) S&S Trade.

—Alberta. (Illus.). 64p. (gr. 3 up). 1991. lib. bdg. 16.95 (*0-7910-1026-0*) Chelsea Hse.

—British Columbia. (Illus.). 64p. (gr. 3 up). 1991. lib. bdg. 16.95 (*0-7910-1033-3*) Chelsea Hse.

—Canada: Facts & Figures. (Illus.). (gr. 3 up). 1992. PLB 16.95 (*0-7910-1035-X*) Chelsea Hse.

—Dominion of Canada. (Illus.). (gr. 3 up). 1992. lib. bdg. 16.95 (*0-7910-1034-1*) Chelsea Hse.

—Doubleday Book of Famous Americans. LC 87-26215. (Illus.). (gr. 5 up). 1989. 16.95 (*0-385-23699-9*) Doubleday.

—Edgar Allan Poe. (Illus.). 112p. (gr. 5 up). 1992. lib. bdg. 17.95 (*0-7910-1640-4*) Chelsea Hse.

—Hillary Rodham Clinton: First Lady. (Illus.). 48p. (gr. 2-4). 1994. 12.40 (*1-56294-432-0*) Millbrook Pr.

—Let's Discover Canada, 14 bks. (Illus.). (gr. 3 up). 1991. PLB 237.30 (*0-7910-1021-X*) Chelsea Hse.

—Manitoba. (Illus.). 64p. (gr. 3 up). 1991. lib. bdg. 16.95 (*0-7910-1025-2*) Chelsea Hse.

—New Brunswick. (Illus.). (gr. 3 up). 1992. lib. bdg. 16. 95 (*0-7910-1029-5*) Chelsea Hse.

—Newfoundland. (Illus.). (gr. 3 up). 1992. lib. bdg. 16.95 (*0-7910-1027-9*) Chelsea Hse.

—Northwest Territories. (Illus.). (gr. 3 up). 1992. lib. bdg. 16.95 (*0-7910-1031-7*) Chelsea Hse.

—Nova Scotia. (Illus.). (gr. 3 up). 1992. lib. bdg. 16.95 (0-7910-1028-7) Chelsea Hse.

—Ontario. Berton, Pierre, intro. by. (Illus.). 64p. (gr. 3 up). 1991. lib. bdg. 16.95 (0-7910-1022-8) Chelsea Hse.

—Prince Edward Island. (Illus.). 69p. (gr. 3 up). 1991. lib. bdg. 16.95 (0-7910-1023-6) Chelsea Hse.

—Quebec. Berton, Pierre, intro. by. (Illus.). 64p. (gr. 3 up). 1991. PLB 16.95 (0-7910-1030-9) Chelsea Hse.

—Saskatchewan. (Illus.). 64p. (gr. 3 up). 1991. lib. bdg. 17.95 (0-7910-1032-5) Chelsea Hse.

—Teens Face to Face with Chronic Illness. LC 92-45819. 1993. lib. bdg. 13.98 (0-671-74540-9, J Messner); lib. bdg. 7.95 (0-671-74541-7, J Messner) S&S Trade.

—Yukon. (Illus.). (gr. 3 up). 1992. lib. bdg. 16.95 (0-7910-1032-5) Chelsea Hse.

LeVert, Suzanne, ed. see Keene, Carolyn.

Levertov, Denise, tr. see Joubert, Jean.

Levey, Judith, ed. The Macmillan First Dictionary. rev. & expanded ed. LC 90-6062. (Illus.). 416p. (gr. k-4). 1990. SBE 12.95 (0-02-761731-9, Macmillan Child Bk) Macmillan Child Grp.

—The Macmillan Picture Wordbook. rev. ed. LC 90-8274. (Illus.). 64p. (ps-1). 1990. SBE 8.95 (0-02-754641-1, Macmillan Child Bk) Macmillan Child Grp.

Levi, Dorothy. A Very Special Friend. Gold, Ethel, illus. LC 88-33410. 40p. (gr. k-3). 1989. 9.95 (0-930323-55-6, Kendall Green Pubns) Gallaudet Univ Pr.

Levi, Dorothy H. A Very Special Friend. Gold, Ethel, illus. 32p. (gr. k-3). 9.95 (1-878363-24-7) Forest Hse.

—A Very Special Sister. Gold, Ethel, illus. LC 88-33410. 32p. (gr. k-3). 1992. 9.95 (0-930323-96-3, Pub. by K Green Pubns) Gallaudet Univ Pr.

—A Very Special Sister. Gold, Ethel, illus. 36p. (gr. k-3). 1992. PLB 11.95 (1-56674-033-9) Forest Hse.

Levi, Herbert W. & Levi, Lorna R. Spiders & Their Kin. rev. ed. Zim, Herbert S. & Fichter, George S., eds. Strekalovsky, Nicholas, illus. (gr. 9 up). 1969. pap. write for info. (0-307-24021-5, Golden Pr) Western Pub.

Levi, Lorna R., jt. auth. see Levi, Herbert W.

Levi, Steven C., jt. auth. see Phillips, Douglas A.

Levicki, Nancy, jt. auth. see Silkwood, Chris.

Levin, Amy, jt. auth. see Wise, Beth A.

Levin, Beatrice. Modern Jewish Stories. (gr. 4-7). 1991. pap. 7.95 (1-56171-079-2) Shapolsky Pubs. Postponed.

Levin, Beatrice & Vanderveld, Marjorie. Me Run Fast Good: Biographies of Tewanima (Hopi), Carlos Montezuma (Apache) & John Horse (Seminole) 32p. (gr. 5-9). 1983. pap. 1.95 (0-89992-087-X) Coun India Ed.

Levin, Betty. Brother Moose. LC 89-34437. (gr. 5 up). 1990. 12.95 (0-688-09266-7) Greenwillow.

—The Ice Bear. LC 86-254. 192p. (gr. 5 up). 1986. reinforced trade ed. 10.25 (0-688-06431-0) Greenwillow.

—The Keeping Room. LC 80-23931. (Illus.). 248p. 1989. Repr. of 1981 ed. 11.95 (0-688-80300-8) Greenwillow.

—Mercy's Mill. LC 91-31483. (gr. 7 up). 1992. 14.00 (0-688-11212-X) Greenwillow.

—Starshine & Sunglow. Smith, Joseph A., illus. LC 93-26672. 1994. write for info. reinforced bdg. (0-688-12806-8) Greenwillow.

—The Trouble With Gramary. LC 87-22702. 192p. (gr. 5up). 1988. 13.95 (0-688-07372-7) Greenwillow.

Levin, Carol. A Rosh Hashanah Walk. Kahn, Katherine J., illus. LC 87-3106. (ps-3). 1987. 4.95 (0-930494-70-9) Kar Ben.

Levin, Harry, ed. see Hawthorne, Nathaniel.

Levin, Ina M. & Sterling, Mary E. Readiness Manipulatives: Counting. Vasconcelles, Keith, illus. 28p. (Orig.). (ps-1). 1992. wkbk. 7.95 (1-55734-179-6) Tchr Create Mat.

—Readiness Manipulatives: Shapes. Vasconcelles, Keith, illus. 28p. (Orig.). (ps-1). 1992. wkbk. 7.95 (1-55734-180-X) Tchr Create Mat.

Levin, Ina M., ed. see Wallace, Annette H.

Levin, Meyer & Kurzband, Toby. Story of the Jewish Way of Life. LC 59-13487. (gr. 4-6). 1959. 6.95 (0-87441-003-7) Behrman.

—Story of the Synagogue. LC 57-13093. (gr. 4-6). 1957. pap. 6.95x (0-87441-006-1); activity bk. 3.50 (0-87441-007-X) Behrman.

Levin, Meyer, jt. auth. see Kripke, Dorothy K.

Levin, Pamela. Susan B. Anthony: Fighter for Women's Rights. (Illus.). 80p. (gr. 3-5). 1993. PLB 13.95 (0-7910-1762-1, Am Art Analog); pap. write for info. (0-7910-1965-9, Am Art Analog) Chelsea Hse.

Levin, Rich. Magic Johnson: Court Magician. rev. ed. LC 80-25814. (Illus.). 48p. (gr. 2-8). 1981. PLB 13.27 (0-516-04313-7); pap. 3.95 (0-516-44313-5) Childrens.

Levin, Rita. Punctuation Partners. 48p. (gr. 2-4). 1983. 6.95 (0-88160-098-9, LW 121) Learning Wks.

Levin, Robert, ed. Y Basketball Dribblers Manual: For 5th-6th Grade Players. Barrett, Jerry, illus. 58p. (gr. 5-6). 1984. pap. text ed. 5.00 (0-931250-84-6, LYMC4666, Pub. by YMCA USA) Human Kinetics.

—Y Basketball Passers Manual: For 3rd-4th Grade Players. Barrett, Jery, illus. 36p. (gr. 3-4). 1984. pap. 5.00x (0-931250-83-8, LYMC4665, Pub. by YMCA USA) Human Kinetics.

Levin, Robert, ed. see YMCA of the U. S. A. Staff.

Levine, Abby. Ollie Knows Everything. Munsinger, Lynn, illus. LC 93-29600. 1994. write for info. (0-8075-6020-0) A Whitman.

—Too Much Mush! Tucker, Kathy, ed. Parkinson, Kathy, illus. LC 88-33906. 32p. (ps-2). 1989. PLB 13.95 (0-8075-8025-2) A Whitman.

—What Did Mommy Do Before You? Fay, Ann, ed. LC 87-27908. (Illus.). 32p. (ps-3). 1988. PLB 13.95 (0-8075-8819-9) A Whitman.

—What Did Mommy Do Before You? (ps-3). 1990. pap. 3.95 (0-14-054215-9, Puffin) Puffin Bks.

—You Push, I Ride. Tucker, Kathleen, ed. Apple, Margot, illus. LC 87-36852. 32p. (ps-k). 1989. PLB 13.95 (0-8075-9444-X) A Whitman.

—You Push, I Ride. (ps). 1990. pap. 3.95 (0-14-054180-2, Puffin) Puffin Bks.

Levine, Abby, ed. see Adorjan, Carol.

Levine, Abby, ed. see Albert, Burton, Jr.

Levine, Abby, ed. see Balterman, Lee.

Levine, Abby, ed. see Bernstein, Joanne E. & Cohen, Paul.

Levine, Abby, ed. see Bernstein, Sharon C.

Levine, Abby, ed. see Brillhart, Julie.

Levine, Abby, ed. see Brown, Drollene.

Levine, Abby, ed. see Chevalier, Christa.

Levine, Abby, ed. see Corey, Dorothy.

Levine, Abby, ed. see Emmert, Michelle.

Levine, Abby, ed. see Fireside, Bryna J.

Levine, Abby, ed. see Freedman, Sally.

Levine, Abby, ed. see Gay, Marie-Louise.

Levine, Abby, ed. see Girard, Linda W.

Levine, Abby, ed. see Goldman, Kelly & Davidson, Ronnie.

Levine, Abby, ed. see Hamilton, Carol.

Levine, Abby, ed. see Hickman, Martha W.

Levine, Abby, ed. see Jordan, MaryKate.

Levine, Abby, ed. see Kite, Patricia.

Levine, Abby, ed. see Krisher, Trudy.

Levine, Abby, ed. see Lawlor, Laurie.

Levine, Abby, ed. see Levine, Caroline.

Levine, Abby, ed. see Limmer, Milly J.

Levine, Abby, ed. see London, Jonathan.

Levine, Abby, ed. see Lydon, Kerry R.

Levine, Abby, ed. see Mathews, Judith & Robinson, Fay.

Levine, Abby, ed. see Monsell, Mary E.

Levine, Abby, ed. see Mueller, Virginia.

Levine, Abby, ed. see Nerlove, Miriam.

Levine, Nancy, ed. see Nikola-Lisa, W.

Levine, Abby, ed. see Ostrow, William & Ostrow, Vivian.

Levine, Abby, ed. see Phillips, Tamara.

Levine, Abby, ed. see Rose, Deborah L.

Levine, Abby, ed. see Schwartz, Mary A.

Levine, Abby, ed. see Seltzer, Meyer.

Levine, Abby, ed. see Sills, Leslie.

Levine, Abby, ed. see Simon, Norma.

Levine, Abby, ed. see Stanek, Muriel.

Levine, Abby, ed. see Stover, Marjorie.

Levine, Abby, ed. see Sussman, Susan.

Levine, Abby, ed. see Vigna, Judith.

Levine, Abby, ed. see West, Dan.

Levine, Abby, ed. see Whitelaw, Nancy.

Levine, Abby, ed. see Williams, Barbara.

Levine, Abby, ed. see Willner-Pardo, Gina.

Levine, Abby, ed. see Wolf, Sallie.

Levine, Abby, ed. see Youdovin, Susan S.

Levine, Arthur A. All the Lights in the Night. Ransome, James, illus. LC 90-47496. 32p. (ps-3). 1991. 14.95 (0-688-10107-0, Tambourine Bks); PLB 14.88 (0-688-10108-9, Tambourine Bks) Morrow.

—The Boardwalk Princess. Guevara, Susan, illus. LC 92-8081. 32p. (ps up). 1993. 14.00 (0-688-10306-5, Tambourine Bks); PLB 13.93 (0-688-10307-3, Tambourine Bks) Morrow.

—Boy Who Drew Cats: A Japanese Folktale. LC 91-46232. (ps-3). 1994. 16.00 (0-8037-1172-7); 15.89 (0-8037-1173-5) Dial Bks Young.

—Pearl Moscowitz's Last Stand. Roth, Rob, illus. LC 91-10652. 32p. (ps up). 1993. 14.00 (0-688-10753-2, Tambourine Bks); PLB 13.93 (0-688-10754-0, Tambourine Bks) Morrow.

—Sheep Dreams. Lanfredi, Judy, illus. LC 91-44929. 32p. (ps-3). 1993. 13.99 (0-8037-1194-8); PLB 13.89 (0-8037-1195-6) Dial Bks Young.

Levine, Arthur A., adapted by see Richard, Francoise.

Levine, Barbara G., jt. auth. see Mogil, H. Michael.

Levine, Bobbie & Lichter, Carolyn. A Child's Walk Through Africa. (Illus.). 38p. (gr. 3-6). 1987. spiral bdg. 1.50 (0-912303-38-7) Michigan Mus.

—A Child's Walk Through Asia. Wu, Marshall, illus. 25p. (gr. 2-6). 1984. spiral bdg. 1.50 (0-912303-31-X) Michigan Mus.

Levine, Bobbie, et al. A Child's Walk Through Twentieth Century American Painting & Sculpture. (Illus.). 29p. (gr. 2-6). 1986. spiral bdg. 1.50 (0-912303-37-9) Michigan Mus.

Levine, Caroline. The Detective Stars & the Case of the Super Soccer Team. Lewin, Betsy, illus. LC 92-28600. 48p. (gr. 1-4). 1994. 11.99 (0-525-65134-9, Cobblehill Bks) Dutton Child Bks.

—Riddles to Tell Your Cat. Grant, Christy, ed. Seltzer, Meyer, illus. 32p. (gr. 1-4). 1992. PLB 8.95 (0-8075-7006-0) A Whitman.

—Silly School Riddles & Other Classroom Crack-Ups. Levine, Abby, ed. Munsinger, Lynn, illus. LC 84-17300. 32p. (gr. 1-5). 1984. 8.95 (0-8075-7359-0) A Whitman.

Levine, Caroline A. The Silly Kid Joke Book. Maestro, Giulio, illus. LC 82-17727. 64p. (gr. 1-3). 1983. 10.95 (0-525-44039-9, DCB) Dutton Child Bks.

Levine, David, selected by. The Fables of Aesop. Gregory, Patrick & Gregory, Justina, trs. Levine, David, illus. LC 84-12894. 108p. (gr. 8). 1984. 13.95 (0-87645-074-5, Pub. by Gambit); pap. 8.95 (0-87645-116-4) Harvard Common Pr.

Levine, Edna S. Lisa & Her Soundless World. Kamen, Gloria, illus. (gr. 1-5). 1984. 14.95 (0-87705-104-6); pap. 9.95 (0-89885-204-8) Human Sci Pr.

Levine, Ellen. Freedom's Children. 1993. 15.95 (0-399-21893-9) Putnam Pub Group.

—Freedom's Children: Young Civil Rights Activists Tell Their Own Stories. large type ed. LC 93-10388. (Illus.). 1993. 16.95 (1-56054-744-8) Thorndike Pr.

—I Hate English! Bjorkman, Steve, illus. (gr. k-2). 1989. pap. 13.95 (0-590-42305-3) Scholastic Inc.

—If You Lived At the Time of Martin Luther King. 1990. pap. 2.95 (0-590-42582-X) Scholastic Inc.

—If You Lived at the Time of the Great San Francisco Earthquake. Williams, Richard, illus. 64p. 1992. pap. 4.95 (0-590-45157-X) Scholastic Inc.

—If You Traveled on the Underground Railroad. (gr. 4-7). 1993. pap. 4.95 (0-590-45156-1) Scholastic Inc.

—If You Traveled West in a Covered Wagon. Freem, Elroy, illus. 80p. (gr. 3-5). 1992. pap. 4.95 (0-590-45158-8) Scholastic Inc.

—If Your Name Was Changed at Ellis Island. Parmenter, Wayne, illus. LC 92-27940. 80p. (gr. 2-5). 1993. 15.95 (0-590-46134-6) Scholastic Inc.

—Ready, Aim, Fire! The Real Adventures of Annie Oakley. (gr. 5-7). 1989. pap. 2.95 (0-590-41877-7) Scholastic Inc.

—Secret Missions: Four True Life Stories. (Illus.). 128p. (gr. 3-7). 1988. pap. 2.50 (0-590-41183-7) Scholastic Inc.

Levine, Evan. Not the Piano, Mrs. Medley! Schindler, S. D., illus. LC 90-29085. 32p. (ps-2). 1991. 14.95 (0-531-05956-1); RLB 14.99 (0-531-08556-2) Orchard Bks Watts.

Levine, Gloria. Anne of Green Gables: A Study Guide. (gr. 6-8). 1989. tchr's ed. & wkbk. 14.95 (0-88122-056-6) LRN Links.

—Children of the Sea. Dillon, Paul, illus. 48p. (Orig.). (gr. 4-8). 1991. pap. 5.95 (0-913839-98-1) Bk Lures.

—Cricket in Times Square: A Study Guide. (gr. 4-7). 1987. tchr's ed. & wkbk. 14.95 (0-88122-073-6) LRN Links.

—Fantastic Mr. Fox: A Study Guide. (gr. 3-5). 1985. tchr's ed. & wkbk. 14.95 (0-88122-076-0) LRN Links.

—Roll of Thunder, Hear My Cry - Study Guide. Friedland, Joyce & Kessler, Rikki, eds. (gr. 6-10). Date not set. pap. text ed. 14.95 (0-88122-126-0) Lrn Links.

Levine, Gloria & Fischer, Kathleen M. The Wave - Study Guide. Friedland, Joyce & Kessler, Rikki, eds. (gr. 6-10). Date not set. pap. text ed. 14.95 (0-88122-132-5) Lrn Links.

Levine, Gloria & Polette, Nancy. The ABCs of Reading Thinking & Literacy. (Illus.). 144p. (gr. 7-12). 1987. pap. 14.95 (0-913839-64-7) Bk Lures.

Levine, I. E. John Kennedy: Young Man in the White House. LC 90-49180. (Illus.). 176p. (gr. 6-10). 1991. PLB 13.95 (1-55905-085-3) Marshall Cavendish.

Levine, Janice R. Microcomputers in Elementary & Secondary Education: A Guide to Resources. 64p. (gr. k-12). 1983. 3.75 (0-937597-06-6, IR-65) ERIC Clear.

Levine, Jennifer. Forever in My Heart: A Story to Help Children Participate in Life As a Parent Dies. Maurer, Jason F., illus. LC 92-50678. 32p. (Orig.). (gr. 1-6). 1992. pap. 6.95 (1-878321-08-0) Rainbow NC.

Levine, Mel. Keeping a Head in School: A Student's Book about Learning Abilities & Learning Disorders. rev. ed. Lord, Anne & Jennings, Ann, illus. 312p. (gr. 4-10). 1991. pap. text ed. 19.35 (0-8388-2069-7, 2069); 6 cassettes 24.50 (0-8388-2070-0, 2070) Ed Pub Serv.

Levine, Saul V. & Wilcox, Kathleen. Dear Doctor. LC 86-21335. 256p. (gr. 7 up). 1987. PLB 12.88 (0-688-07094-9); pap. 6.95 (0-688-07095-7) Lothrop.

Levine, Shar. The Paper Book & Paper Maker. Weissmann, Joe, illus. LC 92-72021. 32p. (gr. k-5). 1993. 12.95 (1-56282-235-7) Hyprn Child.

Levine, Shar & Grafton, Allison. Projects for a Healthy Planet: Simple Environmental Experiments for Kids. 1992. pap. text ed. 9.95 (0-471-55484-7) Wiley.

Levine-Provost, Gail, jt. auth. see Provost, Gary.

Levinger, Elma E. Beautiful Garden & Other Bible Tales. Robinson, Jessie B., illus. (gr. 3-5). 6.95 (0-8197-0253-6) Bloch.

Levinson, Marilyn. The Fourth-Grade Four. Bowman, Leslie, illus. LC 89-31109. 64p. (gr. 2-4). 1989. 12.95 (0-8050-1082-3, Bks Young Read) H Holt & Co.

—The Fourth-Grade Four. Bowman, Leslie, illus. LC 89-31109. 64p. (gr. 2-4). 1991. pap. 4.95 (0-8050-1640-6, Owlet BYR) H Holt & Co.

—No Boys Allowed. Leer, Rebecca, illus. LC 93-22335. 128p. (gr. 5-8). 1993. PLB 13.95 (0-8167-3135-7); pap. write for info. (0-8167-3136-5) BrdgeWater.

Levinson, Nancy S. Christopher Columbus: Voyager to the Unknown. (Illus.). 128p. (gr. 4-7). 1990. 17.00 (0-525-67292-3, Lodestar Bks) Dutton Child Bks.

—Chuck Yeager the Man Who Broke the Sound Barrier. LC 87-25431. 133p. (gr. 5 up). 1988. 13.95 (0-8027-6781-8); PLB 14.85 (0-8027-6799-0) Walker & Co.

—Clara & the Bookwagon. Croll, Carolyn, illus. LC 86-45773. 64p. (gr. k-3). 1988. PLB 13.89 (0-06-023838-0) HarpC Child Bks.

—Clara & the Bookwagon. Croll, Carolyn, illus. LC 86-45773. 64p. (gr. k-3). 1991. pap. 3.50 (*0-06-444134-2*, Trophy) HarpC Child Bks.
—Snowshoe Thompson. Sandin, J., illus. LC 90-37401. 64p. (gr. k-3). 1992. 14.00 (*0-06-023801-1*); PLB 13.89 (*0-06-023802-X*) HarpC Child Bks.
—Sweet Notes, Sour Notes. Peck, Beth, illus. LC 92-19549. 64p. (gr. 2-5). 1993. 12.99 (*0-525-67379-2*, Lodestar Bks) NAL-Dutton.
—Turn of the Century: America One Hundred Years Ago. LC 93-4604. 1994. write for info. (*0-525-67433-0*, Lodestar Bks) Dutton Child Bks.
—Your Friend Natalie Popper. 112p. (gr. 5-9). 1991. 13.95 (*0-525-67307-5*, Lodestar Bks) Dutton Child Bks.
Levinson, Nancy S. & Rocklin, Joanne. Feeling Great: Reaching Out to the World, Reaching in to Yourself--Without Drugs. 2nd ed, rev. ed. LC 92-16217. (Illus.). 112p. (gr. 8-12). 1992. pap. 7.95 (*0-89793-087-8*) Hunter Hse.
Levinson, Riki. Boys Here - Girls There. Ritz, Karen, illus. LC 92-5321. 1993. 13.00 (*0-525-67374-1*, Lodestar Bks) Dutton Child Bks.
—Country Dawn to Dusk. LC 91-34600. (Illus.). 32p. (ps-2). 1992. 14.00 (*0-525-44957-4*, DCB) Dutton Child Bks.
—I Go with My Family to Grandma's. Goode, Diane, illus. LC 86-4490. 32p. (ps-1). 1986. 14.00 (*0-525-44261-8*, DCB); pap. 3.95 (*0-525-44557-9*, DCB) Dutton Child Bks.
—I Go with My Family to Grandma's. (ps-3). 1992. pap. 4.99 (*0-14-054762-2*) Puffin Bks.
—Me Baby! Hafner, Marylin, illus. LC 90-40372. 32p. (ps-1). 1991. 13.95 (*0-525-44693-1*, DCB) Dutton Child Bks.
—Mira Como Salen las Estrellas. (SPA., Illus.). 32p. (ps-3). 1992. 15.00 (*0-525-44958-2*, DCB) Dutton Child Bks.
—Our Home Is the Sea. Luzak, Dennis, illus. LC 87-36419. 32p. (gr. k-3). 1988. pap. 13.95 (*0-525-44406-8*, DCB) Dutton Child Bks.
—Our Home Is the Sea. Luzak, Dennis, illus. 32p. (gr. k-3). 1992. pap. 4.99 (*0-14-054552-2*, Puffin Unicorn) Puffin Bks.
—Soon, Annala. Downing, Julie, photos by. LC 92-44588. (Illus.). 32p. (ps-2). 1993. 14.95 (*0-531-05494-2*); PLB 14.99 (*0-531-08644-5*) Orchard Bks Watts.
—Watch the Stars Come Out. Goode, Diane, illus. LC 84-28672. 32p. (ps-3). 1985. 15.00 (*0-525-44205-7*, DCB) Dutton Child Bks.
Levinson, Riki, retold by see Andersen, Hans Christian.
Levinson, Ronald B., ed. see Plato.
Levit, Rose. With Secrets to Keep. LC 90-20947. 160p. (gr. 7 up). 1991. 12.95 (*1-55870-197-4*) Shoe Tree Pr.
Levite, Christine & Moline, Julie. Princesses. LC 89-8955. (Illus.). 208p. (gr. 5-8). 1989. PLB 15.40 (*0-531-10772-8*) Watts.
Levitin, Sonia. Adam's War. LC 93-13833. Date not set. write for info. (*0-8037-1506-4*); PLB write for info. (*0-8037-1507-2*) Dial Bks Young.
—Annie's Promise. LC 92-16819. 192p. (gr. 5 up). 1993. SBE 14.95 (*0-689-31752-2*, Atheneum Child Bk) Macmillan Child Grp.
—The Golem & the Dragon Girl. LC 92-27665. 176p. (gr. 3-7). 1993. 14.99 (*0-8037-1280-4*); PLB 14.89 (*0-8037-1281-2*) Dial Bks Young.
—Incident at Loring Groves. LC 87-24591. 192p. (gr. 7 up). 1988. 14.95 (*0-8037-0455-0*) Dial Bks Young.
—Journey to America. Robinson, Charles, illus. LC 86-22234. 160p. (gr. 3-6). 1987. pap. 3.95 (*0-689-71130-1*, Aladdin) Macmillan Child Grp.
—Journey to America. 2nd ed. LC 70-98616. (Illus.). 160p. (gr. 3-7). 1993. SBE 13.95 (*0-689-31829-4*, Atheneum Child Bk) Macmillan Child Grp.
—Man Who Kept His Heart in a Bucket. Pinkney, Jerry, illus. (ps-3). 1991. 14.95 (*0-8037-1029-1*); PLB 14.89 (*0-8037-1030-5*) Dial Bks Young.
—The Mark of Conte. 240p. (gr. 7 up). 1987. pap. 3.95 (*0-02-044191-6*, Collier Young Ad) Macmillan Child Grp.
—The Return. LC 86-25891. 224p. (gr. 5 up). 1987. SBE 13.95 (*0-689-31309-8*, Atheneum Child Bk) Macmillan Child Grp.
—Silver Days. LC 88-27491. 192p. (gr. 5 up). 1989. SBE 14.95 (*0-689-31563-5*, Atheneum Child Bk) Macmillan Child Grp.
—Silver Days. LC 91-22581. 192p. (gr. 3-7). 1992. pap. 3.95 (*0-689-71570-6*, Aladdin) Macmillan Child Grp.
—A Single Speckled Egg. Larrecq, John M., illus. LC 75-4189. 40p. (ps-3). 1976. 6.95 (*0-87466-074-2*, Pub. by Parnassus) HM.
Levitt, Paul M., et al. The Weighty Word Book. Stevens, Janet, illus. 99p. (gr. 4-9). 1990. Repr. of 1985 ed. 17.95 (*0-9627979-0-1*) Manuscripts.
Levitt, Saul. Jim Thorpe, All American. (Orig.). (gr. 4 up). 1980. playscript 5.00 (*0-87602-237-9*) Anchorage.
Levitt, Sidney. The Mighty Movers. Levitt, Sidney, illus. 48p. (gr. k-3). 1994. 10.95 (*1-56282-421-X*); PLB 10.89 (*1-56282-422-8*) Hyprn Child.
Levitz, Paul, et al, eds. see O'Neil, Dennis.
Levorsen, Sally, jt. auth. see Kayton, JoAnn.
Levoy, Myron. Alan & Naomi. LC 76-41522. 176p. (gr. 6 up). 1987. pap. 3.95 (*0-06-440209-6*, Trophy) HarpC Child Bks.
—The Hanukkah of Great-Uncle Otto. Ruff, Donna, illus. LC 84-12635. 48p. (gr. 3-7). 1984. 10.95 (*0-8276-0242-1*) JPS Phila.

—Kelly 'n' Me. LC 91-35807. 208p. (gr. 7 up). 1992. 15.00 (*0-06-020838-4*); PLB 14.89 (*0-06-020839-2*) HarpC Child Bks.
—Pictures of Adam. LC 92-24598. 124p. (gr. 7 up). 1993. pap. 4.95 (*0-688-11941-7*, Pub. by Beech Tree Bks) Morrow.
—A Shadow Like a Leopard. LC 79-2812. 192p. (gr. 4-7). 1994. pap. 3.95 (*0-06-440458-7*, Trophy) HarpC Child Bks.
—Three Friends. LC 83-47713. 192p. (gr. 7 up). 1984. HarpC Child Bks.
—Witch of Fourth Street & Other Stories. LC 74-183174. (Illus.). 128p. (gr. 3-7). 1974. pap. 3.95 (*0-06-440059-X*, Trophy) HarpC Child Bks.
—The Witch of Fourth Street & Other Stories. (gr. 3-6). 1991. 16.75 (*0-8446-6450-2*) Peter Smith.
Levy. The Beginners. 1993. pap. 2.75 (*0-590-44050-0*) Scholastic Inc.
—Brian & Pea Brain, No. 2. Date not set. 14.00 (*0-06-023462-8*, Festival); PLB 13.89 (*0-06-023463-6*, Festival) HarpC Child Bks.
—Cleo & Coyote. Date not set. 15.00 (*0-06-024271-X*, Festival); PLB 14.89 (*0-06-024272-8*, Festival) HarpC Child Bks.
—Go for the Gold. 1992. pap. 2.95 (*0-590-45253-3*, Apple Paperbacks) Scholastic Inc.
—If You Were There When They Signed the Constitution. 1992. 4.95 (*0-590-45159-6*) Scholastic Inc.
Levy, Barbara. How to Draw Clowns. LC 91-17171. (Illus.). 1991. PLB 10.65 (*0-8167-2477-6*); pap. text ed. 1.95 (*0-8167-2478-4*) Troll Assocs.
Levy, Constance. I'm Going to Pet a Worm Today: And Other Poems. Himler, Ronald, illus. LC 91-7485. 48p. (gr. k-5). 1991. SBE 12.95 (*0-689-50535-3*, M K McElderry) Macmillan Child Grp.
—A Tree Place & Other Poems. Sabuda, Robert, illus. LC 93-20586. 48p. (gr. k-5). 1994. SBE 13.95 (*0-689-50599-X*, M K McElderry) Macmillan Child Grp.
Levy, Elizabeth. Boys in the Gym. (gr. 4-7). 1990. pap. 2.75 (*0-590-42822-5*) Scholastic Inc.
—The Captain of the Team. 1989. pap. 2.75 (*0-590-42820-9*) Scholastic Inc.
—Case of the Dummy with Cold Eyes. (gr. 4-7). 1991. pap. 10.95 jacketed (*0-671-70543-1*, S&S BFYR) S&S Trade.
—The Case of the Gobbling Squash. Eagle, Ellen, illus. (gr. 2-4). 1989. pap. 10.95 jacketed (*0-671-63655-3*, S&S BFYR); pap. 2.95 (*0-671-68873-1*, S&S BFYR) S&S Trade.
—The Case of the Mind-Reading Mommies. Eagle, Ellen, illus. 1990. pap. 2.95 (*0-671-69435-9*) S&S Trade.
—The Case of the Tattletale Heart. Eagle, Ellen, illus. 64p. (gr. 2-4). 1992. pap. 3.00 (*0-671-74064-4*, S&S BFYR) S&S Trade.
—Cheater, Cheater. LC 92-33455. 1993. 13.95 (*0-590-45865-5*) Scholastic Inc.
—Cold As Ice. LC 88-12898. 176p. (gr. 7 up). 1988. 12.95 (*0-688-06579-1*) Morrow Jr Bks.
—Come Out Smiling: A Novel. LC 80-68734. 192p. (gr. 8-12). 1981. 8.95 (*0-440-01378-X*) Delacorte.
—Crush on the Coach. 1990. pap. 2.75 (*0-590-42821-7*) Scholastic Inc.
—Double Standard. 160p. (gr. 7 up). 1984. pap. 2.25 (*0-380-87379-6*, 87379-6, Flare) Avon.
—Dracula Is a Pain in the Neck. Gerstein, Mordicai, illus. LC 82-47707. 80p. (gr. 2-6). 1983. PLB 12.89 (*0-06-023823-2*) HarpC Child Bks.
—Dracula Is a Pain in the Neck. Gerstein, Mordicai, illus. LC 82-47707. 80p. (gr. k-5). 1984. pap. 3.95 (*0-06-440146-4*, Trophy) HarpC Child Bks.
—Fear of Falling. 128p. (gr. 3-7). 1991. pap. 2.75 (*0-590-43834-4*, Apple Paperbacks) Scholastic Inc.
—First Date. 1990. pap. 2.75 (*0-590-42825-X*) Scholastic Inc.
—Frankenstein Moved in on the Fourth Floor. Gerstein, Mordicai, illus. LC 78-19830. (gr. 1-5). 1979. PLB 12.89 (*0-06-023811-9*) HarpC Child Bks.
—Frankenstein Moved in on the Fourth Floor. Gerstein, Mordecai, illus. LC 78-19830. 64p. (gr. 2-5). 1981. pap. 3.95 (*0-06-440122-7*, Trophy) HarpC Child Bks.
—Gorgonzola Zombies in the Park. Ulrich, George, illus. LC 92-11353. 96p. (gr. 2-5). 1993. 14.00 (*0-06-021461-9*); PLB 13.89 (*0-06-021460-0*) HarpC Child Bks.
—The Gymnasts' Gift. 112p. 1991. pap. 2.75 (*0-590-44693-2*) Scholastic Inc.
—Keep Ms. Sugarman in the Fourth Grade. Henderson, Dave, illus. LC 91-22576. 96p. (gr. 3-6). 1992. 13.00 (*0-06-020426-5*); PLB 12.89 (*0-06-020427-3*) HarpC Child Bks.
—Keep Ms. Sugarman in the Fourth Grade. LC 91-22576. 96p. (gr. 3-6). 1993. pap. 3.95 (*0-06-440487-0*, Trophy) HarpC Child Bks.
—Lizzie Lies a Lot. Wallner, John, illus. LC 75-32914. 80p. (gr. 4-6). 1976. 6.95 (*0-440-04919-9*); PLB 6.46 (*0-440-04920-2*) Delacorte.
—Lizzie Lies a Lot. 112p. (gr. 3-5). 1977. pap. 2.75 (*0-440-44714-3*, YB) Dell.
—Mystery at the Meet. (gr. 4-7). 1990. pap. 2.75 (*0-590-42823-3*) Scholastic Inc.
—Nasty Competition. (gr. 4-7). 1991. pap. 2.75 (*0-590-43833-6*) Scholastic Inc.
—The New Coach? 128p. (gr. 3-7). 1991. pap. 2.75 (*0-590-44695-9*) Scholastic Inc.

—Nice Little Girls. Gerstein, Mordicai, illus. LC 73-15394. (gr. k-3). 1978. pap. 2.75 (*0-440-06360-4*) Delacorte.
—Out of Control. (gr. 4-7). 1990. pap. 2.75 (*0-590-42824-1*) Scholastic Inc.
—Running Out of Time. Mars, W. T., illus. LC 79-28064. 128p. (gr. 3-6). 1980. lib. bdg. 4.99 (*0-394-94422-4*) Knopf Bks Yng Read.
—The Runt. (Orig.). (gr. k-6). 1986. pap. 2.95 (*0-440-47538-4*, YB) Dell.
—School Spirit Sabotage: Brian & Pea Brain Mystery. Ulrich, George, illus. LC 93-23029. 1994. write for info. (*0-06-023407-5*); PLB write for info. (*0-06-023408-3*) HarpC Child Bks.
—Something Queer at the Ball Park. Gerstein, Mordicai, illus. 48p. (gr. 1-4). 1984. pap. 2.99 (*0-440-48116-3*, YB) Dell.
—Something Queer at the Birthday Party. Gerstein, Mordicai, illus. 48p. (gr. 1-4). 1992. pap. 2.99 (*0-440-40687-0*, YB) Dell.
—Something Queer at the Haunted School. Gerstein, Mordicai, illus. LC 81-1940. 48p. (gr. 1-3). 1982. 8.95 (*0-440-08349-4*); pap. 9.95 (*0-385-28992-8*) Delacorte.
—Something Queer at the Haunted School. Gerstein, Mordicai, illus. 48p. (gr. 1-4). 1983. pap. 3.25 (*0-440-48461-8*, YB) Dell.
—Something Queer at the Lemonade Stand. Gerstein, Mordicai, tr. LC 81-69666. (Illus.). 48p. (gr. 1-3). 1982. 7.95 (*0-440-07859-8*); pap. 10.95 (*0-385-28901-4*) Delacorte.
—Something Queer at the Lemonade Stand. Gerstein, Mordicai, illus. 48p. (gr. k-6). 1983. pap. 2.99 (*0-440-48495-2*, YB) Dell.
—Something Queer at the Library. Gerstein, Mordicai, illus. 48p. (gr. 1-4). 1989. pap. 3.25 (*0-440-48120-1*, YB) Dell.
—Something Queer in Outer Space. Gerstein, Mordicai, illus. LC 92-54870. 48p. (gr. 2-5). 1993. pap. 4.95 (*1-56282-279-9*) Hyprn Ppbks.
—Something Queer in Outer Space. Gerstein, Mordicai, illus. LC 92-54870. 48p. (gr. 2-5). 1993. 12.95 (*1-56282-566-6*); PLB 12.89 (*1-56282-280-2*) Hyprn Child.
—Something Queer in Rock N' Roll. Gerstein, Mordicai, illus. LC 86-19772. 48p. (gr. k-3). 1987. pap. 12.95 (*0-385-29547-2*) Delacorte.
—Something Queer in the Cafeteria. Gerstein, Mordicai, illus. LC 93-31343. 1994. write for info. (*0-7868-0001-1*); pap. write for info. (*0-7868-1000-9*) Hyprn Child.
—Something Queer Is Going On. Gerstein, Mordicai, illus. 48p. (gr. 1-4). 1982. pap. 2.99 (*0-440-47974-6*, YB) Dell.
—Something Queer on Vacation. Gerstein, Mordicai, illus. LC 78-72858. (gr. 1-3). 1980. 10.95 (*0-440-08346-X*); pap. 6.95 (*0-385-28987-1*) Delacorte.
—Something Queer on Vacation. Gerstein, Mordicai, illus. 48p. (gr. 1-4). 1982. pap. 2.99 (*0-440-47968-1*, YB) Dell.
—Take Two, They're Small. (Orig.). (gr. k-6). 1986. pap. 2.95 (*0-440-48517-7*, YB) Dell.
—Team Trouble. 128p. 1992. pap. 2.75 (*0-590-45252-5*) Scholastic Inc.
—Tough at the Top. (gr. 4-7). 1991. pap. 2.75 (*0-590-44694-0*) Scholastic Inc.
—Tumbling Ghosts. 1989. pap. 2.75 (*0-590-42221-9*) Scholastic Inc.
—The Winner. 128p. (gr. 3-6). 1989. pap. 2.50 (*0-590-41565-4*, Apple Paperbacks) Scholastic Inc.
—World Class Gymnast. 112p. 1990. pap. 2.75 (*0-590-43832-8*) Scholastic Inc.
Levy, Elizabeth, jt. auth. see Harris, Robbie.
Levy, Elizabeth, adapted by. Fat Albert & the Cosby Kids: Take Two, They're Small. (gr. 2 up). pap. 1.95 (*0-686-74491-8*, YB) Dell.
Levy, Gail, ed. see Stodden, Norma J. & McCormick, Linda.
Levy, H. M., Jr., ed. see Partee, Phillip E.
Levy, Janet, jt. auth. see Levy, Nathan.
Levy, Marilyn. Fitting In. (Orig.). 1991. pap. 3.99 (*0-449-70373-8*, Juniper) Fawcett.
—No Way Home. 160p. 1990. pap. 3.95 (*0-449-70326-6*, Juniper) Fawcett.
—Remember to Remember Me. (gr. 5 up). 1988. pap. 2.95 (*0-449-70278-2*, Juniper) Fawcett.
—Rumors & Whispers. 160p. (gr. 8 up). 1990. pap. 3.95 (*0-449-70327-4*, Juniper) Fawcett.
—Sounds of Silence. (gr. 5 up). 1989. pap. 2.95 (*0-449-70295-2*, Juniper) Fawcett.
—Touching. (gr. 6 up). 1988. pap. 3.50 (*0-449-70267-7*, Juniper) Fawcett.
Levy, Myrna N. The Summer Kid. (gr. 1-5). 1991. pap. 5.95 (*0-929005-20-1*, Pub. by Second Story Pr CN) InBook.
Levy, Nathan. Each Life Is Once. (gr. k up). 1993. pap. 7.95 (*1-878347-15-2*) NL Assocs.
—Nathan Levy's One Hundred Intriguing Questions, Bk. 1. (gr. 3 up). 1993. write for info. (*1-878347-35-7*) NL Assocs.
—Nathan Levy's One Hundred Intriguing Questions, Bk. 2. (gr. 3 up). 1993. write for info. (*1-878347-36-5*) NL Assocs.
—Nathan Levy's One Hundred Intriguing Questions, Bk. 3. (gr. 3 up). 1993. write for info. (*1-878347-37-3*) NL Assocs.
—Personality Probe. (gr. k up). 1990. pap. 19.95 (*1-878347-07-1*) NL Assocs.

—Stories to Stretch Minds, 5 vols., 24 stories ea. (gr. 2 up). 1981. Vol. I. 1.99 (*0-88092-000-9*); Vol. II. 1.99 (*0-88092-001-7*); Vol. III. 1.99 (*0-88092-005-X*); Vol. IV. 1.99 (*0-88092-006-8*); Vol. V. 1.99 (*0-685-55625-5*) Trillium Pr.
—Stories with Holes, Vol. VIII. 20p. (gr. 3 up). 1992. pap. 6.00 (*1-878347-11-X*) NL Assocs.
—Stories with Holes, Vol. I. (gr. 3 up). 1987. 6.00 (*0-685-63374-8*) NL Assocs.
—Stories with Holes, Vol. II. (gr. 3 up). 1990. pap. 6.00 (*1-878347-00-4*) NL Assocs.
—Stories with Holes, Vol. III. (gr. 3 up). 1990. pap. 6.00 (*1-878347-01-2*) NL Assocs.
—Stories with Holes, Vol. IV. (gr. 3 up). 1990. pap. 6.00 (*1-878347-02-0*) NL Assocs.
—Stories with Holes, Vol. V. (gr. 3 up). 1990. pap. 6.00 (*1-878347-03-9*) NL Assocs.
—Stories with Holes, Vol. VI. (gr. 3 up). 1991. pap. 6.00 (*1-878347-09-8*) NL Assocs.
—Stories with Holes, Vol. VII. (gr. 3 up). 1992. pap. 6.00 (*1-878347-10-1*) NL Assocs.
—Stories with Holes, Vol. IX. (gr. 3 up). 1992. pap. 6.00 (*1-878347-17-9*) NL Assocs.
—Stories with Holes, Vol. X. (gr. 3 up). 1992. pap. 6.00 (*1-878347-21-7*) NL Assocs.
—Stories with Holes, Vol. XI. (gr. 3 up). 1992. pap. 6.00 (*1-878347-22-5*) NL Assocs.
—Stories with Holes, Vol. XII. (gr. 3 up). 1993. pap. 6.00 (*1-878347-26-8*) NL Assocs.
—Stories with Holes, Vols. I-XII. (gr. 3 up). 1993. Set. 70.00 (*0-685-63375-6*, NL1970) NL Assocs.
—Stories with Holes, Vol. XIII. (gr. 3 up). 1993. pap. 6.00 (*1-878347-27-6*) NL Assocs.
—Stories with Holes, Vol. XIV. (gr. 3 up). 1993. write for info. (*1-878347-28-4*) NL Assocs.
—Stories with Holes, Vol. XV. (gr. 3 up). 1993. write for info. (*1-878347-29-2*) NL Assocs.
—Stories with Holes, Vol. XVI. (gr. 3 up). 1993. write for info. (*1-878347-30-6*) NL Assocs.
—Stories with Holes, Vol. XVII. (gr. 3 up). 1993. write for info. (*1-878347-31-4*) NL Assocs.
—Stories with Holes, Vol. XVIII. (gr. 3 up). 1993. write for info. (*1-878347-32-2*) NL Assocs.
Levy, Nathan & Burke, Amy M. Tools of the Trade. (gr. 4-12). 1992. pap. 7.95 (*1-878347-18-7*) NL Assocs.
Levy, Nathan & Levy, Janet. There Are Those. Edwards, Joan, illus. LC 82-81111. 32p. (ps up). 1990. 21.95 (*0-9608240-0-6*) NL Assoc Inc.
Levy, Nathan & Mendelowitz, Larry. Who Am I? Music, Vol. 3. (gr. 4-8). 1991. pap. 6.00 (*1-878347-13-6*) NL Assocs.
Levy, Nathan & Moretz, Cheryl. Who Am I? History, Vol. 1. (gr. 4-8). 1990. pap. 6.00 (*1-878347-04-7*) NL Assocs.
Levy, Nathan & Pastis, Steven. Who Am I? Inventors, Vol. 5. (gr. 4-8). 1992. pap. 6.00 (*1-878347-19-5*) NL Assocs.
—Who Am I? Literature Authors, Vol. 2. (gr. 4-8). 1991. pap. 6.00 (*1-878347-12-8*) NL Assocs.
—Who Am I? Literature Characters, Vol. 4. (gr. 2-8). 1991. pap. 6.00 (*1-878347-14-4*) NL Assocs.
Levy, Norman. Essential Math for College-Bound Students. 224p. (Orig.). (gr. 12). 1988. pap. 12.95 wkbk. (*0-13-286436-3*) P-H.
Levy, Patricia. Nigeria. LC 92-38754. 1993. 21.95 (*1-85435-574-0*) Marshall Cavendish.
Levy, Patricia M. Ireland. LC 93-11026. (gr. 5 up). 1993. 21.95 (*1-85435-580-5*) Marshall Cavendish.
—Women in Society: Britain. LC 92-33353. 1993. 22.95 (*1-85435-555-4*) Marshall Cavendish.
Levy, Robert. Clan of the Shape-Changers. LC 92-36010. 1994. write for info. (*0-395-66602-3*) HM.
—Escape from Exile. LC 92-20443. 176p. (gr. 5-9). 1993. 13.95 (*0-395-64379-1*) HM.
—Lost Magic. LC 93-1575. (gr. 10). 1995. write for info. (*0-395-68077-8*) HM.
Levy, Robert & Joseph, Joan. Robert Levy's Magic Book. LC 76-16016. (Illus.). 216p. (gr. 5 up). 1976. 10.95 (*0-87131-219-0*) M Evans.
Levy, Sara G. Mother Goose Rhymes for Jewish Children. Robinson, Jessie B., illus. (ps-2). 1979. pap. 8.95 (*0-8197-0254-4*) Bloch.
Lew, Christina, jt. auth. see Womack, Randy L.
Lew, Gordon, tr. see Lim, Genny.
Lewein, David A. The ABC's of Texas. Lewein, Mary J., ed. Delia, illus. 64p. 1989. pap. 4.95 (*0-685-29420-X*) TX Pride Pubns.
Lewein, Mary J., ed. see Lewein, David A.
Lewellen, John. La Luna, el Sol, y las Estrellas (Moon, Sun, & Stars) Kratky, Lada, tr. from ENG. LC 81-7749. (SPA., Illus.). 48p. (gr. k-4). 1984. PLB 15.27 (*0-516-31637-0*); pap. 4.95 (*0-516-51637-X*) Childrens.
—Moon, Sun & Stars. LC 81-7749. (Illus.). 48p. (gr. k-4). 1981. PLB 15.27 (*0-516-01637-7*); pap. 4.95 (*0-516-41637-5*) Childrens.
Lewin, Hugh. Jafta. Kopper, Lisa, illus. 24p. (ps-3). 1989. pap. 4.95 (*0-87614-494-6*, First Ave Edns) Lerner Pubns.
—Jafta & the Wedding. Kopper, Lisa, illus. LC 82-12836. 24p. (ps-3). 1983. pap. 4.95 (*0-87614-497-0*) Carolrhoda Bks.
—Jafta: The Homecoming. Kopper, Lisa, illus. LC 93-12945. 32p. (ps-2). 1994. 8.99 (*0-679-84722-7*); PLB 9.99 (*0-679-94722-1*) Knopf Bks Yng Read.
—Jafta: The Journey. Kopper, Lisa, illus. LC 84-4326. 24p. (ps-3). 1984. PLB 15.95 (*0-87614-265-X*) Carolrhoda Bks.

—Jafta: The Town. Kopper, Lisa, illus. LC 84-4950. 24p. (ps-3). 1984. PLB 15.95 (*0-87614-266-8*) Carolrhoda Bks.
—Jafta's Father. Kopper, Lisa, illus. 24p. (ps-3). 1989. pap. 4.95 (*0-87614-496-2*, First Ave Edns) Lerner Pubns.
—Jafta's Father. Kopper, Lisa, illus. 24p. (ps-3). 1983. pap. 4.95 (*0-87614-209-9*) Carolrhoda Bks.
—Jafta's Mother. Kopper, Lisa, illus. 24p. (ps-3). 1989. pap. 4.95 (*0-87614-495-4*, First Ave Edns) Lerner Pubns.
—Jafta's Mother. LC 82-12863. (ps-3). 1988. 15.95 (*0-87614-208-0*) Carolrhoda Bks.
Lewin, Larry, jt. auth. see Knight, Tanis.
Lewin, Roger. The Origin of Modern Humans: A Scientific American Library Volume. LC 93-17647. 1993. 32.95 (*0-7167-5039-2*, Sci Am Yng Rdrs) W H Freeman.
Lewin, Simon, retold by see Andersen, Hans Christian.
Lewin, Ted. Amazon Boy. Lewin, Ted, illus. LC 92-15798. 32p. (gr. k-3). 1993. RSBE 14.95 (*0-02-757383-4*, Macmillan Child Bk) Macmillan Child Grp.
—I Was a Teenage Professional Wrestler. Lewin, Ted, illus. LC 92-31523. 128p. (gr. 6-12). 1993. 16.95 (*0-531-05477-2*); RLB 16.99 (*0-531-08627-5*) Orchard Bks Watts.
—The Reindeer People. Lewin, Ted, illus. LC 93-19252. 1994. write for info. (*0-02-757390-7*) Macmillan Child Grp.
—Tiger Trek. Lewin, Ted, illus. LC 89-12710. 40p. (gr. 1-5). 1990. RSBE 14.95 (*0-02-757381-8*, Macmillan Child Bk) Macmillan Child Grp.
—When the Rivers Go Home. LC 90-19937. (Illus.). 40p. (gr. 1 up). 1992. RSBE 14.95 (*0-02-757382-6*, Macmillan Child Bk) Macmillan Child Grp.
Lewington, Anna. Antonio's Rain Forest. Parker, Edward, photos by. (Illus.). 48p. (gr. 2-5). 1993. 21.50 (*0-87614-749-X*) Carolrhoda Bks.
—Rain Forest Amerindians. LC 92-10560. (Illus.). 48p. (gr. 5-6). 1992. PLB 22.80 (*0-8114-2302-6*) Raintree Steck-V.
—What Do We Know about Amazonian Indians? LC 93-1736. (Illus.). 40p. (gr. 3 up). 1993. PLB 16.95 (*0-87226-367-3*); pap. 8.95 (*0-87226-262-6*) P Bedrick Bks.
Lewis. Last Battle. Date not set. PLB 14.89 (*0-06-023494-6*, Festival) HarpC Child Bks.
—Lion Witch & Wardrobe. Date not set. PLB 14.89 (*0-06-023482-2*, Festival) HarpC Child Bks.
—Silver Chair. Date not set. PLB 14.89 (*0-06-023496-2*, Festival) HarpC Child Bks.
Lewis, Barbara A. A Kid's Guide to Social Action: How to Solve the Social Problems You Choose - & Turn Creative Thinking into Positive Action. Espeland, Pamela, ed. LC 90-44297. (Illus.). 208p. (Orig.). (gr. 5 up). 1991. pap. 14.95 (*0-915793-29-6*) Free Spirit Pub.
—Kids with Courage: True Stories about Young People Making a Difference. Espeland, Pamela, ed. LC 91-46726. 184p. (gr. 5-12). 1992. pap. 10.95 (*0-915793-39-3*); write for info. tchr's. guide (*0-915793-40-7*) Free Spirit Pub.
Lewis, Beverley. The Six-Hour Mystery. Johnson, Meredith, illus. LC 93-35020. (gr. 4 up). 1993. 3.99 (*0-8066-2666-6*) Augsburg Fortress.
Lewis, Beverly. Holly's First Love. LC 92-47055. 1993. write for info. (*0-310-38051-0*) Zondervan.
—Mountain Bikes & Garbanzo Beans. Johnson, Meredith, illus. LC 93-4606. 1993. pap. 3.99 (*0-8066-2663-1*, Augsburg) Augsburg Fortress.
—Sealed with a Kiss. 144p. (gr. 6-9). 1993. pap. 4.99 (*0-310-38071-5*, Pub. by Youth Spec) Zondervan.
—Secret Summer Heart. 160p. (gr. 6-9). 1993. pap. 4.99 (*0-310-38061-8*, Pub. by Youth Spec) Zondervan.
—The Trouble with Weddings. 144p. (gr. 6-9). 1993. pap. 4.99 (*0-310-38081-2*, Pub. by Youth Spec) Zondervan.
Lewis, Brenda R. Coins & Currency. LC 92-46359. (Illus.). 80p. (gr. 5 up). 1993. 13.00 (*0-679-82662-9*); PLB 13.99 (*0-679-92662-3*) Random Bks Yng Read.
—Stamps! A Young Collector's Guide. (Illus.). 96p. (gr. 5-9). 1991. 15.00 (*0-525-67341-5*, Lodestar Bks) Dutton Child Bks.
Lewis, Brenda R., jt. auth. see Riordan, James.
Lewis, C. S. C. S. Lewis Letters to Children. 1985. 9.95 (*0-02-570830-9*) Macmillan.
—The Chronicles of Narnia. Baynes, Pauline, illus. (gr. 4 up). 1988. Boxed set. SBE 89.95 (*0-02-758801-7*, Macmillan Child Bk) Macmillan Child Grp.
—The Horse & His Boy. Baynes, Pauline, illus. LC 85-29978. 202p. (gr. 4 up). 1986. pap. 5.95 (*0-02-044410-9*, Collier Young Ad) Macmillan Child Grp.
—The Horse & His Boy. Baynes, Pauline, illus. LC 54-12817. 202p. (gr. 4 up). 1988. SBE 12.95 (*0-02-757650-7*, Macmillan Child Bk); pap. 3.95 (*0-02-044200-9*, Collier) Macmillan Child Grp.
—The Horse & His Boy. Baynes, Pauline, illus. LC 93-14300. (gr. 5 up). Date not set. 15.00 (*0-06-023488-1*); PLB 14.89 (*0-06-023489-X*) HarpC Child Bks.
—The Last Battle. reissued ed. Baynes, Pauline, illus. LC 56-9362. 184p. (gr. 4 up). 1988. SBE 12.95 (*0-02-757900-X*, Macmillan Child Bk) Macmillan Child Grp.
—The Last Battle. Baynes, Pauline, illus. LC 93-14302. Date not set. 15.00 (*0-06-023493-8*) HarpC Child Bks.

—The Lion, the Witch & the Wardrobe. Baynes, Pauline, illus. Incl. The Wardrobe. 160p. (gr. 4 up). 1986. pap. 7.95 (*0-02-044490-7*, Collier Young Ad) Macmillan Child Grp.
—The Lion, the Witch & the Wardrobe. Baynes, Pauline, illus. LC 50-10611. 160p. (gr. 4 up). 1988. 12.95 (*0-02-758120-9*, Macmillan Child Bk) Macmillan Child Grp.
—The Lion. the Witch, & the Wardrobe. Baynes, Pauline, illus. LC 93-8889. (gr. 5 up). 1994. 15.00 (*0-06-023481-4*) HarpC Child Bks.
—The Lion, the Witch, & the Wardrobe: (El Lion, la Bruja y el Armario) (SPA.). 11.95 (*84-204-4564-9*) Santillana.
—The Lion, the Witch & the Wardrobe: Gift Edition. Hague, Michael, illus. LC 83-61572. 192p. (gr. 3 up). 1983. SBE 22.95 (*0-02-758200-0*, Macmillan Child Bk) Macmillan Child Grp.
—The Magician's Nephew. Baynes, Pauline, illus. LC 85-29973. 176p. (gr. 4 up). 1986. pap. 5.95 (*0-02-044390-0*, Collier Young Ad) Macmillan Child Grp.
—The Magician's Nephew. 192p. (gr. 4 up). 1970. pap. 3.50 (*0-02-044230-0*, Collier Young Ad) Macmillan Child Grp.
—The Magician's Nephew. Baynes, Pauline, illus. LC 55-14869. 192p. (gr. 4 up). 1988. SBE 12.95 (*0-02-758340-6*, Macmillan Child Bk) Macmillan Child Grp.
—Prince Caspian. Baynes, Pauline, illus. LC 85-18999. 192p. (gr. 4 up). 1986. pap. 5.95 (*0-02-044430-3*, Collier Young Ad) Macmillan Child Grp.
—Prince Caspian. Baynes, Pauline, illus. LC 51-12799. 192p. (gr. 4 up). 1988. SBE 12.95 (*0-02-758580-8*, Macmillan Child Bk) Macmillan Child Grp.
—The Screwtape Letters. 160p. 1992. pap. text ed. 4.95 (*1-55748-315-9*) Barbour & Co.
—The Silver Chair. Baynes, Pauline, illus. LC 85-29984. 216p. (gr. 4 up). 1986. pap. 5.95 (*0-02-044420-6*, Collier Young Ad) Macmillan Child Grp.
—The Silver Chair. Baynes, Pauline, illus. LC 53-12553. 216p. (gr. 4 up). 1988. SBE 12.95 (*0-02-758780-0*, Macmillan Child Bk); pap. 3.50 (*0-02-044250-5*, Collier) Macmillan Child Grp.
—The Silver Chair. Baynes, Pauline, illus. LC 93-14299. (gr. 5 up). 1994. 15.00 (*0-06-023495-4*) HarpC Child Bks.
—The Voyage of the "Dawn Treader" Baynes, Pauline, illus. LC 85-29979. 218p. (gr. 4 up). 1986. pap. 5.95 (*0-02-044440-0*, Collier Young Ad) Macmillan Child Grp.
—Voyage of the "Dawn Treader" Baynes, Pauline, illus. LC 52-4219. 224p. (gr. 4 up). 1988. SBE 13.95 (*0-02-758820-3*, Macmillan Child Bk); pap. 3.50 (*0-02-044260-2*, Collier) Macmillan Child Grp.
—The Voyage of the Dawn Treader. Baynes, Pauline, illus. LC 93-11515. (gr. 4 up). 1994. 15.00 (*0-06-023486-5*); PLB 14.89 (*0-06-023487-3*) HarpC Child Bks.
Lewis, C. S. & Baynes, Pauline. The Magician's Nephew. LC 93-14301. (gr. 5 up). 1994. 15.00 (*0-06-023497-0*); PLB 14.89 (*0-06-023498-9*) HarpC Child Bks.
Lewis, Cass. Dead Man's Confession. LC 93-71557. 232p. 1993. pap. 3.95 (*1-56969-150-9*) FamilyVision.
Lewis, Cynthia C. Dead End: Understanding Teenage Suicide. LC 93-25010. (gr. 9 up). 1994. write for info. (*0-89490-433-7*) Enslow Pubs.
—Hello, Alexander Graham Bell Speaking. (Illus.). 64p. (gr. 3 up). 1991. RSBE 13.95 (*0-87518-461-8*, Dillon) Macmillan Child Grp.
Lewis, Dallas & Lewis, Lisa. The Planet Yes. Lewis, Dallas, illus. 32p. (Orig.). (gr. 3). 1994. 13.95x (*0-9634087-1-2*); pap. 6.95x (*0-9634087-2-0*) Silly Billys Bks.
Lewis, Dallas & Lewis, Lisa M. The Last Book. (Illus.). 32p. (gr. 1-2). 1992. 16.00 (*0-9634087-0-4*) Silly Billys Bks.
Lewis, Elizabeth F. Young Fu of the Upper Yangtze. new ed. Young, Ed, illus. LC 72-91654. 268p. (gr. 4-6). 1973. 18.95 (*0-8050-0549-8*, Bks Young Read) H Holt & Co.
—Young Fu of the Upper Yangtze. (gr. k-6). 1990. pap. 3.99 (*0-440-49043-X*, YB) Dell.
Lewis, Ernest A. The Great Lost Fremont Cannon Expedition: The Fremont Cannon High Up & Far Back. rev. & 3rd ed. LC 92-60780. (Illus.). 96p. (gr. 10 up). 1992. pap. 12.95 (*0-9633604-2-6*) Western Trails.
Lewis, Glenn A. Dinner at Mario's. Lewis, Glenn A., illus. 19p. (gr. k-3). 1992. pap. 5.95 (*1-895583-53-5*) MAYA Pubs.
—Funny Things. Lewis, Glenn A., illus. 15p. (gr. k-3). 1992. pap. 4.95 (*1-895583-54-3*) MAYA Pubs.
Lewis, Harriet. Pampoody & Max. 72p. 1977. pap. 4.50 (*0-933294-01-8*) Backroads.
Lewis, Hilda. Ship That Flew. Levrin, Nora, illus. LC 58-5903. (gr. 3-7). 1958. 25.95 (*0-87599-067-3*) S G Phillips.
Lewis, J. Patrick. The Christmas of the Reddle Moon. Kelley, Gary, illus. LC 93-28049. 1994. write for info. (*0-8037-1566-8*); PLB write for info. (*0-8037-1567-6*) Dial Bks Young.
—Earth Verses & Water Rhymes. Sabuda, Robert, illus. LC 90-40709. 32p. (gr. 2-5). 1991. SBE 13.95 (*0-689-31693-3*, Atheneum Child Bk) Macmillan Child Grp.
—A Hippopotamusn't: And Other Animal Poems. Chess, Victoria, illus. 40p. (ps-3). 1994. pap. 4.99 (*0-14-055273-1*, Puffin Pied Piper) Puffin Bks.

—July Is a Mad Mosquito. Hall, Melanie W., illus. LC 93-19743. 32p. (gr. 2-5). 1994. SBE 14.95 (*0-689-31813-8*, Atheneum Child Bk) Macmillan Child Grp.
—The Moonbow of Mr. B. Bones. Zimmer, Dirk, illus. LC 88-37107. 40p. (ps-4). 1992. 16.00 (*0-394-85365-2*); PLB 16.99 (*0-394-95365-7*) Knopf Bks Yng Read.
—One Dog Day. Ramsey, Marcy, illus. LC 92-24573. 64p. (gr. 2-5). 1993. SBE 12.95 (*0-689-31808-1*, Atheneum Child Bk) Macmillan Child Grp.
—Two Legged, Four-Legged, No-Legged Rhymes. Paparone, Pamela, illus. LC 90-20651. 40p. (ps-3). 1991. 13.00 (*0-679-80771-3*); lib. bdg. 13.99 (*0-679-90771-8*) Knopf Bks Yng Read.
Lewis, James. Hocus Pocus Stir & Cook, The Kitchen Science Magic Book. LC 91-30403. (Illus.). 79p. 1991. pap. 7.00 (*0-88166-183-X*) Meadowbrook.
—Learn While You Scrub: Science in the Tub. (gr. 5 up). 1989. 7.00 (*0-671-68999-1*) S&S Trade.
Lewis, Jean. Sweet Dreams, Tweety. (ps-3). 1993. pap. 1.95 (*0-307-10552-0*, Golden Pr) Western Pub.
Lewis, Joan, jt. auth. see Heymsfield, Carla.
Lewis, John. Ireland: A Divided Country. LC 89-31550. (Illus.). 32p. (gr. 5-6). 1989. PLB 12.90 (*0-531-17169-8*) Watts.
Lewis, John R., Jr. Dragons Are Lonely. Russell, Judith, illus. 32p. (gr. 1-3). 1993. 14.95 (*0-87797-239-7*) Cherokee.
Lewis, Judy & Yarbrough, Jane. California People & Places. (Illus.). 32p. (gr. 4). 1991. study prints 260.00 (*1-879748-01-0*) Calif Perf Prods.
Lewis, Kathryn, et al, eds. see Evans-Tiller, Jan.
Lewis, Kim. Emma's Lamb. Lewis, Kim, illus. LC 90-3863. 32p. (ps-1). 1991. SBE 13.95 (*0-02-758821-1*, Four Winds) Macmillan Child Grp.
—First Snow. Lewis, Kim, illus. LC 92-54413. 32p. (ps up). 1993. 14.95 (*1-56402-194-7*) Candlewick Pr.
—Floss. LC 91-71853. (Illus.). 32p. (ps up). 1992. 14.95 (*1-56402-010-X*) Candlewick Pr.
—Floss. LC 91-71853. (ps-3). 1994. pap. 4.99 (*1-56402-271-4*) Candlewick Pr.
—The Last Train. LC 93-32370. 1994. PLB write for info. (*1-56402-343-5*) Candlewick Pr.
—The Shepherd Boy. Lewis, Kim, illus. LC 89-23679. 32p. (ps-1). 1990. SBE 13.95 (*0-02-758581-6*, Four Winds) Macmillan Child Grp.
Lewis, Lee A. The Trouble with Dreams. LC 91-27503. 160p. (Orig.). (gr. 4-7). 1991. pap. 5.95 (*0-8361-3571-7*) Herald Pr.
Lewis, Linda. All for the Love of That Boy. 224p. (gr. 7-9). 1989. pap. 2.95 (*0-671-68243-1*, Archway) PB.
—Dedicated to That Boy I Love. 168p. (gr. 6-9). 1990. pap. 2.75 (*0-671-68244-X*, Archway) PB.
—Is There Life after Boys? 165p. (gr. 5-7). 1990. pap. 2.95 (*0-671-69559-2*, Archway) PB.
—Loving Two Is Hard to Do. 160p. (gr. 6-9). 1990. pap. 2.95 (*0-671-70587-3*, Archway) PB.
—Pre-Teen Means Inbetween. MacDonald, Pat, ed. 160p. (Orig.). (gr. 3-6). 1993. pap. 2.99 (*0-671-74535-2*, Minstrel Bks) PB.
—Two Young Two Go Four Boys. (gr. 2-5). 1990. pap. 2.75 (*0-671-69560-6*, Archway) PB.
—We Hate Everything but Boys. (gr. 5-7). 1990. pap. 2.99 (*0-671-72225-5*, Archway) PB.
—We Love only Older Boys. 176p. (Orig.). (gr. 7 up). 1990. pap. 2.95 (*0-671-69558-4*, Archway) PB.
Lewis, Lisa, jt. auth. see Lewis, Dallas.
Lewis, Lisa M., jt. auth. see Lewis, Dallas.
Lewis, Lois F. Carlin School, A History Book: The Story of a School in Ravenna, Ohio, U. S. A. Lewis, William B., illus. 28p. (Orig.). (gr. 5). 1989. pap. text ed. write for info. (*0-9620136-3-3*) L F Lewis.
—Tappan School, a History Book: The Story of a School in Ravenna, Ohio, U. S. A. Lewis, William B., illus. 28p. (Orig.). (gr. 5). 1989. pap. text ed. write for info. (*0-9620136-1-7*) L F Lewis.
—West Main School, a History Book: The Story of a School in Ravenna, Ohio, U. S. A. Lewis, William B., illus. (Orig.). (gr. 5). 1988. pap. text ed. 2.00 (*0-9620136-0-9*) L F Lewis.
Lewis, Luevester. Jackie. Jolly, Cheryl, illus. (gr. k-5). 1970. pap. 1.00 (*0-685-42384-0*) Third World.
Lewis, Margorie, jt. auth. see Mazer, Norma F.
Lewis, Marguerite & Kudla, Pamela. Hooked on Library Skills: A Sequential Activities Program. 288p. (gr. k-6). 1988. pap. 27.95x (*0-87628-408-X*) Ctr Appl Res.
Lewis, Naomi. Cry Wolf & Other Aesop Fables. Castle, Barry, illus. 32p. (ps up) 1988. 18.00 (*0-19-520710-6*) OUP.
—Hans Andersen's Fairy Tales. 1988. pap. 2.99 (*0-14-035085-3*, Puffin Bks.
—Hare & Badger Go to Town. Ross, Tony, illus. 32p. (ps-1). 1987. 9.95 (*0-905478-94-0*, Pub. by Century UK) Trafalgar.
Lewis, Naomi, jt. auth. see Kruss, James.
Lewis, Naomi, ed. Messages: A Book of Poems. LC 85-10326. 255p. (gr. 7 up). 1985. Faber & Faber.
—The Twelve Dancing Princesses & Other Tales from Grimm. Postma, Lidia, illus. LC 85-6964. 100p. (ps up). 1986. 14.95 (*0-8037-0237-X*) Dial Bks Young.
Lewis, Naomi, adapted by see Andersen, Hans Christian.
Lewis, Naomi, retold by see Andersen, Hans Christian.
Lewis, Naomi, tr. Proud Knight, Fair Lady: The Twelve Lais of Marie de France. Barrett, Angela, illus. 128p. (gr. 5 up). 1989. pap. 19.95 (*0-670-82656-1*) Viking Child Bks.

Lewis, Naomi, tr. see Andersen, Hans Christian.
Lewis, Naomi, tr. see Baumann, Kurt.
Lewis, Naomi, tr. see Beisert, Heide H.
Lewis, Naomi, tr. see Grimm, Jacob & Grimm, Wilhelm K.
Lewis, Naomi, tr. see Rupprecht, Siegfried P.
Lewis, O. G. Good News. (Illus.). (gr. k-6). 1978. visualized song 2.99 (*3-90117-005-7*) CEF Press.
Lewis, Patricia, ed. see Blinks, William, et al.
Lewis, Patrick. A Hippopotamusn't: And Other Animal Verses. Fogelman, Phyllis J., ed. Chess, Victoria, illus. LC 87-24579. 40p. (ps-3). 1990. 12.95 (*0-8037-0518-2*); PLB 12.89 (*0-8037-0519-0*) Dial Bks Young.
Lewis, Patrick, retold by. The Frog Princess: A Russian Folktale. Spirin, Gennady, illus. LC 93-10827. 1994. write for info. (*0-8037-1623-0*); lib. bdg. write for info. (*0-8037-1624-9*) Dial Bks Young.
Lewis, Paul O. Davy's Dream. (Illus.). 64p. (ps-6). 1988. 14.95 (*0-941831-32-9*); pap. 9.95 (*0-941831-28-0*) Beyond Words Pub.
—Ever Wondered. Lewis, Paul O., illus. 36p. (gr. 3-6). 1991. pap. 4.95 (*0-941831-67-1*) Beyond Words Pub.
—Grasper: A Young Crab's Discovery out of His Shell. Roehm, Michelle, ed. Lewis, Paul O., illus. 36p. 1993. 13.95 (*0-941831-85-X*) Beyond Words Pub.
—P. Bear's New Years Party - A Counting Book. (Illus.). 24p. (ps-1). 1989. 12.95 (*0-941831-21-3*); pap. 8.95 (*0-941831-29-9*) Beyond Words Pub.
—The Starlight Bride. (Illus.). 40p. (ps-6). 1988. cloth 14.95 (*0-941831-33-7*); pap. 9.95 (*0-941831-25-6*) Beyond Words Pub.
Lewis, R. Aunt Armadillo. (Illus.). 24p. (ps-8). 1985. 12.95 (*0-920303-38-2*, Pub. by Annick CN); pap. 4.95 (*0-920303-39-0*, Pub. by Annick CN) Firefly Bks Ltd.
—All of You Was Singing. Young, Ed, illus. LC 89-18263. 32p. 1991. SBE 13.95 (*0-689-31596-1*, Atheneum Child Bk) Macmillan Child Grp.
—In the Night, Still Dark. Young, Ed, illus. LC 87-11538. 32p. 1988. RSBE 13.95 (*0-689-31310-1*, Atheneum Child Bk) Macmillan Child Grp.
Lewis, Richard, ed. In a Spring Garden. Keats, Ezra J., illus. LC 65-23965. 32p. (ps up). 1989. Repr. of 1965 ed. 13.95 (*0-8037-4024-7*) Dial Bks Young.
—In a Spring Garden. Keats, Ezra J., illus. 32p. (ps up). 1989. pap. 4.95 (*0-8037-4033-6*, Dial Pied Piper) Puffin Bks.
Lewis, Rob. Henrietta's First Winter. (Illus.). 32p. (ps-3). 1990. 11.95 (*0-374-32951-6*) FS&G.
—Tidy up, Trevor. LC 92-30327. (ps-3). 1993. 13.95 (*0-15-200626-5*) HarBrace.
—The White Bicycle. LC 88-45092. (Illus.). 32p. (ps up). 1988. 12.00 (*0-374-38384-7*) FS&G.
Lewis, Rosemary, et al. Reviewbooks for the GED Test. (Illus.). 1992. pap. text ed. 83.65 (*1-56030-089-2*) Comex Systs.
Lewis, Sharen, jt. auth. see LaMorte, Kathy.
Lewis, Shari. Baby Lamb Chop Loves Animals. Beylon, Cathy, illus. 12p. (ps-k). 1991. bds. 3.95 (*0-679-81723-9*) Random Bks Yng Read.
—Baby Lamb Chop Loves Numbers. Beylon, Cathy, illus. 12p. (ps-k). 1991. bds. 3.95 (*0-679-81724-7*) Random Bks Yng Read.
—Baby Lamb Chop Loves Nursery School. Beylon, Cathy, illus. 12p. (ps-k). 1991. bds. 3.95 (*0-679-81725-5*) Random Bks Yng Read.
—Baby Lamb Chop Loves the Beach. Beylon, Cathy, illus. 12p. (ps-k). 1991. bds. 3.95 (*0-679-81726-3*) Random Bks Yng Read.
—The Boat Contest: The Lion & the Mouse. Marshall, Blaine, ed. (Illus.). 32p. (ps-3). 1993. 9.95 (*0-8094-7446-8*) Time-Life.
—One-Minute Bedtime Stories. (ps). 1991. pap. 3.99 (*0-440-40626-9*, YB) Dell.
—One-Minute Bible Stories: New Testament. (ps). 1991. pap. 4.99 (*0-440-40628-5*, YB) Dell.
—One-Minute Bible Stories: Old Testament. Ewing, Carolyn S., illus. LC 86-2011. 48p. (ps-3). 1986. PLB 10.00 (*0-385-19565-6*); pap. 7.99 (*0-385-19566-4*) Doubleday.
—One-Minute Bible Stories: Old Testament. (ps). 1991. pap. 4.99 (*0-440-40627-7*, YB) Dell.
—One-Minute Birthday Stories. (ps-3). 1992. pap. 10.00 (*0-385-41325-4*) Doubleday.
—One Minute Christmas. 1993. pap. 4.99 (*0-440-40856-3*) Dell.
—One Minute Christmas Stories. Palmer, Jan, illus. Matthews, Gerry, contrib. by. LC 86-29146. (Illus.). 48p. (gr. k-3). 1987. pap. 7.95 (*0-385-23424-4*) Doubleday.
—One-Minute Easter Stories. 1990. 8.95 (*0-385-24960-8*) Doubleday.
—One-Minute Easter Stories. (ps-3). 1993. pap. 3.99 (*0-440-40764-8*) Dell.
—One-Minute Favorite Fairy Tales. Mahan, Ben, illus. LC 84-25968. 48p. (ps-3). 1985. pap. 8.95 (*0-385-19322-X*) Doubleday.
—One-Minute Favorite Fairy Tales. (ps). 1991. pap. 3.99 (*0-440-40625-0*, YB) Dell.
—One-Minute Greek Myths. Ewing, Carolyn S., illus. 48p. (ps-3). 1987. 6.95 (*0-385-23849-5*); pap. 9.95 (*0-385-23423-6*) Doubleday.
—One Minute Jewish Stories. 1993. pap. 4.99 (*0-440-40878-4*) Dell.
—One-Minute Scary Stories. (ps-3). 1991. pap. 10.00 (*0-385-41778-0*) Doubleday.

—One-Minute Scary Stories. (ps-3). 1993. 4.99 (*0-440-40833-4*) Dell.
—One Minute Stories of Brothers & Sisters. Oechsli, Kelly, illus. LC 87-20056. 48p. (ps-3). 1988. pap. 7.95 (*0-385-23425-2*) Doubleday.
—One-Minute Stories of Great Americans. (ps-3). 1990. 9.95 (*0-385-24448-7*) Doubleday.
—Shari Lewis Presents One Hundred & One Things for Kids to Do. Buller, Jon, illus. LC 86-43065. 96p. (gr. 1-5). 1987. lib. bdg. 9.99 (*0-394-98966-X*); pap. 7.95 (*0-394-88966-5*) Random Bks Yng Read.
—Shari Lewis Presents One Hundred One Games & Songs for Kids to Play & Sing. LC 92-20572. (Illus.). 96p. (gr. 1-5). 1993. PLB 9.99 (*0-679-92271-7*); pap. 6.99 (*0-679-82271-2*) Random Bks Yng Read.
Lewis, Shari & Henderson, Florence. One-Minute Bible Stories: New Testament. Ewing, Carolyn S., illus. LC 86-6401. 48p. (ps-3). 1986. PLB 10.99 (*0-385-23286-1*) Doubleday.
Lewis, Shari & O'Kun, Lan. One-Minute Bedtime Stories. Cumings, Art, illus. LC 79-8024. 48p. (ps-3). 1982. pap. 10.00 (*0-385-15292-2*) Doubleday.
—One-Minute Teddy Bear Stories. Lisi, Victoria, illus. LC 92-23033. 1993. pap. 12.95 (*0-385-30909-0*) Doubleday.
Lewis, Shari & Oppenheimer, Lillian. Folding Paper Toys. rev. ed. LC 63-20060. (Illus.). 100p. (gr. 4 up). 1992. pap. 11.95 (*0-8128-1953-5*, Scrbrough Hse) Madison Bks UPA.
Lewis, Shari & Zimmerman, Dick. Shari Lewis Presents One Hundred-One Magic Tricks for Kids to Do. Buller, Jon, illus. LC 89-10360. 96p. (Orig.). 1990. PLB 9.99 (*0-394-92059-7*); pap. 6.95 (*0-394-82059-2*) Random Bks Yng Read.
Lewis, Shari, adapted by. One-Minute Jewish Stories. Collier, Roberta, illus. (ps-3). 1989. 10.00 (*0-385-24447-9*) Doubleday.
Lewis, Sherri Y., intro. by see Forte, Imogene & MacKenzie, Joy.
Lewis, Sian. Smoke in the Tunnel. 1991. pap. 23.00x (*0-685-60035-1*, Pub. by Gomer Pr UK) St Mut.
Lewis, Theresa. Caribbean Folk Legends. LC 89-81981. 90p. (gr. 6-12). 1990. 19.95 (*0-86543-158-2*); pap. 7.95 (*0-86543-159-0*) Africa World.
Lewis, Thomas P. Call for Mr. Sniff. Woldin, Beth W., illus. LC 79-2679. 64p. (gr. k-3). 1981. HarpC Child Bks.
—Clipper Ship. Sandin, Joan, illus. LC 77-11858. 64p. (ps-3). 1978. 11.95 (*0-06-023808-9*); PLB 11.89 (*0-06-023809-7*) HarpC Child Bks.
—Clipper Ship. Sandin, Joan, illus. LC 77-11858. 64p. (gr. k-3). 1992. pap. 3.50 (*0-06-444160-1*, Trophy) HarpC Child Bks.
—Hill of Fire. Sandin, Joan, illus. LC 70-121802. 64p. (gr. k-3). 1971. PLB 13.89 (*0-06-023804-6*) HarpC Child Bks.
—Hill of Fire. Sandin, Joan, illus. LC 70-121802. 64p. (gr. k-3). 1987. incl. cassette 5.98 (*0-694-00175-9*, Trophy); pap. 3.50 (*0-06-444040-0*, Trophy) HarpC Child Bks.
Lewis, Tom G. Karate for Kids. 120p. (Orig.). (gr. 2-10). 1980. pap. 3.95 (*0-89826-005-1*) Natl Paperback.
Lewis, Wendy. Sarah Scrap & Her Nature Trail. (Illus.). 32p. 1993. 13.95 (*0-237-51216-5*, Pub. by Evans Bros Ltd) Trafalgar.
—Sarah Scrap & Her Wonderful Heap! (Illus.). 32p. (gr. k-2). 1992. 13.95 (*0-237-51152-5*, Pub. by Evans Bros Ltd) Trafalgar.
—Save the Animals. (Illus.). 32p. (gr. k-2). 1992. 15.95 (*0-237-51153-3*, Pub. by Evans Bros Ltd) Trafalgar.
Lewis, Winfield. Marshmallow World. 1991. 7.95 (*0-533-09536-0*) Vantage.
Lewis-Ferguson, Julinda. Alvin Ailey, Jr. A Life in Dance. LC 93-17906. 1994. 14.95 (*0-8027-8239-6*); PLB 15.85 (*0-8027-8241-8*) Walker & Co.
Lewison. Where's Baby? 1992. 4.95 (*0-685-53516-9*) Scholastic Inc.
Lewison, Wendy. Boo! Peekaboo! Morgan, Mary, illus. LC 90-83244. 24p. (ps). 1991. 2.50 (*0-448-40133-9*, G&D) Putnam Pub Group.
—Buzz Said the Bee. Wilhelm, Hans, illus. 32p. 1992. pap. 2.95 (*0-590-44185-X*, Cartwheel) Scholastic Inc.
—Christmas Cookies. Morgan, Mary, illus. 24p. (ps). 1993. bds. 2.95 (*0-448-40554-7*, G&D) Putnam Pub Group.
—Happy Thanksgiving! Morgan, Mary, illus. 24p. (ps). 1993. bds. 2.95 (*0-448-40552-0*, G&D) Putnam Pub Group.
—Nighty-Night. Orecchia, Giulia, illus. 24p. (ps). 1992. spiral bdg. 9.95 (*0-448-40391-9*, G&D) Putnam Pub Group.
—Say Thank You, Theodore. Kangas, Juli, illus. 32p. (ps-3). 1992. pap. 2.25 (*0-448-40476-1*, G&D) Putnam Pub Group.
Lewison, Wendy, compiled by. Baby's First Mother Goose. Morgan, Mary, illus. 24p. (ps). 1993. bds. 3.50 (*0-307-06143-4*, 6143, Golden Pr) Western Pub.
Lewison, Wendy C. Bye-Bye, Baby. (ps). 1992. 4.95 (*0-590-45172-3*, Cartwheel) Scholastic Inc.
—Going to Sleep on the Farm. Wijngaard, Juan, illus. LC 91-3737. 32p. (ps-2). 1992. 13.00 (*0-8037-1096-8*); PLB 12.89 (*0-8037-1097-6*) Dial Bks Young.
—The Princess & the Potty. Brown, Rick, illus. LC 93-7853. (gr. 2 up). 1994. pap. 14.00 (*0-671-87284-2*, S&S BFYR) S&S Trade.

—The Rooster Who Lost His Crow. Wickstrom, Thor, illus. LC 93-28059. 1994. write for info. (*0-8037-1545-5*); PLB write for info. (*0-8037-1546-3*) Dial Bks Young.
—Shy Vi. Smith, Stephen J., illus. LC 91-39658. 40p. (ps-2). 1993. pap. 14.00 JRT (*0-671-76968-5*, S&S BFYR) S&S Trade.
—Uh-oh, Baby. (ps). 1992. 4.95 (*0-590-45171-5*, Cartwheel) Scholastic Inc.
—Where Is Sammy's Smile: A Lift-the-Flap Book. Bratun, Katy, illus. 24p. (ps-k). 1989. 10.95 (*0-448-40150-9*, G&D) Putnam Pub Group.
—Where's Baby. (ps). 1992. 4.95 (*0-590-45170-7*, Cartwheel) Scholastic Inc.
Lewison, Wendy C., et al. But Why? Reading Workbook. Murdocca, Sal, illus. Pape, Richard, designed by. (Illus.). 32p. (Orig.). (gr. k-2). 1988. wkbk. 1.99 (*0-88743-109-7*) Sch Zone Pub Co.
Lewis-Patrick, Denise. Animal ABC's. Gleeson, Kate, illus. (ps). 1990. bds. write for info. (*0-307-06127-2*) Western Pub.
—How Many Animals. Gleeson, Kate, illus. (ps). 1990. write for info. (*0-307-06129-9*) Western Pub.
—Opposites. (ps). 1990. write for info. (*0-307-06133-7*) Western Pub.
—Shapes & Colors. (ps). 1990. write for info. (*0-307-06134-5*) Western Pub.
—What Does Baby Hear? (ps). 1990. write for info. (*0-307-06132-9*) Western Pub.
—What Does Baby See? (ps). 1990. write for info. (*0-307-06130-2*) Western Pub.
Lewittes. Anne Frank: The Diary of a Young Girl, 2 vols. large type ed. (gr. 10 up). Repr. of 1960 ed. Set. write for info. NAVH.
Lexa-Senning, Susan, jt. auth. see Alden, Laura.
Lexau, Joan. Don't Be My Valentine. Hoff, Syd, illus. LC 85-42621. 64p. (gr. k-3). 1985. PLB 13.89 (*0-06-023873-9*) HarpC Child Bks.
—Striped Ice Cream. LC 68-10774. (Illus.). 96p. (gr. k-3). 1968. PLB 13.89 (*0-397-31047-1*, Lipp Jr Bks) HarpC Child Bks.
Lexau, Joan M. The Dog Food Caper. Hafner, Marylin, illus. LC 84-1904. 48p. (ps-3). 1985. 8.95 (*0-8037-0107-1*) Dial Bks Young.
—Don't Be My Valentine. Hoff, Syd, illus. LC 85-42621. 64p. (gr. k-3). 1988. pap. 3.50 (*0-06-444115-6*, Trophy) HarpC Child Bks.
—Don't Be My Valentine. Hoff, Syd, illus. (gr. 1-4). 1990. incl. cass. 19.95 (*0-87499-150-1*); pap. 12.95 incl. cass. (*0-87499-149-8*); Set; incl. 4 bks., cass., & guide. pap. 27.95 (*0-685-38539-6*) Live Oak Media.
—Emily & the Klunky Baby & the Next-Door Dog. Alexander, Martha, illus. LC 77-181789. 40p. (ps-3). 1972. 5.95 (*0-8037-2309-1*) Dial Bks Young.
—The Poison Ivy Case. Hafner, Marylin, illus. LC 82-22123. 56p. (ps-3). 1984. Dial Bks Young.
—Rooftop Mystery. Hoff, Syd, illus. LC 68-16821. 64p. (gr. k-3). 1968. PLB 13.89 (*0-06-023865-8*) HarpC Child Bks.
—Strawberry Shortcake & Sad Mister Sun. Sustendal, Pat, illus. 40p. (ps-3). 1983. cancelled 5.95 (*0-910313-10-5*) Parker Bros.
—Striped Ice Cream. reissued ed. 1992. 2.75 (*0-590-45729-2*, Little Apple) Scholastic Inc.
—Trouble Will Find You. Chesworth, Michael, illus. LC 93-6813. (ps-6). 1994. write for info. (*0-395-64380-5*) HM.
Leyerle, Anne L. & Leyerle, William D. Song Anthology One. 3rd, rev. ed. LC 79-90829. 159p. (gr. 9 up). 1985. pap. 12.95 plastic comb (*0-9602296-3-9*) Leyerle Pubns.
Leyerle, Anne L. & Leyerle, William D., eds. Song Anthology Two. 159p. (gr. 9 up). 1984. pap. 12.95 plastic comb. (*0-9602296-4-7*) Leyerle Pubns.
Leyerle, William D., jt. auth. see Leyerle, Anne L.
Leyerle, William D., jt. ed. see Leyerle, Anne L.
Leyton, Lawrence. My First Magic Book. LC 93-22104. (Illus.). 48p. (gr. k-4). 1993. 13.95 (*1-56458-319-8*) Dorling Kindersley.
Leyton, Lawrence & Root, Betty. My First Dictionary. Langley, Jonathan, illus. LC 93-20145. 96p. (gr. k-4). 1993. 16.95 (*1-56458-277-9*) Dorling Kindersley.
Lhommedieu, Arthur J. Children of the Sun. (ps-3). 1993. 7.95 (*0-85953-931-8*) Childs Play.
—Metamorphosis: Butterfly. (ps-3). 1993. 5.95 (*0-85953-170-8*) Childs Play.
—Metamorphoses: Egg, Tadpole, Frog. (ps-3). 1993. 5.95 (*0-85953-169-4*) Childs Play.
Li, Xiao M., tr. from CHI. The Mending of the Sky & Other Chinese Myths. Wu, Shan M., illus. Buckley, Cicely, intro. by. (Illus.). 54p. (Orig.). (gr. 5 up). 1989. pap. 9.00 (*0-9617481-3-5*) Oyster River Pr.
Lian, Ann & Lian, Leslie. The Fourteen Carat Caper. LC 88-51031. (Illus.). 44p. 1988. 5.95 (*1-55523-171-3*) Winston-Derek.
Lian, Leslie, jt. auth. see Lian, Ann.
Libb, Melva, see Biros, Florence K.
Libby, Larry. Someday Heaven. 48p. 1993. 13.99 (*0-945564-77-5*, Gold & Honey) Questar Pubs.
Liberati, Bruce D. Bunnylove & the Three Ways to Love. Liberati, Zona, ed. (Illus.). (gr. 1-6). 1989. write for info. Word Dist Intl.
—The King Who Only Loved. Liberati, Zona, ed. (Illus.). (gr. 1-6). 1989. write for info. Word Dist Intl.
Liberati, Zona, ed. see Liberati, Bruce D.
Librairie du Liban Staff. ABC Dictionary I: Arabic & English. (ENG & ARA.). (ps-4). 1983. 6.00x (*0-86685-336-7*) Intl Bk Ctr.

—ABC Dictionary I: Arabic & French. (ARA & FRE.). (ps-4). 1983. 6.00x (*0-86685-310-3*) Intl Bk Ctr.
—ABC Dictionary I: Arabic & German. (ARA & GER.). (ps-4). 1983. 6.00x (*0-86685-309-X*) Intl Bk Ctr.
—ABC Dictionary Tamhidi: Arabic & French. (ARA & FRE.). (ps-4). 1983. 6.00x (*0-86685-315-4*) Intl Bk Ctr.
—ABC Dictionary Tamhidi: Arabic & German. (ARA & GER.). (ps-4). 1983. 6.00x (*0-86685-313-8*) Intl Bk Ctr.
—ABC Dictionary Tamhidi: Arabic & Italian. (ARA & ITA.). (ps-4). 1983. 6.00x (*0-86685-316-2*) Intl Bk Ctr.
—ABC I: Arabic Italian Dictionary. (ps-4). 1983. 6.00x (*0-86685-308-1*) Intl Bk Ctr.
—ABC Tamhidi Arabic-Spanish Dictionary. (ARA & SPA.). (ps-4). 1983. 6.00x (*0-86685-312-X*) Intl Bk Ctr.
—Maroof the Cobbler. 1986. 7.95x (*0-86685-566-1*) Intl Bk Ctr.
—The Mesopotamia. 1991. 7.95x (*0-86685-489-4*) Intl Bk Ctr.
—My Illustrated Dictionary. (ARA & ENG.). (gr. 5-12). 1983. 9.95x (*0-86685-317-0*) Intl Bk Ctr.
—My Illustrated Dictionary. (ARA & GER.). (gr. 5-12). 1983. 9.95x (*0-86685-318-9*) Intl Bk Ctr.
—My Illustrated Dictionary. (ARA & ITA.). (gr. 5-12). 1983. 9.95x (*0-86685-319-7*) Intl Bk Ctr.
—My Illustrated Dictionary. (ARA & SPA.). (gr. 5-12). 1983. 9.95x (*0-86685-320-0*) Intl Bk Ctr.
—My Illustrated Dictionary. (ARA & FRE.). (gr. 5-12). 1983. 9.95x (*0-86685-321-9*) Intl Bk Ctr.
—The Phoenicians. 1991. 7.95x (*0-86685-570-X*) Intl Bk Ctr.
Licata, David P. Advanced Placement Chemistry Student Handbook. (gr. 10-12). 1993. pap. text ed. 12.95 (*0-9636095-0-5*) Licatas Edutype.
Licata, Renora. Everything You Need to Know about Anger. (gr. 7-12). 1992. PLB 13.95 (*0-8239-1320-1*) Rosen Group.
—Princess Diana: Royal Ambassador. (Illus.). 64p. (gr. 3-7). 1993. PLB 14.95 (*1-56711-013-4*) Blackbirch.
—Princess Diana: Royal Ambassador. (Illus.). 64p. (gr. 3-7). 1993. pap. 7.95 (*1-56711-051-7*) Blackbirch.
Lichello, Robert. Enrico Fermi: Father of the Atomic Bomb. Rahmas, D. Steve, ed. LC 70-185667. 32p. (gr. 7-12). 1972. lib. bdg. 4.95 incl. catalog cards (*0-87157-511-6*) SamHar Pr.
Licht, Fred. Shelter the Pilgrim. 48p. (gr. 6). 1990. PLB 13.95s.p. (*0-88682-307-2*) Creative Ed.
Lichter, Carolyn, jt. auth. see Levine, Bobbie.
Lichtman, Wendy. Blew & the Death of the Mag. Mayers, Diane, illus. 74p. (gr. 3-9). 1975. 5.00 (*0-913512-53-2*) Freestone Pub Co.
Lichtner, Schomer. Alphabet Drawings. Lichtner, Schomer, illus. 88p. (Orig.). (gr. k up). 1973. pap. 4.50 (*0-686-97176-0*) Lichtner.
—Ballerina's Holiday. (Illus.). 76p. (Orig.). (gr. 5 up). 1979. pap. 4.95 (*0-941074-04-8*) Lichtner.
Lichtveld, Noni. I Lost My Arrow in a Kan Kan Tree. LC 92-56102. 1993. write for info. (*0-688-12748-7*) Lothrop.
Lick, Sue. The Iberian Americans. Moynihan, Daniel P., intro. by. (Illus.). 112p. (gr. 5 up). 1990. 17.95 (*0-87754-896-X*) Chelsea Hse.
Lickei, Elizabeth, ed. see Rowe, Frank.
Liddell, Janice. Imani & the Flying Africans. Nickiens, Linda, illus. 32p. (gr. 3-8). 1993. 14.95 (*0-685-65590-3*); pap. 6.95 (*0-86543-366-6*) Africa World.
Liddelow, Lorelei. Cook with Me. Forss, Ian, illus. 126p. (Orig.). (gr. k-3). 1989. pap. 11.95 (*0-920541-95-X*) Peguis Pubs Ltd.
—Talk with Me. Hunnum, Cindy, illus. 101p. (Orig.). (gr. k-3). 1984. pap. 11.95 (*0-920541-97-6*) Peguis Pubs Ltd.
Liddle, Matt. Make Your Own Book. (Illus.). 64p. (Orig.). (gr. 3 up). 1993. incl. kit 17.95 (*1-56138-337-6*) Running Pr.
Lidstone, John, ed. Global Issues of Our Time. LC 93-34256. 1994. pap. write for info. (*0-521-42163-2*) Cambridge U Pr.
Liebb, Julius, jt. auth. see Bromberg, Murray.
Lieberman, Joe. Those Amazing Tables: Teaching Multiplication Through Patterns & Color Strips. (gr. 4-7). 1983. pap. 9.95 (*0-201-48019-0*) Addison-Wesley.
—Those Amazing Tables: Teaching Multiplication Through Patterns & Color Strips. 64p. (gr. 3-8). 1983. pap. text ed. 9.95 (*0-914040-98-7*) Cuisenaire.
Lieberman, Lillian. ABC: Board Games. Barr, Marilynn G., illus. 64p. (ps-2). 1991. pap. 7.95 (*1-878279-31-9*) Monday Morning Bks.
—ABC: Box Games. Barr, Marilynn G., illus. 64p. (ps-2). 1991. pap. 7.95 (*1-878279-30-0*) Monday Morning Bks.
—ABC Consonants. 64p. (gr. k-2). 1985. 6.95 (*0-912107-29-4*) Monday Morning Bks.
—ABC: Folder Games. Barr, Marilynn G., illus. 64p. (ps-2). 1991. pap. 7.95 (*1-878279-29-7*) Monday Morning Bks.
—ABC Letters. 64p. (gr. k-2). 1984. 6.95 (*0-912107-10-3*) Monday Morning Bks.
—ABC Order. 64p. (gr. k-3). 1984. 6.95 (*0-912107-12-X*) Monday Morning Bks.
—ABC Rhymes. 64p. (gr. k-3). 1985. 6.95 (*0-912107-28-6*) Monday Morning Bks.
—ABC Sounds. 64p. (gr. k-2). 1984. 6.95 (*0-912107-11-1*) Monday Morning Bks.

—ABC Vowels. 64p. (gr. k-2). 1985. 6.95 (*0-912107-30-8*) Monday Morning Bks.
—Classification. 64p. (gr. 2-5). 1989. 6.95 (*0-912107-89-8*, MM1906) Monday Morning Bks.
—Comprehension. 64p. (gr. 2-5). 1987. 6.95 (*0-912107-66-9*) Monday Morning Bks.
—Following Directions. 64p. (gr. 2-5). 1989. 6.95 (*0-912107-87-1*, MM1904) Monday Morning Bks.
—Making Inferences. 64p. (gr. 2-5). 1989. 6.95 (*0-912107-88-X*, MM1905) Monday Morning Bks.
—Vocabulary. 64p. (gr. 2-5). 1987. 6.95 (*0-912107-68-5*) Monday Morning Bks.
—Word Structure. 64p. (gr. k-3). 1987. 6.95 (*0-912107-67-7*) Monday Morning Bks.
Liebermann, M. Coloring Books on Events of the Jewish Months: Nisan. (ps-2). 1987. 2.50 (*0-914131-86-9*, D712) Torah Umesorah.
—Coloring Books on Events of the Jewish Months: Tishrei, Cheshvan. (ps-2). 1987. 2.50 (*0-914131-84-2*, D710) Torah Umesorah.
—Coloring Books on the Parshas Hashavua: Bereishis. (ps-2). 1987. 2.50 (*0-914131-79-6*, D700) Torah Umesorah.
—Coloring Books on the Parshas Hashavua: Devorim. (ps-2). 1987. 2.50 (*0-914131-83-4*, D704) Torah Umesorah.
—Coloring Books on the Parshas Hashavua: Shemos. (ps-2). 1987. 2.50 (*0-914131-80-X*, D701) Torah Umesorah.
—Coloring Books on the Parshas Hashavua: Vayikrah. (ps-2). 1987. 2.50 (*0-914131-81-8*, D702) Torah Umesorah.
—Learn as You Color Series III: Brachos. (ps-2). 1987. 2.50 (*0-914131-88-5*, D720) Torah Umesorah.
Lieberthal, Edwin M., jt. auth. see Gurau, Peter K.
Liebman, Arthur. Ghosts, Witches & Vampires Quiz Book. LC 91-23371. (Illus.). 128p. (gr. 3-10). 1991. 12.95 (*0-8069-8408-2*) Sterling.
—The Ghosts, Witches & Vampires Quiz Book. Williams, Jack, illus. LC 91-23371. 128p. (gr. 3-10). 1992. pap. 4.95 (*0-8069-8409-0*) Sterling.
Liebowitz, Jay & Zelde, Janet S. Kids & Computers. 2nd ed. Rogers, Nip, illus. 70p. (gr. 3-6). 1989. write for info. (*0-9623252-0-1*); pap. write for info. (*0-9623252-2-8*) J Liebowitz.
Liebowitz, Sol. Argentina. (Illus.). 128p. (gr. 5 up). 1990. 14.95 (*0-7910-1106-2*) Chelsea Hse.
Liedloff, Helmut. Ohne Muhe! LC 79-84596. (Illus.). (gr. 9-10). 1980. pap. 7.84 (*0-395-27931-3*) HM.
Liestman, Vicki. Columbus Day. Hanson, Rick, illus. 56p. (gr. k-4). 1991. PLB 14.95 (*0-87614-444-X*) Carolrhoda Bks.
—Columbus Day. (ps-3). 1992. pap. 5.95 (*0-87614-559-4*) Carolrhoda Bks.
Lifton, Betty J. Joji & the Dragon. Mitsui, Eiichi, illus. LC 88-8434. 64p. (gr. 1-3). 1989. Repr. of 1957 ed. lib. bdg. 16.00 (*0-208-02245-7*, Pub. by Linnet) Shoe String.
Liggett, Clayton E. Concert Theatre. LC 72-104705. (Illus.). (gr. 9 up). 1970. PLB 11.95 (*0-8239-0194-7*) Rosen Group.
Light, John. Beachcombers. LC 91-38130. (gr. 4 up). 1991. 2.95 (*0-85953-502-9*) Childs Play.
—Dig That Hole! LC 91-39036. (gr. 5 up). 1991. 2.95 (*0-85953-503-7*) Childs Play.
—It's Great Outdoors. LC 90-34353. (gr. 5 up). 1991. 2.95 (*0-85953-338-7*) Childs Play.
—Odd Jobs. LC 90-34354. (gr. 4 up). 1991. 2.95 (*0-85953-339-5*) Childs Play.
—Playing at Home. LC 90-34356. (gr. 4 up). 1991. 2.95 (*0-85953-336-0*) Childs Play.
—Race Ace Roger. LC 91-33417. (gr. 4 up). 1991. 2.95 (*0-85953-501-0*) Childs Play.
—Snap Happy. LC 91-36610. (gr. 4 up). 1991. 2.95 (*0-85953-504-5*) Childs Play.
—What's Cooking. LC 90-34355. (gr. 4 up). 1991. 2.95 (*0-85953-337-9*) Childs Play.
Lightbody, Audrey. Faith Is the Journey. 144p. (Orig.). (gr. 7 up). 1987. pap. 5.95 (*0-939925-10-9*) R C Law & Co.
Lightbody, Nancy K. & Malley, Sarah H. Observa-Story: Portland to Cut & Color. Malley, Sarah H., illus. LC 76-54460. (gr. 1-4). 1976. pap. 1.25 (*0-9600612-5-8*) Greater Portland.
Lightbourne, K. A. Grandfather Played the Trumpet: Sailors Fantasies. 375p. (Orig.). 1988. pap. 12.50 (*0-9621212-0-7*) Sailors Fantasies Pub.
Lightfoot, D. J. Trail Fever: The Life of a Texas Cowboy. Bobbish, John, illus. LC 92-5458. 1992. write for info. (*0-688-11537-3*) Lothrop.

Lightfoot, Marge. Cartooning for Kids. Lightfoot, Marge, illus. 64p. 1993. 16. 95 (*1-895688-03-5*, Pub. by Greey dePencier CN); pap. 8.95 (*0-920775-84-5*, Pub. by Greey dePencier CN) Firefly Bks Ltd. All kids love cartoons. CARTOONING FOR KIDS helps them draw their very own! British Columbia cartoonist & cartooning teacher Marge Lightfoot shows kids how to create cartoons like a pro in this easy to follow & delightfully illustrated book. With fun, simple steps & helpful diagrams featuring a cast of colourful characters, Lightfoot answers any questions a budding Charles Schulz or Lynn Johnson might have. Beginners will discover what materials they'll need & how to put them to work drawing animals & people. Other pointers include how to vary facial expressions & show bodies in different positions & how to create wardrobes, fill in backgrounds & work in colour. Lightfoot also shares techniques for coming up with bright ideas, splitting stories into frames, creating captions or speech balloons & developing funny punch lines. And kids can extend their newfound skills by making greeting cards, posters, flip books & other wacky creations. There are hours of fun in CARTOONING FOR KIDS-- the perfect book for every kid who loves cartoons. *Publisher Provided Annotation.*

Lightner, Robert. Triumph Through Tragedy. 70p. (Orig.). (gr. 7 up). 1980. pap. 1.00 (*0-89323-008-1*, 330) Bible Memory.

Lightwood, Donald. Alf's Secret War. 180p. (gr. 5-8). 1994. pap. 7.95 (*0-86241-383-4*, Pub. by Cnngt UK) Trafalgar.

—The Baillie's Daughter. 160p. (gr. 3-5). 1994. pap. 6.95 (*0-86241-285-4*, Pub. by Cnngt UK) Trafalgar.

Ligon, Terry, jt. auth. see Enns, Peter.

Ligou, Jacques P. Elements of Nuclear Engineering. 508p. (gr. 6 up). 1986. text ed. 248.00 (*3-7186-0363-2*, Pub. by Harwood Acad Pubs) Gordon & Breach.

Likken, Laurie. Winner Takes All. 192p. 1987. pap. 2.50 (*0-317-65474-8*, Sweet Dreams) Bantam.

Liles, Maurine. Kitty of Blossom Prairie. (Illus.). 128p. (gr. 4-7). 1992. 14.95 (*0-89015-863-0*) Eakin-Sunbelt.

Liles, Maurine W. Rebecca of Blossom Prairie: Grandmother of a Vice President. Roberts, M., ed. (Illus.). 112p. 1990. 10.95 (*0-89015-754-5*) Eakin-Sunbelt.

Liles, Parker, et al. Typing Mailable Letters. 3rd ed. Rubin, Audrey S., ed. (Illus.). (gr. 9-12). 1978. text ed. 11.24 (*0-07-037855-X*) McGraw.

Lillegard, Dee. Brass. LC 87-32990. (Illus.). 32p. (ps-3). 1988. PLB 15.00 (*0-516-02218-0*); pap. 3.95 (*0-516-42218-9*) Childrens.

—The Day the Daisies Danced. Barron, Rex, photos by. LC 93-30583. 1995. write for info. (*0-399-22661-3*, Putnam) Putnam Pub Group.

—Do Not Feed the Table. (gr. 5 up). 1993. pap. 14.95 (*0-385-30516-8*) Doubleday.

—The Hee Haw River. 1994. write for info. (*0-8050-2375-5*) H Holt & Co.

—I Can Be a Baker. LC 85-27976. (Illus.). 32p. (gr. k-3). 1986. PLB 14.60 (*0-516-01892-2*) Childrens.

—I Can Be a Beautician. LC 87-13835. (Illus.). 32p. (gr. k-3). 1987. PLB 14.60 (*0-516-01910-4*); pap. 3.95 (*0-516-41910-2*) Childrens.

—I Can Be a Carpenter. LC 86-9676. (Illus.). 32p. (gr. k-3). 1986. PLB 14.60 (*0-516-01884-1*); pap. 3.95 (*0-516-41884-X*) Childrens.

—I Can Be a Secretary. LC 86-29947. (Illus.). 32p. (gr. k-3). 1987. PLB 14.60 (*0-516-01907-4*) Childrens.

—James A. Garfield. LC 87-18200. (Illus.). 100p. (gr. 3 up). 1987. PLB 17.27 (*0-516-01394-7*) Childrens.

—James K. Polk. LC 87-35188. (Illus.). 100p. (gr. 3 up). 1988. PLB 17.27 (*0-516-01351-3*) Childrens.

—John Tyler. LC 87-18202. (Illus.). 100p. (gr. 3 up). 1987. PLB 17.27 (*0-516-01393-9*) Childrens.

—My First Columbus Day Book. Raskin, Betty, illus. LC 87-10304. 32p. (ps-2). 1987. PLB 15.00 (*0-516-02909-6*); pap. 3.95 (*0-516-42909-4*) Childrens.

—My First Martin Luther King Book. Endres, Helen, illus. LC 86-31670. 32p. (ps-2). 1987. PLB 15.00 (*0-516-02908-8*); pap. 3.95 (*0-516-42908-6*) Childrens.

—My Yellow Ball. Chamberlain, Sarah, illus. LC 92-27003. (gr. k-3). 1993. 12.99 (*0-525-45078-5*, DCB) Dutton Child Bks.

—Nevada. 195p. 1993. text ed. 15.40 (*1-56956-139-7*) W A T Braille.

—Percussion. LC 87-18217. (Illus.). 32p. (ps-3). 1987. PLB 15.00 (*0-516-02216-4*); pap. 3.95 (*0-516-42216-2*) Childrens.

—Richard Nixon. LC 87-35185. (Illus.). 100p. (gr. 3 up). 1988. PLB 17.27 (*0-516-01356-4*) Childrens.

—Sitting in My Box. Agee, Jon, illus. LC 89-31609. 32p. (ps-2). 1989. 12.95 (*0-525-44528-5*, DCB) Dutton Child Bks.

—Sitting in My Box. Agee, Jon, illus. 32p. (ps-2). 1992. pap. 3.99 (*0-14-054819-X*, Puffin Unicorn) Puffin Bks.

—Sitting in My Box. Agee, Jon, illus. 32p. (ps-2). 1993. pap. 17.99 (*0-14-054886-6*, Puffin Unicorn) Puffin Bks.

—Strings. LC 87-32994. (Illus.). 32p. (ps-3). 1988. PLB 15.00 (*0-516-02219-9*); pap. 3.95 (*0-516-42219-7*) Childrens.

—Where Is It? Sharp, Gene, illus. LC 84-7005. 32p. (ps-2). 1984. lib. bdg. 11.93 (*0-516-02065-X*); pap. 2.95 (*0-516-42065-8*) Childrens.

—Woodwinds. LC 87-18232. (Illus.). 32p. (ps-3). 1987. PLB 15.00 (*0-516-02217-2*); pap. 3.95 (*0-516-42217-0*) Childrens.

Lillegard, Dee & Stoker, Wayne. I Can Be a Plumber. LC 86-30950. (Illus.). 32p. (gr. k-3). 1987. PLB 14.60 (*0-516-01906-6*) Childrens.

—I Can Be a Welder. LC 85-28995. (Illus.). 32p. (gr. k-3). 1986. PLB 14.60 (*0-516-01895-7*) Childrens.

—Nevada. LC 90-34665. (Illus.). 144p. (gr. 4 up). 1990. PlB 26.60 (*0-516-00474-3*) Childrens.

Lillie, Patricia. Everything Has a Place. Tafuri, Nancy, illus. LC 90-23497. 24p. (ps up). 1993. 14.00 (*0-688-10082-1*); PLB 13.93 (*0-688-10083-X*) Greenwillow.

—Jake & Rosie. LC 87-14939. (Illus.). 24p. (ps up). 1989. 11.95 (*0-688-07624-6*); PLB 11.88 (*0-688-07625-4*) Greenwillow.

—Mama Bought Me a Floppy Teddy Bear. Baker, Karen L., illus. LC 93-26516. 1994. write for info. (*0-688-12570-0*); lib. bdg. write for info. (*0-688-12571-9*) Greenwillow.

—When the Rooster Crowed. Parker, Nancy W., illus. LC 90-30783. 32p. (ps up). 1991. 13.95 (*0-688-09378-7*); PLB 13.88 (*0-688-09379-5*) Greenwillow.

—When This Box Is Full. Crews, Donald, illus. LC 92-28743. 24p. 1993. 14.00 (*0-688-12016-4*); PLB 13.93 (*0-688-12017-2*) Greenwillow.

Lillington, Kenneth. Give up the Ghost. 144p. (gr. 7 up). 1991. 15.95 (*0-571-16170-7*) Faber & Faber.

—The Hallowe'en Cat. Floyd, Gareth, illus. 64p. (gr. 3-7). 1987. pap. 3.95 (*0-571-15463-8*) Faber & Faber.

—Jonah's Mirror. 160p. (gr. 7 up). 1992. pap. 6.95 (*0-571-16736-5*) Faber & Faber.

—Josephine. 148p. (gr. 3-6). 1991. pap. 4.95 (*0-571-16118-9*) Faber & Faber.

—The Mad Detective. 160p. (gr. 7 up). 1992. 15.95 (*0-571-16593-1*) Faber & Faber.

—The Real Live Dinosaur & Other Stories. Floyd, Gareth, illus. 144p. (gr. 3-7). 1992. pap. 4.95 (*0-571-16318-1*) Faber & Faber.

Lillington, Kenneth, text by. The Mikado: Easy Piano Picture Book. Sullivan, Arthur, contrib. by. (Illus.). 32p. (gr. k up). 1988. pap. 9.95 (*0-571-10085-6*) Faber & Faber.

Lily Toy Hong. Two of Everything. Mathews, Judith, ed. Hong, Lily T., illus. LC 92-29880. 32p. (gr. k-3). 1993. PLB 14.95 (*0-8075-8157-7*) A Whitman.

Lim, Genny. Wings for Lai Ho. Lew, Gordon, tr. Ja, Andrea, illus. 48p. (Orig.). (gr. 5-8). 1982. pap. 5.95 (*0-934788-01-4*) E-W Pub Co.

Lim, Jessie. China. (Illus.). 32p. (gr. 4-8). 1992. 17.95 (*0-237-60301-2*, Pub. by Evans Bros Ltd) Trafalgar.

Lim, Sing. West Coast Chinese Boy. LC 79-67110. (Illus.). 64p. (gr. 5 up). 1991. pap. 7.95 (*0-88776-270-0*) Tundra Bks.

Limb, Sue. Come Back, Grandma. Munoz, Claudio, illus. LC 92-43534. 32p. (ps-2). 1994. 13.00 (*0-679-84720-0*) Knopf Bks Yng Read.

Limburg, Peter R. Weird! The Complete Book of Halloween Words. Lewin, Betsy, illus. LC 88-38678. 128p. (gr. 4-10). 1989. SBE 13.95 (*0-02-759050-X*, Bradbury Pr) Macmillan Child Grp.

—Weird! The Complete Book of Halloween Words. 176p. 1991. pap. 3.50 (*0-380-71172-9*, Camelot) Avon.

Limmer, Milly J. Where Do Little Girls Grow? Levine, Abby, ed. Hoffman, Rosekrans, illus. LC 92-22936. 32p. (ps-2). 1993. PLB 14.95 (*0-8075-8924-1*) A Whitman.

—Where Will You Swim Tonight? Fay, Ann, ed. Pittman, Helena C., illus. LC 90-38938. 32p. (ps-1). 1991. 14.95 (*0-8075-8949-7*) A Whitman.

Limousin, Odile. The Story of Paper. Matthews, Sarah, tr. from FRE. Brusch, Beat, illus. LC 87-31752. 38p. (gr. k-5). 1988. 4.95 (*0-944589-16-2*, 162) Young Discovery Lib.

Limousin, Odile & Neumann, Daniele. TV & Films: Behind the Scenes. Bogard, Vicki, tr. from FRE. Vincent, Francois, illus. LC 92-966. (gr. k-5). 1992. 4.95 (*0-944589-36-7*) Young Discovery Lib.

—TV & Films: Behind the Scenes. Vincent, Francois, illus. 40p. (gr. k-5). 1993. PLB 9.95 (*1-56674-073-8*, HTS Bks) Forest Hse.

Limpert, Dana. Swan Flyway: The Tundra Swan. Thomas, Peter, narrated by. Bosson, Jo-Ellen, illus. (ps-3). 1993. 11.95 (*0-924483-95-4*); incl. audiocassette tape 16.95 (*0-924483-96-2*); incl. audiocassette tape & 8" toy 25.95 (*0-924483-97-0*); incl. audiocassette tape & 13" toy 39.95 (*0-924483-98-9*); audiocassette tape only avail. (*0-924483-99-7*) Soundprints.

Linam, Gail. God's Fall Gifts. Hester, Ron, illus. (ps). 1992. pap. 3.95 (*0-8054-4159-X*, 4241-59) Broadman.

—God's People: A Book of Children's Sermons. LC 85-25736. (Orig.). (ps-5). 1986. pap. 4.95 (*0-8054-4928-0*) Broadman.

—God's Summer Gifts. Hester, Ron, illus. (ps). 1992. pap. 3.95 (*0-8054-4156-5*, 4241-56) Broadman.

—God's Winter Gifts. (Illus.). (ps). 1992. pap. 3.95 (*0-8054-4158-1*, 4241-58) Broadman.

Lincoln, Abraham. The Hunt Speedball Calligraphy Workbook...: An Italic Notebook. LC 78-56645. (Illus.). 120p. (gr. 7-12). 1978. pap. 9.95 (*0-942032-00-4*) Calligrafree.

—Italic Calligraphy. (Illus.). 112p. (gr. 7-12). 1982. pap. 11.95 (*0-685-08505-8*) Calligrafree.

—Wisdom & Wit. (gr. 8 up). 1965. 6.95 (*0-88088-359-6*) Peter Pauper.

Lincoln, James. Clock. 1992. pap. 15.00 (*0-385-30037-9*, Delta) Delacorte.

Lincoln, Margaret. Amazing Boats. Dunning, Mike & Moller, Ray, photos by. LC 92-3045. (Illus.). 32p. (Orig.). (gr. 1-5). 1992. PLB 9.99 (*0-679-92770-0*); pap. 7.99 (*0-679-82770-6*) Knopf Bks Yng Read.

Lincoln, Wanda. Write Through the Year. (Illus.). 112p. (gr. 2-6). 1989. pap. 9.95 (*0-912107-90-1*, MM1907) Monday Morning Bks.

Lincoln, Wanda & Suid, Murray. For the Love of Letter Writing. 112p. (gr. 2-6). 1983. 9.95 (*0-912107-01-4*) Monday Morning Bks.

Lincoln, Wanda, jt. auth. see Suid, Murray.

Lind, Alan. Black Bear Cub. Lee, Katie, illus. LC 93-31130. 1994. 11.95 (*1-56899-030-8*) Soundprints.

Lind, Levi R., ed. Latin Poetry in Verse Translation. LC 57-59176. (gr. 9 up). 1957. pap. 9.16 (*0-395-05118-5*, RivEd) HM.

—Ten Greek Plays in Contemporary Translations. Incl. Prometheus Bound. Aeschylus; Agamemnon. Aeschylus; Antigone. Sophocles; Oedipus Rex. Sophocles; Philoctetes. Sophocles; Alcestis. Euripides; Suppliants. Euripides; Andromache. Euripides; Bacchae. Euripides; Lysistrata. Aristophanes. LC 57-59175. (gr. 9up). 1972. pap. 9.16 (*0-395-05117-7*, RivEd) HM.

Lind, Mecka. Cackle Goes A-Courting. (ps). 1992. 18.95 (*0-87614-715-5*) Carolrhoda Bks.

Lindamood, Phyllis, jt. auth. see Bell, Nanci.

Lindberg, Anne. The Worry Week. (gr. 3-7). 1988. pap. 2.95 (*0-380-70394-7*, Camelot) Avon.

Lindberg, Becky T. Chelsea Martin Turns Green. Tucker, Kathy, ed. Poydar, Nancy, illus. LC 92-31613. 144p. (gr. 2-4). 1993. PLB 11.95 (*0-8075-1134-X*) A Whitman.

—Speak up, Chelsea Martin! Tucker, Kathleen, ed. Poydar, Nancy, illus. LC 91-313. 128p. (gr. 2-4). 1991. 11.95 (*0-8075-7552-6*) A Whitman.

Lindbergh, Anne. Bailey's Window. 144p. 1991. pap. 3.50 (*0-380-70767-5*, Camelot) Avon.

—Nick of Time. LC 93-20777. 1994. 14.95 (*0-316-52629-0*) Little.

—The People in Pineapple Place. 160p. (gr. 4-5). 1990. pap. 2.95 (*0-380-70766-7*, Camelot) Avon.

—The Prisoner of Pineapple Place. 192p. 1990. pap. 2.95 (*0-380-70765-9*, Camelot) Avon.

—The Shadow on the Dial. LC 86-45783. 160p. (gr. 5-8). 1987. HarpC Child Bks.

—Three Lives to Live. 192p. (gr. 3-7). 1992. 14.95 (*0-316-52628-2*) Little.

—Tidy Lady. Hoguet, Susan, illus. LC 88-10905. 30p. (gr. k-3). 1989. 13.95 (*0-15-287150-0*) HarBrace.

—Travel Far, Pay No Fare. LC 91-35886. 192p. (gr. 5-8). 1992. 14.00 (*0-06-021775-8*); PLB 13.89 (*0-06-021776-6*) HarpC Child Bks.

Lindbergh, Anne M. Bailey's Window. Craft, Kinuko Y., illus. LC 83-18360. 115p. (gr. 3-7). 1984. 14.95 (*0-15-205642-4*, HB Juv Bks) HarBrace.

—The Hunky-Dory Dairy. Brinckloe, Julie, illus. LC 85-16408. 147p. (gr. 4-6). 1986. 14.95 (*0-15-237449-3*, HB Juv Bks) HarBrace.

—Hunky-Dory Dairy. 160p. (gr. 3-7). 1987. pap. 2.75 (*0-380-70320-3*, Camelot) Avon.

—Nobody's Orphan. (gr. 3-7). 1987. pap. 2.95 (*0-380-70395-5*, Camelot) Avon.

—The People in Pineapple Place. LC 82-47935. 153p. (gr. 3-7). 1982. 14.95 (*0-15-260517-7*, HB Juv Bks) HarBrace.

—The Prisoner of Pineapple Place. LC 87-28815. 173p. (gr. 3-7). 1988. 13.95 (*0-15-263559-9*, HB Juv Bks) HarBrace.

—The Shadow on the Dial. (gr. 3-7). 1988. pap. 2.75 (*0-380-70545-1*, Camelot) Avon.

—The Worry Week. Hewitt, Kathryn, illus. LC 84-19299. 144p. (gr. 3-7). 1985. 12.95 (*0-15-299675-3*, HB Juv Bks) HarBrace.

Lindbergh, Anne M. & Hoguet, Susan. Next Time, Take Care. (Illus.). 32p. (ps-3). 1988. 13.95 (*0-15-257200-7*, HB Juv Bks) HarBrace.

Lindbergh, Charles A. Boyhood on the Upper Mississippi: A Reminiscent Letter. LC 72-75804. (Illus.). 50p. (gr. 4-12). 1972. pap. 7.95 (*0-87351-217-0*) Minn Hist.

Lindbergh, Reeve. Benjamin's Barn. Jeffers, Susan, illus. 32p. (ps-3). 1990. 13.95 (*0-8037-0613-8*); PLB 13.89 (*0-8037-0614-6*) Dial Bks Young.

—Day the Goose Got Loose. Kellogg, Steven, illus. LC 87-28959. 32p. (ps-3). 1990. 12.95 (*0-8037-0408-9*); PLB 12.89 (*0-8037-0409-7*) Dial Bks Young.

—Grandfather's Lovesong. Isadora, Rachel, illus. LC 92-22212. 32p. 1993. 14.99 (*0-670-84842-5*) Viking Child Bks.

—If I'd Known Then What I Know Now. Root, Kimberly B., illus. LC 93-24058. 1994. write for info. (*0-670-85351-8*) Viking Child Bks.

—Johnny Appleseed. Jakoben, Kathy, illus. (ps-4). 1990. 14.95 (*0-316-52618-5*, Joy St Bks) Little.

—Johnny Appleseed. (ps-3). 1993. pap. 4.95 (*0-316-52634-7*) Little.

—The Midnight Farm. Jeffers, Susan, illus. LC 86-1722. 32p. (ps-2). 1987. 14.95 (*0-8037-0331-7*); PLB 14.89 (*0-8037-0333-3*) Dial Bks Young.
—There's a Cow in the Road! Pearson, Tracey C., illus. LC 92-34883. 32p. (ps-2). 1993. 13.99 (*0-8037-1335-5*); PLB 13.89 (*0-8037-1336-3*) Dial Bks Young.
—View from the Air: Charles Lindbergh's Earth & Sky. Brown, Richard, photos by. (Illus.). 32p. 1992. 15.00 (*0-670-84660-0*) Viking Child Bks.
—What Is the Sun? Lambert, Stephen, illus. LC 93-3557. 1994. write for info. (*1-56402-146-7*) Candlewick Pr.
Lindblad, Lisa & Lindblad, Sven. Serengeti. (Illus.). 48p. (gr. 3-7). 1994. 15.95 (*1-56282-668-9*); PLB 15.89 (*1-56282-669-7*) Hyprn Child.
Lindblad, Sven, jt. auth. see Lindblad, Lisa.
Lindblom, Steve. Flying the Hot Ones. (gr. 3-7). 1990. write for info. HM.
—Fly the Hot Ones. LC 89-29491. (Illus.). 128p. (gr. 4 up). 1991. 16.45 (*0-395-51075-9*) HM.
Lindblom, Steven. Golden Book of Snakes & Other Reptiles. 1990. write for info. (*0-307-15852-7*, Pub. by Golden Bks) Western Pub.
Lindbloom, James A. Make the Morning. Lindbloom, Nancy, illus. (gr. 3-8). 1977. pap. 3.00 (*0-89409-007-0*) Childrens Art.
Linde, Laurel van der see Van der Linde, Laurel.
Linde, Laurel van der see Van der Linde, Laurel.
Linde, Lavaun & Quishenberry, Mary. Daniel & the Big Cats: Level One. Maniscalco, Joe, illus. 32p. (gr. 1). 1986. pap. text ed. 4.99 (*0-945107-04-8*) Bradshaw Pubs.
—God Adds Oil: Level Two. Maniscalco, Joe, illus. 32p. (Orig.). (gr. 1). 1988. pap. text ed. 4.99 (*0-945107-05-6*) Bradshaw Pubs.
—I Will Help: Level One. Maniscalco, Joe, illus. 32p. (Orig.). (gr. 1). 1986. pap. text ed. 4.99 (*0-945107-01-3*) Bradshaw Pubs.
—Jonah's Ride: Level Two. Maniscalco, Joe, illus. 32p. (Orig.). (gr. 1). 1988. pap. text ed. 4.99 (*0-945107-09-9*) Bradshaw Pubs.
—The Lad's Bag: Level One. Maniscalco, Joe, illus. 32p. (gr. 1). 1986. pap. text ed. 4.99 (*0-945107-03-X*) Bradshaw Pubs.
—Mom & the Lad: Level One. Maniscalco, Joe, illus. 32p. (gr. 1). 1986. pap. text ed. 4.99 (*0-945107-02-1*) Bradshaw Pubs.
—Not a Bed: Level One. Maniscalco, Joe, illus. 32p. (Orig.). (gr. 1). 1986. pap. text ed. 4.99 (*0-945107-00-5*) Bradshaw Pubs.
—Seven Dips: Level Two. Maniscalco, Joe, illus. 32p. (Orig.). (gr. 1). 1988. pap. text ed. 4.99 (*0-945107-08-0*) Bradshaw Pubs.
—Three Brave Men: Level Two. Maniscalco, Joe, illus. 32p. (Orig.). (gr. 1). 1988. pap. text ed. 4.99 (*0-945107-07-2*) Bradshaw Pubs.
—Zacchaeus' Cash Bag: Level Two. Maniscalco, Joe, illus. 32p. (Orig.). (gr. 1). 1988. pap. text ed. 4.99 (*0-945107-06-4*) Bradshaw Pubs.
Linde, Polly Van Der see Van der Linde, Polly & Van der Linde, Tasha.
Linde, Tasha Van Der see Van der Linde, Polly & Van der Linde, Tasha.
Linden, Ann M. One Smiling Grandma: A Caribbean Counting Book. Russell, Lynne, illus. LC 91-30826. 32p. (ps-3). 1992. 15.00 (*0-8037-1132-8*) Dial Bks Young.
Lindenbaum, Pija. Boodil, My Dog. Charbonnet, Gabrielle, retold by. LC 92-13172. (Illus.). 48p. (ps-2). 1992. 14.95 (*0-8050-2444-1*, Bks Young Read) H Holt & Co.
—Else-Marie & Her Seven Little Daddies. LC 91-9077. (Illus.). 32p. (ps-2). 1991. 14.95 (*0-8050-1752-6*, Bks Young Read) H Holt & Co.
Linder, Greg, ed. see Brunke, Dawn B.
Linder, Greg, ed. see Collard, Sneed.
Linder, Greg, ed. see Griffin, Steven & Griffin, Elizabeth.
Linder, Pamela, jt. auth. see Holstead, Christy.
Lindgren, Astrid. Brothers Lionheart. Tate, Joan, tr. Lambert, J. K., illus. LC 85-573. 184p. (gr. 4-6). 1985. pap. 4.95 (*0-14-031955-7*, Puffin) Puffin Bks.
—A Calf for Christmas. Lucas, Barbara, tr. Tornqvist, Marit, illus. 32p. (gr up). 1991. bds. 13.95 (*91-29-59920-2*, Pub. by R & S Bks) FS&G.
—The Children of Noisy Village. (gr. 3-7). 1988. pap. 3.95 (*0-14-032609-X*, Puffin) Puffin Bks.
—The Children on Troublemaker Street. Wikland, Ilon, illus. LC 91-15647. 112p. (gr. 1-4). 1991. pap. 3.50 (*0-689-71515-3*, Aladdin) Macmillan Child Grp.
—Christmas in Noisy Village. LC 64-21473. 32p. (ps-3). 1981. pap. 3.99 (*0-14-050344-7*, Puffin) Puffin Bks.
—Christmas in the Stable. LC 62-14449. (Illus.). (gr. 1-3). 1979. (Coward); pap. text ed. 6.95 (*0-698-20489-1*, Coward) Putnam Pub Group.
—Christmas in the Stable. Wiberg, Harald, illus. 32p. 1991. 5.95 (*0-698-20677-0*, Sandcastle Bks) Putnam Pub Group.
—I Don't Want to Go to Bed. Lucas, Barbara, tr. from SWE. Wikland, Ilon, illus. 32p. (ps up). 1988. 12.95 (*91-29-59066-3*, R & S Bks) FS&G.
—I Want a Brother or Sister. Wikland, Ilon, illus. Bibb, Eric, tr. (Illus.). 32p. (ps up). 1988. 10.95 (*91-29-58778-6*, R & S Bks) FS&G.
—I Want to Go to School, Too! Lucas, Barbara, tr. from SWE. Wikland, Llon, illus. 32p. (ps up). 1987. 10.95 (*91-29-58328-4*, Pub. by R & S Bks) FS&G.

—Lotta on Troublemaker Street. Brinckloe, Julie, illus. Bothmer, Gerry, tr. LC 90-25169. (Illus.). 64p. (gr. 1-4). 1991. pap. 2.95 (*0-689-71443-2*, Aladdin) Macmillan Child Grp.
—Lotta's Christmas Surprise. Wikland, Ilon, illus. 32p. (ps-3). 1990. 13.95 (*91-29-59782-X*, Pub. by R & S Bks) FS&G.
—Lotta's Easter Surprise. Wikland, Ilon, illus. Lucas, Barbara, tr. (Illus.). 32p. (ps up). 1991. bds. 13.95 (*91-29-59862-1*, Pub. by R&S Bks) FS&G.
—Mio My Son. Wikland, Ilon, photos by. (gr. 3-7). 1988. pap. 4.99 (*0-14-032608-1*, Puffin) Puffin Bks.
—Mischievous Meg. Bothmer, Gerry, tr. Domanska, Janina, illus. LC 85-575. (ps-k). 1985. pap. 4.99 (*0-14-031954-9*, Puffin) Puffin Bks.
—Pippi Goes on Board. 192p. 1981. Repr. PLB 16.95x (*0-89966-339-7*) Buccaneer Bks.
—Pippi Goes on Board. 172p. 1980. PLB 12.95x (*0-89967-014-8*) Harmony Raine.
—Pippi Goes on Board. Glanzman, Louis S., illus. (gr. 4-6). 1957. pap. 13.00 (*0-670-55677-7*) Viking Child Bks.
—Pippi Goes on Board. (Orig.). 1977. pap. 3.95 (*0-14-032774-6*, Puffin); pap. 3.99 (*0-14-030959-4*, Puffin) Puffin Bks.
—Pippi in the South Seas. Bothmer, Gerry, tr. Glanzman, Louis S., illus. (gr. 4-6). 1959. pap. 13.00 (*0-670-55711-0*) Viking Child Bks.
—Pippi in the South Seas. (Orig.). 1988. pap. 3.95 (*0-14-032773-8*, Puffin) Puffin Bks.
—Pippi in the South Seas. Bothmer, Gerry, tr. Glanzman, Louis S., illus. 128p. (gr. 3-7). 1977. pap. 3.99 (*0-14-030958-6*, Puffin) Puffin Bks.
—Pippi Longstocking. 192p. 1981. Repr. PLB 21.95 (*0-89966-338-9*) Buccaneer Bks.
—Pippi Longstocking. 175p. 1980. Repr. PLB 12.95x (*0-89967-013-X*) Harmony Raine.
—Pippi Longstocking. Lamborn, Florence, tr. Glanzman, Louis S., illus. (gr. 4-6). 1950. pap. 12.95 (*0-670-55745-5*) Viking Child Bks.
—Pippi Longstocking. (Orig.). 1988. pap. 3.95 (*0-14-032772-X*, Puffin) Puffin Bks.
—Pippi Longstocking. Lamborn, Florence, tr. Glanzman, Louis S., illus. 158p. (gr. 4-6). 1977. pap. 3.99 (*0-14-030957-8*, Puffin) Puffin Bks.
—Pippi Longstocking. large type ed. 127p. 1989. Repr. of 1945 ed. lib. bdg. 13.95 (*1-55736-152-5*, Crnrstn Bks) BDD LT Grp.
—Ronia, the Robber's Daughter. (Illus.). 176p. (gr. 4-7). 1985. pap. 3.99 (*0-14-031720-1*, Puffin) Puffin Bks.
—The Runaway Sleigh Ride. Wikland, Ilon, illus. LC 83-23347. 32p. (ps-3). 1984. pap. 11.95 (*0-670-40454-3*) Viking Child Bks.
—Springtime in Noisy Village. Wikland, Llon, illus. LC 66-15648. 32p. (ps-3). 1988. pap. 11.95 (*0-670-82185-3*) Viking Child Bks.
—The Tomten. Wiberg, Harald, illus. LC 61-10658. (gr. 1-3). 1979. 14.95 (*0-698-20147-7*, Coward); (Coward) Putnam Pub Group.
—The Tomten. Wiberg, Harald, illus. 32p. (ps-3). 1990. pap. 5.95 (*0-698-20680-0*, Coward) Putnam Pub Group.
—The Tomten & the Fox. Wiberg, Harald, illus. 32p. (ps-3). 1989. pap. 5.95 (*0-698-20644-4*, Sandcastle Bks) Putnam Pub Group.
Lindgren, Barbro. Sam's Ball. LC 83-722. (Illus.). 32p. (ps-k). 1983. 6.95 (*0-688-02359-2*) Morrow Jr Bks.
—Sam's Bath. Eriksson, Eva, illus. LC 83-724. 32p. (ps-k). 1983. 6.95 (*0-688-02362-2*) Morrow Jr Bks.
—Sam's Car. Eriksson, Eva, illus. LC 82-3437. 32p. (gr. k-3). 1982. 6.95 (*0-688-01263-9*) Morrow Jr Bks.
—Sam's Cookie. Eriksson, Eva, illus. LC 82-3419. 32p. (gr. k-3). 1982. 6.95 (*0-688-01267-1*) Morrow Jr Bks.
—Sam's Potty. Eriksson, Eva, illus. LC 86-864. 32p. (ps-k). 1986. 6.95 (*0-688-06603-8*) Morrow Jr Bks.
—Sam's Teddy Bear. Eriksson, Eva, illus. LC 82-3418. 32p. (gr. k-3). 1982. 5.95 (*0-688-01270-1*) Morrow Jr Bks.
—Sam's Wagon. Eriksson, Eva, illus. LC 86-865. 32p. (ps-k). 1986. 6.95 (*0-688-05802-7*) Morrow Jr Bks.
—Shorty Takes Off. Fisher, Richard E., tr. Landstrom, Olof, illus. 28p. (ps-3). 1990. 13.95 (*91-29-59770-6*, Pub. by R & S Bks) FS&G.
—The Wild Baby. Prelutsky, Jack, tr. from SWE. Erikkson, Eva, illus. LC 81-2151. (gr. k-3). 1981. PLB 15.88 (*0-688-00601-9*) Greenwillow.
—The Wild Baby Gets a Puppy: Swedish Edition. Prelutsky, Jack, tr. Eriksson, Eva, illus. LC 87-212. 32p. (ps-3). 1988. Repr. of 1985 ed. 11.95 (*0-688-06711-5*); lib. bdg. 11.88 (*0-688-06712-3*) Greenwillow.
Lindman, Maj. Snipp, Snapp, Snurr & the Big Farm. (Illus.). 32p. 1993. Repr. lib. bdg. 14.95x (*1-56849-004-6*) Buccaneer Bks.
—Snipp, Snapp, Snurr & the Big Surprise. (Illus.). 32p. 1993. Repr. lib. bdg. 14.95x (*1-56849-003-8*) Buccaneer Bks.
—Snipp, Snapp, Snurr & the Buttered Bread. (Illus.). 32p. 1993. Repr. lib. bdg. 14.95x (*1-56849-002-X*) Buccaneer Bks.
—Snipp, Snapp, Snurr & the Gingerbread. (Illus.). 30p. 1991. pap. 10.95x (*0-89966-829-1*) Buccaneer Bks.
—Snipp, Snapp, Snurr & the Magic Horse. (Illus.). 32p. 1993. Repr. lib. bdg. 14.95x (*1-56849-001-1*) Buccaneer Bks.
—Snipp, Snapp, Snurr & the Red Shoes. (Illus.). 32p. 1993. Repr. lib. bdg. 14.95x (*1-56849-000-3*) Buccaneer Bks.

—Snipp, Snapp, Snurr & the Reindeer. (Illus.). 32p. 1993. Repr. lib. bdg. 14.95x (*1-56849-005-4*) Buccaneer Bks.
—Snipp, Snapp, Snurr & the Seven Dogs. (Illus.). 32p. 1993. Repr. lib. bdg. 14.95x (*1-56849-007-0*) Buccaneer Bks.
—Snipp, Snapp, Snurr & the Yellow Sled. (Illus.). 30p. 1991. pap. 10.95x (*0-89966-828-3*) Buccaneer Bks.
—Snipp, Snapp, Snurr Learn to Swim. (Illus.). 32p. 1993. Repr. lib. bdg. 14.95x (*1-56849-006-2*) Buccaneer Bks.
Lindo, Howard. Making Dreams Come True. Brand, Jennifer, illus. 1993. 7.95 (*0-533-10406-8*) Vantage.
Lindop, Edmund. Assassinations That Shook America. LC 92-15082. (Illus.). 144p. (gr. 9-12). 1992. PLB 13. 90 (*0-531-11049-4*) Watts.
—The Bill of Rights & Landmark Cases. LC 89-8960. (Illus.). 144p. (gr. 7-9). 1989. PLB 13.90 (*0-531-10790-6*) Watts.
—Birth of the Constitution. LC 86-13380. (Illus.). 160p. (gr. 6 up). 1987. lib. bdg. 18.95 (*0-89490-135-4*) Enslow Pubs.
—Presidents by Accident. LC 91-17056. (Illus.). 208p. (gr. 9-12). 1991. PLB 15.40 (*0-531-11059-1*) Watts.
—Presidents vs. Congress: Conflict & Compromise. LC 93-30784. 1994. write for info. (*0-531-11165-2*) Watts.
Lindow, John. Viking Ships. (gr. 1-9). 1992. pap. 5.95 (*0-88388-078-4*) Bellerophon Bks.
Lindow, Sandra. Rooted in the Earth. Moore, Eugenia & Leiper, Esther M., eds. (Illus.). 32p. (Orig.). (gr. 9 up). 1989. pap. 3.95x (*0-9617284-8-5*) Sand & Silk.
Lindquist, A., jt. auth. see Hanon.
Lindquist, Jennie D. The Little Silver House. Williams, Garth, illus. (gr. 2-6). 15.50 (*0-8446-6190-2*) Peter Smith.
Lindquist, Marie. In a Perfect World. 128p. (gr. 6-12). 1991. pap. 3.95 perfect bdg. (*0-89486-775-X*, T5127) Hazelden.
—Untamed Heart. 160p. (Orig.). (gr. 7-12). 1987. pap. 2.50 (*0-553-26474-5*, Starfire) Bantam.
Lindquist, Susan H. Walking the Rim. LC 91-76966. 144p. (gr. 7 up). 1992. 14.95 (*1-56397-098-8*) Boyds Mills Pr.
Lindsay, A. Brook, III. The Cygnus Conspiracy. Amthor, Terry, ed. Roberts, Tony, illus. 32p. (gr. 10-12). 1987. pap. 12.00 (*0-915795-92-2*, 9102) Iron Crown Ent Inc.
Lindsay, Jeanne W. Do I Have a Daddy? A Story about a Single-Parent Child. 2nd ed. Boeller, Cheryl, illus. LC 90-49676. 48p. 1991. 12.95 (*0-930934-45-8*); pap. 5.95 (*0-930934-44-X*) Morning Glory.
—Pregnant Too Soon: Adoption Is an Option. rev. ed. Morford, Pam P., illus. Monserrat, Catherine, frwd. by. LC 87-22042. (Illus.). 224p. (gr. 7-12). 1987. 9.95 (*0-930934-25-3*); tchr's. guide 2.50 (*0-930934-27-X*) Morning Glory.
—Teen Dads: Rights, Responsibilities & Joys. Crawford, David, photos by. (Illus.). 192p. (Orig.). (gr. 7 up). 1993. 15.95 (*0-930934-77-6*); pap. 9.95 (*0-930934-78-4*); tchr's. guide 2.50 (*0-930934-80-6*); wkbk. 2.50 (*0-930934-79-2*) Morning Glory.
—Teenage Marriage: Coping with Reality. rev. ed. LC 83-19638. (Illus.). 208p. 1988. pap. 9.95 (*0-930934-30-X*) Morning Glory.
—Teens Parenting - Your Baby's First Year: A How-to-Parent Book Especially for Teenage Parents. rev. ed. LC 91-21513. (Illus.). 192p. (gr. 6 up). 1991. text ed. 15.95 (*0-930934-53-9*); pap. text ed. 9.95 (*0-930934-52-0*) wkbk. 2.50 (*0-930934-64-4*) Morning Glory.
—Yo Tengo Papa? Do I Have a Daddy? Un Cuento Sobre Un Nino de Madre Soltera, A Story about a Single-Parent Child. Palacios, Argentina, tr. Boeller, Cheryl, illus. (SPA). 48p. (ps-3). Date not set. 12.95 (*0-930934-83-0*); pap. 5.95 (*0-930934-82-2*) Morning Glory.
Lindsay, Jeanne W. & Brunelli, Jean. Teens Parenting - Your Pregnancy & Newborn Journey (Easier Reading) How to Take Care of Yourself & Your Newborn When You're a Pregnant Teen - Easy Reading Edition. LC 91-3712. (Illus.). 192p. (Orig.). (gr. 6 up). 1992. text ed. 15.95 (*0-930934-62-8*); pap. text ed. 9.95 (*0-930934-61-X*); tchr's. guide 2.50 (*0-930934-68-7*); wkbk. 2.50 (*0-930934-63-6*) Morning Glory.
—Teens Parenting - Your Pregnancy & Newborn Journey: How to Take Care of Yourself & Your Newborn When You're a Pregnant Teen. LC 91-3712. (Illus.). 192p. (Orig.). (gr. 6 up). 1991. text ed. 15.95 (*0-930934-51-2*); pap. text ed. 9.95 (*0-930934-50-4*); wkbk. 2.50 (*0-930934-60-1*) Morning Glory.
Lindsay, Jeanne W. & McCullough, Sally. Teens Parenting - Discipline from Birth to Three: How to Prevent & Deal with Discipline Problems with Babies & Toddlers. LC 91-3711. (Illus.). 192p. (Orig.). (gr. 6 up). 1991. text ed. 15.95 (*0-930934-55-5*); pap. text ed. 9.95 (*0-930934-54-7*); wkbk. 2.50 (*0-930934-66-0*) Morning Glory.
Lindsay, Mela M. The Story of Johann: The Boy Who Longed to Come to Amerika. Gentry, Diane, illus. LC 90-85324. 190p. 1991. 11.50 (*0-914222-18-X*) Am Hist Soc Ger.
Lindsay, Norene. Dream Catchers: Developing Career & Educational Awareness in the Intermediate Grades. Hall, Sara, ed. Gurtzweiler, Michael & Smith, Al, illus. 64p. (gr. k-7). 1993. pap. 2.50 wkbk. (*1-56370-085-9*, DCP); tchr's. guide 14.95 (*1-56370-086-7*, DCTG); reproducible activity sheets 19.95 (*1-56370-087-5*, DCAS) JIST Works.

—Pathfinder - Exploring Career & Educational Paths: Career & Educational Planning for Junior High & High School Students. Adams, Sara, ed. (Illus.). 112p. (gr. 8-12). 1993. pap. 4.95 wkbk. (1-56370-120-0, PFP) JIST Works.
Lindsay, Vachel. Johnny Appleseed & Other Poems. 129p. 1981. Repr. PLB 23.95x (0-89966-365-6) Buccaneer Bks.
—Johnny Appleseed & Other Poems. 138p. 1981. PLB 21.95 (0-89967-039-3) Harmony Raine.
—Una Tortuga Encantadora - Turtle Magic. LC 90-62625. (Illus.). 12p. 1991. bds. 5.95 incl. finger puppet (1-877779-22-9) Schneider Educational.
Lindsay, William. Barosaurus. Norell, Mark, contrib. by. LC 92-52819. (Illus.). 32p. (gr. 3 up). 1993. 12.95 (1-56458-123-3) Dorling Kindersley.
—Corythosaurus. LC 92-54309. (Illus.). 32p. (gr. 3 up). 1993. 12.95 (1-56458-225-6) Dorling Kindersley.
—Great Dinosaur Atlas. Fornari, Giuliano, illus. (gr. 3 up). 1991. 16.00 (0-671-74480-1, J Messner); lib. bdg. 16.98 (0-671-74479-8, J Messner) S&S Trade.
—Prehistoric Life. LC 93-32076. 1994. 15.00 (0-679-86001-0) Knopf Bks Yng Read.
Lindsey, Johanna. Gentle Rogue. 581p. 1992. text ed. 46.48 (1-56956-239-3) W A T Braille.
Lindsey, Marilyn L. The Little Lost Sheep. O'Connell, Ruth, illus. LC 87-91993. (gr. k-2). 1988. 2.50 (0-87403-398-5, 24-03808) Standard Pub.
Lindshell, Sheryl & Alpert, Stanley. Certified Professional Secretary Examination Review (CPSR) 224p. (Orig.). (gr. 12). 1987. pap. 12.95 (0-13-122805-6, Arco Test) P-H Gen Ref & Trav.
Lindskoog, Kathryn, ed. see Alcott, Louisa May.
Lindskoog, Kathryn, ed. see Defoe, Daniel.
Lindskoog, Kathryn, ed. see Sewell, Anna.
Lindsley, Margaret. Andrew Henry: Mine & Mountain Major. (Illus.). 370p. 1990. 19.95 (0-936204-79-6); pap. 15.95 (0-936204-78-8) Jelm Mtn.
Lindstrom, Eva. The Cat Hat. Croall, Stephen, tr. from SWE. (Illus.). 40p. (gr. 1-4). 1989. 12.95 (0-916291-23-5); pap. 6.95 (0-916291-24-3) Kane-Miller Bk.
Lindstrom, Marilyn. The Voice from Inner Space: Answers Who Am I? Why Am I Here? Beckman, Jean, ed. LC 90-35087. 112p. (Orig.). 1990. pap. 7.95 (0-941992-20-9) Los Arboles Pub.
Lindt, Carson Van see Van Lindt, Carson.
Lindvall, Ella K. Bible Illustrated for Little Children. (Illus.). (ps-2). 1991. text ed. 9.99 (0-8024-0569-X) Moody.
—My Friend Jesus. Walles, Dwight, illus. 32p. (Orig.). (gr. 1-3). 1989. pap. 2.99 (0-8024-5949-8) Moody.
—My Teacher Jesus. Walles, Dwight, illus. (ps-2). pap. 2.99 (0-8024-5946-3) Moody.
—Read-Aloud Bible Stories, Vol. 1. LC 82-2114. 160p. (ps-2). 1982. 17.99 (0-8024-7163-3) Moody.
—Read Aloud Bible Stories, Vol. 3. (ps-2). 1990. 17.99 (0-8024-7165-X) Moody.
Lindwall, Bo & Koster, Hans-Curt. The World of Carl Larsson. LC 84-152789. (Illus.). 196p. (Orig.). 1991. 39.95 (0-914676-93-8, Green Tiger) S&S Trade.
Line, Lorie. Selections from Sharing the Season, Vol. 2. Mayberry, Paul, ed. Hinman, Jim, illus. 36p. 1993. pap. text ed. 9.95 (0-9638000-0-0) Time Line Prods.
Linehan, Patricia. See What I Can Do! Rader, Laura, illus. 24p. (ps). 1990. bds. 2.50 (0-448-02259-1, G&D) Putnam Pub Group.
Lineker, Gary. The Young Soccer Player. LC 93-41145. 1994. write for info. (1-56458-592-1) Dorling Kindersley.
Linerode, Darla. Introduction to Art. (Illus., Orig.). (gr. 3-6). 1992. pap. 63.00 (0-935493-29-8) Modern Learn Pr.
—Let's Look at Art. (Illus., Orig.). (gr. 1-6). 1992. pap. write for info. (0-935493-30-1) Modern Learn Pr.
Lines, Kathleen. Lavender's Blue. Jones, Harold, illus. 180p. (ps-7). 1990. pap. 12.00 (0-19-272208-5) OUP.
Lines, Kathleen, ed. The Faber Book of Greek Legends. Jacques, Faith, illus. 268p. (gr. 4 up). 1986. pap. 11.95 (0-571-13920-5) Faber & Faber.
—The Faber Book of Magical Tales. Howard, Alan, illus. LC 85-4437. 176p. (Orig.). (gr. 5-9). 1985. pap. 7.95 (0-571-13648-6) Faber & Faber.
—Lavender's Blue: A Book of Nursery Rhymes. Jones, Harold, illus. 180p. 1987. 22.00 (0-19-279537-6) OUP.
Lines, Kathleen, ed. see Uttley, Alison.
Linforth, Veda. Toy Shop Tales. 1993. 7.95 (0-533-10266-9) Vantage.
Ling, Mary. Amazing Crocodiles & Other Reptiles. Young, Jerry, photos by. LC 90-19239. (Illus.). 32p. (Orig.). (gr. 1-5). 1991. PLB 9.99 (0-679-90689-4); pap. 7.99 (0-679-80689-X) Knopf Bks Yng Read.
—Amazing Fish. Young, Jerry, photos by. LC 90-49651. (Illus.). 32p. (Orig.). (gr. 1-5). 1991. PLB 9.99 (0-679-91516-8); pap. 7.99 (0-679-81516-3) Knopf Bks Yng Read.
—Amazing Wolves, Dogs, & Foxes. Young, Jerry, photos by. LC 91-6514. (Illus.). 32p. (Orig.). (gr. 1-5). 1991. lib. bdg. 9.99 (0-679-91521-4); pap. 7.99 (0-679-81521-X) Knopf Bks Yng Read.
—Butterfly. LC 92-52808. (Illus.). 24p. (ps-1). 1992. 7.95 (1-56458-112-8) Dorling Kindersley.
—Calf. Clayton, Gordon, photos by. LC 92-53486. (Illus.). 24p. (ps-1). 1993. 7.95 (1-56458-205-1) Dorling Kindersley.
—Foal. LC 92-52809. (Illus.). 24p. (ps-1). 1992. 7.95 (1-56458-113-6) Dorling Kindersley.
—Fox. LC 92-52810. (Illus.). 24p. (ps-1). 1992. 7.95 (1-56458-114-4) Dorling Kindersley.
—Giraffe. LC 93-3041. (Illus.). 24p. (ps-1). 1993. 7.95 (1-56458-311-2) Dorling Kindersley.
—Owl. LC 92-52811. (Illus.). 24p. (ps-1). 1992. 7.95 (1-56458-115-2) Dorling Kindersley.
—Penguin. LC 93-22105. (Illus.). 24p. (ps-3). 1993. 7.95 (1-56458-312-0) Dorling Kindersley.
—Pig. Ling, Bill, photos by. LC 92-53487. (Illus.). 24p. (ps-1). 1993. 7.95 (1-56458-204-3) Dorling Kindersley.
Lingard, Joan. Between Two Worlds. 192p. (gr. 7 up). 1991. 14.95 (0-525-67360-1, Lodestar Bks) Dutton Child Bks.
—Between Two Worlds. 192p. (gr. 7 up). 1993. pap. 4.50 (0-14-036505-2, Puffin) Puffin Bks.
—Tug of War. 208p. (gr. 7 up). 1990. 14.95 (0-525-67306-7, Lodestar Bks) Dutton Child Bks.
—Tug of War. 192p. (gr. 5 up). 1992. pap. 4.50 (0-14-036072-7, Puffin) Puffin Bks.
Lingham, Gretchen, ed. see Dunning, Jack.
Lingham, Gretchen, ed. see Rathbone, R. Andrew.
Lingham, Gretchen, ed. see Rathbone, Tina.
Lingham, Gretchen, ed. see Wang, Wally & Millard, Scott.
Lingo, Susan L. & Downey, Melissa C. Abraham. Green, Roy, illus. 32p. (ps-7). 1992. wkbk. 3.99 (0-87403-915-0, 23-02525) Standard Pub.
—Daniel. Green, Roy, illus. 32p. (ps-7). 1992. wkbk. 3.99 (0-87403-919-3, 23-02529) Standard Pub.
—David. Green, Roy, illus. 32p. (ps-7). 1992. wkbk. 3.99 (0-87403-918-5, 23-02528) Standard Pub.
—Joshua. Green, Roy, illus. 32p. (ps-7). 1992. wkbk. 3.99 (0-87403-917-7, 23-02527) Standard Pub.
—Moses. Green, Roy, illus. 112p. (ps-7). 1992. wkbk. 3.99 (0-87403-916-9, 23-02526) Standard Pub.
—Noah. Green, Roy, illus. 32p. (ps-7). 1992. wkbk. 3.99 (0-87403-914-2, 23-02524) Standard Pub.
Lingo, Susan L., jt. auth. see Downey, Melissa C.
LinguiSystems Staff. ACHIEV-Red Sing-a-Longs Manual (Activities for Children Involving Everyday Vocabulary - Home & Family Vocabulary) (ps-3). 1989. 25.95 (1-55999-006-6) LinguiSystems.
Link, Mark. Challenge. 160p. (gr. 9-12). 1987. 6.95 (0-89505-654-2, 22014) Tabor Pub.
—Decision. 160p. 1987. 6.95 (0-89505-655-0, 22015) Tabor Pub.
—Path Through Catholicism. (Illus.). 224p. (Orig.). (gr. 9-12). 1991. pap. 12.50 (1-55924-543-3, 22039) Tabor Pub.
—Path Through Scripture. (Illus.). 288p. (gr. 9-12). 1987. pap. 12.50 (0-89505-402-7, 21095) Tabor Pub.
—Path Through Scripture: Teacher's Resource Manual. 328p. (gr. 9-12). 1987. 24.95 (0-89505-403-5, 253X1) Tabor Pub.
—The Seventh Trumpet: Teacher's Manual. 207p. (gr. 9-12). 1978. 19.95 (0-89505-030-7, 21005) Tabor Pub.
Link, Martin, jt. auth. see Blood, Charles L.
Link, Sarah, et al. Faeries: A Complete Handbook of the Seelie. Dougherty, Charles, et al, illus. 144p. (Orig.). (gr. 11 up). 1991. pap. text ed. 17.95 (0-9627790-5-9) White Wolf.
Link, Sheila, jt. auth. see Dixon, Franklin W.
Linker, Corinne. Circle of Seasons. Kirkeeide, Debi, illus. 32p. (ps-2). Date not set. 11.95 (1-56065-157-1) Capstone Pr. Postponed.
Linklater, Eric. The Wind on the Moon. 302p. (gr. 5-7). 1989. pap. 6.95 (0-86241-131-9, Pub. by Cnngt Pub Ltd) Trafalgar.
Linkletter, Art. Kids Say the Darndest Things. Schulz, Charles, illus. Disney, Walt, intro. by. LC 54-11661. (Illus.). 262p. (gr. 7 up). 1977. pap. 3.50 (0-89559-010-7, Dist. by National Book Network) Green Hill.
Links, Marty. Yes I Can: Yes I Did. Lins, Barbara, ed. Links, Marty & Fudd, Richard, illus. Knight, Marilyn, intro. by. 32p. (Orig.). (ps). 1990. pap. write for info. (1-878079-00-X) Arts Pubns.
Links, Marty & Knight, Marilyn. Yes I Can. (Illus.). 1990. 4.95 (0-685-57229-3); poster 4.95 (0-685-57230-7) Arts Pubns.
Links, Marty & Linse, Barbara. Love the Earth: An Ecology Resource Book. (Illus.). 1991. 5.95 (1-878079-01-8); poster 4.95 (0-685-59046-1) Arts Pubns.
Linksman, Ricki, jt. auth. see Scotti, Juliet.
Linley, Mike. The Frog & the Toad: Masters of Land & Water. Stefoff, Rebecca, ed. LC 92-10246. (Illus.). 31p. (gr. 3-6). 1992. PLB 17.26 (1-56074-050-7) Garrett Ed Corp.
—The Lizard in the Jungle. Oxford Scientific Films, photos by. LC 87-42612. (Illus.). 32p. (gr. 4-6). 1988. PLB 15.93 (1-55532-303-0) Gareth Stevens Inc.
—The Penguin: The Fastest Flightless Birds. Stefoff, Rebecca, ed. LC 92-10245. (Illus.). 31p. (gr. 3-6). 1992. PLB 17.26 (1-56074-052-3) Garrett Ed Corp.
—The Snake in the Grass. Oxford Scientific Films Staff, photos by. LC 89-4621. (Illus.). 32p. (gr. 4-6). 1989. PLB 15.93 (0-8368-0118-0) Gareth Stevens Inc.
—The Snake: Smooth Scaly & Successful. Stefoff, Rebecca, ed. LC 92-10248. (Illus.). 32p. (gr. 3-6). 1992. PLB 17.26 (1-56074-053-1) Garrett Ed Corp.
—Snakes. LC 91-8558. 32p. (gr. 2-5). 1993. 14.95 (1-56847-006-1) Thomson Lrning.
Linn, Christopher. The Everglades: Exploring the Unknown. LC 75-23414. (Illus.). 32p. (gr. 5-10). 1976. PLB 10.79 (0-89375-006-9) Troll Assocs.
Linn, Emily, tr. see Sheffer, Susannah.
Linn, Erin. Children Are Not Paper Dolls: A Visit with Bereaved Siblings. Hargis, Jim, frwd. by. (Illus.). 121p. (Orig.). (gr. k-8). 1982. pap. 8.95 (0-9614636-0-0) Pub Mark.

Linn, James R. The Little Green Hummingbird. Huston, Dwayne L., ed. Benedict, Jennifer S., illus. LC 92-75969. 44p. (gr. 3). 1993. pap. 7.98 (1-882798-01-5) Erth & Sky Pub.
For every child there are times when common day occurrences are magical. They are most magical when the child is first encountering logical thinking but still has a sense of wonderment. This is a story told by an adult but seen through the eyes of his own inner child. Aided by beautifully realistic illustrations from a gifted artist, the author gives a portrayal of two urban families. A family of four follows a hummingbird as she raises two offspring in view of their dining room window. Together with help from their neighbor, the family tries to share the perils of the smallest of all birds. Full of humor & human drama, there are traces of issues important to children who face the start of the next century. Community, schooling, wildlife conservation & instinctive parenting are lightly touched upon. Written so that it is easy reading for third graders & up, it is also a pleasant exercise for adults who will be reading it to younger children. The illustrations will hold the attention of even the most active youngster. The mood will make adults remember their own inner child. *Publisher Provided Annotation.*

Linn, Joseph. Can You Imagine? Date not set. songbk. 5.25 (0-685-68206-4, BCMB-519); coloring bk. 0.50 (0-685-68207-2, BCMU-728); cassette 11.98 (0-685-68208-0, BCTA-9045C) Lillenas.
Linn, Margot. A Trip to the Dentist. Siracusa, Catherine, illus. LC 87-14884. 20p. (ps-k). 1988. HarpC Child Bks.
—A Trip to the Doctor. Siracusa, Catherine, illus. LC 87-15004. 20p. (ps-k). 1988. HarpC Child Bks.
Linnea. A Doll's House & Hedda Gabler (Ibsen) (gr. 9-12). 1985. pap. 2.95 (0-8120-3511-9) Barron.
Linnea, Sharon. Raoul Wallenberg: The Man Who Stopped Death. (Illus.). 168p. (gr. 10 up). 1993. 17.95 (0-8276-0440-8); pap. 9.95 (0-8276-0448-3) JPS Phila.
Linnell, Andrew & Auer, Varvara. The Dance of the Elves. (Illus.). 32p. (Orig.). (ps). 1984. pap. 13.50 (0-936132-68-X) Merc Pr NY.
Linnell, Naomi, jt. auth. see Postgate, Oliver.
Lins, Barbara, ed. see Links, Marty.
Linscott, Jody. Once Upon A to Z: An Alphabet Odyssey. (ps up). 1991. 15.00 (0-385-41893-0); PLB 15.99 (0-385-41907-4) Doubleday.
—The Worthy Wonders Lost at Sea. Holland, Claudia P., illus. LC 92-43367. 1993. pap. 15.00 (0-385-47053-3) Doubleday.
Linse, Barbara. Arts & Crafts for All Seasons. LC 68-57698. (gr. k-6). 1969. pap. 8.95 (0-8224-0490-7) Fearon Teach Aids.
Linse, Barbara & Knight, Marilyn. Love the Earth. Dresser, Ginny, ed. Links, Marty & Clark, Cindy, illus. 32p. 1991. pap. write for info. Arts Pubns.
Linse, Barbara, jt. auth. see Judd, Dick.
Linse, Barbara, jt. auth. see Links, Marty.
Linse, Barbara B. & Kuska, George, eds. Live Again Our Mission Past: California Missions Through Children's Eyes. Clark, Cindy & Kuska, George, illus. 200p. (gr. 7-12). 1984. pap. 13.95 (0-9607458-1-5) Arts Pubns.
Linsenman-Schuh, Norma. Presenting Ali Marie in Cabin Fever. Rogers, Dennis, illus. 32p. (Orig.). (gr. k-5). 1993. pap. 5.95 (1-884073-03-4); pap. 24.95 incl. doll (1-884073-00-X) Esteem Intl.
—Presenting Jessica Lyn in King Purple. Quinlivan, Mary & Snyder, Deborah, illus. 32p. (Orig.). 1993. pap. 5.95 (1-884073-04-2); pap. 24.95 incl. doll (1-884073-01-8) Esteem Intl.
Lint, Charles de. The Dreaming Place. Froud, Brian, illus. LC 90-488. 144p. (gr. 7 up). 1990. SBE 14.95 (0-689-31571-6, Atheneum Child Bk) Macmillan Child Grp.
Lint, Charles de see Lint, Charles de.
Linville, Barbara. Christy's Pouting Again. McCallum, Joanne, created by. & illus. 32p. (gr. k-2). 1989. 2.99 (0-87403-627-5, 3891) Standard Pub.

—God Made the One & Only Me. Heaston, Claudia, illus. LC 76-8737. (ps). 1976. pap. text ed. 3.95 (0-916406-28-8, Chariot Bks) Cook.
—Joey's Too Much TV. McCallum, Joanne, created by. & illus. 32p. (gr. k-2). 1989. 2.99 (0-87403-628-3, 3892) Standard Pub.
—Susie's Afraid of the Dark. McCallum, Joanne, created by. & illus. 32p. (gr. k-2). 1989. 2.99 (0-87403-629-1, 3893) Standard Pub.
—Tommy's Afraid to Try. McCallum, Joanne, created by. & illus. 32p. (gr. k-2). 1989. 2.99 (0-87403-630-5) Standard Pub.
Lion. Best Loved Bible Stories. 1993. pap. 9.99 (0-7814-0136-4) Cook.
Lion Publishing Staff. Jesus Is Born. (ps). 1992. bds. 6.99 (0-7459-2203-1) Lion USA.
Lionni, Leo. Alexander & the Wind-up Mouse. Lionni, Leo, illus. LC 74-2088. 32p. (ps-3). 1974. pap. 4.99 (0-394-82911-5) Pantheon.
—Alexander & the Wind-up Mouse. reissue ed. Lionni, Leo, illus. LC 76-77423. 32p. (ps-2). 1969. 15.00 (0-394-80914-9); lib. bdg. 15.99 (0-394-90914-3) Knopf Bks Yng Read.
—Biggest House in the World. Lionni, Leo, illus. LC 68-12646. (gr. k-3). 1968. lib. bdg. 14.99 (0-394-90944-5) Pantheon.
—The Biggest House in the World. LC 68-12646. (Illus.). 32p. (ps-6). 1987. 3.99 (0-394-82740-6) Knopf Bks Yng Read.
—A Busy Year. LC 91-29149. (Illus.). 36p. (ps-2). 1992. 7.99 (0-679-82464-2); PLB 10.99 (0-679-92464-7) Knopf Bks Yng Read.
—A Color of His Own. Lionni, Leo, illus. LC 75-28456. 40p. (ps-k). 1993. 8.99 (0-679-84197-0); PLB 9.99 (0-679-94197-5) Knopf Bks Yng Read.
—An Extraordinary Egg. LC 93-28565. 1994. write for info. (0-679-85840-7); PLB write for info. (0-679-95840-1) Knopf Bks Yng Read.
—Fish Is Fish. Lionni, Leo, illus. LC 78-117452. (gr. k-3). 1970. lib. bdg. 13.99 (0-394-90440-0) Pantheon.
—Fish Is Fish. LC 78-117452. (Illus.). 32p. (ps-6). 1974. pap. 4.99 (0-394-82799-6) Knopf Bks Yng Read.
—Frederick. Lionni, Leo, illus. LC 66-10355. 40p. (ps-2). 1967. 16.00 (0-394-81040-6); PLB 16.99 (0-394-91040-0) Knopf Bks Yng Read.
—Frederick. Lionni, Leo, illus. LC 66-10355. 32p. (gr. k-3). 1973. pap. 4.99 (0-394-82614-0) Knopf Bks Yng Read.
—Frederick & His Friends. Lionni, Leo, illus. (ps-2). 1989. bk. & cassette 14.95 (0-394-82784-8) Knopf Bks Yng Read.
—Frederick's Fables: A Leo Lionni Treasury of Favorite Stories. reissued ed. Lionni, Leo, illus. Bettelheim, Bruno, intro. by. LC 85-5186. (Illus.). 144p. (ps-3). 1993. 20.00 (0-394-87710-1) Knopf Bks Yng Read.
—Inch by Inch. (Illus.). (gr. k-1). 1962. 10.95 (0-8392-3010-9) Astor-Honor.
—It's Mine. Lionni, Leo, illus. LC 85-190. 32p. (ps-1). 1986. 15.00 (0-394-87000-X); lib. bdg. 15.99 (0-394-97000-4) Knopf Bks Yng Read.
—Let's Make Rabbits. (Illus.). 40p. (ps-3). 1992. 4.99 (0-679-82640-8) Knopf Bks Yng Read.
—Let's Play. Lionni, Leo, illus. 28p. (ps). 1993. 3.25 (0-380-84030-3) Random Bks Yng Read.
—Little Blue & Little Yellow. (Illus.). (gr. k-1). 1959. 10.95 (0-8392-3018-4) Astor-Honor.
—Matthew's Dream. Lionni, Leo, illus. LC 90-34243. 32p. (ps-3). 1991. 15.00 (0-679-81075-7); PLB 15.99 (0-679-91075-1) Knopf Bks Yng Read.
—Mr. McMouse. Lionni, Leo, illus. LC 92-8963. 40p. (ps-1). 1992. 15.00 (0-679-83890-2); PLB 15.99 (0-679-93890-7) Knopf Bks Yng Read.
—Nicolas, Where Have You Been? Rosenthal, Eileen, designed by. LC 86-18574. (Illus.). 32p. (ps-3). 1987. 11.95 (0-394-88370-5); lib. bdg. 11.99 (0-394-98370-X) Knopf Bks Yng Read.
—On My Beach There Are Many Pebbles. (Illus.). (gr. k-1). 1961. 10.95 (0-8392-3024-9) Astor-Honor.
—Pouce par Pouce. (FRE., Illus.). (gr. k-1). 1961. 10.95 (0-8392-3028-1) Astor-Honor.
—Pulgada a Pulgada. (SPA., Illus.). (gr. k-1). 1961. 10.95 (0-8392-3030-3) Astor-Honor.
—Six Crows. LC 87-3141. (Illus.). 32p. (ps-2). 1988. 12.95 (0-394-89572-X); PLB 13.99 (0-394-99572-4) Knopf Bks Yng Read.
—Swimmy. LC 63-8504. (Illus.). 32p. (ps-6). 1987. 4.99 (0-394-82620-5) Knopf Bks Yng Read.
—Swimmy. reissued ed. Lionni, Leo, illus. LC 63-8504. 40p. (ps-2). 1963. 14.95 (0-394-81713-3); lib. bdg. 15.99 (0-394-91713-8) Knopf Bks Yng Read.
—Tico & the Golden Wings. LC 64-18321. (Illus.). 32p. (ps-6). 1975. 4.99 (0-394-83078-4) Knopf Bks Yng Read.
—Tillie & the Wall. Lionni, Leo, illus. LC 88-9316. 32p. (ps-2). 1989. 12.95 (0-394-82155-6); lib. bdg. 13.99 (0-394-92155-0) Knopf Bks Yng Read.
Lion The Printer. Seven Days a Week. (Illus.). (gr. k-5). 1977. spiral 2.00 (0-914080-62-8) Shulsinger Sales.
Lipkind, William. Days to Remember. Snyder, Jerome, illus. (gr. 3 up). 1961. 10.95 (0-8392-3006-0) Astor-Honor.
Lipman, Jean & Aspinwall, Margaret. Alexander Calder & His Magical Mobiles. LC 81-1811. (Illus.). 96p. (ps up). 1981. 17.50 (0-933920-17-2) Hudson Hills.
Lipman, Matthew. Harry Stottlemeier's Discovery. rev. ed. LC 76-9315. 96p. (gr. 5-6). 1982. pap. 9.00 (0-916834-06-9, TX516-633) Inst Advncmnt Philos Child.

—Kio & Gus. LC 79-9315. 77p. (gr. 3-4). 1982. pap. 9.00 (0-916834-19-0, TX942-173) Inst Advncmnt Philos Child.
—Lisa. 96p. (gr. 7-10). 1983. pap. 9.00 (0-916834-21-2) Inst Advncmnt Philos Child.
—Pixie. LC 81-67706. 98p. (Orig.). (gr. 3-4). 1981. pap. 9.00 (0-916834-17-4, TX782-682) Inst Advncmnt Philos Child.
Lipman, Michel & Furniss, Cathy. Legal Eagle Series, 5 novels. Kratoville, Betty L., ed. (Illus.). 240p. (Orig.). (gr. 4-12). 1988. Set. pap. 15.00 (0-87879-594-4) High Noon Bks.
Lipner, jt. auth. see Fredericks.
Lipniacka, Ewa. Asleep at Last. Bogdanowicz, Basia, illus. LC 92-33326. 1993. 6.95 (1-56656-118-3, Crocodile Bks) Interlink Pub.
—It's Mine! Bogdanowicz, Basia, illus. LC 92-33324. 1993. 6.95 (1-56656-119-1, Crocodile Bks) Interlink Pub.
—School Trip. Bogdanowicz, Basia, illus. LC 92-33325. 1993. 6.95 (1-56656-121-3, Crocodile Bks) Interlink Pub.
—To Bed...or Else! Bogdanowicz, Basia, illus. LC 91-22118. 32p. (ps-3). 1992. 13.95 (0-940793-85-7, Crocodile Bks) Interlink Pub.
—Tooth Fairy. Bogdanowicz, Basia, illus. LC 92-33328. 1993. 6.95 (1-56656-120-5, Crocodile Bks) Interlink Pub.
Lippert, Donald F. Mister B. Hedden, Randall, illus. 32p. (ps). 1989. write for info. Pastel Pubns.
—Polly Popcan. Hedden, Randall, illus. 32p. (ps). 1989. write for info. Pastel Pubns.
—Shag & the Bouncing Ball. Hedden, Randall, illus. 32p. (ps). 1989. write for info. Pastel Pubns.
Lippert, Margaret H. La Hija de la Serpiente Marina - the Sea Serpent's Daughter: Una Leyenda Brasilena. (gr. 4-7). 1993. PLB 11.89 (0-8167-3124-1); pap. 3.95 (0-8167-3074-1) Troll Assocs.
—The Sea Serpent's Daughter: A Brazilian Legend. Davalos, Felipe, illus. LC 92-21438. 32p. (gr. 2-5). 1993. lib. bdg. 11.89 (0-8167-3053-9); pap. text ed. 3.95 (0-8167-3054-7) Troll Assocs.
Lippman, Peter. Busy Trains. Lippman, Peter, illus. LC 77-86145. 32p. (ps-3). 1981. lib. bdg. 5.99 (0-394-93748-1); pap. 2.25 (0-394-83748-7) Random Bks Yng Read.
—From Here to There. Lippman, Peter, illus. LC 75-19947. 48p. (gr. 1 up). 1975. pap. 5.00 (0-912846-11-9) Bookstore Pr.
—Little House Books: Old Macdonald's Barn. (Illus.). 20p. (ps). 1993. bds. 9.95 (1-56305-500-7, 3500) Workman Pub.
—Little House Books: Santa's Workshop. (Illus.). 20p. (ps). 1993. bds. 9.95 (1-56305-499-X, 3499) Workman Pub.
Lippman, Sidney, et al. A You're Adorable. Alexander, Martha, illus. LC 93-931. 1994. write for info. (1-56402-237-4) Candlewick Pr.
Lippy, Elsie. God's Story. (Illus.). 10p. (gr. k-6). 1989. pap. text ed. 2.50 (1-55976-128-8) CEF Press.
Lipscomb, Susan D. & Zuanich, Margaret A. BASIC Fun: Computer Games, Puzzles & Problems Children Can Write. 176p. (gr. k-7). 1982. pap. 2.95 (0-380-80606-1, Camelot) Avon.
Lipskerov, M. F. Samy Malenky Gnom (a Very Small Gnome) Kostrina, Irina, illus. (RUS.). 18p. (Orig.). 1991. pap. 14.95 (0-934393-23-0) Rector Pr.
—Volk u Telonok: Wolf & Calf. Kostrina, I. D., illus. (RUS.). 18p. (Orig.). 1989. pap. 14.95 (0-934393-15-X) Rector Pr.
Lipson, Eric, jt. auth. see Lipson, Greta.
Lipson, Greta. A Book for All Seasons. 160p. (gr. 5-9). 1990. 12.95 (0-86653-540-3, GA1153) Good Apple.
—Fact, Fantasy, Folklore. 160p. (gr. 3-12). 1977. 12.95 (0-916456-11-0, GA71) Good Apple.
—Famous Fables for Little Troupers. Kropa, Susan, illus. 168p. (gr. k-6). 1984. 12.95 (0-86653-202-1, GA 554) Good Apple.
Lipson, Greta & Bolkosky, Sidney. Mighty Myth. 152p. (gr. 5-12). 1982. 12.95 (0-86653-064-9, GA 419) Good Apple.
Lipson, Greta & Greenberg, Bernice. Extra! Extra! Read All about It! 160p. (gr. 4-8). 1981. 12.95 (0-86653-006-1, GA234) Good Apple.
Lipson, Greta & Lipson, Eric. Everyday Law for Young Citizens. 160p. (gr. 5 up). 1988. wkbk. 12.95 (0-86653-447-4, GA1056) Good Apple.
Lipson, Greta & Romatowski, Jane. Ethnic Pride. Simmons, Sheri, illus. 152p. (gr. 4-9). 1983. wkbk. 12.95 (0-86653-121-1, GA 464) Good Apple.
Lipson, Greta & Solomon, Susan. Romeo & Juliet: Plainspoken. Kropa, Susan, illus. 256p. (gr. 7-12). 1985. 15.95 (0-86653-283-8, GA 659) Good Apple.
Lipson, Greta B. Audacious Poetry. (Illus.). 128p. (gr. 6-12). 1992. wkbk. 10.95 (0-86653-683-3, 1417) Good Apple.

A Leash on Love: A Book for All Ages. Rundell, Christopher, illus. LC 93-176359. 32p. 1992. 9.95 (0-9630637-0-7) Barclay Bks. Funny & insightful--a look at the enduring bond between humans & dogs as they walk the rocky road of life together, hand in paw. Strikes a chord

---

in the hearts of all dedicated dog lovers. Thirty waggish illustrations. Written in doggerel by Greta B. Lipson, Associate Professor Emeritus of the University of Michigan where she taught Literature for Children & Young Adults. Honored by the Michigan Association of Governing Boards as distinguished Faculty Member for Extraordinary Contributions to Michigan Higher Education. Has authored & co-authored 15 books for teachers & parents: *THE SCOOP ON FROGS & PRINCES: Newspaper Commentaries; * AUDACIOUS POETRY: Reflections on Adolescence; * TALES WITH A TWIST: Ethical Dilemmas; * EVERYDAY LAW FOR YOUNG CITIZENS; * ROMEO & JULIET PLAINSPOKEN; * FAMOUS FABLES FOR LITTLE TROUPERS; * A BOOK FOR ALL SEASONS; * FAST IDEAS FOR BUSY TEACHERS; * ETHNIC PRIDE; * MIGHTY MYTH; * EXTRA! READ ALL ABOUT IT; * CALLIOPE; * FACT, FANTASY & FOLKLORE. Available Good Apple Publisher, Carthage, IL, 1-800-435-7234. Distributed by Publishers Distribution Service, Grawn, MI, 1-800-345-0096. *Publisher Provided Annotation.*

—Tales with a Twist. 160p. (gr. 5-9). 1991. 12.95 (0-86653-609-4, GA1328) Good Apple.
Lipson, Michael. How the Wind Plays. (Illus.). 32p. (ps-1). 1994. 13.95 (1-56282-325-6); PLB 13.89 (1-56282-326-4) Hyprn Child.
Lipson, Michelle. The Fantastic Costume Book: Forty Complete Patterns to Amaze & Amuse. (Illus.). 128p. (gr. 4 up). 1993. pap. 12.95 (0-8069-8377-9, Pub. by Lark Bks) Sterling.
Lipson, Michelle, et al. The Fantastic Costume Book: Forty Complete Patterns to Amaze & Amuse. LC 92-11365. (Illus.). 128p. (gr. 4 up). 1992. 19.95 (0-8069-8376-0) Sterling.
Lipson, Ruth. Modeh Ani Means Thank You. (Illus.). (ps-2). 1986. 7.95 (0-317-42732-6) Feldheim.
Lipsyte. Joe Lewis. Date not set. 14.00 (0-06-023409-1, Festival); PLB 13.89 (0-06-023410-5, Festival) HarpC Child Bks.
—Michael Jordan. Date not set. 14.00 (0-06-024234-5, Festival); PLB 13.89 (0-06-024235-3, Festival) HarpC Child Bks.
Lipsyte, Robert. Arnold Schwarzenegger: Hercules in America. LC 64-46901. (Illus.). 112p. (gr. 5-9). 1993. 14.00 (0-06-023002-9); PLB 13.89 (0-06-023003-7) HarpC Child Bks.
—The Brave. LC 90-25396. 208p. (gr. 7 up). 1991. 15.00 (0-06-023915-8); PLB 14.89 (0-06-023916-6) HarpC Child Bks.
—The Brave. LC 90-25396. 208p. (gr. 7 up). 1993. pap. 3.95 (0-06-447079-2, Trophy) HarpC Child Bks.
—The Chemo Kid. LC 91-55500. 176p. (gr. 7 up). 1992. 14.00 (0-06-020284-X); PLB 13.89 (0-06-020285-8); pap. 3.95 (0-685-59055-0) HarpC Child Bks.
—The Chemo Kid. LC 91-55500. 176p. (gr. 7 up). 1993. pap. 3.95 (0-06-447101-2, Trophy) HarpC Child Bks.
—The Chief. LC 92-54502. 240p. (gr. 7 up). 1993. 15.00 (0-06-021064-8); PLB 14.89 (0-06-021068-0) HarpC Child Bks.
—The Contender. LC 67-19623. 190p. (gr. 7-9). 1967. PLB 14.89 (0-06-023920-4) HarpC Child Bks.
—The Contender. LC 67-19623. 176p. (gr. 7 up). 1987. pap. 3.95 (0-06-447039-3, Trophy) HarpC Child Bks.
—Contender. large type ed. 232p. (gr. 2-7). 1987. Repr. of 1967 ed. lib. bdg. 14.95 (1-55736-024-3, Crnrstn Bks) BDD LT Grp.
—The Contender. LC 67-19623. 190p. (gr. 7 up). 1967. 15.00 (0-06-023919-0) HarpC Child Bks.
—Free to Be Muhammad Ali. LC 77-25640. (gr. 5 up). 1978. PLB 14.89 (0-06-023902-6) HarpC Child Bks.
—Jim Thorpe: Twentieth-Century Jock. LC 92-44069. (Illus.). 112p. (gr. 5-9). 1993. 14.00 (0-06-022988-8); PLB 13.89 (0-06-022989-6) HarpC Child Bks.
—Jock & Jill. LC 81-47723. 160p. (gr. 7 up). 1982. PLB 13.89 (0-06-023900-X) HarpC Child Bks.
—One Fat Summer. LC 76-49746. (gr. 7 up). 1977. PLB 14.89 (0-06-023896-8) HarpC Child Bks.
—One Fat Summer. LC 76-49746. 240p. (gr. 7 up). 1991. pap. 3.95 (0-06-447073-3, Trophy) HarpC Child Bks.
—Summer Rules. LC 79-2816. 160p. (gr. 7 up). 1981. PLB 13.89 (0-06-023898-4) HarpC Child Bks.

—Summer Rules. LC 79-2816. 208p. (gr. 7 up). 1992. pap. 3.95 (*0-06-447071-7*, Trophy) HarpC Child Bks.
—The Summerboy. 160p. 1984. pap. 2.25 (*0-553-24130-3*) Bantam.
—The Summerboy. reissued ed. LC 82-47578. 160p. (gr. 7 up). 1982. PLB 13.89 (*0-06-023889-5*) HarpC Child Bks.
—The Summerboy. LC 82-47578. 208p. (gr. 7 up). 1992. pap. 3.95 (*0-06-447072-5*, Trophy) HarpC Child Bks.
Liptak, Karen. Aerobics Basics. D'Amato, Janet, illus. 48p. (gr. 3-7). 1983. 9.95 (*0-13-018218-4*) P-H.
—Astronomy Basics. (Illus.). 48p. (gr. 3-7). 1986. 10.95 (*0-13-049966-8*) P-H.
—Coming-of-Age: Traditions & Rituals Around the World. LC 93-1414. (Illus.). 128p. (gr. 7 up). 1994. PLB 15.90 (*1-56294-243-3*) Millbrook Pr.
—Dating Dinosaurs & Other Old Things. LC 91-23072. (Illus.). 72p. (gr. 7 up). 1992. PLB 13.90 (*1-56294-134-8*) Millbrook Pr.
—Endangered Peoples. LC 92-41391. 1993. 13.40 (*0-531-10987-9*) Watts.
—Indians of the Pacific Northwest. (Illus.). 96p. (gr. 5-8). 1990. 18.95x (*0-8160-2384-0*) Facts on File.
—Indians of the Southwest. (Illus.). 96p. (gr. 5-8). 1990. 18.95x (*0-8160-2385-9*) Facts on File.
—Inside Biosphere Two: The Rainforest. 64p. (gr. 3 up). 1993. pap. text ed. 8.95 (*1-882428-06-4*) Biosphere Pr.
—North American Indian Ceremonies. Mathews, V., ed. LC 90-12337. (Illus.). 64p. (gr. 3-6). 1992. PLB 12.90 (*0-531-20100-7*) Watts.
—North American Indian Ceremonies. (Illus.). 64p. (gr. 5-8). 1992. pap. 5.95 (*0-531-15639-7*) Watts.
—North American Indian Medicine People. (Illus.). 64p. (gr. 5-8). 1990. PLB 12.90 (*0-531-10868-6*) Watts.
—North American Indian Medicine People. (Illus.). 64p. (gr. 5-8). 1992. pap. 5.95 (*0-531-15640-0*) Watts.
—North American Indian Sign Language. Berry, Don, illus. LC 90-12337. 64p. (gr. 5-8). 1990. PLB 12.90 (*0-531-10869-4*) Watts.
—North American Indian Sign Language. (Illus.). 64p. (gr. 5-8). 1992. pap. 5.95 (*0-531-15641-9*) Watts.
—North American Indian Survival Skills. LC 90-12354. (Illus.). 64p. (gr. 5-8). 1990. PLB 12.90 (*0-531-10870-8*) Watts.
—North American Indian Survival Skills. (Illus.). 64p. (gr. 5-8). 1992. pap. 5.95 (*0-531-15642-7*) Watts.
—North American Indian Tribal Chiefs. Mathews, V., ed. LC 91-30261. (Illus.). 64p. (gr. 3-6). 1992. PLB 12.90 (*0-531-20101-5*) Watts.
—North American Indian Tribal Chiefs. (Illus.). 64p. (gr. 5-8). 1992. pap. 5.95 (*0-531-15643-5*) Watts.
—Out in the Night. Fuller, Sandy F., illus. LC 89-1833. 32p. (Orig.). (gr. 3-5). 1989. pap. 8.95 (*0-943173-31-0*) Harbinger AZ.
—Pangaea: The Mother Continent. Steere, Susan, illus. LC 89-15495. 36p. (Orig.). (gr. 4-6). 1989. pap. 8.95 (*0-943173-42-6*) Harbinger AZ.
—Robotics Basics. Petronella, Michael, illus. 48p. (gr. 3-7). 1984. 10.95 (*0-13-782087-9*) P-H.
—Saving Our Wetlands & Our Wildlife. (Illus.). 64p. (gr. 5-8). 1992. pap. 5.95 (*0-531-15648-6*) Watts.
—Saving Our Wetlands & Their Wildlife. LC 91-4682. (Illus.). 64p. (gr. 5-8). 1991. PLB 12.90 (*0-531-20092-2*) Watts.
Liptak, Karen, jt. auth. see Gentry, Linnea.
Lipton, Alfred. Cinderella, Vol. 512. rev. ed. Caban, Janice, ed. & illus. 10p. (gr. k). 1989. pap. 2.00 (*1-878501-01-1*) Ntrl Science Indus.
—Goldilox & the Three Bears, Vol. 514. rev. ed. Caban, Janice, ed. & illus. 10p. (gr. k). 1989. pap. 2.00 (*1-878501-02-X*) Ntrl Science Indus.
—Jack & the Beanstalk, Vol. 510. rev. ed. Caban, Janice, ed. & illus. 10p. (gr. k). 1989. pap. 2.00 (*1-878501-00-3*) Ntrl Science Indus.
—Little Red Riding Hood, Vol. 520. rev. ed. Caban, Janice, ed. & illus. 10p. (gr. k). 1989. pap. 2.00 (*1-878501-05-4*) Ntrl Science Indus.
—Pinocchio, Vol. 516. rev. ed. Caban, Janice, ed. & illus. 10p. (gr. k). 1989. pap. 2.00 (*1-878501-03-8*) Ntrl Science Indus.
—Sleeping Beauty, Vol. 518. rev. ed. Caban, Janice, ed. & illus. 10p. (gr. k). 1989. pap. 2.00 (*1-878501-04-6*) Ntrl Science Indus.
Lipuma, Anthony, jt. auth. see Rooney, Robert.
Lisandrelli, Elaine, jt. auth. see Bartoletti, Susan.
Lishman, Bill. Father Goose & His Goslings. McMaster, Jack, illus. 72p. (Orig.). (gr. k-8). 1992. pap. 9.95 (*0-9623072-8-9*) S Ink WA.
Li Shufen, ed. Legends of Ten Chinese Traditional Festivals. Zhan, Tong, illus. 54p. (gr. 1-3). 1992. pap. 8.95 (*0-8351-2560-2*) China Bks.
Lisi, Victoria, illus. March of the Wooden Soldiers. 48p. (ps-2). 1992. 5.95 (*0-88101-261-0*) Unicorn Pub.
Lisicky, Paul. Uganda. (Illus.). 96p. (gr. 5 up). 1988. lib. bdg. 14.95 (*1-55546-189-1*) Chelsea Hse.
Lisker, Tom. Terror in the Tropics: The Army Ants. LC 77-10765. (Illus.). 48p. (gr. 4 up). 1983. PLB 18.64 (*0-8172-1060-1*) Raintree Steck-V.
Lisle, Janet T. Afternoon of the Elves. LC 88-35099. 128p. (gr. 4-6). 1989. 13.95 (*0-531-05837-9*); PLB 13.99 (*0-531-08437-X*) Orchard Bks Watts.
—Afternoon of the Elves. LC 91-7375. 1991. pap. 2.75 (*0-590-43944-8*, Apple Paperbacks) Scholastic Inc.
—The Dancing Cats of Applesap. Shefts, Joelle, illus. 1985. pap. 2.50 (*0-553-15348-X*, Skylark) Bantam.
—The Dancing Cats of Applesap. Shefts, Joelle, illus. LC 92-1654. 176p. (gr. 3-7). 1993. pap. 3.95 (*0-689-71687-7*, Aladdin) Macmillan Child Grp.

—Forest. LC 93-9630. 160p. (gr. 5 up). 1993. 15.95 (*0-531-06803-X*); PLB 15.99 (*0-531-08653-4*) Orchard Bks Watts.
—The Gold Dust Letters. LC 93-11806. 128p. (gr. 3-5). 1994. 14.95 (*0-531-06830-7*); lib. bdg. 14.99 RLB (*0-531-08680-1*) Orchard Bks Watts.
—The Great Dimpole Oak. Gammell, Stephen, illus. LC 87-11092. 144p. (gr. 4-6). 1987. 11.95 (*0-531-05716-X*); PLB 11.99 (*0-531-08316-0*) Orchard Bks Watts.
—The Lampfish of Twill. Halperin, Wendy A., illus. LC 91-8279. 176p. (gr. 5 up). 1991. 15.95 (*0-531-05963-4*); RLB 15.99 (*0-531-08563-5*) Orchard Bks Watts.
—The Lampfish of Twill. Halperin, Wendy A., illus. 176p. (gr. 3-7). 1993. pap. 2.75 (*0-590-46040-4*, Apple Paperbacks) Scholastic Inc.
—Sirens & Spies. LC 84-21518. 192p. (gr. 7 up). 1985. SBE 13.95 (*0-02-759150-6*, Bradbury Pr) Macmillan Child Grp.
—Sirens & Spies. LC 90-185. 176p. (gr. 7 up). 1990. pap. 3.95 (*0-02-044341-2*, Collier Young Ad) Macmillan Child Grp.
Liss, Howard. The Giant Book of More Strange but True Sports Stories. Mathieu, Joe, illus. LC 83-13236. 160p. (gr. 5-10). 1983. pap. 8.95 (*0-394-85633-3*) Random Bks Yng Read.
—The Giant Book of Strange but True Sports Stories. Mathieu, Joe, illus. LC 76-8132. (gr. 5-9). 1976. 9.00 (*0-394-83287-6*) Random Bks Yng Read.
—Great Black Americans in Science. (Illus.). 160p. (gr. 3-9). 1990. lib. bdg. 14.95 (*0-87460-392-7*) Lion Bks. Postponed.
—Making of a Rookie. (Illus.). (gr. 5-9). 1968. lib. bdg. 3.69 (*0-394-90199-1*) Random Bks Yng Read.
—Playoff: Professional Football's Great Championship Games. LC 66-10675. (Illus.). (gr. 7 up). 1966. pap. 4.50 (*0-440-06939-4*) Delacorte.
Lissauer, T., jt. auth. see Goldman, Meredith.
Litchfield, Ada B. A Button in Her Ear. Rubin, Caroline, ed. Mill, Eleanor, illus. LC 75-28390. 32p. (gr. 2-4). 1976. PLB 13.95 (*0-8075-0987-6*) A Whitman.
—A Cane in Her Hand. Rubin, Caroline, ed. Mill, Eleanor, illus. LC 77-14255. (gr. 1-3). 1977. PLB 13.95 (*0-8075-1016-8*) A Whitman.
—Making Room for Uncle Joe. Tucker, Kathleen, ed. LC 83-17036. (Illus.). 32p. (gr. 3-5). 1984. PLB 11.95 (*0-8075-4952-5*) A Whitman.
—Words in Our Hands. Tucker, Kathleen, ed. Cogancherry, Helen, illus. LC 79-28402. (gr. 2-4). 1980. PLB 13.95 (*0-8075-9212-9*) A Whitman.
Literski, Nicholas S. Joseph Smith's First Vision: A Book for Little Saints. Brower, R. K., illus. 12p. (ps) 1991. 4.95 (*0-9628778-0-8*) Eagle Gate UT.
Lithgow, John, narrated by see Dr. Seuss.
Lithuanian Photographers Staff. Lithuanian Celebrations: Lietuviu Sventes. Algimantas KEZYS Staff, ed. Bindokiene, Danute, intros. by. (ENG & LIT.). 250p. 1990. pap. text ed. 15.00 (*0-9617756-2-9*) Galerija.
Lithwick, Dahlia, jt. ed. see Berger, Larry B.
Litowinsky, Olga. The High Voyage: The Final Crossing of Christopher Columbus. McKeveny, Tom, illus. 160p. (gr. 5-9). 1992. pap. 3.50 (*0-440-40703-6*, YB) Dell.
Litteral, Linda L. Bobos, Iguanas y Otros Animalejos - Boobies, Iguanas & Other Critters: Historia de la Naturaleza en los Galapagos - Nature's Story in the Galapagos. (SPA.). 72p. (gr. 4-9). 1993. 23.00 (*1-883966-02-7*) Am Kestrel Pr.

—Boobies, Iguanas, & Other Critters: Nature's Story in the Galapagos. (Illus.). 72p. (gr. 5-9). 1994. 23.00 (*1-883966-01-9*) Am Kestrel Pr. BOOBIES, IGUANAS & OTHER CRITTERS describes the wildlife, ecology & volcanic features of the Galapagos Islands as well as Darwin's theory of evolution, bird behavior & recent scientific investigation. It is the first book in a series about Biosphere Reserves--areas set aside by the United Nations to be preserved for the future. Readers will enjoy the 15 illustrations & over 115 enticing color photographs which enhance the clearly written prose. SPECIAL FEATURES: designed, written & audience tested to meet the interests & needs of young readers (Gr. 5-9); appeals to adults; presents both general & in-depth information; gives examples of scientific reasoning & experimental inquiry; includes a special section to help young readers write a science report; index & bibliography, also available in Spanish. ABOUT THE AUTHOR: Dr. Linda Litteral is a biologist & educational specialist in writing science for young readers; she is an award winning nature photographer. AVAILABILITY: Order from American Kestrel Press, Department 7, P.O. Box 774723, Steamboat Springs, CO 80477. *Publisher Provided Annotation.*

Littke, Lael. The Day Bird Almost Flew the Coop at Peanut Butter Pond. Britt, Stephanie M., illus. 36p. (ps-1). 1991. pap. 4.95 incl. audiocassette (*1-55999-145-3*) LinguiSystems.
—The Day Porcupine Put on the Dog at Peanut Butter Pond. Britt, Stephanie M., illus. 36p. (ps-1). 1990. pap. 4.95 incl. audiocassette (*1-55999-123-2*) LinguiSystems.
—The Day Snake Saved Time at Peanut Butter Pond. Britt, Stephanie M., illus. 36p. (ps-1). 1990. pap. 4.95 incl. audiocassette (*1-55999-122-4*) LinguiSystems.
—The Day the Critter Sitters Hung It up at Peanut Butter Pond. Britt, Stephanie M., illus. 36p. (ps-1). 1991. pap. 4.95 incl. audiocassette (*1-55999-146-1*) LinguiSystems.
—The Day They Smelled a Skunk at Peanut Butter Pond. Britt, Stephanie M., illus. 36p. (ps-1). 1991. pap. 4.95 incl. audiocassette (*1-55999-144-5*) LinguiSystems.
—The Day Woodchuck Would Chuck Wood at Peanut Butter Pond. Britt, Stephanie M., illus. 36p. (ps-1). 1990. pap. 4.95 incl. audiocassette (*1-55999-124-0*) LinguiSystems.
—Getting Rid of Rhoda. LC 92-25016. 156p. (Orig.). (gr. 3-7). 1992. pap. 4.95 (*0-87579-636-2*) Deseret Bk.
—Loydene in Love. LC 86-12000. 160p. (gr. 7 up). 1986. 13.95 (*0-15-249888-5*, HB Juv Bks) HarBrace.
—The Mystery of Ruby's Ghost. LC 92-25015. 166p. (Orig.). (gr. 3-7). 1992. pap. 4.95 (*0-87579-656-7*) Deseret Bk.
—Olympia Odette Presents: Annie Oakley's Star Studded Stunt. Newsom, Tom & Newsom, Carol, illus. 36p. (ps-3). 1991. pap. 4.95 incl. audiocassette (*1-55999-155-0*) LinguiSystems.
—Olympia Odette Presents: Betsy Ross's Shag-a-Ragged Rainbow. Newsom, Tom & Newsom, Carol, illus. 36p. (ps-3). 1991. pap. 4.95 incl. audiocassette (*1-55999-148-8*) LinguiSystems.
—Olympia Odette Presents: Davy Crockett's Bear-ly Believable. Newsom, Tom & Newsom, Carol, illus. 36p. (ps-3). 1990. pap. 4.95 incl. audiocassette (*1-55999-130-5*) LinguiSystems.
—Olympia Odette Presents: Nails, Rails, & Donkey Tails. Newsom, Tom & Newsom, Carol, illus. 36p. (ps-3). 1991. pap. 4.95 incl. audiocassette (*1-55999-147-X*) LinguiSystems.
—Olympia Odette Presents: Nellie Bly's "In-a-Jam" Telegram. Newsom, Tom & Newsom, Carol, illus. 36p. (ps-3). 1990. pap. 4.95 incl. audiocassette (*1-55999-131-3*) LinguiSystems.
—Olympia Odette Presents: Paul Bunyan's Blue Ox Blues. Newsom, Tom & Newsom, Carol, illus. 36p. (ps-3). 1990. pap. 4.95 incl. audiocassette (*1-55999-129-1*) LinguiSystems.
—Prom Dress. 176p. (Orig.). (gr. 6-10). 1989. pap. 3.25 (*0-590-44237-6*) Scholastic Inc.
—Shanny on Her Own. LC 85-8451. 179p. (gr. 7 up). 1985. 12.95 (*0-15-273531-3*, HB Juv Bks) HarBrace.
—Star of the Show. (Orig.). (gr. 5-9). 1993. pap. 4.95 (*0-685-66956-4*) Deseret Bk.
—Star of the Show. LC 93-27258. 1993. 4.95 (*0-87579-785-7*) Deseret Bk.
—Trish for President. LC 84-4587. 160p. (gr. 7 up). 1984. 13.95 (*0-15-290512-X*, HB Juv Bks) HarBrace.
—Where the Creeks Meet. LC 87-15592. 132p. (gr. 6-12). 1989. pap. 4.95 (*0-87579-229-4*) Deseret Bk.
Little Brown Staff. George Balanchine's the Nutcracker, Vol. 1: A Keepsake Edition. (gr. 4-7). 1993. 8.95 (*0-316-23154-1*) Little.
Little, Carl, ed. see Farrar, Susan C.
Little, Carl, ed. see Gjelfriend, George E.
Little, Carl, ed. see McMahon, James.
Little, Carl, ed. see May, Daryl & Bansemer, Roger.
Little, Emily. David & the Giant. Wilhelm, Hans, illus. LC 86-22079. 48p. (ps-1). 1987. lib. bdg. 7.99 (*0-394-98867-1*); pap. 3.50 (*0-394-88867-7*) Random Bks Yng Read.
—The Trojan Horse: How the Greeks Won the War. Eagle, Michael, illus. LC 87-43118. 48p. (Orig.). (gr. 2-4). 1988. lib. bdg. 7.99 (*0-394-99674-7*); pap. 2.95 (*0-394-89674-2*) Random Bks Yng Read.
Little, Greta D., ed. see Cranch, Christopher P.
Little, Jack. Moon of Isis. LC 76-8728. (gr. 5 up). 1976. pap. 4.00 (*0-934768-00-5*) Altair Pr.
—Thunder Egg. LC 77-94288. (gr. 5 up). 1978. pap. 4.00 (*0-934768-01-3*) Altair Pr.
Little, Jane. Sneaker Hill. Grossman, Nancy, illus. LC 90-23766. 192p. (gr. 3-7). 1991. pap. 3.95 (*0-689-71477-7*, Aladdin) Macmillan Child Grp.
—Spook. Larsen, Suzanne K., illus. LC 90-31296. 128p. (gr. 2-5). 1990. pap. 3.95 (*0-689-71417-3*, Aladdin) Macmillan Child Grp.
Little, Jean. Different Dragons. (gr. 3-6). 1987. pap. 14.95 (*0-670-80836-9*) Viking Child Bks.
—Different Dragons. Fernandez, Laura, illus. 144p. (gr. 3-7). 1989. pap. 3.95 (*0-14-031998-0*, Puffin) Puffin Bks.

—From Anna. Sandin, Joan, illus. LC 72-76505. 208p. (gr. 4-6). 1972. PLB 14.89 (0-06-023912-3) HarpC Child Bks.

—From Anna. Sandin, Joan, illus. LC 72-76505. 208p. (gr. 4-6). 1973. pap. 3.95 (0-06-440044-1, Trophy) HarpC Child Bks.

—Hey, World, Here I Am! Truesdell, Sue, illus. LC 88-10987. 96p. (gr. 3-7). 1989. 13.00i (0-06-023989-1); PLB 12.89 (0-06-024006-7) HarpC Child Bks.

—Hey World, Here I Am! Truesdell, Sue, illus. LC 88-10987. 96p. (gr. 4 up). 1990. pap. 3.95 (0-06-440384-X, Trophy) HarpC Child Bks.

—Home from Far. Lazare, Jerry, illus. (gr. 5 up). 1989. 14.95 (0-316-52792-0); pap. 4.95 (0-316-52802-1) Little.

—Jess Was the Brave One. Wilson, Janet, illus. 32p. (ps-3). 1992. 13.95 (0-670-83495-5) Viking Child Bks.

—Kate. LC 20-148419. 174p. (gr. 5-8). 1973. pap. 3.95 (0-06-440037-9, Trophy) HarpC Child Bks.

—Listen for the Singing. LC 90-40250. 272p. (gr. 4-7). 1991. pap. 3.95 (0-06-440394-7, Trophy) HarpC Child Bks.

—Listen for the Singing. LC 90-40019. 272p. (gr. 4-7). 1991. PLB 14.89 (0-06-023910-7) HarpC Child Bks.

—Little by Little: A Writer's Childhood. (Illus.). 224p. (gr. 5-9). 1988. pap. 13.95 (0-670-81649-3) Viking Child Bks.

—Little by Little: A Writer's Education. (Illus.). 240p. (gr. 5-9). 1991. pap. 3.95 (0-14-032325-2, Puffin) Puffin Bks.

—Look Through My Window. Sandin, Joan, illus. LC 71-105470. 270p. (gr. 4-7). 1970. PLB 14.89 (0-06-023924-7) HarpC Child Bks.

—Lost & Found. O'Young, Leoung, photos by. (gr. 2-5). 1988. pap. 9.95 (0-14-031997-2, Puffin) Puffin Bks.

—Mama's Going to Buy You a Mockingbird. LC 84-20877. 208p. (gr. 4-6). 1985. pap. 13.95 (0-670-80346-4) Viking Child Bks.

—Mama's Going to Buy You a Mockingbird. 208p. (gr. 5-9). 1986. pap. 3.95 (0-14-031737-6, Puffin) Puffin Bks.

—Mine for Keeps. Parker, Lewis, illus. (gr. 3-7). 1988. pap. 4.95 (0-316-52800-5) Little.

—One to Grow On. (gr. 4-7). 1991. pap. 3.95 (0-14-034667-8, Puffin) Puffin Bks.

—Revenge of the Small Small. Wilson, Janet, illus. 32p. (ps-3). 1993. 14.00 (0-670-84471-3) Viking Child Bks.

—Stars Come Out Within. (gr. 4-7). 1991. 15.00 (0-670-82965-X) Viking Child Bks.

Little, Jean & De Vries, Maggie. Once upon a Golden Apple. Gilman, Phoebe, illus. 32p. (ps-3). 1991. 12.95 (0-670-82963-3) Viking Child Bks.

—Once upon a Golden Apple. Gilman, Phoebe, illus. 32p. (ps-3). 1994. pap. 4.99 (0-14-054164-0) Puffin Bks.

Little, Karen E. Monkey Match. (ps-1). 1981. 4.50 (0-913545-03-1) Moonlight FL.

—Penguin Partners. (Illus.). (ps-1). 1981. 4.50 (0-913545-05-8) Moonlight FL.

—Things on Wheels. (Illus.). 24p. (gr. 2-4). 1987. pap. 3.95 (0-7460-0090-1) EDC.

Little, Karen E. & Thomas, A. Things That Fly. (Illus.). 24p. (gr. 2-4). 1987. pap. 3.95 (0-7460-0104-5) EDC.

—Wings, Wheels & Water. (Illus.). 72p. (gr. 2-4). 1988. 12.95 (0-7460-0106-1) EDC.

Little, Lessie J. Children of Long Ago: Poems. Gilchrist, Jan S., illus. 32p. (gr. 2-5). 1988. 14.95 (0-399-21473-9, Philomel Bks) Putnam Pub Group.

Little, Lessie J. & Greenfield, Eloise. I Can Do It by Myself. Byard, Carole, illus. LC 77-11554. (gr. k-2). 1978. (Crowell Jr Bks); PLB 14.89 (0-690-03851-8) HarpC Child Bks.

Little, Lessie J., jt. auth. see Greenfield, Eloise.

Little, Marjorie. Diabetes. (Illus.). 112p. (gr. 6-12). 1991. 18.95 (0-7910-0061-3) Chelsea Hse.

—The Endocrine System. (Illus.). 112p. (gr. 6-12). 1990. 18.95 (0-7910-0016-8) Chelsea Hse.

—Sexually Transmitted Diseases. (Illus.). 112p. (gr. 6-12). 1991. 18.95 (0-7910-0080-X) Chelsea Hse.

Little, Mary E. Old Cat & the Kitten. 128p. (gr. 3-7). 1994. pap. 3.95 (0-689-71800-4, Aladdin) Macmillan Child Grp.

Littlechild, George. This Land Is My Land. (Illus.). 32p. (gr. 3-8). 1993. 15.95 (0-89239-119-7) Childrens Book Pr.

Littledale, Freya. Brave Little Tailor. 1990. pap. 2.50 (0-590-42797-0) Scholastic Inc.

—The Elves & the Shoemaker. 32p. 1991. pap. 3.95 (0-590-44855-2, Blue Ribbon Bks) Scholastic Inc.

—The Farmer in the Soup. Delaney, Molly, illus. 32p. (Orig.). (gr. k-3). 1987. pap. 2.50 (0-590-42535-8) Scholastic Inc.

—The Magic Fish. Pels, Winslow P., illus. 32p. (Orig.). (gr. k-3). 1986. pap. 2.50 (0-590-41100-4) Scholastic Inc.

—Peter & the North Wind. Howell, Troy, illus. 32p. (gr. k-3). 1989. pap. 2.50 (0-590-40629-9) Scholastic Inc.

—Rip Van Winkle. Dooling, Mike, illus. 40p. 1991. pap. 3.95 (0-590-43113-7) Scholastic Inc.

—The Snow Child. Lavallee, Barbara & Shtainmets, Leon, illus. 32p. (gr. 2-5). 1989. pap. 2.50 (0-590-42141-7) Scholastic Inc.

—Stories of Ghosts, Witches, & Demons. (gr. 4-7). 1992. pap. 2.95 (0-590-45556-7) Scholastic Inc.

Littledale, Freya, adapted by. The Legend of Sleepy Hollow. 1992. 3.95 (0-590-45050-6) Scholastic Inc.

Littledale, Freya, as told by. The Little Mermaid. San Souci, Daniel, illus. 40p. (Orig.). (gr. k-3). 1986. pap. 3.95 (0-590-44358-5) Scholastic Inc.

Littlefield, Bill. Champions: Their Glory & Beyond. Fuchs, Bernie, illus. Deford, Frank, frwd. by. LC 92-31390. 1993. 21.95 (0-316-52805-6) Little.

Littlefield, Kathy M. & Littlefield, Robert S. Let's Debate! Stark, Steve, illus. 36p. (Orig.). (gr. 3-6). 1989. pap. text ed. 8.95 (1-879340-03-8, K0104) Kidspeak.

—Let's Work Together! Stark, Steve, illus. 32p. (Orig.). (gr. 3-6). 1991. pap. text ed. 8.95 (1-879340-08-9, K0109) Kidspeak.

—Read to Me! Stark, Steve, illus. 28p. (Orig.). (gr. 3-6). 1990. pap. text ed. 8.95 (1-879340-04-6, K0105) Kidspeak.

—Speak Up! Stark, Steve, illus. 32p. (Orig.). (gr. 3-6). 1989. pap. text ed. 8.95 (1-879340-00-3, K0101) Kidspeak.

—Tell Me a Story! Stark, Steve, illus. 32p. (Orig.). (gr. 3-6). 1989. pap. text ed. 8.95 (1-879340-02-X, K0103) Kidspeak.

—What Did You Say? Stark, Steve, illus. 32p. (Orig.). (gr. 3-6). 1989. pap. text ed. 8.95 (1-879340-01-1, K0102) Kidspeak.

—What's Your Point? Stark, Steve, illus. 32p. (Orig.). (gr. 3-6). 1990. pap. text ed. 8.95 (1-879340-05-4, K0106) Kidspeak.

Littlefield, Robert S. & Ball, Jane A. Tell Me the Way It Was... Stark, Steve, illus. 32p. (Orig.). (gr. 3-6). 1990. pap. text ed. 8.95 (1-879340-07-0, K0108) Kidspeak.

—Who Am I? Who Are They? Stark, Steve, illus. 28p. (Orig.). (gr. 3-6). 1990. pap. text ed. 8.95 (1-879340-06-2, K0107) Kidspeak.

Littlefield, Robert S., jt. auth. see Littlefield, Kathy M.

Littlejohn, Beth, ed. see Russell, Ching Y.

Littlejohn, Claire, illus. Aesop's Fables: A Pull-the-Tab-Pop-Up-Book. LC 87-24478. 14p. (ps up). 1988. 13.95 (0-8037-0487-9) Dial Bks Young.

Littlejohn, E. G. Texas History Stories. LC 86-62880. (Illus.). 188p. (gr. 3-7). 1986. pap. 9.95 (0-938349-07-4); wkbk. 6.95 (0-938349-10-4) State House Pr.

Littler, A., jt. auth. see Amery, H.

Littler, Angela. What Can You Do-Lib. 1988. 3.95 (0-671-67230-4, J Messner) S&S Trade.

—What Can You Feel-Lib. 1988. 3.95 (0-671-67231-2, J Messner) S&S Trade.

—What Can You Hear-Lib. 1988. 3.95 (0-671-67229-0, J Messner) S&S Trade.

—What Can You See. Galvani, Maureen & Littler, Angela, illus. 20p. (ps-1). 1988. (J Messner); 3.95 (0-671-67228-2) S&S Trade.

—What Can You Series, 4 bks. Galvani, Maureen, illus. 20p. (gr. 2-5). 1988. Set. 15.80 (0-671-93015-X, J Messner) S&S Trade.

Littlesugar, Amy. The Spinster's Daughter. Quackenbush, Robert, illus. 40p. (gr. 1-4). 1993. PLB 14.95 (0-945912-22-6) Pippin Pr.

Littleton, Mark. Filling' Up. Evans, Graci, illus. 168p. 1993. 8.99 (0-945564-72-4, Gold & Honey Books) Questar Pubs.

—Secrets of Moonlight Mountain. 1993. pap. 3.99 (1-56507-960-4) Harvest Hse.

—Tree Fort Wars. LC 92-44181. (gr. 4 up). 1993. write for info. (1-555-13764-4, Chariot Bks) Cook.

—Tunin' Up: Daily Jammin' for Tight Relationships. Heaney, Liz, ed. 208p. 1992. pap. 8.99 (0-88070-454-3, Gold & Honey) Questar Pubs.

—When They Invited Me to Fellowship I Thought They Meant a Cruise. 166p. (Orig.). 1992. pap. 7.99 (0-87509-496-1) Chr Pubns.

—Winter Thunder. LC 92-5433. 1993. pap. 3.99 (1-56507-008-9) Harvest Hse.

Littleton, Mark R. Beefin' Up: Daily Feed for Amazing Grazing. Heaney, Liz, ed. LC 89-29297. 181p. (Orig.). (gr. 7-12). 1992. pap. 9.99 (0-88070-317-2, Gold & Honey) Questar Pubs.

Littlewood, Barbara S., jt. auth. see Hansjurgen Press.

Littlewood, Valerie. Scarecrow. (Illus.). 32p. (gr. 2-6). 1992. 15.00 (0-525-44948-5, DCB) Dutton Child Bks.

Littman, Mark & Willcox, Ken. Totality: Eclipses of the Sun. LC 90-23823. (Illus.). 264p. (Orig.). 1991. pap. 14.95 (0-8248-1371-5) UH Pr.

Litvin, Jay, jt. auth. see Salk, Lee.

Litz, A. Walton, ed. see Hardy, Thomas.

Litzinger, Roseanne. The Old Woman & Her Pig: An Old English Tale. LC 91-38227. (ps). 1993. 13.95 (0-15-257802-1) HarBrace.

Liu, Sarah & Vittitow, Mary L. Learning Games Without Losers. (Illus.). 96p. (gr. 2-6). 1985. guide 8.95 (0-86530-039-9, IP 39-9) Incentive Pubns.

Liu, Sarah, jt. auth. see Vittitow, Mary L.

Liu Qian. Panda Bear Goes Visiting. (Illus.). 22p. (gr. 3-4). 1982. 3.95 (0-8351-1108-3); pap. 2.95 (0-8351-1139-3) China Bks.

Lively, Penelope. The Cat, the Crow, & the Banyan Tree. Milne, Terry, illus. LC 93-22355. (ps-3). write for info. (1-56402-325-7) Candlewick Pr.

—Dragon Trouble. Lively, Penelope, illus. 42p. (gr. 2-4). 1989. 3.95 (0-8120-6136-5) Barron.

—The Ghost of Thomas Kempe. Maitland, Anthony, illus. LC 73-77456. 192p. (gr. 3-6). 1973. 14.95 (0-525-30495-9, DCB) Dutton Child Bks.

—House Inside Out. large type ed. 176p. (gr. 4-7). 1989. lib. bdg. 17.50 (0-7451-0957-8, Lythway Large Print) Hall.

—The Revenge of Samuel Stokes. large type ed. 216p. 1991. 13.95 (0-7451-1406-7, Galaxy Child Lrg Print) Chivers N Amer.

—A Stitch in Time. large type ed. 264p. (gr. 5 up). 1988. 13.95 (0-7451-0726-5, Galaxy Child Lrg Print) Chivers N Amer.

—The Voyage of QV66. large type ed. Jones, Harold, illus. 280p. 1992. 13.95 (0-7451-1548-9, Galaxy Child Lrg Print) Chivers N Amer.

—The Whispering Knights. large type ed. 248p. (gr. 3 up). 1990. 13.95 (0-7451-1153-X, Galaxy Child Lrg Print) Chivers N Amer.

Livezey, Robert, jt. auth. see Brown, Vinson.

Livingston. More Small Stones. Date not set. 14.00 (0-06-023008-8, Festival); PLB 13.89 (0-06-023009-6, Festival) HarpC Child Bks.

Livingston, Carole. Why Was I Adopted? Robins, Arthur, illus. (gr. 1 up). 1978. text ed. 12.00 (0-8184-0257-1) Carol Pub Group.

Livingston, Carole & Ciliotta, Claire. Why Am I Going to the Hospital? Walter, Paul, illus. (gr. 1 up). 1981. 12.00 (0-8184-0316-0) Carol Pub Group.

Livingston, Carole, jt. auth. see Ciliotta, Claire.

Livingston, Cohn. Space Songs. Fisher, Leonard E., illus. (ps-3). 1993. pap. 5.95 (0-8234-1029-3) Holiday.

Livingston, J. B. If I Were a Teenager: Pupil Book, 4 vols. 1966. pap. 2.35 ea. Quality Pubns.

Livingston, Julie, ed. see Sollie, Eddie C.

Livingston, Julie, ed. see Wang, Rosalind.

Livingston, Malcolm, illus. How Many Birds? 16p. (ps). 1986. 3.95 (0-86020-962-8) EDC.

—How Many Monkeys? 16p. (ps). 1986. 3.95 (0-86020-961-X) EDC.

—How Many Monsters? 16p. (ps). 1986. 3.95 (0-86020-960-1) EDC.

Livingston, Myra C. Abraham Lincoln: A Man for All the People: A Ballad. Byrd, Samuel, illus. LC 93-2731. 1993. 15.95 (0-8234-1049-8) Holiday.

—Birthday Poems. Tomes, Margot, illus. LC 89-2114. 32p. (ps-3). 1989. reinforced bdg. 13.95 (0-8234-0783-7) Holiday.

—Celebrations. Fisher, Leonard E., illus. LC 84-19216. 32p. (ps-3). 1985. reinforced bdg. 15.95 (0-8234-0550-8); pap. 5.95 (0-8234-0654-7) Holiday.

—A Circle of Seasons. Fisher, Leonard E., illus. LC 81-20305. 32p. (ps-3). 1982. reinforced bdg. 15.95 (0-8234-0452-8); pap. 5.95 (0-8234-0656-3) Holiday.

—Dilly Dilly Piccalilli: Poems for the Very Young. Christelow, Eileen, illus. (gr. 1 up). 1989. SBE 12.95 (0-689-50466-7, M K McElderry) Macmillan Child Grp.

—Earth Songs. Fisher, Leonard E., illus. LC 86-341. 32p. (ps-4). 1986. reinforced bdg. 14.95 (0-8234-0615-6) Holiday.

—Higgledy-Piggledy: Verses & Pictures. Peter, Sis, illus. LC 86-8789. 32p. (gr. 3-7). 1986. SBE 11.95 (0-689-50407-1, M K McElderry) Macmillan Child Grp.

—I Like You, If You Like Me: Poems of Friendship. LC 86-21108. 160p. (gr. 5 up). 1987. SBE 13.95 (0-689-50408-X, M K McElderry) Macmillan Child Grp.

—I Never Told: And Other Poems. Pinkney, Brian, contrib. by. LC 91-20475. 48p. (gr. 3-7). 1992. SBE 11.95 (0-689-50544-2, M K McElderry) Macmillan Child Grp.

—If the Owl Calls Again: A Collection of Owl Poems. Frasconi, Antonio, illus. LC 89-27659. 128p. (gr. 5 up). 1990. SBE 13.95 (0-689-50501-9, M K McElderry) Macmillan Child Grp.

—Let Freedom Ring: A Ballad of Martin Luther King, Jr. Byrd, Samuel, illus. LC 91-28245. 32p. (ps-3). 1992. reinforced bdg. 15.95 (0-8234-0957-0) Holiday.

—Light & Shadow. Rogasky, Barbara, photos by. LC 91-22355. (Illus.). 32p. (ps-3). 1992. reinforced bdg. 14.95 (0-8234-0931-7) Holiday.

—Monkey Puzzle & Other Poems. Frasconi, Antonio, illus. LC 84-3050. 64p. (gr. 6 up). 1984. SBE 12.95 (0-689-50310-5, M K McElderry) Macmillan Child Grp.

—My Head Is Red & Other Riddle Rhymes. LoPrete, Tere, illus. LC 89-24528. 32p. (ps-3). 1990. reinforced bdg. 12.95 (0-8234-0806-X) Holiday.

—Poem-Making: Ways to Begin Writing Poetry. LC 90-5012. 176p. (gr. 4-8). 1991. 16.00 (0-06-024019-9); PLB 15.89 (0-06-024020-2) HarpC Child Bks.

—Poems for Mothers. Ray, Deborah K., illus. LC 87-19629. 32p. (ps-3). 1988. reinforced bdg. 13.95 (0-8234-0678-4) Holiday.

—Poems of Christmas. LC 80-13627. 132p. (gr. 5 up). 1980. SBE 14.95 (0-689-50180-3, M K McElderry) Macmillan Child Grp.

—Remembering & Other Poems. LC 89-2654. 64p. (gr. 3-7). 1989. SBE 12.95 (0-689-50489-6, M K McElderry) Macmillan Child Grp.

—Sky Songs. Fisher, Leonard E., illus. LC 83-12955. 32p. (ps-4). 1984. reinforced bdg. 14.95 (0-8234-0502-8) Holiday.

—A Song I Sang to You: A Selection of Poems. Tomes, Margot, illus. LC 84-4585. 84p. (ps-3). 1984. 12.95 (0-15-277105-0, HB Juv Bks) HarBrace.

—Space Songs. Fisher, Leonard E., illus. LC 87-19628. 32p. (ps-3). 1988. reinforced bdg. 15.95 (0-8234-0675-X) Holiday.

—There Was a Place: And Other Poems. LC 88-12832. 40p. (gr. 3-7). 1988. SBE 12.95 (0-689-50464-0, M K McElderry) Macmillan Child Grp.

—A Time to Talk: Poems of Friendship. Pinkney, Brian, illus. LC 91-42234. 128p. (gr. 7 up). 1992. SBE 12.95 (0-689-50558-2, M K McElderry) Macmillan Child Grp.

—Up in the Air. Fisher, Leonard E., illus. LC 88-23293. 32p. (ps-3). 1989. reinforced bdg. 14.95 (0-8234-0736-5) Holiday.

—Valentine Poems. Livingston, Myra C., selected by. LC 85-31723. (Illus.). 32p. (ps-3). 1987. reinforced bdg. 14.95 (0-8234-0587-7) Holiday.

—Why Am I Grown So Cold? Poems of the Unknowable. LC 82-6646. 264p. (gr. 5up). 1982. SBE 14.95 (0-689-50242-7, M K McElderry) Macmillan Child Grp.

—Worlds I Know & Other Poems. Arnold, Tim, illus. LC 85-7344. 64p. (gr. 4-7). 1985. SBE 13.95 (0-689-50332-6, M K McElderry) Macmillan Child Grp.

Livingston, Myra C., compiled by. Cat Poems. Hyman, Trina S., illus. LC 86-14810. 32p. (ps-3). 1987. reinforced bdg. 13.95 (0-8234-0631-8) Holiday.

Livingston, Myra C., selected by. Christmas Poems. Hyman, Trina S., illus. LC 83-18559. 32p. (ps-3). 1984. reinforced bdg. 14.95 (0-8234-0508-7) Holiday.

Livingston, Myra C., ed. Dog Poems. Morrill, Leslie, illus. LC 89-2061. 32p. (ps-3). 1990. reinforced 12.95 (0-8234-0776-4) Holiday.

—Easter Poems. Wallner, John, illus. LC 84-15866. 32p. (ps-3). 1985. reinforced bdg. 13.95 (0-8234-0546-X) Holiday.

Livingston, Myra C., selected by. Halloween Poems. Gammell, Stephen, illus. LC 89-1741. 32p. (ps-3). 1989. reinforced bdg. 13.95 (0-8234-0762-4) Holiday.

—If You Ever Meet a Whale: Poems. Fisher, Leonard E., illus. LC 91-36265. 32p. (ps-3). 1992. reinforced bdg. 14.95 (0-8234-0940-6) Holiday.

—Lots of Limericks. Perry, Rebecca, illus. LC 91-329. 144p. (gr. 3 up). 1991. SBE 13.95 (0-689-50531-0, M K McElderry) Macmillan Child Grp.

—New Year's Poems. Tomes, Margot, illus. LC 86-22885. 32p. (ps-3). 1987. reinforced bdg. 12.95 (0-8234-0641-5) Holiday.

—Poems for Brothers, Poems for Sisters. Zallinger, Jean, illus. LC 90-44463. 32p. (ps-3). 1991. reinforced 12.95 (0-8234-0861-2) Holiday.

Livingston, Myra C., ed. Poems for Fathers. Casilla, Robert, illus. LC 88-17010. 32p. (ps-3). 1989. reinforced bdg. 13.95 (0-8234-0729-2) Holiday.

Livingston, Myra C., selected by. Poems for Grandmothers. Cullen-Clark, Patricia, illus. LC 90-55102. 32p. (ps-3). 1990. reinforced 12.95 (0-8234-0830-2) Holiday.

—Poems for Jewish Holidays. Bloom, Lloyd, illus. LC 85-27179. 32p. (ps-4). 1986. reinforced bdg. 13.95 (0-8234-0606-7) Holiday.

—Riddle-Me Rhymes. Perry, Rebecca, illus. LC 93-25179. 96p. (gr. 3-7). 1994. SBE 13.95 (0-689-50602-3, M K McElderry) Macmillan Child Grp.

Livingston, Myra C., ed. Roll Along: Poems on Wheels. LC 92-32714. 80p. (gr. 4 up). 1993. SBE 11.95 (0-689-50585-X, M K McElderry) Macmillan Child Grp.

—Thanksgiving Poems. Gammell, Stephen, illus. LC 85-762. 32p. (ps-4). 1985. reinforced bdg. 14.95 (0-8234-0570-2) Holiday.

Livingston, Myra C., jt. ed. see Farber, Norma.
Livingston, Myra C., tr. see Jimenez, Juan R.
Livingston, P. Gullible the Seagull. (Illus., Orig.). (gr. k-6). 1992. pap. 9.95 (0-9629860-2-X) Sound Pub WA.

Livingstone, Ian & Jackson, Steve. Trial of Champions. (Orig.). (gr. k-12). 1987. pap. 2.50 (0-440-98689-3, LFL) Dell.

Livingstone, Ian, jt. auth. see Jackson, Steve.
Livo, Norma J., ed. see Miller, Teresa & Pellowski, Anne.

Livoni, Cathy. Element of Time. LC 82-48761. 192p. (gr. 7 up). 1983. 12.95 (0-15-225369-6, HB Juv Bks) HarBrace.

Lizon, Karen H. Colonial American Holidays & Entertainment. LC 92-40262. 1993. 12.90 (0-531-12546-7) Watts.

Llewellyn, Claire. First Look at Clothes. LC 91-9425. (Illus.). 32p. (gr. 1-2). 1991. PLB 15.93 (0-8368-0677-8) Gareth Stevens Inc.

—First Look at Growing Food. LC 91-9424. (Illus.). 32p. (gr. 1-2). 1991. PLB 15.93 (0-8368-0678-6) Gareth Stevens Inc.

—First Look at Keeping Warm. LC 91-9423. (Illus.). 32p. (gr. 1-2). 1991. PLB 15.93 (0-8368-0704-9) Gareth Stevens Inc.

—First Look in the Air. (Illus.). 32p. (gr. 1-2). 1991. PLB 15.93 (0-8368-0701-4) Gareth Stevens Inc.

—My First Book of Time. LC 91-58194. (Illus.). 32p. (ps-3). 1992. 14.95 (1-879431-78-5) Dorling Kindersley.

Llewellyn, Grace. The Teenage Liberation Handbook: How to Quit School & Get a Real Life & Education. 401p. (gr. 7-12). 1991. pap. 14.95 (0-9629591-0-3) Lowry Hse.

Llewellyn, Grace, intro. by. Real Lives: Eleven Teenagers Who Don't Go to School. (Illus.). 320p. (gr. 7-12). 1993. pap. 14.95 (0-9629591-3-8, LC32.R) Lowry Hse.

Llorente, Pilar M. Apprentice. (gr. 4-7). 1993. 13.00 (0-374-30389-4) FS&G.

Lloyd, jt. auth. see Guiberson.

Lloyd, Charles, ed. The Roman Family: A Bridge to Roman Culture, Values & Literature. 191p. (Orig.). (gr. 9-12). 1991. spiral bdg. 11.30 (0-939507-35-8, B308) Amer Classical.

Lloyd, Dana O. Ho Chi Minh. (Illus.). 112p. (gr. 5 up). 1987. lib. bdg. 17.95x (0-87754-571-5) Chelsea Hse.

Lloyd, David. Hello, Goodbye. Voce, Louise, illus. LC 87-17110. (ps-1). 1988. 12.95 (0-688-07698-X); lib. bdg. 12.88 (0-688-07699-8) Lothrop.

—My First Library. (ps-3). 1993. 16.00 (0-89577-527-1, Readers Digest Kids) RD Assn.

—The Sneeze. Wegner, Fritz, illus. LC 85-46022. 32p. (ps-2). 1986. PLB 11.89 (0-685-12397-9, Lipp Jr Bks) HarpC Child Bks.

LLoyd, David, jt. auth. see Ormerod, Jan.
Lloyd, Ernest, ed. Scrapbook Stories: Character Building Stories from Yesteryear. (Illus.). 96p. (gr. 5 up). 1990. pap. 5.95 (0-945460-08-2) Upward Way.

Lloyd, Errol. Sasha & the Bicycle Thieves. (Illus.). 42p. (gr. 2-4). 1989. 3.95 (0-8120-6141-1) Barron.

Lloyd, Jeremy. Woodland Gospels: According to Captain Beaky & His Band. Percy, Graham, illus. LC 83-20790. 63p. (gr. k up). 1984. pap. 4.95 (0-571-14285-0) Faber & Faber.

Lloyd, Sue. The Phonics Handbook. Stephen, Lib, illus. 218p. (ps-3). 1993. pap. 19.95 (1-870946-08-1, Pub. by Jolly Lrning UK) Am Intl Dist.

Lloyd, Sue & Wernham, Sara. Finger Phonics, 7 bks. Stephen, Lib, illus. (ps-2). 1994. Set. 39.50 (1-870946-31-6, Pub. by Jolly Lrning UK) Am Intl Dist.

—Finger Phonics, Bk. 1: S, A, T, I, P, N. Stephen, Lib, illus. 14p. (ps-2). 1994. 5.95 (1-870946-24-3, Pub. by Jolly Lrning UK) Am Intl Dist.

—Finger Phonics, Bk. 2: CK, E, H, R, M, D. Stephen, Lib, illus. 14p. (ps-2). 1994. 5.95 (1-870946-25-1, Pub. by Jolly Lrning UK) Am Intl Dist.

—Finger Phonics, Bk. 3: G, O, U, L, F, B. Stephen, Lib, illus. 14p. (ps-2). 1994. 5.95 (1-870946-26-X, Pub. by Jolly Lrning UK) Am Intl Dist.

—Finger Phonics, Bk. 4: AI, J, OA, IE, EE, OR. Stephen, Lib, illus. 14p. (ps-2). 1994. 5.95 (1-870946-27-8, Pub. by Jolly Lrning UK) Am Intl Dist.

—Finger Phonics, Bk. 5: Z, W, NG, V, OO, OO. Stephen, Lib, illus. 14p. (ps-2). 1994. 5.95 (1-870946-28-6, Pub. by Jolly Lrning UK) Am Intl Dist.

—Finger Phonics, Bk. 6: Y, X, CH, SH, TH, TH. Stephen, Lib, illus. 14p. (ps-2). 1994. 5.95 (1-870946-29-4, Pub. by Jolly Lrning UK) Am Intl Dist.

—Finger Phonics, Bk. 7: QU, OU, OI, UE, ER, AR. Stephen, Lib, illus. 14p. (ps-2). 1994. 5.95 (1-870946-30-8, Pub. by Jolly Lrning UK) Am Intl Dist.

—Phonic Wall Frieze. Stephen, Lib, illus. (ps-2). 1994. 8.95 (1-870946-32-4, Pub. by Jolly Lrning UK) Am Intl Dist.

Llywelyn, Morgan. Brian Boru: Emperor of the Irish. 160p. (Orig.). (gr. 4 up). 1990. pap. 8.95 (0-86278-230-9, Pub. by OBrien Pr IE) Dufour.

—Xerxes. Schlesinger, Arthur M., Jr., intro. by. (Illus.). 112p. (gr. 5 up). 1988. lib. bdg. 17.95 (0-87754-447-6) Chelsea Hse.

Loan, Derek van see Keith, Ian & Van Loan, Derek.
Loback, Tom. Halls of the Elven-King. Ruemmler, John D., ed. Martin, David, illus. 32p. (Orig.). (gr. 12). 1988. pap. 6.00 (1-55806-015-4, 8204) Iron Crown Ent Inc.

Lobato, Arcadio. The Greatest Treasure. Lobato, Arcadio, illus. LC 89-3612. 28p. (ps up). 1991. pap. 14.95 (0-88708-093-6) Picture Bk Studio.

—Just One Wish. Clements, Andrew, tr. from GER. Lobato, Arcadio, illus. LC 89-49263. 32p. (ps up). 1991. pap. 14.95 (0-88708-134-7) Picture Bk Studio.

—Paper Bird. Urberuaga, Emilio, illus. LC 93-24469. 1994. 18.95 (0-87614-817-8) Carolrhoda Bks.

Lobban, R. D. Edinburgh & the Medical Revolution. LC 78-51669. (Illus.). 48p. (gr. 7 up). 1980. pap. 6.95 (0-521-22028-9) Cambridge U Pr.

Lobby, Ted. Jessica & the Wolf: A Story for Children Who Have Bad Dreams. Dixon, Tennessee, illus. LC 92-56872. 1993. PLB 17.26 (0-8368-0933-5) Gareth Stevens Inc.

Lobby, Theodore E. Jessica & the Wolf: A Story for Children Who Have Bad Dreams. Dixon, Tennessee, illus. LC 89-29688. 32p. (gr. k-3). 1990. 16.95 (0-945354-22-3); pap. 6.95 (0-945354-21-5) Magination Pr.

Lobe, Mira. Ben & the Child of the Forest. Sklenitzka, Franz S., illus. 96p. (gr. 3-4). 1988. pap. 2.95 (0-8120-3936-X) Barron.

—The Snowman Who Went for a Walk. Opgenoorth, Winifried, illus. LC 83-27298. 32p. (ps-2). 1984. 11.95 (0-688-03865-4); PLB 11.88 (0-688-03866-2) Morrow Jr Bks.

Lobel. On Market Street. 1993. pap. 28.67 (0-590-71697-2) Scholastic Inc.

Lobel, Anita. Alison's Zinnia. LC 89-23700. (Illus.). 32p. (ps up). 1990. 15.00 (0-688-08865-1); PLB 14.93 (0-688-08866-X) Greenwillow.

—The Dwarf Giant. Lobel, Anita, illus. LC 90-39214. 32p. (ps-3). 1991. reinforced 14.95 (0-8234-0852-3) Holiday.

—Pancake. (ps-3). 1992. pap. 2.99 (0-440-40624-2) Dell.

—Pierrot's ABC Garden. (Illus.). 24p. (ps-k). 1992. write for info. (0-307-00139-3, 312-04, Golden Pr) Western Pub.

—Pierrot's ABC Garden. (ps-3). 1993. 12.95 (0-307-17551-0, Artsts Writrs) Western Pub.

—Sven's Bridge. LC 91-29544. (Illus.). 32p. (ps-4). 1992. 14.00 (0-688-11251-X); PLB 13.93 (0-688-11252-8) Greenwillow.

Lobel, Arnold. The Book of Pigericks. Lobel, Arnold, illus. LC 82-47730. 48p. (gr. k-3). 1983. PLB 14.89 (0-06-023983-2) HarpC Child Bks.

—The Book of Pigericks (Pig Limericks) Lobel, Arnold, illus. LC 82-47730. 48p. (ps up). 1988. pap. 5.95 (0-06-443163-0, Trophy) HarpC Child Bks.

—Days with Frog & Toad. LC 78-21786. (Illus.). 64p. (gr. k-3). 1979. 14.00i (0-06-023963-8); PLB 13.89 (0-06-023964-6) HarpC Child Bks.

—Days with Frog & Toad. Lobel, Arnold, illus. LC 78-21786. 64p. (ps-3). 1985. (Trophy); pap. 3.50 (0-06-444058-3, Trophy) HarpC Child Bks.

—Days with Frog & Toad. unabr. ed. (Illus.). (ps-3). 1990. pap. 6.95 incl. cassette (1-55994-227-4, Caedmon) HarperAudio.

—Days with Frog & Toad: (Dios con Sapo y Sepo) (SPA). (gr. 1-6). 8.95 (84-204-3743-3) Santillana.

—Fables. Lobel, Arnold, illus. LC 79-2004. 48p. (gr. 1-4). 1980. 15.00 (0-06-023973-5); PLB 14.89 (0-06-023974-3) HarpC Child Bks.

—Fables. LC 79-2004. (Illus.). 48p. (gr. 1-4). 1983. pap. 5.95 (0-06-443046-4, Trophy) HarpC Child Bks.

—Fables: (Fabulas) (SPA). (gr. 1-6). 21.95 (84-204-4552-5) Santillana.

—Frog & Toad All Year. LC 76-2343. (Illus.). 64p. (gr. k-3). 1976. 14.00 (0-06-023950-6); PLB 13.89 (0-06-023951-4) HarpC Child Bks.

—Frog & Toad All Year. Lobel, Arnold, illus. LC 76-2343. 64p. (ps-3). 1985. (Trophy); pap. 3.50 (0-06-444059-1, Trophy) HarpC Child Bks.

—Frog & Toad All Year. unabr. ed. (Illus.). (ps-3). 1990. pap. 6.95 incl. cassette (1-55994-228-2, Caedmon) HarperAudio.

—Frog & Toad Are Friends. Lobel, Arnold, illus. LC 73-105492. 64p. (gr. k-3). 1970. 14.00 (0-06-023957-3); PLB 13.89 (0-06-023958-1) HarpC Child Bks.

—Frog & Toad Are Friends. Lobel, Arnold, illus. LC 73-105492. 64p. (ps-3). 1985. (Trophy); pap. 3.50 (0-06-444020-6, Trophy) HarpC Child Bks.

—Frog & Toad are Friends. unabr. ed. (Illus.). (ps-3). 1990. pap. 6.95 incl. cassette (1-55994-229-0, Caedmon) HarperAudio.

—Frog & Toad Are Friends: (Sapo y Sepo Son Amigos) (SPA). (gr. 1-6). 9.95 (84-204-3043-9) Santillana.

—Frog & Toad Boxed Set, 4 bks. Lobel, Arnold, illus. (gr. k-3). 1994. pap. 14.00 64p. ea. (0-06-444167-9, Trophy) HarpC Child Bks.

—The Frog & Toad Pop-Up Book. Lobel, Arnold, illus. LC 85-45373. 12p. (ps-3). 1986. 9.95i (0-06-023986-7) HarpC Child Bks.

—Frog & Toad Together. Lobel, Arnold, illus. LC 73-183163. 64p. (gr. k-3). 1972. 14.00 (0-06-023959-X); PLB 13.89 (0-06-023960-3) HarpC Child Bks.

—Frog & Toad Together. Lobel, Arnold, illus. LC 73-183163. 64p. (ps-3). 1985. (Trophy); pap. 3.50 (0-06-444021-4, Trophy) HarpC Child Bks.

—Frog & Toad Together. unabr. ed. (Illus.). (ps-3). 1990. pap. 6.95 incl. cassette (1-55994-230-4, Caedmon) HarperAudio.

—Frog & Toad Together: (Sapo y Sepo Inseparables) (SPA). 8.95 (84-204-3047-1) Santillana.

—Giant John. Lobel, Arnold, illus. LC 64-16639. 32p. (gr. k-3). 1964. PLB 14.89 (0-06-022946-2) HarpC Child Bks.

—Grasshopper on the Road. Lobel, Arnold, illus. LC 77-25653. 64p. (gr. k-3). 1978. 14.00 (0-06-023961-1); PLB 13.89 (0-06-023962-X) HarpC Child Bks.

—Grasshopper on the Road. Lobel, Arnold, illus. LC 77-25653. 64p. (gr. k-3). 1986. pap. 3.50 (0-06-444094-X, Trophy) HarpC Child Bks.

—Great Blueness & Other Predicaments. Lobel, Arnold, illus. LC 68-24323. 32p. (ps-3). 1994. pap. 5.95 (0-06-443316-1, Trophy) HarpC Child Bks.

—Gregory Griggs: And Other Nursery Rhyme People. (ps-3). 1987. pap. 3.95 (0-688-07042-6, Mulberry) Morrow.

—Holiday for Mister Muster. Lobel, Arnold, illus. LC 63-15323. 32p. (gr. k-3). 1963. PLB 12.89 (0-06-023956-5) HarpC Child Bks.

—Lucille. LC 64-11616. (Illus.). 64p. (gr. k-3). 1964. PLB 12.89 (0-06-023966-2) HarpC Child Bks.

—Martha the Movie Mouse. Lobel, Arnold, illus. LC 66-18654. 32p. (ps-3). 1993. pap. 4.95 (0-06-443318-8, Trophy) HarpC Child Bks.

—Ming Lo Moves the Mountain. Lobel, Arnold, illus. LC 81-13327. 32p. (gr. k-3). 1982. PLB 14.93 (0-688-00611-6) Greenwillow.

—Ming Lo Moves the Mountain. (ps-3). 1986. pap. 3.95 (0-590-42902-7) Scholastic Inc.

—Ming Lo Moves the Mountain. (Illus.). 32p. 1993. pap. text ed. 4.95 (0-688-10995-0, Mulberry) Morrow.

—Ming Lo Moves the Mountain. (Illus.). 32p. min. alk. (gr. k-4). 1993. 14.95 (0-685-64815-X); audio cass. 11.00 (1-882869-76-1) Read Advent.

—Mouse Soup. Lobel, Arnold, illus. LC 76-41517. 64p. (gr. k-3). 1977. 14.00 (0-06-023967-0); PLB 13.89 (0-06-023968-9) HarpC Child Bks.

—Mouse Soup. Lobel, Arnold, illus. LC 76-41517. 64p. (gr. k-3). 1986. (Trophy); pap. 3.50 (0-06-444041-9, Trophy) HarpC Child Bks.

—Mouse Tales. Lobel, Arnold, illus. LC 66-18654. 64p. (gr. k-3). 1972. 14.00 (0-06-023941-7); PLB 13.89 (0-06-023942-5) HarpC Child Bks.
—Mouse Tales. Lobel, Arnold, illus. LC 72-76511. 64p. (ps-3). 1978. pap. 3.50 (0-06-444013-3, Trophy) HarpC Child Bks.
—On Market Street. Lobel, Anita, illus. LC 80-21418. 40p. (gr. k-3). 1981. 14.00 (0-688-30309-1); PLB 13.93 (0-688-84309-3); Greenwillow.
—On Market Street. Lobel, Anita, illus. LC 80-21418. (ps up). 1989. pap. 4.95 (0-688-08745-0, Mulberry) Morrow.
—On the Day Peter Stuyvesant Sailed into Town. Lobel, Arnold, illus. LC 75-148420. 48p. (ps-3). 1987. pap. 4.95 (0-06-443144-4, Trophy) HarpC Child Bks.
—Owl at Home. Lobel, Arnold, illus. LC 74-2630. 64p. (gr. k-3). 1975. PLB 13.89 (0-06-023949-2) HarpC Child Bks.
—Owl at Home. Lobel, Arnold, illus. LC 74-2630. 64p. (gr. k-3). 1987. incl. cassette 5.98 (0-694-00176-7, Trophy); pap. 3.50 (0-06-444034-6, Trophy) HarpC Child Bks.
—Prince Bertram the Bad. Lobel, Arnold, illus. LC 63-8741. 32p. (gr. k-3). 1963. PLB 13.89 (0-06-023976-X) HarpC Child Bks.
—The Rose in My Garden. Lobel, Anita, illus. LC 83-14097. 40p. (gr. k-3). 1984. 16.00 (0-688-02586-2); PLB 15.93 (0-688-02587-0) Greenwillow.
—The Rose in My Garden. Lobel, Anita, illus. 40p. (ps-2). 1985. pap. 3.95 (0-590-41530-1) Scholastic Inc.
—The Rose in My Garden. Lobel, Anita, illus. LC 92-24588. 40p. (ps). 1993. pap. 4.95 (0-688-12265-5, Mulberry) Morrow.
—Small Pig. Lobel, Arnold, illus. LC 69-10213. 64p. (gr. k-3). 1969. PLB 13.89 (0-06-023932-8) HarpC Child Bks.
—Small Pig. Lobel, Arnold, illus. LC 69-10213. 64p. (gr. k-3). 1988. pap. 3.50 (0-06-444120-2, Trophy) HarpC Child Bks.
—Treeful of Pigs. LC 78-1810. (Illus.). 32p. (gr. k-3). 1979. PLB 13.88 (0-688-84177-5) Greenwillow.
—A Treeful of Pigs. Lobel, Anita, illus. 32p. (gr. k-3). 1988. pap. 3.95 (0-590-41280-9, Blue Ribbon Bks) Scholastic Inc.
—The Turnaround Wind. Lobel, Arnold, illus. LC 87-45293. 32p. (ps-3). 1988. PLB 12.89 (0-06-023988-3) HarpC Child Bks.
—Uncle Elephant. Lobel, Arnold, illus. LC 80-8944. 64p. (gr. k-3). 1981. 14.00 (0-06-023979-4); PLB 13.89 (0-06-023980-8) HarpC Child Bks.
—Uncle Elephant. LC 80-8944. (Illus.). 64p. (gr. k-3). 1986. pap. 3.50 (0-06-444104-0, Trophy) HarpC Child Bks.
—Whiskers & Rhymes. Lobel, Arnold, illus. LC 83-25424. 48p. (gr. k-3). 1985. 13.00 (0-688-03835-2); lib. bdg. 12.88 (0-688-03836-0) Greenwillow.
—Whiskers & Rhymes. LC 83-25424. 1988. pap. 4.95 (0-688-08291-2, Mulberry) Morrow.
—Zoo for Mister Muster. LC 62-7313. (Illus.). 32p. (ps-3). 1962. PLB 12.89 (0-06-023991-3) HarpC Child Bks.
Lobel, Arnold, jt. auth. see Moore, Lilian.
Lobel, Arnold, jt. auth. see Parish, Peggy.
Lobel, Arnold, selected by. & illus. The Random House Book of Mother Goose: A Treasury of 306 Timeless Nursery Rhymes. LC 86-47532. 176p. (gr. 2-6). 1986. 16.00 (0-394-86799-8); lib. bdg. 16.99 (0-394-96799-2, Random Juv) Random Bks Yng Read.
Lobel, Arnold, illus. The Just Right Mother Goose: Just Right for 3's & 4's. LC 88-43156. 32p. (ps). 1989. PLB 5.99 (0-394-92860-1) Random Bks Yng Read.
Lobstein, Tim. Poisoned Food? 1990. PLB 12.40 (0-531-17208-2, Gloucester Pr) Watts.
Lobus, Catherine O. Careers As a Flight Attendant. Rosen, Ruth, ed. (gr. 7-12). 1991. PLB 13.95 (0-8239-1179-9) Rosen Group.
Lock, Robert D. Student Activities for Taking Charge of Your Career Direction & Job Search: Career Planning Guide, Bk. 3. 2nd ed. 136p. 1992. pap. 12.25 (0-534-13659-1) Brooks-Cole.
Lockborn, Paul, et al. Blood & Lust. Shirley, Sam, ed. Swekel, Arnie, et al, illus. 128p. (Orig.). (gr. 7 up). 1991. pap. 18.95 (0-933635-84-2, 2711) Chaosium.
Locke, Eleanor G., ed. Sail Away. Goodfellow, Robin, illus. 164p. (Orig.). 1987. pap. 17.00 (0-913932-24-8) Boosey & Hawkes.
Locke, Joseph. Game Over. 1993. pap. 3.50 (0-553-29652-3) Bantam.
—Kill the Teacher's Pet. 1991. pap. 2.99 (0-553-29058-4) Bantam.
—Kiss of Death. 1992. pap. 3.50 (0-553-29653-1) Bantam.
—One-Nine-Hundred-Killer. 1994. pap. 3.50 (0-553-56079-4) Bantam.
—Petrified. (gr. 7 up). 1992. pap. 3.50 (0-553-29657-4, Starfire) Bantam.
—Vendetta. (gr. 9-12). 1994. pap. 3.50 (0-553-56080-8) Bantam.
Locke, Mary. Summer the Spies Moved In. (gr. 4-7). 1991. pap. 2.75 (0-590-43723-2, Apple Paperbacks) Scholastic Inc.
Locke, Raymond F. Joachin Murieta. (Orig.). (gr-12). 1980. pap. 2.25 (0-87067-009-3, BH009) Holloway.
Locke, Raymond F., jt. auth. see Ruth, Marianne.
Locke, Raymond F., ed. see Neyland, James.
Locke, Robert. Tracks. (gr. 5 up). 1986. 12.70 (0-395-40571-8) HM.

Locker, Thomas. The Bagpiper. LC 92-42350. 1994. write for info. (0-399-22546-3, Philomel Bks) Putnam Pub Group.
—Boy Who Held Back the Sea. (ps-3). 1991. pap. 4.95 (0-8037-1049-6, Dial Pied Piper) Puffin Bks.
—Family Farm. Locker, Thomas, illus. LC 87-19645. 32p. (ps up). 1988. 16.99 (0-8037-0489-5); PLB 14.89 (0-8037-0490-9) Dial Bks Young.
—The Land of Gray Wolf. Locker, Thomas, illus. LC 90-3915. 32p. (ps up). 1991. 15.95 (0-8037-0936-6); lib. bdg. 15.89 (0-8037-0937-4) Dial Bks Young.
—The Mare on the Hill. Locker, Thomas, illus. LC 85-1684. 32p. (gr. k-12). 1985. 15.95 (0-8037-0207-8); PLB 15.89 (0-8037-0208-6) Dial Bks Young.
—Miranda's Smile. LC 93-28050. 1994. write for info. (0-8037-1688-5); PLB write for info. (0-8037-1689-3) Dial Bks Young.
—Sailing with the Wind. Locker, Thomas, illus. LC 85-23381. 32p. (ps up). 1986. 15.00 (0-8037-0311-2); PLB 14.89 (0-8037-0312-0) Dial Bks Young.
—Sailing with the Wind. (gr. 3 up). 1993. pap. 5.99 (0-14-054698-7, Puffin Pied Piper) Puffin Bks.
—Where the River Begins. LC 84-1709. (Illus.). 32p. (gr. k-3). 1984. 16.95 (0-8037-0089-X); PLB 14.89 (0-8037-0090-3) Dial Bks Young.
—Where the River Begins. (Illus.). 32p. 1993. pap. 4.99 (0-14-054595-6) Puffin Bks.
—The Young Artist. (Illus.). 32p. (ps up). 1989. PLB 15.89 (0-8037-0627-8) Dial Bks Young.
—The Young Artist. (Illus.). 32p. 1993. pap. 4.99 (0-14-054923-4, Puffin Pied Piper) Puffin Bks.
Locker, Thomas, jt. auth. see George, Jean C.
Locker, Thomas, adapted by. & illus. Rip Van Winkle. LC 87-24448. 32p. (ps up). 1988. 15.95 (0-8037-0520-4); PLB 15.89 (0-8037-0521-2) Dial Bks Young.
Lockhart, Barbara. Christmas Tall Books, 3 bks. Lockhart, Lynne, illus. 36p. (ps). 1993. Set, incl. snowman. bds. 14.95 (1-56828-044-0) Red Jacket Pr.
—The Christmas Tree. Lockhart, Lynne, illus. 12p. (ps). 1993. 4.95 (1-56828-025-4) Red Jacket Pr.
—Santa. Lockhart, Lynne, illus. 12p. 1993. 4.95 (1-56828-026-2) Red Jacket Pr.
—The Snowman. Lockhart, Lynne, illus. 12p. (ps). 1993. 4.95 (1-56828-024-6) Red Jacket Pr.
Lockhart, Barbara & Lockhart, Lynne. Once a Pony Time at Chincoteague. Lockhart, Lynne, illus. 30p. (gr. k-5). 1992. 8.95 (0-87033-436-0) Tidewater.
Lockhart, Barbara, jt. auth. see Lockhart, Lynne N.
Lockhart, Charlotte F. Discover Intensive Phonics for Yourself. rev. ed. Griffin, Glen C., frwd. by. LC 83-71502. 452p. 1983. tchrs. ed. 49.95 (0-9605654-1-8) Char-L.
Lockhart, Lynne, jt. auth. see Lockhart, Barbara.
Lockhart, Lynne N. & Lockhart, Barbara. Rambling Raft. LC 89-50761. (Illus.). 30p. (gr. k-5). 1989. 7.95 (0-87033-392-5) Tidewater.
Lockman, Vic. Cartooning for Young Children, Bk. II. Lockman, Vic, illus. 48p. (ps-8). 1992. stapled bdg. 6.95 (0-936175-23-0) V Lockman.
—The Catechism for Young Children with Cartoons, Bk. 1. (Illus.). 45p. (Orig.). (ps-6). 1984. pap. 1.50 (0-936175-01-X); pap. text ed. 1.00 (0-936175-03-6) V Lockman.
—God's Law for Modern Man: Cartoon Illustrated. Lockman, Vic, illus. 60p. 1993. stapled 6.00 (0-936175-25-7) V Lockman.
—Machines. Lockman, Vic, illus. 48p. (Orig.). (gr. 8 up). 1992. pap. 5.95 stapled (0-936175-20-6) V Lockman.
—Miracle Art: Trick Cartoons. Lockman, Vic, illus. 48p. (Orig.). (gr. 8 up). 1992. pap. 5.95 stapled (0-936175-19-2) V Lockman.
—Reading & Understanding the Bible. Lockman, Vic, illus. 56p. (gr. 6). 1992. stapled 5.95 (0-936175-18-4) V Lockman.
—Super Bug Leads Tim Burr to the Gospel in the Woods. Lockman, Vic, illus. 24p. (Orig.). (gr. 8 up). 1991. pap. 2.95 (0-936175-14-1) V Lockman.
Lockridge, Ernest, ed. Twentieth Century Interpretations of The Great Gatsby. (Orig.). (gr. 9-12). 1968. 22.50 (0-13-363820-0, Spec); pap. 2.95 (0-13-363812-X, Spec) P-H.
Lockwood, Barbara & McAuley, Marilyn. Bible Surprises. LC 87-71384. (ps). 1988. bds. 4.99 (1-55513-120-4, Chariot Bks) Cook.
—God Keeps Them Safe. (ps). 1988. bds. 4.99 (1-55513-518-8, Chariot Bks) Cook.
—God Made Little & Big. LC 87-62019. (ps). 1988. bds. 4.99 (1-55513-517-X, Chariot Bks) Cook.
—Good Gifts from God. LC 87-71383. (ps). 1988. bds. 4.99 (1-55513-366-5, Chariot Bks) Cook.
Lockwood, Gayle R. Libbie Sims, Worry Wart. 144p. (gr. 3-7). 1993. 13.99 (0-670-84863-8) Viking Child Bks.
Lockwood, Primrose. One Winter's Night. Mills, Elaine, illus. LC 90-22891. 32p. (ps-1). 1991. SBE 13.95 (0-02-759235-9, Macmillan Child Bk) Macmillan Child Grp.

Loder, Ann. The Wet Hat: And Other Stories from Beyond the Black Stump. Peters, Terry, illus. 102p. (Orig.). (gr. 4 up). 1993. pap. write for info. (0-9636643-0-1) A L Loder.
THE WET HAT, & OTHER STORIES FROM BEYOND THE

BLACK STUMP is a collection of Australian short stories taken from the author's childhood & family album growing up on an Australian sheep ranch. The stories concern family pets; a gutsy pony, two heroic dogs; a kookaburra, (a native Australian bird), a chicken, & a tale about a tiny silkworm. There is a mystery story about a lost ring. Lastly, there is a humorous one. Each story is based on fact & is suitable for children from fourth to eighth grade, up. A dog is featured on the full color cover & there is a black & white illustration with each story. Order from: American Business Communications, 251 Michelle Ct., South San Francisco, CA 94080. FAX: (415) 952-3716 (att: Noel Loder). 415-952-8700. *Publisher Provided Annotation.*

Lodge, Arthur. Opportunities in Accounting Careers. LC 76-42889. (Illus.). (gr. 8 up). 1983. 13.95 (0-8442-6341-9, VGM Career Bks); pap. 10.95 (0-8442-6342-7, VGM Career Bks) NTC Pub Grp.
Lodge, Bernard. Door to Door. Roffey, Maureen, illus. LC 93-22203. 32p. (ps-12). 1993. smythe sewn reinforced 14.95 (1-879085-80-1) Whsprng Coyote Pr.
—There Was an Old Woman Who Lived in a Glove: A Picture Book. Lodge, Bernard, illus. LC 92-12967. 32p. (ps-12). 1992. smythe sewn reinforced 14.95 (1-879085-55-0) Whsprng Coyote Pr.
Lodge, Sally. Cheyenne. (Illus.). 32p. (gr. 5-8). 1990. lib. bdg. 15.94 (0-86625-387-4); lib. bdg. 11.95s.p. (0-685-36388-0) Rourke Corp.
Lodge, Tom see First, Ruth.
Loeffelbein, Robert L. The Recreation Handbook: Three-Hundred Forty-Two Games & Other Activities for Teams & Individuals. LC 92-50310. (Illus.). 240p. 1992. pap. 24.95x (0-89950-744-1) McFarland & Co.
Loehr, Mallory. Trucks. McNaught, Harry, illus. LC 91-75344. 22p. (ps). 1992. 2.95 (0-679-83061-8) Random Bks Yng Read.
Loehring, Wayne. The Athlete's Corner: Megan's Dilemma. 72p. (gr. 6-8). 1992. pap. 3.50 (0-8593-3276-3) Dorrance.
Loehrlein, Myrna & Nylin, Dawn. Preschool Bible Lessons. 96p. (ps-1). 1990. 10.95 (0-86653-541-1, SS1875, Shining Star Pubns) Good Apple.
Loelling, Carol. Whose House Is This? (Illus.). 22p. (ps-4). 1978. 5.95 (0-8431-0444-9) Price Stern.
Looper, John J. Crusade for Kindness: Henry Bergh & the ASPCA. LC 90-27682. (Illus.). 112p. (gr. 3-7). 1991. SBE 12.95 (0-689-31560-0, Atheneum Child Bk) Macmillan Child Grp.
—Going to School in 1776. LC 72-86940. (Illus.). 112p. (gr. 4-7). 1973. SBE 13.95 (0-689-30089-1, Atheneum) Macmillan Child Grp.
—Going to School in 1876. LC 83-15669. (Illus.). 96p. (gr. 4-7). 1984. SBE 13.95 (0-689-31015-3, Atheneum) Macmillan Child Grp.
Loewen. Food in France. 1991. 11.95s.p. (0-86625-344-0) Rourke Pubns.
—Food in Germany. 1991. 11.95s.p. (0-86625-347-5) Rourke Pubns.
—Food in Greece. 1991. 11.95s.p. (0-86625-348-3) Rourke Pubns.
—Food in Israel. 1991. 11.95s.p. (0-86625-349-1) Rourke Pubns.
—Food in Korea. 1991. 11.95s.p. (0-86625-345-9) Rourke Pubns.
—International Food Library, 6 bks, Set II. 1991. 71.70s.p. (0-86625-324-6) Rourke Pubns.
Loewen, L. The Beatles. (Illus.). 112p. (gr. 5 up). 1989. lib. bdg. 18.60 (0-86592-610-7); lib. bdg. 13.95s.p. (0-685-58616-2) Rourke Corp.
—Beethoven. (Illus.). 112p. (gr. 5 up). 1989. lib. bdg. 18.60 (0-86592-609-3); lib. bdg. 13.95s.p. (0-685-58617-0) Rourke Corp.
—Elvis. (Illus.). 112p. (gr. 5 up). 1989. lib. bdg. 18.60 (0-86592-606-9); 13.95 (0-685-58614-6) Rourke Corp.
—James Brown. (Illus.). 112p. (gr. 5 up). 1989. lib. bdg. 18.60 (0-86592-607-7); 13.95 (0-685-58615-4) Rourke Corp.
—Johnny Cash. (Illus.). 112p. (gr. 5 up). 1989. lib. bdg. 18.60 (0-86592-608-5); 13.95s.p. (0-685-58613-8) Rourke Corp.
—Mozart. (Illus.). 112p. (gr. 5 up). 1989. lib. bdg. 18.60 (0-86592-605-0); 13.95 (0-685-58618-9) Rourke Corp.
Loewen, N. Atlanta. (Illus.). 48p. (gr. 5 up). 1989. lib. bdg. 15.94 (0-86592-543-7); PLB 11.95s.p. (0-685-58591-3) Rourke Corp.
—Philadelphia. (Illus.). (gr. 5 up). 1989. lib. bdg. 15.94 (0-86592-542-9); 11.95s.p. (0-685-58593-X) Rourke Corp.
—Seattle. (Illus.). (gr. 5 up). 1989. lib. bdg. 15.94 (0-86592-545-3); 11.95 (0-685-58592-1) Rourke Corp.
—Washington, D. C. (Illus.). (gr. 5 up). 1989. lib. bdg. 15.94 (0-86592-544-5); lib. bdg. 11.95s.p. (0-685-58590-5) Rourke Corp.

Loewen, Nancy. Food in Spain. LC 90-43595. 32p. (gr. 3-5). 1991. 11.95s.p. (0-86625-346-7) Rourke Pubns.
—Mark Twain. LC 93-1177. 1994. write for info. (0-88682-618-7) Creative Ed.
—Pearl Buck. LC 93-17133. 1994. write for info. (0-88682-514-8) Creative Ed.
—Poe. Mucci, Tina, illus. 64p. 1993. 16.95 (1-56846-084-8) Creat Editions.
—Poe. Mucci, Tina, photos by. LC 93-17095. (Illus.). 1993. PLB 16.95 (0-88682-509-1) Creative Ed.
—Profiles in Music, 6 bks, Reading Level 6. (Illus.). 602p. (gr. 5 up). 1989. Set. PLB 111.60 (0-86592-604-2); 83.70s.p. (0-685-58764-9) Rourke Corp.
Loewen, Nancy & Berry, S. L. Robert Frost. (Illus.). 48p. (gr. 5-12). Date not set. lib. bdg. 18.95 RLB smythe-sewn (0-88682-613-6, 97866-098) Creative Ed.
Loewen, Nancy & Stewart, Gail. Great Cities of the U. S, 8 bks, Reading Level 6. (Illus.). 384p. (gr. 5 up). 1989. Set. PLB 127.52 (0-86592-537-2); 95.60s.p. (0-685-58767-3) Rourke Corp.
Loewer, Peter. The Inside-Out Stomach: An Introduction to Animals without Backbones. Jenkins, Jean, illus. LC 89-6499. 64p. (gr. 2 up). 1990. SBE 13.95 (0-689-31432-9, Atheneum Child Bk) Macmillan Child Grp.
—Pond Water Zoo: An Introduction to Microscopic Life. Jenkins, Jean, illus. LC 93-18468. (gr. 1-8). 1995. text ed. 13.95 (0-689-31736-0, Atheneum) Macmillan.
L'Officier, Jean-Marc, jt. auth. see L'Officier, Randy.
L'Officier, Randy & L'Officier, Jean-Marc, eds. Visions of Arzach. Aragones, Sergio, et al, illus. Ellison, Harlan, frwd. by. 64p. (gr. 6 up). 1993. Repr. of 1992 ed. 14.95 (0-87816-233-X) Kitchen Sink.
Lofgren, Ulf. Alvin & the Unruly Elves. (ps-3). 1992. 18.95 (0-87614-590-X) Carolrhoda Bks.
—Alvin the Knight. (ps-3). 1992. 18.95 (0-87614-698-1) Carolrhoda Bks.
—Alvin the Pirate. Lotfren, Ulf, illus. 32p. (ps-3). 1990. PLB 18.95 (0-87614-402-4) Carolrhoda Bks.
—Alvin the Pirate: Picture Book. (ps-3). 1991. pap. 5.95 (0-87614-551-9) Carolrhoda Bks.
—Alvin the Zookeeper. Lofgren, Ulf, illus. 32p. (ps-3). 1991. PLB 18.95 (0-87614-689-2) Carolrhoda Bks.
Loft, Randi, ed. see Aries, Ruby.
Loftin, T. L. Contest for a Capital. (Illus.). 352p. (gr. 9-12). 1989. pap. 19.95 (0-934812-04-7) Tee Loftin.
Loftin, Tee, ed. see Nault, Andy.
Loftin, Tee, tr. see Zarambouka, Sofia.
Lofting, Hugh. Doctor Dolittle: A Treasury. 1990. Repr. lib. bdg. 25.95x (0-89966-674-4) Buccaneer Bks.
—Dr. Dolittle & the Green Canary. (gr. k-6). 1988. pap. 3.50 (0-440-40079-1, YB) Dell.
—Doctor Dolittle & the Green Canary. Lofting, Hugh, illus. (gr. 4 up). 1989. 14.95 (0-318-41607-7) Delacorte.
—Dr. Dolittle in the Moon. (gr. k-6). 1988. pap. 3.25 (0-440-40113-5, YB) Dell.
—Doctor Dolittle's Bag of Books. (gr. 4-7). 1988. pap. 13.45 (0-440-36000-5) Dell.
—Dr. Dolittle's Canary. 1989. pap. 14.95 (0-440-50141-5) Dell.
—Dr. Dolittle's Caravan. (gr. k-6). 1988. pap. 3.50 (0-440-40071-6) Dell.
—Dr. Dolittle's Circus. (gr. k-6). 1988. pap. 3.50 (0-440-40058-9) Dell.
—Doctor Dolittle's Circus. (gr. 3-6). 16.25 (0-8446-6370-0) Peter Smith.
—Gub-Gub's Book. LC 91-4672. (gr. 4-7). 1992. pap. 15.00 (0-671-78355-6, S&S BFYR) S&S Trade.
—The Story of Doctor Dolittle. (gr. k-6). 1988. pap. 2.95 (0-685-18953-8) Dell.
—The Story of Doctor Dolittle. centenary ed. Lofting, Christopher, afterword by. (Illus.). 144p. (gr. 4-6). 1988. pap. 13.95 (0-385-29662-2) Delacorte.
—Story of Dr. Dolittle. (gr. 4-7). 1969. pap. 3.50 (0-440-48307-7) Dell.
—The Twilight of Magic. Kiuchi, Tatsuro, illus. LC 92-15766. 1993. pap. 15.00 (0-671-78358-0, S&S BFYR) S&S Trade.
—The Voyage of Doctor Dolittle. (gr. 4-7). 1988. pap. 3.99 (0-440-44002-3, YB) Dell.
Logan, Anna & Koehler, Ed. The Jesus Tree Activity Book. (Illus.). 48p. (Orig.). (ps-2). 1991. pap. 4.99 (0-570-04197-X) Concordia.
Logan, Joan S. Two Turtles of Paradise: A Love Story for Children & Adults. Smith, Curtis W., illus. 20p. (Orig.). 1988. pap. 1.95 (0-944208-01-0) Seventh-Wing Pubns.
Logan, Les. The Game. 160p. (Orig.). (gr. 7-12). 1986. pap. 2.25 (0-553-25211-9) Bantam.
Logan, Mike. Little Friends: In Verse & Photography. (ps-3). 1992. pap. 7.95 (1-56044-139-9) Falcon Pr MT.
Logue, Frank. Appalachian Trail Fun Book. (ps-3). 1993. pap. 6.95 (0-917953-60-6) Appalachian Trail.
Logue, Mary. The Haunting of Hunter House. (gr. 1-8). 1992. PLB 8.95 (0-89565-877-1); Resale. 12.75 (0-685-60969-3) Childs World.
—The Missing Statue of Minnehaha. (gr. 1-8). 1992. PLB 8.95 (0-89565-902-6); Resale. 12.75 (0-685-60970-7) Childs World.
Loh, Carolyn. Let's Celebrate Valentine's Day: A Book of Things to Draw. Loh, Carolyn, illus. LC 87-50429. 32p. (gr. 2-6). 1988. PLB 10.65 (0-8167-1035-X); pap. text ed. 1.95 (0-8167-1036-8) Troll Assocs.
Loh, Morag. Tucking Mommy In. Rawlins, Donna, illus. LC 87-16740. 40p. (ps-2). 1988. 13.95 (0-531-05740-2); PLB 13.99 (0-531-08340-3) Orchard Bks Watts.

—Tucking Mommy In. LC 87-16740. (Illus.). 40p. (ps-2). 1991. pap. 4.95 (0-531-07025-5) Orchard Bks Watts.
Lohf, Sabine. Building Your Own Toys. LC 89-22276. 64p. (gr. 5 up). 1989. lib. bdg. 19.93 (0-516-09251-0); pap. 8.95 (0-516-49251-9) Childrens.
—Christmas Crafts. LC 89-22255. 64p. 1989. lib. bdg. 19.93 (0-516-09252-9); pap. 8.95 (0-516-49252-7) Childrens.
—I Made It Myself. LC 89-22252. 64p. 1989. lib. bdg. 19.93 (0-516-09254-5); pap. 8.95 (0-516-49254-3) Childrens.
—Making Things for Easter. LC 89-22254. 64p. (gr. 3 up). 1989. PLB 19.93 (0-516-09253-7); pap. 8.95 (0-516-49253-5) Childrens.
—Nature Crafts. LC 89-49552. (Illus.). 64p. 1990. pap. 8.95 (0-516-49257-8) Childrens.
—Things I Can Make with Beads. (Illus.). 32p. (ps-3). 1991. 6.95 (0-87701-837-5) Chronicle Bks.
—Things I Can Make with Boxes. (Illus.). 32p. (ps-3). 1991. 6.95 (0-87701-843-X) Chronicle Bks.
—Things I Can Make with Buttons. (Illus.). 32p. (ps-3). 1990. 6.95 (0-87701-687-9) Chronicle Bks.
—Things I Can Make with Cloth. (Illus.). 28p. (ps-3). 1989. 6.95 (0-87701-666-6) Chronicle Bks.
—Things I Can Make with Cork. (Illus.). 32p. (ps-3). 1990. 6.95 (0-87701-726-3) Chronicle Bks.
—Things I Can Make with Leaves. (Illus.). 32p. (ps-3). 1990. 6.95 (0-87701-763-8) Chronicle Bks.
—Things I Can Make with Paper. (Illus.). 32p. (ps-3). 1989. 6.95 (0-87701-671-2) Chronicle Bks.
—Things I Can Make with Stones. (Illus.). 32p. (ps-2). 1990. 6.95 (0-87701-769-7) Chronicle Bks.
Lohf, Sabine & Schael, Hannelore. Making Things with Yarn. LC 89-22256. 64p. (gr. 2 up). 1989. pap. 8.95 (0-516-49255-1) Childrens.
Lohr, J. E. Your First Budgerigar. (Illus.). 36p. (Orig.). 1991. pap. 1.95 (0-86622-058-5, YF-102) TFH Pubns.
—Your First Cockatiel. (Illus.). 36p. (Orig.). 1991. pap. 1.95 (0-86622-060-7, YF-104) TFH Pubns.
Lois, jt. auth. see Sharon.
Lois, Susan. Reunion Affairs. (Orig.). 1988. pap. 3.95 (0-440-20213-2) Dell.
Lokenvitz, Judith, jt. auth. see Duffy, Karen.
Lokra. The Lady & the Fly. (Illus.). 48p. (gr. k-4). 1990. 12.75 (0-89565-812-7); 8.95s.p. (0-685-55101-6) Childs World.
Lokvig, Gaston. San Diego Coloring Book. (Illus.). 16p. 1985. pap. 1.25 (0-9607696-8-4) Carol Mendel.
Lolling, Atsuko G. Aki & the Banner of Names: And Other Stories from Japan. (Orig.). (gr. 1-6). pap. 4.95 (0-377-00218-6) Friendship Pr.
Loman, Roberta K., illus. All about Hands. 28p. (ps). 1992. 2.50 (0-87403-951-7, 24-03591) Standard Pub.
Lomas Garza, Carmen. Family Pictures (Cuadros de familia) Garza, Carmen L., illus. LC 89-27845. (SPA & ENG.). 32p. (gr. 1-7). 1990. 13.95 (0-89239-050-6) Childrens Book Pr.
—Family Pictures: Cuadros de familia. (SPA & ENG., Illus.). 32p. (gr. 1-7). 1993. pap. 5.95 (0-89239-108-1) Childrens Book Pr.
Lomask, Milton. Great Lives: Exploration. LC 88-15744. (Illus.). 288p. (gr. 4-6). 1988. SBE 22.95 (0-684-18511-3, Scribners Young Read) Macmillan Child Grp.
—Great Lives: Invention & Technology. LC 90-27619. (Illus.). 272p. (gr. 4-6). 1991. SBE 22.95 (0-684-19106-7, Scribners Young Read) Macmillan Child Grp.
—St. Isaac & the Indians. 2nd, rev. ed. Manso, Leo, illus. LC 90-85767. 170p. (gr. 6-8). 1991. pap. 9.95 (0-89870-355-7) Ignatius Pr.
Lomasney, Eileen. What Do You Do with the Rest of the Day, Mary Ann? 1991. pap. 3.95 (0-8091-6601-1) Paulist Pr.
Lomax, John A., jt. auth. see Ledbetter, H.
Lomax, Louis. To Kill a Black Man. (Orig.). (ps-12). 1987. pap. 3.25 (0-87067-731-4) Holloway.
Lombard, Gene. It's Good to Give Thanks. (Illus.). 24p. (gr. k-6). 1991. 4.25 (1-55976-156-3) CEF Press.
Lombardy, William & Marshall, Bette. Chess for Children Step by Step: A New, Easy Way to Learn the Game. (Illus.). 1977. 18.95i (0-316-53091-3); pap. 18.95i (0-316-53090-5) Little.

Lomsky, Gerry. The Beanstalk Bandit: The Giant's Version of "Jack & the Beanstalk" Krug, Ken, illus. 30p. (gr. 2-7). 1993. pap. 4.95 (1-883499-00-3); Story cass. 6.95 (1-883499-01-1) Princess NJ.
For years now, GIANTS, like many other minority groups, have been the target of literary malignment & discrimination. This TRUE story describes the GIANT'S quest for peace & tranquility in a castle in the clouds, his peaceful relationship with his pet hen & his love of harp music. One day, the GIANT'S peaceful life changes as a strange weed sprouts in his garden. Mysterious events confuse the harmless GIANT -- strange noises, footprints in the house, & coins missing from his Gramps' collection. The GIANT experiences true loneliness after his magical friend is "harp-napped." In the exciting climax, the GIANT pursues Jack to regain his stolen pet hen, Cuddles, only to fall off the beanstalk, damaging Jack's house & ending up in jail. The reader is encouraged to be the judge & render the verdict on the GIANT, who is charged with assaulting Jack, stealing coins, pet abuse & house destruction! The reader is also encouraged to join many others who have written to Princess Publishing in support of the GIANT'S case. To order call 609-596-9146. Story cassette also available for $6.95.
Publisher Provided Annotation.

Lonborg, Rosemary. The Quiet Hero - A Baseball Story. Houghton, Diane, illus. 32p. (gr. 2-6). 1993. perfect bound 7.95 (0-8283-1958-8) Branden Pub Co.
Londner, Renee. Morgan's Whistle. Noll, Cheryl K., illus. LC 92-14390. 32p. (ps-2). Date not set. 11.95 (1-56065-162-8) Capstone Pr. Postponed.
London, Carolyn. Adventures of a Jeeponary. (ps-3). 1982. pap. 2.50 (0-915374-19-6) Rapids Christian.
—Stolen Ice Cream Bar. Nielson, Deborah, illus. 12p. (gr. k-6). 1981. pap. text ed. 4.25 (1-55976-151-2) CEF Press.
London, Jack. Call of the Wild. (gr. 6 up). 1964. pap. 2.25 (0-8049-0030-2, CL-30) Airmont.
—The Call of the Wild. Kezer, Karel, illus. LC 63-14831. 144p. (gr. 6 up). 1970. 13.95 (0-02-759510-2, Macmillan Child Bk) Macmillan Child Grp.
—The Call of the Wild. new ed. Platt, Kin, ed. Carrillo, Fred, illus. LC 73-75461. 64p. (Orig.). (gr. 5-10). 1973. pap. 2.95 (0-88301-095-X) Pendulum Pr.
—The Call of the Wild. Nordlicht, Lillian, adapted by. & adapted by. LC 79-24464. (Illus.). 48p. (gr. 4 up). Pub. 1980. PLB 18.64 (0-8172-1656-1) Raintree Steck-V.
—The Call of the Wild. 128p. (gr. 3-7). 1983. pap. 2.99 (0-14-035000-4, Puffin) Puffin Bks.
—Call of the Wild. Hitchner, Earle, ed. De John, Marie, illus. LC 89-33890. 48p. (gr. 3-6). 1990. PLB 12.89 (0-8167-1863-6); pap. text ed. 3.95 (0-8167-1864-4) Troll Assocs.
—Call of the Wild. (gr. 9-12). 1987. pap. 2.95 (0-590-44001-2, NAL) Scholastic Inc.
—Call of the Wild. 128p. (gr. 9-12). 1990. pap. 2.50 (0-8125-0432-1) Tor Bks.
—The Call of the Wild. 1991. 12.99 (0-517-06003-5) Outlet Bk Co.
—Call of the Wild. (Illus.). 1991. pap. 2.95 (1-56156-094-4) Kidsbks.
—The Call of the Wild. (gr. 8). 1991. pap. write for info. (0-663-56265-1) Silver Burdett Pr.
—The Call of the Wild. Moser, Barry, illus. Paulsen, Gary, intro. by. LC 93-18409. (Illus.). 1994. text ed. 19.95 (0-02-759455-6) Macmillan.
—The Call of the Wild & Selected Stories. 176p. (gr. 6). 1960. pap. 2.95 (0-451-52390-3, Sig Classics) NAL-Dutton.
—Jack London in the High School Aegis. Sisson, James E., ed. Lttell, Katherine, pref. by. (Illus.). 125p. (Orig.). (gr. 7-12). 1980. pap. 5.95 (0-932458-01-7) Star Rover.
—Jack London's Stories of the North. 256p. (gr. 4 up). 1989. pap. 2.95 (0-590-44229-5) Scholastic Inc.
—Martin Eden. (gr. 9 up). 1969. pap. 3.50 (0-8049-0209-7, CL-209) Airmont.
—Sea Wolf. Gall, M., intro. by. (gr. 6 up). 1965. pap. 2.50 (0-8049-0064-7, CL-64) Airmont.
—The Sea Wolf & Selected Stories. 352p. (RL 8). 1964. pap. 2.95 (0-451-52356-3, Sig Classics) NAL-Dutton.
—Short Stories. (gr. 9 up). 1969. pap. 2.50 (0-8049-0198-8, CL-198) Airmont.
—To Build a Fire. Neumeier, Marty, illus. 48p. (gr. 6 up). 1980. PLB 13.95s.p. (0-87191-769-6) Creative Ed.
—White Fang. (gr. 6 up). 1964. pap. 2.50 (0-8049-0036-1, CL-36) Airmont.
—White Fang. new & abr. ed. Farr, Naunerle, ed. Carrillo, Fred, illus. (gr. 4-12). 1977. pap. text ed. 2.95 (0-88301-271-5) Pendulum Pr.
—White Fang. LC 85-42971. 272p. (gr. 4-6). 1985. pap. 3.99 (0-14-035045-4, Puffin) Puffin Bks.
—White Fang. 256p. (gr. 6 up). 1986. pap. 3.25 (0-590-42591-9) Scholastic Inc.
—White Fang. 224p. 1989. pap. 2.50 (0-8125-0512-3) Tor Bks.
—White Fang: Illustrated Classics. Arneson, D. J., ed. Walker, Karen, illus. 128p. (Orig.). 1990. pap. 2.95 (0-942025-84-9) Kidsbks.
London, Jack & Conrad, Joseph. Reader's Digest Best Loved Books for Young Readers: The Call of the Wild & Typhoon. Ogburn, Jackie, ed. Schoenherr, John & Mullins, Frank, illus. 136p. (gr. 4-12). 1989. 3.99 (0-945260-28-8) Choice Pub NY.

London, Jonathan. Ali, Child of the Desert. Lewin, Ted, illus. LC 92-44164. (gr. 3 up). 1995. write for info. *(0-688-12560-3)*; PLB write for info. *(0-688-12561-1)* Lothrop.
—The Eyes of Grey Wolf. Van Zale, Jon, illus. LC 92-35987. (gr. 4 up). 1993. 13.95 *(0-8118-0285-X)* Chronicle Bks.
—Froggy Gets Dressed. Remkiewicz, Frank, illus. 32p. (ps-1). 1992. 13.00 *(0-670-84249-4)* Viking Child Bks.
—Gray Fox. Sauber, Robert, illus. LC 92-20653. 32p. (gr. 3-8). 1993. 13.99 *(0-670-84490-X)* Viking Child Bks.
—Hip Cat. Hubbard, Woodleigh, illus. LC 93-1179. 1993. 13.95 *(0-8118-0315-5)* Chronicle Bks.
—Into This Night We Are Rising. Karas, G. Brian, illus. LC 92-27471. (ps-3). 1993. 13.99 *(0-670-84905-7)* Viking Child Bks.
—A Koala for Katie. Jabar, Cynthia, illus. LC 93-16085. 1993. write for info. *(0-8075-4209-1)* A Whitman.
—Let's Go, Froggy! Remkiewicz, Frank, illus. LC 93-24059. 32p. (ps-3). 1994. PLB 12.99 *(0-670-85055-1)* Viking Child Bks.
—The Lion Who Had Asthma. Levine, Abby, ed. Westcott, Nadine B., illus. LC 91-16553. 32p. (ps-1). 1992. PLB 13.95 *(0-8075-4559-7)* A Whitman.
—The Owl Who Became the Moon. Rand, Ted, illus. LC 92-14699. (ps-2). 1993. 13.99 *(0-525-45054-8, DCB)* Dutton Child Bks.
—The Sugaring-off Party. Pelletier, Gilles, illus. LC 93-21911. 1994. write for info. *(0-525-45187-0, DCB)* Dutton Child Bks.
—Voices of the Wild. McLoughlin, Wayne, illus. LC 92-27651. 32p. (ps up). 1993. 15.00 *(0-517-59217-7)*; PLB 15.99 *(0-517-59218-5)* Crown Bks Yng Read.
London, Jonathan & Pinola, Lanny. Fire Race: A Karuk Coyote Tale about How Fire Came to the People. Long, Sylvia, illus. Lang, Julian, afterword by. LC 92-32352. (Illus.). 1993. 13.95 *(0-8118-0241-8)* Chronicle Bks.
London, Jonathan, jt. ed. see Bruchac, Joseph.
London, Robert. Nonroutine Problems: Doing Mathematics. (Illus.). 60p. (Orig.). (gr. 10-12). 1989. pap. text ed. 18.50 *(0-939765-30-6, G117)* Janson Pubns.
Lonergan, Carroll V. Brave Boys of Old Fort Ticonderoga. LC 87-22144. (gr. 6 up). 1987. write for info., 7.95 *(0-932334-57-1, Empire State Bks)*; pap. 7.95, 144 p *(1-55787-018-7, NY16028, Empire State Bks)* Heart of the Lakes.
Long, Carolyn, jt. auth. see Keffer, Christine.
Long, Earlene R. Gone Fishing. Brown, Richard, illus. LC 83-22558. 32p. (ps-3). 1987. 13.95 *(0-395-35570-2, 5-90090)*; pap. 4.80 *(0-395-44236-2)* HM.
Long, Evelyn. Grandma Tellmie about Ant, Wars Snake-Feeders, Blood-Drinking Bugs & Butterfly. Plott, Dave, et al, eds. 31p. 1984. pap. 4.00x *(0-931881-00-5)* Collaborare Pub.
—Grandma Tellmie About...Big Deer, Little Deer... Reindeer. Plott, Dave & Longmeyer, Carole M., eds. 46p. 1985. pap. 3.00 *(0-931881-01-3)* Collaborare Pub.
Long, Hua. The Moon Maiden & Other Asian Folktales. (Illus.). 32p. 1993. 12.95 *(0-8351-2494-0)*; pap. 8.95 *(0-8351-2493-2)* China Bks.
Long, J., ed. Budgeting Know-How. 48p. (gr. 4-5). 1988. pap. text ed. write for info. *(0-8428-7172-1)* Cambridge Bk.
Long, J. O., ed. see Graner, Carl E.
Long, Jack. How Does It Work? rev. ed. McKissack, Vern, illus. 32p. (gr. 2-4). 1990. Repr. of 1988 ed. PLB 9.95 *(1-878363-17-4)* Forest Hse.
—Little Treasury of the Velveteen Rabbit. 1988. 5.99 *(0-517-64371-5)* Outlet Bk Co.
—Why Is the Sky Blue? McKissack, Vern, illus. 32p. (gr. 2-4). 1990. Repr. of 1988 ed. PLB 9.95 *(1-878363-15-8)* Forest Hse.
Long, James A. Oregon Firsts: Oregon's Trailblazing Past & Present. O'Neal, Lauren, illus. 224p. (Orig.). 1993. pap. 24.95 *(1-8826350-0-0)* Pumpkin Ridge.
Long, Jeanne & Mallis, Jackie. Pathways to Poetry Series: Kaleidoscope, Mosaics, Visions. Miller, Jo & Monroe, Laura, eds. (gr. 1-12). 1984. Set of 3. pap. text ed. 39.95 *(0-685-62412-9)* Multi Media TX.
Long, Joann M., ed. see Warren, Betsy.
Long, Jonathan & Paul, Korky. The Dog That Dug. LC 92-15093. (Illus.). 32p. (ps-3). 1993. 13.95 *(0-916291-44-8)* Kane-Miller Bk.
Long, Kathy. Hallelujah the Clown: A Story of Blessing & Discovery. Boddy, Joe, illus. LC 92-70384. 32p. (ps-k). 1992. pap. 4.99 *(0-8066-2560-0, 9-2560, Augsburg)* Augsburg Fortress.
—A Surprise for Mrs. Dodds: A Little Boy's Friendship Changes a Lonely Woman's Life. Rogers, Kathy, illus. LC 89-84939. 32p. (gr. 3-5). 1989. pap. 5.99 *(0-8066-2437-X, 9-2437)* Augsburg Fortress.
Long, Kevin, jt. auth. see Siembieda, Kevin.
Long, Kim. Astronaut Training Book for Kids. (Illus.). 160p. (gr. 5up). 1990. 15.95 *(0-525-67296-6, Lodestar Bks)* Dutton Child Bks.
Long, Lynellyn D. & Podnecky-Spiegel, Janet. In Print: Beginning Literacy Through Cultural Awareness. (Illus.). 192p. 1988. pap. text ed. 9.95 *(0-201-12023-2)*; tchrs., 128 p 7.95 *(0-201-12024-0)* Addison-Wesley.
Long, Lynette. On My Own: The Kids' Self Care Book. Hall, Joann, illus. LC 84-463. 160p. (Orig.). (gr. 1-7). 1984. pap. 7.95 *(0-87491-735-2)* Acropolis.
Long, Mark. The DBS Satellite Handbook. (Illus.). 356p. (gr. 12). 1993. 24.95 *(0-929548-02-7)* MLE Inc.

Long, Olivia. The Dandelion Queen. Long, Olivia, illus. 32p. (ps-4). Date not set. 9.95 *(1-880042-08-8, SL12461)* Shelf-Life Bks.
—Diary of a Dog. Long, Olivia, illus. 32p. (ps-4). Date not set. 9.95 *(1-880042-06-1, SL12456)* Shelf-Life Bks.
—A Horse of a Different Color. Long, Olivia, illus. 32p. (ps-4). Date not set. 9.95 *(1-880042-01-0, SL12451)* Shelf-Life Bks.
Long, Robert A. & Welles, Samuel P. All New Dinosaurs. (gr. 7 up). 1975. pap. 3.95 *(0-88388-031-8)* Bellerophon Bks.
Long, Ron E. & Barrett, Joanne. Hark, the Herald Angel. Fettke, Tom, contrib. by. Date not set. 4.50 *(0-685-68531-4, BCMC-48)*; cassette 9.98 *(0-685-68532-2, BCTA-9039C)* Lillenas.
Long, Sheppard. Carl Yastrzemski. (Illus.). 64p. (gr. 3 up). 1994. PLB 14.95 *(0-7910-1195-X, Am Art Analog)* Chelsea Hse.
Long, Teddy C., jt. auth. see Walter, F. Virginia.
Longanecker, Georgia. Howdy Out There! Phonics Fun. LC 76-62681. (Illus.). (ps-3). 1977. soft cover 6.95 *(0-9601126-1-8)* Longanecker.
Longboat, Dianne, ed. see Green, Richard G.
Longe, Bob. Nutty Challenges & Zany Dares. Longe, Bob, illus. LC 93-32391. 1994. write for info. *(0-8069-0454-2)* Sterling.
—World's Best Card Tricks. LC 90-46641. (Illus.). 128p. 1992. pap. 4.95 *(0-8069-8233-0)* Sterling.
—World's Best Coin Tricks. LC 92-11370. (Illus.). 128p. (gr. 5-10). 1993. pap. 4.95 *(0-8069-8661-1)* Sterling.
Longfellow, Henry Wadsworth. Children's Own Longfellow. (Illus.). 109p. (gr. 4-6). 1908. 16.45 *(0-395-06889-4)* HM.
—Evangeline & Other Poems. Bennet, C. L., intro. by. (gr. 7 up). pap. 1.50 *(0-8049-0094-9, CL-94)* Airmont.
—Hiawatha. Jeffers, Susan, illus. 32p. (gr. k up). 1983. 15.00 *(0-8037-0013-X)*; PLB 14.89 *(0-8037-0014-8)* Dial Bks Young.
—Hiawatha. LC 83-26972. (Illus.). (gr. 2-5). 1984. PLB 17.96 *(0-8172-2106-9)*; PLB 29.28 incl. cassette *(0-8172-2237-5)*; pap. 23.95 incl. cassette *(0-8172-2265-0)* Raintree Steck-V.
—Hiawatha's Childhood. Le Cain, Errol, illus. 32p. (gr. k up). 1984. 15.00 *(0-374-33065-4)* FS&G.
—Hiawatha's Childhood. LeCain, Errol, illus. (ps-3). 1987. pap. 3.99 *(0-14-050562-8, Puffin)* Puffin Bks.
—Paul Revere's Ride. Parker, Nancy W., illus. LC 84-4139. 48p. (gr. 1 up). 1985. 14.95 *(0-688-04014-4)*; PLB 14.88 *(0-688-04015-2)* Greenwillow.
—Paul Revere's Ride. Rand, Ted, illus. LC 89-25630. 40p. (gr. k-4). 1990. 14.95 *(0-525-44610-9, DCB)* Dutton Child Bks.
—Paul Revere's Ride. Parker, Nancy W., illus. LC 92-23319. 48p. (gr. 1 up). 1993. pap. 4.95 *(0-688-12387-2, Mulberry)* Morrow.
Longheed, L. Words More Words, & Ways to Use Them. (gr. 7 up). 1993. pap. text ed. 10.95 *(0-201-53961-6)* Longman.
Longman, C. J. & Walrond, H. Archery: The Badminton Library of Sports & Pastimes. Duck of Beauford, ed. St. Charles, Glenn, frwd. by. (Illus.). 540p. (gr. 10 up). 1992. Repr. of 1894 ed. 39.95 *(1-56416-087-4)* Derrydale Pr.
Longman Staff. Longman Dictionary of English Idioms. 1979. pap. text ed. 24.95 *(0-582-05863-5)* Longman.
—Longman Handy Learner's Dictionary. (gr. 9-12). 1988. pap. text ed. 10.95 *(0-582-96413-X, 78324)* Longman.
Longman, Stanley V. Remus Tales. 40p. (Orig.). 1990. Playscript. pap. 4.50 *(0-87602-293-X)* Anchorage.
Longmeyer, Carole M. An American Mystery: Script. (Orig.). (gr. 3-12). 1983. pap. 24.95 *(0-935326-50-2)* Gallopade Pub Group.
—Clemson Football Mystery. Rhodes, Priscilla, illus. (Orig.). (gr. 3 up). 1983. PLB 24.95 *(1-55609-164-8)*; pap. 14.95 *(0-935326-28-6)* Gallopade Pub Group.
—Deadly Duke Football Mystery. Rhodes, Priscilla, illus. (Orig.). (gr. 3 up). pap. 14.95 *(0-935326-31-6)* Gallopade Pub Group.
—Georgia Tech Football Mystery. Rhodes, Priscilla, illus. (Orig.). (gr. 3 up). 1983. pap. 14.95 *(0-935326-30-8)* Gallopade Pub Group.
—The Lost Colony Activity Book. Rhodes, Priscilla, illus. (Orig.). (gr. 3 up). 1983. pap. 14.95 *(0-935326-41-3)* Gallopade Pub Group.
—The Lost Colony Storybook. Rhodes, Priscilla, illus. (gr. 4 up). 1983. pap. 14.95 *(0-935326-38-3)* Gallopade Pub Group.
—Maryland Football Mystery. Rhodes, Priscilla, illus. 80p. (Orig.). (gr. 3 up). pap. 14.95 *(0-935326-32-4)* Gallopade Pub Group.
—NC State Football Mystery. Rhodes, Priscilla, illus. (Orig.). (gr. 3 up). pap. 14.95 *(0-935326-33-2)* Gallopade Pub Group.
—North Carolina Football Mystery. (Illus., Orig.). (gr. 3 up). 1983. pap. 14.95 *(0-935326-29-4)* Gallopade Pub Group.
—Virginia Football Mystery. Rhodes, Priscilla, illus. 80p. (Orig.). (gr. 3 up). pap. 24.95 *(0-935326-35-9)* Gallopade Pub Group.
—Wake Forest Football Mystery. Rhodes, Priscilla, illus. (Orig.). (gr. 3 up). pap. 14.95 *(0-935326-34-0)* Gallopade Pub Group.
—What Did You Sayeth? Rhodes, Priscilla, illus. (Orig.). (gr. 4 up). 1983. pap. 14.95 *(0-935326-45-6)* Gallopade Pub Group.
Longmeyer, Carole M., ed. see Long, Evelyn.

Longo, Linda. Troll Jokes & Riddles. LC 92-22571. (Illus.). 48p. (gr. 1-7). 1992. pap. 1.95 *(0-8167-2940-9)* Troll Assocs.
Longo, Lucas. Carl Sandburg: Poet & Historian. Rahmas, D. Steve, ed. LC 73-185665. 32p. (gr. 7-12). 1972. lib. bdg. 4.95 incl. catalog cards *(0-87157-509-4)* SamHar Pr.
Longshaw, Robin, tr. see Selden, George.
Longstreet, Stephen. Magic Trumpets: The Story of Jazz for Young People. Longstreet, Stephen, illus. (Orig.). (gr. 6-12). 1989. pap. 16.95 *(0-913705-42-X)* Zephyr Pr AZ.
Longstreet, Stephen, ed. Horse in Art. (Illus., Orig.). (ps). 1965. pap. 4.95 *(0-87505-198-7)* Borden.
Longue, Bob. World's Best Coin Tricks. LC 92-11370. (Illus.). 128p. 1992. 12.95 *(0-8069-8660-3)* Sterling.
Longyear, Barry B. The Homecoming. Clark, Alan M., illus. 224p. 1989. 15.95 *(0-8027-6863-6)* Walker & Co.
Lono, Luz P., ed. see Ozaeta, Pablo.
Lonsdale, Pamela, ed. Spooky: Stories of the Supernatural. Carey, Joanna, illus. LC 84-26425. 144p. (gr. 5 up). 1985. 12.95 *(0-13-835463-4)* P-H.
Looby, Christopher. Benjamin Franklin. Schlesinger, Arthur M., Jr. (Illus.). 112p. (gr. 5 up). 1990. 17.95x *(1-55546-808-X)* Chelsea Hse.
Look, Margaret K. At Home on The Workhouse Farm. (Illus.). 132p. (Orig.). (gr. 7 up). 1986. pap. 6.95 *(0-9616922-0-0)* M K Look.

Loomans, Diane. Lovables in the Kingdom of Self-Esteem. Carleton, Nancy, ed. Howard, Kim, illus. LC 90-52633. 32p. (ps-5). 1991. 14.95 *(0-915811-25-1)* H J Kramer Inc.
THE LOVABLES illuminates the heart of self-esteem! An absolute must for teachers & parents.--Dr. Andrew Mecca, former chairman, California Task Force to Promote Self-Esteem & Personal & Social Responsibility. "A truly outstanding self-esteem book for children. The most beautiful I've seen!" --LeRoy Foster, Executive Director, National Council for Self-Esteem. "I am lovable!" is the magic phrase that opens the gates to the Kingdom of Self-Esteem. Blending an imaginative narrative, charming illustrations, & important lessons in living, this book conducts young readers to the enchanted realm where twenty-four remarkable animals--the Lovables--await them. Each member of the Lovable Team has a special gift to share that gives the child a way of identifying with & creating qualities that make up a positive self-image. 60,000 copies in print. ENDORSED BY THE NEW YORK BOARD OF EDUCATION FOR USE IN ALL SCHOOLS. *Publisher Provided Annotation.*

Loomans, Diane, et al. Positively Mother Goose. Kramer, Linda, ed. Henrichsen, Ronda, illus. LC 90-52634. 32p. (ps-2). 1991. 14.95 *(0-915811-24-3)* H J Kramer Inc.
Loomar, Jane & Friedman, Barbara. Your Balance Sense. Wolf, Elizabeth, illus. 20p. (ps-3). 1992. pap. text ed. 11.00 *(0-910317-88-7)* Am Occup Therapy.
—Your Muscle Senses. Wolf, Elizabeth, illus. 16p. (ps-3). 1992. pap. text ed. 11.00 *(0-910317-89-5)* Am Occup Therapy.
Loomer, Bradley M. & Strege, Maxine G. Useful Spelling: Levels 2-8. (gr. 2-8). 1990. write for info. *(1-878712-03-9)* Useful Lrn.
Loomie, Christine. We're Going on a Trip. Chambliss, Maxie, illus. LC 93-17592. 1994. write for info. *(0-688-10173-9)*; PLB write for info. *(0-688-10172-0)* Morrow Jr Bks.
Loomis, Christine. At the Laundromat. Poydar, Nancy, illus. LC 93-10884. 1993. 14.95 *(0-590-72830-X)*; pap. 4.95 *(0-590-49488-0)* Scholastic Inc.
—At the Library. Poydar, Nancy, illus. LC 93-10882. 1994. 14.95 *(0-590-72831-8)*; pap. 4.95 *(0-590-49489-9)* Scholastic Inc.
—At the Mall. Poydar, Nancy, illus. 1994. 14.95 *(0-590-72832-6)*; pap. 4.95 *(0-590-49490-2)* Scholastic Inc.
—In the Diner. Poydar, Nancy, illus. 32p. (ps-2). 1994. 14.95 *(0-590-46716-6, Scholastic Hardcover)* Scholastic Inc.
—My New Baby-Sitter. Ancona, George, photos by. LC 90-38527. (Illus.). 48p. (ps up). 1991. 13.95 *(0-688-09625-5)*; PLB 13.88 *(0-688-09626-3)* Morrow Jr Bks.

Loon, Borin Van see Van Loon, Borin.
Loon, Joan van see Van Loon, Joan & Van Loon, John.
Loon, John van see Van Loon, Joan & Van Loon, John.
Loon, Paul van see Akkerman, Dinie & Van Loon, Paul.
Loon, Paul Van see Van Loon, Paul.
Loon, Ronald Van see Masuda, Akiko.
Loose, Frances F. Fractions, Book 1: Reusable Edition. (gr. 4). 1973. wkbk. 9.00 (0-87879-795-5, Ann Arbor Div) Acad Therapy.
—Fractions, Book 2: Reusable Edition. (gr. 4-6). 1973. wkbk. 8.00 (0-87879-796-3, Ann Arbor Div) Acad Therapy.
Lopez, Arcadia. Los Animales Del Parque. (Illus.). (gr. k-2). 1973. pap. 2.00 (0-913632-06-6) Am Univ Artforms.
—Barrio Teacher. LC 92-6876. 96p. (Orig.). (gr. 6-12). 1992. pap. text ed. 9.50 (1-55885-051-1) Arte Publico.
Lopez, Arcadia & Smith, John. El Parque Paquete. (Illus.). (gr. k-2). 1976. pap. 86.50 teaching system (0-913632-09-0) Am Univ Artforms.
Lopez, Barry. Crow & Weasel. Pohrt, Tom, illus. LC 90-31500. 64p. (gr. 5 up). 1990. 16.95 (0-86547-439-7, North Pt Pr) FS&G.
Lopez, Gary. Air Pollution. (gr. 5 up). 1992. PLB 18.95 (0-88682-427-3) Creative Ed.
—Air Pollution. (gr. 4-7). 1993. 14.95 (1-56846-050-3) Creat Editions.
—Sharks. 32p. 1991. 22.75 (0-89565-705-8); 15.95s.p. (0-685-55063-X) Childs World.
Lopez, N. C. King Pancho & the First Clock. Gutierrez, M., illus. LC 63-16396. 32p. (gr. 2-7). 1967. PLB 9.95 (0-87783-020-7); pap. 3.94 deluxe ed. (0-87783-098-3); cassette 7.94x (0-685-03701-0) Oddo.
Lopez, Norbert. Cuento Del Rey Pancho y el Primer Reloj. LC 70-108730. (Illus.). 32p. (gr. 2-7). 1970. PLB 9.95 (0-87783-010-X); pap. 3.94 deluxe ed. (0-87783-104-1); cassette 7.94x (0-685-03700-2) Oddo.
Lopez, Ron, ed. see Waller, Wanda W.
Lopez, Ruth K. A Child's Garden Diary: Coloring & Activity Book. Lopez, Ruth K., illus. 56p. (Orig.). (gr. k-6). 1992. pap. 5.95 (0-9627463-4-7) Gardens Growing People.
Lo Pinto, Richard W. Pollution. Head, J. J., ed. Steffen, Ann T., illus. LC 86-72203. 16p. (Orig.). (gr. 10 up). 1987. pap. text ed. 2.75 (0-89278-392-3, 45-9792) Carolina Biological.
LoPresti, Joan. Calendar Capers: A Child's School Year in Celebration. Danner, Robert W., illus. LC 90-36812. 32p. (gr. k-3). 1990. PLB 18.60 (0-8368-0428-7) Gareth Stevens Inc.
Lopshire, Robert. ABC Games. Lopshire, Robert, illus. LC 85-47883. 64p. (ps-1). 1986. (Crowell Jr Bks) HarpC Child Bks.
—I Want to Be Somebody New. Lopshire, Robert, illus. LC 85-43098. 48p. (gr. k-3). 1986. 6.95 (0-394-87616-4); lib. bdg. 7.99 (0-394-97616-9) Beginner.
—Put Me in the Zoo. LC 60-13494. (Illus.). 72p. (gr. 1-2). 1960. 6.95 (0-394-80017-6); lib. bdg. 7.99 (0-394-90017-0) Beginner.
Lorbiecki, Marybeth. Of Things Natural, Wild, & Free: A Story about Aldo Leopold. Maguire, Kerry, illus. LC 92-44049. 1993. 14.95 (0-87614-797-X) Carolrhoda Bks.
Lorbiecki, Marybeth & Lowery, Linda. Earthwise at Play: A Guide to the Care & Feeding of Your Planet. Mataya, David, illus. LC 92-9870. 1993. 19.95 (0-87614-729-5) Carolrhoda Bks.
Lorbiecki, Marybeth, jt. auth. see Lowery, Linda.
Lord. Garbage! The Trashiest Book. 1993. pap. 2.75 (0-590-46024-2) Scholastic Inc.
—One Hundred One Thanksgiving Knock-Knocks, Jokes, & Riddles. 1993. pap. 1.95 (0-590-47163-5) Scholastic Inc.
Lord, Athena V. Today's Special: Z. A. P. & Zoe. Jenkins, Jean, illus. LC 84-9661. 160p. (gr. 4-7). 1984. SBE 13.95 (0-02-761440-9, Macmillan Child Bk) Macmillan Child Grp.
—Z. A. P., Zoe, & the Musketeers. LC 91-31049. 160p. (gr. 3-7). 1992. SBE 13.95 (0-02-759561-7, Macmillan Child Bk) Macmillan Child Grp.
Lord, Bette B. In the Year of the Boar & Jackie Robinson. Simont, Marc, illus. LC 83-48440. 176p. (gr. 3-7). 1984. PLB 13.89 (0-06-024004-0) HarpC Child Bks.
Lord, Betty B. In the Year of the Boar & Jackie Robinson. Simont, Marc, illus. LC 83-48440. 176p. (gr. 3-7). 1986. pap. 3.95 (0-06-440175-8, Trophy) HarpC Child Bks.
Lord, John. Infection, the Immune System, & AIDS. (Illus.). 56p. (Orig.). (gr. 11-12). 1989. pap. 4.95x (0-934653-18-6) Enterprise Educ.
Lord, John V. Mr. Mead & His Garden. LC 74-20766. (Illus.). (gr. k-3). 1975. PLB 6.95 (0-395-20278-7) HM.
Lord, John V. & Burroway, Jane. The Giant Jam Sandwich. (Illus.). 1990. 7.70 (0-395-53966-6) HM.
Lord, John V. & Burroway, Janet. The Giant Jam Sandwich. Lord, John V., illus. LC 72-13578. 32p. (gr. k-3). 1987. 15.45 (0-395-16033-2); pap. 4.80 (0-395-44237-0) HM.
Lord, Suzanne. Drug Enforcement Agents. LC 89-1343. (Illus.). 48p. (gr. 4 up). 1989. RSBE 11.95 (0-89686-428-6, Crestwood Hse) Macmillan Child Grp.

—The Labrador Retriever. LC 90-34198. (Illus.). 48p. (gr. 5-6). 1990. RSBE 12.95 (0-89686-526-6, Crestwood Hse) Macmillan Child Grp.
—Our World of Mysteries: Fascinating Facts about the Planet Earth. 96p. 1991. pap. 2.75 (0-590-44595-2) Scholastic Inc.
—Radio Controlled Model Airplanes. LC 88-7109. (Illus.). 48p. (gr. 5-6). 1988. RSBE 11.95 (0-89686-378-6, Crestwood Hse) Macmillan Child Grp.
—Return of the Unicorn. (gr. 5-7). 1990. pap. 1.95 (0-590-40499-7) Scholastic Inc.
—Superstitions. LC 89-70867. (Illus.). 48p. (gr. 5 up). 1990. RSBE 11.95 (0-89686-512-6, Crestwood Hse) Macmillan Child Grp.
Lord, Trevor. Amazing Bikes. Downs, Peter, photos by. LC 92-911. (Illus.). 32p. (Orig.). (gr. 1-5). 1992. PLB 9.99 (0-679-92772-7); pap. 7.99 (0-679-82772-2) Knopf Bks Yng Read.
—Amazing Cars. King, Dave, photos by. LC 91-53138. (Illus.). 32p. (Orig.). (gr. 1-5). 1992. PLB 9.99 (0-679-92766-2); pap. 6.95 (0-679-82766-8) Knopf Bks Yng Read.
Lord, Walter. Day of Infamy. (gr. 8 up). 1991. pap. 4.99 (0-553-26777-9, Falcon) Bantam.
—Day of Infamy. (Illus.). (gr. 9 up). 1991. Repr. of 1957 ed. 15.00 (0-03-027620-9) Adm Nimitz Foun.
—Night to Remember. (gr. 6-12). 1983. pap. 4.99 (0-553-27827-4) Bantam.
Lord, Wendy. Gorilla on the Midway. LC 93-1051. 1994. write for info. (0-7814-0892-X, Chariot Bks) Cook.
—Pickle Stew. LC 93-19018. 1994. write for info. (0-7814-0886-5, Chariot Bks) Cook.
Lord Baden-Powell. Lessons from the Varsity of Life. (Illus.). 320p. 1992. pap. 17.95 (0-9632054-7-1) Stevens Pub.
—Rovering to Success: A Guide for Young Manhood. Lord Baden-Powell, illus. 247p. (Orig.). 1992. pap. 16.95 (0-9632054-3-9) Stevens Pub.
Lorde, Audre. From a Land Where Other People Live. LC 73-82075. (gr. 12 up). 1973. pap. 5.00 (0-910296-97-9) Broadside Pr.

Loredo, Betsy. Explorers Club Series. (Illus.). (gr. 4-6). 1993. PLB 21.95 (1-881889-47-5) Silver Moon. The four members of the Explorers Club have vowed to go where no kids have gone before. The EXPLORERS CLUB series is being developed in cooperation with the National Oceanic & Atmospheric Administration (NOAA), the U.S. government agency responsible for monitoring global weather, ocean & river activities. Each volume in the series concludes with a geographic activity reflecting the theme of the book & a glossary of terms & each has black & white illustrations throughout by artist Michael Moran. STORM AT THE SHORE, by Betsy Loredo (ISBN 1-881889-10-6), takes the members of the Explorers Club to Fire Island, where they weather a hurricane & see firsthand how nature shapes our shores. In AVALANCHE IN THE ALPS, also by Betsy Loredo (ISBN 1-881889-12-2), the four kids head to Switzerland for a vacation. There they encounter spectacular mountain views, difficult hiking trails, & quaint villages--& an avalanche, too. Each book is $12.95 cloth. *Publisher Provided Annotation.*

—Mystery on the Mississippi. Moran, Michael, illus. 80p. (gr. 4-6). 1994. PLB 12.95 (1-881889-35-1) Silver Moon.
—Storm at the Shore. LC 93-16455. (Illus.). 64p. (Orig.). (gr. 3-5). 1993. PLB 12.95 (1-881889-10-6) Silver Moon.
Loredo, Betsy & Moran, Michael. Avalanche in the Alps. LC 93-11175. (Illus.). 64p. (Orig.). (gr. 4-6). 1993. PLB 12.95 (1-881889-12-2); pap. cancelled (1-881889-13-0) Silver Moon.
Lorenz, Konrad. King Solomon's Ring. 216p. (RL 7). 1991. pap. 3.95 (0-451-62831-4, AE3229, Sig) NAL-Dutton.
Lorenz, Lee. Big Gus & Little Gus. Lorenz, Lee, illus. 32p. (gr. k-3). 1984. pap. 5.95 (0-13-078122-3) P-H.
—The Feathered Ogre. (Illus.). 48p. (gr. 1-4). 1981. 9.95 (0-13-308304-7) P-H.
—The Feathered Ogre. (Illus.). 30p. (gr. 1-4). 1983. pap. 4.95 (0-13-308296-2, Pub. by Treehouse Bks) P-H.
—Hugo & the Spacedog. Lorenz, Lee, illus. LC 82-22960. 30p. (ps-3). 1986. 10.95 (0-13-444497-3); pap. 5.95 (0-13-444480-9) P-H.

—Scornful Simkin. Lorenz, Lee, illus. 30p. (Orig.). (gr. k-3). 1982. pap. 3.95 (0-13-796730-6, Pub. by Treehouse) P-H.
—A Weekend in the City. Lorenz, Lee, illus. 32p. (gr. k-3). 1991. 14.95 (0-945912-15-3) Pippin Pr.
—A Weekend in the Country. Lorenz, Lee, illus. 32p. (gr. k-3). 1985. 11.95 (0-13-947961-9) P-H.
Lorenz, Susan K. The Wag of Their Tails. 1992. 9.95 (0-8062-4266-3) Carlton.
Lorenzen, Anna L. Tiger. Craft, Mary, illus. 22p. (Orig.). (gr. 1-2). 1989. pap. text ed. 2.95 (0-9626133-0-4) ALL Ventura Pub.
Loretan, Sylvia. Bob the Snowman. (ps-3). 1991. 13.95 (0-670-83677-X) Viking Child Bks.
Lorian, Nicole. A Birthday Present for Mama: A Step Two Book. Miller, J. P., illus. LC 83-26849. (ps-2). 1984. pap. 3.50 (0-394-86755-6) Random Bks Yng Read.
Lorimer, Janet. Trouble with Buster: A Day in the Life of a Pilgrim Girl. 1990. pap. 2.50 (0-590-42641-9) Scholastic Inc.
Lorimer, Lawrence. El Arca de Noe. Martin, Charles E., illus. (SPA). 32p. (ps-3). 1993. pap. 2.25 (0-394-85129-3) Random Bks Yng Read.
Lorimer, Lawrence T. El Arca de Noe. (SPA). 1981. 2.25 (0-394-85219-2) Random Bks Yng Read.
Lorimer, Lawrence T., retold by. Noah's Ark. Martin, Charles E., illus. Lerner, Sharon, ed. LC 77-92377. (Illus.). (ps-2). 1978. lib. bdg. 5.99 (0-394-93861-5); pap. 2.25 (0-394-83861-0) Random Bks Yng Read.
Loring, Honey & Harris, John. The Big Good Wolf. Deutsch, Nicholas, illus. 28p. (ps-6). 1990. pap. text ed. 2.75 (0-9626566-0-7) Gone Dogs.
Loring, Philip A. The Miracle of the Blue Horse. (gr. 9-12). 1993. 7.95 (0-8062-4606-5) Carlton.
Los Angeles Children's Museum Staff. Color Your Way Through L. A. Polsky, Carol, ed. U. S.-Japan Cross Culture Center & Opinion Editors, trs. Rubin, Marvin, illus. (ENG, SPA & JPN.). 56p. (Orig.). (gr. k up). 1983. 3.95 (0-914953-00-1) Los Angeles.
Los Angeles Unified School District Staff. Getting a Job. (Illus.). 48p. (Orig.). (gr. 7-12). 1990. Set. 10 wkbks. & tchr's. guide 44.95 (1-56119-095-0); wkbk. 4.95 (1-56119-093-4); tchr's. guide 1.95 (1-56119-094-2) Educ Pr MD.
—Starting Your New Job. (Illus.). 48p. (Orig.). (gr. 7-12). 1990. Set. 10 wkbks. & tchr's. guide 44.95 (1-56119-098-5); wkbk. 4.95 (1-56119-096-9); tchr's. guide 1.95 (1-56119-097-7) Educ Pr MD.
—Working with Others. (Illus.). 48p. (Orig.). (gr. 7-12). 1990. Set. 10 wkbks. & tchr's. guide 44.95 (1-56119-092-6); wkbk. 4.95 (1-56119-090-X); tchr's. guide 1.95 (1-56119-091-8) Educ Pr MD.
—You & Your Attitude. (Illus.). 48p. (Orig.). (gr. 7-12). 1990. Set. 10 wkbks. & tchr's. guide 44.95 (1-56119-089-6); wkbk. 4.95 (1-56119-087-X); tchr's. guide 1.95 (1-56119-088-8) Educ Pr MD.
Losito, Linda. The Ant on the Ground. Oxford Scientific Films Staff, photos by. LC 89-4460. (Illus.). 32p. (gr. 4-6). 1989. PLB 15.93 (0-8368-0111-3) Gareth Stevens Inc.
—Discovering Damselflies & Dragonflies. Caulkins, Janet, ed. (Illus.). 48p. (gr. k-6). 1988. PLB 12.40 (0-531-18168-5, Pub. by Bookwright Pr) Watts.
Losito, Linda, jt. auth. see Harrison, Virginia.
Losito, Linda, et al. Mammals: Small Plant-Eaters. (Illus.). 96p. 1988. 17.95x (0-8160-1958-4) Facts on File.
—Birds: Aerial Hunters. (Illus.). 96p. 1989. 17.95x (0-8160-1963-0) Facts on File.
—Birds: The Plant- & Seed-Eaters. (Illus.). 96p. 1989. 17.95x (0-8160-1964-9) Facts on File.
—Fish. (Illus.). 96p. 1989. 17.95x (0-8160-1966-5) Facts on File.
—Insects & Spiders. (Illus.). 96p. 1989. 17.95x (0-8160-1967-3) Facts on File.
—Pets & Farm Animals. (Illus.). 300p. (gr. 4-9). 1990. 17.95x (0-8160-1969-X) Facts on File.
—Reptiles & Amphibians. (Illus.). 96p. 1989. 17.95x (0-8160-1965-7) Facts on File.
—Simple Animals. (Illus.). 96p. 1989. 17.95x (0-8160-1968-1) Facts on File.
Loss, Kenneth D., ed. see Stotz, Carl E.
Loth, Paul. The Bible Tells Me So. LC 93-18723. 1993. 7.99 (0-8407-9232-8) Nelson.
Loth, Paul J. First Steps. LC 92-11389. 1992. 7.99 (0-8407-9167-4) Oliver-Nelson.
—God's Word in My Heart. LC 93-18774. 1993. 7.99 (0-8407-9233-6) Nelson.
—My Time with God. LC 92-20577. 1992. 7.99 (0-8407-9168-2) Nelson.
Lothrop, Harriet M. The Five Little Peppers & How They Grew. (Orig.). (gr. k-6). 1985. pap. 4.95 (0-440-42505-0, Pub. by Yearling Classics) Dell.
Lottridge, Celia B. One Watermelon Seed. Patkau, Karen, illus. 24p. (ps up). 1990. pap. 6.95 (0-19-540735-0) OUP.
—Ten Small Tales. Fitzgerald, Joanne, illus. LC 92-2878. 64p. (gr. k-4). 1994. SBE 15.95 (0-689-50568-X, M K McElderry) Macmillan Child Grp.
Lottridge, Celia B., retold by. The Name of the Tree: A Bantu Folktale. Wallace, Ian, illus. LC 89-2430. 36p. (gr. 1-5). 1990. SBE 14.95 (0-689-50490-X, M K McElderry) Macmillan Child Grp.
Lotz, Jim. Nova Scotia. LC 91-951128. (Illus.). 144p. (gr. 4 up). 1992. PLB 26.60 (0-516-06613-7) Childrens.

Lotz, Karen E. Can't Sit Still. Browning, Colleen, illus. LC 92-28853. 48p. (ps-3). 1993. 13.99 (0-525-45066-1, DCB) Dutton Child Bks.
—Snowsong Whistling. Kleven, Elisa, illus. LC 92-47117. 32p. (ps-2). 1993. 14.99 (0-525-45145-5, DCB) Dutton Child Bks.
Loudermick, Mary, pref. by see Farmer, Lucile.
Lough, Tom, ed. see Barrowman, Tom, et al.
Loughery, John. John Sloan. (gr. 6 up). 1994. write for info. (0-8050-2878-1) H Holt & Co.
Louie, Al-Ling. Yeh Shen: A Cinderella Story from China. Young, Ed, illus. 32p. (ps-2). 1990. 14.95 (0-399-20900-X, Philomel) Putnam Pub Group.
Louise Hsi Kuo, jt. auth. see Yuan Hsi Kuo.
Louisiana School Students. Ascending. Thornton, Don, intro. by. Louisiana Students, illus. 302p. (Orig.). (gr. 1-12). Date not set. pap. 25.00 (1-882913-00-0) Thornton LA.
Loumaye, Jacqueline. The Tale of the Kite. (Illus.). 32p. (gr. 3-5). 1991. 18.50 (0-89565-759-7); 12.95s.p. (0-685-55093-1) Childs World.
Lourie, Peter. Amazon: A Young Reader's Look at the Last Frontier. Santilli, Marcos, photos by. LC 90-85720. (Illus.). 48p. (gr. 3-7). 1991. 17.95 (1-878093-00-2) Boyds Mills Pr.
—Hudson River: An Adventure from the Mountains to the Sea. LC 91-72870. (Illus.). 48p. (gr. 3-7). 1992. 15.95 (1-878093-01-0) Boyds Mills Pr.
—Yukon River: An Adventure to the Gold Fields of the Klondike. (Illus.). 48p. (gr. 3-7). 1992. PLB 15.95 (1-878093-90-8) Boyds Mills Pr.
Lourie, Richard, tr. see Shulevitz, Uri.
Lousberg, Arlene L. You & Me - Me & You: A Kid's Own Life Story. (Illus.). 40p. (Orig.). (gr. 3-9). 1990. pap. 9.99 (0-9625397-1-6) Memories In Print.
Lovak, Matt, jt. auth. see St. Pierre, Stephanie.
Lovasik, L. G. My Picture Prayer Book. (ps-3). 4.75 (0-89942-134-2) Catholic Bk Pub.
Lovasik, Lawrence G. St. Joseph First Children's Bible. (ps-3). 1983. 4.95 (0-89942-135-0) Catholic Bk Pub.
—The Seven Sacraments. (Illus.). (gr. 1-6). 1978. flexible bdg 0.95 (0-89942-278-0, 278) Catholic Bk Pub.
—The Ten Commandments. (Illus.). (gr. 1-6). 1978. flexible bdg. 0.95 (0-89942-287-X, 287) Catholic Bk Pub.
Love, Ann. The Prince Who Wrote a Letter. Goffe, Toni, illus. LC 92-27587. 1992. write for info. (0-85953-398-0, Pub. by Childs Play UK); pap. write for info. (0-85953-399-9, Pub. by Childs Play UK) Childs Play.
Love, Ann & Drake, Jane. Take Action. LC 92-30412. 1993. pap. 7.95 (0-688-12465-8, Pub. by Beech Tree Bks) Morrow.
—Take Action: An Environmental Book for Kids. Cupples, Pat, illus. LC 92-30412. 96p. (gr. 3 up). 1993. Repr. PLB 13.93 (0-688-12464-X, Tambourine Bks) Morrow.
Love, Ann, jt. auth. see Drake, Jane.
Love, Douglas. Blame It on the Wolf & Be Kind to Your Mother (Earth): Two Original Plays. Zimmerman, Robert, illus. LC 92-4624. 80p. (gr. 5 up). 1993. PLB 13.89 (0-06-021106-7) HarpC Child Bks.
—Holiday in the Rain Forest & Kabuki Gift: Two Plays. Zimmerman, Robert, illus. 112p. (gr. 4 up). 1994. PLB 13.89 (0-06-024276-0) HarpC Child Bks.
—Holiday in the Rain Forest: Theater Kit. Zimmerman, Robert, illus. (gr. 5 up). 1993. 14.95 (0-694-00561-4, Festival) HarpC Child Bks.
—Kabuki Gift: Theater Kit. Zimmerman, Robert, illus. 32p. (gr. 5 up). 1993. 14.95 (0-694-00562-2, Festival) HarpC Child Bks.
—So You Want to Be a Star. Zimmerman, Robert, illus. 32p. (gr. 5 up). 1993. 18.95 (0-694-00428-6, Festival) HarpC Child Bks.
Love, Glen A., intro. by. The World Begins Here: An Anthology of Oregon Short Fiction. LC 92-43642. (Illus.). 320p. (Orig.). (gr. 6 up). 1993. text ed. 32.95x (0-87071-369-8); pap. 18.95t (0-87071-370-1) Oreg St U Pr.
Love, Hallie. A Is for Alligator. Kennedy, Maureen, illus. 64p. (gr. 1 up). 1993. 15.95 (1-879244-02-0) Windom Bks.
Love, Marla. Twenty Decoding Games. (gr. 2-6). 1982. pap. 12.95 (0-8224-5801-2) Fearon Teach Aids.
—Twenty Reading Comprehension Games. (gr. 4-6). 1977. pap. 9.95 (0-8224-5800-4) Fearon Teach Aids.
—Twenty Word Structure Games. (gr. 2-6). 1983. pap. 12.95 (0-8224-5802-0) Fearon Teach Aids.
Love, Marsha L. The Vitamin Parade. LC 89-51346. (Illus.). 44p. (gr. k-3). 1989. 5.95 (1-55523-264-7) Winston-Derek.
Love, Penelope & Morrison, Mark. Terror Australis: Cthulhu down Under. Willis, Lynn & Petersen, Sandy, eds. Sullivan, Tom & Leming, Ron, illus. 136p. (Orig.). (gr. 12 up). 1987. pap. 17.95 (0-933635-40-0, 2319) Chaosium.
Love, Robertus. The Rise & Fall of Jesse James. Fellman, Michael, intro. by. LC 89-24965. xxiv, 446p. 1990. pap. 11.95 (0-8032-7932-9, Bison Books) U of Nebr Pr.
Lovejoy, Addison. The Baseball Song Book. 24p. (gr. 8 up). 1971. 1.95 (0-87884-015-X) Unicorn Ent.
Lovelace, Delos W. King Kong. Conaway, Judith, ed. Van Munching, Paul, illus. LC 87-28354. 96p. (gr. 3-7). 1988. pap. 2.95 (0-394-89789-7) Random Bks Yng Read.

Lovelace, Maud H. Betsy & Joe. Neville, Vera, illus. LC 48-8096. 256p. (gr. 5 up). 1948. 14.95 (0-690-13378-2, Crowell Jr Bks) HarpC Child Bks.
—Betsy & Tacy Go Downtown. reissue ed. Lenski, Lois, illus. LC 43-51264. 192p. (gr. 2-5). 1979. pap. 3.95 (0-06-440098-0, Trophy) HarpC Child Bks.
—Betsy & Tacy Go Downtown. Lenski, Lois, illus. LC 43-51264. 192p. (gr. 2-5). 1966. PLB 14.89 (0-690-13450-9, Crowell Jr Bks) HarpC Child Bks.
—Betsy & Tacy Go over the Big Hill. reissue ed. Lenski, Lois, illus. LC 42-23557. 176p. (gr. 2-5). 1979. pap. 3.95 (0-06-440099-9, Trophy) HarpC Child Bks.
—Betsy & Tacy Go over the Big Hill. Lenski, Lois, illus. LC 42-23557. 176p. (gr. 2-5). 1966. PLB 14.89 (0-690-13521-1, Crowell Jr Bks) HarpC Child Bks.
—Betsy in Spite of Herself. Neville, Vera, illus. LC 46-11995. 272p. (gr. 4-7). 1980. pap. 3.95 (0-06-440111-1, Trophy) HarpC Child Bks.
—Betsy-Tacy. Lenski, Lois, illus. LC 40-30965. 128p. (gr. 2-5). 1979. pap. 3.95 (0-06-440096-4, Trophy) HarpC Child Bks.
—Betsy-Tacy. Lenski, Lois, illus. LC 40-30965. 128p. (gr. 2-5). 1966. PLB 14.89 (0-690-13805-9, Crowell Jr Bks) HarpC Child Bks.
—Betsy-Tacy & Tib. reissue ed. Lenski, Lois, illus. LC 41-18714. 144p. (gr. 2-5). 1979. pap. 3.95 (0-06-440097-2, Trophy) HarpC Child Bks.
—Betsy-Tacy & Tib. Lenski, Lois, illus. LC 41-18714. 144p. (gr. 2-5). 1966. PLB 14.89 (0-690-13876-8, Crowell Jr Bks) HarpC Child Bks.
—Betsy Was a Junior. Neville, Vera, illus. LC 46-11995. 248p. (gr. 5 up). 1947. 14.95 (0-690-13946-2, Crowell Jr Bks) HarpC Child Bks.
—Betsy's Wedding. Neville, Vera, illus. LC 55-11108. 241p. (gr. 5 up). 1955. 14.95 (0-690-13733-8, Crowell Jr Bks) HarpC Child Bks.
—Heaven to Betsy. Neville, Vera, illus. LC 45-9806. 268p. (gr. 4-7). 1980. pap. 3.50 (0-06-440110-3, Trophy) HarpC Child Bks.
Lovelady, J., ed. see Gimbel, Cheryl & Maners, Wendelin.
Lovelady, Janet. Aladdin Literature Mini-Unit. (Illus.). 32p. (gr. 3-5). 1990. wkbk. 4.95 (1-56096-016-7) Mari.
—Annie & the Old One Literature Mini-Unit. (Illus.). 32p. (gr. 3-5). 1990. wkbk. 4.95 (1-56096-018-3) Mari.
—Big Bad Bruce Literature Mini-Unit. (Illus.). 32p. (gr. 2-4). 1989. wkbk. 4.95 (1-56096-001-9) Mari.
—Bread & Jam for Frances Literature Mini-Unit. (Illus.). 32p. (gr. 2-4). 1989. wkbk. 4.95 (1-56096-002-7) Mari.
—Bremen-Town Musicians Literature Mini-Unit. (Illus.). 32p. (gr. 2-4). 1989. wkbk. 4.95 (1-56096-004-3) Mari.
—The Drinking Gourd Literature Mini-Unit. (Illus.). 32p. (gr. 3-5). 1990. wkbk. 4.95 (1-56096-019-1) Mari.
—Hill of Fire Literature Mini Unit. (Illus.). 32p. (gr. 2-4). 1989. wkbk. 4.95 (1-56096-005-1) Mari.
—The Hundred Dresses Literature Mini-Unit. (Illus.). 32p. (gr. 3-5). 1990. wkbk. 4.95 (1-56096-014-0) Mari.
—The Little House Literature Mini-Unit. (Illus.). 32p. (gr. 2-4). 1989. wkbk. 4.95 (1-56096-000-0) Mari.
—Long Way to a New Land Literature Mini-Unit. (Illus.). 32p. (gr. 3-5). 1990. wkbk. 4.95 (1-56096-013-2) Mari.
—Make Way for Ducklings Literature Mini-Unit. (Illus.). 32p. (gr. 2-4). 1989. wkbk. 4.95 (1-56096-006-X) Mari.
—Miss Rumphius Literature Mini-Unit. (Illus.). 32p. (gr. 2-4). 1989. wkbk. 4.95 (1-56096-003-5) Mari.
—Sam, Bangs & Moonshine Literature Mini-Unit. (Illus.). 32p. (gr. 3-5). 1989. wkbk. 4.95 (1-56096-012-4) Mari.
—Shoeshine Girl Literature Mini-Unit. (Illus.). 32p. (gr. 3-5). 1990. wkbk. 4.95 (1-56096-017-5) Mari.
—Song of the Swallows Literature Mini-Unit. (Illus.). 32p. (gr. 2-4). 1989. wkbk. 4.95 (1-56096-007-8) Mari.
—Stone Soup Literature Mini-Unit. (Illus.). 32p. (gr. 2-4). 1989. wkbk. 4.95 (1-56096-008-6) Mari.
—Strega Nona Literature Mini-Unit. (Illus.). 32p. (gr. 2-4). 1989. wkbk. 4.95 (1-56096-009-4) Mari.
—The Ugly Duckling Literature Mini-Unit. (Illus.). 32p. (gr. 3-5). 1990. wkbk. 4.95 (1-56096-015-9) Mari.
—Velveteen Rabbit Literature Mini-Unit. (Illus.). 32p. (gr. 3-5). 1990. wkbk. 4.95 (1-56096-011-6) Mari.
—Wagon Wheels Literature Mini-Unit. (Illus.). 32p. (gr. 3-5). 1990. wkbk. 4.95 (1-56096-010-8) Mari.
Lovelady, Janet, ed. see Drew, Naomi.
Lovelady, Janet, ed. see Fox, C. Lynn.
Loveland Comm. Staff. Discover Animals. 1992. write for info. (1-55513-910-8, Chariot Bks) Cook.
—Discover Colors. 1992. write for info. (1-55513-916-7, Chariot Bks) Cook.
—Discover Families. 1992. write for info. (1-55513-911-6, Chariot Bks) Cook.
—Discover Sizes & Shapes. 1992. write for info. (1-55513-909-4, Chariot Bks) Cook.
Loveland, Nicole. Boogins Gets a Basket. (Illus.). 32p. (ps-2). 1984. PLB 4.95 (0-917107-00-4) Cat-Tales Pr.
—Boogins' Rainy Day. Stebbins, Pat, illus. (ps-3). 1985. PLB 5.95 (0-917107-02-0) Cat-Tales Pr.
Loveless, Ganelle, jt. auth. see Bullock, Waneta B.
Loveless, Liz. One, Two, Buckle My Shoe. Loveless, Liz, illus. LC 92-40947. 32p. (ps). 1993. 13.95 (1-56282-477-5); PLB 13.89 (1-56282-478-3) Hyprn Child.
Lovell, Robert. Probability Activities. 308p. (gr. 9-12). 1993. pap. 18.95 (1-55953-067-7) Key Curr Pr.
Loverance, Rowena. Ancient Greece. (Illus.). 48p. (gr. 3-7). 1993. 14.99 (0-670-84754-2) Viking Child Bks.

Loverseed, Amanda. The Thunder King: A Peruvian Tale. Loverseed, Amanda, illus. 32p. (gr. k-3). 1991. PLB 14.95 (0-87226-450-5, Bedrick Blackie) P Bedrick Bks.
—Tikkatoo's Journey: An Eskimo Folk Tale. Loverseed, Amanda, illus. LC 89-17840. 32p. (gr. k-3). 1990. PLB 14.95 (0-87226-420-3, Bedrick Blackie) P Bedrick Bks.
Loves, June. The Grasshopper. Forss, Ian, illus. LC 92-34263. 1993. 4.25 (0-383-03626-7) SRA Schl Grp.
—I Know That. Smith, Craig, illus. LC 92-34262. 1993. 4.25 (0-383-03633-X) SRA Schl Grp.
—This Is the Book That I Borrowed. McClelland, Linda, illus. LC 92-31955. 1993. 4.25 (0-383-03598-8) SRA Schl Grp.
Lovett, Sarah. Extremely Weird Birds. (gr. 3 up). 1992. pap. 9.95 (1-56261-040-6) John Muir.
—Extremely Weird Endangered Species. (Illus.). 48p. (Orig.). (gr. 3 up). 1992. pap. 9.95 (1-56261-042-2) John Muir.
—Extremely Weird Fish. (Illus.). 48p. (Orig.). (gr. 3 up). 1992. pap. 9.95 (1-56261-041-4) John Muir.
—Extremely Weird Insects. Sundstrom, Mary & Evans, Beth, illus. LC 92-20098. 48p. (gr. 3 up). Date not set. pap. 9.95 (1-56261-076-7) John Muir.
—Extremely Weird Mammals. (Illus.). 48p. (Orig.). (gr. 3 up). 1993. pap. 9.95 (1-56261-107-0) John Muir.
—Extremely Weird Micro Monsters. (Illus.). 48p. (Orig.). (gr. 3 up). 1993. pap. 9.95 (1-56261-120-8) John Muir.
—Extremely Weird Primates. Blakemore, Sally & Sundstrom, Mary, illus. 48p. (Orig.). (gr. 3 up). 1991. pap. 9.95 (1-56261-018-X) John Muir.
—Extremely Weird Reptiles. Blakemore, Sally & Sundstrom, Mary, illus. 48p. (Orig.). (gr. 3 up). 1991. pap. 9.95 (1-56261-036-8) John Muir.
—Extremely Weird Sea Creatures. Sundstrom, Mary & Blakemore, Sally, illus. LC 92-18383. 48p. (Orig.). (gr. 3 up). Date not set. pap. 9.95 (1-56261-077-5) John Muir.
—Extremely Weird Snakes. (Illus.). 48p. (Orig.). (gr. 3 up). 1993. pap. 9.95 (1-56261-108-9) John Muir.
—Kidding Around London: A Young Person's Guide to the City. Taylor, Michael, illus. 64p. (Orig.). (gr. 3 up). 1989. pap. 9.95 (0-945465-24-6) John Muir.
—Kidding Around New York City: A Young Person's Guide. 2nd ed. Blakemore, Sally, illus. 64p. (gr. 3 up). 1993. pap. 9.95 (1-56261-095-3) John Muir.
—Kidding Around the Hawaiian Islands: A Young Person's Guide to the Islands. Taylor, Michael, illus. 64p. (Orig.). (gr. 3 up). 1990. pap. 9.95 (0-945465-37-8) John Muir.
—Kidding Around the National Parks of the Southwest: A Young Person's Guide. Strock, Glen, illus. 108p. (Orig.). (gr. 3 up). 1990. pap. 12.95 (0-945465-72-6) John Muir.
Lovett, Sarah, text by. Extremely Weird Bats. (Illus.). 48p. (gr. 3 up). 1991. 9.95 (1-56261-008-2) John Muir.
—Extremely Weird Frogs. (Illus.). 48p. (gr. 3 up). 1991. 9.95 (1-56261-006-6) John Muir.
—Extremely Weird Spiders. (Illus.). 48p. (gr. 3 up). 1991. 9.95 (1-56261-007-4) John Muir.
Lovik, Craig J. The Exodus. (Illus.). 24p. (gr. k-4). 1987. pap. 1.89 (0-570-09001-6, 59-1429) Concordia.
Lovitt, jt. auth. see Brigandi.
Lovitt, Chip. Magic Johnson Sports Shots. 1991. pap. 1.25 (0-590-47191-0) Scholastic Inc.
—Michael Jordan. (gr. 4-7). 1993. pap. 3.25 (0-590-46094-3) Scholastic Inc.
—Rock On! The Great Rock & Roll Activity Book. (gr. 5-7). 1990. pap. 2.50 (0-590-42973-6) Scholastic Inc.
Low, Alice. The Family Read-Aloud Holiday Treasury. Brown, Marc, illus. 1991. 19.95 (0-316-53368-8) Little.
—The Macmillan Book of Greek Gods & Heroes. Stewart, Arvis, illus. LC 85-7170. 192p. (gr. 2-6). 1985. SBE 16.95 (0-02-761390-9, Macmillan Child Bk) Macmillan Child Grp.
Low, Alice, compiled by. The Family Read-Aloud Christmas Treasury. Brown, Marc, illus. (ps up). 1989. 17.95 (0-316-53371-8, Joy St Bks) Little.
Low, Joseph. A Mad Wet Hen & Other Riddles. LC 76-44329. (Illus.). (gr. 2 up). 1992. pap. 3.95 (0-688-11511-X, Mulberry) Morrow.
—Mice Twice. LC 85-26768. (Illus.). 32p. (ps-3). 1986. pap. 4.95 (0-689-71060-7, Aladdin) Macmillan Child Grp.
Lowdermilk, Karen, ed. see Michael, Linda.
Lowe. Beasts by Bunches. 1987. 10.95 (0-385-23794-4) Doubleday.
Lowe, Darla. Story of Adoption: Why Do I Look Different? Carney, Christina S., illus. LC 87-46273. (Orig.). (gr. 3-6). 1987. pap. 5.95 (0-9606090-2-4) EastWest Pr.
Lowe, Felix C. John Ross. Viola, Herman, intro. by Soper, Patrick, illus. 32p. (gr. 3-6). 1990. PLB 17.96 (0-8172-3407-1); pap. 4.95 (0-8114-4093-1) Raintree Steck-V.
Lowe, George L. B. G., Vol. 1: The Little Drummer Girl Who Drums for the Sun. Montrell, Dan, illus. 21p. (Orig.). (ps). 1988. PLB 5.00x (0-685-22681-6) G L Lowe.
Lowe, Jimmy. Jesse Stuart: the Boy from the Dark Hills: A Boyography. Gifford, James M., et al, eds. Wise, Pamela, designed by. LC 90-62199. (Illus.). 79p. (gr. 4-12). 1990. pap. text ed. 15.00 (0-945084-19-6) J Stuart Found.
Lowe, Malcolm V. Bombers. Gibbons, Tony, et al, illus. 48p. (gr. 5 up). 1987. PLB 13.50 (0-8225-1381-1, First Ave Edns); pap. 4.95 (0-8225-9541-9, First Ave Edns) Lerner Pubns.

—Fighters. Sarson, Peter, et al, illus. LC 84-7941. 48p. (gr. 5 up). 1985. PLB 13.50 (*0-8225-1376-5*, First Ave Edns); pap. 4.95 (*0-8225-9506-0*, First Ave Edns) Lerner Pubns.

Lowe, Steve, ed. see Columbus, Christopher.

Lowe, Steve, ed. see Thoreau, Henry David.

Lowe, William C. Blessings of Liberty: Safeguarding Civil Rights. LC 92-9756. 1992. 22.60 (*0-86593-173-9*); 16. 95s.p. (*0-685-59325-8*) Rourke Corp.

Lowell, Melissa. Breaking the Ice. 1993. pap. 3.50 (*0-553-48134-7*) Bantam.

—Competition. (gr. 4-7). 1994. pap. 3.50 (*0-553-48136-3*, Skylark) Bantam.

—Going for the Gold. (gr. 4-7). 1994. pap. 3.50 (*0-553-48137-1*, Skylark) Bantam.

—In the Spotlight. 1993. pap. 3.50 (*0-553-48135-5*) Bantam.

Lowell, Susan. I Am Lavina Cummings. Mirocha, Paul, illus. 200p. (gr. 2-6). 1993. 14.95 (*0-915943-39-5*); pap. 6.95 (*0-915943-77-8*) Milkweed Ed.

—The Three Little Javelinas. Harris, Jim, illus. LC 92-14232. 32p. (ps-2). 1992. 14.95 (*0-87358-542-9*) Northland AZ.

Lowenberg see Sohn, David A.

Lowerre, George F. Critical Reading: Workbook B: Reusable Edition. 70p. (gr. 3-8). 1973. wkbk. 6.00 (*0-87879-720-3*, Ann Arbor Div) Acad Therapy.

—Critical Reading: Workbook C: Reusable Edition. 78p. (gr. 3-8). 1973. wkbk. 6.00 (*0-87879-721-1*, Ann Arbor Div) Acad Therapy.

Lowerre, George F. & Scandura, Alice M. Critical Reading: Workbook A: Reusable Edition. 54p. (gr. 3-8). 1973. 6.00 (*0-87879-719-X*, Ann Arbor Div); tchr's manual, 28p 2.00 (*0-87879-723-8*) Acad Therapy.

—Critical Reading: Workbook D: Reusable Edition. 68p. (gr. 3-8). 1973. wkbk. 6.00 (*0-87879-722-X*, Ann Arbor Div) Acad Therapy.

Lowery, Lawrence & Verbeeck, Carol. Explorations in Life Science. (gr. 1-3). 1987. pap. 6.95 (*0-8224-2314-6*) Fearon Teach Aids.

—Explorations in Physical Science. (gr. 1-3). 1987. pap. 6.95 (*0-8224-2316-2*) Fearon Teach Aids.

Lowery, Linda. Earth Day. (Illus.). 48p. (gr. k-4). 1991. PLB 14.95 (*0-87614-662-0*) Carolrhoda Bks.

—Earth Day. (ps-3). 1992. pap. 5.95 (*0-87614-560-8*) Carolrhoda Bks.

—Earthwise at Home. (ps-3). 1992. 19.95 (*0-87614-730-9*) Carolrhoda Bks.

—Earthwise at Home: A Guide to the Care & Feeding of Your Planet. (ps-3). 1992. pap. 7.95 (*0-87614-585-3*) Carolrhoda Bks.

—Earthwise at Play: A Guide to the Care & Feeding of Your Planet. (ps-3). 1992. pap. 7.95 (*0-87614-586-1*) Carolrhoda Bks.

—Laurie Tells. Karpinski, John E., illus. LC 93-9786. (gr. 4 up). 1994. 18.95 (*0-87614-790-2*) Carolrhoda Bks.

—Martin Luther King Day. Mitchell, Hetty, illus. 56p. (gr. k-4). 1987. lib. bdg. 14.95 (*0-87614-299-4*) Carolrhoda Bks.

—Martin Luther King Day. Mitchell, Hetty, illus. (gr. 3-5). 1987. incl. cassette 19.95 (*0-87499-071-8*); pap. 12.95 incl. cassette (*0-87499-070-X*); 4 paperbacks, cassette & guide 27.95 (*0-87499-072-6*) Live Oak Media.

—Martin Luther King Day. Mitchell, Hetty, illus. 56p. (gr. k-4). 1987. pap. 5.95 (*0-87614-468-7*, First Ave Edns) Lerner Pubns.

Lowery, Linda & Lorbiecki, Marybeth. Earthwise at School: A Guide to the Care & Feeding of Your Planet. LC 92-11221. (ps-3). 1993. lib. bdg. 19.95 (*0-87614-731-7*); pap. write for info. (*0-87614-587-X*) Carolrhoda Bks.

Lowery, Linda, jt. auth. see Lorbiecki, Marybeth.

Lowesdale School Children. Sarah Snail. Shaw, Peter, illus. LC 92-27084. 1993. 3.75 (*0-383-03592-9*) SRA Schl Grp.

Lowitz, Anson, jt. auth. see Lowitz, Sadyebeth.

Lowitz, Sadyebeth & Lowitz, Anson. Tom Edison Finds Out. 1979. pap. 0.95 (*0-440-48384-0*, YB) Dell.

Lowmiller, Cathie, jt. auth. see Mike, Jan.

Lowrey, Janette S. The Poky Little Puppy. Tenggren, Gustaf, illus. 24p. (ps-k). 1992. Repr. of 1942 ed. write for info. (*0-307-10394-3*, 10394, Pub. by Golden Bks) Western Pub.

—The Poky Little Puppy. Hansen, Rosanna, adapted by. Chandler, Jean, illus. 14p. (ps-k). 1992. bds. write for info. (*0-307-12333-2*, 12333, Golden Pr) Western Pub.

Lowry, James W. In the Whale's Belly & Other Martyr Stories. (Illus.). (gr. 7 up). 1981. pap. 4.70 (*0-87813-513-8*) Christian Light.

—North America Is the Lord's. (gr. 5). 1980. 18.75x (*0-87813-916-8*) Christian Light.

Lowry, Janette S. The Poky Little Puppy. (Illus.). 32p. (ps-k). 1992. write for info. (*0-307-15705-9*, 15705) Western Pub.

Lowry, Lois. All about Sam. (Illus.). 144p. (gr. 1-5). 1988. 13.45 (*0-395-48662-9*) HM.

—All about Sam. DeGroat, Diane, illus. 144p. (gr. k-6). 1989. pap. 3.50 (*0-440-40221-2*, YB) Dell.

—All about Sam. large type ed. 152p. 1993. 13.95 (*0-7451-1659-0*, Galaxy Child Lrg Print) Chivers N Amer.

—Anastasia. write for info. HM.

—Anastasia Again! De Groat, Diane, illus. 160p. (gr. 3-6). 1981. 14.45 (*0-395-31147-0*) HM.

—Anastasia Again! 160p. (gr. 4-7). 1982. pap. 3.50 (*0-440-40009-0*, YB) Dell.

—Anastasia Again. large type ed. (Illus.). 200p. (gr. 3-8). 1988. Repr. of 1981 ed. lib. bdg. 15.95 (*1-55736-074-X*, Crnrstn Bks) BDD LT Grp.

—Anastasia & Her Chosen Career. 192p. (gr. 3-7). 1987. 13.45 (*0-395-42506-9*) HM.

—Anastasia, Ask Your Analyst. LC 83-26687. 128p. (gr. 3-6). 1984. 13.45 (*0-395-36011-0*, 5-90388) HM.

—Anastasia, Ask Your Analyst. 128p. (Orig.). (gr. 4-6). 1992. pap. 3.50 (*0-440-40289-1*, YB) Dell.

—Anastasia, Ask Your Analyst. large type ed. 176p. 1989. Repr. of 1984 ed. lib. bdg. 15.95 (*1-55736-133-9*, Crnrstn Bks) BDD LT Grp.

—Anastasia at This Address. LC 90-48308. 112p. (gr. 3-7). 1991. 13.45 (*0-395-56263-5*) HM.

—Anastasia at This Address. 144p. (gr. 4-7). 1992. pap. 3.50 (*0-440-40652-8*, YB) Dell.

—Anastasia at Your Service. De Groat, Diane, illus. LC 82-9231. 160p. (gr. 3-6). 1982. 13.45 (*0-395-32865-9*) HM.

—Anastasia at Your Service. 160p. (gr. 3-6). 1984. pap. 3.50 (*0-440-40290-5*, YB) Dell.

—Anastasia at Your Service. large type ed. 224p. 1988. lib. bdg. 15.95 (*1-55736-101-0*, Crnrstn Bks) BDD LT Grp.

—Anastasia Has the Answers. (gr. 5 up). 1986. 13.45 (*0-395-41795-3*) HM.

—Anastasia Has the Answers. (gr. k-6). 1987. pap. 3.50 (*0-440-40087-2*, YB) Dell.

—Anastasia Has the Answers. large type ed. 176p. (gr. 3-7). 1991. text ed. 16.95x (*0-7451-1292-7*, Lythway Large Print) Hall.

—Anastasia Krupnik. 128p. 1984. pap. 3.25 (*0-553-15534-2*) Bantam.

—Anastasia Krupnik. 160p. (gr. 3-6). 1979. 13.45 (*0-395-28629-8*) HM.

—Anastasia Krupnik. large type ed. 144p. (gr. 3-7). 1988. Repr. of 1979 ed. lib. bdg. 15.95 (*1-55736-073-1*, Crnrstn Bks) BDD LT Grp.

—Anastasia Krupnik. (gr. 4-7). 1984. pap. 3.50 (*0-440-40852-0*) Dell.

—Anastasia on Her Own. LC 84-22432. 131p. (gr. 5-7). 1985. 13.45 (*0-395-38133-9*) HM.

—Anastasia on Her Own. 144p. (gr. 2-6). 1986. pap. 3.50 (*0-440-40291-3*, YB) Dell.

—Anastasia on Her Own. large type ed. 184p. 1989. Repr. of 1985 ed. lib. bdg. 15.95 (*1-55736-135-5*, Crnrstn Bks) BDD LT Grp.

—Anastasia's Chosen Career. (gr. k-6). 1992. pap. 3.50 (*0-318-33286-8*, YB) Dell.

—Anastasia's Chosen Career. large type ed. 216p. 1992. text ed. 12.95x (*0-7451-1468-7*, Lythway Large Print) Hall.

—Attaboy, Sam! De Groat, Diane, illus. 128p. (gr. 2-6). 1992. 13.45 (*0-395-61588-7*) HM.

—Attaboy, Sam! (gr. 4-7). 1993. pap. 3.50 (*0-440-40816-4*) Dell.

—Autumn Street. 160p. (gr. 5 up). 1980. 13.45 (*0-395-27812-0*) HM.

—Autumn Street. 192p. (gr. 4-7). 1986. pap. 3.50 (*0-440-40344-8*, YB) Dell.

—Find a Stranger, Say Good-Bye. LC 78-1024. 192p. (gr. 5 up). 1978. 14.45 (*0-395-26459-6*) HM.

—Find a Stranger, Say Good-Bye. 1990. pap. 3.50 (*0-440-20541-7*, LFL) Dell.

—The Giver. LC 92-15034. 208p. (gr. 7-9). 1993. 13.45 (*0-395-64566-2*) HM.

—The Giver. LC 93-21002. (gr. 9-12). 1993. 15.95 (*0-7862-0055-3*) Thorndike Pr.

—Number the Stars. LC 88-37134. 160p. (gr. 4-7). 1989. 13.45 (*0-395-51060-0*) HM.

—Number the Stars. (gr. 4-7). 1992. pap. 1.99 (*0-440-21372-X*) Dell.

—The One Hundredth Thing about Caroline. 160p. (gr. 3-6). 1983. 14.45 (*0-395-34829-3*) HM.

—The One Hundredth Thing about Caroline. 160p. (gr. k-6). 1985. pap. 3.50 (*0-440-46625-3*, YB) Dell.

—Rabble Starkey. (gr. 5 up). 1987. 13.95 (*0-395-43607-9*) HM.

—Rabble Starkey. (gr. k-6). 1988. pap. 3.50 (*0-440-40056-2*, YB) Dell.

—A Summer to Die. (gr. 4-10). 1979. pap. 2.95 (*0-553-26297-1*) Bantam.

—A Summer to Die. Oliver, Jenni, illus. (gr. 3-7). 1977. 13.45 (*0-395-25338-1*) HM.

—Summer to Die. 1984. pap. 3.50 (*0-553-27395-7*) Bantam.

—Switcharound. (gr. k-6). 1991. pap. 3.50 (*0-440-48415-4*, YB) Dell.

—Taking Care of Terrific. LC 82-23331. 160p. (gr. 5 up). 1983. 13.95 (*0-395-34070-5*) HM.

—Taking Care of Terrific. 176p. (gr. 4-7). 1984. pap. 3.25 (*0-440-48494-4*, YB) Dell.

—Taking Care of Terrific. large type ed. 208p. 1989. Repr. of 1983 ed. PLB 15.95 (*1-55736-119-3*, Crnrstn Bks) BDD LT Grp.

—Your Move, J. P.! 128p. (gr. 3-7). 1990. 13.45 (*0-395-53639-1*) HM.

—Your Move, J. P. (gr. 4-7). 1991. pap. 3.50 (*0-440-40497-5*) Dell.

—Your Move, J. P. (gr. 4-7). 1991. 3.50 (*0-685-50680-0*, Pub. by Yearling Classics) Dell.

Lowry, Robert. Nothing but the Blood. (Illus.). (gr. k-6). illustrated song 2.99 (*3-90117-009-X*) CEF Press.

Lowry, William B., jt. auth. see Bischof, Larry.

Loxton, Howard. Theater. LC 89-11533. (Illus.). 48p. (gr. 6-11). 1990. PLB 19.92 (*0-8114-2359-X*) Raintree Steck-V.

Loy, Joy A., ed. see Murdock, Michael D.

Loy, Merrie van see Thompson, Denisse & Van Loy, Merrie.

Lubach, Peter. Harry & the Singing Fish. Lubach, Peter, illus. LC 91-73824. 32p. (gr. k-4). 1992. 12.95 (*1-56282-158-X*); PLB 12.89 (*1-56282-159-8*) Hyprn Child.

Lubcker, Donna H. Sameer's Journey. Parado, Arturo H., illus. 40p. (Orig.). (gr. 3-5). 1992. pap. 10.00 (*0-9633803-3-8*) Jasmine Studios.

Lubeck, Maria-Garza & Salinas, Ana M. Mexican Celebrations. 54p. (gr. k-12). 1987. pap. text ed. 3.95x (*0-86728-019-0*) U TX Inst Lat Am Stud.

Lubetkin, Wendy. Deng Xiaoping. Schlesinger, Arthur M., Jr., intro. by. (Illus.). 112p. (gr. 5 up). 1988. 17.95 (*1-55546-830-6*) Chelsea Hse.

—George Marshall. (Illus.). (gr. 5 up). 1990. 17.95 (*1-55546-843-8*) Chelsea Hse.

LuBin, Deanna R. Monster Mother. Fosten, Tom, tr. (Illus.). (ps-9). 1991. lib. bdg. write for info.; text ed. write for info.; pap. write for info. incl. oral tape Lubin Pr.

Lubin, Ernest. A Start at the Piano. LC 78-110975. (Orig.). (gr. 5-8). 1977. pap. 9.95 (*0-8256-2149-6*) Music Sales.

LuBin, L., ed. see Foster, Tom.

Lubin, Leonard. Aladdin & His Wonderful Lamp. Burton, Richard T., tr. from ARA. Lubin, Leonard, illus. LC 82-70308. 48p. (ps-3). 1982. 12.95 (*0-385-28033-5*) Delacorte.

Lubin, Leonard, adapted by. Aladdin & His Wonderful Lamp. Burton, Richard F., tr. from ARA. Lubin, Leonard, illus. LC 82-70308. 48p. (gr. 1-4). 1982. 10. 95 (*0-440-00302-4*); PLB 10.89 (*0-440-00304-0*) Delacorte.

Lubin, Leonard B. Christmas Gift-Bringers. Lubin, Leonard B., illus. LC 89-2292. 32p. (gr. k-4). 1989. 12. 95 (*0-688-07019-1*); PLB 12.88 (*0-688-07020-5*) Lothrop.

Lubiner, Elaine D. Learning about Languages: Upper Elementary Through First Year High School. (SPA.). 128p. pap. text ed. 6.95 (*0-685-62799-3*, F9370-9, Natl Textbk); tchr's. ed., 91p. 14.95 (*0-685-62800-0*, F9371-1, Natl Textbk) NTC Pub Grp.

Luca, Sam De see De Luca, Sam.

Lucadamo, Rhonda, jt. auth. see Dean, Theresa.

Lucado, Max. Just in Case You Ever Wonder. 32p. (ps-2). 1992. 12.99 (*0-8499-0978-3*) Word Inc.

Lucas, Alice. Voices of Liberty. (Illus.). (gr. 5-8). 1990. Complete Package incls. 3 story bks., 3 tchr. discussion guides & 3 audio tapes. pap. text ed. 45.00 (*0-936434-49-X*, Pub. by Zellerbach Fam Fund); pap. text ed. write for info. ea. (Pub. by Zellerbach Fam Fund) SF Study Ctr.

Lucas, Alice, ed. see Northup, Solomon.

Lucas, Barbara. Little People's Mother Goose. LC 87-27261. 1988. 5.99 (*0-517-65860-7*) Outlet Bk Co.

Lucas, Barbara, tr. see Lindgren, Astrid.

Lucas, Barbara M. Snowed In. Stock, Catherine, illus. LC 92-39081. 32p. (ps-3). 1993. RSBE 14.95 (*0-02-761465-4*, Bradbury Pr) Macmillan Child Grp.

Lucas, Daryl. Children. Durham, Robert C., illus. 18p. (gr. 2). 1992. 7.99 (*0-8423-1013-4*) Tyndale.

—Choice Adventures, No. 2: The Smithsonian Connection. (gr. 3-7). 1991. PLB 4.99 (*0-8423-5026-8*) Tyndale.

—Heroes. Durham, Robert C., illus. 18p. (gr. 2). 1992. 8.99 (*0-8423-1009-6*) Tyndale.

—Heroines. Durham, Robert C., illus. 18p. (gr. 2). 1992. 8.99 (*0-8423-1012-6*) Tyndale.

—Prophets. Durham, Robert C., illus. (gr. 2). 1992. 8.99 (*0-8423-1011-8*) Tyndale.

Lucas, Eileen. Acid Rain. LC 91-3879. 128p. (gr. 4-8). 1991. PLB 26.60 (*0-516-05503-8*) Childrens.

—The Cherokees: People of the Southwest. LC 92-40874. (Illus.). 64p. (gr. 4-6). 1993. PLB 14.90 (*1-56294-312-X*) Millbrook Pr.

—Jane Goodall: Friend of the Chimps. LC 91-18060. (Illus.). 48p. (gr. 2-4). 1992. PLB 12.40 (*1-56294-135-6*) Millbrook Pr.

—Jane Goodall: Friend of the Chimps. (gr. 4-7). 1992. pap. 4.95 (*0-395-63570-5*) HM.

—The Mind at Work: How to Make It Work Better for You. LC 92-34663. (Illus.). 96p. (gr. 7 up). 1993. PLB 14.90 (*1-56294-300-6*) Millbrook Pr.

—The Ojibwas: People of the Northern Forests. LC 93-18640. (Illus.). 64p. (gr. 4-6). 1994. PLB 14.90 (*1-56294-313-8*) Millbrook Pr.

—Peace on the Playground: Nonviolent Ways of Problem-Solving. LC 91-12099. (Illus.). 64p. (gr. 5-8). 1991. PLB 12.90 (*0-531-20047-7*) Watts.

—Vincent Van Gogh. LC 90-47222. (Illus.). 64p. (gr. 3-5). 1991. PLB 12.90 (*0-531-20024-8*) Watts.

—Water: A Resource in Crisis. LC 91-36137. 128p. (gr. 4-8). 1991. PLB 26.60 (*0-516-05509-7*) Childrens.

Lucas, Ernest, jt. auth. see Lucas, Hazel.

Lucas, Hazel & Lucas, Ernest. Our World. (Illus.). 48p. (gr. 4 up). 1986. 13.95 (*0-85648-948-4*) Lion USA.

Lucas, Jerry. Becoming a Mental Math Wizard. LC 91-19472. (Illus.). 192p. (Orig.). (gr. 6 up). 1991. pap. 8.95 (*1-55870-216-4*) Shoe Tree Pr.

—Great Unsolved Mysteries of Science: From the End of the Dinosaurs to Interstellar Travel & Life on Other Planets. LC 92-39006. (Illus.). 192p. (Orig.). (gr. 7 up). 1993. pap. 9.95 (*1-55870-291-1*) Betterway Bks.

Lucas, Leanne. Addie McCormick & the Chicago Surprise. 1993. pap. 3.99 (*1-56507-082-8*) Harvest Hse.

—Addie McCormick & the Mystery of the Skeleton Key. (gr. 4-7). 1993. pap. 3.99 (*1-56507-147-6*) Harvest Hse.

—Addie McCormick & the Stolen Statue. (gr. 4 up). 1993. pap. 3.99 (*1-56507-080-1*) Harvest Hse.

Lucas, Leanne C. Addie McCormick & the Computer Pirate. LC 93-32203. (gr. 5 up). 1994. write for info. (*1-56507-165-4*) Harvest Hse.

Lucas, Sally. Twin Monkeys. Lucas, Margeaux, illus. 32p. (ps-2). Date not set. 11.95 (*1-56065-156-3*) Capstone Pr. Postponed.

Lucas, Winafred B., ed. see Blake, Doron W.

Lucas, Zoe. Wild Horses of Sable Island. (Illus.). 36p. (gr. 2 up). 1992. pap. 4.95 (*0-919872-73-5*, Pub. by Greey de Pencier CN) Firefly Bks Ltd.

Luccarelli, Vincent, Jr. Job Revisited. LC 93-60359. 40p. (gr. 5 up). 1994. pap. 5.95 (*1-55523-616-2*) Winston-Derek.

Luce, Celia, jt. auth. see Luce, Willard.

Luce, Willard & Luce, Celia. Jim Bridger: Man of the Mountains. Parrish, George I., Jr., illus. 80p. (gr. 2-6). 1991. Repr. of 1966 ed. lib. bdg. 12.95 (*0-7910-1454-1*) Chelsea Hse.

Luceno, James. The Mata Hari Affair. (gr. 4-6). 1992. pap. 4.99 (*0-345-38009-6*) Ballantine.

Lucero, Faustina H. Little Indians' ABC. LC 73-87800. (Illus.). 32p. (gr. k-2). 1974. PLB 9.95 (*0-87783-129-7*); pap. 3.94 deluxe ed. (*0-87783-130-0*) Oddo.

Lucht, Irmgard. In This Night... Lucht, Irmgard, illus. LC 92-54620. 32p. (ps-3). 1993. 13.95 (*1-56282-408-2*) Hyprn Child.

Luck, Oliver W. Music Is Math. Luck, Oliver W., illus. (Orig.). (gr. 4-12). 1987. pap. 7.00 (*0-9626686-0-5*) Owl Pub CA.

Lucke, Peggy, ed. see Brod, Alexandra.

Luckie, Anita, ed. see Wynn, Mychal.

Lucy, Reda, pseud. The Lord's Prayer for Children. Nannie, illus., pseud. 24p. (Orig.). (ps-3). 1981. pap. 2.25 (*0-87516-437-4*) DeVorss.

Ludden, LaVerne. Job Savvy: How to Be a Success at Work. Hall, Sara, ed. 176p. (gr. 7-12). 1992. pap. 10.95 (*0-942784-79-0*, JS) JIST Works.

Ludier, Carol. Little Mermaid: What's under the Sea? (ps-3). 1993. 9.95 (*0-307-06077-2*, Golden Pr) Western Pub.

Ludlow, Angela. The Fun at Christmas Book. (Illus.). 32p. (gr. 4-8). 1991. pap. 5.99 (*0-7459-1877-8*) Lion USA.

Ludlow, Patricia D., illus. Dear Santa. LC 93-28618. 1993. 11.95 (*0-85953-778-1*) Childs Play.

Ludwig, Charles. George Frideric Handel: Composer of The Messiah. (Illus.). (gr. 3-6). 1987. pap. 6.95 (*0-88062-048-X*) Mott Media.

—Jason Lee. (gr. 3-6). 1992. pap. 6.95 (*0-88062-161-3*) Mott Media.

—Stonewall Jackson: Loved in the South Admired in the North. (Illus.). (gr. 3-6). 1989. pap. 6.95 (*0-88062-157-5*) Mott Media.

—Susanna Wesley. LC 84-60314. 195p. (gr. 3-6). 1984. pap. 6.95 (*0-88062-110-9*) Mott Media.

—The Wright Brothers: They Gave Us Wings. (Illus.). (gr. 3-6). 1985. write for info. (*0-88062-142-7*); pap. 6.95 (*0-88062-141-9*) Mott Media.

Ludwig, Lyndell. The Little White Dragon. Ludwig, Lyndell, illus. 23p. (gr. 5 up). 1989. pap. 4.95 (*0-9621782-0-9*) Star Dust Bks. THE LITTLE WHITE DRAGON - This timeless, well-loved tale from ancient China takes you into the world of a wonderful little dragon intent on exploring everything both inside & outside of his realm. At one point he even changes himself into a little fish so he can dive into the waters of the deep sea. However, after numerous adventures, including a miraculous escape, he decides that, after all, it is much better just to be the dragon he really is, with untold worlds yet to discover. The third in a series of authentic Chinese tales in picture book form, delightfully told & illustrated by the author who is well qualified both as an illustrator & in her knowledge of the Chinese language. ("Like the tales of Rudyard Kipling 'these stories' transport children to another time & a different, fascinating world."--Creative Arts). Children are important! As the world changes cultures are blending. And stories from distant lands such as China are enormously valuable in

broadening the scope for growth & understanding. They are also fun to read. TS'AO CHUNG WEIGHS AN ELEPHANT ("...splendid, vibrantly colored paintings..."--Publishers Weekly) & THE SHOEMAKER'S GIFT are also available from Star Dust Books at $4.95 each. *Publisher Provided Annotation.*

Ludwig, Warren. Good Morning, Granny Rose: An Arkansas Folktale. (Illus.). 32p. (ps-3). 1990. 13.95 (*0-399-21950-1*, Putnam) Putnam Pub Group.

—Old Noah's Elephants. LC 90-35379. (Illus.). 32p. (ps-3). 1991. 14.95 (*0-399-22256-1*, Putnam) Putnam Pub Group.

Ludy, Claude E. The End of the Age: A Commentary on the Revelation. LC 89-92157. (Illus.). 125p. (Orig.). 1989. pap. 7.00 (*0-9625164-1-4*) C E Ludy.

—The Vile & the Holy: A Commentary on the Book of Daniel. LC 77-94874. (Illus.). 100p. (Orig.). 1978. pap. 5.00 (*0-9625164-0-6*) C E Ludy.

Luehrmann, Arthur & Peckham, Herbert. Appleworks Date Bases: A Hands-On Guide. (Illus.). 166p. (Orig.). (gr. 7-12). 1987. pap. text ed. 11.95 (*0-941681-03-3*); tchr's. ed. 24.95 (*0-941681-11-4*); 5.25 inch disk 19.95 (*0-941681-00-9*); tchr's. guide 14.95 (*0-941681-08-4*) Computer Lit Pr.

—Appleworks Spreadsheets: A Hands-On Guide. (Illus.). 160p. (Orig.). (gr. 7-12). 1987. pap. text ed. 11.95 (*0-941681-05-X*); tchr's. set 24.95 (*0-941681-12-2*); tchr's. guide 14.95 (*0-685-67549-1*); 5.25 inch disk 19.95 (*0-685-67550-5*) Computer Lit Pr.

—Appleworks Word Processing: A Hands-On Guide. LC 87-836. (Illus.). 152p. (Orig.). (gr. 7-12). 1987. pap. text ed. 11.95 (*0-941681-01-7*); tchr's. set 24.50 (*0-941681-10-6*); tchr's. guide 14.95 (*0-685-67551-3*); 5.25 inch disk 19.95 (*0-685-67552-1*) Computer Lit Pr.

—Hands-on Appleworks: A Guide to Word Processing, Data Bases & Spreadsheets, 3 bks. LC 87-836. (Illus.). 478p. (Orig.). (gr. 7-12). 1987. Set. pap. text ed. 21.95 (*0-941681-07-6*); Set. tchr's. ed. 34.95 (*0-941681-13-0*); tchr's. guide 14.95 (*0-685-58103-9*); 5.25 inch disk 19.95 (*0-685-67553-X*) Computer Lit Pr.

—Hands-On ClarisWorks: Mac Version 1.0. LC 92-25377. (Illus.). 496p. (gr. 7 up). 1993. text ed. 21.95 spiral bdg. (*0-941681-46-7*); text ed. 27.95 casebound (*0-941681-47-5*); tchr's. ed. 34.95 (*0-941681-49-1*); 3.5 in. disk 19.95 (*0-941681-52-1*); tchr's. guide 14.95 (*0-941681-51-3*) Computer Lit Pr.

Luenn, Nancy. Goldclimbers. LC 90-589. 192p. (gr. 7 up). 1991. SBE 14.95 (*0-689-31585-6*, Atheneum Child Bk) Macmillan Child Grp.

—Mother Earth. Waldman, Neil, illus. LC 90-19134. 32p. (ps-3). 1992. SBE 13.95 (*0-689-31668-2*, Atheneum Child Bk) Macmillan Child Grp.

—Nessa's Fish. Waldman, Neil, illus. LC 89-10548. 32p. (gr. k-3). 1990. SBE 13.95 (*0-689-31477-9*, Atheneum Child Bk) Macmillan Child Grp.

—Nessa's Fish. Waldman, Neil, illus. (gr. k-4). 1993. 13.95 (*0-685-64812-5*); audio cass. 11.00 (*1-882869-81-8*) Read Advent.

—Nessa's Story: El Cuento de Nessa. Ada, Alma F., tr. Waldman, Neil, illus. LC 92-16984. (ENG & SPA.). 32p. (ps-3). 1994. English ed. SBE 14.95 (*0-689-31782-4*, Atheneum Child Bk); Spanish ed. SBE 14.95 (*0-689-31919-3*, Atheneum Child Bk) Macmillan Child Grp.

—Song for the Ancient Forest. Kastner, Jill, illus. LC 91-17187. 32p. (gr. k-3). 1993. SBE 14.95 (*0-689-31719-0*, Atheneum Child Bk) Macmillan Child Grp.

—Unicorn Crossing. Hanson, Peter E., illus. LC 87-995. 64p. (gr. 2-5). 1987. SBE 12.95 (*0-689-31384-5*, Atheneum) Macmillan Child Grp.

—Unicorn Crossing. 64p. (gr. 2-9). 1988. pap. 2.50 (*0-8167-1321-9*) Troll Assocs.

Luenn, Nancy, ed. A Horse's Tale: Ten Adventures in One Hundred Years. Megale, Marina & Schumacher, Sharon, illus. LC 88-61152. 96p. (Orig.). (gr. 2-6). 1988. lib. bdg. 16.95 (*0-943990-51-3*); pap. 7.95 (*0-943990-50-5*) Parenting Pr.

Luft, Ira S. The Student's Guide to Word Processing with WordStar. 90p. (gr. 10 up). 1988. pap. 7.95 (*0-318-23581-1*) Automatic Manuals.

Luger, Harriet. The Elephant Tree. 112p. (gr. 7-11). 1986. pap. 2.25 (*0-440-92394-8*, LFL) Dell.

—Lauren. 176p. (gr. 9 up). 1981. pap. 1.50 (*0-440-94700-6*, LE) Dell.

Lugo, Norma. The Faceless Pumpkin. Quiles, Esther, illus. Mankowitz, Sonia, intro. by. (Illus.). 32p. (Orig.). (gr. k-2). 1989. pap. text ed. write for info. West Side Pubns.

Luhrmann, Winifred B. Only Brave Tomorrows. (gr. 5-9). 1989. 13.45 (*0-395-47983-5*) HM.

Luhrs, Ruth J. Kidding Around San Diego: A Young Person's Guide to the City. Lambert, Mary, illus. 64p. (Orig.). (gr. 3 up). 1991. pap. 9.95 (*1-56261-010-4*) John Muir.

Lukacs, E. & Laha, R. G. Applications of Charateristics Functions. 1964. 17.95 (*0-85264-086-2*) Lubrecht & Cramer.

Lukas, Cynthia K. Center Stage Summer. 157p. (Orig.). (gr. 8-12). 1988. pap. 4.95 (*0-938961-02-0*, Stamp Out Sheep Press) Sq One Pubs.

Lukas, Noah. The Stinky Book. Schindler, S. D., illus. LC 92-22701. 24p. (ps-up). 1993. 6.99 (*0-679-83619-5*) Random Bks Yng Read.

—Tiny Trolls' ABC. Schindler, S. D., illus. LC 92-62940. 24p. (Orig.). (ps-k). 1993. pap. 1.50 (*0-679-84797-9*) Random Bks Yng Read.

—Tiny Trolls' 1, 2, 3. Schindler, S. D., illus. LC 92-62939. 24p. (Orig.). (ps-k). 1993. pap. 1.50 (*0-679-84792-8*) Random Bks Yng Read.

Lukas, Scott E. Amphetamines: Danger in the Fast Lane. (Illus.). 32p. (gr. 5 up). 1991. pap. 4.49 (*0-7910-0003-6*) Chelsea Hse.

—Amphetamines: Danger in the Fast Lane. updated ed. (gr. 5 up). 1992. lib. bdg. 19.95 (*0-685-54573-3*) Chelsea Hse.

Lukasevich, Ann. Favorites, Friendships, Food & Fantasy: Literature-Based Thematic Units for Early Primary. (gr. 1-3). 1993. pap. 24.95 (*0-201-81844-2*) Addison Wesley.

—Food & Fantasy, Vol. 2: Literature-Based Thematic Units for Early Primary. (ps-3). 1993. pap. 18.95 (*0-201-49037-4*) Addison-Wesley.

Lukaszewski, David. Little Ms. Rosey & Friends. 1993. 7.75 (*0-8062-4622-7*) Carlton.

Luke, Melinda, ed. see Blair, Carvel.

Luke, Melinda, ed. see Zallinger, Peter.

Lukes, Bonnie L. How to Be a Reasonably Thin Teenage Girl (Without Starving, Losing Your Friends, or Running Away from Home) Niclaus, Carol, illus. LC 86-3347. 96p. (gr. 6 up). 1986. SBE 13.95 (*0-689-31269-5*, Atheneum) Macmillan Child Grp.

Lukic, Marie. Pasquale's Gift. Kretschmar, Sonia, illus. LC 93-29002. 1994. 4.25 (*0-383-03768-9*) SRA Schl Grp.

Lum, Darrell, jt. ed. see Chock, Eric.

Lum, Peter. Growth of Civilization in East Asia. LC 73-77311. (Illus.). (gr. 8 up). 1969. 32.95 (*0-87599-144-0*) S G Phillips.

Lum, Ray J. The Rebus Escape. LC 91-76970. 64p. (Orig.). (gr. 3-5). 1992. pap. 5.95x (*0-943864-63-1*) Davenport.

Lumbert, Lindy H. Dear Diary. 119p. (gr. 4-10). 1981. pap. 4.25 (*0-943280-00-1*) Blossom Bks.

Lumley, Kathryn W. District of Columbia: In Words & Pictures. Wahl, Richard, illus. LC 80-39645. 48p. (gr. 2-5). 1981. PLB 17.27 (*0-516-03951-2*) Childrens.

—Monkeys & Apes. LC 82-12779. (Illus.). (gr. k-4). 1982. PLB 15.27 (*0-516-01633-4*); pap. 4.95 (*0-516-41633-2*) Childrens.

Lumley, Kay. I Can Be an Animal Doctor. LC 85-12802. 32p. (gr. k-3). 1985. PLB 14.60 (*0-516-01836-1*); pap. 3.95 (*0-516-41836-X*) Childrens.

Lumpkin, Beatrice. Senefer: A Young Genius in Old Egypt. Nickens, Linda, illus. LC 92-71026. 32p. (gr. 2-5). 1992. 16.95 (*0-86543-244-9*); pap. 8.95 (*0-86543-245-7*) Africa World.

Lumpkin, Susan. Big Cats. LC 92-26838. (Illus.). 72p. (gr. 6-9). 1993. 17.95 (*0-8160-2847-8*) Facts on File.

—Small Cats. LC 92-26837. (Illus.). 72p. (gr. 6-9). 1993. 17.95 (*0-8160-2848-6*) Facts on File.

Lumpkin, Susan & Weinberg, Susan. Animals of the National Zoological Park Coloring Book. Weinberg, Lisa F., illus. 24p. (Orig.). (ps-4). 1989. pap. 3.95 (*0-9622062-1-0*) Friends Natl Zoo.

Lumpkin, Susan, jt. auth. see Greenberg, Russell.

Luna, Rose Mary, tr. see Miller, Billie M.

Lund, Charles. Dot Paper Geometry: With or Without a Geoboard. (Illus.). 84p. (gr. 4-8). 1980. pap. text ed. 8.50 (*0-914040-87-1*) Cuisenaire.

—Tricks of the Trade with Cards. new ed. Laycock, Mary, ed. (gr. 2-9). 1978. pap. text ed. 7.95 (*0-918932-57-2*) Activity Resources.

Lund, Charles & Smart, Margaret. Focus on Calculator Math. Kyzer, Martha, illus. Laycock, Mary, intro. by. (Illus.). (gr. 4-12). 1979. pap. text ed. 8.50 (*0-918932-66-1*) Activity Resources.

Lund, Coby, et al. Who Lives in the Igloo? Zilliox, Elaine, illus. 52p. (Orig.). (gr. 4-9). 1984. 6.95 (*0-88047-046-1*, 8402) DOK Pubs.

Lund, Doris. Eric. 268p. (gr. 7 up). 1979. pap. 2.95 (*0-440-94586-0*, LFL) Dell.

Lund, Jillian. Way Out West Lives a Coyote Named Frank. LC 91-46011. (Illus.). 32p. (ps-2). 1993. 13.95 (*0-525-44982-5*, DCB) Dutton Child Bks.

Lundberg, Joy S. Book of Mormon Summer. (gr. 5-8). 1991. 6.95 (*0-915029-00-6*) Cherished Bks.

Lundberg, Leslie, ed. see Abdu'l-Baha.

Lundberg, Louise, ed. see Williams, Selver B.

Lundbergh, Holger, tr. from SWE. Great Swedish Fairy Tales. Bauer, John, illus. LC 73-132364. 224p. (gr. 4-6). 1973. (Sey Lawr); pap. 10.95 (*0-440-03041-2*) Delacorte.

Lundell, Kerth, et al. Criterion Test of Basic Skills. (gr. 1 up). 1974. pap. 53.00 incl. manual, 25 arithmetic recording forms, 25 reading recording forms, 24 math problem sheets, stimulus cards booklet, in vinyl folder (*0-87879-154-X*) Acad Therapy.

Lundell, Margaretta. The Land of Colors. Pazzaglia, Nadia, illus. LC 84-81410. 24p. (gr. 1-8). 1989. 9.95 (*0-448-21028-2*, G&D) Putnam Pub Group.

Lundell, Margo. Disney Babies A to Z. (Illus.). 14p. (ps-k). 1989. write for info. (*0-307-12317-0*, Pub. by Golden Bks) Western Pub.

—Harold Roth's Big Book of Horses. Roth, Harold, photos by. (Illus.). 48p. (gr. 2-5). 1987. 7.95 (0-448-19203-9, G&D) Putnam Pub Group.
—My Book of Funny Valentines. Evans, Nate, illus. 32p. (ps-3). 1993. pap. 2.50 (0-590-44187-6) Scholastic Inc.
—The Wee Mouse Who Was Afraid of the Dark. McQueen, Lucinda, illus. 32p. 1991. pap. 1.95 (0-448-40060-X, Platt & Munk Pubs) Putnam Pub Group.
—The Wee Puppy Who Wet His Bed. McQueen, Lucinda, illus. 32p. (ps-2). 1989. pap. 2.25 (0-448-19114-8, Platt & Munk Pubs) Putnam Pub Group.
—What Does Baby See? Pagnoni, Roberta, illus. 24p. (ps-k). 1990. bds. 9.95 (0-448-19098-2, G&D) Putnam Pub Group.
—Woody, Be Good! A First Book of Manners. Rose, Eve, illus. 24p. (ps-2). 1988. 3.95 (0-448-09288-3, G&D) Putnam Pub Group.
Lundgren, Hal. Ryne Sandberg: The Triple Threat. LC 85-29895. (Illus.). 48p. (gr. 2-8). 1986. PLB 13.27 (0-516-04357-9); pap. 3.95 (0-516-44357-7) Childrens.
Lundy, Alan. Diagnosing & Treating Mental Illness. (Illus.). 136p. (gr. 6-12). 1990. 18.95 (0-7910-0047-8) Chelsea Hse.
Lunn, Carolyn. Bobby's Zoo. Dunnington, Tom, illus. LC 88-36865. 32p. (ps-2). 1989. PLB 11.93 (0-516-02089-7); pap. 2.95 (0-516-42089-5) Childrens.
—Bobby's Zoo Big Book. (Illus.). 32p. (ps-2). 1991. PLB 30.60 (0-516-49501-1) Childrens.
—A Buzz Is Part of a Bee. Dunnington, Tom, illus. LC 89-25434. 32p. (ps-2). 1990. PLB 11.93 (0-516-02062-5); pap. 2.95 (0-516-42062-3) Childrens.
—Un Murmullo Es Silencioso: A Whisper Is Quiet. Martin, Clovis, illus. LC 88-11968. (SPA.). 32p. (ps-2). 1991. PLB 11.93 (0-516-32087-4); pap. 2.95 (0-516-52087-3) Childrens.
—Spiders & Webs. Dunnington, Tom, illus. LC 89-34665. 32p. (ps-2). 1989. PLB 11.93 (0-516-02093-5); pap. 2.95 (0-516-42093-3) Childrens.
—A Whisper Is Quiet. Martin, Clovis, illus. LC 88-11968. 32p. (ps-2). 1988. PLB 11.93 (0-516-02087-0); pap. 2.95 (0-516-42087-9) Childrens.
Lunn, Janet. Amos's Sweater. (ps-3). 1991. 12.95 (0-88899-074-X, Pub. by Groundwood-Douglas & McIntyre CN) Firefly Bks Ltd.
—Double Spell. 144p. (gr. 3-7). 1986. pap. 3.95 (0-14-031858-5, Puffin) Puffin Bks.
—Duck Cakes for Sale. LaFave, Kim, illus. 32p. (ps-2). 1991. 13.95 (0-88899-094-4, Pub. by Groundwood-Douglas & McIntyre CN); pap. 4.95 (0-88899-157-6) Firefly Bks Ltd.
—One Hundred Shining Candles. Grater, Lindsay, illus. LC 90-8892. 32p. (gr. 2-4). 1991. SBE 13.95 (0-684-19280-2, Scribners Young Read) Macmillan Child Grp.
—The Root Cellar. LC 83-3246. 256p. (gr. 5 up). 1983. SBE 14.95 (0-684-17855-9, Scribners Young Read) Macmillan Child Grp.
—The Root Cellar. 230p. (gr. 7 up). 1985. pap. 3.99 (0-14-031835-6, Puffin) Puffin Bks.
—Shadow in Hawthorn Bay. 192p. (gr. 5-9). 1988. pap. 3.95 (0-14-032436-4, Puffin) Puffin Bks.
Luobriel, Marta B., et al, trs. see Resnik, Hank, et al.
Luoma, Jon R. The Air Around Us: An Air Pollution Primer. Copp, Brent, illus. Smith, Richard H., photos by. (Illus.). 20p. (Orig.). (gr. 5 up). 1989. pap. 9.95 (0-935577-10-6) Acid Rain Found.
Lupo, Ann. Being Me & Drug Free Kid-Pak. rev. ed. Fox, Greg, ed. Edwards, Diana, illus. 16p. (gr. k-3). 1991. pap. text ed. 3.95 (1-56230-135-7); pap. text ed. 4.95 incl. audiotape (1-56230-125-X) Syndistar.
—Healthy Bodies Don't Need Drugs Kid-Pak. rev. ed. Fox, Greg, ed. Edwards, Diana, illus. 20p. (gr. 3-5). 1991. pap. text ed. 3.95 (1-56230-138-1); pap. text ed. 4.95 incl. audiotape (1-56230-128-4) Syndistar.
—Red the Firedog's How to Plan for a Safe Escape Kid-Pak. rev. ed. Fox, Greg, ed. Edwards, Diana, illus. 20p. (ps-3). 1991. pap. text ed. 3.95 (1-56230-137-3); pap. text ed. 4.95 incl. audiotape (1-56230-134-9) Syndistar.
Lupo, Ann, ed. see Bosco, James.
Lupoff, Richard A. The Forever City. (Illus.). (gr. 7-12). 1988. 15.95 (0-8027-6742-7) Walker & Co.
Lupsewicz, Veronica-Ann. Misty the Manatee. Weinberger, Jane, ed. (Illus.). 46p. (gr. 1-5). 1993. pap. 10.95 (0-932433-96-0) Windswept Hse.
Luquire, Jerry, ed. see Kempf, Michael J.
Lurie, Alison. Clever Gretchen & Other Forgotten Folktales. Tomes, Margot, illus. LC 78-22512. 128p. (gr. 4-6). 1980. PLB 12.89 (0-690-03944-1, Crowell Jr Bks) HarpC Child Bks.
—Don't Tell the Grown-Ups: Subversive Children's Literature, Vol. 1. 229p. 1990. 19.95 (0-316-53722-5) Little.
Lurie, Morris. The Story of Imelda, Who Was Small. Denton, Terry, illus. 32p. (gr. k-3). 1988. 13.45 (0-395-48663-7) HM.
Lurie, Susan. Ghostwriter Detective Guide: Tools & Tricks of the Trade. (ps-3). 1992. pap. 2.99 (0-553-48069-3) Bantam.
—Nutcracker. (ps-3). 1993. pap. 3.99 (0-553-37293-9) Bantam.
—Rally! (gr. 7-10). 1993. pap. 3.50 (0-553-48092-8) Bantam.
Lusane, Clarence. The Struggle for Equal Education. (Illus.). 144p. (gr. 9-12). 1992. PLB 13.90 (0-531-11121-0) Watts.

Lush, Charles, jt. auth. see Lush, Ron.
Lush, Ron & Lush, Charles. Glorious Easter Day. Date not set. 3.95 (0-685-68658-2, BCME-13) Lillenas.
Lustig, Esther, jt. auth. see Lustig, Michael.
Lustig, Loretta, illus. The Pop-Up Book of the Circus. LC 78-68789. (ps-3). 1979. 8.99 (0-394-84134-4) Random Bks Yng Read.
—The Pop-up Book of Trucks. LC 73-19318. (ps-2). 1974. 8.99 (0-394-82826-7) Random Bks Yng Read.
—Skip to My Lou. 1994. bk. & cassette 6.99 (0-553-45908-2) Bantam.
Lustig, Michael & Lustig, Esther. Willy Whyner, Cloud Designer. Lustig, Michael, illus. LC 93-21957. 40p. (gr. k-4). 1994. RSBE 14.95 (0-02-761365-8, Four Winds) Macmillan Child Grp.
Lutgendorf, Philip & James, Shirley M. The Parts of Speech. Reichmann, Naczinski & Associates, illus. LC 77-730079. (gr. 7-9). 1976. pap. text ed. 219.00 6 filmstrips, 6 cass., 30 skill sheets, Guide (0-89290-118-7, A134-SATC) Soc for Visual.
Luth, Sophie A. The Special Princess. McColgan, Susie, illus. 36p. 1990. glossy cover 5.95 (0-9626153-0-7) Luth & Assocs.
Luther, Luana, ed. see Smith, Sally Ann.
Luther, Rebekah S. The Yoda Family. (Illus.). 16p. (gr. 3). 1994. saddle-stitch 7.95 (0-8059-3486-3) Dorrance.
Luthor. Chico Mendes. Date not set. PLB write for info. (0-8050-2270-8) H Holt & Co.
—George W. Carver. Date not set. PLB write for info. (0-8050-2271-6) H Holt & Co.
—Jacques Costeau. Date not set. PLB write for info. (0-8050-2273-2) H Holt & Co.
—Jane Goodall. Date not set. PLB write for info. (0-8050-2272-4) H Holt & Co.
—Rachel Carson. Date not set. PLB write for info. (0-8050-2291-0) H Holt & Co.
—Theodore Roosevelt. Date not set. PLB write for info. (0-8050-2274-0) H Holt & Co.
Luton, Mildred. Christmas Time in the Mountains. Peattie, Gary, illus. 44p. (Orig.). (gr. 1-6). 1981. pap. 5.00 (0-87516-434-X) DeVorss.
Luttrell, Chuck, illus. Everything's Going Wrong. 74p. (Orig.). (gr. 3-6). 1986. pap. 6.95 (0-9617609-0-7) Shade Tree NV.
Luttrell, Ida. Be Nice to Marilyn. Johnson, Lonnie S., illus. LC 91-25879. 32p. (ps-3). 1992. SBE 13.95 (0-689-31716-6, Atheneum Child Bk) Macmillan Child Grp.
—The Bear Next Door. Stapler, Sarah, illus. LC 90-4153. 64p. (gr. k-3). 1991. 11.95 (0-06-024023-7); PLB 11.89 (0-06-024024-5) HarpC Child Bks.
—Mattie's Little Possum Pet. Lewin, Betsy, illus. LC 91-47709. 40p. (ps-3). 1993. SBE 14.95 (0-689-31786-7, Atheneum Child Bk) Macmillan Child Grp.
—Milo's Toothache. Giannini, Enzo, illus. LC 91-24315. 40p. (ps-3). 1992. 11.00 (0-8037-1034-8); PLB 10.89 (0-8037-1035-6) Dial Bks Young.
—Ottie Slockett. Fogelman, Phyllis J., ed. Krause, Ute, illus. LC 88-30884. 40p. (ps-3). 1990. 9.95 (0-8037-0709-6); PLB 9.89 (0-8037-0711-8) Dial Bks Young.
—Ottie Slockett. LC 88-30884. (Illus.). 40p. (ps-3). 1992. pap. 3.99 (0-8037-1215-4, Dial Easy to Read) Puffin Bks.
—The Star Counters. Pretro, Korinna, illus. LC 93-20342. 32p. 1994. 15.00 (0-688-12149-7, Tambourine Bks); PLB 14.93 (0-688-12150-0, Tambourine Bks) Morrow.
—Three Good Blankets. McDermott, Michael, illus. LC 89-36353. 32p. (ps-2). 1990. SBE 13.95 (0-689-31586-4, Atheneum Child Bk) Macmillan Child Grp.
—Tillie & Mert. Cushman, Doug, illus. LC 85-42641. 64p. (gr. k-3). 1992. pap. 3.50 (0-06-444159-8, Trophy) HarpC Child Bks.
Luttrell, Jean. Winning Isn't Everything. Luttrell, Chuck, illus. 76p. (Orig.). (gr. 3-5). 1990. pap. 6.95 (0-9617609-2-3) Shade Tree NV.
Luttrell, Susan E. Love Was Born at Christmas. (Orig.). (gr. k-4). 1981. pap. 3.40 (0-89536-483-2, 1234) CSS OH.
Lutyk, Carol B., ed. Discover America. (Illus.). 336p. 1989. 26.95 (0-87044-804-8); deluxe ed. 36.95 (0-87044-805-6); lib. bdg. 39.95 incl. flag (0-87044-806-4); lib. bdg. 26.95 (0-87044-807-2) Natl Geog.
Lutz, Arthur, jt. auth. see Lutz, Martha.
Lutz, John. Double Cross. 4p. (Orig.). 1989. pap. 19.95 incls. puzzle (0-922242-14-3) Lombard Mktg.
Lutz, Martha & Lutz, Arthur. Woodville Long Ago. 68p. (gr. 3-7). 1986. pap. write for info. Vimach Assocs.
Lutz, Tim. Gem Hunter's Kit. (Illus.). 64p. (Orig.). (gr. 3 up). 1990. package 16.95 (0-89471-828-2) Running Pr.
Lutzeier, Elizabeth. The Coldest Winter. LC 91-7159. 160p. (gr. 5-9). 1991. 13.95 (0-8234-0899-X) Holiday.
—The Wall. LC 92-52712. 160p. (gr. 5-9). 1992. 14.95 (0-8234-0987-2) Holiday.
Lyall, Elizabeth, ed. see Walley, Susan.
Lydon, Kerry R. A Birthday for Blue. Levine, Abby, ed. Hays, Michael, illus. LC 88-21697. 32p. (gr. k-3). 1989. 13.95g (0-8075-0774-1) A Whitman.
Lye, Keith. Coasts. Furstinger, Nancy, ed. (Illus.). 48p. (gr. 5-8). 1989. PLB 16.98 (0-382-09790-4) Silver Burdett Pr.
—Deserts. (Illus.). 48p. (gr. 5-8). 1987. PLB 16.98 (0-382-09501-4) Silver Burdett Pr.
—The Earth. (Illus.). 64p. (gr. 4-6). 1991. PLB 14.90 (1-56294-025-2) Millbrook Pr.

—Earthquakes. LC 92-31816. (Illus.). 32p. (gr. 2-3). 1992. PLB 18.99 (0-8114-3409-5) Raintree Steck-V.
—Measuring & Maps: Projects with Geography. LC 91-2296. (Illus.). 32p. (gr. 5-8). 1991. PLB 12.40 (0-531-17325-9, Gloucester Pr) Watts.
—Mountains. (Illus.). 48p. (gr. 5-8). 1987. PLB 16.98 (0-382-09498-0) Silver Burdett Pr.
—Mountains. LC 92-31815. (Illus.). 32p. (gr. 2-3). 1992. PLB 18.99 (0-8114-3410-9) Raintree Steck-V.
—The Ocean Floor. LC 90-549. (Illus.). 32p. (gr. 4-7). 1991. PLB 12.40 (0-531-18369-6) Watts.
—Our Planet Earth. LC 92-21675. (Illus.). 128p. (ps-3). 1993. 10.00 (0-679-83696-9); PLB 11.99 (0-679-93696-3) Random Bks Yng Read.
—Our Planet the Earth. LC 79-2346. (Illus.). (gr. 3-6). 1980. PLB 13.50 (0-8225-1182-7, First Ave Edns); pap. 4.95 (0-8225-9510-9, First Ave Edns) Lerner Pubns.
—Passport to Germany. LC 93-26680. (gr. 7 up). 1994. write for info. (0-531-14283-3) Watts.
—Passport to Spain. rev. ed. LC 93-21186. 1994. write for info. (0-531-14294-9) Watts.
—Rocks & Minerals. LC 92-31817. (Illus.). 32p. (gr. 2-3). 1992. PLB 18.99 (0-8114-3411-7) Raintree Steck-V.
—Rocks, Minerals & Fossils. (Illus.). 48p. (gr. 5-8). 1991. PLB 16.98 (0-382-24226-2) Silver Burdett Pr.
—Volcanoes. LC 92-32016. (Illus.). 32p. (gr. 2-3). 1992. PLB 18.99 (0-8114-3412-5) Raintree Steck-V.
—The World Today. (Illus.). 64p. 1985. 12.95x (0-8160-1072-2) Facts on File.
Lye, Keith, jt. auth. see Dempsey, Michael W.
Lye, Keith, jt. auth. see Mason, Antony.
Lyerly, Elaine M., jt. auth. see Neely, Cynthia H.
Lykken, Laurie. The Perfect Catch, No. 153. (gr. 6 up). 1988. pap. 2.50 (0-553-27475-9) Bantam.
—Priceless Love. 192p. (Orig.). (gr. 7 up). 1988. pap. 2.50 (0-553-27174-1) Bantam.
—Programmed for Popularity. 128p. (gr. 5-8). 1992. pap. 2.99 (0-87406-590-9) Willowisp Pr.
—The Truth about Love. 1991. pap. 2.95 (0-553-28862-8) Bantam.
Lyle, Garry. Cyprus. (Illus.). 96p. (gr. 5 up). 1988. 14.95 (0-222-00942-X) Chelsea Hse.
—Pacific Islands. (Illus.). 96p. (gr. 5 up). 1988. 14.95 (0-222-01034-7) Chelsea Hse.
Lyman, et al. Pee Wee Saves Christmas. Curtis, Peggy H., illus. 80p. 1983. 14.95 (0-317-03904-0) Imagination Dust.
Lyman, Alicia G. de see Sheldon, Dyan & De Lyman, Alicia G.
Lyman, Nanci A. Paul Bunyan. new ed. LC 79-66320. (Illus.). 48p. (gr. 3-6). 1980. lib. bdg. 9.89 (0-89375-310-6); pap. 2.95 (0-89375-309-2) Troll Assocs.
—Pecos Bill. LC 79-66319. (Illus.). 48p. (gr. 3-6). 1980. lib. bdg. 9.89 (0-89375-308-4); pap. 2.95 (0-89375-307-6) Troll Assocs.
Lynch. Gypsy Davey. Date not set. 14.00 (0-06-023586-1, Festival); PLB 13.89 (0-06-023587-X, Festival) HarpC Child Bks.
—Walk. Date not set. 14.00 (0-06-023584-5, Festival); PLB 13.89 (0-06-023585-3, Festival) HarpC Child Bks.
Lynch, Amy. Nashville. LC 90-41611. (Illus.). 60p. (gr. 3 up). 1991. RSBE 13.95 (0-87518-453-7, Dillon) Macmillan Child Grp.
Lynch, Chris. Iceman. LC 93-7776. 192p. (gr. 7 up). 1994. 15.00 (0-06-023340-0); PLB 14.89 (0-06-023341-9) HarpC Child Bks.
—Shadow Boxer. LC 92-47490. 224p. (gr. 5 up). 1993. 14.00 (0-06-023027-4); PLB 13.89 (0-06-023028-2) HarpC Child Bks.

Lynch, Don & Thompson, David. Battleborn Nevada: Its People, History & Stories. Bean, James H., ed. Horton, Verne, illus. LC 93-79470. 360p. (gr. 6 up). 1994. 31.00 (0-913205-20-6) Grace Dangberg. A colorful montage by a Nevada artist leads off each of the eight chapters in this 260-page hard cover book. Pictures of characters, places, events, & maps, over 275 illustrations in all, guide the reader through Nevada from prehistoric Indians through statehood during the Civil War & on to modern Nevada with its diverse ethnic & cultural population. The chapters: 1) The Indians, 2) Trailblazers & Emigrants, 3) Railroads, Cities, & Travel, 4) Mining, 5) Agriculture, 6) Government, 7) Business, & 8) The People of Nevada portray Nevada through the use of the land. The book tells of the importance of mining to the state of the nation, the coming of the railroad, & the beginning of Nevada cities. Also told is the development of

gambling in Nevada as a natural heritage of the mining boom towns, & how gaming & tourism developed the communities of Nevada. The reader will see how the geographical influence of the Great Basin & the social & economic influence of gaming as an industry make Nevada different from any other state. *Publisher Provided Annotation.*

Lynch, Don, ed. see Adams, Randy L. & Sodaro, Craig.
Lynch, Don, ed. see Sanger, David.
Lynch, Marietta & Perry, Patricia. No More Monkeys: A Photographic Version of the Children's Finger Game. (Orig.). (ps-3). pap. 2.95 (0-9610962-0-9) M Lynch.
Lynch, Martha E., jt. auth. see Goldman, Ronald.
Lynch, Michael. How Oil Rigs Are Made. (Illus.). 32p. (gr. 7 up). 1986. 12.95x (0-8160-0041-7) Facts on File.
Lynch, P. J., ed. see Andersen, Hans Christian.
Lynch, Patricia. Back of Beyond. 180p. (gr. 4 up). 1993. pap. 8.95 (1-85371-206-X, Pub. by Poolbeg Pr ER) Dufour.
—Brogeen & the Princess of Sheen. (gr. 1 up). 1986. pap. 11.95 (0-85105-905-8, Pub. by Colin Smythe Ltd Britain) Dufour.
—Brogeen Follows the Magic Flute. 191p. (ps-8). 1988. pap. 6.95 (1-85371-022-9, Pub. by Poolbeg Press Ltd Eire) Dufour.
—Tales of Irish Enchantment. (Illus.). 108p. 1986. pap. 8.95 (0-85342-790-9, Pub. by Mercier Press Ltd Eire) Dufour.
—Turf Cutter's Donkey. 243p. (ps-8). 1988. pap. 6.95 (1-85371-016-4, Pub. by Poolbeg Press Ltd Eire) Dufour.
Lynch, Patricia A. Christianity. (Illus.). 128p. (gr. 7-12). 1991. 17.95x (0-8160-2441-3) Facts on File.
Lynch, Patti. Kid's Stuff: Good & Healthy Stuff That's Fun to Cook & Eat. Lynch, Patti, illus. 1993. pap. 12. 95 (0-9620469-2-2) Sweet Inspirations.
Lynd, Alice & Lynd, Staughton, eds. Rank & File: Personal Histories by Working-Class Organizers. Lynd, Alice, intro. by. 320p. (gr. 9-12). 1988. pap. 10. 00 (0-85345-752-2) Monthly Rev.
Lynd, Staughton, jt. ed. see Lynd, Alice.
Lynde, Stan. Stan Lynde's Pardners: The Bonding. (Illus.). (gr. 3 up). 1990. write for info. (0-9626999-1-8) Cttnwd Graphics.
Lyne, Sandy. The Lion & the Boy. Reilly, Kathy, illus. 48p. (gr. 4-7). 1988. 12.95 (0-933905-04-1); pap. 9.95 (0-933905-15-7) Claycomb Pr.
Lyness, James. Multiple Choice Questions in Preparation for the AP Computer Science ("A" & "AB") Examination. 2nd ed. 69p. (gr. 11-12). 1989. wkbk. 15.95 (1-878621-18-1) D & S Mktg Syst.
Lyngheim, Linda. Gold Rush Adventure. Garber, Phyllis, illus. LC 87-82679. 96p. (gr. 3-6). 1988. 12.95 (0-915369-03-6); pap. 9.95 (0-915369-02-8) Langtry Pubns.
—The Indians & the California Missions. rev. ed. Garber, Phyllis, illus. LC 84-80543. 160p. (gr. 4-6). 1990. 14. 95 (0-915369-04-4); pap. 10.95 (0-915369-00-1) Langtry Pubns.
Lyngheim, Linda, et al. Father Junipero Serra, the Traveling Missionary. Garber, Phyllis, illus. LC 85-82131. 64p. (gr. 3-5). 1986. 12.95 (0-915369-01-X) Langtry Pubns.
Lynn, Claire. B-I-B-L-E That's the Book for Me! Lautermilch, John, illus. 18p. (Orig.). (ps-1). 1981. pap. 1.00 (0-89323-013-8) Bible Memory.
—A Cave Is a Deep Dark Hole. 48p. (gr. 1-4). 1978. pap. 1.00 (0-89323-012-X, 100) Bible Memory.
Lynn, Claire, jt. auth. see Ellis, Joyce.
Lynn, Claire, compiled by. Build on the Rock. Lautermilch, John & Fearber, Sharon, illus. 52p. (Orig.). (ps-7). 1979. pap. 1.25 (0-89323-000-6, 707) Bible Memory.
Lynn, Claire, ed. see Philips, Martha & Hadden, Mary.
Lynn, Daryl, et al. Evident Progress. 60p. (Orig.). 1991. pap. 2.25 (0-89323-046-4) Bible Memory.
Lynn, David. More High School Talksheets: Fifty All-New Creative Discussions for High School Youth Groups. 112p. 1992. pap. 9.99 (0-310-57491-9, Pub. by Youth Spec) Zondervan.
—More Junior High Talksheets: Fifty All-New Creative Discussions for Junior High Youth Groups. 112p. 1992. pap. 9.99 (0-310-57481-1, Pub. by Youth Spec) Zondervan.
—More Zingers. 1990. pap. 7.99 (0-310-52521-7) Zondervan.
Lynn, David & Lynn, Kathy. More Zingers for First to Third Graders. 64p. (gr. 1-3). 1993. Saddle stitch. pap. 7.99 (0-310-37231-3, Pub. by Youth Spec) Zondervan.
—Zingers for First to Third Graders: 12 Real-Life Character Builders. 64p. (gr. 1-3). 1993. Saddle stitch. pap. 7.99 (0-310-37221-6, Pub. by Youth Spec) Zondervan.
Lynn, David, jt. ed. see Yaconelli, Mike.
Lynn, Elizabeth. Babe Didrikson Zaharias. Horner, Matina. (Illus.). 112p. (gr. 5 up). 1989. lib. bdg. 17.95 (1-55546-684-2) Chelsea Hse.
Lynn, Kathy, jt. auth. see Lynn, David.

Lynn, Ruth. Ester: The Story of a Small Ghost. Wagner, R. M., ed. Lynn, Ruth, illus. LC 81-69693. 28p. (gr. 5 up). 1981. 12.95 (0-941674-00-2) Woodcock Pr.
Lynn, Sara. Clothes. Lynn, Sara, illus. 14p. (ps). 1986. bds. 2.95 (0-689-71095-X, Aladdin Bks) Macmillan Child Grp.
—I Can Make It! Dress Up. (ps-3). 1994. pap. 4.99 (0-553-37260-2) Bantam.
—I Can Make It! Fun Food. (ps-3). 1994. pap. 4.99 (0-553-37259-0) Bantam.
—Play with Paper. (ps-3). 1992. 18.95 (0-87614-754-6) Carolrhoda Bks.
—Toys. Lynn, Sara, illus. 14p. (ps). 1986. bds. 2.95 (0-689-71096-8, Aladdin) Macmillan Child Grp.
Lynn, Sara & James, Diane. Play with Paint. (Illus.). 24p. (ps-2). 1993. 18.95 (0-87614-755-4) Carolrhoda Bks.
—Rain & Shine. Wright, Joe, illus. LC 93-36420. 32p. (gr. k-2). 1994. 15.95 (1-56847-142-4) Thomson Lrning.
Lynn, Tim & Lynn, Tom. Making Toy Trains in Wood. LC 90-9978. (Illus.). 136p. (Orig.). (gr. 10-12). 1990. pap. 10.95 (0-8069-6989-X) Sterling.
Lynn, Tom, jt. auth. see Lynn, Tim.
Lynnington, M., jt. auth. see Chishom, J.
Lyon, Charleen C. The Tale of Halley's Comet: An Educational Coloring Book. (Illus.). 32p. (Orig.). (gr. 3-6). 1985. pap. 2.95 (0-9614973-0-0) Niota Pr.
Lyon, David. The Biggest Truck. LC 87-22640. (Illus.). 32p. (ps-3). 1988. lib. bdg. 13.88 (0-688-05514-1); 13. 95 (0-688-05513-3) Lothrop.
—The Runaway Duck. LC 84-5677. (Illus.). 32p. (ps-1). 1985. PLB 14.95 (0-688-04003-9); 14.88 (0-688-04002-0) Lothrop.
—The Runaway Duck. LC 84-5677. (ps-1). 1987. pap. 3.95 (0-688-07334-4, Mulberry) Morrow.
Lyon, Elinor. House in Hiding. 126p. (gr. 4-7). 1991. pap. 6.95 (0-86241-338-9, Pub. by Cnngt Pub Ltd) Trafalgar.
Lyon, George E. Father Time & the Day Boxes. Parker, Robert A., illus. LC 93-25201. 32p. (gr. k-3). 1994. pap. 4.95 (0-689-71792-X, Aladdin) Macmillan Child Grp.
—A Regular Rolling Noah. Grammell, Stephen, illus. LC 86-8312. 32p. (ps-2). 1986. RSBE 13.95 (0-02-761330-5, Bradbury Pr) Macmillan Child Grp.
—A Regular Rolling Noah. Gammell, Stephen, illus. LC 90-39984. 32p. (gr. k-3). 1991. pap. 4.95 (0-689-71449-1, Aladdin) Macmillan Child Grp.
Lyon, George-Ella. A B Cedar: An Alphabet of Trees. Parker, Tom, illus. LC 88-22797. 32p. (ps-1). 1989. 14.95 (0-531-05795-X); PLB 14.99 (0-531-08395-0) Orchard Bks Watts.
—Basket. Szilagyi, Mary, illus. LC 89-71011. 32p. (ps-2). 1990. 14.95 (0-531-05886-7); PLB 14.99 (0-531-08486-8) Orchard Bks Watts.
—Borrowed Children. LC 87-22700. 160p. (gr. 5-7). 1988. 14.95 (0-531-05751-8); PLB 14.99 (0-531-08351-9) Orchard Bks Watts.
—Cecil's Story. Catalanotto, Peter, illus. LC 90-7775. 32p. (gr. k-2). 1991. 14.95 (0-531-05912-X); PLB 14. 99 (0-531-08512-0) Orchard Bks Watts.
—Come a Tide. Gammell, Stephen, illus. LC 89-35650. 32p. (ps-2). 1990. 14.95 (0-531-05854-9); PLB 14.99 (0-531-08454-X) Orchard Bks Watts.
—Come a Tide. Gammell, Stephen, illus. LC 89-35650. 32p. (ps-2). 1993. pap. 5.95 (0-531-07036-0) Orchard Bks Watts.
—Dreamplace. Catalanotto, Peter, illus. LC 92-25102. 32p. (ps-2). 1993. 15.95 (0-531-05466-7); PLB 15.99 (0-531-08616-X) Orchard Bks Watts.
—The Outside Inn. Rosenberry, Vera, illus. LC 90-14285. 32p. (ps-1). 1991. 13.95 (0-531-05936-7); RLB 13.99 (0-531-08536-8) Orchard Bks Watts.
—Red Rover, Red Rover. LC 89-42539. 144p. (gr. 6-9). 1989. 12.95 (0-531-05832-8); PLB 12.99 (0-531-08432-9) Orchard Bks Watts.
—Together. LC 89-2892. (Illus.). 32p. (ps-1). 1989. 14.95 (0-531-05831-X); PLB 14.99 (0-531-08431-0) Orchard Bks Watts.
Lyon, George Ella. Together. Rosenberry, Vera, illus. LC 89-2892. 32p. (ps-1). 1994. pap. 5.95 (0-531-07047-6) Orchard Bks Watts.
Lyon, George-Ella. Who Came Down That Road? Catalanotto, Peter, illus. LC 91-20742. 32p. (ps-2). 1992. 15.95 (0-531-05987-1); PLB 15.99 (0-531-08587-2) Orchard Bks Watts.
Lyon, Lucy, jt. auth. see Dewey, Jennifer.
Lyon, Nancy. The Mystery of Stonehenge. LC 77-10044. (Illus.). 48p. (gr. 4 up) 1983. PLB 18.64 (0-8172-1049-0) Raintree Steck-V.
Lyon, Sue, ed. Great Writers of the English Language, 14 vols. LC 88-21077. (Illus.). 1450p. 1991. PLB 449.95 (1-85435-000-5) Marshall Cavendish.
Lyon, Sue, compiled by. Science in Action: Light & Sound: Light & Sound. Berman, Paul, contrib. by. LC 92-36326. (gr. 4-9). 1993. write for info. (0-86307-937-7) Marshall Cavendish.
—Science in Action: The Living World. Berman, Paul, contrib. by. LC 92-36322. (gr. 4-9). 1993. write for info. (0-86307-938-5) Marshall Cavendish.
—Science in Action: The World of Numbers. Berman, Paul, contrib. by. LC 92-36323. (gr. 4-9). 1993. write for info. (0-86307-939-3) Marshall Cavendish.
Lyon, Sue & Lyon, Sue, eds. Science in Action: Experiments in Physics. Berman, Paul, designed by. LC 92-34427. 1993. write for info. (0-86307-342-5) Marshall Cavendish.

—Science in Action: Fun with Chemistry. rev. ed. Berman, Paul, created by. LC 92-36324. (gr. 4-9). 1993. write for info. (0-86307-340-9) Marshall Cavendish.
—Science in Action: Projects in Physics. Berman, Paul, contrib. by. LC 92-36325. (gr. 4-9). 1993. write for info. (0-86307-341-7) Marshall Cavendish.
Lyons, B. Me & My World: Teacher's Guide. 200p. (gr. k). 1993. incl. activity pgs. 95.00 (0-87746-364-6) Graphic Learning.
Lyons, Carole, ed. see Buschman, Janis & Hunley, Debbie.
Lyons, Carole, ed. see Hubbard, Kate & Berlin, Evelyn.
Lyons, Carole, ed. see Jance, Judy.
Lyons, Carole R., ed. see Jance, Judy.
Lyons, Joseph. Clare Booth Luce. Horner, Matina, intro. by. (Illus.). 112p. (gr. 5 up). 1989. lib. bdg. 17.95 (1-55546-665-6) Chelsea Hse.
Lyons, Mark E. Selected Poems. 1992. 7.95 (0-533-09578-6) Vantage.
Lyons, Mary. The Butter Tree. 1994. write for info. (0-8050-2673-8) H Holt & Co.
—Keeping Secrets. 1994. write for info. (0-8050-3065-4) H Holt & Co.
Lyons, Mary E. Letters from a Slave Girl: The Story of Harriet Jacobs. LC 91-45778. (Illus.). 160p. (gr. 7 up). 1992. SBE 13.95 (0-684-19446-5, Scribners Young Read) Macmillan Child Grp.
—Sorrow's Kitchen: The Life & Folklore of Zora Neale Hurston. LC 90-8058. (Illus.). 160p. (gr. 7 up). 1990. SBE 14.95 (0-684-19198-9, Scribners Young Read) Macmillan Child Grp.
—Sorrow's Kitchen: The Life & Folklore of Zora Neale Hurston. LC 92-30600. (Illus.). 160p. (gr. 7 up). 1993. pap. 5.95 (0-02-044445-1, Collier Young Ad) Macmillan Child Grp.
—Starting Home: The Story of Horace Pippin, Painter. LC 92-26990. (Illus.). 48p. (gr. 3-6). 1993. SBE 15.95 (0-684-19534-8, Scribners Young Read) Macmillan Child Grp.
—Stitching Stars: The Story Quilts of Harriet Powers. LC 92-38561. (Illus.). 48p. (gr. 3-6). 1993. SBE 15.95 (0-684-19576-3, Scribners Young Read) Macmillan Child Grp.
Lyons, Mary E., selected by. Raw Head, Bloody Bones: African-American Tales of the Supernatural. LC 91-10690. (Illus.). 96p. (gr. 5 up). 1991. SBE 13.95 (0-684-19333-7, Scribners Young Read) Macmillan Child Grp.
Lyons, Pam. A Boy Called Simon. (Orig.). (gr. k-12). 1987. 2.50 (0-440-91094-3, LFL) Dell.
—Danny's Girl. (Orig.). (gr. 6 up). 1986. pap. 2.50 (0-440-91830-8, LFL) Dell.
—Love Around the Corner. (Orig.). (gr. k-12). 1987. pap. 2.50 (0-440-94726-X, LFL) Dell.
—Tug of Love. (Orig.). (gr. 6 up). 1986. pap. 2.50 (0-440-98818-7, LFL) Dell.
Lysne, Mary. New Testament Match Up. Lysne, Mary E., illus. 32p. 1991. pap. 1.99 saddle stitch (0-87403-876-6, 25-02506) Standard Pub.
—Old Testament Match Up. Lysne, Mary E., illus. 32p. 1991. pap. 1.99 saddle stitch (0-87403-875-8, 25-02505) Standard Pub.
—Read the Pictures: Fun from the New Testament, Bk. 1. Lysne, Mary E., illus. 32p. (gr. k-3). 1991. pap. 1.99 saddle stitch (0-87403-879-0, 23-02509) Standard Pub.
—Read the Pictures: Fun from the Old Testament, Bk. 1. Lysne, Mary E., illus. 32p. (gr. k-3). 1991. pap. 1.99 saddle stitch (0-87403-877-4, 23-02507) Standard Pub.
—Read the Pictures: More Fun from the New Testament, Bk. 2. Lysne, Mary E., illus. 32p. (gr. k-3). 1991. pap. 1.99 saddle stitch (0-87403-880-4, 23-02510) Standard Pub.
—Read the Pictures: More Fun from the Old Testament, Bk. 2. Lysne, Mary E., illus. 32p. (gr. k-3). 1991. pap. 1.99 saddle stitch (0-87403-878-2, 23-02508) Standard Pub.
Lysne, Mary E. Come & See. Gambill, Henrietta, ed. Patterson, Kathleen, illus. 24p. (ps-3). 1993. wkbk. 2.39 (0-7847-0104-0, 23-02584) Standard Pub.
—Mary & Elizabeth. Gambill, Henrietta, ed. Patterson, Kathleen, illus. 24p. (ps-3). 1993. wkbk. 2.39 (0-7847-0101-6, 23-02581) Standard Pub.
—Parables of Jesus. Gambill, Henrietta, ed. Patterson, Kathleen, illus. 24p. (ps-3). 1993. wkbk. 2.39 (0-7847-0102-4, 23-02582) Standard Pub.
—Paul. Gambill, Henrietta, ed. Patterson, Kathleen, illus. 24p. (ps-3). 1993. wkbk. 2.39 (0-7847-0106-7, 23-02586) Standard Pub.
—Peter. Gambill, Henrietta, ed. Patterson, Kathleen, illus. 24p. (ps-3). 1993. wkbk. 2.39 (0-7847-0105-9, 23-02585) Standard Pub.
—What Happened? Gambill, Henrietta, ed. Patterson, Kathleen, illus. 24p. (ps-3). 1993. wkbk. 2.39 (0-7847-0103-2, 23-02583) Standard Pub.
Lyss, Ester, jt. auth. see Kaplan, Carol.
Lyss, Esther, jt. auth. see Kaplan, Carol.
Lytle, Elizabeth S. Exploring Careers in the Construction Industry. Rosen, Ruth, ed. (gr. 7-12). 1992. PLB 13.95 (0-8239-1405-4) Rosen Group.
Lyttle, Richard B. Il Duce: The Rise & Fall of Benito Mussolini. LC 86-28851. 256p. (gr. 7 up). 1987. SBE 15.95 (0-689-31213-X, Atheneum Child Bk) Macmillan Child Grp.
—Ernest Hemingway: The Life & the Legend. LC 91-11218. (Illus.). 224p. (gr. 7 up). 1992. SBE 15.95 (0-689-31670-4, Atheneum Child Bk) Macmillan Child Grp.

—Land Beyond the River: Europe in the Age of
Migration. LC 85-28758. (Illus.). 192p. (gr. 5 up).
1986. SBE 15.95 (0-689-31199-0, Atheneum Child
Bk) Macmillan Child Grp.
—Mark Twain - The Man & His Adventure. LC 93-
11247. 1994. write for info. (0-689-31712-3,
Atheneum Child Bk) Macmillan Child Grp.
—Pablo Picasso: The Man & the Image. LC 89-6561.
(Illus.). 192p. (gr. 7 up). 1989. SBE 15.95
(0-689-31393-4, Atheneum Child Bk) Macmillan
Child Grp.

M

Maartens, Maretha. Paper Bird: A Novel of South
Africa. 144p. (gr. 4-9). 1991. 13.45 (0-395-56490-5,
Clarion Bks) HM.
Maas, Virginia. Niddy Noddy the Noodlemaker.
McIntosh, Carolyn, illus. 12p. (ps-2). 1981. pap. 2.75
(0-933992-15-7) Coffee Break.
Maass, Robert. Fire Fighters. (Illus.). 1992. 3.95
(0-590-41460-7) Scholastic Inc.
—Fire Fighters. Maas, Robert, photos by.
(Illus.). 32p. (gr. k-3). 1989. pap. 12.95
(0-590-41459-3) Scholastic Inc.
—Tugboat Life. 1994. write for info. (0-8050-3116-2) H
Holt & Co.
—When Autumn Comes. Maass, Robert, photos by. LC
90-32069. (Illus.). 32p. (ps-2). 1990. 15.95
(0-8050-1259-1, Owlet BYR) H Holt & Co.
—When Autumn Comes. LC 90-32069. (Illus.). 32p.
(ps-2). 1992. pap. 5.95 (0-8050-2349-6, Bks Young
Read) H Holt & Co.
—When Spring Comes. LC 93-29816. 1994. 14.95
(0-8050-2085-3, Bks Young Read) H Holt & Co.
—When Summer Comes. LC 92-26955. (Illus.). 32p. (gr.
1-3). 1993. PLB 14.95 (0-8050-2087-X, Bks Young
Read) H Holt & Co.
—When Winter Comes. LC 93-7146. (Illus.). 32p. (gr.
1-3). 1993. PLB 14.95 (0-8050-2086-1, Bks Young
Read) H Holt & Co.
Maberly, Norman C. Mastering Speed Reading. 127p.
(gr. 9-12). 1989. pap. 3.50 (0-451-15511-4, Sig) NAL-
Dutton.
—Mastering Speed Reading. 127p. (gr. 7 up). 1966. pap.
4.99 (0-451-16644-2, Sig) NAL-Dutton.
Mabery, D. L. Janet Jackson. (Illus.). 48p. (gr. 4-9). 1988.
pap. 13.50 (0-8225-1618-7) Lerner Pubns.
Mabery, D L. Prince. (Illus.). 48p. (gr. 4-9). 1985. PLB
13.50 (0-8225-1603-9) Lerner Pubns.
Mabery, D. L. This Is Michael Jackson. LC 84-10043.
(Illus.). 48p. (gr. 4-9). 1984. PLB 13.50
(0-8225-1600-4) Lerner Pubns.
Mabie, Grace. A Picture Book of Animal Opposites.
Kinnealy, Janice, illus. LC 91-33596. 24p. (gr. 1-4).
1992. text ed. 9.59 (0-8167-2438-5); 2.50
(0-8167-2439-3) Troll Assocs.
—A Picture Book of Baby Animals. Pistolesi, Roseanna,
illus. LC 92-26264. 24p. (gr. 1-4). 1992. PLB 9.59
(0-8167-2468-7); pap. text ed. 2.50 (0-8167-2469-5)
Troll Assocs.
—A Picture Book of Night-Time Animals. Kinnealy,
Janice, illus. LC 91-33597. 24p. (gr. 1-4). 1992. PLB
9.59 (0-8167-2432-6); pap. text ed. 2.50
(0-8167-2433-4) Troll Assocs.
—A Picture Book of Water Birds. Pistolesi, Roseanna,
illus. LC 91-34129. 24p. (gr. 1-4). 1992. PLB 9.59
(0-8167-2436-9); pap. text ed. 2.50 (0-8167-2437-7)
Troll Assocs.
Mabie, Grace, ed. see Baum, L. Frank.
Mabie, Margot C. Bioethics & the New Medical
Technology. LC 92-22642. 176p. (gr. 7 up). 1993.
SBE 14.95 (0-689-31637-2, Atheneum Child Bk)
Macmillan Child Grp.
McAfee, A. & Browne, A. Visitors Who Came to Stay.
LC 84-40333. 32p. (gr. 4-6). 1985. pap. 11.95
(0-670-74714-9) Viking Child Bks.
McAfee, Carol. Who's the Kid Around Here Anyway?
1992. pap. 3.99 (0-449-70411-4, Juniper) Fawcett.
McAffee, Cheryl W. The U. S. Postal Service.
Schlesinger, Arthur M., Jr., intro. by. (Illus.). 96p. (gr.
5 up). 1987. lib. bdg. 14.95 (0-87754-826-9) Chelsea
Hse.
McAlarv, Florence & Cohen, Judith L. You Can Be a
Woman Marine Biologist. Kate, David A., illus. 40p.
(Orig.). (gr. 4-7). 1992. pap. 6.00 (1-880599-06-6)
Cascade Pass.
McAlary, Florence & Cohen, Judith L. Tu Puedes Ser
Biologa Marina. Katz, David A. & Yanez, Juan, illus.
(SPA.). 40p. (gr. 4-7). 1992. pap. 6.00 (1-880599-07-4)
Cascade Pass.
McAlister, George A. A Time to Love...a Time to Die.
Godfrey, Raymond, illus. 216p. (Orig.). (gr. 10). 1988.
pap. 7.95 (0-924307-01-3) Docutex Inc.
McAlister, George A. & McLeod, Lloyd. Dominoes
Texas Style. (Illus.). (gr. 9). 1977. pap.
5.95 (0-924307-02-1) Docutex Inc.
McAllister. Steven Spielberg, Reading Level 2. (Illus.).
24p. (gr. 1-4). 1989. PLB 14.60 (0-86592-427-9); 10.
95s.p. (0-685-58803-3) Rourke Corp.
McAllister, Angela. The Battle of Sir Cob & Sir Filbert.
McAllister, Angela, illus. LC 91-19023. 32p. (ps-2).
1992. 15.00 (0-517-58730-0) Crown Bks Yng Read.

—Christmas Wish. (ps-3). 1991. 13.95 (0-670-84107-2)
Viking Child Bks.
—Enchanted Flute. 1991. 14.95 (0-385-30326-2)
Delacorte.
—The Honey Festival. Fitzgerald,
Gerald, photos by. LC 92-46079. (gr. 1-8). 1994. 13.
99 (0-8037-1240-5) Dial Bks Young.
—Jessie's Journey. Magill, Ann, illus. LC 92-313. 32p.
(ps-3). 1992. SBE 13.95 (0-02-765366-8, Macmillan
Child Bk) Macmillan Child Grp.
—The King Who Sneezed. Henwood, Simon, illus. LC
88-6858. 32p. (gr. k-3). 1988. 12.95 (0-688-08327-7);
PLB 12.88 (0-688-08328-5, Morrow Jr Bks) Morrow
Jr Bks.
—Matepo. Newton, Jill, illus. LC 90-33113. 32p. (ps-3).
1991. 12.95 (0-8037-0838-6) Dial Bks Young.
—Nesta, the Little Witch. Jenkin-Pearce, Susie, illus. 32p.
(ps-3). 1993. pap. 4.99 (0-14-054266-3, Puffin) Puffin
Bks.
—One Breeze-Scented, Sun-Sparkling Morning. Jenkin-
Pearce, Susie, illus. 32p. (ps-1). 1993. 17.95
(0-09-176363-0, Pub. by Hutchinson UK) Trafalgar.
—Paradise Park. (Illus.). 32p. (ps-2). 1992. 16.95
(0-370-31576-6, Pub. by Bodley Head UK) Trafalgar.
—The Snow Angel. Fletcher, Claire, illus. LC 92-44155.
1993. write for info. (0-688-04569-3) Lothrop.
McAllister, Constance. Creative Writing Activities, 2-6.
32p. (gr. 2-6). 1980. pap. 2.95 (0-87534-176-4)
Highlights.
—Creative Writing for Beginners. 32p. (Orig.). (gr. 1-3).
1976. pap. 2.95 (0-87534-165-9) Highlights.
McAllister, Dawson. Discussion Manual for Student
Relationships, Vol. 2. Lamb, Jim, illus. (gr. 5-12).
1976. pap. 8.75 (0-923417-07-9) Shepherd Minst.
—Discussion Manual for Student Relationships, Vol. 3.
Lamb, Jim, illus. (gr. 5-12). 1978. pap. 8.75
(0-923417-08-7) Shepherd Minst.
—Please Don't Tell My Parents. 176p. 1992. pap. 8.99
(0-8499-3311-0) Word Inc.
—Self Esteem & Loneliness. Lamb, Jim, illus. (gr. 5-12).
1989. pap. 3.95 (0-923417-02-8) Shepherd Minst.
—Student Conference Follow-Up Manual. Lamb, Jim,
illus. (gr. 5-12). 1989. pap. 2.95 (0-923417-10-9)
Shepherd Minst.
—Student Relationships, Vol. 1. (gr. 5-12). 1981. pap.
6.95 tchr's. guide (0-923417-18-4) Shepherd Minst.
—A Walk with Christ Through the Resurrection.
Whitney, Roger, illus. (gr. 5-12). 1981. pap. 8.95
(0-923417-14-1) Shepherd Minst.
—A Walk with Christ to the Cross. Whitney, Roger, illus.
(gr. 5-12). 1980. pap. 8.95 (0-923417-09-5) Shepherd
Minst.
—Who Are You, Jesus? Lewis, Paul, illus. (gr. 5-12).
1986. pap. 7.95 (0-923417-05-2) Shepherd Minst.
McAllister, Dawson & Altman, Tim. You, God & Your
Sexuality. Peterson, Wayne, ed. Trammel, Kim, illus.
(gr. 5-12). 1988. pap. 3.95 (0-923417-01-X) Shepherd
Minst.
McAllister, Dawson & Kimmel, Tim. Student
Relationships, Vol. 2. (gr. 5-12). 1981. pap. 6.95 tchr's.
guide (0-923417-04-4) Shepherd Minst.
—Student Relationships, Vol. 3. (gr. 5-12). 1981. pap.
6.95 tchr's. guide (0-923417-19-2) Shepherd Minst.
McAllister, Dawson & Kimmel, Tim. Walk with Christ to
the Cross. (gr. 5-12). 1981. pap. 5.95 tchr's. guide
(0-923417-20-6) Shepherd Minst.
McAllister, Dawson & May, Tom. Who Are You Jesus?
(gr. 5-12). 1986. pap. 7.95 tchr's. guide
(0-923417-03-6) Shepherd Minst.
McAllister, Dawson & Miller, John. Discussion Manual
for Student Discipleship, Vol. 2. Lamb, Jim, illus. (gr.
5-12). 1978. pap. 8.50 (0-923417-16-8) Shepherd
Minst.
McAllister, Dawson & Miller, Rich. Who Are You,
God? Varner, Charles, illus. (gr. 5-12). 1988. pap. 7.95
(0-923417-11-7) Shepherd Minst.
—Who Are You God? (gr. 5-12). 1990. pap. 5.95 tchr's.
guide (0-923417-13-3) Shepherd Minst.
McAllister, Dawson & Sharp, Floyd. Handbook for
Financial Faithfulness. (Illus.). (gr. 5-12). 1974. pap.
6.95 (0-923417-17-6) Shepherd Minst.
McAllister, Dawson & Webster, Dan. Discussion Manual
for Student Discipleship, Vol. 1. Lamb, Jim, illus. (gr.
5-12). 1975. pap. 8.50 (0-923417-15-X) Shepherd
Minst.
—Discussion Manual for Student Relationships, Vol. 1.
Lamb, Jim, illus. (gr. 5-12). 1975. pap. 8.75
(0-923417-06-0) Shepherd Minst.
McAllister, Fran, jt. auth. see McAllister, Frank.
McAllister, Frank. Tooth Fairy Legend. McAllister,
Stephen, illus. LC 90-28136. 40p. (gr. k-6). 1992. 12.
95 (0-915677-54-7) Roundtable Pub.
McAllister, Frank & McAllister, Fran. The Tooth Fairy
Legend. LC 76-9595. (gr. k-4). 1976. 9.95
(0-916864-01-4) Block.
McAllister, Mimi. Christmas at Gump's. McAllister,
Mimi & Becker, Richard, illus. LC 90-60435. 48p.
1990. 16.95 (0-9624887-4-7) C Salway Pr.
Mcalpine, Helen & Mcalpine, William, eds. Japanese
Tales & Legends. (Illus.). 218p. 1989. pap. 10.95
(0-19-274140-3) OUP.
Mcalpine, William, jt. ed. see Mcalpine, Helen.
McAlvay, Nora & Chorpenning, Charlotte B. The Elves
& the Shoemaker. 1946. 4.50 (0-87602-124-0)
Anchorage.
—Flibbertigibbet. 1952. 4.50 (0-87602-127-5) Anchorage.

MacArthur, Barbara. Canten Navidad. Jensen, Robert,
illus. (ENG & SPA.). 15p. (Orig.). (ps-12). 1993. pap.
12.95 incl. cass. (1-881120-09-0) Frog Pr WI.
—Chantez Noel. Jensen, Robert, illus. (ENG & FRE.).
14p. (ps-12). 1993. pap. 12.95 incl. cass.
(1-881120-10-4) Frog Pr WI.
—Sing, Dance, Laugh & Eat Cheeseburgers. Jensen,
Robert, illus. 35p. (Orig.). (ps-9). 1992. pap. text ed.
17.95 (1-881120-06-6) Frog Pr WI.
—Sing, Dance, Laugh & Eat Quiche. rev. ed. Jensen,
Robert, illus. (FRE.). 35p. (ps-9). 1990. pap. text ed.
17.95 (1-881120-00-7) Frog Pr WI.
—Sing, Dance, Laugh & Eat Quiche 2. Jensen, Robert,
illus. (FRE.). 35p. (ps-9). 1989. pap. text ed.
17.95 incl. cass. (1-881120-01-5) Frog Pr WI.
—Sing, Dance, Laugh, & Eat Quiche 3. Jensen, Robert,
illus. (FRE.). 35p. (Orig.). (ps-12). 1992. pap. 17.95
(1-881120-07-4) Frog Pr WI.
—Sing, Dance, Laugh & Eat Tacos. Jensen, Robert, illus.
(SPA.). 35p. (Orig.). (ps-9). 1990. pap. text ed. 17.95
incl. cass. (1-881120-04-X) Frog Pr WI.
—Sing, Dance, Laugh & Eat Tacos 2. Jensen, Robert,
illus. (SPA.). 36p. (Orig.). (ps-9). 1991. pap. text ed.
17.95 incl. cass. (1-881120-05-8) Frog Pr WI.
—Sing, Dance, Laugh & Learn German. Jensen, Robert,
illus. (ENG & GER.). 18p. (Orig.). (ps-8). 1993. pap.
12.95 incl. cass. (1-881120-11-2) Frog Pr WI.
—Sing, Dance, Laugh & Learn Spanish. Jensen, Robert,
illus. 18p. (Orig.). (ps-4). 1993. pap. 12.95
(1-881120-08-2) Frog Pr WI.
—Singen Weihnachten. Jensen, Robert, illus. (GER.).
14p. (Orig.). (ps-12). 1993. pap. 12.95 (1-881120-12-0)
Frog Pr WI.
McArthur, Dalton R. The First Snowflake. Minson,
Grant L., illus. 32p. (Orig.). (ps-4). 1991. pap. 4.95x
(0-9626111-0-7) McArthur UT.
McArthur, Nancy. The Adventure of the Backyard
Sleepout. 80p. 1992. pap. 2.75 (0-590-45033-6)
Scholastic Inc.
—The Escape of the Plant that Ate Dirty Socks. 128p.
(Orig.). 1992. pap. 3.50 (0-380-76756-2, Camelot)
Avon.
—The Plant That Ate Dirty Socks. 128p. (Orig.). 1988.
pap. 3.50 (0-380-75493-2, Camelot) Avon.
—The Return of the Plant That Ate Dirty Socks. 128p.
(Orig.). (gr. 5-6). 1990. pap. 3.50 (0-380-75873-3,
Camelot) Avon.
—The Secret of the Plant That Ate Dirty Socks. 128p.
(Orig.). 1993. pap. 3.50 (0-380-76757-0, Camelot)
Avon.
McArtot, Marion, jt. auth. see Goss, Louise.
Macaulay, David. BAAA. LC 85-2316. (Illus.). 64p. (gr.
6 up). 1985. 13.45 (0-395-38948-8); pap. 4.80
(0-395-39588-7) HM.
—Black & White. Macaulay, David, illus. 32p. 1990. 14.
45 (0-395-52151-3) HM.
—Castle. Macaulay, David, illus. LC 77-7159. 80p. (gr. 1
up). 1982. 14.45 (0-395-25784-0); pap. 7.70
(0-395-32920-5) HM.
—Cathedral. (Illus.). (gr. k up). 1981. pap. 7.70
(0-395-31668-5) HM.
—Cathedral: The Story of Its Construction. LC 73-6634.
(Illus.). 80p. (gr. 1-5). 1973. 15.45 (0-395-17513-5)
HM.
—City: A Story of Roman Planning & Construction.
Macaulay, David, illus. 112p. (gr. 6 up). 1974. 15.95
(0-395-19492-X); pap. 7.95 (0-395-34922-2) HM.
—Mill. Macaulay, David, illus. 128p. (gr. 6 up). 1983. 15.
45 (0-395-34830-7) HM.
—Mill. 128p. (ps up). 1989. pap. 7.70 (0-395-52019-3,
Sandpiper) HM.
—Pyramid. Macaulay, David, illus. 80p. (gr. 7 up). 1975.
14.95 (0-395-21407-6) HM.
—Pyramid PA. Macaulay, David, illus. (gr. 5 up). 1982.
pap. 7.70 (0-395-32121-2) HM.
—Ship. (gr. 4-7). 1993. 19.95 (0-395-52439-3) HM.
—Unbuilding. (Illus.). (gr. 3 up). 1980. 15.45
(0-395-29457-6) HM.
—Unbuilding. Macaulay, David, illus. LC 80-15491.
128p. (gr. 5 up). 1987. pap. 6.95 (0-395-45360-7) HM.
—Unbuilding. (gr. k-3). 1987. pap. 7.70 (0-395-45425-5)
HM.
—Underground. Macaulay, David, illus. (gr. 1 up). 1976.
16.95 (0-395-24739-X); pap. 8.70 (0-395-34065-9)
HM.
—The Way Things Work. Macaulay, David, illus. 400p.
(ps up). 1988. 29.45 (0-395-42857-2) HM.
—Why the Chicken Crossed the Road. (Illus.). 32p. (gr.
4-6). 1987. 13.45 (0-395-44241-9, Clarion Bks) HM.
—Why the Chicken Crossed the Road. 1991. pap. 4.80
(0-395-58411-6) HM.
Macaulay, Susan S. How to Be Your Own Selfish Pig.
Signorino, Slug, illus. LC 81-70769. 1982. pap. 9.95
(0-89191-530-3) Cook.
McAuley. God Hears Everything. 1992. write for info.
(1-55513-715-6, Chariot Bks) Cook.
—God Made Fireflies. 1992. write for info.
(1-55513-716-4, Chariot Bks) Cook.
McAuley, Karen. Eleanor Roosevelt. Schlesinger, Arthur
M., Jr., intro. by. (Illus.). 112p. (gr. 5 up). 1987. lib.
bdg. 17.95 (0-87754-574-X) Chelsea Hse.
McAuley, Marilyn, jt. auth. see Lockwood, Barbara.
McAulyfe, William E., jt. auth. see Zackon, Fred.
McAvinn, Douglas, jt. auth. see Opie, Brenda.
McBain, Ann F. My Very Own Quilt. 1993. 7.95
(0-8062-4607-3) Carlton.
MacBain, Carol. Heartbreak Hill. 192p. (Orig.). (gr. 7-
12). 1987. pap. 2.50 (0-553-26195-9) Bantam.

—Stand By for Love. 192p. (Orig.). (gr. 7-12). 1987. pap. 2.50 (0-553-26903-8) Bantam.

McBaine, Robert. Student Workbook for Sentence Combining with Exercises & Key. 135p. (Orig.). (gr. 8 up). 1984. pap. 8.90 (0-89420-244-8, 261000) Natl Book.

McBarnet, Gill. Fountain of Fire. McBarnet, Gill, illus. 32p. (gr. k-2). 1987. 7.95 (0-9615102-3-4) Ruwanga Trad.

—Gecko Hide & Seek. McBarnet, Gill, illus. 24p. (ps-2). Date not set. 7.95 (0-9615102-7-7) Ruwanga Trad.

—The Goodnight Gecko. (Illus.). 32p. 1991. 7.95 (0-9615102-6-9) Ruwanga Trad.

—The Pink Parrot. McBarnett, Gill, illus. 40p. (gr. k-2). 1986. 7.95 (0-9615102-1-8) Ruwanga Trad.

—The Shark Who Learned a Lesson. McBarnet, Gill, illus. 32p. (ps-2). 1990. 7.95 (0-9615102-5-0) Ruwanga Trad.

—The Whale Who Wanted to Be Small. McBarnet, Gill, illus. 32p. (gr. k-2). 1985. 7.95 (0-9615102-0-X) Ruwanga Trad.

—A Whale's Tale. McBarnet, Gill, illus. 32p. (ps-2). 1988. 6.95 (0-9615102-4-2) Ruwanga Trad.

—The Wonderful Journey. McBarnet, Gill, illus. 32p. (gr. k-2). 1986. 7.95 (0-9615102-2-6) Ruwanga Trad.

McBratney, Sam. The Ghastly Gertie Swindle: With the Ghosts of Hungryhouse Lane. Thiesing, Lisa, illus. 128p. (gr. 3-6). 1993. PLB 14.95 (0-8050-2614-2, Bks Young Read) H Holt & Co.

—The Ghosts of Hungryhouse Lane. Thiesing, Lisa, illus. 128p. (gr. 4-6). 1989. 13.95 (0-8050-0985-X, Bks Young Read) H Holt & Co.

McBrayer, Brenda. Mom, I Don't Want to Get My Hair Washed: And Other Poems. Phillipps, Julie, illus. 43p. (Orig.). (gr. 2 up). 1992. pap. 7.95 (0-910303-40-1) Writers Pub Serv.

MacBride. Little Farm in the Ozarks. Date not set. 15.00 (0-06-024245-0, Festival); PLB 14.89 (0-06-024246-9, Festival) HarpC Child Bks.

McBride, Rachael, jt. auth. see Adler, Katie.

MacBride, Roger L. Little House on Rocky Ridge. Gilleece, David, illus. LC 92-39132. 368p. (gr. 3-7). 1993. 14.00 (0-06-020842-2); PLB 13.89 (0-06-020843-0) HarpC Child Bks.

—Little House on Rocky Ridge. Gilleece, David, illus. LC 92-39132. 368p. (gr. 3-7). 1993. pap. 3.95 (0-06-440478-1, Trophy) HarpC Child Bks.

MacBride, Roger L., ed. see Wilder, Laura I.

McBrier, Michael. Getting Oliver's Goat. Sims, Blanche, illus. LC 87-13870. 96p. (gr. 3-6). 1988. PLB 9.89 (0-8167-1145-3); pap. text ed. 2.95 (0-8167-1146-1) Troll Assocs.

—Oliver & the Amazing Spy. Sims, Blanche, illus. LC 87-13793. 96p. (gr. 3-6). 1988. PLB 9.89 (0-8167-1143-7); pap. text ed. 2.95 (0-8167-1144-5) Troll Assocs.

—Oliver & the Runaway Alligator. Sims, Blanche, illus. LC 86-7120. 96p. (Orig.). (gr. 3-6). 1987. PLB 9.89 (0-8167-0818-5); pap. text ed. 2.95 (0-8167-0819-3) Troll Assocs.

—Oliver Smells Trouble. Sims, Blanche, illus. LC 87-13954. 96p. (gr. 3-6). 1988. PLB 9.89 (0-8167-1149-6); pap. text ed. 2.95 (0-8167-1150-X) Troll Assocs.

—Oliver's Back-Yard Circus. Sims, Blanche, illus. LC 86-40378. 96p. (Orig.). (gr. 3-6). 1987. PLB 9.89 (0-8167-0822-3); pap. text ed. 2.95 (0-8167-0823-1) Troll Assocs.

—Oliver's Barnyard Blues. Sims, Blanche, illus. LC 87-13864. 96p. (gr. 3-6). 1988. PLB 9.89 (0-8167-1147-X); pap. text ed. 2.95 (0-8167-1148-8) Troll Assocs.

—Oliver's High-Flying Adventure. Sims, Blanche, illus. LC 86-16038. 96p. (Orig.). (gr. 3-6). 1987. PLB 9.89 (0-8167-0820-7); pap. text ed. 2.95 (0-8167-0821-5) Troll Assocs.

McBrier, Page. Adventure in the Haunted House. Sims, Blanche, illus. LC 85-8436. 96p. (gr. 3-6). 1986. PLB 9.89 (0-8167-0539-9); pap. text ed. 2.95 (0-8167-0540-2) Troll Assocs.

—Daphne Takes Charge. 1990. pap. 2.95 (0-380-75899-7, Camelot) Avon.

—First Course: Trouble. 128p. 1990. pap. 2.50 (0-380-75783-4, Camelot) Avon.

—The Great Rip-Off. 128p. 1990. pap. 2.95 (0-380-75902-0, Camelot) Avon.

—The Kickball Crisis. 96p. 1989. pap. 2.50 (0-380-75781-8, Camelot) Avon.

—Oliver & the Lucky Duck. Sims, Blanche, illus. LC 85-8417. 96p. (gr. 3-6). 1986. PLB 9.89 (0-8167-0541-0); pap. text ed. 2.95 (0-8167-0542-9) Troll Assocs.

—Oliver's Lucky Day. Sims, Blanche, illus. LC 85-8437. 96p. (gr. 3-6). 1986. lib. bdg. 9.89 (0-8167-0537-2); pap. text ed. 2.95 (0-8167-0538-0) Troll Assocs.

—The Press Mess. 128p. (Orig.). (gr. 4-5). 1990. pap. 2.95 (0-380-75900-4, Camelot) Avon.

—Rats. 128p. 1990. pap. 2.95 (0-380-75901-2, Camelot) Avon.

—Secret of the Missing Camel. Sims, Blanche, illus. LC 86-887. 96p. (Orig.). (gr. 3-6). 1987. PLB 9.89 (0-8167-0816-9); pap. text ed. 2.95 (0-8167-0817-7) Troll Assocs.

—Secret of the Old Garage. Sims, Blanche, illus. LC 85-16505. 96p. (gr. 3-6). 1986. PLB 9.89 (0-8167-0543-7); pap. text ed. 2.95 (0-8167-0544-5) Troll Assocs.

—Spaghetti Breath. 128p. (gr. 4). 1989. pap. 2.50 (0-380-75782-6, Camelot) Avon.

—Stinky Business. 128p. (Orig.). 1991. pap. 2.95 (0-380-76269-2, Camelot) Avon.

—Under Twelve Not Allowed. 128p. (gr. 4). 1989. pap. 2.50 (0-380-75780-X, Camelot) Avon.

McBrier, Vivian F. R. Nathaniel Dett: His Life & Works (1882-1943) 1990. 15.95 (0-87498-092-5) Assoc Pubs DC.

McBrown, Gertrude P. Picture Poetry Book. Jones, Lois M., illus. 1990. 4.25 (0-87498-007-0) Assoc Pubs DC.

McBurney, Jim. Technopoly. Kraven, Mae, ed. Harris, Linda, illus. 96p. (gr. 4-5). 1991. text ed. 19.95 (0-9629471-0-5) J McBurney.

McCabe, Ann C. & Fairbanks, Eugene B. English Writing: Fifteen-Day Competency Review Text. Gamsey, Wayne H., ed. Fairbanks, Eugene B., illus. 160p. (Orig.). (gr. 7-12). 1992. pap. text ed. 4.95 (0-935487-56-5) N & N Pub Co.

McCabe, Bernard. Bottle Rabbit. (gr. 4-7). 1992. pap. 3.95 (0-571-15339-9) Faber & Faber.

—Bottle Rabbit & Friends. Scheffler, Axel, illus. 136p. (gr. 3-7). 1991. 14.95 (0-571-15318-6) Faber & Faber.

McCabe, Eugene. Cyril: Quest of an Orphaned Squirrel. 72p. (ps-8). 1987. 13.95 (0-86278-116-7, Pub. by O'Brien Press Ltd Eire); pap. 7.95 (0-86278-131-0, Pub. by O'Brien Press Ltd Eire) Dufour.

McCabe, J. L. Everyday Algebra. 133p. (Orig.). 1987. pap. text ed. 13.95 (0-942465-07-5, 2 212 939) Everyday Bks.

—Everyday Mathematics: A Study Guide. (Illus.). 168p. (Orig.). 1988. pap. text ed. 13.95 (0-942465-11-3, 2 323 279) Everyday Bks.

McCabe, Margaret E. & Rhoades, Jacqueline. Cooperative Meeting Management. 40p. (Orig.). (gr. 8 up). 1986. pap. 3.95 (0-933935-03-X) ITA Pubns.

McCabe, Margaret E., jt. auth. see Rhoades, Jacqueline.

McCabe, Michael. Arizona: Studies. (Illus.). 46p. (gr. 4-6). 1994. wkbk. 5.75 (0-911981-59-4) Cloud Pub.

—Arizona: Su Origen. (SPA., Illus.). (gr. 4-6). 1987. text ed. 16.45 (0-911981-54-3) Cloud Pub.

—Colorado: Grassroots. (Illus.). 48p. (gr. 4-6). 1984. Repr. of 1983 ed. wkbk. 5.45 (0-911981-13-6) Cloud Pub.

McCabe, Michael & Brew, Virginia. California: Roots. 28p. (gr. 4-6). 1991. Repr. of 1983 ed. tchr's ed. 7.95 (0-911981-07-1) Cloud Pub.

—California: Roots. (Illus.). 59p. (gr. 4-6). 1983. wkbk. 5.25 (0-911981-05-5) Cloud Pub.

—Colorado: Grassroots. 20p. (gr. 4-6). 1983. tchr's ed. 8.95 (0-911981-14-4) Cloud Pub.

McCabe, Michael, jt. auth. see Brew, Virginia.

McCabe, Michael, jt. auth. see Stacy, Darryl.

McCabe, Robert E. & Goldman, Elizabeth. Getting Started in Developmental Writing. 100p. (gr. 2-9). 1982. 7.60 (0-940444-17-8) Kabyn.

McCafferty, Jim. Holt & the Cowboys. Davis, Florence S., illus. LC 93-16618. 40p. (gr. 4-8). 1993. 12.95 (0-88289-985-6) Pelican.

—Holt & the Teddy Bear. Davis, Florence S., illus. LC 90-44060. 40p. (gr. 4-8). 1991. 12.95 (0-88289-823-X) Pelican.

McCaffrey, Anne. Dragondrums. Marcellino, Fred, illus. LC 78-11318. 256p. (gr. 6 up). 1979. SBE 15.95 (0-689-30685-7, Atheneum Child Bk) Macmillan Child Grp.

—Dragonsinger. Marcellino, Fred, illus. LC 76-40988. 276p. (gr. 5-9). 1977. SBE 15.95 (0-689-30570-2, Atheneum Child Bk) Macmillan Child Grp.

—Dragonsong. Lydecker, Laura, illus. LC 75-30530. 224p. (gr. 5-9). 1976. 16.95 (0-689-30507-9, Atheneum Child Bk) Macmillan Child Grp.

McCaffrey, Kevin, illus. Adventures of Fionn & the Fianna. 40p. (gr. 4 up) 1989. 9.95 (1-871423-05-8) Irish Bks Media.

McCall, B. The Cherokee. (Illus.). 32p. (gr. 5-8). 1989. lib. bdg. 15.94 (0-86625-376-9); lib. bdg. 11.95s.p. (0-685-58583-2) Rourke Corp.

—The Iroquois. (Illus.). 32p. (gr. 5-8). 1989. lib. bdg. 15. 74 (0-86625-378-5); 11.95 (0-685-58582-4) Rourke Corp.

McCall, Barbara. Apache. (Illus.). 32p. (gr. 5-8). 1990. lib. bdg. 15.94 (0-86625-384-X); lib. bdg. 11.95s.p. (0-685-36387-2) Rourke Corp.

—The Three Investigator's Book of Mystery Puzzles. Rao, Anthony, illus. 64p. (gr. 3-7). 1982. pap. 1.50 (0-394-85107-2) Random Bks Yng Read.

McCall, Barbara, et al. Native American People, 6 bks, Reading Level 4. (Illus.). 192p. (gr. 5-8). 1989. Set. PLB 95.64 (0-86625-375-0); lib. bdg. 71.70 (0-685-58768-1) Rourke Corp.

McCall, Barbara A. Los Apache. Lazzarino, Luciano, illus. Marcuse, Aida E., tr. from SPA. LC 92-12177. 1992. 17.26 (0-86625-454-4); 12.95s.p. (0-685-59386-X) Rourke Pubns.

McCall, Dan. Jack the Bear. 224p. (gr. 7 up). 1992. 4.99 (0-449-22142-3) Fawcett.

McCall, Edith. Biography of a River: The Mississippi. (Illus.). (gr. 7 up). 1990. 16.95 (0-8027-6914-4); lib. bdg. 17.85 (0-8027-6915-2) Walker & Co.

—Explorers in a New World. Borja, Robert, illus. LC 60-6675. 128p. (gr. 3-10). 1980. PLB 15.00 (0-516-03318-2) Childrens.

—Forts in the Wilderness. Wiskur, Darrell, illus. LC 68-24378. 128p. (gr. 3-10). 1980. PLB 15.00 (0-516-03324-7) Childrens.

—Message from the Mountains. Nankin, Fran, ed. LC 85-3142. (Illus.). 122p. (gr. 6-9). 1985. 11.95 (0-8027-6582-3) Walker & Co.

—Mississippi Steamboatman: The Story of Henry Miller Shreve. LC 85-13795. (Illus.). 115p. (gr. 5-8). 1986. 11.95 (0-8027-6597-1) Walker & Co.

—Pioneering on the Plains. Rogers, Carol, illus. LC 62-15638. 128p. (gr. 3-10). 1980. PLB 15.00 (0-516-03358-1) Childrens.

—Pioneers on Early Waterways. Rogers, Carl, illus. LC 61-10104. 128p. (gr. 3-10). 1980. PLB 15.00 (0-516-03357-3) Childrens.

—Pirates & Privateers. Palm, Felix, illus. LC 63-15637. 128p. (gr. 3-10). 1980. PLB 15.00 (0-516-03360-3) Childrens.

—Settlers on a Strange Shore. Rogers, Carol, illus. LC 60-11154. 128p. (gr. 3-10). 1980. PLB 15.00 (0-516-03367-0) Childrens.

—Stalwart Men of Early Texas. Aronson, Lou, illus. LC 78-101296. 128p. (gr. 3-10). 1980. PLB 15.00 (0-516-03371-9) Childrens.

—Steamboats to the West. Borja, Robert, illus. LC 59-3665. 128p. (gr. 3-10). 1980. PLB 15.00 (0-516-03368-9) Childrens.

—Wagons Over the Mountains. Rogers, Carol, illus. LC 61-10101. 128p. (gr. 3-10). 1980. PLB 15.00 (0-516-03376-X) Childrens.

McCall, Jody, ed. see Reuther, Ruth E.

McCall, Randy & Siembieda, Kevin. Beyond the Supernatural. Marciniszyn, Alex & Siembieda, Florence, eds. (Illus.). 256p. (Orig.). (gr. 8 up). 1988. pap. 19.95 (0-916211-18-5, 700) Palladium Bks.

McCall, William A. & Harby, Mary L. Test Lessons in Primary Reading. 2nd ed. (gr. 2-3). 1980. pap. text ed. 3.50x (0-8077-5965-1); 2.95x (0-8077-5966-X) Tchrs Coll.

McCall, Yvonne H. The Story of Jacob, Rachel & Leah. (Illus.). 24p. (gr. k-4). 1986. pap. 1.89 saddlestitched (0-570-06205-5, 59-1428) Concordia.

McCallum, George P. Visitor from Another Planet & Other Plays. (gr. 4-6). 1982. student's ed. 7.95x (0-19-502743-4); tchr's. ed. 8.95x (0-19-503167-9) OUP.

McCallum, Joanne, created by. & illu see Linville, Barbara.

McCandless, Bruce see McPhee, Penelope & McPhee, Raymond.

McCandless, Perry & Foley, William E. Missouri: Then & Now. rev. ed. LC 90-32545. (Illus.). 328p. (gr. 4). 1992. text ed. 19.95 (0-8262-0825-8) U of Mo Pr.

McCanlies, Tim. Harlem. (Orig.). (ps-12). 1984. pap. 2.25 (0-87067-245-2, BH245) Holloway.

McCann, Helen. What Do We Do Now, George? Eagle, Ellen, illus. LC 91-2329. 160p. (gr. 4-7). 1993. pap. 2.95 (0-671-86691-5, Half Moon Bks) S&S Trade.

—What's French for Help, George? Eagle, Ellen, illus. LC 91-41563. 460p. (gr. 5-9). 1993. pap. 13.00 JR3 (0-671-74689-8, S&S BFYR) S&S Trade.

McCann, Jennifer, jt. auth. see Kuzmier, Kerrie.

McCann, Sean. Growing Things. LC 89-51018. 138p. (Orig.). 1989. pap. 5.95 (1-85371-029-6, Pub. by Poolbeg Press Ltd Eire) Dufour.

McCants, William D. Anything Can Happen in High School: And It Usually Does. LC 92-32982. 1993. write for info. (0-15-276604-9); pap. write for info. (0-15-276605-7) HarBrace.

McCarney-Muldoon, Eileen & O'Brien, Mary B. Fun with Colors. LC 91-42672. (Illus.). 24p. (ps). 1992. POB 6.95 (0-689-71610-9, Aladdin) Macmillan Child Grp.

—Fun with Numbers. LC 91-39592. (Illus.). 24p. (ps). 1992. POB 6.95 (0-689-71609-5, Aladdin) Macmillan Child Grp.

Maccarone, Grace. Ghost on the Hill. 1990. pap. 2.75 (0-590-42978-7) Scholastic Inc.

—The Haunting of Grade Three. 96p. (Orig.). (gr. 2-5). 1987. pap. 2.75 (0-590-43868-9) Scholastic Inc.

—Itchy, Itchy Chickenpox. Lewin, Betsy, illus. 32p. 1992. pap. 2.95 (0-590-44948-6) Scholastic Inc.

—Pizza Party. LC 93-19732. (Illus.). 48p. (ps-4). 1994. pap. 2.95 (0-590-47563-0, Cartwheel) Scholastic Inc.

—Return of the Third-Grade Ghosthunters. 1989. pap. 2.75 (0-590-41944-7) Scholastic Inc.

—The Sword in the Stone. (Illus.). 1992. pap. 2.95 (0-590-45527-3, 043, Cartwheel) Scholastic Inc.

Maccarone, Grace & Chardiet, Bernice. Brenda's Private Swing. 1992. pap. 2.50 (0-590-43304-0) Scholastic Inc.

—Martin & the Tooth Fairy. Karas, G. Brian, illus. 32p. 1991. pap. 2.50 (0-590-43305-9) Scholastic Inc.

Maccarone, Grace, jt. auth. see Chardiet, Bernice.

McCarthy, Betty. Utah. LC 89-35083. 144p. (gr. 4 up). 1989. PLB 26.60 (0-516-00490-5) Childrens.

—Utah. 199p. 1993. text ed. 15.40 (1-56956-176-1) W A T Braille.

McCarthy, Bobette. Dreaming. LC 93-2882. 1994. write for info. (1-56402-184-X) Candlewick Pr.

—Happy Hiding Hippos. McCarthy, Bobette, illus. LC 92-32599. 32p. (ps-1). 1994. RSBE 13.95 (0-02-765446-X, Bradbury Pr) Macmillan Child Grp.

—Ten Little Hippos: A Counting Book. McCarthy, Bobette, illus. LC 91-17175. 32p. (ps-2). 1992. SBE 13.95 (0-02-765445-1, Bradbury Pr) Macmillan Child Grp.

McCarthy, Colin. Poisonous Snakes. LC 87-80464. (Illus.). 32p. (gr. 1-6). 1987. PLB 12.40 (0-531-17053-5, Gloucester Pr) Watts.

—Poisonous Snakes. (gr. 4-7). 1990. pap. 4.95 (0-531-17260-0) Watts.

McCarthy, Colin & Arnold, Nick. Reptile. Keates, Colin & Arnold, Nick, photos by. LC 90-4890. (Illus.). 64p. (gr. 5 up). 1991. 15.00 (0-679-80783-7); PLB 15.99 (0-679-90783-1) Knopf Bks Yng Read.

McCarthy, Donald. Fun with Math-E-Magic. Cooper, William H., ed. McCarthy, Donald W., illus. 65p. (gr. 4-9). 1984. pap. 2.60 (0-914127-01-2) Univ Class.

—More Fun with Science Magic. LC 91-75095. (Illus.). 80p. (Orig.). 1991. pap. 6.33 (0-914127-12-8) Univ Class.

McCarthy, Donald W. Fun with Science Magic. Cooper, William H., ed. LC 84-50893. (Illus.). 80p. (gr. 4-9). 1984. pap. 5.27 (0-914127-15-2) Univ Class.

McCarthy, Eugene J. Mr. Raccoon & His Friends. Anderson-Miller, Julia, illus. 112p. 1992. 16.00 (0-89733-377-2); pap. 6.95 (0-89733-374-8) Academy Chi Pubs.

McCarthy, Kevin. Saudi Arabia: A Desert Kingdom. LC 85-6941. (Illus.). 128p. (gr. 5 up). 1986. RSBE 14.95 (0-87518-295-X, Dillon) Macmillan Child Grp.

McCarthy, Kevin, jt. auth. see Jones, Maxine D.

MacCarthy, Patricia. Animals Galore. 1989. 11.95 (0-8037-0721-5) Dial Bks Young.

—Herds of Words. MacCarthy, Patricia, illus. LC 90-31537. 32p. (ps-3). 1991. 11.95 (0-8037-0892-0) Dial Bks Young.

—Ocean Parade. 1990. 11.95 (0-8037-0780-0) Dial Bks Young.

McCarthy, Ralph F., et al, eds. Grandfather Cherry Blossom. Kasamatsu, Shiro, illus. LC 93-18301. 48p. 1993. 13.00 (4-7700-1759-6) Kodansha.

—The Inch-High Samurai. Kasamatsu, Shiro, illus. LC 93-16310. 48p. 1993. 13.00 (4-7700-1758-8) Kodansha.

—The Moon Princess. Kasamatsu, Shiro & Oda, Kancho, illus. LC 93-18300. 48p. 1993. 13.00 (4-7700-1756-1) Kodansha.

McCarthy, Rick. Spymaster. (gr. 6-10). 1991. write for info. (0-9629205-0-9) Develop Solutions.

McCartney, Jenny. Grandma's Hospital. Bruere, Julian, illus. LC 92-29958. 1993. 4.25 (0-383-03570-8) SRA Schl Grp.

McCartney, Paul, jt. auth. see Lennon, John.

McCarty, John L. Maverick Town: The Story of Old Tascosa. Bugbee, Harold D., illus. Sonnichsen, C. L., frwd. by. LC 87-5946. (Illus.). 320p. (gr. 6-12). 1968. pap. 12.95 (0-8061-2089-4) U of Okla Pr.

McCaskill, Margaret. Please, Tell Me. 1993. 7.95 (0-8062-4611-1) Carlton.

McCaslin, Nellie. Angel of the Battlefield. LC 93-2604. 20p. 1993. pap. 4.00 (0-88734-430-5) Players Pr.

—Bluebonnets. LC 93-5271. 20p. 1993. pap. 4.00 (0-88734-439-9) Players Pr.

—Brave New Banner. 20p. 1993. pap. 4.00 (0-88734-436-4) Players Pr.

—Cold Face, Warm Heart. LC 93-5273. 20p. 1993. pap. 4.00 (0-88734-440-2) Players Pr.

—The Last Horizon. LC 93-5270. 24p. 1993. pap. 4.00 play script (0-88734-431-3) Players Pr.

—The Legend of Minna Lamourrie. LC 93-2603. 20p. 1993. pap. 4.00 play script (0-88734-438-0) Players Pr.

—Legends in Action: Ten Plays of Ten Lands. Landes, William-Alan, frwd. by. LC 93-22161. 1993. pap. 15.95 (0-88734-633-2) Players Pr.

—A Miracle in the Christmas City. LC 93-2602. 16p. 1993. pap. 4.00 play script (0-88734-437-2) Players Pr.

—Pioneers in Petticoats. (Illus.). 206p. 1993. 19.95 (0-88734-625-1) Players Pr.

—A Straight Shooter. LC 93-5252. 16p. 1993. pap. 4.00 play script (0-88734-429-1) Players Pr.

—Too Many Cooks. LC 93-5250. 20p. 1993. pap. 4.00 play script (0-88734-434-8) Players Pr.

McCaughrean, Geraldine. El Cid. Ambros, Victor G., illus. 128p. (gr. 5 up). 1989. 19.95 (0-19-276077-7) OUP.

—A Little Lower than the Angels. 144p. (gr. 6-9). 1987. 15.00 (0-19-271561-5) OUP.

—The Odyssey. Ambrus, Victor G., illus. 100p. (gr. 4 up). 1993. 14.95 (1-56288-433-6) Checkerboard.

—One Thousand & One Arabian Nights. Lavis, Stephen, illus. 260p. 1987. 18.95 (0-19-274530-1) OUP.

—A Pack of Lies. 168p. (gr. 5-8). 1989. jacketed 14.95 (0-19-271612-3) OUP.

—A Pack of Lies. large type ed. 320p. (gr. 3 up). 1990. lib. bdg. 16.95x (0-7451-1154-8, Lythway Large Print) Hall.

McCaughrean, Geraldine, retold by. Greek Myths. LC 92-61748. (Illus.). 96p. (gr. 4 up). 1993. SBE 18.95 (0-689-50583-3, M K McElderry) Macmillan Child Grp.

McCaughrean, Geraldine, tr. see Ikeda, Daisaku.

McCaughren, Tom. Rainbows of the Moon. 160p. (gr. 9-12). 1989. 13.95 (0-947962-45-X, Pub. by Childrens Pr) Irish Bks Media.

—Run Swift, Run Free. 191p. (ps-8). 1987. 14.95 (0-86327-111-1, Pub. by Wolfhound Pr IE); pap. 7.95 (0-685-25877-7) Dufour.

—Run to Earth. (Illus.). 144p. (ps-8). 1988. pap. 8.95 (0-86327-116-2, Pub. by Wolfhound Press Eire) Dufour.

—Run to the Ark. Dunne, Jeannette, illus. 208p. (gr. 4-8). 1993. 13.95 (0-86327-304-1, Pub. by Wolfhound Pr EIRE); pap. 9.95 (0-86327-342-4, Pub. by Wolfhound Pr EIRE) Dufour.

—Run with the Wind. (Illus.). 160p. (ps-8). 1987. pap. 8.95 (0-86327-071-9, Pub. by Wolfhound Press Eire) Dufour.

—The Silent Sea. Myler, Terry, illus. 111p. (Orig.). 1988. pap. 7.95 (0-947962-20-4, Pub. by Children's Pr) Irish Bks Media.

McCauley, Jane. Africa's Animal Giants. Crump, Donald J., ed. (Illus.). 32p. (ps-3). 1987. 13.95 (0-87044-680-0); lib. bdg. 16.95 (0-87044-685-1) Natl Geog.

McCauley, Jane R. Baby Birds & How They Grow, 4 vols. Crump, Donald J., ed. LC 83-13150. 32p. (ps-3). 1983. Set. 13.95 (0-87044-487-5); lib. bdg. 16.95 (0-87044-492-1) Natl Geog.

—Ways Animals Sleep, 4 vols. LC 83-13189. 32p. (ps-3). 1983. PLB 16.95 (0-87044-494-8) Natl Geog.

McCauley, Jane R; see Crump, Donald J.

McCauslin, Mark. The Homeless. LC 93-24106. Date not set. write for info. (0-89686-805-2, Crestwood Hse) Macmillan Child Grp.

—Lesbian & Gay Rights. LC 91-40863. (Illus.). 48p. (gr. 5-6). 1992. RSBE 12.95 (0-89686-751-X, Crestwood Hse) Macmillan Child Grp.

—Sexually Transmitted Diseases. LC 91-18445. (Illus.). 48p. (gr. 5-6). 1992. RSBE 11.95 (0-89686-720-X, Crestwood Hse) Macmillan Child Grp.

McCaw, Mabel. What Is Loving? Todd, Barbara, illus. 12p. (ps). 1987. 3.25 (0-8378-5208-0) Gibson.

McCay, William. Animals in Danger: A Pop-up Book. Mosley, Keith, illus. 12p. (gr. 1-7). 1990. pap. 12.95 (0-689-71408-4, Aladdin) Macmillan Child Grp.

—Shoot the Works. LC 89-37749. 144p. (gr. 5 up). 1990. pap. 2.95 (0-679-80157-X) Random Bks Yng Read.

—Young Indiana Jones & the Circle of Death, Bk. 3. LC 89-43390. 112p. (Orig.). (gr. 3-7). 1990. PLB 6.99 (0-679-90578-2); pap. 2.95 (0-679-80578-8) Random Bks Yng Read.

—Young Indiana Jones & the Curse of the Ruby Cross, Bk. 8. LC 90-53242. 128p. (Orig.). (gr. 3-7). 1991. PLB 6.99 (0-679-91181-2); pap. 2.95 (0-679-81181-8) Random Bks Yng Read.

—Young Indiana Jones & the Face of the Dragon. Date not set. pap. 3.50 (0-679-85092-9) Random Bks Yng Read.

—Young Indiana Jones & the Ghostly Riders, Bk. 7. LC 90-53241. 128p. (Orig.). (gr. 3-7). 1991. PLB 6.99 (0-679-91180-4); pap. 2.95 (0-679-81180-X) Random Bks Yng Read.

—Young Indiana Jones & the Plantation Treasure, Bk. 1. LC 89-43388. 112p. (Orig.). (gr. 3-7). 1990. PLB 6.99 (0-679-90579-0); pap. 2.95 (0-679-80579-6) Random Bks Yng Read.

McCay, William & Martin, Les. Young Indiana Jones, 4 vols. (gr. 3-7). 1992. Boxed set incls. Young Indiana Jones & The Plantation Treasure, The Gypsy Revenge, The Tomb of Terror & The Ghostly Riders, 128p. ea. 11.80 (0-679-83866-X) Random Bks Yng Read.

McCay, William, adapted by. The Secret Peace. LC 91-58100. (Illus.). 136p. (Orig.). (gr. 4-8). 1992. PLB cancelled (0-679-92777-8); pap. 3.50 (0-679-82777-3) Random Bks Yng Read.

McCay, Winsor. Complete Little Nemo in Slumberland, Vol. II. Marschall, Richard, ed. & intro. by. (Illus.). 96p. (gr. 6 up). 1989. 34.95 (0-924359-02-1) Remco Wrldserv Bks.

—The Complete Little Nemo in Slumberland: In the Land of Wonderful Dreams, Part 2 - 1913-1914, Vol. VI. Marschall, Richard, ed. McCay, Winsor, illus. 96p. (gr. 6 up). 1992. 34.95 (0-924359-36-6) Remco Wrldserv Bks.

—The Complete Little Nemo in Slumberland, Vols. I-IV: 1905-1911. Marschall, Richard, intro. by. (Illus.). 96p. (gr. 6 up). 1991. 139.80 (0-924359-00-5) Remco Wrldserv Bks.

—The Complete Little Nemo in Slumberland, Vol. III: 1908-1910. Marschall, Richard, intro. by. (Illus.). 96p. (gr. 6 up). 1990. 34.95 (0-924359-03-X) Remco Wrldserv Bks.

—The Complete Little Nemo in Slumberland, Vol. IV: 1910-1911. Marschall, Richard, intro. by. (Illus.). 96p. (gr. 6 up). 1990. 34.95 (0-924359-04-8) Remco Wrldserv Bks.

McClain, Cindy, ed. see Kent, Renee.

McClain, Cindy, ed. see McCullough, Mary F.

McClain, Cindy, ed. see Tapp, Sandra.

McClain, Margaret S. Bellboy: A Muletrain Journey. Stuart, Sara B., illus. LC 89-61681. 154p. (gr. 5 up). 1990. 14.95 (0-9622468-1-6) NM Pub Co.

McClain, Mary. Baby's Pockets. McClain, Mary, illus. 8p. (ps). 1981. pap. 3.95 (0-671-43204-4, Little Simon) S&S Trade.

McClanahan, Frank. Christmas with Grandma. Giddings, Noelle, illus. 24p. (Orig.). (gr. k-1). 1990. pap. 0.99 (1-878624-46-6) McClanahan Bk.

—The Little Policeman. Van Wright, Cornelius, illus. 24p. (Orig.). (gr. k-1). 1990. pap. 0.99 (1-878624-38-5) McClanahan Bk.

McClard, Megan. Harriet Tubman: Slavery & the Underground Railroad. (Illus.). 160p. (gr. 5 up). 1990. lib. bdg. 18.98 (0-382-09938-9); pap. 8.95 (0-382-24047-2) Silver Burdett Pr.

McClard, Megan & Ypsilantis, George. Hiawatha. Furstinger, Nancy, ed. (Illus.). 138p. (gr. 5-7). 1989. PLB 12.98 (0-382-09568-5); pap. 7.95 (0-382-09757-2) Silver Burdett Pr.

McClaskey, Marilyn H. What Kind of Name Is Juan? Rosen, Roger, ed. (gr. 7 up). 1989. PLB 12.95 (0-8239-0830-5) Rosen Group.

McCleery, William. Wolf Story. Chappell, Warren, illus. LC 87-25977. 82p. (gr. 1-6). 1988. Repr. of 1947 ed. PLB 15.00 (0-208-02191-4, Linnet) Shoe String.

McClelland, Julia. This Baby. Brooks, Ron, illus. LC 92-43756. 1994. write for info. (0-395-66613-9) HM.

McClenahan, Carolyn, jt. auth. see Getzoff, Ann.

McClenahan, Pat & Jaqua, Ida. Cool Cooking for Kids. LC 75-32841. (ps-k). 1976. pap. 9.95 (0-8224-1614-X) Fearon Teach Aids.

McClernan, James. Hugs from the Refrigerator. Walker, Philip, intro. by. LC 93-24657. 192p. (Orig.). (gr. 7 up). 1994. pap. 12.00 (0-933701-61-6) Westport Pubs.

McClintock, Barbara. The Battle of Luke & Longnose. LC 93-12815. 1994. write for info. (0-395-65751-2) HM.

—The Heartaches of a French Cat. LC 88-45289. (Illus.). 48p. 1989. 14.95 (0-87923-757-0) Godine.

MacClintock, Dorcas. Animals Observed: A Look at Animals in Art. LC 91-36795. (Illus.). 64p. 1993. SBE 18.95 (0-684-19323-X, Scribners Young Read) Macmillan Child Grp.

—Red Pandas: A Natural History. Young, Ellan, illus. LC 88-3528. 112p. (gr. 7 up). 1988. SBE 14.95 (0-684-18677-2, Scribners Young Read) Macmillan Child Grp.

McClintock, Lorene. The McClintock Piano Course: A New Experience in Learning, 11 vols. 2198p. 1992. Set, incl. keyboard concealer & interval keyblocks. wire-o bdg., slipcased 388.00 (1-880556-70-7) McClintock Ent.

McClintock, Mike. Fly Went By. LC 58-9018. (Illus.). (gr. 1-3). 1958. 6.95 (0-394-80003-6); lib. bdg. 7.99 (0-394-90003-0) Beginner.

—Stop That Ball! LC 59-9741. (Illus.). (gr. 1-2). 1959. 6.95 (0-394-80010-9) Beginner.

McCloskey, Kevin. Mrs. Fitz's Flamingos. LC 90-2278. (ps-3). 1992. 14.00 (0-688-10474-6); PLB 13.93 (0-688-10475-4) Lothrop.

—WOWO, the Radio Dog. Primavera, Elise, illus. LC 92-44165. (gr. 3 up). 1994. write for info. (0-688-12657-X); PLB write for info. (0-688-12658-8) Lothrop.

McCloskey, Maris, ed. see Welles, Laura & Welles, Ted.

McCloskey, Patty, illus. Find the Great Mother Goose. 32p. (ps-1). 1993. pap. 5.95 (1-56565-054-9) Lowell Hse.

McCloskey, Robert. Blueberries for Sal. McCloskey, Robert, illus. LC 48-4955. (ps-1). 1976. pap. 3.99 (0-14-050169-X, Puffin) Puffin Bks.

—Blueberries for Sal. McCloskey, Robert, illus. LC 48-4955. 56p. (ps-1). 1948. pap. 14.95 (0-670-17591-9) Viking Child Bks.

—Blueberries for Sal. (Illus.). (ps-3). 1989. pap. 6.95 (0-14-095032-X, Puffin) Puffin Bks.

—Blueberries for Sal. (Illus.). 1993. pap. 6.99 incl. cassette (0-14-095110-5, Puffin) Puffin Bks.

—Burt Dow: Deep-Water Man. McCloskey, Robert, illus. LC 68-364. 64p. (gr. 4-6). 1963. pap. 15.95 (0-670-19748-3) Viking Child Bks.

—Burt Dow, Deep-Water Man. (Illus.). 64p. (ps-3). 1989. pap. 4.99 (0-14-050978-X, Puffin) Puffin Bks.

—Centerburg Tales. (Illus.). (gr. 1-3). 1977. pap. 4.99 (0-14-031072-X, Puffin) Puffin Bks.

—Centerburg Tales. McCloskey, Robert, illus. LC 51-10675. 192p. (gr. 4-6). 1951. pap. 14.95 (0-670-20977-5) Viking Child Bks.

—Homer Price. (Illus.). (gr. 3-7). 1976. pap. 3.99 (0-14-030927-6, Puffin) Puffin Bks.

—Homer Price. McCloskey, Robert, illus. (gr. 4-6). 1943. pap. 14.00 (0-670-37729-5) Viking Child Bks.

—Lentil. (ps-3). 1978. pap. 3.95 (0-14-050287-4, Puffin) Puffin Bks.

—Lentil. McCloskey, Robert, illus. (gr. k-3). 1940. pap. 14.95 (0-670-42357-2) Viking Child Bks.

—Make Way for Ducklings. (Illus.). (gr. 1-3). 1976. pap. 3.99 (0-14-050171-1, Puffin) Puffin Bks.

—Make Way for Ducklings. McCloskey, Robert, illus. (gr. k-3). 1941. pap. 13.99 (0-670-45149-5) Viking Child Bks.

—Make Way for Ducklings. (Illus.). 1993. pap. 6.99 incl. cassette (0-14-095118-0, Puffin) Puffin Bks.

—Make Way for Ducklings: A Giant Book. giant ed. (ps-3). 1991. pap. 17.95 (0-14-054434-8, Puffin) Puffin Bks.

—One Morning in Maine. (ps-3). 1976. pap. 3.99 (0-14-050174-6, Puffin) Puffin Bks.

—One Morning in Maine. McCloskey, Robert, illus. (gr. k-3). 1952. pap. 14.00 (0-670-52627-4) Viking Child Bks.

—Time of Wonder. McCloskey, Robert, illus. 64p. (gr. k-3). 1989. pap. 4.99 (0-14-050201-7, Puffin) Puffin Bks.

—Time of Wonder. McCloskey, Robert, illus. (gr. k-3). 1957. pap. 16.00 (0-670-71512-3) Viking Child Bks.

McCloskey-Padgett, Patty. The Real Mother Goose ABC's. McCloskey-Padgett, Patty, illus. 32p. 1993. pap. 5.95 (1-56565-090-5) Lowell Hse.

McCloud, Scott. Understanding Comics. 2nd ed. Martin, Mark, ed. McCloud, Scott, illus. 224p. (gr. 4 up). 1993. 27.95 (0-87816-244-5); ltd. signed ed. 34.95 (0-87816-245-3); pap. 19.95 (0-87816-243-7) Kitchen Sink.

McCloud, Susan E. A. A. Seagull. pap. 4.95 (0-88494-721-1) Bookcraft Inc.

—I'm Going to Be Baptized. 5.95 (0-88494-512-X) Bookcraft Inc.

—Joseph Smith: A Photobiography. LC 91-76005. (Illus.). 169p. (gr. 4-12). 1992. 12.95 (*1-56236-400-6*) Aspen Bks.

McCloy, James F. & Miller, Ray, Jr. The Jersey Devil. (Illus.). 121p.(gr. 5 up). 1987. pap. 8.95 (*0-912608-11-0*) Mid Atlantic.

McClung. Snakes. 1991. 14.95 (*0-8050-1917-0*) H Holt & Co.

McClung, Cooky. Plugly, the Horse That Could Do Everything. Tyler, Barbara, illus. 48p. 1993. 16.95 (*0-939481-32-4*) Half Halt Pr.

McClung, Robert. Hugh Glass, Mountain Man. LC 90-37814. (Illus.). 224p. (gr. 5 up). 1990. 12.95g (*0-688-08092-8*) Morrow Jr Bks.

—Old Bet & the Start of the American Circus. Kelly, Laura, illus. LC 92-11020. 32p. (gr. k up). 1993. 15.00 (*0-688-10642-0*); PLB 14.93 (*0-688-10643-9*) Morrow Jr Bks.

—Snakes: Their Place in the Sun. Dennis, David M., illus. 64p. (gr. 2-4). 1991. 14.95 (*0-8050-1718-6*, Bks Young Read) H Holt & Co.

McClung, Robert M. America's First Elephant. Janovitz, Marilyn, illus. LC 89-13764. 40p. (gr. k up). 1991. 14. 95 (*0-688-08358-7*); PLB 14.88 (*0-688-08359-5*) Morrow Jr Bks.

—Black Jack: Last of the Big Alligators. Sanford, Lloyd, illus. LC 91-14387. 64p. (gr. 3-7). 1991. Repr. of 1967 ed. PLB 15.00 (*0-208-02326-7*, Linnet) Shoe String.

—Gorilla. Brady, Irene, illus. LC 84-718. 96p. (gr. 3-7). 1984. 11.00 (*0-688-03875-1*) Morrow Jr Bks.

—Left for Dead: The Story of Hugh Glass. LC 92-43790. 176p. (gr. 7 up). 1993. pap. 3.95 (*0-688-04595-2*, Pub. by Beech Tree Bks) Morrow.

—Lili: A Giant Panda of Sichuan. Brady, Irene, illus. LC 87-28271. 96p. (gr. 3-7). 1988. 12.95 (*0-688-06942-8*); PLB 12.88 (*0-688-06943-6*, Morrow Jr Bks) Morrow Jr Bks.

—Lost Wild America: The Story of Our Extinct & Vanishing Wildlife. rev., enl. & updated ed. Mines, Bob, illus. LC 93-15657. 312p. (gr. 6-12). 1993. PLB 25.00 (*0-208-02359-3*, Pub. by Linnet) Shoe String.

—Major: The Story of a Black Bear. McClung, Robert M., illus. LC 87-26126. 64p. (gr. 9-12). 1988. Repr. of 1956 ed. lib. bdg. 15.00 (*0-208-02201-5*, Linnet) Shoe String.

—Samson: Last of the California Grizzlies. Hines, Bob, illus. LC 91-33350. 96p. (gr. 3-6). 1992. Repr. of 1973 ed. lib. bdg. 15.00 (*0-208-02327-5*, Pub. by Linnet) Shoe String.

—Shag: Last of the Plains Buffalo. Darling, Louis, illus. LC 91-7508. 96p. (gr. 3-7). 1991. Repr. of 1960 ed. PLB 15.00 (*0-208-02313-5*, Linnet) Shoe String.

—Snakes: Their Place in the Sun. Dennis, David M., illus. LC 91-692. 64p. (gr. 2-4). 1993. pap. 4.95 (*0-8050-2893-5*, Bks Young Read) H Holt & Co.

—Thor, the Last of the Sperm Whales. Hines, Bob, illus. LC 87-26090. 64p. (gr. 3-7). 1988. Repr. of 1971 ed. PLB 15.00 (*0-208-02186-8*, Linnet) Shoe String.

—The True Adventures of Grizzly Adams. LC 85-8886. (Illus.). 208p. (gr. 5 up). 1985. 11.95 (*0-688-05794-2*) Morrow Jr Bks.

—Whitetail. Brady, Irene, illus. LC 86-18183. 96p. (gr. 3-7). 1987. 12.95 (*0-688-06126-5*); lib. bdg. 12.88 (*0-688-06127-3*, Morrow Jr Bks) Morrow Jr Bks.

McClure, Gillian. Christmas Donkey: A New Version of the Nativity Story. (ps-3). 1993. 15.00 (*0-374-31261-3*) FS&G.

McClure, Nancee. Clip & Copy Art: Creative Curriculum Cutouts. (Illus.). (gr. k-8). 1989. 12.95 (*0-86653-487-3*, GA1086) Good Apple.

—Clip & Copy Art: Holidays, Seasons & Events. (Illus.). (gr. k-8). 1989. 12.95 (*0-86653-486-5*, GA1085) Good Apple.

—Creative Egg Carton Crafts. McClure, Nancee, illus. 64p. (ps-2). 1989. wkbk. 7.95 (*0-86653-471-7*, GA1077) Good Apple.

—The Good Apple Book of Reproducible Patterns. 352p. (gr. 1-6). 1991. 12.95 (*0-86653-622-1*, GA1341) Good Apple.

McClure, Nancee & Rhodes, Janis. Free & Inexpensive Arts & Crafts to Make & Use. 112p. (gr. 2-6). 1987. wkbk. 9.95 (*0-86653-387-7*, GA 1003) Good Apple.

McClure, Nancee, jt. auth. see Orange, Tom.

McClure, Patricia. And You Think You Have Problems: Teen Dilemmas. Bird, Tate, ed. LC 90-70582. (Illus.). 150p. (gr. 8-9). 1990. 13.27 (*0-914127-73-X*); tchr's. guide avail. Univ Class.

—Getting to the Heart of It: Stories about My Friends & Me. 3rd ed. Bard, Tate, ed. LC 85-51062. (Illus.). 110p. (gr. 4-6). 1985. 11.93 (*0-914127-74-8*) Univ Class.

McClure, Patricia, jt. auth. see West Virginia Writers, Inc., Staff.

McClure, Vimala. Bangladesh: Rivers in a Crowded Land. LC 88-35911. (Illus.). 128p. (gr. 5 up). 1989. RSBE 14.95 (*0-87518-404-9*, Dillon) Macmillan Child Grp.

McClurg, Cynthia. No Longer Lost. (gr. k-6). 1985. illustrated song 2.99 (*3-90117-031-6*) CEF Press.

McClurg, Marie, jt. auth. see Wermert, Rosie.

McCluskey, John, ed. see Ceasor, Ebraska, et al.

McCluskey, John A., ed. see Ceasor, Frank, Sr. & Gaines, Edith.

McCluskey, John A., ed. see Johnston, Brenda A., et al.

McCluskey, John A., ed. see Johnston, Brenda A. & Pruitt, Pamela.

McCluskey, John A., ed. see Pruitt, Pamela, et al.

McCluskey, John A., ed. see Shepard, Mary L. & Gaines, Edith.

McClymont, Diane. Books. Young, Richard, ed. LC 91-20532. (Illus.). 32p. (gr. 3-5). 1991. PLB 15.93 (*1-56074-010-8*) Garrett Ed Corp.

—Water. Young, Richard, ed. LC 91-20536. (Illus.). 32p. (gr. 3-5). 1991. PLB 15.93 (*1-56074-006-X*) Garrett Ed Corp.

Maccoll, Gail. The Book of Cards for Kids. LC 91-50962. (ps-3). 1992. pap. 10.95 (*1-56305-240-7*) Workman Pub.

McCollam, Dan, jt. auth. see Betts, Keith.

McColley, Kevin. Pecking Order. LC 93-17768. 224p. (gr. 7 up). 1994. 16.00 (*0-06-023554-3*); PLB 15.89 (*0-06-023555-1*) HarpC Child Bks.

—Walls of Pedro Garcia. LC 91-46264. 1993. 15.00 (*0-385-30806-X*) Doubleday.

MacCombie, Turi, illus. Hush, Little Baby. 1994. pap. 6.99 (*0-553-45907-4*) Bantam.

—My First Book of Animals from A to Z: More Than 150 Animals Every Child Should Know. LC 92-19284. 64p. (ps-2). 1994. 12.95 (*0-590-46305-5*, Cartwheel) Scholastic Inc.

—Velveteen Rabbit. 48p. (ps-3). 1991. 9.95 (*0-88101-114-2*) Unicorn Pub.

—Velveteen Rabbit. 48p. (ps-3). 1992. 12.95 (*0-88101-236-X*) Unicorn Pub.

McCombs, Barbara L. & Brannan, Linda. Adjusting to a New Boss. (Illus.). 32p. (Orig.). (gr. 7-12). 1990. Set. 10 wkbks. & tchr's. guide 44.95 (*1-56119-071-3*); tchr's. guide 1.95 (*1-56119-026-8*); software 39.95 (*1-56119-113-2*) Educ Pr MD.

—Consideration for Co-Worker Rights. (Illus.). 32p. (Orig.). (gr. 7-12). 1990. Set. 10 wkbks. & tchr's. guide 44.95 (*1-56119-063-2*); tchr's. guide 1.95 (*1-56119-010-1*); software 39.95 (*1-56119-105-1*) Educ Pr MD.

—Good Grooming Habits. (Illus.). 32p. (Orig.). (gr. 7-12). 1990. Set. 10 wkbks. & tchr's. guide 44.95 (*1-56119-080-2*); tchr's. guide 1.95 (*1-56119-044-6*); software 39.95 (*1-56119-122-1*) Educ Pr MD.

—Help, Please! (Illus.). 32p. (Orig.). (gr. 7-12). 1990. Set. 10 wkbks. & tchr's. guide 44.95 (*1-56119-077-2*); tchr's. guide 1.95 (*1-56119-038-1*); software 39.95 (*1-56119-119-1*) Educ Pr MD.

—How Does It Work? (Illus.). 32p. (Orig.). (gr. 7-12). 1990. Set. 10 wkbks. & tchr's. guide 44.95 (*1-56119-075-6*); tchr's. guide 1.95 (*1-56119-034-9*); software 39.95 (*1-56119-117-5*) Educ Pr MD.

—How Should I Do It? (Illus.). 32p. (Orig.). (gr. 7-12). 1990. Set. 10 wkbks. & tchr's. guide 44.95 (*1-56119-069-1*); tchr's. guide 1.95 (*1-56119-022-5*); software 39.95 (*1-56119-111-6*) Educ Pr MD.

—Keep Calm! (Illus.). 32p. (Orig.). (gr. 7-12). 1990. Set. 10 wkbks. & tchr's. guide 44.95 (*1-56119-070-5*); tchr's. guide 1.95 (*1-56119-024-1*); software 39.95 (*1-56119-112-4*) Educ Pr MD.

—Late Work. (Illus.). 32p. (Orig.). (gr. 7-12). 1990. Set. 10 wkbks. & tchr's. guide 44.95 (*1-56119-065-9*); tchr's. guide 1.95 (*1-56119-014-4*); software 39.95 (*1-56119-107-8*) Educ Pr MD.

—Leaving Early. (Illus.). 32p. (Orig.). (gr. 7-12). 1990. Set. 10 wkbks. & tchr's. guide 44.95 (*1-56119-078-0*); tchr's. guide 1.95 (*1-56119-040-3*); software 39.95 (*1-56119-120-5*) Educ Pr MD.

—May I Try It? (Illus.). 32p. (Orig.). (gr. 7-12). 1990. Set. 10 wkbks. & tchr's. guide 44.95 (*1-56119-085-3*); tchr's. guide 1.95 (*1-56119-054-3*); software 39.95 (*1-56119-127-2*) Educ Pr MD.

—Neatness Counts. (Illus.). 32p. (Orig.). (gr. 7-12). 1990. Set. 10 wkbks. & tchr's. guide 44.95 (*1-56119-081-0*); tchr's. guide 1.95 (*1-56119-046-2*); software 39.95 (*1-56119-123-X*) Educ Pr MD.

—Notice & Think. (Illus.). 32p. (Orig.). (gr. 7-12). 1990. Set. 10 wkbks. & tchr's. guide 44.95 (*1-56119-059-4*); tchr's. guide 1.95 (*1-56119-002-0*); software 39.95 (*1-56119-101-9*) Educ Pr MD.

—Respect for Property. (Illus.). 32p. (Orig.). (gr. 7-12). 1990. Set. 10 wkbks. & tchr's. guide 44.95 (*1-56119-072-1*); tchr's. guide 1.95 (*1-56119-028-4*); software 39.95 (*1-56119-114-0*) Educ Pr MD.

—Say. (Illus.). 32p. (Orig.). (gr. 7-12). 1990. Set. 10 wkbks. & tchr's. guide 44.95 (*1-56119-060-8*); tchr's. guide 1.95 (*1-56119-004-7*); software 39.95 (*1-56119-102-7*) Educ Pr MD.

—Taking Breaks. (Illus.). 32p. (Orig.). (gr. 7-12). 1990. Set. 10 wkbks. & tchr's. guide 44.95 (*1-56119-079-9*); tchr's. guide 1.95 (*1-56119-042-X*); software 39.95 (*1-56119-121-3*) Educ Pr MD.

—Too Much Talking. (Illus.). 32p. (Orig.). (gr. 7-12). 1990. Set. 10 wkbks. & tchr's. guide 44.95 (*1-56119-064-0*); tchr's. guide 1.95 (*1-56119-012-8*); software 39.95 (*1-56119-106-X*) Educ Pr MD.

—What Should I Do? (Illus.). 32p. (Orig.). (gr. 7-12). 1990. Set. 10 wkbks. & tchr's. guide 44.95 (*1-56119-074-8*); tchr's. guide 1.95 (*1-56119-032-2*); software 39.95 (*1-56119-116-7*) Educ Pr MD.

—What's Next? (Illus.). 32p. (Orig.). (gr. 7-12). 1990. Set. 10 wkbks. & tchr's. guide 44.95 (*1-56119-068-3*); tchr's. guide 1.95 (*1-56119-020-9*); software 39.95 (*1-56119-110-8*) Educ Pr MD.

—What's the Proper Way? (Illus.). 32p. (Orig.). (gr. 7-12). 1990. Set. 10 wkbks. & tchr's. guide 44.95 (*1-56119-067-5*); tchr's. guide 1.95 (*1-56119-018-7*); software 39.95 (*1-56119-109-4*) Educ Pr MD.

—Which Tools to Use? (Illus.). 32p. (Orig.). (gr. 7-12). 1990. Set. 10 wkbks. & tchr's. guide 44.95 (*1-56119-083-7*); tchr's. guide 1.95 (*1-56119-050-0*); software 39.95 (*1-56119-125-6*) Educ Pr MD.

—Which Way Is Right? (Illus.). 32p. (Orig.). (gr. 7-12). 1990. Set. 10 wkbks. & tchr's. guide 44.95 (*1-56119-084-5*); tchr's. guide 1.95 (*1-56119-052-7*); software 39.95 (*1-56119-126-4*) Educ Pr MD.

—Who Can Help? (Illus.). 32p. (Orig.). (gr. 7-12). 1990. Set. 10 wkbks. & tchr's. guide 44.95 (*1-56119-076-4*); tchr's. guide 1.95 (*1-56119-036-5*); software 39.95 (*1-56119-118-3*) Educ Pr MD.

—Will You Do Me a Favor? (Illus.). 32p. (Orig.). (gr. 7-12). 1990. Set. 10 wkbks. & tchr's. guide 44.95 (*1-56119-066-7*); tchr's. guide 1.95 (*1-56119-016-0*); software 39.95 (*1-56119-108-6*) Educ Pr MD.

—Working Too Slowly. (Illus.). 32p. (Orig.). (gr. 7-12). 1990. Set. 10 wkbks. & tchr's. guide 44.95 (*1-56119-062-4*); tchr's. guide 1.95 (*1-56119-008-X*); software 39.95 (*1-56119-104-3*) Educ Pr MD.

McConkey, Lois. Sea & Cedar: How the Northwest Coast Indians Lived. Tait, Douglas, illus. 32p. (gr. 3-7). 1991. pap. 8.95 (*0-88894-371-7*, Pub. by Groundwood-Douglas & McIntyre CN) Firefly Bks Ltd.

McConnachie, Brian. Elmer & the Chickens vs. the Big League. Stevenson, Harvey, illus. LC 91-2914. 32p. (ps-2). 1992. 14.00 (*0-517-57616-3*); PLB 14.99 (*0-517-57617-1*) Crown Bks Yng Read.

McConnell, Anita. The World Beneath Us. (Illus.). 64p. (gr. 7 up). 1993. 15.95x (*0-8160-1068-4*) Facts on File.

McConnell, Anita, jt. auth. see Lambert, David.

McConnell, Christine. Don't Be Mad, Ivy. De Groat, Diane, photos by. (gr. 2-5). 1988. pap. 3.95 (*0-14-032329-5*, Puffin) Puffin Bks.

McConnell, David, jt. auth. see Parker, Lois.

McConnell, David B. Discover Michigan. Rasmussen, George L., illus. LC 81-6722. 144p. (gr. 4). 1989. text ed. 17.45x (*0-910726-07-8*); tchr's. guide 7.45x (*0-910726-33-7*) Hillsdale Educ.

—Explore Michigan A to Z. McConnell, Stella M., ed. Rasmussen, George L., illus. LC 93-17430. 48p. (Orig.). (gr. 3-4). 1993. pap. 7.95 (*0-910726-55-8*) Hillsdale Educ.

—A Puzzle Book for Young Michiganians. Deeter, Theresa, illus. 24p. (Orig.). (gr. 3-6). 1982. pap. 5.50 (*0-910726-17-5*) Hillsdale Educ.

McConnell, Em. The Great Farm Adventure. Moser, Jeanie W., illus. (gr. k-3). Bk. & cassette 4.95 (*0-932715-07-9*) Evans FL.

—Strange Sounds. Moser, Jeanie W., illus. (gr. k-3). Bk. & cassette 4.95 (*0-932715-09-5*) Evans FL.

McConnell, Keith. The AnimAlphabet Encyclopedia. McConnell, Keith A., illus. 48p.(gr. 4 up). 1982. pap. 5.95 (*0-916144-97-6*) Stemmer Hse.

—Dinosaurs from A to Z. (Illus.). 40p. (Orig.). (gr. 2 up). 1988. pap. 5.95 (*0-88045-095-9*) Stemmer Hse.

—The ReptAlphabet Encyclopedia. McConnell, Keith, illus. 48p. (Orig.). (gr. 4 up). 1984. pap. 5.95 (*0-88045-045-2*) Stemmer Hse.

—The SeAlphabet Encyclopedia. McConnell, Keith, illus. 48p. (gr. 4 up). 1982. pap. 5.95 (*0-88045-016-9*) Stemmer Hse.

McConnell, Nancy P. Different & Alike. Duell, Nancy, illus. LC 87-73309. 40p. (gr. 1-6). 1982. pap. text ed. 6.85 (*0-944943-00-4*) Current Inc.

—Different & Alike. 3rd ed. Cliff, Donna, ed. Duell, Nancy, illus. LC 93-70957. 40p. (gr. 1-6). 1993. pap. 6.85 (*0-944943-32-2*, CODE 22164-6*) Current Inc.

—Dusty D. Dawg Has Feelings, Too! Gress, Jonna, ed. (Illus.). 16p. (ps-3). 1992. pap. text ed. 11.60 (*0-944943-15-2*) Current Inc.

—Please Touch the Animals! Gress, Jonna, ed. Ruge, Don, Jr., illus. 12p. (ps-k). 1992. pap. text ed. 16.20 (*0-944943-16-0*) Current Inc.

McConnell, Stella M., ed. see McConnell, David B.

McConoughey, Jana. Bald Eagle. LC 83-5162. (Illus.). 48p. (gr. 5). 1983. RSBE 12.95 (*0-89686-218-6*, Crestwood Hse) Macmillan Child Grp.

—Squirrel. LC 83-2085. (Illus.). 48p. (gr. 5-6). 1983. RSBE 12.95 (*0-89686-223-2*, Crestwood Hse) Macmillan Child Grp.

—The Wolves. LC 83-2086. (Illus.). 48p. (gr. 5-6). 1983. RSBE 12.95 (*0-89686-225-9*, Crestwood Hse) Macmillan Child Grp.

McCord. Dinosaurs. (Illus.). (gr. 4-6). 1977. (Usborne-Hayes); PLB 13.96 (*0-88110-119-2*); pap. 6.95 (*0-86020-126-0*) (*0-685-05980-4*) EDC.

—Early Man. (Illus.). (gr. 4-6). 1977. (Usborne-Hayes); PLB 13.96 (*0-88110-121-4*); pap. 6.95 (*0-86020-130-9*) EDC.

—Prehistoric Mammals. (Illus.). (gr. 4-6). 1977. (Usborne-Hayes); pap. 13.96 (*0-88110-120-6*); pap. 6.95 (*0-86020-128-7*) EDC.

McCord, A. Prehistoric Life (B - U) (Illus.). 96p. (gr. 2-7). 1993. pap. 12.95 (*0-86020-490-1*) EDC.

McCord, Catherine G. Of Butterflies & Buttercups. Scudder, Barbara J., illus. LC 85-61275. 64p. (gr. 5-12). 1985. 12.50 (*0-9614997-0-2*) Buttercup Bks.

McCord, Cindy & Ross, Shirley. Animal Rhythms Alphabet. 64p. (ps-2). 1988. 6.95 (*0-912107-69-3*, MM976) Monday Morning Bks.

—Animal Rhythms Consonants. 64p. (ps-2). 1988. 6.95 (*0-912107-70-7*, MM977) Monday Morning Bks.

—Animal Rhythms Vowels. 64p. (ps-2). 1988. 6.95 (*0-912107-71-5*, MM978) Monday Morning Bks.

McCord, David. All Day Long: Fifty Rhymes of the Never Was & Always Is. (gr. 4-7). 1992. pap. 6.95 (*0-316-55532-0*) Little.

—All Small. Linden, Madelaine G., illus. (gr. 6-8). 1986. lib. bdg. 12.95 (*0-316-55519-3*); pap. 4.95 (*0-316-55520-7*) Little.
—Every Time I Climb a Tree. Simont, Marc, illus. LC 67-25611. 48p. (gr. k-3). 1985. pap. 4.95 (*0-316-55518-5*) Little.
—For Me to Say. Kane, Henry B., illus. (gr. 5 up). 1970. 12.95 (*0-316-55511-8*) Little.
—One at a Time. Kane, Henry B., illus. (gr. 4 up). 1986. 18.95 (*0-316-55516-9*) Little.
—Speak Up: More Rhymes of the Never Was & Always Is. Simont, Marc, illus. 80p. (gr. 5 up). 1980. 13.95 (*0-316-55517-7*) Little.
—Take Sky. Kane, Henry B., illus. (gr. 4 up). 1962. 12.95 (*0-316-55509-6*) Little.
McCorkle, Beth. The Kramurg. Stewart, Alan, illus. 32p. (Orig.). (gr. 1-8). 1991. pap. write for info. (*0-9626729-1-2*) Work Study Assn.
McCormack, Alan. Inventors Workshop. LC 80-84185. (gr. 3-8). 1981. pap. 10.95 (*0-8224-9783-2*) Fearon Teach Aids.
McCormack, Nancy, ed. see Kirby, Jackie M.
McCormick, Anita L. Space Exploration. LC 93-1830. (gr. 4 up). 1994. 14.95 (*1-56006-149-9*) Lucent Bks.
McCormick, Bob. The Story of Tahoe Tessie: The Original Lake Tahoe Monster. 5th, rev. ed. Lambert, Eileen, illus. (gr. 1-4). 1990. pap. 5.95 (*0-9626792-6-7*) Tahoe Tourist.
McCormick, Dell J. Paul Bunyan Swings His Axe. McCormick, Dell J., illus. LC 36-33409. (gr. 4-6). 1936. 11.95 (*0-87004-093-6*) Caxton.
—Tall Timber Tales: More Paul Bunyan Stories. Livesley, Lorna, illus. LC 39-20778. (gr. 4-6). 1939. 11.95 (*0-87004-094-4*) Caxton.
McCormick, John. Acid Rain. (Illus.). 32p. (gr. 5-8). 1991. PLB 12.40 (*0-531-17358-5*, Gloucester Pr) Watts.
McCormick, Linda, jt. auth. see Stodden, Norma J.
McCormick, Maxine. Chimpanzee. LC 89-28272. (Illus.). 48p. (gr. 5). 1990. 12.95 (*0-89686-514-2*, Crestwood Hse) Macmillan Child Grp.
—Pretty As You Please. LC 92-39310. 1994. write for info. (*0-399-22536-6*, Philomel Bks) Putnam Pub Group.
—Sequoia & Kings Canyon. LC 88-20214. (Illus.). 48p. (gr. 4-5). 1988. RSBE 13.95 (*0-89686-409-X*, Crestwood Hse) Macmillan Child Grp.
McCormick, Maxine, jt. auth. see Root, Phyllis.
McCormick, Michele. Designer-Drug Abuse. LC 88-30450. (Illus.). 128p. (gr. 10-12). 1990. 13.40 (*0-531-10660-8*) Watts.
McCoy, Diana L. The Secret: A Child's Story of Sex Abuse, Ages 7-10. Brown, Wynne, illus. Sgroi, Suzanne, intro. by. 32p. (Orig.). (gr. 2-5). 1986. pap. text ed. 6.00 (*0-9619250-1-9*) Magic Lantrn.
—A Special Place: A Child's Story about Entering Counseling for Children Ages 4 Through 6. Brown, Wynne, illus. 24p. (Orig.). (ps-1). 1988. pap. 5.50 (*0-9619250-2-7*) Magic Lantrn.
—A Special Place: A Child's Story about Entering Counseling for Children Ages 7 Through 10. Brown, Wynne, illus. 32p. (gr. 2-5). 1988. pap. text ed. 5.50 (*0-9619250-3-5*) Magic Lantrn.
McCoy, Elin. Cards for Kids: Games, Tricks & Amazing Facts. Huffman, Tom, illus. LC 91-11373. 160p. (gr. 1-7). 1991. SBE 13.95 (*0-02-765461-3*, Macmillan Child Bk) Macmillan Child Grp.
—Secret Spaces, Imaginary Places: Creating Your Own Worlds for Play. Sweat, Lynn, illus. LC 85-23089. 80p. (gr. k-6). 1986. SBE 13.95 (*0-02-765460-5*) Macmillan Child Grp.
McCoy, J. J. Animals in Research: Issues & Conflicts. LC 92-21117. (Illus.). 128p. (gr. 9-12). 1993. PLB 13.90 (*0-531-13023-1*) Watts.
—How Safe Is Our Food Supply? LC 90-35043. (Illus.). 144p. (gr. 9-12). 1990. PLB 13.90 (*0-531-10935-6*) Watts.
McCoy, James C. Darby's Rainbow. Walker, Timothy, illus. Davenport, May, intro. by. LC 88-70551. (Illus.). 32p. (gr. k-3). 1990. pap. 3.50x (*0-943864-52-6*) Davenport.
McCoy, James C., et al. Comic Tales Anthology, No. 2. 2nd ed. Davenport, May, intro. by. Walker, Timothy, et al, illus. LC 88-70551. 100p. (Orig.). (gr. 7-12). 1988. pap. 6.95x (*0-943864-53-4*) Davenport.
McCoy, Karen K. A Tale of Two Tengu. Fossey, Koen, illus. LC 93-2. (gr. 1-3). 1993. 14.95 (*0-8075-7748-0*) A Whitman.
McCoy, Kathy & Wibbelsman, Charles. The New Teenage Body Book. rev. ed. (Illus.). 288p. (Orig.). (gr. 9-12). 1992. pap. 14.95 (*0-399-51725-1*, Body Pr-Perigee) Putnam Pub Group.
McCoy, Leah P. Elementary Math Flipper, Vol. I. 39p. (gr. 3-6). 1989. trade edition 5.95 (*1-878383-13-2*) C Lee Pubns.
McCoy, Lois, et al. The Byte Brothers Input an Investigation. Morrill, Leslie H., illus. 1983. pap. 2.25 (*0-380-85571-2*, 85571, Camelot) Avon.
McCoy, Sandy. Something Happened to Me: Helping a Child to Become a Sexual Abuse Survivor. 18p. (ps-2). 1993. 4.95 (*1-882811-01-1*) Skyline Pubns.
McCracken, Elizabeth, ed. To Mother: An Anthology of Mother Verse. Wiggin, Kate D., intro. by. LC 17-13752. (Illus.). (gr. 7-12). 1976. Repr. of 1917 ed. 17. 50x (*0-89609-051-5*) Roth Pub Inc.
McCracken, Lisa. The Lilies' Edge. Taylor, Neil, illus. LC 86-40282. 48p. (gr. 1-3). 1987. 5.95 (*1-55523-036-9*) Winston-Derek.

McCracken, Marlene J. & McCracken, Robert A. Animals. rev. ed. Colquhoun, Diana, illus. 83p. (gr. k-4). 1985. pap. 11.95 (*0-920541-12-7*) Peguis Pubs Ltd.
—Celebrations. rev. ed. Colquhoun, Diana, illus. 67p. (gr. k-4). 1986. pap. 11.95 (*0-920541-72-0*) Peguis Pubs Ltd.
—Fall. Colquhoun, Diana, illus. 88p. (gr. k-4). 1987. pap. 11.95 (*0-920541-16-X*) Peguis Pubs Ltd.
—Fantasy. 4th ed. Colquhoun, Diana, illus. 39p. (Orig.). (gr. k-4). 1992. pap. 11.95 (*0-920541-02-X*) Peguis Pubs Ltd.
—Halloween. rev. ed. Colquhoun, Diana, illus. 74p. (gr. k-4). 1984. pap. 11.95 (*0-920541-76-3*) Peguis Pubs Ltd.
—Myself. rev. ed. Colquhoun, Diana, illus. 84p. (gr. k-4). 1984. pap. 11.95 (*0-920541-78-X*) Peguis Pubs Ltd.
—The Sea & Other Water. rev. ed. Colquhoun, Diana, illus. 71p. (gr. k-4). 1985. pap. 11.95 (*0-920541-80-1*) Peguis Pubs Ltd.
—Spring. rev. ed. Colquhoun, Diana, illus. 83p. (gr. k-4). 1987. pap. 11.95 (*0-920541-14-3*) Peguis Pubs Ltd.
—Tiger Cub Chants & Poems, 8 bks. rev. ed. (Illus.). 128p. (gr. k-3). 1988. Set. 19.95 (*0-920541-66-6*) Peguis Pubs Ltd.
—Tiger Cub Readers, 8 bks. rev. ed. (Illus.). 128p. (gr. k-1). 1988. Set. 19.95 (*0-920541-62-3*) Peguis Pubs Ltd.
—Tiger Cub Songs, 8 bks. rev. ed. (Illus.). 16p. (gr. k-2). 1988. Set. 19.95 (*0-920541-68-2*) Peguis Pubs Ltd.
—Tiger Cub Stories, 8 bks. rev. ed. (Illus.). 128p. (gr. k-2). 1988. Set. 19.95 (*0-920541-64-X*) Peguis Pubs Ltd.
—Winter. rev. ed. Colquhoun, Diana, illus. 67p. (gr. k-4). 1987. pap. 11.95 (*0-920541-10-0*) Peguis Pubs Ltd.
MacCracken, Mary. A Circle of Children. 224p. (RL 9). 1975. pap. 3.95 (*0-451-14763-4*, Sig) NAL-Dutton.
McCracken, Robert A., jt. auth. see McCracken, Marlene J.
McCrackin, Mark. A Winning Position. 96p. (gr. 7 up). 1982. pap. 1.50 (*0-440-99483-7*, LFL) Dell.
McCraw, Louise H. As the Snow on the High Hills. 198p. (Orig.). 1979. pap. 1.00 (*0-89323-001-4*, 771) Bible Memory.
McCreary, Jane. Story of Christmas: A Trim a Tree Story Six Wonderful Ornaments Tell the Christmas Story. (ps-3). 1992. 10.99 (*0-87403-866-9*, 24-03556) Standard Pub.
McCreary, Paul. The Maze Book. (Illus.). (gr. 2-4). 1979. pap. 7.00 (*0-87879-712-2*, Ann Arbor Div) Acad Therapy.
—Perceptual Activities: A Multitude of Perceptual Actitivies, Level 2-Advanced, Consumeable (Coloring) Edition. (gr. 2-8). 1972. wkbk. 5.00 (*0-87879-711-4*, Ann Arbor Div) Acad Therapy.
—Perceptual Activities: A Multitude of Reusable Perceptual Activities, Level 1-Primary. Reusable Edition ed. (gr. 2-8). 1972. 9.00 (*0-87879-708-4*, Ann Arbor Div) Acad Therapy.
McCrory, G. Jacobs. Softball Rules in Pictures. rev. ed. (Illus.). 80p. (Orig.). 1992. pap. 7.95 (*0-399-51728-6*, Perigee Bks) Putnam Pub Group.
McCrum, Robert. The World Is a Banana. large type ed. 171p. 1992. 13.95 (*0-7451-1611-6*, Galaxy Child Lrg Print) Chivers N Amer.
McCue, jt. auth. see Delton.
McCue, Dick. Baby Elephant's Bedtime. McCue, Lisa, illus. 24p. (ps). 1985. pap. 2.95 (*0-671-55853-6*, Little Simon) S&S Trade.
—Bunny's Numbers. McCue, Lisa, illus. 24p. (ps). 1984. pap. 2.95 (*0-671-50944-6*, Little Simon) S&S Trade.
—Panda's Playtime. McCue, Lisa, illus. 12p. (ps). 1985. 2.95 (*0-671-55850-1*, Little Simon) S&S Trade.
—Raccoon's Hide & Seek. McCue, Lisa, illus. 12p. (ps). 1985. 2.95 (*0-671-55854-4*, Little Simon) S&S Trade.
McCue, Dick & McCue, Lisa. Puppy's Day. (ps). 1984. pap. 2.95 (*0-671-50945-4*, Little Simon) S&S Trade.
McCue, Lisa. Corduroy Goes to the Doctor. (Illus.). (ps). 1987. pap. 3.99 (*0-670-81495-4*) Viking Child Bks.
—Corduroy on the Go. (Illus.). (ps). 1987. pap. 3.50 (*0-670-81497-0*) Viking Child Bks.
—Corduroy's Busy Street. (Illus.). (ps). 1987. pap. 3.99 (*0-670-81496-2*) Viking Child Bks.
—Fuzzytail Bunny. McCue, Lisa, illus. 22p. (ps). 1992. bds. 2.95 (*0-679-81721-2*) Random Bks Yng Read.
—Fuzzytail Lamb. McCue, Lisa, illus. 22p. (ps). 1992. bds. 2.95 (*0-679-81720-4*) Random Bks Yng Read.
—Fuzzytail Bunny Book & Bunny Set. McCue, Lisa, illus. 22p. (ps). 1994. incl. stuffed animal 10.00 (*0-679-85103-8*) Random Bks Yng Read.
—Kittens Love. McCue, Lisa, illus. LC 89-61137. 24p. (ps-1). 1990. 4.95 (*0-394-82876-3*) Random Bks Yng Read.
—The Little Chick. McCue, Lisa, illus. LC 85-63658. 7p. (ps). 1993. bds. 3.95 (*0-394-88017-X*) Random Bks Yng Read.
—Nighty-Night, Little One. McCue, Lisa, illus. LC 87-42786. 28p. (ps). 1988. bds. 2.95 (*0-394-89476-6*) Random Bks Yng Read.
—Puppies Love. McCue, Lisa, illus. LC 89-61140. 24p. (ps-1). 1990. 4.95 (*0-394-82875-5*) Random Bks Yng Read.
McCue, Lisa, jt. auth. see McCue, Dick.
McCue, Lisa, intro. by. Corduroy's Day. (ps-k). 1987. 2 bks. 12.95 (*0-87499-041-6*); cassette incl. Live Oak Media.

McCue, Lisa, illus. Bunnies Love. LC 90-61307. 24p. (ps-1). 1991. 4.95 (*0-679-80385-8*) Random Bks Yng Read.
—Corduroy's Christmas. Freeman, Don & Hennessy, B. G.concept by. (Illus.). 16p. (ps-1). 1992. 10.95 (*0-670-84477-2*) Viking Child Bks.
—Ducklings Love. LC 90-61308. 24p. (ps-1). 1991. 4.95 (*0-679-80386-6*) Random Bks Yng Read.
—Ducky's Seasons. (ps-2). 1983. pap. 2.95 (*0-671-45491-9*, Little Simon) S&S Trade.
—Froggie's Treasure. (ps-2). 1983. 2.95 (*0-671-45488-9*, Little Simon) S&S Trade.
—Kitten's Christmas. 1985. pap. 2.95 (*0-671-55851-X*, Little Simon) S&S Trade.
—Kitty's Colors. (ps-2). 1983. pap. 2.95 (*0-671-45489-7*, Little Simon) S&S Trade.
—Puppy Peek-a-Boo. LC 88-60759. 14p. (ps). 1989. bds. 3.99 (*0-394-81950-0*) Random Bks Yng Read.
—Teddy Dresses. 1983. 2.95 (*0-671-45490-0*, Little Simon) S&S Trade.
—Ten Little Puppy Dogs. LC 86-63577. 28p. (ps). 1987. 2.95 (*0-394-89149-X*) Random Bks Yng Read.
McCuen, Gary E., ed. Born Hooked: Poisoned in the Womb. rev. ed. (Illus.). 163p. (gr. 7-12). 1994. PLB 12.95 (*0-86596-091-7*) GEM McCuen Pubns.
—Crimes of Gender: Violence Against Women. (Illus.). 164p. (gr. 7-12). 1994. PLB 12.95 (*0-86596-092-5*) GEM McCuen Pubns.
—Doctor Assisted Suicide: The Euthanasia Movement. (Illus.). 157p. (gr. 7-12). 1994. PLB 12.95 (*0-86596-093-3*) GEM McCuen Pubns.
—Ending War Against the Earth. (Illus.). 176p. (gr. 7-10). 1991. 12.95 (*0-86596-081-X*) GEM McCuen Pubns.
—Homosexuality & Gay Rights. (Illus.). 152p. (gr. 7-12). 1994. PLB 12.95 (*0-86596-094-1*) GEM McCuen Pubns.
McCulla, Patricia E. Bahamas. (Illus.). 104p. (gr. 5 up). 1988. lib. bdg. 14.95 (*1-55546-191-3*) Chelsea Hse.
—Tanzania. (Illus.). 112p. (gr. 5 up). 1989. lib. bdg. 14.95 (*1-55546-784-9*) Chelsea Hse.
McCullers, Carson. Heart Is a Lonely Hunter. LC 83-61845. (gr. 10-12). 1970. pap. 3.95 (*0-553-25481-2*) Bantam.
—Member of the Wedding. (gr. 9-12). 1985. pap. 4.50 (*0-553-25051-5*) Bantam.
—Sucker. Hayes, James, illus. LC 85-29114. 40p. (gr. 4 up). 1986. PLB 13.95s.p. (*0-88682-053-7*) Creative Ed.
—A Tree, a Rock, a Cloud. (gr. 4-12). Date not set. 13.95 (*0-88682-349-8*, 97225-098) Creative Ed.

McCulloch, Myrna & Madsen, Sharon, eds. Spelling & Usage Vocabulary Builder. large type ed. (Illus.). 478p. (gr. 9-12). 1993. Repr. of 1991 ed. 26. 50 (*0-924277-04-1*) K & M Pub. This picture/word book's 4832 words have been edited with the mnemonic marketing system for precise speech & correct spelling used in Romalda Spalding's WRITING ROAD TO READING (WRTR), Wm. Morrow, N.Y., also distributed through the Riggs Institute. A truly usable, primary-level reference text; covers word explanations, grammar helps (verb forms including tenses, nouns, formation of plurals, adjectives, adverbs), extensive composition "models" with correct usage & word(s) substitutions (homonyms & antonyms), connected writing models, manuscript printing, syllabication, alphabetization practice & 1200 descriptive pictures. Large (14 point) print, 478 pages (4 to 5 words per page). Editing includes a 7-page Introduction for teachers which describes the WRTR system of teaching, the entire phonetic system for correct spelling, the mnemonic marking system, 28 spelling rules & tips for using multi-sensory, direct instruction. Order from: The Riggs Institute, 4185 SW 102nd Ave., Beaverton, OR 97005; 503-646-9459, FAX 503-644-5191. *Publisher Provided Annotation.*

McCullough, Dennis J., tr. Kids Coping with War: How Young People React to Military Conflict. (Illus.). 112p. 1991. pap. 6.95 (*0-933879-37-7*); audio cassette 9.95 (*0-933879-39-3*) Alegra Hse Pubs.
McCullough, Duane K. Spirit of Atlantis, Version 1-E: The Treasure Adventure, 4 vols. LC 88-92585. (Illus.). 100p. (Orig.). (gr. p-12). 1989. pap. text ed. write for info. (*0-9621605-2-0*) D K McCullough.

McCullough, Frances, ed. Earth, Air, Fire & Water. rev. ed. LC 88-45854. 160p. (gr. 7 up). 1989. PLB 13.89 *(0-06-024208-6)* HarpC Child Bks.
—Love Is Like the Lion's Tooth. LC 77-25659. 96p. (gr. 7 up). 1984. PLB 13.89 *(0-06-024139-X)* HarpC Child Bks.
McCullough, Mary F. Brown Eyes, Blue Eyes. Sealy, Kathy, illus. 32p. (Orig.). (ps). 1986. pap. text ed. 3.95 *(0-936625-04-X,* New Hope AL) Womans Mission Union.
—The City: Sights, Sounds, & Smells. McClain, Cindy, ed. (Illus.). 32p. (Orig.). (ps). 1991. pap. text ed. 3.95 *(0-936625-96-1,* New Hope AL) Womans Mission Union.
McCullough, Sally, jt. auth. see Lindsay, Jeanne W.
McCullough, Steven. Becoming Responsible. (Illus.). 48p. (gr. 6-8). 1991. pap. 7.99 *(1-55945-109-2)* Group Pub.
McCully, Emily. I & Sproggy. (gr. 4 up). 1990. pap. 3.95 *(0-14-034542-6,* Puffin) Puffin Bks.
McCully, Emily A. The Amazing Felix. McCully, Emily A., illus. 32p. (ps-3). 1993. 14.95 *(0-685-65234-3,* Putnam) Putnam Pub Group.
—The Christmas Gift. McCully, Emily A., illus. LC 87-45758. 32p. (ps-1). 1988. PLB 12.89 *(0-06-024212-4)* HarpC Child Bks.
—The Christmas Gift. LC 87-45758. (Illus.). 32p. (ps-1). 1992. pap. 3.95 *(0-06-443307-2,* Trophy) HarpC Child Bks.
—Crossing the New Bridge. LC 93-16047. 1994. write for info. *(0-399-22618-4,* Putnam) Putnam Pub Group.
—The Evil Spell. McCully, Emily A., illus. LC 89-24536. 32p. (gr. k-3). 1990. PLB 13.89 *(0-06-024154-3)* HarpC Child Bks.
—First Snow. McCully, Emily A., illus. LC 84-43244. 32p. (ps-1). 1985. PLB 13.89 *(0-06-024129-2)* HarpC Child Bks.
—First Snow. McCully, Emily A., illus. LC 84-43244. 32p. (ps-1). 1988. pap. 4.95 *(0-06-443181-9,* Trophy) HarpC Child Bks.
—The Grandma Mix-Up. McCully, Emily A., illus. LC 87-29378. 64p. (gr. k-3). 1988. PLB 13.89 *(0-06-024202-7)* HarpC Child Bks.
—The Grandma Mix-Up. McCully, Emily A., illus. LC 87-29378. 64p. (gr. k-3). 1991. pap. 3.50 *(0-06-444150-4,* Trophy) HarpC Child Bks.
—Grandmas at Bat. McCully, Emily A., illus. LC 92-8318. 64p. (gr. k-3). 1993. 13.00 *(0-06-021031-1);* PLB 12.89 *(0-06-021032-X)* HarpC Child Bks.
—Grandmas at the Lake. McCully, Emily A., illus. LC 89-26590. 64p. (gr. k-3). 1990. PLB 10.89 *(0-06-024127-6)* HarpC Child Bks.
—Mirette on the Highwire. (Illus.). 32p. (ps-3). 1992. 14.95 *(0-399-22130-1,* Putnam) Putnam Pub Group.
—My Real Family. LC 92-46290. 1994. write for info. *(0-15-277698-2,* Browndeer Pr) HarBrace.
—New Baby. McCully, Emily A., illus. LC 87-45294. 32p. (ps-1). 1988. HarpC Child Bks.
—Picnic. LC 83-47913. (Illus.). 32p. (ps-1). 1984. PLB 14.89 *(0-06-024100-4)* HarpC Child Bks.
—Picnic. McCully, Emily A., illus. LC 83-47913. 32p. (ps-1). 1989. pap. 3.95 *(0-06-443199-1,* Trophy) HarpC Child Bks.
—School. McCully, Emily A., illus. LC 87-156. 32p. (ps-2). 1987. PLB 13.89 *(0-06-024133-0)* HarpC Child Bks.
—School. McCully, Emily A., illus. LC 87-156. 32p. (ps-1). 1990. pap. 4.95 *(0-06-443233-5,* Trophy) HarpC Child Bks.
—Speak up, Blanche! McCully, Emily A., illus. LC 90-36945. 32p. (gr. k-3). 1991. 15.00 *(0-06-024227-2);* PLB 14.89 *(0-06-024228-0)* HarpC Child Bks.
McCully, Ron. Up with Math: Basic Skills Step by Step. Jacobs, Russell F., ed. Haberer, Robert E., illus. (gr. 5-12). 1979. pap. text ed. 6.95 *(0-918272-03-3);* tchr's ed. 6.25 *(0-918272-04-1)* Jacobs.
McCune, Dan. Michael Jordan. LC 87-29021. (Illus.). 48p. (gr. 5-6). 1988. RSBE 11.95 *(0-89686-364-6,* Crestwood Hse) Macmillan Child Grp.
McCune, Dianne, et al. The Welcome Back to School Book. Hierstein, Judy, illus. 112p. (gr. k-4). 1987. pap. 9.95 *(0-86653-383-4,* GA1001) Good Apple.
McCurdy, Michael. The Devils Who Learned to Be Good. McCurdy, Michael, illus. 32p. (gr. 2-5). 1987. 13.95 *(0-316-55527-4,* Joy St Bks) Little.
—Hannah's Farm: Seasons on an Early American Homestead. McCurdy, Michael, illus. LC 87-29631. 32p. (ps-4). 1988. reinforced bdg. 12.95 *(0-8234-0700-4)* Holiday.
—The Old Man & the Fiddle. McCurdy, Michael, illus. 32p. (ps-3). 1992. PLB 14.95 *(0-399-21812-2,* Putnam) Putnam Pub Group.
McCurdy, Michael, ed. & illus. see Douglass, Frederick.
McCusker, Paul. Behind the Locked Door. (gr. 4-7). 1993. pap. 4.99 *(1-56179-133-4)* Focus Family.
—High Flyer with a Flat Tire. (gr. 4-7). 1991. pap. 4.99 *(1-56179-100-8)* Focus Family.
—Lights Out at Camp What a Nut. (gr. 4-7). 1993. pap. 4.99 *(1-56179-134-2)* Focus Family.
—The Secret Cave of Robinwood. (gr. 4-7). 1991. pap. 4.99 *(1-56179-102-4)* Focus Family.
—A Strange Journey Back. (gr. 4-7). 1991. pap. 4.99 *(1-56179-101-6)* Focus Family.
McCutchan, Betty. Rachel's Star. LC 91-75205. 97p. (gr. 6 up). 1992. 8.95 *(1-55523-464-X)* Winston-Derek.
McCutcheon, Elsie. The Rat War. LC 85-4593. 111p. (gr. 4 up). 1986. 13.00 *(0-374-36182-7)* FS&G.

McCutcheon, Randall. Can You Find It? Twenty-Five Library Scavenger Hunts to Sharpen Your Research Skills. rev. ed. LC 91-30105. (Illus.). 208p. (gr. 9 up). pap. 10.95 *(0-915793-38-5)* Free Spirit Pub.
McCutcheon, Randall, et al. Communication Matters. LC 93-10452. 1993. text ed. 41.00 *(0-314-01390-3)* West Pub.
McCutcheon, Randall J. Get off My Brain: A Survival Guide for Lazy Students. Wagner, Pete, illus. LC 84-82166. 120p. (gr. 9 up). 1985. pap. 8.95 *(0-915793-02-4)* Free Spirit Pub.
McDaniel, Becky B. Fue Carmelita (Katie Did It) Axeman, Lois, illus. LC 83-7260. 32p. (ps-2). 1988. PLB 11.93 *(0-516-32043-2);* pap. 2.95 *(0-516-52043-1)* Childrens.
—Fue Carmelita-Libro Grande: Katie Did It-Big Book. (Illus.). 32p. (ps-2). 1988. PLB 30.60 *(0-516-59512-1)* Childrens.
—Katie Can. Axeman, Lois, illus. LC 87-5190. 32p. (ps-2). 1987. PLB 11.93 *(0-516-02082-X);* pap. 2.95 *(0-516-42082-8)* Childrens.
—Katie Couldn't. Axeman, Lois, illus. LC 85-11666. 30p. (gr. 1-2). 1985. PLB 11.93 *(0-516-02069-2);* pap. 2.95 *(0-516-42069-0)* Childrens.
—Katie Did It. LC 83-7260. (Illus.). 32p. (ps-2). 1983. PLB 11.93 *(0-516-02043-9);* pap. 2.95 *(0-516-42043-7)* Childrens.
—Katie Did It Big Book. (Illus.). 32p. (gr. 5-9). 1988. PLB 30.60 *(0-516-49512-7)* Childrens.
—Larry & the Cookie. Martin, Clovis, illus. LC 92-37871. 32p. (ps-2). 1993. PLB 11.93 *(0-516-02014-5);* pap. 2.95 *(0-516-42014-3)* Childrens.
McDaniel, Lurlene. Baby Alicia Is Dying. 1993. pap. 3.50 *(0-553-29605-1)* Bantam.
—Goodbye Doesn't Mean Forever. (gr. 7 up). 1989. pap. 3.50 *(0-553-28007-4,* Starfire) Bantam.
—Happily Ever after. 1992. pap. 3.50 *(0-553-29056-8)* Bantam.
—I Want to Live. 128p. (gr. 5-8). 1987. 2.99 *(0-87406-237-3)* Willowisp Pr.
—If I Should Die Before I Wake. 128p. (gr. 5-8). 1992. pap. 2.99 *(0-87406-486-4)* Willowisp Pr.
—The Legacy: Making Wishes Come True. 1993. pap. 3.50 *(0-553-56134-0)* Bantam.
—Let Him Live. 1993. pap. 3.50 *(0-553-56067-0)* Bantam.
—Mother, Help Me Live: One Last Wish. 1992. pap. 3.50 *(0-553-29811-9)* Bantam.
—Now I Lay Me Down to Sleep. 1991. pap. 3.50 *(0-553-28897-0)* Bantam.
—Please Don't Die. (gr. 10 up). 1993. pap. 3.50 *(0-553-56262-2)* Bantam.
—Sixteen & Dying. 1992. pap. 3.50 *(0-553-29932-8)* Bantam.
—So Much to Live For. 160p. (gr. 5-8). 1991. pap. 2.99 *(0-685-57448-2)* Willowisp Pr.
—Someone Dies, Someone Lives. 1992. pap. 3.50 *(0-553-29842-9)* Bantam.
—Somewhere Between Life & Death. (gr. 5 up). 1991. pap. 3.50 *(0-553-28349-9,* Starfire) Bantam.
—Time to Let Go. (gr. 5 up). 1991. pap. 3.50 *(0-553-28350-2,* Starfire) Bantam.
—Too Young to Die. (gr. 7 up). 1989. pap. 3.50 *(0-553-28008-2,* Starfire) Bantam.
McDaniel, Melissa. Stephen Hawking: Physicist. (Illus.). 1994. 18.95 *(0-7910-2078-9,* Am Art Analog) Chelsea Hse.
McDaniel, Thomas. At Home in South Carolina. (gr. 1-8). 1991. 29.95 *(0-87844-099-2)* Sandlapper Pub Co.
McDaniel, Wilma E. Vito & Zona. Nicholson, Lee, intro. by. 40p. (Orig.). (gr. 10 up). 1993. pap. 4.00 *(0-916155-21-8)* Trout Creek.
McDaniels, William. Abdul & the Designer Tennis Shoes. 1990. pap. 6.95 *(0-913543-15-2)* African Am Imag.
McDermor, Gerald. The Magic Tree. 1994. write for info. *(0-8050-3080-8)* H Holt & Co.
McDermott, Catherine. Design. LC 90-10000. (Illus.). 48p. (gr. 6-11). 1990. PLB 19.92 *(0-8114-2364-6)* Raintree Steck-V.
McDermott, G. Zomo the Rabbit. 1992. 14.95 *(0-15-299967-1,* HB Juv Bks) HarBrace.
McDermott, Gerald. Arrow to the Sun: A Pueblo Indian Tale. McDermott, Gerald, illus. (gr. 1 up). 1977. pap. 4.99 *(0-14-050211-4,* Puffin) Puffin Bks.
—Arrow to the Sun: A Pueblo Indian Tale. LC 73-16172. (Illus.). 48p. (gr. 1 up). 1974. pap. 14.95 *(0-670-13369-8)* Viking Child Bks.
—Daniel O'Rourke. McDermott, Gerald, illus. LC 85-20188. 32p. (ps-3). 1986. pap. 12.95 *(0-670-80924-1)* Viking Child Bks.
—Daniel O'Rourke: An Irish Tale. 1988. pap. 4.99 *(0-14-050673-X,* Puffin) Puffin Bks.
—Daughter of Earth: A Roman Myth. McDermott, Gerald, illus. LC 82-23585. 32p. (ps-3). 1984. pap. 15.00 *(0-385-29294-5)* Delacorte.
—Flecha al Sol. (SPA). (ps-3). 1991. 15.95 *(0-670-83748-2)* Viking Child Bks.
—Flecha al Sol: Un Cuento do Los Indios Pueblo. McDermott, Gerald, illus. (SPA). 48p. (ps-3). 1991. pap. 4.99 *(0-14-054364-3,* Puffin) Puffin Bks.
—Papagayo: The Mischief Maker. LC 91-4036. (ps-3). 1992. write for info. *(0-15-259465-5,* HB Juv Bks); pap. write for info. *(0-15-259464-7,* HB Juv Bks) HarBrace.
—Raven: A Trickster Tale from the Pacific Northwest. LC 91-14563. (ps-3). 1993. 14.95 *(0-15-265661-8,* HB Juv Bks) HarBrace.

—The Stonecutter. (Illus.). (gr. 1-3). 1978. pap. 4.99 *(0-14-050289-0,* Puffin) Puffin Bks.
—Tim O'Toole & the Little People. (ps-3). 1990. pap. 13.95 *(0-670-80393-6)* Viking Child Bks.
—Tim O'Toole & the Wee Folk. McDermott, Gerald, illus. 32p. (ps-3). 1992. pap. 3.99 *(0-14-050675-6)* Puffin Bks.
McDermott, Gerald, jt. auth. see Mayer, Marianna.
McDermott, Gerald, as told by. & illus. Coyote: A Trickster Tale from the Southwest. LC 92-32979. 1992. write for info. *(0-15-220724-4)* HarBrace.
McDermott, Gerald, retold by. & illus. Anansi the Spider: A Tale from the Ashanti. LC 91-150028. 48p. (ps-2). 1972. reinforced bdg. 15.95 *(0-8050-0310-X,* Bks Young Read); pap. 5.95 *(0-8050-0311-8)* H Holt & Co.
McDermott, Kathleen. Peter the Great. (Illus.). 112p. (gr. 5 up). 1991. 17.95 *(1-55546-821-7)* Chelsea Hse.
McDiarmid, T. Making Money. (Illus.). 48p. (gr. 2-6). 1988. pap. 5.95 *(0-88625-152-4)* Durkin Hayes Pub.
MacDonald, Agnes, jt. auth. see MacDonald, Kenneth B.
MacDonald, Alan. The Family Easter Book. LC 92-36602. (Illus.). 96p. 1993. 12.95 *(0-7459-2349-6)* Lion USA.
MacDonald, Amy. Let's Do It. Roffey, Maureen & Roffey, Maureen, illus. LC 91-71836. 12p. (ps). 1992. bds. 4.95 *(1-56402-024-X)* Candlewick Pr.
—Let's Go. Roffey, Maureen, illus. LC 92-46095. 1994. write for info. *(1-56402-202-1)* Candlewick Pr.
—Let's Make a Noise. Roffey, Maureen, illus. LC 91-71837. 12p. (ps). 1992. bds. 4.95 *(1-56402-025-8)* Candlewick Pr.
—Let's Play. Roffey, Maureen, illus. LC 91-71838. 12p. (ps). 1992. bds. 4.95 *(1-56402-023-1)* Candlewick Pr.
—Let's Pretend. Roffey, Maureen, illus. LC 92-47373. 1994. write for info. *(1-56402-233-1)* Candlewick Pr.
—Let's Try. Roffey, Maureen, illus. LC 91-71839. 12p. (ps). 1992. bds. 4.95 *(1-56402-022-3)* Candlewick Pr.
—Little Beaver & the Echo. Fox-Davies, Sarah, illus. 32p. 1990. 14.95 *(0-399-22203-0,* Putnam) Putnam Pub Group.
—Rachel Fister's Blister. Priceman, Marjorie, illus. 32p. (ps-3). 1990. 13.45 *(0-395-52152-1)* HM.
—Rachel Fister's Blister. Priceman, Marjorie, illus. 32p. (gr. k-3). 1993. pap. 4.80 *(0-395-65744-X)* HM.
Mc Donald, Archie. When the Corn Grows Tall in Texas. Peacock, Joe, illus. 96p. (gr. 4-8). 1991. 11.95 *(0-89015-808-8)* Eakin-Sunbelt.
MacDonald, Betty. Hello, Mrs. Piggle-Wiggle. Knight, Hilary, illus. LC 57-5613. (gr. k-3). 1957. 14.00 *(0-397-31715-8,* Lipp Jr Bks) HarpC Child Bks.
—Hello, Mrs. Piggle-Wiggle. LC 57-5613. (Illus.). (gr. 1-3). 1985. pap. 3.95 *(0-06-440149-9,* Trophy) HarpC Child Bks.
—Mrs. Piggle-Wiggle. rev. ed. Knight, Hilary, illus. LC 47-1876. (gr. k-3). 1957. 14.00 *(0-397-31712-3,* Lipp Jr Bks) HarpC Child Bks.
—Mrs. Piggle-Wiggle. rev. ed. LC 47-1876. (Illus.). 120p. (gr. 1-3). 1985. pap. 3.95 *(0-06-440148-0,* Trophy) HarpC Child Bks.
—Mrs. Piggle-Wiggle's Farm. Sendak, Maurice, illus. LC 54-7299. (gr. k-3). 1954. 14.00 *(0-397-31713-1,* Lipp Jr Bks) HarpC Child Bks.
—Mrs. Piggle-Wiggle's Farm. LC 54-7299. (Illus.). 132p. (gr. 1-3). 1985. pap. 3.95 *(0-06-440150-2,* Trophy) HarpC Child Bks.
—Mrs. Piggle-Wiggle's Magic. new ed. Knight, Hilary, illus. LC 49-11124. (gr. k-3). 1957. 14.00 *(0-397-31714-X,* Lipp Jr Bks) HarpC Child Bks.
—Mrs. Piggle-Wiggle's Magic. LC 49-11124. (Illus.). 144p. (gr. 1-3). 1985. pap. 3.95 *(0-06-440151-0,* Trophy) HarpC Child Bks.
MacDonald, Caroline. Hostilities: Nine Bizarre Stories. LC 93-19019. 112p. (gr. 7 up). 1994. 13.95 *(0-590-46063-3)* Scholastic Inc.
—Speaking to Miranda. LC 91-47901. 256p. (gr. 7 up). 1992. 14.00 *(0-06-021102-4);* PLB 13.89 *(0-06-021103-2)* HarpC Child Bks.
MacDonald, Collin. The Chilling Hour. 160p. (gr. 3-7). 1994. pap. 3.95 *(0-06-440493-5,* Trophy) HarpC Child Bks.
—The Chilling Hour: Tales of the Real & Unreal. (Illus.). 128p. (gr. 4 up). 1992. 14.00 *(0-525-65101-2,* Cobblehill Bks) Dutton Child Bks.
—Nightwaves: Scary Tales for after Dark. LC 90-35234. (gr. 4-7). 1990. 12.95 *(0-525-65043-1,* Cobblehill Bks) Dutton Child Bks.
—Nightwaves: Scary Tales for after Dark. 112p. (gr. 3-7). 1992. pap. 3.95 *(0-06-440447-1,* Trophy) HarpC Child Bks.
Macdonald, David S., ed. U. S. Liberty Album. (Illus.). 416p. (gr. 6 up). 1984. text ed. 18.95 *(0-937458-29-5)* Harris & Co.
McDonald, Dick see Hogan, Paula Z.
McDonald, Ed, jt. auth. see Van Deman, Barry A.
MacDonald, Elizabeth. John's Picture. (ps-3). 1991. 13.95 *(0-670-83579-X)* Viking Child Bks.
—Mike's Kite. Kendall, Robert, illus. LC 90-6912. 32p. (ps-3). 1990. 13.95 *(0-531-05876-X);* PLB 13.99 *(0-531-08476-0)* Orchard Bks Watts.
—The Very Windy Day. Summers, Lesley, illus. LC 91-690. 40p. (ps-3). 1992. 15.00 *(0-688-11044-4,* Tambourine Bks); PLB 14.93 *(0-688-11045-2,* Tambourine Bks) Morrow.
MacDonald, Fiona. Ancient Egyptians. (Illus.). 60p. (gr. 4 up). 1993. 15.95 *(0-8120-6378-3)* Barron.
—Aztecs. (Illus.). 60p. (gr. 4 up). 1993. 15.95 *(0-8120-6377-5)* Barron.

—Cities: Citizens & Civilizations. (Illus.). 48p. 1992. 13. 95 (*0-531-15247-2*) Watts.
—A Medieval Castle. Bergin, Mark, illus. 48p. (gr. 5 up). 1993. pap. 8.95 sewn (*0-87226-258-8*) P Bedrick Bks.
—A Medieval Castle: Inside Story. Bergin, Mark, illus. 48p. (gr. 5 up). 1990. 17.95 (*0-87226-340-1*) P Bedrick Bks.
—A Medieval Cathedral. James, John, illus. 48p. (gr. 5 up). 1991. 17.95 (*0-87226-350-9*) P Bedrick Bks.
—The Middle Ages. (Illus.). 80p. (gr. 2-6). 1993. 17.95x (*0-8160-2788-9*) Facts on File.
—A Nineteenth Century Railway Station: Inside Story. James, John, illus. 48p. (gr. 5 up). 1990. 17.95 (*0-87226-341-X*) P Bedrick Bks.
—Plains Indians. (Illus.). 60p. (gr. 4 up). 1993. 15.95 (*0-8120-6376-7*) Barron.
—Rain Forest. Scrace, Carolyn, illus. LC 93-24449. 1994. write for info. (*0-8114-9243-5*) Raintree Steck-V.
—A Roman Fort. Wood, Gerald, illus. LC 93-16397. 48p. (gr. 5 up). 1993. 17.95 (*0-87226-370-3*); pap. 8.95 sewn (*0-87226-259-6*) P Bedrick Bks.
—Vikings. (Illus.). 60p. (gr. 4 up). 1993. 15.95 (*0-8120-6375-9*) Barron.
MacDonald, Fiona & Bergin, Mark. A Greek Temple. LC 92-10712. (Illus.). 48p. (gr. 5 up). 1992. 17.95 (*0-87226-361-4*) P Bedrick Bks.
Macdonald, G. The Little Island. 1993. pap. 4.99 (*0-440-40830-X*) Dell.
MacDonald, George. The Adventures of Ranald Bannerman. rev. ed. Phillips, Michael, ed. 192p. (gr. 3 up). 1991. 10.99 (*1-55661-223-0*) Bethany Hse.
—Alec Forbes & His Friend Annie. Phillips, Michael R., ed. 256p. (gr. 2-7). 1990. 10.99 (*1-55661-140-4*) Bethany Hse.
—At the Back of the North Wind. Thomas, A. M., intro. by. LC 64-21758. (Illus.). (gr. 5 up). 1966. pap. 1.50 (*0-8049-0100-7*, CL-100) Airmont.
—At the Back of the North Wind. LC 64-21758. 336p. (gr. 4-6). 1985. pap. 2.25 (*0-14-035030-6*, Puffin) Puffin Bks.
—At the Back of the North Wind. Mills, Lauren, illus. LC 87-45455. 320p. 1988. 18.95 (*0-87923-703-1*) Godine.
—At the Back of the North Wind. Smith, Jessie W., illus. LC 88-63292. 352p. (gr. 5 up). 1989. 17.95 (*0-688-07808-7*) Morrow Jr Bks.
—At the Back of the North Wind. rev. ed. Phillips, Michael, ed. 176p. (ps-2). 1991. 10.99 (*1-55661-196-X*) Bethany Hse.
—At the Back of the North Wind. 352p. 1990. 12.99 (*0-517-69120-5*) Outlet Bk Co.
—At the Back of the North Wind. Hughes, Arthur, illus. 378p. 1992. Repr. of 1886 ed. 16.00 (*1-881084-07-8*) Johannesen.
—The Christmas Stories of George MacDonald. LC 81-68187. (gr. 3-7). 1981. 12.99 (*0-89191-491-9*, 54916, Chariot Bks) Cook.
—A Daughter's Devotion. rev. ed. Phillips, Michael, ed. LC 88-19256. 320p. (gr. 11 up). 1988. pap. 7.99 (*0-87123-906-X*) Bethany Hse.

—George MacDonald Original Works, 5 vols, Series III. (gr. 5 up). 1993. Repr. Set. 74.00 (*1-881084-18-3*); Per volume, first 3 volumes with color plates. 20.00 (*1-881084-20-5*); Per volume, last 2 volumes with B&W illus. 16.00 (*1-881084-21-3*) Johannesen. Ranald Bannerman's Boyhood, Color-1-881084-13-2; The Princess & the Goblin, Color-1-881084-14-0; The Princess & Curdie, Color-1-881084-15-9; The Light Princess & Other Fairy Tales, B&W-1-881084-16-7; The Wise Woman/Gutta Percha Willie, B&W, (A Duplex)-1-881084-17-5. George MacDonald...the Scotsman who spun daring tales of valiant hearts seeking freedom from English customs & Celtic superstitions of the 19th century, powerfully underscores battles between Divine Wisdom & Earthly Deception. Enchanting, picturesque scenes with Castles, Ghosts, & Treasures backdrop suspenseful plots of tragic & True Love, all-the-while unveiling motives of human behaviour. The fantasy-like-forms realistically speak to the young at heart in Series III. Color Plates & B&W Illustrations by original artists: Stratton, Wheelhouse, Hughes & Humphreys. Hardbound, cotton-cloth covers in original English crown-octavo size, available in Red, Green or Blue. Book length: 300-400 pages & printed on acid-free, recycled paper. Request brochure for other original MacDonald titles & varying discounts from Johannesen, P.O. Box 24, Whitethorn, CA 95589. Phone: 707-986-7465 or FAX: 707-986-1656. *Publisher Provided Annotation.*

—The Golden Key. 2nd ed. Sendak, Maurice, illus. Auden, W. H., afterword by. LC 67-6087. (Illus.). 96p. (gr. 1 up). 1984. 15.00 (*0-374-32706-8*); pap. 4.95 (*0-374-42590-6*) FS&G.
—The Landlady's Master. Phillips, Michael R., ed. 208p. (Orig.). (gr. 11 up). 1989. pap. 7.99 (*0-87123-904-3*) Bethany Hse.
—The Light Princess. rev. ed. Sendak, Maurice, illus. LC 69-14981. 120p. (gr. 1 up). 1969. 15.00 (*0-374-34455-8*); pap. 4.95, 1984 (*0-374-44458-7*) FS&G.
McDonald, George. The Light Princess. McKinley, Robin & Treherne, Katie T., illus. LC 86-53646. 44p. (ps up) 1988. 13.95 (*0-15-245300-8*, HB Juv Bks) HarBrace.
MacDonald, George. The Light Princess. Hughes, Arthur, illus. LC 93-561. 160p. 1993. 6.00 (*1-56957-903-2*) Shambhala Pubns.
—The Light Princess & Other Fairy Tales. Humphrey, Maud, illus. 305p. (gr. 5 up). 1993. Repr. of 1893 ed. 16.00 (*1-881084-16-7*) Johannesen.
—The Light Princess & Other Tales. (Illus.). 288p. (gr. 5-8). 1989. pap. 6.95 (*0-86241-164-5*, Pub. by Cnngt Pub Ltd) Trafalgar.
—Little Daylight. Ingraham, Erick, adapted by. & illus. LC 85-29769. 40p. (gr. 2 up). 1988. 12.95 (*0-688-06300-4*); PLB 12.88 (*0-688-06301-2*, Morrow Jr Bks) Morrow Jr Bks.
—The Lost Princess: A Double Story. Sadler, Glenn E., ed. Oberdieck, Bernhard, illus. 144p. 1992. text ed. 19. 99 (*0-8028-5070-7*) Eerdmans.
—The Peasant Girl's Dream. rev. ed. Phillips, Michael R., ed. LC 88-33336. 224p. (gr. 11 up). 1989. pap. 7.99 (*1-55661-023-8*) Bethany Hse.
—The Princess & Curdie. 306p. 1989. Repr. lib. bdg. 26. 95x (*0-89966-591-8*) Buccaneer Bks.
—The Princess & Curdie. Stratton, Helen, illus. 332p. (gr. 5 up). 1993. Repr. of 1912 ed. 20.00 (*1-881084-15-9*) Johannesen.
—The Princess & the Curdie. (Orig.). (gr. k-6). 1987. pap. 4.95 (*0-440-47182-6*, Pub. by Yearling Clasics) Dell.
—Princess & the Goblin. Hogan, A. H., intro. by. (gr. 3 up). 1967. pap. 1.50 (*0-8049-0156-2*, CL-156) Airmont.
—Princess & the Goblin. (gr. 1 up). 1984. pap. 2.25 (*0-14-035029-2*, Puffin) Puffin Bks.
—The Princess & The Goblin. 1986. pap. 4.95 (*0-440-47189-3*, Yearling Classics) Dell.
—The Princess & the Goblin. Smith, Jesse W., illus. Glassman, Peter, afterword by. LC 86-2532. (Illus.). 208p (ps up) 1986. 17.95 (*0-688-06604-6*) Morrow Jr Bks.
—The Princess & the Goblin. 1989. Repr. lib. bdg. 26.95x (*0-89966-598-5*) Buccaneer Bks.
—The Princess & the Goblin. 208p. (gr. 5-8). 1990. pap. 7.95 (*0-86241-274-9*, Pub. by Cnngt Pub Ltd) Trafalgar.
—The Princess & the Goblin. (gr. 4-7). 1991. pap. 2.95 (*0-590-44025-X*) Scholastic Inc.
—The Princess & the Goblin. Stratton, Helen & Hughes, illus. 320p. (gr. 5 up). 1993. Repr. of 1911 ed. 20.00 (*1-881084-14-0*) Johannesen.
—The Princess & the Goblin. LC 93-11264. (gr. 2 up). 1993. 12.95 (*0-679-42810-0*, Everymans Lib Childs) Knopf.
—Ranald Bannerman's Boyhood. Wheelhouse, A. V. & Houghes, illus. 347p. (gr. 5 up). 1993. Repr. of 1911 ed. 20.00 (*1-881084-13-2*) Johannesen.
—The Son of the Day & the Daughter of the Night. Teeples, Lynn, illus. LC 84-145155. 40p. (gr. 7-9). 1991. pap. 7.95 (*0-914676-45-8*, Green Tiger) S&S Trade.
—Wee Sir Gibbie of the Highlands. Phillips, Michael R., ed. 240p. (gr. 2-7). 1990. 10.99 (*1-55661-139-0*) Bethany Hse.
—The Wise Woman - Gutta Percha Willie, (Duplex) Hughes, Arthur & Willie, Gutta P., illus. 442p. (gr. 5 up). 1993. Repr. of 1901 ed. 16.00 (*1-881084-17-5*) Johannesen.
McDonald, George, jt. ed. see Peterson, Steve.
MacDonald, George, ed. see Robinson, Andrew.
MacDonald, High. Chung Lee Loves Lobsters. Wales, Johnny, illus. 24p. (gr. k-3). 1992. PLB 14.95 (*1-55037-217-3*, Pub. by Annick CN); pap. 4.95 (*1-55037-214-9*, Pub. by Annick CN) Firefly Bks Ltd.
Macdonald, James, jt. auth. see Doyle, Debra.
MacDonald, James, jt. auth. see Kennedy, Sandra.
Macdonald, James D., jt. auth. see Doyle, Debra.
McDonald, Joyce. Mail-Order Kid. 128p. (gr. 3-7). 1988. 13.95 (*0-399-21513-1*, Putnam) Putnam Pub Group.
McDonald, Joyce & Swanson, Karl. Homebody. LC 89-29602. (Illus.). 32p. 1991. 14.95 (*0-399-21939-0*, Putnam) Putnam Pub Group.
McDonald, Julie. Nils Discovers America Adventures with Eric. 96p. (gr. 2-6). 7.95 (*0-941016-74-9*) Penfield.

Macdonald, Kate. The Anne of Green Gables Cookbook. DiLella, Barbara, illus. 48p. 1987. 11.95 (*0-19-540496-3*) OUP.
MacDonald, Kendall. Divers. Stefoff, Rebecca, ed. LC 91-46577. (Illus.). 32p. (gr. 5-9). 1992. PLB 17.26 (*1-56074-043-4*) Garrett Ed Corp.
MacDonald, Kenneth B. & MacDonald, Agnes. The Second Coming: Tough Questions Answered. 300p. (Orig.). 1991. pap. text ed. 9.95 (*0-9626490-0-7*) Revivals & Missions.
McDonald, Mandi. Babes in Toyland. Lisi, Victoria & Lisi, Victoria, illus. 72p. (gr. 3-7). 1990. 11.95 (*0-88101-100-2*) Unicorn Pub.
MacDonald, Margaret R. Peace Tales: World Folktales to Talk About. LC 92-8994. (gr. 1-6). 1992. PLB 22. 50 (*0-208-02328-3*, Linnet); pap. text ed. 13.95 (*0-208-02329-1*, Linnet) Shoe String.
—The Skit Book: One Hundred & One Skits from Kids. LC 89-29654. 152p. (gr. 1-9). 1990. 25.00 (*0-208-02258-9*, Linnet); pap. 15.00 (*0-208-02283-X*, Linnet) Shoe String.
MacDonald, Marianne. The Pirate Queen. Smith, Jan, illus. 32p. (ps-3). 1992. incl. dust jacket 12.95 (*0-8120-6288-4*); pap. 5.95 (*0-8120-4952-7*) Barron.
McDonald, Marilyn. Inspired by a Child of God Called Marilyn. LC 90-71950. 44p. (gr. 9-12). 1991. 5.95 (*1-55523-449-X*) Winston-Derek.
Macdonald, Mary A. Hedgehog Bakes a Cake - Bank Street. (ps-3). 1990. pap. 3.50 (*0-553-34890-6*) Bantam.
McDonald, Mary A. Jupiter. LC 93-3595. (Illus.). 1993. write for info. (*1-56766-022-3*) Childs World.
MacDonald, Maryan. Rabbit's Birthday Kite. (ps-3). 1991. 9.99 (*0-553-05876-2*); pap. 3.50 (*0-553-34908-2*) Bantam.
MacDonald, Maryann. Ben at the Beach. McTaggart, David, illus. 32p. (ps-3). 1991. 14.95 (*0-670-83920-5*) Viking Child Bks.
—Fatso Jean, the Ice Cream Queen. (gr. 4 up). 1990. pap. 2.95 (*0-553-15797-3*) Bantam.
—Little Hippo Gets Glasses. LC 91-11971. (Illus.). 32p. (ps-3). 1992. 11.00 (*0-8037-0964-1*) Dial Bks Young.
—The Pink Party. LC 93-20989. (Illus.). 1994. write for info. (*1-56282-620-4*); PLB write for info. (*1-56282-621-2*) Hyprn Child.
—Rosie & the Poor Rabbits. Sweet, Melissa, illus. LC 92-42766. 32p. (ps-2). 1994. SBE 13.95 (*0-689-31832-4*, Atheneum Child Bk) Macmillan Child Grp.
—Rosie Runs Away. Sweet, Melissa, illus. LC 89-27575. 32p. (ps-2). 1990. SBE 12.95 (*0-689-31625-9*, Atheneum Child Bk) Macmillan Child Grp.
—Rosie's Baby Tooth. Sweet, Melissa, illus. LC 90-35923. 32p. (ps-2). 1991. SBE 12.95 (*0-689-31626-7*, Atheneum Child Bk) Macmillan Child Grp.
—Sam's Worries. Riches, Judith, illus. LC 91-71379. 32p. (ps-3). 1991. 13.95 (*1-56282-081-8*); PLB 13.89 (*1-56282-082-6*) Hyprn Child.
—Sam's Worries. Riches, Judith, illus. 32p. (ps-2). 1994. pap. write for info. (*1-56282-522-4*) Hyprn Ppbks.
—Secondhand Star. (Illus.). 64p. (gr. 2-5). 1994. 11.95 (*1-56282-616-6*); PLB 11.89 (*1-56282-617-4*) Hyprn Child.
McDonald, Megan. The Bridge to Nowhere. LC 92-50844. 160p. (gr. 6 up). 1993. 14.95 (*0-531-05478-0*); PLB 14.99 (*0-531-08628-3*) Orchard Bks Watts.
—The Great Pumpkin Switch. Lewin, Ted, illus. LC 91-39660. 32p. (ps-2). 1992. 14.95 (*0-531-05450-0*); PLB 14.99 (*0-531-08600-3*) Orchard Bks Watts.
—Is This a House for Hermit Crab? Schindler, S. D., illus. LC 89-35653. 32p. (ps-1). 1990. 14.95 (*0-531-05855-7*); PLB 14.99 (*0-531-08455-8*) Orchard Bks Watts.
—Is This a House for Hermit Crab? Schindler, S. D., illus. LC 89-35653. 32p. (ps-1). 1993. pap. 5.95 (*0-531-07041-7*) Orchard Bks Watts.
—The Potato Man. Lewin, Ted, illus. LC 90-7758. 32p. (ps-2). 1991. 14.95 (*0-531-05914-6*); PLB 14.99 (*0-531-08514-7*) Orchard Bks Watts.
—Whoo-oo Is It? Schindler, S. D., illus. LC 91-18494. 32p. (ps-1). 1992. 14.95 (*0-531-05974-X*); lib. bdg. 14. 99 (*0-531-08574-0*) Orchard Bks Watts.
McDonald, Mike, ed. see Gonzales, Rod & Faurot, Chip.
MacDonald, Pat, ed. see Auch, Mary J.
MacDonald, Pat, ed. see Beach, Lynn.
MacDonald, Pat, ed. see Beach, Lynn.
MacDonald, Pat, ed. see Carris, Joan.
MacDonald, Pat, ed. see Cohen, Daniel.
MacDonald, Pat, ed. see Coville, Bruce.
MacDonald, Pat, ed. see Cusick, Richie.
MacDonald, Pat, ed. see Cusick, Richie T.
MacDonald, Pat, ed. see Gilson, Jamie.
MacDonald, Pat, ed. see Gorman, S. S.
MacDonald, Pat, ed. see Haas, Dorothy.
MacDonald, Pat, ed. see Hiser, Constance.
MacDonald, Pat, ed. see Hodgman, Ann.
MacDonald, Pat, ed. see Kehret, Peg.
MacDonald, Pat, ed. see Lewis, Linda.
MacDonald, Pat, ed. see Miller, Judi.
MacDonald, Pat, ed. see Murrow, Liza K.
McDonald, Pat, ed. see Pevsner, Stella.
MacDonald, Pat, ed. see Pike, Christopher.
MacDonald, Pat, ed. see Poploff, Michelle.
MacDonald, Pat, ed. see Posner, Richard.
MacDonald, Pat, ed. see Rubenstein, Gillian.
MacDonald, Pat, ed. see Rubinstein, Gillian.
MacDonald, Pat, ed. see Shirts, Morris A.
MacDonald, Pat, ed. see Siegel, Barbara & Seigel, Scott.
MacDonald, Pat, ed. see Siegel, Barbara & Siegel, Scott.

MacDonald, Pat, ed. see Specter, B. J.
MacDonald, Pat, ed. see Stine, R. L.
McDonald, Pat, ed. see Stine, R. L.
MacDonald, Pat, ed. see Stine, R. L.
MacDonald, Pat, ed. see Thompson, Joan.
MacDonald, Pat, ed. see Wallace, Bill.
MacDonald, Patricia, jt. auth. see Sommer, Robin L.
MacDonald, Patricia, ed. see Baker, Barbara.
MacDonald, Patricia, ed. see Beach, Lynn.
MacDonald, Patricia, ed. see Clifford, Eth.
MacDonald, Patricia, ed. see Cohen, Daniel.
MacDonald, Patricia, ed. see Cone, Molly.
MacDonald, Patricia, ed. see Coville, Bruce.
MacDonald, Patricia, ed. see Cusick, Richie T.
MacDonald, Patricia, ed. see Dillon, Barbara.
MacDonald, Patricia, ed. see Gorman, S. S.
MacDonald, Patricia, ed. see Hermes, Patricia.
MacDonald, Patricia, ed. see Hiser, Constance.
MacDonald, Patricia, ed. see Hollands, Judith.
MacDonald, Patricia, ed. see Kehret, Peg.
MacDonald, Patricia, ed. see Lawlor, Laurie.
MacDonald, Patricia, ed. see Leroe, Ellen.
MacDonald, Patricia, ed. see Nash, Bruce & Zullo, Allan.
MacDonald, Patricia, ed. see Nelson, Peter.
MacDonald, Patricia, ed. see Pike, Christopher.
MacDonald, Patricia, ed. see Ragz, M. M.
MacDonald, Patricia, ed. see Siegal, Barbara & Siegal, Scott.
MacDonald, Patricia, ed. see Stine, R. L.
McDonald, Patricia, ed. see Stine, R. L.
MacDonald, Patricia, ed. see Stine, R. L.
MacDonald, Patricia, ed. see Wallace, Bill.
McDonald, Paula see Hogan, Paula Z.

MacDonald, Reby E. The Ghosts of Austwick Manor. LC 91-22112. 160p. (gr. 3-7). 1991. pap. 3.95 (0-689-71533-1, Aladdin) Macmillan Child Grp.
Macdonald, Robert. Maori. LC 93-35530. (Illus.). 48p. (gr. 6-10). 1994. 16.95 (1-56847-151-3) Thomson Lrning.
—Transitions: Military Pathways to Civilian Careers. Rosen, Roger, ed. (gr. 7 up). 1988. lib. bdg. 14.95 (0-8239-0777-5) Rosen Group.
Macdonald, Robert W. Exploring Careers in the Military Services. rev. ed. Rosen, Ruth, ed. (Illus.). 190p. (gr. 7 up). 1991. 14.95 (0-8239-1358-9) Rosen Group.
McDonald, Roger. Nineteen Fifteen. 434p. (gr. 10 up). 1989. pap. 12.95 (0-7022-2134-1, Pub. by Univ. Queensland Pr AT) Intl Spec Bk.
MacDonald, Sandra. Ben of Colonial Newport. 8p. (gr. k-2). 1993. pap. write for info. (1-882563-08-5) Lamont Bks.
—Birds at the Sanctuary. 8p. (gr. k-2). 1993. pap. write for info. (1-882563-03-4) Lamont Bks.
MacDonald, Sharon. We Learn All about Community Helpers. (ps-1). 1988. pap. 6.95 (0-8224-4599-9) Fearon Teach Aids.
—We Learn All about Dinosaurs. (ps-1). 1988. pap. 6.95 (0-8224-4595-6) Fearon Teach Aids.
—We Learn All about Fall. (ps-1). 1988. pap. 6.95 (0-8224-4596-4) Fearon Teach Aids.
—We Learn All about Farms. (ps-1). 1988. pap. 6.95 (0-8224-4594-8) Fearon Teach Aids.
—We Learn All about Machines. (ps-1). 1991. 6.95 (0-8224-4590-5) Fearon Teach Aids.
—We Learn All about Spring. (ps-1). 1991. 6.95 (0-8224-4591-3) Fearon Teach Aids.
—We Learn all about the Circus. (ps-1). 1988. pap. 6.95 (0-8224-4598-0) Fearon Teach Aids.
—We Learn All about Transportation. (ps-1). 1991. 6.95 (0-8224-4592-1) Fearon Teach Aids.
—We Learn All about Winter. (ps-1). 1988. pap. 6.95 (0-8224-4597-2) Fearon Teach Aids.
McDonald, Stuart. The Adventures of Endill Swift. 180p. (gr. 5-8). 1994. pap. 7.95 (0-86241-352-4, Pub. by Cnngt UK) Trafalgar.
MacDonald, Suse. Alphabatics. LC 85-31429. (Illus.). 64p. (ps up) 1986. SBE 16.95 (0-02-761520-0, Bradbury Pr) Macmillan Child Grp.
—Alphabatics. MacDonald, Suse, illus. LC 91-38497. 56p. (ps-1). 1992. pap. 6.95 (0-689-71625-7, Aladdin) Macmillan Child Grp.
—Puzzlers. LC 88-33392. 1989. 13.89 (0-8037-0690-1); PLB 13.95 (0-8037-0689-8) Dial Bks Young.
—Space Spinners. (ps-3). 1991. 13.95 (0-8037-1008-9); PLB 13.89 (0-8037-1009-7) Dial Bks Young.
McDonald, W. H. Creation Tales from the Salish. (gr. 3-9). 1973. 1.25 (0-89992-061-6) Coun India Ed.
MacDonald, W. Scott & Oden, Chester W., Jr. Moose: The Story of a Very Special Person. 2nd ed. 200p. (Orig.). (gr. 8 up). 1978. pap. 10.95 (0-03-043936-1) Brookline Bks.
McDonnell, Christine. Don't Be Mad, Ivy. DeGroat, Diane, illus. LC 81-65850. 80p. (gr. 1-5). 1981. Dial Bks Young.
—Friends First. 176p. (gr. 4 up). 1990. pap. 11.95 (0-670-81923-9) Viking Child Bks.
—Friends First. LC 92-20290. 176p. (gr. 5 up). 1992. pap. 3.99 (0-14-032477-1) Puffin Bks.
—Just for the Summer. De Groat, Diane, illus. LC 87-8201. (gr. 2-5). 1987. pap. 11.95 (0-670-80059-7) Viking Child Bks.
—Just for the Summer. De Groat, Diane, illus. 128p. (gr. 2-6). 1989. pap. 3.95 (0-14-032147-0, Puffin) Puffin Bks.
—Toad Food & Measle Soup. De Groat, Diane, illus. 112p. 1984. pap. 3.99 (0-14-031724-4, Puffin) Puffin Bks.

McDonnell, Flora. I Love Animals. LC 93-2463. 1994. write for info. (1-56402-387-7) Candlewick Pr.
McDonnell, Janet. Animal Builders. LC 88-36641. (Illus.). 48p. (gr. 2-6). 1989. PLB 21.35 (0-89565-511-X); PLB 14.95s.p. (0-685-55989-0) Childs World.
—Animal Camouflage. LC 88-36642. (Illus.). 48p. (gr. 2-6). 1989. PLB 21.35 (0-89565-512-8); PLB 14.95s.p. (0-685-55988-2) Childs World.
—Animal Camouflage: Hide & Seek Animals. Magnuson, Diana, illus. LC 89-28083. 32p. (ps-2). 1990. PLB 21.35 (0-89565-562-4); PLB 14.95s.p. (0-685-56183-6) Childs World.
—Animal Communication. LC 88-36643. (Illus.). 48p. (gr. 2-6). 1989. PLB 21.35 (0-89565-513-6); PLB 14.95s.p. (0-685-55987-4) Childs World.
—Animal Migration. LC 88-36640. (Illus.). 48p. (gr. 2-6). 1989. PLB 21.35 (0-89565-514-4); PLB 14.95s.p. (0-685-55986-6) Childs World.
—Animal Talk: Barks, Growls, Hisses, Howls. Ching, illus. LC 89-23990. 32p. (ps-2). 1990. PLB 21.35 (0-89565-558-6); PLB 14.95s.p. (0-685-56179-8) Childs World.
—Ape's Adventure in Alphabet Town. Hohag, L., illus. LC 91-20539. 32p. (ps-2). 1992. 14.60 (0-516-05401-5) Childrens.
—Baby Animals: Safe & Sound. Hohag, Linda, illus. LC 89-23978. 32p. (ps-2). 1990. PLB 21.35 (0-89565-554-3); PLB 14.95s.p. (0-685-56175-5) Childs World.
—Bear's Adventure in Alphabet Town. Hohag, L., illus. LC 91-20543. 32p. (ps-2). 1992. PLB 14.60 (0-516-05402-3) Childrens.
—Christmas in Other Lands. Endres, Helen, illus. LC 93-7632. 1993. write for info. (0-516-00682-7) Childrens.
—The Easter Surprise. Hohag, Linda, illus. LC 93-11004. 1993. write for info. (0-516-00683-5) Childrens.
—Fall: A Tale of What's to Come. Hohag, Linda, illus. LC 93-20171. (gr. 2 up). 1993. write for info. (0-516-00676-2) Childrens.
—Fox's Adventure in Alphabet Town. McCallum, J., illus. LC 91-20546. 32p. (ps-2). 1992. PLB 14.60 (0-516-05406-6) Childrens.
—Goat's Adventure in Alphabet Town. Dunnington, T., illus. LC 91-20548. 32p. (ps-2). 1992. PLB 14.60 (0-516-05407-4) Childrens.
—Good Health: A Visit from Droopy. Dunnington, Tom, illus. LC 90-1871. 32p. (ps-2). 1990. PLB 19.95 (0-89565-582-9); PLB 13.95s.p. (0-685-56196-8) Childs World.
—Hippo's Adventure in Alphabet Town. McDonnell, J., illus. LC 91-20549. 32p. (ps-2). 1992. PLB 14.60 (0-516-05408-2) Childrens.
—Ichabod's Adventure in Alphabet Town. Peltier, P., illus. LC 91-20547. 32p. (ps-2). 1992. PLB 14.60 (0-516-05409-0) Childrens.
—Kangaroo's Adventure in Alphabet Town. McCallum, J., illus. LC 91-20540. 32p. (ps-2). 1992. PLB 14.60 (0-516-05411-2) Childrens.
—Martin Luther King Day. Halverson, Lydia, illus. LC 93-13251. 1993. write for info. (0-516-00687-8) Childrens.
—Mouse's Adventure in Alphabet Town. Williams, Jenny, illus. LC 91-47717. 32p. (ps-2). 1992. PLB 14.60 (0-516-05413-9) Childrens.
—Polka-Dot Puppy's New House: A Book about Counting. Hohag, Linda, illus. LC 88-11941. 32p. (ps-2). 1988. PLB 21.35 (0-89565-380-X); PLB 14.95s.p. (0-685-55928-9) Childs World.
—Quarterback's Adventure in Alphabet Town. McCallum, Jodie, illus. LC 91-1067. 32p. (ps-2). 1992. PLB 14.60 (0-516-05417-1) Childrens.
—Raccoon's Adventure in Alphabet Town. Endres, Helen, illus. LC 92-1066. 32p. (ps-2). 1992. PLB 14.60 (0-516-05418-X) Childrens.
—Sharing Hanukkah. Endres, Helen, illus. LC 93-13250. 1993. write for info. (0-516-00685-1) Childrens.
—Space Travel: Blast-Off Day. Collette, Rondi, illus. LC 89-23999. 32p. (ps-2). 1990. PLB 19.95 (0-89565-556-X); PLB 13.95s.p. (0-685-56177-1) Childs World.
—Spring: New Life Everywhere. Hohag, Linda, illus. LC 93-10309. 1993. write for info. (0-516-00677-0) Childrens.
—Success. Hohag, Linda, illus. LC 88-4348. 32p. (gr. k-3). 1988. PLB 21.35 (0-89565-376-1); PLB 14.95s.p. (0-685-55936-X) Childs World.
—Summer, a Growing Time. Hohag, Linda, illus. LC 93-1182. 1993. write for info. (0-516-00678-9) Childrens.
—Thankfulness. Hohag, Linda, illus. LC 88-2657. 32p. (gr. k-3). 1988. PLB 21.35 (0-89565-375-3); PLB 14.95s.p. (0-685-55937-8) Childs World.
—Turtle's Adventure in Alphabet Town. McDonnell, Janet, illus. LC 92-2984. 32p. (ps-2). 1992. PLB 14.60 (0-516-05420-1) Childrens.
—Victor's Adventure in Alphabet Town. Peltier, Pam, illus. LC 92-4036. 32p. (ps-2). 1992. PLB 14.60 (0-516-05422-8) Childrens.
—Wind: What Can It Do? Connelly, Gwen, illus. LC 89-24011. 32p. (ps-2). 1990. PLB 19.95 (0-89565-555-1); PLB 13.95s.p. (0-685-56176-3) Childs World.
—Winter: Tracks in the Snow. Hohag, Linda, illus. LC 93-20172. (ps-6). 1993. write for info. (0-516-00679-7) Childrens.
—An XYZ Adventure in Alphabet Town. Hohag, Linda, illus. LC 92-2985. 32p. (ps-2). 1992. PLB 14.60 (0-516-05424-4) Childrens.

McDonnell, Janet & Ziegler, Sandra. What's So Special about Me? I'm One of a Kind. Friedman, Joy, illus. LC 88-2872. 32p. (ps-2). 1988. PLB 21.35 (0-89565-419-9); PLB 14.95s.p. (0-685-55943-2) Childs World.
McDonnell, Janet, tr. see Andersen, Hans Christian.
McDonnell, Janet, tr. see Jose, Eduard.
McDonough, Barbara. Meet Me at the Fair: A "Choose Your Own Adventure" that lets You Explore the Exciting Treasures of the 1904 St. Louis World's Fair. Wissmann, Joyce, illus. 64p. (Orig.). (gr. 4-6). 1988. pap. 4.50 (0-931821-43-6) Info Res Cons.
McDonough, Chris, illus. Mother Goose Monsters ABC's Sticker Book. 24p. (ps-2). 1992. pap. 2.95 (1-56293-246-2) McClanahan Bk.
—Mother Goose Monsters Counting Sticker Book. 24p. (ps-2). 1992. pap. 2.95 (1-56293-247-0) McClanahan Bk.
McDonough, Jerome. Addict. (Illus.). 47p. (Orig.). (gr. 7-12). 1985. pap. 3.50 (0-88680-241-5); royalty on application 40.00 (0-685-58012-1) I E Clark.
—Alky. 40p. (Orig.). (gr. 7-12). 1991. pap. 3.00 (0-88680-354-3); royalty on application 35.00 (0-685-59145-X) I E Clark.
—Carriers. 34p. (Orig.). (gr. 7-12). 1992. pap. 3.00 (0-88680-370-5); royalty on application 35.00 (0-685-62706-3) I E Clark.
—Hoods. 22p. (Orig.). (gr. 7-12). 1992. pap. 3.00 (0-88680-369-1); royalty on application 35.00 (0-685-62707-1) I E Clark.
—It's Sad, So Sad When an Elf Goes Bad. (Illus.). 24p. (Orig.). (gr. k-6). 1979. pap. 2.00 (0-88680-100-1); royalty on application 20.00 (0-685-59260-X) I E Clark.
—Juvie. (Illus.). 32p. (Orig.). (gr. 7-12). 1982. pap. 3.50 (0-88680-103-6); royalty on application 40.00 (0-685-67533-5) I E Clark.
—Limbo. 28p. (Orig.). (gr. 7 up). 1984. pap. 3.00 (0-88680-219-9); royalty on application 35.00 (0-685-57920-4) I E Clark.
—Mirrors. (Illus.). 32p. (gr. 7 up). 1987. pap. 3.00 (0-88680-278-4); royalty on application 35.00 (0-685-67656-0) I E Clark.
—Not Even A. Mouse: A Chris-Mouse Tale. (Illus.). 20p. (Orig.). (gr. k-9). 1984. pap. 2.00 (0-88680-220-2) royalty on application 15.00 (0-685-57922-0) I E Clark.
—Turners. 40p. (Orig.). (gr. 7-12). 1989. pap. 3.50 (0-88680-320-9); royalty on application 40.00 (0-685-58562-X) I E Clark.
McDonough, Jerome, adapted by. Alice: A One-Act Play. (Illus.). 36p. (Orig.). (gr. 4-12). 1990. pap. 3.00 (0-88680-336-5); royalty on application 25.00 (0-685-58889-0) I E Clark.
McDonough, Kathleen L. School Survival Skills: Student Syllabus. (Illus.). 64p. (gr. 8 up). 1985. pap. 7.95 (0-89420-246-4, 340025) Natl Book.
McDonough, Yona Z. Eve & Her Sisters: Women of the Old Testament. Zeldis, Malcah, illus. LC 93-9378. 32p. (gr. k up). 1994. write for info. (0-688-12512-3); PLB write for info. (0-688-12513-1) Greenwillow.
—Frank Lloyd Wright. (Illus.). 32p. (gr. 5 up). 1992. lib. bdg. 17.95 (0-7910-1626-9) Chelsea Hse.
—Frank Lloyd Wright. (gr. 4-7). 1992. pap. 7.95 (0-7910-1633-1) Chelsea Hse.

MacDougall, Mary-Katherine. Black Jupiter. Gruver, Kate E., ed. Moyers, William, illus. 181p. (gr. 5 up). 1983. 8.95 (0-940175-01-0) Now Comns.
"It was late for the horses to be so high in the mountains. By this time in other years they had already found winter quarters in a lower area. But this fall they were waiting for a colt." That colt was Black Jupiter. Snow came. The horses had to leave through the rock gateway the black mare could not yet get through. The stallion stayed with her. The next dawn the colt came but did not move or make a sound. The horses left the newborn colt alone in the snow. Jim Peters, a prospector, living alone in his cabin, was sensitive to wildlife. He felt something was wrong when he heard two horses leaving a day after the herd. He found Black Jupiter alive but not strong. He took him to his cabin. There are Gregg & Jenine Jordan, children of a mining engineer, a threat to Jim & his mining plans. In turn, Jim is suspected of stealing from the surveying crew. Black Jupiter, set in the Rocky Mountains with a factual copper mining background, is a mystery story of distrust & misunderstanding, healed by

love & a colt. There is a happy Christmas chapter. Black & white illustrations. *Publisher Provided Annotation.*

McDowell, jt. auth. see Martin.
McDowell, Dottie, jt. auth. see McDowell, Josh.
McDowell, John & Hostetler, Bob. The Love Killer. LC 93-25122. (gr. 6 up). 1993. write for info. (0-8499-3509-1) Word Pub.
McDowell, Josh. Under Siege. 192p. 1992. pap. 8.99 (0-8499-3363-3) Word Inc.
McDowell, Josh & Hostetler, Bob. Don't Check Your Brains at the Door. (gr. 7 up). 1992. pap. write for info. (0-8499-3234-3) Word Inc.
—Thirteen Things You Gotta Know: To Make It As a Christian. LC 92-33490. 1992. write for info. (0-8499-3413-3) Word Pub.
McDowell, Josh & McDowell, Dottie. Katie's Adventure at Blueberry Pond. (Illus.). 32p. (ps-2). 1988. 8.99 (1-55513-598-6, Chariot Bks) Cook.
—Pizza for Everyone. LC 88-14041. (Illus.). 32p. (ps-2). 1988. 8.99 (1-55513-596-X, Chariot Bks) Cook.
McDowell, Margaret & Trottier, Maxine. The Big Heart. Trottier, Maxine, illus. 32p. (ps-2). 1991. pap. 29.50 (1-55037-186-X, Pub. by Annick CN) Firefly Bks Ltd.
McDowell, Mildred. The Little People. Whitaker, Arleen, illus. Harman, Sandra L., intro. by. LC 72-133255. (Illus.). 44p. (gr. 1-2). 1971. 2.50 (0-87884-002-8) Unicorn Ent.
—The Squirrel & the Frog. Brennan, Nancy, illus. Harman, Sandra L., intro. by. LC 76-133256. (Illus.). 44p. (gr. 1-2). 1971. 2.50 (0-87884-007-9) Unicorn Ent.
McDowell, N. Hemingway. (Illus.). (gr. 7 up). 1989. lib. bdg. 19.94 (0-86592-298-5); 14.95s.p. (0-685-58634-0) Rourke Corp.
McDowell, Robert, jt. auth. see Lavitt, Edward.
McDowell, Robert E. & Lavitt, Edward, eds. Third World Voices for Children. Isaac, Barbara K., illus. LC 71-169091. 156p. (gr. 5-9). 1981. 7.95 (0-89388-020-5, Odarkai) Okpaku Communications.
Mace, Elisabeth. Under Siege. LC 89-23049. 192p. (gr. 7 up). 1990. 13.95 (0-531-05871-9); PLB 13.99 (0-531-08471-X) Orchard Bks Watts.
—Under Siege. 167p. (gr. 6-9). 1990. pap. 9.95 (0-233-98345-7, Pub. by A Deutsch England) Trafalgar.
Mace, Jean. Home Fairy Tales. Booth, Mary L., tr. from FRE. LC 78-74517. (Illus.). (gr. 4-5). 1979. Repr. of 1867 ed. 24.75x (0-8486-0220-X) Roth Pub Inc.
Mace, Patrick B. The Silver Whistle. (Orig.). (gr. k up). 1985. pap. 4.50 (0-87602-250-6) Anchorage.
McElmurry, Mary A. Appreciating. Herrick, Elizabeth T., illus. 64p. (gr. 2-8). 1983. wkbk. 7.95 (0-9607366-1-1, GA 493) Good Apple.
—Belonging. Herrick, Elizabeth T., illus. 64p. (gr. 2-8). 1983. wkbk. 7.95 (0-9607366-0-3, GA 492) Good Apple.
—Caring. 64p. (gr. 4-8). 1981. 7.95 (0-86653-052-5, GA275) Good Apple.
—Cooperating. Tom, Darcy, illus. 64p. (gr. 3-8). 1985. wkbk. 7.95 (0-86653-334-6, GA 680) Good Apple.
—Feelings. 80p. (gr. 3-8). 1981. 8.95 (0-86653-027-4, GA 276) Good Apple.
—Trivial Pursuit - Language Arts (Jr. High) (Illus.). 64p. (gr. 7-9). 1992. 12.95 (0-86653-650-7, GA1384) Good Apple.
McElrath, Ruth G., tr. see McElrath, William N.
McElrath, William E. Judges & Kings: God's Chosen Leaders. Johnson, Cliff, illus. (gr. 1-6). 1979. 5.99 (0-8054-4249-9, 4242-49) Broadman.
McElrath, William N. Bible Dictionary for Young Readers. Fields, Don, illus. LC 65-15604. (gr. 4-6). 1965. 12.95 (0-8054-4404-1, 4244-04) Broadman.
—Bible Guidebook. LC 72-79174. 144p. (gr. 3-6). 1972. 12.95 (0-8054-4410-6) Broadman.
—Mi Primer Diccionario Biblico. McElrath, Ruth G., tr. from ENG. Fields, Don, illus. (SPA.). 128p. (gr. 4-6). 1991. pap. 4.50 (0-311-03656-2) Casa Bautista.
—Oz & Mary Quick: Taiwan Teammates. LC 84-2962. (gr. 4-6). 1984. pap. 5.95 (0-8054-4287-1, 4242-87) Broadman.
McElroy. Jesus Forgives Peter. 24p. (Orig.). (gr. k-4). 1985. pap. 1.89 (0-570-06192-X, 59-1293) Concordia.
McElroy, Eugene J. Needle-Nosed Ned. LC 89-50144. (gr. 4-6). 1989. pap. 5.00 (0-932433-54-5) Windswept Hse.
McElroy, Janice H., ed. Our Hidden Heritage: Pennsylvania Women in History. LC 83-71272. (Illus.). 440p. (gr. 7-8). 1983. pap. 12.00 (0-9611476-0-1) Am Assoc U Women.
McEntee, Sean. Lectionary for Masses with Children: Cycle C. 192p. (Orig.). (gr. 2-8). 1988. pap. text ed. 19.95 (0-89622-385-X) Twenty-Third.
McEntee, Sean & Breen, Michael. Lectionary for Masses with Children: Cycle A. vi, 216p. (Orig.). (gr. 1-6). 1989. pap. 19.95 (0-89622-411-2) Twenty-Third.
McEvoy, Seth. Between Brothers. 1991. pap. 3.50 (0-671-73941-7, Archway) PB.
—Mission to Microworld. 1984. pap. 1.95 (0-553-24521-X) Bantam.
—On Stage. 1991. pap. 3.50 (0-671-73940-9, Archway) PB.
—Planet Hunters. 128p. (Orig.). (gr. 3 up). 1985. pap. 1.95 (0-553-24532-5) Bantam.

—The Red Rocket. 120p. (Orig.). (gr. 4). 1985. pap. 2.25 (0-553-26676-4) Bantam.
McEvoy, Seth & Smith, Laure. Backstage Surprise. Ashby, Ruth, ed. 144p. (Orig.). (gr. 7 up). 1990. pap. 3.50 (0-671-73170-X, Archway) PB.
—Block Party. Ashby, Ruth, ed. (Orig.). (gr. 5 up). 1991. pap. 3.50 (0-671-73321-4, Archway) PB.
—On Tour. Ashby, Ruth, ed. 160p. (Orig.). 1991. pap. 3.50 (0-671-73939-5, Archway) PB.
McEwan, Chris. The Little Penguin. 1989. pap. 12.95 (0-385-24977-2) Doubleday.
—Pinocchio. 1990. pap. 13.95 (0-385-41327-0) Doubleday.
McEwan, Elaine K. Operation Garbage: A Josh McIntire Book. LC 92-43761. 1993. write for info. (0-7814-0121-6) Cook.
—Underground Hero. LC 92-27104. (gr. 1-6). 1993. write for info. (0-7814-0113-5, Chariot Bks) Cook.
McFadzean, Anita. One Special Star. Jaspers, Kate, illus. LC 90-21485. 32p. (ps-1). 1991. pap. 11.95 jacketed (0-671-74023-7, S&S BFYR); pap. 3.95 (0-671-74024-5, Little Simon) S&S Trade.
McFall, Christie. America Underground. LC 91-8951. (Illus.). 80p. (gr. 5 up). 1992. 14.00 (0-525-65079-2, Cobblehill Bks) Dutton Child Bks.
McFall, Gardner. Naming the Animals. Guarnaccia, Steven, illus. LC 93-14532. (ps-3). 1994. PLB 13.99 (0-670-84814-X) Viking Child Bks.
McFann, Jane. Be Mine. (gr. 12 up). 1994. pap. 3.50 (0-590-46690-9) Scholastic Inc.
—Nothing More, Nothing Less. 176p. (Orig.). (gr. 5). 1993. pap. 3.50 (0-380-76636-1, Flare) Avon.
—One More Chance. 192p. (gr. 6 up). 1988. pap. 2.50 (0-380-75466-5, Flare) Avon.
McFann, Julia B. We Can Play. Wibright, Betsy, illus. 13p. (Orig.). (gr. 1). 1993. pap. text ed. write for info. (1-882225-15-5) Tott Pubns.
MacFarlan, Allan & MacFarlan, Paulette. Knotcraft: The Practical & Entertaining Art of Tying Knots. 186p. (gr. 6up). 1983. pap. 4.50 (0-486-24515-2) Dover.
McFarlan, Donald. White Queen: Mary Slessor. 1982. pap. 3.95 (0-87508-632-2) Chr Lit.
—Wizard of the Great Lakes. (gr. 5-9). 1979. pap. 3.95 (0-87508-631-4) Chr Lit.
MacFarlan, Paulette, jt. auth. see MacFarlan, Allan.
MacFarland, Cynthia. Cows in the Parlor. LC 89-14972. (Illus.). (ps-2). 1990. SBE 13.95 (0-689-31584-8, Atheneum Childrens Bks) Macmillan Child Grp.
McFarland, Cynthia. Hoofbeats: The Story of a Thoroughbred. LC 92-14255. (Illus.). 32p. (gr. 1-3). 1993. SBE 14.95 (0-689-31757-3, Atheneum Child Bk) Macmillan Child Grp.
McFarland, John. The Exploding Frog: & Other Fables from Aesop. Marshall, James, illus. (gr. 3 up). 1981. pap. 8.70i (0-685-03085-7, Pub. by Atlantic Pr) (0-316-55577-0) Little.
McFarland, Kathleen & Larkin, Judy. Colleen Marie. (Illus.). 56p. (Orig.). (ps). 1985. pap. write for info. (0-9621691-1-0, TX 1-705-162) B Bumpers Inc.
—Meet Colleen Marie. (Illus.). 22p. (Orig.). (ps). 1985. pap. write for info. (0-9621691-0-2, TX 1-650-724) B Bumpers Inc.
McFarland, Ken, jt. auth. see Holland, Kenneth J.
McFarland, Philip J., et al. Focus on People. (Illus.). (gr. 8). 1981. HM.
McFarland, Rhoda. Coping Through Assertiveness. rev. ed. (Illus.). 140p. (gr. 7-12). 1992. PLB 13.95 (0-8239-1374-0) Rosen Group.
—Coping Through Self-Esteem. Rosen, Ruth, ed. (gr. 7 up). 1988. PLB 13.95 (0-8239-0790-2) Rosen Group.
—Coping with Stigma. Rosen, Ruth, ed. (gr. 7-12). 1989. PLB 13.95 (0-8239-0998-0) Rosen Group.
—Coping with Substance Abuse. rev. ed. Rosen, Ruth, ed. 144p. (gr. 7 up). 1990. PLB 13.95 (0-8239-1135-7) Rosen Group.
—Drugs & Your Brothers & Sisters. rev. ed. (gr. 7-12). 1993. PLB 14.95 (0-8239-1745-1) Rosen Group.
—The World of Work. Rosen, Ruth, ed. (gr. 7-12). 1993. 12.95 (0-8239-1467-4) Rosen Group.
MacFarlane, Kee & Cunningham, Carolyn. Steps to Healthy Touching. Mortenson, Bob, illus. 144p. (Orig.). (gr. k-7). 1988. wkbk. 19.95 (0-685-20041-8, 1400) Kidsrights.
MacFarlane, Ruth. Making Your Own Nature Museum. Alred, Jean L., illus. LC 89-31826. 128p. (gr. 5 up). 1989. PLB 12.90 (0-531-10809-0) Watts.
McFarlane, Sheryl. Eagle Dreams. Lighburn, Ron, illus. LC 93-21232. 1994. write for info. (0-399-22695-8, Philomel Bks) Putnam Pub Group.
—Waiting for the Whales. Lightburn, Ron, illus. LC 92-25117. 32p. (ps-3). 1993. PLB 14.95 (0-399-22515-3, Philomel Bks) Putnam Pub Group.
McGee, Barbara. Counting Sheep. McGee, Barbara, illus. 24p. (gr. k-3). 1991. 12.95 (1-55037-157-6, Pub. by Annick CN); pap. 4.95 (1-55037-160-6, Pub. by Annick CN) Firefly Bks Ltd.
McGee, Brenda. Felita: A Study Guide. Friedland, Joyce & Kessler, Rikki, eds. (gr. 1-4). 1991. pap. text ed. 14.95 (0-88122-567-3) LRN Links.
McGee, Brenda H. Old Yeller: A Study Guide. Friedland, Joyce & Kessler, Rikki, eds. 21p. (gr. 9-12). 1990. pap. text ed. 14.95 (0-88122-415-4) Lrn Links.
—Rascal: A Study Guide. Friedland, Joyce & Kessler, Rikki, eds. 26p. (gr. 9-12). 1990. pap. text ed. 14.95 (0-88122-416-2) Lrn Links.
McGee, Cecil. Drama for Fun. LC 69-14368. (gr. k up). 1991. 10.95 (0-8054-7505-2) Broadman.

McGee, Charmayne. So Sings the Blue Deer. 160p. (gr. 3-7). 1994. SBE 14.95 (0-689-31888-X, Atheneum Child Bk) Macmillan Child Grp.
McGee, Eddie. The Emergency Handbook. Arico, Diane, ed. Barnes-Murphy, Rowan, illus. 176p. (gr. 8-12). 1985. lib. bdg. 9.79 (0-671-60484-8); pap. 4.95 (0-671-60483-X) S&S Trade.
McGee, Lea, jt. auth. see Jones, Candy.
McGee, Lee, jt. auth. see Jones, Candy.
McGee, Marni. The Alphabet Between. Dennis, Lynne, illus. LC 91-25489. 32p. (ps-1). 1994. SBE 14.95 (0-689-31753-0, Atheneum Child Bk) Macmillan Child Grp.
—Diego Columbus: Adventures on the High Seas. (Illus.). 128p. (Orig.). (gr. 3-7). 1992. pap. 6.99 (0-8007-5433-6) Revell.
—The Forest Child. Banfill, A. Scott, illus. LC 92-37148. 1994. 15.00 (0-671-86608-7, Green Tiger) S&S Trade.
—The Quiet Farmer. Dennis, Lynne, illus. LC 90-37930. 32p. (ps-1). 1991. SBE 12.95 (0-689-31678-X, Atheneum Child Bk) Macmillan Child Grp.
McGee, William & Kabes, Todd. The Basic Guide to Resume Writing & Job Interviews. 75p. (Orig.). 1989. pap. 6.50 (0-9622594-0-3) Advantage Video.
McGeorge, Constance W. Boomer's Big Day. Whyte, Mary, illus. LC 93-27273. 1994. 12.95 (0-8118-0526-3) Chronicle Bks.
McGill, Allyson. The Swedish Americans. Moynihan, Daniel P., intro. by. (Illus.). 112p. (gr. 5 up). 1988. lib. bdg. 17.95 (1-55546-135-2) Chelsea Hse.
Mcgill, Marcy. Louisa May Alcott. (Orig.). (gr. k-6). 1988. pap. 2.95 (0-440-40022-8, YB) Dell.
McGill, Ormond. Paper Magic: Creating Fantasies & Performing Tricks with Paper. LC 91-20996. (Illus.). 64p. (gr. 4-6). 1992. PLB 12.90 (1-56294-136-4) Millbrook Pr.
—Voice Magic: Secrets of Ventriloquism & Voice Conjuring. LC 91-21000. (Illus.). 64p. (gr. 4-6). 1992. PLB 12.90 (1-56294-137-2) Millbrook Pr.
MacGill-Callahan, Sheila. And Still the Turtle Watched. (ps-3). 1991. 14.95 (0-8037-0931-5); PLB 14.89 (0-8037-0932-3) Dial Bks Young.
—The Children of Lir. Spirin, Gennady, illus. LC 91-2712. 32p. (ps-3). 1993. 14.99 (0-8037-1121-2); PLB 14.99 (0-8037-1122-0) Dial Bks Young.
—The Seal Prince. Shi, Jihong, illus. LC 93-16248. 1995. 13.99 (0-8037-1486-6); PLB 13.89 (0-8037-1487-4) Dial Bks Young.
—When Solomon Was King. Johnson, Stephen T., illus. LC 93-28058. 1995. write for info. (0-8037-1589-7); PLB write for info. (0-8037-1590-0) Dial Bks Young.
McGillis, Kelly, read by see Andersen, Hans Christian.
McGilvray, Richard. Don't Climb out of the Window Tonight. Snow, Alan, illus. LC 92-28136. (ps-2). 1993. 13.99 (0-8037-1373-8) Dial Bks Young.
McGinley, Phyllis. Most Wonderful Doll in the World. 1990. 10.95 (0-590-43476-4) Scholastic Inc.
—The Most Wonderful Doll in the World. 1992. 3.95 (0-590-43477-2, Blue Ribbon Bks) Scholastic Inc.
McGinnis, Jeanne, jt. auth. see Eagen, Jane.
McGinnis, Lila S. The Twenty-Four Hour Genie. Sours, Michael, illus. LC 89-77786. 80p. (gr. 2-4). 1990. 12. 95 (0-8050-1303-2, Redfeather BYR) H Holt & Co.
—The Twenty-Four Hour Genie. Sours, Michael, illus. LC 89-77786. 80p. (gr. 2-4). 1991. pap. 4.95 (0-8050-1845-X, Redfeather BYR) H Holt & Co.
McGlothin, Bruce. Great Grooming for Guys. Rosen, Ruth, ed. (gr. 7-12). 1993. 12.95 (0-8239-1468-2) Rosen Group.
McGlothlen, Ken, et al, eds. see Schnurr, Carl.
McGovern, Michael R. Pennsylvania from Wilderness Colony to National Leader. (Illus.). 44p. (gr. 4-6). 1989. pap. text ed. 5.95 (0-939631-15-6) Thomas Publications.
McGough, Roger. The Lighthouse That Ran Away. (Illus.). 32p. (ps-2). 1992. 16.95 (0-370-31471-9, Pub. by Bodley Head UK) Trafalgar.
—The Stowaways. large type ed. (gr. 1-8). 1991. 13.95 (0-7451-1702-3, Galaxy Child Lrg Print) Chivers N Amer.
McGough, Roger, jt. ed. see Tucker, Nicholas.
McGovern. Pilgrims' First Thanksgiving. 1993. pap. 3.95 (0-590-46188-5) Scholastic Inc.
McGovern, Ann. Christopher Columbus. reissued ed. 1992. 4.95 (0-590-45765-9, 051) Scholastic Inc.
—The Defenders. 128p. (Orig.). (gr. 3-7). 1987. pap. 2.95 (0-590-43866-2) Scholastic Inc.
—Desert Beneath the Sea. (gr. 4-7). 1991. 13.95 (0-590-42638-9, Scholastic Hardcover) Scholastic Inc.
—Down Under, Down Under: Diving Adventures on the Great Barrier Reef. McGovern, Ann, et al, illus. LC 88-30530. 48p. (gr. 2-6). 1989. SBE 14.95 (0-02-765770-1, Macmillan Child Bk) Macmillan Child Grp.
—Drop Everything, It's D. E. A. R. Time! (ps-3). 1993. pap. 3.95 (0-590-45802-7) Scholastic Inc.
—Happy Silly Birthday to Me. Bremer, Sue, illus. 32p. (gr. k-3). 1994. pap. 2.50 (0-590-46365-9, Cartwheel Bks) Scholastic Inc.
—If You Grew up with Abraham Lincoln. Turkle, Brinton, illus. 64p. 1992. pap. 3.95 (0-590-45154-5) Scholastic Inc.
—If You Sailed on the May Flower. Devito, Anna, illus. 80p. 1991. pap. 3.95 (0-590-45161-8) Scholastic Inc.
—Nicholas Bentley Stoningpot III. reissue ed. De Paola, Tomie, illus. 32p. (ps-3). 1992. PLB 14.95 (1-56397-104-6) Boyds Mills Pr.

—Night Dive. Scheiner, Martin & Scheiner, James B., photos by. LC 84-7163. (Illus.). 64p. (gr. 2-5). 1984. RSBE 14.95 (0-02-765710-8, Macmillan Child Bk) Macmillan Child Grp.
—The Pilgrim's First Thanksgiving. Lasker, Je, illus. 48p. (gr. k-5). 1984. pap. 2.50 (0-590-40617-5) Scholastic Inc.
—Robin Hood of Sherwood Forest. 128p. (gr. 3-7). 1991. pap. 2.95 (0-590-45441-2) Scholastic Inc.
—The Secret Soldier: The Story of Deborah Sampson. Grifalconi, Ann, illus. LC 75-15819. 64p. (gr. 1-5). 1987. RSBE 13.95 (0-02-765780-9, Pub. by Four Winds Pr) Macmillan Child Grp.
—The Secret Soldier: The Story of Deborah Sampson. 64p. (Orig.). (gr. 3-7). 1990. pap. 2.75 (0-590-43052-1) Scholastic Inc.
—Shark Lady. (Illus.). 96p. (gr. k-3). 1991. pap. 2.50 (0-590-44771-8) Scholastic Inc.
—Shark Lady: True Adventures of Eugenie Clark. reissued ed. Chew, Ruth, illus. LC 78-22126. 96p. (gr. 3-7). 1984. 12.95 (0-02-767060-0, Four Winds) Macmillan Child Grp.
—Sharks. Tinkelman, Murray, illus. 48p. (gr. k-3). 1987. pap. 2.50 (0-590-41360-0) Scholastic Inc.
—Stone Soup. Pels, Winslow P., illus. 32p. (Orig.). (gr. k-2). 1986. pap. 2.50 (0-590-41602-2) Scholastic Inc.
—Swimming with Sea Lions. 48p. 1992. 13.95 (0-590-45282-7, Scholastic Hardcover) Scholastic Inc.
—Too Much Noise. (gr. k-3). 1967. 14.45 (0-395-18110-0) HM.
—Too Much Noise. Taback, Simms, illus. 48p. (gr. k-3). 1992. pap. 4.80 (0-395-62985-3, Sandpiper) HM.
—Wanted Dead Or Alive: The True Story of Harriet Tubman. 64p. (gr. 2-4). 1991. 3.95 (0-590-44212-0) Scholastic Inc.
McGovern, Ann, retold by. Aesop's Fables. 80p. (gr. 4-7). 1990. pap. 2.75 (0-590-43880-8) Scholastic Inc.
McGowan, Chris. Discover Dinosaurs: A Royal Ontario Museum Book. Holdcroft, Tina, illus. (gr. 3-7). 1993. pap. 10.95 (1-55074-048-2) Addison-Wesley.
—Discover Dinosaurs: Become a Dinosaur Detective. Holdcroft, Tina, illus. LC 92-42627. 96p. (gr. 4-7). 1993. pap. 9.95 (0-201-62267-X) Addison-Wesley.
McGowan, E. M. Horses & Ponies, A Photo-Fact Book. (Illus., Orig.). 1988. pap. 1.95 (0-942025-26-1) Kidsbks.
McGowan, Meredith, jt. auth. see McGowan, Tom.
McGowan, Tom & McGowan, Meredith. Children, Literature & Social Studies: Activities for the Intermediate Grades. (Illus.). 218p. (gr. 4-6). 1986. spiral bdg. 18.95 (0-938594-06-0) Spec Lit Pr.
McGowen, Tom. Chemistry: The Birth of a Science. LC 89-8986. (Illus.). 96p. (gr. 6-12). 1989. PLB 12.90 (0-531-10804-X) Watts.
—The Circulatory System: From Harvey to the Artificial Heart. Kline, M., ed. LC 88-231. (Illus.). 72p. (gr. 6-9). 1988. PLB 10.90 (0-531-10574-1) Watts.
—Epilepsy. LC 89-5755. (Illus.). 94p. (gr. 7-12). 1989. PLB 12.90 (0-531-10807-4) Watts.
—The Great Monkey Trial: Science Versus Fundamentalism in America. Gould, Stephen J., frwd. by. LC 90-33610. (Illus.). 128p. (gr. 9-12). 1990. PLB 13.90 (0-531-10965-8) Watts.
—The Korean War. (Illus.). 64p. (gr. 5-8). 1992. PLB 12. 90 (0-531-20040-X) Watts.
—The Korean War. (Illus.). 64p. (gr. 5-8). 1993. pap. 5.95 (0-531-15655-9) Watts.
—The Magical Fellowship. LC 90-45576. 160p. (gr. 5-9). 1991. 14.95 (0-525-67339-3, Lodestar Bks) Dutton Child Bks.
—The Magicians' Challenge. LC 89-32333. 144p. (gr. 5-9). 1989. 13.95 (0-525-67289-3, Lodestar Bks) Dutton Child Bks.
—A Question of Magic. 160p. (gr. 5-9). 1993. 14.99 (0-525-67380-6, Lodestar Bks) Dutton Child Bks.
—A Trial of Magic. 144p. (gr. 5-9). 1992. 15.00 (0-525-67376-8, Lodestar Bks) Dutton Child Bks.
—World War I. LC 92-28329. 1993. 12.90 (0-531-20149-X); pap. 5.95 (0-531-15660-5) Watts.
—World War II. LC 92-28328. 1993. 12.90 (0-531-20150-3) Watts.
—World War II. (Illus.). 64p. (gr. 5-8). 1993. pap. 5.95 (0-531-15661-3) Watts.
McGrain, Eleanore, jt. auth. see Bronstein, Leona B.
McGrath, Carol R., et al. Road Trip. 80p. (gr. 3-6). 1993. pap. text ed. 12.95 (0-944459-71-4) ECS Lrn Systs.
McGrath, Jim, jt. auth. see Doughty, Carolyn.
McGrath, Mary, jt. auth. see Pridmore, Saxby.
McGrath, Meggan. My Grapes. McGrath, Meggan, illus. LC 93-24057. 48p. (Orig.). 1993. pap. 16.95 (0-938586-99-8) Pfeifer-Hamilton.
McGrath, Patrick. The Lewis & Clark Expedition. LC 84-40381. (Illus.). 64p. (gr. 5 up). 1984. PLB 16.98 (0-382-06828-9); pap. 8.98 (0-382-09899-4) Silver Burdett Pr.
McGrath, Susan. How Animals Talk, 4 vols, No. 3. Crump, Donald J., ed. (Illus.). 32p. (ps-3). 1987. Set. 13.95 (0-87044-679-7); Set. lib. bdg. 16.95 (0-87044-684-3) Natl Geog.
—Your World of Pets. Crump, Donald J., ed. LC 85-7288. (Illus.). 104p. (gr. 3-8). 1985. 8.95 (0-87044-517-0); PLB 12.50 (0-87044-522-7) Natl Geog.
McGrath, Susan see Crump, Donald J.
McGrath-Heiss, Arleen. Barbara Bush. (Illus.). 128p. (gr. 5 up). 1992. lib. bdg. 17.95 (0-7910-1627-7) Chelsea Hse.

McGraw, Eloise. The Seventeenth Swap. 160p. (gr. 4-8). 1987. pap. 2.95 (0-8167-1050-3) Troll Assocs.
—The Striped Ships. LC 91-7729. 240p. (gr. 7 up). 1991. SBE 15.95 (0-689-50532-9, M K McElderry) Macmillan Child Grp.
—Tangled Webb. LC 92-27911. 160p. (gr. 5 up). 1993. SBE 13.95 (0-689-50573-6, M K McElderry) Macmillan Child Grp.
—The Trouble with Jacob. LC 87-22719. 288p. (gr. 4-7). 1988. SBE 14.95 (0-689-50447-0, M K McElderry) Macmillan Child Grp.
McGraw, Eloise J. The Golden Goblet. 248p. (gr. 5-9). 1986. pap. 4.99 (0-14-030335-9, Puffin) Puffin Bks.
—Mara, Daughter of the Nile. LC 85-567. 280p. (gr. 5-9). 1985. pap. 4.50 (0-14-031929-8, Puffin) Puffin Bks.
—Master Cornhill. LC 86-30247. 218p. (gr. 5-12). 1987. pap. 4.95 (0-14-032255-8, Puffin) Puffin Bks.
—Moccasin Trail. 256p. (gr. 5-9). 1986. pap. 4.99 (0-14-032170-5, Puffin) Puffin Bks.
—The Money Room. LC 90-26681. 192p. (gr. 7 up). 1991. pap. 3.95 (0-02-044484-2, Collier Young Ad) Macmillan Child Grp.
—A Really Weird Summer. LC 90-31542. 224p. (gr. 7 up). 1990. pap. 3.95 (0-02-044483-4, Collier Young Ad) Macmillan Child Grp.
—The Seventeenth Swap. LC 86-8791. 160p. (gr. 4-7). 1986. SBE 13.95 (0-689-50398-9, M K McElderry) Macmillan Child Grp.
McGraw, Eric. Population Growth. (Illus.). 48p. (gr. 5 up). 1987. Set. PLB 18.60 (0-317-60380-9); 13.95 s.p. (0-86592-276-4) Rourke Corp.
McGraw, Lauren, jt. auth. see Jarvis McGraw, Eloise.

McGraw, Robert. The Rogue & the Horse. McGraw, J. Darrin, illus. 32p. (Orig.). (ps-3). 1993. pap. 5.95 (0-9633385-0-1) Imagin Pr.
Can he really teach a horse to fly? The daring plan is Reynard's only chance to save himself from execution. But is it possible? Nobody thinks so - not even Reynard himself. Set in a kingdom "long ago & far away," this charming modern fairy tale has humor, excitement, & a happy ending with a moral: You CAN start life over again. It's sure to delight young readers for generations to come. To order contact: Imagination Press, 10430 Brookhurst Ave., San Diego, CA 92126. Phone: (619) 578-8444, FAX: (619) 578-8445. *Publisher Provided Annotation.*

McGraw, S. This Old New House. (Illus.). 32p. (ps-8). 1989. 12.95 (1-55037-035-9, Pub. by Annick CN); pap. 4.95 (1-55037-034-0, Pub. by Annick CN) Firefly Bks Ltd.
McGraw, Sheila. Je t'Aimera Toujours. (ps-3). 1988. pap. 4.95 (0-920668-49-6) Firefly Bks Ltd.

—Papier Mache for Kids. (Illus.). 72p. 1991. 17.95 (0-920668-92-5); pap. 9.95 (0-920668-93-3) Firefly Bks Ltd.
Papier Mache expert Sheila McGraw published PAPIER MACHE TODAY in 1990 to great reviews & strong sales. Now she has created a how-to-book for kids that explores this versatile & absorbing craft on levels that are comfortable for children. By experimenting & simplifying, she has created a variety of projects that fit the level of skill, the hand size, & the attention span of kids. All of the projects are bright, engaging & fun. They include monsters, masks, animals, jewellery, & more. While papier mache is the original "recycled" art form, this book takes it a step further, using paper towel & toilet paper tubes, newspaper, bleach bottles, twigs, plastic bags & many other "found" items that are usually doomed to the garbage bag. Each how-to step is matched with a clear full-color photograph. Directions are straightforward, concise, & simple. The introduction to each project features photos of many variations to stimulate the imagination. Each features a sidebar as well, reminding

readers of basic techniques & paste recipe. This alleviates the need to go hunting throughout the book with pasty hands. A chapter on finishing includes collage, decoupage, sponge painting & other painting techniques. Clear symbols denote where an adult's help or supervision may be required. *Publisher Provided Annotation.*

McGraw, Sheila & Cline, Paul. My Father's Hands. McGraw, Sheila, illus. 32p. 1992. 6.95 (0-9625261-6-9, Green Tiger) S&S Trade.
McGreevey, Carla & Kelinson, Roberta. Blooming Health: Fun Health Activities for Language Enrichment Based on Bloom's Taxonomy. 80p. (ps-3). 1991. pap. 14.95 (1-55999-204-2) LinguiSystems.
McGreevey, Carla & Kelinson, Roberta M. Blooming Math: Fun Activities for Beginning Math Based on Benjamin Bloom's Taxonomy. (ps-3). 1988. pap. 14.95 (1-55999-027-9) LinguiSystems.
Mac Gregor, Carol. Storybook Cookbook. Cruz, Ray, illus. (gr. 3-7). pap. 1.95 (0-13-850842-9, Pub. by Treehouse) P-H.
McGregor, Diana, et al. Fizzle, Bubble, Pop & WOW! Simple Science Experiments for Young Children. 63p. (ps-4). 1992. pap. 12.00 (0-9638539-0-2) Exper Print Pr.
MacGregor, Doug. MacGregor's Editorial Cartoons: A Collection of Cartoons Published in the Norwich Bulletin. MacGregor, Doug, illus. 192p. (Orig.). (gr. 6-8). 1988. pap. write for info. Norwich Bulletin.
MacGregor, Douglas. A Collection of MacGregor Editorial Cartoons from the Norwich Bulletin. MacGregor, Douglas, illus. Dodd, Christopher J., intro. by. LC 88-92529. 196p. (Orig.). (gr. 6-8). 1988. pap. text ed. 10.00 (0-9621270-0-0) Norwich Bulletin.
MacGregor, Ellen & Pantell, Dora. Miss Pickerell Meets Mr. H. U. M. new ed. Greer, Charles, illus. 160p. (gr. 2-6). 1974. o.p. (0-07-044577-X) McGraw.
MacGregor, Marilyn. On Top. MacGregor, Marilyn, illus. LC 87-12481. 32p. (gr. 5-7). 1988. 7.95 (0-688-07490-1); PLB 7.88 (0-688-07491-X, Morrow Jr Bks) Morrow Jr Bks.
McGregor, Merideth. Cowgirl. 32p. 1992. 14.95 (0-8027-8170-5); PLB 15.85 (0-8027-8171-3) Walker & Co.
MacGregor, Molly. Sky Goes on Forever: A Book about Death for Children. LC 89-51272. (ps). 1989. pap. 5.95 (0-918801-13-3) Dawn Horse Pr.
McGregor, Philip. The Rigger Black Book: A Shadowrun Sourcebook. Ippolito, Donna & Mulvihill, Sharon T., eds. Knutson, Dana & Nelson, Jim, illus. 136p. (Orig.). (gr. 7 up). 1991. pap. 15.00 (1-55560-169-3) FASA Corp.
MacGrory, Yvonne. Martha & the Ruby Ring. Myler, Terry, illus. 192p. (Orig.). (gr. 4-8). 1993. pap. 7.95 (0-947962-77-8) Irish Bks Media.
—The Secret of the Ruby Ring. Myler, Terry, illus. 160p. (Orig.). 1991. pap. 7.95 (0-947962-64-6, Pub. by Childrens Pr ER) Irish Bks Media.
McGuffey, William H. The Original McGuffey's Eclectic Series, 7 Vols. (gr. k-12). 1982. Repr. of 1837 ed. 89. 95 (0-88062-014-5) Mott Media.
McGugan, Jim. Josepha. (ps-3). 1993. 12.95 (0-88995-101-2, Pub. by Red Deer CN) Empire Pub Srvs.
McGuigan, Mary A. Cloud Dancer. LC 93-5562. 128p. (gr. 6-8). 1994. SBE 14.95 (0-684-19632-8, Scribners Young Read) Macmillan Child Grp.
McGuire, jt. auth. see Harvey.
McGuire, Barry & White, Logan. In the Midst of Wolves. LC 90-80612. 224p. (Orig.). 1990. pap. 8.95 (0-89107-572-0, Crossway Bks) Good News.
McGuire, Donald D. The Country Kids' Encounter with Buttsy. 1992. 7.95 (0-533-10346-0) Vantage.
McGuire, J. Victor. No Negatives: A Positive Guide to Successful Leadership. Prado, Jan, ed. Giblin, Tom, pref. by. 130p. (Orig.). (gr. 9-12). 1989. pap. 7.95 wkbk. (0-685-26846-2) Spice Pr.
McGuire, John E., jt. auth. see Freeman, Chester D.
McGuire, Kevin. Woodworking for Kids: Forty Fabulous, Fun, & Useful Things for Kids to Make. LC 93-20489. (Illus.). 160p. (gr. 4 up). 1993. 19.95 (0-8069-0429-1, Pub. by Lark Bks) Sterling.
McGuire, Leslie. Anastasia: Czarina or Fake? Opposing Viewpoints. LC 89-35584. (Illus.). 112p. (gr. 5-8). 1989. 14.95 (0-89908-074-X) Greenhaven.
—Big Dan's Moving Van. Mathieu, Joe, illus. LC 90-4417. 32p. (Orig.). (ps-1). 1993. pap. 2.25 (0-679-80565-6) Random Bks Yng Read.
—Catherine the Great. (Illus.). 112p. (gr. 5 up). 1986. lib. bdg. 17.95 (0-87754-577-4) Chelsea Hse.
—Death & Illness. (Illus.). 64p. (gr. 7 up). 1990. lib. bdg. 17.27 (0-86593-079-1); lib. bdg. 12.95 s.p. (0-685-46439-3) Rourke Corp.
—Disney Little Q: The Little Mermaid's Treasure Hunt. (ps). pap. 4.95 (0-8431-2865-8) Price Stern.
—Eureeka's Castle: Magellan Saves the Day. Brannon, Tom, illus. (ps-k). 1991. pap. 1.25 (0-307-11512-7, Golden Pr) Western Pub.
—Is There Life after Sixth Grade? Henry, Paul, illus. LC 89-20615. 96p. (gr. 4-6). 1990. PLB 9.89 (0-8167-1706-0); pap. text ed. 2.95 (0-8167-1707-9) Troll Assocs.

—Miss Mopp's Lucky Day. Silver, Jody, illus. LC 81-4879. 48p. (ps-3). 1982. 5.95 (0-8193-1061-1); PLB 5.95 (0-8193-1062-X) Parents.
—Napoleon Bonaparte. (Illus.). 112p. (gr. 5 up). 1986. lib. bdg. 17.95 (0-87754-554-5) Chelsea Hse.
—Suicide. (Illus.). 64p. (gr. 7 up). 1990. lib. bdg. 17.27 (0-86593-069-4); lib. bdg. 12.95s.p. (0-685-46444-X) Rourke Corp.
—The Terrible Truth about Third Grade. Henderson, David F., illus. LC 90-26788. 96p. (gr. 2-4). 1992. lib. bdg. 9.89 (0-8167-2382-6); pap. text ed. 2.95 (0-8167-2383-4) Troll Assocs.
—This Farm Is a Mess. McGuire, Leslie, illus. LC 80-25811. 48p. (ps-3). 1981. 5.95 (0-8193-1045-X); PLB 5.95 (0-8193-1046-8) Parents.
—The Three P. M. Club, No. 1: Get Rich Quick! 1992. pap. 3.50 (0-425-12968-3) Berkley Pub.
—Three P.M. Club, No. 2: My Hair Turned Green & I Feel Blue. 160p. (Orig.). (gr. 4-7). 1992. pap. 3.50 (0-425-12653-6) Berkley Pub.
—Victims. LC 91-11041. 64p. (gr. 5-7). 1991. 12.95s.p. (0-86593-120-8) Rourke Corp.

McGuire, Leslie, jt. auth. see Farrington, Liz.

McGuire, Paula. It Won't Happen to Me: Teenagers Talk about Pregnancy. LC 82-72754. 224p. (gr. 7 up). 1983. 14.95 (0-385-29244-9); pap. 6.95 (0-685-06445-X) Delacorte.
—It Won't Happen to Me: Teenagers Talk about Pregnancy. Ryan, George M., frwd. by. 1923. pap. 6.95 (0-385-29201-5, Delta) Delacorte.
—Putting It Together: Teenagers Talk about Family Breakup. LC 86-29238. 224p. (gr. 7 up). 1987. pap. 15.95 (0-385-29564-2) Delacorte.

McGuire, Paula, jt. auth. see Garver, Susan.

McGuire, Richard. The Orange Book. (Illus.). 32p. (ps-1). 1993. 12.95 (0-87663-798-5) Universe.

McGuire, William. The Final Four (NCAA Basketball) 32p. (gr. 4). 1990. PLB 14.95s.p. (0-88682-310-2) Creative Ed.
—Southeast Asians. LC 90-12996. (Illus.). (gr. 5-10). 1991. PLB 13.40 (0-531-11108-3) Watts.
—The Stanley Cup. 32p. (gr. 4). 1990. PLB 14.95s.p. (0-88682-316-1) Creative Ed.
—The Summer Olympics. 32p. (gr. 4). 1990. PLB 14.95s.p. (0-88682-318-8) Creative Ed.
—The World Series. 32p. (gr. 4). 1990. PLB 14.95s.p. (0-88682-313-7) Creative Ed.

McGuire-Turcotte, Casey A. How Honu the Turtle Got His Shell. (Illus.). 32p. (gr. 2-4). 1990. PLB 29.28 clipper (0-8172-2788-1) Raintree Steck-V.
—How Honu the Turtle Got His Shell. Sakahara, Dick, illus. 30p. (gr. k up). 1991. PLB 17.96 (0-8172-2783-0); pap. 3.95 (0-8114-4304-3) Raintree Steck-V.

Machac, Kathy, jt. auth. see McWaid, Helen.

Machado, Antonio A., et al. Our Lady at Fatima: Prophecies of Tragedy or Hope for America & the World? LC 85-70673. (Illus.). 128p. (Orig.). (gr. 8). 1986. pap. 8.95 (1-877-90510-0) TFFACC.

MacHaffie, Ingeborg. Henry: The Heron. Blumenstein, Amy, illus. Mouck, Mike, frwd. by. (Illus.). 55p. (Orig.). (ps). 1988. lib. bdg. 7.95 (0-9609374-3-9) Skribent.

MacHale, Des, jt. auth. see Sloane, Paul.

MacHale, Don. East of the Sun, West of the Moon. Flesher, Vivienne, illus. LC 91-15220. 40p. (gr. k up). 1992. pap. 14.95 (0-88708-192-4, Rabbit Ears); incl. cass. 19.95 (0-88708-193-2, Rabbit Ears) Picture Bk Studio.

Machamer, Gene. The Illustrated Black American Profiles. Sager, Linda C., ed. LC 90-82937. (Illus.). 192p. (Orig.). 1991. pap. 9.95 (0-9627369-0-2) Carlisle Pr.
—The Illustrated Hispanic American Profiles. Acevedo, Maria, ed. LC 93-91377. (Illus.). 176p. (Orig.). 1993. pap. 12.00 (0-9627369-2-9) Carlisle Pr.

Machan, Wayne & Bruggen, Bill. The Corvair, 1960-1969. LC 89-63378. (Illus.). 128p. (Orig.). 1991. pap. 19.95 (0-929758-07-2) Beeman Jorgensen.

McHargue, Georgess. Beastie. (gr. 4-7). 1992. pap. 14.00 (0-385-30589-3) Doubleday.
—The Beasts of Never. Bozzo, Frank, illus. LC 86-29374. 128p. (gr. 7 up). 1987. pap. 14.95 (0-385-29573-1) Delacorte.
—The Horseman's Word. LC 80-68736. 272p. (gr. 7 up). 1981. pap. 9.95 (0-385-28472-1) Delacorte.
—The Horseman's Word. (gr. k-12). 1988. pap. 2.95 (0-440-20126-8, LFL) Dell.
—See You Later, Crocodile. 192p. (gr. 5-9). 1988. 14.95 (0-440-50052-4) Delacorte.
—The Turquoise Toad Mystery. LC 81-69664. 160p. (gr. 4-6). 1982. 9.95 (0-385-29057-8) Delacorte.

MacHaster, Eve B. God Comforts His People. Converse, James, illus. LC 95-835. 176p. (Orig.). (gr. 3 up). 1985. pap. 5.95 (0-8361-3393-5) Herald Pr.

McHattie, Grace. Going Live! Cat Book. (Illus.). 94p. 1992. pap. 3.95 (0-563-20880-5, BBC-Parkwest) Parkwest Pubns.

McHenry, Ellen J. Inside a Freight Train. McHenry, Ellen J., illus. LC 92-23225. (ps-3). 1993. 9.99 (0-525-65099-7, Cobblehill Bks) Dutton Child Bks.

McHenry, Martha J. Time to Read: Short Stories for Young People. McManus, Joseph F., ed. & illus. 96p. 1991. 12.50 (0-929443-06-3) Quali-Type.

Machiavelli, Niccolo. Prince. Detmold, C. E., intro. by. (gr. 11 up). 1965. pap. 2.25 (0-8049-0056-6, CL-56) Airmont.

—Prince. Bull, George, tr. (Orig.). (gr. 9 up). 1961. pap. 3.50 (0-14-044107-7, Penguin Classics) Viking Penguin.

Machlas, Sally, jt. auth. see Field, Nancy.
Machlis, Sally, jt. auth. see Field, Nancy.

Machotka, Hana. Breathtaking Noses. Machotka, Hana, photos by. LC 91-12252. (Illus.). 32p. (gr. k up). 1992. 15.00 (0-688-09526-7); PLB 14.93 (0-688-09527-5) Morrow Jr Bks.
—Magic Ring: A Year With The Big Apple Circus. Machotka, Hana, illus. Binder, Paul, intro. by. LC 87-28230. (Illus.). 80p. (gr. 3 up). 1988. 13.95 (0-688-07449-9); pap. 8.95 (0-688-08222-X, Pub. by Beech Tree Bks) Morrow.
—Outstanding Outsides. LC 92-19517. (Illus.). 32p. (gr. k up). 1993. 15.00 (0-688-11752-X); PLB 14.96 (0-688-11753-8) Morrow Jr Bks.
—Pasta Factory. Machotka, Hana, illus. LC 92-4333. 32p. (ps-3). 1992. 14.45 (0-395-60197-5) HM.
—Terrific Tails. LC 93-17687. 1994. write for info. (0-688-04562-6); PLB write for info. (0-688-04563-4) Morrow Jr Bks.
—What Do You Do at a Petting Zoo? Machotka, Hana, photos by. LC 89-34478. (Illus.). 32p. (gr. k up). 1990. 13.95 (0-688-08737-X); PLB 13.88 (0-688-08738-8, Morrow Jr Bks) Morrow Jr Bks.
—What Neat Feet! Machotka, Hana, photos by. LC 90-40886. (Illus.). 32p. (gr. k up). 1991. 13.95 (0-688-09474-0); PLB 13.88 (0-688-09475-9, Morrow Jr Bks) Morrow Jr Bks.

MacHovec, et al. The Aware Bears. Downey, John & Cohen, Lois, eds. (Illus., Orig.). (gr. k-2). 1991. Set. pap. 39.50 (0-89976-236-0) Oceana Educ Comm.

Macht, Norm. Babe Ruth. Murray, Jim, intro. by. (Illus.). 64p. (gr. 3 up). 1991. lib. bdg. 14.95 (0-7910-1189-5) Chelsea Hse.
—Christy Mathewson. Murray, Jim, intro. by. (Illus.). 64p. (gr. 3 up). 1991. lib. bdg. 14.95 (0-7910-1182-8) Chelsea Hse.
—Frank Robinson. Murray, Jim, intro. by. (Illus.). 64p. (gr. 3 up). 1991. lib. bdg. 14.95 (0-7910-1187-9) Chelsea Hse.
—Jimmie Foxx. Murray, Jim, intro. by. (Illus.). 64p. (gr. 3 up). 1991. PLB 14.95 (0-7910-1175-5) Chelsea Hse.
—Satchel Paige. Murray, Jim, intro. by. (Illus.). 64p. (gr. 3 up). 1991. lib. bdg. 14.95 (0-7910-1185-2) Chelsea Hse.

Macht, Norman L. Christopher Columbus. (Illus.). 72p. (gr. 3-5). 1992. lib. bdg. 12.95 (0-7910-1752-4) Chelsea Hse.
—Christopher Columbus: Junior World Biographies. (gr. 4-7). 1992. pap. 4.95 (0-7910-1953-5) Chelsea Hse.
—Cy Young. (Illus.). 64p. (gr. 3 up). 1992. PLB 14.95 (0-7910-1196-8) Chelsea Hse.
—Jim Abbott: Baseball Star. LC 93-31838. (Illus.). 1994. 18.95 (0-7910-2079-7, Am Art Analog); pap. write for info. (0-7910-2092-4, Am Art Analog) Chelsea Hse.
—Lou Gehrig. (Illus.). 64p. (gr. 3 up). 1992. lib. bdg. 14.95 (0-7910-1176-3) Chelsea Hse.
—Roberto Clemente: Baseball Great. LC 93-26178. (Illus.). 1993. 13.95 (0-7910-1764-8, Am Art Analog); pap. write for info. (0-7910-2541-1) Chelsea Hse.
—Sandra Day O'Connor. (Illus.). 80p. (gr. 3-5). 1992. lib. bdg. 12.95 (0-7910-1756-7) Chelsea Hse.
—Sojourner Truth: Crusader for Civil Rights. (Illus.). 80p. 1993. 13.95 (0-7910-1754-0, Am Art Analog); pap. 4.95 (0-7910-1998-5, Am Art Analog) Chelsea Hse.
—Ty Cobb. (Illus.). 64p. (gr. 3 up). 1992. lib. bdg. 14.95 (0-685-48322-3) Chelsea Hse.

Macht, Philip. Circles in the Sand. Rosenthal, Linda, illus. LC 84-90597. 64p. (gr. 7 up). 1985. 12.95 (0-930339-00-2) Maxrom Pr.
—Great Mountain. Field, Ann, illus. 30p. (Orig.). 1991. pap. 15.00 (0-930339-01-0) Maxrom Pr.
—Wonderpup. Faust, Jeff, illus. 40p. (gr. 4-6). 1992. 15.00 (0-930339-03-7) Maxrom Pr.

McHugh, Christopher. Animals. LC 93-43265. (Illus.). 32p. (gr. 4-6). 1993. 14.95g (1-56847-025-8) Thomson Lrning.
—Faces. LC 93-20400. 32p. (gr. 4-6). 1993. 14.95 (1-56847-071-1) Thomson Lrning.
—Food. LC 93-20399. 32p. (gr. 4-6). 1993. 14.95 (1-56847-070-3) Thomson Lrning.
—People at Work. LC 93-20405. 32p. (gr. 4-6). 1993. 14.95 (1-56847-111-4) Thomson Lrning.
—Town & Country. LC 93-20401. 32p. (gr. 4-6). 1993. 14.95 (1-56847-110-6) Thomson Lrning.
—Water. LC 92-43266. (Illus.). 32p. (gr. 4-6). 1993. 14.95g (1-56847-024-X) Thomson Lrning.

McHugh, Denise. Discover George Mason: Home, State, & Country: A Sampler of Lesson Plans, Activities, & Resources for Teachers of Students in Grades 3 Through 6. rev. ed. Sarecky, Melody, illus. vi, 101p. (gr. 3-6). 1993. pap. 9.50 (1-884085-02-4) Bd Regents.
—George Mason, Planter & Patriot: A Sampler of Lesson Plans Exploring Primary Sources for Teachers of Students in Grades 7 Through 12. Sarecky, Melody, illus. viii, 200p. (Orig.). (gr. 7-12). 1992. pap. 14.00 (1-884085-00-8) Bd Regents.

McHugh, Elisabet. Beethoven's Cat. (gr. k-6). 1991. pap. 3.50 (0-440-40398-7) Dell.
—The Real Thing. 1991. pap. 2.99 (0-553-29186-6) Bantam.
—Wiggie Wins the West. (gr. 4-7). 1991. pap. 3.25 (0-440-40457-6) Dell.

McHugh, Fiona. Of Corsets & Secrets & True, True Love. (gr. 4-7). 1993. pap. 3.99 (0-553-48040-5) Bantam.

—Song of the Night, No. 3. (gr. 3-7). 1992. pap. 3.99 (0-553-48029-4, Skylark) Bantam.

McHugh, Joe. Better Than Money: Tales to Treasure for a Lifetime. McHugh, Paula, illus. LC 91-70909. 125p. (gr. 1-8). 1991. 11.95g (0-9619943-1-2) Catalpa Pr.

Machutta, Stephen T., Sr. Acne? Try Nature's Remedy. LC 88-92625. 90p. (Orig.). (gr. 3-11). 1991. pap. 9.95 (0-9621489-0-3) New Begin Life.

Macias, Benjamin. One Hundred One Bible Riddles for All Ages. Macias, Daniel, illus. 112p. (Orig.). 1993. pap. 7.95 (0-9638277-0-7); pap. 7.95 (0-9638277-1-5) Fam of God.
This Bible riddle book is the most complete collection of fully illustrated Bible riddles for children, adolescents & adults. Each humorous Bible riddle has its own unique, creative & vivid illustration that perfectly describes the riddle. These Bible riddles have been shared with young & old & all agree that it is a treasure of wit & humor for ages to come. You will certainly find this Bible riddle book worthy of sharing with those who also have an appreciation for wholesome & clean riddles. In addition, this witty book can be used in children's activities & programs & young people can also incorporate it in their social activities. Parents can also share it as a gift to their children, knowing satisfactorily that the riddles are children oriented. This Bible riddle indeed is for all ages & ages to come. Family of God Publishing House, P.O. Box 758, Vista, CA 92083-0758. (619) 598-3629, FAX (619) 966-0312.
Publisher Provided Annotation.

Macias, Regina, ed. see Burrill, Richard.

McIlhaney, Joe S., Jr. Sexuality & Sexually Transmitted Diseases: A Doctor Confronts the Myth of "Safe" Sex. LC 90-649. 176p. (Orig.). 1990. pap. 8.99 (0-8010-6274-8) Baker Bk.

McIlhenny, Robyn. Our Baby. Smith, Craig, illus. LC 92-27268. 1993. 3.75 (0-383-03646-1) SRA Schl Grp.

McIlveen, J. F. Fundamentals of Weather & Climate. (gr. 5 up). 1991. pap. 39.95 (0-442-31476-0) Van Nos Reinhold.

McIndoo, Ethel. Discover Girls in Action. (SPA.). 22p. (Orig.). (gr. 4-6). 1988. pap. text ed. 1.50 (0-936625-74-0) Womans Mission Union.
—Discover Girls in Action. 22p. (Orig.). (gr. 4-6). 1988. pap. text ed. 1.50 (0-936625-41-4) Womans Mission Union.
—Freeda Harris: Woman of Prayer. LC 84-2978. (gr. 4-6). 1984. 5.95 (0-8054-4286-3, 4242-86) Broadman.
—Missions Adventures 1. Massey, Barbara, ed. 32p. (Orig.). (gr. 1-6). 1991. pap. text ed. 1.50 (1-56309-026-0) Womans Mission Union.
—Missions Adventures 2. Massey, Barbara, ed. 32p. (Orig.). (gr. 1-6). 1991. pap. text ed. 1.50 (1-56309-027-9) Womans Mission Union.
—Missions Adventures 3. Massey, Barbara, ed. 32p. (Orig.). (gr. 1-6). 1991. pap. text ed. 1.50 (1-56309-028-7) Womans Mission Union.
—Missions Adventures 4. Massey, Barbara, ed. 32p. (Orig.). (gr. 1-6). 1991. pap. text ed. 1.50 (1-56309-029-5) Womans Mission Union.
—Missions Adventures 5. Massey, Barbara, ed. 32p. (Orig.). (gr. 1-6). 1991. pap. text ed. 1.50 (1-56309-030-9) Womans Mission Union.
—Missions Adventures 6. Massey, Barbara, ed. 32p. (Orig.). (gr. 1-6). 1991. pap. text ed. 1.50 (1-56309-031-7) Womans Mission Union.

McInerney, Claire. Find It! The Inside Story at Your Library. Pulver, Harry, illus. 56p. (gr. 4-6). 1989. PLB 14.95 (0-8225-2425-2) Lerner Pubns.
—Tracking the Facts: How to Develop Research Skills. Pulver, Harry, illus. 64p. (gr. 4 up). 1990. PLB 14.95 (0-8225-2426-0) Lerner Pubns.

McInerney, Judith W. Judge Benjamin: The Superdog Gift. Morrill, Leslie, illus. 128p. (gr. 2-4). 1987. pap. 2.95 (0-8167-1043-0) Troll Assocs.
—Judge Benjamin: The Superdog Rescue. Morrill, Leslie, illus. (gr. 4-6). pap. 2.75 (0-317-66178-7, Minstrel Bks) PB.

McInnes, Celia. Projects for Spring & Holiday Activities. Young, Richard G., ed. Walker, Malcom, illus. LC 88-33514. 32p. (gr. 3-5). 1989. PLB 15.93 (0-944483-40-2) Garrett Ed Corp.
—Projects for Summer & Holiday Activities. Young, Richard G., ed. Wheele, Stephen, illus. LC 89-11791. 32p. (gr. 3-5). 1989. PLB 15.93 (0-944483-39-9) Garrett Ed Corp.

McIntire, Donald. The Pemaquid Loon from Temple. Bull, Kris F., illus. 1988. pap. 5.99 (*0-317-92307-2*) Herit Print Co.

McIntire, Jamie. Santa's Christmas Surprise. Henry, Steve, illus. LC 93-24843. (gr. k-3). 1993. pap. text ed. 2.95 (*0-8167-3257-4*) Troll Assocs.

MacIntosh, Craig & Sack, Steve. Professor Doodle's Upside Down Sideways Puzzle Book. (Illus.). (gr. 4-7). 1992. pap. 4.95 (*0-941263-56-8*) Tribune FL.

McIntosh, Scott. How to Be an Angel: The Book the Devil Did Not Want Published. (Illus.). 80p. (Orig.). 1993. pap. 9.95 (*0-9632879-1-5*) McIntosh Pubns.

McIntyre, Rick. Grizzly Cub: Five Years in the Life of a Bear. LC 90-35587. (Illus.). 104p. (Orig.). (gr. 4 up). 1990. pap. 14.95 (*0-88240-373-7*) Alaska Northwest.

McIntyre, Vonda N. Dreamsnake. 320p. 1986. pap. 3.95 (*0-440-11729-1*) Dell.

Mack, Grace C. My Special Book of Jewish Celebrations. (Illus.). 36p. (Orig.). (ps-2). 1984. pap. 8.95 (*0-9602338-4-9*) Rockdale Ridge.

Mack, Jacqueline. Tales about Tails. Halloway, Jan, illus. 24p. (ps-k). 1985. 10.95 (*0-88625-089-7*) Durkin Hayes Pub.

Mack, Karen. The Magical Adventures of Sun Beams. Johnson, Tani B., illus. 32p. (ps-4). 1992. pap. 5.95 (*0-9631644-0-6*) Shooting Star.

Mack, Maynard, ed. see Shakespeare, William.

Mack, Stan. The King's Cat Is Coming. Mack, Stan, illus. (ps-1). 1976. lib. bdg. 4.99 (*0-394-93302-8*) Pantheon.

—Ten Bears in My Bed: A Goodnight Countdown. Mack, Stan, illus. LC 74-151. 32p. (ps-1). 1974. lib. bdg. 11.99 (*0-394-92902-0*) Pantheon.

Mackall, Dandi D. Christmas Gifts That Didn't Need Wrapping. Mathers, Dawn, illus. LC 89-82553. 32p. (ps-2). 1990. pap. 5.99 (*0-8066-2466-3*, 9-2466) Augsburg Fortress.

—Kay's Birthday Surprise. Mathers, Dawn, illus. LC 89-82554. 32p. (ps-2). 1990. pap. 5.99 (*0-8066-2467-1*, 9-2467) Augsburg Fortress.

Mackall, Phyllis, ed. see Barkey, Tom.

Mackan, Donald, tr. see Sehlin, Gunhild.

McKaughan, Larry. Why Are Your Fingers Cold? Keenan, Joy D., illus. LC 92-16549. 32p. (Orig.). (ps-1). 1992. 14.95 (*0-8361-3604-7*) Herald Pr. Childlike questions & reassuring answers are complemented by exquisite illustrations. Several family groupings including African American & Caucasian people appear, as children & adults interact. This delightful picture book helps children to become more sensitive to the needs of others. It fosters a strong sense of extended family & community. For children ages 2 to 6 & the adults that love them. *Publisher Provided Annotation.*

McKay, Bob. How to Draw Funny People. McKay, Bob, illus. LC 81-69658. 32p. (gr. 2-6). 1981. PLB 10.65 (*0-89375-688-1*); pap. text ed. 1.95 (*0-89375-408-0*) Troll Assocs.

MacKay, Claire. The Toronto Story. Wales, Johnny, illus. 112p. (Orig.). (gr. 5 up). 1991. 34.95 (*1-55037-137-1*, Pub. by Annick CN) Firefly Bks Ltd.; pap. 24.95 (*1-55037-135-5*, Pub. by Annick CN) Firefly Bks Ltd.

McKay, David. American Politics & Society. 3rd ed. LC 93-7211. (Illus.). 340p. (gr. 10 up). 1993. 44.95 (*0-631-18813-4*); pap. text ed. 19.95 (*0-631-18814-2*) Blackwell Pubs.

—Space Science Projects for Young Scientists. 1989. pap. 5.95 (*0-531-15134-4*) Watts.

McKay, David, jt. auth. see Smith, Bruce.

McKay, David W. & Smith, Bruce G. Space Science Projects for Young Scientists. LC 86-7745. (Illus.). 128p. (gr. 7-12). 1986. PLB 13.90 (*0-531-10244-0*) Watts.

McKay, George, jt. auth. see McKay, Louise.

McKay, Hilary. The Exiles. McKeating, Eileen, illus. LC 91-38220. 208p. (gr. 4-7). 1992. SBE 14.95 (*0-689-50555-8*, M K McElderry) Macmillan Child Grp.

MacKay, Judy F. Tales of a Nuf in the Land of Doon. Langley, William A., illus. 84p. (Orig.). (gr. 4-7). 1992. pap. 9.95 perfect bdg. (*1-882748-00-X*) MacKay-Langley. McKay-Langley Publishing is dedicated to producing children's books that educate, enlighten & provoke laughter. TALES OF A NUF IN THE LAND OF DOON is their Premier Edition. The six-color cover introduces the reader to the Land of Doon: a land filled with love & light, & just a hint of darkness in the form of chocolate-eating Murcs & their leader Tsol Eno. The story begins with a struggling, cantankerous Nuf (Htrim) who has been sent to find a boy, a creature unknown to him. As the story unfolds, Htrim & the boy (Anthony) discover that their destinies are intertwined. With great difficulty Anthony succeeds in adjusting to Htrim: who turns his ears off & on at will so that he can "go within"; who is not an elf; who turns the color of whatever vegetable he is eating. With the help of Xela the Dream Merchant, Uncle Twinkle, Htrim's mentor & the colorful Nam Wobniar, a prophecy is fulfilled; a Nuf learns what love is; a boy learns what inner peace is; & the reader learns that children's literature can be non-violent, & still be an adventure in reading. *Publisher Provided Annotation.*

MacKay, Kathryn. Ontario. (Illus.). 144p. (gr. 5-8). 1992. PLB 26.60 (*0-516-06614-5*) Childrens.

McKay, Louise & McKay, George. Marny's Ride with the Wind. Smetana, Margaret, illus. (gr. k-3). 1979. 6.95 (*0-934986-00-2*) New Harbinger.

McKay, Robert. The Troublemaker. 192p. (gr. 7 up). 1972. pap. 1.50 (*0-440-99122-6*, LFL) Dell.

McKay, Sharon & MacLeod, David. Chalk Around the Block: A Somerville House Book. Mets, Marilyn, illus. LC 92-41495. 48p. 1993. incl. 5 pieces of sidewalk chalk 8.95 (*0-8362-4502-4*) Andrews & McMeel.

McKay, Sindy. Color Crazy. Alchemy II, Inc., illus. 26p. (ps up). 1987. 12.95 (*1-55578-609-X*) Worlds Wonder.

—Something's Fishy. Alchemy II, Inc., illus. 26p. (ps up). 1986. 12.95 (*1-55578-610-3*) Worlds Wonder.

McKay, Sindy & Swerdlove, Larry. Radio Station K-E-R-M. Alchemy II, Inc., illus. 26p. (ps up). 1987. 12.95 (*1-55578-607-3*) Worlds Wonder.

McKay, William. Funny Business. LC 88-45879. 144p. (Orig.). (gr. 5 up). 1989. pap. 2.95 (*0-394-89981-4*) Knopf Bks Yng Read.

MacKay-Robinson, Christina. Edd the Astronaut. Ellis, Andy, illus. 32p. (gr. k-3). 1992. pap. 4.95 (*0-563-36062-3*, BBC-Parkwest) Parkwest Pubns.

—Edd's Ghost Story. Johnson, Paul, illus. 32p. (gr. k-3). 1992. pap. 4.95 (*0-563-36063-1*, BBC-Parkwest) Parkwest Pubns.

MacKay-Robinson, Christina & Faulkner, Keith. Edd the Duck in Storyland. Johnson, Paul, illus. 32p. (gr. k-3). 1992. 12.95 (*0-563-36046-1*, BBC-Parkwest) Parkwest Pubns.

McKeage, Jeff. Hillmen of the Trollshaws. (Illus.). 36p. (gr. 10-12). 1984. pap. 7.00 (*0-915795-24-8*, 8040) Iron Crown Ent Inc.

—The Lost Realm of Cardolan. Fenlon, Peter C., Jr., ed. 64p. (Orig.). (gr. 10-12). 1987. pap. 12.00 (*0-915795-95-7*, 3700) Iron Crown Ent Inc.

—Raiders of Cardolan. Charlton, Coleman, ed. Horne, Daniel, illus. 32p. (Orig.). (gr. 10-12). 1988. pap. 6.00 (*1-55806-005-7*, 8108) Iron Crown Ent Inc.

McKeage, Jeff & Fenlon, Peter C., Jr. Woses of the Black Wood. McBride, Angus, illus. 32p. (gr. 10-12). 1987. pap. 6.00 (*0-915795-99-X*, 8107) Iron Crown Ent Inc.

McKeage, Jeffrey. Dark Mage of Rhudaur. Ney, Jessica, ed. McBride, Angus & Danforth, Liz, illus. 40p. (Orig.). (gr. 12). 1989. pap. 7.00 (*1-55806-072-3*, 8013) Iron Crown Ent Inc.

McKean, Barb. Birds. Migliore, Ron, illus. 32p. (gr. 3-7). 1985. pap. 3.50 (*0-88625-116-8*) Durkin Hayes Pub.

—Wild Animals. Rowden, Rick & Winik, J. T., illus. 32p. (gr. 3-7). 1985. pap. 3.50 (*0-88625-117-6*) Durkin Hayes Pub.

McKean, Thomas. The Haunted Circus. LC 92-32713. 176p. (gr. 4-7). 1993. pap. 13.00 JRT (*0-671-72998-5*, S&S BFYR) S&S Trade.

—Hooray for Grandma Jo! Demarest, Chris, illus. LC 93-16376. (ps-6). 1994. 14.00 (*0-517-57842-5*); PLB 14.99 (*0-517-57843-3*) Crown Bks Yng Read.

—The Search for Sara Sanderson. 160p. (gr. 3-7). 1987. pap. 2.50 (*0-380-75295-6*, Camelot) Avon.

—Secret of the Seven Willows. LC 91-4447. 160p. 1991. pap. 12.95 3-pc. bdg. (*0-671-72997-7*) S&S Trade.

—Secret of the Seven Willows. LC 91-4447. 160p. (gr. 4-7). 1993. pap. 2.95 (*0-671-86690-7*, Half Moon Bks) S&S Trade.

McKee, Chuck & McKee, David. The Mystery of the Blue Arrows. (Illus.). 32p. (ps-1). 1991. 15.95 (*0-86264-267-1*, Pub. by Andersen Pr UK) Trafalgar.

McKee, David. Elmer. McKee, David, illus. LC 89-2285. 32p. (ps-2). 1989. Repr. of 1968 ed. 12.95 (*0-688-09171-7*); PLB 12.88 (*0-688-09172-5*) Lothrop.

—Elmer Again. Pearson, Susan, ed. LC 91-38901. (Illus.). 32p. (ps up). 1992. reinforced bdg. 14.00 (*0-688-11596-9*) Lothrop.

—King Rollo's Letter: And Other Stories. (Illus.). 28p. (gr. k-3). 1989. 13.95 (*0-86264-076-8*, Pub. by Anderson Pr UK) Trafalgar.

—The Sad Story of Veronica Who Played the Violin. (Illus.). 32p. (gr. k-4). 1991. 10.95 (*0-916291-37-5*) Kane-Miller Bk.

—The School Bus Comes at Eight O'Clock. (Illus.). 32p. (ps-3). 1994. write for info. (*1-56282-662-X*); PLB write for info. (*1-56282-663-8*) Hyprn Child.

—Snow Woman. LC 87-116996. (Illus.). 32p. (gr. 1-3). 1988. 12.95 (*0-688-07674-2*); PLB 12.88 (*0-688-07675-0*) Lothrop.

—Tusk Tusk. (Illus.). 32p. (ps-3). 1990. pap. 6.95 (*0-916291-28-6*) Kane-Miller Bk.

—Two Can Toucan. McKee, David, illus. 32p. (gr. k-3). 1987. 15.95 (*0-86264-094-6*, Pub. by Anderson Pr UK) Trafalgar.

—Who's a Clever Baby? Briley, D., ed. McKee, D., illus. LC 88-22966. 32p. (gr. 1-3). 1989. 12.95 (*0-688-08595-4*); PLB 12.88 (*0-688-08596-2*) Lothrop.

—Zebra's Hiccups. LC 92-14453. 1993. pap. 14.00 (*0-671-79440-X*, S&S BYR) S&S Trade.

McKee, David, jt. auth. see McKee, Chuck.

McKee, Jesse O. The Choctaw. (Illus.). 104p. (gr. 5 up). 1989. 17.95 (*1-55546-699-0*) Chelsea Hse.

McKee, Karen A., illus. How to Draw Airplanes. 32p. (Orig.). 1990. 2.95 (*0-942025-73-3*) Kidsbks.

—How to Draw Airplanes. 32p. 1991. 3.98 (*1-56156-021-9*) Kidsbks.

—How to Draw Cars. 32p. 1991. 3.98 (*1-56156-017-0*) Kidsbks.

—How to Draw Cars. 32p. 1991. pap. 2.95 (*1-56156-026-X*) Kidsbks.

—How to Draw Trucks. 48p. 1992. pap. 2.95 (*1-56156-145-2*) Kidsbks.

MacKeen, Leslie A. Who Can Fix It? Thatch, Nancy R., ed. MacKeen, Leslie A., illus. Melton, David, intro. by. LC 89-31819. (Illus.). 26p. (gr. k-3). 1989. PLB 14.95 (*0-933849-19-2*) Landmark Edns.

McKeever, Catherine. A Place for Owls. Kassian, Olena, illus. 96p. (gr. 3 up). 1992. pap. 7.95 (*0-920775-24-1*, Pub. by Greey de Pencier CN) Firefly Bks Ltd.

McKeever, Michael & Irvine, Georgeanne. A Day in the Life of a Test Pilot. Garrison, Ron, photos by. LC 90-37439. (Illus.). 32p. (gr. 4-8). 1991. lib. bdg. 11.79 (*0-8167-2224-2*); pap. text ed. 2.95 (*0-8167-2225-0*) Troll Assocs.

McKellar, Shona, selected by. Counting Rhymes. LC 93-12383. (Illus.). 32p. (ps-3). 1993. 12.95 (*1-56458-309-0*) Dorling Kindersley.

McKelvey, David. Bobby the Mostly Silky. LC 83-73327. (Illus.). 32p. (gr. 1-3). 1984. lib. bdg. 10.95 (*0-931722-28-4*); pap. 3.95 (*0-931722-27-6*) Corona Pub.

—Commander the Gander. Asklin, William O., illus. LC 84-72455. 48p. (gr. 4-6). 1984. lib. bdg. 10.95 (*0-931722-31-4*); pap. 3.95 (*0-931722-30-6*) Corona Pub.

—Maverick the Lucky Longhorn. McKelvey, David, illus. 32p. (gr. k-3). 1986. lib. bdg. 10.95 (*0-931722-48-9*); pap. 3.95 (*0-931722-47-0*) Corona Pub.

McKelvey, Robbie. A Frog on a Log. McKelvey, Robbie, illus. 22p. (Orig.). (gr. k-4). 1993. pap. 3.95 plastic laminate (*1-884525-00-8*) Whimsical Pubns.

McKelvy, Charles. Kids in the Woods. Sova, Mike & Sova, Mike, illus. LC 89-50591. 24p. (gr. 1-4). 1993. 14.95x (*0-944771-03-3*) Dunery Pr.

McKelway, Margaret. A World of Things to Do. Crump, Donald J., ed. (Illus.). 104p. 1987. 8.95 (*0-87044-610-X*); PLB 12.50 (*0-87044-615-0*) Natl Geog.

Macken, Walter. Flight of the Doves. LC 91-3922. 1992. pap. 14.00 (*0-671-73801-1*, S&S BFYR) S&S Trade.

—Island of the Great Yellow Ox. LC 90-22515. 192p. (gr. 5-9). 1991. pap. 14.00 jacketed, 3-pc. bdg. (*0-671-73800-3*, S&S BFYR) S&S Trade.

—Island of the Great Yellow Ox. LC 90-22515. 192p. (gr. 5-9). 1993. pap. 2.95 (*0-671-86689-3*, Half Moon Bks) S&S Trade.

McKend, H. Moving Gives Me a Stomach Ache. (Illus.). 32p. (ps-8). 1988. pap. 4.95 (*0-88753-178-4*, Pub. by Black Moss Pr CN) Firefly Bks Ltd.

McKenna, jt. auth. see O'Shaughnessy.

McKenna, Colleen. The Truth about Sixth Grade. 192p. (gr. 3-7). 1992. pap. 2.75 (*0-590-44392-5*, Apple Paperbacks) Scholastic Inc.

McKenna, Colleen M. Merry Christmas, Miss McConnell. 160p. 1991. pap. 2.95 (*0-590-43555-8*, Apple Paperbacks) Scholastic Inc.

—Mother Murphy. 160p. (gr. 4-7). 1993. 13.95 (*0-590-44820-X*, Scholastic Hardcover); pap. 3.25 (*0-590-44856-0*, Scholastic Hardcover) Scholastic Inc.

—Murphy's Island. 208p. 1991. pap. 2.95 (*0-590-43553-1*, Apple Paperbacks) Scholastic Inc.

McKenna, Colleen O. The Brightest Light. 1992. 13.95 (*0-590-45347-5*, Scholastic Hardcover) Scholastic Inc.

—Camp Murphy. LC 92-12691. 160p. (gr. 3-7). 1993. 13.95 (*0-590-45807-8*) Scholastic Inc.

—Cousins: Not Quite Sisters. (gr. 4-7). 1993. pap. 2.95 (*0-590-49428-7*) Scholastic Inc.

—Cousins: Stuck in the Middle. (gr. 4-7). 1993. pap. 2.95 (*0-590-49429-5*) Scholastic Inc.

—Fifth Grade: Here Comes Trouble. 128p. (gr. 3-7). 1991. pap. 2.95 (*0-590-41734-7*, Apple Paperbacks) Scholastic Inc.

—Fourth Grade Is a Jinx. LC 88-23897. 176p. (gr. 4-6). 1989. pap. 10.95 (*0-590-41735-5*) Scholastic Inc.

—Fourth Grade Is a Jinx. (ps-3). 1990. pap. 2.95 (*0-590-41736-3*, Apple Paperbacks) Scholastic Inc.

—Good Grief, Third Grade. LC 92-33457. 1993. 13.95 (*0-590-45123-5*) Scholastic Inc.

—Merry Christmas Miss McConnell. (ps-3). 1990. 12.95
  (*0-590-43554-X*, Scholastic Hardcover) Scholastic Inc.
—Murphy's Island. (gr. 4-7). 1990. 12.95 (*0-590-43552-3*)
  Scholastic Inc.
—Roger Friday: Live from the Fifth Grade. LC 93-
  13706. (gr. 5 up). 1994. write for info.
  (*0-590-46684-4*) Scholastic Inc.
—Too Many Murphys. 144p. (gr. 3-7). 1988. pap. 13.95
  (*0-590-41731-2*, Pub. by Scholastic Hardcover)
  Scholastic Inc.
—Too Many Murphys. (gr. 5-7). 1989. pap. 2.95
  (*0-590-41732-0*) Scholastic Inc.
—The Truth about Sixth Grade. 1991. pap. 12.95
  (*0-590-44388-7*) Scholastic Inc.
McKenna, David. East Germany. (Illus.). 96p. (gr. 5 up).
  1988. 14.95 (*1-55546-197-2*) Chelsea Hse.
McKenna, Helen. Young Hickory. (gr. 1-7). 1940. 4.50
  (*0-87602-225-5*) Anchorage.
McKenna, Nancy D. A Family in Hong Kong. (Illus.).
  32p. (gr. 2-5). 1987. 13.50 (*0-8225-1676-4*) Lerner
  Pubns.
—A Zulu Family. (Illus.). 32p. (gr. 2-5). 1986. PLB 13.50
  (*0-8225-1666-7*) Lerner Pubns.
MacKenthun, Carole. Biblical Bulletin Boards. Henson,
  Grace, illus. 48p. (gr. k-4). 1984. wkbk. 6.95
  (*0-86653-197-1*, SS 814, Shining Star Pubns) Good
  Apple.
—Celebrate Summer. Grossman, Dan, illus. 144p. (gr.
  k-3). 1985. wkbk. 11.95 (*0-86653-265-X*, SS 837,
  Shining Star Pubns) Good Apple.
MacKenthun, Carole & Dwyer, Paulinus. Faith. Filkins,
  Vanessa, illus. 48p. (gr. 2-7). 1986. wkbk. 6.95
  (*0-86653-361-3*, SS 874, Shining Star Pubns) Good
  Apple.
—Gentleness. Filkins, Vanessa, illus. 48p. (gr. 2 up).
  1987. pap. 6.95 (*0-86653-395-8*, SS879, Shining Star
  Pubns) Good Apple.
—Goodness. Filkins, Vanessa, illus. 48p. (gr. 2-7). 1986.
  wkbk. 6.95 (*0-86653-363-X*, SS 875, Shining Star
  Pubns) Good Apple.
—Joy. Filkins, Vanessa, illus. 48p. (gr. 2-7). 1986. wkbk.
  6.95 (*0-86653-360-5*, SS 873, Shining Star Pubns)
  Good Apple.
—Kindness. Filkins, Vanessa, illus. 48p. (gr. 2 up). 1987.
  pap. 6.95 (*0-86653-379-6*, SS880, Shining Star Pubns)
  Good Apple.
—Love. Filkins, Vanessa, illus. 48p. (gr. 2-7). 1986. wkbk.
  6.95 (*0-86653-359-1*, SS 872, Shining Star Pubns)
  Good Apple.
—Patience. Filkins, Vanessa, illus. 48p. (gr. 2-7). 1986.
  wkbk. 6.95 (*0-86653-364-8*, SS 876, Shining Star
  Pubns) Good Apple.
—Peace. Filkins, Vanessa, illus. 48p. (gr. 2-7). 1986.
  wkbk. 6.95 (*0-86653-365-6*, SS 877, Shining Star
  Pubns) Good Apple.
—Self-Control. Filkins, Vanessa, illus. 48p. (gr. 2 up).
  1987. pap. 6.95 (*0-86653-396-6*, SS878, Shining Star
  Pubns) Good Apple.
Mackenzie. ABC House. 1992. 14.95 (*0-8050-1946-4*) H
  Holt & Co.
Mackenzie, Donald, ed. see Kipling, Rudyard.
McKenzie, Earl. A Boy Named Ossie: A Jamaican
  Childhood. (Illus.). 104p. (Orig.). 1991. pap. 8.95
  (*0-435-98816-6*, 98816) Heinemann.
McKenzie, Edna C. Freedom in the Midst of a Slave
  Society. 1990. 12.50 (*0-87498-003-8*) Assoc Pubs DC.
McKenzie, Ellen K. A Bowl of Mischief. LC 92-24246.
  240p. (gr. 4-7). 1992. 14.95 (*0-8050-2090-X*, Bks
  Young Read) H Holt & Co.
—The King, the Princess, & the Tinker. Low, William,
  illus. LC 91-31316. 80p. (gr. 2-4). 1992. 14.95
  (*0-8050-1773-9*, Redfeather BYR) H Holt & Co.
—The King, the Princess, & the Tinker. Low, William,
  illus. LC 91-31316. 64p. (gr. 2-4). 1993. pap. 4.95
  (*0-8050-2951-6*, Bks Young Read) H Holt & Co.
—Stargone John. Low, William, illus. LC 90-34119. 80p.
  (gr. 2-4). 1990. 13.95 (*0-8050-1451-9*, Redfeather
  BYR) H Holt & Co.
—Stargone John. Low, William, illus. LC 90-34119. 64p.
  (gr. 2-4). 1992. pap. 4.95 (*0-8050-2069-1*, Redfeather
  BYR) H Holt & Co.
—Taash & the Jesters. LC 92-12378. 245p. (gr. 5 up).
  1992. 15.95 (*0-8050-2381-X*, Bks Young Read) H
  Holt & Co.
McKenzie, Helen B. The Sassenach. 166p. (gr. 5-7).
  1989. pap. 5.95 (*0-86241-115-7*, Pub. by Cnngt Pub
  Ltd) Trafalgar.
Mackenzie, Jill W. The Golden Fairy. LC 90-70311.
  (Illus.). 44p. (gr. 1-6). 1990. 6.95 (*1-55523-336-8*)
  Winston-Derek.
MacKenzie, Joy. Bible Read-to-Me: ABC. LC 87-18337.
  48p. (ps-1). 1988. 9.99 (*1-55513-861-6*, Chariot Bks)
  Cook.
—Bible Read-to-Me: 1-2-3. LC 87-18334. 48p. (ps-1).
  1988. 9.99 (*1-55513-480-7*, Chariot Bks) Cook.
—The Big Book of Bible Crafts & Projects. Flint, Russ,
  illus. 212p. (Orig.). (ps-4). 1981. pap. 15.99
  (*0-310-70151-1*, 14019P) Zondervan.
McKenzie, Joy. Solving Bible Mysteries. 96p. 1994. pap.
  9.99 (*0-310-59761-7*, Pub. by Youth Spec) Zondervan.
MacKenzie, Joy & Bledsoe, Shirley. A Big Book of Bible
  Games & Puzzles. 192p. (gr. 1-6). 1982. pap. 15.99
  (*0-310-70271-2*, 14029P) Zondervan.
MacKenzie, Joy, jt. auth. see Forte, Imogene.
McKenzie, Linda, jt. auth. see Childress, Casey.
McKenzie, Marni S. Alphabet of Bible Creatures.
  Patterson, Karen T., illus. 56p. (ps-8). 1993. 14.95
  (*1-882630-00-9*) Mercy Pr.

McKeown, Charles, jt. auth. see Gilliam, Terry.
McKeown, Martha F. Come to Our Salmon Feast. LC
  59-9823. (Illus.). (gr. 4-9). 1959. 7.95 (*0-8323-0157-4*)
  Binford Mort.
—Linda's Indian Home. LC 56-8826. (Illus.). (gr. 3-7).
  1969. 7.95 (*0-8323-0151-5*) Binford Mort.
McKerchar, Marit, jt. auth. see Spellerberg, Ian.
McKernan, Llewellyn. More Songs of Gladness (Suppl.)
  (Illus.). 24p. (gr. k-4). 1987. pap. 1.89 (*0-570-09004-0*,
  59-1432) Concordia.
Mackie, D. Undersea. (Illus.). 32p. (gr. 4-9). 1987. pap.
  5.95 (*0-88625-156-7*) Durkin Hayes Pub.
Mackie, Dan. Communications. (Illus.). 32p. (gr. 4-9).
  1987. pap. 5.95 (*0-88625-135-4*) Durkin Hayes Pub.
—Electricity. Goshorn, Bill, ed. Bastien, Charles, illus.
  32p. (gr. 4). 1986. PLB 14.65 (*0-88625-133-8*); pap.
  5.95 (*0-685-30764-6*) Durkin Hayes Pub.
—Flight. Shulist, Steve, illus. 32p. (gr. 5-9). 1985. pap.
  5.95 (*0-88625-112-5*) Durkin Hayes Pub.
—Planets & Galaxies. Bastien, Charles & Livingston,
  Richard, illus. 32p. (gr. 5-9). 1985. pap. 5.95
  (*0-88625-102-8*) Durkin Hayes Pub.
—Space Tour. Hughes, Mark, illus. 32p. (gr. 5-9). 1985.
  pap. 5.95 (*0-88625-103-6*) Durkin Hayes Pub.
Mackie, David, jt. auth. see Mackie, Dean.
Mackie, Dean & Mackie, David. BASIC. Migliore, Ron,
  illus. 48p. (gr. 1-5). 1985. pap. 3.95 (*0-88625-085-4*)
  Durkin Hayes Pub.
McKie, Roy. The Alphabet Block Book. McKie, Roy,
  illus. LC 79-63611. (ps-1). 1979. 3.95 (*0-394-84269-3*)
  Random Bks Yng Read.
—The Joke Book. McKie, Roy, illus. LC 78-62699.
  (ps-2). 1979. pap. 2.25 (*0-394-84077-1*) Random Bks
  Yng Read.
—The Riddle Book. LC 77-85237. (ps-2). 1978. lib. bdg.
  5.99 (*0-394-93732-5*); pap. 2.25 (*0-394-83732-0*)
  Random Bks Yng Read.
McKie, Roy & Eastman, Philip D. Snow. LC 62-15114.
  (Illus.). 72p. (gr. 1-2). 1962. 6.95 (*0-394-80027-3*); lib.
  bdg. 7.99 (*0-394-90027-8*) Beginner.
McKiernan, Dennis L. Trek to Kraagen-Cor. (gr. 9-12).
  1989. pap. 3.95 (*0-451-15563-7*, Sig) NAL-Dutton.
McKillip, Patricia. The House on Parchment Street.
  Robinson, Charles, illus. LC 90-27119. 192p. (gr. 3-7).
  1991. pap. 3.95 (*0-689-71471-8*, Aladdin) Macmillan
  Child Grp.
McKillip, Patricia A. The Changeling Sea. LC 88-3435.
  160p. (gr. 5 up). 1988. SBE 13.95 (*0-689-31436-1*,
  Atheneum Child Bk) Macmillan Child Grp.
McKinley, Nancy L. Signs of Survival. Joles, Richard &
  Joles, Michael, illus. (gr. 5-12). 1986. Box 30 4x6
  cards. 12.00 (*0-930599-10-1*) Thinking Pubns.
—Signs of Survival. Joles, Richard & Joles, Michael, illus.
  (gr. 5-12). 1987. Box 30 4x6 cards. 12.00
  (*0-930599-15-2*) Thinking Pubns.
—Signs of Survival. (Illus.). (gr. 5-12). 1991. 12.00
  (*0-930599-69-1*) Thinking Pubns.
McKinley, Nancy L. & Schwartz, Linda.
  Make-It-Yourself Barrier Activities. 210p. (gr. k-12).
  1987. pap. 33.00 (*0-930599-16-0*) Thinking Pubns.
—Referential Communication: Barrier Activities for
  Speakers & Listeners, 2 pts. 100p. (Orig.). (gr. k-12).
  1985. Pt. I, Grades K-8. pap. text ed. 85.00x
  (*0-930599-00-4*); Pt. II, Grades 5-Adult. 89.00x
  (*0-930599-01-2*) Thinking Pubns.
McKinley, Nancy L., jt. auth. see Larson, Vicki L.
McKinley, Nancy L., jt. auth. see Schwartz, Linda.
McKinley, Olive, tr. see Garst, Hitjo.
McKinley, Robin. Beauty: A Retelling of the Story of
  Beauty & the Beast. LC 77-25636. 256p. (gr. 7-9).
  1978. 16.00 (*0-06-024149-7*); PLB 15.89
  (*0-06-024150-0*) HarpC Child Bks.
—Beauty: A Retelling of the Story of Beauty & the Beast.
  LC 77-25636. 256p. (gr. 5 up). 1993. pap. 4.95
  (*0-06-440477-3*, Trophy) HarpC Child Bks.
—The Blue Sword. LC 82-2895. 288p. (gr. 7 up). 1982.
  reinforced 16.00 (*0-688-00938-7*) Greenwillow.
—The Door in the Hedge. LC 80-21903. 224p. (gr. 7 up).
  1981. reinforced bdg. 11.75 (*0-688-00312-5*)
  Greenwillow.
—The Hero & the Crown. LC 84-4074. 256p. (gr. 7 up).
  1984. reinforced 15.00 (*0-688-02593-5*) Greenwillow.
—The Hero & the Crown. 1987. pap. 4.99
  (*0-441-32809-1*) Ace Bks.
—Hero & the Crown. large type ed. (gr. 3-7). 1988. Repr.
  of 1984 ed. lib. bdg. 15.95 (*1-55736-078-2*, Crnrstn
  Bks) BDD LT Grp.
—Imaginary Lands. LC 85-21867. 160p. (gr. 7 up). 1986.
  reinforced bdg. 11.75 (*0-688-05213-4*) Greenwillow.
—A Knot in the Grain & Other Stories. LC 93-17557.
  (gr. 6 up). 1994. write for info. (*0-688-09201-2*)
  Greenwillow.
—My Father Is in the Navy. Gourbault, Martine, illus.
  LC 91-12566. 24p. (ps up). 1992. 14.00
  (*0-688-10639-0*); PLB 13.93 (*0-688-10640-4*)
  Greenwillow.
—Outlaws of Sherwood. LC 88-45227. 256p. (gr. 7 up).
  1988. 12.95 (*0-688-07178-3*) Greenwillow.
—Rowan. Ruff, Donna, illus. LC 91-33809. 24p. (gr. 4).
  1992. 14.00 (*0-688-10682-X*); PLB 13.93
  (*0-688-10683-8*) Greenwillow.
McKinley, Robin, adapted by see Kipling, Rudyard.
McKinley, Robin, adapted by see Sewell, Anna.
McKinney, Cecilia B. Clif's Special Day. 1995. 7.95
  (*0-8062-4867-X*) Carlton.
McKinney, Jack. Death Dance. (gr. 10 up). 1988. pap.
  4.95 (*0-345-35302-1*, Del Rey) Ballantine.

McKinney, Phyliss. Revelations. 20p. (Orig.). (gr. 5 up).
  1992. pap. text ed. 4.95 (*1-877860-09-3*) Eula Intl
  Pub.
McKinney, Roberta, ed. Songs for Children of the World.
  16p. (Orig.). (gr. 1-8). 1984. pap. 12.95 set of 10
  (*0-87487-740-7*, Suzuki Method) Summy-Birchard.
MacKinnon, Bernie. Meantime. 1992. pap. 4.95
  (*0-395-61622-0*) HM.
—Song for a Shadow. LC 90-39647. 320p. (gr. 7 up).
  1991. 16.45 (*0-395-55419-5*) HM.
MacKinnon, Christy. Silent Observer. (Illus.). 48p. 1993.
  15.95 (*1-56368-022-X*) Gallaudet Univ Pr.
MacKinnon, Debbie. Baby's First Year. Sieveking,
  Anthea, photos by. LC 92-21830. 26p. (ps). 1993. 11.
  95 (*0-8120-6334-1*) Barron.
—How Many? Sieveking, Anthea, photos by. LC 91-
  46720. (Illus.). 24p. (ps-k). 1993. 10.99
  (*0-8037-1253-7*) Dial Bks Young.
—My First ABC. Sieveking, Anthea, photos by. LC 92-
  11500. (Illus.). (ps). 1992. 11.95 (*0-8120-6331-7*)
  Barron.
—What Noise? Sieveking, Anthea, photos by. LC 92-
  43651. (Illus.). (gr. 4 up). 1994. 10.99 (*0-8037-1510-2*)
  Dial Bks Young.
—What Shape? Sieveking, Anthea, photos by. LC 91-
  34700. (Illus.). 24p. (ps-k). 1992. 10.99
  (*0-8037-1244-8*) Dial Bks Young.
MacKinnon, Debbie & Sieveking, Anthea. All about Me.
  LC 93-23143. (Illus.). 32p. (ps). 1994. 11.95
  (*0-8120-6348-1*) Barron.
MacKinnon, Elizabeth. Great Big Holiday Celebrations:
  Activities for Celebrating Major Holidays with Young
  Children. Bittinger, Gayle, ed. Ekberg, Marion, illus.
  LC 91-65045. 224p. (Orig.). (ps-1). 1991. pap. text ed.
  16.95 (*0-911019-43-X*) Warren Pub Hse.
—Play & Learn with Rubber Stamps. Warren, Jean, ed.
  Mohrmann, Gary, illus. LC 93-61083. 64p. (Orig.).
  1994. pap. text ed. 7.95 (*0-911019-93-6*) Warren Pub
  Hse.
—Special Day Celebrations: Seasonal Mini Celebrations
  to Enjoy with Young Children. Bittinger, Gayle, ed.
  Ekberg, Marion H., illus. LC 89-50765. 128p. (Orig.).
  (ps-1). 1989. pap. text ed. 14.95 (*0-911019-24-3*)
  Warren Pub Hse.
—Yankee Doodle Birthday Celebrations: All-American
  Birthdays to Celebrate with Young Children. Bittinger,
  Gayle, ed. Ekberg, Marion H., illus. LC 90-70414.
  128p. (Orig.). (ps-1). 1990. pap. text ed. 12.95
  (*0-911019-32-4*) Warren Pub Hse.
MacKinnon, Elizabeth, ed. see Bittinger, Gayle.
MacKinnon, Elizabeth, ed. see Warren, Jean.
McKinnon, Elizabeth, jt. ed. see Warren, Jean.
McKinnon, Elizabeth S., jt. auth. see Warren, Jean.
McKinnon, Elizabeth S., ed. One-Two-Three Colors:
  Activities for Introducing Color to Young Children.
  Warren, Jean, compiled by. Ekberg, Marion H., illus.
  LC 87-51241. 160p. (Orig.). (ps-1). 1988. pap. 14.95
  (*0-911019-17-0*) Warren Pub Hse.
McKinnon, Elizabeth S. & Warren, Jean, eds. Piggyback
  Songs for Infants & Toddlers. Ekberg, Marion H.,
  illus. LC 85-50433. 80p. (Orig.). (ps-k). 1985. pap.
  7.95 (*0-911019-07-3*) Warren Pub Hse.
—Short-Short Stories: Simple Stories for Young Children
  Plus Seasonal Activities. Ekberg, Marion, illus. LC 86-
  51509. 80p. (Orig.). (ps-1). 1987. pap. 7.95
  (*0-911019-13-8*) Warren Pub Hse.
McKinnon, Elizabeth S., compiled by see Warren, Jean.
McKinnon, Elizabeth S., ed. see Warren, Jean.
McKinstry, Anne P. Can You Come with Me?
  McKinstry-Peterson, Laurel, illus. 44p. (gr. 4-8). 1986.
  5.95 (*1-55523-034-2*) Winston-Derek.
Mackintosh, Barry. The National Park Service.
  Schlesinger, Arthur M., Jr., intro. by. (Illus.). 96p. (gr.
  5 up). 1988. lib. bdg. 14.95 (*1-55546-116-6*) Chelsea
  Hse.
Mackintosh, William H. & Goliwas, Ruth M. The
  Stained Glass Coloring Book. (Illus.). 48p. (ps-2).
  1990. pap. 2.95 (*0-671-69477-4*, Little Simon) S&S
  Trade.
McKinzie, Harry & Tindimwebwa, Issy. Names from
  East Africa. Campbell, Elisabeth, ed. 42p. (Orig.).
  1980. pap. 4.95 (*0-86626-007-2*) McKinzie Pub.
McKissack. One Family's Story. 1993. 19.95
  (*0-8050-1671-6*) H Holt & Co.
McKissack, Frederick & McKissack, Patricia C.
  Sojourner Truth: Ain't I a Woman? (gr. 8-12). 1994.
  pap. 3.50 (*0-590-44691-6*) Scholastic Inc.
McKissack, Frederick, jt. auth. see McKissack, Patricia.
Mckissack, Frederick, jt. auth. see McKissack, Patricia.
McKissack, Frederick, jt. ed. see McKissack, Patricia.
McKissack, Fredrick, jt. auth. see McKissack, Patricia.
Mckissack, Fredrick, jt. auth. see McKissack, Patricia.
McKissack, Fredrick, jt. auth. see McKissack, Patricia.
**McKissack, Fredrick, jt. auth. see McKissack, Patricia
  C.**

McKissack, Fredrick, ed. see Bartholomew.
McKissack, Fredrick, ed. see Chapman, Mary W.
McKissack, Fredrick, ed. see Chodkowski, Dick.
McKissack, Fredrick, ed. see Collins, David R.
McKissack, Fredrick, ed. see Duyff, Roberta L.
McKissack, Fredrick, ed. see Frankel, Julie.
McKissack, Fredrick, ed. see Greene, Carol.
McKissack, Fredrick, ed. see Halloran, Phyllis.
McKissack, Fredrick, ed. see Moore, Elaine.
McKissack, Fredrick, ed. see Polette, Keith.
**McKissack, Fredrick, ed. see Roop, Peter & Roop,
  Connie.**
McKissack, Fredrick, ed. see Singerman, Ellen.

McKissack, Fredrick, ed. see Van Woerkom, Dorothy.
McKissack, Fredrick, ed. see Witter, Evelyn.
McKissack, Fredrick, Jr., jt. auth. see McKissack, Patricia C.
McKissack, Patricia. The Apache. LC 84-7803. (Illus.). 48p. (gr. k-4). 1984. PLB 15.27 (*0-516-01925-2*); pap. 4.95 (*0-516-41925-0*) Childrens.
—The Aztec. LC 84-23142. (Illus.). 48p. (gr. k-4). 1985. PLB 15.27 (*0-516-01936-8*); pap. 4.95 (*0-516-41936-6*) Childrens.
—The Dark-Thirty: Southern Tales of the Supernatural. Pinkney, Brian, illus. LC 92-3021. 128p. (gr. 3-7). 1992. 15.00 (*0-679-81863-4*); PLB 15.99 (*0-679-91863-9*) Knopf Bks Yng Read.
—Give It with Love, Christopher: Christopher Learns about Gifts & Giving. Batholomew, illus. LC 87-73524. 32p. (ps-3). 1988. pap. 5.99 (*0-8066-2354-3*, 10-2554, Augsburg) Augsburg Fortress.
—Tne Inca. LC 85-6712. (Illus.). 45p. (gr. 2-3). 1985. PLB 15.27 (*0-516-01268-1*); pap. 4.95 (*0-516-41268-0*) Childrens.
—Los Incas (The Inca) LC 85-6712. (SPA.). 48p. (gr. k-4). 1987. PLB 15.27 (*0-516-31268-5*); pap. 4.95 (*0-516-51268-4*) Childrens.
—Martin Luther King, Jr. A Man to Remember. LC 83-23933. (Illus.). 128p. (gr. 4 up). 1984. PLB 18.60 (*0-516-03206-2*); pap. 5.95 (*0-516-43206-0*) Childrens.
—The Maya. LC 85-9927. (Illus.). 45p. (gr. 2-3). 1985. PLB 15.27 (*0-516-01270-3*); pap. 4.95 (*0-516-41270-1*) Childrens.
—Los Mayas (The Maya) LC 85-9927. (Illus.). 48p. (gr. k-4). 1987. PLB 15.27 (*0-516-31270-7*); pap. 4.95 (*0-516-51270-6*) Childrens.
—Monkey-Monkey's Trick. Meisel, Paul, illus. LC 88-3072. 48p. (Orig.). (gr. 1-3). 1988. lib. bdg. 7.99 (*0-394-99173-7*); pap. 3.50 (*0-394-89173-2*) Random Bks Yng Read.
—Our Martin Luther King Book. Endres, Helen, illus. LC 86-6785. 32p. (ps-3). 1986. PLB 19.95 (*0-89565-342-7*); PLB 13.95s.p. (*0-685-55831-2*) Childs World.
—Paul Laurence Dunbar: A Poet to Remember. LC 84-7625. (Illus.). 112p. (gr. 4 up). 1984. PLB 18.60 (*0-516-03209-7*); pap. 5.95 (*0-516-43209-5*) Childrens.
—Quien Viene? (Who Is Coming?) Martin, Clovis, illus. LC 86-11805. (SPA & ENG.). 32p. (ps-2). 1989. PLB 11.93 (*0-516-32073-4*); pap. 2.95 (*0-516-52073-3*) Childrens.
—Royal Kingdoms of Ghana, Mali, & Soghay: Life in Medieval Africa. (Illus.). 128p. (gr. 5-9). 1993. PLB 15.95 (*0-8050-1670-8*, Bks Young Read) H Holt & Co.
—Speak Up, Christopher: Christopher Learns the Difference Between Right & Wrong. Bartholomew, illus. LC 87-73523. 32p. (ps-6). 1988. pap. 5.99 (*0-8066-2355-1*, 10-5966, Augsburg) Augsburg Fortress.
—Who Is Coming? Martin, Clovis, illus. LC 86-11805. 32p. (ps-3). 1990. PLB 11.93 (*0-516-02073-0*); pap. 2.95 (*0-516-42073-9*); pap. 30.60 big bk. (*0-516-49458-9*) Childrens.
—Who Is Who? LC 83-7361. (Illus.). 32p. (ps-2). 1983. PLB 11.93 (*0-516-02042-0*); pap. 2.95 (*0-516-42042-9*) Childrens.
McKissack, Patricia & McKissack, Fredrick. Ada, la Desordenada - Libro Grande: Messey Bessey-Big Book. 32p. (ps-2). 1988. PLB 30.60 (*0-516-59508-3*) Childrens.
—Ada, la Desordenada (Messey Bessey) Hackney, Richard, illus. LC 87-15079. (SPA.). 32p. (ps-2). 1988. PLB 11.93 (*0-516-32083-1*); pap. 2.95 (*0-516-52083-0*) Childrens.
—African-American Scientists. LC 93-11226. (Illus.). 80p. (gr. 4-6). 1994. PLB 17.90 (*1-56294-372-3*) Millbrook Pr.
—African Americans. (Illus.). 48p. (gr. 4-7). 1991. pap. 5.95 (*0-88335-345-8*) Milliken Pub Co.
—All Paths Lead to Bethlehem. Shoemaker, Kathryn E., illus. LC 87-70472. 32p. (Orig.). (ps-3). 1987. pap. 5.99 (*0-8066-2265-2*, 10-0220, Augsburg) Augsburg Fortress.
McKissack, Patricia & McKissack, Fredrick. Big Bug Book of Counting. Bartholomew, illus. LC 87-61655. 24p. (Orig.). (gr. k-1). 1987. spiral bdg. 14.95 (*0-88335-762-3*); pap. text ed. 4.95 (*0-88335-772-0*) Milliken Pub Co.
—Big Bug Book of Opposites. Bartholomew, illus. LC 87-61654. 24p. (Orig.). (gr. k-1). 1987. spiral bdg. 14.95 (*0-88335-763-1*); pap. text ed. 4.95 (*0-88335-773-9*) Milliken Pub Co.
—Big Bug Book of Places to Go. Bartholomew, illus. LC 87-61652. 24p. (Orig.). (gr. k-1). 1987. spiral bdg. 14. 95 (*0-88335-765-8*); pap. text ed. 4.95 (*0-88335-775-5*) Milliken Pub Co.
—Big Bug Book of the Alphabet. Bartholomew, illus. LC 87-61653. 24p. (Orig.). (gr. k-1). 1987. spiral bdg. 14. 95 (*0-88335-764-X*); pap. text ed. 4.95 (*0-88335-774-7*) Milliken Pub Co.
—Big Bug Book of Things to Do. Bartholomew, illus. LC 87-61651. 24p. (Orig.). (gr. k-1). 1987. spiral bdg. 14. 95 (*0-88335-766-6*); pap. text ed. 4.95 (*0-88335-776-3*) Milliken Pub co.
—Booker T. Washington: Leader & Educator. LC 92-5356. (Illus.). 32p. (gr. 1-4). 1992. lib. bdg. 12.95 (*0-89490-314-4*) Enslow Pubs.

—Bugs! Martin, Clovis, illus. LC 88-22875. 32p. (ps-2). 1988. PLB 11.93 (*0-516-02088-9*); pap. 2.95 (*0-516-42088-7*) Childrens.
—Carter G. Woodson: The Father of Black History. Ostendorf, Ned, illus. LC 91-8813. 32p. (gr. 1-4). 1991. lib. bdg. 12.95 (*0-89490-309-8*) Enslow Pubs.
—The Children's ABC Christmas. Rogers, Kathy, illus. LC 87-73525. 32p. (ps-6). 1988. pap. 5.99 (*0-8066-2356-X*, 10-1046, Augsburg) Augsburg Fortress.
McKissack, Patricia & McKissack, Fredrick. Cinderella. Dunnington, Tom, illus. LC 85-12764. (gr. 1-2). 1985. PLB 11.93 (*0-516-02361-6*); pap. 3.95 (*0-516-42361-4*) Childrens.
—The Civil Rights Movement in America from 1865 to the Present. 2nd ed. LC 86-9636. (Illus.). 352p. (gr. 4 up). 1991. 39.93 (*0-516-00579-0*) Childrens.
—Constance Stumbles. Dunnington, Tom, illus. 32p. (ps-2). 1988. PLB 11.93 (*0-516-02086-2*); pap. 2.95 (*0-516-42086-0*) Childrens.
—Country Mouse & City Mouse. Sikorski, Anne, illus. LC 85-12759. (ps-2). 1985. PLB 11.93 (*0-516-02362-4*); pap. 3.95 (*0-516-42362-2*) Childrens.
—Frederick Douglass: Leader Against Slavery. Ostendorf, Ned, illus. LC 91-3084. 32p. (gr. 1-4). 1991. lib. bdg. 12.95 (*0-89490-306-3*) Enslow Pubs.
—Frederick Douglass: The Black Lion. LC 86-32695. (Illus.). 136p. (gr. 4 up). 1987. PLB 18.60 (*0-516-03221-6*); pap. 5.95 (*0-516-43221-4*) Childrens.
—From Heaven Above: The Story of Christmas Proclaimed by the Angels. Knutson, Barbara, illus. LC 92-70385. 32p. (ps-2). 1992. pap. 4.99 (*0-8066-2609-7*, 9-2609, Augsburg) Augsburg Fortress.
—La Gallinita Roja: The Little Red Hen. LC 86-20801. (Illus.). 32p. (ps-2). 1986. PLB 11.93 (*0-516-32363-6*); pap. 4.95 (*0-516-52363-5*) Childrens.
—George Washington Carver: The Peanut Scientist. Ostendorf, Ned, illus. LC 91-8814. 32p. (gr. 1-4). 1991. lib. bdg. 12.95 (*0-89490-308-X*) Enslow Pubs.
—God Made Something Wonderful. Ching, illus. LC 89-84938. 32p. (Orig.). (gr. 3-5). 1989. pap. 5.99 (*0-8066-2434-5*, 9-2434) Augsburg Fortress.
—Great African Americans Series, 18 bks. (Illus.). (gr. 1-4). Set, 32p. ea. lib. bdg. 233.10 (*0-89490-376-4*) Enslow Pubs.
—Ida B. Wells-Barnett: A Voice Against Violence. Ostendorf, Ned, illus. LC 90-49848. 32p. (gr. 1-4). 1991. lib. bdg. 12.95 (*0-89490-301-2*) Enslow Pubs.
—Insectos! Bugs! LC 88-22875. (SPA., Illus.). 32p. (ps-2). 1991. PLB 11.93 (*0-516-32088-2*); pap. 2.95 (*0-516-52088-1*) Childrens.
—James Weldon Johnson: Lift Every Voice & Sing. LC 89-77273. (Illus.). 32p. (gr. 2-5). 1990. PLB 14.60 (*0-516-04174-6*); pap. text ed. 3.95 (*0-516-44174-4*) Childrens.
—Jesse Owens: Olympic Star. LC 92-3584. (Illus.). 32p. (gr. 1-4). 1992. lib. bdg. 12.95 (*0-89490-312-8*) Enslow Pubs.
—King Midas & His Gold. Dunnington, Tom, illus. LC 86-11744. 32p. (ps-2). 1986. PLB 11.93 (*0-516-03984-9*); pap. 3.95 (*0-516-43984-7*) Childrens.
—The King's New Clothes. Connelly, Gwen, illus. LC 86-33422. 32p. (ps-3). 1987. PLB 11.93 (*0-516-02365-9*); pap. 3.95 (*0-516-42365-7*) Childrens.
—Langston Hughes: Great American Poet. LC 92-2583. (Illus.). 32p. (gr. 1-4). 1992. lib. bdg. 12.95 (*0-89490-315-2*) Enslow Pubs.
—The Little Red Hen. Hockerman, Dennis, illus. LC 85-12760. (ps-2). 1985. PLB 11.93 (*0-516-02363-2*); pap. 3.95 (*0-516-42363-0*) Childrens.
—A Long Hard Journey. 144p. (gr. 7-9). 1990. 17.95 (*0-8027-6884-9*); PLB 18.85 (*0-8027-6885-7*) Walker & Co.
McKissack, Patricia & McKissack, Fredrick. Lorraine Hansberry: Dramatist & Activist. Davis, Thulani, intro. by. LC 93-31086. 1994. write for info. (*0-385-31164-8*) Delacorte.
—Louis Armstrong: Jazz Musician. Ostendorf, Ned, illus. LC 91-12420. 32p. (gr. 1-4). 1991. lib. bdg. 12.95 (*0-89490-307-1*) Enslow Pubs.
—Madam C. J. Walker: Self-Made Millionaire. LC 92-6189. (Illus.). 32p. (gr. 1-4). 1992. lib. bdg. 12.95 (*0-89490-311-X*) Enslow Pubs.
—Marian Anderson: A Great Singer. Ostendorf, Ned, illus. LC 90-19163. 32p. (gr. 1-4). 1991. lib. bdg. 12.95 (*0-89490-303-9*) Enslow Pubs.
—Martin Luther King, Jr. Man of Peace. Ostendorf, Ned, illus. LC 90-19156. 32p. (gr. 1-4). 1991. lib. bdg. 12.95 (*0-89490-302-0*) Enslow Pubs.
—Mary Church Terrell: Leader for Equality. Ostendorf, Ned, illus. LC 91-3083. 32p. (gr. 1-4). 1991. lib. bdg. 12.95 (*0-89490-305-5*) Enslow Pubs.
—Mary McLeod Bethune. LC 92-12098. (Illus.). 32p. (gr. 3-6). 1992. PLB 15.27 (*0-516-06658-7*) Childrens.
—Mary McLeod Bethune. LC 92-12098. (Illus.). 32p. (gr. 3-6). 1993. pap. 3.95 (*0-516-46658-5*) Childrens.
—Mary McLeod Bethune: A Great Teacher. Ostendorf, Ned, illus. LC 91-8818. 32p. (gr. 1-4). 1991. lib. bdg. 12.95 (*0-89490-304-7*) Enslow Pubs.
—Messey Bessey Big Book. (Illus.). 32p. (ps-2). 1988. PLB 30.60 (*0-516-49508-9*) Childrens.
—Messy Bessey. Hackney, illus. LC 87-15079. (Illus.). (ps-2). 1987. PLB 11.93 (*0-516-02083-8*); pap. 2.95 (*0-516-42083-6*) Childrens.

—Messy Bessey's Garden. Hackney, Richard, illus. LC 91-15333. 32p. (ps-2). 1991. PLB 11.93 (*0-516-02008-0*); pap. 2.95 (*0-516-42008-9*) Childrens.
—My Bible ABC Book. Merrill, Reed, illus. LC 87-70473. 32p. (Orig.). (ps-3). 1987. pap. 5.99 (*0-8066-2271-7*, 10-4588, Augsburg) Augsburg Fortress.
McKissack, Patricia & McKissack, Fredrick. No Need for Alarm. Smith, Phil, illus. LC 88-60388. 32p. (Orig.). (gr. 1-3). 1990. text ed. 8.95 (*0-88335-783-6*); pap. text ed. 4.95 (*0-88335-795-X*) Milliken Pub Co.
—Oh, Happy, Happy Day! A Child's Easter in Story, Song, & Prayer. Swisher, Elizabeth, illus. LC 88-83017. 32p. 1989. pap. 5.99 (*0-8066-2394-2*, 10-4733, Augsburg) Augsburg Fortress.
McKissack, Patricia & McKissack, Fredrick. Paul Robeson: A Voice to Remember. LC 92-2582. (Illus.). 32p. (gr. 1-4). 1992. lib. bdg. 12.95 (*0-89490-310-1*) Enslow Pubs.
—Ralph J. Bunche: Peacemaker. Ostendorf, Ned, illus. LC 90-49849. 32p. (gr. 1-4). 1991. lib. bdg. 12.95 (*0-89490-300-4*) Enslow Pubs.
—El Ratoncito del Campo y el Ratoncito de la Ciudad: Country Mouse & City Mouse. LC 86-21565. 32p. (ps-2). 1986. PLB 11.93 (*0-516-32362-8*); pap. 3.95 (*0-516-52362-7*) Childrens.
—Reading Well Softcover Package, 24 bks. (Illus., Orig.). (gr. 1-3). 1989. Set, 32p. ea. pap. 107.00 (*0-88335-739-9*) Milliken Pub Co.
McKissack, Patricia & McKissack, Fredrick. A Real Winner. Jones, Ken & Thompson, Quentin, illus. LC 88-61637. 32p. (Orig.). (gr. 1-3). 1987. text ed. 8.95 (*0-88335-732-1*); pap. text ed. 4.95 (*0-88335-752-6*) Milliken Pub Co.
—Satchel Paige: The Best Arm in Baseball. LC 92-3583. (Illus.). 32p. (gr. 1-4). 1992. lib. bdg. 12.95 (*0-89490-317-9*) Enslow Pubs.
—Sojourner Truth: A Voice for Freedom. LC 92-6190. (Illus.). 32p. (gr. 1-4). 1992. lib. bdg. 12.95 (*0-89490-313-6*) Enslow Pubs.
—The Story of Booker T. Washington. LC 91-15895. (Illus.). 32p. (gr. 3-6). 1991. PLB 13.27 (*0-516-04758-2*); pap. 3.95 (*0-516-44758-0*) Childrens.
—Taking a Stand Against Racism & Racial Discrimination. LC 89-28627. 1990. PLB 14.40 (*0-531-10924-0*) Watts.
McKissack, Patricia & McKissack, Fredrick. Tall Phil & Small Bill. Mitter, Kathy, illus. LC 87-61644. 32p. (Orig.). (gr. 1-3). 1987. text ed. 8.95 (*0-88335-727-5*); pap. text ed. 4.95 (*0-88335-747-X*) Milliken Pub Co.
—Tennessee Trailblazers. 96p. (gr. 4-7). 1993. 13.95 (*0-9634824-0-8*) March Media.
—The Three Bears. LC 85-12765. (Illus.). 32p. (ps-2). 1985. PLB 11.93 (*0-516-02364-0*); pap. 3.95 (*0-516-42364-9*) Childrens.
—Three Billy Goats Gruff. Dunnington, Tom, illus. LC 86-33450. 32p. (ps-2). 1987. PLB 11.93 (*0-516-02366-7*); pap. 3.95 (*0-516-42366-5*) Childrens.
—El Traje Nuevo del Emperador: (The King's New Clothes) LC 86-33422. (ENG & SPA., Illus.). 32p. (ps-2). 1989. PLB 11.93 (*0-516-32365-2*); pap. 3.95 (*0-516-52365-1*) Childrens.
—Los Tres Chivitos. Dunnington, Tom, illus. LC 86-33450. 32p. (SPA.). 32p. (ps-2). 1988. PLB 11.93 (*0-516-32366-0*); pap. 3.95 (*0-516-52366-X*) Childrens.
—A Troll in a Hole. Bartholomew, illus. LC 88-60384. 32p. (Orig.). (gr. 1-3). 1988. text ed. 8.95 (*0-88335-782-8*); pap. text ed. 4.95 (*0-88335-794-1*) Milliken Pub Co.
—The Ugly Little Duck. Anderson, Peggy P., illus. LC 85-31428. 32p. (ps-2). 1986. PLB 11.93 (*0-516-03982-2*); pap. 3.95 (*0-516-43982-0*) Childrens.
—W. E. B. Dubois. LC 90-37823. (Illus.). 128p. (gr. 9-12). 1990. PLB 14.40 (*0-531-10939-9*) Watts.
—When Do You Talk to God? Prayers for Small Children. Gumble, Gary, illus. LC 86-71903. 32p. (Orig.). (gr. 3-8). 1986. pap. 5.99 (*0-8066-2239-3*, 10-7078, Augsburg) Augsburg Fortress.
—Zora Neale Hurston: Writer & Storyteller. LC 92-2588. (Illus.). 32p. (gr. 1-4). 1992. lib. bdg. 12.95 (*0-89490-316-0*) Enslow Pubs.
McKissack, Patricia & McKissack, Fredrick, eds. Reading Well Hardcover Package, 24 bks. (Illus.). (gr. 1-3). 1989. Set, 32p. ea. 190.00 (*0-88335-717-8*) Milliken Pub Co.
McKissack, Patricia, ed. see Bartholomew.
McKissack, Patricia, ed. see Chapman, Mary W.
McKissack, Patricia, ed. see Chodkowski, Dick.
McKissack, Patricia, ed. see Collins, David R.
McKissack, Patricia, ed. see Duyff, Roberta L.
McKissack, Patricia, ed. see Frankel, Julie.
McKissack, Patricia, ed. see Greene, Carol.
McKissack, Patricia, ed. see Halloran, Phyllis.
McKissack, Patricia, ed. see Moore, Elaine.
McKissack, Patricia, ed. see Polette, Keith.
McKissack, Patricia, ed. see Roop, Peter & Roop, Connie.
McKissack, Patricia, ed. see Singerman, Ellen.
McKissack, Patricia, ed. see Van Woerkom, Dorothy.
McKissack, Patricia, ed. see Witter, Evelyn.
McKissack, Patricia A. Lights Out, Christopher. Bartholomew, illus. LC 84-71375. 32p. (Orig.). (ps-1). 1984. pap. 5.99 (*0-8066-2110-9*, 10-3870, Augsburg) Augsburg Fortress.

McKissack, Patricia C. Flossie & the Fox. Isadora, Rachel, illus. LC 86-2024. 32p. (ps-3). 1986. 14.00 (0-8037-0250-7); PLB 13.89 (0-8037-0251-5) Dial Bks Young.

—It's the Truth, Christopher. Bartholomew, illus. LC 84-71376. 32p. (Orig.). (ps-1). 1984. pap. 5.99 (0-8066-2111-7, 10-3457, Augsburg) Augsburg Fortress.

—Mary McLeod Bethune: A Great American Educator. LC 85-12843. (Illus.). 111p. (gr. 4 up). 1985. PLB 18.60 (0-516-03218-6); pap. 5.95 (0-516-43218-4) Childrens.

—A Million Fish...More or Less. Schutzer, Dena, illus. LC 90-34322. 40p. (ps-3). 1992. 14.00 (0-679-80692-X); PLB 14.99 (0-679-90692-4) Knopf Bks Yng Read.

—Mirandy & Brother Wind. Pinkney, Jerry, illus. LC 87-349. 32p. (ps-3). 1988. 15.00 (0-394-88765-4); lib. bdg. 15.99 (0-394-98765-9) Knopf Bks Yng Read.

—Mirandy & Brother Wind. Tyson, Cicely, narrated by. Pinkney, Jerry, illus. LC 87-349. 32p. (ps up). 1992. incl. cassette 17.00 (0-679-82668-8) Knopf Bks Yng Read.

—Nettie Jo's Friends. Cook, Scott, illus. LC 87-14080. 40p. (ps-4). 1989. 15.00 (0-394-89158-9); lib. bdg. 15.99 (0-394-99158-3) Knopf Bks Yng Read.

—Quien Es Quien? (Who Is Who?) Allen, Elizabeth M., illus. LC 83-7361. (SPA). 32p. (ps-2). 1989. pap. 2.95 (0-516-52042-3) Childrens.

McKissack, Patricia C. & McKissack, Fredrick, Jr. Black Diamond: The Story of the Negro Baseball Leagues. LC 93-22691. (Illus.). 192p. (gr. 3-9). 1994. 13.95 (0-590-45809-4) Scholastic Inc.

McKissack, Patricia C. & McKissack, Fredrick. Messy Bessey's Closet. Hackney, Rick, illus. LC 89-34667. 32p. (ps-2). 1989. PLB 11.93 (0-516-02091-9); pap. 2.95 (0-516-42091-7) Childrens.

—Sojourner Truth: Ain't I a Woman. 1992. 13.95 (0-590-44690-8, Scholastic Hardcover) Scholastic Inc.

—Los Tres Osos: (The Three Bears) Bala, Virginia, illus. LC 85-12765. (SPA). 32p. (ps-2). 1989. PLB 11.93 (0-516-32364-4); pap. 3.95 (0-516-52364-3) Childrens.

McKissack, Patricia C., jt. auth. see McKissack, Frederick.

McKissak, Patricia. Jesse Jackson: A Biography. 112p. (gr. 3-7). 1990. 2.95 (0-590-42395-9) Scholastic Inc.

Macklin, John. World's Most Bone-Chilling "True" Ghost Stories. LC 93-16616. (gr. 3 up). 1993. 12.95 (0-8069-0390-2) Sterling.

—The World's Strangest "True" Ghost Stories. Chanowitz, Elise, illus. LC 89-26125. 96p. 1990. 12.95 (0-8069-5784-0) Sterling.

—World's Strangest "True" Ghost Stories. Chanowitz, Elise, illus. LC 89-26125. 96p. (gr. 4 up). 1991. pap. 3.95 (0-8069-5785-9) Sterling.

Mackness, Brian, jt. auth. see Saunders, Richard.

McKowen, K. D. Wildlife Activity & Coloring Book. rev. ed. McKowen, K. D., illus. 32p. (gr. 2-6). 1987. workbook 1.50 (0-913635-02-2) Aspen Prods.

Mack-Williams, Kibibi. Malcolm X. LC 92-46767. 1993. 19.93 (0-86625-493-5); 14.95s.p. (0-685-66548-8) Rourke Pubns.

MacLachlan, Patricia. All the Places to Love. Wimmer, Mike, illus. LC 92-794. 32p. (gr. 1 up). 1994. 15.00 (0-06-021098-2); PLB 14.89 (0-06-021099-0) HarpC Child Bks.

—Arthur, for the Very First Time. Bloom, Lloyd, illus. LC 79-2007. 128p. (gr. 4-7). 1980. PLB 13.89 (0-06-024047-4) HarpC Child Bks.

—Arthur for the Very First Time. Bloom, Lloyd, illus. LC 79-2007. 128p. (gr. 3-6). 1989. pap. 3.95 (0-06-440288-6, Trophy) HarpC Child Bks.

—Arthur for the Very First Time. large type ed. 160p. 1990. Repr. lib. bdg. 15.95 (1-55736-169-X, Crnrstn Bks) BDD LT Grp.

—Baby. LC 93-22117. (gr. 1-8). 1993. 13.95 (0-385-31133-8) Delacorte.

—Cassie Binegar. LC 81-48641. 128p. (gr. 3-7). 1982. PLB 11.89 (0-06-024034-2) HarpC Child Bks.

—Cassie Binegar. LC 81-48641. 128p. (gr. 3-7). 1987. pap. 3.95 (0-06-440195-2, Trophy) HarpC Child Bks.

—The Facts & Fictions of Minna Pratt. LC 85-45388. 144p. (gr. 3-7). 1988. 12.00 (0-06-024114-4); PLB 11.89 (0-06-024117-9) HarpC Child Bks.

—The Facts & Fictions of Minna Pratt. LC 85-45388. 144p. (gr. 3-7). 1990. pap. 3.95 (0-06-440265-7, Trophy) HarpC Child Bks.

—Journey. (gr. 4-7). 1993. pap. 3.50 (0-440-40809-1) Dell.

—Mama One, Mama Two. Bornstein, Ruth, illus. LC 81-47795. 32p. (gr. 1-3). 1982. 13.00 (0-06-024081-4); PLB 13.89 (0-06-024082-2) HarpC Child Bks.

—Sarah, Plain & Tall. LC 83-49481. 64p. (gr. 3-5). 1985. 12.00 (0-06-024101-2); PLB 11.89 (0-06-024102-0) HarpC Child Bks.

—Sarah, Plain & Tall. LC 83-49481. 64p. (gr. 3 up). 1987. pap. 3.95 (0-06-440205-3, Trophy) HarpC Child Bks.

—Sarah, Plain & Tall. large type ed. (gr. 4-7). 1988. lib. bdg. 15.95 (1-55736-080-4, Crnrstn Bks) BDD LT Grp.

—Seven Kisses in a Row. Marella, Maria P., illus. LC 82-47718. 64p. (gr. 2-5). 1983. 13.00 (0-06-024083-0); PLB 12.89 (0-06-024084-9) HarpC Child Bks.

—Seven Kisses in a Row. Marrella, Maria P., illus. LC 82-47718. 64p. (gr. 2-5). 1988. pap. 3.95 (0-06-440231-2, Trophy) HarpC Child Bks.

—The Sick Day. Du Bois, William P., illus. LC 78-11686. (gr. k-3). 1979. 6.95 (0-394-83876-9) Pantheon.

—Skylark. 64p. (gr. 5-8). 1994. 12.00 (0-06-023328-1); PLB 11.89 (0-06-023333-8) HarpC Child Bks.

—Three Names. Pertzoff, Alexander, illus. LC 90-4444. 32p. (gr. k-4). 1991. 14.95 (0-06-024035-0); PLB 14.89 (0-06-024036-9) HarpC Child Bks.

—Through Grandpa's Eyes. Ray, Deborah, illus. LC 79-2019. 48p. (gr. 2-4). 1971. PLB 13.89 (0-06-022560-2) HarpC Child Bks.

—Through Grandpa's Eyes. Ray, Deborah, illus. LC 79-2019. 48p. (gr. k-3). 1983. pap. 4.95 (0-06-443041-3, Trophy) HarpC Child Bks.

—Tomorrow's Wizard. Jacobi, Kathy, illus. LC 81-47733. 96p. (gr. 3-6). 1982. 12.95 (0-06-024073-3); PLB 12.89 (0-06-024074-1) HarpC Child Bks.

—Unclaimed Treasures. LC 83-47714. 128p. (gr. 5-7). 1984. 13.00 (0-06-024093-8); PLB 12.89 (0-06-024094-6) HarpC Child Bks.

—Unclaimed Treasures. LC 83-47714. 128p. (gr. 5-7). 1987. pap. 3.95 (0-06-440189-8, Trophy) HarpC Child Bks.

McLain, Gary. The Indian Way: Learning to Communicate with Mother Earth. (Illus.). 114p. (Orig.). (gr. 3 up). 1990. pap. 9.95 (0-945465-73-4) John Muir.

McLanathan, Richard. Leonardo Da Vinci. (Illus.). 72p. (gr. 7 up). 1990. 19.95 (0-8109-1256-2) Abrams.

—Michelangelo. LC 92-27688. (Illus.). 92p. 1993. 19.95 (0-8109-3634-8) Abrams.

McLane, Gretel B. Kailia & the King's Horse. Kenyon, Tony, illus. 96p. (gr. 4-6). 1982. 7.95 (0-916630-28-5) Pr Pacifica.

McLaren, Clemence. Women of Destiny: A Story of the Trojan War. LC 93-8127. 1994. write for info. (0-689-31820-0, Atheneum Child Bk) Macmillan Child Grp.

MacLaren, Dorothy. Esopus Hodie, Aesop Today, Vol. II. (LAT). 68p. (Orig.). (gr. 6-12). 1991. pap. text ed. 9.50 (0-939507-25-0, B21) Amer Classical.

MacLaren, Dorothy H. Esopus Hodie, Vol. 1: Aesop Today. (LAT & ENG). 64p. (gr. 9-12). 6.70 (0-939507-06-4, B703) Amer Classical.

McLaren, Ian. Young Barbarians. 112p. (gr. 5-8). 1990. pap. 6.95 (0-86241-076-2, Pub. by Cnngt Pub Ltd) Trafalgar.

McLaughlin, Jack. People Piece Puzzles. (Illus.). (gr. 2-8). 1973. pap. 7.95 (0-918932-38-6) Activity Resources.

McLaughlin, Maria. Gymnastics. (Illus.). 64p. (gr. 7-12). 1984. 24.95 (0-7134-4283-2, Pub. by Batsford UK) Trafalgar.

McLaughlin, Michael, ed. see Howard, Lati, et al.

McLaughlin, Molly. Dragonflies. (gr. 1-5). 1989. 14.95 (0-8027-6846-6); PLB 15.85 (0-8027-6847-4) Walker & Co.

—Earthworms, Dirt, & Rotten Leaves. Shetterly, Robert, illus. 96p. 1990. pap. 3.50 (0-380-71074-9, Camelot) Avon.

—Earthworms, Dirt & Rotten Leaves: An Exploration in Ecology. Shetterly, Robert, illus. LC 86-3318. 96p. (gr. 3-7). 1986. SBE 13.95 (0-689-31215-6, Atheneum Child Bk) Macmillan Child Grp.

McLaughlin, Patrick F. The Practical Musical Instrument Owner's Guide Series, 4 bks. (Illus.). 40p. (gr. 7 up). 1992. Set. pap. text ed. write for info. (1-881158-04-7); A Practical Owner's Guide to the B flat Clarinet. pap. text ed. 5.95 (1-881158-00-4); A Practical Owner's Guide to the Saxophone. pap. text ed. 5.95 (1-881158-02-0); A Practical Owner's Guide to the Flute. pap. text ed. 5.95 (1-881158-01-2); A Practical Owner's Guide to the Brasswinds. pap. text ed. 5.95 (1-881158-03-9) Instrument Pr.

McLaughlin, Tim, jt. ed. see Rice, Wayne.

MacLaurin, Diane. The Magick Horn. Karcher, Pamela, ed. Garrity, Gloria J., illus. 75p. (Orig.). (gr. 6 up). 1993. pap. write for info. (0-934549-01-X) Laurin Hse.

Mac Laverty, Bernard. Andrew McAndrew. Smith, Duncan, illus. LC 92-52993. 80p. (gr. k-3). 1993. 13.95 (1-56402-173-4) Candlewick Pr.

MacLean, Alistair, ed. see Bowser, Milton.

McLean, Bill. The Best Peanut Butter Sandwich in the Whole World. Helmer, Katherine, illus. 28p. (ps-2). 1990. pap. 4.95 (0-88753-207-1, Pub. by Black Moss Pr CN) Firefly Bks Ltd.

Maclean, Colin & Maclean, Moira. Albert & Albertine. (Illus.). 32p. (gr. k-3). 1990. 13.95 (0-09-173486-X, Pub. by Hutchinson UK) Trafalgar.

—Albert & Albertine at the Seaside. (Illus.). 32p. (gr. k-3). 1990. 14.95 (0-09-173481-9, Pub. by Hutchinson UK) Trafalgar.

—King Cole's Castle. Maclean, Colin & Maclean, Moira, illus. LC 92-53098. 24p. (ps-1). 1992. 9.95 (1-85697-819-2) Kingfisher Bks.

—Peter's Pumpkin House. Maclean, Colin & Maclean, Moira, illus. LC 92-53099. 24p. (ps-1). 1992. 9.95 (1-85697-820-6) Kingfisher Bks.

Maclean, Colin & Maclean, Moira, illus. Mother Goose Rhymes. LC 92-26443. 32p. (ps-1). 1993. 9.95 (1-85697-898-2) Kingfisher Bks.

Maclean, Donald, tr. see Reinckens, Sunnhild.

McLean, Edwin, ed. see Faber, Nancy & Faber, Randall.

McLean, Gill. Time to Get Up. Willey, Lynne, illus. LC 93-18114. 1993. 7.95 (1-870516-11-7) Childs Play.

McLean, Gill, jt. ed. see Wilkins, Verna.

McLean, J., jt. auth. see Smith, J. C.

McLean, Janet. Fire-Engine Lil. McLean, Andrew, illus. 32p. (Orig.). (gr. k-2). 1993. pap. 6.95 (0-04-928067-8, Pub. by Allen & Unwin Aust Pty AT) IPG Chicago.

—Hector & Maggie. McLean, Andrew, illus. 32p. (Orig.). (gr. k-2). 1993. 16.95 (0-04-442162-1, Pub. by Allen & Unwin Aust Pty AT); pap. 6.95 (0-04-442245-8, Pub. by Allen & Unwin Aust Pty AT) IPG Chicago.

—Oh, Kipper! McLean, Andrew, illus. 32p. (Orig.). (gr. k-2). 1993. 16.95 (1-86373-013-3, Pub. by Allen & Unwin Aust Pty AT); pap. 6.95 (1-86373-080-X, Pub. by Allen & Unwin Aust Pty AT) IPG Chicago.

MacLean, John. Mac. 192p. (gr. 7 up). 1987. 13.45 (0-395-43080-1) HM.

—When the Mountain Sings. LC 91-26720. 212p. (gr. 5-9). 1992. 14.95 (0-395-59917-2) HM.

McLean, Margaret. Make Your Own Musical Instruments. Stott, Ken, illus. 32p. (gr. 4-7). 1988. PLB 14.95 (0-8225-0895-8, First Ave Edns); pap. 4.95 (0-8225-9558-3, First Ave Edns) Lerner Pubns.

Maclean, Moira, jt. auth. see Maclean, Colin.

McLean, Mollie & Wiseman, Anne. The Adventures of Greek Heroes. Mars, Witold T., illus. LC 61-10628. 192p. (ps-3). 1973. 15.45 (0-395-06913-0, Sandpiper); pap. 5.95 (0-685-42189-9, Sandpiper) HM.

MacLean, Norman. Hockey Basics. Gow, Bill, illus. LC 83-9451. 48p. (gr. 4-6). 1983. 10.95 (0-13-392506-4) P-H.

—Ice Skating Basics. Gow, Bill, illus. LC 84-6933. 48p. (gr. 3-7). 1984. 9.95 (0-13-448762-1) P-H.

McLean, P., et al. Building Understanding (Primary) (gr. 1-3). 1990. 7.95 (0-918932-96-3) Activity Resources.

McLean, Peggy. Mirror Explorations. (gr. k-4). 1994. pap. text ed. 7.95 (1-882293-01-0) Activity Resources.

McLean, Peggy & Sternberg, Betty. People Piece Primer. (Orig.). (gr. k-3). 1975. pap. 7.50 (0-918932-37-8) Activity Resources.

McLean, Peggy, jt. auth. see Jenkins, Lee.

McLean, Peggy, et al. Let's Pattern Block It. (Illus., Orig.). (gr. k-8). 1973. pap. 12.50 (0-918932-26-2) Activity Resources.

—Multilink Explorations. (Illus.). 48p. (gr. 1-6). 1986. pap. 7.95 (0-918932-88-2) Activity Resources.

McLean, Susan. Pennies for the Piper. 1993. pap. 4.50 (0-374-45754-9, Sunburst) FS&G.

McLean, Virginia O. Chasing the Moon to China. Cheairs, Nancy & Robinson, Susan, illus. Mitler, Ellen, et al, photos by. LC 87-60411. 40p. (gr. k-6). 1987. PLB 15.95 incl. record (0-9606046-1-8) Redbird.

—Pastatively Italy. (Illus.). 40p. (gr. k-6). 1994. incl. cassette 15.95 (0-9606046-6-9) Redbird.

McLean, Virginia O. & Klyce, Katherine P. Kenya, Jambo! LC 88-63987. (Illus.). 36p. (gr. k-6). 1989. 15.95 (0-9606046-4-2); Incl. cassette. pap. 11.95 (0-9606046-5-0) Redbird.

McLeish, Ewan. Spread of Deserts. LC 90-10018. (Illus.). 48p. (gr. 4-9). 1990. PLB 19.92 (0-8114-2390-5); pap. 5.95 (0-8114-3456-7) Raintree Steck-V.

McLeish, Kenneth. The Seven Wonders of the World. 32p. (gr. 4-7). 1986. 14.95 (0-521-26538-X) Cambridge U Pr.

—The Seven Wonders of the World. (Illus.). 1989. pap. 7.95 (0-521-37911-3) Cambridge U Pr.

McLeish, Kenneth & McLeish, Valerie. Famous People. LC 90-37910. (Illus.). 96p. (gr. 3-6). 1991. PLB 14.89 (0-8167-2238-2); pap. text ed. 6.95 (0-8167-2239-0) Troll Assocs.

McLeish, Kenneth, ed. see Buchanan, David.

McLeish, Kenneth, jt. ed. see Nichols, Roger.

McLeish, Kenneth, ed. see Nichols, Roger & Nichols, Sarah.

McLeish, Kenneth, adapted by see Vautier, Ghislaine.

McLeish, Valerie, jt. auth. see McLeish, Kenneth.

McLeish, Valerie, ed. see Buchanan, David.

McLeish, Valerie, ed. see Nichols, Roger & Nichols, Sarah.

McLellan, Vern. Wise Words from a Wise Guy. (Illus., Orig.). (gr. 7-12). 1989. pap. 3.99 (0-89081-775-8) Harvest Hse.

McLenighan, Valjean. China: A History to Nineteen Forty-Nine. LC 83-14260. (Illus.). 128p. (gr. 5-9). 1983. PLB 26.60 (0-516-02754-9) Childrens.

—One Whole Doughnut...One Doughnut Hole. LC 82-12838. (Illus.). 32p. (ps-2). 1982. PLB 11.93 (0-516-02031-5); pap. 2.95 (0-516-42031-3) Childrens.

—People's Republic of China. LC 84-7025. (Illus.). 128p. (gr. 5-9). 1984. PLB 26.60 (0-516-02781-6) Childrens.

—Stop-Go, Fast-Slow. Fiddle, Margrit, illus. LC 81-17080. 32p. (ps-2). 1982. PLB 11.93 (0-516-03617-3); pap. text ed. 2.95 (0-516-43617-1) Childrens.

MacLeod, David, jt. auth. see McKay, Sharon.

McLeod, Emilie W. The Bear's Bicycle. McPhail, David, illus. 32p. (gr. k-3). 1986. (Joy St Bks); pap. 5.95 (0-316-56206-8, Joy St Bks) Little.

—The Bear's Bicycle. McPhail, David, illus. (gr. 1-3). 1986. incl. cassette 19.95 (0-87499-025-4); pap. 12.95 incl. cassette (0-87499-023-8); 4 paperbacks, cassette & guide 27.95 (0-87499-024-6) Live Oak Media.

McLeod, Lloyd, jt. auth. see McAlister, George A.

McLeod, W. H. Way of the Sikh. (gr. 4-8). 1986. pap. 7.95 (0-7175-0731-9) Dufour.

McLerran, Alice. Dreamsong. Vasiliev, Valery, illus. LC 91-32622. 32p. (gr. k up). 1992. 14.00 (0-688-10105-4, Tambourine Bks); PLB 13.93 (0-688-10106-2, Tambourine Bks) Morrow.

—Hugs. Morgan, Mary, illus. 32p. (ps-3). 1993. 4.95 (0-590-44637-1) Scholastic Inc.

—I Want to Go Home. Kastner, Jill, illus. LC 91-9599. 32p. (ps-3). 1992. 15.00 (0-688-10144-5, Tambourine Bks); PLB 14.93 (0-688-10145-3, Tambourine Bks) Morrow.
—Kisses. Morgan, Mary, illus. 32p. (ps-3). 1993. 4.95 (0-590-44711-4) Scholastic Inc.
—The Mountain That Loved a Bird. Carle, Eric, illus. LC 85-9391. 32p. (ps up). 1991. pap. 15.95 (0-88708-000-6) Picture Bk Studio.
—Roxaboxen. (ps-3). 1991. 14.95 (0-688-07592-4) Lothrop.
—Roxaboxen. (ps-3). 1991. PLB 14.88 (0-688-07593-2) Lothrop.
—Roxaboxen. Cooney, Barbara, illus. 32p. (ps-3). 1992. pap. 4.99 (0-14-054475-5, Puffin) Puffin Bks.
—Secrets. 128p. 1990. 12.95 (0-688-09545-3) Lothrop.
McLoone, Margo, jt. auth. see Siegel, Alice.
McLoone-Basta, Margo & Siegel, Alice. The Second Kids' World Almanac of Records & Facts. World Almanac Staff, ed. 288p. (gr. 3-9). 1987. 14.95 (0-88687-397-5, World Almanac); pap. 7.95 (0-88687-317-7, World Almanac) F&W Inc NJ.
McLoughland, Beverly. Hippo's a Heap: And Other Animal Poems. 32p. (gr. 3-5). 1993. 14.95 (1-56397-017-1) Boyds Mills Pr.
McMahan, Candace. Easy-to-Use, Fun-to-Do Junior High Meetings. LC 93-37144. 1994. 14.99 (1-55945-284-6) Group Pub.
McMahan, Dean. Ajuna's Star. LC 90-82569. (SPA., Illus.). 24p. (ps-2). 1990. pap. 4.95 (0-9626254-3-4) Ajuna Unlimited.
McMahan, Dean & Rose, Willi. Ajuna's Star. rev. ed. McMahan, Dean, illus. LC 90-80841. 24p. (ps-2). 1990. pap. 4.95 (0-9626254-1-8); write for info. audio-cassette (0-9626254-2-6) Ajuna Unlimited.
MacMahon, Bryan. Patsy-O. LC 89-51016. 128p. (Orig.). (gr. 4-7). 1989. pap. 5.95 (1-85371-036-9, Pub. by Poolbeg Press Ltd Eire) Dufour.
Macmahon, Horace. Stereogram Book of Contours. LC 74-188860. 32p. (gr. 1 up). 1972. pap. 5.10 plastic comb bdg. (0-8331-1705-X) Hubbard Sci.
McMahon, James. Forty-Seven Alligators. Little, Carl, ed. Martin, Shawna, illus. 48p. (Orig.). (ps-3). 1993. pap. 10.95 (0-932433-95-2) Windswept Hse.
McMahon, James P. The Walking Fish. Weinberger, Jane, ed. LC 90-70520. (Illus.). 54p. (Orig.). (ps-3). 1990. pap. 8.95 (0-932433-70-7) Windswept Hse.
McMahon, Patricia. Chi-Hoon: A Korean Girl. O'Brien, Michael, photos by. LC 92-81331. (Illus.). 48p. (gr. 4-7). 1993. 16.95 (1-56397-026-0) Boyds Mills Pr.
McMahon, Sean. The Poolbeg Book of Irish Placenames. 113p. (Orig.). (gr. 10-12). 1990. pap. 8.95 (1-85371-087-3, Pub. by Poolbeg Pr ER) Dufour.
—The Three Seals. 181p. (Orig.). (gr. 7-9). 1992. pap. 7.95 (1-85371-148-9, Pub. by Poolbeg Pr ER) Dufour.
McMahon, Sean, jt. auth. see Byrne, Art.
McMahon, Sean, ed. Poolbeg Book of Children's Verse. 240p. 1987. pap. 9.95 (0-905169-88-3, Pub. by Poolbeg Press Ltd Eire) Dufour.
McMahon, William. Pine Barrens Legends, Lore & Lies. (Illus.). 149p. (gr. 6 up). 1986. pap. 8.95 (0-912608-19-6) Mid Atlantic.
McMane, Fred. Track & Field Basics. Seiden, Art, illus. LC 82-21458. 48p. (gr. 3-7). 1983. 9.95 (0-13-925966-X) P-H.
McMane, Fred & Wolf, Cathrine. The Worst Day I Ever Had. Hamann, Brad, illus. (gr. 3-7). 1991. pap. 8.95 (0-316-55354-9, Spts Illus Kids) Little.
McManus, Dorothy. Song of Sirius. Myhre, M., ed. McManus, Michael, illus. 155p. (Orig.). 1990. pap. 8.00 (0-929646-01-2) Temple Golden Pubns.
McManus, Joseph F., ed. & illus. see McHenry, Martha J.
McManus, Patrick F. Kid Camping from Aaaaiii! to Zip. Doty, Roy, illus. LC 79-13152. (gr. 3-8). 1979. 12.95 (0-688-41910-0) Lothrop.
—Kid Camping from AAAAIII! to Zip. Doty, Roy, illus. 144p. (gr. 6-7). 1991. pap. 3.50 (0-380-71311-X, Camelot) Avon.
—Real Ponies Don't Go Oink! large type ed. 242p. 1992. text ed. 18.95x (0-8161-5343-4, Large Print Bks) Hall.
MacManus, Seumas, ed. Donegal Fairy Stories. Verbeck, Frank, illus. xii, 256p. (gr. 4-6). 1968. pap. 5.95 (0-486-21971-2) Dover.
McMaster, Clara W. Sing a Happy Song: Beloved Children's Favorites. 1992. 8.95 (0-88290-451-5) Horizon Utah.
Macmaster, Eve. God Gives the Land. Converse, James, photos by. LC 83-182. (Illus.). 168p. (Orig.). (ps-1). 1983. pap. 5.95 (0-8361-3332-3) Herald Pr.
—God Rescues His People: Stories of God & His People: Exodus, Leviticus, Numbers & Deuteronomy. Converse, James, illus. LC 82-2849. 176p. (Orig.). (ps-1). 1982. pap. 5.95 (0-8361-1994-0) Herald Pr.
—God's Chosen King. Converse, James, illus. LC 83-12736. 190p. (Orig.). (gr. 5-6). 1983. pap. 5.95 (0-8361-3344-7) Herald Pr.
—God's Family. Converse, James, illus. LC 81-6551. 168p. (gr. 3 up). 1981. pap. 5.95 (0-8361-1964-9) Herald Pr.
—God's Justice. Converse, James, illus. LC 84-20514. 168p. (Orig.). (ps-1). 1984. pap. 5.95 (0-8361-3381-1) Herald Pr.
—God's Wisdom & Power. Converse, James, illus. LC 84-8974. 168p. (gr. 3-8). 1984. pap. 5.95 (0-8361-3362-5) Herald Pr.

MacMaster, Eve B. God Builds His Church. Converse, James, illus. LC 87-2875. 184p. (Orig.). (gr. 3 up). 1987. pap. 5.95 (0-8361-3446-X) Herald Pr.
—God Sends His Son. Converse, James, illus. LC 86-18342. 160p. (Orig.). (gr. 3-9). 1986. pap. 5.95 (0-8361-3420-6) Herald Pr.
—God's Suffering Servant. Converse, James, illus. LC 86-19526. 120p. (Orig.). (gr. 3-9). 1987. pap. 5.95 (0-8361-3422-2) Herald Pr.
MacMath, Fiona. Coming of the King. (Illus.). 24p. (gr. 3). 1991. 9.99 (0-8407-9607-2) Oliver-Nelson.
McMillan. Eating Fractions. 1993. pap. 19.95 (0-590-72732-X) Scholastic Inc.
McMillan, Brett, jt. auth. see McMillan, Bruce.
McMillan, Bruce. The Alphabet Symphony. (Illus.). 32p. (gr. k-2). 1989. 15.00 (0-317-09544-5) Apple Isl Bks.
—Apples, How They Grow. (Illus.). 48p. (ps-3). 1979. 17.45 (0-395-27806-6) HM.
—The Baby Zoo. 32p. 1992. 13.95 (0-590-44634-7, Scholastic Hardcover) Scholastic Inc.
—Beach Ball - Left, Right. McMillan, Bruce, illus. LC 91-32802. 32p. (ps-3). 1992. reinforced bdg. 14.95 (0-8234-0946-5) Holiday.
—A Beach for the Birds. McMillan, Bruce, illus. LC 92-10920. 32p. (gr. 2-5). 1993. 15.45 (0-395-64050-4) HM.
—Becca Backward, Becca Frontward: A Book of Concept Pairs. LC 86-7221. (Illus.). 32p. (ps-1). 1986. 12.95 (0-688-06282-2); PLB 12.88 (0-688-06283-0) Lothrop.
—Counting Wildflowers. LC 85-16607. (Illus.). 32p. (ps-1). 1986. 13.95 (0-688-02859-4); PLB 13.88 (0-688-02860-8) Lothrop.
—Dry or Wet? LC 86-27345. (Illus.). 32p. (ps-2). 1988. 12.95 (0-688-07100-7); PLB 12.88 (0-688-07101-5) Lothrop.
—Eating Fractions. (ps-3). 1991. 14.95 (0-590-43770-4, Scholastic Hardcover) Scholastic Inc.
—Finestkind O'Day, Lobstering in Maine. (Illus.). 48p. (gr. 3-8). 1990. 15.00 (0-685-35117-3) Apple Isl Bks.
—Fire Engine Shapes. McMillan, Bruce, photos by. LC 87-38145. (Illus.). 32p. (ps-2). 1988. 12.95 (0-688-07842-7); PLB 12.88 (0-688-07843-5) Lothrop.
—Ghost Doll. (Illus.). 32p. (gr. k-6). 1989. 15.00 (0-317-93062-1) Apple Isl Bks.
—Going on a Whale Watch. (Illus.). (ps up). 1992. 14.95 (0-590-45768-3, 016, Scholastic Hardcover) Scholastic Inc.
—Growing Colors. McMillan, Bruce, photos by. LC 88-2767. (Illus.). 40p. (ps-2). 1988. 13.95 (0-688-07844-3); PLB 13.88 (0-688-07845-1) Lothrop.
—Growing Colors. McMillan, Bruce, photos by. (Illus.). 32p. (ps up). 1994. pap. 4.95 (0-688-13112-3, Mulberry) Morrow.
—Here a Chick, There a Chick. McMillan, Bruce, photos by. LC 82-20348. (Illus.). 32p. (ps-1). 1983. 15.95 (0-688-02000-3); PLB 15.88 (0-688-02001-1) Lothrop.
—Kitten Can...a Concept Book. McMillan, Bruce, illus. LC 83-19539. 32p. (ps-1). 1984. 12.95 (0-688-02668-0); PLB 12.88 (0-688-02669-9) Lothrop.
—Making Sneakers. (Illus.). 32p. (gr. 3-12). 1989. 15.00 (0-317-93063-X) Apple Isl Bks.
—Mouse Views: What the Class Pet Saw. LC 92-25921. (Illus.). 32p. (ps-3). 1993. reinforced bdg. 15.95 (0-8234-1008-0) Holiday.
—One Sun: A Book of Terse Verse. McmMillan, Bruce, illus. LC 89-24625. 32p. (ps-3). reinforced bdg. 15.95 (0-8234-0810-8); pap. 5.95 (0-8234-0951-1) Holiday.
—One Two One Pair. McMillan, Bruce, illus. LC 90-37410. 32p. (ps-3). 1991. 12.95 (0-590-43767-4, Scholastic Hardcover) Scholastic Inc.
—Penguins at Home: Gentoos of Antarctica. McMillan, Bruce, illus. LC 92-34769. 1993. 15.95 (0-395-66560-4) HM.
—Play Day: A Book of Terse Verse. McMillan, Bruce, illus. LC 90-29077. 32p. (ps-3). 1991. reinforced 14.95 (0-8234-0894-9) Holiday.
—The Remarkable Riderless Runaway Tricycle. rev. ed. (Illus.). 48p. (gr. k-4). 1985. pap. 10.00 (0-934313-00-8) Apple Isl Bks.
—Sense Suspense. McMillan, Bruce, photos by. LC 93-30272. (Illus.). 1994. 14.95 (0-590-47904-0) Scholastic Inc.
—Step by Step. McMillan, Bruce, illus. LC 87-4195. 32p. (ps-2). 1987. 13.95 (0-688-07233-X) Lothrop.
—Step by Step. (Illus.). 28p. (ps-2). 1990. PLB 15.00 (0-685-35118-1) Apple Isl Bks.
—Super, Super, Superwords. Briley, D., ed. McMillan, Bruce, illus. LC 88-9342. 32p. (ps-3). 1989. 12.95 (0-688-08098-7); PLB 12.88 (0-688-08099-5) Lothrop.
—Time to... McMillan, Bruce, photos by. LC 89-2325. (Illus.). 32p. (ps-2). 1989. 13.95 (0-688-08855-4); PLB 13.88 (0-688-08856-2) Lothrop.
—The Weather Sky. (Illus.). 40p. (gr. 5 up). 1991. 16.95 (0-374-38261-1) FS&G.
McMillan, Bruce & McMillan, Brett. Puniddles. McMillan, Bruce, illus. (gr. 2 up). 1982. pap. 4.80 (0-395-32076-3) HM.
McMillan, Dana. Language Boosters. 64p. (gr. 2-6). 1988. 6.95 (0-912107-83-9, MM999) Monday Morning Bks.
McMillan, Dana & Martin, Shirley. Science Boosters. 64p. (gr. 2-6). 1988. 6.95 (0-912107-82-0, MM998) Monday Morning Bks.
McMillan, Dana, jt. auth. see Martin, Sidney.
McMillan, Daniel. Winning the Battle Against Drugs: Rehabilitation Programs. LC 91-16344. (Illus.). 160p. (gr. 9-12). 1991. PLB 14.40 (0-531-11063-X) Watts.

MacMillan, Dianne & Freeman, Dorothy. My Best Friend Martha Rodriquez: Meeting a Mexican-American Family. Fricke, Warren, illus. LC 86-5342. 48p. (gr. 3-6). 1986. lib. bdg. 9.98 (0-671-61973-X, J Messner) S&S Trade.
—My Best Friend Mee-Yung Kim: Meeting a Korean-American Family. Steltenpohl, Jane, ed. Marstall, Bob, illus. 48p. (gr. 3-5). 1989. lib. bdg. 9.98 (0-671-65691-0, J Messner) S&S Trade.
MacMillan, Dianne M. Easter. LC 92-18970. (Illus.). 48p. (gr. 1-4). 1993. lib. bdg. 14.95 (0-89490-405-1) Enslow Pubs.
—Elephants: Our Last Land Giants. LC 92-35268. 1993. 19.95 (0-87614-770-8) Carolrhoda Bks.
—Jewish Holidays in the Fall. LC 92-30952. (Illus.). 48p. (gr. 1-4). 1993. lib. bdg. 14.95 (0-89490-406-X) Enslow Pubs.
—Martin Luther King, Jr. Day. LC 91-43097. (Illus.). 48p. (gr. 1-4). 1992. lib. bdg. 14.95 (0-89490-382-9) Enslow Pubs.
MacMillan, Dianne M., jt. auth. see Freeman, Dorothy R.
Macmillan Educational Company Staff. Macmillan Encyclopedia of Science, 12 vols. (Illus.). 1991. Set. text ed. 360.00 (0-02-941346-X) Macmillan.
McMillan, Kate. Great Advice from Lila Fenwick. DeGroat, Diane, illus. LC 87-24513. 160p. (gr. 3-7). 1988. PLB 11.89 (0-8037-0532-8) Dial Bks Young.
McMillan, Kent. Hydroslide Kneeboarding: An Illustrated Guide to Learning & Mastering the Sport. Robertson, Jo, ed. LC 88-50672. (Illus.). 166p. (Orig.). 1988. pap. 12.95 (0-944406-03-3) World Pub FL.
McMillan, Mary. Baby Jesus. Grossman, Dan, illus. 48p. (ps-1). 1986. wkbk. 6.95 (0-86653-369-9, SS 1800, Shining Star Pubns) Good Apple.
—Bible Story Bulletin Boards. 96p. (ps-3). 1988. 10.95 (0-86653-430-X, SS1828, Shining Star Pubns) Good Apple.
—Christian Celebrations for Autumn & Winter. 96p. (gr. 2-7). 1990. 9.95 (0-86653-546-2, SS1821, Shining Star Pubns) Good Apple.
—Christian Crafts from Hand-Shaped Art. 64p. (ps-5). 1991. 8.95 (0-86653-629-9, SS1886, Shining Star Pubns) Good Apple.
—Christian Parties for Autumn & Winter. 96p. (ps-3). 1989. 9.95 (0-86653-497-0, SS1815, Shining Star Pubns) Good Apple.
—Christian Parties for Spring & Summer. (Illus.). 96p. (ps-3). 1989. 9.95 (0-86653-473-3, SS1814, Shining Star Pubns) Good Apple.
—God's ABC Zoo. Grossman, Dan, illus. 48p. (ps-1). 1987. pap. 6.95 (0-86653-405-9, SS1802, Shining Star Pubns) Good Apple.
—Joseph & His Brothers. 48p. (ps-1). 1988. 6.95 (0-86653-451-2, SS1803, Shining Star Pubns) Good Apple.
—King David. Grossman, Dan, illus. 48p. (ps-1). 1987. pap. 6.95 (0-86653-392-3, SS 1801, Shining Star Pubns) Good Apple.
—The Story of Jesus. 48p. (ps-1). 1988. 6.95 (0-86653-454-7, SS1804, Shining Star Pubns) Good Apple.
McMillan, Naomi. Wish You Were Here. LC 90-85435. (Illus.). 32p. (gr. k-3). 1991. 5.95 (1-56282-036-2) Disney Pr.
Macmillan Publishing Company Staff. Macmillan Dictionary for Students. LC 84-3880. (Illus.). 1216p. (gr. 6-12). 1984. SBE 16.95 (0-02-761560-X, Macmillan Child Bk) Macmillan Child Grp.
—Macmillan Very First Dictionary: A Magic World of Words. rev. ed. LC 82-22901. (Illus.). 280p. (ps-2). 1983. 10.95 (0-02-761730-0) Macmillan.
McMillion, Mac. Who'll Sing For Me. LC 87-91267. 130p. (Orig.). 1987. pap. 10.00 (0-9619399-0-7) M McMillion Pub.
McMinn, Tom. Prophets: Preachers for God. Fields, Don, illus. (gr. 1-6). 1979. 5.95 (0-8054-4250-2, 4242-50) Broadman.
McMullan, Jim, jt. auth. see McMullan, Kate.
McMullan, Kate. The Biggest Mouth in Baseball. DiVito, Anna, illus. LC 92-24467. 48p. (gr. 2-4). 1993. lib. bdg. 7.99 (0-448-40516-4, G&D); pap. 3.50 (0-448-40515-6, G&D) Putnam Pub Group.
—Dinosaur Hunters. Jones, John R., illus. LC 88-30742. 48p. (Orig.). (gr. 2-4). 1989. PLB 7.99 (0-394-91150-4); 3.50 (0-394-81150-X) Random Bks Yng Read.
—Goodnight, Stella. Clark, Emma C., illus. LC 93-876. Date not set. write for info. (1-56402-065-7) Candlewick Pr.
—The Great Eggspectations of Lila Fenwick. De Groat, Diane, illus. 148p. (gr. 3-7). 1991. bds. 13.95 jacketed (0-374-32774-2) FS&G.
—The Great Ideas of Lila Fenwick. De Groat, Diane, illus. (gr. 2-5). 1988. pap. 3.95 (0-14-032499-2, Puffin) Puffin Bks.
—Nutcracker Noel. McMullan, Jim, illus. LC 93-77115. 32p. (ps up). 1993. 15.00 (0-06-205039-7); PLB 14.89 (0-06-205040-0) HarpC Child Bks.
—Under the Mummy's Spell. 176p. (gr. 5 up). 1992. 16.00 (0-374-38033-3) FS&G.
McMullan, Kate & McMullan, Jim. The Noisy Giants' Tea Party. LC 92-52692. (Illus.). 32p. (ps-3). 1992. 15.00 (0-06-205017-6); PLB 14.89 (0-06-205018-4) HarpC Child Bks.
McMullan, Kate, adapted by see Leroux, Gaston.
McMullan, Kate, ed. see Stevenson, Robert Louis.

McMullen, David. Atlantis: The Missing Continent. LC 77-22138. (Illus.). 48p. (gr. 4 up). 1983. PLB 18.64 (*0-8172-1047-4*) Raintree Steck-V.
—Mystery in Peru: The Lines of Nazca. LC 77-10456. (Illus.). 48p. (gr. 4 up). 1983. PLB 18.64 (*0-8172-1058-X*) Raintree Steck-V.
McMullen, Eunice & McMullen, Nigel. Dragon for Breakfast. (Illus.). 28p. (ps-3). 1990. PLB 18.95 (*0-87614-650-7*) Carolrhoda Bks.
McMullen, Nigel, jt. auth. see McMullen, Eunice.
McMullen, Shawn. A New Home. Haley, Amanda, illus. LC 91-43071. 32p. (gr. 4-8). 1992. saddle-stitched 5.99 (*0-87403-976-2*, 24-03866) Standard Pub.
—That's What Friends Are For. Haley, Amanda, illus. LC 91-43656. (gr. 4-8). 1992. saddle-stitched 5.99 (*0-87403-975-4*, 24-03865) Standard Pub.
McMullen, Shawn A. It's What's Inside That Counts. Haley, Amanda, illus. 32p. (ps-2). 1991. pap. text ed. 3.99 (*0-87403-808-1*, 24-03898) Standard Pub.
—Justin Ordinary Squirrel. Haley, Amanda, illus. 32p. (ps-2). 1991. pap. text ed. 3.99 (*0-87403-807-3*, 24-03897) Standard Pub.
McMurtrey, Martin. Loose to the Wilds. 2nd ed. 162p. pap. 6.00 (*0-9623961-0-9*) M A McMurtrey.
McMurtry, Ken. A History Mystery: The Mystery of the Roswell UFO. 96p. (Orig.). 1992. pap. 3.50 (*0-380-76843-7*, Camelot) Avon.
—Manhunt. 1992. pap. 3.25 (*0-553-29841-0*) Bantam.
—Mystery on the Trans-Siberian Express. 1992. pap. 3.25 (*0-553-29686-8*) Bantam.
—Survival! in the Mountains. 112p. (Orig.). 1993. pap. 3.50 (*0-380-76602-7*, Camelot) Avon.
McNail, Stanley, ed. Sorcerer's Samplecase: Selected Poems in a Jugular Vein. (Illus.). 26p. (Orig.). (gr. 7 up). 1986. pap. 3.00 (*0-940945-00-2*) Embassy Hall Edns.
McNair, Joseph. Commander Coatrack Returns. 192p. (gr. 6-9). 1989. 13.45 (*0-395-48295-X*) HM.
McNair, S. New Hampshire. LC 91-540. 144p. (gr. 4 up). 1991. PLB 26.60 (*0-516-00475-1*) Childrens.
McNair, Sylvia. Alabama. LC 88-11744. (Illus.). 144p. (gr. 4 up). 1988. PLB 26.60 (*0-516-00447-6*) Childrens.
—Alabama. 178p. 1993. text ed. 15.40 (*1-56956-159-1*) W A T Braille.
—Hawaii. LC 89-35084. 144p. (gr. 4 up). 1989. PLB 26.60 (*0-516-00457-3*) Childrens.
—Hawaii. 187p. 1993. text ed. 15.40 (*1-56956-177-X*) W A T Braille.
—India. LC 89-25435. (Illus.). 128p. (gr. 5-9). 1990. PLB 26.60 (*0-516-02719-0*) Childrens.
—Indonesia. LC 93-3401. (Illus.). 128p. (gr. 5-9). 1993. PLB 26.60 (*0-516-02618-6*) Childrens.
—Kentucky. LC 87-34150. (Illus.). 144p. (gr. 4 up). 1988. PLB 26.60 (*0-516-00463-8*) Childrens.
—Kentucky. 199p. 1993. text ed. 15.40 (*1-56956-163-X*) W A T Braille.
—Korea. LC 85-23273. (Illus.). 127p. (gr. 5-6). 1986. PLB 26.60 (*0-516-02771-9*) Childrens.
—New Hampshire. 197p. 1993. text ed. 15.40 (*1-56956-156-7*) W A T Braille.
—Tennessee. LC 89-25285. (Illus.). 144p. (gr. 4 up). 1990. PLB 26.60 (*0-516-00488-3*) Childrens.
—Tennessee. 202p. 1993. text ed. 15.40 (*1-56956-162-1*) W A T Braille.
—Thailand. LC 86-29933. (Illus.). 128p. (gr. 5-9). 1987. PLB 26.60 (*0-516-02792-1*) Childrens.
—Vermont. LC 90-21117. (Illus.). 144p. (gr. 4 up). 1991. PLB 26.60 (*0-516-00491-3*) Childrens.
—Vermont. 208p. 1993. text ed. 15.40 (*1-56956-160-5*) W A T Braille.
—Virginia. LC 88-38203. (Illus.). 144p. (gr. 4 up). 1989. PLB 26.60 (*0-516-00492-1*) Childrens.
—Virginia. 195p. 1993. text ed. 15.40 (*1-56956-170-2*) W A T Braille.
McNair, Wallace Y. Black & Beautiful: A Self-Discovery Coloring Book. Caldwell, Herschel V., illus. 26p. (Orig.). (gr. 2 up). 1992. pap. 10.00 (*0-9627600-3-X*) Wstrn Images.
McNally, Bruce. Beasty Bits: Cereal Box Joke Book. Ruiz, Aristides, illus. LC 92-60580. 400p. (gr. 1-6). 1993. pap. 2.99 (*0-679-83456-7*) Random Bks Yng Read.
McNally, Darcie, adapted by. In a Cabin in a Wood. Koontz, Robin M., illus. LC 89-25192. 32p. (ps-3). 1991. 12.95 (*0-525-65035-0*, Cobblehill Bks) Dutton Child Bks.
McNamara, Brooks. The Merry Muldoons & the Brighteyes Affair. LC 91-46923. 160p. (gr. 5-12). 1992. 14.95 (*0-531-05454-3*); PLB 14.99 (*0-531-08604-6*) Orchard Bks Watts.
McNamara, John. Model Behavior. (gr. k-12). 1987. pap. 2.75 (*0-440-95569-6*, LFL) Dell.
—Revenge of the Nerd. 128p. (gr. 5 up). 1985. pap. 2.50 (*0-440-97353-8*, LFL) Dell.
McNamara, Rita. Fourteen Basic Roots & the Key to 100,000 English Words. 52p. (gr. 9-12). 1991. spiral 3.95 (*0-939507-18-8*, B117) Amer Classical.
McNamee, Daniel, ed. TAAS Quick Review Mathematics: Grade 9. (Illus.). 112p. (gr. 9). 1992. pap. text ed. 14.95 (*0-944459-34-X*) ECS Lrn Systs.
McNaught, Denise. When a Parent Loses a Job: A Workbook about My Parent's Job Loss. 1993. pap. 7.95 wkbk. (*0-385-30931-7*) Doubleday.
McNaught, Harry. Animal Babies. LC 76-24175. (Illus.). (ps-1). 1977. 2.25 (*0-394-83570-0*) Random Bks Yng Read.

—Baby Animals. McNaught, Harry, illus. LC 75-36462. 14p. (ps-1). 1976. Repr. of 1976 ed. bds. 3.95 (*0-394-83241-8*) Random Bks Yng Read.
—Los Camiones. McNaught, Harry, illus. (SPA.). 32p. (ps-3). 1993. 2.25 (*0-394-85220-6*) Random Bks Yng Read.
—Five Hundred Words to Grow on. LC 73-2442. (Illus.). (ps-1). 1973. pap. 2.25 (*0-394-82668-X*) Random Bks Yng Read.
—Muppets in My Neighborhood. McNaught, Harry, illus. LC 77-74472. (ps-k). 1977. bds. 3.95 (*0-394-83593-X*) Random Bks Yng Read.
—The Truck Book. LC 77-79851. (ps-2). 1978. pap. 2.25 (*0-394-83703-7*) Random Bks Yng Read.
—Trucks. McNaught, Harry, illus. LC 75-36463. 14p. (ps-1). 1976. Repr. of 1976 ed. bds. 3.95 (*0-394-83240-X*) Random Bks Yng Read.
McNaught, Harry, illus. Words to Grow On. LC 84-6880. 24p. (ps-1). 1984. 3.95 (*0-394-86103-5*); lib. bdg. 4.99 (*0-394-96103-X*) Random Bks Yng Read.
McNaughton, Colin. Captain Abdul's Pirate School. McNaughton, Colin, illus. LC 93-21293. 1994. write for info. (*1-56402-429-6*) Candlewick Pr.
—Guess Who's Just Moved in Next Door? McNaughton, Colin, illus. 32p. (ps-2). 1991. 15.00 (*0-679-81802-2*) Random Bks Yng Read.
—If Dinosaurs Were Cats & Dogs. rev. ed. McNaughton, Colin, illus. LC 90-22870. 32p. (ps-3). 1991. SBE 13.95 (*0-02-765785-X*, Four Winds) Macmillan Child Grp.
—Making Friends with Frankenstein: A Book of Monstrous Poems & Pictures. LC 93-20027. (Illus.). 1994. write for info. (*1-56402-308-7*) Candlewick Pr.
—Walk Rabbit Walk. McNaughton, Colin, illus. LC 91-32608. 32p. (ps-3). 1992. Repr. of 1977 ed. 13.00 (*0-688-11410-5*, Tambourine Bks) Morrow.
—Who's That Banging on the Ceiling? McNaughton, Colin, illus. LC 91-58768. 32p. (ps up). 1992. 13.95 (*1-56402-105-X*) Candlewick Pr.
McNear, Robert & Glassman, Bruce. The Marathon Race Mystery. Rogers, Jackie, illus. LC 84-16395. 128p. (gr. 3-7). 1985. lib. bdg. 9.49 (*0-8167-0444-9*) Troll Assocs.
McNeer, May. America's Abraham Lincoln. LC 90-48982. (Illus.). 128p. (gr. 6-10). 1991. PLB 13.95 (*1-55905-090-X*) Marshall Cavendish.
—The California Gold Rush. LC 87-4685. 160p. (gr. 5-9). 1987. lib. bdg. 8.99 (*0-394-90306-4*); pap. 4.99 (*0-394-89177-5*) Random Bks Yng Read.
McNeese, Tim. America's Early Canals. LC 91-41353. (Illus.). 48p. (gr. 5 up). 1993. lib. bdg. 11.95 RSBE (*0-89686-730-7*, Crestwood Hse) Macmillan Child Grp.
—America's First Railroads. LC 91-738. (Illus.). 48p. (gr. 5). 1993. RSBE 11.95 (*0-89686-729-3*, Crestwood Hse) Macmillan Child Grp.
—Clippers & Whaling Ships. LC 91-27187. (Illus.). 48p. (gr. 5). 1993. RSBE 11.95 (*0-89686-735-8*, Crestwood Hse) Macmillan Child Grp.
—Conestogas & Stagecoaches. LC 91-24064. (Illus.). 48p. (gr. 5). 1993. RSBE 11.95 (*0-89686-732-3*, Crestwood Hse) Macmillan Child Grp.
—Early River Travel. LC 91-42302. (Illus.). 48p. (gr. 5 up). 1993. lib. bdg. 11.95 RSBE (*0-89686-733-1*, Crestwood Hse) Macmillan Child Grp.
—From Trails to Turnpikes. LC 91-41352. (Illus.). 48p. (gr. 5 up). 1993. lib. bdg. 11.95 RSBE (*0-89686-731-5*, Crestwood Hse) Macmillan Child Grp.
—West by Steamboat. LC 91-22822. (Illus.). 48p. (gr. 5). 1993. RSBE 11.95 (*0-89686-728-5*, Crestwood Hse) Macmillan Child Grp.
—Western Wagon Trains. LC 91-42076. (Illus.). 48p. (gr. 5 up). 1993. lib. bdg. 11.95 RSBE (*0-89686-734-X*, Crestwood Hse) Macmillan Child Grp.
McNeil. How Things Began. (gr. 2-5). 1975. (Usborne-Hayes); PLB 13.96 (*0-88110-114-1*); pap. 6.95 (*0-86020-199-6*) EDC.
McNeil, A. Galactic War: With Four Realistic Space Wargames. (Illus.). 48p. (gr. 5 up). 1975. pap. 2.95 (*0-86020-164-3*) EDC.
McNeil, M. E. The Magic Storysinger: From the Finnish Epic Kalevala. (Illus.). 96p. (gr. 4-8). 1993. 16.95 (*0-88045-128-9*) Stemmer Hse.
McNeil, M. J. Flying Models. (Illus.). 32p. (gr. 3-6). 1977. pap. 5.95 (*0-86020-007-8*) EDC.
McNeil, M. J., jt. auth. see Philpott, V.

McNeil, Mary. Earth Sciences Reference. 709p. (gr. 6 up). 1991. 55.00 (*0-938905-00-7*); pap. 49.00 (*0-938905-01-5*) Flamingo Pr. CHOICE notes that, "There is no other single volume that combines the wealth of knowledge found in this work...Definitions are concise but informative & they are indexed geographically & by subject... Appropriate...especially for those libraries with small earth science collections or tight budgets." October, 1991. LIBRARY JOURNAL..." McNeil's bibliography of books & journal articles published through 1990 is exhaustive. Special emphasis has been given to the Southern Hemisphere since it has often been underrepresented. Appropriate for large public or academic library reference collections...More detailed coverage of earth science than a multi-volume encyclopedia." June 1, 1991. The reference has been found useful for curriculum development from middle school to college level. *Publisher Provided Annotation.*

McNeil, Nellie, et al, eds. see Wolfe, Thomas, et al.
McNickle, D'Arcy. Runner in the Sun. Houser, Allan C., illus. LC 87-5986. 260p. 1987. pap. 11.95 (*0-8263-0974-7*) U of NM Pr.
Macnow, Glen. Sports Great Cal Ripken, Jr. LC 92-24158. (Illus.). 64p. (gr. 4-10). 1993. lib. bdg. 15.95 (*0-89490-387-X*) Enslow Pubs.
—Sports Great Charles Barkley. LC 91-45827. (Illus.). 64p. (gr. 4-10). 1992. lib. bdg. 15.95 (*0-89490-386-1*) Enslow Pubs.
McNulty, Edward. Hazardous to Your Health. 48p. (Orig.). (gr. 9-12). 1990. pap. 7.99 (*1-55945-200-5*) Group Pub.
McNulty, Faith. Dancing with Manatees. Shiffman, Lena, illus. LC 93-7593. 48p. (ps-4). 1994. pap. 2.95 (*0-590-46401-9*) Scholastic Inc.
—The Elephant Who Couldn't Forget. Reissue. ed. Simont, Marc, illus. LC 79-2741. 64p. (gr. k-3). 1980. PLB 13.89 (*0-06-024146-2*) HarpC Child Bks.
—The Elephant Who Couldn't Forget. Simont, Mark, illus. LC 79-2741. 64p. (gr. k-3). 1989. pap. 3.50 (*0-06-444128-8*, Trophy) HarpC Child Bks.
—How to Dig a Hole to the Other Side of the World. Simont, Marc, illus. LC 78-22479. 32p. (ps-3). 1979. PLB 14.89 (*0-06-024148-9*) HarpC Child Bks.
—How to Dig a Hole to the Other Side of the World. Simont, Marc, illus. LC 78-22479. 32p. (gr. k-3). 1990. pap. 4.95 (*0-06-443218-1*, Trophy) HarpC Child Bks.
—The Lady & the Spider. Marstall, Bob, illus. LC 85-5427. 48p. (gr. 1-4). 1986. PLB 14.89 (*0-06-024192-6*) HarpC Child Bks.
—The Lady & the Spider. Marstall, Bob, illus. LC 85-5427. 48p. (gr. 1-4). 1987. pap. 4.95 (*0-06-443152-5*, Trophy) HarpC Child Bks.
—The Orphan. 48p. 1992. 11.95 (*0-590-43838-7*, Scholastic Hardcover) Scholastic Inc.
—Peeping in the Shell: A Whooping Crane Is Hatched. Brady, Irene, illus. LC 85-45837. 64p. (gr. 3-7). 1986. PLB 11.89 (*0-06-024135-7*) HarpC Child Bks.
—A Snake in the House. Rand, Ted, illus. LC 92-27939. 32p. (ps-3). 1994. 14.95 (*0-590-44758-0*) Scholastic Inc.
—With Love from Koko. (gr. k up). 1990. pap. 12.95 (*0-590-42774-1*) Scholastic Inc.
McNutt, Nan. Archeology for the Classroom: Teacher's Guide. (gr. 5-8). 1988. tchr's. ed. 14.50 (*0-944584-00-4*) Sopris.
—The Artifact, Unit One: Field Notebook. (gr. 5-8). 1987. wkbk. 1.25 (*0-944584-01-2*) Sopris.
—The Bentwood Box. 3rd ed. Osawa, Yasu & Jackson, Nathan, illus. 36p. (Orig.). (gr. 3-8). 1989. pap. text ed. 9.95 (*0-9614534-0-0*) N McNutt Assocs.
—The Button Blanket. 2nd ed. Osawa, Yasu & Dawson, Nancy, illus. 44p. (gr. k-3). 1989. pap. 7.95 (*0-9614534-1-9*) N McNutt Assocs.
—The Button Blanket. 2nd ed. (Illus.). 44p. (gr. k-3). 1989. pap. 7.95 (*0-9614534-3-5*) Workshop Pubns.
—The Cedar Plank Mask. (Illus.). 34p. (gr. 3-6). 1991. pap. 9.95 (*0-9614534-2-7*) N McNutt Assocs.
—The Culture, Unit Three: Field Notebook. (gr. 5-8). 1987. wkbk. 1.25 (*0-944584-03-9*) Sopris.
—Northwest Coast Indian Art Series, 3 bks. rev. ed. Yasu Osawa, illus. 118p. (gr. k-8). 1992. Set. pap. text ed. 29.95 (*0-9614534-5-1*) N McNutt Assocs.
—The Site, Unit Two: Field Notebook. (gr. 5-8). 1987. wkbk. 1.25 (*0-944584-02-0*) Sopris.
McOmber, Rachel B., ed. McOmber Phonics Storybooks: A Box. rev. ed. (Illus.). write for info. (*0-944991-13-0*) Swift Lrn Res.
—McOmber Phonics Storybooks: A Game for Champions. rev. ed. (Illus.). write for info. (*0-944991-77-7*) Swift Lrn Res.
—McOmber Phonics Storybooks: A Hum-Bug. rev. ed. (Illus.). write for info. (*0-944991-20-3*) Swift Lrn Res.
—McOmber Phonics Storybooks: A Nifty Ball of String. rev. ed. (Illus.). write for info. (*0-944991-50-5*) Swift Lrn Res.
—McOmber Phonics Storybooks: A Night to Celebrate. rev. ed. (Illus.). write for info. (*0-944991-69-6*) Swift Lrn Res.
—McOmber Phonics Storybooks: A Package from Hong Kong. rev. ed. (Illus.). write for info. (*0-944991-61-0*) Swift Lrn Res.
—McOmber Phonics Storybooks: A Red Hen. rev. ed. (Illus.). write for info. (*0-944991-25-4*) Swift Lrn Res.
—McOmber Phonics Storybooks: A Trip to China. rev. ed. (Illus.). write for info. (*0-944991-68-8*) Swift Lrn Res.
—McOmber Phonics Storybooks: At the Fair. rev. ed. (Illus.). write for info. (*0-944991-60-2*) Swift Lrn Res.

—McOmber Phonics Storybooks: Bags... Bags (Animals) rev. ed. (Illus.). write for info. *(0-944991-97-1)* Swift Lrn Res.
—McOmber Phonics Storybooks: Bags... Bags (Holidays) rev. ed. (Illus.). write for info. *(0-944991-98-X)* Swift Lrn Res.
—McOmber Phonics Storybooks: Ben Has a Pet. rev. ed. (Illus.). write for info. *(0-944991-26-2)* Swift Lrn Res.
—McOmber Phonics Storybooks: Ben in Bed. rev. ed. (Illus.). write for info. *(0-944991-29-7)* Swift Lrn Res.
—McOmber Phonics Storybooks: Ben Will Get Well. rev. ed. (Illus.). write for info. *(0-944991-30-0)* Swift Lrn Res.
—McOmber Phonics Storybooks: Boe E. Toad. rev. ed. (Illus.). write for info. *(0-944991-54-8)* Swift Lrn Res.
—McOmber Phonics Storybooks: Boyer's Toy Store. rev. ed. (Illus.). write for info. *(0-944991-66-1)* Swift Lrn Res.
—McOmber Phonics Storybooks: Bug. rev. ed. (Illus.). write for info. *(0-944991-19-X)* Swift Lrn Res.
—McOmber Phonics Storybooks: Choose Which One - 1. rev. ed. (Illus.). write for info. *(0-944991-67-X)* Swift Lrn Res.
—McOmber Phonics Storybooks: Choose Which One - 2. rev. ed. (Illus.). write for info. *(0-944991-70-X)* Swift Lrn Res.
—McOmber Phonics Storybooks: Everyone Knows a Pitcher. rev. ed. (Illus.). write for info. *(0-944991-79-3)* Swift Lrn Res.
—McOmber Phonics Storybooks: Fizz in the Pit. rev. ed. (Illus.). write for info. *(0-944991-12-2)* Swift Lrn Res.
—McOmber Phonics Storybooks: Fizz Mix. rev. ed. (Illus.). write for info. *(0-944991-11-4)* Swift Lrn Res.
—McOmber Phonics Storybooks: Fizz Mud. rev. ed. (Illus.). write for info. *(0-944991-21-1)* Swift Lrn Res.
—McOmber Phonics Storybooks: Hello Again. rev. ed. (Illus.). write for info. *(0-944991-84-X)* Swift Lrn Res.
—McOmber Phonics Storybooks: Hen Pox. rev. ed. (Illus.). write for info. *(0-944991-28-9)* Swift Lrn Res.
—McOmber Phonics Storybooks: Humps & Lumps. rev. ed. (Illus.). write for info. *(0-944991-62-9)* Swift Lrn Res.
—McOmber Phonics Storybooks: In the Dell. rev. ed. (Illus.). write for info. *(0-944991-32-7)* Swift Lrn Res.
—McOmber Phonics Storybooks: Jud & Nell. rev. ed. (Illus.). write for info. *(0-944991-33-5)* Swift Lrn Res.
—McOmber Phonics Storybooks: Kim. rev. ed. (Illus.). write for info. *(0-944991-07-6)* Swift Lrn Res.
—McOmber Phonics Storybooks: Kim & the Lion. rev. ed. (Illus.). write for info. *(0-944991-74-2)* Swift Lrn Res.
—McOmber Phonics Storybooks: Max. rev. ed. (Illus.). write for info. *(0-944991-01-7)* Swift Lrn Res.
—McOmber Phonics Storybooks: Max is Six. rev. ed. (Illus.). write for info. *(0-944991-43-2)* Swift Lrn Res.
—McOmber Phonics Storybooks: Max Ran. rev. ed. (Illus.). write for info. *(0-944991-02-5)* Swift Lrn Res.
—McOmber Phonics Storybooks: Max the Grand. rev. ed. (Illus.). write for info. *(0-944991-57-2)* Swift Lrn Res.
—McOmber Phonics Storybooks: Max's Treasure Hunt. rev. ed. (Illus.). write for info. *(0-944991-73-4)* Swift Lrn Res.
—McOmber Phonics Storybooks: Me & the Bee. rev. ed. (Illus.). write for info. *(0-944991-46-7)* Swift Lrn Res.
—McOmber Phonics Storybooks: Miss Vie. rev. ed. (Illus.). write for info. *(0-944991-48-3)* Swift Lrn Res.
—McOmber Phonics Storybooks: Mom & Dad Hop-Jig. rev. ed. (Illus.). write for info. *(0-944991-16-5)* Swift Lrn Res.
—McOmber Phonics Storybooks: Number Fun. rev. ed. (Illus.). write for info. *(0-944991-58-0)* Swift Lrn Res.
—McOmber Phonics Storybooks: On TV. rev. ed. (Illus.). write for info. *(0-944991-17-3)* Swift Lrn Res.
—McOmber Phonics Storybooks: Pete's Bike Ride. rev. ed. (Illus.). write for info. *(0-944991-40-8)* Swift Lrn Res.
—McOmber Phonics Storybooks: Razz. rev. ed. (Illus.). write for info. *(0-944991-06-8)* Swift Lrn Res.
—McOmber Phonics Storybooks: Razz Visits Raz in Israel. rev. ed. (Illus.). write for info. *(0-944991-75-0)* Swift Lrn Res.
—McOmber Phonics Storybooks: Robin Hood's Cook. rev. ed. (Illus.). write for info. *(0-944991-64-5)* Swift Lrn Res.
—McOmber Phonics Storybooks: Snores & More. rev. ed. (Illus.). write for info. *(0-944991-59-9)* Swift Lrn Res.
—McOmber Phonics Storybooks: Starfish of Norway. rev. ed. (Illus.). write for info. *(0-944991-72-6)* Swift Lrn Res.
—McOmber Phonics Storybooks: String Art, Vol. 1. rev. ed. (Illus.). write for info. *(0-944991-96-3)* Swift Lrn Res.
—McOmber Phonics Storybooks: String Art, Vol. 2. rev. ed. (Illus.). write for info. *(0-944991-95-5)* Swift Lrn Res.
—McOmber Phonics Storybooks: Tale of the Green Glob. rev. ed. (Illus.). write for info. *(0-944991-65-3)* Swift Lrn Res.
—McOmber Phonics Storybooks: Ten in the Hut. rev. ed. (Illus.). write for info. *(0-944991-27-0)* Swift Lrn Res.
—McOmber Phonics Storybooks: The Bag. rev. ed. (Illus.). write for info. *(0-944991-03-3)* Swift Lrn Res.
—McOmber Phonics Storybooks: The Big Deal. rev. ed. (Illus.). write for info. *(0-944991-47-5)* Swift Lrn Res.
—McOmber Phonics Storybooks: The Big Hole. rev. ed. (Illus.). write for info. *(0-944991-38-6)* Swift Lrn Res.

—McOmber Phonics Storybooks: The Bon-Bon Box. rev. ed. (Illus.). write for info. *(0-944991-14-9)* Swift Lrn Res.
—McOmber Phonics Storybooks: The Box Mix. rev. ed. (Illus.). write for info. *(0-944991-15-7)* Swift Lrn Res.
—McOmber Phonics Storybooks: The Cake. rev. ed. (Illus.). write for info. *(0-944991-44-0)* Swift Lrn Res.
—McOmber Phonics Storybooks: The Confection Connection. rev. ed. (Illus.). write for info. *(0-944991-71-8)* Swift Lrn Res.
—McOmber Phonics Storybooks: The Cove of Gloom. rev. ed. (Illus.). write for info. *(0-944991-83-1)* Swift Lrn Res.
—McOmber Phonics Storybooks: The Fumes. rev. ed. (Illus.). write for info. *(0-944991-39-4)* Swift Lrn Res.
—McOmber Phonics Storybooks: The Gal Pals. rev. ed. (Illus.). write for info. *(0-944991-42-4)* Swift Lrn Res.
—McOmber Phonics Storybooks: The Haircut. rev. ed. (Illus.). write for info. *(0-944991-53-X)* Swift Lrn Res.
—McOmber Phonics Storybooks: The Hum-Bug Hop. rev. ed. (Illus.). write for info. *(0-944991-31-9)* Swift Lrn Res.
—McOmber Phonics Storybooks: The Invisible Crocodiles. rev. ed. (Illus.). write for info. *(0-944991-80-7)* Swift Lrn Res.
—McOmber Phonics Storybooks: The Kit. rev. ed. (Illus.). write for info. *(0-944991-08-4)* Swift Lrn Res.
—McOmber Phonics Storybooks: The Land of Morning. rev. ed. (Illus.). write for info. *(0-944991-82-3)* Swift Lrn Res.
—McOmber Phonics Storybooks: The Lemonade Sale. rev. ed. (Illus.). write for info. *(0-944991-41-6)* Swift Lrn Res.
—McOmber Phonics Storybooks: The Magic e. rev. ed. (Illus.). write for info. *(0-944991-37-8)* Swift Lrn Res.
—McOmber Phonics Storybooks: The Map. rev. ed. (Illus.). write for info. *(0-944991-05-X)* Swift Lrn Res.
—McOmber Phonics Storybooks: The Neat Trick. rev. ed. (Illus.). write for info. *(0-944991-55-6)* Swift Lrn Res.
—McOmber Phonics Storybooks: The Pit Kit. rev. ed. (Illus.). write for info. *(0-944991-09-2)* Swift Lrn Res.
—McOmber Phonics Storybooks: The Prime Time Trick. rev. ed. (Illus.). write for info. *(0-944991-56-4)* Swift Lrn Res.
—McOmber Phonics Storybooks: The Prize. rev. ed. (Illus.). write for info. *(0-944991-49-1)* Swift Lrn Res.
—McOmber Phonics Storybooks: The Quiz Is (1) rev. ed. (Illus.). write for info. *(0-944991-34-3)* Swift Lrn Res.
—McOmber Phonics Storybooks: The Quiz Is (2) rev. ed. (Illus.). write for info. *(0-944991-35-1)* Swift Lrn Res.
—McOmber Phonics Storybooks: The Rope. rev. ed. (Illus.). write for info. *(0-944991-45-9)* Swift Lrn Res.
—McOmber Phonics Storybooks: The Sub. rev. ed. (Illus.). write for info. *(0-944991-43-2X)* Swift Lrn Res.
—McOmber Phonics Storybooks: The Tan Cab. rev. ed. (Illus.). write for info. *(0-944991-04-1)* Swift Lrn Res.
—McOmber Phonics Storybooks: The Time Box. rev. ed. (Illus.). write for info. *(0-944991-52-1)* Swift Lrn Res.
—McOmber Phonics Storybooks: The Tin Lid. rev. ed. (Illus.). write for info. *(0-944991-10-6)* Swift Lrn Res.
—McOmber Phonics Storybooks: The Tub. rev. ed. (Illus.). write for info. *(0-944991-24-6)* Swift Lrn Res.
—McOmber Phonics Storybooks: The TV Box. rev. ed. (Illus.). write for info. *(0-944991-18-1)* Swift Lrn Res.
—McOmber Phonics Storybooks: The Video Show. rev. ed. (Illus.). write for info. *(0-944991-63-7)* Swift Lrn Res.
—McOmber Phonics Storybooks: The Wizz Kid. rev. ed. (Illus.). write for info. *(0-944991-23-8)* Swift Lrn Res.
—McOmber Phonics Storybooks: Tid Bits. rev. ed. (Illus.). write for info. *(0-944991-36-X)* Swift Lrn Res.
—McOmber Phonics Storybooks: Under the Rainbow. rev. ed. (Illus.). write for info. *(0-944991-81-5)* Swift Lrn Res.
—McOmber Phonics Storybooks: Writing Book No. 1. rev. ed. (Illus.). write for info. *(0-944991-93-9)* Swift Lrn Res.
—McOmber Phonics Storybooks: Writing Book No. 2. rev. ed. (Illus.). write for info. *(0-944991-94-7)* Swift Lrn Res.
—McOmber Phonics Storybooks: Yellow Crocodile. rev. ed. (Illus.). write for info. *(0-944991-76-9)* Swift Lrn Res.
—McOmber Phonics Storybooks: You Can Make It. rev. ed. (Illus.). write for info. *(0-944991-51-3)* Swift Lrn Res.

McPartland, Scott. Edwin Land. LC 93-22077. (gr. 7-8). 1993. 15.93 *(0-86592-150-4)*; 11.95s.p. *(0-685-66592-5)* Rourke Enter.
—Gordon Gould. LC 93-2819. 1993. 15.93 *(0-86592-079-6)*; 11.95s.p. *(0-685-66585-2)* Rourke Enter.

McPartland, Suzy. Good Morning, Sun. Neeper, William, illus. 12p. (ps-k). 1994. bds. 4.95 *(0-689-71747-4,* Aladdin) Macmillan Child Grp.
—Sleepy-Time Moon. Neeper, William, illus. 12p. (ps-k). 1994. bds. 4.95 *(0-689-71748-2,* Aladdin) Macmillan Child Grp.
—Toy-Shop Surprise. Neeper, William, illus. 12p. (ps-k). 1994. bds. 4.95 *(0-689-71749-0,* Aladdin) Macmillan Child Grp.
—Zoom, Car, Zoom. Neeper, William, illus. 12p. (ps-k). 1994. bds. 4.95 *(0-689-71750-4,* Aladdin) Macmillan Child Grp.

McPhail, David. Andrew's Bath. McPhail, David, illus. (ps-3). 1984. 13.95 *(0-316-56319-6,* Joy St Bks) Little.

—Annie & Co. LC 90-34119. 40p. (gr. 2-4). 1991. 13.95 *(0-8050-1596-5,* Bks Young Read); PLB 13.89 *(0-8050-1686-4)* H Holt & Co.
—Annie & Company II. 1994. write for info. *(0-8050-2819-6)* H Holt & Co.
—The Bear's Toothache. (Illus.). 32p. (gr. k-3). 1972. lib. bdg. 14.95 *(0-316-56312-9,* Joy St Bks) Little.
—The Bear's Toothache. McPhail, David, illus. (gr. k-2). 1986. incl. cassette 19.95 *(0-87499-081-5)*; pap. 12.95 incl. cassette *(0-87499-080-7)*; 4 paperbacks, cassette & guide 27.95 *(0-87499-082-3)* Live Oak Media.
—The Bear's Toothache. McPhail, David, illus. (ps-3). 1988. pap. 5.95 *(0-316-56325-0,* Joy St Bks) Little.
—David Mcphail's Animals A to Z. 1989. pap. 2.50 *(0-590-40347-8)* Scholastic Inc.
—David McPhail's Animals A to Z. (Illus.). 32p. (ps-1). 1993. 2.50 *(0-590-46462-0,* Cartwheel) Scholastic Inc.
—The Dream Child. McPhail, David, illus. LC 84-18755. 32p. (ps-3). 1988. pap. 4.95 *(0-525-44366-5,* 0383-120, DCB) Dutton Child Bks.
—Ed & Me. LC 86-3175. (Illus.). 32p. (ps-3). 1990. 13.95 *(0-15-224888-9)* HarBrace.
—Emma's Pet. McPhail, David, illus. LC 85-4414. 24p. (ps-k). 1985. 9.95 *(0-525-44210-3,* DCB) Dutton Child Bks.
—Emma's Pet. McPhail, David, illus. (ps-2). 1988. bk. & cassette 19.95 *(0-87499-107-2)*; bk. & cassette 12.95 *(0-87499-106-4)*; 4 cassettes & guide 27.95 *(0-87499-108-0)* Live Oak Media.
—Emma's Pet. McPhail, David, illus. LC 85-4414. 24p. (ps-k). 1988. pap. 3.95 *(0-525-44430-0,* DCB) Dutton Child Bks.
—Emma's Vacation. McPhail, David, illus. LC 86-24066. 24p. (ps-k). 1987. 7.95 *(0-525-44315-0,* DCB) Dutton Child Bks.
—Emma's Vacation. LC 86-24066. (Illus.). 24p. (ps-k). 1991. pap. 3.95 *(0-525-44737-7,* Puffin) Puffin Bks.
—Farm Boy's Year. McPhail, David, illus. LC 91-4982. 32p. (gr. k-3). 1992. SBE 13.95 *(0-689-31679-8,* Atheneum Child Bk) Macmillan Child Grp.
—Farm Morning. McPhail, David, illus. LC 84-19167. 32p. (ps-3). 1985. 15.95 *(0-15-227299-2,* HB Juv Bks) HarBrace.
—Farm Morning. D'Andrade, Diane, ed. (Illus.). 32p. (Orig.). (ps-3). 1991. pap. 3.95 *(0-15-227300-X,* HB Juv Bks) HarBrace.
—First Flight. McPhail, David, illus. LC 86-28804. (ps-3). 1987. 14.95i *(0-316-56323-4,* Joy St Bks) Little.
—First Flight. (Illus.). (ps-3). 1991. Repr. 4.95 *(0-316-56332-3,* Joy St Bks) Little.
—Fix-It. McPhail, David, illus. LC 83-16459. 24p. (ps-k). 1984. 11.00 *(0-525-44093-3,* DCB) Dutton Child Bks.
—Fix-It. McPhail, David, illus. (gr. k-3). 1988. bk. & cassette 19.95 *(0-87499-084-X)*; bk. & cassette 12.95 *(0-87499-083-1)*; 4 cassettes & guide 27.95 *(0-87499-085-8)* Live Oak Media.
—Fix-It. McPhail, David, illus. LC 83-16459. 24p. (ps-k). 1987. pap. 3.95 *(0-525-44323-1,* 0383-120, DCB) Dutton Child Bks.
—Fix-It. (Illus.). 24p. (ps-k). 1993. pap. 17.99 *(0-14-054931-5,* Puffin Unicorn) Puffin Bks.
—Fix It All. (ps). 1992. pap. 4.99 *(0-14-054752-5)* Puffin Bks.
—Great Cat. LC 81-12654. (Illus.). 32p. (gr. k up). 1986. pap. 4.95 *(0-525-44273-1,* DCB) Dutton Child Bks.
—Henry Bear's Park. McPhail, David, illus. 48p. (gr. 1-3). 1976. lib. bdg. 14.95 *(0-316-56315-3,* Joy St Bks) Little.
—Lost! (gr. 4-8). 1993. pap. 5.95 *(0-316-56336-6,* Joy St Bks) Little.
—Lost, Vol. 1. (ps-3). 1990. 14.95 *(0-316-56329-3,* Joy St Bks) Little.
—Moony B. Finch, Fastest Draw in the West. LC 93-37408. 1994. lib. bdg. 12.95 *(0-307-17554-5,* Artsts Writrs) Western Pub.
—The Party. (ps-4). 1990. 14.95 *(0-316-56330-7,* Joy St Bks) Little.
—Pig Pig & the Magic Photo Album. McPhail, David, illus. LC 85-20459. 24p. (ps-3). 1986. 10.95 *(0-525-44238-3,* DCB) Dutton Child Bks.
—Pig Pig & the Magic Photo Album. LC 85-20459. (Illus.). 24p. (ps-3). 1989. pap. 3.95 *(0-525-44539-0,* DCB) Dutton Child Bks.
—Pig Pig Gets a Job. LC 89-25606. (Illus.). 24p. (ps-3). 1990. 12.95 *(0-525-44619-2,* DCB) Dutton Child Bks.
—Pig Pig Goes to Camp. LC 83-1412. (Illus.). 24p. (ps-3). 1983. 12.95 *(0-525-44064-X,* 0966-290, DCB) Dutton Child Bks.
—Pig Pig Goes to Camp. McPhail, David, illus. LC 83-1412. 24p. (ps-3). 1987. pap. 3.95 *(0-525-44302-9,* DCB) Dutton Child Bks.
—Pig Pig Grows Up. LC 80-377. (Illus.). 32p. (ps-2). 1980. 13.95 *(0-525-37027-7,* DCB); pap. 3.95 *(0-525-44195-6,* DCB) Dutton Child Bks.
—Pig Pig Grows Up. McPhail, David, illus. (ps-2). 1985. pap. 12.95 incl. cassette *(0-941078-94-9)*; incl. cassette 19.95 *(0-941078-96-5)*; incl. cassette 4 paperbacks guide 27.95 *(0-941078-95-7)* Live Oak Media.
—Pig Pig Rides. McPhail, David, illus. LC 82-9777. 24p. (ps-3). 1982. 14.00 *(0-525-44024-0,* DCB) Dutton Child Bks.
—Pig Pig Rides. McPhail, David, illus. (gr. 1-3). 1988. bk. & cassette 19.95 *(0-87499-090-4)*; bk. & cassette 12.95 *(0-87499-089-0)*; 4 cassettes & guide 27.95 *(0-87499-091-2)* Live Oak Media.
—Pig Pig Rides. McPhail, David, illus. LC 82-9777. 24p. (ps-3). 1985. pap. 3.95 *(0-525-44222-7,* DCB) Dutton Child Bks.

—Pig Pig Rides Again. (ps-3). 1992. pap. 4.99
(*0-14-054781-9*) Puffin Bks.
—Pigs Aplenty, Pigs Galore. LC 92-27986. (ps-2). 1993.
13.99 (*0-525-45079-3*, DCB) Dutton Child Bks.
—Santa's Book of Names. LC 92-37279. 1993. 14.95
(*0-316-56335-8*, Joy St Bks) Little.
—Sisters. LC 84-3775. (Illus.). 32p. (ps-3). 1984. 12.95
(*0-15-275319-2*, HB Juv Bks) HarBrace.
—Sisters. 32p. (ps-3). 1990. pap. 3.95 (*0-15-275320-6*,
Voyager Bks) HarBrace.
—Snow Lion. McPhail, David, illus. LC 82-8119. 48p.
(ps-3). 1987. 5.95 (*0-8193-1097-2*); PLB 5.95
(*0-8193-1098-0*) Parents.
—Snow Lion. McPhail, David, illus. 48p. (gr. 3-7). 1990.
pap. 2.95 (*0-448-04335-1*, G&D) Putnam Pub Group.
—Something Special. McPhail, David, illus. 32p. (ps-3).
1988. 12.95 (*0-316-56324-2*) Little.
—Something Special. (ps-3). 1992. pap. 4.95
(*0-316-56333-1*, Joy St Bks) Little.
—Story of James. LC 89-30549. (Illus.). 32p. (ps-3).
1989. 11.95 (*0-525-44529-3*, DCB) Dutton Child Bks.
—Those Terrible Toy-Breakers. McPhail, David, illus. LC
80-10450. 48p. (ps-3). 1980. 5.95 (*0-8193-1019-0*);
PLB 5.95 (*0-8193-1020-4*) Parents.
—Those Terrible Toy Breakers. McPhail, David, illus.
48p. (ps-2). 1990. pap. 2.95 (*0-448-04343-2*, G&D)
Putnam Pub Group.
—The Train. (gr. 3-6). 1977. lib. bdg. 14.95
(*0-316-56316-1*, Joy St Bks) Little.
—Train. (ps-3). 1990. write for info.;(Joy St Bks); pap.
5.95 (*0-316-56331-5*, Joy St Bks) Little.
McPhail, Mac. Emma's Pet. (ps) 1988. pap. 4.50
(*0-14-054749-5*, DCB) Dutton Child Bks.
McPhee, John, ed. Tu Fe. Diaz, Olimpia, tr. (SPA.). (gr.
9-12). 1979. pap. 3.95 (*0-89243-124-5*, 48290) Liguori
Pubns.
McPhee, Penelope & McPhee, Raymond. Your Future in
Space: The U. S. Space Camp Training Program.
Schulke, Flip & Schulke, Debra, photos by.
McCandless, Bruce & Sullivan, Kathryn D.frwd. by.
LC 86-9003. (Illus.). 128p. (gr. 7 up). 1986. pap. 14.95
(*0-517-56418-1*) Crown Bks Yng Read.
McPhee, Raymond, jt. auth. see McPhee, Penelope.
McPherson, Betty. A Mayflower Adventure. Stefano,
Nancy Di, illus. 32p. (ps-1). 1985. 6.00
(*0-918823-00-5*) Boyce-Pubns.
—The Small Patriot. (Illus.). 32p. (ps-1). 1987. 6.00
(*0-918823-01-3*) Boyce-Pubns.
McPherson, J. G. Fun with Electronics. 64p. (gr. 3-6).
1983. nap. 9.95 (*0-86020-525-8*); lib. bdg. 11.96
(*0-88110-160-5*) EDC.
McPherson, James M. Marching Toward Freedom:
Blacks in the Civil War, 1861-1865. (Illus.). 128p. (gr.
7-12). 1990. 16.95x (*0-8160-2337-9*) Facts on File.
McPherson, Jan. The Dog School. LC 90-10085. (Illus.).
24p. (gr. 1-4). 1990. PLB 15.96 (*0-8114-2697-1*)
Raintree Steck-V.
—In the Cold, Cold Dawn. LC 92-31918. 1993. 4.25
(*0-383-03578-3*) SRA Schl Grp.
MacPherson, Jennifer B. To Attempt a Tower. LC 85-
90339. 84p. (gr. 9-12). 1985. 16.95 (*0-9614949-0-X*);
pap. 8.95 (*0-9614849-1-8*) MacPherson Pub.
MacPherson, Margaret. The Rough Road. 226p. (gr.
5-8). 1990. nap. 6.95 (*0-86241-177-7*, Pub. by Cnngt
Pub Ltd) Trafalgar.
McPherson, Mark. Caring for Your Cat. Bernstein,
Marianne, illus. LC 84-223. 48p. (gr. 3-7). 1985. PLB
9.89 (*0-8167-0115-6*); pap. text ed. 2.95
(*0-8167-0116-4*) Troll Assocs.
—Caring for Your Dog. Bernstein, Marianne, illus. LC
84-222. 48p. (gr. 3-7). 1985. PLB 9.89
(*0-8167-0113-X*); pap. 2.95 (*0-8167-0114-8*) Troll
Assocs.
—Caring for Your Fish. Bernstein, Marianne, illus. LC
84-8563. 48p. (gr. 3-7). 1985. PLB 9.89
(*0-8167-0109-1*); pap. text ed. 2.95 (*0-8167-0110-5*)
Troll Assocs.
—Choosing Your Pet. Bernstein, Dianne, illus. LC 84-
226. 48p. (gr. 3-7). 1985. PLB 9.89 (*0-8167-0111-3*)
Troll Assocs.
MacPherson, Mary. Birdwatch: A Young Person's
Introduction to Birding. Douglas, Virginia, illus. 144p.
(Orig.). (gr. 6 up). 1989. pap. 9.95 (*0-920197-57-4*,
Pub. by Summerhill CN) Sterling.
McPherson, Stephanie. Rooftop Astronomer: A Story
about Maria Mitchell. Mitchell, Hetty, illus. 32p. (gr.
3-6). 1990. PLB 14.95 (*0-87614-410-5*) Carolrhoda
Bks.
McPherson, Stephanie S. Genius: The Story of Albert
Einstein. LC 93-1408. 1993. 17.50 (*0-87614-788-0*)
Carolrhoda Bks.
—I Speak for the Women: A Story about Lucy Stone.
Liedahl, Brian, illus. LC 92-13786. 1992. 14.95
(*0-87614-740-6*) Carolrhoda Bks.
—Workers' Detective: A Story about Alice Hamilton.
(ps-3). 1992. 14.95 (*0-87614-699-X*) Carolrhoda Bks.
McPhillips, Martin. The Battle of Trenton. LC 84-40382.
(Illus.). 64p. (gr. 5 up). 1984. PLB 16.98
(*0-382-06823-8*); pap. 8.95 (*0-382-09900-1*) Silver
Burdett Pr.
—The Constitutional Convention. LC 85-40169. (Illus.).
64p. (gr. 5 up). 1985. PLB 16.98 (*0-382-06827-0*); pap.
8.95 (*0-382-09435-2*) Silver Burdett Pr.
—Hiroshima. LC 85-40170. (Illus.). 64p. (gr. 5 up). 1985.
PLB 16.98 (*0-382-06829-7*); pap. 8.95 (*0-382-06976-5*)
Silver Burdett Pr.

McQuade, Susan. Great-Grandpa. Rogers, Gregory, illus.
LC 92-27235. 1993. 3.75 (*0-383-03622-4*) SRA Schl
Grp.
McQueen. La Gallinita Roja. (SPA.). 1993. pap. 28.67
(*0-590-71879-7*) Scholastic Inc.
—What Does Sunny Bunny Love? (gr. 2 up). 1988. 2.50
(*0-448-09252-2*, G&D) Putnam Pub Group.
McQueen, John T. A World Full of Monsters. Brown,
Marc, illus. LC 85-48257. 32p. (ps-3). 1986. (Crowell
Jr Bks) HarpC Child Bks.
McQueen, Kelly & Fassler, David. Let's Talk Trash: The
Kids' Book about Recycling. LC 90-21400. (Illus.).
168p. (ps-6). 1991. pap. 14.95g (*0-914525-19-0*);
plastic comb 18.95 (*0-914525-20-4*) Waterfront Bks.
McQueen, Kelly, jt. auth. see Fassler, David.
McQueen, Lucinda. Counting Bears. (Illus.). 24p. (gr.
1-3). 1990. bds. 2.50 (*0-448-02263-X*, G&D) Putnam
Pub Group.
—Little Lamb's Easter Surprise. (Illus.). 10p. (ps). 1994.
bds. 4.95 (*0-590-47803-6*, Cartwheel) Scholastic Inc.
—Pet the Baby Farm Animals: Their Fur Feels Real!
(Illus.). 16p. (ps). 1994. 8.95 (*0-590-47687-4*,
Cartwheel) Scholastic Inc.
McQueen, Lucinda, illus. Coloring Bears. LC 90-83242.
24p. (ps) 1991. 2.50 (*0-448-40126-6*, G&D) Putnam
Pub Group.
—The Little Red Hen. 32p. (Orig.). (gr. k-2). 1985. Big
book. 19.95 (*0-590-71718-9*); pap. 2.50
(*0-590-41145-4*) Scholastic Inc.
—Pudgy Zoo Babies. 16p. 1989. bds. 2.95
(*0-448-02256-7*, G&D) Putnam Pub Group.
—Xavier's Fantastic Discovery. LC 83-20446. 1984. incl.
cassette 7.95 (*0-910313-60-1*); 5.95 (*0-910313-25-3*)
Parker Bros.
McQueen, Lucinda & Guitar, Jeremy, illus. Otis Lee.
12p. (gr. 1-5). 1984. 4.00 (*0-910313-33-4*) Parker
Bros.
—Sybil Sadie. 12p. (gr. 1-5). 1984. 4.00 (*0-910313-32-6*)
Parker Bros.
McQueen, Priscilla L. How Many. Walter, Mary W.,
illus. (gr. k). 1968. pap. 2.54 (*0-685-16725-9*)
McQueen.
—We Can Read: Story Pack-54 Little Stories. 1973. pap.
18.66 (*0-685-47089-X*) McQueen.
—What Kind. Walter, Mary W., illus. (gr. k). 1968. pap.
2.07 (*0-685-16726-7*) McQueen.
—Which One. Walter, Mary W., illus. (gr. k). 1968. pap.
6.15 (*0-685-16727-5*) McQueen.
McQueen, Tiffany, jt. auth. see Grubbs, Tabitha.
McQuilkin, Frank. Forgottenville: The Town That
Arrested Santa Claus. Doros Animations, Inc., illus.
48p. (gr. k-7). 1982. 11.95 (*0-941316-00-9*) TSM
Books.
MacQuitty, Miranda. Desert. LC 93-21068. 1994. 15.00
(*0-679-86003-7*); PLB 15.99 (*0-679-96003-1*) Knopf
Bks Yng Read.
—Discovering Foxes. Caulkins, Janet, ed. (Illus.). 48p.
(gr. 1-6). 1988. PLB 12.40 (*0-531-18197-9*, Pub. by
Bookwright Pr) Watts.
—Discovering Jellyfish. (Illus.). 48p. (gr. k-6). 1989. PLB
12.40 (*0-531-18281-9*, Pub. by Bookwright Pr) Watts.
—Discovering Weasels. (Illus.). 48p. (gr. k-6). 1989. PLB
12.40 (*0-531-18282-7*, Pub. by Bookwright Pr) Watts.
—Shark. Greenaway, Frank & King, Dave, photos by. LC
92-4712. (Illus.). 64p. 1992. 15.00 (*0-679-81683-6*);
PLB 16.99 (*0-679-91683-0*) Knopf Bks Yng Read.
McRae, Patrick, illus. Peter Cottontail. 24p. (Orig.). (gr.
k-6). 1986. pap. 2.95 (*0-8249-8106-5*, Ideals Child)
Hambleton-Hill.
McRae, Rodney. Cry Me a River. (ps-3). 1992. 12.00
(*0-207-17197-1*, Pub. by Angus & Robertson AT)
HarpC.
—Who Killed Cock Robin? 1990. 13.95 (*0-385-30085-9*)
Doubleday.
MacRaois, Cormac. Dance of the Midnight Fire. LC 89-
82284. (Illus.). 144p. (gr. 4-8). 1990. 12.95
(*0-86327-241-X*, Pub. by Wolfhound Pr EIRE); pap.
8.95 (*0-685-33034-6*, Pub. by Wolfhound Pr IE)
Dufour.
—Lightning over Giltspur. Dunne, Jeanette, illus. 139p.
(gr. 4-6). 1991. 14.95 (*0-86327-308-4*, Pub. by
Wolfhound Pr EIRE) Dufour.
—Lightning over Giltspur. Dunne, Jeannette, illus. 144p.
(gr. 4-8). 1993. pap. 9.95 (*0-86327-332-7*, Pub. by
Wolfhound Pr EIRE) Dufour.
McRay, Ron. The Last Days. 150p. (Orig.). (gr. 9-12).
1990. pap. 5.95 (*0-9621311-3-X*) E E Stevens Pub.
McShane, Barbara, tr. see Rodgers, Mary.
McSharry, Patra & Rosen, Roger, eds. Apartheid:
Calibrations of Color. (Illus.). 176p. (gr. 7-12). 1991.
PLB 16.95 (*0-8239-1330-9*); pap. 8.95 (*0-8239-1331-7*)
Rosen Group.
—Coca Cola Culture: Icons of Pop. (gr. 7-12). 1993. 16.
95 (*0-8239-1593-X*); pap. 8.95 (*0-8239-1594-8*) Rosen
Group.
—On Heroes & the Heroic: In Search of Good Deeds.
(gr. 7-12). 1993. 16.95 (*0-8239-1384-8*); pap. 8.95
(*0-8239-1385-6*) Rosen Group.
—The People of This Place: Natural & Unnatural
Habitats. (gr. 7-12). 1993. 16.95 (*0-8239-1381-3*); pap.
8.95 (*0-8239-1382-1*) Rosen Group.
—Urbanities: Visions of the Metropolis. (gr. 7-12). 1993.
16.95 (*0-8239-1387-2*); pap. 8.95 (*0-8239-1388-0*)
Rosen Group.
McSherry, Frank D., Jr., et al, eds. Western Ghosts. LC
90-8072. 224p. (Orig.). (gr. 8 up). 1990. pap. 9.95
(*1-55853-069-X*) Rutledge Hill Pr.

Macsolis. Baile de Luna: Dance Moon. Macsolis, illus.
(SPA.). 25p. (ps-2). 1991. 12.95 (*84-261-2583-2*)
Donars.
McSpadden, J. Walker. Robin Hood. Hildebrandt, Greg,
illus. 160p. 1991. 14.95 (*0-88101-272-6*) Unicorn Pub.
McSweeney, Sean & Bunnett, Chris. Gymnastics. (Illus.).
64p. (gr. 7-10). 1993. 1994. 24.95 (*0-7134-7129-8*, Pub. by
Batsford UK) Trafalgar.
McSweeney, Sean & Sampson, Rebecca. Swimming.
(Illus.). 64p. (gr. 7-10). 1993. 1994. 24.95 (*0-7134-7128-X*,
Pub. by Batsford UK) Trafalgar.
McSweeney, Terry, illus. Great Gift & the Wish-
Fulfilling Gem. Tulku, Tarthang, intro. by. LC 86-
19767. (Illus.). 32p. (gr. k-5). 1987. PLB 14.95
(*0-89800-157-9*); pap. 7.95 (*0-89800-143-9*) Dharma
Pub.
McSwigan, Marie. Snow Treasure. 160p. (gr. 3-7). 1986.
pap. 2.95 (*0-590-42537-4*) Scholastic Inc.
McTavish, Douglas. Isaac Newton. (Illus.). 48p. (gr. 5-8).
1990. PLB 12.40 (*0-531-18351-3*, Pub. by Bookwright
Pr) Watts.
—Joseph Lister. LC 91-22572. (Illus.). 48p. (gr. 5-8).
1992. PLB 12.40 (*0-531-18461-7*, Pub. by Bookwright
Pr) Watts.
McTigue, Bernard, compiled by. A Child's Garden of
Delights: Pictures, Poems, & Stories for Children from
the Collections of the New York Public Library.
(Illus.). 271p. 1987. 35.00 (*0-8109-0791-7*) NY Pub
Lib.
McTigue, Bernard, frwd. by. Kate Greenways' Mother
Goose: The Complete Facsimile Sketchbooks from the
Arents Collections. Engen, Rodney, intro. by. (Illus.).
96p. 1988. 19.95 (*0-685-65645-4*) NY Pub Lib.
Mactire, Sean P. Lyme Disease. Rich, Mary P., ed. LC
91-40895. (Illus.). 112p. (gr. 7-12). 1991. PLB 12.90
(*0-531-12523-8*) Watts.
MacUistin, Liam. The Tain: The Great Celtic Epic.
Teskey, Donald, illus. 93p. (Orig.). (gr. 5-12). 1991.
pap. 9.95 (*0-86278-238-4*, Pub. by OBrien Pr IE)
Dufour.
McVaugh, Julia A., ed. see Swalin, Benjamin.
McVeigh, Amy, jt. auth. see Jolliffe, Susan D.
McVey, R. Parker. The Missing Rock Star Caper.
Rogers, Jackie, illus. LC 84-8721. 128p. (gr. 3-7).
1985. lib. bdg. 9.49 (*0-8167-0398-1*); pap. text ed. 2.95
(*0-8167-0399-X*) Troll Assocs.
—Mystery at the Ball Game. Rogers, Jackie, illus. LC 84-
8486. 128p. (gr. 3-7). 1985. lib. bdg. 9.49
(*0-8167-0336-1*); pap. text ed. 2.95 (*0-8167-0337-X*)
Troll Assocs.
McVey, Vicki. Sierra Club Book of Weatherwisdom. (gr.
4-7). 1991. 16.95 (*0-316-56341-2*) Little.
—The Sierra Club Kid's Guide to Planet Care & Repair.
Weston, Martha, illus. LC 91-38307. 96p. (gr. 4-7).
1993. 16.95 (*0-87156-567-6*) Sierra.
—The Sierra Club Wayfinding Book. Weston, Martha,
illus. 96p. (gr. 4-7). 1991. 14.95 (*0-316-56340-4*); pap.
7.95 (*0-316-56342-0*) Little.
McWaid, Helen & Machac, Kathy. Home Stuff: Teach-
away with Toss-away. (Illus.). 159p. (Orig.). (gr. 1-6).
1982. pap. text ed. 8.95 (*0-9611480-0-4*) Custom
Curriculum.
McWilliams, Karen. Pirates. LC 87-23711. (Illus.). 64p.
(gr. 3-5). 1989. PLB 12.90 (*0-531-10464-8*) Watts.
Macy, Sue. A Whole New Ball Game: The Story Behind
A League of Their Own. LC 92-31813. (Illus.). 144p.
(gr. 7 up). 1993. PLB 14.95 (*0-8050-1942-1*, Bks
Young Read) H Holt & Co.
Madama, John. Desktop Publishing: The Art of
Communication. (Illus.). 80p. (gr. 5-12). 1993. PLB
19.95 (*0-8225-2303-5*) Lerner Pubns.
Madame d'Aulnoy's Collection Staff. Jack & the
Beanstalk. Francois, Andre, illus. 32p. (gr. 4 up). 1983.
PLB 13.95s.p. (*0-87191-947-8*) Creative Ed.
Madame de Villeneuve. Beauty & the Beast. Delessert,
Etienne, illus. 48p. (gr. 4 up). 1984. PLB 13.95s.p.
(*0-87191-946-X*) Creative Ed.
Madaras, Area, jt. auth. see Madaras, Lynda.
Madaras, Lynda. Lynda Madaras Talks to Teens about
AIDS: An Essential Guide for Parents, Teachers &
Young People. LC 87-31567. (Illus.). 128p. (gr. 7 up).
1988. 14.95 (*1-55704-010-9*); pap. 6.95
(*1-55704-009-5*) Newmarket.
—Lynda Madaras Talks to Teens about AIDS: An
Essential Guide for Parents, Teachers & Young
People. rev. ed. Levin, Linda, frwd. by. (Illus.). 128p.
(gr. 9-12). 1993. 16.95 (*1-55704-188-1*); pap. 7.95
(*1-55704-180-6*) Newmarket.
Madaras, Lynda & Madaras, Area. My Body, My Self:
The What's Happening Workbook for Girls. (Illus.).
128p. (Orig.). (gr. 3-10). 1993. pap. 9.95
(*1-55704-150-4*) Newmarket.
—My Feelings, My Self: Lynda Madaras' Growing-Up
Guide for Girls. Aher, Jackie, illus. LC 86-23719.
160p. (gr. 3-10). 1993. cancelled (*0-937858-87-0*); pap.
9.95 (*1-55704-157-1*) Newmarket.
Madavan, Vijay. Cooking the Indian Way. (Illus.). 52p.
(gr. 5 up). 1985. lib. bdg. 14.95 (*0-8225-0911-3*)
Lerner Pubns.
Madden, Andrea C., tr. see Hoffmann, E. T.
Madden, Don. The Wartville Wizard. LC 92-22246.
(Illus.). 32p. (gr. k-3). 1993. nap. 4.95 (*0-689-71667-2*,
Aladdin) Macmillan Child Grp.
Madden, John. The First Book of Football. (gr. 3 up).
1988. bds. 10.95 (*0-517-56981-7*) Crown Bks Yng
Read.

—First Book of Football. LC 87-37981. (Illus.). 128p. (gr. 4-9). 1991. pap. 4.99 (*0-517-58593-6*) Crown Bks Yng Read.
—I've Got Your Nose! Bentley, Nancy, illus. 1991. 12.00 (*0-685-59973-6*) Dell.

Madden, Margaret L., jt. auth. see Herda, D. J.
Madden, Paul. Fidel Castro. LC 92-46482. 1993. 19.93 (*0-86625-479-X*); 14.95s.p. (*0-685-67776-1*) Rourke Pubns.
Maddern, Eric. Curious Clownfish. (ps-3). 1990. 14.95 (*0-316-48894-1*, Joy St Bks) Little.
—Life Story. Duff, Leo, illus. LC 87-73253. 32p. (gr. 1 up). 1988. 11.95 (*0-8120-5941-9*) Barron.
—Rainbow Bird. (gr. 4-8). 1993. 14.95 (*0-316-54314-4*) Little.

Maddern, Eric, retold by. The Fire Children: A West African Creation Tale. Lessac, Frane, illus. LC 92-34685. (ps-3). 1993. 14.50 (*0-8037-1477-7*) Dial Bks Young.

Maddox, Linda C., jt. auth. see Maddox, Robert L.
Maddox, Linda G. Step Toward Freedom. LC 88-8154. (Orig.). (gr. 12). 1991. 7.95 (*0-8054-5070-X*) Broadman.
Maddox, Robert L. & Maddox, Linda C. Get off My Back. (Orig.). (gr. 7 up). 1987. pap. 5.95 (*0-8054-5344-X*) Broadman.
Maddox, Tony. Fergus the Farmyard Dog. (Illus.). 28p. 12.95 (*0-8120-6373-2*); pap. 4.95 (*0-8120-1763-3*) Barron.
Maddux, Bob, et al. The Dog That Went Too Fast. French, Marty, et al, illus. 26p. (ps up). 1987. 7.95 (*1-55578-104-7*); cass. incl. Worlds Wonder.
Madenski, Melissa. Some of the Pieces. Ray, Deborah K., illus. (ps-3). 1991. 15.95 (*0-316-54324-1*) Little.
Madgett, Naomi L. Deep Rivers, A Portfolio: Twenty Contemporary Black American Poets-with Teachers' Guide. 46p. (gr. 7-12). 1978. pap. 11.00 (*0-916418-02-2*) Lotus.
—Exits & Entrances. Enright, Beverley R., illus. LC 77-91712. 69p. (gr. 9-12). 1978. 5.00 perfect bdg. (*0-916418-13-8*) Lotus.
—Octavia & Other Poems. Duskin, Leisia, illus. LC 87-51637. 117p. (Orig.). (gr. 9-12). 1988. pap. 8.00 (*0-88378-121-2*) Third World.
—Pink Ladies in the Afternoon. 2nd ed. LC 90-60605. 75p. (gr. 7-10). 1990. pap. 7.00 (*0-916418-78-2*) Lotus.
—Star by Star. 2nd ed. LC 77-143900. 61p. (gr. 7-12). 1970. pap. 5.00 perf. bdg. (*0-916418-06-6*) Lotus.

Madgett, Naomi L., intro. by. Adam of Ife: Black Women in Praise of Black Men. LC 91-61410. (Illus.). 235p. (Orig.). (gr. 7-12). 1992. pap. 15.00 (*0-916418-80-4*) Lotus.

Madgett, Naomi L., ed. A Milestone Sampler: Fifteenth Anniversary Anthology. (Illus.). 130p. (Orig.). (gr. 9-12). 1988. pap. 9.00 perfect bdg. (*0-916418-74-X*) Lotus.

Madgwick, Wendy. Animaze! A Collection of Amazing Nature Mazes. Hussey, Lorna, illus. LC 91-46892. 40p. (ps-3). 1992. 13.00 (*0-679-82665-3*); PLB 13.99 (*0-679-92665-8*) Knopf Bks Yng Read.
—Behold! Spot the Difference Bible Stories. Alles, Hemesh, illus. LC 93-5506. 48p. (gr. k-3). 1994. 12.00 (*0-679-85333-2*) Knopf Bks Yng Read.
—Cacti & Other Succulents. LC 91-14934. (Illus.). 48p. (gr. 5-9). 1992. PLB 19.92 (*0-8114-2737-4*) Raintree Steck-V.
—Flowering Plants. LC 90-9572. (Illus.). 48p. (gr. 5-9). 1990. PLB 19.92 (*0-8114-2730-7*) Raintree Steck-V.
—Fungi & Lichens. LC 90-9571. (Illus.). 48p. (gr. 5-9). 1990. PLB 19.92 (*0-8114-2728-5*) Raintree Steck-V.

Madhu Bazaz Wangu. Hinduism. (Illus.). 128p. (gr. 7-12). 1991. 17.95x (*0-8160-2447-2*) Facts on File.
Madhubuti, Haki R. Killing Memory, Seeking Ancestors. LC 85-82523. 58p. (Orig.). (gr. 9-12). 1987. pap. 8.00 perfect bdg. (*0-916418-63-4*) Lotus.
Madhubuti, Safisha. Story of Kwanzaa. (gr. 1). 1989. pap. 5.95 (*0-88378-001-1*) Third World.
Madigan, Carol O., jt. auth. see Elwood, Ann.
Madinaveitia, Horacio. La Gran Aventura de Don Roberto. Madinaveitia, Horacio, illus. (SPA.). 32p. (gr. k-4). 1992. PLB 13.95 (*1-879567-02-4*, Valeria Bks) Wonder Well.
—Sir Robert's Little Outing. Madinaveitia, Horacio, illus. 32p. (gr. k-4). 1991. PLB 13.95 (*1-879567-01-6*, Valeria Bks); pap. text ed. 7.95 (*1-879567-00-8*) Wonder Well.

Madis, George. The Winchester Handbook. (Illus.). 320p. 1981. 19.50 (*0-910156-04-2*) Art & Ref.
Madison, Arnold. Drugs & You. rev. ed. LC 82-3450. (Illus.). 80p. (gr. 4 up). 1984. lib. bdg. 9.79 (*0-671-43986-3*, J Messner); lib. bdg. 4.95 (*0-671-49477-5*) S&S Trade.
—Drugs & You. rev. ed. Steltenpohl, Jane, ed. (Illus.). 128p. (gr. 4-6). 1990. lib. bdg. 13.98 (*0-671-69147-3*, J Messner); lib. bdg. 5.95 (*0-671-69148-1*) S&S Trade.
—How the Colonists Lived. (gr. 7 up). 1980. 8.95 (*0-679-20685-X*) McKay.
—Suicide & Young People. LC 77-13240. 144p. (gr. 6 up). 1979. (Clarion Bks); (Clarion) HM.

Madison, Curt & Yarber, Yvonne Y. Edgar Kallands-A Biography: Kaltag. 64p. (Orig.). 1983. pap. 6.95 (*0-910871-00-0*) Spirit Mount Pr.
—Josephine Roberts - A Biography: Tanana. 64p. (Orig.). (gr. 6-8). 1983. pap. 6.95 (*0-910871-02-7*) Spirit Mount Pr.

Madison, Kathy. Fun Guide to Anchorage. Lauzen, Elizabeth, ed. Burrus, Sue, illus. 32p. (gr. 1-6). 1987. pap. 3.50 incl. wkbk. (*0-942553-00-4*) Madison Aves.

Madler, Trudy. Why Did Grandma Die? Lewis, Gloria, intro. by. LC 79-23892. (Illus.). 32p. (gr. k-6). 1980. PLB 17.96 (*0-8172-1354-6*) Raintree Steck-V.
—Why Did Grandma Die? (ps-3). 1993. pap. 3.95 (*0-8114-7156-X*) Raintree Steck-V.

Mado, Michio. The Animals: Selected Poems. HRM the Empress of Japan, tr. Mitsumasa Anno, illus. LC 92-10356. (ENG & JPN.). 48p. (ps up). 1992. SBE 16.95 (*0-689-50574-4*, M K McElderry) Macmillan Child Grp.

Madokoro, Hisako. The Adventures of Buster the Puppy, 6 vols. Kuroi, Ken, illus. 96p. (gr. k-2). 1991. Set. PLB 87.60 (*0-8368-0488-0*) Gareth Stevens Inc.
—Buster & the Dandelions. Karoi, Ken, illus. LC 90-47926. 24p. (gr. k-2). 1991. PLB 14.60 (*0-8368-0491-0*) Gareth Stevens Inc.
—Buster & the Little Kitten. Kuroi, Ken, illus. LC 90-47947. 24p. (gr. k-2). 1991. PLB 14.60 (*0-8368-0490-2*) Gareth Stevens Inc.
—Buster Catches a Cold. Kuroi, Ken, illus. LC 90-47948. 24p. (gr. k-2). 1991. PLB 14.60 (*0-8368-0489-9*) Gareth Stevens Inc.
—Buster's Blustery Day. Kuroi, Ken, illus. LC 90-47927. 24p. (gr. k-2). 1991. PLB 14.60 (*0-8368-0494-5*) Gareth Stevens Inc.
—Buster's First Snow. Kuroi, Ken, illus. LC 90-47946. 24p. (gr. k-2). 1991. PLB 14.60 (*0-8368-0492-9*) Gareth Stevens Inc.
—Buster's First Thunderstorm. Kuroi, Ken, illus. LC 90-47869. 24p. (gr. k-2). 1991. PLB 14.60 (*0-8368-0493-7*) Gareth Stevens Inc.

Madrigal, Margarita. Open Door to Spanish, Bk. 2. 222p. (gr. 7-12). 1981. pap. text ed. 5.25 (*0-88345-427-0*, 18470); cassettes 45.00 (*0-686-77684-4*, 58472); ans. key Bk 1, 2 1.50 (*0-88345-487-4*, 18474) Prentice ESL.

Madsen, Christine. Drinking & Driving. LC 89-31584. (Illus.). 62p. (gr. 6-10). 1989. PLB 12.40 (*0-531-10799-X*) Watts.
Madsen, Ross M. Perrywinkle & the Book of Magic Spells. Zimmer, Dirk, illus. LC 85-15932. 48p. (ps-3). 1988. pap. 4.95 (*0-8037-0501-8*) Dial Bks Young.
—Stewart Stork. Halsey, Megan, illus. LC 92-30730. 40p. (ps-3). 1993. 11.99 (*0-8037-1325-8*); PLB 11.89 (*0-8037-1326-6*) Dial Bks Young.

Madsen, Sharon, jt. ed. see McCulloch, Myrna.
Madsen, Sheila & Gould, Bette. The Teacher's Book of Lists. 2nd ed. (Illus.). 336p. (gr. k-6). 1994. pap. 19.95 (*0-673-36074-1*) GdYrBks.
Madsen, Susan A. The Lord Needed a Prophet. LC 90-81829. (Illus.). 234p. (gr. 3-6). 1990. 10.95 (*0-87579-276-6*) Deseret Bk.

Maecha, Alberto, ed. see Bourgeois, Jean-Francois.
Maeda, Jun. Let's Study Japanese. LC 64-24949. (Illus.). 130p. (gr. 9 up). 1965. pap. 6.95 (*0-8048-0362-5*) C E Tuttle.
Maehlis, Sally, jt. auth. see Field, Nancy.
Maestro. Riddle City USA. Date not set. 12.00 (*0-06-023368-0*, Festival); PLB 11.89 (*0-06-023369-9*, Festival) HarpC Child Bks.
Maestro, Betsy. All Aboard Overnight: A Book of Compound Words. Maestro, Giulio, illus. 32p. (ps-2). 1992. 14.45 (*0-395-51120-8*, Clarion Bks) HM.
—Bike Trip. Maestro, Giulio, illus. LC 90-35935. 32p. (gr. k-4). 1992. 16.00 (*0-06-022731-1*); PLB 15.89 (*0-06-022732-X*) HarpC Child Bks.
—Delivery Van: Words for Town & Country. Maestro, Giulio, illus. 32p. (ps-2). 1990. 14.45 (*0-395-51119-4*, Clarion Bks) HM.
—Discovery of the Americas. (ps-3). 1991. PLB 14.88 (*0-688-06838-3*) Lothrop.
—The Discovery of the Americas Activities Book. Bodnar, Judit Z., ed. Maestro, Guilio, illus. 92p. (gr. 1-6). 1992. pap. 7.95 (*0-688-08590-3*) Lothrop.
—Ferryboat. Maestro, Giulio, illus. LC 85-47887. 32p. (ps-3). 1986. (Crowell Jr Bks); PLB 14.89 (*0-690-04520-4*) HarpC Child Bks.
—How Do Apples Grow? Maestro, Giulio, illus. LC 91-9468. 32p. (gr. k-4). 1992. 14.00 (*0-06-020055-3*); PLB 13.89 (*0-06-020056-1*) HarpC Child Bks.
—How Do Apples Grow? Maestro, Giulio, illus. LC 91-9468. 32p. (ps-3). 1993. pap. 4.95 (*0-06-445117-8*, Trophy) HarpC Child Bks.
—Leaves Change Color. Krupinski, Loretta, illus. LC 93-9611. (gr. k-3). 1994. 14.00 (*0-06-022873-3*); PLB 13.89 (*0-06-022874-1*) HarpC Child Bks.
—A More Perfect Union: The Story of Our Constitution. Maestro, Giulio, illus. LC 87-4083. 48p. (gr. 1-5). 1987. 15.95 (*0-688-06839-1*); PLB 15.88 (*0-688-06840-5*) Lothrop.
—Sea Full of Sharks. (ps-3). 1990. 12.95 (*0-590-43100-5*) Scholastic Inc.
—The Story of Money. Maestro, Giulio, illus. 48p. (gr. 4-7). 1993. 15.45 (*0-395-56242-2*, Clarion Bks) HM.
—The Story of Religion. Weihs, Erika, illus. LC 92-38980. 1994. write for info (*0-395-62364-2*, Clarion Bks) HM.
—The Story of the Statue of Liberty. Maestro, Giulio, illus. LC 85-11324. 40p. (ps-3). 1986. PLB 12.88 (*0-688-05774-8*) Lothrop.
—The Story of the Statue of Liberty. LC 85-11324. (Illus.). (gr. 1 up). 1989. pap. 5.95 (*0-688-08746-9*, Mulberry) Morrow.

—Take a Look at Snakes. (Illus.). 1992. 14.95 (*0-590-44935-4*, Scholastic Hardcover) Scholastic Inc.
—Taxi: A Book of City Words. Maestro, Giulio, illus. LC 88-22867. (ps-2). 1989. 13.95 (*0-89919-528-8*, Clarion Bks) HM.
—Taxi: A Book of City Words. Maestro, Giulio, illus. LC 88-22867. (ps-3). 1990. pap. 5.70 (*0-395-54811-X*, Clarion Bks) HM.
—Where Is My Friend? A Word Concept Book. Maestro, Giulio, illus. LC 75-15902. 32p. (ps-1). 1986. PLB 12.95 (*0-517-52436-8*) Crown Bks Yng Read.

Maestro, Betsy & DelVecchio, Ellen. Big City Port. Maestro, Giulio, illus. LC 83-4339. 32p. (gr. k-3). 1984. RSBE 14.95 (*0-02-762110-3*, Four Winds) Macmillan Child Grp.
—Big City Port. Maestro, Giulio, illus. 32p. (gr. k-3). 1984. pap. 3.95 (*0-590-41577-8*) Scholastic Inc.

Maestro, Betsy & Maestro, Giulio. El Descubrimiento de las Americas. Arturo, Juan G., tr. (Illus.). 48p. (gr. 5-8). 1992. 13.95 (*0-9625162-9-5*) Lectorum Pubns.
—Discovery of the Americas. (gr. 4-7). 1991. 14.95 (*0-688-06837-5*) Lothrop.
—Discovery of the Americas. LC 89-32375. (Illus.). 48p. (gr. 1 up). 1992. pap. 5.95 (*0-688-11512-8*, Mulberry) Morrow.
—Dollars & Cents for Harriet. (ps-1). 1988. PLB 12.95 (*0-517-56958-2*) Crown Bks Yng Read.
—A More Perfect Union: The Story of Our Constitution. LC 87-4083. (Illus.). 48p. (ps-2). 1990. pap. 5.95 (*0-688-10192-5*, Mulberry) Morrow.
—Traffic: A Book of Opposites. reissued ed. Maestro, Betsy & Maestro, Giulio, illus. LC 80-29641. 32p. (ps-1). 1991. 16.00 (*0-517-54427-X*) Crown Bks Yng Read.
—Una Union Mas Perfecta: La Historia de Nuestra Constitucion. Marcuse, Aida, tr. (Illus.). 48p. (gr. 5). 1992. 13.95 (*0-9625162-8-7*) Lectorum Pubns.

Maestro, Giulio. Halloween Howls: Riddles That Are a Scream. Maestro, Giulio, illus. LC 83-1419. 64p. (gr. 3-7). 1983. 10.95 (*0-525-44059-3*, DCB) Dutton Child Bks.
—Halloween Howls: Riddles That Are a Scream. LC 83-1419. (Illus.). 64p. (gr. 2-7). 1992. pap. 4.99 (*0-14-036115-4*, Puffin Unicorn) Puffin Bks.
—More Halloween Howls: Riddles That Come Back to Haunt You. LC 91-23505. (Illus.). 64p. (gr. 2-7). 1992. 12.00 (*0-525-44899-3*, DCB) Dutton Child Bks.
—Razzle-Dazzle Riddles. Maestro, Giulio, illus. LC 85-3785. 64p. (Orig.). (gr. 2-5). 1985. 11.95 (*0-89919-382-X*, Clarion Bks); pap. 5.95 (*0-89919-405-2*, Clarion Bks) HM.
—Riddle Romp. LC 83-2067. (Illus.). 64p. (gr. k-3). 1983. (Clarion Bks); pap. 4.95 (*0-89919-207-6*, Clarion Bks) HM.
—Riddle Roundup: A Wild Bunch to Beef up Your Word Power. Maestro, Giulio, illus. LC 86-33404. 64p. (gr. 2-5). 1989. (Clarion Bks); pap. 5.70 (*0-89919-537-7*, Clarion Bks) HM.
—What's a Frank Frank? Tasty Homograph Riddles. Maestro, Giulio, illus. LC 84-5021. 64p. (gr. 2-5). 1984. 13.95 (*0-89919-297-1*, Clarion Bks); pap. 5.95 (*0-89919-317-X*, Clarion Bks) HM.
—What's Mite Might? Homophone Riddles to Boost Your Word Power! Maestro, Giulio, illus. LC 86-2665. 64p. (gr. 2-5). 1986. 11.95 (*0-89919-434-6*, Clarion Bks); pap. 4.95 (*0-89919-435-4*, Clarion Bks) HM.

Maestro, Giulio, jt. auth. see Maestro, Betsy.
Maeterlinck, Maurice. The Blue Bird. Goscinsky, Michael, illus. Poesnecker, Gerald E. & Poesnecker, Gerald E.intro. by. Bd. with The Betrothal. 304p. (gr. 1 up). 1985. 16.95 (*0-932785-02-6*); pap. 10.95 (*0-932785-01-8*) Philos Pub.
Maez, Frances. Come See What God Made. Maez, Frances, illus. 16p. (gr. k). 1991. pap. text ed. 3.95 (*1-880047-02-0*) Creative Des.

Magarian, Judith. Spelling Skills. (gr. 4-7). 1986. pap. 2.95 (*0-8431-2517-9*) Price Stern.
Magarian-Gold, jt. auth. see Mogensen.
Magarian-Gold, Judi, jt. auth. see Mogensen, Sandra.
Magee, Doug & Newman, Robert. All Aboard ABC. LC 89-29852. (Illus.). (ps). 1990. 13.95 (*0-525-65036-9*, Cobblehill Bks) Dutton Child Bks.
—Let's Fly from A to Z. LC 91-39774. (Illus.). 48p. (ps-3). 1992. 14.00 (*0-525-65105-5*, Cobblehill Bks) Dutton Child Bks.

Magee, James E. Your Place in the Cosmos, Vol. I: A Layman's Book of Astronomy & the Mythology of the Eighty-Eight Celestial Constellations & Registry. Hevelius, Johannes, illus. 530p. 1985. text ed. 34.45 (*0-9614354-0-2*) Mosele & Assocs.
—Your Place in the Cosmos, Vol. II: A Layman's Book of Astronomy & the Mythology of the Eighty-Eight Celestial Constellations & Registry. Hevelius, Johannes, illus. 508p. 1988. text ed. 34.45 (*0-9614354-1-0*) Mosele & Assocs.
—Your Place in the Cosmos, Vol. III: A Layman's Book of Astronomy & the Mythology of the Eighty-Eight Celestial Constellations & Registry. Hevelius, Johannes, illus. 388p. 1992. text ed. 49.45 (*0-9614354-2-9*) Mosele & Assocs.

Magee, Wes. Legend of the Ragged Boy. Hennessy, Linda, illus. 32p. (ps-3). 1993. 14.95 (*1-55970-228-1*) Arcade Pub Inc.
Magellan, Mauro. Cambio Chameleon. Magellan, Mauro, illus. LC 89-19995. 32p. 1990. 12.95 (*0-89334-118-5*) Humanics Ltd.

—Home at Last. Magellan, Mauro, illus. LC 89-19994. 32p. 1989. 12.95 (*0-89334-119-3*) Humanics Ltd.
—Max, the Apartment Cat. Magellan, Mauro, illus. LC 88-32067. 32p. 1989. 12.95 (*0-89334-117-7*) Humanics Ltd.
Magers, Pat, illus. Sing with Me Animal Songs. (ps-1). 1987. incl. cassette 5.95 (*0-394-88809-X*) Random Bks Yng Read.
Maggi, Tolstoy M. Fables & Folk Tales. (Illus.). 30p. (ps-1). 1986. 3.95 (*0-8120-5727-9*) Barron.
Maggio, Rosalie. The Music Box Christmas. LC 90-38529. 128p. (gr. 5 up). 1990. 12.95g (*0-688-08851-1*) Morrow Jr Bks.
Magill, Frank N., ed. Critical Survey of Drama, 7 vols. rev. ed. 3500p. (gr. 9-12). 1994. Set. PLB 425.00 (*0-89356-851-1*, Magill Bks) Salem Pr.
—Magill's Literary Annual 1994, 2 vols. 1000p. (gr. 9-12). 1994. Set. PLB 70.00 (*0-89356-294-7*) Salem Pr.
—Masterplots, 3 vols, No. II. 1500p. (gr. 9-12). 1994. Set. PLB 275.00 (*0-89356-594-6*, Magill Bks) Salem Pr.
—Masterplots II, 4 vols. LC 92-44708. 1695p. (gr. 8 up). 1991. Set. PLB 365.00 (*0-89356-579-2*, Magill Bks); CD-ROM avail.; Vol. 1. write for info. (*0-89356-580-6*); Vol. 2. write for info. (*0-89356-581-4*); Vol. 3. write for info. (*0-89356-582-2*); Vol. 4. write for info. 335 (*0-89356-583-0*) Salem Pr.
—Masterplots II, 4 vols. 2000p. (gr. 8 up). 1993. Set. lib. bdg. 365.00x (*0-89356-700-0*) Salem Pr.
Maginnis, Matthew, jt. auth. see Carpenter, Allan.
Magley, Beverly. Arizona Wildflowers. Dowden, D. D., illus. 32p. (gr. 1-8). 1991. pap. 5.95 (*1-56044-096-1*) Falcon Pr MT.
—California Wildflowers. Dowden, D. D., illus. LC 88-83883. 32p. (Orig.). (gr. 3-6). 1989. pap. 4.95 (*0-937959-58-8*) Falcon Pr MT.
—The Fire Mountains: The Story of the Cascade Volcanos. Dowden, D. D., illus. LC 88-83884. 32p. (Orig.). (gr. 3-6). 1989. pap. 5.95 (*0-937959-57-X*) Falcon Pr MT.
—Minnesota Wildflowers: Childrens Field Guide. Dowden, D. D., illus. 32p. (Orig.). (gr. 4-7). 1992. pap. 5.95 (*1-56044-117-8*) Falcon Pr MT.
—Montana Wildflowers. Dowden, D. D., illus. 32p. (Orig.). (gr. 4-7). 1992. pap. 5.95 (*1-56044-118-6*) Falcon Pr MT.
—North Carolina Wildflowers: A Children's Field Guide to the State's Most Common Flowers. Dowden, D. D., illus. 32p. (Orig.). 1993. pap. 5.95 (*1-56044-184-4*) Falcon Pr MT.
—Oregon Wildflowers: Childrens Field Guide. Dowden, D. D., illus. 32p. (Orig.). (gr. 4-7). 1992. pap. 5.95 (*1-56044-035-X*) Falcon Pr MT.
—Texas Wildflowers: A Children's Field Guide to the State's Most Common Flowers. Dowden, D. D., illus. 32p. (Orig.). 1993. pap. 5.95 (*1-56044-183-6*) Falcon Pr MT.
Maglione, Robin S. Alyndoria: Tales of Inner Magic. Wheeling, Darren, illus. 71p. (Orig.). (gr. k-12). 1986. pap. 12.00 (*0-910609-11-X*) Gifted Educ Pr.
Magni, Laura. Come to the Park. Cluet, Jaume, illus. 16p. (ps up) 1989. 8.95 (*0-8120-5994-8*) Barron.
—Goodnight Stories from the Big Tree. (Illus.). 192p. (ps-6). 1990. 9.99 (*0-517-69687-8*) Outlet Bk Co.
—Two Little Monkeys. Bosni, Nella, illus. 18p. (ps-k). 1992. Set of 3 books. bds. 11.85 (*1-56397-159-3*); bds. 3.95 (*1-56397-154-2*) Boyds Mills Pr.
Magnus, Erica. Around Me. Pearson, Susan, ed. Magnus, Erica, illus. LC 90-26459. 32p. (ps-3). 1992. 13.00 (*0-688-09756-1*); PLB 12.93 (*0-688-09753-7*) Lothrop.
—My Secret Place. LC 93-8701. 1994. write for info. (*0-688-11859-3*); PLB write for info. (*0-688-11860-7*) Lothrop.
Magnusson, Magnus see Zevin, Jack.
Magocsi, Paul R. Carpatho-Rusyn Americans. Moynihan, Daniel P., intro. by. (Illus.). 112p. (gr. 5 up). 1990. 17. 95 (*0-87754-866-8*) Chelsea Hse.
Magoldi, Mary. Daily Close-Ups for Spring. McClure, Nancee, illus. Russell, Bruce, ed. 96p. (gr. k-6). 1984. wkbk. 9.95 (*0-86653-255-2*, GA 563) Good Apple.
—Daily Close-Ups for Winter. Hall, Robyn, illus. Russell, Bruce, ed. 96p. (gr. k-6). 1984. wkbk. 9.95 (*0-86653-256-0*, GA 562) Good Apple.
Magoldi, Mary & Russell, Bruce. Daily Close-Ups for Fall. 96p. (gr. k-6). 1984. wkbk. 9.95 (*0-86653-254-4*, GA 561) Good Apple.
Magorian, James. At the City Limits. LC 86-72766. (Illus.). 34p. (gr. 3-5). 1987. pap. 3.00 (*0-930674-22-7*) Black Oak.
—The Beautiful Music. LC 88-71142. (Illus.). 12p. (gr. 2-5). 1988. pap. 3.00 (*0-930674-25-1*) Black Oak.
—The Bonkly Dribblefink Fables. LC 87-70706. (Illus.). 16p. (gr. 1-4). 1987. pap. 3.00 (*0-930674-24-3*) Black Oak.
—Fimperings & Torples. LC 81-69872. (Illus.). 44p. (gr. 4-6). 1981. pap. 3.00 (*0-930674-06-5*) Black Oak.
—Griddlemort Loses His Birthday. LC 88-71604. (Illus.). 32p. (gr. 1-4). 1988. pap. 3.00 (*0-930674-29-4*) Black Oak.
—Ground-Hog Day. LC 87-70705. (Illus.). 22p. (gr. 3-5). 1987. pap. 3.00 (*0-930674-23-5*) Black Oak.
—Imaginary Radishes. LC 79-53857. (Illus.). 32p. (gr. 3-5). 1980. 5.00 (*0-930674-03-0*) Black Oak.
—The Invention of the Afternoon Nap. LC 89-62222. (Illus.). 20p. (gr. 2-5). 1989. pap. 3.00 (*0-930674-32-4*) Black Oak.

—Keeper of Fire. Hardgrove, Tanya, illus. 78p. (Orig.). (gr. 4-12). 1984. pap. 6.95 (*0-89992-088-8*) Coun India Ed.
—The Kingdom of Junk Bonds. LC 88-71143. (Illus.). 24p. (gr. 5-9). 1988. pap. 3.00 (*0-930674-27-8*) Black Oak.
—The Magic Pretzel. LC 88-71603. (Illus.). 32p. (gr. 2-5). 1988. pap. 3.00 (*0-930674-28-6*) Black Oak.
—Mud Pies. Summers, Wendy H., illus. LC 91-70218. 24p. (Orig.). (gr. 4-6). 1991. pap. 3.00 (*0-930674-35-9*) Black Oak.
—The Palace of Water. LC 90-81003. (Illus.). 16p. (gr. 2-5). 1990. pap. 3.00 (*0-930674-33-2*) Black Oak.
—Plucked Chickens. LC 80-68263. (Illus.). 32p. (gr. 4-6). 1981. 5.00 (*0-930674-04-9*) Black Oak.
—Spoonproof Jello & Other Poems. LC 90-81004. (Illus.). 16p. (gr. 2-5). 1990. pap. 3.00 (*0-930674-34-0*) Black Oak.
—The Three Diminutive Pigs. LC 88-71605. (Illus.). 20p. (gr. 1-4). 1988. pap. 3.00 (*0-930674-30-8*) Black Oak.
—The Witches' Olympics. LC 83-71262. 44p. (gr. 4-7). 1983. pap. 5.00 (*0-930674-10-3*) Black Oak.
Magorian, Michelle. Back Home. LC 84-47629. 352p. (gr. 7 up). 1984. 14.95 (*0-685-08449-3*) HarpC Child Bks.
—Back Home. LC 84-47629. 384p. (gr. 7 up). 1992. pap. 4.95 (*0-06-440411-0*, Trophy) HarpC Child Bks.
—Good Night, Mr. Tom. LC 80-8444. 336p. (gr. 7 up). 1982. PLB 15.89 (*0-06-024079-2*) HarpC Child Bks.
—Good Night, Mr. Tom. LC 80-8444. 336p. (gr. 5-9). 1986. pap. 3.95 (*0-06-440174-X*, Trophy) HarpC Child Bks.
—Not a Swan. LC 91-19507. 416p. (gr. 7 up). 1992. 18. 00 (*0-06-024214-0*); PLB 17.89 (*0-06-024215-9*) HarpC Child Bks.
Magosci, Paul R. The Russian Americans. Moynihan, Daniel P., intro. by. (Illus.). 112p. (gr. 5 up). 1989. 17. 95x (*0-87754-899-4*) Chelsea Hse.
Magoun, Christine, jt. auth. see Danielson, Jan.
Maguire, Arlene. Life's Changes. Holtman, Noel, illus. LC 91-9353. 32p. (Orig.). (ps-5). 1991. 6.95 (*0-941992-26-8*) Los Arboles Pub.
Maguire, Gregory. I Feel Like the Morning Star. LC 88-21544. 288p. (gr. 7 up). 1989. HarpC Child Bks.
—Missing Sisters. LC 93-8300. 160p. (gr. 5-9). 1994. SBE 14.95 (*0-689-50590-6*, M K McElderry) Macmillan Child Grp.
—The Peace & Quiet Diner. Perry, David, illus. LC 87-36865. 48p. (ps-3). 1988. 5.95 (*0-8193-1176-6*) Parents.
—The Peace-&-Quiet Diner. Perry, David, illus. LC 93-7770. 1994. PLB 13.27 (*0-8368-0971-8*) Gareth Stevens Inc.
—Seven Spiders Spinning. LC 93-30478. 1994. write for info. (*0-395-68965-1*, Clarion Bks) HM.
Maguire, Jesse. Breaking the Rules, No. 6: Nowhere High. (Orig.). 1992. pap. 3.99 (*0-8041-0849-8*) Ivy Books.
—Nowhere High No. 4: On the Edge. 192p. 1991. pap. 3.50 (*0-8041-0447-6*) Ivy Books.
—Starting Over. (Orig.). 1992. pap. 3.99 (*0-8041-0848-X*) Ivy Books.
—Starting Over. 1992. 3.99 (*0-8041-1016-X*) Ivy Books.
Mah, Ronald. Dinosaur Masks & Puppets. (gr. 2 up). pap. 4.50 (*0-8431-1952-7*) Price Stern.
—North America Animal Masks & Hats. Werges, Rosanne, ed. (Illus.). 48p. (Orig.). (gr. k-4). 1988. pap. 4.95 (*0-9615903-2-7*) Symbiosis Bks.
—Predator Prey Puppets & Toys: Eight Paper Animal Projects to Make. Mah, Ronald, illus. 32p. (ps-3). 1986. pap. 3.95 (*0-9615903-1-9*) Symbiosis Bks.
Mahajan, Carlee S. Ghost's New Old Home. LC 91-65247. (Illus.). 44p. (gr. k-3). 1992. 6.95 (*1-55523-430-5*) Winston-Derek.
Mahak, Francine T., tr. see Martinez, Eliseo R. & Martinez, Irma C.
Mahan, Ben, illus. Addition. 6p. (gr. k-1). 1992. bds. 3.95 (*1-56293-183-0*) McClanahan Bk.
—All Around. 12p. (ps-k). 1993. bds. 2.50 (*1-56293-316-7*) McClanahan Bk.
—Counting. 12p. (ps-k). 1993. bds. 2.50 (*1-56293-313-2*) McClanahan Bk.
—Little Bits. 12p. (ps-k). 1993. bds. 2.50 (*1-56293-315-9*) McClanahan Bk.
—See a Circle. 10p. (ps-k). 1992. bds. 1.95 (*1-56293-206-3*) McClanahan Bk.
—See a Square. 10p. (ps-k). 1992. bds. 1.95 (*1-56293-207-1*) McClanahan Bk.
—See a Star. 10p. (ps-k). 1992. bds. 1.95 (*1-56293-208-X*) McClanahan Bk.
—See a Triangle. 10p. (ps-k). 1992. bds. 1.95 (*1-56293-209-8*) McClanahan Bk.
—Shapes. 12p. (ps-k). 1993. bds. 2.50 (*1-56293-314-0*) McClanahan Bk.
Mahan, Benton, illus. Goldilocks & the Three Bears. LC 80-27631. 32p. (gr. k-2). 1981. PLB 9.79 (*0-89375-470-6*); pap. text ed. 1.95 (*0-89375-471-4*) Troll Assocs.
Maher, Alan, ed. see Dewazien, Karl.
Maher, Robert. Leadership: Self, School, Community. Bruce, C., ed. 96p. (Illus.). (gr. 9-12). 1988. pap. 10.00 (*0-88210-217-6*) Natl Assn Student.
Mahfouz, Naguib. Autumn Quail (Siman wa Khareef) Arabic Novel. (ARA.). (gr. 4-7). 1985. 8.95x (*0-86685-162-3*) Intl Bk Ctr.
Mahiri, Jabari. The Day They Stole the Letter J. Carter, Dorothy, illus. (Orig.). (gr. 3-5). 1981. pap. 3.95 (*0-88378-084-4*) Third World.

Mahon, Thomas J. Say, Kids! Always Say No to That Junky Stuff, Drugs! 1992. 7.95 (*0-533-09698-7*) Vantage.
Mahone-Lonesome, Robyn. Charles R. Drew. King, Coretta Scott, intro. by. (Illus.). (gr. 5 up). 1990. 17.95 (*1-55546-581-1*) Chelsea Hse.
Mahoney, Bateman & Mahoney, Bill. Macho: Is This What I Really Want? 1986. pap. 6.00 (*0-87738-024-4*) Youth Ed.
Mahoney, Bill, jt. auth. see Mahoney, Bateman.
Mahoney, Carole, jt. auth. see Staples, Danny.
Mahoney, Ellen. Button Tales: Fluffy Gets Dressed. Mahoney, Ellen, illus. 8p. (ps). 1993. 6.99 (*0-8431-3543-3*) Price Stern.
—Pocketales: In My Pocket. Mahoney, Ellen, illus. 8p. (ps). 1993. 6.99 (*0-8431-3544-1*) Price Stern.
Mahoney, Ellen V. Animals. Mahoney, Ellen V., illus. 8p. (ps). 1993. vinyl 4.99 (*0-8431-3545-X*) Price Stern.
—Coping with Safer Sex. Rosen, Ruth, ed. (gr. 7-12). 1989. PLB 13.95 (*0-8239-0999-9*) Rosen Group.
—Food. Mahoney, Ellen V., illus. 8p. (ps). 1993. vinyl 4.99 (*0-8431-3546-8*) Price Stern.
—Now You've Got Your Period. rev. ed. Rosen, Roger, ed. (gr. 7 up). 1993. PLB 13.95 (*0-8239-1662-6*) Rosen Group.
—The Sea. Mahoney, Ellen V., illus. 8p. (ps). 1993. vinyl 4.99 (*0-8431-3547-6*) Price Stern.
—Toys. Mahoney, Ellen V., illus. 8p. (ps). 1993. vinyl 4.99 (*0-8431-3548-4*) Price Stern.
Mahoney, Judy. Teach Me English. (Illus.). 20p. (ps-6). 1993. pap. 11.95 incl. audiocassette (*0-934633-60-6*); tchr's. ed. 5.95 (*0-934633-25-8*) Teach Me.
—Teach Me Hebrew. Horowitz, Shelly, tr. (Illus.). 20p. (ps-6). 1991. pap. 11.95 incl. audiocassette (*0-934633-54-1*); tchr's. ed. 5.95 (*0-934633-28-2*) Teach Me.
—Teach Me Italian. Grifoni, Maria C., tr. (ITA., Illus.). 20p. (ps-6). 1992. pap. 11.95 incl. audiocassette (*0-934633-57-6*); tchr's. ed. 5.95 (*0-934633-29-0*) Teach Me.
—Teach Me Japanese. Satoh, Naomi, tr. Bennett, Charlotte, illus. 20p. (ps-6). 1990. pap. 11.95 incl. audiocassette (*0-934633-17-7*); tchr's. ed. 5.95 (*0-934633-30-4*) Teach Me.
—Teach Me More English. (Illus.). 20p. (Orig.). (ps-6). 1994. pap. 13.95 incl. audiocassette (*0-934633-66-5*); tchr's. ed. 6.95 (*0-934633-38-X*) Teach Me.
—Teach Me More French. (FRE., Illus.). 20p. (ps-6). 1989. pap. 13.95 incl. audiocassette (*0-934633-11-8*); tchr's. ed. 6.95 (*0-934633-33-9*) Teach Me.
—Teach Me More German. Kamstra, Angela, illus. (GER.). 20p. (ps-6). 1990. pap. 13.95 incl. audiocassette (*0-934633-23-1*); tchr's. ed. 6.95 (*0-934633-34-7*) Teach Me.
—Teach Me More Italian. Grifoni, Maria C., tr. (Illus.). 20p. (Orig.). (ps-6). 1993. pap. 13.95 incl. audio cass. (*0-934633-63-0*); tchr's. ed. 6.95 (*0-934633-35-5*) Teach Me.
—Teach Me More Japanese. Satoh, Naomi, tr. Kamstra, Angela, illus. (JPN.). 20p. (ps-6). 1991. pap. 13.95 incl. audiocassette (*0-934633-20-7*); tchr's. ed. 6.95 (*0-934633-36-3*) Teach Me.
—Teach Me More Spanish. (Illus.). 20p. (ps-6). 1989. pap. 13.95 incl. audiocassette (*0-934633-14-2*); tchr's. ed. 6.95 (*0-934633-37-1*) Teach Me.
—Teach Me Russian. Gybin, Sasha, tr. 20p. (Orig.). (ps-6). 1991. pap. 11.95 incl. audiocassette (*0-934633-51-7*); tchr's. ed. 5.95 (*0-934633-31-2*) Teach Me.
Mahoney, Judy, compiled by. Sing with Me in English: A Teach Me Tapes Songbook. Thiede, Carla R., contrib. by. (Illus.). 32p. (Orig.). (ps-6). 1994. pap. 7.95 (*0-934633-90-8*) Teach Me.
—Sing with Me in French: A Teach Me Tapes Songbook. Thiede, Carla R., contrib. by. (FRE., Illus.). 32p. (Orig.). (ps-6). 1994. pap. 7.95 (*0-934633-91-6*) Teach Me.
—Sing with Me in Spanish: A Teach Me Tapes Songbook. Thiede, Carla R., contrib. by. (SPA., Illus.). 32p. (Orig.). (ps-6). 1994. pap. 7.95 (*0-934633-92-4*) Teach Me.
Mahuika, A. T., tr. see Smith, Miriam.
Mahy, Margaret. Aliens in the Family. LC 86-3908. 192p. (gr. 7 up). 1986. pap. 12.95 (*0-590-40320-6*, Scholastic Hardcover) Scholastic Inc.
—Aliens in the Family. (gr. 4-7). 1991. pap. 2.95 (*0-590-44898-6*, Apple Paperbacks) Scholastic Inc.
—The Birthday Burglar & a Very Wicked Head Mistress. large type ed. Chamberlain, Margaret, illus. 184p. 1991. 13.95 (*0-7451-1407-5*, Galaxy Child Lrg Print) Chivers N Amer.
—The Birthday Burglar: And A Very Wicked Headmistress. Chamberlain, Margaret, illus. LC 92-43777. 144p. (gr. 5 up). 1993. pap. 4.95 (*0-688-12470-4*, Pub. by Beech Tree Bks) Morrow.
—The Blood-&-Thunder Adventure on Hurricane Peak. Smith, Wendy, illus. LC 89-8098. 144p. (gr. 4-7). 1989. SBE 13.95 (*0-689-50488-8*, M K McElderry) Macmillan Child Grp.
—The Blood-&-Thunder Adventure on Hurricane Peak. (gr. 4-7). 1991. pap. 3.25 (*0-440-40422-3*) Dell.
—The Blood-&-Thunder Adventure on Hurricane Peak. large type ed. Smith, Wendy, illus. 192p. (gr. 3-7). 1990. 13.95 (*0-7451-1230-7*, Galaxy Child Lrg Print) Chivers N Amer.
—Boy Who Was Followed Home. Kellogg, Steven, illus. LC 75-2866. 32p. (gr. 3-5). 1986. 13.95 (*0-8037-0286-8*) Dial Bks Young.

—The Boy Who Was Followed Home. Kellogg, Steven, illus. 32p. (ps-3). 1983. pap. 4.95 (0-8037-0903-X) Dial Bks Young.
—The Boy with Two Shadows. Williams, Jenny, illus. LC 87-17160. 32p. (ps-3). 1988. (Lipp Jr Bks) HarpC Child Bks.
—Bubble Trouble: And Other Poems & Stories. Mahy, Margaret, illus. LC 92-3540. 80p. (gr. 3-7). 1992. SBE 13.95 (0-689-50557-4, M K McElderry) Macmillan Child Grp.
—A Busy Day for a Good Grandmother. Chamberlain, Margaret, illus. LC 93-77331. 32p. (ps-3). 1993. SBE 14.95g (0-689-50595-7, M K McElderry) Macmillan Child Grp.
—The Catalogue of the Universe. LC 85-72262. 192p. (gr. 9 up). 1986. SBE 15.95 (0-689-50391-1, M K McElderry) Macmillan Child Grp.
—The Catalogue of the Universe. 192p. (gr. 7 up). 1994. pap. 3.99 (0-14-036600-8) Puffin Bks.
—The Changeover. 224p. (gr. 7 up). 1994. pap. 3.99 (0-14-036599-0) Puffin Bks.
—The Changeover: A Supernatural Romance. LC 83-83446. 224p. (gr. 7 up). 1984. SBE 14.95 (0-689-50303-2, M K McElderry) Macmillan Child Grp.
—The Chewing Gum Rescue. (gr. 5 up). 1994. pap. 3.95 (0-688-12798-3, Pub. by Beech Tree Bks) Morrow.
—The Chewing-Gum Rescue & Other Stories. Ormerod, Jan, illus. 142p. (gr. 3-7). 1991. 12.95 (0-87951-424-8) Overlook Pr.
—Dangerous Spaces. 1991. 12.95 (0-670-83734-2) Viking Child Bks.
—Dangerous Spaces. large type ed. 217p. 1992. 13.95 (0-7451-1622-1, Galaxy Child Lrg Print) Chivers N Amer.
—Dangerous Spaces. 160p. (gr. 5 up). 1993. pap. 3.99 (0-14-036362-9, Puffin) Puffin Bks.
—Door in the Air. (gr. 4-7). 1993. pap. 3.50 (0-440-40774-5) Dell.
—The Dragon of an Ordinary Family. LC 91-2513. (Illus.). 48p. (ps-3). 1992. 14.00 (0-8037-1062-3) Dial Bks Young.
—A Fortunate Name. Young, Marion, illus. LC 93-560. 1993. 13.95 (0-385-31135-4) Delacorte.
—A Fortune Branches Out. Young, Marian, illus. LC 93-11441. 1994. 13.95 (0-385-32037-X) Delacorte.
—The Girl with the Green Ear: Stories about Magic in Nature. Hughes, Shirley, illus. LC 91-14992. 112p. (gr. 3-7). 1992. 15.00 (0-679-82231-3); PLB 15.99 (0-679-92231-8) Knopf Bks Yng Read.
—The Girl with the Green Ear: Stories about Magic in Nature. Hughes, Shirley, illus. LC 91-14992. 112p. (gr. 3-7). 1993. pap. 3.25 (0-679-84000-1, Bullseye Bks) Knopf Bks Yng Read.
—The Good Fortunes Gang. Young, Marion, illus. LC 92-38784. (gr. 5 up). 1993. 13.95 (0-385-31015-3) Delacorte.
—The Great Piratical Rumbustification & The Librarian & The Robbers. Blake, Quentin, illus. LC 92-46599. 64p. (gr. 5 up). 1993. pap. 3.95 (0-688-12469-0, Pub. by Beech Tree Bks) Morrow.
—Great Piratical Rumbustification the Librarian & the Robbers. Blake, Quentin, illus. LC 85-45966. 64p. 1986. 11.95 (0-87923-629-9) Godine.
—The Great White Man-Eating Shark: A Cautionary Tale. Allen, Jonathan, illus. (ps-3). 1990. 13.00 (0-8037-0749-5) Dial Bks Young.
—The Haunting. LC 82-3983. 144p. (gr. 5-9). 1982. SBE 13.95 (0-689-50243-5, M K McElderry) Macmillan Child Grp.
—The Horrendous Hullabaloo. MacCarthy, Patricia, illus. 32p. (ps-3). 1992. 13.00 (0-670-84547-7) Viking Child Bks.
—The Horrible Story & Others. large type ed. 216p. (gr. 3-7). 1991. 13.95 (0-7451-1293-5, Galaxy Child Lrg Print) Chivers N Amer.
—Jam. Craig, Helen, illus. 32p. (ps-3). 1986. 12.95 (0-316-54396-9, 543969, Joy St Bks) Little.
—Keeping House. Smith, Wendy, illus. LC 90-37591. 32p. (gr. k-4). 1991. SBE 13.95 (0-689-50515-9, M K McElderry) Macmillan Child Grp.
—A Lion in the Meadow. Williams, Jenny, illus. 32p. (ps-3). 1992. 13.95 (0-87951-446-9) Overlook Pr.
—Making Friends. LC 89-13246. (Illus.). 32p. (gr. k-3). 1990. SBE 13.95 (0-689-50498-5, M K McElderry) Macmillan Child Grp.
—Memory. LC 87-21427. 288p. (gr. 9 up). 1988. SBE 14.95 (0-689-50446-2, M K McElderry) Macmillan Child Grp.
—Memory. (gr. k-12). 1989. pap. 3.50 (0-440-20433-X, LFL) Dell.
—Nonstop Nonsense. Blake, Quentin, illus. LC 88-8401. 128p. (gr. 1-5). 1989. SBE 12.95 (0-689-50483-7, M K McElderry) Macmillan Child Grp.
—The Pirates' Mixed-up Voyage. Chamberlain, Margaret, illus. LC 92-3931. 192p. (gr. 4-8). 1993. 13.99 (0-8037-1350-9) Dial Bks Young.
—Pumpkin Man & the Crafty Creeper. (ps-3). 1991. 14.95 (0-688-10347-2) Lothrop.
—Pumpkin Man & the Crafty Creeper. (ps-3). 1991. 14.88 (0-688-10348-0) Lothrop.
—The Queen's Goat. LC 90-46717. (Illus.). 32p. (ps-3). 1991. 12.95 (0-8037-0938-2) Dial Bks Young.
—Raging Robots & Unruly Uncles. large type ed. Stevenson, Peter, illus. 160p. 1992. 13.95 (0-7451-1526-8, Galaxy Child Lrg Print) Chivers N Amer.

—Raging Robots & Unruly Uncles. Stevenson, Peter, illus. 94p. (gr. 3-7). 1993. 13.95 (0-87951-469-8) Overlook Pr.
—The Rattlebang Picnic. Kellogg, Steven, illus. LC 93-36294. (gr. 3 up). 1994. write for info. (0-8037-1318-5); PLB write for info. (0-8037-1319-3) Dial Bks Young.
—Seven Chinese Brothers. Tseng, Jean & Mou-sien Tseng, illus. (ps-3). 1990. pap. 13.95 (0-590-42055-0) Scholastic Inc.
—Seven Chinese Brothers. 1992. pap. 3.95 (0-590-42057-7) Scholastic Inc.
—Seventeen Kings & Forty-Two Elephants. MacCarthy, Patricia, illus. LC 87-5311. 32p. (ps-3). 1987. 13.99 (0-8037-0458-5) Dial Bks Young.
—Seventeen Kings & Forty-Two Elephants. Fogelman, Phyllis J., ed. MacCarthy, Patricia, illus. LC 87-5311. 32p. (ps-3). 1990. pap. 4.95 (0-8037-0781-9) Dial Bks Young.
—A Tall Story & Other Tales. Nesbitt, Jan, illus. LC 91-62222. 96p. (gr. 3-7). 1992. SBE 15.95 (0-689-50547-7, M K McElderry) Macmillan Child Grp.
—The Three-Legged Cat. Allen, Jonathan, illus. 32p. (ps-3). 1993. 13.99 (0-670-85015-2) Viking Child Bks.
—Tick Tock Tales. Smith, Wendy, illus. 96p. (gr. k-4). 1994. SBE 16.95 (0-689-50604-X, M K McElderry) Macmillan Child Grp.
—The Tricksters. LC 86-33761. 272p. (gr. 9 up). 1987. 14.95 (0-689-50400-4, M K McElderry) Macmillan Child Grp.
—Underrunners. 192p. (gr. 5-9). 1992. 14.00 (0-670-84179-X) Viking Child Bks.
—Underrunners. large type ed. 217p. 1993. 13.95 (0-7451-1671-X, Galaxy Child Lrg Print) Chivers N Amer.

Mahy, Margaret & Chamberlain, Margaret. The Man Whose Mother Was a Pirate. (Illus.). (gr. 3-7). 1987. pap. 3.99 (0-14-050624-1, Puffin) Puffin Bks.

Maiben, Dina, jt. auth. see Zlotowitz, Bernard M.

Maiboroda, Tanya. Fairy Tales. (Illus.). 48p. (gr. 4-7). 1987. pap. 2.95 (0-8431-1882-2) Price Stern.
—Farm. (Illus.). 48p. (gr. 4-7). 1987. pap. 2.95 (0-8431-1880-6) Price Stern.
—Zoo. (Illus.). 48p. (gr. 4-7). 1987. pap. 2.95 (0-8431-1879-2) Price Stern.

Maid, Amy. Mindscapes. LC 82-9904. 67p. (gr. 3-8). 1983. pap. 11.95x (0-8290-1001-7) Irvington.
—Write, from the Beginning. (Illus.). 92p. (Orig.). (gr. 2-4). 1982. pap. 11.95x (0-8290-0993-0) Irvington.

Maidat, Rita. The Twins Visit Israel. (Illus.). (gr. 3-10). 1978. pap. 2.00 (0-914080-72-5) Shulsinger Sales.

Maidoff, Ilka. Let's Explore the Shore. (Illus.). (gr. 5 up). 1962. 9.95 (0-8392-3017-6) Astor-Honor.

Maifair, Linda, jt. auth. see Sussman, Ellen.

Maifair, Linda L. The Case of the Choosey Cheater. 64p. (gr. 2-5). 1993. pap. 2.99 (0-310-57901-5, Pub. by Youth Spec) Zondervan.
—The Case of the Giggling Ghost. 64p. (gr. 2-5). 1993. pap. 2.99 (0-310-57911-2, Pub. by Youth Spec) Zondervan.
—The Case of the Mixed-up Monsters. 64p. 1993. pap. 0.99 (0-310-57921-X, Pub. by Youth Spec) Zondervan.
—The Case of the Pampered Poodler. 64p. (gr. 2-5). 1993. pap. 2.99 (0-310-57891-4, Pub. by Youth Spec) Zondervan.
—Eighteen-Wheelers. 48p. (gr. 3-4). 1991. PLB 11.95 (1-56065-073-7) Capstone Pr.

Maifair, Linda L., jt. auth. see Roth, David.

Maifair, Linda L. see Tada, Joni E.

Maifair, Linda Lee. Brothers Don't Know Everything. Johnson, Meredith, illus. LC 93-4605. 1993. pap. 3.99 (0-8066-2635-6, Augsburg) Augsburg Fortress.

Maile, jt. auth. see Wren.

Main, Katy. Baby Animals of the North. Main, Katy, illus. 36p. (ps-k). 1992. bds. 12.95 (0-88240-395-8) Alaska Northwest.

Maine, Diana, ed. Science. LC 92-54482. (Illus.). 1993. 12.95 (1-56458-248-5) Dorling Kindersley.

Mainwaring, Jane. My Feather. 1990. pap. 6.95 (0-385-41129-4) Doubleday.

Mainwaring, S. Learning Through Sewing & Pattern Design. 35p. (gr. k-3). 1976. pap. 8.00 (0-931114-86-1) High-Scope.

Mainwaring, S. & Shouse, C. Learning Through Construction. 43p. (gr. k-3). 1983. pap. 8.00 (0-685-51017-4) High-Scope.

Mair, Jacqui, illus. Merry-Go-Round. Philip, Ned, compiled by. LC 93-32620. (Illus.). (gr. 2 up). 1994. write for info. (0-688-13367-3) Lothrop.

Maisner, Heather. Find Mouse in the House. Hard, Charlotte, illus. LC 93-3638. 1994. write for info. (1-56402-351-6) Candlewick Pr.

Maison, Della. The Care Bears' Garden. Bracken, Carolyn, illus. LC 82-61566. 32p. (gr. 1-6). 1983. pap. 1.25 saddle-stitched (0-394-85827-1) Random Bks Yng Read.

Maitland, Sandra M. The Cedar Glen Secret. Leon, Linda, illus. 24p. (ps-8). 1983. 6.95 (0-920806-44-9, Pub. by Penumbra Pr CN) U of Toronto Pr.

Maitland, William J. Beginning Weight Training for Young Athletes. (Illus.). 84p. (gr. 7 up). 1987. pap. 9.95 (0-936759-00-3) Maitland Enter.
—Weight Training for Gifted Athletes. Mollen, Art, intro. by. LC 89-90833. (Illus.). 147p. (Orig.). (gr. 8 up). 1990. pap. 17.95 (0-936759-01-1) Maitland Enter.

—Young Ball Player's Guide to Safe Pitching: Ages Eight Thru Adult with Conditioning, Strengthening. (Illus.). 140p. (gr. 3 up). 1993. pap. 14.95 (0-936759-14-3) Maitland Enter.
—Young Ballplayers Guide to Safe Pitching - Ages 8 through Adult. Barclay, John, ed. Molen, Art, intro. by. (Illus.). 150p. (gr. 4 up). 1991. pap. write for info. (0-936759-02-X) Maitland Enter.

Majeski, Bill. Fifty Great Monologs for Student Actors. Zapel, Arthur L., ed. LC 87-14103. 144p. (Orig.). (gr. 10 up). 1987. pap. 9.95 (0-916260-43-7, B-197) Meriwether Pub.

Majewski, Joe. A Friend for Oscar Mouse. Majewski, Maria, illus. LC 87-5365. 32p. (ps-2). 1991. pap. 3.99 (0-8037-0913-7, Dial Pied Piper) Puffin Bks.

Major, Beverly. The Magic Pizza. Shortall, Leonard, illus. LC 77-26993. (gr. 2-5). 1978. 5.95 (0-13-545202-3) P-H.
—Over Back. Allen, Thomas B., illus. LC 91-19696. 32p. (gr. k-4). 1993. 15.00 (0-06-020286-6); PLB 14.89 (0-06-020287-4) HarpC Child Bks.

Major, Henriette, jt. auth. see Boucher, Helene.

Major, John S. The Land & People of China. LC 88-23427. (Illus.). 288p. (gr. 6 up). 1989. (Lipp Jr Bks); PLB 18.89 (0-397-32337-9, Lipp Jr Bks) HarpC Child Bks.
—The Land & People of Malaysia & Brunei. LC 90-20124. (Illus.). 272p. (gr. 6 up). 1991. 17.95 (0-06-022488-6); PLB 17.89 (0-06-022489-4) HarpC Child Bks.
—The Land & People of Mongolia. LC 89-37790. (Illus.). 224p. (gr. 6 up). 1990. 15.95 (0-397-32386-7, Lipp Jr Bks); (Lipp Jr Bks) HarpC Child Bks.

Major, John. S. The Silk Route. Fieser, Stephen, illus. LC 92-38169. 1994. 15.00 (0-06-022924-1); PLB 14.89 (0-06-022926-8) HarpC.

Major, Kevin. Blood Red Ochre. 147p. (gr. 7-9). 1989. 14.95 (0-385-29794-7) Delacorte.
—Blood Red Ochre. (gr. k up). 1990. pap. 3.25 (0-440-20730-4, LFL) Dell.
—Dear Bruce Springsteen. (gr. k-12). 1989. pap. 3.25 (0-440-20410-0) Dell.
—Far from Shore. 224p. (gr. 7 up). 1983. pap. 2.95 (0-440-92585-1, LFL) Dell.
—Far from Shore: A Novel. LC 81-65495. 192p. (gr. 7 up). 1981. 12.95 (0-385-28266-4) Delacorte.
—Hold Fast. LC 79-17544. (gr. 9-12). 1980. 9.95 (0-440-03506-6) Delacorte.
—Hold Fast. 176p. (gr. 7 up). 1981. pap. 3.50 (0-440-93756-6, LE) Dell.
—Thirty-Six Exposures. LC 84-4995. (gr. 7 up). 1984. 14.95 (0-385-29347-X) Delacorte.

Major, Ted, jt. auth. see Williams, Terry T.

Majumdar, Lila. Jorasanko House. (Illus.). (gr. 1-9). 1979. pap. 2.50 (0-89744-176-1) Auromere.

Makela, Chuck. After You've Tried Everything Else: A "More Excellent Way" to Freedom from Addictions. 32p. (Orig.). (gr. 7 up). 1987. pap. 1.00 (0-9618532-0-4) Just Pub Hse.

Makela, Constance E. Iron Mining Fun Book for Children: Featuring Orville Ore. Makela, Constance E., illus. 44p. (Orig.). (gr. k-6). 1982. pap. 2.00x (0-9608686-0-7) Happy Thoughts & Rainbow.

Makhanlall, David. Brer Anansi & the Boat Race: A Folk Tale from the Caribbean. Rosato, Amelio, illus. LC 88-925. 32p. (gr. k-3). 1988. PLB 14.95 (0-87226-184-0, Bedrick Blackie) P Bedrick Bks.

Makhlouf, Georgia. The Rise of Major Religions. Moeller, Walter O., tr. from FRE. Welply, Michael, illus. 77p. (gr. 7 up). 1988. 17.98 (0-382-09482-4) Silver Burdett Pr.

Maki, Chu. Snowflakes, Sugar, & Salt: Crystals up Close. Sekido, Isamu, photos by. LC 92-18538. (Illus.). 1993. 17.50 (0-8225-2903-3) Lerner Pubns.

Makris, Kathryn. Almost Sisters, No. 2: The Sisters War. 160p. (Orig.). 1991. pap. 3.50 (0-380-76055-X, Camelot) Avon.
—Almost Sisters: The Sisters Scheme. 144p. (Orig.). 1991. pap. 2.99 (0-380-76035-5, Camelot) Avon.
—Almost Sisters: The Sisters Team. 176p. (Orig.). (gr. 5 up). 1992. pap. 3.50 (0-380-76056-8, Camelot) Avon.
—Crosstown. 176p. 1993. pap. 3.50 (0-380-76226-9, Flare) Avon.
—A Different Way. 192p. 1989. pap. 2.95 (0-380-75728-1, Flare) Avon.
—Mission: Love. 192p. (Orig.). (gr. 7-12). 1986. pap. 2.25 (0-553-25470-7) Bantam.

Malam, John. Indiana Jones Explores Egypt. (Illus.). 48p. (gr. 3-7). 1992. 13.95 (1-55970-183-8) Arcade Pub Inc.
—Indiana Jones Explores the Incas. (Illus.). 48p. (gr. 3-7). 1993. 14.95 (1-55970-199-4) Arcade Pub Inc.
—Pop-Up Dinosaurs. Everitt-Stewart, Andy & Moseley, Dudley, illus. LC 90-60818. 10p. (gr. 1 up). 1991. 7.95 (0-679-80871-X) Random Bks Yng Read.
—Pop-Up Machines. Everitt-Stewart, Andy & Mutimer, Ray, illus. LC 90-60819. 10p. (gr. 1 up). 1991. 7.95 (0-679-80872-8) Random Bks Yng Read.

Malcarne, Vanessa, jt. auth. see Holden, Lorraine.

Malcolm, Andrew H. The Land & People of Canada. LC 90-47560. (Illus.). 240p. (gr. 6 up). 1991. 17.95 (0-06-022494-0); PLB 17.89 (0-06-022495-9) HarpC Child Bks.

Malcolm, Dorothea C. Design: Elements & Principles. LC 71-148087. (Illus.). (gr. 5-12). 1972. 14.95 (0-87192-039-5) Davis Mass.

Malcolm, Jahnna N. Too Hot to Handle. 1991. pap. 2.99 (0-553-28262-X) Bantam.

Malcolm, Jahnna N. Bad News Ballet, No. 7: The King & Us. 1990. pap. 2.75 (*0-590-43395-4*) Scholastic Inc.
—Freak Show. (gr. 4-7). 1993. pap. 2.95 (*0-590-45853-1*) Scholastic Inc.
—The House of Fear. 1991. pap. 2.99 (*0-553-28392-8*) Bantam.
—Makin' the Grade. 1991. pap. 2.99 (*0-553-15955-0*) Bantam.
—Run for Your Life. 1991. pap. 2.99 (*0-553-28794-X*) Bantam.
—Scared Stiff. 128p. 1991. pap. 2.75 (*0-590-44996-6*, Apple Paperbacks) Scholastic Inc.
—Scared to Death. 144p. 1992. pap. 2.95 (*0-590-44995-8*, Apple Paperbacks) Scholastic Inc.
—Signed, Sealed, Delivered. 160p. (gr. 7 up). 1991. pap. 2.99 (*0-553-28314-6*) Bantam.
—The Slime That Ate Crestview. 1992. 2.95 (*0-590-45852-3*, Apple Paperbacks) Scholastic Inc.
—Sticking Together. 1991. pap. 2.99 (*0-553-15956-9*) Bantam.
Malcolm, Peter. Libya. LC 92-38756. 1993. 21.95 (*1-85435-573-2*); Set. write for info. (*1-85435-571-6*) Marshall Cavendish.
Male, Lydia S. The Amazing Book of Shapes. LC 93-34260. 1994. write for info. (*1-56458-514-X*) Dorling Kindersley.
Malecki, Maryann. Mom & Dad & I Are Having a Baby! Malecki, Maryann, illus. LC 82-81707. 70p. (Orig.). (ps-3). 1982. pap. 6.95 (*0-937604-03-8*) Pennypress.
Malerba-Foran, Joan. When You Look in the Mirror, What Do You See? 24p. (Orig.). (gr. 7 up). 1985. pap. 2.50 (*0-89486-262-6*) Hazelden.
Males, Carolyn & Feigen, Roberta. Life after High School: A Career Planning Guide. LC 85-43383. 176p. (gr. 7 up). 1986. lib. bdg. 11.98 (*0-671-54664-3*, J Messner) S&S Trade.
Maleska, Eugene T. Children's Word Games & Crossword Puzzles, Vol. 2. (gr. 2-4). 1988. pap. 7.50 (*0-8129-1692-1*) Random.
—Children's Word Games & Crossword Puzzles, Vol. 3. (gr. 2-4). 1992. pap. 7.00 (*0-8129-1980-7*, Times Bks) Random.
Maleska, Eugene T., ed. Children's Word Games & Puzzles. 2nd ed. LC 86-886. 80p. (gr. 3 up). 1986. pap. 7.00 (*0-8129-1308-6*) Random.
Maletis, Margaret, jt. auth. see Patton, Sally.
Maletsky, Evan & Hirsch, Christian, eds. Activities from the "Mathematics Teacher" LC 81-4028. (Illus.). 140p. (gr. 7 up). 1981. pap. 10.00 (*0-87353-173-6*) NCTM.
Malfatti, Patrizia. Look Inside the Ocean. Crema, Laura, illus. 16p. (ps-3). 1993. bds. 11.95 (*0-448-40488-5*, G&D) Putnam Pub Group.
Malfatti, Patrizia, tr. Look Around the City. Montanari, Donata, illus. 16p. (ps-3). 1993. bds. 11.95 (*0-448-40187-8*, G&D) Putnam Pub Group.
Mali, Jane L., jt. auth. see Herzig, Alison C.
Malin, Stuart. Story of the Earth. LC 90-11019. (Illus.). 32p. (gr. 4-6). 1991. lib. bdg. 11.89 (*0-8167-2134-3*); pap. text ed. 3.95 (*0-8167-2135-1*) Troll Assocs.
Malinowski, Stanley B. & Melodia, Thomas V. The Easter Bunny Comes to Forgottenville. 48p. (ps-3). 1988. 11.95 (*0-941316-02-5*) TSM Books.
Malkevitch, Joseph, ed. see Guy, Richard K.
Malkin, Michele. Blanche & Smitty, No. 1. 1988. pap. 3.95 (*0-553-05424-4*) Bantam.
—Blanche & Smitty, No. 2. 1988. 3.50 (*0-553-05478-3*) Bantam.
Mallett, David. Garden Song. Eitan, Ora, photos by. 1995. write for info. (*0-06-024303-1*, Festival); PLB write for info. (*0-06-024304-X*, Festival) HarpC Child Bks.
Mallett, Jerry & Bartch, Marian. Bellyful of Ballet. Smith, Mark D., illus. 56p. (gr. 2-5). 1986. PLB 7.35 (*0-8479-9926-2*, 027155) Perma-Bound.
—Booker's Bunch, Bk. 1. 80p. (gr. 3-4). 1988. PLB 9.44 (*0-8000-4735-4*, 036417) Perma-Bound.
—Booker's Bunch, Bk. 2. 88p. (gr. 3-4). 1988. PLB 9.44 (*0-8000-4736-2*, 036418) Perma-Bound.
—Clearly Old Ernie. 151p. (gr. 4-7). 1989. PLB 8.15 (*0-8000-3303-5*, 055786) Perma-Bound.
—Close the Curtains. Smith, Mark D., illus. 54p. (gr. 2-5). 1986. PLB 7.35 (*0-8479-9927-0*, 056115) Perma-Bound.
—First-Last Gravelsburg Elementary School Spelling Bee. Smith, Mark D., illus. 55p. (gr. 2-5). 1986. PLB 7.35 (*0-8479-9928-9*, 101440) Perma-Bound.
—Good Old Ernie. 127p. (gr. 4-7). 1978. PLB 7.35 (*0-8479-1992-7*, 120716) Perma-Bound.
—Goodbye to Camp Crumb. Smith, Mark D., illus. 59p. (gr. 2-5). 1986. PLB 7.35 (*0-8479-9929-7*, 120950) Perma-Bound.
—Just Old Ernie. 108p. (gr. 4-7). 1988. PLB 8.15 (*0-8000-5352-4*, 167580) Perma-Bound.
—The Mystery at Chung's Chinese Restaurant. Smith, Mark D., illus. 61p. (gr. 4-7). 1987. PLB 7.65 (*0-8000-1699-8*, 207909) Perma-Bound.
—Mystery at Madame Darkle's Wax Museum. Smith, Mark D., illus. 57p. (gr. 4-7). 1987. PLB 7.65 (*0-8000-0506-6*, 207916) Perma-Bound.
—Mystery at the Hollender Hotel. Smith, Mark D., illus. 57p. (gr. 4-7). 1987. PLB 7.65 (*0-8000-0507-4*, 207918) Perma-Bound.
—Mystery at the Laff-a-Lott Amusement Park. Smith, Mark D., illus. 59p. (gr. 4-7). 1987. PLB 7.65 (*0-8000-0509-0*, 207923) Perma-Bound.
—Mystery at the Seesaw Cinema Company. Smith, Mark D., illus. 60p. (gr. 4-7). 1987. PLB 7.65 (*0-8000-0508-2*, 207922) Perma-Bound.

—On Your Mark...Get Set... Help! Smith, Mark D., illus. 55p. (gr. 2-5). 1986. PLB 7.35 (*0-8479-9931-9*, 222340) Perma-Bound.
—Poor Old Ernie. 96p. (gr. 4-7). 1988. Repr. of 1983 ed. PLB 8.15 (*0-8479-9036-2*, 239600) Perma-Bound.
Mallett, Jerry J. Library Skills Activity Puzzles Series, 5 bks. Incl. Book Bafflers. 1982; Dictionary Puzzlers. 1982; Lively Locators. 1982; Reading Incentives. 1982; Resource Rousers. 1982. (gr. 2-6). 1988. pap. text ed. 32.95x ea., 64 pgs. ea. (*0-87628-537-X*) Ctr Appl Res.
Mallett, Jerry J. & Ervin, Timothy S. Elevator. Johnston, Clinton, illus. 23p. (ps-2). 1992. 9.10 (*0-7804-3989-9*, 088542) Perma-Bound.
—Elevator: Paper Big Book. Johnston, Clinton, illus. 23p. (Orig.). (ps-2). 1992. pap. 22.00 (*0-7804-3988-0*, 088544) Perma-Bound.
—Elevator: Perma Big Book. Johnston, Clinton, illus. 23p. (ps-2). 1992. 47.50 (*0-7804-3987-2*, 088543) Perma-Bound.
—Good Day, Blue Goose. Feraris, Kathy, illus. 28p. (ps-2). 1992. 9.10 (*0-7804-3992-9*, 120051) Perma-Bound.
—Good Day, Blue Goose: Paper Big Book. Feraris, Kathy, illus. 28p. (Orig.). (ps-2). 1992. pap. 22.00 (*0-7804-3990-2*, 120052) Perma-Bound.
—Good Day, Blue Goose: Perma Big Book. Feraris, Kathy, illus. 28p. (ps-2). 1992. 47.50 (*0-7804-3991-0*, 120053) Perma-Bound.
Malley, Barbara & Allen, Frances. Poetry with a Purpose. Lawrence, Grace, illus. 128p. (gr. 4-7). 1987. pap. 10.95 (*0-86653-415-6*, GA 1018) Good Apple.
Malley, Sarah H., jt. auth. see Lightbody, Nancy K.
Malley, Stephen. A Kid's Guide to the Nineteen Ninety-Four Winter Olympics. (Illus.). (gr. 4-7). 1994. pap. 9.95 (*0-553-48159-2*) Bantam.
—The Kids' Guide to the Nineteen Ninety-Two Summer Olympics. (Illus.). 80p. (gr. 3-7). 1992. pap. 12.95 (*0-316-54534-1*, Spts Illus Kids) Little.
Mallick, Joan. Anorexia. Head, J. J., ed. Steffen, Ann T. & Slifko, Fran, illus. LC 86-72198. 16p. (Orig.). (gr. 10 up). 1987. pap. text ed. 2.75 (*0-89278-373-7*, 45-9773*) Carolina Biological.
Mallis, Jackie, jt. auth. see Long, Jeanne.
Mallory, Ken. Water Hole: And the Rebirth of a Tropical Forest. LC 92-14360. (Illus.). 56p. (gr. 5-8). 1992. 15.95 (*0-531-15250-2*); PLB 15.90 (*0-531-11154-7*) Watts.
Mallory, Ken, jt. auth. see Kraus, Scott.
Mallory, Kenneth. The Red Sea. (Illus.). 48p. (gr. 5-7). 1991. 14.95 (*0-531-15213-8*); PLB 14.90 (*0-531-10993-3*) Watts.
Mallory, Kenneth & Conley, Andrea. Rescue of the Stranded Whales. Prescott, John H., intro. by. 48p. (gr. 3 up). 1989. pap. 14.95 jacketed (*0-671-67122-7*, S&S BFYR) S&S Trade.
—Rescue of the Stranded Whales. (gr. 6). 1991. pap. write for info. (*0-663-56248-1*) Silver Burdett Pr.
Mallory, Thomas. King Arthur & His Knights of the Round Table. Lanier, Sidney & Pyle, Howard, eds. Florian, illus. 288p. (gr. 4-6). 1950. (G&D); 13.95 (*0-448-06016-7*, G&D) Putnam Pub Group.
Malmgren, Dallin. The Ninth Issue. LC 88-22881. (gr. 7 up). 1989. pap. 14.95 (*0-440-50124-5*) Delacorte.
—The Whole Nine Yards. LC 85-16222. 192p. (gr. 7 up). 1986. 14.95 (*0-385-29452-2*) Delacorte.
—The Whole Nine Yards. (gr. 7 up). 1987. pap. 2.95 (*0-440-99575-2*, LFL) Dell.
Malnig, Anita. Where the Waves Break: Life at the Edge of the Sea. LC 84-9614. (Illus.). 48p. (gr. 2-5). 1985. PLB 19.95 (*0-87614-226-9*) Carolrhoda Bks.
—Where the Waves Break: Life at the Edge of the Sea. (Illus.). 48p. (gr. 1-5). 1987. pap. 6.95 (*0-87614-477-6*, First Ave Edns) Lerner Pubns.
Malone, James H. No-Job Dad. LC 92-15873. (Illus.). 30p. (gr. 1-2). 1992. 13.95 (*1-878217-06-2*) Victory Press.
Malone, Maggie. Christmas Scrapcrafts. (Illus.). 136p. (gr. 5-10). 1992. pap. 12.95 (*0-8069-6805-2*) Sterling.
Malone, Mary. Connie Chung: Broadcast Journalist. LC 91-25396. (Illus.). 128p. (gr. 6 up). 1992. lib. bdg. 17.95 (*0-89490-332-2*) Enslow Pubs.
—Dorothea L. Dix: Hospital Founder. Sampson, Katharine, illus. 80p. (gr. 2-6). 1991. Repr. of 1968 ed. lib. bdg. 12.95 (*0-7910-1436-3*) Chelsea Hse.
—Liliuokalani: Queen of Hawaii. (Illus.). 80p. (gr. 2-6). 1993. Repr. of 1975 ed. lib. bdg. 12.95 (*0-7910-1413-4*) Chelsea Hse.
Malone, Nola L. A Home. LC 87-17849. (Illus.). 24p. (ps-2). 1988. SBE 12.95 (*0-02-751440-4*, Bradbury Pr) Macmillan Child Grp.
Malone, P. M. Into the High Branches. Lewison, Terry, illus. 196p. (Orig.). (gr. 1-8). 1992. pap. text ed. 11.95 (*0-9631957-1-9*) Raspberry Hill.
—Out of the Nest. Lewison, Terry, illus. 198p. (Orig.). (gr. 1-8). 1991. pap. text ed. 11.95 (*0-9631957-0-0*) Raspberry Hill.
—To Find a Way Home. Lewison, Terry, illus. 200p. (Orig.). (gr. 1-8). 1993. pap. text ed. 11.95 (*0-9631957-2-7*) Raspberry Hill.
Maloney, Marina. The Knight of the Sand Castle. LC 92-85410. (Illus.). 44p. (gr. k-4). 1993. pap. 5.95 (*1-55523-553-0*) Winston-Derek.
Maloney, Michael. Straight Talk about Anxiety & Depression. 1993. pap. 3.99 (*0-440-21472-6*) Dell.
—Straight Talk about Eating Disorders. 1993. pap. 3.99 (*0-440-21350-9*) Dell.

Maloney, Michael & Kranz, Rachel. Straight Talk about Anxiety & Depression. 128p. (gr. 5-12). 1991. lib. bdg. 16.95x (*0-8160-2434-0*) Facts on File.
—Straight Talk about Eating Disorders. 128p. (gr. 7-12). 1991. 16.95x (*0-8160-2414-6*) Facts on File.
Maloney, P. Dennis, ed. see Lehner, Devony.
Maloney, Ray. Impact Zone. LC 85-16156. 256p. (gr. 7 up). 1986. 14.95 (*0-385-29447-6*) Delacorte.
—The Impact Zone. (gr. k-12). 1987. pap. 2.95 (*0-440-94013-3*, LFL) Dell.
Malot, Hector. En Famille, Tome 1. Lanot, H., illus. (FRE.). 220p. (gr. 5-10). 1980. pap. 8.95 (*2-07-033131-8*) Schoenhof.
—En Famille, Tome 2. Lanos, H., illus. (FRE.). 221p. (gr. 5-10). 1980. pap. 8.95 (*2-07-033132-6*) Schoenhof.
—Sans Famille, Tome 1. Bayard, E., illus. (FRE.). 351p. (gr. 5-10). 1990. pap. 10.95 (*2-07-033612-3*) Schoenhof.
—Sans Famille, Tome 2. Bayard, E., illus. (FRE.). 417p. (gr. 5-10). 1991. pap. 10.95 (*2-07-033617-4*) Schoenhof.
Malotki, Ekkehart, retold by. The Mouse Couple. Lacapa, Michael, illus. LC 88-60916. 64p. (gr. 2-7). 1988. 14.95 (*0-87358-473-2*) Northland AZ.
Malovitzki, Sinai. Parshas Lech. (YID., Illus.). 160p. 1987. tchr's. ed. 10.00 (*0-944704-03-4*) Sinai Heritage.
—Parshas Nitzuvim. (YID., Illus.). 150p. 1988. pap. 5.00 (*0-944704-61-1*) Sinai Heritage.
—Parshas Yisroy. (YID., Illus.). 400p. 1988. PLB 25.00 (*0-944704-19-0*) Sinai Heritage.
—Parshaw Va'Yeilech. (YID., Illus.). 95p. 1988. pap. 5.00 (*0-944704-62-X*) Sinai Heritage.
Malowicky, Sinai, ed. & illus. see Teitelbaum, Eli.
Maloy, Jacqueline. Teeth. (Illus.). 32p. (gr. 1-4). 1989. PLB 15.96 (*0-8172-3520-5*); pap. 3.95 (*0-8114-6722-8*) Raintree Steck-V.
Malterre, Elona. The Last Wolf of Ireland. (gr. 4-9). 1990. 13.45 (*0-395-54381-9*, Clarion Bks) HM.
Malve, Eduardo, jt. auth. see Ureta, Floreal.
Mamet, David. Three Children's Plays: The Poet & the Rent; The Frog Prince; The Revenge of the Space Pandas or Binky Rudich & the Two-Speed Clock. 144p. (gr. 3-7). pap. 8.95 (*0-8021-5173-6*) Grove-Atltic.
Mamin-Sibiryak, D. N. Grey Neck. Rudolph, Marguerita, adapted by. Kronz, Leslie S., illus. LC 88-2100. 32p. (gr. k-3). 1988. 13.95 (*0-88045-068-1*) Stemmer Hse.
Mammana, Dennis. Start Exploring Space: A Fact-Filled Coloring Book. Driggs, Helen, illus. 128p. (Orig.). (gr. 3 up). 1991. pap. 8.95 (*0-89471-864-9*) Running Pr.
Mammen, Lori. Passageways: Vocabulary Activities to Build Writing Skills. 96p. (gr. 4-9). 1992. pap. text ed. 12.95 (*0-944459-62-5*) ECS Lrn Systs.
—Springboards for Reading, Grades 3-6: 48 Strategic Reading Lessons. 96p. (gr. 3-6). 1993. pap. text ed. 11.95 (*0-944459-69-2*) ECS Lrn Systs.
—Springboards for Reading, Grades 7-12: 38 Strategic Reading Lessons. 80p. (gr. 7-12). 1993. pap. text ed. 10.95 (*0-944459-70-6*) ECS Lrn Systs.
—TAAS Master Reading Teacher Training Manual - Elementary. (Illus.). 64p. (gr. 2-5). 1992. pap. text ed. 7.95 (*0-944459-41-2*) ECS Lrn Systs.
—TAAS Master Reading Teacher Training Manual - Secondary. 64p. (gr. 6-12). 1992. pap. text ed. 7.95 (*0-944459-42-0*) ECS Lrn Systs.
—TAAS Master Social Studies Grade Four. (Illus.). 144p. (gr. 1-4). 1993. pap. text ed. 19.95 (*0-944459-92-7*) ECS Lrn Systs.
—TAAS Quick Review Reading: Exit Level. (Illus.). 96p. (gr. 9). 1992. pap. text ed. 12.95 (*0-944459-39-0*) ECS Lrn Systs.
—TAAS Quick Review Writing: Exit Level. 64p. (gr. 11). 1991. pap. text ed. 9.95 (*0-944459-30-7*) ECS Lrn Systs.
—TAAS Quick Review Writing: Grade 3. (Illus.). 64p. (gr. 3). 1991. pap. text ed. 9.95 (*0-944459-26-9*) ECS Lrn Systs.
—TAAS Quick Review Writing: Grade 5. (Illus.). 64p. (gr. 5). 1991. pap. text ed. 9.95 (*0-944459-27-7*) ECS Lrn Systs.
—TAAS Quick Review Writing: Grade 7. 64p. (gr. 7). 1991. pap. text ed. 9.95 (*0-944459-28-5*) ECS Lrn Systs.
—TAAS Quick Review Writing: Grade 9. 64p. (gr. 9). 1991. pap. text ed. 9.95 (*0-944459-29-3*) ECS Lrn Systs.
—TEAMS Vocabulary Plus: Learning & Using TEAMS Vocabulary Words, 3 vols. (Illus.). 120p. 1988. pap. text ed. 7.95 ea. Grade 3 (*0-944459-00-5*) Grade 5 (*0-944459-01-3*) Grade 7 (*0-944459-02-1*) ECS Lrn Systs.
—Writing Prompts Plus: Preparing Students for the TEAMS Composition Test, 4 vols. (Illus.). 160p. 1988. pap. text ed. 7.95 ea. Grade 3 (*0-944459-03-X*) Grade 5 (*0-944459-04-8*) Grade 7 (*0-944459-05-6*) Grade 9 (*0-944459-06-4*) ECS Lrn Systs.
—Writing Warm-Ups. 80p. (gr. 7-12). 1989. pap. text ed. 9.95 (*0-944459-08-0*) ECS Lrn Systs.
—Writing Warm-ups Two K-6: Quick, Creative, & Challenging Writing Exercises. 80p. (gr. k-6). 1992. pap. text ed. 9.95 (*0-944459-45-5*) ECS Lrn Systs.
—Writing Warm-ups Two 7-12: Quick, Creative, & Challenging Writing Exercises. 80p. (gr. 7-12). 1992. pap. text ed. 9.95 (*0-944459-46-3*) ECS Lrn Systs.
Mammen, Lori, jt. auth. see Parker, Violette.

Man, John. Exploration & Discovery. LC 89-11376. (Illus.). 64p. (gr. 4-6). 1990. PLB 19.93 (*0-8368-0007-9*) Gareth Stevens Inc.
—Exploring the World. LC 89-11285. (Illus.). 64p. (gr. 2-3). 1990. PLB 19.93 (*0-8368-0032-X*) Gareth Stevens Inc.

Mana, Tawa & Youyouseyah. When Hopi Children Were Bad: A Monster Story. Coates, Ross, illus. 41p. (Orig.). (gr. k-5). 1989. pap. 6.95 (*0-940113-20-1*) Sierra Oaks Pub.

Manber, David. Zachary of the Wings. 88p. (gr. 9-12). 1993. PLB 10.95 (*1-879567-27-X*) Wonder Well.

Manci, William E. Farming & the Environment. LC 93-13046. 1993. write for info. (*0-8368-0731-6*) Gareth Stevens Inc.

Mancini, Richard. Everything You Need to Know about Living with a Single Parent. (gr. 7-12). 1992. PLB 13.95 (*0-8239-1323-6*) Rosen Group.

Mancini, Richard E. Indians of the Southeast. (Illus.). 96p. (gr. 5-8). 1991. lib. bdg. 18.95x (*0-8160-2390-5*) Facts on File.

Mancuso, Robert A. Question the Direction: A Program for Teaching Careful Listening & the Questioning of Unclear Directions. (gr. 1-7). 1988. manual & reproducible wkbk. 29.95 (*1-55999-065-1*) LinguiSystems.

Mandel, Gerry, ed. see Schwartzman, Lee T.

Mandel, Peter. Ballerina Bunny Loves to Dance. 1987. pap. 2.50 (*0-89954-674-9*) Antioch Pub Co.
—Red Cat, White Cat. 1994. write for info. (*0-8050-2929-X*) H Holt & Co.

Mandel, Suzy. Make Your Own Calendar, 1994. Mandel, Suzy, illus. (gr. 1-5). 1993. 5.95 (*0-316-54559-7*) Little.

Mandelbaum, Pili. You Be Me, I'll Be You. (Illus.). 40p. (ps-3). 1990. 13.95 (*0-916291-27-8*) Kane-Miller Bk.
—You Be Me, I'll Be You. (Illus.). 40p. (ps-3). pap. 6.95 (*0-916291-47-2*) Kane-Miller Bk.

Mandelkern, Nicholas, ed. see Bamberger, David.

Mandell, Judy, jt. auth. see Rochester, Lois.

Mandell, Muriel. Physics Experiments for Children. Matsuda, S., illus. LC 68-9308. (gr. 3-10). 1968. pap. 2.95 (*0-486-22033-8*) Dover.
—Simple Science Experiments with Everyday Materials. Zweifel, Frances W., illus. LC 88-31201. 128p. (gr. 4-10). 1989. 12.95 (*0-8069-6794-3*) Sterling.
—Simple Science Experiments with Everyday Materials. LC 88-31201. (Illus.). 128p. (gr. 4-10). 1990. pap. 4.95 (*0-8069-5764-6*) Sterling.
—Simple Weather Experiments with Everyday Materials. LC 90-37915. (Illus.). 128p. (gr. 4-10). 1990. 12.95 (*0-8069-7296-3*) Sterling.
—Simple Weather Experiments with Everyday Materials. Zweifel, Frances, illus. LC 90-37915. 128p. (gr. 4 up). 1991. pap. 4.95 (*0-8069-7295-5*) Sterling.
—Two Hundred & Twenty Easy-to-Do Science Experiments for Young People: Three Complete Books. 287p. (gr. 3 up). 1985. pap. 8.85 (*0-486-24874-7*) Dover.

Mandell, Steven L., jt. auth. see Baumann, Susan K.
Mandell, Steven L., jt. auth. see Brenan, Kathleen M.
Mandeville, Jerry, tr. see Dolson, Gina.

Mandino, Og. Greatest Salesman in the World. LC 68-10798. (gr. 9 up). 1987. 12.95 (*0-8119-0067-3*) Lifetime.
—Og Mandino's Great Trilogy. 1993. 12.98 (*0-8119-0428-8*) Lifetime.

Mandrell, Louise. All American Hero: A Story about the Meaning of Veterans Day. (gr. 4-7). 1993. 12.95 (*1-56530-010-6*) Summit TX.
—All in a Day's Work: A Story about the Meaning of Mother's Day. (ps-3). 1993. 12.95 (*1-56530-036-X*) Summit TX.
—All in a Day's Work: A Story about the Meaning of Mother's Day. (gr. 4-7). 1993. 12.95 (*1-56540-036-4*) Impact Photograph.
—Best Man for the Job: A Story about the Meaning of Father's Day. (ps-3). 1993. 12.95 (*1-56530-039-4*) Summit TX.
—Candy's Frog Prince: A Story about the Meaning of Valentines Day. (gr. 4-7). 1993. 12.95 (*1-56530-046-7*) Summit TX.
—Eddie Finds a Hero: A Story about the Meaning of Memorial Day. (ps-3). 1993. 12.95 (*1-56530-037-8*) Summit TX.
—End of the Rainbow: A Story about the Meaning of St. Patrick's Day. (gr. 4-7). 1993. 12.95 (*1-56530-047-5*) Summit TX.
—Eye of an Eagle: A Story about the Meaning of Columbus Day, Lo. (gr. 4-7). 1993. 12.95 (*1-56530-009-2*) Summit TX.
—Kimis American Dream: A Story about the Meaning of Martin Luther King Day. (gr. 4-7). 1993. 12.95 (*1-56530-045-9*) Summit TX.
—Mission for Jenny: A Story about the Meaning of Flag Day. (ps-3). 1993. 12.95 (*1-56530-038-6*) Summit TX.
—Peril in Evans Woods: A Story about the Meaning of Easter. (ps-3). 1993. 12.95 (*1-56530-035-1*) Summit TX.
—Peril in Evans Woods: A Story about the Meaning of Easter. (ps-3). 1993. 12.95 (*1-56530-053-X*) Summit TX.
—Sunrise over the Harbor: A Story about the Meaning. (ps-3). 1993. 12.95 (*1-56530-048-3*) Summit TX.
—Twin Disasters: A Story about the Meaning of Labor Day. (gr. 4-7). 1993. 12.95 (*1-56530-041-6*) Summit TX.

Mandrell, Louise & Collins, Ace. Jonathan's Gift. 32p. 1992. 12.95 (*1-56530-012-2*) Summit TX.
—Runaway Thanksgiving: A Story About the Meaning of Thanksgiving. 32p. 1992. 12.95 (*1-56530-011-4*) Summit TX.
—Sunrise over the Harbor: A Story About the Meaning. Gale, Mark, illus. LC 93-310. 1993. 12.95 (*1-56530-040-8*) Summit TX.

Maners, Wendelin, jt. auth. see Gimbel, Cheryl.

Manes, Stephen. Be a Perfect Person. 1983. pap. 3.50 (*0-553-15580-6*) Bantam.
—Be a Perfect Person in Just Three Days! Huffman, Tom, illus. 64p. (gr. 3-6). 1982. 13.45 (*0-89919-064-2*, Clarion Bks) HM.
—Be a Perfect Person in Just Three Days. (ps-7). 1987. pap. 2.95 (*0-553-15367-6*) Bantam.
—The Boy Who Turned into a TV Set. Bass, Michael, illus. 32p. (Orig.). (gr. 2-5). 1983. pap. 2.50 (*0-380-62000-6*, Camelot) Avon.
—Chocolate-Covered Ants. 1990. 13.95 (*0-590-40960-3*) Scholastic Inc.
—Chocolate-Covered Ants. (gr. 4-7). 1993. pap. 2.95 (*0-590-40961-1*) Scholastic Inc.
—Comedy High. 176p. (gr. 7 up). 1992. 13.95 (*0-590-44436-0*, Scholastic Hardcover) Scholastic Inc.
—The Great Gerbil Roundup. McKinley, John, illus. 105p. (gr. 3-7). 1988. 13.95 (*0-15-232490-9*, HB Juv Bks) HarBrace.
—The Great Gerbil Roundup. McKinley, John, illus. LC 88-2266. 112p. (gr. 3-7). 1991. pap. 3.95 (*0-06-440375-0*, Trophy) HarpC Child Bks.
—The Hooples' Haunted House. Weston, Martha, illus. LC 81-2216. 128p. (gr. 4-6). 1981. pap. 11.95 (*0-385-28416-0*) Delacorte.
—The Hooples' Haunted House. Weston, Martha, illus. 112p. (gr. 3-7). 1983. pap. 2.25 (*0-440-43794-6*, YB) Dell.
—The Hooples' Horrible Holiday. 108p. (Orig.). (gr. 3-7). 1986. pap. 2.50 (*0-380-89740-7*, Camelot) Avon.
—It's New!, It's Improved!, It's Terrible! (gr. 2-6). 1989. pap. 3.50 (*0-553-15682-9*, Skylark) Bantam.
—Make Four Million Dollars. (gr. 4-7). 1991. 14.95 (*0-553-07050-9*) Bantam.
—Make Four Million Dollars by Next Thursday! Ulrich, George, illus. (gr. 3-7). 1992. pap. 3.50 (*0-553-15908-9*, Skylark) Bantam.
—Monstra vs. Irving. Sours, Michael, illus. LC 89-33423. 80p. (gr. 2-4). 1991. pap. 4.95 (*0-8050-1642-2*, Bks Young Read) H Holt & Co.
—The Obnoxious Jerks. 160p. (gr. 7 up). 1988. 13.95 (*0-553-05488-0*) Bantam.
—Some of the Adventures of Rhode Island Red. Joyce, William, illus. LC 89-35397. 128p. (gr. 3-7). 1990. (Lipp Jr Bks); PLB 10.89 (*0-397-32348-4*, Lipp Jr Bks) HarpC Child Bks.
—Some of the Adventures of Rhode Island Red. Joyce, William, illus. LC 89-35397. 128p. (gr. 3-7). 1993. pap. 3.95 (*0-06-440358-0*, Trophy) HarpC Child Bks.

Maness, Malia. Curious Kimo. Hall, Pat, illus. LC 93-86143. 32p. (ps-3). 1993. 9.95 (*0-9633493-0-9*) Pacific Greetings.
—The Toad That Taught Flying. Hall, Patt, illus. LC 93-86144. 32p. (ps-3). 1993. 9.95 (*0-9633493-1-7*) Pacific Greetings.

Maney, D. C. Our Changing Landscape. LC 89-11340. (Illus.). 64p. (gr. 4-6). 1990. PLB 19.93 (*0-8368-0008-7*) Gareth Stevens Inc.

Manfred, Frederick. Conquering Horse. 352p. 1965. pap. 4.50 (*0-451-08739-9*, W8739, Sig) NAL-Dutton.
—Duke's Mixture. 230p. (gr. 8). 1993. pap. 12.95 (*0-931170-55-9*) Ctr Western Studies.

Mangan, Velda B., ed. see Bair, Elmer O.

Mangas, Brian. Carrot Delight. 1990. pap. 5.95 (*0-671-67886-8*, S&S BFYR) S&S Trade.
—Carrot Delight. Levitt, Sidney, illus. 32p. (ps-1). 1991. pap. 2.25 (*0-671-73278-1*, Little Simon) S&S Trade.
—Follow that Puppy. (ps-6). 1993. pap. 4.95 (*0-671-87171-4*, S&S BFYR) S&S Trade.
—A Nice Surprise for Father Rabbit. Levitt, Sidney, illus. 32p. (ps-1). 1991. pap. 2.25 (*0-671-73277-3*, Little Simon) S&S Trade.
—Sshaboom! Bratun, Katy, illus. LC 91-24764. 40p. (ps-1). 1993. pap. 14.00 JRT (*0-671-75538-2*, S&S BFYR) S&S Trade.
—You Don't Get a Carrot Unless You're a Bunny. Levitt, Sidney, illus. 1989. pap. 5.95 (*0-671-67201-0*, Little Simon) S&S Trade.
—You Don't Get a Carrot Unless You're a Bunny. Levitt, Sidney, illus. LC 88-19763. 32p. (ps-k). 1991. pap. 2.25 (*0-671-74200-0*, Little Simon) S&S Trade.

Mangieri, Rose M. My Companion to Know, Love, & Serve. LC 73-158919. (Illus.). 85p. (Orig.). (ps-1). 1977. pap. 5.50 (*0-913382-45-0*, 103-7) Prow Bks-Franciscan.

Mango, Karin N. Codes, Ciphers & Other Secrets. Rosoff, Iris, ed. LC 88-5638. (Illus.). 96p. (gr. 4-6). 1988. PLB 10.90 (*0-531-10575-X*) Watts.
—Hearing Loss. Perrotta, Mary, ed. LC 90-19746. (Illus.). 144p. (gr. 7-12). 1991. PLB 13.90 (*0-531-12519-X*) Watts.
—Mapmaking. Corwin, Judith H., illus. LC 83-25084. 112p. (gr. 4 up). 1984. lib. bdg. 9.29 (*0-671-45518-4*, J Messner) S&S Trade.
—Portrait of Miranda. LC 92-8191. 240p. (gr. 7 up). 1993. 16.00 (*0-06-021777-4*); PLB 15.89 (*0-06-021778-2*) HarpC Child Bks.

Mangold, Paul, jt. auth. see Gipson, Morrell.

Mangrum, Charles T., II. Learning to Study, Bks. B-C. 2nd ed. 80p. (gr. 2-3). 1994. pap. 8.00 (*0-89061-725-2*); tchr's. guide 3.95 (*0-89061-732-5*) Jamestown Pubs.
—Learning to Study, Bk. D. 2nd ed. 80p. (gr. 4). 1994. pap. 8.00 (*0-89061-726-0*); tchr's. guide 3.95 (*0-89061-733-3*) Jamestown Pubs.
—Learning to Study, Bk. E. 2nd ed. 96p. (gr. 5). 1994. pap. 8.00 (*0-89061-727-9*); tchr's. guide 3.95 (*0-89061-734-1*) Jamestown Pubs.
—Learning to Study, Bk. F. 2nd ed. 96p. (gr. 6). 1994. pap. 8.00 (*0-89061-728-7*); tchr's. guide 3.95 (*0-89061-735-X*) Jamestown Pubs.
—Learning to Study, Bk. G. 2nd ed. 96p. (gr. 7). 1994. pap. 8.00 (*0-89061-729-5*); tchr's. guide 3.95 (*0-89061-736-8*) Jamestown Pubs.
—Learning to Study, Bk. H. 2nd ed. 96p. (gr. 8). 1994. pap. 8.00 (*0-89061-730-9*); tchr's. guide 3.95 (*0-89061-737-6*) Jamestown Pubs.
—Learning to Study, 6 bks, Bks.B-H. 2nd ed. (gr. 2-8). 1994. Set. pap. 48.00 (*0-89061-724-4*); tchr's. guide 23.70 (*0-89061-731-7*) Jamestown Pubs.

Mangrum, Charles T., II, et al. Fell's Guide to College Money for the Asking in Florida. 224p. (Orig.). (gr. 9-12). 1988. pap. 13.95 (*0-8119-0706-6*) Lifetime.

Manheim, Ralph, tr. see Ende, Michael.
Manheim, Ralph, tr. see Grimm, Jacob & Grimm, Wilhelm K.
Manheim, Ralph, tr. see Grimm, Wilhelm K.
Manheim, Ralph, tr. see Heine, Helme.
Manheim, Ralph, tr. see Hoffmann, E. T.

Maniscalco, Joe. Old Barn: Springtime. Wheeler, Penny E., ed. 32p. (gr. 2-4). 1988. pap. 3.95 (*0-8280-0423-4*) Review & Herald.

Manley, D. Look & Learn about People, Places & Things. (Illus.). (gr. 2-6). 5.98 (*0-517-45795-4*) Outlet Bk Co.

Manley, Dean V., ed. see Asham, Roger & Ford, Horace.

Manley, Deborah. Bible Times. 48p. 1990. 4.99 (*0-517-69616-9*) Outlet Bk Co.
—How to Make a Rainbow: Forty Great Things to Make & Do for Seven Year Olds. LC 93-23331. 1994. 2.95 (*1-85697-929-6*) Kingfisher Bks.
—Long Ago. (Illus.). 48p. (ps-6). 1990. 4.99 (*0-517-69615-0*) Outlet Bk Co.
—People & Places. (Illus.). 48p. (ps-6). 1990. 4.99 (*0-517-69614-2*) Outlet Bk Co.
—Peppermint Mice: Forty Great Things to Make & Do for Six Year Olds. LC 93-23330. 1994. 2.95 (*1-85697-928-8*) Kingfisher Bks.

Manley, Molly. Talkaty Talker. Marshall, Janet, illus. 24p. (ps-1). 1994. prepub. 9.95 (*1-56397-195-X*) Boyds Mills Pr.

Manley, Robert N. Nebraska: Our Pioneer Heritage. Warp, Eric & Elley, Charles, illus. 197p. (gr. 4-6). 1981. text ed. 7.50 (*0-939644-00-2*); tchr's. guide 50 pgs. 4.00 (*0-939644-01-0*) Media Pub.

Manley, Rosie, jt. auth. see Brackett, Karen.

Manley, Stephen. More Than Words. 32p. 1988. pap. 1.95 (*0-8341-1236-1*) Beacon Hill.

Mann, Angela La see La Mann, Angela.

Mann, Barry. Sigmund Freud. LC 92-42548. 1993. 19.93 (*0-86625-491-9*); 14.95s.p. (*0-685-66534-8*) Rourke Pubns.

Mann, Kenny. I Am Not Afraid! Based on a Masai Tale. Leonard, Richard, illus. LC 92-13811. 1993. 9.99 (*0-553-09119-0*, Little Rooster); 3.50 (*0-553-37108-8*, Little Rooster) Bantam.

Mann, Marek. Annie's City Adventures. Max, Jill, ed. Verlag, Mangold, tr. from GER. Mann, Marek, illus. LC 91-21302. 24p. (gr. k-3). 1991. PLB 14.60 (*1-56074-031-0*) Garrett Ed Corp.
—Annie's High Sea Adventure. Max, Jill & Bradford, Elizabeth, eds. Verlag, Mangold, tr. from GER. Mann, Marek, illus. LC 91-21305. 24p. (gr. k-3). 1991. PLB 14.60 (*1-56074-027-2*) Garrett Ed Corp.
—Dino, the Star Keeper. Max, Jill, ed. Verlag, Mangold, tr. from GER. Mann, Marek, illus. LC 91-21304. 24p. (gr. k-3). 1991. PLB 14.60 (*1-56074-028-0*) Garrett Ed Corp.

Mann, Marek, jt. auth. see Gipson, Morrell.

Mann, P. Z. Bees Buzz. Reasoner, Chuck, illus. 14p. (ps-1). 1992. bds. 1.95 (*1-56293-203-9*) McClanahan Bk.
—Frogs Fiddle. Reasoner, Chuck, illus. 14p. (ps-2). 1992. bds. 1.95 (*1-56293-202-0*) McClanahan Bk.
—Spiders Spin. Reasoner, Chuck, illus. 14p. (ps-1). 1992. bds. 1.95 (*1-56293-205-5*) McClanahan Bk.
—Turtles Tiptoe. Reasoner, Chuck, illus. 14p. (ps-2). 1992. bds. 1.95 (*1-56293-204-7*) McClanahan Bk.

Mann, Peggy. La Historia de Maria Wanna: O Como te Dana la Marihuana. Ramirez, Gloria & Gatti, Maria N., trs. from ENG. Lind, Naomi, illus. (SPA.). 44p. (Orig.). (gr. 1-6). 1990. pap. text ed. 3.95 (*0-942493-15-X*) Woodmere Press.
—Pot Safari: A Visit to the Top Marijuana Researchers. Rev. ed. LC 82-91050. 133p. (Orig.). (gr. 9-12). 1987. pap. 6.95 (*0-942493-01-X*) Woodmere Press.
—The Sad Story of Mary Wanna or How Marijuana Harms You. rev. ed. 40p. (gr. 1-6). 1990. pap. 3.95 (*0-318-50073-6*) Woodmere Press.
—Twelve Is Too Old. updated ed. 140p. (gr. 6-9). 1987. pap. 6.95 (*0-942493-00-1*) Woodmere Press.

Mann, Peggy & Houlton, Betsy. Ms. Cramm on Pot: The Real Story about Marijuana. Hanson, Eric, illus. 21p. (gr. 6-12). 1991. pap. 1.75 (*0-89486-738-5*) Hazelden.

Mann, Peggy, jt. auth. see Moran, Bill.

Mann, Roland. Cat & Mouse Collection. Ulm, Chris, ed. Byrd, Mitch & Butler, Steven, illus. 139p. 1990. pap. 9.95 (0-944735-70-3) Malibu Graphics.
Mann, Victor. He Remembered to Say "Thank You" (Illus.). 32p. (ps-4). 1976. pap. 1.89 (0-570-06103-2, 59-1221) Concordia.
Mannetti, William. Dinosaurs in Your Backyard. Mannetti, William, illus. LC 81-7998. 160p. (gr. 4-7). 1982. SBE 13.95 (0-689-30906-6, Atheneum Child Bk) Macmillan Child Grp.
Manniche, Lise. The Ancient Egyptians. (Illus.). (gr. 2-6). pap. 3.95 (0-7141-0941-X, Pub. by Brit Mus UK) Parkwest Pubns.
Mannin, Ethel. The Saga of Sammy-Cat. Kesteven, Peter, illus. (gr. 1-3). 1969. Repr. of 1969 ed. 2.59 (0-08-013397-5) Pergamon.
Manning, Linda. Animal Hours. Van Kampen, Vlasta, illus. 32p. (ps-2). 1991. bds. 13.95 (0-19-540771-7) OUP.
—Dinosaur Days. Van Kampen, Vlasta, illus. LC 93-28443. 32p. (ps-2). 1993. PLB 12.95 (0-8167-3315-5); pap. 3.95 (0-8167-3316-3) Troll Assocs.
Manning, Mick. A Ruined House. LC 93-21295. 1994. write for info. (1-56402-453-9) Candlewick Pr.
Manning, Rosemary. Green Smoke. large type ed. 224p. (gr. 3-7). 1991. 13.95 (0-7451-1318-4, Galaxy Child Lrg Print) Chivers N Amer.
—Heraldry. (Illus.). (gr. 7 up). 1975. 14.95 (0-7136-0108-6) Dufour.
Mannino, Angelica L., jt. auth. see Mannino, Marc P.
Mannino, Marc P. & Mannino, Angelica L. La Cola Magico De Marjorie. Norman-Grumbley, Patricia, tr. from ENG. Mannino, Angelica L., illus. LC 93-86116. (SPA.). 32p. (Orig.). (gr. k-3). 1993. pap. 7.95 (0-9638340-1-0) Sugar Sand.

—Marjorie's Magical Tail. LC 93-86041. (Illus.). 32p. (Orig.). (ps-5). 1993. pap. 7.95 (0-9638340-0-2) Sugar Sand. MAJORIE'S MAGICAL TAIL is a children's picture book fantasy designed to entertain & educate children of all ages about the plight of the endangered West Indian Manatee. In addition to the delightful story & colorful illustrations, MAJORIE'S MAGICAL TAIL contains facts about manatees, information on organizations working to ensure the survival of the species & places where manatees can be seen in their natural habitat, as well as captive environments. A Spanish version, LA COLA MAGICO DE MARJORIE is also available. MARJORIE'S MAGICAL TAIL is used by teachers & zoos to educate young children about this magnificent animal. Various zoos & aquariums are ordering. Synopsis: A young boy befriends a gentle manatee named Marjorie. Marjorie's magical powers enable the boy to become a manatee & experience the joys & hazards of these endangered mammals. This environmental tale enlightens young readers to the plight of this nearly extinct mammal & leaves them with the hope that the reader can make a difference in saving this gentle giant of the sea. To order contact: Sugar Sand, Inc., P.O. Box 1857, Anna Maria, FL 34216 or 1911 41st Street West, Bradenton, FL 34205, (813) 747-6258. *Publisher Provided Annotation.*

Mannion, Sean. Ireland's Friendly Dolphin. (Illus.). 128p. (Orig.). (gr. 7-11). 1991. pap. 9.95 (0-86322-122-X, Pub. by Brandon Bk Pubs ER) Irish Bks Media.
Manovrier, Lynne. Animal Farm: A Study Guide. (gr. 6-10). 1983. tchr's. ed. & wkbk. 14.95 (0-88122-021-3) LRN Links.
Manrique, Beatriz. Hola Bebe. (SPA., Illus., Orig.). 1987. pap. 5.00x (0-944499-23-6) Editorial Amer.
Manry, Douglas. The Land the Cleves Built. Sloan, Stephen, ed. Manry, Douglas, illus. 32p. (gr. 2-5). 1989. write for info. (0-9622316-0-6) Sloan Manry Pubs.
Mansell, Dom. Dinosaurs Came to Town. (ps-3). 1991. 12.95 (0-316-54584-8) Little.
—My Old Teddy. Mansell, Dom, illus. LC 91-71830. 32p. (ps). 1992. 12.95 (1-56402-035-5) Candlewick Pr.
—My Old Teddy. LC 91-71830. (ps). 1994. pap. 3.99 (1-56402-282-X) Candlewick Pr.
Mansfield, Katherine. The Doll's House. 32p. (gr. 4 up). 1986. PLB 13.95s.p. (0-88682-056-1) Creative Ed.

—The Garden Party. (gr. 4-12). Date not set. 13.95 (0-88682-342-0, 97216-098) Creative Ed.
Mansmann, Patricia A. & Neuhausel, Patricia A. Life after Survival: A Therapeutic Approach for Adult Children of Alcoholics. Thorpe, Karen E., illus. Bowden, Julie & Gravitz, Herbertfrwd. by. (Illus.). 56p. (gr. 9 up). 1986. pap. text ed. 6.95 (0-940967-00-6) Genesis Pub PA.
Manson, Ainslie. A Dog Came, Too: A True Story. Blades, Ann, illus. LC 91-44891. 32p. (gr. 1-5). 1993. SBE 13.95 (0-689-50567-1, M K McElderry) Macmillan Child Grp.
Manson, Christopher. The Crab Prince. Manson, Christopher, illus. LC 90-26626. 32p. (gr. k-3). 1991. 14.95 (0-8050-1215-X, Bks Young Read) H Holt & Co.
—A Farmyard Song. Manson, Christopher, illus. LC 91-46238. 32p. (gr. k). 1992. 14.95 (1-55858-169-3); PLB 14.88 (1-55858-170-7) North-South Bks NYC.
—The Marvellous Blue Mouse. Manson, Christopher, illus. LC 91-29131. 32p. (gr. k-3). 1992. 15.95 (0-8050-1622-8, Bks Young Read) H Holt & Co.
Manson, Christopher, adapted by. & illus. The Tree in the Wood: An Old Nursery Song. LC 92-23524. 32p. (gr. k-3). 1993. 14.95 (1-55858-192-8); PLB 14.88 (1-55858-193-6) North-South Bks NYC.
Manson, Cynthia, jt. ed. see Jordan, Cathleen.
Manson, Cynthia, jt. ed. see Sullivan, Eleanor.
Manson, Cynthia, jt. ed. see Williams, Sheila.
Manson, Frank A. The Adventures of Prince Albert & the Royal Dinosaurs. Henley, Joan, illus. 144p. (gr. 2-7). 1990. 11.95 (0-918339-17-0) Vandamere.
Manson, G., jt. auth. see Cherryholmes, C.
Mantegazza, Giovanna. The Cat. Mesturini, Cristina, illus. LC 91-73872. 12p. (ps-1). 1992. 6.95 (1-56397-032-5) Boyds Mills Pr.
—Dog. (ps). 1993. 6.95 (1-56397-200-X) Boyds Mills Pr.
—The Hippopotamus. Mesturini, Cristina, illus. LC 91-73871. 12p. (ps-1). 1992. 6.95 (1-56397-033-3) Boyds Mills Pr.
Mantell, Paul, jt. auth. see Hart, Avery.
Manthey, Cynthia M. With Respect, Vol. 1P: Successful Primary Theme Activities. 100p. (ps-1). 1992. pap. text ed. 11.95 (0-9634651-0-4); audio music cass. 9.95 (0-9634651-1-2) Qual Instruct.
Mantin, Peter & Pulley, Richard. The Roman World: From Republic to Empire. (Illus.). 80p. (gr. 6 up). 1993. pap. 10.95 (0-521-40608-0) Cambridge U Pr.
Mantinband, Gerda. Blabbermouths. LC 91-3006. (ps-3). 1992. 14.00 (0-688-10602-1); PLB 13.93 (0-688-10604-8) Greenwillow.
Mantinband, Gerda, retold by. & illus. Three Clever Mice. LC 91-48171. 32p. (gr. k up). 1993. 14.00 (0-688-11369-9); PLB 13.93 (0-688-11370-2) Greenwillow.
Mantione, Denise A. Speech-Language In-Services for Colleagues in Education (SLICE) 112p. (ps-12). 1992. 22.95 (0-937857-33-5, 1510) Speech Bin.
Manton, Denis. Tigers in the Park. (Illus.). 32p. (ps-2). 1992. 15.95 (0-09-174525-X, Pub. by Hutchinson UK) Trafalgar.
Manton, Thomas. The Works of Thomas Manton, 3 vols. 1993. 25.95 ea. Vol. 1, 500p (0-85151-648-3) Vol. 2, 500p (0-85151-649-1) Vol. 3, 500p (0-85151-650-5) Banner of Truth.
Manuelian, Peter Der see Der Manuelian, Peter.
Manus, Ron, jt. auth. see Hall, Steve.
Manushkin, Fran. Baby, Come Out! Himler, Ronald, illus. LC 78-183159. 32p. (ps-3). 1984. pap. 3.95 (0-06-443050-2, Trophy) HarpC Child Bks.
—The Best Toy of All. LC 91-34589. (Illus.). 24p. (ps-1). 1992. 11.00 (0-525-44897-7, DCB) Dutton Child Bks.
—Buster Loves Buttons! Zimmer, Dirk, illus. LC 84-48332. 64p. (gr. k-3). 1985. HarpC Child Bks.
—Hello World. Ortiz, Juan & Bliss, Phil, illus. LC 91-71337. 32p. (ps-1). 1991. 8.95 (1-56282-059-1) Disney Pr.
—Latkes & Applesauce. (Illus.). 1992. 4.95 (0-590-42265-0, Blue Ribbon Bks) Scholastic Inc.
—Latkes & Applesauce: A Hanukkah Story. Spowart, Robin, illus. (ps-3). 1990. 12.95 (0-590-42261-8, Scholastic Hardcover) Scholastic Inc.
—Let's Go Riding in Our Strollers. Huang, Benrei, illus. LC 92-72935. 32p. (ps-k). 1993. 13.95 (1-56282-390-6); PLB 13.89 (1-56282-391-4) Hyprn Child.
—My Christmas Safari. Alley, R. W., illus. LC 92-28643. 32p. (ps-1). 1993. 13.99 (0-8037-1294-4); PLB 13.89 (0-8037-1295-2) Dial Bks Young.
—One Hundred One Dalmatas: Un Libro Para Contar. Santacruz, Daniel M., tr. from ENG. Hicks, Russell, illus. (SPA.). 32p. 1994. pap. 4.95 (1-56282-568-2) Disney Pr.
—One Hundred One Dalmatians Counting Book & Puppy. Hicks, Russell, illus. 32p. (ps-1). 1993. Boxed set incl. plush puppy. 16.95 (1-56282-572-0) Disney Pr.
—The Perfect Christmas Picture. Weinhaus, Karen A., illus. LC 79-2678. 64p. (ps-3). 1987. pap. 3.50 (0-06-444112-1, Trophy) HarpC Child Bks.
—Puppies & Kittens. (Illus.). 24p. (ps-k). 1989. pap. write for info. (0-307-11806-1, Pub. by Golden Bks) Western Pub.
—Walt Disney's One Hundred One Dalmatians: A Counting Book. Hicks, Russell, illus. LC 90-85426. 32p. (ps-k). 1991. 9.95 (1-56282-012-5); PLB 9.89 (1-56282-032-X) Disney Pr.

Manushkin, Fran, compiled by. Somebody Loves You: Poems of Friendship & Love. Shelly, Jeff, illus. LC 92-53436. 32p. (ps-k). 1993. 9.95 (1-56282-370-1) Disney Pr.
Many, Margaret. Non-Stop Nonsense. (gr. k-6). 1991. pap. 3.25 (0-440-40399-5, Pub. by Yearling Classics) Dell.
Manzano, Roy R. Pelly's Exciting Adventures. (Illus.). 1993. 9.95 (0-533-10526-9) Vantage.
Mao Wall, Lina & Spagnoli, Cathy, eds. Judge Rabbit & the Tree Spirit: A Folktale from Cambodia. LC 90-26240. (Illus.). 32p. (gr. k-5). 1991. 13.95 (0-89239-071-9) Childrens Book Pr.
Maple, Marilyn. On the Wings of a Butterfly: A Story about Life & Death. Haight, Sandy, illus. Grollman, Earl, afterword by. LC 91-50854. (Illus.). 32p. (gr. 1-6). 1992. 18.95 (0-943990-69-6); pap. 9.95 (0-943990-68-8) Parenting Pr.
Mapstone, Bryan. Making Wooden Toys for All Ages. LC 92-44019. (Illus.). 172p. (gr. 10-12). 1993. pap. 17.95 (0-7153-9809-1, Pub. by David & Charles Pub UK) Sterling.
Mapstone, Edna. Footsteps of Faith. Means, Gary & Cook, Beth A., illus. 32p. (Orig.). (gr. 1-5). 1993. wkbk. 2.99 (0-87509-528-3) Chr Pubns.
Mara, Pam. The Greeks Pop-up. (Illus.). 32p. (Orig.). (gr. 3 up). 1985. pap. 7.95 (0-906212-33-2, Pub. by Tarquin UK) Parkwest Pubns.
Mara, Thalia. First Steps in Ballet: Basic Exercises at the Barre. LC 75-37100. (Illus.). 64p. (Orig.). (gr. 2-5). 1987. pap. 6.95 (0-916622-53-3) Princeton Bk Co.
—Fourth Steps in Ballet: On Your Toes! Basic Pointe Work. LC 74-181476. (Illus.). 64p. (gr. 9-12). 1987. pap. 6.95 (0-916622-56-8) Princeton Bk Co.
—Second Steps in Ballet: Basic Center Exercises. LC 75-37101. (Illus.). 64p. (Orig.). (gr. 4-6). 1987. pap. 6.95 (0-916622-54-1) Princeton Bk Co.
—Third Steps in Ballet: Basic Allegro Steps. LC 70-181475. (Illus.). 64p. (Orig.). (gr. 6-9). 1987. pap. 6.95 (0-916622-55-X) Princeton Bk Co.
Maran, Meredith, jt. auth. see Heron, Ann.
Maran, Richard & Feistmantl, Eric. Computers Simplified: MaranGraphics Simplified Computer Guide. LC 93-12260. 160p. 1993. Academic edition. pap. text ed. 10.00 (0-13-095324-5) P-H Gen Ref & Trav.
MaranGraphics Development Group Staff. MaranGraphics Learn at First Sight Lotus 1-2-3 for Windows Release 4. LC 93-34098. 1994. write for info. (0-13-458233-0) P-H.
Maraniss, Linda, ed. see Center for Environmental Education Staff.
Marar, Eve. More Haunted House Stories. (Illus.). 96p. (Orig.). 1988. pap. 1.95 (0-942025-64-4) Kidsbks.
Marbach, Ellen S., et al. Nutrition in a Changing World: A Curriculum for Primary Level. LC 79-11776. (Illus., Orig.). (gr. 1-3). 1979. pap. 8.95 (0-8425-1660-3) Brigham.
Marbach, Ethel. The Cabbage Moth & the Shamrock. Hague, Michael, illus. LC 91-575. 32p. (ps-2). 1991. jacketed, reinforced bdg. 9.00 (0-671-74864-5, Green Tiger) S&S Trade.
Marcantel, David E., jt. auth. see Gelhay, Patrick.
Marcel Socias Studio Staff, ed. see Julivert, Maria A.
Marcellino. Picture Book 2. (Illus.). Date not set. 15.00 (0-06-205064-8); lib. bdg. 14.89 (0-06-205065-6) HarpC Child Bks.
—Picture Book 3. (Illus.). Date not set. 15.00 (0-06-205066-4); PLB 14.89 (0-06-205067-2) HarpC Child Bks.
Marcey, Sally. Choice Adventures, No. 11: The Silverlake Stranger. LC 92-36889. 1993. 4.99 (0-8423-5048-9) Tyndale.
—Choice Adventures, No. 3: The Underground Railroad. (gr. 3-7). 1991. PLB 4.99 (0-8423-5027-6) Tyndale.
March, Rita N., jt. auth. see Shires, H. Bess.
Marchand, Leslie A., ed. see Byron, George Gordon.
Marchand, Roger. Meeting Jesus in Holy Communion. 32p. (gr. 1-3). 1984. pap. 2.95 (0-89243-202-0) Liguori Pubns.
Marchetti, Tony. Automative Engine Overhaul. Gorham, Kelly, ed. 23p. (gr. 10 up). Date not set. wkbk. 7.00 (0-8064-0009-9) Bergwall.
Marchisio, Linda. With a Little of Both. (Illus.). 19p. (gr. k-5). 1987. tchr's. guide, incl. 50 min. tape 15.95 (0-9624224-1-X); tape only 8.95 (0-9624224-0-1) Rainbow Bend.
Marciniszyn, Alex, ed. see Greenberg, Daniel & Siembieda, Kevin.
Marciniszyn, Alex, ed. see McCall, Randy & Siembieda, Kevin.
Marciniszyn, Alex, ed. see Reed, Gary.
Marciniszyn, Alex, ed. see Siembieba, Kevin.
Marciniszyn, Alex, ed. see Siembieda, Kevin.
Marciniszyn, Alex, ed. see Siembieda, Kevin, et al.
Marciniszyn, Alex, ed. see Siembieda, Kevin & Bartold, Thomas.
Marciniszyn, Alex, ed. see Siembieda, Kevin & Long, Kevin.
Marciniszyn, Alex, ed. see Wallis, James & Siembieda, Kevin.
Marciniszyn, Alex, ed. see Wujcik, Erick.
Marciniszyn, Alex, ed. see Wujcik, Erick & Balent, Matthew.
Marciniszyn, Alex, ed. see Wujcik, Erick & Siembieda, Kevin.
Marciniszyn, Alex, et al, eds. see Siembieda, Kevin.

Marciniszyn, Alex, et al, eds. see Siembieda, Kevin & Long, Kevin.
Marciniszyn, Alex, et al, eds. see Siembieda, Kevin & Siembieda, Maryann.
Marciniszyn, Alex, et al, eds. see Siembieda, Kevin & Truman, Timothy.
Marciniszyn, Alex, et al, eds. see Wallis, James & Sienbieda, Kevin.
Marcinsizyn, Alex, ed. see Siembieda, Kevin.
Marcroft, Karen. Fulbert Firefly. Marcroft, Renee, illus. LC 85-90463. 48p. (gr. 3-8). 1986. 14.95 (0-935849-00-9) Marcroft Prods.
Marcus. Letters Ursula Nordstrom. Date not set. 17.00 (0-06-023625-6, Festival); PLB 17.00 (0-06-023624-8, Festival) HarpC Child Bks.
Marcus, Audrey F. & Zwerin, Raymond A. Like a Maccabee. Carmi, Giora, illus. (gr. k-3). 1991. 11.95 (0-8074-0445-4, 102564) UAHC.
—Shabbat Can Be. Saltzman, Yuri, illus. Syme, Daniel B., ed. (Illus.). (gr. k-3). 1979. 10.95 (0-8074-0023-8) UAHC.
Marcus, Audrey F., jt. auth. see Zwerin, Raymond A.
Marcus, Audrey F., jt. auth. see Zwerm, Raymond A.
Marcus, Elizabeth. All about Mountains & Volcanoes. Veno, Joseph, illus. LC 83-4834. 32p. (gr. 3-6). 1984. lib. bdg. 10.59 (0-89375-969-4); pap. text ed. 2.95 (0-89375-970-8) Troll Assocs.
—Amazing World of Plants. Boyd, Patti, illus. LC 83-4836. 32p. (gr. 3-6). 1984. lib. bdg. 10.59 (0-89375-967-8); pap. text ed. 2.95 (0-89375-968-6) Troll Assocs.
—Our Wonderful Seasons. Boyd, Patti, illus. LC 82-17372. 32p. (gr. 3-6). 1983. PLB 10.59 (0-89375-896-5); pap. text ed. 2.95 (0-89375-897-3) Troll Assocs.
—Rocks & Minerals. Lawler, Dan, illus. LC 82-17424. 32p. (gr. 3-6). 1983. PLB 10.59 (0-89375-876-0); pap. text ed. 2.95 (0-89375-877-9) Troll Assocs.
Marcus, Irene W. Into the Great Forest: A Story for Children Away from Parents for the First Time. LC 91-37636. 32p. (ps-3). 1992. pap. 6.95 (0-945354-40-1); 16.95 (0-945354-39-8) Magination Pr.
Marcus, Irene W. & Marcus, Paul. Into the Great Forest: A Story for Children Away from Parents for the First Time. Jeschke, Susan, illus. LC 92-56871. 1993. PLB 17.26 (0-8368-0932-7) Gareth Stevens Inc.
—Scary Night Visitors: A Story for Children with Bedtime Fears. Jeschke, Susan, illus. LC 90-41919. 32p. (ps-2). 1990. 16.95 (0-945354-26-6); pap. 6.95 (0-945354-25-8) Magination Pr.
—Scary Night Visitors: A Story for Children with Bedtime Fears. Jeschke, Susan, illus. LC 92-56874. 1993. PLB 17.26 (0-8368-0935-1) Gareth Stevens Inc.
Marcus, Laurie R., ed. see Scott, Carlton.
Marcus, Leonard S. Petrouchka: A Ballet Cut-Out Book. Kendall, Jane F., illus. 16p. (gr. 3-6). 1983. pap. 12.95 cutout bk. (0-87923-469-5) Godine.
Marcus, Leonard S., jt. auth. see Schwartz, Amy.
Marcus, Leonard S., selected by. Lifelines: A Poetry Anthology Patterned on the Stages of Life. LC 93-26413. 112p. (gr. 6 up). 1994. 16.99 (0-525-45164-1, DCB) Dutton Child Bks.
Marcus, Paul, jt. auth. see Marcus, Irene W.
Marcus Aurelius. Meditations. Staniforth, Maxwell, tr. (Orig.). (gr. 9 up). 1964. pap. 6.95 (0-14-044140-9, Penguin Classics) Viking Penguin.
Marcuse, Aida, tr. from ENG. Lizard's Song. Aruego, Jose & Dewey, Ariane, illus. (SPA.). 32p. (ps up). 1994. pap. 3.95 (0-688-13201-4, Mulberry) Morrow.
Marcuse, Aida, tr. see Cowcher, Helen.
Marcuse, Aida, tr. see Dr. Seuss.
Marcuse, Aida, tr. see Joyce, James.
Marcuse, Aida, tr. see Kellogg, Steven.
Marcuse, Aida, tr. see Maestro, Betsy & Maestro, Giulio.
Marcuse, Aida, tr. see Perrault, Charles.
Marcuse, Aida, tr. see Potter, Beatrix.
Marcuse, Aida, tr. see Singer, Isaac Bashevis.
Marcuse, Aida, tr. see Williams, Vera.
Marcuse, Aida, tr. see Zemach, Margot.

Marcuse, Aida E. Caperucita Roja y la Luna de Papel. Torrecilla, Pablo, illus. (SPA.). 24p. (Orig.). (gr. k-6). 1993. PLB 9.95x (1-56492-103-4) Laredo. A modern adaptation of the original Little Red Riding Hood through rhyme. Rich illustrations & text will entertain young & older readers alike. Written in play format in Spanish. *Publisher Provided Annotation.*

Marcuse, Aida E., tr. see Dr. Seuss.
Marcuse, Aida E., tr. see McCall, Barbara A.
Mare, Walter De La see De La Mare, Walter.
Mare, Walter de la see De La Mare, Walter.
Mare, Walter De La see De La Mare, Walter.
Mare, Walter De La se De la Mare, Walter.
Maren, Michael. The Land & People of Kenya. LC 88-22959. (Illus.). 208p. (gr. 6 up). 1989. 18.00 (0-397-32334-4, Lipp Jr Bks); PLB 14.89 (0-397-32335-2, Lipp Jr Bks) HarpC Child Bks.

Margeson, Sue. Viking. LC 93-32593. 1994. 15.00 (0-679-86002-9); PLB 15.99 (0-679-96002-3) Knopf Bks Yng Read.
Margolies, Barbara A. Kanu of Kathmandu: A Journey to Nepal. Margolies, Barbara, illus. LC 92-12482. 40p. (gr. 1-4). 1992. RSBE 14.95 (0-02-762282-7, Four Winds) Macmillan Child Grp.
—Olbalbal: A Day in Maasailand. Margolies, Barbara A., illus. LC 93-19744. 32p. (gr. 1-4). 1994. RSBE 15.95 (0-02-762284-3, Four Winds) Macmillan Child Grp.
—Warriors, Wigmen, & Crocodile People: Journeys in Papua New Guinea. Margolies, Barbara, illus. LC 92-27475. 40p. (gr. 1-5). 1993. RSBE 14.95 (0-02-762283-5, Four Winds) Macmillan Child Grp.
Margolies, Jacob. Hank Aaron: Home Run King. Mathews, V., ed. LC 91-29776. (Illus.). 64p. (gr. 3-6). 1992. PLB 12.90 (0-531-20075-2) Watts.
—Kareem Abdul-Jabbar: Basketball Great. Mathews, V., ed. LC 91-31662. (Illus.). 64p. (gr. 3-6). 1992. PLB 12.90 (0-531-20076-0) Watts.
—The Negro Leagues: The Story of Black Baseball. (Illus.). 160p. (gr. 7-12). 1993. PLB 13.90 (0-531-11130-X) Watts.
Margolis, Matthew, jt. auth. see Sendak, Maurice.
Margolis, Richard J. Secrets of a Small Brother. Carrick, Donald, illus. LC 84-3478. 40p. (gr. 1-4). 1984. RSBE 12.95 (0-02-762280-0, Macmillan Child Bk) Macmillan Child Grp.
Margoshes, David. Saskatchewan. (Illus.). 144p. (gr. 4 up). 1992. PLB 26.60 (0-516-06618-8) Childrens.
Margulies, Alice. Compassion. (Illus.). 64p. (gr. 7-12,RL 4-6). 1990. PLB 13.95 (0-8239-1108-X) Rosen Group.
Margulies, Teddy S. Walt Disney's Snow White & the Seven Dwarfs. Guell, illus. 24p. (ps-3). 1993. pap. 1.95 (0-307-12686-2, 12686, Golden Pr) Western Pub.
Margulis, et al. The Five Kingdom Coloring Book. (Illus.). 1993. 19.00 (0-06-500843-X) HarpCollege.
Margulis, Lynn. Diversity of Life: The Five Kingdoms. LC 91-44773. (Illus.). 80p. (gr. 6 up). 1992. lib. bdg. 16.95 (0-89490-278-4) Enslow Pubs.
Mariama Ba. So Long a Letter. Modupe' Bode'-Thomas, tr. from FRE. 96p. (Orig.). 1989. pap. 8.95 (0-435-90555-4, 90555) Heinemann.
Mariana. Miss Flora McFlimsey & the Baby New Year. rev ed ed. Mariana & Howe, Caroline W., illus. LC 86-15339. 40p. (ps-2). 1988. 11.95 (0-688-04533-2); PLB 11.88 (0-688-04534-0) Lothrop.
—Miss Flora McFlimsey's Birthday. rev. ed. Mariana, illus. LC 86-15269. 40p. (ps-2). 1987. 11.95 (0-688-04537-5) Lothrop.
—Miss Flora McFlimsey's Christmas Eve. rev ed ed. Mariana & Howe, Caroline W., illus. LC 86-15259. 40p. (ps-2). 1988. 11.95 (0-688-04282-1); PLB 11.88 (0-688-04283-X) Lothrop.
—Miss Flora McFlimsey's Easter Bonnet. rev. ed. Mariana, illus. LC 86-15268. 40p. (gr. k-3). 1987. 9.95 (0-688-04535-9); PLB 8.88 (0-688-04536-7) Lothrop.
—Miss Flora McFlimsey's Halloween. rev. ed. Mariana, illus. LC 86-15270. 40p. (ps-2). 1987. 11.95 (0-688-04549-9) Lothrop.
—Miss Flora McFlimsey's May Day. rev. ed. Mariana, illus. LC 86-15252. 40p. (ps-3). 1987. 9.95 (0-688-04545-6) Lothrop.
—Miss Flora McFlimsey's Valentine. rev. ed. Mariana, illus. LC 86-15254. 40p. (gr. k-3). 1987. 9.95 (0-688-04547-2) Lothrop.
Marias, Julian. History of Philosophy. 22nd. ed. (gr. 7-12). 1966. pap. 9.95 (0-486-21739-6) Dover.
Marie, D. Tears for Ashan. Childers, Norman, illus. LC 88-63766. 32p. (ps-3). 1989. 11.95 (0-9621681-0-6) Creative Pr Works.
Marie, Evelyn. My Tree. Beveren, Margaret V., illus. 24p. (gr. k-2). 1987. pap. 3.95 (0-9614746-5-3) Berry Bks.
Marie, Jeanne. Moving Through Your ABC's. Drum, Stacy, illus. LC 92-9944. 32p. (ps-2). Date not set. 11.95 (1-56065-166-0) Capstone Pr. Postponed.
Marie, Nancy. Country Christmas. Ryan, Delores, illus. 36p. (gr. k-5). 1979. 5.95 (0-941595-00-5) Heldreth Pub.
Marie, Sharon. Granny's Crooked Teeth. 1993. 7.95 (0-533-10602-8) Vantage.
Mariella, Cinzia. Passport to Italy. rev. ed. LC 93-21189. 1994. write for info. (0-531-14295-7) Watts.
Maril, Nadja. Me, Molly Midnight, the Artist's Cat. Maril, Herman, illus. LC 77-22708. 40p. (gr. k up). 1977. 9.95 (0-916144-15-1); pap. 3.95 (0-916144-16-X) Stemmer Hse.
—Runaway Molly Midnight, the Artist's Cat. Maril, Herman, illus. LC 80-17097. 40p. (gr. k up). 1980. 9.95 (0-916144-62-3) Stemmer Hse.
Marilue. Bobby Bear & the Friendly Ghost. LC 85-61830. (Illus.). 32p. (ps-1). 1985. 6.95 (0-87783-204-8) Oddo.
—Bobby Bear at the Circus. Marilue, illus. LC 89-62708. 32p. (ps-2). 1990. PLB 12.95 (0-87783-252-8) Oddo.
—Bobby Bear Meets Cousin Boo. LC 80-82952. (Illus.). 32p. (ps-1). 1981. PLB 9.95 (0-87783-155-6) Oddo.
—Bobby Bear's Christmas. LC 77-83628. (Illus.). 32p. (ps-1). 1978. PLB 9.95 (0-87783-142-4); cassette o.p. 7.94x (0-87783-182-3) Oddo.
—Bobby Bear's Kite Contest. Marilue, illus. LC 87-62507. 32p. (ps-1). 1988. PLB 11.45 (0-87783-219-6) Oddo.
—Bobby Bear's Magic Show. Marilue, illus. LC 89-62707. 32p. (ps-2). 1990. PLB 12.95 (0-87783-253-6) Oddo.
—Bobby Bear's New Home. LC 78-190265. (Illus.). 32p. (ps-1). 1973. PLB 9.95 (0-87783-054-1); cassette 7.94x (0-87783-184-X) Oddo.

—Bobby Bear's Red Raft. LC 71-190266. (Illus.). 32p. (ps-1). 1973. PLB 9.95 (0-87783-055-X); cassette 7. 94x (0-87783-185-8) Oddo.
—Bobby Bear's Thanksgiving. LC 77-83623. (Illus.). 32p. (ps-1). 1978. PLB 9.95 (0-87783-143-2); cassette o.s.i. 7.94x (0-87783-187-4) Oddo.
Marin, Albert. Unconditional Surrender: U. S. Grant & the Civil War. LC 93-20041. (Illus.). 32p. (gr. 5-9). 1994. SBE 19.95 (0-689-31837-5, Atheneum Child Bk) Macmillan Child Grp.
Marin, Cheech. My Name Is Cheech the School Bus Driver. 16p. 1992. pap. 13.98 incl. CD (1-56668-178-2, 70508-2); pap. 9.98 incl. audio cass. (1-56668-177-4, 70508-4) Rincon Child Ent.
Mariner, Tom. Continents. LC 89-17285. (Illus.). 32p. (gr. 3-8). 1990. PLB 9.95 (1-85435-195-8) Marshall Cavendish.
—Deserts. LC 89-17278. (Illus.). 32p. (gr. 3-8). 1990. PLB 9.95 (1-85435-192-3) Marshall Cavendish.
—Earth in Action Series, 6 vols. (Illus.). (gr. 3-8). 1990. PLB 59.70 (1-85435-189-3) Marshall Cavendish.
—Mountains. LC 89-17280. (Illus.). 32p. (gr. 3-8). 1990. PLB 9.95 (1-85435-193-1) Marshall Cavendish.
—Oceans. LC 89-9823. (Illus.). 32p. (gr. 3-8). 1990. PLB 9.95 (1-85435-190-7) Marshall Cavendish.
—Rivers. LC 89-9824. (Illus.). 32p. (gr. 3-8). 1990. PLB 9.95 (1-85435-191-5) Marshall Cavendish.
—Rocks. LC 89-17321. (Illus.). 32p. (gr. 3-8). 1990. PLB 9.95 (1-85435-194-X) Marshall Cavendish.
Marino, Barbara P. Eric Needs Stitches. Rudinski, Richard, illus. LC 84-40753. 32p. (gr. k-3). 1989. PLB 12.89 (0-397-32374-3, Lipp Jr Bks) HarpC Child Bks.
Marino, Jan. The Day That Elvis Came to Town. 208p. (gr. 5). 1993. pap. 3.50 (0-380-71672-0, Camelot) Avon.
—Day That Elvis Came to Town, Vol. 1. (gr. 9-12). 1991. 15.95 (0-316-54618-6) Little.
—Eighty-Eight Steps to September. 162p. (gr. 3-6). 1989. 14.95 (0-316-54620-8) Little.
—Eighty-Eight Steps to September. 160p. (gr. 3-7). 1991. pap. 2.95 (0-380-71001-3, Camelot) Avon.
—For the Love of Pete: A Novel. LC 92-36465. 1993. 14.95 (0-316-54627-5) Little.
—Like Some Kind of Hero. (gr. 7 up). 1992. 14.95 (0-316-54626-7) Little.
—Like Some Kind of Hero. 224p. 1993. pap. 3.50 (0-380-72010-8, Flare) Avon.
Marino, Tony. Intergalatic Grudge Match. LC 92-12845. (gr. 2). 1992. 13.99 (1-56239-154-2) Abdo & Dghtrs.
—Ratchet Hood. LC 92-12841. 1992. 13.99 (1-56239-152-6) Abdo & Dghtrs.
—Scraboolee Jubilee. LC 92-12840. 1992. 13.99 (1-56239-153-4) Abdo & Dghtrs.
Marion, Craig A., ed. see Renfro, Nancy & Sullivan, Debbie.
Marion, Jeff D. Hello, Crow. Bowman, Leslie, illus. LC 91-18561. 32p. (ps-2). 1992. 13.95 (0-531-05975-8); PLB 13.99 (0-531-08575-9) Orchard Bks Watts.
Marion, Kenneth P. Volunteer Firefighter. Beyer, Beverly, illus. 32p. (ps-2). 1990. pap. 4.00 (0-945878-00-1) JK Pub.
Mariotti, Mario. Hand Games. (Illus.). 32p. (ps-4). 1992. 11.95 (0-916291-43-X) Kane-Miller Bk.
—Hands Off! (Illus.). 40p. (ps-4). 1990. 10.95 (0-916291-29-4) Kane-Miller Bk.
—Hanimations. (Illus.). 40p. (ps-4). 1989. 10.95 (0-916291-22-7) Kane-Miller Bk.
—Humages. Marchiori, Roberto, illus. (Orig.). 1991. pap. 8.95 (0-671-75233-2, Green Tiger) S&S Trade.
—Humands. Marchiori, Roberto, photos by. (Illus.). 1991. pap. 8.95 (0-671-75235-9, Green Tiger) S&S Trade.
Mariotti, Mario & Marchiori, Roberto, illus. Hanimals. 40p. (Orig.). (gr. 4 up). 1991. pap. 8.95 (0-671-75232-4, Green Tiger) S&S Trade.
Maris. I Wish I Could Fly. 1993. pap. 28.67 (0-590-72461-4) Scholastic Inc.
Maris, Ron. Are You There, Bear? LC 84-4180. (Illus.). 32p. (ps-1). 1985. 15.00 (0-688-03997-9); PLB 14.93 (0-688-03998-7) Greenwillow.
—Are You There, Bear? Maris, Ron, illus. 32p. (ps-1). 1986. pap. 3.50 (0-14-050524-5, Puffin) Puffin Bks.
—Bernard's Boring Day. 1990. 12.95 (0-385-29948-6) Doubleday.
—Ducks Quack. Maris, Ron, illus. LC 91-58726. 14p. (ps). 1992. 4.95 (1-56402-080-0) Candlewick Pr.
—Frogs Jump. Maris, Ron, illus. LC 91-58730. 14p. (ps). 1992. 4.95 (1-56402-081-9) Candlewick Pr.
—Hello, Baby Badger. (Illus.). 1993. Date not set. 16.95 (1-85681-261-8, Pub. by J MacRae UK) Trafalgar.
—Hold Tight, Bear! (ps-1). 1989. 12.95 (0-440-50152-0) Delacorte.
—I Wish I Could Fly. Maris, Ron, illus. LC 86-9797. 32p. (ps-1). 1987. 13.95 (0-688-06654-2); PLB 13.88 (0-688-06655-0) Greenwillow.
—In My Garden. LC 87-8773. (Illus.). 32p. (ps-1). 1988. Repr. of 1987 ed. 13.00 (0-688-07631-9) Greenwillow.
—Is Anyone Home? Maris, Ron, illus. LC 85-5436. 32p. (ps-2). 1986. 16.00 (0-688-05899-X) Greenwillow.
—My Book. Maris, Ron, illus. 32p. (ps-1). 1986. pap. 3.95 (0-14-050523-7, Puffin) Puffin Bks.
—Rescuing Robot. (Illus.). 32p. (ps-k). 1992. 16.95 (1-85681-260-X, Pub. by J MacRae UK) Trafalgar.
Mark, Jan. Fun with Mrs. Thumb & Ginger Paw. Bayley, Nicola, illus. LC 92-54955. 32p. (ps up). 1993. 9.95 (1-56402-247-1) Candlewick Pr.
—Handles. LC 86-43076. 160p. (gr. 5-9). 1987. pap. 3.95 (0-14-031587-X, Puffin) Puffin Bks.

—Handles. large type ed. (gr. 1-8). 1991. 13.95
(*0-7451-0760-5*, Galaxy Child Lrg Print) Chivers N
Amer.
—In Black & White & Other Stories. large type ed. 216p.
(gr. 3-7). 1992. 13.95 (*0-7451-1584-5*, Galaxy Child
Lrg Print) Chivers N Amer.
—Silly Tails. LC 92-38679. (Illus.). 32p. (gr. k-3). 1993.
SBE 13.95 (*0-689-31843-X*, Atheneum Child Bk)
Macmillan Child Grp.
Mark, Jan, ed. The Oxford Book of Children's Stories.
472p. 1993. 25.00 (*0-19-214228-3*) OUP.
Mark, Sara, ed. Mystery Mansion: House Math. LC 93-
25398. (Illus.). 64p. (gr. k-2). 1993. write for info.
(*0-8094-9986-X*) Time-Life.
—The Mystery of the Sunken Treasure: Sea Math.
(Illus.). 64p. 1993. write for info. (*0-8094-9994-0*)
Time-Life.
Mark, Sara, et al, eds. see Time-Life Bks. Editors.
Mark, Sara, et al, eds. see Time-Life Inc. Editors.
Markels, Bobby. How to Be a Human Bean. Leek,
Kenny, illus. 24p. (gr. 3 up). 1989. pap. 3.50
(*1-880991-01-2*) Stone Pub.
Marker, Sherry. London. (Illus.). 64p. (gr. 3-7). PLB 14.
95 (*1-56711-023-1*) Blackbirch.
Markert, Jenny. Arctic Foxes. 32p. 1991. 22.75
(*0-89565-710-4*); 15.95s.p. (*0-685-55045-1*) Childs
World.
—Camels. 32p. 1991. 22.75 (*0-89565-719-8*); 15.95s.p.
(*0-685-55049-4*) Childs World.
—Cheetahs. 32p. 1991. 22.75 (*0-89565-716-3*); 15.95s.p.
(*0-685-55050-8*) Childs World.
—Clouds. (gr. 4-7). 1993. 14.95 (*1-56846-060-0*) Creat
Editions.
—Elephants. 32p. 1991. 22.75 (*0-89565-724-4*); 15.95s.p.
(*0-685-55052-4*) Childs World.
—Giraffes. 32p. 1991. 22.75 (*0-89565-723-6*); 15.95s.p.
(*0-685-55054-0*) Childs World.
—Glacier National Park. (gr. 1-8). 1992. PLB 15.95
(*0-89565-858-5*); Resale. 22.75 (*0-685-60998-7*) Childs
World.
—Glaciers & Icebergs. LC 92-324498. 1993. write for info.
(*1-56766-004-5*, Pub. by Childs World) Childs World.
—Grand Canyon. (gr. 1-8). 1992. PLB 15.95
(*0-89565-856-9*); Resale. 22.75 (*0-685-61000-4*) Childs
World.
—Kangaroos. 32p. 1991. 22.75 (*0-89565-715-5*); 15.95s.p.
(*0-685-55056-7*) Childs World.
—Moose. 32p. 1991. 22.75 (*0-89565-713-9*); 15.95s.p.
(*0-685-55058-3*) Childs World.
—Ocean Resources. LC 93-12204. (gr. 5 up). 1993. PLB
18.95s.p. (*0-88682-599-7*) Creative Ed.
—Octopuses. (gr. 1-8). 1992. PLB 15.95 (*0-89565-836-4*);
Resale. 22.75 (*0-685-61016-0*) Childs World.
—Penguins. 32p. 1991. 22.75 (*0-89565-709-0*); 15.95s.p.
(*0-685-55060-5*) Childs World.
—Polar Bears. 32p. 1991. 22.75 (*0-89565-708-2*); 15.
95s.p. (*0-685-55061-3*) Childs World.
—Reptiles. (gr. 1-8). 1992. PLB 15.95 (*0-89565-850-X*);
Resale. 22.75 (*0-685-61003-9*) Childs World.
—Tigers. 32p. 1991. 22.75 (*0-89565-722-8*); 15.95s.p.
(*0-685-55064-8*) Childs World.
—Water. (gr. 5 up). 1992. PLB 18.95 (*0-88682-431-1*)
Creative Ed.
—Wildcats. 32p. 1991. 22.75 (*0-89565-704-X*); 15.95s.p.
(*0-685-55066-4*) Childs World.
—Wolves. 32p. 1991. 22.75 (*0-89565-711-2*); 15.95s.p.
(*0-685-55067-2*) Childs World.
—Yellowstone. (gr. 1-8). 1992. PLB 15.95
(*0-89565-859-3*); Resale. 22.75 (*0-685-60997-9*) Childs
World.
—Yosemite. (gr. 1-8). 1992. PLB 15.95 (*0-89565-857-7*);
Resale. 22.75 (*0-685-60999-5*) Childs World.
—Zebras. (gr. 1-8). 1992. PLB 15.95 (*0-89565-839-9*);
Resale. 22.75 (*0-685-66168-7*) Childs World.
Markert, Jenny M. Hippos. LC 92-29743. 1993. PLB 14.
95 (*1-56766-003-7*); Resale. 21.35 (*0-685-61654-1*)
Childs World.
Markham, Adam. The Environment. (Illus.). 48p. (gr. 5
up). 1988. PLB 18.60 (*0-86592-286-1*); 13.95
(*0-685-58320-1*) Rourke Corp.
Markham, Lois. Helen Keller. LC 92-24942. (Illus.). 64p.
(gr. 5-8). 1993. PLB 12.90 (*0-531-20104-X*) Watts.
—Inventions That Changed Modern Life. Gerstle, Gary,
contrib. by. LC 93-17022. (Illus.). 48p. (gr. 5-7). 1993.
PLB 22.80 (*0-8114-4930-0*) Raintree Steck-V.
—Theodore Roosevelt. (Illus.). 112p. (gr. 5 up). 1985. lib.
bdg. 17.95x (*0-87754-553-7*) Chelsea Hse.
—Theodore Roosevelt. LC 90-48981. (Illus.). 96p. (gr. 6-
10). 1991. PLB 13.95 (*1-55905-098-5*) Marshall
Cavendish.
Markham, Marion M. The April Fool's Day Mystery.
Estrada, Pau, illus. LC 90-41318. 48p. (gr. 2-6). 1991.
13.45 (*0-395-56235-X*) HM.
—The April Fool's Day Mystery. 64p. 1993. pap. 3.50
(*0-380-71716-6*, Camelot Young) Avon.
—The Birthday Party Mystery. Estrada, Pau, illus. (gr. 2
up). 1989. 13.45 (*0-395-49698-5*) HM.
—The Birthday Party Mystery. 64p. (gr. 1-4). 1990. pap.
2.95 (*0-380-70968-6*, Camelot Young) Avon.
—The Christmas Present Mystery. McCully, Emily A.,
illus. LC 84-4557. 48p. (gr. 2-5). 13.45
(*0-395-36383-7*) HM.
—The Christmas Present Mystery. McCully, Emily A.,
illus. 64p. 1990. pap. 2.95 (*0-380-70966-X*, Camelot)
Avon.
—The Halloween Candy Mystery. McCully, Emily A.,
illus. LC 82-6059. 48p. (gr. 2-5). 1982. 9.95
(*0-395-32437-8*) HM.

—The Halloween Candy Mystery. 64p. (gr. 1-4). 1990.
pap. 2.95 (*0-380-70965-1*, Camelot Young) Avon.
—The Thanksgiving Day Parade Mystery. Cassidy,
Dianne, illus. LC 86-4618. 48p. (gr. 2-5). 1986. 10.95
(*0-395-41855-0*) HM.
—The Thanksgiving Day Parade Mystery. Cassidy,
Dianne, illus. 64p. 1990. pap. 2.95 (*0-380-70967-8*,
Camelot) Avon.
—The Valentine's Day Mystery. Jerome, Karen A., illus.
LC 92-8391. 48p. (gr. 2-5). 1992. 13.45
(*0-395-61589-5*) HM.
Markham-David, Sally. Hands & Feet. Fleming, Leanne,
illus. LC 93-28978. 1994. 4.25 (*0-383-03746-8*) SRA
Schl Grp.
—It Takes All Kinds. Ruth, Trevor, illus. LC 93-21246.
1994. 4.25 (*0-383-03753-0*) SRA Schl Grp.
—Mouths & Noses. Ruth, Trevor, illus. LC 93-29008.
1994. 4.25 (*0-383-03764-6*) SRA Schl Grp.
—The Secrets of a Garden. Russell-Arnot, Elizabeth,
illus. LC 93-29003. 1994. 4.25 (*0-383-03773-5*) SRA
Schl Grp.
Markle, Sandra. Digging Deeper: Investigations into
Rocks, Shocks, Quakes, & Other Earthy Matters. LC
86-27412. (Illus.). 128p. (gr. 4-9). 1987. 13.00
(*0-688-05986-4*) Lothrop.
—Earth Alive! (gr. 4-7). 1991. 14.95 (*0-688-09360-4*)
Lothrop.
—Earth Alive! (ps). 1991. PLB 14.88 (*0-688-09361-2*)
Lothrop.
—Exploring Autumn. 160p. 1993. pap. 3.50
(*0-380-71910-X*, Camelot) Avon.
—Exploring Autumn: A Season of Science Activities,
Puzzlers, & Games. Markle, Sandra, illus. LC 90-
24209. 160p. (gr. 3-7). 1991. SBE 14.95
(*0-689-31620-8*, Atheneum Child Bk) Macmillan
Child Grp.
—Exploring Spring. 128p. (gr. 4-7). 1992. pap. 2.99
(*0-380-71319-5*, Camelot) Avon.
—Exploring Spring: A Season of Science Activities,
Puzzlers & Games. LC 89-394. (Illus.). 128p. (gr. 3-7).
1990. SBE 14.95 (*0-689-31341-1*, Atheneum Child
Bk) Macmillan Child Grp.
—Exploring Summer. 176p. (gr. 7-8). 1991. pap. 2.95
(*0-380-71320-9*, Camelot) Avon.
—Exploring Summer: A Season of Science Activities,
Puzzlers, & Games. Markle, Sandra, illus. LC 86-
17322. 176p. (gr. 3-7). 1987. SBE 14.95
(*0-689-31212-1*, Atheneum Child Bk) Macmillan
Child Grp.
—Exploring Winter. Markle, Sandra, illus. LC 84-3049.
160p. (gr. 3-7). 1984. SBE 14.95 (*0-689-31065-X*,
Atheneum Child Bk) Macmillan Child Grp.
—Exploring Winter. 160p. (gr. 7 up). 1992. pap. 2.99
(*0-380-71321-7*, Camelot) Avon.
—The Fledglings. (gr. 7 up). 1992. 16.00 (*0-553-07729-5*,
Starfire) Bantam.
—The Kids' Earth Handbook. Markle, Sandra, illus. LC
90-27478. 48p. (gr. 3-7). 1991. SBE 13.95
(*0-689-31707-7*, Atheneum Child Bk) Macmillan
Child Grp.
—Math Mini-Mysteries. Markle, Sandra, illus. LC 92-
11217. 64p. (gr. 3-7). 1993. SBE 14.95
(*0-689-31700-X*, Atheneum Child Bk) Macmillan
Child Grp.
—Outside & Inside Spiders. Markle, Sandra, illus. LC 93-
22643. 40p. (ps-3). 1994. SBE 15.95 (*0-02-762314-9*,
Bradbury Pr) Macmillan Child Grp.
—Outside & Inside Trees. LC 92-5145. (Illus.). 40p.
(ps-3). 1993. RSBE 15.95 (*0-02-762313-0*, Bradbury
Pr) Macmillan Child Grp.
—Outside & Inside You. Kuklin, Susan, illus. LC 90-
37791. 40p. (ps-3). 1991. RSBE 14.95 (*0-02-762311-4*,
Bradbury Pr) Macmillan Child Grp.
—Pioneering Space. LC 91-24936. (Illus.). 40p. (gr. 3-7).
1992. SBE 14.95 (*0-689-31748-4*, Atheneum Child
Bk) Macmillan Child Grp.
—Power Up: Experiments, Puzzles & Games Exploring
Electricity. LC 88-7772. (Illus.). 48p. (gr. 3-7). 1989.
SBE 14.95 (*0-689-31442-6*, Atheneum Child Bk)
Macmillan Child Grp.
—Primary Science Sampler. 112p. (gr. 1-3). 1980. 9.95
(*0-88160-008-3*, LW 110) Learning Wks.
—A Rainy Day. Johnson, Cathy, illus. LC 91-17059. 32p.
(ps-2). 1993. 14.95 (*0-531-05976-6*); PLB 14.99
(*0-531-08576-7*) Orchard Bks Watts.
—Science Mini-Mysteries. LC 87-17420. (Illus.). 72p. (gr.
3-7). 1988. SBE 13.95 (*0-689-31291-1*, Atheneum
Child Bk) Macmillan Child Grp.
—Science Sampler. 112p. (gr. 4-8). 1980. 9.95
(*0-88160-031-8*, LW 216) Learning Wks.
—Science to the Rescue. LC 92-41096. (Illus.). 48p. (gr.
3-7). 1994. SBE 15.95 (*0-689-31783-2*, Atheneum
Child Bk) Macmillan Child Grp.
—Weather, Electricity, Environmental Investigations.
112p. (gr. 4-6). 1982. 9.95 (*0-88160-082-2*, LW 902)
Learning Wks.
—The Young Scientist's Guide to Successful Science
Projects. Byrd, Bob, photos by. LC 89-45290. (Illus.).
128p. (gr. 3-7). lib. bdg. 12.88 (*0-688-07217-8*)
Lothrop. Postponed.
—The Young Scientist's Guide to Successful Science
Projects. Byrd, Bob, photos by. LC 89-45290. (Illus.).
128p. (gr. 3-7). 1990. pap. 6.95 (*0-688-09137-7*, Pub.
by Beech Tree Bks) Morrow.

Markmann, Erika. Grow It! An Indoor - Outdoor
Gardening Guide for Kids. Konemund, Gisela, illus.
LC 90-45043. 48p. (gr. 2-7). 1991. PLB 11.99
(*0-679-91528-1*); pap. 6.95 (*0-679-81528-7*) Random
Bks Yng Read.
Marko, Katherine M. Animals in Orbit: Monkeynauts &
Other Pioneers in Space. LC 90-47226. (Illus.). 64p.
(gr. 3-5). 1991. PLB 12.90 (*0-531-20003-5*) Watts.
—Away to Fundy Bay. LC 84-25680. (Illus.). 128p. (gr. 4
up). 1985. 11.95 (*0-8027-6576-9*); PLB 12.85
(*0-8027-6594-7*) Walker & Co.
—Hang Out the Flag. LC 92-349. 160p. (gr. 3-7). 1992.
SBE 13.95 (*0-02-762320-3*, Macmillan Child Bk)
Macmillan Child Grp.
Markosian, Becky T. & Thayne, Emma L. Hope &
Recovery: A Mother-Daughter Story about Anorexia
Nervosa, Bulimia, & Manic Depression. Rosoff, Iris,
ed. LC 91-36619. (Illus.). 176p. (gr. 9-12). 1992. PLB
14.40 (*0-531-11140-7*) Watts.
Markowitz, Endel. Kid-Ish Yiddish. Klein, Debby, illus.
44p. 1993. PLB 16.95 (*0-933910-05-3*) Haymark.
Marks, A., jt. auth. see Tingay, G.
Marks, Alan. Nowhere to be Found. Marks, Alan, illus.
LC 87-32729. 28p. (ps up). 1991. pap. 14.95
(*0-88708-062-6*) Picture Bk Studio.
Marks, Alan. ed. & illus. Ring-a-Ring o' Roses & a Ding,
Dong Bell: A Collection of Nursery Rhymes. LC 91-
15222. 96p. (gr. k up). 1991. pap. 19.95
(*0-88708-187-8*) Picture Bk Studio.
Marks, Burton. Animal Antics. (Illus.). 24p. (ps-3). 1992.
3.98 (*0-8317-7187-9*) Smithmark.
—Animals. Harvey, Paul, illus. LC 91-3656. 24p. (gr.
k-2). 1992. PLB 9.89 (*0-8167-2415-6*); pap. text ed.
2.50 (*0-8167-2416-4*) Troll Assocs.
—Bear's Boat. (ps-3). 1993. 4.99 (*0-89577-516-6*, Readers
Digest Kids) RD Assn.
—Colors & Numbers. Harvey, Paul, illus. LC 91-17493.
24p. (gr. k-2). 1992. PLB 8.89 (*0-8167-2411-3*); pap.
text ed. 2.50 (*0-8167-2412-1*) Troll Assocs.
—Let's Go. Harvey, Paul, illus. LC 91-9986. 24p. (gr.
k-2). 1992. lib. bdg. 8.89 (*0-8167-2413-X*); pap. text
ed. 2.50 (*0-8167-2414-8*) Troll Assocs.
—Off We Go. (Illus.). 24p. (ps-3). 1992. 3.98
(*0-8317-7189-5*) Smithmark.
—Penguin's Plane. (ps-3). 1993. 4.99 (*0-89577-517-4*,
Readers Digest Kids) RD Assn.
—Rhymes & Stories. Harvey, Paul, illus. LC 91-3663.
24p. (gr. k-2). 1992. PLB 9.89 (*0-8167-2409-1*); pap.
2.50 (*0-8167-2410-5*) Troll Assocs.
Marks, Graham. Webster & the Witch. (Illus.). 40p. (gr.
k-3). 1987. 15.95 (*0-340-35564-6*, Pub. by Hodder &
Stoughton UK) Trafalgar.
Marks, Leonard. Make a Model Starship Enterprise.
1990. pap. 5.99 (*0-517-06030-2*) Outlet Bk Co.
Marksbury, Tina, illus. Nighty-Night, Teddy Beddy Bear.
12p. (ps). 1986. 4.99 (*0-394-88244-X*) Random Bks
Yng Read.
Markun, Patricia M. The Little Painter of Sabana
Grande. Casilla, Robert, illus. LC 91-35230. 32p.
(ps-2). 1993. RSBE 14.95 (*0-02-762205-3*, Bradbury
Pr) Macmillan Child Grp.
Markus, Julia. Friends along the Way. (gr. k-12). 1987.
pap. 4.95 (*0-440-32761-X*, LE) Dell.
—Uncle. 1987. pap. 3.95 (*0-440-39187-3*, LE) Dell.
Marlette, Doug. The Before & After Book. Marlette,
Doug, illus. 48p. (ps-8). 1992. pap. 5.70
(*0-395-60905-4*) HM.
—Before & after Book. (ps). 1992. 16.95 (*0-395-63198-X*)
HM.
Marlor Editors. Kid's Vacation Diary: A Fun Diary &
Vacation Book for Use While Traveling! Bree, Marlin,
illus. 96p. (Orig.). (gr. 1-7). 1991. pap. 6.95
(*0-943400-56-2*) Marlor Pr.
Marlowe, Christopher see Bald, Robert C.
Marney, Dean. The Computer That Ate My Brother.
128p. (Orig.). (gr. 6-8). 1987. pap. 2.75
(*0-590-44005-5*) Scholastic Inc.
—Dirty Socks Don't Win Games. 128p. (gr. 3-7). 1992.
pap. 2.95 (*0-590-44880-3*, Apple Paperbacks)
Scholastic Inc.
Marolda, Maria. Cuisenaire Alphabet Book. 64p. (gr.
k-4). 1980. pap. text ed. 8.50 (*0-914040-78-2*)
Cuisenaire.
Marolles, Chantal de see De Marolles, Chantal.
Marozzi, Alfred. Skiing Basics. Gow, Bill, illus. 48p. (gr.
3-7). 1984. pap. 4.95 (*0-13-812264-4*) P-H.
Marquand, John P. The Late George Apley: A Novel in
the Form of a Memoir. (gr. 7 up). 1937. 18.95
(*0-685-03075-X*) Little.
Marquardt, Marsha. Colorful Ghost. 16p. (gr. 1). 1989.
pap. text ed. 3.00 (*1-882225-05-8*) Tott Pubns.
—Little Ghost Goes to School. Marquardt, Marsha, illus.
12p. (Orig.). (gr. 1). 1993. pap. text ed. write for info.
(*1-882225-12-0*) Tott Pubns.
—Little Ghost's Vacation. 8p. (gr. 1). 1990. pap. text ed.
2.50 (*1-882225-01-5*) Tott Pubns.
—Rotten Reggie. 12p. (gr. 1). 1990. pap. text ed. 3.00
(*1-882225-00-7*) Tott Pubns.
—Tommy Snake. 8p. (gr. 1). 1989. pap. text ed. 3.00
(*1-882225-02-3*) Tott Pubns.
Marquardt, Max. Wilbur, Orville & the Flying Machine.
(Illus.). 32p. (gr. 1-4). 1989. PLB 15.96
(*0-8172-3530-2*); pap. 3.95 (*0-8114-6735-X*) Raintree
Steck-V.
—Working Dogs. (Illus.). 32p. (gr. 1-4). 1989. PLB 15.96
(*0-8172-3506-X*); pap. 3.95 (*0-8114-6711-2*) Raintree
Steck-V.

Marquardt, Mervin A. The Temptation of Jesus. (Illus.). 24p. (gr. k-4). 1986. pap. 1.89 saddlestitched (0-570-06204-7, 59-1427) Concordia.

Marquart, M. Jesus' Second Family. (gr. k-2). 1977. pap. 1.89 (0-570-06111-3, 59-1229) Concordia.

Marquez, Gabriel G. The Handsomest Drowned Man in the World: A Tale for Children. Rabazza, Gregory, tr. LC 92-44055. 1994. write for info. (0-88682-587-3) Creative Ed.

Marquez, Nancy & Perez, Theresa. Portraits of Mexican Americans. 96p. (gr. 4-8). 1991. 9.95 (0-86653-605-1, GA1324) Good Apple.

Marquez, Nieves del Rosario see Del Rosario Marquez, Nieves.

Marquis, M. Ann & Addy-Trout, Elaine. CASE Study: Communication & Self-Esteem. LC 92-21826. (gr. 5-12). 1992. pap. 35.00 (0-930599-75-6) Thinking Pubns.

Marr, John S. A Breath of Air & a Breath of Smoke. Sweat, Lynn, illus. LC 70-161362. 48p. (gr. 3 up). 1970. 4.95 (0-87131-038-4) M Evans.

Marr, Molly. I Wonder Where Butterflies Go in Winter & Other Neat Facts about Insects. (Illus.). 36p. (ps-3). 1992. write for info. (0-307-11324-8, 11324) Western Pub.

Marrapodi, Betty. Clock That Went Meow. (Illus.). 31p. (gr. k up). 1970. pap. 7.50 director's script (0-88680-030-7); pap. 2.00 bk. (0-88680-029-3); royalty on application 20.00 (0-685-57885-2) I E Clark.

—Doctor Hoo. (Illus.). 22p. (gr. 1-6). 1973. pap. 7.50 director's script (0-88680-039-0); pap. 1.75 bk. (0-88680-038-2); royalty on application 15.00 (0-685-57888-7) I E Clark.

Marrin, Albert. America in Vietnam: The Elephant & the Tiger. (Illus.). 256p. (gr. 7 up). 1992. 16.00 (0-670-84063-7) Viking Child Bks.

—Aztecs & Spaniards: Cortes & the Conquest of Mexico. LC 85-28782. (Illus.). 224p. (gr. 5 up). 1986. SBE 15.95 (0-689-31176-1, Atheneum Child Bk) Macmillan Child Grp.

—Cowboys, Indians, & Gunfighters: The Story of the Cattle Kingdom. LC 92-5727. (Illus.). 208p. (gr. 5 up). 1993. SBE 22.95 (0-689-31774-3, Atheneum Child Bk) Macmillan Child Grp.

—Eighteen Twelve: The War Nobody Won. LC 84-21623. (Illus.). 190p. (gr. 5 up). 1985. SBE 14.95 (0-689-31075-7, Atheneum Child Bk) Macmillan Child Grp.

—Hitler. LC 93-13057. 256p. (gr. 7 up). 1993. pap. 5.99 (0-14-036526-5, Puffin) Puffin Bks.

—Hitler: A Portrait of a Tyrant. (gr. 7 up). 1987. pap. 15.00 (0-670-81546-2) Viking Child Bks.

—Inca & Spaniard: Pizarro & the Conquest of Peru. LC 88-29372. (Illus.). 192p. (gr. 5 up). 1989. SBE 14.95 (0-689-31481-7, Atheneum Child Bk) Macmillan Child Grp.

—Mao Tse-Tung & His China. (Illus.). 284p. (gr. 7 up). 1989. pap. 14.95 (0-670-82940-4) Viking Child Bks.

—Mao Tse-Tung & His China. LC 93-3799. 288p. (gr. 7 up). 1993. pap. 5.99 (0-14-036478-1, Puffin) Puffin Bks.

—Napoleon & the Napoleonic Wars. 1991. 14.95 (0-670-83480-7) Viking Child Bks.

—Napoleon & the Napoleonic Wars. LC 93-13067. 288p. (gr. 7 up). 1993. pap. 5.99 (0-14-036479-X, Puffin) Puffin Bks.

—The Sea Rovers: Pirates, Privateers & Buccaneers. LC 83-15886. (Illus.). 224p. (gr. 6 up). 1984. SBE 14.95 (0-689-31029-3, Atheneum Child Bk) Macmillan Child Grp.

—The Secret Armies: Spies, Counterspies, & Saboteurs in World War II. LC 85-7944. (Illus.). 192p. (gr. 5 up). 1985. SBE 14.95 (0-689-31165-6, Atheneum Child Bk) Macmillan Child Grp.

—The Spanish-American War. LC 90-935. (Illus.). 192p. (gr. 5 up). 1991. SBE 14.95 (0-689-31663-1, Atheneum Child Bk) Macmillan Child Grp.

—Stalin: Russia's Man of Steel. 256p. (gr. 7 up). 1988. pap. 14.95 (0-670-82102-0) Viking Child Bks.

—Stalin: Russia's Man of Steel. LC 93-3798. 256p. (gr. 7 up). 1993. pap. 5.99 (0-14-032605-7, Puffin) Puffin Bks.

—Struggle for a Continent: The French & Indian Wars: 1690-1760. LC 86-26508. (Illus.). 232p. (gr. 5 up). 1987. SBE 15.95 (0-689-31313-6, Atheneum Child Bk) Macmillan Child Grp.

—Victory in the Pacific. LC 82-6707. (Illus.). 224p. (gr. 6 up). 1983. SBE 14.95 (0-689-30948-1, Atheneum Child Bk) Macmillan Child Grp.

—The War for Independence: The Story of the American Revolution. LC 87-13711. (Illus.). 288p. (gr. 5 up). 1988. SBE 15.95 (0-689-31390-X, Atheneum Child Bk) Macmillan Child Grp.

—The Yanks Are Coming: The United States in the First World War. LC 86-3585. (Illus.). 256p. (gr. 5 up). 1986. SBE 15.95 (0-689-31209-1, Atheneum Child Bk) Macmillan Child Grp.

Marriott. Amazing Fact Book of Balloons. (Illus.). 32p. (gr. 4-8). 1987. PLB 14.95s.p. (0-87191-841-2) Creative Ed.

Marriott, Michelle. Old King Cole & Friends. (gr. 4 up). 1990. 9.95 (0-85953-446-4) Childs Play.

Marrocha, Jean, jt. auth. see Haasl, Beth.

Marron, Carol. Yellowstone. LC 88-18643. (Illus.). 48p. (gr. 4-8). 1988. RSBE 13.95 (0-89686-405-7, Crestwood Hse) Macmillan Child Grp.

Marron, Carol A. Just One of the Family. (ps-3). 1993. pap. 4.95 (0-8114-8404-1) Raintree Steck-V.

—Someone Just Like Me. (ps-3). 1993. pap. 4.95 (0-8114-8407-6) Raintree Steck-V.

Marrone, Russell. The Wizard's Quest. Marrone, Russell, illus. LC 87-50268. 102p. (gr. 3-5). 1987. 7.95 (1-55523-078-4) Winston-Derek.

Marrs, Carol R. Pet Cobwebs. Marrs, Greg, illus. 112p. (gr. 1 up). 1988. 12.95 (0-9621234-0-4) Funny Farm Pr.

Marrs, Texe W. The Great Robot Book. (Illus.). 112p. (gr. 3-9). 1985. (J Messner); 9.59 (0-671-60178-4) S&S Trade.

Marryat, Captain. Mr. Midshipman Easy. 432p. (gr. 2 up). 1991. pap. 2.95 (0-14-035118-3, Puffin) Puffin Bks.

Mars, Dominique de Saint see De Saint Mars, Dominique.

Marsano, Daniel T. Sir Day the Knight. Stroschin, Jane H., illus. 48p. (gr. k-6). 1993. 15.00 (1-883960-11-8) Henry Quill.

Marschall, Richard, intros. by see Caniff, Milton.

Marschall, Richard, intros. by see Herriman, George.

Marschall, Richard, ed. & intro. by see McCay, Winsor.

Marschall, Richard, intro. by see McCay, Winsor.

Marschall, Richard, ed. see McCay, Winsor.

Marschall, Richard, intros. by see Sterrett, Cliff.

Marsden, John. So Much to Tell You. 112p. (gr. 7 up). 1989. 14.95 (0-316-54877-4, Joy St Bks) Little.

—So Much to Tell You. (gr. 7 up). 1990. pap. 3.50 (0-449-70374-6, Juniper) Fawcett.

Marsh, Carole. A-Plus Very Good! Secrets of Good Writing for Students. (Orig.). (gr. 4-12). 1986. 24.95 (1-55609-272-5); pap. text ed. 14.95 (0-935326-63-4) Gallopade Pub Group.

—Abstinence Makes the Heart Grow Fonder. (gr. 2-12). 1987. 24.95 (1-55609-273-3); pap. 14.95 (1-55609-208-3) Gallopade Pub Group.

—AIDS-Zits: A "Sextionary" for Kids. (Orig.). (gr. 2-12). 1987. 24.95 (1-55609-263-6); pap. 14.95 (1-55609-210-5) Gallopade Pub Group.

—Alabama & Other State Greats (Biographies) (Illus.). (gr. 3-12). 1990. PLB 24.95 (1-55609-469-8); pap. 14.95 (1-55609-468-X); computer disk 29.95 (0-7933-1338-4) Gallopade Pub Group.

—Alabama Bandits, Bushwackers, Outlaws, Crooks, Devils, Ghosts, Desperadoes & Other Assorted & Sundry Characters! (Illus.). (gr. 3-12). 1990. PLB 24.95 (0-7933-0041-X); pap. 14.95 (0-7933-0040-1); computer disk 29.95 (0-7933-0042-8) Gallopade Pub Group.

—Alabama Classic Christmas Trivia: Stories, Recipes, Activities, Legends, Lore & More! (Illus.). (gr. 3-12). 1990. PLB 24.95 (0-7933-0044-4); pap. 14.95 (0-7933-0043-6); computer disk 29.95 (0-7933-0045-2) Gallopade Pub Group.

—Alabama Coastales. (Illus.). (gr. 3-12). 1990. PLB 24.95 (1-55609-465-5); pap. 14.95 (1-55609-120-6); computer disk 29.95 (0-7933-1334-1) Gallopade Pub Group.

—Alabama Coastales! 1992. lib. bdg. 24.95 (0-7933-6938-X) Gallopade Pub Group.

—Alabama "Crinkum-Crankum" A Funny Word Book about Our State. (Illus.). 1992. lib. bdg. 24.95 (0-7933-4810-2); pap. 14.95 (0-7933-4811-0); disk 29.95 (0-7933-4812-9) Gallopade Pub Group.

—Alabama Dingbats! Bk. 1: A Fun Book of Games, Stories, Activities & More about Our State That's All in Code! for You to Decipher. (Illus.). (gr. 3-12). 1991. PLB 24.95 (0-7933-3773-9); pap. 14.95 (0-7933-3774-7); computer disk 29.95 (0-7933-3775-5) Gallopade Pub Group.

—Alabama Festival Fun for Kids! (Illus.). (gr. 3-12). 1991. lib. bdg. 24.95 (0-7933-3926-X); pap. 14.95 (0-7933-3927-8); disk 29.95 (0-7933-3928-6) Gallopade Pub Group.

—The Alabama Hot Air Balloon Mystery. (Illus.). (gr. 2-9). 1990. 24.95 (0-7933-2318-5); pap. 14.95 (0-7933-2319-3); computer disk 29.95 (0-7933-2320-7) Gallopade Pub Group.

—Alabama Jeopardy! Answers & Questions about Our State! (Illus.). (gr. 3-12). 1991. PLB 24.95 (0-7933-4079-9); pap. 14.95 (0-7933-4080-2); computer disk 29.95 (0-7933-4081-0) Gallopade Pub Group.

—Alabama "Jography" A Fun Run Thru Our State! (Illus.). (gr. 3-12). 1990. PLB 24.95 (1-55609-461-2); pap. 14.95 (1-55609-092-7); computer disk 29.95 (0-7933-1327-9) Gallopade Pub Group.

—Alabama Kid's Cookbook: Recipes, How-to, History, Lore & More! (Illus.). (gr. 3-12). 1990. PLB 24.95 (0-7933-0082-7); pap. 14.95 (0-7933-0081-9); computer disk 29.95 (0-7933-0083-5) Gallopade Pub Group.

—The Alabama Mystery Van Takes Off! Book 1: Handicapped Alabama Kids Sneak Off on a Big Adventure. (Illus.). (gr. 3-12). 1992. 24.95 (0-7933-4964-8); pap. 14.95 (0-7933-4965-6); computer disk 29.95 (0-7933-4966-4) Gallopade Pub Group.

—Alabama Quiz Bowl Crash Course! (Illus.). (gr. 3-12). 1990. PLB 24.95 (1-55609-467-1); pap. 14.95 (1-55609-466-3); computer disk 29.95 (0-7933-1333-3) Gallopade Pub Group.

—Alabama Rollercoasters! (Illus.). (gr. 3-12). 1992. PLB 24.95 (0-7933-5224-X); pap. 14.95 (0-7933-5225-8); computer disk 29.95 (0-7933-5226-6) Gallopade Pub Group.

—Alabama School Trivia: An Amazing & Fascinating Look at Our State's Teachers, Schools & Students! (Illus.). (gr. 3-12). 1990. PLB 24.95 (0-7933-0079-7); pap. 14.95 (0-7933-0049-5); computer disk 29.95 (0-7933-0080-0) Gallopade Pub Group.

—Alabama Silly Basketball Sportsmysteries, Vol. I. (Illus.). (gr. 3-12). 1990. PLB 24.95 (0-7933-0047-9); pap. 14.95 (0-7933-0046-0); computer disk 29.95 (0-7933-0048-7) Gallopade Pub Group.

—Alabama Silly Basketball Sportsmysteries, Vol. II. (Illus.). (gr. 3-12). 1990. PLB 24.95 (0-7933-1562-X); pap. 14.95 (0-7933-1563-8); computer disk 29.95 (0-7933-1564-6) Gallopade Pub Group.

—Alabama Silly Football Sportsmysteries, Vol. I. (Illus.). (gr. 3-12). 1990. PLB 24.95 (1-55609-464-7); pap. 14.95 (1-55609-463-9); computer disk 29.95 (0-7933-1329-5) Gallopade Pub Group.

—Alabama Silly Football Sportsmysteries, Vol. II. (Illus.). (gr. 3-12). 1990. PLB 24.95 (0-7933-1339-2); pap. 14.95 (0-7933-1340-6); computer disk 29.95 (0-7933-1341-4) Gallopade Pub Group.

—Alabama Silly Trivia! (Illus.). (gr. 3-12). 1990. PLB 24.95 (1-55609-460-4); pap. 14.95 (1-55609-038-2); computer disk 29.95 (0-7933-1326-0) Gallopade Pub Group.

—Alabama Timeline: A Chronology of Alabama History, Mystery, Trivia, Legend, Lore & More! (Illus.). (gr. 3-12). 1992. PLB 24.95 (0-7933-5875-2); pap. 14.95 (0-7933-5876-0); computer disk 29.95 (0-7933-5877-9) Gallopade Pub Group.

—Alabama's (Most Devastating!) Disasters & (Most Calamitous!) Catastrophies! (Illus.). (gr. 3-12). 1990. PLB 24.95 (0-7933-0038-X); pap. 14.95 (0-7933-0037-1); computer disk 29.95 (0-7933-0039-8) Gallopade Pub Group.

—Alabama's Unsolved Mysteries (& Their "Solutions") Includes Scientific Information & Other Activities for Students. (Illus.). (gr. 3-12). 1992. PLB 24.95 (0-7933-5722-5); pap. 14.95 (0-7933-5723-3); computer disk 29.95 (0-7933-5724-1) Gallopade Pub Group.

—Alaska & Other State Greats (Biographies). (Illus.). (gr. 3-12). 1990. PLB 24.95 (1-55609-483-3); pap. 14.95 (1-55609-482-X); computer disk 29.95 (0-7933-1354-6) Gallopade Pub Group.

—Alaska Bandits, Bushwackers, Outlaws, Crooks, Devils, Ghosts, Desperadoes & Other Assorted & Sundry Characters! (Illus.). (gr. 3-12). 1990. PLB 24.95 (0-7933-0094-0); pap. 14.95 (0-7933-0093-2); computer disk 29.95 (0-7933-0095-9) Gallopade Pub Group.

—Alaska Classic Christmas Trivia: Stories, Recipes, Activities, Legends, Lore & More! (Illus.). (gr. 3-12). 1990. PLB 24.95 (0-7933-0097-5); pap. 14.95 (0-7933-0096-7); computer disk 29.95 (0-7933-0098-3) Gallopade Pub Group.

—Alaska Coastales. (Illus.). (gr. 3-12). 1990. PLB 24.95 (1-55609-479-5); pap. 14.95 (1-55609-478-7); computer disk 29.95 (0-7933-1353-8) Gallopade Pub Group.

—Alaska Coastales. 1992. lib. bdg. 24.95 (0-7933-7266-6) Gallopade Pub Group.

—Alaska "Crinkum-Crankum" A Funny Word Book about Our State. (Illus.). 1992. lib. bdg. 24.95 (0-7933-4813-7); pap. 14.95 (0-7933-4814-5); disk 29.95 (0-7933-4815-3) Gallopade Pub Group.

—Alaska Dingbats! Bk. 1: A Fun Book of Games, Stories, Activities & More about Our State That's All in Code! for You to Decipher. (Illus.). (gr. 3-12). 1991. PLB 24.95 (0-7933-3776-3); pap. 14.95 (0-7933-3777-1); computer disk 29.95 (0-7933-3778-X) Gallopade Pub Group.

—Alaska Festival Fun for Kids! (Illus.). (gr. 3-12). 1991. lib. bdg. 24.95 (0-7933-3929-4); pap. 14.95 (0-7933-3930-8); disk 29.95 (0-7933-3931-6) Gallopade Pub Group.

—The Alaska Hot Air Balloon Mystery. (Illus.). (gr. 2-9). 1990. 24.95 (0-7933-2327-4); pap. 14.95 (0-7933-2328-2); computer disk 29.95 (0-7933-2329-0) Gallopade Pub Group.

—Alaska Jeopardy! Answers & Questions about Our State! (Illus.). (gr. 3-12). 1991. PLB 24.95 (0-7933-4082-9); pap. 14.95 (0-7933-4083-7); computer disk 29.95 (0-7933-4084-5) Gallopade Pub Group.

—Alaska "Jography" A Fun Run Thru Our State! (Illus.). (gr. 3-12). 1990. PLB 24.95 (0-7933-4173-6); pap. 14.95 (0-7933-4172-8); computer disk 29.95 (0-7933-1343-0) Gallopade Pub Group.

—Alaska Kid's Cookbook: Recipes, How-to, History, Lore & More! (Illus.). (gr. 3-12). 1990. PLB 24.95 (0-7933-0106-8); pap. 14.95 (0-7933-0105-X); computer disk 29.95 (0-7933-0107-6) Gallopade Pub Group.

—The Alaska Mystery Van Takes Off! Book 1: Handicapped Alaska Kids Sneak Off on a Big Adventure. (Illus.). (gr. 3-12). 1992. 24.95 (0-7933-4967-2); pap. 14.95 (0-7933-4968-0); computer disk 29.95 (0-7933-4969-9) Gallopade Pub Group.

—Alaska Quiz Bowl Crash Course! (Illus.). (gr. 3-12). 1990. PLB 24.95 (1-55609-481-7); pap. 14.95 (1-55609-480-9); computer disk 29.95 (0-7933-1352-X) Gallopade Pub Group.

—Alaska Rollercoasters! (Illus.). (gr. 3-12). 1992. PLB 24.95 (0-7933-5227-4); pap. 14.95 (0-7933-5228-2); computer disk 29.95 (0-7933-5229-0) Gallopade Pub Group.

—Alaska School Trivia: An Amazing & Fascinating Look at Our State's Teachers, Schools & Students! (Illus.). (gr. 3-12). 1990. PLB 24.95 (*0-7933-0103-3*); pap. 14.95 (*0-7933-0102-5*); computer disk 29.95 (*0-7933-0104-1*) Gallopade Pub Group.

—Alaska Silly Basketball Sportsmysteries, Vol. I. (Illus.). (gr. 3-12). 1990. PLB 24.95 (*0-7933-0100-9*); pap. 14.95 (*0-7933-0099-1*); computer disk 29.95 (*0-7933-0101-7*) Gallopade Pub Group.

—Alaska Silly Basketball Sportsmysteries, Vol. II. (Illus.). (gr. 3-12). 1990. PLB 24.95 (*0-7933-1565-4*); pap. 14.95 (*0-7933-1566-2*); computer disk 29.95 (*0-7933-1567-0*) Gallopade Pub Group.

—Alaska Silly Football Sportsmysteries, Vol. I. (Illus.). (gr. 3-12). 1990. PLB 24.95 (*1-55609-477-9*); pap. 14.95 (*1-55609-476-0*); computer disk 29.95 (*0-7933-1345-7*) Gallopade Pub Group.

—Alaska Silly Football Sportsmysteries, Vol. II. (Illus.). (gr. 3-12). 1990. PLB 24.95 (*0-7933-1346-5*); pap. 14.95 (*0-7933-1347-3*); computer disk 29.95 (*0-7933-1348-1*) Gallopade Pub Group.

—Alaska Silly Trivia! (Illus.). (gr. 3-12). 1990. PLB 24.95 (*1-55609-471-X*); pap. 14.95 (*1-55609-470-1*); computer disk 29.95 (*0-7933-1342-2*) Gallopade Pub Group.

—Alaska Timeline: A Chronology of Alaska History, Mystery, Trivia, Legend, Lore & More. (Illus.). (gr. 3-12). 1992. PLB 24.95 (*0-7933-5878-7*); pap. 14.95 (*0-7933-5879-5*); computer disk 29.95 (*0-7933-5880-9*) Gallopade Pub Group.

—Alaska's (Most Devastating!) Disasters & (Most Calamitous!) Catastrophies! (Illus.). (gr. 3-12). 1990. PLB 24.95 (*0-7933-0091-6*); pap. 14.95 (*0-7933-0090-8*); computer disk 29.95 (*0-7933-0092-4*) Gallopade Pub Group.

—Alaska's Unsolved Mysteries (& Their "Solutions") Includes Scientific Information & Other Activities for Students. (Illus.). (gr. 3-12). 1992. PLB 24.95 (*0-7933-5725-X*); pap. 14.95 (*0-7933-5726-8*); computer disk 29.95 (*0-7933-5727-6*) Gallopade Pub Group.

—Arizona: A(dama) to Z(oroaster) 1992. PLB 24.95 (*0-7933-7317-4*); pap. text ed. 14.95 (*0-7933-7316-6*); disk 29.95 (*0-7933-7318-2*) Gallopade Pub Group.

—Arizona & Other State Greats (Biographies) (Illus.). (gr. 3-12). 1990. PLB 24.95 (*1-55609-507-4*); pap. 14.95 (*1-55609-506-6*); computer disk 29.95 (*0-7933-1373-2*) Gallopade Pub Group.

—Arizona Bandits, Bushwackers, Outlaws, Crooks, Devils, Ghosts, Desperadoes & Other Assorted & Sundry Characters! (Illus.). (gr. 3-12). 1990. PLB 24.95 (*0-7933-0118-1*); pap. 14.95 (*0-7933-0117-3*); computer disk 29.95 (*0-7933-0119-X*) Gallopade Pub Group.

—Arizona Classic Christmas Trivia: Stories, Recipes, Activities, Legends, Lore & More! (Illus.). (gr. 3-12). 1990. PLB 24.95 (*0-7933-0121-1*); pap. 14.95 (*0-7933-0122-X*) Gallopade Pub Group.

—Arizona Coastales. (Illus.). (gr. 3-12). 1990. PLB 24.95 (*1-55609-503-1*); pap. 14.95 (*1-55609-502-3*); computer disk 29.95 (*0-7933-1369-4*) Gallopade Pub Group.

—Arizona Coastales! 1992. lib. bdg. 24.95 (*0-7933-7267-4*) Gallopade Pub Group.

—Arizona "Crinkum-Crankum" A Funny Word Book about Our State. (Illus.). 1992. lib. bdg. 24.95 (*0-7933-4816-1*); pap. 14.95 (*0-7933-4817-X*); disk 29.95 (*0-7933-4818-8*) Gallopade Pub Group.

—Arizona Dingbats! Bk. 1: A Fun Book of Games, Stories, Activities & More about Our State That's All in Code! for You to Decipher. (Illus.). (gr. 3-12). 1991. PLB 24.95 (*0-7933-3779-8*); pap. 14.95 (*0-7933-3780-1*); computer disk 29.95 (*0-7933-3781-X*) Gallopade Pub Group.

—Arizona Festival Fun for Kids! (Illus.). (gr. 3-12). 1991. lib. bdg. 24.95 (*0-7933-3932-4*); pap. 14.95 (*0-7933-3933-2*); disk 29.95 (*0-7933-3934-0*) Gallopade Pub Group.

—The Arizona Hot Air Balloon Mystery. (Illus.). (gr. 2-9). 1990. 24.95 (*0-7933-2336-3*); pap. 14.95 (*0-7933-2337-1*); computer disk 29.95 (*0-7933-2338-X*) Gallopade Pub Group.

—Arizona Jeopardy! Answers & Questions about Our State! (Illus.). (gr. 3-12). 1991. PLB 24.95 (*0-7933-4085-3*); pap. 14.95 (*0-7933-4086-1*); computer disk 29.95 (*0-7933-4087-X*) Gallopade Pub Group.

—Arizona "Jography" A Fun Run Thru Our State! (Illus.). (gr. 3-12). 1990. PLB 24.95 (*1-55609-498-1*); pap. 14.95 (*1-55609-497-3*); computer disk 29.95 (*0-7933-1359-7*) Gallopade Pub Group.

—Arizona Kid's Cookbook: Recipes, How-to, History, Lore & More! (Illus.). (gr. 3-12). 1990. PLB 24.95 (*0-7933-0130-0*); pap. 14.95 (*0-7933-0129-7*); computer disk 29.95 (*0-7933-0131-9*) Gallopade Pub Group.

—The Arizona Mystery Van Takes Off! Book 1: Handicapped Arizona Kids Sneak Off on a Big Adventure. (Illus.). (gr. 3-12). 1992. 24.95 (*0-7933-4970-2*); pap. 14.95 (*0-7933-4971-0*); computer disk 29.95 (*0-7933-4972-9*) Gallopade Pub Group.

—Arizona Quiz Bowl Crash Course! (Illus.). (gr. 3-12). 1990. PLB 24.95 (*1-55609-505-8*); pap. 14.95 (*1-55609-504-X*); computer disk 29.95 (*0-7933-1368-6*) Gallopade Pub Group.

—Arizona Rollercoasters! (Illus.). (gr. 3-12). 1992. PLB 24.95 (*0-7933-5230-4*); pap. 14.95 (*0-7933-5231-2*); computer disk 29.95 (*0-7933-5232-0*) Gallopade Pub Group.

—Arizona School Trivia: An Amazing & Fascinating Look at Our State's Teachers, Schools & Students! (Illus.). (gr. 3-12). 1990. PLB 24.95 (*0-7933-0127-0*); pap. 14.95 (*0-7933-0126-2*); computer disk 29.95 (*0-685-45932-2*) Gallopade Pub Group.

—Arizona Silly Basketball Sportsmysteries, Vol. I. (Illus.). (gr. 3-12). 1990. PLB 24.95 (*0-7933-0124-6*); pap. 14.95 (*0-7933-0123-8*); computer disk 29.95 (*0-7933-0125-4*) Gallopade Pub Group.

—Arizona Silly Basketball Sportsmysteries, Vol. II. (Illus.). (gr. 3-12). 1990. PLB 24.95 (*0-7933-1568-9*); pap. 14.95 (*0-7933-1569-7*); computer disk 29.95 (*0-7933-1570-0*) Gallopade Pub Group.

—Arizona Silly Football Sportsmysteries, Vol. I. (Illus.). (gr. 3-12). 1990. PLB 24.95 (*1-55609-501-5*); pap. 14.95 (*1-55609-500-7*); computer disk 29.95 (*0-7933-1361-9*) Gallopade Pub Group.

—Arizona Silly Football Sportsmysteries, Vol. II. (Illus.). (gr. 3-12). 1990. PLB 24.95 (*0-7933-1362-7*); pap. 14.95 (*0-7933-1363-5*); computer disk 29.95 (*0-7933-1364-3*) Gallopade Pub Group.

—Arizona Silly Trivia! (Illus.). (gr. 3-12). 1990. PLB 24.95 (*1-55609-496-5*); pap. 14.95 (*1-55609-495-7*); computer disk 29.95 (*0-7933-1358-9*) Gallopade Pub Group.

—Arizona Timeline: A Chronology of Arizona History, Mystery, Trivia, Legend, Lore & More. (Illus.). (gr. 3-12). 1992. PLB 24.95 (*0-7933-5881-7*); pap. 14.95 (*0-7933-5882-5*); computer disk 29.95 (*0-7933-5883-3*) Gallopade Pub Group.

—Arizona's (Most Devastating!) Disasters & (Most Calamitous!) Catastrophies! (Illus.). (gr. 3-12). 1990. PLB 24.95 (*0-7933-0115-7*); pap. 14.95 (*0-7933-0114-9*); computer disk 29.95 (*0-7933-0116-5*) Gallopade Pub Group.

—Arizona's Unsolved Mysteries (& Their "Solutions") Includes Scientific Information & Other Activities for Students. (Illus.). (gr. 3-12). 1992. PLB 24.95 (*0-7933-5728-4*); pap. 14.95 (*0-7933-5729-2*); computer disk 29.95 (*0-7933-5730-6*) Gallopade Pub Group.

—Arkansas & Other State Greats (Biographies) (Illus.). (gr. 3-12). 1990. PLB 24.95 (*0-7933-0494-9*); pap. 14.95 (*1-55609-493-0*); computer disk 29.95 (*0-7933-1389-9*) Gallopade Pub Group.

—Arkansas Bandits, Bushwackers, Outlaws, Crooks, Devils, Ghosts, Desperadoes & Other Assorted & Sundry Characters! (Illus.). (gr. 3-12). 1990. PLB 24.95 (*0-7933-0142-4*); pap. 14.95 (*0-7933-0141-6*); computer disk 29.95 (*0-7933-0143-2*) Gallopade Pub Group.

—Arkansas Classic Christmas Trivia: Stories, Recipes, Activities, Legends, Lore & More! (Illus.). (gr. 3-12). 1990. PLB 24.95 (*0-7933-0145-9*); pap. 14.95 (*0-7933-0144-0*); computer disk 29.95 (*0-7933-0146-7*) Gallopade Pub Group.

—Arkansas Coastales. (Illus.). (gr. 3-12). 1990. PLB 24.95 (*1-55609-490-6*); pap. 14.95 (*1-55609-489-2*); computer disk 29.95 (*0-7933-1385-6*) Gallopade Pub Group.

—Arkansas Coastales! 1992. lib. bdg. 24.95 (*0-7933-7268-2*) Gallopade Pub Group.

—Arkansas "Crinkum-Crankum" A Funny Word Book about Our State. (Illus.). 1992. lib. bdg. 24.95 (*0-7933-4819-6*); pap. 14.95 (*0-7933-4820-X*); disk 29.95 (*0-7933-4821-8*) Gallopade Pub Group.

—Arkansas Dingbats! Bk. 1: A Fun Book of Games, Stories, Activities & More about Our State That's All in Code! for You to Decipher. (Illus.). (gr. 3-12). 1991. PLB 24.95 (*0-7933-3782-8*); pap. 14.95 (*0-7933-3783-6*); computer disk 29.95 (*0-7933-3784-4*) Gallopade Pub Group.

—Arkansas Festival Fun for Kids! (Illus.). (gr. 3-12). 1991. lib. bdg. 24.95 (*0-7933-3935-9*); pap. 14.95 (*0-7933-3936-7*); disk 29.95 (*0-7933-3937-5*) Gallopade Pub Group.

—The Arkansas Hot Air Balloon Mystery. (Illus.). (gr. 2-9). 1990. 24.95 (*0-7933-2345-2*); pap. 14.95 (*0-7933-2346-0*); computer disk 29.95 (*0-7933-2347-9*) Gallopade Pub Group.

—Arkansas Jeopardy! Answers & Questions about Our State! (Illus.). (gr. 3-12). 1991. PLB 24.95 (*0-7933-4088-8*); pap. 14.95 (*0-7933-4089-6*); computer disk 29.95 (*0-7933-4090-X*) Gallopade Pub Group.

—Arkansas "Jography" A Fun Run Thru Our State! (Illus.). (gr. 3-12). 1990. PLB 24.95 (*1-55609-485-X*); pap. 14.95 (*1-55609-088-9*); computer disk 29.95 (*0-7933-1375-9*) Gallopade Pub Group.

—Arkansas Kid's Cookbook: Recipes, How-to, History, Lore & More! (Illus.). (gr. 3-12). 1990. PLB 24.95 (*0-7933-0154-8*); pap. 14.95 (*0-7933-0153-X*); computer disk 29.95 (*0-7933-0155-6*) Gallopade Pub Group.

—The Arkansas Mystery Van Takes Off! Book 1: Handicapped Arkansas Kids Sneak Off on a Big Adventure. (Illus.). (gr. 3-12). 1992. 24.95 (*0-7933-4973-7*); pap. 14.95 (*0-7933-4974-5*); computer disk 29.95 (*0-7933-4975-3*) Gallopade Pub Group.

—Arkansas Quiz Bowl Crash Course! (Illus.). (gr. 3-12). 1990. PLB 24.95 (*1-55609-492-2*); pap. 14.95 (*1-55609-491-4*); computer disk 29.95 (*0-7933-1384-8*) Gallopade Pub Group.

—Arkansas Rollercoasters! (Illus.). (gr. 3-12). 1992. PLB 24.95 (*0-7933-5233-9*); pap. 14.95 (*0-7933-5234-7*); computer disk 29.95 (*0-7933-5235-5*) Gallopade Pub Group.

—Arkansas School Trivia: An Amazing & Fascinating Look at Our State's Teachers, Schools & Students! (Illus.). (gr. 3-12). 1990. PLB 24.95 (*0-7933-0151-3*); pap. 14.95 (*0-7933-0150-5*); computer disk 29.95 (*0-7933-0152-1*) Gallopade Pub Group.

—Arkansas Silly Basketball Sportsmysteries, Vol. I. (Illus.). (gr. 3-12). 1990. PLB 24.95 (*0-7933-0149-1*); pap. 14.95 (*0-7933-0147-5*); computer disk 29.95 (*0-685-45933-0*) Gallopade Pub Group.

—Arkansas Silly Basketball Sportsmysteries, Vol. II. (Illus.). (gr. 3-12). 1990. PLB 24.95 (*0-7933-1571-9*); pap. 14.95 (*0-685-45934-9*); computer disk 29.95 (*0-7933-1573-5*) Gallopade Pub Group.

—Arkansas Silly Football Sportsmysteries, Vol. I. (Illus.). (gr. 3-12). 1990. PLB 24.95 (*1-55609-488-4*); pap. 14.95 (*1-55609-487-6*); computer disk 29.95 (*0-7933-1377-5*) Gallopade Pub Group.

—Arkansas Silly Football Sportsmysteries, Vol. II. (Illus.). (gr. 3-12). 1990. PLB 24.95 (*0-7933-1378-3*); pap. 14.95 (*0-7933-1379-1*); computer disk 29.95 (*0-7933-1380-5*) Gallopade Pub Group.

—Arkansas Silly Trivia! (Illus.). (gr. 3-12). 1990. PLB 24.95 (*1-55609-484-1*); pap. 14.95 (*1-55609-083-8*); computer disk 29.95 (*0-7933-1374-0*) Gallopade Pub Group.

—Arkansas Timeline: A Chronology of Arkansas History, Mystery, Trivia, Legend, Lore & More. (Illus.). (gr. 3-12). 1992. PLB 24.95 (*0-7933-5884-1*); pap. 14.95 (*0-7933-5885-X*); computer disk 29.95 (*0-7933-5886-8*) Gallopade Pub Group.

—Arkansas's (Most Devastating!) Disasters & (Most Calamitous!) Catastrophies! (Illus.). (gr. 3-12). 1990. PLB 24.95 (*0-7933-0139-4*); pap. 14.95 (*0-7933-0138-6*); computer disk 29.95 (*0-7933-0140-8*) Gallopade Pub Group.

—Arkansas's Unsolved Mysteries (& Their "Solutions") Includes Scientific Information & Other Activities for Students. (Illus.). (gr. 3-12). 1992. PLB 24.95 (*0-7933-5731-4*); pap. 14.95 (*0-7933-5732-2*); computer disk 29.95 (*0-7933-5733-0*) Gallopade Pub Group.

—Astronomy for Kids: Milky Way & Mars Bars. (Illus.). 1990. 24.95 (*0-7933-0012-6*); pap. 14.95 (*0-7933-0013-4*); computer disk 29.95 (*0-7933-0014-2*) Gallopade Pub Group.

—Autumn: Silly Trivia. Marsh, Carole, illus. (Orig.). (gr. 2-9). 1986. 24.95 (*1-55609-274-1*); pap. 14.95 (*0-685-14606-5*) Gallopade Pub Group.

—Avast, Ye Slobs! Alabama Pirate Trivia. (Illus.). (gr. 3-12). 1990. PLB 24.95 (*0-7933-0088-6*); pap. 14.95 (*0-7933-0087-8*); computer disk 29.95 (*0-7933-0089-4*) Gallopade Pub Group.

—Avast, Ye Slobs! Alaska Pirate Trivia. (Illus.). (gr. 3-12). 1990. PLB 24.95 (*0-7933-0112-2*); pap. 14.95 (*0-7933-0111-4*); computer disk 29.95 (*0-7933-0113-0*) Gallopade Pub Group.

—Avast, Ye Slobs! Arizona Pirate Trivia. (Illus.). (gr. 3-12). 1990. PLB 24.95 (*0-7933-0136-X*); pap. 14.95 (*0-7933-0135-1*); computer disk 29.95 (*0-7933-0137-8*) Gallopade Pub Group.

—Avast, Ye Slobs! Arkansas Pirate Trivia. (Illus.). (gr. 3-12). 1990. PLB 24.95 (*0-7933-0160-2*); pap. 14.95 (*0-7933-0159-9*); computer disk 29.95 (*0-7933-0161-0*) Gallopade Pub Group.

—Avast, Ye Slobs! California Pirate Trivia. (Illus.). (gr. 3-12). 1990. PLB 24.95 (*0-7933-0184-X*); pap. 14.95 (*0-7933-0183-1*); computer disk 29.95 (*0-7933-0185-8*) Gallopade Pub Group.

—Avast, Ye Slobs! Colorado Pirate Trivia. (Illus.). (gr. 3-12). 1990. PLB 24.95 (*0-7933-0208-0*); pap. 14.95 (*0-7933-0207-2*); computer disk 29.95 (*0-7933-0209-9*) Gallopade Pub Group.

—Avast, Ye Slobs! Connecticut Pirate Trivia. (Illus.). (gr. 3-12). 1990. PLB 24.95 (*0-7933-0232-3*); pap. 14.95 (*0-7933-0231-5*); computer disk 29.95 (*0-7933-0233-1*) Gallopade Pub Group.

—Avast, Ye Slobs! Delaware Pirate Trivia. (Illus.). (gr. 3-12). 1990. PLB 24.95 (*0-7933-0256-0*); pap. 14.95 (*0-7933-0255-2*); computer disk 29.95 (*0-7933-0257-9*) Gallopade Pub Group.

—Avast, Ye Slobs! Florida Pirate Trivia. (Illus.). (gr. 3-12). 1990. PLB 24.95 (*0-7933-0304-4*); pap. 14.95 (*0-7933-0303-6*); computer disk 29.95 (*0-7933-0305-2*) Gallopade Pub Group.

—Avast, Ye Slobs! Georgia Pirate Trivia. (Illus.). (gr. 3-12). 1990. PLB 24.95 (*0-7933-0328-1*); pap. 14.95 (*0-7933-0327-3*); computer disk 29.95 (*0-7933-0329-X*) Gallopade Pub Group.

—Avast, Ye Slobs! Hawaii Pirate Trivia. (Illus.). (gr. 3-12). 1990. PLB 24.95 (*0-7933-0352-4*); pap. 14.95 (*0-7933-0351-6*); computer disk 29.95 (*0-7933-0353-2*) Gallopade Pub Group.

—Avast, Ye Slobs! Idaho Pirate Trivia. (Illus.). (gr. 3-12). 1990. PLB 24.95 (*0-7933-0376-1*); pap. 14.95 (*0-7933-0375-3*); computer disk 29.95 (*0-7933-0377-X*) Gallopade Pub Group.

—Avast, Ye Slobs! Illinois Pirate Trivia. (Illus.). (gr. 3-12). 1990. PLB 24.95 (*0-7933-0400-8*); pap. 14.95 (*0-7933-0399-0*); computer disk 29.95 (*0-7933-0401-6*) Gallopade Pub Group.

—Avast, Ye Slobs! Indiana Pirate Trivia. (Illus.). (gr. 3-12). 1990. PLB 24.95 (*0-7933-0424-5*); pap. 14.95 (*0-7933-0423-7*); computer disk 29.95 (*0-685-45926-8*) Gallopade Pub Group.

—Avast, Ye Slobs! Iowa Private Trivia. (Illus.). (gr. 3-12). 1990. PLB 24.95 (*0-7933-0448-2*); pap. 14.95 (*0-7933-0447-4*); computer disk 29.95 (*0-7933-0449-0*) Gallopade Pub Group.
—Avast, Ye Slobs! Kansas Pirate Trivia. (Illus.). (gr. 3-12). 1990. PLB 24.95 (*0-7933-0472-5*); pap. 14.95 (*0-7933-0471-7*); computer disk 29.95 (*0-7933-0473-3*) Gallopade Pub Group.
—Avast, Ye Slobs! Kentucky Pirate Trivia. (Illus.). (gr. 3-8). 1990. PLB 24.95 (*0-7933-0496-2*); pap. 14.95 (*0-7933-0495-4*); disk 29.95 (*0-685-45938-1*) Gallopade Pub Group.
—Avast, Ye Slobs! Louisiana Pirate Trivia. (Illus.). (gr. 3-8). 1990. PLB 24.95 (*0-7933-0520-9*); pap. 14.95 (*0-7933-0519-5*); disk 29.95 (*0-7933-0521-7*) Gallopade Pub Group.
—Avast, Ye Slobs! Maine Pirate Trivia. (Illus.). (gr. 3-8). 1990. PLB 24.95 (*0-7933-0545-4*); pap. 14.95 (*0-7933-0544-6*); disk 29.95 (*0-7933-0546-2*) Gallopade Pub Group.
—Avast, Ye Slobs! Maryland Pirate Trivia. (Illus.). (gr. 3-8). 1990. PLB 24.95 (*0-7933-0569-1*); pap. 14.95 (*0-7933-0568-3*); disk 29.95 (*0-7933-0570-5*) Gallopade Pub Group.
—Avast, Ye Slobs! Massachusetts Pirate Trivia. (Illus.). (gr. 3-8). 1990. PLB 24.95 (*0-7933-0593-4*); pap. 14.95 (*0-7933-0592-6*); disk 29.95 (*0-7933-0594-2*) Gallopade Pub Group.
—Avast, Ye Slobs!: Michigan Pirate Trivia. (Illus.). (gr. 3 up). 1990. PLB 24.95 (*0-7933-0617-5*); pap. 14.95 (*0-7933-0616-7*); computer disk 29.95 (*0-7933-0618-3*) Gallopade Pub Group.
—Avast, Ye Slobs!: Minnesota Pirate Trivia. (Illus.). (gr. 3 up). 1990. PLB 24.95 (*0-7933-0641-8*); pap. 14.95 (*0-7933-0640-X*); computer disk 29.95 (*0-7933-0642-6*) Gallopade Pub Group.
—Avast, Ye Slobs!: Mississippi Pirate Trivia. (Illus.). (gr. 3 up). 1990. PLB 24.95 (*0-7933-0666-3*); pap. 14.95 (*0-7933-0665-5*); computer disk 29.95 (*0-7933-0667-1*) Gallopade Pub Group.
—Avast, Ye Slobs!: Missouri Pirate Trivia. (Illus.). (gr. 3 up). 1990. PLB 24.95 (*0-7933-0690-6*); pap. 14.95 (*0-7933-0689-2*); computer disk 29.95 (*0-7933-0691-4*) Gallopade Pub Group.
—Avast, Ye Slobs!: Montana Pirate Trivia. (Illus.). (gr. 3 up). 1990. PLB 24.95 (*0-7933-0715-5*); pap. 14.95 (*0-7933-0714-7*); computer disk 29.95 (*0-7933-0716-3*) Gallopade Pub Group.
—Avast, Ye Slobs!: Nebraska Pirate Trivia. (Illus.). (gr. 3 up). 1990. PLB 24.95 (*0-7933-0739-2*); pap. 14.95 (*0-7933-0738-4*); computer disk 29.95 (*0-7933-0740-6*) Gallopade Pub Group.
—Avast, Ye Slobs! Nevada Pirate Trivia. (Illus.). 1990. PLB 24.95 (*0-7933-0763-5*); pap. 14.95 (*0-7933-0762-7*); computer disk 29.95 (*0-7933-0764-3*) Gallopade Pub Group.
—Avast, Ye Slobs! New Hampshire Pirate Trivia. (Illus.). 1990. PLB 24.95 (*0-7933-0787-2*); pap. 14.95 (*0-7933-0786-4*); computer disk 29.95 (*0-7933-0788-0*) Gallopade Pub Group.
—Avast, Ye Slobs! New Jersey Pirate Trivia. (Illus.). 1990. PLB 24.95 (*0-7933-1809-2*); pap. 14.95 (*0-7933-1810-6*); computer disk 29.95 (*0-7933-1811-4*) Gallopade Pub Group.
—Avast, Ye Slobs! New Mexico Pirate Trivia. (Illus.). 1990. PLB 24.95 (*0-7933-0811-9*); pap. 14.95 (*0-7933-0810-0*); computer disk 29.95 (*0-7933-0812-7*) Gallopade Pub Group.
—Avast, Ye Slobs! New York Pirate Trivia. (Illus.). 1990. PLB 24.95 (*0-7933-0835-6*); pap. 14.95 (*0-7933-0834-8*); computer disk 29.95 (*0-7933-0836-4*) Gallopade Pub Group.
—Avast, Ye Slobs! North Carolina Pirate Trivia. (Illus.). 1990. PLB 24.95 (*0-7933-0859-3*); pap. 14.95 (*0-7933-0858-5*); computer disk 29.95 (*0-7933-0860-7*) Gallopade Pub Group.
—Avast, Ye Slobs! North Dakota Pirate Trivia. (Illus.). 1990. PLB 24.95 (*0-7933-0883-6*); pap. 14.95 (*0-7933-0882-8*); computer disk 29.95 (*0-7933-0884-4*) Gallopade Pub Group.
—Avast, Ye Slobs! Ohio Pirate Trivia. (Illus.). 1990. PLB 24.95 (*0-7933-0908-5*); pap. 14.95 (*0-7933-0907-7*); computer disk 29.95 (*0-7933-0909-3*) Gallopade Pub Group.
—Avast, Ye Slobs! Oklahoma Pirate Trivia. (Illus.). 1990. PLB 24.95 (*0-7933-0932-8*); pap. 14.95 (*0-7933-0931-X*); computer disk 29.95 (*0-7933-0933-6*) Gallopade Pub Group.
—Avast, Ye Slobs! Oregon Pirate Trivia. (Illus.). 1990. PLB 24.95 (*0-7933-0956-5*); pap. 14.95 (*0-7933-0955-7*); computer disk 29.95 (*0-685-45979-9*) Gallopade Pub Group.
—Avast, Ye Slobs! Pennsylvania Pirate Trivia. (Illus.). 1990. PLB 24.95 (*0-7933-0980-8*); pap. 14.95 (*0-7933-0979-4*); computer disk 29.95 (*0-7933-0981-6*) Gallopade Pub Group.
—Avast, Ye Slobs! Rhode Island Pirate Trivia. (Illus.). 1990. PLB 24.95 (*0-7933-1004-0*); pap. 14.95 (*0-7933-1003-2*); computer disk 29.95 (*0-7933-1005-9*) Gallopade Pub Group.
—Avast, Ye Slobs! South Carolina Pirate Trivia. (Illus.). 1990. PLB 24.95 (*0-7933-1028-8*); pap. 14.95 (*0-7933-1027-X*); computer disk 29.95 (*0-7933-1029-6*) Gallopade Pub Group.
—Avast, Ye Slobs! South Dakota Pirate Trivia. (Illus.). 1990. PLB 24.95 (*0-7933-1052-0*); pap. 14.95 (*0-7933-1051-2*); computer disk 29.95 (*0-7933-1053-9*) Gallopade Pub Group.

—Avast, Ye Slobs! Tennessee Pirate Trivia. (Illus.). 1990. PLB 24.95 (*0-7933-1076-8*); pap. 14.95 (*0-7933-1075-X*); computer disk 29.95 (*0-7933-1077-6*) Gallopade Pub Group.
—Avast, Ye Slobs! Texas Pirate Trivia. (Illus.). 1990. PLB 24.95 (*0-7933-1100-4*); pap. 14.95 (*0-7933-1099-7*); computer disk 0-7933-1101-2 29.95 (*0-685-45953-5*) Gallopade Pub Group.
—Avast, Ye Slobs! The Book of Silly Pirate Trivia. (Illus., Orig.). (gr. 1-12). 1986. PLB 24.95 (*1-55609-281-4*); pap. 14.95 (*0-935326-82-0*) Gallopade Pub Group.
—Avast, Ye Slobs! Utah Pirate Trivia. (Illus.). 1990. PLB 24.95 (*0-7933-1124-1*); pap. 14.95 (*0-7933-1123-3*); computer disk 29.95 (*0-7933-1125-X*) Gallopade Pub Group.
—Avast, Ye Slobs! Vermont Pirate Trivia. (Illus.). 1990. PLB 24.95 (*0-7933-1148-9*); pap. 14.95 (*0-685-45958-6*); computer disk 29.95 (*0-7933-1149-7*) Gallopade Pub Group.
—Avast, Ye Slobs! Virginia Pirate Trivia. (Illus.). 1990. PLB 24.95 (*0-7933-1172-1*); pap. 14.95 (*0-7933-1171-3*); computer disk 29.95 (*0-7933-1173-X*) Gallopade Pub Group.
—Avast, Ye Slobs! Washington, D.C. (Illus.). (gr. 3-12). 1990. PLB 24.95 (*0-7933-0280-3*); pap. 14.95 (*0-7933-0279-X*); computer disk 29.95 (*0-7933-0281-1*) Gallopade Pub Group.
—Avast, Ye Slobs! Washington Pirate Trivia. (Illus.). 1990. PLB 24.95 (*0-7933-1196-9*); pap. 14.95 (*0-7933-1195-0*); computer disk 29.95 (*0-7933-1197-7*) Gallopade Pub Group.
—Avast, Ye Slobs! West Virginia Pirate Trivia. (Illus.). 1990. PLB 24.95 (*0-7933-1220-5*); pap. 14.95 (*0-7933-1219-1*); computer disk 29.95 (*0-7933-1221-3*) Gallopade Pub Group.
—Avast, Ye Slobs! Wisconsin Pirate Trivia. (Illus.). 1990. PLB 24.95 (*0-7933-1244-2*); pap. 14.95 (*0-7933-1243-4*); computer disk 29.95 (*0-7933-1245-0*) Gallopade Pub Group.
—Avast, Ye Slobs! Wyoming Pirate Trivia. (Illus.). 1990. PLB 24.95 (*0-7933-1268-X*); pap. 14.95 (*0-7933-1267-1*); computer disk 29.95 (*0-7933-1269-8*) Gallopade Pub Group.
—The Backyard Searcher's Extra Terrestrial Log Book. (Illus.). (gr. 4-9). 1983. PLB 24.95 (*1-55609-282-2*); pap. 14.95 (*0-935326-27-8*) Gallopade Pub Group.
—Bat Cave Mystery. (Orig.). (gr. 3-8). 1986. PLB 24.95 (*1-55609-154-0*); pap. 14.95 (*0-935326-72-3*)
—The Beast & the Kansas Bed & Breakfast. (gr. 3-12). 1989. PLB 24.95 (*1-55609-371-3*); pap. 14.95 (*1-55609-372-1*); bk. on computer disk 29.95 (*1-55609-373-X*) Gallopade Pub Group.
—The Beast of the Alabama Bed & Breakfast. (Illus.). (gr. 3-12). 1990. PLB 24.95 (*0-7933-1332-5*); pap. 14.95 (*0-7933-1331-7*); computer disk 29.95 (*0-7933-1330-9*) Gallopade Pub Group.
—The Beast of the Arizona Bed & Breakfast. (Illus.). (gr. 3-12). 1990. PLB 24.95 (*0-7933-1365-1*); pap. 14.95 (*0-7933-1366-X*); computer disk 29.95 (*0-7933-1367-8*) Gallopade Pub Group.
—The Beast of the Arkansas Bed & Breakfast. (Illus.). (gr. 3-12). 1990. PLB 24.95 (*0-7933-1381-3*); pap. 14.95 (*0-7933-1382-1*); computer disk 29.95 (*0-7933-1383-X*) Gallopade Pub Group.
—The Beast of the Colorado Bed & Breakfast. (Illus.). (gr. 3-12). 1990. PLB 24.95 (*0-7933-1413-5*); pap. 14.95 (*0-7933-1414-3*); computer disk 29.95 (*0-7933-1415-1*) Gallopade Pub Group.
—The Beast of the Connecticut Bed & Breakfast. (Illus.). (gr. 3-12). 1990. PLB 24.95 (*0-7933-1429-1*); pap. 14.95 (*0-7933-1430-5*); computer disk 29.95 (*0-7933-1431-3*) Gallopade Pub Group.
—The Beast of the Delaware Bed & Breakfast. (Illus.). (gr. 3-12). 1990. PLB 24.95 (*0-7933-1447-X*); pap. 14.95 (*0-7933-1448-8*); computer disk 29.95 (*0-7933-1449-6*) Gallopade Pub Group.
—The Beast of the Florida Bed & Breakfast. (Illus.). (gr. 3-12). 1990. PLB 24.95 (*0-7933-1493-3*); pap. 14.95 (*0-7933-1494-1*); computer disk 29.95 (*0-7933-1495-X*) Gallopade Pub Group.
—The Beast of the Georgia Bed & Breakfast. (Illus.). (gr. 3-12). 1990. PLB 24.95 (*0-7933-1512-3*); pap. 14.95 (*0-7933-1513-1*); computer disk 29.95 (*0-7933-1514-X*) Gallopade Pub Group.
—The Beast of the Hawaii Bed & Breakfast. (Illus.). (gr. 3-12). 1990. PLB 24.95 (*0-7933-1531-X*); pap. 14.95 (*0-7933-1532-8*); computer disk 29.95 (*0-7933-1533-6*) Gallopade Pub Group.
—The Beast of the Idaho Bed & Breakfast. (Illus.). (gr. 3-12). 1990. PLB 24.95 (*0-7933-1550-6*); pap. 14.95 (*0-7933-1551-4*); computer disk 29.95 (*0-7933-1552-2*) Gallopade Pub Group.
—The Beast of the Illinois Bed & Breakfast. (Illus.). (gr. 3-12). 1990. PLB 24.95 (*0-7933-1590-5*); pap. 14.95 (*0-7933-1591-3*); computer disk 29.95 (*0-7933-1592-1*) Gallopade Pub Group.
—The Beast of the Indiana Bed & Breakfast. (Illus.). (gr. 3-12). 1990. PLB 24.95 (*0-7933-1609-X*); pap. 14.95 (*0-7933-1610-3*); computer disk 29.95 (*0-7933-1611-1*) Gallopade Pub Group.
—The Beast of the Iowa Bed & Breakfast. (Illus.). (gr. 3-12). 1990. PLB 24.95 (*0-7933-1628-6*); pap. 14.95 (*0-7933-1629-4*); computer disk 29.95 (*0-7933-1630-8*) Gallopade Pub Group.

—The Beast of the Kentucky Bed & Breakfast. (Illus.). (gr. 3-8). 1990. PLB 24.95 (*0-7933-1650-2*); pap. 14.95 (*0-7933-1651-0*); disk 29.95 (*0-7933-1652-9*) Gallopade Pub Group.
—The Beast of the Louisiana Bed & Breakfast. (Illus.). (gr. 3-8). 1990. PLB 24.95 (*0-7933-1669-3*); pap. 14.95 (*0-7933-1670-7*); disk 29.95 (*0-7933-1671-5*) Gallopade Pub Group.
—The Beast of the Maine Bed & Breakfast. (Illus.). (gr. 3-8). 1990. PLB 24.95 (*0-7933-1681-2*); pap. 14.95 (*0-7933-1682-0*) (*0-7933-1683-9*) Gallopade Pub Group.
—The Beast of the Maryland Bed & Breakfast. (Illus.). (gr. 3-8). 1990. PLB 24.95 (*0-7933-1690-1*); pap. 14.95 (*0-7933-1691-X*); disk 29.95 (*0-7933-1692-8*) Gallopade Pub Group.
—The Beast of the Massachusetts Bed & Breakfast. (Illus.). (gr. 3-8). 1990. PLB 24.95 (*0-7933-1699-5*); pap. 14.95 (*0-7933-1700-2*); disk 29.95 (*0-7933-1701-0*) Gallopade Pub Group.
—The Beast of the Michigan Bed & Breakfast. (Illus.). (gr. 3 up). 1990. PLB 24.95 (*0-7933-1708-8*); pap. 14.95 (*0-7933-1709-6*); computer disk 29.95 (*0-7933-1710-X*) Gallopade Pub Group.
—The Beast of the Minnesota Bed & Breakfast. (Illus.). (gr. 3 up). 1990. PLB 24.95 (*0-7933-1714-2*); pap. 14.95 (*0-7933-1715-0*); computer disk 29.95 (*0-7933-1716-9*) Gallopade Pub Group.
—The Beast of the Mississippi Bed & Breakfast. (Illus.). (gr. 3 up). 1990. PLB 24.95 (*0-7933-0644-2*); pap. 14.95 (*0-7933-1726-6*); computer disk 29.95 (*0-7933-1727-4*) Gallopade Pub Group.
—The Beast of the Missouri Bed & Breakfast. (Illus.). (gr. 3 up). 1990. PLB 24.95 (*0-7933-1734-7*); pap. 14.95 (*0-7933-1735-5*); computer disk 29.95 (*0-685-45946-2*) Gallopade Pub Group.
—The Beast of the Montana Bed & Breakfast. (Illus.). (gr. 3 up). 1990. PLB 24.95 (*0-7933-1743-6*); pap. 14.95 (*0-7933-1744-4*); computer disk 29.95 (*0-7933-1745-2*) Gallopade Pub Group.
—The Beast of the Nebraska Bed & Breakfast. (Illus.). (gr. 3 up). 1990. PLB 24.95 (*0-7933-1752-5*); pap. 14.95 (*0-7933-1753-3*); computer disk 29.95 (*0-7933-1754-1*) Gallopade Pub Group.
—The Beast of the Nevada Bed & Breakfast. (Illus.). 1990. PLB 24.95 (*0-7933-1761-4*); pap. 14.95 (*0-7933-1762-2*); computer disk 29.95 (*0-7933-1763-0*) Gallopade Pub Group.
—The Beast of the New Hampshire Bed & Breakfast. (Illus.). 1990. PLB 24.95 (*0-7933-1770-3*); pap. 14.95 (*0-7933-1771-1*); computer disk 29.95 (*0-7933-1772-X*) Gallopade Pub Group.
—The Beast of the New Jersey Bed & Breakfast. (Illus.). 1990. PLB 24.95 (*0-7933-1779-7*); pap. 14.95 (*0-7933-1780-0*); computer disk 29.95 (*0-7933-1781-9*) Gallopade Pub Group.
—The Beast of the New Mexico Bed & Breakfast. (Illus.). 1990. PLB 24.95 (*0-7933-1812-2*); pap. 14.95 (*0-7933-1813-0*); computer disk 29.95 (*0-7933-1814-9*) Gallopade Pub Group.
—The Beast of the New York Bed & Breakfast. (Illus.). 1990. PLB 24.95 (*0-7933-1821-1*); pap. 14.95 (*0-7933-1822-X*); computer disk 29.95 (*0-7933-1823-8*) Gallopade Pub Group.
—The Beast of the North Dakota Bed & Breakfast. (Illus.). 1990. PLB 24.95 (*0-7933-1839-4*); pap. 14.95 (*0-7933-1840-8*); computer disk 29.95 (*0-7933-1841-6*) Gallopade Pub Group.
—The Beast of the Ohio Bed & Breakfast. (Illus.). 1990. PLB 24.95 (*0-7933-0905-0*); pap. 14.95 (*0-7933-1848-3*); computer disk 29.95 (*0-7933-1849-1*) Gallopade Pub Group.
—The Beast of the Oklahoma Bed & Breakfast. (Illus.). 1990. PLB 24.95 (*0-7933-1869-6*); pap. 14.95 (*0-7933-1870-X*); computer disk 29.95 (*0-7933-1871-8*) Gallopade Pub Group.
—The Beast of the Oregon Bed & Breakfast. (Illus.). 1990. PLB 24.95 (*0-7933-1901-3*); pap. 14.95 (*0-7933-1902-1*); computer disk 29.95 (*0-7933-1903-X*) Gallopade Pub Group.
—The Beast of the Pennsylvania Bed & Breakfast. (Illus.). 1990. PLB 24.95 (*0-7933-1933-1*); pap. 14.95 (*0-7933-1934-X*); computer disk 29.95 (*0-7933-1935-8*) Gallopade Pub Group.
—The Beast of the Rhode Island Bed & Breakfast. (Illus.). 1990. PLB 24.95 (*0-7933-1965-X*); pap. 14.95 (*0-7933-1966-8*); computer disk 29.95 (*0-7933-1967-6*) Gallopade Pub Group.
—The Beast of the South Carolina Bed & Breakfast. (Illus.). 1990. PLB 24.95 (*0-7933-1995-1*); pap. 14.95 (*0-7933-1996-X*); computer disk 29.95 (*0-7933-1997-8*) Gallopade Pub Group.
—The Beast of the South Dakota Bed & Breakfast. (Illus.). 1990. PLB 24.95 (*0-7933-2026-7*); pap. 14.95 (*0-7933-2027-5*); computer disk 29.95 (*0-7933-2028-3*) Gallopade Pub Group.
—The Beast of the Tennessee Bed & Breakfast. (Illus.). 1990. PLB 24.95 (*0-7933-2056-9*); pap. 14.95 (*0-7933-2057-7*); computer disk 29.95 (*0-7933-2058-5*) Gallopade Pub Group.
—The Beast of the Texas Bed & Breakfast. (Illus.). 1990. PLB 24.95 (*0-7933-2086-0*); pap. 14.95 (*0-7933-2087-9*); computer disk 29.95 (*0-7933-2088-7*) Gallopade Pub Group.
—The Beast of the Utah Bed & Breakfast. (Illus.). 1990. PLB 24.95 (*0-7933-2117-4*); pap. 14.95 (*0-7933-2118-2*); computer disk 29.95 (*0-7933-2119-0*) Gallopade Pub Group.

—The Beast of the Vermont Bed & Breakfast. (Illus.). 1990. PLB 24.95 (0-7933-2149-2); pap. 14.95 (0-7933-2150-6); computer disk 29.95 (0-7933-2151-4) Gallopade Pub Group.
—The Beast of the Virginia Bed & Breakfast. (Illus.). 1990. PLB 24.95 (0-7933-2179-4); pap. 14.95 (0-7933-2180-8); computer disk 29.95 (0-7933-2181-6) Gallopade Pub Group.
—The Beast of the Washington Bed & Breakfast. (Illus.). 1990. PLB 24.95 (0-7933-2212-X); pap. 14.95 (0-7933-2213-8); computer disk 29.95 (0-7933-2214-6) Gallopade Pub Group.
—The Beast of the Washington, D.C. Bed & Breakfast. (Illus.). (gr. 3-12). 1990. PLB 24.95 (0-7933-1468-2); pap. 14.95 (0-7933-1469-0); computer disk 29.95 (0-7933-1470-4) Gallopade Pub Group.
—The Beast of the West Virginia Bed & Breakfast. (Illus.). 1990. PLB 24.95 (0-7933-2244-8); pap. 14.95 (0-7933-2245-6); computer disk 29.95 (0-7933-2246-4) Gallopade Pub Group.
—The Beast of the Wisconsin Bed & Breakfast. (Illus.). 1990. PLB 24.95 (0-7933-2276-6); pap. 14.95 (0-7933-2277-4); computer disk 29.95 (0-7933-2278-2) Gallopade Pub Group.
—The Beast of the Wyoming Bed & Breakfast. (Illus.). 1990. PLB 24.95 (0-7933-2300-2); pap. 14.95 (0-7933-2301-0); computer disk 29.95 (0-7933-2302-9) Gallopade Pub Group.
—The Best Book of Black Biographies. (gr. 3-12). 1989. PLB 24.95 (1-55609-330-6); pap. 14.95 (1-55609-329-2); computer disk 29.95 (1-55609-331-4) Gallopade Pub Group.
—The Best of the Alaska Bed & Breakfast. (Illus.). (gr. 3-12). 1990. PLB 24.95 (0-7933-1349-X); pap. 14.95 (0-7933-1350-3); computer disk 29.95 (0-7933-1351-1) Gallopade Pub Group.
—The Best of the California Bed & Breakfast. (Illus.). (gr. 3-12). 1990. PLB 24.95 (0-7933-1397-X); pap. 14.95 (0-7933-1398-8); computer disk 29.95 (0-7933-1399-6) Gallopade Pub Group.
—The Best of the North Carolina Bed & Breakfast. (Illus.). 1990. PLB 24.95 (0-7933-1830-0); pap. 14.95 (0-7933-1831-9); computer disk 29.95 (0-7933-1832-7) Gallopade Pub Group.
—The Big Rio of Ross Perot! 1992. lib. bdg. 24.95 (0-7933-6942-8); pap. text ed. 14.95 (0-7933-6943-6); disk 29.95 (0-7933-6941-X) Gallopade Pub Group.
—Bill S: Shakespeare for Kids. (Illus.). (gr. 4-12). 1983. PLB 24.95 (1-55609-156-7); pap. 14.95 (0-935326-10-3) Gallopade Pub Group.
—The Biltmore House Classroom Gamebook. (Illus., Orig.). (gr. 1-12). 1986. PLB 24.95 (0-935326-83-9) Gallopade Pub Group.
—Black Business. (gr. 4-12). 1989. PLB 24.95 (1-55609-327-6); pap. 14.95 (1-55609-326-8); computer disk 29.95 (1-55609-328-4) Gallopade Pub Group.
—Black "Jography" The Paths of Our Black Pioneers. (gr. 3-12). 1989. PLB 24.95 (1-55609-321-7); pap. 14.95 (1-55609-320-9); computer disk 29.95 (1-55609-322-5) Gallopade Pub Group.
—Black Trivia, A-Z. (gr. 3-12). 1989. PLB 24.95 (1-55609-318-7); pap. 14.95 (1-55609-317-9); computer disk 29.95 (1-55609-319-5) Gallopade Pub Group.
—Blackbeard the Pirate's Missing Head Mystery Spook Kit. (Illus.). (ps-6). 1986. PLB 24.95 (0-935326-19-7) Gallopade Pub Group.
—The Blood & Guts Dingbats Book. (Illus.). (gr. 3-12). 1992. PLB 24.95 (0-7933-5398-X); pap. 14.95 (0-7933-5399-8); computer disk 29.95 (0-7933-5400-5) Gallopade Pub Group.
—Bow Wow! Alabama Dogs in History, Mystery, Legend, Lore, Humor & More! (Illus.). (gr. 3-12). 1991. PLB 24.95 (0-7933-3467-5); pap. 14.95 (0-7933-3468-3); computer disk 29.95 (0-7933-3469-1) Gallopade Pub Group.
—Bow Wow! Alaska Dogs in History, Mystery, Legend, Lore, Humor & More! (Illus.). (gr. 3-12). 1991. PLB 24.95 (0-7933-3470-5); pap. 14.95 (0-7933-3471-3); computer disk 29.95 (0-7933-3472-1) Gallopade Pub Group.
—Bow Wow! Arizona Dogs in History, Mystery, Legend, Lore, Humor & More! (Illus.). (gr. 3-12). 1991. PLB 24.95 (0-7933-3473-X); pap. 14.95 (0-7933-3474-8); computer disk 29.95 (0-7933-3475-6) Gallopade Pub Group.
—Bow Wow! Arkansas Dogs in History, Mystery, Legend, Lore, Humor & More! (Illus.). (gr. 3-12). 1991. PLB 24.95 (0-7933-3476-4); pap. 14.95 (0-7933-3477-2); computer disk 29.95 (0-7933-3478-0) Gallopade Pub Group.
—Bow Wow! California Dogs in History, Mystery, Legend, Lore, Humor & More! (Illus.). (gr. 3-12). 1991. PLB 24.95 (0-7933-3479-9); pap. 14.95 (0-7933-3480-2); computer disk 29.95 (0-7933-3481-0) Gallopade Pub Group.
—Bow Wow! Colorado Dogs in History, Mystery, Legend, Lore, Humor & More! (Illus.). (gr. 3-12). 1991. PLB 24.95 (0-7933-3482-9); pap. 14.95 (0-7933-3483-7); computer disk 29.95 (0-7933-3484-5) Gallopade Pub Group.
—Bow Wow! Connecticut Dogs in History, Mystery, Legend, Lore, Humor & More! (Illus.). (gr. 3-12). 1991. PLB 24.95 (0-7933-3485-3); pap. 14.95 (0-7933-3486-1); computer disk 29.95 (0-7933-3487-X) Gallopade Pub Group.

—Bow Wow! Delaware Dogs in History, Mystery, Legend, Lore, Humor & More! (Illus.). (gr. 3-12). 1991. PLB 24.95 (0-7933-3488-8); pap. 14.95 (0-7933-3489-6); computer disk 29.95 (0-7933-3490-X) Gallopade Pub Group.
—Bow Wow! Florida Dogs in History, Mystery, Legend, Lore, Humor & More! (Illus.). (gr. 3-12). 1991. PLB 24.95 (0-7933-3494-2); pap. 14.95 (0-7933-3495-0); computer disk 29.95 (0-7933-3496-9) Gallopade Pub Group.
—Bow Wow! Georgia Dogs in History, Mystery, Legend, Lore, Humor & More! (Illus.). (gr. 3-12). 1991. PLB 24.95 (0-7933-3497-7); pap. 14.95 (0-7933-3498-5); computer disk 29.95 (0-7933-3499-3) Gallopade Pub Group.
—Bow Wow! Hawaii Dogs in History, Mystery, Legend, Lore, Humor & More! (Illus.). (gr. 3-12). 1991. PLB 24.95 (0-7933-3500-0); pap. 14.95 (0-7933-3501-9); computer disk 29.95 (0-7933-3502-7) Gallopade Pub Group.
—Bow Wow! Idaho Dogs in History, Mystery, Legend, Lore, Humor & More! (Illus.). (gr. 3-12). 1991. PLB 24.95 (0-7933-3503-5); pap. 14.95 (0-7933-3504-3); computer disk 29.95 (0-7933-3505-1) Gallopade Pub Group.
—Bow Wow! Illinois Dogs in History, Mystery, Legend, Lore, Humor & More! (Illus.). (gr. 3-12). 1991. PLB 24.95 (0-7933-3506-X); pap. 14.95 (0-7933-3507-8); computer disk 29.95 (0-7933-3508-6) Gallopade Pub Group.
—Bow Wow! Indiana Dogs in History, Mystery, Legend, Lore, Humor & More! (Illus.). (gr. 3-12). 1991. PLB 24.95 (0-7933-3509-4); pap. 14.95 (0-7933-3510-8); computer disk 29.95 (0-7933-3511-6) Gallopade Pub Group.
—Bow Wow! Iowa Dogs in History, Mystery, Legend, Lore, Humor & More! (Illus.). (gr. 3-12). 1991. PLB 24.95 (0-7933-3512-4); pap. 14.95 (0-7933-3513-2); computer disk 29.95 (0-7933-3514-0) Gallopade Pub Group.
—Bow Wow! Kansas Dogs in History, Mystery, Legend, Lore, Humor & More! (Illus.). (gr. 3-12). 1991. PLB 24.95 (0-7933-3515-9); pap. 14.95 (0-7933-3516-7); computer disk 29.95 (0-7933-3517-5) Gallopade Pub Group.
—Bow Wow! Kentucky Dogs in History, Mystery, Legend, Lore, Humor & More! (Illus.). (gr. 3-12). 1991. PLB 24.95 (0-7933-3518-3); pap. 14.95 (0-7933-3519-1); computer disk 29.95 (0-7933-3520-5) Gallopade Pub Group.
—Bow Wow! Louisiana Dogs in History, Mystery, Legend, Lore, Humor & More! (Illus.). (gr. 3-12). 1991. PLB 24.95 (0-7933-3521-3); pap. 14.95 (0-7933-3522-1); computer disk 29.95 (0-7933-3523-X) Gallopade Pub Group.
—Bow Wow! Maine Dogs in History, Mystery, Legend, Lore, Humor & More! (Illus.). (gr. 3-12). 1991. PLB 24.95 (0-7933-3524-8); pap. 14.95 (0-7933-3525-6); computer disk 29.95 (0-7933-3526-4) Gallopade Pub Group.
—Bow Wow! Maryland Dogs in History, Mystery, Legend, Lore, Humor & More! (Illus.). (gr. 3-12). 1991. PLB 24.95 (0-7933-3527-2); pap. 14.95 (0-7933-3528-0); computer disk 29.95 (0-7933-3529-9) Gallopade Pub Group.
—Bow Wow! Massachusetts Dogs in History, Mystery, Legend, Lore, Humor & More! (Illus.). (gr. 3-12). 1991. PLB 24.95 (0-7933-3530-2); pap. 14.95 (0-7933-3531-0); computer disk 29.95 (0-7933-3532-9) Gallopade Pub Group.
—Bow Wow! Michigan Dogs in History, Mystery, Legend, Lore, Humor & More! (Illus.). (gr. 3-12). 1991. PLB 24.95 (0-7933-3533-7); pap. 14.95 (0-7933-3534-5); computer disk 29.95 (0-7933-3535-3) Gallopade Pub Group.
—Bow Wow! Minnesota Dogs in History, Mystery, Legend, Lore, Humor & More! (Illus.). (gr. 3-12). 1991. PLB 24.95 (0-7933-3536-1); pap. 14.95 (0-7933-3537-X); computer disk 29.95 (0-7933-3538-8) Gallopade Pub Group.
—Bow Wow! Mississippi Dogs in History, Mystery, Legend, Lore, Humor & More! (Illus.). (gr. 3-12). 1991. PLB 24.95 (0-7933-3539-6); pap. 14.95 (0-7933-3540-X); computer disk 29.95 (0-7933-3541-8) Gallopade Pub Group.
—Bow Wow! Missouri Dogs in History, Mystery, Legend, Lore, Humor & More! (Illus.). (gr. 3-12). 1991. PLB 24.95 (0-7933-3542-6); pap. 14.95 (0-7933-3543-4); computer disk 29.95 (0-7933-3544-2) Gallopade Pub Group.
—Bow Wow! Montana Dogs in History, Mystery, Legend, Lore, Humor & More! (Illus.). (gr. 3-12). 1991. PLB 24.95 (0-7933-3545-0); pap. 14.95 (0-7933-3546-9); computer disk 29.95 (0-7933-3547-7) Gallopade Pub Group.
—Bow Wow! Nebraska Dogs in History, Mystery, Legend, Lore, Humor & More! (Illus.). (gr. 3-12). 1991. PLB 24.95 (0-7933-3548-5); pap. 14.95 (0-7933-3549-3); computer disk 29.95 (0-7933-3550-7) Gallopade Pub Group.
—Bow Wow! Nevada Dogs in History, Mystery, Legend, Lore, Humor & More! (Illus.). (gr. 3-12). 1991. PLB 24.95 (0-7933-3551-5); pap. 14.95 (0-7933-3552-3); computer disk 29.95 (0-7933-3553-1) Gallopade Pub Group.

—Bow Wow! New Hampshire Dogs in History, Mystery, Legend, Lore, Humor & More! (Illus.). (gr. 3-12). 1991. PLB 24.95 (0-7933-3554-X); pap. 14.95 (0-7933-3555-8); computer disk 29.95 (0-7933-3556-6) Gallopade Pub Group.
—Bow Wow! New Jersey Dogs in History, Mystery, Legend, Lore, Humor & More! (Illus.). (gr. 3-12). 1991. PLB 24.95 (0-7933-3557-4); pap. 14.95 (0-7933-3558-2); computer disk 29.95 (0-7933-3559-0) Gallopade Pub Group.
—Bow Wow! New Mexico Dogs in History, Mystery, Legend, Lore, Humor & More! (Illus.). (gr. 3-12). 1991. PLB 24.95 (0-7933-3560-4); pap. 14.95 (0-7933-3561-2); computer disk 29.95 (0-7933-3562-0) Gallopade Pub Group.
—Bow Wow! New York Dogs in History, Mystery, Legend, Lore, Humor & More! (Illus.). (gr. 3-12). 1991. PLB 24.95 (0-7933-3563-9); pap. 14.95 (0-7933-3564-7); computer disk 29.95 (0-7933-3565-5) Gallopade Pub Group.
—Bow Wow! North Carolina Dogs in History, Mystery, Legend, Lore, Humor & More! (Illus.). (gr. 3-12). 1991. PLB 24.95 (0-7933-3566-3); pap. 14.95 (0-7933-3567-1); computer disk 29.95 (0-7933-3568-X) Gallopade Pub Group.
—Bow Wow! North Dakota Dogs in History, Mystery, Legend, Lore, Humor & More! (Illus.). (gr. 3-12). 1991. PLB 24.95 (0-7933-3569-8); pap. 14.95 (0-7933-3570-1); computer disk 29.95 (0-7933-3571-X) Gallopade Pub Group.
—Bow Wow! Ohio Dogs in History, Mystery, Legend, Lore, Humor & More! (Illus.). (gr. 3-12). 1991. PLB 24.95 (0-7933-3572-8); pap. 14.95 (0-7933-3573-6); computer disk 29.95 (0-7933-3574-4) Gallopade Pub Group.
—Bow Wow! Oklahoma Dogs in History, Mystery, Legend, Lore, Humor & More! (Illus.). (gr. 3-12). 1991. PLB 24.95 (0-7933-3575-2); pap. 14.95 (0-7933-3576-0); computer disk 29.95 (0-7933-3577-9) Gallopade Pub Group.
—Bow Wow! Oregon Dogs in History, Mystery, Legend, Lore, Humor & More! (Illus.). (gr. 3-12). 1991. PLB 24.95 (0-7933-3578-7); pap. 14.95 (0-7933-3579-5); computer disk 29.95 (0-7933-3580-9) Gallopade Pub Group.
—Bow Wow! Pennsylvania Dogs in History, Mystery, Legend, Lore, Humor & More! (Illus.). (gr. 3-12). 1991. PLB 24.95 (0-7933-3581-7); pap. 14.95 (0-7933-3582-5); computer disk 29.95 (0-7933-3583-3) Gallopade Pub Group.
—Bow Wow! Rhode Island Dogs in History, Mystery, Legend, Lore, Humor & More! (Illus.). (gr. 3-12). 1991. PLB 24.95 (0-7933-3584-1); pap. 14.95 (0-7933-3585-X); computer disk 29.95 (0-7933-3586-8) Gallopade Pub Group.
—Bow Wow! South Carolina Dogs in History, Mystery, Legend, Lore, Humor & More! (Illus.). (gr. 3-12). 1991. PLB 24.95 (0-7933-3587-6); pap. 14.95 (0-7933-3588-4); computer disk 29.95 (0-7933-3589-2) Gallopade Pub Group.
—Bow Wow! South Dakota Dogs in History, Mystery, Legend, Lore, Humor & More! (Illus.). (gr. 3-12). 1991. PLB 24.95 (0-7933-3590-6); pap. 14.95 (0-7933-3591-4); computer disk 29.95 (0-7933-3592-2) Gallopade Pub Group.
—Bow Wow! Tennessee Dogs in History, Mystery, Legend, Lore, Humor & More! (Illus.). (gr. 3-12). 1991. PLB 24.95 (0-7933-3593-0); pap. 14.95 (0-7933-3594-9); computer disk 29.95 (0-7933-3595-7) Gallopade Pub Group.
—Bow Wow! Texas Dogs in History, Mystery, Legend, Lore, Humor & More! (Illus.). (gr. 3-12). 1991. PLB 24.95 (0-7933-3596-5); pap. 14.95 (0-7933-3597-3); computer disk 29.95 (0-7933-3598-1) Gallopade Pub Group.
—Bow Wow! Utah Dogs in History, Mystery, Legend, Lore, Humor & More! (Illus.). (gr. 3-12). 1991. PLB 24.95 (0-7933-3599-X); pap. 14.95 (0-7933-3600-7); computer disk 29.95 (0-7933-3601-5) Gallopade Pub Group.
—Bow Wow! Vermont Dogs in History, Mystery, Legend, Lore, Humor & More! (Illus.). (gr. 3-12). 1991. PLB 24.95 (0-7933-3602-3); pap. 14.95 (0-7933-3603-1); computer disk 29.95 (0-7933-3604-X) Gallopade Pub Group.
—Bow Wow! Virginia Dogs in History, Mystery, Legend, Lore, Humor & More! (Illus.). (gr. 3-12). 1991. PLB 24.95 (0-7933-3605-8); pap. 14.95 (0-7933-3606-6); computer disk 29.95 (0-7933-3607-4) Gallopade Pub Group.
—Bow Wow! Washington DC Dogs in History, Mystery, Legend, Lore, Humor & More! (Illus.). (gr. 3-12). 1991. PLB 24.95 (0-7933-3491-8); pap. 14.95 (0-7933-3492-6); computer disk 29.95 (0-7933-3493-4) Gallopade Pub Group.
—Bow Wow! Washington Dogs in History, Mystery, Legend, Lore, Humor & More! (Illus.). (gr. 3-12). 1991. PLB 24.95 (0-7933-3608-2); pap. 14.95 (0-7933-3609-0); computer disk 29.95 (0-7933-3610-4) Gallopade Pub Group.
—Bow Wow! West Virginia Dogs in History, Mystery, Legend, Lore, Humor & More! (Illus.). (gr. 3-12). 1991. PLB 24.95 (0-7933-3611-2); pap. 14.95 (0-7933-3612-0); computer disk 29.95 (0-7933-3613-9) Gallopade Pub Group.

—Bow Wow! Wisconsin Dogs in History, Mystery, Legend, Lore, Humor & More! (Illus.). (gr. 3-12). 1991. PLB 24.95 (0-7933-3614-7); pap. 14.95 (0-7933-3615-5); computer disk 29.95 (0-7933-3616-3) Gallopade Pub Group.

—Bow Wow! Wyoming Dogs in History, Mystery, Legend, Lore, Humor & More! (Illus.). (gr. 3-12). 1991. PLB 24.95 (0-7933-3617-1); pap. 14.95 (0-7933-3618-X); computer disk 29.95 (0-7933-3619-8) Gallopade Pub Group.

—The Boy-Is-This-Place-Big Biltmore House Spark Kit. (Illus., Orig.). (gr. 3-12). 1986. PLB 24.95 (0-935326-22-7) Gallopade Pub Group.

—California & Other State Greats (Biographies) (Illus.). (gr. 3-12). 1990. PLB 24.95 (1-55609-521-X); pap. 14.95 (1-55609-520-1); computer disk 29.95 (0-7933-1405-4) Gallopade Pub Group.

—California Bandits, Bushwackers, Outlaws, Crooks, Devils, Ghosts, Desperadoes & Other Assorted & Sundry Characters! (Illus.). (gr. 3-12). 1990. PLB 24.95 (0-7933-0166-1); pap. 14.95 (0-7933-0165-3); computer disk 29.95 (0-7933-0167-X) Gallopade Pub Group.

—California Classic Christmas Trivia: Stories, Recipes, Activities, Legends, Lore & More! (Illus.). (gr. 3-12). 1990. PLB 24.95 (0-7933-0169-6); pap. 14.95 (0-7933-0168-8); computer disk 29.95 (0-7933-0170-X) Gallopade Pub Group.

—California Coastales. (Illus.). (gr. 3-12). 1990. PLB 24.95 (1-55609-517-1); pap. 14.95 (1-55609-516-3); computer disk 29.95 (0-7933-1401-1) Gallopade Pub Group.

—California Coastales! 1992. lib. bdg. 24.95 (0-7933-7269-0) Gallopade Pub Group.

—California "Crinkum-Crankum" A Funny Word Book about Our State. (Illus.). 1992. lib. bdg. 24.95 (0-7933-4822-6); pap. 14.95 (0-7933-4823-4); disk 29.95 (0-7933-4824-2) Gallopade Pub Group.

—California Dingbats! Bk. 1: A Fun Book of Games, Stories, Activities & More about Our State That's All in Code! for You to Decipher. (Illus.). (gr. 3-12). 1991. PLB 24.95 (0-7933-3785-2); pap. 14.95 (0-7933-3786-0); computer disk 29.95 (0-7933-3787-9) Gallopade Pub Group.

—California Festival Fun for Kids! (Illus.). (gr. 3-12). 1991. lib. bdg. 24.95 (0-7933-3938-3); pap. 14.95 (0-7933-3939-1); disk 29.95 (0-7933-3940-5) Gallopade Pub Group.

—The California Hot Air Balloon Mystery. (Illus.). (gr. 2-9). 1990. 24.95 (0-7933-2354-1); pap. 14.95 (0-7933-2355-X); computer disk 29.95 (0-7933-2356-8) Gallopade Pub Group.

—California Jeopardy! Answers & Questions about Our State! (Illus.). (gr. 3-12). 1991. PLB 24.95 (0-7933-4091-8); pap. 14.95 (0-7933-4092-6); computer disk 29.95 (0-7933-4093-4) Gallopade Pub Group.

—California "Jography" A Fun Run Thru Our State! (Illus.). (gr. 3-12). 1990. PLB 24.95 (1-55609-511-2); pap. 14.95 (1-55609-510-4); computer disk 29.95 (0-685-45935-7) Gallopade Pub Group.

—California Kid's Cookbook: Recipes, How-to, History, Lore & More! (Illus.). (gr. 3-12). 1990. PLB 24.95 (0-7933-0178-5); pap. 14.95 (0-7933-0177-7); computer disk 29.95 (0-7933-0179-3) Gallopade Pub Group.

—The California Mystery Van Takes Off! Book 1: Handicapped California Kids Sneak Off on a Big Adventure. (Illus.). (gr. 3-12). 1992. 24.95 (0-7933-4976-1); pap. 14.95 (0-7933-4977-X); computer disk 29.95 (0-7933-4978-8) Gallopade Pub Group.

—California Quiz Bowl Crash Course! (Illus.). (gr. 3-12). 1990. PLB 24.95 (1-55609-519-8); pap. 14.95 (1-55609-518-X); computer disk 29.95 (0-7933-1400-3) Gallopade Pub Group.

—California Rollercoasters! (Illus.). (gr. 3-12). 1992. PLB 24.95 (0-7933-5236-3); pap. 14.95 (0-7933-5237-1); computer disk 29.95 (0-7933-5238-X) Gallopade Pub Group.

—California School Trivia: An Amazing & Fascinating Look at Our State's Teachers, Schools & Students! (Illus.). (gr. 3-12). 1990. PLB 24.95 (0-7933-0175-0); pap. 14.95 (0-7933-0174-2); computer disk 29.95 (0-7933-0176-9) Gallopade Pub Group.

—California Silly Basketball Sportsmysteries, Vol. I. (Illus.). (gr. 3-12). 1990. lib. 24.95 (0-7933-0172-6); pap. 14.95 (0-7933-0171-8); computer disk 29.95 (0-7933-0173-4) Gallopade Pub Group.

—California Silly Basketball Sportsmysteries, Vol. II. (Illus.). (gr. 3-12). 1990. PLB 24.95 (0-7933-1574-3); pap. 14.95 (0-7933-1575-1); computer disk 29.95 (0-7933-1576-X) Gallopade Pub Group.

—California Silly Football Sportsmysteries, Vol. I. (Illus.). (gr. 3-12). 1990. PLB 24.95 (1-55609-515-5); pap. 14.95 (1-55609-514-7); computer disk 29.95 (0-7933-1396-1) Gallopade Pub Group.

—California Silly Football Sportsmysteries, Vol. II. (Illus.). (gr. 3-12). 1990. PLB 24.95 (0-7933-1394-5); pap. 14.95 (0-7933-1395-3); computer disk 29.95 (0-685-45936-5) Gallopade Pub Group.

—California Silly Trivia! (Illus.). (gr. 3-12). 1990. PLB 24.95 (1-55609-509-0); pap. 14.95 (1-55609-508-2); computer disk 29.95 (0-7933-1390-2) Gallopade Pub Group.

—California Timeline: A Chronology of California History, Mystery, Trivia, Legend, Lore & More. (Illus.). (gr. 3-12). 1992. PLB 24.95 (0-7933-5887-6); pap. 14.95 (0-7933-5888-4); computer disk 29.95 (0-7933-5889-2) Gallopade Pub Group.

—California's (Most Devastating!) Disasters & (Most Calamitous!) Catastrophies! (Illus.). (gr. 3-12). 1990. PLB 24.95 (0-7933-0163-7); pap. 14.95 (0-7933-0162-9); computer disk 29.95 (0-7933-0164-5) Gallopade Pub Group.

—California's Unsolved Mysteries (& Their "Solutions") Includes Scientific Information & Other Activities for Students. (Illus.). (gr. 3-12). 1992. PLB 24.95 (0-7933-5734-9); pap. 14.95 (0-7933-5735-7); computer disk 29.95 (0-7933-5736-5) Gallopade Pub Group.

—Carole Marsh Kentucky Books, 31 bks. (Illus.). (gr. 3-8). 1990. Set. PLB 638.45 (0-7933-1292-2) Gallopade Pub Group.

—Carole Marsh Louisiana Books, 31 bks. (Illus.). (gr. 3-8). 1990. Set. PLB 638.45 (0-7933-1293-0) Gallopade Pub Group.

—Carole Marsh Maine Books, 31 bks. (Illus.). (gr. 3-8). 1990. Set. PLB 638.45 (0-7933-1294-9) Gallopade Pub Group.

—Carole Marsh Massachusetts Books, 31 bks. (Illus.). (gr. 3-8). 1990. Set. PLB 638.45 (0-7933-1296-5) Gallopade Pub Group.

—Castle Hayne. (Illus.). 60p. (gr. 4-12). 1988. PLB 19.95 (1-55609-159-1); pap. 14.95 (1-55609-241-5) Gallopade Pub Group.

—Chill Out: Scary Alabama Tales Based on Frightening Alabama Truths. (Illus.). 1992. lib. bdg. 24.95 (0-7933-4657-6); pap. 14.95 (0-7933-4658-4); disk 29.95 (0-7933-4659-2) Gallopade Pub Group.

—Chill Out: Scary Alaska Tales Based on Frightening Alaska Truths. (Illus.). 1992. lib. bdg. 24.95 (0-7933-4660-6); pap. 14.95 (0-7933-4661-4); disk 29.95 (0-7933-4662-2) Gallopade Pub Group.

—Chill Out: Scary Arizona Tales Based on Frightening Arizona Truths. (Illus.). 1992. lib. bdg. 24.95 (0-7933-4663-0); pap. 14.95 (0-7933-4664-9); disk 29.95 (0-7933-4665-7) Gallopade Pub Group.

—Chill Out: Scary Arkansas Tales Based on Frightening Arkansas Truths. (Illus.). 1992. lib. bdg. 24.95 (0-7933-4666-5); pap. 14.95 (0-7933-4667-3); disk 29.95 (0-7933-4668-1) Gallopade Pub Group.

—Chill Out: Scary California Tales Based on Frightening California Truths. (Illus.). 1992. lib. bdg. 24.95 (0-7933-4669-X); pap. 14.95 (0-7933-4670-3); disk 29.95 (0-7933-4671-1) Gallopade Pub Group.

—Chill Out: Scary Colorado Tales Based on Frightening Colorado Truths. (Illus.). 1992. lib. bdg. 24.95 (0-7933-4672-X); pap. 14.95 (0-7933-4673-8); disk 29.95 (0-7933-4674-6) Gallopade Pub Group.

—Chill Out: Scary Connecticut Tales Based on Frightening Connecticut Truths. (Illus.). 1992. lib. bdg. 24.95 (0-7933-4675-4); pap. 14.95 (0-7933-4676-2); disk 29.95 (0-7933-4677-0) Gallopade Pub Group.

—Chill Out: Scary Delaware Tales Based on Frightening Delaware Truths. (Illus.). 1992. lib. bdg. 24.95 (0-7933-4678-9); pap. 14.95 (0-7933-4679-7); disk 29.95 (0-7933-4680-0) Gallopade Pub Group.

—Chill Out: Scary Florida Tales Based on Frightening Florida Truths. (Illus.). 1992. lib. bdg. 24.95 (0-7933-4681-9); pap. 14.95 (0-7933-4682-7); disk 29.95 (0-7933-4683-5) Gallopade Pub Group.

—Chill Out: Scary Georgia Tales Based on Frightening Georgia Truths. (Illus.). 1992. lib. bdg. 24.95 (0-7933-4684-3); pap. 14.95 (0-7933-4685-1); disk 29.95 (0-7933-4686-X) Gallopade Pub Group.

—Chill Out: Scary Hawaii Tales Based on Frightening Hawaii Truths. (Illus.). 1992. lib. bdg. 24.95 (0-7933-4687-8); pap. 14.95 (0-7933-4688-6); disk 29.95 (0-7933-4689-4) Gallopade Pub Group.

—Chill Out: Scary Idaho Tales Based on Frightening Idaho Truths. (Illus.). 1992. lib. bdg. 24.95 (0-7933-4690-8); pap. 14.95 (0-7933-4691-6); disk 29.95 (0-7933-4692-4) Gallopade Pub Group.

—Chill Out: Scary Illinois Tales Based on Frightening Illinois Truths. (Illus.). 1992. lib. bdg. 24.95 (0-7933-4693-2); pap. 14.95 (0-7933-4694-0); disk 29.95 (0-7933-4695-9) Gallopade Pub Group.

—Chill Out: Scary Indiana Tales Based on Frightening Indiana Truths. (Illus.). 1992. lib. bdg. 24.95 (0-7933-4696-7); pap. 14.95 (0-7933-4697-5); disk 29.95 (0-7933-4698-3) Gallopade Pub Group.

—Chill Out: Scary Iowa Tales Based on Frightening Iowa Truths. (Illus.). 1992. lib. bdg. 24.95 (0-7933-4699-1); pap. 14.95 (0-7933-4700-9); disk 29.95 (0-7933-4701-7) Gallopade Pub Group.

—Chill Out: Scary Kansas Tales Based on Frightening Kansas Truths. (Illus.). 1992. lib. bdg. 24.95 (0-7933-4702-5); pap. 14.95 (0-7933-4703-3); disk 29.95 (0-7933-4704-1) Gallopade Pub Group.

—Chill Out: Scary Kentucky Tales Based on Frightening Kentucky Truths. (Illus.). 1992. lib. bdg. 24.95 (0-7933-4705-X); pap. 14.95 (0-7933-4706-8); disk 29.95 (0-7933-4707-6) Gallopade Pub Group.

—Chill Out: Scary Louisiana Tales Based on Frightening Louisiana Truths. (Illus.). 1992. lib. bdg. 24.95 (0-7933-4708-4); pap. 14.95 (0-7933-4709-2); disk 29.95 (0-7933-4710-6) Gallopade Pub Group.

—Chill Out: Scary Maine Tales Based on Frightening Maine Truths. (Illus.). 1992. lib. bdg. 24.95 (0-7933-4711-4); pap. 14.95 (0-7933-4712-2); disk 29.95 (0-7933-4713-0) Gallopade Pub Group.

—Chill Out: Scary Maryland Tales Based on Frightening Maryland Truths. (Illus.). 1992. lib. bdg. 24.95 (0-7933-4714-9); pap. 14.95 (0-7933-4715-7); disk 29.95 (0-7933-4716-5) Gallopade Pub Group.

—Chill Out: Scary Massachusetts Tales Based on Frightening Massachusetts Truths. (Illus.). 1992. lib. bdg. 24.95 (0-7933-4717-3); pap. 14.95 (0-7933-4718-1); disk 29.95 (0-7933-4719-X) Gallopade Pub Group.

—Chill Out: Scary Michigan Tales Based on Frightening Michigan Truths. (Illus.). 1992. lib. bdg. 24.95 (0-7933-4720-3); pap. 14.95 (0-7933-4721-1); disk 29.95 (0-7933-4722-X) Gallopade Pub Group.

—Chill Out: Scary Minnesota Tales Based on Frightening Minnesota Truths. (Illus.). 1992. lib. bdg. 24.95 (0-7933-4723-8); pap. 14.95 (0-7933-4724-6); disk 29.95 (0-7933-4725-4) Gallopade Pub Group.

—Chill Out: Scary Mississippi Tales Based on Frightening Mississippi Truths. (Illus.). 1992. lib. bdg. 24.95 (0-7933-4726-2); pap. 14.95 (0-7933-4727-0); disk 29.95 (0-7933-4728-9) Gallopade Pub Group.

—Chill Out: Scary Missouri Tales Based on Frightening Missouri Truths. (Illus.). 1992. lib. bdg. 24.95 (0-7933-4729-7); pap. 14.95 (0-7933-4730-0); disk 29.95 (0-7933-4731-9) Gallopade Pub Group.

—Chill Out: Scary Montana Tales Based on Frightening Montana Truths. (Illus.). 1992. lib. bdg. 24.95 (0-7933-4732-7); pap. 14.95 (0-7933-4733-5); disk 29.95 (0-7933-4734-3) Gallopade Pub Group.

—Chill Out: Scary Nebraska Tales Based on Frightening Nebraska Truths. (Illus.). 1992. lib. bdg. 24.95 (0-7933-4735-1); pap. 14.95 (0-7933-4736-X); disk 29.95 (0-7933-4737-8) Gallopade Pub Group.

—Chill Out: Scary Nevada Tales Based on Frightening Nevada Truths. (Illus.). 1992. lib. bdg. 24.95 (0-7933-4738-6); pap. 14.95 (0-7933-4739-4); disk 29.95 (0-7933-4740-8) Gallopade Pub Group.

—Chill Out: Scary New Hampshire Tales Based on Frightening New Hampshire Truths. (Illus.). 1992. lib. bdg. 24.95 (0-7933-4741-6); pap. 14.95 (0-7933-4742-4); disk 29.95 (0-7933-4743-2) Gallopade Pub Group.

—Chill Out: Scary New Jersey Tales Based on Frightening New Jersey Truths. (Illus.). 1992. lib. bdg. 24.95 (0-7933-4744-0); pap. 14.95 (0-7933-4745-9); disk 29.95 (0-7933-4746-7) Gallopade Pub Group.

—Chill Out: Scary New Mexico Tales Based on Frightening New Mexico Truths. (Illus.). 1992. lib. bdg. 24.95 (0-7933-4747-5); pap. 14.95 (0-7933-4748-3); disk 29.95 (0-7933-4749-1) Gallopade Pub Group.

—Chill Out: Scary New York Tales Based on Frightening New York Truths. (Illus.). 1992. lib. bdg. 24.95 (0-7933-4750-5); pap. 14.95 (0-7933-4751-3); disk 29.95 (0-7933-4752-1) Gallopade Pub Group.

—Chill Out: Scary North Carolina Tales Based on Frightening North Carolina Truths. (Illus.). 1992. lib. bdg. 24.95 (0-7933-4753-X); pap. 14.95 (0-7933-4754-8); disk 29.95 (0-7933-4755-6) Gallopade Pub Group.

—Chill Out: Scary North Dakota Tales Based on Frightening North Dakota Truths. (Illus.). 1992. lib. bdg. 24.95 (0-7933-4756-4); pap. 14.95 (0-7933-4757-2); disk 29.95 (0-7933-4758-0) Gallopade Pub Group.

—Chill Out: Scary Ohio Tales Based on Frightening Ohio Truths. (Illus.). 1992. lib. bdg. 24.95 (0-7933-4759-9); pap. 14.95 (0-7933-4760-2); disk 29.95 (0-7933-4761-0) Gallopade Pub Group.

—Chill Out: Scary Oklahoma Tales Based on Frightening Oklahoma Truths. (Illus.). 1992. lib. bdg. 24.95 (0-7933-4762-9); pap. 14.95 (0-7933-4763-7); disk 29.95 (0-7933-4764-5) Gallopade Pub Group.

—Chill Out: Scary Oregon Tales Based on Frightening Oregon Truths. (Illus.). 1992. lib. bdg. 24.95 (0-7933-4765-3); pap. 14.95 (0-7933-4766-1); disk 29.95 (0-7933-4767-X) Gallopade Pub Group.

—Chill Out: Scary Pennsylvania Tales Based on Frightening Pennsylvania Truths. (Illus.). 1992. lib. bdg. 24.95 (0-7933-4768-8); pap. 14.95 (0-7933-4769-6); disk 29.95 (0-7933-4770-X) Gallopade Pub Group.

—Chill Out: Scary Rhode Island Tales Based on Frightening Rhode Island Truths. (Illus.). 1992. lib. bdg. 24.95 (0-7933-4771-8); pap. 14.95 (0-7933-4772-6); disk 29.95 (0-7933-4773-4) Gallopade Pub Group.

—Chill Out: Scary South Carolina Tales Based on Frightening South Carolina Truths. (Illus.). 1992. lib. bdg. 24.95 (0-7933-4774-2); pap. 14.95 (0-7933-4775-0); disk 29.95 (0-7933-4776-9) Gallopade Pub Group.

—Chill Out: Scary South Dakota Tales Based on Frightening South Dakota Truths. (Illus.). 1992. lib. bdg. 24.95 (0-7933-4777-7); pap. 14.95 (0-7933-4778-5); disk 29.95 (0-7933-4779-3) Gallopade Pub Group.

—Chill Out: Scary Tennessee Tales Based on Frightening Tennessee Truths. (Illus.). 1992. lib. bdg. 24.95 (0-7933-4780-7); pap. 14.95 (0-7933-4781-5); disk 29.95 (0-7933-4782-3) Gallopade Pub Group.

—Chill Out: Scary Texas Tales Based on Frightening Texas Truths. (Illus.). 1992. lib. bdg. 24.95 (0-7933-4783-1); pap. 14.95 (0-7933-4784-X); disk 29.95 (0-7933-4785-8) Gallopade Pub Group.

—Chill Out: Scary Utah Tales Based on Frightening Utah Truths. (Illus.). 1992. lib. bdg. 24.95 (*0-7933-4786-6*); pap. 14.95 (*0-7933-4787-4*); disk 29.95 (*0-7933-4788-2*) Gallopade Pub Group.

—Chill Out: Scary Vermont Tales Based on Frightening Vermont Truths. (Illus.). 1992. lib. bdg. 24.95 (*0-7933-4789-0*); pap. 14.95 (*0-7933-4790-4*); disk 29.95 (*0-7933-4791-2*) Gallopade Pub Group.

—Chill Out: Scary Virginia Tales Based on Frightening Virginia Truths. (Illus.). 1992. lib. bdg. 24.95 (*0-7933-4792-0*); pap. 14.95 (*0-7933-4793-9*); disk 29.95 (*0-7933-4794-7*) Gallopade Pub Group.

—Chill Out: Scary Washington DC Tales Based on Frightening Washington DC Truths. (Illus.). 1992. lib. bdg. 24.95 (*0-7933-4798-X*); pap. 14.95 (*0-7933-4799-8*); disk 29.95 (*0-7933-4800-5*) Gallopade Pub Group.

—Chill Out: Scary Washington Tales Based on Frightening Washington Truths. (Illus.). 1992. lib. bdg. 24.95 (*0-7933-4795-5*); pap. 14.95 (*0-7933-4796-3*); disk 29.95 (*0-7933-4797-1*) Gallopade Pub Group.

—Chill Out: Scary West Virginia Tales Based on Frightening West Virginia Truths. (Illus.). 1992. lib. bdg. 24.95 (*0-7933-4801-3*); pap. 14.95 (*0-7933-4802-1*); disk 29.95 (*0-7933-4803-X*) Gallopade Pub Group.

—Chill Out: Scary Wisconsin Tales Based on Frightening Wisconsin Truths. (Illus.). 1992. lib. bdg. 24.95 (*0-7933-4804-8*); pap. 14.95 (*0-7933-4805-6*); disk 29.95 (*0-7933-4806-4*) Gallopade Pub Group.

—Chill Out: Scary Wyoming Tales Based on Frightening Wyoming Truths. (Illus.). 1992. lib. bdg. 24.95 (*0-7933-4807-2*); pap. 14.95 (*0-7933-4808-0*); disk 29.95 (*0-7933-4809-9*) Gallopade Pub Group.

—Christopher Columbus Comes to Alabama! Includes Reproducible Activities for Kids! (Illus.). (gr. 3-12). 1991. PLB 24.95 (*0-7933-3620-1*); pap. 14.95 (*0-7933-3621-X*); computer disk 29.95 (*0-7933-3622-8*) Gallopade Pub Group.

—Christopher Columbus Comes to Alaska! Includes Reproducible Activities for Kids! (Illus.). (gr. 3-12). 1991. PLB 24.95 (*0-7933-3623-6*); pap. 14.95 (*0-7933-3624-4*); computer disk 29.95 (*0-7933-3625-2*) Gallopade Pub Group.

—Christopher Columbus Comes to Arizona! Includes Reproducible Activities for Kids! (Illus.). (gr. 3-12). 1991. PLB 24.95 (*0-7933-3626-0*); pap. 14.95 (*0-7933-3627-9*); computer disk 29.95 (*0-7933-3628-7*) Gallopade Pub Group.

—Christopher Columbus Comes to Arkansas! Includes Reproducible Activities for Kids! (Illus.). (gr. 3-12). 1991. PLB 24.95 (*0-7933-3629-5*); pap. 14.95 (*0-7933-3630-9*); computer disk 29.95 (*0-7933-3631-7*) Gallopade Pub Group.

—Christopher Columbus Comes to California! Includes Reproducible Activities for Kids! (Illus.). (gr. 3-12). 1991. PLB 24.95 (*0-7933-3632-5*); pap. 14.95 (*0-7933-3633-3*); computer disk 29.95 (*0-7933-3634-1*) Gallopade Pub Group.

—Christopher Columbus Comes to Colorado! Includes Reproducible Activities for Kids! (Illus.). (gr. 3-12). 1991. PLB 24.95 (*0-7933-3635-X*); pap. 14.95 (*0-7933-3636-8*); computer disk 29.95 (*0-7933-3637-6*) Gallopade Pub Group.

—Christopher Columbus Comes to Connecticut! Includes Reproducible Activities for Kids! (Illus.). (gr. 3-12). 1991. PLB 24.95 (*0-7933-3638-4*); pap. 14.95 (*0-7933-3639-2*); computer disk 29.95 (*0-7933-3640-6*) Gallopade Pub Group.

—Christopher Columbus Comes to Delaware! Includes Reproducible Activities for Kids! (Illus.). (gr. 3-12). 1991. PLB 24.95 (*0-7933-3641-4*); pap. 14.95 (*0-7933-3642-2*); computer disk 29.95 (*0-7933-3643-0*) Gallopade Pub Group.

—Christopher Columbus Comes to Florida! Includes Reproducible Activities for Kids! (Illus.). (gr. 3-12). 1991. PLB 24.95 (*0-7933-3647-3*); pap. 14.95 (*0-7933-3648-1*); computer disk 29.95 (*0-7933-3649-X*) Gallopade Pub Group.

—Christopher Columbus Comes to Georgia! Includes Reproducible Activities for Kids! (Illus.). (gr. 3-12). 1991. PLB 24.95 (*0-7933-3650-3*); pap. 14.95 (*0-7933-3651-1*); computer disk 29.95 (*0-7933-3652-X*) Gallopade Pub Group.

—Christopher Columbus Comes to Hawaii! Includes Reproducible Activities for Kids! (Illus.). (gr. 3-12). 1991. PLB 24.95 (*0-7933-3653-8*); pap. 14.95 (*0-7933-3654-6*); computer disk 29.95 (*0-7933-3655-4*) Gallopade Pub Group.

—Christopher Columbus Comes to Idaho! Includes Reproducible Activities for Kids! (Illus.). (gr. 3-12). 1991. PLB 24.95 (*0-7933-3656-2*); pap. 14.95 (*0-7933-3657-0*); computer disk 29.95 (*0-7933-3658-9*) Gallopade Pub Group.

—Christopher Columbus Comes to Illinois! Includes Reproducible Activities for Kids! (Illus.). (gr. 3-12). 1991. PLB 24.95 (*0-7933-3659-7*); pap. 14.95 (*0-7933-3660-0*); computer disk 29.95 (*0-7933-3661-9*) Gallopade Pub Group.

—Christopher Columbus Comes to Indiana! Includes Reproducible Activities for Kids! (Illus.). (gr. 3-12). 1991. PLB 24.95 (*0-7933-3662-7*); pap. 14.95 (*0-7933-3663-5*); computer disk 29.95 (*0-7933-3664-3*) Gallopade Pub Group.

—Christopher Columbus Comes to Iowa! Includes Reproducible Activities for Kids! (Illus.). (gr. 3-12). 1991. PLB 24.95 (*0-7933-3665-1*); pap. 14.95 (*0-7933-3666-X*); computer disk 29.95 (*0-7933-3667-8*) Gallopade Pub Group.

—Christopher Columbus Comes to Kansas! Includes Reproducible Activities for Kids! (Illus.). (gr. 3-12). 1991. PLB 24.95 (*0-7933-3668-6*); pap. 14.95 (*0-7933-3669-4*); computer disk 29.95 (*0-7933-3670-8*) Gallopade Pub Group.

—Christopher Columbus Comes to Kentucky! Includes Reproducible Activities for Kids! (Illus.). (gr. 3-12). 1991. PLB 24.95 (*0-7933-3671-6*); pap. 14.95 (*0-7933-3672-4*); computer disk 29.95 (*0-7933-3673-2*) Gallopade Pub Group.

—Christopher Columbus Comes to Louisiana! Includes Reproducible Activities for Kids! (Illus.). (gr. 3-12). 1991. PLB 24.95 (*0-7933-3674-0*); pap. 14.95 (*0-7933-3675-9*); computer disk 29.95 (*0-7933-3676-7*) Gallopade Pub Group.

—Christopher Columbus Comes to Maine! Includes Reproducible Activities for Kids! (Illus.). (gr. 3-12). 1991. PLB 24.95 (*0-7933-3677-5*); pap. 14.95 (*0-7933-3678-3*); computer disk 29.95 (*0-7933-3679-1*) Gallopade Pub Group.

—Christopher Columbus Comes to Maryland! Includes Reproducible Activities for Kids! (Illus.). (gr. 3-12). 1991. PLB 24.95 (*0-7933-3680-5*); pap. 14.95 (*0-7933-3681-3*); computer disk 29.95 (*0-7933-3682-1*) Gallopade Pub Group.

—Christopher Columbus Comes to Massachusetts! Includes Reproducible Activities for Kids! (Illus.). (gr. 3-12). 1991. PLB 24.95 (*0-7933-3683-X*); pap. 14.95 (*0-7933-3684-8*); computer disk 29.95 (*0-7933-3685-6*) Gallopade Pub Group.

—Christopher Columbus Comes to Michigan! Includes Reproducible Activities for Kids! (Illus.). (gr. 3-12). 1991. PLB 24.95 (*0-7933-3686-4*); pap. 14.95 (*0-7933-3687-2*); computer disk 29.95 (*0-7933-3688-0*) Gallopade Pub Group.

—Christopher Columbus Comes to Minnesota! Includes Reproducible Activities for Kids! (Illus.). (gr. 3-12). 1991. PLB 24.95 (*0-7933-3689-9*); pap. 14.95 (*0-7933-3690-2*); computer disk 29.95 (*0-7933-3691-0*) Gallopade Pub Group.

—Christopher Columbus Comes to Mississippi! Includes Reproducible Activities for Kids! (Illus.). (gr. 3-12). 1991. PLB 24.95 (*0-7933-3692-9*); pap. 14.95 (*0-7933-3693-7*); computer disk 29.95 (*0-7933-3694-5*) Gallopade Pub Group.

—Christopher Columbus Comes to Missouri! Includes Reproducible Activities for Kids! (Illus.). (gr. 3-12). 1991. PLB 24.95 (*0-7933-3695-3*); pap. 14.95 (*0-7933-3696-1*); computer disk 29.95 (*0-7933-3697-X*) Gallopade Pub Group.

—Christopher Columbus Comes to Montana! Includes Reproducible Activities for Kids! (Illus.). (gr. 3-12). 1991. PLB 24.95 (*0-7933-3698-8*); pap. 14.95 (*0-7933-3699-6*); computer disk 29.95 (*0-7933-3700-3*) Gallopade Pub Group.

—Christopher Columbus Comes to Nebraska! Includes Reproducible Activities for Kids! (Illus.). (gr. 3-12). 1991. PLB 24.95 (*0-7933-3701-1*); pap. 14.95 (*0-7933-3702-X*); computer disk 29.95 (*0-7933-3703-8*) Gallopade Pub Group.

—Christopher Columbus Comes to Nevada! Includes Reproducible Activities for Kids! (Illus.). (gr. 3-12). 1991. PLB 24.95 (*0-7933-3704-6*); pap. 14.95 (*0-7933-3705-4*); computer disk 29.95 (*0-7933-3706-2*) Gallopade Pub Group.

—Christopher Columbus Comes to New Hampshire! Includes Reproducible Activities for Kids! (Illus.). (gr. 3-12). 1991. PLB 24.95 (*0-7933-3707-0*); pap. 14.95 (*0-7933-3708-9*); computer disk 29.95 (*0-7933-3709-7*) Gallopade Pub Group.

—Christopher Columbus Comes to New Jersey! Includes Reproducible Activities for Kids! (Illus.). (gr. 3-12). 1991. PLB 24.95 (*0-7933-3710-0*); pap. 14.95 (*0-7933-3711-9*); computer disk 29.95 (*0-7933-3712-7*) Gallopade Pub Group.

—Christopher Columbus Comes to New Mexico! Includes Reproducible Activities for Kids! (Illus.). (gr. 3-12). 1991. PLB 24.95 (*0-7933-3713-5*); pap. 14.95 (*0-7933-3714-3*); computer disk 29.95 (*0-7933-3715-1*) Gallopade Pub Group.

—Christopher Columbus Comes to New York! Includes Reproducible Activities for Kids! (Illus.). (gr. 3-12). 1991. PLB 24.95 (*0-7933-3716-X*); pap. 14.95 (*0-7933-3717-8*); computer disk 29.95 (*0-7933-3718-6*) Gallopade Pub Group.

—Christopher Columbus Comes to North Carolina! Includes Reproducible Activities for Kids! (Illus.). (gr. 3-12). 1991. PLB 24.95 (*0-7933-3719-4*); pap. 14.95 (*0-7933-3720-8*); computer disk 29.95 (*0-7933-3721-6*) Gallopade Pub Group.

—Christopher Columbus Comes to North Dakota! Includes Reproducible Activities for Kids! (Illus.). (gr. 3-12). 1991. PLB 24.95 (*0-7933-3722-4*); pap. 14.95 (*0-7933-3723-2*); computer disk 29.95 (*0-7933-3724-0*) Gallopade Pub Group.

—Christopher Columbus Comes to Ohio! Includes Reproducible Activities for Kids! (Illus.). (gr. 3-12). 1991. PLB 24.95 (*0-7933-3725-9*); pap. 14.95 (*0-7933-3726-7*); computer disk 29.95 (*0-7933-3727-5*) Gallopade Pub Group.

—Christopher Columbus Comes to Oklahoma! Includes Reproducible Activities for Kids! (Illus.). (gr. 3-12). 1991. PLB 24.95 (*0-7933-3728-3*); pap. 14.95 (*0-7933-3729-1*); computer disk 29.95 (*0-7933-3730-5*) Gallopade Pub Group.

—Christopher Columbus Comes to Oregon! Includes Reproducible Activities for Kids! (Illus.). (gr. 3-12). 1991. PLB 24.95 (*0-7933-3731-3*); pap. 14.95 (*0-7933-3732-1*); computer disk 29.95 (*0-7933-3733-X*) Gallopade Pub Group.

—Christopher Columbus Comes to Pennsylvania! Includes Reproducible Activities for Kids! (Illus.). (gr. 3-12). 1991. PLB 24.95 (*0-7933-3734-8*); pap. 14.95 (*0-7933-3735-6*); computer disk 29.95 (*0-7933-3736-4*) Gallopade Pub Group.

—Christopher Columbus Comes to Rhode Island! Includes Reproducible Activities for Kids! (Illus.). (gr. 3-12). 1991. PLB 24.95 (*0-7933-3737-2*); pap. 14.95 (*0-7933-3738-0*); computer disk 29.95 (*0-7933-3739-9*) Gallopade Pub Group.

—Christopher Columbus Comes to South Carolina! Includes Reproducible Activities for Kids! (Illus.). (gr. 3-12). 1991. PLB 24.95 (*0-7933-3740-2*); pap. 14.95 (*0-7933-3741-0*); computer disk 29.95 (*0-7933-3742-9*) Gallopade Pub Group.

—Christopher Columbus Comes to South Dakota! Includes Reproducible Activities for Kids! (Illus.). (gr. 3-12). 1991. PLB 24.95 (*0-7933-3743-7*); pap. 14.95 (*0-7933-3744-5*); computer disk 29.95 (*0-7933-3745-3*) Gallopade Pub Group.

—Christopher Columbus Comes to Tennessee! Includes Reproducible Activities for Kids! (Illus.). (gr. 3-12). 1991. PLB 24.95 (*0-7933-3746-1*); pap. 14.95 (*0-7933-3747-X*); computer disk 29.95 (*0-7933-3748-8*) Gallopade Pub Group.

—Christopher Columbus Comes to Texas! Includes Reproducible Activities for Kids! (Illus.). (gr. 3-12). 1991. PLB 24.95 (*0-7933-3749-6*); pap. 14.95 (*0-7933-3750-X*); computer disk 29.95 (*0-7933-3751-8*) Gallopade Pub Group.

—Christopher Columbus Comes to Utah! Includes Reproducible Activities for Kids! (Illus.). (gr. 3-12). 1991. PLB 24.95 (*0-7933-3752-6*); pap. 14.95 (*0-7933-3753-4*); computer disk 29.95 (*0-7933-3754-2*) Gallopade Pub Group.

—Christopher Columbus Comes to Vermont! Includes Reproducible Activities for Kids! (Illus.). (gr. 3-12). 1991. PLB 24.95 (*0-7933-3755-0*); pap. 14.95 (*0-7933-3756-9*); computer disk 29.95 (*0-7933-3757-7*) Gallopade Pub Group.

—Christopher Columbus Comes to Virginia! Includes Reproducible Activities for Kids! (Illus.). (gr. 3-12). 1991. PLB 24.95 (*0-7933-3758-5*); pap. 14.95 (*0-7933-3759-3*); computer disk 29.95 (*0-7933-3760-7*) Gallopade Pub Group.

—Christopher Columbus Comes to Washington DC! Includes Reproducible Activities for Kids! (Illus.). (gr. 3-12). 1991. PLB 24.95 (*0-7933-3644-9*); pap. 14.95 (*0-7933-3645-7*); computer disk 29.95 (*0-7933-3646-5*) Gallopade Pub Group.

—Christopher Columbus Comes to Washington! Includes Reproducible Activities for Kids! (Illus.). (gr. 3-12). 1991. PLB 24.95 (*0-7933-3761-5*); pap. 14.95 (*0-7933-3762-3*); computer disk 29.95 (*0-7933-3763-1*) Gallopade Pub Group.

—Christopher Columbus Comes to West Virginia! Includes Reproducible Activities for Kids! (Illus.). (gr. 3-12). 1991. PLB 24.95 (*0-7933-3764-X*); pap. 14.95 (*0-7933-3765-8*); computer disk 29.95 (*0-7933-3766-6*) Gallopade Pub Group.

—Christopher Columbus Comes to Wisconsin! Includes Reproducible Activities for Kids! (Illus.). (gr. 3-12). 1991. PLB 24.95 (*0-7933-3767-4*); pap. 14.95 (*0-7933-3768-2*); computer disk 29.95 (*0-7933-3769-0*) Gallopade Pub Group.

—Christopher Columbus Comes to Wyoming! Includes Reproducible Activities for Kids! (Illus.). (gr. 3-12). 1991. PLB 24.95 (*0-7933-3770-4*); pap. 14.95 (*0-7933-3771-2*); computer disk 29.95 (*0-7933-3772-0*) Gallopade Pub Group.

—The Color Purple & All That Jazz. (gr. 3-12). 1989. PLB 24.95 (*1-55609-315-2*); pap. 14.95 (*1-55609-314-4*); computer disk 29.95 (*1-55609-316-0*) Gallopade Pub Group.

—Colorado & Other State Greats (Biographies) (Illus.). (gr. 3-12). 1990. PLB 24.95 (*1-55609-534-1*); pap. 14.95 (*1-55609-533-3*); computer disk 29.95 (*0-7933-1421-6*) Gallopade Pub Group.

—Colorado Bandits, Bushwackers, Outlaws, Crooks, Devils, Ghosts, Desperadoes & Other Assorted & Sundry Characters! (Illus.). (gr. 3-12). 1990. PLB 24.95 (*0-7933-0190-4*); pap. 14.95 (*0-7933-0189-0*); computer disk 29.95 (*0-7933-0191-2*) Gallopade Pub Group.

—Colorado Classic Christmas Trivia: Stories, Recipes, Activities, Legends, Lore & More! (Illus.). (gr. 3-12). 1990. PLB 24.95 (*0-7933-0193-9*); pap. 14.95 (*0-7933-0192-0*); computer disk 29.95 (*0-7933-0194-7*) Gallopade Pub Group.

—Colorado Coastales. (Illus.). (gr. 3-12). 1990. PLB 24.95 (*1-55609-530-9*); pap. 14.95 (*1-55609-529-5*); computer disk 29.95 (*0-7933-1417-8*) Gallopade Pub Group.

—Colorado Coastales! 1992. lib. bdg. 24.95 (*0-7933-7270-4*) Gallopade Pub Group.

—Colorado "Crinkum-Crankum" A Funny Word Book about Our State. (Illus.). 1992. lib. bdg. 24.95 (0-7933-4825-0); pap. 14.95 (0-7933-4826-9); disk 29.95 (0-7933-4827-7) Gallopade Pub Group.
—Colorado Dingbats! Bk. 1: A Fun Book of Games, Stories, Activities & More about Our State That's All in Code! for You to Decipher. (Illus.). (gr. 3-12). 1991. PLB 24.95 (0-7933-3788-7); pap. 14.95 (0-7933-3789-5); computer disk 29.95 (0-7933-3790-9) Gallopade Pub Group.
—Colorado Festival Fun for Kids! (Illus.). (gr. 3-12). 1991. lib. bdg. 24.95 (0-7933-3941-3); pap. 14.95 (0-7933-3942-1); disk 29.95 (0-7933-3943-X) Gallopade Pub Group.
—The Colorado Hot Air Balloon Mystery. (Illus.). (gr. 2-9). 1990. 24.95 (0-7933-2363-0); pap. 14.95 (0-7933-2364-9); computer disk 29.95 (0-7933-2365-7) Gallopade Pub Group.
—Colorado Jeopardy! Answers & Questions about Our State! (Illus.). (gr. 3-12). 1991. PLB 24.95 (0-7933-4094-2); pap. 14.95 (0-7933-4095-0); computer disk 29.95 (0-7933-4096-9) Gallopade Pub Group.
—Colorado "Jography" A Fun Run Thru Our State! (Illus.). (gr. 3-12). 1990. PLB 24.95 (1-55609-525-2); pap. 14.95 (1-55609-524-4); computer disk 29.95 (0-7933-1407-0) Gallopade Pub Group.
—Colorado Kid's Cookbook: Recipes, How-to, History, Lore & More! (Illus.). (gr. 3-12). 1990. PLB 24.95 (0-7933-0202-1); pap. 14.95 (0-7933-0201-3); computer disk 29.95 (0-7933-0203-X) Gallopade Pub Group.
—The Colorado Mystery Van Takes Off! Book 1: Handicapped Colorado Kids Sneak Off on a Big Adventure. (Illus.). (gr. 3-12). 1992. 24.95 (0-7933-4979-6); pap. 14.95 (0-7933-4980-X); computer disk 29.95 (0-7933-4981-8) Gallopade Pub Group.
—Colorado Quiz Bowl Crash Course! (Illus.). (gr. 3-12). 1990. PLB 24.95 (0-685-45927-6); pap. 14.95 (1-55609-531-7); computer disk 29.95 (0-7933-1416-X) Gallopade Pub Group.
—Colorado Rollercoasters! (Illus.). (gr. 3-12). 1992. PLB 24.95 (0-7933-5239-8); pap. 14.95 (0-7933-5240-1); computer disk 29.95 (0-7933-5241-X) Gallopade Pub Group.
—Colorado School Trivia: An Amazing & Fascinating Look at Our State's Teachers, Schools & Students! (Illus.). (gr. 3-12). 1990. PLB 24.95 (0-7933-0199-8); pap. 14.95 (0-7933-0198-X); computer disk 29.95 (0-7933-0200-5) Gallopade Pub Group.
—Colorado Silly Basketball Sportsmysteries, Vol. I. (Illus.). (gr. 3-12). 1990. PLB 24.95 (0-7933-0196-3); pap. 14.95 (0-7933-0195-5); computer disk 29.95 (0-7933-0197-1) Gallopade Pub Group.
—Colorado Silly Basketball Sportsmysteries, Vol. II. (Illus.). (gr. 3-12). 1990. PLB 24.95 (0-7933-1577-8); pap. 14.95 (0-7933-1578-6); computer disk 29.95 (0-7933-1579-4) Gallopade Pub Group.
—Colorado Silly Football Sportsmysteries, Vol. I. (Illus.). (gr. 3-12). 1990. PLB 24.95 (1-55609-528-7); pap. 14.95 (1-55609-527-9); computer disk 29.95 (0-7933-1409-7) Gallopade Pub Group.
—Colorado Silly Football Sportsmysteries, Vol. II. (Illus.). (gr. 3-12). 1990. PLB 24.95 (0-7933-1410-0); pap. 14.95 (0-7933-1411-9); computer disk 29.95 (0-7933-1412-7) Gallopade Pub Group.
—Colorado Silly Trivia! (Illus.). (gr. 3-12). 1990. PLB 24.95 (1-55609-523-6); pap. 14.95 (1-55609-522-8); computer disk 29.95 (0-7933-1406-2) Gallopade Pub Group.
—Colorado Timeline: A Chronology of Colorado History, Mystery, Trivia, Legend, Lore & More. (Illus.). (gr. 3-12). 1992. PLB 24.95 (0-7933-5890-6); pap. 14.95 (0-7933-5891-4); computer disk 29.95 (0-7933-5892-2) Gallopade Pub Group.
—Colorado's (Most Devastating!) Disasters & (Most Calamitous!) Catastrophies! (Illus.). (gr. 3-12). 1990. PLB 24.95 (0-7933-0187-4); pap. 14.95 (0-7933-0186-6); computer disk 29.95 (0-7933-0188-2) Gallopade Pub Group.
—Colorado's Unsolved Mysteries (& Their "Solutions") Includes Scientific Information & Other Activities for Students. (Illus.). (gr. 3-12). 1992. PLB 24.95 (0-7933-5737-3); pap. 14.95 (0-7933-5738-1); computer disk 29.95 (0-7933-5739-X) Gallopade Pub Group.
—Columbia Lastname: The Schwarzchild Radius, Bk. 1. (Orig.). (gr. 4 up). 1986. PLB 24.95 (1-55609-284-9); pap. text ed. 14.95 (0-935326-62-6) Gallopade Pub Group.
—Connecticut & Other State Greats (Biographies) (Illus.). (gr. 3-12). 1990. PLB 24.95 (1-55609-547-3); pap. 14.95 (1-55609-546-5); computer disk 29.95 (0-7933-1437-9) Gallopade Pub Group.
—Connecticut Bandits, Bushwackers, Outlaws, Crooks, Devils, Ghosts, Desperadoes & Other Assorted & Sundry Characters! (Illus.). (gr. 3-12). 1990. PLB 24.95 (0-7933-0214-5); pap. 14.95 (0-7933-0213-7); computer disk 29.95 (0-7933-0215-3) Gallopade Pub Group.
—Connecticut Classic Christmas Trivia: Stories, Recipes, Activities, Legends, Lore & More! (Illus.). (gr. 3-12). 1990. PLB 24.95 (0-7933-0217-X); pap. 14.95 (0-7933-0216-1); computer disk 29.95 (0-7933-0218-8) Gallopade Pub Group.

—Connecticut Coastales. (Illus.). (gr. 3-12). 1990. PLB 24.95 (1-55609-543-0); pap. 14.95 (1-55609-542-2); computer disk 29.95 (0-7933-1433-X) Gallopade Pub Group.
—Connecticut Coastales! 1992. lib. bdg. 24.95 (0-7933-7271-2) Gallopade Pub Group.
—Connecticut "Crinkum-Crankum" A Funny Word Book about Our State. (Illus.). 1992. lib. bdg. 24.95 (0-7933-4828-5); pap. 14.95 (0-7933-4829-3); disk 29.95 (0-7933-4830-7) Gallopade Pub Group.
—Connecticut Dingbats! Bk. 1: A Fun Book of Games, Stories, Activities & More about Our State That's All in Code! for You to Decipher. (Illus.). (gr. 3-12). 1991. PLB 24.95 (0-7933-3791-7); pap. 14.95 (0-7933-3792-5); computer disk 29.95 (0-7933-3793-3) Gallopade Pub Group.
—Connecticut Festival Fun for Kids! (Illus.). (gr. 3-12). 1991. lib. bdg. 24.95 (0-7933-3944-8); pap. 14.95 (0-7933-3945-6); disk 29.95 (0-7933-3946-4) Gallopade Pub Group.
—The Connecticut Hot Air Balloon Mystery. (Illus.). (gr. 2-9). 1990. 24.95 (0-7933-2372-X); pap. 14.95 (0-7933-2373-8); computer disk 29.95 (0-7933-2374-6) Gallopade Pub Group.
—Connecticut Jeopardy! Answers & Questions about Our State! (Illus.). (gr. 3-12). 1991. PLB 24.95 (0-7933-4097-7); pap. 14.95 (0-7933-4098-5); computer disk 29.95 (0-7933-4099-3) Gallopade Pub Group.
—Connecticut "Jography" A Fun Run Thru Our State! (Illus.). (gr. 3-12). 1990. PLB 24.95 (1-55609-538-4); pap. 14.95 (1-55609-537-6); computer disk 29.95 (0-7933-1423-2) Gallopade Pub Group.
—Connecticut Kid's Cookbook: Recipes, How-to, History, Lore & More! (Illus.). (gr. 3-12). 1990. PLB 24.95 (0-7933-0226-9); pap. 14.95 (0-7933-0225-0); computer disk 29.95 (0-7933-0227-7) Gallopade Pub Group.
—The Connecticut Mystery Van Takes Off! Book 1: Handicapped Connecticut Kids Sneak Off on a Big Adventure. (Illus.). (gr. 3-12). 1992. 24.95 (0-7933-4982-6); pap. 14.95 (0-7933-4983-4); computer disk 29.95 (0-7933-4984-2) Gallopade Pub Group.
—Connecticut Quiz Bowl Crash Course! (Illus.). (gr. 3-12). 1990. PLB 24.95 (1-55609-545-7); pap. 14.95 (1-55609-544-9); computer disk 29.95 (0-7933-1432-1) Gallopade Pub Group.
—Connecticut Rollercoasters! (Illus.). (gr. 3-12). 1992. PLB 24.95 (0-7933-5242-8); pap. 14.95 (0-7933-5243-6); computer disk 29.95 (0-7933-5244-4) Gallopade Pub Group.
—Connecticut School Trivia: An Amazing & Fascinating Look at Our State's Teachers, Schools & Students! (Illus.). (gr. 3-12). 1990. PLB 24.95 (0-7933-0223-4); pap. 14.95 (0-7933-0222-6); computer disk 29.95 (0-7933-0224-2) Gallopade Pub Group.
—Connecticut Silly Basketball Sportsmysteries, Vol. I. (Illus.). (gr. 3-12). 1990. PLB 24.95 (0-7933-0220-X); pap. 14.95 (0-7933-0219-6); computer disk 29.95 (0-7933-0221-8) Gallopade Pub Group.
—Connecticut Silly Basketball Sportsmysteries, Vol. II. (Illus.). (gr. 3-12). 1990. PLB 24.95 (0-7933-1580-8); pap. 14.95 (0-7933-1581-6); computer disk 29.95 (0-685-45929-2) Gallopade Pub Group.
—Connecticut Silly Football Sportsmysteries, Vol. I. (Illus.). (gr. 3-12). 1990. PLB 24.95 (1-55609-541-4); pap. 14.95 (1-55609-540-6); computer disk 29.95 (0-7933-1425-9) Gallopade Pub Group.
—Connecticut Silly Football Sportsmysteries, Vol. II. (Illus.). (gr. 3-12). 1990. PLB 24.95 (0-7933-1426-7); pap. 14.95 (0-7933-1427-5); computer disk 29.95 (0-7933-1428-3) Gallopade Pub Group.
—Connecticut Silly Trivia! (Illus.). (gr. 3-12). 1990. PLB 24.95 (1-55609-536-8); pap. 14.95 (1-55609-535-X); computer disk 29.95 (0-7933-1422-4) Gallopade Pub Group.
—Connecticut Timeline: A Chronology of Connecticut History, Mystery, Trivia, Legend, Lore & More. (Illus.). (gr. 3-12). 1992. PLB 24.95 (0-7933-5893-0); pap. 14.95 (0-7933-5894-9); computer disk 29.95 (0-7933-5895-7) Gallopade Pub Group.
—Connecticut's (Most Devastating!) Disasters & (Most Calamitous!) Catastrophies! (Illus.). (gr. 3-12). 1990. PLB 24.95 (0-7933-0211-0); pap. 14.95 (0-7933-0210-2); computer disk 29.95 (0-7933-0212-9) Gallopade Pub Group.
—Connecticut's Unsolved Mysteries (& Their "Solutions") Includes Scientific Information & Other Activities for Students. (Illus.). (gr. 3-12). 1992. PLB 24.95 (0-7933-5740-3); pap. 14.95 (0-7933-5741-1); computer disk 29.95 (0-7933-5742-X) Gallopade Pub Group.
—Crazy Comet Classroom Gamebook. (Illus., Orig.). (gr. 3-12). 1986. pap. 19.95 (0-935326-87-1) Gallopade Pub Group.
—The Crazy Comet Silly Trivia Book. (Illus.). 60p. (Orig.). (gr. 2-12). 1985. pap. 14.95 (0-935326-64-2) Gallopade Pub Group.
—Crosstaff: Journal Writing Activity Kit. (Illus., Orig.). (gr. 4-12). 1985. pap. 14.95 (0-935326-23-5) Gallopade Pub Group.
—Delaware & Other State Greats (Biographies) (Illus.). (gr. 3-12). 1990. PLB 24.95 (1-55609-558-9); pap. 14.95 (1-55609-557-0); computer disk 29.95 (0-7933-1455-0) Gallopade Pub Group.

—Delaware Bandits, Bushwackers, Outlaws, Crooks, Devils, Ghosts, Desperadoes & Other Assorted & Sundry Characters! (Illus.). (gr. 3-12). 1990. PLB 24.95 (0-7933-0238-2); pap. 14.95 (0-7933-0237-4); computer disk 29.95 (0-7933-0239-0) Gallopade Pub Group.
—Delaware Classic Christmas Trivia: Stories, Recipes, Activities, Legends, Lore & More! (Illus.). (gr. 3-12). 1990. PLB 24.95 (0-7933-0240-4); computer disk 29.95 (0-7933-0242-0) Gallopade Pub Group.
—Delaware Coastales. (Illus.). (gr. 3-12). 1990. PLB 24.95 (1-55609-554-6); pap. 14.95 (1-55609-553-8); computer disk 29.95 (0-7933-1451-8) Gallopade Pub Group.
—Delaware Coastales! 1992. lib. bdg. 24.95 (0-7933-7272-0) Gallopade Pub Group.
—Delaware "Crinkum-Crankum" A Funny Word Book about Our State. (Illus.). 1992. lib. bdg. 24.95 (0-7933-4831-5); pap. 14.95 (0-7933-4832-3); disk 29.95 (0-7933-4833-1) Gallopade Pub Group.
—Delaware Dingbats! Bk. 1: A Fun Book of Games, Stories, Activities & More about Our State That's All in Code! for You to Decipher. (Illus.). (gr. 3-12). 1991. PLB 24.95 (0-7933-3794-1); pap. 14.95 (0-7933-3795-X); computer disk 29.95 (0-7933-3796-8) Gallopade Pub Group.
—Delaware Festival Fun for Kids! (Illus.). (gr. 3-12). 1991. lib. bdg. 24.95 (0-7933-3947-2); pap. 14.95 (0-7933-3948-0); disk 29.95 (0-7933-3949-9) Gallopade Pub Group.
—The Delaware Hot Air Balloon Mystery. (Illus.). (gr. 2-9). 1990. 24.95 (0-685-37849-7); pap. 14.95 (0-7933-2382-7); computer disk 29.95 (0-7933-2383-5) Gallopade Pub Group.
—Delaware Jeopardy! Answers & Questions about Our State! (Illus.). (gr. 3-12). 1991. PLB 24.95 (0-7933-4100-0); pap. 14.95 (0-7933-4101-9); computer disk 29.95 (0-7933-4102-7) Gallopade Pub Group.
—Delaware "Jography" A Fun Run Thru Our State! (Illus.). (gr. 3-12). 1990. PLB 24.95 (1-55609-551-1); pap. 14.95 (1-55609-550-3); computer disk 29.95 (0-7933-1439-9) Gallopade Pub Group.
—Delaware Kid's Cookbook: Recipes, How-to-, History, Lore & More! (Illus.). (gr. 3-12). 1990. PLB 24.95 (0-7933-0250-1); pap. 14.95 (0-7933-0249-8); computer disk 29.95 (0-7933-0251-X) Gallopade Pub Group.
—The Delaware Mystery Van Takes Off! Book 1: Handicapped Delaware Kids Sneak Off on a Big Adventure. (Illus.). (gr. 3-12). 1992. 24.95 (0-7933-4985-0); pap. 14.95 (0-7933-4986-9); computer disk 29.95 (0-7933-4987-7) Gallopade Pub Group.
—Delaware Quiz Bowl Crash Course! (Illus.). (gr. 3-12). 1990. PLB 24.95 (1-55609-556-2); pap. 14.95 (1-55609-555-4); computer disk 29.95 (0-7933-1450-X) Gallopade Pub Group.
—Delaware Rollercoasters! (Illus.). (gr. 3-12). 1992. PLB 24.95 (0-7933-5245-2); pap. 14.95 (0-7933-5246-0); computer disk 29.95 (0-7933-5247-9) Gallopade Pub Group.
—Delaware School Trivia: An Amazing & Fascinating Look at Our State's Teachers, Schools & Students! (Illus.). (gr. 3-12). 1990. PLB 24.95 (0-7933-0247-1); pap. 14.95 (0-7933-0246-3); computer disk 29.95 (0-7933-0248-X) Gallopade Pub Group.
—Delaware Silly Basketball Sportsmysteries, Vol. I. (Illus.). (gr. 3-12). 1990. PLB 24.95 (0-7933-0244-7); pap. 14.95 (0-7933-0243-9); computer disk 29.95 (0-7933-0245-5) Gallopade Pub Group.
—Delaware Silly Basketball Sportsmysteries, Vol. II. (Illus.). (gr. 3-12). 1990. PLB 24.95 (0-7933-1456-9); pap. 14.95 (0-7933-1457-7); computer disk 29.95 (0-7933-1458-5) Gallopade Pub Group.
—Delaware Silly Football Sportsmysteries, Vol. I. (Illus.). (gr. 3-12). 1990. PLB 24.95 (0-7933-1441-0); pap. 14.95 (0-7933-1442-9); computer disk 29.95 (0-7933-1443-7) Gallopade Pub Group.
—Delaware Silly Football Sportsmysteries, Vol. II. (Illus.). (gr. 3-12). 1990. PLB 24.95 (0-7933-1444-5); pap. 14.95 (0-7933-1445-3); computer disk 29.95 (0-7933-1446-1) Gallopade Pub Group.
—Delaware Silly Trivia! (Illus.). (gr. 3-12). 1990. PLB 24.95 (1-55609-549-X); pap. 14.95 (1-55609-548-1); computer disk 29.95 (0-7933-1438-0) Gallopade Pub Group.
—Delaware Timeline: A Chronology of Delaware History, Mystery, Trivia, Legend, Lore & More. (Illus.). (gr. 3-12). 1992. PLB 24.95 (0-7933-5896-5); pap. 14.95 (0-7933-5897-3); computer disk 29.95 (0-7933-5898-1) Gallopade Pub Group.
—Delaware's (Most Devastating!) Disasters & (Most Calamitous!) Catastrophies! (Illus.). (gr. 3-12). 1990. PLB 24.95 (0-7933-0235-8); pap. 14.95 (0-7933-0234-X); computer disk 29.95 (0-7933-0236-6) Gallopade Pub Group.
—Delaware's Unsolved Mysteries (& Their "Solutions") Includes Scientific Information & Other Activities for Students. (Illus.). (gr. 3-12). 1992. PLB 24.95 (0-7933-5743-8); pap. 14.95 (0-7933-5744-6); computer disk 29.95 (0-7933-5745-4) Gallopade Pub Group.
—Dinosaur Trivia for Kids: I'm Saury! (Illus., Orig.). (gr. 2 up). 1986. PLB 24.95 (1-55609-162-1); pap. 14.95 (0-935326-54-5) Gallopade Pub Group.

—The Dragons & Dungeons Dingbats Book. (Illus.). (gr. 3-12). 1992. PLB 24.95 (*0-7933-5395-5*); pap. 14.95 (*0-7933-5396-3*); computer disk 29.95 (*0-7933-5397-1*) Gallopade Pub Group.
—The Drawers of Ocracoke. (Illus., Orig.). (ps-7). 1988. 24.95 (*1-55609-163-X*); pap. 14.95 (*1-55609-236-9*) Gallopade Pub Group.
—Florida & Other State Greats (Biographies) Florida Bks. (Illus.). (gr. 3-12). 1990. PLB 24.95 (*1-55609-426-4*); pap. 14.95 (*1-55609-425-6*); computer disk 29.95 (*0-7933-1501-8*) Gallopade Pub Group.
—Florida Bandits, Bushwackers, Outlaws, Crooks, Devils, Ghosts, Desperadoes & Other Assorted & Sundry Characters! (Illus.). (gr. 3-12). 1990. PLB 24.95 (*0-7933-0286-2*); pap. 14.95 (*0-7933-0285-4*); computer disk 29.95 (*0-7933-0287-0*) Gallopade Pub Group.
—Florida Classic Christmas Trivia: Stories, Recipes, Activities, Legends, Lore & More! (Illus.). (gr. 3-12). 1990. PLB 24.95 (*0-7933-0289-7*); pap. 14.95 (*0-7933-0288-9*); computer disk 29.95 (*0-7933-0290-0*) Gallopade Pub Group.
—Florida Coastales. (Illus.). (gr. 3-12). 1990. PLB 24.95 (*1-55609-422-1*); pap. 14.95 (*1-55609-118-4*); computer disk 29.95 (*0-7933-1497-6*) Gallopade Pub Group.
—Florida Coastales! 1992. lib. bdg. 24.95 (*0-7933-7274-7*) Gallopade Pub Group.
—Florida "Crinkum-Crankum" A Funny Word Book about Our State. (Illus.). 1992. lib. bdg. 24.95 (*0-7933-4834-X*); pap. 14.95 (*0-7933-4835-8*); disk 29.95 (*0-7933-4836-6*) Gallopade Pub Group.
—Florida Dingbats! Bk. 1: A Fun Book of Games, Stories, Activities & More about Our State That's All in Code! for You to Decipher. (Illus.). (gr. 3-12). 1991. PLB 24.95 (*0-7933-3800-X*); pap. 14.95 (*0-7933-3801-8*); computer disk 29.95 (*0-7933-3802-6*) Gallopade Pub Group.
—Florida Festival Fun for Kids! (Illus.). (gr. 3-12). 1991. lib. bdg. 24.95 (*0-7933-3953-7*); pap. 14.95 (*0-7933-3954-5*); disk 29.95 (*0-7933-3955-3*) Gallopade Pub Group.
—The Florida Hot Air Balloon Mystery. (Illus.). (gr. 2-9). 1990. 24.95 (*0-7933-2399-1*); pap. 14.95 (*0-7933-2400-9*); computer disk 29.95 (*0-7933-2401-7*) Gallopade Pub Group.
—Florida Jeopardy! Answers & Questions about Our State! (Illus.). (gr. 3-12). 1991. PLB 24.95 (*0-7933-4106-X*); pap. 14.95 (*0-7933-4107-8*); computer disk 29.95 (*0-7933-4108-6*) Gallopade Pub Group.
—Florida "Jography" A Fun Run Thru Our State! (Illus.). (gr. 3-12). 1990. PLB 24.95 (*1-55609-418-3*); pap. 14.95 (*1-55609-048-X*); computer disk 29.95 (*0-7933-1487-9*) Gallopade Pub Group.
—Florida Kid's Cookbook: Recipes, How-To, History, Lore & More! (Illus.). (gr. 3-12). 1990. PLB 24.95 (*0-7933-0298-6*); pap. 14.95 (*0-7933-0297-8*); computer disk 29.95 (*0-7933-0299-4*) Gallopade Pub Group.
—The Florida Mystery Van Takes Off! Book 1: Handicapped Florida Kids Sneak Off on a Big Adventure. (Illus.). (gr. 3-12). 1992. 24.95 (*0-7933-4988-5*); pap. 14.95 (*0-7933-4989-3*); computer disk 29.95 (*0-7933-4990-7*) Gallopade Pub Group.
—Florida Quiz Bowl Crash Course! (Illus.). (gr. 3-12). 1990. PLB 24.95 (*1-55609-424-8*); pap. 14.95 (*1-55609-423-X*); computer disk 29.95 (*0-7933-1496-8*) Gallopade Pub Group.
—Florida Rollercoasters! (Illus.). (gr. 3-12). 1992. PLB 24.95 (*0-7933-5251-7*); pap. 14.95 (*0-7933-5252-5*); computer disk 29.95 (*0-7933-5253-3*) Gallopade Pub Group.
—Florida School Trivia: An Amazing & Fascinating Look at Our State's Teachers, Schools & Students! (Illus.). (gr. 3-12). 1990. PLB 24.95 (*0-7933-0295-1*); pap. 14.95 (*0-7933-0294-3*); computer disk 29.95 (*0-7933-0296-X*) Gallopade Pub Group.
—Florida Silly Basketball Sportsmysteries, Vol. I. (Illus.). (gr. 3-12). 1990. PLB 24.95 (*0-7933-0292-7*); pap. 14.95 (*0-7933-0291-9*); computer disk 29.95 (*0-7933-0293-5*) Gallopade Pub Group.
—Florida Silly Basketball Sportsmysteries, Vol. II. (Illus.). (gr. 3-12). 1990. PLB 24.95 (*0-7933-1502-6*); pap. 14.95 (*0-7933-1503-9*); computer disk 29.95 (*0-7933-1504-2*) Gallopade Pub Group.
—Florida Silly Football Sportsmysteries, Vol. I. (Illus.). (gr. 3-12). 1990. PLB 24.95 (*1-55609-421-3*); pap. 14.95 (*1-55609-420-5*); computer disk 29.95 (*0-7933-1489-5*) Gallopade Pub Group.
—Florida Silly Football Sportsmysteries, Vol. II. (Illus.). (gr. 3-12). 1990. PLB 24.95 (*0-7933-1490-9*); pap. 14.95 (*0-7933-1491-7*); computer disk 29.95 (*0-7933-1492-5*) Gallopade Pub Group.
—Florida Silly Trivia! (Illus.). (gr. 3-12). 1990. PLB 24.95 (*1-55609-417-5*); pap. 14.95 (*1-55609-037-4*); computer disk 29.95 (*0-7933-1486-0*) Gallopade Pub Group.
—Florida Timeline: A Chronology of Florida History, Mystery, Trivia, Legend, Lore & More. (Illus.). (gr. 3-12). 1992. PLB 24.95 (*0-7933-5902-3*); pap. 14.95 (*0-7933-5903-1*); computer disk 29.95 (*0-7933-5904-X*) Gallopade Pub Group.

—Florida's (Most Devastating!) Disasters & (Most Calamitous!) Catastrophies! (Illus.). (gr. 3-12). 1990. PLB 24.95 (*0-7933-0283-8*); pap. 14.95 (*0-7933-0282-X*); computer disk 29.95 (*0-7933-0284-6*) Gallopade Pub Group.
—Florida's Unsolved Mysteries (& Their "Solutions") Includes Scientific Information & Other Activities for Students. (Illus.). (gr. 3-12). 1992. PLB 24.95 (*0-7933-5749-7*); pap. 14.95 (*0-7933-5750-0*); computer disk 29.95 (*0-7933-5751-9*) Gallopade Pub Group.
—For Your Eyes Only: Silly, Secret & Scary Code & Spy Trivia for Kids. (Illus.). (gr. 3-12). 1992. PLB 24.95 (*0-7933-5413-7*); pap. 14.95 (*0-7933-5414-5*); computer disk 29.95 (*0-7933-5415-3*) Gallopade Pub Group.
—The Fortune Cookie Christmas. (Illus., Orig.). (gr. 3 up). 1986. 24.95 (*1-55609-285-7*); pap. 14.95 (*0-935326-53-7*) Gallopade Pub Group.
—A Fun Book of Olympic Trivia A-Z: 1886-1996! 1992. lib. bdg. 24.95 (*0-7933-6876-6*); pap. text ed. 14.95 (*0-7933-6875-8*); disk 29.95 (*0-7933-6877-4*) Gallopade Pub Group.
—Gee! Ology: Trivia for Kids. (Illus.). (gr. 3-12). 1989. PLB 24.95 (*1-55609-305-5*); pap. 14.95 (*1-55609-306-3*); computer disk 29.95 (*1-55609-307-1*) Gallopade Pub Group.
—Georgia & Other State Greats (Biographies) (Illus.). (gr. 3-12). 1990. PLB 24.95 (*1-55609-392-6*); pap. 14.95 (*1-55609-391-8*); computer disk 29.95 (*0-7933-1520-4*) Gallopade Pub Group.
—Georgia Bandits, Bushwackers, Outlaws, Crooks, Devils, Ghosts, Desperadoes & Other Assorted & Sundry Characters! (Illus.). (gr. 3-12). 1990. PLB 24.95 (*0-7933-0310-9*); pap. 14.95 (*0-7933-0309-5*); computer disk 29.95 (*0-7933-0311-7*) Gallopade Pub Group.
—Georgia Classic Christmas Trivia: Stories, Recipes, Activities, Legends, Lore & More! (Illus.). (gr. 3-12). 1990. PLB 24.95 (*0-7933-0313-3*); pap. 14.95 (*0-7933-0312-5*); computer disk 29.95 (*0-7933-0314-1*) Gallopade Pub Group.
—Georgia Coastales. (Illus.). (gr. 3-12). 1990. PLB 24.95 (*1-55609-233-4*); pap. 14.95 (*1-55609-117-6*); computer disk 29.95 (*0-7933-1516-6*) Gallopade Pub Group.
—Georgia Coastales! 1992. lib. bdg. 24.95 (*0-7933-7275-5*) Gallopade Pub Group.
—Georgia "Crinkum-Crankum" A Funny Word Book about Our State. (Illus.). 1992. lib. bdg. 24.95 (*0-7933-4837-4*); pap. 14.95 (*0-7933-4838-2*); disk 29.95 (*0-7933-4839-0*) Gallopade Pub Group.
—Georgia Dingbats! Bk. 1: A Fun Book of Games, Stories, Activities & More about Our State That's All in Code! for You to Decipher. (Illus.). (gr. 3-12). 1991. PLB 24.95 (*0-7933-3803-4*); pap. 14.95 (*0-7933-3804-2*); computer disk 29.95 (*0-7933-3805-0*) Gallopade Pub Group.
—Georgia Festival Fun for Kids! (Illus.). (gr. 3-12). 1991. lib. bdg. 24.95 (*0-7933-3956-1*); pap. 14.95 (*0-7933-3957-X*); disk 29.95 (*0-7933-3958-8*) Gallopade Pub Group.
—The Georgia Hot Air Balloon Mystery. (Illus.). (gr. 2-9). 1990. 24.95 (*0-7933-2408-4*); pap. 14.95 (*0-7933-2409-2*); computer disk 29.95 (*0-7933-2410-6*) Gallopade Pub Group.
—Georgia Jeopardy! Answers & Questions about Our State! (Illus.). (gr. 3-12). 1991. PLB 24.95 (*0-7933-4109-4*); pap. 14.95 (*0-7933-4110-8*); computer disk 29.95 (*0-7933-4111-6*) Gallopade Pub Group.
—Georgia Jography: A Fun Run Through the Peach State. (Illus.). 50p. (Orig.). (gr. 4-8). 1986. pap. 14.95 (*0-935326-93-6*) Gallopade Pub Group.
—Georgia Kid's Cookbook: Recipes, How-To, History, Lore & More! (Illus.). (gr. 3-12). 1990. PLB 24.95 (*0-7933-0322-2*); pap. 14.95 (*0-7933-0321-4*); computer disk 29.95 (*0-7933-0323-0*) Gallopade Pub Group.
—The Georgia Mystery Van Takes Off! Book 1: Handicapped Georgia Kids Sneak Off on a Big Adventure. (Illus.). (gr. 3-12). 1992. 24.95 (*0-7933-4991-5*); pap. 14.95 (*0-7933-4992-3*); computer disk 29.95 (*0-7933-4993-1*) Gallopade Pub Group.
—Georgia Quiz Bowl Crash Course! (Illus.). (gr. 3-12). 1990. PLB 24.95 (*1-55609-384-5*); pap. 14.95 (*1-55609-383-7*); computer disk 29.95 (*0-7933-1515-8*) Gallopade Pub Group.
—Georgia Rollercoasters! (Illus.). (gr. 3-12). 1992. PLB 24.95 (*0-7933-5254-1*); pap. 14.95 (*0-7933-5255-X*); computer disk 29.95 (*0-7933-5256-8*) Gallopade Pub Group.
—Georgia School Trivia: An Amazing & Fascinating Look at Our State's Teachers, Schools & Students! (Illus.). (gr. 3-12). 1990. PLB 24.95 (*0-7933-0319-2*); pap. 14.95 (*0-7933-0318-4*); computer disk 29.95 (*0-7933-0320-6*) Gallopade Pub Group.
—Georgia Silly Basketball Sportsmysteries, Vol. I. (Illus.). (gr. 3-12). 1990. PLB 24.95 (*0-7933-0315-X*); pap. 14.95 (*0-7933-0317-6*) Gallopade Pub Group.
—Georgia Silly Basketball Sportsmysteries, Vol. II. (Illus.). (gr. 3-12). 1990. PLB 24.95 (*0-7933-1521-2*); pap. 14.95 (*0-7933-1522-0*); computer disk 29.95 (*0-7933-1523-9*) Gallopade Pub Group.

—Georgia Silly Football Sportsmysteries, Vol. I. (Illus.). (gr. 3-12). 1990. PLB 24.95 (*0-7933-5394-2*); pap. 14.95 (*1-55609-393-4*); computer disk 29.95 (*0-7933-1508-5*) Gallopade Pub Group.
—Georgia Silly Football Sportsmysteries, Vol. II. (Illus.). (gr. 3-12). 1990. PLB 24.95 (*0-7933-1509-3*); pap. 14.95 (*0-7933-1510-7*); computer disk 29.95 (*0-7933-1511-5*) Gallopade Pub Group.
—Georgia Silly Trivia Book. (Illus.). 48p. (Orig.). (gr. 2-12). 1985. pap. 14.95 (*0-935326-61-8*) Gallopade Pub Group.
—Georgia Timeline: A Chronology of Georgia History, Mystery, Trivia, Legend, Lore & More. (Illus.). (gr. 3-12). 1992. PLB 24.95 (*0-7933-5906-6*); computer disk 29.95 (*0-7933-5907-4*) Gallopade Pub Group.
—Georgia's (Most Devastating!) Disasters & (Most Calamitous!) Catastrophies! (Illus.). (gr. 3-12). 1990. PLB 24.95 (*0-7933-0307-9*); pap. 14.95 (*0-7933-0306-0*); computer disk 29.95 (*0-7933-0308-7*) Gallopade Pub Group.
—Georgia's Unsolved Mysteries (& Their "Solutions") Includes Scientific Information & Other Activities for Students. (Illus.). (gr. 3-12). 1992. PLB 24.95 (*0-7933-5752-7*); pap. 14.95 (*0-7933-5753-5*); computer disk 29.95 (*0-7933-5754-3*) Gallopade Pub Group.
—The Ghost & Graveyards Dingbats Book. (Illus.). (gr. 3-12). 1992. PLB 24.95 (*0-7933-5386-6*); pap. 14.95 (*0-7933-5387-4*); computer disk 29.95 (*0-7933-5388-2*) Gallopade Pub Group.
—Ghost of the Bed & Breakfast. (Illus.). 48p. (ps-7). 1988. 24.95 (*1-55609-155-9*); pap. 14.95 (*1-55609-239-3*) Gallopade Pub Group.
—Go Queen Go! Chess for Kids. (Illus.). 48p. (gr. k-12). 1983. 24.95 (*1-55609-160-5*); pap. 14.95 (*0-935326-14-6*) Gallopade Pub Group.
—Gold Shines Forever! The Treasure Ship Atocha A-Z. 1992. pap. 7.95 (*0-7933-7319-0*) Gallopade Pub Group.
—The Hairy Horrors Dingbats Book. (Illus.). (gr. 3-12). 1992. PLB 24.95 (*0-7933-5404-8*); pap. 14.95 (*0-7933-5405-6*); computer disk 29.95 (*0-7933-5406-4*) Gallopade Pub Group.
—Halloween: Silly Trivia. Marsh, Carole, illus. (Orig.). (gr. 2-9). 1986. PLB 24.95 (*1-55609-169-9*); pap. 14.95 (*0-685-14605-7*) Gallopade Pub Group.
—The Hard-to-Believe-But-True! Book of Alabama History, Mystery, Trivia, Legend, Lore, Humor & More. (Illus.). (gr. 3-12). 1990. PLB 24.95 (*0-7933-0085-1*); pap. 14.95 (*0-7933-0084-3*); computer disk 29.95 (*0-7933-0086-X*) Gallopade Pub Group.
—The Hard-to-Believe-But-True! Book of Alaska History, Mystery, Trivia, Legend, Lore, Humor & More. (Illus.). (gr. 3-12). 1990. PLB 24.95 (*0-7933-0109-2*); pap. 14.95 (*0-7933-0108-4*); computer disk 29.95 (*0-7933-0110-6*) Gallopade Pub Group.
—The Hard-to-Believe-But-True! Book of Arizona History, Mystery, Trivia, Legend, Lore, Humor & More. (Illus.). (gr. 3-12). 1990. PLB 24.95 (*0-7933-0133-5*); pap. 14.95 (*0-7933-0132-7*); computer disk 29.95 (*0-7933-0134-3*) Gallopade Pub Group.
—The Hard-to-Believe-But-True! Book of Arkansas History, Mystery, Trivia, Legend, Lore, Humor & More. (Illus.). (gr. 3-12). 1990. PLB 24.95 (*0-7933-0157-2*); pap. 14.95 (*0-7933-0156-4*); computer disk 29.95 (*0-7933-0158-0*) Gallopade Pub Group.
—The Hard-to-Believe-But-True! Book of California History, Mystery, Trivia, Legend, Lore, Humor & More. (Illus.). (gr. 3-12). 1990. PLB 24.95 (*0-7933-0181-5*); pap. 14.95 (*0-7933-0180-7*); computer disk 29.95 (*0-7933-0182-3*) Gallopade Pub Group.
—The Hard-to-Believe-But-True! Book of Colorado History, Mystery, Trivia, Legend, Lore, Humor & More. (Illus.). (gr. 3-12). 1990. PLB 24.95 (*0-7933-0205-6*); pap. 14.95 (*0-7933-0204-8*); computer disk 29.95 (*0-7933-0206-4*) Gallopade Pub Group.
—The Hard-to-Believe-But-True! Book of Connecticut History, Mystery, Trivia, Legend, Lore, Humor & More. (Illus.). (gr. 3-12). 1990. PLB 24.95 (*0-7933-0229-3*); pap. 14.95 (*0-7933-0228-5*); computer disk 29.95 (*0-7933-0230-7*) Gallopade Pub Group.
—The Hard-to-Believe-But-True! Book of Delaware History, Mystery, Trivia, Legend, Lore, Humor & More. (Illus.). (gr. 3-12). 1990. PLB 24.95 (*0-7933-0253-6*); pap. 14.95 (*0-7933-0252-8*); computer disk 29.95 (*0-7933-0254-4*) Gallopade Pub Group.
—The Hard-to-Believe-But-True! Book of Florida History, Mystery, Trivia, Legend, Lore, Humor & More. (Illus.). (gr. 3-12). 1990. PLB 24.95 (*0-7933-0301-X*); pap. 14.95 (*0-7933-0300-1*); computer disk 29.95 (*0-7933-0302-8*) Gallopade Pub Group.
—The Hard-to-Believe-But-True! Book of Georgia History, Mystery, Trivia, Legend, Lore, Humor & More. (Illus.). (gr. 3-12). 1990. PLB 24.95 (*0-7933-0325-7*); pap. 14.95 (*0-7933-0324-9*); computer disk 29.95 (*0-7933-0326-5*) Gallopade Pub Group.

—The Hard-to-Believe-But-True! Book of Hawaii History, Mystery, Trivia, Legend, Lore, Humor & More. (Illus.). (gr. 3-12). 1990. PLB 24.95 (0-7933-0349-4); pap. 14.95 (0-7933-0348-6); computer disk 29.95 (0-7933-0350-8) Gallopade Pub Group.

—The Hard-to-Believe-But-True! Book of Idaho History, Mystery, Trivia, Legend, Lore, Humor & More. (Illus.). (gr. 3-12). 1990. PLB 24.95 (0-7933-0373-7); pap. 14.95 (0-7933-0372-9); computer disk 29.95 (0-7933-0374-5) Gallopade Pub Group.

—The Hard-to-Believe-But-True! Book of Illinois History, Mystery, Trivia, Legend, Lore, Humor & More. (Illus.). (gr. 3-12). 1990. PLB 24.95 (0-7933-0397-4); pap. 14.95 (0-7933-0396-6); computer disk 29.95 (0-7933-0398-2) Gallopade Pub Group.

—The Hard-to-Believe-But-True! Book of Indiana History, Mystery, Trivia, Legend, Lore, Humor & More. (Illus.). (gr. 3-12). 1990. PLB 24.95 (0-7933-0421-0); pap. 14.95 (0-7933-0420-2); computer disk 29.95 (0-7933-0422-9) Gallopade Pub Group.

—The Hard-to-Believe-But-True! Book of Iowa History, Mystery, Trivia, Legend, Lore, Humor & More. (Illus.). (gr. 3-12). 1990. PLB 24.95 (0-7933-0445-8); pap. 14.95 (0-7933-0444-X); computer disk 29.95 (0-7933-0446-6) Gallopade Pub Group.

—The Hard-to-Believe-But-True! Book of Kansas History, Mystery, Trivia, Legend, Lore, Humor & More. (Illus.). (gr. 3-12). 1990. PLB 24.95 (0-7933-0469-5); pap. 14.95 (0-7933-0468-7); computer disk 29.95 (0-7933-0470-9) Gallopade Pub Group.

—The Hard-to-Believe-But-True! Book of Kentucky History, Mystery, Trivia, Legend, Lore, Humor & More. (Illus.). (gr. 3-8). 1990. PLB 24.95 (0-7933-0493-8); pap. 14.95 (0-7933-0492-X); disk 29.95 (0-7933-0494-6) Gallopade Pub Group.

—The Hard-to-Believe-But-True! Book of Louisiana History, Mystery, Trivia, Legend, Lore, Humor & More. (Illus.). (gr. 3-8). 1990. PLB 24.95 (0-7933-0517-9); pap. 14.95 (0-7933-0516-0); disk 29.95 (0-7933-0518-7) Gallopade Pub Group.

—The Hard-to-Believe-But-True! Book of Maine History, Mystery, Trivia, Legend, Lore, Humor & More. (Illus.). (gr. 3-8). 1990. PLB 24.95 (0-7933-0542-X); pap. 14.95 (0-7933-0541-1); disk 29.95 (0-7933-0543-8) Gallopade Pub Group.

—The Hard-to-Believe-But-True! Book of Maryland History, Mystery, Trivia, Legend, Lore, Humor & More. (Illus.). (gr. 3-8). 1990. PLB 24.95 (0-7933-0566-7); pap. 14.95 (0-7933-0565-9); disk 29.95 (0-7933-0567-5) Gallopade Pub Group.

—The Hard-to-Believe-But-True! Book of Massachusetts History, Mystery, Trivia, Legend, Lore, Humor & More. (Illus.). (gr. 3-8). 1990. PLB 24.95 (0-7933-0590-X); pap. 14.95 (0-7933-0589-6); disk 29.95 (0-7933-0591-8) Gallopade Pub Group.

—The Hard-to-Believe-But-True! Book of Michigan History, Mystery, Trivia, Legend, Lore, Humor & More. (Illus.). (gr. 3 up). 1990. PLB 24.95 (0-7933-0614-0); pap. 14.95 (0-7933-0613-2); computer disk 29.95 (0-7933-0615-9) Gallopade Pub Group.

—The Hard-to-Believe-But-True! Book of Minnesota History, Mystery, Trivia, Legend, Lore, Humor & More. (Illus.). (gr. 3 up). 1990. PLB 24.95 (0-7933-0638-8); pap. 14.95 (0-7933-0637-X); computer disk 29.95 (0-7933-0639-6) Gallopade Pub Group.

—The Hard-to-Believe-But-True! Book of Mississippi History, Mystery, Trivia, Legend, Lore, Humor & More. (Illus.). (gr. 3 up). 1990. PLB 24.95 (0-7933-0663-9); pap. 14.95 (0-7933-0662-0); computer disk 29.95 (0-7933-0664-7) Gallopade Pub Group.

—The Hard-to-Believe-But-True! Book of Missouri History, Mystery, Trivia, Legend, Lore, Humor & More. (Illus.). (gr. 3 up). 1990. PLB 24.95 (0-7933-0687-6); pap. 14.95 (0-7933-0686-8); computer disk 29.95 (0-7933-0688-4) Gallopade Pub Group.

—The Hard-to-Believe-But-True! Book of Montana History, Mystery, Trivia, Legend, Lore, Humor & More. (Illus.). (gr. 3 up). 1990. PLB 24.95 (0-7933-0712-0); pap. 14.95 (0-7933-0711-2); computer disk 29.95 (0-7933-0713-9) Gallopade Pub Group.

—The Hard-to-Believe-But-True! Book of Nebraska History, Mystery, Trivia, Legend, Lore, Humor & More. (Illus.). (gr. 3 up). 1990. PLB 24.95 (0-7933-0736-8); pap. 14.95 (0-7933-0735-X); computer disk 29.95 (0-7933-0737-6) Gallopade Pub Group.

—The Hard-to-Believe-But-True! Book of Nevada History, Mystery, Trivia, Legend, Lore, Humor & More. (Illus.). 1990. PLB 24.95 (0-7933-0760-0); pap. 14.95 (0-7933-0759-7); computer disk 29.95 (0-7933-0761-9) Gallopade Pub Group.

—The Hard-to-Believe-But-True! Book of New Hampshire History, Mystery, Trivia, Legend, Lore, Humor & More. (Illus.). 1990. PLB 24.95 (0-7933-0784-8); pap. 14.95 (0-7933-0783-X); computer disk 29.95 (0-7933-0785-6) Gallopade Pub Group.

—The Hard-to-Believe-But-True! Book of New Jersey History, Mystery, Trivia, Legend, Lore, Humor & More. (Illus.). 1990. PLB 24.95 (0-7933-1806-8); pap. 14.95 (0-7933-1807-6); computer disk 29.95 (0-7933-1808-4) Gallopade Pub Group.

—The Hard-to-Believe-But-True! Book of New Mexico History, Mystery, Trivia, Legend, Lore, Humor & More. (Illus.). 1990. PLB 24.95 (0-7933-0808-9); pap. 14.95 (0-7933-0807-0); computer disk 29.95 (0-7933-0809-7) Gallopade Pub Group.

—The Hard-to-Believe-But-True! Book of New York History, Mystery, Trivia, Legend, Lore, Humor & More. (Illus.). 1990. PLB 24.95 (0-7933-0832-1); pap. 14.95 (0-7933-0831-3); computer disk 29.95 (0-7933-0833-X) Gallopade Pub Group.

—The Hard-to-Believe-But-True! Book of North Carolina History, Mystery, Trivia, Legend, Lore, Humor & More. (Illus.). 1990. PLB 24.95 (0-7933-0856-9); pap. 14.95 (0-7933-0855-0); computer disk 29.95 (0-7933-0857-7) Gallopade Pub Group.

—The Hard-to-Believe-But-True! Book of North Dakota History, Mystery, Trivia, Legend, Lore, Humor & More. (Illus.). 1990. PLB 24.95 (0-7933-0880-1); pap. 14.95 (0-7933-0879-8); computer disk 29.95 (0-7933-0881-X) Gallopade Pub Group.

—The Hard-to-Believe-But-True! Book of Ohio History, Mystery, Trivia, Legend, Lore, Humor & More. (Illus.). 1990. PLB 24.95 (0-7933-0904-2); pap. 14.95 (0-7933-0903-4); computer disk 29.95 (0-7933-0906-9) Gallopade Pub Group.

—The Hard-to-Believe-But-True! Book of Oklahoma History, Mystery, Trivia, Legend, Lore, Humor & More. (Illus.). 1990. PLB 24.95 (0-7933-0929-8); pap. 14.95 (0-7933-0928-X); computer disk 29.95 (0-7933-0930-1) Gallopade Pub Group.

—The Hard-to-Believe-But-True! Book of Oregon History, Mystery, Trivia, Legend, Lore, Humor & More. (Illus.). 1990. PLB 24.95 (0-7933-0953-0); pap. 14.95 (0-7933-0952-2); computer disk 29.95 (0-7933-0954-9) Gallopade Pub Group.

—The Hard-to-Believe-But-True! Book of Pennsylvania History, Mystery, Trivia, Legend, Lore. Humor & More. (Illus.). 1990. PLB 24.95 (0-7933-0977-8); pap. 14.95 (0-7933-0976-X); computer disk 29.95 (0-7933-0978-6) Gallopade Pub Group.

—The Hard-to-Believe-But-True! Book of Rhode Island History, Mystery, Trivia, Legend, Lore, Humor & More. (Illus.). 1990. PLB 24.95 (0-7933-1001-6); pap. 14.95 (0-7933-1000-8); computer disk 29.95 (0-7933-1002-4) Gallopade Pub Group.

—The Hard-to-Believe-But-True! Book of South Carolina History, Mystery, Trivia, Legend, Lore, Humor & More. (Illus.). 1990. PLB 24.95 (0-7933-1025-3); pap. 14.95 (0-7933-1024-5); computer disk 29.95 (0-7933-1026-1) Gallopade Pub Group.

—The Hard-to-Believe-But True! Book of South Dakota History, Mystery, Trivia, Legend, Lore, Humor & More. (Illus.). 1990. PLB 24.95 (0-7933-1049-0); pap. 14.95 (0-7933-1048-2); computer disk 29.95 (0-7933-1050-4) Gallopade Pub Group.

—The Hard-to-Believe-But-True! Book of Tennessee History, Mystery, Trivia, Legend, Lore, Humor & More. (Illus.). 1990. PLB 24.95 (0-7933-1073-3); pap. 14.95 (0-7933-1072-5); computer disk 29.95 (0-7933-1074-1) Gallopade Pub Group.

—The Hard-to-Believe-But-True! Book of Texas History, Mystery, Trivia, Legend, Lore, Humor & More. (Illus.). 1990. PLB 24.95 (0-7933-1097-0); pap. 14.95 (0-7933-1096-2); computer disk 29.95 (0-7933-1098-9) Gallopade Pub Group.

—The Hard-to-Believe-But-True! Book of Utah History, Mystery, Trivia, Legend, Lore, Humor & More. (Illus.). 1990. PLB 24.95 (0-7933-1121-7); pap. 14.95 (0-7933-1120-9); computer disk 29.95 (0-7933-1122-5) Gallopade Pub Group.

—The Hard-to-Believe-But-True! Book of Vermont History, Mystery, Trivia, Legend, Lore, Humor & More. (Illus.). 1990. PLB 24.95 (0-7933-1145-4); pap. 14.95 (0-7933-1144-6) (0-7933-1146-2) Gallopade Pub Group.

—The Hard-to-Believe-But-True! Book of Virginia History, Mystery, Trivia, Legend, Lore, Humor & More. (Illus.). 1990. PLB 24.95 (0-7933-1169-1); pap. 14.95 (0-7933-1168-3); computer disk 29.95 (0-7933-1170-5) Gallopade Pub Group.

—The Hard-to-Believe-But-True! Book of Washington, D.C. History, Mystery, Trivia, Legend, Lore, Humor & More. (Illus.). (gr. 3-12). 1990. PLB 24.95 (0-685-45931-4); pap. 14.95 (0-7933-0276-5); computer disk 29.95 (0-7933-0278-1) Gallopade Pub Group.

—The Hard-to-Believe-But-True! Book of Washington History, Mystery, Trivia, Legend, Lore, Humor & More. (Illus.). 1990. PLB 24.95 (0-7933-1193-4); pap. 14.95 (0-7933-1192-6); computer disk 29.95 (0-7933-1194-2) Gallopade Pub Group.

—The Hard-to-Believe-But-True! Book of West Virginia History, Mystery, Trivia, Legend, Lore, Humor & More. (Illus.). 1990. PLB 24.95 (0-7933-1217-5); pap. 14.95 (0-7933-1216-7); computer disk 29.95 (0-7933-1218-3) Gallopade Pub Group.

—The Hard-to-Believe-But-True! Book of Wisconsin History, Mystery, Trivia, Legend, Lore, Humor & More. (Illus.). 1990. PLB 24.95 (0-7933-1241-8); pap. 14.95 (0-7933-1240-X); computer disk 29.95 (0-7933-1242-6) Gallopade Pub Group.

—The Hard-to-Believe-But-True! Book of Wyoming History, Mystery, Trivia, Legend, Lore, Humor & More. (Illus.). 1990. PLB 24.95 (0-7933-1265-5); pap. 14.95 (0-7933-1264-7); computer disk 29.95 (0-7933-1266-3) Gallopade Pub Group.

—The Haunt of Hope Plantation. Marsh, Carole, illus. (Orig.). (gr. 3-9). 1982. 24.95 (1-55609-170-2); pap. 14.95 (0-935326-03-0) Gallopade Pub Group.

—The Haunt of Hope Plantation S. P. A. R. K. Kit. (Illus., Orig.). (gr. 3-12). 1986. pap. 24.95 (0-935326-21-9) Gallopade Pub Group.

—Hawaii & Other State Greats (Biographies) (Illus.). (gr. 3-12). 1990. PLB 24.95 (1-55609-577-5); pap. 14.95 (1-55609-576-7); computer disk 29.95 (0-7933-1539-5) Gallopade Pub Group.

—Hawaii Bandits, Bushwackers, Outlaws, Crooks, Devils, Ghosts, Desperadoes & Other Assorted & Sundry Characters! (Illus.). (gr. 3-12). 1990. PLB 24.95 (0-7933-0334-6); pap. 14.95 (0-7933-0333-8); computer disk 29.95 (0-7933-0335-4) Gallopade Pub Group.

—Hawaii Classic Christmas Trivia: Stories, Recipes, Activities, Legends, Lore & More! (Illus.). (gr. 3-12). 1990. PLB 24.95 (0-7933-0337-0); pap. 14.95 (0-7933-0336-2); computer disk 29.95 (0-7933-0338-9) Gallopade Pub Group.

—Hawaii Coastales. (Illus.). (gr. 3-12). 1990. PLB 24.95 (1-55609-573-2); pap. 14.95 (1-55609-572-4); computer disk 29.95 (0-7933-1535-2) Gallopade Pub Group.

—Hawaii Coastales! 1992. lib. bdg. 24.95 (0-7933-7276-3) Gallopade Pub Group.

—Hawaii "Crinkum-Crankum" A Funny Word Book about Our State. (Illus.). 1992. lib. bdg. 24.95 (0-7933-4840-4); pap. 14.95 (0-7933-4841-2); disk 29.95 (0-7933-4842-0) Gallopade Pub Group.

—Hawaii Dingbats! Bk. 1: A Fun Book of Games, Stories, Activities & More about Our State That's All in Code! for You to Decipher. (Illus.). (gr. 3-12). 1991. PLB 24.95 (0-7933-3806-9); pap. 14.95 (0-7933-3807-7); computer disk 29.95 (0-7933-3808-5) Gallopade Pub Group.

—Hawaii Festival Fun for Kids! (Illus.). (gr. 3-12). 1991. lib. bdg. 24.95 (0-7933-3959-6); pap. 14.95 (0-7933-3960-X); disk 29.95 (0-7933-3961-8) Gallopade Pub Group.

—The Hawaii Hot Air Balloon Mystery. (Illus.). (gr. 2-9). 1990. 24.95 (0-7933-2417-3); pap. 14.95 (0-7933-2418-1); computer disk 29.95 (0-7933-2419-X) Gallopade Pub Group.

—Hawaii Jeopardy! Answers & Questions about Our State! (Illus.). (gr. 3-12). 1991. PLB 24.95 (0-7933-4112-4); pap. 14.95 (0-7933-4113-2); computer disk 29.95 (0-7933-4114-0) Gallopade Pub Group.

—Hawaii "Jography" A Fun Run Thru Our State! (Illus.). (gr. 3-12). 1990. PLB 24.95 (1-55609-568-6); pap. 14.95 (1-55609-567-8); computer disk 29.95 (0-7933-1525-5) Gallopade Pub Group.

—Hawaii Kid's Cookbook: Recipes, How-to, History, Lore & More! (Illus.). (gr. 3-12). 1990. PLB 24.95 (0-7933-0346-X); pap. 14.95 (0-7933-0345-1); computer disk 29.95 (0-7933-0347-8) Gallopade Pub Group.

—The Hawaii Mystery Van Takes Off! Book 1: Handicapped Hawaii Kids Sneak Off on a Big Adventure. (Illus.). (gr. 3-12). 1992. 24.95 (0-7933-4994-X); pap. 14.95 (0-7933-4995-8); computer disk 29.95 (0-7933-4996-6) Gallopade Pub Group.

—Hawaii Quiz Bowl Crash Course! (Illus.). (gr. 3-12). 1990. PLB 24.95 (1-55609-575-9); pap. 14.95 (1-55609-574-0); computer disk 29.95 (0-7933-1534-4) Gallopade Pub Group.

—Hawaii Rollercoasters! (Illus.). (gr. 3-12). 1992. PLB 24.95 (0-7933-5257-6); pap. 14.95 (0-7933-5258-4); computer disk 29.95 (0-7933-5259-2) Gallopade Pub Group.

—Hawaii School Trivia: An Amazing & Fascinating Look at Our State's Teachers, Schools & Students! (Illus.). (gr. 3-12). 1990. PLB 24.95 (0-7933-0343-5); pap. 14.95 (0-7933-0342-7); computer disk 29.95 (0-7933-0344-3) Gallopade Pub Group.

—Hawaii Silly Basketball Sports Mysteries. (Illus.). (gr. 3-12). 1990. PLB 24.95 (0-7933-1540-9); pap. 14.95 (0-7933-1541-7); computer disk 29.95 (0-7933-1542-5) Gallopade Pub Group.

—Hawaii: Silly Basketball Sportsmysteries, Vol. I. (Illus.). (gr. 3-12). 1990. PLB 24.95 (0-7933-0340-0); pap. 14.95 (0-7933-0339-7); computer disk 29.95 (0-7933-0341-9) Gallopade Pub Group.

—Hawaii Silly Football Sportsmysteries, Vol. I. (Illus.). (gr. 3-12). 1990. PLB 24.95 (1-55609-571-6); pap. 14.95 (1-55609-570-8); computer disk 29.95 (0-7933-1527-1) Gallopade Pub Group.

—Hawaii Silly Football Sportsmysteries, Vol. II. (Illus.). (gr. 3-12). 1990. PLB 24.95 (0-7933-1528-X); pap. 14.95 (0-7933-1529-8); computer disk 29.95 (0-7933-1530-1) Gallopade Pub Group.

—Hawaii Silly Trivia! (Illus.). (gr. 3-12). 1990. PLB 24.95 (1-55609-566-X); pap. 14.95 (1-55609-565-1); computer disk 29.95 (0-7933-1524-7) Gallopade Pub Group.

—Hawaii Timeline: A Chronology of Hawaii History, Mystery, Trivia, Legend, Lore & More. (Illus.). (gr. 3-12). 1992. PLB 24.95 (0-7933-5908-2); pap. 14.95 (0-7933-5909-0); computer disk 29.95 (0-7933-5910-4) Gallopade Pub Group.

—Hawaii's (Most Devastating!) Disasters & (Most Calamitous!) Catastrophies! (Illus.). (gr. 3-12). 1990. PLB 24.95 (0-7933-0331-1); pap. 14.95 (0-7933-0330-3); computer disk 29.95 (0-7933-0332-X) Gallopade Pub Group.
—Hawaii's Unsolved Mysteries (& Their "Solutions") Includes Scientific Information & Other Activities for Students. (Illus.). (gr. 3-12). 1992. PLB 24.95 (0-7933-5755-1); pap. 14.95 (0-7933-5756-X); computer disk 29.95 (0-7933-5757-8) Gallopade Pub Group.
—Ho Lee Chow! Chinese for Kids. (gr. k-6). Date not set. 24.95 (0-7933-7355-7); bk.-in-a-bag 14.95 (0-7933-7357-3); pap. 14.95 (0-7933-7356-5); computer disk 14.95 (0-7933-7358-1); video 14.95 (0-7933-7359-X); audiobk. 14.95 (0-7933-7360-3); CD-ROM 14.95 (0-7933-7361-1) Gallopade Pub Group.
—Hot Shot: Photography for Kids. (Illus., Orig.). (gr. 3-12). 1986. 24.95 (1-55609-171-0); pap. 14.95 (0-935326-79-0) Gallopade Pub Group.
—How to Find an Extra Terrestrial in Your Own Backyard. (Illus.). 1983. 24.95 (0-935326-09-X) Gallopade Pub Group.
—How to Start a California Library: At Home or School - A Book for All Ages. (Illus.). (gr. 3 up). 1992. PLB 24.95 (0-7933-4247-3); pap. 14.95 (0-7933-4248-1); computer disk 29.95 (0-7933-4249-X) Gallopade Pub Group.
—How to Start a Colorado Library: At Home or School - A Book for All Ages. (Illus.). (gr. 3 up). 1992. PLB 24.95 (0-7933-4250-3); pap. 14.95 (0-7933-4251-1); computer disk 29.95 (0-7933-4252-X) Gallopade Pub Group.
—How to Start a Connecticut Library: At Home or School - A Book for All Ages. (Illus.). (gr. 3 up). 1992. PLB 24.95 (0-7933-4253-8); pap. 14.95 (0-7933-4254-6); computer disk 29.95 (0-7933-4255-4) Gallopade Pub Group.
—How to Start a Delaware Library: At Home or School - A Book for All Ages. (Illus.). (gr. 3 up). 1992. PLB 24.95 (0-7933-4256-2); pap. 14.95 (0-7933-4257-0); computer disk 29.95 (0-7933-4258-9) Gallopade Pub Group.
—How to Start a Florida Library: At Home or School - A Book for All Ages. (Illus.). (gr. 3 up). 1992. PLB 24.95 (0-7933-4259-7); pap. 14.95 (0-7933-4260-0); computer disk 29.95 (0-7933-4261-9) Gallopade Pub Group.
—How to Start a Georgia Library: At Home or School - A Book for All Ages. (Illus.). (gr. 3 up). 1992. PLB 24.95 (0-7933-4262-7); pap. 14.95 (0-7933-4263-5); computer disk 29.95 (0-7933-4264-3) Gallopade Pub Group.
—How to Start a Hawaii Library: At Home or School - A Book for All Ages. (Illus.). (gr. 3 up). 1992. PLB 24.95 (0-7933-4265-1); pap. 14.95 (0-7933-4266-X); computer disk 29.95 (0-7933-4267-8) Gallopade Pub Group.
—How to Start a Kansas Library: At Home or School - A Book for All Ages. (Illus.). (gr. 3 up). 1992. PLB 24.95 (0-7933-4280-5); pap. 14.95 (0-7933-4281-3); computer disk 29.95 (0-7933-4282-1) Gallopade Pub Group.
—How to Start a Kentucky Library: At Home or School - A Book for All Ages. (Illus.). (gr. 3 up). 1992. PLB 24.95 (0-7933-4283-X); pap. 14.95 (0-7933-4284-8); computer disk 29.95 (0-7933-4285-6) Gallopade Pub Group.
—How to Start a Louisiana Library: At Home or School - A Book for All Ages. (Illus.). (gr. 3 up). 1992. PLB 24.95 (0-7933-4286-4); pap. 14.95 (0-7933-4287-2); computer disk 29.95 (0-7933-4288-0) Gallopade Pub Group.
—How to Start a Maine Library: At Home or School - A Book for All Ages. (Illus.). (gr. 3 up). 1992. PLB 24.95 (0-7933-4289-9); pap. 14.95 (0-7933-4290-2); computer disk 29.95 (0-7933-4291-0) Gallopade Pub Group.
—How to Start a Maryland Library: At Home or School - A Book for All Ages. (Illus.). (gr. 3 up). 1992. PLB 24.95 (0-7933-4292-9); pap. 14.95 (0-7933-4293-7); computer disk 29.95 (0-7933-4294-5) Gallopade Pub Group.
—How to Start a Massachusetts Library: At Home or School - A Book for All Ages. (Illus.). (gr. 3 up). 1992. PLB 24.95 (0-7933-4295-3); pap. 14.95 (0-7933-4296-1); computer disk 29.95 (0-7933-4297-X) Gallopade Pub Group.
—How to Start a Michigan Library: At Home or School - A Book for All Ages. (Illus.). (gr. 3 up). 1992. PLB 24.95 (0-7933-4298-8); pap. 14.95 (0-7933-4299-6); computer disk 29.95 (0-7933-4300-3) Gallopade Pub Group.
—How to Start a Minnesota Library: At Home or School - A Book for All Ages. (Illus.). (gr. 3 up). 1992. PLB 24.95 (0-7933-4301-1); pap. 14.95 (0-7933-4302-X); computer disk 29.95 (0-7933-4303-8) Gallopade Pub Group.
—How to Start a Mississippi Library: At Home or School - A Book for All Ages. (Illus.). (gr. 3 up). 1992. PLB 24.95 (0-7933-4304-6); pap. 14.95 (0-7933-4305-4); computer disk 29.95 (0-7933-4306-2) Gallopade Pub Group.

—How to Start a Missouri Library: At Home or School - A Book for All Ages. (Illus.). (gr. 3 up). 1992. PLB 24.95 (0-7933-4307-0); pap. 14.95 (0-7933-4308-9); computer disk 29.95 (0-7933-4309-7) Gallopade Pub Group.
—How to Start a Montana Library: At Home or School - A Book for All Ages. (Illus.). (gr. 3 up). 1992. PLB 24.95 (0-7933-4310-0); pap. 14.95 (0-7933-4311-9); computer disk 29.95 (0-7933-4312-7) Gallopade Pub Group.
—How to Start a Nebraska Library: At Home or School - A Book for All Ages. (Illus.). (gr. 3 up). 1992. PLB 24.95 (0-7933-4313-5); pap. 14.95 (0-7933-4314-3); computer disk 29.95 (0-7933-4315-1) Gallopade Pub Group.
—How to Start a Nevada Library: At Home or School - A Book for All Ages. (Illus.). (gr. 3 up). 1992. PLB 24.95 (0-7933-4316-X); pap. 14.95 (0-7933-4317-8); computer disk 29.95 (0-7933-4319-4) Gallopade Pub Group.
—How to Start a New Hampshire Library: At Home or School - A Book for All Ages. (Illus.). (gr. 3 up). 1992. PLB 24.95 (0-685-49562-0); pap. 14.95 (0-7933-4320-8); computer disk 29.95 (0-685-49563-9) Gallopade Pub Group.
—How to Start a New Jersey Library: At Home or School - A Book for All Ages. (Illus.). (gr. 3 up). 1992. PLB 24.95 (0-7933-4322-4); pap. 14.95 (0-7933-4323-2); computer disk 29.95 (0-7933-4324-0) Gallopade Pub Group.
—How to Start a New Mexico Library: At Home or School - A Book for All Ages. (Illus.). (gr. 3 up). 1992. PLB 24.95 (0-7933-4325-9); pap. 14.95 (0-7933-4326-7); computer disk 29.95 (0-7933-4327-5) Gallopade Pub Group.
—How to Start a New York Library: At Home or School - A Book for All Ages. (Illus.). (gr. 3 up). 1992. PLB 24.95 (0-7933-4328-3); pap. 14.95 (0-7933-4329-1); computer disk 29.95 (0-7933-4330-5) Gallopade Pub Group.
—How to Start a North Carolina Library: At Home or School - A Book for All Ages. (Illus.). (gr. 3 up). 1992. PLB 24.95 (0-7933-4331-3); pap. 14.95 (0-7933-4332-1); computer disk 29.95 (0-7933-4333-X) Gallopade Pub Group.
—How to Start a North Dakota Library: At Home or School - A Book for All Ages. (Illus.). (gr. 3 up). 1992. PLB 24.95 (0-7933-4334-8); pap. 14.95 (0-7933-4335-6); computer disk 29.95 (0-7933-4336-4) Gallopade Pub Group.
—How to Start a Pennsylvania Library: At Home or School - A Book for All Ages. (Illus.). (gr. 3 up). 1992. PLB 24.95 (0-7933-4346-1); pap. 14.95 (0-7933-4347-X); computer disk 29.95 (0-7933-4348-8) Gallopade Pub Group.
—How to Start a Rhode Island Library: At Home or School - A Book for All Ages. (Illus.). (gr. 3 up). 1992. PLB 24.95 (0-7933-4349-6); pap. 14.95 (0-7933-4350-X); computer disk 29.95 (0-7933-4351-8) Gallopade Pub Group.
—How to Start a South Carolina Library: At Home or School - A Book for All Ages. (Illus.). (gr. 3 up). 1992. PLB 24.95 (0-7933-4352-6); pap. 14.95 (0-7933-4353-4); computer disk 29.95 (0-7933-4354-2) Gallopade Pub Group.
—How to Start a South Dakota Library: At Home or School - A Book for All Ages. (Illus.). (gr. 3 up). 1992. PLB 24.95 (0-7933-4355-0); pap. 14.95 (0-7933-4356-9); computer disk 29.95 (0-7933-4357-7) Gallopade Pub Group.
—How to Start a Tennessee Library: At Home or School - A Book for All Ages. (Illus.). (gr. 3 up). 1992. PLB 24.95 (0-7933-4358-5); pap. 14.95 (0-7933-4359-3); computer disk 29.95 (0-7933-4360-7) Gallopade Pub Group.
—How to Start a Texas Library: At Home or School - A Book for All Ages. (Illus.). (gr. 3 up). 1992. PLB 24.95 (0-7933-4361-5); pap. 14.95 (0-7933-4362-3); computer disk 29.95 (0-7933-4363-1) Gallopade Pub Group.
—How to Start a Utah Library: At Home or School - A Book for All Ages. (Illus.). (gr. 3 up). 1992. PLB 24.95 (0-7933-4364-X); pap. 14.95 (0-7933-4365-8); computer disk 29.95 (0-7933-4366-6) Gallopade Pub Group.
—How to Start a Vermont Library: At Home or School - A Book for All Ages. (Illus.). (gr. 3 up). 1992. PLB 24.95 (0-7933-4367-4); pap. 14.95 (0-685-49564-7); computer disk 29.95 (0-7933-4369-0) Gallopade Pub Group.
—How to Start a Virginia Library: At Home or School - A Book for All Ages. (Illus.). (gr. 3 up). 1992. PLB 24.95 (0-7933-4370-4); pap. 14.95 (0-7933-4371-2); computer disk 29.95 (0-7933-4372-0) Gallopade Pub Group.
—How to Start a Washington DC Library: At Home or School - A Book for All Ages. (Illus.). (gr. 3 up). 1992. PLB 24.95 (0-7933-4376-3); pap. 14.95 (0-7933-4377-1); computer disk 29.95 (0-7933-4378-X) Gallopade Pub Group.
—How to Start a Washington Library: At Home or School - A Book for All Ages. (Illus.). (gr. 3 up). 1992. PLB 24.95 (0-7933-4373-9); pap. 14.95 (0-7933-4374-7); computer disk 29.95 (0-7933-4375-5) Gallopade Pub Group.

—How to Start a West Virginia Library: At Home or School - A Book for All Ages. (Illus.). (gr. 3 up). 1992. PLB 24.95 (0-7933-4379-8); pap. 14.95 (0-7933-4380-1); computer disk 29.95 (0-7933-4381-X) Gallopade Pub Group.
—How to Start a Wisconsin Library: At Home or School - A Book for All Ages. (Illus.). (gr. 3 up). 1992. PLB 24.95 (0-7933-4382-8); pap. 14.95 (0-7933-4383-6); computer disk 29.95 (0-7933-4384-4) Gallopade Pub Group.
—How to Start a Wyoming Library: At Home or School - A Book for All Ages. (Illus.). (gr. 3 up). 1992. PLB 24.95 (0-7933-4385-2); pap. 14.95 (0-7933-4386-0); computer disk 29.95 (0-7933-4387-9) Gallopade Pub Group.
—How to Start an Alabama Library: At Home or School - A Book for All Ages. (Illus.). (gr. 3 up). 1992. PLB 24.95 (0-7933-4235-X); pap. 14.95 (0-7933-4236-8); computer disk 29.95 (0-7933-4237-6) Gallopade Pub Group.
—How to Start an Alaska Library: At Home or School - A Book for All Ages. (Illus.). (gr. 3 up). 1992. PLB 24.95 (0-7933-4238-4); pap. 14.95 (0-7933-4239-2); computer disk 29.95 (0-7933-4240-6) Gallopade Pub Group.
—How to Start an Arizona Library: At Home or School - A Book for All Ages. (Illus.). (gr. 3 up). 1992. PLB 24.95 (0-7933-4241-4); pap. 14.95 (0-7933-4242-2); computer disk 29.95 (0-7933-4243-0) Gallopade Pub Group.
—How to Start an Arkansas Library: At Home or School - A Book for All Ages. (Illus.). (gr. 3 up). 1992. PLB 24.95 (0-7933-4244-9); pap. 14.95 (0-7933-4245-7); computer disk 29.95 (0-7933-4246-5) Gallopade Pub Group.
—How to Start an Idaho Library: At Home or School - A Book for All Ages. (Illus.). (gr. 3 up). 1992. PLB 24.95 (0-7933-4268-6); pap. 14.95 (0-7933-4269-4); computer disk 29.95 (0-7933-4270-8) Gallopade Pub Group.
—How to Start an Illinois Library: At Home or School - A Book for All Ages. (Illus.). (gr. 3 up). 1992. PLB 24.95 (0-7933-4271-6); pap. 14.95 (0-7933-4272-4); computer disk 29.95 (0-7933-4273-2) Gallopade Pub Group.
—How to Start an Indiana Library: At Home or School - A Book for All Ages. (Illus.). (gr. 3 up). 1992. PLB 24.95 (0-7933-4274-0); pap. 14.95 (0-7933-4275-9); computer disk 29.95 (0-7933-4276-7) Gallopade Pub Group.
—How to Start an Iowa Library: At Home or School - A Book for All Ages. (Illus.). (gr. 3 up). 1992. PLB 24.95 (0-7933-4277-5); pap. 14.95 (0-7933-4278-3); computer disk 29.95 (0-7933-4279-1) Gallopade Pub Group.
—How to Start an Ohio Library: At Home or School - A Book for All Ages. (Illus.). (gr. 3 up). 1992. PLB 24.95 (0-7933-4337-2); pap. 14.95 (0-7933-4338-0); computer disk 29.95 (0-7933-4339-9) Gallopade Pub Group.
—How to Start an Oklahoma Library: At Home or School - A Book for All Ages. (Illus.). (gr. 3 up). 1992. PLB 24.95 (0-7933-4340-2); pap. 14.95 (0-7933-4341-0); computer disk 29.95 (0-7933-4342-9) Gallopade Pub Group.
—How to Start an Oregon Library: At Home or School - A Book for All Ages. (Illus.). (gr. 3 up). 1992. PLB 24.95 (0-7933-4343-7); pap. 14.95 (0-7933-4344-5); computer disk 29.95 (0-7933-4345-3) Gallopade Pub Group.
—How You Know When Your Tush Is Turf. 1992. PLB 24.95 (0-7933-6924-X); pap. text ed. 14.95 (0-7933-6923-1); disk 29.95 (0-7933-6925-8) Gallopade Pub Group.
—Idaho & Other State Greats (Biographies) (Illus.). (gr. 3-12). 1990. PLB 24.95 (1-55609-592-9); pap. 14.95 (1-55609-591-0); computer disk 29.95 (0-7933-1558-1) Gallopade Pub Group.
—Idaho Bandits, Bushwackers, Outlaws, Crooks, Devils, Ghosts, Desperadoes & Other Assorted & Sundry Characters! (Illus.). (gr. 3-12). 1990. PLB 24.95 (0-7933-0358-3); pap. 14.95 (0-7933-0357-5); computer disk 29.95 (0-7933-0359-1) Gallopade Pub Group.
—Idaho Classic Christmas Trivia: Stories, Recipes, Activities, Legends, Lore & More! (Illus.). (gr. 3-12). 1990. PLB 24.95 (0-7933-0361-3); pap. 14.95 (0-7933-0360-5); computer disk 29.95 (0-7933-0362-1) Gallopade Pub Group.
—Idaho Coastales. (Illus.). (gr. 3-12). 1990. PLB 24.95 (1-55609-588-0); pap. 14.95 (1-55609-587-2); computer disk 29.95 (0-7933-1554-9) Gallopade Pub Group.
—Idaho Coastales! 1992. lib. bdg. 24.95 (0-7933-7277-1) Gallopade Pub Group.
—Idaho "Crinkum-Crankum" A Funny Word Book about Our State. (Illus.). 1992. lib. bdg. 24.95 (0-7933-4843-9); pap. 14.95 (0-7933-4844-7); disk 29.95 (0-7933-4845-5) Gallopade Pub Group.
—Idaho Dingbats! Bk. 1: A Fun Book of Games, Stories, Activities & More about Our State That's All in Code! for You to Decipher. (Illus.). (gr. 3-12). 1991. PLB 24.95 (0-7933-3809-3); pap. 14.95 (0-7933-3810-7); computer disk 29.95 (0-7933-3811-5) Gallopade Pub Group.

—Idaho Festival Fun for Kids! (Illus.). (gr. 3-12). 1991. lib. bdg. 24.95 (0-7933-3962-6); pap. 14.95 (0-7933-3963-4); disk 29.95 (0-7933-3964-2) Gallopade Pub Group.

—The Idaho Hot Air Balloon Mystery. (Illus.). (gr. 2-9). 1990. 24.95 (0-7933-2426-2); pap. 14.95 (0-7933-2427-0); computer disk 29.95 (0-7933-2428-9) Gallopade Pub Group.

—Idaho Jeopardy! Answers & Questions about Our State! (Illus.). (gr. 3-12). 1991. PLB 24.95 (0-7933-4115-9); pap. 14.95 (0-7933-4116-7); computer disk 29.95 (0-7933-4117-5) Gallopade Pub Group.

—Idaho "Jography" A Fun Run Thru Our State! (Illus.). (gr. 3-12). 1990. PLB 24.95 (1-55609-583-X); pap. 14.95 (1-55609-582-1); computer disk 29.95 (0-7933-1544-1) Gallopade Pub Group.

—Idaho Kid's Cookbook: Recipes, How-to, History, Lore & More! (Illus.). (gr. 3-12). 1990. PLB 24.95 (0-7933-0370-2); pap. 14.95 (0-7933-0369-9); computer disk 29.95 (0-7933-0371-0) Gallopade Pub Group.

—The Idaho Mystery Van Takes Off! Book 1: Handicapped Idaho Kids Sneak Off on a Big Adventure. (Illus.). (gr. 3-12). 1992. 24.95 (0-7933-4997-4); pap. 14.95 (0-7933-4998-2); computer disk 29.95 (0-7933-4999-0) Gallopade Pub Group.

—Idaho Quiz Bowl Crash Course! (Illus.). (gr. 3-12). 1990. PLB 24.95 (1-55609-590-2); pap. 14.95 (1-55609-589-9); computer disk 29.95 (0-685-45925-X) Gallopade Pub Group.

—Idaho Rollercoasters! (Illus.). (gr. 3-12). 1992. PLB 24.95 (0-7933-5260-6); pap. 14.95 (0-7933-5261-4); computer disk 29.95 (0-7933-5262-2) Gallopade Pub Group.

—Idaho School Trivia: An Amazing & Fascinating Look at Our State's Teachers, School & Students! (Illus.). (gr. 3-12). 1990. PLB 24.95 (0-7933-0367-2); pap. 14.95 (0-7933-0366-4); computer disk 29.95 (0-7933-0368-0) Gallopade Pub Group.

—Idaho Silly Basketball Sportsmysteries, Vol. I. (Illus.). (gr. 3-12). 1990. PLB 24.95 (0-7933-0364-8); pap. 14.95 (0-7933-0363-X); computer disk 29.95 (0-7933-0365-6) Gallopade Pub Group.

—Idaho Silly Basketball Sportsmysteries. (Illus.). (gr. 3-12). 1990. PLB 24.95 (0-7933-1559-X); pap. 14.95 (0-7933-1560-3); computer disk 29.95 (0-7933-1561-1) Gallopade Pub Group.

—Idaho Silly Football Sportsmysteries, Vol. I. (Illus.). (gr. 3-12). 1990. PLB 24.95 (1-55609-586-4); pap. 14.95 (1-55609-585-6); computer disk 29.95 (0-7933-1546-8) Gallopade Pub Group.

—Idaho Silly Football Sportsmysteries, Vol. II. (Illus.). (gr. 3-12). 1990. PLB 24.95 (0-7933-1547-6); pap. 14.95 (0-7933-1548-4); computer disk 29.95 (0-7933-1549-2) Gallopade Pub Group.

—Idaho Silly Trivia! (Illus.). (gr. 3-12). 1990. PLB 24.95 (1-55609-581-3); pap. 14.95 (1-55609-580-5); computer disk 29.95 (0-7933-1543-3) Gallopade Pub Group.

—Idaho Timeline: A Chronology of Idaho History, Mystery, Trivia, Legend, Lore & More. (Illus.). (gr. 3-12). 1992. PLB 24.95 (0-7933-5911-2); pap. 14.95 (0-7933-5912-0); computer disk 29.95 (0-7933-5913-9) Gallopade Pub Group.

—Idaho's (Most Devastating!) Disasters & (Most Calamitous!) Catastrophies! (Illus.). (gr. 3-12). 1990. PLB 24.95 (0-7933-0355-9); pap. 14.95 (0-7933-0354-0); computer disk 29.95 (0-7933-0356-7) Gallopade Pub Group.

—Idaho's Unsolved Mysteries (& Their "Solutions") Includes Scientific Information & Other Activities for Students. (Illus.). (gr. 3-12). 1992. PLB 24.95 (0-7933-5758-6); pap. 14.95 (0-7933-5759-4); computer disk 29.95 (0-7933-5760-8) Gallopade Pub Group.

—If My Alabama Mama Ran the World! (Illus.). (gr. 3-12). 1990. PLB 24.95 (0-7933-1335-X); pap. 14.95 (0-7933-1336-8); computer disk 29.95 (0-7933-1337-6) Gallopade Pub Group.

—If My Alaska Mama Ran the World! (Illus.). (gr. 3-12). 1990. PLB 24.95 (0-7933-1355-4); pap. 14.95 (0-7933-1356-2); computer disk 29.95 (0-7933-1357-0) Gallopade Pub Group.

—If My Arizona Mama Ran the World! (Illus.). (gr. 3-12). 1990. PLB 24.95 (0-7933-1370-8); pap. 14.95 (0-7933-1371-6); computer disk 29.95 (0-7933-1372-4) Gallopade Pub Group.

—If My Arkansas Mama Ran the World! (Illus.). (gr. 3-12). 1990. PLB 24.95 (0-7933-1386-4); pap. 14.95 (0-7933-1387-2); computer disk 29.95 (0-7933-1388-0) Gallopade Pub Group.

—If My California Mama Ran the World! (Illus.). (gr. 3-12). 1990. PLB 24.95 (0-7933-1402-X); pap. 14.95 (0-7933-1403-8); computer disk 29.95 (0-7933-1404-6) Gallopade Pub Group.

—If My Colorado Mama Ran the World! (Illus.). (gr. 3-12). 1990. PLB 24.95 (0-7933-1418-6); pap. 14.95 (0-7933-1419-4); computer disk 29.95 (0-7933-1420-8) Gallopade Pub Group.

—If My Connecticut Mama Ran the World! (Illus.). (gr. 3-12). 1990. PLB 24.95 (0-7933-1434-8); pap. 14.95 (0-7933-1435-6); computer disk 29.95 (0-7933-1436-4) Gallopade Pub Group.

—If My Delaware Mama Ran the World! (Illus.). (gr. 3-12). 1990. PLB 24.95 (0-7933-1452-6); pap. 14.95 (0-7933-1453-4); computer disk 29.95 (0-7933-1454-2) Gallopade Pub Group.

—If My Florida Mama Ran the World! (Illus.). (gr. 3-12). 1990. PLB 24.95 (0-7933-1498-4); pap. 14.95 (0-7933-1499-2); computer disk 29.95 (0-7933-1500-X) Gallopade Pub Group.

—If My Georgia Mama Ran the World! (Illus.). (gr. 3-12). 1990. PLB 24.95 (0-7933-1517-4); pap. 14.95 (0-7933-1518-2); computer disk 29.95 (0-7933-1519-0) Gallopade Pub Group.

—If My Hawaii Mama Ran the World! (Illus.). (gr. 3-12). 1990. PLB 24.95 (0-7933-1536-0); pap. 14.95 (0-7933-1537-9); computer disk 29.95 (0-7933-1538-7) Gallopade Pub Group.

—If My Idaho Mama Ran the World! (Illus.). (gr. 3-12). 1990. PLB 24.95 (0-7933-1555-7); pap. 14.95 (0-7933-1556-5); computer disk 29.95 (0-7933-1557-3) Gallopade Pub Group.

—If My Illinois Mama Ran the World! (Illus.). (gr. 3-12). 1990. PLB 24.95 (0-7933-1595-6); pap. 14.95 (0-7933-1596-4); computer disk 29.95 (0-7933-1597-2) Gallopade Pub Group.

—If My Indiana Mama Ran the World! (Illus.). (gr. 3-12). 1990. PLB 24.95 (0-7933-1613-8); pap. 14.95 (0-7933-1614-6); computer disk 29.95 (0-7933-1615-4) Gallopade Pub Group.

—If My Iowa Mama Ran the World! (Illus.). (gr. 3-12). 1990. PLB 24.95 (0-7933-1633-2); pap. 14.95 (0-7933-1634-0); computer disk 29.95 (0-7933-1635-9) Gallopade Pub Group.

—If My Kansas Mama Ran the World. (gr. 3-12). 1989. 24.95 (1-55609-374-8); pap. 14.95 (1-55609-375-6); bk. on computer disk 29.95 (1-55609-376-4) Gallopade Pub Group.

—If My Kentucky Mama Ran the World! (Illus.). (gr. 3-8). 1990. lib. bdg. 24.95 (0-7933-1655-3); pap. 14.95 (0-7933-1656-1); disk 29.95 (0-7933-1657-X) Gallopade Pub Group.

—If My Louisiana Mama Ran the World! (Illus.). (gr. 3-8). 1990. lib. bdg. 24.95 (0-7933-1674-X); pap. 14.95 (0-7933-1675-8); disk 29.95 (0-7933-1676-6) Gallopade Pub Group.

—If My Maine Mama Ran the World! (Illus.). (gr. 3-8). 1990. lib. bdg. 24.95 (0-7933-1687-1); pap. 14.95 (0-7933-1688-X); disk 29.95 (0-7933-1689-8) Gallopade Pub Group.

—If My Mama Ran the World. 1989. 24.95 (1-55609-287-3); pap. 14.95 (0-318-37385-8) Gallopade Pub Group.

—If My Maryland Mama Ran the World! (Illus.). (gr. 3-8). 1990. lib. bdg. 24.95 (0-7933-1693-6); pap. 14.95 (0-7933-1694-4); disk 29.95 (0-7933-1695-2) Gallopade Pub Group.

—If My Massachusetts Mama Ran the World! (Illus.). (gr. 3-8). 1990. lib. bdg. 24.95 (0-7933-1702-9); pap. 14.95 (0-7933-1703-7); disk 29.95 (0-7933-1704-5) Gallopade Pub Group.

—If My Michigan Mama Ran the World! (Illus.). (gr. 3 up). 1990. lib. bdg. 24.95 (0-7933-1723-1); pap. 14.95 (0-7933-1724-X); computer disk 29.95 (0-7933-1725-8) Gallopade Pub Group.

—If My Minnesota Mama Ran the World! (Illus.). (gr. 3 up). 1990. lib. bdg. 24.95 (0-7933-1717-7); pap. 14.95 (0-7933-1718-5); computer disk 29.95 (0-7933-1719-3) Gallopade Pub Group.

—If My Mississippi Mama Ran the World! (Illus.). (gr. 3 up). 1990. lib. bdg. 24.95 (0-7933-1728-2); pap. 14.95 (0-7933-1729-0); computer disk 29.95 (0-7933-1730-4) Gallopade Pub Group.

—If My Missouri Mama Ran the World! (Illus.). (gr. 3 up). 1990. lib. bdg. 24.95 (0-7933-1737-1); pap. 14.95 (0-7933-1738-X); computer disk 29.95 (0-7933-1739-8) Gallopade Pub Group.

—If My Montana Mama Ran the World! (Illus.). (gr. 3 up). 1990. lib. bdg. 24.95 (0-7933-1746-0); pap. 14.95 (0-7933-1747-9); computer disk 29.95 (0-7933-1748-7) Gallopade Pub Group.

—If My Nebraska Mama Ran the World! (Illus.). (gr. 3 up). 1990. PLB 24.95 (0-7933-1755-X); pap. 14.95 (0-7933-1756-8); computer disk 29.95 (0-7933-1757-6) Gallopade Pub Group.

—If My Nevada Mama Ran the World! (Illus.). 1990. lib. bdg. 24.95 (0-7933-1764-9); pap. 14.95 (0-7933-1765-7); computer disk 29.95 (0-7933-1766-5) Gallopade Pub Group.

—If My New Hampshire Mama Ran the World! (Illus.). 1990. lib. bdg. 24.95 (0-7933-1773-8); pap. 14.95 (0-7933-1774-6); computer disk 29.95 (0-7933-1775-4) Gallopade Pub Group.

—If My New Jersey Mama Ran the World! (Illus.). 1990. lib. bdg. 24.95 (0-7933-1782-7); pap. 14.95 (0-7933-1783-5); computer disk 29.95 (0-7933-1784-3) Gallopade Pub Group.

—If My New Mexico Mama Ran The World! (Illus.). 1990. lib. bdg. 24.95 (0-7933-1815-7); pap. 14.95 (0-7933-1816-5); computer disk 29.95 (0-7933-1817-3) Gallopade Pub Group.

—If My New York Mama Ran the World! (Illus.). 1990. lib. bdg. 24.95 (0-7933-1827-0); pap. 14.95 (0-7933-1828-9); computer disk 29.95 (0-7933-1829-7) Gallopade Pub Group.

—If My North Carolina Mama Ran the World! (Illus.). 1990. lib. bdg. 24.95 (0-7933-1833-5); pap. 14.95 (0-7933-1834-3); computer disk 29.95 (0-7933-1835-1) Gallopade Pub Group.

—If My North Dakota Mama Ran the World! (Illus.). 1990. lib. bdg. 24.95 (0-7933-1842-4); pap. 14.95 (0-7933-1843-2); computer disk 29.95 (0-7933-1844-0) Gallopade Pub Group.

—If My Ohio Mama Ran the World! (Illus.). 1990. lib. bdg. 24.95 (0-7933-1850-5); pap. 14.95 (0-7933-1851-3); computer disk 29.95 (0-7933-1852-1) Gallopade Pub Group.

—If My Oklahoma Mama Ran the World! (Illus.). 1990. lib. bdg. 24.95 (0-7933-1875-0); pap. 14.95 (0-7933-1876-9); computer disk 29.95 (0-7933-1877-7) Gallopade Pub Group.

—If My Oregon Mama Ran the World! (Illus.). 1990. lib. bdg. 24.95 (0-7933-1910-2); pap. 14.95 (0-7933-1911-0); computer disk 29.95 (0-7933-1912-9) Gallopade Pub Group.

—If My Pennsylvania Mama Ran the World! (Illus.). 1990. lib. bdg. 24.95 (0-7933-1939-0); pap. 14.95 (0-7933-1940-4); computer disk 29.95 (0-7933-1941-2) Gallopade Pub Group.

—If My Rhode Island Mama Ran the World! (Illus.). 1990. lib. bdg. 24.95 (0-7933-1974-9); pap. 14.95 (0-7933-1975-7); computer disk 29.95 (0-7933-1976-5) Gallopade Pub Group.

—If My South Carolina Mama Ran the World! (Illus.). 1990. lib. bdg. 24.95 (0-7933-2003-8); pap. 14.95 (0-7933-2004-6); computer disk 29.95 (0-7933-2005-4) Gallopade Pub Group.

—If My South Dakota Mama Ran the World! (Illus.). 1990. lib. bdg. 24.95 (0-7933-2035-6); pap. 14.95 (0-7933-2036-4); computer disk 29.95 (0-7933-2037-2) Gallopade Pub Group.

—If My Tennessee Mama Ran the World! (Illus.). 1990. lib. bdg. 24.95 (0-7933-2065-8); pap. 14.95 (0-7933-2066-6); computer disk 29.95 (0-7933-2067-4) Gallopade Pub Group.

—If My Texas Mama Ran the World! (Illus.). 1990. PLB 24.95 (0-7933-2094-1); pap. 14.95 (0-7933-2095-X); computer disk 29.95 (0-7933-2096-8) Gallopade Pub Group.

—If My Utah Mama Ran the World! (Illus.). 1990. PLB 24.95 (0-7933-2126-3); pap. 14.95 (0-7933-2127-1); computer disk 29.95 (0-7933-2128-X) Gallopade Pub Group.

—If My Vermont Mama Ran the World! (Illus.). 1990. PLB 24.95 (0-7933-2158-1); pap. 14.95 (0-7933-2159-X); computer disk 29.95 (0-7933-2160-3) Gallopade Pub Group.

—If My Virginia Mama Ran the World! (Illus.). 1990. PLB 24.95 (0-7933-2187-5); pap. 14.95 (0-7933-2188-3); computer disk 29.95 (0-7933-2189-1) Gallopade Pub Group.

—If My Washington, D.C. Mama Ran the World! (Illus.). (gr. 3-12). 1990. PLB 24.95 (0-7933-1477-1); pap. 14.95 (0-7933-1478-X); computer disk 29.95 (0-7933-1479-8) Gallopade Pub Group.

—If My Washington Mama Ran the World! (Illus.). 1990. PLB 24.95 (0-7933-2221-9); pap. 14.95 (0-7933-2222-7); computer disk 29.95 (0-7933-2223-5) Gallopade Pub Group.

—If My West Virginia Mama Ran the World! (Illus.). 1990. PLB 24.95 (0-7933-2253-7); pap. 14.95 (0-7933-2254-5); computer disk 29.95 (0-7933-2255-3) Gallopade Pub Group.

—If My Wisconsin Mama Ran the World! (Illus.). 1990. PLB 24.95 (0-7933-2285-5); pap. 14.95 (0-7933-2286-3); computer disk 29.95 (0-7933-2287-1) Gallopade Pub Group.

—If My Wyoming Mama Ran the World. (Illus.). 1990. PLB 24.95 (0-7933-2309-6); pap. 14.95 (0-7933-2310-X); computer disk 29.95 (0-7933-2311-8) Gallopade Pub Group.

—Illinois & Other State Greats (Biographies) (Illus.). (gr. 3-12). 1990. PLB 24.95 (1-55609-416-7); pap. 14.95 (1-55609-415-9); computer disk 29.95 (0-7933-1598-0) Gallopade Pub Group.

—Illinois Bandits, Bushwackers, Outlaws, Crooks, Devils, Ghosts, Desperadoes & Other Assorted & Sundry Characters! (Illus.). (gr. 3-12). 1990. PLB 24.95 (0-7933-0382-6); pap. 14.95 (0-7933-0381-8); computer disk 29.95 (0-7933-0383-4) Gallopade Pub Group.

—Illinois Classic Christmas Trivia: Stories, Recipes, Activities, Legends, Lore & More! (Illus.). (gr. 3-12). 1990. PLB 24.95 (0-7933-0385-0); pap. 14.95 (0-7933-0384-2); computer disk 29.95 (0-7933-0386-9) Gallopade Pub Group.

—Illinois Coastales. (Illus.). (gr. 3-12). 1990. PLB 24.95 (1-55609-412-4); pap. 14.95 (1-55609-411-6); computer disk 29.95 (0-7933-1594-8) Gallopade Pub Group.

—Illinois Coastales. 1992. lib. bdg. 24.95 (0-7933-7278-X) Gallopade Pub Group.

—Illinois "Crinkum-Crankum" A Funny Word Book about Our State. (Illus.). 1992. lib. bdg. 24.95 (0-7933-4846-3); pap. 14.95 (0-7933-4847-1); disk 29.95 (0-7933-4848-X) Gallopade Pub Group.

—Illinois Dingbats! Bk. 1: A Fun Book of Games, Stories, Activities & More about Our State That's All in Code! for You to Decipher. (Illus.). (gr. 3-12). 1991. PLB 24.95 (0-7933-3812-3); pap. 14.95 (0-7933-3813-1); computer disk 29.95 (0-7933-3814-X) Gallopade Pub Group.

—Illinois Festival Fun for Kids! (Illus.). (gr. 3-12). 1991. lib. bdg. 24.95 (0-7933-3965-0); pap. 14.95 (0-7933-3966-9); disk 29.95 (0-7933-3967-7) Gallopade Pub Group.

—The Illinois Hot Air Balloon Mystery. (Illus.). (gr. 2-9). 1990. 24.95 (*0-7933-2435-1*); pap. 14.95 (*0-7933-2436-X*); computer disk 29.95 (*0-7933-2437-8*) Gallopade Pub Group.
—Illinois Jeopardy! Answers & Questions about Our State! (Illus.). (gr. 3-12). 1991. PLB 24.95 (*0-7933-4118-3*); pap. 14.95 (*0-7933-4119-1*); computer disk 29.95 (*0-7933-4120-5*) Gallopade Pub Group.
—Illinois "Jography" A Fun Run Thru Our State! (Illus.). (gr. 3-12). 1990. PLB 24.95 (*1-55609-407-8*); pap. 14.95 (*1-55609-406-X*); computer disk 29.95 (*0-7933-1584-0*) Gallopade Pub Group.
—Illinois Kid's Cookbook: Recipes, How-to, History, Lore & More! (Illus.). (gr. 3-12). 1990. PLB 24.95 (*0-7933-0394-X*); pap. 14.95 (*0-7933-0393-1*); computer disk 29.95 (*0-7933-0395-8*) Gallopade Pub Group.
—The Illinois Mystery Van Takes Off! Book 1: Handicapped Illinois Kids Sneak Off on a Big Adventure. (Illus.). (gr. 3-12). 1992. 24.95 (*0-7933-5000-X*); pap. 14.95 (*0-7933-5001-8*); computer disk 29.95 (*0-7933-5002-6*) Gallopade Pub Group.
—Illinois Quiz Bowl Crash Course! (Illus.). (gr. 3-12). 1990. PLB 24.95 (*1-55609-414-0*); pap. 14.95 (*1-55609-413-2*); computer disk 29.95 (*0-7933-1593-X*) Gallopade Pub Group.
—Illinois Rollercoasters! (Illus.). (gr. 3-12). 1992. PLB 24.95 (*0-7933-5263-0*); pap. 14.95 (*0-7933-5264-9*); computer disk 29.95 (*0-7933-5265-7*) Gallopade Pub Group.
—Illinois School Trivia: An Amazing & Fascinating Look at Our State's Teachers, Schools & Students! (Illus.). (gr. 3-12). 1990. PLB 24.95 (*0-7933-0391-5*); pap. 14.95 (*0-7933-0390-7*); computer disk 29.95 (*0-7933-0392-3*) Gallopade Pub Group.
—Illinois Silly Basketball Sportsmysteries, Vol. I. (Illus.). (gr. 3-12). 1990. PLB 24.95 (*0-7933-0388-5*); pap. 14.95 (*0-7933-0387-7*); computer disk 29.95 (*0-7933-0389-3*) Gallopade Pub Group.
—Illinois Silly Basketball Sportsmysteries, Vol. II. (Illus.). (gr. 3-12). 1990. PLB 24.95 (*0-7933-1599-9*); pap. 14.95 (*0-7933-1600-6*); computer disk 29.95 (*0-7933-1601-4*) Gallopade Pub Group.
—Illinois Silly Football Sportsmysteries, Vol. I. (Illus.). (gr. 3-12). 1990. PLB 24.95 (*1-55609-410-8*); pap. 14.95 (*1-55609-409-4*); computer disk 29.95 (*0-7933-1586-7*) Gallopade Pub Group.
—Illinois Silly Football Sportsmysteries. (Illus.). (gr. 3-12). 1990. PLB 24.95 (*0-7933-1587-5*); pap. 14.95 (*0-7933-1588-3*); computer disk 29.95 (*0-7933-1589-1*) Gallopade Pub Group.
—Illinois Silly Trivia! (Illus.). (gr. 3-12). 1990. PLB 24.95 (*1-55609-405-1*); pap. 14.95 (*1-55609-113-3*); computer disk 29.95 (*0-7933-1583-2*) Gallopade Pub Group.
—Illinois Timeline: A Chronology of Illinois History, Mystery, Trivia, Legend, Lore & More. (Illus.). (gr. 3-12). 1992. PLB 24.95 (*0-7933-5914-7*); pap. 14.95 (*0-7933-5915-0*); computer disk 29.95 (*0-7933-5916-3*) Gallopade Pub Group.
—Illinois's (Most Devastating!) Disasters & (Most Calamitous!) Catastrophies! (Illus.). (gr. 3-12). 1990. PLB 24.95 (*0-7933-0379-6*); pap. 14.95 (*0-7933-0378-8*); computer disk 29.95 (*0-7933-0380-X*) Gallopade Pub Group.
—Illinois's Unsolved Mysteries (& Their "Solutions") Includes Scientific Information & Other Activities for Students. (Illus.). (gr. 3-12). 1992. PLB 24.95 (*0-7933-5761-6*); pap. 14.95 (*0-7933-5762-4*); computer disk 29.95 (*0-7933-5763-2*) Gallopade Pub Group.
—Indiana & Other State Greats (Biographies) (Illus.). (gr. 3-12). 1990. PLB 24.95 (*1-55609-437-X*); pap. 14.95 (*1-55609-436-1*); computer disk 29.95 (*0-7933-1616-2*) Gallopade Pub Group.
—Indiana Bandits, Bushwackers, Outlaws, Crooks, Devils, Ghosts, Desperadoes & Other Assorted & Sundry Characters! (Illus.). (gr. 3-12). 1990. PLB 24.95 (*0-7933-0406-7*); pap. 14.95 (*0-7933-0405-9*); computer disk 29.95 (*0-7933-0407-5*) Gallopade Pub Group.
—Indiana Classic Christmas Trivia: Stories, Recipes, Activities, Legends, Lore & More! (Illus.). (gr. 3-12). 1990. PLB 24.95 (*0-7933-0409-1*); pap. 14.95 (*0-7933-0408-3*); computer disk 29.95 (*0-7933-0410-5*) Gallopade Pub Group.
—Indiana Coastales. (Illus.). (gr. 3-12). 1990. PLB 24.95 (*1-55609-433-7*); pap. 14.95 (*1-55609-432-9*); computer disk 29.95 (*0-7933-1617-0*) Gallopade Pub Group.
—Indiana Coastales! 1992. lib. bdg. 24.95 (*0-7933-7279-8*) Gallopade Pub Group.
—Indiana "Crinkum-Crankum" A Funny Word Book about Our State. (Illus.). 1992. lib. bdg. 24.95 (*0-7933-4849-8*); pap. 14.95 (*0-7933-4851-X*); disk 29.95 (*0-7933-4852-8*) Gallopade Pub Group.
—Indiana Dingbats! Bk. 1: A Fun Book of Games, Stories, Activities & More about Our State That's All in Code! for You to Decipher. (Illus.). (gr. 3-12). 1991. PLB 24.95 (*0-7933-3815-8*); pap. 14.95 (*0-7933-3816-6*); computer disk 29.95 (*0-7933-3817-4*) Gallopade Pub Group.
—Indiana Festival Fun for Kids! (Illus.). (gr. 3-12). 1991. lib. bdg. 24.95 (*0-7933-3968-5*); pap. 14.95 (*0-7933-3969-3*); disk 29.95 (*0-7933-3970-7*) Gallopade Pub Group.

—The Indiana Hot Air Balloon Mystery. (Illus.). (gr. 2-9). 1990. 24.95 (*0-7933-2444-0*); pap. 14.95 (*0-7933-2445-9*); computer disk 29.95 (*0-7933-2446-7*) Gallopade Pub Group.
—Indiana Jeopardy! Answers & Questions about Our State! (Illus.). (gr. 3-12). 1991. PLB 24.95 (*0-7933-4121-3*); pap. 14.95 (*0-7933-4122-1*); computer disk 29.95 (*0-7933-4123-X*) Gallopade Pub Group.
—Indiana "Jography" A Fun Run Thru Our State! (Illus.). (gr. 3-12). 1990. PLB 24.95 (*1-55609-428-0*); pap. 14.95 (*1-55609-102-8*); computer disk 29.95 (*0-7933-1603-0*) Gallopade Pub Group.
—Indiana Kid's Cookbook: Recipes, How-to, History, Lore & More! (Illus.). (gr. 3-12). 1990. PLB 24.95 (*0-7933-0418-0*); pap. 14.95 (*0-7933-0417-2*); computer disk 29.95 (*0-7933-0419-9*) Gallopade Pub Group.
—The Indiana Mystery Van Takes Off! Book 1: Handicapped Indiana Kids Sneak Off on a Big Adventure. (Illus.). (gr. 3-12). 1992. 24.95 (*0-7933-5003-4*); pap. 14.95 (*0-7933-5004-2*); computer disk 29.95 (*0-7933-5005-0*) Gallopade Pub Group.
—Indiana Quiz Bowl Crash Course! (Illus.). (gr. 3-12). 1990. PLB 24.95 (*1-55609-435-3*); pap. 14.95 (*1-55609-434-5*); computer disk 29.95 (*0-7933-1612-X*) Gallopade Pub Group.
—Indiana Rollercoasters! (Illus.). (gr. 3-12). 1992. PLB 24.95 (*0-7933-5266-5*); pap. 14.95 (*0-7933-5267-3*); computer disk 29.95 (*0-7933-5268-1*) Gallopade Pub Group.
—Indiana School Trivia: An Amazing & Fascinating Look at Our State's Teachers, Schools & Students! (Illus.). (gr. 3-12). 1990. PLB 24.95 (*0-7933-0415-6*); pap. 14.95 (*0-7933-0414-8*); computer disk 29.95 (*0-7933-0416-4*) Gallopade Pub Group.
—Indiana Silly Basketball Sportsmysteries, Vol. I. (Illus.). (gr. 3-12). 1990. PLB 24.95 (*0-7933-0412-1*); pap. 14.95 (*0-7933-0411-3*); computer disk 29.95 (*0-7933-0413-X*) Gallopade Pub Group.
—Indiana Silly Basketball Sportsmysteries, Vol. II. (Illus.). (gr. 3-12). 1990. PLB 24.95 (*0-7933-1618-9*); pap. 14.95 (*0-7933-1619-7*); computer disk 29.95 (*0-7933-1620-0*) Gallopade Pub Group.
—Indiana Silly Football Sportsmysteries, Vol. I. (Illus.). (gr. 3-12). 1990. PLB 24.95 (*1-55609-431-0*); pap. 14.95 (*1-55609-430-2*); computer disk 29.95 (*0-7933-1605-7*) Gallopade Pub Group.
—Indiana Silly Football Sportsmysteries, Vol. II. (Illus.). (gr. 3-12). 1990. PLB 24.95 (*0-7933-1606-5*); pap. 14.95 (*0-7933-1607-3*); computer disk 29.95 (*0-7933-1608-1*) Gallopade Pub Group.
—Indiana Silly Trivia! (Illus.). (gr. 3-12). 1990. PLB 24.95 (*1-55609-427-2*); pap. 14.95 (*1-55609-101-X*); computer disk 29.95 (*0-7933-1602-2*) Gallopade Pub Group.
—Indiana Timeline: A Chronology of Indiana History, Mystery, Trivia, Legend, Lore & More. (Illus.). (gr. 3-12). 1992. PLB 24.95 (*0-7933-5917-1*); pap. 14.95 (*0-7933-5918-X*); computer disk 29.95 (*0-7933-5919-8*) Gallopade Pub Group.
—Indiana's (Most Devastating!) Disasters & (Most Calamitous!) Catastrophies! (Illus.). (gr. 3-12). 1990. PLB 24.95 (*0-7933-0403-2*); pap. 14.95 (*0-7933-0402-4*); computer disk 29.95 (*0-7933-0404-0*) Gallopade Pub Group.
—Indiana's Unsolved Mysteries (& Their "Solutions") Includes Scientific Information & Other Activities for Students. (Illus.). (gr. 3-12). 1992. PLB 24.95 (*0-7933-5764-0*); pap. 14.95 (*0-7933-5765-9*); computer disk 29.95 (*0-7933-5766-7*) Gallopade Pub Group.
—Iowa & Other State Greats (Biographies) (Illus.). (gr. 3-12). 1990. PLB 24.95 (*1-55609-459-0*); pap. 14.95 (*1-55609-458-2*); computer disk 29.95 (*0-7933-1636-7*) Gallopade Pub Group.
—Iowa Bandits, Bushwackers, Outlaws, Crooks, Devils, Ghosts, Desperadoes & Other Assorted & Sundry Characters! (Illus.). (gr. 3-12). 1990. PLB 24.95 (*0-7933-0430-X*); pap. 14.95 (*0-7933-0429-6*); computer disk 29.95 (*0-7933-0431-8*) Gallopade Pub Group.
—Iowa Classic Christmas Trivia: Stories, Recipes, Activities, Legends, Lore & More! (Illus.). (gr. 3-12). 1990. PLB 24.95 (*0-7933-0433-4*); pap. 14.95 (*0-7933-0432-6*); computer disk 29.95 (*0-7933-0434-2*) Gallopade Pub Group.
—Iowa Coastales. (Illus.). (gr. 3-12). 1990. PLB 24.95 (*1-55609-455-8*); pap. 14.95 (*1-55609-454-X*); computer disk 29.95 (*0-7933-1632-4*) Gallopade Pub Group.
—Iowa Coastales! 1992. lib. bdg. 24.95 (*0-7933-7280-1*) Gallopade Pub Group.
—Iowa "Crinkum-Crankum" A Funny Word Book about Our State. (Illus.). 1992. lib. bdg. 24.95 (*0-7933-4853-6*); pap. 14.95 (*0-7933-4854-4*); disk 29.95 (*0-7933-4855-2*) Gallopade Pub Group.
—Iowa Dingbats! Bk. 1: A Fun Book of Games, Stories, Activities & More about Our State That's All in Code! for You to Decipher. (Illus.). (gr. 3-12). 1991. PLB 24.95 (*0-7933-3818-2*); pap. 14.95 (*0-7933-3819-0*); computer disk 29.95 (*0-7933-3820-4*) Gallopade Pub Group.
—Iowa Festival Fun for Kids! (Illus.). (gr. 3-12). 1991. lib. bdg. 24.95 (*0-7933-3971-5*); pap. 14.95 (*0-7933-3972-3*); disk 29.95 (*0-7933-3973-1*) Gallopade Pub Group.

—The Iowa Hot Air Balloon Mystery. (Illus.). (gr. 2-9). 1990. 24.95 (*0-7933-2453-X*); pap. 14.95 (*0-7933-2454-8*); computer disk 29.95 (*0-7933-2455-6*) Gallopade Pub Group.
—Iowa Jeopardy! Answers & Questions about Our State! (Illus.). (gr. 3-12). 1991. PLB 24.95 (*0-7933-4124-8*); pap. 14.95 (*0-7933-4125-6*); computer disk 29.95 (*0-7933-4126-4*) Gallopade Pub Group.
—Iowa "Jography" A Fun Run Thru Our State! (Illus.). (gr. 3-12). 1990. PLB 24.95 (*1-55609-450-7*); pap. 14.95 (*1-55609-085-4*); computer disk 29.95 (*0-7933-1622-7*) Gallopade Pub Group.
—Iowa Kid's Cookbook: Recipes, How-to, History, Lore & More! (Illus.). (gr. 3-12). 1990. PLB 24.95 (*0-7933-0442-3*); pap. 14.95 (*0-7933-0441-5*); computer disk 29.95 (*0-7933-0443-1*) Gallopade Pub Group.
—The Iowa Mystery Van Takes Off! Book 1: Handicapped Iowa Kids Sneak Off on a Big Adventure. (Illus.). (gr. 3-12). 1992. 24.95 (*0-7933-5006-9*); pap. 14.95 (*0-7933-5007-7*); computer disk 29.95 (*0-7933-5008-5*) Gallopade Pub Group.
—Iowa Quiz Bowl Crash Course! (Illus.). (gr. 3-12). 1990. PLB 24.95 (*1-55609-457-4*); pap. 14.95 (*1-55609-456-6*); computer disk 29.95 (*0-7933-1631-6*) Gallopade Pub Group.
—Iowa Rollercoasters! (Illus.). (gr. 3-12). 1992. PLB 24.95 (*0-7933-5269-X*); pap. 14.95 (*0-7933-5270-3*); computer disk 29.95 (*0-7933-5271-1*) Gallopade Pub Group.
—Iowa School Trivia: An Amazing & Fascinating Look at Our State's Teachers, Schools & Students! (Illus.). (gr. 3-12). 1990. PLB 24.95 (*0-7933-0439-3*); pap. 14.95 (*0-7933-0438-5*); computer disk 29.95 (*0-7933-0440-7*) Gallopade Pub Group.
—Iowa Silly Basketball Sportsmysteries, Vol. I. (Illus.). (gr. 3-12). 1990. PLB 24.95 (*0-7933-0436-9*); pap. 14.95 (*0-7933-0435-0*); computer disk 29.95 (*0-7933-0437-7*) Gallopade Pub Group.
—Iowa Silly Basketball Sportsmysteries, Vol. II. (Illus.). (gr. 3-12). 1990. PLB 24.95 (*0-7933-1637-5*); pap. 14.95 (*0-7933-1638-3*); computer disk 29.95 (*0-7933-1639-1*) Gallopade Pub Group.
—Iowa Silly Football Sportsmysteries, Vol. I. (Illus.). (gr. 3-12). 1990. PLB 24.95 (*1-55609-453-1*); pap. 14.95 (*1-55609-452-3*); computer disk 29.95 (*0-7933-1624-3*) Gallopade Pub Group.
—Iowa Silly Football Sportsmysteries, Vol. II. (Illus.). (gr. 3-12). 1990. PLB 24.95 (*0-7933-1625-1*); pap. 14.95 (*0-7933-1626-X*); computer disk 29.95 (*0-7933-1627-8*) Gallopade Pub Group.
—Iowa Silly Trivia! (Illus.). (gr. 3-12). 1990. PLB 24.95 (*1-55609-449-3*); pap. 14.95 (*1-55609-084-6*); computer disk 29.95 (*0-7933-1621-9*) Gallopade Pub Group.
—Iowa Timeline: A Chronology of Iowa History, Mystery, Trivia, Legend, Lore & More. (Illus.). (gr. 3-12). 1992. PLB 24.95 (*0-7933-5920-1*); pap. 14.95 (*0-7933-5921-X*); computer disk 29.95 (*0-7933-5922-8*) Gallopade Pub Group.
—Iowa's (Most Devastating!) Disasters & (Most Calamitous!) Catastrophies! (Illus.). (gr. 3-12). 1990. PLB 24.95 (*0-7933-0426-1*); pap. 14.95 (*0-7933-0427-X*); computer disk 29.95 (*0-7933-0428-8*) Gallopade Pub Group.
—Iowa's Unsolved Mysteries (& Their "Solutions") Includes Scientific Information & Other Activities for Students. (Illus.). (gr. 3-12). 1992. PLB 24.95 (*0-7933-5767-5*); pap. 14.95 (*0-7933-5768-3*); computer disk 29.95 (*0-7933-5769-1*) Gallopade Pub Group.
—Island of the Calamari. (Illus., Orig.). (ps-7). 1988. 24.95 (*1-55609-172-9*); pap. 14.95 (*0-317-66069-1*) Gallopade Pub Group.
—Jason Hewitt! German for Kids. 1992. lib. bdg. 24.95 (*0-7933-6879-0*); pap. text ed. 14.95 (*0-7933-6878-2*); disk 29.95 (*0-7933-6880-4*) Gallopade Pub Group.
—Jungle Gym! A Monkey's Eye View of the World's Jungles Yesterday, Today & Tomorrow? 36p. (gr. 3-5). 1993. PLB 24.95 (*0-7933-7346-8*); pap. 14.95 (*0-7933-7347-6*); disk 29.95 (*0-7933-7348-4*) Gallopade Pub Group.
—Jurassic Ark! Alabama Dinosaurs & Other Prehistoric Creatures. (gr. k-12). 1993. PLB 24.95 (*0-7933-7428-6*); pap. 14.95 (*0-7933-7429-4*); computer disk 29.95 (*0-7933-7430-8*) Gallopade Pub Group.
—Jurassic Ark! Alaska Dinosaurs & Other Prehistoric Creatures. (gr. k-12). 1993. PLB 24.95 (*0-7933-7431-6*); pap. 14.95 (*0-7933-7432-4*); computer disk 29.95 (*0-7933-7433-2*) Gallopade Pub Group.
—Jurassic Ark! Arizona Dinosaurs & Other Prehistoric Creatures. (gr. k-12). 1993. PLB 24.95 (*0-7933-7434-0*); pap. 14.95 (*0-7933-7435-9*); computer disk 29.95 (*0-7933-7436-7*) Gallopade Pub Group.
—Jurassic Ark! Arkansas Dinosaurs & Other Prehistoric Creatures. (gr. k-12). 1993. PLB 24.95 (*0-7933-7437-5*); pap. 14.95 (*0-7933-7438-3*); computer disk 29.95 (*0-7933-7439-1*) Gallopade Pub Group.
—Jurassic Ark! California Dinosaurs & Other Prehistoric Creatures. (gr. k-12). 1993. PLB 24.95 (*0-7933-7440-5*); pap. 14.95 (*0-7933-7441-3*); computer disk 29.95 (*0-7933-7442-1*) Gallopade Pub Group.

—Jurassic Ark! Colorado Dinosaurs & Other Prehistoric Creatures. (gr. k-12). 1993. PLB 24.95 (0-7933-7443-X); pap. 14.95 (0-7933-7444-8); computer disk 29.95 (0-7933-7445-6) Gallopade Pub Group.

—Jurassic Ark! Connecticut Dinosaurs & Other Prehistoric Creatures. (gr. k-12). 1993. PLB 24.95 (0-7933-7446-4); pap. 14.95 (0-7933-7447-2); computer disk 29.95 (0-7933-7448-0) Gallopade Pub Group.

—Jurassic Ark! Delaware Dinosaurs & Other Prehistoric Creatures. (gr. k-12). 1993. PLB 24.95 (0-7933-7449-9); pap. 14.95 (0-7933-7450-2); computer disk 29.95 (0-7933-7451-0) Gallopade Pub Group.

—Jurassic Ark! Florida Dinosaurs & Other Prehistoric Creatures. (gr. k-12). 1993. PLB 24.95 (0-7933-7455-3); pap. 14.95 (0-7933-7456-1); computer disk 29.95 (0-7933-7457-X) Gallopade Pub Group.

—Jurassic Ark! Georgia Dinosaurs & Other Prehistoric Creatures. (gr. k-12). 1993. PLB 24.95 (0-7933-7458-8); pap. 14.95 (0-7933-7459-6); computer disk 29.95 (0-7933-7460-X) Gallopade Pub Group.

—Jurassic Ark! Hawaii Dinosaurs & Other Prehistoric Creatures. (gr. k-12). 1993. PLB 24.95 (0-7933-7461-8); pap. 14.95 (0-7933-7462-6); computer disk 29.95 (0-7933-7463-4) Gallopade Pub Group.

—Jurassic Ark! Idaho Dinosaurs & Other Prehistoric Creatures. (gr. k-12). 1993. PLB 24.95 (0-7933-7464-2); pap. 14.95 (0-7933-7465-0); computer disk 29.95 (0-7933-7466-9) Gallopade Pub Group.

—Jurassic Ark! Illinois Dinosaurs & Other Prehistoric Creatures. (gr. k-12). 1993. PLB 24.95 (0-7933-7467-7); pap. 14.95 (0-7933-7468-5); computer disk 29.95 (0-7933-7469-3) Gallopade Pub Group.

—Jurassic Ark! Indiana Dinosaurs & Other Prehistoric Creatures. (gr. k-12). 1993. PLB 24.95 (0-7933-7470-7); pap. 14.95 (0-7933-7471-5); computer disk 29.95 (0-7933-7472-3) Gallopade Pub Group.

—Jurassic Ark! Iowa Dinosaurs & Other Prehistoric Creatures. (gr. k-12). 1993. PLB 24.95 (0-7933-7473-1); pap. 14.95 (0-7933-7474-X); computer disk 29.95 (0-7933-7475-8) Gallopade Pub Group.

—Jurassic Ark! Kansas Dinosaurs & Other Prehistoric Creatures. (gr. k-12). 1993. PLB 24.95 (0-7933-7476-6); pap. 14.95 (0-7933-7477-4); computer disk 29.95 (0-7933-7478-2) Gallopade Pub Group.

—Jurassic Ark! Kentucky Dinosaurs & Other Prehistoric Creatures. (gr. k-12). 1993. PLB 24.95 (0-7933-7479-0); pap. 14.95 (0-7933-7480-4); computer disk 29.95 (0-7933-7481-2) Gallopade Pub Group.

—Jurassic Ark! Louisiana Dinosaurs & Other Prehistoric Creatures. (gr. k-12). 1993. PLB 24.95 (0-7933-7482-0); pap. 14.95 (0-7933-7483-9); computer disk 29.95 (0-7933-7484-7) Gallopade Pub Group.

—Jurassic Ark! Maine Dinosaurs & Other Prehistoric Creatures. (gr. k-12). 1993. PLB 24.95 (0-7933-7485-5); pap. 14.95 (0-7933-7486-3); computer disk 29.95 (0-7933-7487-1) Gallopade Pub Group.

—Jurassic Ark! Maryland Dinosaurs & Other Prehistoric Creatures. (gr. k-12). 1993. PLB 24.95 (0-7933-7488-X); pap. 14.95 (0-7933-7489-8); computer disk 29.95 (0-7933-7490-1) Gallopade Pub Group.

—Jurassic Ark! Massachusetts Dinosaurs & Other Prehistoric Creatures. (gr. k-12). 1993. PLB 24.95 (0-7933-7491-X); pap. 14.95 (0-7933-7492-8); computer disk 29.95 (0-7933-7493-6) Gallopade Pub Group.

—Jurassic Ark! Michigan Dinosaurs & Other Prehistoric Creatures. (gr. k-12). 1993. PLB 24.95 (0-7933-7494-4); pap. 14.95 (0-7933-7495-2); computer disk 29.95 (0-7933-7496-0) Gallopade Pub Group.

—Jurassic Ark! Minnesota Dinosaurs & Other Prehistoric Creatures. (gr. k-12). 1993. PLB 24.95 (0-7933-7497-9); pap. 14.95 (0-7933-7498-7); computer disk 29.95 (0-7933-7499-5) Gallopade Pub Group.

—Jurassic Ark! Mississippi Dinosaurs & Other Prehistoric Creatures. (gr. k-12). 1993. PLB 24.95 (0-7933-7500-2); pap. 14.95 (0-7933-7501-0); computer disk 29.95 (0-7933-7502-9) Gallopade Pub Group.

—Jurassic Ark! Missouri Dinosaurs & Other Prehistoric Creatures. (gr. k-12). 1993. PLB 24.95 (0-7933-7503-7); pap. 14.95 (0-7933-7504-5); computer disk 29.95 (0-7933-7505-3) Gallopade Pub Group.

—Jurassic Ark! Montana Dinosaurs & Other Prehistoric Creatures. (gr. k-12). 1993. PLB 24.95 (0-7933-7506-1); pap. 14.95 (0-7933-7507-X); computer disk 29.95 (0-7933-7508-8) Gallopade Pub Group.

—Jurassic Ark! Nebraska Dinosaurs & Other Prehistoric Creatures. (gr. k-12). 1993. PLB 24.95 (0-7933-7509-6); pap. 14.95 (0-7933-7510-X); computer disk 29.95 (0-7933-7511-8) Gallopade Pub Group.

—Jurassic Ark! Nevada Dinosaurs & Other Prehistoric Creatures. (gr. k-12). 1993. PLB 24.95 (0-7933-7512-6); pap. 14.95 (0-7933-7513-4); computer disk 29.95 (0-7933-7514-2) Gallopade Pub Group.

—Jurassic Ark! New Hampshire Dinosaurs & Other Prehistoric Creatures. (gr. k-12). 1993. PLB 24.95 (0-7933-7515-0); pap. 14.95 (0-7933-7516-9); computer disk 29.95 (0-7933-7517-7) Gallopade Pub Group.

—Jurassic Ark! New Jersey Dinosaurs & Other Prehistoric Creatures. (gr. k-12). 1993. PLB 24.95 (0-7933-7518-5); pap. 14.95 (0-7933-7519-3); computer disk 29.95 (0-7933-7520-7) Gallopade Pub Group.

—Jurassic Ark! New Mexico Dinosaurs & Other Prehistoric Creatures. (gr. k-12). 1993. PLB 24.95 (0-7933-7521-5); pap. 14.95 (0-7933-7522-3); computer disk 29.95 (0-7933-7523-1) Gallopade Pub Group.

—Jurassic Ark! New York Dinosaurs & Other Prehistoric Creatures. (gr. k-12). 1993. PLB 24.95 (0-7933-7524-X); pap. 14.95 (0-7933-7525-8); computer disk 29.95 (0-7933-7526-6) Gallopade Pub Group.

—Jurassic Ark! North Carolina Dinosaurs & Other Prehistoric Creatures. (gr. k-12). 1993. PLB 24.95 (0-7933-7527-4); pap. 14.95 (0-7933-7528-2); computer disk 29.95 (0-7933-7529-0) Gallopade Pub Group.

—Jurassic Ark! North Dakota Dinosaurs & Other Prehistoric Creatures. (gr. k-12). 1993. PLB 24.95 (0-7933-7530-4); pap. 14.95 (0-7933-7531-2); computer disk 29.95 (0-7933-7532-0) Gallopade Pub Group.

—Jurassic Ark! Ohio Dinosaurs & Other Prehistoric Creatures. (gr. k-12). 1993. PLB 24.95 (0-7933-7533-9); pap. 14.95 (0-7933-7534-7); computer disk 29.95 (0-7933-7535-5) Gallopade Pub Group.

—Jurassic Ark! Oklahoma Dinosaurs & Other Prehistoric Creatures. (gr. k-12). 1993. PLB 24.95 (0-7933-7536-3); pap. 14.95 (0-7933-7537-1); computer disk 29.95 (0-7933-7538-X) Gallopade Pub Group.

—Jurassic Ark! Oregon Dinosaurs & Other Prehistoric Creatures. (gr. k-12). 1993. PLB 24.95 (0-7933-7539-8); pap. 14.95 (0-7933-7540-1); computer disk 29.95 (0-7933-7541-X) Gallopade Pub Group.

—Jurassic Ark! Pennsylvania Dinosaurs & Other Prehistoric Creatures. (gr. k-12). 1993. PLB 24.95 (0-7933-7542-8); pap. 14.95 (0-7933-7543-6); computer disk 29.95 (0-7933-7544-4) Gallopade Pub Group.

—Jurassic Ark! Rhode Island Dinosaurs & Other Prehistoric Creatures. (gr. k-12). 1993. PLB 24.95 (0-7933-7545-2); pap. 14.95 (0-7933-7546-0); computer disk 29.95 (0-7933-7547-9) Gallopade Pub Group.

—Jurassic Ark! South Carolina Dinosaurs & Other Prehistoric Creatures. (gr. k-12). 1993. PLB 24.95 (0-7933-7548-7); pap. 14.95 (0-7933-7549-5); computer disk 29.95 (0-7933-7550-9) Gallopade Pub Group.

—Jurassic Ark! South Dakota Dinosaurs & Other Prehistoric Creatures. (gr. k-12). 1993. PLB 24.95 (0-7933-7551-7); pap. 14.95 (0-7933-7552-5); computer disk 29.95 (0-7933-7553-3) Gallopade Pub Group.

—Jurassic Ark! Tennessee Dinosaurs & Other Prehistoric Creatures. (gr. k-12). 1993. PLB 24.95 (0-7933-7554-1); pap. 14.95 (0-7933-7555-X); computer disk 29.95 (0-7933-7556-8) Gallopade Pub Group.

—Jurassic Ark! Texas Dinosaurs & Other Prehistoric Creatures. (gr. k-12). 1993. PLB 24.95 (0-7933-7557-6); pap. 14.95 (0-7933-7558-4); computer disk 29.95 (0-7933-7559-2) Gallopade Pub Group.

—Jurassic Ark! Utah Dinosaurs & Other Prehistoric Creatures. (gr. k-12). 1993. PLB 24.95 (0-7933-7560-6); pap. 14.95 (0-7933-7561-4); computer disk 29.95 (0-7933-7562-2) Gallopade Pub Group.

—Jurassic Ark! Vermont Dinosaurs & Other Prehistoric Creatures. (gr. k-12). 1993. PLB 24.95 (0-7933-7563-0); pap. 14.95 (0-7933-7564-9); computer disk 29.95 (0-7933-7565-7) Gallopade Pub Group.

—Jurassic Ark! Virginia Dinosaurs & Other Prehistoric Creatures. (gr. k-12). 1993. PLB 24.95 (0-7933-7566-5); pap. 14.95 (0-7933-7567-3); computer disk 29.95 (0-7933-7568-1) Gallopade Pub Group.

—Jurassic Ark! Washington, D. C. Dinosaurs & Other Prehistoric Creatures. (gr. k-12). 1993. PLB 24.95 (0-7933-7452-9); pap. 14.95 (0-7933-7453-7); computer disk 29.95 (0-7933-7454-5) Gallopade Pub Group.

—Jurassic Ark! Washington Dinosaurs & Other Prehistoric Creatures. (gr. k-12). 1993. PLB 24.95 (0-7933-7569-X); pap. 14.95 (0-7933-7570-3); computer disk 29.95 (0-7933-7571-1) Gallopade Pub Group.

—Jurassic Ark! West Virginia Dinosaurs & Other Prehistoric Creatures. (gr. k-12). 1993. PLB 24.95 (0-7933-7572-X); pap. 14.95 (0-7933-7573-8); computer disk 29.95 (0-7933-7574-6) Gallopade Pub Group.

—Jurassic Ark! Wisconsin Dinosaurs & Other Prehistoric Creatures. (gr. k-12). 1993. PLB 24.95 (0-7933-7575-4); pap. 14.95 (0-7933-7576-2); computer disk 29.95 (0-7933-7577-0) Gallopade Pub Group.

—Jurassic Ark! Wyoming Dinosaurs & Other Prehistoric Creatures. (gr. k-12). 1993. PLB 24.95 (0-7933-7578-9); pap. 14.95 (0-7933-7579-7); computer disk 29.95 (0-7933-7580-0) Gallopade Pub Group.

—Kansas & Other State Greats (Biographies) (gr. 3-12). 1989. 24.95 (1-55609-362-4); pap. 14.95 (1-55609-363-2); bk. on computer disk 29.95 (1-55609-364-0) Gallopade Pub Group.

—Kansas Bandits, Bushwackers, Outlaws, Crooks, Devils, Ghosts, Desperadoes & Other Assorted & Sundry Characters! (Illus.). (gr. 3-12). 1990. PLB 24.95 (0-7933-0454-7); pap. 14.95 (0-7933-0453-9); computer disk 29.95 (0-7933-0455-5) Gallopade Pub Group.

—Kansas Classic Christmas Trivia: Stories, Recipes, Activities, Legends, Lore & More! (Illus.). (gr. 3-12). 1990. PLB 24.95 (0-7933-0457-1); pap. 14.95 (0-7933-0456-3); computer disk 29.95 (0-7933-0458-X) Gallopade Pub Group.

—Kansas Coastales. 1989. PLB 24.95 (1-55609-365-9); pap. 14.95 (1-55609-366-7); bk. on computer disk 29. 95 (1-55609-367-5) Gallopade Pub Group.

—Kansas Coastales! 1992. lib. bdg. 24.95 (0-7933-7281-X) Gallopade Pub Group.

—Kansas "Crinkum-Crankum" A Funny Word Book about Our State. (Illus.). 1992. lib. bdg. 24.95 (0-7933-4856-0); pap. 14.95 (0-7933-4857-9); disk 29. 95 (0-7933-4858-7) Gallopade Pub Group.

—Kansas Dingbats! Bk. 1: A Fun Book of Games, Stories, Activities & More about Our State That's All in Code! for You to Decipher. (Illus.). (gr. 3-12). 1991. PLB 24.95 (0-7933-3821-2); pap. 14.95 (0-7933-3822-0); computer disk 29.95 (0-7933-3823-9) Gallopade Pub Group.

—Kansas Festival Fun for Kids! (Illus.). (gr. 3-12). 1991. lib. bdg. 24.95 (0-7933-3974-X); pap. 14.95 (0-7933-3975-8); disk 29.95 (0-7933-3976-6) Gallopade Pub Group.

—The Kansas Hot Air Balloon Mystery. (Illus.). (gr. 2-9). 1990. 24.95 (0-7933-2462-9); pap. 14.95 (0-7933-2463-7); computer disk 29.95 (0-7933-2464-5) Gallopade Pub Group.

—Kansas Jeopardy! Answers & Questions about Our State! (Illus.). (gr. 3-12). 1991. PLB 24.95 (0-7933-4127-2); pap. 14.95 (0-7933-4128-0); computer disk 29.95 (0-7933-4129-9) Gallopade Pub Group.

—Kansas "Jography" A Fun Run Thru Your State. (gr. 3-12). 1989. PLB 24.95 (1-55609-353-5); pap. 14.95 (1-55609-354-3); bk. on computer disk 29.95 (1-55609-355-1) Gallopade Pub Group.

—Kansas Kid's Cookbook: Recipes, How-to, History, Lore & More! (Illus.). (gr. 3-12). 1990. PLB 24.95 (0-7933-0466-0); pap. 14.95 (0-7933-0465-2); computer disk 29.95 (0-7933-0467-9) Gallopade Pub Group.

—The Kansas Mystery Van Takes Off! Book 1: Handicapped Kansas Kids Sneak Off on a Big Adventure. (Illus.). (gr. 3-12). 1992. 24.95 (0-7933-5009-3); pap. 14.95 (0-7933-5010-7); computer disk 29.95 (0-7933-5011-5) Gallopade Pub Group.

—Kansas Quiz Bowl Crash Course. (gr. 3-12). 1989. PLB 24.95 (1-55609-359-4); pap. 14.95 (1-55609-360-8); bk. on computer disk 29.95 (1-55609-361-6) Gallopade Pub Group.

—Kansas Rollercoasters! (Illus.). (gr. 3-12). 1992. PLB 24.95 (0-7933-5272-X); pap. 14.95 (0-7933-5273-8); computer disk 29.95 (0-7933-5274-6) Gallopade Pub Group.

—Kansas School Trivia: An Amazing & Fascinating Look at Our State's Teachers, Schools & Students! (Illus.). (gr. 3-12). 1990. PLB 24.95 (0-7933-0463-6); pap. 14. 95 (0-7933-0462-8); computer disk 29.95 (0-7933-0464-4) Gallopade Pub Group.

—Kansas Silly Basketball Sportsmysteries, Vol. I. (Illus.). (gr. 3-12). 1990. PLB 24.95 (0-7933-0460-1); pap. 14. 95 (0-7933-0459-8); computer disk 29.95 (0-7933-0461-X) Gallopade Pub Group.

—Kansas Silly Basketball Sportsmysteries, Vol. II. (Illus.). (gr. 3-12). 1990. PLB 24.95 (0-7933-1640-5); pap. 14. 95 (0-7933-1641-3); computer disk 29.95 (0-7933-1642-1) Gallopade Pub Group.

—Kansas Silly Football Mystery, Vol. I. (gr. 3-12). 1989. PLB 24.95 (1-55609-368-3); pap. 14.95 (1-55609-369-1); bk. on computer disk 29.95 (1-55609-370-5) Gallopade Pub Group.

—Kansas Silly Football Mystery, Vol. II. (gr. 3-12). 1989. PLB 24.95 (1-55609-377-2); pap. 14.95 (0-318-41972-6); bk. on computer disk 29.95 (1-55609-379-9) Gallopade Pub Group.

—Kansas Silly Trivia. (gr. 3-12). 1989. PLB 24.95 (*0-318-41973-4*); pap. 14.95 (*1-55609-351-9*); bk. on computer disk 29.95 (*1-55609-352-7*) Gallopade Pub Group.

—Kansas Timeline: A Chronology of Kansas History, Mystery, Trivia, Legend, Lore & More. (Illus.). (gr. 3-12). 1992. PLB 24.95 (*0-7933-5923-6*); pap. 14.95 (*0-7933-5924-4*); computer disk 29.95 (*0-7933-5925-2*) Gallopade Pub Group.

—Kansas's (Most Devastating!) Disasters & (Most Calamitous!) Catastrophies! (Illus.). (gr. 3-12). 1990. PLB 24.95 (*0-7933-0451-2*); pap. 14.95 (*0-7933-0450-4*); computer disk 29.95 (*0-7933-0452-0*) Gallopade Pub Group.

—Kansas's Unsolved Mysteries (& Their "Solutions") Includes Scientific Information & Other Activities for Students. (Illus.). (gr. 3-12). 1992. PLB 24.95 (*0-7933-5770-5*); pap. 14.95 (*0-7933-5771-3*); computer disk 29.95 (*0-7933-5772-1*) Gallopade Pub Group.

—Kentucky & Other State Greats (Biographies) (Illus.). (gr. 3-8). 1990. PLB 24.95 (*1-55609-448-3*); pap. 14.95 (*1-55609-447-7*); disk 29.95 (*0-7933-1658-8*) Gallopade Pub Group.

—Kentucky Bandits, Bushwackers, Outlaws, Crooks, Devils, Ghosts, Desperadoes & Other Assorted & Sundry Characters! (Illus.). (gr. 3-8). 1990. PLB 24.95 (*0-7933-0478-4*); pap. 14.95 (*0-7933-0477-6*); disk 29.95 (*0-7933-0479-2*) Gallopade Pub Group.

—Kentucky Classic Christmas Trivia: Stories, Recipes, Activities, Legends, Lore & More! (Illus.). (gr. 3-8). 1990. PLB 24.95 (*0-7933-0481-4*); pap. 14.95 (*0-7933-0480-6*); disk 29.95 (*0-7933-0482-2*) Gallopade Pub Group.

—Kentucky Coastales. (Illus.). (gr. 3-8). 1990. PLB 24.95 (*1-55609-444-2*); pap. 14.95 (*1-55609-443-4*); disk 29.95 (*0-7933-1654-5*) Gallopade Pub Group.

—Kentucky Coastales! 1992. lib. bdg. 24.95 (*0-7933-7282-8*) Gallopade Pub Group.

—Kentucky "Crinkum-Crankum" A Funny Word Book about Our State. (Illus.). 1992. lib. bdg. 24.95 (*0-7933-4859-5*); pap. 14.95 (*0-7933-4860-9*); disk 29.95 (*0-7933-4861-7*) Gallopade Pub Group.

—Kentucky Dingbats! Bk. 1: A Fun Book of Games, Stories, Activities & More about Our State That's All in Code! for You to Decipher. (Illus.). (gr. 3-12). 1991. PLB 24.95 (*0-7933-3824-7*); pap. 14.95 (*0-7933-3825-5*); computer disk 29.95 (*0-7933-3826-3*) Gallopade Pub Group.

—Kentucky Festival Fun for Kids! (Illus.). (gr. 3-12). 1991. lib. bdg. 24.95 (*0-7933-3977-4*); pap. 14.95 (*0-7933-3978-2*); disk 29.95 (*0-7933-3979-0*) Gallopade Pub Group.

—The Kentucky Hot Air Balloon Mystery. (Illus.). (gr. 2-9). 1990. 24.95 (*0-7933-2471-8*); pap. 14.95 (*0-7933-2472-6*); computer disk 29.95 (*0-7933-2473-4*) Gallopade Pub Group.

—Kentucky Jeopardy! Answers & Questions about Our State! (Illus.). (gr. 3-12). 1991. PLB 24.95 (*0-7933-4130-2*); pap. 14.95 (*0-7933-4131-0*); computer disk 29.95 (*0-7933-4132-9*) Gallopade Pub Group.

—Kentucky "Jography" A Fun Run Thru Our State! (Illus.). (gr. 3-8). 1990. PLB 24.95 (*1-55609-439-6*); pap. 14.95 (*1-55609-109-5*); disk 29.95 (*0-7933-1644-8*) Gallopade Pub Group.

—Kentucky Kid's Cookbook: Recipes, How-To, History, Lore & More! (Illus.). (gr. 3-8). 1990. PLB 24.95 (*0-7933-0490-3*); pap. 14.95 (*0-7933-0489-X*); disk 29.95 (*0-7933-0491-1*) Gallopade Pub Group.

—The Kentucky Mystery Van Takes Off! Book 1: Handicapped Kentucky Kids Sneak Off on a Big Adventure. (Illus.). (gr. 3-12). 1992. 24.95 (*0-7933-5012-3*); pap. 14.95 (*0-7933-5013-1*); computer disk 29.95 (*0-7933-5014-X*) Gallopade Pub Group.

—Kentucky Quiz Bowl Crash Course! (Illus.). (gr. 3-8). 1990. PLB 24.95 (*1-55609-446-9*); pap. 14.95 (*1-55609-445-0*); disk 29.95 (*0-7933-1653-7*) Gallopade Pub Group.

—Kentucky Rollercoasters! (Illus.). (gr. 3-12). 1992. PLB 24.95 (*0-7933-5275-4*); pap. 14.95 (*0-7933-5276-2*); computer disk 29.95 (*0-7933-5277-0*) Gallopade Pub Group.

—Kentucky School Trivia: An Amazing & Fascinating Look at Our State's Teachers, Schools & Students! (Illus.). (gr. 3-8). 1990. PLB 24.95 (*0-7933-0487-3*); pap. 14.95 (*0-7933-0486-5*); disk 29.95 (*0-7933-0488-1*) Gallopade Pub Group.

—Kentucky Silly Basketball Sportsmysteries, Vol. I. (Illus.). (gr. 3-8). 1990. PLB 24.95 (*0-7933-0484-9*); pap. 14.95 (*0-7933-0483-0*); disk 29.95 (*0-7933-0485-7*) Gallopade Pub Group.

—Kentucky Silly Basketball Sportsmysteries, Vol. II. (Illus.). (gr. 3-8). 1990. PLB 24.95 (*0-7933-1659-6*); pap. 14.95 (*0-7933-1660-X*); disk 29.95 (*0-7933-1661-8*) Gallopade Pub Group.

—Kentucky Silly Football Sportsmysteries, Vol. I. (Illus.). (gr. 3-8). 1990. PLB 24.95 (*1-55609-442-6*); pap. 14.95 (*1-55609-441-8*); disk 29.95 (*0-7933-1646-4*) Gallopade Pub Group.

—Kentucky Silly Football Sportsmysteries, Vol. II. (Illus.). (gr. 3-8). 1990. PLB 24.95 (*0-7933-1647-2*); pap. 14.95 (*0-7933-1648-0*); disk 29.95 (*0-7933-1649-9*) Gallopade Pub Group.

—Kentucky Silly Trivia! (gr. 3-8). 1990. PLB 24.95 (*1-55609-438-8*); pap. 14.95 (*1-55609-040-4*); disk 29.95 (*0-7933-1643-X*) Gallopade Pub Group.

—Kentucky Timeline: A Chronology of Kentucky History, Mystery, Trivia, Legend, Lore & More. (Illus.). (gr. 3-12). 1992. PLB 24.95 (*0-7933-5926-0*); pap. 14.95 (*0-7933-5927-9*); computer disk 29.95 (*0-7933-5928-7*) Gallopade Pub Group.

—Kentucky's (Most Devastating!) Disasters & (Most Calamitous!) Catastrophies! LC 7933000476000008. (Illus.). (gr. 3-8). 1990. PLB 24.95 (*0-7933-0475-X*); pap. 14.95 (*0-7933-0474-1*); disk 29.95 (*0-685-45937-3*) Gallopade Pub Group.

—Kentucky's Unsolved Mysteries (& Their "Solutions") Includes Scientific Information & Other Activities for Students. (Illus.). (gr. 3-12). 1992. PLB 24.95 (*0-7933-5773-X*); pap. 14.95 (*0-7933-5774-8*); computer disk 29.95 (*0-7933-5775-6*) Gallopade Pub Group.

—Kids & Space: Look Forward, Plan, Prepare, Go! (Illus.). (gr. 3-8). 1990. PLB 24.95 (*0-7933-0003-7*); pap. 14.95 (*0-7933-0004-5*); computer disk 29.95 (*0-7933-0005-3*) Gallopade Pub Group.

—A Kid's Book of Smarts: How to Think, Make Decisions, Figure Things Out, Budget Your Time, Money, Plan Your Day, Week, Life & Other Things Adults Wish They'd Learned When They Were Kids! (Illus.). 68p. (gr. 4-12). 1983. PLB 24.95 (*1-55609-173-7*); pap. 14.95 (*0-935326-18-9*) Gallopade Pub Group.

—The Kitchen House: How Yesterdays Black Women Created Todays American Foods. (gr. 3-12). 1989. PLB 24.95 (*1-55609-309-8*); pap. 14.95 (*1-55609-308-X*); computer disk 29.95 (*1-55609-310-1*) Gallopade Pub Group.

—Latin for Kids: Of All the Gaul. (Illus.). (gr. 2-10). 1983. 24.95 (*0-935326-17-0*) Gallopade Pub Group.

—The Legend of the Devil's Hoofprints. (Illus., Orig.). (gr. 2 up). 1986. PLB 24.95 (*1-55609-177-X*); pap. 14.95 (*0-935326-57-X*) Gallopade Pub Group.

—Let's Find Out about Florida! In the Yellow Pages, Dictionary, Encyclopedia, Almanac, Atlas, Who's Who, Bartlett's Quotations & Other Reference Sources! 36p. (gr. 3-5). 1993. PLB 24.95 (*0-7933-7349-2*); pap. 14.95 (*0-7933-7350-6*); disk 29.95 (*0-7933-7351-4*) Gallopade Pub Group.

—Let's Quilt Alabama & Stuff It Topographically! (Illus.). (gr. 3-12). 1990. PLB 24.95 (*1-55609-462-0*); pap. 14.95 (*1-55609-073-0*); computer disk 29.95 (*0-7933-1328-7*) Gallopade Pub Group.

—Let's Quilt Alaska & Stuff It Topographically! (Illus.). (gr. 3-12). 1990. PLB 24.95 (*1-55609-475-2*); pap. 14.95 (*1-55609-094-3*); computer disk 29.95 (*0-7933-1344-9*) Gallopade Pub Group.

—Let's Quilt Arizona & Stuff It Topographically! (Illus.). (gr. 3-12). 1990. PLB 24.95 (*1-55609-499-X*); pap. 14.95 (*1-55609-128-1*); computer disk 29.95 (*0-7933-1360-0*) Gallopade Pub Group.

—Let's Quilt Arkansas & Stuff It Topographically! (Illus.). (gr. 3-12). 1990. PLB 24.95 (*1-55609-486-8*); pap. 14.95 (*1-55609-078-1*); computer disk 29.95 (*0-7933-1376-7*) Gallopade Pub Group.

—Let's Quilt California & Stuff It Topographically! (Illus.). (gr. 3-12). 1990. PLB 24.95 (*1-55609-513-9*); pap. 14.95 (*1-55609-512-0*); computer disk 29.95 (*0-7933-1392-9*) Gallopade Pub Group.

—Let's Quilt Colorado & Stuff It Topographically! (Illus.). (gr. 3-12). 1990. PLB 24.95 (*1-55609-526-0*); pap. 14.95 (*1-55609-126-5*); computer disk 29.95 (*0-7933-1408-9*) Gallopade Pub Group.

—Let's Quilt Connecticut & Stuff It Topographically! (Illus.). (gr. 3-12). 1990. PLB 24.95 (*1-55609-539-2*); pap. 14.95 (*0-685-45928-4*); computer disk 29.95 (*0-7933-1424-0*) Gallopade Pub Group.

—Let's Quilt Delaware & Stuff It Topographically! (Illus.). (gr. 3-12). 1990. PLB 24.95 (*1-55609-552-X*); pap. 14.95 (*1-55609-063-3*); computer disk 29.95 (*0-7933-1440-2*) Gallopade Pub Group.

—Let's Quilt Florida & Stuff It Topographically! (Illus.). (gr. 3-12). 1990. PLB 24.95 (*1-55609-419-1*); pap. 14.95 (*1-55609-055-2*); computer disk 29.95 (*0-7933-1488-7*) Gallopade Pub Group.

—Let's Quilt Georgia & Stuff It Topographically! (Illus.). (gr. 3-12). 1990. PLB 24.95 (*1-55609-382-9*); pap. 14.95 (*1-55609-054-4*); computer disk 29.95 (*0-7933-1507-7*) Gallopade Pub Group.

—Let's Quilt Hawaii & Stuff It Topographically! (Illus.). (gr. 3-12). 1990. PLB 24.95 (*1-55609-569-4*); pap. 14.95 (*1-55609-093-5*); computer disk 29.95 (*0-7933-1526-3*) Gallopade Pub Group.

—Let's Quilt Idaho & Stuff It Topographically! (Illus.). (gr. 3-12). 1990. PLB 24.95 (*1-55609-584-8*); pap. 14.95 (*1-55609-139-7*); computer disk 29.95 (*0-7933-1545-X*) Gallopade Pub Group.

—Let's Quilt Illinois & Stuff It Topographically! (Illus.). (gr. 3-12). 1990. PLB 24.95 (*1-55609-408-6*); pap. 14.95 (*1-55609-097-8*); computer disk 29.95 (*0-7933-1585-9*) Gallopade Pub Group.

—Let's Quilt Indiana & Stuff It Topographically! (Illus.). (gr. 3-12). 1990. PLB 24.95 (*1-55609-429-9*); pap. 14.95 (*1-55609-096-X*); computer disk 29.95 (*0-7933-1604-9*) Gallopade Pub Group.

—Let's Quilt Iowa & Stuff It Topographically! (Illus.). (gr. 3-12). 1990. PLB 24.95 (*1-55609-451-5*); pap. 14.95 (*1-55609-072-2*); computer disk 29.95 (*0-7933-1623-5*) Gallopade Pub Group.

—Lets Quilt Kansas. (gr. 3-12). 1989. PLB 24.95 (*1-55609-356-X*); pap. 14.95 (*1-55609-357-8*); bk. on computer disk 29.95 (*1-55609-358-6*) Gallopade Pub Group.

—Let's Quilt Louisiana & Stuff It Topographically! (Illus.). (gr. 3-8). 1990. PLB 24.95 (*1-55609-397-7*); pap. 14.95 (*1-55609-075-7*); disk 29.95 (*0-7933-1664-2*) Gallopade Pub Group.

—Let's Quilt Maine & Stuff It Topographically! (Illus.). (gr. 3-8). 1990. PLB 24.95 (*1-55609-599-6*); pap. 14.95 (*1-55609-068-4*); disk 29.95 (*1-55609-601-1*) Gallopade Pub Group.

—Let's Quilt Maryland & Stuff It Topographically! (Illus.). (gr. 3-8). 1990. PLB 24.95 (*1-55609-622-4*); pap. 14.95 (*1-55609-058-7*); disk 29.95 (*1-55609-623-2*) Gallopade Pub Group.

—Let's Quilt Massachusetts & Stuff It Topographically! (Illus.). (gr. 3-8). 1990. PLB 24.95 (*1-55609-684-4*); pap. 14.95 (*1-55609-685-2*); disk 29.95 (*1-55609-686-0*) Gallopade Pub Group.

—Let's Quilt Michigan & Stuff It Topographically! (Illus.). (gr. 3 up). 1990. PLB 24.95 (*1-55609-669-0*); pap. 14.95 (*1-55609-138-9*); computer disk 29.95 (*1-55609-670-4*) Gallopade Pub Group.

—Let's Quilt Minnesota & Stuff It Topographically! (Illus.). (gr. 3 up). 1990. PLB 24.95 (*1-55609-645-3*); pap. 14.95 (*1-55609-099-4*); computer disk 29.95 (*1-55609-647-X*) Gallopade Pub Group.

—Let's Quilt Mississippi & Stuff It Topographically! (Illus.). (gr. 3 up). 1990. PLB 24.95 (*1-55609-710-7*); pap. 14.95 (*1-55609-074-9*); computer disk 29.95 (*1-55609-716-6*) Gallopade Pub Group.

—Let's Quilt Missouri & Stuff It Topographically! (Illus.). (gr. 3 up). 1990. PLB 24.95 (*1-55609-733-6*); pap. 14.95 (*1-55609-734-4*); computer disk 29.95 (*1-55609-735-2*) Gallopade Pub Group.

—Let's Quilt Montana & Stuff It Topographically! (Illus.). (gr. 3 up). 1990. PLB 24.95 (*1-55609-757-3*); pap. 14.95 (*1-55609-131-1*); computer disk 29.95 (*1-55609-759-X*) Gallopade Pub Group.

—Let's Quilt Nebraska & Stuff It Topographically! (Illus.). (gr. 3 up). 1990. PLB 24.95 (*1-55609-781-6*); pap. 14.95 (*1-55609-779-4*); computer disk 29.95 (*1-55609-783-2*) Gallopade Pub Group.

—Let's Quilt Nevada & Stuff It Topographically! (Illus.). 1990. PLB 24.95 (*1-55609-805-7*); pap. 14.95 (*1-55609-130-3*); computer disk 29.95 (*1-55609-807-3*) Gallopade Pub Group.

—Let's Quilt New Hampshire & Stuff It Topographically! (Illus.). 1990. PLB 24.95 (*1-55609-829-4*); pap. 14.95 (*1-55609-067-6*); computer disk 29.95 (*1-55609-831-6*) Gallopade Pub Group.

—Let's Quilt New Jersey & Stuff It Topographically! (Illus.). 1990. PLB 24.95 (*1-55609-853-7*); pap. 14.95 (*1-55609-069-2*); computer disk 29.95 (*1-55609-855-3*) Gallopade Pub Group.

—Let's Quilt New Mexico & Stuff It Topographically! (Illus.). 1990. PLB 24.95 (*1-55609-877-4*); pap. 14.95 (*1-55609-127-3*); computer disk 29.95 (*1-55609-879-0*) Gallopade Pub Group.

—Let's Quilt New York & Stuff It Topographically! (Illus.). 1990. PLB 24.95 (*1-55609-904-5*); pap. 14.95 (*1-55609-060-9*); computer disk 29.95 (*1-55609-905-3*) Gallopade Pub Group.

—Let's Quilt North Carolina & Stuff It Topographically! (Illus.). 1990. PLB 24.95 (*1-55609-925-8*); pap. 14.95 (*1-55609-050-1*); computer disk 29.95 (*1-55609-926-6*) Gallopade Pub Group.

—Let's Quilt North Dakota & Stuff It Topographically! (Illus.). 1990. PLB 24.95 (*1-55609-946-0*); pap. 14.95 (*1-55609-135-4*); computer disk 29.95 (*1-55609-947-9*) Gallopade Pub Group.

—Let's Quilt Ohio & Stuff It Topographically! (Illus.). 1990. PLB 24.95 (*0-685-45975-6*); pap. 14.95 (*1-55609-095-1*); computer disk 29.95 (*1-55609-985-1*) Gallopade Pub Group.

—Let's Quilt Oklahoma & Stuff It Topographically! (Illus.). 1990. PLB 24.95 (*0-7933-1860-2*); pap. 14.95 (*0-7933-1861-0*); computer disk 29.95 (*0-7933-1862-9*) Gallopade Pub Group.

—Let's Quilt Oregon & Stuff It Topographically! (Illus.). 1990. PLB 24.95 (*0-7933-1893-9*); pap. 14.95 (*1-55609-132-X*); computer disk 29.95 (*0-7933-1894-7*) Gallopade Pub Group.

—Let's Quilt Our Alabama County. 1992. lib. bdg. 24.95 (*0-7933-6936-3*); pap. text ed. 14.95 (*0-7933-6935-5*); disk 29.95 (*0-7933-6937-1*) Gallopade Pub Group.

—Let's Quilt Our Alabama Town. 1992. lib. bdg. 24.95 (*0-7933-6933-9*); pap. text ed. 14.95 (*0-7933-6932-0*); disk 29.95 (*0-7933-6934-7*) Gallopade Pub Group.

—Let's Quilt Our Alaska County. 1992. lib. bdg. 24.95 (*0-7933-7116-3*); pap. text ed. 14.95 (*0-7933-7117-1*); disk 29.95 (*0-7933-7118-X*) Gallopade Pub Group.

—Let's Quilt Our Alaska Town. 1992. lib. bdg. 24.95 (*0-685-60854-9*); pap. text ed. 14.95 (*0-7933-6967-3*); disk 29.95 (*0-7933-6968-1*) Gallopade Pub Group.

—Let's Quilt Our Arizona County. 1992. lib. bdg. 24.95 (*0-7933-7119-8*); pap. text ed. 14.95 (*0-7933-7120-1*); disk 29.95 (*0-7933-7121-X*) Gallopade Pub Group.

—Let's Quilt Our Arizona Town. 1992. lib. bdg. 24.95 (*0-7933-6969-X*); pap. text ed. 14.95 (*0-7933-6970-3*); disk 29.95 (*0-7933-6971-1*) Gallopade Pub Group.

—Let's Quilt Our Arkansas County. 1992. lib. bdg. 24.95 (*0-7933-7122-8*); pap. text ed. 14.95 (*0-7933-7123-6*); disk 29.95 (*0-7933-7124-4*) Gallopade Pub Group.

—Let's Quilt Our Arkansas Town. 1992. lib. bdg. 24.95 (*0-7933-6972-X*); pap. text ed. 14.95 (*0-7933-6973-8*); disk 29.95 (*0-7933-6974-6*) Gallopade Pub Group.

—Let's Quilt Our California County. 1992. lib. bdg. 24.95 (*0-7933-7125-2*); pap. text ed. 14.95 (*0-7933-7126-0*); disk 29.95 (*0-7933-7127-9*) Gallopade Pub Group.

—Let's Quilt Our California Town. 1992. lib. bdg. 24.95 (0-7933-6975-4); pap. text ed. 14.95 (0-7933-6976-2); disk 29.95 (0-7933-6977-0) Gallopade Pub Group.
—Let's Quilt Our Colorado County. 1992. lib. bdg. 24.95 (0-7933-7128-7); pap. text ed. 14.95 (0-7933-7129-5); disk 29.95 (0-7933-7130-9) Gallopade Pub Group.
—Let's Quilt Our Colorado Town. 1992. lib. bdg. 24.95 (0-7933-6978-9); pap. text ed. 14.95 (0-7933-6979-7); disk 29.95 (0-7933-6980-0) Gallopade Pub Group.
—Let's Quilt Our Connecticut County. 1992. lib. bdg. 24.95 (0-7933-7131-7); pap. text ed. 14.95 (0-7933-7132-5); disk 29.95 (0-7933-7133-3) Gallopade Pub Group.
—Let's Quilt Our Connecticut Town. 1992. lib. bdg. 24.95 (0-7933-6981-9); pap. text ed. 14.95 (0-7933-6982-7); disk 29.95 (0-7933-6983-5) Gallopade Pub Group.
—Let's Quilt Our Delaware County. 1992. lib. bdg. 24.95 (0-7933-7134-1); pap. text ed. 14.95 (0-7933-7135-X); disk 29.95 (0-7933-7136-8) Gallopade Pub Group.
—Let's Quilt Our Delaware Town. 1992. lib. bdg. 24.95 (0-7933-6984-3); pap. text ed. 14.95 (0-7933-6985-1); disk 29.95 (0-7933-6986-X) Gallopade Pub Group.
—Let's Quilt Our Florida County. 1992. lib. bdg. 24.95 (0-7933-7140-6); pap. text ed. 14.95 (0-7933-7141-4); disk 29.95 (0-7933-7142-2) Gallopade Pub Group.
—Let's Quilt Our Florida Town. 1992. lib. bdg. 24.95 (0-7933-6990-8); pap. text ed. 14.95 (0-7933-6991-6); disk 29.95 (0-7933-6992-4) Gallopade Pub Group.
—Let's Quilt Our Georgia County. 1992. lib. bdg. 24.95 (0-7933-7143-0); pap. text ed. 14.95 (0-7933-7144-9); disk 29.95 (0-7933-7145-7) Gallopade Pub Group.
—Let's Quilt Our Georgia Town. 1992. lib. bdg. 24.95 (0-7933-6993-2); pap. text ed. 14.95 (0-7933-6994-0); disk 29.95 (0-7933-6995-9) Gallopade Pub Group.
—Let's Quilt Our Hawaii County. 1992. lib. bdg. 24.95 (0-7933-7146-5); pap. text ed. 14.95 (0-7933-7147-3); disk 29.95 (0-7933-7148-1) Gallopade Pub Group.
—Let's Quilt Our Hawaii Town. 1992. lib. bdg. 24.95 (0-7933-6996-7); pap. text ed. 14.95 (0-7933-6997-5); disk 29.95 (0-7933-6998-3) Gallopade Pub Group.
—Let's Quilt Our Idaho County. 1992. lib. bdg. 24.95 (0-7933-7149-X); pap. text ed. 14.95 (0-7933-7150-3); disk 29.95 (0-7933-7151-1) Gallopade Pub Group.
—Let's Quilt Our Idaho Town. 1992. lib. bdg. 24.95 (0-7933-6999-1); pap. text ed. 14.95 (0-7933-7000-0); disk 29.95 (0-7933-7001-9) Gallopade Pub Group.
—Let's Quilt Our Illinois County. 1992. lib. bdg. 24.95 (0-7933-7152-X); pap. text ed. 14.95 (0-7933-7153-8); disk 29.95 (0-7933-7154-6) Gallopade Pub Group.
—Let's Quilt Our Illinois Town. 1992. lib. bdg. 24.95 (0-7933-7002-7); pap. text ed. 14.95 (0-7933-7003-5); disk 29.95 (0-7933-7004-3) Gallopade Pub Group.
—Let's Quilt Our Indiana County. 1992. lib. bdg. 24.95 (0-7933-7155-4); pap. text ed. 14.95 (0-7933-7156-2); disk 29.95 (0-7933-7157-0) Gallopade Pub Group.
—Let's Quilt Our Indiana Town. 1992. lib. bdg. 24.95 (0-7933-7005-1); pap. text ed. 14.95 (0-7933-7006-X); disk 29.95 (0-7933-7007-8) Gallopade Pub Group.
—Let's Quilt Our Iowa County. 1992. lib. bdg. 24.95 (0-7933-7158-9); pap. text ed. 14.95 (0-7933-7159-7); disk 29.95 (0-7933-7160-0) Gallopade Pub Group.
—Let's Quilt Our Iowa Town. 1992. lib. bdg. 24.95 (0-7933-7008-6); pap. text ed. 14.95 (0-7933-7009-4); disk 29.95 (0-7933-7010-8) Gallopade Pub Group.
—Let's Quilt Our Kansas County. 1992. lib. bdg. 24.95 (0-7933-7161-9); pap. text ed. 14.95 (0-7933-7162-7); disk 29.95 (0-7933-7163-5) Gallopade Pub Group.
—Let's Quilt Our Kansas Town. 1992. lib. bdg. 24.95 (0-7933-7011-6); pap. text ed. 14.95 (0-7933-7012-4); disk 29.95 (0-7933-7013-2) Gallopade Pub Group.
—Let's Quilt Our Kentucky County. 1992. lib. bdg. 24.95 (0-7933-7164-3); pap. text ed. 14.95 (0-7933-7165-1); disk 29.95 (0-7933-7166-X) Gallopade Pub Group.
—Let's Quilt Our Kentucky Town. 1992. lib. bdg. 24.95 (0-7933-7014-0); pap. text ed. 14.95 (0-7933-7015-9); disk 29.95 (0-7933-7016-7) Gallopade Pub Group.
—Let's Quilt Our Louisiana Parish. 1992. lib. bdg. 24.95 (0-7933-7167-8); pap. text ed. 14.95 (0-7933-7168-6); disk 29.95 (0-7933-7169-4) Gallopade Pub Group.
—Let's Quilt Our Louisiana Town. 1992. lib. bdg. 24.95 (0-7933-7017-5); pap. text ed. 14.95 (0-7933-7018-3); disk 29.95 (0-7933-7019-1) Gallopade Pub Group.
—Let's Quilt Our Maine County. 1992. lib. bdg. 24.95 (0-7933-7170-8); pap. text ed. 14.95 (0-7933-7171-6); disk 29.95 (0-7933-7172-4) Gallopade Pub Group.
—Let's Quilt Our Maine Town. 1992. lib. bdg. 24.95 (0-7933-7020-5); pap. text ed. 14.95 (0-7933-7021-3); disk 29.95 (0-7933-7022-1) Gallopade Pub Group.
—Let's Quilt Our Maryland County. 1992. lib. bdg. 24.95 (0-7933-7173-2); pap. text ed. 14.95 (0-7933-7174-0); disk 29.95 (0-7933-7175-9) Gallopade Pub Group.
—Let's Quilt Our Maryland Town. 1992. lib. bdg. 24.95 (0-7933-7023-X); pap. text ed. 14.95 (0-7933-7024-8); disk 29.95 (0-7933-7025-6) Gallopade Pub Group.
—Let's Quilt Our Massachusetts County. 1992. lib. bdg. 24.95 (0-7933-7176-7); pap. text ed. 14.95 (0-7933-7177-5); disk 29.95 (0-7933-7178-3) Gallopade Pub Group.
—Let's Quilt Our Massachusetts Town. 1992. lib. bdg. 24.95 (0-7933-7026-4); pap. text ed. 14.95 (0-7933-7027-2); disk 29.95 (0-7933-7028-0) Gallopade Pub Group.
—Let's Quilt Our Michigan County. 1992. lib. bdg. 24.95 (0-7933-7179-1); pap. text ed. 14.95 (0-7933-7180-5); disk 29.95 (0-7933-7181-3) Gallopade Pub Group.

—Let's Quilt Our Michigan Town. 1992. lib. bdg. 24.95 (0-7933-7029-9); pap. text ed. 14.95 (0-7933-7030-2); disk 29.95 (0-7933-7031-0) Gallopade Pub Group.
—Let's Quilt Our Minnesota County. 1992. lib. bdg. 24.95 (0-7933-7182-1); pap. text ed. 14.95 (0-7933-7183-X); disk 29.95 (0-7933-7184-8) Gallopade Pub Group.
—Let's Quilt Our Minnesota Town. 1992. lib. bdg. 24.95 (0-7933-7032-9); pap. text ed. 14.95 (0-7933-7033-7); disk 29.95 (0-7933-7034-5) Gallopade Pub Group.
—Let's Quilt Our Mississippi County. 1992. lib. bdg. 24.95 (0-7933-7185-6); pap. text ed. 14.95 (0-7933-7186-4); disk 29.95 (0-7933-7187-2) Gallopade Pub Group.
—Let's Quilt Our Mississippi Town. 1992. lib. bdg. 24.95 (0-7933-7035-3); pap. text ed. 14.95 (0-7933-7036-1); disk 29.95 (0-7933-7037-X) Gallopade Pub Group.
—Let's Quilt Our Missouri County. 1992. lib. bdg. 24.95 (0-7933-7188-0); pap. text ed. 14.95 (0-7933-7189-9); disk 29.95 (0-7933-7190-2) Gallopade Pub Group.
—Let's Quilt Our Missouri Town. 1992. lib. bdg. 24.95 (0-7933-7038-8); pap. text ed. 14.95 (0-7933-7039-6); disk 29.95 (0-7933-7040-X) Gallopade Pub Group.
—Let's Quilt Our Montana County. 1992. lib. bdg. 24.95 (0-7933-7191-0); pap. text ed. 14.95 (0-7933-7192-9); disk 29.95 (0-7933-7193-7) Gallopade Pub Group.
—Let's Quilt Our Montana Town. 1992. lib. bdg. 24.95 (0-7933-7041-8); pap. text ed. 14.95 (0-7933-7042-6); disk 29.95 (0-7933-7043-4) Gallopade Pub Group.
—Let's Quilt Our Nebraska County. 1992. lib. bdg. 24.95 (0-7933-7194-5); pap. text ed. 14.95 (0-7933-7195-3); disk 29.95 (0-7933-7196-1) Gallopade Pub Group.
—Let's Quilt Our Nebraska Town. 1992. lib. bdg. 24.95 (0-7933-7044-2); pap. text ed. 14.95 (0-7933-7045-0); disk 29.95 (0-7933-7046-9) Gallopade Pub Group.
—Let's Quilt Our Nevada County. 1992. lib. bdg. 24.95 (0-7933-7197-X); pap. text ed. 14.95 (0-7933-7198-8); disk 29.95 (0-7933-7199-6) Gallopade Pub Group.
—Let's Quilt Our Nevada Town. 1992. lib. bdg. 24.95 (0-7933-7047-7); pap. text ed. 14.95 (0-7933-7048-5); disk 29.95 (0-7933-7049-3) Gallopade Pub Group.
—Let's Quilt Our New Hampshire County. 1992. lib. bdg. 24.95 (0-7933-7200-3); pap. text ed. 14.95 (0-7933-7201-1); disk 29.95 (0-685-60853-0) Gallopade Pub Group.
—Let's Quilt Our New Hampshire Town. 1992. lib. bdg. 24.95 (0-7933-7050-7); pap. text ed. 14.95 (0-7933-7051-5); disk 29.95 (0-7933-7052-3) Gallopade Pub Group.
—Let's Quilt Our New Jersey County. 1992. lib. bdg. 24.95 (0-7933-7203-8); pap. text ed. 14.95 (0-7933-7204-6); disk 29.95 (0-7933-7205-4) Gallopade Pub Group.
—Let's Quilt Our New Jersey Town. 1992. lib. bdg. 24.95 (0-7933-7053-1); pap. text ed. 14.95 (0-7933-7054-X); disk 29.95 (0-7933-7055-8) Gallopade Pub Group.
—Let's Quilt Our New Mexico County. 1992. lib. bdg. 24.95 (0-7933-7206-2); pap. text ed. 14.95 (0-7933-7207-0); disk 29.95 (0-7933-7208-9) Gallopade Pub Group.
—Let's Quilt Our New Mexico Town. 1992. lib. bdg. 24.95 (0-7933-7056-6); pap. text ed. 14.95 (0-7933-7057-4); disk 29.95 (0-7933-7058-2) Gallopade Pub Group.
—Let's Quilt Our New York County. 1992. lib. bdg. 24.95 (0-7933-7209-7); pap. text ed. 14.95 (0-7933-7210-0); disk 29.95 (0-7933-7211-9) Gallopade Pub Group.
—Let's Quilt Our New York Town. 1992. lib. bdg. 24.95 (0-7933-7059-0); pap. text ed. 14.95 (0-7933-7060-4); disk 29.95 (0-7933-7061-2) Gallopade Pub Group.
—Let's Quilt Our North Carolina County. 1992. lib. bdg. 24.95 (0-7933-7212-7); pap. text ed. 14.95 (0-7933-7213-5); disk 29.95 (0-7933-7214-3) Gallopade Pub Group.
—Let's Quilt Our North Carolina Town. 1992. lib. bdg. 24.95 (0-7933-7062-0); pap. text ed. 14.95 (0-7933-7063-9); disk 29.95 (0-7933-7064-7) Gallopade Pub Group.
—Let's Quilt Our North Dakota County. 1992. lib. bdg. 24.95 (0-7933-7215-1); pap. text ed. 14.95 (0-7933-7216-X); disk 29.95 (0-7933-7217-8) Gallopade Pub Group.
—Let's Quilt Our North Dakota Town. 1992. lib. bdg. 24.95 (0-7933-7065-5); pap. text ed. 14.95 (0-7933-7066-3); disk 29.95 (0-7933-7067-1) Gallopade Pub Group.
—Let's Quilt Our Ohio County. 1992. lib. bdg. 24.95 (0-7933-7218-6); pap. text ed. 14.95 (0-7933-7219-4); disk 29.95 (0-7933-7220-8) Gallopade Pub Group.
—Let's Quilt Our Ohio Town. 1992. lib. bdg. 24.95 (0-7933-7068-X); pap. text ed. 14.95 (0-7933-7069-8); disk 29.95 (0-7933-7070-1) Gallopade Pub Group.
—Let's Quilt Our Oklahoma County. 1992. lib. bdg. 24.95 (0-7933-7221-6); pap. text ed. 14.95 (0-7933-7222-4); disk 29.95 (0-7933-7223-2) Gallopade Pub Group.
—Let's Quilt Our Oklahoma Town. 1992. lib. bdg. 24.95 (0-7933-7071-X); pap. text ed. 14.95 (0-7933-7072-8); disk 29.95 (0-7933-7073-6) Gallopade Pub Group.
—Let's Quilt Our Oregon County. 1992. lib. bdg. 24.95 (0-7933-7224-0); pap. text ed. 14.95 (0-7933-7225-9); disk 29.95 (0-7933-7226-7) Gallopade Pub Group.
—Let's Quilt Our Oregon Town. 1992. lib. bdg. 24.95 (0-7933-7074-4); pap. text ed. 14.95 (0-7933-7075-2); disk 29.95 (0-7933-7076-0) Gallopade Pub Group.

—Let's Quilt Our Pennsylvania County. 1992. lib. bdg. 24.95 (0-7933-7227-5); pap. text ed. 14.95 (0-7933-7228-3); disk 29.95 (0-7933-7229-1) Gallopade Pub Group.
—Let's Quilt Our Pennsylvania Town. 1992. lib. bdg. 24.95 (0-7933-7077-9); pap. text ed. 14.95 (0-7933-7078-7); disk 29.95 (0-7933-7079-5) Gallopade Pub Group.
—Let's Quilt Our Rhode Island County. 1992. lib. bdg. 24.95 (0-7933-7230-5); pap. text ed. 14.95 (0-7933-7231-3); disk 29.95 (0-7933-7232-1) Gallopade Pub Group.
—Let's Quilt Our Rhode Island Town. 1992. lib. bdg. 24.95 (0-7933-7080-9); pap. text ed. 14.95 (0-7933-7081-7); disk 29.95 (0-7933-7082-5) Gallopade Pub Group.
—Let's Quilt Our South Carolina County. 1992. lib. bdg. 24.95 (0-7933-7233-X); pap. text ed. 14.95 (0-7933-7234-8); disk 29.95 (0-7933-7235-6) Gallopade Pub Group.
—Let's Quilt Our South Carolina Town. 1992. lib. bdg. 24.95 (0-7933-7083-3); pap. text ed. 14.95 (0-7933-7084-1); disk 29.95 (0-7933-7085-X) Gallopade Pub Group.
—Let's Quilt Our South Dakota County. 1992. lib. bdg. 24.95 (0-7933-7236-4); pap. text ed. 14.95 (0-7933-7237-2); disk 29.95 (0-7933-7238-0) Gallopade Pub Group.
—Let's Quilt Our South Dakota Town. 1992. lib. bdg. 24.95 (0-7933-7086-8); pap. text ed. 14.95 (0-7933-7087-6); disk 29.95 (0-7933-7088-4) Gallopade Pub Group.
—Let's Quilt Our Tennessee County. 1992. lib. bdg. 24.95 (0-7933-7239-9); pap. text ed. 14.95 (0-7933-7240-2); disk 29.95 (0-7933-7241-0) Gallopade Pub Group.
—Let's Quilt Our Tennessee Town. 1992. lib. bdg. 24.95 (0-7933-7089-2); pap. text ed. 14.95 (0-7933-7090-6); disk 29.95 (0-7933-7091-4) Gallopade Pub Group.
—Let's Quilt Our Texas County. 1992. lib. bdg. 24.95 (0-7933-7242-9); pap. text ed. 14.95 (0-7933-7243-7); disk 29.95 (0-7933-7244-5) Gallopade Pub Group.
—Let's Quilt Our Texas Town. 1992. lib. bdg. 24.95 (0-7933-7092-2); pap. text ed. 14.95 (0-7933-7093-0); disk 29.95 (0-7933-7094-9) Gallopade Pub Group.
—Let's Quilt Our Utah County. 1992. lib. bdg. 24.95 (0-7933-7245-3); pap. text ed. 14.95 (0-7933-7246-1); disk 29.95 (0-7933-7247-X) Gallopade Pub Group.
—Let's Quilt Our Utah Town. 1992. lib. bdg. 24.95 (0-7933-7095-7); pap. text ed. 14.95 (0-7933-7096-5); disk 29.95 (0-7933-7097-3) Gallopade Pub Group.
—Let's Quilt Our Vermont County. 1992. lib. bdg. 24.95 (0-7933-7248-8); pap. text ed. 14.95 (0-7933-7249-6); disk 29.95 (0-7933-7250-X) Gallopade Pub Group.
—Let's Quilt Our Vermont Town. 1992. lib. bdg. 24.95 (0-7933-7098-1); pap. text ed. 14.95 (0-7933-7099-X); disk 29.95 (0-7933-7100-7) Gallopade Pub Group.
—Let's Quilt Our Virginia County. 1992. lib. bdg. 24.95 (0-7933-7251-8); pap. text ed. 14.95 (0-7933-7252-6); disk 29.95 (0-7933-7253-4) Gallopade Pub Group.
—Let's Quilt Our Virginia Town. 1992. lib. bdg. 24.95 (0-7933-7101-5); pap. text ed. 14.95 (0-7933-7102-3); disk 29.95 (0-7933-7103-1) Gallopade Pub Group.
—Let's Quilt Our Washington County. 1992. lib. bdg. 24.95 (0-7933-7254-2); pap. text ed. 14.95 (0-7933-7255-0); disk 29.95 (0-7933-7256-9) Gallopade Pub Group.
—Let's Quilt Our Washington Town. 1992. lib. bdg. 24.95 (0-7933-7104-X); pap. text ed. 14.95 (0-7933-7105-8); disk 29.95 (0-7933-7106-6) Gallopade Pub Group.
—Let's Quilt Our West Virginia County. 1992. lib. bdg. 24.95 (0-7933-7257-7); pap. text ed. 14.95 (0-7933-7258-5); disk 29.95 (0-7933-7259-3) Gallopade Pub Group.
—Let's Quilt Our West Virginia Town. 1992. lib. bdg. 24.95 (0-7933-7107-4); pap. text ed. 14.95 (0-7933-7108-2); disk 29.95 (0-7933-7109-0) Gallopade Pub Group.
—Let's Quilt Our Wisconsin County. 1992. lib. bdg. 24.95 (0-7933-7260-7); pap. text ed. 14.95 (0-7933-7261-5); disk 29.95 (0-7933-7262-3) Gallopade Pub Group.
—Let's Quilt Our Wisconsin Town. 1992. lib. bdg. 24.95 (0-7933-7110-4); pap. text ed. 14.95 (0-7933-7111-2); disk 29.95 (0-7933-7112-0) Gallopade Pub Group.
—Let's Quilt Our Wyoming County. 1992. lib. bdg. 24.95 (0-7933-7263-1); pap. text ed. 14.95 (0-7933-7264-X); disk 29.95 (0-7933-7265-8) Gallopade Pub Group.
—Let's Quilt Our Wyoming Town. 1992. lib. bdg. 24.95 (0-7933-7113-9); pap. text ed. 14.95 (0-7933-7114-7); disk 29.95 (0-7933-7115-5) Gallopade Pub Group.
—Let's Quilt Pennsylvania & Stuff It Topographically! (Illus.). 1990. PLB 24.95 (0-7933-1925-0); pap. 14.95 (1-55609-059-5); computer disk 29.95 (0-7933-1926-9) Gallopade Pub Group.
—Let's Quilt Rhode Island & Stuff it Topographically! (Illus.). 1990. PLB 24.95 (0-7933-1957-9); pap. 14.95 (1-55609-065-X); computer disk 29.95 (0-7933-1958-7) Gallopade Pub Group.
—Let's Quilt South Carolina & Stuff It Topographically! (Illus.). 1990. PLB 24.95 (0-7933-1987-0); pap. 14.95 (1-55609-053-X); computer disk 29.95 (0-7933-1988-9) Gallopade Pub Group.
—Let's Quilt South Dakota & Stuff It Topographically! (Illus.). 1990. lib. bdg. 24.95 (0-7933-2018-6); pap. 14.95 (1-55609-136-2); computer disk 29.95 (0-7933-2019-4) Gallopade Pub Group.

—Let's Quilt Tennessee & Stuff It Topographically! (Illus.). 1990. PLB 24.95 (*0-7933-2048-8*); pap. 14.95 (*1-55609-079-X*); computer disk 29.95 (*0-7933-2049-6*) Gallopade Pub Group.
—Let's Quilt Texas & Stuff It Topographically! (Illus.). 1990. PLB 24.95 (*0-7933-2078-X*); pap. 14.95 (*1-55609-077-3*); computer disk 29.95 (*0-7933-2079-8*) Gallopade Pub Group.
—Let's Quilt Utah & Stuff It Topographically! (Illus.). 1990. PLB 24.95 (*0-7933-2109-3*); pap. 14.95 (*1-55609-129-X*); computer disk 29.95 (*0-7933-2110-7*) Gallopade Pub Group.
—Let's Quilt Vermont & Stuff It Topographically! (Illus.). 1990. PLB 24.95 (*0-7933-2141-7*); pap. 14.95 (*1-55609-066-8*); computer disk 29.95 (*0-7933-2142-5*) Gallopade Pub Group.
—Let's Quilt Virginia & Stuff It Topographically! (Illus.). 1990. PLB 24.95 (*0-7933-2171-9*); pap. 14.95 (*1-55609-051-X*); computer disk 29.95 (*0-7933-2172-7*) Gallopade Pub Group.
—Let's Quilt Washington & Stuff It Topographically! (Illus.). 1990. PLB 24.95 (*0-7933-2204-9*); pap. 14.95 (*1-55609-133-8*); computer disk 29.95 (*0-7933-2205-7*) Gallopade Pub Group.
—Let's Quilt Washington, D.C. & Stuff it Topographically! (Illus.). (gr. 3-12). 1990. PLB 24.95 (*1-55609-564-3*); pap. 14.95 (*0-685-45930-4*); computer disk 29.95 (*0-7933-1461-5*) Gallopade Pub Group.
—Let's Quilt West Virginia & Stuff It Topographically! (Illus.). 1990. PLB 24.95 (*0-7933-2236-7*); pap. 14.95 (*0-7933-052-8*); computer disk 29.95 (*0-7933-2237-5*) Gallopade Pub Group.
—Let's Quilt Wisconsin & Stuff It Topographically! (Illus.). 1990. PLB 24.95 (*0-7933-2268-5*); pap. 14.95 (*1-55609-098-6*); computer disk 29.95 (*0-7933-2269-3*) Gallopade Pub Group.
—Let's Quilt Wyoming & Stuff Topographically! (Illus.). 1990. PLB 24.95 (*1-55609-290-3*); pap. 14.95 (*1-55609-134-6*); computer disk 29.95 (*1-55609-291-1*) Gallopade Pub Group.
—Life Isn't Fair: Murphy's Laws for Kids. (Illus.). (gr. 4-12). 1983. 14.95 (*0-935326-08-1*) Gallopade Pub Group.
—The Lost Colony Classroom Gamebook. (Illus., Orig.). (gr. 3-12). 1986. pap. 19.95 (*0-935326-86-3*) Gallopade Pub Group.
—Louisiana! A(lligator) to Z(ydeco) 1992. PLB 24.95 (*0-7933-7321-2*); pap. text ed. 14.95 (*0-7933-7320-4*); disk 29.95 (*0-7933-7322-0*) Gallopade Pub Group.
—Louisiana & Other State Greats (Biographies) (Illus.). (gr. 3-8). 1990. lib. bdg. 24.95 (*1-55609-404-3*); pap. 14.95 (*1-55609-403-5*); disk 29.95 (*0-685-45939-X*) Gallopade Pub Group.
—Louisiana Bandits, Bushwackers, Outlaws, Crooks, Devils, Ghosts, Desperadoes & Other Assorted & Sundry Characters! (Illus.). (gr. 3-8). 1990. PLB 24.95 (*0-7933-0502-0*); pap. 14.95 (*0-7933-0501-2*); disk 29.95 (*0-7933-0503-9*) Gallopade Pub Group.
—Louisiana Classic Christmas Trivia: Stories, Recipes, Activities, Legends, Lore & More! (Illus.). (gr. 3-8). 1990. PLB 24.95 (*0-7933-0505-5*); pap. 14.95 (*0-7933-0504-7*); disk 29.95 (*0-7933-0506-3*) Gallopade Pub Group.
—Louisiana Coastales. (Illus.). (gr. 3-8). 1990. PLB 24.95 (*1-55609-400-0*); pap. 14.95 (*1-55609-119-2*); disk 29.95 (*0-7933-1673-1*) Gallopade Pub Group.
—Louisiana Coastales. 1992. lib. bdg. 24.95 (*0-7933-7283-6*) Gallopade Pub Group.
—Louisiana "Crinkum-Crankum" A Funny Word Book about Our State. (Illus.). 1992. lib. bdg. 24.95 (*0-7933-4862-5*); pap. 14.95 (*0-7933-4863-3*); disk 29.95 (*0-7933-4864-1*) Gallopade Pub Group.
—Louisiana Dingbats! Bk. 1: A Fun Book of Games, Stories, Activities & More about Our State That's All in Code! for You to Decipher. (Illus.). (gr. 3-12). 1991. PLB 24.95 (*0-7933-3827-1*); pap. 14.95 (*0-7933-3828-X*); computer disk 29.95 (*0-7933-3829-8*) Gallopade Pub Group.
—Louisiana Festival Fun for Kids! (Illus.). (gr. 3-12). 1991. lib. bdg. 24.95 (*0-7933-3980-4*); pap. 14.95 (*0-7933-3981-2*); disk 29.95 (*0-7933-3982-0*) Gallopade Pub Group.
—The Louisiana Hot Air Balloon Mystery. (Illus.). (gr. 2-9). 1990. 24.95 (*0-685-37850-0*); pap. 14.95 (*0-7933-2481-5*); computer disk 29.95 (*0-7933-2482-3*) Gallopade Pub Group.
—Louisiana Jeopardy! Answers & Questions about Our State! (Illus.). (gr. 3-12). 1991. PLB 24.95 (*0-7933-4133-7*); pap. 14.95 (*0-7933-4134-5*); computer disk 29.95 (*0-7933-4135-3*) Gallopade Pub Group.
—Louisiana "Jography" A Fun Run Thru Our State! (Illus.). (gr. 3-8). 1990. lib. bdg. 24.95 (*1-55609-396-9*); pap. 14.95 (*1-55609-108-7*); disk 29.95 (*0-7933-1663-4*) Gallopade Pub Group.
—Louisiana Kid's Cookbook: Recipes, How-to, History, Lore & More! (Illus.). (gr. 3-8). 1990. PLB 24.95 (*0-7933-0514-4*); pap. 14.95 (*0-7933-0513-6*); disk 29.95 (*0-7933-0515-2*) Gallopade Pub Group.
—The Louisiana Mystery Van Takes Off! Book 1: Handicapped Louisiana Kids Sneak Off on a Big Adventure. (Illus.). (gr. 3-12). 1992. 24.95 (*0-7933-5015-8*); pap. 14.95 (*0-7933-5016-6*); computer disk 29.95 (*0-7933-5017-4*) Gallopade Pub Group.

—Louisiana Quiz Bowl Crash Course! (Illus.). (gr. 3-8). 1990. PLB 24.95 (*1-55609-402-7*); pap. 14.95 (*1-55609-401-9*); disk 29.95 (*0-7933-1672-3*) Gallopade Pub Group.
—Louisiana Rollercoasters! (Illus.). (gr. 3-12). 1992. PLB 24.95 (*0-7933-5278-9*); pap. 14.95 (*0-7933-5279-7*); computer disk 29.95 (*0-7933-5280-0*) Gallopade Pub Group.
—Louisiana School Trivia: An Amazing & Fascinating Look at Our State's Teachers, Schools & Students! (Illus.). (gr. 3-8). 1990. PLB 24.95 (*0-7933-0511-X*); pap. 14.95 (*0-7933-0510-1*); disk 29.95 (*0-7933-0512-8*) Gallopade Pub Group.
—Louisiana Silly Basketball Sportsmysteries, Vol. I. (Illus.). (gr. 3-8). 1990. PLB 24.95 (*0-7933-0508-X*); pap. 14.95 (*0-7933-0507-1*); disk 29.95 (*0-7933-0509-8*) Gallopade Pub Group.
—Louisiana Silly Basketball Sportsmysteries, Vol. II. (Illus.). (gr. 3-8). 1990. PLB 24.95 (*0-7933-1678-2*); pap. 14.95 (*0-7933-1679-0*); disk 29.95 (*0-7933-1680-4*) Gallopade Pub Group.
—Louisiana Silly Football Sportsmysteries, Vol. I. (Illus.). (gr. 3-8). 1990. PLB 24.95 (*1-55609-399-3*); pap. 14.95 (*1-55609-398-5*); disk 29.95 (*0-7933-1665-0*) Gallopade Pub Group.
—Louisiana Silly Football Sportsmysteries, Vol. II. (Illus.). (gr. 3-8). 1990. PLB 24.95 (*0-7933-1666-9*); pap. 14.95 (*0-7933-1667-7*); disk 29.95 (*0-7933-1668-5*) Gallopade Pub Group.
—Louisiana Silly Trivia! (Illus.). (gr. 3-8). 1990. PLB 24.95 (*1-55609-395-0*); pap. 14.95 (*1-55609-041-2*); disk 29.95 (*0-7933-0522-5*) Gallopade Pub Group.
—Louisiana Timeline: A Chronology of Louisiana History, Mystery, Trivia, Legend, Lore & More. (Illus.). (gr. 3-12). 1992. PLB 24.95 (*0-7933-5929-5*); pap. 14.95 (*0-7933-5930-9*); computer disk 29.95 (*0-7933-5931-7*) Gallopade Pub Group.
—Louisiana's (Most Devastating!) Disasters & (Most Calamitous!) Catastrophies! (Illus.). (gr. 3-8). 1990. PLB 24.95 (*0-7933-0499-7*); pap. 14.95 (*0-7933-0498-9*); disk 29.95 (*0-685-45940-3*) Gallopade Pub Group.
—Louisiana's Unsolved Mysteries (& Their "Solutions") Includes Scientific Information & Other Activities for Students. (Illus.). (gr. 3-12). 1992. PLB 24.95 (*0-7933-5776-4*); pap. 14.95 (*0-7933-5777-2*); computer disk 29.95 (*0-7933-5778-0*) Gallopade Pub Group.
—The Magic & Sorcery Dingbats Book. (Illus.). (gr. 3-12). 1992. PLB 24.95 (*0-7933-5377-7*); pap. 14.95 (*0-7933-5378-5*); computer disk 29.95 (*0-7933-5379-3*) Gallopade Pub Group.
—Maine & Other State Greats (Biographies) (Illus.). (gr. 3-8). 1990. PLB 24.95 (*1-55609-614-3*); pap. 14.95 (*1-55609-615-1*); disk 29.95 (*1-55609-616-X*) Gallopade Pub Group.
—Maine Bandits, Bushwackers, Outlaws, Crooks, Devils, Ghosts, Desperadoes & Other Assorted & Sundry Characters! (Illus.). (gr. 3-8). 1990. PLB 24.95 (*0-7933-0527-0*); pap. 14.95 (*0-7933-0526-8*); disk 29.95 (*0-7933-0528-4*) Gallopade Pub Group.
—Maine Classic Christmas Trivia: Stories, Recipes, Activities, Legends, Lore & More! (Illus.). (gr. 3-8). 1990. PLB 24.95 (*0-7933-0530-6*); pap. 14.95 (*0-7933-0529-2*); disk 29.95 (*0-7933-0531-4*) Gallopade Pub Group.
—Maine Coastales. (Illus.). (gr. 3-8). 1990. PLB 24.95 (*1-55609-608-9*); pap. 14.95 (*1-55609-609-7*); disk 29.95 (*1-55609-610-0*) Gallopade Pub Group.
—Maine Coastales! 1992. lib. bdg. 24.95 (*0-7933-7284-4*) Gallopade Pub Group.
—Maine "Crinkum-Crankum" A Funny Word Book about Our State. (Illus.). 1992. lib. bdg. 24.95 (*0-7933-4865-X*); pap. 14.95 (*0-7933-4866-8*); disk 29.95 (*0-7933-4867-6*) Gallopade Pub Group.
—Maine Dingbats! Bk. 1: A Fun Book of Games, Stories, Activities & More about Our State That's All in Code! for You to Decipher. (Illus.). (gr. 3-12). 1991. PLB 24.95 (*0-7933-3830-1*); pap. 14.95 (*0-7933-3831-X*); computer disk 29.95 (*0-7933-3832-8*) Gallopade Pub Group.
—Maine Festival Fun for Kids! (Illus.). (gr. 3-12). 1991. lib. bdg. 24.95 (*0-7933-3983-9*); pap. 14.95 (*0-7933-3984-7*); disk 29.95 (*0-7933-3985-5*) Gallopade Pub Group.
—The Maine Hot Air Balloon Mystery. (Illus.). (gr. 2-9). 1990. 24.95 (*0-7933-2489-0*); pap. 14.95 (*0-7933-2490-4*); computer disk 29.95 (*0-7933-2491-2*) Gallopade Pub Group.
—Maine Jeopardy! Answers & Questions about Our State! (Illus.). (gr. 3-12). 1991. PLB 24.95 (*0-7933-4136-1*); pap. 14.95 (*0-7933-4137-X*); computer disk 29.95 (*0-7933-4138-8*) Gallopade Pub Group.
—Maine "Jography" A Fun Run Thru Our State! (Illus.). (gr. 3-8). 1990. PLB 24.95 (*1-55609-596-1*); pap. 14.95 (*1-55609-597-X*); disk 29.95 (*1-55609-598-8*) Gallopade Pub Group.
—Maine Kid's Cookbook: Recipes, How-to, History, Lore & More! (Illus.). (gr. 3-8). 1990. PLB 24.95 (*0-7933-0539-X*); pap. 14.95 (*0-7933-0538-1*); disk 29.95 (*0-7933-0540-3*) Gallopade Pub Group.
—The Maine Mystery Van Takes Off! Book 1: Handicapped Maine Kids Sneak Off on a Big Adventure. (Illus.). (gr. 3-12). 1992. 24.95 (*0-7933-5018-2*); pap. 14.95 (*0-7933-5019-0*); computer disk 29.95 (*0-7933-5020-4*) Gallopade Pub Group.

—Maine Quiz Bowl Crash Course! (Illus.). (gr. 3-8). 1990. PLB 24.95 (*1-55609-611-9*); pap. 14.95 (*1-55609-612-7*); disk 29.95 (*1-55609-613-5*) Gallopade Pub Group.
—Maine Rollercoasters! (Illus.). (gr. 3-12). 1992. PLB 24.95 (*0-7933-5281-9*); pap. 14.95 (*0-7933-5282-7*); computer disk 29.95 (*0-7933-5283-5*) Gallopade Pub Group.
—Maine School Trivia: An Amazing & Fascinating Look at Our State's Teachers, Schools & Students! (Illus.). (gr. 3-8). 1990. PLB 24.95 (*0-7933-0536-5*); pap. 14.95 (*0-7933-0535-7*); disk 29.95 (*0-7933-0537-3*) Gallopade Pub Group.
—Maine Silly Basketball Sportsmysteries, Vol. I. (Illus.). (gr. 3-8). 1990. PLB 24.95 (*0-7933-0533-0*); pap. 14.95 (*0-7933-0532-2*); disk 29.95 (*0-7933-0534-9*) Gallopade Pub Group.
—Maine Silly Basketball Sportsmysteries, Vol. II. (Illus.). (gr. 3-8). 1990. PLB 24.95 (*0-7933-1684-7*); pap. 14.95 (*0-7933-1685-5*); disk 29.95 (*0-7933-1686-3*) Gallopade Pub Group.
—Maine Silly Football Sportsmysteries, Vol. I. (Illus.). (gr. 3-8). 1990. PLB 24.95 (*1-55609-602-X*); pap. 14.95 (*1-55609-604-6*); disk 29.95 (*1-55609-606-2*) Gallopade Pub Group.
—Maine Silly Football Sportsmysteries, Vol. II. (Illus.). (gr. 3-8). 1990. PLB 24.95 (*1-55609-603-8*); pap. 14.95 (*1-55609-605-4*); disk 29.95 (*1-55609-607-0*) Gallopade Pub Group.
—Maine Silly Trivia! (Illus.). (gr. 3-8). 1990. PLB 24.95 (*1-55609-593-7*); pap. 14.95 (*1-55609-594-5*); disk 29.95 (*1-55609-595-3*) Gallopade Pub Group.
—Maine Timeline: A Chronology of Maine History, Mystery, Trivia, Legend, Lore & More. (Illus.). (gr. 3-12). 1992. PLB 24.95 (*0-7933-5932-3*); pap. 14.95 (*0-7933-5933-3*); computer disk 29.95 (*0-7933-5934-1*) Gallopade Pub Group.
—Maine's (Most Devastating!) Disasters & (Most Calamitous!) Catastrophies! (Illus.). (gr. 3-8). 1990. PLB 24.95 (*0-7933-0524-1*, *0-7933-0525-X*); pap. 14.95 (*0-7933-0523-3*); disk 29.95 (*0-685-45941-1*) Gallopade Pub Group.
—Maine's Unsolved Mysteries (& Their "Solutions") Includes Scientific Information & Other Activities for Students. (Illus.). (gr. 3-12). 1992. PLB 24.95 (*0-7933-5779-9*); pap. 14.95 (*0-7933-5780-2*); computer disk 29.95 (*0-7933-5781-0*) Gallopade Pub Group.
—Mariner's & More! Virginia People, Places & Things Everyone Should Know. (Illus.). (gr. 9-12). 1990. PLB 24.95 (*0-7933-0000-2*); pap. 14.95 (*0-7933-0001-0*); computer disk 29.95 (*0-7933-0002-9*) Gallopade Pub Group. Postponed.
—Maryland & Other State Greats (Biographies) (Illus.). (gr. 3-8). 1990. PLB 24.95 (*1-55609-636-4*); pap. 14.95 (*1-55609-637-2*); disk 29.95 (*1-55609-638-0*) Gallopade Pub Group.
—Maryland Bandits, Bushwackers, Outlaws, Crooks, Devils, Ghosts, Desperadoes & Other Assorted & Sundry Characters! (Illus.). (gr. 3-8). 1990. PLB 24.95 (*0-7933-0551-9*); pap. 14.95 (*0-7933-0550-0*); disk 29.95 (*0-7933-0552-7*) Gallopade Pub Group.
—Maryland Books, 19 bks. (Illus.). (gr. 3-8). 1990. Set. PLB 379.00 (*0-7933-1295-7*) Gallopade Pub Group.
—Maryland Classic Christmas Trivia: Stories, Recipes, Activities, Legends, Lore & More! (Illus.). (gr. 3-8). 1990. PLB 24.95 (*0-7933-0554-3*); pap. 14.95 (*0-7933-0553-5*); disk 29.95 (*0-7933-0555-1*) Gallopade Pub Group.
—Maryland Coastales. (Illus.). (gr. 3-8). 1990. PLB 24.95 (*1-55609-630-5*); pap. 14.95 (*1-55609-631-3*); disk 29.95 (*1-55609-632-1*) Gallopade Pub Group.
—Maryland Coastales! 1992. lib. bdg. 24.95 (*0-7933-7285-2*) Gallopade Pub Group.
—Maryland "Crinkum-Crankum" A Funny Word Book about Our State. (Illus.). 1992. lib. bdg. 24.95 (*0-7933-4868-4*); pap. 14.95 (*0-7933-4869-2*); disk 29.95 (*0-7933-4870-6*) Gallopade Pub Group.
—Maryland Dingbats! Bk. 1: A Fun Book of Games, Stories, Activities & More about Our State That's All in Code! for You to Decipher. (Illus.). (gr. 3-12). 1991. PLB 24.95 (*0-7933-3833-6*); pap. 14.95 (*0-7933-3834-4*); computer disk 29.95 (*0-7933-3835-2*) Gallopade Pub Group.
—Maryland Festival Fun for Kids! (Illus.). (gr. 3-12). 1991. lib. bdg. 24.95 (*0-7933-3986-3*); pap. 14.95 (*0-7933-3987-1*); disk 29.95 (*0-7933-3988-X*) Gallopade Pub Group.
—The Maryland Hot Air Balloon Mystery. (Illus.). (gr. 2-9). 1990. 24.95 (*0-7933-2498-X*); pap. 14.95 (*0-7933-2499-8*); computer disk 29.95 (*0-7933-2500-5*) Gallopade Pub Group.
—Maryland Jeopardy! Answers & Questions about Our State! (Illus.). (gr. 3-12). 1991. PLB 24.95 (*0-7933-4139-6*); pap. 14.95 (*0-7933-4140-X*); computer disk 29.95 (*0-7933-4141-8*) Gallopade Pub Group.
—Maryland "Jography" A Fun Run Thru Our State! (Illus.). (gr. 3-8). 1990. PLB 24.95 (*1-55609-619-4*); pap. 14.95 (*1-55609-620-8*); disk 29.95 (*1-55609-621-6*) Gallopade Pub Group.
—Maryland Kid's Cookbook: Recipes, How-to, History, Lore & More! (Illus.). (gr. 3-8). 1990. PLB 24.95 (*0-7933-0563-2*); pap. 14.95 (*0-7933-0562-4*); disk 29.95 (*0-7933-0564-0*) Gallopade Pub Group.

—The Maryland Mystery Van Takes Off! Book 1: Handicapped Maryland Kids Sneak Off on a Big Adventure. (Illus.). (gr. 3-12). 1992. 24.95 (0-7933-5021-2); pap. 14.95 (0-7933-5022-0); computer disk 29.95 (0-7933-5023-9) Gallopade Pub Group.
—Maryland Quiz Bowl Crash Course! (Illus.). (gr. 3-8). 1990. PLB 24.95 (1-55609-633-X); pap. 14.95 (1-55609-634-8); disk 29.95 (1-55609-635-6) Gallopade Pub Group.
—Maryland Rollercoasters! (Illus.). (gr. 3-12). 1992. PLB 24.95 (0-7933-5284-3); pap. 14.95 (0-7933-5285-1); computer disk 29.95 (0-7933-5286-X) Gallopade Pub Group.
—Maryland School Trivia: An Amazing & Fascinating Look at Our State's Teachers, Schools & Students! (Illus.). (gr. 3-8). 1990. PLB 24.95 (0-7933-0560-8); pap. 14.95 (0-7933-0559-4); disk 29.95 (0-7933-0561-6) Gallopade Pub Group.
—Maryland Silly Basketball Sportsmysteries, Vol. I. (Illus.). (gr. 3-8). 1990. PLB 24.95 (0-7933-0557-8); pap. 14.95 (0-7933-0556-X); disk 29.95 (0-7933-0558-6) Gallopade Pub Group.
—Maryland Silly Basketball Sportsmysteries, Vol. II. (Illus.). (gr. 3-8). 1990. PLB 24.95 (0-7933-1696-9); pap. 14.95 (0-7933-1697-9); disk 29.95 (0-7933-1698-7) Gallopade Pub Group.
—Maryland Silly Football Sportsmysteries, Vol. I. (Illus.). (gr. 3-8). 1990. PLB 24.95 (1-55609-624-0); pap. 14.95 (1-55609-625-9); disk 29.95 (1-55609-626-7) Gallopade Pub Group.
—Maryland Silly Football Sportsmysteries, Vol. II. (Illus.). (gr. 3-8). 1990. PLB 24.95 (1-55609-627-5); pap. 14.95 (1-55609-628-3); disk 29.95 (1-55609-629-1) Gallopade Pub Group.
—Maryland Silly Trivia! (Illus.). (gr. 3-8). 1990. PLB 24.95 (1-55609-617-8); pap. 14.95 (1-55609-042-0); disk 29.95 (1-55609-618-6) Gallopade Pub Group.
—Maryland Timeline: A Chronology of Maryland History, Mystery, Trivia, Legend, Lore & More. (Illus.). (gr. 3-12). 1992. PLB 24.95 (0-7933-5935-X); pap. 14.95 (0-7933-5936-8); computer disk 29.95 (0-7933-5937-6) Gallopade Pub Group.
—Maryland's (Most Devastating!) Disasters & (Most Calamitous) Catastrophies! (Illus.). (gr. 3-8). 1990. PLB 24.95 (0-7933-0548-9); pap. 14.95 (0-7933-0547-0); disk 29.95 (0-7933-0549-7) Gallopade Pub Group.
—Maryland's Unsolved Mysteries (& Their "Solutions") Includes Scientific Information & Other Activities for Students. (Illus.). (gr. 3-12). 1992. PLB 24.95 (0-7933-5782-9); pap. 14.95 (0-7933-5783-7); computer disk 29.95 (0-7933-5784-5) Gallopade Pub Group.
—Massachusetts & Other State Greats (Biographies) (Illus.). (gr. 3-8). 1990. PLB 24.95 (1-55609-699-2); pap. 14.95 (1-55609-700-X); disk 29.95 (1-55609-701-8) Gallopade Pub Group.
—Massachusetts Bandits, Bushwackers, Outlaws, Crooks, Devils, Ghosts, Desperadoes & Other Assorted & Sundry Characters! (Illus.). (gr. 3-8). 1990. PLB 24.95 (0-7933-0575-6); pap. 14.95 (0-7933-0574-8); disk 29.95 (0-7933-0576-4) Gallopade Pub Group.
—Massachusetts Classic Christmas Trivia: Stories, Recipes, Activities, Legends, Lore & More! (Illus.). (gr. 3-8). 1990. PLB 24.95 (0-7933-0578-0); pap. 14.95 (0-7933-0577-2); disk 29.95 (0-7933-0579-9) Gallopade Pub Group.
—Massachusetts Coastales. (Illus.). (gr. 3-8). 1990. PLB 24.95 (1-55609-693-3); pap. 14.95 (1-55609-694-1); disk 29.95 (1-55609-695-X) Gallopade Pub Group.
—Massachusetts Coastales! 1992. lib. bdg. 24.95 (0-7933-7286-0) Gallopade Pub Group.
—Massachusetts "Crinkum-Crankum" A Funny Word Book about Our State. (Illus.). 1992. lib. bdg. 24.95 (0-7933-4871-4); pap. 14.95 (0-7933-4872-2); disk 29.95 (0-7933-4873-0) Gallopade Pub Group.
—Massachusetts Dingbats! Bk. 1: A Fun Book of Games, Stories, Activities & More about Our State That's All in Code! for You to Decipher. (Illus.). (gr. 3-12). 1991. PLB 24.95 (0-7933-3836-0); pap. 14.95 (0-7933-3837-9); computer disk 29.95 (0-7933-3838-7) Gallopade Pub Group.
—Massachusetts Festival Fun for Kids! (Illus.). (gr. 3-12). 1991. lib. bdg. 24.95 (0-7933-3989-8); pap. 14.95 (0-7933-3990-1); disk 29.95 (0-7933-3991-X) Gallopade Pub Group.
—The Massachusetts Hot Air Balloon Mystery. (Illus.). (gr. 2-9). 1990. 24.95 (0-7933-2507-2); pap. 14.95 (0-7933-2508-0); computer disk 29.95 (0-7933-2509-9) Gallopade Pub Group.
—Massachusetts Jeopardy! Answers & Questions about Our State! (Illus.). (gr. 3-12). 1991. PLB 24.95 (0-7933-4142-6); pap. 14.95 (0-7933-4143-4); computer disk 29.95 (0-7933-4144-2) Gallopade Pub Group.
—Massachusetts "Jography" A Fun Run Thru Our State! (Illus.). (gr. 3-8). 1990. PLB 24.95 (1-55609-682-8); pap. 14.95 (1-55609-111-7); disk 29.95 (1-55609-683-6) Gallopade Pub Group.
—Massachusetts Kid's Cookbook: Recipes, How-to, History, Lore & More! (Illus.). (gr. 3-8). 1990. PLB 24.95 (0-7933-0587-X); pap. 14.95 (0-7933-0586-1); disk 29.95 (0-7933-0588-8) Gallopade Pub Group.

—Massachusetts' (Most Devastating!) Disasters & (Most Calamitous!) Catastrophies! (Illus.). (gr. 3-8). 1990. PLB 24.95 (0-7933-0572-1); pap. 14.95 (0-7933-0571-3); disk 29.95 (0-7933-0573-X) Gallopade Pub Group.
—The Massachusetts Mystery Van Takes Off! Book 1: Handicapped Massachusetts Kids Sneak Off on a Big Adventure. (Illus.). (gr. 3-12). 1992. 24.95 (0-7933-5024-7); pap. 14.95 (0-7933-5025-5); computer disk 29.95 (0-7933-5026-3) Gallopade Pub Group.
—Massachusetts Quiz Bowl Crash Course! (Illus.). (gr. 3-8). 1990. PLB 24.95 (1-55609-696-8); pap. 14.95 (1-55609-697-6); disk 29.95 (1-55609-698-4) Gallopade Pub Group.
—Massachusetts Rollercoasters! (Illus.). (gr. 3-12). 1992. PLB 24.95 (0-7933-5287-8); pap. 14.95 (0-7933-5288-6); computer disk 29.95 (0-7933-5289-4) Gallopade Pub Group.
—Massachusetts School Trivia: An Amazing & Fascinating Look at Our State's Teachers, Schools & Students! (Illus.). (gr. 3-8). 1990. PLB 24.95 (0-7933-0584-5); pap. 14.95 (0-7933-0583-7); disk 29.95 (0-7933-0585-3) Gallopade Pub Group.
—Massachusetts Silly Basketball Sportsmysteries, Vol. I. (Illus.). (gr. 3-8). 1990. PLB 24.95 (0-7933-0581-0); pap. 14.95 (0-7933-0580-2); disk 29.95 (0-7933-0582-9) Gallopade Pub Group.
—Massachusetts Silly Basketball Sportsmysteries, Vol. II. (Illus.). (gr. 3-8). 1990. PLB 24.95 (0-7933-1705-3); pap. 14.95 (0-7933-1706-1); disk 29.95 (0-7933-1707-X) Gallopade Pub Group.
—Massachusetts Silly Football Sportsmysteries, Vol. I. (Illus.). (gr. 3-8). 1990. PLB 24.95 (1-55609-687-9); pap. 14.95 (1-55609-688-7); disk 29.95 (1-55609-689-5) Gallopade Pub Group.
—Massachusetts Silly Football Sportsmysteries, Vol. II. (Illus.). (gr. 3-8). 1990. PLB 24.95 (1-55609-690-9); pap. 14.95 (1-55609-691-7); disk 29.95 (1-55609-692-5) Gallopade Pub Group.
—Massachusetts Silly Trivia! (Illus.). (gr. 3-8). 1990. PLB 24.95 (1-55609-680-1); pap. 14.95 (1-55609-110-9); disk 29.95 (1-55609-681-X) Gallopade Pub Group.
—Massachusetts Timeline: A Chronology of Massachusetts History, Mystery, Trivia, Legend, Lore & More. (Illus.). (gr. 3-12). 1992. PLB 24.95 (0-7933-5938-4); pap. 14.95 (0-7933-5939-2); computer disk 29.95 (0-7933-5940-6) Gallopade Pub Group.
—Massachusetts's Unsolved Mysteries (& Their "Solutions") Includes Scientific Information & Other Activities for Students. (Illus.). (gr. 3-12). 1992. PLB 24.95 (0-7933-5785-3); pap. 14.95 (0-7933-5786-1); computer disk 29.95 (0-7933-5787-X) Gallopade Pub Group.
—Math for Boys: A Book with the Number or Getting Boys to Love & Excel in Math! (Illus.). (gr. 4-12). 1989. PLB 24.95 (1-55609-806-5); pap. 14.95 (1-55609-830-8); computer disk 29.95 (1-55609-878-2) Gallopade Pub Group.
—Math for Girls: The Book with the Number to Get Girls to Love & Excel in Math! (Illus.). 60p. (gr. 3-9). 1989. PLB 24.95 (1-55609-343-8); pap. 14.95 (1-55609-344-6); computer disk 29.95 (1-55609-345-4) Gallopade Pub Group.
—Meet in the Middle: The Parents Test - The Kids Test. (Illus.). (gr. 4 up). 1983. 24.95 (0-935326-24-3) Gallopade Pub Group.
—Meow! Alabama Cats in History, Mystery, Legend, Lore, Humor & More! (Illus.). (gr. 3-12). 1991. PLB 24.95 (0-7933-3314-8); pap. 14.95 (0-7933-3315-6); computer disk 29.95 (0-7933-3316-4) Gallopade Pub Group.
—Meow! Alaska Cats in History, Mystery, Legend, Lore, Humor & More! (Illus.). (gr. 3-12). 1991. PLB 24.95 (0-7933-3317-2); pap. 14.95 (0-7933-3318-0); computer disk 29.95 (0-7933-3319-9) Gallopade Pub Group.
—Meow! Arizona Cats in History, Mystery, Legend, Lore, Humor & More! (Illus.). (gr. 3-12). 1991. PLB 24.95 (0-7933-3320-2); pap. 14.95 (0-7933-3321-0); computer disk 29.95 (0-7933-3322-9) Gallopade Pub Group.
—Meow! Arkansas Cats in History, Mystery, Legend, Lore, Humor & More! (Illus.). (gr. 3-12). 1991. PLB 24.95 (0-7933-3323-7); pap. 14.95 (0-7933-3324-5); computer disk 29.95 (0-7933-3325-3) Gallopade Pub Group.
—Meow! California Cats in History, Mystery, Legend, Lore, Humor & More! (Illus.). (gr. 3-12). 1991. PLB 24.95 (0-7933-3326-1); pap. 14.95 (0-7933-3327-X); computer disk 29.95 (0-7933-3328-8) Gallopade Pub Group.
—Meow! Colorado Cats in History, Mystery, Legend, Lore, Humor & More! (Illus.). (gr. 3-12). 1991. PLB 24.95 (0-7933-3329-6); pap. 14.95 (0-7933-3330-X); computer disk 29.95 (0-7933-3331-8) Gallopade Pub Group.
—Meow! Connecticut Cats in History, Mystery, Legend, Lore, Humor & More! (Illus.). (gr. 3-12). 1991. PLB 24.95 (0-7933-3332-6); pap. 14.95 (0-7933-3333-4); computer disk 29.95 (0-7933-3334-2) Gallopade Pub Group.
—Meow! Delaware Cats in History, Mystery, Legend, Lore, Humor & More! (Illus.). (gr. 3-12). 1991. PLB 24.95 (0-7933-3335-0); pap. 14.95 (0-7933-3336-9); computer disk 29.95 (0-7933-3337-7) Gallopade Pub Group.

—Meow! Florida Cats in History, Mystery, Legend, Lore, Humor & More! (Illus.). (gr. 3-12). 1991. PLB 24.95 (0-7933-3341-5); pap. 14.95 (0-7933-3342-3); computer disk 29.95 (0-7933-3343-1) Gallopade Pub Group.
—Meow! Georgia Cats in History, Mystery, Legend, Lore, Humor & More! (Illus.). (gr. 3-12). 1991. PLB 24.95 (0-7933-3344-X); pap. 14.95 (0-7933-3345-8); computer disk 29.95 (0-7933-3346-6) Gallopade Pub Group.
—Meow! Hawaii Cats in History, Mystery, Legend, Lore, Humor & More! (Illus.). (gr. 3-12). 1991. PLB 24.95 (0-7933-3347-4); pap. 14.95 (0-7933-3348-2); computer disk 29.95 (0-7933-3349-0) Gallopade Pub Group.
—Meow! Idaho Cats in History, Mystery, Legend, Lore, Humor & More! (Illus.). (gr. 3-12). 1991. PLB 24.95 (0-7933-3350-4); pap. 14.95 (0-7933-3351-2); computer disk 29.95 (0-7933-3352-0) Gallopade Pub Group.
—Meow! Illinois Cats in History, Mystery, Legend, Lore, Humor & More! (Illus.). (gr. 3-12). 1991. PLB 24.95 (0-7933-3353-9); pap. 14.95 (0-7933-3354-7); computer disk 29.95 (0-7933-3355-5) Gallopade Pub Group.
—Meow! Indiana Cats in History, Mystery, Legend, Lore, Humor & More! (Illus.). (gr. 3-12). 1991. PLB 24.95 (0-7933-3356-3); pap. 14.95 (0-7933-3357-1); computer disk 29.95 (0-7933-3358-X) Gallopade Pub Group.
—Meow! Iowa Cats in History, Mystery, Legend, Lore, Humor & More! (Illus.). (gr. 3-12). 1991. PLB 24.95 (0-7933-3359-8); pap. 14.95 (0-7933-3360-1); computer disk 29.95 (0-7933-3361-X) Gallopade Pub Group.
—Meow! Kansas Cats in History, Mystery, Legend, Lore, Humor & More! (Illus.). (gr. 3-12). 1991. PLB 24.95 (0-7933-3362-8); pap. 14.95 (0-7933-3363-6); computer disk 29.95 (0-7933-3364-4) Gallopade Pub Group.
—Meow! Kentucky Cats in History, Mystery, Legend, Lore, Humor & More! (Illus.). (gr. 3-12). 1991. PLB 24.95 (0-7933-3365-2); pap. 14.95 (0-7933-3366-0); computer disk 29.95 (0-7933-3367-9) Gallopade Pub Group.
—Meow! Louisiana Cats in History, Mystery, Legend, Lore, Humor & More! (Illus.). (gr. 3-12). 1991. PLB 24.95 (0-7933-3368-7); pap. 14.95 (0-7933-3369-5); computer disk 29.95 (0-7933-3370-9) Gallopade Pub Group.
—Meow! Maine Cats in History, Mystery, Legend, Lore, Humor & More! (Illus.). (gr. 3-12). 1991. PLB 24.95 (0-7933-3371-7); pap. 14.95 (0-7933-3372-5); computer disk 29.95 (0-7933-3373-3) Gallopade Pub Group.
—Meow! Maryland Cats in History, Mystery, Legend, Lore, Humor & More! (Illus.). (gr. 3-12). 1991. PLB 24.95 (0-7933-3374-1); pap. 14.95 (0-7933-3375-X); computer disk 29.95 (0-7933-3376-8) Gallopade Pub Group.
—Meow! Massachusetts Cats in History, Mystery, Legend, Lore, Humor & More! (Illus.). (gr. 3-12). 1991. PLB 24.95 (0-7933-3377-6); pap. 14.95 (0-7933-3378-4); computer disk 29.95 (0-7933-3379-2) Gallopade Pub Group.
—Meow! Michigan Cats in History, Mystery, Legend, Lore, Humor & More! (Illus.). (gr. 3-12). 1991. PLB 24.95 (0-7933-3380-6); pap. 14.95 (0-7933-3381-4); computer disk 29.95 (0-7933-3382-2) Gallopade Pub Group.
—Meow! Minnesota Cats in History, Mystery, Legend, Lore, Humor & More! (Illus.). (gr. 3-12). 1991. PLB 24.95 (0-7933-3383-0); pap. 14.95 (0-7933-3384-9); computer disk 29.95 (0-7933-3385-7) Gallopade Pub Group.
—Meow! Mississippi Cats in History, Mystery, Legend, Lore, Humor & More! (Illus.). (gr. 3-12). 1991. PLB 24.95 (0-7933-3386-5); pap. 14.95 (0-7933-3387-3); computer disk 29.95 (0-7933-3388-1) Gallopade Pub Group.
—Meow! Missouri Cats in History, Mystery, Legend, Lore, Humor & More! (Illus.). (gr. 3-12). 1991. PLB 24.95 (0-7933-3389-X); pap. 14.95 (0-7933-3390-3); computer disk 29.95 (0-7933-3391-1) Gallopade Pub Group.
—Meow! Montana Cats in History, Mystery, Legend, Lore, Humor & More! (Illus.). (gr. 3-12). 1991. PLB 24.95 (0-7933-3392-X); pap. 14.95 (0-7933-3393-8); computer disk 29.95 (0-7933-3394-6) Gallopade Pub Group.
—Meow! Nebraska Cats in History, Mystery, Legend, Lore, Humor & More! (Illus.). (gr. 3-12). 1991. PLB 24.95 (0-7933-3395-4); pap. 14.95 (0-7933-3396-2); computer disk 29.95 (0-7933-3397-0) Gallopade Pub Group.
—Meow! Nevada Cats in History, Mystery, Legend, Lore, Humor & More! (Illus.). (gr. 3-12). 1991. PLB 24.95 (0-7933-3398-9); pap. 14.95 (0-7933-3399-7); computer disk 29.95 (0-685-41935-5) Gallopade Pub Group.
—Meow! New Hampshire Cats in History, Mystery, Legend, Lore, Humor & More! (Illus.). (gr. 3-12). 1991. PLB 24.95 (0-7933-3400-4); pap. 14.95 (0-7933-3401-2); computer disk 29.95 (0-7933-3402-0) Gallopade Pub Group.

—Meow! New Jersey Cats in History, Mystery, Legend, Lore, Humor & More! (Illus.). (gr. 3-12). 1991. PLB 24.95 (0-7933-3404-7); pap. 14.95 (0-685-48034-8); computer disk 29.95 (0-7933-3406-3) Gallopade Pub Group.

—Meow! New Mexico Cats in History, Mystery, Legend, Lore, Humor & More! (Illus.). (gr. 3-12). 1991. PLB 24.95 (0-7933-3407-1); pap. 14.95 (0-7933-3408-X); computer disk 29.95 (0-7933-3409-8) Gallopade Pub Group.

—Meow! New York Cats in History, Mystery, Legend, Lore, Humor & More! (Illus.). (gr. 3-12). 1991. PLB 24.95 (0-7933-3410-1); pap. 14.95 (0-7933-3411-X); computer disk 29.95 (0-7933-3412-8) Gallopade Pub Group.

—Meow! North Carolina Cats in History, Mystery, Legend, Lore, Humor & More! (Illus.). (gr. 3-12). 1991. PLB 24.95 (0-7933-3413-6); pap. 14.95 (0-7933-3414-4); computer disk 29.95 (0-7933-3415-2) Gallopade Pub Group.

—Meow! North Dakota Cats in History, Mystery, Legend, Lore, Humor & More! (Illus.). (gr. 3-12). 1991. PLB 24.95 (0-7933-3416-0); pap. 14.95 (0-7933-3417-9); computer disk 29.95 (0-7933-3418-7) Gallopade Pub Group.

—Meow! Ohio Cats in History, Mystery, Legend, Lore, Humor & More! (Illus.). (gr. 3-12). 1991. PLB 24.95 (0-7933-3419-5); pap. 14.95 (0-7933-3420-9); computer disk 29.95 (0-7933-3421-7) Gallopade Pub Group.

—Meow! Oklahoma Cats in History, Mystery, Legend, Lore, Humor & More! (Illus.). (gr. 3-12). 1991. PLB 24.95 (0-7933-3422-5); pap. 14.95 (0-7933-3423-3); computer disk 29.95 (0-7933-3424-1) Gallopade Pub Group.

—Meow! Oregon Cats in History, Mystery, Legend, Lore, Humor & More! (Illus.). (gr. 3-12). 1991. PLB 24.95 (0-7933-3425-X); pap. 14.95 (0-7933-3426-8); computer disk 29.95 (0-7933-3427-6) Gallopade Pub Group.

—Meow! Pennsylvania Cats in History, Mystery, Legend, Lore, Humor & More! (Illus.). (gr. 3-12). 1991. PLB 24.95 (0-7933-3428-4); pap. 14.95 (0-7933-3429-2); computer disk 29.95 (0-7933-3430-6) Gallopade Pub Group.

—Meow! Rhode Island Cats in History, Mystery, Legend, Lore, Humor & More! (Illus.). (gr. 3-12). 1991. PLB 24.95 (0-7933-3431-4); pap. 14.95 (0-7933-3432-2); computer disk 29.95 (0-7933-3433-0) Gallopade Pub Group.

—Meow! South Carolina Cats in History, Mystery, Legend, Lore, Humor & More! (Illus.). (gr. 3-12). 1991. PLB 24.95 (0-7933-3434-9); pap. 14.95 (0-7933-3435-7); computer disk 29.95 (0-7933-3436-5) Gallopade Pub Group.

—Meow! South Dakota Cats in History, Mystery, Legend, Lore, Humor & More! (Illus.). (gr. 3-12). 1991. PLB 24.95 (0-7933-3437-3); pap. 14.95 (0-7933-3438-1); computer disk 29.95 (0-7933-3439-X) Gallopade Pub Group.

—Meow! Tennessee Cats in History, Mystery, Legend, Lore, Humor & More! (Illus.). (gr. 3-12). 1991. PLB 24.95 (0-7933-3440-5); pap. 14.95 (0-7933-3441-1); computer disk 29.95 (0-7933-3442-X) Gallopade Pub Group.

—Meow! Texas Cats in History, Mystery, Legend, Lore, Humor & More! (Illus.). (gr. 3-12). 1991. PLB 24.95 (0-7933-3443-8); pap. 14.95 (0-7933-3444-6); computer disk 29.95 (0-7933-3445-4) Gallopade Pub Group.

—Meow! Utah Cats in History, Mystery, Legend, Lore, Humor & More! (Illus.). (gr. 3-12). 1991. PLB 24.95 (0-7933-3446-2); pap. 14.95 (0-7933-3447-0); computer disk 29.95 (0-7933-3448-9) Gallopade Pub Group.

—Meow! Vermont Cats in History, Mystery, Legend, Lore, Humor & More! (Illus.). (gr. 3-12). 1991. PLB 24.95 (0-7933-3449-7); pap. 14.95 (0-7933-3450-0); computer disk 29.95 (0-7933-3451-9) Gallopade Pub Group.

—Meow! Virginia Cats in History, Mystery, Legend, Lore, Humor & More! (Illus.). (gr. 3-12). 1991. PLB 24.95 (0-7933-3452-7); pap. 14.95 (0-7933-3453-5); computer disk 29.95 (0-7933-3454-3) Gallopade Pub Group.

—Meow! Washington Cats in History, Mystery, Legend, Lore, Humor & More! (Illus.). (gr. 3-12). 1991. PLB 24.95 (0-7933-3455-1); pap. 14.95 (0-7933-3456-X); computer disk 29.95 (0-7933-3457-8) Gallopade Pub Group.

—Meow! Washington DC Cats in History, Mystery, Legend, Lore, Humor & More! (Illus.). (gr. 3-12). 1991. PLB 24.95 (0-7933-3338-5); pap. 14.95 (0-7933-3339-3); computer disk 29.95 (0-7933-3340-7) Gallopade Pub Group.

—Meow! West Virginia Cats in History, Mystery, Legend, Lore, Humor & More! (Illus.). (gr. 3-12). 1991. PLB 24.95 (0-7933-3458-6); pap. 14.95 (0-7933-3459-4); computer disk 29.95 (0-7933-3460-8) Gallopade Pub Group.

—Meow! Wisconsin Cats in History, Mystery, Legend, Lore, Humor & More! (Illus.). (gr. 3-12). 1991. PLB 24.95 (0-7933-3461-6); pap. 14.95 (0-7933-3462-4); computer disk 29.95 (0-7933-3463-2) Gallopade Pub Group.

—Meow! Wyoming Cats in History, Mystery, Legend, Lore, Humor & More! (Illus.). (gr. 3-12). 1991. PLB 24.95 (0-7933-3464-0); pap. 14.95 (0-7933-3465-9); computer disk 29.95 (0-7933-3466-7) Gallopade Pub Group.

—Michigan & Other State Greats (Biographies) (Illus.). (gr. 3 up). 1990. PLB 24.95 (1-55609-677-1); pap. 14.95 (1-55609-678-X); computer disk 29.95 (1-55609-679-8) Gallopade Pub Group.

—Michigan Bandits, Bushwackers, Outlaws, Crooks, Devils, Ghosts, Desperadoes & Other Assorted & Sundry Characters! (Illus.). (gr. 3 up). 1990. PLB 24.95 (0-7933-0599-3); pap. 14.95 (0-7933-0598-5); computer disk 29.95 (0-7933-0600-0) Gallopade Pub Group.

—Michigan Classic Christmas Trivia: Stories, Recipes, Activities, Legends, Lore & More! (Illus.). (gr. 3 up). 1990. PLB 24.95 (0-685-45942-X); pap. 14.95 (0-7933-0601-9); computer disk 29.95 (0-7933-0603-5) Gallopade Pub Group.

—Michigan Coastales. (Illus.). (gr. 3 up). 1990. PLB 24.95 (1-55609-671-2); pap. 14.95 (1-55609-672-0); computer disk 29.95 (1-55609-673-9) Gallopade Pub Group.

—Michigan Coastales! 1992. lib. bdg. 24.95 (0-7933-7287-9) Gallopade Pub Group.

—Michigan "Crinkum-Crankum" A Funny Word Book about Our State. (Illus.). 1992. lib. bdg. 24.95 (0-7933-4874-9); pap. 14.95 (0-7933-4875-7); disk 29.95 (0-7933-4876-5) Gallopade Pub Group.

—Michigan Dingbats! Bk. 1: A Fun Book of Games, Stories, Activities & More about Our State That's All in Code! for You to Decipher. (Illus.). (gr. 3-12). 1991. PLB 24.95 (0-7933-3839-5); pap. 14.95 (0-7933-3840-9); computer disk 29.95 (0-7933-3841-7) Gallopade Pub Group.

—Michigan Festival Fun for Kids! (Illus.). (gr. 3-12). 1991. lib. bdg. 24.95 (0-7933-3992-8); pap. 14.95 (0-7933-3993-6); disk 29.95 (0-7933-3994-4) Gallopade Pub Group.

—The Michigan Hot Air Balloon Mystery. (Illus.). (gr. 2-9). 1990. 24.95 (0-7933-2516-1); pap. 14.95 (0-7933-2517-X); computer disk 29.95 (0-7933-2518-8) Gallopade Pub Group.

—Michigan Jeopardy! Answers & Questions about Our State! (Illus.). (gr. 3-12). 1991. PLB 24.95 (0-7933-4145-0); pap. 14.95 (0-7933-4146-9); computer disk 29.95 (0-7933-4147-7) Gallopade Pub Group.

—Michigan "Jography" A Fun Run Thru Our State. (Illus.). (gr. 3 up). 1990. PLB 24.95 (1-55609-666-6); pap. 14.95 (1-55609-667-4); computer disk 29.95 (1-55609-668-2) Gallopade Pub Group.

—Michigan Kid's Cookbook: Recipes, How-To, History, Lore & More! (Illus.). (gr. 3 up). 1990. PLB 24.95 (0-7933-0611-6); pap. 14.95 (0-7933-0610-8); computer disk 29.95 (0-7933-0612-4) Gallopade Pub Group.

—The Michigan Mystery Van Takes Off! Book 1: Handicapped Michigan Kids Sneak Off on a Big Adventure. (Illus.). (gr. 3-12). 1992. 24.95 (0-7933-5027-1); pap. 14.95 (0-7933-5028-X); computer disk 29.95 (0-7933-5029-8) Gallopade Pub Group.

—Michigan Quiz Bowl Crash Course! (Illus.). (gr. 3 up). 1990. PLB 24.95 (1-55609-674-7); pap. 14.95 (1-55609-675-5); computer disk 29.95 (1-55609-676-3) Gallopade Pub Group.

—Michigan Rollercoasters! (Illus.). (gr. 3-12). 1992. PLB 24.95 (0-7933-5290-8); pap. 14.95 (0-7933-5291-6); computer disk 29.95 (0-7933-5292-4) Gallopade Pub Group.

—Michigan School Trivia: An Amazing & Fascinating Look at Our State's Teachers, Schools & Students! (Illus.). (gr. 3 up). 1990. PLB 24.95 (0-7933-0608-6); pap. 14.95 (0-7933-0607-8); computer disk 29.95 (0-7933-0609-4) Gallopade Pub Group.

—Michigan Silly Basketball Sportsmysteries, Vol. I. (Illus.). (gr. 3 up). 1990. PLB 24.95 (0-7933-0605-1); pap. 14.95 (0-7933-0604-3); computer disk 29.95 (0-7933-0606-X) Gallopade Pub Group.

—Michigan Silly Basketball Sportsmysteries, Vol. II. (Illus.). (gr. 3 up). 1990. PLB 24.95 (0-7933-1711-8); pap. 14.95 (0-7933-1712-6); computer disk 29.95 (0-7933-1713-4) Gallopade Pub Group.

—Michigan Silly Football Sportsmysteries, Vol. I. (Illus.). (gr. 3 up). 1990. PLB 24.95 (1-55609-702-6); pap. 14.95 (1-55609-703-4); computer disk 29.95 (1-55609-704-2) Gallopade Pub Group.

—Michigan Silly Football Sportsmysteries, Vol. II. (Illus.). (gr. 3 up). 1990. PLB 24.95 (1-55609-705-0); pap. 14.95 (1-55609-706-9); computer disk 29.95 (1-55609-707-7) Gallopade Pub Group.

—Michigan Silly Trivia! (Illus.). (gr. 3 up). 1990. PLB 24.95 (1-55609-663-1); pap. 14.95 (1-55609-664-X); computer disk 29.95 (1-55609-665-8) Gallopade Pub Group.

—Michigan Timeline: A Chronology of Michigan History, Mystery, Trivia, Legend, Lore & More. (Illus.). (gr. 3-12). 1992. PLB 24.95 (0-7933-5941-4); pap. 14.95 (0-7933-5942-2); computer disk 29.95 (0-7933-5943-0) Gallopade Pub Group.

—Michigan's (Most Devastating!) Disasters & (Most Calamitous!) Catastrophies! (Illus.). (gr. 3 up). 1990. PLB 24.95 (0-7933-0596-9); pap. 14.95 (0-7933-0595-0); computer disk 29.95 (0-7933-0597-7) Gallopade Pub Group.

—Michigan's Unsolved Mysteries (& Their "Solutions") Includes Scientific Information & Other Activities for Students. (Illus.). (gr. 3-12). 1992. PLB 24.95 (0-7933-5788-8); pap. 14.95 (0-7933-5789-6); computer disk 29.95 (0-7933-5790-X) Gallopade Pub Group.

—Minnesota & Other State Greats (Biographies) (Illus.). (gr. 3 up). 1990. PLB 24.95 (1-55609-660-7); pap. 14.95 (1-55609-661-5); computer disk 29.95 (1-55609-662-3) Gallopade Pub Group.

—Minnesota Bandits, Bushwackers, Outlaws, Crooks, Devils, Ghosts, Desperadoes & Other Assorted & Sundry Characters! (Illus.). (gr. 3 up). 1990. PLB 24.95 (0-7933-0623-X); pap. 14.95 (0-7933-0622-1); computer disk 29.95 (0-7933-0624-8) Gallopade Pub Group.

—Minnesota Classic Christmas Trivia: Stories, Recipes, Activities, Legends, Lore & More! (Illus.). (gr. 3 up). 1990. PLB 24.95 (0-7933-0626-4); pap. 14.95 (0-7933-0625-6); computer disk 29.95 (0-7933-0627-2) Gallopade Pub Group.

—Minnesota Coastales. (Illus.). (gr. 3 up). 1990. PLB 24.95 (1-55609-654-2); pap. 14.95 (1-55609-655-0); computer disk 29.95 (1-55609-656-9) Gallopade Pub Group.

—Minnesota Coastales! 1992. lib. bdg. 24.95 (0-7933-7288-7) Gallopade Pub Group.

—Minnesota "Crinkum-Crankum" A Funny Word Book about Our State. (Illus.). 1992. lib. bdg. 24.95 (0-7933-4877-3); pap. 14.95 (0-7933-4878-1); disk 29.95 (0-7933-4879-X) Gallopade Pub Group.

—Minnesota Dingbats! Bk. 1: A Fun Book of Games, Stories, Activities & More about Our State That's All in Code! for You to Decipher. (Illus.). (gr. 3-12). 1991. PLB 24.95 (0-7933-3842-5); pap. 14.95 (0-7933-3843-3); computer disk 29.95 (0-7933-3844-1) Gallopade Pub Group.

—Minnesota Festival Fun for Kids! (Illus.). (gr. 3-12). 1991. lib. bdg. 24.95 (0-7933-3995-2); pap. 14.95 (0-7933-3996-0); disk 29.95 (0-7933-3997-9) Gallopade Pub Group.

—The Minnesota Hot Air Balloon Mystery. (Illus.). (gr. 2-9). 1990. 24.95 (0-7933-2525-0); pap. 14.95 (0-7933-2526-9); computer disk 29.95 (0-7933-2527-7) Gallopade Pub Group.

—Minnesota Jeopardy! Answers & Questions about Our State! (Illus.). (gr. 3-12). 1991. PLB 24.95 (0-7933-4148-5); pap. 14.95 (0-7933-4149-3); computer disk 29.95 (0-7933-4150-7) Gallopade Pub Group.

—Minnesota "Jography" A Fun Run Thru Our State. (Illus.). (gr. 3 up). 1990. PLB 24.95 (1-55609-642-9); pap. 14.95 (1-55609-643-7); computer disk 29.95 (1-55609-644-5) Gallopade Pub Group.

—Minnesota Kid's Cookbook: Recipes, How-To, History, Lore & More. (Illus.). (gr. 3 up). 1990. PLB 24.95 (0-7933-0635-3); pap. 14.95 (0-7933-0634-5); computer disk 29.95 (0-7933-0636-1) Gallopade Pub Group.

—The Minnesota Mystery Van Takes Off! Book 1: Handicapped Minnesota Kids Sneak Off on a Big Adventure. (Illus.). (gr. 3-12). 1992. 24.95 (0-7933-5030-1); pap. 14.95 (0-7933-5031-X); computer disk 29.95 (0-7933-5032-8) Gallopade Pub Group.

—Minnesota Quiz Bowl Crash Course! (Illus.). (gr. 3 up). 1990. PLB 24.95 (1-55609-657-7); pap. 14.95 (1-55609-658-5); computer disk 29.95 (1-55609-659-3) Gallopade Pub Group.

—Minnesota Rollercoasters! (Illus.). (gr. 3-12). 1992. PLB 24.95 (0-7933-5293-2); pap. 14.95 (0-7933-5294-0); computer disk 29.95 (0-7933-5295-9) Gallopade Pub Group.

—Minnesota School Trivia: An Amazing & Fascinating Look at Our State's Teachers, Schools & Students! (Illus.). (gr. 3 up). 1990. PLB 24.95 (0-7933-0632-9); pap. 14.95 (0-7933-0631-0); computer disk 29.95 (0-7933-0633-7) Gallopade Pub Group.

—Minnesota Silly Basketball Sportsmysteries, Vol. I. (Illus.). (gr. 3 up). 1990. PLB 24.95 (0-7933-0629-9); pap. 14.95 (0-7933-0628-0); computer disk 29.95 (0-7933-0630-2) Gallopade Pub Group.

—Minnesota Silly Basketball Sportsmysteries, Vol. II. (Illus.). (gr. 3 up). 1990. PLB 24.95 (0-7933-1720-7); pap. 14.95 (0-7933-1721-5); computer disk 29.95 (0-7933-1722-3) Gallopade Pub Group.

—Minnesota Silly Football Sportsmysteries, Vol. I. (Illus.). (gr. 3 up). 1990. PLB 24.95 (1-55609-648-8); pap. 14.95 (1-55609-649-6); computer disk 29.95 (1-55609-650-X) Gallopade Pub Group.

—Minnesota Silly Football Sportsmysteries, Vol. II. (Illus.). (gr. 3 up). 1990. PLB 24.95 (1-55609-651-8); pap. 14.95 (1-55609-652-6); computer disk 29.95 (1-55609-653-4) Gallopade Pub Group.

—Minnesota Silly Trivia! (Illus.). (gr. 3 up). 1990. PLB 24.95 (1-55609-639-9); pap. 14.95 (1-55609-640-2); computer disk 29.95 (1-55609-641-0) Gallopade Pub Group.

—Minnesota Timeline: A Chronology of Minnesota History, Mystery, Trivia, Legend, Lore & More. (Illus.). (gr. 3-12). 1992. PLB 24.95 (0-7933-5944-9); pap. 14.95 (0-7933-5945-7); computer disk 29.95 (0-7933-5946-5) Gallopade Pub Group.

—Minnesota's (Most Devastating!) Disasters & (Most Calamitous!) Catastrophies! (Illus.). (gr. 3 up). 1990. PLB 24.95 (0-7933-0620-5); pap. 14.95 (0-7933-0619-1); computer disk 29.95 (0-7933-0621-3) Gallopade Pub Group.

—Minnesota's Unsolved Mysteries (& Their "Solutions") Includes Scientific Information & Other Activities for Students. (Illus.). (gr. 3-12). 1992. PLB 24.95 (0-7933-5791-8); pap. 14.95 (0-7933-5792-6); computer disk 29.95 (0-7933-5793-4) Gallopade Pub Group.

—The Missing Head Mystery. LC 79-55447. (Illus., Orig.). (gr. 3-9). 1980. 24.95 (1-55609-179-6); pap. 14.95 (0-935326-01-4) Gallopade Pub Group.

—The Missing Head Mystery Classroom Gamebook. (Illus., Orig.). (gr. 3-6). 1986. pap. 19.95 (0-935326-84-7) Gallopade Pub Group.

—Mississippi & Other State Greats (Biographies) (Illus.). (gr. 3 up). 1990. PLB 24.95 (1-55609-725-5); pap. 14.95 (1-55609-726-3); computer disk 29.95 (1-55609-727-1) Gallopade Pub Group.

—Mississippi Bandits, Bushwackers, Outlaws, Crooks, Devils, Ghosts, Desperadoes & Other Assorted & Sundry Characters! (Illus.). (gr. 3 up). 1990. PLB 24.95 (0-7933-0648-5); pap. 14.95 (0-7933-0647-7); computer disk 29.95 (0-7933-0649-3) Gallopade Pub Group.

—Mississippi Classic Christmas Trivia: Stories, Recipes, Activities, Legends, Lore & More. (Illus.). (gr. 3 up). 1990. PLB 24.95 (0-7933-0651-5); pap. 14.95 (0-7933-0650-7); computer disk 29.95 (0-7933-0652-3) Gallopade Pub Group.

—Mississippi Coastales. (Illus.). (gr. 3 up). 1990. PLB 24.95 (1-55609-720-4); pap. 14.95 (1-55609-122-2); computer disk 29.95 (1-55609-721-2) Gallopade Pub Group.

—Mississippi Coastales! 1992. lib. bdg. 24.95 (0-7933-7289-5) Gallopade Pub Group.

—Mississippi "Crinkum-Crankum" A Funny Word Book about Our State. (Illus.). 1992. lib. bdg. 24.95 (0-7933-4880-3); pap. 14.95 (0-7933-4881-1); disk 29.95 (0-7933-4882-X) Gallopade Pub Group.

—Mississippi Dingbats! Bk. 1: A Fun Book of Games, Stories, Activities & More about Our State That's All in Code! for You to Decipher. (Illus.). (gr. 3-12). 1991. PLB 24.95 (0-7933-3845-X); pap. 14.95 (0-7933-3846-8); computer disk 29.95 (0-7933-3847-6) Gallopade Pub Group.

—Mississippi Festival Fun for Kids! (Illus.). (gr. 3-12). 1991. lib. bdg. 24.95 (0-7933-3998-7); pap. 14.95 (0-7933-3999-5); disk 29.95 (0-7933-4000-4) Gallopade Pub Group.

—The Mississippi Hot Air Balloon Mystery. (Illus.). (gr. 2-9). 1990. 24.95 (0-7933-2534-X); pap. 14.95 (0-7933-2535-8); computer disk 29.95 (0-7933-2536-6) Gallopade Pub Group.

—Mississippi Jeopardy! Answers & Questions about Our State! (Illus.). (gr. 3-12). 1991. PLB 24.95 (0-7933-4151-5); pap. 14.95 (0-7933-4152-3); computer disk 29.95 (0-7933-4153-1) Gallopade Pub Group.

—Mississippi "Jography" A Fun Run Thru Our State. (Illus.). (gr. 3 up). 1990. PLB 24.95 (1-55609-709-3); pap. 14.95 (1-55609-091-9); computer disk 29.95 (1-55609-715-8) Gallopade Pub Group.

—Mississippi Kid's Cookbook: Recipes, How-To, History, Lore & More. (Illus.). (gr. 3 up). 1990. PLB 24.95 (0-7933-0660-4); pap. 14.95 (0-7933-0659-0); computer disk 29.95 (0-7933-0661-2) Gallopade Pub Group.

—The Mississippi Mystery Van Takes Off! Book 1: Handicapped Mississippi Kids Sneak Off on a Big Adventure. (Illus.). (gr. 3-12). 1992. 24.95 (0-7933-5033-6); pap. 14.95 (0-7933-5034-4); computer disk 29.95 (0-7933-5035-2) Gallopade Pub Group.

—Mississippi Quiz Bowl Crash Course! (Illus.). (gr. 3 up). 1990. PLB 24.95 (1-55609-722-0); pap. 14.95 (1-55609-723-9); computer disk 29.95 (1-55609-724-7) Gallopade Pub Group.

—Mississippi Rollercoasters! (Illus.). (gr. 3-12). 1992. PLB 24.95 (0-7933-5296-7); pap. 14.95 (0-7933-5297-5); computer disk 29.95 (0-7933-5298-3) Gallopade Pub Group.

—Mississippi School Trivia: An Amazing & Fascinating Look at Our State's Teachers, Schools & Students! (Illus.). (gr. 3 up). 1990. PLB 24.95 (0-7933-0657-4); pap. 14.95 (0-7933-0656-6); computer disk 29.95 (0-7933-0658-2) Gallopade Pub Group.

—Mississippi Silly Basketball Sports Mysteries, Vol. II. (Illus.). (gr. 3 up). 1990. PLB 24.95 (0-7933-1731-2); pap. 14.95 (0-7933-1732-0); computer disk 29.95 (0-685-45944-6) Gallopade Pub Group.

—Mississippi Silly Basketball Sportsmysteries, Vol. I. (Illus.). (gr. 3 up). 1990. PLB 24.95 (0-7933-0654-X); pap. 14.95 (0-7933-0653-1); computer disk 29.95 (0-7933-0655-8) Gallopade Pub Group.

—Mississippi Silly Football Sportsmysteries, Vol. I. (Illus.). (gr. 3 up). 1990. PLB 24.95 (1-55609-711-5); pap. 14.95 (1-55609-712-3); computer disk 29.95 (1-55609-713-1) Gallopade Pub Group.

—Mississippi Silly Football Sportsmysteries, Vol. II. (Illus.). (gr. 3 up). 1990. PLB 24.95 (1-55609-717-4); pap. 14.95 (1-55609-718-2); computer disk 29.95 (1-55609-719-0) Gallopade Pub Group.

—Mississippi Silly Trivia! (Illus.). (gr. 3 up). 1990. PLB 24.95 (1-55609-708-5); pap. 14.95 (1-55609-039-0); computer disk 29.95 (1-55609-714-X) Gallopade Pub Group.

—Mississippi Timeline: A Chronology of Mississippi History, Mystery, Trivia, Legend, Lore & More. (Illus.). (gr. 3-12). 1992. PLB 24.95 (0-7933-5947-3); pap. 14.95 (0-7933-5948-1); computer disk 29.95 (0-7933-5949-X) Gallopade Pub Group.

—Mississippi's (Most Devastating!) Disasters & (Most Calamitous!) Catastrophies! (Illus.). (gr. 3 up). 1990. PLB 24.95 (0-7933-0645-0); pap. 14.95 (0-7933-0643-4); computer disk 29.95 (0-7933-0646-9) Gallopade Pub Group.

—Mississippi's Unsolved Mysteries (& Their "Solutions") Includes Scientific Information & Other Activities for Students. (Illus.). (gr. 3-12). 1992. PLB 24.95 (0-7933-5794-2); pap. 14.95 (0-7933-5795-0); computer disk 29.95 (0-7933-5796-9) Gallopade Pub Group.

—Missouri & Other State Greats (Biographies) (Illus.). (gr. 3 up). 1990. PLB 24.95 (1-55609-748-4); pap. 14.95 (1-55609-749-2); computer disk 29.95 (1-55609-750-6) Gallopade Pub Group.

—Missouri Bandits, Bushwackers, Outlaws, Crooks, Devils, Ghosts, Desperadoes & Other Assorted & Sundry Characters! (Illus.). (gr. 3 up). 1990. PLB 24.95 (0-7933-0672-8); pap. 14.95 (0-7933-0671-X); computer disk 29.95 (0-7933-0673-6) Gallopade Pub Group.

—Missouri Classic Christmas Trivia: Stories, Recipes, Activities, Legends, Lore & More. (Illus.). (gr. 3 up). 1990. PLB 24.95 (0-7933-0675-2); pap. 14.95 (0-7933-0674-4); computer disk 29.95 (0-7933-0676-0) Gallopade Pub Group.

—Missouri Coastales. (Illus.). (gr. 3 up). 1990. PLB 24.95 (1-55609-742-5); pap. 14.95 (1-55609-743-3); computer disk 29.95 (1-55609-744-1) Gallopade Pub Group.

—Missouri Coastales! 1992. lib. bdg. 24.95 (0-7933-7290-9) Gallopade Pub Group.

—Missouri "Crinkum-Crankum" A Funny Word Book about Our State. (Illus.). 1992. lib. bdg. 24.95 (0-7933-4883-8); pap. 14.95 (0-7933-4884-6); disk 29.95 (0-7933-4885-4) Gallopade Pub Group.

—Missouri Dingbats! Bk. 1: A Fun Book of Games, Stories, Activities & More about Our State That's All in Code! for You to Decipher. (Illus.). (gr. 3-12). 1991. PLB 24.95 (0-7933-3848-4); pap. 14.95 (0-7933-3849-2); computer disk 29.95 (0-7933-3850-6) Gallopade Pub Group.

—Missouri Festival Fun for Kids! (Illus.). (gr. 3-12). 1991. lib. bdg. 24.95 (0-7933-4001-2); pap. 14.95 (0-7933-4002-0); disk 29.95 (0-7933-4003-9) Gallopade Pub Group.

—The Missouri Hot Air Balloon Mystery. (Illus.). (gr. 2-9). 1990. 24.95 (0-7933-2543-9); pap. 14.95 (0-7933-2544-7); computer disk 29.95 (0-7933-2545-5) Gallopade Pub Group.

—Missouri Jeopardy! Answers & Questions about Our State! (Illus.). (gr. 3-12). 1991. PLB 24.95 (0-7933-4154-X); pap. 14.95 (0-7933-4155-8); computer disk 29.95 (0-7933-4156-6) Gallopade Pub Group.

—Missouri "Jography" A Fun Run Thru Our State. (Illus.). (gr. 3 up). 1990. PLB 24.95 (1-55609-730-1); pap. 14.95 (1-55609-731-X); computer disk 29.95 (1-55609-732-8) Gallopade Pub Group.

—Missouri Kid's Cookbook: Recipes, How-To, History, Lore & More. (Illus.). (gr. 3 up). 1990. PLB 24.95 (0-7933-0684-1); pap. 14.95 (0-7933-0683-3); computer disk 29.95 (0-7933-0685-X) Gallopade Pub Group.

—The Missouri Mystery Van Takes Off! Book 1: Handicapped Missouri Kids Sneak Off on a Big Adventure. (Illus.). (gr. 3-12). 1992. 24.95 (0-7933-5036-0); pap. 14.95 (0-7933-5037-9); computer disk 29.95 (0-7933-5038-7) Gallopade Pub Group.

—Missouri Quiz Bowl Crash Course! (Illus.). (gr. 3 up). 1990. PLB 24.95 (1-55609-745-X); pap. 14.95 (1-55609-746-8); computer disk 29.95 (1-55609-747-6) Gallopade Pub Group.

—Missouri Rollercoasters! (Illus.). (gr. 3-12). 1992. PLB 24.95 (0-7933-5299-1); pap. 14.95 (0-7933-5300-9); computer disk 29.95 (0-7933-5301-7) Gallopade Pub Group.

—Missouri School Trivia: An Amazing & Fascinating Look at Our State's Teachers, Schools & Students! (Illus.). (gr. 3 up). 1990. PLB 24.95 (0-7933-0681-7); pap. 14.95 (0-7933-0680-9); computer disk 29.95 (0-7933-0682-5) Gallopade Pub Group.

—Missouri Silly Basketball Sportsmysteries, Vol. I. (Illus.). (gr. 3 up). 1990. PLB 24.95 (0-7933-0678-7); pap. 14.95 (0-7933-0677-9); computer disk 29.95 (0-685-45947-0) Gallopade Pub Group.

—Missouri Silly Basketball Sportsmysteries, Vol. II. (Illus.). (gr. 3 up). 1990. PLB 24.95 (0-7933-1740-1); pap. 14.95 (0-7933-1741-X); computer disk 29.95 (0-7933-1742-8) Gallopade Pub Group.

—Missouri Silly Football Sportsmysteries, Vol. I. (Illus.). (gr. 3 up). 1990. PLB 24.95 (1-55609-736-0); pap. 14.95 (1-55609-737-9); computer disk 29.95 (0-685-45945-4) Gallopade Pub Group.

—Missouri Silly Football Sportsmysteries, Vol. II. (Illus.). (gr. 3 up). 1990. PLB 24.95 (1-55609-739-5); pap. 14.95 (1-55609-740-9); computer disk 29.95 (1-55609-741-7) Gallopade Pub Group.

—Missouri Silly Trivia! (Illus.). (gr. 3 up). 1990. PLB 24.95 (1-55609-728-X); pap. 14.95 (1-55609-100-1); computer disk 29.95 (1-55609-729-8) Gallopade Pub Group.

—Missouri Timeline: A Chronology of Missouri History, Mystery, Trivia, Legend, Lore & More. (Illus.). (gr. 3-12). 1992. PLB 24.95 (0-7933-5950-3); pap. 14.95 (0-7933-5951-1); computer disk 29.95 (0-7933-5952-X) Gallopade Pub Group.

—Missouri's (Most Devastating!) Disasters & (Most Calamitous!) Catastrophies! (Illus.). (gr. 3 up). 1990. PLB 24.95 (0-7933-0669-8); pap. 14.95 (0-7933-0668-X); computer disk 29.95 (0-7933-0670-1) Gallopade Pub Group.

—Missouri's Unsolved Mysteries (& Their "Solutions") Includes Scientific Information & Other Activities for Students. (Illus.). (gr. 3-12). 1992. PLB 24.95 (0-7933-5797-7); pap. 14.95 (0-7933-5798-5); computer disk 29.95 (0-7933-5799-3) Gallopade Pub Group.

—The Monsters, Vampires & Werewolves Dingbats Book. (Illus.). (gr. 3-12). 1992. PLB 24.95 (0-7933-5392-0); pap. 14.95 (0-7933-5393-9); computer disk 29.95 (0-7933-5394-7) Gallopade Pub Group.

—Montana & Other State Greats (Biographies) (Illus.). (gr. 3 up). 1990. PLB 24.95 (1-55609-772-7); pap. 14.95 (1-55609-773-5); computer disk 29.95 (1-55609-774-3) Gallopade Pub Group.

—Montana Bandits, Bushwackers, Outlaws, Crooks, Devils, Ghosts, Desperadoes & Other Assorted & Sundry Characters! (Illus.). (gr. 3 up). 1990. PLB 24.95 (0-7933-0697-3); pap. 14.95 (0-7933-0696-5); computer disk 29.95 (0-7933-0698-1) Gallopade Pub Group.

—Montana Classic Christmas Trivia. (gr. 3 up). 1990. PLB 24.95 (0-7933-0700-7); pap. 14.95 (0-7933-0699-X); computer disk 29.95 (0-7933-0701-5) Gallopade Pub Group.

—Montana Coastales. (Illus.). (gr. 3 up). 1990. PLB 24.95 (1-55609-766-2); pap. 14.95 (1-55609-767-0); computer disk 29.95 (1-55609-768-9) Gallopade Pub Group.

—Montana Coastales! 1992. lib. bdg. 24.95 (0-7933-7291-7) Gallopade Pub Group.

—Montana "Crinkum-Crankum" A Funny Word Book about Our State. (Illus.). 1992. lib. bdg. 24.95 (0-7933-4886-2); pap. 14.95 (0-7933-4887-0); disk 29.95 (0-7933-4888-9) Gallopade Pub Group.

—Montana Dingbats! Bk. 1: A Fun Book of Games, Stories, Activities & More about Our State That's All in Code! for You to Decipher. (Illus.). (gr. 3-12). 1991. PLB 24.95 (0-7933-3851-4); pap. 14.95 (0-7933-3852-2); computer disk 29.95 (0-7933-3853-0) Gallopade Pub Group.

—Montana Festival Fun for Kids! (Illus.). (gr. 3-12). 1991. lib. bdg. 24.95 (0-7933-4004-7); pap. 14.95 (0-7933-4005-5); disk 29.95 (0-7933-4006-3) Gallopade Pub Group.

—The Montana Hot Air Balloon Mystery. (Illus.). (gr. 2-9). 1990. 24.95 (0-7933-2552-8); pap. 14.95 (0-7933-2553-6); computer disk 29.95 (0-7933-2554-4) Gallopade Pub Group.

—Montana Jeopardy! Answers & Questions about Our State! (Illus.). (gr. 3-12). 1991. PLB 24.95 (0-7933-4157-4); pap. 14.95 (0-7933-4158-2); computer disk 29.95 (0-7933-4159-0) Gallopade Pub Group.

—Montana "Jography" A Fun Run Thru Our State. (Illus.). (gr. 3 up). 1990. PLB 24.95 (1-55609-754-9); pap. 14.95 (1-55609-755-7); computer disk 29.95 (1-55609-756-5) Gallopade Pub Group.

—Montana Kid's Cookbook: Recipes, How-To, History, Lore & More. (Illus.). (gr. 3 up). 1990. PLB 24.95 (0-7933-0709-0); pap. 14.95 (0-7933-0708-2); computer disk 29.95 (0-7933-0710-4) Gallopade Pub Group.

—The Montana Mystery Van Takes Off! Book 1: Handicapped Montana Kids Sneak Off on a Big Adventure. (Illus.). (gr. 3-12). 1992. 24.95 (0-7933-5039-5); pap. 14.95 (0-7933-5040-9); computer disk 29.95 (0-7933-5041-7) Gallopade Pub Group.

—Montana Quiz Bowl Crash Course! (Illus.). (gr. 3 up). 1990. PLB 24.95 (1-55609-769-7); pap. 14.95 (1-55609-770-0); computer disk 29.95 (1-55609-771-9) Gallopade Pub Group.

—Montana Rollercoasters! (Illus.). (gr. 3-12). 1992. PLB 24.95 (0-7933-5302-5); pap. 14.95 (0-7933-5303-3); computer disk 29.95 (0-7933-5304-1) Gallopade Pub Group.

—Montana School Trivia: An Amazing & Fascinating Look at Our State's Teachers, Schools & Students! (Illus.). (gr. 3 up). 1990. PLB 24.95 (0-7933-0706-6); pap. 14.95 (0-7933-0705-8); computer disk 29.95 (0-7933-0707-4) Gallopade Pub Group.

—Montana Silly Basketball Sportsmysteries, Vol. I. (Illus.). (gr. 3 up). 1990. PLB 24.95 (0-7933-0703-1); pap. 14.95 (0-7933-0702-3); computer disk 29.95 (0-7933-0704-X) Gallopade Pub Group.

—Montana Silly Basketball Sportsmysteries, Vol. II. (Illus.). (gr. 3 up). 1990. PLB 24.95 (0-7933-1749-5); pap. 14.95 (0-7933-1750-9); computer disk 29.95 (0-7933-1751-7) Gallopade Pub Group.

—Montana Silly Football Sportsmysteries, Vol. I. (Illus.). (gr. 3 up). 1990. PLB 24.95 (1-55609-760-3); pap. 14.95 (1-55609-761-1); computer disk 29.95 (1-55609-762-X) Gallopade Pub Group.

—Montana Silly Football Sportsmysteries, Vol. II. (Illus.). (gr. 3 up). 1990. PLB 24.95 (1-55609-763-8); pap. 14.95 (1-55609-764-6); computer disk 29.95 (1-55609-765-4) Gallopade Pub Group.

—Montana Silly Trivia! (Illus.). (gr. 3 up). 1990. PLB 24.
95 (*1-55609-751-4*); pap. 14.95 (*1-55609-752-2*);
computer disk 29.95 (*1-55609-753-0*) Gallopade Pub
Group.
—Montana Timeline: A Chronology of Montana History,
Mystery, Trivia, Legend, Lore & More. (Illus.). (gr. 3-
12). 1992. PLB 24.95 (*0-7933-5953-8*); pap. 14.95
(*0-7933-5954-6*); computer disk 29.95 (*0-7933-5955-4*)
Gallopade Pub Group.
—Montana's (Most Devastating!) Disasters & (Most
Calamitous!) Catastrophies! (Illus.). (gr. 3 up). 1990.
PLB 24.95 (*0-685-45943-8*); pap. 14.95
(*0-7933-0692-2*); computer disk 29.95 (*0-7933-0695-7*)
Gallopade Pub Group.
—Montana's Unsolved Mysteries (& Their "Solutions")
Includes Scientific Information & Other Activities for
Students. (Illus.). (gr. 3-12). 1992. PLB 24.95
(*0-7933-5800-0*); pap. 14.95 (*0-7933-5801-9*);
computer disk 29.95 (*0-7933-5802-7*) Gallopade Pub
Group.
—My First Book about Alabama. (gr. k-4). 1992. PLB 24.
95 (*0-7933-5569-9*); pap. 14.95 (*0-7933-5570-2*);
computer disk 29.95 (*0-7933-5571-0*) Gallopade Pub
Group.
—My First Book about Alaska. (gr. k-4). 1992. PLB 24.
95 (*0-7933-5572-9*); pap. 14.95 (*0-7933-5573-7*);
computer disk 29.95 (*0-7933-5574-5*) Gallopade Pub
Group.
—My First Book about Arizona. (gr. k-4). 1992. PLB 24.
95 (*0-7933-5575-3*); pap. 14.95 (*0-7933-5576-1*);
computer disk 29.95 (*0-7933-5577-X*) Gallopade Pub
Group.
—My First Book about Arkansas. (gr. k-4). 1992. PLB
24.95 (*0-7933-5578-8*); pap. 14.95 (*0-7933-5579-6*);
computer disk 29.95 (*0-7933-5580-X*) Gallopade Pub
Group.
—My First Book about California. (gr. k-4). 1992. PLB
24.95 (*0-7933-5581-8*); pap. 14.95 (*0-7933-5582-6*);
computer disk 29.95 (*0-7933-5583-4*) Gallopade Pub
Group.
—My First Book about Colorado. (gr. k-4). 1992. PLB
24.95 (*0-7933-5584-2*); pap. 14.95 (*0-7933-5585-0*);
computer disk 29.95 (*0-7933-5586-9*) Gallopade Pub
Group.
—My First Book about Connecticut. (gr. k-4). 1992. PLB
24.95 (*0-7933-5587-7*); pap. 14.95 (*0-7933-5588-5*);
computer disk 29.95 (*0-7933-5589-3*) Gallopade Pub
Group.
—My First Book about Delaware. (gr. k-4). 1992. PLB
24.95 (*0-7933-5590-7*); pap. 14.95 (*0-7933-5591-5*);
computer disk 29.95 (*0-7933-5592-3*) Gallopade Pub
Group.
—My First Book about Florida. (gr. k-4). 1992. PLB 24.
95 (*0-7933-5596-6*); pap. 14.95 (*0-7933-5597-4*);
computer disk 29.95 (*0-7933-5598-2*) Gallopade Pub
Group.
—My First Book about Georgia. (gr. k-4). 1992. PLB 24.
95 (*0-7933-5599-0*); pap. 14.95 (*0-7933-5600-8*);
computer disk 29.95 (*0-7933-5601-6*) Gallopade Pub
Group.
—My First Book about Hawaii. (gr. k-4). 1992. PLB 24.
95 (*0-7933-5602-4*); pap. 14.95 (*0-7933-5603-2*);
computer disk 29.95 (*0-7933-5604-0*) Gallopade Pub
Group.
—My First Book about Idaho. (gr. k-4). 1992. PLB 24.95
(*0-7933-5605-9*); pap. 14.95 (*0-7933-5606-7*);
computer disk 29.95 (*0-7933-5607-5*) Gallopade Pub
Group.
—My First Book about Illinois. (gr. k-4). 1992. PLB 24.
95 (*0-7933-5608-3*); pap. 14.95 (*0-7933-5609-1*);
computer disk 29.95 (*0-7933-5610-5*) Gallopade Pub
Group.
—My First Book about Indiana. (gr. k-4). 1992. PLB 24.
95 (*0-7933-5611-3*); pap. 14.95 (*0-7933-5612-1*);
computer disk 29.95 (*0-7933-5613-X*) Gallopade Pub
Group.
—My First Book about Iowa. (gr. k-4). 1992. PLB 24.95
(*0-7933-5614-8*); pap. 14.95 (*0-7933-5615-6*);
computer disk 29.95 (*0-7933-5616-4*) Gallopade Pub
Group.
—My First Book about Kansas. (gr. k-4). 1992. PLB 24.
95 (*0-7933-5617-2*); pap. 14.95 (*0-7933-5618-0*);
computer disk 29.95 (*0-7933-5619-9*) Gallopade Pub
Group.
—My First Book about Kentucky. (gr. k-4). 1992. PLB
24.95 (*0-7933-5620-2*); pap. 14.95 (*0-7933-5621-0*);
computer disk 29.95 (*0-7933-5622-9*) Gallopade Pub
Group.
—My First Book about Louisiana. (gr. k-4). 1992. PLB
24.95 (*0-7933-5623-7*); pap. 14.95 (*0-7933-5624-5*);
computer disk 29.95 (*0-7933-5625-3*) Gallopade Pub
Group.
—My First Book about Maine. (gr. k-4). 1992. PLB 24.95
(*0-7933-5626-1*); pap. 14.95 (*0-7933-5627-X*);
computer disk 29.95 (*0-7933-5628-8*) Gallopade Pub
Group.
—My First Book about Maryland. (gr. k-4). 1992. PLB
24.95 (*0-7933-5629-6*); pap. 14.95 (*0-7933-5630-X*);
computer disk 29.95 (*0-7933-5631-8*) Gallopade Pub
Group.
—My First Book about Massachusetts. (gr. k-4). 1992.
PLB 24.95 (*0-7933-5632-6*); pap. 14.95
(*0-7933-5633-4*); computer disk 29.95 (*0-7933-5634-2*)
Gallopade Pub Group.
—My First Book about Michigan. (gr. k-4). 1992. PLB
24.95 (*0-7933-5635-0*); pap. 14.95 (*0-7933-5636-9*);
computer disk 29.95 (*0-7933-5637-7*) Gallopade Pub
Group.

—My First Book about Minnesota. (gr. k-4). 1992. PLB
24.95 (*0-7933-5638-5*); pap. 14.95 (*0-7933-5639-3*);
computer disk 29.95 (*0-7933-5640-7*) Gallopade Pub
Group.
—My First Book about Mississippi. (gr. k-4). 1992. PLB
24.95 (*0-7933-5641-5*); pap. 14.95 (*0-7933-5642-3*);
computer disk 29.95 (*0-7933-5643-1*) Gallopade Pub
Group.
—My First Book about Missouri. (gr. k-4). 1992. PLB 24.
95 (*0-7933-5644-X*); pap. 14.95 (*0-7933-5645-8*);
computer disk 29.95 (*0-7933-5646-6*) Gallopade Pub
Group.
—My First Book about Montana. (gr. k-4). 1992. PLB 24.
95 (*0-7933-5647-4*); pap. 14.95 (*0-7933-5648-2*);
computer disk 29.95 (*0-7933-5649-0*) Gallopade Pub
Group.
—My First Book about Nebraska. (gr. k-4). 1992. PLB
24.95 (*0-7933-5650-4*); pap. 14.95 (*0-7933-5651-2*);
computer disk 29.95 (*0-7933-5652-0*) Gallopade Pub
Group.
—My First Book about Nevada. (gr. k-4). 1992. PLB 24.
95 (*0-7933-5653-9*); pap. 14.95 (*0-7933-5654-7*);
computer disk 29.95 (*0-7933-5655-5*) Gallopade Pub
Group.
—My First Book about New Hampshire. (gr. k-4). 1992.
PLB 24.95 (*0-7933-5656-3*); pap. 14.95
(*0-7933-5657-1*); computer disk 29.95
(*0-7933-5658-X*) Gallopade Pub Group.
—My First Book about New Jersey. (gr. k-4). 1992. PLB
24.95 (*0-7933-5659-8*); pap. 14.95 (*0-7933-5660-1*);
computer disk 29.95 (*0-7933-5661-X*) Gallopade Pub
Group.
—My First Book about New Mexico. (gr. k-4). 1992.
PLB 24.95 (*0-7933-5662-8*); pap. 14.95
(*0-7933-5663-6*); computer disk 29.95 (*0-7933-5664-4*)
Gallopade Pub Group.
—My First Book about New York. (gr. k-4). 1992. PLB
24.95 (*0-7933-5665-2*); pap. 14.95 (*0-7933-5666-0*);
computer disk 29.95 (*0-7933-5667-9*) Gallopade Pub
Group.
—My First Book about North Carolina. (gr. k-4). 1992.
PLB 24.95 (*0-7933-5668-7*); pap. 14.95
(*0-7933-5669-5*); computer disk 29.95 (*0-7933-5670-9*)
Gallopade Pub Group.
—My First Book about North Dakota. (gr. k-4). 1992.
PLB 24.95 (*0-7933-5671-7*); pap. 14.95
(*0-7933-5672-5*); computer disk 29.95 (*0-7933-5673-3*)
Gallopade Pub Group.
—My First Book about Ohio. (gr. k-4). 1992. PLB 24.95
(*0-7933-5674-1*); pap. 14.95 (*0-7933-5675-X*);
computer disk 29.95 (*0-7933-5676-8*) Gallopade Pub
Group.
—My First Book about Oklahoma. (gr. k-4). 1992. PLB
24.95 (*0-7933-5677-6*); pap. 14.95 (*0-7933-5678-4*);
computer disk 29.95 (*0-7933-5679-2*) Gallopade Pub
Group.
—My First Book about Oregon. (gr. k-4). 1992. PLB 24.
95 (*0-7933-5680-6*); pap. 14.95 (*0-7933-5681-4*);
computer disk 29.95 (*0-7933-5682-2*) Gallopade Pub
Group.
—My First Book about Pennsylvania. (gr. k-4). 1992.
PLB 24.95 (*0-7933-5683-0*); pap. 14.95
(*0-7933-5684-9*); computer disk 29.95 (*0-7933-5685-7*)
Gallopade Pub Group.
—My First Book about Rhode Island. (gr. k-4). 1992.
PLB 24.95 (*0-7933-5686-5*); pap. 14.95
(*0-7933-5687-3*); computer disk 29.95 (*0-7933-5688-1*)
Gallopade Pub Group.
—My First Book about South Carolina. (gr. k-4). 1992.
PLB 24.95 (*0-7933-5689-X*); pap. 14.95
(*0-7933-5690-3*); computer disk 29.95 (*0-7933-5691-1*)
Gallopade Pub Group.
—My First Book about South Dakota. (gr. k-4). 1992.
PLB 24.95 (*0-7933-5692-X*); pap. 14.95
(*0-7933-5693-8*); computer disk 29.95 (*0-7933-5694-6*)
Gallopade Pub Group.
—My First Book about Tennessee. (gr. k-4). 1992. PLB
24.95 (*0-7933-5695-4*); pap. 14.95 (*0-7933-5696-2*);
computer disk 29.95 (*0-7933-5697-0*) Gallopade Pub
Group.
—My First Book about Texas. (gr. k-4). 1992. PLB 24.95
(*0-7933-5698-9*); pap. 14.95 (*0-7933-5699-7*);
computer disk 29.95 (*0-7933-5700-4*) Gallopade Pub
Group.
—My First Book about Utah. (gr. k-4). 1992. PLB 24.95
(*0-7933-5701-2*); pap. 14.95 (*0-7933-5702-0*);
computer disk 29.95 (*0-7933-5703-9*) Gallopade Pub
Group.
—My First Book about Vermont. (gr. k-4). 1992. PLB 24.
95 (*0-7933-5704-7*); pap. 14.95 (*0-7933-5705-5*);
computer disk 29.95 (*0-7933-5706-3*) Gallopade Pub
Group.
—My First Book about Virginia. (gr. k-4). 1992. PLB 24.
95 (*0-7933-5707-1*); pap. 14.95 (*0-7933-5708-X*);
computer disk 29.95 (*0-7933-5709-8*) Gallopade Pub
Group.
—My First Book about Washington. (gr. k-4). 1992. PLB
24.95 (*0-7933-5710-1*); pap. 14.95 (*0-7933-5711-X*);
computer disk 29.95 (*0-7933-5712-8*) Gallopade Pub
Group.
—My First Book about Washington DC. (gr. k-4). 1992.
PLB 24.95 (*0-7933-5593-1*); pap. 14.95
(*0-7933-5594-X*); computer disk 29.95
(*0-7933-5595-8*) Gallopade Pub Group.
—My First Book about West Virginia. (gr. k-4). 1992.
PLB 24.95 (*0-7933-5713-6*); pap. 14.95
(*0-7933-5714-4*); computer disk 29.95 (*0-7933-5715-2*)
Gallopade Pub Group.

—My First Book about Wisconsin. (gr. k-4). 1992. PLB
24.95 (*0-7933-5716-0*); pap. 14.95 (*0-7933-5717-9*);
computer disk 29.95 (*0-7933-5718-7*) Gallopade Pub
Group.
—My First Book about Wyoming. (gr. k-4). 1992. PLB
24.95 (*0-7933-5719-5*); pap. 14.95 (*0-7933-5720-9*);
computer disk 29.95 (*0-7933-5721-7*) Gallopade Pub
Group.
—My Lifetime of Sex & How to Handle It. (Orig.). (ps-
12). 1987. pap. 14.95 (*1-55609-211-3*) Gallopade Pub
Group.
—Mystery of Old Salem Activity Book. 12p. (Orig.). (gr.
4-8). 1986. pap. 12.00 (*0-935326-67-7*) Gallopade Pub
Group.
—Mystery of Old Salem Gamebook. (Orig.). (gr. 4-8).
1986. pap. 19.95 (*0-935326-66-9*) Gallopade Pub
Group.
—Mystery of Old Salem S. P. A. R. K. Kit. (Illus., Orig.).
(gr. 3-9). 1986. pap. 24.95 (*0-935326-74-X*) Gallopade
Pub Group.
—Mystery of Stone Mountain. (Orig.). (gr. 3-7). 1983.
PLB 24.95 (*1-55609-180-X*); pap. 14.95
(*0-935326-25-1*) Gallopade Pub Group.
—The Mystery of the Biltmore House. (Illus., Orig.). (gr.
3-9). 1982. 14.95 (*0-935326-07-3*) Gallopade Pub
Group.
—Mystery of the Lost Colony. (Illus.). (gr. 4-9). 1983.
PLB 24.95 (*1-55609-182-6*); pap. 14.95
(*0-935326-05-7*) Gallopade Pub Group.
—Mystery of the World's Fair. Marsh, Carol, illus.
(Orig.). (gr. 3-9). 1982. pap. 14.95 (*0-935326-04-9*)
Gallopade Pub Group.
—Mystery of Tryon Palace Activity Book. (Orig.). (gr.
3-6). 1986. pap. 14.95 (*0-935326-69-3*) Gallopade Pub
Group.
—Mystery of Tryon Palace Gamebook. (Orig.). (gr. 2-6).
1986. pap. 14.95 (*0-935326-70-7*) Gallopade Pub
Group.
—Mystery of Tryon Palace S. P. A. R. K. Kit. (Illus.,
Orig.). (gr. 3-8). 1986. pap. 24.95 (*0-317-44654-1*)
Gallopade Pub Group.
—Nebraska & Other State Greats (Biographies) (Illus.).
(gr. 3 up). 1990. PLB 24.95 (*1-55609-796-4*); pap. 14.
95 (*1-55609-797-2*); computer disk 29.95
(*1-55609-798-0*) Gallopade Pub Group.
—Nebraska Bandits, Bushwackers, Outlaws, Crooks,
Devils, Ghosts, Desperadoes & Other Assorted &
Sundry Characters! (Illus.). (gr. 3 up). 1990. PLB 24.
95 (*0-7933-0721-X*); pap. 14.95 (*0-7933-0720-1*);
computer disk 29.95 (*0-7933-0722-8*) Gallopade Pub
Group.
—Nebraska Bandits, Bushwackers, Outlaws, Crooks,
Devils, Ghosts, Desperadoes & Other Assorted &
Sundry Characters. 1992. wkbk. 6.95 (*0-7933-6811-1*)
Gallopade Pub Group.
—Nebraska Books Series: Student Workbooks, 3 bks.
1992. Set. 20.85 (*0-7933-6812-X*) Gallopade Pub
Group.
—Nebraska Classic Christmas Trivia: Stories, Recipes,
Activities, Legends, Lore & More! (Illus.). (gr. 3 up).
1990. PLB 24.95 (*0-7933-0724-4*); pap. 14.95
(*0-7933-0723-6*); computer disk 29.95 (*0-7933-0725-2*)
Gallopade Pub Group.
—Nebraska Coastales. (Illus.). (gr. 3 up). 1990. PLB 24.
95 (*1-55609-790-5*); pap. 14.95 (*1-55609-791-3*);
computer disk 29.95 (*1-55609-792-1*) Gallopade Pub
Group.
—Nebraska Coastales. 1992. lib. bdg. 24.95
(*0-7933-7292-5*) Gallopade Pub Group.
—Nebraska "Crinkum-Crankum" A Funny Word Book
about Our State. (Illus.). 1992. lib. bdg. 24.95
(*0-7933-4889-7*); pap. 14.95 (*0-7933-4890-0*); disk 29.
95 (*0-7933-4891-9*) Gallopade Pub Group.
—Nebraska Dingbats! Bk. 1: A Fun Book of Games,
Stories, Activities & More about Our State That's All
in Code! for You to Decipher. (Illus.). (gr. 3-12).
1991. PLB 24.95 (*0-7933-3854-9*); pap. 14.95
(*0-7933-3855-7*); computer disk 29.95 (*0-7933-3856-5*)
Gallopade Pub Group.
—Nebraska Festival Fun for Kids! (Illus.). (gr. 3-12).
1991. lib. bdg. 24.95 (*0-7933-4007-1*); pap. 14.95
(*0-7933-4008-X*); disk 29.95 (*0-7933-4009-8*)
Gallopade Pub Group.
—The Nebraska Hot Air Balloon Mystery. (Illus.). (gr.
2-9). 1990. 24.95 (*0-7933-2561-7*); pap. 14.95
(*0-7933-2562-5*); computer disk 29.95 (*0-7933-2563-3*)
Gallopade Pub Group.
—Nebraska Jeopardy! Answers & Questions about Our
State! (Illus.). (gr. 3-12). 1991. PLB 24.95
(*0-7933-4160-4*); pap. 14.95 (*0-7933-4161-2*);
computer disk 29.95 (*0-7933-4162-0*) Gallopade Pub
Group.
—Nebraska "Jography" A Fun Run Thru Our State.
(Illus.). (gr. 3 up). 1990. PLB 24.95 (*1-55609-778-6*);
pap. 14.95 (*0-685-45948-9*); computer disk 29.95
(*1-55609-780-8*) Gallopade Pub Group.
—Nebraska Jography: Answers & Questions about Our
State. 1992. wkbk. 6.95 (*0-7933-6810-3*) Gallopade
Pub Group.
—Nebraska Kid's Cookbook: Recipes, How-To, History,
Lore & More! (Illus.). (gr. 3 up). 1990. PLB 24.95
(*0-7933-0733-3*); pap. 14.95 (*0-7933-0732-5*);
computer disk 29.95 (*0-7933-0734-1*) Gallopade Pub
Group.

—The Nebraska Mystery Van Takes Off! Book 1: Handicapped Nebraska Kids Sneak Off on a Big Adventure. (Illus.). (gr. 3-12). 1992. 24.95 (*0-7933-5042-5*); pap. 14.95 (*0-7933-5043-3*); computer disk 29.95 (*0-7933-5044-1*) Gallopade Pub Group.

—Nebraska Quiz Bowl Crash Course! (Illus.). (gr. 3 up). 1990. PLB 24.95 (*1-55609-793-X*); pap. 14.95 (*1-55609-794-8*); computer disk 29.95 (*1-55609-795-6*) Gallopade Pub Group.

—Nebraska Rollercoasters! (Illus.). (gr. 3-12). 1992. PLB 24.95 (*0-7933-5305-X*); pap. 14.95 (*0-7933-5306-8*); computer disk 29.95 (*0-7933-5307-6*) Gallopade Pub Group.

—Nebraska School Trivia: An Amazing & Fascinating Look at Our State's Teachers, Schools & Students! (Illus.). (gr. 3 up). 1990. PLB 24.95 (*0-7933-0730-9*); pap. 14.95 (*0-7933-0729-5*); computer disk 29.95 (*0-7933-0731-7*) Gallopade Pub Group.

—Nebraska Silly Basketball Sportsmysteries, Vol. I. (Illus.). (gr. 3 up). 1990. PLB 24.95 (*0-7933-0727-9*); pap. 14.95 (*0-7933-0726-0*); computer disk 29.95 (*0-7933-0728-7*) Gallopade Pub Group.

—Nebraska Silly Basketball Sportsmysteries, Vol. II. (Illus.). (gr. 3 up). 1990. PLB 24.95 (*0-7933-1758-4*); pap. 14.95 (*0-7933-1759-2*); computer disk 29.95 (*0-7933-1760-6*) Gallopade Pub Group.

—Nebraska Silly Football Sportsmysteries, Vol. I. (Illus.). (gr. 3 up). 1990. PLB 24.95 (*1-55609-784-0*); pap. 14. 95 (*1-55609-785-9*); computer disk 29.95 (*1-55609-786-7*) Gallopade Pub Group.

—Nebraska Silly Football Sportsmysteries, Vol. II. (Illus.). (gr. 3 up). 1990. PLB 24.95 (*1-55609-787-5*); pap. 14.95 (*1-55609-788-3*); computer disk 29.95 (*1-55609-789-1*) Gallopade Pub Group.

—Nebraska Silly Trivia! (Illus.). (gr. 3 up). 1990. PLB 24. 95 (*1-55609-775-1*); pap. 14.95 (*1-55609-776-X*); computer disk 29.95 (*1-55609-777-8*) Gallopade Pub Group.

—Nebraska Silly Trivia. 1992. wkbk. 6.95 (*0-7933-6809-X*) Gallopade Pub Group.

—Nebraska Timeline: A Chronology of Nebraska History, Mystery, Trivia, Legend, Lore & More. (Illus.). (gr. 3-12). 1992. PLB 24.95 (*0-7933-5956-2*); pap. 14.95 (*0-7933-5957-0*); computer disk 29.95 (*0-7933-5958-9*) Gallopade Pub Group.

—Nebraska's (Most Devastating!) Disasters & (Most Calamitous!) Catastrophies! (Illus.). (gr. 3 up). 1990. PLB 24.95 (*0-7933-0718-X*); pap. 14.95 (*0-7933-0717-1*) (*0-7933-0719-8*) Gallopade Pub Group.

—Nebraska's Unsolved Mysteries (& Their "Solutions") Includes Scientific Information & Other Activities for Students. (Illus.). (gr. 3-12). 1992. PLB 24.95 (*0-7933-5803-5*); pap. 14.95 (*0-7933-5804-3*); computer disk 29.95 (*0-7933-5805-1*) Gallopade Pub Group.

—Nevada & Other State Greats (Biographies) (Illus.). 1990. PLB 24.95 (*1-55609-820-0*); pap. 14.95 (*1-55609-821-9*); computer disk 29.95 (*1-55609-822-7*) Gallopade Pub Group.

—Nevada Bandits, Bushwackers, Outlaws, Crooks, Devils, Ghosts, Desperadoes & Other Assorted & Sundry Characters! (Illus.). 1990. PLB 24.95 (*0-7933-0745-7*); pap. 14.95 (*0-7933-0744-9*); computer disk 29.95 (*0-7933-0746-5*) Gallopade Pub Group.

—Nevada Classic Christmas Trivia: Stories, Recipes, Activities, Legends, Lore & More! (Illus.). 1990. PLB 24.95 (*0-7933-0748-1*); pap. 14.95 (*0-7933-0747-3*); computer disk 29.95 (*0-7933-0749-X*) Gallopade Pub Group.

—Nevada Coastales. (Illus.). 1990. PLB 24.95 (*1-55609-814-6*); pap. 14.95 (*1-55609-815-4*); computer disk 29.95 (*1-55609-816-2*) Gallopade Pub Group.

—Nevada Coastales! 1992. lib. bdg. 24.95 (*0-7933-7293-3*) Gallopade Pub Group.

—Nevada "Crinkum-Crankum" A Funny Word Book about Our State. (Illus.). 1992. lib. bdg. 24.95 (*0-7933-4892-7*); pap. 14.95 (*0-7933-4893-5*); disk 29. 95 (*0-7933-4894-3*) Gallopade Pub Group.

—Nevada Dingbats! Bk. 1: A Fun Book of Games, Stories, Activities & More about Our State That's All in Code! for You to Decipher. (Illus.). (gr. 3-12). 1991. PLB 24.95 (*0-7933-3857-3*); pap. 14.95 (*0-7933-3858-1*); computer disk 29.95 (*0-7933-3859-X*) Gallopade Pub Group.

—Nevada Festival Fun for Kids! (Illus.). (gr. 3-12). 1991. lib. bdg. 24.95 (*0-7933-4010-1*); pap. 14.95 (*0-7933-4011-X*); disk 29.95 (*0-7933-4012-8*) Gallopade Pub Group.

—The Nevada Hot Air Balloon Mystery. (Illus.). (gr. 2-9). 1990. 24.95 (*0-7933-2570-6*); pap. 14.95 (*0-7933-2571-4*); computer disk 29.95 (*0-7933-2572-2*) Gallopade Pub Group.

—Nevada Jeopardy! Answers & Questions about Our State! (Illus.). (gr. 3-12). 1991. PLB 24.95 (*0-7933-4163-9*); pap. 14.95 (*0-7933-4164-7*); computer disk 29.95 (*0-7933-4165-5*) Gallopade Pub Group.

—Nevada "Jography" A Fun Run Thru Our State! (Illus.). 1990. PLB 24.95 (*1-55609-802-2*); pap. 14.95 (*1-55609-803-0*); computer disk 29.95 (*1-55609-804-9*) Gallopade Pub Group.

—Nevada Kid's Cookbook: Recipes, How-to, History, Lore & More! (Illus.). 1990. PLB 24.95 (*0-7933-0757-0*); pap. 14.95 (*0-7933-0756-2*); computer disk 29.95 (*0-7933-0758-9*) Gallopade Pub Group.

—The Nevada Mystery Van Takes Off! Book 1: Handicapped Nevada Kids Sneak Off on a Big Adventure. (Illus.). (gr. 3-12). 1992. 24.95 (*0-7933-5045-X*); pap. 14.95 (*0-7933-5046-8*); computer disk 29.95 (*0-7933-5047-6*) Gallopade Pub Group.

—Nevada Quiz Bowl Crash Course! (Illus.). 1990. PLB 24.95 (*1-55609-817-0*); pap. 14.95 (*1-55609-818-9*); computer disk 29.95 (*1-55609-819-7*) Gallopade Pub Group.

—Nevada Rollercoasters! (Illus.). (gr. 3-12). 1992. PLB 24.95 (*0-7933-5308-4*); pap. 14.95 (*0-7933-5309-2*); computer disk 29.95 (*0-7933-5310-6*) Gallopade Pub Group.

—Nevada School Trivia: An Amazing & Fascinating Look at Our State's Teachers, Schools & Students! (Illus.). 1990. PLB 24.95 (*0-7933-0754-6*); pap. 14.95 (*0-7933-0753-8*); computer disk 29.95 (*0-7933-0755-4*) Gallopade Pub Group.

—Nevada Silly Basketball Sportsmystereis, Vol. 2. (Illus.). 1990. PLB 24.95 (*0-7933-1767-3*); pap. 14.95 (*0-7933-1768-1*); computer disk 29.95 (*0-7933-1769-X*) Gallopade Pub Group.

—Nevada Silly Basketball Sportsmysteries, Vol. 1. (Illus.). 1990. PLB 24.95 (*0-7933-0751-1*); pap. 14.95 (*0-7933-0750-3*); computer disk 29.95 (*0-7933-0752-X*) Gallopade Pub Group.

—Nevada Silly Football Sportsmysteries, Vol. 1. (Illus.). 1990. PLB 24.95 (*1-55609-808-1*); pap. 14.95 (*1-55609-809-X*); computer disk 29.95 (*1-55609-810-3*) Gallopade Pub Group.

—Nevada Silly Football Sportsmysteries, Vol. 2. (Illus.). 1990. PLB 24.95 (*1-55609-811-1*); pap. 14.95 (*1-55609-812-X*); computer disk 29.95 (*1-55609-813-8*) Gallopade Pub Group.

—Nevada Silly Trivia! (Illus.). 1990. PLB 24.95 (*1-55609-799-9*); pap. 14.95 (*1-55609-800-6*); computer disk 29.95 (*1-55609-801-4*) Gallopade Pub Group.

—Nevada Timeline: A Chronology of Nevada History, Mystery, Trivia, Legend, Lore & More. (Illus.). (gr. 3-12). 1992. PLB 24.95 (*0-7933-5959-7*); pap. 14.95 (*0-7933-5960-0*); computer disk 29.95 (*0-7933-5961-9*) Gallopade Pub Group.

—Nevada's (Most Devastating!) Disasters & (Most Calamitous!) Castastrophies! (Illus.). 1990. PLB 24.95 (*0-7933-0742-2*); pap. 14.95 (*0-7933-0741-4*); computer disk 29.95 (*0-7933-0743-0*) Gallopade Pub Group.

—Nevada's Unsolved Mysteries (& Their "Solutions") Includes Scientific Information & Other Activities for Students. (Illus.). (gr. 3-12). 1992. PLB 24.95 (*0-7933-5806-X*); pap. 14.95 (*0-7933-5807-8*); computer disk 29.95 (*0-7933-5808-6*) Gallopade Pub Group.

—New Hampshire & Other State Greats (Biographies) (Illus.). 1990. PLB 24.95 (*0-685-45980-2*); pap. 14.95 (*1-55609-845-6*); computer disk 29.95 (*1-55609-846-4*) Gallopade Pub Group.

—New Hampshire Bandits, Bushwackers, Outlaws, Crooks, Devils, Ghosts, Desperadoes & Other Assorted & Sundry Characters! (Illus.). 1990. PLB 24. 95 (*0-7933-0769-4*); pap. 14.95 (*0-7933-0768-6*); computer disk 29.95 (*0-7933-0770-8*) Gallopade Pub Group.

—New Hampshire Classic Christmas Trivia: Stories, Recipes, Activities, Legends, Lore & More! (Illus.). 1990. PLB 24.95 (*0-7933-0772-4*); pap. 14.95 (*0-7933-0771-6*); computer disk 29.95 (*0-7933-0773-2*) Gallopade Pub Group.

—New Hampshire Coastales. (Illus.). 1990. PLB 24.95 (*1-55609-838-3*); pap. 14.95 (*1-55609-839-1*); computer disk 29.95 (*1-55609-840-5*) Gallopade Pub Group.

—New Hampshire Coastales! 1992. lib. bdg. 24.95 (*0-7933-7294-1*) Gallopade Pub Group.

—New Hampshire "Crinkum-Crankum" A Funny Word Book about Our State. (Illus.). 1992. lib. bdg. 24.95 (*0-7933-4895-1*); pap. 14.95 (*0-7933-4896-X*); disk 29. 95 (*0-7933-4897-8*) Gallopade Pub Group.

—New Hampshire Dingbats! Bk. 1: A Fun Book of Games, Stories, Activities & More about Our State That's All in Code! for You to Decipher. (Illus.). (gr. 3-12). 1991. PLB 24.95 (*0-7933-3860-3*); pap. 14.95 (*0-7933-3861-1*); computer disk 29.95 (*0-7933-3862-X*) Gallopade Pub Group.

—New Hampshire Festival Fun for Kids! (Illus.). (gr. 3-12). 1991. lib. bdg. 24.95 (*0-7933-4013-8*); pap. 14.95 (*0-7933-4014-4*); disk 29.95 (*0-7933-4015-2*) Gallopade Pub Group.

—The New Hampshire Hot Air Balloon Mystery. (Illus.). (gr. 2-9). 1990. 24.95 (*0-7933-2579-X*); pap. 14.95 (*0-7933-2580-3*); computer disk 29.95 (*0-7933-2581-1*) Gallopade Pub Group.

—New Hampshire Jeopardy! Answers & Questions about Our State! (Illus.). (gr. 3-12). 1991. PLB 24.95 (*0-7933-4166-3*); pap. 14.95 (*0-7933-4167-1*); computer disk 29.95 (*0-7933-4168-X*) Gallopade Pub Group.

—New Hampshire "Jography" A Fun Run Thru Our State! (Illus.). 1990. PLB 24.95 (*1-55609-826-X*); pap. 14.95 (*1-55609-827-8*); computer disk 29.95 (*1-55609-828-6*) Gallopade Pub Group.

—New Hampshire Kid's Cookbook: Recipes, How-to, History, Lore & More! (Illus.). 1990. PLB 24.95 (*0-7933-0781-3*); pap. 14.95 (*0-7933-0780-5*); computer disk 29.95 (*0-7933-0782-1*) Gallopade Pub Group.

—The New Hampshire Mystery Van Takes Off! Book 1: Handicapped New Hampshire Kids Sneak Off on a Big Adventure. (Illus.). (gr. 3-12). 1992. 24.95 (*0-7933-5048-4*); pap. 14.95 (*0-7933-5049-2*); computer disk 29.95 (*0-7933-5050-6*) Gallopade Pub Group.

—New Hampshire Quiz Bowl Crash Course! (Illus.). 1990. PLB 24.95 (*1-55609-841-3*); pap. 14.95 (*1-55609-842-1*); computer disk 29.95 (*1-55609-843-X*) Gallopade Pub Group.

—New Hampshire Rollercoasters! (Illus.). (gr. 3-12). 1992. PLB 24.95 (*0-7933-5311-4*); pap. 14.95 (*0-7933-5312-2*); computer disk 29.95 (*0-7933-5313-0*) Gallopade Pub Group.

—New Hampshire School Trivia: An Amazing & Fascinating Look at Our State's Teachers, Schools & Students! (Illus.). 1990. PLB 24.95 (*0-7933-0778-3*); pap. 14.95 (*0-7933-0777-5*); computer disk 29.95 (*0-7933-0779-1*) Gallopade Pub Group.

—New Hampshire Silly Basketball Sportsmysteries, Vol. I. (Illus.). 1990. PLB 24.95 (*0-7933-0775-9*); pap. 14. 95 (*0-7933-0774-0*); computer disk 29.95 (*0-7933-0776-7*) Gallopade Pub Group.

—New Hampshire Silly Basketball Sportsmysteries, Vol. II. (Illus.). 1990. PLB 24.95 (*0-7933-1776-2*); pap. 14. 95 (*0-7933-1777-0*); computer disk 29.95 (*0-7933-1778-9*) Gallopade Pub Group.

—New Hampshire Silly Football Sportsmysteries, Vol. 1. (Illus.). 1990. PLB 24.95 (*1-55609-832-4*); pap. 14.95 (*1-55609-833-2*); computer disk 29.95 (*1-55609-834-0*) Gallopade Pub Group.

—New Hampshire Silly Football Sportsmysteries, Vol. 2. (Illus.). 1990. PLB 24.95 (*1-55609-835-9*); pap. 14.95 (*1-55609-836-7*); computer disk 29.95 (*1-55609-837-5*) Gallopade Pub Group.

—New Hampshire Silly Trivia! (Illus.). 1990. PLB 24.95 (*1-55609-823-5*); pap. 14.95 (*1-55609-824-3*); computer disk 29.95 (*1-55609-825-1*) Gallopade Pub Group.

—New Hampshire Timeline: A Chronology of New Hampshire History, Mystery, Trivia, Legend, Lore & More. (Illus.). (gr. 3-12). 1992. PLB 24.95 (*0-7933-5962-7*); pap. 14.95 (*0-7933-5963-5*); computer disk 29.95 (*0-7933-5964-3*) Gallopade Pub Group.

—New Hampshire's (Most Devastating!) Disasters & (Most Calamitous!) Catastrophies! (Illus.). 1990. PLB 24.95 (*0-7933-0766-X*); pap. 14.95 (*0-7933-0765-1*); computer disk 29.95 (*0-7933-0767-8*) Gallopade Pub Group.

—New Hampshire's Unsolved Mysteries (& Their "Solutions") Includes Scientific Information & Other Activities for Students. (Illus.). (gr. 3-12). 1992. PLB 24.95 (*0-7933-5809-4*); pap. 14.95 (*0-7933-5810-8*); computer disk 29.95 (*0-7933-5811-6*) Gallopade Pub Group.

—New Jersey & Other State Greats (Biographies) (Illus.). 1990. PLB 24.95 (*1-55609-868-5*); pap. 14.95 (*1-55609-869-3*); computer disk 29.95 (*1-55609-870-7*) Gallopade Pub Group.

—New Jersey Bandits, Bushwackers, Outlaws, Crooks, Devils, Ghosts, Desperadoes & Other Assorted & Sundry Characters! (Illus.). 1990. PLB 24.95 (*0-7933-1788-6*); pap. 14.95 (*0-7933-1789-4*); computer disk 29.95 (*0-7933-1790-8*) Gallopade Pub Group.

—New Jersey Classic Christmas Trivia: Stories, Recipes, Activities, Legends, Lore & More! (Illus.). 1990. PLB 24.95 (*0-7933-1791-6*); pap. 14.95 (*0-7933-1792-4*); computer disk 29.95 (*0-7933-1793-2*) Gallopade Pub Group.

—New Jersey Coastales. (Illus.). 1990. PLB 24.95 (*1-55609-862-6*); pap. 14.95 (*1-55609-863-4*); computer disk 29.95 (*1-55609-864-2*) Gallopade Pub Group.

—New Jersey Coastales! 1992. lib. bdg. 24.95 (*0-7933-7295-X*) Gallopade Pub Group.

—New Jersey "Crinkum-Crankum" A Funny Word Book about Our State. (Illus.). 1992. lib. bdg. 24.95 (*0-7933-4898-6*); pap. 14.95 (*0-7933-4899-4*); disk 29. 95 (*0-7933-4900-1*) Gallopade Pub Group.

—New Jersey Dingbats! Bk. 1: A Fun Book of Games, Stories, Activities & More about Our State That's All in Code! for You to Decipher. (Illus.). (gr. 3-12). 1991. PLB 24.95 (*0-7933-3863-8*); pap. 14.95 (*0-7933-3864-6*); computer disk 29.95 (*0-7933-3865-4*) Gallopade Pub Group.

—New Jersey Festival Fun for Kids! (Illus.). (gr. 3-12). 1991. lib. bdg. 24.95 (*0-7933-4016-0*); pap. 14.95 (*0-7933-4017-9*); disk 29.95 (*0-7933-4018-7*) Gallopade Pub Group.

—The New Jersey Hot Air Balloon Mystery. (Illus.). (gr. 2-9). 1990. 24.95 (*0-7933-2588-9*); pap. 14.95 (*0-7933-2589-7*); computer disk 29.95 (*0-7933-2590-0*) Gallopade Pub Group.

—New Jersey Jeopardy! Answers & Questions about Our State! (Illus.). (gr. 3-12). 1991. PLB 24.95 (*0-7933-4169-8*); pap. 14.95 (*0-7933-4170-1*); computer disk 29.95 (*0-7933-4171-X*) Gallopade Pub Group.

—New Jersey "Jography" A Fun Run Thru Our State!
(Illus.). 1990. PLB 24.95 (*1-55609-850-2*); pap. 14.95
(*1-55609-851-0*); computer disk 29.95 (*1-55609-852-9*)
Gallopade Pub Group.
—New Jersey Kid's Cookbook: Recipes, How-to, History,
Lore & More. (Illus.). 1990. PLB 24.95
(*0-7933-1803-3*); pap. 14.95 (*0-7933-1804-1*);
computer disk 29.95 (*0-7933-1805-X*) Gallopade Pub
Group.
—The New Jersey Mystery Van Takes Off! Book 1:
Handicapped New Jersey Kids Sneak Off on a Big
Adventure. (Illus.). 1992. 24.95
(*0-7933-5051-4*); pap. 14.95 (*0-7933-5052-2*)
computer disk 29.95 (*0-7933-5053-0*) Gallopade Pub
Group.
—New Jersey Quiz Bowl Crash Course! (Illus.). 1990.
PLB 24.95 (*1-55609-865-0*); pap. 14.95
(*1-55609-866-9*); computer disk 29.95 (*1-55609-867-7*)
Gallopade Pub Group.
—New Jersey Rollercoasters! (Illus.). (gr. 3-12). 1992.
PLB 24.95 (*0-7933-5314-9*); pap. 14.95
(*0-7933-5315-7*); computer disk 29.95 (*0-7933-5316-5*)
Gallopade Pub Group.
—New Jersey School Trivia: An Amazing & Fascinating
Look at Our State's Teachers, Schools & Students!
(Illus.). 1990. PLB 24.95 (*0-7933-1800-9*); pap. 14.95
(*0-7933-1801-7*); computer disk 29.95 (*0-7933-1802-5*)
Gallopade Pub Group.
—New Jersey Silly Basketball Sportsmysteries, Vol. 1.
(Illus.). 1990. PLB 24.95 (*0-7933-1794-0*); pap. 14.95
(*0-7933-1795-9*); computer disk 29.95 (*0-7933-1796-7*)
Gallopade Pub Group.
—New Jersey Silly Basketball Sportsmysteries, Vol. 2.
(Illus.). 1990. PLB 24.95 (*0-7933-1797-5*); pap. 14.95
(*0-7933-1798-3*); computer disk 29.95 (*0-7933-1799-1*)
Gallopade Pub Group.
—New Jersey Silly Football Sportsmysteries, Vol. 1.
(Illus.). 1990. PLB 24.95 (*1-55609-856-1*); pap. 14.95
(*1-55609-857-X*); computer disk 29.95
(*1-55609-858-8*) Gallopade Pub Group.
—New Jersey Silly Football Sportsmysteries, Vol. 2.
(Illus.). 1990. PLB 24.95 (*1-55609-859-6*); pap. 14.95
(*1-55609-860-X*); computer disk 29.95
(*1-55609-861-8*) Gallopade Pub Group.
—New Jersey Silly Trivia! (Illus.). 1990. PLB 24.95
(*1-55609-847-2*); pap. 14.95 (*1-55609-848-0*);
computer disk 29.95 (*1-55609-849-9*) Gallopade Pub
Group.
—New Jersey Timeline: A Chronology of New Jersey
History, Mystery, Trivia, Legend, Lore & More.
(Illus.). (gr. 3-12). 1992. PLB 24.95 (*0-7933-5965-1*);
pap. 14.95 (*0-7933-5966-X*); computer disk 29.95
(*0-7933-5967-8*) Gallopade Pub Group.
—New Jersey's (Most Devastating!) Disasters & (Most
Calamitous!) Catastrophies! (Illus.). 1990. PLB 24.95
(*0-685-45981-0*); pap. 14.95 (*0-7933-1786-X*);
computer disk 29.95 (*0-7933-1787-8*) Gallopade Pub
Group.
—New Jersey's Unsolved Mysteries (& Their "Solutions")
Includes Scientific Information & Other Activities for
Students. (Illus.). (gr. 3-12). 1992. PLB 24.95
(*0-7933-5812-4*); pap. 14.95 (*0-7933-5813-2*);
computer disk 29.95 (*0-7933-5814-0*) Gallopade Pub
Group.
—New Mexico & Other State Greats (Biographies)
(Illus.). 1990. PLB 24.95 (*1-55609-892-9*); pap. 14.95
(*1-55609-893-6*); computer disk 29.95 (*1-55609-894-4*)
Gallopade Pub Group.
—New Mexico Bandits, Bushwackers, Outlaws, Crooks,
Devils, Ghosts, Desperadoes & Other Assorted &
Sundry Characters! (Illus.). 1990. PLB 24.95
(*0-7933-0793-7*); pap. 14.95 (*0-7933-0792-9*);
computer disk 29.95 (*0-7933-0794-5*) Gallopade Pub
Group.
—New Mexico Classic Christmas Trivia: Stories, Recipes,
Activities, Legends, Lore & More! (Illus.). 1990. PLB
24.95 (*0-7933-0796-1*); pap. 14.95 (*0-7933-0795-3*);
computer disk 29.95 (*0-7933-0797-X*) Gallopade Pub
Group.
—New Mexico Coastales. (Illus.). 1990. PLB 24.95
(*1-55609-886-3*); pap. 14.95 (*1-55609-887-1*);
computer disk 29.95 (*1-55609-888-X*) Gallopade Pub
Group.
—New Mexico Coastales! 1992. lib. bdg. 24.95
(*0-7933-7296-8*) Gallopade Pub Group.
—New Mexico "Crinkum-Crankum" A Funny Word
Book about Our State. (Illus.). 1992. lib. bdg. 24.95
(*0-7933-4901-X*); pap. 14.95 (*0-7933-4902-8*); disk 29.
95 (*0-7933-4903-6*) Gallopade Pub Group.
—New Mexico Dingbats! Bk. 1: A Fun Book of Games,
Stories, Activities & More about Our State That's All
in Code! for You to Decipher. (Illus.). (gr. 3-12).
1991. PLB 24.95 (*0-7933-3866-2*); pap. 14.95
(*0-7933-3867-0*); computer disk 29.95 (*0-7933-3868-9*)
Gallopade Pub Group.
—New Mexico Festival Fun for Kids! (Illus.). (gr. 3-12).
1991. lib. bdg. 24.95 (*0-7933-4019-5*); pap. 14.95
(*0-7933-4020-9*); disk 29.95 (*0-7933-4021-7*)
Gallopade Pub Group.
—The New Mexico Hot Air Balloon Mystery. (Illus.).
(gr. 2-9). 1990. 24.95 (*0-7933-2597-8*); pap. 14.95
(*0-7933-2598-6*); computer disk 29.95 (*0-7933-2599-4*)
Gallopade Pub Group.
—New Mexico Jeopardy! Answers & Questions about
Our State! (Illus.). (gr. 3-12). 1991. PLB 24.95
(*0-7933-4172-8*); pap. 14.95 (*0-7933-4173-6*);
computer disk 29.95 (*0-7933-4174-4*) Gallopade Pub
Group.

—New Mexico "Jography" A Fun Run Thru Our State!
(Illus.). 1990. PLB 24.95 (*1-55609-874-X*); pap. 14.95
(*1-55609-875-8*); computer disk 29.95 (*1-55609-876-6*)
Gallopade Pub Group.
—New Mexico Kid's Cookbook: Recipes, How-to,
History, Lore & More! (Illus.). 1990. PLB 24.95
(*0-7933-0805-4*); pap. 14.95 (*0-7933-0804-6*);
computer disk 29.95 (*0-7933-0806-2*) Gallopade Pub
Group.
—The New Mexico Mystery Van Takes Off! Book 1:
Handicapped New Mexico Kids Sneak Off on a Big
Adventure. (Illus.). (gr. 3-12). 1992. 24.95
(*0-7933-5054-9*); pap. 14.95 (*0-7933-5055-7*);
computer disk 29.95 (*0-7933-5056-5*) Gallopade Pub
Group.
—New Mexico Quiz Bowl Crash Course! (Illus.). 1990.
PLB 24.95 (*1-55609-889-8*); pap. 14.95
(*1-55609-890-1*); computer disk 29.95
(*1-55609-891-X*) Gallopade Pub Group.
—New Mexico Rollercoasters! (Illus.). (gr. 3-12). 1992.
PLB 24.95 (*0-7933-5317-3*); pap. 14.95
(*0-7933-5318-1*); computer disk 29.95
(*0-7933-5319-X*) Gallopade Pub Group.
—New Mexico School Trivia: An Amazing & Fascinating
Look at Our State's Teachers, Schools & Students!
(Illus.). 1990. PLB 24.95 (*0-7933-0802-X*); pap. 14.95
(*0-7933-0801-1*); computer disk 29.95 (*0-7933-0803-8*)
Gallopade Pub Group.
—New Mexico Silly Basketball Sportsmystereis, Vol. 1.
(Illus.). 1990. PLB 24.95 (*0-7933-0799-6*); pap. 14.95
(*0-7933-0798-8*); computer disk 29.95 (*0-7933-0800-X*)
Gallopade Pub Group.
—New Mexico Silly Basketball Sportsmysteries, Vol. 2.
(Illus.). 1990. PLB 24.95 (*0-7933-1818-1*); pap. 14.95
(*0-7933-1819-X*); computer disk 29.95
(*0-7933-1820-3*) Gallopade Pub Group.
—New Mexico Silly Football Sportsmysteries. (Illus.).
1990. PLB 24.95 (*1-55609-880-4*); pap. 14.95
(*1-55609-881-2*); computer disk 29.95 (*1-55609-882-0*)
Gallopade Pub Group.
—New Mexico Silly Football Sportsmysteries, Vol. 2.
1990. pap. 14.95 (*1-55609-884-7*); computer disk 29.
95 (*1-55609-885-5*) Gallopade Pub Group.
—New Mexico Silly Trivia! (Illus.). 1990. PLB 24.95
(*1-55609-871-5*); pap. 14.95 (*1-55609-872-3*);
computer disk 29.95 (*1-55609-873-1*) Gallopade Pub
Group.
—New Mexico Timeline: A Chronology of New Mexico
History, Mystery, Trivia, Legend, Lore & More.
(Illus.). (gr. 3-12). 1992. PLB 24.95 (*0-7933-5968-6*);
pap. 14.95 (*0-7933-5969-4*); computer disk 29.95
(*0-7933-5970-8*) Gallopade Pub Group.
—New Mexico's (Most Devastating!) Disasters & (Most
Calamitous!) Catastrophies! (Illus.). 1990. PLB 24.95
(*0-7933-0790-2*); pap. 14.95 (*0-7933-0789-9*);
computer disk 29.95 (*0-7933-0791-0*) Gallopade Pub
Group.
—New Mexico's Unsolved Mysteries (& Their
"Solutions") Includes Scientific Information & Other
Activities for Students. (Illus.). (gr. 3-12). 1992. PLB
24.95 (*0-7933-5815-9*); pap. 14.95 (*0-7933-5816-7*);
computer disk 29.95 (*0-7933-5817-5*) Gallopade Pub
Group.
—New York & Other State Greats (Biographies) (Illus.).
1990. PLB 24.95 (*1-55609-918-5*); pap. 14.95
(*1-55609-919-3*); computer disk 29.95 (*1-55609-920-7*)
Gallopade Pub Group.
—New York Bandits, Bushwackers, Outlaws, Crooks,
Devils, Ghosts, Desperadoes & Other Assorted &
Sundry Characters! (Illus.). 1990. PLB 24.95
(*0-7933-0817-8*); pap. 14.95 (*0-7933-0816-X*);
computer disk 29.95 (*0-7933-0818-6*) Gallopade Pub
Group.
—New York Classic Christmas Trivia: Stories, Recipes,
Activities, Legends, Lore & More! (Illus.). 1990. PLB
24.95 (*0-7933-0820-8*); pap. 14.95 (*0-685-45982-9*);
computer disk 29.95 (*0-7933-0821-6*) Gallopade Pub
Group.
—New York Coastales. (Illus.). 1990. PLB 24.95
(*1-55609-912-6*); pap. 14.95 (*1-55609-913-4*);
computer disk 29.95 (*1-55609-914-2*) Gallopade Pub
Group.
—New York Coastales! 1992. lib. bdg. 24.95
(*0-7933-7297-6*) Gallopade Pub Group.
—New York "Crinkum-Crankum" A Funny Word Book
about Our State. (Illus.). 1992. lib. bdg. 24.95
(*0-7933-4904-4*); pap. 14.95 (*0-7933-4905-2*); disk 29.
95 (*0-7933-4906-0*) Gallopade Pub Group.
—New York Dingbats! Bk. 1: A Fun Book of Games,
Stories, Activities & More about Our State That's All
in Code! for You to Decipher. (Illus.). (gr. 3-12).
1991. PLB 24.95 (*0-7933-3869-7*); pap. 14.95
(*0-7933-3870-0*); computer disk 29.95 (*0-7933-3871-9*)
Gallopade Pub Group.
—New York Festival Fun for Kids! (Illus.). (gr. 3-12).
1991. lib. bdg. 24.95 (*0-7933-4022-5*); pap. 14.95
(*0-7933-4023-3*); disk 29.95 (*0-7933-4024-1*)
Gallopade Pub Group.
—The New York Hot Air Balloon Mystery. (Illus.). (gr.
2-9). 1990. 24.95 (*0-7933-2606-0*); pap. 14.95
(*0-7933-2607-9*); computer disk 29.95 (*0-7933-2608-7*)
Gallopade Pub Group.
—New York Jeopardy! Answers & Questions about Our
State! (Illus.). (gr. 3-12). 1991. PLB 24.95
(*0-7933-4175-2*); pap. 14.95 (*0-7933-4176-0*);
computer disk 29.95 (*0-7933-4177-9*) Gallopade Pub
Group.

—New York "Jography" A Fun Run Thru Our State!
(Illus.). 1990. PLB 24.95 (*1-55609-897-9*); pap. 14.95
(*1-55609-898-7*); computer disk 29.95 (*1-55609-899-5*)
Gallopade Pub Group.
—New York Kid's Cookbook: Recipes, How-to, History,
Lore & More! (Illus.). 1990. PLB 24.95
(*0-7933-0829-1*); pap. 14.95 (*0-7933-0828-3*);
computer disk 29.95 (*0-7933-0830-5*) Gallopade Pub
Group.
—The New York Mystery Van Takes Off! Book 1:
Handicapped New York Kids Sneak Off on a Big
Adventure. (Illus.). (gr. 3-12). 1992. 24.95
(*0-7933-5057-3*); pap. 14.95 (*0-7933-5058-1*);
computer disk 29.95 (*0-7933-5059-X*) Gallopade Pub
Group.
—New York Quiz Bowl Crash Course! (Illus.). 1990.
PLB 24.95 (*1-55609-915-0*); pap. 14.95
(*1-55609-916-9*); computer disk 29.95 (*1-55609-917-7*)
Gallopade Pub Group.
—New York Rollercoasters! (Illus.). (gr. 3-12). 1992.
PLB 24.95 (*0-7933-5320-3*); pap. 14.95
(*0-7933-5321-1*); computer disk 29.95
(*0-7933-5322-X*) Gallopade Pub Group.
—New York School Trivia: An Amazing & Fascinating
Look at Our State's Teachers, Schools & Students!
(Illus.). 1990. PLB 24.95 (*0-7933-0826-7*); pap. 14.95
(*0-7933-0825-9*); computer disk 29.95 (*0-7933-0827-5*)
Gallopade Pub Group.
—New York Silly Basketball Sportsmysteries, Vol. 1.
(Illus.). 1990. PLB 24.95 (*0-7933-0823-2*); pap. 14.95
(*0-7933-0822-4*); computer disk 29.95 (*0-7933-0824-0*)
Gallopade Pub Group.
—New York Silly Basketball Sportsmysteries, Vol. 2.
(Illus.). 1990. PLB 24.95 (*0-685-45983-7*); pap. 14.95
(*0-7933-1825-4*); computer disk 29.95 (*0-7933-1826-2*)
Gallopade Pub Group.
—New York Silly Football Sportsmysteries, Vol. 1.
(Illus.). 1990. PLB 24.95 (*1-55609-906-1*); pap. 14.95
(*1-55609-907-X*); computer disk 29.95
(*1-55609-908-8*) Gallopade Pub Group.
—New York Silly Football Sportsmysteries, Vol. 2.
(Illus.). 1990. PLB 24.95 (*1-55609-909-6*); pap. 14.95
(*1-55609-910-X*); computer disk 29.95
(*1-55609-911-8*) Gallopade Pub Group.
—New York Silly Trivia! (Illus.). 1990. PLB 24.95
(*1-55609-895-2*); pap. 14.95 (*1-55609-103-6*);
computer disk 29.95 (*1-55609-896-0*) Gallopade Pub
Group.
—New York Timeline: A Chronology of New York
History, Mystery, Trivia, Legend, Lore & More.
(Illus.). (gr. 3-12). 1992. PLB 24.95 (*0-7933-5971-6*);
pap. 14.95 (*0-7933-5972-4*); computer disk 29.95
(*0-7933-5973-2*) Gallopade Pub Group.
—New York's (Most Devasting!) Disasters & (Most
Calamitous!) Catastrophies! (Illus.). 1990. PLB 24.95
(*0-7933-0814-3*); pap. 14.95 (*0-7933-0813-5*);
computer disk 29.95 (*0-7933-0815-1*) Gallopade Pub
Group.
—New York's Unsolved Mysteries (& Their "Solutions")
Includes Scientific Information & Other Activities for
Students. (Illus.). (gr. 3-12). 1992. PLB 24.95
(*0-7933-5818-3*); pap. 14.95 (*0-7933-5819-1*);
computer disk 29.95 (*0-7933-5820-5*) Gallopade Pub
Group.
—North Carolina & Other State Greats (Biographies)
(Illus.). 1990. PLB 24.95 (*1-55609-937-1*); pap. 14.95
(*1-55609-938-X*); computer disk 29.95
(*1-55609-939-8*) Gallopade Pub Group.
—North Carolina Bandits, Bushwackers, Outlaws,
Crooks, Devils, Ghosts, Desperadoes & Other
Assorted & Sundry Characters! (Illus.). 1990. PLB 24.
95 (*0-7933-0841-0*); pap. 14.95 (*0-7933-0840-2*);
computer disk 29.95 (*0-7933-0842-9*) Gallopade Pub
Group.
—North Carolina Classic Christmas Trivia: Stories,
Recipes, Activities, Legends, Lore & More. (Illus.).
1990. PLB 24.95 (*0-7933-0844-5*); pap. 14.95
(*0-7933-0843-7*); computer disk 29.95 (*0-7933-0845-3*)
Gallopade Pub Group.
—North Carolina Coastales! 1992. lib. bdg. 24.95
(*0-7933-7298-4*) Gallopade Pub Group.
—North Carolina "Crinkum-Crankum" A Funny Word
Book about Our State. (Illus.). (gr. 3-12). 1992. 24.95
(*0-7933-4907-9*); pap. 14.95 (*0-7933-4908-7*);
computer disk 29.95 (*0-7933-4909-5*) Gallopade Pub
Group.
—North Carolina Dingbats! Bk. 1: A Fun Book of
Games, Stories, Activities & More about Our State
That's All in Code! for You to Decipher. (Illus.). (gr.
3-12). 1991. PLB 24.95 (*0-7933-3872-7*); pap. 14.95
(*0-7933-3873-5*); computer disk 29.95 (*0-7933-3874-3*)
Gallopade Pub Group.
—North Carolina Festival Fun for Kids! (Illus.). (gr. 3-
12). 1991. lib. bdg. 24.95 (*0-7933-4025-X*); pap. 14.95
(*0-7933-4026-8*); disk 29.95 (*0-7933-4027-6*)
Gallopade Pub Group.
—The North Carolina Hot Air Balloon Mystery. (Illus.).
(gr. 2-9). 1990. 24.95 (*0-7933-2615-X*); pap. 14.95
(*0-7933-2616-8*); computer disk 29.95 (*0-7933-2617-6*)
Gallopade Pub Group.
—North Carolina Jeopardy! Answers & Questions about
Our State! (Illus.). (gr. 3-12). 1991. PLB 24.95
(*0-7933-4178-7*); pap. 14.95 (*0-7933-4179-5*);
computer disk 29.95 (*0-7933-4180-9*) Gallopade Pub
Group.
—North Carolina Jography: A Fun Run Through the
Tarheel State. (Illus.). 50p. (Orig.). (gr. 4-8). 1986.
pap. 14.95 (*0-935326-81-2*) Gallopade Pub Group.

—North Carolina Kid's Cookbook: Recipes, How-to, History, Lore & More. (Illus.). 1990. PLB 24.95 (0-7933-0853-4); pap. 14.95 (0-7933-0852-6); computer disk 29.95 (0-7933-0854-2) Gallopade Pub Group.

—The North Carolina Mystery Van Takes Off! Book 1: Handicapped North Carolina Kids Sneak Off on a Big Adventure. (Illus.). (gr. 3-12). 1992. 24.95 (0-7933-5060-3); pap. 14.95 (0-7933-5061-1); computer disk 29.95 (0-7933-5062-X) Gallopade Pub Group.

—North Carolina Quiz Bowl Crash Course! (Illus.). 1990. PLB 24.95 (1-55609-934-7); pap. 14.95 (1-55609-935-5); computer disk 29.95 (1-55609-936-3) Gallopade Pub Group.

—North Carolina Rollercoasters! (Illus.). (gr. 3-12). 1992. PLB 24.95 (0-7933-5323-8); pap. 14.95 (0-7933-5324-6); computer disk 29.95 (0-7933-5325-4) Gallopade Pub Group.

—North Carolina School Trivia: An Amazing & Fascinating Look at Our State's Teachers, Schools & Students! (Illus.). 1990. PLB 24.95 (0-7933-0850-X); pap. 14.95 (0-7933-0849-6); computer disk 29.95 (0-7933-0851-8) Gallopade Pub Group.

—North Carolina Silly Basketball Sportsmysteries, Vol. 1. (Illus.). 1990. PLB 24.95 (0-7933-0847-X); pap. 14.95 (0-7933-0846-1); computer disk 29.95 (0-7933-0848-8) Gallopade Pub Group.

—North Carolina Silly Basketball Sportsmysteries, Vol. 2. (Illus.). 1990. PLB 24.95 (0-7933-1836-X); pap. 14.95 (0-7933-1837-8); computer disk 29.95 (0-7933-1838-6) Gallopade Pub Group.

—North Carolina Silly Football Sportmysteries, Vol. 2. (Illus.). 1990. PLB 24.95 (1-55609-930-4); pap. 14.95 (1-55609-931-2); computer disk 29.95 (1-55609-932-0) Gallopade Pub Group.

—North Carolina Silly Football Sportmysteries, Vol. 1. (Illus.). 1990. PLB 24.95 (1-55609-927-4); pap. 14.95 (1-55609-928-2); computer disk 29.95 (1-55609-929-0) Gallopade Pub Group.

—North Carolina Silly Trivia! (Illus.). 1990. PLB 24.95 (1-55609-921-5); pap. 14.95 (0-685-45984-X); computer disk 29.95 (1-55609-922-3) Gallopade Pub Group.

—North Carolina Timeline: A Chronology of North Carolina History, Mystery, Trivia, Legend, Lore & More. (Illus.). (gr. 3-12). 1992. PLB 24.95 (0-7933-5974-0); pap. 14.95 (0-7933-5975-9); computer disk 29.95 (0-7933-5976-7) Gallopade Pub Group.

—North Carolina's (Most Devastating!) Disasters & (Most Calamitous!) Catastrophies! (Illus.). 1990. PLB 24.95 (0-7933-0838-0); pap. 14.95 (0-7933-0837-2); computer disk 29.95 (0-7933-0839-9) Gallopade Pub Group.

—North Carolina's Scariest Swamp: The Great Dismal. (Illus.). (gr. 3 up). 1990. lib. bdg. 24.95 (0-7933-1270-1); pap. 14.95 (0-7933-1271-X); computer disk 29.95 (0-7933-1272-8) Gallopade Pub Group.

—North Carolina's Unsolved Mysteries (& Their "Solutions") Includes Scientific Information & Other Activities for Students. (Illus.). (gr. 3-12). 1992. PLB 24.95 (0-7933-5821-3); pap. 14.95 (0-7933-5822-1); computer disk 29.95 (0-7933-5823-X) Gallopade Pub Group.

—The North Dakota Air Balloon Mystery. (Illus.). (gr. 2-9). 1990. 24.95 (0-7933-2624-9); pap. 14.95 (0-7933-2625-7); computer disk 29.95 (0-7933-2626-5) Gallopade Pub Group.

—North Dakota & Other State Greats (Biographies) (Illus.). 1990. PLB 24.95 (1-55609-976-2); pap. 14.95 (1-55609-977-0); computer disk 29.95 (0-685-45973-X) Gallopade Pub Group.

—North Dakota Bandits, Bushwackers, Outlaws, Crooks, Devils, Ghosts, Desperadoes & Other Assorted & Sundry Characters! (Illus.). 1990. PLB 24.95 (0-7933-0865-8); pap. 14.95 (0-7933-0864-X); computer disk 29.95 (0-7933-0866-6) Gallopade Pub Group.

—North Dakota Classic Christmas Trivia: Stories, Recipes, Activities, Legends, Lore & More! (Illus.). 1990. PLB 24.95 (0-7933-0868-2); pap. 14.95 (0-7933-0867-4); computer disk 29.95 (0-7933-0869-0) Gallopade Pub Group.

—North Dakota Coastales. (Illus.). 1990. PLB 24.95 (0-685-45972-1); pap. 14.95 (1-55609-971-0); computer disk 29.95 (1-55609-972-X) Gallopade Pub Group.

—North Dakota Coastales! 1992. lib. bdg. 24.95 (0-7933-7299-2) Gallopade Pub Group.

—North Dakota "Crinkum-Crankum" A Funny Word Book about Our State. (Illus.). (gr. 3-12). 1992. 24.95 (0-7933-4910-9); pap. 14.95 (0-7933-4911-7); computer disk 29.95 (0-7933-4912-5) Gallopade Pub Group.

—North Dakota Dingbats! Bk. 1: A Fun Book of Games, Stories, Activities & More about Our State That's All in Code! for You to Decipher. (Illus.). (gr. 3-12). 1991. PLB 24.95 (0-7933-3875-1); pap. 14.95 (0-7933-3876-X); computer disk 29.95 (0-7933-3877-8) Gallopade Pub Group.

—North Dakota Festival Fun for Kids! (Illus.). (gr. 3-12). 1991. lib. bdg. 24.95 (0-7933-4028-4); pap. 14.95 (0-7933-4029-2); disk 29.95 (0-7933-4030-6) Gallopade Pub Group.

—North Dakota Jeopardy! Answers & Questions about Our State! (Illus.). (gr. 3-12). 1991. PLB 24.95 (0-7933-4181-7); pap. 14.95 (0-7933-4182-5); computer disk 29.95 (0-7933-4183-3) Gallopade Pub Group.

—North Dakota "Jography" A Fun Run Thru Our State! (Illus.). 1990. PLB 24.95 (1-55609-943-6); pap. 14.95 (1-55609-944-4); computer disk 29.95 (1-55609-945-2) Gallopade Pub Group.

—North Dakota Kid's Cookbook: Recipes, How-to, History, Lore & More! (Illus.). 1990. PLB 24.95 (0-7933-0877-1); pap. 14.95 (0-7933-0876-3); computer disk 29.95 (0-7933-0878-X) Gallopade Pub Group.

—The North Dakota Mystery Van Takes Off! Book 1: Handicapped North Dakota Kids Sneak Off on a Big Adventure. (Illus.). (gr. 3-12). 1992. 24.95 (0-7933-5063-8); pap. 14.95 (0-7933-5064-6); computer disk 29.95 (0-7933-5065-4) Gallopade Pub Group.

—North Dakota Quiz Bowl Crash Course! (Illus.). 1990. PLB 24.95 (1-55609-973-8); pap. 14.95 (1-55609-974-6); computer disk 29.95 (1-55609-975-4) Gallopade Pub Group.

—North Dakota Rollercoasters! (Illus.). (gr. 3-12). 1992. PLB 24.95 (0-7933-5326-2); pap. 14.95 (0-7933-5327-0); computer disk 29.95 (0-7933-5328-9) Gallopade Pub Group.

—North Dakota School Trivia: An Amazing & Fascinating Look at Our State's Teachers, Schools & Students! (Illus.). 1990. PLB 24.95 (0-7933-0874-7); pap. 14.95 (0-7933-0873-9); computer disk 29.95 (0-7933-0875-5) Gallopade Pub Group.

—North Dakota Silly Basketball Sportsmysteries, Vol. 1. (Illus.). 1990. PLB 24.95 (0-7933-0871-2); pap. 14.95 (0-7933-0870-4); computer disk 29.95 (0-7933-0872-0) Gallopade Pub Group.

—North Dakota Silly Basketball Sportsmysteries, Vol. 2. (Illus.). 1990. PLB 24.95 (0-685-45974-8); pap. 14.95 (0-7933-1846-7); computer disk 29.95 (0-7933-1847-5) Gallopade Pub Group.

—North Dakota Silly Football Sportsmysteries, Vol. 1. (Illus.). 1990. PLB 24.95 (1-55609-948-7); pap. 14.95 (1-55609-949-5); computer disk 29.95 (0-685-45971-3) Gallopade Pub Group.

—North Dakota Silly Football Sportsmysteries, Vol. 2. (Illus.). 1990. PLB 24.95 (1-55609-967-3); pap. 14.95 (1-55609-968-1); computer disk 29.95 (1-55609-969-X) Gallopade Pub Group.

—North Dakota Silly Trivia! (Illus.). 1990. PLB 24.95 (1-55609-940-1); pap. 14.95 (1-55609-941-X); computer disk 29.95 (1-55609-942-8) Gallopade Pub Group.

—North Dakota Timeline: A Chronology of North Dakota History, Mystery, Trivia, Legend, Lore & More. (Illus.). (gr. 3-12). 1992. PLB 24.95 (0-7933-5977-5); pap. 14.95 (0-7933-5978-3); computer disk 29.95 (0-7933-5979-1) Gallopade Pub Group.

—North Dakota's (Most Devastating!) Disasters & (Most Calamitous!) Catastrophies! (Illus.). 1990. PLB 24.95 (0-7933-0862-3); pap. 14.95 (0-7933-0861-5); computer disk 29.95 (0-7933-0863-1) Gallopade Pub Group.

—North Dakota's Unsolved Mysteries (& Their "Solutions") Includes Scientific Information & Other Activities for Students. (Illus.). (gr. 3-12). 1992. PLB 24.95 (0-7933-5824-8); pap. 14.95 (0-7933-5825-6); computer disk 29.95 (0-7933-5826-4) Gallopade Pub Group.

—Ohio & Other State Greats (Biographies) (Illus.). 1990. PLB 24.95 (1-55609-998-3); pap. 14.95 (1-55609-999-1); computer disk 29.95 (1-55609-854-5) Gallopade Pub Group.

—Ohio Bandits, Bushwackers, Outlaws, Crooks, Devils, Ghosts, Desperadoes & Other Assorted & Sundry Characters! (Illus.). 1990. PLB 24.95 (0-7933-0889-5); pap. 14.95 (0-7933-0888-7); computer disk 29.95 (0-7933-0890-9) Gallopade Pub Group.

—Ohio Classic Christmas Trivia: Stories, Recipes, Activities, Legends, Lore & More! (Illus.). 1990. PLB 24.95 (0-7933-0892-5); pap. 14.95 (0-7933-0891-7); computer disk 29.95 (0-7933-0893-3) Gallopade Pub Group.

—Ohio Coastales. (Illus.). 1990. PLB 24.95 (1-55609-992-4); pap. 14.95 (1-55609-993-2); computer disk 29.95 (1-55609-994-0) Gallopade Pub Group.

—Ohio Coastales! 1992. lib. bdg. 24.95 (0-7933-7300-X) Gallopade Pub Group.

—Ohio "Crinkum-Crankum" A Funny Word Book about Our State. (Illus.). (gr. 3-12). 1992. 24.95 (0-7933-4913-3); pap. 14.95 (0-7933-4914-1); computer disk 29.95 (0-7933-4915-X) Gallopade Pub Group.

—Ohio Dingbats! Bk. 1: A Fun Book of Games, Stories, Activities & More about Our State That's All in Code! for You to Decipher. (Illus.). (gr. 3-12). 1991. PLB 24.95 (0-7933-3878-6); pap. 14.95 (0-7933-3879-4); computer disk 29.95 (0-7933-3880-8) Gallopade Pub Group.

—Ohio Festival Fun for Kids! (Illus.). (gr. 3-12). 1991. lib. bdg. 24.95 (0-7933-4031-4); pap. 14.95 (0-7933-4032-2); disk 29.95 (0-7933-4033-0) Gallopade Pub Group.

—The Ohio Hot Air Balloon Mystery. (Illus.). (gr. 2-9). 1990. 24.95 (0-7933-2633-8); pap. 14.95 (0-7933-2634-6); computer disk 29.95 (0-7933-2635-4) Gallopade Pub Group.

—Ohio Jeopardy! Answers & Questions about Our State! (Illus.). (gr. 3-12). 1991. PLB 24.95 (0-7933-4184-1); pap. 14.95 (0-7933-4185-X); computer disk 29.95 (0-7933-4186-8) Gallopade Pub Group.

—Ohio "Jography" A Fun Run Thru Our State! (Illus.). 1990. PLB 24.95 (1-55609-981-9); pap. 14.95 (1-55609-982-7); computer disk 29.95 (1-55609-983-5) Gallopade Pub Group.

—Ohio Kid's Cookbook: Recipes, How-to, History, Lore & More! (Illus.). 1990. PLB 24.95 (0-7933-0901-8); pap. 14.95 (0-7933-0900-X); computer disk 29.95 (0-7933-0902-6) Gallopade Pub Group.

—The Ohio Mystery Van Takes Off! Book 1: Handicapped Ohio Kids Sneak Off on a Big Adventure. (Illus.). (gr. 3-12). 1992. 24.95 (0-7933-5066-2); pap. 14.95 (0-7933-5067-0); computer disk 29.95 (0-7933-5068-9) Gallopade Pub Group.

—Ohio Quiz Crash Course! (Illus.). 1990. PLB 24.95 (1-55609-995-9); pap. 14.95 (1-55609-996-7); computer disk 29.95 (1-55609-997-5) Gallopade Pub Group.

—Ohio Rollercoasters! (Illus.). (gr. 3-12). 1992. PLB 24.95 (0-7933-5329-7); pap. 14.95 (0-7933-5330-0); computer disk 29.95 (0-7933-5331-9) Gallopade Pub Group.

—Ohio School Trivia: An Amazing & Fascinating Look at Our State's Teachers, Schools & Students! (Illus.). 1990. PLB 24.95 (0-7933-0898-4); pap. 14.95 (0-7933-0897-6); computer disk 29.95 (0-7933-0899-2) Gallopade Pub Group.

—Ohio Silly Basketball Sportsmysteries, Vol. 1. (Illus.). 1990. PLB 24.95 (0-7933-0895-X); pap. 14.95 (0-7933-0894-1); computer disk 29.95 (0-7933-0896-8) Gallopade Pub Group.

—Ohio Silly Basketball Sportsmysteries, Vol. 2. (Illus.). 1990. PLB 24.95 (0-685-45976-4); pap. 14.95 (0-7933-1854-8); computer disk 29.95 (0-7933-1855-6) Gallopade Pub Group.

—Ohio Silly Football Sportsmysteries, Vol. 1. (Illus.). 1990. PLB 24.95 (1-55609-986-X); pap. 14.95 (1-55609-987-8); computer disk 29.95 (1-55609-988-6) Gallopade Pub Group.

—Ohio Silly Football Sportsmysteries, Vol. 2. (Illus.). 1990. PLB 24.95 (1-55609-989-4); pap. 14.95 (1-55609-990-8); computer disk 29.95 (1-55609-991-6) Gallopade Pub Group.

—Ohio Silly Trivia1. (Illus.). 1990. PLB 24.95 (1-55609-979-7); pap. 14.95 (1-55609-112-5); computer disk 29.95 (1-55609-980-0) Gallopade Pub Group.

—Ohio Timeline: A Chronology of Ohio History, Mystery, Trivia, Legend, Lore & More. (Illus.). (gr. 3-12). 1992. PLB 24.95 (0-7933-5980-5); pap. 14.95 (0-7933-5981-3); computer disk 29.95 (0-7933-5982-1) Gallopade Pub Group.

—Ohio's (Most Devastating!) Disasters & (Most Calamitous!) Catastrophies! (Illus.). 1990. PLB 24.95 (0-7933-0886-0); pap. 14.95 (0-7933-0885-2); computer disk 29.95 (0-7933-0887-9) Gallopade Pub Group.

—Ohio's Unsolved Mysteries (& Their "Solutions") Includes Scientific Information & Other Activities for Students. (Illus.). (gr. 3-12). 1992. PLB 24.95 (0-7933-5827-2); pap. 14.95 (0-7933-5828-0); computer disk 29.95 (0-7933-5829-9) Gallopade Pub Group.

—Oklahoma & Other State Greats (Biographies) (Illus.). 1990. PLB 24.95 (0-7933-1878-5); pap. 14.95 (0-7933-1879-3); computer disk 29.95 (0-7933-1880-7) Gallopade Pub Group.

—Oklahoma Bandits, Bushwackers, Outlaws, Crooks, Devils, Ghosts, Desperadoes & Other Assorted & Sundry Characters! (Illus.). 1990. PLB 24.95 (0-7933-0914-X); pap. 14.95 (0-7933-0913-1); computer disk 29.95 (0-7933-0915-8) Gallopade Pub Group.

—Oklahoma Classic Christmas Trivia: Stories, Recipes, Activities, Legends, Lore & More! (Illus.). 1990. PLB 24.95 (0-7933-0917-4); pap. 14.95 (0-7933-0916-6); computer disk 29.95 (0-7933-0918-2) Gallopade Pub Group.

—Oklahoma Coastales. (Illus.). 1990. PLB 24.95 (0-7933-1872-6); pap. 14.95 (0-7933-1873-4); computer disk 29.95 (0-7933-1874-2) Gallopade Pub Group.

—Oklahoma Coastales. 1992. lib. bdg. 24.95 (0-7933-7301-8) Gallopade Pub Group.

—Oklahoma "Crinkum-Crankum" A Funny Word Book about Our State. (Illus.). (gr. 3-12). 1992. 24.95 (0-7933-4916-8); pap. 14.95 (0-7933-4917-6); computer disk 29.95 (0-7933-4918-4) Gallopade Pub Group.

—Oklahoma Dingbats! Bk. 1: A Fun Book of Games, Stories, Activities & More about Our State That's All in Code! for You to Decipher. (Illus.). (gr. 3-12). 1991. PLB 24.95 (0-7933-3881-6); pap. 14.95 (0-7933-3882-4); computer disk 29.95 (0-7933-3883-2) Gallopade Pub Group.

—Oklahoma Festival Fun for Kids! (Illus.). (gr. 3-12). 1991. lib. bdg. 24.95 (0-7933-4034-9); pap. 14.95 (0-7933-4035-7); disk 29.95 (0-7933-4036-5) Gallopade Pub Group.

—The Oklahoma Hot Air Balloon Mystery. (Illus.). (gr. 2-9). 1990. 24.95 (*0-7933-2642-7*); pap. 14.95 (*0-7933-2643-5*); computer disk 29.95 (*0-7933-2644-3*) Gallopade Pub Group.
—Oklahoma Jeopardy! Answers & Questions about Our State! (Illus.). (gr. 3-12). 1991. PLB 24.95 (*0-7933-4187-6*); pap. 14.95 (*0-7933-4188-4*); computer disk 29.95 (*0-7933-4189-2*) Gallopade Pub Group.
—Oklahoma "Jography" A Fun Run Thru Our State! (Illus.). 1990. PLB 24.95 (*0-7933-1858-0*); pap. 14.95 (*1-55609-086-2*); computer disk 29.95 (*0-7933-1859-9*) Gallopade Pub Group.
—Oklahoma Kid's Cookbook: Recipes, How-to, History, Lore & More! (Illus.). 1990. PLB 24.95 (*0-7933-0926-3*); pap. 14.95 (*0-7933-0925-5*); computer disk 29.95 (*0-7933-0927-1*) Gallopade Pub Group.
—The Oklahoma Mystery Van Takes Off! Book 1: Handicapped Oklahoma Kids Sneak Off on a Big Adventure. (Illus.). (gr. 3-12). 1992. 24.95 (*0-7933-5069-7*); pap. 14.95 (*0-7933-5070-0*); computer disk 29.95 (*0-7933-5071-9*) Gallopade Pub Group.
—Oklahoma Quiz Bowl Crash Course! (Illus.). 1990. PLB 24.95 (*0-7933-1881-5*); pap. 14.95 (*0-7933-1882-3*); computer disk 29.95 (*0-7933-1883-1*) Gallopade Pub Group.
—Oklahoma Rollercoasters! (Illus.). (gr. 3-12). 1992. PLB 24.95 (*0-7933-5332-7*); pap. 14.95 (*0-7933-5333-5*); computer disk 29.95 (*0-7933-5334-3*) Gallopade Pub Group.
—Oklahoma School Trivia: An Amazing & Fascinating Look at Our State's Teachers, Schools & Students! (Illus.). 1990. PLB 24.95 (*0-7933-0923-9*); pap. 14.95 (*0-7933-0922-0*); computer disk 29.95 (*0-7933-0924-7*) Gallopade Pub Group.
—Oklahoma Silly Basketball Sportsmysteries, Vol. 1. (Illus.). 1990. PLB 24.95 (*0-7933-0920-4*); pap. 14.95 (*0-7933-0919-0*); computer disk 29.95 (*0-7933-0921-2*) Gallopade Pub Group.
—Oklahoma Silly Basketball Sportsmysteries: Oklahoma Bks, Vol. 2. (Illus.). 1990. PLB 24.95 (*0-7933-1884-X*); pap. 14.95 (*0-7933-1885-8*); computer disk 29.95 (*0-7933-1886-6*) Gallopade Pub Group.
—Oklahoma Silly Football Sportsmysteries, Vol. 1. (Illus.). 1990. PLB 24.95 (*0-7933-1863-7*); pap. 14.95 (*0-7933-1864-5*); computer disk 29.95 (*0-7933-1865-3*) Gallopade Pub Group.
—Oklahoma Silly Football Sportsmysteries, Vol. 2. (Illus.). 1990. PLB 24.95 (*0-7933-1866-1*); pap. 14.95 (*0-7933-1867-X*); computer disk 29.95 (*0-7933-1868-8*) Gallopade Pub Group.
—Oklahoma Silly Trivia! (Illus.). 1990. PLB 24.95 (*0-685-45977-2*); pap. 14.95 (*1-55609-082-X*); computer disk 29.95 (*0-7933-1857-2*) Gallopade Pub Group.
—Oklahoma Timeline: A Chronology of Oklahoma History, Mystery, Trivia, Legend, Lore & More. (Illus.). (gr. 3-12). 1992. PLB 24.95 (*0-7933-5983-X*); pap. 14.95 (*0-7933-5984-8*); computer disk 29.95 (*0-7933-5985-6*) Gallopade Pub Group.
—Oklahoma's (Most Devastating!) Disasters & (Most Calamitous!) Catastrophies! (Illus.). 1990. PLB 24.95 (*0-7933-0911-5*); pap. 14.95 (*0-7933-0910-7*); computer disk 29.95 (*0-7933-0912-3*) Gallopade Pub Group.
—Oklahoma's Unsolved Mysteries (& Their "Solutions") Includes Scientific Information & Other Activities for Students. (Illus.). (gr. 3-12). 1992. PLB 24.95 (*0-7933-5830-2*); pap. 14.95 (*0-7933-5831-0*); computer disk 29.95 (*0-7933-5832-9*) Gallopade Pub Group.
—Old Salem Mystery. (Orig.). (gr. 3-12). 1986. 24.95 (*1-55609-184-2*); pap. 14.95 (*0-935326-59-6*) Gallopade Pub Group.
—Oregon & Other State Greats (Biographies) (Illus.). 1990. PLB 24.95 (*0-7933-1913-7*); pap. 14.95 (*0-7933-1914-5*); computer disk 29.95 (*0-7933-1915-3*) Gallopade Pub Group.
—Oregon Bandits, Bushwackers, Outlaws, Crooks, Devils, Ghosts, Desperadoes & Other Assorted & Sundry Characters! (Illus.). 1990. PLB 24.95 (*0-7933-0938-7*); pap. 14.95 (*0-7933-0937-9*); computer disk 29.95 (*0-7933-0939-5*) Gallopade Pub Group.
—Oregon Classic Christmas Trivia: Stories, Recipes, Activities, Legends, Lore & More! (Illus.). 1990. PLB 24.95 (*0-7933-0941-7*); pap. 14.95 (*0-7933-0940-9*); computer disk 29.95 (*0-7933-0942-5*) Gallopade Pub Group.
—Oregon Coastales. (Illus.). 1990. PLB 24.95 (*0-7933-1907-2*); pap. 14.95 (*0-685-45978-0*) Gallopade Pub Group.
—Oregon Coastales! 1992. lib. bdg. 24.95 (*0-7933-7302-6*) Gallopade Pub Group.
—Oregon "Crinkum-Crankum" A Funny Word Book about Our State. (Illus.). (gr. 3-12). 1992. 24.95 (*0-7933-4919-2*); pap. 14.95 (*0-7933-4920-6*); computer disk 29.95 (*0-7933-4921-4*) Gallopade Pub Group.
—Oregon Dingbats! Bk. 1: A Fun Book of Games, Stories, Activities & More about Our State That's All in Code! for You to Decipher. (Illus.). (gr. 3-12). 1991. PLB 24.95 (*0-7933-3884-0*); pap. 14.95 (*0-7933-3885-9*); computer disk 29.95 (*0-7933-3886-7*) Gallopade Pub Group.

—Oregon Festival Fun for Kids! (Illus.). (gr. 3-12). 1991. lib. bdg. 24.95 (*0-7933-4037-3*); pap. 14.95 (*0-7933-4038-1*); disk 29.95 (*0-7933-4039-X*) Gallopade Pub Group.
—The Oregon Hot Air Balloon Mystery. (Illus.). (gr. 2-9). 1990. 24.95 (*0-7933-2651-6*); pap. 14.95 (*0-7933-2652-4*); computer disk 29.95 (*0-7933-2653-2*) Gallopade Pub Group.
—Oregon Jeopardy! Answers & Questions about Our State! (Illus.). (gr. 3-12). 1991. PLB 24.95 (*0-7933-4190-6*); pap. 14.95 (*0-7933-4191-4*); computer disk 29.95 (*0-7933-4192-2*) Gallopade Pub Group.
—Oregon "Jography" A Fun Run Thru Our State. (Illus.). 1990. PLB 24.95 (*0-7933-1890-4*); pap. 14.95 (*0-7933-1891-2*); computer disk 29.95 (*0-7933-1892-0*) Gallopade Pub Group.
—Oregon Kid's Cookbook: Recipes, How-to, History, Lore & More! (Illus.). 1990. PLB 24.95 (*0-7933-0950-6*); pap. 14.95 (*0-7933-0949-2*); computer disk 29.95 (*0-7933-0951-4*) Gallopade Pub Group.
—The Oregon Mystery Van Takes Off! Book 1: Handicapped Oregon Kids Sneak Off on a Big Adventure. (Illus.). (gr. 3-12). 1992. 24.95 (*0-7933-5072-7*); pap. 14.95 (*0-7933-5073-5*); computer disk 29.95 (*0-7933-5074-3*) Gallopade Pub Group.
—Oregon Quiz Bowl Crash Course! (Illus.). 1990. PLB 24.95 (*0-7933-1904-8*); pap. 14.95 (*0-7933-1905-6*); computer disk 29.95 (*0-7933-1906-4*) Gallopade Pub Group.
—Oregon Rollercoasters! (Illus.). (gr. 3-12). 1992. PLB 24.95 (*0-7933-5335-1*); pap. 14.95 (*0-7933-5336-X*); computer disk 29.95 (*0-7933-5337-8*) Gallopade Pub Group.
—Oregon School Trivia: An Amazing & Fascinating Look at Our State's Teachers, Schools & Students. (Illus.). 1990. PLB 24.95 (*0-7933-0947-6*); pap. 14.95 (*0-7933-0946-8*); computer disk 29.95 (*0-7933-0948-4*) Gallopade Pub Group.
—Oregon Silly Basketball Sportsmysteries, Vol. 1. (Illus.). 1990. PLB 24.95 (*0-7933-0944-1*); pap. 14.95 (*0-7933-0943-3*); computer disk 29.95 (*0-7933-0945-X*) Gallopade Pub Group.
—Oregon Silly Basketball Sportsmysteries, Vol. 2. (Illus.). 1990. PLB 24.95 (*0-7933-1916-1*); pap. 14.95 (*0-7933-1917-X*); computer disk 29.95 (*0-7933-1918-8*) Gallopade Pub Group.
—Oregon Silly Football Sportsmysteries, Vol. 1. (Illus.). 1990. PLB 24.95 (*0-7933-1895-5*); pap. 14.95 (*0-7933-1896-3*); computer disk 29.95 (*0-7933-1897-1*) Gallopade Pub Group.
—Oregon Silly Football Sportsmysteries, Vol. 2. (Illus.). 1990. PLB 24.95 (*0-7933-1898-X*); pap. 14.95 (*0-7933-1899-8*); computer disk 29.95 (*0-7933-1900-5*) Gallopade Pub Group.
—Oregon Silly Trivia! (Illus.). 1990. PLB 24.95 (*0-7933-1887-4*); pap. 14.95 (*0-7933-1888-2*); computer disk 29.95 (*0-7933-1889-0*) Gallopade Pub Group.
—Oregon Timeline: A Chronology of Oregon History, Mystery, Trivia, Legend, Lore & More. (Illus.). (gr. 3-12). 1992. PLB 24.95 (*0-7933-5986-4*); pap. 14.95 (*0-7933-5987-2*); computer disk 29.95 (*0-7933-5988-0*) Gallopade Pub Group.
—Oregon's (Most Devastating!) Disasters & (Most Calamitous!) Catastrophies! (Illus.). 1990. PLB 24.95 (*0-7933-0935-2*); pap. 14.95 (*0-7933-0934-4*); computer disk 29.95 (*0-7933-0936-0*) Gallopade Pub Group.
—Oregon's Unsolved Mysteries (& Their "Solutions") Includes Scientific Information & Other Activities for Students. (Illus.). (gr. 3-12). 1992. PLB 24.95 (*0-7933-5833-7*); pap. 14.95 (*0-7933-5834-5*); computer disk 29.95 (*0-7933-5835-3*) Gallopade Pub Group.
—Out of the Mouths of Slaves. (gr. 3-12). 1989. PLB 24.95 (*1-55609-312-8*); pap. 14.95 (*1-55609-311-X*); computer disk 29.95 (*1-55609-313-6*) Gallopade Pub Group.
—Palm Fever. (Illus.). (gr. 4-12). 1988. 24.95 (*1-55609-185-0*); pap. 14.95 (*1-55609-237-7*) Gallopade Pub Group.
—Patch, the Pirate Dog: A California Pet Story. (ps-4). 1992. PLB 24.95 (*0-7933-5428-5*); pap. 14.95 (*0-7933-5429-3*); computer disk 29.95 (*0-7933-5430-7*) Gallopade Pub Group.
—Patch, the Pirate Dog: A Colorado Pet Story. (ps-4). 1992. PLB 24.95 (*0-7933-5431-5*); pap. 14.95 (*0-7933-5432-3*); computer disk 29.95 (*0-7933-5433-1*) Gallopade Pub Group.
—Patch, the Pirate Dog: A Connecticut Pet Story. (ps-4). 1992. PLB 24.95 (*0-7933-5434-X*); pap. 14.95 (*0-7933-5435-8*); computer disk 29.95 (*0-7933-5436-6*) Gallopade Pub Group.
—Patch, the Pirate Dog: A Delaware Pet Story. (ps-4). 1992. PLB 24.95 (*0-7933-5437-4*); pap. 14.95 (*0-7933-5438-2*); computer disk 29.95 (*0-7933-5439-0*) Gallopade Pub Group.
—Patch, the Pirate Dog: A Florida Pet Story. (ps-4). 1992. PLB 24.95 (*0-7933-5443-9*); pap. 14.95 (*0-7933-5444-7*); computer disk 29.95 (*0-7933-5445-5*) Gallopade Pub Group.
—Patch, the Pirate Dog: A Georgia Pet Story. (ps-4). 1992. PLB 24.95 (*0-7933-5446-3*); pap. 14.95 (*0-7933-5447-1*); computer disk 29.95 (*0-7933-5448-X*) Gallopade Pub Group.

—Patch, the Pirate Dog: A Hawaii Pet Story. (ps-4). 1992. PLB 24.95 (*0-7933-5449-8*); pap. 14.95 (*0-7933-5450-1*); computer disk 29.95 (*0-7933-5451-X*) Gallopade Pub Group.
—Patch, the Pirate Dog: A Kansas Pet Story. (ps-4). 1992. PLB 24.95 (*0-7933-5464-1*); pap. 14.95 (*0-7933-5465-X*); computer disk 29.95 (*0-7933-5466-8*) Gallopade Pub Group.
—Patch, the Pirate Dog: A Kentucky Pet Story. (ps-4). 1992. PLB 24.95 (*0-7933-5467-6*); pap. 14.95 (*0-7933-5468-4*); computer disk 29.95 (*0-7933-5469-2*) Gallopade Pub Group.
—Patch, the Pirate Dog: A Louisiana Pet Story. (ps-4). 1992. PLB 24.95 (*0-7933-5470-6*); pap. 14.95 (*0-7933-5471-4*); computer disk 29.95 (*0-7933-5472-2*) Gallopade Pub Group.
—Patch, the Pirate Dog: A Maine Pet Story. (ps-4). 1992. PLB 24.95 (*0-7933-5473-0*); pap. 14.95 (*0-7933-5474-9*); computer disk 29.95 (*0-7933-5475-7*) Gallopade Pub Group.
—Patch, the Pirate Dog: A Maryland Pet Story. (ps-4). 1992. PLB 24.95 (*0-7933-5476-5*); pap. 14.95 (*0-7933-5477-3*); computer disk 29.95 (*0-7933-5478-1*) Gallopade Pub Group.
—Patch, the Pirate Dog: A Massachusetts Pet Story. (ps-4). 1992. PLB 24.95 (*0-7933-5479-X*); pap. 14.95 (*0-7933-5480-3*); computer disk 29.95 (*0-7933-5481-1*) Gallopade Pub Group.
—Patch, the Pirate Dog: A Michigan Pet Story. (ps-4). 1992. PLB 24.95 (*0-7933-5482-X*); pap. 14.95 (*0-7933-5483-8*); computer disk 29.95 (*0-7933-5484-6*) Gallopade Pub Group.
—Patch, the Pirate Dog: A Minnesota Pet Story. (ps-4). 1992. PLB 24.95 (*0-7933-5485-4*); pap. 14.95 (*0-7933-5486-2*); computer disk 29.95 (*0-7933-5487-0*) Gallopade Pub Group.
—Patch, the Pirate Dog: A Mississippi Pet Story. (ps-4). 1992. PLB 24.95 (*0-7933-5488-9*); pap. 14.95 (*0-7933-5489-7*); computer disk 29.95 (*0-7933-5490-0*) Gallopade Pub Group.
—Patch, the Pirate Dog: A Missouri Pet Story. (ps-4). 1992. PLB 24.95 (*0-7933-5491-9*); pap. 14.95 (*0-7933-5492-7*); computer disk 29.95 (*0-7933-5493-5*) Gallopade Pub Group.
—Patch, the Pirate Dog: A Montana Pet Story. (ps-4). 1992. PLB 24.95 (*0-7933-5494-3*); pap. 14.95 (*0-7933-5495-1*); computer disk 29.95 (*0-7933-5496-X*) Gallopade Pub Group.
—Patch, the Pirate Dog: A Nebraska Pet Story. (ps-4). 1992. PLB 24.95 (*0-7933-5497-8*); pap. 14.95 (*0-7933-5498-6*); computer disk 29.95 (*0-7933-5499-4*) Gallopade Pub Group.
—Patch, the Pirate Dog: A Nevada Pet Story. (ps-4). 1992. PLB 24.95 (*0-7933-5500-1*); pap. 14.95 (*0-7933-5501-X*); computer disk 29.95 (*0-7933-5502-8*) Gallopade Pub Group.
—Patch, the Pirate Dog: A New Hampshire Pet Story. (ps-4). 1992. PLB 24.95 (*0-7933-5503-6*); pap. 14.95 (*0-7933-5504-4*); computer disk 29.95 (*0-7933-5505-2*) Gallopade Pub Group.
—Patch, the Pirate Dog: A New Jersey Pet Story. (ps-4). 1992. PLB 24.95 (*0-7933-5506-0*); pap. 14.95 (*0-7933-5507-9*); computer disk 29.95 (*0-7933-5508-7*) Gallopade Pub Group.
—Patch, the Pirate Dog: A New Mexico Pet Story. (ps-4). 1992. PLB 24.95 (*0-7933-5509-5*); pap. 14.95 (*0-7933-5510-9*); computer disk 29.95 (*0-7933-5511-7*) Gallopade Pub Group.
—Patch, the Pirate Dog: A New York Pet Story. (ps-4). 1992. PLB 24.95 (*0-7933-5512-5*); pap. 14.95 (*0-7933-5513-3*); computer disk 29.95 (*0-7933-5514-1*) Gallopade Pub Group.
—Patch, the Pirate Dog: A North Carolina Pet Story. (ps-4). 1992. PLB 24.95 (*0-7933-5515-X*); pap. 14.95 (*0-7933-5516-8*); computer disk 29.95 (*0-7933-5517-6*) Gallopade Pub Group.
—Patch, the Pirate Dog: A North Dakota Pet Story. (ps-4). 1992. PLB 24.95 (*0-7933-5518-4*); pap. 14.95 (*0-7933-5519-2*); computer disk 29.95 (*0-7933-5520-6*) Gallopade Pub Group.
—Patch, the Pirate Dog: A Ohio Pet Story. (ps-4). 1992. PLB 24.95 (*0-7933-5521-4*); pap. 14.95 (*0-7933-5522-2*); computer disk 29.95 (*0-7933-5523-0*) Gallopade Pub Group.
—Patch, the Pirate Dog: A Oklahoma Pet Story. (ps-4). 1992. PLB 24.95 (*0-7933-5524-9*); pap. 14.95 (*0-7933-5525-7*); computer disk 29.95 (*0-7933-5526-5*) Gallopade Pub Group.
—Patch, the Pirate Dog: A Oregon Pet Story. (ps-4). 1992. PLB 24.95 (*0-7933-5527-3*); pap. 14.95 (*0-7933-5528-1*); computer disk 29.95 (*0-7933-5529-X*) Gallopade Pub Group.
—Patch, the Pirate Dog: A Pennsylvania Pet Story. (ps-4). 1992. PLB 24.95 (*0-7933-5530-3*); pap. 14.95 (*0-7933-5531-1*); computer disk 29.95 (*0-7933-5532-X*) Gallopade Pub Group.
—Patch, the Pirate Dog: A Rhode Island Pet Story. (ps-4). 1992. PLB 24.95 (*0-7933-5533-8*); pap. 14.95 (*0-7933-5534-6*); computer disk 29.95 (*0-7933-5535-4*) Gallopade Pub Group.
—Patch, the Pirate Dog: A South Carolina Pet Story. (ps-4). 1992. PLB 24.95 (*0-7933-5536-2*); pap. 14.95 (*0-7933-5537-0*); computer disk 29.95 (*0-7933-5538-9*) Gallopade Pub Group.
—Patch, the Pirate Dog: A South Dakota Pet Story. (ps-4). 1992. PLB 24.95 (*0-7933-5539-7*); pap. 14.95 (*0-7933-5540-0*); computer disk 29.95 (*0-7933-5541-9*) Gallopade Pub Group.

—Patch, the Pirate Dog: A Tennessee Pet Story. (ps-4).
1992. PLB 24.95 (*0-7933-5542-7*); pap. 14.95
(*0-7933-5543-5*); computer disk 29.95 (*0-7933-5544-3*)
Gallopade Pub Group.
—Patch, the Pirate Dog: A Texas Pet Story. (ps-4). 1992.
PLB 24.95 (*0-7933-5545-1*); pap. 14.95
(*0-7933-5546-X*); computer disk 29.95
(*0-7933-5547-8*) Gallopade Pub Group.
—Patch, the Pirate Dog: A Utah Pet Story. (ps-4). 1992.
PLB 24.95 (*0-7933-5548-6*); pap. 14.95
(*0-7933-5549-4*); computer disk 29.95 (*0-7933-5550-8*)
Gallopade Pub Group.
—Patch, the Pirate Dog: A Vermont Pet Story. (ps-4).
1992. PLB 24.95 (*0-7933-5551-6*); pap. 14.95
(*0-7933-5552-4*); computer disk 29.95 (*0-7933-5553-2*)
Gallopade Pub Group.
—Patch, the Pirate Dog: A Virginia Pet Story. (ps-4).
1992. PLB 24.95 (*0-7933-5554-0*); pap. 14.95
(*0-7933-5555-9*); computer disk 29.95 (*0-7933-5556-7*)
Gallopade Pub Group.
—Patch, the Pirate Dog: A Washington DC Pet Story.
(ps-4). 1992. PLB 24.95 (*0-7933-5440-4*); pap. 14.95
(*0-7933-5441-2*); computer disk 29.95 (*0-7933-5442-0*)
Gallopade Pub Group.
—Patch, the Pirate Dog: A Washington Pet Story. (ps-4).
1992. PLB 24.95 (*0-7933-5557-5*); pap. 14.95
(*0-7933-5558-3*); computer disk 29.95 (*0-7933-5559-1*)
Gallopade Pub Group.
—Patch, the Pirate Dog: A West Virginia Pet Story.
(ps-4). 1992. PLB 24.95 (*0-7933-5560-5*); pap. 14.95
(*0-7933-5561-3*); computer disk 29.95 (*0-7933-5562-1*)
Gallopade Pub Group.
—Patch, the Pirate Dog: A Wisconsin Pet Story. (ps-4).
1992. PLB 24.95 (*0-7933-5563-X*); pap. 14.95
(*0-7933-5564-8*); computer disk 29.95 (*0-7933-5565-6*)
Gallopade Pub Group.
—Patch, the Pirate Dog: A Wyoming Pet Story. (ps-4).
1992. PLB 24.95 (*0-7933-5566-4*); pap. 14.95
(*0-7933-5567-2*); computer disk 29.95 (*0-7933-5568-0*)
Gallopade Pub Group.
—Patch, the Pirate Dog: An Alabama Pet Story. (ps-4).
1992. PLB 24.95 (*0-7933-5416-1*); pap. 14.95
(*0-7933-5417-X*); computer disk 29.95
(*0-7933-5418-8*) Gallopade Pub Group.
—Patch, the Pirate Dog: An Alaska Pet Story. (ps-4).
1992. PLB 24.95 (*0-7933-5419-6*); pap. 14.95
(*0-7933-5420-X*); computer disk 29.95
(*0-7933-5421-8*) Gallopade Pub Group.
—Patch, the Pirate Dog: An Arizona Pet Story. (ps-4).
1992. PLB 24.95 (*0-7933-5422-6*); pap. 14.95
(*0-7933-5423-4*); computer disk 29.95 (*0-7933-5424-2*)
Gallopade Pub Group.
—Patch, the Pirate Dog: An Arkansas Pet Story. (ps-4).
1992. PLB 24.95 (*0-7933-5425-0*); pap. 14.95
(*0-7933-5426-9*); computer disk 29.95 (*0-7933-5427-7*)
Gallopade Pub Group.
—Patch, the Pirate Dog: An Idaho Pet Story. (ps-4).
1992. PLB 24.95 (*0-7933-5452-8*); pap. 14.95
(*0-7933-5453-6*); computer disk 29.95 (*0-7933-5454-4*)
Gallopade Pub Group.
—Patch, the Pirate Dog: An Illinois Pet Story. (ps-4).
1992. PLB 24.95 (*0-7933-5455-2*); pap. 14.95
(*0-7933-5456-0*); computer disk 29.95 (*0-7933-5457-9*)
Gallopade Pub Group.
—Patch, the Pirate Dog: An Indiana Pet Story. (ps-4).
1992. PLB 24.95 (*0-7933-5458-7*); pap. 14.95
(*0-7933-5459-5*); computer disk 29.95 (*0-7933-5460-9*)
Gallopade Pub Group.
—Patch, the Pirate Dog: An Iowa Pet Story. (ps-4). 1992.
PLB 24.95 (*0-7933-5461-7*); pap. 14.95
(*0-7933-5462-5*); computer disk 29.95 (*0-7933-5463-3*)
Gallopade Pub Group.
—Pennsylvania & Other State Greats (Biographies)
(Illus.). 1990. PLB 24.95 (*0-7933-1942-0*); pap. 14.95
(*0-7933-1943-9*); computer disk 29.95 (*0-7933-1944-7*)
Gallopade Pub Group.
—Pennsylvania Bandits, Bushwackers, Outlaws, Crooks,
Devils, Ghosts, Desperadoes & Other Assorted &
Sundry Characters! (Illus.). 1990. PLB 24.95
(*0-7933-0962-X*); pap. 14.95 (*0-7933-0961-1*);
computer disk 29.95 (*0-7933-0963-8*) Gallopade Pub
Group.
—Pennsylvania Classic Christmas Trivia: Stories, Recipes,
Activities, Legends, Lore & More! (Illus.). 1990. PLB
24.95 (*0-7933-0965-4*); pap. 14.95 (*0-7933-0964-6*);
computer disk 29.95 (*0-7933-0966-2*) Gallopade Pub
Group.
—Pennsylvania Coastales. (Illus.). 1990. PLB 24.95
(*0-7933-1936-6*); pap. 14.95 (*0-7933-1937-4*);
computer disk 29.95 (*0-7933-1938-2*) Gallopade Pub
Group.
—Pennsylvania Coastales. 1992. lib. bdg. 24.95
(*0-7933-7303-4*) Gallopade Pub Group.
—Pennsylvania "Crinkum-Crankum" A Funny Word
Book about Our State. (Illus.). (gr. 3-12). 1992. 24.95
(*0-7933-4922-2*); pap. 14.95 (*0-7933-4923-0*);
computer disk 29.95 (*0-7933-4924-9*) Gallopade Pub
Group.
—Pennsylvania Dingbats! Bk. 1: A Fun Book of Games,
Stories, Activities & More about Our State That's All
in Code! for You to Decipher. (Illus.). (gr. 3-12).
1991. PLB 24.95 (*0-7933-3887-5*); pap. 14.95
(*0-7933-3888-3*); computer disk 29.95 (*0-7933-3889-1*)
Gallopade Pub Group.
—Pennsylvania Festival Fun for Kids! (Illus.). (gr. 3-12).
1991. lib. bdg. 24.95 (*0-7933-4040-3*); pap. 14.95
(*0-7933-4041-1*); disk 29.95 (*0-7933-4042-X*)
Gallopade Pub Group.

—The Pennsylvania Hot Air Balloon Mystery. (Illus.).
(gr. 2-9). 1990. 24.95 (*0-7933-2660-5*); pap. 14.95
(*0-7933-2661-3*); computer disk 29.95 (*0-7933-2662-1*)
Gallopade Pub Group.
—Pennsylvania Jeopardy! Answers & Questions about
Our State! (Illus.). (gr. 3-12). 1991. PLB 24.95
(*0-7933-4193-0*); pap. 14.95 (*0-7933-4194-9*);
computer disk 29.95 (*0-7933-4195-7*) Gallopade Pub
Group.
—Pennsylvania "Jography" A Fun Run Thru Our State!
(Illus.). PLB 24.95 (*0-7933-1922-6*); pap. 14.95
(*0-7933-1923-4*); computer disk 29.95 (*0-7933-1924-2*)
Gallopade Pub Group.
—Pennsylvania Kid's Cookbook: Recipes, How-to,
History, Lore & More! (Illus.). 1990. PLB 24.95
(*0-7933-0974-3*); pap. 14.95 (*0-7933-0973-5*);
computer disk 29.95 (*0-7933-0975-1*) Gallopade Pub
Group.
—The Pennsylvania Mystery Van Takes Off! Book 1:
Handicapped Pennsylvania Kids Sneak Off on a Big
Adventure. (Illus.). (gr. 3-12). 1992. 24.95
(*0-7933-5075-1*); pap. 14.95 (*0-7933-5076-X*);
computer disk 29.95 (*0-7933-5077-8*) Gallopade Pub
Group.
—Pennsylvania Quiz Bowl Crash Course! (Illus.). 1990.
PLB 24.95 (*0-7933-1945-5*); pap. 14.95
(*0-7933-1946-3*); computer disk 29.95 (*0-7933-1947-1*)
Gallopade Pub Group.
—Pennsylvania Rollercoasters! (Illus.). (gr. 3-12). 1992.
PLB 24.95 (*0-7933-5338-6*); pap. 14.95
(*0-7933-5339-4*); computer disk 29.95 (*0-7933-5340-8*)
Gallopade Pub Group.
—Pennsylvania School Trivia: An Amazing & Fascinating
Look at Ou State's Teachers, Schools & Students!
(Illus.). 1990. PLB 24.95 (*0-7933-0971-9*); pap. 14.95
(*0-7933-0970-0*); computer disk 29.95 (*0-7933-0972-7*)
Gallopade Pub Group.
—Pennsylvania Silly Basketball Sportsmysteries, Vol. 1.
(Illus.). 1990. PLB 24.95 (*0-7933-0968-9*); pap. 14.95
(*0-7933-0967-0*); computer disk 29.95 (*0-7933-0969-7*)
Gallopade Pub Group.
—Pennsylvania Silly Basketball Sportsmysteries, Vol. 2.
(Illus.). 1990. PLB 24.95 (*0-7933-1948-X*); pap. 14.95
(*0-7933-1949-8*); computer disk 29.95 (*0-7933-1950-1*)
Gallopade Pub Group.
—Pennsylvania Silly Football Sportsmysteries, Vol. 1.
(Illus.). 1990. PLB 24.95 (*0-7933-1927-7*); pap. 14.95
(*0-7933-1928-5*); computer disk 29.95 (*0-7933-1929-3*)
Gallopade Pub Group.
—Pennsylvania Silly Football Sportsmysteries, Vol. 2.
(Illus.). 1990. PLB 24.95 (*0-7933-1930-7*); pap. 14.95
(*0-7933-1931-5*); computer disk 29.95 (*0-7933-1932-3*)
Gallopade Pub Group.
—Pennsylvania Silly Trivia! (Illus.). 1990. PLB 24.95
(*0-7933-1919-6*); pap. 14.95 (*0-7933-1920-X*);
computer disk 29.95 (*0-7933-1921-8*) Gallopade Pub
Group.
—Pennsylvania Timeline: A Chronology of Pennsylvania
History, Mystery, Trivia, Legend, Lore & More.
(Illus.). (gr. 3-12). 1992. PLB 24.95 (*0-7933-5989-9*);
pap. 14.95 (*0-7933-5990-2*); computer disk 29.95
(*0-7933-5991-0*) Gallopade Pub Group.
—Pennsylvania's (Most Devastating!) Disasters & (Most
Calamitous!) Catastrophies! (Illus.). 1990. PLB 24.95
(*0-7933-0959-X*); pap. 14.95 (*0-7933-0958-1*);
computer disk 29.95 (*0-7933-0960-3*) Gallopade Pub
Group.
—Pennsylvania's Unsolved Mysteries (& Their
"Solutions") Includes Scientific Information & Other
Activities for Students. (Illus.). (gr. 3-12). 1992. PLB
24.95 (*0-7933-5836-1*); pap. 14.95 (*0-7933-5837-X*);
computer disk 29.95 (*0-7933-5838-8*) Gallopade Pub
Group.
—Phyzzics for Kids. (gr. 4-9). 1989. 24.95
(*1-55609-258-X*); pap. 14.95 (*1-55609-245-8*);
computer disk 29.95 (*1-55609-340-3*) Gallopade Pub
Group.
—The Pirate & Treasure Dingbats Book. (Illus.). (gr. 3-
12). 1992. PLB 24.95 (*0-7933-5407-2*); pap. 14.95
(*0-7933-5408-0*); computer disk 29.95 (*0-7933-5409-9*)
Gallopade Pub Group.
—Quiz Bowl Crash Course. (gr. 5 up). 1989. 24.95
(*1-55609-288-1*); pap. 14.95 (*1-55609-195-8*);
computer disk 29.95 (*1-55609-289-X*) Gallopade Pub
Group.
—Rhode Island & Other State Greats (Biographies)
(Illus.). 1990. PLB 24.95 (*0-7933-1977-3*); pap. 14.95
(*0-7933-1978-1*); computer disk 29.95
(*0-7933-1979-X*) Gallopade Pub Group.
—Rhode Island Bandits, Bushwackers, Outlaws, Crooks,
Devils, Ghosts, Desperadoes & Other Assorted &
Sundry Characters! (Illus.). 1990. PLB 24.95
(*0-7933-0986-7*); pap. 14.95 (*0-685-45967-5*);
computer disk 29.95 (*0-7933-0987-5*) Gallopade Pub
Group.
—Rhode Island Classic Christmas Trivia: Stories,
Recipes, Activities, Legends, Lore & More! (Illus.).
1990. PLB 24.95 (*0-7933-0989-1*); pap. 14.95
(*0-7933-0988-3*); computer disk 29.95 (*0-7933-0990-5*)
Gallopade Pub Group.
—Rhode Island Coastales. (Illus.). 1990. PLB 24.95
(*0-7933-1971-4*); pap. 14.95 (*0-7933-1972-2*);
computer disk 29.95 (*0-7933-1973-0*) Gallopade Pub
Group.
—Rhode Island Coastales! 1992. lib. bdg. 24.95
(*0-7933-7304-2*) Gallopade Pub Group.

—Rhode Island "Crinkum-Crankum" A Funny Word
Book about Our State. (Illus.). (gr. 3-12). 1992. 24.95
(*0-7933-4925-7*); pap. 14.95 (*0-7933-4926-5*);
computer disk 29.95 (*0-7933-4927-3*) Gallopade Pub
Group.
—Rhode Island Dingbats! Bk. 1: A Fun Book of Games,
Stories, Activities & More about Our State That's All
in Code! for You to Decipher. (Illus.). (gr. 3-12).
1991. PLB 24.95 (*0-7933-3890-5*); pap. 14.95
(*0-7933-3891-3*); computer disk 29.95 (*0-7933-3892-1*)
Gallopade Pub Group.
—Rhode Island Festival Fun for Kids! (Illus.). (gr. 3-12).
1991. lib. bdg. 24.95 (*0-7933-4043-8*); pap. 14.95
(*0-7933-4044-6*); disk 29.95 (*0-7933-4045-4*)
Gallopade Pub Group.
—The Rhode Island Hot Air Balloon Mystery. (Illus.).
(gr. 2-9). 1990. 24.95 (*0-7933-2669-9*); pap. 14.95
(*0-7933-2670-2*); computer disk 29.95 (*0-7933-2671-0*)
Gallopade Pub Group.
—Rhode Island Jeopardy! Answers & Questions about
Our State! (Illus.). (gr. 3-12). 1991. PLB 24.95
(*0-7933-4196-5*); pap. 14.95 (*0-7933-4197-3*);
computer disk 29.95 (*0-7933-4198-1*) Gallopade Pub
Group.
—Rhode Island "Jography" A Fun Run Thru Our State!
(Illus.). 1990. PLB 24.95 (*0-7933-1954-4*); pap. 14.95
(*0-7933-1955-2*); computer disk 29.95 (*0-7933-1956-0*)
Gallopade Pub Group.
—Rhode Island Kid's Cookbook: Recipes, How-to,
History Lore & More! (Illus.). 1990. PLB 24.95
(*0-7933-0998-0*); pap. 14.95 (*0-7933-0997-2*);
computer disk 29.95 (*0-7933-0999-9*) Gallopade Pub
Group.
—The Rhode Island Mystery Van Takes Off! Book 1:
Handicapped Rhode Island Kids Sneak Off on a Big
Adventure. (Illus.). (gr. 3-12). 1992. 24.95
(*0-7933-5078-6*); pap. 14.95 (*0-7933-5079-4*);
computer disk 29.95 (*0-7933-5080-8*) Gallopade Pub
Group.
—Rhode Island Quiz Bowl Crash Course! (Illus.). 1990.
PLB 24.95 (*0-7933-1968-4*); pap. 14.95
(*0-7933-1969-2*); computer disk 29.95 (*0-7933-1970-6*)
Gallopade Pub Group.
—Rhode Island Rollercoasters! (Illus.). (gr. 3-12). 1992.
PLB 24.95 (*0-7933-5341-6*); pap. 14.95
(*0-7933-5342-4*); computer disk 29.95 (*0-7933-5343-2*)
Gallopade Pub Group.
—Rhode Island School Trivia: An Amazing &
Fascinating Look at Our State's Teachers, Schools &
Students! (Illus.). 1990. PLB 24.95 (*0-7933-0995-6*);
pap. 14.95 (*0-7933-0994-8*); computer disk 29.95
(*0-7933-0996-4*) Gallopade Pub Group.
—Rhode Island Silly Basketball Sportsmysteries, Vol. 1.
(Illus.). 1990. PLB 24.95 (*0-7933-0992-1*); pap. 14.95
(*0-7933-0991-3*); computer disk 29.95 (*0-685-45968-3*)
Gallopade Pub Group.
—Rhode Island Silly Basketball Sportsmysteries, Vol. 2.
(Illus.). 1990. PLB 24.95 (*0-7933-1980-3*); pap. 14.95
(*0-7933-1981-1*); computer disk 29.95
(*0-7933-1982-X*) Gallopade Pub Group.
—Rhode Island Silly Football Sportsmysteries, Vol. 1.
(Illus.). 1990. PLB 24.95 (*0-7933-1959-5*); pap. 14.95
(*0-7933-1960-9*); computer disk 29.95 (*0-7933-1961-7*)
Gallopade Pub Group.
—Rhode Island Silly Football Sportsmysteries, Vol. 2.
(Illus.). 1990. PLB 24.95 (*0-7933-1962-5*); pap. 14.95
(*0-7933-1963-3*); computer disk 29.95 (*0-7933-1964-1*)
Gallopade Pub Group.
—Rhode Island Silly Trivia! (Illus.). 1990. PLB 24.95
(*0-7933-1951-X*); pap. 14.95 (*0-7933-1952-8*);
computer disk 29.95 (*0-7933-1953-6*) Gallopade Pub
Group.
—Rhode Island Timeline: A Chronology of Rhode Island
History, Mystery, Trivia, Legend, Lore & More.
(Illus.). (gr. 3-12). 1992. PLB 24.95 (*0-7933-5992-9*);
pap. 14.95 (*0-7933-5993-7*); computer disk 29.95
(*0-7933-5994-5*) Gallopade Pub Group.
—Rhode Island's (Most Devastating!) Disasters & (Most
Calamitous!) Catastrophies! (Illus.). 1990. PLB 24.95
(*0-7933-0983-2*); pap. 14.95 (*0-7933-0982-4*);
computer disk 29.95 (*0-685-45966-7*) Gallopade Pub
Group.
—Rhode Island's Unsolved Mysteries (& Their
"Solutions") Includes Scientific Information & Other
Activities for Students. (Illus.). (gr. 3-12). 1992. PLB
24.95 (*0-7933-5839-6*); pap. 14.95 (*0-7933-5840-X*);
computer disk 29.95 (*0-7933-5841-8*) Gallopade Pub
Group.
—River Rogues! Natchez Pirates, Playboys, & the Rest of
the Cock-o-the-Walk Crowd under-the-Hill & along
the Trace. 1992. pap. 14.95 (*0-7933-7323-9*)
Gallopade Pub Group.
—Saturnalia. (Illus., Orig.). (gr. 4-12). 1988. 24.95
(*1-55609-187-7*); pap. 14.95 (*1-55609-238-5*)
Gallopade Pub Group.
—The Secret Mysteries Dingbats Book. (Illus.). (gr. 3-12).
1992. PLB 24.95 (*0-7933-5383-1*); pap. 14.95
(*0-7933-5384-X*); computer disk 29.95
(*0-7933-5385-8*) Gallopade Pub Group.
—The Secret of Somerset Place S. P. A. R. K. Kit. (Illus.,
Orig.). (gr. 3-9). 1986. pap. 24.95 (*0-935326-20-0*)
Gallopade Pub Group.
—Sex Stuff: A Book of Practical Information & Ideas for
Kids 7-17, & Their Teachers & Parents, Contains
Chapter on 'AIDS' (gr. 2-12). 1987. 24.95
(*1-556092-00-8*); pap. 14.95 (*1-556092-01-6*); tchr's.
ed. 24.95 (*1-55609-204-0*) Gallopade Pub Group.

—The Sinister Spies Dingbats Book. (Illus.). (gr. 3-12). 1992. PLB 24.95 (*0-7933-5389-0*); pap. 14.95 (*0-7933-5390-4*); computer disk 29.95 (*0-7933-5391-2*) Gallopade Pub Group.
—Six Puppy Feet: Bridge for Kids. (Illus.). (gr. k-12). 1983. 24.95 (*1-55609-157-5*); pap. 14.95 (*0-935326-13-8*) Gallopade Pub Group.
—Snowshoe & Earmuff Go North. (Illus.). (ps-4). 1989. 24.95 (*1-55609-646-1*); pap. 14.95 (*1-55609-758-1*) Gallopade Pub Group.
—Snowshoe & Earmuff Go West. (Illus.). (ps-3). 1989. 24.95 (*1-55609-304-7*); pap. 14.95 (*1-55609-303-9*) Gallopade Pub Group.
—Sorta Silly, Smart-Aleck Study Tips Even Teens Will Like. (gr. 7-12). 1992. PLB 24.95 (*0-7933-7352-2*); pap. 14.95 (*0-7933-7353-0*); computer disk 29.95 (*0-7933-7354-9*) Gallopade Pub Group.
—South Carolina & Other State Greats (Biographies) (Illus.). 1990. PLB 24.95 (*0-7933-2006-2*); pap. 14.95 (*0-7933-2007-0*); computer disk 29.95 (*0-7933-2008-9*) Gallopade Pub Group.
—South Carolina Bandits, Bushwackers, Outlaws, Crooks, Devils, Ghosts, Desperadoes & Other Assorted & Sundry Characters! (Illus.). 1990. PLB 24.95 (*0-7933-1010-5*); pap. 14.95 (*0-7933-1009-1*); computer disk 29.95 (*0-7933-1011-3*) Gallopade Pub Group.
—South Carolina Classic Christmas Trivia: Stories, Recipes, Activities, Legends, Lore & More! (Illus.). 1990. PLB 24.95 (*0-7933-1013-X*); pap. 14.95 (*0-7933-1012-1*); computer disk 29.95 (*0-7933-1014-8*) Gallopade Pub Group.
—South Carolina Coastales. (Illus.). 1990. PLB 24.95 (*0-7933-2001-1*); pap. 14.95 (*1-55609-115-X*); computer disk 29.95 (*0-7933-2002-X*) Gallopade Pub Group.
—South Carolina Coastales! 1992. lib. bdg. 24.95 (*0-7933-7305-0*) Gallopade Pub Group.
—South Carolina "Crinkum-Crankum" A Funny Word Book about Our State. (Illus.). (gr. 3-12). 1992. 24.95 (*0-7933-4928-1*); pap. 14.95 (*0-7933-4929-X*); computer disk 29.95 (*0-7933-4930-3*) Gallopade Pub Group.
—South Carolina Dingbats! Bk. 1: A Fun Book of Games, Stories, Activities & More about Our State That's All in Code! for You to Decipher. (Illus.). (gr. 3-12). 1991. PLB 19.95 (*0-7933-3893-X*); pap. 14.95 (*0-7933-3894-8*); computer disk 29.95 (*0-7933-3895-6*) Gallopade Pub Group.
—South Carolina Festival Fun for Kids! (Illus.). (gr. 3-12). 1991. lib. bdg. 24.95 (*0-7933-4046-2*); pap. 14.95 (*0-7933-4047-0*); disk 29.95 (*0-7933-4048-9*) Gallopade Pub Group.
—The South Carolina Hot Air Balloon Mystery. (Illus.). (gr. 2-9). 1990. 24.95 (*0-7933-2678-8*); pap. 14.95 (*0-7933-2679-6*); computer disk 29.95 (*0-7933-2680-X*) Gallopade Pub Group.
—South Carolina Jeopardy! Answers & Questions about Our State! (Illus.). (gr. 3-12). 1991. PLB 24.95 (*0-7933-4199-X*); pap. 14.95 (*0-7933-4200-7*); computer disk 29.95 (*0-7933-4201-5*) Gallopade Pub Group.
—South Carolina "Jography" A Fun Run Thru Our State! (Illus.). 1990. PLB 24.95 (*0-7933-1985-4*); pap. 14.95 (*1-55609-049-8*); computer disk 29.95 (*0-7933-1986-2*) Gallopade Pub Group.
—South Carolina Jography: A Fun Run Through the Palmetto State. (Illus.). 50p. (Orig.). (gr. 3-9). 1986. pap. 14.95 (*0-935326-96-0*) Gallopade Pub Group.
—South Carolina Kid's Cookbook: Recipes, How-to, History, Lore & More! (Illus.). 1990. PLB 24.95 (*0-7933-1022-9*); pap. 14.95 (*0-7933-1021-0*); computer disk 29.95 (*0-7933-1023-7*) Gallopade Pub Group.
—The South Carolina Mystery Van Takes Off! Book 1: Handicapped South Carolina Kids Sneak Off on a Big Adventure. (Illus.). (gr. 3-12). 1992. 24.95 (*0-7933-5081-6*); pap. 14.95 (*0-7933-5082-4*); computer disk 29.95 (*0-7933-5083-2*) Gallopade Pub Group.
—South Carolina Quiz Bowl Crash Course! (Illus.). 1990. PLB 24.95 (*0-7933-1998-6*); pap. 14.95 (*0-7933-1999-4*); computer disk 29.95 (*0-7933-2000-3*) Gallopade Pub Group.
—South Carolina Rollercoasters! (Illus.). (gr. 3-12). 1992. PLB 24.95 (*0-7933-5344-0*); pap. 14.95 (*0-7933-5345-9*); computer disk 29.95 (*0-7933-5346-7*) Gallopade Pub Group.
—South Carolina School Trivia: An Amazing & Fascinating Look at Our State's Teachers, Schools & Students! (Illus.). 1990. PLB 24.95 (*0-7933-1019-9*); pap. 14.95 (*0-7933-1018-0*); computer disk 29.95 (*0-7933-1020-2*) Gallopade Pub Group.
—South Carolina Silly Basketball Sportsmysteries, Vol. 1. (Illus.). 1990. PLB 24.95 (*0-7933-1016-4*); pap. 14.95 (*0-7933-1015-6*); computer disk 29.95 (*0-7933-1017-2*) Gallopade Pub Group.
—South Carolina Silly Basketball Sportsmysteries, Vol. 2. (Illus.). 1990. PLB 24.95 (*0-7933-2009-7*); pap. 14.95 (*0-7933-2010-0*); computer disk 29.95 (*0-7933-2011-9*) Gallopade Pub Group.
—South Carolina Silly Football Sportsmysteries, Vol. 1. (Illus.). 1990. PLB 24.95 (*0-7933-1989-7*); pap. 14.95 (*0-7933-1990-0*); computer disk 29.95 (*0-7933-1991-9*) Gallopade Pub Group.

—South Carolina Silly Football Sportsmysteries, Vol. 2. (Illus.). 1990. PLB 24.95 (*0-7933-1992-7*); pap. 14.95 (*0-7933-1993-5*); computer disk 29.95 (*0-7933-1994-3*) Gallopade Pub Group.
—South Carolina Silly Trivia! (Illus.). 1990. PLB 24.95 (*0-7933-1983-8*); pap. 14.95 (*0-685-54060-X*); computer disk 29.95 (*0-7933-1984-6*) Gallopade Pub Group.
—South Carolina Timeline: A Chronology of South Carolina History, Mystery, Trivia, Legend, Lore & More. (Illus.). (gr. 3-12). 1992. PLB 24.95 (*0-7933-5995-3*); pap. 14.95 (*0-7933-5996-1*); computer disk 29.95 (*0-7933-5997-X*) Gallopade Pub Group.
—South Carolina's (Most Devastating!) Disasters & (Most Calamitous!) Catastrophies! (Illus.). 1990. PLB 24.95 (*0-7933-1007-5*); pap. 14.95 (*0-7933-1006-7*); computer disk 29.95 (*0-7933-1008-3*) Gallopade Pub Group.
—South Carolina's Unsolved Mysteries (& Their "Solutions") Includes Scientific Information & Other Activities for Students. (Illus.). (gr. 3-12). 1992. PLB 24.95 (*0-7933-5842-6*); pap. 14.95 (*0-7933-5843-4*); computer disk 29.95 (*0-7933-5844-2*) Gallopade Pub Group.
—South Dakota & Other State Greats (Biographies) (Illus.). 1990. PLB 24.95 (*0-7933-2038-0*); pap. 14.95 (*0-7933-2039-9*); computer disk 29.95 (*0-7933-2040-2*) Gallopade Pub Group.
—South Dakota Bandits, Bushwackers, Outlaws, Crooks, Devils, Ghosts, Desperadoes & Other Assorted & Sundry Characters! (Illus.). 1990. PLB 24.95 (*0-7933-1034-2*); pap. 14.95 (*0-7933-1033-4*); computer disk 29.95 (*0-7933-1035-0*) Gallopade Pub Group.
—South Dakota Classic Christmas Trivia: Stories, Recipes, Activities, Legends, Lore & More! (Illus.). 1990. PLB 24.95 (*0-7933-1037-7*); pap. 14.95 (*0-7933-1036-9*); computer disk 29.95 (*0-7933-1038-5*) Gallopade Pub Group.
—South Dakota Coastales. (Illus.). 1990. PLB 24.95 (*0-7933-2032-1*); pap. 14.95 (*0-7933-2033-X*); computer disk 29.95 (*0-7933-2034-8*) Gallopade Pub Group.
—South Dakota Coastales! 1992. lib. bdg. 24.95 (*0-7933-7306-9*) Gallopade Pub Group.
—South Dakota "Crinkum-Crankum" A Funny Word Book about Our State. (Illus.). (gr. 3-12). 1992. 24.95 (*0-7933-4931-1*); pap. 14.95 (*0-7933-4932-X*); computer disk 29.95 (*0-7933-4933-8*) Gallopade Pub Group.
—South Dakota Dingbats! Bk. 1: A Fun Book of Games, Stories, Activities & More about Our State That's All in Code! for You to Decipher. (Illus.). (gr. 3-12). 1991. PLB 19.95 (*0-7933-3896-4*); pap. 14.95 (*0-7933-3897-2*); computer disk 29.95 (*0-7933-3898-0*) Gallopade Pub Group.
—South Dakota Festival Fun for Kids! (Illus.). (gr. 3-12). 1991. lib. bdg. 19.95 (*0-7933-4049-7*); pap. 14.95 (*0-7933-4050-0*); disk 29.95 (*0-7933-4051-9*) Gallopade Pub Group.
—The South Dakota Hot Air Balloon Mystery. (Illus.). (gr. 2-9). 1990. 24.95 (*0-7933-2687-7*); pap. 14.95 (*0-7933-2688-5*); computer disk 29.95 (*0-7933-2689-3*) Gallopade Pub Group.
—South Dakota Jeopardy! Answers & Questions about Our State! (Illus.). (gr. 3-12). 1991. PLB 24.95 (*0-7933-4202-3*); pap. 14.95 (*0-7933-4203-1*); computer disk 29.95 (*0-7933-4204-X*) Gallopade Pub Group.
—South Dakota "Jography" A Fun Run Thru Our State! (Illus.). 1990. PLB 24.95 (*0-7933-2015-1*); pap. 14.95 (*0-7933-2016-X*); computer disk 29.95 (*0-7933-2017-8*) Gallopade Pub Group.
—South Dakota Kid's Cookbook: Recipes, How-to, History, Lore & More! (Illus.). 1990. PLB 24.95 (*0-7933-1046-6*); pap. 14.95 (*0-7933-1045-8*); computer disk 29.95 (*0-7933-1047-6*) Gallopade Pub Group.
—The South Dakota Mystery Van Takes Off! Book 1: Handicapped South Dakota Kids Sneak Off on a Big Adventure. (Illus.). (gr. 3-12). 1992. 24.95 (*0-7933-5084-0*); pap. 14.95 (*0-7933-5085-9*); computer disk 29.95 (*0-7933-5086-7*) Gallopade Pub Group.
—South Dakota Quiz Bowl Crash Course! (Illus.). 1990. PLB 24.95 (*0-7933-2029-1*); pap. 14.95 (*0-7933-2030-5*); computer disk 29.95 (*0-7933-2031-3*) Gallopade Pub Group.
—South Dakota Rollercoasters! (Illus.). (gr. 3-12). 1992. PLB 24.95 (*0-7933-5347-5*); pap. 14.95 (*0-7933-5348-3*); computer disk 29.95 (*0-7933-5349-1*) Gallopade Pub Group.
—South Dakota School Trivia: An Amazing & Fascinating Look at Our State's Teachers, Schools & Students! (Illus.). 1990. PLB 24.95 (*0-7933-1043-1*); pap. 14.95 (*0-7933-1042-3*); computer disk 29.95 (*0-7933-1044-X*) Gallopade Pub Group.
—South Dakota Silly Basketball Sportsmysteries, Vol. 1. (Illus.). 1990. PLB 24.95 (*0-7933-1040-7*); pap. 14.95 (*0-7933-1039-3*); computer disk 29.95 (*0-7933-1041-5*) Gallopade Pub Group.
—South Dakota Silly Basketball Sportsmysteries, Vol. 2. (Illus.). 1990. PLB 24.95 (*0-7933-2041-0*); pap. 14.95 (*0-7933-2042-9*); computer disk 29.95 (*0-7933-2043-7*) Gallopade Pub Group.

—South Dakota Silly Football Sportsmysteries, Vol. 1. (Illus.). 1990. PLB 24.95 (*0-7933-2020-8*); pap. 14.95 (*0-7933-2021-6*); computer disk 29.95 (*0-7933-2022-4*) Gallopade Pub Group.
—South Dakota Silly Football Sportsmysteries, Vol. 2. (Illus.). 1990. PLB 24.95 (*0-7933-2023-2*); pap. 14.95 (*0-685-45970-5*); computer disk 29.95 (*0-7933-2025-9*) Gallopade Pub Group.
—South Dakota Silly Trvia! (Illus.). 1990. PLB 24.95 (*0-7933-2012-7*); pap. 14.95 (*0-7933-2013-5*); computer disk 29.95 (*0-7933-2014-3*) Gallopade Pub Group.
—South Dakota Timeline: A Chronology of South Dakota History, Mystery, Trivia, Legend, Lore & More. (Illus.). (gr. 3-12). 1992. PLB 24.95 (*0-7933-5998-8*); pap. 14.95 (*0-7933-5999-6*); computer disk 29.95 (*0-7933-6000-5*) Gallopade Pub Group.
—South Dakota's (Most Devastating!) Disasters & (Most Calamitous!) Catastrophies! (Illus.). 1990. PLB 24.95 (*0-7933-1031-8*); pap. 14.95 (*0-7933-1030-X*); computer disk 29.95 (*0-7933-1032-6*) Gallopade Pub Group.
—South Dakota's Unsolved Mysteries (& Their "Solutions") Includes Scientific Information & Other Activities for Students. (Illus.). (gr. 3-12). 1992. PLB 24.95 (*0-7933-5845-0*); pap. 14.95 (*0-7933-5846-9*); computer disk 29.95 (*0-7933-5847-7*) Gallopade Pub Group.
—State Greats. (gr. 4-9). 1988. 24.95 (*1-55609-254-7*); pap. 14.95 (*0-318-37389-0*); computer disk 29.95 (*1-55609-341-1*) Gallopade Pub Group.
—Stone Mountain Mystery Gamebook. (Illus., Orig.). (gr. 3-9). 1985. pap. 19.95 (*0-935326-80-4*) Gallopade Pub Group.
—The Super Silly Riddles Dingbats Book. (Illus.). (gr. 3-12). 1992. PLB 24.95 (*0-7933-5410-2*); pap. 14.95 (*0-7933-5411-0*); computer disk 29.95 (*0-7933-5412-9*) Gallopade Pub Group.
—The Super Silly Sports Trivia Dingbats Book. (Illus.). (gr. 3-12). 1992. PLB 24.95 (*0-7933-5380-7*); pap. 14.95 (*0-7933-5381-5*); computer disk 29.95 (*0-7933-5382-3*) Gallopade Pub Group.
—The Teddy Bear Company: Economics for Kids. (Illus.). (gr. 4-8). 1983. 14.95 (*0-935326-16-2*); tchr's. ed. o.p. 6.00 (*0-935326-90-1*) Gallopade Pub Group.
—Teddy Bear's Annual Report. (Illus.). (gr. 4-8). 1983. 14.95 (*0-935326-26-X*) Gallopade Pub Group.
—Tennessee & Other State Greats (Biographies) (Illus.). 1990. PLB 24.95 (*0-7933-1055-5*); pap. 14.95 (*0-7933-1054-7*); computer disk 29.95 (*0-7933-1056-3*) Gallopade Pub Group.
—Tennessee Bandits, Bushwackers, Outlaws, Crooks, Devils, Ghosts, Desperadoes & Other Assorted & Sundry Characters! (Illus.). 1990. PLB 24.95 (*0-7933-1058-X*); pap. 14.95 (*0-7933-1057-1*); computer disk 29.95 (*0-7933-1059-8*) Gallopade Pub Group.
—Tennessee Classic Christmas Trivia: Stories, Recipes, Activities, Legends, Lore & More! (Illus.). 1990. PLB 24.95 (*0-7933-1061-X*); pap. 14.95 (*0-7933-1060-1*); computer disk 29.95 (*0-7933-1062-8*) Gallopade Pub Group.
—Tennessee Coastales. (Illus.). 1990. PLB 24.95 (*0-7933-2062-3*); pap. 14.95 (*0-7933-2063-1*); computer disk 29.95 (*0-7933-2064-X*) Gallopade Pub Group.
—Tennessee Coastales! 1992. lib. bdg. 24.95 (*0-7933-7307-7*) Gallopade Pub Group.
—Tennessee "Crinkum-Crankum" A Funny Word Book about Our State. (Illus.). (gr. 3-12). 1992. 24.95 (*0-7933-4934-6*); pap. 14.95 (*0-7933-4935-4*); computer disk 29.95 (*0-7933-4936-2*) Gallopade Pub Group.
—Tennessee Dingbats! Bk. 1: A Fun Book of Games, Stories, Activities & More about Our State That's All in Code! for You to Decipher. (Illus.). (gr. 3-12). 1991. PLB 24.95 (*0-7933-3899-9*); pap. 14.95 (*0-7933-3900-6*); computer disk 29.95 (*0-7933-3901-4*) Gallopade Pub Group.
—Tennessee Festival Fun for Kids! (Illus.). (gr. 3-12). 1991. lib. bdg. 24.95 (*0-7933-4052-7*); pap. 14.95 (*0-7933-4053-5*); disk 29.95 (*0-7933-4054-3*) Gallopade Pub Group.
—The Tennessee Hot Air Balloon Mystery. (Illus.). (gr. 2-9). 1990. 24.95 (*0-7933-2696-6*); pap. 14.95 (*0-7933-2697-4*); computer disk 29.95 (*0-7933-2698-2*) Gallopade Pub Group.
—Tennessee Jeopardy! Answers & Questions about Our State! (Illus.). (gr. 3-12). 1991. PLB 24.95 (*0-7933-4205-8*); pap. 14.95 (*0-7933-4206-6*); computer disk 29.95 (*0-7933-4207-4*) Gallopade Pub Group.
—Tennessee "Jography" A Fun Run Thru Our State! (Illus.). 1990. PLB 24.95 (*0-7933-2046-1*); pap. 14.95 (*1-55609-089-7*); computer disk 29.95 (*0-7933-2047-X*) Gallopade Pub Group.
—Tennessee Kid's Cookbook: Recipes, How-to, History, Lore & More! (Illus.). 1990. PLB 24.95 (*0-7933-1070-9*); pap. 14.95 (*0-7933-1069-5*); computer disk 29.95 (*0-7933-1071-7*) Gallopade Pub Group.
—The Tennessee Mystery Van Takes Off! Book 1: Handicapped Tennessee Kids Sneak Off on a Big Adventure. (Illus.). (gr. 3-12). 1992. 24.95 (*0-7933-5087-5*); pap. 14.95 (*0-7933-5088-3*); computer disk 29.95 (*0-7933-5089-1*) Gallopade Pub Group.

—Tennessee Quiz Bowl Crash Course! (Illus.). 1990. PLB 24.95 (0-7933-2059-3); pap. 14.95 (0-7933-2060-7); computer disk 29.95 (0-7933-2061-5) Gallopade Pub Group.
—Tennessee Rollercoasters! (Illus.). (gr. 3-12). 1992. PLB 24.95 (0-7933-5350-5); pap. 14.95 (0-7933-5351-3); computer disk 29.95 (0-7933-5352-1) Gallopade Pub Group.
—Tennessee School Trivia: An Amazing & Fascinating Look at Our State's Teachers, Schools & Students! (Illus.). 1990. PLB 24.95 (0-7933-1067-9); pap. 14.95 (0-7933-1066-0); computer disk 29.95 (0-7933-1068-7) Gallopade Pub Group.
—Tennessee Silly Basketball Sportsmysteries, Vol. 1. (Illus.). 1990. PLB 24.95 (0-7933-1064-4); pap. 14.95 (0-7933-1063-6); computer disk 29.95 (0-7933-1065-2) Gallopade Pub Group.
—Tennessee Silly Basketball Sportsmysteries, Vol. 2. (Illus.). 1990. PLB 24.95 (0-7933-2071-2); pap. 14.95 (0-7933-2072-0); computer disk 29.95 (0-7933-2073-9) Gallopade Pub Group.
—Tennessee Silly Football Sportsmysteries, Vol. 1. (Illus.). 1990. PLB 24.95 (0-7933-2050-X); pap. 14.95 (0-7933-2051-8); computer disk 29.95 (0-7933-2052-6) Gallopade Pub Group.
—Tennessee Silly Football Sportsmysteries, Vol. 2. (Illus.). 1990. PLB 24.95 (0-7933-2053-4); pap. 14.95 (0-7933-2054-2); computer disk 29.95 (0-7933-2055-0) Gallopade Pub Group.
—Tennessee Silly Trivia! (Illus.). 1990. PLB 24.95 (0-7933-2044-5); pap. 14.95 (1-55609-036-6); computer disk 29.95 (0-7933-2045-3) Gallopade Pub Group.
—Tennessee Timeline: A Chronology of Tennessee History, Mystery, Trivia, Legend, Lore & More. (Illus.). (gr. 3-12). 1992. PLB 24.95 (0-7933-6001-3); pap. 14.95 (0-7933-6002-1); computer disk 29.95 (0-7933-6003-X) Gallopade Pub Group.
—Tennessee's (Most Devastating!) Disasters & (Most Calamitous!) Catastrophies! (Illus.). 1990. PLB 24.95 (0-7933-2068-2); pap. 14.95 (0-7933-2069-0); computer disk 29.95 (0-7933-2070-4) Gallopade Pub Group.
—Tennessee's Unsolved Mysteries (& Their "Solutions") Includes Scientific Information & Other Activities for Students. (Illus.). (gr. 3-12). 1992. PLB 24.95 (0-7933-5848-5); pap. 14.95 (0-7933-5849-3); computer disk 29.95 (0-7933-5850-7) Gallopade Pub Group.
—The Terror & Tombstones Dingbats Book. (Illus.). (gr. 3-12). 1992. PLB 24.95 (0-7933-5401-3); pap. 14.95 (0-7933-5402-1); computer disk 29.95 (0-7933-5403-X) Gallopade Pub Group.
—Texas & Other State Greats (Biographies) (Illus.). 1990. PLB 24.95 (0-7933-2097-6); pap. 14.95 (0-7933-2098-4); computer disk 29.95 (0-7933-2099-2) Gallopade Pub Group.
—Texas Bandits, Bushwackers, Outlaws, Crooks, Devils, Ghosts, Desperadoes & Other Assorted & Sundry Characters! (Illus.). 1990. PLB 24.95 (0-7933-1082-2); pap. 14.95 (0-7933-1081-4); computer disk 29.95 (0-7933-1083-0) Gallopade Pub Group.
—Texas Classic Christmas Trivia: Stories, Recipes, Activities, Legends, Lore & More! (Illus.). 1990. PLB 24.95 (0-7933-1085-7); pap. 14.95 (0-7933-1084-9); computer disk 29.95 (0-7933-1086-5) Gallopade Pub Group.
—Texas Coastales. (Illus.). 1990. PLB 24.95 (0-7933-2092-5); pap. 14.95 (1-55609-121-4); computer disk 29.95 (0-7933-2093-3) Gallopade Pub Group.
—Texas Coastales! 1992. lib. bdg. 24.95 (0-7933-7308-5) Gallopade Pub Group.
—Texas "Crinkum-Crankum" A Funny Word Book about Our State. (Illus.). (gr. 3-12). 1992. 24.95 (0-7933-4937-0); pap. 14.95 (0-7933-4938-9); computer disk 29.95 (0-7933-4939-7) Gallopade Pub Group.
—Texas Dingbats! Bk. 1: A Fun Book of Games, Stories, Activities & More about Our State That's All in Code! for You to Decipher. (Illus.). (gr. 3-12). 1991. PLB 24.95 (0-7933-3902-2); pap. 14.95 (0-7933-3903-0); computer disk 29.95 (0-7933-3904-9) Gallopade Pub Group.
—Texas Festival Fun for Kids! (Illus.). (gr. 3-12). 1991. lib. bdg. 24.95 (0-7933-4055-1); pap. 14.95 (0-7933-4056-X); disk 29.95 (0-7933-4057-8) Gallopade Pub Group.
—The Texas Hot Air Balloon Mystery. (Illus.). (gr. 2-9). 1990. 24.95 (0-7933-2705-9); pap. 14.95 (0-7933-2706-7); computer disk 29.95 (0-7933-2707-5) Gallopade Pub Group.
—Texas Jeopardy! Answers & Questions about Our State! (Illus.). (gr. 3-12). 1991. PLB 24.95 (0-7933-4208-2); pap. 14.95 (0-7933-4209-0); computer disk 29.95 (0-7933-4210-4) Gallopade Pub Group.
—Texas "Jography" A Fun Run Thru Our State! (Illus.). 1990. PLB 24.95 (0-7933-2076-3); pap. 14.95 (1-55609-087-0); computer disk 29.95 (0-7933-2077-1) Gallopade Pub Group.
—Texas Kid's Cookbook: Recipes, How-To, History, Lore & More! (Illus.). 1990. PLB 24.95 (0-7933-1094-6); pap. 14.95 (0-7933-1093-8); computer disk 29.95 (0-7933-1095-4) Gallopade Pub Group.

—The Texas Mystery Van Takes Off! Book 1: Handicapped Texas Kids Sneak Off on a Big Adventure. (Illus.). (gr. 3-12). 1992. 24.95 (0-7933-5090-5); pap. 14.95 (0-7933-5091-3); computer disk 29.95 (0-7933-5092-1) Gallopade Pub Group.
—Texas Quiz Bowl Crash Course! (Illus.). 1990. PLB 24.95 (0-7933-2089-5); pap. 14.95 (0-7933-2090-9); computer disk 29.95 (0-7933-2091-7) Gallopade Pub Group.
—Texas Rollercoasters! (Illus.). (gr. 3-12). 1992. PLB 24.95 (0-7933-5353-X); pap. 14.95 (0-7933-5354-8); computer disk 29.95 (0-7933-5355-6) Gallopade Pub Group.
—Texas School Trivia: An Amazing & Fascinating Look at Our State's Teachers, Schools & Students! (Illus.). 1990. PLB 24.95 (0-7933-1091-1); pap. 14.95 (0-7933-1090-3); computer disk 29.95 (0-7933-1092-X) Gallopade Pub Group.
—Texas Silly Basketball Sportsmysteries, Vol. 1. (Illus.). 1990. PLB 24.95 (0-7933-1088-1); pap. 14.95 (0-7933-1087-3); computer disk 29.95 (0-7933-1089-X) Gallopade Pub Group.
—Texas Silly Basketball Sportsmysteries, Vol. 2. (Illus.). 1990. PLB 24.95 (0-7933-2100-X); pap. 14.95 (0-7933-2101-8); computer disk 29.95 (0-7933-2102-6) Gallopade Pub Group.
—Texas Silly Football Sportsmysteries, Vol. 1. (Illus.). 1990. PLB 24.95 (0-7933-2080-1); pap. 14.95 (0-7933-2081-X); computer disk 29.95 (0-7933-2082-8) Gallopade Pub Group.
—Texas Silly Football Sportsmysteries, Vol. 2. (Illus.). 1990. PLB 24.95 (0-7933-2083-6); pap. 14.95 (0-7933-2084-4); computer disk 29.95 (0-7933-2085-2) Gallopade Pub Group.
—Texas Silly Trivia! (Illus.). 1990. PLB 24.95 (0-7933-2074-7); pap. 14.95 (1-55609-081-1); computer disk 29.95 (0-7933-2075-5) Gallopade Pub Group.
—Texas Timeline: A Chronology of Texas History, Mystery, Trivia, Legend, Lore & More. (Illus.). (gr. 3-12). 1992. PLB 24.95 (0-7933-6004-8); pap. 14.95 (0-7933-6005-6); computer disk 29.95 (0-7933-6006-4) Gallopade Pub Group.
—Texas's (Most Devastating!) Disasters & (Most Calamitous!) Catastrophies! (Illus.). 1990. PLB 24.95 (0-7933-1079-2); pap. 14.95 (0-7933-1078-4); computer disk 29.95 (0-7933-1080-6) Gallopade Pub Group.
—Texas's Unsolved Mysteries (& Their "Solutions") Includes Scientific Information & Other Activities for Students. (Illus.). (gr. 3-12). 1992. PLB 24.95 (0-7933-5851-5); pap. 14.95 (0-7933-5852-3); computer disk 29.95 (0-7933-5853-1) Gallopade Pub Group.
—Thirty Days Has September: Calendar Trivia & Activities for Kids. (gr. 3-9). 1990. 24.95 (0-7933-0015-0); pap. 14.95 (0-7933-0016-9); computer disk 29.95 (0-7933-0017-7) Gallopade Pub Group.
—Those Whose Names Were Terrible. Rhodes, Priscilla, illus. (Orig.). (gr. 4-8). 1983. pap. 14.95 (0-935326-48-0) Gallopade Pub Group.
—Tryon Palace Mystery. (Orig.). (gr. 3-12). 1986. 24.95 (1-55609-193-1); pap. 14.95 (0-935326-58-8) Gallopade Pub Group.
—Typing in Ten Minutes: On Any Keyboard - At Any Age. (Illus.). (gr. k-12). 1983. 24.95 (1-55609-194-X); pap. 14.95 (0-935326-12-X) Gallopade Pub Group.
—Tyrannosaurus & Other Wrecks: Fossil Trivia for Kids. (Illus., Orig.). (gr. 2 up). 1986. 24.95 (1-55609-166-4); pap. 14.95 (0-935326-56-1) Gallopade Pub Group.
—U. S. A. Jography: A Fun Run Thru the United States, Vol. II. (Illus.). (gr. k-12). 1989. 60p. (gr. k-12). PLB 24.95 (1-55609-301-2); pap. 14.95 (1-55609-300-4); computer disk 29.95 (1-55609-302-0) Gallopade Pub Group.
—Uncle Rebus: Alabama Picture Stories for Computer Kids. (Illus.). (gr. k-3). 1992. PLB 24.95 (0-7933-4504-9); pap. 14.95 (0-7933-4505-7); disk 29.95 (0-7933-4506-5) Gallopade Pub Group.
—Uncle Rebus: Alaska Picture Stories for Computer Kids. (Illus.). (gr. k-3). 1992. PLB 24.95 (0-7933-4507-3); pap. 14.95 (0-7933-4508-1); disk 29.95 (0-7933-4509-X) Gallopade Pub Group.
—Uncle Rebus: Arizona Picture Stories for Computer Kids. (Illus.). (gr. k-3). 1992. PLB 24.95 (0-7933-4510-3); pap. 14.95 (0-7933-4511-1); disk 29.95 (0-7933-4512-X) Gallopade Pub Group.
—Uncle Rebus: Arkansas Picture Stories for Computer Kids. (Illus.). (gr. k-3). 1992. PLB 24.95 (0-7933-4513-8); pap. 14.95 (0-7933-4514-6); disk 29.95 (0-7933-4515-4) Gallopade Pub Group.
—Uncle Rebus: California Picture Stories for Computer Kids. (Illus.). (gr. k-3). 1992. PLB 24.95 (0-7933-4516-2); pap. 14.95 (0-7933-4517-0); disk 29.95 (0-7933-4518-9) Gallopade Pub Group.
—Uncle Rebus: Colorado Picture Stories for Computer Kids. (Illus.). (gr. k-3). 1992. PLB 24.95 (0-7933-4519-7); pap. 14.95 (0-7933-4520-0); disk 29.95 (0-7933-4521-9) Gallopade Pub Group.
—Uncle Rebus: Connecticut Picture Stories for Computer Kids. (Illus.). (gr. k-3). 1992. PLB 24.95 (0-7933-4522-7); pap. 14.95 (0-7933-4523-5); disk 29.95 (0-7933-4524-3) Gallopade Pub Group.

—Uncle Rebus: Delaware Picture Stories for Computer Kids. (Illus.). (gr. k-3). 1992. PLB 24.95 (0-7933-4525-1); pap. 14.95 (0-7933-4526-X); disk 29.95 (0-7933-4527-8) Gallopade Pub Group.
—Uncle Rebus: Florida Picture Stories for Computer Kids. (Illus.). (gr. k-3). 1992. PLB 24.95 (0-7933-4528-6); pap. 14.95 (0-7933-4529-4); disk 29.95 (0-7933-4530-8) Gallopade Pub Group.
—Uncle Rebus: Georgia Picture Stories for Computer Kids. (Illus.). (gr. k-3). 1992. PLB 24.95 (0-7933-4531-6); pap. 14.95 (0-7933-4532-4); disk 29.95 (0-7933-4533-2) Gallopade Pub Group.
—Uncle Rebus: Hawaii Picture Stories for Computer Kids. (Illus.). (gr. k-3). 1992. PLB 24.95 (0-7933-4534-0); pap. 14.95 (0-7933-4535-9); disk 29.95 (0-7933-4536-7) Gallopade Pub Group.
—Uncle Rebus: Idaho Picture Stories for Computer Kids. (Illus.). (gr. k-3). 1992. PLB 24.95 (0-7933-4537-5); pap. 14.95 (0-7933-4538-3); disk 29.95 (0-7933-4539-1) Gallopade Pub Group.
—Uncle Rebus: Illinois Picture Stories for Computer Kids. (Illus.). (gr. k-3). 1992. PLB 24.95 (0-7933-4540-5); pap. 14.95 (0-7933-4541-3); disk 29.95 (0-7933-4542-1) Gallopade Pub Group.
—Uncle Rebus: Indiana Picture Stories for Computer Kids. (Illus.). (gr. k-3). 1992. PLB 24.95 (0-7933-4543-X); pap. 14.95 (0-7933-4544-8); disk 29.95 (0-7933-4545-6) Gallopade Pub Group.
—Uncle Rebus: Iowa Picture Stories for Computer Kids. (Illus.). (gr. k-3). 1992. PLB 24.95 (0-7933-4546-4); pap. 14.95 (0-7933-4547-2); disk 29.95 (0-7933-4548-0) Gallopade Pub Group.
—Uncle Rebus: Kansas Picture Stories for Computer Kids. (Illus.). (gr. k-3). 1992. PLB 24.95 (0-7933-4549-9); pap. 14.95 (0-7933-4550-2); disk 29.95 (0-7933-4551-0) Gallopade Pub Group.
—Uncle Rebus: Kentucky Picture Stories for Computer Kids. (Illus.). (gr. k-3). 1992. PLB 24.95 (0-7933-4552-9); pap. 14.95 (0-7933-4553-7); disk 29.95 (0-7933-4554-5) Gallopade Pub Group.
—Uncle Rebus: Louisiana Picture Stories for Computer Kids. (Illus.). (gr. k-3). 1992. PLB 24.95 (0-7933-4555-3); pap. 14.95 (0-7933-4556-1); disk 29.95 (0-7933-4557-X) Gallopade Pub Group.
—Uncle Rebus: Maine Picture Stories for Computer Kids. (Illus.). (gr. k-3). 1992. PLB 24.95 (0-7933-4558-8); pap. 14.95 (0-7933-4559-6); disk 29.95 (0-7933-4560-X) Gallopade Pub Group.
—Uncle Rebus: Maryland Picture Stories for Computer Kids. (Illus.). (gr. k-3). 1992. PLB 24.95 (0-7933-4561-8); pap. 14.95 (0-7933-4562-6); disk 29.95 (0-7933-4563-4) Gallopade Pub Group.
—Uncle Rebus: Massachusetts Picture Stories for Computer Kids. (Illus.). (gr. k-3). 1992. PLB 24.95 (0-7933-4564-2); pap. 14.95 (0-7933-4565-0); disk 29.95 (0-7933-4566-9) Gallopade Pub Group.
—Uncle Rebus: Michigan Picture Stories for Computer Kids. (Illus.). (gr. k-3). 1992. PLB 24.95 (0-7933-4567-7); pap. 14.95 (0-7933-4568-5); disk 29.95 (0-7933-4569-3) Gallopade Pub Group.
—Uncle Rebus: Minnesota Picture Stories for Computer Kids. (Illus.). (gr. k-3). 1992. PLB 24.95 (0-7933-4570-7); pap. 14.95 (0-7933-4571-5); disk 29.95 (0-7933-4572-3) Gallopade Pub Group.
—Uncle Rebus: Mississippi Picture Stories for Computer Kids. (Illus.). (gr. k-3). 1992. PLB 24.95 (0-7933-4573-1); pap. 14.95 (0-7933-4574-X); disk 29.95 (0-7933-4575-8) Gallopade Pub Group.
—Uncle Rebus: Missouri Picture Stories for Computer Kids. (Illus.). (gr. k-3). 1992. PLB 24.95 (0-7933-4576-6); pap. 14.95 (0-7933-4577-4); disk 29.95 (0-7933-4578-2) Gallopade Pub Group.
—Uncle Rebus: Montana Picture Stories for Computer Kids. (Illus.). (gr. k-3). 1992. PLB 24.95 (0-7933-4579-0); pap. 14.95 (0-7933-4580-4); disk 29.95 (0-7933-4581-2) Gallopade Pub Group.
—Uncle Rebus: Nebraska Picture Stories for Computer Kids. (Illus.). (gr. k-3). 1992. PLB 24.95 (0-7933-4582-0); pap. 14.95 (0-7933-4583-9); disk 29.95 (0-7933-4584-7) Gallopade Pub Group.
—Uncle Rebus: Nevada Picture Stories for Computer Kids. (Illus.). (gr. k-3). 1992. PLB 24.95 (0-7933-4585-5); pap. 14.95 (0-7933-4586-3); disk 29.95 (0-7933-4587-1) Gallopade Pub Group.
—Uncle Rebus: New Hampshire Picture Stories for Computer Kids. (Illus.). (gr. k-3). 1992. PLB 24.95 (0-7933-4588-X); pap. 14.95 (0-7933-4589-8); disk 29.95 (0-7933-4590-1) Gallopade Pub Group.
—Uncle Rebus: New Jersey Picture Stories for Computer Kids. (Illus.). (gr. k-3). 1992. PLB 24.95 (0-7933-4591-X); pap. 14.95 (0-7933-4592-8); disk 29.95 (0-7933-4593-6) Gallopade Pub Group.
—Uncle Rebus: New Mexico Picture Stories for Computer Kids. (Illus.). (gr. k-3). 1992. PLB 24.95 (0-7933-4594-4); pap. 14.95 (0-7933-4595-2); disk 29.95 (0-7933-4596-0) Gallopade Pub Group.
—Uncle Rebus: New York Picture Stories for Computer Kids. (Illus.). (gr. k-3). 1992. PLB 24.95 (0-7933-4597-9); pap. 14.95 (0-7933-4598-7); disk 29.95 (0-7933-4599-5) Gallopade Pub Group.
—Uncle Rebus: North Carolina Picture Stories for Computer Kids. (Illus.). (gr. k-3). 1992. PLB 24.95 (0-7933-4600-2); pap. 14.95 (0-7933-4601-0); disk 29.95 (0-7933-4602-9) Gallopade Pub Group.
—Uncle Rebus: North Dakota Picture Stories for Computer Kids. (Illus.). (gr. k-3). 1992. PLB 24.95 (0-7933-4603-7); pap. 14.95 (0-7933-4604-5); disk 29.95 (0-7933-4605-3) Gallopade Pub Group.

—Uncle Rebus: Ohio Picture Stories for Computer Kids. (Illus.). (gr. k-3). 1992. PLB 24.95 (0-7933-4606-1); pap. 14.95 (0-7933-4607-X); disk 29.95 (0-7933-4608-8) Gallopade Pub Group.

—Uncle Rebus: Oklahoma Picture Stories for Computer Kids. (Illus.). (gr. k-3). 1992. PLB 24.95 (0-7933-4609-6); pap. 14.95 (0-7933-4610-X); disk 29.95 (0-7933-4611-8) Gallopade Pub Group.

—Uncle Rebus: Oregon Picture Stories for Computer Kids. (Illus.). (gr. k-3). 1992. PLB 24.95 (0-7933-4612-6); pap. 14.95 (0-7933-4613-4); disk 29.95 (0-7933-4614-2) Gallopade Pub Group.

—Uncle Rebus: Pennsylvania Picture Stories for Computer Kids. (Illus.). (gr. k-3). 1992. PLB 24.95 (0-7933-4615-0); pap. 14.95 (0-7933-4616-9); disk 29.95 (0-7933-4617-7) Gallopade Pub Group.

—Uncle Rebus: Rhode Island Picture Stories for Computer Kids. (Illus.). (gr. k-3). 1992. PLB 24.95 (0-7933-4618-5); pap. 14.95 (0-7933-4619-3); disk 29.95 (0-7933-4620-7) Gallopade Pub Group.

—Uncle Rebus: South Carolina Picture Stories for Computer Kids. (Illus.). (gr. k-3). 1992. PLB 24.95 (0-7933-4621-5); pap. 14.95 (0-7933-4622-3); disk 29.95 (0-7933-4623-1) Gallopade Pub Group.

—Uncle Rebus: South Dakota Picture Stories for Computer Kids. (Illus.). (gr. k-3). 1992. PLB 24.95 (0-7933-4624-X); pap. 14.95 (0-7933-4625-8); disk 29.95 (0-7933-4626-6) Gallopade Pub Group.

—Uncle Rebus: Tennessee Picture Stories for Computer Kids. (Illus.). (gr. k-3). 1992. PLB 24.95 (0-7933-4627-4); pap. 14.95 (0-7933-4628-2); disk 29.95 (0-7933-4629-0) Gallopade Pub Group.

—Uncle Rebus: Texas Picture Stories for Computer Kids. (Illus.). (gr. k-3). 1992. PLB 24.95 (0-7933-4630-4); pap. 14.95 (0-7933-4631-2); disk 29.95 (0-7933-4632-0) Gallopade Pub Group.

—Uncle Rebus: Utah Picture Stories for Computer Kids. (Illus.). (gr. k-3). 1992. PLB 24.95 (0-7933-4633-9); pap. 14.95 (0-7933-4634-7); disk 29.95 (0-7933-4635-5) Gallopade Pub Group.

—Uncle Rebus: Vermont Picture Stories for Computer Kids. (Illus.). (gr. k-3). 1992. PLB 24.95 (0-7933-4636-3); pap. 14.95 (0-7933-4637-1); disk 29.95 (0-7933-4638-X) Gallopade Pub Group.

—Uncle Rebus: Virginia Picture Stories for Computer Kids. (Illus.). (gr. k-3). 1992. PLB 24.95 (0-7933-4639-8); pap. 14.95 (0-7933-4640-1); disk 29.95 (0-7933-4641-X) Gallopade Pub Group.

—Uncle Rebus: Washington, DC Picture Stories for Computer Kids. (Illus.). (gr. k-3). 1992. PLB 24.95 (0-7933-4645-2); pap. 14.95 (0-7933-4646-0); disk 29.95 (0-7933-4647-9) Gallopade Pub Group.

—Uncle Rebus: Washington Picture Stories for Computer Kids. (Illus.). (gr. k-3). 1992. PLB 24.95 (0-7933-4642-8); pap. 14.95 (0-7933-4643-6); disk 29.95 (0-7933-4644-4) Gallopade Pub Group.

—Uncle Rebus: West Virginia Picture Stories for Computer Kids. (Illus.). (gr. k-3). 1992. PLB 24.95 (0-7933-4648-7); pap. 14.95 (0-7933-4649-5); disk 29.95 (0-7933-4650-9) Gallopade Pub Group.

—Uncle Rebus: Wisconsin Picture Stories for Computer Kids. (Illus.). (gr. k-3). 1992. PLB 24.95 (0-7933-4651-7); pap. 14.95 (0-7933-4652-5); disk 29.95 (0-7933-4653-3) Gallopade Pub Group.

—Uncle Rebus: Wyoming Picture Stories for Computer Kids. (Illus.). (gr. k-3). 1992. PLB 24.95 (0-7933-4654-1); pap. 14.95 (0-7933-4655-X); disk 29.95 (0-7933-4656-8) Gallopade Pub Group.

—Utah & Other State Greats (Biographies) (Illus.). 1990. PLB 24.95 (0-7933-2129-8); pap. 14.95 (0-7933-2130-1); computer disk 29.95 (0-7933-2131-X) Gallopade Pub Group.

—Utah Bandits, Bushwackers, Outlaws, Crooks, Devils, Ghosts, Desperadoes & Other Assorted & Sundry Characters! (Illus.). 1990. PLB 24.95 (0-7933-1106-3); pap. 14.95 (0-685-45955-1); computer disk 29.95 (0-7933-1107-1) Gallopade Pub Group.

—Utah Classic Christmas Trivia: Stories, Recipes, Activities, Legends, Lore & More! (Illus.). 1990. PLB 24.95 (0-7933-1109-8); pap. 14.95 (0-7933-1108-X); computer disk 29.95 (0-7933-1110-1) Gallopade Pub Group.

—Utah Coastales. (Illus.). 1990. PLB 24.95 (0-7933-2123-9); pap. 14.95 (0-7933-2124-7); computer disk 29.95 (0-685-45954-3) Gallopade Pub Group.

—Utah Coastales! 1992. lib. bdg. 24.95 (0-7933-7309-3) Gallopade Pub Group.

—Utah "Crinkum-Crankum" A Funny Word Book about Our State. (Illus.). (gr. 3-12). 1992. 24.95 (0-7933-4940-0); pap. 14.95 (0-7933-4941-9); computer disk 29.95 (0-7933-4942-7) Gallopade Pub Group.

—Utah Dingbats! Bk. 1: A Fun Book of Games, Stories, Activities & More about Our State That's All in Code! for You to Decipher. (Illus.). (gr. 3-12). 1991. PLB 24.95 (0-7933-3905-7); pap. 14.95 (0-7933-3906-5); computer disk 29.95 (0-7933-3907-3) Gallopade Pub Group.

—Utah Festival Fun for Kids! (Illus.). (gr. 3-12). 1991. PLB 24.95 (0-7933-4058-6); pap. 14.95 (0-7933-4059-4); disk 29.95 (0-7933-4060-8) Gallopade Pub Group.

—The Utah Hot Air Balloon Mystery. (Illus.). (gr. 2-9). 1990. 24.95 (0-7933-2714-8); pap. 14.95 (0-7933-2715-6); computer disk 29.95 (0-7933-2716-4) Gallopade Pub Group.

—Utah Jeopardy! Answers & Questions about Our State! (Illus.). (gr. 3-12). 1991. PLB 24.95 (0-7933-4211-2); pap. 14.95 (0-7933-4212-0); computer disk 29.95 (0-7933-4213-9) Gallopade Pub Group.

—Utah "Jography" A Fun Run Thru Our State! (Illus.). 1990. PLB 24.95 (0-7933-2106-9); pap. 14.95 (0-7933-2107-7); computer disk 29.95 (0-7933-2108-5) Gallopade Pub Group.

—Utah Kid's Cookbook: Recipes, How-to, History, Lore & More! (Illus.). 1990. PLB 24.95 (0-7933-1118-7); pap. 14.95 (0-7933-1117-9); computer disk 29.95 (0-7933-1119-5) Gallopade Pub Group.

—The Utah Mystery Van Takes Off! Book 1: Handicapped Utah Kids Sneak Off on a Big Adventure. (Illus.). (gr. 3-12). 1992. 24.95 (0-7933-5093-X); pap. 14.95 (0-7933-5094-8); computer disk 29.95 (0-7933-5095-6) Gallopade Pub Group.

—Utah Quiz Bowl Crash Course! (Illus.). 1990. PLB 24.95 (0-7933-2120-4); pap. 14.95 (0-7933-2121-2); computer disk 29.95 (0-7933-2122-0) Gallopade Pub Group.

—Utah Rollercoasters! (Illus.). (gr. 3-12). 1992. PLB 24.95 (0-7933-5356-4); pap. 14.95 (0-7933-5357-2); computer disk 29.95 (0-7933-5358-0) Gallopade Pub Group.

—Utah School Trivia: An Amazing & Fascinating Look at Our State's Teachers, Schools & Students! (Illus.). 1990. PLB 24.95 (0-7933-1115-2); pap. 14.95 (0-7933-1114-4); computer disk 29.95 (0-7933-1116-0) Gallopade Pub Group.

—Utah Silly Basketball Sportsmysteries, Vol. 1. (Illus.). 1990. PLB 24.95 (0-7933-1112-8); pap. 14.95 (0-7933-1111-X); computer disk 29.95 (0-7933-1113-6) Gallopade Pub Group.

—Utah Silly Basketball Sportsmysteries, Vol. 2. (Illus.). 1990. PLB 24.95 (0-7933-2132-8); pap. 14.95 (0-7933-2133-6); computer disk 29.95 (0-7933-2134-4) Gallopade Pub Group.

—Utah Silly Football Sportsmysteries, Vol. 1. (Illus.). 1990. PLB 24.95 (0-7933-2111-5); pap. 14.95 (0-7933-2112-3); computer disk 29.95 (0-7933-2113-1) Gallopade Pub Group.

—Utah Silly Football Sportsmysteries, Vol. 2. (Illus.). 1990. PLB 24.95 (0-7933-2114-X); pap. 14.95 (0-7933-2115-8); computer disk 29.95 (0-7933-2116-6) Gallopade Pub Group.

—Utah Silly Trivia! (Illus.). 1990. PLB 24.95 (0-7933-2103-4); pap. 14.95 (0-7933-2104-2); computer disk 29.95 (0-7933-2105-0) Gallopade Pub Group.

—Utah Timeline: A Chronology of Utah History, Mystery, Trivia, Legend, Lore & More. (Illus.). (gr. 3-12). 1992. PLB 24.95 (0-7933-6007-2); pap. 14.95 (0-7933-6008-0); computer disk 29.95 (0-7933-6009-9) Gallopade Pub Group.

—Utah's (Most Devastating!) Disasters & (Most Calamitous!) Catastrophies! (Illus.). 1990. PLB 24.95 (0-7933-1103-9); pap. 14.95 (0-7933-1102-0) (0-7933-1104-7) Gallopade Pub Group.

—Utah's Unsolved Mysteries (& Their "Solutions") Includes Scientific Information & Other Activities for Students. (Illus.). (gr. 3-12). 1992. PLB 24.95 (0-7933-5854-X); pap. 14.95 (0-7933-5855-8); computer disk 29.95 (0-7933-5856-6) Gallopade Pub Group.

—Vermont & Other State Greats (Biographies) (Illus.). 1990. PLB 24.95 (0-7933-2161-1); pap. 14.95 (0-7933-2162-X); computer disk 29.95 (0-7933-2163-8) Gallopade Pub Group.

—Vermont Bandits, Bushwackers, Outlaws, Crooks, Devils, Ghosts, Desperadoes & Other Assorted & Sundry Characters! (Illus.). 1990. PLB 24.95 (0-7933-1130-6); pap. 14.95 (0-7933-1129-2) (0-7933-1131-4) Gallopade Pub Group.

—Vermont Classic Christmas Trivia: Stories, Recipes, Activities, Legends, Lore & More! (Illus.). 1990. PLB 24.95 (0-7933-1133-0); pap. 14.95 (0-7933-1132-2); computer disk 29.95 (0-7933-1134-9) Gallopade Pub Group.

—Vermont Coastales. (Illus.). 1990. PLB 24.95 (0-7933-2155-7); pap. 14.95 (0-7933-2156-5); computer disk 29.95 (0-7933-2157-3) Gallopade Pub Group.

—Vermont Coastales! 1992. lib. bdg. 24.95 (0-7933-7310-7) Gallopade Pub Group.

—Vermont "Crinkum-Crankum" A Funny Word Book about Our State. (Illus.). (gr. 3-12). 1992. 24.95 (0-7933-4943-5); pap. 14.95 (0-7933-4944-3); computer disk 29.95 (0-7933-4945-1) Gallopade Pub Group.

—Vermont Dingbats! Bk. 1: A Fun Book of Games, Stories, Activities & More about Our State That's All in Code! for You to Decipher. (Illus.). (gr. 3-12). 1991. PLB 24.95 (0-7933-3908-1); pap. 14.95 (0-7933-3909-X); computer disk 29.95 (0-7933-3910-3) Gallopade Pub Group.

—Vermont Festival Fun for Kids! (Illus.). (gr. 3-12). 1991. lib. bdg. 24.95 (0-7933-4061-6); pap. 14.95 (0-7933-4062-4); disk 29.95 (0-7933-4063-2) Gallopade Pub Group.

—The Vermont Hot Air Balloon Mystery. (Illus.). (gr. 2-9). 1990. 24.95 (0-7933-2723-7); pap. 14.95 (0-7933-2724-5); computer disk 29.95 (0-7933-2725-3) Gallopade Pub Group.

—Vermont Jeopardy! Answers & Questions about Our State! (Illus.). (gr. 3-12). 1991. PLB 24.95 (0-7933-4214-7); pap. 14.95 (0-7933-4215-5); computer disk 29.95 (0-7933-4216-3) Gallopade Pub Group.

—Vermont "Jography" A Fun Run Thru Our State! (Illus.). 1990. PLB 24.95 (0-7933-2138-7); pap. 14.95 (0-7933-2139-5); computer disk 29.95 (0-7933-2140-9) Gallopade Pub Group.

—Vermont Kids' Cookbook: Recipes, How-to, History, Lore & More! (Illus.). 1990. PLB 24.95 (0-7933-1142-X); pap. 14.95 (0-685-45957-8); computer disk 29.95 (0-7933-1143-8) Gallopade Pub Group.

—The Vermont Mystery Van Takes Off! Book 1: Handicapped Vermont Kids Sneak Off on a Big Adventure. (Illus.). (gr. 3-12). 1992. 24.95 (0-7933-5096-4); pap. 14.95 (0-7933-5097-2); computer disk 29.95 (0-7933-5098-0) Gallopade Pub Group.

—Vermont Quiz Bowl Crash Course! (Illus.). 1990. PLB 24.95 (0-7933-2152-2); pap. 14.95 (0-7933-2153-0); computer disk 29.95 (0-7933-2154-9) Gallopade Pub Group.

—Vermont Rollercoasters! (Illus.). (gr. 3-12). 1992. PLB 24.95 (0-7933-5359-9); pap. 14.95 (0-7933-5360-2); computer disk 29.95 (0-7933-5361-0) Gallopade Pub Group.

—Vermont School Trivia: An Amazing & Fascinating Look at Our State's Teachers, Schools & Students! (Illus.). 1990. PLB 24.95 (0-7933-1139-X); pap. 14.95 (0-7933-1138-1); computer disk 29.95 (0-7933-1140-3) Gallopade Pub Group.

—Vermont Silly Basketball Sportsmysteries, Vol. 1. (Illus.). 1990. PLB 24.95 (0-7933-1136-5); pap. 14.95 (0-7933-1135-7); computer disk 29.95 (0-7933-1137-3) Gallopade Pub Group.

—Vermont Silly Basketball Sportsmysteries, Vol. 2. (Illus.). 1990. PLB 24.95 (0-7933-2164-6); pap. 14.95 (0-7933-2165-4); 29.95 (0-7933-2166-2) Gallopade Pub Group.

—Vermont Silly Football Sportsmysteries, Vol. 1. (Illus.). 1990. PLB 24.95 (0-7933-2143-3); pap. 14.95 (0-7933-2144-1); computer disk 29.95 (0-7933-2145-X) Gallopade Pub Group.

—Vermont Silly Football Sportsmysteries, Vol. 2. (Illus.). 1990. PLB 24.95 (0-685-45956-X); pap. 14.95 (0-7933-2147-6); computer disk 29.95 (0-7933-2148-4) Gallopade Pub Group.

—Vermont Silly Trivia! (Illus.). 1990. PLB 24.95 (0-7933-2135-2); pap. 14.95 (0-7933-2136-0); computer disk 29.95 (0-7933-2137-9) Gallopade Pub Group.

—Vermont Timeline: A Chronology of Vermont History, Mystery, Trivia, Legend, Lore & More. (Illus.). (gr. 3-12). 1992. PLB 24.95 (0-7933-6010-2); pap. 14.95 (0-7933-6011-0); computer disk 29.95 (0-7933-6012-9) Gallopade Pub Group.

—Vermont's (Most Devastating!) Disasters & (Most Calamitous!) Catastrophies! (Illus.). 1990. PLB 24.95 (0-7933-1127-6); pap. 14.95 (0-7933-1126-8); computer disk 29.95 (0-7933-1128-4) Gallopade Pub Group.

—Vermont's Unsolved Mysteries (& Their "Solutions") Includes Scientific Information & Other Activities for Students. (Illus.). (gr. 3-12). 1992. PLB 24.95 (0-7933-5857-4); pap. 14.95 (0-7933-5858-2); computer disk 29.95 (0-7933-5859-0) Gallopade Pub Group.

—Virginia & Other State Greats (Biographies) (Illus.). 1990. PLB 24.95 (0-7933-2190-5); pap. 14.95 (0-7933-2191-3); computer disk 29.95 (0-7933-2192-1) Gallopade Pub Group.

—Virginia Bandits, Bushwackers, Outlaws, Crooks, Devils, Ghosts, Desperadoes & Other Assorted & Sundry Characters! (Illus.). 1990. PLB 24.95 (0-7933-1154-3); pap. 14.95 (0-7933-1153-5); computer disk 29.95 (0-7933-1155-1) Gallopade Pub Group.

—Virginia Classic Christmas Trivia: Stories, Recipes, Activities, Legends, Lore & More. (Illus.). 1990. PLB 24.95 (0-7933-1157-8); pap. 14.95 (0-7933-1156-X); computer disk 29.95 (0-7933-1158-6) Gallopade Pub Group.

—Virginia Coastales. (Illus.). 1990. PLB 24.95 (0-685-45962-4); pap. 14.95 (1-55609-116-8); computer disk 29.95 (0-7933-2186-7) Gallopade Pub Group.

—Virginia Coastales! 1992. lib. bdg. 24.95 (0-7933-7311-5) Gallopade Pub Group.

—Virginia "Crinkum-Crankum" A Funny Word Book about Our State. (Illus.). (gr. 3-12). 1992. 24.95 (0-7933-4946-X); pap. 14.95 (0-7933-4947-8); computer disk 29.95 (0-7933-4948-6) Gallopade Pub Group.

—Virginia Dingbats! Bk. 1: A Fun Book of Games, Stories, Activities & More about Our State That's All in Code! for You to Decipher. (Illus.). (gr. 3-12). 1991. PLB 24.95 (0-7933-3911-1); pap. 14.95 (0-7933-3912-X); computer disk 29.95 (0-7933-3913-8) Gallopade Pub Group.

—Virginia Festival Fun for Kids! (Illus.). (gr. 3-12). 1991. lib. bdg. 24.95 (0-7933-4064-0); pap. 14.95 (0-7933-4065-9); disk 29.95 (0-685-41938-X) Gallopade Pub Group.

—The Virginia Hot Air Balloon Mystery. (Illus.). (gr. 2-9). 1990. 24.95 (0-7933-2732-6); pap. 14.95 (0-7933-2733-4); computer disk 29.95 (0-7933-2734-2) Gallopade Pub Group.

—Virginia Jeopardy! Answers & Questions about Our State! (Illus.). (gr. 3-12). 1991. PLB 24.95 (0-7933-4217-1); pap. 14.95 (0-7933-4218-X); computer disk 29.95 (0-7933-4219-8) Gallopade Pub Group.

—Virginia Jography: A Fun Run Through the Old Dominion State. (Illus.). 50p. (Orig.). (gr. 3-12). 1986. pap. 24.95 (0-935326-99-5) Gallopade Pub Group.

—Virginia "Jography" A Fun Run Thru Our State. (Illus.). 1990. PLB 24.95 (0-685-45960-8); pap. 14.95 (1-55609-057-9); computer disk 29.95 (0-7933-2170-0) Gallopade Pub Group.

—Virginia Kid's Cookbook: Recipes, How-to, History, Lore & More! (Illus.). 1990. PLB 24.95 (0-7933-1166-7); pap. 14.95 (0-7933-1165-9); computer disk 29.95 (0-7933-1167-5) Gallopade Pub Group.

—The Virginia Mystery Van Takes Off! Book 1: Handicapped Virginia Kids Sneak Off on a Big Adventure. (Illus.). (gr. 3-12). 1992. 24.95 (0-7933-5099-9); pap. 14.95 (0-7933-5100-6); computer disk 29.95 (0-7933-5101-4) Gallopade Pub Group.

—Virginia Quiz Bowl Crash Courses! (Illus.). 1990. PLB 24.95 (0-7933-2182-4); pap. 14.95 (0-7933-2183-2); computer disk 29.95 (0-7933-2184-0) Gallopade Pub Group.

—Virginia Rollercoasters! (Illus.). (gr. 3-12). 1992. PLB 24.95 (0-7933-5362-9); pap. 14.95 (0-7933-5363-7); computer disk 29.95 (0-7933-5364-5) Gallopade Pub Group.

—Virginia School Trivia: An Amazing & Fascinating Look at Our State's Teachers, Schools & Students! (Illus.). 1990. PLB 24.95 (0-7933-1163-2); pap. 14.95 (0-7933-1162-4); computer disk 29.95 (0-7933-1164-0) Gallopade Pub Group.

—Virginia Silly Basketball Sportsmysteries, Vol. 1. (Illus.). 1990. PLB 24.95 (0-7933-1160-8); pap. 14.95 (0-7933-1159-4); computer disk 29.95 (0-7933-1161-6) Gallopade Pub Group.

—Virginia Silly Basketball Sportsmysteries, Vol. 2. (Illus.). 1990. PLB 24.95 (0-7933-2195-6); pap. 14.95 (0-7933-2196-4); computer disk 29.95 (0-7933-2197-2) Gallopade Pub Group.

—Virginia Silly Football Sportsmysteries, Vol. 1. (Illus.). 1990. PLB 24.95 (0-685-45961-6); pap. 14.95 (0-7933-2174-3); computer disk 29.95 (0-7933-2175-1) Gallopade Pub Group.

—Virginia Silly Football Sportsmysteries, Vol. 2. (Illus.). 1990. PLB 24.95 (0-7933-2176-X); pap. 14.95 (0-7933-2177-8); computer disk 29.95 (0-7933-2178-6) Gallopade Pub Group.

—Virginia Silly Trivia. (Illus.). 60p. (Orig.). (gr. 3-12). 1986. pap. 14.95 (0-935326-94-4) Gallopade Pub Group.

—Virginia Silly Trivia! (Illus.). 1990. PLB 24.95 (0-7933-2167-0); pap. 14.95 (0-685-45959-4); computer disk 29.95 (0-7933-2168-9) Gallopade Pub Group.

—Virginia Timeline: A Chronology of Virginia History, Mystery, Trivia, Legend, Lore & More. (Illus.). (gr. 3-12). 1992. PLB 24.95 (0-7933-6013-7); pap. 14.95 (0-7933-6014-5); computer disk 29.95 (0-7933-6015-3) Gallopade Pub Group.

—Virginia's (Most Devastating!) Disasters & (Most Calamitous!) Catastrophies! (Illus.). 1990. PLB 24.95 (0-7933-2193-X); pap. 14.95 (0-7933-1150-0); computer disk 29.95 (0-7933-2194-8) Gallopade Pub Group.

—Virginia's Unsolved Mysteries (& Their "Solutions") Includes Scientific Information & Other Activities for Students. (Illus.). (gr. 3-12). 1992. PLB 24.95 (0-7933-5860-4); pap. 14.95 (0-7933-5861-2); computer disk 29.95 (0-7933-5862-0) Gallopade Pub Group.

—Washington & Other State Greats (Biographies)! (Illus.). 1990. PLB 24.95 (0-7933-2224-3); pap. 14.95 (0-7933-2225-1); computer disk 29.95 (0-7933-2226-X) Gallopade Pub Group.

—Washington Bandits, Bushwackers, Outlaws, Crooks, Devils, Ghosts, Desperadoes & Other Assorted & Sundry Characters! (Illus.). 1990. PLB 24.95 (0-7933-1178-0); pap. 14.95 (0-7933-1177-2); computer disk 29.95 (0-7933-1179-9) Gallopade Pub Group.

—Washington Classic Christmas Trivia: Stories, Recipes, Activities, Legends, Lore & More! (Illus.). 1990. PLB 24.95 (0-7933-1181-0); pap. 14.95 (0-7933-1180-2); computer disk 29.95 (0-7933-1182-9) Gallopade Pub Group.

—Washington Coastales. (Illus.). 1990. PLB 24.95 (0-7933-2218-9); pap. 14.95 (0-7933-2219-7); computer disk 29.95 (0-7933-2220-0) Gallopade Pub Group.

—Washington Coastales! 1992. lib. bdg. 24.95 (0-7933-7312-3) Gallopade Pub Group.

—Washington "Crinkum-Crankum" A Funny Word Book about Our State. (Illus.). (gr. 3-12). 1992. 24.95 (0-7933-4949-4); pap. 14.95 (0-7933-4950-8); computer disk 29.95 (0-7933-4951-6) Gallopade Pub Group.

—Washington, D. C. Coastales! 1992. lib. bdg. 24.95 (0-7933-7273-9) Gallopade Pub Group.

—Washington D. C. "Crinkum-Crankum" A Funny Word Book about Our State. (Illus.). (gr. 3-12). 1992. 24.95 (0-7933-4952-4); pap. 14.95 (0-7933-4953-2); computer disk 29.95 (0-7933-4954-0) Gallopade Pub Group.

—The Washington D. C. Hot Air Balloon Mystery. (Illus.). (gr. 2-9). 1990. 24.95 (0-7933-2390-8); pap. 14.95 (0-7933-2391-6); computer disk 29.95 (0-7933-2392-4) Gallopade Pub Group.

—The Washington D. C. Mystery Van Takes Off! Book 1: Handicapped Washington D. C. Kids Sneak Off on a Big Adventure. (Illus.). (gr. 3-12). 1992. 24.95 (0-7933-5105-7); pap. 14.95 (0-7933-5106-5); computer disk 29.95 (0-7933-5107-3) Gallopade Pub Group.

—Washington D. C. Timeline: A Chronology of Washington D. C. History, Mystery, Trivia, Legend, Lore & More. (Illus.). (gr. 3-12). 1992. PLB 24.95 (0-7933-5899-X); pap. 14.95 (0-7933-5900-7); computer disk 29.95 (0-7933-5901-5) Gallopade Pub Group.

—Washington D. C.'s Unsolved Mysteries (& Their "Solutions") Includes Scientific Information & Other Activities for Students. (Illus.). (gr. 3-12). 1992. PLB 24.95 (0-7933-5746-2); pap. 14.95 (0-7933-5747-0); computer disk 29.95 (0-7933-5748-9) Gallopade Pub Group.

—Washington, D.C. & Other State Greats (Biographies) (Illus.). (gr. 3-12). 1990. PLB 24.95 (0-7933-1480-1); pap. 14.95 (0-7933-1481-X); computer disk 29.95 (0-7933-1482-8) Gallopade Pub Group.

—Washington, D.C. Bandits, Bushwackers, Outlaws, Crooks, Devils, Ghosts, Desperadoes & Other Assorted & Sundry Characters! (Illus.). (gr. 3-12). 1990. PLB 24.95 (0-7933-0262-5); pap. 14.95 (0-7933-0261-7); computer disk 29.95 (0-7933-0263-3) Gallopade Pub Group.

—Washington, D.C. Classic Christmas Trivia: Stories, Recipes, Activities, Legends, Lore & More! (Illus.). (gr. 3-12). 1990. PLB 24.95 (0-7933-0265-X); pap. 14. 95 (0-7933-0264-1); computer disk 29.95 (0-7933-0266-8) Gallopade Pub Group.

—Washington, D.C. Coastales. (Illus.). (gr. 3-12). 1990. PLB 24.95 (0-7933-1474-7); pap. 14.95 (0-7933-1475-5); computer disk 29.95 (0-7933-1476-3) Gallopade Pub Group.

—Washington DC Dingbats! Bk. 1: A Fun Book of Games, Stories, Activities & More about Our State That's All in Code! for You to Decipher. (Illus.). (gr. 3-12). 1991. PLB 24.95 (0-7933-3797-6); pap. 14.95 (0-7933-3798-4); computer disk 29.95 (0-7933-3799-2) Gallopade Pub Group.

—Washington DC Festival Fun for Kids! Includes Reproducible Activities for Kids! (Illus.). (gr. 3-12). 1991. PLB 24.95 (0-7933-3950-2); pap. 14.95 (0-7933-3951-0); computer disk 29.95 (0-7933-3952-9) Gallopade Pub Group.

—Washington DC Jeopardy! Answers & Questions about Our State! (Illus.). (gr. 3-12). 1991. PLB 24.95 (0-7933-4103-5); pap. 14.95 (0-7933-4104-3); computer disk 29.95 (0-7933-4105-1) Gallopade Pub Group.

—Washington, D.C. "Jography" A Fun Run Thru Our State! (Illus.). 1990. PLB 24.95 (1-55609-562-7); pap. 14.95 (1-55609-561-9); computer disk 29.95 (0-7933-1460-7) Gallopade Pub Group.

—Washington, D.C. Kid's Cookbook: Recipes, How-to, History, Lore & More! (Illus.). (gr. 3-12). 1990. PLB 24.95 (0-7933-0274-9); pap. 14.95 (0-7933-0273-0); computer disk 29.95 (0-7933-0275-7) Gallopade Pub Group.

—Washington, D.C. Quiz Bowl Crash Course! (Illus.). (gr. 3-12). 1990. PLB 24.95 (0-7933-1471-2); pap. 14. 95 (0-7933-1472-0); computer disk 29.95 (0-7933-1473-9) Gallopade Pub Group.

—Washington DC Rollercoasters! (Illus.). (gr. 3-12). 1992. PLB 24.95 (0-7933-5248-7); pap. 14.95 (0-7933-5249-5); computer disk 29.95 (0-7933-5250-9) Gallopade Pub Group.

—Washington, D.C. School Trivia: An Amazing & Fascinating Look at Our State's Teachers, Schools & Students! (Illus.). (gr. 3-12). 1990. PLB 24.95 (0-7933-0271-4); pap. 14.95 (0-7933-0270-6); computer disk 29.95 (0-7933-0272-2) Gallopade Pub Group.

—Washington, D.C. Silly Basketball Sportsmysteries, Vol. 1. (Illus.). (gr. 3-12). 1990. PLB 24.95 (0-7933-0268-4); pap. 14.95 (0-7933-0267-6); computer disk 29.95 (0-7933-0269-2) Gallopade Pub Group.

—Washington, D.C. Silly Basketball Sportsmysteries, Vol. 2. (Illus.). (gr. 3-12). 1990. PLB 24.95 (0-7933-1483-6); pap. 14.95 (0-7933-1484-4); computer disk 29.95 (0-7933-1485-2) Gallopade Pub Group.

—Washington, D.C. Silly Football Sportsmysteries, Vol. 1. (Illus.). (gr. 3-12). 1990. PLB 24.95 (0-7933-1462-3); pap. 14.95 (0-7933-1463-1); computer disk 29.95 (0-7933-1464-X) Gallopade Pub Group.

—Washington, D.C. Silly Football Sportsmysteries, Vol. 2. (Illus.). (gr. 3-12). 1990. PLB 24.95 (0-7933-1465-8); pap. 14.95 (0-7933-1466-6); computer disk 29.95 (0-7933-1467-4) Gallopade Pub Group.

—Washington, D.C. Silly Trivia! (Illus.). (gr. 3-12). 1990. PLB 24.95 (1-55609-560-0); pap. 14.95 (1-55609-559-7); computer disk 29.95 (0-7933-1459-3) Gallopade Pub Group.

—Washington, D.C.'s (Most Devastating!) Disasters & (Most Calamitous!) Catastrophies! (Illus.). (gr. 3-12). 1990. PLB 24.95 (0-7933-0259-5); pap. 14.95 (0-7933-0258-7); computer disk 29.95 (0-7933-0260-9) Gallopade Pub Group.

—Washington Dingbats! Bk. 1: A Fun Book of Games, Stories, Activities & More about Our State That's All in Code! for You to Decipher. (Illus.). (gr. 3-12). 1991. PLB 24.95 (0-7933-3914-6); pap. 14.95 (0-7933-3915-4); computer disk 29.95 (0-7933-3916-2) Gallopade Pub Group.

—Washington Festival Fun for Kids! Includes Reproducible Activities for Kids! (Illus.). (gr. 3-12). 1991. PLB 24.95 (0-7933-4067-5); pap. 14.95 (0-7933-4068-3); computer disk 29.95 (0-7933-4069-1) Gallopade Pub Group.

—The Washington Hot Air Balloon Mystery. (Illus.). (gr. 2-9). 1990. 24.95 (0-7933-2741-5); pap. 14.95 (0-7933-2742-3); computer disk 29.95 (0-7933-2743-1) Gallopade Pub Group.

—Washington Jeopardy! Answers & Questions about Our State! (Illus.). (gr. 3-12). 1991. PLB 24.95 (0-7933-4220-1); pap. 14.95 (0-7933-4221-X); computer disk 29.95 (0-7933-4222-8) Gallopade Pub Group.

—Washington "Jography" A Fun Run Thru Our State! (Illus.). 1990. PLB 24.95 (0-7933-2201-4); pap. 14.95 (0-7933-2202-2); computer disk 29.95 (0-7933-2203-0) Gallopade Pub Group.

—Washington Kid's Cookbook: Recipes, How-to, History, Lore & More! (Illus.). 1990. PLB 24.95 (0-7933-1190-X); pap. 14.95 (0-7933-1189-6); computer disk 29.95 (0-7933-1191-8) Gallopade Pub Group.

—The Washington Mystery Van Takes Off! Book 1: Handicapped Washington Kids Sneak Off on a Big Adventure. (Illus.). (gr. 3-12). 1992. 24.95 (0-7933-5102-2); pap. 14.95 (0-7933-5103-0); computer disk 29.95 (0-7933-5104-9) Gallopade Pub Group.

—Washington Quiz Bowl Crash Course! (Illus.). 1990. PLB 24.95 (0-7933-2215-4); pap. 14.95 (0-7933-2216-2); computer disk 29.95 (0-7933-2217-0) Gallopade Pub Group.

—Washington Rollercoasters! (Illus.). (gr. 3-12). 1992. PLB 24.95 (0-7933-5365-3); pap. 14.95 (0-7933-5366-1); computer disk 29.95 (0-7933-5367-X) Gallopade Pub Group.

—Washington School Trivia: An Amazing & Fascinating Look at Our State's Teachers, Schools & Students! (Illus.). 1990. PLB 24.95 (0-685-45964-0); pap. 14.95 (0-7933-1186-1); computer disk 29.95 (0-7933-1188-8) Gallopade Pub Group.

—Washington Silly Basketball Sportsmysteries, Vol. 1. (Illus.). 1990. PLB 24.95 (0-7933-1184-5); pap. 14.95 (0-7933-1183-7); computer disk 29.95 (0-7933-1185-3) Gallopade Pub Group.

—Washington Silly Basketball Sportsmysteries, Vol. 2. (Illus.). 1990. PLB 24.95 (0-7933-2227-8); pap. 14.95 (0-7933-2228-6); computer disk 29.95 (0-7933-2229-4) Gallopade Pub Group.

—Washington Silly Football Sportsmysteries, Vol. 1. (Illus.). 1990. PLB 24.95 (0-7933-2206-5); pap. 14.95 (0-7933-2207-3); computer disk 29.95 (0-7933-2208-1) Gallopade Pub Group.

—Washington Silly Football Sportsmysteries, Vol. 2. (Illus.). 1990. PLB 24.95 (0-685-45963-2); pap. 14.95 (0-7933-2210-3); computer disk 29.95 (0-7933-2211-1) Gallopade Pub Group.

—Washington Silly Trivia! (Illus.). 1990. PLB 24.95 (0-7933-2198-0); pap. 14.95 (0-7933-2199-9); computer disk 29.95 (0-7933-2200-6) Gallopade Pub Group.

—Washington Timeline: A Chronology of Washington History, Mystery, Trivia, Legend, Lore & More. (Illus.). (gr. 3-12). 1992. PLB 24.95 (0-7933-6016-1); pap. 14.95 (0-7933-6017-X); computer disk 29.95 (0-7933-6018-8) Gallopade Pub Group.

—Washington's (Most Devastating!) Disasters & (Most Calamitous!) Catastrophies! (Illus.). 1990. PLB 24.95 (0-7933-1175-6); pap. 14.95 (0-7933-1174-8); computer disk 29.95 (0-7933-1176-4) Gallopade Pub Group.

—Washington's Unsolved Mysteries (& Their "Solutions") Includes Scientific Information & Other Activities for Students. (Illus.). (gr. 3-12). 1992. PLB 24.95 (0-7933-5863-9); pap. 14.95 (0-7933-5864-7); computer disk 29.95 (0-7933-5865-5) Gallopade Pub Group.

—West Virginia & Other State Greats (Biographies) (Illus.). 1990. PLB 24.95 (0-7933-2256-1); pap. 14.95 (0-7933-2257-X); computer disk 29.95 (0-7933-2258-8) Gallopade Pub Group.

—West Virginia Bandits, Bushwackers, Outlaws, Crooks, Devils, Ghosts, Desperadoes & Other Assorted & Sundry Characters! (Illus.). 1990. PLB 24.95 (0-7933-1202-7); pap. 14.95 (0-7933-1201-9); computer disk 29.95 (0-7933-1203-5) Gallopade Pub Group.

—West Virginia Classic Christmas Trivia: Stories, Recipies, Activities, Legends, Lore & More! (Illus.). 1990. PLB 24.95 (0-7933-1205-1); pap. 14.95 (0-7933-1204-3); computer disk 29.95 (0-7933-1206-X) Gallopade Pub Group.

—West Virginia Coastales. (Illus.). 1990. PLB 24.95 (0-7933-2250-2); pap. 14.95 (0-7933-2251-0); computer disk 29.95 (0-7933-2252-9) Gallopade Pub Group.

—West Virginia Coastales! 1992. lib. bdg. 24.95 (0-7933-7313-1) Gallopade Pub Group.

—West Virginia "Crinkum-Crankum" A Funny Word Book about Our State. (Illus.). (gr. 3-12). 1992. 24.95 (0-7933-4955-9); pap. 14.95 (0-7933-4956-7); computer disk 29.95 (0-7933-4957-5) Gallopade Pub Group.

—West Virginia Dingbats! Bk. 1: A Fun Book of Games, Stories, Activities & More about Our State That's All in Code! for You to Decipher. (Illus.). (gr. 3-12). 1991. PLB 24.95 (0-7933-3917-0); pap. 14.95 (0-7933-3918-9); computer disk 29.95 (0-7933-3919-7) Gallopade Pub Group.

—West Virginia Festival Fun for Kids! Includes Reproducible Activities for Kids! (Illus.). (gr. 3-12). 1991. PLB 24.95 (0-7933-4070-5); pap. 14.95 (0-7933-4071-3); computer disk 29.95 (0-7933-4072-1) Gallopade Pub Group.

—The West Virginia Hot Air Balloon Mystery. (Illus.). (gr. 2-9). 1990. 24.95 (0-7933-2750-4); pap. 14.95 (0-7933-2751-2); computer disk 29.95 (0-7933-2752-0) Gallopade Pub Group.

—West Virginia Jeopardy! Answers & Questions about Our State! (Illus.). (gr. 3-12). 1991. PLB 24.95 (0-7933-4223-6); pap. 14.95 (0-7933-4224-4); computer disk 29.95 (0-7933-4225-2) Gallopade Pub Group.

—West Virginia "Jography" A Fun Run Thru Our State! (Illus.). 1990. PLB 24.95 (0-7933-2233-2); pap. 14.95 (0-7933-2234-0); computer disk 29.95 (0-7933-2235-9) Gallopade Pub Group.

—West Virginia Kid's Cookbook: Recipes, How-to, History, Lore & More! (Illus.). 1990. PLB 24.95 (0-7933-1214-0); pap. 14.95 (0-7933-1213-2); computer disk 29.95 (0-7933-1215-9) Gallopade Pub Group.

—The West Virginia Mystery Van Takes Off! Book 1: Handicapped West Virginia Kids Sneak Off on a Big Adventure. (Illus.). (gr. 3-12). 1992. 24.95 (0-7933-5108-1); pap. 14.95 (0-7933-5109-X); computer disk 29.95 (0-7933-5110-3) Gallopade Pub Group.

—West Virginia Quiz Bowl Crash Course! (Illus.). 1990. PLB 24.95 (0-7933-2247-2); pap. 14.95 (0-7933-2248-0); computer disk 29.95 (0-7933-2249-9) Gallopade Pub Group.

—West Virginia Rollercoasters! (Illus.). (gr. 3-12). 1992. PLB 24.95 (0-7933-5368-8); pap. 14.95 (0-7933-5369-6); computer disk 29.95 (0-7933-5370-X) Gallopade Pub Group.

—West Virginia School Trivia: An Amazing & Fascinating Look at Our State's Teachers, Schools & Students! (Illus.). 1990. PLB 24.95 (0-7933-1211-6); pap. 14.95 (0-7933-1210-8); computer disk 29.95 (0-7933-1212-4) Gallopade Pub Group.

—West Virginia Silly Basketball Sportsmysteries, Vol. 1. (Illus.). 1990. PLB 24.95 (0-7933-1208-6); pap. 14.95 (0-7933-1207-8); computer disk 29.95 (0-7933-1209-4) Gallopade Pub Group.

—West Virginia Silly Basketball Sportsmysteries, Vol. 2. (Illus.). 1990. PLB 24.95 (0-7933-2259-6); pap. 14.95 (0-7933-2260-X); computer disk 29.95 (0-7933-2261-8) Gallopade Pub Group.

—West Virginia Silly Football Sportsmysteries, Vol. 1. (Illus.). 1990. PLB 24.95 (0-7933-2238-3); pap. 14.95 (0-7933-2239-1); computer disk 29.95 (0-7933-2240-5) Gallopade Pub Group.

—West Virginia Silly Football Sportsmysteries, Vol. 2. (Illus.). 1990. PLB 24.95 (0-7933-2241-3); pap. 14.95 (0-7933-2242-1); computer disk 29.95 (0-685-45965-9) Gallopade Pub Group.

—West Virginia Silly Trivia! (Illus.). 1990. PLB 24.95 (0-7933-2230-8); pap. 14.95 (0-7933-2231-6); computer disk 29.95 (0-7933-2232-4) Gallopade Pub Group.

—West Virginia Timeline: A Chronology of West Virginia History, Mystery, Trivia, Legend, Lore & More. (Illus.). (gr. 3-12). 1992. PLB 24.95 (0-7933-6019-6); pap. 14.95 (0-7933-6020-X); computer disk 29.95 (0-7933-6021-8) Gallopade Pub Group.

—West Virginia's (Most Devastating!) Disasters & (Most Calamitous!) Catastrophies! (Illus.). 1990. PLB 24.95 (0-7933-1199-3); pap. 14.95 (0-7933-1198-5); computer disc 29.95 (0-7933-1200-0) Gallopade Pub Group.

—West Virginia's Unsolved Mysteries (& Their "Solutions") Includes Scientific Information & Other Activities for Students. (Illus.). (gr. 3-12). 1992. PLB 24.95 (0-7933-5866-3); pap. 14.95 (0-7933-5867-1); computer disk 29.95 (0-7933-5868-X) Gallopade Pub Group.

—What the Heck Are Ethics? (gr. 4-9). 1988. 24.95 (1-55609-342-X); pap. 14.95 (0-318-37388-2) Gallopade Pub Group.

—Will Somebody Hold This Thing a Minute? Statue of Liberty Silly Trivia Book. (Illus.). 60p. (Orig.). (gr. 3-12). 1986. 24.95 (1-55609-192-3); pap. 14.95 (0-935326-75-8) Gallopade Pub Group.

—Wisconsin & Other State Greats (Biographies) (Illus.). 1990. PLB 24.95 (0-7933-2288-X); pap. 14.95 (0-7933-2289-8); computer Disk 29.95 (0-7933-2290-1) Gallopade Pub Group.

—Wisconsin Bandits, Bushwackers, Outlaws, Crooks, Devils, Ghosts, Desperadoes & Other Assorted & Sundry Characters! (Illus.). 1990. PLB 24.95 (0-7933-1226-4); pap. 14.95 (0-7933-1225-6); computer disk 29.95 (0-7933-1227-2) Gallopade Pub Group.

—Wisconsin Classic Christmas Trivia: Stories, Recipes, Activities, Legends, Lore & More. (Illus.). 1990. PLB 24.95 (0-7933-1229-9); pap. 14.95 (0-7933-1228-0); computer disk 29.95 (0-7933-1230-2) Gallopade Pub Group.

—Wisconsin Coastales. (Illus.). 1990. 24.95 (0-7933-2282-0); pap. 14.95 (0-7933-2283-9); computer disk 29.95 (0-7933-2284-7) Gallopade Pub Group.

—Wisconsin Coastales! 1992. lib. bdg. 24.95 (0-7933-7314-X) Gallopade Pub Group.

—Wisconsin "Crinkum-Crankum" A Funny Word Book about Our State. (Illus.). (gr. 3-12). 1992. 24.95 (0-7933-4958-3); pap. 14.95 (0-7933-4959-1); computer disk 29.95 (0-7933-4960-5) Gallopade Pub Group.

—Wisconsin Dingbats! Bk. 1: A Fun Book of Games, Stories, Activities & More about Our State That's All in Code! for You to Decipher. (Illus.). (gr. 3-12). 1991. PLB 24.95 (0-7933-3920-0); pap. 14.95 (0-7933-3921-9); computer disk 29.95 (0-7933-3922-7) Gallopade Pub Group.

—Wisconsin Festival Fun for Kids! Includes Reproducible Activities for Kids! (Illus.). (gr. 3-12). 1991. PLB 24.95 (0-7933-4073-X); pap. 14.95 (0-7933-4074-8); computer disk 29.95 (0-7933-4075-6) Gallopade Pub Group.

—The Wisconsin Hot Air Balloon Mystery. (Illus.). (gr. 2-9). 1990. 24.95 (0-7933-2759-8); pap. 14.95 (0-7933-2760-1); computer disk 29.95 (0-7933-2761-X) Gallopade Pub Group.

—Wisconsin Jeopardy! Answers & Questions about Our State! (Illus.). (gr. 3-12). 1991. PLB 24.95 (0-7933-4226-0); pap. 14.95 (0-7933-4227-9); computer disk 29.95 (0-7933-4228-7) Gallopade Pub Group.

—Wisconsin "Jography" A Fun Run Thru Our State! (Illus.). 1990. PLB 24.95 (0-7933-2265-0); pap. 14.95 (0-7933-2266-9); computer disk 29.95 (0-7933-2267-7) Gallopade Pub Group.

—Wisconsin Kid's Cookbook: Recipes, How-To, History, Lore & More! (Illus.). 1990. PLB 24.95 (0-7933-1238-8); pap. 14.95 (0-7933-1237-X); computer disk 29.95 (0-7933-1239-6) Gallopade Pub Group.

—The Wisconsin Mystery Van Takes Off! Book 1: Handicapped Wisconsin Kids Sneak Off on a Big Adventure. (Illus.). (gr. 3-12). 1992. 24.95 (0-7933-5111-1); pap. 14.95 (0-7933-5112-X); computer disk 29.95 (0-7933-5113-8) Gallopade Pub Group.

—Wisconsin Quiz Bowl Crash Course! (Illus.). 1990. PLB 24.95 (0-7933-2279-0); pap. 14.95 (0-7933-2280-4); computer disk 29.95 (0-7933-2281-2) Gallopade Pub Group.

—Wisconsin Rollercoasters! (Illus.). (gr. 3-12). 1992. PLB 24.95 (0-7933-5371-8); pap. 14.95 (0-7933-5372-6); computer disk 29.95 (0-7933-5373-4) Gallopade Pub Group.

—Wisconsin School Trivia: An Amazing & Fascinating Look at Our State's Teachers, Schools & Students! (Illus.). 1990. PLB 24.95 (0-7933-1235-3); pap. 14.95 (0-7933-1234-5); computer disk 29.95 (0-7933-1236-1) Gallopade Pub Group.

—Wisconsin Silly Basketball Sportsmysteries, Vol. 1. (Illus.). 1990. PLB 24.95 (0-7933-1232-9); pap. 14.95 (0-7933-1231-0); computer disk 29.95 (0-7933-1233-7) Gallopade Pub Group.

—Wisconsin Silly Basketball Sportsmysteries, Vol. 2. (Illus.). 1990. PLB 24.95 (0-7933-2291-X); pap. 14.95 (0-7933-2292-8); computer disk 29.95 (0-7933-2293-6) Gallopade Pub Group.

—Wisconsin Silly Football Sportsmysteries, Vol. 1. (Illus.). 1990. PLB 24.95 (0-7933-2270-7); pap. 14.95 (0-7933-2271-5); computer disk 29.95 (0-7933-2272-3) Gallopade Pub Group.

—Wisconsin Silly Football Sportsmysteries, Vol. 2. (Illus.). 1990. PLB 24.95 (0-7933-2273-1); pap. 14.95 (0-7933-2274-X); computer disk 29.95 (0-7933-2275-8) Gallopade Pub Group.

—Wisconsin Silly Trivia! (Illus.). 1990. PLB 24.95 (0-7933-2262-6); pap. 14.95 (0-7933-2263-4); computer disk 29.95 (0-7933-2264-2) Gallopade Pub Group.

—Wisconsin Timeline: A Chronology of Wisconsin History, Mystery, Trivia, Legend, Lore & More. (Illus.). (gr. 3-12). 1992. PLB 24.95 (0-7933-6022-6); pap. 14.95 (0-7933-6023-4); computer disk 29.95 (0-7933-6024-2) Gallopade Pub Group.

—Wisconsin's (Most Devastating!) Disasters & (Most Calamitous!) Catastrophies! (Illus.). 1990. PLB 24.95 (0-7933-1223-X); pap. 14.95 (0-7933-1222-1); computer disk 29.95 (0-7933-1224-8) Gallopade Pub Group.

—Wisconsin's Unsolved Mysteries (& Their "Solutions") Includes Scientific Information & Other Activities for Students. (Illus.). (gr. 3-12). 1992. PLB 24.95 (0-7933-5869-8); pap. 14.95 (0-7933-5870-1); computer disk 29.95 (0-7933-5871-X) Gallopade Pub Group.

—World's Fair Fun Trivia Book. Marsh, Carole, illus. (Orig.). (gr. 4 up). 1982. pap. 4.95 (0-935326-06-5) Gallopade Pub Group.

—Worlds Fair Kit S. P. A. R. K. (Illus., Orig.). (gr. 3-12). 1986. pap. 24.95 (0-935326-85-5) Gallopade Pub Group.

—Write Your Own Sports Mystery Kit. (Illus., Orig.). (gr. 3-12). 1986. pap. 24.00 (0-935326-11-1) Gallopade Pub Group.

—Wyoming & Other State Greats (Biographies) (Illus.). 1990. PLB 24.95 (0-7933-2312-6); pap. 14.95 (0-7933-2313-4); computer disk 29.95 (0-7933-2314-2) Gallopade Pub Group.

—Wyoming Bandits, Bushwackers, Outlaws, Crooks, Devils, Ghosts, Desperadoes & Other Assorted & Sundry Characters! (Illus.). 1990. PLB 24.95 (0-7933-1250-7); pap. 14.95 (0-7933-1249-3); computer disk 29.95 (0-7933-1251-5) Gallopade Pub Group.

—Wyoming Classic Christmas Trivia: Stories, Recipes, Activities, Legends, Lore & More! (Illus.). 1990. PLB 24.95 (0-7933-1253-1); pap. 14.95 (0-7933-1252-3); computer disk 29.95 (0-7933-1254-X) Gallopade Pub Group.

—Wyoming Coastales. (Illus.). 1990. PLB 24.95 (0-7933-2306-1); pap. 14.95 (0-7933-2307-X); computer disk 29.95 (0-7933-2308-8) Gallopade Pub Group.

—Wyoming Coastales! 1992. lib. bdg. 24.95 (0-7933-7315-8) Gallopade Pub Group.

—Wyoming "Crinkum-Crankum" A Funny Word Book about Our State. (Illus.). (gr. 3-12). 1992. 24.95 (0-7933-4961-3); pap. 14.95 (0-7933-4962-1); computer disk 29.95 (0-7933-4963-X) Gallopade Pub Group.

—Wyoming Dingbats! Bk. 1: A Fun Book of Games, Stories, Activities & More about Our State That's All in Code! for You to Decipher. (Illus.). (gr. 3-12). 1991. PLB 24.95 (0-7933-3923-5); pap. 14.95 (0-7933-3924-3); computer disk 29.95 (0-7933-3925-1) Gallopade Pub Group.

—Wyoming Festival Fun for Kids! Includes Reproducible Activities for Kids! (Illus.). (gr. 3-12). 1991. PLB 24.95 (0-7933-4076-4); pap. 14.95 (0-7933-4077-2); computer disk 29.95 (0-7933-4078-0) Gallopade Pub Group.

—The Wyoming Hot Air Balloon Mystery. (Illus.). (gr. 2-9). 1990. 24.95 (0-7933-2768-7); pap. 14.95 (0-7933-2769-5); computer disk 29.95 (0-7933-2770-9) Gallopade Pub Group.

—Wyoming Jeopardy! Answers & Questions about Our State! (Illus.). (gr. 3-12). 1991. PLB 24.95 (0-7933-4229-5); pap. 14.95 (0-7933-4230-9); computer disk 29.95 (0-7933-4231-7) Gallopade Pub Group.

—Wyoming "Jography" A Fun Run Thru Our State! (Illus.). (gr. 3-12). 1990. PLB 24.95 (1-55609-295-4); pap. 14.95 (1-55609-296-2); computer disk 29.95 (1-55609-297-0) Gallopade Pub Group.

—Wyoming Kid's Cookbook: Recipes, How-To, History, Lore & More. (Illus.). 1990. PLB 24.95 (0-7933-1262-0); pap. 14.95 (0-7933-1261-2); 29.95 (0-7933-1263-9) Gallopade Pub Group.

—The Wyoming Mystery Van Takes Off! Book 1: Handicapped Wyoming Kids Sneak Off on a Big Adventure. (Illus.). (gr. 3-12). 1992. 24.95 (0-7933-5114-6); pap. 14.95 (0-7933-5115-4); computer disk 29.95 (0-7933-5116-2) Gallopade Pub Group.

—Wyoming Quiz Bowl Crash Course! (Illus.). 1990. PLB 24.95 (0-7933-2303-7); pap. 14.95 (0-7933-2304-5); computer disk 29.95 (0-7933-2305-3) Gallopade Pub Group.

—Wyoming Rollercoasters! (Illus.). (gr. 3-12). 1992. PLB 24.95 (0-7933-5374-2); pap. 14.95 (0-7933-5375-0); computer disk 29.95 (0-7933-5376-9) Gallopade Pub Group.

—Wyoming School Trivia: An Amazing & Fascinating Look at Our State's Teachers, Schools & Students! (Illus.). 1990. PLB 24.95 (0-7933-1259-0); pap. 14.95 (0-7933-1258-2); computer disk 29.95 (0-7933-1260-4) Gallopade Pub Group.

—Wyoming Silly Basketball Sportsmysteries, Vol. 1. (Illus.). 1990. PLB 24.95 (0-7933-1256-6); pap. 14.95 (0-7933-1255-8); computer disk 29.95 (0-7933-1257-4) Gallopade Pub Group.

—Wyoming Silly Basketball Sportsmysteries, Vol. 2. (Illus.). 1990. PLB 24.95 (0-7933-2315-0); pap. 14.95 (0-7933-2316-9); computer disk 29.95 (0-7933-2317-7) Gallopade Pub Group.

—Wyoming Silly Football Sportsmysteries, Vol. 1. (Illus.). 1990. PLB 24.95 (0-7933-2294-4); pap. 14.95 (0-7933-2295-2); computer disk 29.95 (0-7933-2296-0) Gallopade Pub Group.

—Wyoming Silly Football Sportsmysteries, Vol. 2. (Illus.). 1990. PLB 24.95 (0-7933-2297-9); pap. 14.95 (0-7933-2298-7); computer disk 29.95 (0-7933-2299-5) Gallopade Pub Group.

—Wyoming Silly Trivia. (Illus.). (gr. 3-12). 1990. PLB 24.95 (1-55609-292-X); pap. 14.95 (1-55609-293-8); computer disk 29.95 (1-55609-294-6) Gallopade Pub Group.

—Wyoming Timeline: A Chronology of Wyoming History, Mystery, Trivia, Legend, Lore & More. (Illus.). (gr. 3-12). 1992. PLB 24.95 (0-7933-6025-0); pap. 14.95 (0-7933-6026-9); computer disk 29.95 (0-7933-6027-7) Gallopade Pub Group.

—Wyoming's (Most Devastating!) Disasters & (Most Calamitous!) Catastrophies! (Illus.). 1990. PLB 24.95 (*0-7933-1247-7*); pap. 14.95 (*0-7933-1246-9*); computer disk 29.95 (*0-7933-1248-5*) Gallopade Pub Group.
—Wyoming's Unsolved Mysteries (& Their "Solutions") Includes Scientific Information & Other Activities for Students. (Illus.). (gr. 3-12). 1992. PLB 24.95 (*0-7933-5872-8*); pap. 14.95 (*0-7933-5873-6*); computer disk 29.95 (*0-7933-5874-4*) Gallopade Pub Group.
—Yes, You Have to Wipe Your Feet! White House Trivia. 1992. lib. bdg. 24.95 (*0-7933-6873-1*); pap. text ed. 14.95 (*0-7933-6872-3*); disk 29.95 (*0-7933-6874-X*) Gallopade Pub Group.

Marsh, Chuck, ed. see Basow, Lynn.

Marsh, Fabienne. The Moralist of the Alphabet Streets. 252p. (gr. 10 up). 1991. 17.95 (*0-945575-47-5*) Algonquin Bks.

Marsh, Frank L. Life, Man & Time. 2nd ed. James, Elden & Baerg, Harry, illus. LC 66-21121. (gr. 7 up). 1967. 8.95 (*0-911080-15-5*) Outdoor Pict.

Marsh, James. Bizarre Birds & Beasts: Animal Verses. 1991. 12.95 (*0-8037-1046-1*) Dial Bks Young.
—From the Heart: Light-Hearted Verse. LC 92-17912. (Illus.). 32p. 1993. 6.99 (*0-8037-1449-1*) Dial Bks Young.

Marsh, Jerry, ed. see Breakstone, Steve.

Marsh, Jessie. Chinook. 32p. (ps-9). 1976. 4.95 (*0-89992-041-1*) Coun India Ed.
—Indian Folk Tales from Coast to Coast. Cunningham, Tanya, illus. (gr. 3-6). 1978. 1.95 (*0-89992-068-3*) Coun India Ed.

Marsh, Joan. Martha Washington. LC 92-24531. (Illus.). 64p. (gr. 5-8). 1993. PLB 12.90 (*0-531-20145-7*) Watts.

Marsh, Norma. The Chocolate Touch: A Study Guide. (gr. 2-4). 1989. tchr's. ed. & wkbk. 14.95 (*0-88122-043-4*) Lrn Links.
—Follow My Leader: A Study Guide. Friedland, Joyce & Kessler, Rikki, eds. 18p. (gr. 9-12). 1990. pap. text ed. 14.95 (*0-88122-403-0*) Lrn Links.
—A Gift for Mama: A Study Guide. (gr. 2-4). 1989. tchr's. ed. & wkbk. 14.95 (*0-88122-045-0*) LRN Links.
—Park's Quest: A Study Guide. Friedland, Joyce & Kessler, Rikki, eds. (gr. 5-8). 1991. pap. text ed. 14.95 (*0-88122-581-9*) LRN Links.

Marsh, Richard S. Reading & Understanding Technical Information. (Illus.). (gr. 5). 1986. wkbk. 4.95 (*0-89525-758-0*) Ed Activities.

Marshak, Samuel. Hail to Mail. Pevear, Richard, tr. from RUS. Radunsky, Vladimir, illus. LC 89-7605. 32p. (ps-2). 1990. 14.95 (*0-8050-1132-3*, Bks Young Read) H Holt & Co.
—The Month Brothers: A Slavic Tale. Whitney, Thomas P., tr. from RUS. Stanley, Diane, illus. LC 82-7927. 32p. (gr. k up). 1983. PLB 12.88 (*0-688-01510-7*) Morrow Jr Bks.
—The Pup Grew Up! Pevear, Richard, tr. from RUS. Radunsky, Vladimir, illus. LC 88-28428. 32p. (ps-2). 1989. 13.95 (*0-8050-0952-3*, Bks Young Read) H Holt & Co.

Marshak, Sondra & Culbreath, Myrna. Star Trek, the New Voyages 2. 288p. (Orig.). 1985. pap. 2.95 (*0-553-27933-5*, Spectra) Bantam.

Marshak, Suzanne. The Wizard's Promise. Rand, Ted, illus. LC 92-36507. 1994. pap. 15.00 (*0-671-78431-5*, S&S BFYR) S&S Trade.

Marshal, Edward. Four on the Shore. (ps-3). 1993. pap. 4.99 (*0-14-036186-3*, Puffin) Puffin Bks.

Marshall, Ann E. Woven with Love. DeLapp, Tom & Whittaker, Jessica A., illus. 36p. (Orig.). (gr. 2-5). 1988. pap. 4.50 (*0-934351-02-3*) Heard Mus.

Marshall, Anthony. George's Story. LC 89-50143. (gr. 6-12). 1989. 9.95 (*0-932433-58-8*) Windswept Hse.

Marshall, Bette, jt. auth. see Lombardy, William.

Marshall, Blaine, ed. see Lewis, Shari.

Marshall, Blaine, ed. see Time-Life Books Editors.

Marshall, Brian. The Secret of Getting Straight A's: Learn More in Less Time with Little Effort. Ferguson, Bill, illus. 182p. (Orig.). (gr. 8 up). 1993. pap. 12.95 (*0-9633357-9-0*) Hathaway Intl.

Marshall, Catherine. Catherine Marshall's Story Bible. 200p. (ps-5). 1985. pap. 10.95 (*0-380-69961-3*) Avon.

Marshall, D. J. A Little Duck's Christmas Wish. 1992. 6.95 (*0-533-08777-5*) Vantage.

Marshall, David. Food. Young, Richard, ed. LC 91-20535. (Illus.). 32p. (gr. 3-5). 1991. PLB 15.93 (*1-56074-011-6*) Garrett Ed Corp.

Marshall, Donald R. The Enchantress of Crumbledown. LC 90-81830. 229p. (gr. 3-6). 1990. 9.95 (*0-87579-352-5*) Deseret Bk.

Marshall, Edward. Four on the Shore. Marshall, James, illus. LC 84-1708. 48p. (ps-3). 1985. 9.95 (*0-8037-0155-1*); PLB 9.89 (*0-8037-0142-X*) Dial Bks Young.
—Fox All Week. Marshall, James, illus. LC 84-1708. (ps-3). 1984. 10.95 (*0-8037-0062-8*) Dial Bks Young.
—Fox All Week. Marshall, James, illus. LC 84-1708. 48p. (ps-3). 1987. pap. 4.95 (*0-8037-0008-3*) Dial Bks Young.
—Fox & His Friends. Marshall, James, illus. LC 81-68769. 56p. (ps-3). 1982. PLB 10.89 (*0-8037-2669-4*); pap. 4.95 (*0-8037-2668-6*) Dial Bks Young.
—Fox & His Friends. (ps-3). 1993. pap. 4.99 (*0-14-036188-X*) Puffin Bks.

—Fox at School. Marshall, James, illus. LC 82-45506. 48p. (ps-3). 1983. PLB 9.89 (*0-8037-2675-9*); pap. 4.95 (*0-8037-2674-0*) Dial Bks Young.
—Fox at School. Marshall, James, illus. LC 93-2721. (gr. 1-4). 1993. pap. 3.25 (*0-14-036544-3*, Puffin) Puffin Bks.
—Fox in Love. Marshall, James, illus. LC 82-70190. 56p. (ps-3). 1982. PLB 10.89 (*0-8037-2433-0*) Dial Bks Young.
—Fox on Wheels. Marshall, James, illus. LC 83-5254. 48p. (ps-3). 1983. PLB 10.89 (*0-8037-0002-4*) Dial Bks Young.
—Fox on Wheels. Marshall, James, illus. (gr. 1-4). 1993. pap. 3.25 (*0-14-036541-9*, Puffin) Puffin Bks.
—La Pandilla en la Orilla - Four on the Shore. Marshall, James, illus. (SPA.). 52p. (gr. 2-4). 1990. pap. write for info. (*84-204-4678-5*) Santillana.
—Space Case. Marshall, James, illus. LC 80-13369. 32p. (ps-3). 1980. 14.00 (*0-8037-8005-2*); PLB 12.89 (*0-8037-8007-9*) Dial Bks Young.
—Space Case. Marshall, James, illus. 40p. (gr. k-3). 1982. pap. 4.99 (*0-8037-8431-7*) Dial Bks Young.
—Three by the Sea. Marshall, James, illus. 48p.(ps-3). 1981. PLB 10.89 (*0-8037-8687-5*) Dial Bks Young.
—Troll Country. Marshall, James, illus. LC 79-19324. 56p. (ps-3). 1980. pap. 4.95 (*0-8037-6210-0*) Dial Bks Young.

Marshall, Eliot. Legalization: A Debate. Mendelson, Jack & Mello, Nancy intro. by. (Illus.). 128p. (gr. 5 up). 1988. lib. bdg. 19.95 (*1-55546-229-4*) Chelsea Hse.

Marshall, Eliot & Finn, Jeffrey. Medical Ethics. (Illus.). 128p. (gr. 6-12). 1990. 18.95 (*0-7910-0086-9*) Chelsea Hse.

Marshall, Grace L. & Haggblade, Berle. Keyboarding & Computer Applications. LC 92-35186. 1994. write for info. (*0-538-61877-9*) S-W Pub.

Marshall, James. The Cut-ups. (Illus.). 32p. (gr. 3-8). 1984. pap. 14.00 (*0-670-25195-X*) Viking Child Bks.
—The Cut-Ups. Marshall, James, illus. 32p. (ps-3). 1986. pap. 3.95 (*0-14-050637-3*, Puffin) Puffin Bks.
—The Cut-ups at Camp Custer. (Illus.). 32p. (ps-3). 1989. pap. 12.95 (*0-670-82051-2*) Viking Child Bks.
—The Cut-ups at Camp Custer. (Illus.). 32p. (ps-3). 1991. pap. 3.99 (*0-14-050817-1*, Puffin) Puffin Bks.
—The Cut-ups Carry On. (Illus.). 32p. (ps-2). 1990. pap. 12.95 (*0-670-81645-0*) Viking Child Bks.
—The Cut-ups Carry On. LC 92-40721. (Illus.). 32p. (ps-3). 1993. pap. 4.99 (*0-14-050726-4*, Puffin) Puffin Bks.
—The Cut-ups Crack Up. (Illus.). 32p. (ps-3). 1992. RB 14.00 (*0-670-84486-1*) Viking Child Bks.
—The Cut-ups Cut Loose. (Illus.). 32p. (ps-3). 1987. pap. 12.95 (*0-670-80740-0*) Viking Child Bks.
—The Cut-ups Cut Loose. (Illus.). 32p. (ps-3). 1989. pap. 4.99 (*0-14-050672-1*, Puffin) Puffin Bks.
—Fox Be Nimble. Fogelman, Phyllis J., ed. Marshall, James, illus. LC 89-7933. 48p. (ps-3). 1990. 10.95 (*0-8037-0760-6*); PLB 10.89 (*0-8037-0761-4*) Dial Bks Young.
—Fox Be Nimble. (Illus.). (gr. 1-4). 1994. pap. 3.25 (*0-14-036842-6*) Puffin Bks.
—Fox in Love. (Illus.). (gr. 1-4). 1994. pap. 3.25 (*0-14-036843-4*) Puffin Bks.
—Fox on Stage. Marshall, James, illus. LC 91-46740. 48p. (ps-3). 1993. 10.99 (*0-8037-1356-8*); PLB 10.89 (*0-8037-1357-6*) Dial Bks Young.
—Fox on the Job. Marshall, James, illus. LC 87-15589. 48p. (gr. k-3). 1988. 10.99 (*0-8037-0350-3*); PLB 9.89 (*0-8037-0351-1*) Dial Bks Young.
—Fox on the Job. 1990. pap. 4.99 (*0-8037-0746-0*, Dial Easy to Read) Puffin Bks.
—Fox Outfoxed. Marshall, James, illus. LC 91-21815. 48p. (ps-3). 1992. 11.00 (*0-8037-1036-4*); PLB 10.89 (*0-8037-1037-2*) Dial Bks Young.
—George & Martha. LC 74-184250. (Illus.). 48p. (gr. k-3). 1974. pap. 4.80 (*0-395-19972-7*, Sandpiper) HM.
—George & Martha. Marshall, James, illus. LC 74-184250. 48p. (gr. k-3). 1972. 13.45 (*0-395-16619-5*) HM.
—George & Martha. (gr. 3 up). 1993. pap. 7.95 incl. cass. (*0-395-45739-4*) HM.
—George & Martha Back in Town. Marshall, James, illus. LC 83-22842. 32p. (gr. k-3). 1984. 14.45 (*0-395-35386-6*, 5-90939); pap. 3.95 (*0-685-07886-8*) HM.
—George & Martha Encore. LC 73-5845. (Illus.). 48p. (gr. k-3). 1977. 13.45 (*0-395-17512-7*); pap. 4.80 (*0-395-25379-9*) HM.
—George & Martha One Fine Day. Marshall, James, illus. 48p. (gr. k-3). 1978. 14.45 (*0-395-27154-1*); pap. 4.80 (*0-395-32921-3*) HM.
—George & Martha Rise & Shine. Marshall, James, illus. (gr. k-3). 1979. 13.45 (*0-395-24738-1*); pap. 4.80 (*0-395-28006-0*) HM.
—George & Martha Round & Round. Marshall, James, illus. LC 88-14739. 48p. (gr. k-3). 1988. 13.45 (*0-395-46763-2*) HM.
—George & Martha Round & Round. (ps-3). 1991. pap. 4.80 (*0-395-58410-8*) HM.
—George & Martha Tons of Fun. (Illus.). 48p. (gr. k-3). 1986. 13.45 (*0-395-29524-6*); pap. 4.80 (*0-395-42646-4*) HM.
—Goldilocks & the Three Bears. Marshall, James, illus. LC 87-32983. 32p. (ps-3). 1988. 14.00 (*0-8037-0542-5*); PLB 13.89 (*0-8037-0543-3*) Dial Bks Young.

—Hansel & Gretel. LC 89-26011. (Illus.). 32p. (ps-3). 1990. 12.95 (*0-8037-0827-0*); PLB 12.89 (*0-8037-0828-9*) Dial Bks Young.
—James Marshall's Mother Goose. Marshall, James, illus. LC 79-2574. 40p. (ps-6). 1986. pap. 5.95 (*0-374-43723-8*) FS&G.
—Merry Christmas, Space Case. Marshall, James, illus. LC 85-1664. 32p. (ps-3). 1986. 11.95 (*0-8037-0215-9*) Dial Bks Young.
—Merry Christmas Space Case. 1989. pap. 4.95 (*0-8037-0653-7*, Dial) Doubleday.
—The Night Before Christmas. (Illus.). 1992. 4.95 (*0-590-45977-5*, Blue Ribbon Bks) Scholastic Inc.
—Old Mother Hubbard & Her Wonderful Dog. (ps-3). 1991. 13.95 (*0-374-35621-1*) FS&G.
—Old Mother Hubbard & Her Wonderful Dog. (ps-3). 1993. pap. 4.95 (*0-374-45611-9*) FS&G.
—Pocketful of Nonsense. (Illus.). 24p. (ps-k). 1992. write for info. (*0-307-00140-7*, 312-05, Golden Pr) Western Pub.
—Rats on the Range & Other Stories. LC 92-28918. (gr. 1-5). 1993. 12.99 (*0-8037-1384-3*); PLB 12.89 (*0-8037-1385-1*) Dial Bks Young.
—Rats on the Roof: And Other Stories. Marshall, James, illus. LC 90-44084. 80p. (gr. 1-5). 1991. 13.00 (*0-8037-0834-3*); lib. bdg. 12.89 (*0-8037-0835-1*) Dial Bks Young.
—Red Riding Hood. LC 86-16722. (Illus.). 32p. (ps-3). 1987. 13.99 (*0-8037-0344-9*); PLB 10.89 (*0-8037-0345-7*) Dial Bks Young.
—Red Riding Hood. (ps-3). 1991. pap. 4.95 (*0-8037-1054-2*, Dial Pied Piper) Puffin Bks.
—Red Riding Hood. (Illus.). 32p. (ps-3). 1993. pap. 17.99 (*0-14-054976-5*, Puffin Pied Piper) Puffin Bks.
—Taking Care of Carruthers. (Illus.). (gr. 4-6). 1981. 14.45 (*0-395-28593-3*) HM.
—Three up a Tree. Marshall, James, illus. LC 86-2163. 48p. (ps-3). 1986. 9.95 (*0-8037-0328-7*); PLB 9.89 (*0-685-13452-0*) Dial Bks Young.
—Tres en un Arbol - Three up a Tree. Baro, Ana B., tr. Marshall, James, illus. (SPA.). 48p. (gr. 2-4). 1990. pap. write for info. (*84-204-4637-8*) Santillana.
—What's the Matter with Carruthers? Marshall, James, illus. LC 72-75607. 32p. (gr. k-3). 1972. 16.95 (*0-395-13895-7*) HM.
—Willis. Marshall, James, illus. LC 74-5259. (gr. k-3). 1974. 13.95 (*0-395-19494-6*) HM.
—Willis. Marshall, James, illus. (ps-3). 1989. pap. 4.95 (*0-395-51008-2*, Sandpiper) HM.
—Wings: A Tale of Two Chickens. (ps up). 1988. pap. 4.99 (*0-14-050579-2*, Puffin) Puffin Bks.
—Yummers! Marshall, James, illus. LC 72-5400. 32p. (gr. k-3). 1973. 13.45 (*0-395-14757-3*) HM.
—Yummers! (Illus.). (gr. 4-8). 1986. pap. 4.80 (*0-395-39590-9*, Sandpiper) HM.
—Yummers Too. Marshall, James, illus. LC 86-10667. 32p. (gr. k-3). 1986. 12.95 (*0-395-38990-9*) HM.
—Yummers Too: The Second Course. Marshall, James, illus. 32p. (gr. k-3). 1990. pap. 4.95 (*0-395-53967-6*) HM.

Marshall, James, jt. auth. see Allard, Harry.

Marshall, James, compiled by. & illus. Pocketful of Nonsense. LC 93-18297. 1993. 12.95 (*0-307-17552-9*, Golden Pr) Western Pub.

Marshall, James, retold by. & illus. The Three Little Pigs. LC 88-33411. (ps-3). 1989. 12.95 (*0-8037-0591-3*); PLB 12.89 (*0-8037-0594-8*) Dial Bks Young.

Marshall, James, illus. James Marshall's Mother Goose. LC 79-2574. 40p. (ps-3). 1979. 15.00 (*0-374-33653-9*) FS&G.

Marshall, Janet P. My Camera: At the Aquarium, Vol. 1. 1989. 12.95 (*0-316-54713-1*) Little.
—My Camera: At the Zoo. Marshall, Janet P., illus. 32p. (ps-2). 1989. 12.95 (*0-316-54687-9*) Little.
—Ohmygosh My Pocket. Marshall, Janet P., illus. 24p. (ps-k). 1992. bds. 7.95 (*1-56397-044-9*) Boyds Mills Pr.

Marshall, Kirk. Backboard Battle. 144p. (gr. 4 up). 1989. pap. 2.95 (*0-345-35910-0*) Ballantine.
—Fast Breaks. (gr. 4 up). 1989. pap. 3.99 (*0-345-35908-9*) Ballantine.
—Longshot Center. (gr. 4 up). 1989. pap. 3.95 (*0-345-35909-7*) Ballantine.
—Pressure Play. (gr. 6-10). 1989. pap. 2.95 (*0-345-35913-5*) Ballantine.

Marshall, Laura. The Girl Who Changed Her Fate. Marshall, Laura, illus. LC 91-23137. 32p. (ps-3). 1992. SBE 14.95 (*0-689-31742-5*, Atheneum Child Bk) Macmillan Child Grp.

Marshall, Linda D. What Is a Step? Marshall, Linda D., et al, illus. LC 91-67511. 48p. (Orig.). 5). 1992. pap. 10.00 (*1-879289-00-8*) Native Sun Pubs.

Marshall, Mary A. Music. LC 93-14832. (Illus.). 48p. (gr. 5-6). 1994. RSBE 14.95 (*0-89686-793-5*, Crestwood Hse) Macmillan Child Grp.

Marshall, Mollie. Ready for Romance. 192p. (Orig.). (gr. 6-12). 1982. pap. 1.95 (*0-8439-1129-8*) Dorchester Pub Co.

Marshall, Norman F. & Ripamonti, Aldo. Leonardo da Vinci. (Illus.). 104p. (gr. 5-8). 1990. 16.98 (*0-382-09982-6*); pap. 8.95 (*0-382-24007-3*) Silver Burdett Pr.

Marshall, Peter, et al. From Sea to Shining Sea for Children: Discovering God's Plan for America in Her First Half-Century of Independence. 176p. (gr. 3-6). 1993. pap. 9.99 (*0-8007-5484-0*) Revell.

—The Light & the Glory for Children. LC 92-11727.
(Illus.). 160p. (Orig.). (gr. 4-7). 1992. pap. 9.99
(0-8007-5448-4) Revell.
Marshall, Ray & Bradley, John. The Car: Watch It Work
by Operating the Moving Diagrams! Marshall, Ray &
Bradley, John, illus. LC 83-40569. 10p. 1984. pap. 14.
95 (0-670-20371-8) Viking Child Bks.
—The Train: Watch It Work. Marshall, Ray & Bradley,
John, illus. 1986. pap. 13.95 (0-670-81134-3) Viking
Child Bks.
Marshall, Rita. I Hate to Read. Delessert, Etienne, illus.
1992. PLB 16.95 (0-88682-531-8) Creative Ed.
Marshall, Val & Tester, Bronwyn. And Grandpa Sat on
Friday. Spavern, Marilyn, illus. LC 92-34159. 1993.
4.25 (0-383-03610-0) SRA Schl Grp.
—The Cat's Whiskers. Knuckey, Cam, illus. LC 93-11737.
1994. 4.25 SRA Schl Grp.
—The Old Car. Axelsen, Stephen, illus. LC 92-27264.
1993. 3.75 (0-383-03644-5) SRA Schl Grp.
Marshall, William. Adam's Island. (Illus.). (gr. 1-8).
1992. PLB 8.95 (0-89565-889-5); Resale. 12.75
(0-685-60990-1) Childs World.
Marshall-Noke, Dorothy. Feathers. Weinberger, Jane, ed.
Christian, Marilynn V., illus. LC 88-51278. 64p. (gr.
1-4). 1990. pap. 7.95 (0-932433-52-9) Windswept Hse.
Marshbum, Sandra, jt. auth. see RanDelle, B. J.
Marson, Ron. Balancing. LC 81-90443. (Illus.). 80p. (gr.
5-10). 1981. 13.95 (0-941008-31-2) Tops Learning.
—Electricity. Marson, Peg, illus. LC 81-90444. 80p. (gr.
5-10). 1983. 13.95 (0-941008-32-0) Tops Learning.
—Green Thumbs: Corn & Beans. Marson, Peg, illus. 80p.
(gr. 5-10). 1989. tchr's ed. 13.95 (0-941008-39-8) Tops
Learning.
—Green Thumbs: Radishes. Marson, Peg, illus. 80p. (gr.
5-10). 1986. tchr's ed. 13.95 (0-941008-38-X) Tops
Learning.
—Magnetism. Marson, Peg, illus. LC 81-90445. 78p. (gr.
5-10). 1983. 13.95 (0-941008-33-9) Tops Learning.
—Metric Measuring. Marson, Peg, illus. LC 81-90446.
80p. (gr. 5-10). 1984. 13.95 (0-941008-35-5) Tops
Learning.
—More Metrics. LC 81-90448. (Illus.). 80p. (gr. 5-10).
1985. 13.95 (0-941008-36-3) Tops Learning.
—Pendulums. Marson, Peg, illus. LC 81-90447. 80p. (gr.
5-10). 1983. 13.95 (0-941008-34-7) Tops Learning.
Marson, Ron, jt. auth. see Metcalf, Doris.
Marson, Ron, ed. see Balick, Don.
Marson, Ron, ed. see Fellers, Pat & Gritzmacher, Kathy.
Marston, Bernice & Swiecki, Mark. In Plain English: A
Game of Figurative Language. 1991. instr's manual 34.
95 (1-55999-210-7) LinguiSystems.
Marston, Elsa. Cynthia & the Runaway Gazebo. Henstra,
Friso, illus. LC 91-32548. 32p. (gr. k-4). 1992. 14.00
(0-688-10282-4, Tambourine Bks); PLB 13.93
(0-688-10283-2, Tambourine Bks) Morrow.
—A Griffin in the Garden. Daste, Larry, illus. LC 92-
35399. 32p. (gr. k up). 1993. 15.00 (0-688-10981-0,
Tambourine Bks); PLB 14.93 (0-688-10982-9,
Tambourine Bks) Morrow.
—Lebanon: New Light in an Ancient Land. LC 93-5402.
(Illus.). 128p. (gr. 4). 1994. RSBE 14.95
(0-87518-584-3, Dillon) Macmillan Child Grp.
—Mysteries in American Archaeology. LC 85-20259.
(Illus.). 115p. (gr. 7 up). 1986. 13.95 (0-8027-6608-0);
lib. bdg. 13.85 (0-8027-6627-7) Walker & Co.
Marston, Hope I. Big Rigs. rev. & updated ed. LC 92-
39881. (Illus.). 48p. (gr. 2-5). 1993. 14.99
(0-525-65123-3, Cobblehill Bks) Dutton Child Bks.
—To the Rescue. LC 90-2575. (Illus.). 48p. (gr. 2-5).
1991. 14.95 (0-525-65059-8, Cobblehill Bks) Dutton
Child Bks.
Martchenko, Michael. Bird Feeder Banquet. Martchenko,
Michael, illus. 24p. (Orig.). (gr. k-3). 1990. 14.95
(1-55037-147-9, Pub. by Annick CN); pap. 4.95
(1-55037-146-0, Pub. by Annick CN) Firefly Bks Ltd.
Martchenko, Michael, jt. auth. see Munsch, Robert.
Martel, Jane, ed. Smashed Potatoes: A Kid's Eye View of
the Kitchen. LC 74-10947. 96p. (gr. 2 up). 1974. HM.
Martell, Hazel see Zevin, Jack.
Martell, Hazel M. The Age of Discovery, 1500-1650.
LC 92-18621. (Illus.). 80p. (gr. 2-6). 1993. 17.95x
(0-8160-2789-7) Facts on File.
—Everyday Life in Viking Times. LC 93-36128. 1994.
write for info. (0-531-14287-6) Watts.
—Native Americans & Mesa Verde. LC 92-27758.
(Illus.). 32p. (gr. 5 up). 1993. RSBE 13.95
(0-87518-540-1, Dillon) Macmillan Child Grp.
—The Normans. LC 91-40970. (Illus.). 64p. (gr. 6 up).
1992. RSBE 14.95 (0-02-762428-5, New Discovery)
Macmillan Child Grp.
—Over Nine Hundred Years Ago: With the Vikings.
Payne, Roger, illus. LC 93-2647. 32p. (gr. 6 up). 1993.
RSBE 13.95 (0-02-726325-8, New Discovery Bks)
Macmillan Child Grp.
—Over Six Thousand Years Ago: In the Stone Age. LC
91-39458. (Illus.). 32p. (gr. 6 up). 1992. RSBE 13.95
(0-02-762429-3, New Discovery) Macmillan Child
Grp.
—The Vikings. LC 91-507. (Illus.). 64p. (gr. 6 up). 1992.
RSBE 14.95 (0-02-762427-7, New Discovery)
Macmillan Child Grp.
—The Vikings & Jorvik. LC 92-25215. (Illus.). 32p. (gr. 5
up). 1993. RSBE 13.95 (0-87518-541-X, Dillon)
Macmillan Child Grp.
—What Do We Know about the Celts? (Illus.). 40p. (gr.
3-6). 1993. 16.95 (0-87226-363-0) P Bedrick Bks.

Martell, Helen M. What Do We Know about the
Vikings? LC 92-7893. (Illus.). 40p. (gr. 3-6). 1992.
PLB 16.95 (0-87226-355-X) P Bedrick Bks.
Martell, Mary H. The Ancient Chinese. LC 92-9052.
(Illus.). 64p. (gr. 6 up). 1992. RSBE 14.95
(0-02-730653-4, New Discovery) Macmillan Child
Grp.
Martell, Ralph. Aesop's Fables in Song. Martell, Ralph,
illus. 21p. (gr. k-5). 1987. bk. & cassette 9.95
(0-941977-00-5, RTB-1) Ralmar Enter.
Marten, Elizabeth H., jt. auth. see Crosby, Nina E.
Marten, Phyllis. Why Papa Went Away & Other Stories.
112p. (gr. 8 up). 1987. pap. 4.95 (0-919797-45-8)
Kindred Pr.
Martens, Frederick H., tr. see Flesch, Carl.
Martens, Sheri. Adam & Andrea Learn & Grow:
Understanding Church Words from a Kid's Viewpoint.
Penner, Kathy, illus. 80p. (ps-5). 1989. pap. 7.95
(0-919797-81-4) Kindred Pr.
Marti, Donald B., Jr., jt. auth. see Kouhoupt, Rudy.
Martignoni, Margaret E., ed. & intro. by. Illustrated
Treasury of Children's Literature. (Illus.). 512p. (gr.
5-8). 1955. 18.95 (0-448-04101-4, G&D) Putnam Pub
Group.
Martin. Baby-Sitters' Summer Vacation Super Special,
No. 2. 1993. pap. 3.95 (0-590-44239-2) Scholastic Inc.
—Baby-Sitters' Winter Vacation Super Special, No. 3.
1993. pap. 3.95 (0-590-43973-1) Scholastic Inc.
—Brown Bear Ltd. 1992. 100.00 (0-8050-2308-9) H Holt
& Co.
—Claudia & the Mystery at the Museum. 1993. pap. 3.50
(0-590-47049-3) Scholastic Inc.
—Hello Mallory. 1993. pap. 3.25 (0-590-43385-7)
Scholastic Inc.
—Knots on a Counting. 1987. 14.95 (0-8050-1932-4) H
Holt & Co.
—Logan Likes Mary Anne! 1993. pap. 3.50
(0-590-43387-3) Scholastic Inc.
—Mallory & the Trouble with Twins. 1993. pap. 3.25
(0-590-43507-8) Scholastic Inc.
—Monkey Mothers. Date not set. 15.00 (0-06-023515-2,
Festival); PLB 14.89 (0-06-023516-0, Festival) HarpC
Child Bks.
—Reaching Your Goal, 8 bks, Set I, Reading Level 2.
(Illus.). 192p. (gr. 1-4). 1987. Set. PLB 116.80
(0-86592-166-0); 87.60s.p. (0-685-58796-7) Rourke
Corp.
Martin & McDowell. Life & Works, 4 bks, Set I, Reading
Level 8. (Illus.). 448p. (gr. 7 up). 1989. Set. PLB 79.76
(0-86592-295-0); 59.80s.p. (0-685-58807-6) Rourke
Corp.
Martin, Alexander C. Weeds. Zallinger, Jean, illus. 160p.
(gr. 7 up). 1973. pap. write for info. (0-307-24353-2,
Golden Pr) Western Pub.
Martin, Alexander C., jt. auth. see Zim, Herbert S.
Martin, Ana. Prehistoric Stone Monuments. LC 93-756.
(ENG & SPA., Illus.). 36p. (gr. 3 up). 1993. PLB 19.
93 (0-516-08386-4) Childrens.
—Romanesque Art & Architecture. LC 93-3436. (Illus.).
36p. (gr. 3 up). 1993. PLB 19.93 (0-516-08387-2)
Childrens.
Martin, Ann. Rachel Parker Kindergarten Show-Off.
Poydar, Nancy, illus. 1993. pap. 6.95 (0-8234-1067-6)
Holiday.
Martin, Ann A. Get Well Soon, Mallory. (gr. 4-7). 1993.
pap. 3.50 (0-590-47007-8) Scholastic Inc.
Martin, Ann M. Baby-Sitters at Shadow Lake Super
Special. 1992. pap. 3.50 (0-590-44962-1) Scholastic
Inc.
—Baby-Sitter's Club. (gr. 4 up). 1989. Set no. 5. pap. 11.
00 (0-590-63344-9, SCHOLASTIC) Scholastic Inc.
—Baby-Sitters Club, Bks. 5-8. (gr. 4-7). 1990. 13.00
boxed set (0-590-63672-3) Scholastic Inc.
—The Baby-Sitters Club, Bks. 9-12. (gr. 3-7). 1991. pap.
13.00 boxed set (0-590-63701-0) Scholastic Inc.
—The Baby-Sitters Club, Bks. 13-16. (gr. 3-7). 1991. pap.
13.00 boxed set (0-590-63705-3) Scholastic Inc.
—The Baby-Sitters Club, Bks. 17-20. (gr. 3-7). 1991. pap.
13.00 boxed set (0-590-63704-5) Scholastic Inc.
—The Baby-Sitters Club, Bks. 21-24. (gr. 3-7). 1991. pap.
13.00 boxed set (0-590-63703-7) Scholastic Inc.
—The Baby-Sitters Club, Bks. 25-28. (gr. 3-7). 1991. pap.
13.00 boxed set (0-590-63702-9) Scholastic Inc.
—Baby-Sitters Club, Bks. 29-32. (gr. 4-7). 1990. pap. 13.
00 boxed set (0-590-63583-2) Scholastic Inc.
—Baby-Sitters Club, 4 vols, Bks. 33-36. (gr. 4-7). 1990.
Boxed set. pap. 13.00 (0-590-63669-3) Scholastic Inc.
—Baby-Sitters Club, No. 45-48. (gr. 4-7). 1991. pap. 13.
00 boxed set (0-590-63963-3) Scholastic Inc.
—Baby-Sitters Club Guide to Baby-Sitting. (gr. 4-7).
1993. pap. 3.25 (0-590-47686-6) Scholastic Inc.
—Baby-Sitters Club Postcard Book. (gr. 4-7). 1991. pap.
4.95 (0-590-44783-1) Scholastic Inc.
—The Baby-Sitters Little Sister, Bks. 5-12. (gr. 2-4).
1990. pap. 11.00 boxed set (0-590-63668-5) Scholastic
Inc.
—The Baby-Sitters Little Sister, Bks. 17-20. 1991. pap.
11.00 boxed set (0-590-63950-1) Scholastic Inc.
—Baby-Sitters Little Sister Boxed Set, 4 bks, Bks. 25-28.
1992. Set. 11.00 (0-590-66125-6) Scholastic Inc.
—The Baby-Sitters Little Sister: School Scrapbook. (gr.
7-9). 1993. pap. 2.95 (0-590-47677-7) Scholastic Inc.
—Baby-Sitters Little Sisters: Secret Diary. (gr. 4-7). 1991.
pap. 2.50 (0-590-45010-7) Scholastic Inc.
—Baby-Sitters on Board! (gr. 3-6). 1988. pap. 3.95
(0-590-44240-6) Scholastic Inc.
—Beware Dawn! 160p. 1991. pap. 3.25 (0-590-44085-3)
Scholastic Inc.

—Boy-Crazy Stacey. (gr. 4-7). 1989. pap. 3.50
(0-590-43509-4) Scholastic Inc.
—Bummer Summer. LC 82-48755. 160p. (gr. 5-9). 1983.
14.95 (0-8234-0483-8) Holiday.
—Bummer Summer. (gr. 4-7). 1990. pap. 2.95
(0-590-43622-8) Scholastic Inc.
—California Girls! 240p. (gr. 3-7). 1990. pap. 3.75
(0-590-43575-2) Scholastic Inc.
—Claudia & Mean Janine. (gr. 4-7). 1987. pap. 3.50
(0-590-43719-4) Scholastic Inc.
—Claudia & Middle School. (gr. 4-7). 1991. pap. 3.25
(0-590-44082-9) Scholastic Inc.
—Claudia & the Bad Joke. 160p. (gr. 3-7). 1988. pap.
3.50 (0-590-43510-8) Scholastic Inc.
—Claudia & the Bad Joke. large type ed. 176p. (gr. 4 up).
1993. PLB 14.60 (0-8368-1023-6) Gareth Stevens Inc.
—Claudia & the New Girl. large type ed. LC 93-15969.
176p. (gr. 4 up). 1993. PLB 14.60 (0-8368-1016-3)
Gareth Stevens Inc.
—Claudia & the Phantom Phone Calls. 160p. (Orig.). (gr.
3-7). 1986. pap. 3.25 (0-590-43513-2) Scholastic Inc.
—Claudia: The Genius of Elm Street. 1991. pap. 3.25
(0-590-44970-2) Scholastic Inc.
—Claudia's Freind Friend. (gr. 4-7). 1993. pap. 3.50
(0-590-45665-2) Scholastic Inc.
—Dawn & the Big Sleepover. (gr. 4-7). 1991. pap. 3.50
(0-590-43573-6) Scholastic Inc.
—Dawn & the Disappearing Dogs. (gr. 4-7). 1993. pap.
3.50 (0-590-44960-5) Scholastic Inc.
—Dawn & the Impossible Three. 144p. (Orig.). (gr. 4-6).
1987. pap. 3.50 (0-590-43720-8) Scholastic Inc.
—Dawn & the Older Boy. (gr. 4-7). 1990. pap. 3.25
(0-590-43566-3) Scholastic Inc.
—Dawn & the Surfer Ghost. (gr. 4-7). 1993. pap. 3.50
(0-590-47050-7) Scholastic Inc.
—Dawn on the Coast. 1989. pap. 3.50 (0-590-43900-6)
Scholastic Inc.
—Dawn Saves the Planet. 1992. 3.25 (0-590-45658-X,
052) Scholastic Inc.
—Dawn's Big Move. (gr. 4-7). 1993. pap. 3.50
(0-590-47005-1) Scholastic Inc.
—Dawn's Family Feud. (gr. 4-7). 1993. pap. 3.50
(0-590-45666-0) Scholastic Inc.
—Dawn's Wicked Stepsister. (gr. 4-7). 1990. pap. 3.25
(0-590-42497-1) Scholastic Inc.
—Eleven Kids, One Summer. LC 91-55025. 160p. (gr.
3-7). 1991. 14.95 (0-8234-0912-0) Holiday.
—Eleven Kids, One Summer. (gr. 4-7). 1993. pap. 2.95
(0-590-45917-1) Scholastic Inc.
—Ghost at Dawn's House. 1993. pap. 3.50
(0-590-43508-6) Scholastic Inc.
—Good-Bye, Stacy, Good-Bye. large type ed. LC 93-
4345. 176p. (gr. 4 up). 1993. PLB 14.60
(0-8368-1017-1) Gareth Stevens Inc.
—Goodbye Stacey, Goodbye. 1993. pap. 3.25
(0-590-43386-5) Scholastic Inc.
—Hello, Mallory. large type ed. 176p. (gr. 4 up). 1993.
PLB 14.60 (0-8368-1018-X) Gareth Stevens Inc.
—Inside Out. LC 83-18631. 160p. (gr. 4-9). 1984. 13.95
(0-8234-0512-5) Holiday.
—Inside Out. (gr. 5-7). 1990. pap. 2.95 (0-590-43621-X)
Scholastic Inc.
—Jessi & the Awful Secret. (gr. 4-7). 1993. pap. 3.50
(0-590-45663-6) Scholastic Inc.
—Jessi & the Bad Baby-Sitter. 1993. pap. 3.50
(0-590-47006-X) Scholastic Inc.
—Jessi & the Dance School Phantom. 160p. (gr. 3-7).
1991. pap. 3.50 (0-590-44083-7, Apple Paperbacks)
Scholastic Inc.
—Jessi and the Jewel Thieves: Baby-sitters Club Mystery
Ser. (gr. 4-7). 1993. pap. 3.50 (0-590-44959-1)
Scholastic Inc.
—Jessi & the Superbrat. (gr. 5 up). 1989. pap. 3.25
(0-590-42502-1, Apple Paperbacks) Scholastic Inc.
—Jessi's Baby Sitter. (gr. 4-7). 1990. pap. 3.50
(0-590-43565-5) Scholastic Inc.
—Jessi's Gold Medal. 1992. pap. 3.25 (0-590-44964-8,
Apple Paperbacks) Scholastic Inc.
—Jessi's Secret Language. 1993. pap. 3.50
(0-590-44234-1) Scholastic Inc.
—Jessi's Secret Language. large type ed. LC 93-15971.
176p. (gr. 4 up). 1993. PLB 14.60 (0-8368-1020-1)
Gareth Stevens Inc.
—Jessi's Wish. (gr. 4 up). 1993. pap. 3.50
(0-685-66003-6) Scholastic Inc.
—Just a Summer Romance. LC 86-46201. 170p. (gr. 7
up). 1987. 13.95 (0-8234-0649-0) Holiday.
—Just a Summer Romance. 1988. pap. 2.75
(0-590-43999-5, NAL) Scholastic Inc.
—Karen, Hannie, & Nancy: The Three Musketeers. 128p.
(gr. 2-4). 1992. pap. 2.95 (0-590-45644-X, Little
Apple) Scholastic Inc.
—Karen's Baby. (gr. 4-7). 1992. pap. 3.25
(0-590-45649-0) Scholastic Inc.
—Karen's Big Joke. 1992. pap. 2.95 (0-590-44829-3)
Scholastic Inc.
—Karen's Big Lie. (gr. 4-7). 1993. pap. 2.95
(0-590-45655-5) Scholastic Inc.
—Karen's Big Weekend. (gr. 4-7). 1993. pap. 2.95
(0-590-47043-4) Scholastic Inc.
—Karen's Birthday. (gr. 4-7). 1990. pap. 2.95
(0-590-44257-0) Scholastic Inc.
—Karen's Brothers. (gr. 4-7). 1991. pap. 2.75
(0-590-43643-0) Scholastic Inc.
—Karen's Bully. 1992. 2.95 (0-590-45646-6, 053)
Scholastic Inc.
—Karens Campout. (gr. 3-7). 1993. pap. 3.25
(0-590-46911-8) Scholastic Inc.

—Karen's Carnival. 112p. (gr. 2-4). 1991. 2.75 (0-590-44823-4) Scholastic Inc.
—Karen's Cartwheel. 1992. pap. 2.75 (0-590-44825-0) Scholastic Inc.
—Karen's Doll. 112p. 1991. pap. 2.95 (0-590-44832-3) Scholastic Inc.
—Karen's Doll House. (gr. 4-7). 1993. pap. 2.95 (0-590-45652-0) Scholastic Inc.
—Karen's Ducklings. 96p. 1992. pap. 2.75 (0-590-44830-7) Scholastic Inc.
—Karen's Ghost. 96p. (gr. 2-4). 1990. pap. 2.95 (0-590-43649-X) Scholastic Inc.
—Karen's Goldfish. 112p. (gr. 2-4). 1991. pap. 2.75 (0-590-44844-9) Scholastic Inc.
—Karen's Good-Bye. (gr. 4-7). 1991. pap. 2.95 (0-590-43641-4) Scholastic Inc.
—Karen's Grandmother. (gr. 4-7). 1990. pap. 2.75 (0-590-43651-1) Scholastic Inc.
—Karen's Haircut. (gr. 4-7). 1990. pap. 2.75 (0-590-42670-2) Scholastic Inc.
—Karen's Home Run. (gr. 4-7). 1991. pap. 2.75 (0-590-43642-2) Scholastic Inc.
—Karen's in Love. (gr. 4-7). 1991. pap. 2.75 (0-590-43645-7) Scholastic Inc.
—Karen's Kittens. 1992. pap. 2.75 (0-590-45645-8) Scholastic Inc.
—Karen's Kittycat Club. 112p. (gr. 2-4). 1989. pap. 2.75 (0-590-44264-3) Scholastic Inc.
—Karen's Little Sister. 96p. (gr. 2-4). 1989. pap. 2.95 (0-590-44298-8) Scholastic Inc.
—Karen's Little Witch. 112p. 1991. pap. 2.95 (0-590-44833-1) Scholastic Inc.
—Karen's Mystery. 144p. 1991. pap. 2.95 (0-590-44827-7) Scholastic Inc.
—Karen's New Friend. (gr. 4-7). 1993. pap. 2.95 (0-590-45651-2) Scholastic Inc.
—Karen's New Teacher. (gr. 4-7). 1991. pap. 2.95 (0-590-44824-2) Scholastic Inc.
—Karen's New Year. (gr. 4-7). 1991. pap. 2.75 (0-590-43646-5) Scholastic Inc.
—Karen's Newspaper. (gr. 4-7). 1993. pap. 2.95 (0-590-47040-X) Scholastic Inc.
—Karen's Pen Pal. 96p. 1992. pap. 2.95 (0-590-44831-5) Scholastic Inc.
—Karen's Pizza Party. 1993. pap. 2.95 (0-590-47042-6) Scholastic Inc.
—Karen's Plane Trip. 144p. (gr. 2-4). 1991. pap. 3.25 (0-590-44834-X) Scholastic Inc.
—Karen's Prize. 1990. pap. 2.95 (0-590-43650-3) Scholastic Inc.
—Karen's Roller Skates. 64p. (gr. 2-4). 1988. pap. 2.95 (0-590-44259-7) Scholastic Inc.
—Karen's School. (gr. 4-7). 1993. pap. 2.95 (0-590-47041-8) Scholastic Inc.
—Karen's School Picture. 112p. (gr. 2-4). 1989. pap. 2.95 (0-590-44258-9) Scholastic Inc.
—Karen's Secret. 1992. 2.95 (0-590-45648-2) Scholastic Inc.
—Karen's Sleepover. (gr. 4-7). 1990. pap. 2.95 (0-590-43652-X) Scholastic Inc.
—Karen's Snowy Day. (gr. 4-7). 1993. pap. 2.95 (0-590-45650-4) Scholastic Inc.
—Karen's Surprise. 112p. (gr. 2-4). 1990. pap. 2.75 (0-590-43648-1) Scholastic Inc.
—Karen's Tea Party. 96p. 1992. pap. 2.75 (0-590-44828-5) Scholastic Inc.
—Karen's Toothache. (gr. 4-7). 1993. pap. 2.95 (0-590-46912-6) Scholastic Inc.
—Karen's Tuba. (gr. 4-7). 1993. pap. 2.95 (0-590-45653-9) Scholastic Inc.
—Karen's Wedding. (gr. 4-7). 1993. pap. 2.95 (0-590-45654-7) Scholastic Inc.
—Karen's Wish. 128p. (gr. 2-4). 1990. pap. 3.25 (0-590-43647-3) Scholastic Inc.
—Karen's Witch. 112p. (gr. 2-4). 1988. pap. 2.95 (0-590-44300-3) Scholastic Inc.
—Karen's Worst Day. 1993. pap. 2.95 (0-590-44299-6) Scholastic Inc.
—Keep Out, Claudia! 160p. (gr. 3-7). 1992. pap. 3.50 (0-590-45657-1, Apple Paperbacks) Scholastic Inc.
—Kristy & the Baby Parade. 160p. (gr. 3-7). 1991. pap. 3.50 (0-590-43574-4) Scholastic Inc.
—Kristy & the Baby Parade. 154p. 1992. text ed. 11.60 (1-56956-118-4) W A T Braille.
—Kristy and the Haunted Mansion. (gr. 4-7). 1993. pap. 3.50 (0-590-44958-3) Scholastic Inc.
—Kristy & the Missing Child: Baby-Sitters Club Mystery, No. 4. 160p. 1992. pap. 3.25 (0-590-44800-5) Scholastic Inc.
—Kristy & the Mother's Day Surprise. (gr. 4-7). 1989. pap. 3.50 (0-590-43506-X) Scholastic Inc.
—Kristy & the Snobs. 1993. pap. 3.50 (0-590-43660-0) Scholastic Inc.
—Kristy & the Snobs. large type ed. LC 93-15968. 176p. (gr. 4 up). 1993. PLB 14.60 (0-8368-1015-5) Gareth Stevens Inc.
—Kristy & the Walking Disaster. 1993. pap. 3.50 (0-590-43722-4) Scholastic Inc.
—Kristy & the Walking Disaster. large type ed. 176p. (gr. 4 up). 1993. PLB 14.60 (0-8368-1024-4) Gareth Stevens Inc.
—Kristy and the Worst Kid Ever. (gr. 4-7). 1993. pap. 3.50 (0-590-45664-4) Scholastic Inc.
—Kristy for President. 160p. 1992. pap. 3.25 (0-590-44967-2) Scholastic Inc.
—Kristy's Big Day. (gr. 4-7). 1987. pap. 3.25 (0-590-43899-9) Scholastic Inc.

—Kristy's Great Idea. 1991. collector's ed. 9.95 (0-590-44816-1, Scholastic Hardcover) Scholastic Inc.
—Kristy's Great Idea. 1993. pap. 3.25 (0-590-43388-1) Scholastic Inc.
—Kristy's Mystery Admirer. (gr. 4-7). 1990. pap. 3.25 (0-590-43567-1) Scholastic Inc.
—Little Miss Stoneybrook-- & Dawn. large type ed. LC 93-8100. 176p. (gr. 4 up). 1993. PLB 14.60 (0-8368-1019-8) Gareth Stevens Inc.
—Little Miss Stoneybrook & Dawn. 160p. (gr. 3-7). 1988. pap. 3.25 (0-590-43717-8) Scholastic Inc.
—Logan Bruno, Boy Baby-Sitter. (gr. 3-7). 1993. pap. 3.50 (0-590-47118-X) Scholastic Inc.
—Logan Likes Maryanne. 160p. (Orig.). (gr. 4-6). 1988. pap. 2.75 (0-590-41124-1, Apple Paperbacks) Scholastic Inc.
—Logan's Story (Special Edition Reader's Request) 1992. pap. 3.25 (0-590-44575-3, Apple Paperbacks) Scholastic Inc.
—Ma & Pa Dracula. Zimmer, Dirk, illus. LC 89-2081. 128p. (gr. 3-7). 1989. 13.95 (0-8234-0781-0) Holiday.
—Ma & Pa Dracula. 128p. 1991. pap. 2.95 (0-590-43828-X) Scholastic Inc.
—Maid Mary Anne. (gr. 4-7). 1993. pap. 3.50 (0-590-47004-3) Scholastic Inc.
—Mallory & the Ghost Cat. 160p. 1992. pap. 3.25 (0-590-44799-8) Scholastic Inc.
—Mallory & the Secret Diary. (gr. 5 up). 1989. pap. 3.25 (0-590-42500-5, Apple Paperbacks) Scholastic Inc.
—Mallory Hates Boys (& Gym) 1992. 3.25 (0-590-45660-1) Scholastic Inc.
—Mallory on Strike. (gr. 4-7). 1991. pap. 3.50 (0-590-44971-0) Scholastic Inc.
—Mallory's Dream Horse. 160p. 1992. pap. 3.25 (0-590-44965-6) Scholastic Inc.
—Mary Anne & the Search for Tigger. 1993. pap. 3.50 (0-590-43347-4) Scholastic Inc.
—Mary Anne & the Secret in the Attic. 160p. (gr. 3-7). 1992. pap. 3.25 (0-590-44801-3, Apple Paperbacks) Scholastic Inc.
—Mary Anne & Too Many Babies. 160p. 1992. pap. 3.25 (0-590-44966-4) Scholastic Inc.
—Mary Anne & Too Many Boys. (gr. 4-7). 1990. pap. 3.25 (0-590-42494-7) Scholastic Inc.
—Mary Anne Misses Logan. 160p. (gr. 3-7). 1991. pap. 3.50 (0-590-43569-8) Scholastic Inc.
—Mary Anne Saves the Day. 1993. pap. 3.50 (0-590-43512-4) Scholastic Inc.
—Mary Anne vs. Logan. (gr. 4-7). 1991. pap. 3.50 (0-590-43570-1) Scholastic Inc.
—Mary Anne's Bad Luck Mystery. 144p. (gr. 3-7). 1988. 3.50 (0-590-43659-7) Scholastic Inc.
—Mary Anne's Bad-Luck Mystery. large type ed. LC 93-4346. 176p. (gr. 4 up). 1993. PLB 14.60 (0-8368-1021-X) Gareth Stevens Inc.
—Mary Anne's Makeover. (gr. 4-7). 1993. pap. 3.50 (0-590-45662-8) Scholastic Inc.
—Me & Katie (the Pest) Sims, Blanche, illus. LC 85-5558. 160p. (gr. 4-7). 1985. 13.95 (0-8234-0580-X) Holiday.
—Me & Katie the Pest. 1990. pap. 2.95 (0-590-43618-X) Scholastic Inc.
—Missing since Monday. LC 86-45390. 176p. (gr. 7 up). 1986. 14.95 (0-8234-0626-1) Holiday.
—Missing since Monday. 176p. (gr. 7 up). 1987. pap. 2.95 (0-590-43136-6) Scholastic Inc.
—The Mystery at Claudia's House. 1992. 3.25 (0-590-44961-3) Scholastic Inc.
—New York, New York. (gr. 4-7). 1991. pap. 3.50 (0-590-43576-0) Scholastic Inc.
—Poor Mallory. 160p. 1990. pap. 3.25 (0-590-43568-X) Scholastic Inc.
—Rachel Parker, Kindergarten Show-Off. Poydar, Nancy, illus. LC 91-25793. 40p. (ps-3). 1992. reinforced bdg. 15.95 (0-8234-0935-X) Holiday.
—Sea City, Here We Come! (gr. 3-7). 1993. pap. 3.95 (0-590-45674-1) Scholastic Inc.
—Slam Book. LC 87-45335. 160p. (gr. 7 up). 1987. 12.95 (0-8234-0666-0) Holiday.
—Snowbound. 240p. 1991. pap. 3.95 (0-590-44963-X) Scholastic Inc.
—Stacey & the Cheerleaders. (gr. 4-7). 1993. pap. 3.50 (0-590-47008-6) Scholastic Inc.
—Stacey & the Missing Ring. 160p. (gr. 3-7). 1991. pap. 3.50 (0-590-44084-5) Scholastic Inc.
—Stacey & the Mystery. (gr. 4-7). 1993. pap. 3.50 (0-590-45696-2) Scholastic Inc.
—Stacey & the Mystery of Stoneybrook. (gr. 4-7). 1990. pap. 3.50 (0-590-42508-0) Scholastic Inc.
—Stacey's Big Crush. (gr. 4-7). 1993. pap. 3.50 (0-590-45667-9) Scholastic Inc.
—Stacey's Emergency. (gr. 4-7). 1991. pap. 3.50 (0-590-43572-8) Scholastic Inc.
—Stacey's Ex-Best Friend. 160p. 1992. pap. 3.25 (0-590-44968-0) Scholastic Inc.
—Stacey's Mistake. 1993. pap. 3.50 (0-590-43718-6) Scholastic Inc.
—Stacey's Mistake. large type ed. LC 93-8086. 176p. (gr. 4 up). 1993. PLB 14.60 (0-8368-1022-8) Gareth Stevens Inc.
—Stage Fright. Sims, Blanche, illus. LC 84-47834. 144p. (gr. 3-7). 1984. 13.95 (0-8234-0541-9) Holiday.
—Stage Fright. (gr. 5-7). 1990. pap. 2.95 (0-590-43619-8) Scholastic Inc.
—Starring the Baby-Sitters Club. (gr. 4-7). 1992. pap. 3.95 (0-590-45661-X) Scholastic Inc.
—Ten Kids, No Pets. LC 87-25206. 184p. (gr. 3-7). 1988. 14.95 (0-8234-0691-1) Holiday.

—Ten Kids No Pets. (gr. 5-7). 1990. pap. 2.75 (0-590-43620-1) Scholastic Inc.
—The Truth about Stacey. 1993. pap. 3.25 (0-590-43511-6) Scholastic Inc.
—Welcome Back, Stacey. (gr. 5 up). 1989. pap. 3.25 (0-590-42501-3, Apple Paperbacks) Scholastic Inc.
—With You & Without You. LC 85-21990. 192p. (gr. 4-8). 1986. 14.95 (0-8234-0601-6) Holiday.
—Your Turly, Shirley. (gr. 5-7). 1990. pap. 2.95 (0-590-42809-8) Scholastic Inc.
—Yours Turly, Shirley. LC 88-6460. 144p. (gr. 3-7). 1988. 14.95 (0-8234-0719-5) Holiday.
Martin, Ann The BabySitters Club, 10 titles. large type ed. (gr. 4 up). 1993. Set. PLB 146.00 (0-8368-1025-2) Gareth Stevens Inc.
Martin, Antoinette T. Famous Seaweed Soup. Mathews, Judith, ed. Westcott, Nadine B., illus. LC 92-31612. 32p. (ps-2). 1993. PLB 13.95 (0-8075-2263-5) A Whitman.
Martin, B. Yo, Grocer. (gr. 4 up). 1990. 12.95 (0-8050-0329-0) H Holt & Co.
Martin, B. Jay. Conundrum, Vol. 1: A Cartoon Collection of Concepts, College, & Confounded Connotations. Martin, B. Jay, illus. Lillard, Ross E., intro. by. (Illus.). 160p. (Orig.). (gr. 12 up). 1988. pap. 5.95 (0-922073-00-7) Thought Wave Pr.
Martin, Bengt. Olaf the Ship's Cat. Friberger, Anna, illus. 32p. (ps-3). 1992. 7.95 (1-56288-266-X) Checkerboard.
Martin, Bette. The Children's Material. (Illus.). 100p. (gr. k-4). 1980. pap. write for info. (1-880436-02-7) Miracle Exper.
—Help Is on the Way. (Illus.). 61p. (gr. 5-7). 1986. pap. write for info. (1-880436-01-9) Miracle Exper.
Martin, Bill. Calendar Lion. 1993. write for info. (0-8050-2417-4) H Holt & Co.
—Chicka Chicka ABC. (ps-6). 1993. 4.95 (0-671-87893-X, Little Simon) S&S Trade.
—Fit for the King. Haynes, Glenda, ed. Sweeney, Hazel, illus. 384p. (Orig.). (gr. 7 up). 1985. pap. 11.50 (0-89114-154-5) Baptist Pub Hse.
—Happy Hippopotami. 30p. (ps-3). 1991. pap. 19.95 (0-15-233381-9, HB Juv Bks) HarBrace.
—Happy Hippopotami. (ps-3). 1992. pap. 4.95 (0-15-233382-7) HarBrace.
—Knots on a Counting Rope. Rand, Ted, illus. 32p. (gr. k-3). 1993. pap. 19.95 (0-8050-2955-9, Bks Young Read) H Holt & Co.
—Little Woodland Books: The Bears & the Bees; The Doe & the Fawn; The Earthworm & the Underground; The Fox & the Fleas; The Gray Squirrel & the Red Intruder; The Owl & the Mouse; The Rabbit & the Cat; The Skunk & Its Swoosher; The Wild Turkey & Her Poults; The Bird & the Snake, 10 vols. (Illus.). (gr. 1-6). 1979. incl. cassettes 149.00 (0-87827-322-0) Ency Brit Ed.
—Words. (ps-6). 1993. 4.95 (0-671-87174-9, Little Simon) S&S Trade.
Martin, Bill, Jr. Brown Bear, Brown Bear, What Do You See? Carle, Eric, illus. LC 83-12779. 24p. (ps-k). 1983. 14.95 (0-8050-0201-4, Bks Young Read) H Holt & Co.
—Brown Bear, Brown Bear, What Do You See? 25th Anniversary Edition. Carle, Eric, illus. LC 91-29115. 32p. (ps-k). 1992. 14.95 (0-8050-1744-5, Bks Young Read) H Holt & Co.
—The Happy Hippopotami. Johnston, Allyn, ed. Everitt, Betsy, illus. 32p. (ps-3). 1991. 12.95 (0-15-233380-0) HarBrace.
—Little Nature Books. Incl. Poppies Afield; Frogs in a Pond; Butterflies Becoming; Germination; Ants Underground; A Mushroom Is Growing; A Hydra Goes Walking; Moon Cycle; Messenger Bee; June Bugs. (Illus.). (gr. 1-6). 1975. 149.00 (0-87827-196-1); tchr's. guide incl. (0-685-55948-3); cassettes incl. Ency Brit Ed.
—Old Devil Wind. Root, Barry, illus. LC 92-37908. 1993. 13.95 (0-15-257768-8) HarBrace.
—Polar Bear, Polar Bear, What Do You Hear? Carle, Eric, illus. 32p. (ps). 1991. 14.95 (0-8050-1759-3, Bks Young Read) H Holt & Co.
—Polar Bear, Polar Bear, What Do You Hear? Carle, Eric, illus. 32p. (ps-2). 1993. PLB 16.95 incl. plush toy (0-8050-2815-3, Bks Young Read) H Holt & Co.
—Polar Bear, Polar Bear, What Do You Hear? Big Book. Carle, Eric, illus. LC 91-13322. 32p. (ps-2). 1993. pap. 18.95 (0-8050-2346-1, Bks Young Read) H Holt & Co.
—The Wizard. Schaefer, Alex, illus. LC 93-15521. 1994. write for info. (0-15-298926-9) HarBrace.
Martin, Bill, Jr. & Archambault, John. Barn Dance! Rand, Ted, illus. LC 86-14225. 32p. (ps-2). 1986. 13.95 (0-8050-0089-5, Bks Young Read); pap. 4.95 (0-8050-0799-7) H Holt & Co.
—Chicka Chicka Boom Boom. Ehlert, Lois, illus. (gr. 2-6). 1989. pap. 13.95 jacketed (0-671-67949-X, S&S BFYR) S&S Trade.
—The Ghost-Eye Tree. Rand, Ted, illus. LC 85-8422. 32p. (Orig.). (ps-2). 1985. 13.95 (0-8050-0208-1, Bks Young Read); pap. 5.95 (0-8050-0947-7) H Holt & Co.
—Here Are My Hands. Rand, Ted, illus. LC 86-25842. 32p. (ps-2). 1987. 14.95 (0-8050-0328-2, Bks Young Read) H Holt & Co.
—Here Are My Hands. Rand, Ted, illus. LC 86-25842. 32p. (ps-2). 1989. pap. 5.95 (0-8050-1168-4, Owlet BYR) H Holt & Co.

—Knots on a Counting Rope. Rand, Ted, illus. LC 87-14832. 32p. (ps-2). 1987. 14.95 (*0-8050-0571-4*, Bks Young Read) H Holt & Co.
—Listen to the Rain. Endicott, James, illus. LC 88-6502. 32p. (ps-2). 1988. 14.95 (*0-8050-0682-6*, Bks Young Read) H Holt & Co.
—The Magic Pumpkin. Lee, Robert J., illus. LC 89-11162. 32p. (ps-2). 1989. 14.95 (*0-8050-1134-X*, Bks Young Read) H Holt & Co.
—Up & down on the Merry-Go-Round. Rand, Ted, illus. LC 87-28836. 32p. (ps-2). 1988. 12.95 (*0-8050-0681-8*, Bks Young Read) H Holt & Co.
—Up & Down on the Merry-Go-Round. Rand, Ted, illus. LC 87-28836. 32p. (ps-2). 1991. pap. 4.95 (*0-8050-1638-4*, Bks Young Read) H Holt & Co.
—White Dynamite & Curly Kidd. Rand, Ted, illus. LC 85-27214. 48p. (ps-2). 1986. 12.95 (*0-8050-0658-3*, Bks Young Read) H Holt & Co.
—White Dynamite & Curly Kidd. Rand, Ted, illus. LC 85-27214. 48p. (ps-2). 1989. pap. 5.95 (*0-8050-1018-1*, Bks Young Read) H Holt & Co.
Martin, Bill, Jr., jt. auth. see Archambault, John.
Martin, C. Brontes. (Illus.). 112p. (gr. 7 up). 1989. lib. bdg. 19.94 (*0-86592-299-3*); 14.95s.p. (*0-685-58635-9*) Rourke Corp.
—H. G. Wells. (Illus.). 112p. (gr. 7 up). 1989. lib. bdg. 19.94 (*0-86592-297-7*); 14.95s.p. (*0-685-58636-7*) Rourke Corp.
—Shakespeare. (Illus.). 112p. (gr. 7 up). 1989. lib. bdg. 19.94 (*0-86592-296-9*); 14.95s.p. (*0-685-58633-2*) Rourke Corp.
Martin, C. L. Down Dairy Farm Road. Hearn, Diane D., illus. LC 92-42848. 32p. (gr. k-3). 1994. RSBE 14.95 (*0-02-762450-1*, Macmillan Child Bk) Macmillan Child Grp.
—The Dragon Nanny. Rayevsky, Robert, illus. LC 87-7674. 32p. (gr. k-3). 1988. RSBE 14.95 (*0-02-762440-4*, Macmillan Child Bk) Macmillan Child Grp.
—The Dragon Nanny. Rayevsky, Robert, illus. LC 90-39985. 32p. (gr. k-3). 1991. pap. 3.95 (*0-689-71451-3*, Aladdin) Macmillan Child Grp.
Martin, C. L. G. Three Brave Women. Elwell, Peter, illus. LC 89-77770. 32p. (gr. k-3). 1991. RSBE 13.95 (*0-02-762445-5*, Macmillan Child Bk) Macmillan Child Grp.
Martin, Charles E. For Rent. Martin, Charles E., illus. LC 85-864. 32p. (gr. k-3). 1986. 11.75 (*0-688-05716-0*); PLB 11.88 (*0-688-05717-9*) Greenwillow.
—Island Rescue. Martin, Charles E., illus. LC 84-13672. 32p. (gr. k-3). 1985. 11.75 (*0-688-04257-0*); PLB 11.88 (*0-688-04258-9*) Greenwillow.
—Island Winter. Marten, Charles E., illus. LC 83-14098. 32p. (gr. k-3). 1984. 13.95 (*0-688-02590-0*); PLB 13.88 (*0-688-02592-7*) Greenwillow.
—Sams Saves the Day. Martin, Charles E., illus. LC 86-19594. 32p. (gr. k-3). 1987. 11.75 (*0-688-06814-6*); lib. bdg. 11.88 (*0-688-06815-4*) Greenwillow.
—Summer Business. Martin, Charles E., illus. LC 83-25422. 32p. (gr. k-3). 1984. PLB 14.88 (*0-688-03864-6*) Greenwillow.
Martin, Christopher. Dickens. (Illus.). 112p. (gr. 7 up). 1990. lib. bdg. 19.94 (*0-86593-016-3*); lib. bdg. 14.95s.p (*0-685-36352-X*) Rourke Corp.
Martin, Claire. I Can Be a Weather Forecaster. LC 86-31763. (Illus.). 32p. (gr. k-3). 1987. PLB 14.60 (*0-516-01908-2*); pap. 3.95 (*0-516-41908-0*) Childrens.
—The Race of the Golden Apples. Dillon, Leo & Dillon, Diane, illus. LC 85-16290. 32p. (ps-3). 1991. 14.95 (*0-8037-0248-5*); PLB 14.89 (*0-8037-0249-3*) Dial Bks Young.
Martin, Claire & Martin, Steve. My Best Book: A Year-Long Record of "Personal Bests" Martin, Diane, illus. 40p. (Orig). (gr. 3-5). 1988. pap. 7.95 (*0-929545-00-1*) Black Birch Bks.
Martin, Claire, retold by. Boots & the Glass Mountain. Spirin, Gennady, illus. LC 91-9724. 32p. (ps-3). 1992. 15.00 (*0-8037-1110-7*); PLB 14.89 (*0-8037-1111-5*) Dial Bks Young.
Martin, Cyd. A Yellowstone ABC. (Illus.). 16p. 1992. pap. 5.95 (*1-879373-12-2*) R Rinehart.
Martin, D. E. Fabula Ranae. (LAT & ENG.). 56p. (gr. 6-12). 3.95 (*0-939507-07-2*, B705) Amer Classical.
Martin, Debbie. Lizzie & Her Dolly. Gliori, Debi, illus. LC 92-54404. 24p. (ps). 1993. 6.95 (*1-56402-060-6*) Candlewick Pr.
—Lizzie & Her Friend. Gliori, Debi, illus. LC 92-53009. 24p. (ps). 1993. 5.95 (*1-56402-061-4*) Candlewick Pr.
—Lizzie & Her Kitty. Gliori, Debi, illus. LC 92-54405. (ps). 1993. 5.95 (*1-56402-058-4*) Candlewick Pr.
—Lizzie & Her Puppy. Gliori, Debi, illus. LC 92-53008. 24p. (ps). 1993. 5.95 (*1-56402-059-2*) Candlewick Pr.
Martin, David & Sampugna, Joe. Molecules in Living Systems: A Biochemistry Module. Gardner, Marjorie, intro. by. (Illus.). 122p. (Orig). (gr. 9-12). 1991. pap. text ed. 8.20 (*1-879827-02-6*) Vistas.
Martin, David, tr. see Soloukhin, Vladimir.
Martin, David S., jt. auth. see Gewirtz, Herman.
Martin, Dick. Cut & Assemble the Emerald City. 1980. pap. 4.50 (*0-486-24053-3*) Dover.
—Cut & Assemble Wizard of Oz Theatre. 1985. pap. 4.95 (*0-486-24799-6*) Dover.
Martin, Donald. How to Be a Successful Student. 2nd ed. (Illus.). 48p. (gr. 8-12). 1991. pap. text ed. 5.95 (*0-9617044-2-X*) Martin Press.

Martin, E. A Student's Notebook: A Cooking Manual for Teenagers Who Like to Cook. large type ed. 96p. (gr. 9 up). 1973. 24.00 (*0-317-01945-7*, J-24530-00) Am Printing Hse.
Martin, Ernest L. The Original Bible Restored. 2nd ed. (Illus.). 336p. (gr. 10). 1991. pap. text ed. 14.95 (*0-945657-89-7*) Acad Scriptural Knowledge.
—The Star that Astonished the World. Griffith Observatory Sky & Telescope Staff, illus. 220p. (Orig). (gr. 10). 1991. pap. 14.95x (*0-945657-88-9*) Acad Scriptural Knowledge.
Martin, Francesca. Honey Hunters. LC 91-58736. (ps-3). 1994. pap. 5.99 (*1-56402-276-5*) Candlewick Pr.
Martin, Francesca, retold by. The Honey Hunters. LC 91-58736. (Illus.). 32p. (ps up) 1992. 14.95 (*1-56402-086-X*) Candlewick Pr.
Martin, Gene L. & Boyd, Aaron. Bill Clinton: President from Arkansas. (Illus.). 104p. (gr. 7-12). 1993. PLB 17.95 (*0-936389-31-1*) Tudor Pubs.
Martin, George. Wild Oakie. LC 92-85412. 76p. (gr. 2-6). 1993. 6.95 (*1-55523-552-2*) Winston-Derek.
Martin, George R. Aces High, No. 2. 288p. (Orig). 1987. pap. 5.50 (*0-553-26464-8*, Spectra) Bantam.
Martin, Guenn. Remember the Eagle Day. Converse, James, illus. LC 83-26376. 128p. (gr. 7-9). 1983. pap. 4.95 (*0-8361-3351-X*) Herald Pr.
Martin, Jacqueline B. Bizzy Bones & the Lost Quilt. Qrmai, Stella, illus. LC 87-13577. (ps-3). 1988. 12.95 (*0-688-07407-3*); PLB 12.88 (*0-688-07408-1*) Lothrop.
—Bizzy Bones & Uncle Ezra. Ormai, Stella, illus. LC 83-25618. 32p. (ps-2). 1984. PLB 12.88 (*0-688-03782-8*) Lothrop.
—The Finest Horse in Town. Gaber, Susan, illus. LC 90-38596. 32p. (gr. k-5). 1992. 15.00 (*0-06-024151-9*); PLB 14.89 (*0-06-024152-7*) HarpC Child Bks.
—Good Times on Grandfather Mountain. Gaber, Susan, illus. LC 91-17058. 32p. (ps-1). 1992. 14.95 (*0-531-05977-4*); lib. bdg. 14.99 (*0-531-08577-5*) Orchard Bks Watts.
Martin, James. Chameleons: Dragons in the Trees. Wolfe, Art, photos by. LC 91-8736. (Illus.). 36p. (gr. 1-5). 1991. 13.00 (*0-517-58388-7*); lib. bdg. 13.99 (*0-517-58389-5*) Crown Bks Yng Read.
—Hiding Out: Camouflage in the Wild. Wolfe, Art, illus. LC 92-38211. 32p. (gr. 2-6). 1993. 13.00 (*0-517-59392-0*); PLB 13.99 (*0-517-59393-9*) Crown Bks Yng Read.
—Tentacles: Octopus, Squid, & Their Relatives. LC 92-22234. 32p. (gr. 2-6). 1993. 14.00 (*0-517-59149-9*); PLB 14.99 (*0-517-59150-2*) Crown Bks Yng Read.
Martin, Jan, ed. see Gilbert, Ann.
Martin, Jane R. & Marx, Patricia. Now Everybody Really Hates Me. Chast, Roz, illus. LC 93-13075. 32p. (gr. k-3). 1993. 14.00 (*0-06-021293-4*); PLB 13.89 (*0-06-021294-2*) HarpC Child Bks.
Martin, Jerome. Carrot-Parrot. (ps). 1991. pap. 9.95 (*0-671-69555-X*, S&S BFYR) S&S Trade.
—Mitten-Kitten. (ps). 1991. pap. 9.95 (*0-671-69556-8*, S&S BFYR) S&S Trade.
Martin, Jo. Drugs & the Family. Mendelson, Jack H. & Mello, Nancyintro. by. (Illus.). (gr. 5 up). 1988. lib. bdg. 19.95 (*1-55546-220-0*); pap. 9.95 (*0-7910-0797-9*) Chelsea Hse.
Martin, John. In-Line Skating: Extreme Blading. 48p. (gr. 3-10). 1994. PLB 17.27 (*1-56065-202-0*) Capstone Pr.
—Jet Watercraft. 48p. (gr. 3-10). 1994. PLB 17.27 (*1-56065-201-2*) Capstone Pr.
—The World's Fastest Motorcycles. 48p. (gr. 3-10). 1994. PLB 17.27 (*1-56065-208-X*) Capstone Pr.
—The World's Most Exotic Cars. 48p. (gr. 3-10). 1994. PLB 17.27 (*1-56065-209-8*) Capstone Pr.
Martin, John D. Living Together on God's Earth. (gr. 3). 1974. 15.00x (*0-87813-915-X*); tchr's. guide 19.65x (*0-87813-910-9*) Christian Light.
Martin, John H. A Day in the Life of a Ballet Dancer. Jann, Gayle, illus. LC 84-2424. 32p. (gr. 4-8). 1985. PLB 11.79 (*0-8167-0089-3*); pap. text ed. 2.95 (*0-8167-0090-7*) Troll Assocs.
—A Day in the Life of a Carpenter. Wells, Sarah, illus. LC 84-2420. 32p. (gr. 4-8). 1985. PLB 11.79 (*0-8167-0093-1*); pap. text ed. 2.95 (*0-8167-0094-X*) Troll Assocs.
—A Day in the Life of a High-Iron Worker. Jann, Gayle, illus. LC 84-2449. 32p. (gr. 4-8). 1985. PLB 11.79 (*0-8167-0107-5*); pap. text ed. 2.95 (*0-8167-0108-3*) Troll Assocs.
—A Day in the Life of a Police Cadet. Jann, Gayle, illus. LC 84-2578. 32p. (gr. 4-8). 1985. PLB 11.79 (*0-8167-0103-2*); pap. text ed. 2.95 (*0-8167-0104-0*) Troll Assocs.
Martin, John J., ed. see Schiller, Alexandra.
Martin, Judith. Dandelion. Martin, Judith, illus. (Orig). (gr. 1-5). 1978. pap. 4.50 (*0-9606662-0-6*) Paper Bag.
—Reasons to Be Cheerful. (Illus.). 80p. (ps-4). 1985. pap. 4.50 (*0-9606662-1-4*) Paper Bag.
Martin, Judith & Ashwander, Donald. Christmas All over the Place. 22p. (Orig). (ps-12). 1977. playscript 3.50 (*0-87602-113-5*) Anchorage.
—The Lost & Found Christmas. 14p. (Orig). (ps up). 1977. playscript 3.50 (*0-87602-152-6*) Anchorage.
—The Runaway Presents. 16p. (Orig). (ps up). 1977. playscript 3.50 (*0-87602-197-6*) Anchorage.
—Wiggle Worm's Surprise. 16p. (Orig). (ps up). 1977. playscript 3.50 (*0-87602-218-2*) Anchorage.
Martin, Judith & Charlip, Remy. The Tree Angel. Charlip, Remy, illus. 40p. (gr. k-3). 1992. pap. 3.25 (*0-440-40725-7*, YB) Dell.

Martin, Julia. Hellsgate. 64p. (Orig). 1992. pap. 10.00 (*1-55878-097-1*) Game Designers.
—Rotten to the Core. Aulisio, Janet, illus. 64p. (Orig). 1990. pap. 8.00 (*1-55878-059-9*) Game Designers.
Martin, Kathy. Party Shakers. Biancalana, Tim, illus. Martin, Kathy. LC 82-21729. (Illus.). 47p. (gr. k-8). 1982. pap. 3.95 (*0-942752-00-7*) C A M Co.
Martin, Kerry, illus. Walt Disney's Dumbo. LC 91-71354. 12p. 1991. 9.95 (*1-56282-056-7*) Disney Pr.
—Walt Disney's One Hundred One Dalmatians Play Hide-&-Seek. LC 92-52972. 18p. (ps-1). 1992. 9.95 (*1-56282-270-5*) Disney Pr.
Martin, Kerry & Wakeman, Diana, illus. Walt Disney's Sleeping Beauty. LC 92-53435. 12p. (ps-k). 1993. 11.95 (*1-56282-369-8*) Disney Pr.
Martin, L. Alligators. (Illus.). 24p. (gr. k-5). 1989. lib. bdg. 11.94 (*0-86592-579-8*) Rourke Corp.
—Bird Eating Spiders. (Illus.). 24p. (gr. k-5). 1988. PLB 11.94 (*0-86592-966-1*) Rourke Corp.
—Black Widow Spiders. (Illus.). 24p. (gr. k-5). 1988. PLB 11.94 (*0-86592-965-3*) Rourke Corp.
—Chameleons. (Illus.). 24p. (gr. k-5). 1989. lib. bdg. 11.94 (*0-86592-576-3*) Rourke Corp.
—Elephants. (Illus.). 24p. (gr. k-5). 1988. PLB 11.94 (*0-86592-998-X*); 8.95s.p. (*0-685-58306-6*) Rourke Corp.
—Fishing Spiders. (Illus.). 24p. (gr. k-5). 1988. PLB 11.94 (*0-86592-964-5*); 8.95s.p. (*0-685-58305-8*) Rourke Corp.
—Funnel Web Spiders. (Illus.). 24p. (gr. k-5). 1988. PLB 11.94 (*0-86592-962-9*); 8.95s.p. (*0-685-58304-X*) Rourke Corp.
—Iguanas. (Illus.). 24p. (gr. k-5). 1989. lib. bdg. 11.94 (*0-86592-575-5*); 8.95s.p. (*0-685-58606-5*) Rourke Corp.
—Komodo Dragons. (Illus.). 24p. (gr. k-5). 1989. lib. bdg. 11.94 (*0-86592-574-7*); 8.95s.p. (*0-685-58604-9*) Rourke Corp.
—Lizards. (Illus.). 24p. (gr. k-5). 1989. lib. bdg. 11.94 (*0-86592-577-1*); 8.95s.p. (*0-685-58605-7*) Rourke Corp.
—Panda. (Illus.). 24p. (gr. k-5). 1988. PLB 11.94 (*0-86592-996-3*) Rourke Corp.
—Rhinoceros. (Illus.). 24p. (gr. k-5). 1988. PLB 11.94 (*0-86592-997-1*) Rourke Corp.
—Seals. (Illus.). 24p. (gr. k-5). 1988. PLB 11.94 (*0-86592-999-8*) Rourke Corp.
—Tarantulas. (Illus.). 24p. (gr. k-5). 1988. PLB 11.94 (*0-86592-967-X*); PLB 8.95s.p. (*0-685-58302-3*) Rourke Corp.
—Tigers. (Illus.). 24p. (gr. k-5). 1988. PLB 11.94 (*0-86592-995-5*); PLB 8.95s.p. (*0-685-58307-4*) Rourke Corp.
—Trapdoor Spiders. (Illus.). 24p. (gr. k-5). 1988. PLB 11.94 (*0-86592-963-7*); PLB 8.95s.p. (*0-685-58303-1*) Rourke Corp.
—Turtles. (Illus.). 24p. (gr. k-5). 1989. lib. bdg. 11.94 (*0-86592-578-X*); lib. bdg. 8.95s.p. (*0-685-58607-3*) Rourke Corp.
—Whales. (Illus.). 24p. (gr. k-5). 1988. PLB 11.94 (*0-86592-988-2*); PLB 8.95s.p. (*0-685-67679-X*) Rourke Corp.
Martin, LaJoyce. Heart-Shaped Pieces. Agnew, Tim, illus. LC 90-22517. 160p. (Orig). (gr. 9 up). 1991. pap. 6.99 (*0-932581-78-1*) Word Aflame.
—Love's Golden Wings. Agnew, Tim & Kirchoff, Art, illus. LC 87-17346. 256p. (Orig). (gr. 7 up). 1987. pap. 6.99 (*0-932581-19-6*) Word Aflame.
Martin, Laurence W. Nuclear Warfare. Gibbons, Tony, et al, illus. 48p. (gr. 5 up). 1989. 14.95 (*0-8225-1384-6*) Lerner Pubns.
Martin, Les. Prisoner of War. LC 92-56395. 136p. (Orig). (gr. 4-8). 1993. pap. 3.50 (*0-679-84389-2*) Random Bks Yng Read.
—Young Indiana Jones & the Gypsy Revenge, Bk. 6. LC 90-52818. 128p. (Orig). (gr. 3-7). 1991. PLB 6.99 (*0-679-91179-0*); pap. 2.95 (*0-679-81179-6*) Random Bks Yng Read.
—Young Indiana Jones & the Princess of Peril, Bk. 5. LC 90-52817. 128p. (Orig). (gr. 3-7). 1991. PLB 6.99 (*0-679-91178-2*); pap. 2.95 (*0-679-81178-8*) Random Bks Yng Read.
—Young Indiana Jones & the Secret City, Bk. 4. LC 89-43391. 112p. (Orig). (gr. 3-7). 1990. PLB 6.99 (*0-679-90580-4*); pap. 2.95 (*0-679-80580-X*) Random Bks Yng Read.
—Young Indiana Jones & the Titanic Adventure. 132p. (Orig). (gr. 3-7). 1993. pap. 2.99 (*0-679-84925-4*) Random Bks Yng Read.
—Young Indiana Jones & the Tomb of Terror, Bk. 2. LC 89-43389. 112p. (Orig). (gr. 3-7). 1990. PLB 6.99 (*0-679-90581-2*); pap. 2.95 (*0-679-80581-8*) Random Bks Yng Read.
Martin, Les, jt. auth. see McCay, William.
Martin, Les, adapted by. Field of Death. LC 91-53164. (Illus.). 136p. (Orig). (gr. 4-8). 1992. PLB cancelled (*0-679-92775-1*); pap. 3.50 (*0-679-82775-7*) Random Bks Yng Read.
—Trek of Doom. (Illus.). 136p. (Orig). (gr. 4-8). 1992. pap. 3.50 (*0-679-83237-8*) Random Bks Yng Read.
Martin, Les, adapted by see Cooper, James Fenimore.
Martin, Les, adapted by see Dickens, Charles.
Martin, Les, adapted by see Poe, Edgar Allan.
Martin, Les, adapted by see Polidori, John.
Martin, Les, adapted by see Wells, H. G.
Martin, Lillian. Nosey Rides the Train. Martin, J. V., illus. 22p. (ps-4). 1992. pap. 3.95 (*1-881079-04-X*) Antex Corp.

Martin, Linda. When Dinosaurs Go Visiting. LC 93-10207. 1993. 12.95 (*0-8118-0122-5*) Chronicle Bks.

Martin, Linda R. The Witch's Pearl. 1991. 7.95 (*0-533-09491-7*) Vantage.

Martin, Louise. Reptile Discovery Library, 6 bks, Reading Level 2. (Illus.). 144p. (gr. k-5). 1989. Set. PLB 71.60 (*0-86592-573-9*) Rourke Corp.

Martin, Lynne. Puffin, Bird of the Open Seas. Lewin, Ted, illus. LC 76-3486. (gr. 3-7). 1976. PLB 12.88 (*0-688-32074-0*) Morrow Jr Bks.

Martin, M. W. Let's Talk about the New World of Medicine. LC 72-91738. (Illus.). 76p. (gr. 3-6). 1973. PLB 4.95 (*0-8246-0149-1*) Jonathan David.

Martin, Marilyn. Pedro. 152p. (gr. 3 up). 1980. 6.55 (*0-686-30765-8*) Rod & Staff.

Martin, Marilyn, ed. see Vercillo, Tony.

Martin, Marilyn G. Shawn's Search for True Love. (Illus.). 24p. (gr. k-6). 1991. 4.25 (*1-55976-154-7*) CEF Press.

Martin, Mark, ed. see McCloud, Scott.

Martin, Marla. A Sweet Singer. (gr. 2-4). 1976. 2.55 (*0-686-15487-8*) Rod & Staff.

Martin, Mary & Zorn, Steven. Start Exploring Masterpieces: A Fact-Filled Coloring Book. rev. ed. (Illus.). 128p. (gr. 2 up). 1990. pap. 8.95 (*0-89471-801-0*) Running Pr.

Martin, Melanie. Itsy-Bitsy Giant. Cushman, Doug, illus. LC 88-1234. 48p. (Orig.). (gr. 1-4). 1989. PLB 10.59 (*0-8167-1335-9*); pap. text ed. 3.50 (*0-8167-1336-7*) Troll Assocs.

—Madison Moves to the Country. Karas, G. Brian, illus. LC 88-1313. 48p. (Orig.). (gr. 1-4). 1989. PLB 10.59 (*0-8167-1345-6*); pap. text ed. 3.50 (*0-8167-1346-4*) Troll Assocs.

—Morris, the Millionaire Mouse. LC 88-1235. (Illus.). 48p. (Orig.). (gr. 1-4). 1989. PLB 10.59 (*0-8167-1339-1*); pap. text ed. 3.50 (*0-8167-1340-5*) Troll Assocs.

Martin, Michael. The Good Behavior Book. Harris, Stephen & Brower, Nancy, eds. Shea, Mikki, illus. (Orig.). (ps up). 1988. pap. 10.95 (*0-9621191-7-2*) Behavior Products.

Martin, Mildred A. Missionary Stories & the Millers. Burkholder, Edith, illus. 208p. (gr. 3 up). 1993. pap. 6.00 (*0-9627643-4-5*) Green Psturs Pr.

—Prudence & the Millers. 190p. (Orig.). (gr. 3-8). 1993. 9.50 (*0-9627643-9-6*); pap. 6.00 (*0-9627643-8-8*) Green Psturs Pr.

—Storytime with the Millers. Baker, Anthony, illus. 96p. (Orig.). (ps-3). 1992. pap. 4.50 (*0-9627643-1-0*) Green Psturs Pr.

—Wisdom & the Millers: Proverbs for Children. rev. ed. (Illus.). 159p. (gr. 2-8). 1990. pap. 6.00 (*0-9627643-0-2*) Green Psturs Pr.

—Wisdom & the Millers: Proverbs for Children. 2nd ed. Burkholder, Edith, illus. 159p. (gr. 2-8). 1993. 9.50 (*0-685-68129-7*); pap. 6.00 (*0-9627643-5-3*) Green Psturs Pr.

Martin, Nancie S. Miss America: Through the Looking Glass. LC 85-13038. (Illus.). 128p. (gr. 5 up). 1985. (J Messner) S&S Trade.

Martin, Patricia S. Beverly Cleary: She Makes Reading Fun. (Illus.). 24p. (gr. 1-4). 1987. PLB 14.60 (*0-86592-171-7*); 10.95s.p. (*0-685-67568-8*) Rourke Corp.

—Bill Cosby: Superstar. (Illus.). 24p. (gr. 1-4). 1987. PLB 14.60 (*0-86592-169-5*); 10.95s.p. (*0-685-67569-6*) Rourke Corp.

—Christine McAuliffe: Reach for the Stars. (Illus.). 24p. (gr. 1-4). 1987. PLB 14.60 (*0-86592-172-5*); Set. lib. bdg. 10.95s.p. (*0-685-67566-1*) Rourke Corp.

—Dale Murphy: Baseball's Gentle Giant. (Illus.). 24p. (gr. 1-4). 1987. PLB 14.60 (*0-86592-167-9*); 10.95 (*0-685-67567-X*) Rourke Corp.

—Dr. Seuss: We Love You. (Illus.). 24p. (gr. 1-4). 1987. PLB 14.60 (*0-86592-168-7*); Set. 10.95s.p. (*0-685-67570-X*) Rourke Corp.

—Jesse Jackson: A Black Leader. (Illus.). 24p. (gr. 1-4). 1987. PLB 14.60 (*0-86592-170-9*); 10.95s.p. (*0-685-67565-3*) Rourke Corp.

—Samantha Smith: Little Ambassador. (Illus.). 24p. (gr. 1-4). 1987. PLB 14.60 (*0-86592-173-3*); 10.95 (*0-685-58131-4*) Rourke Corp.

—Ted Kennedy Jr. He Faced His Challenge. (Illus.). 24p. (gr. 1-4). 1987. PLB 14.60 (*0-86592-174-1*); 10.95s.p. (*0-685-58129-2*) Rourke Corp.

Martin, Paul D. Messengers to the Brain: Your Fantastic Five Senses. Crump, Donald J., ed. LC 82-45636. 104p. (gr. 3-8). 1984. 8.95 (*0-87044-499-9*); PLB 12.50 (*0-87044-504-9*) Natl Geog.

—Science: It's Changing Your World. Crump, Donald J., ed. LC 85-2936. (Illus.). 104p. (gr. 3-8). 1985. 8.95 (*0-87044-516-2*); PLB 12.50 (*0-87044-521-9*) Natl Geog.

Martin, Peggy, ed. see Fifth Period LEAP & Honors English Classes.

Martin, Phyllis. Job-Hunt Success Plan, High School Edition. rev. & abr. ed. Savage, Kent V., contrib. by. (Illus.). 118p. (gr. 11-12). 1989. pap. text ed. 8.50 (*0-685-31060-4*) Ctr Career Dev.

Martin, Prisha. The Poor People of England & Other Works. (Orig.). 1991. pap. write for info. (*1-879019-04-3*) Amer Edit Servs.

Martin, Rafe. The Boy Who Lived with Seals. Shannon, David, illus. 32p. (ps-3). 1993. PLB 14.95 (*0-399-22413-0*, Putnam) Putnam Pub Group.

—Foolish Rabbit's Big Mistake. (Illus.). 32p. (ps-3). 1991. pap. 6.95 (*0-399-21778-9*, Sandcastle Bks) Putnam Pub Group.

—The Rough-Face Girl. Shannon, David, illus. 32p. (ps-3). 1992. PLB 14.95 (*0-399-21859-9*, Putnam) Putnam Pub Group.

—A Storyteller's Story. Krementz, Jill, illus. 32p. (gr. 2-5). 1992. 12.95 (*0-913461-03-2*) R Owen Pubs.

—Will's Mammoth. Grammell, Stephen, illus. 32p. (ps-3). 1989. 15.95 (*0-399-21627-8*, Putnam) Putnam Pub Group.

—Will's Mammoth. Gammell, Stephen, illus. 32p. (ps-1). 1993. pap. 4.95 (*0-399-22603-6*, Putnam) Putnam Pub Group.

Martin, Rafe, rev. by. Foolish Rabbit's Big Mistake. Young, Ed, illus. LC 84-11665. 32p. (gr. k-3). 1985. 14.95 (*0-399-21178-0*, Putnam) Putnam Pub Group.

Martin, Rodney. The Making of a Picture Book. Siow, John, illus. LC 88-42911. 32p. (gr. 3-4). 1989. PLB 18.60 (*1-555̲2-958-6*) Gareth Stevens Inc.

—There's a Dinosaur in the Park! Siow, John, illus. LC 86-42811. 31p. (gr. 2-3). 1987. PLB 18.60 (*1-55532-151-8*) Gareth Stevens Inc.

Martin, Rose. Mary Mouse Has Her Baby. 1992. 6.95 (*0-8062-4228-0*) Carlton.

Martin, Samuel E. Easy Japanese: A Direct Approach to Immediate Conversation. LC 57-6763. 272p. (gr. 9 up). 1965. pap. 6.95 (*0-8048-0157-6*) C E Tuttle.

Martin, Shirley, jt. auth. see McMillan, Dana.

Martin, Sidney & McMillan, Dana. Learning Ideas Through the Year. 112p. (gr. 2-6). 1989. 9.95 (*0-912107-91-X*, MM1908) Monday Morning Bks.

Martin, Steve, jt. auth. see Martin, Claire.

Martin, Sue, jt. auth. see Green, Harriet.

Martin, Sue G., jt. auth. see Green, Harriet H.

Martin, Susan. Duran Duran. 1984. 8.29 (*0-685-09673-4*) S&S Trade.

Martin, Susan & Green, Harriet. Research Workout. Melton, Gerald, illus. 144p. (gr. 4-9). 1984. wkbk. 11.95 (*0-86653-194-7*, GA 551) Good Apple.

Martin, Teri. Junipero Serra: God's Pioneer. Novack, Kevin, illus. 64p. (gr. 7-9). 1990. pap. 4.95 (*0-8091-6589-9*) Paulist Pr.

Martin, Thomas. Private High. 25p. (Orig.). (gr. 7 up). 1986. pap. 4.50 playscript (*0-87602-267-0*) Anchorage.

Martinello, Marian & Field, William T., Jr. Who Are the Chinese Texans? Ricks, Thorn, illus. 84p. (Orig.). (gr. 5-8). 8.95 (*0-933164-36-X*); pap. 5.95 (*0-933164-46-7*) U of Tex Inst Tex Culture.

Martinello, Marian, et al. Hopes, Prayers & Promises. Shelton, Caroline, illus. 48p. (gr. k-8). 1986. 12.95 (*0-935857-05-2*); pap. write for info. (*0-935857-06-0*) Texart.

Martinello, Marian L. Cedar Fever: Story of a German-Texan Girl During World War I. Hudgins, Paul, illus. LC 92-73295. 212p. (gr. 7-9). 1992. 15.95 (*0-931722-90-X*); pap. 7.95 (*0-931722-95-0*) Corona Pub.

Martinello, Marian L. & Nesmith, Samuel P. With Domingo Leal in San Antonio, 1734. Institute of Texan Cultures Staff, ed. Lowther, Marilyn, illus. 78p. (Orig.). (gr. 5-8). 1980. pap. 6.95 (*0-933164-40-8*) U of Tex Inst Tex Culture.

Martinello, Marian L. & Sance, Melvin M. A Personal History: The Afro-American Texans. (Illus.). 104p. (gr. 5-8). 8.95 (*0-86701-005-3*) U of Tex Inst Tex Culture.

Martinet, Jeanne. The Year You Were Born, 1983. Lanfredi, Judy, illus. LC 91-31605. 56p. 1992. PLB 13.93 (*0-688-11078-9*, Tambourine Bks); pap. 7.95 (*0-688-11077-0*, Tambourine Bks) Morrow.

—The Year You Were Born, 1984. Lanfredi, Judy & Lanfredi, Judy, illus. LC 91-34577. 56p. 1992. PLB 13.93 (*0-688-11080-0*, Tambourine Bks); pap. 7.95 (*0-688-11079-7*, Tambourine Bks) Morrow.

—The Year You Were Born, 1985. Lanfredi, Judy, illus. LC 91-37439. 56p. 1992. PLB 13.93 (*0-688-11082-7*, Tambourine Bks); pap. 7.95 (*0-688-11081-9*, Tambourine Bks) Morrow.

—The Year You Were Born, 1986. Lanfredi, Judy, illus. 56p. (gr. 2 up). 1993. PLB 13.93 (*0-688-11969-7*, Tambourine Bks); pap. 7.95 (*0-688-11968-9*, Tambourine Bks) Morrow.

—The Year You Were Born, 1987. Lanfredi, Judy, illus. 56p. (gr. 2 up). 1993. PLB 13.93 (*0-688-11971-9*, Tambourine Bks); pap. 7.95 (*0-688-11970-0*, Tambourine Bks) Morrow.

Martinez, Alejandro C. The Woman Who Outshone the Sun: The Legend of Lucia Zenteno. LC 91-16646. (Illus.). 32p. (gr. k-5). 1991. 13.95 (*0-89239-101-4*) Childrens Book Pr.

Martinez, Alicia. Feeling Fit. Richey, Donald, illus. LC 90-10846. 128p. (gr. 5-9). 1991. PLB 10.89 (*0-8167-2140-8*); pap. text ed. 2.95 (*0-8167-2141-6*) Troll Assocs.

Martinez, Carla, et al, eds. see Punches, Laurie C.

Martinez, Carol. Paco y Ana Aprenden Acerca de la Amabilidad. Stillman, Peter, illus. (SPA.). 32p. (Orig.). (gr. 2-4). 1988. pap. 1.50 (*0-311-38590-7*, Edit Mundo) Casa Bautista.

—Paco y Ana Aprenden Acerca de la Amistad. Stillman, Peter, illus. (SPA., Orig.). (gr. 2-4). 1988. pap. 1.50 (*0-311-38589-3*, Edit Mundo) Casa Bautista.

—Paco y Ana Aprenden Acerca de la Honradez. Stillman, Peter, illus. (SPA.). 32p. (Orig.). (gr. 2-4). 1988. pap. 1.50 (*0-311-38587-7*, Edit Mundo) Casa Bautista.

—Paco y Ana Aprenden Acerca de la Obediencia. Stillman, Peter, illus. (SPA.). 32p. (Orig.). (gr. 2-4). 1988. pap. 1.50 (*0-311-38588-5*, Edit Mundo) Casa Bautista.

Martinez, Eliseo R. & Martinez, Irma C. French Readiness Skills, Vol. 1. Mahak, Francine T., tr. (Illus.). 87p. 1987. wkbk. 9.50 (*1-878300-02-4*) Childrens Work.

—Spanish Readiness Skills, Vol. 1. (Illus.). 78p. (ps-3). 1986. wkbk. 8.75 (*1-878300-01-6*) Childrens Work.

—Supplemental Studies in Math, Vol. 1. (Illus.). 73p. (ps-1). 1985. wkbk. 8.75 (*1-878300-00-8*) Childrens Work.

Martinez, Elizabeth C. Edward James Olmos: Committed Actor. LC 93-37659. Date not set. PLB write for info. (*1-56294-410-X*) Millbrook Pr.

—Henry Cisneros: Mexican-American Leader. LC 92-21384. (Illus.). 32p. (gr. 2-4). 1993. PLB 12.40 (*1-56294-368-5*) Millbrook Pr.

—Sor Juana: A Trailblazing Woman. (Illus.). 32p. (gr. 2-4). 1994. 12.40 (*1-56294-406-1*) Millbrook Pr.

Martinez, Estefanita, as told by. The Naughty Little Rabbit & Old Man Coyote: A Tewa Story from San Juan Pueblo. Regan, Rick, illus. LC 92-8992. 24p. (ps-3). 1992. PLB 15.53 (*0-516-05141-5*); pap. 4.95 (*0-516-45141-3*) Childrens.

Martinez, Gayle R. Journey into Light: The Story of a Woman's Struggle to Heal, Love, & Forgive. 182p. 1992. pap. 10.95 (*0-87604-292-2*) ARE Pr.

Martinez, Irma C., jt. auth. see Martinez, Eliseo R.

Martinez, Larry, jt. auth. see Caggiano, Rosemary.

Martinez, Lourdes, tr. see Kipling, Rudyard.

Martinez, Luz M. de see Hooker, Irene H. & Brindle, Susan A.

Martinez, Mario, tr. see Lea, Thomas D. & Latham, Bill.

Martinez, Ruth. Mrs. McDockerty's Knitting. O'Neill, Catharine, illus. 32p. (ps-3). 1990. 13.45 (*0-395-51591-2*) HM.

Martinez, Violeta S. de see Stowell, Gordon.

Martinez, Yvonne. From Victim to Victor: A Biblical Guide for Turning Hurting into Healing. LC 93-13946. 128p. (gr. 12 up). 1993. pap. 9.95 (*0-941405-24-9*) Recovery CA.

Martini, Teri. Christmas for Andy. (gr. 3 up). 1991. pap. 3.95 (*0-8091-6603-8*) Paulist Pr.

—Christopher Columbus: The Man Who Unlocked the Secrets of the World. LC 91-44755. 96p. (gr. 4-7). 1992. pap. 4.95 (*0-8091-6604-6*) Paulist Pr.

—Cowboys. LC 81-10049. (Illus.). 48p. (gr. k-4). 1981. PLB 15.27 (*0-516-01611-3*) Childrens.

—Feliz Navidad, Pablo. McNichols, William H., illus. (gr. 4 up). 1990. 2.95 (*0-8091-6597-X*) Paulist Pr.

—Indians. LC 81-15442. (Illus.). 48p. (gr. k-4). 1982. pap. 4.95 (*0-516-41628-6*) Childrens.

—Secret Is Out. (gr. 4-7). 1990. 14.95 (*0-316-54864-2*, Joy St Bks) Little.

—The Secret Is Out. 144p. (gr. 5). 1992. pap. 2.99 (*0-380-71465-5*, Camelot) Avon.

Martino, Teresa. Pizza! (Illus.). 32p. (gr. 1-4). 1989. PLB 15.96 (*0-8172-3533-7*); pap. 3.95 (*0-8114-6730-9*) Raintree Steck-V.

Martinson, Thomas. Super Course for the SAT. 784p. (Orig.). (gr. 7-8). 1988. pap. 15.95 (*0-13-788506-7*) S&S Trade.

Martinson, Tom. The Christmas Loon. (Illus.). 48p. (gr. 1-3). 1990. 14.95 (*1-55971-092-6*); pap. 6.95 (*1-55971-124-8*) NorthWord.

Marton, Betty. Ruben Blades. (Illus.). (gr. 5 up). 1992. lib. bdg. 17.95 (*0-7910-1235-2*) Chelsea Hse.

Marton, Jirina. Amelia's Celebration. Marton, Jirina, illus. 24p. (ps-3). 1992. PLB 15.95 (*1-55037-221-1*, Pub. by Annick CN); pap. 5.95 (*1-55037-220-3*, Pub. by Annick CN) Firefly Bks Ltd.

—Flowers for Mom. Marton, Jirina, illus. 24p. (ps-3). 1991. PLB 15.95 (*1-55037-155-X*, Pub. by Annick CN); pap. 5.95 (*1-55037-158-4*, Pub. by Annick CN) Firefly Bks Ltd.

—I'll Do It Myself. Marton, Jirina, illus. 1990. 14.95 (*1-550370-63-4*, Pub. by Annick CN); pap. 5.95 (*1-550370-62-6*, Pub. by Annick CN) Firefly Bks Ltd.

—Midnight Visit at Molly's House. (Illus.). 24p. (ps-8). 1988. 12.95 (*0-920303-99-4*, Pub. by Annick CN); pap. 4.95 (*0-920303-98-6*, Pub. by Annick CN) Firefly Bks Ltd.

Martorana, Barbara, jt. auth. see Kane, Andrea L.

Martre Audrey de, la see De la Martre, Audrey.

Martz, John, ed. see Bowling, David L. & Bowling, Patricia H.

Maruki, Toshi. Hiroshima No Pika. Maruki, Toshi, illus. LC 82-15365. 48p. (gr. 7 up). 1982. 14.95 (*0-688-01297-3*) Lothrop.

Marulanda, Sandra, tr. see Avery, Charles.

Maruska, Edward J. Amphibians. LC 93-29843. 1994. write for info. (*0-531-11158-X*) Watts.

Maruya, Saiichi. Rain in the Wind: Four Stories. Keene, Dennis, tr. from JPN. 190p. 1990. 18.95 (*0-87011-940-0*) Kodansha.

Marvel Staff. Juggernaut's Rampage. (gr. 4-7). 1993. pap. 2.50 (*0-679-85709-5*) Random Bks Yng Read.

—Morlock Madness. (gr. 4-7). 1993. pap. 2.50 (*0-679-85710-9*) Random Bks Yng Read.

—Night of the Sentinels, Pt. 1: Meet the X-Men. (gr. 4-7). 1993. pap. 2.50 (*0-679-85707-9*) Random Bks Yng Read.

—Night of the Sentinels, Pt. 2: Wolverine's Vengeance. (gr. 4-7). 1993. pap. 2.50 (*0-679-85708-7*) Random Bks Yng Read.

Marvin, Fred, illus. Bambi: The New Prince. LC 93-71377. 10p. (ps-k). 1994. 4.95 (*1-56282-601-8*) Disney Pr.

—The Little Mermaid Novels. (gr. 1-4). 1993. Boxed set incl. Green-Eyed Pearl, Nefazia Visits the Palace, Reflections of Arsulu & The Same Old Song. 15.80 (*1-56282-562-3*) Disney Pr.

—Snow White & the Seven Dwarfs: Suppertime. LC 93-71376. 10p. (gr. 2-5). 1994. 4.95 (*1-56282-600-X*) Disney Pr.

Marvin, Isabel. Bridge to Freedom. 148p. (gr. 5-9). 1991. 14.95 (*0-8276-0377-0*) JPS Phila.

Marvin, Isabel R. Josefina & the Hanging Tree. LC 91-34501. 128p. (gr. 6-9). 1992. pap. 9.95 (*0-87565-103-8*) Tex Christian.

—Shipwrecked on Padre Island. Miller, Lyle L., illus. 160p. (gr. 4 up). 1993. 14.95 (*0-937460-83-4*) Hendrick-Long.

Marvin, Isabelle. The Tenth Rifle. Costner, Howard, illus. 128p. (Orig.). (gr. 3-8). 1993. pap. 9.95 (*0-89896-109-2*) Larksdale.

Marvis, Barbara J. Contemporary American Success Stories, Vol. I: Famous People of Asian Ancestry. 96p. (gr. 4-7). 1993. pap. 8.95 (*1-883845-06-8*) M Lane Pubs.

—Contemporary American Success Stories, Vol. II: Famous People of Asian Ancestry. 96p. (gr. 5-7). 1993. pap. text ed. 8.95 (*1-883845-07-6*) M Lane Pubs.

Marx. Gold Gloves. 1991. 12.50s.p. (*0-86593-130-5*); PLB 16.67 (*0-685-59188-3*) Rourke Corp.

—Relief Pitchers. 1991. 12.50s.p. (*0-86593-131-3*); lib. bdg. 16.67 (*0-685-66096-6*) Rourke Corp.

—Rookies. 1991. 12.50s.p. (*0-86593-132-1*); lib. bdg. 16.67 (*0-685-66097-4*) Rourke Corp.

Marx, Doug. Homeless. (Illus.). 64p. (gr. 7 up). 1990. lib. bdg. 17.27 (*0-86593-071-6*); lib. bdg. 12.95s.p. (*0-685-36326-0*) Rourke Corp.

—Mythical Beasts. 48p. (gr. 3-4). 1991. PLB 11.95 (*1-56065-046-X*) Capstone Pr.

—Running Backs. LC 92-8764. 1992. 17.26 (*0-86593-151-8*); lib. bdg. 12.95s.p. (*0-685-59321-5*) Rourke Corp.

—Track & Field. LC 93-27154. 1993. write for info. (*0-86593-345-6*) Rourke Corp.

—Wrestling. LC 93-36544. 1993. write for info. (*0-86593-347-2*) Rourke Corp.

Marx, Fonda. Who's Hot! Nirvana. (gr. 4-7). 1993. pap. 1.49 (*0-440-21478-5*) Dell.

Marx, Jacqueline A., jt. auth. see Arnoldt, Robert P.

Marx, Jacqueline A., ed. see Arnoldt, Robert P.

Marx, Pamela. Classroom Museums: Touchable Tables for Kids! Grades 3-6. (Illus.). 184p. (Orig.). 1992. pap. 12.95 (*0-673-36040-7*) GdYrBks.

—Practical Plays. (Illus.). 128p. (Orig.). (gr. 1-5). 1993. pap. 9.95 (*0-673-36049-0*) GdYrBks.

Marx, Patricia, jt. auth. see Martin, Jane R.

Marx, Robert F. Following Columbus: The Voyage of the Nina II. (Illus.). 80p. 1991. 17.95 (*0-88415-004-6*, 5004) Gulf Pub.

Marx, Trish. Echoes of World War Two. LC 92-47369. 1993. 19.95 (*0-8225-4898-4*) Lerner Pubns.

—Hanna's Cold Winter. Knutson, Barbara, illus. LC 92-27143. 1993. 18.95 (*0-87614-772-4*) Carolrhoda Bks.

Marxhausen, Evelyn. Simeon & the Baby Jesus. (Illus.). 24p. (gr. k-4). 1986. pap. 1.89 saddlestitched (*0-570-06202-0*, 59-1425) Concordia.

—When God Laid Down the Law. (gr. k-4). 1981. pap. 1.89 (*0-570-06142-3*) Concordia.

Marxhausen, J. If I Should Die-If I Should Live. (Illus.). 48p. (ps). 1987. pap. 4.99 (*0-570-07793-1*, 56HH1317) Concordia.

Marxhausen, Joanne. Some of My Best Friends Are Trees. LC 56-1640. (Illus., Orig.). 24p. (gr. 4). 1990. pap. 7.99 (*0-570-04182-1*, 56-1640) Concordia.

Marydass, C. A Compendium of Shakespeare. 180p. (gr. 7 up). 1988. text ed. 25.00x (*81-207-0713-3*, Pub. by Sterling Pubs IA) Apt Bks.

Marzilli, Vincent, II. Return of the Nighthawks. Marzilli, Roanne A., illus. 56p. (Orig.). (gr. k-6). 1987. pap. 7.95 (*0-9617809-1-6*) Vincent Marzilli.

—Where Ravens Fly. Skalski, Margaret, illus. 64p. (Orig.). (gr. k-6). 1987. pap. 7.95 (*0-9617809-0-8*) Vincent Marzilli.

Marzollo & Bjorkman. In 1492. 1993. pap. 19.95 (*0-590-72737-0*) Scholastic Inc.

Marzollo, Claude, jt. auth. see Marzollo, Jean.

Marzollo, Claudio. Kenny & the Little Kickers. Rogers, Jacqueline, illus. 32p. 1992. pap. 2.95 (*0-590-45417-X*) Scholastic Inc.

Marzollo, Claudio, jt. auth. see Marzollo, Jean.

Marzollo, Jean. Best Present Ever. 1989. pap. 2.50 (*0-590-42724-5*) Scholastic Inc.

—Cannonball Chris. Sims, Blanche, illus. LC 86-31512. 48p. (gr. 2-3). 1987. lib. bdg. 6.99 (*0-394-98512-5*); pap. 3.50 (*0-394-88512-0*, Random Juv) Random Bks Yng Read.

—Close Your Eyes. Jeffers, Susan, illus. LC 76-42935. (ps-2). 1978. PLB 12.89 (*0-8037-1610-9*) Dial Bks Young.

—Close Your Eyes. Jeffers, Susan, illus. (ps-k). 1981. 4.95 (*0-8037-1617-6*) Dial Bks Young.

—Feliz Cumpleanos, Martin Luther King: Happy Birthday, Martin Luther King. Romo, Alberto, tr. from ENG. Pinkney, J. Brian, illus. (SPA.). (gr. 3-7). 1994. pap. 4.95 (*0-590-47507-X*) Scholastic Inc.

—Getting Your Period. (gr. 4-7). 1993. pap. 6.99 (*0-14-036193-6*) Puffin Bks.

—Getting Your Period: A Book about Menstruation. Williams, Kent, illus. Storch, Marcia, intro. by. LC 88-3986. (Illus.). 112p. (gr. 4 up). 1989. 13.95 (*0-8037-0355-4*); 6.95 (*0-8037-0356-2*) Dial Bks Young.

—Halloween Cats. (ps-3). 1992. pap. 2.50 (*0-590-46026-9*) Scholastic Inc.

—Happy Birthday, Martin Luther King. Pinkney, J. Brian, illus. LC 91-42137. 32p. (ps-3). 1993. 14.95 (*0-590-44065-9*) Scholastic Inc.

—I Spy Funhouse. Wick, Walter, photos by. Carson, Carol D., designed by. LC 92-16425. (Illus.). 40p. 1993. 12.95 (*0-590-46293-8*) Scholastic Inc.

—I Spy, Mystery: A Book of Picture Riddles. Wick, Walter, photos by. LC 92-40863. (Illus.). 1993. 12.95 (*0-590-46294-6*) Scholastic Inc.

—I'm Tyrannosaurus! A Book of Dinosaur Rhymes. Wilhelm, Hans, illus. 32p. (ps-1). 1993. pap. 2.50 (*0-590-44641-X*, Cartwheel) Scholastic Inc.

—In Fourteen Ninety-Two. Bjorkman, Steven, illus. 40p. 1991. 14.95 (*0-590-44413-1*, Scholastic Hardcover) Scholastic Inc.

—Jed & the Space Bandits. 1989. pap. 4.95 (*0-8037-0682-0*, Dial Pied Piper) Puffin Bks.

—My Sister, the Blabbermouth. (gr. 4-7). 1990. pap. 2.50 (*0-590-42728-8*) Scholastic Inc.

—The Pizza Pie Slugger. Sims, Blanche, illus. LC 88-33379. 64p. (Orig.). (gr. 2-4). 1989. PLB 6.99 (*0-394-92881-4*); pap. 2.50 (*0-394-82881-X*) Random Bks Yng Read.

—Pretend You're a Cat. Fogelman, Phyllis J., ed. Pinkney, Jerry, illus. LC 89-34546. 32p. (ps-3). 1990. PLB 12.89 (*0-8037-0774-6*) Dial Bks Young.

—The Rebus Treasury. Carson, Carol D., illus. LC 85-16133. 64p. (ps up). 1986. Dial Bks Young.

—Red Ribbon Rosie. Sims, Blanche, illus. LC 87-29641. 64p. (Orig.). (gr. 2-4). 1988. lib. bdg. 5.99 (*0-394-99608-9*); pap. 2.50 (*0-394-89608-4*) Random Bks Yng Read.

—Soccer Sam. Sims, Blanche, illus. LC 86-47533. 48p. (gr. 1-3). 1987. lib. bdg. 7.99 (*0-394-98406-4*); pap. 3.50 (*0-394-88406-X*) Random Bks Yng Read.

—The Teddy Bear Book. Schweninger, Ann, illus. LC 87-24538. 32p. (ps-2). 1989. 11.95 (*0-8037-0524-7*); PLB 11.89 (*0-8037-0632-4*) Dial Bks Young.

—The Teddy Bear Book. Schweninger, Ann, illus. LC 87-24538. 32p. (ps-2). 1992. pap. 3.99 (*0-14-054546-8*, Puffin Pied Piper) Puffin Bks.

—Thirty-Nine Kids on the Block, No. 1: A Curious George Activity Book. (gr. 5-7). 1989. pap. 2.75 (*0-590-42723-7*) Scholastic Inc.

—Three Little Kittens. Thornton, Shelley, illus. 32p. (Orig.). (ps-k). 1986. pap. 2.50 (*0-590-43713-5*) Scholastic Inc.

—Uproar on Holler Cat Hill. Kellogg, Steven, illus. LC 79-22201. (ps-2). 1981. Dial Bks Young.

Marzollo, Jean & Carson, Carol D. I Spy: A Book of Picture Riddles. Wick, Walter, illus. 48p. 1992. 12.95 (*0-590-45087-5*, Cartwheel) Scholastic Inc.

Marzollo, Jean & Marzollo, Claude. Ruthie's Rude Friends. 14p. 1991. Braille. 1.12 (*1-56956-311-X*) W A T Braille.

Marzollo, Jean & Marzollo, Claudio. Jed's Junior Space Patrol. Rose, David, illus. LC 81-12483. 56p. (ps-3). 1982. Dial Bks Young.

—Ruthie's Rude Friends. Meddaugh, Susan, illus. LC 84-1707. (ps-3). 1984. Dial Bks Young.

—Ruthie's Rude Friends. Meddaugh, Susan, illus. LC 84-1707. 48p. (ps-3). 1987. pap. 4.95 (*0-8037-0378-3*) Dial Bks Young.

—Ruthie's Rude Friends. 14p. (gr. 2-4). 1984. pap. 1.12 (*0-685-66379-5*, BR8065) W A T Braille.

Marzollo, Jean & Wick, Walter. I Spy Christmas. 1992. bds. 12.95 (*0-590-45846-9*, Cartwheel) Scholastic Inc.

Marzollo, Jean, jt. auth. see Adams, Patricia.

Marzollo, Jean, compiled by. The Rebus Treasury. Carson, Carol D., illus. LC 85-16133. 64p. (ps up). 1989. pap. 5.95 (*0-8037-0644-8*) Dial Bks Young.

Masaomi Kanzaki. Xenon, Vol. 2: Heavy Metal Warrior. Seiji Horibuchi, ed. Satoru Fujii, tr. from JPN. Masaomi Kanzaki, illus. 192p. 1991. pap. 14.95 (*0-929279-41-7*) Viz Commns Inc.

—Xenon, Vol. 4: Heavy Metal Warrior. Seiji Horibuchi, ed. Satoru Fujii, tr. from JPN. Masaomi Kanzaki, illus. 176p. 1992. pap. 14.95 (*0-929279-47-6*) Viz Commns Inc.

Mascetta, Joseph A. How to Prepare for the SAT II: Chemistry. 5th ed. LC 93-21075. 1994. pap. 11.95 (*0-8120-1702-1*) Barron.

Maschke, Ruby. Bible Puzzles for Children, Vol. 2. 64p. 1991. pap. 9.00 (*0-8170-1165-X*) Judson.

Maschke, Ruby A. Bible Puzzles for Children. 64p. (gr. 4-6). 1986. pap. 8.00 (*0-8170-1095-5*) Judson.

Masciantonio, Rudolph. Greco Roman Sports & Games. 64p. (gr. 7-12). 1991. spiral bdg. 4.50 (*0-939507-28-5*, B 314) Amer Classical.

—Latin, the Language of the Health Sciences. (Illus.). 42p. (Orig.). (gr. 7-12). 1992. spiral bound 3.10 (*0-939507-43-9*, B313) Amer Classical.

Masco, Steve De see De Masco, Steve & Simmons, Alex.

Mascola. Charles Schulz, Reading Level 2. (Illus.). 24p. (gr. 1-4). 1989. PLB 14.60 (*0-86592-429-5*) Rourke Corp.

—Ray Kroc, Reading Level 2. (Illus.). 24p. (gr. 1-4). 1989. PLB 14.60 (*0-86592-433-3*); 10.95s.p. (*0-685-58802-5*) Rourke Corp.

Mascola, et al. Reaching Your Goal, 8 bks, Set II, Reading Level 2. (Illus.). 192p. (gr. 1-4). 1989. Set. PLB 116.80 (*0-86592-425-2*); 87.60s.p. (*0-685-58797-5*) Rourke Corp.

Mase, Thomas. What's Gnu? Riddles from the Zoo. Burke, Susan S., illus. 32p. (gr. 1-4). 1989. PLB 11.95 (*0-8225-2330-2*) Lerner Pubns.

Masefield, John. The Box of Delights: Or, When the Wolves Were Running. Crampton, Patricia, abridged by. Jaques, Faith, illus. 176p. (gr. k up). 1984. pap. 2.95 (*0-440-40853-9*, YB) Dell.

—The Midnight Folk. (gr. k-6). 1985. pap. 4.95 (*0-440-45631-2*, Pub. by Yearling Classics) Dell.

Masek, Linda E. Mag-ni-fi-cat & the Christmas Tree Mystery. 1992. 10.95 (*0-533-10173-5*) Vantage.

Mashat, Mazal, jt. auth. see Dvir, Azriel.

Mashburn, William H. A Mountain Summer. Gayheart, Willard, illus. LC 88-11782. 140p. (Orig.). (gr. 9-12). 1990. pap. 8.95 (*0-936015-14-4*) Pocahontas Pr.

Masihlall, Kamala. Drug Card. Masihlall, Kamala, illus. 13p. (gr. k-3). 1993. pap. 12.95 (*1-895583-61-6*) MAYA Pubs.

—Rozan with Personnel. Masihlall, Kamala, illus. 16p. (gr. k-3). 1993. pap. 9.95 (*1-895583-60-8*) MAYA Pubs.

Masin, Herman L. The Funniest Moments in Sports. Callahan, Kevin, illus. LC 73-86219. 128p. (gr. 4 up). 1973. 5.95 (*0-87131-133-X*) M Evans.

Mask, Michael, et al. Off to a Good Start. LC 93-6942. Date not set. 7.99 (*0-8407-7823-6*) Nelson.

Maskowski, Alice, jt. auth. see Hauswald, Carol.

Masland, Skip. William Willya & the Washing Machine. Sheppard, Scott O., illus. 40p. (gr. k-5). 1993. 15.95 (*1-883016-01-0*) Moonglow Pubns. WILLIAM WILLYA & THE WASHING MACHINE, written by Skip Masland, illustrated by Scott Sheppard. What happens when a working mother asks her son to stay home & do the laundry on a Saturday morning & a mischievous little girl stops by to give him a hand? Throw in a couple cupfuls of Spurt, his mother's white blouse & a checkerboard shirt & you'll have some good, clean fun with WILLIAM WILLYA & THE WASHING MACHINE. Scheduled to be published in June of 1993, WILLIAM WILLYA & THE WASHING MACHINE introduces a memorable new character to the ranks of classic children's literature: William Willya, an impressionable young lad with a heart of gold who always tries to do exactly what he's told but, quite often, manages to make a well-meaning mess of it all. WILLIAM WILLYA & THE WASHING MACHINE is delightfully illustrated by Scott Sheppard & written by Skip Masland in a lyrical rhythm reminiscent of the legendary Dr. Seuss. WILLIAM WILLYA & THE WASHING MACHINE - the first installment in the new William Willya series from Moonglow Publishing - is certain to become a favorite of children & parents alike. *Publisher Provided Annotation.*

Maslen, Bobby L. Bob Books, Beginning Readers, 12 bks, Set I. (Illus.). 144p. (ps). 1983. pap. 14.95 (*0-9612104-0-0*) Bob Bks.

—Bob Books, Even More for Young Readers, 8 bks, Set III. Maslen, John R., illus. 144p. 1987. pap. 14.95 incl. teaching guide (*0-9612104-2-7*) Bob Bks.

—Bob Books, More for Young Readers, Set II. Maslen, John R., illus. 144p. 1987. Set of 8 books & teaching guide. 13.95 (*0-9612104-1-9*) Bob Bks.

Masom, Caroline, jt. auth. see Alexander, Pat.

Mason, jt. auth. see Vervoort.

Mason, Ann M. The Weird Things in Nanna's House. Wilcox, Cathy, illus. LC 91-16208. 32p. (ps-1). 1992. 13.95 (*0-531-05970-7*); lib. bdg. 13.99 (*0-531-08570-8*) Orchard Bks Watts.

Mason, Anthony. Soccer. 1990. 7.95 (*0-86685-475-4*) Intl Bk Ctr.

Mason, Antony. The Caribbean. (Illus.). 48p. (gr. 4-8). 1989. PLB 14.98 (*0-382-09823-4*) Silver Burdett Pr.

—The Children's Atlas of Civilizations. LC 93-23564. 1994. PLB write for info. (*1-56294-494-0*) Millbrook Pr.

—Middle East. LC 88-18312. (Illus.). 48p. (gr. 4-8). 1988. PLB 14.98 (*0-382-09514-6*) Silver Burdett pr.

—Southeast Asia. (Illus.). 48p. (gr. 4-8). 1989. lib. bdg. 14.98 (*0-382-09796-3*) Silver Burdett Pr.

—Southeast Asia. LC 91-24807. (Illus.). 96p. (gr. 6-12). 1992. PLB 19.92 (*0-8114-2447-2*) Raintree Steck-V.

Mason, Antony & Lye, Keith. The Children's Atlas of Exploration. LC 92-28856. (Illus.). 96p. (gr. 2-6). 1993. PLB 18.95 (*1-56294-256-5*); pap. 10.95 (*1-56294-711-7*) Millbrook Pr.

Mason, Bernard S. Boomerangs: How to Make & Throw Them. (Illus.). (gr. 5 up). 17.25 (*0-8446-5062-5*) Peter Smith.

—Drums, Tomtoms & Rattles: Primitive Percussion Instruments for Modern Use. (Illus.). (gr. 5 up). 18.25 (*0-8446-5063-3*) Peter Smith.

Mason, Cherie. Wild Fox: A True Story. Stammen, JoEllen M., illus. LC 92-74622. 32p. (gr. 2-5). 1993. 15.95 (*0-89272-319-X*) Down East.

Mason, Eileen. Witty Words: A Hilarious Collection of Outrageous Quotations for Every Day of the Year. Miller, Myron, illus. LC 92-25145. 224p. (gr. 10-12). 1992. 18.95 (*0-8069-8604-2*) Sterling.

Mason, Evelyn. The Baby Hugs Bear & Baby Tugs Bear Look & Find Book. Cooke, Tom, illus. 40p. (ps) 1984. 5.95 (*0-910313-73-3*) Parker Bros.

Mason, George, jt. auth. see Alberti, Delbert.

Mason, George F. Animal Tracks. LC 87-31124. (Illus.). 95p. (gr. 4-11). 1988. Repr. of 1943 ed. lib. bdg. 14.50 (*0-208-02213-9*, Linnet) Shoe String.

Mason, Helen. Great Careers for People Who Like Being Outdoors, 6 vols. LC 93-78075. (Illus.). 48p. (gr. 6-9). 1993. 16.95 (*0-8103-9390-5*, 102108, UXL) Gale.

—Life at the Seashore. (Illus.). 32p. (gr. 2-5). 1990. PLB 14.25 (*0-88625-270-9*); pap. 3.50 (*0-88625-269-5*) Durkin Hayes Pub.

—Life in a Forest. Rodgers, Gregg, illus. 32p. (Orig.). (gr. 3-6). 1992. pap. 3.50 (*0-88625-260-1*) Durkin Hayes Pub.

—Life in a Pond. Rodgers, Gregg, illus. 32p. (Orig.). (gr. 3-6). 1992. pap. 3.50 (*0-88625-255-5*) Durkin Hayes Pub.

Mason, Jane. A Family Affair. (gr. 4-8). 1993. pap. 2.50 (*0-448-40464-8*, G&D) Putnam Pub Group.

—River Day. Sorensen, Henri, illus. LC 93-26573. 32p. (gr. k-3). 1994. RSBE 14.95 (*0-02-762869-8*, Macmillan Child Bk) Macmillan Child Grp.

—Theater. LC 93-5744. 1994. write for info. (*0-89686-792-7*, Crestwood Hse) Macmillan Child Grp.

Mason, John. Autumn Weather. LC 90-34585. (Illus.). 32p. (gr. 1-5). 1991. PLB 11.90 (*0-531-18357-2*, Pub. by Bookwright Pr) Watts.

—Power Station Sun: The Story of Energy. (Illus.). 48p. (gr. 1-4). 1987. 12.95x (*0-8160-1778-6*) Facts on File.

—Spacecraft Technology. 1990. PLB 12.90 (*0-531-18328-9*, Pub. by Bookwright Pr) Watts.

—Spring Weather. LC 90-14397. (Illus.). 32p. (gr. 1-5). 1991. PLB 11.90 (*0-531-18437-4*, Pub. by Bookwright Pr) Watts.

—Summer Weather. LC 90-41063. (Illus.). 32p. (gr. 1-4). 1991. PLB 11.90 (*0-531-18382-3*, Pub. by Bookwright Pr) Watts.

—Weather & Climate. (Illus.). 48p. (gr. 5-8). 1991. PLB 16.98 (*0-382-24225-4*) Silver Burdett Pr.

—Winter Weather. LC 90-828. (Illus.). 32p. (gr. 1-5). 1991. PLB 11.90 (*0-531-18358-0*, Pub. by Bookwright Pr) Watts.

Mason, Judy S. Mr. Farmer & His Animals. Scoggan, Nita, ed. Wilson, Krista, illus. Shaw, Gwen, intro. by. (Illus.). 52p. (Orig.). (gr. 3 up). 1987. pap. 3.95 (*0-910487-11-1*) Royalty Pub.

Mason, Laura L. Lots of Ways to Win. LC 91-68087. (Illus.). 44p. (gr. k-3). 1992. 7.95 (*1-55523-500-X*) Winston-Derek.

Mason, Margo. Are We There Yet? (ps-3). 1990. 9.99 (*0-553-05870-3*) Bantam.

—Are We There Yet? (ps-3). 1990. pap. 3.50 (*0-553-34886-8*) Bantam.

—Go Away, Crows! Prebenna, David, illus. 32p. (ps-1). 1989. 3.50 (*0-553-34725-X*) Bantam.

—Go Away, Crows. 1989. pap. 8.95 (*0-553-05817-7*, Little Rooster) Bantam.

—Ready, Alice? (ps-3). 1990. 9.99 (*0-553-05816-9*) Bantam.

—Ready, Alice? (gr. 4 up). 1990. pap. 3.50 (*0-553-34741-1*) Bantam.

—Rover. Hoffman, Sandy, illus. 32p. (ps-1). write for info. Bantam.

—Two Good Friends. (ps-3). 1990. 9.99 (*0-553-05869-X*) Bantam.

—Two Good Friends. (ps-3). 1990. pap. 3.50 (*0-553-34885-X*) Bantam.

—Winter Coats. (ps-k). 1989. 8.95 (*0-553-05818-5*) Bantam.

—Winter Coats. 1989. pap. 3.50 (*0-553-34726-8*) Bantam.

Mason, Mary, jt. auth. see Goldin, Stephen.

Mason, Michael. How to Write a Winning College-Application Essay. 250p. (Orig.). (gr. 10 up). 1991. pap. 8.95 (*1-55958-083-6*) Prima Pub.

Mason, Miriam E. Mark Twain: Young Writer. Gillette, Henry S., illus. LC 90-23768. 192p. (gr. 3-7). 1991. pap. 3.95 (*0-689-71480-7*, Aladdin) Macmillan Child Grp.

Mason, Patrice G., jt. auth. see Rosenberg, Amye.

Mason, Patrice G., jt. auth. see Rossel, Karen T.

Mason, Tom, ed. see Bellem, Robert L.

Mason, Tom, ed. see Matsumoto, Leiji.

Mass, Lynne. Kids Working with Computers: The Texas Instruments LOGO Manual. Schlendorf, Lori, illus. 64p. (gr. 4-7). 1983. pap. 4.99 (*0-89824-074-3*) Trillium Pr.

Mass, Lynne, jt. auth. see Kemnitz, T. M.

Mass, Lynne, jt. auth. see Kemnitz, Thomas M.

Mass, Lynne, jt. auth. see Kemntz, T. M.

Massare, Judy A. Prehistoric Marine Reptiles: Sea Monsters During the Age of Dinosaurs. LC 91-17057. (Illus.). 64p. (gr. 5-8). 1991. PLB 14.90 (*0-531-11022-2*) Watts.

Massasati, Ahmad. Islamic Calligraphy Coloring Book. (Illus.). 57p. (Orig.). (gr. 3-6). 1991. pap. 4.95 (*0-89259-120-X*) Am Trust Pubns.

Massey, Barbara. Virginia Wingo: Teacher & Friend. LC 82-73665. (gr. k-3). 1983. 5.95 (*0-8054-4282-0*, 4242-82) Broadman.

Massey, Barbara, ed. see McIndoo, Ethel.

Massey, Grace C. Black Science Activity Books Teacher's Guide. Ivery, Evelyn L., ed. Chandler, Alton, intro. by. (Illus., Orig.). (gr. 1-6). 1988. pap. text ed. 2.95 (*0-685-26064-X*) Chandler White.

Massey, Grace C., jt. auth. see Howell, Ann C.

Massey Weddle, Linda. T. J. & the Big Trout River Vandals. LC 91-14678. 94p. (Orig.). (gr. 4-7). 1991. pap. 3.95 (*0-87227-148-X*, RBP5180) Reg Baptist.

—T. J. & the Nobody House. LC 90-8702. 95p. (Orig.). (gr. 3-7). 1990. pap. text ed. 3.95 (*0-87227-145-5*, RBP5174) Reg Baptist.

—T. J. & the Somebody Club. LC 92-5342. 108p. 1992. 3.95 (*0-87227-176-5*, RBP5210) Reg Baptist.

Massi, Jeri. Abandoned. 136p. (Orig.). (gr. 5-8). 1989. pap. 4.95 (*0-89084-467-4*) Bob Jones Univ Pr.

—The Bridge. (Illus.). 122p. (Orig.). (gr. 2-4). 1986. pap. 4.95 (*0-89084-348-1*) Bob Jones Univ Pr.

—Courage by Darkness. 157p. (Orig.). 1987. pap. 4.95 (*0-89084-412-7*) Bob Jones Univ Pr.

—Crown & Jewel. (Illus.). 160p. (Orig.). (gr. 5). 1987. pap. 4.95 (*0-89084-390-2*) Bob Jones Univ Pr.

—A Dangerous Game. 121p. (Orig.). (gr. 4-6). 1986. pap. 4.95 (*0-89084-347-3*) Bob Jones Univ Pr.

—Derwood, Inc. 288p. (Orig.). (gr. 4-6). 1986. pap. 6.94 (*0-89084-323-6*) Bob Jones Univ Pr.

—The Lesser Brother. 124p. (Orig.). (gr. 11). 1989. pap. 5.95 (*1-877778-02-8*) Llama Bks.

—The Myth of the Llama. Thompson, Del & Thompson, Dana, illus. 118p. (Orig.). (gr. 6). 1989. pap. 5.95 (*1-877778-00-1*) Llama Bks.

—Treasure in the Yukon. (Illus.). 136p. (Orig.). (gr. 4-6). 1986. pap. 4.95 (*0-89084-365-1*) Bob Jones Univ Pr.

Massie, Diane R. Chameleon Was a Spy. Massie, Diane R., illus. LC 78-19510. (gr. 2-6). 1979. (Crowell Jr Bks) HarpC Child Bks.

Masson, A. The Magic of Marionettes. Kinney, Pamela, illus. 88p. (gr. 6 up). 1989. Repr. 9.95 (*1-55037-042-1*, Pub. by Annick CN) Firefly Bks Ltd.

Masson, Marcelle. A Bag of Bones: Legends of the Wintu Indians of Northern California. LC 66-23398. 130p. (gr. 4 up). 1966. 16.95 (*0-911010-27-0*); pap. 8.95 (*0-911010-26-2*) Naturegraph.

Mast, Coleen K. Sex Respect: The Option of True Sexual Freedom: A Public Health Manual for Teachers. Evans, Wendy M. & Evans, Dolly B., illus. 61p. (Orig.). (gr. 7-9). 1986. pap. 12.95 (*0-945745-00-1*) Respect Inc.

—Sex Respect: The Option of True Sexual Freedom: A Public Health Guide for Parents. Evans, Wendy M. & Evans, Dolly B., illus. 61p. (Orig.). (gr. 7-9). 1986. pap. text ed. 8.95 (*0-945745-01-X*) Respect Inc.

—Sex Respect: The Option of True Sexual Freedom: A Public Health Workbook for Students. Evans, Wendy M. & Evans, Dolly B., illus. 61p. (Orig.). (gr. 7-9). 1986. pap. text ed. 7.95 (*0-945745-02-8*) Respect Inc.

—Sex Respect: The Option of True Sexual Freedom: A Public Health Workbook for Students. rev. ed. Forrestal, Julienne, ed. Greiner, William, illus. 118p. (gr. 7-9). 1990. pap. text ed. 8.95 (*0-945745-05-2*) Respect Inc.

Mast, Edward, adapted by. Jungalbook. 60p. (Orig.). 1990. Playscript. pap. 4.50 (*0-87602-291-3*) Anchorage.

Masterman-Smith, Virginia. The Treasure Trap. Litzinger, Roseanne, illus. LC 91-45217. 208p. (gr. 3-7). 1992. pap. 3.95 (*0-689-71578-1*, Aladdin) Macmillan Child Grp.

Masters, Anthony. Klondyker. LC 92-351. 1992. pap. 15. 00 (*0-671-79173-7*, S&S BFYR) S&S Trade.

Masters, Brien, ed. The Waldorf Song Book. 1988. pap. 8.50 (*0-86315-059-4*, 20243) Gryphon Pub.

Masters, James I., ed. North Fork & Shelter Island Guidebook. 3rd ed. LC 81-67384. (Illus.). 320p. (gr. 9-12). 1981. pap. 4.95 (*0-89808-007-X*, Pub. by Blue Claw) Masters Pubns.

Masters, Nanvy R. The Horrible, Homemade Halloween Costume. Maver, Debra H., illus. 32p. (gr. 2-4). 1993. 14.95 (*0-9623563-3-6*) J R Matthews.

Masterson, Audrey. The Day the Gypsies Came to Town. Oudekerk, Douglas, illus. LC 83-7319. 32p. (gr. 3-6). 1983. PLB 14.65 (*0-940742-22-5*) Raintree Steck-V.

Masterson, James J., jt. auth. see Gaetano, Ronald J.

Masterson, Richard. Exploring Careers in Computer Graphics. (gr. 7-12). 1990. 13.95 (*0-8239-1149-7*) Rosen Group.

Masterton, David S. Get Out of My Face. LC 90-24096. 160p. (gr. 5-9). 1991. SBE 13.95 (*0-689-31675-5*, Atheneum Child Bk) Macmillan Child Grp.

Maston, T. B. & Pinson, William M., Jr. Right or Wrong. rev. 14th ed. LC 75-143282. (gr. 8 up). 1971. pap. 3.95 (*0-8054-6116-7*, 6241-16); 4.50 (*0-685-00856-8*, 4825-37) Broadman.

Mastrangelo, Judy & Mastrangelo, Judy, illus. The Sandman: And Other Sleepy-Time Rhymes. LC 90-34513. 48p. (ps-2). 1990. 4.95 (*0-88101-105-3*) Unicorn Pub.

Masuda, Akiko. The Adventures of Kalakoa: A Hawaiian Rainbow Fantasy. Van Loon, Roland, illus. 32p. (gr. k-7). 1991. 7.95 (*0-9629842-1-3*) Stew & Rice.

Masui, Mitsuko. Pandas of the World. Ooka, Diane, tr. (Illus.). 32p. (gr. k-2). 1989. 11.95 (*0-89346-314-0*) Heian Intl.

Masurel, Claire. Good Night! Henry, Marie H., illus. LC 93-30198. 1994. 12.95 (*0-8118-0644-8*) Chronicle Bks.

Mataka, Laini. Never As Strangers. LC 88-82280. 60p. (Orig.). 1988. pap. 7.95 (*0-933121-75-X*) Black Classic.

Matalon, David. Target: Hero. Bell, Robert, ed. Lyle, Tom, illus. 32p. (Orig.). (gr. 10-12). 1988. pap. 6.00 (*1-55806-004-9*, 34) Iron Crown Ent Inc.

Matanah. Love Bones. Ridge, Delores F., ed. 75p. (Orig.). (gr. 9). 1974. pap. text ed. 4.95 (*0-9600978-1-3*) Knees Pbk.

Matarasso, Janet. Angela's New Sister. Chamberlain, Margaret, illus. 24p. 1988. 11.95 (*0-521-35640-7*) Cambridge U Pr.

—Why Can't You Grow Up? Chambers, Margaret, illus. LC 85-25539. 24p. (ps-2). 1986. 11.95 (*0-521-32125-5*) Cambridge U Pr.

Matas, Carol. Adventure in Legoland. (ps-3). 1992. pap. 2.50 (*0-590-43875-1*) Scholastic Inc.

—Code Name Kris. LC 90-32656. 160p. (gr. 7 up). 1990. SBE 13.95 (*0-684-19208-X*, Scribners Young Read) Macmillan Child Grp.

—Daniel's Story. LC 92-27537. 144p. (gr. 4-9). 1993. 13. 95 (*0-590-46920-7*) Scholastic Inc.

—Daniel's Story. (gr. 4-7). 1993. pap. 3.95 (*0-590-46588-0*) Scholastic Inc.

—Kris's War. 176p. 1992. pap. 3.25 (*0-590-45034-4*, Point) Scholastic Inc.

—Lisa's War. LC 88-29525. 128p. (gr. 7 up). 1989. SBE 13.95 (*0-684-19010-9*, Scribners Young Read) Macmillan Child Grp.

—Lisa's War. 1991. pap. 2.95 (*0-590-43517-5*) Scholastic Inc.

—Safari Adventure in Legoland. (gr. 4-7). 1993. pap. 2.75 (*0-590-45876-0*) Scholastic Inc.

—Sworn Enemies. LC 92-6188. 1993. 16.00 (*0-553-08326-0*) Bantam.

Mateer, Charlotte F. Let's Go to the Arctic: A Story & Activities Book about Arctic People & Animals. Witt, Linda A., illus. 64p. (gr. 4-6). 1993. pap. text ed. 7.95 (*1-879373-24-6*) R Rinehart.

Matens, Margaret H. Mandy & the Kookalocka. Matens, Margaret H., illus. LC 93-77130. 32p. (gr. k-5). 1993. 14.95 (*1-882959-53-1*) Foxglove TN.

—Wuzzy the Witch. Matens, Margaret H., illus. LC 93-77128. 42p. (gr. k-5). 1993. 14.95 (*1-882959-54-X*) Foxglove TN.

Mateo, Mary A. Portraits of Native American Indians. (Illus.). 96p. (gr. 4-7). 1992. 9.95 (*0-86653-669-8*, GA1322) Good Apple.

Matero, Robert. Eyes on Nature: Reptiles. (Illus.). 32p. 1992. pap. 4.95 (*1-56156-151-7*) Kidsbks.

Math, Irwin. More Wires & Watts: Understanding & Using Electricity. Keith, Hal, illus. LC 88-15767. 96p. (gr. 7 up). 1988. SBE 14.95 (*0-684-18914-3*, Scribners Young Read) Macmillan Child Grp.

—Tomorrow's Technology: Experimenting with the Science of the Future. Keith, Hal, illus. LC 91-32341. 80p. (gr. 7 up). 1992. SBE 13.95 (*0-684-19294-2*, Scribners Young Read) Macmillan Child Grp.

—Wires & Watts: Understanding & Using Electricity. Keith, Hal, illus. LC 88-15767. 96p. (gr. 7 up). 1981. RSBE 15.95 (*0-684-16854-5*, Scribners Young Read) Macmillan Child Grp.

—Wires & Watts: Using & Understanding Electricity. Math, Irwin, illus. LC 81-2255. 96p. (gr. 7 up). 1989. pap. 4.95 (*0-689-71298-7*, Aladdin) Macmillan Child Grp.

Matheny, James F. & Matheny, Marjorie B. Is There a Russian Connection? An Exposition of Ezekiel 37 & 39. 76p. (Orig.). 1987. pap. 3.95 (*0-939422-01-8*) Jay & Assocs.

Matheny, Marjorie B., jt. auth. see Matheny, James F.

Mather, Anne D. & Weldon, Louise B. The Cat at the Door: And Other Stories to Live By. Martin, Lyn, illus. 192p. (ps-2). 1991. pap. 12.00 perfect bdg. (*0-89486-758-X*, T5131) Hazelden.

Mather, Maurice W. & Hewitt, Joseph W. Xenophon's Anabasis, Bks. 1-4. (Illus.). 528p. (gr. 12 up). 1976. pap. 21.95x (*0-8061-1347-2*) U of Okla Pr.

Mather, Melissa. Rough Road Home. LC 58-9537. 256p. 1988. pap. 9.95 (*0-8397-7237-8*) Eriksson.

Mather, Pamela, ed. see Cairis, Nicholas T.

Mathers, Douglas. Brain. Farmer, Andrew & Green, Robina, illus. LC 90-42883. 32p. (gr. 4-6). 1992. PLB 11.89 (*0-8167-2090-8*); pap. 3.95 (*0-8167-2091-6*) Troll Assocs.

—Ears. Farmer, Andrew & Green, Robina, illus. LC 90-42176. 32p. (gr. 4-6). 1992. lib. bdg. 11.89 (*0-8167-2092-4*); pap. text ed. 3.95 (*0-8167-2093-2*) Troll Assocs.

Mathers, Pamela, ed. see Cairis, Nicholas T.

Mathers, Petra. Maria Theresa. Mathers, Petra, illus. LC
84-48346. 32p. (ps-3). 1985. PLB 13.89
(0-06-024112-8) HarpC Child Bks.
—Maria Theresa. Mathers, Petra, illus. LC 84-48346.
32p. (gr. k-3). 1992. pap. 4.95 (0-06-443282-3,
Trophy) HarpC Child Bks.
—Sophie & Lou. Mathers, Petra, illus. LC 90-37562. 32p.
(ps-3). 1991. 15.00 (0-06-024071-7); PLB 14.89
(0-06-024072-5) HarpC Child Bks.
—Sophie & Lou. LC 90-37562. (Illus.). 32p. (ps-3). 1993.
pap. 4.95 (0-06-443331-5, Trophy) HarpC Child Bks.
—Victor & Christabel. Mathers, Petra, illus. LC 92-
33468. 40p. (ps-3). 1993. 15.00 (0-679-83060-X); PLB
15.99 (0-679-93060-4) Knopf Bks Yng Read.
Mathes, Patricia G. & Irby, Beverly J. Teen Pregnancy
& Parenting Handbook. LC 92-85264. 440p. (Orig.).
1993. pap. text ed. 19.95 (0-87822-333-9, 4660) Res
Press.
Mathews, jt. auth. see Kramer, Janice.
Mathews, Judith. An Egg & Seven Socks. Hafner,
Marylin, illus. LC 91-11476. 32p. (ps-2). 1993. 14.00
(0-06-020207-6); PLB 13.89 (0-06-020208-4) HarpC
Child Bks.
—Knock-Knock Knees & Funny Bones: Riddles for
Every Body. (ps-3). 1993. 8.95 (0-8075-4203-2) A
Whitman.
—Tuti, Blue Horse, & the Nipnope Man. Powers, Daniel,
illus. LC 93-1. 1993. write for info. (0-8075-8130-5) A
Whitman.
Mathews, Judith & Robinson, Fay. Oh, How Waffle!
Riddles You Can Eat. Levine, Abby, ed. Whiting,
Carl, illus. LC 92-13478. 32p. (gr. 1-4). 1992. 8.95g
(0-8075-5907-5) A Whitman.
Mathews, Judith, ed. see Asher, Sandy.
Mathews, Judith, ed. see Baden, Robert.
Mathews, Judith, ed. see Berleth, Richard.
**Mathews, Judith, ed. see Bernstein, Joanne E. & Cohen,
Paul.**
**Mathews, Judith, ed. see Bernstein, Joanne E. &
Fireside, Bryna.**
Mathews, Judith, ed. see Brillhart, Julie.
Mathews, Judith, ed. see Coleman, Mary A.
Mathews, Judith, ed. see Green, Phyllis.
Mathews, Judith, ed. see Hamm, Diane J.
Mathews, Judith, ed. see Helfman, Elizabeth.
Mathews, Judith, ed. see Ketteman, Helen.
Mathews, Judith, ed. see Kroll, Virginia L.
Mathews, Judith, ed. see Lily Toy Hong.
Mathews, Judith, ed. see Martin, Antoinette T.
**Mathews, Judith, ed. see Molnar, Dorothy E. & Fenton,
Stephen H.**
Mathews, Judith, ed. see Muldoon, Kathleen M.
Mathews, Judith, ed. see Nerlove, Miriam.
Mathews, Judith, ed. see Nims, Bonnie L.
Mathews, Judith, ed. see Nodar, Carmen M.
Mathews, Judith, ed. see Patneaude, David.
Mathews, Judith, ed. see Seltzer, Meyer.
Mathews, Judith, ed. see Shepard, Aaron.
Mathews, Judith, ed. see Vigna, Judith.
**Mathews, Judith, ed. see White, Laurence B., Jr. &
Broekel, Ray.**
Mathews, Judith, ed. see Zimelman, Nathan.
Mathews, Louise. Bunches & Bunches of Bunnies.
Bassett, Jeni, illus. 32p. (gr. k-3). 1991. pap. 3.95
(0-590-44766-1) Scholastic Inc.
Mathews, Nancy. Friends of Jesus: The Animals Tell
Their Stories. (Illus.). 24p. (gr. 2-3). 1991. 9.99
(0-8407-9609-9) Oliver-Nelson.
Mathews, Sally. Travel & Learn Florida: A Children's
Activity Book. (Illus.). 48p. (ps-8). 1991. pap. 7.95
(0-941263-24-X) Tribune FL.
Mathews, Sally S. The Sad Night: The Story of an Aztec
Victory & a Spanish Loss. Mathews, Sally S., illus. LC
92-25119. 1993. write for info. (0-395-63035-5,
Clarion Bks) HM.
Mathews, V., ed. see Arnold, Caroline.
Mathews, V., ed. see Greenberg, Lorna.
Mathews, V., ed. see Koral, April.
Mathews, V., ed. see Liptak, Karen.
Mathews, V., ed. see Margolies, Jacob.
Mathews, V., ed. see Nourse, Alan E.
Mathews-Deacon, Saundra. Magic Theatre I: Children's
Musical. Date not set. 3.75 (0-87129-230-0, M12)
Dramatic Pub.
Mathias, Beverly, selected by. Reader's Digest Children's
Book of Poetry. Snow, Alan, illus. LC 92-14698. 48p.
(ps-1). 1992. 13.00 (0-89577-442-9, Readers Digest
Kids) RD Assn.
Mathias, Robert. Beauty & the Beast. 1991. 4.99
(0-517-06693-9) Outlet Bk Co.
Mathiesen, Egon. Jungle in the Wheat Field. (Illus.). (gr.
k-3). 1960. 9.95 (0-8392-3014-1) Astor-Honor.
—Oswald the Monkey. (Illus.). (gr. k-3). 1959. 9.95
(0-8392-3025-7) Astor-Honor.
Mathieson, David. Trial by Wilderness. 1990. pap. 3.95
(0-395-56456-5) HM.
Mathieu, Joe. Big Bird's Big Book. Mathieu, Joe, illus.
12p. (ps-1). 1987. 29.95 (0-394-89128-7) Random Bks
Yng Read.
—Elmo Wants a Bath. Mathieu, Joe, illus. 10p. (ps).
1992. vinyl 3.95 (0-679-83066-9) Random Bks Yng
Read.
—The Olden Days. Mathieu, Joe, illus. 32p. (ps-3). 1981.
lib. bdg. 4.99 (0-394-94085-7) Random Bks Yng Read.
—Sesame Street One Two Three: A Counting Book from
1 to 100. Mathieu, Joe, illus. LC SY-1992. 32p. (ps-1).
1991. 9.00 (0-679-81230-X); lib. bdg. 10.99
(0-679-91230-4) Random Bks Yng Read.

Mathieu, Joe, illus. Pop Goes the Santa! A Sesame Street
Thumb Fun Book. LC 91-68546. 48p. (ps). 1992. pap.
2.50 (0-679-83065-0) Random Bks Yng Read.
—Rocking Reindeer: A Sesame Street Thumb Fun Book.
LC 91-68545. 48p. (Orig.). (ps). 1992. pap. 2.50
(0-679-83064-2) Random Bks Yng Read.
—Sesame Street Fire Trucks. 14p. (ps-k). 1988. bds. 3.99
(0-394-89952-0) Random Bks Yng Read.
—Trucks in Your Neighborhood. 14p. (ps-k). 1988. bds.
3.99 (0-394-89951-2) Random Bks Yng Read.
Mathieu, Joseph. Big Joe's Trailer Truck. reissued ed.
Mathieu, Joseph, illus. LC 74-2538. 32p. (Orig.).
(ps-1). 1993. pap. 2.95 (0-394-82925-5) Random Bks
Yng Read.
Mathis, Danny E., compiled by see Mathis, Quincy D.
Mathis, Quincy D. Brudder & the Babe. Mathis, Danny
E., compiled by. LC 93-60735. 92p. (gr. 1-4). 1994.
8.95 (1-55523-636-7) Winston-Derek.
Mathis, Sharon B. The Hundred-Penny Box. Dillon, Leo
& Dillon, Diane, illus. 48p. (gr. k-3). 1975. pap. 15.00
(0-670-38787-8) Viking Child Bks.
—The Hundred-Penny Box. Dillon, Leo & Dillon, Diane,
illus. 48p. (gr. 1-4). 1986. pap. 3.99 (0-14-032169-1,
Puffin) Puffin Bks.
—Listen for the Fig Tree. 176p. (gr. 7 up). 1990. pap.
4.99 (0-14-034364-4, Puffin) Puffin Bks.
—Red Dog - Blue Fly: Poems for a Football Season.
(ps-3). 1991. 13.95 (0-670-83623-0) Viking Child Bks.
—Sidewalk Story. 64p. (gr. 2-6). 1986. pap. 3.99
(0-14-032165-9, Puffin) Puffin Bks.
—Teacup Full of Roses. (gr. 3-7). 1987. pap. 3.99
(0-14-032328-7, Puffin) Puffin Bks.
Matiella, Ana C. Cultural Pride Student Workbook.
Salinas, Ron, illus. 96p. (Orig.). (gr. 5-8). 1988. pap.
7.95 (0-941816-68-0) ETR Assocs.
—La Familia Student Workbook. Salinas, Ron, illus. 96p.
(Orig.). (gr. 5-8). 1988. pap. 7.95 (0-941816-70-2)
ETR Assocs.
Matov, G. Tales of Tzaddikim: Bereishis. Weinbach,
Shaindel, tr. from HEB. Bardugo, Miriam, illus. 320p.
(gr. 7-12). 1987. 14.95 (0-89906-825-1); pap. 10.95
(0-89906-826-X) Mesorah Pubns.
—Tales of Tzaddikim: Devarim. Weinbach, Shaindel, tr.
Bardugo, Miriam, illus. 320p. (gr. 7-12). 1988. 14.95
(0-89906-833-2); pap. 10.95 (0-89906-834-0) Mesorah
Pubns.
—Tales of Tzaddikim: Sh'emos. Weinbach, Shaindel, tr.
from HEB. Bardvgo, Miriam, illus. 320p. (gr. 7-12).
1988. 14.95 (0-89906-827-8); pap. 10.95
(0-89906-828-6) Mesorah Pubns.
Matovcik, Gerard. Academic Sportfolio: Excuse Notes
Are No Excuse. Pranzo, Donard, ed. (Illus.). (gr. 9-
12). 1989. portfolio ser. 50.00 (0-924086-11-4) Acad
Sportfolio.
Matozzi, Patricia R. God Is Love. LC 92-12769. (Illus.).
1992. 3.99 (0-517-08143-1, Pub. by Derrydale Bks)
Outlet Bk Co.
Matranga, Frances C. One Step at a Time. (Illus.). (gr.
4-7). 1987. pap. 3.99 (0-570-03642-9, 39-1126)
Concordia.
—The Perfect Friend. 80p. (Orig.). (gr. 5-7). 1985. pap.
3.99 (0-570-04112-0, 56-1523) Concordia.
**Matre, Nancy A. Van see Poppe, Carol A. & Van Matre,
Nancy A.**
Matricardi, Connie. Preschool Puppet Plays. (Illus.). 36p.
(Orig.). (gr. k). 1993. pap. 9.95 (1-884555-00-4) P
Depke Bks.
Matson, Emerson N. Legends of the Great Chiefs.
(Illus.). 144p. (gr. 8-12). pap. 5.95 (0-9609940-0-9)
Storypole.
Matson, Sue, ed. see Bowkett, Gerald E.
Matsui, Susan, tr. see Akio, Terumasa.
Matsui, Susan, tr. see Tejima, Keizaburo.
Matsumoto, Leiji. Captain Harlock Television Scripts,
Vol. 1. Villa, Mickie & Mason, Tom, eds. Dunn, Ben,
illus. Gibson, Robert, intro. by. (Illus.). 135p. 1990.
pap. 19.95 (0-944735-63-0) Malibu Graphics.
Matsuoka, Kyoko. There's a Hippo in My Bath! Hayashi,
Akiko, illus. 1989. 12.95 (0-385-26188-8); PLB 12.95
(0-385-26189-6) Doubleday.
Mattel Inc. Staff. Hot Wheels Model Set. (Illus.). 24p.
(gr. 1-6). 1993. play set 7.99 (0-8431-3472-0)
Troubador Pr.
Mattern, Joanne. Australian Animals. LC 92-41033.
(Illus.). 24p. (gr. k-2). 1993. 1.95 (0-8167-3096-2)
Troll Assocs.
—Baby Animals. Stone, Lynn M., illus. LC 91-40282.
24p. (gr. 4-7). 1993. pap. text ed. 1.95
(0-8167-2958-1) Troll Assocs.
—Bears. Leeson, Tom & Leeson, Pat, illus. LC 92-20176.
24p. (gr. 4-7). 1992. (Pub. by Watermill Pr); pap. 1.95
(0-8167-2952-2, Pub. by Watermill Pr) Troll Assocs.
—Lions & Tigers. Stone, Lynn M., illus. LC 92-19053.
24p. (gr. 4-7). 1992. (Pub. by Watermill Pr); pap. 1.95
(0-8167-2956-5, Pub. by Watermill Pr) Troll Assocs.
—Monkeys & Apes. LC 92-28080. (Illus.). 24p. (gr. 4-7).
1992. pap. text ed. 1.95 (0-8167-2962-X) Troll Assocs.
—A Picture Book of Butterflies & Moths. Pistolesi,
Roseanna, illus. LC 92-5225. 24p. (gr. 1-4). 1992. PLB
9.59 (0-8167-2796-1); pap. 2.50 (0-8167-2797-X) Troll
Assocs.
—Picture Book of Cats. Pistolesi, Roseanna, illus. LC 90-
42548. 24p. (gr. 1-4). 1991. PLB 9.59
(0-8167-2146-7); pap. 2.50 (0-8167-2147-5) Troll
Assocs.

—A Picture Book of Insects. Kinnealy, Janice, illus. LC
90-11211. 24p. (gr. 1-4). 1991. PLB 9.59
(0-8167-2154-8); pap. 2.50 (0-8167-2155-6) Troll
Assocs.
—Reptiles & Amphibians. Stone, Lynn M., illus. LC 92-
20189. 24p. (gr. 4-7). 1992. pap. 1.95 (0-8167-2954-9,
Pub. by Watermill Pr) Troll Assocs.
—Young Martin Luther King, Jr. I Have a Dream.
Eitzen, Allan, illus. LC 91-26478. 32p. (gr. k-2). 1992.
text ed. 11.59 (0-8167-2544-6); pap. text ed. 2.95
(0-8167-2545-4) Troll Assocs.
Mattern, Joanne, ed. see Montgomery, Lucy M.
Mattern, Joanne, ed. see Pyle, Howard.
Mattern, Joanne, retold by see Stevenson, Robert Louis.
Matthews. Bunches & Bunches of Bunnies. 1993. pap. 28.
67 (0-590-71572-0) Scholastic Inc.
Matthews, Andrew. Crackling Brat. Bogacki, Tomek,
illus. LC 93 (gr. k-3). 1993. PLB 15.95 (0-8050-2608-8,
Bks Young Read) H Holt & Co.
—Mallory Cox & His Interstellar Socks. Ross, Tony, illus.
96p. (gr. 4-6). 1993. 18.95 (0-460-88126-4, Pub. by J
M Dent & Sons) Trafalgar.
Matthews, Andrew & Todd, Justin. The Jar of the Sun.
(Illus.). 32p. (gr. k-3). 1992. 16.95 (0-09-176400-9,
Pub. by Hutchinson UK) Trafalgar.
Matthews, Andrew, retold by. Stories from Hans
Christian Andersen. Snow, Alan, illus. LC 92-45627.
96p. (gr. 2-5). 1993. 18.95 (0-531-05463-2) Orchard
Bks Watts.
Matthews, Billie L. & Hurlburt, Virginia E. Davy's
Dawg. Welch, Karen E., ed. Boyce, Kenneth, illus. LC
88-32832. 64p. (gr. 3-8). 1989. PLB 9.95
(0-937460-58-3) Hendrick-Long.
Matthews, Billie P. & Chichester, A. Lee. Secret of the
Cibolo. Roberts, Melissa, ed. (Illus.). 104p. (gr. 4-7).
1988. 9.95 (0-89015-638-7, Pub. by Panda Bks) Eakin-
Sunbelt.
Matthews, Cecily. Mr. Clutterbus. Hunnam, Lucinda,
illus. LC 92-34257. 1993. 4.25 (0-383-03642-9) SRA
Schl Grp.
—My Dog Ben. Cullo, Ned, illus. LC 92-31946. 1993.
3.75 (0-383-03585-6) SRA Schl Grp.
—Why Not? Culic, Ned, illus. LC 93-9280. 1994. write
for info. (0-383-03727-1) SRA Schl Grp.
Matthews, Downs. Arctic Summer. Guravich, Dan,
photos by. LC 92-25376. (Illus.). 40p. (gr. 2-5). 1993.
pap. 14.00 JRT (0-671-79539-2, S&S BFYR) S&S
Trade.
—Polar Bear Cubs. Guravich, Dan, photos by. (Illus.).
(gr. 2 up). 1989. pap. 13.95 jacketed (0-671-66757-2,
S&S BFYR) S&S Trade.
—Polar Bear Cubs. Guravich, Dan, photos by. LC 88-
10284. (Illus.). 32p. (gr. 2-5). 1991. pap. 4.00
(0-671-74493-3, S&S BFYR) S&S Trade.
—Polar Bear Cubs. (gr. 3). pap. write for info.
(0-663-56236-8) Silver Burdett Pr.
—Wetlands. Guravich, Dan, photos by. LC 93-3439.
1994. pap. 14.00 (0-671-86562-5, S&S BFYR) S&S
Trade.
Matthews, Gordon. Madonna. Arico, Diane, ed. LC 85-
10587. (Illus.). 64p. (gr. 8-12). 1985. pap. 3.50
(0-685-10385-4) S&S Trade.
—Michael Jackson. LC 84-725. (Illus.). 64p. (gr. 4 up).
1984. lib. bdg. 8.79 (0-671-50636-6, J Messner) S&S
Trade.
—Prince. Arico, Diane, ed. (Illus.). 64p. (gr. 3 up). 1985.
pap. 3.50 (0-685-09758-7) S&S Trade.
Matthews, Graham P., Jr. Children's Bible Stories with
Questions. LeDee, Kim, illus. LC 93-19623. (gr. 3 up).
1993. write for info. (0-910683-18-2) Townsnd Pr.
Matthews, John R. Eating Disorders. (Illus.). 240p. (gr.
9-12). 1990. 21.95x (0-8160-1911-8) Facts on File.
Matthews, Judith & Robinson, Fay. Nathaniel Willy,
Scared Silly. Natchev, Alexi, illus. LC 92-4052. 32p.
(ps-3). 1994. RSBE 14.95 (0-02-765285-8, Bradbury
Pr) Macmillan Child Grp.
Matthews, Kay. An Anasazi Welcome. Belknap, Barbara,
illus. LC 92-796. 40p. (gr. 1-6). 1992. pap. 8.95
(1-878610-27-9) Red Crane Bks.
Matthews, L. Cowboys. (Illus.). 32p. (gr. 3-8). 1989. PLB
18.00 (0-86625-363-7); lib. bdg. 13.50s.p.
(0-685-58277-9) Rourke Corp.
—Gunfighters. (Illus.). 32p. (gr. 3-8). 1989. PLB 18.00
(0-86625-361-0); 13.50s.p. (0-685-58278-7) Rourke
Corp.
—Indians. (Illus.). 32p. (gr. 3-8). 1989. PLB 18.00
(0-86625-364-5); 13.50s.p. (0-685-58279-5) Rourke
Corp.
—Pioneers. (Illus.). 32p. (gr. 3-8). 1989. PLB 18.00
(0-86625-362-9); 13.50s.p. Rourke Corp.
—Railroaders. (Illus.). 32p. (gr. 3-8). 1989. PLB 18.00
(0-86625-366-1); 13.50s.p. (0-685-67677-3) Rourke
Corp.
—Soldiers. (Illus.). 32p. (gr. 3-8). 1989. PLB 18.00
(0-86625-365-3); 13.50 (0-685-67678-1) Rourke Corp.
Matthews, Leonard J. Pioneers & Trailblazers:
Adventures of the Old West, 6 vols. 1990. 9.99
(0-517-02537-X) Outlet Bk Co.
Matthews, Liz. Teeny Witch & Christmas Magic. Loh,
Carolyn, illus. LC 90-11206. 48p. (gr. k-1). 1991. PLB
11.89 (0-8167-2270-6); pap. 3.50 (0-8167-2271-4)
Troll Assocs.
—Teeny Witch & the Great Halloween Ride. Loh,
Carolyn, illus. LC 90-11207. 48p. (gr. k-1). 1991. PLB
11.89 (0-8167-2274-9); pap. text ed. 3.50
(0-8167-2275-7) Troll Assocs.

—Teeny Witch & the Perfect Valentine. Loh, Carolyn, illus. LC 90-11204. 48p. (gr. k-1). 1991. PLB 11.89 (0-8167-2280-3); pap. text ed. 3.50 (0-8167-2281-1) Troll Assocs.

—Teeny Witch & the Terrible Twins. Loh, Carolyn, illus. LC 90-11139. 48p. (gr. k-1). 1991. PLB 11.89 (0-8167-2266-8); pap. text ed. 3.50 (0-8167-2267-6) Troll Assocs.

—Teeny Witch & the Tricky Easter Bunny. Loh, Carolyn, illus. LC 90-11205. 48p. (gr. k-1). 1991. PLB 11.89 (0-8167-2272-2); pap. text ed. 3.50 (0-8167-2273-0) Troll Assocs.

—Teeny Witch Goes on Vacation. Loh, Carolyn, illus. LC 90-11141. 48p. (gr. k-1). 1991. lib. bdg. 11.89 (0-8167-2278-1); pap. text ed. 3.50 (0-8167-2279-X) Troll Assocs.

—Teeny Witch Goes to School. Loh, Carolyn, illus. LC 90-11208. 48p. (gr. k-1). 1991. PLB 11.89 (0-8167-2276-5); pap. 3.50 (0-8167-2277-3) Troll Assocs.

—Teeny Witch Goes to the Library. Loh, Carolyn, illus. LC 90-11140. 48p. (gr. k-1). 1991. PLB 11.89 (0-8167-2268-4); pap. text ed. 3.50 (0-8167-2269-2) Troll Assocs.

Matthews, Mary. Jacob & the Star. LC 86-12505. (Orig.). (gr. 4-7). 1986. pap. 7.95 (0-8192-1384-5) Morehouse Pub.

Matthews, Morgan. The Big Race. Schindler, S. D., illus. LC 88-1287. 48p. (Orig.). (gr. 1-4). 1989. PLB 10.59 (0-8167-1329-4); pap. text ed. 3.50 (0-8167-1330-8) Troll Assocs.

—Brave Sir Laughalot. Baer, Mary A., illus. LC 85-14010. 48p. (Orig.). (gr. 1-3). 1986. PLB 10.59 (0-8167-0594-1); pap. text ed. 3.50 (0-8167-0595-X) Troll Assocs.

—Chuck, the Unlucky Duck. Harvey, Paul, illus. LC 88-1284. 48p. (Orig.). (gr. 1-4). 1989. PLB 10.59 (0-8167-1333-2); pap. text ed. 3.50 (0-8167-1334-0) Troll Assocs.

—Fish for Supper. Miller, Susan, illus. LC 85-14056. 48p. (Orig.). (gr. 1-3). 1986. PLB 10.59 (0-8167-0588-7); pap. text ed. 3.50 (0-8167-0589-5) Troll Assocs.

—Houdini, the Vanishing Hare. Gustafson, Dana, illus. LC 88-1286. 48p. (Orig.). (gr. 1-4). 1989. PLB 10.59 (0-8167-1343-X); pap. text ed. 3.50 (0-8167-1344-8) Troll Assocs.

—Icky, Sticky Gloop. Victor, Ymonne, illus. LC 85-14013. 48p. (Orig.). (gr. 1-3). 1986. lib. bdg. 10.59 (0-8167-0616-6); pap. text ed. 3.50 (0-8167-0617-4) Troll Assocs.

—One Hundred Two Goofy Jokes. LC 91-35176. (Illus.). 64p. (gr. 2-6). 1992. pap. text ed. 2.95 (0-8167-2697-3) Troll Assocs.

—One Hundred Two Out of This World Jokes. Matthews, Morgan, illus. LC 91-45021. 64p. (gr. 2-6). 1992. pap. text ed. 2.95 (0-8167-2789-9) Troll Assocs.

—One Hundred Two School Cafeteria Jokes. LC 91-30055. (Illus.). 64p. (gr. 2-6). 1991. pap. text ed. 2.95 (0-8167-2611-6) Troll Assocs.

—Silly Sidney. Kolding, Richard M., illus. LC 85-14063. 48p. (Orig.). (gr. 1-3). 1986. PLB 10.59 (0-8167-0610-7); pap. text ed. 3.50 (0-8167-0611-5) Troll Assocs.

—Squeaky Shoes. Karas, Brian, illus. LC 85-14014. 48p. (Orig.). (gr. 1-3). 1986. PLB 10.59 (0-8167-0642-5); pap. text ed. 3.50 (0-8167-0643-3) Troll Assocs.

—Tricky Alex. Mahan, Ben, illus. LC 85-14018. 48p. (Orig.). (gr. 1-3). 1986. PLB 10.59 (0-8167-0598-4); pap. text ed. 3.50 (0-8167-0599-2) Troll Assocs.

—What's It Like to Be a Farmer. Kennedy, Anne, illus. LC 89-34386. 32p. (gr. k-3). 1990. lib. bdg. 10.89 (0-8167-1803-2); pap. text ed. 2.95 (0-8167-1804-0) Troll Assocs.

—What's It Like to Be a Postal Worker. Hicks, Mark A., illus. LC 89-34385. 32p. (gr. k-3). 1990. lib. bdg. 10.89 (0-8167-1813-X); pap. text ed. 2.95 (0-8167-1814-8) Troll Assocs.

—What's It Like to Be a Railroad Worker. Sweat, Lynn, illus. LC 89-34389. 32p. (gr. k-3). 1989. lib. bdg. 10.89 (0-8167-1815-6); pap. text ed. 2.95 (0-8167-1816-4) Troll Assocs.

—Which Way, Hugo? Miller, Susan, illus. LC 85-14132. 48p. (Orig.). (gr. 1-3). 1986. PLB 10.59 (0-8167-0648-4); pap. text ed. 3.50 (0-8167-0649-2) Troll Assocs.

—Whoo's Too Tired? Kolding, Richard M., illus. LC 88-1285. 48p. (Orig.). (gr. 1-4). 1988. PLB 10.59 (0-8167-1331-6); pap. text ed. 3.50 (0-8167-1332-4) Troll Assocs.

Matthews, Nancy. Wilderness Preservation. (Illus.). 112p. (gr. 5 up). 1991. PLB 19.95 (0-7910-1580-7); pap. write for info. (0-7910-1605-6) Chelsea Hse.

Matthews, Penny, compiled by. Amazing & Bizarre: Ten Wonderfully Weird Stories. 80p. (Orig.). (gr. 4-7). 1992. pap. 3.50 (0-440-40705-2, YB) Dell.

Matthews, Phoebe. The Boy on the Cover. (gr. 7 up). 1988. pap. 2.75 (0-380-75407-X, Flare) Avon.

—Switchstance. 176p. (Orig.). (gr. 7 up). 1989. pap. 2.95 (0-380-75729-X, Flare) Avon.

Matthews, Rupert. Age of Mammals. (ps-3). 1990. PLB 12.40 (0-531-18311-4) Watts.

—The Dinosaur Age. LC 88-39047. (Illus.). 32p. (gr. 5-6). 1989. PLB 12.40 (0-531-18280-0) Watts.

—Explorer. Stevenson, Jim, illus. LC 91-8428. 64p. (gr. 5 up). 1991. 15.00 (0-679-81460-4); lib. bdg. 15.99 (0-679-91460-9) Knopf Bks Yng Read.

—The First People. (Illus.). 32p. (gr. 5-8). 1990. PLB 12.40 (0-531-18298-3) Watts.

—The First Settlements. (Illus.). 32p. (gr. 5-8). 1990. PLB 12.40 (0-531-18299-1) Watts.

—Let's Look At Ships & Boats. (ps-3). 1990. PLB 11.40 (0-531-18322-X, Pub. by Bookwright Pr) Watts.

—The Race to the South Pole. Post, Doug, illus. LC 88-7534. 32p. (gr. 5-8). 1989. PLB 11.90 (0-531-18273-8, Pub. by Bookwright Pr) Watts.

—Record Breakers of the Air. LC 89-5212. (Illus.). 32p. (gr. 2-6). 1990. PLB 9.59 (0-8167-1921-7); pap. text ed. 2.50 (0-8167-1922-5) Troll Assocs.

—Record Breakers of the Land. LC 89-5202. (Illus.). 32p. (gr. 2-6). 1990. PLB 9.59 (0-8167-1923-3); pap. text ed. 2.50 (0-8167-1924-1) Troll Assocs.

—Record Breakers of the Sea. LC 89-35503. (Illus.). 32p. (gr. 2-6). 1990. PLB 9.59 (0-8167-1925-X); pap. text ed. 2.50 (0-8167-1926-8) Troll Assocs.

—Roman Soldiers. LC 90-47. (Illus.). 24p. (gr. k-4). 1990. PLB 10.90 (0-531-18345-9, Pub. by Bookwright Pr) Watts.

—Viking Explorers. LC 90-178. (Illus.). 24p. (gr. k-4). 1990. PLB 10.90 (0-531-18346-7, Pub. by Bookwright Pr) Watts.

Matthews, Sarah, tr. see Bombarde, Odile & Moatti, Claude.

Matthews, Sarah, tr. see Brice, Raphaelle.

Matthews, Sarah, tr. see De Sairigne, Catherine.

Matthews, Sarah, tr. see Farre, Marie.

Matthews, Sarah, tr. see Jobin, Claire.

Matthews, Sarah, tr. see Limousin, Odile.

Matthews, Sarah, tr. see Pfeffer, Pierre.

Matthews, Sarah, tr. see Planche, Bernard.

Matthews, Sarah, tr. see Ruffault, Charlotte.

Matthews, Sarah, tr. see Singh, Anne.

Matthews, Velda & Beard, Ray. Basic Bible Dictionary. Korth, Bob, ed. Wahl, Dick, illus. 128p. (Orig.). (gr. 4-12). 1984. pap. 12.99 (0-87239-720-3, 2770) Standard Pub.

Matthias, Catherine. Arriba y Abajo (Over-Under) Sharp, Gene, illus. LC 83-21005. (SPA). 32p. (ps-2). 1989. PLB 11.93 (0-516-52048-3); pap. 2.95 (0-516-52048-2) Childrens.

—Demasiados Globos (Too Many Balloons) Sharp, Gene, illus. LC 81-15520. (SPA). 32p. (ps-2). 1990. PLB 11.93 (0-516-33633-9); pap. 2.95 (0-516-53633-8) Childrens.

—Los Gatos Me Gustan Mas (I Love Cats) Dunnington, Tom, illus. LC 83-7215. (SPA). 32p. (ps-2). 1988. pap. 2.95 (0-516-52041-5) Childrens.

—I Can Be a Computer Operator. LC 84-23281. (Illus.). 32p. (gr. k-3). 1985. PLB 14.60 (0-516-01838-8); pap. 3.95 (0-516-41838-6) Childrens.

—I Can Be a Police Officer. LC 84-12106. (Illus.). 32p. (gr. k-3). 1984. PLB 14.60 (0-516-01840-X); pap. 3.95 (0-516-41840-8) Childrens.

—I Love Cats. LC 83-7215. (Illus.). 32p. (ps-2). 1983. PLB 11.93 (0-516-02041-2); pap. 2.95 (0-516-42041-0) Childrens.

—I Love Cats Big Book. (Illus.). 32p. (ps-2). 1987. PLB 30.60 (0-516-49503-8) Childrens.

—Out the Door. Neill, Eileen M., illus. LC 81-17060. 32p. (ps-2). 1982. PLB 11.93 (0-516-03560-6); pap. 2.95 (0-516-43560-4) Childrens.

—Over-Under. Sharp, Gene, illus. LC 83-21005. 32p. (ps-2). 1984. lib. bdg. 11.93 (0-516-02048-X); pap. 2.95 (0-516-42048-8) Childrens.

—Puedo Ser un Policia (I Can Be a Police Officer) LC 84-12106. (SPA., Illus.). 32p. (gr. k-3). 1987. PLB 13.93 (0-516-31840-3); pap. 3.95 (0-516-51840-2) Childrens.

—Sal y Entra (Out the Door) Neill, Eileen M., illus. LC 81-17060. (SPA). 32p. (ps-2). 1989. PLB 11.93 (0-516-33560-X); pap. 2.95 (0-516-53560-9) Childrens.

—Too Many Balloons. Sharp, Gene, illus. LC 81-15520. 32p. (ps-2). 1982. PLB 11.93 (0-516-03563-5); pap. text ed. 2.95 (0-516-43633-3) Childrens.

Matthies, Susanna. Egyptians, Maya, Minoans. (Illus.). 112p. (gr. 4-6). 1986. 9.95 (0-88160-122-5, LW 906) Learning Wks.

Matthiessen, F. O., ed. Oxford Book of American Verse. (gr. 9 up). 1950. 45.00x (0-19-500049-8) OUP.

Mattingley, Christobel. The Miracle Tree. Yamaguchi, Marianne, illus. LC 86-4541. 28p. (gr. 3 up). 1986. 11.95 (0-15-200530-7, Gulliver Bks) HarBrace.

Mattingly, Christobel. Rummage. (gr. 4-7). 1992. pap. 7.00 (0-207-17135-1, Pub. by Angus & Robertson AT) HarpC.

Mattingly, Jennie, ed. see Nelson, Theresa M.

Mattingly, Jennie, ed. see Stauffer, Patricia I.

Mattingly, Jennie, ed. see Tyler, Jan.

Mattox, Cheryl. My Play a Tune Book: Shake It to the One That You Love the Best. 1991. 15.95 (0-938971-11-5) JTG Nashville.

Mattox, Cheryl W., ed. Shake It to the One That You Love the Best: Play Songs & Lullabies from Black Musical Traditions. Honeywood, Varnette P. & Joysmith, Brenda, illus. (Orig.). (ps-6). 1990. pap. 7.95 (0-9623381-0-9) Warren-Mattox.

Mattozzi, Patricia R. Eastertime. Mattozzi, Patricia R., illus. 1992. 3.95 (0-8378-2459-1) Gibson.

—The Greatest Gift. 1990. 3.95 (0-8378-1887-7) Gibson.

—My Shepherd Is the Lord: Inspirational Treasures. LC 92-12768. (Illus.). 1992. 3.99 (0-517-08145-8, Pub. by Derrydale Bks) Outlet Bk Co.

Mattozzi, Patti. Little Lessons for Little Learners: Angels. 32p. (gr. 2 up). 1989. pap. 3.95 (0-8378-1843-5) Gibson.

—Little Lessons for Little Learners: Heaven. (gr. 3 up). 1991. 3.95 (0-8378-1986-5) Gibson.

—Little Lessons for Little Learners: Prayer. 32p. (gr. 1 up). 1989. 3.95 (0-8378-1844-3) Gibson.

Mattson, Robert A. The Living Ocean. LC 89-25791. (Illus.). 64p. (gr. 6 up). 1991. lib. bdg. 15.95 (0-89490-277-6) Enslow Pubs.

Matula, Joyce. A Friend in Winter. LC 91-68091. (Illus.). 44p. (gr. k-4). 1992. 6.95 (1-55523-504-2) Winston-Derek.

Matunis, Joe, jt. auth. see Hammond, Anna.

Matus, Joel. Leroy & the Caveman. LC 92-24647. 144p. (gr. 3-7). 1993. SBE 13.95 (0-689-31812-X, Atheneum Child Bk) Macmillan Child Grp.

Matusky, Gregory & Hayes, John P. The U. S. Secret Service. Schlesinger, Arthur M., Jr., intro. by. (Illus.). 96p. (gr. 5 up). 1988. lib. bdg. 14.95 (1-55546-130-1) Chelsea Hse.

Matusky, Gregory & Hayes, John P., Jr. Hussein. (Illus.). 112p. (gr. 5 up). 1987. lib. bdg. 17.95 (0-87754-533-2) Chelsea Hse.

Matz, Dale, jt. auth. see Edgar, Pamela.

Matz, Terry, rev. by see Lee, Frank.

Mauck, Sue I., jt. auth. see Clapp, Steve.

Maugham, W. Somerset. Appointment. Benjamin, Alan, adapted by. Essley, Roger, illus. LC 92-391. (ps-3). 1993. 16.00 (0-671-75887-X, Green Tiger) S&S Trade.

Maughan, Joyce B. Talks for Tots. LC 85-70993. xviii, 152p. (ps-9). 1985. 9.95 (0-87747-804-X) Deseret Bk.

Maupassant. Mon Oncle Jules. (gr. 7-12). pap. 5.95 (0-88436-044-X, 40281) EMC.

Maupassant, Guy De see De Maupassant, Guy.

Maupassant, Guy de see De Maupassant, Guy.

Maupassant, Guy De see De Maupassant, Guy.

Maurer, Donna. Annie, Bea, & Chi Chi Dolores: A School Day Alphabet. Cazet, Denys, illus. LC 92-25104. 32p. (ps-k). 1993. 14.95 (0-531-05467-5); PLB 14.99 (0-531-08617-8) Orchard Bks Watts.

Maurer, Judy A., tr. see Sandberg, Inger.

Maurer, Richard. Airborne: The Search for the Secret of Flight. (Illus.). 48p. (gr. 5 up). 1990. (S&S BFYR); pap. 5.95 (0-671-69423-5, S&S BFYR) S&S Trade.

—Junk in Space. (gr. 3 up). 1989. pap. 14.95 jacketed (0-671-67768-3, S&S BFYR); pap. 5.95 (0-671-67747-0, S&S BFYR) S&S Trade.

—The NOVA Space Explorer's Guide: Where to Go & What to See. NASA Staff, photos by. LC 90-20074. (Illus.). 128p. (gr. 3-7). 1991. 20.00 (0-517-57758-5, Clarkson Potter) Crown Bks Yng Read.

Mauriette, Gail, jt. ed. see Dolmetsch, Paul.

Maury, Inez. My Mother & I Are Growing Strong. (SPA & ENG., Illus.). (ps-4). 1978. 6.95 (0-938678-06-X) New Seed.

—My Mother the Mail Carrier - Mi Mama la Cartera. Alemany, Norah, tr. McCrady, Lady, illus. LC 76-14275. (ENG & SPA.). 32p. (Orig.). (gr. k-4). 1976. 7.95 (0-935312-23-4) Feminist Pr.

Maury, Jean-Pierre. The Atmosphere. 80p. (gr. 8 up). 1989. pap. 4.95 (0-8120-4213-1) Barron.

—Heat & Cold. 80p. (gr. 8 up). 1989. pap. 4.95 (0-8120-4211-5) Barron.

—The Turtleons Are Coming. (Illus.). 48p. (gr. k-4). 1990. 12.75 (0-89565-810-0); 8.95s.p. (0-685-55104-0) Childs World.

Maury, Jean-Pierre, jt. auth. see Balibar, Françoise.

Mauser, Pat R. A Bundle of Sticks. Owens, Gail, illus. LC 87-1074. 176p. (gr. 3-6). 1987. pap. 3.95 (0-689-71169-7, Aladdin) Macmillan Child Grp.

—How I Found Myself at the Fair. Howell, Kathleen C., illus. LC 90-30630. 64p. (gr. 1-4). 1990. pap. 2.95 (0-689-71414-9, Aladdin) Macmillan Child Grp.

—Love Is for the Dogs. 1989. pap. 2.50 (0-380-75723-0, Flare) Avon.

—Patti's Pet Gorilla. 64p. 1991. pap. 2.95 (0-380-71039-0, Camelot) Avon.

—Rip-Off. LC 90-31543. 160p. (gr. 7 up). 1990. pap. 3.95 (0-02-044471-0, Collier Young Ad) Macmillan Child Grp.

Mauser, Patricia R. Patti's Pet Gorilla. Palmisciano, Diane, illus. LC 86-20546. 64p. (gr. 2-4). 1987. SBE 11.95 (0-689-31279-2, Atheneum Child Bk) Macmillan Child Grp.

Mauver, Judy A., tr. see Sandberg, Inger.

Maves, Carolyn, jt. auth. see Maves, Paul.

Maves, Paul & Maves, Carolyn. Finding Your Way Through the Bible: Revised NRSV Edition. 176p. (Orig.). (gr. 2-5). 1992. pap. 4.95 (0-687-13046-8) Abingdon.

Max, Jill, ed. see Bohlke, Dorothee.

Max, Jill, ed. see Mann, Marek.

Maxey, Kathleen. The Duck That Was a Chicken. 1993. 7.00 (0-8062-4675-8) Carlton.

Maxfield, Christine. Christmas in Water Village. Colquhoun, Jean, illus. 32p. (ps-5). 1989. 15.95 (0-9621029-0-3) Prima Design.

Maxfield, Michael & Maxfield, Myrica. The Sound of Success: Musical Motivation. 32p. 1992. 19.95 (0-9634682-1-9, 232822) Myrichael Way.

Maxfield, Myrica, jt. auth. see Maxfield, Michael.

Maxner, Joyce. Lady Bugatti. Hawkes, Kevin, illus. LC 90-19127. 32p. (gr. k up). 1991. 13.95 (0-688-10340-5); PLB 13.88 (0-688-10341-3) Lothrop.

—Lady Bugatti. Hawkes, Kevin, illus. 32p. (ps-3). 1993. pap. 4.99 (0-14-054832-7) Puffin Bks.

—Nicholas Cricket. Joyce, William, illus. LC 88-33076. 32p. (gr. k-3). 1989. 14.00 (0-06-024216-7); PLB 13.89 (0-06-024222-1) HarpC Child Bks.

—Nicholas Cricket. Joyce, William, illus. LC 88-33076. 28p. (gr. k-3). 1991. pap. 4.95 (0-06-443275-0, Trophy) HarpC Child Bks.

Maxon, Dianne, jt. auth. see Patton, Sally.
Maxwell, Arthur S. & Holloway, Cheryl W. Uncle Arthur's Storytime. Mull, Christy, et al, illus. 128p. 1989. 29.90 (*1-877773-03-4*) Family Media.
—Uncle Arthur's Storytime, Vol. 1. Tank, Darrel, et al, illus. 128p. 1989. PLB 29.90 (*1-877773-01-8*) Family Media.
—Uncle Arthur's Storytime, Vol. 2. Mull, Christ, et al, illus. 128p. 1989. PLB 29.90 (*1-877773-02-6*) Family Media.
Maxwell, Cassandre. Bright Star, Bright Star, What Do You See? Maxwell, Cassandre, illus. LC 89-82551. 32p. (ps-k). 1990. pap. 5.99 (*0-8066-2462-0, 9-2462*) Augsburg Fortress.
—Yosef's Gift of Many Colors: An Easter Story. Maxwell, Cassandre, illus. LC 92-44189. 32p. (ps-3). 1993. 14.99 (*0-8066-2627-5, 9-2627*) Augsburg Fortress.
Maxwell, Colin. Model Making. Kline, Marjory, ed. (Illus.). 48p. (gr. 5-8). 1992. PLB 12.40 (*0-531-14195-0*) Watts.
Maxwell, Judith. The Feminist Revised Mother Goose Rhymes: A 21st Century Childrens Edition. LC 92-81770. 32p. (gr. 1-9). 1992. pap. 7.95 (*0-9632698-1-X*) Veda Vangarde.
Maxwell, William. Heavenly Tenants. (gr. 4-7). 1992. 13.95 (*0-930407-25-3*) Parabola Bks.
May. Halloween, Reading Level 4. (Illus.). 48p. (gr. 3-8). 1989. PLB 15.94 (*0-86592-983-1*); 11.95s.p. (*0-685-58773-8*) Rourke Corp.
May, Bob & Tibbetts, Cristopher. The Andrew Is Dead Story. 26p. (Orig.). (gr. 7-12). 1991. pap. 3.00 (*0-88680-345-4*); royalty on application 35.00 (*0-685-59141-7*) I E Clark.
May, Chris. Bob Geldof. (Illus.). 64p. (gr. 5-9). 1991. 11.95 (*0-237-60031-5*, Pub. by Evans Bros Ltd) Trafalgar.
—Bob Marley. (Illus.). 64p. (gr. 5-9). 1991. 11.95 (*0-317-04244-0*, Pub. by Evans Bros Ltd) Trafalgar.
May, D. J. Mr. Marble's Moose. LC 93-1494. 1993. 9.99 (*0-8499-1068-4*) Word Pub.
May, Darcy. Twelve Days of Christmas. 1993. 9.95 (*1-55670-336-8*) Stewart Tabori & Chang.
May, Daryl & Bansemer, Roger. Rachael's Splendifilous Adventure. Little, Carl, ed. Bansemer, Roger, illus. LC 91-66032. 40p. (Orig.). (ps-4). 1992. PLB 10.95 (*0-932433-83-9*) Windswept Hse.
May, Elaine T. Young Oxford History of Women in the United States, Vol. 9: Pushing the Limits: American Women 1940-1961. (Illus.). 144p. 1993. PLB 19.95 (*0-19-508084-X*) OUP.
May, Ingrid. Magic Ears Sandy. 1991. 7.95 (*0-533-09382-1*) Vantage.
May, Jim. The Boo Baby Girl Meets the Ghost of Mable's Gable. Finley, Shawn, illus. LC 92-72702. 32p. (ps-5). 1992. PLB 14.95 (*1-878925-03-2*) Brotherstone Pubs.
May, John, ed. The Greenpeace Book of Dolphins. LC 90-38836. (Illus.). 160p. (gr. 10-12). 1992. pap. 19.95 (*0-8069-7485-0*) Sterling.
May, Kara. Big Brave Brother Ben. LC 91-530234. (ps-3). 1992. PLB 13.93 (*0-688-11235-8*) Lothrop.
—Big Brave Brother Ben. LC 91-530234. (ps-3). 1992. 14.00 (*0-688-11234-X*) Lothrop.
May, Lawrence, tr. see Groth, Lynn.
May, Robert. Rudolph the Red Nosed Reindeer. LC 91-156221. (ps-3). 1990. 9.95 (*1-55709-139-0*) Applewood.
May, Robert E. How Billy Joe Bobtail Met Texas Slim. McQueen, Don, illus. 32p. (gr. k-7). 1987. lib. bdg. 11.89 (*0-87397-303-8*); pap. 5.95 (*0-87397-300-3*) Strode.
—Poppa & Elizabeth: A Bobtail Romance. McQueen, Don, illus. 32p. (Orig.). (ps-3). 1988. PLB 11.89 (*0-87397-314-3*); pap. 5.95 (*0-87397-313-5*) Strode.
May, Robert L. Rudolph the Red-Nosed Reindeer. (ps) 1993. 4.95 (*0-307-12396-0*, Golden Pr) Western Pub.
—Rudolph's Second Christmas. Emberley, Michael, illus. LC 92-18416. (ps-3). 1992. 9.95 (*1-55709-192-7*) Applewood.
May, Robin. Looking at Theater. LC 89-7155. 48p. (gr. 4-8). 1990. 13.95 (*1-85435-103-6*) Marshall Cavendish.
—Plains Indians of North America. (Illus.). 48p. (gr. 4-8). 1987. PLB 16.67 (*0-86625-258-4*); 12.50s.p. (*0-685-67607-2*) Rourke Corp.
May, Rollo. The Courage to Create. (gr. 9 up). 1984. pap. 4.95 (*0-553-26361-7*) Bantam.
May, Tom, jt. auth. see McAllister, Dawson.
Mayakovsky, Stanislaw, pseud. Cyberantics. Geary, Rick, illus. 56p. 1992. 14.95 (*1-878574-29-9*) Dark Horse Comics.
Mayall, R. Newton, et al. Sky Observer's Guide. rev. ed. Polgreen, John, illus. (gr. 9 up). 1985. pap. write for info. (*0-307-24009-6*, Golden Pr) Western Pub.
Mayard. Ghosts. 32p. (gr. k-6). 1977. pap. 5.95 (*0-86020-148-1*) EDC.
Mayberry, Claude. Discovering Seeds of Change. (ps-3). 1993. pap. 4.95 (*0-201-49001-3*) Addison-Wesley.
—Discovering Seeds of Change. (gr. 4-7). 1993. pap. 4.95 (*0-201-49002-1*) Addison-Wesley.
—Discovering Seeds of Change. 1993. pap. 4.95 (*0-201-49003-X*) Addison-Wesley.
Mayberry, Jodine. Chinese. Daniels, Roger, contrib. by. LC 90-17223. (Illus.). 64p. (gr. 5-8). 1990. PLB 13.40 (*0-531-10977-1*) Watts.
—Eastern Europeans. Culleton, P., ed. LC 90-12995. (Illus.). 64p. (gr. 5-8). 1991. PLB 13.40 (*0-531-11109-1*) Watts.

—Filipinos. Daniels, Roger, contrib. by. (Illus.). 64p. (gr. 5-8). 1990. PLB 13.40 (*0-531-10978-X*) Watts.
—Koreans. LC 90-12987. (Illus.). 64p. (gr. 5-10). 1991. PLB 13.40 (*0-531-11106-7*) Watts.
—Leaders Who Changed the Twentieth Century. LC 93-19032. (Illus.). 48p. (gr. 5-7). 1993. PLB 22.80 (*0-8114-4926-2*) Raintree Steck-V.
—Mexicans. Daniels, Roger, contrib. by. LC 90-32095. (Illus.). 64p. (gr. 5-8). 1990. PLB 12.40 (*0-531-10979-8*) Watts.
Maybery, Paul, ed. see Line, Lorie.
Maybury, Anne. The Terracotta Palace. large type ed. LC 89-27151. 475p. 1989. lib. bdg. 16.95 (*0-89621-898-8*) Thorndike Pr.
Maybury, Richard J. Whatever Happened to Justice? Williams, Jane A., ed. (Illus.). 256p. (Orig.). (gr. 7 up). 1993. pap. 14.95 (*0-942617-10-X*) Blstckng Pr.
Maybury, Richard J. see Uncle Eric, pseud.
Mayer, jt. auth. see Becker.
Mayer, Albert I. Mystery at Seabreeze. (gr. 6-10). 1965. PLB 7.19 (*0-8313-0077-9*) Lantern.
Mayer, Albert I., Jr. Olympiad. LC 61-12875. (Illus.). (gr. 7 up). 1938. 18.00 (*0-8196-0115-2*) Biblo.
Mayer, Andy, jt. auth. see Becker, Jim.
Mayer, Gina. Trick or Treat, Little Critter. (ps-3). 1993. pap. 2.25 (*0-307-12791-5*, Golden Pr) Western Pub.
Mayer, Gina & Mayer, Mercer. Just a Thunderstorm. (Illus.). 24p. (ps-k). 1993. pap. 1.45 (*0-307-11540-2*, 11540, Golden Pr) Western Pub.
—The New Potty. (Illus.). 24p. (ps-k). 1992. write for info. (*0-307-11523-2*, 11523) Western Pub.
—Rosie's Mouse. (Illus.). 24p. (gr. 2-4). 1992. pap. write for info. (*0-307-11468-6*, 11468, Golden Pr) Western Pub.
—This Is My Family. (Illus.). 24p. (ps-k). 1992. write for info. (*0-307-00137-7*, 312-02, Golden Pr) Western Pub.
—A Very Special Critter. (Illus.). 24p. (ps-3). 1993. pap. 1.95 (*0-307-12763-X*, 12763, Golden Pr) Western Pub.
Mayer, Jan, et al, trs. see Evans, Joy & Moore, Jo E.
Mayer, Lene, jt. auth. see Gipson, Morrell.
Mayer, Marianna. Beauty & the Beast. Mayer, Marianna, illus. LC 78-54679. 48p. (gr. k up). 1984. SBE 15.95 (*0-02-765270-X*, Four Winds) Macmillan Child Grp.
—Beauty & the Beast. Mayer, Mercer, illus. LC 87-1095. 48p. (ps up). 1987. pap. 5.95 (*0-689-71151-4*, Aladdin) Macmillan Child Grp.
—Black Horse. Thamer, Katie, illus. LC 83-25271. 42p. (ps-3). 1987. pap. 4.95 (*0-8037-0181-0*) Dial Bks Young.
—The Golden Swan. Sauber, Robert, illus. (gr. 3 up). 1990. 14.95 (*0-553-07054-1*, Skylark) Bantam.
—Iduna & the Magic Apples. Gal, Laszlo, illus. LC 88-2494. 40p. (gr. k-4). 1988. RSBE 16.95 (*0-02-765120-7*, Macmillan Child Bk) Macmillan Child Grp.
—The Little Jewel Box. Torres, Margot, illus. (ps-3). 1990. pap. 3.95 (*0-8037-0737-1*, Dial Pied Piper) Puffin Bks.
—Marcel the Pastry Chef. McDermott, Gerald, illus. 32p. (ps-3). 1991. 14.95 (*0-553-05192-X*) Bantam.
—My First Book of Nursery Tales: Five Favorite Bedtime Tales. reissue ed. Joyce, William, illus. Mayer, Marianna, retold by. LC 82-20452. (Illus.). 48p. (ps-1). 1992. text ed. 10.00 (*0-394-85396-2*) Random Bks Yng Read.
—Noble-Hearted Kate. Pels, Winslow, illus. (gr. 3 up). 1990. 14.95 (*0-553-07049-5*, Skylark) Bantam.
—The Prince & the Princess: A Bohemian Fairy Tale. Rogers, Jacqueline, illus. 64p. (gr. 3 up). 1989. 13.95 (*0-553-05843-6*) Bantam.
—The Sorcerer's Apprentice: A Greek Fable. Wiesner, David, illus. (gr. 3 up). 1989. 13.95 (*0-553-05844-4*) Bantam.
—The Spirit of the Blue Light. Gal, Laszlo, illus. LC 86-12524. 40p. (gr. k-3). 1990. RSBE 15.95 (*0-02-765350-1*, Macmillan Child Bk) Macmillan Child Grp.
—Turandot. Pels, Winslow, illus. LC 93-27033. Date not set. write for info. (*0-688-09073-7*); lib. bdg. write for info. (*0-688-09074-5*) Morrow.
—Twelve Dancing Princess. Craft, Kinuko Y., illus. LC 83-1034. 40p. (ps up). 1989. 14.95 (*0-688-08051-0*); PLB 14.88 (*0-688-02026-7*, Morrow Jr Bks) Morrow Jr Bks.
—The Unicorn Alphabet. Hague, Michael, illus. 32p. (gr. 1 up). 1989. 14.95 (*0-8037-0372-4*); PLB 14.89 (*0-8037-0373-2*) Dial Bks Young.
—The Unicorn Alphabet. Hague, Michael, illus. 32p. 1993. pap. 5.99 (*0-14-054922-6*, Puffin Pied Piper) Puffin Bks.
—The Unicorn & the Lake. Hague, Michael, illus. LC 82-71356. 32p. (gr. k up). 1982. PLB 13.89 (*0-8037-9338-3*) Dial Bks Young.
—Unicorn & the Lake. giant ed. (ps-3). 1990. 17.99 (*0-8037-0844-0*) Dial Bks Young.
—Unicorn & the Lake. LC 81-5469. (Illus.). 32p. (gr. k up). 1987. pap. 4.95 (*0-8037-0436-4*) Dial Bks Young.
Mayer, Marianna & McDermott, Gerald. The Brambleberrys Animal Alphabet. LC 91-70420. (Illus.). 32p. (ps up). 1991. 3.95 (*1-878093-78-9*); Set of 3 bks. 11.85 (*1-878093-96-7*) Boyds Mills Pr.
—The Brambleberrys Animal Book of Colors. LC 91-70418. (Illus.). 32p. (ps up). 1991. 3.95 (*1-878093-76-2*); Set of 3 bks. 11.85 (*1-878093-97-5*) Boyds Mills Pr.

—The Brambleberrys Animal Book of Counting. LC 91-70419. (Illus.). 32p. (ps up). 1991. 3.95 (*1-878093-75-4*); Set of 3 bks. 11.85 (*1-878093-98-3*) Boyds Mills Pr.
—The Brambleberrys Animal Book of Shapes. LC 91-70421. (Illus.). 32p. (ps up). 1991. 3.95 (*1-878093-77-0*); Set of 3 bks. 11.85 (*1-878093-99-1*) Boyds Mills Pr.
Mayer, Marianna, jt. auth. see Mayer, Mercer.
Mayer, Marianna, retold by see Andersen, Hans Christian.
Mayer, Mercer. Ah-Choo. (Illus.). (gr. k-2). 1977. PLB 4.58 (*0-8037-4895-7*) Dial Bks Young.
—All By Myself. Mayer & Mercer, illus. 24p. (ps-3). 1985. pap. write for info. (*0-307-11938-6*, Pub. by Golden Bks) Western Pub.
—Appeland & Liverwurst. Kellogg, Steven, illus. LC 89-13803. 40p. (gr. k up). 1990. 13.95 (*0-688-09659-X*); PLB 13.88 (*0-688-09660-3*, Morrow Jr Bks) Morrow Jr Bks.
—Baby Sister Says No. Mayer, Mercer, illus. LC 86-82368. 24p. (gr. 4-8). 1987. pap. write for info. (*0-307-11949-1*, Pub. by Golden Bks) Western Pub.
—A Boy, a Dog, a Frog & a Friend. LC 70-134857. (ps-2). 1978. 8.95 (*0-8037-0754-1*); PLB 8.89 (*0-8037-0755-X*); pap. 2.95 (*0-8037-0804-1*) Dial Bks Young.
—A Boy, a Dog & a Frog. LC 67-22254. (Illus.). (ps-3). 1985. 9.95 (*0-8037-0763-0*); PLB 8.89 (*0-8037-0767-3*) Dial Bks Young.
—A Boy, a Dog & a Frog. Mayer, Mercer, illus. LC 67-22254. 32p. (ps-3). 1985. pap. 3.50 (*0-8037-0769-X*) Dial Bks Young.
—Boy, a Dog, & a Frog. (ps-3). 1992. pap. 3.50 (*0-14-054611-1*) Viking Child Bks.
—Bubble Bubble. rev. ed. Mayer, Mercer, illus. 48p. 1992. pap. 5.95 (*1-879920-03-4*) Rain Bird Prods.
—East of the Sun & West of the Moon. Mayer, Mercer, illus. LC 80-11496. 48p. (gr. k up). 1984. SBE 15.95 (*0-02-765190-8*, Four Winds) Macmillan Child Grp.
—East of the Sun & West of the Moon. Mercer, Mayer, illus. LC 86-20578. 48p. (ps-3). 1987. pap. 5.95 (*0-689-71113-1*, Aladdin) Macmillan Child Grp.
—Eight Favorite Little Critter Books Just for You. (Illus.). (ps-3). 1993. Incls. Just Me & My Dad, Just Grandma & Me, When I Get Bigger, Just Go to Bed, I Was So Mad, The New Baby, & Me Too! 24p. ea. bk. pap. 15.95 shrink-wrapped slipcase (*0-307-16205-2*, 16205-0, Golden Pr) Western Pub.
—Frog Goes to Dinner. Mayer, Mercer, illus. LC 74-2881. 32p. (ps-2). 1974. 8.95 (*0-8037-3386-0*); PLB 8.89 (*0-8037-3381-X*) Dial Bks Young.
—Frog Goes to Dinner. Mayer, Mercer, illus. (gr. k-2). 1977. pap. 2.95 (*0-8037-2733-X*) Dial Bks Young.
—Frog Goes to Dinner. (ps). 1992. 3.99 (*0-14-054633-2*) Puffin Bks.
—Frog on His Own. Mayer, Mercer, illus. LC 73-6018. 32p. (ps-2). 1973. 8.95 (*0-8037-2701-1*); PLB 8.89 (*0-8037-2695-3*) Dial Bks Young.
—Frog on His Own. Mayer, Mercer, illus. LC 73-6018. 32p. (ps-2). 1980. pap. 2.95 (*0-8037-2716-X*) Dial Bks Young.
—Frog, Where Are You? Mayer, Mercer, illus. LC 72-85544. (ps-3). 1969. 9.95 (*0-8037-2737-2*); PLB 9.89 (*0-8037-2732-1*) Dial Bks Young.
—Frog, Where Are You? Mayer, Mercer, illus. LC 72-85544. 32p. (ps-2). 1980. pap. 2.95 (*0-8037-2729-1*) Dial Bks Young.
—Happy Easter, Little Critter. Mayer, Mercer, illus. LC 87-81759. 24p. (ps-3). 1988. pap. write for info. (*0-307-11723-5*, Pub. by Golden Bks) Western Pub.
—Hiccup. LC 76-2284. (Illus.). (ps-2). 1976. Dial Bks Young.
—Hiccup. LC 76-2284. (Illus.). (ps-2). 1978. pap. 3.95 (*0-8037-3590-1*, 0383-120) Dial Bks Young.
—Hiccup. (gr. 4-7). 1993. pap. 3.99 (*0-14-054641-3*) Puffin Bks.
—I Just Forgot. Mayer, Mercer, illus. LC 87-81779. 24p. (Orig.). (ps-3). 1988. pap. write for info. (*0-307-11975-0*) Western Pub.
—Just a Daydream. (Illus.). 24p. (ps-3). 1989. pap. write for info. (*0-307-11973-4*, Pub. by Golden Bks) Western Pub.
—Just a Mess. Mayer, Mercer, illus. LC 86-82369. 24p. (gr. 4-8). 1987. pap. write for info. (*0-307-11948-3*, Pub. by Golden Bks) Western Pub.
—Just a Nap. (Illus.). 24p. (ps-k). 1989. pap. write for info. (*0-307-11713-8*, Pub. by Golden Bks) Western Pub.
—Just a Rainy Day. (ps). 1990. pap. write for info. (*0-307-11682-4*) Western Pub.
—Just a Snowy Day. (Illus.). 20p. (gr. k). 1983. write for info. comb. bdg. (*0-307-12156-9*, 12156, Golden Bks) Western Pub.
—Just Camping Out. (Illus.). 24p. (ps-3). 1989. pap. write for info. (*0-307-11714-6*, Pub. by Golden Bks) Western Pub.
—Just for You. Mayer, Mercer, illus. 24p. (ps-3). 1975. pap. write for info. (*0-307-11838-X*, Golden Bks.) Western Pub.
—Just Go to Bed. rev. ed. Mayer, Mercer, illus. 24p. (ps-3). 1985. pap. write for info. (*0-307-11940-8*, 11940, Pub. by Golden Bks) Western Pub.
—Just Going to the Dentist. (ps-3). 1990. pap. write for info. (*0-307-12583-1*) Western Pub.
—Just Grandma & Me. (Illus.). 24p. (ps-3). 1985. pap. write for info. (*0-307-11893-2*, Golden Bks) Western Pub.

—Just Grandpa & Me. Mayer, Mercer, illus. 24p. (ps-3). 1985. pap. write for info. (0-307-11936-X, Pub. by Golden Bks) Western Pub.
—Just Me & My Babysitter. Mayer, Mercer, illus. 24p. (Orig.). (ps-3). 1986. pap. write for info. (0-307-11945-9, Pub. by Golden Bks) Western Pub.
—Just Me & My Cousin. Mayer, Mercer, illus. 24p. (ps-3). 1992. pap. write for info. (0-307-12688-9, 12688, Golden Pr) Western Pub.
—Just Me & My Dad. (Illus.). 24p. (ps-3). 1977. pap. write for info. (0-307-11839-8, Golden Bks) Western Pub.
—Just Me & My Little Sister. Mayer, Mercer, illus. 24p. (Orig.). (ps-3). 1986. pap. write for info. (0-307-11946-7, Pub. by Golden Bks) Western Pub.
—Just Me & My Mom. (ps-3). 1990. pap. write for info. (0-307-12584-X) Western Pub.
—Just Me & My Puppy. Mayer, Mercer, illus. 24p. (ps-3). 1985. pap. write for info. (0-307-11937-8, Pub. by Golden Bks) Western Pub.
—Just My Friend & Me. Mayer, Mercer, illus. 1988. write for info. (0-307-11947-5, 11947, Pub. by Golden Bks) Western Pub.
—Just Shopping with Mom. (Illus.). 24p. (ps-3). 1989. pap. write for info. (0-307-11972-6, Pub. by Golden Bks) Western Pub.
—Little Critter's Joke Book. (ps-3). 1993. pap. 2.25 (0-307-12790-7, Golden Pr) Western Pub.
—Little Critter's Read-It-Yourself Storybook: Six Funny Easy-to-Read Stories. (Illus.). 196p. (gr. k-2). 1993. 11.95 (0-307-16840-9, 16840, Golden Pr) Western Pub.
—Little Critter's: This Is My School. (ps-3). 1990. write for info. (0-307-11589-5) Western Pub.
—Little Critter's This Is My School. (Illus.). 32p. (ps-2). 1992. pap. write for info. (0-307-15963-9, 15963) Western Pub.
—Little Critter's This Is My Town. (ps-3). 1993. pap. 3.50 (0-307-11567-4, Golden Pr) Western Pub.
—Liverwurst Is Missing. Kellogg, Steven, illus. LC 90-5435. 32p. (gr. k up) 1990. 13.95 (0-688-09657-3); lib. bdg. 13.88 (0-688-09658-1, Morrow Jr Bks) Morrow Jr Bks.
—Liza Lou & the Yeller Belly Swamp. Mayer, Mercer, illus. LC 80-16605. 48p. (gr. k-3). 1980. Repr. of 1976 ed. RSBE 14.95 (0-02-765220-3, Four Winds) Macmillan Child Grp.
—Me Too! Mayer, Mercer, illus. 24p. (ps-3). 1985. pap. write for info. (0-307-11941-6, Pub. by Golden Bks) Western Pub.
—Mercer Mayer's Super Critter to the Rescue. (Illus.). 20p. (ps up) 1992. write for info. incl. long-life batteries (0-307-74708-5, 64708, Golden Pr) Western Pub.
—Mercer Mayer's What a Bad Dream. (Illus.). 24p. (ps-3). 1992. write for info. (0-307-12685-4, 12685) Western Pub.
—Merry Christmas Mom & Dad. Mayer, Mercer, illus. 24p. (ps-3). 1982. pap. write for info. (0-307-11886-X, Golden Bks.) Western Pub.
—The New Baby. Mayer, Mercer, illus. 24p. (ps-3). 1985. pap. write for info. (0-307-11942-4, Pub. by Golden Bks) Western Pub.
—One Monster after Another. (ps-3). 1993. pap. 5.95 (1-879920-05-0) Rain Bird Prods.
—The Pied Piper of Hamlin. Mayer, Mercer, illus. LC 87-1167. 48p. (gr. k up). 1987. RSBE 16.95 (0-02-765361-7, Macmillan Child Bk) Macmillan Child Grp.
—Professor Wormbog in Search for the Zipperump-a-Zoo. Mayer, Mercer, illus. 48p. (ps up). 1992. pap. 5.95 (1-879920-04-2) Rain Bird Prods.
—A Silly Story: Nothing Less Nothing More. Mayer, Mercer, illus. 48p. 1992. pap. 5.95 (1-879920-02-6) Rain Bird Prods.
—A Special Trick. LC 69-18220. (Illus.). (gr. k-3). 1976. pap. 4.95 (0-8037-8103-2) Dial Bks Young.
—Staying Overnight. Mayer, Mercer, illus. LC 87-83014. 40p. (gr. k-2). 1988. write for info. (0-307-11662-X) Western Pub.
—Terrible Troll. Mayer, Mercer, illus. LC 68-28730. (gr. k-3). 1968. Dial Bks Young.
—There's a Nightmare in My Closet. giant ed. Mayer, Mercer, illus. LC 68-15250. (ps-3). 1985. 12.95 (0-8037-8682-4); PLB 12.89 (0-8037-8683-2); pap. 4.95 (0-8037-8574-7); guide 17.99 (0-8037-0843-2) Dial Bks Young.
—There's a Nightmare in My Closet. 1992. pap. 4.99 (0-14-054712-6, Puffin) Puffin Bks.
—There's an Alligator under My Bed. LC 86-19944. (Illus.). 32p. (ps-3). 1987. 14.00 (0-8037-0374-0); PLB 13.89 (0-8037-0375-9) Dial Bks Young.
—There's Something in My Attic. Mayer, Mercer, illus. LC 86-32875. 32p. (ps-3). 1988. 11.95 (0-8037-0414-3); PLB 11.89 (0-8037-0415-1) Dial Bks Young.
—There's Something in My Attic. Mayer, Mercer, illus. 32p. (ps-3). 1992. pap. 3.99 (0-14-054813-0, Puffin) Puffin Bks.
—These Are My Pets. Mayer, Mercer, illus. LC 87-83016. 40p. (gr. k-2). 1988. write for info. (0-307-11664-6) Western Pub.
—These Are My Pets, Level 2. Mayer, Mercer, illus. 32p. (gr. 1-2). 1992. pap. 3.00 (0-307-15962-0, 15962, Golden Pr) Western Pub.
—This Is My Friend. (Illus.). 40p. (gr. k-2). 1989. write for info. (0-307-11685-9, Pub. by Golden Bks) Western Pub.

—This Is My Friend. (Illus.). 32p. (gr. k-2). 1993. pap. 3.25 (0-307-15977-9, 15977, Golden Pr) Western Pub.
—This Is My House. Mayer, Mercer, illus. LC 87-116603. 40p. (gr. k-2). 1988. write for info. (0-307-11660-3) Western Pub.
—The Trip. Mayer, Mercer, illus. LC 87-83013. 40p. (gr. k-2). 1988. write for info. (0-307-11661-1) Western Pub.
—Two-Minute Little Critter Stories. (ps). 1990. write for info. (0-307-12192-5) Western Pub.
—What Do You Do with a Kangaroo. (ps-3). 1987. pap. 3.95 (0-590-44850-1) Scholastic Inc.
—When I Get Bigger. Mayer, Mercer, illus. 24p. (ps-3). 1985. pap. write for info. (0-307-11943-2, Pub. by Golden Bks) Western Pub.
—Whinnie the Lovesick Dragon. Hearn, Diane D., illus. LC 85-18886. 32p. (gr. k-3). 1986. RSBE 14.95 (0-02-765180-0, Macmillan Child Bk) Macmillan Child Grp.
—The Wizard Comes to Town. Mayer, Mercer, illus. 40p. 1991. pap. 5.95 (1-879920-00-X) Rain Bird Prods.
—You're the Scaredy-Cat. Mayer, Mercer, illus. 40p. 1991. pap. 5.95 (1-879920-01-8) Rain Bird Prods.
Mayer, Mercer & Mayer, Marianna. One Frog Too Many. Mayer, Mercer, illus. LC 75-6325. 32p. (ps-2). 1985. 9.95 (0-8037-4838-8); PLB 9.89 (0-8037-4858-2) Dial Bks Young.
—One Frog Too Many. LC 75-6325. (Illus.). (ps-2). 1977. pap. 3.50 (0-8037-6734-X) Dial Bks Young.
Mayer, Mercer, jt. auth. see Mayer, Gina.
Mayer, Mercer, retold by. The Sleeping Beauty. LC 84-7195. (Illus.). 48p. (gr. k up). 1984. SBE 14.95 (0-02-765340-4, Macmillan Child Bk) Macmillan Child Grp.
Mayer, Mercer, illus. & abridged by. A Christmas Carol: Being a Ghost Story of Christmas. LC 86-12651. 48p. (ps up). 1986. SBE 16.95 (0-02-730310-1, Macmillan Child Bk) Macmillan Child Grp.
Mayer, Robert, et al. Opportunities in Photography Careers. rev. ed. LC 90-50737. 160p. (gr. 7 up). 1991. 13.95 (0-8442-8152-2, VGM Career Bks); pap. 10.95 (0-8442-8153-0, VGM Career Bks) NTC Pub Grp.
Mayers, Florence C. ABC: National Museum of American History. (Illus.). 32p. 1989. 12.95 (0-8109-1875-7) Abrams.
—ABC: the Alef-Bet Book: The Israel Museum, Jerusalem. LC 88-27501. (Illus.). 32p. (gr. k up). 1989. 12.95 (0-8109-1885-4) Abrams.
—ABC: The Wild West Buffalo Bill Historical Center, Cody, Wyoming. LC 90-440. (Illus.). 32p. 1990. 12.95 (0-8109-1903-6) Abrams.
—A Russian ABC: Featuring Masterpieces from the Hermitage, St. Petersburg. (Illus.). 36p. 1992. 12.95 (0-8109-1919-2) Abrams.
Mayer-Skumanz, Lene. Caroline Moves In. Sklenitzka, Franz S., illus. 96p. (gr. 1-3). 1988. pap. 2.95 (0-8120-3938-6) Barron.
—The Tower. (gr. 2-5). 1993. 12.95 (0-685-68827-5) Yllw Brick Rd.
Mayerson, Evelyn W. The Cat Who Escaped from Steerage. LC 90-32890. 80p. (gr. 4-6). 1990. SBE 13.95 (0-684-19209-8, Scribners Young Read) Macmillan Child Grp.
Mayes, Dave, jt. auth. see Davis, Kathleen.
Mayes, S. How Do Animals Talk? (Illus.). 24p. (gr. 1 up). 1991. PLB 11.96 (0-88110-549-X, Usborne); pap. 3.95 (0-7460-0600-4, Usborne) EDC.
—How Does a Bird Fly? (Illus.). 24p. (gr. 1 up). 1991. PLB 11.96 (0-88110-546-5, Usborne); pap. 3.95 (0-7460-0694-2, Usborne) EDC.
—Starting Point Science. (Illus.). 96p. (gr. 1-4). 1989. 11.95 (0-7460-0481-8, Usborne) EDC.
—What Makes a Flower Grow? (Illus.). 24p. (gr. 1-4). 1989. lib. bdg. 11.96 (0-88110-381-0, Usborne); pap. 3.95 (0-7460-0275-0, Usborne) EDC.
—What Makes It Rain? (Illus.). 24p. (gr. 1-4). 1989. lib. bdg. 11.96 (0-88110-379-9, Usborne); pap. 3.95 (0-7460-0274-2, Usborne) EDC.
—What's Inside You? (Illus.). 24p. (gr. 1 up). 1991. PLB 11.96 (0-88110-550-3, Usborne); pap. 3.95 (0-7460-0602-0, Usborne) EDC.
—What's Out in Space? (Illus.). 24p. (gr. 1-4). 1990. lib. bdg. 11.96 (0-88110-443-4, Usborne); pap. 3.95 (0-7460-0430-3, Usborne) EDC.
—What's under the Ground? (Illus.). 24p. (gr. 1-4). 1989. (Usborne); pap. 3.95 (0-7460-0357-9, Usborne) EDC.
—Where Do Babies Come From? (Illus.). 24p. (gr. 1 up). 1992. PLB 11.96 (0-88110-547-3, Usborne); pap. 3.95 (0-7460-0690-X, Usborne) EDC.
—Where Does Electricity Come From? (Illus.). 24p. (gr. 1-4). 1989. (Usborne); pap. 3.95 (0-7460-0358-7, Usborne) EDC.
—Where Does Rubbish Go? (Illus.). 24p. (gr. 1 up). 1992. PLB 11.96 (0-88110-551-1, Usborne); pap. 3.95 (0-7460-0627-6, Usborne) EDC.
—Why Is Night Dark? (Illus.). 24p. (gr. 1-4). 1990. lib. bdg. 11.96 (0-88110-442-6, Usborne); pap. 3.95 (0-7460-0428-1, Usborne) EDC.
Mayes, S., et al. Starting Point Science, Vol. 2. (gr. 4-7). 1992. 11.95 (0-7460-0655-1, Usborne) EDC.
Mayes, Sue. Dinosaurs. (Illus.). 32p. (gr. k-1). 1993. lib. bdg. 13.96 (0-88110-641-0, Usborne); pap. 5.95 (0-7460-1020-6, Usborne) EDC.

Mayfield, Barbara J. The Kid's Club Cubs & the Search for the Treasures of the Pyramid. Gold, Ethel, illus. 40p. (ps-2). 1994. pap. 24.95 (1-883983-15-0) Noteworthy Creat.
Barbara Mayfield, Registered Dietician & nutrition educator, author of KID'S CLUB: NUTRITION LEARNING ACTIVITIES FOR YOUNG CHILDREN, & NUTRITION NOTES: MUSICAL NUTRITION EDUCATION TO SING & COLOR, has written a delightful adventure story to teach young children about the new Food Guide Pyramid. The beautiful color illustrations show the Kid's Club Cubs & their friend Picky Piggy in their search for the treasures of the Pyramid, learning the difference between healthy & less-healthy foods, food groups, & the nutrient treasures they provide. The book invites participation from the reader & comes with a puzzle for the child to build their own Food Guide Pyramid & a cassette tape of the story & 11 original songs. Activity ideas for parents are included in the book as well as lyrics to the 11 songs & camera-ready artwork of the Food Guide Pyramid. The book-puzzle-tape may be ordered directly from the publisher. Noteworthy Creations, Inc., P.O. Box 335, 112 W. Main St., Delphi, IN 46923; phone 317-564-4167. *Publisher Provided Annotation.*

—Nutrition Notes: Musical Nutrition Education to Sing & Color. (Illus.). 80p. (ps-2). 1992. pap. 12.00 incl. cass. tape (1-883983-02-9) Noteworthy Creat.
Mayfield, Larry. God's Power. (Illus.). (gr. k-6). 1980. visualized song 5.99 (3-90117-017-0) CEF Press.
—Jesus Is Caring for You. Behl, Deborah, illus. 20p. (gr. k-6). 1982. visualized song 5.99 (3-90117-026-X) CEF Press.
Mayfield, Larry, jt. auth. see Hawthorne, Grace.
Mayfield, Sue. I Carried You on Eagles' Wings. LC 90-28554. 128p. (gr. 6 up). 1991. text ed. 12.95 (0-688-10597-1) Lothrop.
Mayfield, Susan. Timeline: Women & Power. (Illus.). 64p. (gr. 7-9). 1989. 19.95 (0-85219-768-3, Pub. by Batsford UK) Trafalgar.
Mayhar, Ardath. A Place of Silver Silence. Ortega, Pat, illus. (gr. 7 up). 1988. 15.95 (0-8027-6825-3) Walker & Co.
Mayhar, Ardath & Fortier, Ron. Monkey Station. LC 88-51729. 320p. (Orig.). 1989. pap. 3.95 (0-88038-743-2) TSR Inc.
Mayhew, James. Dare You! LC 92-18862. 1993. 13.45 (0-395-65013-5, Clarion Bks) HM.
—Katie & the Dinosaurs. Mayhew, James, illus. (ps-3). 1992. 15.00 (0-553-08129-2, Little Rooster) Bantam.
—Katie's Picture Show. (ps-3). 1989. 14.95 (0-553-05846-0) Bantam.
—Koshka's Tales: Stories from Russia. LC 92-41185. (Illus.). 80p. (gr. k up). 1993. 16.95 (1-85697-943-1) Kingfisher Bks.
—Madame Nightingale Will Sing. (ps-3). 1991. 13.95 (0-553-07100-9) Bantam.
Mayhew, Nicholas. Coinage in France from the Dark Ages to Napoleon. (Illus.). 163p. (gr. 10 up). 1988. 39.95 (0-900652-87-X, Pub. by Seaby UK) Trafalgar.
Mayle, Peter. Sweet Dreams & Monsters: A Beginner's Guide to Dreams & Nightmares & Things That Go Bump under the Bed. Robins, Arthur, illus. (gr. k up). 1986. 9.95 (0-517-55972-2, Harmony) Crown Pub Group.
—What's Happening to Me? Walter, Paul & Robins, Arthur, illus. LC 75-14410. 56p. (gr. 3 up). 1975. 12.00 (0-8184-0221-0); pap. 6.95 (0-8184-0312-8) Carol Pub Group.
—Where Did I Come From. Robbins, Arthur & Walter, Paul, illus. 48p. (gr. 3 up). 1973. 12.00 (0-8184-0161-3); pap. 6.95 (0-8184-0253-9) Carol Pub Group.
—Why Are We Getting a Divorce? Robins, Arthur, illus. LC 87-12105. 32p. (gr. k-3). 1988. 15.00 (0-517-56527-7, Harmony) Crown Pub Group.
Maynard. Stars & Planets. (Illus.). 32p. (gr. 4-8). 1976. PLB 13.96 (0-88110-313-6); pap. 6.95 (0-86020-094-9) EDC.
Maynard, Chris. Amazing Animal Babies. LC 92-23736. 32p. (Orig.). (gr. 1-5). 1993. PLB 10.99 (0-679-93924-5); pap. 7.99 (0-679-93924-0) Knopf Bks Yng Read.
—I Wonder Why Planes Have Wings & Other Questions about Transport. Quigley, Sebastian, illus. LC 92-42373. 32p. (gr. k-3). 1993. 8.95 (1-85697-877-X) Kingfisher Bks.

—I Wonder Why Stars Twinkle & Other Questions about Space: And Other Questions about Space. Forsey, Chris & Kenyon, Tony, illus. LC 92-44259. 32p. (gr. k-3). 1993. 8.95 (*1-85697-881-8*) Kingfisher Bks.
Maynard, Christopher. Airplanes. LC 92-32843. 32p. (gr. 1-4). 1993. 3.95 (*1-85697-895-8*) Kingfisher Bks.
—Amazing Animal Facts. (Illus.). (gr. 1-5). 1993. 18.00 (*0-679-85085-6*) Knopf Bks Yng Read.
—Ballet. LC 92-32055. 32p. (gr. 1-4). 1993. 3.95 (*1-85697-890-7*) Kingfisher Bks.
—Castles. LC 92-32844. 32p. (gr. 1-4). 1993. 3.95 (*1-85697-891-5*) Kingfisher Bks.
—Dinosaurs. LC 92-32265. 1993. 3.95 (*1-85697-892-3*) Kingfisher Bks.
—Guide to Germany. LC 93-39021. 1994. 3.95 (*1-85697-959-8*) Kingfisher Bks.
—Helicopters. LC 92-32924. 32p. (gr. 1-4). 1993. 3.95 (*1-85697-893-1*) Kingfisher Bks.
—Horses. LC 92-32264. 32p. (gr. 1-4). 1993. 3.95 (*1-85697-894-X*) Kingfisher Bks.
—Jungle Animals. LC 92-32845. 32p. (gr. 1-4). 1993. 3.95 (*1-85697-896-6*) Kingfisher Bks.
—Space. LC 92-32266. (Illus.). 32p. (gr. 1-4). 1993. 3.95 (*1-85697-897-4*) Kingfisher Bks.
—War Vehicles. LC 79-5063. (Illus.). 36p. (gr. 3-6). 1980. PLB 13.50 (*0-8225-1185-1*) Lerner Pubns.
Maynard, Frankie. A Tree! for Me! LC 86-51132. (Illus.). 68p. 15.00 (*0-912783-07-9*) Upton Sons.
Maynard, Joan. Mud Pies. 8p. (gr. 1). 1988. pap. text ed. 2.50 (*1-882225-09-0*) Tott Pubns.
—Mud Puddles. 7p. (gr. 1). 1989. pap. text ed. 2.50 (*1-882225-06-6*) Tott Pubns.
Maynard, Joyce. Camp-Out. Bethel, Steve, illus. LC 85-5504. 32p. (ps-3). 1985. 12.95 (*0-15-214077-8*, HB Juv Bks) HarBrace.
—New House. Bethel, Steve, illus. 32p. (gr. k-3). 1987. 12.95 (*0-15-257042-X*) HarBrace.
Maynard, Morlee. Happy Times with People. LC 85-25555. (ps). 1986. 4.95 (*0-8054-4165-4*) Broadman.
Maynard, Roy. A Quick Thirty Seconds. LC 93-10829. 192p. 1993. pap. 7.99 (*0-89107-745-6*, Crossway Bks) Good News.
Maynard, Thane. Animal Inventors. LC 91-14749. (Illus.). 64p. (gr. 5-8). 1991. PLB 12.90 (*0-531-20051-5*) Watts.
—Animal Olympians. LC 93-30769. 1994. write for info. (*0-531-11159-8*) Watts.
—Endangered Animal Babies: Saving Species One Birth at a Time. LC 92-33220. (Illus.). 56p. (gr. 5-8). 1993. 15.95 (*0-531-15257-X*); PLB 15.90 (*0-531-11077-X*) Watts.
—A Rhino Comes to America. (Illus.). 40p. (gr. 4-8). 1993. 15.95 (*0-531-15258-8*); PLB 15.90 (*0-531-11173-3*) Watts.
—Saving Endangered Birds: Ensuring a Future in the Wild. (Illus.). 56p. (gr. 5-7). 1993. 15.95 (*0-531-15260-X*); PLB 15.90 (*0-531-11094-X*) Watts.
—Saving Endangered Mammals: A Field Guide to Some of the Earth's Rarest Animals. (Illus.). 64p. (gr. 5-8). 1992. PLB 15.90 (*0-531-11076-1*) Watts.
Mayne, William. All the King's Men. LC 87-25659. 192p. (gr. 3-7). 1988. pap. 14.95 (*0-385-29626-6*) Delacorte.
—Drift. 1990. pap. 3.25 (*0-440-40381-2*, Pub. by Yearling Classics) Dell.
—Earthfasts. (gr. 4-7). 19.75 (*0-8446-6430-8*) Peter Smith.
—The Farm That Ran Out of Names. 88p. (gr. 4-6). 1991. 17.95 (*0-224-02757-3*, Pub. by Jonathan Cape UK) Trafalgar.
—Gideon Ahoy! (gr. 5-9). 1989. pap. 13.95 (*0-440-50126-1*) Delacorte.
—Low Tide. LC 92-24717. 1993. 14.00 (*0-385-30904-X*) Delacorte.
—Mousewing. Baynton, Martin, illus. 32p. (ps-3). 1988. 9.95 (*0-13-604240-6*) P-H.
—A Year & a Day. (gr. 4-7). 18.75 (*0-8446-6431-6*) Peter Smith.
Maynes, William. Corbie. (Illus.). 1986. 9.95 (*0-13-172602-1*) P-H.
Mayo, Cynthia R. Developing Tomorrow's Leaders Today: A Global Perspective: Leadership Development for Youths. 200p. (gr. 8 up). 1991. pap. 25.00 (*0-9630519-0-3*) M&M Pub.
Mayo, Gretchen W. Earthmaker's Tales: North American Indian Stories about Earth Happenings. Mayo, Gretchen W., illus. LC 88-20515. 96p. (gr. 5 up). 1989. 12.95 (*0-8027-6839-3*); PLB 13.85 (*0-8027-6840-7*) Walker & Co.
—Meet Tricky Coyote! LC 92-12424. (Illus.). 35p. (gr. 6-10). 1993. 12.95 (*0-8027-8198-5*); PLB 13.85 (*0-8027-8199-3*) Walker & Co.
—North American Indian Stories, 4 vols. Mayo, Gretchen W., illus. 256p. (gr. 5 up). 1990. Set. pap. 23.80 (*0-8027-7341-9*) Walker & Co.
—North American Indian Stories: Earthmaker's Tales. Mayo, Gretchen W., illus. 48p. (gr. 5 up). 1990. pap. 5.95 (*0-8027-7343-5*) Walker & Co.
—North American Indian Stories: More Earthmaker's Tales. Mayo, Gretchen W., illus. 48p. (gr. 5 up). 1990. pap. 5.95 (*0-8027-7344-3*) Walker & Co.
—North American Indian Stories: More Star Tales. Mayo, Gretchen W., illus. 48p. (gr. 5 up). 1990. pap. 5.95 (*0-8027-7347-8*) Walker & Co.
—North American Indian Stories: Star Tales. Mayo, Gretchen W., illus. 48p. (gr. 5 up). 1990. pap. 5.95 (*0-8027-7345-1*) Walker & Co.

—Star Tales: North American Indian Stories about the Stars. 96p. (gr. 5 up). 1987. 12.95 (*0-8027-6672-2*); PLB 13.85 (*0-8027-6673-0*) Walker & Co.
—That Tricky Coyote! LC 92-12440. (Illus.). 32p. (gr. 1-5). 1993. 12.95 (*0-8027-8200-0*); PLB 13.85 (*0-8027-8201-9*) Walker & Co.
Mayo, Gretchen W., retold by. Big Trouble for Tricky Rabbit! LC 93-29749. 1994. write for info. (*0-8027-8275-2*); PLB write for info. (*0-8027-8276-0*) Walker & Co.
—Here Comes Tricky Rabbit. LC 93-29763. 1994. write for info. (*0-8027-8273-6*); lib. bdg. write for info. (*0-8027-8274-4*) Walker & Co.
Mayo, Margaret, retold by. Magical Tales from Many Lands. Ray, Jane, illus. LC 93-12164. 128p. 1993. 19.99 (*0-525-45017-3*, DCB) Dutton Child Bks.
Mayo, P., jt. auth. see Gajewski, N.
Mayo, Patty & Gajewski, Nancy. SSS: Social Skill Strategies, Book B: A Curriculum for Adolescents. Krause, Brad, illus. 350p. (Orig.). (gr. 5-12). 1989. pap. text ed. 33.00x (*0-930599-52-7*) Thinking Pubns.
—Transfer Activities: Thinking Skill Vocabulary Development. Baker, Robert T., illus. 202p. (gr. 5-12). 1987. pap. text ed. 31.00 (*0-930599-13-6*) Thinking Pubns.
Mayo, Patty & Waldo, Pattii. Communicate. (Orig.). (gr. 5-12). 1986. 39.00x (*0-930599-04-7*) Thinking Pubns.
—Communicate Expansion Cards. (gr. 5-12). 1988. 21.00 (*0-930599-22-5*) Thinking Pubns.
—Scripting: Social Communication for Adolescents. 292p. (gr. 5-12). 1986. pap. text ed. 31.00 spiral bdg. (*0-930599-08-X*) Thinking Pubns.
Mayo, Patty, jt. auth. see Gajewski, Nancy.
Mayo, Patty, et al. Communicate Junior. Madsen, Kris, illus. 60p. (gr. 1-4). 1991. incl. game board 35.00 (*0-930599-68-3*) Thinking Pubns.
—Social Star: General Interaction Skills, Bk. 1. LC 92-39097. 485p. (gr. 2-5). 1993. pap. 35.00 (*0-930599-79-9*) Thinking Pubns.
—Study Smart. Madsen, Kris, illus. 59p. (gr. 5-12). 1990. bd. game 39.00 (*0-930599-64-0*) Thinking Pubns.
Mayo, Virginia. Dont' Forget Me Santa Claus. (ps). 1993. 12.95 (*0-8120-6391-0*) Barron.
—The Swan. (Illus.). 32p. (ps-3). 1994. 12.95 (*0-8120-6408-9*); pap. 5.95 (*0-8120-1938-5*) Barron.
Mayorga, Dolores. David Plays Hide-&-Seek in Celebrations: David Juega Al Escondite y Celebra. Mayorga, Dolores, illus. (ENG & SPA.). 24p. (gr. 2-5). 1992. PLB 18.95 (*0-8225-2001-X*) Lerner Pubns.
—David Plays Hide-&-Seek in Folktales: David Juega Al Escondite En Cuentos Folkloricos. Mayorga, Dolores, illus. (ENG & SPA.). 24p. (gr. 2-5). 1992. PLB 18.95 (*0-8225-2003-6*) Lerner Pubns.
—David Plays Hide-&-Seek in the City: David Juega Al Escondite En la Ciudad. Mayorga, Dolores, illus. (ENG & SPA.). 24p. (gr. 2-5). 1992. PLB 18.95 (*0-8225-2002-8*) Lerner Pubns.
—David Plays Hide-&-Seek on Vacation: David Juega Al Escondite En Vacaciones. Mayorga, Dolores, illus. (ENG & SPA.). 24p. (gr. 2-5). 1992. PLB 18.95 (*0-8225-2004-4*) Lerner Pubns.
Mayper, Monica. Come & See. Date not set. 15.00 (*0-06-023526-8*, Festival); PLB 14.89 (*0-06-023527-6*, Festival) HarpC Child Bks.
Mayper, Monica. After Good-Night. Sis, Peter, illus. LC 86-45766. 32p. (ps-3). 1987. HarpC Child Bks.
—Oh Snow. Otani, June, illus. LC 90-42088. 32p. (ps-1). 1991. PLB 14.89 (*0-06-024204-3*) HarpC Child Bks.
Mayr-Pletschen, Heide, illus. A Christmas Carol Book. (gr. 3 up). 2.75 (*0-685-24603-5*) Merry Thoughts.
Mazak, Lisa. One, Two, Three, Jesus Loves Me. (Illus.). (gr. k-6). 1982. illustrated song 3.99 (*3-90117-018-9*) CEF Press.
Mazar, Peter, ed. Take-Me-Home: Notes on the Church Year for Children. (Illus.). 128p. (Orig.). (gr. 1-8). 1991. pap. 15.00 (*0-929650-52-2*) Liturgy Tr Pubns.
Mazer, Anne. Moose Street. LC 91-36534. (gr. 4-7). 1992. 13.00 (*0-679-83233-5*); PLB 13.99 (*0-679-93233-X*) Knopf Bks Yng Read.
—The Oxboy. LC 92-37199. 112p. (gr. 3-7). 1993. 13.00 (*0-679-84191-1*); PLB cancelled (*0-679-94119-3*) Knopf Bks Yng Read.
—The Salamander Room. Johnson, Steve, illus. LC 90-33301. 32p. (ps-3). 1991. 14.00 (*0-394-82945-X*); PLB 14.99 (*0-394-92945-4*) Knopf Bks Yng Read.
—Watch Me. Schuett, Stacey, illus. LC 89-34920. 40p. (ps-k). 1990. lib. bdg. 13.99 (*0-394-92946-2*) Knopf Bks Yng Read.
Mazer, Anne, intro. by. America Street: A Multicultural Anthology of Stories. 1993. 14.95 (*0-89255-190-9*); pap. 4.95 (*0-89255-191-7*) Persea Bks.
Mazer, Harry. Cave under the City. LC 86-45008. 160p. (gr. 3-7). 1986. (Crowell Jr Bks); PLB 13.89 (*0-690-04559-X*, Crowell Jr Bks) HarpC Child Bks.
—City Light. LC 87-23486. 192p. (gr. 9 up). 1988. pap. 12.95 (*0-590-40511-X*) Scholastic Inc.
—The Dollar Man. (gr. 6-12). 16.00 (*0-8446-6415-4*) Peter Smith.
—Guy Lenny. (gr. 4-8). 15.00 (*0-8446-6369-7*) Peter Smith.
—The Island Keeper. 176p. (gr. k-12). 1982. pap. 3.25 (*0-440-94774-X*, LFL) Dell.
—The Island Keeper: A Tale of Courage & Survival. LC 80-39762. 192p. (gr. 7 up). 1981. pap. 11.95 (*0-385-28446-2*) Delacorte.
—The Last Mission. 192p. (gr. 7 up). 1981. pap. 3.50 (*0-440-94797-9*, LE) Dell.

—Snow Bound. 144p. (gr. 5 up). 1975. pap. 3.50 (*0-440-96134-3*, LFL) Dell.
—Someone's Mother Is Missing. 1991. pap. 3.50 (*0-440-21097-6*, YB) Dell.
—The War on Villa Street. 128p. (gr. 7 up). 1979. pap. 2.95 (*0-440-99062-9*, LFL) Dell.
—When the Phone Rang. LC 84-6098. (Illus.). 192p. (gr. 7 up). 1985. pap. 11.95 (*0-590-32167-6*, Scholastic Hardcover) Scholastic Inc.
—When the Phone Rang. 192p. (gr. 7 up). 1986. pap. 2.95 (*0-590-44773-4*) Scholastic Inc.
—Who Is Eddie Leonard? LC 93-22114. (gr. 4 up). 1993. 14.95 (*0-385-31136-2*) Delacorte.
Mazer, Harry, jt. auth. see Mazer, Norma F.
Mazer, Norma F. After the Rain. LC 86-33270. 304p. (gr. 7 up). 1987. 12.95 (*0-688-06867-7*) Morrow Jr Bks.
—After the Rain. large type ed. 408p. (gr. 7 up). 1989. lib. bdg. 14.95 (*0-8161-4807-4*, Large Print Bks) Hall.
—Babyface. LC 90-6485. 176p. (gr. 7 up). 1990. 12.95 (*0-688-08752-3*) Morrow Jr Bks.
—Babyface. 176p. 1991. pap. 3.50 (*0-380-75720-6*, Flare) Avon.
—Bright Days, Stupid. 1993. pap. 3.50 (*0-553-56253-3*) Bantam.
—C My Name Is Cal. 144p. 1990. 13.95 (*0-590-41833-5*, Point); pap. 2.95 (*0-685-49598-1*, Point) Scholastic Inc.
—D, My Name Is Danita. (gr. 7 up). 1991. 13.95 (*0-590-43655-4*) Scholastic Inc.
—Downtown. LC 84-91105. 192p. (gr. 7 up). 1984. 11.95 (*0-688-03859-X*) Morrow Jr Bks.
—E, My Name is Emily. 176p. 1991. 13.95 (*0-590-43653-8*, Scholastic Hardcover) Scholastic Inc.
—Mrs. Fish, Ape & Me, the Dump Queen. 144p. (Orig.). (gr. 4 up). 1981. pap. 3.50 (*0-380-69153-1*, Flare) Avon.
—Out of Control. LC 92-32516. 224p. (gr. 7 up). 1993. 14.00 (*0-688-10208-5*) Morrow Jr Bks.
—Silver. LC 88-18652. 272p. (gr. 7 up). 1988. 12.95 (*0-688-06865-0*) Morrow Jr Bks.
—Silver. 208p. 1989. pap. 3.50 (*0-380-75026-0*, Flare) Avon.
—Someone to Love. LC 82-72755. 256p. (gr. 7 up). 1983. 13.95 (*0-685-06446-8*) Delacorte.
—Summer Girls, Love Boys & Other Short Stories. LC 82-70320. 192p. (gr. 7 up). 1982. pap. 11.95 (*0-385-28930-8*) Delacorte.
—Taking Terri Mueller. 192p. (gr. 8 up). 1981. pap. 3.50 (*0-380-79004-1*, Flare) Avon.
—Taking Terri Mueller. LC 82-18849. 224p. (gr. 7 up). 1983. 12.95 (*0-688-01732-0*) Morrow Jr Bks.
—Three Sisters. (gr. 7 up). 1991. pap. 2.95 (*0-590-43817-4*, Point) Scholastic Inc.
—Up in Seth's Room. LC 79-2102. 208p. (gr. 7 up). 1979. pap. 7.95 (*0-385-29058-6*) Delacorte.
—When We First Met. 1991. pap. 2.95 (*0-590-43823-9*) Scholastic Inc.
Mazer, Norma F. & Lewis, Margorie. Waltzing on Water: Poetry by Women. (Orig.). (gr. k-12). 1989. pap. 3.50 (*0-440-20257-4*, LFL) Dell.
Mazer, Norma F. & Mazer, Harry. Bright Days, Stupid Nights. 1992. 16.00 (*0-553-08126-8*) Bantam.
—Heartbeat. 1989. 16.00 (*0-553-05808-8*, Starfire) Bantam.
—Heartbeat. (gr. 7 up). 1990. pap. 3.50 (*0-553-28779-6*, Starfire) Bantam.
—The Solid Gold Kid. 224p. (gr. 7 up). 1978. pap. 1.50 (*0-440-98080-1*, LE) Dell.
—The Solid Gold Kid. (gr. 7 up). 1989. pap. 3.50 (*0-553-27851-7*, Starfire) Bantam.
Mazour, A., et al. People & Nations: A World History, 7 vols. large type ed. 2000p. (gr. 9-12). 1984. Repr. of 1983 ed. Set. 414.00 (*0-317-01920-1*, J-21590-00) Am Printing Hse.
Mazzarella, Mimi. Alphabatty Animals & Funny Foods. Mazzarella, Mimi & Mazzarella, James, illus. LC 83-81449. 96p. (Orig.). (gr. k-3). 1984. pap. 5.95 (*0-89059-045-4*) Liberty Pub.
Mazzenga, Isabel B. Compromise or Confrontation: Dealing with the Adults in Your Life. Green, Anne C., illus. LC 89-5711. 96p. (gr. 6-10). 1989. PLB 13.40 (*0-531-10805-8*) Watts.
Mazzio, Joann. Leaving Eldorado. LC 92-13853. 176p. (gr. 5-9). 1993. 13.95 (*0-395-64381-3*) HM.
—The One Who Came Back. 208p. (gr. 5-9). 1992. 13.45 (*0-395-59506-1*) HM.
Mazzocchi, Paul, jt. auth. see Jarvis, Bruce.
Mazzola, Toni & Guten, Mimi. Wally Koala & Friends. Cohen, Keri, ed. McCoy, William M., illus. LC 93-94001. 24p. (ps-3). 1993. saddlestitch bdg. incl. cassette 9.95 (*1-883747-00-7*) WK Prods.
—Wally Koala & the Little Green Peach. Cohen, Keri, ed. McCoy, William M., illus. 24p. (ps-3). 1993. saddlestitch bdg. incl. cassette 9.95 (*1-883747-02-3*) WK Prods.
Mbengue, Demba, illus. Aesop: Tales of Aethiop the African, Vol. 1. 64p. (gr. 2-9). 1991. 6.95 (*1-877610-03-8*); cass. 6.95 (*0-685-50185-X*) Sea Island.
Meacham, Margaret. Boy on the Beach. Ramsey, Marcy D., illus. 144p. (Orig.). (gr. 4-8). 1992. pap. 8.95 (*0-87033-441-7*) Tidewater.
—The Secret of Heron Creek. LC 90-50373. 136p. (Orig.). (gr. 5-8). 1991. pap. 7.95 (*0-87033-414-X*) Tidewater.

Mead, Alice. Crossing the Starlight Bridge. 128p. (gr. 3-6). 1994. SBE 14.95 (0-02-765950-X, Bradbury Pr) Macmillan Child Grp.

Mead, Margaret, jt. auth. see Baldwin, James.

Mead, Robin, et al. The Fifty States. LC 92-9404. (Illus.). 64p. (gr. 2-6). 1993. 7.98 (0-8317-2317-3) Smithmark.

—Our National Parks. LC 92-9460. (Illus.). 64p. (gr. 2-6). 1993. 7.98 (0-8317-2314-9) Smithmark.

Meade, Everard. Dragonfly. 1992. pap. 7.95 (0-933905-20-3) Claycomb Pr.

Meador, Nancy, jt. auth. see Harman, Betty.

Meador, Nancy, jt. ed. see Harman, Betty.

Meadows, Jayne, jt. auth. see Allen, Steve.

Meadway, Wendy. Let's Look at Birds. (Illus.). 32p. (gr. k-4). 1990. PLB 11.40 (0-531-18340-8, Pub. by Bookwright Pr) Watts.

Mealer, Tamara. My World in French Coloring Book. (FRE., Illus.). 64p. 1991. pap. 4.95 (0-8442-1393-4, Passport Bks) NTC Pub Grp.

—My World in German Coloring Book. (GER., Illus.). 96p. 1991. pap. 4.95 (0-8442-2169-4, Passport Bks) NTC Pub Grp.

—My World in Italian Coloring Book. (ITA., Illus.). 96p. 1991. pap. 4.95 (0-8442-8067-4, Passport Bks) NTC Pub Grp.

—My World in Spanish Coloring Book. (SPA., Illus.). 64p. 1991. pap. 4.95 (0-8442-7552-2, Passport Bks) NTC Pub Grp.

Mealy, Virginia, jt. auth. see Polette, Nancy.

Mealy, Virginia T. Happy Birthday Author. (Illus.). 128p. (gr. k-4). 1986. pap. 12.95 (0-913839-50-7) Bk Lures.

—Newbery Book. rev. ed. (Illus.). 128p. (gr. 4-8). 1991. pap. 12.95 (1-879287-02-1) Bk Lures.

Means, Florence. Carvers' George. LC 90-59179. (Illus.). 160p. (gr. 6-10). 1991. PLB 13.95 (1-55905-075-6) Marshall Cavendish.

Means, Florence C. The Moved-Outers. LC 92-13706. 156p. 1993. pap. 6.95 (0-8027-7386-9) Walker & Co.

Mearian, Judy F. Two Ways About It. LC 79-10029. (gr. 5 up). 1985. Dial Bks Young.

Meastro, Betsy. Snow Day. (ps-3). 1992. pap. 4.95 (0-590-46083-8) Scholastic Inc.

Mebane, Robert. Air & Gasses. 1994. PLB write for info. (0-8050-2839-0) H Holt & Co.

—Metals. 1994. PLB write for info. (0-8050-2842-0) H Holt & Co.

—Plastics & Polymers. 1994. PLB write for info. (0-8050-2843-9) H Holt & Co.

—Salts & Solids. 1994. PLB write for info. (0-8050-2841-2) H Holt & Co.

—Water & Liquids. 1994. PLB write for info. H Holt & Co.

Mebane, Robert C. & Rybolt, Thomas R. Adventures with Atoms & Molecules, Bk. I: Chemistry Experiments for Young People. Perkins, Ronald I., intro. by. LC 85-10177. (Illus.). 96p. (gr. 4-9). 1985. lib. bdg. 16.95 (0-89490-120-6) Enslow Pubs.

—Adventures with Atoms & Molecules, Bk. II: Chemistry Experiments for Young People. Perkins, Ronald I., intro. by. LC 85-10177. (Illus.). 96p. (gr. 4-9). 1987. lib. bdg. 16.95 (0-89490-164-8) Enslow Pubs.

—Adventures with Atoms & Molecules, Bk. III: Chemistry Experiments for Young People. LC 85-10177. (Illus.). 96p. (gr. 4-9). 1991. lib. bdg. 16.95 (0-89490-254-7) Enslow Pubs.

—Adventures with Atoms & Molecules, Bk. IV: Chemistry Experiments for Young People. LC 85-10177. (Illus.). 96p. (gr. 4-9). 1992. lib. bdg. 16.95 (0-89490-336-5) Enslow Pubs.

Mebane, Robert C., jt. auth. see Rybolt, Thomas R.

Mebs, Gudren. Sunday's Child. (gr. k-6). 1989. pap. 2.95 (0-440-40167-4, YB) Dell.

Mecklenberg, Jan. Alphabet Animals. Mecklenberg, Jan, illus. LC 93-35479. 1994. write for info. (0-7852-8218-1) Oliver-Nelson.

—Counting God's Creatures. Mecklenberg, Jan, illus. LC 93-36019. 1994. write for info. (0-7852-8217-3) Nelson.

Meddaugh, Susan. Beast. Meddaugh, Susan, illus. 32p. (gr. k-3). 1985. 13.95 (0-395-30349-4); pap. 3.95 (0-317-18511-X) HM.

—Beast Pa. (ps-3). 1985. pap. 5.70 (0-395-38366-8) HM.

—Martha Speaks. Meddaugh, Susan, illus. LC 91-48455. 32p. (ps-3). 1992. 13.45 (0-395-63313-3) HM.

—Tree of Birds. Meddaugh, Susan, illus. 32p. (gr. k-3). 1990. 13.45 (0-395-53147-0) HM.

—The Witches' Supermarket. Meddaugh, Susan, illus. 32p. (gr. k-3). 1991. 13.95 (0-395-57034-4, Sandpiper) HM.

Meddick, James. Robotman Takes Off, No. 1. 128p. (gr. 6 up). 1986. pap. 4.95 (0-88687-250-2, Pharos) F&W Inc NJ.

Meddick, Jim. Robotman II: The Untold Story. (Illus.). 128p. (gr. 6 up). 1986. pap. 5.95 (0-88687-279-0, Pharos) F&W Inc NJ.

Medearis. Poppa's New Pants. 1994. 14.95 (0-8050-1840-9) H Holt & Co.

Medearis, Angela S. Annie's Gifts. Richa, Anna, illus. LC 92-71998. 32p. (gr. 1-4). 1993. 14.95 (0-940975-30-0); pap. 6.95 (0-940975-31-9) Just Us Bks.

—Come This Far to Freedom: A History of African Americans. Shaffer, Terea D., illus. LC 92-31251. 144p. (gr. 3-7). 1993. SBE 14.95 (0-689-31522-8, Atheneum Child Bk) Macmillan Child Grp.

—Dancing with the Indians. Byrd, Samuel, illus. LC 90-28666. 32p. (ps-3). 1991. reinforced 14.95 (0-8234-0893-0) Holiday.

—Dancing with the Indians: A Reading Rainbow Review Book. Byrd, Samuel, illus. (ps-3). 1993. pap. 5.95 (0-8234-1023-4) Holiday.

—Our People. Bryant, Micheal, illus. LC 92-44499. 32p. (gr. k-3). 1994. SBE 14.95 (0-689-31826-X, Atheneum Child Bk) Macmillan Child Grp.

—Picking Peas for a Penny. Shaw, Charles, illus. LC 89-49754. 36p. (gr. 1-4). 1990. 11.95 (0-938349-54-6) State House Pr.

Medearis, Angela S., adapted by. The Christmas Riddle. Ward, John, illus. LC 93-10713. (gr. 2 up). 1994. write for info. (0-525-67469-1, Lodestar Bks) Dutton Child Bks.

Medearis, Angela S., compiled by. The Zebra-Riding Cowboy: A Folk Song of the Old West. Brusca, Maria C., illus. LC 91-27941. 32p. (ps-2). 1992. 14.95 (0-8050-1712-7, Bks Young Read) H Holt & Co.

Medearis, Angela Shelf. Picking Peas for a Penny. Shaw, Charles, illus. 40p. (gr. 1-4). 1993. pap. 4.95 (0-590-45942-2) Scholastic Inc.

Medearis, Mary. Big Doc's Girl. LC 84-45641. 142p. (gr. 7-12). 1985. pap. 7.95 (0-87483-105-9) August Hse.

Medeiros, Selene de see De Medeiros, Selene.

Medema, K. Gorgles. Vreeman, J., ed. (Orig.). 1985. pap. 3.95 (0-918789-05-2) FreeMan Prods.

—Rennis the Nam. Vreeman, J., ed. (Illus.). 16p. (Orig.). 1985. pap. 3.95 (0-918789-04-4) FreeMan Prods.

Medicine Story. Children of the Morning Light: Wampanoag Tales As Told by Manitonquat. Arquette, Mary F., illus. LC 92-32328. 80p. (gr. 1). 1994. SBE 18.95 (0-02-765905-4, Macmillan Child Bk) Macmillan Child Grp.

Medland, Mary. The Red Badge of Courage: A Study Guide. (gr. 9-12). 1990. pap. text ed. 14.95 (0-88122-414-6) Lrn Links.

—Where the Lilies Bloom: A Study Guide. Friedland, Joyce & Kessler, Rikki, eds. 30p. (gr. 9-12). 1990. pap. text ed. 14.95 (0-88122-399-9) Lrn Links.

Medley, Steven P., ed. see Ross, Michael E.

Medlicott, Mary, ed. Tales for Telling: From Around the World. Williams, Sue, illus. LC 92-53095. 96p. (gr. k-5). 1992. 16.95 (1-85697-824-9) Kingfisher Bks.

Medoff, Francine. The Mouse in the Matzah Factory. Goldstein, David, illus. LC 82-23349. 40p. (ps-3). 1983. pap. 4.95 (0-930494-19-9) Kar Ben.

Medvene, Mark. Foilrigami. (Illus.). (gr. 4-7). 1968. 10.95 (0-685-06619-3) Astor-Honor.

Meek, James. The Land & People of Scotland. LC 88-27215. (Illus.). 256p. (gr. 6 up). 1990. 18.00 (0-397-32332-8, Lipp Jr Bks); PLB 14.89 (0-397-32333-6, Lipp Jr Bks) HarpC Child Bks.

Meek, Mary E., jt. auth. see David, Alfred.

Meeks, Arone R. Enora & the Black Crane. LC 92-32123. 1993. 14.95 (0-590-46375-6) Scholastic Inc.

Meeks, Christopher. Arnold Schwarzenegger: Hard Work Brought Success. LC 92-42288. 1993. 14.60 (0-86593-260-3); 10.95s.p. (0-685-66328-0) Rourke Corp.

—Japan. (Illus.). 64p. (gr. 7 up). 1990. lib. bdg. 12.95s.p. (0-685-36366-X) Rourke Corp.

—Roald Dahl. LC 92-42286. (gr. 3-7). 1993. 14.60 (0-86593-259-X); 10.95s.p. (0-685-66357-4) Rourke Corp.

—Skydiving. 48p. (gr. 3-4). 1991. PLB 11.95 (1-56065-051-6) Capstone Pr.

Meer, Altie van der see Van der Meer, Ron & Van der Meer, Altie.

Meer, Atie Van Der see Van Der Meer, Ron & Van Der Meer, Atie.

Meer, Jeff. Drugs & Sports. Mendelson, Jack H. & Mello, Nancyintro. by. (Illus.). 136p. (gr. 5 up). 1988. lib. bdg. 19.95 (1-55546-226-X); pap. 9.95 (0-7910-0794-4) Chelsea Hse.

—Drugs & Sports. (Illus.). 32p. (gr. 5 up). 1991. pap. 4.49 (1-55546-996-5) Chelsea Hse.

Meer, Mara van der see Van der Meer, Mara.

Meer, Ron Van Der see Cole, Babette & Van Der Meer, Ron.

Meer, Ron van Der see Van der Meer, Ron.

Meer, Ron Van Der see Van Der Meer, Ron.

Meer, Ron van der see Van der Meer, Ron.

Meer, Ron Van Der see Van Der Meer, Ron.

Meer, Ron van der see Van der Meer, Ron & Ivory, Lesley A.

Meer, Ron van der see Van der Meer, Ron & Van der Meer, Altie.

Meer, Ron van Der see Van Der Meer, Ron & Van Der Meer, Atie.

Meer, Ron van der see Van der Meer, Ron & Van der Meer, Atie.

Meer Ron, Van Der see Van Der Meer, Ron.

Mees, Walter H., Jr. Who Is God? (Illus.). 48p. (gr. 9-12). 1991. pap. 7.99 (1-55945-218-8) Group Pub.

Mega-Books of N.Y. Award Night, No. 8. 176p. (gr. 7 up). 1988. pap. 2.50 (0-553-26794-9) Bantam.

Mega-Books Staff. My Friend Fang. 1992. pap. 3.99 (0-553-37116-9) Bantam.

—Shadow & the Ghosts. 1992. pap. 3.99 (0-553-37115-0) Bantam.

Megakinetics Staff. Baby Loves... (gr. k-5). 1991. pap. text ed. 15.00 (1-56495-007-7) Megakinetics.

Megale, Marina see Meyer, Linda D.

Meggendorfer, Lothar. The Doll's House: A Reproduction of the Antique Pop-up Book. Meggendorfer, Lothar, illus. Shiller, Justin G., notes by. LC 79-5072. (Illus.). (gr. k-3). 1989. pap. 8.95 (0-670-27761-4) Viking Child Bks.

Mehew, Karen, jt. auth. see Mehew, Randall.

Mehew, Randall & Mehew, Karen. The Best Manners Book Ever. Bales, Marcia, illus. 68p. 1990. pap. text ed. 5.95 (0-929985-55-9) Sonos.

—Gospel Basic Busy Book, Vol. II. Bales, Marcia, illus. 100p. 1990. pap. text ed. 6.95 (0-910613-08-7) Millenial Pr.

—Gospel Basic Busy Book, Vol. I. Christopherson, Jerry, illus. 100p. 1989. pap. text ed. 6.95 (0-910613-13-3) Millenial Pr.

Mehl, Ron, Jr. & Gunderson, Sandy. The Littlest Shepherd. (Illus.). 36p. (ps-3). 1991. pap. 4.99 (0-88070-449-7, Gold & Honey) Questar Pubs.

Mehrabi, Jacqueline. Song in the Ground. (Illus.). 48p. (Orig.). (gr. k-4). 1986. pap. text ed. 4.00 (0-85398-225-2) G Ronald Pub.

Mehrens, Gloria & Wick, Karen. Bagging It with Puppets. (gr. k-2). 1988. pap. 16.95 (0-8224-0677-2) Fearon Teach Aids.

Mehta, Hansa. Prince of Ayodhya. (Illus.). (gr. 1-9). 1979. pap. 2.50 (0-89744-178-8) Auromere.

Mehta, Rama, jt. auth. see Galbraith, Catherine A.

Meiczinger, John. How to Draw Indian Arts & Crafts. Meiczinger, John, illus. LC 88-50807. 32p. (gr. 2-6). 1989. lib. bdg. 10.65 (0-8167-1537-8, Pub. by Watermill Pr); pap. text ed. 1.95 (0-8167-1515-7, Pub. by Watermill Pr) Troll Assocs.

Meier, Gisela. Ghosts & Poltergeists. 48p. (gr. 3-4). 1991. PLB 11.95 (1-56065-040-0) Capstone Pr.

—Minorities. LC 91-11651. 64p. (gr. 5-7). 1991. 12.95s.p. (0-86593-124-0); lib. bdg. 17.27 (0-685-59203-0) Rourke Corp.

—Teenage Pregnancy. LC 93-14169. 1993. write for info. (1-85435-611-9) Marshall Cavendish.

Meigs, Cornelia. Invincible Louisa. LC 68-21174. (Illus.). (gr. 7 up). 1968. 16.95 (0-316-56590-3) Little.

—Invisible Louisa. (gr. 4-7). 1988. pap. 2.95 (0-590-44818-8) Scholastic Inc.

Meigs, Mildred P. Moon Song. Conover, Chris, illus. LC 89-32942. 32p. (ps up). 1990. 14.95 (0-688-08160-6); PLB 14.88 (0-688-08707-8, Morrow Jr Bks) Morrow Jr Bks.

Meinders, LaDonna K. Leaves in the Wind. Loftin, Beth, illus. Wheeler, J. Clyde, intro. by. LC 89-81374. (Illus.). 152p. 1989. 15.95 (0-934188-31-9) Evans Pubns.

Meir, Mira. Alina: A Russian Girl Comes to Israel. Shapiro, Zeva, tr. from HEB. Rozen, Yael, illus. 48p. (gr. 2-4). 1982. 7.95 (0-8276-0208-1) JPS Phila.

Meisenheimer, Sharon. Color Days. (gr. k-3). 1988. pap. 8.95 (0-8224-1641-7) Fearon Teach Aids.

—Special Ways with Ordinary Days. (gr. k-3). 1988. pap. 12.95 (0-8224-6347-4) Fearon Teach Aids.

Meissel, Chris. Young Children Rap to Learn about Famous African-Americans. Keeling, Jan, ed. Eaddy, Susan, illus. 80p. (Orig.). 1993. pap. text ed. 8.95 (0-86530-265-0) Incentive Pubns.

Meister, Teddy & Simpson, Ann M. Independent Study Enrichment Projects: Ready-to-Use Projects. 272p. (gr. 3-8). 1988. pap. 22.95x (0-87628-447-0) Ctr Appl Res.

Meisterfeld, C. W. Psychological Dog Training: Behavior Conditioning with Respect & Trust. (Illus.). 232p. (Orig.). (gr. 6 up). 1991. pap. 18.00 (0-9601292-6-X) M R K.

Mejia, Eileen. From Inside Our Mountain. (Illus.). 24p. 1984. pap. 2.95 (0-87595-166-X) Oregon Hist.

Mejo, Oscar de see De Mejo, Oscar.

Melanos, Jack. Rapunzel & the Witch. 1950. 4.50 (0-87602-186-0) Anchorage.

—Sinbad & the Evil Genii. (Orig.). (gr. k up). 1985. pap. 4.50 (0-87602-251-4) Anchorage.

Melendez, Francisco. The Mermaid & the Major: or, the True Story of the Invention of the Submarine. Melendez, Francisco, illus. 64p. 1991. 24.95 (0-8109-3619-4) Abrams.

Melger, Boyd A., jt. auth. see Re'lem, Dyob.

Mell, Jan. Atlantic Gray Whale. LC 89-7868. (Illus.). 48p. (gr. 5-6). 1989. RSBE 12.95 (0-89686-458-8, Crestwood Hse) Macmillan Child Grp.

—Grand Canyon. LC 88-18707. (Illus.). (gr. 4-8). 1988. RSBE 13.95 (0-89686-406-5, Crestwood Hse) Macmillan Child Grp.

—Scorpion. LC 89-28273. (Illus.). 48p. (gr. 4-5). 1990. RSBE 12.95 (0-89686-520-7, Crestwood Hse) Macmillan Child Grp.

Melle, Julie. My 911 Book for Help. Collas, Daniel, illus. LC 92-71606. 16p. (ps-6). 1992. pap. text ed. 9.99g (1-881402-00-2) CA Storybook.

Mellecker, Judith. The Fox & the Kingfisher. Parker, Robert A., illus. LC 89-27180. 48p. (gr. k-4). 1990. 14.95 (0-679-80539-7); lib. bdg. 15.99 (0-679-90539-1) Knopf Bks Yng Read.

Mellen, Stephanie. The Crystal Rabbit. Mellen, Stephanie, illus. 52p. (gr. k-12). 1993. pap. 5.95 (0-9637414-0-3) Meltec.

Mellen, Stephanie, jt. auth. see Polakiewicz, David M.

Mellet, Peter, et al. Transportation. Smith, Guy & Bull, Peter, illus. LC 89-11358. 48p. (gr. 4-5). 1989. PLB 17.27 (0-8368-0134-2) Gareth Stevens Inc.

Mellett, Peter & Rossiter, Jane. Air on the Move. LC 92-14719. 1993. 12.40 (0-531-14244-2) Watts.

—Food Energy. LC 92-11238. 1993. 12.40 (0-531-14247-7) Watts.

—Hot & Cold. LC 92-5141. (Illus.). 32p. (gr. 5-8). 1993. PLB 12.40 (0-531-14236-1) Watts.

—Liquids in Action. LC 92-7649. (Illus.). 32p. (gr. 5-8). 1993. PLB 12.40 (0-531-14235-3) Watts.

Mellett, Peter, et al, eds. Science & Technology. LC 92-16694. (Illus.). 160p. (gr. 4-10). 1992. pap. 19.00 *(0-13-681727-0)* P-H Gen Ref & Trav.
Mellick, J. S., ed. see Kingsley, Henry.
Melling, Orla. The Druid's Tune. rev. ed. (Illus.). 195p. (gr. 7 up). 1993. pap. 9.95 *(0-86278-285-6,* Pub. by OBrien Pr IE) Dufour.
Mello, Nancy see August, Paul.
Mello, Nancy see Avraham, Regina.
Mello, Nancy see Check, William A.
Mello, Nancy see Grauer, Neil.
Mello, Nancy see Hoobler, Dorothy & Hoobler, Thomas.
Mello, Nancy see Knox, Jean M.
Mello, Nancy see Marshall, Eliot.
Mello, Nancy see Martin, Jo.
Mello, Nancy see Meer, Jeff.
Mello, Nancy see Miller, Mark.
Mello, Nancy see Rodgers, Joann.
Mello, Nancy see Theodore, Alan.
Mellor, Grant. Flying Tinsel. (Illus.). 80p. (gr. 5-8). 1993. pap. text ed. 9.50 *(0-938587-33-1)* Cuisenaire.
Mello Vianna, Fernando de see Webster's New World Dictionaries Staff.
Melmed, Laura. The Rainbabies. Pearson, Susan, ed. LaMarche, Jim, illus. LC 91-16877. 32p. (gr. 1 up). 1992. 15.00 *(0-688-10755-9)*; PLB 14.93 *(0-688-10756-7)* Lothrop.
Melmed, Laura K. First Song Ever Sung. LC 91-28528. (ps-3). 1993. 15.00 *(0-688-08230-0)*; PLB 14.93 *(0-688-08231-9)* Lothrop.
—I Love You As Much... Sorensen, Henri, illus. LC 92-27677. 1993. write for info. *(0-688-11718-X)*; PLB write for info. *(0-688-11719-8)* Lothrop.
—The Marvelous Market on Mermaids. LC 93-32621. (gr. 4 up). 1995. write for info. *(0-688-13053-4)*; lib. bdg. write for info. *(0-688-13054-2)* Lothrop.
Melodia, Thomas V., jt. auth. see Malinowski, Stanley B.
Melody, Michael E. The Apache. Porter, Frank, intro. by. (Illus.). 112p. (gr. 5 up). 1989. 17.95 *(1-55546-689-3)*; pap. 9.95 *(0-7910-0352-3)* Chelsea Hse.
Meloy, J. Reid, jt. auth. see Gacono, Carl B.
Meltabarger, P. J. The Ballad of Padre Island, Vol. 1. Samuelson, Arnold & Samuelson, Billie, eds. Becher, Ivy, illus. Miller, Jesse A., intro. by. (Illus.). 28p. (Orig.). (gr. 1-5). 1987. pap. text ed. 3.95 *(0-923133-00-3)* JM Pub.
—The Karankawa Indians, Pt. 2. Samuelson, Arnold & Samuelson, Billie, eds. Becher, Ivy, illus. Miller, Jesse A., intro. by. (Illus.). 28p. (Orig.). (gr. 1-5). 1988. pap. text ed. 3.95 *(0-923133-01-1)* JM Pub.
—Livingston: The Pedigreed Pooch of Padre Island. Samuelson, Arnold & Samuelson, Billie, eds. Becher, Ivy, illus. Lynn, E. Russell, intro. by. (Illus.). 150p. (gr. 7-10). 1988. 19.95 *(0-923133-02-X)* JM Pub.
Melton, Dana D. & Ledbetter, Frances M. Hooked on Games. Melton, Dana D., illus. 150p. (Orig.). (gr. k-6). 1989. pap. 9.95 *(0-685-29409-9)* Hooked Games.
Melton, David. A Boy Called Hopeless. Melton, Todd, illus. LC 86-27557. 232p. (gr. 4 up). 1986. pap. 5.95 *(0-933849-07-9)* Landmark Edns.
—A Boy Called Hopeless. Melton, Todd, illus. LC 86-27557. 231p. (gr. 4-8). 1986. Repr. of 1976 ed. PLB 13.95 *(0-933849-32-X)* Landmark Edns.
—The One & Only Autobiography of Ralph Miller: The Dog Who Knew He Was A Boy. Melton, David, illus. LC 86-27551. 104p. (gr. 2-6). 1986. pap. 5.95 *(0-933849-05-2)* Landmark Edns.
—The One & Only Autobiography of Ralph Miller: The Dog Who Knew He Was a Boy. LC 86-27551. (Illus.). 90p. (gr. 2-6). 1987. Repr. of 1979 ed. PLB 13.95 *(0-933849-30-3)* Landmark Edns.
—The One & Only Second Autobiography of Ralph Miller: The Dog Who Knew He Was a Boy. Melton, David, illus. LC 86-27556. 128p. (gr. 2-6). 1986. pap. 5.95 *(0-933849-06-0)* Landmark Edns.
—The One & Only Second Autobiography of Ralph Miller: The Dog Who Knew He Was a Boy. LC 86-27556. (Illus.). 116p. (gr. 2-6). 1986. Repr. of 1983 ed. PLB 13.95 *(0-933849-31-1)* Landmark Edns.
Melton, David, jt. auth. see Teachers of the School District of Independence, Missouri Staff.
Melton, David, illus. Images of Greatness: A Celebration of Life. LC 87-26300. 64p. (gr. 4 up). 1987. 15.95 *(0-933849-11-7)* Landmark Edns.
Melton, Lisa & Ladizinsky, Eric. Fifty Nifty Science Experiments. Yamamoto, Neal, illus. 64p. (ps-3). 1992. pap. 3.95 *(0-929923-92-8)* Lowell Hse.
Meltzer, Lisa. One-Two-Three Look at Me. Gilchrest, Mary, illus. 28p. (ps). 1990. 2.95 *(0-02-689486-6)* Checkerboard.
Meltzer, Maxine. Pups Speak Up. Schmidt, Karen L., illus. LC 92-33687. 32p. (ps-3). 1994. RSBE 13.95 *(0-02-766710-3,* Bradbury Pr) Macmillan Child Grp.
Meltzer, Milton. Ain't Gonna Study War No More: The Story of America's Peace Seekers. LC 84-48337. (Illus.). 288p. (gr. 7 up). 1985. PLB 14.89 *(0-06-024200-0)* HarpC Child Bks.
—All Times, All Peoples: A World History of Slavery. Fisher, Leonard E., illus. LC 79-2810. 80p. (gr. 5-9). 1980. PLB 15.89 *(0-06-024187-X)* HarpC Child Bks.
—The Amazing Potato: A Story in Which the Incas, Conquistadors, Marie Antoinette, Thomas Jefferson, Wars, Famines, Immigrants, & French Fries All Play a Part. LC 91-29610. (Illus.). 128p. (gr. 3-7). 1992. 15.00 *(0-06-020806-6)*; PLB 14.89 *(0-06-020807-4)* HarpC Child Bks.

—American Politics: How It Really Works. LC 88-26635. (Illus.). 192p. (gr. 7 up). 1989. 12.95 *(0-688-07494-4)* Morrow Jr Bks.
—The American Promise: Voices of a Changing Nation, 1945-Present. (Illus.). (gr. 7 up). 1990. 15.95 *(0-553-07020-7,* Starfire) Bantam.
—The American Revolutionaries: A History in Their Own Words. LC 86-47846. (Illus.). 256p. (gr. 7 up). 1987. 14.00 *(0-690-04641-3,* Crowell Jr Bks); PLB 13.89 *(0-690-04643-X,* Crowell Jr Bks) HarpC Child Bks.
—American Revolutionaries: A History in Their Own Words 1750-1800. (Illus.). 224p. (gr. 7 up). 1993. pap. 6.95 *(0-06-446145-9,* Trophy) HarpC Child Bks.
—Andrew Jackson: And His America. (Illus.). 208p. (gr. 7-12). 1993. PLB 16.40 *(0-531-11157-1)* Watts.
—Benjamin Franklin: The New American. Vestal, Jeanne, ed. LC 88-17015. (Illus.). 176p. (gr. 6-9). 1988. PLB 15.40 *(0-531-10582-2)* Watts.
—Betty Friedan: A Voice for Women's Rights. Marchesi, Stephen, illus. LC 85-40441. 57p. (gr. 5 up). 1985. 10.95 *(0-670-81249-8)* Viking Child Bks.
—The Bill of Rights: How We Got It & What It Means. LC 90-1537. 180p. (gr. 7 up). 1990. 15.00 *(0-690-04805-X,* Crowell Jr Bks); PLB 14.89 *(0-690-04807-6,* Crowell Jr Bks) HarpC Child Bks.
—The Black Americans: A History in Their Own Words. rev. ed. LC 83-46160. (Illus.). 320p. (gr. 7 up). 1984. (Crowell Jr Bks); PLB 15.89 *(0-690-04418-6,* Crowell Jr Bks) HarpC Child Bks.
—The Black Americans: A History in Their Own Words, 1619-1983. rev. ed. LC 83-46160. (Illus.). 320p. (gr. 7 up). 1987. pap. 9.95 *(0-06-446055-X,* Trophy) HarpC Child Bks.
—A Book about Names. Richter, Mischa, illus. LC 83-45241. 128p. (gr. 7 up). 1984. (Crowell Jr Bks); PLB 13.89 *(0-690-04381-3,* Crowell Jr Bks) HarpC Child Bks.
—Bread & Roses: The Struggle of American Labor, 1865-1915. (Illus.). 192p. 1990. 17.95x *(0-8160-2371-9)* Facts on File.
—Brother, Can You Spare a Dime. 192p. (gr. 7). 1977. pap. 3.95 *(0-451-62442-4,* ME2178, Ment) NAL-Dutton.
—Brother, Can You Spare a Dime: The Great Depression 1929-1933. (Illus.). 144p. 1990. 16.95x *(0-8160-2372-7)* Facts on File.
—Cheap Raw Material: How Our Youngest Workers Are Exploited & Abused. LC 93-31478. (Illus.). 192p. (gr. 7 up). 1994. 14.99 *(0-670-83128-X)* Viking Child Bks.
—The Chinese Americans. LC 79-3419. (Illus.). 192p. (gr. 5 up). 1980. PLB 13.89 *(0-690-04039-3,* Crowell Jr Bks) HarpC Child Bks.
—Columbus & the World Around Him. 1990. 15.45 *(0-531-15148-4)* Watts.
—Columbus & the World Around Him. (gr. 4-7). 1990. PLB 15.40 *(0-531-10899-6)* Watts.
—Columbus & the World Around Him. 245p. (gr. 6 up). 1990. 19.60 *(0-685-63798-0,* BR8496) W A T Braille.
—Crime in America. LC 90-5698. 176p. (gr. 7 up). 1990. 12.95g *(0-688-08513-X)* Morrow Jr Bks.
—Dorothea Lange: Life Through the Camera. Diamond, Donna, illus. Lange, Dorothea, photos by. 64p. (gr. 2-6). 1986. pap. 3.95 *(0-14-032105-5,* Puffin) Puffin Bks.
—George Washington & the Birth of Our Nation. LC 86-9222. 176p. (gr. 7 up). 1986. PLB 14.40 *(0-531-10253-X)* Watts.
—Gold: The True Story of Why People Search for It, Mine It, Trade It, Fight for It, Mint It, Display It, Steal It, & Kill for It. LC 92-44497. (Illus.). 128p. (gr. 3-7). 1993. 15.00 *(0-06-022983-7)*; PLB 14.89 *(0-06-022984-5)* HarpC Child Bks.
—The Hispanic Americans. Noren, Catherine & Camhi, Morrie, illus. LC 81-43314. 160p. (gr. 5 up). 1982. 15.00 *(0-690-04110-1,* Crowell Jr Bks); PLB 14.89 *(0-690-04111-X,* Crowell Jr Bks) HarpC Child Bks.
—The Jewish Americans: A History in Their Own Words. LC 81-43886. (Illus.). 192p. (gr. 5 up). 1982. PLB 14.89 *(0-690-04228-0,* Crowell Jr Bks) HarpC Child Bks.
—Langston Hughes: A Biography. LC 68-21925. 296p. (gr. 7 up). 1988. PLB 13.89 *(0-690-04762-2,* Crowell Jr Bks) HarpC Child Bks.
—Mary McCleod Bethune. Marchesi, Stephen, illus. (gr. 2-6). 1988. pap. 3.50 *(0-317-69647-5,* Puffin) Puffin Bks.
—Mary McLeod Bethune: Voice of Black Hope. Marchesi, Stephen, illus. LC 86-15923. (gr. 2-6). 1987. pap. 11.95 *(0-670-80744-3)* Viking Child Bks.
—Never to Forget: The Jews of the Holocaust. LC 75-25409. (gr. 7 up). 1976. PLB 15.89 *(0-06-024175-6)* HarpC Child Bks.
—Never to Forget: The Jews of the Holocaust. LC 75-25409. (Illus.). 240p. (gr. 7 up). 1991. pap. 6.95 *(0-06-446118-1,* Trophy) HarpC Child Bks.
—Poverty in America. LC 85-31963. 128p. (gr. 7 up). 1986. 12.95 *(0-688-05911-2)* Morrow Jr Bks.
—Rescue: The Story of How Gentiles Saved Jews in the Holocaust. LC 87-47816. (Illus.). 224p. (gr. 7 up). 1988. 16.00 *(0-06-024209-4)*; PLB 15.89 *(0-06-024210-8)* HarpC Child Bks.
—Rescue: The Story of How Gentiles Saved Jews in the Holocaust. LC 87-47816. (Illus.). 176p. (gr. 7 up). 1991. pap. 6.95 *(0-06-446117-3,* Trophy) HarpC Child Bks.
—Starting from Home: A Writer's Beginnings. (Illus.). 160p. (gr. 7 up). 1991. pap. 3.95 *(0-14-032299-X,* Puffin) Puffin Bks.

—The Terrorists. LC 82-48858. (Illus.). 192p. (gr. 7 up). 1983. HarpC Child Bks.
—Thomas Jefferson: The Revolutionary Aristocrat. LC 91-15943. (Illus.). 256p. (gr. 9-12). 1991. 16.45 *(0-531-15227-8)*; PLB 16.40 *(0-531-11069-9)* Watts.
—Underground Man. 261p. (gr. 3-7). 1990. 14.95 *(0-15-200617-6,* Gulliver Bks) HarpBrace.
—Underground Man. 261p. (gr. 3-7). 1990. pap. 4.95 *(0-15-292846-4,* Odyssey) HarBrace.
—Voices from the Civil War: A Documentary History of the Great American Conflict. LC 88-34067. (Illus.). 224p. (gr. 7 up). 1989. 15.00 *(0-690-04800-9,* Crowell Jr Bks); PLB 14.89 *(0-690-04802-5,* Crowell Jr Bks) HarpC Child Bks.
—Voices from the Civil War: A Documentary of the Great American Conflict. LC 88-34067. (Illus.). 224p. (gr. 6 up). 1992. pap. 6.95 *(0-06-446124-6,* Trophy) HarpC Child Bks.
—Winnie Mandela: The Soul of South Africa. Marchesi, Stephen, illus. LC 86-5531. 64p. (gr. 2-6). 1986. pap. 10.95 *(0-670-81249-8)* Viking Child Bks.
—Winnie Mandela: The Soul of South Africa. Marchesi, Stephen, illus. (gr. 2-6). 1987. pap. 3.99 *(0-14-032181-0,* Puffin) Puffin Bks.
Melville, Herman. Billy Budd. Fisher, N. H., intro. by. Bd. with The Encantadas. (gr. 9 up). 1966. pap. 1.75 *(0-8049-0116-3,* CL-116) Airmont.
—Billy Budd. (Illus.). 64p. (gr. 4-12). 1979. pap. text ed. 2.95 *(0-88301-385-1)*; student activity bk. 1.25 *(0-88301-409-2)* Pendulum Pr.
—Catskill Eagle. Locker, Thomas, illus. 32p. (ps-3). 1991. 15.95 *(0-399-21857-2,* Philomel) Putnam Pub Group.
—Confidence Man. Grube, J., intro. by. (gr. 11 up). 1966. pap. 1.95 *(0-8049-0121-X,* CL-121) Airmont.
—Moby Dick. (gr. 11 up). 1964. pap. 3.95 *(0-8049-0033-7,* CL-33) Airmont.
—Moby Dick. Kazin, Alfred, ed. LC 56-14087. (gr. 9 up). 1956. pap. 9.16 *(0-395-05108-8,* RivEd) HM.
—Moby Dick. new ed. Shapiro, Irwin, ed. Nino, Alex, illus. LC 73-75458. 64p. (Orig.). (gr. 5-10). 1973. pap. 2.95 *(0-88301-099-2)* Pendulum Pr.
—Moby Dick. Daniels, Patricia, adapted by. LC 81-15386. (Illus.). 48p. (gr. 4 up). 1983. PLB 18.64 *(0-8172-1679-0)* Raintree Steck-V.
—Moby Dick. Kirn, Elaine, adapted by. (Illus.). 62p. (gr. 7 up). 1987. pap. text ed. write for info. *(0-13-586272-8,* 20381) Prentice ESL.
—Moby Dick. Selden, Bernice, adapted by. Gianni, Gary, illus. LC 87-16788. 48p. (gr. 3-6). 1988. PLB 12.89 *(0-8167-1207-7)*; pap. text ed. 3.95 *(0-8167-1208-5)* Troll Assocs.
—Moby Dick. Carlson, Donna, ed. (Illus.). 128p. 1992. pap. 2.95 *(1-56156-093-6)* Kidsbks.
—Moby Dick. (gr. 4-7). 1993. pap. 4.95 *(0-8114-6834-8)* Raintree Steck-V.
—Typee. Thomas, C., intro. by. (gr. 10 up). 1965. pap. 1.50 *(0-8049-0053-1,* CL-53) Airmont.
Melzer, Milton, ed. Lincoln, in His Own Words. Alcorn, Stephen, illus. LC 92-17431. 1993. 22.95 *(0-15-245437-3)* HarpBrace.
Memling, Lise, jt. auth. see Golder, Stephen.
Mendel, Kathleen L. Whispering Clay. LC 92-71598. (Illus.). 40p. (Orig.). 1992. pap. 9.50x *(1-878142-29-1)* Telstar TX.
Mendel, Kathleen L., ed. Lions, Lizards & Ladybugs. Harrison, Judy A., illus. LC 89-51485. 80p. (gr. k-6). 1989. pap. 9.95g *(0-9624384-2-1)* Telstar TX.
Mendell, Olga K., tr. see Hammond, Anna & Matunis, Joe.
Mendelowitz, Larry, jt. auth. see Levy, Nathan.
Mendelsohn, A. Pocket Guide to Job Interviewing. rev. ed. Chavez, Joseph, ed. 45p. (gr. 8 up). 1981. text ed. 1.50 *(0-918443-00-8,* AJDBI101) Job Data.
Mendelson, Jack see Marshall, Eliot.
Mendelson, Jack see Theodore, Alan.
Mendelson, Jack H. see August, Paul.
Mendelson, Jack H. see Avraham, Regina.
Mendelson, Jack H. see Check, William A.
Mendelson, Jack H. see Grauer, Neil.
Mendelson, Jack H. see Hoobler, Dorothy & Hoobler, Thomas.
Mendelson, Jack H. see Knox, Jean M.
Mendelson, Jack H. see Martin, Jo.
Mendelson, Jack H. see Meer, Jeff.
Mendelson, Jack H. see Miller, Mark.
Mendelson, Jack H. see Rodgers, Joann.
Mendelson, Lee. Rock-a-Bye Snoopy. Hill, Frank, illus. 26p. (ps up). 1986. 12.95 *(1-55578-011-3)* Worlds Wonder.
—Snoopy & the Great Pumpkin. Hill, Frank, illus. 26p. (ps up). 1986. 12.95 *(1-55578-006-7)* Worlds Wonder.
—Snoopy at the Dog Show. Hill, Frank, illus. 26p. (ps up). 1986. 12.95 *(1-55578-008-3)* Worlds Wonder.
—Snoopy Goes Camping. Hill, Frank, illus. 26p. (ps up). 1986. 12.95 *(1-55578-002-4)* Worlds Wonder.
—Snoopy Hits the Beach. Hill, Frank, illus. 26p. (ps up). 1986. 12.95 *(1-55578-004-0)* Worlds Wonder.
—Snoopy, Spike & the Cat Next Door. Hill, Frank, illus. 26p. (ps up). 1986. 12.95 *(1-55578-010-5)* Worlds Wonder.
—Snoopy's America. Hill, Frank, illus. 26p. (ps up). 1986. 12.95 *(1-55578-007-5)* Worlds Wonder.
—Snoopy's Band. Hill, Frank, illus. 26p. (ps up). 1986. 12.95 *(1-55578-009-1)* Worlds Wonder.
—Snoopy's Baseball Game. Hill, Frank, illus. 26p. (ps up). 1986. 12.95 *(1-55578-012-1)* Worlds Wonder.
—Snoopy's Birthday Party. Hill, Frank, illus. 26p. (ps up). 1986. 12.95 *(1-55578-001-6)* Worlds Wonder.

—Snoopy's Land of Make Believe. Hill, Frank, illus. 26p. (ps up). 1986. 12.95 (*1-55578-003-2*) Worlds Wonder.
—Snoopy's Show & Tell. Hill, Frank, illus. 26p. (ps up). 1986. 12.95 (*1-55578-005-9*) Worlds Wonder.
—Snoopy's Talent Show. Hill, Frank, illus. 26p. (ps up). 1986. 12.95 (*1-55578-006-8*) Worlds Wonder.
Mendelson, S. T. Stupid Emilien. Mendelson, S. T., illus. LC 90-28780. 32p. (gr. k-3). 1991. 14.95 (*1-55670-213-2*) Stewart Tabori & Chang.
Mendelson, Steve, retold by. & illus. The Emperor's New Clothes. LC 91-42606. 32p. 1992. 14.95 (*1-55670-232-9*) Stewart Tabori & Chang.
Mendez, Adriana. Cubans in America. LC 93-14339. 1993. lib. bdg. 15.95 (*0-8225-1953-4*); pap. 5.95 (*0-8225-1039-1*) Lerner Pubns.
Mendez, Phil. The Black Snowman. Byard, Carole, illus. (gr. 2-5). 1989. 14.95 (*0-590-40552-7*) Scholastic Inc.
—The Black Snowman. Byard, Carole, illus. 48p. 1991. pap. 4.95 (*0-590-44873-0*, Blue Ribbon Bks) Scholastic Inc.
Mendoza, George. The Gillygoofang. Mayer, Mercer, illus. 32p. (ps-2). 1982. Dial Bks Young.
—Hunter I Might Have Been. (Illus.). (gr. 3-5). 1968. 10.95 (*0-8392-3064-8*) Astor-Honor.
—The Hunter I Might Have Been. (Illus.). 48p. (gr. 3-6). 1989. pap. 6.95 (*0-89815-333-6*) Ten Speed Pr.
—Traffic Jam. Stoltz, David, illus. LC 89-28597. 32p. 1990. PLB 14.95 (*1-55670-135-7*) Stewart Tabori & Chang.
—Were You a Wild Duck, Where Would You Go? Osborn-Smith, Jane, illus. LC 89-28596. 32p. 1990. PLB 14.95 (*1-55670-136-5*) Stewart Tabori & Chang.
Mendoza, George & Wilson, Gahan. Hairticklers. (Illus.). 128p. (gr. 5 up). 1989. cloth 13.95 (*0-89815-332-8*); pap. 8.95 (*0-89815-330-1*) Ten Speed Pr.
Meneely, Janie. Santa & the Skipjack. Ramsey, Marcy D., illus. 32p. (gr. k-6). 1991. write for info. (*0-9618461-1-9*) BaySailor Bks.
Mengel, Gail E. The Homework Organizer: Assignment Notebook & Guide. 96p. (gr. 7-12). 1991. 9.95 (*0-9631705-0-3*) Get Organized.
Menkart, Deborah & Sunshine, Catherine A., eds. Caribbean Connections: Puerto Rico. LC 90-62779. (Illus.). 108p. (Orig.). (gr. 7-12). 1990. pap. text ed. 12.00 (*1-878554-04-2*) NECA.
Menkart, Deborah, jt. ed. see Sunshine, Catherine A.
Menkart, Deborah, jt. ed. see Sunshine, Catherine H.
Menke, E. Grand & Spinet Pianos. large type ed. 176p. (gr. 10 up). 1961. 23.49 (*0-317-01896-5*, 4-08980-00) Am Printing Hse.
Menken, John. Grandpa's Gizmos. Skaggs, Keith A., ed. Davis, Tim, illus. 28p. (Orig.). (gr. 2-6). 1992. pap. 4.95 (*0-89084-663-4*) Bob Jones Univ Pr.
Mennella, Roxanna. Roxanna Mennella, in Search of a Song, Vol. 6. Fisher, Barbara & Spiegel, Richard, eds. 40p. (Orig.). (gr. 4-7). 1984. pap. 2.00 (*0-934830-32-0*) Ten Penny.
—Roxanna Mennella, in Search of a Song: Inner Clockwork, Vol. 8. Fisher, Barbara, ed. (Illus.). 10p. (Orig.). (gr. 5-9). 1985. pap. 2.00 (*0-934830-36-3*) Ten Penny.
Mennella, Roxanna, jt. auth. see Wilkins, Sarah.
Mennella, Roxanna, et al. Fairies, Elves & Gnomes. (Illus.). 32p. (Orig.). (gr. 3-8). 1985. pap. 2.00x (*0-934830-38-X*, Dist. by Waterways Project) Ten Penny.
Mennen, Ingrid. One Round Moon & a Star for Me. Daly, Niki, illus. LC 93-9628. 32p. (ps-2). 1994. 14.95 (*0-531-06804-8*); PLB 14.99 (*0-531-08654-2*) Orchard Bks Watts.
Mennen, Ingrid & Daly, Niki. Somewhere in Africa. Maritz, Nicolaas, illus. LC 91-19379. 32p. (ps-3). 1992. 13.00 (*0-525-44848-9*, DCB) Dutton Child Bks.
Menning, Viiu. Great Dancers. Conkle, Nancy & Neary, D., illus. (Orig.). (gr. 8). 1978. pap. 3.95 (*0-88388-065-2*) Bellerophon Bks.
Menotti, Gian-Carlo. Amahl & the Night Visitors. Lemieux, Michele, illus. LC 84-27196. 64p. (ps up) 1986. 15.00 (*0-688-05426-9*); lib. bdg. 14.88 (*0-688-05427-7*, Morrow Jr Bks) Morrow Jr Bks.
Menten, Ted. Cut & Use Stencil Bunny Rabbit. 1985. pap. 4.95 (*0-486-24909-3*) Dover.
—Folk Art Cut & Use Stencils. 1985. pap. 4.95 (*0-486-24838-0*) Dover.
—Ships & Boats Punch Out Stencils. 1986. pap. 3.50 (*0-486-25049-0*) Dover.
—Teddy Bear-Cut & Use Stencils. 1983. pap. 4.95 (*0-486-24595-0*) Dover.
—Teddy Bear Punch Out Stencils. 1985. pap. 3.50 (*0-486-24832-1*) Dover.
Menten, Ted, compiled by. The Teddy Bear Lover's Postcard Book. (Illus.). 64p. (Orig.). 1988. pap. 7.95 (*0-89471-646-8*) Running Pr.
Menten, Theodore. Art Deco Cut & Use Stencils. 1977. pap. 4.95 (*0-486-23551-3*) Dover.
—Victorian Fashion Paper Dolls from Harper's Bazar, 1867-1898. 1979. pap. 3.95 (*0-486-23453-3*) Dover.
Menville, Douglas, jt. ed. see Reginald, R.
Menzel, Barbara J. Would You Rather? Brahm, Sumishta, illus. LC 81-6810. 32p. (ps-3). 1982. 16.95 (*0-89885-076-2*) Human Sci Pr.
Menzel-Gerrie, Sharon. Careers in Comedy. LC 93-4962. 1993. 13.95 (*0-8239-1517-4*); pap. 9.95 (*0-8239-1713-4*) Rosen Group.
Menzies, Linda. Teen's Guide to Business: The Secret to a Successful Enterprise. 1992. pap. 7.95 (*0-942361-50-4*) MasterMedia Ltd.

Menzies, Linda, et al. A Teen's Guide to Business: The Secrets to a Successful Enterprise. LC 93-30254. (gr. 9-12). 1993. 15.95 (*0-7862-0061-8*) Thorndike Pr.
Mercer, Deborah B., jt. auth. see Burkhart, Joyce L.
Mercer, Denis, tr. see Keckeis, M. B., et al.
Mercier, Sheryl, jt. auth. see Hoover, Evalyn.
Mercuri, Carmela. Toot-in-Time Band: Introducing Children to the World of Music. Smith, Robin A., illus. (gr. 1-6). 1993. pap. 10.95 (*0-935474-21-8*) Carousel Pub Corp.
Mercurio, Helen C. The Miracle Santa's Beard. Mercurio, Mary M., ed. Adjoian, Eva M., illus. 29p. 1985. 12.00 (*0-9616079-0-4*) Tiffany Pub.
Mercurio, Mary M., ed. see Mercurio, Helen C.
Meredith. Films & Special Effects. 32p. (gr. 6up). PLB 13.96 (*0-88110-164-8*); pap. 5.95 (*0-86020-749-8*) EDC.
Meredith Corporation-Better Homes & Gardens Staff. At the Circus. (Illus.). 32p. (ps-12). 1991. PLB 10.95 (*1-878363-57-3*) Forest Hse.
Meredith Corporation, Better Homes & Gardens Staff. At the Zoo. Meredith Corporation, Better Homes & Gardens Staff, illus. 32p. (ps-12). 1991. Repr. of 1989 ed. PLB 10.95 (*1-878363-30-1*) Forest Hse.
—Bird Buddies. Meredith Corporation, Better Homes & Gardens Staff, illus. 32p. (ps-12). 1991. Repr. of 1989 ed. PLB 10.95 (*1-878363-31-X*) Forest Hse.
Meredith Corporation-Better Homes & Gardens Staff. Let's Go Exploring. (Illus.). 32p. (ps-12). 1991. PLB 10.95 (*1-878363-58-1*) Forest Hse.
Meredith Corporation, Better Homes & Gardens Staff. Make Believe. Meredith Corporation, Better Homes & Gardens Staff, illus. 32p. (ps-12). 1991. Repr. of 1989 ed. PLB 10.95 (*1-878363-32-8*) Forest Hse.
—On the Farm. Meredith Corporation, Better Homes & Gardens Staff, illus. 32p. (ps-12). 1991. Repr. of 1989 ed. PLB 10.95 (*1-878363-33-6*) Forest Hse.
Meredith Corporation-Better Homes & Gardens Staff. Trains & Railroads. (Illus.). 32p. (ps-12). 1991. PLB 10.95 (*1-878363-59-X*) Forest Hse.
—Water Wonders. (Illus.). 32p. (ps-12). 1991. PLB 10.95 (*1-878363-60-3*) Forest Hse.
Meredith, Mary, ed. see Demou, Doris B.
Meredith, Paul, jt. auth. see Landin, Leslie.
Meredith, S. & Tahta, S. Starting Point Science, Vol. 3. (Illus.). 96p. (gr. 2-7). 1992. 11.95 (*0-7460-0970-4*, Usborne) EDC.
Meredith, S., jt. auth. see Gee, R.
Meredith, Sue. Why Are People Different? (Illus.). 24p. (gr. 1-5). 1993. lib. bdg. 11.96 (*0-88110-642-9*, Usborne); pap. 5.95 (*0-7460-1014-1*, Usborne) EDC.
Meredith, Susan H. Nature Walk. 2nd ed. Meredith, Susan H., illus. 25p. 1993. pap. text ed. 4.95 (*1-880666-09-X*) Oughten Hse.
—Wonder Walk. Meredith, Susan H., illus. 25p. (Orig.). 1993. pap. text ed. 4.95 (*1-880666-02-2*) Oughten Hse.
Meretzky, S. Eric. Zork: The Cavern of Doom, No. 3. Harris, Dell, illus. (gr. 4-6). 1984. pap. 1.95 (*0-8125-7985-2*, Pinnacle Bks) Tor Bks.
—Zork: The Malifestro Quest, No. 2. (Illus.). 127p. (gr. 4-6). 1984. pap. 1.95 (*0-8125-7980-1*, Pinnacle Bks) Tor Bks.
Merfield, LeAnn. Surrounded by Wild Hogs. Van Treese, James B., ed. 30p. 1993. pap. 6.95 (*1-56901-135-4*) NW Pub.
Merino, Jose M. The Gold of Dreams. Lane, Helen, tr. 224p. (gr. 7 up). 1992. 15.00 (*0-374-32692-4*) FS&G.
Merlin, Lester. Courage for a Cross, Teacher's Guide To. (gr. 1-6). 1987. pap. 9.95 (*0-377-00169-4*) Friendship Pr.
Mernit, Susan. Everything You Need to Know about Changing Schools. (gr. 7-12). 1992. PLB 13.95 (*0-8239-1326-0*) Rosen Group.
Merrell, Barbara. Sign of Death. (gr. 7 up). 1981. pap. 2.50 (*0-89083-781-3*) Zebra.
Merrell, James H. The Catawbas. Porter, Frank W., III, intro. by. (Illus.). 112p. (gr. 5 up). 1989. 17.95 (*1-55546-694-X*) Chelsea Hse.
Merrell, Karen D. Baptism. 24p. (ps-2). 1975. pap. 4.95 (*0-87747-559-8*) Deseret Bk.
—Joseph Smith. 24p. (ps-2). 1975. pap. 4.95 (*0-87747-561-X*) Deseret Bk.
—Prayer. 23p. (ps-2). 1975. pap. 4.95 (*0-87747-562-8*) Deseret Bk.
—Tithing. 22p. (ps-2). 1975. pap. 4.95 (*0-87747-560-1*) Deseret Bk.
Merriam, Eve. Blackberry Ink. Wilhelm, Hans, illus. LC 84-16633. 40p. (ps-2). 1985. 12.95 (*0-688-04150-7*); PLB 12.88 (*0-688-04151-5*, Morrow Jr Bks) Morrow Jr Bks.
—Chortles: New & Selected Wordplay Poems. Hamanaka, Sheila, illus. LC 88-29129. 64p. (gr. 3-7). 1989. 11.95 (*0-688-08152-5*); PLB 11.88 (*0-688-08153-3*, Morrow Jr Bks) Morrow Jr Bks.
—The Christmas Box. Small, David, illus. LC 85-5666. 32p. (ps-3). 1985. 12.95 (*0-688-05255-X*); lib. bdg. 12.88 (*0-688-05256-8*, Morrow Jr Bks) Morrow Jr Bks.
—Daddies at Work. Fernandes, Eugenie, illus. (ps-2). 1989. pap. 5.95 (*0-671-64873-X*, S&S BFYR) S&S Trade.
—Daddies at Work. Fernandes, Eugenie, illus. 32p. (ps-2). 1991. pap. 2.50 (*0-671-73276-5*, Little Simon) S&S Trade.
—Fighting Words. Small, David, illus. 32p. (gr. k up). 1992. 15.00 (*0-688-09676-X*); PLB 14.93 (*0-688-09677-8*) Morrow Jr Bks.

—Fresh Paint: New Poems. Frampton, David, illus. LC 85-23742. 48p. (gr. 5 up). 1986. RSBE 13.95 (*0-02-766860-6*, Macmillan Child Bk) Macmillan Child Grp.
—Goodnight to Annie. Schwartz, Carol, illus. LC 92-7111. 32p. (ps-1). 1992. Repr. of 1990 ed. 14.95 (*1-56282-205-5*); PLB 14.89 (*1-56282-206-3*) Hyprn Child.
—Halloween ABC. Smith, Lane, illus. LC 86-23772. 32p. (gr. k up). 1987. RSBE 14.95 (*0-02-766870-3*, Macmillan Child Bk) Macmillan Child Grp.
—Higgle Wiggle. Wilhelm, Hans, illus. LC 92-29795. 1994. write for info. (*0-688-11948-4*); PLB write for info. (*0-688-11949-2*) Morrow Jr Bks.
—The Inner City Mother Goose. LC 93-19735. (Illus.). 1994. pap. 15.00 (*0-671-88033-0*, S&S BFYR) S&S Trade.
—Jamboree. 96p. (Orig.). (ps-6). 1984. pap. 2.50 (*0-440-44199-4*, YB) Dell.
—Mommies at Work. Fernandes, Eugenie, illus. (ps-2). 1989. pap. 5.95 (*0-671-64386-X*, S&S BFYR) S&S Trade.
—Mommies at Work. (ps-3). 1991. pap. 2.50 (*0-671-73275-7*, Little Simon) S&S Trade.
—A Poem for a Pickle: Funnybone Verses. Hamanaka, Sheila, illus. LC 88-22047. 40p. (gr. k up). 1989. 12.95 (*0-688-08137-1*); PLB 12.88 (*0-688-08138-X*, Morrow Jr Bks) Morrow Jr Bks.
—Shhh! Hamanaka, Sheila, illus. LC 92-44110. (gr. 4 up). 1993. pap. 14.00 (*0-671-79816-2*, S&S BFYR) S&S Trade.
—The Singing Green: New & Selected Poems for All Seasons. Howell, Kathleen C., illus. LC 91-31205. 112p. (gr. 3 up). 1992. 14.00 (*0-688-11025-8*) Morrow Jr Bks.
—A Sky Full of Poems. Gaffney-Kessell, Walter, illus. (Orig.). (gr. k-6). 1986. pap. 3.25 (*0-440-47986-X*, YB) Dell.
—Train Leaves the Station. Gottlieb, Dale, illus. LC 91-28009. 32p. (ps-k). 1992. 14.95 (*0-8050-1934-0*, B Martin BYR) H Holt & Co.
—Twelve Ways to Get to Eleven. Karlin, Bernie, illus. LC 92-25810. 40p. (ps-1). 1993. pap. 14.00 JRT (*0-671-75544-7*, S&S BFYR) S&S Trade.
—Where Is Everybody? DeGroat, Diane, illus. LC 88-19800. (ps-1). 1992. pap. 14.95 jacketed (*0-671-64964-7*, S&S BFYR); pap. 4.95 (*0-671-77821-8*, S&S BFYR) S&S Trade.
—Wise Woman & Her Secret. LC 90-42406. 1991. pap. 13.95 (*0-671-72603-X*, S&S BFYR) S&S Trade.
—The Wise Woman & Her Secret. (gr. 3). 1991. write for info. (*0-663-56231-7*) Silver Burdett Pr.
—You Be Good & I'll Be Night: Jump-on-the-Bed-Poems. Schmidt, Karen L., illus. LC 87-24859. 40p. (ps-2). 1988. 13.95 (*0-688-06742-5*); PLB 13.88 (*0-688-06743-3*, Morrow Jr Bks) Morrow Jr Bks.
Merriam, Eve, retold by. That Noodlehead Epaminondas. (Illus.). 1992. pap. 8.95x (*0-89966-962-X*) Buccaneer Bks.
Merriam, Robert L. Abigail Challenges the Telephone Company. Merriam, Robert L., illus. 8p. (Orig.). (ps-6). 1972. pap. 1.50x (*0-686-32483-8*) R L Merriam.
—Santa Claus' Snack. Roberts, William, illus. 14p. (ps-6). 1970. pap. 2.00x (*0-686-32491-9*) R L Merriam.
Merriam-Webster Editorial Staff. Webster's Elementary Dictionary. (Illus.). (gr. 1-6). 1986. 14.95 (*0-87779-475-8*) Merriam-Webster Inc.
Merrians, Deborah. I Can Read About Earthquakes & Volcanoes. LC 74-24966. (Illus.). (gr. 2-4). 1975. pap. 1.95 (*0-89375-067-0*) Troll Assocs.
—I Can Read About Insects. Nodel, Norman, illus. LC 76-54493. (gr. 2-5). 1977. pap. 1.95 (*0-89375-040-9*) Troll Assocs.
—I Can Read About Spiders. McKeown, Gloria, illus. LC 76-54576. (gr. 2-5). 1977. pap. 1.95 (*0-89375-043-3*) Troll Assocs.
Merrick, Paul, ed. see Bureloff, Morris, et al.
Merrick, Sandra. Whole Language Units for Math. Vasconcelles, Keith & Fullam, Sue, illus. 144p. (ps-1). 1993. wkbk. 12.95 (*1-55734-200-8*) Tchr Create Mat.
Merrill, Arthur A. Battle of White Plains. (Illus.). (gr. 7 up). 1976. pap. 3.00 (*0-911894-27-6*) Analysis.
—Revolutionary War: An Outline & Calendar. (Illus.). (gr. 7 up). 1976. pap. 2.00 (*0-911894-35-7*) Analysis.
Merrill, Jean. The Girl Who Loved Caterpillars. Cooper, Floyd, illus. 32p. (ps up). 1992. PLB 14.95 (*0-399-21871-8*, Philomel Bks) Putnam Pub Group.
—The Pushcart War. 224p. 1987. pap. 3.99 (*0-440-47147-8*, YB) Dell.
—The Pushcart War. Solbert, Ronni, illus. LC 84-43131. 224p. (gr. 5-8). 1992. PLB 14.89 (*0-06-020822-8*) HarpC Child Bks.
—The Toothpaste Millionaire. Palmer, Jan, illus. LC 73-22055. 96p. (gr. 2-5). 1974. 13.95 (*0-395-18511-4*) HM.
—Toothpaste Millionaire. (gr. 4-7). 1993. pap. 4.95 (*0-395-66954-5*) HM.
Merrill, John N. Legends of Derbyshire. 2nd ed. Merrill, John N., illus. 71p. (Orig.). (gr. 6 up). 1975. pap. 3.00 (*0-913714-15-1*) Legacy Bks.
Merrill, Linda. The Princess & the Peacocks: Or, the Story of the Room. Dixon, Tennessee, illus. LC 92-72019. 32p. (gr. k-4). 1993. 14.95 (*1-56282-327-2*); PLB 14.89 (*1-56282-328-0*) Hyprn Child.

Merriman, Nick. Early Humans. King, Dave, photos by. LC 88-13431. (Illus.). 64p. (gr. 5 up). 1989. 15.00 (*0-394-82257-9*); lib. bdg. 15.99 (*0-394-92257-3*) Knopf Bks Yng Read.

Merrins. Golf for the Young. 1983. pap. 9.95 (*0-689-70659-6*, Atheneum) Macmillan.

Merrison, Lynne. Rice. Yeats, John, illus. 32p. (gr. 1-4). 1990. PLB 13.50 (*0-87614-417-2*) Carolrhoda Bks.

Merrison, Tim. Books. Stefoff, Rebecca, ed. LC 90-13868. (Illus.). 32p. (gr. 4-8). 1991. PLB 17.26 (*0-944483-96-8*) Garrett Ed Corp.

—Comics & Magazines. Stefoff, Rebecca, ed. LC 90-13985. (Illus.). 32p. (gr. 4-8). 1991. PLB 17.26 (*0-944483-97-6*) Garrett Ed Corp.

—Field Athletics. LC 90-27451. (Illus.). 48p. (gr. 5-6). 1991. RSBE 13.95 (*0-89686-665-3*, Crestwood Hse) Macmillan Child Grp.

—Movies. Stefoff, Rebecca, ed. LC 90-3964. (Illus.). 32p. (gr. 4-8). 1991. PLB 17.26 (*0-944483-94-1*) Garrett Ed Corp.

Merrison, Tim, jt. auth. see Sandelson, Robert.

Merriss, William E. & Griswold, David H. A Composition Handbook. 3rd ed. 1985. tchr's. guide 10. 84 (*0-8013-0074-6*, 75738); pap. text ed. 17.28 (*0-88334-186-7*, 76152) Longman.

Merton, D. & Yun-Kan, Shio. China: The Land & Its People. rev. ed. LC 85-72107. (Illus.). 48p. (gr. 5 up). 1991. PLB 16.98 (*0-382-24242-4*) Silver Burdett Pr.

Mervan, Leroy. Your First Gerbil. (Illus.). 34p. (Orig.). 1991. pap. 1.95 (*0-86622-063-1*, YF-037) TFH Pubns.

Merveille, David. Thomas the Circus Boy. Merveille, David, illus. 32p. (ps-1). 1993. PLB 14.95 (*0-8050-2953-2*, Bks Young Read) H Holt & Co.

Merwin, Richard. Mega-Slank from Titanium. LC 92-12842. (gr. 2). 1992. 13.99 (*1-56239-151-8*) Abdo & Dghtrs.

Meryl, Debra. Baby's Peek-a-Boo Album. Kelley, True, illus. 24p. (ps). 1989. 11.95 (*0-448-15375-0*, G&D) Putnam Pub Group.

Meryman, Richard. Andrew Wyeth. (Illus.). 92p. (gr. 7 up). 1991. 19.95 (*0-8109-3956-8*) Abrams.

Meschel, Susan V., jt. auth. see Handler, Andrew.

Meservy, Jay. The Terrible, Horrible, Awful, Deplorable, Lovable, Little Troll. Lucas, Sheila, illus. LC 91-41387. 32p. (ps-2). 1992. pap. 6.95 (*0-89802-586-9*) Beautiful Am.

Mesner, Susan, jt. ed. see Davison, Rebecca.

Messenger, Jannat. Lullaby & Goodnight: A Bedtime Book with Music. Messenger, Jannat, illus. 12p. (ps-1). 1988. POB 10.95 (*0-689-71268-5*, Aladdin) Macmillan Child Grp.

—Twinkle Twinkle Little Star: A Lullaby Book with Lights & Music. Messenger, Jannat, illus. 12p. (ps-1). 1987. bds. 10.95 (*0-689-71136-0*, Aladdin) Macmillan Child Grp.

Messenger, Norman. Annabel's House. LC 88-60089. (Illus.). 28p. 1989. 18.95 (*0-531-05764-X*) Orchard Bks Watts.

—Making Faces. (Illus.). 16p. 1993. 14.95 (*1-56458-111-X*) Dorling Kindersley.

Messent, Jan. Wool 'n Magic: Creative Uses of Yarn... Knitting, Crochet, Embroidery. Dawson, Pam, ed. Search Press Studios Staff, illus. 144p. 1989. 32.95 (*0-85532-614-X*, Pub. by Search Pr UK) A Schwartz & Co.

Messerly, Laura. The Weirdest, Wackiest, Craziest Practical Joke Book in the Universe. Tisserand, Rose-Ann & Huculak, Greg, illus. LC 90-24598. 96p. (gr. 2-10). 1991. pap. 3.95 (*0-8069-8258-6*) Sterling.

Messick, Linda S. Through My Day with the 'L', 'R', 'S', 'SH' Sounds, 4 bks. (Illus.). (gr. k-6). 1975. Set. pap. text ed. 24.50x (*0-87015-218-1*) Pacific Bks.

—Through My Day with the 'L' Sound. (Illus.). 120p. (Orig.). (gr. k-6). 1975. pap. text ed. 6.95x (*0-87015-212-2*) Pacific Bks.

—Through My Day with the 'R' Sound. (Illus.). 112p. (Orig.). (gr. k-6). 1975. pap. text ed. 6.95x (*0-87015-213-0*) Pacific Bks.

—Through My Day with the 'S' Sound. (Illus.). 120p. (Orig.). (gr. k-6). 1975. pap. text ed. 6.95x (*0-87015-214-9*) Pacific Bks.

—Through My Day with the 'SH' Sound. (Illus.). 112p. (Orig.). (gr. k-6). 1975. pap. text ed. 6.95x (*0-87015-215-7*) Pacific Bks.

Messina, Kathlyn & Dacquino, Vinny. Proud That I'm Still Me. Maley, Matthew & Benjamin, Ann, illus. LC 92-70002. 21p. (Orig.). (ps-5). 1992. pap. 7.95 shrinkwrapped (*0-910569-05-3*) Hampton Court Pub.

Messmer, Barbara A. The Starshiners & the Gloomies. 1991. 7.95 (*0-533-08634-5*) Vantage.

Meston, Zach & Arnold, J. Douglas. Awesome Sega Genesis Secrets 4. (Illus.). 352p. 1994. pap. 11.95 (*0-9624676-2-6*) Sandwich Islands.

Metaxas, Eric. David & Goliath. Fraser, Douglas, illus. 40p. (gr. k up). 1993. incl. cass. 19.95 (*0-88708-295-5*, Rabbit Ears); 14.95 (*0-88708-294-7*, Rabbit Ears) Picture Bk Studio.

—The Fool & the Flying Ship. Drescher, Henrik, illus. LC 91-40669. 40p. (gr. k up). 1992. pap. 14.95 (*0-88708-228-9*, Rabbit Ears); incl. cass. 19.95 (*0-88708-229-7*, Rabbit Ears) Picture Bk Studio.

—Jack & the Beanstalk. Sorel, Ed, illus. LC 91-14176. 40p. (gr. k up). 1991. pap. 14.95 (*0-88708-188-6*, Rabbit Ears); incls. cassette 19.95 (*0-88708-189-4*, Rabbit Ears) Picture Bk Studio.

—King Midas & the Golden Touch. Prato, Rodica, illus. LC 91-40670. 40p. (gr. k up). 1992. pap. 14.95 (*0-88708-234-3*, Rabbit Ears); incl. cass. 19.95 (*0-88708-235-1*, Rabbit Ears) Picture Bk Studio.

—Puss in Boots. Le-Tan, Pierre, illus. LC 92-7789. 40p. 1992. pap. 14.95 (*0-88708-285-8*, Rabbit Ears); pap. 19.95 incl. cass. (*0-88708-286-6*, Rabbit Ears) Picture Bk Studio.

Metaxas, Eric, jt. ed. see Harris, Joel C.

Metaxas, Eric, tr. see Andersen, Hans Christian.

Metaxas, Eric, tr. see Grimm, Jacob & Grimm, Wilhelm K.

Metcalf, Calvin S. Voices from the Bible: Dramatic Monologs in Worship. LC 90-53277. (Illus.). 144p. (Orig.). 1990. pap. 9.95 (*0-916260-70-4*, B173) Meriwether Pub.

Metcalf, Doris. African Americans: Their Impact on U. S. History. (Illus.). 240p. (gr. 5-9). 1992. 15.95 (*0-86653-670-1*, GA1345) Good Apple.

Metcalf, Doris & Marson, Ron. Rocks & Minerals. Marson, Peg, illus. 88p. (gr. 7-12). 1989. tchr's. ed. 15. 70 (*0-941008-23-1*) Tops Learning.

Metcalf, Florence E. A Peek at Japan: A Lighthearted Look at Japan's Language & Culture. 2nd, rev. ed. Tomoko, illus. 133p. (gr. 1-5). 1992. pap. text ed. 14. 95 (*0-9631684-3-6*) Metco Pub.

Metcalf, Rosamond S. The Sugar Maple. Hearn, James, photos by. LC 82-595. (Illus.). 40p. (gr. 3-5). 1982. pap. 3.50x (*0-914016-87-3*) Phoenix Pub.

Metil, Luana & Townsend, Jace. The Story of Karate: From Ancient Legends to Modern Heroes. LC 93-32006. 1994. 18.95 (*0-8225-3325-1*) Lerner Pubns.

Metos, Thomas H. Communicable Diseases. (Illus.). 96p. (gr. 4-9). 1987. PLB 10.90 (*0-531-10380-3*) Watts.

—The Human Mind: How We Think & Learn. (Illus.). 128p. (gr. 9-12). 1990. PLB 13.40 (*0-531-10885-6*) Watts.

Metoyer, Patrick G. I'm Rattle-Me-Bones III, Esquire. Manchee, Bruce N., illus. LC 87-90349. 24p. (Orig.). (gr. 1-6). 1988. pap. 3.95 (*0-944523-02-1*) Western Slope Pubns.

—No Bones! No Bones! Manchee, Bruce N., illus. LC 87-90350. 24p. (Orig.). (gr. k-2). 1988. pap. 3.95 (*0-944523-03-X*) Western Slope Pubns.

Metropolitan Museum of Art Staff. Baby's First Year Calendar. Franc-Nohain, Marie M., illus. 24p. 1984. pap. 9.95 (*0-684-18258-0*, Scribners Young Read) Macmillan Child Grp.

—Fun with Hieroglyphs Stationary. 1991. 12.95 (*0-670-84207-9*) Viking Child Bks.

—Go in & out the Window: An Illustrated Songbook for Children. Marks, Claude, commentary by. LC 87-752208. (Illus.). 144p. (gr. k up). 1987. 24.95 (*0-8050-0628-1*, Bks Young Read) H Holt & Co.

Metten, Patricia. The Power of Attitude. LC 81-50865. (gr. k-7). lib. bdg. write for info. (*0-911712-91-7*) Eagle Mktg Corp.

—The Power of Being Creative. LC 81-50863. (gr. k-7). lib. bdg. write for info. (*0-911712-89-5*) Eagle Mktg Corp.

—The Power of Family. LC 81-50867. (gr. k-7). lib. bdg. write for info. (*0-911712-93-3*) Eagle Mktg Corp.

Metter, Bert. Bar Mitzvah, Bat Mitzvah: How Jewish Boys & Girls Come of Age. Friedman, Marvin, illus. LC 83-23230. 64p. (Orig.). (gr. 4 up). 1984. (Clarion Bks) HM.

Mettger, Zak. Till Victory Is Won: Black Soldiers in the Civil War. (Illus.). 96p. (gr. 5-9). 1994. 16.99 (*0-525-67412-8*, Lodestar Bks) Dutton Child Bks.

Mettler, Rene. The Rain Forest. (Illus.). 24p. (ps-2). 1994. 11.95 (*0-590-47728-5*, Cartwheel) Scholastic Inc.

Mettler, Rene, illus. Birds. Jeunesse, Gallimard, et al. LC 92-15956. (Illus.). 1993. 10.95 (*0-590-46367-5*) Scholastic Inc.

—Flowers. Jeunesse, Gallimard, created by. LC 92-15957. (Illus.). 1993. 10.95 (*0-590-46383-7*) Scholastic Inc.

Metzger, Barbara, jt. auth. see Schlank, Carol H.

Metzger, Lois. Barry's Sister. LC 91-23738. 240p. (gr. 5 up). 1992. SBE 15.95 (*0-689-31521-X*, Atheneum Child Bk) Macmillan Child Grp.

—Barry's Sister. LC 93-7760. 240p. (gr. 5 up). 1993. pap. 4.50 (*0-14-036484-6*, Puffin) Puffin Bks.

Metzler, Rosemary M. Snooty the Fox. 28p. 1993. pap. write for info. (*0-9637381-0-0*) Snooty Prods.

Metzner, Seymour. One-Minute Game Guide. LC 67-29157. (gr. 1-6). 1968. pap. 5.95 (*0-8224-5070-4*) Fearon Teach Aids.

Metzner, Seymour, jt. auth. see Sharp, Richard M.

Meuli, Judith, jt. auth. see Carabillo, Toni.

Meyer, Alice, jt. auth. see Meyer, David.

Meyer, Alice, jt. ed. see Meyer, David.

Meyer, Carolyn. Because of Lissa. (gr. 7 up). 1990. pap. 2.95 (*0-553-28802-4*, Starfire) Bantam.

—Gillian's Choice. 1991. pap. 2.95 (*0-553-28835-0*) Bantam.

—Killing the Kudu. LC 90-6089. 208p. (gr. 9 up). 1990. SBE 14.95 (*0-689-50508-6*, M K McElderry) Macmillan Child Grp.

—The Problem with Sidney. (gr. 7 up). 1990. pap. 2.95 (*0-553-28803-2*, Starfire) Bantam.

—The Two Faces of Adam. 1991. pap. 2.99 (*0-553-28859-8*) Bantam.

—A Voice from Japan: An Outsider Looks In. (Illus.). 212p. (gr. 7 up). 1988. 14.95 (*0-15-200633-8*, Gulliver Bks) HarBrace.

—Voice from Japan: An Outsider Looks In. 1992. pap. 9.95 (*0-15-200634-6*) HarBrace.

—Voices of Northern Ireland: Growing up in a Troubled Land. LC 87-199. (Illus.). 212p. (gr. 7 up). 1987. 15. 95 (*0-15-200635-4*, Gulliver Bks) HarBrace.

—Voices of Northern Ireland: Growing up in a Troubled Land. 1992. pap. 9.95 (*0-15-200636-2*) HarBrace.

—Voices of Northern Ireland: Growing Up in a Troubled Land. (gr. 7 up). 1992. pap. 9.95 (*0-15-200638-9*) HarBrace.

—Voices of South Africa: Growing up in a Troubled Land. LC 86-45059. 244p. (gr. 7 up). 1986. 16.95 (*0-15-200637-0*) HarBrace.

—Where the Broken Heart Still Beats. LC 92-257. (gr. 4-7). 1992. pap. write for info. (*0-15-295602-6*) HarBrace.

—Where the Broken Heart Still Beats. LC 92-257. (gr. 4-7). 1992. write for info. (*0-15-200639-7*) HarBrace.

—White Lilacs. LC 92-30503. 1993. write for info. (*0-15-200641-9*) HarBrace.

—White Lilacs. (gr. 4-7). 1993. pap. 3.95 (*0-15-295876-2*, HB Juv Bks) HarBrace.

Meyer, Carolyn & Gallenkamp, Charles. The Mystery of the Ancient Maya. LC 84-24209. (Illus.). 160p. (gr. 7 up). 1985. SBE 14.95 (*0-689-50319-9*, M K McElderry) Macmillan Child Grp.

Meyer, Carolyn & Pickens, Kel. Sing & Learn. Hayes, Steve, illus. 144p. (ps-3). 1989. wkbk. 11.95 (*0-86653-476-8*, GA1078) Good Apple.

Meyer, Charles R. How to Be a Juggler. (Illus.). (gr. 4-7). 1977. 6.95 (*0-679-20407-5*) McKay.

Meyer, David & Meyer, Alice. The Ten Commandments: An Illustrated Bible Passage for Young Children. Katsma, Candi, illus. LC 90-71557. 40p. (Orig.). (ps-4). 1991. pap. 11.95 incl. cassette (*1-879099-02-0*) Thy Word.

Meyer, David & Meyer, Alice, eds. First Corinthians Thirteen: An Illustrated Bible Chapter for Young Children. DeWind, June & Katsma, Candi, illus. LC 90-71555. 48p. (Orig.). (ps-4). 1990. pap. 12.95 incl. cassette (*1-879099-01-2*) Thy Word.

—Isaiah Fifty-Three: An Illustrated Bible Chapter for Young Children. Katsma, Candi, illus. LC 91-90827. 40p. (Orig.). (ps-4). 1992. pap. 11.95 incl. cassette (*1-879099-06-3*) Thy Word.

—The Lord's Prayer: An Illustrated Bible Passage for Young Children. Katsma, Candi, illus. LC 91-90826. 32p. (Orig.). (ps-4). 1991. pap. 10.95 incl. cassette (*1-879099-05-5*) Thy Word.

—Psalm One Hundred Thirty-Nine: An Illustrated Bible Chapter for Young Children. Crews, Terry, illus. LC 91-90825. 48p. (Orig.). (ps-4). 1991. pap. 12.95 incl. cassette (*1-879099-03-9*) Thy Word.

—Psalm Twenty-Three: An Illustrated Bible Chapter for Young Children. Katsma, Candi, illus. 32p. (Orig.). (ps-4). 1990. pap. 9.95 incl. cassette (*1-879099-00-4*) Thy Word.

Meyer, Henye. The Exiles of Crocodile Island. Dershowitz, Yosef, illus. 224p. (gr. 6-12). 1984. 12.95 (*0-89906-772-7*); pap. 9.95 (*0-89906-773-5*) Mesorah Pubns.

Meyer, Kathleen. Little Bear Finds a Friend. Boerke, Carole, illus. 32p. (gr. k-2). 1991. pasted 2.50 (*0-87403-815-4*, 24-03915) Standard Pub.

Meyer, Kathleen A. Bear, Your Manners Are Showing. Creative Studios 1, Inc. Staff, illus. 32p. (gr. k-2). 1987. 2.50 (*0-87403-271-7*, 3771) Standard Pub.

—Father Serra: Traveler on the Golden Chain. LC 89-63335. (Illus.). 72p. (Orig.). 1990. 9.95 (*0-87973-139-7*); pap. 6.50 (*0-87973-141-9*) Our Sunday Visitor.

—God Sends the Seasons. McIlrath, James, illus. LC 81-80712. 32p. (ps-2). 1981. 7.50 (*0-87973-668-2*, 668) Our Sunday Visitor.

—Little Bear's Big Adventure. Boerke, Carole, illus. 32p. (gr. k-2). 1990. pasted 2.50 (*0-87403-706-9*, 24-03906) Standard Pub.

—Tul-Tok-A-Na: The Small One. Hardgrove, Tanya, illus. 32p. (Orig.). (gr. 1-5). 1992. pap. 6.95 (*0-89992-105-1*) Coun India Ed.

Meyer, Linda D. Harriet Tubman: They Called Me Moses. Kerstetter, J., illus. LC 87-43308. 32p. (Orig.). (ps-4). 1988. lib. bdg. 16.95 (*0-943990-33-5*); pap. 5.95 (*0-943990-32-7*) Parenting Pr.

—I Take Good Care of Me! I Take Good Care of Us! Peaker, Denelle, illus. Meyer, Linda D., intro. by. (Illus.). 64p. (Orig.). (ps-4). 1987. pap. 2.95 (*0-9603516-9-8*) Franklin Pr Wa.

—Safety Zone: A Book Teaching Children Abduction Prevention Skills. Megale, Marina & Walsh, John. (Illus.). 32p. (Orig.). (gr. k-6). 1984. PLB 9.00 (*0-9603516-8-X*) Franklin Pr WA.

Meyer, Linda D., ed. see Buschman, Janis & Hunley, Debbie.

Meyer, Linda D., ed. see Hubbard, Kate & Berlin, Evelyn.

Meyer, Linda D., ed. see Jance, Judy.

Meyer, Mary. Fahrenheit 451: A Study Guide. 1984. tchr's. ed. & wkbk. 14.95 (*0-88122-114-7*) LRN Links.

Meyer, Miriam W. The Blind Guards of Easter Island. LC 77-14528. (Illus.). 48p. (gr. 4 up). 1983. PLB 18.64 (*0-8172-1048-2*) Raintree Steck-V.

Meyer, Nancy. Endangered Species Coloring-Learning Books Adventure Series. Meyer, George, illus. (ps-3). 1993. write for info. (*1-883408-05-9*) Meyer Pub FL.

ENDANGERED SPECIES COLORING/LEARNING BOOKS... ADVENTURE SERIES teaches children the importance of protecting our endangered species. Each adventure story is factorial & details the dangers the animal faces, not only from man, but from nature, & what are we doing to help protect the animal from extinction. The stories are action packed & recommended for preschoolers to age eight. The pictures are large & fun to color challenging children's creative ability & continuing to make learning fun. The book includes 16 pages plus a colorful cover which depicts the endangered species in its natural habitat. The series is written so that our children will grow up with an insight into the plight of our wildlife giving them a concern & caring nature for all living things. Titles include: The Adventures of Mortie the Manatee (1-883408-00-8), The Adventures of Susie the Green Sea Turtle (1-883408-01-6), The Adventures of Wally the Right Whale (1-883408-02-4), The Adventures of Dimples the Dolphin (1-883408-03-2), The Adventures of Peter the Florida Panther (1-883408-04-0). Retail Price $4.50 each. Order from: Meyer Publishing, Inc., 10991-55 San Jose Blvd., Suite 149, Jacksonville, FL 32223.
Publisher Provided Annotation.

Meyer, Nicholas E. Magic in the Dark: A Young Viewer's History of the Movies. (Illus.). 292p. (gr. 5-11). 1985. 17.95x (*0-8160-1256-3*) Facts on File.

Meyer, Rich. Thieves of Tharbad. (Illus.). 36p. (gr. 10-12). 1985. 7.00 (*0-915795-35-3*, 8050) Iron Crown Ent Inc.

Meyer, Susan E. Mary Cassatt. (Illus.). 80p. (gr. 7 up). 1990. 19.95 (*0-8109-3154-0*) Abrams.

Meyer, Ursula & Wolfson, Alice. Abenteuer in Deutschland. (Illus.). (gr. 9-12). 1976. pap. text ed. 4.75 (*0-88345-276-6*, 18485) Prentice ESL.
—Workbook in Everyday German. (gr. 9-10). 1976. pap. text ed. 4.75 (*0-88345-277-4*, 18600); pap. text ed. 14.55 (*0-13-965138-1*) Prentice ESL.

Meyer, Verne, jt. auth. see Sebranek, Patrick.

Meyerowitz, Joel. George Balanchine's the Nutcracker. (Illus.). 1993. 29.95 (*0-316-56921-6*) Little.

Meyers, Arthur. The Cheyenne. (Illus.). 64p. (gr. 5-8). 1992. pap. 5.95 (*0-531-15636-2*) Watts.

Meyers, Carole T. Miles of Smiles: One Hundred One Great Car Games & Activities. (Illus.). 128p. (Orig.). 1992. pap. 8.95 (*0-917120-11-6*) Carousel Pr.

Meyers, Madeleine, intro. by. Cherokee Nation: Life Before the Tears. (Illus.). 64p. (Orig.). (gr. 5-12). 1993. pap. 4.95 (*1-878668-26-9*) Disc Enter Ltd.
—Forward into Light: The Struggle for Women's Suffrage. (Illus.). 64p. (Orig.). (gr. 5-12). 1994. pap. 4.95 (*1-878668-25-0*) Disc Enter Ltd.

Meyers, Marsha A. A Child's Fear: Vision of Hope. 1993. pap. 12.95 (*0-9637083-9-2*) Myi-Way Prod. A Child Begs To Stay Home From School. Debbie's Sick. No Stomach Ache. No Sore Throat. She's Sick With Fear. An Epidemic Of Fear Has Gripped The Children Of Freedom Elementary School. Learning On The Inner City Campus Is An Impossibility As Neighborhood Children Are Dropping Dead Victims Of Drive By Shooting. Education Is A Must. The School Officials At Freedom Elementary School Are Helpless To Stop The Violence. The Police Are Burned Out & Confused. Debbie Sparks A Class Discussion In Which Students Agree To Form An "Anti-Gang" Named VISION OF HOPE, To Confront The Various Youth "Sets" That Are Terrorizing The Community. The Idea Snowballs When Teachers,

Police & Parents Follow The Children's Lead. But It Takes A CHILD'S FEAR To Overcome Helplessness & Become A Beacon By Which A Path Of Hope Is Lit. A CHILD'S FEAR Is A Gripping Tale Of Faith Overcoming Despair & Optimism Overcoming Apathy. MYI-WAY PRODUCTIONS, P.O. BOX 203, HAWTHORNE, CA. 90251-0203. PHONE: 310-973-1625.
Publisher Provided Annotation.

Meyers, Odette. The Enchanted Umbrella: With a Short History of the Umbrella. Zemach, Margot, illus. 28p. (ps-3). 1988. 13.95 (*0-15-200448-3*, Gulliver Bks) HarBrace.

Meyers, Susan. Insect Zoo. Hewett, Richard, photos by. (Illus.). 48p. (gr. 3-7). 1991. 16.95 (*0-525-67325-3*, Lodestar Bks) Dutton Child Bks.
—P. J. Clover, Private Eye: The Case of the Halloween Hoot. Fiammenghi, Gioia, illus. 128p. (gr. 4-6). 1990. 13.95 (*0-525-67297-4*, Lodestar Bks) Dutton Child Bks.

Meyers, Susan, ed. see Koosman, Jerry.

Meyrick, Bette. Invasion! 70p. 1991. pap. 23.00x (*0-86383-773-5*, Pub. by Gomer Pr UK) St Mut.

Meyrick, Kathryn. Hazel's Healthy Halloween. LC 90-46517. 1989. 11.95 (*0-85953-296-8*); pap. 5.95 (*0-85953-308-5*) Childs Play.
—The Lost Music: Gustav Mole's War on Noise. LC 91-33555. (Illus.). (ps-5). 1992. 11.95 (*0-85953-304-2*); pap. 5.95 (*0-85953-327-1*) Childs Play.
—Musical Life of Gustav Mole. LC 90-49100. (ps-3). 1990. 11.95 (*0-85953-303-4*); pap. 5.95 (*0-85953-347-6*) Childs Play.

Meyzlisch, Saul, ed. A Child's Passover Haggadah. (Illus.). 76p. (gr. 1-6). 1987. 9.95 (*0-915361-70-1*) Modan-Adama Bks.

Miasek, Meryl A., ed. see Miller, Heather S.

Micallef, Mary. Floods & Droughts. Micallef, Mary, illus. 48p. (gr. 4-8). 1985. wkbk. 6.95 (*0-86653-323-0*, GA 632) Good Apple.
—Listening: The Basic Connection. Micallef, Mary, illus. 96p. (gr. 3-8). 1984. wkbk. 9.95 (*0-86653-188-2*, GA 555) Good Apple.
—Storms & Blizzards. Micallef, Mary, illus. 48p. (gr. 4-8). 1985. wkbk. 6.95 (*0-86653-321-4*, GA 683) Good Apple.

Michael, Duncan. How Skyscrapers Are Made. (Illus.). 32p. (gr. 5-12). 1987. 12.95x (*0-8160-1692-5*) Facts on File.

Michael, Emory H. Androcles & the Lion. Hatchem, Mia, illus. LC 87-51492. 44p. (gr. k-4). 1988. 6.95 (*1-55523-132-2*) Winston-Derek.

Michael, Linda. Big As Texas: The A to Z Tour of Texas Cities & Places. Lowdermilk, Karen, ed. Lewis, Patrick, illus. LC 87-36793. 64p. (gr. k-3). 1988. pap. 6.95 (*0-937460-34-6*) Hendrick-Long.

Michael, ed. see Schneider, D. Douglas.

Michaels, Fran. Mr. Wonderful. 192p. (Orig.). (gr. 7-12). 1987. pap. 2.50 (*0-553-26340-4*) Bantam.

Michaels, Judy, jt. auth. see Stevens, Jared.

Michaels, Scott, ed. Freddy & Betty, Vol. 1. Morton, Tom, illus. (gr. 1-6). 1989. tchr's. ed. 2.50 (*0-317-93682-4*) S Michaels Pub.

Michaels, Serge, jt. auth. see Uchitel, Sandra.

Michaels, Ski. The Baseball Bat. Guzzi, George, illus. LC 85-14065. 48p. (Orig.). (gr. 1-3). 1986. PLB 10.59 (*0-8167-0596-8*); pap. text ed. 3.50 (*0-8167-0597-6*) Troll Assocs.
—The Big Surprise. Paterson, Diane, illus. LC 85-14017. 48p. (gr. 1-3). 1986. PLB 10.59 (*0-8167-0576-3*); pap. text ed. 3.50 (*0-8167-0577-1*) Troll Assocs.
—Felix, the Funny Fox. Mahan, Ben, illus. LC 85-14097. 48p. (Orig.). (gr. 1-3). 1986. PLB 10.59 (*0-8167-0590-9*); pap. text ed. 3.50 (*0-8167-0591-7*) Troll Assocs.
—Fun in the Sun. Paterson, Diane, illus. LC 85-14055. 48p. (Orig.). (gr. 1-3). 1986. PLB 10.59 (*0-8167-0568-2*); pap. text ed. 3.50 (*0-8167-0569-0*) Troll Assocs.
—Mystery of the Missing Fuzzy. Smolinski, Dick, illus. LC 85-14084. 48p. (Orig.). (gr. 1-3). 1986. PLB 10.59 (*0-8167-0646-8*); pap. text ed. 3.50 (*0-8167-0647-6*) Troll Assocs.
—Mystery of the Windy Meadow. Atkinson, Allen, illus. LC 85-14019. 48p. (Orig.). (gr. 1-3). 1986. PLB 10.59 (*0-8167-0630-1*); pap. text ed. 3.50 (*0-8167-0631-X*) Troll Assocs.
—One Hundred Two Animal Jokes. LC 91-30061. (Illus.). 64p. (gr. 2-6). 1991. pap. text ed. 2.95 (*0-8167-2613-2*) Troll Assocs.
—One Hundred Two Creepy, Crawly Bug Jokes. Michaels, Ski, illus. LC 91-14254. 64p. (gr. 2-6). 1992. pap. text ed. 2.95 (*0-8167-2745-7*) Troll Assocs.
—One Hundred Two Haunted House Jokes. LC 91-21891. (Illus.). 64p. (gr. 2-6). 1991. pap. 2.95 (*0-8167-2578-0*) Troll Assocs.
—Something New to Do. Palmer, Jan, illus. LC 85-14021. 48p. (Orig.). (gr. 1-3). 1986. PLB 10.59 (*0-8167-0634-4*); pap. text ed. 3.50 (*0-8167-0635-2*) Troll Assocs.

—Wake up, Sam! Garry-McCord, Kathi, illus. LC 85-14115. 48p. (Orig.). (gr. 1-3). 1986. PLB 10.59 (*0-8167-0580-1*); pap. text ed. 3.50 (*0-8167-0581-X*) Troll Assocs.

Michaels, William. Clare & Her Shadow. Michaels, William, illus. LC 90-8487. 32p. (ps-k). 1991. lib. bdg. 15.00 (*0-208-02301-1*, Linnet) Shoe String.

Michals, Duane. Upside down, Inside Out, & Backwards. 80p. Date not set. pap. 19.95 (*0-685-68802-X*) Sonny Boy Bks.

Michalski, Tilman, jt. auth. see Michalski, Ute.

Michalski, Ute & Michalski, Tilman. Wind Crafts. LC 89-49553. (Illus.). 64p. 1991. 19.93 (*0-516-09258-8*); pap. 8.95 (*0-516-49258-6*) Childrens.

Michel, Francois. Water. Larvor, Yves, illus. LC 92-9715. 1993. write for info. (*0-688-11427-X*) Lothrop.

Michel, Sandra S., ed. see Smith, Viola B.

Michels, Penny & Tropea, Judith. A Day in the Life of a Beekeeper. Halpern, John, photos by. LC 90-11078. (Illus.). 32p. (gr. 4-8). 1991. lib. bdg. 11.79 (*0-8167-2206-4*); pap. text ed. 2.95 (*0-8167-2207-2*) Troll Assocs.

Michels, Tilde. At the Frog Pond. Ignatowicz, Nina, tr. from GER. Michl, Reinhard, illus. LC 88-37835. 32p. (ps-4). 1989. (Lipp Jr Bks) HarpC Child Bks.
—Rabbit Spring. Bhend, Kathi, illus. LC 87-18107. 96p. (gr. 1-4). 1990. pap. 2.95 (*0-679-80153-7*) Knopf Bks Yng Read.
—Rabbit Spring. James, J. Alison & Bhend, Kathi, illus. LC 87-18107. 85p. (gr. 2-6). 1989. 11.95 (*0-15-200568-4*, Gulliver Bks) HarBrace.
—Sophie the Rag Picker. Michels, Tilde, illus. (gr. k-1). 1962. 10.95 (*0-8392-3036-2*) Astor-Honor.
—Who's That Knocking at My Door? Michl, Reinhard, illus. 28p. (ps-3). 1986. 10.95 (*0-8120-5732-5*) Barron.
—Who's That Knocking at My Door? Michl, Reinhard, illus. 28p. (ps-3). 1992. pap. 4.95 (*0-8120-1486-3*) Barron.

Michelson, Richard. Did You Say Ghosts? Baskin, Leonard, illus. LC 92-30134. 32p. (ps up). 1993. RSBE 14.95 (*0-02-766915-7*, Macmillan Child Bk) Macmillan Child Grp.

Michelson, Sonia. New Dimensions in Classical Guitar for Children. 1993. 7.95 (*0-685-63855-3*, 94537); cass. 9.98 (*0-685-63856-1*, 94537) Mel Bay.

Michener, Dorothy & Muschlitz, Beverly. Bulletin Board Bonanza. (Illus.). 96p. (gr. 2-6). 1981. pap. 7.95 (*0-86530-028-3*, IP-283) Incentive Pubns.

Michener, J. A. South Pacific. Hague, M., ed. 1992. write for info. (*0-15-200618-4*, Gulliver Bks) HarBrace.

Michener, James A. The Eagle & the Raven. Shaw, Charles, illus. LC 90-9684. 228p. 1990. 19.95 (*0-938349-57-0*); ltd. ed. o.p. 100.00 (*0-938349-58-9*) State House Pr.

Michio Hoshino. The Grizzly Bear Family Book. Colligan-Taylor, Karen, tr. from JPN. (Illus.). 52p. (gr. 2 up). 1993. 15.95 (*0-88708-309-9*) Picture Bk Studio.

Michunas, Lynn. Kalculator Kids. 64p. (gr. 3-7). 1982. 7.95 (*0-86653-076-2*, GA 410) Good Apple.

Micklethwait, Lucy, selected by. A Child's Book of Art: Great Pictures, First Words. LC 93-54320. (Illus.). 64p. (gr. k up). 1993. 16.95 (*1-56458-203-5*) Dorling Kindersley.
—I Spy a Lion: Animals in Art. LC 93-30017. 1994. write for info. (*0-688-13230-8*); PLB write for info. (*0-688-13231-6*) Greenwillow.
—I Spy: An Alphabet in Art. LC 91-42212. (Illus.). 1992. 19.00 (*0-688-11679-5*) Greenwillow.

Micklethwait, Lucy, selected by. & created by. I Spy Two Eyes: Numbers in Art. LC 92-35641. (Illus.). 48p. (ps-3). 1993. 19.00 (*0-688-12640-5*); PLB 18.93 (*0-688-12642-1*) Greenwillow.

Micklos, John, Jr. Leonard Nimoy: A Stars Trek. LC 87-32457. (Illus.). 64p. (gr. 3 up). 1988. RSBE 13.95 (*0-87518-376-X*, Dillon) Macmillan Child Grp.

Micocci, Harriet. Captain Orkle's Treasure. Dora, illus. (gr. 3-7). 1961. 10.95 (*0-8392-3003-6*) Astor-Honor.

Micucci, Charles. Cabbie Who Stole New York City. (ps-3). 1992. 16.00 (*0-553-08114-4*) Random.
—The Life & Times of the Apple. LC 90-22779. (Illus.). 32p. (ps-3). 1992. 14.95 (*0-531-05939-1*); lib. bdg. 14.99 (*0-531-08539-2*) Orchard Bks Watts.
—Life & Times of the Honey Bee. LC 93-8135. (gr. 4 up). 1994. 14.95 (*0-395-65968-X*) Ticknor & Fields.
—A Little Night Music. Micucci, Charles, illus. LC 88-505. 32p. (ps-3). 1989. 10.95 (*0-688-07900-8*); PLB 10.88 (*0-688-07901-6*, Morrow Jr Bks) Morrow Jr Bks.

Middlebrooks-Hutcherson, Gracie. How Many Vehicles Can You Name? I Can Name These Objects! Can You? What Animals Do You See, 3 vols. Clowney, Earle D., tr. Hutcherson, Matthew, III, illus. (SPA & ENG., Orig.). 1992. Set. 25.00 (*1-882485-05-X*); Set. pap. 12.00 (*1-882485-07-6*); write for info. cass. tape (*1-882485-06-8*) Enhance Your Chlds.

Middleton, Barth & Middleton, Sally. Living God's Way. Bates, Steve, illus. 64p. (gr. k-6). 1985. pap. text ed. 11.99 (*1-55976-031-1*) CEF Press.
—Loving God's Way. Bates, Stephen, illus. 55p. (gr. k-6). 1988. pap. text ed. 7.50 (*1-55976-033-8*) CEF Press.

Middleton, Gayle. Glim the Glorious or How the Little Folk Bested the Gubgoblins. Pangrazio, Micheal, illus. LC 86-2978. 64p. (gr. k-5). 1987. 12.95 (*0-394-88081-1*) Knopf Bks Yng Read.

Middleton, Hayden & Heater, Derek, eds. The Atlas of Modern History. (Illus.). 64p. (gr. 7 up). 1991. bds. 15.95 (*0-19-831677-1*) OUP.

Middleton, Haydn. Island of the Mighty. 80p. (gr. 5-8). 1987. 18.95 (0-19-274133-0) OUP.
Middleton, Nick. Atlas of Environmental Issues. (Illus.). 64p. (gr. 6 up). 1989. 16.95x (0-8160-2023-X) Facts on File.
—Atlas of Social Issues. (Illus.). 64p. 1990. 16.95x (0-8160-2024-8) Facts on File.
—Atlas of the Natural World. (Illus.). 64p. 1990. 16.95x (0-8160-2131-7) Facts on File.
—Atlas of World Issues. (Illus.). 64p. (gr. 6 up). 1989. 16. 95x (0-8160-2022-1) Facts on File.
Middleton, Pat. Mississippi River Activity Guide. (Illus.). 32p. (gr. 4-7). 1993. pap. 5.50 (0-9620823-5-X) Heritage WI.
Middleton, Sally, jt. auth. see Middleton, Barth.
Midgley, David A. & Lefton, Phillip. How to Prepare for SAT II: American History & Social Studies. 9th ed. LC 93-5987. 1994. pap. 11.95 (0-8120-1757-9) Barron.
Miescke, Lori. Christian Crafts from Construction Paper. 64p. (ps-5). 1992. 8.95 (0-86653-707-4, SS2843, Shining Star Pubns) Good Apple.
Migan, Helen. Nell's Story of Long Ago. LC 92-84106. 60p. (gr. 2-6). 1993. pap. 5.95 (1-55523-593-X) Winston-Derek.
Migneco, Ronald & Biel, Timothy L. The Crash of 1929. LC 89-33556. (Illus.). 64p. (gr. 5-8). 1989. PLB 11.95 (1-56006-007-7) Lucent Bks.
Mignolli, Marisa. Hosanna to You, Jesus! A Palm Sunday Experience. Benigni, M. Luisa, illus. 32p. (Orig.). (ps-3). 1993. pap. 3.95 (0-8198-3368-1) St Paul Bks.
Mihalik, Paul A. Patagonia Profile. (Illus.). 93p. (Orig.). (gr. 7-12). 1985. pap. text ed. 9.95 (0-9615916-0-9) Padre Pio Pubs.
Mijares, David P. Modern Samurai Training. Mijares, David P., illus. 100p. (Orig.). 1989. pap. 9.95 (0-9623400-0-6) Group M Probelications.
Mikaelsen, Ben. Rescue Josh McGuire. LC 91-71386. 272p. (gr. 5-9). 1991. 14.95 (1-56282-099-0); PLB 14. 89 (1-56282-100-8) Hyprn Child.
—Rescue Josh McGuire. LC 91-71386. 272p. (gr. 5-9). 1993. pap. 4.50 (1-56282-523-2) Hyprn Ppbks.
—Sparrow Hawk Red. 224p. (gr. 5-9). 1993. 14.95 (1-56282-387-6); PLB 14.89 (1-56282-388-4) Hyprn Child.
Mikalac, Miriam, jt. auth. see Carter, Eneida.
Mike, Jan. Chana, An Anasazi Girl: Historical Paperdoll Books to Read, Color & Cut. Lowmiller, Cathy, illus. 32p. (Orig.). (gr. k-4). 1991. pap. 3.95 (0-918080-61-4) Treasure Chest.
—New Mexico, Land of Enchantment Alphabet Book. Lowmiller, Cathie, illus. 32p. (Orig.). (gr. k-5). 1993. pap. 7.95 (0-918080-55-X) Treasure Chest.
—La Zariguerya y el Gran Creador de Fuego - Opossum & the Great Filmmaker: Una Leyenda Mexicana. (gr. 4-7). 1993. PLB 11.89 (0-8167-3125-X); pap. 3.95 (0-8167-3073-3) Troll Assocs.
Mike, Jan & Lowmiller, Cathie. Bizagolaa; Apache Cut & Color Book. Lowmiller, Cathie, illus. 32p. (Orig.). (gr. k-6). 1989. pap. 3.95 (0-918080-46-0) Treasure Chest.
Mike, Jan M. Desert Seasons. Mike, Samuel A., illus. 32p. (gr. k-8). 1991. pap. 7.95 (0-918080-49-5) Treasure Chest.
—Dolii; a Navajo Girl: Historical Paper Doll Book to Read, Color & Cut. Lowmiller, Cathie, illus. 32p. (gr. k-6). 1990. pap. 3.95 (0-918080-54-1) Treasure Chest.
—Gift of the Nile: An Ancient Egyptian Legend. Reasoner, Charles, illus. 32p. (gr. 2-5). 1992. PLB 11.89 (0-8167-2813-5); pap. text ed. 3.95 (0-8167-2814-3) Troll Assocs.
—Kachi; a Hopi Girl: Historical Paper Doll Book to Read, Color & Cut. Lowmiller, Cathie, illus. 32p. (gr. k-6). 1989. pap. 3.95 (0-918080-47-9) Treasure Chest.
—Opossum & the Great Firemaker: A Mexican Legend. Reasoner, Charles, illus. 32p. (gr. 2-5). 1993. lib. bdg. 11.89 (0-8167-3055-5); tchr's ed. 3.95 (0-8167-3056-3) Troll Assocs.
Miklowitz, Gloria. The Killing Boy. 1993. pap. 3.50 (0-553-56037-9) Bantam.
Miklowitz, Gloria D. After the Bomb. 156p. (gr. 7 up). 1987. pap. 2.95 (0-590-43483-7) Scholastic Inc.
—Anything to Win. 1989. pap. 14.95 (0-440-50142-3) Dell.
—The Day the Senior Class Got Married. 160p. (gr. 6 up). 1985. pap. 2.75 (0-440-92096-5, LFL) Dell.
—Desperate Pursuit. (gr. 7 up). 1992. pap. 3.99 (0-553-29746-5, Starfire) Bantam.
—Did You Hear What Happened to Andrea? LC 78-72972. 1979. 7.95 (0-440-01923-0) Delacorte.
—Did You Hear What Happened to Andrea? 176p. (gr. 7 up). 1986. pap. 1.75 (0-440-91853-7, LE) Dell.
—The Emerson High Vigilantes. LC 87-25657. 160p. (gr. 7 up). 1988. 14.95 (0-385-29637-1) Delacorte.
—Goodbye Tomorrow. LC 86-23948. 192p. (gr. 7 up). 1987. 13.95 (0-385-29562-6) Delacorte.
—Goodbye Tomorrow. (gr. k-12). 1988. pap. 3.25 (0-440-20081-4, LFL) Dell.
—The Love Bombers. LC 80-65836. 160p. (gr. 7 up). 1980. pap. 8.95 (0-385-28545-0) Delacorte.
—Love Story, Take Three. (gr. k-12). 1987. pap. 2.75 (0-440-95084-8, LFL) Dell.
—Secrets Not Meant to Be Kept. (gr. k up). 1989. pap. 2.75 (0-440-20334-1, LFL) Dell.
—Standing Tall, Looking Good. 160p. 1992. pap. 3.50 (0-440-21263-4, LFL) Dell.
—Suddenly Super Rich. (gr. 7 up). 1989. 13.95 (0-553-05845-2, Starfire) Bantam.

—The War Between the Classes. (gr. 6 up). 1986. pap. 3.50 (0-440-99406-3, LFL) Dell.
Mikolaycak, C. Orpheus. 1992. write for info. (0-15-258804-3, HB Juv Bks) HarBrace.
Mikolaycak, C., ed. see Hopkins, L. B.
Mikolaycak, Charles. Babushka: An Old Russian Folktale. Mikolaycak, Charles, illus. LC 84-500. 32p. (ps-3). 1984. reinforced bdg. 15.95 (0-8234-0520-6); pap. 5.95 (0-8234-0712-8) Holiday.
Mila, jt. auth. see Amery.
Milano, Keri E., jt. auth. see Ossorio, Nelson A.
Milard, A. & Chisholm, J. Early Civilizations. (Illus.). 96p. 1992. PLB 16.96 (0-88110-438-8); pap. 10.95 (0-7460-0328-5) EDC.
Milburn, Constance. Let's Look at the Seasons. Caulkins, Janet, ed. (Illus.). (gr. k-6). 1988. PLB 11.40 (0-531-18179-0, Pub. by Bookwright Pr) Watts.
Milcsik, Margie. Cupid Computer. LC 91-46152. 128p. (gr. 3-7). 1993. pap. 3.95 (0-689-71569-2, Aladdin) Macmillan Child Grp.
Miles, A. Marie. Bible: Chain of Truth. 168p. (gr. 5 up). pap. 2.00 (0-686-29101-8) Faith Pub Hse.
Miles, Bernard. Favorite Tales from Shakespeare. Ambrus, Victor G., illus. 128p. (gr. 4-7). 1993. Repr. of 1976 ed. 14.95 (1-56288-257-0) Checkerboard.
—Robin Hood: His Life & Legend. Ambrus, Victor G., illus. LC 79-64615. 128p. (gr. 4 up). 12.95 (1-56288-412-3) Checkerboard.
—Well-Loved Tales from Shakespeare. Ambrus, Victor G., illus. LC 85-63829. 128p. (gr. 2 up). 1986. 12.95 (0-528-82758-8) Checkerboard.
Miles, Betty. All It Takes Is Practice. LC 76-13057. 128p. (gr. 3-7). 1989. pap. 3.99 (0-394-82053-3) Knopf Bks Yng Read.
—All It Takes Is Practice. LC 76-13057. (gr. 4-8). 1976. lib. bdg. 10.99 (0-394-93325-7) Knopf Bks Yng Read.
—How to Read: A Book for Beginners. LC 93-25884. Date not set. write for info. (0-679-85644-7) Knopf.
—I Would If I Could. LC 81-8458. 128p. (gr. 3-6). 1982. Repr. PLB 11.99 (0-394-93929-8) Knopf Bks Yng Read.
—I Would If I Could. 120p. (gr. 3-6). 1983. pap. 2.95 (0-380-63438-4, Camelot) Avon.
—Just the Beginning. 148p. (gr. 3 up). 1978. pap. 2.50 (0-380-01913-2, Camelot) Avon.
—Looking On. LC 77-15946. (gr. 4-8). 1978. lib. bdg. 10. 99 (0-394-93582-9) Knopf Bks Yng Read.
—Maudie & Me & the Dirty Book. 140p. (gr. 4-7). 1981. pap. 2.95 (0-380-55541-7, Camelot) Avon.
—The Real Me. 124p. (gr. 4-7). 1978. pap. 2.75 (0-380-00347-3, Camelot) Avon.
—The Real Me. LC 74-160. 128p. (gr. 3-7). 1989. 2.95 (0-394-82588-8) Knopf Bks Yng Read.
—The Real Me. LC 74-160. 144p. (gr. 3 up). 1974. lib. bdg. 9.99 (0-394-92838-5) Knopf Bks Yng Read.
—Save the Earth: An Action Handbook for Kids. Davis, Nelle, illus. LC 90-46514. 128p. (Orig.). (gr. 5 up). 1991. 13.99 (0-679-91731-4); pap. 6.95 (0-679-81731-X) Knopf Bks Yng Read.
—The Secret Life of the Underwear Champ. Jones, Dan, illus. LC 80-15651. (gr. 3-7). 1981. PLB 8.99 256p. (0-394-94563-8); pap. 3.50 128p. (0-394-84563-3) Knopf Bks Yng Read.
—Sink or Swim. 208p. (gr. 3-7). 1987. pap. 2.95 (0-380-69913-3, Camelot) Avon.
—The Trouble with Thirteen. LC 78-31678. (gr. 4-7). 1979. PLB 12.99 (0-394-93930-1) Knopf Bks Yng Read.
—The Trouble with Thirteen. LC 78-31678. 112p. (gr. 3-7). 1989. pap. 2.95 (0-394-82043-6) Knopf Bks Yng Read.
Miles, Calvin. Calvin's Christmas Wish. Johnson, Dolores, illus. 32p. (ps-3). 1993. 13.99 (0-670-84295-8) Viking Child Bks.
Miles, J. C. First Book of the Keyboard. (Illus.). 64p. (gr. 2 up). 1993. PLB 14.96 (0-88110-622-4); pap. 8.95 (0-7460-0962-3) EDC.
Miles, John C., ed. Treasury of Animal Stories. Oak-Rhind, Mary & Dennison, Graham, illus. LC 90-11158. 96p. (gr. 2-5). 1991. lib. bdg. 14.89 (0-8167-2240-4); pap. text ed. 6.95 (0-8167-2241-2) Troll Assocs.
—Treasury of Christmas. De Lisle, Elizabeth, et al, illus. LC 90-39372. 96p. (gr. 2-5). 1991. lib. bdg. 14.89 (0-8167-2236-6); pap. text ed. 6.95 (0-8167-2237-4) Troll Assocs.
Miles, John C., ed. see Dempsey, Michael.
Miles, Leona, ed. see Hamilton, Mary M.

Miles, Mary. What's So Special about Nantucket? Locke, Barbara K., illus. LC 98-71418. 36p. (ps up). 1993. PLB 17.00 (0-9636885-0-2) Faraway Pub. This is the story of "Tuck," traveling by ferry with his mother to Nantucket Island where he was born. They will spend the summer with his Gram there while Mom writes a book. Tuck doesn't remember the island at all, but people have told him that he'll love it because "there's something so special about Nantucket." As he visits famous scenic, & historic island sites with his Gram he keeps wondering if THIS or THAT is the special thing. Is it the peppermint-striped lighthouse? Is it bubble-blowing at sunset at Steps Beach? Is it band concerts with balloons & tubas & dancing kids & ice cream cones? Tuck scarcely realizes that he's learning a lot about the history & environment of Nantucket as he enjoys day after day of exploring with Gram & her dog Emma. But finally he discovers the answer to the big question: it's not only boats & lighthouses, flowers & birds & cobblestones & scallops that make the island special--it's seeing your Dad arriving on the ferry as it rounds Brant Point & suddenly knowing that the most special thing of all is sharing the Nantucket Island with the people you love. To order: Faraway Publishing Group, Box 792, Nantucket, MA 02554. *Publisher Provided Annotation.*

Miles, Miska. Annie & the Old One. Parnall, Peter, illus. (gr. 1-3). 1972. lib. bdg. 14.95i (0-316-57117-2, Joy St Bks) Little.
—Annie & the Old One. Parnall, Peter, illus. (gr. 1-3). 1985. pap. 6.95 (0-316-57120-2) Little.
—Gertrude's Pocket. McCully, Emily, illus. (gr. 2-5). 1984. 15.25 (0-8446-6164-3) Peter Smith.
Miles, Patrick, jt. auth. see Westfall, Tanja.
Miles, Sally. Alfi & the Dark. Le Cain, Errol, illus. LC 88-1043. 32p. (ps-1). 1988. 13.95 (0-87701-527-9) Chronicle Bks.
Milgrim, Shirley. Haym Salomon: Liberty's Son. Fish, Richard, illus. LC 75-17349. 120p. (gr. 5-8). 1975. 7.95 (0-8276-0073-9) JPS Phila.
Milhous, Katherine. The Egg Tree. Milhous, Katherine, illus. LC 50-6817. 32p. (gr. 1-4). 1971. RSBE 13.95 (0-684-12716-4, Scribners Young Read) Macmillan Child Grp.
—The Egg Tree. LC 91-15854. (Illus.). 32p. (gr. k-3). 1992. pap. 4.95 (0-689-71568-4, Aladdin) Macmillan Child Grp.
Milhous, Katherine & Dalgiesh, Alice. The Turnip: An Old Russian Folktale. Morgan, Pierr, illus. 32p. (ps-3). 1990. 14.95 (0-399-22229-4, Philomel Bks) Putnam Pub Group.
Milios, Rita. Bears, Bears Everywhere. (ps-2). 1988. PLB 11.93 (0-516-02085-4); pap. 2.95 (0-516-42085-2) Childrens.
—A Desert Cactus Comes to Life. Stoffregen, Jill A., illus. LC 92-12895. 24p. (ps-3). Date not set. 11.95 (1-56065-168-7) Capstone Pr. Postponed.
—Discovering How to Make Good Choices. 64p. (gr. 8 up). PLB 14.95 (0-8239-1281-7) Rosen Group.
—Discovering Positive Thinking. (gr. 7-12). 1992. PLB 14.95 (0-8239-1280-9) Rosen Group.
—Donde Esta Pedro? Sneaky Pete. Martin, Clovis, illus. LC 89-34666. (SPA). 32p. (ps-2). 1991. PLB 11.93 (0-516-32092-0); pap. 2.95 (0-516-52092-X) Childrens.
—The Hungry Billy Goat. Walters, Mary C., illus. LC 88-673. 32p. (ps-2). 1989. PLB 11.93 (0-516-02090-0); pap. 2.95 (0-516-42090-9) Childrens.
—I Am. Martin, Clovis, illus. LC 87-5163. 32p. (ps-2). 1987. PLB 11.93 (0-516-02081-1); pap. 2.95 (0-516-42081-X) Childrens.
—Imagi-size: Activities to Exercise Your Students' Imaginations. (Illus.). 80p. (gr. k-4). 1993. pap. 8.95 (1-880505-05-3) Pieces of Lrning.
—Independent Living. Rosen, Ruth, ed. (gr. 7-12). 1992. 12.95 (0-8239-1454-2) Rosen Group.
—Mean Words. Lemeiux, Margo, illus. LC 92-10837. 32p. (ps-2). Date not set. 11.95 (1-56065-163-6) Capstone Pr. Postponed.
—Osos, osos, aqui y alli: (Bears, Bears, Everywhere) Dunnington, Tom, illus. LC 87-33780. (ENG & SPA). 32p. (ps-2). 1989. PLB 11.93 (0-516-32085-8); pap. 2.95 (0-516-52085-7) Childrens.
—Shopping Savvy. Rosen, Ruth, ed. (gr. 7-12). 1992. 12. 95 (0-8239-1455-0) Rosen Group.
—Sneaky Pete. Martin, Clovis, illus. LC 89-34666. 32p. (ps-2). 1989. PLB 11.93 (0-516-02092-7); pap. 2.95 (0-516-42092-5) Childrens.
—The Value of Trust. Rosen, Ruth, ed. (gr. 7-12). 1991. PLB 15.95 (0-8239-1285-X) Rosen Group.
—Yo Soy (I Am) Martin, Clovis, illus. LC 87-5163. (SPA). 32p. (ps-2). 1990. PLB 11.93 (0-516-32081-5); pap. 2.95 (0-516-52081-4) Childrens.
Milkins, Colin S. Discovering Pond Life. (Illus.). 48p. (gr. 5-8). 1990. PLB 12.40 (0-531-18304-1, Pub. by Bookwright Pr) Watts.
—Fish. LC 91-6726. (Illus.). 32p. (gr. 2-6). 1993. 14.95g (1-56847-008-8) Thomson Lrning.
Millais, Raoul. Elijah & Pin-Pin. LC 91-20032. (Illus.). 48p. (ps-1). 1992. pap. 14.00 jacketed (0-671-75543-9, S&S BFYR) S&S Trade.
Millang, Steve, jt. auth. see Scelsa, Greg.

Millar, Alejandra, tr. see Zollars, Jean A.
Millard. The Age of Revolutions. (Illus.). (gr. 4-9). 1979. (Usborne-Hayes); PLB 13.96 (*0-88110-112-5*); pap. 6.95 (*0-86020-263-1*) EDC.
—Crusaders, Aztecs & Samurai. (Illus.). (gr. 4-6). 1978. (Usborne-Hayes); PLB 13.96 (*0-88110-110-9*); pap. 6.95 (*0-86020-194-5*) EDC.
—Exploration & Discovery. (Illus.). (gr. 4-9). 1979. (Usborne-Hayes); PLB 13.96 (*0-88110-111-7*); pap. 6.95 (*0-86020-261-5*) EDC.
—The First Civilization. (Illus.). (gr. 4-9). 1977. (Usborne-Hayes); PLB 13.96 (*0-88110-107-9*); pap. 6.95 (*0-86020-138-4*) EDC.
—Warriors & Seafarers. (Illus.). (gr. 4-9). 1977. (Usborne-Hayes); PLB 13.96 (*0-88110-108-7*); pap. 6.95 (*0-86020-140-6*) EDC.
—World History, Book Of. (Illus.). 195p. (gr. 3-9). 1986. 19.95 (*0-86020-959-8*) EDC.
Millard, jt. auth. see Evans.
Millard, A. Round the World Cookbook. (Illus.). 48p. 1993. pap. 7.95 (*0-7460-0966-6*, Usborne) EDC.
Millard, A. & Peach, S. The Greeks. (Illus.). 96p. 1990. PLB 16.96 (*0-88110-415-9*); pap. 10.95 (*0-7460-0342-0*) EDC.
Millard, A., jt. auth. see Evans, C.
Millard, A., et al. Ancient World. (Illus.). 288p. (gr. 7-12). 1992. pap. 23.95 (*0-7460-1233-0*) EDC.
Millard, Anne. Eric the Red: The Vikings Sail the Atlantic. LC 93-26113. 1994. write for info. (*0-8114-7252-3*) Raintree Steck-V.
—How People Lived. Sergio, illus. LC 92-54315. 64p. (gr. 3-7). 1993. 12.95 (*1-56458-237-X*) Dorling Kindersley.
—Pyramids. LC 88-83093. (Illus.). 32p. (gr. 5-7). 1989. PLB 12.40 (*0-531-17154-X*, Gloucester Pr) Watts.
Millard, Catherine. A Children's Companion Guide to America's History. (Illus.). 96p. (Orig.). 1993. wkbk. 9.99 (*0-88965-102-7*) Chr Pubns.
Millard, Scott, jt. auth. see Wang, Wally.
Millay, Edna St. Vincent. The Ballad of the Harp Weaver. Peck, Beth, illus. 32p. (ps-3). 1991. 14.95 (*0-399-21611-1*, Philomel) Putnam Pub Group.
—Collected Poems. Millay, Norma, ed. LC 75-6348. 760p. 1981. pap. 20.00 (*0-06-090889-0*, CN-889, PL) HarpC.
—Edna St. Vincent Millay's Poems Selected for Young People. Keller, Ronald, illus. LC 77-25671. 120p. (gr. 7 up). 1979. 14.00 (*0-06-024218-3*) HarpC Child Bks.
Millay, Norma, ed. see Millay, Edna St. Vincent.
Millea, Nicholas. Settlements. LC 93-24680. (Illus.). 32p. (gr. 4-6). 1993. 14.95 (*1-56847-057-6*) Thomson Lrning.
Millender, Dharathula H. Crispus Attucks: Black Leader of Colonial Patriots. Morrow, Gray, illus. LC 86-10779. 192p. (gr. 2-6). 1986. pap. 3.95 (*0-02-041810-8*, Aladdin) Macmillan Child Grp.
—Martin Luther King, Jr. Young Man with a Dream. Fiorentino, Al, illus. LC 86-10739. 192p. (gr. 2-6). 1986. pap. 3.95 (*0-02-042010-2*, Aladdin) Macmillan Child Grp.
Millen-Posner, Barbara, jt. auth. see Hyman, Jane.
Miller. Monsters. Francis, John, illus. 32p. (gr. k-6). 1977. PLB write for info. (*0-86020-146-5*); pap. 5.95 (*0-685-42639-4*) EDC.
—Soviet Navy. LC 88-11327. (Illus.). 48p. (gr. 3-8). 1988. PLB 18.60 (*0-86625-336-X*); PLB 13.95s.p. (*0-685-58300-7*) Rourke Corp.
—Soviet Rocket Forces. LC 88-11367. (Illus.). 48p. (gr. 3-8). 1988. PLB 18.60 (*0-86625-333-5*); PLB 13.95s.p. (*0-685-58297-3*) Rourke Corp.
—Soviet Submarines. (Illus.). 48p. (gr. 3-8). 1987. PLB 18.60 (*0-86625-332-7*); PLB 13.95s.p. (*0-685-58296-5*) Rourke Corp.
—You Be the Jury: Courtroom Two. 1992. pap. 2.50 (*0-590-45727-6*) Scholastic Inc.
—Your Own Christmas Magic Show. 1993. pap. 6.95 (*0-590-47558-4*) Scholastic Inc.
—Your Own Super Magic Show. 1993. pap. 4.95 (*0-590-33044-6*) Scholastic Inc.
Miller, A. G. Walt Disney's Bambi Gets Lost. (ps-3). 1973. 6.95 (*0-394-82520-9*); lib. bdg. 4.99 (*0-394-92520-3*) Random Bks Yng Read.
Miller, Albert G. Captain Whopper. Komisarow, Donald, illus. (gr. 3-7). 1968. 10.95 (*0-8392-3058-3*) Astor-Honor.
—More Captain Whopper Tales. Komisarow, Don, illus. (gr. 3-7). 1968. 10.95 (*0-8392-3060-5*) Astor-Honor.
—Sesame Street Storybook. 1986. pap. 6.95 (*0-394-88301-2*) Random Bks Yng Read.
Miller, Alice. Young Girl's Diary. 1991. pap. 10.95 (*0-385-41596-6*, Anchor Pr) Doubleday.
Miller, Allan, jt. auth. see Winn, Marie.
Miller, Angela, jt. auth. see Norman, David.
Miller, Arlene D. What's What. Gilbert, Carol, ed. (Illus.). 21p. (Orig.). (ps-6). 1985. pap. 4.00 (*0-9614209-0-1*) Adam Pub Co.
Miller, Arthur. Spain. (Illus.). 112p. (gr. 5 up). 1989. lib. bdg. 14.95 (*1-55546-795-4*) Chelsea Hse.
Miller, Barbara, jt. auth. see Newman, Marsha.
Miller, Betty. Sign Language House. 32p. 1984. 4.50 (*0-915035-03-0*, 4162) Dawn Sign.
Miller, Billie M. Soo Ling: The Story of the Silkworm. Guerra, Mauricio, illus. Luna, Rose Mary, tr. (SPA & ENG, Illus.). 12p. 1991. 12.00 (*1-878742-01-9*); pap. 6.00 (*1-878742-02-7*) Kidship Assoc.
Miller, C., et al. Mysteries of Unknown (B - U) (Illus.). 96p. (gr. 5 up). 1992. pap. 12.95 (*0-86020-492-8*) EDC.

Miller, Calvin. The Singer Trilogy: A Mythic Retelling of the Story of the New Testament. LC 90-39944. (Illus.). 496p. 1990. 19.99 (*0-8308-1300-4*, 1300) InterVarsity.
Miller, Christina G. & Berry, Louise A. Acid Rain. LC 86-8605. (Illus.). 128p. (gr. 7 up). 1986. lib. bdg. 12.98 (*0-671-60177-6*, J Messner) S&S Trade.
—Coastal Rescue: Preserving Our Seashores. LC 88-27520. (Illus.). 144p. (gr. 5-9). 1989. SBE 13.95 (*0-689-31288-1*, Atheneum Child Bk) Macmillan Child Grp.
—Jungle Rescue: Saving the New World Tropical Rain Forests. LC 90-1150. (Illus.). 128p. (gr. 5-9). 1991. SBE 14.95 (*0-689-31487-6*, Atheneum Child Bk) Macmillan Child Grp.
Miller, Cynthia P. Challenges of the Heart. Agnew, Tim, illus. LC 90-21432. 144p. (Orig.). 1991. pap. 6.99 (*0-932581-79-X*) Word Aflame.
Miller, Dawn. David Robinson: Backboard Admiral. (Illus.). 64p. (gr. 4-9). 1991. PLB 13.50 (*0-8225-0494-4*) Lerner Pubns.
—David Robinson: Backboard Admiral. 1992. pap. 4.95 (*0-8225-9600-8*) Lerner Pubns.
Miller, Debbie S. A Caribou Journey. Van Zyle, Jon, illus. LC 93-9777. (gr. 2-5). 1995. 14.95 (*0-316-57380-9*) Little.
Miller, Deborah. Coping When a Parent Is Gay. Rosen, Ruth, ed. (gr. 7-12). 1993. 13.95 (*0-8239-1404-6*) Rosen Group.
—Coping with Incest. (gr. 4-7). 1992. 12.95 (*0-8239-1422-4*) Rosen Group.
Miller, Deborah & Ostrove, Karen. Fins & Scales: A Kosher Tale. Ostrove, Karen, illus. LC 90-24388. 32p. (gr. 1-3). 1992. 12.95 (*0-929371-25-9*); pap. 5.95 (*0-929371-26-7*) Kar Ben.
Miller, Deborah A. & Waigandt, Alex. Coping with Your Sexual Orientation. Rosen, Ruth, ed. (gr. 7-12). 1990. PLB 13.95 (*0-8239-1158-6*) Rosen Group.
Miller, Deborah U. My Siddur. Paiss, Jana, illus. 35p. (gr. k-2). 1984. pap. text ed. 4.25 (*0-87441-389-3*) Behrman.
—Only Nine Chairs-A Tall Tale for Passover. LC 82-80035. (Illus.). 40p. (ps-3). 1982. pap. 4.95 (*0-930494-13-X*) Kar Ben.
Miller, Don. Calculator Explorations & Problems. 1992. pap. 9.95 (*0-201-48038-7*) Addison-Wesley.
—Calculator Explorations & Problems. 108p. (gr. 5 up). 1979. pap. text ed. 9.95 (*0-914040-75-8*) Cuisenaire.
—Mental Math & Estimation. 80p. (gr. 3-8). 1993. pap. text ed. 9.50 (*0-938587-30-7*) Cuisenaire.
Miller, Donald C., jt. auth. see Davis, Arnold R.
Miller, Douglas. Henry David Thoreau. Scott, John A., ed. (Illus.). 144p. (gr. 6-10). 1991. lib. bdg. 16.95x (*0-8160-2478-2*) Facts on File.
Miller, Douglas T. Frederick Douglass & the Fight for Freedom. (Illus.). 144p. (gr. 5 up). 1988. 16.95x (*0-8160-1617-8*) Facts on File.
Miller, E. Lorraine. Free with Biz Bee. LC 77-82754. (Illus.). (gr. k up). 1977. 6.50 (*0-89566-350-3*) Miller Ent.
—Friendship. Browne, Rob, illus. LC 77-79105. (ps up). 1977. 5.00 (*0-89566-000-8*) Miller Ent.
—Rooney Crooney's Second Chance. Stuker, Chris, illus. LC 77-88334. (ps-4). 1978. perfect bdg. 6.50x (*0-89566-351-1*) Miller Ent.
Miller, Edna. Duck Duck. (ps-3). 1981. pap. 3.95 (*0-685-03845-9*) P-H.
—Mousekin Finds a Friend. Miller, Edna, illus. (ps-3). 1971. (Pub. by Treehouse) P-H.
—Mousekin Finds a Friend. 1987. pap. 5.95 (*0-13-604216-3*) P-H.
—Mousekin Finds a Friend. LC 67-18924. (Illus.). 32p. (gr. k-4). 1967. PLB 11.95 (*0-13-604224-4*) P-H.
—Mousekin Finds a Friend. LC 67-18924. (Illus.). 32p. (gr. k-4). 1987. pap. 5.95 (*0-671-66973-7*, S&S BFYR) S&S Trade.
—Mousekin Takes a Trip. (Illus.). (ps-3). 1976. 9.95x (*0-13-604363-1*, Pub. by Treehouse) P-H.
—Mousekin's ABC. LC 72-176159. (Illus.). 32p. (gr. k-4). 1972. PLB 11.95 (*0-13-604125-6*) P-H.
—Mousekin's ABC. LC 72-176159. (Illus.). 32p. (gr. k-4). 1974. pap. 5.95 (*0-671-66473-5*, S&S BFYR) S&S Trade.
—Mousekin's Birth. Miller, Edna, illus. 32p. (gr. k-3). 1982. pap. 2.50 (*0-13-604132-9*, Pub. by Treehouse) P-H.
—Mousekin's Christmas Eve. Miller, Edna, illus. (gr. k-3). 1972. 11.95 (*0-13-604454-9*, Pub. by Treehouse) P-H.
—Mousekin's Christmas Eve. LC 65-25244. (Illus.). 32p. (gr. k-4). 1972. pap. 5.95 (*0-671-66479-4*, S&S BFYR) S&S Trade.
—Mousekin's Close Call. Miller, Edna, illus. LC 77-27571. (gr. k-3). 1980. 9.95x (*0-13-604207-4*, Pub. by Treehouse); pap. 3.95 (*0-13-604199-X*) P-H.
—Mousekin's Easter Basket. Miller, Edna, illus. LC 86-22511. 32p. (ps-3). 1989. pap. 12.95 jacketed (*0-671-66803-X*, S&S BFYR); pap. 5.95 (*0-671-67439-0*, S&S BFYR) S&S Trade.
—Mousekin's Fables. Miller, Edna, illus. 28p. (ps-3). 1982. 11.95 (*0-13-604165-5*) P-H.
—Mousekin's Family. Miller, Edna, illus. (gr. k-3). 1972. PLB 9.95x (*0-13-604462-X*, Pub. by Treehouse); pap. 5.95 (*0-13-604157-4*) P-H.
—Mousekins Family. (ps up). 1987. 11.95 (*0-13-604182-5*) P-H.
—Mousekin's Family. LC 69-12673. (Illus.). 32p. (gr. k-4). 1972. pap. 5.95 (*0-671-66477-8*, S&S BFYR) S&S Trade.

—Mousekin's Frosty Friend. LC 89-29892. (Illus.). 32p. (gr. k-4). 1990. pap. 12.95 jacketed (*0-671-70445-1*, S&S BFYR) S&S Trade.
—Mousekin's Golden House. Miller, Edna, illus. (gr. k-3). 1971. PLB 9.95x (*0-13-604421-2*, Pub. by Treehouse) P-H.
—Mousekin's Golden House. 1987. 11.95 (*0-13-604232-5*) P-H.
—Mousekin's Golden House. LC 64-16429. (Illus.). 32p. (gr. k-4). 1971. pap. 5.95 (*0-671-66972-9*, S&S BFYR) S&S Trade.
—Mousekin's Golden House. LC 87-32111. (ps-3). 1990. pap. 12.95 (*0-671-66282-1*, S&S BFYR) S&S Trade.
—Mousekin's Lost Woodland. LC 91-4201. (Illus.). 40p. (ps-3). 1992. pap. 13.00 jacketed (*0-671-74938-2*, S&S BFYR) S&S Trade.
—Mousekin's Mystery. LC 83-9622. (Illus.). 32p. (gr. k-3). 1983. 11.95 (*0-13-604330-5*) P-H.
—Mousekin's Thanksgiving. Miller, Edna, illus. 32p. (ps-3). 1988. pap. 5.95 (*0-671-66859-5*, S&S BFYR) S&S Trade.
—Mousekin's Woodland Sleepers. (Illus.). (gr. k-3). 1977. (Pub. by Treehouse); pap. 3.95 (*0-13-604561-8*) P-H.
—Mousekin's Woodland Sleepers. 1987. 11.95 (*0-13-604505-7*) P-H.
—Mousekins Woodland Sleepers. (ps-3). 1988. pap. 5.95 (*0-13-604497-2*) P-H.
—Patches Finds a New Home. Miller, Edna, illus. (ps-4). 1989. pap. 12.95 jacketed (*0-671-66266-X*, S&S BFYR) S&S Trade.
—Patches Finds a New Home. LC 87-32355. (Illus.). 40p. (gr. k-4). 1993. pap. 5.95 (*0-671-79677-1*, S&S BFYR) S&S Trade.
—Scamper: A Gray Tree Squirrel. Miller, Edna, illus. 32p. (gr. k-3). 1991. PLB 14.95 (*0-945912-12-9*) Pippin Pr.
Miller, Elizabeth G., tr. see Balcells, Jacqueline.
Miller, Frances A. Aren't You the One Who...? 187p. 1987. pap. 3.99 (*0-449-70286-3*, Juniper) Fawcett.
—Cutting Loose. 240p. (gr. 9-12). 1991. pap. 3.95 (*0-449-70384-3*, Juniper) Fawcett.
—The Truth Trap. 187p. 1986. pap. 3.95 (*0-449-70247-2*, Juniper) Fawcett.
Miller, Gary. Mind Bogglers for Juniors. 38p. 1991. wkbk. 1.95 (*1-882449-00-2*) Messenger Pub.
Miller, Heather S. Children & Gardens: An Annotated Bibliography of Children's Garden Books, 1829-1988. Miasek, Meryl A., ed. 60p. (Orig.). pap. write for info. (*0-9621791-1-0*) CBHL Inc.
Miller, Helen L. Everyday Plays for Boys & Girls. LC 86-8884. (Orig.). (gr. 1-6). 1986. pap. 12.00 (*0-8238-0274-4*) Plays.
—First Plays for Children. 295p. (gr. 1-3). 1985. pap. 12.00 (*0-8238-0268-X*) Plays.
—Special Plays for Holidays. LC 86-9332. (Orig.). (gr. 1-6). 1986. pap. 12.00 (*0-8238-0275-2*) Plays.
Miller, Howard. Abraham Lincoln's Flag: We Won't Give up a Star. Heiser, John, illus. 26p. (gr. 4-6). 1990. pap. text ed. 4.95 (*0-939631-19-9*) Thomas Publications.
Miller, J. E., Jr., ed. see Whitman, Walt.
Miller, J. P. Farmer John's Animals. Miller, J. P., illus. LC 79-63900. (ps-1). 1979. 3.95 (*0-394-84270-7*) Random Bks Yng Read.
—Good Night, Little Rabbit. Miller, J. P., illus. LC 85-62017. 7p. (ps). 1993. bds. 3.95 (*0-394-87992-9*) Random Bks Yng Read.
—Learn about Colors with Little Rabbit. Miller, J. P., illus. LC 84-6943. (ps-1). 1984. 3.95 (*0-394-86671-1*); lib. bdg. 4.99 (*0-394-96671-6*) Random Bks Yng Read.
—Learn to Count with Little Rabbit. Miller, J. P., illus. LC 83-21100. 24p. (ps-1). 1984. 3.95 (*0-394-86149-3*) Random Bks Yng Read.
—Little Duckling's Surprise. LC 86-62052. (Illus.). 24p. (ps-1). 1987. bk. & doll pkg. 4.95 (*0-394-88682-8*) Random Bks Yng Read.
—Little Rabbit Takes a Walk. Miller, J. P., illus. LC 86-61525. 24p. (ps-1). 1987. bk. & doll pkg. 4.95 (*0-394-88667-4*) Random Bks Yng Read.
—Yoo-Hoo Little Rabbit. Miller, J. P., illus. LC 85-61529. 16p. (ps). 1986. 3.99 (*0-394-87884-1*) Random Bks Yng Read.
Miller, J. P., illus. The Cow Says Moo. (ps). 1979. 3.50 (*0-394-84131-X*) Random Bks Yng Read.
Miller, Jane. The Farm Alphabet Book. Miller, Jane, illus. 32p. (ps-2). 1987. pap. 2.50 (*0-590-31991-4*) Scholastic Inc.
—Farm Alphabet Book. 32p. (ps-2). 1984. 8.95 (*0-13-304767-9*) P-H.
—Farm Counting Book. Miller, Jane, illus. 24p. (ps-3). 1986. 8.95 (*0-13-304790-3*); pap. 4.95 (*0-13-304809-8*) P-H.
—Farm Counting Book. (Illus.). 24p. (ps-4). 1992. pap. 5.00 (*0-671-66552-9*, S&S BFYR) S&S Trade.
—Farm Noises. Miller, Jane, photos by. (ps-3). 1989. 8.95 (*0-671-67450-1*, Little Simon) S&S Trade.
—Farm Noises. (Illus.). 24p. (ps-4). 1992. pap. 5.00 (*0-671-75976-0*, S&S BFYR) S&S Trade.
—Seasons on the Farm. Miller, Jane, illus. 32p. (gr. k-3). 1986. 10.95 (*0-13-797275-X*) P-H.
Miller, Jay. The Delawares. 1994. write for info. (*0-516-01053-0*) Childrens.
—Native Americans. (Illus.). 48p. (gr. k-4). 1993. PLB 16.60 (*0-516-01192-8*) Childrens.

Miller, Jayne. Too Much Trick or Treat. Thatch, Nancy R., ed. Miller, Jayna, illus. Melton, David, intro. by. LC 91-14930. (Illus.). 26p. (gr. k-4). 1991. PLB 14.95 (0-933849-37-0) Landmark Edns.

Miller, Jim W. Newfound. LC 89-42540. 256p. (gr. 7 up). 1989. 14.95 (0-531-05845-X); PLB 14.99 (0-531-08445-0) Orchard Bks Watts.

Miller, Jim W., ed. see Stuart, Jesse.

Miller, Jim W., et al, eds. see Stuart, Jesse.

Miller, Jo, ed. see Long, Jeanne & Mallis, Jackie.

Miller, John, jt. auth. see McAllister, Dawson.

Miller, Jonathan. The Human Body. Pelham, David, ed. Willock, Harry, illus. LC 83-80311. 1983. pap. 22.50 (0-670-38605-7, Studio) Viking Child Bks.

Miller, Joseph. Wandering Gypsies. LC 72-87908. (Illus.). (gr. 6-12). 1969. text ed. 10.00 (0-912472-08-1) Miller Bks.

Miller, Judi. Confessions of an Eleven-Year Old Ghost. (gr. 4-7). 1991. pap. 2.99 (0-553-15932-1) Bantam.

—Ghost a La Mode. (gr. 3-7). 1989. pap. 2.75 (0-553-15755-8, Skylark) Bantam.

—Ghost in My Soup. (gr. 3-7). 1985. pap. 2.99 (0-553-15622-5, Skylark) Bantam.

—How I Kept the U. S. Out of War. 112p. (Orig.). (gr. 7-12). 1987. pap. 2.50 (0-553-15522-9, Skylark) Bantam.

—How to be Friends with a Boy - How to be Friends with a Girl. 96p. (gr. 5-9). 1990. pap. 2.50 (0-590-42806-3) Scholastic Inc.

—My Crazy Cousin Courtney. MacDonald, Pat, ed. 160p. (Orig.). (gr. 4-6). 1993. pap. 2.99 (0-671-73821-6, Minstrel Bks) PB.

—Vampire Named Murray. (gr. 4-7). 1991. pap. 2.99 (0-553-15885-6) Bantam.

Miller, Julano. Life Line Series, 5 in 1 set. (Illus.). 48p. (gr. 3-9). 1985. Set. pap. 15.00 (0-87879-484-0) High Noon Bks.

Miller, Kathryn S. Poe! Poe! Poe! (Illus.). 24p. (gr. 4-12). 1984. pap. 2.50 (0-88680-224-5); royalty on application 25.00 (0-685-57938-7) I E Clark.

—The Shining Moment: (Musical) 1989. Playscript. 4.50 (0-87602-286-7) Anchorage.

Miller, Kenneth. Energy & Life. Head, J. J., ed. Steffen, Ann T., illus. LC 86-72192. 16p. (Orig.). (gr. 10 up). 1988. pap. text ed. 2.75 (0-89278-168-8, 45-9768) Carolina Biological.

Miller, Leo. Ghost Stories. Costa, Gwen, ed. LC 91-33874. 1992. pap. 13.95 (0-87949-358-5) Ashley Bks.

Miller, Libby & Rothlein, Liz. Read It Again! Introducing Literature to Young Children, Preschool - Kindergarten, Bk. 1. (Illus.). 112p. (reinf.). (ps-k). 1991. pap. 9.95 (0-673-36008-3) GdYrBks.

—Read It Again! Preschool - Kindergarten, Bk. 2. (Illus.). 144p. (Orig.). (ps-k) 1993. pap. 9.95 (0-673-36042-3) GdYrBks.

Miller, Linda F. An Introduction to the Literature & Personalities of the Bible. 89p. (gr. 7-12). 1985. curriculum guide 14.00 (1-881678-10-5) CRIS.

Miller, Louise. Careers for Animal Lovers: And Other Zoological Types. LC 90-50725. 160p. (Orig.). (gr. 7 up). 1991. pap. 9.95 (0-8442-8125-5, VGM Career Bks) NTC Pub Grp.

Miller, Lucille. Heidi. 1936. 4.50 (0-87602-136-4) Anchorage.

Miller, Luree & Miller, Scott. Alaska: Pioneer Stories of a Twentieth-Century Frontier. LC 91-10744. (Illus.). 144p. (gr. 6 up). 1991. 14.95 (0-525-65050-4, Cobblehill Bks) Dutton Child Bks.

Miller, Lynne, ed. Ten Tales of Christmas. 112p. (gr. 4-6). 1988. pap. 2.50 (0-590-41447-X) Scholastic Inc.

Miller, M. L. Dizzy from Fools. Tharlet, Eve, illus. LC 85-9390. 32p. (gr. 1 up). 1991. pap. 13.95 (0-88708-004-9) Picture Bk Studio.

Miller, Madge. Alice in Wonderland. 1953. 4.50 (0-87602-104-6) Anchorage.

—Hansel & Gretel. 1954. 4.50 (0-87602-135-6) Anchorage.

—The Land of the Dragon. 1946. 4.50 (0-87602-148-8) Anchorage.

—OPQRS, Etc. (Orig.). (gr. 4 up). 1984. pap. 4.50 (0-87602-246-8) Anchorage.

—The Pied Piper of Hamelin. 1951. 4.50 (0-87602-174-7) Anchorage.

—Pinocchio. 1954. 4.00 (0-87602-175-5) Anchorage.

—The Princess & the Swineherd. 1946. 4.50 (0-87602-181-X) Anchorage.

—Puss in Boots: Miniature Play. 37p. (Orig.). 1954. 4.00 (0-87602-184-4) Anchorage.

—Robinson Crusoe. (gr. 1-9). 1954. 4.00 (0-87602-193-3) Anchorage.

—The Unwicked Witch. (gr. 1-7). 1964. 4.50 (0-87602-216-6) Anchorage.

Miller, Marc W. ASW Forms. Venters, Steve, illus. 49p. (Orig.). 1990. pap. 8.00 (1-55878-057-2) Game Designers.

—Fighting Ships. Ellis, Kevin, illus. 96p. (Orig.). 1990. pap. 10.00 (1-55878-050-5) Game Designers.

—Sub Forms. Venters, Steve, illus. 49p. (Orig.). 1989. pap. 8.00 (1-55878-019-X) Game Designers.

Miller, Margaret. Can You Guess? LC 92-29406. (Illus.). 40p. (ps-up). 1993. 14.00 (0-688-11180-7); PLB 13.93 (0-688-11181-5) Greenwillow.

—More First Words: My Birthday. Miller, Margaret, illus. LC 89-82635. 14p. (ps-1). 1991. 3.95 (0-694-00302-6) HarpC Child Bks.

—My Five Senses. LC 93-1956. 1993. write for info. (0-671-79168-0, S&S BFYR) S&S Trade.

—Where Does It Go? LC 91-30160. (Illus.). 40p. (ps-4). 1992. 14.00 (0-688-10928-4); PLB 13.93 (0-688-10929-2) Greenwillow.

—Where's Jenna? LC 93-13981. 1994. pap. 14.00 (0-671-79167-2, S&S BFYR) S&S Trade.

—Who Uses This? LC 89-30456. (Illus.). 40p. (ps up). 1990. 12.95 (0-688-08278-5); PLB 12.88 (0-688-08279-3) Greenwillow.

—Whose Hat? LC 86-18324. (Illus.). 40p. (ps-1). 1988. 14.00 (0-688-06906-1); lib. bdg. 13.93 (0-688-06907-X) Greenwillow.

—Whose Shoe? LC 90-38491. (Illus.). 40p. (ps up) 1991. 13.95 (0-688-10008-2); PLB 13.88 (0-688-10009-0) Greenwillow.

Miller, Marge, ed. see Burke, Patricia A., et al.

Miller, Marge, ed. see Carl, Angela R. & Holmes, Alice C.

Miller, Margery S., jt. auth. see Allen, Karen K.

Miller, Marianne M. Too Busy: A Days of the Week Story. Wray, Rhonda, ed. Miller, Marianne M., illus. LC 93-11657. 36p. (Orig.). (gr. k-3). 1993. pap. 8.95 (0-916260-96-8, B114) Meriwether Pub.

Miller, Marilyn. The Bridge at Selma. LC 84-40379. (Illus.). 64p. (gr. 5 up). 1984. PLB 16.98 (0-382-06826-2); pap. 8.95 (0-382-06973-0) Silver Burdett Pr.

—D-Day. LC 84-40380. (Illus.). 64p. (gr. 5 up). 1984. PLB 16.98 (0-382-06825-4); pap. 8.95 (0-382-06972-2) Silver Burdett Pr.

—The Trans-Continental Railroad. LC 85-40167. (Illus.). 64p. (gr. 5 up). 1985. PLB 8.95 (0-382-06824-6); pap. 8.95 (0-382-09912-5) Silver Burdett Pr.

Miller, Mark. Bad Trips. Mendelson, Jack H. & Mello, Nancyintro. by. (Illus.). 112p. (gr. 5 up). 1987. lib. bdg. 19.95 (1-55546-218-9) Chelsea Hse.

Miller, Mark S. The Physically Handicapped. (Illus.). (gr. 6-12). 1994. 19.95 (0-7910-0073-7, Am Art Analog) Chelsea Hse.

Miller, Martha. Kidney Disorders. (Illus.). (gr. 6-12). 1992. 18.95 (0-7910-0066-4) Chelsea Hse.

Miller, Marvin. Who Dunnnit? How to Be a Detective in Ten Easy Lessons. (gr. 4-7). 1992. pap. 2.75 (0-590-44717-3) Scholastic Inc.

—You Be the Detective. (gr. 4-7). 1991. pap. 2.50 (0-590-42731-8) Scholastic Inc.

—You Be the Detective, No. II. 1992. 2.50 (0-590-45690-3) Scholastic Inc.

—You Be the Jury: Courtroom Four. 1992. 2.50 (0-590-45723-3, 066) Scholastic Inc.

—You Be the Jury: Courtroom Three. 96p. (gr. 4 up). 1992. pap. 2.50 (0-590-45724-1) Scholastic Inc.

—You Be the Jury: Courtroom Two. (gr. 4-7). 1992. pap. 2.50 (0-590-45725-X) Scholastic Inc.

Miller, Mary B. & Charlip, Remy. Handtalk Birthday: A Number & Story Book in Sign Language. Ancona, George, illus. LC 91-1967. 48p. (ps-3). 1991. pap. 4.95 (0-689-71531-5, Aladdin) Macmillan Child Grp.

Miller, Mary B., jt. auth. see Ancona, George.

Miller, Mary B., jt. auth. see Charlip, Remy.

Miller, Mary Beth & Ancona, George. Handtalk School. LC 90-24030. (Illus.). 32p. (gr. k-6). 1991. RSBE 14.95 (0-02-700912-2, Four Winds) Macmillan Child Grp.

Miller, Mary J. Fast Forward. 144p. (gr. 3-7). 1993. 13.99 (0-670-84339-3) Viking Child Bks.

—Me & My Name. LC 92-20302. 128p. (gr. 5 up). 1992. pap. 3.99 (0-14-034374-1) Puffin Bks.

—Upside Down. 128p. (gr. 3-7). 1992. 13.00 (0-670-83648-6) Viking Child Bks.

Miller, Mary Jane. Me & My Name. (gr. 4-7). 1990. 11.95 (0-670-83196-4) Viking Child Bks.

Miller, Maryann. Coping with a Bigoted Parent. (gr. 7-12). 1992. PLB 13.95 (0-8239-1345-7) Rosen Group.

—Coping with Weapons & Violence in School & on Your Streets. Rosen, Ruth, ed. (gr. 7-12). 1993. 13.95 (0-8239-1435-6) Rosen Group.

Miller, May. Collected Poems. LC 88-83172. 235p. (gr. 7-12). 1989. 18.00 (0-916418-70-7) Lotus.

—Dust of Uncertain Journey. LC 75-40977. 67p. (gr. 9-12). 1975. pap. 5.00 (0-916418-05-7) Lotus.

—Halfway to the Sun. Pauker, John, intro. by. LC 81-50427. (Illus.). 50p. (Orig.). (gr. 6). 1981. pap. text ed. 7.00 (0-931846-17-X) Wash Writers Pub.

—Halfway to the Sun. (Illus.). 52p. (gr. 2-5). 1988. pap. 5.00 (0-916418-75-8) Lotus.

—The Ransomed Wait. LC 82-83856. 77p. (gr. 9-12). 1983. pap. 4.50x perf. bnd (0-916418-40-5) Lotus.

Miller, Miamon. How to Play Romanian Folk Violin. Fraenkel, Eran, ed. (Illus.). 31p. (Orig.). 1990. pap. 19.95 (0-9626468-0-6) Fuge Imaginea.

Miller, Michael. Dare to Live: A Guide to the Prevention & Understanding of Teenage Suicide & Depression. (gr. 7-12). 1989. pap. 9.95 (0-941831-22-1) Beyond Words Pub.

Miller, Minnie T. Grandma's Tiny Kitty. 130p. (gr. k-3). 1975. 5.95 (0-87881-014-5) Mojave Bks.

—Why the March Hare Went Mad & Other Stories. 55p. (gr. k-4). 1972. 5.00 (0-87881-002-1) Mojave Bks.

Miller, Moira. Oscar Mouse Finds a Home. (ps-3). 1992. pap. 4.99 (0-14-054682-0) Viking Child Bks.

—The Proverbial Mouse. LC 86-16737. (Illus.). 32p. (ps-3). 1992. pap. 4.99 (0-8037-1072-0, Dial Pied Piper) Puffin Bks.

Miller, Moshe L., tr. see Steinberg, Shalom D.

Miller, Natalie. The Statue of Liberty. LC 91-44647. (Illus.). 32p. (gr. 3-6). 1992. PLB 15.27 (0-516-06655-2) Childrens.

—The Statue of Liberty. LC 91-44647. (Illus.). 32p. (gr. 3-6). 1993. pap. 3.95 (0-516-46655-0) Childrens.

—Story of the Liberty Bell. Warren, B., illus. LC 65-12215. 32p. (gr. 2-5). 1965. PLB 13.27 (0-516-04622-5) Childrens.

—Story of the Star-Spangled Banner. Wilde, G., illus. LC 65-1221. (gr. 2-5). 1965. pap. 3.95 (0-516-44636-3) Childrens.

Miller, Ned. Emmett's Snowball. Guevara, Susan, illus. LC 89-77787. 40p. (ps-2). 1990. 14.95 (0-8050-1394-6, Bks Young Read) H Holt & Co.

Miller, Olive B., compiled by. My Storytime Treasury. (Illus.). 224p. (gr. k-3). 1991. 14.45 (0-395-59423-5, Sandpiper) HM.

Miller, Paul M. Christmas Comes to Lone Star Gulch. Linn, Joseph, contrib. by. Date not set. 4.50 (0-685-68523-3, BCMC-67); song charts 29.95 (0-685-68524-1, BCMC-67C); cassette 9.98 (0-685-68525-X, BCTA-9106C) Lillenas.

Miller, Philip, jt. auth. see LeBaron, John.

Miller, R. Edward. The Flaming Flame. 95p. (Orig.). (gr. 12). 1973. pap. 2.50 (0-945818-03-3) Peniel Pubns.

—I Looked & I Saw Mysteries. Schisler, Jack, intro. by. 106p. (gr. 12). 1988. pap. 3.50 (0-945818-01-7) Peniel Pubns.

—I Looked & I Saw the Lord. Schisler, Jack, intro. by. 95p. (Orig.). (gr. 12). 1988. pap. 3.50 (0-945818-00-9) Peniel Pubns.

—I Looked & I Saw Visions of God. 147p. (Orig.). (gr. 12). 1974. pap. 3.50 (0-945818-04-1) Peniel Pubns.

—I Looked & Saw the Heavens Opened... 96p. (Orig.). (gr. 12). 1972. pap. 3.50 (0-945818-05-X) Peniel Pubns.

—The Prince & the Three Beggars. 33p. (Orig.). (gr. 12). 1975. pap. 2.50 (0-945818-04-1) Peniel Pubns.

—Romance of Redemption. 213p. (Orig.). (gr. 10). 1990. pap. 7.95 (0-945818-09-2) Peniel Pubns.

—Secrets of the Kingdom. 180p. (Orig.). (gr. 10). 1989. pap. 5.25 (0-945818-08-4) Peniel Pubns.

—Thy God Reigneth. Frodsham, Stanley, intro. by. 58p. (gr. 12). 1964. pap. 2.50 (0-945818-02-5) Peniel Pubns.

—Victory in Adversity. 168p. (Orig.). (gr. 10). 1988. pap. 4.95 (0-945818-07-6) Peniel Pubns.

Miller, Ralph, Sr. Sign Language Clowns. 32p. 1983. 4.50 (0-915035-00-6, 4160) Dawn Sign.

Miller, Ray, Jr., jt. auth. see McCloy, James F.

Miller, Rich, jt. auth. see McAllister, Dawson.

Miller, Robert. Buffalo Soldiers. Leonard, Richard, illus. 104p. (gr. 4-7). 1992. PLB 13.98 (0-382-24080-4); pap. 7.95 (0-382-24085-5) (0-685-47034-2) Silver Burdett Pr.

—Cowboys. Leonard, Richard, illus. 104p. (gr. 4-7). 1992. PLB 13.98 (0-382-24079-0); pap. 7.95 (0-382-24084-7) Silver Burdett Pr.

—Mountain Men. Leonard, Richard, illus. 104p. (gr. 4-7). 1991. PLB 13.98 (0-382-24082-0); pap. 7.95 (0-382-24087-1) Silver Burdett Pr.

—Pioneers. Leonard, Richard, illus. 104p. (gr. 4-7). 1991. PLB 13.98 (0-382-24081-2); pap. 7.95 (0-382-24086-3) Silver Burdett Pr.

—Reflections of a Black Cowboy Series, 4 vols. Leonard, Richard, illus. 416p. (gr. 4-7). 1991. Set. PLB 55.92 (0-382-24078-2); Set. pap. 31.80 (0-382-24083-9) Silver Burdett Pr.

Miller, Robert D. Spelling Games & Puzzles for Junior High. (gr. 6-8). 1976. pap. 9.95 (0-8224-6460-8) Fearon Teach Aids.

—Tommy the Toothbrush. Palsa, Soozee, illus. 16p. (gr. 2-4). 1982. write for info Miller OH.

Miller, Robert F. Travel: Careers Without College. Colton, Kitty, ed. Schmidt, Peggy, contrib. by. 96p. (Orig.). (gr. 10-12). 1993. pap. 7.95 (1-56079-249-3) Petersons Guides.

Miller, Robert H. Reflections of a Black Cowboy. Miller, Robert H., illus. 9p. (Orig.). (gr. 5-7). 1988. pap. text ed. 9.95x (0-929592-01-8) Waterline Prodns.

Miller, Robin J. see Scribbles, R. J., pseud.

Miller, Rose. The Old Barn. Enik, Ted, illus. LC 92-35283. 32p. (gr. 2-6). 1992. PLB 17.96 (0-8114-3581-4) Raintree Steck-V.

Miller, Russell. Continents in Collision. (Illus.). 176p. (gr. 7 up). 1983. 18.60 (0-8094-4326-0); lib. bdg. 24.60 (0-8094-4325-2) Time-Life.

Miller, Russell A., jt. auth. see Shuster, Albert H.

Miller, S. My Book about Hudson. 1989. 5.95 (9971-972-69-7) OMF Bks.

Miller, Sandy. Smart Girl. 160p. (gr. 7 up). 1982. pap. 2.25 (0-451-11887-1, Sig Vista) NAL-Dutton.

Miller, Sarah W. Bible Dramas for Older Boys & Girls. LC 75-95409. (gr. 3-6). 1970. pap. 4.95 (0-8054-7506-0) Broadman.

—Christmas Drama for Youth. LC 76-20255. 96p. (Orig.). (gr. 7 up). 1976. pap. 4.95 (0-8054-7511-7) Broadman.

Miller, Scott. Loon Journal. (Illus.). 40p. (Orig.). (gr. 4 up). 1989. pap. 5.98 (0-926147-01-3) Loonfeather.

Miller, Scott, jt. auth. see Miller, Luree.

Miller, Sheila & Murray, Ian. The Gods Must Be Angry. Chung, Simon T., illus. 34p. (gr. 1-4). 1990. 2.95 (9971-972-93-X) OMF Bks.

Miller, Sherry. The Day Happy E. Bunny Lost His Cotton Tail. Martinez, Jesse, illus. 16p. (Orig.). (gr. k-5). 1983. pap. 0.49 saddle-stitched (0-685-43303-X) Double M Pub.

—Lost in the Arctic with Pal Bear. Martinez, Jesse, illus. 32p. (Orig.). (gr. k-5). 1984. pap. 1.95 saddle-stitched (0-913379-01-8) Double M Pub.

—Santa's Helper. Martinez, Jesse, illus. LC 83-72493. 32p. (gr. k-5). 1983. pap. 1.95 saddle-stitched (*0-913379-00-X*) Double M Pub.
—Snowskate Goes for Gold. Martinez, Jesse, illus. 32p. (Orig.). (gr. k-5). 1984. pap. 1.95 saddle-stitched (*0-913379-02-6*) Double M Pub.
Miller, Sherry C. Snowharry Takes a Vacation (with Arctic Friends) Martinez, Jesse, illus. 32p. (gr. k-5). 1985. pap. write for info. saddle-stitched (*0-913379-03-4*) Double M Pub.
Miller, Shirley J. Billy. Casey, Marjorie, illus. 60p. (Orig.). (gr. 2-6). 1993. pap. 6.95 (*1-878580-92-2*) Asylum Arts.
—My House, Your House. Casey, Marjorie, illus. 60p. (Orig.). (gr. 2-6). 1993. pap. 6.95 (*1-878580-91-4*) Asylum Arts.
—School Days. Casey, Marjorie, illus. 80p. (Orig.). (gr. 2-6). 1993. pap. 6.95 (*1-878580-90-6*) Asylum Arts.
Miller, Susan M. Elijah. (Illus.). (gr. 3 up). pap. 2.50 perfect bdg. (*1-55748-189-X*) Barbour & Co.
—Esther. (gr. 3 up). 1992. pap. 2.50 perfect bdg. (*1-55748-260-8*) Barbour & Co.
—Hudson Taylor. (gr. 3-10). 1993. pap. 4.95 (*1-55748-338-8*) Barbour & Co.
Miller, Susanna. Beans & Peas. Yeats, John, illus. 32p. (gr. 1-4). 1990. PLB 14.95 (*0-87614-428-8*) Carolrhoda Bks.
Miller, Susanne S. Prehistoric Mammals. Santoro, Christopher, illus. (ps-5). 1984. pap. 7.95 (*0-671-47976-8*, S&S BFYR) S&S Trade.
Miller, Suzanne S. Whales & Sharks. Klimo, Kate, ed. Bonforte, Lisa, illus. 48p. 1982. pap. 9.95 (*0-671-45148-0*, S&S BFYR) S&S Trade.
Miller, Teresa & Pellowski, Anne. Joining In: An Anthology of Audience Participation Stories & How to Tell Them. Livo, Norma J., ed. Simms, Laura, intro. by. 125p. (Orig.). 1988. pap. text ed. 11.95 (*0-938756-21-4*) Yellow Moon.
Miller, Timothy B. Just in the Nick of Time. LC 87-72303. 90p. (Orig.). (gr. 5 up). 1989. pap. 6.00 (*0-916383-48-2*) Aegina Pr.
Miller, Tom. This Path of Scattered Glass: A Collection of Poems. Miller, Tom, illus. LC 92-84067. 96p. (Orig.). (gr. 7 up). 1993. pap. 6.95 (*1-878893-39-4*) Telcraft Bks.
Miller, Viola P. & Blodgett, Elizabeth G. Practice Power for Phonology: An Easy Does It Approach. 180p. (ps-2). 1991. wkbk. spiral bdg. 25.95 (*1-55999-207-7*) LinguiSystems.
Miller, Virginia. Eat Your Dinner! LC 91-58728. (Illus.). 32p. (ps up). 1992. 14.95 (*1-56402-121-1*) Candlewick Pr.
—Go to Bed! Miller, Virginia, illus. LC 92-54958. 32p. (ps up). 1993. 14.95 (*1-56402-244-7*) Candlewick Pr.
—On Your Potty! LC 90-49221. (Illus.). 32p. (ps up). 1991. 13.95 (*0-688-10617-X*); PLB 13.88 (*0-688-10618-8*) Greenwillow.
Miller, Virginia, jt. auth. see Waddell, Martin.
Miller, Vousette T. Color Me Beautiful Color Me Black. (Illus.). 32p. (ps-6). 1988. wkbk. 4.00 (*0-9619641-0-3*) Vous Etes Tres Belle.
—Poems by Shining Star: The Voice of Shining Star. 16p. (Orig.). (ps-6). 1990. pap. write for info. wkbk. (*0-9619641-1-1*) Vous Etes Tres Belle.
Miller, W. Wesley. Blain's Woods. Kratoville, Betty L., ed. (Illus.). 64p. (gr. 3-9). 1989. PLB 4.95 (*0-87879-618-5*) High Noon Bks.
—Connections, 5 novels. Kratoville, Betty L., ed. Heidinger, Herbert H., illus. 240p. (Orig.). (gr. 4-12). 1988. Set. pap. 15.00 (*0-87879-556-1*) High Noon Bks.
—Dark Secret. Kratoville, Betty L., ed. (Illus.). (gr. 3-9). 1989. PLB 4.95 (*0-87879-620-7*) High Noon Bks.
Miller, Wendy. Around the World with God's Friends: Mission Education Activity Book - Elementary Grades. Frailey, Joy, illus. 24p. (Orig.). (gr. 1-5). 1990. pap. text ed. 1.50g (*1-877736-06-6*, Mission Focus) MB Missions.
Miller, Wynne, ed. see Ratner-Gantshar, Barbara.
Miller-Lachmann, Lyn. Hiding Places. 206p. (Orig.). (gr. 9-12). 1987. pap. 4.95 (*0-938961-00-4*, Stamp Out Sheep Pr) Sq One Pubs.
Millet, C. & Millet, D., illus. Castles. Jeunesse, Gallimard, et al. LC 92-15955. 1993. 10.95 (*0-590-46377-2*) Scholastic Inc.
Millhouse, Nicholas, jt. auth. see Bowman, Margret.
Millicer, Jan. When It Rains. Swearingen, Karen M., illus. LC 92-31136. 1993. 2.50 (*0-383-03667-4*) SRA Schl Grp.
Milligan, Bryce. Comanche Captive: You Are There. Shaw, Charles, illus. 156p. (gr. 5 up). 1989. pap. 3.95 (*0-87719-157-3*, Lone Star Bks) Gulf Pub.
—With the Wind, Kevin Dolan. LC 86-70018. (Illus.). 194p. (gr. 7 up). 1992. pap. 7.95 (*0-931722-45-4*) Corona Pub.
Milligan, Lynda, jt. auth. see Smith, Nancy.
Milligan, Lynda, jt. auth. see Smith, Nancy J.
Milliken, Linda. Frontier American Activity Book: Art, Crafts, Ccooking. Lorseyedi, Barb, illus. (gr. k-6). 1990. pap. text ed. 5.95 (*1-56472-017-9*) Edupress.
Millman, Dan. Quest for the Crystal Castle. Bruce, T. Taylor, illus. LC 92-70302. 32p. (ps-5). 1992. 13.95 (*0-915811-41-3*) H J Kramer Inc.
Mills. Secret Carousel. (ps-7). 1987. pap. 2.50 (*0-553-15499-0*, Skylark) Bantam.
Mills, Adam. Cold Chills. (gr. 4 up). 1989. pap. 2.95 (*0-345-35929-1*) Ballantine.
Mills, Bart. Melrose Place - Off the Record. 1992. pap. 3.99 (*0-06-106787-3*, Harp PBks) HarpC.

Mills, Brenda. My Bible Story Picture Book. (Illus.). 128p. (gr. k-5). 1982. text ed. 12.99 (*0-89081-319-1*) Harvest Hse.
Mills, Bronwyn. The Mexican War. Bowman, John, ed. (Illus.). 128p. (gr. 6-12). 1992. lib. bdg. 17.95x (*0-8160-2393-X*) Facts on File.
Mills, Charles. My Talents for Jesus; When I Grow Up. LC 92-26393. 1993. 8.95 (*0-8163-1115-3*) Pacific Pr Pub Assn.
—Voyager, II. Coffen, Richard, ed. 192p. (Orig.). (gr. 5-8). 1991. pap. 9.95 (*0-8280-0595-8*) Review & Herald.
Mills, Claudia. After Fifth Grade, the World! LC 88-26664. 128p. (gr. 3-7). 1989. SBE 12.95 (*0-02-767041-4*, Macmillan Child Bk) Macmillan Child Grp.
—After Fifth Grade, the World! (gr. 3-7). 1991. pap. 2.95 (*0-380-70894-9*, Camelot) Avon.
—Boardwalk with Hotel. 144p. (gr. 7-12). 1986. pap. 2.50 (*0-553-15397-8*, Skylark) Bantam.
—Cally's Enterprise. LC 87-36471. 128p. (gr. 3-7). 1988. SBE 13.95 (*0-02-767100-3*, Macmillan Child Bk) Macmillan Child Grp.
—Cally's Enterprise. 128p. (gr. 5 up). 1989. pap. 2.75 (*0-380-70693-8*, Camelot) Avon.
—Dinah for President. LC 91-34839. 128p. (gr. 3-7). 1992. SBE 12.95 (*0-02-766999-8*, Macmillan Child Bk) Macmillan Child Grp.
—Dinah in Love. 144p. (gr. 4-7). 1993. SBE 13.95 (*0-02-766998-X*, Macmillan Child Bk) Macmillan Child Grp.
—Dynamite Dinah. LC 89-13300. 128p. (gr. 3-7). 1990. SBE 13.95 (*0-02-767101-1*, Macmillan Child Bk) Macmillan Child Grp.
—Dynamite Dinah. LC 91-20651. 128p. (gr. 3-7). 1992. pap. 3.95 (*0-689-71591-9*, Aladdin) Macmillan Child Grp.
—Hannah on Her Way. LC 90-46532. 144p. (gr. 3-7). 1991. SBE 13.95 (*0-02-767011-2*, Macmillan Child Bk) Macmillan Child Grp.
—Hannah on Her Way. LC 92-42534. 160p. (gr. 3-7). 1993. pap. 3.95 (*0-689-71754-7*, Aladdin) Macmillan Child Grp.
—Melanie Magpie. 96p. (Orig.). 1987. pap. 2.50 (*0-553-15524-5*, Skylark) Bantam.
—The One & Only Cynthia Jane Thornton. LC 86-12629. 120p. (gr. 3-7). 1986. SBE 12.95 (*0-02-767090-2*, Macmillan Child Bk) Macmillan Child Grp.
—Phoebe's Parade. Ewing, Carolyn, illus. LC 93-21861. 32p. (gr. k-3). 1994. RSBE 14.95 (*0-02-767012-0*, Macmillan Child Bk) Macmillan Child Grp.
—A Visit to Amy-Claire. Hamanaka, Sheila, illus. LC 91-280. 32p. (gr. k-3). 1992. RSBE 14.95 (*0-02-766991-2*, Macmillan Child Bk) Macmillan Child Grp.
—What about Annie? LC 84-20862. 128p. (gr. 5 up). 1985. 9.95 (*0-8027-6573-4*) Walker & Co.
Mills, Diana. Crazy Hattie. (Illus.). 12p. (gr. 3-7). 1986. pap. 7.95 (*0-9616555-0-X*) Berry Good Child Bks.
Mills, Dick. Encyclopedia of the Marine Aquarium. 1988. 12.99 (*0-517-63378-7*) Outlet Bk Co.
Mills, Earl. Dorothy Dandridge. rev. ed. 1991. pap. 3.95 (*0-87067-580-X*) Holloway.
Mills, Elaine, jt. auth. see Wilkins, Verna.
Mills, Elaine, jt. auth. see Wilkins, Verna A.
Mills, George, jt. auth. see Aitken, John.
Mills, Jackie. Sirena of Salado. Mills, Jackie, illus. 32p. (gr. 2-7). 1991. 10.95 (*0-9629284-0-2*) Indian Trail.
Mills, Jane L. & Johnson, Larry D. Arnie's Surprise. Hebert, Kim T., illus. LC 86-60363. 14p. (Orig.). (ps). 1986. pap. 4.00 (*0-938155-05-9*); pap. 12.00 set of 3 bks. (*0-685-13523-3*) Read A Bol.
—Build Like Me. Hebert, Kim T., illus. LC 86-60362. 13p. (Orig.). (ps). 1986. pap. 4.00 (*0-938155-01-6*); pap. 12.00 set of 3 bks. (*0-685-13524-1*) Read A Bol.
—Peek-a-Boo. Hebert, Kim T., illus. LC 86-60380. 13p. (Orig.). (ps). 1986. pap. 3.50 (*0-938155-04-0*); pap. 12.00 set of 3 bks. (*0-685-13530-6*) Read A Bol.
Mills, Jane L., jt. auth. see Johnson, Larry D.
Mills, Joyce C. Gentle Willow: A Story for Children about Dying. Chesworth, Michael, illus. LC 93-22770. 1993. 16.95 (*0-945354-54-1*); pap. 8.95 (*0-945354-53-3*) Magination Pr.
—Little Tree: A Story for Children with Serious Medical Problems. Chesworth, Michael, illus. LC 92-19654. 32p. 1992. 16.95 (*0-945354-52-5*); pap. 6.95 (*0-945354-51-7*) Magination Pr.
Mills, Joyce C. & Crowley, Richard J. Sammy the Elephant & Mr. Camel: A Story to Help Children Overcome Bedwetting While Discovering Self-Appreciation. Cook, Germaine, illus. LC 88-13581. 48p. (gr. 1 up). 1988. PLB 16.95 (*0-945354-09-6*); pap. 6.95 (*0-945354-08-8*) Magination Pr.
Mills, Judie. John F. Kennedy. Kline, M., ed. LC 87-29470. (Illus.). 384p. (gr. 7-12). 1988. PLB 17.40 (*0-531-10520-2*) Watts.
Mills, Kathi, ed. see Dobson, James.
Mills, Kathleen. Fairy Wings. LC 92-37168. 1992. 14.95 (*0-316-57397-3*) Little.
—The Rag Coat. (Illus.). (ps-3). 1991. 15.95 (*0-316-57407-4*) Little.
Mills, Lauren, retold by. Tatterhood & the Hobgoblins: A Norwegian Folktale, Vol. 1. (Illus.). (ps-3). 1993. 15.95 (*0-316-57406-6*) Little.
Mills, Louise, ed. see Haaland, Lynn.

Mills, Patricia. Until the Cows Come Home. Mills, Patricia, illus. LC 92-31049. 32p. (gr. k-3). 1993. 14.95 (*1-55858-190-1*); PLB 14.88 (*1-55858-191-X*) North-South Bks NYC.
Mills, Perry, ed. see Shakespeare, William.
Mills, Peter. Jonah's Adventure with the Big Fish: Bible Adventures. Mills, Peter, illus. 1991. bds. 8.99 with flaps (*0-8007-7121-4*) Revell.
—The Lost Coin. (Illus.). 24p. (ps-k). 1994. 3.99 (*0-8499-1088-9*) Word Inc.
—The Lost Pearl. (Illus.). 24p. (ps-k). 1994. 3.99 (*0-8499-1087-0*) Word Inc.
—The Lost Sheep. (Illus.). 24p. (ps-5). 1994. 3.99 (*0-8499-1089-7*) Word Inc.
—The Lost Son. (Illus.). 24p. (ps-k). 1994. 3.99 (*0-8499-1086-2*) Word Inc.
Mills, Reita. Santa's Ups & Downs. 1992. 6.95 (*0-533-10307-X*) Vantage.
Millspaugh, Ben. Aviation & Space Science Projects. 1991. 16.95 (*0-8306-2157-1*); pap. 9.95 (*0-8306-2156-3*) TAB Bks.
Mills-Thornton, Serena G. Mentor Wisdom: Requisites for Living. Allen, Sharon, ed. Thornton, John H., illus. 31p. (Orig.). 1993. write for info. (*0-9614338-0-9*) Ideas.
Millward, David W. Jenny & Bob. (ps). 1991. 15.00 (*0-385-30431-5*) Delacorte.
Millyard, Anne W., jt. auth. see Wilks, Rick J.
Milne, A. A. Christopher Robin Gives Pooh a Party. Shepard, Ernest H., illus. 32p. (ps up). 1992. incl. charm 13.95 (*0-525-44871-3*, DCB) Dutton Child Bks.
—Christopher Robin Gives Pooh a Party. Shepard, Ernest H., illus. 32p. 1993. 4.99 (*0-525-45144-7*, DCB) Dutton Child Bks.
—Christopher Robin Leads an Expotition. Shepard, Ernest H., illus. 32p. 1993. 4.99 (*0-525-45142-0*, DCB) Dutton Child Bks.
—Eeyore Loses a Tail. Shepard, Ernest H., illus. 32p. 1993. 4.99 (*0-525-45137-4*, DCB) Dutton Child Bks.
—Eeyore Loses a Tail. Shepard, Ernest H., illus. 32p. 1993. incl. charm 13.99 (*0-525-45045-9*, DCB) Dutton Child Bks.
—Eyeore Has a Birthday. Shepard, Ernest H., illus. 32p. 1993. 4.99 (*0-525-45043-2*, DCB) Dutton Child Bks.
—House at Pooh Corner. Shepard, Ernest H., illus. (gr. k up). 1985. 9.95 (*0-525-32302-3*, Dutton) NAL-Dutton.
—The House at Pooh Corner. Shepard, Ernest H., illus. 192p. (ps up). 1988. 9.95 (*0-525-44444-0*, DCB) Dutton Child Bks.
—The House at Pooh Corner. Shepard, Ernest H., illus. LC 91-29462. 192p. (ps up). 1991. Full-color Gift Edition. 20.00 (*0-525-44774-1*, DCB) Dutton Child Bks.
—The House at Pooh Corner. Shepard, Ernest H., illus. 192p. 1992. pap. 3.99 (*0-14-036122-7*, Puffin) Puffin Bks.
—The House at Pooh Corner. 1923. pap. 1.75 (*0-440-73795-8*) Dell.
—House at Pooh Corner: A Pop-Up Book. (Illus.). 12p. (ps up). 1986. 12.95 (*0-525-44245-6*, DCB) Dutton Child Bks.
—Kanga & Baby Roo Come to the Forest. Shepard, Ernest H., illus. 32p. 1993. 4.99 (*0-525-45141-2*, DCB) Dutton Child Bks.
—Le Meilleur des Ours. (FRE.). (gr. 3-8). 9.95 (*0-685-23403-7*) Fr & Eur.
—Now We Are Six. Shepard, Ernest H., illus. 112p. (ps up). 1988. 9.95 (*0-525-44446-7*, DCB) Dutton Child Bks.
—Now We Are Six. Shepard, Ernest H., illus. 112p. (ps-6). 1992. full-color gift ed. 17.50 (*0-525-44960-4*, DCB) Dutton Child Bks.
—Now We Are Six. Shepard, Ernest H., illus. 112p. 1992. pap. 3.99 (*0-14-036124-3*, Puffin) Puffin Bks.
—Piglet Is Entirely Surrounded by Water. Shepard, Ernest H., illus. 16p. (ps up). 1991. 7.95 (*0-525-44784-9*, DCB) Dutton Child Bks.
—Piglet Is Entirely Surrounded by Water. Shepard, Ernest H., illus. 32p. 1993. 4.99 (*0-525-45143-9*, DCB) Dutton Child Bks.
—Piglet Meets a Heffalump. Shepard, Ernest H., illus. 32p. 1993. 4.99 (*0-525-45042-4*, DCB) Dutton Child Bks.
—The Poems & Hums of Winnie-the-Pooh. Shepard, Ernest H., illus. 10p. (gr. 4-7). 1994. pap. 5.99 (*0-525-45205-2*, DCB) Dutton Child Bks.
—Pooh & Piglet Go Hunting. Shepard, Ernest H., illus. 32p. (ps up). 1992. incl. charm 13.95 (*0-525-44872-1*, DCB) Dutton Child Bks.
—Pooh & Piglet Go Hunting. Shepard, Ernest H., illus. 32p. 1993. 4.99 (*0-525-45136-6*, DCB) Dutton Child Bks.
—Pooh & Some Bees. Cremins, Robert, illus. 10p. (ps up). 1987. 7.95 (*0-525-44339-8*, 0674-210, DCB) Dutton Child Bks.
—Pooh Goes Visiting. Cremins, Robert, illus. 10p. (ps up). 1987. 7.95 (*0-525-44337-1*, 0674-210, DCB) Dutton Child Bks.
—Pooh Goes Visiting. Shepard, Ernest H., illus. 32p. 1993. 4.99 (*0-525-45040-8*, DCB) Dutton Child Bks.
—Pooh Invents a New Game. Shepard, Ernest H., illus. 16p. (ps up). 1991. 7.95 (*0-525-44783-0*, DCB) Dutton Child Bks.
—The Pooh Story Book. Shepard, Ernest H., illus. LC 65-19580. 80p. (gr. k-4). 1965. 13.00 (*0-525-37546-5*, DCB) Dutton Child Bks.

—Pooh's Adventures with Eeyore & Tigger. (Illus.). 18p. (ps-4). 1986. 2.98 (0-525-44263-4, DCB) Dutton Child Bks.
—Pooh's Adventures with Piglet. (Illus.). 18p. (ps-4). 1986. 2.98 (0-525-44264-2, DCB) Dutton Child Bks.
—Pooh's Birthday Book. Shepard, Ernest H., illus. 160p. (gr. 1-3). 1991. pap. 3.50 (0-440-46934-1, YB) Dell.
—Pooh's Library, 4 bks. Shepard, Ernest H., illus. (ps up). 1988. Set. 39.95 (0-525-44451-3, DCB) Dutton Child Bks.
—Pooh's Library, 4 bks. Shepard, Ernest H., illus. 1992. Set. pap. 16.00 slipcased (0-14-095560-7, Puffin) Puffin Bks.
—Pooh's Pot O'Honey, 4 vols. Shepard, Ernest H., illus. (ps up). 1985. Boxed Set. 10.95 (0-525-37518-X, DCB) Dutton Child Bks.
—Prince Rabbit. 1991. PLB 13.95s.p. (0-88682-480-X) Creative Ed.
—The Songs of Winnie-the-Pooh. Shepard, Ernest H., illus. 10p. (gr. 4-7). 1994. pap. 5.99 (0-525-45206-0, DCB) Dutton Child Bks.
—A Treasury of Winnie-the-Pooh, 4 bks. Shepard, Ernest H., illus. Incl. Winnie-the-Pooh; The House at Pooh Corner; Now We Were Six; When We Were Very Young. (Illus.). 1987. Boxed set. pap. 13.00 (0-440-49580-6) Dell.
—When We Were Very Young. Shepard, Ernest H., illus. 112p. (gr. 2-5). 1970. pap. 3.50 (0-440-49485-0, YB) Dell.
—When We Were Very Young. Shepard, Ernest H., illus. 112p. (ps up). 1988. 9.95 (0-525-44445-9, DCB) Dutton Child Bks.
—When We Were Very Young. (Illus.). 112p. (ps-6). 1992. full-color gift ed. 17.50 (0-525-44961-2, DCB) Dutton Child Bks.
—When We Were Very Young. Shepard, Ernest H., illus. 112p. 1992. pap. 3.99 (0-14-036123-5, Puffin) Puffin Bks.
—Winnie l'Ourson. (FRE., Illus.). (gr. 3-8). 9.95 (0-685-23402-9) Fr & Eur.
—Winnie-the-Pooh. Shepard, Ernest H., illus. (gr. 1-5). 1961. 9.95 (0-525-43035-0, Dutton) NAL-Dutton.
—Winnie-the-Pooh. (gr. k-6). 1988. pap. 5.95 (0-440-40116-X, Pub. by Yearling Classics) Dell.
—Winnie-the-Pooh. Shepard, Ernest H., illus. 176p. (ps up). 1988. 9.95 (0-525-44443-2, DCB) Dutton Child Bks.
—Winnie-the-Pooh. Shepard, Ernest H., illus. LC 91-26203. 176p. (ps up). 1991. Full-color Gift Edition. 20.00 (0-525-44776-8, DCB) Dutton Child Bks.
—Winnie-the-Pooh. Shepard, Ernest H., illus. 176p. 1992. pap. 3.99 (0-14-036121-9, Puffin) Puffin Bks.
—Winnie the Pooh, 4 vols. 1992. Set. slipcased 75.00 (0-525-45004-1, DCB) Dutton Child Bks.
—Winnie-the-Pooh: A Pop-Up Book. (Illus.). 12p. (ps up). 1984. 13.00 (0-525-44119-0, DCB) Dutton Child Bks.
—Winnie the Pooh & Some Bees. Shepard, Ernest H., illus. 32p. 1993. incl. charm 13.99 (0-525-45044-0, DCB) Dutton Child Bks.
—Winnie the Pooh & Some Bees Storybooks. 128p. (ps-2). 1993. (DCB); pap. 4.99 (0-525-45033-5, DCB) Dutton Child Bks.
—Winnie-the-Pooh Goes Exploring. (ps-4). 1986. 2.98 (0-525-44269-3, DCB) Dutton Child Bks.
—The Winnie-the-Pooh Journal. Shepard, Ernest H., illus. 64p. (ps up). 1986. 7.99 (0-525-44237-5, DCB) Dutton Child Bks.
—Winnie-the-Pooh Lift-the-Flap Rebus Book. (Illus.). 16p. (ps-3). 1992. 12.95 (0-525-44987-6, DCB) Dutton Child Bks.
—Winnie-the-Pooh's Calendar Book 1987. Shepard, Ernest H., illus. (ps up). 1986. 4.95 (0-525-44235-9, Dutton) NAL-Dutton.
—Winnie-the-Pooh's Calendar Book 1988. Shepard, Ernest H., illus. (ps up). 1987. spiral bd. 4.95 (0-525-44311-8, Dutton) NAL-Dutton.
—Winnie-the-Pooh's Calendar Book 1989. Shepard, Ernest H., illus. 32p. (ps up). 1988. spiral bd. 5.95 (0-525-44398-3, Dutton) NAL-Dutton.
—Winnie-the-Pooh's Friendship Book. Shepard, Ernest H., illus. 48p. (gr. 4-7). 1994. 8.99 (0-525-45204-4, DCB) Dutton Child Bks.
—Winnie-the-Pooh's Little Book about Food. Shepard, Ernest H., illus. 10p. (ps up). 1992. 4.95 (0-525-44875-6, DCB) Dutton Child Bks.
—Winnie-the-Pooh's Little Book about Friends. Shepard, Ernest H., illus. 10p. (ps up). 1992. 4.95 (0-525-44874-8, DCB) Dutton Child Bks.
—Winnie-the-Pooh's Little Book about Parties. Shepard, Ernest H., illus. 10p. (ps up). 1992. 4.95 (0-525-44876-4, DCB) Dutton Child Bks.
—Winnie-the-Pooh's Little Book about Weather. Shepard, Ernest H., illus. 10p. (ps up). 1992. 4.95 (0-525-44877-2, DCB) Dutton Child Bks.
—Winnie the Pooh's Pop-up Theater Book. (Illus.). 12p. 1993. 15.95 (0-525-44990-6, DCB) Dutton Child Bks.
—Winnie-the-Pooh's Revolving Picture Book. (Illus.). 12p. (ps up). 1990. 13.00 (0-525-44645-1, DCB) Dutton Child Bks.
—Winnie-the-Pooh's Story Box, 10 bks. Shepard, Ernest H., illus. 1993. Set. 49.90 (0-525-45168-4, DCB) Dutton Child Bks.
—Winnie-the-Pooh's Teatime Cookbook. Shepard, Ernest H., illus. LC 92-35650. 64p. 1993. 9.99 (0-525-45135-8, DCB) Dutton Child Bks.
—Winny de Puh. (SPA.). 7.50 (0-685-31015-9) Santillana.

—Winny De Puh. (SPA., Illus.). 176p. (ps-3). 1992. 11.00 (0-525-44986-8, DCB) Dutton Child Bks.
—World of Christopher Robin. (gr. 1-4). 1958. Boxed with "World of Pooh" 29.95 (0-525-43348-1, Dutton) NAL-Dutton.
—The World of Christopher Robin. Shepard, Ernest H., illus. 256p. (ps up). 1988. 17.50 (0-525-44448-3, DCB) Dutton Child Bks.
—The World of Pooh. Shepard, Ernest H., illus. 320p. (ps up). 1988. 17.50 (0-525-44447-5, DCB) Dutton Child Bks.
—The World of Pooh. (Illus.). (gr. 1-4). 1957. 13.95 (0-525-43320-1, 01258-370, Dutton); Incl. "World of Christopher" boxed 29.95 (0-685-46952-2, 01258-370) NAL-Dutton.
—The World of Winnie-the-Pooh, 2 bks. Shepard, Ernest H., illus. (ps up). 1988. Set. 33.95 (0-525-44452-1, DCB) Dutton Child Bks.
Milne, A. A. & Fraser-Simon, H. The Pooh Song Book. Shepard, E. H., illus. LC 61-1021. 154p. 1985. pap. 8.95 (0-87923-557-8) Godine.
Milne, A. A. & Shepard. Pooh's Bedtime Book. LC 80-65523. (Illus.). 48p. (ps-3). 1980. 9.95 (0-525-44895-0, DCB) Dutton Child Bks.
Milne, Lorus J. Insects & Spiders. (gr. 4-7). 1992. 13.00 (0-385-26396-1) Doubleday.
Milne, Lorus J. & Milne, Margery. Understanding Radioactivity. Hiscock, Bruce, illus. LC 88-7382. 80p. (gr. 4 up). 1989. SBE 13.95 (0-689-31362-4, Atheneum Child Bk) Macmillan Child Grp.
Milne, Margery, jt. auth. see Milne, Lorus J.
Milne, Teddy. Anthony. LC 86-62446. 197p. (Orig.). (gr. 5 up). 1986. pap. 5.00 (0-938875-01-9) Pittenbrauch Pr.
—The Candy Puzzle: An Alexa Powell Mystery. LC 89-60248. 172p. (gr. 6-8). 1988. pap. 6.95 (0-938875-16-7) Pittenbrauch Pr.
—Shambala Warriors: Non-Violent Fighters for Peace. Milne, James A., illus. LC 86-64054. 150p. (Orig.). (gr. 4 up). 1987. pap. 7.95 (0-938875-07-8) Pittenbrauch Pr.
Milner, Cate. France. LC 89-21783. (Illus.). 96p. (gr. 6-12). 1990. PLB 19.92 (0-8114-2427-8) Raintree Steck-V.
Milner, Cedric. Desert Trek. LC 88-42906. (Illus.). 32p. (gr. 4-5). 1989. PLB 15.93 (1-55532-919-5) Gareth Stevens Inc.
Milner, Richard. Charles Darwin. 128p. (gr. 5 up). 1993. PLB 16.95x (0-8160-2557-6) Facts on File.
Milnes, Gerald. Granny Will Your Dog Bite? And Other Mountain Rhymes. Root, Kimberly, illus. LC 88-27350. 48p. 1990. 14.95 (0-394-84749-0) Knopf Bks Yng Read.
—Granny Will Your Dog Bite? And Other Mountain Rhymes. Root, Kimberly, illus. Bird, Sonja, contrib. by. LC 88-27350. (Illus.). 48p. 1990. Incl. 40 min. cassette. slipcase 18.95 (0-394-85363-6) Knopf Bks Yng Read.
Milone, Karen, illus. Beauty & the Beast. LC 81-612. 32p. (gr. k-4). 1981. PLB 9.79 (0-89375-464-1); pap. text ed. 1.95 (0-89375-465-X) Troll Assocs.
Milord, Susan. Adventures in Art: Art & Crafts Experiences for 7- to 14-Year Olds. Williamson, Susan, ed. Milord, Susan, illus. LC 90-39031. 160p. (Orig.). (gr. 2-8). 1990. pap. 12.95 (0-913589-54-3) Williamson Pub Co.
—Hands Around the World: Three Hundred Sixty-Five Creative Ways to Build Cultural Awareness & Global Respect. LC 92-21753. (Illus.). 176p. (Orig.). (gr. 1-8). 1992. pap. 12.95 (0-913589-65-9) Williamson Pub Co.
—The Kids' Nature Book: Three Hundred Sixty-Five Indoor - Outdoor Activities & Experiences. Williamson, Susan, ed. LC 89-14724. (Illus.). 160p. (Orig.). (ps-3). 1989. pap. 12.95 (0-913589-42-X) Williamson Pub Co.
Milsome, John. Sierra Leone. (Illus.). 96p. (gr. 5 up). 1988. 14.95 (0-7910-0106-7) Chelsea Hse.
Milstein, Linda. Grandma's Jewelry Box. Hirashima, Jean, illus. LC 91-66738. 24p. (ps-3). 1992. 8.00 (0-679-81973-8) Random Bks Yng Read.
Milstein, Linda B. Amanda's Perfect Hair. Meddaugh, Susan, illus. LC 92-34314. 32p. (ps up). 1993. 14.00 (0-688-11153-X, Tambourine Bks); PLB 13.93 (0-688-11154-8, Tambourine Bks) Morrow.
—Miami-Nanny Stories. Han, Oki, illus. LC 93-28680. 1994. write for info. (0-688-11151-X, Tambourine Bks); PLB write for info. (0-688-11152-1, Tambourine Bks) Morrow.
Milton, Hilary. Escape from High Doom. Schwartz, Betty, ed. Frame, Paul, illus. 128p. (Orig.). (gr. 3-7). 1984. PLB 5.97 (0-685-08595-3) S&S Trade.
—Fun House Terrors! Frame, Paul, illus. 128p. (gr. 3-7). 1984. (J Messner); pap. 2.95 (0-685-09678-5) S&S Trade.
Milton, John. Paradise Lost. new ed. Tromley, F., intro. by. Bd. with Paradise Regained. (gr. 11up). 1968. pap. 2.50 (0-8049-0173-2, CL-173) Airmont.
Milton, Joyce. Bats! Creatures of the Night. Moffatt, Judith, illus. LC 92-43198. 48p. (ps-1). 1993. 7.99g (0-448-40194-0, G&D); pap. 3.50 (0-448-40193-2, G&D) Putnam Pub Group.
—Dinosaur Days. Roe, Richard, illus. LC 84-17861. 48p. (gr. k-3). 1985. lib. bdg. 7.99 (0-394-97023-3); pap. 3.50 (0-394-87023-9) Random Bks Yng Read.
—Dinosaur Days. Roe, Richard, illus. 48p. (gr. k-3). 1988. pap. 5.95 bk. & cassette pkg. (0-394-89774-9) Random Bks Yng Read.

—Don Quixote (Miguel de Cervantes) (gr. 9-12). 1985. pap. 2.50 (0-8120-3512-7) Barron.
—George Washington. (Orig.). (gr. k-6). 1988. pap. 2.95 (0-440-40020-1, YB) Dell.
—Marching to Freedom: The Story of Martin Luther King Jr. (Orig.). (gr. k-6). 1987. pap. 3.25 (0-440-45433-6, YB) Dell.
—Whales & Other Creatures of the Sea. Deal, Jim, illus. LC 92-2409. 32p. (ps-4). 1993. PLB 7.99 (0-679-93899-0); pap. 2.25 (0-679-83899-6) Random Bks Yng Read.
—Whales: The Gentle Giants. Langford, Alton, illus. LC 88-15616. 48p. (Orig.). (gr. k-3). 1989. lib. bdg. 7.99 (0-394-99809-X); pap. 3.50 (0-394-89809-5) Random Bks Yng Read.
—Wild, Wild Wolves. Schwinger, Larry, illus. LC 90-8807. 48p. (Orig.). (gr. 1-3). 1992. PLB 7.99 (0-679-91052-2); pap. 3.50 (0-679-81052-8) Random Bks Yng Read.
Milton, Nancy. The Giraffe That Walked to Paris. Roth, Roger, illus. LC 91-31767. 32p. (gr. k-4). 1992. 15.00 (0-517-58132-9); PLB 15.99 (0-517-58133-7) Crown Bks Yng Read.
Miluck, Nancy C. Nevada History Coloring Books: Nevada's Native Americans. Miluck, Nancy C., illus. 48p. (gr. k-5). 1992. pap. text ed. 3.50 (0-9606382-4-5) Dragon Ent.
—Nevada History Coloring Books: The First Settlers. Miluck, Nancy C., illus. 48p. (gr. k-6). 1993. pap. 3.50 (0-9606382-5-3) Dragon Ent. Postponed.
—Nevada History Coloring Books: The 20th Century. Miluck, Nancy C., illus. 48p. (Orig.). (gr. k-5). 1992. pap. text ed. 3.50 (0-9606382-3-7) Dragon Ent.
Min, Kellet I. Modern Informative Nursery Rhymes: American History, Book I. Hansen, Heidi, illus. LC 89-91719. 64p. (Orig.). (gr. 2-5). 1992. pap. 10.95 (0-9623411-2-6) Rhyme & Reason.
—Modern Informative Nursery Rhymes: General Science, Book I. Hansen, Heidi, illus. LC 89-91719. 64p. (Orig.). (gr. 2-5). 1993. pap. 10.95 (0-9623411-4-2) Rhyme & Reason.
—Modern Informative Nursery Rhymes: Values. Hansen, Heidi, illus. 32p. (Orig.). (ps-3). 1989. pap. 7.95 (0-685-26431-9) Rhyme & Reason.
—Modern Informative Nursery Rhymes: Values, Book I. Hansen, Heidi, illus. LC 89-91719. 32p. (ps-3). 1989. pap. 7.95 (0-9623411-3-4) Rhyme & Reason.
Minar, Barbra. Lamper's Meadow. Bishop, Lila, ed. 160p. (gr. 4-7). 1992. pap. 6.99 (0-89107-663-8) Good News.
Minard, Rosemary, ed. Womenfolk & Fairy Tales. LC 74-26555. (Illus.). 176p. (gr. 2-5). 1975. 14.45 (0-395-20276-0) HM.
Minarik, Elsa H. Percy & the Five Houses. (ps-3). 1990. pap. 3.95 (0-14-054209-4, Puffin) Puffin Bks.
Minarik, Else. Father Bear Comes Home: (Papa Oso Vuele a Casa) (SPA). 9.95 (84-204-3048-X) Santillana.
Minarik, Else H. Am I Beautiful? Abolafia, Yossi, illus. LC 91-32562. 24p. (ps-4). 1992. 14.00 (0-688-09911-4); PLB 13.93 (0-688-09912-2) Greenwillow.
—Cat & Dog. Siebel, Fritz, illus. LC 60-14998. 32p. (gr. k-2). 1960. PLB 13.89 (0-06-024221-3) HarpC Child Bks.
—Father Bear Comes Home. Sendak, Maurice, illus. LC 59-5794. 64p. (gr. k-3). 1959. 14.00 (0-06-024230-2); PLB 13.89 (0-06-024231-0) HarpC Child Bks.
—Father Bear Comes Home. Sendak, Maurice, illus. LC 59-5794. (ps-3). 1978. pap. 3.50 (0-06-444014-1, Trophy) HarpC Child Bks.
—It's Spring! Graham, Margaret B., illus. LC 87-37202. 24p. (ps up). 1989. 11.95 (0-688-07619-X); PLB 11.88 (0-688-07620-3) Greenwillow.
—Kiss for Little Bear. Sendak, Maurice, illus. LC 57-9263. 32p. (gr. k-3). 1968. 14.00 (0-06-024298-1); PLB 13.89 (0-06-024299-X) HarpC Child Bks.
—A Kiss for Little Bear. Sendak, Maurice, illus. LC 68-16820. 32p. (ps-3). 1984. pap. 3.50 (0-06-444050-8, Trophy) HarpC Child Bks.
—A Kiss for Little Bear. unabr. ed. Sendak, Maurice, illus. (ps-3). 1991. pap. 6.95 incl. cassette (1-55994-263-0, Caedmon) HarperAudio.
—A Kiss for Little Bear. 6p. (gr. 2-4). 1968. pap. 0.48 (0-685-63776-X, BR7951) W A T Braille.
—Kiss for Little Bear. 6p. 1992. Braille. 0.48 (1-56956-271-7) W A T Braille.
—Little Bear. Sendak, Maurice, illus. 64p. (gr. k-3). 1957. 14.00i (0-06-024240-X); PLB 13.89 (0-06-024241-8) HarpC Child Bks.
—Little Bear. LC 57-9263. (Illus.). 64p. (gr. k-3). 1986. incl. cassette 5.98 (0-694-00113-9, Trophy); pap. 3.50 (0-06-444004-4, Trophy) HarpC Child Bks.
—Little Bear. unabr. ed. Sendak, Maurice, illus. (ps-3). 1990. pap. 6.95 incl. cassette (1-55994-234-7, Caedmon) HarperAudio.
—Little Bear, 3 bks. Sendak, Maurice, contrib. by. (Illus.). (gr. k-3). 1992. Boxed set. pap. 10.50 (0-06-444197-0, Trophy) HarpC Child Bks.
—Little Bear's Friend. Sendak, Maurice, illus. LC 60-6370. 64p. (gr. k-3). 1960. 14.00i (0-06-024255-8); PLB 13.89 (0-06-024256-6) HarpC Child Bks.
—Little Bear's Friend. Sendak, Maurice, illus. LC 60-6370. 64p. (ps-3). 1985. incl. cassette 5.98 (0-694-00031-0, Trophy); pap. 3.50 (0-06-444051-6, Trophy) HarpC Child Bks.

—Little Bear's Friend. unabr. ed. Sendak, Maurice, illus. (ps-3). 1990. pap. 6.95 incl. cassette (*1-55994-235-5*, Caedmon) HarperAudio.
—Little Bear's Visit. Sendak, Maurice, illus. LC 61-11451. 64p. (ps-3). 1961. 14.00 (*0-06-024265-5*); PLB 13.89 (*0-06-024266-3*) HarpC Child Bks.
—Little Bear's Visit. Sandal, Maurice, illus. LC 61-11451. 64p. (gr. k-3). 1979. pap. 3.50 (*0-06-444023-0*, Trophy) HarpC Child Bks.
—Little Bear's Visit. Sendak, Maurice, illus. LC 61-11451. 64p. (ps-3). 1985. incl. cassette 5.98 (*0-694-00032-9*, Trophy) HarpC Child Bks.
—Little Bear's Visit. unabr. ed. Sendak, Maurice, illus. (ps-3). 1990. pap. 6.95 incl. cassette (*1-55994-236-3*, Caedmon) HarperAudio.
—The Little Girl & the Dragon. Gourlault, Martine, illus. LC 90-38495. 24p. (ps up) 1991. 13.95 (*0-688-09913-0*); PLB 13.88 (*0-688-09914-9*) Greenwillow.
—No Fighting, No Biting! Sendak, Maurice, illus. LC 58-5293. 64p. (gr. k-3). 1958. 13.00 (*0-06-024290-6*); PLB 13.89 (*0-06-024291-4*) HarpC Child Bks.
—No Fighting, No Biting! Sendak, Maurice, illus. LC 58-5293. 64p. (ps-3). 1978. pap. 3.50 (*0-06-444015-X*, Trophy) HarpC Child Bks.
—Osito. LC 69-14452. (SPA., Illus.). 64p. (ps-3). 1969. PLB 10.89 (*0-06-024244-2*) HarpC Child Bks.
—Percy & the Five Houses. Stevenson, James, illus. LC 88-4804. 24p. (gr. k up). 1989. 11.95 (*0-688-08104-5*); PLB 11.88 (*0-688-08105-3*) Greenwillow.
—Visita de Osito: (La Visita de Osito) Sendak, Maurice, illus. (SPA.). (gr. 1-6). pap. 9.50 (*84-204-3051-X*) Santillana.
—What If? LC 86-7649. (Illus.). 24p. (ps-2). 1987. 11.75 (*0-688-06473-6*); PLB 11.88 (*0-688-06474-4*) Greenwillow.
Minasian, Stanley M., jt. auth. see Balcomb, Kenneth C., III.
Minchin-Comm, Dorothy. Gates of Promise. Wheeler, Gerald, ed. 96p. (gr. 7 up). 1989. pap. 6.95 (*0-8280-0470-6*) Review & Herald.
Mineau, Charles. The Flowers. (Illus.). 24p. (ps-8). 1988. pap. 4.95 (*0-88753-171-7*, Pub. by Black Moss Pr CN) Firefly Bks Ltd.
Minelli, Giuseppe. Amphibians. (Illus.). 64p. 1987. 15.95x (*0-8160-1557-0*) Facts on File.
—Dinosaurs & Birds. (Illus.). 64p. 1988. 15.95x (*0-8160-1559-7*) Facts on File.
—Mammals. (Illus.). 64p. 1988. 15.95x (*0-8160-1560-0*) Facts on File.
Miner. Veronica. 1993. pap. 2.75 (*0-590-42134-4*) Scholastic Inc.
Miner, Jane C. Alcohol & Teens. LC 84-658. (Illus.). 64p. (gr. 7-11). 1984. lib. bdg. 9.29 (*0-671-44890-0*, J Messner) S&S Trade.
—Margaret. 224p. (Orig.). (gr. 7 up) 1988. pap. 2.75 (*0-590-41191-8*) Scholastic Inc.
—Roxanne, Vol. 15. 368p. (Orig.). (gr. 11 up) 1985. pap. 2.95 (*0-590-33686-X*) Scholastic Inc.
—Winter Love Story. 1993. pap. 3.50 (*0-590-47610-6*) Scholastic Inc.
Miner, Julia, illus. The Shepherd's Song: The Twenty-Third Psalm. LC 91-31067. 32p. 1993. 14.99 (*0-8037-1196-4*) Dial Bks Young.
Miner, O. Irene. Plants We Know. LC 81-9929. 48p. (gr. k-4). 1981. PLB 15.27 (*0-516-01642-3*) Childrens.
Miner, Ron, jt. auth. see Benjamin, Don-Paul.
Miner, Sharon. The Delmarva Conspiracy. LC 92-72680. 125p. (gr. 7-9). 1993. 13.95 (*1-880851-06-7*) Greene Bark Pr.
Mines, Jeanette. Risking It. 160p. 1988. pap. 2.75 (*0-380-75401-0*, Flare) Avon.
Mink, Len. Gospel Duck. Strand, David, illus. 20p. (ps-5). 1988. pap. text ed. write for info. Mink Ministries.
—Gospel Duck Goes to School. Strand, David, illus. 24p. (ps-6). 1988. pap. text ed. write for info. Mink Ministries.
Minkin, Rita, tr. see Salaz, Ruben D.
Minks, Benton, jt. auth. see Minks, Louise.
Minks, Louise & Minks, Benton. The Revolutionary War. (Illus.). 128p. (gr. 7 up). 1992. PLB 16.95x (*0-8160-2508-8*) Facts on File.
Minks, Louise & Minks, Leah, illus. Memorial Hall Coloring Book. 24p. (Orig.). (gr. 3-4). 1989. pap. 2.95 (*0-9612876-7-5*) Pocumtuck Valley Mem.
Minn, Loretta. Teach Speech. 64p. (gr. 3-7). 1982. 7.95 (*0-86653-058-4*, GA 418) Good Apple.
Minn, Loretta B. Trek for Trivia. Jurgens, Steve, illus. 48p. (gr. 3-8). 1985. wkbk. 6.95 (*0-86653-291-9*, GA 646) Good Apple.
Minnesota Humanities Commission Staff, ed. Braided Lives: An Anthology of Multicultural American Writing. 288p. (gr. 9-12). 1991. pap. text ed. 12.95 (*0-9629298-0-8*) MN Humanities.
Minnick, Molly A. Divorce Illustrated: Workbook. Minnick, Molly A., illus. 60p. (Orig.). 1990. pap. 5.00 (*1-878526-03-0*) Pineapple MI.
Mino, Frank Di see Di Mino, Frank.
Minor, Lee. Table in the Sky. LC 88-51386. 53p. (gr. k-3). 1989. 5.95 (*1-55523-197-7*) Winston-Derek.
Minor, Mary Ed. see Perry, Katy.
Minor, Nancy & Bradley, Patricia. Coping with School-Age Motherhood. (gr. 7-12). 1979. PLB 13.95 (*0-8239-0923-9*) Rosen Group.
Minsberg, David. The Bookmonster. Matheis, Shelley, illus. 32p. (ps-k). 1981. 7.50 (*0-940674-00-9*); incl. bookmonster doll 27.95 (*0-685-03087-3*) Littlebee.

Minshull, Evelyn. The Cornhusk Doll. Wallace, Edwin B., illus. LC 86-27125. 72p. (ps). 1987. 14.95 (*0-8361-3431-1*) Herald Pr.
Minshull, Evelyn W. But I Thought You Really Loved Me. LC 76-14992. 150p. (gr. 7 up). 1976. 8.00 (*0-664-32600-5*, Westminster) Westminster John Knox.
Minters, Frances. Cinder-Elly. Karas, G. Brian, illus. LC 93-14533. 32p. (ps-3). 1994. PLB 13.99 (*0-670-84417-9*) Viking Child Bks.
Minton, Janis. Basic Skills Map Workbook. 32p. (gr. 4-7). 1983. 1.98 (*0-8209-0540-2*, SSW-4) ESP.
Mintz, Barbara, jt. auth. see Katan, Norma J.
Mirable, Lisa. The Berlin Wall. (Illus.). 64p. (gr. 7 up). 1991. PLB 16.98 (*0-382-24133-9*); pap. 8.95 (*0-382-24140-1*) Silver Burdett Pr.
Miranda, Altina. Love on an Animal Farm. (Illus.). 32p. (Orig.). 1993. pap. 8.95 (*0-86534-202-4*) Sunstone Pr.
Miranda, Anne. Baby-Sit, Vol. 1. (ps). 1990. 9.95 (*0-316-57454-6*, Joy St Bks) Little.
—Baby Talk. Stott, Dorothy, illus. 16p. (ps). 1987. 9.95 (*0-525-44319-3*, 0772-230, DCB) Dutton Child Bks.
—Baby Walk. Stott, Dorothy, illus. 14p. (ps). 1988. 8.95 (*0-525-44421-1*, DCB) Dutton Child Bks.
—Night Songs. Miranda, Anne, illus. LC 92-251. 32p. (ps-1). 1993. RSBE 13.95 (*0-02-767250-6*, Bradbury Pr) Macmillan Child Grp.
Miranda, Anne M. Does a Mouse Have a House? LC 93-20587. Date not set. write for info. (*0-02-767251-4*, Bradbury Pr) Macmillan Child Grp.
Miranda, Lydia. Redheads: Stories & Narrations for School Students. 1993. 9.95 (*0-8062-4521-2*) Carlton.
Mire, Betty. It's Funny How Things Change. LC 84-1164. 155p. (gr. 5-10). 1985. 12.95 (*0-88289-431-5*) Pelican.
Miriani, Patricia, ed. see Nakajima, Caroline.
Mirikitani, Janice, jt. ed. see Williams, Cecil.
Mirko, Vincent W. Grandpa Says. 300p. (illus.). (gr. 10). 1989. pap. 25.00 (*0-9623257-0-8*) Millsmont Pub.
Miro, Norma S., tr. see Elliott, Dan.
Mirpuri, Gouri. Indonesia. LC 89-25457. (Illus.). 128p. (gr. 5-9). 1991. PLB 21.95 (*1-85435-294-6*) Marshall Cavendish.
Mischel, Florence. How to Write a Letter. rev. ed. Greenberg, Lorna, ed. Green, Anne C., illus. LC 88-10263. 72p. (gr. 5-9). 1988. PLB 10.90 (*0-531-10587-3*) Watts.
Mishica, Clare. Billions of Bugs. Loman, Roberta K., illus. 28p. (ps). 1993. 4.99 (*0-7847-0039-7*, 24-03829) Standard Pub.
—Charlie the Champ. (Illus.). 48p. (gr. k-3). 1994. pap. 3.99 (*0-7847-0138-5*, 24-03958) Standard Pub.
—The Penguin's Big Win. (Illus.). 48p. (Orig.). (gr. k-3). 1994. pap. 3.99 (*0-7847-0139-3*, 24-03959) Standard Pub.
Miskowski, Mike. Applianoidal Grphcus Birthday Elaps 4-89. (Illus.). 44p. 1989. pap. text ed. 4.00 (*0-944215-04-1*) Abscond Pubs.
MisKowski, Mike & Foley, Jack. Artifact Collective - Texts, No. 1. Berry, Jake, ed. 20p. (Orig.). (gr. 7 up). 1988. pap. 3.00 (*0-944215-02-5*) Abscond Pubs.
Misla, Victor M. Little Anabo from Boriken. Misla, Victor M., illus. 32p. (Orig.). (gr. 6-7). 1987. pap. 5.00 (*0-9626870-0-6*) NW Monarch Pr.
—The Treasure of Camuy's Cave. Misla, Victor M., illus. 30p. (Orig.). (gr. 6-7). 1987. pap. 5.00 (*0-9626870-1-4*) NW Monarch Pr.

Miss Lori. Shapeless & the Magic Box, Bk. 1. White, Lori G., ed. Miss Lori, illus. 18p. (Orig.). (ps-1). 1990. pap. 11.99 (*0-9623368-3-1*) Shapeless Enterprises.

It is the intention of Shapeless Enterprises to develop, design & produce top quality early childhood literature through various media outlets. Individual stories feature texts, videos, & sound recordings. Each storyline represents an educational concept as well as a valuable moral stepping stone for personal success. We are striving to provide a service to the youth of our communities by nurturing their most positive attributes. By captivating the senses of sight, sound & imagination we facilitate a positive, nonviolent image. SHAPELESS & THE MAGIC BOX, Book 1, ISBN 0-9623368-3-1. This exciting, full color, fictional children's text is rendered in poetic verse. Its educational basis features self-image, shapes & colors. Cassette available. JUVENILE 2-7. SHAPE UP THE EARTH/LOVE IS SHAPELESS, ISBN 0-923368-4-X. What a fun way to remember how important earth conservation is. Our

poster is filled with smiles & poetic phrases to soften every global heart. BEE SAFE'S SWAT THE DRUG BUG POSTER, ISBN 0-9623368-1-5. Help your little champions become a success with our newest hero Bee Safe. This attractive full color delight is a must for your little poster bug. Shapless Enterprises, P.O. Box 297, Harbor City, CA 90710. *Publisher Provided Annotation.*

—Shapeless & the Magic Box, Bk. 2. White, Lori G., ed. Miss Lori, illus. 18p. (Orig.). (ps-1). 1991. pap. 11.99 (*0-9623368-8-2*) Shapeless Enterprises.
Mister Tom. Fuzzy Buzzard. Bretlinger, Ted, illus. 32p. (gr. 2-4). 1978. write for info. Oddo.
—Gilly the Goose. Bonnett, Niki, illus. 32p. (gr. 2-4). 1978. write for info. Oddo.
—Gilly the Goose. Bonnett, Niki, illus. 32p. (Orig.). (gr. k-4). 1989. pap. 5.95 (*0-925237-02-7*) Ten Pubns.
—The Little Computer. Spivey, Elvera, illus. 32p. (gr. 2-4). 1978. write for info. Oddo.
—Messycat. Spivey, Elvera, illus. LC 77-85397. 36p. (gr. k-4). 1989. pap. 4.95 (*0-925237-00-0*) Ten Pubns.
—Queen Fussy. Spivey, Elvera, illus. 48p. (gr. 2-4). 1973. Cassette. write for info. Oddo.
—Six Silly Puppet Plays, Vol. I. Neely, David, ed. Neely, Heather, illus. LC 89-50784. 44p. (Orig.). (gr. 4-6). 1989. spiral bdg. 6.95 (*0-925237-05-1*) Ten Pubns.
—Six Silly Puppet Plays, Vol. 2. Neely, David, ed. Neely, Heather, illus. 32p. (Orig.). (gr. k-3). 1989. pap. 6.95 spiral bdg. (*0-925237-06-X*) Ten Pubns.
Mitchard, Jacquelyn. Jane Addams: Pioneer in Social Reform & Activist for World Peace. LC 89-49624. (Illus.). 64p. (gr. 5-6). 1991. PLB 18.60 (*0-8368-0144-X*) Gareth Stevens Inc.
Mitchel, Sue A. & Hughes, Barbara A. From the Bridegroom with Love. 144p. (gr. 8 up). 1992. pap. 6.95 (*0-9634469-0-8*) Chereb Pub.
Mitchell, A. The Young Naturalist. (Illus.). 32p. (gr. 5-10). 1984. PLB 13.96 (*0-88110-235-0*); pap. 6.95 (*0-86020-653-X*) EDC.
Mitchell, Adrian. Our Mammoth. Lamont, Priscilla, illus. (ps-3). 1987. 11.95 (*0-15-258838-8*) HarBrace.
—The Ugly Duckling. Heale, Jonathan, illus. LC 93-39962. (gr. 2 up). 1994. Repr. of 1994 ed. write for info (*1-564585-57-3*) Dorling Kindersley.
Mitchell, Barbara. America, I Hear You: A Story about George Gershwin. Smith, Jan H., illus. 64p. (gr. 3-6). 1987. PLB 14.95 (*0-87614-309-5*) Carolrhoda Bks.
—Between Two Worlds: A Story about Pearl Buck. Ritz, Karen, illus. 56p. (gr. 3-6). 1988. PLB 14.95 (*0-87614-332-X*) Carolrhoda Bks.
—Click! A Story about George Eastman. Hosking-Smith, Jan, illus. 64p. (gr. 3-6). 1986. PLB 14.95 (*0-87614-289-7*) Carolrhoda Bks.
—Click! A Story about George Eastman. Smith, Jan H., illus. (gr. 3-6). 1987. pap. 5.95 (*0-87614-472-5*, First Ave Edns) Lerner Pubns.
—Cornstalks & Cannonballs. (ps-3). 1991. pap. 2.99 (*0-440-40533-5*, YB) Dell.
—Down Buttermilk Lane. LC 90-46876. (ps-3). 1993. 15.00 (*0-688-10114-3*); PLB 14.93 (*0-688-10115-1*) Lothrop.
—Good Morning Mr. President: A Story about Carl Sandburg. Collins, Dane, illus. LC 88-7265. 56p. (gr. 3-6). 1988. PLB 14.95 (*0-87614-329-X*) Carolrhoda Bks.
—Hush, Puppies. Wyman, Cherie R., illus. LC 82-4465. 48p. (gr. k-4). 1983. PLB 14.95 (*0-87614-201-3*) Carolrhoda Bks.
—A Pocketful of Goobers: A Story about George Washington Carver. Hanson, Peter, illus. 64p. (gr. 3-6). 1986. PLB 14.95 (*0-87614-292-7*) Carolrhoda Bks.
—A Pocketful of Goobers: A Story about George Washington Carver. Hanson, Peter E., illus. (gr. 3-6). 1987. pap. 5.95 (*0-87614-474-1*, First Ave Edns) Lerner Pubns.
—The Pyramids: Opposing Viewpoints. LC 87-8392. (Illus.). 96p. (gr. 5-8). 1988. lib. bdg. 14.95 (*0-89908-051-0*) Greenhaven.
—Raggin' A Story about Scott Joplin. Mitchell, Hetty, illus. 64p. (gr. 3-6). 1987. PLB 14.95 (*0-87614-310-9*) Carolrhoda Bks.
—Raggin' A Story about Scott Joplin. (gr. 4-7). 1992. pap. 5.95 (*0-87614-589-6*) Carolrhoda Bks.
—Shoes for Everyone: A Story about Jan Matzeliger. Mitchell, Hetty, illus. 64p. (gr. 3-6). 1986. PLB 14.95 (*0-87614-290-0*) Carolrhoda Bks.
—Shoes for Everyone: A Story about Jan Matzeliger. Mitchell, Hetty, illus. (gr. 3-6). 1987. pap. 5.95 (*0-87614-473-3*, First Ave Edns) Lerner Pubns.
—We'll Race You, Henry: A Story about Henry Ford. Haubrich, Kathy, illus. 64p. (gr. 3-6). 1986. PLB 14.95 (*0-87614-291-9*) Carolrhoda Bks.
—We'll Race You, Henry: A Story about Henry Ford. Haubrich, Kathy, illus. (gr. 3-6). 1987. pap. 5.95 (*0-87614-471-7*, First Ave Edns) Lerner Pubns.
—The Wizard of Sound: A Story about Thomas Edison. Mitchell, Hetty, illus. 64p. (gr. 3-6). 1991. PLB 14.95 (*0-87614-445-8*) Carolrhoda Bks.

Mitchell, Cindy. Happy Hands & Feet. LC 88-82903. (Illus.). 80p. (ps-3). 1989. pap. text ed 7.95 (0-86530-062-3, IP 166-0) Incentive Pubns.
Mitchell, Crohan. The Napoleonic Wars. (Illus.). 72p. (gr. 7-10). 1989. 19.95 (0-7134-5729-5, Pub. by Batsford UK) Trafalgar.
Mitchell, Cynthia, ed. Here a Little Child I Stand: Poems of Prayer & Praise for Children. Ichikawa, Satomi, illus. LC 85-3450. 32p. (gr. k-3). 1985. 12.95 (0-399-21244-2, Philomel) Putnam Pub Group.
Mitchell, Darby. Blue Eye of a Pond. Harris, Andrew S., illus. 10p. (ps-5). 1991. 8.00 (0-9631809-0-8) Castle MI.
Mitchell, David. The Complete Book of Freestyle Karate. (Illus.). 192p. (gr. 3 up). 1992. 24.95 (0-7063-7053-8, Pub. by Ward Lock UK) Sterling.
—The Young Martial Artist. (Illus.). 128p. 1992. 19.95 (0-87951-422-1) Overlook Pr.
Mitchell, Debbie. Diary of a First Class Jerk. LC 87-50267. 96p. (gr. 6-8). 1987. 8.95 (1-55523-079-2) Winston-Derek.
Mitchell, Don, jt. auth. see Grimm, Gary.
Mitchell, Greg. Going Fishing. Ridgway, Jo A., illus. LC 92-14449. 1993. 3.75 (0-383-03625-9) SRA Schl Grp.
—Our Playhouse. Ridgway, Jo A., illus. LC 92-21451. 1993. 3.75 (0-383-03647-X) SRA Schl Grp.
—Simply Sam. Ridgway, Jo A., illus. LC 92-21452. 1993. 3.75 (0-383-03652-6) SRA Schl Grp.
Mitchell, Janis & Baron, Stanley. The Hamster Ballet Company. LC 85-52135. (Illus.). 64p. (ps up). 1986. 12.95 (0-500-01382-9) Thames Hudson.
Mitchell, John C. Great Lakes & Great Ships: An Illustrated History for Children. Woodruff, Thomas R., illus. 52p. (gr. 2-7). 1991. 15.95 (0-9621466-1-7) Suttons Bay Pubns.
—Michigan: An Illustrated History for Children. 2nd ed. Woodrutt, Thomas R., illus. 52p. (gr. 1-6). 1987. Repr. 14.95 (0-9621466-0-9) Suttons Bay Pubns.
Mitchell, Joni. Both Sides Now. (Illus.). 1992. 14.95 (0-590-45668-7, Scholastic Hardcover) Scholastic Inc.
Mitchell, Joyce. Other Choices for Becoming a Woman. (gr. 7 up). 1975. pap. 6.00 (0-912786-34-5) Know Inc.
Mitchell, Joyce S. The Best Guide to the Top Colleges: How to Get into the Ivies or Nearly Ivies. LC 90-24012. (Illus.). 111p. (Orig.). (gr. 11-12). 1991. pap. 10.95 (0-912048-85-9) Garrett Pk.
—Free to Choose: Decision Making for Young Men. LC 76-5589. (gr. 7 up). 1976. 8.95 (0-440-02723-3) Delacorte.
—Mitchell Express: The Fast Track to the Top Colleges. LC 93-16962. 269p. (Orig.). 1993. pap. 15.00 (1-880774-03-8) Garrett Pk.
Mitchell, Julie, compiled by. A Christmas Garland. Orr, Kathy, illus. 40p. 1991. lib. bdg. 8.95 (0-8378-2069-3) Gibson.
Mitchell, Kathy. Silent Night: A Christmas Book with Lights & Music. Mitchell, Kathy, illus. 12p. (ps-3). 1989. bds. 10.95 (0-689-71330-4, Aladdin) Macmillan Child Grp.
Mitchell, Lorayne. And the Winner Is... A Book about Inner Beauty. Lee, Jeff, illus. 32p. (ps-4). 1987. PLB 12.95 (0-943491-00-2) Valued Pubns.
—Beautiful Feathers: A Book about Selflessness. Lee, Jeff, illus. 32p. (ps-4). 1987. PLB 12.95 (0-943491-01-0) Valued Pubns.
—The Shadow in the Window: A Book about Caring. Lee, Jeff, illus. 32p. (ps-4). 1987. PLB 12.95 (0-943491-02-9) Valued Pubns.
Mitchell, Lucy S., et al. The Taxi That Hurried. reissued ed. Gergely, Tibor, illus. 24p. (ps-k). 1992. write for info. (0-307-00144-X, 312-09, Golden Pr) Western Pub.
Mitchell, Lyn, illus. Animals. 10p. (ps). 1992. 4.95 (0-448-40304-8, G&D) Putnam Pub Group.
—Clothes. 10p. (ps). 1992. 4.95 (0-448-40307-2, G&D) Putnam Pub Group.
—Eating. 10p. (ps). 1992. 4.95 (0-448-40305-6, G&D) Putnam Pub Group.
—Playing. 10p. (ps). 1992. 4.95 (0-448-40306-4, G&D) Putnam Pub Group.
Mitchell, Margaree K. Uncle Jed's Barbershop. (ps-6). 1993. pap. 15.00 (0-671-76969-3, S&S BFYR) S&S Trade.
Mitchell, Mark. The Mustang Professor: The Story of J. Frank Dobie. Mitchell, Mark, illus. 96p. (gr. 4-7). 1993. 12.95 (0-89015-823-1) Eakin-Sunbelt.
Mitchell, Pratima. Dance of Shiva. (Illus.). 25p. (gr. 2-4). 1991. 12.95 (0-237-60148-6, Pub. by Evans Bros Ltd) Trafalgar.
Mitchell, Rita P. Hue Boy. Binch, Caroline, illus. LC 92-18560. (ps-3). 1993. 13.99 (0-8037-1448-3) Dial Bks Young.
Mitchell, Robert & Zim, Herbert S. Butterflies & Moths. Durenceau, Andre, illus. (gr. 5 up). 1964. PLB write for info. (0-307-24052-5); pap. write for info. (Golden Pr) Western Pub.
Mitchell, Robert E. Jesus the Good Shepherd. (Illus.). 24p. (ps-2). 1989. pap. 1.89 (0-570-09018-0, 59-1441) Concordia.
Mitchell, Sarah, ed. see Dugas-Bonds, Pat.
Mitchell, Stephen. Creation. LC 89-39726. (Illus.). 40p. 1990. 15.95 (0-8037-0617-0); PLB 15.89 (0-8037-0618-9) Dial Bks Young.
Mitchell, Suzanne, ed. see Alpine Partners Staff.
Mitchell, Tucker. The Crystal Whizzard. Graves, Helen, ed. LC 88-50120. 64p. (gr. 2-5). 1988. 12.00 (1-55523-146-2) Winston-Derek.

—You're Not Alone When You're Alone. LC 92-70981. (Illus.). 130p. 1992. 12.95 (1-55523-522-0) Winston-Derek.
Mitchell, Victor. Birds. Mitchell, Victor, illus. 16p. (gr. k up). 1988. pap. 1.99 (0-7459-1467-5) Lion USA.
—Butterflies. (Illus.). 16p. (gr. k up). 1988. pap. 1.99 (0-7459-1466-7) Lion USA.
—Fish. Mitchell, Victor, illus. 16p. (gr. k up). 1988. pap. 1.99 (0-7459-1468-3) Lion USA.
—Flowers. Mitchell, Victor, illus. 16p. (gr. k up). 1988. pap. 1.99 (0-7459-1470-5) Lion USA.
—Jungles. Mitchell, Victor, illus. 16p. (gr. k up). 1988. pap. 1.99 (0-7459-1473-X) Lion USA.
—Pets. Mitchell, Victor, illus. 16p. (gr. k up). 1988. pap. 1.99 (0-7459-1469-1) Lion USA.
—Seashore. Mitchell, Victor, illus. 16p. (gr. k up). 1988. pap. 1.99 (0-7459-1471-3) Lion USA.
—Woodlands. Mitchell, Victor, illus. 16p. (gr. k up). 1988. pap. 1.99 (0-7459-1472-1) Lion USA.
Mitchetz, Marc. The Bloody Lotus. Hansom, Dick, tr. from FRE. Bosmans, Serge, illus. 49p. (Orig.). (gr. 12 up). 1990. pap. 7.95 (0-87416-103-7, Comcat Comics) Catalan Communs.
Mitgutsch, Ali. From Blossom to Honey. Mitgutsch, Ali, illus. 24p. (ps-3). 1981. PLB 10.95 (0-87614-146-7) Carolrhoda Bks.
—From Cacao Bean to Chocolate: Translation of Vom Kakao Zur Schokolade. Mitgutsch, Ali, illus. LC 80-29588. 24p. (ps-3). 1981. PLB 10.95 (0-87614-147-5) Carolrhoda Bks.
—From Cement to Bridge. Mitgutsch, Ali, illus. LC 81-334. 24p. (ps-3). 1981. PLB 10.95 (0-87614-148-3) Carolrhoda Bks.
—From Clay to Bricks. Mitgutsch, Ali, illus. LC 80-29567. 24p. (ps-3). 1981. PLB 10.95 (0-87614-149-1) Carolrhoda Bks.
—From Cotton to Pants. Mitgutsch, Ali, illus. LC 80-29552. 24p. (ps-3). 1981. PLB 10.95 (0-87614-150-5) Carolrhoda Bks.
—From Cow to Shoe. LC 80-29587. (Illus.). 24p. (ps-3). 1981. PLB 10.95 (0-87614-151-3) Carolrhoda Bks.
—From Fruit to Jam. Mitgutsch, Ali, illus. LC 81-58. 24p. (ps-3). 1981. PLB 10.95 (0-87614-154-8) Carolrhoda Bks.
—From Gold to Money. Mitgutsch, Ali, illus. LC 84-17488. 24p. (ps-3). 1985. PLB 10.95 (0-87614-230-7) Carolrhoda Bks.
—From Grain to Bread. Mitgutsch, Ali, illus. LC 80-28592. 24p. (ps-3). 1981. PLB 10.95 (0-87614-155-6) Carolrhoda Bks.
—From Graphite to Pencil. Mitgutsch, Ali, illus. LC 84-17469. 24p. (ps-3). 1985. PLB 10.95 (0-87614-231-5) Carolrhoda Bks.
—From Grass to Butter. Mitgutsch, Ali, illus. LC 80-28588. 24p. (ps-3). 1981. PLB 10.95 (0-87614-156-4) Carolrhoda Bks.
—From Idea to Toy. (Illus.). 24p. (ps-3). 1988. PLB 10.95 (0-87614-352-4) Carolrhoda Bks.
—From Milk to Ice Cream. Mitgutsch, Ali, illus. LC 81-81. 24p. (ps-3). 1981. PLB 10.95 (0-87614-158-0) Carolrhoda Bks.
—From Oil to Gasoline. Mitgutsch, Ali, illus. LC 80-29562. 24p. (ps-3). 1981. PLB 10.95 (0-87614-160-2) Carolrhoda Bks.
—From Ore to Spoon. Mitgutsch, Ali, illus. LC 80-28862. 24p. (ps-3). 1981. PLB 10.95 (0-87614-161-0) Carolrhoda Bks.
—From Picture to Picture Book. (Illus.). 24p. (ps-3). 1988. PLB 10.95 (0-87614-353-2) Carolrhoda Bks.
—From Rubber Tree to Tire. Lerner, Mark, tr. from GER. Mitgutsch, Ali, illus. 24p. (ps-3). 1986. lib. bdg. 10.95 (0-87614-297-8) Carolrhoda Bks.
—From Sand to Glass. Mitgutsch, Ali, illus. LC 80-29572. 24p. (ps-3). 1981. PLB 10.95 (0-87614-162-9) Carolrhoda Bks.
—From Sea to Salt. Mitgutsch, Ali, illus. LC 84-17466. 24p. (ps-3). 1985. PLB 10.95 (0-87614-232-3) Carolrhoda Bks.
—From Seed to Pear. Mitgutsch, Ali, illus. LC 81-83. 24p. (ps-3). 1981. PLB 10.95 (0-87614-163-7) Carolrhoda Bks.
—From Sheep to Scarf. Mitgutsch, Ali, illus. LC 80-29557. 24p. (ps-3). 1981. PLB 10.95 (0-87614-164-5) Carolrhoda Bks.
—From Swamp to Coal. Mitgutsch, Ali, illus. LC 84-17465. 24p. (ps-3). 1985. PLB 10.95 (0-87614-233-1) Carolrhoda Bks.
—From Tree to Table. Mitgutsch, Ali, illus. LC 81-672. 24p. (ps-3). 1981. PLB 10.95 (0-87614-165-3) Carolrhoda Bks.
—From Wood to Paper. Lerner, Mark, tr. from GER. Mitgutsch, Ali, illus. 24p. (ps-3). 1986. lib. bdg. 10.95 (0-87614-296-X) Carolrhoda Bks.
—A Knight's Book. Crawford, Elizabeth D., tr. Mitgutsch, Ali, illus. 40p. (gr. 2-5). 1991. 16.45 (0-395-58103-6, Clarion Bks) HM.
Mitra, Annie. Penguin Moon. Mitra, Annie, illus. LC 88-32797. 32p. (ps-1). 1989. reinforced bdg. 13.95 (0-8234-0749-7) Holiday.
—Tusk! Tusk! Mitra, Annie, illus. LC 89-77508. 32p. (ps-2). 1990. reinforced 13.95 (0-8234-0819-1) Holiday.
Mitsch, Ray, jt. auth. see Brown, Kevin.
Mittelstaedt, Robert C. Chai. Browne, James, illus. LC 93-80043. 32p. (ps-2). 1994. 15.00 (0-9630976-3-6) Morgin Pr.

Mitter. Hindu Festivals, Reading Level 4. (Illus.). 48p. (gr. 3-8). 1989. PLB 14.60 (0-86592-986-6) Rourke Corp.
Mitton, David & Permane, Terry, photos by. Edward's Exploit. LC 92-23189. (Illus.). 32p. (ps-3). 1993. pap. 2.25 (0-679-83896-1) Random Bks Yng Read.
Mitton, David, et al, photos by. James in a Mess & Other Thomas the Tank Engine Stories. LC 92-25654. (Illus.). 32p. (ps-3). 1993. pap. 2.25 (0-679-83895-3) Random Bks Yng Read.
Mitton, Jacqueline. Discovering the Planets. LC 90-11020. (Illus.). 32p. (gr. 4-6). 1991. lib. bdg. 11.89 (0-8167-2130-0); pap. text ed. 3.95 (0-8167-2131-9) Troll Assocs.
Miyazaki, Hayao. Nausicaa of the Valley of the Wind, Vols. 1-2. (Illus.). (gr. 7-12). 1993. 19.95 ea. Vol. 1 (4-19-086975-9) Vol. 2 (4-19-086976-7) Tokuma Pub.
—Tokuma's Magical Adventure Series. Zimmerman, Maureen, ed. Saburi, Eugene, tr. from JPN. Miyazaki, Hayao, illus. 112p. (gr. 3-6). 1992. PLB 44.85 (4-19-086974-0) Tokuma Pub.
Miyazima, Yasuhiko. Children of the World: China. LC 87-42576. (Illus.). 64p. (gr. 5-6). 1988. PLB 19.93 (1-55532-207-7) Gareth Stevens Inc.
Mizell, Linda. Racism. 160p. (gr. 7 up). 1992. PLB 15.85 (0-8027-8113-6); pap. 9.95 (0-8027-7365-6) Walker & Co.
Mizumura, Kazue, jt. auth. see Stamm, Claus.
Mlawer, Teresa, tr. see Adler, David A.
Mlawer, Teresa, tr. see Aliki.
Mlawer, Teresa, tr. see Brown, Marcia.
Mlawer, Teresa, tr. see Eastman, P. D.
Mlawer, Teresa, tr. see Grunsell, Angela.
Mlawer, Teresa, tr. see Hoff, Syd.
Mlawer, Teresa, tr. see Jonas, Ann.
Mlawer, Teresa, tr. see Nodar, Carmen M.
Mlawer, Teresa, tr. see Price, Mathew.
Mlawer, Teresa, tr. see Steig, William.
Moak, Allen. A Big City ABC. (Illus.). 32p. (ps up). 1989. text ed. 14.95 (0-88776-161-5, Dist. by U of Toronto Pr); pap. 6.95 (0-88776-238-7) Tundra Bks.
Moats, Lillian S. The Gate of Dreams. 116p. 1993. 21.95 (0-9636492-0-5) Cranbrook Educ.
Moatti, Claude, jt. auth. see Bombarde, Odile.
Moche. What's Down There? Questions & Answers about the Oceans. 1993. pap. 2.50 (0-590-42855-1) Scholastic Inc.
Moche, Dinah. Amazing Space Facts. Alley, R. W., illus. & photos by LC 87-82370. 24p. (ps-3). 1992. pap. write for info. (0-307-11815-0, 11815-02, Golden Pr) Western Pub.
—The Astronauts. LC 78-54955. (Illus.). (ps-3). 1979. pap. 2.25 (0-394-83901-3) Random Bks Yng Read.
—Astronomy Today: Planets, Stars, Space Exploration. McNaught, Harry, illus. LC 82-5211. 96p. (gr. 5 up). 1982. lib. bdg. 12.99 (0-394-94423-2); pap. 12.00 (0-394-84423-8) Random Bks Yng Read.
—The Golden Book of Space Exploration. LaPadula, Tom, illus. (ps-7). 1990. write for info. (0-307-15855-1, Pub. by Golden Bks) Western Pub.
—If You Were an Astronaut. (Illus.). 24p. (ps-3). 1992. pap. write for info. (0-307-11896-7, 11896-02, Golden Pr) Western Pub.
Mochizuki, Ken. Baseball Saved Us. Lee, Dom, illus. LC 92-73215. 32p. (gr. k-8). 1993. 14.95 (1-880000-01-6) Lee & Low Bks.
Mochnick, Beth R. New Holiday Songs for Children: A Creative Approach. Davis, Barbara, ed. (Illus.). iv, 44p. 1988. pap. text ed. 14.95 (0-916656-25-X) Mark Foster Mus.
Mock, Dorothy. Aqua Kid Saves the Day: The Good News Kids Learn about Peace. (Illus.). 32p. (Orig.). (ps-2). 1992. pap. 5.99 (0-570-04718-8) Concordia.
—Fire Truck Friends: The Good News Kids Learn about Joy. (Illus.). 32p. (Orig.). (ps-2). 1992. pap. 5.99 (0-570-04717-X) Concordia.
—One Big Family: The Good News Kids Learn about Kindness. Mitter, Kathy, illus. LC 92-27012. 32p. (Orig.). (ps-2). 1993. pap. 5.99 (0-570-04737-4) Concordia.
—Springtime Special: The Good News Kids Learn about Patience. Mitter, Kathy, illus. LC 92-27010. 32p. (Orig.). (ps-2). 1993. pap. 5.99 (0-570-04736-6) Concordia.
—The Trouble with Trevor: The Good News Kids Learn about Goodness. Mitter, Kathy, illus. LC 92-27013. 32p. (Orig.). (ps-2). 1993. pap. 5.99 (0-570-04738-2) Concordia.
—Worms for Winston: The Good News Kids Learn about Love. (Illus.). 32p. (Orig.). (ps-2). 1992. pap. 5.99 (0-570-04716-1) Concordia.
Mock, Dorothy K. The Big Secret: The Good News Kids Learn about Gentleness. Mitter, Kathy, illus. LC 93-6865. 32p. (Orig.). (ps-2). 1993. pap. 5.99 (0-570-04744-7) Concordia.
—God Is Everywhere: The Good News Kids Learn about Self-Control. Mitter, Kathy, illus. LC 93-22311. 32p. (Orig.). (ps-2). 1993. pap. 5.99 (0-570-04745-5) Concordia.
—The Thanksgiving Parade: The Good News Kids Learn about Faithfulness. Mitter, Kathy, illus. LC 93-2988. 32p. (Orig.). (ps-2). 1993. pap. 5.99 (0-570-04743-9) Concordia.
Mock, Valerie E. A.S.M.D. Multi-Graded Arithmetic Practice & Drill Sheets. (gr. 1-6). 1977. pap. 20.95 (0-8224-0462-1) Fearon Teach Aids.

Mockler, Anthony. King Arthur & His Knights. Harris, Nick, illus. 308p. 1987. jacketed 18.95 (*0-19-274531-X*) OUP.

Mockrin, Ida. The Big Parade. Brodsky, Harry, illus. 16p. (ps-1). 1983. pap. 2.00 (*0-9612244-0-1*) Honeycomb Pr.

Modan, Shula. Why Jonathan Doesn't Cry. Leon, Yael, illus. (ps-2). 1988. 7.95 (*1-55774-022-4*, Dist. by Watts) Modan-Adama Bks.

Modell, Frank. Ice Cream Soup. LC 87-21097. (Illus.). 24p. (ps-3). 1988. 11.95 (*0-688-07770-6*); lib. bdg. 11.88 (*0-688-07771-4*) Greenwillow.
—Look Out, It's April Fools' Day. Modell, Frank, illus. LC 84-4138. 24p. (ps up). 1985. 13.00 (*0-688-04016-0*); PLB 12.88 (*0-688-04017-9*) Greenwillow.
—One Zillion Valentines. LC 81-2215. (Illus.). 32p. (gr. k-3). 1981. 12.93 (*0-688-00565-9*); PLB 11.88 (*0-688-00569-1*) Greenwillow.
—One Zillion Valentines. LC 81-2215. (ps-3). 1987. pap. 3.95 (*0-688-07329-8*, Mulberry) Morrow.
—Skeeter & the Computer. LC 84-1585. (Illus.). 24p. (ps-3). 1988. 11.95 (*0-688-03703-8*); lib. bdg. 11.88 (*0-688-03706-2*) Greenwillow.

Modesitt, Jeanne. Mama, If You Had a Wish. Spowart, Robin, illus. LC 91-31354. 40p. (ps-1). 1993. JRT 14.00 (*0-671-75437-8*, Green Tiger) S&S Trade.
—Night Call. (ps). 1991. pap. 3.95 (*0-14-050944-5*, Puffin) Puffin Bks.
—Sometimes I Feel Like a Mouse. (Illus.). 1992. 14.95 (*0-590-44835-8*, Scholastic Hardcover) Scholastic Inc.
—Songs of Chanukah. (ps-3). 1992. 15.95 (*0-316-57739-1*) Little.
—The Story of Z. Johnson, Lonnie S., illus. LC 89-3923. 28p. (ps up). 1991. pap. 14.95 (*0-88708-105-3*) Picture Bk Studio.
—The Story of Z. Johnson, Lonnie S., illus. LC 92-6626. 28p. 1992. pap. 4.95 (*0-88708-278-5*) Picture Bk Studio.
—Vegetable Soup. Spowart, Robin, illus. LC 87-11169. 32p. (ps-1). 1988. 13.95 (*0-02-767630-7*, Macmillan Child Bk) Macmillan Child Grp.
—Vegetable Soup. Spowart, Robin, illus. LC 91-247. 32p. (ps-3). 1991. pap. 4.50 (*0-689-71523-4*, Aladdin) Macmillan Child Grp.

Modest, Diane & Cymerman, Sandra. SAGE: Teacher Training & Implementation Manual. (gr. 1-6). 1986. tchr's. ed. 35.00 (*0-944584-05-5*) Sopris.

Modiano, Patrick. Aventure de Choura. Zehrfuss, D., illus. (FRE.). 36p. 1986. 24.95 (*2-07-056294-8*) Schoenhof.
—Catherine Certitude. Sempe, Jean-Jacques, illus. 64p. (gr. 3 up). 1993. 17.95 (*0-87923-959-X*) Godine.

Modiano, Patrick & Sempe, J. J. Catherine Certitude. (FRE.). 95p. (gr. 5-10). 1988. pap. 8.95 (*2-07-033600-X*) Schoenhof.

Modica, Terry A. The Dark Secret of the Ouija. Bohl, Al, illus. 224p. (gr. 9-12). 1990. pap. text ed. 2.50 (*1-55748-138-5*) Barbour & Co.

Modl, Tom, ed. America's Elections: Opposing Viewpoints. LC 87-36788. (Illus.). (gr. 10 up). 1988. lib. bdg. 17.95 (*0-89908-433-8*); pap. text ed. 9.95 (*0-89908-408-7*) Greenhaven.

Modl, Tom, jt. ed. see Bach, Julie.

Modupe' Bode'-Thomas, tr. see Mariama Ba.

Moe, Barbara. Coping with Chronic Illness. Rosen, Ruth, ed. LC 92-15377. (gr. 7-12). 1992. 13.95 (*0-8239-1464-X*) Rosen Group.
—Coping with Eating Disorders. (gr. 7-12). 1991. PLB 13.95 (*0-8239-1343-0*) Rosen Group.

Moe, J. E., jt. auth. see Asbjornsen, P. C.

Moe, Mary, ed. see Sullivan, Mick.

Moeller, Jack R., jt. auth. see Drath, Viola.

Moeller, Walter O., tr. see Makhlouf, Georgia.

Moerbeek, Kees. Fancy That! LC 91-39451. 1992. 9.95 (*0-85953-543-6*) Childs Play.
—Four Courageous Climbers. (Illus.). 12p. 1991. 9.95 (*0-8431-2915-8*) Price Stern.
—Four Courageous Climbers: Mini-Triangles Pop-Up. (ps-3). 1992. 5.99 (*0-8431-3448-8*) Price Stern.
—Have You Seen a Pog? (Illus.). 10p. (ps up) 1988. 9.95 (*0-8431-2261-7*) Price Stern.
—Hi Mom, I'm Home. Moerbeek, Kees, illus. 20p. 1992. 9.95 (*0-8431-3393-7*) Price Stern.
—Let's Go. LC 91-38117. 1992. 9.95 (*0-85953-542-8*) Childs Play.
—New at the Zoo: A Mix-&-Match Pop-up Book. Moerbeek, Kees, illus. LC 89-60077. 10p. (ps-1). 1989. bds. 8.99 (*0-679-80076-X*) Random Bks Yng Read.
—New at the Zoo Two: A Mix-&-Match Pop-up Book. Moerbeek, Kees, illus. LC 92-60763. 10p. (ps-1). 1993. 8.99 (*0-679-83711-6*) Random Bks Yng Read.
—Night Before Christmas: Pop-Up. 1992. 10.99 (*0-8431-3445-3*) Price Stern.
—Oh No, Santa! (Illus.). 12p. 1991. 9.95 (*0-8431-2984-0*) Price Stern.
—Penguins Slide. LC 91-42040. 1992. 9.95 (*0-85953-544-4*) Childs Play.
—Six Brave Explorers: Mini-Triangles Pop-Up. (ps-3). 1992. 5.99 (*0-8431-3449-6*) Price Stern.
—When the Wild Pirates Go Sailing: Mini-Triangles Pop-Up. (ps-3). 1992. 5.99 (*0-8431-3450-X*) Price Stern.
—Who's Peeking at Me: A Pop-Up Book. (Illus.). 12p. (ps-3). 1989. 8.95 (*0-8431-2410-5*) Price Stern.

Moerbeek, Kees & Dijs, Carla. Six Brave Explorers. (Illus.). 12p (ps up). 9.95 (*0-8431-2253-6*) Price Stern.

Moerbeek, Kees, jt. auth. see Dijs, Carla.

Moeri, Louise. Downwind. (gr. k-12). 1987. pap. 2.75 (*0-440-92132-5*, LFL) Dell.
—The Forty-Third War. 208p. (gr. 5-9). 1989. 13.45 (*0-395-50215-2*) HM.
—Forty-Third War. 1993. 1993. pap. 4.95 (*0-395-66955-3*) HM.
—Save Queen of Sheba. 112p. 1990. (pap. 3.50 (*0-380-71154-0*, Camelot) Avon.
—Star Mother's Youngest Child. Hyman, Trina S., illus. 48p. (ps-2). 1980. 14.45 (*0-395-21406-8*, Sandpiper); pap. 4.95 (*0-395-29929-2*) HM.

Moers, Hermann. Annie's Dancing Day. Unzner-Fischer, Christa, illus. Lanning, Rosemary, tr. from GER. LC 92-3612. (Illus.). 32p. (gr. k-3). 1992. 14.95 (*1-55858-160-X*); PLB 14.88 (*1-55858-161-8*) North-South Bks NYC.
—Hugo's Baby Brother. Wilkon, Jozef, illus. Lanning, Rosemary, tr. from GER. LC 91-7775. (Illus.). 32p. (gr. k-3). 1992. 14.95 (*1-55858-137-5*); lib. bdg. 14.88 (*1-55858-146-4*) North-South Bks NYC.
—Little Ben. Corderoc'h, Jean-Pierre, illus. Lanning, Rosemary, tr. from GER. LC 90-47030. (Illus.). 32p. (gr. k-3). 1991. 14.95 (*1-55858-105-7*) North-South Bks NYC.

Moers, Hermann, jt. auth. see Wilkon, Jozef.

Moeschl, Richard. Exploring the Sky: Projects for Beginning Astronomers. rev. ed. LC 92-18863. (Illus.). 320p. (gr. 9-12). 1992. pap. 14.95 (*1-55652-160-X*) Chicago Review.

Moeskops, J., jt. auth. see Leeuwen, M.

Moessinger, Pierre. Socrates. Boix, Manuel, illus. LC 92-44060. 1993. 14.95 (*0-88682-606-3*) Creative Ed.

Moffatt, M. Children's Word Liturgies, Vol. 2. 112p. (gr. k-6). 1987. pap. 9.95 (*0-8146-1538-4*) Liturgical Pr.

Moffatt, Marjorie. Children's Word Liturgies, Vol. 3. (Illus.). 112p. 1988. pap. 9.95 (*0-8146-1539-2*) Liturgical Pr.

Moffett, Berdell, ed. see Chaney, Casey.

Moffett, Carol G. & Strydesky, Rebecca. The Receiving-Checking-Marking-Stocking Clerk. 2nd ed. (Illus.). 160p. (gr. 10-12). 1979. text ed. 13.32 (*0-07-042667-8*) McGraw.

Moffett, Eileen. Korean Ways. Moffett, Eileen, illus. 55p. (gr. k up). 1986. 10.95 (*0-8048-7013-6*, Pub. by Seoul Intl Tourist SK) C E Tuttle.

Moffett, James & Tashlik, Phyllis. Active Voices, II: A Writer's Reader. 317p. (gr. 7-9). 1987. pap. text ed. 14.50x (*0-86709-111-8*); Rational and Teaching Guide 1.75x (*0-86709-182-7*) Boynton Cook Pubs.

Moffett, James, et al. Active Voices, I: A Writer's Reader. 265p. (gr. 4-6). 1987. text ed. 14.50x (*0-86709-091-X*); Rationale and Teaching Guide 1.75x (*0-86709-184-3*) Boynton Cook Pubs.
—Active Voices, III: A Writer's Reader. 414p. (gr. 10-12). 1987. pap. text ed. 14.50x (*0-86709-113-4*); Rationale and Teaching Guide 1.75x (*0-86709-180-0*) Boynton Cook Pubs.

Moffit, Linda L. The Magic Mirror. LC 89-50125. (Illus.). 80p. (Orig.). (gr. k-7). 1989. pap. 8.95 (*0-87516-615-6*) DeVorss.

Mofid, Bijan. The Butterfly. 1974. 4.50 (*0-87602-111-9*) Anchorage.

Moga, Jerome. Mikhail Gorbachev. (gr. 4-7). 1991. pap. 3.50 (*0-553-15898-8*) Bantam.

Mogensen & Magarian-Gold. Pattern Animals: Puzzles for Pattern Blocks. Liberatore, Michael, illus. 48p. (gr. 1-4). 1986. pap. text ed. 7.95 (*0-914040-46-4*) Cuisenaire.

Mogensen, Jan. The Forty-Six Little Men. LC 90-36470. (Illus.). 28p. (ps up). 1991. 13.95 (*0-688-09283-7*); PLB 13.88 (*0-688-09284-5*) Greenwillow.
—The Forty-Six Little Men. LC 92-25329. (Illus.). 1993. pap. 4.99 (*0-14-054831-9*) Puffin Bks.
—The Land of the Big. Mogensen, Jan, illus. LC 92-18302. 32p. (ps-3). 1993. 14.95 (*1-56656-111-6*, Crocodile Bks) Interlink Pub.
—Teddy & the Chinese Dragon. LC 85-26091. (Illus.). 32p. (gr. 3-4). 1985. PLB 18.60 (*1-55532-002-3*) Gareth Stevens Inc.
—Teddy Runs Away. Mogensen, Jan, illus. LC 90-36069. 32p. (gr. 3-4). 1990. PLB 18.60 (*0-8368-0371-X*) Gareth Stevens Inc.
—Teddy's Birthday Bugle. Mogensen, Jan, illus. LC 90-10071. 32p. (gr. 3-4). 1990. PLB 18.60 (*0-8368-0372-8*) Gareth Stevens Inc.
—The Tiger's Breakfast. LC 91-3606. (Illus.). 32p. (ps-3). 1991. 14.95 (*0-940793-83-0*, Crocodile Bks) Interlink Pub.

Mogensen, Sandra & Magarian-Gold, Judi. Exploring with Color Tiles. 48p. (gr. k-3). 1990. pap. text ed. 7.95 (*0-938587-17-X*) Cuisenaire.

Mogil, H. Michael & Levine, Barbara G. The Amateur Meteorologist: Explorations & Investigations. LC 93-17506. (Illus.). 144p. (gr. 6-9). 1993. PLB 12.90 (*0-531-11045-1*) Watts.

Moguet, Pamela J., jt. auth. see Belchez, Chito.

Mohan, Claire J. Kaze's True Home: The Young Life of a Modern Day Saint, Mother Maria Kaupas. Thomer, Susannah, illus. Xuzmickus, Marilyn, intro. by. LC 91-66722. (Illus.). 64p. (gr. 4-9). 1992. 8.95 (*0-9621500-5-3*) Young Sparrow Pr.
—Mother Teresa's Someday: The Young Life of Mother Teresa of Calcutta. Gallagher, Patricia C., ed. Thomes, Susannah H., illus. 60p. (Orig.). (gr. k-6). 1990. PLB 14.95 (*0-9621500-6-1*); pap. 6.95 (*0-9621500-7-X*) Young Sparrow Pr.

—A Red Rose for Francis: A Story of the Young Life of Francis Siedlisha. 2nd ed. Thomas, Susannah, illus. (gr. 4-7). 1990. lib. bdg. write for info. (*0-9621500-9-6*) Young Sparrow Pr.
—A Red Rose for Frania: A Story of the Young Life of Francis Siedliska. Thomer, Susannah, illus. (gr. 4-7). 1989. PLB 5.95 (*0-9621500-8-8*) Young Sparrow Pr.

Mohr, Carole. Freud & Freud, Inc. (gr. 4-7). 1991. pap. 2.75 (*0-553-15915-1*) Bantam.

Mohr, Joseph. Silent Night. Jeffers, Susan, illus. LC 84-8113. 32p. (ps up) 1984. 14.95 (*0-525-44144-1*, DCB); pap. 4.95 (*0-8037-4443-9*, DCB) Dutton Child Bks.
—Silent Night. LC 84-8113. 1988. pap. 4.95 (*0-685-57131-9*, DCB) Dutton Child Bks.

Mohr, Nicholasa. All for the Better: A Story of el Barrio. Gutierrez, Rudy, illus. LC 92-23639. 56p. (gr. 2-5). 1992. PLB 21.34 (*0-8114-7220-5*) Raintree Steck-V.
—El Bronx Remembered. LC 75-6306. 288p. (gr. 7 up). 1993. pap. 4.95 (*0-06-447100-4*, Trophy) HarpC Child Bks.
—Felita. Cruz, Ray, illus. LC 79-50149. (gr. 3-6). 1979. Dial Bks Young.
—Going Home. LC 85-20621. 176p. (gr. 5-8). 1986. 14.95 (*0-8037-0269-8*); PLB 13.89 (*0-8037-0338-4*) Dial Bks Young.
—Going Home. (gr. 4-7). 1989. pap. 3.50 (*0-553-15699-3*, Skylark) Bantam.

Mohr-Stephens, Judy. Please Understand Us! Is the World As I See It?; My Little World Book; Open Minded Kids!; Fence Me In...with Understanding, 33 vols. Riegert, Evelyn, ed. Bruce, Michael, illus. 500p. (gr. k-8). 1990. Set. 139.95 (*0-935323-00-7*) Barrington Hse.

Mohun, Janet. Drugs Steroids & Sports. FS-Aladdin Staff, ed. LC 88-50494. (Illus.). 64p. (gr. 6-12). 1988. PLB 12.40 (*0-531-10626-8*) Watts.

Moir, Hughes, ed. Collected Perspectives: Choosing & Using Books for the Classroom. 2nd ed. 417p. (Orig.). (gr. k-8). 1991. pap. text ed. 32.95 (*0-926842-12-9*) CG Pubs Inc.

Mokosso, Henry E. My First Pair of Shoes & the Little Altar Boy: Two Childhood Memories. LC 91-33536. 90p. (gr. 6-12). 1992. 7.95 (*0-944957-08-0*) Rivercross Pub.

Mokrinskaia, Nina. Moia Zhizn' (My Life) Detstvo v Sibiri, junost' v Shankkhaie 1914-1392 godq. Valk, Gabriel, ed. LC 90-85815. (RUS., Illus.). 224p. (Orig.). 1991. pap. 16.00 (*0-911971-61-0*) Effect Pub.

Moktefi, Mokhtar. The Arabs: In the Golden Age. LaRose, Mary K., tr. Ageorges, Veronique, illus. LC 92-4989. 64p. (gr. 4-6). 1992. PLB 14.90 (*1-56294-201-8*) Millbrook Pr.

Molan, Chris, as told by. The Viking Saga. (Illus.). 32p. (gr. k-5). 1985. PLB 17.96 (*0-8172-2503-X*) Raintree Steck-V.

Molan, Chris, illus. The First Easter: Retold by Catherine Storr. 32p. (gr. k-4). 1984. 14.65 (*0-8172-1987-0*, Raintree Childrens Books Belitha Press Ltd. - London) Raintree Steck-V.
—Joseph the Dream Teller: Retold by Catererine Storr. 32p. (gr. k-4). 1984. 14.65 (*0-8172-1989-7*, Raintree Children's Books Belitha Press Ltd. - London) Raintree Steck-V.

Moldenhauer, Janice. Developing Dictionary Skills. 64p. (gr. 3-8). 1979. 7.95 (*0-916456-48-X*, GA120) Good Apple.

Mole, Elsie H. A Christmas Tree from Puddin' Stone Hill. Hahn, Sylvia, illus. 36p. (ps-8). 1985. 6.95 (*0-920806-74-0*, Pub. by Penumbra Pr CN) U of Toronto Pr.

Molesworth, M. L. The Cuckoo Clock. (Orig.). (gr. k-6). 1987. pap. 4.95 (*0-440-41618-3*, Pub. by Yearling Classics) Dell.

Molgard, jt. auth. see Burgess.

Molgard, Max, jt. auth. see Burgess, Allan.

Moliere. Misanthrope & Other Plays. Wood, John, tr. Incl. Tartuffe; Imaginary Invalid; Doctor in Spite of Himself; Sicilian. (Orig.). (gr. 9 up). 1959. pap. 7.95 (*0-14-044089-5*, Penguin Classics) Viking Penguin.
—Miser & Other Plays. Wood, John, tr. Incl. Would-Be Gentleman; That Scoundrel Scapin; Don Juan; Love's the Best Doctor. (Orig.). (gr. 9 up). 1953. pap. 6.95 (*0-14-044036-4*, Penguin Classics) Viking Penguin.

Moline, Julie, jt. auth. see Levite, Christine.

Moll, Hans G., jt. auth. see Cumming, James T.

Moll, Louise B. Great Book of Cryptograms. Sharpe, Jim, illus. LC 92-39447. 128p. (gr. 10-12). 1993. pap. 5.95 (*0-8069-8784-7*) Sterling.

Moll, Patricia B. Children & Books I: African American Storybooks & Activities for all Children. 218p. (ps-3). 1991. pap. 14.95 (*0-9616511-2-1*); spiral bdg. 14.95 (*0-9616511-3-X*) Hampton Mae.

Mollel, Tololwa M. The King & the Tortoise. Blankley, Kathy, illus. LC 92-12485. 32p. (gr. k-3). 1993. 14.45 (*0-395-64480-1*, Clarion Bks) HM.
—Orphan Boy. Morin, Paul, illus. 32p. (gr. k-3). 1991. 15.45 (*0-89919-985-2*, Clarion Bks) HM.
—The Orphan Boy. Morin, Paul, illus. 1991. 14.95 (*0-685-53587-8*) HM.
—A Promise to the Sun: A Story of Africa. Vidal, Beatriz, illus. 32p. (ps-3). 1992. 15.95 (*0-316-57813-4*, Joy St Bks) Little.
—Rhinos for Lunch & Elephants for Supper! Spurll, Barbara, illus. 32p. (ps-3). 1992. 15.95 (*0-395-60734-5*, Clarion Bks) HM.

Mollel, Tololwa M., retold by. The Flying Tortoise: An Igbo Tale. Spurll, Barbara, illus. LC 93-14349. 1994. write for info. (*0-395-68845-0*) HM.

—The Princess Who Lost Her Hair: An Akamba Legend. Reasoner, Charles, illus. LC 92-13273. 32p. (gr. 2-5). 1992. lib. bdg. 11.89 (*0-8167-2815-1*); pap. 3.95 (*0-8167-2816-X*) Troll Assocs.

Moller, James, jt. auth. see American Heart Association Staff.

Moller, Linda. The Great Pig Escape. 112p. (gr. 3-5). 1994. pap. 6.95 (*0-86241-408-3*, Pub. by Cnngt UK) Trafalgar.

—The Great Pig Escape: A Green Story - A Wild Adventure. (Illus.). 111p. (Orig.). (gr. 2-6). 1990. pap. 8.95 (*0-86278-213-9*, Pub. by OBrien Pr IE) Dufour.

Molleson, Diane. Easy Science Experiments. (ps-3). 1993. pap. 3.95 (*0-590-45304-1*) Scholastic Inc.

—How Ducklings Grow. Kuhn, Dwight, photos by. 32p. (ps-2). 1993. pap. 2.50 (*0-590-45201-0*) Scholastic Inc.

—Secret Garden, with Charm, Key-Shaped. (Illus.). (ps-3). 1993. pap. 12.95 (*0-590-47173-2*) Scholastic Inc.

Mollica, Anthony & Northup, Bill. Those Wonderful Chriscraft Speedboats. (Illus.). 28p. 1992. wkbk. 3.95 (*1-883029-02-3*) CHP NY.

Mollica, Tony & Northup, Bill. Those Wonderful Garwood Speedboats. (Illus.). 28p. 1992. wkbk. 3.95 (*1-883029-01-5*) CHP NY.

—Those Wonderful Old Racing Boats. (Illus.). 28p. 1992. wkbk. 3.95 (*1-883029-00-7*) CHP NY.

—Touring the One Thousand Islands. (Illus.). 28p. 1993. wkbk. 3.95 (*1-883029-03-1*) CHP NY.

Molnar, Dorothy E. & Fenton, Stephen H. Who Will Pick Me up When I Fall? Mathews, Judith, ed. Trivas, Irene, illus. LC 90-28250. 32p. (ps-2). 1991. 13.95 (*0-8075-9072-X*) A Whitman.

Molnar, Ralph E., jt. auth. see Farlow, James O.

Moloney, James. Dougy. 1993. pap. 10.95 (*0-7022-2499-5*, Pub. by Univ Queensland Pr AT) Intl Spec Bk.

Molyneux, Lynn. Active Learning for Young Children. Park, Rosemary, illus. 228p. (ps-3). 1989. 19.95 (*0-685-29143-X*) Trellis Bks Inc.

—Get It Together: Group Projects for Creative Bulletin Boards. Bucur, Mike, illus. 160p. (gr. k-4). 1983. perfect bdg. 9.95 (*0-685-29141-3*) Trellis Bks Inc.

Molyneux, Lynn & Bucur, Mike. Your Own Thing: Individual Art Projects for Primary Grades. Bucur, Mike, illus. 160p. (gr. k-6). 1983. perfect bdg. 9.95 (*0-685-29140-5*) Trellis Bks Inc.

Molyneux, Lynn & Gordner, Brad. Act It Out: Original Plays Plus Crafts for Costumes & Scenery. Marasco, Pam, illus. 192p. (gr. 2-6). 1986. spiral bdg. 12.95 (*0-685-29139-1*) Trellis Bks Inc.

Momaday, Natachee S. Owl in the Cedar Tree. Perceval, Don, illus. LC 91-41866. viii, 117p. 1992. pap. 9.95 (*0-8032-8184-6*, Bison) U of Nebr Pr.

Momiyama, Nanae. Sumi-E: An Introduction to Ink Painting. LC 67-15320. (Illus.). 1967. pap. 6.95 (*0-8048-0554-7*) C E Tuttle.

Monahan, Patricia. Beginner's Guides: Oil Painting. (Illus.). 96p. (gr. 10-12). 1992. pap. 17.95 (*0-289-80058-7*, Pub. by Studio Vista UK) Sterling.

—Beginner's Guides: Painting in Acrylics. (Illus.). 96p. (gr. 10-12). 1993. pap. 17.95 (*0-289-80072-2*, Pub. by Cassell UK) Sterling.

Monceaux, Morgan. Jazz. Monceaux, Morgan, illus. LC 93-38177. 1994. write for info. (*0-679-86518-7*); PLB write for info. (*0-679-96518-1*) Knopf Bks Yng Read.

Moncure, Jane. Apes Find Shapes. Friedman, Joy, illus. 32p. (gr. 1-3). 1993. pap. text ed. 5.95 (*1-56189-347-1*) Amer Educ Pub.

—The Biggest Snowball of All. Friedman, Joy, illus. 32p. (gr. 1-3). 1993. pap. text ed. 5.95 (*1-56189-348-X*) Amer Educ Pub.

—Butterfly Express. Hohag, Linda, illus. 32p. (gr. 1-3). 1993. pap. text ed. 5.95 (*1-56189-377-3*) Amer Educ Pub.

—Here We Go 'Round the Year. Hohag, Linda & Jacobson, Lori, illus. 32p. (gr. 1-3). 1993. pap. text ed. 5.95 (*1-56189-378-1*) Amer Educ Pub.

—How Many Ways Can You Cut a Pie? Hohag, Linda & Jacobson, Lori, illus. 32p. (gr. 1-3). 1993. pap. text ed. 5.95 (*1-56189-349-8*) Amer Educ Pub.

—Ice-Cream Cows & Mitten Sheep. Friedman, Joy, illus. 32p. (gr. 1-3). 1993. pap. text ed. 5.95 (*1-56189-379-X*) Amer Educ Pub.

—The Magic Moon Machine. Hohag, Linda & Spoden, Dan, illus. 32p. (gr. 1-3). 1993. pap. text ed. 5.95 (*1-56189-375-7*) Amer Educ Pub.

—My "A" Sound Box. Beltier, Pam, illus. 32p. (gr. k-2). 1993. pap. text ed. 5.95 (*1-56189-384-6*) Amer Educ Pub.

—My "E" Sound Box. Gohman, Vera, illus. 32p. (gr. k-2). 1993. pap. text ed. 5.95 (*1-56189-385-4*) Amer Educ Pub.

—My "I" Sound Box. Gohman, Vera, illus. 32p. (gr. k-2). 1993. pap. text ed. 5.95 (*1-56189-386-2*) Amer Educ Pub.

—My "O" Sound Box. Gohman, Vera, illus. 32p. (gr. k-2). 1993. pap. text ed. 5.95 (*1-56189-387-0*) Amer Educ Pub.

—My Sound Parade. Sommers, Linda, illus. 32p. (gr. k-2). 1993. pap. text ed. 5.95 (*1-56189-389-7*) Amer Educ Pub.

—My "U" Sound Box. Beltier, Pam, illus. 32p. (gr. k-2). 1993. pap. text ed. 5.95 (*1-56189-383-8*) Amer Educ Pub.

—One Tricky Monkey up on Top. Hohag, Linda & Jacobson, Lori, illus. 32p. (gr. 1-3). 1993. pap. text ed. 5.95 (*1-56189-376-5*) Amer Educ Pub.

—Peter Pan: A Classic Tale. (Illus.). 32p. 1988. PLB 19.95 (*0-89565-469-5*); PLB 13.95s.p. (*0-685-66236-5*) Childs World.

—A Pocketful of Pets. Hohag, Linda & Jacobson, Lori, illus. 32p. (gr. 1-3). 1993. pap. text ed. 5.95 (*1-56189-380-3*) Amer Educ Pub.

—Where Is Baby Bear? Friedman, Joy, illus. 32p. (gr. 1-3). 1993. pap. text ed. 5.95 (*1-56189-381-1*) Amer Educ Pub.

Moncure, Jane B. Apes Find Shapes. Freidman, Joy, illus. LC 87-11747. 32p. (ps-2). 1987. PLB 21.35 (*0-89565-364-8*); PLB 14.95s.p. (*0-685-55867-3*) Childs World.

—Away Went the Farmer's Hat. Hohag, Linda, illus. LC 87-11742. 32p. (ps-2). 1987. PLB 21.35 (*0-89565-367-2*); PLB 14.95s.p. (*0-685-55868-1*) Childs World.

—The Bears Upstairs. Knipper, Sue, illus. LC 87-11715. 32p. (ps-2). 1987. PLB 21.35 (*0-89565-373-7*); PLB 14.95s.p. (*0-685-55876-2*) Childs World.

—Biggest Snowball of All. Friedman, Joy, illus. LC 88-25600. 32p. (ps-2). 1989. PLB 21.35 (*0-89565-391-5*); PLB 14.95s.p. (*0-685-56001-5*) Childs World.

—Butterfly Express. Hohag, Linda, illus. LC 88-22944. 32p. (ps-2). 1989. PLB 21.35 (*0-89565-392-3*); PLB 14.95s.p. (*0-685-55985-8*) Childs World.

—Caring. rev. ed. Endes, Helen, illus. LC 80-27506. (gr. k-3). 1981. PLB 21.35 (*0-89565-201-3*); PLB 14.95s.p. (*0-685-55475-9*) Childs World.

—Caring for My Baby Sister. Martin, Clovis, illus. 32p. (ps-2). 1990. PLB 18.50 (*0-89565-669-8*); PLB 12.95s.p. (*0-685-58738-X*) Childs World.

—Caring for My Body. McCallum, Jodie, illus. 32p. (ps-2). 1990. PLB 18.50 (*0-89565-668-X*); PLB 12.95s.p. (*0-685-58737-1*) Childs World.

—Caring for My Home. Connelly, Gwen, illus. 32p. (ps-2). 1990. PLB 18.50 (*0-89565-667-1*); PLB 12.95s.p. (*0-685-56168-2*) Childs World.

—Caring for My Kitty. Rigo, Christina, illus. 32p. (ps-2). 1990. PLB 18.50 (*0-89565-666-3*); PLB 12.95s.p. (*0-685-56167-4*) Childs World.

—Caring for My Things. Collette, Rondi, illus. 32p. (ps-2). 1990. PLB 18.50 (*0-89565-670-1*); PLB 12.95s.p. (*0-685-58739-8*) Childs World.

—A Color Clown Comes to Town. Hohag, Linda, illus. LC 87-11605. 32p. (ps-2). 1987. PLB 21.35 (*0-89565-369-9*); PLB 14.95s.p. (*0-685-55869-X*) Childs World.

—Courage. rev. ed. Endes, Helen, illus. LC 80-39515. 32p. (gr. k-3). 1981. PLB 21.35 (*0-89565-202-1*); PLB 14.95s.p. (*0-685-55478-3*) Childs World.

—Dinosaurs: Back in Time. Hohag, Linda, illus. LC 89-38469. 32p. (ps-2). 1990. PLB 21.35 (*0-89565-550-0*) Childs World.

—A Dragon in a Wagon. Hohag, Linda, illus. LC 87-11755. 32p. (ps-2). 1987. PLB 21.35 (*0-89565-400-8*); PLB 14.95s.p. (*0-685-55870-3*) Childs World.

—The Five Senses: Treasures Outside. Axeman, Lois, illus. LC 90-30635. 32p. (ps-2). 1990. PLB 19.95 (*0-89565-575-6*); PLB 13.95s.p. (*0-685-56191-7*) Childs World.

—Growing Strong Inside. Hohag, Linda, illus. LC 85-10341. 32p. (gr. k-2). 1985. PLB 21.35 (*0-89565-333-8*); PLB 14.95s.p. (*0-685-55765-0*) Childs World.

—Happy Birthday, Word Bird. Hohag, Linda, illus. LC 83-15256. 32p. (gr. k-2). 1983. PLB 21.35 (*0-89565-256-0*); PLB 14.95s.p. (*0-685-55678-6*) Childs World.

—Happy Healthkins. Axeman, Lois, illus. LC 82-14794. (ps-2). 1982. PLB 19.95 (*0-89565-243-9*); PLB 13.95s.p. (*0-685-55640-9*) Childs World.

—The Healthkin Food Train. Endres, Helen, illus. LC 82-14710. 32p. (ps-2). 1982. PLB 19.95 (*0-89565-240-4*); PLB 13.95s.p. (*0-685-55643-3*) Childs World.

—Healthkins Exercise! Endres, Helen, illus. LC 82-14712. 32p. (ps-2). 1982. PLB 19.95 (*0-89565-241-2*); PLB 13.95s.p. (*0-685-55641-7*) Childs World.

—Healthkins Help. Axeman, Lois, illus. LC 82-14713. 32p. (ps-2). 1982. PLB 19.95 (*0-89565-242-0*); PLB 13.95s.p. (*0-685-55642-5*) Childs World.

—Here We Go 'Round the Year. Hohag, Linda, illus. LC 87-13257. 32p. (ps-2). 1987. PLB 21.35 (*0-89565-402-4*); PLB 14.95s.p. (*0-685-55920-3*) Childs World.

—Hi, Word Bird. Hohag, Linda S., illus. LC 80-15919. 32p. (ps-2). 1981. PLB 21.35 (*0-89565-159-9*); PLB 14.95s.p. (*0-685-55485-6*) Childs World.

—Hide-&-Seek Word Bird. Hohag, Linda S., illus. LC 81-18068. (ps-2). 1982. PLB 21.35 (*0-89565-218-8*); PLB 14.95s.p. (*0-685-55486-4*) Childs World.

—Honesty. rev. ed. Karch, Paul, illus. LC 80-39571. 32p. (gr. k-3). 1981. PLB 21.35 (*0-89565-203-X*); PLB 14.95s.p. (*0-685-55487-2*) Childs World.

—Hop-skip-jump-a-roo Zoo. Hohag, Linda, illus. LC 87-11743. 32p. (ps-2). 1987. PLB 21.35 (*0-89565-371-0*); PLB 14.95s.p. (*0-685-55871-1*) Childs World.

—How Many Ways Can You Cut a Pie? Hohag, Linda, illus. LC 87-15807. 32p. (ps-2). 1987. PLB 21.35 (*0-89565-408-3*); PLB 14.95s.p. (*0-685-55921-1*) Childs World.

—How Seeds Travel: Popguns & Parachutes. Endres, Helen, illus. LC 89-71171. 32p. (ps-2). 1990. PLB 19.95 (*0-89565-569-1*); PLB 13.95s.p. (*0-685-56185-2*) Childs World.

—I Never Say I'm Thankful, But I Am. Hook, Frances, illus. LC 78-21577. (ps-3). 1979. PLB 21.35 (*0-89565-023-1*); PLB 14.95s.p. (*0-685-55488-0*) Childs World.

—Ice-Cream Cows & Mitten Sheep. Friedman, Joy, illus. LC 87-14603. 32p. (ps-2). 1987. PLB 21.35 (*0-89565-403-2*); PLB 14.95s.p. (*0-685-55922-X*) Childs World.

—John's Choice. Halverson, Lydia, illus. LC 82-19897. 32p. (gr. 1-3). 1982. PLB 19.95 (*0-89565-252-8*); PLB 13.95 (*0-685-57930-1*) Childs World.

—Joy. (Illus.). 32p. (ps-3). 1980. PLB 21.35 (*0-89565-224-2*); PLB 14.95s.p. (*0-685-62607-5*) Childs World.

—Julie's New Home. Karch, Pat, illus. LC 82-19900. 32p. (gr. 3-4). 1983. lib. bdg. 8.45 (*0-89565-254-4*) Childs World.

—Kindness. rev. ed. Hohag, Linda S., illus. LC 80-39535. 32p. (gr. k-3). 1981. PLB 21.35 (*0-89565-204-8*); PLB 14.95s.p. (*0-685-55491-0*) Childs World.

—Kinds of Animals: Flyers, Leapers, Crawlers, Creepers. Hohag, Linda, illus. LC 89-71172. 32p. (ps-2). 1990. PLB 21.35 (*0-89565-567-5*); PLB 14.95s.p. (*0-89565-596-9*) Childs World.

—Let's Take a Walk in the Zoo. Axeman, Lois, illus. LC 86-20744. 32p. (ps-2). 1986. PLB 21.35 (*0-89565-356-7*); PLB 14.95s.p. (*0-685-55821-5*) Childs World.

—Life Cycles: The Singing Mailbox. Lexa-Senning, Susan, illus. LC 89-24000. 32p. (ps-2). 1990. PLB 21.35 (*0-89565-552-7*); PLB 14.95s.p. (*0-685-56173-9*) Childs World.

—Little Too-Tall. Hohag, Linda, illus. LC 87-11632. 32p. (ps-2). 1987. PLB 21.35 (*0-89565-374-5*); PLB 14.95s.p. (*0-685-55872-X*); pap. 6.96 (*0-89565-448-2*) Childs World.

—The Look Book. Axeman, Lois, illus. LC 82-4517. 32p. (ps-3). 1982. pap. 3.95 (*0-516-43251-6*) Childrens.

—Love. rev. ed. Hohag, Linda, illus. LC 80-27479. 32p. (gr. k-3). 1981. PLB 21.35 (*0-89565-205-6*); PLB 14.95s.p. (*0-685-55492-9*) Childs World.

—Magic Monsters Act the Alphabet. Endres, Helen, illus. LC 79-23841. (ps-3). 1980. PLB 21.35 (*0-89565-116-5*); PLB 14.95s.p. (*0-685-55493-7*) Childs World.

—Magic Monsters Count to Ten. Fudala, Rosemary, illus. LC 78-23634. (ps-3). 1979. PLB 21.35 (*0-89565-058-4*); PLB 14.95s.p. (*0-685-55495-3*) Childs World.

—Magic Monsters Learn about Health. Endres, Helen, illus. LC 79-24240. (ps-3). 1980. PLB 21.35 (*0-89565-117-3*); PLB 14.95s.p. (*0-685-57681-7*) Childs World.

—Magic Monsters Learn about Manners. Sommers, Linda, illus. LC 79-24528. (ps-3). 1980. PLB 21.35 (*0-89565-118-1*); PLB 14.95s.p. (*0-685-57682-5*) Childs World.

—Magic Monsters Learn about Space. Sommers, Linda, illus. LC 79-25765. (ps-3). 1980. PLB 21.35 (*0-89565-119-X*); PLB 14.95s.p. (*0-685-55500-3*) Childs World.

—Magic Monsters Look for Colors. Magnuson, Diana, illus. LC 78-23792. (ps-3). 1979. PLB 21.35 (*0-89565-056-8*); PLB 14.95s.p. (*0-685-55502-X*) Childs World.

—Magic Monsters Look for Shapes. Magnuson, Diana, illus. LC 78-21529. (ps-3). 1979. PLB 21.35 (*0-89565-057-6*); PLB 14.95s.p. (*0-685-55503-8*) Childs World.

—The Magic Moon Machine. Hohag, Linda, illus. LC 87-30959. 32p. (ps-2). 1987. PLB 21.35 (*0-89565-410-5*); PLB 14.95s.p. (*0-685-55923-8*); pap. 6.96 (*0-89565-438-5*) Childs World.

—Mr. Doodle Had a Poodle. Hohag, Linda, illus. LC 87-15808. 32p. (ps-2). 1987. PLB 21.35 (*0-89565-409-1*); PLB 14.95s.p. (*0-685-55924-6*) Childs World.

—Mousekin's Special Day. Williams, Jenny, illus. LC 87-11750. 32p. (ps-2). 1987. PLB 21.35 (*0-89565-366-4*); PLB 14.95s.p. (*0-685-67590-4*) Childs World.

—My "a" Sound Box. Peltier, Pam, illus. LC 84-17024. 32p. (ps-2). 1984. PLB 21.35 (*0-89565-296-X*); PLB 14.95s.p. (*0-685-55767-7*) Childs World.

—My "b" Sound Box. Sommers, Linda, illus. LC 77-23588. (ps-2). 1977. PLB 21.35 (*0-913778-92-3*); PLB 14.95s.p. (*0-685-55506-2*) Childs World.

—My Baby Brother Needs a Friend. Hook, Frances, illus. LC 78-21935. (ps-3). 1979. PLB 21.35 (*0-89565-019-3*) Childs World.

—My "c" Sound Box. Sommers, Linda, illus. LC 78-23638. (ps-2). 1979. PLB 21.35 (*0-89565-052-5*); PLB 14.95s.p. (*0-685-55507-0*) Child's World.

—My "d" Sound Box. Sommers, Linda, illus. LC 78-8450. (ps-2). 1978. PLB 21.35 (*0-89565-044-4*); PLB 14.95s.p. (*0-685-55508-9*) Childs World.

—My "e" Sound Box. Gohman, Vera, illus. LC 84-17021. 32p. (ps-2). 1984. PLB 21.35 (*0-89565-297-8*); PLB 14.95s.p. (*0-685-57951-4*) Childs World.

—My Eight Book. Hohag, Linda, illus. LC 85-30962. 32p. (ps-2). 1986. PLB 21.35 (*0-89565-319-2*); PLB 14.95s.p. (*0-685-55823-1*) Childs World.

—My "f" Sound Box. Sommers, Linda, illus. LC 77-9377. (ps-2). 1977. PLB 21.35 (*0-913778-93-1*); PLB 14.95s.p. (*0-685-55509-7*); pap. 6.96 (*0-685-57684-1*) Childs World.

—My First Book. Hutton, Kathryn, illus. LC 84-17455. 32p. (ps-2). 1984. PLB 21.35 (*0-89565-271-4*); PLB 14.95s.p. (*0-685-57948-4*) Childs World.

—My First Presidents' Day Book. Halverson, Lydia, illus. LC 87-10309. 32p. (ps-2). 1987. pap. 3.95 (0-516-42910-8) Childrens.
—My First Thanksgiving Book. Connelly, Gwen, illus. LC 84-9433. 32p. (ps-2). 1984. PLB 15.00 (0-516-02903-7); pap. 3.95 (0-516-42903-5) Childrens.
—My Five Book. Hohag, Linda, illus. LC 85-9699. 32p. (ps-2). 1985. PLB 21.35 (0-89565-316-8); PLB 14.95s.p. (0-685-55768-5) Childs World.
—My Four Book. Hohag, Linda, illus. LC 85-9700. 32p. (ps-2). 1985. PLB 21.35 (0-89565-315-X); PLB 14.95s.p. (0-685-55769-3) Childs World.
—My "g" Sound Box. Sommers, Linda, illus. LC 78-22037. (ps-2). 1979. PLB 21.35 (0-89565-053-3); PLB 14.95s.p. (0-685-55510-0) Childs World.
—My "h" Sound Box. Sommers, Linda, illus. LC 77-8977. (ps-2). 1977. PLB 21.35 (0-913778-94-X); PLB 14.95s.p. (0-685-55511-9) Childs World.
—My "I" Sound Box. Gohman, Vera K., illus. LC 84-17022. 32p. (ps-2). 1984. PLB 21.35 (0-89565-298-6); PLB 14.95s.p. (0-685-57949-2) Childs World.
—My "j" Sound Box. Sommers, Linda, illus. LC 78-23178. (ps-2). 1979. PLB 21.35 (0-89565-049-5); PLB 14.95s.p. (0-685-55512-7) Childs World.
—My "k" Sound Box. Sommers, Linda, illus. LC 78-22034. (ps-2). 1979. PLB 21.35 (0-89565-050-9); PLB 14.95s.p. (0-685-55513-5) Childs World.
—My "l" Sound Box. Sommers, Linda, illus. LC 78-8373. (ps-2). 1978. PLB 21.35 (0-89565-045-2); PLB 14.95s.p. (0-685-55514-3) Childs World.
—My "m" Sound Box. Sommers, Linda, illus. LC 78-24458. (ps-2). 1979. PLB 21.35 (0-89565-051-7); PLB 14.95s.p. (0-685-55515-1) Childs World.
—My "n" Sound Box. Sommers, Linda, illus. LC 78-22053. (ps-2). 1979. PLB 21.35 (0-89565-054-1) Childs World.
—My Nine Book. Hohag, Linda, illus. LC 85-30959. 32p. (ps-2). 1986. PLB 21.35 (0-89565-320-6); PLB 14.95s.p. (0-685-55824-X) Childs World.
—My "O" Sound Box. Gohman, Vera, illus. LC 84-17023. 32p. (ps-2). 1984. PLB 21.35 (0-89565-299-4); PLB 14.95s.p. (0-685-57950-6) Childs World.
—My One Book. Peltier, Pam, illus. LC 85-5897. 32p. (ps-2). 1985. PLB 21.35 (0-89565-312-5); PLB 14.95s.p. (0-685-55770-7) Childs World.
—My "p" Sound Box. Sommers, Linda, illus. LC 78-7841. (ps-2). 1978. PLB 21.35 (0-89565-047-9); PLB 14.95s.p. (0-685-55516-X) Childs World.
—My "q" Sound Box. Sommers, Linda, illus. LC 79-13085. (ps-2). 1979. PLB 21.35 (0-89565-100-9); PLB 14.95s.p. (0-685-55517-8) Childs World.
—My "r" Sound Box. Sommers, Linda, illus. LC 78-7842. (ps-2). 1978. PLB 21.35 (0-89565-048-7); PLB 14.95s.p. (0-685-55518-6) Childs World.
—My "s" Sound Box. Sommers, Linda, illus. LC 77-8970. (ps-2). 1977. PLB 21.35 (0-913778-95-8); PLB 14.95s.p. (0-685-55519-4) Childs World.
—My Seven Book. Hohag, Linda, illus. LC 86-2594. 32p. (ps-2). 1986. PLB 21.35 (0-89565-318-4); PLB 14.95s.p. (0-685-55825-8) Childs World.
—My Six Book. Hohag, Linda, illus. LC 85-30961. 32p. (ps-2). 1986. PLB 21.35 (0-89565-317-6); PLB 14.95s.p. (0-685-55826-6) Childs World.
—My Sound Parade. Sommers, Linda, illus. LC 79-15930. (ps-2). 1979. PLB 21.35 (0-89565-103-3); PLB 14.95s.p. (0-685-55520-8) Childs World.
—My "t" Sound Box. Sommers, Linda, illus. LC 77-23587. (ps-2). 1977. PLB 21.35 (0-913778-96-6); PLB 14.95s.p. (0-685-55521-6) Childs World.
—My Ten Book. Hohag, Linda, illus. LC 86-2293. 32p. (ps-2). 1986. PLB 21.35 (0-89565-321-4); PLB 14.95s.p. (0-685-55827-4) Childs World.
—My Three Book. Hohag, Linda, illus. LC 85-5898. 32p. (ps-2). 1985. PLB 21.35 (0-89565-314-1); PLB 14.95s.p. (0-685-55771-5) Childs World.
—My Two Book. Peltier, Pam, illus. LC 85-7885. 32p. (ps-2). 1985. PLB 21.35 (0-89565-313-3); PLB 14.95s.p. (0-685-55772-3) Childs World.
—My "u" Sound Box. Peltier, Pam, illus. LC 84-17012. 32p. (ps-2). 1984. PLB 21.35 (0-89565-300-1); PLB 14.95s.p. (0-685-55773-1) Childs World.
—My "v" Sound Box. Sommers, Linda, illus. LC 79-13084. (ps-2). 1979. PLB 21.35 (0-89565-101-7); PLB 14.95s.p. (0-685-55522-4) Childs World.
—My "w" Sound Box. Sommers, Linda, illus. LC 78-8614. (ps-2). 1978. PLB 21.35 (0-89565-046-0); PLB 14.95s.p. (0-685-55523-2) Childs World.
—My "x, y, z" Sound Box. Sommers, Linda, illus. LC 79-13086. (ps-2). 1979. PLB 21.35 (0-89565-102-5); PLB 14.95s.p. (0-685-55524-0) Childs World.
—Nanny Goat's Boat. Friedman, Joy, illus. LC 87-12839. 32p. (ps-2). 1987. PLB 21.35 (0-89565-404-0); PLB 14.95s.p. (0-685-55925-4) Childs World.
—Night Animals: Wake-Up, Little Owl! Halverson, Lydia, illus. LC 89-71173. 32p. (ps-2). 1990. PLB 21.35 (0-89565-568-3); PLB 14.95s.p. (0-685-56184-4) Childs World.
—Now I Am Five! Endres, Helen, illus. LC 83-25264. 32p. (ps-2). 1984. pap. 3.95 (0-516-41879-3) Childrens.
—Now I Am Four! Hutton, Kathryn, illus. LC 83-25270. 32p. (ps-2). 1984. pap. 3.95 (0-516-41878-5) Childrens.
—Now I Am Three! Hohag, Linda, illus. LC 83-20892. 32p. (ps). 1984. pap. 3.95 (0-516-41877-7) Childrens.
—Now I Am Two! Hutton, Kathryn, illus. LC 83-20891. 32p. (ps). 1984. pap. 3.95 (0-516-41876-9) Childrens.

—One Tricky Monkey Up on Top. Freidman, Joy, illus. LC 87-11612. 32p. (ps-2). 1987. PLB 21.35 (0-89565-365-6); PLB 14.95s.p. (0-685-55874-6) Childs World.
—Our Birthday Book. Endres, Helen, illus. LC 86-30976. 32p. (ps-3). 1987. PLB 19.95 (0-89565-349-4); PLB 13.95s.p. (0-685-55999-8) Childs World.
—Our Christmas Book. rev. ed. Stasiak, Krystyna & Connelly, Gwen, illus. LC 85-29132. 32p. (ps-3). 1986. PLB 19.95 (0-89565-341-9); PLB 13.95s.p. (0-685-55828-2) Childs World.
—Our Columbus Day Book. Shackelford, Jean, illus. LC 86-6818. 32p. (ps-3). 1986. PLB 19.95 (0-89565-347-8); PLB 13.95s.p. (0-685-55829-0) Childs World.
—Our Easter Book. Rev. ed. Endres, Helen, illus. LC 86-29876. 32p. (ps-3). 1987. PLB 19.95 (0-89565-345-1); PLB 13.95s.p. (0-685-55850-9) Childs World.
—Our Halloween Book. rev. ed. Peltier, Pam, illus. LC 85-30868. 32p. (ps-3). 1986. PLB 19.95 (0-89565-348-6); PLB 13.95s.p. (0-685-55830-4) Childs World.
—Our Mother's Day Book. Rev. ed. Lexa, Susan, illus. LC 86-29980. (ps-3). 1987. PLB 19.95 (0-89565-346-X); PLB 13.95s.p. (0-685-55537-2) Childs World.
—Our Thanksgiving Book. rev. ed. Gohman, Vera, illus. LC 85-29077. 32p. (ps-3). 1986. PLB 19.95 (0-89565-340-0); PLB 13.95s.p. (0-685-55832-0) Childs World.
—Our Valentine's Day Book. Rev. ed. McLean, Mina G., illus. LC 86-28387. 32p. (ps-3). 1987. PLB 19.95 (0-89565-343-5); PLB 13.95s.p. (0-685-55852-5) Childs World.
—Play with A & T. McCallum, Jodi, illus. LC 89-774. 32p. (gr. k-2). 1989. PLB 21.35 (0-89565-505-5); PLB 14.95s.p. (0-685-56019-8) Childs World.
—Play with E & D. (Illus.). 32p. (gr. k-2). 1989. PLB 21.35 (0-89565-508-X); PLB 14.95s.p. (0-685-56017-1) Childs World.
—Play with I & G. (Illus.). 32p. (gr. k-2). 1989. PLB 21.35 (0-89565-507-1); PLB 14.95s.p. (0-685-56016-3) Childs World.
—Play with O & G. (Illus.). 32p. (gr. k-2). 1989. PLB 21.35 (0-89565-506-3); PLB 14.95s.p. (0-685-56018-X) Childs World.
—Play with U & G. (Illus.). 32p. (gr. k-2). 1989. PLB 21.35 (0-89565-509-8); PLB 14.95s.p. (0-685-56020-1) Childs World.
—Please? Thanks! I'm Sorry. Axeman, Lois, illus. LC 85-11664. 32p. (gr. k-2). 1985. PLB 21.35 (0-89565-331-1); PLB 14.95s.p. (0-685-55774-X) Childs World.
—A Pocketful of Pets. Hohag, Linda, illus. LC 87-11748. 32p. (ps-2). 1987. PLB 21.35 (0-89565-370-2); PLB 14.95s.p. (0-685-55875-4) Childs World.
—Polka-Dot Puppy. Endres, Helen, illus. LC 87-15813. 32p. (ps-2). 1987. PLB 21.35 (0-89565-407-5); PLB 14.95s.p. (0-685-55926-2) Childs World.
—Rabbits' Habits. Peltier, Pam, illus. LC 87-12841. 32p. (ps-2). 1987. PLB 21.35 (0-89565-406-7); PLB 14.95s.p. (0-685-55931-9) Childs World.
—Rain: A Great Day for Ducks. Friedman, Joy, illus. LC 89-24010. 32p. (ps-2). 1990. PLB 19.95 (0-89565-553-5); PLB 13.95s.p. (0-685-56174-7) Childs World.
—Saying Please. Inderieden, Nancy, illus. LC 82-19927. 32p. (ps-2). 1983. PLB 21.35 (0-89565-248-X); PLB 14.95s.p. (0-685-55661-1) Childs World.
—Short A & Long A Play a Game. Endres, Helen, illus. LC 79-10300. (gr. k-2). 1979. PLB 21.35 (0-89565-089-4); PLB 14.95s.p. (0-685-55544-5) Childs World.
—Short E & Long E Play a Game. Endres, Helen, illus. LC 79-10305. (gr. k-2). 1979. PLB 21.35 (0-89565-090-8); PLB 14.95s.p. (0-685-55545-3) Childs World.
—Short I & Long I Play a Game. Endres, Helen, illus. LC 79-10303. (gr. k-2). 1979. PLB 21.35 (0-89565-091-6); PLB 14.95s.p. (0-685-55546-1) Childs World.
—Short O & Long O Play a Game. Endres, Helen, illus. LC 79-10304. (gr. k-2). 1979. PLB 21.35 (0-89565-092-4); PLB 14.95s.p. (0-685-55547-X) Childs World.
—Short U & Long U Play a Game. Endres, Helen, illus. LC 79-10306. (gr. k-2). 1979. PLB 21.35 (0-89565-093-2); PLB 14.95s.p. (0-685-55548-8) Childs World.
—Smile, Says Little Crocodile. Hohag, Linda, illus. LC 87-13833. 32p. (ps-2). 1987. PLB 21.35 (0-89565-401-6); PLB 14.95s.p. (0-685-55935-1); pap. 6.96 (0-89565-449-0) Childs World.
—Sounds All Around. Axeman, Lois, illus. LC 82-4516. 32p. (ps-3). 1982. pap. 3.95 (0-516-43252-4) Childrens.
—Step into Fall: A New Season. Lexa-Senning, Susan, illus. LC 90-30637. 32p. (ps-2). 1990. PLB 19.95 (0-89565-573-X); PLB 13.95s.p. (0-685-56189-5) Childs World.
—Step into Spring: A New Season. Williams, Jenny, illus. LC 90-30375. 32p. (ps-2). 1990. PLB 19.95 (0-89565-571-3); PLB 13.95s.p. (0-685-56187-9) Childs World.
—Step into Summer: A New Season. McCallum, Jodie, illus. LC 90-30456. 32p. (ps-2). 1990. PLB 19.95 (0-89565-572-1); PLB 13.95s.p. (0-685-56188-7) Childs World.

—Step into Winter: A New Season. Hohag, Linda, illus. LC 90-30636. 32p. (ps-2). 1990. PLB 19.95 (0-89565-574-8); PLB 13.95s.p. (0-685-56190-9) Childs World.
—Stop! Go! Word Bird. Hohag, Linda S., illus. LC 80-16273. 32p. (ps-2). 1981. PLB 21.35 (0-89565-160-2); PLB 14.95s.p. (0-685-55552-6) Childs World.
—The Sun: Our Daytime Star. Endres, Helen, illus. LC 89-24009. 32p. (ps-2). 1990. PLB 19.95 (0-89565-551-9); PLB 13.95s.p. (0-685-56172-0) Childs World.
—A Tasting Party. Axeman, Lois, illus. LC 82-4411. 32p. (ps-3). 1982. pap. 3.95 (0-516-43253-2) Childrens.
—Terry's Turn-Around. Endres, Helen, illus. LC 82-19898. 32p. (gr. 3-4). 1982. 19.95 (0-89565-250-1); PLB 13.95 (0-685-57929-8) Childs World.
—The Touch Book. Axeman, Lois, illus. LC 82-4154. (ps-3). 1982. pap. 3.95 (0-516-43254-0) Childrens.
—Watch Out! Word Bird. Hohag, Linda S., illus. (ps-2). 1982. PLB 21.35 (0-89565-219-6); PLB 14.95s.p. (0-685-55555-0) Childs World.
—What Can We Play Today? Hohag, Linda, illus. LC 87-32565. 32p. (ps-2). 1987. PLB 21.35 (0-89565-412-1); PLB 14.95s.p. (0-89565-940-8); pap. 6.96 (0-89565-441-5) Childs World.
—What Do You Do with a Grumpy Kangaroo? Hohag, Linda, illus. LC 87-11731. 32p. (ps). 1987. PLB 21.35 (0-89565-372-9); PLB 14.95s.p. (0-685-55877-0) Childs World.
—What Do You Say When a Monkey Acts This Way? Super, Terri, illus. LC 87-11736. 32p. (ps-2). 1987. PLB 21.35 (0-89565-368-0); PLB 14.95s.p. (0-685-55878-9) Childs world.
—What Does Word Bird See? Gohman, Vera, illus. LC 81-21594. (ps-2). 1982. PLB 21.35 (0-89565-220-X); PLB 14.95s.p. (0-685-55557-7) Childs World.
—What Plants Need: The Rabbit Who Knew. Dunnington, Tom, illus. LC 89-24001. 32p. (ps-2). 1990. PLB 19.95 (0-89565-559-4); PLB 13.95s.p. (0-685-56180-1) Childs World.
—What Was It Before It Was Bread? Hygaard, Elizabeth, illus. LC 85-11402. 32p. (ps-2). 1985. PLB 21.35 (0-89565-323-0); PLB 14.95s.p. (0-685-55775-8) Childs World.
—What Was It Before It Was Orange Juice? Lexa, Susan, illus. LC 85-11396. 32p. (ps-2). 1985. PLB 21.35 (0-89565-322-2); PLB 14.95s.p. (0-685-55779-0) Childs World.
—What Your Nose Knows! Axeman, Lois, illus. LC 82-9464. 32p. (ps-3). 1982. pap. 3.95 (0-516-43255-9) Childrens.
—What's So Special about Lauren? She's My Baby Sister. Williams, Jenny, illus. LC 87-21927. 32p. (ps-2). 1987. PLB 21.35 (0-89565-413-X); PLB 14.95s.p. (0-685-55942-4) Childs World.
—What's So Special about This Fall? I'm Going to School: I'm Going to School. Williams, Jenny, illus. LC 88-2868. 32p. (ps-2). 1988. PLB 21.35 (0-89565-420-2); PLB 14.95s.p. (0-685-55941-6) Childs World.
—What's So Special about Today? It's My Birthday. Williams, Jenny, illus. LC 87-21907. 32p. (ps-2). 1987. PLB 21.35 (0-89565-414-8); PLB 14.95s.p. (0-685-55944-0) Childs World.
—Where? Axeman, Lois, illus. LC 83-7307. 32p. (gr. k-2). 1983. pap. 3.95 (0-516-46593-7) Childrens.
—Where Is Baby Bear? Friedman, Joy, illus. LC 87-12840. 32p. (ps-2). 1987. PLB 21.35 (0-89565-405-9); PLB 14.95s.p. (0-685-55945-9) Childs World.
—A Wish-for Dinosaur. Gohman, Vera, illus. LC 88-20302. 32p. (ps-2). 1989. PLB 21.35 (0-89565-393-1); PLB 14.95s.p. (0-685-56000-7) Childs World.
—Wishes, Whispers & Secrets. Hook, Frances, illus. LC 78-31295. (ps-3). 1979. PLB 21.35 (0-89565-024-X); PLB 14.95s.p. (0-685-55560-7) Childs World.
—Word Bird Asks: What? What? What? Gohman, Vera, illus. LC 83-15258. 32p. (gr. k-2). 1983. PLB 21.35 (0-89565-258-7); PLB 14.95s.p. (0-685-55680-8) Childs World.
—Word Bird Builds a City. Gohman, Vera, illus. LC 83-15275. 32p. (ps-2). 1983. PLB 21.35 (0-89565-257-9); PLB 14.95s.p. (0-685-55677-8) Childs World.
—Word Bird Makes Words with Cat. Hohag, Linda, illus. LC 83-23948. 32p. (gr. k-2). 1984. PLB 21.35 (0-89565-259-5); PLB 14.95s.p. (0-685-55684-0) Childs World.
—Word Bird Makes Words with Dog. Gohman, Vera, illus. LC 83-23946. 32p. (gr. k-1). 1984. PLB 21.35 (0-89565-263-3); PLB 14.95s.p. (0-685-55687-5) Childs World.
—Word Bird Makes Words with Duck. Hohag, Linda, illus. LC 83-23943. 32p. (gr. k-2). 1984. PLB 21.35 (0-89565-261-7); PLB 14.95s.p. (0-685-55686-7) Childs World.
—Word Bird Makes Words with Hen. Hohag, Linda, illus. LC 83-23944. 32p. (gr. k-2). 1984. PLB 21.35 (0-89565-260-9); PLB 14.95s.p. (0-685-55685-9) Childs World.
—Word Bird Makes Words with Pig. LC 83-23945. (Illus.). 32p. (gr. k-2). 1984. PLB 21.35 (0-89565-262-5); PLB 14.95s.p. (0-685-55690-5) Childs World.
—Word Bird's Christmas Words. Gohman, Vera, illus. LC 86-31666. 32p. (gr. k-2). 1987. PLB 21.35 (0-89565-361-3); PLB 14.95s.p. (0-685-55879-7) Childs World.

—Word Bird's Circus Surprise. Hohag, Linda, illus. LC 80-29528. 32p. (gr. k-2). 1981. PLB 21.35 (*0-89565-162-9*); PLB 14.95.s.p. (*0-685-55561-5*) Childs World.

—Word Bird's Dinosaur Day. Hohag, Linda, illus. 32p. (ps-2). 1990. PLB 21.35 (*0-89565-617-5*); PLB 14. 95.s.p. (*0-685-56204-2*) Childs World.

—Word Bird's Easter Words. Axeman, Lois, illus. 32p. (gr. k-2). 1987. PLB 21.35 (*0-89565-363-X*); PLB 14. 95.s.p. (*0-685-55880-0*) Childs World.

—Word Bird's Fall Words. Miracle, Ric, illus. LC 85-5935. 32p. (gr. k-2). 1985. PLB 21.35 (*0-89565-308-7*); PLB 14.95.s.p. (*0-685-55735-9*) Childs World.

—Word Bird's Halloween Words. Gohman, Vera, illus. LC 86-31024. 32p. (gr. k-2). 1987. PLB 21.35 (*0-89565-359-1*); PLB 14.95.s.p. (*0-685-55881-9*) Childs World.

—Word Bird's Hats. Gohman, Vera, illus. LC 81-18065. (ps-2). 1982. PLB 21.35 (*0-89565-221-8*); PLB 14. 95.s.p. (*0-685-55562-3*) Childs World.

—Word Bird's Magic Wand. Hohag, Linda, illus. LC 90-1645. 32p. (ps-2). 1990. PLB 21.35 (*0-89565-580-2*); PLB 14.95.s.p. (*0-685-56202-6*) Childs World.

—Word Bird's New Friend. Hohag, Linda, illus. LC 90-37002. 32p. (ps-2). 1990. PLB 21.35 (*0-89565-616-7*); PLB 14.95.s.p. (*0-685-56203-4*) Childs World.

—Word Bird's Rainy-Day Dance. Hohag, Linda, illus. LC 90-31693. 32p. (ps-2). 1990. PLB 21.35 (*0-89565-579-9*); PLB 14.95.s.p. (*0-685-56201-8*) Childs World.

—Word Bird's School Words. Hohag, Linda, illus. LC 89-7179. 32p. (ps-2). 1989. PLB 21.35 (*0-89565-510-1*); PLB 14.95.s.p. (*0-685-56082-1*) Childs World.

—Word Bird's Shapes. Hohag, Linda, illus. LC 83-15255. 32p. (gr. k-2). 1983. PLB 21.35 (*0-89565-255-2*); PLB 14.95.s.p. (*0-685-55679-4*) Childs World.

—Word Bird's Spring Words. Gohman, Vera, illus. LC 85-5902. 32p. (gr. k-2). 1985. PLB 21.35 (*0-89565-310-9*); PLB 14.95.s.p. (*0-685-55736-7*) Childs World.

—Word Bird's Summer Words. Miracle, Ric, illus. LC 85-5930. 32p. (gr. k-2). 1985. PLB 21.35 (*0-89565-311-7*); PLB 14.95.s.p. (*0-685-55737-5*) Childs World.

—Word Bird's Thanksgiving Words. Hohag, Linda, illus. LC 86-32639. 32p. (gr. k-2). 1987. PLB 21.35 (*0-89565-360-5*); PLB 14.95.s.p. (*0-685-55882-7*) Childs World.

—Word Bird's Valentine Day Words. Fullam, Sue M., illus. 32p. (gr. k-2). 1987. PLB 21.35 (*0-89565-362-1*); PLB 14.95.s.p. (*0-685-55883-5*) Childs World.

—Word Bird's Winter Words. Gohman, Vera, illus. LC 85-5942. 32p. (gr. k-2). 1985. PLB 21.35 (*0-89565-309-5*); PLB 14.95.s.p. (*0-685-55738-3*) Childs World.

—Yes, No, Little Hippo. Gohman, Vera, illus. LC 87-21211. 32p. (ps-2). 1987. PLB 21.35 (*0-89565-411-3*); PLB 14.95.s.p. (*0-685-55946-7*) Childs World.

—You & Me. Bolt, John, illus. LC 81-17009. 112p. (gr. 2-6). 1980. PLB 21.35 (*0-89565-212-9*); PLB 14.95.s.p. (*0-685-55563-1*) Childs World.

Moncure, Jane B., tr. see **Andersen, Hans Christian.**
Moncure, Jane B., tr. see **Collodi, Carlo.**
Moncure, Jane B., tr. see **Grimm, Jacob & Grimm, Wilhelm K.**
Moncure, Jane B., tr. see **Jose, Eduard.**
Moncure, Jane B., tr. see **Perrault, Charles.**
Mondo. Morning of the Bright Bird. Akinlana, Marcus, illus. 48p. 1993. pap. 8.95 (*0-88378-136-0*) Third World.

Moner, John G. The Animal Cell. Head, J. J., ed. Steffen, Ann T., illus. LC 83-70597. 32p. (gr. 10 up). 1987. pap. text ed. 3.00 (*0-89278-347-8*, 45-9747) Carolina Biological.

Monesson, Harry S. The World's Biggest Tummy. Monesson, Harry S., illus. LC 92-96830. 40p. (Orig.). (gr. k-3). 1992. pap. 6.95 (*0-9633735-0-1*) H S Monesson.

Money, D. C. The Changing Face of the Earth. LC 89-11339. (Illus.). 64p. (gr. 2-3). 1990. PLB 19.93 (*0-8368-0033-8*) Gareth Stevens Inc.

Monfried, Lucia. The Daddie's Boat. LC 89-25689. (Illus.). (ps-3). 1990. 12.95 (*0-525-44584-6*, DCB) Dutton Child Bks.

—The Daddies Boat. Chessare, Michele, illus. 32p. (ps-3). 1993. pap. 4.99 (*0-14-054938-2*, Puffin Unicorn) Puffin Bks.

Mongo, C. Uncle Happy's Cat. (Illus., Orig.). (gr. 2-3). pap. 1.25 (*0-8198-0167-4*) St Paul Bks.

Monjo, F. N. The Drinking Gourd. newly illustrated ed. Brenner, Fred, illus. LC 92-10823. 64p. (gr. k-3). 1983. pap. 3.50 (*0-06-444042-7*, Trophy) HarpC Child Bks.

—The Drinking Gourd. newly illus. ed. Brenner, Fred, photos by. LC 92-10823. (Illus.). 64p. (gr. k-3). 1970. 14.00 (*0-06-024329-5*); PLB 13.89 (*0-06-024330-9*) HarpC Child Bks.

—Grand Papa & Ellen Aroon. (gr. k-6). 1990. pap. 2.75 (*0-440-43004-6*, YB) Dell.

—House on Stink Alley. (gr. 4-7). 1991. pap. 3.25 (*0-440-43376-2*, YB) Dell.

—Indian Summer. Lobel, Anita, illus. LC 78-20264. 192p. (gr. k-3). 1968. PLB 13.89 (*0-06-024328-7*) HarpC Child Bks.

—Letters to Horseface: Young Mozart's Travels in Italy. Bolognese, Don & Raphael, Elaine, illus. 96p. (gr. 3 up). 1991. pap. 7.95 (*0-14-034801-8*, Puffin) Puffin Bks.

—The One Bad Thing about Father. Negri, Rocco, illus. LC 71-85036. 64p. (gr. k-3). 1987. pap. 3.50 (*0-06-444110-5*, Trophy) HarpC Child Bks.

—The Secret of the Sachem's Tree. Tomes, Margot, illus. 64p. (gr. 1-5). 1973. pap. 0.75 (*0-440-47634-8*, Yearling) Dell.

Monk, Donny, jt. auth. see **Hernandez, Betsy.**
Monk, Lenore, ed. see **Pelzel, Vernise E.**
Monke, Ingrid. Boston. LC 88-20202. (Illus.). 60p. (gr. 3 up). 1988. RSBE 13.95 (*0-87518-382-4*, Dillon) Macmillan Child Grp.

Monnig, Judith, jt. auth. see **Carter, Sharon.**
Monos, Dimitri. The Greek Americans. Moynihan, Daniel P., intro. by. 112p. (Orig.). (gr. 5 up). 1988. 17. 95 (*0-87754-880-3*); pap. 9.95 (*0-7910-0266-7*) Chelsea Hse.

Monrad, Jean. How Many Kisses Goodnight: Just Right for 2's & 3's. Wilkin, Eloise, illus. LC 88-6453. 24p. (ps). 1986. 6.00 (*0-394-88253-9*) Random Bks Yng Read.

Monro, Louise. Forest of Fear. Packard, Edward, created by. 128p. (Orig.). (gr. 4). 1986. pap. 2.25 (*0-553-25490-1*) Bantam.

Monroe, Betsy. My Visit to My Doctor: A Coloring Book for Kids. Monroe, Betsy, illus. 24p. (gr. k-4). 1989. pap. write for info. (*1-878083-01-5*) Color Me Well.

—My Visit to the Emergency Room: A Coloring Book for Kids. Monroe, Betsy, illus. (SPA.). 32p. (gr. k-4). 1990. pap. write for info. (*1-878083-03-1*) Color Me Well.

—My Visit to the Hospital: A Coloring Book for Kids. Monroe, Betsy, illus. 32p. (Orig.). (gr. k-4). 1986. pap. write for info. (*1-878083-02-3*) Color Me Well.

—My Visit to the Outpatient Department: A Coloring Book for Kids. Monroe, Betsy, illus. 24p. (gr. k-4). 1986. pap. write for info. (*1-878083-04-X*) Color Me Well.

—Sibling Scrapbook: An Activity Book for the New Big Brother & Big Sister. Monroe, Betsy, illus. 24p. (Orig.). (gr. k-4). 1989. pap. write for info. (*1-878083-00-7*) Color Me Well.

Monroe, Jean G., jt. auth. see **Williamson, Ray A.**
Monroe, John B., ed. Blood Brothers: B-Movie Monsters & Adventures. (Illus.). 128p. (Orig.). (gr. 12 up). 1990. pap. 18.95 (*0-933635-69-9*, 2329) Chaosium.

Monroe, John B., ed. see **Hargrave, et al.**
Monroe, John B., ed. see **St. Andre, Ken & Perrin, Steve.**
Monroe, Judy. Alcohol. LC 93-28607. Date not set. write for info. (*0-89490-470-1*) Enslow Pubs.

—Censorship. LC 89-25407. (Illus.). 48p. (gr. 4 up). 1990. RSBE 12.95 (*0-89686-490-1*, Crestwood Hse) Macmillan Child Grp.

—Dave Winfield. LC 87-30503. (Illus.). 48p. (gr. 5-6). 1988. RSBE 11.95 (*0-89686-370-0*, Crestwood Hse) Macmillan Child Grp.

—Drug Testing. LC 89-25425. (Illus.). 48p. (gr. 4 up). 1990. RSBE 12.95 (*0-89686-492-8*, Crestwood Hse) Macmillan Child Grp.

—John Elway. LC 87-27430. (Illus.). 48p. (gr. 5-6). 1988. RSBE 11.95 (*0-89686-367-0*, Crestwood Hse) Macmillan Child Grp.

—Latchkey Children. LC 89-1383. (Illus.). 48p. (gr. 4 up). 1989. RSBE 12.95 (*0-89686-438-3*, Crestwood Hse) Macmillan Child Grp.

—Leukemia. LC 90-33663. (Illus.). 48p. (gr. 5-6). 1990. RSBE 12.95 (*0-89686-532-0*, Crestwood Hse) Macmillan Child Grp.

—Prescription Drugs. LC 88-22911. (Illus.). 48p. (gr. 5-6). 1988. RSBE 12.95 (*0-89686-414-6*, Crestwood Hse) Macmillan Child Grp.

—Steffi Graf. LC 87-30115. (Illus.). 48p. (gr. 5-6). 1988. RSBE 11.95 (*0-89686-368-9*, Crestwood Hse) Macmillan Child Grp.

—Stimulants & Hallucinogens. LC 88-20350. (Illus.). 48p. (gr. 5-6). 1988. RSBE 12.95 (*0-89686-415-4*, Crestwood Hse) Macmillan Child Grp.

Monroe, Judy, jt. auth. see **Chung, Okwha.**
Monroe, Judy, jt. auth. see **Harrison, Supenn.**
Monroe, Judy M., jt. auth. see **Nguyen, Chi.**
Monroe, Laura, ed. see **Long, Jeanne & Mallis, Jackie.**
Monroe, Lucy. Creepy Cuisine. Burke, Dianne O., illus. LC 92-41654. 80p. (gr. 4-7). 1993. pap. 4.99 (*0-679-84402-3*) Random Bks Yng Read.

—Fifty Nifty Ways to Paint Your Face. Nolte, Larry, illus. LC 92-549. 1992. pap. 3.95 (*1-56565-029-8*) Lowell Hse.

Monseau, Virginia R. & Salvner, Gary M., eds. Reading Their World: The Young Adult Novel in the Classroom. LC 92-22108. 185p. (gr. 9-12). 1992. pap. text ed. 17.50 (*0-86709-306-4*) Boynton Cook Pubs.

Monsell, Helen A. Robert E. Lee: Young Confederate. Arthur, James & Morrow, Gray, illus. LC 86-10736. 192p. (gr. 2-6). 1986. pap. 3.95 (*0-02-042020-X*, Aladdin) Macmillan Child Grp.

—Susan B. Anthony: Champion of Women's Rights. Fiorentino, Al, illus. LC 86-10716. 192p. (gr. 2-6). 1986. pap. 3.95 (*0-02-041800-0*, Aladdin) Macmillan Child Grp.

—Tom Jefferson: The Third President of the United States. LC 89-37841. (Illus.). 192p. (gr. 2-6). 1989. pap. 3.95 (*0-689-71347-9*, Aladdin) Macmillan Child Grp.

Monsell, Mary E. Armadillo. Wickstrom, Sylvie, illus. LC 90-19135. 32p. (ps-1). 1991. SBE 13.95 (*0-689-31676-3*, Atheneum Child Bk) Macmillan Child Grp.

—Crackle Creek. McCord, Kathleen G., illus. LC 89-15105. 64p. (gr. 2-4). 1990. SBE 12.95 (*0-689-31564-3*, Atheneum Child Bk) Macmillan Child Grp.

—A Fish Named Yum: Mr. Pin, Vol. IV. Christelow, Eileen, illus. LC 93-25731. 64p. (ps-4). 1994. SBE 13. 95 (*0-689-31882-0*, Atheneum Child Bk) Macmillan Child Grp.

—Mr. Pin: The Chocolate Files. Christelow, Eileen, illus. LC 89-78228. 64p. (gr. 2-5). 1990. SBE 12.95 (*0-689-31639-9*, Atheneum Child Bk) Macmillan Child Grp.

—The Mysterious Cases of Mr. Pin. Christelow, Eileen, illus. LC 88-8102. 64p. (gr. 2-5). 1989. SBE 12.95 (*0-689-31435-3*, Atheneum Child Bk) Macmillan Child Grp.

—The Spy Who Came North from the Pole: Mr. Pin, Vol. III. Christelow, Eileen, illus. LC 92-24646. 64p. (gr. 1-4). 1993. SBE 12.95 (*0-689-31754-9*, Atheneum Child Bk) Macmillan Child Grp.

—Toohy & Wood. Tryon, Leslie, illus. LC 91-38217. 64p. (gr. 2-5). 1992. SBE 12.95 (*0-689-31721-2*, Atheneum Child Bk) Macmillan Child Grp.

—Underwear! Levine, Abby, ed. Munsinger, Lynn, illus. LC 87-25419. 24p. (ps-2). 1988. PLB 11.95 (*0-8075-8308-1*) A Whitman.

—Underwear! (ps-3). 1993. pap. 4.95 (*0-8075-8309-X*) A Whitman.

Monserrat, Catherine, jt. auth. see **Barr, Linda.**
Monson, A. M. The Deer Stand. Pearson, Susan, ed. LC 91-32122. 160p. (gr. 4 up). 1992. reinforced bdg. 13. 00 (*0-688-11057-6*) Lothrop.

—The Secret of Sanctuary Island. LC 90-6479. 128p. (gr. 4-7). 1991. 12.95 (*0-688-10111-9*) Lothrop.

—The Secret of Sanctuary Island. ALC Staff, ed. LC 90-6479. 176p. (gr. 4-12). 1992. pap. 3.95 (*0-688-11693-0*, Pub. by Beech Tree Bks) Morrow.

Montagna, William. Human Skin. Head, J. J., ed. Ito, Joel, illus. LC 84-45831. 16p. (Orig.). (gr. 10 up). 1986. pap. text ed. 2.75 (*0-89278-159-9*, 45-9759) Carolina Biological.

Montague, William A. Little Mouse: The Mouse Who Lived with Henry David Thoreau at Walden Pond. Roof, Christopher, ed. Payne, Maxine & Montague, William A., illus. LC 93-73231. 56p. (Orig.). (gr. 2-4). 1993. pap. text ed. 7.95 (*0-9638644-0-8*) Concord MouseTrap.
The book introduces young people to one of America's great figures, Henry David Thoreau! The story is based on the little mouse that Thoreau describes in Walden, under "Brute Neighbors." It follows Walden chronologically along with the detail building of his little house, skating, showshoeing, planting beans, writing in his journal, & translates some of his more complex statements into "Mouse Talk." After Walden, Thoreau moves into Emerson house & takes Little Mouse along, & meets the Emerson children, Ellen, Edith & Edward. She sleeps in the doll house that you can see today. The book includes a map of Thoreau's house site, where the story took place at Walden Pond. A guide map, to find The Emerson House, to see the doll house. The Concord Museums, to see Thoreau's actual furniture & the Thoreau Lyceum, for information on Thoreau.
Publisher Provided Annotation.

Montana, LeRoy, jt. auth. see **Waldron, Linda.**
Montano, Macrina C., ed. see **Zollars, Jean A.**
Montavon, Jay. A History Mystery: The Curse of King Tut's Tomb. 96p. (Orig.). 1991. pap. 3.50 (*0-380-76220-X*, Camelot) Avon.

Monteith, Jay. ABC's African Art Coloring Book. Monteith, Jay, illus. 32p. (ps-3). 1992. pap. text ed. 6.95 (*0-9627366-3-5*) Arts & Comns NY.

—African Art: Activity Workbook. (Illus.). 24p. (Orig.). 1993. pap. text ed. 8.75 (*0-9627366-4-3*) Arts & Comns NY.

—A Multicultural Activity Workbook: Africa, Asia & the Americas. (Illus.). 72p. (Orig.). (gr. 1 up). 1991. pap. text ed. 7.95 (*0-9627366-1-9*) Arts & Comns NY.

Montejo, Victor. The Bird Who Cleans the World: And Other Mayan Fables. Perera, Victor & Kaufman, Wallace, trs. from SPA. LC 90-52757. (Illus.). 128p. (Orig.). 1991. 22.95 (*0-915306-93-X*); pap. 13.95 (*1-880684-03-9*) Curbstone.

Monteleone, John. A Day in the Life of a Major League Baseball Player. Plunkett, Michael, photos by. LC 90-36052. (Illus.). 32p. (gr. 4-8). 1991. PLB 11.79 (*0-8167-2216-1*); pap. text ed. 2.95 (*0-8167-2217-X*) Troll Assocs.

Montenegro, Laura N. One Stuck Drawer. Montenegro, Laura N., illus. LC 90-46139. 32p. (gr. k-3). 1991. 14. 45 (*0-395-57319-X*) HM.

Monterey Bay Aquarium Education Department Staff, ed. see Thompson, Frances.

Montero, Jaime A. Gatan & Talaw. (Illus., Orig.). (gr. 1-3). 1984. pap. 3.50 (*971-10-0164-0*, Pub. by New Day Pub PI) Cellar.

Montero, Miguel, tr. see Ronnholm, Ursula O.

Montes, Elizabeth, jt. auth. see Aisenberg, Gino.

Montfort, Elizabeth S. That Special Magic. LC 87-71719. (Illus.). 53p. (Orig.). (gr. 2-3). 1988. pap. 5.00 (*0-916383-37-7*) Aegina Pr.

Montgomerie, N., jt. auth. see Montgomerie, W.

Montgomerie, W. & Montgomerie, N. Well at the World's End. (Illus.). 150p. (gr. 5-8). 1989. pap. 6.95 (*0-86241-093-2*, Pub. by Cnngt Pub Ltd) Trafalgar.

Montgomery. Help! You're Shrinking. (gr. 2-4). 1987. pap. 2.25 (*0-553-15532-6*, Skylark) Dell.

—Indian Trail. (gr. 2-4). 1987. pap. 2.25 (*0-553-15496-6*, Skylark) Dell.

—Railway Children. 1994. write for info. (*0-8050-3129-4*) H Holt & Co.

Montgomery & Gillig. Home in Time for Christmas. 1987. pap. 2.99 (*0-553-15709-4*) Bantam.

Montgomery, Becky, jt. auth. see Grimm, Carol.

Montgomery, Bertha & Nabwire, Constance. Cooking the African Way. (Illus.). 48p. (gr. 5 up). 1988. PLB 14.95 (*0-8225-0919-9*) Lerner Pubns.

Montgomery, Charlotte B. Como Darle una Mano a los Perros y los Gatos: (How to Be a Helping Hand for Dogs & Cats) Armstrong, Beverly, illus. (SPA & ENG.). 32p. (Orig.). (gr. k). Date not set. wkbk. 3.00 (*0-941246-07-8*) NAHEE.

Montgomery, Charlotte B., illus. & intro. by see Wilson, Karle B.

Montgomery, Dorothy. Countdown. (Illus.). (gr. k-6). 1966. visualized song 4.50 (*3-90117-010-3*) CEF Press.

—Knowing Christ Song. Lautermilch, John, illus. 19p. (gr. k-6). 1981. visualized song 2.99 (*3-90117-025-1*) CEF Press.

Montgomery, Frances T. Billy Whiskers: Autobiography of a Goat. Fry, W. H., illus. 159p. (gr. 2 up). 1985. pap. 4.50 (*0-486-22345-0*) Dover.

Montgomery, H. Mongoose Magoo. LC 68-56822. (Illus.). 64p. (gr. 2-5). 1968. PLB 10.95 (*0-87783-026-6*); pap. 3.94 deluxe ed. (*0-87783-100-9*) Oddo.

Montgomery, Herb, jt. auth. see Montgomery, Mary.

Montgomery, K. C., jt. auth. see Holmes, Frank, Jr.

Montgomery, L. M. Anne of Avonlea. 288p. (gr. 5-8). 1976. pap. 2.95 (*0-553-24740-9*) Bantam.

—Anne of Avonlea. (gr. 8 up). 1984. pap. 0.75 (*0-8049-0219-4*) Airmont.

—Anne of Green Gables. 320p. (gr. 7-12). 1976. pap. 2.95 (*0-553-24295-4*) Bantam.

—Anne of Green Gables. Lee, Jody, illus. (gr. 4 up). 1983. deluxe ed. 13.95 (*0-448-06030-2*, G&D) Putnam Pub Group.

—Anne of Green Gables. (gr. 7 up). 1984. pap. 1.95 (*0-8049-0218-6*) Airmont.

—Anne of Green Gables, 3 vols. (gr. 7-12). 1987. Boxed Set. pap. 8.85 (*0-553-33307-0*); pap. 8.85 (*0-553-30838-6*) Bantam.

—Anne of Green Gables. 384p. (gr. 4-7). 1989. pap. 2.95 (*0-590-42243-X*, Apple Classics) Scholastic Inc.

—Anne of Green Gables. 1982. pap. 3.25 (*0-553-21313-X*, Bantam Classics) Bantam.

—Anne of Green Gables. 256p. (gr. 5 up). 1994. pap. 2.99 (*0-14-035148-5*) Puffin Bks.

—Anne of Green Gables Address Book. Mills, Lauren, illus. 1990. 8.95 (*0-7704-2363-9*) Bantam.

—Anne of Green Gables Birthday Book. Mills, Lauren, illus. 1990. 8.95 (*0-7704-2362-0*) Bantam.

—Anne of Ingleside, No. 6. 1984. pap. 2.95 (*0-553-21315-6*, Bantam Classics) Bantam.

—Anne of the Island. 256p. (gr. 5 up). 1976. pap. 2.95 (*0-553-24158-3*) Bantam.

—Anne of the Island. (gr. 3-7). 1992. pap. 3.25 (*0-553-48066-9*) Bantam.

—Anne of the Island. (gr. 4-7). 1993. pap. 3.25 (*0-590-46163-X*) Scholastic Inc.

—Anne of Windy Poplars, No. 4. 1984. pap. 2.95 (*0-553-21316-4*, Bantam Classics) Bantam.

—Anne's House of Dreams, No. 5. 240p. (gr. 7-9). 1981. pap. 2.95 (*0-553-24195-8*) Bantam.

—The Blue Castle. (gr. 7 up). 1989. pap. 3.50 (*0-553-28051-1*, Starfire) Bantam.

—Chronicles of Avonlea. Rubio, Mario, afterword by. 224p. 1988. pap. 2.95 (*0-451-52233-8*, Sig Classics) NAL-Dutton.

—Doctor's Sweetheart. 1993. pap. 3.99 (*0-553-56330-0*) Bantam.

—Emily of New Moon. 352p. (Orig.). 1988. pap. 3.50 (*0-318-33019-9*, Starfire) Bantam.

—Further Chronicles of Avonlea. 208p. (Orig.). 1989. pap. 2.95 (*0-553-21381-4*, Starfire) Bantam.

—Jane of Lantern, Magic for Marigold. (gr. 7 up). 1989. pap. 2.95 (*0-318-41644-1*, Starfire) Bantam.

—Rainbow Valley. 240p. (gr. 6 up). 1985. pap. 2.95 (*0-553-25213-5*) Bantam.

—Rainbow Valley. 422p. 1992. text ed. 33.76 (*1-56956-121-4*) W A T Braille.

—Road to Yesterday. 1993. pap. 3.99 (*0-553-56068-9*) Bantam.

Montgomery, Lucy M. Among the Shadows. 1991. pap. 3.99 (*0-553-28959-4*) Bantam.

—Anne of Avonlea. (gr. 4-7). 1991. pap. 3.25 (*0-590-44556-1*, Apple Classics) Scholastic Inc.

—Anne of Avonlea. 1992. 3.25 (*0-553-15114-2*) Bantam.

—Anne of Avonlea. Hunter, Stan, illus. LC 92-10199. 1992. 12.99 (*0-517-08127-X*, Child Classics) Outlet Bk Co.

—Anne of Avonlea. large type ed. LC 93-22574. 1993. write for info. (*1-56054-780-4*) Thorndike Pr.

—Anne of Avonlea: An Anne of Green Gables Story. Sieffert, Clare, illus. 320p. 1990. 13.95 (*0-448-40063-4*, G&D) Putnam Pub Group.

—Anne of Green Gables. 1987. Boxed set. pap. 8.95 (*0-553-33306-2*) Bantam.

—Anne of Green Gables. Mattern, Joanne, ed. Graef, Renee, illus. LC 92-12703. 48p. (gr. 3-6). 1992. PLB 12.89 (*0-8167-2866-6*); pap. text ed. 3.95 (*0-8167-2867-4*) Troll Assocs.

—Anne of Green Gables. facsimile ed. 352p. 1992. Repr. of 1908 ed. 16.95 (*1-55109-013-9*, Pub. by Nimbus Publishing Ltd CN) Chelsea Green Pub.

—Anne of Green Gables. Atwood, Margaret, afterword by. 338p. 1993. pap. 4.95 (*0-7710-9883-9*) Firefly Bks Ltd.

—Anne of Green Gables. large type ed. LC 92-43772. 484p. 1993. Repr. lib. bdg. 15.95 (*1-56054-643-3*) Thorndike Pr.

—Anne of Green Gables. 240p. (gr. 4 up). 1993. 5.98 (*1-56138-324-4*) Courage Bks.

—Anne of Green Gables, Vol. 1. (gr. 4-7). 1984. pap. 3.50 (*0-553-15327-7*) Bantam.

—Anne of Green Gables Storybook. (Illus.). 80p. (gr. 3 up). 1987. 16.95 (*0-920668-43-7*); pap. 9.95 (*0-920668-42-9*) Firefly Bks Ltd.

—Anne of the Island. 1983. pap. 2.95 (*0-553-21317-2*, Bantam Classics) Bantam.

—Anne of the Island. Graham, Mark, illus. 288p. (gr. 4 up). 1992. 14.95 (*0-448-40311-0*, G&D) Putnam Pub Group.

—Anne of the Island & Other Tales of Avonlea. 1991. 10.99 (*0-517-03705-X*) Outlet Bk Co.

—Anne of Windy Poplars. (gr. 3-7). 1992. pap. 3.25 (*0-553-48065-0*) Bantam.

—Anne's House of Dreams. 1983. pap. 2.95 (*0-553-21318-0*, Bantam Classics) Bantam.

—Chronicles of Avonlea. 1988. pap. 2.95 (*0-553-21378-4*, Bantam Classics) Bantam.

—Days of Dreams & Laughter: The Story Girl & Other Tales. 1990. 10.99 (*0-517-05137-0*) Outlet Bk Co.

—Emily, 3 vols. (gr. 9-12). 1990. Boxed set. pap. 10.50 (*0-553-33308-9*) Bantam.

—Emily Climbs. 336p. (Orig.). 1983. pap. 3.50 (*0-553-26214-9*, Starfire) Bantam.

—Rainbow Valley. 1985. pap. 3.50 (*0-553-26921-6*) Bantam.

—Rilla of Ingleside. 1985. pap. 3.50 (*0-553-26922-4*) Bantam.

—The Story Girl. 1989. pap. 2.95 (*0-553-21366-0*, Bantam Classics) Bantam.

Montgomery, Lucy M., text by. The Avonlea Album. (Illus.). 72p. 1991. PLB 16.95 (*0-920668-96-8*); pap. 9.95 (*0-920668-97-6*) Firefly Bks Ltd.

Montgomery, Mary & Baraldi, Severino. Marie Curie. (Illus.). 104p. (gr. 5-8). 1990. lib. bdg. 16.98 (*0-382-09981-8*); pap. 8.95 (*0-382-24006-5*) Silver Burdett Pr.

Montgomery, Mary & Montgomery, Herb. Our Bible Story: A Celebration of God's Gift of Love. rev. ed. (Illus.). (ps-1). 1992. pap. text ed. 9.51 student pack (*1-55944-017-1*, 2538734); tchr's. ed. 15.75 (*1-55944-018-X*, 2538726) Franciscan Comns.

Montgomery, Monty. The One & Only Original Sanibel-Captiva Alphabet Coloring Book. Nagata, Thomas, illus. 32p. (Orig.). (gr. 7 up). 1988. pap. 6.95 (*0-945026-00-5*) SME Pr.

Montgomery, Paul J. Nutritional Analysis of Ready-to-Eat Cereal. rev. ed. 274p. (gr. 7 up). 1989. pap. text ed. 19.95 (*0-9621865-0-3*) Prod Info Analysis.

—Nutritional Cereal Counter. (Illus.). 92p. (Orig.). (gr. 9 up). 1989. pap. 2.95 (*0-9621865-1-1*) Prod Info Analysis.

Montgomery, R. A. Abominable Snowman. (ps-7). 1987. pap. 2.25 (*0-553-25965-2*) Bantam.

—Blood on the Handle. 1989. pap. 2.75 (*0-553-28076-7*) Bantam.

—Chinese Dragons. (gr. 9-12). 1991. pap. 2.95 (*0-553-28828-8*) Bantam.

—Dream Trips. (gr. 2-4). 1987. pap. 2.25 (*0-553-15506-7*, Skylark) Bantam.

—Everest Attempt. 1994. pap. 3.50 (*0-553-56005-0*) Bantam.

—Genie in the Bottle. (gr. 2-4). 1987. pap. 2.25 (*0-553-15495-8*, Skylark) Bantam.

—The Haunted House. 1983. pap. 2.99 (*0-553-15679-0*) Bantam.

—Inside UFO 54-40. (ps-7). 1987. pap. 2.25 (*0-553-25987-3*) Bantam.

—The Island of Time. 1991. pap. 3.25 (*0-553-29057-6*) Bantam.

—Journey to the Sea. 1982. pap. 3.25 (*0-553-27393-0*) Bantam.

—Motocross Mania. (gr. 4-6). 1993. pap. 3.25 (*0-553-56002-6*) Bantam.

—Passport, Bk. 1. 1992. pap. 3.25 (*0-553-29443-1*) Bantam.

—Passport, Bk. 2. 1992. pap. 3.25 (*0-553-29444-X*) Bantam.

—The Race Forever. 1987. pap. 2.25 (*0-553-25988-1*) Bantam.

—Secret of Ninja, No. 66. 1987. pap. 2.99 (*0-553-27565-8*) Bantam.

—Secret of the Ninja. (ps-7). 1987. pap. 2.25 (*0-553-26484-2*) Bantam.

—Silver Wings. 1992. pap. 3.25 (*0-553-29293-5*) Bantam.

—Smoke Jumper. 1991. pap. 2.95 (*0-553-28861-X*) Bantam.

—Space & Beyond. (ps-7). 1982. pap. 3.25 (*0-553-27453-8*) Bantam.

—Stock Car Champion. 1989. pap. 3.25 (*0-553-28294-8*) Bantam.

—Survival at Sea. (ps-7). 1987. pap. 2.25 (*0-553-26560-1*) Bantam.

Montgomery, R. A. see Gilligan, Shannon, pseud.

Montgomery, Ramsey. Grave Robbers. 1990. pap. 2.95 (*0-553-28554-8*) Bantam.

—Outlaw Gulch. (gr. 4-7). 1992. pap. 3.25 (*0-553-29295-1*) Bantam.

Montgomery, Raymond A. The Abominable Snowman. large type ed. Granger, Paul, illus. 116p. (gr. 2-7). 1987. 8.95 (*0-942545-02-8*); PLB 9.95 (*0-942545-08-7*, Dist. by Grolier) Grey Castle.

—Behind the Wheel. 1992. pap. 3.25 (*0-553-29401-6*) Bantam.

—Beyond Escape. 128p. (gr. 4). 1986. pap. 2.25 (*0-553-26169-X*) Bantam.

—Caravan. 64p. (Orig.). (gr. 4). 1987. pap. 2.25 (*0-553-15477-X*, Skylark) Bantam.

—Danger Zones. 176p. (Orig.). (gr. 4). 1987. pap. 2.95 (*0-553-26791-4*) Bantam.

—Exiled to Earth. 176p. (Orig.). 1989. pap. 2.50 (*0-553-27651-4*) Bantam.

—Fire. 64p. (Orig.). (gr. 2 up). 1985. pap. 2.25 (*0-553-15462-1*) Bantam.

—The Haunted House. 64p. 1981. pap. 2.25 (*0-553-15428-1*) Bantam.

—Home in Time for Christmas. 64p. (gr. 1-4). 1987. pap. 2.25 (*0-553-15553-9*, Skylark) Bantam.

—House of Danger. 128p. (gr. 1-8). 1982. pap. 2.25 (*0-553-26181-9*) Bantam.

—Journey under the Sea. large type ed. Granger, Paul, illus. 117p. (gr. 3-7). 1987. Repr. of 1977 ed. 8.95 (*0-942545-04-4*); PLB 9.95 (*0-942545-10-9*, Dist. by Grolier) Grey Castle.

—Lost Dog! 64p. (Orig.). 1985. pap. 2.25 (*0-553-15508-3*) Bantam.

—Mystery of the Maya. large type ed. Anderson, Richard, illus. 134p. (gr. 3-7). 1987. Repr. of 1977 ed. 8.95 (*0-942545-00-1*); PLB 9.95 (*0-942545-06-0*, Dist. by Grolier) Grey Castle.

—The Owl Tree. 64p. (Orig.). (gr. 4). 1986. pap. 2.25 (*0-553-15449-4*) Bantam.

—Prisoner of the Ant People. Reese, Ralph, illus. 115p. (gr. 4). 1983. pap. 2.25 (*0-553-25763-3*) Bantam.

—The Race Forever. large type ed. Illus. (gr. 3-7). 1987. Repr. of 1983 ed. 8.95 (*0-942545-12-5*); PLB 9.95 (*0-942545-17-6*, Dist. by Grolier) Grey Castle.

—Race of the Year. 1989. pap. 2.99 (*0-553-15696-9*) Bantam.

—Return to Atlantis, No. 78. 176p. (Orig.). (gr. 5 up). 1988. pap. 2.75 (*0-553-27123-7*) Bantam.

—Sand Castle. 64p. (Orig.). (gr. 4). 1986. pap. 2.25 (*0-553-15458-3*) Bantam.

—Space & Beyond. large type ed. Granger, Paul, illus. 117p. (gr. 3-7). 1987. Repr. of 1979 ed. 8.95 (*0-942545-11-7*); PLB 9.95 (*0-942545-16-8*, Dist. by Grolier) Grey Castle.

—Spooky Thanksgiving. 64p. (gr. 2). 1988. pap. 2.75 (*0-553-15672-1*, Skylark) Bantam.

—Track of the Bear. 64p. (gr. 2). 1988. pap. 2.50 (*0-553-27533-X*) Bantam.

—Trouble on Planet Earth. Reese, Ralph, illus. (Orig.). (gr. 4). 1984. pap. text ed. 2.25 (*0-553-26308-0*) Bantam.

—War with the Evil Power Master. 128p. (Orig.). (gr. 4). 1984. pap. 2.25 (*0-553-25778-1*) Bantam.

Montgomery, Robert. Grand Slam. Reese, Ralph, illus. LC 89-5198. 176p. (gr. 5-8). 1991. PLB 9.89 (*0-8167-1988-8*); pap. text ed. 2.95 (*0-8167-1989-6*) Troll Assocs.

—Hitting Streak. Reese, Ralph, illus. LC 90-10968. 176p. (gr. 5-8). 1991. PLB 9.89 (*0-8167-1982-9*); pap. text ed. 2.95 (*0-8167-1983-7*) Troll Assocs.

—Home Run! Reese, Ralph, illus. LC 89-5190. 176p. (gr. 5-8). 1991. PLB 9.89 (*0-8167-1986-1*); pap. text ed. 2.95 (*0-8167-1987-X*) Troll Assocs.

—MVP. Reese, Ralph, illus. LC 89-20180. 176p. (gr. 5-8). 1991. lib. bdg. 9.89 (*0-8167-1992-6*); pap. text ed. 2.95 (*0-8167-1993-4*) Troll Assocs.

—The Show! Reese, Ralph, illus. LC 90-20586. 176p. (gr. 5-8). 1991. PLB 9.89 (*0-8167-1984-5*); pap. text ed. 2.95 (*0-8167-1985-3*) Troll Assocs.

—Triple Play. Reese, Ralph, illus. LC 89-20179. 176p. (gr. 5-8). 1991. lib. bdg. 9.89 (*0-8167-1990-X*); pap. text ed. 2.95 (*0-8167-1991-8*) Troll Assocs.

Montgomery, Rutherford. Kildee House: Newbery Honor Book 1950. (gr. 4-7). 1993. pap. 7.95 (0-8027-7388-5) Walker & Co.

Montgomery, Rutherford G. Carcajou. Cram, L. D., illus. LC 36-6665. (gr. 6-8). 1936. 4.95 (0-87004-105-3) Caxton.

—High Country. (Illus.). 248p. (gr. 10 up). 1993. Repr. of 1938 ed. 40.00 (1-56416-043-2) Derrydale Pr.

—Pekan the Shadow. Nenninger, Jerome D., illus. LC 78-84779. (gr. 8-12). 1970. 3.95 (0-87004-132-0) Caxton.

—Rufus. Nenninger, J. D., illus. LC 78-150819. (Orig.). (gr. 4-8). 1973. 4.95 (0-87004-227-0) Caxton.

Montresor, Beni. The Dragon Drummer: A Story ABC. LC 92-27684. 1993. Repr. of 1969 ed. write for info. (0-385-30845-0) Doubleday.

—The Witches of Venice. (Illus.). (ps-3). 1989. 13.95 (0-385-26354-6, Zephyr-BFYR); (Zephyr-BFYR) Doubleday.

Montroll, Andrew, ed. see Montroll, John.

Montroll, John. African Animals in Origami. Montroll, John, illus. LC 91-76400. 160p. (Orig.). 1993. pap. 9.95 (1-877656-09-7) Antroll Pub.

—Origami American Style. 2p. (gr. 2 up). 1990. pap. 6.00 (0-9627254-0-4) Zenagraf.

—Origami Inside-Out. Montroll, John, illus. LC 95-90214. 120p. (Orig.). 1993. pap. 9.95 (1-877656-08-9) Antroll Pub.

—Origami Sculptures. 2nd ed. Montroll, Andrew, ed. Montroll, John, illus. 144p. 1990. pap. text ed. 9.95 (1-877656-02-X) Antroll Pub.

Moodie, Fiona. Boy & the Giants. (ps-3). 1993. 15.00 (0-374-30927-2) FS&G.

—The Sugar Prince. (Illus.). (ps-3). 1987. 12.95 (1-55774-005-4) Modan-Adama Bks.

Moody, Debra L. Youth Training Leadership Program. (Illus.). 92p. (Orig.). (gr. 6-12). 1989. tchrs. ed. 25.00 (0-9618164-3-0) PA Coun Churches.

Moody, Richard T. Over Sixty-Five Million Years Ago: Before the Dinosaurs Died. LC 91-44774. (Illus.). 32p. (gr. 6 up). 1992. RSBE 13.95 (0-02-767270-0, New Discovery) Macmillan Child Grp.

Moon, Dolly. My Very First Piano Book of Cowboy Songs: Twenty-Two Favorite Songs Easy in Piano Arrangement. (Illus.). 32p. (gr. 2 up). 1983. pap. 3.50 (0-486-24311-7) Dover.

Moon, Marjorie, ed. A Is for Art. (Illus., Orig.). (ps-2). 1988. pap. 10.95 (0-317-91187-2) M Moon.

Moon, Pat. Earth Lines: Poems for the Green Age. LC 92-27570. 64p. (gr. 5 up). 1993. 14.00 (0-688-11853-4) Greenwillow.

Moon, Sheila. Deepest Roots. Renfrew, Susan, illus. LC 86-19578. 240p. (gr. 8-12). 1986. pap. 8.95 (0-917479-10-6) Guild Psy.

—Hunt down the Prize. Renfrew, Susan, illus. LC 86-19576. 245p. (gr. 8-12). 1986. pap. 8.95 (0-917479-09-2) Guild Psy.

—Knee-Deep in Thunder. Parnell, Peter, illus. LC 86-19534. 307p. (gr. 8-12). 1986. pap. 8.95 (0-917479-08-4) Guild Psy.

Moon, Teresa, jt. auth. see Davis, Nancy M.

Mooney, Ann J. The Sock Animals: Tiger's New Friends. Mooney, Ann J., photos by. LC 91-76359. (Illus.). 32p. (Orig.). (ps-2). 1992. pap. 7.95 (0-9631035-0-4) Jamondas Pr.

Mooney, Chuck, III. The Recruiting Survival Guide: How to Be a Smart Recruit. Bucheit, Kelly S., ed. Swan, Kyle, illus. 84p. (Orig.). (gr. 11-12). 1991. pap. 9.95 (0-9630239-0-X) C Mooney.

Mooney, Martin. The Comanche Indians. (Illus.). 80p. (gr. 2-5). 1993. PLB 12.95 (0-7910-1653-6) Chelsea Hse.

Mooney, T. Arithmetic That We Need. large type ed. 148p. (gr. 7-12). 1983. Repr. of 1969 ed. 25.91 (0-317-01871-X, 4-01700-00) Am Printing Hse.

Moorbeek, Kees. Boo Whoo: Pop-up Book. Moorbeek, Kees, illus. 10p. 1993. 9.99 (0-8431-3623-5) Price Stern.

—Museum of Unnatural History. Moorbeek, Kees, illus. 6p. (gr. k-4). 1993. 14.99 (0-8431-3541-7) Price Stern.

Moore, Adam. Broken Arrow Boy. Thatch, Nancy R., ed. Melton, David, intro. by. LC 90-5933. (Illus.). 26p. (gr. 3-8). 1990. PLB 14.95 (0-933849-24-9) Landmark Edns.

Moore, Albert. Gabriel's Odyssey. 210p. (Orig.). (gr. 12). 1990. pap. 15.95 (1-85371-081-4, Pub. by Poolbeg Pr ER) Dufour.

Moore, April. The Earth & You: Eating for Two. Stark, Elizabeth, ed. Francoeur, Janet, illus. 165p. (Orig.). (gr. 8-12). 1993. write for info. (0-938443-05-4) Potomac Val Pr.

Moore, Beverly. Echo's Song. Moore, Beverly, illus. 40p. (gr. k-3). 1993. PLB 13.95g (0-9637288-7-3) River Walker Bks.

The setting & characters in ECHO'S SONG are all real. This beautifully illustrated children's story is told through the daily adventures of ECHO, a tropical bird who happens to live in the Colorado Rocky Mountains between the high-country & the meadow. He lives contentedly in a log home with a ferret named TWIRP, a girl named TRACY, & TYLER, a big, yellow dog. This lovely story is as simple & safe as the woodland meadow where they live & play. ECHO sings his own unique song to express his love for the life he lives & to joyfully communicate that love to the broader world around him. The events described in this book are recorded & interpreted by artist Beverly Moore. A native of the Colorado mountain country, Beverly Moore lives & works in the Roaring Fork Valley near Aspen. For many years a professional artist, she has won awards for graphic design & illustration, & as an art director & magazine publisher. Her paintings, drawings, & sculpture have been widely exhibited. ECHO'S SONG is dedicated to the extraordinary creatures who live among us as our friends & teachers, & are commonly referred to as "pets." Volume discounts available from publisher--River Walker Books, 3334 Wyandot St., Denver, CO 80211; 303-480-5009.
Publisher Provided Annotation.

Moore, Charles. Beauty & the Beast. LC 90-26307. (Illus.). 32p. 1991. 17.95 (0-8478-1368-1) Rizzoli Intl.

Moore, Chris. The Oceans & the Jungles. 1988. write for info. (Puffin) Puffin Bks.

Moore, Clement. Night Before Christmas Pop-Ups. 1991. 4.99 (0-517-06127-9) Outlet Bk Co.

Moore, Clement C. Disney Babies the Night Before Christmas. LC 91-58969. (Illus.). 1992. incls 6 ornaments 11.95 (1-56282-244-6) Disney Pr.

—The Grandma Moses Night before Christmas. 2nd ed. Moses, Grandma, illus. LC 90-24145. 32p. 1991. 15.00 (0-679-81526-0); lib. bdg. 15.99 (0-679-91526-5) Random Bks Yng Read.

—The Night Before Christmas. Trimby, Elisa, illus. LC 77-71994. (gr. 1 up). 1977. pap. 5.95 (0-385-13615-3) Doubleday.

—The Night Before Christmas. (Illus.). 16p. (gr. 1-8). 1970. pap. 4.00 (0-914510-01-0) Evergreen.

—The Night Before Christmas. De Paola, Tomie, illus. LC 80-11758. 32p. (ps up). 1980. reinforced bdg. 14.95 (0-8234-0414-5); pap. 5.95 (0-8234-0417-X) Holiday.

—The Night Before Christmas. Hague, Michael, illus. LC 80-84842. 12p. (gr. k up). 1981. 12.95 (0-8050-0900-0, Bks Young Read) H Holt & Co.

—The Night Before Christmas. Gorsline, Douglas, illus. LC 75-7511. 32p. (gr. 2-6). 1975. 2.25 (0-394-83019-9) Random Bks Yng Read.

—The Night Before Christmas. Lobel, Anita, illus. LC 84-4342. 32p. (ps-5). 1984. 12.00 (0-394-86863-3); lib. bdg. 12.99 (0-394-96863-8) Knopf Bks Yng Read.

—The Night Before Christmas. De Paola, Tomie, illus. (gr. k-3). 1984. incl. cassette 19.95 (0-317-07112-2); pap. 12.95 incl. cassette (0-941078-37-X); incl. 4 bks., cassette, & guide 27.95 (0-685-08869-3) Live Oak Media.

—The Night Before Christmas. Wilburn, Kathy, illus. 24p. (ps-1). 1985. write for info. (0-307-10202-5, Pub. by Golden Bks) Western Pub.

—The Night Before Christmas. Gustafson, Scott, illus. LC 85-40334. 32p. (ps-3). 1985. 12.95 (0-394-54809-4) Knopf Bks Yng Read.

—The Night Before Christmas. Gorsline, Douglas, illus. 32p. (ps-1). 1985. incl. cassette 5.95 (0-394-87658-X) Random Bks Yng Read.

—The Night Before Christmas. Tien, illus. 32p. (ps-1). 1986. pap. 5.95 (0-671-62209-9, Little Simon) S&S Trade.

—The Night Before Christmas. LC 87-15343. (Illus.). 48p. (gr. k-3). 1988. PLB 12.89 (0-8167-1209-3); pap. text ed. 3.95 (0-8167-1210-7) Troll Assocs.

—The Night Before Christmas. Holt, Shirley, illus. 28p. 16.95 (0-9613476-2-7) Shirlee.

—The Night Before Christmas. Goode, Diane, illus. LC 82-62171. 32p. 1988. pap. 1.25 (0-394-81938-1) Random Bks Yng Read.

—The Night Before Christmas. Foreman, Michael, illus. LC 88-50097. (ps up). 1988. pap. 11.95 (0-670-82388-0) Viking Child Bks.

—The Night Before Christmas. Amoss, Berthe, illus. 10p. (ps-7). 1989. pap. 3.95 (0-922589-06-2) More Than Card.

—The Night Before Christmas. LC 89-42998. (Illus.). 80p. 1989. 4.95 (0-89471-754-5) Running Pr.

—The Night Before Christmas. Harness, Cheryl, illus. LC 88-35019. 40p. (ps-8). 1990. 6.99 (0-394-82698-1) Random Bks Yng Read.

—The Night Before Christmas. Clonan, Paula, illus. LC 89-6560. 28p. (gr. k-3). 1990. PLB 12.95 (0-87226-416-5, Bedrick Blackie) P Bedrick Bks.

—Night Before Christmas. Szekeres, Cyndy, illus. (ps up). 1986. write for info. (0-307-13724-4, Golden Bks) Western Pub.

—The Night Before Christmas. Rice, James, illus. LC 89-34789. 32p. 1990. 14.95 (0-88289-755-1) Pelican.

—Night Before Christmas. 1989. pap. 2.25 (0-671-68408-6, Little Simon) S&S Trade.

—The Night Before Christmas. Pollard, Nan, illus. 24p. (Orig.). (gr. k-1). 1990. pap. 0.99 (1-878624-49-0) McClanahan Bk.

—The Night Before Christmas. Watson, Wendy, illus. 32p. (ps-1). 1990. 13.95 (0-395-53624-3, Clarion Bks) HM.

—The Night Before Christmas. Marshall, James, illus. 32p. (ps-3). 1989. pap. 5.95 incl. cass. (0-590-63489-5); pap. 2.50 (0-590-42758-X) Scholastic Inc.

—The Night Before Christmas. Regan, Dana, illus. LC 90-22388. 24p. (ps up). 1991. 2.95 (0-694-00365-4) HarpC Child Bks.

—Night Before Christmas. (Illus.). 32p. (ps-2). 1985. 2.95 (0-89542-498-3, Ideals Child) Hambleton-Hill.

—The Night Before Christmas. Ferris, Lynn B., illus. 24p. 1991. 6.95 (0-8362-4917-8) Andrews & McMeel.

—The Night Before Christmas. Marshall, James, illus. 32p. 1991. 13.95 (0-590-45075-1, Scholastic Hardcover) Scholastic Inc.

—The Night Before Christmas. Patti, Joyce, illus. LC 92-9084. 6p. 1992. 10.95 (1-55670-274-4) Stewart Tabori & Chang.

—The Night Before Christmas. Regan, Dana, illus. LC 91-46766. 26p. (ps). 1992. 4.95 (0-694-00424-3, Festival) HarpC Child Bks.

—The Night Before Christmas. Cone, William, illus. LC 92-22712. 40p. 1992. 14.95 (0-88708-261-0, Rabbit Ears); incl. cassette 19.95 (0-88708-260-2, Rabbit Ears) Picture Bk Studio.

—Night Before Christmas. (ps). 1992. 3.99 (0-553-37118-5) Bantam.

—The Night Before Christmas. Hirashima, Jean, illus. LC 92-27138. 32p. (ps-3). 1993. pap. 2.25 (0-448-40482-6, G&D) Putnam Pub Group.

—Night Before Christmas. (ps-3). 1986. 4.95 (0-307-13750-3) Western Pub.

—The Night Before Christmas. (ps-3). 1993. pap. 5.95 (0-395-66508-6, Clarion Bks) HM.

—The Night Before Christmas: A Pop-Up Book. Harris, Denise & Cote, Nancy, illus. Costello, Linda, designed by. (ps-1). 1993. 9.95 (1-56397-003-1) Boyds Mills Pr.

—The Night Before Christmas: A Reproduction of an Antique Christmas Classic. LC 88-19600. (Illus.). 32p. 1989. 15.95 (0-399-21614-6, Philomel Bks) Putnam Pub Group.

—The Night Before Christmas: A Revolving Picture & Lift-the-Flap Book. Ives, Penny, illus. 14p. 1988. 14.95 (0-399-21544-1, Putnam) Putnam Pub Group.

—Night Before Christmas Coloring Book. 1986. pap. 2.95 (0-671-62959-X, Little Simon) S&S Trade.

—The Night Before Christmas Hidden Picture Book. Manning, Maurie J., illus. 32p. 1992. bds. 7.95 (1-56397-116-X) Boyds Mills Pr.

—The Night Before Christmas in Hawaii. Lee, Michael S., illus. 32p. 1991. text ed. write for info. (0-9627294-2-6) Hawaiian Resources.

—The Night Before Christmas: Or: Account of a Visit from St. Nicholas. Bevis, Phillip & Irwin, Colin, eds. Henley, Clark, illus. 22p. 1984. 150.00 (0-923980-03-2) Arundel Pr.

—Twas the Night Before Christmas. (Illus.). 24p. (gr. k-3). 1992. pap. 2.50 (1-56144-163-5, Honey Bear Bks) Modern Pub NYC.

—Twas the Night Before Christmas. 1992. pap. 3.95 (0-395-64374-0) HM.

—Twas the Night Before Christmas: A Visit from St. Nicholas. Smith, Jessie W., illus. (ps-2). 1912. 14.95 (0-395-06952-1) HM.

—Two Little Christmas Classics. Goode, Diane, illus. 32p. (ps up). 1989. pap. 4.95 incl. cassette (0-394-84629-X) Random Bks Yng Read.

—A Visit from St. Nicholas. Hader, Berta & Hader, Elmer, illus. LC 93-33703. (gr. 2 up). 1994. pap. write for info. (0-486-27978-2) Dover.

Moore, Clement C., jt. auth. see Wolf, Jill.

Moore, Douglas. Entertainment: Movies. Baker, Syd, illus. 50p. (Orig.). (gr. 7 up). 1986. incl. cass. 22.00 (0-939990-48-2) Intl Linguistics.

Moore, Douglas, jt. auth. see Lennon, Patricia.

Moore, Earl F. Western Echoes. LC 23-939860. (Illus.). 198p. (gr. 4-12). 1980. 12.95 (0-939860-00-7) Tremaine Graph & Pub.

Moore, Elaine. Deep River. Sorensen, Henri, illus. LC 93-23043. 1994. pap. 14.00 (0-671-86534-X, S&S BFYR) S&S Trade.

—Grandma's House. Primavera, Elise, illus. LC 84-11233. 32p. (gr. k up). 1985. PLB 14.88 (0-688-04116-7); 14.95 (0-688-04115-9) Lothrop.

—Grandma's Promise. Primavera, Elise, illus. LC 86-33762. (gr. k-3). 1988. 14.88 (0-688-06740-9); lib. bdg. 14.88 (0-688-06741-7) Lothrop.

—Mixed-Up Sam. McKissack, Patricia & McKissack, Fredrick, eds. Boddy, Joe, illus. LC 88-60390. 32p. (Orig.). (gr. 1-3). 1988. text ed. 8.95 (0-88335-786-0); pap. text ed. 4.95 (0-88335-798-4) Milliken Pub Co.

—The Substitute Teacher from Mars. LC 93-37527. 1993. pap. 2.95 (0-8167-3283-3) Troll Assocs.

Moore, Elizabeth, jt. auth. see Couvillon, Alice.

Moore, Elizabeth B. & Couvillon, Alice W. Louisiana Indian Tales. LC 89-71060. 112p. 1990. 11.95 (*0-88289-756-X*) Pelican.

Moore, Emily. Just My Luck: Meet Olivia & Jeffrey, Canine Detectives. 112p. (gr. 3-7). 1991. pap. 3.99 (*0-14-034790-9*, Puffin) Puffin Bks.
—Something to Count On. 112p. (gr. 3-7). 1991. pap. 3.99 (*0-14-034791-7*, Puffin) Puffin Bks.
—Whose Side Are You On? 128p. (gr. 3-7). 1988. 14.00 (*0-374-48373-6*) FS&G.
—Whose Side Are You On? 128p. (gr. 3-7). 1990. pap. 3.50 (*0-374-48373-6*, Sunburst) FS&G.

Moore, Eugenia. In a Minute! Leiper, Esther M., ed. 32p. (Orig.). (gr. 9 up). 1988. pap. 3.95x (*0-9617284-9-3*) Sand & Silk.
—Kidnapped by an Angel. Leiper, Esther M., ed. Moore, Eugenia, illus. 32p. (Orig.). (gr. 3-4). 1988. pap. 3.95x (*0-9617284-4-2*) Sand & Silk.

Moore, Eugenia, ed. see Lindow, Sandra.

Moore, Eva. The Fairy Tale Life of Hans Christian Andersen. Hyman, Trina S., illus. 80p. 1992. pap. 2.75 (*0-590-45225-8*, Apple Paperbacks) Scholastic Inc.
—Johnny Appleseed. (Orig.). (gr. 2-3). pap. 2.50 (*0-590-40297-8*) Scholastic Inc.
—Story of George Washington Carver. 1990. pap. 2.95 (*0-590-42660-5*) Scholastic Inc.

Moore, Frank G. The Roman's World. LC 65-23486. (Illus.). 502p. (gr. 7 up). 1936. 25.00 (*0-8196-0155-1*) Biblo.

Moore, Frank J. The Incredible Moving Picture Book. 32p. (gr. 1 up). 1987. pap. 3.95 (*0-486-25374-0*) Dover.

Moore, Inga. A Big Day for Little Jack. LC 93-6272. 1994. text ed. write for info. RTE (*1-56402-418-0*) Candlewick Pr.
—Little Dog Lost. Moore, Inga, illus. LC 90-24483. 32p. (ps-3). 1991. SBE 14.95 (*0-02-767648-X*, Macmillan Child Bk) Macmillan Child Grp.
—Oh, Little Jack. Moore, Inga, illus. LC 91-71827. 32p. (ps up). 1992. 14.95 (*1-56402-028-2*) Candlewick Pr.
—Oh, Little Jack. LC 91-71827. (ps-3). 1994. pap. 4.99 (*1-56402-273-0*) Candlewick Pr.
—Six Dinner Sid. LC 90-42749. (gr. k-3). 1991. pap. 13.95 (*0-671-73199-8*, S&S BFYR) S&S Trade.
—Six-Dinner Sid. LC 90-42749. (gr. k-3). (ps-3). 1993. pap. 4.95 (*0-671-79613-5*, S&S BFYR) S&S Trade.
—The Sorcerer's Apprentice. Moore, Inga, illus. LC 88-27195. 32p. (gr. k-3). 1989. SBE 14.95 (*0-02-767645-5*, Macmillan Child Bk) Macmillan Child Grp.
—The Truffle Hunter. (Illus.). 32p. (ps-3). 1987. 10.95 (*0-916291-09-X*) Kane-Miller Bk.

Moore, J. Thomas. Night after Christmas. (gr. k up). 1990. pap. 5.95 (*0-925928-07-0*) Tiny Thought.

Moore, Jo E. Africa. Shipman, Gary, illus. 16p. (gr. 3-6). 1993. pap. 5.95 (*1-55799-247-9*) Evan-Moor Corp.
—Antarctica. Shipman, Gary, illus. 16p. (gr. 3-6). 1993. pap. 5.95 (*1-55799-246-0*) Evan-Moor Corp.
—Asia. Shipman, Gary, illus. 16p. (gr. 3-6). 1993. pap. 5.95 (*1-55799-244-4*) Evan-Moor Corp.
—Australia. Shipman, Gary, illus. 16p. (gr. 3-6). 1993. pap. 5.95 (*1-55799-243-6*) Evan-Moor Corp.
—Beginning Geography, Vol. 2: Landforms & Bodies of Water. (Illus.). 16p. (gr. k-2). 1993. pap. text ed. 5.95 incl. poster (*1-55799-253-3*) Evan-Moor Corp.
—Beginning Geography, Vol. 3: Continents & Oceans. (Illus.). 16p. (gr. k-2). 1993. pap. text ed. 5.95 incl. poster (*1-55799-254-1*) Evan-Moor Corp.
—Children Around the World-Writing Forms. Supancich, Jo, illus. 48p. (gr. k-3). 1992. pap. 5.95 (*1-55799-239-8*) Evan-Moor Corp.
—Dinosaurs & Other Prehistoric Animals. (Illus.). 48p. (ps-1). 1991. pap. 9.95 (*1-55799-213-4*) Evan-Moor Corp.
—Dragons. (Illus.). 48p. (gr. 2-5). 1989. pap. 5.95 (*1-55799-161-8*) Evan-Moor Corp.
—Endangered Species. (Illus.). 48p. (gr. 2-5). 1991. pap. 5.95 (*1-55799-217-7*) Evan-Moor Corp.
—Europe. Shipman, Gary, illus. 16p. (gr. 3-6). 1993. pap. 5.95 (*1-55799-245-2*) Evan-Moor Corp.
—Families Around the World. (Illus.). 48p. (ps-1). 1991. pap. 9.95 (*1-55799-214-2*) Evan-Moor Corp.
—Making Books with Beginning Writers. (Illus.). 48p. (gr. k-2). 1992. pap. 6.95 (*1-55799-225-8*) Evan-Moor Corp.
—My Pets. (Illus.). 48p. (ps-1). 1988. pap. 9.95 (*1-55799-131-6*) Evan-Moor Corp.
—North America. Shipman, Gary, illus. 16p. (gr. 3-6). 1993. pap. 5.95 (*1-55799-241-X*) Evan-Moor Corp.
—Sharks. (Illus.). 48p. (gr. 2-5). 1991. pap. 5.95 (*1-55799-215-0*) Evan-Moor Corp.
—Shoebox Center: Math Activities. (Illus.). 64p. (gr. 1-3). 1993. pap. text ed. 7.95 (*1-55799-252-5*) Evan-Moor Corp.
—South America. Shipman, Gary, illus. 16p. (gr. 3-6). 1993. pap. 5.95 (*1-55799-242-8*) Evan-Moor Corp.
—Stories about Children from Many Lands. Supancich, Jo, illus. 64p. (gr. k-2). 1993. pap. text ed. 11.95 (*1-55799-248-7*) Evan-Moor Corp.
—Who Discovered America? (Illus.). 48p. (gr. 2-5). 1991. pap. 5.95 (*1-55799-218-5*) Evan-Moor Corp.
—Writing Activities: Shoe Box Centers. (Illus.). 64p. (gr. 1-3). 1992. pap. 7.95 (*1-55799-224-X*) Evan-Moor Corp.

Moore, Jo E. & Evans, Joy. El Agua. Ficklin, Dora & Wolfe, Liz, trs. from ENG. (SPA., Illus.). 16p. (gr. 1-3). 1992. pap. text ed. 5.95 incl. poster (*1-55799-234-7*) Evan-Moor Corp.
—Beginning Geography. (Illus.). 16p. (gr. k-2). 1991. pap. text ed. 5.95 (*1-55799-219-3*) Evan-Moor Corp.
—Categorias. Wolfe, Liz & Ficklin, Dora, trs. from ENG. (SPA., Illus.). 32p. (gr. 1-2). 1990. pap. text ed. 4.95 (*1-55799-180-4*) Evan-Moor Corp.
—Creative Writing Ideas. (Illus.). 78p. (gr. 1-6). 1987. pap. text ed. 9.95 (*1-55799-060-3*) Evan-Moor Corp.
—How Is It Made? (Illus.). 48p. (gr. 2-5). 1989. pap. 5.95 (*1-55799-162-6*) Evan-Moor Corp.
—Read Long Vowel Words. (Illus.). 32p. (gr. 1-2). 1988. pap. text ed. 4.95 (*1-55799-119-7*) Evan-Moor Corp.
—Write a SUPER Sentence. (Illus.). 32p. (gr. 1-3). 1988. pap. text ed. 4.95 (*1-55799-059-X*) Evan-Moor Corp.
—Writing Poetry with Children. (Illus.). 64p. (gr. 1-6). 1988. pap. 6.95 (*1-55799-129-4*) Evan-Moor Corp.

Moore, Jo E. & Tryon, Leslie. Bears Bears Bears. (Illus.). 48p. (gr. k-1). 1988. pap. 8.95 (*1-55799-130-8*) Evan-Moor Corp.
—The Big Book of Science Rhymes & Chants. (Illus.). 64p. (gr. k-2). 1991. pap. 11.95 (*1-55799-211-8*) Evan-Moor Corp.
—The Big Book of Science Stories. (Illus.). 64p. (gr. k-2). 1991. pap. 11.95 (*1-55799-210-X*) Evan-Moor Corp.

Moore, Jo E., jt. auth. see Evans, Jo.
Moore, Jo E., jt. auth. see Evans, Joy.

Moore, Jo E., et al. A Happy, Healthy Me. (Illus.). 48p. (ps-1). 1990. pap. text ed. 9.95 (*1-55799-170-7*) Evan-Moor Corp.
—Making Seasonal Big Books with Children. (Illus.). 64p. (gr. k-3). 1990. pap. 11.95 (*1-55799-194-4*) Evan-Moor Corp.
—A Unit about Whales. (Illus.). 48p. (gr. 2-5). 1989. pap. 5.95 (*0-685-50705-X*) Evan-Moor Corp.
—Write Every Day. (Illus.). 48p. (gr. 1-6). 1988. pap. 4.95 (*1-55799-128-6*) Evan-Moor Corp.

Moore, John C., jt. ed. see Sheringham, Hugh.

Moore, John T., et al. Christmas Classics for Children. (ps-k). 1981. 14.99 (*0-570-04058-2*, 56-1351) Concordia.

Moore, Kathryn C. My First Flight. rev. ed. Hutson, Ronald, ed. Grant, Leslie, illus. (ps-4). 1991. PLB 3.95 (*0-9633295-0-2*) K Cs Bks N Stuff. "This looks just like a real airplane!" "This is exactly what happens on an airplane trip, I know a lot of adults who need this book." "It's so easy to understand - & it's fun! These are just a few of the comments about MY FIRST FLIGHT - a children's coloring activities book. MY FIRST FLIGHT describes what goes on when you take an airplane trip from the time that you arrive at the airport until the time that you land. It is written in narrative rhyme & illustrated in coloring book style. The reader is acquainted with airline personnel, the airplane - its safety features & travel comforts & things that you can do to facilitate your own comfort (i.e. pressurization, etc.). In addition to the story there are travel related games, a flight log page, & a flight facts page. This activities book is the perfect travel companion for the unaccompanied minor. A number of parents & teachers have reviewed MY FIRST FLIGHT. They have found it to be creative, comprehensive, educational & entertaining. Welcome aboard with MY FIRST FLIGHT. Sit back enjoy the ride & have fun. Retail price $2.95. *Publisher Provided Annotation.*

Moore, Leonard. Enciclopedia Juvenil De la Naturaleza. (SPA). 256p. 1976. 59.95 (*0-8288-5666-4*, S50476) Fr & Eur.

Moore, Lilian. Adam Mouse's Book of Poems. McCord, Kathleen G., illus. LC 91-42223. 64p. (gr. 5-8). 1992. SBE 11.95 (*0-689-31765-4*, Atheneum Child Bk) Macmillan Child Grp.
—Don't Be Afraid, Amanda. McCord, Kathleen, illus. LC 91-19661. 64p. (gr. 2-5). 1992. SBE 12.95 (*0-689-31725-5*, Atheneum Child Bk) Macmillan Child Grp.
—I'll Meet You at the Cucumbers. Wooding, Sharon, illus. LC 87-15195. 72p. (gr. 2-6). 1988. SBE 12.95 (*0-689-31243-1*, Atheneum Child Bk) Macmillan Child Grp.
—I'll Meet You at the Cucumbers. Wooding, Sharon, illus. (gr. 1-4). 1989. pap. 2.75 (*0-553-15705-1*, Skylark) Bantam.
—Junk Day on Easy Street & Other Easy-To-Read Stories. Lobel, Arnold, illus. (gr. 1-4). 1991. pap. 2.75 (*0-553-15627-6*, Skylark) Bantam.
—The Magic Spectacles & Other Easy-to-Read Stories. Lobel, Arnold, illus. 1992. pap. 2.99 (*0-553-48026-X*) Bantam.
—Something New Begins: New & Selected Poems. Dunton, Mary J., illus. LC 82-1723. 128p. (gr. 3 up). 1982. SBE 12.95 (*0-689-30818-3*, Atheneum Child Bk) Macmillan Child Grp.

Moore, Lilian & Lobel, Arnold. The Magic Spectacles & Other Easy to Read Stories. 80p. (Orig.). (gr. 6). 1985. pap. 2.25 (*0-553-15329-3*) Bantam.

Moore, Lilian, selected by. Sunflakes: Poems for Children. Ormerod, Jan, illus. 96p. (ps-3). 1992. 18.45 (*0-395-58833-2*, Clarion Bks) HM.

Moore, Lilian, retold by see Andersen, Hans Christian.
Moore, Malcolm, jt. auth. see Bassett, Patrick F.

Moore, Mary S. Fireside Tales. Clay, Cliff, illus. 21p. (Orig.). (gr. 5-12). 1990. pap. 7.95 (*0-913678-18-X*); paper & audiocassette 10.00 (*0-913678-19-8*) New Day Pr.

Moore, Melissa, ed. see Lafferty, Jerry.

Moore, Peggy A. Neighbors & Family Coloring Book. Adoma, Afua, illus. 20p. (Orig.). (gr. k up). 1989. pap. 2.50 (*0-9613078-4-6*) Detroit Black.

Moore, Peggy S. The Case of the Missing Bike & Other Things. 2nd, rev. ed. Adome, Afua, illus. 40p. (Orig.). (gr. 4-6). 1992. pap. 5.95 (*0-9613078-1-1*) Detroit Black.
—My Very First book of Poetry & Other Things. Moore, Peggy S., illus. 16p. (gr. 3-5). 1982. pap. 1.98 (*0-9613078-0-3*) Detroit Black.

Moore, Randy & Vodopich, Darrell S. The Living Desert. LC 90-42243. (Illus.). 64p. (gr. 6-9). 1991. lib. bdg. 15.95 (*0-89490-182-6*) Enslow Pubs.

Moore, Reavis. Native Artists of Africa. 48p. (gr. 4-7). 1994. 14.95 (*1-56261-147-X*) John Muir.
—Native Artists of North America. Burton, LeVar, frwd. by. (Illus.). 48p. (gr. 3 up). 1993. 14.95 (*1-56261-105-4*) John Muir.

Moore, Rebecca, ed. see Thomson, Andy.

Moore, Richard. Portugal. LC 91-26998. (Illus.). 96p. (gr. 6-12). 1992. PLB 19.92 (*0-8114-2451-0*) Raintree Steck-V.

Moore, Robert B. Violence, the KKK & the Struggle for Equality. 72p. (Orig.). (gr. 9 up). 1981. pap. 5.95 (*0-930040-38-4*) CIBC.

Moore, Robin. The Bread Sister of Sinking Creek. LC 89-36400. (Illus.). 160p. (gr. 4-7). 1990. 15.00 (*0-397-32418-9*, Lipp Jr Bks); PLB 14.89 (*0-397-32419-7*, Lipp Jr Bks) HarpC Child Bks.
—The Bread Sister of Sinking Creek. LC 89-36400. 160p. (gr. 4-7). 1992. pap. 3.95 (*0-06-440357-2*, Trophy) HarpC Child Bks.
—Maggie among the Seneca. rev. ed. LC 89-77110. 112p. (gr. 4-7). 1990. (Lipp Jr Bks); PLB 13.89 (*0-397-32456-1*, Lipp Jr Bks) HarpC Child Bks.

Moore, Rosalind, ed. The Dell Big Book of Crosswords & Pencil Puzzles, No. 7. (Orig.). 1989. pap. 9.99 (*0-440-50161-X*, Dell Trade Pbks) Dell.

Moore, Ruth N. The Christmas Surprise. Eitzen, Allen, illus. 160p. (Orig.). (gr. 4-8). 1989. pap. 5.95 (*0-8361-3499-0*) Herald Pr.
—Danger in the Pines. LC 82-15770. 160p. (gr. 4-9). 1983. text ed. 7.95 (*0-8361-3313-7*); pap. 4.95 (*0-8361-3314-5*) Herald Pr.
—Distant Thunder: A Sequel to the Christmas Surprise. LC 91-10845. 160p. (Orig.). (gr. 4-8). 1991. pap. 5.95 (*0-8361-3557-1*) Herald Pr.
—Ghost Town Mystery. Gerig, Sibyl G., illus. LC 87-2874. 144p. (gr. 4 up). 1987. pap. 5.95 (*0-8361-3445-1*) Herald Pr.
—In Search of Liberty, Vol. 1. Converse, James, illus. LC 83-10827. 168p. (Orig.). (gr. 7-10). 1983. pap. 4.95 (*0-8361-3340-4*) Herald Pr.
—Mystery at Camp Ichthus. Gerig, Sibyl G., illus. LC 86-25637. 128p. (Orig.). (gr. 3-9). 1986. pap. 5.95 (*0-8361-3421-4*) Herald Pr.
—Mystery at Captain's Cove. 160p. (Orig.). (gr. 4-7). 1992. pap. 5.95 (*0-8361-3581-4*) Herald Pr.
—Mystery at Indian Rocks. Bond, Magi, illus. LC 80-25803. 192p. (gr. 5-10). 1981. pap. 4.95 (*0-8361-1944-4*) Herald Pr.
—Mystery at the Spanish Castle. 112p. (Orig.). (gr. 4-8). 1990. pap. 5.95 (*0-8361-3515-6*) Herald Pr.
—Mystery of the Lost Heirloom. Converse, James, illus. LC 85-27334. 152p. (Orig.). (gr. 6-9). 1985. pap. 5.95 (*0-8361-3408-7*) Herald Pr.
—Mystery of the Missing Stallions. Converse, James, illus. LC 84-19. 136p. (Orig.). (gr. 3-8). 1984. pap. 5.95 (*0-8361-3376-5*) Herald Pr.
—Mystery of the Secret Code. Converse, James, illus. LC 85-5441. 128p. (Orig.). (gr. 7-9). 1985. pap. 5.95 (*0-8361-3394-3*) Herald Pr.
—The Sorrel Horse. LC 82-3136. 144p. (Orig.). (gr. 5-10). 1982. pap. 3.95 (*0-8361-3303-X*) Herald Pr.

Moore, Shirley, ed. see Corbett, Julia.

Moore, Silas. Scarlet Arena 30303. Oddo, Genevieve, ed. Luering, Jacqueline M., illus. LC 74-190272. 196p. (gr. 8-12). 1972. PLB 3.95 (*0-87783-063-0*) Oddo.

Moore, Stanley B. Ornamental Horticulture As a Vocation. 2nd ed. Moore, Stanley B., illus. 1988. text ed. 11.95x (*0-912178-01-9*) Mor-Mac.

Moore, Susan, ed. see Roach, Margaret J.

Moore, Yvette. Freedom Songs. LC 88-43073. 176p. (gr. 7 up). 1991. 14.95 (*0-531-05812-3*); PLB 14.99 (*0-531-08412-4*) Orchard Bks Watts.
—Freedom Songs. LC 92-20289. 176p. (gr. 7 up). 1992. pap. 3.99 (*0-14-036017-4*) Puffin Bks.
—Jubilee Year Bible Stories: The Birth of Christ. 16p. 1993. pap. 9.00 (*0-9637273-0-3*) Jubilee Yr Bks.
Moore-Betty, Maurice, jt. auth. see Travers, Pamela L.
Moore-Slater, Carole. Dana Doesn't Like Guns Anymore. (Illus., Orig.). 1991. 10.95 (*0-377-00246-1*) Friendship Pr.
Moorhead, Carol A. Colorado's Backyard Wildlife. Moorhead, Carol A., illus. 96p. (Orig.). (gr. 6-8). 1992. pap. 10.95 (*1-879373-08-4*) R Rinehart.
Moorhouse, Karin. A Child's Story of Canada. 72p. (ps-8). 1987. 6.95 (*0-920806-50-3*, Pub. by Penumbra Pr CN) U of Toronto Pr.
Moos, Michael, jt. ed. see Bradford, Gigi.
Mooser, Stephen. Amazing Stories. (gr. 4-7). 1993. pap. 3.25 (*0-440-40646-3*) Dell.
—April Fools. (gr. 4-7). 1993. pap. 3.25 (*0-440-40651-X*) Dell.
—Babe Ruth & the Home Run Derby. Ulrich, George, illus. 80p. (Orig.). (gr. 2-5). 1992. pap. 3.25 (*0-440-40486-X*, YB) Dell.
—The Case of the Slippery Sharks. Morrill, Leslie, illus. LC 87-3490. 96p. (gr. 3-6). 1988. PLB 9.89 (*0-8167-1177-1*); pap. text ed. 2.95 (*0-8167-1178-X*) Troll Assocs.
—Crazy Mixed-up Valentines. (gr. k-6). 1990. pap. 2.99 (*0-440-40269-7*, YB) Dell.
—Creepy Creature Club, No. 3: Monster Holiday. 1989. pap. 2.75 (*0-440-40251-4*) Dell.
—Disaster in Room One Hundred One. MacDougall, Rob, illus. LC 93-24055. 80p. (gr. 2-4). 1993. PLB 9.89 (*0-8167-3278-7*); pap. text ed. 2.95 (*0-8167-3279-5*) Troll Assocs.
—The Fright-Face Contest. (gr. k-6). 1989. pap. 2.75 (*0-685-26138-7*, YB) Dell.
—The Ghost with the Halloween Hiccups. De Paola, Tomie, illus. 32p. (gr. k-3). 1978. pap. 2.95 (*0-380-04287-4*, Camelot) Avon.
—The Headless Snowman. Ulrich, George, illus. 80p. (Orig.). (gr. 2-5). 1992. pap. 3.25 (*0-440-40542-4*, YB) Dell.
—The Hitchhiking Vampire. (gr. 5 up). 1989. 13.95 (*0-385-29725-4*) Delacorte.
—Hitchhiking Vampire. 1989. pap. 13.95 (*0-440-50134-2*) Dell.
—It's a Weird, Weird School. 1989. 13.95 (*0-385-29812-9*) Doubleday.
—It's a Weird, Weird School. (gr. 4-7). 1991. pap. 3.25 (*0-440-40500-9*) Dell.
—The Man Who Ate a Car. (ps-3). 1991. pap. 2.99 (*0-440-40460-6*) Dell.
—Monster of the Year. 1990. pap. 2.75 (*0-440-40363-4*, YB) Dell.
—Monsters in the Outfield. (gr. k-6). 1989. pap. 2.75 (*0-440-40219-0*, YB) Dell.
—The Mummy's Secret. Morrill, Leslie, illus. LC 87-16152. 96p. (gr. 3-6). 1988. PLB 9.89 (*0-8167-1181-X*); pap. text ed. 2.95 (*0-8167-1182-8*) Troll Assocs.
—Muscle Mania. (ps-3). 1993. pap. 3.25 (*0-440-40564-5*) Dell.
—My Halloween Boyfriend. (gr. k-6). 1989. pap. 2.75 (*0-440-40231-X*, YB) Dell.
—Night of the Vampire Kitty. (ps-3). 1991. pap. 2.95 (*0-440-40329-4*) Dell.
—Scary Scraped-up Skaters. Ulrich, George, illus. 80p. (Orig.). (gr. 2-5). 1992. pap. 3.25 (*0-440-40488-6*, YB) Dell.
—The Secret Gold Mine. Morrill, Leslie, illus. LC 87-16151. 96p. (gr. 3-6). 1988. PLB 9.89 (*0-8167-1179-8*); pap. text ed. 2.95 (*0-8167-1180-1*) Troll Assocs.
—Secret in the Old Mansion. Morrill, Leslie, illus. LC 87-15456. 96p. (gr. 3-6). 1988. PLB 9.89 (*0-8167-1175-5*); pap. text ed. 2.95 (*0-8167-1176-3*) Troll Assocs.
—Secrets of Scary Fun. (Orig.). (gr. k-6). 1990. pap. 2.99 (*0-440-40338-3*, YB) Dell.
—Shadows on the Graveyard Trail. (Orig.). (gr. 5-7). 1986. pap. 2.75 (*0-440-40805-9*, YB) Dell.
—The Snow Bowl. Ulrich, George, illus. 80p. (gr. 2-5). 1992. pap. 3.25 (*0-440-40563-7*, YB) Dell.
—The Terrible Tickler. Ulrich, George, illus. 80p. (Orig.). (gr. 2-5). 1992. pap. 3.25 (*0-440-40487-8*, YB) Dell.
—That's So Funny, I Forgot to Laugh. (gr. k-6). 1990. pap. 2.99 (*0-440-40262-X*, YB) Dell.
Mooser, Stephen & Oliver, Lin. Tad & Dad. Day, Susan, illus. LC 87-40340. (ps-2). 1990. 4.95 (*1-55782-023-6*, Pub. by Warner Juvenile Bks) Little.
Mooyaart, B. M., tr. see Frank, Anne.
Mora, E., jt. auth. see Pezzoli, F.
Mora, Emma. Animals of the Forest. (Illus.). 30p. (ps-1). 1986. 3.95 (*0-8120-5722-8*) Barron.
—Cyril the Lion. 30p. (ps-1). 1987. 3.95 (*0-8120-5811-9*) Barron.
—Gideon the Little Bear Cub. (Illus.). 30p. (ps-1). 1986. 3.95 (*0-8120-5728-7*) Barron.
—Mortimer Visits Santa Claus. Kennedy, illus. 1987. 3.95 (*0-8120-5808-9*) Barron.
—Snow White & the Seven Dwarfs. (Illus.). 30p. (ps-1). 1986. 3.95 (*0-8120-5815-1*) Barron.
Mora, Francisco X. The Coyote Rings the Wrong Bell. LC 91-13163. (Illus.). 24p. (ps-3). 1991. PLB 15.53 (*0-516-05136-9*); pap. 4.95 (*0-516-45136-7*) Childrens.

—La Gran Fiesta. Mora, Francisco X., illus. LC 92-44365. 32p. (ps-k). 1993. PLB 19.00 (*0-917846-19-2*, 95518) Highsmith Pr.
—Juan Tuza & the Magic Pouch. Mora, Francisco X., illus. 32p. (ps-1). 1993. PLB 19.00 (*0-917846-24-9*, 95563) Highsmith Pr.
—The Legend of the Two Moons. Mora, Francisco X., illus. LC 93-21552. 32p. (ps-k). 1993. PLB 19.00 (*0-917846-15-X*, 95517) Highsmith Pr.
—The Tiger & the Rabbit: A Puerto Rican Folk Tale. Mora, Francisco X., illus. LC 91-3500. 32p. (ps-3). 1991. PLB 16.93 (*0-516-05137-7*); pap. 5.95 (*0-516-45137-5*) Childrens.
Mora, Pat. A Birthday Basket for Tia. Lang, Cecily, illus. LC 91-15753. 32p. (ps-1). 1992. RSBE 13.95 (*0-02-767400-2*, Macmillan Child Bk) Macmillan Child Grp.
—A Birthday Basket for Tia. Lang, Cecily, illus. (gr. k-4). 1993. 13.95 (*0-685-64816-8*); audio cass. 11.00 (*1-882869-78-8*) Read Advent.
—Listen to the Desert - Que Dice el Desierto? Mora, Francisco X., illus. LC 93-31463. (ENG & SPA.). 1994. write for info. (*0-395-67292-9*, Clarion Bks) HM.
—Pablo's Tree. Mora, Francisco X., illus. LC 92-27145. 32p. (ps-1). 1993. RSBE 13.95 (*0-02-767401-0*, Macmillan Child Bk) Macmillan Child Grp.
Morales, Edgar O., tr. see Houk, Margaret.
Moran, Barbara, ed. see San Diego County School Children.
Moran, Bill. The Mary Wanna Student Activity Book. Lind, Naomi, illus. Mann, Peggy, intro. by. (Illus.). 23p. (gr. 4-6). 1989. pap. 2.50 (*0-942493-10-9*) Woodmere Press.
Moran, Bill & Mann, Peggy. The Mary Wanna Student Activity Book: Based Upon: The Sad Story of Mary Wanna Or How Marijuana Harms You. rev. ed. Lind, Naomi, illus. 26p. (gr. 4-6). 1990. pap. text ed. 2.95 (*0-942493-11-7*) Woodmere Press.
Moran, John, et al. Term Paper Study Aids. 1986. pap. 2.25 (*0-87738-025-2*) Youth Ed.
Moran, Michael, jt. auth. see Loredo, Betsy.
Moran, Patrick R. Lexicarry: An Illustrated Vocabulary-Builder for Second Languages. 2nd, rev. ed. LC 84-1007. (Illus.). 128p. (gr. 6 up). 1989. pap. text ed. 9. 95x (*0-86647-032-8*) Pro Lingua.
Moran, Tom. Canoeing Is for Me. Wolfe, Robert L., illus. LC 83-19957. 48p. (gr. 2-5). 1984. PLB 13.50 (*0-8225-1142-8*) Lerner Pubns.
—A Family in Ireland. (Illus.). 32p. (gr. 2-5). 1986. lib. bdg. 13.50 (*0-8225-1668-3*) Lerner Pubns.
—A Family in Mexico. (Illus.). 32p. (gr. 2-5). 1987. 13.50 (*0-8225-1677-2*) Lerner Pubns.
—The U. S. Army. (Illus.). 88p. (gr. 5 up). 1990. PLB 22. 95 (*0-8225-1434-6*) Lerner Pubns.
Moravia. Sette Racconti. (gr. 7-12). pap. 5.95 (*0-88436-060-1*, 55258) EMC.
Morberg, Mary, jt. auth. see Kinghorn, Harriet.
Mordechai, Tova. Good Night My Friend Aleph. Mordechai, Tova, illus. 32p. (ps-1). 1989. 9.95 (*0-922613-12-5*); pap. 7.95 (*0-922613-13-3*) Hachai Pubns.
Morehead, Albert H. & Mott-Smith, Geoffrey, eds. Hoyle's Rules of Games. (RL 7). 1946. pap. 4.99 (*0-451-16309-5*, Sig) NAL-Dutton.
Morehead, Ruth J. The Christmas Story with Holly Babies. Morehead, Ruth J., illus. LC 85-32305. 32p. (ps-1). 1987. 2.25 (*0-394-88051-X*); cassette pkg. 5.95 (*0-394-89058-2*) Random Bks Yng Read.
Morehead, Ruth J., illus. A Christmas Countdown with Ruth J. Morehead's Holly Babes. LC 90-61905. 22p. (ps). 1991. bds. 2.95 (*0-679-81417-5*) Random Bks Yng Read.
—Christmas Is Coming with Ruth J. Morehead's Holly Babes: A Book of Poems & Songs. LC 89-3717. 32p. (Orig.). (ps-1). 1990. pap. 2.25 (*0-679-80075-1*) Random Bks Yng Read.
Morehouse, Joyce M. In Search of Yesterday. Agnew, Tim, illus. LC 87-14741. 136p. (Orig.). (gr. 9 up). 1987. pap. 4.99 (*0-932581-17-X*) Word Aflame.
Morel, Gaud. Nature's Timekeeper - The Tree. Bogard, Vicki, tr. from FRE. Perols, Sylvaine, illus. LC 92-2710. 38p. (gr. k-5). 1992. 4.95 (*0-944589-43-X*) Young Discovery Lib.
—Nature's Timekeeper: The Tree. Perols, Sylvaine, illus. 40p. (gr. k-5). 1993. PLB 9.95 (*1-56674-072-X*, HTS Bks) Forest Hse.
Morelli, Susan. Mrs. Funnywinkle. Weinberger, Jane, ed. (Illus.). 54p. (gr. 1-4). 1994. pap. 9.95 (*0-932433-62-6*) Windswept Hse.
Moreno, Leslie B. Companeros: Activity Book in Spanish & English for Children. 144p. (gr. 7-11). 1983. pap. 5.95 (*0-917168-09-7*) Executive Comm.
Moretti, Stephanie. The An Book. (Illus.). 16p. (ps-1). 1993. large format easle bk. 18.95 (*1-879567-09-1*) Wonder Well.
—The At Book. (Illus.). 18p. (ps-1). 1991. large format easle book 18.95 (*1-879567-08-3*, Valeria Bks) Wonder Well.
Moretz, Cheryl, jt. auth. see Levy, Nathan.
Morey, Cathy, ed. see Newlin, Lana S.
Morey, Janet & Dunn, Wendy. Famous Mexican Americans. LC 89-7218. (Illus.). (gr. 5 up). 1989. 14. 99 (*0-525-65012-1*, Cobblehill Bks) Dutton Child Bks.
Morey, Janet N. & Dunn, Wendy. Famous Asian Americans. (Illus.). 192p. (gr. 5 up). 1992. 15.00 (*0-525-65080-6*, Cobblehill Bks) Dutton Child Bks.

Morey, Shaun. Incredible Fishing Stories for Kids. Martin, Rick, illus. LC 93-77082. 96p. (Orig.). 1993. pap. 11.95 (*0-9633691-1-3*) Incrdble Fish.
Morey, Walt. Angry Waters. Spillman, Fredicka, illus. (Orig.). (gr. 5-9). 1990. Repr. 6.95 (*0-936085-10-X*) Blue Heron OR.
—Canyon Winter. 208p. (gr. 5 up). 1994. pap. 3.99 (*0-14-036856-6*) Puffin Bks.
—Death Walk. Spillman, Fredrika, illus. (gr. 5-12). 1991. 13.95 (*0-936085-18-5*) Blue Heron OR.
—Death Walk. 176p. 1993. pap. 7.95 (*0-936085-55-X*) Blue Heron OR.
—Deep Trouble. Spillman, Fredrika, contrib. by. (gr. 5-9). 1989. pap. 6.95 (*0-936085-15-0*) Blue Heron OR.
—Gentle Ben. 192p. (gr. 4 up). 1976. pap. 2.95 (*0-380-00743-6*, Camelot) Avon.
—Gentle Ben. Schoenherr, John, illus. LC 65-21290. 192p. (gr. 4 up). 1965. 12.95 (*0-525-30429-0*, DCB) Dutton Child Bks.
—Gentle Ben. Schoenherr, John, illus. 192p. (gr. 5 up). 1992. pap. 3.99 (*0-14-036035-2*, Puffin) Puffin Bks.
—Gloomy Gus. Spillman, Fredrika, illus. 192p. (gr. 4-8). 1989. pap. 6.95 (*0-936085-17-7*) Blue Heron OR.
—Home Is the North. Spillman, Fredrika, contrib. by. (gr. 4-9). 1989. pap. 6.95 (*0-936085-11-8*) Blue Heron OR.
—Kavik, the Wolf Dog. Parnall, Peter, illus. LC 68-24727. (gr. 5-9). 1977. 14.95 (*0-525-33093-3*, DCB); (DCB) Dutton Child Bks.
—Run Far, Run Fast. Spillman, Fredrika, contrib. by. (gr. 4-9). 1989. pap. 6.95 (*0-936085-16-9*) Blue Heron OR.
—Runaway Stallion. Spillman, Fredrika, illus. 176p. (gr. 4-8). 1989. pap. 6.95 (*0-936085-12-6*) Blue Heron OR.
—Sandy & the Rock Star. LC 78-12375. (gr. 4-7). 1979. 13.95 (*0-525-38785-4*, DCB) Dutton Child Bks.
—Scrub Dog of Alaska. Spillman, Fredrika, illus. 160p. (gr. 4-9). 1989. pap. 6.95 (*0-936085-13-4*) Blue Heron OR.
—Year of the Black Pony. Spillman, Fredrika, illus. 160p. (gr. 4-8). 1989. pap. 6.95 (*0-936085-14-2*) Blue Heron OR.
Morgan, et al. What Made Them Great Series, 8 bks. (Illus.). 832p. (gr. 5-8). 1990. Set. PLB 135.84 (*0-382-09983-4*); Set. pap. 71.60 (*0-382-09984-2*) Silver Burdett Pr.
Morgan, A. Daddy-Care. (Illus.). 24p. (ps-8). 1986. 12.95 (*0-920303-58-7*, Pub. by Annick CN); pap. 4.95 (*0-920303-59-5*, Pub. by Annick CN) Firefly Bks Ltd.
—Matthew & the Midnight Money Van. (Illus.). 24p. (ps-8). 1987. PLB 14.95 (*0-920303-75-7*, Pub. by Annick CN); pap. 4.95 (*0-920303-72-2*, Pub. by Annick CN) Firefly Bks Ltd.
—Matthew & the Midnight Tow Truck. (Illus.). 24p. (ps-8). 1984. 12.95 (*0-920303-00-5*, Pub. by Annick CN); pap. 4.95 (*0-920303-01-3*, Pub. by Annick CN) Firefly Bks Ltd.
—Matthew & the Midnight Turkeys. (Illus.). 24p. (ps-8). 1985. PLB 14.95 (*0-920303-36-6*, Pub. by Annick CN); pap. 4.95 (*0-920303-37-4*, Pub. by Annick CN) Firefly Bks Ltd.
—Nicole's Boat. (Illus.). 24p. (ps-8). 1986. 12.95 (*0-920303-60-9*, Pub. by Annick CN); pap. 4.95 (*0-920303-61-7*, Pub. by Annick CN) Firefly Bks Ltd.
Morgan, Adrian, jt. auth. see Morgan, Sally.
Morgan, Allan. Sadie & the Snowman. Clark, Brenda, illus. 32p. (ps-2). 1987. pap. 2.50 (*0-590-41826-2*) Scholastic Inc.
Morgan, Allen. Andrew & the Wild Bikes. Beinicke, Steve, illus. 32p. (ps-2). 1990. 12.95 (*1-55037-083-9*, Pub. by Annick CN); pap. 4.95 (*1-55037-082-0*, Pub. by Annick CN) Firefly Bks Ltd.
—Ellie & the Ivy. Beinieke, Steven, illus. 32p. (gr. 2 up). 1990. bds. 12.95 laminated (*0-19-540726-1*) OUP.
—Mateo y los Pavos de Medianoche: (Matthew & the Midnight Turkeys) Langer, Shirley, tr. Martchenko, Michael, illus. (SPA.). 32p. 1991. pap. 5.95 (*1-55037-188-6*, Pub. by Annick CN) Firefly Bks Ltd.
—Matthew & the Midnight Money Van. Martchenko, Michael, illus. 24p. (ps-2). 1991. pap. 0.99 (*1-55037-194-0*, Pub. by Annick CN) Firefly Bks Ltd.
—Matthew & the Midnight Tow Truck. Martchenko, Michael, illus. 24p. (ps-2). 1991. pap. 0.99 (*1-55037-192-4*, Pub. by Annick CN) Firefly Bks Ltd.
—Matthew & the Midnight Turkeys. Martchenko, Michael, illus. 24p. (ps-2). 1991. pap. 0.99 (*1-55037-193-2*, Pub. by Annick CN) Firefly Bks Ltd.
Morgan, Bill. Incredible Captures. (gr. 4-7). 1993. pap. 2.95 (*0-590-47142-2*) Scholastic Inc.
—The Magic: Earvin Johnson. 1992. 2.95 (*0-590-46050-1*, 063) Scholastic Inc.
Morgan, Buford. Quest for Quivera: Coronado's Exploration into Southern U. S. 189p. (gr. 10 up). 1990. 15.95 (*0-89992-425-5*); pap. 9.95 (*0-89992-125-6*) Coun India Ed.
Morgan, Cheryl K. The Everglades. Morgan, Cheryl K., illus. LC 89-5175. 32p. (gr. 3-6). 1990. PLB 10.79 (*0-8167-1733-8*); pap. text ed. 2.95 (*0-8167-1734-6*) Troll Assocs.
Morgan, Edith, jt. auth. see Jasper, James M.
Morgan, Elizabeth D. Jane Long: A Child's Pictorial History. Johnson, Nancy D., photos by. Richards, Ann, intro. by. LC 92-17739. (Illus.). 96p. (gr. 4-7). 1992. 12.95 (*0-89015-861-4*) Eakin-Sunbelt.
Morgan, Gareth, jt. auth. see Harlow, Rosie.
Morgan, Geoffrey. Tea with Mr. Timothy. 2nd, large type ed. (Illus.). 111p. 1993. 18.95 (*1-85695-300-9*, Pub. by ISIS UK) Transaction Pubs.

Morgan, Hal & Tucker, Kerry. Jack & the Beanstalk; with an Inflatable Beanstalk. Marsh, Susan, illus. 10p. (ps-3). 1987. pap. 4.95 (0-942820-21-5) Steam Pr MA.
Morgan, Hal, jt. ed. see Tucker, Kerry.
Morgan, Helen. The Witch Doll. (Illus.). 144p. (gr. 3-7). 1992. 14.00 (0-670-84285-0) Viking Child Bks.
Morgan, Jenny. Herbs for Horses, No. 27: Threshold Picture Guide. Vincer, Carole, illus. 24p. (Orig.). 1993. pap. 12.00 (1-872082-46-7, Pub. by Kenilworth Pr UK) Half Halt Pr.
Morgan, Judith. Art Text-Workbook: Calligraphy (Introduction) Wallace, Dorathye, ed. (Illus.). 134p. (Orig.). (gr. 8-10). 1990. pap. 13.27 (0-914127-31-4); tchr's. ed. avail. Univ Class.
—An Art Text-Workbook: Ceramics (Introduction) Wallace, Dorathye, ed. (Illus.). 123p. (gr. 8-10). 1990. pap. 13.27 (0-914127-24-1); tchr's. ed. avail. Univ Class.
—Art Text-Workbook: Drawing (Introduction) Wallace, Dorathye, ed. (Illus.). 150p. (Orig.). (gr. 8-10). 1990. pap. 13.27 (0-914127-51-9); tchr's. ed. avail. Univ Class.
—Art Text-Workbook: Film Making (Introduction) Wallace, Dorathye, ed. (Illus.). 146p. (Orig.). (gr. 8-10). 1990. pap. 13.27 (0-914127-36-5); tchr's. ed. avail. Univ Class.
—An Art Text-Workbook: Metalsmithing (Introduction) Wallace, Dorothy, ed. (Illus.). 142p. (Orig.). (gr. 8-10). 1990. pap. 13.27 (0-914127-33-0); tchr's. ed. avail. Univ Class.
—Art Text-Workbook: Painting (Introduction) Wallace, Dorathye, ed. (Illus.). 127p. (Orig.). (gr. 8-10). 1990. pap. 13.27 (0-914127-57-8); tchr's. ed. avail. Univ Class.
—An Art Text-Workbook: Photography (Introduction) Baird, Tate, ed. (Illus.). 178p. (Orig.). (gr. 8-10). 1990. pap. text ed. 13.27 (0-914127-23-3); tchr's. ed. avail. Univ Class.
—Art Text-Workbook: Printmaking (Introduction) Wallace, Dorathye, ed. (Illus.). 124p. (Orig.). (gr. 8-10). 1990. pap. 13.27 (0-914127-27-6); tchr's. ed. avail. Univ Class.
—Art Text-Workbook: Sculpture (Introduction) Wallace, Dorathye, ed. (Illus.). 113p. (gr. 8-10). 1990. 13.27 (0-914127-34-9); tchr's. ed. avail. Univ Class.
—Art Text-Workbook: Weaving (Introduction) Wallace, Dorathye, ed. (Illus.). 144p. (Orig.). (gr. 8-10). 1990. pap. 13.27 (0-914127-61-6); tchr's. ed. avail. Univ Class.
Morgan, Kate. The Story of Things. De Puthod, Daisy, illus. 32p. (gr. 3-7). 1991. 14.95 (0-8027-6918-7); lib. bdg. 15.85 (0-8027-6919-5) Walker & Co.
Morgan, Kathleen. Math Readiness. (Illus.). 48p. (ps-1). 1989. pap. text ed. 5.95 (1-55799-157-X) Evan-Moor Corp.
—Simple Games for Practicing Basic Skills. (Illus.). 48p. (ps-1). 1989. pap. text ed. 5.95 (1-55799-147-2) Evan-Moor Corp.
Morgan, Lael. Art & Eskimo Power: The Life & Times of Alaskan Howard Rock. Sims, Virginia, ed. LC 88-24408. (Illus.). 260p. (Orig.). (gr. 9-12). 1988. 24.95 (0-945397-02-X); pap. 16.95 (0-945397-03-8) Epicenter Pr.
Morgan, Lee & Cattaneo, Pietro. Abraham Lincoln. (Illus.). 104p. (gr. 5-8). 1990. 16.98 (0-382-09973-7); pap. 8.95 (0-382-24000-6) Silver Burdett Pr.
Morgan, Lee & Solarino, Claudio. Christopher Columbus. (Illus.). 104p. (gr. 5-8). 1990. 16.98 (0-382-09974-5); pap. 8.95 (0-382-24001-4) Silver Burdett Pr.
Morgan, Lenore. Dragons & Stuff. LC 70-108725. (Illus.). 32p. (gr. 2-4). 1970. PLB 9.95 (0-87783-012-6); pap. 3.94 deluxe ed. (0-87783-091-6) Oddo.
—Peter's Pockets. LC 65-27622. (Illus.). 32p. (gr. k-2). 1968. PLB 9.95 (0-87783-029-0) Oddo.
—Peter's Pockets. Lysaker, Gene, illus. (gr. k-2). 1978. pap. 1.25 (0-89508-063-X) Rainbow Bks.
Morgan, Les. Pulling Weeds. Hartley, Fred, frwd. by. LC 88-93031. 124p. (Orig.). (gr. 9-12). 1989. pap. 5.99 (0-87509-414-7) Chr Pubns.
—Taming the Lions in Your Life. 160p. (Orig.). (gr. 8-12). 1992. pap. 6.99 (0-87509-479-1) Chr Pubns.
Morgan, Marcia K. My Feelings. 2nd ed. Hilty, Christi S., illus. (ps-5). 1984. pap. text ed. 3.95 (0-930413-00-8, TX-1-361-947) Equal Just Con.
Morgan, Marian & Preston, Izola. The Arkansas African-American Quizbook. 40p. (Orig.). 1993. pap. 10.00x (0-938041-12-6) Arc Pr AR.
Morgan, Mary. Benjamin's Bugs. Morgan, Mary, illus. LC 93-22911. 44p. (ps-1). 1994. RSBE 12.95 (0-02-767450-9, Bradbury Pr) Macmillan Child Grp.
—Wee Seasons. (Illus.). 24p. (ps-1). 1990. bds. 2.50 (0-448-02261-3, G&D) Putnam Pub Group.
Morgan, Mary, illus. Guess Who I Love? 18p. (ps). 1992. bds. 2.95 (0-448-40313-7) Putnam Pub Group.
—The Pudgy Merry Christmas Book. 16p. 1989. bds. 2.95 (0-448-02262-1, G&D) Putnam Pub Group.
—Sleepy Time. LC 89-63997. 14p. (ps). 1990. bds. 3.95 (0-679-80753-5) Random Bks Yng Read.
Morgan, Mary H. How to Dress an Old-Fashioned Doll. LC 72-93612. (Illus.). 96p. (gr. 5-8). 1973. pap. 2.95 (0-486-22912-2) Dover.
Morgan, Michaela. Dinostory. Kelley, True, illus. LC 90-44935. 32p. (ps-4). 1991. 13.95 (0-525-44726-1, DCB) Dutton Child Bks.
—Helpful Betty to the Rescue. Kemp, Moira, illus. LC 93-39885. 1994. 18.95 (0-87614-831-1) Carolrhoda Bks.

Morgan, Michaela & Kemp, Moira. Helpful Betty Solves a Mystery. LC 93-39050. (gr. 3 up). 1994. 18.95 (0-87614-832-1) Carolrhoda Bks.
Morgan, Nicola. Louis & the Night Sky. (Illus.). 32p. 1991. bds. 13.95 laminated (0-19-540746-6) OUP.
—Once in a Blue Moon. (Illus.). 32p. (ps-3). 1992. bds. 12.95 (0-19-540831-4) OUP.
Morgan, Nina. Guglielmo Marconi. (Illus.). 48p. (gr. 5-7). 1991. PLB 12.40 (0-531-18417-X, Pub. by Bookwright Pr) Watts.
—The Human Cycle. LC 93-5265. (Illus.). 32p. (gr. 2-5). 1993. 12.95 (1-56847-094-0) Thomson Lrning.
—Louis Pasteur. (Illus.). 48p. (gr. 5-9). 1992. PLB 12.40 (0-531-18459-5, Pub. by Bookwright Pr) Watts.
—The Mississippi. Fordyce, Lawrence, illus. LC 92-39950. 48p. (gr. 5-6). 1993. PLB 22.80 (0-8114-3103-7) Raintree Steck-V.
—The Plant Cycle. Yates, John, illus. LC 93-977. 32p. (gr. 2-5). 1993. 12.95 (1-56847-091-6) Thomson Lrning.
—Thomas Edison. LC 90-27784. (Illus.). 48p. (gr. 5-8). 1991. RLB 12.40 (0-531-18406-4, Pub. by Bookwright Pr) Watts.
Morgan, Patricia G. A Mountain Adventure. Herde, Tom, illus. LC 87-3486. 32p. (gr. 3-6). 1988. PLB 10.79 (0-8167-1173-9); pap. text ed. 2.95 (0-8167-1174-7) Troll Assocs.
—A River Adventure. Plunkett, Micheal, illus. LC 87-3485. 32p. (gr. 3-6). 1988. PLB 10.79 (0-8167-1171-2); pap. text ed. 2.95 (0-8167-1172-0) Troll Assocs.
Morgan, Peggy. Being a Buddhist. (Illus.). 72p. (gr. 7-10). 1989. 19.95 (0-7134-6015-6, Pub. by Batsford UK) Trafalgar.
Morgan, Robin. The Mer-Child: A Legend for Children & Other Adults. (Illus.). 64p. 1991. 17.95 (1-55861-053-7); 8.95 (1-55861-054-5) Feminist Pr.
Morgan, Sally. The Flying Emu & Other Australian Stories. Morgan, Sally, illus. LC 92-37880. 128p. (gr. k-7). 1993. 18.00 (0-679-84705-7) Knopf Bks Yng Read.
—The Super Science Book of the Environment. Lloyd, Frances, illus. 32p. (gr.-8). 1994. 14.95 (1-56847-095-9) Thomson Lrning.
Morgan, Sally & Morgan, Adrian. Materials. LC 93-31722. 1994. write for info. (0-8160-2985-7) Facts on File.
—Movement. LC 93-20162. 1993. write for info. (0-8160-2979-2) Facts on File.
—Structures. LC 93-20164. 1993. write for info. (0-8160-2983-0) Facts on File.
—Using Energy. LC 93-20407. (gr. 4 up). 1993. write for info. (0-8160-2984-9) Facts on File.
—Using Light. LC 93-21535. 1993. write for info. (0-8160-2980-6) Facts on File.
—Using Sound. LC 93-31720. 1994. write for info. (0-8160-2981-4) Facts on File.
—Water. LC 93-31721. 1994. write for info. (0-8160-2982-2) Facts on File.
Morgan, Stephanie. The Witch down the Street. Cooke, Tom, illus. 40p. (ps-3). 1983. cancelled 5.95 (0-910313-02-4, 7003) Parker Bros.
Morgan, Terri. Photography: Terri Morgan. 1991. pap. 8.95 (0-8225-9605-9) Lerner Pubns.
Morgan, Terri & Thaler, Shmuel. Photography: Take Your Best Shot. 80p. (gr. 5 up). 1991. PLB 19.95 (0-8225-2302-7) Lerner Pubns.
Morgan, William. Navajo Coyote Tales. Thompson, Hildegard, ed. & tr. Lind, Jenny, illus. LC 88-72048. 50p. (gr. 1-3). 1988. pap. 8.95 (0-941270-52-1) Ancient City Pr.
Morgan, William, tr. see Crowder, Jack L. & Hill, Faith.
Morgan-Williams, Louise. I Can Sing En Francais! Fun Songs for Learning French. (gr. 4-7). 1993. 8.95 (0-8442-1457-4, Passport Bks) NTC Pub Grp.
—I Can Sing Ien Espanol! Fun Songs for Learning Spanish. (gr. 4-7). 1993. 8.95 (0-8442-7168-3, Passport Bks) NTC Pub Grp.
Morgen, Howard. Ten from Guitar Player. Stang, Aaron, ed. 72p. (Orig.). 1992. pap. text ed. 12.95 (0-89898-575-7) CPP Belwin.
Morgenroth, Barbara. Inside an American Ranch. 64p. (gr. 4-6). 1994. PLB 12.95 (1-881889-56-4) Silver Moon.
Morgenstern, Constance. Good Night, Feet. Smith, Cat B., illus. LC 90-42170. 32p. (ps-2). 1991. PLB 14.95 (0-8050-1453-5, Bks Young Read) H Holt & Co.
Morgenstern, Susie. Oukele la Tele. Pef, illus. (FRE.). 54p. (gr. 1-5). 1991. pap. 9.95 (2-07-031190-2) Schoenhof.
Mori, Hana. Jirohattan. Kurosaki, Tamiko & Crowe, Elizabeth, trs. from JPN. Crowe, Elizabeth, illus. LC 93-72833. 80p. (gr. 4-8). 1993. pap. 5.95 (1-880188-69-4) Bess Pr.
Mori, Kyoko. Shizuko's Daughter. LC 92-26956. 256p. (gr. 7-up). 1993. PLB 15.95 (0-8050-2557-X, Bks Young Read) H Holt & Co.
Moriarty, Kathleen M. A Shaker Sampler: Coloring Book. 2nd ed. Orrin, Mary, illus. 30p. (gr. k-6). 1991. pap. 4.95 (0-915836-15-7) United Soc Shakers.
Moriarty, Mary & Sweeney, Catherine. Bob Geldof. LC 89-50965. (Illus.). 80p. (Orig.). (gr. 9-12). 1990. pap. 8.95 (0-86278-163-9, Pub. by O'Brien Press Ltd Eire) Dufour.
—The Rebel Countess. Teskey, Donald, illus. 80p. (Orig.). (gr. 1-7). 1992. pap. 8.95 (0-86278-211-2, Pub. by OBrien Pr EIRE) Dufour.

—Theobald Wolfe Tone. (Illus.). 64p. 1989. pap. 8.95 (0-86278-160-4, Pub. by O'Brien Press Ltd Eire) Dufour.
Moriarty, Nancy, ed. see Boles, Lisa P., et al.
Morieda, Takashi. Children of the World: Burma. LC 86-42799. (Illus.). 64p. (gr. 5-6). 1987. PLB 19.93 (1-55532-159-3) Gareth Stevens Inc.
Morimoto, Junko. The Inch Boy. (ps-3). 1988. pap. 3.95 (0-14-050677-2, Puffin) Puffin Bks.
—Kenju's Forest. (Illus.). 32p. (gr. k-3). 1991. pap. 7.95 (0-7322-7358-7, Pub. by Angus & Robertson AT) HarpC.
—Kojura. (Illus.). 32p. (gr. k-3). 1991. pap. 7.95 (0-7322-7228-9, Pub. by Angus & Robertson AT) HarpC.
—Mouse's Marriage. (Illus.). 32p. (Orig.). (ps-1). 1988. pap. 4.99 (0-14-050678-0, Puffin) Puffin Bks.
—My Hiroshima. (Illus.). 32p. (ps up). 1990. pap. 13.95 (0-670-83181-6) Viking Child Bks.
—My Hiroshima. (Illus.). 32p. (ps-3). 1992. pap. 5.99 (0-14-054524-7, Puffin) Puffin Bks.
Morin, Alice. Newspaper Theatre. (gr. 1-8). 1989. pap. 8.95 (0-8224-6349-0) Fearon Teach Aids.
Morin, Isobel V. Women of the U. S. Congress. LC 93-26068. (Illus.). 160p. (gr. 5-12). 1994. PLB 14.95 (1-881508-12-9) Oliver Pr MN.
Morin, John B. Sea-Lords of Gondor. McBride, Angus, illus. Fenlon, Peter C., Jr., ed. 64p. (Orig.). (gr. 10-12). 1987. pap. 12.00 (0-915795-88-4, 3400) Iron Crown Ent Inc.
Morin, Virginia K. Messy Activities & More. Sokoloff, David, illus. Jernberg, Ann M., intro. by. LC 92-41453. (Illus.). 144p. (Orig.). (ps-5). 1993. pap. 9.95 (1-55652-173-1) Chicago Review.
Morison, Samuel E. Christopher Columbus, Mariner. (Illus.). 192p. (gr. 9-12). 1983. pap. 9.00 (0-452-00992-8, Mer) NAL-Dutton.
—Oxford History of the American People. (gr. 9 up). 1965. OUP.
Morison, Samuel E., ed. Sources & Documents Illustrating the American Revolution, 1764-1788, & the Formation of the Federal Constitution. 2nd ed. (gr. 9 up). 1965. pap. 15.95x (0-19-500262-8) OUP.
Morissette, Oliver, et al. Prey. Morissette, Oliver, illus. (Orig.). Date not set. pap. 19.95 (0-938782-29-0) Fantaco.
Moritz, Nadia, intro. by see Institute for Women's Policy Research, The Young Women's Project Staff.
Moriwaki, Glenda. Love for Priscilla. Mendez, Gerardo, illus. 28p. (Orig.). (ps-3). 1991. pap. 4.95 (0-9627956-7-4) Meadora Pub.
Morland, John, et al. Classroom Learning Centers. LC 73-77592. (gr. 1-6). 1973. pap. 10.95 (0-8224-1410-4) Fearon Teach Aids.
Morley, Carol. Dots & Spots. Morley, Carol, illus. LC 92-24526. 32p. (ps-3). 1993. 14.00 (0-06-021526-7); PLB 13.89 (0-06-021527-5) HarpC Child Bks.
—A Spider & a Pig. LC 92-53215. 1993. 14.95 (0-316-58405-3) Little.
Morley, Jacqueline. Clothes for Work, Play & Display. LC 92-4852. 1992. 13.95 (0-531-15249-9) Watts.
—An Egyptian Pyramid. Bergin, Mark & James, John, illus. 48p. (gr. 5 up). 1993. pap. 8.95 (0-87226-255-3) P Bedrick Bks.
—An Egyptian Pyramid: Inside Story. Bergin, Mark & James, John, illus. 48p. (gr. 5 up). 1991. 17.95 (0-87226-346-0) P Bedrick Bks.
Morley, Jacqueline & James, John. A Roman Villa: Inside Story. LC 92-15279. (Illus.). 48p. (gr. 5 up). 1992. 17.95 (0-87226-360-6) P Bedrick Bks.
Morneau, Sharon see Katherine, Sharon.
Morninghouse, Sundaira. Habari Gani? What's the News? Kim, Jody, illus. 32p. (gr. k-4). 1992. 14.95 (0-940880-39-3) Open Hand.
—Nightfeathers: Black Goose Rhymes. Kim, Jody, illus. LC 89-84866. 32p. (gr. 1-4). 1989. 9.95 (0-940880-27-X); pap. text ed. 4.95 (0-940880-28-8) Open Hand.
Morningstar, Amadea, jt. auth. see Gagnon, Daniel.
Morolez-de Anda, Martha, tr. see Pugh, Ann & Anderson, Joan F.
Moroney, Lynn, adapted by. Elinda Who Danced in the Sky: An Eastern European Folktale from Estonia. Reisberg, Veg, illus. LC 99-2247. 32p. (gr. 1-7). 1990. 13.95 (0-89239-066-2) Childrens Book Pr.
Moroney, Lynn, jt. ed. see Ata, Te.
Morozumi, Atsuko. One Gorilla. (ps). 1993. pap. 4.95 (0-374-45646-1, Sunburst) FS&G.
—One Gorilla: A Counting Book. Morozumi, Atsuko, illus. 26p. (ps-1). 1990. 15.00 (0-374-35644-0) FS&G.
Morpurgo, Michael. King of the Cloud Forest. (Illus.). 160p. (gr. 5-9). 1991. pap. 3.95 (0-14-032586-7, Puffin) Puffin Bks.
—King of the Cloud Forests. (gr. 10 up). 1988. pap. 12.95 (0-670-82069-5) Viking Child Bks.
—My Friend Walter. large type ed. 216p. 1991. 13.95 (0-7451-1408-3, Galaxy Child Lrg Print) Chivers N Amer.
—Twist of Gold. LC 92-25928. 224p. (gr. 5-9). 1993. 14.99 (0-670-84851-4) Viking Child Bks.
—Waiting for Anya. 1991. 13.00 (0-670-83735-0) Viking Child Bks.
—Waiting for Anya. large type ed. 240p. 1992. 13.95 (0-7451-1527-6, Galaxy Child Lrg Print) Chivers N Amer.
—Why the Whales Came. (gr. 5-7). 1990. pap. 10.95 (0-590-42911-6) Scholastic Inc.

—Why the Whales Came. 144p. 1992. pap. 2.75 (*0-590-42912-4*, Apple Paperbacks) Scholastic Inc.
Morreale, Vin, Jr. The Day the Woods Were One. (Orig.). (gr. 3 up). 1985. pap. 6.00 play script (*0-88734-507-7*) Players Pr.
Morreim, Dennis C. Changed Lives: The Story of Alcoholics Anonymous. (ps-3). 1991. pap. 8.99 (*0-8066-2548-1*) Augsburg Fortress.
Morrice, Polly. The French Americans. Moynihan, Daniel P. (Illus.). 112p. (gr. 5 up) 1988. lib. bdg. 17.95 (*0-87754-878-1*) Chelsea Hse.
Morris, A. Earl. The Long Road. Jones, M. L., ed. 336p. (Orig.). 1993. pap. text ed. 12.95 (*1-882270-10-X*) Old Rugged Cross.
Morris, Ann. Bread, Bread, Bread. Heyman, Ken, photos by. LC 82-26677. (Illus.). 32p. (ps-2). 1989. 14.95 (*0-688-06334-9*); PLB 14.88 (*0-688-06335-7*) Lothrop.
—Bread, Bread, Bread. Heyman, Ken, photos by. LC 92-25547. (Illus.). 32p. (gr. k). 1993. pap. 4.95 (*0-688-12275-2*, Mulberry) Morrow.
—Bread, Bread, Bread: Big Book Edition. (ps-3). 1993. pap. 18.95 (*0-688-12939-0*, Mulberry) Morrow.
—The Cinderella Rebus Book. Rylands, Ljiljana, illus. LC 88-1451. 32p. (ps-3). 1989. 13.95 (*0-531-05761-5*); PLB 13.99 (*0-531-08361-6*) Orchard Bks Watts.
—Hats, Hats, Hats. Heyman, Ken, photos by. LC 88-26676. (Illus.). 32p. (ps-2). 1989. 13.95 (*0-688-06338-1*); PLB 13.88 (*0-688-06339-X*) Lothrop.
—Hats, Hats, Hats. Heyman, Ken, photos by. LC 92-25548. (Illus.). 32p. (gr. k). 1993. pap. 4.95 (*0-688-12274-4*, Mulberry) Morrow.
—Hats, Hats, Hats: Big Book Edition. (ps-3). 1993. pap. 18.95 (*0-688-12938-2*, Mulberry) Morrow.
—Houses & Homes. Pearson, Susan, ed. Heyman, Ken, photos by. LC 92-1365. (Illus.). 32p. (ps-2). 1992. 14.00 (*0-688-10168-2*); PLB 13.93 (*0-688-10169-0*) Lothrop.
—The Little Red Riding Hood Rebus Book. Rylands, Ljiljana, illus. LC 87-7696. 32p. (ps-3). 1987. 11.95 (*0-531-05730-5*); PLB 11.99 (*0-531-08330-6*) Orchard Bks Watts.
—Loving. 32p. 1990. 13.95 (*0-688-06340-3*); PLB 13.88 (*0-688-06341-1*) Lothrop.
—On Their Toes: A Russian Ballet School. Heyman, Ken, photos by. LC 91-11903. (Illus.). 48p. (gr. 3-7). 1991. SBE 14.95 (*0-689-31660-7*, Atheneum Child Bk) Macmillan Child Grp.
—On with the Show. (Illus.). 25p. (gr. 2-4). 1991. 12.95 (*0-237-60144-3*, Pub. by Evans Bros Ltd) Trafalgar.
—Seven Hundred Kids on Grandpa's Farm. Heyman, Ken, photos by. (Illus.). 32p. (ps-3). 1994. 14.99 (*0-525-45162-5*, DCB) Dutton Child Bks.
—Tools. Pearson, Susan, ed. Heyman, Ken, photos by. LC 92-3871. (Illus.). 32p. (ps-2). 1992. 14.00 (*0-688-10170-4*); PLB 13.93 (*0-688-10171-2*) Lothrop.
—When Will the Fighting Stop? A Child's View of Jerusalem. Rivlin, Lilly, illus. LC 88-34181. 64p. (gr. 3-7). 1989. SBE 13.95 (*0-689-31508-2*, Atheneum Child Bk) Macmillan Child Grp.
Morris, Brenda. Friends Help Me. LC 86-18769. (ps). 1987. 5.95 (*0-8054-4179-4*) Broadman.
Morris, C. Spencer, jt. auth. see Beers, V. Gilbert.
Morris, Campbell. Fold Your Own Dinosaurs. Jackson, Paul, illus. LC 92-32894. 48p. (Orig.). 1993. pap. 7.95 (*0-399-51794-4*, Perigee Bks) Putnam Pub Group.
Morris, Christopher, et al, eds. The HBJ Student Thesaurus. (Illus.). 312p. (gr. 2-7). 1991. 14.95 (*0-15-232880-7*) HarBrace.
Morris, Dave. Buried Treasure. (gr. 4 up). 1990. pap. 2.95 (*0-440-40391-X*) Dell.
—Dinosaur Farm. (gr. 4-7). 1991. pap. 3.50 (*0-440-40491-6*) Dell.
—Red Herrings. (gr. 4 up). 1990. pap. 2.95 (*0-440-40390-1*) Dell.
—Six Guns & Shurikens. (gr. 4-7), 1990. pap. 2.95 (*0-440-40392-8*) Dell.
—Sky High. (gr. 4 up). 1990. pap. 2.95 (*0-440-40389-8*) Dell.
—Splinter to the Fore. (gr. 4-7). 1991. pap. 3.50 (*0-440-40492-4*) Dell.
Morris, Dean. Animals That Burrow. rev. ed. LC 87-16694. (Illus.). 48p. (gr. 2-6). 1987. PLB 18.64 (*0-8172-3201-X*) Raintree Steck-V.
—Animals That Live in Shells. rev. ed. LC 87-20556. (Illus.). 48p. (gr. 2-6). 1987. PLB 18.64 (*0-8172-3202-8*) Raintree Steck-V.
—Birds. rev. ed. LC 87-16672. (Illus.). 48p. (gr. 2-6). 1987. PLB 18.64 (*0-8172-3203-6*) Raintree Steck-V.
—Butterflies & Moths. rev. ed. LC 87-16666. (Illus.). 48p. (gr. 2-6). 1987. PLB 18.64 (*0-8172-3204-4*) Raintree Steck-V.
—Cats. rev. ed. LC 87-16699. (Illus.). 48p. (gr. 2-6). 1987. PLB 18.64 (*0-8172-3205-2*) Raintree Steck-V.
—Dinosaurs & Other First Animals. rev. ed. LC 87-16670. (Illus.). 48p. (gr. 2-6). 1987. PLB 18.94 (*0-8172-3206-0*) Raintree Steck-V.
—Endangered Animals. rev. ed. LC 87-20459. (Illus.). 48p. (gr. 2-6). 1987. PLB 18.64 (*0-8172-3207-9*) Raintree Steck-V.
—Endangered Animals. (ps-3). 1990. pap. 4.49 (*0-8114-8220-0*) Raintree Steck-V.
—Frogs & Toads. rev. ed. LC 87-16698. (Illus.). 48p. (gr. 2-6). 1987. PLB 18.64 (*0-8172-3208-7*) Raintree Steck-V.
—Horses. rev. ed. LC 87-16690. (Illus.). 48p. (Orig.). (gr. 2-6). 1987. PLB 18.64 (*0-8172-3209-5*) Raintree Steck-V.

—Insects That Live in Families. rev. ed. LC 87-16696. (Illus.). 48p. (gr. 2-6). 1987. PLB 18.64 (*0-8172-3210-9*) Raintree Steck-V.
—Monkeys & Apes. rev. ed. LC 87-16688. (Illus.). 48p. (gr. 3). 1987. PLB 18.64 (*0-8172-3211-7*) Raintree Steck-V.
—Snakes & Lizards. rev. ed. LC 87-16697. (Illus.). 48p. (gr. 2-6). 1987. PLB 18.64 (*0-8172-3212-5*) Raintree Steck-V.
—Spiders. rev. ed. LC 87-16695. (Illus.). 48p. (gr. 2-6). 1987. PLB 18.64 (*0-8172-3213-3*) Raintree Steck-V.
—Spiders. (ps-3). 1990. pap. 11.99 (*0-8172-3238-9*) Raintree Steck-V.
—Underwater Life. rev. ed. LC 87-16693. (Illus.). 48p. (gr. 2-6). 1987. PLB 18.64 (*0-8172-3214-1*) Raintree Steck-V.
—Underwater Life. (ps-3). 1990. pap. 4.49 (*0-8114-8219-7*) Raintree Steck-V.
Morris, Deborah. Trapped In A Cave! A True Story. LC 92-40731. 1993. 6.99 (*0-8054-4003-8*) Broadman.
Morris, Desmond. The World of Animals. Barrett, Peter, illus. 128p. 1993. 22.50 (*0-670-85184-1*) Viking Child Bks.
Morris, Dixie G. Who is Santa? Medrano, JoAnn, illus. Robinson, Deborah L., intro. by. (Illus.). 25p. (Orig.). (ps-3). 1988. spiral bdg. 7.50 (*0-929946-04-9*) L P T C.
Morris, E. & Sadler, T. Our Rainforests & the Issues. (Illus.). 54p. (gr. 6-11). 1991. pap. 14.95x (*0-643-05141-4*, Pub. by CSIRO) Intl Spec Bk.
Morris, Eileen. Crafts Kids Can Eat, Play with, or Wear. (gr. k-3). 1991. pap. 11.95 (*0-86653-979-4*) Fearon Teach Aids.
Morris, Emily. Cuba. LC 90-10354. (Illus.). 96p. (gr. 6-12). 1991. PLB 19.92 (*0-8114-2439-1*) Raintree Steck-V.
Morris, George W., et al. Russian: Face to Face: Beginning. (RUS.). 1993. text ed. 24.95 (*0-685-62838-8*, F4300-0, Natl Textbk); annotated tchr's ed. 30.95 (*0-685-62839-6*, F4302-7, Natl Textbk); student wkbk. 6.95 (*0-685-62840-X*, F4301-9, Natl Textbk); student wkbk. (tchr's ed.) 9.95 (*0-685-62841-8*, F4307-8, Natl Textbk); 3 60-min. audiocassettes 79.95 (*0-685-62842-6*, F4303-X, Natl Textbk) NTC Pub Grp.
Morris, Gilbert. The Crossed Sabres. 304p. (Orig.). 1993. pap. 8.99 (*1-55661-309-1*) Bethany Hse.
—The Dixie Widow. 302p. (Orig.). (gr. 9-12). 1991. text ed. 8.99 (*1-55661-115-3*) Bethany Hse.
—House of Winslow, Vols. 6-10. (Orig.). 1993. 44.99 (*1-55661-768-2*) Bethany Hse.
—The Saintly Buccaneer. LC 88-33337. 288p. (Orig.). (gr. 11 up) 1989. pap. 8.99 (*1-55661-048-3*) Bethany Hse.
—The Union Belle. 302p. (Orig.). 1992. pap. 8.99 (*1-55661-186-2*) Bethany Hse.
Morris, Greggory. Basketball Basics. Engelland, Tim, illus. LC 75-34142. (gr. 2-6). 1979. 6.95 (*0-13-072256-1*, Pub. by Treehouse) P-H.
Morris, Hazel. My Family. LC 85-24334. (Illus.). (ps). 1986. 4.95 (*0-8054-4164-6*) Broadman.
Morris, John. From Coronado to Escalante: The Explorers of the Spanish Southwest. (Illus.). 112p. (gr. 5 up). 1992. lib. bdg. 18.95 (*0-7910-1300-6*) Chelsea Hse.
—Noah's Ark & the Lost World. (Illus.). 64p. (gr. 3-5). 1988. 10.95 (*0-89051-138-1*) Master Bks.
Morris, John, et al. What Really Happened to the Dinosaurs? (Illus.). 24p. (ps-2). 1990. pap. 9.95 (*0-89051-159-4*) Master Bks.
Morris, Johnny. Animal-Go-Round. LC 93-12376. (Illus.). 18p. (gr. 3 up). 1993. 12.95 (*1-56458-329-5*) Dorling Kindersley.
—Lifecycles. LC 93-25426. 1994. 14.95 (*1-56458-458-5*) Dorling Kindersley.
Morris, Judy K. The Kid Who Ran for Principal. LC 89-2729. 224p. (gr. 3-7). 1989. (Lipp Jr Bks) PLB 12.89 (*0-397-32360-3*, Lipp Jr Bks) HarpC Child Bks.
Morris, Kimberly. Wild Hearts. 1992. pap. 3.50 (*0-06-106781-4*, Harp PBks) HarpC.
Morris, Laurence. Pilgrim's Progress (Retold for Children) (gr. 1-5). 1993. pap. 3.95 (*0-87508-747-7*) Chr Lit.
Morris, Linda L. Morning Milking. DeRan, David, illus. LC 91-13103. 32p. (gr. k up). 1991. pap. 16.95 (*0-88708-173-8*) Picture Bk Studio.
Morris, M. C., jt. auth. see Bosschere, Jean de.
Morris, Martha. Katherine & the Garbage Dump. Cathcart, Yvonne, illus. 24p. (gr. 1-4). 1992. 12.95 (*0-929005-39-2*, Pub. by Second Story Pr CN); pap. 5.95 (*0-929005-38-4*, Second Story Pr CN) InBook.
Morris, Neil. Feel! A Fun Book of Touch. Stevenson, Peter, illus. 32p. (ps-2). 1991. PLB 13.50 (*0-87614-672-8*) Carolrhoda Bks.
—Feel! A Fun Book of Touch. (ps). 1992. pap. 6.95 (*0-87614-569-1*) Carolrhoda Bks. Postponed.
—The Golden Atlas for Children. Studio Illustratori Associati Boni Galante Staff, illus. 48p. (gr. 1-6). 1992. 8.95 (*0-307-17876-5*, 17876, Golden Pr) Western Pub.
—Holly & Harry: A Fun Book of Sizes. Stevenson, Peter, illus. 32p. (ps-2). 1991. PLB 13.50 (*0-87614-673-6*) Carolrhoda Bks.
—Holly & Harry: A Fun Book of Sizes. (ps). 1992. pap. 6.95 (*0-87614-570-5*) Carolrhoda Bks. Postponed.
—Home on the Prairie. LC 89-987. (Illus.). 32p. (gr. 4-8). 1989. PLB 9.95 (*1-85435-165-6*) Marshall Cavendish.

—I'm Big: A Fun Book of Opposites. Stevenson, Peter, illus. 32p. (ps-2). 1991. PLB 13.50 (*0-87614-674-4*) Carolrhoda Bks.
—I'm Big: A Fun Book of Opposites. (ps). 1992. pap. 6.95 (*0-87614-571-3*) Carolrhoda Bks. Postponed.
—Jump Along: A Fun Book of Movement. Stevenson, Peter, illus. 32p. (ps-2). 1991. PLB 13.50 (*0-87614-671-X*) Carolrhoda Bks.
—Linda's Late: A Fun Book of Time. Stevenson, Peter, illus. 32p. (ps-2). 1991. PLB 13.50 (*0-87614-675-2*) Carolrhoda Bks.
—Longhorn on the Move. LC 89-7153. (Illus.). 32p. (gr. 3-8). 1989. PLB 9.95 (*1-85435-166-4*) Marshall Cavendish.
—Magic Monkey: A Fun Book of Numbers. Stevenson, Peter, illus. 32p. (ps-2). 1991. PLB 13.50 (*0-87614-677-9*) Carolrhoda Bks.
—Magic Monkey: A Fun Book of Shapes & Colors. (ps). 1992. pap. 6.95 (*0-87614-574-8*) Carolrhoda Bks. Postponed.
—On the Trapping Trail. LC 89-989. (Illus.). 32p. (gr. 3-8). 1989. PLB 9.95 (*1-85435-164-8*) Marshall Cavendish.
—Rummage Sale: A Fun Book of Shapes & Colors. Stevenson, Peter, illus. 32p. (ps-2). 1991. PLB 13.50 (*0-87614-676-0*) Carolrhoda Bks.
—Rummage Sale: A Fun Book of Shapes & Colors. (ps). 1992. pap. 6.95 (*0-87614-575-6*) Carolrhoda Bks. Postponed.
—The Student's Activity Atlas. Walker, Roger, illus. 48p. (gr. 3 up). 1993. PLB 19.93 (*0-8368-1041-4*) Gareth Stevens Inc.
—Wagon Wheels Roll West. LC 89-988. (Illus.). 32p. (gr. 3-8). 1989. PLB 9.95 (*1-85435-167-2*) Marshall Cavendish.
—What a Noise: A Fun Book of Sounds. Stevenson, Peter, illus. 32p. (ps-2). 1991. PLB 13.50 (*0-87614-670-1*) Carolrhoda Bks.
—What a Noise: A Fun Book of Sounds. (ps). 1992. pap. 6.95 (*0-87614-576-4*) Carolrhoda Bks. Postponed.
Morris, Neil & Morris, Ting. Battle of the Gladiators. (Illus.). 24p. (gr. 3-5). 1991. 13.95 (*0-237-51021-9*, Pub. by Evans Bros Ltd) Trafalgar.
—Heidi. (Illus.). 48p. (gr. 2-5). 1991. 13.95 (*0-237-50935-0*, Pub. by Evans Bros Ltd) Trafalgar.
—In the Slave Market. (Illus.). 24p. (gr. 3-5). 1991. 13.95 (*0-237-51019-7*, Pub. by Evans Bros Ltd) Trafalgar.
Morris, Neil, jt. auth. see Morris, Ting.
Morris, Oradel N. Le Monde Acadien de Ti-Jean. LC 81-107884. (FRE & ENG., Illus.). 81p. (gr. k-8). 1980. Repr. of 1981 ed. 8.95 (*0-944064-01-9*) Paupieres Pub.
Morris, R. Ocean Life. Jackson, Ian, et al, illus. 32p. (gr. 3-6). 1983. (Usborne-Haynes); PLB 13.96 (*0-88110-149-4*, Usborne-Haynes); pap. 5.95 (*0-86020-753-6*, Usborne-Haynes) EDC.
Morris, R., jt. auth. see Cork, Barbara.
Morris, Richard B. The American Revolution. rev. ed. Fisher, Leonard E., illus. LC 85-12878. 72p. (gr. 5-10). 1985. PLB 13.50 (*0-8225-1701-9*) Lerner Pubns.
—The Constitution. rev. ed. Fisher, Leonard E., illus. 72p. (gr. 5-10). 1985. PLB 13.50 (*0-8225-1702-7*) Lerner Pubns.
—The Founding of the Republic. rev. ed. Fisher, Richard B., illus. 72p. (gr. 5-10). 1985. PLB 13.50 (*0-8225-1704-3*) Lerner Pubns.
—The War of Eighteen Twelve. rev. ed. Fisher, Leonard E., illus. 72p. (gr. 5-10). 1985. PLB 13.50 (*0-8225-1705-1*) Lerner Pubns.
Morris, Robert. Bare Ruined Choirs: The Fate of a Welsh Abbey. 52p. (gr. 11 up). 1987. pap. 7.95 (*0-85950-544-8*, Pub. by S Thornes UK) Dufour.
Morris, Robert A. Dolphin. Funai, Mamoru, illus. LC 75-6292. 64p. (gr. k-3). 1975. PLB 13.89 (*0-06-024342-2*) HarpC Child Bks.
—Dolphin. Funai, Mamoru, illus. LC 75-6292. 64p. (gr. k-3). 1983. pap. 3.50 (*0-06-444043-5*, Trophy) Irwin Prof Pubng.
Morris, Scott. How to Read a Map. De Blij, Harm J., intro. by. LC 92-22824. (Illus.). 1993. 15.95 (*0-7910-1812-1*, Am Art Analog); pap. write for info. (*0-7910-1825-3*, Am Art Analog) Chelsea Hse.
Morris, Scott, ed. Agriculture & Vegetation of the World. De Blij, Harm J., intro. by. LC 92-22290. (Illus.). 1993. 15.95 (*0-7910-1804-0*, Am Art Analog); pap. write for info. (*0-7910-1817-2*, Am Art Analog) Chelsea Hse.
—The Economy of the World. De Blij, Harm J., intro. by. LC 92-22291. (Illus.). 1993. 15.95 (*0-7910-1809-1*, Am Art Analog); pap. write for info. (*0-7910-1822-9*, Am Art Analog) Chelsea Hse.
—The Endangered World. De Blij, Harm J., intro. by. LC 92-22289. (Illus.). 1993. 15.95 (*0-7910-1806-7*, Am Art Analog); pap. write for info. (*0-7910-1819-9*, Am Art Analog) Chelsea Hse.
—Industry of the World. De Blij, Harm J., intro. by. LC 92-22288. (Illus.). 1993. 15.95 (*0-7910-1807-5*, Am Art Analog); pap. write for info. (*0-7910-1820-2*, Am Art Analog) Chelsea Hse.
—Languages of the World. De Blij, Harm J., intro. by. LC 92-22287. (Illus.). 1993. 15.95 (*0-7910-1811-3*, Am Art Analog); pap. write for info. (*0-7910-1824-5*, Am Art Analog) Chelsea Hse.
—The Military World. De Blij, Harm J., intro. by. LC 92-22286. (Illus.). 1993. 15.95 (*0-7910-1808-3*, Am Art Analog); pap. write for info. (*0-7910-1821-0*, Am Art Analog) Chelsea Hse.

—The Physical World. De Blij, Harm J., intro. by. LC 92-22285. (Illus.). 1993. 15.95 (0-7910-1801-6, Am Art Analog); pap. write for info. (0-7910-1814-8, Am Art Analog) Chelsea Hse.
—The Political World. De Blij, Harm J., intro. by. LC 92-22284. (Illus.). 1993. 15.95 (0-7910-1802-4, Am Art Analog); pap. write for info. (0-7910-1815-6, Am Art Analog) Chelsea Hse.
—Populations of the World. De Blij, Harm J., intro. by. LC 92-22283. (Illus.). 1993. 15.95 (0-7910-1805-9, Am Art Analog) Chelsea Hse.
—Religions of the World. De Blij, Harm J., intro. by. LC 92-22282. (Illus.). 1993. 15.95 (0-7910-1810-5, Am Art Analog); pap. write for info. (0-7910-1823-7, Am Art Analog) Chelsea Hse.
—Rocks & Minerals of the World. De Blij, Harm J., intro. by. LC 92-22910. (Illus.). 1993. 15.95 (0-7910-1803-2, Am Art Analog); pap. write for info. (0-7910-1816-4, Am Art Analog) Chelsea Hse.
Morris, Stephanie, jt. auth. see Crilly, Eileen.
Morris, Stephen. Edward Jenner. LC 91-22574. (Illus.). 48p. (gr. 5-8). 1992. PLB 12.40 (0-531-18460-9, Pub. by Bookwright Pr) Watts.
Morris, Susan, jt. auth. see Cooper, John.
Morris, Ting & Morris, Neil. Animals. LC 93-20415. (Illus.). 32p. (gr. 2-4). 1993. PLB 12.40 (0-531-14268-X) Watts.
—Dinosaurs. LC 92-32915. 1993. 12.40 (0-531-14258-2) Watts.
—Masks. LC 92-32916. 1993. 12.40 (0-531-14259-0) Watts.
—Music. LC 93-20424. (Illus.). 32p. (gr. 2-4). 1993. PLB 12.40 (0-531-14269-8) Watts.
—No-Cook Cooking. LC 93-31801. 1994. write for info. Watts.
—Space. Levy, Ruth, illus. LC 93-24435. 1994. write for info. (0-531-14282-5) Watts.
Morris, Ting, jt. auth. see Morris, Neil.
Morris, Ting, et al. Germany. LC 93-14701. 1993. write for info. (0-531-14265-5) Watts.
—Germany. (Illus.). 32p. (gr. 5-7). 1993. PLB 11.90 (0-531-14296-5) Watts.
Morris, Tony. Papa Panovs Special Day. (ps-3). 1993. pap. 4.99 (0-7459-2261-9) Lion USA.
Morris, Victoria S. More Mobiles: Math Shapes & Forms. (gr. 1-8). 1977. pap. 3.00 (0-914318-03-9) V S Morris.
—String Along with Me: The Math Way. (gr. 4 up). 1976. pap. 3.00 (0-914318-05-5) V S Morris.
Morris, Winifred. The Future of Yen-tzu. Henstra, Friso, illus. LC 90-26989. 32p. (ps-3). 1992. SBE 13.95 (0-689-31501-5, Atheneum Child Bk) Macmillan Child Grp.
—The Jell-O Syndrome. LC 90-1437. 176p. (gr. 7 up). 1990. pap. 3.95 (0-02-044712-4, Collier Young Ad) Macmillan Child Grp.
—What If the Shark Wears Tennis Shoes? Lewin, Betsy, illus. LC 89-38150. 32p. (gr. k-3). 1990. SBE 13.95 (0-689-31587-2, Atheneum Child Bk) Macmillan Child Grp.
Morris-McKinsey, Jill, ed. Religiously Speaking: Plays & Poems for Children's Church. 48p. (Orig.). 1992. pap. 7.98 (1-877588-03-2) Creatively Yours.
Morrison, Ann, jt. ed. see Black, Patti.
Morrison, Bill. Squeeze a Sneeze. Morrison, Bill, illus. LC 76-62503. (gr. k-3). 1987. pap. 3.80 (0-395-44238-9) HM.
Morrison, Blake. The Yellow House. Craig, Helen, illus. 32p. (ps-3). 1987. 12.95 (0-15-299820-9, HB Juv Bks) HarBrace.
Morrison, Dorothy N. Chief Sarah: Sarah Winnemucca's Fight for Indian Rights. (Illus.). 192p. (gr. 4 up). 1990. pap. 7.95 (0-87595-204-6) Oregon Hist.
—Somebody's Horse. 224p. (gr. 4-8). 1987. pap. 2.95 (0-8167-1046-5) Troll Assocs.
—Under a Strong Wind: The Adventures of Jessie Benton Fremont. LC 83-6356. (Illus.). 224p. (gr. 5-9). 1983. SBE 14.95 (0-689-31004-8, Atheneum Child Bk) Macmillan Child Grp.
—Whisper Again. 208p. (gr. 2-9). 1989. pap. 2.95 (0-8167-1307-3) Troll Assocs.
—Whisper Goodbye. 192p. (gr. 2-9). 1988. pap. 2.95 (0-8167-1045-7) Troll Assocs.
Morrison, Ellen E. The Church That Keeps Memories Alive: The Story of Christ Church, Alexandria, Virginia. 2nd, rev. ed. LC 79-114253. (Illus.). 12p. (gr. 6). 1979. saddle-stitched 1.75 (0-9622537-0-7) Morielle Pr.
—Gentle Man of Destiny: A Portrait of Robert E. Lee. 2nd, rev. ed. LC 80-201289. (Illus.). 16p. (gr. 6). 1984. saddle-stitched 1.75 (0-9622537-1-5) Morielle Pr.
—Guardian of the Forest: A History of the Smokey Bear Program. 2nd, rev. ed. LC 89-60719. (Illus.). 144p. (gr. 6). 1989. 12.95 (0-9622537-3-1) Morielle Pr.
—Lady of Legend: The Mystery of the Female Stranger of Gadsby's Tavern. 2nd, rev. ed. LC 87-460803. (Illus.). 16p. (gr. 6). 1986. saddle-stitched 1.75 (0-9622537-2-3) Morielle Pr.
Morrison, Gordon, jt. auth. see Kricher, John.
Morrison, Gordon, jt. auth. see Kricher, John C.
Morrison, Gordon, jt. auth. see Walton, Richard K.
Morrison, Ian. Play the Game: Golf. (Illus.). 80p. (gr. 10-12). 1991. pap. 6.95 (0-7063-6661-1, Pub. by Ward Lock UK) Sterling.
Morrison, Ian A. Egypt. LC 91-7791. (Illus.). 96p. (gr. 6-12). 1991. PLB 19.92 (0-8114-2445-6) Raintree Steck-V.

—Middle East. LC 90-24433. (Illus.). 96p. (gr. 6-12). 1991. PLB 19.92 (0-8114-2440-5) Raintree Steck-V.
Morrison, James, jt. auth. see Morrison, Rob.
Morrison, Jan. A Safe Place: Beyond Sexual Abuse. 180p. (Orig.). 1990. pap. 7.99 (0-87788-747-0) Shaw Pubs.
Morrison, Jaydene, jt. auth. see Clayton, Lawrence.
Morrison, Lillian. At the Crack of the Bat. (Illus.). 1994. pap. write for info. (1-56282-670-0) Hyprn Ppbks.
—The Break Dance Kids Poems of Sport, Motion & Locomotion. LC 84-23396. (Illus.). 64p. (gr. 5 up). 1985. PLB 11.88 (0-688-04554-5) Lothrop.
—Rhythm Road: Poems to Move To. LC 87-4071. (gr. 4 up). 1988. PLB 13.95 (0-688-07098-1) Lothrop.
—Whistling the Morning in New Poems by Lillian Morrison: New Poems. Cook, Joel, illus. 40p. 1992. PLB 16.95 (1-56397-035-X) Boyds Mills Pr.
Morrison, Lillian, ed. At the Crack of the Bat. Cieslawski, Steve, illus. LC 91-28946. 64p. (gr. 2-5). 1992. 14.95 (1-56282-176-8); lib. bdg. 14.89 (1-56282-177-6) Hyprn Child.
Morrison, Marion. The Amazon Rain Forest & Its People. LC 93-20410. 48p. (gr. 5-8). 1993. 15.95 (1-56847-087-8) Thomson Lrning.
—Argentina. (Illus.). 48p. (gr. 4-8). 1989. lib. bdg. 14.98 (0-382-09793-9) Silver Burdett Pr.
—Bolivia. LC 88-10877. (Illus.). 128p. (gr. 5-9). 1988. PLB 26.60 (0-516-02705-0) Childrens.
—Brazil. LC 88-18294. (Illus.). 48p. (gr. 4-8). 1988. PLB 14.98 (0-382-09516-2) Silver Burdett Pr.
—Brazil. LC 93-26100. 1993. write for info. (0-8114-1842-1) Raintree Steck-V.
—Central America. (Illus.). 48p. (gr. 4-8). 1989. lib. bdg. 14.98 (0-382-09824-2) Silver Burdett Pr.
—Central America. LC 92-14537. 96p. (gr. 5-9). 1992. lib. bdg. 19.92 (0-8114-2458-8) Raintree Steck-V.
—Colombia. LC 90-36528. (Illus.). 128p. (gr. 5-9). 1990. PLB 26.60 (0-516-02722-0) Childrens.
—Ecuador, Peru, Bolivia. (Illus.). 96p. (gr. 6-12). 1992. PLB 19.92 (0-8114-2453-7) Raintree Steck-V.
—Indians of the Andes. (Illus.). 48p. (gr. 4-8). 1987. PLB 16.67 (0-86625-260-6); 12.50s.p. (0-685-67605-6) Rourke Corp.
—Italy. LC 88-18317. (Illus.). 48p. (gr. 4-8). 1988. PLB 14.98 (0-382-09517-0) Silver Burdett Pr.
—Paraguay. LC 93-754. (Illus.). 128p. (gr. 5-9). 1993. PLB 26.60 (0-516-02619-4) Childrens.
—Uruguay. LC 91-35144. 128p. (gr. 5-9). 1992. PLB 26. 60 (0-516-02607-0) Childrens.
—Venezuela. LC 88-30493. (Illus.). 128p. (gr. 5-9). 1989. PLB 26.60 (0-516-02711-5) Childrens.
Morrison, Mark, jt. auth. see Herber, Keith.
Morrison, Mark, jt. auth. see Love, Penelope.
Morrison, Penelope, jt. auth. see Morrison, Rob.
Morrison, Rob. X-Rays. Black, Don, illus. LC 93-28983. 1994. 4.25 (0-383-03789-1) SRA Schl Grp.
Morrison, Rob & Morrison, James. Monsters! Just Imagine. Crossett, Warren, illus. LC 93-26927. 1994. 4.25 (0-383-03763-8) SRA Schl Grp.
Morrison, Rob & Morrison, Penelope. Snorkels for Tadpoles. Morrison, Penelope, illus. LC 93-28967. 1994. 4.25 (0-383-03775-1) SRA Schl Grp.
Morrison, Susan D. The Passenger Pigeon. LC 89-31839. (Illus.). 48p. (gr. 5-6). 1989. RSBE 12.95 (0-89686-457-X, Crestwood Hse) Macmillan Child Grp.
Morrison, Toni. Song of Solomon. 352p. (RL 7). 1978. pap. 4.50 (0-451-12933-4, AE2003, Sig) NAL-Dutton.
Morrissette, Mikki. Jennifer Capriati. (Illus.). (gr. 3-7). 1991. pap. 3.95 (0-316-59979-4, Spts Illus Kids) Little.
Morris-Vann, Artie M. My Dad Is Unemployed... But. Orlowski, Dennis, illus. 40p. (Orig.). (ps-5). 1981. pap. 6.50 (0-940370-01-8); counseling activity guide-unemployed families 6.50 (0-685-00149-0) Aid-U Pub.
—My Mom Keeps Hitting Me...But. Orlowski, Dennis, illus. 32p. (Orig.). (ps-5). 1981. pap. 6.50x (0-940370-02-6); counseling activity guide-abused children 6.50 (0-940370-06-9) Aid-U Pub.
—My Parents Are Drug Abusers. 40p. (Orig.). (ps-5). pap. 6.50 (0-317-02490-6) Aid-U Pub.
Morrow, Barbara. Edward's Portrait. Morrow, Barbara, illus. LC 90-45008. 32p. (ps-3). 1991. RSBE 13.95 (0-02-767591-2, Macmillan Child Bk) Macmillan Child Grp.
—Help for Mr. Peale. Morrow, Barbara, illus. LC 89-39273. 32p. (gr. k-3). 1990. RSBE 13.95 (0-02-767590-4, Macmillan Child Bk) Macmillan Child Grp.
Morrow, Catherine. The Jellybean Principal. Wummer, Amy, illus. LC 93-26537. (gr. 3 up). 1994. write for info. (0-679-94743-4); pap. write for info. (0-679-84743-X) Random Bks Yng Read.
Morrow, Honore. On to Oregon. Shenton, Edward, illus. (gr. 5-9). 1946. Repr. of 1926 ed. 16.00 (0-688-21639-0) Morrow Jr Bks.
—On to Oregon. Shenton, Edward, illus. LC 26-16049. 240p. (gr. 4-6). 1991. pap. 4.95 (0-688-10494-0, Pub. by Beech Tree Bks) Morrow.
Morrow, Mary F. Sarah Winnemucca. Viola, Herman, intro. by. (Illus.). 32p. (gr. 3-6). 1990. PLB 17.69 (0-8172-3402-0); pap. 4.95 (0-8114-4095-8) Raintree Steck-V.
Morrow, Roger & Glenn, Monica. Let's Talk. 160p. (Orig.). (gr. 7-12). 1991. pap. 4.95 (0-8474-6625-6) Back to Bible.
Mors, A. & Williams, J. Americans at School. 1991. pap. text ed. 5.25 (0-582-01714-9) Longman.
Morse, J. Thomas, ed. see Gouge, Betty, et al.

Morse, J. Thomas, et al. KidSkills Interpersonal Skill Series, An Island Adventure: Self-Esteem: Being a Friend to Myself. Gouge, Betty, et al, eds. Bleck, Cathie, illus. LC 85-45429. 47p. (gr. 2-3). 1985. PLB 9.95 (0-934275-01-7); bk. & cassette 13.95 (0-934275-14-9) Fam Skills.
—KidSkills Interpersonal Skill Series, A Lasting Friend: Friendship: Making Friends. Gouge, Betty, et al, eds. Bleck, Cathie, illus. LC 85-45422. 45p. (gr. 2-3). 1985. PLB 9.95 (0-934275-06-8); bk. & cassette 13.95 (0-934275-20-3) Fam Skills.
—KidSkills Interpersonal Skill Series, Lair of the Jade Tiger: Friendship: Keeping Friends. Gouge, Betty, et al, eds. Bleck, Cathie, illus. LC 85-81270. 48p. (gr. 2-3). 1986. PLB 9.95 (0-934275-07-6); bk. & cassette 13.95 (0-934275-21-1) Fam Skills.
—KidSkills Interpersonal Skill Series, The Feeling Fun House: Feelings: Dealing with Feelings. Gouge, Betty, et al, eds. Bleck, Cathie, illus. LC 85-45423. 45p. (gr. 2-3). 1985. PLB 9.95 (0-934275-03-3); bk. & cassette 13.95 (0-934275-17-3) Fam Skills.
—KidSkills Interpersonal Skill Series, The Land of Listening: Listening: Getting & Giving Attention. Gouge, Betty, et al, eds. Bleck, Cathie, illus. LC 85-45429. 45p. (gr. 2-3). 1985. PLB 9.95 (0-934275-00-9); bk. & cassette 13.95 (0-934275-15-7) Fam Skills.
Morse, J. Thomas, et al, eds. see Gouge, Betty, et al.
Morse, Joyce. Peter Sinks in the Water. 32p. (Orig.). (gr. 2). 1980. pap. 1.95 (0-8127-0281-6) Review & Herald.
Morse, Mary, ed. see Kincher, Jonni.
Morse, Robert E. Fabulae Latinae. (LAT.). 36p. (Orig.). (gr. 9-12). 1992. pap. 2.50 spiral bdg. (0-939507-42-0, B729) Amer Classical.
Morse, Sarah, jt. auth. see Cross, David.
Morss, Martha. When Dinosaurs Ruled the Earth. (Illus.). 32p. (gr. 1-2). 1991. pap. 2.99 (0-87406-560-7) Willowisp Pr.
Morss, Willard N. & Herren, Janet M. Stolen Princess: A Northwest Indian Legend. Millard, Carolyn, illus. LC 83-82920. 79p. (Orig.). (gr. 4-8). 1983. pap. 8.95 (0-9613025-0-X) J M Herren.
Mortensen, Carl M. Flea & Gang & the Tube Dogs. 1993. 6.95 (0-8062-4437-2) Carlton.
Mortenson, William P. Modern Marketing of Farm Products. 3rd ed. LC 76-14650. (Illus.). (gr. 9-12). 1977. 18.60 (0-8134-1816-X); text ed. 13.95x (0-685-02553-5) Interstate.
Morton, Christine. The Pig That Barked. (Illus.). 32p. (gr. 2-4). 1994. 11.895 (0-340-56814-3, Pub. by Hodder & Stoughton UK); pap. 6.95 (0-340-58659-1, Pub. by Hodder & Stoughton UK) Trafalgar.
Morton, Jane. No Place for Cal. 112p. (Orig.). 1989. pap. 2.75 (0-380-75548-3, Camelot) Avon.
—What Babies Can Do. Arnsteen, Katy K., illus. 12p. (ps). 1993. bds. 2.99 (1-56476-081-2, Victor Books) SP Pubns.
—What Ones Can Do. Arnsteen, Katy K., illus. 12p. (ps). 1993. bds. 2.99 (1-56476-082-0, Victor Books) SP Pubns.
—What Threes Can Do. Arnsteen, Katy K., illus. 12p. (ps). 1993. bds. 2.99 (1-56476-084-7, Victor Books) SP Pubns.
—What Twos Can Do. Arnsteen, Katy K., illus. 12p. (ps). 1993. bds. 2.99 (1-56476-083-9, Victor Books) SP Pubns.
Morton, Leith D. The Fox. Murakami, Yukuo, illus. LC 91-43003. (ENG & JPN.). 32p. (ps-6). 1992. 14.95 (0-87358-534-8) Northland AZ.
Morton, Lone. My First Design Book: Projects to Make with Stencil Shapes. (Illus.). 24p. (gr. 1-4). pap. 4.95 (0-8120-1744-7) Barron.
Morton, Lone, jt. auth. see Bruzzone, Catherine.
Morton, Miriam. The Moon Is like a Silver Sickle: A Celebration of Poetry by Russian Children. LC 72-77768. (Illus.). (gr. 5 up). 1972. 4.95 (0-671-65198-6) S&S Trade.
Morton, Miriam, ed. A Harvest of Russian Children's Literature. Viguers, Ruth H., frwd. by. LC 67-21384. (Illus.). (ps up). 1967. 47.50x (0-520-00886-3); pap. 12.95 (0-520-01745-5, CAL199) U CA Pr.
Morton, Miriam, ed. & tr. see Chukovsky, Kornei.
Mosca, Frank. All American Boys. 116p. (Orig.). (gr. 7-12). 1983. pap. 5.95 (0-932870-44-9) Alyson Pubns.
Moscinski, Sharon. Tracing Our Irish Roots. Butler, Nate & Evans, Beth, illus. LC 93-2070. 48p. 1993. text ed. 12.95 (1-56261-148-8) John Muir.
Moscovich, Ivan. The Magic Cylinder Book: Hidden Pictures to Color & Discover. 1991. pap. 6.95 (0-906212-67-9, Pub. by Tarquin UK) Parkwest Pubns.
—Puzzling Reflections: Test Your Thinking Powers with Mirror-Cubes. 1991. pap. 6.95 (0-906212-72-3, Pub. by Tarquin UK) Parkwest Pubns.
Mosel, Arlene. The Funny Little Woman. Lent, Blair, illus. LC 75-179046. 40p. (ps-4). 1972. 16.00 (0-525-30265-4, 01258-370, DCB); pap. 4.95 (0-525-45036-X, DCB) Dutton Child Bks.
—Funny Little Woman. (Illus.). 1993. pap. 4.99 (0-14-054753-3, Puffin) Puffin Bks.
—Tikki Tikki Tembo. Lent, Blair, illus. LC 68-11839. 32p. (ps-2). 1968. 14.95 (0-8050-0662-1, Bks Young Read) H Holt & Co.
—Tikki Tikki Tembo: Big Book. Lent, Blair, illus. LC 68-11839. 32p. (ps-2). 1993. pap. 18.95 (0-8050-2345-3, Bks Young Read) H Holt & Co.
Mosel, Arlene, retold by. Tikki Tikki Tembo. Lent, Blair, illus. LC 68-11839. 32p. (ps-2). 1989. pap. 5.95 (0-8050-1166-8, Bks Young Read) H Holt & Co.

Moseley, Elizabeth R. Davy Crockett: Hero of the Wild Frontier. Beecham, Thomas, illus. 80p. (gr. 2-6). 1991. Repr. of 1967 ed. lib. bdg. 12.95 (*0-7910-1409-6*) Chelsea Hse.

Moseley, Keith. Dinosaur Skeletons. (ps-3). 1992. 15.00 (*0-440-40597-1*) Dell.

—The Ghosts of Creepy Castle. (gr. 2 up). 1988. 7.95 (*0-448-09290-5*, G&D) Putnam Pub Group.

—It Was a Dark & Stormy Night: A Pop-up Mystery Whodunit. Birkinshaw, Linda, illus. 14p. (gr. 1-4). 1991. 12.95 (*0-8037-1021-6*) Dial Bks Young.

Moseley, Keith & Everitt-Stewart, Andy. The Door under the Stairs. (Illus.). 12p. 1990. 8.95 (*0-448-40044-8*, G&D) Putnam Pub Group.

—Some Bodies in the Attic. (Illus.). 12p. 1990. 8.95 (*0-448-40043-X*, G&D) Putnam Pub Group.

Moseley, Keith, jt. auth. see Katz, Bobbi.

Mosenthal, Basil. Young Sailor: An Introduction to Sailing & the Sea. (Illus.). 48p. (gr. 8 up). 1993. 13.95 (*0-924486-61-9*) Sheridan.

Moser, Adolph. Don't Feed the Monster on Tuesdays! The Children's Self-Esteem Book. Thatch, Nancy R., ed. Melton, David, illus. Moser, Adolph, intro. by. LC 91-12941. (Illus.). 55p. (gr. k-12). 1991. PLB 14.95 (*0-933849-38-9*) Landmark Edns.

Moser, Adolph J. Don't Pop Your Cork on Mondays! The Children's Anti-Stress Book. Pilkey, Dav, illus. LC 88-13912. 48p. (gr. k up). 1988. PLB 14.95 (*0-933849-18-4*) Landmark Edns.

Moser, Barry. Fly! A Brief History of Flight Illustrated. Moser, Barry, illus. LC 92-30960. 56p. (gr. 1 up). 1993. 16.00 (*0-06-022893-8*); PLB 15.89 (*0-06-022894-6*) HarpC Child Bks.

—Tales of Edgar Allan Poe. Glassman, Peter, afterword by. LC 91-3277. (Illus.). 312p. 1991. 19.95 (*0-688-07509-6*) Morrow Jr Bks.

—Tucker Pfeffercorn. LC 92-34340. 1993. 15.95 (*0-316-58542-4*) Little.

Moser, Barry, retold by. & illus. Polly Vaughn: A Traditional British Ballad. 32p. (gr. 2 up). 1992. 15.95 (*0-316-58541-6*) Little.

Moser, Barry, adapted by see Andersen, Hans Christian.

Moser, Barry, illus. & adapted by see Harris, Joel C.

Moser, Cindy & Hummel, Nancy. Dinosaurs Don't Wear Diapers. Parker, Sherry, illus. 16p. (Orig.). (ps). 1990. pap. text ed. 9.95 (*0-9628204-0-7*) Stopher.

Moser, Diane, jt. auth. see Spangenberg, Ray.

Moser, Diane, jt. auth. see Spangenburg, Ray.

Moser, Diane K., jt. auth. see Spangenburg, Ray.

Moser, Erwin. The Crow in the Snow & Other Bedtime Stories. Agee, Joel, tr. from GER. Moser, Erwin, illus. LC 86-10740. 48p. (ps up). 1986. 10.95 (*0-915361-49-3*) Modan-Adama Bks.

—Wilma the Elephant. Agee, Joel, tr. LC 86-1145. (gr. 3-8). 1986. 9.95 (*0-915361-45-0*) Modan-Adama Bks.

Moses, Amy. I Am an Explorer. Hackney, Richard, illus. LC 90-38374. 32p. (ps-2). 1990. PLB 11.93 (*0-516-02029-5*); pap. 2.95 (*0-516-42059-3*) Childrens.

—I Am an Explorer Big Book. (Illus.). 32p. (ps-2). 1991. PLB 30.60 (*0-516-49517-8*) Childrens.

—If I Were an Ant. Dunnington, Tom, illus. LC 92-12947. 32p. (ps-2). 1992. PLB 11.93 (*0-516-02011-0*) Childrens.

—If I Were an Ant. Dunnington, Tom, illus. LC 92-12947. 32p. (ps-2). 1993. pap. 2.95 (*0-516-42011-9*) Childrens.

Moses, Elbert R. Beating the Odds: A Mini Autobiography. Peters, Claude D., intro. by. (Illus.). 50p. (Orig.). 1992. pap. text ed. 3.95 (*0-922484-03-1*) Poligion Pub.

Moses, Will, as told by see Irving, Washington.

Moshzisker, Felix Von see Von Moshzisker, Felix.

Moskin, Marietta D. Margaret Thatcher. (Illus.). 128p. 1990. lib. bdg. 13.98 (*0-671-69632-7*, J Messner); pap. 7.95 (*0-671-69633-5*) S&S Trade.

Moskin, Marietta D., jt. auth. see Worth, Richard.

Moskowitz, Addie A., jt. auth. see Laskin, Pamela L.

Moskowitz, Nachama S. A Bridge to Prayer: The Jewish Worship Workbook: God, Prayer, & the Shema, Vol. 1. (gr. 4-6). 1988. pap. text ed. 6.00 (*0-8074-0417-9*, 123594) UAHC.

—Bridge to Prayer: The Jewish Worship Workbook, Vol. II. (Illus.). 144p. (gr. 6-7). 1989. pap. text ed. 6.00 (*0-8074-0432-2*, 123596) UAHC.

—Games, Games, & More Games for the Jewish Classroom. (Orig.). (gr. 4-6). 1994. pap. 8.00 (*0-8074-0504-3*, 201000) UAHC.

Moskowitz, Stewart. Patchwork Fish Tale. Klimo, Kate, ed. Moskowitz, Stewart, illus. 32p. 1982. 4.95 (*0-671-45327-0*) S&S Trade.

Mosley, Francis. The Dinosaur Eggs. (Illus.). 32p. (ps-2). 1992. pap. 5.95 (*0-8120-4959-4*) Barron.

Mosley, Marilyn C. Dachshund Tails Down the Yukon. Ross, Sueellen, illus. 112p. (Orig.). (gr. 5). 1988. pap. 5.95 (*0-9614850-2-7*) M C Mosley.

—Dachshund Tails North. Mosley, Rob & Lingle, Bea, illus. LC 82-90167. 50p. (Orig.). (gr. 5). 1982. pap. 4.95 (*0-9614850-0-0*) M C Mosley.

—Dachshund Tails up the Inside Passage. LC 84-90672. (Illus.). 95p. (Orig.). (gr. 5). 1984. pap. 4.95 (*0-9614850-1-9*) M C Mosley.

Moss, Anne, jt. auth. see Zimmer-Loew, Helene.

Moss, Carol. Science in Ancient Mesopotamia. Rasof, Henry, ed. LC 88-2649. (Illus.). 72p. (gr. 5-8). 1988. PLB 10.90 (*0-531-10594-6*) Watts.

Moss, David. Colors. 10p. 1989. 4.99 (*0-517-69421-2*) Outlet Bk Co.

—Numbers. 10p. (ps). 1989. 4.99 (*0-517-69423-9*) Outlet Bk Co.

—Shapes. (Illus.). 10p. (ps). 1989. 4.99 (*0-517-69422-0*) Outlet Bk Co.

Moss, Deborah. Lee, the Rabbit with Epilepsy. Schwartz, Carol, illus. LC 88-40249. 32p. (gr. k-4). 1989. PLB 12.95 (*0-933149-32-8*) Woodbine House.

—Shelley, the Hyperactive Turtle. Schwartz, Carol, illus. LC 88-40248. 24p. (gr. k up) 1989. PLB 12.95 (*0-933149-31-X*) Woodbine House.

Moss, Elaine. Polar. LC 89-2115. (Illus.). 32p. (ps up). 1990. 13.95 (*0-688-09176-8*); lib. bdg. 13.88 (*0-688-09177-6*) Greenwillow.

Moss, Graveyard. Graveyard Moss Is Still Alive. 48p. (Orig.). (gr. 9). 1988. pap. 5.00 (*0-945237-00-6*) Morgan Virginia Pub.

Moss, Helen. Silky, the Woods Cat. Arkinstall, Eva, illus. 80p. (gr. 2-4). 1993. 10.95 (*0-89015-867-3*) Eakin-Sunbelt.

Moss, Jeff. Bob & Jack: A Boy & His Yak. Demarest, Chris, illus. LC 92-17458. 64p. (gr. 4 up). 1992. 15.00 (*0-553-08931-5*) Bantam.

—Other Side of the Door. (gr. k up). 1991. 15.00 (*0-553-07259-5*) Bantam.

—The Sesame Street Book of Poetry. McNally, Bruce, illus. LC 90-8994. 48p. (ps-3). 1992. 10.00 (*0-679-80774-8*); PLB 10.99 (*0-679-90774-2*) Random Bks Yng Read.

Moss, Jeffrey. The Butterfly Jar. Demarest, Chris, illus. (ps up) 1989. 15.00 (*0-553-05704-9*) Bantam.

—Sesame Street: ABC Storybook. 1986. pap. 5.95 (*0-394-88303-9*) Random Bks Yng Read.

Moss, Marissa. After-School Monster. LC 90-49416. (Illus.). 32p. (gr. k up) 1991. 13.95 (*0-688-10116-X*); PLB 13.88 (*0-688-10117-8*) Lothrop.

—After-School Monster. 32p. (ps-3). 1993. pap. 4.99 (*0-14-054829-7*, Puffin) Puffin Bks.

—But Not Kate. Donovan, Melanie, ed. Moss, Marissa, illus. LC 90-25751. 32p. (ps-3). 1992. 14.00 (*0-688-10600-5*); PLB 13.93 (*0-688-10601-3*) Lothrop.

—In America. Moss, Marissa, illus. LC 93-26885. 1994. write for info. (*0-525-45152-8*, DCB) Dutton Child Bks.

—Knick Knack Paddywack. Moss, Marissa, illus. 32p. (ps-3). 1992. 13.45 (*0-395-54701-6*) HM.

—Regina's Big Mistake. Moss, Marissa, illus. 32p. (gr. k-3). 1990. 13.45 (*0-395-55330-X*) HM.

—Want to Play? Moss, Marissa, illus. 32p. (ps-3). 1990. 13.45 (*0-395-52022-3*) HM.

—Who Was It? Moss, Marissa, illus. (gr. k-3). 1989. 13.45 (*0-395-49699-3*) HM.

Moss, Miriam. Be Positive. LC 92-26717. (Illus.). 32p. (gr. 6). 1993. RSBE 13.95 (*0-89686-786-2*, Crestwood Hse) Macmillan Child Grp.

—Eat Well. LC 92-28738. (Illus.). 32p. (gr. 6). 1993. RSBE 13.95 (*0-89686-785-4*, Crestwood Hse) Macmillan Child Grp.

—Eggs. Stefoff, Rebecca, ed. Pickett, Robert, photos by. LC 91-18186. (Illus.). 32p. (gr. 3-5). 1991. PLB 15.93 (*1-56074-005-1*) Garrett Ed Corp.

—Fashion Designer. LC 90-48323. (Illus.). 32p. (gr. 5-6). 1991. RSBE 13.95 (*0-89686-610-6*, Crestwood Hse) Macmillan Child Grp.

—Fashion Model. LC 90-15082. (Illus.). 32p. (gr. 5-6). 1991. RSBE 13.95 (*0-89686-609-2*, Crestwood Hse) Macmillan Child Grp.

—Fashion Photographer. LC 90-15059. (Illus.). 32p. (gr. 5-6). 1991. RSBE 13.95 (*0-89686-608-4*, Crestwood Hse) Macmillan Child Grp.

—Forts & Castles. Forsey, Chris, illus. LC 93-11167. 32p. (gr. 4-6). 1993. PLB 19.97 (*0-8114-6157-2*) Raintree Steck-V.

—Keep Fit. LC 92-13916. (Illus.). 32p. (gr. 6). 1993. RSBE 13.95 (*0-89686-788-9*, Crestwood Hse) Macmillan Child Grp.

—Street Fashion. LC 90-48913. (Illus.). 32p. (gr. 5-6). 1991. RSBE 13.95 (*0-89686-611-4*, Crestwood Hse) Macmillan Child Grp.

Moss, Nathaniel. Ron Kovic: Antiwar Activist. LC 93-16373. (Illus.). 1994. 18.95 (*0-7910-2076-2*, Am Art Analog); pap. write for info. (*0-7910-2089-4*, Am Art Analog) Chelsea Hse.

Moss, Pamela, ed. see Rogler, Ingrid.

Moss, Peter & Palmer, Thelma. France. LC 86-9628. (Illus.). 128p. (gr. 5-9). 1986. PLB 26.60 (*0-516-02761-1*) Childrens.

Moss, Thylias. I Want to Be. Pinkney, Jerry, illus. LC 92-28965. 32p. (ps-3). 1993. 14.99 (*0-8037-1286-3*); PLB 14.89 (*0-8037-1287-1*) Dial Bks Young.

Mosse, Richard. Bun-Bun's Brook Trout. Sonstegard, Jeff, ed. Mosse, Richard, illus. 32p. (gr. 6-10). 1992. 9.95 (*0-9630328-1-X*) SDPI.

—Bun-Bun's Garden. Sonstegard, Jeff, ed. (Illus.). 24p. (gr. 6-10). 1993. text ed. 12.95 (*0-9630328-4-4*) SDPI.

Most, B. Happy Holidaysaurus! 1992. 13.95 (*0-15-233386-X*, HB Juv Bks) HarBrace.

—Zoodles. 1992. write for info. (*0-15-299969-8*, HB Juv Bks) HarBrace.

Most, Bernard. Boo! LC 80-18984. (Illus.). 31p. 1980. 7.95 (*0-13-079780-4*) P-H.

—Can You Find It? LC 92-33691. (Illus.). 1993. 13.95 (*0-15-292872-3*) HarBrace.

—The Cow That Went Oink. (Illus.). 32p. (ps-k). 1990. 9.95 (*0-15-220195-5*) HarBrace.

—Cow That Went Oink. 30p. (ps-1). 1991. pap. 19.95 (*0-15-220196-3*, HB Juv Bks) HarBrace.

—Dinosaur Cousins? LC 86-18485. (Illus.). 40p. (ps-3). 1987. 13.95 (*0-15-223497-7*, HB Juv Bks) HarBrace.

—Dinosaur Cousins? 32p. (ps-3). 1990. pap. 4.95 (*0-15-223498-5*, Voyager Bks) HarBrace.

—A Dinosaur Named after Me. D'Andrade, Diane, ed. Most, Bernard, illus. 32p. (ps-3). 1991. 12.95 (*0-15-223494-2*) HarBrace.

—Four & Twenty Dinosaurs. Most, Bernard, illus. LC 89-34472. 40p. (ps-3). 1990. PLB 13.89 (*0-06-024377-5*) HarpC Child Bks.

—How Big Were the Dinosaurs? LC 93-19152. (Illus.). 1994. write for info. (*0-15-236800-0*, HB Juv Bks) HarBrace.

—If the Dinosaurs Came Back. Most, Bernard, illus. LC 77-23911. (ps-2). 1978. 13.95 (*0-15-238020-5*, HB Juv Bks) HarBrace.

—If the Dinosaurs Came Back. Most, Bernard, illus. LC 77-23911. 32p. (ps-2). 1984. pap. 4.95 (*0-15-238021-3*, Voyager Bks) HarBrace.

—If the Dinosaurs Came Back. Most, Bernard, illus. 32p. (ps-2). 1991. pap. 19.95 (*0-15-238022-1*) HarBrace.

—The Littlest Dinosaurs. Most, Bernard, illus. 30p. (ps-3). 1989. 13.95 (*0-15-248125-7*) HarBrace.

—Littlest Dinosaurs. LC 88-30063. (ps-3). 1993. pap. 5.95 (*0-15-248126-5*) HarBrace.

—My Very Own Octopus. D'Andrade, Diane, ed. (Illus.). 32p. (Orig.). (ps-3). 1991. pap. 4.95 (*0-15-256345-8*, Voyager Bks) HarBrace.

—Pets in Trumpets & Other Word-Play Riddles. (ps-3). 1991. 12.95 (*0-15-261210-6*, HB Juv Bks) HarBrace.

—There's an Ant in Anthony. Most, Bernard, illus. LC 79-23089. 32p. (gr. k-3). 1980. PLB 12.88 (*0-688-32226-3*) Morrow Jr Bks.

—There's an Ant in Anthony. LC 79-23089. (Illus.). 32p. (ps up). 1992. pap. 3.95 (*0-688-11513-6*, Mulberry) Morrow.

—Whatever Happened to the Dinosaurs? Most, Bernard, illus. LC 84-3779. 30p. (ps-3). 1984. 13.95 (*0-15-295295-0*, HB Juv Bks) HarBrace.

—Whatever Happened to the Dinosaurs? LC 84-37795. (Illus.). 32p. (Orig.). (ps-3). 1987. pap. 4.95 (*0-15-295296-9*, Voyager Bks) HarBrace.

—Where to Look for a Dinosaur. LC 92-19443. 1993. 12.95 (*0-15-295616-6*, HB Juv Bks) HarBrace.

Mostoller, Dwight E. & Campbell, Margaret F. Ready-to-Use Computer Literacy Activities Kits, Level I. 64p. (gr. 4-6). 1987. student wkbk. 5.95 (*0-317-66399-2*); tchr's. manual 24.95 (*0-13-762022-5*) P-H.

—Ready-to-Use Computer Literacy Activities Kits Level II. 64p. (gr. 7-10). 1987. student wkbk. 5.95 (*0-317-66401-8*); tchr's. manual 24.95 (*0-13-762048-9*) P-H.

Motai, L. & Boone, E. Strategies in Reading: Developing Essential Reading Skills. 112p. 1988. pap. text ed. 10.50 (*0-8013-0515-2*, 78361); tchr's. ed. 14.50 (*0-8013-0516-0*, 78362) Longman.

Mother. Tales of All Times. (Illus.). 138p. (gr. 3-8). 1983. pap. 4.95 (*0-89071-321-9*, Pub. by Sri Aurobindo Ashram IA) Aurobindo Assn.

Mother Goose Staff. Little Red Riding Hood. Facsimile ed. LC 86-11772. (Illus.). 56p. (gr. k-5). 1986. Repr. of 1924 ed. 11.95 (*0-916410-35-8*) A D Bragdon.

Mother Goof. The Sheep Who Was Allergic to Wool. Mother Goof, illus. LC 92-60096. 32p. (gr. 3 up). 1992. 8.95 (*0-9623184-1-8*) Sunflower Hill.

Motomora, Mitchell. Happy Birthday! (Illus.). 32p. (gr. 1-4). 1989. PLB 15.96 (*0-8172-3510-8*); pap. 3.95 (*0-8114-6706-6*) Raintree Steck-V.

—Lazy Jack & the Silent Princess. (Illus.). 32p. (gr. 1-4). 1989. PLB 15.96 (*0-8172-3529-9*); pap. 3.95 (*0-8114-6726-0*) Raintree Steck-V.

—Peach Boy. (Illus.). 32p. (gr. 1-3). 1989. PLB 12.33 (*0-8172-3513-2*) Raintree Steck-V.

—Specs: The True Story of Baseball Player George Toporcer. Barbaresi, Nina, illus. 24p. (ps-2). 1990. 14.60 (*0-8172-3585-X*); PLB 10.95 pkg. of 3 (*0-685-58557-3*) Raintree Steck-V.

Mott, Evelyn C. Balloon Ride. Mott, Evelyn C., illus. 32p. (ps-1). 1991. 13.95 (*0-8027-8124-1*); PLB 14.85 (*0-8027-8126-8*) Walker & Co.

—A Day at the Races with Austin & Kyle Petty. LC 92-10947. 32p. (ps-3). 1993. pap. 2.25 (*0-679-83258-0*) Random Bks Yng Read.

—Steam Train Ride. (Illus.). 32p. (gr. 4-8). 1991. 13.95 (*0-8027-6995-0*); lib. bdg. 14.85 (*0-8027-6996-9*) Walker & Co.

Mott, Michael. Master Entrick. (gr. 3-6). 1986. pap. 2.95 (*0-440-45818-8*, YB) Dell.

Mott-Smith, Geoffrey, jt. ed. see Morehead, Albert H.

Mouillesseaux, Claire & Seger, Doris. Devil-Kings & Cannibals. (Illus.). 52p. (gr. k-4). 1962. pap. text ed. 8.99 (*1-55976-053-2*) CEF Press.

Moulton, Deborah. Children of Time. (gr. 7 up). 1989. 14.95 (*0-8037-0607-3*) Dial Bks Young.

—Summer Girl. LC 91-15790. 128p. (gr. 5-9). 1992. 15.00 (*0-8037-1153-0*) Dial Bks Young.

Moulton, Dwayne. The Mystery of the Pink Waterfall. Headley, Adriane M., illus. LC 80-84116. 192p. (gr. 3-8). 1980. 14.95 (*0-9605236-0-X*) Pandoras Treasures.

Moulton, Gary. Lewis & Clark & the Route to the Pacific. Goetzmann, William H., ed. Collins, Michael, intro. by. (Illus.). 112p. (gr. 5 up). 1991. lib. bdg. 18.95 (*0-7910-1327-8*) Chelsea Hse.

Mound, Laurence. Amazing Insects. LC 92-26735. 32p. (Orig.). (gr. 1-5). 1993. PLB 10.99 (*0-679-93925-3*); pap. 7.99 (*0-679-83925-9*) Knopf Bks Yng Read.

—Insect. Keates, Colin, et al, photos by. LC 89-15603. (Illus.). 64p. (gr. 5 up). 1990. 15.00 (0-679-80441-2); PLB 15.99 (0-679-90441-7) Knopf Bks Yng Read.
—Paper Predators Spider & Fly. (gr. 4-7). 1993. pap. 8.00 (0-440-40766-4) Dell.
Mount, Guy. How Steelhead Lost His Stripes: A Children's Story & Coloring Book. (Illus.). (gr. k-6). 1984. pap. 3.00 (0-9604462-1-4) Sweetlight.
—Lady Ocean: A Love Story for Children. (Illus.). (gr. k-6). 1986. pap. 3.00 (0-9604462-2-2) Sweetlight.
Mountain, Lee. Bobby Bear & Uncle Sam's Riddle. Marilue, illus. 32p. (ps-1). 1988. PLB 11.45 (0-87783-221-8) Oddo.
—El Fuego del Dragon - Dragon Fire. (ENG & SPA., Illus.). 23p. (gr. k-1). 1992. pap. 23.75 (0-89061-720-1) Jamestown Pubs.
—Pelea con Dragon - Dragon Fight. (ENG & SPA., Illus.). 24p. (gr. k-1). 1992. pap. 23.75 (0-89061-719-8) Jamestown Pubs.
—Uncle Sam & the Flag. LC 77-83633. (Illus.). 32p. (gr. 2-3). 1978. PLB 9.95 (0-87783-145-9); pap. 3.94 deluxe ed (0-87783-148-3); cassette o.s.i. 7.94x (0-87783-232-3) Oddo.
Mountain, Lee, et al. The Gingerbread Man. (Illus.). 20p. (gr. k-1). 1993. pap. write for info. (0-89061-740-6) Jamestown Pubs.
—Goldilocks & the Three Bears. (Illus.). 16p. (gr. k-1). 1993. pap. write for info. (0-89061-739-2) Jamestown Pubs.
—The Little Red Hen. (Illus.). 12p. (gr. k-1). 1993. pap. write for info. (0-89061-738-4) Jamestown Pubs.
—Mother Goose Tea Party. (Illus.). 16p. (gr. k-1). 1993. pap. write for info. (0-89061-741-4) Jamestown Pubs.
—The Gingerbread Man. (Illus.). 20p. (gr. k-1). 1991. pap. 18.75 (0-89061-943-3) Jamestown Pubs.
—Goldilocks & the Three Bears. (Illus.). 16p. (gr. k-1). 1991. pap. 18.75 (0-89061-942-5) Jamestown Pubs.
—Jamestown Heritage Reader, Bk. A. (Illus.). 160p. (gr. 1). 1991. 12.10 (0-89061-710-4); pap. 9.10 (0-89061-951-4); tchr's. ed. 22.10 (0-89061-961-1) Jamestown Pubs.
—Jamestown Heritage Reader, Bk. C. 256p. (gr. 3). 1991. 14.95 (0-89061-712-0); pap. 11.95 (0-89061-953-0); tchr's. ed. 24.95 (0-89061-963-8) Jamestown Pubs.
—Jamestown Heritage Reader, Bk. D. 256p. (gr. 4). 1991. 15.75 (0-89061-713-9); pap. 12.75 (0-89061-954-9); tchr's. ed. 25.75 (0-89061-964-6) Jamestown Pubs.
—Jamestown Heritage Reader, Bk. E. 256p. (gr. 5). 1991. 16.50 (0-89061-714-7); pap. 13.50 (0-89061-955-7); tchr's. ed. 26.50 (0-89061-965-4) Jamestown Pubs.
—Jamestown Heritage Reader, Bk. F. 246p. (gr. 6). 1991. 17.20 (0-89061-715-5); pap. 14.20 (0-89061-956-5); tchr's. ed. 27.20 (0-89061-966-2) Jamestown Pubs.
—The Little Red Hen. (Illus.). 12p. (gr. k-1). 1991. pap. 18.75 (0-89061-941-7) Jamestown Pubs.
—Mother Goose Tea Party. (Illus.). 16p. (gr. k-1). 1991. pap. 18.75 (0-89061-944-1) Jamestown Pubs.
Mountford, Christine. Kids Can Type Too! 32p. (gr. 3-7). 1987. pap. 6.95 (0-8120-3780-4) Barron.
Mounishkin, Fran. Walt Disney's One Hundred One Dalmatians: A Counting Book. Hicks, Russell, illus. LC 92-53493. 32p. (ps-k). 1993. pap. 4.95 (1-56282-324-8) Disney Pr.
Mouse, Timothy D., tr. see Tudor, Tasha.
Moutoussamy-Ashe, Jeanne. Daddy & Me. Moutoussamy-Ashe, Jeanne, photos by. LC 93-11513. (Illus.). 40p. (ps-3). 1993. 12.00 (0-679-85096-1); PLB 13.99 (0-679-95096-6) Knopf Bks Yng Read.
Moutran, Julia S. Collecting Bugs & Things: A Science Activity Storybook. (Illus.). 48p. (gr. k up). 1988. pap. 2.95 (0-8431-2226-9) Price Stern.
—The Story of Punxsutawney Phil, "The Fearless Forecaster" Dubnansky, Marsha L., illus. LC 86-82950. 64p. (ps-5). 1987. 14.95 (0-9617819-2-0); pap. 8.95 (0-9617819-0-4); audiocassette 10.95 (0-9617819-3-9) Lit Pubns.
—Will Spring Ever Come to Gobbler's Knob? A Punxsutawney Phil Adventure Story. Sweetland, Marsha L., illus. 64p. (ps-5). 1992. Incl. Phil's Field Guide to Woodland Animals. 15.95 (0-9617819-5-5); Incl. Phil's Field Guide to Woodland Animals. pap. 9.95 (0-9617819-4-7); audiocass. 10.95 (0-685-48131-X) Lit Pubns.
Mouw, Richard J. Reasons Three, Objections to Christianity. (Orig.). (gr. 10-12). 1981. pap. text ed. 5.75 (0-933140-27-4); tchr's. manual, 64p. 5.75 (0-933140-28-2) CRC Pubns.
Mowat, Farley. The Boat That Wouldn't Float. 1984. pap. 3.99 (0-553-27788-X) Bantam.
—The Dog Who Wouldn't Be. (Illus.). (gr. 3-7). 1957. 18.95 (0-316-58636-6, Joy St Bks) Little.
—The Dog Who Wouldn't Be. 1984. pap. 3.99 (0-553-27928-9) Bantam.
—Lost in the Barrens. (Illus.). (gr. 7 up). 1956. 15.95 (0-316-58638-2, Joy St Bks) Little.
—Never Cry Wolf. 1963. 18.95 (0-316-58639-0, Joy St. Bks) Little.
—Owls in the Family. (gr. 4-7). 1985. pap. 3.50 (0-553-15585-7) Bantam.
Mowdy, Sharon, ed. see Van Horn, Brian & Van Horn, Chris.
Mower, Nancy. Tutu Kane & Granpa. Wozniak, Patricia, illus. 32p. (ps). 1989. 7.95 (0-916630-66-8) Pr Pacifica.
Mower, Nancy A. I Visit My Tutu & Grandma. Wozniak, Patricia A., illus. LC 84-3280. (ps). 1984. 7.95 (0-916630-41-2) Pr Pacifica.
Mowrey, Joe, ed. see Hayes, Joe.

Mowry, Jess. Rats in the Trees: Stories. LC 89-27909. 160p. (Orig.). 1990. pap. 8.95 (0-936784-81-4) J Daniel.
Moxley, Sheila, illus. The Christmas Story: A Lift-the-Flap Advent Calendar. LC 92-29520. 24p. 1993. 15.99 (0-8037-1351-7) Dial Bks Young.
Moxon, Julian. How Jet Engines Are Made. LC 85-21049. (Illus.). 32p. (gr. 7 up). 12.95x (0-8160-0037-9) Facts on File.
Moyer, Inez. Responding to Infants. LC 83-71345. 200p. (Orig.). (ps). 1983. pap. 18.95 (0-513-01769-0) Denison.
Moynihan, Daniel P., ed. Japanese Americans. (Illus.). 112p. (gr. 7-12). PLB 16.95 (0-685-44179-2, 047831) Know Unltd.
Mozeleski, Paul M., ed. see Mozeleski, Peter A.
Mozeleski, Peter A. The Rubber Bros AIDS Educational Publications. Mozeleski, Paul M. & Pinatti, Gloria J, eds. (Illus.). (gr. 6-12). 1992. Set of Vol. 1, Nos. 1-4 in English or Spanish. pap. 5.00 (1-880058-00-6); pap. 0.85 ea. Rubbers Bros Comics.
—The Rubbers Bros. Comics, Vol. 1, No. 2. Mozeleski, Paul M. & Pinatti, Gloria J., eds. Pagan, Margarita, tr. (Illus.). 16p. (gr. 6-12). 1991. pap. 0.85 ea. English. Spanish (1-880058-14-6) Rubbers Bros Comics.
—The Rubbers Bros. Comics, Vol. 1, No. 4. Mozeleski, Paul M. & Pinatti, Gloria J., eds. Castalanas, Guadalupe, tr. (Illus.). 16p. (Orig.). (gr. 6-12). 1992. pap. text ed. 0.85 ea. English. Spanish. Rubbers Bros Comics.
—The Rubbers Bros. Comics, Vol. 1, No. 3. Mozeleski, Paul M. & Pinatti, Gloria J., eds. Pagan, Margarita, tr. Wilda, Fred, illus. 16p. (Orig.). (gr. 6-12). 1992. pap. text ed. 0.85 ea. English (1-880058-03-0) Spanish (1-880058-15-4) Rubbers Bros Comics.
—The Rubbers Bros. Comics, Vol. 1, No. 1: Purpose: AIDS Prevention, Condom Awareness, AIDS Education. Mozelski, Paul M. & Pinatti, Gloria J., eds. Pagan, Margarita, tr. (Illus.). 16p. (gr. 6-12). 1990. pap. text ed. 0.85 ea. English. Spanish. Rubbers Bros Comics.
Mozeleski, Peter A. & Mozelski, Paul M. When AIDS Strikes, Vol. 1, No. 2. Pinatti, Gloria J., eds. 8p. 1992. Set of Vol. 1, No. 1 & Vol. 1, No. 2 avail. pap. 0.55 (0-685-60121-8) Rubbers Bros Comics.
Mozelle, Shirley. Bridget Goes to School. Watts, James, illus. LC 92-29871. 1994. 13.00 (0-06-022887-3); PLB 12.89 (0-06-022888-1) HarpC Child Bks.
—Zack's Alligator. Watts, James, illus. LC 88-32069. 64p. (gr. k-3). 1989. 14.00 (0-06-024309-0); PLB 13.89 (0-06-024310-4) HarpC Child Bks.
Mozelski, Paul M., jt. auth. see Mozeleski, Peter A.
Mozelski, Paul M., ed. see Mozeleski, Peter A.
Mrowicki, Linda, ed. see Terdy, Dennis.
Mrs. Moose. Raymond Floyd Goes to Africa: or There Are No Bears in Africa. Christa, illus. 32p. (gr. 1-4). 1993. 14.95 (0-86543-375-5); pap. 6.95 (0-86543-376-3) Africa World.
Muchene, Barbara S. & Muchene, Munene. Suzanne's African Adventure: A Visit to Cucu's Land. Wagner, Shirley L., ed. Jarvis, David, illus. LC 92-75821. 90p. (Orig.). (gr. 3-6). 1993. pap. 9.95 (1-878398-18-0) Blue Note Pubns.
Muchene, Munene, jt. auth. see Muchene, Barbara S.
Muchnik, Michael. The Cuckoo Clock Castle of Shir. LC 79-55560. (Illus.). (ps-3). 1980. 9.95 (0-8197-0476-8) Bloch.
Mudd, Maria M. The Beetle. Smith-Griswold, Wendy, illus. 14p. 1992. 14.95 (1-55670-255-8) Stewart Tabori & Chang.
—The Butterfly. Smith-Griswold, Wendy, illus. 14p. (gr. 2 up). 1991. 12.95 (1-55670-219-1) Stewart Tabori & Chang.
Mueller, A. C. My Good Shepherd Bible Story Book. LC 70-89876. (gr. 3-5). 1969. bds. 15.99 (0-570-03400-0, 56-1126) Concordia.
Mueller, Amelia. Jeremy's Jack-O-Lantern. Barb, Arlene, illus. 24p. (ps). (gr. k-3). 1992. pap. 5.95 (0-945530-06-4) Wordsworth KS.
Mueller, Charles. Almost Adult: Devotions for 9-12 Year Olds. LC 92-27014. 160p. (Orig.). (gr. 4-7). 1993. pap. 6.99 (0-570-04598-3) Concordia.
Mueller, Charles S. & Bardill, Donald R. Thank God, I'm a Teenager. rev. ed. LC 88-6215. (Illus.). 144p. (gr. 7-12). 1988. pap. 8.99 (0-8066-2351-9, 10-6242, Augsburg) Augsburg Fortress.
Mueller, Kate. Antimatter Universe: Young Readers Ser. (gr. 6 up). 1994. pap. 3.50 (0-553-56391-2) Bantam.
Mueller, M. Let's Color Korea: Traditional Games. 24p. (gr. k-3). 1989. oversized 7.95x (0-930878-95-7) Hollym Intl.
Mueller, Marge, jt. auth. see Diamond, Lynnell.
Mueller, Mark, jt. auth. see Vorhees, Duance.
Mueller, Mark, jt. ed. see Vorhees, Duance.
Mueller, Thomas. What a Beautiful Day! (ps-3). 1992. 18.95 (0-87614-739-2) Carolrhoda Bks.
Mueller, Tobin J. Danger, Dinosaurs! A Musical Comedy about the Evolution & Extinction of the Dinosaurs. Heller, Joe, illus. (ps-8). 1990. Audio tape incl. pap. 14.95 (1-56213-003-X) Ctr Stage Prodns.
—Music of the Planet: A Musical Journey about the World & Wonders of Our Solar System. (ps-8). 1990. pap. 14.95 (1-56213-017-X) Ctr Stage Prodns.
—Say Yes! to Life: A Musical Drama about the Dangers Drugs Pose to the Joys of Living. Patros, Ann & Patros, Dan, photos by. (Illus.). (gr. 4-9). 1990. Audio tape incl. pap. 14.95 (1-56213-045-5) Ctr Stage Prodns.

—The Sound of Money: A Musical Adventure about Economics & the Building of Community. Vanderlinden, Kathy, illus. (ps-8). Audio tape incl. pap. 14.95 (1-56213-031-5) Ctr Stage Prodns.
—To Save the Planet: A Musical Fable about the Global Environment; Performed at the United Nations for the Earth Summit. Heller, Joe, illus. 54p. (gr. 4-9). 1991. Audio tape Incl. pap. 14.95 (1-56213-078-1) Ctr Stage Prodns.
Mueller, Tobin J., jt. auth. see Pulaski High School Drama Club Staff.
Mueller, Virginia. A Halloween Mask for Monster. Fay, Ann, ed. Munsinger, Lynn, illus. LC 86-1569. 24p. (ps-1). 1986. 11.95 (0-8075-3134-0) A Whitman.
—A Halloween Mask for Monster. Munsinger, Lynn, illus. (ps-1). 1988. pap. 3.95 (0-14-050879-1, Puffin) Puffin Bks.
—Jacob's Ladder. LC 59-1444. (Illus.). 24p. (ps-4). 1990. pap. 1.89 (0-570-09021-0) Concordia.
—Monster & the Baby. Fay, Ann, ed. Munsinger, Lynn, illus. LC 85-3127. 24p. (ps-1). 1985. PLB 11.95 (0-8075-5253-4) A Whitman.
—Monster & the Baby. Munsinger, Lynn, illus. (ps-1). 1988. pap. 3.95 (0-14-050880-5, Puffin) Puffin Bks.
—Monster Can't Sleep. Fay, Ann, ed. Munsinger, Lynn, illus. LC 86-1568. 24p. (ps-1). 1986. PLB 11.95 (0-8075-5261-5) A Whitman.
—Monster Can't Sleep. Munsinger, Lynn, illus. (ps-1). 1988. pap. 3.95 (0-14-050878-3, Puffin) Puffin Bks.
—Monster Goes to School. Levine, Abby, ed. Munsinger, Lynn, illus. LC 90-29873. 24p. (ps-1). 1991. 11.95 (0-8075-5264-X) A Whitman.
—Monster's Birthday Hiccups. Levine, Abby, ed. Munsinger, Lynn, illus. LC 91-2118. 24p. (ps-1). 1991. 11.95 (0-8075-5267-4) A Whitman.
—A Playhouse for Monster. Fay, Ann, ed. Munsinger, Lynn, illus. LC 85-3144. 24p. (ps-1). 1985. PLB 11.95 (0-8075-6541-5) A Whitman.
—A Playhouse for Monster. Munsinger, Lynn, illus. (ps-1). 1988. pap. 3.95 (0-14-050877-5, Puffin) Puffin Bks.
Mufassir, Sulaiman S. Jesus, a Prophet of Islam. Ahmad, Anis, pref. by. 23p. (Orig.). (gr. 10-12). 1980. pap. 1.25 (0-89259-089-0) Am Trust Pubns.
Mufassir, Sulayman. Biblical Studies from a Muslim Perspective. Obaba, Al I., ed. 49p. (Orig.). 1991. pap. text ed. 2.00 (0-916157-61-X) African Islam Miss Pubns.
Mufson, Susan. Straight Talk about Child Abuse. 1993. pap. 3.99 (0-440-21349-5) Dell.
Mufson, Susan & Kranz, Rachel. Straight Talk about Child Abuse. 128p. 1991. 16.95x (0-8160-2376-X) Facts on File.
—Straight Talk about Date Rape. Ryan, Elizabeth A., ed. 128p. (gr. 9-12). 1993. 16.95x (0-8160-2863-X) Facts on File.
Muhaiyaddeen, M. R. Treasures of the Heart: Sufi Stories for Young Children. Steele, Christine, ed. Balamore, Usha, tr. Deis, Ishaq, et al, illus. 110p. (ps). 1993. 10.00 (0-914390-33-5) Fellowship Pr PA.
Muhaiyaddeen, M. R. Bawa. Come to the Secret Garden: Sufi Tales of Wisdom. LC 83-49210. (Illus.). 450p. 1985. 20.00 (0-914390-27-9) Fellowship Pr PA.
Muhammad, Nimat A. The Mysterious Bag. 1992. 6.95 (0-533-09723-4) Vantage.
Muhammad, S. Ifetayo. The Goals of a Polygamous Woman. 16p. (Orig.). 1987. pap. 0.50 (0-916157-11-3) African Islam Miss Pubns.
—Vitamin A Through Zinc: An Alphabet of Good Health. 16p. (Orig.). 1985. pap. 1.00 (0-916157-13-X) African Islam Miss Pubns.
Muhlberger, Richard, text by. What Makes a Bruegel a Bruegel? (Illus.). 48p. (gr. 5 up). 1993. 9.95 (0-670-85203-1) Viking Child Bks.
—What Makes a Degas a Degas? (Illus.). 48p. (gr. 5 up). 1993. 9.95 (0-670-85205-8) Viking Child Bks.
—What Makes a Monet a Monet? (Illus.). 48p. (gr. 5 up). 1993. 9.95 (0-670-85200-7) Viking Child Bks.
—What Makes a Raphael a Raphael? (Illus.). 48p. (gr. 5 up). 1993. 9.95 (0-670-85204-X) Viking Child Bks.
—What Makes a Rembrandt a Rembrandt? (Illus.). 48p. (gr. 5 up). 1993. 9.95 (0-670-85199-X) Viking Child Bks.
—What Makes a van Gogh a van Gogh? (Illus.). 48p. (gr. 5 up). 1993. 9.95 (0-670-85198-1) Viking Child Bks.
Muillo. Enciclopedia Juvenil, 10 vols. (SPA.). 1500p. 1974. Set. 295.00 (0-8288-6034-3, S50472) Fr & Eur.
Muir, Alison, jt. auth. see Sinclair-House, Elizabeth.
Muir, Jim. Little Girls Have to Sleep. Barwick, Mary, illus. Moore, Robert, contrib. by. LC 92-37456. (Illus.). 1992. 19.50 (1-881320-03-0) Black Belt Pr.
Muir, Michael. Fantastic Journey Through Minds & Machines. (gr. 9-12). 1990. pap. text ed. 19.95 incl. 2 5.25 inch disks (0-924667-74-5) Intl Society Tech Educ.
Muir, Virginia J. The One Year Bible Story Book. Hook, Richard & Hook, Frances, illus. 384p. (gr. 5 up). 1988. 12.99 (0-8423-2631-6) Tyndale.
Muirden, James. Stars & Planets. LC 93-20104. (Illus.). 96p. (gr. 5 up). 1993. 15.95 (1-85697-852-4); pap. 9.95 (1-85697-851-6) Kingfisher Bks.
Mukerji, Dhan G. Gay-Neck: The Story of a Pigeon. Artzybasheff, Boris, illus. LC 68-13419. 192p. (gr. 4 up). 1968. 15.00 (0-525-30400-2, DCB) Dutton Child Bks.
—Gay-Neck, the Story of a Pigeon. 190p. (gr. 4 up). 1927. 15.27 (0-685-66378-7, BR8403) W A T Braille.

—Gay-Neck: The Story of a Pigeon. 190p. 1991. text ed. 15.27 (*1-56956-238-5*) W A T Braille.
Mukherjee, Meenakshi, tr. see Tagore, Rabindranath.
Mulder, Linnea. Sarah & Puffle: A Story for Children about Diabetes. Friar, Joanne H., illus. LC 92-25638. 32p. 1992. 16.95 (*0-945354-41-X*); pap. 6.95 (*0-945354-42-8*) Imagination Pr.
Muldoon, Kathleen M. Princess Pooh. Mathews, Judith, ed. Shute, Linda, illus. LC 88-33978. 32p. (gr. 2-5). 1989. PLB 13.95 (*0-8075-6627-6*) A Whitman.
Muldron, Diane. Walt Disney's Bambi: Count to Five. Langley, Bill & Wakeraw, Diana, illus. (ps-k). 1991. bds. write for info. (*0-307-06114-0*, Golden Pr) Western Pub.
Muldrow, Diane. Dearest Baby. Lundell, Margo & Lanza, Barbara, illus. 14p. (ps). 1993. bds. 3.95 (*0-307-12394-4*, 12394, Golden Pr) Western Pub.
—Walt Disney's Dumbo the Circus Baby. (ps). 1993. 4.95 (*0-307-12397-9*, Golden Pr) Western Pub.
Muldrow, Diane, selected by. My Little Book of Mother Goose Rhymes. Lubin, Leonard, illus. 24p. (ps-k). 1992. pap. write for info. (*0-307-11756-1*, 11756, Pub. by Golden Bks) Western Pub.
Muldrow, Diane, adapted by. Walt Disney's Pinocchio. Marvin, Fred, illus. 28p. (ps). 1992. bds. write for info. (*0-307-12532-7*, 12532, Golden Pr) Western Pub.
Mule, Marty & Remy, Bob. Louisiana Athletes: The Top Twenty. LC 81-4601. (Illus.). 160p. (gr. 6 up). 1981. 11.95 (*0-88289-282-7*) Pelican.
Mulford, Carolyn. Elizabeth Dole: Public Servant. LC 91-25396. (Illus.). 144p. (gr. 6 up). 1992. lib. bdg. 18.95 (*0-89490-331-4*) Enslow Pubs.
Mulford, Philippa G. Everything I Hoped For. 192p. (Orig.). (gr. 8-12). 1990. pap. 2.95 (*0-380-76074-6*, Flare) Avon.
—If It's Not Funny, Why Am I Laughing. LC 82-70321. 144p. (gr. 7 up). 1982. pap. 10.95 (*0-385-28441-1*) Delacorte.
—If It's Not Funny, Why Am I Laughing? LC 82-70321. 144p. (gr. 7 up). 1982. 9.95 (*0-440-03961-4*) Delacorte.
—Perfect Past Tense. 160p. (gr. 5-9). 1994. SBE 14.95 (*0-02-767652-8*, Macmillan Child Bk) Macmillan Child Grp.
—The World Is My Eggshell. LC 85-16198. (gr. 7 up). 1986. pap. 14.95 (*0-385-29432-8*) Delacorte.
—The World Is My Eggshell. (gr. k-12). 1989. pap. 2.95 (*0-440-20243-4*, LFL) Dell.
Mulherin, Jennifer. As You Like It: Shakespeare for Everyone. Thompson, George, illus. LC 90-478. 32p. (gr. 3-7). 1990. PLB 12.95 (*0-87226-339-8*) P Bedrick Bks.
—Hamlet. (Illus.). 32p. (gr. 6-12). 1988. 10.96g (*0-382-09697-5*); 8.22s.p. (*0-685-58840-8*) Silver Burdett Pr.
—Julius Caesar: Shakespeare for Everyone. Payne, Roger, illus. LC 90-476. 32p. (gr. 3-7). 1990. 12.95 (*0-87226-338-X*) P Bedrick Bks.
—Macbeth. Scoble, Lesley, illus. LC 87-37225. 32p. (gr. 6-12). 1988. PLB 10.96 (*0-382-09693-2*) Silver Burdett Pr.
—The Merchant of Venice. (Illus.). 32p. (gr. 6-12). 1988. 10.96g (*0-382-09692-4*) Silver Burdett Pr.
—A Midsummer Night's Dream. Bancroft-Hunt, Norman, illus. LC 87-37229. 32p. (gr. 6-12). 1988. 10. 96g (*0-382-09690-8*) Silver Burdett Pr.
—Romeo & Juliet. Thompson, George, illus. LC 87-37222. 32p. (gr. 6-12). 1988. 10.96 (*0-382-09688-6*) Silver Burdett Pr.
—Twelfth Night. Thompson, George, illus. 32p. (gr. 6-12). 1988. 10.96g (*0-382-09689-4*) Silver Burdett Pr.
Mulherin, Jennifer, retold by see Shakespeare, William.
Mulherin, Jenny, jt. auth. see Barrett, Norman.
Mullen, Michael. Sea Wolves from the North. Dunne, Jeanette, illus. 112p. (gr. 3-9). 1989. 10.95 (*0-905473-94-9*, Pub. by Wolfhound Pr EIRE); pap. 7.95 (*0-86327-023-9*, Pub. by Wolfhound Pr IE) Dufour.
Mullen, Sharon. When Jesus Was Born. LC 86-17558. (ps). 1987. 5.95 (*0-8054-4177-8*) Broadman.
Mulleneux, Jane. Discovering Bats. (Illus.). 48p. (gr. k-6). 1989. PLB 12.40 (*0-531-18277-0*, Pub. by Bookwright Pr) Watts.
Muller, Brenda, jt. auth. see Muller, Carrel.
Muller, Brunhild. Painting with Children. 1988. pap. 8.50 (*0-86315-052-7*, 20240) Gryphon Hse.
Muller, Carrel & Jacques, Ethel M. Dinosaur Discovery. Muller, Carrel, illus. 32p. (gr. 4-6). 1987. wkbk. 3.75 (*0-915785-02-1*) Bonjour Books.
Muller, Carrel & Muller, Brenda. Explore Louisiana. (Illus.). 32p. (gr. 4 up). 1984. 5.50 (*0-915785-00-5*) Bonjour Books.
—Louisiana Indians. Muller, Carrel & Muller, Brenda, illus. 64p. (gr. 3 up). 1985. 7.50 (*0-915785-01-3*) Bonjour Books.
Muller, Cynthia, et al. Apples for Teachers Series, 5 bks. (ps-k). 1988. pap. 10.95 (*0-685-18080-8*) Letters A-Z (*0-8224-0456-7*) Numbers 0-10 (*0-8224-0457-5*) Time (*0-8224-0458-3*) Colors & Shapes (*0-8224-0459-1*) Fearon Teach Aids.
Muller, Gerald. Gentle Giants. LC 87-24537. (Illus.). (gr. 6-9). 1988. pap. 7.95 (*0-8198-3045-3*) St Paul Bks.
Muller, Gerda. Around the Oak. LC 93-32310. (gr. 3 up). 1994. write for info. (*0-525-45239-7*, DCB) Dutton Child Bks.
—The Garden in the City. Muller, Gerda, illus. 40p. (gr. k-5). 1992. 13.50 (*0-525-44697-4*, DCB) Dutton Child Bks.

Muller, Gerda, illus. The Adventures of Tom Thumb. 48p. (gr. 2-6). 1991. 2.99 (*0-517-02418-7*) Outlet Bk Co.
—Jack & the Beanstalk. 48p. (gr. 2-6). 1991. 2.99 (*0-517-02421-7*) Outlet Bk Co.
—The Ugly Duckling. 48p. (gr. 2-6). 1991. 2.99 (*0-517-02422-5*) Outlet Bk Co.
Muller, Jim. One-Two-Three My Computer & Me: A LOGO Funbook for Kids. (gr. 3 up). 1984. (Reston); Commodore 64. pap. 15.95 (*0-8359-5244-4*) P-H.
Muller, Jim, jt. auth. see Bearden, Donna.
Muller, Jorg. The Changing City. Muller, Jorg, illus. LC 76-46646. 8p. (gr. 4 up). 1977. portfolio 18.95 (*0-689-50084-X*, M K McElderry) Macmillan Child Grp.
Muller, Robin. Hickory, Dickory, Dock. Duranceau, Suzanne, illus. LC 92-37588. 32p. (ps-6). 1994. 15.95 (*0-590-47278-X*) Scholastic Inc.
—The Magic Paintbrush. LC 89-51265. (Illus.). 32p. 1990. pap. 13.95 (*0-670-83167-0*) Viking Child Bks.
—The Magic Paintbrush. 1992. pap. 8.50 (*0-385-25373-7*) Doubleday.
Mulligan, Mark. Ghost of Black's Island: The Screenplay. Thomas, Tim & Zorn, Vic, illus. 121p. (Orig.). (gr. 6-8). 1993. pap. 9.95x (*1-882444-01-9*) Blvd Bks FL.
—Manatee: The Screenplay. Thomas, Tim & Zorn, Vic, illus. 121p. (Orig.). (gr. 9-12). 1993. pap. 9.95x (*1-882444-00-0*) Blvd Bks FL.

Mullin. Postcards from Europe Series, 5 bks. Kratoville, B. L., ed. Rarey, D., illus. 48p. (gr. 6-10). 1994. pap. text ed. 15.00 (*0-87879-976-1*) Acad Therapy. Four multi-cultural junior high students & their teacher are treated to a trip to Europe by an anonymous benefactor. The four young travelers never stop learning as facts about the historical & cultural treasures of each country are woven into the fast-paced, exciting stories: THE LONDON CONNECTION, The kids climb on board a double-decker bus to see the sights: Buckingham Palace, Westminster Abbey, the Tower of London, & more. PASSPORT TO PARIS, The history of the Arc de Triomphe & the Eiffel Tower, fine art at the Louvre, & folklore & facts about Notre Dame are all part of this whirlwind tour. RIDDLES IN ROME, The kids roam through the ruins at the Forum & the Coliseum, marvel at Michaelangelo's Pieta & Sistine Chapel at Vatican City, & enjoy gelato. THE CLUES TO MADRID, In Madrid, the kids are dazzled by the Prado Museum, Picasso's Guernica, & the Plaza Mayor, & end up at the bullfights. SECRETS OF THE MATTERHORN, A fondue dinner & a hike to a Swiss hut on the slopes of the Matterhorn are only a part of this entertaining excursion.
Publisher Provided Annotation.

Mullin, Penn. Ghosts of Black Point. Kratoville, Betty L., ed. (Illus.). 64p. (gr. 3-9). 1989. PLB 4.95 (*0-87879-653-3*) High Noon Bks.
—High-Five Series: Whale Summer, Spirits of the Canyon & Trail to Danger, 3 bks. (Orig.). (gr. 6-11). 1991. Set, 64 p. ea. pap. text ed. 12.50 ea. (*0-87879-913-3*); wkbk. 8.50 (*0-87879-924-9*) High Noon Bks.
—Message from Outer Space. Kratoville, Betty L., ed. (Illus.). 64p. (gr. 3-9). 1989. PLB 4.95 (*0-87879-616-9*) High Noon Bks.

—Postcards from America Series: The White House Mystery, High Time in New York, Windy City Whirl, Trouble in the Black Hills, San Francisco Adventure. Kratoville, B. L., ed. Rarey, Damon, illus. (Orig.). (gr. 4-12). 1992. pap. 15.00 (*0-87879-957-5*, 957-5) High Noon Bks.
Lisa, Juan, Amy & Justin could hardly believe that they won the national essay contest that awarded them a three-week trip across America. At each spot they visit, the group manages to encounter an adventure that adds

considerable spice to these high-interest novels. Sites seen include: The White House Mystery-the White House, Washington Monument & the Lincoln Memorial; High Time in New York-the Statue of Liberty & Ellis Island; Windy City Whirl-Sears Tower & Wrigley Field; Trouble in the Black Hills-Mount Rushmore & the site of an ancient Indian reservation; & San Francisco Adventure-Chinatown & Fisherman's Wharf, among other locales. A multicultural mix of central characters (African-American, Mexican-American, Asian-American & Caucasian) is featured. For recreational reading, these books offer a great mix of reading for fun & knowledge at a comfortable (2nd grade) reading level. Because these captivating fictional accounts are filled with interesting facts about each location, the novels also are a great way for classroom teachers to engage student interest in elements of American history for further study. Each adult-size paperback book in the five title series features a full-color & full-page illustrations of the sites.
Publisher Provided Annotation.

Mullin, Virginia L. Chemistry Experiments for Children. Case, Bernard, illus. LC 68-9306. (gr. 3-10). 1968. pap. 2.95 (*0-486-22031-1*) Dover.
Mulliner, Stephen. Play the Game: Croquet. (Illus.). 80p. (gr. 10-12). 1991. pap. 6.95 (*0-7063-6776-6*, Pub. by Ward Lock UK) Sterling.
Mullins, Patricia. Dinosaur Encore. Mullins, Patricia, illus. LC 92-19848. 32p. (ps-2). 1993. 15.00 (*0-06-021069-9*); PLB 14.89 (*0-06-021073-7*) HarpC Child Bks.
—Planet Earth: An Alphabet of Endangered Species. LC 93-8181. (Illus.). 1994. 15.00 (*0-06-023556-X*, HarpT); PLB 14.89 (*0-06-023557-8*, HarpT) HarpC.
Mullins, Patricia, jt. auth. see Vaughan, Marcia.
Mullins, Tom, ed. Irish Stories for Children. 111p. (gr. 5 up). 1993. pap. 11.95 (*1-85635-027-4*, Pub. by Mercier Pr Eire) Dufour.
Mullvihill, Sharon T., ed. see Nystul, Mike & Smith, Lester.
Mulqueen, Jack & Chatton, Ray. God's Mother Is My Mother. Chatton, Ray, illus. 28p. (Orig.). (gr. 1-3). 1978. pap. 2.50 (*0-913382-49-3*, 103-13) Prow Bks-Franciscan.
Mulvihill, Margaret. The French Revolution. Wood, Gerald, illus. LC 88-31564. 32p. (gr. 3-6). 1989. PLB 12.40 (*0-531-17167-1*, Gloucester Pr) Watts.
—Mussolini: And Italian Fascism. (Illus.). 64p. (gr. 5-8). 1990. PLB 12.40 (*0-531-17253-8*) Watts.
—Roman Forts. 1990. PLB 12.40 (*0-531-17201-5*, Gloucester Pr) Watts.
—Viking Longboats. Smith, Tony, illus. LC 89-31565. 32p. (gr. 3-6). 1989. PLB 12.40 (*0-531-17168-X*, Gloucester Pr) Watts.
Mulvihill, Margaret, ed. People in the Past. LC 92-54483. 1993. 12.95 (*1-56458-217-5*) Dorling Kindersley.
Mulvihill, Sharon T., ed. see Dowd, Tom & Kubasik, Chris.
Mulvihill, Sharon T., ed. see Findley, Nigel D.
Mulvihill, Sharon T., ed. see McGregor, Philip.
Mulvihill, Sharon T., ed. see Sargent, Carl.
Mumaw, Catherine & Voran, Marilyn. The Whole Thing. 24p. (gr. 6-11). 1981. pap. 1.50 (*0-8361-1962-2*) Herald Pr.
Mumford, Amy & Danhauer, Karen E. Love Away my Hurt: A Child's Book about Death. 24p. (gr. 1-6). 1983. gift bk. 4.95 (*0-89636-109-8*, Chariot Bks) Cook.
Mumford, Claire, illus. The Nile. 32p. (gr. 3-5). 1983. 7. 95x (*0-86685-447-9*) Intl Bk Ctr.
Mumford, Donald & Mumford, Esther. From Africa to the Arctic: Five Explorers. Lee, Nancy, illus. 48p. (gr. 1-3). 1992. 9.95 (*0-9605670-6-2*) Ananse Pr.
Mumford, Esther, jt. auth. see Mumford, Donald.
Mumford, Esther H. The Man Who Founded a Town. Kim, Jody, illus. 32p. (Orig.). (gr. 2-5). 1990. 8.95 (*0-9605670-2-X*); pap. 4.95 (*0-9605670-3-8*) Ananse Pr.
Mumma, Barbara J. Two to Tango. (gr. 6 up). 1989. pap. 2.95 (*0-449-13466-0*) Fawcett.
Munan, Heidi. Malaysia. LC 89-25464. (Illus.). 128p. (gr. 5-9). 1991. PLB 21.95 (*1-85435-296-2*) Marshall Cavendish.
Munch, Helen, ed. see Haverson, Wayne W. & Haverson, Susan.
Munchhausen, Angelita Von see Von Munchhausen, Angelita.

Mundale, Susan. Mopeds: The Go-Everywhere Bikes. LC 79-165511. (Illus.). 48p. (gr. 4-9). 1979. PLB 14.95 *(0-8225-0428-6)* Lerner Pubns.

Munday, Marianne F. Opportunities in Word Processing Careers. rev. ed. LC 90-50735. 160p. (gr. 7 up). 1991. 13.95 *(0-8442-8164-6,* VGM Career Bks); pap. 10.95 *(0-8442-8165-4,* VGM Career Bks) NTC Pub Grp.

Mundy. Story of Music. (gr. 6-9). 1980. (Usborne-Hayes); PLB 13.96 *(0-88110-031-5)*; pap. 6.95 *(0-86020-443-X)* EDC.

Munger, Anne R. The Not-So-Witchy Witch. (Illus.). 32p. (gr. 1-3). 1991. pap. 2.99 *(0-87406-583-6)* Willowisp Pr.

Munger, Carol V. Billy Groat. Decker, Tim, illus. LC 87-71679. 23p. (Orig.). 1990. pap. 4.00 *(0-916383-45-8)* Aegina Pr.

Mungin, Horace. Sleepy Willie. Orange, Charlotte, ed. LC 90-82440. 128p. (Orig.). (gr. 8-12). 1991. pap. 8.95 *(0-936026-24-3)* R&M Pub Co.

Munro, Alice. Dance of the Happy Shades & Other Stories. 240p. 1990. pap. 7.95 *(0-14-012408-X)* Viking Child Bks.

—Lives of Girls & Women. (RL 10). 1974. pap. 4.95 *(0-451-15352-9,* Sig) NAL-Dutton.

Munro, Bob. Aircraft. Moores, Ian, illus. LC 93-19868. 32p. (gr. 4-6). 1993. PLB 19.97 *(0-8114-6161-0)* Raintree Steck-V.

Munro, David, jt. auth. see Wood, Jenny.

Munro, Roxie. Blimps. Munro, Roxie, illus. LC 88-18138. 32p. (gr. 2-7). 1988. 12.95 *(0-525-44441-6,* DCB) Dutton Child Bks.

—The Inside-Outside Book of London. LC 89-12023. (Illus.). 48p. (ps up). 1989. 13.95 *(0-525-44522-6,* DCB) Dutton Child Bks.

—The Inside-Outside Book of New York City. (Illus.). 48p. (gr. k-3). 1985. 14.95 *(0-396-08513-X,* Putnam) Putnam Pub Group.

—The Inside-Outside Book of Paris. Munro, Roxie, illus. LC 91-29318. 48p. (ps up). 1992. 15.00 *(0-525-44863-2,* DCB) Dutton Child Bks.

—The Inside-Outside Book of Washington, D. C. (Illus.). 48p. 1993. pap. 4.99 *(0-14-054940-4,* Puffin Unicorn) Puffin Bks.

—Inside Outside Book of Washington D.C. Munro, Roxie, illus. LC 86-24267. 48p. (ps up). 1987. 13.95 *(0-525-44298-7,* DCB) Dutton Child Bks.

Munro, Roxie, illus. Architects Make Zigzags: Looking at Architecture from A to Z. Maddex, Diane, contrib. by. LC 84-9679. (Illus.). 64p. (Orig.). (gr. 3 up). 1986. pap. 8.95 *(0-89133-121-2)* Preservation Pr.

—The Great American Landmarks Adventure. Weeks, Kay, created by. LC 92-31806. (Illus.). 1992. 3.25 *(0-16-038003-0)* USGPO.

Munro, Sandra H., jt. auth. see Shelley, Mary V.

Munsch, Robert. Agu, Agu, Agu: Murmel, Murmel, Murmel. Martchenko, Michael, illus. (SPA). 32p. (ps-2). 1991. pap. 5.95 *(1-55037-095-2,* Pub. by Annick CN) Firefly Bks Ltd.

—Angela's Airplane. Martchenko, Michael, illus. 24p. (gr. k-3). 1988. PLB 14.95 *(1-55037-27-8,* Pub. by Annick CN); pap. 4.95 *(1-550370-26-X,* Pub. by Annick CN) Firefly Bks Ltd.

—Angela's Airplane. Martchenko, Michael, illus. 24p. (ps-1). 1986. pap. 0.99 *(0-920236-75-8,* Pub. by Annick CN) Firefly Bks Ltd.

—Angela's Airplane. (CHI., Illus.). 32p. 1993. pap. 5.95 *(1-55037-295-5,* Pub. by Annick CN) Firefly Bks Ltd.

—El Avion de Angela: (Angela's Airplane) Langer, Shirley, tr. Martchenko, Michael, illus. (SPA). 32p. 1991. pap. 5.95 *(1-55037-189-4,* Pub. by Annick CN) Firefly Bks Ltd.

—Boy in the Drawer. Martchenko, Michael, illus. 32p. (gr. k-3). 1982. 12.95 *(0-920236-34-0,* Pub. by Annick CN); pap. 4.95 *(0-920236-36-7,* Pub. by Annick CN) Firefly Bks Ltd.

—The Boy in the Drawer. Martchenko, Michael, illus. 24p. (ps-1). 1987. pap. 0.99 *(0-920303-50-1,* Pub. by Annick CN) Firefly Bks Ltd.

—The Boy in the Drawer. (CHI., Illus.). 32p. 1993. pap. 5.95 *(1-55037-296-3,* Pub. by Annick CN) Firefly Bks Ltd.

—Los Cochinos: (Pigs) Langer, Shirley, tr. Martchenko, Michael, illus. (SPA). 32p. 1991. pap. 5.95 *(1-55037-191-6,* Pub. by Annick CN) Firefly Bks Ltd.

—El Cumpleanos de Mariela: Moira's Birthday. Martchenko, Michael, illus. (SPA). 32p. (ps-1). 1992. pap. 5.95 *(1-55037-269-6,* Pub. by Annick CN) Firefly Bks Ltd.

—The Dark. Suomalainen, Sami, illus. 32p. (gr. k-3). 1984. pap. 4.95 *(0-920236-85-5,* Pub. by Annick CN) Firefly Bks Ltd.

—The Dark. Suomalainen, Sami, illus. 24p. (ps-1). 1987. pap. 0.99 *(0-920303-47-1,* Pub. by Annick CN) Firefly Bks Ltd.

—David's Father. Martchenko, Michael, illus. 32p. (gr. k-3). 1983. PLB 14.95 *(0-920236-62-6,* Pub. by Annick CN); pap. 4.95 *(0-920236-64-2,* Pub. by Annick CN) Firefly Bks Ltd.

—David's Father. Martchenko, Michael, illus. 24p. (Orig.). (ps-2). 1989. pap. 0.99 *(1-55037-011-1,* Pub. by Annick CN) Firefly Bks Ltd.

—David's Father. (CHI., Illus.). 32p. 1993. pap. 5.95 *(1-55037-297-1,* Pub. by Annick CN) Firefly Bks Ltd.

—La Estacion de Bomberos: The Fire Station. Martchenko, Michael, illus. (SPA). 32p. (ps-1). 1992. pap. 5.95 *(1-55037-268-8,* Pub. by Annick CN) Firefly Bks Ltd.

—Fifty Below Zero. Martchenko, Michael, illus. 24p. (gr. k-3). 1986. PLB 14.95 *(0-920236-86-3,* Pub. by Annick CN); pap. 4.95 *(0-920236-91-X,* Pub. by Annick CN) Firefly Bks Ltd.

—Fifty Below Zero. (CHI., Illus.). 32p. 1993. pap. 5.95 *(1-55037-298-X,* Pub. by Annick CN) Firefly Bks Ltd.

—The Fire Station. Martchenko, Michael, illus. 24p. (Orig.). (gr. k-3). 1991. PLB 14.95 *(1-55037-170-3,* Pub. by Annick CN); pap. 4.95 *(1-55037-171-1,* Pub. by Annick CN) Firefly Bks Ltd.

—The Fire Station. Martchenko, Michael, illus. 24p. (ps-1). 1986. pap. 0.99 *(0-920236-77-4,* Pub. by Annick CN) Firefly Bks Ltd.

—Giant. Tibo, Gilles, illus. 32p. (gr. k-3). 1989. PLB 15. 95 *(1-550370-71-5,* Pub. by Annick CN); pap. 4.95 *(1-550370-70-7,* Pub. by Annick CN) Firefly Bks Ltd.

—I Have to Go! Martchenko, Michael, illus. 24p. (gr. k-2). 1987. PLB 14.95 *(0-920303-77-3,* Pub. by Annick CN); pap. 4.95 *(0-920303-74-9,* Pub. by Annick CN) Firefly Bks Ltd.

—I Have to Go! Martchenko, Michael, illus. 24p. (ps-1). 1987. pap. 0.99 *(0-920303-51-X,* Pub. by Annick CN) Firefly Bks Ltd.

—I Have to Go! (CHI., Illus.). 32p. 1993. pap. 5.95 *(1-55037-299-8,* Pub. by Annick CN) Firefly Bks Ltd.

—Jonathan Cleaned Up. Martchenko, Michael, illus. 24p. (ps-1). 1986. pap. 0.99 *(0-920236-21-9,* Pub. by Annick CN) Firefly Bks Ltd.

—Jonathan Cleaned up - Then He Heard a Sound. (CHI., Illus.). 32p. 1993. pap. 5.95 *(1-55037-300-5,* Pub. by Annick CN) Firefly Bks Ltd.

—Jonathan Cleaned-up: Then He Heard a Sound. Martchenko, Michael, illus. 32p. (gr. 4-7). 1981. PLB 14.95 *(0-920236-22-7,* Pub. by Annick CN); pap. 4.95 *(0-920236-20-0,* Pub. by Annick CN) Firefly Bks Ltd.

—Love You Forever. Mcgraw, Sheila, illus. 32p. (gr. 4-10). 1986. 12.95 *(0-920668-36-4)*; pap. 4.95 *(0-920668-37-2)* Firefly Bks Ltd.

—Mateo y la Grua de Medianoche: (Matthew & the Midnight Tow Truck) Langer, Shirley, tr. Martchenko, Michael, illus. (SPA). 32p. 1991. pap. 5.95 *(1-55037-190-8,* Pub. by Annick CN) Firefly Bks Ltd.

—Millicent & the Wind. Duranceau, Suzanne, illus. 32p. (gr. k-3). 1984. PLB 14.95 *(0-920236-98-7,* Pub. by Annick CN); pap. 4.95 *(0-920236-93-6,* Pub. by Annick CN) Firefly Bks Ltd.

—Millicent & the Wind. Duranceau, Suzanne, illus. 24p. (Orig.). (ps-2). 1989. pap. 0.99 *(1-55037-010-3,* Pub. by Annick CN) Firefly Bks Ltd.

—Moira's Birthday. Martchenko, Michael, illus. 32p. (gr. k-3). 1987. 12.95 *(0-920303-85-4,* Pub. by Annick CN); pap. 4.95 *(0-920303-83-8,* Pub. by Annick CN) Firefly Bks Ltd.

—Moira's Birthday. (CHI., Illus.). 32p. 1993. pap. 5.95 *(1-55037-301-3,* Pub. by Annick CN) Firefly Bks Ltd.

—Mortimer. Martchenko, Michael, illus. 24p. (gr. k-3). 1985. PLB 14.95 *(0-920303-12-9,* Pub. by Annick CN); pap. 4.95 *(0-920303-11-0,* Pub. by Annick CN) Firefly Bks Ltd.

—Mortimer. Martchenko, Michael, illus. 24p. (ps-1). 1986. pap. 0.99 *(0-920236-68-5,* Pub. by Annick CN) Firefly Bks Ltd.

—Mortimer. (CHI., Illus.). 32p. 1993. pap. 5.95 *(1-55037-302-1,* Pub. by Annick CN) Firefly Bks Ltd.

—El Muchacho en la Gaveta: The Boy in the Drawer. Martchenko, Michael, illus. (SPA). 32p. (ps-2). 1989. pap. 5.95 *(1-55037-097-9,* Pub. by Annick CN) Firefly Bks Ltd.

—Mud Puddle. Suomalaimen, Sami, illus. 32p. (gr. k-3). 1982. pap. 4.95 *(0-920236-28-6,* Pub. by Annick CN) Firefly Bks Ltd.

—Mud Puddle. Suomalainen, Sami, illus. 24p. (ps-1). 1986. pap. 0.99 *(0-920236-23-5,* Pub. by Annick CN) Firefly Bks Ltd.

—Murmel, Murmel, Murmel. Martchenko, Michael, illus. 32p. (gr. k-3). 1982. PLB 14.95 *(0-920236-29-4,* Pub. by Annick CN); pap. 4.95 *(0-920236-31-6,* Pub. by Annick CN) Firefly Bks Ltd.

—Murmel, Murmel, Murmel. Martchenko, Michael, illus. 24p. (Orig.). (ps-2). 1989. pap. 0.99 *(1-55037-012-X,* Pub. by Annick CN) Firefly Bks Ltd.

—Murmel Murmel Murmel. (CHI., Illus.). 32p. 1993. pap. 5.95 *(1-55037-303-X,* Pub. by Annick CN) Firefly Bks Ltd.

—El Papa de David: David's Father. Martchenko, Michael, illus. (SPA). 32p. (ps-2). 1991. pap. 5.95 *(1-55037-096-0,* Pub. by Annick CN) Firefly Bks Ltd.

—Paper Bag Princess. Martchenko, Michael, illus. 32p. (gr. k-3). 1980. PLB 14.95 *(0-920236-82-0,* Pub. by Annick CN); pap. 4.95 *(0-920236-16-2,* Pub. by Annick CN) Firefly Bks Ltd.

—The Paper Bag Princess. Martchenko, Michael, illus. 24p. (ps-1). 1986. pap. 0.99 *(0-920236-25-1,* Pub. by Annick CN) Firefly Bks Ltd.

—Pigs. Martchenko, Michael, illus. 24p. (gr. k-2). 1989. 12.95 *(1-550370-39-1,* Pub. by Annick CN); pap. 4.95 *(1-550370-38-3,* Pub. by Annick CN) Firefly Bks Ltd.

—Pigs. (CHI., Illus.). 32p. 1993. pap. 5.95 *(1-55037-304-8,* Pub. by Annick CN) Firefly Bks Ltd.

—La Princesa Vestida Con Una Bolsa De Papel: The Paperbag Princess. Martchenko, Michael, illus. (SPA). 32p. (ps-2). 1991. pap. 5.95 *(1-55037-098-7,* Pub. by Annick CN) Firefly Bks Ltd.

—Purple, Green & Yellow. Desputeaux, Helene, illus. 32p. (ps-2). 1992. PLB 14.95 *(1-55037-255-6,* Pub. by Annick Pr); pap. 4.95 *(1-55037-256-4,* Pub. by Annick Pr) Firefly Bks Ltd.

—Siempre Te Querre (Love You Forever) McGraw, Sheila, illus. 32p. 1992. pap. 4.95 *(1-895565-01-4)* Firefly Bks Ltd.

—Something Good. Martchenko, Michael, illus. 24p. (ps-2). 1990. PLB 14.95 *(1-55037-099-5,* Pub. by Annick CN); pap. 4.95 *(1-55037-100-2,* Pub. by Annick CN) Firefly Bks Ltd.

—Something Good. (CHI., Illus.). 32p. 1993. pap. 5.95 *(1-55037-305-6,* Pub. by Annick CN) Firefly Bks Ltd.

—Thomas' Snowsuit. Martchenko, Michael, illus. 24p. (gr. k-3). 1985. PLB 14.95 *(0-920303-32-3,* Pub. by Annick CN); pap. 4.95 *(0-920303-33-1,* Pub. by Annick CN) Firefly Bks Ltd.

—Thomas' Snowsuit. (CHI., Illus.). 32p. 1993. pap. 5.95 *(1-55037-306-4,* Pub. by Annick CN) Firefly Bks Ltd.

—Violet, Vert et Jaune: Purple, Green & Yellow in French. Desputeaux, Helene, illus. 32p. 1992. pap. 5.95 *(1-55037-272-6,* Pub. by Annick Pr) Firefly Bks Ltd.

Munsch, Robert & Kusugak, M. A Promise Is a Promise. Krykorka, Vladyana, illus. 32p. (gr. k-3). 1988. PLB 14.95 *(1-550370-09-X,* Pub. by Annick CN); pap. 4.95 *(1-550370-08-1,* Pub. by Annick CN) Firefly Bks Ltd.

Munsch, Robert & Martchenko, Michael. Show & Tell. (ps-2). 1991. 14.95 *(1-55037-195-9,* Pub. by Annick CN); pap. 4.95 *(1-55037-197-5,* Pub. by Annick CN) Firefly Bks Ltd.

—Wait & See. 24p. 1993. PLB 14.95 *(1-55037-335-8,* Pub. by Annick CN); pap. 4.95 *(1-55037-334-X,* Pub. by Annick CN) Firefly Bks Ltd.

Munsen, Sylvia. Cooking the Norwegian Way. LC 82-259. (Illus.). 48p. (gr. 5 up). 1982. PLB 14.95 *(0-8225-0901-6)* Lerner Pubns.

Munsil, Janet. Dinner at Auntie Rose's. Ritchie, Scot, illus. 24p. (Orig.). (ps-2). 1989. pap. 0.99 *(1-55037-047-2,* Pub. by Annick CN) Firefly Bks Ltd.

—Il N'y a Pas de Fumee - Where There's Smoke. Martchenko, Michael, illus. (ENG & FRE.). 24p. 1993. PLB 14.95 *(1-55037-291-2,* Pub. by Annick CN); French ed. pap. 4.95 *(1-55037-311-0,* Pub. by Annick CN); English ed. pap. 4.95 *(1-55037-290-4,* Pub. by Annick CN) Firefly Bks Ltd.

Munsil, Ritchie. Dinner at Auntie Rose's. (Illus.). 24p. (ps-8). 1984. 12.95 *(0-920236-66-9,* Pub. by Annick CN); pap. 4.95 *(0-920236-63-4,* Pub. by Annick CN) Firefly Bks Ltd.

Munson, Howard R. Science Activities with Simple Things. (gr. 4-8). 1972. pap. 7.95 *(0-8224-6320-2)* Fearon Teach Aids.

—Science Experiences with Everyday Things. (gr. 4-8). 1988. pap. 9.95 *(0-8224-6846-8)* Fearon Teach Aids.

Munson, Sammye. Our Tejano Heroes: Outstanding Mexican-Americans. Eakin, Edwin M., ed. (Illus.). 96p. (gr. 4-6). 1989. 10.95 *(0-89015-691-3,* Pub. by Panda Bks) Eakin-Sunbelt.

Muntean, Michaela. All about Me. Appleby, Ellen, illus. 48p. (ps-3). 1984. 5.95 *(0-8193-1123-5)* Parents.

—Baby Fozzie Goes Camping. Wilson, Ann, illus. 26p. (ps up). 1987. 12.95 *(1-55578-604-9)* Worlds Wonder.

—Bert & the Magic Lamp & Other Good-Night Stories. (Illus.). 24p. (ps-1). 1989. write for info. *(0-307-12073-2,* Pub. by Golden Bks) Western Pub.

—Bicycle Bear. Cushman, Doug, illus. LC 83-3980. 48p. (ps-3). 1983. 5.95 *(0-8193-1103-0)*; PLB 5.95 *(0-8193-1104-9)* Parents.

—Bicycle Bear. Cushman, Doug, illus. LC 93-15458. 1994. PLB 13.27 *(0-8368-0963-7)* Gareth Stevens Inc.

—Bicycle Bear Rides Again. Cushman, Doug, illus. LC 89-27823. 48p. (ps-3). 1989. 5.95 *(0-8193-1193-6)* Parents.

—Bicycle Bear Rides Again. Cushman, Doug, illus. LC 93-15470. 1993. write for info. *(0-8368-0964-5)* Gareth Stevens Inc.

—Cookie Soup & Other Good-night Stories. (ps-3). 1990. write for info. *(0-307-12114-3)* Western Pub.

—A Garden for Miss Mouse. Santoro, Christopher, illus. LC 82-2135. 48p. (ps-3). 1982. 5.95 *(0-8193-1083-2)*; lib. bdg. 5.95 *(0-8193-1084-0)* Parents.

—Grouchs Christmas. (ps). 1990. write for info. *(0-307-12049-X)* Western Pub.

—I Want to Be a Veterinarian. Cooke, Tom, illus. 24p. (ps-k). 1992. pap. write for info. *(0-307-13116-5,* 13116, Golden Pr) Western Pub.

—I Want to Be President. Brannon, Tom, illus. 24p. (ps-k). 1993. pap. 1.95 *(0-307-13118-1,* 13118, Golden Pr) Western Pub.

—Imagine: Ernie Is King. (ps-3). 1993. pap. 2.25 *(0-307-13123-8,* Golden Pr) Western Pub.

—Imagine: Grover's Magic Carpet Ride. (ps-3). 1993. pap. 2.25 *(0-307-13120-3,* Golden Pr) Western Pub.

—The Little Engine That Could & the Big Snow. Graham, Florence, illus. 32p. (ps-2). 1988. pap. 1.95 *(0-448-19095-8,* Platt & Munk Pubs) Putnam Pub Group.

—The Old Man & the Afternoon Cat. Weissman, Bari, illus. LC 81-11047. 48p. (ps-3). 1982. 5.95 *(0-8193-1071-9)*; PLB 5.95 *(0-8193-1072-7)* Parents.

—Sesame Street: Ernie & His Merry Monsters & Other Good-Night Stories. Leigh, Tom, illus. 34p. (ps-3). 1992. write for info. *(0-307-12336-7,* 12336, Golden Pr) Western Pub.

—The Very Bumpy Bus Ride. Wiseman, Bernard, illus. LC 81-16905. 48p. (ps-3). 1982. 5.95 *(0-8193-1079-4)*; 5.95 *(0-8193-1080-8)* Parents.

—The Very Bumpy Bus Ride. Wiseman, Bernard, illus. 48p. (gr. 3-7). 1990. pap. 2.95 *(0-448-04337-8,* G&D) Putnam Pub Group.

—The Very Bumpy Bus Ride. Wiseman, Bernard, illus. LC 93-13042. 1993. PLB 13.27 (0-8368-0980-7) Gareth Stevens Inc.
—We're Counting on You, Grover! Ewers, Joe, illus. (ps-k). 1991. write for info. (0-307-12050-3, Golden Pr) Western Pub.
—What's in Oscar's Trash Can? And Other Good-Night Stories. Cooke, Tom, illus. (ps-1). 1991. 3.25 (0-307-12342-1, Golden Pr) Western Pub.
Murad, Maria B. The Magic Words. Margodo, Dick, illus. 40p. (ps-3). 1984. 5.95 (0-910313-17-2) Parker Bros.
Murail, Marie-Aude. Mystere. Bloch, Serge, illus. (FRE.). 64p. (gr. 1-5). 1987. pap. 8.95 (2-07-031217-8) Schoenhof.
—Uncle Giorgio. (Illus.). 48p. (gr. k-4). 1990. 12.75 (0-89565-809-7); 8.95s.p. (0-685-55105-9) Childs World.
Murakami, Haruki. A Wild Sheep Chase: A Novel. Birnbaum, Alfred, tr. 272p. 1989. 18.95 (0-87011-905-2) Kodansha.
Muramaru, N. Japanese Folktales. (Illus.). 160p. (gr. 4-9). 1993. pap. 11.95 (4-89684-228-6, Pub. by Yohan Pubns JP) Weatherhill.
Murata, Michinori. Water & Light: Looking Through Lenses. Sekido, Isamu, illus. LC 92-19969. 1993. 17.50 (0-8225-2904-1) Lerner Pubns.
Muratore, Carol. Scooter Goes to the Hospital. (Illus., Orig.). 1992. pap. text ed. 3.75 (0-9628084-2-3) Hlth Mngmnt Pubns.
Murchie, Guy. Music of the Spheres: The Material Universe from Atom to Quasar, Simply Explained, 2 Vols. rev. ed. (Illus.). (gr. 7-12). Vol. 1. pap. 8.95 (0-486-21809-0); Vol. 2. pap. 6.95 (0-486-21810-4) Dover.
Murdocca, Sal. Christmas Bear. (gr. k-3). 1990. (Little Simon). pap. 3.95 (0-671-70849-X) S&S Trade.
Murdocca, Sal, illus. & designed by see Bendick, Jeanne & Bendick, Robert.
Murdoch, David H. Cowboy. Brightling, Geoff, illus. LC 93-12768. 64p. (gr. 5 up). 1993. 15.00 (0-679-84014-1); PLB 15.99 (0-679-94014-6) Knopf Bks Yng Read.
Murdoch, Kathleen, jt. auth. see Ray, Stephen.
Murdock, Hy. Jack & the Beanstalk. 1989. pap. 3.95 (0-7214-5061-X) Ladybird Bks.
Murdock, M. S. Armageddon off Vesta. LC 88-51716. (Illus.). 288p. (Orig.). 1989. pap. 3.95 (0-88038-761-0) TSR Inc.
—Hammer of Mars. LC 88-51715. (Illus.). 288p. (Orig.). 1989. pap. 3.95 (0-88038-751-3) TSR Inc.
—Rebellion 2456. LC 88-51714. 288p. (Orig.). 1989. pap. 3.95 (0-88038-728-9) TSR Inc.
Murdock, M. S., et al. Arrival. LC 88-50404. 320p. (Orig.). 1988. pap. 3.95 (0-88038-582-0) TSR Inc.
Murdock, Michael D. The God-Book. Loy, Joy A., ed. 250p. (Orig.). 1991. pap. text ed. 4.95 (1-56394-004-3) Wisdom Intl.
—The Teenager's One Minute Bible. Loy, Joy A., ed. 365p. (Orig.). 1991. pap. text ed. 5.95 (1-56394-003-1) Wisdom Intl.
Murdock, Tony & Stuart, Nik. Gymnastics: A Practical Guide for Beginners. LC 89-8870. (Illus.). 112p. (gr. 7-12). 1989. PLB 14.90 (0-531-10770-1) Watts.
Murez, Diane. A Day on the Boat with Captain Betty. Murez, Steve, illus. LC 92-11428. 32p. (gr. 2 up). 1993. RSBE 14.95 (0-02-767430-4, Macmillan Child Bk) Macmillan Child Grp.
Murphy see Sohn, David A.
Murphy, Barbara, jt. auth. see Hoover, Rosalie.
Murphy, Barbara B. Annie At the Ranch. (gr. 4-7). 1991. pap. 2.99 (0-553-15960-7) Bantam.
—Eagles in Their Flight. LC 93-11438. 1994. write for info. (0-385-32035-3) Delacorte.
—One Another. LC 91-15651. 160p. (gr. 7 up). 1991. pap. 3.95 (0-02-042015-3, Collier Young Ad) Macmillan Child Grp.
Murphy, Bryan. Experiment with Air. 32p. (gr. 2-5). 1991. PLB 17.50 (0-8225-2452-X) Lerner Pubns.
—Experiment with Light. 32p. (gr. 2-5). 1991. PLB 17.50 (0-8225-2454-6) Lerner Pubns.
—Experiment with Movement. 32p. (gr. 2-5). 1991. PLB 17.50 (0-8225-2451-1) Lerner Pubns.
—Experiment with Water. 32p. (gr. 2-5). 1991. PLB 17.50 (0-8225-2453-8) Lerner Pubns.
Murphy, Campbell. David & I Talk to God. (gr. 3-7). 1983. pap. 2.95 each (0-686-45018-3) Cook.
Murphy, Carol. Christopher Columbus. Reese, Bob, illus. (gr. k-6). 1991. 11.95 (0-89868-228-2) ARO Pub.
—Christopher Columbus. Reese, Bob, illus. (gr. k-6). 1991. pap. 20.00 (0-89868-229-0) ARO Pub.
—Martin Luther King, Jr. Reese, Bob, illus. (gr. k-6). 1991. 11.95 (0-89868-230-4) ARO Pub.
—Martin Luther King, Jr. Reese, Bob, illus. (gr. k-6). 1991. pap. 20.00 (0-89868-231-2) ARO Pub.
Murphy, Catherine F. Alice Dodd & the Spirit of Truth. LC 92-32039. 176p. (gr. 3-7). 1993. SBE 14.95 (0-02-767702-8, Macmillan Child Bk) Macmillan Child Grp.
—Songs in the Silence. LC 93-26947. 192p. (gr. 3-7). 1994. SBE 14.95 (0-02-767730-3, Macmillan Child Bk) Macmillan Child Grp.
Murphy, Cecil see Carson, Ben.
Murphy, Chuck. My First Book of Colors. (ps). 1991. 5.95 (0-590-44481-6) Scholastic Inc.
—My First Book of Counting. (ps). 1991. 5.95 (0-590-44471-9) Scholastic Inc.

—My First Book of Shapes. (Illus.). 12p. 1993. 6.95 (0-590-46303-9) Scholastic Inc.
—My First Book of the Alphabet. (Illus.). 12p. 1993. 6.95 (0-590-46304-7) Scholastic Inc.
Murphy, Claire R. Friendship Across Arctic Waters: Alaskan Cub Scouts Visit Their Soviet Neighbors. Mason, Charles, photos by. (Illus.). 48p. (gr. 3-8). 1991. 15.95 (0-525-67348-2, Lodestar Bks) Dutton Child Bks.
—To the Summit. 160p. (gr. 7 up). 1992. 15.00 (0-525-67383-0, Lodestar Bks) Dutton Child Bks.
Murphy, Claire R., retold by. The Prince & the Salmon People. Pasco, Duane, illus. LC 92-38394. 48p. 1993. 19.95 (0-8478-1662-1) Rizzoli Intl.
Murphy, Corinne. Exploring the Hand Arts: For Juniors, Cadettes, Seniors, & Leaders. 112p. (gr. 4-12). 1955. pap. 5.00 (0-88441-140-0, 19-994) Girl Scouts USA.
Murphy, Daniel O. Salinas Pueblo Missions National Monument. Priehs, T. J. & Foreman, Ronald, eds. LC 91-60459. 16p. 1992. pap. write for info. (0-911408-98-3) SW Pks Mnmts.
Murphy, Deborah A., et al. Exceptions: A Handbook for Teachers of Mainstreamed Students. (gr. k-6). 1988. tchr's. ed. 11.95 (0-944584-06-3) Sopris.
Murphy, Elspeth C. Barney Wigglesworth & the Birthday Surprise. Yakovetic, illus. LC 88-4346. 32p. (ps-2). 1988. 7.99 (1-55513-696-6, Chariot Bks) Cook.
—Barney Wigglesworth & the Church Flood. Yakovetic, illus. LC 88-5008. 32p. (ps-2). 1988. 7.99 (1-55513-685-0, Chariot Bks) Cook.
—Barney Wigglesworth & the Party That Almost Wasn't. Yakovetic, illus. LC 88-4342. 32p. (ps-2). 1988. 7.99 (1-55513-684-2, Chariot Bks) Cook.
—Barney Wigglesworth & the Smallest Christmas Pageant. Yakovetic, illus. LC 88-5009. 32p. (ps-2). 1989. 7.99 (1-55513-686-9, Chariot Bks) Cook.
—Becky Garcia. Kenyon, Tony, illus. LC 86-8877. 108p. (gr. 3-7). 1986. pap. 4.49 (1-55513-029-1, Chariot Bks) Cook.
—Curtis Anderson. Kenyon, Tony, illus. LC 86-8819. 120p. (gr. 3-7). 1986. pap. 4.49 (1-55513-027-5, Chariot Bks) Cook.
—Danny Petrowski. LC 85-16568. 120p. (Orig.). (gr. 3-7). 1985. pap. 4.49 (0-89191-730-6, Chariot Bks) Cook.
—Do You See Me God? Duca, Bill, illus. 32p. (ps). 1989. text ed. 7.95 (1-55513-457-2, Chariot Bks) Cook.
—Everybody, Shout Hallelujah! Nelson, Jane, illus. LC 81-65525. 24p. (ps-2). 1981. pap. 2.99 (0-89191-369-6, 53694, Chariot Bks) Cook.
—God You Fill Us up with Joy. LC 86-4140. (Illus.). (ps-2). 1987. pap. 2.99 (1-55513-037-2, Chariot Bks) Cook.
—I'm Listening, God. Nelson, Jane, illus. LC 81-71813. (ps-2). 1983. misc. format 2.99 (0-89191-583-4, Chariot Bks) Cook.
—It's My Birthday, God: Psalm 90. Nelson, Jane, illus. (ps-2). 1983. misc. format 2.99 (0-89191-580-X, Chariot Bks) Cook.
—Julie Chang. 107p. (gr. 3-7). 1986. 4.49 (0-89191-720-9, 57208, Chariot Bks) Cook.
—Kids Can Be Wise Too. LC 87-35539. 24p. (ps-2). 1988. pap. 3.79 (1-55513-893-4, Chariot Bks) Cook.
—The Littlest One. LC 87-7106. (ps). 1987. 3.95 (1-55513-268-5, Chariot Bks) Cook.
—Make Way for the King: Psalm 145 & 24. Nelson, Jane, illus. (ps-2). 1983. 2.99 (0-89191-581-8, Chariot Bks) Cook.
—Mary Jo Bennett. 107p. (Orig.). (gr. 3-7). 1985. pap. 4.49 (0-89191-711-X, 57117, Chariot Bks) Cook.
—The Mystery of the Carousel Horse. LC 87-16722. (gr. 3-7). 1988. pap. 2.79 (1-55513-163-8, Chariot Bks) Cook.
—The Mystery of the Clumsy Juggler. 48p. (gr. 3-7). 1991. pap. 2.79 (1-55513-897-7, 38976, Chariot Bks) Cook.
—The Mystery of the Double Trouble. LC 87-26461. (gr. 3-7). 1988. pap. 2.79 (1-55513-545-5, Chariot Bks) Cook.
—The Mystery of the Gravestone Riddle. LC 87-16721. (gr. 3-7). 1988. pap. 2.79 (1-55513-800-4, Chariot Bks) Cook.
—The Mystery of the Hidden Egg. 48p. (gr. 3-7). 1991. pap. 2.79 (1-55513-915-9, 39156, Chariot Bks) Cook.
—The Mystery of the Laughing Cat. LC 87-16719. (gr. 3-7). 1988. pap. 2.79 (1-55513-649-4, Chariot Bks) Cook.
—Mystery of the Messed-Up Wedding. LC 87-16720. (gr. 3-7). 1988. pap. 2.79 (1-55513-687-7, Chariot Bks) Cook.
—The Mystery of the Second Map. LC 87-24919. (gr. 3-7). 1988. pap. 2.79 (1-55513-526-9, Chariot Bks) Cook.
—The Mystery of the Silent Idol. LC 87-24285. (gr. 3-7). 1988. pap. 2.79 (1-55513-527-7, Chariot Bks) Cook.
—The Mystery of the Silver Dolphin. LC 87-24285. (gr. 3-7). 1988. pap. 2.79 (1-55513-515-3, Chariot Bks) Cook.
—Mystery of the Tattletale Parrot. LC 87-26460. (gr. 3-7). 1988. pap. 2.79 (1-55513-528-5, Chariot Bks) Cook.
—The Mystery of the Vanishing Present. LC 87-20852. (gr. 3-7). 1988. pap. 2.79 (1-55513-364-9, Chariot Bks) Cook.
—Pug McConnell. LC 85-26922. 107p. (gr. 3-7). 1986. 4.49 (0-89191-728-4, Chariot Bks) Cook.

—Some Words Help, Some Words Hurt. LC 87-31474. 24p. (ps-1). 1988. pap. 3.79 (1-55513-164-6, Chariot Bks) Cook.
—Sometimes Everything Feels Just Right. (Illus.). (ps-2). 1987. pap. 2.99 (1-55513-038-0, Chariot Bks) Cook.
—Sometimes I Get Lonely. Nelson, Jane, illus. LC 80-70251. 24p. (ps-2). 1981. pap. 2.99 (0-89191-367-X, 53678, Chariot Bks) Cook.
—Sometimes I Get Mad. (ps-2). 1981. pap. 2.99 (0-89191-493-5, 54932, Chariot Bks) Cook.
—Sometimes I Get Scared. Nelson, Jane E., illus. (ps-2). 1980. pap. 2.99 (0-89191-275-4, 52753, Chariot Bks) Cook.
—Sometimes I Have to Cry. Nelson, Jane, illus. (ps-2). 1981. pap. 2.99 (0-89191-494-3, 54940, Chariot Bks) Cook.
—Sometimes I Need to Be Hugged. (Illus.). (ps-2). 1981. pap. 2.99 (0-89191-492-7, 54924, Chariot Bks) Cook.
—Sometimes I Think "What If?" LC 86-2273. (Illus.). (ps-2). 1987. pap. 2.99 (1-55513-036-4, Chariot Bks) Cook.
—Sometimes I'm Good, Sometimes I'm Bad. Nelson, Jane, illus. 24p. (ps-2). 1981. pap. 2.99 (0-89191-368-8, 53686, Chariot Bks) Cook.
—That's Not Fair. LC 87-35458. 24p. (ps-1). 1988. pap. 3.79 (1-55513-354-1, Chariot Bks) Cook.
—Too Many Bunnies. LC 87-70609. (ps). 1987. pap. 2.99 (1-55513-247-2, Chariot Bks) Cook.
—What Can I Say to You, God? Nelson, Jane E., illus. (ps-2). 1980. pap. 2.99 (0-89191-276-2, Chariot Bks) Cook.
—Where Are You, God? Nelson, Jane E., illus. (ps-2). 1980. pap. 2.99 (0-89191-274-6, Chariot Bks) Cook.
—Where's My Lamb. LC 87-70608. (ps). 1987. 2.99 (1-55513-248-0, Chariot Bks) Cook.
—Who Lost a Mitten. LC 87-70615. (ps). 1987. 2.99 (1-55513-578-1, Chariot Bks) Cook.
Murphy, Emmy L. Who Made God. (ps-3). 1978. 2.50 (0-915374-07-2, 07-2) Rapids Christian.
Murphy, Fred. Radio-Controlled Action Cars. (Illus.). 24p. (Orig.). 1990. pap. 2.50 (0-942025-87-3) Kidsbks.
Murphy, J. Feelings. (Illus.). 24p. (ps-8). 1985. pap. 4.95 (0-88753-129-6, Pub. by Black Moss Pr CN) Firefly Bks Ltd.
Murphy, Jack, jt. auth. see Murphy, Wendy.
Murphy, Jane. My Pet Tyrannosaurus. LC 88-81468. (Illus.). 32p. (Orig.). (ps-2). 1988. pap. 8.95 (0-937124-17-6) Kimbo Educ.
Murphy, Jill. Bad Spell for the Worst Witch. (gr. 4-7). 1991. pap. 3.95 (0-14-031446-6, Puffin) Puffin Bks.
—A Bad Spell for the Worst Witch. large type ed. Murphy, Jill, illus. 1993. 15.95 (0-7451-1809-7, Galaxy Child Lrg Print) Chivers N Amer.
—Five Minutes' Peace: Miniature Edition. Murphy, Jill, illus. 32p. (ps-3). 1989. 4.95 (0-399-21938-2, Putnam) Putnam Pub Group.
—Jeffrey Strangeways. Murphy, Jill, illus. LC 91-71844. 144p. (gr. 3-6). 1992. 14.95 (1-56402-018-5) Candlewick Pr.
—Jeffrey Strangeways. LC 91-71844. (gr. 4-7). 1994. pap. 4.50 (1-56402-283-8) Candlewick Pr.
—Peace at Last. Murphy, Jill, illus. LC 80-66743. 32p. (ps-2). 1980. 13.95 (0-8037-6757-9) Dial Bks Young.
—Peace at Last. Murphy, Jill, illus. LC 80-66743. 32p. (ps-2). 1982. pap. 3.95 (0-8037-6964-4) Dial Bks Young.
—A Quiet Night In. LC 93-875. Date not set. write for info. (1-56402-248-X) Candlewick Pr.
—What Next, Baby Bear! Murphy, Jill, illus. LC 83-7316. 32p. (ps-2). 1984. 13.95 (0-8037-0027-X) Dial Bks Young.
—What Next, Baby Bear! Murphy, Jill, illus. LC 83-7316. 32p. (ps-2). 1986. pap. 3.95 (0-685-37306-1) Dial Bks Young.
—What Next, Baby Bear! LC 83-7316. (Illus.). 32p. (ps-3). 1992. pap. 17.99 giant size (0-14-054539-5, Puffin Pied Piper) Puffin Bks.
—The Worst Witch. (Illus.). 80p. (gr. 3-7). 1982. pap. 2.50 (0-380-60665-8, Camelot) Avon.
—Worst Witch. (gr. 4-7). 1991. pap. 3.99 (0-14-031108-4, Puffin) Puffin Bks.
—The Worst Witch. large type ed. Murphy, Jill, illus. 96p. 1992. 13.95 (0-7451-1549-7, Galaxy Child Lrg Print) Chivers N Amer.
—The Worst Witch Strikes Again. 80p. (gr. 3-7). 1982. pap. 2.50 (0-380-60673-9, Camelot) Avon.
—Worst Witch Strikes Again. (gr. 4-7). 1991. pap. 3.99 (0-14-031348-6, Puffin) Puffin Bks.
—The Worst Witch Strikes Again. large type ed. Murphy, Jill, illus. 96p. 1993. 13.95 (0-7451-1672-8, Galaxy Child Lrg Print) Chivers N Amer.
Murphy, Jim. Across America on an Emigrant Train. LC 92-38650. 1993. 16.95 (0-395-63390-7, Clarion Bks) HM.
—Backyard Bear. Greene, Jeffrey, illus. LC 92-15479. 32p. (gr. k-3). 1993. 15.95 (0-590-44375-5) Scholastic Inc.
—The Boys' War: Confederate & Union Soldiers Talk about the Civil War. (Illus.). 128p. (gr. 4-9). 1990. 15.95 (0-89919-893-7, Clarion Bks) HM.
—The Boys' War: Confederate & Union Soldiers Talk about the Civil War. (Illus.). 128p. (gr. 4-7). 1993. pap. 7.70 (0-395-66412-8, Clarion Bks) HM.
—The Call of the Wolves. Weatherby, Mark A., illus. 32p. (gr. k-3). 1989. pap. 13.95 (0-590-41941-2) Scholastic Inc.
—Dinosaur for a Day. (Illus.). 1992. 15.95 (0-590-42866-7, Scholastic Hardcover) Scholastic Inc.

—Guess Again: More Weird & Wacky Inventions. LC 85-24320. (Illus.). 64p. (gr. 3-6). 1986. SBE 13.95 (0-02-767720-6, Bradbury Pr) Macmillan Child Grp.
—The Last Dinosaur. Weatherby, Mark A., illus. LC 87-3008. 32p. (gr. 1-3). 1988. pap. 14.95 (0-590-41097-0, Scholastic Hardcover) Scholastic Inc.
—The Last Dinosaur. Weatherby, Mark A., illus. 1991. pap. 3.95 (0-590-44875-7, Blue Ribbon Bks) Scholastic Inc.
—The Long Road to Gettysburg. (Illus.). 128p. (gr. 4-7). 1992. 15.45 (0-395-55965-0, Clarion Bks) HM.
Murphy, John D., ed. see Feghali, Habaka J.
Murphy, Linda. Computer Entrepreneurs: People Who Built Successful Businesses Around Computers. Berke, Tina, ed. Verougstraete, Randy, contrib. by. 128p. (Orig.). 1990. pap. text ed. 7.95 (0-945776-14-4) Comptr Pub Enterprises.
Murphy, Lois. Story Clay. Wilson, Karen, illus. 8p. (gr. 1-8). 1990. pap. write for info. (0-9620672-0-2) Dragon Studio.
Murphy, Lorraine. The Prize. 192p. (gr. 8). 1993. pap. text ed. 7.95 (1-883511-02-X) Veritas Pr CA.
Murphy, Louise S. A Teenager Who Dared Obey God. 97p. (Orig.). 1985. pap. text ed. 3.95 (0-937580-44-9) LeSEA Pub Co.
Murphy, Marge. Monsters. 11p. (gr. 1). 1989. pap. text ed. 2.50 (1-882225-07-4) Tott Pubns.
—Work. 9p. (gr. 1). 1988. pap. text ed. 2.50 (1-882225-08-2) Tott Pubns.
Murphy, Marion F., jt. auth. see Murphy, Raymond E.

Murphy, Marsha A. Secrets of Making A's the Easy Speedlearning Way: Powerful Learning Tools & Study Techniques Revealed. LC 92-75555. (Illus., Orig.). 1993. pap. 33.00 incl. audio tape (0-9635508-0-2) DataQuest VA.

The author has coupled a learning resource guide & explanatory audio tape into a "learning kit" containing richly-informative tips for students of all ages on actually HOW to learn what they are INSTRUCTED to learn. Audio, visual, & tactile/kinesthetic techniques are clearly explained, showing students how to learn by circumventing rote memory alone. Mind pictures & mental movies are some of the powerful learning tools described here. These techniques are easy, fun, & will dramatically shorten learning time. This three-part guide contains clear explanations & illustrations, making it highly readable & easy to use. To order: write DataQuest, P.O. Box 62692, Virginia Beach, VA 23466.
Publisher Provided Annotation.

Murphy, Mary. Mary Had a Baby. Amen! 16p. (Orig.). (ps-8). 1991. pap. text ed. 14.95 (0-89243-339-6); pap. text ed. 1.00 coloring bk. (0-89243-340-X) Liguori Pubns.
—The Way We Feel Inside: With the Song "How I'm Made" Freitag, Jim, illus. 28p. (gr. k-4). 1990. pap. 9.00 (0-89486-618-4) Hazelden.
Murphy, Michael. My Brother Sam Is Dead - Study Guide. Friedland, Joyce & Kessler, Rikki, eds. (gr. 5-8). Date not set. pap. text ed. 14.95 (0-88122-119-8) Lrn Links.
Murphy, Pat. Pigasus. Percy, Graham, photos by. LC 93-32214. 16p. (gr. 3 up). 1995. write for info. (0-8037-1587-0); lib. bdg. write for info. (0-8037-1588-9) Dial Bks Young.
Murphy, Pat, et al. Bending Light: An Exploratorium Toolbook. Osborn, Stephen, illus. LC 92-20336. 1993. 15.95 (0-316-25851-2) Little.
Murphy, Peter, jt. auth. see Broukal, Milada.
Murphy, Raymond E. & Murphy, Marion F. Pennsylvania Landscapes: A Geography of the Commonwealth. LC 73-77560. (gr. 8-10). 1974. 7.95 (0-931992-19-2); teachers guide o.p. 1.00 (0-931992-20-6) Penns Valley.
Murphy, S. Wind Child. Date not set. 15.00 (0-06-024351-1, Festival); PLB 14.89 (0-06-024352-X, Festival) HarpC Child Bks.
Murphy, Shirley R. The Dragonbards. LC 87-45295. 256p. (gr. 7 up). 1988. PLB 12.89 (0-06-024367-8) HarpC Child Bks.
—Nightpool. LC 85-42626. 256p. (gr. 7 up). 1985. PLB 12.89 (0-06-024361-9) HarpC Child Bks.
—Nightpool. LC 85-42626. 256p. (gr. 7 up). 1987. pap. 2.95 (0-06-447041-5, Trophy) HarpC Child Bks.
—Silver Woven in My Hair. Tiegreen, Alan, illus. LC 91-23144. 128p. (gr. 3-7). 1992. pap. 3.95 (0-689-71525-0, Aladdin) Macmillan Child Grp.

—The Song of the Christmas Mouse. Diamond, Donna, illus. LC 89-19744. 96p. (gr. 2-5). 1990. 13.00 (0-06-024357-0); PLB 12.89 (0-06-024358-9) HarpC Child Bks.
—Tattie's River Journey. De Paola, Tomie, illus. LC 82-45508. 32p. (ps-3). 1983. 11.95 (0-8037-8767-7) Dial Bks Young.
Murphy, Stephen. Donatello, the Radical Robot. (ps-3). 1993. 3.50 (0-440-40860-1) Dell.
—Monsters among Us: Teenage Mutant Ninja Turtles. 16p. (ps-2). 1993. write for info. (1-883366-09-7) YES Ent.
—The Mystery of the Missing Pizza: Teenage Mutant Ninja Turtles. 16p. (ps-2). 1993. write for info. (1-883366-08-9) YES Ent.
—Raphael, Big Trouble in Chinatown. (ps-3). 1993. pap. 3.50 (0-440-40863-6) Dell.
Murphy, Steven. Leonardo, the Wilderness Adventure. (ps-3). 1993. pap. 3.50 (0-440-40866-0) Dell.
—Michaelangelo, the Haunted Mansion. (ps-3). 1993. pap. 3.50 (0-440-40869-5) Dell.
Murphy, Thomas, jt. auth. see Christen, William.
Murphy, Wendy. Frank Lloyd Wright. (Illus.). 128p. (gr. 7-9). 1990. 14.95 (0-382-24033-2); lib. bdg. 17.98 (0-382-09905-2) Silver Burdett Pr.
Murphy, Wendy & Murphy, Jack. Hong Kong. (Illus.). 64p. (gr. 3-7). PLB 14.95 (1-56711-021-5) Blackbirch.
—Nuclear Medicine. Garell, Dale C. & Snyder, Solomon H., eds. (Illus.). (gr. 6-12). 1994. 19.95 (0-7910-0070-2, Am Art Analog); pap. write for info. (0-7910-0497-X, Am Art Analog) Chelsea Hse.
—Toronto. (Illus.). 64p. (gr. 3-7). 1994. PLB 14.95 (1-56711-025-8) Blackbirch.
Murray, Beth. Thanksgiving Fun: A Bountiful Harvest of Crafts, Recipes, & Games. Matsick, Anni, illus. 32p. (Orig.). (gr. 2-7). 1993. pap. 3.95 (1-56397-280-8) Boyds Mills Pr.
Murray, Beth, ed. Animal Craft Fun: Indoor & Outdoor Activities & Projects. LeHew, Ron, illus. 32p. (gr. k-5). 1994. pap. 3.95 (1-56397-314-6) Boyds Mills Pr.
Murray, Cleitus O. Stories of the Southern Mountains & Swamps. Murray, Cleitus O., illus. 192p. (Orig.). 1992. pap. 9.95 (0-9632132-0-2) Murray Pubns.
Murray, D. M. & Wong, T. W. Noodle Words: An Introduction to Chinese & Japanese Characters. LC 79-147179. (Illus.). (gr. 9 up). 1971. pap. 6.95 (0-8048-0948-8) C E Tuttle.
Murray, Eleanor B. Cherokee County Summer. Murray, Hubert, photos by. (Illus.). 48p. (Orig.). (gr. 9-12). 1981. pap. 3.98 (1-879313-01-4) Murrays Leprechaun Bks.
Murray, Eleanor H. Bend Like the Bamboo. Murray, Eleanor H., illus. 91p. (Orig.). (gr. 9-12). 1982. pap. 8.95 (1-879313-02-2) Murrays Leprechaun Bks.
—Growing up in Aunt Molly's Omaha, 1920-1965: And Facing the World Beyond. (Illus.). 140p. (Orig.). (gr. 9-12). 1990. pap. 8.95 (1-879313-00-6) Murrays Leprechaun Bks.
Murray, Francis. World's Wildest Animal Jokes. LC 91-47701. (Illus.). 96p. (gr. 3-8). 1992. 12.95 (0-8069-8538-0) Sterling.
—World's Wildest Animal Jokes. Hoffman, Sanford, illus. 96p. (gr. 2-6). 1993. pap. 3.95 (0-8069-8539-9) Sterling.
Murray, Ian, jt. auth. see Miller, Sheila.
Murray, Jean, jt. auth. see Darin, Bobby.
Murray, Jocelyn. Africa. 96p. 1990. 17.95 (0-8160-2209-7) Facts on File.
Murray, John. Lake Superior, Wow! A Kid's Guide to 99 Fun Things to Do in Duluth, Superior, & along Lake Superior's North Shore. (Illus.). 96p. 1993. pap. 7.95 (0-943400-73-2) Marlor Pr.
—Modern Monologues for Young People. rev. ed. 150p. (gr. 7-12). 1982. pap. 12.00 (0-8238-0255-8) Plays.
—Mystery Plays for Young Actors. (Orig.). (gr. 5-12). 1984. pap. 13.95 (0-8238-0265-5) Plays.
Murray, Linda. How to Draw Prehistoric Animals. Shi Chen, illus. LC 93-23058. 32p. (gr. k-6). 1993. PLB 10.65 (0-8167-3287-6); pap. text ed. 1.95 (0-8167-3288-4) Troll Assocs.
Murray, Marjorie D. Saturday with Little Rabbit. Britt, Stephanie, illus. LC 91-48362. 48p. (gr. k-3). 1993. RSBE 13.95 (0-02-767753-2, Macmillan Child Bk) Macmillan Child Grp.
Murray, Neil, jt. auth. see Beglar, David.
Murray, Patricia A. Let's Learn the Hawaiian Alphabet. Tanaka, Cliff, illus. 24p. (ps-k). 1987. 7.95 (0-89610-075-8) Island Heritage.
—Let's Learn the Hawaiian Alphabet. Tanaka, Cliff, illus. 24p. (ps-k). 1988. incls. cass. 11.95 (0-89610-079-0) Island Heritage.
Murray, Peter. The Amazon. LC 93-7617. 1993. write for info. (1-56766-021-5) Childs World.
—Beavers. (gr. 1-8). 1992. PLB 15.95 (0-89565-844-5); Resale. 22.75 (0-685-61009-8) Childs World.
—Beetles. LC 92-29742. 1993. PLB 15.95 (1-56766-000-2); Resale. 22.75 (0-685-61653-3) Childs World.
—Black Widows. (gr. 1-8). 1992. PLB 15.95 (0-89565-845-3); Resale. 22.75 (0-685-61008-X) Childs World.
—Chameleons. LC 92-41543. 1993. write for info. (1-56766-016-9) Childs World.
—Dirt, Wonderful Dirt! Dann, Penny, illus. LC 92-42741. Date not set. write for info. (1-56766-079-7) Childs World. Postponed.
—Dogs. (gr. 1-8). 1992. PLB 15.95 (0-89565-848-8); Resale. 22.75 (0-685-61005-5) Childs World.

—Earth. LC 92-8412. (gr. 1-8). 1992. PLB 15.95 (0-89565-854-2); Resale. 22.75 (0-685-59393-2) Childs World.
—The Everglades. LC 92-37962. 1993. write for info. (1-56766-012-6) Childs World.
—Frogs. LC 92-32499. 1993. write for info. (1-56766-010-X) Childs World.
—Gorillas. LC 93-13649. 1993. write for info. (Pub. by Childs World) Standard Pub.
—Hummingbirds. LC 92-32320. 1993. write for info. (1-56766-011-8) Childs World.
—La Lanzadera Espacial. LC 93-17916. (gr. 3 up). 1993. write for info. (1-56766-038-5) Childs World.
—Parrots. LC 92-44265. (gr. 3 up). 1993. write for info. (1-56766-015-0) Childs World.
—The Perfect Pizza. Dann, Penny, illus. LC 93-4032. (gr. 7-8). Date not set. write for info. (1-56766-080-0) Childs World. Postponed.
—The Planets. LC 92-20016. (Illus.). (gr. 1-8). 1992. PLB 14.95 (0-89565-975-1); Resale. 21.35 (0-685-60105-6) Childs World.
—Porcupines. LC 93-22833. 1993. write for info. (1-56766-019-3) Childs World.
—Professor Solomon Snickerdoodle Looks at Water. Mitchell, Anastasia, illus. LC 93-1322. 1993. write for info. (1-56766-081-9) Childs World.
—The Sahara. LC 93-25782. 1993. write for info. (1-56766-023-1) Childs World.
—Saturn. LC 92-41542. 1993. write for info. (1-56766-014-2) Childs World.
—Sea Otters. LC 93-42. 1993. write for info. (1-56766-007-X) Childs World.
—Silly Science Tricks. LC 92-18903. 1992. PLB 14.95 (0-89565-976-X); Resale. 21.35 (0-685-60110-2) Childs World.
—Snakes. (gr. 1-8). 1992. PLB 15.95 (0-89565-849-6); Resale. 22.75 (0-685-61004-7) Childs World.
—The Space Shuttle. LC 93-7064. 1993. write for info. (1-56766-018-5, Childs World) Standard Pub.
—Spiders. (gr. 1-8). 1992. PLB 15.95 (0-89565-847-X); Resale. 22.75 (0-685-61006-3) Childs World.
—Tarantulas. 1993. write for info. (1-56766-060-6) Childs World.
—World's Greatest Chocolate Chip Cookies. (Illus.). (gr. 1-8). 1992. PLB 14.95 (0-89565-892-5); Resale. 21.35 (0-685-60978-2) Childs World.
—World's Greatest Paper Airplanes. (Illus.). (gr. 1-8). 1992. PLB 14.95 (0-89565-963-8); Resale. 21.35 (0-685-60977-4) Childs World.
—You Can Juggle. LC 92-9504. 1992. PLB 14.95 (0-89565-966-2); Resale. 22.75 (0-89565-906-9) Childs World.
—Your Bones: An Inside Look at Skeletons. LC 92-7460. (Illus.). (gr. 1-8). 1992. PLB 14.95 (0-89565-968-9); Resale. 21.35 (0-685-59288-X) Childs World.
Murray, Raymond L. & Powell, Judith A. Understanding Radioactive Waste. 3rd, rev. ed. LC 88-22134. (Illus.). 184p. (gr. 6-12). 1989. pap. 12.50 (0-935470-42-5) Battelle.
Murray, Steve, tr. see Newth, Mette.
Murray, Steven T., tr. see Pettersson, Bertil.
Murray, Terry & Anderson, Jeff. Cutting Edge, Legends of Larian, Bk. 1. (Illus.). 48p. (Orig.). (gr. 9 up). 1992. pap. 5.99 (0-7459-2369-0) Lion USA.
Murray, Thompson C. License Plate Book. 1993. 5.99 (0-517-08802-9) Outlet Bk Co.
Murray, Tom. Estimation Exploration. (gr. 3-8). 1994. pap. text ed. 7.95 (1-882293-02-9) Activity Resources.
Murray, William. Picture Dictionary. Matthews, Anne, illus. 28p. (ps-2). 1991. 3.50 (0-7214-1416-8, 9112-1) Ladybird Bks.
—Picture Word Cards. (ps-2). 1991. flash cards 9.95 (0-7214-3232-8, 9113) Ladybird Bks.
Murray, William D. & Rigney, Francis J. Paper Folding for Beginners. (Illus.). (gr. 1 up). pap. 2.95 (0-486-20713-7) Dover.
Murrow, Liza K. Allergic to My Family. LC 91-31529. (Illus.). 160p. (gr. 2-6). 1992. 13.95 (0-8234-0959-7) Holiday.
—Dancing on the Table. Himler, Ronald, illus. LC 89-46066. 128p. (gr. 3-7). 1990. 13.95 (0-8234-0808-6) Holiday.
—Fire in the Heart. LC 88-45864. 264p. 1989. 15.95 (0-8234-0750-0) Holiday.
—Fire in the Heart. 255p. (gr. 5-9). 1990. pap. 2.95 (0-8167-2261-7) Troll Assocs.
—The Ghost of Lost Island. LC 90-47671. 176p. (gr. 3-7). 1991. 14.95 (0-8234-0874-4) Holiday.
—The Ghost of Lost Island. MacDonald, Pat, ed. 176p. (gr. 3-6). 1993. pap. 2.99 (0-671-75368-1, Minstrel Bks) PB.
—Good-Bye, Sammy. Owens, Gail, illus. LC 88-17011. 32p. (ps-3). 1989. reinforced bdg. 13.95 (0-8234-0726-8) Holiday.
—Lolly Cochran: Veterinarian. Schwarz, Marsha, photos by. LC 88-51682. (Illus.). 64p. (Orig.). (gr. 4-8). 1989. pap. text ed. 6.95 (0-9621820-0-1) Teachers Lab.
—Susan Humphris: Geologist. Woods Hole Oceanographic Institution Staff, photos by. LC 88-51681. (Illus.). 64p. (Orig.). (gr. 4-8). 1989. pap. text ed. 6.95 (0-9621820-1-X) Teachers Lab.
—Twelve Days in August: A Novel. LC 92-54489. 160p. (gr. 7 up). 1993. 14.95 (0-8234-1012-9) Holiday.
—West Against the Wind. LC 87-45337. 240p. (gr. 7 up). 1987. 15.95 (0-8234-0668-7) Holiday.
—West Against the Wind. 240p. (gr. 7 up). 1988. pap. 2.50 (0-8167-1324-3) Troll Assocs.

Murtha, Philly. Blank Books Series, 8 bks. (Illus.). Date not set. Set. 20 or more 2.55 ea. (*0-88682-117-7,* 31196-098) Creative Ed.
—Creative Reading: You Can Be a Free Reader. Redpath, Ann, ed. 32p. (gr. 6 up). 1984. PLB 11.95s.p. (*0-87191-997-4*) Creative Ed.
—Library: Your Teammate. Redpath, Ann, ed. 32p. (gr. 4 up). 1984. PLB 11.95s.p. (*0-87191-999-0*) Creative Ed.
—Reading Fast: You Can Be a Reading Athlete. Redpath, Ann, ed. 32p. (gr. 4 up). 1984. PLB 11.95s.p. (*0-87191-996-6*) Creative Ed.
—Writing: You Can Be an Author. Redpath, Ann, ed. 32p. (gr. 4 up). 1984. PLB 11.95s.p. (*0-87191-998-2*) Creative Ed.
Muschlitz, Beverly, jt. auth. see Michener, Dorothy.
Musee en Herbe Staff. Livre de la Tour Eiffel. (FRE.). 96p. (gr. 4-9). 1983. 13.95 (*2-07-039502-2*) Schoenhof.
Musgrove, Margaret W. Ashanti to Zulu: African Traditions. Dillon, Diane & Dillon, Leo, illus. LC 76-6610. (gr. k-4). 1976. 17.00 (*0-8037-0357-0*); PLB 15.89 (*0-8037-0358-9*) Dial Bks Young.
—Ashanti to Zulu: African Traditions. Dillon, Leo & Dillon, Diane, illus. LC 76-6610. 32p. (gr. k up). 1980. pap. 4.95 (*0-8037-0308-2,* Dial Pied Piper) Puffin Bks.
Mushkat, Jerome. Aaron Burr: Controversial Politician of Early America. Rahmas, D. Steve & Kurland, Gerald, eds. 32p. (gr. 7-12). 1974. lib. bdg. 4.75 incl. catalog cards (*0-87157-571-X*) SamHar Pr.
Musical Lynn. The Early Poems. 5p. (Orig.). (gr. 12). 1990. pap. 7.95 (*1-880718-05-7*) Genius New.
—Musical Lynn Essays, Vol. I: A Baker's Dozen. 13p. (Orig.). (gr. 12). 1990. pap. 8.95 (*1-880718-02-2*); pap. text ed. 8.95 (*1-880718-03-0*) Genius New.
Musil, Rosemary G. The Ghost of Mr. Penny. 1940. 4.50 (*0-87602-129-1*) Anchorage.
Mussari, Mark. The Danish Americans. Moynihan, Daniel P., intro. by. (Illus.). 112p. (gr. 5 up). 1988. lib. bdg. 17.95 (*0-87754-871-4*) Chelsea Hse.
—Suzanne De Passe: Motown's Boss Lady. Young, Richard G., ed. LC 91-28541. (Illus.). 64p. (gr. 4-8). 1992. PLB 17.26 (*1-56074-026-4*) Garrett Ed Corp.
Musselman, Don, ed. O Ye Jigs & Juleps! 1992. pap. 5.50 playscript (*0-87602-315-4*) Anchorage.
Musser, Joe see Tada, Joni E.
Mussiett, Salomon R., ed. Cancionero para Preescolares. (SPA.). 54p. (ps). 1989. pap. 3.50 (*0-311-32226-3*) Casa Bautista.
Musson, Cyril D., jt. auth. see Musson, Gloria J.
Musson, Gloria J. & Musson, Cyril D. RAPmetic, the Arithmetic Rap. Miller, Benjamin S., illus. 48p. (Orig.). (gr. 3 up). 1988. pap. text ed. 3.50 (*0-9619321-0-4*); cass. 6.50 (*0-9619321-1-2*) Sq One Pubns.
Mutel, Cornelia F. Tropical Rain Forests: Our Endangered Planet. (gr. 4-7). 1993. pap. 8.95 (*0-8225-9629-6*) Lerner Pubns.
Muth, Jillian De see De Muth, Jillian.
Muzik, Katy. At Home on the Coral Reef. (Illus.). 32p. (ps-3). 1992. 14.95 (*0-88106-487-4*) Charlesbridge Pub.
—Dentro del Arrecife de Coral (At Home in the Coral Reef). (Illus.). 32p. (ps-3). 1993. pap. 6.95 (*0-88106-422-X*) Charlesbridge Pub.
Mwangudza, Johnson A. Mijikenda. (Illus.). 37p. (gr. 6-9). 1991. pap. 4.95 (*0-237-50490-1,* Pub. by Evans Bros Ltd) Trafalgar.
Myer, Rick, jt. auth. see Ottens, Allen.
Myers. Story of Three Kingdoms. Date not set. 15.00 (*0-06-024286-8,* Festival); PLB 14.89 (*0-06-024287-6,* Festival) HarpC Child Bks.
Myers, Albert C., ed. William Penn's Own Account of Lenni Lenape or Delaware Indians. (Illus.). 96p. (gr. 7 up). 1986. pap. 6.95 (*0-912608-13-7*) Mid Atlantic.
Myers, Anna. Red-Dirt Jessie. 107p. 1992. 13.95 (*0-8027-8172-1*) Walker & Co.
Myers, Arthur. The Cheyenne. Rich, Mary P., ed. LC 91-31010. (Illus.). 48p. (gr. 3-6). 1992. PLB 12.90 (*0-531-20069-8*) Watts.
—The Pawnee. LC 93-18369. (Illus.). 64p. (gr. 4-6). 1993. PLB 12.90 (*0-531-20165-1*) Watts.
—Sea Creatures Do Amazing Things. Zallinger, Jean D., illus. LC 80-20089. 72p. (gr. 2-5). 1981. 7.95 (*0-394-84487-4*); lib. bdg. 8.99 (*0-394-94487-9*) Random Bks Yng Read.
Myers, Bernice. Cry Baby. Myers, Bernice, illus. LC 89-12342. 32p. (ps-2). 1990. 12.95 (*0-688-09083-4*); lib. bdg. 12.88 (*0-688-09084-2*) Lothrop.
—Ding-a-Ling-a-Ling. 16p. (ps-2). 1992. pap. 14.95 (*1-56784-055-8*) Newbridge Comms.
—The Flying Shoes. LC 91-335. (ps up). 1992. 15.00 (*0-688-01695-1*); PLB 14.93 (*0-688-10696-X*) Lothrop.
—The Gold Watch. LC 90-45764. (Illus.). 32p. (gr. k up). 1991. 13.95 (*0-688-09888-6*); PLB 13.88 (*0-688-09889-4*) Lothrop.
—It Happens to Everyone. 1990. 12.95 (*0-688-09081-8*); PLB 12.88 (*0-688-09082-6*) Lothrop.
—The Millionth Egg. (gr. k-3). 1991. 13.95 (*0-688-09886-X*) Lothrop.
—Millionth Egg. (ps-3). 1991. 13.88 (*0-688-09887-8*) Lothrop.
—Sidney Rella & the Glass Sneaker. Myers, Bernice, illus. LC 85-3044. 32p. (gr. k-3). 1985. RSBE 14.95 (*0-02-767790-7,* Macmillan Child Bk) Macmillan Child Grp.
Myers, Bill. The Experiment. Jorgenson, Andrea, illus. 160p. (Orig.). (gr. 3 up). 1991. pap. 5.99 (*1-55661-214-1*) Bethany Hse.

—More Hot Topics. 144p. 1989. pap. 5.99 (*0-89693-670-8*) SP Pubns.
—My Life As a Broken Bungee Cord. (gr. 4-7). 1993. pap. 4.99 (*0-8499-3404-4*) Word Inc.
—My Life As a Smashed Burrito with Extra Hot Sauce. 1993. pap. 4.99 (*0-8499-3402-8*) Word Inc.
—My Life As Alien Monster Bait. (gr. 3-7). 1993. pap. 4.99 (*0-8499-3403-6*) Word Inc.
—My Life As Crocodile Junk Food. (gr. 3-7). 1993. pap. 4.99 (*0-8499-3405-2*) Word Inc.
—The Portal. Jorgenson, Andrea, illus. 160p. (Orig.). (gr. 3 up). 1991. pap. 5.99 (*1-55661-163-3*) Bethany Hse.
—The Tablet. Jorgenson, Andrea, illus. LC 92-34301. 160p. (Orig.). (gr. 3 up). 1992. pap. 5.99 (*1-55661-299-0*) Bethany Hse.
—The Whirlwind. 160p. (Orig.). (gr. 4-8). 1992. pap. 5.99 (*1-55661-258-3*) Bethany Hse.
Myers, Bill & Johnson, Ken. McGee & Me! No. 2: Star in the Breaking. 1989. pap. 3.99 (*0-8423-4168-4*); video 19.95 (*0-8423-4153-6*) Tyndale.
—McGee & Me! No. 3: Not-So-Great Escape. 1989. video 19.95 (*0-8423-4154-4*) Tyndale.
—McGee & Me! No. 4: Skate Expectations. 1989. pap. 3.99 (*0-8423-4165-X*); video 19.95 (*0-8423-4155-2*) Tyndale.
—McGee & Me: The Big Lie. 1989. pap. 3.95 (*0-8423-4169-2*) Tyndale.
Myers, Bill & West, Robert. The Blunder Years. LC 93-964. (Illus.). 1993. 3.99 (*0-8423-4117-X*) Tyndale.
—In the Nick of Time. LC 93-16107. (Illus.). 1993. 3.99 (*0-8423-4122-6*) Tyndale.
Myers, Bill & West, Robert E. Beauty in the Least. LC 93-14026. 1993. 3.99 (*0-8423-4124-2*) Tyndale.
Myers, Bill, jt. auth. see Focus on the Family Staff.
Myers, Christopher A. & Myers, Lynne B. Forest of the Clouded Leopard. LC 93-350. (gr. 4 up). 1994. write for info. (*0-395-67408-5*) HM.
—McCrephy's Field. Chartier, Normand, illus. 32p. (gr. 2-5). 1991. 14.45 (*0-395-53807-6,* Sandpiper) HM.
Myers, Christopher A., jt. auth. see Myers, Lynne B.
Myers, Edward. Forri the Baker. Natchev, Alexi, photos by. LC 93-2468. 1994. write for info. (*0-8037-1396-7*); PLB write for info. (*0-8037-1397-5*) Dial Bks Young.
Myers, Gail A. A World of Sports for Girls. LC 81-10440. (Illus.). 160p. (gr. 5-9). 1981. 11.00 (*0-664-32683-8,* Westminster) Westminster John Knox.
Myers, Garry C. Creative Thinking Activities. Rev. ed. 32p. (gr. 2-6). 1980. pap. 2.95 (*0-87534-113-6*) Highlights.
Myers, Jack. Can Birds Get Lost? And Other Questions about Animals. LC 90-85911. (Illus.). 64p. (gr. 1-5). 1991. 10.95 (*1-878093-32-0*) Boyds Mills Pr.
—Do Cats Really Have Nine Lives? And Other Questions about Your World. (gr. 4-7). 1993. 12.95 (*1-56397-089-9*) Boyds Mills Pr.
—Do Cats Really Have Nine Lives? And Other Questions about Your World. (gr. 4-7). 1993. pap. 7.95 (*1-56397-215-8*) Boyds Mills Pr.
—How Do We Dream? And Other Questions about Your Body. (Illus.). 64p. (gr. 1-5). 1992. bds. 10.95 (*1-56397-091-0*) Boyds Mills Pr.
—What Makes Popcorn Pop? And Other Questions about the World Around Us. Gardner, Charles, et al, illus. LC 90-85912. 64p. (gr. 1-5). 1991. 10.95 (*1-878093-33-9*) Boyds Mills Pr.
Myers, Laurie. Earthquake in the Third Grade. LC 92-26609. 1993. 13.95 (*0-395-65360-6,* Clarion Bks) HM.
—Garage Sale Fever. Howell, Kathleen C., illus. LC 92-40342. 80p. (gr. 1-5). 1993. 13.00 (*0-06-022905-5*); PLB 12.89 (*0-06-022908-X*) HarpC.
—Guinea Pigs Don't Talk. Taylor, Cheryl, illus. LC 93-39642. Date not set. write for info. (*0-395-68967-8,* Clarion Bks) HM.
Myers, Lynne B. & Myers, Christopher A. Turnip Soup. (Illus.). 32p. (ps-2). 1994. 13.95 (*1-56282-445-7*); PLB 13.89 (*1-56282-446-5*) Hyprn Child.
Myers, Lynne B., jt. auth. see Myers, Christopher A.
Myers, Ruth S. & Banfield, Beryle, eds. Embers: Stories for a Changing World. LC 82-73499. (Illus.). 175p. (gr. 3-6). 1983. pap. 8.95 (*0-930040-47-3*); tchr's manual 18.95 (*0-930040-46-5*) CIBC.
Myers, Tim. Let's Call Him Lau-Wili-Wili-Humu-Humu-Nukuauku-Nukunukai-Apuaa-Oioi. Arakaki, Daryl, illus. LC 93-72767. 24p. (ps-3). 1993. 12.95 (*1-880188-67-8*); pap. 5.95 (*0-685-68878-X*) Bess Pr.
Myers, Walter D. Brown Angels: An Album of Pictures & Verse. LC 92-36792. (Illus.). 40p. (gr. 2 up). 1993. 16.00 (*0-06-022917-9*); PLB 15.89 (*0-06-022918-7*) HarpC Child Bks.
—Crystal. LC 86-15958. (gr. 5-9). 1987. pap. 14.95 (*0-670-80426-6*) Viking Child Bks.
—Crystal. (gr. k-8). 1990. pap. 3.25 (*0-440-20538-7,* LFL) Dell.
—Dangerous Games. 1993. pap. 3.50 (*0-553-56269-X*) Bantam.
—Fallen Angels. 336p. (gr. 8 up). 1988. pap. 13.95 (*0-590-40942-5*) Scholastic Inc.
—Fallen Angels. (gr. 8 up). 1989. pap. 3.95 (*0-590-40943-3*) Scholastic Inc.
—Fashion by Tasha. 1993. pap. 3.50 (*0-553-29724-4*) Bantam.
—Fast Sam, Cool Clyde & Stuff. (gr. 5-9). 1988. pap. 3.99 (*0-14-032613-8,* Puffin) Puffin Bks.
—Hoops. LC 81-65497. 224p. (gr. 7 up). 1981. 13.95 (*0-385-28142-0*) Delacorte.
—Hoops. 192p. (gr. 7 up). 1983. pap. 3.50 (*0-440-93884-8,* LFL) Dell.

—Intensive Care. 1993. pap. 3.50 (*0-553-56268-1*) Bantam.
—The Legend of Tarik. 180p. (gr. 7 up). 1991. pap. 2.95 (*0-590-44426-3*) Scholastic Inc.
—Me, Mop, & the Moondance Kid. Pate, Rodney, illus. LC 88-6503. 128p. (gr. 3-7). 1988. 13.95 (*0-440-50065-6*) Delacorte.
—Me, Mop, & the Moondance Kid. (gr. 4-7). 1988. 13.95 (*0-385-30147-2*) Doubleday.
—Me, Mop & the Moondance Kid. (gr. k-6). 1991. pap. 3.50 (*0-440-40396-0,* Pub. by Yearling Classics) Dell.
—Mop, Moondance, & the Nagasaki Knights. LC 91-36824. 160p. (gr. 3-7). 1992. 14.00 (*0-385-30687-3*) Delacorte.
—Mop, Moondance, & the Nagasaki Knights. (gr. 4-7). 1994. pap. 3.50 (*0-440-40914-4*) Dell.
—Motown & Didi. (gr. k-12). 1987. pap. 3.50 (*0-440-95762-1,* LFL) Dell.
—Motown & Didi: A Love Story. LC 84-3632. 192p. (gr. 7 up). 1984. pap. 14.95 (*0-670-49062-8*) Viking Child Bks.
—The Mouse Rap. LC 89-36419. 192p. (gr. 5-9). 1990. 14.00 (*0-06-024343-0*); PLB 13.89 (*0-06-024344-9*) HarpC Child Bks.
—The Mouse Rap. Bacha, Andy. LC 89-35419. 192p. (gr. 5-9). 1992. pap. 3.95 (*0-06-440356-4,* Trophy) HarpC Child Bks.
—Now Is Your Time! The African-American Struggle for Freedom. LC 91-314. (Illus.). 304p. (gr. 6 up). 1992. 18.00 (*0-06-024370-8*); PLB 17.89 (*0-06-024371-6*) HarpC Child Bks.
—Now Is Your Time! The African-American Struggle for Freedom. LC 91-314. (Illus.). 320p. (gr. 6 up). 1992. pap. 10.95 (*0-06-446120-3,* Trophy) HarpC Child Bks.
—The Outside Shot. (gr. k-12). 1987. pap. 3.50 (*0-440-96784-8,* LFL) Dell.
—A Place Called Heartbreak: A Story of Vietnam. Porter, Frederick, illus. LC 92-14428. 71p. (gr. 2-5). 1992. PLB 21.34 (*0-8114-7237-X*) Raintree Steck-V.
—The Righteous Revenge of Artemis Bonner. LC 42401. 144p. (gr. 5-9). 1992. 14.00 (*0-06-020844-9*); PLB 13.89 (*0-06-020846-5*) HarpC Child Bks.
—Scorpions. LC 85-45815. 160p. (gr. 7 up). 1988. 13.00 (*0-06-024364-3*); PLB 12.89 (*0-06-024365-1*) HarpC Child Bks.
—Scorpions. LC 85-45815. 224p. (gr. 7 up). 1990. pap. 3.95 (*0-06-447066-0,* Trophy) HarpC Child Bks.
—Somewhere in the Darkness. 224p. 1992. 14.95 (*0-590-42411-4,* Scholastic Hardcover) Scholastic Inc.
—Somewhere in the Darkness. (gr. 10 up). 1993. pap. 3.25 (*0-590-42412-2*) Scholastic Inc.
—Sweet Illusions. 146p. (Orig.). 1987. 14.95 (*0-915924-14-5*); pap. 7.95 (*0-915924-15-3*) Tchrs & Writers Coll.
—The Test. 1993. pap. 3.50 (*0-553-29722-8*) Bantam.
—Won't Know Till I Get There. LC 87-7340. (gr. 3 up). 1988. pap. 3.99 (*0-14-032612-X,* Puffin) Puffin Bks.
—Won't Know Till I Get There. large type ed. 188p. (gr. 6-9). Repr. of 1982 ed. 49.94 (*0-317-01969-4,* 4-27630-00) Am Printing Hse.
—The Young Landlords. 208p. (gr. 5-9). 1989. pap. 4.99 (*0-14-034244-3,* Puffin) Puffin Bks.
—The Young Landlords. (gr. 6-10). 1992. 17.00 (*0-8446-6569-X*) Peter Smith.
—Young Martin's Promise. Bond, Barbara H., illus. LC 92-18070. 32p. (gr. 2-5). 1992. PLB 21.34 (*0-8114-7210-8*) Raintree Steck-V.
Myers, Walter Dean. Malcolm X: By Any Means Necessary. LC 92-13480. 224p. (gr. 5 up). 1993. 13.95 (*0-590-46484-1*) Scholastic Inc.
Myers, William A., jt. auth. see Donaldson, Stephen E.
Myerson, A. Lee. Seawater: A Delicate Balance. LC 88-10961. (Illus.). 64p. (gr. 6 up). 1988. lib. bdg. 15.95 (*0-89490-157-5*) Enslow Pubs.
Myerson, Joel, ed. see Cranch, Christopher P.
Myhre, M., ed. see McManus, Dorothy.
Myles, Glenn, ed. see Lehman, Yvette K.
Mylet, Trish. Children, Today's Joy & Tomorrow's Hope, 8 bks, Set 2. Sheffield, Antoinette, illus. 224p. (ps-3). 1991. Set. pap. text ed. 16.00 (*0-945590-62-8*) Pals 1, Pals 2, Pals 3, Pals 4, Pals 5, Pals 6, Pals 7, Pals 8. Sizzy Bks.

—Children, Today's Joy & Tomorrow's Hope Series, 19 bks. Sheffield, Antoinette, illus. 448p. (ps-3). 1991. Set 1 & 2. pap. text ed. 32.00 (*0-945590-74-1*) Set 1: Jan & Pam, The Van, Rex & Tex, The Bed, Siz & Liz, The Pit, Dod & Bob, The Box, Hun & Sun, The Hut, Pals. Set 2: Pals 1, Pals 2, Pals, 3, Pals 4, Pals 5, Pals, 6, Pals 7, Pals 8. Sizzy Bks. CHILDREN, TODAY'S JOY & TOMORROW'S HOPE SERIES: Set 1 & Set 2, 19 books. This SERIES consists of two Sets of books. Set 1 contains 11 beginning reader & activity books. Set 2 contains 8 books of short stories & activity books. The CHILDREN SERIES consists of positive global readers incorporating

geography (the fifty United States & the District of Columbia), phonics (short & long vowels, blends & digraphs), number recognition & self expression & explores the areas of zoology, botany, history & global unity. Each pair of books in Set 1 & each story in Set 2 contain a state reference page with a dot-to-dot exercise in the shape of that state's outline. The first sixteen books include sentence completion exercises & that story's word list. In Set 2 at least one story in each book has an O. Henry-type ending in which the child decides how the story ends. The SERIES includes a Reference Guide. Building on Set 1's themes of fun & fantasy, Set 2 expands & concludes with joy, fact & hope. This warmly written & illustrated series has been well received worldwide by Early Education, Special Education & English as a Second Language teachers, parents & most importantly, children. $32.00 (ISBN 0-945590-74-1). Trish Mylet, author. Antoinette Sheffield, illustrator. Sizzy Books. Write for brochure. *Publisher Provided Annotation.*

—Phonetic Readers for the Short Vowels, 11 bks, Set 1. Sheffield, Antoinette, illus. 224p. (ps-2). 1988. Set. pap. text ed. 16.00 (*0-945590-00-8*) Jan & Pam, The Van, Rex & Tex, The Bed, Siz & Liz, The Pit, Dod & Bob, The Box, Hun & Sun, The Hut, Pals. Sizzy Bks.
Myller, Rolf. How Big Is a Foot? 1991. pap. 2.99 (*0-440-40495-9*) Dell.
Myra, Harold. Easter Bunny, Are You for Real? LC 78-21268. (Illus.). (gr. 5-8). 1979. 8.99 (*0-8407-5148-6*) Nelson.
—Halloween, Is It For Real? Walles, Dwight, illus. LC 82-6323. 32p. (gr. 2-4). 1982. 8.99 (*0-8407-5268-7*) Nelson.
Myrick, David F. Montecito & Santa Barbara, Vol. 2. LC 87-30188. (Illus.). 320p. (gr. 11). 1991. 54.95 (*0-87046-100-1*, Pub. by Trans-Anglo) Interurban.
Myrick, Mildred. Secret Three. Lobel, Arnold, illus. LC 63-13323. 64p. (gr. k-3). 1963. PLB 13.89 (*0-06-024356-2*) HarpC Child Bks.
Myrick, Robert D. & Folk, Betsy E. Peervention: Training Peer Facilitators for Prevention Education. Swenson, Paula, illus. LC 90-86235. 210p. (Orig.). (gr. 9-12). 1991. pap. text ed. 13.95x (*0-932796-35-4*) Ed Media Corp.
Myrick, Robert D. & Sorenson, Don L. Helping Skills for Middle School Students. Mitchell, Hetty, illus. LC 92-70820. 160p. (Orig.). (gr. 6-8). 1992. pap. text ed. 7.95x (*0-932796-40-0*) Ed Media Corp.
**Myring, First Guide to the Universe. (gr. 2-5). 1982. 11. 95 (*0-86020-611-4*, Usborne-Hayes) EDC.
—Rockets & Spaceflight. (gr. 2-5). 1982. (Usborne-Hayes); pap. 3.95 (*0-86020-584-3*) EDC.
Myring, L. & Graham, I. Information Revolution. Ashman, Iain, illus. 48p. (gr. 6 up). 1983. lib. bdg. 13. 96 (*0-88110-153-2*); pap. 6.95 (*0-86020-726-9*) EDC.
Myring, Lynn. Sun, Moon & Planets. (gr. 2-5). 1982. (Usborne-Hayes); pap. 3.95 (*0-86020-580-0*) EDC.
Mystic Jhamon Publishers Staff, ed. Is Man a Free Agent? (Illus.). 128p. (gr. 6 up). 1985. pap. 9.95 (*0-933961-01-4*) Mystic Jhamom.

N

Naava. The Golden Goose. LC 93-11681. 1994. write for info. (*0-688-11302-8*, Tambourine Bks); PLB write for info. (*0-688-11303-6*, Tambourine Bks) Morrow.
Nabb, Magdalen. The Enchanted Horse. Heller, Julek, illus. LC 93-18423. 96p. (gr. 3-7). 1993. 14.95 (*0-531-06805-6*); PLB 14.99 (*0-531-08655-0*) Orchard Bks Watts.
—Josie Smith. Vainio, Pirkko, illus. LC 88-8301. 80p. (gr. 1-4). 1989. SBE 12.95 (*0-689-50485-3*, M K McElderry) Macmillan Child Grp.
—Josie Smith. large type ed. Vainio, Pirkko, illus. 88p. 1993. 13.95 (*0-7451-1673-6*, Galaxy Child Lrg Print) Chivers N Amer.
—Josie Smith & Eileen. Vainio, Pirkko, illus. LC 91-31848. 96p. (gr. 1-5). 1992. SBE 12.95 (*0-689-50534-5*, M K McElderry) Macmillan Child Grp.

—Josie Smith at School. Vainio, Pirkko, illus. LC 91-10970. 112p. (gr. 1-5). 1991. SBE 12.95 (*0-689-50533-7*, M K McElderry) Macmillan Child Grp.
—Josie Smith at the Seashore. Vainio, Pirkko, illus. LC 89-8168. 96p. (gr. 1-5). 1990. SBE 12.95 (*0-689-50492-6*, M K McElderry) Macmillan Child Grp.
—Josie Smith at the Seaside. large type ed. Vainio, Pirkko, illus. 1993. 15.95 (*0-7451-1808-9*, Galaxy Child Lrg Print) Chivers N Amer.
Nabham, Marty. Skateboarding. LC 93-23317. 1993. write for info. (*0-86593-346-4*) Rourke Corp.
Nabhan. Cy Young Winners. 1991. 12.50s.p. (*0-86593-133-X*) Rourke Corp.
Nabhan, Gary. Desert Life. 1994. write for info. (*0-8050-3100-6*) H Holt & Co.
Nabhan, Martin. Australia. (Illus.). 64p. (gr. 7 up) 1990. lib. bdg. 17.27 (*0-86593-088-0*); PLB 12.95s.p. (*0-685-36362-7*) Rourke Corp.
—White Water Rafting. 48p. (gr. 3-4). 1991. PLB 11.95 (*1-56065-053-2*) Capstone Pr.
Nabhan, Martin, et al. World Partners, 6 bks. (Illus.). 384p. (gr. 7 up). 1990. Set. lib. bdg. 95.58 (*0-86593-087-2*); Set. lib. bdg. 77.70s.p. (*0-685-36361-9*) Rourke Corp.
Nabhan, Marty. Fabulous Forwards. LC 92-9479. 1992. PLB 17.26 (*0-86593-161-5*); lib. bdg. 12.95s.p. (*0-685-59298-7*) Rourke Corp.
Nabwire, Constance. Cooking the African Way. 1990. pap. 5.95 (*0-8225-9564-8*) Lerner Pubns.
Nabwire, Constance, jt. auth. see Montgomery, Bertha.
Nachman of Breslov. The Fixer. Succot, Miriam & Succot, Eliyah, trs. from HEB. Succot, Miriam & Succot, Eliyah, illus. (gr. 3-12). 1977. pap. 1.50 (*0-917246-04-7*) Maimes.
Nadel, Laurie. Corazon Aquino: Journey to Power. LC 86-33266. 93p. (gr. 6 up). 1987. lib. bdg. 13.98 (*0-671-63950-1*, J Messner) S&S Trade.
—The Great Stream of History: A Biography of Richard M. Nixon. LC 90-920. (Illus.). 144p. (gr. 5-9). 1991. SBE 14.95 (*0-689-31559-7*, Atheneum Child Bk) Macmillan Child Grp.
—The Kremlin Coup. LC 91-36892. (Illus.). 64p. (gr. 5-8). 1992. PLB 15.90 (*1-56294-170-4*) Millbrook Pr.
—Kremlin Coup. 1992. pap. 4.95 (*0-395-62468-1*) HM.
Naden, C. J. Cycle Chase. LC 79-64638. (Illus.). 32p. (gr. 4-9). 1980. PLB 10.79 (*0-89375-249-5*); pap. 2.95 (*0-89375-263-0*) Troll Assocs.
—I Can Read About All Kinds of Giants. LC 78-65833. (Illus.). (gr. 2-4). 1979. pap. 1.95 (*0-89375-201-0*) Troll Assocs.
—I Can Read About Caves. new ed. LC 78-66271. (Illus.). (gr. 2-5). 1979. pap. 1.95 (*0-89375-205-3*) Troll Assocs.
—I Can Read About Creepy Crawly Creatures. LC 78-68469. (Illus.). (gr. 3-6). 1979. pap. 1.95 (*0-89375-207-X*) Troll Assocs.
—I Can Read About Elephants. LC 78-65834. (Illus.). (gr. 2-5). 1979. pap. 1.95 (*0-89375-208-8*) Troll Assocs.
—I Can Read About Motorcycles. LC 78-74657. (Illus.). (gr. 3-6). 1979. pap. 1.95 (*0-89375-212-6*) Troll Assocs.
—I Can Read About Pioneers. LC 78-65835. (Illus.). (gr. 3-6). 1979. pap. 1.95 (*0-89375-214-2*) Troll Assocs.
—I Can Read About Racing Cars. LC 78-74658. (Illus.). (gr. 3-6). 1979. pap. 1.95 (*0-89375-216-9*) Troll Assocs.
—I Can Read About Sharks. LC 78-73736. (Illus.). (gr. 2-6). 1979. pap. 1.95 (*0-89375-218-5*) Troll Assocs.
—John Henry, the Steeldriving Man. new ed. LC 79-66317. (Illus.). 48p. (gr. 3-6). 1980. lib. bdg. 9.89 (*0-89375-304-1*); pap. 2.95 (*0-89375-303-3*) Troll Assocs.
—Motorcycle Challenge, Trials & Races. LC 79-52178. (Illus.). 32p. (gr. 4-9). 1980. PLB 10.79 (*0-89375-252-5*); pap. 2.95 (*0-89375-253-3*) Troll Assocs.
—Rough Rider. LC 79-52177. (Illus.). 32p. (gr. 4-9). 1980. PLB 10.79 (*0-89375-250-9*); pap. 2.95 (*0-89375-251-7*) Troll Assocs.
Naden, C. J., adapted by. Jason & the Golden Fleece. Baxter, Robert, illus. LC 80-50068. 32p. (gr. 4-8). 1980. PLB 11.79 (*0-89375-360-2*); pap. 2.95 (*0-89375-364-5*) Troll Assocs.
—Pegasus, the Winged Horse. new ed. LC 80-50069. (Illus.). 32p. (gr. 4-8). 1980. PLB 11.79 (*0-89375-361-0*); pap. 2.95 (*0-89375-365-3*) Troll Assocs.
—Perseus & Medusa. Baxter, Robert, illus. LC 80-50083. 32p. (gr. 4-8). 1980. PLB 11.79 (*0-89375-362-9*); pap. 2.95 (*0-89375-366-1*) Troll Assocs.
—Theseus & the Minotaur. Baxter, Robert, illus. LC 80-50067. 32p. (gr. 4-8). 1980. PLB 11.79 (*0-89375-363-7*); pap. 2.95 (*0-89375-367-X*) Troll Assocs.
Naden, Corinne. Ronald McNair. King, Coretta Scott, intro. by. (Illus.). 112p. (gr. 5 up). 1991. lib. bdg. 17.95 (*0-7910-1133-X*) Chelsea Hse.
—Ronald McNair. (gr. 4-7). 1993. pap. 7.95 (*0-7910-1158-5*) Chelsea Hse.
Naden, Corinne J. John Muir: Saving the Wilderness. (gr. 4-7). 1992. pap. 4.95 (*0-395-63569-1*) HM.
Naden, Corinne J. & Blue, Rose. Christa McAuliffe: Teacher in Space. (Illus.). 48p. (gr. 2-4). 1991. PLB 12.40 (*1-56294-046-5*) Millbrook Pr.

—John Muir: Saving the Wilderness. LC 91-18106. (Illus.). 48p. (gr. 2-4). 1992. PLB 12.40 (*1-56294-110-0*) Millbrook Pr.
—The U. S. Coast Guard. LC 92-31042. (Illus.). 64p. (gr. 3-6). 1993. PLB 14.90 (*1-56294-321-9*) Millbrook Pr.
—The U. S. Navy. LC 92-13430. (Illus.). 64p. (gr. 3-6). 1993. PLB 14.90 (*1-56294-216-6*) Millbrook Pr.
Naden, Corinne J., jt. auth. see Blue, Rose.
Nadja. Little Nina & Baby Bear. LC 91-18464. (Illus.). 32p. (ps-1). 1992. 4.99 (*0-679-82468-5*); PLB 6.99 (*0-679-92468-X*) Knopf Bks Yng Read.
—Little Nina & the Radio. LC 91-18465. (Illus.). 32p. (ps-1). 1992. 4.99 (*0-679-82466-9*); PLB 6.99 (*0-679-92466-3*) Knopf Bks Yng Read.
—Little Nina Plays Ball. LC 91-18466. (Illus.). 32p. (ps-1). 1992. 4.99 (*0-679-82467-7*); PLB 6.99 (*0-679-92467-1*) Knopf Bks Yng Read.
Nadler, Ellis. The Bee's Sneeze. LC 92-32470. (Illus.). 32p. (ps-1). 1993. pap. 12.00 POB (*0-671-86575-7*, S&S BFYR) S&S Trade.
Nadler, Ellis, jt. auth. see Porritt, Jonathon.
Naeb, Yuli, tr. see Lehman, Yvette K.
Naegelin, Lanny. Getting Started in Oral Interpretation. 128p. (gr. 7-12). 1993. pap. text ed. 8.95 (*0-685-62771-3*, C5403-7, Natl Textbk); tchr's. manual 7.95 (*0-685-62772-1*, C5404-5, Natl Textbk) NTC Pub Grp.
Naether, Carl & Vriends, Matthew M. Building an Aviary. (Illus.). 160p. (gr. 8 up). 1989. PLB 12.95 (*0-685-28494-8*, PS-763) TFH Pubns.
Naff, Alixa. The Arab Americans. Moynihan, Daniel P., intro. by. (Illus.). 112p. (gr. 5 up). 1988. lib. bdg. 17.95 (*0-87754-861-7*) Chelsea Hse.
Nagaoki, Kobun, tr. see Hober, David.
Nagel, Karen. Two Crazy Pigs. Schatell, Brian, illus. 32p. 1992. pap. 2.95 (*0-590-44972-9*, Cartwheel) Scholastic Inc.
Nagel, Karen B. Norfin Trolls Campout Adventure. (ps-3). 1993. pap. 2.50 (*0-590-46630-5*) Scholastic Inc.
—The Three Young Maniacs & the Red Rubber Boots. Gullikson, Sandy, illus. LC 91-30842. 32p. (ps-3). 1993. 15.00 (*0-06-020777-9*); PLB 14.89 (*0-06-020778-7*) HarpC Child Bks.
Nagel, Stephan, ed. see Newland, Mary R.
Nagel, Steve, ed. see Ahlers, Julia, et al.
Nagy, Janet R., ed. Good Health Guides Library, 7 vols. (Illus.). 1990. Set. lib. bdg. 355.00 (*0-931013-79-8*) Moonbeam Pubns.
—Healing & Herbs Library. (Illus.). 1990. lib. bdg. 50.00 (*0-931013-85-2*) Moonbeam Pubns.
—Healthy Foods & Recipes Library. (Illus.). 1990. lib. bdg. 50.00 (*0-931013-83-6*) Moonbeam Pubns.
—Nutrients Library. (Illus.). 1990. lib. bdg. 50.00 (*0-931013-82-8*) Moonbeam Pubns.
—Nutrition Library. (Illus.). 1990. lib. bdg. 50.00 (*0-931013-86-0*) Moonbeam Pubns.
—Prevention Guides Library, Pt. 1. (Illus.). 1990. lib. bdg. 55.00 (*0-931013-80-1*) Moonbeam Pubns.
—Prevention Guides Library, Pt. 2. (Illus.). 1990. lib. bdg. 50.00 (*0-931013-81-X*) Moonbeam Pubns.
—Vitamins & Minerals Library. (Illus.). 1990. lib. bdg. 50.00 (*0-931013-84-4*) Moonbeam Pubns.
Naha, Ed. Breakdown. (Orig.). 1988. pap. 3.50 (*0-440-20210-8*) Dell.
Nahm, Andrew C., et al, eds. I Love Korea! (Illus.). 86p. 1992. 22.50x (*0-930878-87-6*) Hollym Intl.
Nahrstadt, Jennifer, ed. see Stahl, Hilda.
Nahum, Andrew. Flying Machine. King, Dave, et al, photos by. LC 90-4007. (Illus.). 64p. (gr. 5 up). 1990. 15.00 (*0-679-80744-6*); PLB 15.99 (*0-679-90744-0*) Knopf Bks Yng Read.
Nahum-Valensi, Maya. Mom's Sore Throat. (Illus.). 48p. (gr. k-4). 1990. 12.75 (*0-89565-807-0*); 8.95s.p. (*0-685-55102-4*) Childs World.
Nai'an, Shi & Guanzhong, Luo. Outlaws of the Marsh, 4 vols. Shapiro, Sidney, tr. from CHI. (Illus.). 4144p. (Orig.). (gr. 12 up). 1988. pap. 29.95 (*0-8351-2289-1*) China Bks.
Naidoo, Beverley. Chain of Fire. Velasquez, Eric, illus. LC 89-27551. 256p. (gr. 6 up). 1990. 14.00 (*0-397-32426-X*, Lipp Jr Bks); PLB 13.89 (*0-397-32427-8*, Lipp Jr Bks) HarpC Child Bks.
—Chain of Fire. LC 89-27551. 256p. (gr. 6 up). 1993. pap. 3.95 (*0-06-440468-4*, Trophy) HarpC Child Bks.
—Journey to Jo'burg: A South African Story. reissued ed. Velasquez, Eric, illus. LC 85-45508. 96p. (gr. 4-7). 1986. 14.00 (*0-397-32168-6*, Lipp Jr Bks); PLB 13.89 (*0-397-32169-4*) HarpC Child Bks.
—Journey to Jo'burg: A South African Story. Velasquez, Eric, illus. LC 85-45508. 96p. (gr. 4-7). 1988. pap. 3.95 (*0-06-440237-1*, Trophy) HarpC Child Bks.
Naish, Jack. Philip: Traveling Preacher. Hester, Ron, illus. (gr. 1-6). 1978. 5.95 (*0-8054-4241-3*, 4242-41) Broadman.
Nakajima, Caroline. A Literature Unit: Tuck Everlasting. Miriani, Patricia, ed. Fullam, Sue, illus. 48p. (Orig.). (gr. 5-8). 1992. pap. 5.95 wkbk. (*1-55734-408-6*) Tchr Create Mat.
Nakano, Dokuihtei. Easy Origami. Kenneway, Eric, tr. Nakano, Dokuihtei, illus. LC 85-40644. 64p. (gr. k-12). 1986. pap. 13.00 (*0-670-80382-0*) Viking Child Bks.
—Easy Origami. Kenneway, Eric, tr. (Illus.). 64p. (gr. 2-5). 1994. pap. 4.99 (*0-14-036525-7*) Puffin Bks.
Nakano, Mei T. Riko Rabbit. LC 82-81737. (gr. 2-5). 1982. pap. 5.95 (*0-942610-00-8*) Mina Pr.

Nakatani, Herbert Y. Photosynthesis. Head, J. J., ed. Steffen, Ann T., illus. LC 84-45838. 16p. (Orig.). (gr. 10 up). 1988. pap. text ed. 2.75 (0-89278-109-2, 45-9793) Carolina Biological.

Nakawatari, Harutaka. The Sea & I. (Illus.). 32p. (ps-3). 1992. 15.00 (0-374-36428-1) FS&G.

Nakosteen, Mehdi. Mulla's Donkey & Other Friends. LC 74-620109. (Illus.). 150p. 1988. 20.00 (0-317-90546-5); pap. 8.50 (0-317-90547-3) Iran Bks.

Name Game Staff. Hanukkah Alphabet. (Illus.). (ps-5). 1977. pap. 2.50 (0-914080-63-6) Shulsinger Sales.

Namioka, Lensey. April & the Dragon Lady. LC 93-27958. 1994. write for info. (0-15-276644-8, Browndeer Pr) HarBrace.

—The Coming of the Bear. LC 91-17331. 192p. (gr. 7 up). 1992. 14.00 (0-06-020288-2); PLB 13.89 (0-06-020289-0) HarpC Child Bks.

—Island of Ogres. LC 88-22058. 208p. (gr. 7 up) 1989. PLB 13.89 (0-06-024373-2) HarpC Child Bks.

—Valley of the Broken Cherry Trees. LC 79-53605. (gr. 7 up). 1980. 8.95 (0-440-09325-2) Delacorte.

—Village of the Vampire Cat: A Novel. LC 80-68737. 224p. (gr. 8-12). 1981. 9.95 (0-440-09377-5) Delacorte.

—Yang the Youngest & His Terrible Ear. De Kiefte, Kees, illus. 112p. (gr. 3-7). 1992. 14.95 (0-316-59701-5, Joy St Bks) Little.

—Yang the Youngest & His Terrible Ear. (gr. 4-7). 1994. pap. 3.50 (0-440-40917-9) Dell.

Namjoshi, Suniti. Aditi & the One-Eyed Monkey. Hassan, Hanife, illus. LC 88-19058. 96p. (gr. 2-5). 1989. lib. bdg. 10.95 (0-8070-8314-3); pap. 3.95 (0-8070-8315-1) Beacon Pr.

Namm, D. Little Bear. (Illus.). 28p. (ps-2). 1990. PLB 12.33 (0-516-05356-6); pap. 3.95 (0-516-45356-4) Childrens.

—Monsters! (Illus.). 28p. (ps-2). 1990. PLB 12.33 (0-516-05358-2); pap. 3.95 (0-516-45358-0) Childrens.

Nanao, Jun. Life of the Ant. Pohl, Kathy, ed. LC 85-28198. (Illus.). 32p. (gr. 3-7). 1986. PLB 17.96 (0-8172-2539-0) Raintree Steck-V.

Nance, Douglas W. Pascal: Introduction to Programming & Problem Solving. (Illus.). 639p. (gr. 9-12). 1989. Repr. of 1986 ed. text ed. 34.25 (0-314-93206-2) West Pub.

Nance, John. Lobo of the Tasaday: A Stone Age Boy Meets the Modern World. Nance, John, illus. LC 81-14113. 56p. (gr. 3-7). 1982. 9.95 (0-394-85077-7) Pantheon.

Nankin, Fran, ed. see McCall, Edith.

Nannini, Roger, illus. Josephine's Toy Shop: A Look-&-Play Book with a Special Fold-Out Toy Shop. (ps-2). 1991. 15.95 (0-8037-1004-6) Dial Bks Young.

Nanus, Susan & Kornblatt, Marc. Mission to World War Two. 144p. (Orig.). (gr. 4 up). 1986. pap. 2.25 (0-553-25431-6) Bantam.

Napa, Amy. Dealing with Disappointment. (Illus.). 48p. (gr. 6-8). 1992. pap. 7.99 (1-55945-139-4) Group Pub.

Naples, Marge. A Step-by-Step Book about Siamese Cats. (Illus.). 64p. (gr. 9-12). 1988. pap. 3.95 (0-86622-473-4, SK-021) TFH Pubns.

Napoli, Donna J. Hero of Barletta. (ps-3). 1992. pap. 2.99 (0-440-40562-9) Dell.

—The Magic Circle. LC 92-27008. 112p. (gr. 7 up). 1993. 14.99 (0-525-45127-7, DCB) Dutton Child Bks.

—Prince of the Pond. LC 91-40340. (Illus.). 112p. (gr. 2-5). 1992. 13.00 (0-525-44976-0, DCB) Dutton Child Bks.

—Soccer Shock. Johnson, Meredith, illus. LC 91-20706. 192p. (gr. 4-7). 1991. 13.95 (0-525-44827-6, DCB) Dutton Child Bks.

—Soccer Shock. Johnson, Meredith, illus. LC 93-7483. 192p. (gr. 3-7). 1993. pap. 3.99 (0-14-036482-X, Puffin) Puffin Bks.

—When the Water Closes over My Head. Poydar, Nancy, illus. LC 93-14486. 60p. (gr. 2-5). 1994. 13.99 (0-525-45083-1) Dutton Child Bks.

Napp, John L. United States History, Bk. I: To 1877. (Illus.). 344p. (gr. 7-12). 1988. text ed. 18.49 (0-86601-692-9); tchr's. ed. 12.99 (0-86601-693-7); wkbk. 4.99 (0-86601-694-5) Media Materials.

Nappa, Amy. Exodus: Following God. (Illus.). 48p. (gr. 9-12). 1992. pap. 7.99 (1-55945-226-9) Group Pub.

—Love or Infatuation? (Illus.). 48p. (gr. 6-8). 1992. pap. 7.99 (1-55945-128-9) Group Pub.

Nappa, Amy, jt. auth. see Nappa, Mike.

Nappa, Mike. Accepting Other: Beyond Barriers & Stereotypes. (Illus.). 48p. (gr. 6-8). 1992. pap. 7.99 (1-55945-126-2) Group Pub.

—Reaching Out to a Hurting World. (Illus.). 48p. (gr. 6-8). 1992. pap. 7.99 (1-55945-140-8) Group Pub.

Nappa, Mike & Nappa, Amy. Student Plan-it Calendar 1993-1994 Daily Organizer. (Illus.). 120p. (gr. 9-12). 1993. spiral bdg. 6.99 (1-55945-163-7) Group Pub.

Narahashi, Keiko. I Have a Friend. Narahashi, Keiko, illus. LC 86-27628. 32p. (ps-3). 1987. SBE 13.95 (0-689-50432-2, M K McElderry) Macmillan Child Grp.

Narain, Aditya, jt. auth. see Khurelblat, B.

Narang, Rajanini, ed. see Barber, Ezekiel.

Naranjo, Rafael S. Great Animal Refuges. LC 93-3437. (Illus.). 36p. (gr. 3 up). 1993. PLB 19.93 (0-516-08385-6) Childrens.

Naranjo, Tito. Native Americans of the Southwest. (Illus.). 64p. (Orig.). (gr. 2 up). 1993. pap. 17.95 incl. kit (1-56138-241-8) Running Pr.

Narayana, T. R. Bheesma. Sharma, Mukesh, illus. (gr. 1-8). 1979. 3.00 (0-89744-151-6) Auromere.

Nardi, James B. Once upon a Tree: Life from Treetop to Root Tips. Nardi, James B., illus. LC 92-36444. 104p. (gr. 5-10). 1993. 16.95x (0-8138-0917-7) Iowa St U Pr.

Nardi, Thomas J. Bowling Basics. Gow, Bill, illus. LC 83-22893. 48p. (gr. 3-7). 1984. PLB 10.95 (0-13-080516-5) P-H.

Nardo, Don. Ancient Greece. 1994. 14.95 (1-56006-229-0) Lucent Bks.

—Animation: Drawings Spring to Life. LC 92-5151. (Illus.). 96p. (gr. 5-8). 1992. PLB 15.95 (1-56006-218-5) Lucent Bks.

—Anxiety & Phobias. (Illus.). 112p. (gr. 6-12). 1992. 18.95 (0-7910-0041-9) Chelsea Hse.

—Charles Darwin. (Illus.). 112p. (gr. 5 up). 1993. 18.95 (0-7910-1729-X, Am Art Analog); pap. write for info. (0-7910-1730-3, Am Art Analog) Chelsea Hse.

—Chernobyl. McGovern, Brian, illus. LC 90-33567. 64p. (gr. 5-8). 1990. PLB 11.95 (1-56006-008-5) Lucent Bks.

—Computers: Mechanical Minds. LC 90-6648. (Illus.). 96p. (gr. 5-8). 1990. PLB 15.95 (1-56006-206-1) Lucent Bks.

—Death Penalty. LC 92-20366. (Illus.). 112p. (gr. 5-8). 1992. PLB 14.95 (1-56006-132-4) Lucent Bks.

—Dinosaurs. LC 93-4314. (gr. 5 up). 1994. write for info. (1-56510-154-5) Lucent Bks.

—Drugs & Sports. LC 90-6686. (Illus.). 112p. (gr. 5-8). 1990. PLB 14.95 (1-56006-112-X) Lucent Bks.

—Eating Disorders. LC 91-15563. (Illus.). 112p. (gr. 5-8). 1991. PLB 14.95 (1-56006-129-4) Lucent Bks.

—Exercise. (Illus.). 112p. (gr. 6-12). 1992. 18.95 (0-7910-0017-6) Chelsea Hse.

—Germs: Mysterious Microorganisms. LC 91-15569. (Illus.). 96p. (gr. 5-8). 1991. PLB 15.95 (1-56006-214-2) Lucent Bks.

—Gravity: The Universal Force. LC 90-6413. (Illus.). 96p. (gr. 5-8). 1990. PLB 15.95 (1-56006-204-5) Lucent Bks.

—H. G. Wells. LC 92-19870. (Illus.). 112p. (gr. 5-8). 1992. PLB 14.95 (1-56006-025-5) Lucent Bks.

—Hygiene. (Illus.). (gr. 7-12). 1994. 19.95 (0-7910-0020-6, Am Art Analog) Chelsea Hse.

—Hygiene. Koop, C. Everett, intro. by. LC 92-32086. 1993. pap. write for info. (0-7910-0460-0) Chelsea Hse.

—The Indian Wars. LC 91-23068. (Illus.). 112p. (gr. 5-8). 1991. PLB 17.95 (1-56006-403-X) Lucent Bks.

—The Irish Potato Famine. McGovern, Brian, illus. LC 90-6246. 64p. (gr. 5-8). 1990. PLB 11.95 (1-56006-012-3) Lucent Bks.

—Jim Thorpe. LC 93-41138. 1994. 14.95 (1-56006-045-X) Lucent Bks.

—Krakatoa. McGovern, Brian, illus. LC 90-6003. 64p. (gr. 5-8). 1990. PLB 11.95 (1-56006-011-5) Lucent Bks.

—Lasers: Humanity's Magic Light. LC 90-6269. (Illus.). 96p. (gr. 5-8). 1990. PLB 15.95 (1-56006-200-2) Lucent Bks.

—Medical Diagnosis. (Illus.). (gr. 6-12). 1993. 18.95 (0-7910-0067-2) Chelsea Hse.

—The Mexican-American War. LC 91-16728. (Illus.). 112p. (gr. 5-8). 1991. PLB 17.95 (1-56006-402-1) Lucent Bks.

—Oil Spills. LC 90-23524. (Illus.). 112p. (gr. 5-8). 1991. PLB 14.95 (1-56006-151-0) Lucent Bks.

—Ozone. LC 91-6275. (Illus.). 112p. (gr. 5-8). 1991. PLB 14.95 (1-56006-101-4) Lucent Bks.

—The Persian Gulf War. LC 91-23064. (Illus.). 112p. (gr. 5-8). 1991. PLB 17.95 (1-56006-411-0) Lucent Bks.

—Population. LC 90-23525. (Illus.). 112p. (gr. 5-8). 1991. PLB 14.95 (1-56006-123-5) Lucent Bks.

—Recycling. LC 92-27849. (Illus.). 112p. (gr. 5-8). 1992. PLB 14.95 (1-56006-135-9) Lucent Bks.

—The Roman Empire. 1994. 14.95 (1-56006-231-2) Lucent Bks.

—The Roman Republic. 1994. 14.95 (1-56006-230-4) Lucent Bks.

—Thomas Jefferson. (Illus.). 111p. (gr. 5-8). 1993. PLB 14.95 (1-56006-037-9) Lucent Bks.

—The U. S. Congress. LC 93-41137. 1994. 14.95 (1-56006-155-3) Lucent Bks.

—Vitamins & Minerals. (Illus.). (gr. 7-12). 1994. 19.95 (0-7910-0032-X, Am Art Analog) Chelsea Hse.

—The War of 1812. LC 91-29501. (Illus.). 112p. (gr. 5-8). 1991. PLB 17.95 (1-56006-401-3) Lucent Bks.

—World War Two: The War in the Pacific. LC 91-16727. (Illus.). 112p. (gr. 5-8). 1991. PLB 17.95 (1-56006-408-0) Lucent Bks.

Nardo, Don & Belgum, Erik. Voodoo: Opposing Viewpoints. LC 91-14497. (Illus.). 112p. (gr. 5-8). 1991. PLB 14.95 (0-89908-089-8) Greenhaven.

Narell, Irena. Joshua: Fighter for Bar Kochba. LC 78-55959. (gr. 6-12). 1979. pap. 5.95 (0-934764-01-8) Akiba Pr.

Nargi, Ben J. Are You He Who Is to Come. LC 88-51027. 138p. 1989. pap. 6.95 (1-55523-177-2) Winston-Derek.

Narney, Dean. The Christmas Tree That Ate My Mother. 1992. 2.95 (0-590-44881-1, Apple Paperbacks) Scholastic Inc.

Nasaw, Jonathan. Shakedown Street. LC 92-43046. 1993. 14.95 (0-385-31071-4) Delacorte.

Nash, Amy. North Korea. (Illus.). 128p. (gr. 5 up). 1990. 14.95 (0-7910-0157-1) Chelsea Hse.

Nash, Bartleby. Mother Nature's Greatest Hits: The Top 40 Wonders of the Animal World. (Illus.). 144p. (Orig.). 1991. pap. 5.95 (0-9626072-7-4) Living Planet Pr.

Nash, Bruce. Little Big Leaguers: Amazing Boyhood Stories of Today's Baseball Stars. (gr. 4-7). 1990. pap. 7.95 (0-671-69360-3, Little Simon) S&S Trade.

Nash, Bruce & Zullo, Allan. Baseball Hall of Shame Two: Young Fans' Edition. Clancy, Lisa, ed. 144p. (Orig.). 1991. pap. 2.99 (0-671-73533-0, Archway) PB.

—The Baseball Hall of Shame's Funtastic Trivia & Sticker Book. Maul, Bill, illus. 24p. (gr. 1 up). 1992. pap. 3.95 (0-671-74439-9, Little Simon) S&S Trade.

—The Basketball Hall of Shame: Young Fans' Edition. Clancy, Lisa, ed. 160p. (Orig.). 1993. pap. 2.99 (0-671-75356-8, Archway) PB.

—The Football Hall of Shame Two: Young Fans' Edition. Clancy, Lisa, ed. 160p. (Orig.). (gr. 3-6). 1991. pap. 2.99 (0-671-73534-9, Archway) PB.

—The Football Hall of Shame: Young Fans' Edition. (Illus.). 144p. (gr. 5 up). 1990. pap. 2.95 (0-671-72922-5, Archway) PB.

—Freebies for Sports Fans. Doty, Roy, illus. 96p. (gr. 1 up). 1990. pap. 4.95 (0-671-70339-0, S&S BFYR) S&S Trade.

—The Greatest Sports Stories Never Told. Ward, Bernie, compiled by. Gampert, John, illus. LC 92-15352. 1993. pap. 13.00 (0-671-79527-9); pap. 8.95 (0-671-75938-8) S&S Trade.

—Little Basketball Big Leaguers: Amazing Boyhood Stories of Today's Basketball Stars. (Illus.). 96p. (gr. 1 up). 1991. pap. 7.95 (0-671-73445-8, Little Simon) S&S Trade.

—More Little Big Leaguers: Amazing Boyhood Stories of Today's Baseball Stars. (Illus.). 96p. (gr. 1 up). 1991. pap. 7.95 incl. baseball cards (0-671-73394-X, Little Simon) S&S Trade.

—The Sports Hall of Shame: Young Fans Edition. MacDonald, Patricia, ed. 176p. 1990. pap. 2.95 (0-671-69355-7, Archway) PB.

—The Sports Hall of Shame's Funtastic Trivia & Sticker Book. Maul, Bill, illus. 24p. (gr. 1 up). 1992. pap. 3.95 incl. 24 stickers (0-671-74438-0, Little Simon) S&S Trade.

Nash, Bruce, et al. Haunted Kids: True Ghost Stories. LC 93-14489. (Illus.). (gr. 4-9). 1993. pap. 2.95 (0-8167-3266-3) Troll Assocs.

Nash, Corey. I'm Growing Up! Things I Can Do by Myself. Wells, Chrissie, illus. (ps-k). 1990. 4.95 (1-55782-028-7, Pub. by Warner Juvenile Bks) Little.

—Little Treasury of Beatrix Potter, 6 vols. in 1. 1988. boxed 5.99 (0-517-46667-8) Outlet Bk Co.

—Little Treasury of Fairy Tales, 6 vols. in 1. 1988. boxed 5.99 (0-517-43616-7) Outlet Bk Co.

—Little Treasury of Mother Goose, 6 vols. in 1. 1988. boxed 5.99 (0-517-38571-6) Outlet Bk Co.

—Little Treasury of Nursery Rhymes, 6 vols. in 1. 1988. 5.99 (0-517-49203-2) Outlet Bk Co.

—Little Treasury of Raggedy Ann & Andy. Gruelle, Johnny, illus. (ps-1). 1984. 5.99 (0-517-44730-4) Outlet Bk Co.

—Little Treasury of Walt Disney: Mickey & Friends. 1988. 5.99 (0-517-61639-4) Outlet Bk Co.

Nash, Corey, retold by. Little Treasury of Peter Rabbit, 6 vols. Potter, Beatrix, illus. (ps). 1983. 5.99 (0-517-41069-9, Chatham River Pr) Outlet Bk Co.

Nash, Corey & Nash, Corey, eds. My Gingerbread Fairy Tale House, 4 bks. Durrell, Julie, illus. LC 87-40689. (ps). 1990. Set. bds. 6.95 (1-55782-056-2, Pub. by Warner Juvenile Bks) Little.

Nash, Grace C. & Rapley, Janice. Holidays & Special Days. Feldstein, Sandy, et al, eds. (Illus.). 260p. (gr. k-6). 1988. tchr's. ed. 24.95 (0-88284-368-0, 3517); student, 136p. 9.95 (0-88284-369-9, 3516) Alfred Pub.

Nash, Margaret & Brodley, Sue. Josh's Expedition. (Illus.). 32p. (ps-1). 1993. 17.95 (0-370-31572-3, Pub. by Bodley Head UK) Trafalgar.

Nash, Ogden. The Adventures of Isabel. Marshall, James, illus. (ps-3). 1991. 14.95 (0-316-59874-7) Little.

—The Animal Garden. Knight, Hilary, illus. LC 65-21772. 48p. (gr. 10 up). 1988. pap. 5.95 (0-87131-568-8) M Evans.

—The Cruise of the Aardvark. Watson, Wendy, illus. LC 67-27296. 48p. (ps up). 1989. pap. 5.95 (0-87131-570-X) M Evans.

—Custard & Company. Blake, Quentin, illus. 128p. (gr. 2-6). 1985. pap. 6.95 (0-316-59855-0) Little.

—Custard the Dragon. Nash, Linell, illus. (gr. k-3). 1973. lib. bdg. 14.95 (0-316-59841-0) Little.

Nash, Ogden, jt. auth. see Lear, Edward.

Nash, Paul. Colossal Constructions. Young, Richard G., ed. LC 89-11714. (Illus.). 32p. (gr. 3-5). 1989. PLB 13.26 (0-944483-35-6) Garrett Ed Corp.

—Super Structures. Harris, Peter, ed. LC 89-12009. (Illus.). 32p. (gr. 2-4). 1989. PLB 13.26 (0-944483-37-2) Garrett Ed Corp.

Nash, Renea D. Coping with Interracial Dating. LC 93-6895. 1993. 13.95 (0-8239-1606-5) Rosen Group.

Nash, Rod. In Germany. (GER.). 80p. (gr. 7-12). 1984. pap. text ed. 8.95 (0-8219-0056-0, 45285); tchr's. wkbk. 5.95 (0-8219-0274-1, 45820); 4.95 (0-8219-0273-3, 45660) EMC.

Nash, Sue, jt. auth. see Khdir, Kate.

Nashone. Grandmother Stories: Northwestern Indian Tales. (Illus.). (gr. 5-12). 1987. pap. 6.95 (0-940113-06-6) Sierra Oaks Pub.

—Where Indians Live: American Indian Houses. Smith, Louise, illus. 37p. (Orig.). (gr. k-6). 1989. pap. 6.95 (*0-940113-16-3*) Sierra Oaks Pub.

Nason, Janet. Little Women Paper Dolls. 8p. (gr. 8-12). 1982. pap. 4.00 (*0-914510-13-4*) Evergreen.

Nast, Thomas, jt. auth. see Webster, George P.

Nasta, Cynthia V. Peter & His Pick-up Truck: A Southwestern Children's Tale. Zilka, Pat, illus. LC 89-80351. 24p. (ps-8). 1989. pap. 6.95 (*0-9622064-0-7*) Little Buckaroo.

—Peter & His Pick-up Truck: An Arizona Children's Tale. Zilka, Pat, illus. LC 89-80352. 24p. (ps-8). 1989. PLB 6.95 (*0-9622064-1-5*); pap. 6.95 (*0-9622064-2-3*) Little Buckaroo.

Nasta, Phyllis. Aaron Goes to the Shelter: A Story & Workbook Guide about Abuse, Placement & Protective Services. Williams, Mary L., illus. 37p. (Orig.). (gr. k-6). 1992. pap. text ed. 5.95 (*1-880702-00-2*) Whole Child.

Nathan, Adele G. First Transatlantic Cable. (Illus.). (gr. 5-9). 1963. lib. bdg. 8.99 (*0-394-90388-9*) Random Bks Yng Read.

Nathan, Beverly & Bizer, Linda. The Huddles Jumbo Activity & Coloring Book. Kong, Emilie, illus. 128p. (ps-8). pap. write for info (*0-910313-78-4*) Parker Bros.

—King Size Coloring & Activity Book. Paris, Pat & Kong, Emilie, illus. 128p. (ps-8). 1984. pap. 2.50 (*0-910313-57-1*) Parker Bros.

Nathan, Robert. Portrait of Jennie. 293p. 1981. Repr. PLB 18.95x (*0-89966-356-7*) Buccaneer Bks.

—Portrait of Jennie. 234p. 1981. Repr. PLB 16.95x (*0-89967-030-X*) Harmony Raine.

Nathan, Ruth, ed. Writers in the Classroom. Kirby, Dan, frwd. by. 288p. (gr. k-12). 1990. text ed. 22.50 (*0-926842-05-6*) CG Pubs Inc.

Nathanson, Laura. The Trouble with Wednesdays. 176p. (gr. 7-12). 1987. pap. 2.95 (*0-553-26337-4*, Starfire) Bantam.

National Archives Staff, ed. Kennedy's Inaugural Address of 1961. LC 86-600367. (Illus.). 30p. (Orig.). 1987. pap. text ed. 3.50x (*0-911333-53-3*, 200110) Natl Archives & Records.

National Conference of Catholic Bishops Staff, jt. auth. see Bishops' Committee for Pastoral Research Staff.

National Council of Teachers of Mathematics Staff. Organizing Data & Dealing with Uncertainty. rev. ed. LC 79-9281. (Illus.). 135p. (gr. 5-8). 1979. pap. 10.00 (*0-87353-141-8*) NCTM.

National Curriculum Editors. The English Book: A Perma-Bound Teach & Use Handbook for the Secondary Level. Snodgrass, Mary E., ed. (Illus.). 252p. (gr. 7 up). 1991. text ed. 13.25 (*0-7804-1950-2*, 089669) Perma-Bound.

National Curriculum Publishing Editors. Great American English Handbook. rev. ed. Snodgrass, Mary E., ed. Booten, Kevin, illus. 235p. (gr. 7 up). 1991. Repr. of 1987 ed. lib. bdg. 10.80 (*0-8000-2426-5*, 122550) Perma-Bound.

National Dairy Council Staff. Food...Early Choices Program. rev. ed. (ps-k). 1979. write for info. (*1-55647-491-1*) Natl Dairy Coun.

—Growth Record. (Illus.). 8p. (gr. 3-4). 1988. pap. text ed. write for info. (*1-55647-003-7*) Natl Dairy Coun.

—Uncle Jim's Dairy Farm: A Summer Visit with Aunt Helen & Uncle Jim. (Illus.). 4p. (gr. 3-6). 1980. Set incls. 12 user's guides & 1 tchr's. guide. write for info. (*1-55647-611-6*); write for info. 1/2 inch VHS tape (*1-55647-634-5*) Natl Dairy Coun.

National Dairy Council Staff & Dairy Council of California Staff. Smart Moves. (Illus.). 1990. write for info. tchr's ed. (*1-556-47172-6*); write for info. wkbk. (*1-556-47173-4*); write for info. videotape (*1-556-47171-8*); write for info. poster (*1-556-47174-2*) Natl Dairy Coun.

National Gallery, London. Christmas Decorations. (Illus.). (gr. 8 up). 1993. pap. 12.95 (*0-316-59890-9*) Little.

National Gallery of Art Staff. A Renaissance Christmas. (Illus.). 64p. 1991. 19.95 (*0-8212-1875-1*) Bulfinch Pr.

National Geographic Society, ed. Books for Young Explorers, 4 vols, Set 5. Incl. Camping Adventures. LC 76-2116; Wonders of the Desert World. LC 76-2221; The Playful Dolphins. LC 76-2118; Animals That Build Their Homes. LC 76-2117. avail. only from Natl Geog 13.95 (*0-87044-200-7*); PLB 16.95 (*0-87044-205-8*) Natl Geog.

National Geographic Society, Special Publications Division Staff, ed. Exploring Your World: The Adventure of Geography. rev. ed. LC 93-1849. (ps-6). 1993. write for info. Natl Geog.

National Geographic Society Staff. Books for Young Explorers, 4 vols., set 8. Incl. Wild Cats. Winston, Peggy D. LC 81-47742; Amazing Animal Groups. LC 81-47743; Koalas & Kangaroos: Strange Animals of Australia. Eugene, Toni. LC 81-607859; Life in Ponds & Streams. Amos, William H. LC 81-47745. (Illus.). (ps-3). 1981. Set. lib. bdg. 16.95 (*0-87044-405-0*); Set. PLB 13.95 (*0-87044-410-5*) Natl Geog.

—Books for Young Explorers, 4 vols, set 9. Incl. Animals That Travel. Urquhart, Jennifer C. LC 82-47856; Puppies. Rinard, Judith E. LC 82-47857; Animals in Winter. Fisher, Ronald M. LC 82-47859; What Happens in the Autumn. Venino, Suzanne. LC 82-47858. 1982. lib. bdg. 16.95 (*0-87044-966-4*) Natl Geog.

National Geographic Society Staff, ed. Books for Young Explorers, 4 vols, Set 2. Incl. Honeybees. LC 73-7111; How Animals Hide. LC 73-7112; Namu. LC 73-7113; Pandas. LC 73-7114. (ps-3). 1973. PLB 16.95 avail. only from Natl Geog (*0-87044-305-4*) Natl Geog.

—Books for Young Explorers, 4 vols, Set 3. Incl. Spiders. LC 74-10109; Creepy Crawly Things. LC 74-10110; Three Little Indians. LC 74-10111; Cats. LC 74-10112. (Illus.). (ps-3). 1974. PLB 16.95 (*0-87044-310-0*) Natl Geog.

—Books for Young Explorers, 4 vols, Set 4. Incl. Cowboys. LC 75-6067; A Day in the Woods. LC 75-6068; Tricks Animals Play. LC 75-6066; The Wild Ponies of Assategue Island. LC 75-6065. PLB 16.95 avail. only from Natl Geog (*0-87044-175-2*) Natl Geog.

—Books for Young Explorers, 4 vols, Set 6. Incl. Creatures of the Night. LC 77-76968; The Blue Whale. LC 77-76971; Let's Go to the Moon. LC 77-76972; What Happens in the Spring. LC 77-76970. 13.95 (*0-87044-245-7*); PLB 16.95 (*0-87044-250-3*) Natl Geog.

—Books for Young Explorers, 4 vols, Set 7. Incl. Animals in Danger. Winston, Peggy D. LC 77-95411; Animals That Live in the Sea. Straker, Joan A. LC 77-95415; Explore a Spooky Swamp. Cortesi, Wendy W. Bailey, Joseph H., illus. LC 77-95414; Zoo Babies. Grosvenor, Donna K. Grosvenor, Donna K., illus. LC 77-95413. (Illus.). (gr. 4-8). 1978. 13.95 (*0-87044-265-1*) Natl Geog.

—Books for Young Explorers, 4 vols, Set 15. (gr. k-4). 1988. Set. 13.95 (*0-87044-737-8*); Set. PLB 16.95 (*0-87044-742-4*) No. 1: Animals in Summer. No. 2: Animals at Play. No. 3: Busy Beavers. No. 4: Let's Explore a River. Natl Geog.

National Geographic Society Staff, ed. Around My Town. (ps) 1993. 5.00 (*0-7922-1968-6*) Natl Geog.

—At the Zoo. (ps-3). 1993. 16.00 (*0-87044-872-2*) Natl Geog.

—Fun at the Fair. (ps). 1993. 4.50 (*0-7922-1919-8*) Natl Geog.

—My House. (ps). 1993. 4.50 (*0-7922-1835-3*) Natl Geog.

—Pile of Puppies. (ps). 1993. 4.50 (*0-7922-1834-5*) Natl Geog.

National Geographical Society Staff, ed. Books for Young Explorers, 4 vols, Set 1. Incl. Dinosaurs. LC 72-91418; Treasures in the Sea. LC 72-91419; Dogs Working for People. LC 72-91419; Lion Cubs. LC 72-91420. (ps-3). 1972. PLB 16.95 avail. only from Natl Geog (*0-87044-300-3*) Natl Geog.

National Museum of American Art Staff, jt. auth. see Everett, Gwen.

National Safety Council Staff. Learn to Swim, Journey One. 1993. pap. 5.00 (*0-86720-788-4*) Jones & Bartlett.

National TCA Book Committee Staff, et al. Lionel Trains: Standard of the World, 1900-1943. 2nd ed. Witalis-Burke Agency Staff, illus. (Illus.). 256p. 1989. Repr. of 1976 ed. 34.95 (*0-917896-02-5*); prepub. 24.95 (*0-317-93968-8*) TCA PA.

National Trust Staff. Investigating Gardens. (Illus.). 32p. (gr. 5-8). 1993. pap. 6.95 (*0-7078-0146-X*, Pub. by Natl Trust UK) Trafalgar.

—Investigating the Civil War. (Illus.). 32p. (gr. 5-8). 1993. pap. 6.95 (*0-7078-0111-7*, Pub. by Natl Trust UK) Trafalgar.

—Investigating the Victorians. (Illus.). 32p. (gr. 3-6). 1994. pap. 6.95 (*0-7078-0167-2*, Pub. by Natl Trust UK) Trafalgar.

National Wildlife Federation Staff. Amazing Mammals I. (gr. k-8). 1991. pap. 7.95 (*0-945051-29-8*, 75023) Natl Wildlife.

—Amazing Mammals II. (gr. k-8). 1991. pap. 7.95 (*0-945051-30-1*, 75024) Natl Wildlife.

—Astronomy Adventures. (gr. k-8). 1991. pap. 7.95 (*0-945051-31-X*, 75022) Natl Wildlife.

—Birds, Birds, Birds. (gr. k-8). 1991. pap. 7.95 (*0-945051-32-8*, 75004) Natl Wildlife.

—Digging into Dinosaurs. (gr. k-8). 1991. pap. 7.95 (*0-945051-33-6*, 75002) Natl Wildlife.

—Discovering Deserts. (gr. k-8). 1991. pap. 7.95 (*0-945051-34-4*, 75005) Natl Wildlife.

—Diving into Oceans. (gr. k-8). 1991. pap. 7.95 (*0-945051-36-0*, 75042) Natl Wildlife.

—Endangered Species. (gr. k-8). 1991. pap. 7.95 (*0-945051-37-9*, 75033) Natl Wildlife.

—Geology: The Active Earth. (gr. k-8). 1991. pap. 7.95 (*0-945051-38-7*, 75032) Natl Wildlife.

—Incredible Insects. (gr. k-8). 1991. pap. 7.95 (*0-945051-39-5*, 75001) Natl Wildlife.

—Let's Hear It for Herps. (gr. k-8). 1991. pap. 7.95 (*0-945051-42-5*, 75043) Natl Wildlife.

—Pollution: Problems & Solutions. (gr. k-8). 1991. pap. 7.95 (*0-945051-40-9*, 75045) Natl Wildlife.

—Rain Forests: Tropical Treasures. (gr. k-8). 1991. pap. 7.95 (*0-945051-41-7*, 75044) Natl Wildlife.

—Trees Are Terrific. (gr. k-8). 1991. pap. 7.95 (*0-945051-43-3*, 75021) Natl Wildlife.

—Wading into Wetlands. (gr. k-8). 1991. pap. 7.95 (*0-945051-44-1*, 75025) Natl Wildlife.

—Wild about Weather. (gr. k-8). 1991. pap. 7.95 (*0-945051-45-X*, 75003) Natl Wildlife.

—Wild & Crafty. (gr. k-8). 1991. pap. 7.95 (*0-945051-46-8*, 75043) Natl Wildlife.

Natti, Susanna, jt. auth. see Abler, David A.

Natural History Museum, London, England Staff, compiled by. Creepy Crawlies: Ladybugs, Lobsters, & Other Amazing Arthropods. LC 90-27531. (Illus.). 108p. 1991. 14.95 (*0-8069-8336-1*) Sterling.

Natural History Museum Staff. Rocks & Minerals. Keates, Colin & Einsiedel, Andreas, photos by. LC 87-26514. (Illus.). 64p. (gr. 5 up). 1988. 15.00 (*0-394-89621-1*); lib. bdg. 15.99 (*0-394-99621-6*) Knopf Bks Yng Read.

Natural History Museum Staff, compiled by. Creepy Crawlies, Lobsters & Other Amazing Arthropods. LC 90-27531. (Illus.). 108p. (gr. 4-10). 1992. pap. 9.95 (*0-8069-8337-X*) Sterling.

Nau, Douglas S. The New CRIS Case Studies. 57p. (gr. k up). 1982. pap. 15.50 (*1-881678-03-2*) CRIS.

Nau, Patrick. State Patrol. Nau, Pat, photos by. LC 83-2716. (Illus.). 32p. (gr. k-4). 1984. PLB 13.50 (*0-87614-264-1*) Carolrhoda Bks.

Naughton, Jim. My Brother Stealing Second. LC 88-22035. 224p. (gr. 7 up). 1989. PLB 13.89 (*0-06-024375-9*) HarpC Child Bks.

—My Brother Stealing Second. LC 88-22035. 288p. (gr. 7 up). 1991. pap. 3.95 (*0-06-447017-2*, Trophy) HarpC Child Bks.

Nault, Andy. Staying Alive in Alaska's Wild. Loftin, Tee, ed. (Illus.). 224p. (Orig.). (gr. 5 up). 1980. pap. 8.95 (*0-934812-01-2*) Tee Loftin.

Naumann, Cynthia E., ed. see Cutburth, Ronald W.

Naumenko, Maria. The Life of Saint Seraphim Wonderworkerof Sarov. Naumenko, Maria, illus. 24p. (Orig.). (gr. 5-10). 1992. pap. 3.00 (*0-88465-049-9*) Holy Trinity.

—The Life of Saint Seraphim Wonderworkerof Sarov: (Zhitie Prepodobnovo Serpahima, Sarovskovo Chudotvortsa) Naumenko, Maria, illus. (RUS.). 22p. (Orig.). (gr. 5-10). 1992. pap. 3.00 (*0-88465-052-9*) Holy Trinity.

Naumoff, Olga. About the Splendid Macedonians: A Coloring Book & Much, Much More. Schindler, A. A., illus. 64p. 1982. pap. 4.95 (*0-941983-00-5*) Splendid Assocs.

Nauta Staff. Mi Primera Enciclopedia, 2 vols. 7th ed. (SPA.). 420p. 1978. Set. 65.00 (*0-8288-5254-5*, S26910) Fr & Eur.

Navaroo, Jose G., jt. auth. see Reit, Seymour V.

Navarra, Jean E. Willowood. (gr. 3-5). 1990. 7.95 (*0-533-08923-9*) Vantage.

Navarra, Tova. On My Own: Helping Kids Help Themselves. Kerr, Tom, illus. 128p. (gr. 2-8). 1993. pap. 6.95 (*0-8120-1563-0*) Barron.

—Playing It Smart: What to Do When You're on Your Own. Kerr, Tom, illus. 128p. (gr. 2-8). 1989. 12.95 (*0-8120-6131-4*) Barron.

Navarro, C. F. Early Geometry. (Illus.). 64p. (Orig.). (gr. 2-3). 1990. pap. text ed. 6.50 (*1-878694-04-8*) Start Smart Bks.

Navarro, Carlos. Categories. (gr. k-2). 1990. wkbk. 4.50 (*1-878396-02-1*) Start Smart Bks.

—Verbal Correspondences. (gr. k-2). 1990. wkbk. 4.50 (*1-878396-00-5*) Start Smart Bks.

Navasky, Bruno P., selected by. & tr. Festival in My Heart: Poems by Japanese Children. LC 93-18251. 1993. 29.95 (*0-8109-3314-4*) Abrams.

Navazelskis, Ina. Alexander Dubcek. (Illus.). 112p. (gr. 5 up). 1991. 17.95 (*1-55546-831-4*) Chelsea Hse.

—Leonid Brezhnev. Schlesinger, Arthur M., Jr., intro. by. (Illus.). 112p. (gr. 5 up). 1988. lib. bdg. 17.95 (*0-87754-513-8*) Chelsea Hse.

Nave, Yolanda. Goosebumps & Butterflies. LC 89-48987. (Illus.). 32p. (ps-2). 1990. 12.95 (*0-531-05904-9*); PLB 12.99 (*0-531-08504-X*) Orchard Bks Watts.

Naveen, Ron. Antarctica. (Illus.). 16p. (Orig.). (gr. 10 up). 1992. pap. text ed. 2.75 (*0-89278-124-6*, 45-9624) Carolina Biological.

Naver, Judith E., ed. see Wise, Beth A. & Levin, Amy.

Navon, Ziva B., ed. The Glorious Sephardic Heritage. 120p. (Orig.). (gr. 6-12). 1992. pap. text ed. 10.00 (*0-685-57455-5*) Central Agency.

Nayer, Judith E., ed. see Block, Arlene.

Nayer, Judith E., ed. see Evans, Karen.

Nayer, Judith E., ed. see Jonson, Liz & Silliman, Emery.

Nayer, Judith E., ed. see Silliman, Emery & Jonson, Liz.

Nayer, Judith E., ed. see Wise, Beth A.

Nayer, Judith E., ed. see Wise, Beth A. & Block, Arlene.

Nayer, Judith E., ed. see Wise, Beth A. & Sokoloff, Myka-Lynne.

Nayer, Judy. Dinosaurs. Goldberg, Grace, illus. 12p. (ps-2). 1993. bds. 6.95 (*1-56293-336-1*) McClanahan Bk.

—The Happy Little Dinosaur. Goldberg, Grace, illus. 24p. (Orig.). (gr. k-1). 1990. pap. 0.99 (*1-878624-34-2*) McClanahan Bk.

—The Happy Little Engine. Allert, Kathy, illus. 24p. (Orig.). (gr. k-1). 1990. pap. 0.99 (*1-878624-43-1*) McClanahan Bk.

—Insects. Goldberg, Grace, illus. 12p. (ps-2). 1993. bds. 6.95 (*1-56293-335-3*) McClanahan Bk.

—Jungle Life. Goldberg, Grace, illus. 10p. (ps-2). 1992. bds. 6.95 (*1-56293-221-7*) McClanahan Bk.

—Mammals. Goldberg, Grace, illus. 12p. (ps-2). 1993. bds. 6.95 (*1-56293-337-X*) McClanahan Bk.

—My First Numbers. Cocca-Leffler, Maryann, illus. 32p. (ps). 1991. wkbk. 1.95 (*1-56293-166-0*) McClanahan Bk.

—My First Picture Dictionary. Schanzer, Roz, illus. 24p. (ps-2). 1992. pap. 0.99 (*1-56293-110-5*) McClanahan Bk.

—Night Animals. Goldberg, Grace, illus. 10p. (ps-2). 1992. bds. 6.95 (*1-56293-223-3*) McClanahan Bk.
—Reptiles. Goldberg, Grace, illus. 10p. (ps-2). 1992. bds. 6.95 (*1-56293-220-9*) McClanahan Bk.
—Sea Creatures. Goldberg, Grace, illus. 10p. (ps-2). 1992. bds. 6.95 (*1-56293-222-5*) McClanahan Bk.
—Space. Goldberg, Grace, illus. 12p. (ps-2). 1993. bds. 6.95 (*1-56293-338-8*) McClanahan Bk.
Nayer, Judy, ed. Mother Goose. Brodie, Cynthia, illus. 24p. (ps-2). 1992. pap. 0.99 (*1-56293-105-9*) McClanahan Bk.
—My First Book of Christmas Carols. Severn, Jeff, illus. 24p. (ps-2). 1991. pap. 0.99 (*1-56293-117-2*) McClanahan Bk.
—Rhymes to Count On. Bates, Louise, illus. 24p. (ps-2). 1992. pap. 0.99 (*1-56293-104-0*) McClanahan Bk.
Naylor, Bob. Yesterday in the Nineteen Twenties. Piequet, Miriam, illus. LC 83-61988. 62p. (Orig.). 1983. pap. 6.95 (*0-914275-00-3*) Anyone Can Read Bks.
Naylor, Keith, jt. auth. see St. Clair, Barry.
Naylor, Kim. Mali. (Illus.). 96p. (gr. 5 up). 1988. 14.95 (*1-55546-181-6*) Chelsea Hse.
Naylor, Phyllis R. The Agony of Alice. LC 85-7957. 144p. (gr. 4-9). 1985. SBE 13.95 (*0-689-31143-5*, Atheneum Child Bk) Macmillan Child Grp.
—Alice in April. LC 92-17016. 176p. (gr. 4-8). 1993. SBE 14.95 (*0-689-31805-7*, Atheneum Child Bk) Macmillan Child Grp.
—Alice In-Between. LC 93-8167. 160p. (gr. 5-9). 1994. SBE 14.95 (*0-689-31890-1*, Atheneum Child Bk) Macmillan Child Grp.
—Alice in Rapture, Sort Of. LC 88-8174. 176p. (gr. 3-7). 1989. SBE 13.95 (*0-689-31466-3*, Atheneum Child Bk) Macmillan Child Grp.
—Alice in Rapture Sort Of. (gr. 4-7). 1991. pap. 3.50 (*0-440-40462-2*) Dell.
—All but Alice. LC 91-28722. 160p. (gr. 4-8). 1992. SBE 13.95 (*0-689-31773-5*, Atheneum Child Bk) Macmillan Child Grp.
—Beetles, Lightly Toasted. LC 87-911. 144p. (gr. 3-7). 1987. SBE 13.95 (*0-689-31355-1*, Atheneum Child Bk) Macmillan Child Grp.
—Bernie & the Bessledorf Ghost. LC 88-29389. 144p. (gr. 3-7). 1990. SBE 13.95 (*0-689-31499-X*, Atheneum Child Bk) Macmillan Child Grp.
—Bernie & the Bessledorf Ghost. 144p. 1992. pap. 3.50 (*0-380-71351-9*, Camelot) Avon.
—The Bodies in the Bessledorf Hotel. LC 86-3602. 144p. (gr. 3-7). 1986. SBE 13.95 (*0-689-31304-7*, Atheneum Child Bk) Macmillan Child Grp.
—The Boy with the Helium Head. Choroa, Kay, illus. (ps-3). 1992. 2.99 (*0-440-40644-7*, YB) Dell.
—Boys Against Girls. LC 93-37683. (Illus.). 1994. write for info. (*0-385-32081-7*) Delacorte.
—Boys Start the War. LC 92-249. (gr. 4-7). 1993. 14.00 (*0-385-30814-0*) Doubleday.
—The Dark of the Tunnel. LC 84-20441. 216p. (gr. 8 up). 1985. SBE 14.95 (*0-689-31098-6*, Atheneum Child Bk) Macmillan Child Grp.
—Eddie, Incorporated. Sims, Blanche, illus. LC 79-22589. (gr. 4-6). 1980. SBE 12.95 (*0-689-30754-3*, Atheneum Child Bk) Macmillan Child Grp.
—The Face in the Bessledorf Funeral Parlor. LC 92-32613. 144p. (gr. 3-7). 1993. SBE 13.95 (*0-689-31802-2*, Atheneum Child Bk) Macmillan Child Grp.
—The Girls Got Even. LC 92-43047. 1993. 13.95 (*0-385-31029-3*) Delacorte.
—The Grand Escape. Daniel, Alan, illus. LC 91-40816. 160p. (gr. 3-7). 1993. SBE 13.95 (*0-689-31722-0*, Atheneum Child Bk) Macmillan Child Grp.
—How I Came to Be a Writer. LC 86-32283. (Illus.). 144p. (gr. 4). 1987. pap. 4.95 (*0-689-71129-8*, Aladdin) Macmillan Child Grp.
—How Lazy Can You Get? (gr. 4-7). 1992. pap. 3.25 (*0-440-40608-0*) Dell.
—Josie's Troubles. Matheis, Shelley, illus. LC 90-47641. 128p. (gr. 3-7). 1992. SBE 12.95 (*0-689-31659-3*, Atheneum Child Bk) Macmillan Child Grp.
—The Keeper. LC 85-20029. 228p. (gr. 5 up). 1986. SBE 14.95 (*0-689-31204-0*, Atheneum Child Bk) Macmillan Child Grp.
—Keeping a Christmas Secret. Shiffman, Lena, illus. LC 88-29277. 32p. (ps-2). 1989. RSBE 13.95 (*0-689-31447-7*, Atheneum Child Bk) Macmillan Child Grp.
—Keeping a Christmas Secret. Shiffman, Lena, illus. LC 93-12248. 32p. (gr. k-2). 1993. pap. 4.95 (*0-689-71760-1*, Aladdin) Macmillan Child Grp.
—King of the Playground. Malone, Nola L., illus. 32p. (ps-3). 1991. SBE 13.95 (*0-689-31558-9*, Atheneum Child Bk) Macmillan Child Grp.
—The King of the Playground. Malone, Nola L., illus. LC 93-25125. 32p. (gr. k-3). 1994. pap. 4.95 (*0-689-71802-0*, Aladdin) Macmillan Child Grp.
—The Mad Gasser of Bessledorf Street. 112p. 1992. pap. 2.99 (*0-380-71350-0*, Camelot) Avon.
—Maudie in the Middle. 1990. pap. 3.25 (*0-440-40324-3*, Pub. by Yearling Classics) Dell.
—Night Cry. LC 83-15569. 168p. (gr. 5-9). 1984. SBE 13.95 (*0-689-31017-X*, Atheneum Child Bk) Macmillan Child Grp.
—Old Sadie & the Christmas Bear. LC 84-2995. (Illus.). 32p. (ps-2). 1984. RSBE 13.95 (*0-689-31052-8*, Atheneum Child Bk) Macmillan Child Grp.

—One of the Third-Grade Thonkers. Gaffney-Kessell, Walter, illus. LC 88-3130. 144p. (gr. 3-7). 1988. SBE 13.95 (*0-689-31424-8*, Atheneum Child Bk) Macmillan Child Grp.
—One of the Third Thonkers. (gr. 4-7). 1991. pap. 3.50 (*0-440-40407-X*) Dell.
—Reluctantly Alice. LC 90-37956. 192p. (gr. 3-7). 1991. SBE 13.95 (*0-689-31681-X*, Atheneum Child Bk) Macmillan Child Grp.
—Reluctantly Alice. 196p. (gr. 5 up). 1992. pap. 3.25 (*0-440-40685-4*, YB) Dell.
—Send No Blessings. LC 89-28024. 240p. (gr. 7 up). 1990. SBE 14.95 (*0-689-31582-1*, Atheneum Child Bk) Macmillan Child Grp.
—Send No Blessings. 240p. (gr. 5 up). 1992. pap. 3.99 (*0-14-034859-X*) Puffin Bks.
—Shiloh. LC 90-603. 144p. (gr. 3-7). 1991. SBE 12.95 (*0-689-31614-3*, Atheneum Child Bk) Macmillan Child Grp.
—Shiloh. 144p. (gr. 3-7). 1992. pap. 3.99 (*0-440-40752-4*, YB) Dell.
—The Solomon System. LC 86-21758. 216p. (gr. 5-9). 1987. pap. 3.95 (*0-689-71128-X*, Aladdin) Macmillan Child Grp.
—A String of Chances. LC 82-1790. 252p. (gr. 6 up). 1982. SBE 13.95 (*0-689-30935-X*, Atheneum Childrens Bks) Macmillan Child Grp.
—To Walk the Skypath. (gr. 4-7). 1992. 3.50 (*0-440-40636-6*, YB) Dell.
—The Witch Returns. Burleson, Joe, illus. LC 91-32370. 192p. (gr. 3-6). 1992. 14.00 (*0-385-30601-6*) Delacorte.
—Witch Returns. (gr. 4-7). 1993. pap. 3.50 (*0-440-40815-6*) Dell.
—Witch Weed. Burleson, Joe, illus. 192p. (gr. 4-7). 1992. pap. 3.50 (*0-440-40708-7*, YB) Dell.
—Witch's Eye. 1990. 13.95 (*0-385-30157-X*) Delacorte.
—Witch's Eye. (gr. 4-7). 1991. pap. 3.25 (*0-440-40514-9*, YB) Dell.
—The Year of the Gopher. LC 86-17317. 224p. (gr. 7 up). 1987. SBE 14.95 (*0-689-31333-0*, Atheneum Child Bk) Macmillan Child Grp.
—The Year of the Gopher. 208p. (gr. 7 up). 1988. pap. 3.50 (*0-553-27131-8*, Starfire) Bantam.
Naylor, Phyllis R. & Reynolds, Lura S. Maudie in the Middle. Brown, Judith G., illus. LC 87-3470. 176p. (gr. 2-6). 1988. SBE 13.95 (*0-689-31395-0*, Atheneum Child Bk) Macmillan Child Grp.
Naylor-Reynolds, Phyllis. The Agony of Alice. (gr. k-6). 1988. pap. 3.50 (*0-440-40051-1*, YB) Dell.
—The Witch Herself. (gr. k-6). 1988. pap. 3.50 (*0-440-40044-9*, TB) Dell.
—Witch Water. (gr. k-6). 1988. pap. 3.50 (*0-440-40038-4*, YB) Dell.
Ndachi, Teresa, ed. see True, Adiaha.
NEA Staff, jt. auth. see Kaufman, Les.
Neal, Judith. Fun Projects for Kids: A Teacher's Guide to Classroom Art. Bellew, Mike, illus. LC 83-7657. 136p. (gr. k-6). 1983. PLB 21.27 (*0-516-00821-8*) Childrens.
Neal, Philip. Acid Rain. (Illus.). 48p. (gr. 7-12). 1986. 19.95 (*0-85219-784-5*, Pub. by Batsford UK) Trafalgar.
—Energy, Power Sources & Electricity. (Illus.). 48p. (gr. 6-9). 1989. 19.95 (*0-85219-776-4*, Pub. by Batsford UK) Trafalgar.
—The Greenhouse Effect. (Illus.). 64p. (gr. 7-10). 1989. 19.95 (*0-85219-822-1*, Pub. by Batsford UK) Trafalgar.
—Greenhouse Effect. 56p. (gr. 8-11). 1991. pap. 13.95 (*0-7134-6697-9*, Pub. by Batsford UK) Trafalgar.
—The Oceans. (Illus.). 64p. (gr. 6-9). 1993. 24.95 (*0-7134-6712-6*, Pub. by Batsford UK) Trafalgar.
—The Ozone Layer: Conservation 2000. (Illus.). 64p. (gr. 7-10). 1994. 24.95 (*0-7134-6713-4*, Pub. by Batsford UK) Trafalgar.
Neale, J. M. Good King Wenceslas. Henterly, Jamichael, illus. LC 88-3633. 24p. (ps up) 1988. 11.95 (*0-525-44420-3*, DCB) Dutton Child Bks.
—Good King Wenceslas. Henterly, Jamichael, illus. 24p. 1993. pap. 4.99 (*0-14-054942-0*, Puffin Unicorn) Puffin Bks.
Nealy, Kenneth. Multiple Choice Questions in Preparation for the AP Chemistry Examination. 2nd ed. 116p. (gr. 11-12). 1992. wkbk. 15.95 (*1-878621-19-X*); student's solns. manual, 129p. 12.95 (*1-878621-20-3*) D & S Mktg Syst.
Neamen, Mimi & Strong, Mary. Literature Circles: Cooperative Learning for Grades 3-8. (Illus.). 175p. (gr. 3-8). 1992. pap. text ed. 18.00 (*0-87287-987-9*) Libs Unl.
Near, Holly. The Great Peace March. Desimini, Lisa, illus. LC 92-25170. 32p. (gr. 2-5). 1993. PLB 15.95 (*0-8050-1941-3*, Bks Young Read) H Holt & Co.
Neasi, Barbara. Just Like Me. Axeman, Lois, illus. LC 83-23154. 32p. (ps-2). 1984. lib. bdg. 11.93 (*0-516-02047-1*); pap. 2.95 (*0-516-42047-X*) Childrens.
—Just Like Me Big Book. (Illus.). 32p. (ps-2). 1988. PLB 30.60 (*0-516-49506-2*) Childrens.
—Listen to Me. Sharp, Gene, illus. LC 86-10664. 32p. (ps-2). 1986. PLB 11.93 (*0-516-02072-2*); pap. 2.95 (*0-516-42072-0*) Childrens.
—Listen To Me Big Book. (Illus.). 32p. (ps-2). 1988. PLB 30.60 (*0-516-49507-0*) Childrens.
—Sweet Dreams. Martin, Clovis, illus. LC 87-15083. 32p. (ps-2). 1987. PLB 11.93 (*0-516-02084-6*); pap. 2.95 (*0-516-42084-4*) Childrens.

Neasi, Barbara J. Dulces Suenos: Sweet Dreams. Martin, Clovis, illus. LC 87-15083. (SPA.). 32p. (ps-2). 1991. PLB 11.93 (*0-516-32084-X*); pap. 2.95 (*0-516-52084-9*) Childrens.
—Escuchame (Listen to Me) Sharp, Gene, illus. LC 86-10665. (SPA.). 32p. (ps-2). 1988. PLB 11.93 (*0-516-32072-6*); PLB 30.60 big bk. (*0-516-59507-5*); pap. 2.95 (*0-516-52072-5*) Childrens.
—Igual Que Yo (Just Like Me) Axeman, Lois, illus. LC 83-23154. (SPA.). 32p. (ps-2). 1988. PLB 11.93 (*0-516-32047-5*); PLB 30.60 big bk. (*0-516-59506-7*); pap. 2.95 (*0-516-52047-4*) Childrens.
—A Minute Is a Minute. Martin, Clovis, illus. 32p. (ps-3). 1988. pap. 3.95 (*0-516-43491-8*) Childrens.
Nebor, Leos. Children of the World: Czechoslovakia. LC 87-42638. (Illus.). 64p. (gr. 5-6). 1988. PLB 19.93 (*1-55532-216-6*) Gareth Stevens Inc.
Nebraska Library Commission Staff. Our Books, Our Wings: Books that Nebraskans Read & Treasure. 300p. (Orig.). (gr. 7). 1989. pap. 8.95 (*0-685-29054-9*) NE Library Commission.
Nechodom, Kerry, adapted by. & illus. The Rainbow Bridge: A Chumash Legend. 32p. (Orig.). (gr. k-3). 1992. pap. 6.95 (*0-944627-36-6*) Sand River Pr.
Nicholson, John. Chi-la-pe & the White Buffalo. 44p. (gr. 2-10). 1981. pap. 2.95 (*0-89992-064-0*) Coun India Ed.
Nederhood, Joel. Promises, Promises, Promises. LC 79-18889. (Orig.). (gr. 10-12). 1979. pap. text ed. 6.25 (*0-933140-09-6*); tchr's. manual 8.50 (*0-933140-78-9*) CRC Pubns.

Nedobeck, Don. Nedobeck's Alphabet Book. (Illus.). 26p. (gr. 1-8). 1993. Repr. of 1981 ed. 9.95 (*0-944314-00-7*) New Wrinkle.
Wonderful, wacky, whimsical watercolors join always amusing & amazing alliterations. A creative, compelling new way to view the alphabet from the popular artist/author/musician Don Nedobeck, whose other titles include NEDOBECK'S NUMBERS BOOK, THE TWELVE DAYS OF CHRISTMAS, & NO KNOWN ENGLISH TRANSLATION. NEDOBECK'S ALPHABET BOOK will delight those young & young at heart, as the alphabet we know comes alive with lively, lovable characters. You'll meet Henrietta Hen with the Horrendous Hairdo & Darryl the Daring, Diving Duck. NEDOBECK'S ALPHABET BOOK is a fascinating & fun journey into the magical world of Don Nedobeck's imagination. Of Nedobeck's creations, the Washington Post says, "they are animals who might be dukes or marchionesses-played by Alec Guinness & Margaret Rutherford -in costume." The Kansas City Star: "The overstuffed animals of Don Nedobeck's imagination are as endearing as can be, with grown lions hugging teddy bears & alligators on leashes aloose bright splashes of color." To order: 1-800-642-9953.
Publisher Provided Annotation.

—Nedobeck's Numbers Book. 26p. (gr. 1-8). 1988. 9.95 (*0-944314-01-5*) New Wrinkle.
Nedobeck, Don, illus. Nedobecks Twelve Days of Christmas. (gr. 1-8). 1988. Repr. lib. bdg. 9.95 (*0-944314-02-3*) New Wrinkle.
Needham, K. Origami Kit. (Illus.). 32p. (gr. 2-6). 1993. pap. 12.95 incl. origami paper (*0-88110-657-7*, Usborne) EDC.
Needham, K., et al. Things to Make with Paper. (Illus.). 96p. (gr. 2-6). 1992. pap. 12.95 (*0-7460-0669-1*) EDC.
Needham, Kate. Why Do People Eat? (Illus.). 24p. (gr. 1-5). 1993. lib. bdg. 11.96 (*0-88110-638-0*, Usborne); pap. 3.95 (*0-7460-1302-7*, Usborne) EDC.
Neeley, Deta P. A Child's Story of the Book of Mormon. LC 87-19903. 382p. (gr. 1-6). 1987. 12.95 (*0-87579-101-8*) Deseret Bk.
Neeley, Gwen C. Miss Ima & the Hogg Family. LaFreniere, Annette, intro. by. (Illus.). 96p. (gr. 4 up). 1992. PLB 12.95 (*0-937460-78-8*); pap. 8.95 (*0-937460-79-6*) Hendrick-Long.
Neely, Cynthia H. & Lyerly, Elaine M. Mister Cookie Breakfast Cookbook. Lyerly, Elaine M., illus. LC 86-2386. 32p. (gr. k-4). 1986. pap. 2.95 (*0-88289-493-5*) Pelican.
Neely, David, ed. see Mister Tom.

Neely, David, ed. see Tom, Mister.
Neeves, D'Reen, illus. God Cares for Me. 12p. (ps-2). 1991. bds. 6.99 (*0-7459-2059-4*) Lion USA.
—God Cares for the Earth. 12p. (ps-2). 1991. bds. 6.99 (*0-7459-2060-8*) Lion USA.
Neeves, Robert, ed. see Sweetgall, Rob.
Neff, Fred. Basic Karate Handbook. Reid, James, illus. LC 75-38471. 56p. (gr. 5 up). 1976. PLB 14.95 (*0-8225-1150-9*) Lerner Pubns.
—Basic Self-Defense Manual. Reid, James, illus. LC 75-38473. 56p. (gr. 5 up). 1976. PLB 14.95 (*0-8225-1152-5*) Lerner Pubns.
—Foot-Fighting Manual for Self-Defense & Sport Karate. Reid, James, illus. LC 75-38474. 56p. (gr. 5 up). 1977. PLB 14.95 (*0-8225-1153-3*) Lerner Pubns.
—Hand-Fighting Manual for Self-Defense & Sport Karate. Reid, James, illus. LC 75-38475. 56p. (gr. 5 up). 1977. PLB 11.95 (*0-8225-1154-1*) Lerner Pubns.
—Karate Is for Me. Reid, James E., photos by. LC 79-16900. (Illus.). 48p. (gr. 2-5). 1980. PLB 13.50 (*0-8225-1090-1*) Lerner Pubns.
—Keeping Fit Handbook for Physical Conditioning & Better Health. Reid, James, illus. LC 75-38478. 56p. (gr. 5 up). 1977. PLB 14.95 (*0-8225-1157-6*) Lerner Pubns.
—Lessons from the Art of Kempo: Subtle & Effective Self-Defense. Wolfe, Bob & Wolfe, Diane, photos by. (Illus.). 96p. (gr. 5 up). 1987. PLB 14.95 (*0-8225-1160-6*, First Ave Edns); pap. 4.95 (*0-8225-9532-X*, First Ave Edns) Lerner Pubns.
—Lessons from the Eastern Warriors. O'Leary, Patrick, photos by. (Illus.). 96p. (gr. 5-12). 1992. PLB 14.95 (*0-8225-1166-5*) Lerner Pubns.
—Lessons from the Fighting Commandos. O'Leary, Patrick, photos by. (Illus.). 96p. (gr. 5-12). 1992. PLB 14.95 (*0-8225-1165-7*) Lerner Pubns.
—Lessons from the Japanese Masters. O'Leary, Patrick, photos by. (Illus.). 96p. (gr. 5-12). 1992. PLB 14.95 (*0-8225-1164-9*) Lerner Pubns.
—Lessons from the Samurai: Ancient Self-Defense Strategies & Techniques. Wolfe, Bob & Wolfe, Diane, illus. 96p. (gr. 5 up). 1987. PLB 14.95 (*0-8225-1161-4*, First Ave Edns); pap. 4.95 (*0-8225-9531-1*, First Ave Edns) Lerner Pubns.
—Lessons from the Western Warriors: Dynamic Self-Defense Techniques. Wolfe, Bob & Wolfe, Diane, illus. 96p. (gr. 5 up). 1987. PLB 14.95 (*0-8225-1159-2*, First Ave Edns); pap. 4.95 (*0-8225-9533-8*, First Ave Edns) Lerner Pubns.
—Manual of Throws for Sport Judo & Self-Defense. Reid, James, illus. LC 75-38476. 56p. (gr. 5 up). 1976. PLB 14.95 (*0-8225-1155-X*) Lerner Pubns.
—Running Is for Me. Reid, James E., illus. LC 79-16789. 48p. (gr. 2-5). 1980. PLB 13.50 (*0-8225-1093-6*) Lerner Pubns.
—Self-Protection Guide-Book for Girls & Women. Reid, James, illus. LC 75-38477. 56p. (gr. 5 up). 1977. PLB 11.95 (*0-8225-1156-8*) Lerner Pubns.
Neff, Lavonne. God's Gift Baby. (gr. k-4). 1977. pap. 1.89 (*0-570-06113-X*, 59-1230) Concordia.
Neff, LaVonne, retold by. Jesus Is Risen! Goffe, Toni, illus. LC 92-34972. 1993. 6.99 (*0-8423-1880-1*) Tyndale.
—Stories Jesus Told. Goffe, Toni, illus. LC 92-34973. 1993. 6.99 (*0-8423-5943-5*) Tyndale.
Negash, Askale. Haile Selassie. Schlesinger, Arthur M., intro. by. (Illus.). 112p. (gr. 5 up). 1989. 17.95x (*1-55546-850-0*) Chelsea Hse.
Negishi, Takashi, jt. auth. see Itoh, Motoshige.
Negroni, Maria, tr. see Ransome, Arthur.
Negroni, Maria, tr. see Shulevitz, Uri.
Nehemias, Paulette. A Tree in Sprocket's Pocket: Stories about God's Green Earth. Harris, Jim, illus. LC 92-26033. 128p. (Orig.). (gr. 3-5). 1993. pap. 4.95 (*0-570-04730-7*) Concordia.
—Wiggler's Worms: Stories about God's Green Earth. Harris, Jim, illus. LC 92-28486. 128p. (Orig.). (gr. 3-5). 1993. pap. 4.95 (*0-570-04731-5*) Concordia.
Neidorf, Mary. Operantics with Wolfgang Amadeus Mozart. LC 86-14435. 32p. (Orig.). (gr. 3-6). 1987. pap. 4.95 (*0-86534-092-7*) Sunstone Pr.
Neighbour, Ralph W., Jr. Sigueme, Edicion para Ninos. Geiger, Mary J. & Ditmore, Shirley, trs. from ENG. (SPA., Illus.). 64p. (Orig.). 1989. pap. 2.65 (*0-311-13848-9*) Casa Bautista.
Neil, Marilyn. Stars, Wings, & Fun Things: Three Hundred Sixty-Five Activities for Children. (Illus.). 68p. (Orig.). (gr. k-3). 1991. pap. text ed. 8.95 (*0-945301-05-7*) Druid Pr.
Neill, John R. Lucky Bucky in Oz. (Illus.). (gr. 3 up). 1992. 24.95 (*0-929605-17-9*) Books Wonder.
—The Scalawagons in Oz. Neill, John R., illus. 309p. (gr. 3 up). 1991. 24.95 (*0-929605-12-8*) Books Wonder.
—The Wonder City of Oz. Neill, John R., illus. 318p. (gr. 2 up). 1990. text ed. 24.95 (*0-929605-07-1*) Books Wonder.
Neill, Peter see Hellman, Nina & Brouwer, Norman.
Neill, Robert H. Beware the Barking Bumblebees: And Forty-Three More Nature Talks. Rolfes, Ellen, ed. 96p. (gr. k-6). 1993. spiral top-bound 5.95 (*1-879958-18-X*) Tradery Hse.
Neilsen, Shelly. I Love Animals. Berg, Julie, ed. LC 93-18955. 1993. 14.96 (*1-56239-191-7*) Abdo & Dghtrs.
Neilson, Gena. Favorite Rhymes. (Illus.). (ps-1). 1986. pap. 9.95 (*0-937763-02-0*) Lauri Inc.
Neilson, Gena, illus. Dinosaurs. (ps-1). 1986. spiral bdg. 9.95 (*0-937763-00-4*) Lauri Inc.

—It's Your Birthday. (ps-1). 1986. spiral bdg. 9.95 (*0-937763-03-9*) Lauri Inc.
—Noah's Ark. (ps-1). 1986. spiral bdg. 9.95 (*0-937763-01-2*) Lauri Inc.
Neilson, Stefan & Thoelke, Shay. Color Me Winning. (Illus.). 50p. (gr. 4-6). 1989. spiral bdg., adult wkbk. 20.00 (*1-880830-02-7*) Aeon-Hierophant.
Neimark, Anne E. A Deaf Child Listened: Thomas Gallaudet, Pioneer in American Education. LC 82-23942. 160p. (gr. 7up). 1983. 11.95 (*0-688-01719-3*) Morrow Jr Bks.
—Diego Rivera, Artist of the People. LC 91-25209. (Illus.). 128p. (gr. 3-7). 1992. 17.00 (*0-06-021783-9*); PLB 16.89 (*0-06-021784-7*) HarpC Child Bks.
—One Man's Valor: Leo Baeck & the Holocaust. LC 85-27366. (Illus.). 128p. (gr. 5-9). 1986. 14.95 (*0-525-67175-7*, Lodestar Bks) Dutton Child Bks.
Neimark, Jill. Ice Cream. Milone, Karen, illus. LC 84-10915. (gr. 2-6). 1986. 11.95 (*0-8038-3440-3*); pap. 11.95 (*0-8038-9290-X*) Hastings.
Neitzel, Shirley. The Dress I'll Wear to the Party. Parker, Nancy W., illus. LC 91-30906. 32p. (ps-4). 1992. 14.00 (*0-688-09959-9*); PLB 13.93 (*0-688-09960-2*) Greenwillow.
—Jacket I Wear in the Snow. LC 88-18767. (Illus.). 32p. (ps up). 1989. 15.00 (*0-688-08028-6*); PLB 13.93 (*0-688-08030-8*) Greenwillow.
—The Jacket I Wear in the Snow. Parker, Nancy W., photos by. LC 92-43789. Date not set. write for info. (*0-688-04587-1*, Mulberry) Morrow. Postponed.
Nelesen, J. H. Mr. Washington's Travelling Music. 32p. (ps-4). 1987. 7.99 (*0-570-04151-1*, 56-1611) Concordia.
Nelesen, James H. The Most Important Christmas. 32p. (gr. 5-9). 1985. 7.99 (*0-570-04110-4*, 56-1521) Concordia.
Nelken, Andrea, ed. see Van Hook, Beverly.
Nellist, Cassandra L. Child's First Book about Hawaii. Nellist, Cassandra L., illus. 24p. (ps). 1987. 7.95 (*0-916630-58-7*) Pr Pacifica.
Nelsen, Karen. Books by Kids! Helping Young Children Create Their Own Books. (gr. k-3). 1993. pap. 9.95 (*0-86653-930-1*) Fearon Teach Aids.
Nelson, A. A Long Hard Day on the Ranch. (Illus.). 24p. (ps-8). 1989. pap. 4.95 (*0-88753-184-9*, Pub. by Black Moss Pr CN) Firefly Bks Ltd.
Nelson, Andy. The Carl Larsson Coloring Book. (Illus.). 96p. (Orig.). (gr. 1-6). 1990. 5.95 (*0-929636-07-4*) Culpepper Pr.
—The Impressionists Coloring Book. Nelson, Andy, illus. 96p. (Orig.). (gr. 1-6). 1990. pap. 5.95 (*0-929636-06-6*) Culpepper Pr.
—The Renaissance Painters Coloring Book: Donatello, Raphael, Leonardo & Michelangelo. (Illus.). 96p. (gr. 1-6). 1991. pap. 5.95 (*0-929636-10-4*) Culpepper Pr.
Nelson, Becky, ed. see Brown, Pam.
Nelson, Becky, ed. see Browning, James.
Nelson, Becky, ed. see Dickson, Charles.
Nelson, Becky, ed. see Dockrey, Karen.
Nelson, Becky, ed. see Howard, David.
Nelson, Becky, ed. see Serratt, Mary L.
Nelson, Becky, ed. see Smith, Melanie.
Nelson, Becky, ed. see Sutton, Jan, et al.
Nelson, Becky, ed. see Taylor, Laurie.
Nelson, Becky, ed. see Wood, Randy.
Nelson, Bonnie E. Science & Computer Activities for Children 3 to 9 Years Old. 2nd, rev. ed. (Illus.). 146p. (gr. k-3). 1988. 28.00x (*0-931642-21-3*) Lintel.
Nelson, Colin. American Football. (Illus.). 80p. (gr. 5 up). 1991. pap. 6.95 (*0-7063-6666-2*, Pub. by Ward Lock UK) Sterling.
—American Football. rev. ed. (Illus.). 80p. (gr. 10-12). 1993. pap. 7.95 (*0-7137-2414-5*, Pub. by Blandford Pr UK) Sterling.
Nelson, Cordner. Careers in Pro Sports. rev. ed. Rosen, Ruth, ed. LC 89-37641. (Illus.). 143p. (gr. 7-12). 1992. PLB 13.95 (*0-8239-1456-9*) Rosen Group.
Nelson, Drew. Wild Voices. Schoenherr, John, illus. 96p. (gr. 3 up). 1991. 15.95 (*0-399-21798-3*, Philomel) Putnam Pub Group.
Nelson, Eileen, ed. see Redleaf, Rhoda.
Nelson, Elizabeth. Coping with Drugs & Sports. (gr. 7-12). 1992. PLB 13.95 (*0-8239-1342-9*) Rosen Group.
Nelson, Esther. World's Best Funny Songs. Behr, Joyce, illus. LC 87-753871. 128p. (gr. 1-8). 1989. pap. 4.95 (*0-8069-6893-1*) Sterling.
Nelson, Esther L. Musical Games for Children of All Ages. (Illus.). 72p. (gr. k-5). 1981. pap. 10.95 (*0-8069-7520-2*) Sterling.
Nelson, Esther L., ed. The Fun-to-Sing Songbook. LC 86-752869. (Illus.). 96p. (gr. k-6). 1986. 14.95 (*0-8069-4760-8*); pap. 10.95 (*0-8069-4762-4*) Sterling.
Nelson, G. K. To Be a Farmer's Boy. (gr. 5-12). 1991. 30.00 (*0-86299-872-7*); pap. 18.00 (*0-7509-0182-9*) A Sutton Pub.
Nelson, Ginger K. Pirate's Revenge. Kratoville, Betty L., ed. (Illus.). 64p. (gr. 3-9). 1989. PLB 4.95 (*0-87879-654-1*) High Noon Bks.
Nelson, Gladys T. War Drums at Eden Prairie. Nelson, Gladys T., illus. (gr. 5-9). 1977. 5.95 (*0-87839-023-5*) North Star.
Nelson, Harold D., ed. Morocco: A Country Study. LC 85-600265. (Illus.). 476p. (gr. 9-12). 1986. 15.00 (*0-16-001640-1*, S/N 008-020-01072-3) USGPO.
Nelson, Jack & Halpern-Segal, Janice. My Trip. Schoonover, Annette, illus. 24p. (Orig.). (ps-3). 1989. pap. 6.95 (*0-685-29177-4*) Take Along Pubns.
Nelson, Jane, jt. auth. see Childress, Valerie.

Nelson, Jeffrey. The Dinosaur Hunt Activity Book. (Orig.). 1994. pap. 2.99 (*0-8125-9439-8*) Tor Bks.
—Dinosaur Jokes & Riddles Book. (Illus.). 24p. (gr. 3 up). 1988. pap. 1.95 (*1-56288-341-0*) Checkerboard.
—Monster Jokes & Riddles. (Illus.). 24p. (gr. 3 up). 1988. pap. 1.95 (*1-56288-342-9*) Checkerboard.
—Outerspace Jokes & Riddles Book. (Illus.). 24p. (gr. 3 up). 1988. pap. 1.95 (*1-56288-343-7*) Checkerboard.
—Spooky Jokes & Riddles Book. (Illus.). 24p. (gr. 3 up). 1988. pap. 1.95 (*1-56288-344-5*) Checkerboard.
Nelson, Jeffrey S. Animal Jokes & Riddles. Nelson, Jeffrey S., illus. LC 90-27676. 24p. (gr. 3 up). 1991. pap. 1.95 (*1-56288-016-0*) Checkerboard.
—Family Jokes & Riddles. Nelson, Jeffrey S., illus. 24p. (gr. 3 up). 1991. pap. 1.95 (*1-56288-015-2*) Checkerboard.
—Jungle Jokes & Riddles. Nelson, Jeffrey S., illus. 24p. (gr. 3 up). 1991. pap. 1.95 (*1-56288-017-9*) Checkerboard.
—Yucky Jokes & Riddles. Nelson, Jeffrey S., illus. 24p. (gr. 3 up). 1991. pap. 1.95 (*1-56288-014-4*) Checkerboard.
Nelson, Jenny. Archibald & the Crunch Machine. Battersby, Sarah, illus. 40p. (gr. 2-4). 1990. pap. 5.95 (*1-55037-114-2*, Pub. by Annick CN) Firefly Bks Ltd.
Nelson, Joan. Abortion. LC 91-15566. (Illus.). 112p. (gr. 5-8). 1992. PLB 14.95 (*1-56006-128-6*) Lucent Bks.
Nelson, Joan E. Kids Who Kill Kids. 284p. (Orig.). (gr. 8-12). 1993. pap. 12.95 (*0-9637293-1-4*) Storm Pub.
Nelson, JoAnne. Count by Twos. Beylon, Cathy, illus. 16p. (Orig.). (gr. k-2). 1990. pap. 3.95 (*1-878624-10-5*) McClanahan Bk.
—Feeling Fit, That's It! McKinnell, Michael, illus. LC 92-37719. 1994. pap. 5.95 (*0-935529-58-6*) Comprehen Health Educ.
—Friends All Around. DuCharme, Tracy, illus. LC 92-4657. 24p. (Orig.). (gr. k-2). 1993. pap. 5.95 (*0-935529-17-9*) Comprehen Health Educ.
—Good Grief! Good Grief! Thomsen, Ernie, illus. LC 92-6685. 24p. (Orig.). (gr. k-2). 1993. pap. 5.95 (*0-935529-18-7*) Comprehen Health Educ.
—How Do You Feel? Vance, R. Scott, illus. LC 91-36336. 24p. (Orig.). (gr. k-2). 1993. pap. write for info. (*0-935529-15-2*) Comprehen Health Educ.
—It's up to Me! Magnuson, Diana, illus. LC 93-9349. 1994. 5.95 (*0-935529-63-2*) Comprehen Health Educ.
—Nose to Toes. Keith, Doug, illus. LC 91-34706. 24p. (Orig.). (gr. k-2). 1993. pap. 5.95 (*0-935529-16-0*) Comprehen Health Educ.
—Our Friend, the Earth. Thomsen, Ernie, illus. LC 92-37716. 1994. pap. 5.95 (*0-935529-59-4*) Comprehen Health Educ.
—Play It Safe. Meier, Melissa, illus. LC 93-12173. 1994. 5.95 (*0-935529-62-4*) Comprehen Health Educ.
—We Are Family. Woolf, Marie W., illus. LC 93-12176. 1994. 5.95 (*0-935529-60-8*) Comprehen Health Educ.
—What Next? Katayama, Mits, illus. LC 91-35731. 24p. (Orig.). (gr. k-2). 1993. pap. 5.95 (*0-935529-19-5*) Comprehen Health Educ.
—When I'm Sick. Keith, Doug, illus. LC 93-9348. 1994. 5.95 (*0-935529-61-6*) Comprehen Health Educ.
—Where's Mittens? Du Charme, Tracy, illus. LC 91-9373. 24p. (Orig.). (gr. k-2). 1993. pap. 5.95 (*0-935529-14-4*) Comprehen Health Educ.
Nelson, Johnnierence. Positive Passage: Everyday Kwanzaa Poems. (Illus.). 48p. (Orig.). (gr. 1 up). 1991. pap. 6.00 (*0-9623205-1-X*) House Nia.
Nelson, Lisa M. Bright Smiles & Blue Skies: Positive Music for Today's Kids. (Illus.). 16p. (Orig.). (gr. k-6). 1990. pap. 9.95 incl. audio tape (*0-9627863-0-6*) Brght Ideas CA.
Nelson, Lynn A. Learning to Print Animal Alphabet Book. 1990. 9.95 (*0-88047-221-9*, D9007) DOK Pubs.
Nelson, Mary, ed. see Abbey, Nancy & Wagman, Ellen.
Nelson, Mary, ed. see Quackenbush, Marcia & Villarreal, Sylvia.
Nelson, Mary, ed. see Stronck, David.
Nelson, Mary, ed. see Strong, Bryan & DeVault, Christine.
Nelson, Nigel. Body Talk. De Saulles, Tony, illus. LC 93-27780. 32p. (gr. k-2). 1993. 12.95 (*1-56847-099-1*) Thomson Lrning.
—Signs & Symbols. De Saulles, Tony, illus. LC 93-27779. 32p. (gr. k-2). 1993. 12.95 (*1-56847-100-9*) Thomson Lrning.
—Space. LC 93-7257. 32p. (gr. k-2). 1993. 14.95 (*1-56847-109-2*) Thomson Lrning.
Nelson, O. T. The Girl Who Owned a City. 192p. (gr. 6 up). 1977. pap. 3.50 (*0-440-92893-1*, LFL) Dell.
Nelson, P. C. Bible Doctrines. Zimmerman, Thomas F., intro. by. LC 81-82738. 128p. (gr. 9-12). 1981. pap. 2.95 (*0-88243-479-9*, 02-0479) Gospel Pub.
Nelson, Patty. Teacher's Bag of Tricks. 80p. (gr. 2-6). 1986. pap. text ed. 7.95 (*0-86530-132-8*) Incentive Pubns.
Nelson, Peter. Deadly Games. 240p. 1992. pap. 2.99 (*0-671-74890-4*, Archway) PB.
—Death Threat. (gr. 9-12). 1993. pap. 3.50 (*0-06-106104-2*, Harp PBks) HarpC.
—Double Dose. 1992. pap. 3.50 (*0-06-106101-8*, Harp PBks) HarpC.
—First to Die. (gr. 7 up). 1992. pap. 3.50 (*0-06-106100-X*, Harp PBks) HarpC.
—Fourth-Quarter Fix. 1992. pap. 3.50 (*0-06-106103-4*, Harp PBks) HarpC.
—Melrose Place. 1992. pap. 3.99 (*0-06-106788-1*, Harp PBks) HarpC.

—Scarface. MacDonald, Patricia, ed. 224p. (Orig.). 1991. pap. 2.99 (0-671-70585-7, Archway) PB.
—Six Deadly Lies. 1993. pap. 3.50 (0-06-106110-7, Harp PBks) HarpC.
—Sylvia Smith-Smith. (gr. 6 up). 1987. 2.25 (0-373-98007-8) S&S Trade.
—Third Degree. 1992. pap. 3.50 (0-06-106102-6, Harp PBks) HarpC.
Nelson, Ray. I Never Met One Stranger. 450p. (Orig.). (gr. 12). 1989. pap. write for info. Raynel.
Nelson, Ray, Jr. Greetings from America: Postcards from Donovan Willoughby. Nelson, Ray, Jr. & Kelly, Douglas, illus. LC 92-14819. 48p. (ps-6). 1992. 12.95 (0-89802-590-7) Beautiful Am.
—Incredible Adventures of Donovan Willoughby. LC 90-42652. (Illus.). (ps-7). 1990. 12.95 (0-89802-551-6) Beautiful Am.
—The Internal Adventures of Donovan Willoughby. LC 91-18810. (Illus.). 48p. (ps-7). 1991. 12.95 (0-89802-572-9) Beautiful Am.
Nelson, Ray, Jr. & Kelly, Doug. The Seven Seas of Billy's Bathtub. (Illus.). 48p. (gr. 1-5). 1993. 12.95 (1-883772-00-1) Flying Rhino.
Nelson, Ray R. I Never Met One Stranger: A Personal Journey. 435p. (Orig.). (gr. 12). 1989. pap. 410.45 (0-9623068-0-0) Raynel.
Nelson, Rebecca S. Games & Activities with Base Ten Blocks, Bk. 1. (Illus.). 64p. (Orig.). (gr. 1-4). 1987. pap. text ed. 8.50 (0-914040-57-X) Cuisenaire.
—Games & Activities with Base Ten Blocks, Bk. 2. 64p. (gr. 1-4). 1987. pap. text ed. 8.50 (0-914040-58-8) Cuisenaire.
Nelson, Steve & Rollins, Jack. Frosty the Snowman: Book & Cookie Cutter Set. Zimmerman, Jerry, illus. 17p. (ps-2). 1993. Incl. 2 cookie cutters. pap. 3.95 (0-590-69016-7, Cartwheel) Scholastic Inc.
Nelson, Theresa. And One for All. LC 88-22490. 192p. (gr. 6-8). 1989. 12.95 (0-531-05804-2); PLB 12.99 (0-531-08404-3) Orchard Bks Watts.
—And One for All. (gr. 4-7). 1991. pap. 3.50 (0-440-40456-8) Dell.
—The Beggars' Ride. LC 90-52515. 256p. (gr. 6-12). 1992. 15.95 (0-531-05896-4); PLB 15.99 (0-531-08496-5) Orchard Bks Watts.
—Devil Storm. LC 87-5493. 224p. (gr. 5-7). 1987. 12.95 (0-531-05711-9); PLB 12.99 (0-531-08311-X) Orchard Bks Watts.
—Devil Storm. (gr. 4-7). 1991. pap. 3.25 (0-440-40409-6) Dell.
—The Twenty-Five Cent Miracle. LC 85-17061. 224p. (gr. 7 up). 1986. SBE 14.95 (0-02-724370-2, Bradbury Pr) Macmillan Child Grp.
—The Twenty-Five Cent Miracle. LC 89-6822. 224p. (gr. 4-7). 1989. pap. 3.95 (0-689-71326-6, Aladdin) Macmillan Child Grp.
Nelson, Theresa M. For the Love of Casey. Mattingly, Jennie, ed. LC 87-50991. 230p. (Orig.). (gr. 7 up). 1987. pap. 8.95 (1-55587-083-0) Winston-Derek.
Nelson, Tina & Lanza, Janet. An Illustrated Guide to Northeastern Forest Trees. (Illus.). 50p. 1983. pap. 3.00 (0-942788-11-7) Marginal Med.
Nelson, Vaunda M. Always Gramma. Uhler, Kimanne, illus. 32p. (ps-3). 1988. PLB 14.95 (0-399-21542-5, Putnam) Putnam Pub Group.
—Mayfield Crossing. Jenkins, Leonard, illus. LC 92-10564. 96p. (gr. 3-7). 1993. 14.95 (0-399-22331-2, Putnam) Putnam Pub Group.
Nelson, Vaunda Micheaux. Mayfield Crossing. 96p. 1994. pap. 3.50 (0-380-72179-1, Camelot) Avon.
Nelson, Yvette. Celebrating the Eucharist. Proof Positive-Farrowlyne Associates, Inc. Staff, illus. 73p. (Orig.). (gr. 7-8). 1992. pap. text ed. 2.80 (0-88489-269-7); tchr's ed. 6.00 (0-88489-270-0) St Marys.
Nelson, Yvette, jt. auth. see Bitney, James.
Nelson-Erichsen, Jean. Copito: The Christmas Chihuahua. Atcheson, Marguerite, illus. Davenport, May, intro. by. LC 82-72080. (Illus.). 80p. (gr. k-5). 1982. pap. 3.50x (0-943864-07-0) Davenport.
Nemaneic, Allison, et al. Diabetes Care Made Easy: A Simple Step-by-Step Guide for Controlling Your Diabetes. LC 92-11193. 1992. 9.95 (1-56561-013-X) Chronimed.
Nemcova, B. Fairy Tales from Czechoslovakia, Vol. I. Velinsky, L., tr. Kabel Pub Staff, illus. Absolon, Karel B., intro. by. (CZE., Illus.). 305p. (Orig.). (gr. 4 up). 1987. pap. 39.50 (0-685-19314-4) KABEL Pubs.
Nemes, Claire. A Picture Book of Dinosaurs. Kinnealy, Janice, illus. LC 89-37331. 24p. (gr. 1-4). 1990. lib. bdg. 9.59 (0-8167-1900-4); pap. text ed. 2.50 (0-8167-1901-2) Troll Assocs.
Nemetz, Rowena. Bo's Search for Love & Understanding. LC 86-10379. (Illus.). 48p. (Orig.). (gr. 1-6). 1986. pap. 5.95 (0-941992-09-8) Los Arboles Pub.
Nemiroff, Marc A. & Annunziata, Jane. A Child's First Book about Play Therapy. Scott, Margaret, illus. LC 90-49954. 60p. (Orig.). 1990. 19.95 (1-55798-112-4, 4317180); pap. text ed. write for info. (1-55798-089-6, 4317200) Am Psychol.
Nentl, Jerolyn. Beaver. LC 83-5323. (Illus.). 48p. (gr. 5). 1983. RSBE 12.95 (0-89686-219-4, Crestwood Hse) Macmillan Child Grp.
—The Caribou. LC 83-26254. (Illus.). 48p. (gr. 5-6). 1984. RSBE 12.95 (0-89686-244-5, Crestwood Hse) Macmillan Child Grp.
—The Grizzly. LC 83-22354. (Illus.). 48p. (gr. 5-6). 1984. RSBE 12.95 (0-89686-245-3, Crestwood Hse) Macmillan Child Grp.

—The Mallard. LC 83-2087. (Illus.). 48p. (gr. 4-5). 1983. RSBE 12.95 (0-89686-221-6, Crestwood Hse) Macmillan Child Grp.
—Raccoon. LC 83-21072. (Illus.). 48p. (gr. 5-6). 1984. RSBE 12.95 (0-89686-246-1, Crestwood Hse) Macmillan Child Grp.
—The Wild Cats. LC 83-22506. (Illus.). 48p. (gr. 4-5). 1984. RSBE 12.95 (0-89686-249-6, Crestwood Hse) Macmillan Child Grp.
Nentl, Jerolyn, jt. auth. see East, Ben.
Nerbun, Ann. Our Power to Love. Conway, Robin & Nguyen, Peter, illus. LC 91-73633. 100p. 1990. pap. 6.00 (0-89870-382-4) Ignatius Pr.
Nerlove, Miriam. Christmas. Tucker, Kathy, ed. Nerlove, Miriam, illus. LC 89-70737. 24p. (ps-1). 1990. 11.95 (0-8075-1148-X) A Whitman.
—Christmas: An Albert Whitman Prairie Book. (ps-3). 1993. pap. 4.95 (0-8075-1147-1) A Whitman.
—Easter. Mathews, Judith, ed. Nerlove, Miriam, illus. LC 89-35394. 24p. (ps-1). 1989. 11.95 (0-8075-1871-9); pap. 4.95 (0-8075-1872-7) A Whitman.
—Halloween. Levine, Abby, ed. Nerlove, Miriam, illus. LC 88-36858. 24p. (ps-1). 1989. PLB 11.95 (0-8075-3131-6); pap. 4.95 (0-8075-3130-8) A Whitman.
—Hanukkah. Levine, Abby, ed. Nerlove, Miriam, illus. LC 88-36648. 24p. (ps-1). 1989. PLB 11.95 (0-8075-3143-X); pap. 4.95 (0-8075-3142-1) A Whitman.
—I Made a Mistake. Nerlove, Miriam, illus. LC 85-6018. 32p. (ps-2). 1985. SBE 13.95 (0-689-50327-X, M K McElderry) Macmillan Child Grp.
—I Meant to Clean My Room Today. LC 87-16968. (Illus.). 32p. (ps-3). 1988. 13.95 (0-689-50438-1, M K McElderry) Macmillan Child Grp.
—If All the World Were Paper. Tucker, Kathy, ed. Nerlove, Miriam, illus. LC 90-39217. 32p. (gr. k-3). 1991. 13.95 (0-8075-3535-4) A Whitman.
—Just One Tooth. Nerlove, Miriam, illus. LC 88-19488. 32p. (ps-3). 1989. SBE 13.95 (0-689-50465-9, M K McElderry) Macmillan Child Grp.
—Passover. Levine, Abby, ed. Nerlove, Miriam, illus. LC 89-35393. 24p. (ps-1). 1989. 11.95 (0-8075-6360-9); pap. 4.95 (0-8075-6361-7) A Whitman.
—Purim. Levine, Abby, ed. Nerlove, Miriam, illus. LC 91-19516. 24p. (ps-1). 1992. PLB 11.95 (0-8075-6682-9) A Whitman.
—Thanksgiving. Mathews, Judith, ed. Nerlove, Meriam, illus. LC 89-49363. 24p. (ps-1). 1990. PLB 11.95 (0-8075-7818-5) A Whitman.
—Thanksgiving: An Albert Whitman Prairie Book. (ps-3). 1993. pap. 4.95 (0-8075-7817-7) A Whitman.
—Valentine's Day. Mathews, Judith, ed. Nerlove, Miriam, illus. LC 91-19289. 24p. (ps-1). 1992. PLB 11.95 (0-8075-8454-1) A Whitman.
Nero, Ann B. Essential Skills in Geography. Radner, Barbara, ed. (Illus.). 94p. (Orig.). (gr. 4-9). 1987. pap. text ed. 3.96 (0-528-17918-7); tchrs. ed 7.92 (0-528-17919-5) Rand McNally.
Nesbit, E. The Enchanted Castle. Zelinsky, Paul O., illus. Glassman, Peter, afterword by. LC 91-46267. (Illus.). 304p. 1992. 20.00 (0-688-05435-8) Morrow Jr Bks.
—Melisande. 41p. (gr. k-3). 1989. 13.95 (0-15-253164-5) HarBrace.
—Railway Children. (gr. 4-7). 1992. pap. 3.50 (0-440-40602-1) Dell.
—Whereyouwantogoto: And Other Unlikely Tales. Millar, H. R. & Shepperson, Claude, illus. LC 93-18685. 224p. 1993. 6.00 (1-56957-904-0) Shambhala Pubns.
Nesbit, Edith. The Book of Dragons. (gr. 4-6). 1986. pap. 4.95 (0-440-40696-X, Pub. by Yearling Classics) Dell.
—The Deliverers of Their Country. Zwerger, Lisbeth, illus. LC 85-9389. 32p. (gr. 3-5). 1991. pap. 15.95 (0-88708-005-7) Picture Bk Studio.
—Enchanted Castle. 231p. 1981. Repr. PLB 10.95x (0-89966-361-3) Buccaneer Bks.
—Enchanted Castle. 179p. 1981. Repr. PLB 16.95x (0-89967-035-0) Harmony Raine.
—The Enchanted Castle. (gr. 5 up). 1986. pap. 2.99 (0-14-035057-8, Puffin) Puffin Bks.
—Five Children & It. 188p. 1981. Repr. PLB 21.95 (0-89966-362-1) Buccaneer Bks.
—Five Children & It. 182p. 1981. Repr. PLB 21.95 (0-89967-036-9) Harmony Raine.
—Five Children & It. Millar, H. R., illus. 224p. (gr. 4-6). 1985. pap. 2.95 (0-14-035061-6, Puffin) Puffin Bks.
—The Five Children & It. (gr. 4-6). 1986. pap. 3.50 (0-440-42586-7, Pub. by Yearling Classics) Dell.
—Five Children & It. 208p. (gr. 4-7). 1988. pap. 3.25 (0-590-42146-8, Apple Classics) Scholastic Inc.
—The House of Arden. (gr. 4-6). 1986. pap. 2.95 (0-14-035073-X, Puffin) Puffin Bks.
—The Last of the Dragons & Some Others. LC 85-42967. 60p. (gr. 6 up). 1985. pap. 2.25 (0-14-035069-1, Puffin) Puffin Bks.
—The Magic World. (gr. 4 up). 1989. pap. 2.95 (0-14-035094-2, Puffin) Puffin Bks.
—New Treasure Seekers. 219p. (gr. 5 up). 1986. pap. 2.25 (0-14-035060-8, Puffin) Puffin Bks.
—New Treasure Seekers. (gr. 5-8). 1988. 15.50 (0-8446-6348-4) Peter Smith.
—Phoenix & the Carpet. Millar, H. R., illus. (gr. 4-6). 1985. pap. 2.25 (0-14-035062-4, Puffin) Puffin Bks.
—The Railway Children. 240p. (gr. 3-7). 1983. pap. 2.95 (0-14-035005-5, Puffin) Puffin Bks.
—The Railway Children. (gr. 5-8). 1988. 16.00 (0-8446-6345-X) Peter Smith.

—The Railway Children. Butts, Dennis, intro. by. 224p. 1991. pap. 3.95 (0-19-282659-X, 11912) OUP.
—The Railway Children. (Illus.). 192p. 1991. 16.95 (0-399-21819-X, Philomel Bks) Putnam Pub Group.
—The Railway Children. 1993. 12.95 (0-679-42534-9, Everymans Lib) Knopf.
—Railway Children. (gr. 4 up). 1993. pap. 3.25 (0-553-21415-2, Bantam Classics) Bantam.
—Story of the Amulet. 1986. pap. 2.95 (0-14-035063-2, Puffin) Puffin Bks.
—Story of the Treasure Seekers. (gr. 4-6). 1987. pap. 2.25 (0-685-03990-0, Puffin) Puffin Bks.
—Story of the Treasure Seekers. (gr. 3 up). 1987. pap. 2.99 (0-14-035058-6, Puffin) Puffin Bks.
—The Wouldbegoods. 283p. (gr. 5 up). 1986. pap. 2.95 (0-14-035059-4, Puffin) Puffin Bks.
—The Wouldbegoods. (gr. 5-8). 1988. 15.75 (0-8446-6347-6) Peter Smith.
Nesbit, Evelyn. Railway Children. Dryhurst, Dinal, illus. 192p. 1992. 9.99 (0-517-07011-1, Pub. by Derrydale Bks) Outlet Bk Co.
Nesbit, Jeffrey A. Absolutely Perfect Summer. 211p. (Orig.). (gr. 9-12). 1990. pap. 6.99 (0-87788-005-0) Shaw Pubs.
—All the King's Horses. 192p. (Orig.). (gr. 9-12). 1990. pap. 6.99 (0-87788-040-9) Shaw Pubs.
—Crosscourt Winner. 132p. 1991. pap. 4.99 (0-89693-129-3) SP Pubns.
—The Great Nothing Strikes Back. 256p. (Orig.). (gr. 9-12). 1991. pap. 6.99 (0-87788-323-8) Shaw Pubs.
—The Lost Canoe. 130p. 1991. pap. 4.99 (0-89693-130-7) SP Pubns.
—The Puzzled Prodigy. (Orig.). (gr. 3-6). 1992. pap. 4.99 (0-89693-075-0, Victor Books) SP Pubns.
—The Reluctant Runaway. 120p. 1991. pap. 4.99 (0-89693-131-5) SP Pubns.
—The Sioux Society. LC 92-20199. 1992. 6.99 (0-87788-748-9) Shaw Pubs.
—Struggle with Silence. 129p. 1991. pap. 4.99 (0-89693-132-3) SP Pubns.
—A War of Words. LC 92-27663. (Illus.). 1992. pap. 4.99 (0-89693-076-9, Victor Books) SP Pubns.
Nesbitt, W. H. & Reneau, Jack, eds. Records of North American Elk & Mule Deer, 1991. LC 91-73121. (Illus.). viii, 264p. (Orig.). 1991. pap. 16.95 (0-940864-18-5) Boone & Crockett.
—Records of North American Whitetail Deer, 1991. 2nd ed. LC 91-973120. (Illus.). viii, 312p. (Orig.). 1991. pap. 16.95 (0-940864-17-7) Boone & Crockett.
Nesmith, Samuel P., jt. auth. see Callihan, D. Jeanne.
Nesmith, Samuel P., jt. auth. see Martinello, Marian L.
Ness, E. Sam Bang & Moonshine. (gr. 4 up). 1971. pap. 3.95 (0-03-080111-7) HR&W Schl Div.
Ness, Evaline. Sam, Bangs & Moonshine. Ness, Evaline, illus. LC 66-10113. 48p. (ps-2). 1966. 14.95 (0-8050-0314-2, Bks Young Read); pap. 5.95 (0-8050-0315-0) H Holt & Co.
Ness Seymour, Tryntje Van see Van Ness Seymour, Tryntje.
Nestingen, Jan, ed. see Brandt, Betty.
Nestlebaum, Chora. The Mookster's Mitzvah Mishaps. 32p. (gr. k-4). 1991. 11.95 (0-910818-26-6); pap. 8.95 (0-910818-27-4) Judaica Pr.
Nethery, Mary. Hannah & Jack. Morgan, Mary, illus. LC 93-4651. 1995. write for info. (0-02-768125-4, Bradbury Pr) Macmillan Child Grp.
Netzel, Sally. Cinderella. (Illus.). 32p. (ps up) 1981. pap. 3.00 (0-88680-028-5); royalty on application 25.00 (0-317-03605-X) I E Clark.
—Puss in Boots. (Illus.). 32p. (gr. k up). 1979. pap. 3.00 (0-88680-157-5); royalty on application 35.00 (0-317-03611-4) I E Clark.
Netzley, Patricia D. The Assassination of President John F. Kennedy. LC 93-20818. (Illus.). 96p. (gr. 6 up). 1994. RSBE 14.95 (0-02-768127-0, New Discovery Bks) Macmillan Child Grp.
Neubacher, G. Little Red Riding Hood. (Illus.). 32p. (gr. 1-4). 1989. PLB 6.95 (0-88625-214-8) Durkin Hayes Pub.
Neubacher, Gerda. Tales from the Beechy Woods: Fluff's Birthday. Neubacher, Gerda, illus. 32p. (ps-k). 1983. 10.95 (0-88625-044-7) Durkin Hayes Pub.
Neuberger, Julia. The Story of the Jews. (Illus.). 32p. (gr. 4-8). 1986. 7.95 (0-521-30601-9) Cambridge U Pr.
Neuberger, Phyllis J. Suppose You Were a Kitten. LC 82-91105. (Illus.). 32p. (gr. 1-3). 1982. pap. 2.95 (0-9610050-0-9) P J Neuberger.
Neuburg, Norman. California Missions to Cut Out, Vol. I. (gr. 4-9). 1993. pap. 4.95 (0-88388-177-2) Bellerophon Bks.
—California Missions to Cut Out, Vol. 2. (gr. 4-9). 1993. pap. 4.95 (0-88388-185-3) Bellerophon Bks.
Neufeld, Evelyn. Homework! 64p. (ps-2). 1987. pap. text ed. 8.50 (0-914040-56-1) Cuisenaire.
Neufeld, Herm & Chaffin, Charles. Climate in Three-D. (Orig.). (gr. 4-9). 1973. pap. 5.50 (0-918932-04-1) Activity Resources.
Neufeld, John. Edgar Allan. Dunlap, Loren, illus. LC 68-31175. (gr. 5-8). 1968. 21.95 (0-87599-149-1) S G Phillips.
—Lisa, Bright & Dark. (RL 7). 1970. pap. 2.95 (0-451-16093-2, AE1983, Sig) NAL-Dutton.
—Lisa, Bright & Dark. (gr. 7 up). 1969. 21.95 (0-87599-153-X) S G Phillips.
—Twink. 128p. (RL 7). 1971. pap. 2.95 (0-451-15955-1, Sig) NAL-Dutton.
Neufeldt, Victoria, ed. see Webster's New World Dictionaries Staff.

Neufld, Rose. Exploring Nontraditional Jobs for Women. rev. ed. Rosen, Ruth, ed. (gr. 7-12). 1989. PLB 13.95 (0-8239-0971-9) Rosen Group.

Neugeboren, Jay. Poli - a Mexican Boy in Early Texas. Leamon, Tom, illus. LC 88-64094. 120p. (gr. 7 up). 1992. pap. 7.95 (0-931722-74-8) Corona Pub.

Neuhausel, Patricia A., jt. auth. see Mansmann, Patricia A.

Neuman, Pearl. When Winter Comes. (Illus.). 32p. (gr. 1-4). 1989. PLB 15.96 (0-8172-3519-1); pap. 3.95 (0-8114-6723-6) Raintree Steck-V.

Neumann, Daniele, jt. auth. see Limousin, Odile.

Neumann, Peter J. Playing a Virginia Moon. LC 93-25563. 1994. write for info. (0-395-66562-0) HM.

Neumann- Cosel-Nebe, Isabelle von see Von Neumann-Cosel-Nebe, Isabelle.

Neumayr, Sharon. World Literature Activities Kit: Ready-to-Use Worksheets. 288p. (gr. 7-12). 1994. 27. 95x (0-87628-948-0) Ctr Appl Res.

Neumeier, Marty & Glaser, Byron. Action Alphabet. Neumeier, Marty & Glaser, Byron, illus. LC 84-25322. 56p. (gr-1). 1985. 14.00 (0-688-05703-9); lib. bdg. 13. 93 (0-688-05704-7) Greenwillow.

Neusner, Jacob. Learn Mishnah. Hellmuth, Jim, illus. LC 78-5482. (gr. 5-6). 1978. pap. 5.95x (0-87441-310-9) Behrman.

—Meet Our Sages. Hellmuth, Jim, illus. LC 80-12771. 128p. (gr. 5-8). 1980. pap. text ed. 5.95x (0-87441-327-3) Behrman.

—Mitzvah. (gr. 6-8). 5.95 (0-317-70156-8); tchr's guide 14.95 (0-317-70157-6) Behrman.

Neutens, James J. Healthy Sexual Development, Course I. (Illus.). 144p. (gr. 6-8). 1993. text ed. 7.50 wkbk. (1-56269-056-6); tchr's. manual, 152p. 17.50 (1-56269-057-4) Educ Assess Pub.

—Healthy Sexual Development, Course II. (Illus.). 144p. (gr. 9-12). 1993. text ed. 7.50 wkbk. (1-56269-058-2); tchr's. manual, 152p. 17.50 (1-56269-059-0) Educ Assess Pub.

Neve, Herbert. A Student Reader on Africa. LC 93-28433. 1993. write for info. (0-86543-407-7); pap. write for info. (0-86543-408-5) Africa World.

Nevfield, Len. Skystalker. Rivoche, Paul & Humphrey, Brian, illus. 128p. (Orig.). 1985. pap. 1.95 (0-553-24894-4) Bantam.

Neville, Emily C. Berries Goodman. LC 65-19485. (gr. 5-9). 1975. pap. 3.95 (0-06-440072-7, Trophy) HarpC Child Bks.

—Berries Goodman. (gr. 5-9). 1992. 16.75 (0-8446-6584-3) Peter Smith.

—The China Year. LC 90-39899. 256p. (gr. 5-9). 1991. PLB 15.89 (0-06-024384-8) HarpC Child Bks.

—It's Like This, Cat. Weiss, Emil, illus. LC 62-21292. 192p. (gr. 5-9). 1964. 15.00 (0-06-024390-2); PLB 14. 89 (0-06-024391-0) HarpC Child Bks.

—It's Like This, Cat. Weiss, Emil, illus. LC 62-21292. 192p. (gr. 5-9). 1975. pap. 3.95 (0-06-440073-5, Trophy) HarpC Child Bks.

—Newbery Award Library I: It's Like This Cat - Julie of the Wolves - Onion John - Sounder, 4 bks. (gr. 4-6). 1985. Boxed set. pap. 15.80 (0-06-440162-6) HarpC Child Bks.

Neville, Mary. The Christmas Tree Ride. Lloyd, Megan, illus. LC 91-28853. 32p. (ps-3). 1992. reinforced bdg. 14.95 (0-8234-0965-2) Holiday.

Neville, Mary, ed. If a Poem Bothers You. (Illus.). 64p. (Orig.). (gr. 2-6). 1991. pap. 3.75x (0-913678-14-7) New Day Pr.

Nevins, Albert J. Called to Serve: A Guidebook for Altar Servers. LC 81-82546. 48p. (gr. 4 up). 1981. pap. 13. 95 pkg. of six (0-87973-663-1, 663) Our Sunday Visitor.

—My Baptismal Book. 20p. (ps). 1971. pap. 4.95 (0-87973-360-8, 360) Our Sunday Visitor.

—A Saint for Your Name: Saints for Boys. McIlrath, James, illus. LC 79-92504. 120p. (gr. 7 up). 1980. pap. 5.95 (0-87973-320-9, 320) Our Sunday Visitor.

—A Saint for Your Name: Saints for Girls. McIlrath, James, illus. LC 79-92502. 104p. (gr. 7 up). 1980. pap. 5.95 (0-87973-321-7, 321) Our Sunday Visitor.

Nevins, Dan. More Three-D Mouse Mazes. (Illus.). 48p. (Orig.). (gr. 2-5). 1989. pap. 2.95 (0-8431-2337-0) Price Stern.

—Three-D Mouse Mazes. (Illus.). 48p. (gr. 8-11). 1987. pap. 2.95 (0-8431-1883-0) Price Stern.

Nevins, Kathy. Dot-to-Dot Dinos. (Illus.). 48p. (Orig.). (gr. k-3). 1989. pap. 2.95 (0-8431-2338-9) Price Stern.

New England Aquarium Staff. Dive to the Coral Reefs. New England Aquarium Staff, photos by. LC 86-4565. (Illus.). 36p. (gr. k up). 1990. pap. 4.95 (0-517-58210-4) Crown Bks Yng Read.

New England Aquarium Staff & Kaufman, Les. Do Fishes Get Thirsty? Questions Answered by the New England Aquarium. (Illus.). 40p. (gr. 5 up). 1991. 14. 95 (0-531-15214-6); PLB 14.90 (0-531-10992-5) Watts.

New International Version of Bible Staff. The Lost Boy. (Illus., Orig.). 1986. pap. 4.95 (0-918789-07-9) FreeMan Prods.

—The Stowaway. (Illus., Orig.). 1986. pap. 4.95 (0-918789-09-5) FreeMan Prods.

New International Version of the Bible Staff. Daniel & the Lions. (Orig.). 1986. pap. 4.95 (0-918789-08-7) FreeMan Prods.

—The Giant & the Boy. (Illus., Orig.). 1986. pap. 4.95 (0-918789-06-0) FreeMan Prods.

New Mexico People & Energy Collective Staff, et al. Red Ribbons for Emma. LC 80-83883. (Illus.). 48p. (Orig.). (gr. 3 up). 1981. limited ed. 12.00 (0-938678-07-8) New Seed.

New Seed Press Collective Staff. A Book about Us. (Illus.). (ps-5). 1977. 4.95 (0-938678-04-3) New Seed.

New York Book Fair Staff. In Search of Song, Vol. 5. Fisher, Barbara & Spiegel, Richard, eds. (Illus.). 40p. (Orig.). (gr. k-9). 1983. pap. 2.00 (0-934830-30-4) Ten Penny.

New York State League of Women Voters Staff. A Guide to New York State Government. 6th ed. Fairbanks, Mary Jo, ed. 191p. (gr. 12). 1989. text ed. 14.95x (0-936826-33-9) PS Assocs Croton.

New York Transit Museum Staff. I've Been Working on the Subway: The Folklore & Oral History of Transit. Webb, William, illus. 54p. (Orig.). (gr. 5-10). 1991. pap. 5.00 incl. curriculum guide (0-9637492-9-3) NY Transit Mus.

Newberger, Devra. Full House Family Scrapbook. (gr. 4-7). 1992. pap. 3.95 (0-590-45706-3) Scholastic Inc.

Newberger, Joe & Hendricks, Elrod. The Ultimate Baseball Players Yearbook. Benscoter, Robert, illus. 96p. (gr. 3-9). 1991. wkbk. 12.95 (0-9629307-0-9) Batboy Pr.

Newberger-Speregen, Devra. Hip Hop Till You Drop. 1994. pap. 3.50 (0-671-88291-0, Minstrel Bks) PB.

—Stephanie: Phone Call from a Flamingo. 128p. (Orig.). (gr. 5 up). 1993. pap. 3.50 (0-671-88004-7, Minstrel Bks) PB.

Newberry, C. Kittens ABC. Date not set. 14.95 (0-06-024450-X, Festival); PLB 14.89 (0-06-024451-8, Festival) HarpC Child Bks.

Newberry, Clare T. April's Kittens. Newberry, Clare T., illus. LC 40-32442. 32p. (ps-1). 1940. 17.00 (0-06-024400-3); PLB 16.89 (0-06-024401-1) HarpC Child Bks.

—Marshmallow. reissued ed. LC 89-20052. (Illus.). 32p. (ps-3). 1990. 17.00 (0-06-024460-7); PLB 16.89 (0-06-024461-5) HarpC Child Bks.

Newberry, Tina T. Kelli Tyler Extraordinaire. 120p. (Orig.). (gr. 4-6). 1990. pap. text ed. 3.50 (0-936625-91-0, New Hope AL) Womans Mission Union.

Newbery Library Award Staff. The Newbery Library Award. Incl. The Twenty-One Balloons. Pene du Bois, William; The Witch of Blackbird Pond. Speare, Elizabeth; Johnny Tremain. Forbes, Esther; Island of the Blue Dolphins. O'Dell, Scott. (gr. 5 up). 1983. pap. 12.30 boxed set (0-440-46256-8) Dell.

Newbold, Patt & Diebel, Anne. Paper Hat Tricks, Vol. 4: A Big Book of Hat Patterns, Fairytales, Foreign Lands & History Hats. 39p. (ps-5). 1992. pap. text ed. 13.95 (1-56422-996-3, Pub. by Paper Hat) Start Reading.

—Paper Hat Tricks, Vol. 5: A Big Book of Hat Patterns, Sports, Good Health, & Safety Hats. 39p. (ps-5). 1992. pap. text ed. 13.95 (1-56422-995-5, Pub. by Paper Hat) Start Reading.

Newbury, Kenneth. Life Skills Handbook. (Illus.). 48p. (gr. 9-12). 1993. text ed. 6.00 wkbk. (1-56269-060-4); tchr's. manual, 72p. 9.00 (1-56269-061-2) Educ Assess Pub.

Newby, Robert. King Midas. Majewski, Dawn & Cozzolino, Sandra, illus. 64p. (gr. 1-6). 1990. PLB 15. 95 (1-87863-25-5) Forest Hse.

—King Midas: With Selected Sentences in American Sign Language. Majewski, Dawn & Cozzolino, Sandra, illus. LC 90-4908. 64p. (gr. 1-5). 1990. 14.95 (0-930323-75-0, Pub. by K Green Pubns); incl. video 38.20 (0-930323-77-7, Pub. by K Green Pubns); video 29.95 (0-930323-71-8) Gallaudet Univ Pr.

—Sleeping Beauty. Steiner, Pat & Cozzolino, Sandra, illus. 64p. (gr. k-3). 1992. PLB 15.95 (1-56674-035-5) Forest Hse.

—Sleeping Beauty: With Selected Sentences in American Sign Language. Steiner, Pat & Cozzolino, Sandra, illus. LC 91-29729. 64p. (gr. 1-7). 1992. 14.95 (0-930323-97-1, Pub. by K Green Pubns) video 29.95 (0-930323-98-X) Gallaudet Univ Pr.

Newcomb, Everett W., Jr. The Creatures Nobody Loves. Grotke, Christopher, illus. LC 91-66375. 48p. (gr. 4-6). 1991. pap. 3.95 (0-9627974-3-X) Tabby Hse Bks.

Newcombe, Barry. Tennis: Tactics of Success. (Illus.). 80p. (gr. 10-12). 1992. pap. 8.95 (0-7063-7098-8, Pub. by Ward Lock UK) Sterling.

Newcome, Robert & Newcome, Zita. Little Lion. (Illus.). 32p. (ps-1). 1993. 17.95 (1-85681-181-6, Pub. by J MacRae UK) Trafalgar.

Newcome, Zita. Rosie Goes Exploring. (Illus.). 32p. (ps-k). 1992. 11.95 (1-85681-170-0, Pub. by J MacRae UK) Trafalgar.

—Rosie Goes Shopping. (Illus.). 32p. (ps-k). 1992. 11.95 (1-85681-160-3, Pub. by J MacRae UK) Trafalgar.

Newcome, Zita, jt. auth. see Newcome, Robert.

Newell, George E. & Durst, Russel K., eds. Exploring Texts: The Role of Discussion & Writing in the Teaching & Learning of Literature. 352p. (gr. 8-12). 1992. text ed. 31.95 (0-926842-24-2) CG Pubs Inc.

Newell, John, jt. auth. see Calder, Nigel.

Newell, Mindy. The Catwoman: Her Sister's Keeper. O'Neil, Dennis, ed. Birch, J. J. & Bair, Michael, illus. 104p. (Orig.). 1991. pap. 9.95 (0-930289-97-8) DC Comics.

Newell, Peter. The Hole Book. LC 84-52396. (Illus.). 50p. (gr. k-4). 1985. Repr. of 1902 ed. 14.95 (0-8048-1948-8) C E Tuttle.

—The Rocket Book. Newell, Peter, illus. LC 69-12080. 52p. (gr. k-4). 1969. Repr. of 1912 ed. 14.95 (0-8048-0505-9) C E Tuttle.

—The Rocket Book. (Illus.). 48p. (gr. 4-7). 1992. pap. 3. 95t (0-685-52838-3) Dover.

—Rocket Book. LC 91-3120. (gr. 4-7). 1992. pap. 3.95 (0-486-26961-2) Dover.

—The Slant Book. Newell, Peter, illus. LC 67-12304. 50p. (gr. k-4). 1967. Repr. of 1910 ed. 16.95 (0-8048-0532-6) C E Tuttle.

Newell, Peter S. Topsys & Turvys. (Illus.). 76p. (gr. 3-7). pap. 3.50 (0-486-21231-9) Dover.

—Topsys & Turvys. LC 87-51208. (gr. k-4). 1988. 12.95 (0-8048-1551-8) C E Tuttle.

—Topsys & Turvys, No. 2. LC 87-51208. (gr. k-4). 1988. 12.95 (0-8048-1552-6) C E Tuttle.

Newfield, Marcia. The Life of Louis Pasteur. Castro, Antonio, illus. 84p. (gr. 4-7). 1991. PLB 13.95 (0-941477-67-3) TFC Bks NY.

—Where Did You Put Your Sleep? Da Rif, Andrea, illus. LC 83-2785. 32p. (gr. k-4). 1983. SBE 13.95 (0-689-50286-9, M K McElderry) Macmillan Child Grp.

Newhouse, Dora. The Encyclopedia of Homonyms-Sound Alikes: Condensed & Abridged Edition. LC 76-50944. (Illus.). (gr. 6-12). 1978. pap. 6.95 (0-918050-00-6) Newhouse Pr.

Newhouse, Dora, illus. Homonyms Plus. (gr. 6-12). 1979. wkbk 6.95 (0-918050-42-1); tchr's guide 6.95 (0-918050-41-3); activity cards 4.95 (0-918050-44-8) Newhouse Pr.

Newhouse, Elizabeth L., ed. see Scott, John A.

Newhouse, George, jt. auth. see Ezell, Elaine.

Newhouse, Sue. Creative Hand Embroidery. (Illus.). 64p. (Orig.). 1993. pap. 14.95 (0-85532-727-8, Pub. by Search Pr UK) A Schwartz & Co.

Newland, Mary R. The Hebrew Scriptures: The Biblical Story of God's Promise to Israel & to Us. Nagel, Stephan, ed. Abrahamson, Evie, illus. 261p. (Orig.). (gr. 10-11). 1990. pap. text ed. 12.00 (0-88489-231-X); tchr's. ed. 18.95 (0-88489-232-8) St Marys.

Newlin, Lana S. Surviving Sixth Grade. Morey, Cathy, ed. Newlin, Lana S., illus. 90p. (gr. 5-7). 1990. 16.95 (0-9625413-0-3); pap. 9.95 (0-9625413-1-1) Christmans.

Newman, Al. Fibber E. Frog. Doody, Jim, illus. LC 93-77685. 32p. (ps-3). 1993. text ed. 13.95 (0-89334-213-0); pap. 4.95 (0-89334-217-3) Humanics Ltd.

—Fraid E. Cat. Doody, Jim, illus. LC 93-77687. 32p. (ps-3). 1993. 13.95 (0-89334-215-7); pap. 4.95 (0-89334-219-X) Humanics Ltd.

—Giggle E. Goose. Doody, Jim, illus. LC 93-77684. 32p. (ps-3). 1993. 13.95 (0-89334-212-2); pap. 4.95 (0-89334-216-5) Humanics Ltd.

—Grub E. Dog. Doody, Jim, illus. LC 93-77686. 32p. (ps-3). 1993. 13.95 (0-89334-214-9); pap. 4.95 (0-89334-218-1) Humanics Ltd.

Newman, Chris. Phillip's Dream World: A Coloring Book. Newman, Chris, illus. 52p. (Orig.). 1992. pap. 5.95 (0-9635004-3-0) Flying Heart.

Newman, Ed. Hot Air & Gas: The Basics of Balloons. Newman, Ed, illus. LC 92-70713. 52p. (gr. 4-12). 1992. pap. 6.95 (0-9632038-0-0) Greenway Pub.

Newman, Elanor W., jt. auth. see Newman, Gerald.

Newman, Ernest, tr. see Schweitzer, Albert.

Newman, Gerald. Happy Birthday, Little League. LC 88-38158. 64p. (gr. 3-6). 1989. PLB 12.90 (0-531-10687-X) Watts.

Newman, Gerald & Layfield, Eleanor N. Allergies. Cohn, Tom, ed. LC 91-33862. 112p. (gr. 7-12). 1992. PLB 13.40 (0-531-12516-5) Watts.

Newman, Gerald & Newman, Elanor W. Writing Your College Admissions Essay. LC 87-10411. (Illus.). 128p. (gr. 7-12). 1987. PLB 13.90 (0-531-10428-1) Watts.

Newman, Jerry. Green Earrings & a Felt Hat. Hewitt, Margaret, illus. LC 92-29056. 48p. (gr. 1-3). 1993. PLB 14.95 (0-8050-2392-5, Bks Young Read) H Holt & Co.

Newman, Leslea. Belinda's Bouquet. Willhoite, Michael, illus. 24p. (gr. k-3). 1991. pamphlet 6.95 (1-55583-154-0) Alyson Pubns.

—Gloria Goes to Gay Pride. Crocker, Russell, illus. 48p. (Orig.). (ps-2). 1991. pap. 7.95 (1-55583-185-0) Alyson Pubns.

—Heather Has Two Mommies. Souza, Diana, illus. 38p. (ps-3). 1991. pap. 7.95 (1-55583-180-X) Alyson Pubns.

—Saturday Is Pattyday. Hegel, Annette, illus. 24p. (ps-5). 1993. PLB 14.95 (0-934678-52-9); pap. 6.95 (0-934678-51-0) New Victoria Pubs.

—Too Far Away to Touch, Close Enough to See. Stock, Catherine, illus. LC 93-30327. 1995. write for info. (0-395-68968-6, Clarion Bks) HM.

Newman, Louis, ed. see Newman, Shirley.

Newman, Marc. Longhorn Territory. 128p. (Orig.). (gr. 4). 1987. pap. 2.50 (0-553-26904-6) Bantam.

Newman, Marjorie. A Child's First Book of Prayers. Dadd, Elvira, illus. 24p. (ps-1). 1991. 10.00 (0-8007-7129-X) Revell.

Newman, Marjorie, retold by. The Christmas Story. (Illus.). 32p. (gr. 1-7). 1992. 3.98 (0-8317-1265-1) Smithmark.

Newman, Marjorie, ed. My Book of Favorite Prayers. Pasifull, Linda, illus. LC 89-82555. 28p. (ps-2). 1990. pap. 9.99 (0-8066-2469-8, 9-2469) Augsburg Fortress.

Newman, Marsha & Miller, Barbara. The Jewels of Vicarey Harbor. 208p. (Orig.). (gr. 11-12). 1993. pap. 5.95 (*0-9608658-8-8*) Wellspring Utah.

Newman, Matt & Lemay, Nita K. Human Reproductive Systems. Green, James, et al, illus. (gr. 5-8). 1980. pap. text ed. 165.00 4 filmstrips, 4 cass., 24 skill sheets, Guide (*0-89290-101-2, A794-SATC*) Soc for Visual.

Newman, Matthew. Dwight Gooden. LC 86-16527. (Illus.). 48p. (gr. 5-6). 1986. RSBE 11.95 (*0-89686-317-4*, Crestwood Hse) Macmillan Child Grp.

—Larry Bird. LC 86-16524. (Illus.). 48p. (gr. 5-6). 1986. RSBE 11.95 (*0-89686-314-X*, Crestwood Hse) Macmillan Child Grp.

—Lynette Woodard. LC 86-19737. (Illus.). 48p. (gr. 5-6). 1986. RSBE 11.95 (*0-89686-316-6*, Crestwood Hse) Macmillan Child Grp.

—Mary Decker Slaney. LC 86-16525. (Illus.). 48p. (gr. 5-6). 1986. RSBE 11.95 (*0-89686-319-0*, Crestwood Hse) Macmillan Child Grp.

—Patrick Ewing. LC 86-16522. (Illus.). 48p. (gr. 5-6). 1986. RSBE 11.95 (*0-89686-315-8*, Crestwood Hse) Macmillan Child Grp.

—Watch Guard Dogs. LC 85-19542. (Illus.). 48p. (gr. 5-6). 1985. RSBE 11.95 (*0-89686-287-9*, Crestwood Hse) Macmillan Child Grp.

Newman, Nanette. Sharing. 1990. 13.95 (*0-385-41104-9*) Doubleday.

—Spider the Horrible Cat. Foreman, Michael, illus. LC 92-17242. 1993. write for info. (*0-15-277972-8*) HarBrace.

—That Dog! Hafner, Marylin, contrib. by. LC 81-43892. (Illus.). 48p. (gr. 1-4). 1992. pap. 3.95 (*0-06-440363-7*, Trophy) HarpC Child Bks.

—There's a Bear in the Bath! Foreman, Michael, illus. LC 93-12877. 1994. write for info. (*0-15-285512-2*) HarBrace.

Newman, Nanette & Foreman, Michael. A Cat & Mouse Love Story. Foreman, Michael, illus. 32p. (gr. k-3). 1985. 14.95 (*0-434-98045-5*, Pub. by W Heinemann Ltd) Trafalgar.

Newman, Pamela, et al. Egyptian Peaks. (Illus.). 60p. (Orig.). (gr. 4-12). 1988. pap. 24.95 (*0-943804-66-3*) U of Denver Teach.

Newman, Robert. The Case of the Baker Street Irregular. LC 77-15463. (gr. 3-7). 1984. pap. 4.95 (*0-689-70766-5*, Aladdin) Macmillan Child Grp.

—The Case of the Vanishing Corpse. LC 79-22078. 228p. (gr. 4-6). 1985. pap. 4.95 (*0-689-71037-2*, Aladdin) Macmillan Child Grp.

—The Case of the Watching Boy. LC 86-28859. 192p. (gr. 3-7). 1987. SBE 13.95 (*0-689-31317-9*, Atheneum Child Bk) Macmillan Child Grp.

—Merlin's Mistake. Lebenson, Richard, illus. (gr. 5-9). 15.75 (*0-8446-6187-2*) Peter Smith.

—The Testing of Tertius. Cuffani, Richard, illus. (gr. 5-9). 19.75 (*0-8446-6188-0*) Peter Smith.

Newman, Robert, jt. auth. see Magee, Doug.

Newman, Roger C. Murtagh & the Vikings. (Illus.). 96p. (Orig.). (gr. 5-8). 1986. 9.95 (*0-947962-05-0*, Pub. by Childrens Pr); pap. 5.95 (*0-947962-06-9*, Pub. by Childrens Pr) Irish Bks Media.

Newman, Shirlee P. The Incas. Rosoff, Iris, ed. LC 91-31378. (Illus.). 64p. (gr. 3-5). 1992. PLB 12.90 (*0-531-20004-3*) Watts.

—The Incas. (Illus.). 64p. (gr. 5-8). 1992. pap. 5.95 (*0-531-15637-0*) Watts.

—The Inuits. LC 93-18370. (Illus.). 64p. (gr. 4-6). 1993. PLB 12.90 (*0-531-20073-6*) Watts.

Newman, Shirley. A Child's Introduction to the Early Prophets. LC 75-14052. (Illus.). 128p. (gr. 2-3). 1975. 6.95x (*0-87441-244-7*); tchr's guide 12.50x (*0-87441-227-7*); wkbk. 1, Amye Rosenberg 2.75 (*0-87441-268-4*); wkbk. 2 2.75x (*0-87441-269-2*) Behrman.

—A Child's Introduction to Torah. Newman, Louis, ed. Zemsky, Jessica, illus. 128p. (Orig.). (gr. 4). 1972. pap. text ed. 12.50 (*0-87441-067-3*) Behrman.

—Introduction to Kings, Later Prophets & Writings, Vol. 3. Rossel, Seymour, ed. Hoban, Brom, illus. 160p. (Orig.). (gr. 4-5). 1981. pap. text ed. 6.95x (*0-87441-336-2*); wkbk. by Morris Sugarman 3.95 (*0-685-00733-2*); tchr's ed. 14.95x (*0-685-41994-0*) Behrman.

Newman, Susan. Dont Be S. A. D. A Teenage Guide to Handling Stress, Anxiety & Depression. 1991. lib. bdg. 12.98 (*0-671-72610-2*, J Messner); lib. bdg. 7.95 (*0-671-72611-0*, J Messner) S&S Trade.

Newman, Winifred B. The Secret in the Garden. (Illus.). 32p. (Orig.). (gr. k-5). 1980. Bahai.

Newmark, Ann. Chemistry. LC 92-54480. (Illus.). 64p. (gr. 7 up). 1993. 15.95 (*1-56458-231-0*) Dorling Kindersley.

Newsom, D. Earl. The Birth of Oklahoma. (Illus.). 178p. (gr. 5-12). 1983. 14.95 (*0-934188-08-4*) Evans Pubns.

Newsome, Arden. Cork & Wood Crafts. Coner, Nancy, illus. LC 72-112370. 64p. (gr. k-3). 1971. PLB 12.95 (*0-87460-229-7*) Lion Bks.

Newth, Mette. The Abduction. Nunnally, Tiina & Murray, Steve, trs. (gr. 7 up). 1989. 15.00 (*0-374-30008-9*) FS&G.

—Abduction. 1993. pap. 3.95 (*0-374-40009-1*) FS&G.

Newton, David. James Watson & Francis Crick. (Illus.). 128p. (gr. 7-12). 1992. lib. bdg. 16.95x (*0-8160-2558-4*) Facts on File.

Newton, David E. AIDS Issues: A Handbook. LC 92-10071. 144p. (gr. 6 up). 1992. lib. bdg. 18.95 (*0-89490-338-1*) Enslow Pubs.

—The Chemical Elements. LC 93-30044. 1994. write for info. (*0-531-12501-7*) Watts.

—Consumer Chemistry Projects for Young Scientists. LC 90-48499. (Illus.). 128p. (gr. 9-12). 1991. PLB 13.90 (*0-531-11011-7*) Watts.

—Earthquakes. LC 92-23291. 1993. 12.90 (*0-531-20054-X*) Watts.

—Earthquakes. (Illus.). 64p. (gr. 5-8). 1993. pap. 5.95 (*0-531-15664-8*) Watts.

—Gun Control: An Issue for the Nineties. LC 91-23352. (Illus.). 128p. (gr. 6 up). 1992. lib. bdg. 17.95 (*0-89490-296-2*) Enslow Pubs.

—Hunting. (Illus.). 144p. (gr. 9-12). 1992. PLB 13.40 (*0-531-13022-3*) Watts.

—Land Use A-Z. LC 89-78119. 128p. (gr. 6 up). 1991. lib. bdg. 17.95 (*0-89490-260-1*) Enslow Pubs.

—Linus Pauling: Scientist & Advocate. LC 93-31719. 1994. write for info. (*0-8160-2959-8*) Facts on File.

—Making & Using Scientific Equipment. LC 92-38039. (Illus.). 128p. (gr. 9-12). 1993. PLB 13.90 (*0-531-11176-8*); pap. 6.95 (*0-531-15663-X*) Watts.

—Particle Accelerations: From the Cyclotron to the Superconducting Super Collider. LC 88-31375. (Illus.). 128p. (gr. 10-12). 1990. 13.40 (*0-531-10671-3*) Watts.

—Population: Too Many People? LC 92-14306. (Illus.). 128p. (gr. 6 up). 1992. lib. bdg. 18.95 (*0-89490-295-4*) Enslow Pubs.

—Science - Technology - Society Projects for Young Scientists. LC 91-17825. (Illus.). 144p. (gr. 9-12). 1991. PLB 13.90 (*0-531-11047-8*) Watts.

Newton, Derek, jt. auth. see Smith, David.

Newton, James R. Rain Shadow. Bonners, Susan, illus. LC 82-45927. 32p. (gr. 2-6). 1983. (Crowell Jr Bks); (Crowell Jr Bks) HarpC Child Bks.

Newton, Jane. Good Morning Dogs! Edgell, Kyle, illus. 20p. (Orig.). (ps). 1991. pap. text ed. 4.95 (*0-931571-08-1*) Lifetime Pr.

Newton, Jill. Cat-Fish. Pearson, Susan, ed. LC 91-42858. (Illus.). 32p. (ps up). 1992. 14.00 (*0-688-11423-7*); PLB 13.93 (*0-688-11424-5*) Lothrop.

—Our New Sofa. LC 93-23538. 1994. write for info. (*0-688-13309-6*) Lothrop.

—Polar Bear Scare. LC 91-5304. (ps-3). 1992. PLB 14.93 (*0-688-11233-1*) Lothrop.

—Polar Scare. (Illus.). (ps-3). 1992. 15.00 (*0-688-11232-3*) Lothrop.

Newton, Joe, jt. auth. see Durkin, John F.

Newton, Laura. Me & My Aunts. Fay, Ann, ed. Oz, Robin, illus. LC 86-15950. 32p. (gr. 2-5). 1986. PLB 13.95 (*0-8075-5029-9*) A Whitman.

Newton, Laura P. William the Vehicle King. Rogers, Jackie, illus. LC 86-33412. 32p. (ps-2). 1987. RSBE 13.95 (*0-02-768230-7*, Bradbury Pr) Macmillan Child Grp.

Newton, Lucilda A. Big Peanuts. (ps-3). 1976. pap. 2.50 (*0-915374-17-X*, 17-X) Rapids Christian.

—Big Peanuts in Trouble. (ps-3). 1976. pap. 2.50 (*0-915374-18-8*, 18-8) Rapids Christian.

Newton, Michael. The King Conspiracy. (Orig.). (ps-12). 1987. pap. 3.25 (*0-87067-729-2*) Holloway.

Newton, Pam, retold by. & illus. The Stonecutter: An Indian Folktale. 32p. (ps-3). 1990. 14.95 (*0-399-22187-5*, Putnam-Whitebird) Putnam Pub Group.

Newton, Rebecca, ed. see LaMorte, Kathy & Lewis, Sharen.

Newton, Robert. Tokyo. LC 92-2498. (Illus.). 96p. (gr. 6 up). 1992. RSBE 13.95 (*0-02-768235-8*, New Discovery) Macmillan Child Grp.

Newton, Suzanne. I Will Call It Georgie's Blues. (gr. 7 up). 1986. pap. 2.75 (*0-440-94090-7*, LFL) Dell.

—I Will Call It Georgie's Blues. 1990. pap. 3.95 (*0-14-034536-1*, Puffin) Puffin Bks.

—M. V. Sexton Speaking. 198p. (ps up) 1990. pap. 3.95 (*0-14-032356-2*, Puffin) Puffin Bks.

—Reubella & the Old Focus Home. LC 78-18336. 200p. (gr. 7-10). 1978. 8.00 (*0-664-32635-8*, Westminster) Westminster John Knox.

—Where Are You When I Need You? 1991. 14.00 (*0-670-81702-3*) Viking Child Bks.

—Where Are You When I Need You? LC 92-31360. 208p. (gr. 7 up). 1993. pap. 3.99 (*0-14-034454-3*) Puffin Bks.

Newton-John, Olivia & Hurst, Brian S. A Pig Tale. Murdocca, Sal, illus. LC 92-44116. 1993. pap. 12.00 (*0-671-78778-0*, S&S BFYR) S&S Trade.

Nexo, John B. Camels. 24p. (gr. 3). 1989. PLB 14.95s.p. (*0-88682-222-X*) Creative Ed.

Ney, Jessica, ed. The Necromancer's Lieutenant. Danforth, Liz & Martin, David, illus. 32p. (Orig.). (gr. 12). 1990. pap. 7.00 (*1-55806-113-4*, 8113) Iron Crown Ent Inc.

Ney, Jessica, ed. see Birkner, Malthias & Birkner, Karen.

Ney, Jessica, ed. see Cooke, Tim.

Ney, Jessica, ed. see Crowdis, John.

Ney, Jessica, ed. see Crutchfield, Charles.

Ney, Jessica, ed. see Feild, William B., Jr. & Stassun, Peter G.

Ney, Jessica, ed. see Ferrone, John M.

Ney, Jessica, ed. see McKeage, Jeffrey.

Neyland, James. Booker T. Washington, Educator. Locke, Raymond F., ed. (Illus.). 192p. 1993. pap. 3.95 (*0-87067-599-0*, Melrose Sq) Holloway.

—W. E. B. DuBois, Scholar & Activist. Locke, Raymond F., ed. (Illus.). 192p. 1993. pap. 3.95 (*0-87067-588-5*, Melrose Sq) Holloway.

Ng, Franklin. Chinese Amerian Struggle for Equality. LC 92-7472. 1992. 22.60 (*0-86593-181-X*); lib. bdg. 16. 95s.p. (*0-685-59290-1*) Rourke Corp.

Ngugi wa Thiong'o. Njamba Nene & the Flying Bus. Wangui wa Goro, tr. Kariuki, Emmanuel, illus. LC 88-70433. 34p. (gr. 2-7). 1989. 12.95 (*0-86543-079-9*); pap. 5.95 (*0-86543-080-2*) Africa World.

—Njamba Nene's Pistol. Wangui wa Goro, tr. Kariuki, Emmanuel, illus. LC 88-70432. 32p. (gr. 2-7). 1989. 12.95 (*0-86543-081-0*); pap. 5.95 (*0-86543-082-9*) Africa World.

Nguyen, Chi. Cooking the Vietnamese Way. (gr. 4-7). 1993. pap. 5.95 (*0-8225-9647-4*) Lerner Pubns.

Nguyen, Chi & Monroe, Judy M. Cooking the Vietnamese Way. (Illus.). 48p. (gr. 5 up). 1985. PLB 14.95 (*0-8225-0914-8*) Lerner Pubns.

Nguyen, Dinh H. Two Hundred One Vietnamese Verbs Fully Conjugated in All the Tenses. new ed. LC 79-14200. (gr. 10-12). 1979. pap. text ed. 9.95 (*0-8120-2019-7*) Barron.

Nguyen, Kim-Anh. Vietnamese Word Book. My Ly, Ha, illus. LC 93-73560. (VIE & ENG.). 144p. (gr. k-6). 1994. 15.95 (*1-880188-70-8*); pap. 11.95 (*1-880188-51-1*) Bess Pr.

Ng'Weno, Fleur. Kenya. (Illus.). 32p. (gr. 7-10). 1992. 17. 95 (*0-237-60194-X*, Pub. by Evans Bros Ltd) Trafalgar.

Nhuong. Land I Lost. Date not set. 12.95 (*0-06-024592-1*, Festival); PLB 12.89 (*0-06-024593-X*, Festival) HarpC Child Bks.

Nhuong, Nuynh Quang. The Land I Lost: Adventures of a Boy in Vietnam. LC 80-8437. (Illus.). 128p. (gr. 4-7). 1990. (Lipp Jr Bks); PLB 13.89 (*0-397-32448-0*, Lipp Jr Bks) HarpC Child Bks.

Nichelason, Margery G. Homelessness. LC 92-19675. 1993. 17.50 (*0-8225-2606-9*) Lerner Pubns.

Nichol, B. P. Once: A Lullaby. Lobel, Anita, illus. LC 85-9942. 24p. (ps-1). 1986. 11.95 (*0-688-04284-8*); PLB 11.88 (*0-688-04285-6*) Greenwillow.

—Once: A Lullaby. Lobel, Anita, illus. LC 85-9942. 24p. (ps up). 1992. pap. 4.95 (*0-688-04286-4*, Mulberry) Morrow.

Nichol, Barbara. Beethoven Lives Upstairs. Cameron, Scott, illus. LC 93-5774. 1994. 15.95 (*0-531-06828-5*) Orchard Bks Watts.

Nicholas, jt. auth. see Scott, Sharon.

Nicholas, Anna K. The Great Dane. (Illus.). 319p. (gr. 7 up). 1988. 19.95 (*0-86622-122-0*, PS-826) TFH Pubns.

Nicholas, Charles, illus. Banner in the Sky. Gifford, Mary, adapted by. (Illus.). (gr. 4-12). 1978. pap. text ed. 2.25 (*0-88301-301-0*) Pendulum Pr.

—God Is My Co-Pilot. Cadrain, Linda A., adapted by. LC 78-50959. (Illus.). (gr. 4-12). 1978. pap. text ed. 2.25 (*0-88301-302-9*) Pendulum Pr.

—Hiroshima. Cadrain, Linda A., adapted by. LC 78-50861. (Illus.). (gr. 4-12). 1978. pap. text ed. 2.25 (*0-88301-304-5*) Pendulum Pr.

—Hot Rod. Cadrain, Linda A., adapted by. LC 78-50957. (Illus.). (gr. 4-12). 1978. pap. text ed. 2.25 (*0-88301-305-3*) Pendulum Pr.

—Just Dial a Number. Gifford, Mary, adapted by. LC 78-50860. (Illus.). (gr. 4-12). 1978. pap. text ed. 2.25 (*0-88301-306-1*) Pendulum Pr.

Nicholas, Robert J. Fifty Creative Exercises, 2 bks. (gr. 7 up). 1991. Set. pap. 24.00 (*1-879777-02-9*); Bk. I. pap. 12.95 (*1-879777-00-2*); Bk. II. pap. 12.95 (*1-879777-01-0*) Leonardos Work.

Nicholaus, J. Air Defence Weapons. (Illus.). 48p. (gr. 3-8). 1989. lib. bdg. 18.60 (*0-86592-423-6*); lib. bdg. 13.95s.p. (*0-685-58578-6*) Rourke Corp.

—Army Air Support. (Illus.). 48p. (gr. 3-8). 1989. lib. bdg. 18.60 (*0-86592-421-X*) Rourke Corp.

—Artillery. (Illus.). 48p. (gr. 3-8). 1989. lib. bdg. 18.60 (*0-86592-419-8*) Rourke Corp.

—Main Battle Tanks. (Illus.). 48p. (gr. 3-8). 1989. lib. bdg. 18.60 (*0-86592-420-1*); 13.95s.p. (*0-685-58576-X*) Rourke Corp.

—Rockets & Missiles. (Illus.). 48p. (gr. 3-8). 1989. lib. bdg. 18.60 (*0-86592-418-X*); lib. bdg. 13.95s.p. (*0-685-58577-8*) Rourke Corp.

—Tracked Vehicles. (Illus.). 48p. (gr. 3-8). 1989. lib. bdg. 18.60 (*0-86592-422-8*); lib. bdg. 13.95s.p. (*0-685-58579-4*) Rourke Corp.

Nicholaus, John. The Army Library, 6 bks, Reading Level 5. (Illus.). 288p. (gr. 3-8). 1989. Set. PLB 111.60 (*0-86592-417-1*) Rourke Corp.

Nicholls, Delia, jt. auth. see Hatherly, Janelle.

Nicholls, Judith, ed. Sing Freedom! Children's Poetry. (Illus.). 132p. (gr. 3 up). 1993. 16.95 (*0-571-16513-3*); pap. 9.95 (*0-571-16514-1*) Faber & Faber.

—What on Earth? Poems with a Conservation Theme. Baker, Alan, illus. 132p. (gr. 2 up). 1989. pap. 8.95 (*0-571-15262-7*) Faber & Faber.

Nicholson, Michael. Mahatma Gandhi: Champion of Human Rights. Birch, Beverley, adapted by. LC 89-77589. (Illus.). 64p. (gr. 3-4). 1990. PLB 18.60 (*0-8368-0390-6*) Gareth Stevens Inc.

Nichols, Belia, jt. auth. see Nichols, Peter.

Nichols, Eugene D. & Schwartz, Sharon L. Mathematics Dictionary & Handbook. 464p. (gr. 5-10). 1993. text ed. 28.95 (*1-882269-00-4*) N Schwartz Pub.

Nichols, Frank. Curves. 1989. pap. 2.95 (*0-85953-049-3*) Childs Play.

—Stencils. 1989. pap. 3.95 (*0-85953-048-5*) Childs Play.

—Tangrams. 1989. pap. 3.95 (0-85953-050-7) Childs Play.
Nichols, Frank, illus. Circles. (Orig.). (ps-2). 1976. pap. 2.95 (0-85953-047-7) Childs Play.
Nichols, Freeda B. Little Bug Eyes: The Little Frog Who Did. 2nd ed. LC 89-91965. (Illus.). 24p. (Orig.). (gr. k-6). 1991. pap. 4.95 (0-9623980-0-4) Baker Seaforth.
Nichols, Janet. American Music Makers. (Illus.). 232p. (gr. 7 up). 1990. 19.95 (0-8027-6957-8); lib. bdg. 19.85 (0-8027-6958-6) Walker & Co.
—Casey Wooster's Pet Care Service. LC 93-7041. 112p. (gr. 4-7). 1993. SBE 12.95 (0-689-31879-0, Atheneum Child Bk) Macmillan Child Grp.
—Women Music Makers. 224p. (gr. 7 up). 1992. 18.95 (0-8027-8168-3); lib. bdg. 19.85 (0-8027-8169-1) Walker & Co.
Nichols, Joan K. A Matter of Conscience: The Trial of Anne Hutchinson. Krovatin, Dan, illus. LC 92-18087. 101p. (gr. 2-5). 1992. PLB 21.34 (0-8114-7233-7) Raintree Steck-V.
—New Orleans. LC 88-35915. (Illus.). 60p. (gr. 3 up). 1989. RSBE 13.95 (0-87518-403-0, Dillon) Macmillan Child Grp.
Nichols, Kathie. Sarah: A Story of Love & Adoption. Nichols, Fran, illus. 32p. (Orig.). (gr. 2-4). 1992. pap. 6.95 (0-943861-21-7) Lone Tree.
Nichols, Kim, jt. auth. see Nichols, Wendy.
Nichols, Nick. The Comfort Fairy Story. 24p. (gr. k-4). 1990. 19.95 (0-9632531-0-7) N Squared Ent.
Nichols, Paul. Blitz: Rookie Quarterback, No. 1. (gr. 3 up). 1988. pap. 3.99 (0-345-35108-8) Ballantine.
—Tough Tackle. 1988. pap. 2.95 (0-345-35109-6) Ballantine.
—Where in the World Did You Come From? Stallings, Scott, illus. 32p. (ps up). 1993. 17.95g (1-884507-00-X) Boyer-Caswell.
Nichols, Peter & Nichols, Belia. Mastodon Hunters to Mound Builders: North American Archaeology. Battles-Herron, Linda & Newman, Beth, illus. 112p. (gr. 4-7). 1992. 12.95 (0-89015-748-0) Eakin-Sunbelt.
Nichols, Roger & Nichols, Sarah. Greek Everyday Life. McLeish, Kenneth & McLeish, Valerie, eds. (Illus.). 48p. (gr. 7-12). 1978. pap. text ed. 9.00 (0-582-20672-3, 70819) Longman.
Nichols, Roger & McLeish, Kenneth, eds. Through Greek Eyes. LC 74-80353. (Illus.). 144p. (gr. 7-12). 1975. pap. 10.95 (0-521-08560-8) Cambridge U Pr.
Nichols, Sarah, jt. auth. see Nichols, Roger.
Nichols, Terri V. Francis: The Knight of Assisi. CCC of America Staff, illus. 61p. (Illus.). (ps-6). 1990. incl. video 21.95 (1-56814-002-9); pap. text ed. 4.95 book (0-685-62404-8) CCC of America.
Nichols, Wendy & Nichols, Kim. Wonderscience: A Developmentally Appropriate Guide to Hands-on Science for Young Children. LC 90-60081. 60p. (Orig.). (ps-3). 1990. pap. 14.95 (0-9625907-0-3) Learning Expo.
Nicholson, Alasdair. The Cold War. Yapp, Malcolm, et al, eds. (Illus.). 32p. (gr. 6-11). 1980. pap. text ed. 3.45 (0-89908-211-4) Greenhaven.
Nicholson, Darrell. Wild Boars. Blacklock, Craig, photos by. (Illus.). 48p. (gr. 2-5). 1987. PLB 19.95 (0-87614-308-7) Carolrhoda Bks.
Nicholson, Dorinda M. Pearl Harbor Child: A Child's View of Pearl Harbor-From Attack to Peace. Nicholson, Larry, illus. 60p. 1993. pap. write for info. (0-9631388-6-3) AZ Mem Mus.

Nicholson, Lois. Cal Ripken, Jr. Quiet Hero. LC 93-22741. (Illus.). 112p. (gr. 4-8). 1993. bds. 12.95 (0-87033-445-X) Tidewater.

"In an era of one-shot prima donnas, Cal Ripken, Jr., is an athlete of stamina, humility & uncommon talent. Lois Nicholson's biography of the Orioles iron man is more than simply the story of a great ballplayer; it is a testimonial to the most appealing virtues of baseball itself."--David Plaut, USA TODAY BASEBALL WEEKLY. Cal Ripken, Jr., has always strived to be the best--in school, in baseball, & as a role model for young people who, like himself, love the game of baseball. He has turned a lifelong study of baseball into a staggeringly successful career, with a playing streak of consecutive games second only to that of Lou Gehrig. With the help of Vi Ripken, Cal's mother; Johnny Oates, manager of the Orioles; Cal's minor league & high school coaches; former teammates; & many others who have watched Cal Ripken, Jr., become the baseball hero he is today, Lois Nicholson has written a book that young fans will enjoy. *Publisher Provided Annotation.*

—George Washington Carver: Scientist. (Illus.). 80p. 1993. 13.95 (0-7910-1763-X, Am Art Analog) Chelsea Hse.
Nicholson, Loren. Old Picture Postcards: A Historic Journey along California's Central Coast. (Illus.). 144p. (Orig.). (gr. 9-12). 1989. pap. 12.95 (0-9623233-1-4) CA HPA.
—Rails Across the Ranchos: The Pacific Coastline of Southern Pacific Railroad. (Illus.). 197p. (gr. 10-12). 1980. text ed. 18.95 (0-913548-72-3) CA HPA.
—Romualdo Pacheco's California! The Mexican-American Who Won. (Illus.). 112p. (Orig.). (gr. 10-12). 1991. pap. text ed. 12.95 (0-9623233-2-2) CA HPA.
Nicholson, Michael. Across the Limpopo: A Family's Hazardous Journey Through Africa. 196p. 1991. pap. 6.95 (0-86051-369-6, Robson-Parkwest) Parkwest Pubns.
—Mahatma Gandhi: The Man Who Freed India & Led the World in Nonviolent Change. Sherwood, Rhoda, ed. LC 88-2098. (Illus.). 68p. (gr. 5-6). 1988. PLB 18.60 (1-55532-813-X) Gareth Stevens Inc.
Nicholson, Michael & Winner, David. Raoul Wallenberg. LC 88-2078. (Illus.). 68p. (Orig.). (gr. 5-6). 1990. pap. 7.95 (0-8192-1525-2) Morehouse Pub.
—Raoul Wallenberg: The Swedish Diplomat Who Saved 100,000 Jews from the Nazi Holocaust Before Mysteriously Disappearing. Sherwood, Rhoda, ed. LC 88-2078. (Illus.). 68p. (gr. 5-6). 1989. PLB 18.60 (1-55532-820-2) Gareth Stevens Inc.
Nicholson, Robert. Ancient Greece. LC 93-29442. 1994. write for info. (0-7910-2703-1); write for info. (0-7910-2727-9) Chelsea Hse.

—Los Siux. Araluce, Jose R., tr. from ENG. (SPA., Illus.). 32p. 1993. PLB 16.95x (1-56492-092-5) Laredo. The history, culture, & traditions of the Sioux are lively presented in this book through an exploration of their rituals, beliefs, artifacts, daily life activities & customs. Each title contains maps, full-color photographs & illustrations, as well as factual texts, activities & the retelling of a traditional story which will stimulate & engage the reader's curiosity. *Publisher Provided Annotation.*

Nicholson, Robert & Watts, Claire. La Antigua China: Hechos, Historias, Actividades. Araluce, Jose R., tr. (SPA., Illus.). 32p. (gr. 6-10). 1993. 14.95x (1-56492-093-3) Laredo.
—El Antiguo Egipto: Hechos - Historias - Actividades. Araluce, Jose R., tr. (SPA., Illus.). 32p. (gr. 6-10). 1993. 14.95x (1-56492-094-1) Laredo.

—Los Aztecas. Araluce, Jose R., tr. from ENG. (SPA., Illus.). 24p. 1993. PLB 16.95x (1-56492-091-7) Laredo. The history, culture, & traditions of the Aztecs are lively presented in this book through an exploration of their rituals, beliefs, artifacts, daily life activities & customs. This book contains maps, full-color photographs & illustrations, as well as factual texts, activities & the retelling of a traditional story which will stimulate & engage the reader's curiosity. *Publisher Provided Annotation.*

Nicieza, Mariano. Space: 34-24-34: The Exciting Adventures of the Nova Girls. O'Connor, Thom, et al, illus. 64p. (Orig.). (gr. 9). 1989. write for info. MN DPPD Inc.
Nickell, Joe. The Magic Detectives: Join Them in Solving Strange Mysteries. (Illus.). 115p. (gr. 4-9). 1989. 8.95 (0-87975-547-4) Prometheus Bks.
—Wonderworkers! How They Perform the Impossible. Nickell, Joe, illus. 80p. (Orig.). 1991. pap. 11.95 (0-87975-688-8) Prometheus Bks.
Nickelodeon Staff. Postcards over the Edge. 1992. pap. 5.95 (0-448-40502-4, G&D) Putnam Pub Group.
—Rugrats at the Movies. 1992. pap. 2.25 (0-448-40500-8, G&D) Putnam Pub Group.
—Rugrats Monster in the Garage. 1992. pap. 2.25 (0-448-40501-6, G&D) Putnam Pub Group.
Nickelson, Harry. Vietnam. LC 89-13100. (Illus.). 80p. (gr. 5-8). 1989. PLB 14.95 (1-56006-110-3) Lucent Bks.
Nickerson, Betty, ed. All about Us - Nous Autres: Creative Writing & Painting by & for Young People. (ENG & FRE., Illus.). 36p. 1992. pap. 4.95 (0-685-61052-7) All About Us.
Nickerson, Sara. Martin the Cavebine. Weller, Don, illus. LC 88-71369. 28p. (Orig.). (gr. 1-4). 1989. pap. 8.00 (0-935529-06-3) Comprehen Health Educ.
—Peter Parrot, Private Eye. Bagley, Michael, illus. Counts, Sandra J., frwd. by. LC 88-63800. (Illus.). 43p. (Orig.). (gr. 2-6). 1988. pap. 8.00 (0-935529-07-1) Comprehen Health Educ.
Nickl, Peter. Crocodile, Crocodile. Schroeder, Binnette, illus. Cutler, Ebbitt, tr. (Illus.). 32p. 1989. 11.95 (0-940793-33-4, Pub. by Crocodile Bks); pap. 6.95 (0-940793-32-6, Pub. by Crocodile Bks) Interlink Pub.
—The Story of the Kind Wolf. Wilkon, Jozef, illus. LC 87-42923. 32p. (gr. k-3). 1988. 13.95 (1-55858-066-2); pap. 4.95 (1-55858-058-1) North-South Bks NYC.
—The Wonderful Travels & Adventures of Baron Munchhausen: As Told by Himself in the Company of His Friends & Washed down by Many a Good Bottle of Wine - The Adventures on Land. Schroeder, Binette, illus. Taylor, Elizabeth B., tr. from GER. LC 91-16510. (Illus.). 32p. (gr. 5 up). 1992. 17.95 (1-55858-134-0) North-South Bks NYC.
Nicklaus, Carol. Come Dance with Me. Nicklaus, Carol, illus. 32p. (ps-1). 1991. PLB 8.98 (0-671-73503-9); pap. 9.98 (0-671-73507-1) Silver Pr.
—The Go Club. Nicklaus, Carol, illus. 32p. (ps-1). 1991. PLB 8.98 (0-671-73500-4); pap. 3.95 (0-671-73505-5) Silver Pr.
—Silver Sports Series, 4 vols. Nicklaus, Carol, illus. (ps-1). 1991. Set, 32p. ea. lib. bdg. 35.92 (0-671-31271-5); Set, 32p. ea. pap. 15.80 (0-671-31272-3) Silver Pr.
Nicklaus, Carol, jt. auth. see Ziefert, Harriet.
Nicklaus, Carol, illus. see Bunny Shines. LC 91-68458. 48p. (Orig.). (ps up). 1993. pap. 2.50 (0-679-83449-4) Random Bks Yng Read.
—Eggs-O-Poppin' LC 91-68547. 48p. (Orig.). (ps up). 1993. pap. 2.50 (0-679-83448-6) Random Bks Yng Read.
Nickman, Steven L. The Adoption Experiences. LC 85-8957. 192p. (gr. 7 up). 1985. lib. bdg. 14.98 (0-671-50817-2, J Messner) S&S Trade.
—When Mom & Dad Divorce. De Groat, Diane, illus. 80p. (gr. 3-6). 1986. lib. bdg. 10.98 (0-671-60153-9, J Messner); pap. 4.95 (0-671-62878-X) S&S Trade.
Nicks, Mel J., jt. auth. see Ortwerth, John.
Nic Leodhas, Sorche. Always Room for One More. Hogrogian, Nonny, illus. LC 65-12881. 32p. (ps-2). 1965. reinforced bdg. 14.95 (0-8050-0331-2, Bks Young Read); pap. 5.95 (Owlet Bk.) (0-8050-0330-4) H Holt & Co.
Nicol, Mary M. & Roth, Pamela K., eds. Ready, Set... Sing! (Songs for Sunday & Everyday) 96p. (Orig.). 1989. pap. 9.00 (0-8170-1155-2) Judson.
Nicolai, D. Miles. The Summer the Flowers Had No Scent. (Illus.). 1978. pap. 2.75 (0-933992-00-9) Coffee Break.
—The Summer the Flowers Had No Scent. 3rd ed. Poyser, Victoria, illus. 28p. (gr. 3-5). 1977. pap. 2.75 (0-933992-19-X) Coffee Break.
Nicolas, jt. auth. see Will.
Nicole, David. The Crusades. (gr. 1-9). 1992. pap. 3.95 (0-88388-096-2) Bellerophon Bks.
—The Hundred Years War. (gr. 1-9). 1992. pap. 3.95 (0-88388-142-X) Bellerophon Bks.
Nicoll, Helen & Pienkowski, Jan. Meg & Mog. (Illus.). (ps-2). 1976. pap. 3.50 (0-14-050117-7, Puffin) Puffin Bks.
—Meg on the Moon. (Illus.). 32p. (ps). 1980. 15.95 (0-434-95424-1, Pub. by W Heinemann Ltd) Trafalgar.
—Mog's Box. (Illus.). 32p. (ps-k). 1987. 15.95 (0-434-95658-9, Pub. by W Heinemann Ltd) Trafalgar.
—Mog's Mumps. (Illus.). 32p. (ps-1). 1983. 15.95 (0-434-95640-6, Pub. by W Heinemann Ltd) Trafalgar.
—Owl at School. (Illus.). 32p. (ps). 1984. 15.95 (0-434-95434-9, Pub. by W Heinemann Ltd) Trafalgar.
Nicolson, Iain. Explore the World of Space & the Universe. Quigley, Sebastian, illus. 48p. (gr. 3-7). 1992. write for info. (0-307-15608-7, 15608, Golden Pr) Western Pub.
—Illustrated World of Space. (gr. 4-7). 1991. pap. 12.95 (0-671-74127-6, S&S BFYR) S&S Trade.
Nida, Patricia C. & Heller, Wendy M. The Teenager's Survival Guide to Moving. LC 87-1134. 148p. 1987. pap. 2.95 (0-02-044510-5, Collier Young Ad) Macmillan Child Grp.
Niedergeses, Catherine. Peter the Ship Eater. LC 88-51703. (Illus.). 44p. (gr. k-3). 1988. pap. 5.95 (1-55523-210-8) Winston-Derek.
Niederhauser, Hans R. & Frohlich, Margaret. Form Drawing. Niederhauser, Hans R. & Frohlich, Margaret, illus. 57p. (Orig.). 1974. pap. 10.00 (0-318-41110-5) Merc Pr NY.
Niedermayer, Walter. Into the Deep Misty Woods of the Ardennes. (Illus.). 170p. (Orig.). (gr. 12). 1990. pap. text ed. 13.50 (0-935648-30-5) Halldin Pub.
Nielsen, Laura F. Jeremy's Muffler. Desch, Christine, illus. 1994. write for info. (0-02-768135-1, Bradbury Pr) Macmillan Child Grp.
Nielsen, Lisa C., tr. see Amir, Tami.
Nielsen, Lisa C., tr. see Assaf, Yael.
Nielsen, Lisa C., tr. see Bar, Amos.
Nielsen, Lisa C., tr. see Baram, Bella.
Nielsen, Lisa C., tr. see Blatchford, Claire.
Nielsen, Lisa C., tr. see Burla, Oded.
Nielsen, Lisa C., tr. see Eitan, Ora.
Nielsen, Lisa C., tr. see Fleisher, Gila M.
Nielsen, Lisa C., tr. see Gelbart, Ofra.
Nielsen, Lisa C., tr. see Gelbert, Ofra.
Nielsen, Lisa C., tr. see Griffin, Gail M.
Nielsen, Lisa C., tr. see Harel, Nira.
Nielsen, Lisa C., tr. see Ofek, Uriel.

Nielsen, Lisa C., tr. see Sherrow, Victoria.
Nielsen, Lisa C., tr. see Shinhav, Chaya.
Nielsen, Nancy. Black Widow Spider. LC 89-28271.
(Illus.). 48p. (gr. 5). 1990. 12.95 (0-89686-513-4,
Crestwood Hse) Macmillan Child Grp.
—Teen Alcoholism. LC 90-66. (Illus.). 96p. (gr. 5-8).
1990. PLB 14.95 (1-56006-121-9) Lucent Bks.
Nielsen, Nancy, ed. see Fisher, Gary & Cummings,
Rhoda.
Nielsen, Nancy J. Animal Migration. (Illus.). 64p. (gr.
5-8). 1991. PLB 12.90 (0-531-20044-2) Watts.
—Bicycle Racing. LC 87-30489. (Illus.). 48p. (gr. 5-6).
1988. RSBE 11.95 (0-89686-361-1, Crestwood Hse)
Macmillan Child Grp.
—Carnivorous Plants. Cohn, Tom, ed. LC 91-34422.
(Illus.). 64p. (gr. 3-6). 1992. PLB 12.90
(0-531-20056-6) Watts.
—Carnivorous Plants. (Illus.). 64p. (gr. 5-8). 1992. pap.
5.95 (0-531-15644-3) Watts.
—Helicopter Pilots. LC 88-12007. (Illus.). 48p. (gr. 5-6).
1988. RSBE 11.95 (0-89686-399-9, Crestwood Hse)
Macmillan Child Grp.
Nielsen, Shelly. Caring. Wallner, Rosemary, ed. LC 91-
73044. 1992. 13.99 (1-56239-064-3) Abdo & Dghtrs.
—Christmas. Wallner, Rosemary, ed. LC 91-73034. 1992.
13.99 (1-56239-067-8) Abdo & Dghtrs.
—Easter. Wallner, Rosemary, ed. LC 91-73032. 1992. 13.
99 (1-56239-069-4) Abdo & Dghtrs.
—Fun with A - a. LC 92-16038. 1992. 13.99
(1-56239-134-8) Abdo & Dghtrs.
—Fun with E - e. LC 92-16041. 1992. 13.99
(1-56239-135-6) Abdo & Dghtrs.
—Fun with I - i. LC 92-16040. 1992. 13.99
(1-56239-136-4) Abdo & Dghtrs.
—Fun with O - o. LC 92-16039. 1992. 13.99
(1-56239-137-2) Abdo & Dghtrs.
—Fun with U - u. LC 92-16042. 1992. 13.99
(1-56239-138-0) Abdo & Dghtrs.
—Halloween. Wallner, Rosemary, ed. LC 91-73031.
1992. 13.99 (1-56239-070-8) Abdo & Dghtrs.
—Hanukkah. Wallner, Rosemary, ed. LC 91-73029. 1992.
13.99 (1-56239-072-4) Abdo & Dghtrs.
—I Love Air. LC 93-7597. 1993. 14.96 (1-56239-189-5)
Abdo & Dghtrs.
—I Love Dirt. Berg, Julie, ed. LC 93-18956. (gr. 3 up).
1993. 14.96 (1-56239-188-7) Abdo & Dghtrs.
—Independence Day. Wallner, Rosemary, ed. LC 91-
73030. 1992. 13.99 (1-56239-071-6) Abdo & Dghtrs.
—Just Victoria. 130p. (gr. 3-7). 1986. pap. 4.49
(0-89191-609-1, Chariot Bks) Cook.
—Manners. Wallner, Rosemary, ed. LC 91-73042. 1992.
13.99 (1-56239-066-X) Abdo & Dghtrs.
—More Victoria. 130p. (gr. 3-7). 1986. pap. 4.49
(0-89191-453-6, Chariot Bks) Cook.
—Only Kidding, Victoria. 130p. (gr. 3-7). 1986. pap. 4.49
(0-89191-474-9, Chariot Bks) Cook.
—Playing Fair. Wallner, Rosemary, ed. LC 92-73043.
1992. 13.99 (1-56239-065-1) Abdo & Dghtrs.
—Self Esteem. Wallner, Rosemary, ed. LC 91-73047.
1992. 13.99 (1-56239-061-9) Abdo & Dghtrs.
—Sharing. Wallner, Rosemary, ed. LC 91-73045. 1992.
13.99 (1-56239-063-5) Abdo & Dghtrs.
—Take a Bow, Victoria. 130p. (gr. 3-7). 1986. pap. 4.49
(0-89191-470-6, Chariot Bks) Cook.
—Telling the Truth. Wallner, Rosemary, ed. LC 91-
73046. 1992. 13.99 (1-56239-062-7) Abdo & Dghtrs.
—Thanksgiving. Wallner, Rosemary, ed. LC 91-73033.
1992. 13.99 (1-56239-068-6) Abdo & Dghtrs.
—Trash! Trash! Trash! Berg, Julie, ed. LC 93-18952.
1993. PLB 14.96 (1-56239-192-5) Abdo & Dghtrs.
Nielsen, Shelly & Berg, Julie. I Love Water. LC 93-
18957. 1993. PLB 14.96 (1-56239-190-9) Abdo &
Dghtrs.
—Love Earth: The Beauty Makeover. LC 93-18954.
1993. lib. bdg. 14.96 (1-56239-198-4) Abdo & Dghtrs.
Nielsen, Virginia. La Sauvage. (Orig.). 1988. pap. 3.95
(0-440-20190-X) Dell.
Nielsen-McLellan, Karen L. Ginger Bear's Christmas
Cookie Mystery. Nielsen-McLellan, Karen L., illus.
32p. (ps-1). 1992. 12.95 (0-9634851-0-5) Scand
Descent.
Nielson, Johnj M. & Skillings, Otis. Bible Walk. Date
not set. 4.50 (0-685-68193-9, BCMB-492); cassette
9.98 (0-685-68194-7, BCTA-9016C); Choral Preview
Pack 5.00 (0-685-68195-5, BCL-9016C) Lillenas.
Niemi, Matt, jt. auth. see Sharp, Mary.

Nierman, Lewis G. Lefty's Place.
Nierman, Lewis G., illus. 32p. (gr. 1-4).
1994. 18.95g (0-9636820-0-8) Kindness
Pubns.
LEFTY'S PLACE; a factual &
inspiring story of a young child's hard
work to give an injured wild animal a
chance at life. EXPLORES a loving
relationship & the rewards of kindness
& courage. SHOWS how the child,
from this experience, will never again
look at animals without thinking &
caring more about their lives &
feelings. FOSTERS in children a
greater tolerance & appreciation for all
living things. HELPS develop a greater

ability to face the challenges of injury,
illness, or hardship in their own lives.
SHOWS how every single child &
every act of kindness can make a
difference. Uniquely illustrated in
artwork combined with original
photography for dramatic impact.
ORDER FROM KINDNESS
PUBLICATIONS, INC., 1859 North
Pine Island Rd., Suite # 135,
Plantation, FL 33322. (305) 424-9323;
FAX (305) 721-0910. From
KINDNESS: Children's reading to
educate, entertain & inspire a more
sensitive & caring future generation of
adults.
Publisher Provided Annotation.

Nies, Kevin A. From Sorceress to Scientist: Biographies
of Women Physical Scientists. Neis, Kevin A., illus.
95p. (Orig.). (gr. 8 up). 1991. 30.00 (1-880211-00-9);
pap. 14.99 (1-880211-01-7); tchr's. ed. 14.99
(1-880211-02-5) Calif Video.
Nietzel, Shirley. Jacket I Wear in the Snow. (ps-3). 1992.
pap. 19.95 (0-590-72613-7) Scholastic Inc.
Nighswander, Ada. The Little Martins Learn to Love.
(ps-4). 1982. 6.95 (0-686-30775-5) Rod & Staff.
Nightingale, S. A Giraffe on the Moon. (ps-1). 1992. 13.
95 (0-15-230950-0, HB Juv Bks) HarBrace.
—Pink Pigs A-Plenty. (ps-3). 1992. pap. 14.95
(0-15-261882-1, HB Juv Bks) HarBrace.
Nightingale, Sandy. Cat's Knees & Bee's Whiskers.
Nightingale, Sandy, illus. LC 92-39811. 1993. 14.95
(0-15-215364-0) HarBrace.
Nightingale, Sandy A., illus. Hansel & Gretel. LC 85-
2222. 24p. (ps-1). 1985. lib. bdg. 4.99 (0-394-97022-5)
Random Bks Yng Read.
Nii-owoo, Ife. A Is for Africa: Looking at Africa Through
the Alphabet. Nii-owoo, Ife, illus. LC 90-81575. 32p.
(ps-k). 1992. 12.95 (0-86543-182-5); pap. 5.95
(0-86543-183-3) Africa World.
Nikolai. Frog Princess Tales. 1988. 12.95
(0-385-24624-2) Doubleday.
Nikola-Lisa, W. Bein' with You This Way. Bryant,
Michael, illus. LC 93-5164. 1994. 14.95
(1-880000-05-9) Lee & Low Bks.
—Night Is Coming. Henterly, Jamichael, illus. LC 90-
3806. 32p. (ps-2). 1991. 13.95 (0-525-44687-7, DCB)
Dutton Child Bks.
—No Babies Asleep. Palagonia, Peter, illus. LC 93-20589.
Date not set. write for info. (0-689-31841-3,
Atheneum) Macmillan Child Grp.
—One, Two, Three Thanksgiving! Levine, Abby, ed.
Kramer, Robin, illus. LC 90-28638. 32p. (ps-1). 1991.
13.95 (0-8075-6109-6) A Whitman.
—Storm. Hays, Michael, illus. LC 92-22775. 32p. (ps-2).
1993. SBE 14.95 (0-689-31704-2, Atheneum Child
Bk) Macmillan Child Grp.
Niland, Kilmeny. A Bellbird in a Flame Tree: The Twelve
Days of Christmas. LC 90-25869. 32p. (ps-3). 1991.
12.95 (0-688-10797-4, Tambourine Bks); PLB 12.88
(0-688-10798-2) Morrow.
Nile, Richard. Australian Aborigines. LC 92-17044.
(Illus.). 48p. (gr. 5-6). 1992. PLB 22.80
(0-8114-2303-4) Raintree Steck-V.
Niles, Steve, jt. auth. see Barker, Clive.
Nilsen, Alleen P. Presenting M. E. Kerr. (gr. k-8). 1990.
pap. 3.95 (0-440-20540-9, LFL) Dell.
Nilsen, David. Ranger. Bostick, Angela, illus. 64p.
(Orig.). 1989. pap. 8.00 (1-55878-016-5) Game
Designers.
Nilsen, Frances S. & Salter, James L. Amerigo: The
Amerigo Vespucci Story. Salter, Marsha C., illus. LC
92-93878. 253p. (gr. 10-12). 1992. 14.95
(0-9633937-6-6) Shamrock TN.
Nilsson, Lennart. How Was I Born? Reproduction &
Birth for Children. LC 75-24725. (Illus.). 32p. (ps-3).
1975. pap. 14.95 (0-385-28624-4, Sey Lawr)
Delacorte.
Nilsson, Ulf. If You Didn't Have Me. Eriksson, Eva,
illus. Blecher, Lone T. & Blecher, George, trs. LC 86-
21327. (Illus.). 128p. (gr. 2-5). 1987. SBE 12.95
(0-689-50406-3, M K McElderry) Macmillan Child
Grp.
Nimeth, Albert J. I Like You, Just Because. LC 79-
139971. (Illus.). (gr. 5 up). 1971. 5.00 (0-8199-0422-8,
Frncscn Herld) Franciscan Pr.
Nimmo, Jenny. The Chestnut Soldier. LC 90-21532.
164p. (gr. 6 up). 1991. 14.95 (0-525-44656-7, DCB)
Dutton Child Bks.
—The Chestnut Soldier. large type ed. 312p. (gr. 3-7).
1991. lib. bdg. 18.50x (0-7451-1178-5, Lythway Large
Print) Hall.
—Orchard of the Crescent Moon. 170p. (gr. 5-9). 1990.
pap. 2.95 (0-8167-2265-X) Troll Assocs.
—The Snow Spider. large type ed. 208p. (gr. 3-7). 1987.
lib. bdg. 13.95x (0-7451-0590-4, Pub. by Chivers Pr
UK) Hall.
—The Snow Spider. LC 87-5429. 144p. (gr. 5 up). 1987.
11.95 (0-525-44306-1, DCB) Dutton Child Bks.
—The Snow Spider. 136p. (gr. 5-9). 1990. pap. 2.95
(0-8167-2264-1) Troll Assocs.

—Ultramarine. LC 91-43642. 192p. (gr. 6 up). 1992. 15.
00 (0-525-44869-1, DCB) Dutton Child Bks.
—Ultramarine. large type ed. 296p. 1992. 13.95
(0-7451-1554-3, Galaxy Child Lrg Print) Chivers N
Amer.
Nimmo, Jenny, retold by. The Starlight Cloak. Todd,
Justin, photos by. LC 92-26186. (Illus.). (ps-3). 1993.
14.99 (0-8037-1508-0) Dial Bks Young.
—The Witches & the Singing Mice: A Celtic Tale.
Barrett, Angela, illus. LC 92-37642. 32p. (gr. 1 up).
1993. 14.99 (0-8037-1509-9) Dial Bks Young.
Nims, Bonnie L. Just Beyond Reach. Anema, George,
illus. 48p. 1992. 13.95 (0-590-44077-2, Scholastic
Hardcover) Scholastic Inc.
—Where Is the Bear? Fay, Ann, ed. Wallner, John, illus.
LC 87-25321. 24p. (ps-2). 1988. PLB 11.95
(0-8075-8933-0) A Whitman.
—Where Is the Bear at School? Tucker, Kathy, ed. Gill,
Madelaine, illus. LC 89-37903. 24p. (ps-1). 1989. 11.
95 (0-8075-8935-7) A Whitman.
—Where Is the Bear in the City? Mathews, Judith, ed.
Gill, Madelaine, illus. LC 92-3390. 24p. (ps-1). 1992.
11.95g (0-8075-8937-3) A Whitman.
Ninojosa, Ida N. De see Georgiady, Nicholas P. &
Romano, Louis G.
Nintendo Staff. Super Mario Bros. Adventures. Nintendo
Staff, illus. 32p. (gr. 1-7). 1991. pap. 6.95 incl.
cassette (0-679-81822-7) Random Bks Yng Read.
Nipp, Susan, jt. auth. see Beall, Pamela C.
Nipp, Susan H., jt. auth. see Beall, Pamela C.
Niquette, Alan & Niquette, Beth. Building Your
Christian Defense System. (Orig.). (gr. 9-12). 1988.
pap. text ed. 6.99 (1-55661-015-7); tchr's. guide 7.99
(1-55661-016-5) Bethany Hse.
Niquette, Beth, jt. auth. see Niquette, Alan.
Nirgiotis, Nicholas. Erie Canal: Gateway to the West. LC
92-24547. (Illus.). 64p. (gr. 5-8). 1993. PLB 12.90
(0-531-20146-5) Watts.
Nishiyama, Hidetaka & Brown, Richard C. Karate: Art
of Empty-Hand Fighting. (Illus.). 246p. (gr. 9 up).
1991. pap. 17.95 (0-8048-1668-9) C E Tuttle.
Nispen, Doug Van see Haubrich-Casperson, Jane & Van
Nispen, Doug.
Nister, Ernest. Animal Playmates. (Illus.). 10p. 1990.
5.95 (0-399-21957-9, Philomel Bks) Putnam Pub
Group.
—The Children's Picture Book. Nister, Ernest, illus. LC
80-7613. 18p. (ps-3). 1980. pop-up bk. 9.95
(0-385-28173-0) Delacorte.
—Christmas Surprises: An Antique Revolving Picture
Book. (Illus.). 20p. 1990. 16.95 (0-399-22160-3,
Philomel Bks) Putnam Pub Group.
—Christmas Toys. (Illus.). 10p. (ps up) 1992. 4.95
(0-399-21995-1, Philomel Bks) Putnam Pub Group.
—A Day in the Country. (Illus.). 10p. 1990. 5.95
(0-399-21959-5, Philomel Bks) Putnam Pub Group.
—Ernest Nister's Book of Christmas. Intervisual Staff,
illus. 12p. 1991. 12.95 (0-399-21799-1, Philomel)
Putnam Pub Group.
—Farmyard Friends. Intervisual Staff, illus. 10p. (ps up).
1991. 4.95 (0-399-22110-7, Philomel) Putnam Pub
Group.
—Favorite Animals. (Illus.). 10p. 1989. 5.95
(0-399-21728-2, Philomel Bks) Putnam Pub Group.
—Golden Tales from Long Ago, 3 vols. Nister, Ernest,
illus. LC 80-7614. (24p. ea.). 1980. Set. 6.95
(0-440-03015-3) Delacorte.
—Good Friends. (Illus.). 1989. 5.95 (0-399-21729-0,
Philomel Bks) Putnam Pub Group.
—The Great Panorama Picture Book. Nister, Ernest,
illus. LC 82-70305. 18p. (ps-3). 1982. pop-up bk. 8.95
(0-385-28327-X) Delacorte.
—Hide-&-Seek. (Illus.). 20p. (ps-8). 1992. 14.95
(0-399-21810-6, Philomel Bks) Putnam Pub Group.
—Keepsake Carousel. 1993. 7.95 (1-56397-081-3) Boyds
Mills Pr.
—Land of Sweet Surprises: An Antique Revolving Picture
Books. Nister, Ernest, illus. (gr. k up). 1983. 12.95
(0-399-20993-X, Philomel) Putnam Pub Group.
—Little Dolls. Intervisual Staff, illus. 10p. (ps up). 1991.
4.95 (0-399-22107-7, Philomel) Putnam Pub Group.
—Magic Windows: An Antique Revolving Picture Book.
(Illus.). 14p. (ps up) 1981. 12.95 (0-399-20773-2,
Philomel) Putnam Pub Group.
—Merry Magic-Go-Round. (Illus.). (gr. k up). 1983. PLB
12.95 (0-399-20946-8, Philomel Bks) Putnam Pub Group.
—Mother & Me. (Illus.). 10p. 1990. 5.95 (0-399-21958-7,
Philomel Bks) Putnam Pub Group.
—My Best Friend. (Illus.). 10p. 1990. 5.95
(0-399-21960-9, Philomel Bks) Putnam Pub Group.
—My Little Pets. Intervisual Staff, illus. 10p. (ps up).
1991. 4.95 (0-399-22109-3, Philomel) Putnam Pub
Group.
—My Picture Puzzle Book: Reproductions of Antique
Pictures. (Illus.). 10p. 1991. incl. 40 puzzle pieces 12.
95 (0-399-21855-6, Philomel Bks) Putnam Pub Group.
—Our Baby. (Illus.). 32p. 1991. 15.95 (0-399-21856-4,
Philomel Bks) Putnam Pub Group.
—Our Farmyard: A Pop-up Book with Punch-out Play
Figures. Nister, Ernest, illus. 12p. (ps-3). 1991. 13.95
(0-525-44689-3, DCB) Dutton Child Bks.
—Playtime Delights. (Illus.). 26p. (ps up) 1993. pop-up
15.95 (0-399-21898-X, Philomel Bks) Putnam Pub
Group.
—Pop up Mother Goose Favorites. (Illus.). 18p. (ps up).
1989. 13.50 (0-525-44504-8, DCB) Dutton Child Bks.
—Rainbow Round-a-Bout. 10p. 1993. 7.95
(1-56397-088-0) Boyds Mills Pr.

—Santa's Surprises. (Illus.). 10p. (ps up). 1992. 4.95 (0-399-21996-X, Philomel Bks) Putnam Pub Group.
—Snowy Days. (Illus.). 10p. (ps up). 1992. 4.95 (0-399-21997-8, Philomel Bks) Putnam Pub Group.
—Special Days. Nister, Ernest, illus. (gr. k up). 1989. 5.95 (0-399-21694-4, Philomel Bks) Putnam Pub Group.
—Tiny Tots. Intervisual Staff, illus. 10p. (ps up). 1991. 4.95 (0-399-22108-5, Philomel) Putnam Pub Group.
—Visiting Grandma. Nister, Ernest, illus. (gr. k up). 1989. 5.95 (0-399-21695-2, Philomel Bks) Putnam Pub Group.
—We Visit the Farm. Nister, Ernest, illus. (gr. k up). 1989. 13.95 (0-399-21724-X, Philomel Bks) Putnam Pub Group.
—Yuletide Delights. (Illus.). 10p. (ps up). 1992. 4.95 (0-399-21998-6, Philomel Bks) Putnam Pub Group.
Nister, Ernest & Bingham, Clifton. Revolving Pictures. LC 79-12438. (Illus.). (ps-4). 1981. 12.95 (0-399-20802-X, Philomel) Putnam Pub Group.
Nister, Ernest, illus. Moving Pictures: An Antique Picture Book. 12p. (gr up). 1985. 11.95 (0-399-21272-8, Philomel) Putnam Pub Group.
—Playtime Delights. 26p. 1993. 15.95 (0-685-66598-4, Philomel Bks) Putnam Pub Group.
Nivedita, Sr. Cradle Tales of Hinduism. (Illus.). 329p. (gr. 3-12). 1972. pap. 5.95 (0-87481-170-8); pap. 5.95 (0-87481-131-7) Vedanta Pr.
Nivedita, Sr., jt. auth. see Coomaraswamy, Ananda K.
Nix, Garth. The Ragwitch. 1994. pap. 3.99 (0-8125-3506-5) Tor Bks.
Nixon. Edgar Winners Collection. Date not set. 14.00 (0-06-023650-7, Festival); PLB 13.89 (0-06-023651-5, Festival) HarpC Child Bks.
Nixon, Jean L. A Deadly Game of Magic. LC 83-8379. 148p. (gr. 7 up). 1983. 13.95 (0-15-222954-X, HB Juv Bks) HarBrace.
—A Deadly Game of Magic. (gr. 6-12). 1985. pap. 3.50 (0-440-92102-3, LFL) Dell.
Nixon, Joan L. And Maggie Makes Three. LC 85-16389. 112p. (gr. 3-7). 1986. 12.95 (0-15-250355-2, HB Juv Bks) HarBrace.
—And Maggie Makes Three. (gr. k-6). 1987. pap. 2.75 (0-440-40127-5, YB) Dell.
—Beats Me, Claude. Pearson, Tracey C., illus. LC 86-5465. 32p. (ps-3). 1986. 11.95 (0-670-80781-8) Viking Child Bks.
—Beats Me, Claude. Pearson, Tracey C., illus. (ps-3). 1988. pap. 3.95 (0-14-050847-3, Puffin) Puffin Bks.
—Before You Were Born. McIlrath, James, illus. LC 79-91741. 32p. (ps up). 1980. pap. 5.95 (0-87973-343-8) Our Sunday Visitor.
—Candidate for Murder. 1991. 14.95 (0-385-30257-6) Delacorte.
—Candidate for Murder. 1992. pap. 3.50 (0-440-21212-X) Dell.
—Caught in the Act. 160p. (gr. 9 up). 1988. 14.95 (0-553-05443-0, Starfire) Bantam.
—Caught in the Act. (gr. 7 up). 1989. pap. 3.50 (0-553-27912-2, Starfire) Bantam.
—The Christmas Eve Mystery. Fay, Ann, ed. Cummins, Jim, illus. LC 81-345. 32p. (gr. 1-3). 1981. PLB 8.95 (0-8075-1150-1) A Whitman.
—The Dark & Deadly Pool. LC 87-6723. 192p. (gr. 7 up). 1987. 14.95 (0-385-29585-5) Delacorte.
—The Dark & Deadly Pool. 196p. (gr. 6 up). 1989. pap. 3.50 (0-440-20348-1, LFL) Dell.
—Deadly Promise. 1993. pap. 3.50 (0-553-56177-4) Bantam.
—Encore: Hollywood Daughters: A Family Trilogy, Bk. 3. (gr. 7 up). 1990. 14.95 (0-553-07024-X, Starfire) Bantam.
—A Family Apart. 176p. (gr. 5 up). 1988. pap. 3.99 (0-553-27478-3, Starfire) Bantam.
—Fat Chance, Claude. Pearson, Tracey C., illus. 32p. (ps-3). 1989. pap. 4.95 (0-14-050679-9, Puffin) Puffin Bks.
—Fat Chance Claude. Pearson, Tracey, illus. (ps-3). 1987. 11.95 (0-670-81459-8) Viking Child Bks.
—The Ghosts of Now. 192p. (gr. 7 up). 1986. pap. 3.50 (0-440-93115-0, LFL) Dell.
—The Gift. Glass, Andrew, illus. LC 82-17994. 96p. (gr. 4-7). 1983. SBE 13.95 (0-02-768160-2, Macmillan Child Bk) Macmillan Child Grp.
—The Gift. Glass, Andrew, illus. LC 87-22764. 96p. (gr. 3-7). 1988. pap. 3.95 (0-689-71217-0, Aladdin) Macmillan Child Grp.
—The Happy Birthday Mystery. Ann, Fay, ed. Cummins, Jim, illus. LC 79-18362. 32p. (gr. 1-3). 1980. PLB 8.95 (0-8075-3150-2) A Whitman.
—Haunted House on Honeycutt Street. (gr. 4-7). 1991. pap. 2.99 (0-440-40472-X) Dell.
—Haunted Island. 128p. (Orig.). (gr. 3-7). 1987. pap. 2.95 (0-590-43134-X) Scholastic Inc.
—High Trail To Danger. 1991. 16.00 (0-553-07314-1) Bantam.
—High Trail to Danger. (gr. 4-7). 1992. pap. 3.50 (0-553-29602-7) Bantam.
—Hollywood Daughters, No. 3. 1992. pap. 3.50 (0-553-29287-0) Bantam.
—Hollywood Daughters: Star Baby. 1991. pap. 3.50 (0-553-28957-8) Bantam.
—If You Were a Writer. Degen, Bruce, illus. LC 88-402. 32p. (gr. k-3). 1988. RSBE 14.95 (0-02-768210-2, Four Winds) Macmillan Child Grp.
—In the Face of Danger. (gr. 7 up). 1989. 3.99 (0-553-28196-8, Starfire) Bantam.

—In the Face of Danger: The Orphan Train Quartet, No. 3. 160p. (gr. 7 up). 1988. 16.00 (0-553-05490-2, Starfire) Bantam.
—The Island of Dangerous Dreams. 196p. (Orig.). (gr. k-12). 1989. pap. 3.50 (0-440-20258-2, LFL) Dell.
—The Kidnapping of Christina Lattimore. 196p. (gr. 7 up). 1992. pap. 3.50 (0-440-94520-8, LFL) Dell.
—Land of Dreams. LC 93-8734. 1994. 14.95 (0-385-31170-2) Delacorte.
—Land of Hope. 1992. 16.00 (0-553-08110-1) Bantam.
—Land of Promise. LC 92-28591. (gr. 4-7). 1993. 16.00 (0-553-08111-X) Bantam.
—Maggie Forevermore. LC 86-20135. 112p. (gr. 3-7). 1987. 13.95 (0-15-250345-5) HarBrace.
—Maggie, Too. LC 84-19766. 101p. (gr. 3-7). 1985. 11.95 (0-15-250350-1, HB Juv Bks) HarBrace.
—Maggie Too. (gr. k-6). 1987. pap. 2.50 (0-440-45288-0, YB) Dell.
—Mystery Box. (gr. 4-7). 1991. pap. 2.99 (0-440-40458-4) Dell.
—The Name of the Game Was Murder. LC 92-8392. 1993. 15.00 (0-385-30864-7) Delacorte.
—The New Year's Mystery. Pacini, Kathy, ed. Cummins, Jim, illus. (gr. 1-3). 1979. PLB 8.95 (0-8075-5592-4) A Whitman.
—The Other Side of Dark. 1987. pap. 3.50 (0-440-96638-8, LFL) Dell.
—A Place to Belong. 1990. pap. 3.50 (0-553-28485-1) Bantam.
—The Seance. 176p. (gr. 7 up). 1981. pap. 3.50 (0-440-97937-4, LFL) Dell.
—Secret, Silent Screams. LC 88-417. (gr. 7 up). 1988. 14.95 (0-440-50059-1) Delacorte.
—Secret Silent Screams. (gr. k-8). 1990. pap. 3.50 (0-440-20539-5, LFL) Dell.
—Shadowmaker. LC 93-32314. 1994. write for info. (0-385-32030-2) Delacorte.
—The Specter. LC 82-70322. 160p. (gr. 7 up). 1982. pap. 12.95 (0-385-28948-0) Delacorte.
—Specter. 1993. pap. 3.50 (0-440-97740-1) Dell.
—The Stalker. LC 84-16962. (gr. 7 up). 1985. 14.95 (0-385-29376-3) Delacorte.
—The Stalker. (gr. 7 up). 1987. pap. 3.50 (0-440-97753-3, LFL) Dell.
—Star Baby. (gr. 7 up). 1989. 14.95 (0-553-05838-X, Starfire) Bantam.
—The Thanksgiving Mystery. Fay, Ann, ed. Cummins, Jim, illus. LC 79-27346. 32p. (gr. 1-3). 1979. PLB 8.95 (0-8075-7820-7) A Whitman.
—That's the Spirit, Claude. Pearson, Tracey C., illus. 32p. (ps-3). 1992. 13.00 (0-670-83434-3) Viking Child Bks.
—The Valentine Mystery. Tucker, Kathleen, ed. Cummins, Jim, illus. LC 79-17055. 32p. (gr. 1-3). 1979. PLB 8.95 (0-8075-8450-9) A Whitman.
—Watch Out for Dinosaurs. (gr. 4-7). 1991. pap. 2.99 (0-440-40459-2) Dell.
—The Weekend Was Murder. 1992. 15.00 (0-385-30531-1) Doubleday.
—When I Am Eight. LC 93-20023. (ps-3). 1994. 13.89 (0-8037-1500-5) Dial Bks Young.
—Whispers from the Dead. (gr. 7 up). 1989. 14.95 (0-385-29809-9) Delacorte.
—Whispers from the Dead. 192p. 1991. pap. 3.50 (0-440-20809-2, LFL) Dell.
—Will You Give Me a Dream? Degen, Bruce, illus. LC 91-19581. 40p. (ps-1). 1994. RSBE 14.95 (0-02-768211-0, Four Winds) Macmillan Child Grp.
—You Bet Your Britches, Claude. Pearson, Tracey C., illus. 32p. (ps-3). 1989. pap. 11.95 (0-670-82310-4) Viking Child Bks.
—You Bet Your Britches, Claude. Pearson, Tracey C., illus. 32p. (ps-3). 1991. pap. 3.95 (0-14-050900-3, Puffin) Puffin Bks.
Nixon, Joan Lowery. When I am Eight. Gackenbach, Dick, photos by. LC 93-20023. (gr. 1-3). 1994. 13.99 (0-8037-1499-8) Dial Bks Young.
Njoku, Scholastica I. Dog What? Fergurson, Meg, illus. 49p. (gr. k up). 1989. perfect bdg. 6.95x (0-9617833-1-1) S I NJOKU.
—The Miracle of a Christmas Doll. McKay, Suzanne, illus. 29p. (gr. k up). 1986. perfect bdg. 5.95x (0-9617833-0-3) S I NJOKU.
NK Lawn & Garden Co. Staff. My First Garden Book. (Illus.). 80p. (Orig.). 1992. pap. 6.95 (0-380-76667-1) Avon.
Noakes, Polly, jt. auth. see Kennedy, Fiona.
Nobens, C. A. Montgomery's Time Zone. Nobens, C. A., illus. 32p. (ps-4). 1990. PLB 18.95 (0-87614-398-2) Carolrhoda Bks.
Nobile, Jeanett. Portrait of Love. 166p. (gr. 6-8). 1983. pap. 2.25 (0-553-17846-6) Bantam.
Nobisso, Joi, jt. auth. see Lehmann, Terry.
Nobisso, Josephine. Grandma's Scrapbook. LC 91-23309. (Illus.). 1991. 12.95 (0-671-74976-5, Green Tiger) S&S Trade.
—Grandpa Loved. Hyde, Maureen, illus. 32p. 1991. 12.95 (0-88138-119-5, Green Tiger) S&S Trade.
—Shh! The Whale Is Smiling. Hyde, Maureen, illus. LC 91-21521. 40p. (gr. k-1). 1992. 14.00 (0-671-74908-0, Green Tiger) S&S Trade.
Nobisso, Josephine & Krajnc, Anton C. For the Sake of a Cake. LC 92-38391. (Illus.). 28p. 1993. 9.95 (0-8478-1685-0) Rizzoli Intl.
Noble, David, ed. Houses Beneath the Rock: The Anasazi of Canyon de Chelly & Navajo National Monument. LC 91-78069. (Illus.). 56p. (gr. 9 up). 1992. pap. 8.95 (0-941270-72-6) Ancient City Pr.

—Understanding the Anasazi of Mesa Verde & Hovenweep. LC 92-9279. (Illus.). 48p. (Orig.). (gr. 9 up). 1992. pap. 8.95 (0-941270-71-8) Ancient City Pr.
Noble, Dennis L. & O'Brien, Mike. U. S. Life-Saving Service 1889-1915, U. S. Coast Guard Service 1915-1989. (Illus.). 24p. (Orig.). (gr. 8 up). 1989. pap. text ed. 2.00 (0-935549-12-9) MI City Hist.
Noble, Jim. Swimming. LC 91-6314. (Illus.). 32p. (gr. k-4). 1991. 11.90 (0-531-18466-8, Pub. by Bookwright Pr) Watts.
Noble, Kate. Bubble Gum. Bass, Rachel, illus. 32p. (ps-3). 1992. 14.95 (0-9631798-0-2) Silver Seahorse.

—Oh Look, It's a Nosserus. Bass, Rachel, illus. 32p. (ps-4). 1993. 14.95 (0-9631798-2-9) Silver Seahorse. Robbi is a young rhino who lives in a game park in Africa. He can't wait to have a horn as beautiful as his Mama's; he gets teased for being clumsy, & he sets out to save his friends from terrible danger. Children who loved & laughed with Kimbi in BUBBLE GUM will be delighted to meet Robbi & his zebra & giraffe friends. Once again, Rachel Bass creates the beauty of Africa & the charm of its animals in her vivid paintings. BUBBLE GUM. Kate Noble (Africa Stories Ser.) (Illus. by Rachel Bass). 32p. 1992. 14.95 (0-9631798-0-2) Silver Seahorse Press. Kimbi is a young baboon who lives in a park in Africa. He wishes tourists didn't pay so much attention to lions. He loves sweets, & he stumbles into an amazing adventure. The illustrations for this delightful story capture the magic of the African landscape. There's also a learning plus: the details of animal behavior are correct, & the pictures show both black & white children & adults. A kindergarten teacher who previewed the boards writes "I can't wait to read it to children."
Publisher Provided Annotation.

Noble, Margaret see Nivedita, Sr.
Noble, Mary, jt. ed. see Hobbs, Anne S.
Noble, Trinka H. Apple Tree Christmas. Noble, Trinka H., illus. LC 84-1901. 32p. (ps-2). 1988. 13.50 (0-8037-0102-0); PLB 12.89 (0-8037-0103-9) Dial Bks Young.
—The Day Jimmy's Boa Ate the Wash. Kellogg, Steven, illus. LC 80-15098. 32p. (ps-3). 1980. 13.95 (0-8037-1723-7); PLB 13.89 (0-8037-1724-5); pap. 4.95 (0-8037-0094-6) Dial Bks Young.
—Day Jimmy's Boa Ate the Wash. giant ed. (ps-3). 1991. pap. 17.95 (0-8037-1073-9, Dial Pied Piper) Puffin Bks.
—The Day Jimmy's Boa Ate the Wash. Kellogg, Steven, illus. 32p. (ps-3). 1993. pap. 4.99 (0-14-054623-5, Puffin Pied Piper) Puffin Bks.
—Hansy's Mermaid. Noble, Trinka H., illus. LC 82-45509. 32p. (ps-2). 1983. PLB 10.89 (0-8037-3606-1) Dial Bks Young.
—Jimmy's Boa & the Big Splash Birthday Bash. Kellog, Steven, illus. LC 88-10933. 32p. (ps-3). 1989. 13.95 (0-8037-0539-5); PLB 13.89 (0-8037-0540-9) Dial Bks Young.
—Jimmy's Boa & the Big Splash Birthday Bash. Kellogg, Steven, illus. 32p. (ps-3). 1993. pap. 4.99 (0-14-054921-8, Puffin Pied Piper) Puffin Bks.
—Jimmy's Boa Bounces Back. Kellog, Steven, illus. LC 83-14289. 32p. (ps-3). 1984. 13.95 (0-8037-0049-0); PLB 13.89 (0-8037-0050-4) Dial Bks Young.
—Jimmy's Boa Bounces Back. Kellogg, Steven, illus. 32p. (ps-3). 1993. pap. 4.99 (0-14-054654-5, Puffin Pied Piper) Puffin Bks.
—Meanwhile Back at the Ranch. Ross, Tony, illus. LC 86-11651. 32p. (ps-3). 1987. 13.95 (0-8037-0353-8); PLB 13.89 (0-8037-0354-6) Dial Bks Young.
—Meanwhile Back at the Ranch. Ross, Tony, illus. 32p. (ps-3). 1992. pap. 3.99 (0-14-054564-6, Puffin Pied Piper) Puffin Bks.
Noble, Trudy V. God Answers Children's Prayers Too. Carmen, Dave, illus. LC 85-217377. 30p. (ps-4). 1990. write for info. (0-9620133-0-7) Joy Deliverance.
Nobleman, Louis R. Second Dreams. Nobleman, Louis R., illus. (gr. k-6). 1993. pap. 9.95 (1-56883-010-6) Colonial Pr AL.
Nodar, Carmen M. Abuelita's Paradise. Mathews, Judith, ed. Paterson, Diane, illus. LC 91-42330. 32p. (gr. k-3). 1992. 13.95g (0-8075-0129-8) A Whitman.

—El Paraiso de Abuelita. Mathews, Judith, ed. Mlawer, Teresa, tr. Paterson, Diane, illus. LC 92-3767. (SPA.). 32p. (gr. k-3). 1992. 13.95g (*0-8075-6346-3*) A Whitman.

Nodar, Carmen S. Abuelita's Paradise. Paterson, Diane, illus. (gr. k-4). 1993. 13.95 (*0-685-66422-8*); audio cass. 11.00 (*1-882869-79-6*) Read Advent.

Nodel, Maxine. Moral or Less: An Adventure in Addition & Subtraction. Nodel, Norman, illus. 32p. (ps-3). 1990. 8.95 (*0-922613-25-7*); pap. 6.95 (*0-922613-26-5*); 4.95 (*0-922613-27-3*); cass. 9.00 (*0-922613-28-1*) Hachai Pubns.

Nodelman, Perry. The Same Place but Different. LC 93-29514. Date not set. 15.00 (*0-06-024258-2*, Festival); PLB 14.89 (*0-06-024259-0*, Festival) HarpC Child Bks.

Nodset, Joan L. Come Here, Cat. Kellog, Steven, illus. LC 92-39005. (ps-3). 1973. 10.00 (*0-06-024557-3*); PLB 9.89 (*0-06-024558-1*) HarpC Child Bks.
—Go Away, Dog. Bonsall, Crosby, illus. LC 63-11162. 32p. (ps-3). 1963. PLB 9.89 (*0-06-024556-5*) HarpC Child Bks.
—Go Away, Dog! reissued ed. Bonsall, Crosby, illus. LC 63-11162. (ps-3). 1963. 10.00 (*0-06-024555-7*) HarpC Child Bks.
—Who Took the Farmer's Hat? Siebel, Fritz, illus. LC 62-17964. 32p. (gr. k-3). 1963. PLB 14.89 (*0-06-024566-2*) HarpC Child Bks.
—Who Took the Farmer's Hat? Siebel, Fritz, illus. LC 62-17964. 32p. (ps-2). 1988. pap. 5.95 (*0-06-443174-6*, Trophy) HarpC Child Bks.

Noel, Christopher. Rumpelstiltskin. Sis, Peter, illus. LC 92-4592. 40p. (gr. k up) 1993. incl. cass. 19.95 (*0-88708-280-7*, Rabbit Ears); 14.95 (*0-88708-279-3*, Rabbit Ears) Picture Bk Studio.

Noffs, David & Noffs, Laurie. The Daily Harold, Bk. 6. Lynch, Reg, illus. 24p. (Orig.). (gr. 6). 1987. wkbk. 2.50 (*0-929875-07-9*) Noffs Assocs.
—The Daily Harold, Bk. 7. (Illus.). 24p. (Orig.). (gr. 7). 1988. wkbk. 2.50 (*0-929875-08-7*) Noffs Assocs.
—The Daily Harold, Bk. 8. Noffs, Lauri, illus. 24p. (Orig.). (gr. 8). 1991. wkbk. 2.50 (*0-929875-09-5*) Noffs Assocs.
—Day of the Dinosaur. Noffs, Laurie, illus. 24p. (Orig.). (gr. 4-8). 1989. wkbk. 2.50 (*0-929875-12-5*) Noffs Assocs.
—The Happy Healthy Harold, Bk. 1. Noffs, Laurie, illus. 24p. (Orig.). (gr. 1). 1987. wkbk. 2.50 (*0-929875-02-8*) Noffs Assocs.
—A Happy Healthy Harold, Bk. 2. Noffs, Laurie, illus. 24p. (Orig.). (gr. 2). 1987. wkbk. 2.50 (*0-929875-03-6*) Noffs Assocs.
—Harold, Bk. 3: You Are Special. Hilliard, Kristin, illus. 24p. (Orig.). (gr. 3). 1987. wkbk. 2.50 (*0-929875-04-4*) Noffs Assocs.
—Harold Magazine, Bk. 4: Let's Be Friends. Noffs, Lauri A., illus. 24p. (Orig.). (gr. 4). 1987. wkbk. 2.50 (*0-929875-05-2*) Noffs Assocs.
—Harold Magazine, Bk. 5: Watching the Stars at Night. Noffs, Lauri A., illus. 24p. (Orig.). (gr. 5). 1987. wkbk. 2.50 (*0-929875-06-0*) Noffs Assocs.
—Harold: Revista. rev. ed. Noffs, Laurie, illus. (SPA.). 24p. 1991. wkbk. 2.50 (*0-929875-11-7*) Noffs Assocs.
—Kindergarten - Introductory, Bk. K: The Happy Healthy Harold. Noffs, Laurie, illus. 24p. (Orig.). (gr. k). 1987. wkbk. 2.50 (*0-929875-01-X*) Noffs Assocs.

Noffs, Laurie, jt. auth. see Noffs, David.

Nofsinger, Ray & Hargrove, Jim. Pigeons & Doves. LC 92-12948. (Illus.). 48p. (gr. k-4). 1992. PLB 15.27 (*0-516-02196-6*) Childrens.
—Pigeons & Doves. LC 92-12948. (Illus.). 48p. (gr. k-4). 1993. pap. 4.95 (*0-516-42196-4*) Childrens.

Nofziger, Harold H., illus. And It Was Good. 36p. (ps up). 1993. 12.95 (*0-8361-3634-9*) Herald Pr.

Nohl, Frederick. Martin Luther: Hero of Faith. LC 62-14146. (Illus.). (gr. 4-6). 1962. pap. 5.99 (*0-570-03727-1*, 12-2629) Concordia.

Nolan, Cecile A. Journey West, on the Oregon Trail. (gr. 5 up). 1993. 16.95 (*0-9633168-2-6*) Rain Dance Pub. JOURNEY WEST, ON THE OREGON TRAIL is an intriguing children's story dealing with trauma, turmoil, friendship, & delights meted out daily on the arduous pioneer trail. This book comprises the poignant struggles of children & their families suffering from "Oregon Fever" & their valiant efforts to survive & reach their goal. The fictional characters in the story proceed on the journey dealing with actual events that happened to unwary travelers. Every child in America should be aware of the hardships endured on their wagon trip to the Oregon Territories, for this is their heritage. Can be ordered from Rain Dance Publishing, P.O. Box

---

301428, Portland, OR 97230.
Publisher Provided Annotation.

Nolan, D., jt. auth. see Yolen, J.

Nolan, Dennis. The Castle Builder. Nolan, Dennis, illus. LC 86-23784. 32p. (gr. k-3). 1987. RSBE 13.95 (*0-02-768240-4*, Macmillan Child Bk) Macmillan Child Grp.
—The Castle Builder. Nolan, Dennis, illus. LC 92-29563. 32p. (gr. k-3). 1993. pap. 4.95 (*0-689-71703-2*, Aladdin) Macmillan Child Grp.
—Dinosaur Dream. Nolan, Dennis, illus. LC 89-78208. 32p. (ps-2). 1990. RSBE 14.95 (*0-02-768145-9*, Macmillan Child Bk) Macmillan Child Grp.
—Wolf Child. Nolan, Dennis, illus. LC 88-35955. 40p. (gr. 1-5). 1989. RSBE 13.95 (*0-02-768141-6*, Macmillan Child Bk) Macmillan Child Grp.

Nolan, Han. If I Should Die Before I Wake. LC 93-30720. 1994. write for info. (*0-15-238040-X*, HB Juv Bks); pap. write for info. (*0-15-238041-8*, HB Juv Bks) HarBrace.

Nolan, Jeannette C. La Salle & the Grand Enterprise. LC 90-48978. (Illus.). 176p. (gr. 6-10). 1991. PLB 13.95 (*1-55905-087-X*) Marshall Cavendish.

Nolan, Paul T. Folk Tale Plays Round the World. (gr. 3-5). 1982. pap. 12.95 (*0-8238-0253-1*) Plays.

Nolan, Virginia J. & Terry, Phyllis D. Gingerbread & Friends. rev. ed. Terry, Phyllis D., illus. 22p. 1987. pap. 3.50 (*0-9624497-0-9*) Planet Playmates.

Nolasco-Carrandi, Guadalupe, tr. see Thompson-Peters, Flossie E.

Noll, Sally. I Have a Loose Tooth. LC 91-31456. (Illus.). 32p. (ps-4). 1992. 14.00 (*0-688-11191-2*); PLB 13.93 (*0-688-11192-0*) Greenwillow.
—Jiggle Wiggle Prance. Noll, Sally, illus. LC 86-18322. 24p. (ps-1). 1987. 11.75 (*0-688-06760-3*); PLB 11.88 (*0-688-06761-1*) Greenwillow.
—Jiggle, Wiggle, Prance. LC 92-25332. 1993. pap. 3.99 (*0-14-054883-1*) Puffin Bks.
—Lucky Morning. (Illus.). (ps up). 1994. write for info. (*0-688-12474-7*); PLB write for info. (*0-688-12475-5*) Greenwillow.
—Off & Counting. LC 84-17943. (Illus.). 32p. (ps). 1985. pap. 3.95 (*0-14-050502-4*, Puffin) Puffin Bks.
—That Bothered Kate. LC 90-38488. (Illus.). 32p. (ps up). 1991. 13.95 (*0-688-10095-3*); PLB 13.88 (*0-688-10096-1*) Greenwillow.
—That Bothered Kate. LC 92-40167. (Illus.). 32p. (ps-3). 1993. pap. 4.99 (*0-14-054885-8*, Puffin) Puffin Bks.
—Watch Where You Go. LC 88-35591. (Illus.). 32p. (ps up). 1990. 12.95 (*0-688-08498-2*); lib. bdg. 12.88 (*0-688-08499-0*) Greenwillow.
—Watch Where You Go. LC 92-25333. 1993. pap. 3.99 (*0-14-054884-X*) Puffin Bks.

Nolt, Marilyn, jt. auth. see Peifer, Jane.

Nomura, Takaaki. Grandpa's Town. Stinchecum, Amanda M., tr. from JPN. (Illus.). 32p. (ps-3). 1991. 13.95 (*0-916291-36-7*) Kane-Miller Bk.

Non. Animal Art Book. (Illus.). 1986. pap. 2.81 (*0-385-24227-1*) Doubleday.

Nones, Eric J. Caleb's Friend. (ps-3). 1993. 15.00 (*0-374-31017-3*) FS&G.
—Canary Prince. (ps up). 1991. 14.95 (*0-374-31029-7*) FS&G.
—Wendell. (ps up). 1989. 13.95 (*0-374-38266-2*) FS&G.

Noonan, Diana. Donkeys. Black, Don, illus. LC 93-28998. 1994. 4.25 (*0-383-03741-7*) SRA Schl Grp.
—Fat Cat Tompkin. Smith, Craig, illus. LC 92-34273. 1993. 3.75 (*0-383-03623-2*) SRA Schl Grp.
—Shooting It Straight. LC 93-21248. 1994. 4.25 (*0-383-03731-X*) SRA Schl Grp.

Noonan, Diane. Houses That Move. Black, Don, illus. LC 92-27085. 1993. 14.00 (*0-383-03574-0*) SRA Schl Grp.

Noonan, Geoffrey J. Nineteenth-Century Inventors. 128p. (gr. 6-9). 1992. lib. bdg. 16.95x (*0-8160-2480-4*) Facts on File.

Noonan, Janet & Calvert, Jacquelyn. Berries for the Queen. LC 92-32336. (gr. 4 up). 1993. write for info. (*0-7814-0903-9*, Chariot Bks) Cook.
—A Crown for Sir Conrad. LC 92-32337. 1993. write for info. (*0-7814-0317-0*, Chariot Bks) Cook.
—Millicent Eats Her Supper. Bartholomew, illus. (ps-2). 1990. 3.79 (*1-55513-984-1*, Chariot Bks) Cook.
—Millicent Goes to the Shopping Mall. Bartholomew, illus. (ps-2). 1990. 3.79 (*1-55513-970-1*, Chariot Bks) Cook.
—Millicent Has a Party. Bartholomew, illus. (ps-2). 1990. 3.79 (*1-55513-983-3*, Chariot Bks) Cook.
—Millicent Plays at the Park. Bartholomew, illus. (ps-2). 1990. 3.79 (*1-55513-982-5*, Chariot Bks) Cook.

Noonan, Jon. Captain Cook. LC 92-8231. (Illus.). 48p. (gr. 5). 1993. RSBE 12.95 (*0-89686-709-9*, Crestwood Hse) Macmillan Child Grp.
—Ferdinand Magellan. (Illus.). 48p. (gr. 5). 1993. RSBE 12.95 (*0-89686-706-4*, Crestwood Hse) Macmillan Child Grp.
—Lewis & Clark. LC 92-9381. (Illus.). 48p. (gr. 5). 1993. RSBE 12.95 (*0-89686-707-2*, Crestwood Hse) Macmillan Child Grp.
—Marco Polo. LC 91-38219. (Illus.). 48p. (gr. 5). 1993. RSBE 12.95 (*0-89686-704-8*, Crestwood Hse) Macmillan Child Grp.

Noonan, Michael. McKenzie's Boots. LC 87-25031. 240p. (gr. 6 up). 1988. 13.95 (*0-531-05748-8*); PLB 13.99 (*0-531-08348-9*) Orchard Bks Watts.

Noonan, R. A. Critters. LC 90-45819. (Illus.). 48p. (gr. 5-6). 1991. RSBE 13.95 (*0-89686-575-4*, Crestwood Hse) Macmillan Child Grp.

Noorlun, Lyle J. I Can-Can. 131p. (gr. 9 up). 1989. incl. cassette 16.95 (*1-877616-00-1*) Wholeness Intl.

Nora, Clarke. The Christmas Collection. Rouwntree, Julia, et al, illus. 24p. (ps up). 1992. 9.95 (*1-85697-833-8*) Kingfisher Bks.

Noraas, Margaret. Math Activities for Preschool. 93p. (ps). Date not set. pap. text ed. 12.95 (*0-9637985-0-2*) Penguin Family.

Norback, Craig. VGM's Careers Encyclopedia. 3rd ed. LC 90-50726. 464p. (gr. 7 up). 1991. 39.95 (*0-8442-8692-3*, VGM Career Bks) NTC Pub Grp.

Norberg, Jon. Academic Sportfolio. Gallup, Beth, ed. Norberg, Jon, illus. 1200p. (gr. 3-6). 1987. 495.00 (*0-685-24265-X*) Acad Sportfolio.
—Academic Sportfolio: Excuse Notes Are No Excuse. Pranzo, Donard, ed. Norberg, Jon, illus. (gr. 3-6). 1987. portfolio ser. 50.00 (*0-924086-00-9*) Acad Sportfolio.

Norbrook, Dominique. Passport to France. rev. ed. LC 93-21188. 1994. write for info. (*0-531-14293-0*) Watts.

Norby, Lisa, adapted by see Sewell, Anna.

Norby, Lisa, adapted by see Stevenson, Robert Louis.

Nord, Barry M. The Spaceship Earth. Palmer, Norman D., illus. 64p. (Orig.). (gr. 6 up). pap. 9.95 (*0-935656-09-X*) Nords Studio.

Nordberg, Marion, jt. auth. see Jenkins, Lee.

Norden, Beth. The Bee. Hansen, Biruta A., illus. 14p. (gr. 2 up). 1991. 12.95 (*1-55670-218-3*) Stewart Tabori & Chang.

Norden, Beth B., jt. auth. see Ruschak, Lynette.

Norden, Carroll R. Deserts. rev. ed. LC 87-23224. (Illus.). 48p. (gr. 2-6). 1987. PLB 18.64 (*0-8172-3252-4*) Raintree Steck-V.
—The Jungle. rev. ed. LC 87-20820. (Illus.). 48p. (gr. 2-6). 1987. PLB 18.64 (*0-8172-3256-7*) Raintree Steck-V.

Nordhoff, Charles & Hall, James N. The Bounty Trilogy. (Illus.). (gr. 9 up). 1982. 29.95 (*0-316-61161-1*, Pub. by Atlantic Monthly Pr) Little.

Nordic, Rolla. Let's Talk about the Tarot: A Story for Children & the Young at Heart. 1992. 12.95 (*0-533-09686-3*) Vantage.

Nordlicht, Lillian. I Love to Laugh. Davis, Allen, illus. Silverman, Manuel, intro. by. LC 80-14399. (Illus.). 32p. 1980. 17.96 (*0-8172-1364-3*) Raintree Steck-V.

Nordlicht, Lillian, adapted by. & adapted see London, Jack.

Nordmark, Magdalene L. Moss, a Border Collie. Miller, Robert W., illus. Miller, Janus W., prologue by. (Illus.). 37p. (Orig.). 1988. pap. 7.00 (*0-685-21901-1*) Willow Run UT.

Nordqvist, Sven. Festus & Mercury: Ruckus in the Garden. Nordqvist, Sven, illus. 24p. (ps-3). 1991. PLB 18.95 (*0-87614-678-7*) Carolrhoda Bks.
—Festus & Mercury: Wishing to Go Fishing. Nordqvist, Sven, illus. 24p. (ps-3). 1991. PLB 18.95 (*0-87614-658-2*) Carolrhoda Bks.
—Festus & Mercury Go Camping. LC 92-43181. 1993. 18.95 (*0-87614-802-X*) Carolrhoda Bks.
—The Fox Hunt. Nordqvist, Sven, illus. LC 87-28197. 32p. (ps-2). 1988. 12.95 (*0-688-06881-2*); PLB 12.88 (*0-688-06882-0*, Morrow Jr Bks) Morrow Jr Bks.
—Merry Christmas, Festus & Mercury. (Illus.). 24p. (ps-3). 1989. PLB 18.95 (*0-87614-383-4*) Carolrhoda Bks.
—Pancake Pie. Wilhelm, Hans, illus. LC 84-16640. 32p. (ps-3). 1985. 11.95 (*0-688-04141-8*); PLB 11.88 (*0-688-04142-6*, Morrow Jr Bks) Morrow Jr Bks.
—Porker Finds a Chair. (Illus.). 24p. (ps-3). 1989. PLB 13.50 (*0-87614-367-2*) Carolrhoda Bks.
—Tomten's Christmas Porridge. Haug, Arden, tr. from SWE. Nordqvist, Sven, illus. 26p. (ps-3). 1991. 14.95 (*0-9615394-2-9*) Skandisk.

Nordstrom, Judy. Concord & Lexington. LC 92-23392. (Illus.). 72p. (gr. 4 up). 1993. RSBE 14.95 (*0-87518-567-3*, Dillon) Macmillan Child Grp.

Nordstrom, Ursula. Secret Language. Chalmers, Mary, illus. LC 60-7701. 192p. (gr. 3-5). 1960. PLB 12.89 (*0-06-024576-X*) HarpC Child Bks.
—Secret Language. LC 60-7701. (Illus.). 192p. (gr. 3-5). 1972. pap. 3.95 (*0-06-440022-0*, Trophy) HarpC Child Bks.

Nordtvedt, Matilda. Ladybugs Bees & Butterfly Trees. LC 84-24343. 160p. (Orig.). (ps). 1985. pap. 5.99 (*0-87123-820-9*) Bethany Hse.

Noreen, George W. Your First Finch. (Illus.). 36p. (Orig.). 1991. pap. 1.95 (*0-86622-062-3*, YF-106) TFH Pubns.

Norell, Mark. All You Need to Know about Dinosaurs. LC 91-21701. (Illus.). 96p. (gr. 2-9). 1991. 12.95 (*0-8069-8396-5*) Sterling.

Norlen, Paul, tr. see Lagercrantz, Rose & Lagercrantz, Samuel.

Norman, C. J. Aircraft Carriers. LC 85-51452. (Illus.). 32p. (gr. 3-6). 1989. pap. 4.95 (*0-531-15136-0*) Watts.
—Buques de Guerra. LC 85-51458. (SPA., Illus.). 32p. (gr. k-4). 1991. PLB 11.90 (*0-531-07921-X*) Watts.
—Combat Aircraft. LC 85-51453. (Illus.). 32p. (gr. 1-6). 1986. PLB 11.90 (*0-531-10089-8*) Watts.
—The Picture World of Motorcycles. (Illus.). 32p. (gr. k-4). 1989. PLB 12.40 (*0-531-10727-2*) Watts.
—Tanks. (Illus.). 32p. (gr. 2 up). 1990. pap. 4.95 (*0-531-15145-X*) Watts.

Norman, D. Dinosaurs. (Illus.). 64p. (gr. 10 up). 1993. pap. 4.50 (*0-86020-458-8*) EDC.

Norman, David. When Dinosaurs Ruled the Earth. 1985. 6.98 *(0-671-07522-5)* S&S Trade.

Norman, David & Miller, Angela. Dinosaur. Keates, Colin, illus. LC 88-27167. 64p. (gr. 5 up). 1989. 15.00 *(0-394-82253-6)*; PLB 15.99 *(0-394-92253-0)* Knopf Bks Yng Read.

Norman, Floyd. Afro-Classic Folk Tales, Bk. 4: High John. Stewart, lyn, ed. Sullivan, Leo, illus. & intro. by. 28p. (Orig.). (gr. 4-7). 1992. pap. 9.95 *(1-881368-21-1)* Vignette.

Norman, Floyd & Sullivan, Leo. Afro-Classic Folk Tales, Bk. 6: Work-Let-Me-See. Stewart, Lyn, ed. Sullivan, Leo, illus. 28p. (Orig.). (gr. 4-7). 1992. pap. 9.95 *(1-881368-23-8)* Vignette.

Norman, Floyd, jt. auth. see Sullivan, Leo.

Norman, Floyd E. Afro-Classic Folk Tales, Bk. 1: A Rattlesnake Tale. Stewart, Lyn, ed. Norman, Floyd, illus. Sullivan, Leo, intro. by. (Illus.). 28p. (Orig.). (gr. 4-7). 1992. pap. 9.95 *(1-881368-00-9)* Vignette.

Norman, Howard. How Glooskap Outwits the Ice Giants: And Other Tales of the Maritime Indians, Vol. 1. 1989. 14.95 *(0-316-61181-6,* Joy St Bks) Little.

Norman, Howard, ed. see Strauss, Susan.

Norman, Jane & Beazley, Frank. Big Purr to the Rescue. 24p. (ps-3). 1993. pap. write for info. *(1-883585-11-2)* Pixanne Ent.

—The Case of the Missing Shoes. 24p. (ps-3). 1993. pap. write for info. *(1-883585-07-4)* Pixanne Ent.

—It's Raining Vegetables! 24p. (ps-3). 1993. pap. write for info. *(1-883585-08-2)* Pixanne Ent.

—Maxi's Big Adventure. 24p. (ps-3). 1993. pap. write for info. *(1-883585-04-X)* Pixanne Ent.

—The Mumble Mystery. 24p. (ps-3). 1993. pap. write for info. *(1-883585-12-0)* Pixanne Ent.

—The Mysterious Light. 24p. (ps-3). 1993. pap. write for info. *(1-883585-05-8)* Pixanne Ent.

—The Mystery of the Flying Elephants. 24p. (ps-3). 1993. pap. write for info. *(1-883585-02-3)* Pixanne Ent.

—The Night the Moon Fell. 24p. (ps-3). 1993. pap. write for info. *(1-883585-06-6)* Pixanne Ent.

—The Search for the Peanut Butter King. 24p. (ps-3). 1993. pap. write for info. *(1-883585-00-7)* Pixanne Ent.

—The Tale of the Tickle Bug. 24p. (ps-3). 1993. pap. write for info. *(1-883585-03-1)* Pixanne Ent.

—Tick-i-ty Ted Joins the Circus. 24p. (ps-3). 1993. pap. write for info. *(1-883585-01-5)* Pixanne Ent.

—Tick-i-ty Ted Meets the Rude Rabbits. 24p. (ps-3). 1993. pap. write for info. *(1-883585-09-0)* Pixanne Ent.

—The Voice from Nowhere. 24p. (ps-3). 1993. pap. write for info. *(1-883585-10-4)* Pixanne Ent.

—Who Lives There? 24p. (ps-3). 1993. pap. write for info. *(1-883585-13-9)* Pixanne Ent.

Norman, Lilith. The Paddock: A Story in Praise of the Earth. Roennfeldt, Robert, illus. LC 92-15013. 32p. (ps-3). 1993. 12.00 *(0-679-83887-2)* Knopf Bks Yng Read.

Norman, Louise. God's Power Versus Satan's Power: Christian Life Lessons. Snader, Barbara, illus. 64p. (Orig.). (gr. 1-8). 1985. pap. text ed. 11.50 *(0-86508-062-3)* BCM Pubn.

Norman, Philip R. The Carrot War. Norman, Philip R., illus. 32p. (ps-3). 1992. 13.95 *(0-316-61200-6)* Little.

—A Mammoth Imagination. LC 92-53455. 1992. 14.95 *(0-316-61201-4)* Little.

Norman, Roger. Albion's Dream. LC 91-693. 192p. (gr. 7 up). 1992. 15.00 *(0-385-30533-8)* Delacorte.

Norman, Winifred L. & Patterson, Lily. Lewis Latimer: Scientist. LC 93-185. (Illus.). (gr. 5 up). 1994. PLB 18.95 *(0-7910-1977-2,* Am Art Analog); pap. write for info. *(0-7910-1978-0,* Am Art Analog) Chelsea Hse.

Norman-Grumbley, Patricia, tr. see Mannino, Marc P. & Mannino, Angelica L.

Norrell, Robert J. The Alabama Story: State History & Geography. (Illus.). 304p. (gr. 4). 1993. 22.95x *(1-882700-00-7)* Yellowhammer.

—We Want Jobs! A Story of the Great Depression. Jones, Jan N., illus. LC 92-18082. 40p. (gr. 2-5). 1992. PLB 21.34 *(0-8114-7229-9)* Raintree Steck-V.

Norris, Ann. On the Go. 32p. 1990. 13.95 *(0-688-06336-5)*; PLB 13.88 *(0-688-06337-3)* Lothrop.

Norris, Carolyn. In Our House: Story for Young Children in Sign Language. Norris, Carolyn, illus. 32p. (Orig.). (ps-3). 1984. 4.95 *(0-916708-11-X)* Modern Signs.

—Jeans Christmas Stocking. Norris, Carolyn, illus. 24p. (Orig.). (ps-4). 1982. pap. 3.95 *(0-916708-10-1)* Modern Signs.

Norris, Crystal. Flowers for Algernon: A Study Guide. (gr. 9-11). 1985. tchr's. ed. & wkbk. 14.95 *(0-88122-115-5)* LRN Links.

—Great Expectations: A Study Guide. (gr. 9-12). 1987. tchr's. ed. & wkbk. 14.95 *(0-88122-116-3)* LRN Links.

—I Am the Cheese - Study Guide. Friedland, Joyce & Kessler, Rikki, eds. (gr. 7-10). Date not set. pap. text ed. 14.95 *(0-88122-101-5)* Lrn Links.

—Julie of the Wolves - Study Guide. Friedland, Joyce & Kessler, Rikki, eds. (gr. 6-9). Date not set. pap. text ed. 14.95 *(0-88122-099-X)* Lrn Links.

—Julius Caesar - Study Guide. Friedland, Joyce & Kessler, Rikki, eds. (gr. 9-12). Date not set. pap. text ed. 14.95 *(0-88122-102-X)* Lrn Links.

—The Light in the Forest - Study Guide. Friedland, Joyce & Kessler, Rikki, eds. (gr. 6-9). Date not set. pap. text ed. 14.95 *(0-88122-117-1)* Lrn Links.

—One Flew over the Cuckoo's Nest - Study Guide. Friedland, Joyce & Kessler, Rikki, eds. (gr. 10-12). Date not set. pap. text ed. 14.95 *(0-88122-121-X)* Lrn Links.

—Ordinary People - Study Guide. Friedland, Joyce & Kessler, Rikki, eds. (gr. 9-12). Date not set. pap. text ed. 14.95 *(0-88122-122-8)* Lrn Links.

—The Picture of Dorian Gray - Study Guide. Friedland, Joyce & Kessler, Rikki, eds. (gr. 10-12). Date not set. pap. text ed. 14.95 *(0-88122-123-6)* Lrn Links.

—Shane - Study Guide. Friedland, Joyce & Kessler, Rikki, eds. (gr. 7-10). Date not set. pap. text ed. 14.95 *(0-88122-129-5)* Lrn Links.

Norris, Frank. Octopus. (gr. 11 up). 1968. pap. 1.95 *(0-8049-0179-1,* CL-179) Airmont.

Norris, Gunilla. Learning from the Angel. LC 85-80140. 62p. (Orig.). (gr. 9-12). 1985. pap. 5.00 perf. bdg. *(0-916418-59-6)* Lotus.

Norris, James. Aladdin & the Wonderful Lamp. 1940. 4.50 *(0-87602-102-X)* Anchorage.

—Robin Hood. (gr. 1-9). 1952. 4.50 *(0-87602-191-7)* Anchorage.

Norris, Jerrie. Presenting Rosa Guy. 1992. pap. 3.99 *(0-440-21133-6)* Dell.

Norris, Leslie. Norris's Ark. LC 87-50520. (Illus.). 64p. (gr. k-8). 1988. 15.00 *(0-930954-28-9)*; pap. 10.00 *(0-930954-29-7)*; cassette 6.95 *(0-930954-32-7)* Tidal Pr.

Norsgaard, E. Jaediker. Nature's Great Balancing Act: In Our Own Backyard. Norsgaard, Campbell, photos by. LC 89-38589. (Illus.). 64p. (gr. 4 up). 1990. 14.95 *(0-525-65028-8,* Cobblehill Bks) Dutton Child Bks.

Norsgaard, Jaediker E. How to Raise Butterflies. Norsgaard, Campbell, photos by. (Illus.). 48p. (gr. 2-5). 1988. 11.99 *(0-396-09144-X,* Putnam) Putnam Pub Group.

Norskog, Howard L. High Country Ballads: Cowboy Poetry. 80p. (Orig.). (gr. 8 up). 1988. pap. 6.99 *(0-685-30409-4)* H L Norskog.

—Yesterdays Trails: Cowboy Poetry. 49p. (gr. 8 up). 1989. pap. 6.99 *(0-685-30410-8)* H L Norskog.

North, A. C. & Attwood, Teresa K. Protein Structure. 3rd ed. Head, J. J., ed. (Illus.). 32p. (gr. 10 up). 1991. pap. 3.00 *(0-89278-434-2,* 45-9634) Carolina Biological.

North, Carol. Disney Babies: What Does Baby Mickey Find? Baker, Darrell, illus. (ps-k). 1991. bds. 1.80 *(0-307-06113-2,* Golden Pr) Western Pub.

—Frosty the Snowman. (ps-3). 1990. write for info. *(0-307-10039-1)* Western Pub.

—Hansel & Gretel. 1990. pap. write for info. *(0-307-10033-2,* Golden Pr) Western Pub.

—Jungle Book: Mowgli's Noisy Jungle. (ps). 1993. 9.95 *(0-307-06076-4,* Golden Pr) Western Pub.

—Walt Disney's Winnie the Pooh: Pooh Can... Can You? Baker, Darrell, illus. 12p. (ps). 1993. bds. 1.95 *(0-307-06081-0,* 6081, Golden Pr) Western Pub.

North Carolina School of Science & Mathematics, Department of Mathematics & Computer Science Staff. Data Analysis. LC 88-5305. (Illus.). 132p. (Orig.). (gr. 11-12). 1988. pap. 12.00 *(0-87353-263-5)* NCTM.

—Geometric Probability. LC 88-5305. (Illus.). 40p. (Orig.). (gr. 11-12). 1988. pap. 11.00 *(0-87353-259-7)* NCTM.

North, Margie. To Chase a Dream. 418p. (gr. 8-12). 1989. 14.95 *(0-934188-26-2)* Evans Pubns.

North, Rick. Young Astronauts No. 1, No. 1. 1990. pap. 2.95 *(0-8217-3000-2)* Zebra.

—Young Astronauts No. 2. 1990. pap. 2.95 *(0-8217-3173-4)* Zebra.

—Young Astronauts No. 3. 1990. pap. 2.95 *(0-8217-3178-5)* Zebra.

North, Sterling. Abe Lincoln: Log Cabin to White House. LC 87-4654. (Illus.). 160p. (gr. 5-9). 1987. lib. bdg. 8.99 *(0-394-90361-7)*; pap. 4.99 *(0-394-89179-1)* Random Bks Yng Read.

—Rascal. (gr. 5 up). 1976. pap. 2.75 *(0-380-01518-8,* Flare) Avon.

—Rascal. Schoenherr, John, illus. 192p. (ps up). 1990. pap. 3.99 *(0-14-034445-4,* Puffin) Puffin Bks.

—Rascal: A Memoir of a Better Era. Shoenherr, John, illus. LC 63-13882. (gr. 4 up). 1984. 13.95 *(0-525-18839-8,* DCB) Dutton Child Bks.

—The Wolfling. Schoenherr, John, illus. 224p. (gr. 5-9). 1992. pap. 3.99 *(0-14-036166-9,* Puffin) Puffin Bks.

Northrop, Nancy. Mystari. St. James, Jim, illus. 16p. 1991. bds. 5.95 spiral bdg. *(0-9627894-1-0)* LNR Pubns.

Northup, Bill, jt. auth. see Mollica, Anthony.

Northup, Bill, jt. auth. see Mollica, Tony.

Northup, Soloman. Twelve Years a Slave, Eighteen Forty-One to Eighteen Fifty-Three. Eakin, Sue, retold by. Dean, W. A., illus. LC 89-82295. 205p. (gr. 6-12). 1990. lib. bdg. 16.50 *(0-944419-27-5)*; pap. text ed. 9.95x *(0-944419-17-8)* Everett Cos Pub.

Northup, Solomon. Twelve Years a Slave: Excerpts from the Narrative of Solomon Northup. abr. ed. Lucas, Alice, ed. (Illus.). 48p. (Orig.). (gr. 5-12). 1992. pap. text ed. 25.00 incl. 3 audio tapes *(0-936434-39-2,* Pub. by Zellerbach Fam Fund); pap. text ed. 5.00 tchr's. guide *(0-936434-59-7)* SF Study Ctr.

Excerpts in print & on audiotape from the true story of Solomon Northup, a free African American from New York who was kidnapped & sold into slavery in Louisiana. He lived as a slave for 12 years before regaining his freedom in 1853. Northup told of his harrowing experiences in a full-length book which Frederick Douglass called truth that is "stranger than fiction." African American actor/singer Wendell Brooks dramatically retells this moving story, enhancing the text by singing work songs & spirituals from the period. Actor Ossie Davis calls it "a powerful work. I recommend it without reservation." Reviewed in SLJ, 5/93, p. 71, BOOKLIST, 5/15/93, p. 1716, calls this 48-page illustrated excerpt: "excellent primary source material for the study of slavery in the United States." Also recorded on three 30-minute audiocassettes, TWELVE YEARS A SLAVE is excellent for schools, fifth grade through junior college. Also for church groups, other adult settings. Make checks payable to Many Cultures Publishing, P.O. Box 425646, San Francisco, CA 94142-5646. Toll Free 1-800-484-4173, ext. 1073, FAX 415-626-7276. California purchasers add sales tax. *Publisher Provided Annotation.*

Northway, Del L. Kirida. LC 86-62054. 216p. (gr. 10-12). 1987. 12.95 *(0-939137-00-3)* Mirage Bks.

Norton, Ann. Brooke's Little Lies. 112p. (gr. 4-9). 1992. pap. 2.95 *(0-448-40491-5,* G&D) Putnam Pub Group.

Norton, Bettina A. Neighborhood Trivia Hunt for Concord, Massachusetts. (Illus.). 20p. (gr. 7-12). 1985. pap. 4.95 *(0-938357-02-6)* BAN Pub Boston.

Norton, M. & Hague, M. The Borrowers. 177p. (ps up). 1991. 22.95 *(0-15-209991-3,* HB Juv Bks) HarBrace.

Norton, Margaret. Brantub the Dancing Bear. Widdowson, Kay, illus. 32p. (ps-2). 1992. 15.95 *(0-370-31409-3,* Pub. by Bodley Head UK) Trafalgar.

Norton, Mary. Are All the Giants Dead? Froud, Brian, illus. LC 78-6622. 123p. (gr. 3-7). 1978. pap. 9.95 *(0-15-607888-0,* Voyager Bks) HarBrace.

—Bed-Knob & Broomstick. large type ed. Blegvad, Erik, illus. 296p. (gr. 3-7). 1989. lib. bdg. 14.95 *(0-8161-4786-8,* Large Print Bks) Hall.

—Bed-Knob & Broomstick. Gaber, Susan, contrib. by. 229p. (gr. 3-7). 1990. pap. 3.95 *(0-15-206231-9,* Odyssey) HarBrace.

—Borrowers. Krush, Beth & Krush, Joe, illus. LC 53-7870. 180p. (gr. 3 up). 1953. 13.95 *(0-15-209987-5,* HB Juv Bks) HarBrace.

—The Borrowers. Krush, Beth & Krush, Joe, illus. 200p. (gr. 3-7). 1989. pap. 4.95 *(0-15-209990-5,* Odyssey) HarBrace.

—Borrowers Afield. Krush, Beth & Krush, Joe, illus. LC 55-11011. 215p. (gr. 3 up). 1955. 13.95 *(0-15-210166-7,* HB Juv Bks) HarBrace.

—The Borrowers Afield. Krush, Beth, contrib. by. 238p. (gr. 5-7). 1990. pap. 3.95 *(0-15-210535-2,* Odyssey) HarBrace.

—Borrowers Afloat. Krush, Beth & Krush, Joe, illus. LC 59-5630. 191p. (gr. 3 up). 1959. 12.95 *(0-15-210345-7,* HB Juv Bks) HarBrace.

—The Borrowers Afloat. Krush, Beth, contrib. by. 205p. (gr. 3-7). 1990. pap. 3.95 *(0-15-210534-4,* Odyssey) HarBrace.

—Borrowers Aloft. Krush, Beth & Krush, Joe, illus. LC 61-11751. 192p. (gr. 3 up). 1961. 12.95 *(0-15-210524-7,* HB Juv Bks) HarBrace.

—The Borrowers Aloft. Krush, Beth & Krush, Joe, illus. 196p. (gr. 3-7). 1990. pap. 4.95 *(0-15-210533-6,* Odyssey) HarBrace.

—The Borrowers Avenged. (gr. 3-6). 1988. 17.25 *(0-8446-6358-1)* Peter Smith.

—The Borrowers Avenged. 365p. (gr. 3-7). 1990. pap. 4.95 *(0-15-210532-8,* Odyssey) HarBrace.

—Poor Stainless. Krush, Beth & Krush, Joe, illus. LC 70-140781. 32p. (gr. 3 up). 1985. 7.95 *(0-15-263221-2,* HB Juv Bks) HarBrace.

Norton, Miriam. Kitten Who Thought He Was a Mouse. (ps-3). 1993. 11.95 *(0-307-17553-7,* Artsts Writrs) Western Pub.

Norton, Penny. Earth Watch. (Illus.). 48p. (gr. 7-9). 1992. 13.95 *(0-563-34407-5,* BBC-Parkwest); pap. 6.95 *(0-563-34408-3,* BBC-Parkwest) Parkwest Pubns.

Norwood, D. Chess Puzzles. (Illus.). 64p. (gr. 5 up). 1992. PLB 12.96 *(0-88110-464-7)*; pap. text ed. 6.95 *(0-7460-0950-X)* EDC.

Norwood, David, et al, illus. Children's Tour of Red Stick City. 32p. (gr. 1-6). 1980. pap. text ed. 2.00 (0-9608282-2-2) YWCO.

Norworth, Jack. Take Me Out to the Ballgame. LC 91-18555. (Illus.). 40p. (ps up) 1992. RSBE 14.95 (0-02-735991-X, Four Winds) Macmillan Child Grp.

Nostlinger, Christine. Conrad, the Factory-Made Boy. large type ed. 308p. (gr. 1-7). 1991. 13.95 (0-7451-1249-8, Galaxy Child Lrg Print) Chivers N Amer.

—The Cucumber King. Bell, Anthea, tr. 126p. (gr. 3-7). 1984. 9.95 (0-930267-01-X) Bergh Pub.

Nottingham, Ted, et al. Chess for Children. LC 93-24832. (Illus.). 128p. (gr. 3 up). 1993. 14.95 (0-8069-0452-6) Sterling.

Nottridge, Rhoda. Additives. LC 92-33083. 1993. PLB 14.95 (0-87614-794-5); pap. 5.95 (0-87614-609-4) Carolrhoda Bks.

—Adventure Films. LC 91-25839. (Illus.). 32p. (gr. 5-6). 1992. RSBE 13.95 (0-89686-718-8, Crestwood Hse) Macmillan Child Grp.

—Animated Films. LC 91-36041. (Illus.). 32p. (gr. 5-6). 1992. RSBE 13.95 (0-89686-717-X, Crestwood Hse) Macmillan Child Grp.

—Apples. (Illus.). 32p. (gr. 1-4). 1991. PLB 14.95 (0-87614-655-8) Carolrhoda Bks.

—Care for Your Body. LC 92-13917. (Illus.). 32p. (gr. 6). 1993. RSBE 13.95 (0-89686-787-0, Crestwood Hse) Macmillan Child Grp.

—Fats. LC 92-26758. 1993. 14.95 (0-87614-779-1); pap. 5.95 (0-87614-606-X) Carolrhoda Bks.

—Horror Films. LC 91-23328. (Illus.). 32p. (gr. 5-6). 1992. RSBE 13.95 (0-89686-719-6, Crestwood Hse) Macmillan Child Grp.

—Let's Look At Big Cats. (ps-3). 1990. PLB 11.40 (0-531-18285-1) Watts.

—Sea Disasters. LC 93-6830. 48p. (gr. 4-6). 1993. 15.95 (1-56847-084-3) Thomson Lrning.

—Sugar. Yeats, John, illus. 32p. (gr. 1-4). 1990. PLB 14.95 (0-87614-418-0) Carolrhoda Bks.

—Sugars. LC 92-21414. 1993. PLB 14.95 (0-87614-796-1); pap. 5.95 (0-87614-611-6) Carolrhoda Bks.

—Vitamins. LC 92-21415. 1993. PLB 14.95 (0-87614-795-3); pap. 5.95 (0-87614-610-8) Carolrhoda Bks.

Nourse, Alan. The Tooth Book. (gr. 6up) 1977. 6.95 (0-679-20376-1) McKay.

Nourse, Alan E. Lumps, Bumps, & Rashes: A Look at Kids' Diseases. rev. ed. LC 90-32785. (Illus.). 64p. (gr. 5-8). 1990. PLB 12.90 (0-531-10865-1) Watts.

—Radio Astronomy. LC 89-32405. (Illus.). 96p. (gr. 6 up). 1989. PLB 12.90 (0-531-10811-2) Watts.

—Sexually Transmitted Diseases. Mathews, V., ed. LC 91-21707. (Illus.). 144p. (gr. 9-12). 1992. PLB 14.40 (0-531-11065-6) Watts.

—Teen Guide to AIDS Prevention. LC 90-12750. (Illus.). 64p. (gr. 9-12). 1990. PLB 13.40 (0-531-10966-6) Watts.

—Teen Guide to Safe Sex. Kline, M., ed. (Illus.). 64p. (gr. 6-12). 1988. PLB 13.40 (0-531-10592-X) Watts.

—Teen Guide to Safe Sex. 1990. pap. 4.95 (0-531-15211-1) Watts.

—Teen Guide to Survival. LC 90-12267. (Illus.). 64p. (gr. 9-12). 1990. PLB 13.40 (0-531-10968-2) Watts.

—The Virus Invaders. Mathews, V., ed. LC 91-36650. (Illus.). 96p. (gr. 9-12). 1992. PLB 12.90 (0-531-12511-4) Watts.

—Your Immune System. rev. ed. LC 89-8925. (Illus.). 128p. (gr. 7-12). 1989. PLB 12.90 (0-531-10817-1) Watts.

Novak, Greg. Over the Top. Doubet, Amy, illus. 120p. (Orig.). (gr. 9-12). 1990. pap. 12.00 (1-55878-012-2) Game Designers.

Novak, Joyce R. One Hundred One Wooden Clock Patterns. LC 90-9853. (Illus.). 132p. (Orig.). (gr. 10-12). 1990. pap. text ed. 12.95 (0-8069-5776-X) Sterling.

Novak, Matt. Elmer Blunt's Open House. LC 91-38424. (Illus.). 24p. (ps-1). 1992. 14.95 (0-531-05998-7); PLB 14.99 (0-531-08598-8) Orchard Bks Watts.

—The Last Christmas Present. Novak, Matt, illus. LC 92-44513. 32p. (ps-1). 1993. 14.95 (0-531-05495-0); PLB 14.99 (0-531-08645-3) Orchard Bks Watts.

—Mr. Floop's Lunch. LC 89-22963. (Illus.). 32p. (ps-1). 1990. 12.95 (0-531-05826-3); PLB 12.99 (0-531-08426-4) Orchard Bks Watts.

—While the Shepherd Slept. LC 90-7733. (Illus.). 32p. (ps-2). 1991. 13.95 (0-531-05915-4); PLB 13.99 (0-531-08515-5) Orchard Bks Watts.

Novelly, Maria C. Theatre Games for Young Performers. Pijanowski, Kathy & Zapel, Arthur L., eds. LC 85-60572. (Illus.). 160p. (Orig.). (gr. 6-10). 1985. pap. text ed. 9.95 (0-916260-31-3, B-188) Meriwether Pub.

Nover, Elizabeth Z. My Land of Israel. Rosenblum, Richard, illus. 35p. (Orig.). (gr. 1-2). 1987. pap. text ed. 4.25 (0-87441-447-4) Behrman.

—Reading Workbook for the Hebrew Primer. 60p. (gr. 4-7). 1987. pap. 2.95 (0-317-60046-X) Behrman.

Novis, Constance, ed. see Dempsey, Michael.

Novit, Renee Z. Alphabet Aa to Zz. R. Z. Novit Graphic Design Staff, illus. 16p. (ps-k). Date not set. pap. 7.95 (1-883371-00-7) Kidz & Katz.

—Counting by Tens & Fives. Novit, R. Z., Graphic Design Staff, illus. 16p. (ps-k). Date not set. pap. 7.95 (1-883371-02-3) Kidz & Katz.

—Counting One to Twenty. Novit, R. Z., Graphic Design Staff, illus. 16p. (ps-k). Date not set. pap. 7.95 (1-883371-01-5) Kidz & Katz.

Novotny, Ann. Alice's World: The Life & Photography of an American Original: Alice Austen, 1866-1952. Austen, Alice, illus. LC 76-18489. (gr. 7-9). 1976. 22.50 (0-85699-128-7) Chatham Pr.

Nowiszewski, Nancy. Olympia Odette Presents: My Think-Along Funbook. DeRosa, Dee, illus. 100p. (ps-4). 1991. wkbk. 3.95 (1-55999-157-7) LinguiSystems.

—Olympia Odette Presents: My Think 'n' Do Adventure Book. DeRosa, Dee, illus. 100p. (ps-3). 1990. spiral bdg., wkbk. 3.95 (1-55999-132-1) LinguiSystems.

Nowlin, Susan & Sterling, Mary E. Think & Do Bulletin Boards. Wright, Terry, illus. 96p. (gr. k-4). 1988. wkbk. 9.95 (1-55734-063-3) Tchr Create Mat.

Nowlin, Susan S. Fall Time Savers. Spence, Paula, et al, illus. 48p. (gr. k-6). 1989. wkbk. 5.95 (1-55734-123-0) Tchr Create Mat.

—Holiday Crossword Puzzles. Spence, Paula, illus. 48p. (gr. 2-5). 1988. wkbk. 5.95 (1-55734-366-7) Tchr Create Mat.

—Spring Time Savers. Spence, Paula, et al, illus. 48p. (gr. k-6). 1989. wkbk. 5.95 (1-55734-125-7) Tchr Create Mat.

—Winter Time Savers. Spence, Paula, et al, illus. 48p. (gr. k-6). 1989. wkbk. 5.95 (1-55734-124-9) Tchr Create Mat.

—Year-Round Open Worksheets. Spence, Paula, et al, illus. 48p. (gr. k-6). 1989. wkbk. 5.95 (1-55734-126-5) Tchr Create Mat.

Nowlin, Susan S., jt. auth. see Sterling, Mary E.

Noyes, Alfred. The Highwayman. Mikolaycak, Charles, illus. LC 83-725. 40p. (gr. 5 up). 1983. 11.95 (0-688-02117-4) Lothrop.

—The Highwayman. Keeping, Charles, illus. 32p. 1987. 16.00 (0-19-279748-4); pap. 7.50 (0-19-272133-X) OUP.

—Highwayman. Waldman, Neil, illus. 28p. (ps-3). 1990. 14.95 (0-15-234340-7) HarBrace.

Noyes, Beppie. Wigglesworth. Noyes, Beppie, illus. LC 85-62022. 74p. (gr. k-4). 1985. pap. 5.95 (0-932433-08-1) Windswept Hse.

Nozaki, Akihiro & Anno, Mitsumasa. Anno's Hat Tricks. LC 84-18900. (Illus.). 44p. (gr. 3 up). 1985. 15.95 (0-399-21212-4, Philomel Bks) Putnam Pub Group.

NPS Staff, ed. see Gilmore, Jackie.

NPS Staff, ed. see Salts, Bobbi.

Nudelman, Edward D., frwd. by. The Jessie Willcox Smith Mother Goose. enhanced ed. LC 90-19903. (Illus.). 192p. (gr. k up). 1991. 24.95 (0-88289-844-2); deluxe ed. 75.00 (0-88289-830-2) Pelican.

Nuebacher, G. The Frog Prince. (Illus.). 32p. (gr. 1-4). 1989. 6.95 (0-88625-216-4) Durkin Hayes Pub.

—Pinocchio. (Illus.). 32p. (gr. 1-4). 1989. 6.95 (0-88625-218-0) Durkin Hayes Pub.

—Sleeping Beauty. (Illus.). 32p. (gr. 1-4). 1989. 6.95 (0-88625-220-2) Durkin Hayes Pub.

Nugent, Nicholas. India. LC 90-25300. (Illus.). 96p. (gr. 6-12). 1991. PLB 19.92 (0-8114-2441-3) Raintree Steck-V.

—Pakistan & Bangladesh. LC 92-10765. 96p. 1992. lib. bdg. 19.92 (0-8114-2456-1) Raintree Steck-V.

Null, Cheryl J. & Gad, Carol L. The Barnyard Buddies. (Illus.). 32p. (gr. 2-6). 1989. pap. 5.95 (1-880171-00-7) Stardom.

—The Barnyard Buddies in Circus Champions. (Illus.). 36p. (gr. 2-6). 1990. pap. 5.95 (1-880171-01-5) Stardom.

—The Barnyard Buddies in Finders Keepers. (Illus.). 36p. (gr. 2-6). 1992. pap. 5.95 (1-880171-04-X) Stardom.

Numani, Shibli. Umar the Great, Vol. II. Saleem, M., tr. 200p. (gr. 7-12). 1985. 14.50 (1-56744-407-5) Kazi Pubns.

Numeroff. Fathers & Mothers. 1993. 15.95 (0-8050-2056-X) H Holt & Co.

—If You Give a Mouse a Cookie. 1993. pap. 28.67 (0-590-71885-1) Scholastic Inc.

Numeroff, Laura. Dogs Don't Wear Sneakers. Mathieu, Joe, illus. LC 92-27007. 1993. pap. 14.00 (0-671-79525-2, S&S BFYR) S&S Trade.

—Why a Disguise? McPhail, David M., illus. LC 93-19025. 1994. pap. 14.00 (0-671-87006-8, S&S BFYR) S&S Trade.

Numeroff, Laura J. If You Give a Moose a Muffin. Bond, Felicia, illus. LC 91-2207. 32p. (ps-2). 1991. 14.00 (0-06-024405-4); PLB 13.89 (0-06-024406-2) HarpC Child Bks.

—If You Give a Moose a Muffin Big Book. Bond, Felicia, illus. LC 91-2207. 32p. (ps-2). 1994. pap. 19.95 (0-06-443366-8, Trophy) HarpC Child Bks.

—If You Give a Mouse a Cookie. Bond, Felicia, illus. LC 84-48343. 32p. (ps-2). 1985. 13.00 (0-06-024586-7); PLB 12.89 (0-06-024587-5) HarpC Child Bks.

—If You Give a Mouse a Cookie Box & Doll. Bond, Felicia, illus. LC 91-46093. 32p. (ps-2). 1992. 16.95 (0-694-00416-2, Festival) HarpC Child Bks.

Numrick, Carol. Face the Issues: Intermediate Listening & Critical Thinking Skills. (Orig.). (gr. 7 up). 1990. pap. text ed. 13.50 (0-8013-0300-1, 75950); 2 cassettes 37.95 (0-8013-0301-X, 75945); bk. & cassette 46.50 (0-8013-0535-7, 78411) Longman.

Nunes, Lygia B. My Friend the Painter. Pontiero, Giovanni, tr. from POR. 85p. (gr. 3-7). 1991. 13.95 (0-15-256340-7) HarBrace.

Nunes, Susan. Coyote Dreams. Himler, Ronald, illus. LC 87-30288. 32p. (ps-3). 1988. SBE 13.95 (0-689-31398-5, Atheneum Child Bk) Macmillan Child Grp.

—Coyote Dreams. Himler, Ronald, illus. LC 93-22931. 32p. (gr. k-3). 1994. pap. 4.95 (0-689-71804-7, Aladdin) Macmillan Child Grp.

—Tiddalick the Frog. Chen, Ju-Hong, illus. LC 89-1. 32p. (gr. k-3). 1989. SBE 13.95 (0-689-31502-3, Atheneum Child Bk) Macmillan Child Grp.

—To Find the Way. Gray, Cissy, illus. LC 91-31334. 48p. (gr. 4-8). 1992. 12.95 (0-8248-1376-6) UH Pr.

Nunes, Susan M. The Last Dragon. Soentpiet, Chris K., illus. LC 93-30631. 1996. write for info. (0-395-67020-9, Clarion Bks) HM.

Nunez, Ana R. Antologia de Poesia Infantil. LC 85-81795. (SPA). 180p. (Orig.). (gr. 3-12). 1985. pap. 9.95 (0-89729-369-X) Ediciones.

Nunis & Knill, Harry. Tales of Mexican California. (gr. 1-9). 1993. pap. 8.95 (0-88388-161-6) Bellerophon Bks.

Nunis, Doyce B., Jr. Great Doctors. Conkle, Nancy, illus. 64p. (Orig.). (gr. 8). 1991. pap. 3.95 (0-88388-144-6) Bellerophon Bks.

Nunn, Abigail. The Land of Tuppitry. (Illus.). 96p. (gr. 3-4). 1991. pap. 4.95 (0-9620765-3-8) Victory Press.

Nunnally, Tiina, tr. see Alfredson, Hans.

Nunnally, Tiina, tr. see Newth, Mette.

Nurland, Patricia. Vietnam. Vu Viet Dung, photos by. LC 89-43178. (Illus.). 64p. (gr. 5-6). 1991. PLB 19.93 (0-8368-0230-6) Gareth Stevens Inc.

Nurnberg, Maxwell & Rosenblum, Morris. All about Words: An Adult Approach to Vocabulary Building. (gr. 7 up). 1968. pap. 4.95 (0-451-62598-6, Ment) NAL-Dutton.

Nursey-Bray, Rosemary. Through the Looking Glass & What Alice Found There. (Orig.). (ps up). 1987. playscript 5.00 (0-87602-276-X) Anchorage.

Nussbaum, Hedda. Animals Build Amazing Homes. Santoro, Christopher, illus. LC 79-11326. (gr. 2-5). 1979. 7.95 (0-394-83850-5) Random Bks Yng Read.

—Plants Do Amazing Things. Mathieu, Joe, illus. LC 75-36471. 72p. (gr. 2-3). 1977. 9.95 (0-394-83232-9); lib. bdg. 8.99 (0-394-93232-3) Random Bks Yng Read.

Nutkins, Terry & Corwin, Marshall. Pets. (Illus.). 48p. (gr. 7-9). 1992. 13.95 (0-563-34523-3, BBC-Parkwest); pap. 6.95 (0-563-34524-1, BBC-Parkwest) Parkwest Pubns.

Nutt, Robert van see Irving, Washington.

Nuwer, Hank. Recruiting in Sports. LC 89-9151. (Illus.). 144p. (gr. 9 up). 1989. PLB 13.90 (0-531-10796-5) Watts.

—Sports Scandals. LC 93-26317. 1994. write for info. (0-531-11183-0) Watts.

—Steroids. LC 90-32757. (Illus.). 144p. (gr. 9-12). 1990. PLB 13.90 (0-531-10946-1) Watts.

Nwabugwu, Frank. Antalo the Antelope, B-era the Bear, C-esto the Cheetah, D-opicooko the Deer. 18p. 1992. write for info. (1-881687-04-X); lib. bdg. write for info. (1-881687-05-8); pap. write for info. (1-881687-06-6); write for info. tchr's. ed. (1-881687-07-4) F Nwabugwu.

—Sparo; the Wild & Crazy Pretty Dog. 2nd ed. 26p. (gr. 2-8). 1993. write for info. 1-881687-08-2) F Nwabugwu.

Nyberg, Judy. Just Pretend! Creating Dramatic Play Centers with Young Children. (Illus.). 104p. (Orig.). (ps-1). 1994. pap. 8.95 (0-673-36116-0) GdYrBks.

Nye, Bill. Bill Nye the Science Guy's Big Blast of Science. (Illus.). 176p. 1993. pap. write for info. (0-201-60864-2) Addison-Wesley.

Nye, Julie. Every Perfect Gift. Vogt, Carla, ed. Weikel, Cheryl, illus. 201p. (Orig.). (gr. 9 up). 1990. pap. 4.95 (0-89084-499-2) Bob Jones Univ Pr.

—In My Uncle's House. 117p. (Orig.). (gr. 4-6). 1986. pap. 4.95 (0-89084-349-X) Bob Jones Univ Pr.

—Scout. 177p. (Orig.). 1987. pap. 4.95 (0-89084-413-5) Bob Jones Univ Pr.

Nye, Naomi S. Sitti's Secrets. Carpenter, Nancy, illus. LC 93-19742. 32p. (ps-3). 1994. RSBE 15.95 (0-02-768460-1, Four Winds) Macmillan Child Grp.

—This Same Sky: A Collection of Poems from Around the World. LC 92-11617. (Illus.). 224p. (gr. 5 up). 1992. SBE 15.95 (0-02-768440-7, Four Winds) Macmillan Child Grp.

Nye, Robert. Beowulf. 96p. (gr. 5 up). 1982. pap. 3.50 (0-440-90560-5, LFL) Dell.

Nye, Russel B., ed. see Franklin, Benjamin.

Nygren, Tord. The Red Thread. (Illus.). 32p. (ps up) 1988. 12.95 (91-29-59005-1, R & S Bks) FS&G.

Nylin, Dawn, jt. auth. see Loehrlein, Myrna.

Nystrom, Carolyn. Angels & Me. (Illus.). (ps-2). 1984. pap. 4.99 (0-8024-6150-6) Moody.

—Children's Bible Basics Ser, 11 bks. Hanna, Wayne, illus. (ps-2). Set. pap. 54.89 (0-8024-5988-9) Moody.

—Emma Says Goodbye. (Illus.). 48p. (gr. 4-8). 1990. 7.99 (0-7459-1826-3) Lion USA.

—Growing Jesus' Way. (ps-2). 1982. 4.99 (0-8024-6151-4) Moody.

—The Holy Spirit in Me. 32p. (ps-2). 1980. pap. 4.99 (0-8024-6152-2) Moody.

—Holy Spirit in Me: Children's Bible Basics. (ps-3). 1993. 5.99 (0-8024-7858-1) Moody.

—Jesus Is No Secret. Hanna, Wayne, illus. (ps-2). pap. 4.99 (0-8024-6153-0) Moody.

—The Lark Who Had No Song. McElrath-Eslick, Lori, illus. 32p. (ps-6). 1991. 11.95 (0-7459-1879-4) Lion USA.

—Mark: God on the Move. 96p. (gr. 7-12). 1978. saddle-stitched tchr's. ed. 4.99 (*0-87788-312-2*); student ed. 3.99 (*0-87788-311-4*) Shaw Pubs.
—Mike's Lonely Summer. Baum, Ann, illus. 48p. (gr. 1-6). 1986. 7.99 (*0-7459-1016-5*) Lion USA.
—The Trouble with Josh. Rees, Gary, illus. 48p. (gr. 6-12). 1989. text ed. 7.99 (*0-7459-1621-X*) Lion USA.
—What Happens When We Die? 32p. (ps-2). 1981. pap. 4.99 (*0-8024-6154-9*) Moody.
—What Is a Christian? Children's Bible Basics. (ps). 1992. 5.99 (*0-8024-7854-9*) Moody.
—What Is Prayer? 32p. (ps-2). 1980. pap. 4.99 (*0-8024-6156-5*) Moody.
—What Is Prayer. (ps-3). 1993. 5.99 (*0-8024-7859-X*) Moody.
—What Is the Bible? 32p. (gr. 3-7). 1982. pap. 4.99 (*0-8024-6157-3*) Moody.
—Who Is God? 32p. (ps-2). 1980. pap. 4.99 (*0-8024-6158-1*) Moody.
—Who Is Jesus? 32p. (ps-2). 1980. pap. 4.99 (*0-8024-6159-X*) Moody.
—Why Do I Do Things Wrong? 32p. (ps-2). 1981. pap. 4.99 (*0-8024-6160-3*) Moody.
Nystrom, Carolyn & Floding, Matthew. Relationships: Face to Face. (Illus.). 64p. (Orig.). (gr. 7 up). 1986. saddle-stitched student ed. 3.99 (*0-87788-722-5*); saddle-stitched tchr's. ed. 4.99 (*0-87788-723-3*) Shaw Pubs.
—Sexuality: God's Good Idea. (Illus.). 64p. (Orig.). (gr. 9-12). 1988. saddle-stitched student ed. 3.99 (*0-87788-764-0*); saddle-stitched tchr's. ed. 4.99 (*0-87788-765-9*) Shaw Pubs.
Nystrom, Carolyn, jt. auth. see Fromer, Margaret.
Nystrom, Carolyn. Jenny & Grandpa: What Is It Like to Grow Old? Bellwood, Shirley, illus. 48p. (gr. 9-12). 1988. 7.99 (*0-7459-1396-2*) Lion USA.
Nystul, Mike & Smith, Lester. Mechwarrior. 2nd ed. Ippolito, Donna & Mullvihill, Sharon T., eds. Venters, Steve & Knutson, Dana, illus. 167p. (Orig.). (gr. 7 up). 1991. pap. 15.00 (*1-55560-129-4*) FASA Corp.

O

Oakes, Catherine. The Middle Ages. Biesty, Stephen, illus. 28p. (gr. 3-7). 1989. 14.95 (*0-15-200451-3*, Gulliver Bks) HarBrace.
Oakes, Donald T., ed. see Irving, Washington.
Oakes, Terry, illus. A Pull-the-Tab Pop-Up Book of Classic Tales of Horror. Marshall, Ray, designed by. (Illus.). 10p. (gr. 5 up). 1988. 13.95 (*0-525-44418-1*, DCB) Dutton Child Bks.
Oakeshott, R. Ewart. Knight & His Castle. Oakeshott, R. Ewart, illus. 108p. 1992. 16.95 (*0-8023-1294-2*) Dufour.
Oakland, Don. Wildwoods Dad. Schley, Cynthia, illus. 220p. (Orig.). (gr. 5 up). 1987. pap. 6.95 (*0-9615242-1-9*) Oak Pr.
Oakley, Don. The Adventure of Christian Fast. Wiggins, D. Kevin, illus. LC 88-8001. 279p. (Orig.). (gr. 9 up). 1989. 12.95 (*0-9619465-1-2*); pap. 8.95 (*0-9619465-2-0*) Eyrie Pr.
Oakley, Graham. The Church Mice & the Moon. Oakley, Graham, illus. LC 74-75569. 40p. (gr. k-3). 1974. SBE 13.95 (*0-689-30437-4*, Atheneum Childrens Bks) Macmillan Child Grp.
—The Church Mice & the Ring. Oakley, Graham, illus. LC 91-45273. 32p. (ps up). 1992. SBE 14.95 (*0-689-31790-5*, Atheneum Child Bk) Macmillan Child Grp.
—The Church Mice in Action. LC 82-11394. (Illus.). 32p. (gr. k-3). 1983. SBE 13.95 (*0-689-30949-X*, Atheneum Child Bk) Macmillan Child Grp.
—The Church Mice Spread Their Wings. Oakley, Graham, illus. LC 75-15102. 40p. (gr. k-3). 1976. SBE 13.95 (*0-689-30496-X*, Atheneum Child Bk) Macmillan Child Grp.
—The Church Mouse. Oakley, Graham, illus. LC 72-75276. 40p. (gr. k-3). 1972. SBE 13.95 (*0-689-30058-1*, Atheneum Child Bk) Macmillan Child Grp.
—The Church Mouse. (Illus.). 40p. (gr. k-4). 1980. pap. 4.95 (*0-689-70475-5*, Aladdin) Macmillan Child Grp.
—Hetty & Harriet. Oakley, Graham, illus. LC 81-8024. 32p. (gr. k-3). 1982. SBE 13.95 (*0-689-30888-4*, Atheneum Child Bk) Macmillan Child Grp.
Oakley, Ruth. Board & Card Games. LC 88-28710. (Illus.). 48p. (gr. 4-8). 1990. PLB 15.95 (*1-85435-082-X*) Marshall Cavendish.
—Chanting Games. LC 88-28774. (Illus.). 48p. (gr. 3-8). 1990. PLB 15.95 (*1-85435-080-3*) Marshall Cavendish.
—Games with Papers & Pencils. LC 88-28711. (Illus.). 48p. (gr. 3-8). 1989. PLB 15.95 (*1-85435-083-8*) Marshall Cavendish.
—Games with Sticks, Stones & Shells. LC 88-28773. (Illus.). 48p. (gr. 3-8). 1989. PLB 15.95 (*1-85435-079-X*) Marshall Cavendish.
—Presidents of the United States: The Illustrated History of the, 8 vols. (Illus.). 512p. 1990. Set. PLB 149.95 (*1-85435-144-3*) Marshall Cavendish.
Oana. Bobby Bear & the Blizzard. LC 80-82950. (Illus.). 32p. (ps-1). 1981. PLB 9.95 (*0-87783-151-3*) Oddo.
—Bobby Bear Goes to the Beach. LC 80-82951. (Illus.). 32p. (ps-1). 1981. PLB 9.95 (*0-87783-153-X*) Oddo.

—Timmy Tiger & the Butterfly Net. LC 80-82954. (Illus.). 32p. (ps-4). 1981. PLB 9.95 (*0-87783-160-2*) Oddo.
—Timmy Tiger & the Masked Bandit. LC 80-82955. (Illus.). 32p. (ps-4). 1981. PLB 9.95x (*0-87783-161-0*) Oddo.
Oana, Katherine. Chirpy Chipmunk. Baird, Tate, ed. Butrick, Lyn M., illus. LC 88-51854. 16p. (Orig.). (ps). 1989. pap. 4.52 (*0-914127-08-X*) Univ Class.
—Kippy Koala. Cooper, William, ed. Butrick, Lyn M., illus. LC 85-51823. 16p. (Orig.). (ps up). 1985. pap. text ed. 3.72 (*0-914127-21-7*) Univ Class.
—Learning the Words of Color. Baird, Tate, ed. Wallace, Dorathye B., illus. LC 86-50866. 32p. (Orig.). (ps-1). 1986. pap. 2.65 (*0-914127-79-9*) Univ Class.
—Lori Lamb. Baird, Tate, ed. Burtick, Lyn M., illus. 16p. (Orig.). (ps-k). 1989. pap. 4.52 (*0-914127-09-8*) Univ Class.
—Minnie Muskrat. Baird, Tate, ed. Butrick, Lyn M., illus. LC 88-51856. 16p. (Orig.). (ps-k). 1989. pap. 4.52 (*0-914127-10-1*) Univ Class.
—Spacebear Lands on Earth. Baird, Tate, ed. Wallace, Dorathye, illus. LC 86-51210. 16p. (Orig.). (ps up). 1988. pap. 3.72 (*0-914127-26-8*) Univ Class.
—The Sporting Way to Reading Comprehension. Cooper, William H., ed. Shuster, Dorarhye, illus. LC 84-51195. 68p. (Orig.). (gr. 3-8). 1984. 5.27 (*0-914127-17-9*) Univ Class.
—Zippy Zebra. Baird, Tate, ed. Butrick, Lyn M., illus. LC 88-51853. 16p. (Orig.). (ps). 1989. pap. 4.52 (*0-914127-11-X*) Univ Class.
Oana, Katy D. The Little Dog Who Wouldn't Be. LC 77-18351. (Illus.). 32p. (gr. 2-4). 1978. PLB 9.95 (*0-87783-150-5*) Oddo.
—Robbie & the Raggedy Scarecrow. LC 77-18349. (Illus.). 32p. (gr. 2-4). 1978. PLB 9.95 (*0-87783-154-8*) Oddo.
—Robbie & the Raggedy Scarecrow. Stephens, Jacquelyn S., illus. LC 77-18349. (gr. k-2). 1978. PLB 5.95 (*0-89508-065-6*) Rainbow Bks.
—Shasta & the Shebang Machine. LC 77-18350. (Illus.). 32p. (gr. 2-4). 1978. PLB 9.95 (*0-87783-152-1*) Oddo.
—Shasta & the Shebang Machine. Stephens, Jacquelyn S., illus. LC 77-18350. (gr. k-2). 1978. PLB 5.95 (*0-89508-066-4*) Rainbow Bks.
Oates, Eddie. Garden Hose Trumpet: and 5 Other Musical Instruments You Can Make. Koelsch, Michael, illus. LC 92-20060. 32p. (gr. 2-5). 1995. 14.00 (*0-06-021478-3*); PLB 13.89 (*0-06-021479-1*) HarpC Child Bks.
Obaba, Al I., ed. Sayings of the Honorable Elijah Muhammad, Vol. II. 49p. 1991. pap. text ed. 3.95 (*0-916157-86-5*) African Islam Miss Pubns.
Obaba, Al I., ed. see African Islamic Mission Staff.
Obaba, Al I., ed. see Deedat, Ahmed.
Obaba, Al I., ed. see Douglass, Frederick.
Obaba, Al I., ed. see Mufassir, Sulayman.
Obaba, Al I., ed. see Osei, G. K.
Obaba, Al I., ed. see Owaida, Mohammad T.
Obaba, Al I., ed. see Perry, Rufus L.
Obaba, Al I., ed. see Westbrook, Henry S.
Obaba, Al-Imam. Adam Clayton Powell, Jr. (Illus.). 43p. (Orig.). 1989. pap. 3.95 (*0-916157-06-7*) African Islam Miss Pubns.
—The Aware Pages: Economic Unity a Must. (Illus.). 43p. (Orig.). 1988. pap. text ed. 2.50 (*0-916157-05-9*) African Islam Miss Pubns.
—Dr. Martin Luther King, Jr. (Illus.). 43p. (Orig.). 1989. pap. 3.95 (*0-916157-14-8*) African Islam Miss Pubns.
—Emperor Haile Selassie. (Illus.). 43p. (Orig.). 1989. pap. 3.95 (*0-916157-07-5*) African Islam Miss Pubns.
—Harriet Tubman Great Nubian Quiz. (Illus.). 43p. (Orig.). 1989. pap. 3.95 (*0-916157-09-1*) African Islam Miss Pubns.
—Malcolm X Great Nubian Quiz. (Illus.). 43p. (Orig.). 1988. pap. 3.95 (*0-916157-16-4*) African Islam Miss Pubns.
—Marcus Mosiah Garvey, Jr. Great Nubian Quiz. (Illus.). 43p. (Orig.). 1989. pap. 3.95 (*0-916157-15-6*) African Islam Miss Pubns.
—Sojourner Truth Great Nubian Quiz. (Illus.). 43p. (Orig.). 1989. pap. 3.95 (*0-916157-08-3*) African Islam Miss Pubns.
Obaba, Al-Imam & Abdullah. The Why & How of Burial & Death of a Muslim. (Illus.). 24p. (Orig.). 1985. pap. 1.50 (*0-916157-03-2*) African Islam Miss Pubns.
Obaba, Al-Imam & Chisa. The Name Book: The One You've Been Waiting For. 48p. (Orig.). 1977. pap. 3.95 (*0-916157-12-1*) African Islam Miss Pubns.
O'Banyon, Constance. Song of the Nightingale. 1992. pap. 8.99 (*0-06-104122-X*, Harp PBks) HarpC.
Obedin, Harry. Peter Penguin & the Polar Sea. Strecker, Rebekah J., illus. LC 88-63171. 32p. (Orig.). (ps-4). 1989. pap. 4.95 (*0-943990-54-8*) Parenting Pr.
Ober, Hal, retold by. How Music Came into the World. Ober, Carol, illus. LC 93-11330. Date not set. write for info. (*0-395-67523-5*) HM.
Oberg, Pearl, jt. auth. see Stanley, Samuel.
Obergfoll, Michael. Super Santa of All Space & Beyond Assisted by His Galaxy Elves. Jew, Flora, illus. 38p. (gr. 2-12). 1988. 2.95 (*0-929052-00-5*) Super Santa Prodns.
—Super Santa of All Space & Beyond Assisted by His Galaxy Elves: Coloring Activity Book. Obergfoll, Michael, illus. LC 72-847. 34p. (gr. 2-12). 1988. 10.95 (*0-929052-01-3*) Super Santa Prodns.

Oberkotter, Mildred, et al, eds. The Possible Dream: Mainstream Experiences of Hearing-Impaired Students. 68p. (Orig.). 1990. pap. text ed. 7.95 (*0-88200-171-X*) Alexander Graham.
Oberle, Joseph G. Anchorage. LC 89-26068. (Illus.). 60p. (gr. 3 up). 1990. RSBE 13.95 (*0-87518-420-0*, Dillon) Macmillan Child Grp.
Oberman, Sheldon. The Always Prayer Shawl. Lewin, Ted, illus. 32p. (gr. 2 up). 1994. 14.95 (*1-878093-22-3*) Boyds Mills Pr.
—Lion in the Lake - Le Lion dans le Lac. Barham, Scott, illus. (ENG & FRE.). 56p. (gr. k-3). 1988. 14.95 (*0-920541-36-4*) Peguis Pub Ltd.
—TV Sal & the Game Show from Outer Space. (gr. 4-7). 1993. 12.95 (*0-88995-093-8*, Pub. by Red Deer CN) Empire Pub Srvs.
Oberman, Sheldon, jt. auth. see Penner, Fred.
Obligado, Lilian. The Chocolate Cow. LC 91-27464. (Illus.). 48p. (ps-2). 1993. pap. 14.00 JRT (*0-671-73852-6*, S&S BFYR) S&S Trade.
—Guess the Animal! 1990. pap. write for info. (*0-307-12165-8*, Golden Pr) Western Pub.
Obligado, Lillian. Faint Frogs Feeling Feverish. (Illus.). 32p. (ps-3). 1986. pap. 3.95 (*0-14-050507-5*, Puffin) Puffin Bks.
Obojski, Robert. Baseball Bloopers & Diamond Oddities. LC 89-31270. (Illus.). 128p. 1991. pap. 4.95 (*0-8069-6981-4*) Sterling.
Obojski, Robert, ed. see Hobson, Burton H.
Obold, Ruth. Prepare for Peace, Pt. I. (Illus.). 40p. (gr. 1-3). 1986. 6.25 (*0-87303-116-4*) Faith & Life.
—Prepare for Peace, Pt. II. (Illus.). 48p. (gr. 4-6). 1986. 6.25 (*0-87303-117-2*) Faith & Life.
—Prepare for Peace, Pt. III. (Illus.). 55p. (gr. 7-8). 1986. 6.25 (*0-87303-118-0*) Faith & Life.
O'Brian, Michael. I Helped Save the Earth! (gr. 4-7). 1991. pap. 3.95 (*0-425-12830-X*, Berkley Trade) Berkley Pub.
O'Brian, Steven. Ulysses S. Grant. Schlesinger, Arthur M., intro. by. (Illus.). 112p. (gr. 5 up). 1991. 17.95x (*1-55546-809-8*) Chelsea Hse.
O'Brien, Anne S. I Don't Want to Go. O'Brien, Anne S., illus. LC 85-82108. 14p. (ps-2). 1986. bds. 3.95 (*0-8050-0051-8*, Bks Young Read) H Holt & Co.
—The Princess & the Beggar: A Korean Folktale. LC 92-11988. (Illus.). 32p. (gr. k-4). 1993. 14.95 (*0-590-46092-7*) Scholastic Inc.
O'Brien, Edna. Tales for the Telling. Foreman, Michael, illus. LC 87-62364. 128p. (ps up). 1988. pap. 8.95 (*0-14-032293-0*, Puffin) Puffin Bks.
O'Brien, Elaine F. Anita of Rancho del Mar. Cunningham, Richard W., illus. LC 90-19711. 176p. (Orig.). (gr. 4-8). 1991. pap. 8.95 (*0-931832-79-9*) Fithian Pr.
O'Brien, Jane. Alien. (Illus.). 48p. (gr. 5-6). 1991. RSBE 13.95 (*0-89686-573-8*, Crestwood Hse) Macmillan Child Grp.
O'Brien, John. The Twelve Days of Christmas. (Illus.). 32p. 1993. 14.95 (*1-56397-142-9*) Boyds Mills Pr.
O'Brien, John & Taylor-Boyd, Susan, eds. Children of the World: England. Kato, Setsvo, photos by. LC 89-4462. (Illus.). 64p. (gr. 5-6). 1989. PLB 19.93 (*1-55532-211-5*) Gareth Stevens Inc.
O'Brien, Marie, jt. auth. see Kearns, Kimberly.
O'Brien, Mary. Counting Sheep to Sleep. (ps-3). 1992. 13.95 (*0-316-62206-0*) Little.
O'Brien, Mary B., jt. auth. see McCarney-Muldoon, Eileen.
O'Brien, Mike, jt. auth. see Noble, Dennis L.
O'Brien, P. M. The Promoter: His Life & Times. (Illus.). 118p. (gr. 10-12). 1988. pap. 5.65 (*0-9620540-0-3*) P M O'Brien.
O'Brien, Richard. Evil. (Orig.). (gr. 7 up). 1989. pap. 3.50 (*0-440-20226-4*) Dell.
O'Brien, Robert C. Mrs. Frisby & the Rats of NIMH. Bernstein, Zena, illus. LC 74-134818. 240p. (gr. 3-7). 1971. SBE 14.95 (*0-689-20651-8*, Atheneum Child Bk) Macmillan Child Grp.
—Mrs. Frisby & the Rats of NIMH. 248p. (gr. 3-7). 1986. pap. 3.95 (*0-689-71068-2*, Aladdin) Macmillan Child Grp.
—Secret of Nimh. 1988. pap. 2.75 (*0-590-41708-8*) Scholastic Inc.
—The Silver Crown. LC 88-2837. 272p. (gr. 7 up). 1988. pap. 3.95 (*0-02-044651-9*, Collier Young Ad) Macmillan Child Grp.
—Z for Zachariah. LC 74-76736. 256p. (gr. 7 up). 1975. SBE 14.95 (*0-689-30442-0*, Atheneum Child Bk) Macmillan Child Grp.
—Z for Zachariah. LC 86-23228. 256p. (gr. 7 up). 1987. pap. 3.95 (*0-02-044650-0*, Collier Young Ad) Macmillan Child Grp.
O'Brien, Steve. Alexander Hamilton. Schlesinger, Arthur M., Jr., intro. by. (Illus.). 112p. (gr. 5 up). 1989. 17.95 (*1-55546-810-1*) Chelsea Hse.
O'Brien, Steven. Pancho Villa: Mexican Revolutionary. (Illus.). 112p. (gr. 6-12). 1994. PLB 18.95 (*0-7910-1257-3*, Am Art Analog) Chelsea Hse.
O'Brien, Teresa. I Love You Shyly. LC 91-40298. (gr. 4 up). 1985. 5.95 (*0-85953-318-2*) Childs Play.
—Memories. LC 90-46155. 1985. 5.95 (*0-85953-310-1*) Childs Play.
O'Brien, Theresa. Little Fish in a Big Pond. LC 90-46519. (ps-3). 1990. 7.95 (*0-85953-390-5*); pap. 3.95 (*0-85953-391-3*) Childs Play.
O'Brien, Thomas C. Puzzle Tables: Number Problems with Computational Skills. (gr. 4-7). 1980. pap. 8.50 (*0-201-48011-5*) Addison-Wesley.

O'Brien, Thomas C. Wollygoggles & Other Creatures: Problems for Developing Thinking Skills. 64p. (gr. 3 up). 1980. pap. text ed. 8.50 (*0-914040-85-5*) Cuisenaire.
—Woolygoggles & Other Creatures: Problems for Developing Thinking Skills. (gr. 4-7). 1992. pap. 8.50 (*0-201-48018-2*) Addison-Wesley.
O'Brien-Palmer, Michelle. Book-Write: A Creative Bookmaking Guide for Young Authors. Rubin, Shannon, illus. LC 91-68412. 128p. (gr. k-6). 1992. pap. 16.95 (*1-879235-01-3*) MicNik Pubns.
O'Bries, Thomas C. Puzzle Tables. 64p. (gr. 3-8). 1980. pap. text ed. 8.50 (*0-914040-83-9*) Cuisenaire.
Obstfeld, Raymond. The Joker & the Thief. LC 92-9823. 1993. 15.00 (*0-385-30855-8*) Delacorte.
O'Byrne-Pelham, Fran & Balcer, Bernadette. The Search for the Atocha Treasure. LC 88-20201. (Illus.). 128p. (gr. 4 up). 1988. RSBE 14.95 (*0-87518-399-9*, Dillon) Macmillan Child Grp.
O'Byrne-Pelham, Fran, jt. auth. see Balcer, Bernadette.
O'Callaghan, Myrnie. A Boy Called Mish Mash. LC 91-92177. 100p. (Orig.). (gr. 5-8). 1991. pap. 9.95 (*0-9630075-0-5*) Creole Connect.
O'Callahan, Jay. Orange Cheeks. Raine, Patricia, illus. LC 92-43509. 40p. (ps-3). 1983. 15.95 (*1-56145-073-1*) Peachtree Pubs.
—Tulips. Santini, Debrah, illus. LC 91-41704. 28p. (gr. k up). 1992. pap. 14.95 (*0-88708-223-8*) Picture Bk Studio.
Ochieng, William R. People of the South-Western Highlands: Gusii. (Illus.). 34p. (gr. 6-9). 1991. pap. 4.95 (*0-237-49898-7*, Pub. by Evans Bros Ltd) Trafalgar.
—People Round the Lake: Luo. (Illus.). 32p. (gr. 6-9). 1991. pap. 4.95 (*0-237-50924-5*, Pub. by Evans Bros Ltd) Trafalgar.
Ochoa, George. The Assassination of Julius Caesar. (Illus.). 64p. (gr. 7 up). 1991. PLB 16.98 (*0-382-24130-4*); pap. 8.95 (*0-382-24136-3*) Silver Burdett Pr.
—The Fall of Mexico City. (Illus.). 64p. (gr. 5 up). 1989. PLB 16.98 (*0-382-09836-0*); pap. 8.95 (*0-382-09853-6*) Silver Burdett Pr.
—The Fall of Quebec & the French & Indian War. (Illus.). 64p. (gr. 5 up). 1990. PLB 16.98 (*0-382-09954-0*); pap. 8.95 (*0-382-09950-8*) Silver Burdett Pr.
—Let's Visit a Bicycle Factory. Fisher, Jon & Halpern, John, illus. LC 89-35714. 32p. (gr. 2-4). 1990. PLB 10.79 (*0-8167-1739-7*); pap. text ed. 2.95 (*0-8167-1740-0*) Troll Assocs.
Ochs, Bill. The Clarke Learn to Play Tin Whistle Set. (Illus.). 80p. (Orig.). (gr. 3 up). 1988. pap. 6.95 (*0-9623456-0-1*); pap. 14.95 incl. cassette (*0-9623456-5-2*); Incl. tin whistle & cassette in blister package. pap. 24.95 (*0-9623456-2-8*) Pnnywhstlrs Pr.
Ochs, Carol P. Moose on the Loose. Mitchell, Anastasia, illus. 32p. (ps-4). 1991. PLB 18.95 (*0-87614-448-2*) Carolrhoda Bks.
—When I'm Alone. (ps-3). 1993. 18.95 (*0-87614-752-X*) Carolrhoda Bks.
—When I'm Alone. (ps-3). 1993. pap. 6.95 (*0-87614-620-5*) Carolrhoda Bks.
Ockenga, Earl & Rucker, Walt. Money. Dawson, Dave, illus. 16p. (gr. 1). 1990. pap. text ed. 1.25 (*1-56281-125-8*, M125) Extra Eds.
—Place Value to One Hundred. Dawson, Dave, illus. 16p. (gr. 1). 1990. pap. text ed. 1.25 (*1-56281-115-0*, M115) Extra Eds.
—Subtracting from Eighteen or Less. Dawson, Dave, illus. 16p. (gr. 1). 1990. pap. text ed. 1.25 (*1-56281-135-5*, M135) Extra Eds.
—Subtracting from Ten or Less. Dawson, Dave, illus. 16p. (gr. 1). 1990. pap. text ed. 1.25 (*1-56281-110-X*, M110) Extra Eds.
—Sums Through Eighteen. Dawson, Dave, illus. 16p. (gr. 1). 1990. pap. text ed. 1.25 (*1-56281-130-4*, M130) Extra Eds.
—Sums Through Ten. Dawson, Dave, illus. 16p. (gr. 1). 1990. pap. text ed. 1.25 (*1-56281-105-3*, M105) Extra Eds.
—Telling Time. Dawson, Dave, illus. 16p. (gr. 1). 1990. pap. text ed. 1.25 (*1-56281-120-7*, M120) Extra Eds.
O'Collins, Gerald. Friends in Faith. 112p. (gr. 10-12). 1989. pap. 4.95 (*0-8091-3086-6*) Paulist Pr.
O'Connell, Frances H. Giving & Growing: A Student's Guide for Service Projects. Stamschror, Robert P., ed. Mediawerks Staff, illus. 79p. (Orig.). (gr. 7-12). 1990. text ed. 3.50 stitched (*0-88489-224-7*); tchr's. ed. 3.95 (*0-88489-225-5*) St Marys.
O'Connell, June. His & Hers. 1993. pap. 2.99 (*0-553-29980-8*) Bantam.
—Love on the Upbeat. 1992. pap. 2.99 (*0-553-29455-5*) Bantam.
—Time Out for Love. 1991. pap. 2.99 (*0-553-29059-2*) Bantam.
—Why Must I Choose? 143p. (gr. 5-8). 1992. pap. 2.75 (*0-87406-631-X*) Willowisp Pr.
O'Connell, Lily H., et al. Nutrition in a Changing World: Grade Five. 152p. (Illus.). (gr. 5). 1981. pap. text ed. 11.95 (*0-8425-1916-5*) Brigham.
O'Connell, Margaret. The Magic Cauldron: Witchcraft for Good & Evil. LC 75-26757. (Illus.). 256p. (gr. 9-12). 1975. 32.95 (*0-87599-187-4*) S G Phillips.
O'Connor, Barbara. Barefoot Dancer: The Story of Isadora Duncan. LC 93-14312. (gr. 5 up). 1994. 17.50 (*0-87614-807-0*) Carolrhoda Bks.

—Mammolina: A Story about Maria Montessori. LC 92-415. 1993. lib. bdg. 14.95 (*0-87614-743-0*); pap. 5.95 (*0-87614-602-7*) Carolrhoda Bks.
O'Connor, Daniel, adapted by see Barrie, James M.
O'Connor, Edmund. Darwin. Yapp, Malcolm, et al, eds. (Illus.). 32p. (gr. 6-11). 1980. pap. text ed. 3.45 (*0-89908-022-7*) Greenhaven.
—Education. Yapp, Malcolm & O'Connor, Edmund, eds. (Illus.). 32p. (gr. 6-10). 1980. pap. text ed. 3.45 (*0-89908-122-3*) Greenhaven.
—Japan's Modernization. Yapp, Malcolm & Killingray, Marget, eds. (Illus.). (gr. 6-11). 1980. pap. text ed. 3.45 (*0-89908-207-6*) Greenhaven.
—Roosevelt. Yapp, Malcolm & Killingray, Margaret, eds. (Illus.). 32p. (gr. 6-11). 1980. pap. text ed. 3.45 (*0-89908-100-2*) Greenhaven.
—The Wealth of Japan. Yapp, Malcolm, et al, eds. (Illus.). 32p. (gr. 6-11). 1980. pap. text ed. 3.45 (*0-89908-212-2*) Greenhaven.
O'Connor, Edmund, ed. see Doncaster, Islay.
O'Connor, Edmund, ed. see Killingray, David.
O'Connor, Edmund, ed. see Killingray, Margaret.
O'Connor, Edmund, ed. see O'Connor, Edmund.
O'Connor, Edmund, ed. see Read, James & Yapp, Malcolm.
O'Connor, Edmund, ed. see Yapp, Malcolm.
O'Connor, Edwin. Benjy: A Ferocious Fairy Tale. LC 88-46131. (Illus.). 128p. (gr. 5 up). 1988. 14.95 (*0-87923-795-3*) Godine.
O'Connor, Francine. You & God: Friends Forever - A Faith Book for Catholic Children. (Illus.). 64p. (gr. 1-4). 1993. pap. text ed. 2.95 (*0-89243-515-1*) Liguori Pubns.
O'Connor, Francine & Boswell, Kathryn. ABC's of the Ten Commandments. (Illus.). 32p. (gr. 1-4). 1980. pap. 2.95 (*0-89243-125-3*) Liguori Pubns.
O'Connor, Francine M. The ABC's Lessons of Love: Sermon on the Mount for Children. Boswell, Kathryr, illus. 48p. (gr. 6-8). 1991. pap. text ed. 4.95 (*0-89243-345-0*) Liguori Pubns.
—The ABC's of Prayer...for Children. Boswell, Kathryn, illus. 32p. (gr. 1-5). 1989. pap. 2.95 (*0-89243-317-5*) Liguori Pubns.
—ABCs of the Mass...for Children. Boswell, Kathryn, illus. 32p. (Orig.). (ps-4). 1988. pap. text ed. 2.95 (*0-89243-291-8*) Liguori Pubns.
—ABCs of the Old Testament...for Children. Boswell, Kathryn, illus. 32p. (gr. 1-5). 1989. pap. 2.95 (*0-89243-310-8*) Liguori Pubns.
—ABCs of the Sacraments...for Children. Nolte, Larry, illus. 32p. (gr. k-3). 1989. pap. 2.95 (*0-89243-298-5*) Liguori Pubns.
—My Lenten Walk with Jesus. (Illus.). 32p. (gr. 1-3). 1992. pap. 1.95 incl. cut-out Lenten calendar (*0-89243-421-X*); pap. 9.95 incl. tchr's packet (*0-89243-420-1*) Liguori Pubns.
—Wait & Wonder. (Illus.). 16p. (gr. 1-3). 1991. pap. 1.95 (*0-89243-419-8*); incl. tchr's. packet 9.95 (*0-89243-418-X*) Liguori Pubns.
O'Connor, Francine M. & Boswell, Kathryn. The ABC's of Faith: God & You. (gr. 1-4). 1979. Bk. 1. pap. 2.95 (*0-89243-113-X*) Liguori Pubns.
—The ABC'S of the Rosary. (Illus.). 32p. (gr. 1-4). 1984. pap. 2.95 (*0-89243-221-7*) Liguori Pubns.
O'Connor, Frank. First Confessions. 32p. (gr. 3 up). 1986. 13.95 (*0-88682-058-8*) Creative Ed.
—My Oedipus Complex. Delessert, Etienne, illus. LC 85-32526. 40p. (gr. 4 up). 1986. PLB 13.95s.p. (*0-88682-062-6*) Creative Ed.
O'Connor, Genevieve A. The Admiral & the Deck Boy: One Boy's Journey with Christopher Columbus. LC 91-17978. (Illus.). 168p. (gr. 5 up). 1991. 12.95 (*1-55870-218-0*) Shoe Tree Pr.
O'Connor, Jane. Amy's (Not So) Great Camp-Out. Long, Laurie S., illus. LC 92-45881. 64p. (gr. 1-4). 1993. 7.99 (*0-448-40167-3*, G&D); pap. 3.95 (*0-448-40166-5*, G&D) Putnam Pub Group.
—The Care Bears' Party Cookbook. Sustendal, Pat, illus. LC 84-18252. 48p. (gr. k-3). 1985. pap. 2.95 (*0-394-87305-X*) Random Bks Yng Read.
—Corrie's Secret Pal. Long, Laurie S., illus. LC 92-35602. 64p. (gr. 1-4). 1993. 7.99 (*0-448-40161-4*, G&D); pap. 3.95 (*0-448-40160-6*, G&D) Putnam Pub Group.
—Eek! Stories to Make You Shriek. Karas, Brian, illus. 48p. (gr. 1-3). 1992. (G&D); pap. 3.50 (*0-448-40382-X*, G&D) Putnam Pub Group.
—Lulu & the Witch Baby. McCully, Emily A., illus. LC 85-45832. 64p. (gr. k-3). 1986. PLB 13.89 (*0-06-024627-8*) HarpC Child Bks.
—Lulu & the Witch Baby. LC 85-45832. (Illus.). 64p. (gr. k-3). 1989. pap. 3.50 (*0-06-444130-X*, Trophy) HarpC Child Bks.
—Lulu Goes to Witch School. McCully, Emily A., illus. LC 87-37. 64p. (gr. k-3). 1987. HarpC Child Bks.
—Lulu Goes to Witch School. McCully, Emily A., illus. LC 87-37. 64p. (gr. k-3). 1990. pap. 3.50 (*0-06-444138-5*, Trophy) HarpC Child Bks.
—Make up Your Mind, Marsha! Long, Laurie S., illus. LC 92-45880. 64p. (gr. 1-4). 1993. 7.99 (*0-448-40165-7*, G&D); pap. 3.95 (*0-448-40164-9*, G&D) Putnam Pub Group.
—Molly the Brave & Me. Hamanaka, Sheila, illus. LC 89-10864. 48p. (Orig.). (gr. 1-3). 1990. lib. bdg. 7.99 (*0-394-94175-6*); pap. 3.50 (*0-394-84175-1*) Random Bks Yng Read.

—Nina, Nina, Ballerina. DiSalvo-Ryan, DyAnne, illus. LC 92-24465. 32p. (ps-1). 1993. lib. bdg. 7.99 (*0-448-40512-1*, G&D); pap. 3.50 (*0-448-40511-3*, G&D) Putnam Pub Group.
—Sarah's Incredible Idea. Long, Laurie S., illus. LC 92-36803. 64p. (gr. 1-4). 1993. 7.99g (*0-448-40163-0*, G&D); pap. 3.95 (*0-448-40162-2*, G&D) Putnam Pub Group.
—Sir Small & the Dragonfly. O'Brien, John, illus. LC 87-35309. 32p. (Orig.). (ps-1). 1988. lib. bdg. 7.99 (*0-394-99625-9*); 3.50 (*0-394-89625-4*, Random Juv) Random Bks Yng Read.
—Splat! Mets, Marilyn, illus. LC 93-34127. (gr. 3 up). 1994. 3.50 (*0-448-40220-3*, G&D); pap. write for info. (*0-448-40219-X*) Putnam Pub Group.
—Yours till Niagara Falls, Abby. 128p. (Orig.). (gr. 3-7). 1991. pap. 2.75 (*0-590-42854-3*) Scholastic Inc.
O'Connor, Jane & O'Connor, Jim. The Ghost in Tent Nineteen. Williams, Richard, illus. LC 87-82372. 64p. (Orig.). (gr. 2-4). 1988. lib. bdg. 6.99 (*0-394-99800-6*); pap. 2.50 (*0-394-89800-1*) Random Bks Yng Read.
O'Connor, Jane & O'Connor, Robert. Super Cluck. Lloyd, Megan, illus. LC 90-32832. 64p. (ps-3). 1991. 11.95 (*0-06-024594-8*); PLB 11.89 (*0-06-024595-6*) HarpC Child Bks.
—Super Cluck. Lloyd, Megan, illus. LC 90-32832. 64p. (gr. k-3). 1993. pap. 3.50 (*0-06-444162-8*, Trophy) HarpC Child Bks.
O'Connor, Jane, jt. auth. see O'Connor, Jim.
O'Connor, Jane, retold by. The Teeny Tiny Woman. Alley, R. W., illus. LC 86-485. 32p. (ps-1). 1986. lib. bdg. 7.99 (*0-394-98320-3*); pap. 3.50 (*0-394-88320-9*, Random Juv) Random Bks Yng Read.
O'Connor, Jim. Comeback! Four True Stories. Campbell, Jim, illus. LC 91-25028. 48p. (Orig.). (gr. 2-4). 1992. PLB 7.99 (*0-679-92666-6*); pap. 3.50 (*0-679-82666-1*) Random Bks Yng Read.
—Jackie Robinson & the Story of All-Black Baseball. Butcher, Jim, illus. LC 88-18466. 48p. (Orig.). (gr. 2-4). 1989. PLB 7.99 (*0-394-92456-8*); pap. 3.50 (*0-394-82456-3*) Random Bks Yng Read.
—Story of Roberto Clemente. (gr. 4-7). 1991. pap. 2.95 (*0-440-40425-8*) Dell.
O'Connor, Jim & O'Connor, Jane. Slime Time. Porter, Pat, illus. LC 89-77324. 64p. (Orig.). (gr. 2-4). 1990. PLB 6.99 (*0-679-90714-9*); pap. 2.50 (*0-679-80714-4*) Random Bks Yng Read.
O'Connor, Jim, jt. auth. see O'Connor, Jane.
O'Connor, Karen. Dan Thuy's New Life in America. (Illus.). 40p. (gr. 4-8). 1992. PLB 17.50 (*0-8225-2555-0*) Lerner Pubns.
—The Feather Book. LC 90-2959. (Illus.). 60p. (gr. 4 up). 1991. RSBE 14.95 (*0-87518-445-6*, Dillon) Macmillan Child Grp.
—Garbage. LC 89-9382. (Illus.). 96p. (gr. 5-8). 1989. PLB 14.95 (*1-56006-100-6*) Lucent Bks.
—The Green Team: The Adventures of Mitch & Molly. Chapin, Patrick O., illus. LC 92-24643. 80p. (Orig.). (gr. 1-4). 1993. pap. 4.95 (*0-570-04726-9*) Concordia.
—The Herring Gull. LC 91-40856. (Illus.). 60p. (gr. 4 up). 1992. RSBE 13.95 (*0-87518-506-1*, Dillon) Macmillan Child Grp.
—Homeless Children. LC 89-37553. (Illus.). 96p. (gr. 5-8). 1989. PLB 14.95 (*1-56006-109-X*) Lucent Bks.
—Let's Take a Walk on the Beach. Axeman, Lois, illus. LC 86-9551. 32p. (ps-2). 1986. PLB 21.35 (*0-89565-354-0*); PLB 14.95s.p. (*0-685-55822-3*) Childs World.
—San Diego. (Illus.). 60p. (gr. 3 up). 1990. RSBE 13.95 (*0-87518-439-1*, Dillon) Macmillan Child Grp.
—The Water Detectives: The Adventures of Mitch & Molly. Chapin, Patrick O., illus. LC 92-24649. 80p. (Orig.). (gr. 1-4). 1993. pap. 4.95 (*0-570-04727-7*) Concordia.
O'Connor, Karen & Crowdy, Deborah. Let's Take a Walk in the City. Axeman, Lois, illus. LC 86-20746. 32p. (ps-2). 1986. PLB 21.35 (*0-89565-355-9*); PLB 14.95s.p. (*0-685-55819-3*) Childs World.
O'Connor, Patricia. Hitting the Nail on the Head. Trotter, Candace L., ed. 112p. (Orig.). (gr. 8 up). 1991. pap. text ed. 9.95 (*0-9622684-0-2*) Nugget Pub.
O'Connor, Robert, jt. auth. see O'Connor, Jane.
O'Connor, Thomas H. Bibles, Brahmins, & Bosses: A Short History of Boston. 3rd, rev. ed. (Illus.). 271p. (Orig.). 1991. 12.00 (*0-89073-082-2*) Boston Public Lib.
O'Connor-Mikolai, Marie. Ginny, a Friend for All Seasons, Bk. One: Winter in Ginny's World. 1991. 14.95 (*0-533-09490-9*) Vantage.
Oda, Hidetomo. Animals of the Seashore. LC 85-28192. (Illus.). 32p. (gr. 3-7). 1986. PLB 17.96 (*0-8172-2543-9*) Raintree Steck-V.
—Butterflies. Pohl, Kathy, ed. LC 85-28196. (Illus.). 32p. (gr. 3-7). 1986. text ed. 17.96 (*0-8172-2531-5*) Raintree Steck-V.
—The Diving Beetle. Pohl, Kathy, ed. LC 85-28300. (Illus.). 32p. (gr. 3-7). 1986. PLB 17.96 (*0-8172-2533-1*) Raintree Steck-V.
—Dragonflies. Pohl, Kathy, ed. LC 85-28197. (Illus.). 32p. (gr. 3-7). 1986. text ed. 17.96 (*0-8172-2534-X*) Raintree Steck-V.
—Insect Hibernation. Pohl, Kathy, ed. LC 85-2892. (Illus.). 32p. (gr. 3-7). 1986. text ed. 17.96 (*0-8172-2526-9*) Raintree Steck-V.
—Insects & Flowers. Pohl, Kathy, ed. LC 85-28206. (Illus.). 32p. (gr. 3-7). 1986. text ed. 17.96 (*0-8172-2527-7*) Raintree Steck-V.

—Insects & Their Homes. Pohl, Kathleen, ed. LC 85-28226. (Illus.). 32p. (gr. 3-7). 1986. PLB 17.96 (*0-8172-2528-5*) Raintree Steck-V.
—Insects in the Pond. Pohl, Kathy, ed. LC 85-28227. (Illus.). 32p. (gr. 3-7). 1986. text ed. 17.96 (*0-8172-2529-3*) Raintree Steck-V.
—The Ladybug. Pohl, Kathy, ed. LC 85-28199. (Illus.). 32p. (gr. 3-7). 1986. text ed. 17.96 (*0-8172-2538-2*) Raintree Steck-V.
—Observing Bees & Wasps. Pohl, Kathy, ed. LC 85-28195. (Illus.). 32p. (gr. 3-7). 1986. PLB 17.96 (*0-8172-2540-4*) Raintree Steck-V.
—Snails. LC 85-28211. (Illus.). 32p. (gr. 3-7). 1986. PLB 17.96 (*0-8172-2544-7*) Carlton.
—The Swallowtail Butterfly. Pohl, Kathy, ed. LC 85-28229. (Illus.). 32p. (gr. 3-7). 1986. PLB 17.96 (*0-8172-2542-0*) Raintree Steck-V.
—The Tadpole. Pohl, Kathy, ed. LC 85-28202. (Illus.). 32p. (gr. 3-7). 1986. PLB 17.96 (*0-8172-2545-5*) Raintree Steck-V.
—The Tree Frog: Annual. annual Pohl, Kathy, ed. LC 85-28194. (Illus.). 32p. (gr. 3-7). 1986. PLB 17.96 (*0-8172-2546-3*) Raintree Steck-V.
—The Turtle. Pohl, Kathy, ed. LC 85-28234. (Illus.). 32p. (gr. 3-7). 1986. PLB 17.96 (*0-8172-2547-1*) Raintree Steck-V.
Oda, Stephanie C. My Nighttime Book. 12p. (ps). 1986. 3.25 (*0-8378-5091-6*) Gibson.
—One-Two-Three God Is Good to Me. 12p. (ps). 1986. 2.95 (*0-8378-5092-4*) Gibson.
Oddo, Eileen, jt. auth. see Patella, Chris.
Oddo, Genevieve, ed. see Moore, Silas.
O'Dell, Scott. Alexandra. LC 83-26590. 160p. (gr. 7 up). 1984. 13.45 (*0-395-35571-0*, 5-92366) HM.
—Alexandra. 128p. (gr. 7 up). 1985. pap. 2.25 (*0-449-70135-2*, Juniper) Fawcett.
—The Amethyst Ring. LC 82-23388. 224p. (gr. 7 up). 1983. 14.45 (*0-395-33886-7*) HM.
—Black Pearl. Johnson, Milton, illus. LC 67-23311. 160p. (gr. 7 up). 1967. 13.45 (*0-395-06961-0*) HM.
—Black Star, Bright Dawn. LC 87-35351. 144p. (gr. 5-9). 1988. 14.95 (*0-395-47778-6*) HM.
—The Captive. 244p. (gr. 7 up). 1979. 14.95 (*0-395-27811-2*) HM.
—Carlota. O'Dell, Scott, illus. LC 77-9468. 176p. (gr. 5-9). 1977. 13.45 (*0-395-25487-6*) HM.
—Carlotta. 144p. (gr. k-12). 1989. pap. 3.50 (*0-440-90928-7*, LFL) Dell.
—The Castle in the Sea. 192p. (gr. 7up). 1983. 13.95 (*0-395-34831-5*) HM.
—The Castle in the Sea. 160p. (gr. 7 up). 1984. pap. 3.50 (*0-449-70123-9*, Juniper) Fawcett.
—Dark Canoe. LC 68-29334. (Illus.). 160p. (gr. 7 up). 1968. 13.45 (*0-395-06960-2*) HM.
—The Feathered Serpent. 224p. (gr. 7 up). 1981. 16.95 (*0-395-30851-8*) HM.
—The Hawk That Dare Not Hunt by Day. (Illus.). 192p. (gr. 4-6). 1986. pap. 4.95 (*0-89084-368-6*) Bob Jones Univ Pr.
—Island of the Blue Dolphins. (gr. 7 up). 1960. 13.45 (*0-395-06962-9*) HM.
—Island of the Blue Dolphins. 192p. (gr. k-6). 1987. pap. 3.99 (*0-440-43988-4*, YB) Dell.
—Island of the Blue Dolphins. large type ed. 161p. (gr. 2-6). 1987. Repr. of 1960 ed. lib. bdg. 14.95 (*1-55736-002-2*, Crnrstn Bks) BDD LT Grp.
—Island of the Blue Dolphins. Lewin, Ted, illus. 192p. (gr. 5 up). 1990. 18.45 (*0-395-53680-4*) HM.
—Janey. (gr. 7-12). 1986. write for info. HM.
—Kathleen, Please Come Home. 224p. (gr. 7 up). 1980. pap. 2.25 (*0-440-94283-7*, LFL) Dell.
—King's Fifth. Bryant, Samuel, illus. (gr. 7-10). 1966. 14. 45 (*0-395-06963-7*) HM.
—My Name Is Not Angelica. 144p. (gr. 5-9). 1989. 14.95 (*0-395-51061-9*) HM.
—My Name Is Not Angelica. (gr. k-6). 1990. pap. 3.50 (*0-440-40379-0*, YB) Dell.
—The Road to Damietta. 256p. (gr. 6 up). 1985. 14.45 (*0-395-38923-2*) HM.
—The Road to Damietta. 240p. 1987. pap. 3.99 (*0-449-70233-2*, Juniper) Fawcett.
—Sarah Bishop. (gr. 7 up). 1980. 14.45 (*0-395-29185-2*) HM.
—Sarah Bishop. 240p. (gr. 7up). 1991. pap. 3.25 (*0-590-44651-7*, Point) Scholastic Inc.
—The Serpent Never Sleeps: A Novel of Jamestown & Pocahontas. Lewin, Ted, illus. 240p. (gr. 5 up). 1987. 16.95 (*0-395-44242-7*) HM.
—The Serpent Never Sleeps: A Novel of Jamestown & Pocahontas. (gr. 8 up). 1988. pap. 3.99 (*0-449-70328-2*, Juniper) Fawcett.
—Sing Down the Moon. LC 71-98513. (gr. 5 up). 1970. 13.45 (*0-395-10919-1*) HM.
—Sing Down the Moon. large type ed. 176p. (gr. 9-12). 1989. Repr. of 1970 ed. lib. bdg. 15.95 (*1-55736-142-8*, Crnrstn Bks) BDD LT Grp.
—Sing Down the Moon. 144p. (gr. 5 up). 1992. pap. 3.99 (*0-440-40673-0*, YB) Dell.
—The Spanish Smile. (gr. 7 up). 1982. 13.95 (*0-395-32867-5*) HM.
—Streams to the River, River to the Sea: A Novel of Sacagawea. 1986. 14.45 (*0-395-40430-4*) HM.
—Streams to the River, River to the Sea: A Novel of Sacagawea. large type ed. 312p. (gr. 7 up). 1989. lib. bdg. 14.95 (*0-8161-4811-2*, Large Print Bks) Hall.
—Thunder Rolling in the Mountains. 1993. pap. 3.99 (*0-440-40879-2*) Dell.

—The Two Hundred Ninety. (gr. 5-9). 1976. 15.45 (*0-395-24737-3*) HM.
—Zia. 144p. (gr. 4 up). 1978. pap. 3.50 (*0-440-99904-9*, LFL) Dell.
—Zia. Lewin, Ted, illus. LC 75-44156. 224p. (gr. 4-8). 1976. 14.95 (*0-395-24393-9*) HM.
O'Dell, Scott & Hall, Elizabeth. Thunder Rolling in the Mountains. (Illus.). 144p. (gr. 5-9). 1992. 14.45 (*0-395-59966-0*) HM.
O'Dell, Scott see Newbery Library Award Staff.
Oden, Chester W., Jr., jt. auth. see MacDonald, W. Scott.
Oden, Fay. Calvin & His Video Camera. 1993. 7.95 (*0-8062-4565-4*) Carlton.
Odgers, Sally F. Dog Went for a Walk. Shaw, Peter, illus. LC 92-27100. (gr. 3 up). 1993. 2.50 (*0-383-03564-3*) SRA Schl Grp.
—Drummond: The Search for Sarah. Jones, Carol, illus. LC 90-55198. 112p. (gr. 2-6). 1990. reinforced 16.95 (*0-8234-0851-5*) Holiday.
—Up the Stairs. Hunnam, Lucinda, illus. LC 92-21395. 1993. 4.25 (*0-383-03601-1*) SRA Schl Grp.
—Wiz. Sofilas, Mark, illus. LC 92-31952. 1993. 3.75 (*0-383-03608-9*) SRA Schl Grp.
Odijk, Pamela. The Ancient World, 12 bks. (Illus.). (gr. 5-8). 1991. Set, 48p. ea. lib. bdg. 203.76 (*0-382-09883-8*) Silver Burdett Pr.
—The Aztecs. (Illus.). 48p. (gr. 5-8). 1990. PLB 16.98 (*0-382-09887-0*) Silver Burdett Pr.
—The Chinese. (Illus.). 48p. (gr. 5-8). 1991. PLB 16.98 (*0-382-09894-3*) Silver Burdett Pr.
—The Egyptians. (Illus.). 48p. (gr. 5-8). 1989. PLB 16.98 (*0-382-09886-2*) Silver Burdett Pr.
—The Greeks. (Illus.). 48p. (gr. 5-8). 1989. PLB 16.98 (*0-382-09884-6*) Silver Burdett Pr.
—The Incas. (Illus.). 48p. (gr. 5-8). 1990. PLB 16.98 (*0-382-09889-7*) Silver Burdett Pr.
—The Israelites. (Illus.). 48p. (gr. 5-8). 1990. PLB 16.98 (*0-382-09888-9*) Silver Burdett Pr.
—The Japanese. (Illus.). 48p. (gr. 5-8). 1991. PLB 16.98 (*0-382-09898-6*) Silver Burdett Pr.
—The Mayas. (Illus.). 48p. (gr. 5-8). 1990. PLB 16.98 (*0-382-09890-0*) Silver Burdett Pr.
—The Phoenicians. (Illus.). 48p. (gr. 5-8). 1989. PLB 16. 98 (*0-382-09891-9*) Silver Burdett Pr.
—The Romans. (Illus.). 48p. (gr. 5-8). 1989. PLB 16.98 (*0-382-09885-4*) Silver Burdett Pr.
—The Sumerians. (Illus.). 48p. (gr. 5-8). 1990. PLB 16.98 (*0-382-09892-7*) Silver Burdett Pr.
—The Vikings. Easton, Emily, ed. (Illus.). 48p. (gr. 5-8). 1990. PLB 16.98 (*0-382-09893-5*) Silver Burdett Pr.
Odom, Melissa. A Medal for Murphy. Rice, James, illus. LC 86-25369. 32p. (gr. 1-6). 1987. 12.95 (*0-88289-635-0*) Pelican.
Odom, Melissa W. No Regard Beauregard & the Golden Rule. Rice, James, illus. LC 87-36118. 132p. (gr. k-6). 1988. 12.95 (*0-88289-686-5*) Pelican.
O'Donnell, Elizabeth L. Are You Flying, Charlie Duncan? Milone, Karen, illus. LC 92-39876. 96p. (gr. 4 up). 1993. 14.00 (*0-688-09027-3*) Morrow Jr Bks.
—I Can't Get My Turtle to Move. Chambliss, Maxie, illus. LC 88-22046. 32p. (ps-1). 1989. 11.95 (*0-688-07323-9*); PLB 11.88 (*0-688-07324-7*, Morrow Jr Bks) Morrow Jr Bks.
—Maggie Doesn't Want to Move. Schwartz, Amy, illus. LC 86-23684. 32p. (gr. k-3). 1987. RSBE 13.95 (*0-02-768830-5*, Pub. by Four Winds Pr) Macmillan Child Grp.
—Maggie Doesn't Want to Move. LC 89-18207. (Illus.). 32p. (gr. k-3). 1990. pap. 3.95 (*0-689-71375-4*, Aladdin) Macmillan Child Grp.
—Patrick's Day. Rogers, Jacqueline, illus. LC 92-27421. 1993. write for info. (*0-688-07853-2*); lib. bdg. write for info. (*0-688-07854-0*) Morrow Jr Bks.
—Sing Me a Window. Sweet, Melissa, illus. LC 92-10719. (ps up). 1993. 15.00 (*0-688-09500-3*); PLB 14.93 (*0-688-09501-1*) Morrow Jr Bks.
—The Twelve Days of Summer. Schmidt, Karen L., illus. LC 89-35161. 32p. (ps up). 1991. 13.95 (*0-688-08202-5*); PLB 13.88 (*0-688-08203-3*, Morrow Jr Bks) Morrow Jr Bks.
O'Donnell, Joe, jt. auth. see Doherty, Jim.
O'Donnell, Peggy, jt. auth. see Ingram, Anne.
O'Donnell, Peter. Carnegie's Excuse. O'Donnell, Peter, illus. LC 92-17617. 32p. (ps-3). 1993. 14.95 (*0-590-46435-3*) Scholastic Inc.
—Dizzy. (Illus.). (ps up). 1992. 14.95 (*0-590-45475-7*, 021, Scholastic Hardcover) Scholastic Inc.
—Moonlit Journey. (ps-3). 1991. 13.95 (*0-590-44655-X*) Scholastic Inc.
—Pinkie Leaves Home. 1992. 13.95 (*0-590-45485-4*, Scholastic Hardcover) Scholastic Inc.
O'Donohoe, Nick. Too, Too Solid Flesh. LC 88-51731. 352p. (Orig.). 1989. pap. 3.95 (*0-88038-767-X*) TSR Inc.
O'Donovan, Dermot. Silas Rat & the Nuclear Tail. Booth, Tim, illus. 125p. 1988. pap. 7.95 (*0-947962-22-0*, Pub. by Children's Pr) Irish Bks Media.
Odor, Harold & Odor, Ruth. Becoming a Christian. Greene, Tom, illus. 16p. (gr. 3-7). 1985. 0.99 (*0-87203-901-X*, 3301) Standard Pub.
—Sharing Your Faith. Greene, Tom, illus. 16p. (gr. 3-7). 1985. 0.75 (*0-87239-902-8*, 3302) Standard Pub.
Odor, Ruth, jt. auth. see Odor, Harold.
Odor, Ruth S. Bigfoot. Magnuson, Diana, illus. LC 88-7882. 100p. (gr. 3-7). 1989. PLB 21.35 (*0-89565-455-5*); PLB 14.95s.p. (*0-685-55994-7*) Childs World.

—A Child's Book of Manners. McCallum, Joanne, illus. 32p. (gr. k-2). 1990. pasted 2.50 (*0-87403-701-8*, 24-03901) Standard Pub.
—Followers of Jesus. Williams, Karin, illus. LC 91-67210. 32p. (gr. 5-7). 1992. saddle-stitch 5.99 (*0-87403-933-9*, 24-03563) Standard Pub.
—Glad. Indereiden, Nancy, illus. LC 79-26076. (ps-2). 1980. PLB 18.50 (*0-89565-114-9*); PLB 12.95s.p. (*0-685-55483-X*) Childs World.
—God Answers Prayers. Leisner, Kurt, illus. LC 91-67209. 32p. (gr. 5-7). 1992. saddle-stitch 5.99 (*0-87403-932-0*, 24-03562) Standard Pub.
—God Keeps His Promises. Chase, Andra, illus. LC 91-67212. 32p. (gr. 5-7). 1992. saddle-stitch 5.99 (*0-87403-931-2*, 24-03561) Standard Pub.
—Jesus Loves Us. Fagan, Wendy, illus. LC 91-67211. 32p. (gr. 5-7). 1992. saddle-stitched 5.99 (*0-87403-934-7*, 24-03564) Standard Pub.
—Moods & Emotions. Bolt, John, illus. LC 81-17008. 112p. (gr. 2-6). 1980. PLB 21.35 (*0-89565-210-2*); PLB 14.95s.p. (*0-685-55505-4*) Childs World.
—Please. Indereiden, Nancy, illus. LC 79-25319. (ps-2). 1980. PLB 18.50 (*0-89565-115-7*); PLB 12.95s.p. (*0-685-55538-0*) Childs World.
—Thanks. Indereiden, Nancy, illus. LC 79-23926. (ps-2). 1980. PLB 18.50 (*0-89565-113-0*); PLB 12.95s.p. (*0-685-55553-4*) Childs World.
—The Very Special Night. Karch, Pat, illus. 32p. (gr. k-2). 1990. pasted 2.50 (*0-87403-709-3*, 24-03909) Standard Pub.
—The Very Special Visitors. Clarke, Karen, illus. 28p. (ps). 1992. 2.50 (*0-87403-955-X*, 24-03595) Standard Pub.
—What's a Body to Do? Letwenko, Ed, illus. LC 81-17031. 112p. (gr. 2-6). 1980. PLB 21.35 (*0-89565-209-9*); PLB 14.95s.p. (*0-685-55559-3*) Childs World.
Oechsle, Robert. Ducky, Ucky & Mucky. (Illus.). 40p. (ps). 1985. pap. 7.95 (*0-9603376-0-1*) Flourtown Pub.
Oechsli, Helen & Oechsli, Kelly. In My Garden: A Child's Gardening Book. Oechsli, Kelly, illus. LC 84-21285. 32p. (ps-2). 1985. RSBE 12.95 (*0-02-768510-1*, Macmillan Child Bk) Macmillan Child Grp.
Oechsli, Kelly. Mice at Bat. Oechsli, Kelly, illus. LC 85-45266. 64p. (gr. 1-3). 1986. HarpC Child Bks.
—Mice at Bat. Oechsli, Kelly, illus. LC 85-45266. 64p. (gr. k-3). 1990. pap. 3.50 (*0-06-444139-3*, Trophy) HarpC Child Bks.
Oechsli, Kelly, jt. auth. see Oechsli, Helen.
Oelerich, Marjorie, ed. see Sandell, Elizabeth.
Oestreicher, James. Choice Adventures: Monumental Discovery. 160p. 1992. pap. 4.99 (*0-8423-5030-6*) Tyndale.
Oetker. Let's Bake. LC 91-45595. (Illus.). 48p. (gr. 8-12). 1992. 12.95 (*0-8069-8534-8*) Sterling.
—Let's Cook. LC 91-46336. (Illus.). 48p. (gr. 8-12). 1992. 12.95 (*0-8069-8532-1*) Sterling.
Oetting. The Chieftain of Chaucer. LC 73-87806. (Illus.). 32p. (gr. 2-5). 1974. PLB 9.95 (*0-87783-137-8*); pap. 3.94 deluxe ed. (*0-87783-138-6*) Oddo.
—The Gray Ghosts of Gotham. LC 73-87804. (Illus.). 32p. (gr. 2-5). 1974. PLB 9.95 (*0-87783-135-1*); pap. 3.94 deluxe ed. (*0-87783-136-X*) Oddo.
—Keiki of the Islands. LC 71-108728. (Illus.). 96p. (gr. 3 up). 1970. PLB 10.95 (*0-87783-018-5*); pap. 3.94 deluxe ed. (*0-87783-096-7*) Oddo.
Oetting, R. Orderly Cricket. Marilue, illus. LC 68-16395. 32p. (gr. 2-3). 1967. PLB 9.95 (*0-87783-028-2*) Oddo.
—Prairie Dog Town. LC 68-56829. (Illus.). 48p. (gr. 2-5). 1968. PLB 10.95 (*0-87783-030-4*); pap. 3.94 deluxe ed. (*0-87783-157-2*) Oddo.
—Quetico Wolf. LC 71-190274. (Illus.). 48p. (gr. 4 up). 1972. PLB 9.95 (*0-87783-059-2*); pap. 3.94 deluxe ed. (*0-87783-103-3*) Oddo.
—When Jesus Was a Lad. LC 68-56816. (Illus.). 32p. (gr. 2-3). 1968. PLB 9.95x (*0-87783-047-9*) Oddo.
Oetting, Rae. Bobby Bear's Birthday. Marilue, illus. LC 87-62508. 32p. (ps-1). 1988. PLB 11.45 (*0-87783-220-X*) Oddo.
—Timmy Tiger & the Elephant. LC 73-108730. (Illus.). 32p. (ps-2). 1970. PLB 9.95 (*0-87783-041-X*); pap. 3.94 deluxe ed (*0-87783-111-4*); cassette 7.94x (*0-87783-277-3*) Oddo.
—Timmy Tiger to the Rescue. LC 70-108733. (Illus.). 32p. (ps-4). 1970. PLB 9.95x (*0-87783-043-6*); pap. 3. 94x deluxe ed (*0-87783-112-2*); cassette 7.94x (*0-87783-229-3*) Oddo.
—Timmy Tiger's New Coat. LC 74-108734. (Illus.). 32p. (ps-2). 1970. PLB 9.95 (*0-87783-044-4*); pap. 3.94 deluxe ed (*0-87783-113-0*); cassette 7.94x (*0-87783-230-7*) Oddo.
—Timmy Tiger's New Friend. LC 77-108732. (Illus.). (ps-2). 1970. PLB 9.95 (*0-87783-042-8*); pap. 3.94 deluxe ed (*0-87783-114-9*); cassette 7.94x (*0-87783-231-5*) Oddo.
—Wrongway Santa. Shardin, Art, illus. LC 90-62546. 32p. 1991. PLB 15.95 (*0-87783-254-4*) Oddo.
Ofek, Uriel. Beware! Ducks Crossing. Kriss, David, tr. from HEB. Elchanan, illus. 24p. (Orig.). 1992. pap. text ed. 3.00x (*1-56134-145-2*) Dushkin Pub.
—Cuidado! Patos Cruzando. Writer, C. C. & Nielsen, Lisa C., trs. Elchanan, illus. (SPA.). 24p. (Orig.). (ps). 1992. pap. text ed. 3.00x (*1-56134-155-X*) Dushkin Pub.
Offen, Hilda. Elephant Pie. Offen, Hilda, illus. 32p. (ps-2). 1993. 13.99 (*0-525-45123-4*, DCB) Dutton Child Bks.

—A Fox Got My Socks. LC 92-7380. (ps-2). 1993. 10.00 (*0-525-44991-4*, DCB) Dutton Child Bks.
—Nice Work, Little Wolf! LC 91-23741. (Illus.). 32p. (ps-2). 1992. 14.00 (*0-525-44880-2*, DCB) Dutton Child Bks.
—The Sheep Made a Leap. Offen, Hilda, illus. 32p. (ps-2). 1994. 10.99 (*0-525-45174-9*, DCB) Dutton Child Bks.
Offen, Hilda, illus. My Favorite Nursery Rhymes. (ps-5). 1987. pap. 12.95 (*0-671-64705-9*, S&S BFYR) S&S Trade.
—A Treasury of Bedtime Stories. Yeatman, Linda, compiled by. (Illus.). 160p. (ps-3). 1981. pap. 13.00 (*0-671-44463-8*, S&S BFYR) S&S Trade.
—A Treasury of Mother Goose. (gr. 1 up). 1984. pap. 13.00 (*0-671-50118-6*, S&S BFYR) S&S Trade.
Officer, Robyn, illus. Mother Goose's Nursery Rhymes. 32p. (ps-3). 1992. 6.95 (*0-8362-4907-0*) Andrews & McMeel.
Offit, Sidney. What Kind of Guy Do You Think I Am? 160p. (gr. 9 up). 1979. pap. 1.50 (*0-440-99455-1*, LFL) Dell.
Ofosu-Appiah, L. H. People in Bondage. (gr. 4-7). 1992. 15.95 (*0-8225-3150-X*) Lerner Pubns.
—People in Bondage: African Slavery in the Modern Era. (Illus.). 132p. (gr. 5-12). 1993. PLB 19.95 (*0-8225-1437-0*) Lerner Pubns.
Ogawa, ed. see Quackenbush, Hiroko C.
Ogawa, ed. see Quackenbush, Hiroko C.
Ogawa, Brian K., et al. To Tell the Truth. Wagstaff, Bob, illus. LC 88-51256. 40p. (gr. 4-6). 1988. text ed. write for info. (*0-9621260-0-4*) VWAP.
Ogawa, Hiroshi. The Potter Wasp. Pohl, Kathy, ed. (Illus.). 32p. (gr. 3-7). 1986. PLB 17.96 (*0-8172-2541-2*) Raintree Steck-V.
Ogburn, Jackie, ed. see Alcott, Louisa May.
Ogburn, Jackie, ed. see Carroll, Lewis.
Ogburn, Jackie, ed. see Crane, Stephen.
Ogburn, Jackie, ed. see Defoe, Daniel.
Ogburn, Jackie, ed. see Doyle, Arthur Conan.
Ogburn, Jackie, ed. see Kipling, Rudyard.
Ogburn, Jackie, ed. see London, Jack & Conrad, Joseph.
Ogburn, Jackie, ed. see Poe, Edgar Allan.
Ogburn, Jackie, ed. see Pyle, Howard.
Ogburn, Jackie, ed. see Stevenson, Robert Louis.
Ogburn, Jackie, ed. see Twain, Mark.
Ogburn, Jackie, ed. see Verne, Jules.
Ogburn, Jackie, ed. see Wren, Percival C.
Ogburn, Jacqueline. The Masked Marvel. Carlson, Nancy, illus. LC 92-1669. 1994. write for info. (*0-688-11049-5*); PLB write for info. (*0-688-11050-9*) Lothrop.
Ogburn, Jacqueline K. Scarlett Angelina Wolverton-Manning. Ajhar, Brian, illus. LC 92-41930. 1994. write for info. (*0-8037-1376-2*); PLB write for info. (*0-8037-1377-0*) Dial Bks Young.
Ogden, Betina, illus. The Ugly Duckling. 18p. (ps). 1994. bds. 3.95 (*0-448-40184-3*, G&D) Putnam Pub Group.
Ogden, Dale. Hoosier Sports Heroes. Day, Richard, illus. LC 90-84308. 192p. 1990. 19.95 (*1-878208-01-2*) Guild Pr In.
Ogden, John A. The Medibears Guide to the Doctor's Exam: For Children & Parents. Ogden, Ethel F., illus. (gr. k-5). 1991. 10.95 (*0-8130-1082-9*) U Press Fla.
Ogden, Peggy, ed. see Vrooman, Christine W.
Ogg, Diana. Coll: Island of the Hebrides. (Illus.). 63p. (gr. 7-9). 1988. 17.95 (*0-85219-728-4*, Pub. by Batsford UK) Trafalgar.
Ogilvy, Carol & Tinkham, Trudy. Classy Christmas Concerts. Renard, Jan, illus. 112p. (gr. k-7). 1986. wkbk. 9.95 (*0-86653-349-4*, GA 795) Good Apple.
—Primary Christmas Concerts. Renard, Jan, illus. (gr. k-3). 1989. 9.95 (*0-86653-485-7*, GA1091) Good Apple.
Ogle, Lucille & Thoburn, Tina. The Golden Picture Dictionary. Knight, Hilary, illus. (gr. 3). 1989. write for info. (*0-307-17861-7*, Pub. by Golden Bks) Western Pub.
O'Grady, Jim. Dorothy Day: With Love for the Poor. (Illus.). 128p. (gr. 4 up). 1993. pap. 10.95 (*0-9623380-6-0*) Ward Hill Pr.
—Dorothy Day: With Love for the Poor. (Illus.). 128p. (gr. 4 up). 1993. PLB 14.95 (*0-9623380-2-8*) Ward Hill Pr.
O'Hair, Madalyn M. Atheist Primer: Did You Know All the Gods Came from the Same Place? (Illus.). 30p. (Orig.). (gr. 2-4). 1978. saddle-stitched 4.00 (*0-911826-10-6*, 5372) Am Atheist.
O'Halloran, Tim. Know Your Numbers. O'Halloran, Tim, illus. 38p. (ps-1). 1983. 10.95 (*0-88625-045-5*) Durkin Hayes Pub.
—Words Around Us. O'Halloran, Tim, illus. 48p. (ps-k). 1985. 10.95 (*0-88625-124-9*) Durkin Hayes Pub.
—Words Around Us in French. O'Halloran, Tim, illus. (FRE.). 48p. (ps-k). 1985. 10.95 (*0-88625-125-7*) Durkin Hayes Pub.
Ohanesian, Diane. Let's Pretend Bunny: Playtime Pals. (Illus.). (ps). 1993. Incl. bunny. bds. 9.95 (*0-89577-451-8*, Readers Digest Kids) RD Assn.
—Let's Pretend Teddy: Playtime Pals Board Book. (ps). 1992. bds. 9.95 gift boxed (*0-89577-450-X*, Readers Digest Kids) RD Assn.
Ohanian, Susan. All about Bears. Ruth, Trevor, illus. LC 93-28988. 1994. 4.25 (*0-383-03735-2*) SRA Schl Grp.
—Wolves. Ruth, Trevor, illus. LC 93-28973. 1994. 4.25 (*0-383-03742-5*) SRA Schl Grp.
O'Hara, Mary. My Friend Flicka. LC 87-45654. 272p. (gr. 7 up). 1988. pap. 5.00 (*0-06-080902-7*, P-902, PL) HarpC.

—Thunderhead. 320p. (gr. 5-9). 1967. pap. 1.75 (*0-440-98875-6*, LFL) Dell.
—Thunderhead. LC 87-45653. 320p. (gr. 7 up). 1988. pap. 6.00 (*0-06-080903-5*, P-903, PL) HarpC.
O'Hare, Jeff. Globe Probe: Exciting Geographical Adventures All Around the World. 32p. (gr. 4-7). 1993. 10.95 (*1-56397-037-6*) Boyds Mills Pr.
—Searchin' Safari: Looking for Camouflaged Creatures. Nadel, Marc, illus. LC 91-72974. 32p. (ps-3). 1992. 8.95 (*1-56397-016-3*) Boyds Mills Pr.
O'Hare, Jeff, ed. Cat & Dog Mysteries: Fourteen Exciting Mini-Mysteries with Hidden Pictures. Palan, R. Michael, illus. 32p. (Orig.). (gr. 2-7). 1993. pap. 4.95 (*1-56397-019-8*) Boyds Mills Pr.
—Knee Slappers, Side Splitters & Tummy Ticklers: A Book of Riddles & Jokes. LC 91-76204. (Illus.). 48p. (ps-7). 1992. pap. 6.95 (*1-56397-019-8*) Boyds Mills Pr.
O'Hearn, Michael. Hercules the Harbor Tug. (Illus.). 32p. (ps-4). 1994. 15.95 (*0-88106-889-6*); PLB 16.00 (*0-88106-890-X*); pap. 7.95 (*0-88106-888-8*) Charlesbridge Pub.
O. Henry. Four Million & Other Stories. (gr. 8 up). 1964. pap. 1.25 (*0-8049-0025-6*, CL-25) Airmont.
—The Gift of the Magi. King, Kevin, illus. 32p. (gr. 5 up). 1988. pap. 12.95 (*0-671-64706-7*, Little Simon) S&S Trade.
—Gift of the Magi. Wheeler, Jody, illus. 24p. (ps-3). 1989. pap. 2.95 (*0-8249-8388-2*, Ideals Child) Hambleton-Hill.
—The Gift of the Magi. Sauber, Robert, illus. LC 91-7313. 48p. (gr. 1-6). 1991. 9.95 (*0-88101-116-9*) Unicorn Pub.
—The Gift of the Magi. Zwerger, Lisbeth, illus. LC 92-6632. 28p. 1992. pap. 5.95 (*0-88708-276-9*) Picture Bk Studio.
—The Gift of the Magi: A Special Christmas Edition. rev. ed. Marshall, Rita, illus. 32p. (gr. 4 up). 1984. PLB 13.95s.p. (*0-87191-954-0*) Creative Ed.
—The Last Leaf. (Illus.). 32p. (gr. 6 up). 1980. PLB 13.95s.p. (*0-87191-774-2*) Creative Ed.
—The Last Leaf. rev. ed. (gr. 6 up). 1989. Repr. of 1906 ed. multi-media kit 35.00 (*0-685-31126-0*) Balance Pub.
—The Ransom of Red Chief. (Illus.). 40p. (gr. 4 up). 1980. PLB 13.95s.p. (*0-87191-776-9*) Creative Ed.
O'Huigin, Sean. The Ghost Horse of the Mounties. Moser, Barry, illus. LC 87-46287. (gr. 4-6). 1991. 14.95 (*0-87923-721-X*) Godine.
—King of the Birds. Dixon, Tom, illus. 36p. (ps-5). 1992. pap. 4.95 (*0-88753-168-7*, Pub. by Black Moss Pr CN) Firefly Bks Ltd.
Oivardi, Anne & Philpot, Graham. My First Picture Dictionary. (Illus.). 64p. (gr. 1-3). 1989. incl. dust jacket 7.95 (*0-8120-5961-1*) Barron.
Ojaide, Tanure. The Eagle's Vision. LC 87-46316. 104p. (Orig.). (gr. 9-12). 1987. pap. 8.00 perfect bdg. (*0-916418-66-9*) Lotus.
Ojeda, Linda. Safe Dieting for Teens. 128p. (Orig.). (gr. 7-12). 1992. pap. 7.95 (*0-89793-113-0*) Hunter Hse.
Ojibway Curriculum Committee Staff. The Land of the Ojibway. (Illus.). 48p. (gr. 9 up). 1991. pap. 1.50 (*0-685-53561-4*, E-11-B) Minn Hist.
Okawa, Essei. The Adventures of the One Inch Boy. Ooka, D. T., tr. from JPN. Endo, Teruyo, illus. 32p. (gr. k-6). 1985. 11.95 (*0-89346-258-6*) Heian Intl.
—The Fisherman & the Grateful Turtle. Ooka, D. T., tr. from JPN. Murakami, Koichi, illus. 32p. (gr. k-6). 1985. PLB 11.95 (*0-89346-257-8*) Heian Intl.
Okaze, Kunio, ed. see Hober, David.
Oke, Janette. A Bride for Donnigan. 224p. (Orig.). 1993. pap. 7.99 (*1-55661-327-X*) Bethany Hse.
—A Bride for Donnigan. large type ed. 224p. (Orig.). 1993. pap. 9.99 (*1-55661-328-8*) Bethany Hse.
—A Cote of Many Colors. Mann, Brenda, illus. 128p. (Orig.). (gr. 3 up). 1987. pap. 4.99 (*0-934998-27-2*) Bethel Pub.
—Ducktails. Mann, Brenda, illus. 131p. (gr. 3 up). 1985. pap. 4.99 (*0-934998-20-5*) Bethel Pub.
—The Impatient Turtle. Peterson, Pete, ed. Mann, Brenda, illus. 110p. (Orig.). (gr. 3-6). 1986. pap. 4.99 (*0-934998-24-8*) Bethel Pub.
—Julia's Last Hope. large type ed. 224p. (Orig.). (gr. 8 up). 1990. pap. 8.99 (*1-55661-157-9*) Bethany Hse.
—Julia's Last Hope. 224p. (Orig.). (gr. 8 up). 1990. pap. 7.99 (*1-55661-153-6*) Bethany Hse.
—Love Comes Softly. large type ed. 188p. (gr. 4 up). 1985. pap. 8.99 (*0-87123-828-4*) Bethany Hse.
—Love Comes Softly, 4 bks, Vols. 5-8. 1993. Set. 27.96 (*1-55661-778-X*) Bethany Hse.
—Love Finds a Home. large type ed. 224p. (Orig.). 1989. Large type. pap. 8.99 (*1-55661-093-9*); pap. 6.99 (*1-55661-086-6*) Bethany Hse.
—Love Takes Wing. LC 88-19276. 224p. (Orig.). (gr. 8 up). 1988. pap. 6.99 (*1-55661-035-1*) Bethany Hse.
—Love's Unending Legacy. large type ed. LC 84-18412. 224p (gr. 4 up). 1985. pap. 8.99 (*0-87123-855-1*) Bethany Hse.
—Maury Had a Little Lamb. Mann, Brenda, illus. 137p. (Orig.). (gr. 3 up). 1989. pap. 4.99 (*0-934998-34-5*) Bethel Pub.
—New Kid in Town. Mann, Brenda, illus. 125p. (Orig.). (gr. 3 up). 1983. pap. 4.99 (*0-934998-16-7*) Bethel Pub.
—Once upon a Summer. large type ed. LC 81-10183. (gr. 7 up). 1987. pap. 8.99 (*0-87123-981-7*) Bethany Hse.
—Pordy's Prickly Problem. Mann, Brenda, illus. 1993. pap. 4.99 (*0-934998-50-7*) Bethel Pub.

—Prairie Dog Town. Mann, Brenda, illus. 140p. (gr. 3 up). 1988. pap. 4.99 (*0-934998-31-0*) Bethel Pub.
—The Prodigal Cat. 160p. (Orig.). (gr. 3). 1984. pap. 4.99 (*0-934998-19-1*) Bethel Pub.
—Spring's Gentle Promise. LC 89-22. 224p. (Orig.). (gr. 4 up). 1989. pap. 6.99 (*1-55661-059-9*) Bethany Hse.
—Spring's Gentle Promise. large type ed. 224p. (Orig.). 1989. pap. 8.99 (*1-55661-074-2*) Bethany Hse.
—Spunky's Diary. 99p. (gr. 5-12). 1982. pap. 4.99 (*0-934998-11-6*) Bethel Pub.
—They Called Her Mrs. Doc. 224p. 1992. pap. 7.99 (*1-55661-246-X*) Bethany Hse.
—They Called Her Mrs. Doc. large type ed. 224p. 1992. pap. 9.99 (*1-55661-247-8*) Bethany Hse.
—This Little Pig. Mann, Brenda, illus. 145p. (Orig.). (gr. 1-6). 1991. pap. 4.99 (*0-934998-43-4*) Bethel Pub.
—Trouble in a Fur Coat. Mann, Brenda, illus. 152p. (Orig.). (gr. 1-6). 1990. pap. 4.99 (*0-934998-38-8*) Bethel Pub.
—When Breaks the Dawn. LC 86-3405. 250p. (Orig.). (gr. 4 up). 1986. pap. 6.99 (*0-87123-882-9*) Bethany Hse.
—When Breaks the Dawn. large type ed. 219p. (gr. 4 up). 1986. pap. 8.99 (*0-87123-895-0*) Bethany Hse.
—When Comes the Spring. LC 85-11261. 224p. (Orig.). (gr. 6). 1985. pap. 6.99 (*0-87123-795-4*) Bethany Hse.
—When Hope Springs New. LC 86-13664. 224p. (Orig.). (gr. 4 up). 1986. pap. 6.99 (*0-87123-657-5*) Bethany Hse.
—When Hope Springs New. large type ed. 216p. (gr. 4 up). 1986. pap. 8.99 (*0-87123-675-3*) Bethany Hse.
—Winter Is Not Forever. large type ed. LC 88-2882. 224p. (gr. 4 up). 1988. 6.99 (*1-55661-002-5*); pap. 8.99 (*1-55661-008-4*) Bethany Hse.
—A Woman Named Damaris. large type ed. 224p. (Orig.). (gr. 9 up). 1991. pap. 9.99 (*1-55661-226-5*) Bethany Hse.
O'Keef, Richard D. How to Make More Money Babysitting: What Works, What Doesn't, & Why. LC 91-92960. (Illus.). 136p. (Orig.). (gr. 6-10). 1992. pap. 8.95 (*0-9630531-3-2*) Diamond Bks UT.
O'Keefe, Candace. Texas Women - A Celebration of History: A Multicultural Guide. Shaw, Charles, illus. 60p. (gr. 4 up). 1991. pap. 8.95 (*0-685-51123-5*) Hendrick-Long.
O'Keefe, Susan H. A Bug from Aunt Tillie. LC 91-3094. 32p. (Orig.). 1991. pap. 3.95 (*0-8091-6602-X*) Paulist Pr.
—One Hungry Monster: A Counting Book in Rhyme. Munsinger, Lynn, illus. 32p. (ps-3). 1989. 12.95 (*0-316-63385-2*, Joy St Bks) Little.
—One Hungry Monster: A Counting Book in Rhyme. Munsinger, Lynn, illus. 32p. (ps-3). 1992. pap. 4.95 (*0-316-63388-7*, Joy St Bks) Little.
—A Season for Giving. Keating, Pamela T., illus. 1990. 2.95 (*0-8091-6592-9*) Paulist Pr.
—Who Will Miss Me If I Don't Go to Church? Keating, Pam, illus. LC 92-28347. 32p. 1993. pap. 3.95 (*0-8091-6608-9*) Paulist Pr.
O'Kelley, Mattie L. From the Hills of Georgia: An Autobiography in Paintings. LC 83-9414. (Illus.). 32p. (ps-3). 1986. 14.95 (*0-316-63800-5*, Joy St Bks); (Joy St Bks) Little.
—Moving to Town. (Illus.). (ps-3). 1991. 15.95 (*0-316-63805-6*) Little.
Okie, Susan, jt. auth. see Ride, Sally.
Okimoto, Jean D. Blumpoe Grumpoe Meets Arnold C, Vol. 1. (ps-3). 1990. 13.95 (*0-316-63811-0*, Joy St Bks) Little.
—Jason's Women. LC 85-28655. 210p. (gr. 7up). 1986. 14.95 (*0-316-63809-9*, 638099, Joy St Bks) Little.
—Jason's Women. (gr. k-12). 1988. pap. 2.95 (*0-440-20000-8*) Dell.
—A Place for Grace. Keith, Doug, illus. 32p. (gr. 1 up). 1993. 14.95 (*0-912365-73-0*) Sasquatch Bks.
—Take a Chance, Gramps, Vol. 1. (gr. 4-7). 1990. 14.95 (*0-316-63812-9*, Joy St Bks) Little.
—Talent Night. LC 93-34591. 1995. 13.95 (*0-590-47809-5*) Scholastic Inc.
Okon, Bern, jt. auth. see Otumokala, Jean.
O'Kun, Lan, jt. auth. see Lewis, Shari.
Okun, Milton, ed. Cabbage Patch Dreams: Piano - Vocal. (Illus.). 64p. (Orig.). 1990. pap. text ed. 9.95 (*0-89524-268-0*) Cherry Lane.
Okun, Milton & Sosin, Donald, eds. Magic of Music - Children's Song: Piano - Vocal. Payor, Terry, illus. 80p. (Orig.). 1988. pap. text ed. 9.95 (*0-89524-372-5*) Cherry Lane.
Olah, Suzann M. My Phone Book. 18p. (ps-2). 1991. pap. 6.95 (*0-9630985-0-0*) RJB Enter.
Oldcoyote, Sally, ed. Teepees are Folded: American Indian Poetry. (gr. 4 up). 1991. pap. 5.95 (*0-89992-133-7*) Coun India Ed.
Olden, Diana J. & Smith, Vicki. Pendleton Pennywise Presents the Money Book - Just for You: A Budget Book for Children. 44p. (gr. 3-5). 1991. wirebound 11.95 (*0-9630463-0-6*) S & D.
Older, Jules. Ben & Jerry...The Real Scoop! Severance, Lyn, illus. 80p. (Orig.). (gr. 3-8). 1993. pap. 6.95 (*1-881527-04-2*) Chapters Pub.
Oldershaw, Callie. Oceans. Burns, Robert, illus. LC 91-45079. 32p. (gr. 4-6). 1993. PLB 11.59 (*0-8167-2753-8*); pap. text ed. 3.95 (*0-8167-2754-6*) Troll Assocs. Postponed.
Oldfield, Jenny. Misfits & Rebels. 112p. (gr. 8-11). 1991. pap. 9.95 (*1-85381-155-6*, Pub. by Virago Pr UK) Trafalgar.

Oldfield, Margaret J. Costumes & Customs of Many Lands. (Illus.). (gr. k-3). 1982. pap. 2.95 (0-934876-19-3) Creative Storytime.
—Fat Cat & Ebenezer Geezer: The Teeny Tiny Mouse. 2nd ed. Oldfield, Margaret J., illus. (gr. k-2). 1980. pap. 3.00 (0-934876-13-4) Creative Storytime.
—Finger Puppets & Finger Plays. (Illus.). (ps-3). 1982. pap. 3.00 (0-934876-18-5) Creative Storytime.
—Lots More Tell & Draw Stories. (Illus.). (ps-3). 1973. PLB 11.95 (0-934876-07-X); pap. 6.95 (0-934876-06-1); pap. 6.95 (0-934876-02-9) Creative Storytime.
—More Tell & Draw Stories. (Illus.). (ps-3). 1969. PLB 11.95 (0-934876-06-1); pap. 6.95 (0-934876-02-9) Creative Storytime.
—Tell & Draw Paper Bag Puppet Book. 2nd ed. Oldfield, Margaret J., illus. (gr. k-2). 1981. pap. 5.95 (0-934876-16-9) Creative Storytime.
—Tell & Draw Paper Cut-Outs. Oldfield, Margaret J., illus. (gr. k-2). 1988. pap. 3.50 (0-934876-23-1, 23) Creative Storytime.
Oldfield, Wendy, jt. auth. see Davies, Kay.
Oldgate, Karl. Karate. rev. ed. (Illus.). 80p. (gr. 10-12). 1993. pap. 7.95 (0-7137-2410-2, Pub. by Blandford Pr UK) Sterling.
Oldham, Bruce, ed. Footprints: Following Jesus for Junior Highers. 144p. (Orig.). (gr. 7-9). 1983. pap. 4.50 (0-8341-0863-1) Beacon Hill.
Oldham, June. Grow Up Cupid. (gr. k-12). 1989. pap. 2.95 (0-440-20256-6, LFL) Dell.
Oldham, Linda, jt. auth. see Lee, Nancy.
Oldham, Robert K. The Cure. LC 90-92322. 343p. (Orig.). 1991. pap. write for info. (0-9628850-0-2) Pulse Pubns.
Oldsfield, Wendy, jt. auth. see Davis, Kay.
O'Leary, Daniel J. & Dalton, Kathleen. Where Is God? Sabatte, Frank, illus. (gr. 4 up). 1991. pap. 2.95 (0-8091-6598-8) Paulist Pr.
O'Leary, Sean C. Christmas Wonder: From Ireland - For Children: Craftwork, Lore, Poems, Songs & Stories. LC 89-50972. (Illus.). 98p. (Orig.). 1989. pap. 12.95 (0-86278-177-9, Pub. by O'Brien Press Ltd Eire) Dufour.
—Whizz Quiz: Quiz & Puzzle Book. (Illus.). 92p. (gr. 2-6). 1993. pap. 7.95 (0-86278-287-2, Pub. by OBrien Pr IE) Dufour.
Oleksy, Walter. The Boston Tea Party. LC 92-26247. (Illus.). 64p. (gr. 4-6). 1993. PLB 12.90 (0-531-20193-7) Watts.
—Entertainers. (Illus.). 128p. (gr. 3-6). Date not set. 19. 95 (1-56065-120-2) Capstone Pr. Postponed.
—Experiments with Heat. LC 85-30860. (Illus.). 48p. (gr. k-4). 1986. PLB 15.27 (0-516-01277-0); pap. 4.95 (0-516-41277-9) Childrens.
—Inventors. (Illus.). 128p. (gr. 3-6). Date not set. 19.95 (1-56065-118-0) Capstone Pr. Postponed.
—Mikhail Gorbachev: A Leader for Soviet Change. LC 88-36960. (Illus.). 152p. (gr. 4 up). 1989. PLB 18.60 (0-516-03265-8) Childrens.
—Musicians. (Illus.). 128p. (gr. 3-6). Date not set. 19.95 (0-685-57489-X) Capstone Pr. Postponed.
—Sports Legends. (Illus.). 128p. (gr. 3-6). Date not set. 19.95 (1-56065-121-0) Capstone Pr. Postponed.
Olesen, Jens. Snail. LC 86-10084. (Illus.). 25p. (gr. k-4). 1986. 6.95 (0-382-09304-6); PLB 9.98 (0-382-09289-9) pap. 3.95 (0-382-24019-7) Silver Burdett Pr.
Olesky, Walter. Boston Tea Party. LC 92-26247. (gr. 4-7). 1993. 18.43 (0-531-20147-3) Watts.
Olfers, Sibylle von see Von Olfers, Sibylle.
Olfson, Lewy. Fifty Great Scenes for Student Actors. (gr. 9 up). 1990. pap. 4.95 (0-553-25520-7) Bantam.
Olgin, Joseph. Illustrated Football Dictionary for Young People. Sutton, Larry, illus. (gr. 4 up). 1978. pap. 2.50 (0-13-450874-2, Pub. by Treehouse) P-H.
Olin, Caroline & Dutton, Bertha P. Southwest Indians, Bk. 1: (Navajo, Pima, Apache, Bk. 1. (Illus.). (gr. 5). 1978. pap. 3.95 (0-88388-049-0) Bellerophon Bks.
Oliphant, Margaret. The Earliest Civilizations. (Illus.). 80p. (gr. 2-6). 1993. 17.95x (0-8160-2785-4) Facts on File.
Olitzky, Kerry M., jt. auth. see Kasakove, David P.
Olivarez, Anna & Rohmer, Harriet, eds. Mr. Sugar Came to Town Read-Along. (SPA & ENG.). (ps-7). 1990. incl. audiocassette 22.95 (0-89239-062-X) Childrens Book Pr.
Olivarez, Anna, jt. ed. see Rohmer, Harriet.
Olive, Teresa. Joseph & His Brothers. (Illus.). 24p. (Orig.). (ps-4). 1993. pap. 1.89 (0-570-09030-X) Concordia.
Oliver. Ankylosaurus. (Illus.). 24p. 1984. PLB 14.00 (0-86592-212-8) Rourke Enter.
—Archaeopteryx. (Illus.). 24p. 1984. PLB 14.00 (0-86592-209-8) Rourke Enter.
—Brachiosaurus. (Illus.). 24p. 1986. PLB 14.00 (0-86592-219-5) Rourke Enter.
—Chasmosaurus. (Illus.). 24p. 1986. PLB 14.00 (0-86592-218-7) Rourke Enter.
—Deinonychus. (Illus.). 24p. 1984. PLB 14.00 (0-86592-213-6) Rourke Enter.
—Dilophosaurus. (Illus.). 24p. 1984. PLB 14.00 (0-86592-215-2) Rourke Enter.
—Dimetrodon. (Illus.). 24p. 1984. PLB 14.00 (0-86592-210-1) Rourke Enter.
—Dimorphodon. (Illus.). 24p. 1986. PLB 14.00 (0-86592-217-9) Rourke Enter.
—Dinosaur Library, 6 bks, Set III. (Illus.). 144p. 1986. Set. PLB write for info. (0-86592-214-4) Rourke Enter.

—Mamenchisaurus. (Illus.). 24p. 1986. PLB 14.00 (0-86592-220-9) Rourke Enter.
—Plesiosaurus. (Illus.). 24p. 1984. PLB 14.00 (0-86592-211-X) Rourke Enter.
—Protoceratops. (Illus.). 24p. 1986. PLB 14.00 (0-86592-216-0) Rourke Enter.
Oliver & Wilson. Dinosaur Library, 13 bks, Set II. (Illus.). 312p. 1984. Set. PLB write for info. (0-86592-200-4) Rourke Enter.
Oliver, ed. Iguanodon. (Illus.). 24p. 1984. PLB 14.00 (0-86592-207-1) Rourke Enter.
—Nothosaurus. (Illus.). 24p. 1984. PLB 14.00 (0-86592-208-X) Rourke Enter.
Oliver, Barbara. Mission Stories for Young Children. 48p. (Orig.). (gr. 1-3). 1990. pap. 2.95 (0-936625-93-7, New Hope AL) Womans Mission Union.
Oliver, Carl R. Panama's Canal. LC 90-34273. (Illus.). 128p. (gr. 9-12). 1990. PLB 14.40 (0-531-10958-5) Watts.
Oliver, Cookie D. Come Comet Come Cupid. Goodin, Sallie B., illus LC 91-65161. 44p. (gr. k-3). 1991. 6.95 (1-55523-426-7) Winston-Derek.
Oliver, Dana M. California Game Book. Oliver, Rice D., ed. (Illus.). 32p. (gr. 4-12). 1993. pap. 7.00 (0-936778-69-5) Calif Weekly.
Oliver, Diana. Annie's Rainbow. 120p. (Orig.). (gr. 3-7). 1993. pap. 3.50 (0-679-85006-6) Random Bks Yng Read.
—Desdemona Acts Up. 120p. (Orig.). (gr. 3-7). 1993. pap. 3.50 (0-679-85293-X) Random Bks Yng Read.
—Get Lost, Sylvie! (Orig.). (gr. 3-7). 1993. pap. 3.50 (0-679-84988-2) Random Bks Yng Read.
—Kathleen, Karate Queen. 120p. (Orig.). (gr. 3-7). 1993. pap. 3.50 (0-679-85327-8) Random Bks Yng Read.
—Tough Luck, Nonnie. 132p. (gr. 3-5). Date not set. pap. 3.50 (0-679-85475-4) Random Bks Yng Read.
Oliver, Elizabeth M. Black Mother Goose Book. 2nd ed. Stockett, Thomas A., illus. LC 81-83427. 48p. (gr. k-3). Repr. of 1981 ed. 12.95 (0-912444-35-5) DARE Bks.
Oliver, James E. Educational Interest Inventory & Career Guidance Inventory Examiner's Manual. 41p. (Orig.). (gr. 12). 1989. pap. 6.00x tchr's. ed. (0-685-35798-8) Orchard Hse MA.
—Educational Interest Inventory Answer Sheet, Profile & Interpretation Guide. 9p. (Orig.). (gr. 12). 1989. pap. 35.00x wkbk., 25 copies (0-685-35796-1) Orchard Hse MA.
—Educational Interest Inventory Booklet. 12p. (Orig.). (gr. 12). 1989. pap. 3.00x wkbk. (0-685-35797-X) Orchard Hse MA.
Oliver, June. Polysymmetrics: The Art of Making Geometric Patterns. (Illus.). 32p. (Orig.). (gr. 5-9). 1986. pap. 7.50 (0-906212-09-X, Pub. by Tarquin UK) Parkwest Pubns.
Oliver, Lin, jt. auth. see Mooser, Stephen.
Oliver, M. Agent Arthur's Arctic Adventure. (Illus.). 48p. 1990. PLB 11.96 (0-88110-408-6); pap. 4.95 (0-7460-0145-2) EDC.
—Agent Arthur's Jungle Journey. (Illus.). 48p. 1989. PLB 11.96 (0-88110-334-9); pap. 4.95 (0-7460-0141-X) EDC.
—The Intergalactic Bus Trip. (Illus.). 48p. (gr. 3-5). 1988. PLB 11.96 (0-88110-301-2); pap. 4.95 (0-7460-0151-7) EDC.
—Search for the Sunken City. (Illus.). 48p. 1989. PLB 11. 96 (0-88110-409-4); pap. 4.95 (0-7460-0304-8) EDC.
Oliver, M. & Waters, G. Agent Arthur's Puzzle Adventures. (Illus.). 1990. pap. 9.95 (0-7460-0147-9) EDC.
Oliver, Ray. Rocks & Fossils. LC 92-44791. (Illus.). 80p. (gr. 5 up). 1993. 13.00 (0-679-82661-0); PLB 13.99 (0-679-92661-5) Random Bks Yng Read.
Oliver, Rice D. California Student Resource File. (Illus.). 158p. (gr. 4). 1993. 25.00 (0-936778-66-0) Calif Weekly.
—Lone Woman of Ghalas-hat. Zafuto, Charles, illus. 32p. (gr. 4-8). 1993. PLB 12.00 (0-936778-52-0); pap. 6.00 (0-936778-51-2) Calif Weekly.
—Lone Woman of Ghalas-Hat: The True Story of the Island of the Blue Dolphins. (Illus.). 48p. (gr. 4-8). 1986. PLB 9.95x (0-936778-96-2); pap. 3.95x (0-936778-95-4) Calif Weekly.
—Student Atlas of California. 3rd ed. (Illus.). 72p. (gr. 4 up). 1988. 7.95 (0-936778-98-9); tchr's ed. 8.95 (0-936778-99-7) Calif Weekly.
—Student Atlas of California. 4th, rev. ed. (Illus.). 66p. (gr. 4-8). 1993. pap. text ed. 11.00 (0-936778-63-6); tchr's. ed. 13.00 (0-936778-64-4) Calif Weekly.
Oliver, Rice D., ed. see Oliver, Dana M.
Oliver, Rick, ed. see Shanower, Eric.
Oliver, Rupert. Brontosaur. (gr. 4-7). 1991. 4.95 (0-8167-1303-0) Troll Assocs.
—Tyrannosaurus. (gr. 4-7). 1991. 4.95 (0-8167-1305-7) Troll Assocs.
Oliver, Stephen, photos by. Clothes. LC 90-23999. (Illus.). 24p. (ps-k). 1991. 7.00 (0-679-81806-5) Random Bks Yng Read.
—Counting. LC 90-8577. (Illus.). 24p. (ps-k). 1991. 6.95 (0-679-81163-X) Random Bks Yng Read.
—Home. LC 89-63092. (Illus.). 24p. (ps-k). 1990. 6.95 (0-679-80622-9) Random Bks Yng Read.
—My First Look at Colors. LC 89-63091. (Illus.). 24p. (ps-k). 1990. 7.00 (0-679-80535-4) Random Bks Yng Read.
—My First Look at Numbers. LC 89-63088. (Illus.). 24p. (ps-k). 1990. 7.00 (0-679-80533-8) Random Bks Yng Read.

—My First Look at Shapes. LC 89-63087. (Illus.). 24p. (ps-k). 1990. 7.00 (0-679-80534-6) Random Bks Yng Read.
—My First Look at Sizes. LC 89-63086. (Illus.). 24p. (ps-k). 1990. 7.00 (0-679-80532-X) Random Bks Yng Read.
—Nature. LC 90-23568. (Illus.). 24p. (ps-k). 1991. 7.00 (0-679-81805-7) Random Bks Yng Read.
—Noises. LC 90-8587. (Illus.). 24p. (ps-k). 1991. 6.95 (0-679-81161-3) Random Bks Yng Read.
—Opposites. LC 89-63093. (Illus.). 24p. (ps-k). 1990. 6.95 (0-679-80620-2) Random Bks Yng Read.
—Seasons. LC 89-63094. (Illus.). 24p. (ps-k). 1990. 6.95 (0-679-80621-0) Random Bks Yng Read.
—Shopping. LC 90-23567. (Illus.). 24p. (ps-k). 1991. 7.00 (0-679-81803-0) Random Bks Yng Read.
—Sorting. LC 90-8575. (Illus.). 24p. (ps-k). 1991. 6.95 (0-679-81162-1) Random Bks Yng Read.
—Things That Go. LC 90-23562. (Illus.). 24p. (ps-k). 1991. 7.00 (0-679-81804-9) Random Bks Yng Read.
—Time. LC 90-8576. (Illus.). 24p. (ps-k). 1991. 6.95 (0-679-81164-8) Random Bks Yng Read.
—Touch. LC 89-63095. (Illus.). (ps-k). 1990. 6.95 (0-679-80623-7) Random Bks Yng Read.
Oliver, Tony, ed. see Kipling, Rudyard.
Oliver, Vickie. Kalyn's Life Adventures: Not Even in a Book. 32p. (gr. 4-10). 1991. 4.95 (1-877610-07-0) Sea Island.
Olivier, Pierre & Wessels, Florence. My Body. (Illus.). 128p. (ps-3). 1993. 10.00 (0-679-84160-1); PLB 11.99 (0-679-94160-6) Random Bks Yng Read.
Oliviero, Jamie. The Fish Skin. Morriseau, Brent, illus. LC 92-85509. 40p. (ps-2). 1993. 14.95 (1-56282-401-5); PLB 14.89 (1-56282-402-3) Hyprn Child.
Ollivant, Alfred. Bob, Son of Battle. (Illus.). (gr. 5 up). 1967. pap. 2.50 (0-8049-0141-4, CL-141) Airmont.
—Bob, Son of Battle. Hinkle, Don, ed. Riccio, Frank, illus. LC 87-15477. 48p. (gr. 3-6). 1988. PLB 12.89 (0-8167-1211-5); pap. text ed. 3.95 (0-8167-1212-3) Troll Assocs.
—Bob, Son of Battle. (Illus.). 306p. (gr. 5 up). 1988. 16. 95 (0-9616844-2-9) GreenHouse Pub.
Olliver, Jane, ed. Doubleday Children's Atlas. LC 86-67523. (Illus.). 96p. (gr. k-6). 1987. pap. 14.00 (0-385-23760-X) Doubleday.
—A Treasury of Animal Stories. Spenceley, Annabel, illus. LC 92-53110. 160p. (Orig.). (gr. k-5). 1992. pap. 5.95 (1-85697-831-1) Kingfisher Bks.
—A Treasury of Giant & Monster Stories. Spenceley, Annabel, illus. LC 92-53112. 160p. (Orig.). (gr. k-5). 1992. pap. 5.95 (1-85697-832-X) Kingfisher Bks.
—A Treasury of Spooky Stories. Spenceley, Annabel, illus. LC 92-53111. 160p. (Orig.). (gr. k-5). 1992. pap. 5.95 (1-85697-830-3) Kingfisher Bks.
Olmsted, Cheryl. Alphabet Cooking Cards. (gr. k-1). 1990. pap. 11.95 (0-8224-0454-0) Fearon Teach Aids.
Olney, Ross R. The Farm Combine. (Illus.). 64p. (gr. 4 up). 1984. PLB 10.85 (0-8027-6568-8) Walker & Co.
Olofsdotter, Marie. Sofia & the Heartmender. Olofsdotter, Marie, illus. LC 92-46200. 32p. (gr. k up). 1993. 14.95 (0-915793-50-4) Free Spirit Pub.
Olsav Lautenschlaeger, Susan J. Blooming Discoveries: Fun Language Activities to Explore Everyday Wonders Based on Bloom's Taxonomy. 80p. (gr. k-5). 1991. pap. 14.95 (1-55999-206-9) LinguiSystems.
Olsen, Alfa-Betty & Efron, Marshall. Gabby the Shrew. Chast, Roz, illus. LC 92-31902. 1994. lib. bdg. write for info. (0-679-94467-2) Random.
Olsen, Alfa-Betty, jt. auth. see Efron, Marshall.
Olsen, Carol. Left-Over Louie. (Illus.). 169p. (Orig.). 1993. 29.95 (1-883078-75-X); pap. 11.95 (1-883078-76-8) Gig Harbor Pr.
Olsen, David C., ed. The Greatest Songs of 1890-1920. 112p. (Orig.). 1990. pap. text ed. 9.95 (0-89898-599-4) CPP Belwin.
—The Greatest Songs of 1940-1960. 112p. (Orig.). 1990. pap. text ed. 9.95 (0-89898-601-X) CPP Belwin.
—The Greatest Songs of 1975-1990. 112p. (Orig.). 1993. pap. text ed. 9.95 (0-89898-603-6) CPP Belwin.
—Life of the Christmas Party. 160p. (Orig.). 1988. pap. text ed. 19.95 (0-89898-645-1) CPP Belwin.
—One Hundred Seventy Christmas Songs & Carols. 232p. (Orig.). 1987. pap. text ed. 19.95 (0-89898-644-3) CPP Belwin.
—Songs of Judy Garland. 80p. (Orig.). 1990. pap. text ed. 11.95 (0-89898-611-7) CPP Belwin.
—The World's Best Piano. 280p. (Orig.). 1991. pap. text ed. 19.95 (0-89898-598-6) CPP Belwin.
Olsen, David C., ed. see Charles, Ray.
Olsen, E. A. Adrift on a Raft. Le Blanc, L., illus. LC 68-16397. 48p. (gr. 3 up). 1970. PLB 10.95 (0-87783-000-2); pap. 3.94 deluxe ed. (0-87783-078-9); cassette 10.60x (0-87783-176-9) Oddo.
—Killer in the Trap. Le Blanc, L., illus. LC 68-16399. 48p. (gr. 3 up). 1970. PLB 10.95 (0-87783-019-3); pap. 3.94 deluxe ed. (0-87783-097-5); cassette 10.60x (0-87783-190-4) Oddo.
—Lobster King. LC 68-16400. (Illus.). 48p. (gr. 3 up). 1970. PLB 10.95 (0-87783-024-X); pap. 3.94 deluxe ed. (0-87783-099-1); cassette 10.60x (0-87783-192-0) Oddo.
—Mystery at Salvage Rock. LC 68-16401. (Illus.). 48p. (gr. 3 up). 1970. PLB 10.95 (0-87783-027-4); pap. 3.94 deluxe ed. (0-87783-101-7); cassette 10.60x (0-87783-195-5) Oddo.

Olsen, Frank H. Inventors Who Left Their Brand on America. 1991. pap. 3.50 (0-553-29211-0) Bantam.

Olsen, Glenda P. Birds of Prey. LC 93-2670. 1993. write for info. (1-56766-059-2) Childs World.

Olsen, Ib S. The Grown-up Trap. LC 91-35251. (Illus.). 32p. (ps-3). 1992. 13.95 (0-934738-96-3) Thomasson-Grant.

Olsen, Larry D. Outdoor Survival Skills. rev. ed. (Illus.). (gr. 6 up). 1988. pap. 9.95 (0-9620429-0-0) Salmon Falls Pub.

Olsen, Penny. Falcons & Hawks. LC 92-11986. (Illus.). 72p. (gr. 5 up). 1992. PLB 17.95 (0-8160-2843-5) Facts on File.

Olsen, Roger E., ed. see Seward, Bernard.

Olsen, Tillie. Yonnondio: From the Thirties. 144p. (gr. 9 up). 1975. pap. 1.95 (0-440-39881-9, LE) Dell.

Olsen, Victoria. Emily Dickinson. Horner, Matina S., intro. by. (Illus.). 112p. (gr. 5 up). 1990. 17.95 (1-55546-649-4) Chelsea Hse.

Olsen, Warren & Rinden, David. Explanation of Luther's Small Catachism. 128p. (gr. 7-8). 1988. text ed. 7.95 (0-943167-12-4) Faith & Fellowship Pr.

Olsen, Warren & Rinden, David, eds. Explanation of Luther's Small Catechism. 2nd ed. 128p. (gr. 7-8). 1992. text ed. 7.95 (0-943167-20-5) Faith & Fellowship Pr.

Olshansky, Joanne. The Pizza Boogie Songbook. Colucci, Kristina & Boughton, Narda, illus. 33p. (Orig.). (gr. k-6). 1990. pap. 9.95 (0-9626239-0-3) JHO Music.

Olshtain, Elite, et al. The Junior Files, File 1: English for Today & Tomorrow. rev. ed. Berman, Aaron & Chapman, Charles, eds. (Illus.). 270p. (gr. 6-10). 1991. pap. write for info. (1-878598-02-3) Alta Bk Co Pubs.

Olson, Arielle N. Hurry Home, Grandma! Dabcovich, Lydia, illus. LC 84-1529. 32p. (ps-1). 1984. 9.95 (0-525-44113-1, DCB) Dutton Child Bks.

—Hurry Home, Grandma! LC 84-1529. (Illus.). 32p. (ps-1). 1990. pap. 3.95 (0-525-44650-8, DCB) Dutton Child Bks.

—The Lighthouse Keeper's Daughter. Wentworth, Elaine, illus. 32p. (ps-3). 1987. 14.95 (0-316-65057-9) Little.

—Noah's Cats & the Devil's Fire. Moser, Barry, illus. LC 91-17408. 32p. (ps-2). 1992. 14.95 (0-531-05984-7); lib. bdg. 14.99 (0-531-08584-8) Orchard Bks Watts.

Olson, Eleanor. Wayne Estes: A Hero's Legacy. (Illus.). (gr. 7-12). 1991. pap. text ed. 6.00 (0-9628317-0-0) E Olson.

Olson, Gene, jt. auth. see Olson, Joan.

Olson, Jim. The Reindeer & the Easter Bunny. Van Vleck, Jane & Olson, Sally, eds. (Illus.). 18p. (Orig.). (gr. 1-4). 1981. pap. 4.95 (0-943806-00-3) Neahtawanta Pr.

Olson, Joan & Olson, Gene. Washington Times & Trails. rev. ed. LC 75-83521. (Illus.). (gr. 7-12). 1983. pap. 8.97x (0-913366-01-3) Windyridge.

Olson, Kenfield & Houghton, Cleo, eds. Collected Memoirs of Central School: Kirkland, Washington, 1890-1980. 67p. (Orig.). (gr. 9-12). 1982. pap. 5.00 (0-685-28866-8) Marymoor Mus.

Olson, Margaret J. Aloysious Alligator. 2nd ed. Olson, Margaret J., illus. (gr. k-2). 1980. pap. 3.00 (0-934876-14-2) Creative Storytime.

—Tell & Draw Animal Cut-outs. 3rd ed. (gr. k-2). 1963. pap. 3.00 (0-934876-15-0) Creative Storytime.

—Tell & Draw Stories. (Illus.). (ps-3). 1963. PLB 11.95 (0-934876-05-3); pap. 6.95 (0-934876-01-0) Creative Storytime.

Olson, Marjorie E. Art Activities: To Encourage Perceptual Development. 64p. (gr. 1-4). 1977. Level C. 5.00 (0-87879-831-5, Ann Arbor Div) Acad Therapy.

—Benji the Bug: Directionality Concepts for Children. (Illus.). 48p. (gr. k-1). 1973. pap. text ed. 4.00 (0-87879-693-2, Ann Arbor Div) Acad Therapy.

—Finton the Fish: Visual Discriminations for Children. (Illus.). 29p. (gr. k-1). 1974. pap. text ed. 4.00 (0-87879-692-4, Ann Arbor Div) Acad Therapy.

—Itty the Inchworm: Motor Coordination Experiences for Children. (Illus.). 31p. (gr. k-1). 1974. pap. text ed. 4.00 (0-87879-694-0, Ann Arbor Div) Acad Therapy.

—Roxy the Robin: Sequence Relationships for Children. (Illus.). 48p. (gr. k-1). 1974. pap. text ed. 4.00 (0-87879-695-9, Ann Arbor Div) Acad Therapy.

Olson, Marjorie T. The Sly Spy & Other Stories. Reusable ed. (Illus.). 64p. (gr. 2-3). 1979. pap. 6.50 (0-87879-830-7, Ann Arbor Div) Acad Therapy.

Olson, Michelle. The Adventures of Eggbert Egghead. Van Treese, James B., ed. (Illus.). 1992. 9.95 (1-880416-27-1) NW Pub.

Olson, Norman. I Can Read About Trucks & Cars. LC 72-96957. (Illus.). 32p. (gr. 2-4). 1973. pap. 1.95 (0-89375-055-7) Troll Assocs.

Olson, Rachel. Twas the Night Before: A Picture-Story of the Nativity. Wray, Rhonda, ed. Zapel, Arthur L., illus. LC 93-26740. 24p. (Orig.). (gr. k-3). 1993. 14.95 (0-916260-85-2, B143) Meriwether Pub.

Olson, Sally, ed. see Olson, Jim.

Olson, Wayne, ed. see Schwartz, Frederick J.

Olswanger, Anna. Big Mistreatin' Bittersweet'n' Blues. Moser, Barry, illus. LC 92-24430. 1994. write for info. (0-553-09184-0) Bantam.

Olszewski, Lema J., ed. see Ward, Fred & Ward, Betty.

Olu Easmon, Carol. Bisi & the Golden Disc. LC 89-77347. (Illus.). 32p. 1990. 13.95 (0-940793-56-3, Pub. by Crocodile Bks) Interlink Pub.

Olujic, Grozdana. Rose of Mother-of-Pearl. Kessler, Jascha, tr. Jacobi, Kathy, illus. LC 83-18254. (SER & CRO.). 19p. (Orig.). (gr. 4 up). 1983. pap. 6.00 (0-915124-90-4, Pub. by Toothpaste) Coffee Hse.

O'Mahony, Kieran, ed. see Brinn, Ross.

O'Mahony, Kieran, ed. see Jacobson, Sheldon A.

O'Malley, Brian. Secret of the Mountains. 28p. (gr. 2-5). 1993. 14.95 (0-7634-4460-X) Westcliffe Pubs Inc.

O'Malley, Kevin. The Box. O'Malley, Kevin, illus. LC 92-25153. 32p. 1993. 8.95 (1-55670-275-2) Stewart Tabori & Chang.

—Bruno, You're Late for School. LC 92-44498. 1993. write for info. (1-55670-287-6) Stewart Tabori & Chang.

—Froggy Went A-Courtin' O'Malley, Kevin, illus. LC 91-41449. 32p. 1992. 14.95 (1-55670-260-4) Stewart Tabori & Chang.

—Miss Mary Mack. (gr. 4-7). 1993. 4.95 (1-55670-346-5) Stewart Tabori & Chang.

—Who Killed Cock Robin? LC 92-40340. (Illus.). (gr. k-3). 1993. write for info. (0-688-12430-5); PLB write for info. (0-688-12431-3) Lothrop.

Omar, N. Bradley. My Toy Box. 16p. 1980. pap. 2.95 (0-671-41343-0) S&S Trade.

O'Mara, Lesley, ed. Classic Animal Stories. Dominguez, Angel, illus. 160p. (gr. 1 up). 1991. 18.95 (1-55970-143-9) Arcade Pub Inc.

O'Meara, Jan. Kids' Guide to Common Alaska Critters. O'Meara, Michael, illus. 32p. (Orig.). 1993. pap. text ed. 7.95 (0-9621543-3-4) Wizard Works.

Omer, Devorah. Once There Was a Hassid. Shvo, Aaron, illus. 28p. (gr. 4 up). 1987. 9.95 (0-915361-73-6) Modan-Adama Bks.

Omodt, Jimm. The Chronicles of Caroltune: Scherzo Finds a Home. Omodt, Mary, ed. & illus. 40p. (Orig.). (gr. 3-8). 1993. pap. text ed. 10.00 (1-881026-05-1) Scherzo Pub.

Omodt, Jimm A. The Huge Hairy Horse Comes Back with Twenty-Six More. Omodt, Mary, ed. & illus. 40p. (Orig.). (ps-5). 1993. pap. text ed. 10.00 (1-881026-03-5); pap. text ed. 20.00 incl. cassette (1-881026-02-7) Scherzo Pub.

Omodt, Mary, ed. & illus. see Omodt, Jimm.

Omodt, Mary, ed. & illus. see Omodt, Jimm A.

Omoleye, Amoke. Yoruba Children's Tales. Omoleye, Amoke, illus. 33p. (Orig.). (gr. k-8). 1990. pap. 5.95 (0-9625699-1-7) Amoke Omoleye Pub.

Omond, Roger. Steve Biko & Apartheid. (Illus.). 95p. (gr. 9-12). 1991. 16.95 (0-237-60041-2, Pub. by Evans Bros Ltd) Trafalgar.

Omotani, Les M. Konnichi Wa, Japan. 1992. pap. 15.95 (0-8442-8497-1, Passport Bks) NTC Pub Grp.

—Konnichi Wa, Japan: Middle School Through High School. (JPN.). 120p. (gr. 7-12). 1993. pap. 15.95 (0-685-62857-4, F8497-1, Natl Textbk) NTC Pub Grp.

Ondori Publishing Company Staff. Desserts You Can Make: Children's Cookbook, Vol. 2. (Illus.). 64p. (Orig.). (gr. 7 up). 1984. pap. 9.95 (0-87040-561-6) Japan Pubns USA.

O'Neal, Debbie T. My Read-&-Do Bible Storybook. Ebert, Len, illus. LC 89-15184. 128p. (Orig.). (gr. 3-8). 1989. pap. 14.99 kivar (0-8066-2431-0, 9-2431) Augsburg Fortress.

O'Neal, Debbie T. & Rosato, Amelia. The Lost Coin. Rosato, Amelia, illus. LC 92-46610. 14p. 1993. 7.00 (0-8170-1194-3) Judson.

—The Lost Sheep. Rosato, Amelia, illus. LC 92-46612. 14p. 1993. 7.00 (0-8170-1193-5) Judson.

O'Neal, Esther. Knowing Christ. (Illus.). 64p. (gr. k-6). 1962. pap. text ed. 8.99 (1-55976-026-5) CEF Press.

O'Neal, Kathleen, jt. auth. see Polette, Nancy.

O'Neal, Michael. The Assassination of Abraham Lincoln: Opposing Viewpoints. LC 91-13682. (Illus.). 112p. (gr. 5-8). 1991. PLB 14.95 (0-89908-092-8) Greenhaven.

—Haunted Houses. 1994. 14.95 (1-56510-095-6) Greenhaven.

—King Arthur: Opposing Viewpoints. LC 92-11421. (Illus.). 112p. (gr. 5-8). 1992. 14.95 (0-89908-095-2) Greenhaven.

—President Truman & the Atomic Bomb: Opposing Viewpoints. LC 90-35611. (Illus.). 112p. (gr. 5-8). 1990. PLB 14.95 (0-89908-079-0) Greenhaven.

O'Neal, Scott. Theory on the Major Scales. (Illus.). 64p. (Orig.). 1993. pap. 6.95 (0-8059-3414-6) Dorrance.

O'Neal, Zibby. A Formal Feeling. LC 82-2018. (Illus.). 168p. (gr. 7 up). 1982. pap. 12.95 (0-670-32488-4) Viking Child Bks.

—Grandma Moses. 1987. pap. 4.99 (0-14-032220-5, Puffin) Puffin Bks.

—Grandma Moses: Painter of Rural. Ruff, Donna & Moses, Grandma, illus. LC 86-4071. 64p. (gr. 2-6). 1986. pap. 10.95 (0-670-80664-1) Viking Child Bks.

—Grandma Moses: Painter of Rural America. Ruff, Donna, illus. (gr. 2-6). pap. 3.50 (0-317-62289-7, Puffin) Puffin Bks.

—In Summer Light. LC 85-50806. 180p. (gr. 7 up). 1985. pap. 6.00 (0-670-80784-2) Viking Child Bks.

—In Summer Light. 160p. (gr. 6 up). 1986. pap. 3.50 (0-553-25940-7) Bantam.

—The Language of Goldfish. LC 79-19167. (gr. 6 up). 1980. pap. 14.95 (0-670-41785-8) Viking Child Bks.

—The Language of Goldfish. large type ed. PLB 15.95 (0-685-29758-6, Crnrstn Bks) BDD LT Grp.

—Language of Goldfish. 1990. pap. 3.99 (0-14-034540-X, Puffin) Puffin Bks.

—A Long Way to Go. Dooling, Michael, illus. 64p. (gr. 2-6). 1990. pap. 11.95 (0-670-82532-8) Viking Child Bks.

—A Long Way to Go: A Story of Women's Right to Vote. Dooling, Michael, illus. 64p. (gr. 2-6). 1992. pap. 3.99 (0-14-032950-1, Puffin) Puffin Bks.

O'Neil, Catherine. How & Why? A Kid's Book about the Body. Barr, Loel, illus. 144p. (Orig.). (gr. 2 up). 1987. pap. 9.95 (0-89043-099-3) Consumer Reports.

O'Neil, Dennis. Batman: Tales of the Demon. Levitz, Paul, et al, eds. Brown, Bob, et al, illus. 208p. (Orig.). 1991. pap. 17.95 (0-930289-94-3) DC Comics.

O'Neil, Dennis, ed. see Barr, Mike.

O'Neil, Dennis, ed. see Newell, Mindy.

O'Neil, Dennis, ed. see Starlin, Jim.

O'Neil, Dennis, ed. see Wagner, John & Grant, Alan.

O'Neil, Karen E. Health & Medicine Projects for Young Scientists. (Illus.). 128p. (gr. 8-9). 1993. PLB 13.90 (0-531-11050-8); pap. 6.95 (0-531-15668-0) Watts.

O'Neil, R., et al. New Dimensions: Advanced Level. (Illus.). 1993. pap. text ed. 13.50 (0-8013-0607-8); tchr's. ed. 18.95 (0-8013-0921-2); wkbk. 7.50 (0-8013-0927-1); 2 cassettes 24.95 (0-8013-0926-3) Longman.

O'Neill, Catharine. Mrs. Dunphy's Dog. (Illus.). 32p. (ps-3). 1989. pap. 3.95 (0-14-050622-5, Puffin) Puffin Bks.

O'Neill, Catherine. Amazing Mysteries of the World. Crump, Donald J., ed. LC 83-13444. 104p. (gr. 3-8). 1983. 8.95 (0-87044-497-2); PLB 12.50 (0-87044-502-2) Natl Geog.

—Dogs on Duty. LC 88-15933. (Illus.). 104p. (gr. 4 up). 1988. 8.95 (0-87044-659-2); lib. bdg. 12.50 (0-87044-664-9) Natl Geog.

—Focus on Alcohol. Neuahaus, David, illus. 56p. (gr. 2-4). 1990. PLB 14.95 (0-941477-96-7) TFC Bks NY.

—Let's Visit a Chocolate Factory. Parker, James W., illus. LC 87-3460. 32p. (gr. 2-4). 1988. PLB 10.79 (0-8167-1161-5); pap. text ed. 2.95 (0-8167-1162-3) Troll Assocs.

—Let's Visit a Printing Plant. Parker, James W., illus. LC 87-3484. 32p. (gr. 2-4). 1988. PLB 10.79 (0-8167-1163-1); pap. text ed. 2.95 (0-8167-1164-X) Troll Assocs.

—Natural Wonders of North America. Crump, Donald J., ed. LC 84-16614. (Illus.). 104p. (gr. 3-8). 1984. 8.95 (0-87044-514-6); PLB 12.50 (0-87044-519-7) Natl Geog.

O'Neill, Judith. Transported to Van Diemen's Land. (Illus.). 48p. (gr. 7 up). 1977. pap. 7.50 (0-521-21231-6) Cambridge U Pr.

O'Neill, Laura. No More Little Miss Perfect. 112p. (gr. 4-9). 1992. pap. 2.95 (0-448-40490-7, G&D) Putnam Pub Group.

—The Ski Trip. 128p. (Orig.). (gr. 3-9). 1993. pap. 2.95 (0-448-40494-X, G&D) Putnam Pub Group.

O'Neill, Laurie. Wounded Knee: Death of a Dream. LC 92-12998. (Illus.). 64p. (gr. 4-6). 1993. 14.40 (1-56294-253-0) Millbrook Pr.

O'Neill, Martha, jt. auth. see Snyder, Thomas F.

O'Neill, Martha, ed. see Snyder, Thomas F.

O'Neill, Martha, ed. see Tsumura, Ted K. & Jones, Lorraine H.

O'Neill, Mary. Air Scare. Bindon, John, illus. LC 89-49626. 32p. (gr. 3-6). 1991. lib. bdg. 12.89 (0-8167-2082-7); pap. text ed. 3.95 (0-8167-2083-5) Troll Assocs.

—Dinosaur Mysteries. Bindon, John, illus. LC 89-4789. 32p. (gr. 3-7). 1989. lib. bdg. 12.89 (0-8167-1635-8); pap. text ed. 3.95 (0-8167-1636-6) Troll Assocs.

—A Family of Dinosaurs. Bindon, John, illus. LC 89-4792. 32p. (gr. 3-7). 1989. lib. bdg. 12.89 (0-8167-1633-1); pap. text ed. 3.95 (0-8167-1634-X) Troll Assocs.

—Hailstones & Halibut Bones: Adventures in Color. Wallner, John, illus. 1989. 12.95 (0-385-24484-3) Doubleday.

—Life after the Dinosaurs. Bindon, John, illus. LC 89-31164. 32p. (gr. 3-7). 1989. lib. bdg. 12.89 (0-8167-1639-0); pap. text ed. 3.95 (0-8167-1640-4) Troll Assocs.

—Nature in Danger. Bindon, John, illus. LC 90-37437. 32p. (gr. 3-6). 1991. lib. bdg. 12.89 (0-8167-2285-4); pap. text ed. 3.95 (0-8167-2286-2) Troll Assocs.

—Power Failure. Bindon, John, illus. LC 90-11148. 32p. (gr. 3-6). 1991. PLB 12.89 (0-8167-2288-9); pap. text ed. 3.95 (0-8167-2289-7) Troll Assocs.

—Water Squeeze. Bindon, John, illus. LC 89-77456. 32p. (gr. 3-6). 1989. PLB 12.89 (0-8167-2080-0); pap. text ed. 3.95 (0-8167-2081-9) Troll Assocs.

—Where Are All the Dinosaurs? Bindon, John, illus. LC 89-31165. 32p. (gr. 2-6). 1989. lib. bdg. 12.89 (0-8167-1637-4); pap. text ed. 3.95 (0-8167-1638-2) Troll Assocs.

O'Neill, R., et al. New Dimensions: Intermediate Level. (Illus.). 1993. pap. text ed. 13.50 (0-8013-0459-8); tchr's. ed. 18.95 (0-8013-0852-6); wkbk. 7.50 (0-8013-0851-8); 2 cassettes 24.95 (0-8013-0856-9) Longman.

O'Neill, Richard & Bryan, Antonia D. Presidents of the U. S. LC 92-9401. (Illus.). 64p. (gr. 2-6). 1993. 7.98 (0-8317-2310-6) Smithmark.

O'Neill, Teresa, ed. Immigration: Opposing Viewpoints. LC 92-21794. 288p. 1992. lib. bdg. 17.95 (1-56510-007-7); pap. 9.95 (1-56510-006-9) Greenhaven.

O'Neill, Terry. The Homeless: Distinguishing Between Fact & Opinion. LC 90-45283. (Illus.). 32p. (gr. 3-6). 1990. PLB 10.95 (0-89908-605-5) Greenhaven.
—Zoos: Identifying Propaganda Techniques. LC 90-3247. (Illus.). 32p. (gr. 3-6). 1990. pap. text ed. 10.95 (0-89908-600-4) Greenhaven.
O'Neill, Terry, ed. Paranormal Phenomena: Opposing Viewpoints. LC 90-24081. (Illus.). 240p. (gr. 10 up). 1991. PLB 17.95 (0-89908-487-7); pap. 9.95 (0-89908-462-1) Greenhaven.
O'Neill, Terry & Bernards, Neal, eds. Male-Female Roles: Opposing Viewpoints. LC 89-23419. (Illus.). 261p. (gr. 10 up). 1989. lib. bdg. 17.95 (0-89908-446-X); pap. 9.95 (0-89908-421-4) Greenhaven.
O'Neill, Terry & Swisher, Karin, eds. Economics in America: Opposing Viewpoints. LC 91-42802. (Illus.). 264p. (gr. 10 up). 1992. PLB 17.95 (0-89908-187-8); pap. text ed. 9.95 (0-89908-162-2) Greenhaven.
Ong, Cristina, illus. The Little Engine That Could ABC. 20p. (ps-3). 1994. bds. 2.95 (0-448-40262-9, Platt & Munk Pubs) Putnam Pub Group.
—The Little Engine That Could Colors. 20p. (ps-3). 1994. bds. 2.95 (0-448-40264-5, Platt & Munk Pubs) Putnam Pub Group.
—The Little Engine That Could: Let's Sing ABC. 24p. (ps). 1993. 9.95 (0-448-40509-1, Platt & Munk Pubs) Putnam Pub Group.
—The Little Engine That Could: Little Library, 3 bks. (Set incls. Colors, ABC & Numbers, 20 pgs. ea. bk.). (ps). 1992. Set. bds. 7.95 slipcased (0-448-40261-0, Platt & Munk Pubs) Putnam Pub Group.
—The Little Engine That Could Numbers. 20p. (ps-3). 1994. bds. 2.95 (0-448-40263-7, Platt & Munk Pubs) Putnam Pub Group.
Ongaro, A. St. Pancratius. (gr. 4-8). 1977. 2.00 (0-8198-0220-4); pap. 1.25 (0-8198-0221-2) St Paul Bks.
Onge, Susan St. see St. Onge, Susan, et al.
Oni, Sauda. What Kwanzaa Means to Me. Brother Theo, illus. 36p. (gr. k-3). Date not set. pap. 3.95 (0-912444-38-X) DARE Bks.
Ono, Koichi. Little Panda Bear. McClain, Mary, illus. 12p. (ps-2). 1982. 4.95 (0-671-42549-8, Little Simon) S&S Trade.

Ontario Science Center Staff. Foodworks: Over One Hundred Science Activities & Fascinating Facts That Explore the Magic of Food. LC 87-1796. 96p. (gr. 7-12). 1987. pap. 8.61 (0-201-11470-4) Addison-Wesley.
—Scienceworks: Sixty-Five Experiments That Introduce the Fun & Wonder of Science. Holdcroft, Tina, illus. (gr. 2-7). 1986. pap. 8.61 (0-201-16780-8) Addison-Wesley.

Onyefulu, Ifeoma. A Is for Africa. Onyefulu, Ifeoma, photos by. LC 92-39964. (Illus.). 32p. (ps-3). 1993. 14.99 (0-525-65147-0, Cobblehill Bks) Dutton Child Bks.
Ooka, D. T., tr. see Horio, Seishi.
Ooka, D. T., tr. see Okawa, Essei.
Ooka, D. T., tr. see Shibano, Tamizo.
Ooka, D. T., tr. see Watanabe, Yuichi.
Ooka, D. T., tr. see Yazaki, Setsuo.
Ooka, Diane, tr. see Masui, Mitsuko.
Oomen, Francine. Come Outside. Oomen, Francine, illus. 8p. (ps). 1993. 4.99 (0-8431-3535-2) Price Stern.
—I Can Do It, Too! Oomen, Francine, illus. 8p. (ps). 1993. 4.99 (0-8431-3534-4) Price Stern.
—Moo, Says the Cow. Oomen, Francine, illus. 8p. (ps). 1993. 4.99 (0-8431-3532-8) Price Stern.
—My Day! Oomen, Francine, illus. 8p. (ps). 1993. 4.99 (0-8431-3533-6) Price Stern.
Opfell, Olga S. Women Prime Ministers & Presidents, 1960-1992. LC 92-56675. (Illus.). 237p. (gr. 9-12). 1993. lib. bdg. 29.95x (0-89950-790-5) McFarland & Co.
Opheim, Teresa. AIDS: Distinguishing Between Fact & Opinion. LC 89-12006. (Illus.). 32p. (gr. 3-6). 1990. PLB 10.95 (0-89908-633-0) Greenhaven.
Opie, Brenda & McAvinn, Douglas. Effective Language Arts Techniques for Middle Grades (4-8) An Integrated Approach. McAvinn, Douglas, illus. 84p. (Orig.). (gr. 4-8). 1989. pap. text ed. 7.95 (0-685-26803-9) Masterminds Pubns.
Opie, I. & Opie, P. Tail Feathers from Mother Goose: The Opie Rhyme Book. (Illus.). 124p. 1991. 7.99 (0-517-05555-4) Outlet Bk Co.
Opie, Iona, jt. auth. see Opie, Peter.
Opie, Iona & Opie, Peter, eds. Oxford Dictionary of Nursery Rhymes. (Illus.). (ps-3). 1951. 47.50x (0-19-869111-4) OUP.
—Oxford Nursery Rhyme Book. Hassall, Joan, illus. (ps-3). 1955. 29.95x (0-19-869112-2) OUP.
Opie, Iona, jt. ed. see Opie, Peter.
Opie, Iona, et al. The Treasures of Childhood: Books, Toys & Games from the Opie Collection. (Illus.). 192p. 1990. 40.00 (1-55970-047-5); pre Dec. 1990 45.00 (0-685-31105-8) Arcade Pub Inc.
Opie, P., jt. auth. see Opie, I.
Opie, Peter & Opie, Iona. I Saw Esau. Sendak, Maurice, illus. LC 91-71845. 160p. (ps-up). 1992. 19.95 (1-56402-046-0) Candlewick Pr.
Opie, Peter & Opie, Iona, eds. Tail Feathers from Mother Goose: The Opie Rhyme Book. (Illus.). (ps up). 1988. 15.95 (0-316-65081-1) Little.
Opie, Peter, jt. ed. see Opie, Iona.
Opie, William. Shenandoah Spector. 120p. (Orig.). 1989. pap. write for info. Opie Pub.

Opinion Editors, tr. see Los Angeles Children's Museum Staff.
Opler, Paul. Butterflies East & West: A Book to Color. Strawn, Susan, illus. 96p. (Orig.). (gr. 1-6). 1993. pap. 8.95 (1-879373-45-9) R Rinehart.
Opler, Paul & Strawn, Susan. Butterflies of Eastern North America: A Coloring Album & Activity Book. Strawn, Susan, illus. (gr. 1-6). 1989. pap. 4.95 (0-911797-53-X) R Rinehart.
Oppel, Kenneth. Dead Water Zone. LC 92-37282. 1993. 14.95 (0-316-65102-8, Joy St Bks) Little.
Oppenheim, Carol. Science Is Fun Activity Package: For Families & Classroom Groups - Sing a Song of Science with Carol & the Kids. 1993. incl. song tape 23.90 (0-9633555-6-2) Cracom.
—Science Is Fun! For Families & Classroom Groups. Schmitt, Judy & Cooney, Cynthia D., illus. LC 92-35717. 198p. (Orig.). (ps up). 1993. pap. 14.95 (0-9633555-1-1) Cracom.
Oppenheim, Joanne. Black Hawk, Frontier Warrior. new ed. LC 78-18049. (Illus.). 48p. (gr. 4-6). 1979. PLB 10.59 (0-89375-157-X); pap. 3.50 (0-89375-147-2) Troll Assocs.
—Could It Be - Bank Street. (ps-3). 1990. PLB 9.99 (0-553-05893-2, Little Rooster); pap. 3.50 (0-553-34924-4) Bantam.
—Do You Like Cats? Newsom, Carol, illus. LC 92-14113. 1993. 9.99 (0-553-09116-6, Little Rooster); pap. 3.50 (0-553-37107-X, Little Rooster) Bantam.
—Eency Weency Spider. (ps-3). 1991. 9.99 (0-553-07316-8); pap. 3.50 (0-553-35304-7) Bantam.
—Floratorium. Schindler, S. D., illus. Eberbach, Catherine, intro. by. LC 92-17886. (Illus.). 1994. 15.95 (0-553-09365-7); PLB 9.95 (0-553-37145-2) Bantam.
—Have You Seen Birds? Reid, Barbara, illus. (ps-2). 1988. pap. 2.95 (0-590-40890-9) Scholastic Inc.
—Left & Right. Litzinger, Rosanne, illus. LC 87-22939. 153p. (ps-3). 1989. 13.95 (0-15-200505-6, Gulliver Bks) HarBrace.
—The Not Now! Said the Cow-Bank Street. (ps-3). 1989. pap. 3.50 (0-553-34691-1) Bantam.
—Not Now! Said the Cow: Level 2. Demarest, Chris, illus. 1989. 9.99 (0-553-05826-6) Bantam.
—One Gift Deserves Another. (Illus.). 32p. (ps-1). 1992. 13.00 (0-525-44975-2, DCB) Dutton Child Bks.
—Osceola, Seminole Warrior. LC 78-60116. (Illus.). 48p. (gr. 4-6). 1979. PLB 10.59 (0-89375-158-8); pap. 3.50 (0-89375-148-0) Troll Assocs.
—Rooter Remembers. (ps-3). 1991. 11.95 (0-670-82865-3) Viking Child Bks.
—Row, Row, Row Your Boat. O'Malley, Kevin, illus. LC 92-29015. 1993. 9.99 (0-553-09498-X) Bantam.
—Sequoyah, Cherokee Hero. new ed. LC 78-60117. (Illus.). 48p. (gr. 4-6). 1979. PLB 10.59 (0-89375-159-6); pap. 3.50 (0-89375-149-9) Troll Assocs.
—The Story Book Prince. Litzinger, Rosanne, illus. LC 85-31745. 32p. (ps-3). 1987. 12.95 (0-15-200590-0, Gulliver Bks) HarBrace.
—Uh-oh! Cawed the Crow. Demarest, Chris, illus. LC 92-1629. 1993. 9.99 (0-553-09387-8, Little Rooster); pap. 3.50 (0-553-37186-X, Little Rooster) Bantam.
—Wake Up, Baby. (ps-3). 1990. PLB 9.99 (0-685-54065-0, Little Rooster); pap. 3.50 (0-685-46039-8) Bantam.
—Wake up, Baby! Sweat, Lynn, illus. (ps-3). 1990. PLB 9.99 (0-553-05907-6); pap. 3.50 (0-553-34914-7) Bantam.
Oppenheim, Joanne F. You Can't Catch Me! Shachat, Andrew, illus. LC 86-7211. 32p. (gr. k). 1986. 13.45 (0-395-41452-0) HM.
Oppenheim, Shulamith. Iblis: An Islamic Tale. Young, Ed, illus. LC 92-15060. 1993. write for info. (0-15-238016-7) HarBrace.
Oppenheim, Shulamith L. Appleblossom. Yolen, Jane, ed. Yardley, Joanna, illus. 28p. (gr. 1-7). 1991. 14.95 (0-15-203750-0, HB Juv Bks) HarBrace.
—The Lily Cupboard. Himler, Ronald, illus. LC 90-38592. 32p. (gr. 1-3). 1992. 15.00 (0-06-024669-3); PLB 14.89 (0-06-024670-7) HarpC Child Bks.
—Waiting for Noah. Hoban, Lillian, illus. LC 89-35561. 32p. (ps-2). 1990. 12.95 (0-06-024633-2); PLB 12.89 (0-06-024634-0) HarpC Child Bks.
Oppenheimer, Evelyn. Tilli Comes to Texas. Haverfield, Mary, illus. LC 86-3089. 40p. (gr. k-3). 1986. PLB 9.95 (0-937460-21-4) Hendrick-Long.
Oppenheimer, Joan F. Working on It. 144p. (gr. 7 up). 1986. pap. 2.25 (0-440-99514-0, LFL) Dell.
Oppenheimer, Joan L. Toughing It Out. (gr. 7 up). 1987. pap. 2.25 (0-373-98003-5) S&S Trade.
Oppenheimer, Lillian, jt. auth. see Lewis, Shari.
Oppenlem, Joanne. Donkey's Tale. (ps-3). 1991. 9.99 (0-553-07090-8); pap. 3.50 (0-553-35208-3) Bantam.
Oppenneer, Betsy. Betsy's Breads. rev. ed. (Illus.). 70p. (gr. 8 up). 1991. pap. 7.95 (0-9627665-2-6) Breadworks.
Oram, Hiawyn. Angry Arthur. Kitamura, Satoshi, illus. LC 88-31695. 32p. (ps-1). 1989. (DCB); pap. 3.95 (0-525-44472-6) Dutton Child Bks.
—A Boy Wants a Dinosaur. (ps-3). 1991. bds. 13.95 jacketed (0-374-30939-6) FS&G.
—Boy Wants a Dinosaur. (ps-3). 1993. pap. 4.95 (0-374-40889-0) FS&G.
—Creepy Crawly Song Book. (ps-3). 1993. 17.00 (0-374-31639-2) FS&G.
—In the Attic. Kitamura, Satoshi, illus. LC 84-15570. 32p. (ps-2). 1985. 13.95 (0-8050-0779-2, Bks Young Read) H Holt & Co.

—In the Attic. Kitamura, Satoshi, illus. LC 84-15570. 32p. (Orig.). (ps-2). 1988. pap. 4.95 (0-8050-0780-6, Bks Young Read) H Holt & Co.
—Mine! Rees, Mary, illus. 16p. (ps-k). 1992. with dust jacket 12.95 (0-8120-6303-1); pap. 5.95 (0-8120-4905-5) Barron.
—Ned & the Joybaloo. Kitamura, Satoshi, illus. 28p. (ps up). 1989. 11.95 (0-374-35501-0) FS&G.
—Out of the Blue: Poems about Color. McKee, David, illus. LC 92-55044. 64p. (gr. 1-5). 1993. 18.95 (1-56282-469-4); PLB 18.89 (1-56282-470-8) Hyprn Child.
—Reckless Ruby. Ross, Tony, illus. LC 91-20124. 32p. (ps-2). 1992. 12.00 (0-517-58744-0) Crown Bks Yng Read.
Oram, Hiawyn & Baird, Daniel. Just Like Us. (Illus.). 32p. (gr. 2-4). 1988. 11.95 (0-8192-1472-8) Morehouse Pub.
Oram, Hiawyn & Ross, Tony. Anyone Seen Harry Lately? (Illus.). 32p. (gr. 1-4). 1989. 13.95 (0-86264-198-5, Pub. by Anderson Pr UK) Trafalgar.
Oram, Liz & Baker, R. Robin. Bird Migration. LC 91-12120. (Illus.). 48p. (gr. 4-8). 1992. PLB 19.92 (0-8114-2925-3) Raintree Steck-V.
—Insect Migration. LC 91-12776. (Illus.). 48p. (gr. 4-8). 1992. PLB 19.92 (0-8114-2926-1) Raintree Steck-V.
—Mammal Migration. LC 91-12181. (Illus.). 48p. (gr. 4-8). 1992. PLB 19.92 (0-8114-2927-X) Raintree Steck-V.
—Migration in the Sea. LC 91-12765. (Illus.). 48p. (gr. 4-8). 1992. PLB 19.92 (0-8114-2928-8) Raintree Steck-V.
Orange, Anne. The Flower Book. Lerner, Sharon, illus. LC 74-12743. 32p. (gr. k-3). 1975. PLB 10.95 (0-8225-0294-1) Lerner Pubns.
—The Leaf Book. Lerner, Sharon, illus. LC 74-12745. 32p. (gr. k-3). 1975. PLB 10.95 (0-8225-0296-8) Lerner Pubns.
Orange, Charlotte, ed. see Mungin, Horace.
Orange County Association Staff. Frases Fundamentales para Comunicarse. (gr. k-12). 1975. 5.15 (0-89075-200-1) Bilingual Ed Serv.
Orange, Tom. Scripture Bulletin Boards. 96p. (gr. 2-7). 1987. 10.95 (0-86653-397-4, SS1826, Shining Star Pubns) Good Apple.
Orange, Tom & McClure, Nancee. Bulletin Boards That Bless. 48p. (gr. 4-8). 1984. wkbk. 6.95 (0-86653-201-3, SS 821, Shining Star Pubns) Good Apple.
Orczy, Emmuska. Beau Brocade. 275p. (gr. 4 up). 1980. Repr. of 1905 ed. lib. bdg. 13.95x (0-89968-194-8) Lightyear.
—Lord Tony's Wife. 1986. Repr. lib. bdg. 19.95x (0-89966-553-5) Buccaneer Bks.
—Scarlet Pimpernel. (gr. 7 up). 1964. pap. 2.95 (0-8049-0028-0, CL-28) Airmont.
—The Scarlet Pimpernel. 256p. (RL 7). 1974. pap. 3.95 (0-451-52315-6, Sig Classics) NAL-Dutton.
—The Scarlet Pimpernel. 256p. (gr. 5 up). 1989. pap. 4.99 (0-14-035056-X, Puffin) Puffin Bks.
Orden, J. Hannah. In Real Life. LC 92-31359. 192p. (gr. 7 up). 1993. pap. 3.99 (0-14-034039-4) Puffin Bks.
Orden, M. D. Van see Van Orden, M. D.
O'Rear, Sybil J. Charles Goodnight: Pioneer Cowman. LC 89-48652. (Illus.). 69p. (gr. 5-8). 1990. 10.95 (0-89015-741-3) Eakin-Sunbelt.
O'Reilly, Edward. Brown Pelican at the Pond. Strange, Florence, illus. LC 78-58689. (gr. k-4). 1979. 7.95 (0-931644-01-1) Manzanita Pr.
O'Reilly, John, ed. see DeCesare, Ruth.
O'Reilly, Susie. Batik & Tie-Die. 32p. (gr. 4-6). 1993. 14.95 (1-56847-064-9) Thomson Lrning.
—Block Printing. Mukhida, Zul, photos by. LC 92-43263. 32p. (gr. 4-6). 1993. 14.95 (1-56847-065-7) Thomson Lrning.
—Modeling. Mukhida, Zul, photos by. LC 93-7517. (Illus.). 32p. (gr. 4-6). 1993. 14.95 (1-56847-066-5) Thomson Lrning.
—Papermaking. LC 93-24397. (Illus.). 32p. (gr. 4-6). 1994. 14.95 (1-56847-069-X) Thomson Lrning.
—Stencils & Screens. LC 93-28349. (Illus.). 32p. (gr. 4-6). 1994. 14.95 (1-56847-068-1) Thomson Lrning.
—Textiles. (Illus.). 48p. (gr. 5-8). 1991. 12.90 (0-531-18441-2, Pub. by Bookwright Pr) Watts.
—Weaving. Mukhida, Zul, photos by. LC 93-18935. (Illus.). 32p. (gr. 4-6). 1993. 14.95 (1-56847-067-3) Thomson Lrning.
Oren, Rony. The Animated Haggadah (1990 Edition) (Illus.). 54p. 1990. 14.95 (0-944007-43-0) Shapolsky Pubs.
Organ, Sue. Salt Dough Models. (Illus.). 48p. 1993. pap. 12.95 (0-85532-756-1, Pub. by Search Pr UK) A Schwartz & Co.
Orgel, Doris. Ariadne, Awake! Moser, Barry, illus. LC 93-24123. 80p. (ps-3). 1994. PLB 15.99 (0-670-85158-2) Viking Child Bks.
—Button Soup. Estrada, Pau, illus. LC 93-14087. 1994. write for info. (0-553-09045-3); pap. write for info. (0-553-37341-2) Bantam.
—Crack in the Heart. (gr. 7 up). 1989. pap. 2.95 (0-449-70204-9, Juniper) Fawcett.
—Devil in Vienna. 1988. pap. 4.99 (0-14-032500-X, Puffin) Puffin Bks.
—Flower of Sheba. LC 92-33477. (ps-3). 1994. 10.95 (0-553-09041-0) Bantam.
—Midnight Soup & a Witch's Hat. Newsom, Carol, illus. (gr. 2-5). 1987. pap. 10.95 (0-670-81440-7) Viking Child Bks.

—Nobodies & Somebodies. 160p. (gr. 3-7). 1991. 13.95 (*0-670-82754-1*) Viking Child Bks.
—Nobodies & Somebodies. 160p. (gr. 3-7). 1993. pap. 3.99 (*0-14-034098-X*, Puffin) Puffin Bks.
—Sarah's Room. LC 63-13675. (Illus.). (gr. k-3). 1963. 11.95 (*0-06-024605-7*) HarpC Child Bks.
—Sarah's Room. Sendak, Maurice, illus. LC 63-13675. 48p. (ps-3). 1991. pap. 3.95 (*0-06-443238-6*, Trophy) HarpC Child Bks.
—Sarah's Room. reissued ed. Sendak, Maurice, illus. LC 63-13675. 48p. (gr. k-3). 1963. PLB 14.89 (*0-06-024606-5*) HarpC Child Bks.
—Starring Becky Suslow. (gr. 4-7). 1991. pap. 3.95 (*0-14-034063-7*, Puffin) Puffin Bks.
—Whiskers, Once & Always. Newsom, Carol, illus. 96p. (gr. 2-5). 1989. pap. 3.95 (*0-14-032038-5*, Puffin) Puffin Bks.
Orgel, Doris & Schecter, Ellen. The Flower of Sheba. Kelly, Laura, illus. LC 92-33477. 1994. pap. 3.50 (*0-553-37235-1*, Little Rooster, Little Rooster) Bantam.
Orgel, Doris, retold by. Next Time I Will: An Old English Tale. Day, Betsy, illus. LC 92-10772. 1993. 9.99 (*0-553-09031-3*); pap. 3.50 (*0-553-37147-9*) Bantam.
Oriev, Uri. Island on Bird Street. (gr. 4-7). 1992. pap. 3.80 (*0-395-61623-9*) HM.
Orihara, Kei. Children of the World: Thailand. LC 88-21050. (Illus.). 64p. (gr. 5-6). 1988. PLB 19.93 (*1-55532-223-9*) Gareth Stevens Inc.
Orii, Eijo & Orii, Masako. Simple Science Experiments with Circles. Fujishima, Kaoru, et al, illus. Knopp, Jonathan, contrib. by. LC 88-23295. 32p. (gr. 2-3). 1989. PLB 15.93 (*1-55532-857-1*) Gareth Stevens Inc.
—Simple Science Experiments with Light. Fujishima, Kaoru, et al, illus. Knopp, Jonathan, contrib. by. LC 88-23306. 32p. (gr. 2-3). 1989. PLB 15.93 (*1-55532-858-X*) Gareth Stevens Inc.
—Simple Science Experiments with Marbles. Fujishima, Kaoru, et al, illus. Knopp, Jonathan, contrib. by. LC 88-23297. 32p. (gr. 2-3). 1989. PLB 15.93 (*1-55532-856-3*) Gareth Stevens Inc.
—Simple Science Experiments with Optical Illusions. LC 88-24756. (Illus.). 32p. (gr. 2-3). 1989. PLB 15.93 (*1-55532-853-9*) Gareth Stevens Inc.
—Simple Science Experiments with Ping-Pong Balls. Fujishima, Kaoru, et al, illus. Knopp, Jonathan, contrib. by. LC 88-22508. 32p. (gr. 2-3). 1989. PLB 15.93 (*1-55532-852-0*) Gareth Stevens Inc.
—Simple Science Experiments with Starting & Stopping. Fujishima, Kaoru, et al, illus. Knopp, Jonathan, contrib. by. LC 88-20156. 32p. (gr. 2-3). 1989. PLB 15.93 (*1-55532-855-5*) Gareth Stevens Inc.
—Simple Science Experiments with Straws. Fujishima, Kaoru, et al, illus. Knopp, Jonathan, contrib. by. LC 88-23298. 32p. (gr. 2-3). 1989. PLB 15.93 (*1-55532-854-7*) Gareth Stevens Inc.
—Simple Science Experiments with Water. Fujishima, Kaoru, et al, illus. Knopp, Jonathan, contrib. by. LC 88-23304. 32p. (gr. 2-3). 1989. PLB 15.93 (*1-55532-859-8*) Gareth Stevens Inc.
Orii, Masako, jt. auth. see Orii, Eijo.
Orkand, Robert, jt. auth. see Bogot, Howard.
Orlandi, Mario & Prue, Donald. Substance Abuse. (gr. 5 up). 1989. 18.95x (*0-8160-1669-0*) Facts On File.
Orlandi, Mario, et al. Maintaining Good Health. 128p. (gr. 5 up). 1989. 18.95x (*0-8160-1667-4*) Facts On File.
—Human Sexuality. (Illus.). 128p. 1989. 18.95x (*0-8160-1666-6*) Facts on File.
—Nutrition. (Illus.). 128p. 1988. 18.95x (*0-8160-1670-4*) Facts on File.
Orlev, Uri. The Island on Bird Street. Halkin, Hillel, tr. from HEB. 176p. (gr. 5 up). 1984. 13.45 (*0-395-33887-5*, 5-92515) HM.
—Lydia: Queen of Palestine. Halkin, Hillel, tr. from HEB. LC 93-12488. 1993. 13.95 (*0-395-65660-5*) HM.
—The Man from the Other Side. Halkin, Hillel, tr. LC 90-47898. 144p. (gr. 5 up). 1991. 13.45 (*0-395-53808-4*) HM.
Ormerod, Jan. Come Back, Kittens: A Hide & Seek Book with See-Through Pages. Pearson, Susan, ed. Ormerod, Jan, illus. LC 91-30426. 32p. (ps up) 1992. 13.00 (*0-688-09134-2*) Lothrop.
—Come Back, Puppies: A Hide & Seek Book with See-Through Pages. Pearson, Susan, ed. Ormerod, Jan, illus. LC 91-30424. 32p. (ps up) 1992. 13.00 (*0-688-09135-0*) Lothrop.
—Dad's Back. LC 84-12614. (Illus.). 24p. (ps). 1985. 4.95 (*0-688-04126-4*) Lothrop.
—Joe Can Count. LC 92-43781. (Illus.). 24p. (ps up) 1993. pap. 3.95 (*0-688-04588-X*, Mulberry) Morrow.
—Just Like Me. LC 85-18056. (Illus.). 24p. (ps). 1986. 4.95 (*0-688-04211-2*) Lothrop.
—Kitten Day. Ormerod, Jan, illus. LC 88-26687. 22p. (ps-1). 1989. 13.95 (*0-688-08536-9*); PLB 13.88 (*0-688-08537-7*) Lothrop.
—Messy Baby. LC 84-12610. (Illus.). 24p. (ps). 1985. 4.95 (*0-688-04128-0*) Lothrop.
—Midnight Pillow Fight. Ormerod, Jan, illus. LC 92-53011. 32p. (ps-3). 1993. 14.95 (*1-56402-169-6*) Candlewick Pr.
—Mom's Home. Ormerod, Jan, illus. LC 87-2712. 24p. (ps). 1987. 5.95 (*0-688-07274-7*) Lothrop.
—Moonlight. Ormerod, Jan, illus. LC 81-8290. 32p. (ps-1). 1982. 14.95 (*0-688-00846-1*); PLB 14.88 (*0-688-00847-X*) Lothrop.

—One Hundred One Things to Do with a Baby. LC 84-4401. (Illus.). 32p. (ps-2). 1984. lib. bdg. 13.88 (*0-688-03802-6*) Lothrop.
—One Hundred One Things to Do with a Baby. Ormerod, Jan, illus. 32p. (ps-3). 1986. pap. 3.50 (*0-14-050447-8*, Puffin) Puffin Bks.
—One Hundred One Things to Do with a Baby. (Illus.). 32p. (ps). 1994. pap. 4.95 (*0-688-12770-3*, Mulberry) Morrow.
—Our Ollie. LC 85-17133. (Illus.). 24p. (ps). 1986. 4.95 (*0-688-04208-2*) Lothrop.
—Reading. LC 84-12628. (Illus.). 24p. (ps). 1985. 4.95 (*0-688-04127-2*) Lothrop.
—The Saucepan Game. Briley, D., ed. Ormerod, Jan, illus. LC 88-12893. 32p. (ps). 1989. 10.95 (*0-688-08518-0*); PLB 10.88 (*0-688-08519-9*) Lothrop.
—Silly Goose. LC 85-17131. (Illus.). 24p. (ps). 1986. 4.95 (*0-688-04209-0*) Lothrop.
—The Story of Chicken Licken. Ormerod, Jan, illus. LC 85-7911. 32p. (ps-1). 1986. 13.00 (*0-688-06058-7*) Lothrop.
—Sunshine. LC 80-84971. (Illus.). 32p. (ps-1). 1981. PLB 13.88 (*0-688-00553-5*) Lothrop.
—Sunshine. (Illus.). 32p. (ps-k). 1984. pap. 3.50 (*0-14-050362-5*, Puffin) Puffin Bks.
—Sunshine. LC 80-84971. (Illus.). 32p. (ps-3). 1990. pap. 3.95 (*0-688-09353-1*, Mulberry) Morrow.
—This Little Nose. Ormerod, Jan, illus. LC 87-2605. 24p. (ps). 1987. 5.95 (*0-688-07276-3*) Lothrop.
—To Baby with Love. LC 93-8093. 1994. write for info. (*0-688-12558-1*); lib. bdg. write for info. (*0-688-12559-X*) Lothrop.
—When We Went to the Zoo. (ps-3). 1991. 13.95 (*0-688-09878-9*) Lothrop.
—When We Went to the Zoo. (ps-3). 1991. 13.88 (*0-688-09879-7*) Lothrop.
—Young Joe. LC 85-17128. (Illus.). 24p. (ps). 1985. 4.95 (*0-688-04210-4*) Lothrop.
Ormerod, Jan & LLoyd, David. The Frog Prince. Omerod, Jan, illus. LC 89-12977. 32p. (ps-3). 1990. 12.95 (*0-688-09568-2*); lib. bdg. 12.88 (*0-688-09569-0*) Lothrop.
Ormondroyd, Edward. Broderick. Larrecq, John M., illus. LC 77-83752. (gr. k-3). 1969. (Pub. by Parnassus); PLB 4.77 (*0-686-86580-4*) HM.
—Broderick. Larrecq, John M., illus. LC 77-83752. 40p. (ps-3). 1984. pap. 4.95 (*0-395-36170-2*, 4-92538) HM.
—Castaways on Long Ago. 1983. pap. 2.25 (*0-553-15457-5*) Bantam.
—Johnny Castleseed. Thewlis, Diana, illus. LC 85-8189. 32p. (gr. k-3). 1988. 12.95 (*0-395-38355-2*); pap. 4.80 (*0-395-47947-9*) HM.
—Theodore. Larrecq, John M., illus. LC 66-10352. 40p. (ps-3). 1984. pap. 5.95 (*0-395-36610-0*) HM.
—Theodore's Rival. Larrecq, John M., illus. LC 76-156876. 40p. (ps-3). 1971. (Pub. by Parnassus); PLB 4.59 (*0-87466-001-7*) HM.
—Theodore's Rival. Larrecq, John M., illus. (gr. 4-8). 1986. pap. 3.80 (*0-395-41669-8*, Sandpiper) HM.
—Time at the Top. 1990. pap. 2.95 (*0-553-15420-6*) Bantam.
O'Rourke, Everett V. The Highest School in California: A Story of Bodie, California. O'Rourke, Michael E., photos by. (Illus.). 32p. (gr. 1-4). 1978. 4.00 (*0-685-22567-4*) E ORourke.
O'Rourke, Frank. Burton & Stanley. Allen, Jonathan, illus. (gr. 4-7). 1993. 15.95 (*0-87923-824-0*) Godine.
O'Rourke, Page, illus. Rub-a-Dub-Dub. 9p. (ps-1). 1993. bds. 4.95 (*0-448-40521-0*, G&D) Putnam Pub Group.
O'Rourke, Page E., illus. See & Say: A Book of First Words. 12p. (ps). 1993. bds. 4.95 (*0-448-40540-7*, G&D) Putnam Pub Group.
O'Rourke, Robert. What God Did for Zeke the Fuzzy Caterpillar. Loman, Roberta K., illus. 32p. (gr. k-2). 1991. pasted 2.50 (*0-87403-824-3*, 24-03924) Standard Pub.
Orovitz, Norma A. Puzzled! The Jewish Word Search. LC 77-83177. (gr. 3 up). 1977. pap. 3.95 (*0-8197-0022-3*) Bloch.
Orr, Anne. Tatting with Anne Orr. 1989. pap. 2.50 (*0-486-25982-X*) Dover.
Orr, C. Rob & Tyler, Jane B. Swimming Basics. Gow, Bill, illus. 48p. 1984. pap. 4.95 (*0-13-879594-0*) P-H.
Orr, Frank. Great Moments in Auto Racing. LC 73-18087. (Illus.). 160p 1974. lib. bdg. 3.69 (*0-394-92763-X*) Random Bks Yng Read.
Orr, Jack. Black Athlete: His Story in American History. Robinson, Jackie, intro. by. (gr. 6 up). 1969. PLB 14.95 (*0-87460-104-5*) Lion Bks.
Orr, Katherine. The Coral Reef Coloring Book. Orr, Katherine, illus. 48p. (gr. 2 up). 1988. pap. 5.95 (*0-88045-090-8*) Stemmer Hse.
—The Hawaiian Coral Reef Coloring Book. Orr, Katherine, illus. 48p. (Orig.). (gr. 1-6). 1992. pap. 5.95 (*0-88045-122-X*) Stemmer Hse.
—My Grandpa & the Sea. Orr, Katherine, illus. LC 89-23876. 32p. (gr. 1-4). 1990. PLB 18.95 (*0-87614-409-1*) Carolrhoda Bks.
—My Grandpa & the Sea. (ps-3). 1991. pap. 5.95 (*0-87614-525-X*) Carolrhoda Bks.
—Story of a Dolphin. Orr, Katherine, illus. LC 92-28656. 1993. 18.95 (*0-87614-777-5*) Carolrhoda Bks.
Orr, Leonard D. Physical Immortality. (gr. 7 up). 1988. pap. 10.00 (*0-945793-01-4*) Inspir Univ.
Orr, Lernard D. Breath Awareness: Breath Awareness for Public Schools, Medical Profession. (gr. 7 up). 1988. pap. 10.00 (*0-945793-02-2*) Inspir Univ.

Orr, Lisa, ed. Censorship: Opposing Viewpoints. LC 90-42854. (Illus.). 240p. (gr. 10 up). 1990. PLB 17.95 (*0-89908-479-6*); pap. text ed. 9.95 (*0-89908-454-0*) Greenhaven.
—The Homeless: Opposing Viewpoints. LC 89-25734. (Illus.). 216p. (gr. 10 up). 1990. lib. bdg. 17.95 (*0-89908-476-1*); pap. text ed. 9.95 (*0-89908-451-6*) Greenhaven.
—Sexual Values: Opposing Viewpoints. LC 89-36527. (Illus.). 214p. (gr. 10 up). 1989. lib. bdg. 17.95 (*0-89908-445-1*); pap. 9.95 (*0-89908-420-6*) Greenhaven.
Orr, Richard. The Bird Atlas. Orr, Richarad, illus. LC 93-18225. 64p. (gr. 4 up). 1993. 19.95 (*1-56458-327-9*) Dorling Kindersley.
Orr, Wendy. Aa-Choo! Ohi, Ruth, illus. 32p. (ps-3). 1992. PLB 14.95 (*1-55037-209-2*, Pub. by Annick CN); pap. 4.95 (*1-55037-208-4*, Pub. by Annick CN) Firefly Bks Ltd.
—Pegasus & Ooloo-Moo-loo. Ohi, Ruth, illus. 32p. 1993. lib. bdg. 14.95 (*1-55037-278-5*, Pub. by Annick CN); pap. 4.95 (*1-55037-279-3*, Pub. by Annick CN) Firefly Bks Ltd.
Orsetti, Marion. The Computer Zone. LC 87-42912. 44p. (ps-2). 1988. 8.95 (*1-55523-111-X*) Winston-Derek.
Orska, Kr. Illustrated Poems for Children. (Illus.). 1985. 12.95 (*0-02-689410-6*) Macmillan.
Ortega, Pedro R., tr. see Chapman, Al.
Ortega, Pedro R., tr. see Dressman, John.
Ortego, Pedro R., tr. see LaFarge, Oliver.
Orthner, Donald P. Wellsprings of Life: Understanding Proverbs. Thompson, Del, illus. Minnick, Mark, pref. by. (Illus.). xii, 228p. (Orig.). (gr. 9 up). 1989. pap. 7.95 (*0-317-93833-9*) Adon Bks.
Ortiz, Alfonso. The Pueblo: Southwest. (Illus.). (gr. 5 up). 1994. 18.95 (*1-55546-727-X*, Am Art Analog); pap. 7.95 (*0-7910-0396-5*, Am Art Analog) Chelsea Hse.
Ortiz, Elizabeth. Fantasia. Iscaro, Nancy L., ed. Figueroa, Mariano, illus. 58p. (Orig.). (gr. 9-12). 1989. pap. text ed. write for info. West Side Pubns.
Ortiz, Lucio. Sus Derechos de Credito en Estados Unidos. Garcia, Santos, intro. by. (SPA., Orig.). (gr. 9-12). 1989. pap. 6.00 (*0-685-28998-2*) Publicaciones Nuevos.
Ortiz, Mamie. My Grandfather & the Boys. Aragon, Sherry, illus. 14p. (Orig.). (ps-7). 1982. pap. 3.75 (*0-915347-03-2*) Pueblo Acoma Pr.
Ortiz, Simon. Blue & Red. Aragon, Hilda, illus. 14p. (Orig.). (ps-7). 1981. pap. 3.75 (*0-915347-08-3*) Pueblo Acoma Pr.
—The Importance of Childhood. Gracia, Fred D., illus. 16p. (Orig.). (ps-7). 1982. pap. 3.75 (*0-915347-01-6*) Pueblo Acoma Pr.
—The People Shall Continue. Graves, Sharol, illus. LC 88-18929. 24p. (gr. 2-7). 1988. 13.95 (*0-89239-041-7*) Childrens Book Pr.
Ortiz, Victoria. Sojourner Truth: A Self-Made Woman. LC 73-22290. (Illus.). 160p. (gr. 7 up). 1986. PLB 12.89 (*0-397-32134-1*, Lipp Jr Bks) HarpC Child Bks.
Orton, Helen F. The Gold-Laced Coat. rev. ed. Ball, Robert, illus. 226p. (gr. 4-8). 1988. pap. 5.95 (*0-941967-07-7*) Old Fort Niagara Assn.
—The Treasure in the Little Trunk. Ball, Robert, illus. 208p. (gr. 4). 1989. pap. text ed. 5.95 (*0-685-29125-1*) Niagara Cnty Hist Soc.
Orton, Stephen A. Pan the Man. 36p. (Orig.). (gr. 7-12). 1991. pap. 8.95 (*0-88680-355-1*); royalty on application 35.00 (*0-685-59135-2*) I E Clark.
Ortwerth, John & Nicks, Mel J. P. E. Curriculum Guide. Nobis, Kevin, illus. 160p. (gr. 1-6). 1984. wkbk. 12.95 (*0-86653-262-5*, GA 599) Good Apple.
Orwell, George. Animal Farm. 128p. (RL 10). 1986. pap. 4.95 (*0-451-52466-7*, Sig Classics) NAL-Dutton.
—Animal Farm. 122p. (Orig.). 1945. pap. text ed. 5.95 (*0-582-53008-3*) Longman.
Osawa, Yasu, jt. auth. see Schatz, Dennis.
Osband, Gillian. Boysie's First Birthday. Allen, Jonathan, illus. 32p. (gr. k-2). 1990. PLB 14.95 (*0-87614-404-0*) Carolrhoda Bks.
—Boysie's Kitten. Allen, Jonathan, illus. 32p. (ps-2). 1990. PLB 14.95 (*0-87614-403-2*) Carolrhoda Bks.
—Castles. Andrew, Robert, illus. LC 91-60082. 16p. 1991. 15.95 (*0-531-05949-9*) Orchard Bks Watts.
Osberg, Susan, jt. auth. see Duden, Jane.
Osborn, Kevin. A Day in the Life of a Seeing Eye Dog Trainer. Halpern, John, photos by. LC 90-11076. (Illus.). 32p. (gr. 4-8). 1991. lib. bdg. 11.79 (*0-8167-2218-8*); pap. text ed. 2.95 (*0-8167-2219-6*) Troll Assocs.
—Everything You Need to Know about Bias Incidents. Rosen, Ruth, ed. (gr. 7-12). 1993. PLB 13.95 (*0-8239-1530-1*) Rosen Group.
—The Peoples of the Arctic. Moynihan, Daniel P., intro. by. (Illus.). 112p. (gr. 5 up). 1990. 17.95 (*0-685-18912-0*) Chelsea Hse.
—Tolerance. rev. ed. (gr. 7-12). 1993. 12.95 (*0-8239-1508-5*) Rosen Group.
—The Ukrainian Americans. Moynihan, Daniel P., intro. by. (Illus.). 112p. (gr. 5 up). 1989. PLB 17.95 (*1-55546-138-7*) Chelsea Hse.
Osborn, Marvin. Dynamic Devotions for Teens. Spear, Cindy G., ed. (Orig.). (gr. 7-12). 1993. pap. 9.95 spiral bound (*0-941005-90-9*) Chrch Grwth VA.
Osborn, Susan T. & Tangvald, Christine H. Children Around the World Celebrate Christmas! McCallum, Jodie, illus. LC 93-6683. (gr. 4 up). 1993. 10.00 (*0-87403-799-9*, 24-03664) Standard Pub.

Osborne, Angela. Abigail Adams. Horner, Matina S., intro. by. (Illus.). 112p. (gr. 5 up). 1989. 17.95 *(1-55546-635-4)*; pap. 9.95 *(0-7910-0405-8)* Chelsea Hse.

Osborne, Christine. The Netherlands. (Illus.). 48p. (gr. 5-8). 1990. PLB 13.90 *(0-531-18336-X)* Watts.
—People at Work in the Middle East. (gr. 6 up). 1988. 19.95 *(0-7134-5571-3,* Pub. by Batsford UK) Trafalgar.

Osborne, Denise. Murder Offscreen. (gr. 6 up). 1994. write for info. *(0-8050-3113-8)* H Holt & Co.

Osborne, Dwight. The Squiggly Wiggly Head Family. Ablin, Barry, illus. 16p. 1992. pap. 5.95 *(0-9632817-0-4)* Osborne Bks.

Osborne, Jill. Baby Animals Dot-To-Dot Activity Book. 1989. pap. 1.25 *(0-89375-904-X)* Troll Assocs.
—Dinosaur Dot-To-Dot Activity Book. 32p. 1989. pap. 1.25 *(0-89375-837-X)* Troll Assocs.
—Wild Animals Dot-To-Dot Activity Book. 1989. pap. 1.25 *(0-89375-836-1)* Troll Assocs.

Osborne, Jill E. Make Color & Halloween Decoration. (ps-3). 1989. pap. 1.95 *(0-89375-644-X)* Troll Assocs.

Osborne, John, et al. Global Studies: A Competency Review Text. 3rd ed. Gamsey, Wayne & Stich, Paul, eds. Fairbanks, Eugene B., illus. 384p. (gr. 7-12). 1992. pap. text ed. 8.33 *(0-935487-37-9)* N & N Pub Co.
—Global Studies: A Regents Review Text. 6th ed. Gamsey, Wayne & Stich, Paul, eds. Fairbanks, Eugene B., illus. 448p. (gr. 7-12). 1992. pap. text ed. 6.22 *(0-935487-35-2)* N & N Pub Co.
—Global Studies: Ten Day Competency Review. 2nd ed. Gamsey, Wayne & Stich, Paul, eds. Fairbanks, Eugene B., illus. 128p. (gr. 7-12). 1992. pap. text ed. 4.95 *(0-935487-53-0)* N & N Pub Co.
—Global Studies: Ten Day Regents Review. 2nd ed. Gamsey, Wayne & Stich, Paul, eds. Fairbanks, Eugene B., illus. 128p. (gr. 7-12). 1992. pap. text ed. 4.95 *(0-935487-48-4)* N & N Pub Co.

Osborne, John T. Miracles. Osborne, John T., illus. 90p. 1988. pap. text ed. 5.75 *(0-929918-00-2)* Midstates Pub.

Osborne, Judy. My Teacher Said Goodbye Today: Planning for the End of the School Year. 2nd ed. Osborne, John, photos by. (Illus.). 39p. (ps-6). 1987. pap. text ed. 9.95 *(0-9618303-8-7)* Emijo Pubns.

Osborne, Mary P. American Tall Tales. McCurdy, Michael, illus. LC 89-37235. 128p. (gr. 1 up). 1991. 18.00 *(0-679-80089-1)*; lib. bdg. 18.99 *(0-679-90089-6)* Knopf Bks Yng Read.
—Christopher Columbus: Admiral of the Sea. (Orig.). (gr. k-6). 1987. pap. 3.25 *(0-440-41275-7,* YB) Dell.
—Dinosaurs Before Dark. Murdocca, Sal, illus. LC 91-51106. 80p. (Orig.). (gr. 1-4). 1992. PLB 9.99 *(0-679-92411-6)*; pap. 2.99 *(0-679-82411-1)* Random Bks Yng Read.
—Favorite Greek Myths. Howell, Troy, illus. (gr. 2-6). 1989. pap. 15.95 *(0-590-41338-4)* Scholastic Inc.
—George Washington: Leader of a New Nation. LC 90-42601. (Illus.). 96p. (gr. 4-7). 1991. 14.00 *(0-8037-0947-1)*; lib. bdg. 13.89 *(0-8037-0949-8)* Dial Bks Young.
—The Knight at Dawn. Murdocca, Sal, illus. LC 92-13075. 80p. (Orig.). (gr. 1-4). 1993. PLB 9.99 *(0-679-92412-4)*; pap. 2.99 *(0-679-82412-X)* Random Bks Yng Read.
—The Many Lives of Benjamin Franklin. (Illus.). (gr. 5 up). 1990. 13.95 *(0-685-31008-6)* Dial Bks Young.
—The Many Lives of Benjamin Franklin. LC 88-38369. (Illus.). 144p. (gr. 4-7). 1990. PLB 13.89 *(0-8037-0680-4)* Dial Bks Young.
—Mo & His Friends. (ps-3). 1991. pap. 3.95 *(0-8037-0924-2,* Dial Easy to Read) Puffin Bks.
—Molly & the Prince. Sayles, Elizabeth, illus. LC 92-25305. 1993. write for info. *(0-679-81941-X)*; PLB write for info. *(0-679-91941-4)* Knopf.
—Moonhorse. Saelig, S. M., illus. LC 87-3818. 40p. (ps-3). 1991. 14.95 *(0-394-88960-6)*; lib. bdg. 15.99 *(0-394-98960-0)* Knopf Bks Yng Read.
—Mummies in the Morning. Murdocca, Sal, illus. 1993. PLB 9.99 *(0-679-92424-8)*; pap. 2.99 *(0-679-82424-3)* Random Bks Yng Read.
—Pirates Past Noon. Murdocca, Sal, illus. LC 93-2039. Date not set. PLB write for info. *(0-679-92425-6)*; pap. write for info. *(0-679-82425-1)* Random.
—Run, Run, As Fast As You Can. LC 81-68781. 156p. (gr. 3-7). 1993. pap. 3.99 *(0-679-84649-2)* Random Bks Yng Read.
—Spider Kane & the Mystery at Jumbo Nightcrawler's. Chess, Victoria, illus. LC 91-10983. 128p. (gr. 1-5). 1993. 14.00 *(0-679-80856-6)* Knopf Bks Yng Read.
—Spider Kane & the Mystery under the May-Apple. Chess, Victoria, illus. LC 90-33524. 128p. (gr. 1-7). 1992. 13.00 *(0-679-80855-8)*; PLB 13.99 *(0-679-90855-2)* Knopf Bks Yng Read.
—Spider Kane & the Mystery under the May-Apple. Chess, Victoria, illus. LC 90-33524. 128p. (gr. 1-7). 1993. pap. 3.50 *(0-679-84174-1,* Bullseye Bks) Knopf Bks Yng Read.

Osborne, Mary P., jt. auth. see Osborne, Will.

Osborne, Mary P., compiled by. Bears, Bears, Bears. Schmidt, Karen L., illus. 96p. (ps-2). 1990. pap. 14.95 *(0-671-69631-9,* S&S BYR); pap. 18.98 *(0-671-69630-0)* S&S Trade.

Osborne, Mary P., retold by. Beauty & the Beast. Pels, Winslow P., illus. 40p. (gr. 1-4). 1988. pap. 3.95 *(0-590-40166-1)* Scholastic Inc.

Osborne, Richard, compiled by. Proverbs for Kids from the Book. VanRoon, Terry & Kielesinski, Chris, illus. 240p. (gr. k). 1987. 12.99 *(0-8423-4975-8)* Tyndale.

Osborne, Thelma. The Adventures of Speedy. Caroland, Mary, ed. LC 90-71229. (Illus.). 44p. (gr. k-3). 1991. 5.95 *(1-55523-383-X)* Winston-Derek.

Osborne, Victor. Moondream. LC 88-13654. 128p. (gr. 3-7). 1989. 11.95 *(0-688-08778-7)* Lothrop.
—Rex, the Most Special Car in the World. Anderson, Scoular, illus. 24p. (ps-3). 1989. PLB 17.50 *(0-87614-357-5)* Carolrhoda Bks.

Osborne, Will & Osborne, Mary P. The Deadly Power of Medusa. 96p. (gr. 3-7). 1992. pap. 2.75 *(0-590-45580-X,* Apple Paperbacks) Scholastic Inc.

Osei, G. K. The African Concept of Life & Death. Obaba, Al I., ed. (Illus.). 49p. (Orig.). 1991. pap. text ed. 3.00 *(0-916157-64-4)* African Islam Miss Pubns.

O'Shaughnessy & McKenna. Eenie, Meenie, Murphy, No! 1992. pap. 2.95 *(0-590-42900-0,* Apple Paperbacks) Scholastic Inc.

O'Shaughnessy, Ellen. Somebody Called Me a Retard Today - & My Heart Felt Sad. Garner, David, illus. LC 92-10812. 24p. 1992. 13.95 *(0-8027-8196-9)*; PLB 14.85 *(0-8027-8197-7)* Walker & Co.

O'Shaughnessy, Peter. Con's Fabulous Journey to the Land of Gobel O'Glug. rev. ed. Myler, Terry, illus. 104p. (gr. 6-10). 1992. pap. 5.95 *(0-947962-68-9,* Pub. by Anvil Bks Ltd ER) Irish Bks Media.

O'Shaughnessy, Tam, jt. auth. see Ride, Sally.

O'Shea, Brandy. The Black Cat Inn. O'Shea, Bronwyn C., illus. LC 91-67920. Date not set. 8.00 *(1-56002-180-2,* Univ Edtns) Aegina Pr.

O'Shea, Farrell. Play the Game: Windsurfing. (Illus.). 80p. (gr. 10-12). 1991. pap. 6.95 *(0-7063-6971-8,* Pub. by Ward Lock UK) Sterling.

O'Shea, Pat. The Hounds of the Morrigan. LC 85-16435. 469p. (gr. 4 up). 1986. 15.95 *(0-8234-0595-8)* Holiday.

Oshihara, Yuzuro. Children of the World: Malaysia. LC 86-42802. (Illus.). 64p. (gr. 5-6). 1987. PLB 19.93 *(1-55532-160-7)* Gareth Stevens Inc.

Osinski, Alice. Andrew Jackson. LC 86-29983. (Illus.). 100p. (gr. 3 up). 1987. PLB 17.27 *(0-516-01387-4)*; pap. 6.95 *(0-516-41387-2)* Childrens.
—The Chippewa. LC 86-32687. (Illus.). 48p. (gr. k-4). 1987. PLB 15.27 *(0-516-01230-4)*; pap. 4.95 *(0-516-41230-2)* Childrens.
—The Eskimo: Inuit & Yupik. LC 85-9691. (Illus.). 45p. (gr. 2-3). 1985. PLB 15.27 *(0-516-01267-3)*; pap. 4.95 *(0-516-41267-1)* Childrens.
—Franklin D. Roosevelt. (Illus.). 100p. (gr. 3 up). 1987. PLB 17.27 *(0-516-01395-5)*; pap. 6.95 *(0-516-41395-3)* Childrens.
—The Navajo. (Illus.). 48p. (gr. k-4). 1987. PLB 15.27 *(0-516-01236-3)*; pap. 4.95 *(0-516-41236-1)* Childrens.
—The Nez Perce. LC 88-11822. (Illus.). 48p. (gr. k-4). 1988. PLB 15.27 *(0-516-01154-5)*; pap. 4.95 *(0-516-41154-3)* Childrens.
—The Sioux. LC 84-7629. (Illus.). 48p. (gr. k-4). 1984. PLB 15.27 *(0-516-01929-5)*; pap. 4.95 *(0-516-41929-3)* Childrens.
—The Tlingit. LC 89-25345. (Illus.). 48p. (gr. k-4). 1990. PLB 15.27 *(0-516-01189-8)*; pap. 4.95 *(0-516-41189-6)* Childrens.
—Woodrow Wilson. LC 88-8678. (Illus.). 100p. (gr. 3 up). 1989. PLB 17.27 *(0-516-01367-X)* Childrens.

Osius, Alison. Second Ascent: The Story of Hugh Herr. LC 91-13171. (Illus.). 240p. (gr. 7 up). 1991. 19.95 *(0-8117-1794-1)* Stackpole.

Osman, Karen. Gangs. LC 92-28009. (Illus.). 112p. (gr. 5-8). 1992. PLB 14.95 *(1-56006-131-6)* Lucent Bks.

Osmond, Tony, jt. auth. see Cooper, Chris.

Osofsky, Audrey. Dreamcatcher. Young, Ed, illus. LC 91-20029. 32p. (ps-2). 1992. 14.95 *(0-531-05988-X)*; lib. bdg. 14.99 *(0-531-08588-0)* Orchard Bks Watts.
—My Buddy. Rand, Ted, illus. LC 92-3028. 32p. (gr. k-3). 1992. 14.95 *(0-8050-1747-X,* Bks Young Read) H Holt & Co.

Ossorio, Nelson A. & Milano, Keri E. The Blind Man at the Alhambra. (Illus.). 98p. (gr. 4-8). 1993. pap. 6.95 *(1-56721-016-3)* Twenty-Fifth Cent Pr.
—Bobtail's Invention. (Illus.). 72p. (gr. 4-8). 1993. pap. 8.95 *(1-56721-019-8)* Twenty-Fifth Cent Pr.
—The Lake That Talked. (Illus.). 80p. (gr. 4-7). 1993. pap. 6.95 *(1-56721-015-5)* Twenty-Fifth Cent Pr.
—Maid Lightning & the Spirit of Speed. (Illus.). 84p. (gr. 4-8). 1993. pap. 6.95 *(1-56721-017-1)* Twenty-Fifth Cent Pr.
—The Skunk's New Perfume. (Illus.). 48p. (gr. 1-3). 1993. pap. 7.95 *(1-56721-020-1)* Twenty-Fifth Cent Pr.
—The Three. (Illus.). 96p. (gr. 4-7). 1993. pap. 14.95 *(1-56721-021-X)* Twenty-Fifth Cent Pr.
—The Upstairs Window. (Illus.). 96p. (gr. 4-8). 1993. pap. 6.95 *(1-56721-018-X)* Twenty-Fifth Cent Pr.

Ossowski, Leonie. Star Without a Sky. LC 84-21834. 216p. (gr. 5 up). 1985. 19.95 *(0-8225-0771-4)* Lerner Pubns.

Ostarch, Judy. I Love Pets. Nex, Anthony, illus. 10p. (ps). 1993. bds. 4.99 *(0-8431-3656-1)* Price Stern.
—Let's Get Dressed. Nex, Anthony, illus. 10p. (ps). 1993. bds. 4.99 *(0-8431-3654-5)* Price Stern.
—My Family. Nex, Anthony, illus. 10p. (ps). 1993. bds. 4.99 *(0-8431-3655-3)* Price Stern.
—Playtime. Nex, Anthony, illus. 10p. (ps). 1993. bds. 4.99 *(0-8431-3657-X)* Price Stern.

Osten, James, ed. see Siembieda, Kevin & Bartold, Thomas.

Osterberg, Susan S. & Jackson, R. Eugene. Bumper Snickers. 30p. (Orig.). (gr. 6-12). 1978. pap. 2.00 *(0-88680-015-3)*; royalty on application 20.00 *(0-685-59247-2)* I E Clark.

Osterink, Carol. My Sticker Dictionary. Morgado, Richard, illus. 64p. (ps-2). 1992. pap. 5.95 *(1-56293-250-0)* McClanahan Bk.

Osterman, Joe. The Old El Toro Reader: A Guide to the Past. Walker, Doris & Osterman, Tim, eds. Schepp, Warren & Dodson, Deborah, illus. LC 92-96902. 112p. 1992. pap. 9.95 *(1-881129-02-0)* Old El Toro Pr.

Osterman, Tim, ed. see Osterman, Joe.

Osterritter, John F., jt. auth. see Elgin, Kathleen.

Osterwald, Doris B. High Line to Leadville: A Mile by Mile Guide for the Leadville, Colorado & Southern Railroad. (Illus.). 160p. (Orig.). 1991. pap. 9.95 *(0-931788-70-6)* Western Guideways.
—Rocky Mountain Splendor: A Mile by Mile Guide for Rocky Mountain National Park. (Illus.). 272p. (Orig.). 1989. pap. 13.95 *(0-931788-89-7)* Western Guideways.

Ostheeren, Ingrid. Coriander's Easter Adventure. Corderoc'h, Jean-Pierre, illus. Lanning, Rosemary, tr. from GER. LC 91-26867. (Illus.). 32p. (gr. k-3). 1992. 14.95 *(1-55858-136-7)*; lib. bdg. 14.88 *(1-55858-150-2)* North-South Bks NYC.
—Fabian Youngpig Sails the World. Romanelli, Serena, illus. James, Alison, tr. from GER. LC 91-16531. (Illus.). 32p. (gr. k-3). 1992. 14.95 *(1-55858-125-1)*; lib. bdg. 14.88 *(1-55858-145-6)* North-South Bks NYC.
—Jonathan Mouse. Lanning, Rosemary, tr. from GER. LC 85-10501. (Illus.). 32p. (gr. k-3). 1986. 13.95 *(1-55858-064-6)* North-South Bks NYC.
—Jonathan Mouse & the Baby Bird. Mathieu, Agnes, illus. Lanning, Rosemary, tr. from GER. LC 91-6614. (Illus.). 32p. (gr. k-3). 1991. 14.95 *(1-55858-108-1)* North-South Bks NYC.
—Jonathan Mouse & the Magic Box. Mathieu, Agnes, illus. Lanning, Rosemary, tr. from GER. LC 89-43248. (Illus.). 32p. (gr. k-3). 1990. 13.95 *(1-55858-087-5)* North-South Bks NYC.
—Jonathan Mouse at the Circus. Lanning, Rosemary, tr. from GER. Mathieu, Agnes, illus. LC 87-42980. 32p. (gr. k-3). 1988. 12.95 *(1-55858-055-7)* North-South Bks NYC.
—Jonathan Mouse, Detective. Mathieu, Agnes, illus. Lanning, Rosemary, tr. from GER. LC 92-29023. (Illus.). 32p. (gr. k-3). 1993. 14.95 *(1-55858-164-2)*; pap. 14.95 *(1-55858-141-3)* North-South Bks NYC.
—The New Dog. Corderoc'h, Jean-Pierre, illus. James, J. Alison, tr. from GER. (Illus.). 32p. (gr. k-3). 1993. 14.95 *(1-55858-218-5)*; lib. bdg. 14.88 *(1-55858-219-3)* North-South Bks NYC.

Ostrom, John. Dinosaurs. 2nd ed. Head, J. J., ed. LC 84-71139. (Illus.). 32p. (gr. 10 up). 1984. pap. 3.00 *(0-89278-201-3,* 45-9698) Carolina Biological.

Ostrove, Karen, jt. auth. see Miller, Deborah.

Ostrovsky, Alexsandr. Birthday (Den Rosdenia) Ostrovsky, Alexsandr, illus. (RUS.). 16p. (Orig.). 1982. pap. 14.95 *(0-934393-17-6)* Rector Pr.
—Clouds (Oblaka) Ostrovsky, Alexsandr, illus. (RUS.). 16p. (Orig.). 1984. pap. 14.95 *(0-934393-20-6)* Rector Pr.
—Paper Kite (Bumazhni Emei) Ostrovsky, Alexsandr, illus. (RUS.). 30p. (Orig.). 1987. pap. 14.95 *(0-934393-18-4)* Rector Pr.

Ostrovsky, Alexsandr & Ostrovsky, Alexsandr. Besely Clon (Merry Elephant) (RUS.). (Illus.). 32p. (Orig.). 1991. pap. 14.95 *(0-934393-22-2)* Rector Pr.

Ostrow, Vivian, jt. auth. see Ostrow, William.

Ostrow, William & Ostrow, Vivian. All about Asthma. Levine, Abby, ed. Sims, Blanche, illus. LC 89-5254. 32p. (gr. 2-6). 1989. PLB 11.95 *(0-8075-0276-6)*; pap. 4.95 *(0-8075-0275-8)* A Whitman.

O'Sullivan, Anna-Margaret. The Green Bank Year. LC 88-62114. 255p. 1989. pap. 6.95 *(1-55523-183-7)* Winston-Derek.

O'Sullivan, Carol. Alcohol: Understanding Words in Context. (Illus.). 32p. (gr. 3-6). 1990. PLB 10.95 *(0-89908-634-9)* Greenhaven.
—Death Penalty: Identifying Propaganda Techniques. LC 89-11033. (Illus.). 32p. (gr. 3-6). 1990. PLB 10.95 *(0-89908-636-5)* Greenhaven.
—Drugs & Sports: Locating the Author's Main Idea. LC 89-36322. (Illus.). 32p. (gr. 3-6). 1990. PLB 10.95 *(0-89908-637-3)* Greenhaven.
—Gun Control: Distinguishing Between Fact & Opinion. LC 89-2226. (Illus.). 32p. (gr. 3-6). 1990. PLB 10.95 *(0-89908-638-1)* Greenhaven.
—Poverty: Locating the Authors Main Idea. LC 89-17069. (Illus.). 32p. (gr. 3-6). 1990. PLB 10.95 *(0-89908-641-1)* Greenhaven.

Otani, Takeshi. The Honeybee. Pohl, Kathy, ed. LC 85-28230. (Illus.). 32p. (gr. k-3). 1986. text ed. 17.96 *(0-8172-2537-4)* Raintree Steck-V.

Otero, George G., jt. auth. see West, Patricia M.

Otey, Mimi. Blue Moon Soup Spoon. (ps-3). 1993. 15.00 *(0-374-30851-9)* FS&G.
—Daddy Has a Pair of Striped Shorts. LC 90-55289. (Illus.). 32p. (ps-3). 1990. 13.95 *(0-374-31675-9)* FS&G.

Otfinoski. Blizzards. 1994. PLB write for info. *(0-8050-3093-X)* H Holt & Co.

Otfinoski, Stephen. Nineteenth Century Writers. (Illus.). 128p. (gr. 7-12). 1991. 16.95x *(0-8160-2486-3)* Facts on File.

Otfinoski, Steve. Gun Control: Is It a Right or a Danger to Bear Arms? (Illus.). 64p. (gr. 5-8). 1993. PLB 14.95 *(0-8050-2570-7)* TFC Bks NY.

—Marian Wright Edelman: Defender of Children's Rights. (Illus.). 64p. (gr. 3-7). PLB 14.95 (*1-56711-029-0*) Blackbirch.
—Marion Wright Edelman: Defender of Children's Rights. (Illus.). 64p. (gr. 3-7). 1993. pap. 7.95 (*1-56711-060-6*) Blackbirch.
—Oprah. (Illus.). 64p. (gr. 3-7). 1993. pap. 7.95 (*1-56711-061-4*) Blackbirch.
—Oprah Winfrey: Television Star. (Illus.). 64p. (gr. 3-7). 1993. PLB 14.95 (*1-56711-015-0*) Blackbirch.
Otfinoski, Steven. Alexander Fleming: Conquering Disease with Penicillin. LC 92-9910. (Illus.). 128p. (gr. 5 up). 1993. PLB 16.95 (*0-8160-2752-8*) Facts on File.
—Bill Gaines. LC 93-16177. 1993. write for info. (*0-86592-080-X*) Rourke Enter.
—Joseph Stalin: Russia's Last Czar. LC 92-41143. (Illus.). 128p. (gr. 2-4). 1992. 15.90 (*1-56294-240-9*) Millbrook Pr.
—Nelson Mandela: The Fight Against Apartheid. LC 91-35031. (Illus.). 128p. (gr. 7 up). 1992. PLB 15.90 (*1-56294-067-8*) Millbrook Pr.
—The Stolen Signs. Dodson, Bert, illus. Lewis, Glenn. (Illus.). 112p. (gr. 2-6). 1992. (S&S BFYR); pap. 2.95 (*0-671-72930-6*, S&S BFYR) S&S Trade.
—Triumph & Terror: The French Revolution. LC 92-37131. (Illus.). 128p. (gr. 6-9). 1993. 16.95x (*0-8160-2762-5*) Facts on File.
—Who Stole Home Plate? Dodson, Bert, illus. Lewis, Glenn. (Illus.). 112p. (gr. 2-6). 1992. (S&S BFYR); pap. 2.95 (*0-671-72932-2*, S&S BFYR) S&S Trade.
Otfinski, Steven. Igor Sikorsky. LC 93-2822. 1993. 15.93 (*0-86592-100-8*); 11.95s.p. (*0-685-66610-7*) Rourke Enter.
Otis, James. Toby Tyler. 152p. 1981. Repr. PLB 21.95x (*0-89966-363-X*) Buccaneer Bks.
—Toby Tyler. 188p. 1981. Repr. PLB 19.95 (*0-89967-037-7*) Harmony Raine.
—Toby Tyler, or, Ten Weeks with a Circus. (gr. 4 up). 1990. pap. 3.50 (*0-440-40358-8*) Dell.
Otis, Sharon & Walker, Lois. Jeffrey's Laugh. Hawk, Lee, illus. Goldman, Howard, intro. by. (Illus., Orig.). (ps-6). 1987. wkbk. 6.50 (*0-9617737-2-3*) Total Lrn.
—Tammy's Smile. Porter, Debbie, illus. Goldman, Howard, pref. by. (Illus., Orig.). (ps-7). 1985. wkbk. 6.00 (*0-9617737-0-7*) Total Lrn.
O'Toole, Christopher. Discovering Bees & Wasps. LC 85-72247. (Illus.). 48p. (gr. k-6). 1986. lib. PLB 12.40 (*0-531-18047-6*, Pub. by Bookwright Pr) Watts.
—The Dragonfly over the Water. Oxford Scientific Films, photos by. LC 87-42613. (Illus.). 32p. (gr. 4-6). 1988. PLB 15.93 (*1-55532-306-5*) Gareth Stevens Inc.
—The Honeybee in the Meadow. Oxford Scientific Films Staff, photos by. LC 89-33935. (Illus.). 32p. (gr. 4-6). 1989. PLB 15.93 (*0-8368-0117-2*) Gareth Stevens Inc.
O'Toole, Christopher & Stidworthy, John. Mammals: The Hunters. (Illus.). 96p. 1988. 17.95x (*0-8160-1959-2*) Facts on File.
O'Toole, Donna. Aarvy Aardvark Finds Hope: A Read-Aloud Story for People of All Ages. McWhirter, Mary Lou, illus. 80p. (Orig.). (ps up) 1989. pap. 9.95 (*1-878321-25-0*, Mntn Rainbow); tchr's. guide 6.95 (*1-878321-26-9*, Mntn Rainbow); audio tape 9.95 (*0-685-20985-7*, Mntn Rainbow) Rainbow NC.
—Healing & Growing Through Grief. (Illus.). 20p. 1986. pap. 3.25 (*0-685-31273-9*, HG-02-4) Rainbow NC.
O'Toole, Donna R. Growing Through Grief: A K-Twelve Curriculum to Help Young People Through All Kinds of Loss. rev. ed. McWhirter, Kore L., illus. 392p. (gr. k-12). 1989. pap. 59.95 3-ring bdr. (*1-878321-00-5*, Mntn Rainbow) Rainbow NC.
O'Toole, Maureen A. Ama & the White Crane. (Orig.). 1991. Playscript. pap. 5.50 (*0-87602-295-6*) Anchorage.
O'Toole, Sharon S. Brave Dog Blizzard. 1992. pap. 2.75 (*0-590-44409-3*) Scholastic Inc.
O'Toole, Thomas. Economic History of the United States. (Illus.). 88p. (gr. 5 up). 1990. 21.50 (*0-8225-1776-0*) Lerner Pubns.
—Global Economics. (Illus.). 80p. (gr. 5 up). 1991. PLB 21.50 (*0-8225-1782-5*) Lerner Pubns.
Otten, Charlotte. Months: A Book of Poems for Children. Lewin, Ted, illus. LC 92-44159. 1995. write for info. (*0-688-12556-5*); PLB write for info. (*0-688-12557-3*) Lothrop.
Ottenheimer. Martin Luther King, Jr. (gr. 2-5). 1987. pap. 2.50 (*0-671-63632-4*, Little Simon) S&S Trade.
Ottenheimer, Laurence. Japan: Land of Samurai & Robots. Nikly, Michelle, illus. LC 87-34524. 38p. (gr. k-5). 1988. 4.95 (*0-944589-11-1*, 111) Young Discovery Lib.
—Livre d'Automne. Galeron, Henri, illus. (FRE.). 90p. (gr. 4-9). 1983. 8.95 (*2-07-039506-5*) Schoenhof.
—Livre d'Ete. Claverie, Jean, illus. (FRE.). 88p. (gr. 4-9). 1983. 13.95 (*2-07-039508-1*) Schoenhof.
—Livre d'Hiver. Bour, Daniele, illus. (FRE.). 93p. (gr. 4-9). 1983. 14.95 (*2-07-039505-7*) Schoenhof.
—Livre du Printemps. (FRE.). 96p. (gr. 4-9). 1983. 14.95 (*2-07-039507-3*) Schoenhof.
Ottens, Allen & Myer, Rick. Coping with Satanism. Rosen, Ruth, ed. (gr. 7-12). 1993. 13.95 (*0-8239-1423-2*) Rosen Group.
Ottens, Allen J. Coping with Romantic Breakup. 147p. (gr. 7-12). 1987. PLB 13.95 (*0-8239-0649-3*) Rosen Group.
Ottenstein, Claire. Catch a Whiffle-Pooflee! Ottenstein, Claire & Cogbill, Catherine, illus. 64p. (Orig.). 1991. lib. bdg. 8.95 (*1-878149-03-2*) Counterpoint Pub.

—The Poetry Fun Book. (Illus.). 40p. (Orig.). 1992. pap. 7.95 (*1-878149-20-2*) Counterpoint Pub.
Ottewell, Guy. To Know the Stars. (Illus.). 41p. (gr. 3 up). 1983. pap. 7.00 (*0-934546-12-6*) Astron Wkshp.
Otting, Rae. When Jesus Was a Lad. Marilue, illus. (gr. 1-2). 1978. pap. 1.25 (*0-89508-055-9*) Rainbow Bks.
Otto. Animal Camouflage. Date not set. 14.00 (*0-06-023342-7*, Festival); PLB 13.89 (*0-06-023343-5*, Festival) HarpC Child Bks.
Otto, Carolyn. Dinosaur Chase. Hurd, Thacher, illus. LC 90-2021. 32p. (ps-1). 1991. 15.00 (*0-06-021613-1*); PLB 14.89 (*0-06-021614-X*) HarpC Child Bks.
—Dinosaur Chase. Hurd, Thacher, illus. LC 90-2021. 32p. (ps-1). 1993. pap. 4.95 (*0-06-443330-7*, Trophy) HarpC Child Bks.
—First Church. 1994. write for info. (*0-8050-2554-5*) H Holt & Co.
—I Can Tell by Touching. Westcott, Nadine B., illus. LC 93-18630. (gr. 4 up). 1994. 14.00 (*0-06-023324-9*); PLB 13.89 (*0-06-023325-7*) HarpC Child Bks.
—One Dog Twenty Stars. 1994. write for info. (*0-8050-2369-0*) H Holt & Co.
—That Sky, That Rain. Lloyd, Megan, illus. LC 89-36582. 32p. (ps-3). 1990. (Crowell Jr Bks); PLB 12.89 (*0-690-04765-7*, Crowell Jr Bks) HarpC Child Bks.
—That Sky, That Rain. Lloyd, Megan, illus. LC 89-36582. 32p. (ps-3). 1992. pap. 4.95 (*0-06-443290-4*, Trophy) HarpC Child Bks.
Otto, Carolyn B. Ducks, Ducks, Ducks. Coxe, Molly, illus. LC 90-42089. 32p. (ps-1). 1991. PLB 14.89 (*0-06-024639-1*) HarpC Child Bks.
Otto, Simon. Walk in Peace: Legends & Stories of the Michigan Indians. 2nd ed. Bussey, M. T., ed. Crampton, Kaylie, illus. 50p. (gr. 3-4). 1992. pap. 9.95 (*0-9617707-5-9*) Grnd Rpds Intertribal.
Ottow, Harriett. Ruth's Adventures in Israel. LC 87-51493. 44p. (gr. k-2). 1988. 5.95 (*1-55523-133-0*) Winston-Derek.
Ottum, Bob & Wood, JoAnne. Santa's Beard Is Soft & Warm. Ruth, Rod, illus. (ps). 1974. write for info. (*0-307-12148-8*, Golden Bks) Western Pub.
Otumokala, Jean & Okon, Bern. Black-American Women African Men: Myths Misconceptions & Misunderstandings. Ettah, Geneieve, ed. 197p. (Orig.). 1994. pap. 19.95 (*0-9629214-4-0*) Intl Spectrum.
Otway, Thomas see Wilson, John H.
Oudheusden, Susan. Go for It! A Student's Guide to Independent Projects. 75p. (gr. 3-9). pap. 14.95 (*0-936386-51-7*) Creative Learning.
Oughten, Jerrie. The Magic Weaver of Rugs. Desimini, Lisa, illus. LC 93-4850. 1994. write for info. (*0-395-66140-4*) HM.
Oughton, Jerrie. How the Stars Fell into the Sky. Desimini, Lisa, illus. 32p. (gr. k-3). 1992. 14.45 (*0-395-58798-0*) HM.
Ouida, pseud. A Dog of Flanders. (Illus.). 80p. 1992. pap. 1.00t (*0-486-27087-4*) Dover.
Ourada, Patricia K. The Menominee. (Illus.). 112p. (gr. 5 up). 1990. 17.95 (*1-55546-715-6*) Chelsea Hse.
Ourth, John & Sawitz, Mike. Hooray, It's Raining. 48p. (gr. k-6). 1979. 5.95 (*0-916456-50-1*, GA110) Good Apple.
Ourth, John & Tamarri, Kathie T. Career Caravan. 64p. (gr. 4-8). 1979. 7.95 (*0-916456-52-8*, GA121) Good Apple.
Outlet Staff. At the Farm. 1991. bds. 3.99 (*0-517-05401-9*) Outlet Bk Co.
—At the Zoo. 1991. bds. 3.99 (*0-517-05402-7*) Outlet Bk Co.
—Beauty & the Beast. 1992. 3.99 (*0-517-08665-4*) Outlet Bk Co.
—Black Beauty. 1993. 6.99 (*0-517-08777-4*) Outlet Bk Co.
—Cinderella. 1993. 12.99 (*0-517-03707-6*) Outlet Bk Co.
—Go to Sleep Little Pig. 1991. 3.99 (*0-517-05684-4*) Outlet Bk Co.
—In the Garden: A Book about Numbers. 1992. 2.99 (*0-517-03596-0*) Outlet Bk Co.
—The Kids' Cookbook. 1993. 7.99 (*0-517-05589-9*) Outlet Bk Co.
—Little Red Riding Hood. 1992. 3.99 (*0-517-08664-6*) Outlet Bk Co.
—Lost in the Haunted Mansion. 1991. pap. 3.99 (*0-517-06138-4*) Outlet Bk Co.
—Missing Snowman: Look & Look Again. 1991. 3.99 (*0-517-06142-2*) Outlet Bk Co.
—More Five Minute Bunny Tales for Bedtime. 1993. 7.99 (*0-517-08769-3*) Outlet Bk Co.
—Pinocchio. 1992. 3.99 (*0-517-08666-2*) Outlet Bk Co.
—Puss-n-Boots. 1992. 3.99 (*0-517-08667-0*) Outlet Bk Co.
—Tabby Cat Wants That. 1991. 3.99 (*0-517-05682-8*) Outlet Bk Co.
—That's My Hat: Dial the Answer. 1992. 3.99 (*0-517-06617-3*) Outlet Bk Co.
Ovecka, Janice. Cave of Falling Water. Fadden, David K., illus. LC 92-56713. 1992. 9.95 (*0-933050-98-4*) New Eng Pr VT.
Overbeck, Cynthia. Ants. LC 81-17216. (Illus.). 48p. (gr. 4 up). 1982. PLB 19.95 (*0-8225-1468-0*, First Ave Edns); pap. 5.95 (*0-8225-9525-7*, First Ave Edns) Lerner Pubns.
—The Butterfly Book. LC 78-7235. (Illus.). 32p. (gr. k-3). 1978. PLB 10.95 (*0-8225-1111-8*) Lerner Pubns.
—Cactus. Hani, Shabo, illus. LC 82-211. 48p. (gr. 4 up). 1982. lib. bdg. 19.95 (*0-8225-1469-9*, First Ave Edns); pap. 5.95 (*0-8225-9556-7*, First Ave Edns) Lerner Pubns.

—Carnivorous Plants. LC 81-17234. (Illus.). 48p. (gr. 4 up). 1982. PLB 19.95 (*0-8225-1470-2*, First Ave Edns); pap. 5.95 (*0-8225-9535-4*, First Ave Edns) Lerner Pubns.
—Cats. Yoshino, Shin, illus. LC 83-17530. 48p. (gr. 4 up). 1983. PLB 19.95 (*0-8225-1480-X*) Lerner Pubns.
—Elephants. LC 80-27550. (Illus.). 48p. (gr. 4-10). 1981. PLB 19.95 (*0-8225-1452-4*) Lerner Pubns.
—The Fish Book. Lerner, Sharon, illus. LC 78-7205. 32p. (gr. k-3). 1978. PLB 10.95 (*0-8225-1110-X*) Lerner Pubns.
—The Fruit Book. Lerner, Sharon, illus. LC 74-12744. 32p. (gr. k-3). 1975. PLB 10.95 (*0-8225-0295-X*) Lerner Pubns.
—How Seeds Travel. LC 81-17217. (Illus.). 48p. (gr. 4 up). 1982. PLB 19.95 (*0-8225-1474-5*) Lerner Pubns.
—How Seeds Travel. Hani, Shabo, photos by. (Illus.). 48p. (gr. 4 up). Repr. of 1982 ed. 5.95g (*0-8225-9569-9*) Lerner Pubns.
—Monkeys. LC 81-1961. (Illus.). 48p. (gr. 4 up). 1981. PLB 19.95 (*0-8225-1464-8*) Lerner Pubns.
—The Vegetable Book. Lerner, Sharon, illus. LC 74-12746. 32p. (gr. k-3). 1975. PLB 10.95 (*0-8225-0297-6*) Lerner Pubns.
Overbeck, Cynthia, jt. auth. see Thompson, Brenda.
Overholt, Jim, jt. ed. see Children's Museum of Oak Ridge, Tennessee Staff.
Overholtzer, Ruth. Elijah. Butcher, Sam, illus. 36p. (gr. k-6). 1967. pap. text ed. 9.45 (*1-55976-009-5*) CEF Press.
—Elisha. Biel, Bill, illus. 33p. (gr. k-6). 1967. pap. text ed. 9.45 (*1-55976-010-9*) CEF Press.
—Joshua. Butcher, Sam & Anderasen, Norma, illus. 62p. (gr. k-6). 1987. pap. text ed. 9.45 (*1-55976-012-5*) CEF Press.
—Moses, Vol. I. Andreasen, Norma, illus. 50p. (gr. k-6). 1957. pap. text ed. 9.45 (*1-55976-007-9*) CEF Press.
—Moses, Vol. II. Andreasen, Norma, illus. 50p. (gr. k-6). 1967. pap. text ed. 9.45 (*1-55976-008-7*) CEF Press.
—Salvation Songs, Vol. I. 100p. (gr. k-6). 1975. pap. text ed. 2.99 (*3-90117-100-2*) CEF Press.
—Salvation Songs, Vol. II. 105p. (gr. k-4). 1979. pap. text ed. 2.99 (*1-55976-201-2*) CEF Press.
—Salvation Songs, Vol. III. 100p. (gr. k-6). 1975. pap. text ed. 2.99 (*1-55976-202-0*) CEF Press.
—Salvation Songs, Vol. IV. (Illus.). 96p. (gr. k-6). 1979. pap. text ed. 2.99 (*1-55976-203-9*) CEF Press.
—Wordless Book Visualized. (Illus.). 54p. (gr. k-6). 1979. pap. text ed. 8.99 (*1-55976-027-3*) CEF Press.
Overholtzer, Ruth P. Life of Peter. Beerhorst, Adrian, illus. 21p. (gr. k-6). 1964. pap. text ed. 9.45 (*1-55976-013-3*) CEF Press.
Overson, David. Perspectives from the Passenger Seat. Jones, M. L., ed. 105p. (Orig.). 1993. pap. text ed. 6.95 (*1-882270-09-6*) Old Rugged Cross.
Overstreet, Charles. Indian & Mountain Man Crafts: Cuttin' & Stitchin' Smith, Monte, ed. Overstreet, Charles, illus. 106p. (Orig.). (gr. 8-12). 1994. pap. 10.95 perfect bdg. (*0-943604-41-9*) Eagles View.
Overton, Jenny. The Ship from Simnel Street. LC 85-21965. 224p. (gr. 5 up). 1986. reinforced trade ed. 10.25 (*0-688-06182-6*) Greenwillow.
Owaida, Mohammad T. Glimpses of Islam. Obaba, Al I., ed. 49p. (Orig.). 1977. pap. text ed. 1.50 (*0-916157-70-9*) African Islam Miss Pubns.
Owen, Barbara. Look, I'm Cooking! Simple Recipes for Preschoolers. Gross, Karen, ed. 64p. (Orig.). (ps). 1993. pap. text ed. 5.95 (*1-56309-079-1*, New Hope) Womans Mission Union.
Owen, Cheryl. My Naturecrafts Book. LC 92-10187. (Illus.). 1993. 14.95 (*0-316-67715-9*) Little.
Owen, Gwyneth, jt. auth. see Heater, Derek.
Owen, Jackie, jt. auth. see Laemmlen, Ann.
Owen, Jennifer. Insect Life. Jackson, Ian & Harris, Alan, illus. 32p. (gr. 4-7). 1985. PLB 13.96 (*0-88110-173-7*, Pub. by Usborne); pap. 5.95 (*0-86020-843-5*) EDC.
Owen, Oliver S. Eco-Solutions: How We Can Make Our Sick Earth Well. LC 93-19132. 1993. 14.96 (*1-56239-203-4*) Abdo & Dghtrs.
—Intro to Your Environment. Italia, Bob, ed. LC 93-7746. 1993. 14.96 (*1-56239-204-2*) Abdo & Dghtrs.
Owen, Roy. The Ibis & the Egret. Sabuda, Robert, illus. LC 92-26220. 32p. (ps-3). 1993. 14.95 (*0-399-22504-8*, Philomel Bks) Putnam Pub Group.
Owen, Wilfred, Jr., ed. see Carpenter, Allan.
Owen, William B. & Goodspeed, Edgar J. Homeric Vocabularies: Greek & English Word-Lists for the Study of Homer. Pharr, C., frwd. by. LC 68-31669. (GRE & ENG.). (gr. 9 up). 1969. pap. 9.95x (*0-8061-0828-2*) U of Okla Pr.
Owens, Carolyn. Color Me...Going! McLaughlin, Dorthy, illus. 32p. (ps-4). 1982. pap. 1.19 (*0-87123-695-8*) Bethany Hse.
Owens, Carolyn, jt. auth. see Roggow, Linda.
Owens, Laurella, jt. auth. see Brown, Virginia P.
Owens, Mary B. A Caribou Alphabet. McCollough, Mark, contrib. by. (Illus.). 40p. (gr. k-6). 1988. 16.95 (*0-937966-25-8*) Tilbury Hse.
—A Caribou Alphabet. McCollough, Mark, contrib. by. (Illus.). 40p. (ps-3). 1990. pap. 4.95 (*0-374-41043-7*, Sunburst) FS&G.
—Counting Cranes. (ps-3). 1993. 14.95 (*0-316-67719-1*) Little.
Owens, Rochelle, tr. see Atlan, Liliane.
Owens, Thomas S. Collecting Baseball Cards. LC 92-18166. (Illus.). 80p. (gr. 4 up). 1993. PLB 14.90 (*1-56294-254-9*); pap. 9.95 (*1-56294-713-3*) Millbrook Pr.

Owens, Tom. Collecting Sports Autographs: Fun & Profit from This Easy-to-Learn Hobby. 131p. (Orig.). (gr. 7 up). 1989. pap. 6.95 (*0-933893-79-5*) Bonus Books.

Owens-Knudsen, Vic. Photography Basics: An Introduction for Young People. Petronella, Michael, illus. LC 83-9775. 48p. (gr. 5-9). 1983. 9.95 (*0-13-664995-5*) P-H.

Owl Editors & Chicadee Editors. Kitchen Fun. (Illus.). 32p. (gr. 1-5). 1989. 10.95 (*0-316-67734-5*, Joy St Bks) Little.

Owl Magazine Editors. Amazing but True. (Illus.). 96p. (gr. 3 up). 1992. pap. 3.95 (*0-920775-69-1*, Pub. by Greey dePencier CN) Firefly Bks Ltd.

—Bee Hives & Bat Caves: Amazing Animal Homes. Plewes, Andrew, illus. 48p. (gr. 1 up). 1992. pap. 6.95 (*0-920775-46-2*, Pub. by Greey dePencier CN) Firefly Bks Ltd.

—Jokes & Riddles. (Illus.). 96p. (gr. 3 up). 1992. pap. 3.95 (*0-919872-85-9*, Pub. by Greey dePencier CN) Firefly Bks Ltd.

—The Kids' Question & Answer Book. (Illus.). 80p. (gr. 3-7). 1988. 11.95 (*0-448-19221-7*, G&D) Putnam Pub Group.

—My Summer Book. (Illus.). 64p. (gr. 3 up). 1992. pap. 8.95 (*0-920775-36-5*, Pub. by Greey dePencier CN) Firefly Bks Ltd.

—Nature What's It? Creatures, Plants, Nature's Oddities & More. (Illus.). 32p. (gr. 4 up). 1992. pap. 4.95 (*0-920775-38-1*, Pub. by Greey dePencier CN) Firefly Bks Ltd.

—Puzzles & Puzzlers. (Illus.). 96p. (gr. 3 up). 1992. pap. 3.95 (*0-920775-67-5*, Pub. by Greey dePencier CN) Firefly Bks Ltd.

—Singing Fish & Flying Rhinos: Amazing Animal Habits. Sisco, Sam, illus. 48p. (gr. 2 up). 1992. pap. 6.95 (*0-920775-45-4*, Pub. by Greey dePencier CN) Firefly Bks Ltd.

—Summer Fun. (Illus.). 128p. (gr. 4 up). 1992. pap. 8.95 (*0-919872-87-5*, Pub. by Greey dePencier CN) Firefly Bks Ltd.

—Weird & Wonderful. (Illus.). 96p. (gr. 3 up). 1992. pap. 3.95 (*0-919872-81-6*, Pub. by Greey dePencier CN) Firefly Bks Ltd.

—What's It? Gadgets, Objects, Machines & More. (Illus.). 32p. (gr. 3 up). 1992. pap. 4.95 (*0-920775-30-6*, Pub. by Greey dePencier CN) Firefly Bks Ltd.

Owl Magazine Editors & Chickadee Magazine Editors. Party Fun. (Illus.). 32p. (gr. 3 up). 1992. pap. 7.95 (*0-920775-41-1*, Pub. by Greey dePencier CN) Firefly Bks Ltd.

Owl Magazine Editors, ed. The Kids' Cat Book. (Illus.). 96p. (gr. 3 up). 1992. pap. 9.95 (*0-920775-51-9*, Pub. by Greey de Pencier CN) Firefly Bks Ltd.

—The Kids' Dog Book. (Illus.). 96p. (gr. 3 up). 1992. pap. 9.95 (*0-920775-50-0*, Pub. by Greey de Pencier CN) Firefly Bks Ltd.

OWL Magazine Editors Staff. The Kids' Question & Answer Book Two. (Illus.). 80p. (gr. 3-7). 1988. 11.95 (*0-448-09276-X*, G&D) Putnam Pub Group.

Owl Magazine Staff. Dinosaur Question & Answer Book: Everything Kids Want to Know about Dinosaurs, Fossils, And... (gr. 4-7). 1992. 16.95 (*0-316-67736-1*, Joy St Bks) Little.

—The Kids' Question & Answer Book Three. 80p. 1990. 11.95 (*0-448-40057-X*, G&D) Putnam Pub Group.

—Winter Fun: A Book Full of Things to Do in Cold Weather. (Illus.). 128p. (gr. 3 up). 1992. pap. 9.95 (*0-919872-86-7*, Pub. by Greey de Pencier CN) Firefly Bks Ltd.

OWL Magazine Staff & Chickadee Magazine Staff. Magic Fun: Mystery Potions, Card Magic, Vanishing Tricks Plus Puzzles, Treats, & Much More. 32p. (gr. 1-5). 1992. pap. 5.95 (*0-316-67739-6*, Joy St Bks) Little.

Owl Magazine Staff, ed. see Funston, Sylvia.

Owre, J. Riis, ed. see Casona, Alejandro.

Oxenbury, Helen. All Fall Down. Oxenbury, Helen, illus. 10p. (ps-1). 1987. bds. 5.95 (*0-02-769040-7*, Aladdin) Macmillan Child Grp.

—Beach Day. LC 81-69273. (Illus.). 14p. (ps-k). 1991. bds. 3.95 (*0-8037-0992-7*) Dial Bks Young.

—The Birthday Party. (Illus.). 24p. (ps-1). 1993. pap. 3.99 (*0-14-054947-1*, Puffin Pied Piper) Puffin Bks.

—The Car Trip. Oxenbury, Helen, illus. 24p. (ps-1). 1983. 3.95 (*0-8037-0009-1*, 0383-120) Dial Bks Young.

—The Checkup. (Illus.). 24p. (ps-1). 1994. pap. 3.99 (*0-14-055275-8*, Puffin Pied Piper) Puffin Bks.

—Clap Hands. Oxenbury, Helen, illus. 10p. (ps). 1987. bds. 5.95 (*0-02-769030-X*, Aladdin) Macmillan Child Grp.

—The Dancing Class. Oxenbury, Helen, illus. LC 82-19791. 24p. (ps-1). 1983. 5.95 (*0-8037-1651-6*, 0383-120) Dial Bks Young.

—The Dancing Class. (Illus.). 24p. (ps-1). 1993. pap. 3.99 (*0-14-054934-X*, Puffin Pied Piper) Puffin Bks.

—Dressing. Oxenbury, Helen, illus. 14p. (ps-k). 1981. 3.95 (*0-671-42113-1*, Little Simon) S&S Trade.

—Eating Out. (Illus.). 24p. (ps-1). 1994. pap. 3.99 (*0-14-054948-X*, Puffin Pied Piper) Puffin Bks.

—Family. (Illus.). 14p. (ps-k). 1981. 3.95 (*0-671-42110-7*, Little Simon) S&S Trade.

—First Day of School. (Illus.). 24p. (ps-1). 1993. pap. 3.99 (*0-14-054917-3*, Puffin Pied Piper) Puffin Bks.

—Friends. Oxenbury, Helen, illus. 14p. (ps-k). 1981. 3.95 (*0-671-42111-5*, Little Simon) S&S Trade.

—Good Night, Good Morning. LC 81-69272. (Illus.). 14p. (ps-k). 1991. bds. 3.95 (*0-8037-0993-5*) Dial Bks Young.

—Grandma & Grandpa. (Illus.). 24p. (ps-1). 1993. pap. 3.99 (*0-14-054978-1*, Puffin Pied Piper) Puffin Bks.

—Helen Oxebury's Numbers of Things. Oxenbury, Helen, illus. LC 83-5263. 32p. (ps-3). 1983. pap. 9.95 (*0-385-29288-0*); pap. 9.95 (*0-385-29289-9*) Delacorte.

—The Helen Oxenbury Nursery Storybook. LC 84-28887. (Illus.). 80p. (ps-1). 1985. 17.00 (*0-394-87519-2*); PLB 17.99 (*0-394-97519-7*) Knopf Bks Yng Read.

—Helen Oxenbury's ABC of Things. Oxenbury, Helen, illus. LC 83-5263. 56p. (ps-3). 1983. PLB 13.95 (*0-385-29291-0*); pap. 12.95 (*0-385-29290-2*) Delacorte.

—Helen Oxenbury's ABC of Things. Oxenbury, Helen, illus. 28p. (ps). 1993. Repr. bds. 3.95 (*0-689-71761-X*, Aladdin) Macmillan Child Grp.

—Helen Oxenbury's First Nursery Stories. Oxenbury, Helen, illus. 32p. (ps-k). 1994. bds. 3.95 (*0-689-71825-X*, Aladdin) Macmillan Child Grp.

—I Hear. Oxenbury, Helen, illus. LC 85-61367. 14p. (ps). 1986. 3.95 (*0-394-87481-1*) Random Bks Yng Read.

—I See. Oxenbury, Helen, illus. LC 85-61365. 14p. (ps). 1986. Repr. of 1986 ed. bds. 3.95 (*0-394-87479-X*) Random Bks Yng Read.

—Monkey See, Monkey Do. LC 81-69271. (Illus.). 14p. (ps-k). 1991. bds. 3.95 (*0-8037-0994-3*) Dial Bks Young.

—Mother's Helper. LC 81-68773. (Illus.). 14p. (ps-k). 1991. bds. 3.95 (*0-8037-0995-1*) Dial Bks Young.

—Pippo Gets Lost. Oxenbury, Helen, illus. LC 89-340. 14p. (ps-k). 1989. bds. 5.95 (*0-689-71336-3*, Aladdin) Macmillan Child Grp.

—Playing. Oxenbury, Helen, illus. 14p. (ps-k). 1981. 3.95 (*0-671-42109-3*, Little Simon) S&S Trade.

—Say Goodnight. Oxenbury, Helen, illus. 10p. (ps). 1987. bds. 5.95 (*0-02-769010-5*, Aladdin) Macmillan Child Grp.

—Shopping Trip. LC 81-69274. 14p. (ps-k). 1982. bds. 3.50 (*0-8037-7939-9*) Dial Bks Young.

—Shopping Trip. LC 81-69274. (Illus.). 14p. (ps-k). 1991. bds. 3.95 (*0-8037-0997-8*) Dial Bks Young.

—Tickle, Tickle. Oxenbury, Helen, illus. 10p. (ps). 1987. bds. 5.95 (*0-02-769020-2*, Aladdin) Macmillan Child Grp.

—Tom & Pippo & the Dog. Oxenbury, Helen, illus. LC 89-341. 14p. (ps-k). 1989. bds. 5.95 (*0-689-71338-X*, Aladdin) Macmillan Child Grp.

—Tom & Pippo & the Washing Machine. Oxenbury, Helen, illus. LC 89-37431. 14p. (ps-k). 1988. bds. 5.95 (*0-689-71255-3*, Aladdin) Macmillan Child Grp.

—Tom & Pippo Go for a Walk. Oxenbury, Helen, illus. LC 87-37432. 14p. (ps-k). 1988. bds. 5.95 (*0-689-71254-5*, Aladdin) Macmillan Child Grp.

—Tom & Pippo Go Shopping. Oxenbury, Helen, illus. LC 88-10497. 14p. (ps-1). 1989. Repr. of 1989 ed. bds. 5.95 (*0-689-71278-2*, Aladdin) Macmillan Child Grp.

—Tom & Pippo in the Garden. Oxenbury, Helen, illus. LC 88-9145. 14p. (ps-1). 1989. Repr. of 1989 ed. bds. 5.95 (*0-689-71275-8*, Aladdin) Macmillan Child Grp.

—Tom & Pippo in the Snow. Oxenbury, Helen, illus. LC 89-3306. 14p. (ps-k). 1989. bds. 5.95 (*0-689-71337-1*, Aladdin) Macmillan Child Grp.

—Tom & Pippo Make a Friend. Oxenbury, Helen, illus. LC 89-337. 14p. (ps-k). 1989. bds. 5.95 (*0-689-71339-8*, Aladdin) Macmillan Child Grp.

—Tom & Pippo Make a Mess. Oxenbury, Helen, illus. LC 87-37437. 14p. (ps-k). 1988. bds. 5.95 (*0-689-71253-7*, Aladdin) Macmillan Child Grp.

—Tom & Pippo on the Beach. Oxenbury, Helen, illus. LC 92-53130. 24p. (ps). 1993. 5.95 (*1-56402-181-5*) Candlewick Pr.

—Tom & Pippo Read a Story. Oxenbury, Helen, illus. LC 87-37438. 14p. (ps-k). 1988. bds. 5.95 (*0-689-71252-9*, Aladdin) Macmillan Child Grp.

—Tom & Pippo See the Moon. Oxenbury, Helen, illus. 14p. (ps-1). 1989. Repr. of 1989 ed. bds. 5.95 (*0-689-71277-4*, Aladdin) Macmillan Child Grp.

—Tom & Pippo's Day. Oxenbury, Helen, illus. 14p. (ps-1). 1989. Repr. of 1989 ed. bds. 5.95 (*0-689-71276-6*, Aladdin) Macmillan Child Grp.

—Working. Oxenbury, Helen, illus. 7p. (ps). 1981. 3.95 (*0-671-42112-3*, Little Simon) S&S Trade.

Oxenbury, Helen & Bennett, Jim. Tiny Tim: Verses for Children. (ps-2). 1992. 3.99 (*0-440-40521-1*, YB) Dell.

Oxenbury, Helen, illus. Tiny Tim. Bennett, Jill, selected by. LC 81-68916. (Illus.). 32p. (ps-3). 1982. PLB 10.95 (*0-685-01402-9*); pap. 10.95 (*0-385-29055-1*) Delacorte.

Oxendine, Bess H. Miriam. LC 93-61292. (Illus.). 44p. (gr. 2-6). 1994. 6.95 (*1-55523-665-0*) Winston-Derek.

Oxendine, Reginald. Our Family Can Read, 2 bks. Scott, Ricky, illus. 76p. (Orig.). (gr. k up). 1992. Set. pap. text ed. 29.95 incl. audio cass. (*0-944049-00-1*); 29.95 (*0-944049-01-X*); 29.95 (*0-944049-02-8*) Arrow Pub NC.

Oxford, Mariesa. Going to Grandma's. (Illus.). (gr. 2-6). 1992. PLB 17.96 (*0-8114-3575-X*) Raintree Steck-V.

Oxford Staff, ed. Oxford Children's Encyclopedia, 7 vols. (Illus.). 2928p. (gr. 3-8). 1992. Set. laminated boards 200.00 (*0-19-910139-6*) OUP.

Oxlade, C. & Stockley, C. The World of the Microscope. (Illus.). 48p. 1989. PLB 13.96 (*0-88110-364-0*); pap. 7.95 (*0-7460-0289-0*) EDC.

Oxlade, C., jt. auth. see Wertheim, J.

Oxley, Dorothy. Quest. 144p. (Orig.). (gr. 7-10). 1990. pap. 4.99 (*0-7459-1846-8*) Lion USA.

Oxman, Fannie-Rose, jt. auth. see Harnett, Juli O.

Oyama, Kaikilani E. The Kaua'i Guide on Ni'ihau: UniNi'ihau: M-m-m, What a Sweet Potato. Archives of the Kauai Museum Staff & Bernice P. Bishop Museum Staff, illus. (Orig.). 1988. pap. 2.50 (*0-942255-04-6*, G3) Magic Fishes Pr.

Oyer, Sharron, et al. Seekers in Sneakers: A Children's Devotional, Vol. 1. 128p. (Orig.). (gr. 2-5). 1988. pap. 6.99 (*0-89081-611-5*) Harvest Hse.

Oyster Books Staff. My Fairy Tale Library. LC 90-84674. (Illus.). 32p. (ps-3). 1991. 15.95 (*0-448-40144-4*, G&D) Putnam Pub Group.

Ozaeta, Pablo. Mis Primeros Cuentos. Frank, Marjorie & Lono, Luz P., eds. Sussman, Dee, illus. LC 75-16546. (gr. 4-8). 1975. pap. 6.60 student ed. (*0-8325-9642-6*, Natl Textbk); tchr's. ed. 10.60 (*0-8325-9641-8*, Natl Textbk); program pkg. (1 tchr's. ed. & 10 student wkbks.) 76.60 (*0-8325-9640-X*, Natl Textbk) NTC Pub Grp.

Ozaki, Yei T., compiled by. The Japanese Fairy Book. LC 70-109415. (Illus.). 320p. (gr. 3-8). 1970. pap. 12.95 (*0-8048-0885-6*) C E Tuttle.

Ozer, Elizabeth M. & Toure, Nkenge. Staying Safe: How to Protect Yourself Against Sexual Assault. Hamilton, Linda, illus. 23p. (Orig.). (gr. 2-6). 1984. pap. text ed. 3.00 (*0-318-04650-4*) Rape Crisis Ctr.

Ozer, Steven. Netherlands. (Illus.). 104p. (gr. 5 up). 1990. 14.95 (*0-7910-1107-0*) Chelsea Hse.

Ozman. Jennifer's Birthday Present. LC 73-87798. (Illus.). 32p. (gr. k-3). 1974. PLB 9.95 (*0-87783-125-4*); pap. 3.94 deluxe ed. (*0-87783-126-2*) Oddo.

Ozmon, H. Twelve Great Western Philosophers. Steinbauer, S., illus. LC 68-16403. 48p. (gr. 4 up). 1967. PLB 9.95 (*0-87783-046-0*); pap. 3.94 deluxe ed (*0-87783-115-7*) Oddo.

P

Paamoni, Zev. Aaron, the High Priest. (Illus.). (gr. 5-10). 1970. 3.00 (*0-914080-27-X*) Shulsinger Sales.

—The Adventures of Jacob. (Illus.). (gr. 5-10). 1970. 3.00 (*0-914080-26-1*) Shulsinger Sales.

—Benjamin, the Littlest Brother. (Illus.). (gr. 5-10). 1970. 3.00 (*0-914080-28-8*) Shulsinger Sales.

—Yitzchak, Son of Abraham. (Illus.). (gr. 5-10). 1970. 4.00 (*0-914080-25-3*) Shulsinger Sales.

Paananen, Eloise. The Military. LC 92-29008. (Illus.). 48p. (gr. 5-6). 1992. PLB 21.34 (*0-8114-7353-8*) Raintree Steck-V.

Pace, Betty. Chris Gets Ear Tubes. Hutton, Katherine, illus. LC 87-26759. 48p. (ps-2). 1987. 5.95 (*0-930323-36-X*, Kendall Green Pubns) Gallaudet Univ Pr.

Pace, Mildred M. Kentucky Derby Champion. rev. ed. Gifford, James M., et al, eds. Dennis, Wesley, illus. 144p. (gr. 3 up). 1993. Repr. of 1955 ed. 12.00 (*0-945084-36-6*) J Stuart Found.

Pace, Sue. The Last Oasis. LC 92-20223. 1993. 15.00 (*0-385-30881-7*) Delacorte.

Pacheco, Anne M. My Other Dad. LC 90-7170. 138p. 1991. pap. 6.95 (*1-55523-404-6*) Winston-Derek.

Pacheco, M. A., jt. auth. see Sanchez, J. L.

Pacific Press Staff. Before I Was a Kid. 1991. pap. 5.95 (*0-8163-1043-2*) Pacific Pr Pub Assn.

Pacinelli, Donna, illus. Heidi. 48p. (gr. 2-5). 1991. 6.95 (*0-88101-112-6*) Unicorn Pub.

Pacini, Kathy, ed. see Nixon, Joan L.

Pack, Janet. Fueling the Future. LC 91-34602. 128p. (gr. 4-8). 1992. PLB 26.60 (*0-516-05512-7*) Childrens.

Pack, Robert. The Octopus Who Wanted to Juggle. Willard, Nancy, illus. (Orig.). (ps-7). 1990. text ed. 13.95 (*0-913123-26-9*) Galileo.

Packager, Belgian, tr. see Pittau, Francisco.

Packard, Andrea. The Evil Wizard. 64p. 1984. pap. 2.25 (*0-553-15418-4*) Bantam.

Packard, Ann & Stafford, Shirley. Holidays. 116p. 1983. write for info. (*0-9607580-4-6*) S Stafford.

—Space. 58p. (ps-3). 1981. write for info. (*0-9607580-2-X*) S Stafford.

—Time of the Dinosaurs. 92p. (ps-3). 1981. write for info. (*0-9607580-1-1*) S Stafford.

Packard, Edward. The Castle of Frome. 144p. (Orig.). (gr. 7-12). 1986. pap. 2.50 (*0-553-26089-8*) Bantam.

—The Cave of Time. (gr. 4-8). 1982. pap. 3.25 (*0-553-26965-8*) Bantam.

—The Cave of Time. large type ed. (Illus.). 115p. (gr. 3-7). 1987. 8.95 (*0-942545-01-X*); PLB 9.95 (*0-942545-07-9*, Dist. by Grolier) Grey Castle.

—The Circus. 64p. 1983. pap. 2.25 (*0-553-15426-5*) Bantam.

—Comet Crash. (gr. 4-7). 1994. pap. 3.50 (*0-553-56009-3*) Bantam.

—The Comet Masters. (gr. 4-7). 1991. pap. 2.99 (*0-553-28961-6*) Bantam.

—The Curse of the Haunted Mansion. 1982. pap. 3.25 (*0-553-27419-8*) Bantam.

—A Day with the Dinosaurs, No. 46. 64p. (Orig.). 1988. pap. 2.99 (*0-553-15612-8*, Skylark) Bantam.

—Deadwood City. 128p. (gr. 4). 1989. pap. 2.50 (*0-553-26213-0*) Bantam.

—Dinosaur Island. (gr. 4-7). 1993. pap. 3.25 (*0-553-56007-7*) Bantam.

—The Fiber People. (gr. 4-7). 1991. pap. 2.99 (*0-553-29355-9*) Bantam.

—Ghost Hunter. 128p. (Orig.). (gr. 4). 1986. pap. 3.25 (0-553-26983-6) Bantam.
—The Great Easter Bunny Adventure. 64p. (Orig.). (gr. 4). 1987. pap. 2.50 (0-553-15492-3, Skylark) Bantam.
—Horror House. 1993. pap. 3.25 (0-553-56008-5) Bantam.
—Journey to the Year Three Thousand: Cyoa Superadventure. (Orig.). (gr. 4). 1987. pap. 3.50 (0-553-26157-6) Bantam.
—Jungle Safari. Tomei, Lorna, illus. 51p. (gr. 4). 1983. pap. 2.25 (0-553-15403-6) Bantam.
—Kidnapped. 1991. pap. 3.25 (0-553-29143-2) Bantam.
—The Luckiest Day of Your Life. (gr. 4-7). 1993. pap. 3.25 (0-553-29304-4) Bantam.
—Magic Master. 1992. pap. 3.25 (0-553-29606-X) Bantam.
—Mountain Survival. 128p. (gr. 4-6). pap. text ed. 2.25 (0-553-26252-1) Bantam.
—Mutiny. 1989. pap. 2.75 (0-553-27854-1) Bantam.
—Mystery-Chimney Rock. (gr. 3-7). 1979. pap. 2.25 (0-553-26307-2) Bantam.
—The Polar Bear Express. 64p. (Orig.). 1984. pap. 2.25 (0-553-15409-5) Bantam.
—The Power Dome. (gr. 9-12). 1991. pap. 3.25 (0-553-28837-7) Bantam.
—Reality Machine. 1993. pap. 3.25 (0-553-56401-3) Bantam.
—Return to the Cave of Time. 128p. (Orig.). (gr. 4). 1985. pap. 2.25 (0-553-25495-2) Bantam.
—Roller Star. (gr. 4-7). 1993. pap. 3.25 (0-553-56006-9) Bantam.
—Secret of the Dolphins. (gr. 4-7). 1993. pap. 3.25 (0-553-29300-1) Bantam.
—Secret of the Sun God. (ps-7). 1987. pap. 2.25 (0-553-26529-6) Bantam.
—Skateboard Champion. 1991. pap. 3.25 (0-553-28898-9) Bantam.
—Soccer Star. 1994. pap. 3.50 (0-553-56011-5) Bantam.
—The Space Fortress. (gr. 4-7). 1991. pap. 2.99 (0-553-28899-7) Bantam.
—Space Hawks, Bk. 1: Faster Than Light. 96p. 1991. lib. bdg. 21.28 (0-553-28838-5) Bantam.
—Space Hawks, Bk. 2: Alien Invaders. 128p. 1991. pap. 2.99 (0-553-28839-3) Bantam.
—Space Vampire. 128p. 1987. pap. 2.99 (0-553-26723-X) Bantam.
—Spy Trap (Your Code Name Is Jonah, Vol. 1. 1989. pap. 2.50 (0-553-23182-0) Bantam.
—Sugarcane Island. 128p. (gr. 4). 1986. pap. 2.25 (0-553-26040-5) Bantam.
—Sunken Treasure. 1982. pap. 6.95 (0-553-05018-4) Bantam.
—Superbike. (gr. 4-7). 1992. pap. 3.25 (0-553-29294-3) Bantam.
—Supercomputer. 128p. (Orig.). (gr. 4). 1984. pap. 2.25 (0-553-25818-4) Bantam.
—Teropia Island. 128p. (Orig.). 1986. pap. 2.25 (0-553-25472-3, Starfire) Bantam.
—The Third Planet from Altair. 128p. (Orig.). (gr. 5 up). 1989. pap. 2.50 (0-553-23185-5) Bantam.
—Through the Black Hole. 1990. pap. 3.25 (0-553-28440-1) Bantam.
—Underground Kingdom. (ps-7). 1983. pap. 2.25 (0-553-25989-X) Bantam.
—Vampire Invaders. (gr. 4-7). 1991. pap. 3.25 (0-553-29212-9) Bantam.
—Viking Raiders. (gr. 4-7). 1992. pap. 3.25 (0-553-29302-8) Bantam.
—Who Killed Harlowe Thrombey, Vol. 1. 1989. pap. 2.50 (0-553-23181-2) Bantam.
—Who Killed Harlowe Thrombey, No. 9. large type ed. Granger, Paul, illus. 121p. (gr. 3-7). 1987. Repr. of 1981 ed. 8.95 (0-942545-13-3); PLB 9.95 (0-942545-18-4, Dist. by Grolier) Grey Castle.
—Worst Day of Your Life. 1990. pap. 3.25 (0-553-28316-2) Bantam.
—You Are a Genius. 1989. pap. 3.25 (0-553-28155-0) Bantam.
—You Are a Monster. 128p. (gr. 4). 1988. pap. 2.75 (0-553-27474-0) Bantam.
—You Are a Shark. (gr. 5-12). 1985. pap. 2.25 (0-553-26386-2) Bantam.
—You Are Microscopic. (gr. 4-7). 1992. pap. 3.25 (0-553-29298-6) Bantam.
—Your Code Name Is Jonah. large type ed. Granger, Paul, illus. 114p. (gr. 3-7). 1987. Repr. of 1979 ed. 8.95 (0-942545-15-X); PLB 9.95 (0-942545-20-6, Dist. by Grolier) Grey Castle.
Packard, Edward, jt. auth. see Saunders, Susan.
Packard, Gwen K. Coping in an Interfaith Family. LC 92-39454. 1993. 13.95 (0-8239-1452-6) Rosen Group.
Packard, M. The Kite. (Illus.). 28p. (ps-2). 1990. PLB 12.33 (0-516-05355-8); pap. 3.95 (0-516-45355-6) Childrens.
—Surprise! (Illus.). 28p. (ps-2). 1990. PLB 12.33 (0-516-05360-4); pap. 3.95 (0-516-45360-2) Childrens.
—Where Is Jake? (Illus.). 28p. (ps-2). 1990. PLB 12.33 (0-516-05361-2); pap. 3.95 (0-516-45361-0) Childrens.
Packard, Mary. Dinosaurs. Santoro, Chris, illus. 48p. (ps-3). 1981. pap. 9.95 (0-671-43040-8, S&S BFYR) S&S Trade.
—Disney's Two-Minute Good Night Stories. Langley, Bill, et al, illus. LC 87-83200. 36p. (ps-1). 1988. write for info. (0-307-12181-X) Western Pub.
—Fairest of All. McCue, Lisa, illus. LC 93-11056. (gr. 5 up). 1993. write for info. (0-516-00826-9) Childrens.
—Fun Factory. Barish, Wendy, ed. 64p. (Orig.). (gr. 3-8). 1984. pap. 2.95 (0-671-47729-3) S&S Trade.

—I Wonder How Parrots Can Talk & Other Neat Facts about Birds. (Illus.). 36p. (ps-3). 1992. write for info. (0-307-11320-5, 11320) Western Pub.
—Mickey's Riddles, Codes, & Games Book. Barish, Wendy, ed. 64p. (gr. 7 up). 1984. pap. 2.95 (0-671-47731-5) S&S Trade.
—My First Answer Book. Allert, Kathy, illus (ps-5). 1984. pap. 7.95 (0-671-49312-4, Little Simon) S&S Trade.
—Playing by the Rules. McCue, Lisa, illus. LC 93-4423. 1993. write for info. (0-516-00827-7) Childrens.
—Puzzle Party. Barish, Wendy, ed. 64p. (gr. 7 up). 1984. pap. 2.95 (0-671-47730-7) S&S Trade.
—Safe & Sound. McCue, Lisa, illus. LC 93-11058. 1993. write for info. (0-516-00828-5) Childrens.
—Save the Swamp. McCue, Lisa, illus. LC 93-11059. 1993. write for info. (0-516-00829-3) Childrens.
—Scaredy Ghost. Williams, Jennifer H., illus. LC 93-24845. 24p. (gr. k-2). 1993. pap. text ed. 1.50 (0-8167-3246-9) Troll Assocs.
—Spike & Mike & the Treasure Hunt. McCue, Lisa, illus. LC 92-50295. 1993. write for info. (0-679-93936-9); lib. bdg. write for info. (0-679-83936-4) Knopf Bks Yng Read.
—Starting Over. McCue, Lisa & Scribner, Toni, illus. LC 93-11060. 1993. write for info. (0-516-00831-5) Childrens.
—Two-Minute Bedtime Stories. Wilburn, Kathy, illus. LC 87-83202. 36p. (ps-1). 1988. write for info. (0-307-12183-6) Western Pub.
Packard, Mary, adapted by. Disney's Two-Minute Classics. LC 87-83199. (Illus.). 36p. (ps-1). 1988. write for info. (0-307-12180-1) Western Pub.
Packard, Mary, retold by. The Nutcracker Story Book Set & Advent Calendar, 24 bks. Brooks, Nan, illus. 96p. 1993. miniature ed. 16.95 (1-56305-503-1, 3503) Workman Pub.
Packard, Mary E. The Witch Who Couldn't Fly. Cushman, Douglas E., illus. LC 93-2212. (gr. k-3). 1993. pap. 2.95 (0-8167-3256-6) Troll Assocs.
Packer, Alex J. Bringing up Parents: The Teenager's Handbook. Espeland, Pamela, ed. Pulver, Harry, Jr., illus. LC 92-36625. 272p. (gr. 7 up). 1993. pap. 12.95 (0-915793-48-2) Free Spirit Pub.
Packer, Kenneth L. Puberty: The Story of Growth & Change. Green, Anne C., illus. LC 89-5665. 109p. (gr. 6-9). 1989. PLB 13.40 (0-531-10810-4) Watts.
Pacovska, Kveta. The Little Flower King. Bell, Anthea, tr. from GER. LC 92-6046. (Illus.). 36p. 1992. pap. 15.95 (0-88708-221-1) Picture Bk Studio.
—The Midnight Play. Clements, Andrew, adapted by. LC 93-16258. (Illus.). (ps-8). 1993. 15.95 (0-88708-317-X) Picture Bk Studio.
—One Five Many. (ps-3). 1990. 16.95 (0-685-54064-2) HM.
—One, Five, Many. Pacovska, Kveta, illus. 30p. (gr. k-3). 1990. 16.45 (0-395-54997-3, Clarion Bks) HM.
Paddington Bear. Childhood Memories. large type ed. 194p. 1991. 21.95 (1-85089-456-6, Pub. by ISIS UK) Transaction Pubs.
Padgett, Ron, ed. The Teachers & Writers Handbook of Poetic Forms. 230p. 1987. 21.95 (0-915924-24-2); pap. 12.95 (0-915924-23-4) Tchrs & Writers Coll.
Padilla, Jaime & Taylor, Maurie. Easy Spanish Word Games. (SPA., Illus.). 64p. (gr. 4 up). 1983. pap. 4.95 (0-8442-7242-6, Passport Bks) NTC Pub Grp.
Padoan, Gianni. Danger Kid. LC 90-48381. 1989. 10.95 (0-85953-312-3) Childs Play.
—Remembering Grandad. 1989. 10.95 (0-85953-311-5) Childs Play.
Padoan, Gianni & Collini, Emanuela. Follow My Leader. (gr. 4 up). 1989. 10.95 (0-85953-313-1) Childs Play.
Padzik, Alicja, jt. ed. see Lehman, Patricia J.
Paek, Min. Aekyung's Dream. Paek, Min, illus. LC 88-18928. (ENG & KOR). 24p. (gr. 2-7). 1988. 13.95 (0-89239-042-5) Childrens Book Pr.
Paelo, Tomie De see De Paola, Tomie.
Pagan, Margarita, tr. see Mozeleski, Peter A.
Page, Andrea C. Student Success Tutor Directory: Sarasota & Manatee County Edition, 1991-92. (Illus.). 64p. (gr. k-12). 1991. pap. write for info. Computer Pr.
—Student Success Tutor Directory (TM) Manatee & Sarasota County, 1990-91 Edition. (Illus.). 128p. (gr. k-12). 1990. pap. write for info. (0-9621214-2-8) Computer Pr.
Page, Bispham. Tea At Miss Jean's. LC 91-65465. (Illus.). 36p. (Orig.). (gr. k-4). 1991. pap. text ed. 9.95 (0-9628129-1-9) Sagebrush Bks.
Page, Brian. Franc-Parler. (FRE.). 208p. 1988. pap. 10.95 (0-8219-0340-3, 40306); tchr's. guide 5.95 (0-8219-0341-1, TG-40825) EMC.
Page, Burdys. Learning to Color with Rhymes. Yamashita, Mina, illus. 32p. (Orig.). 1990. pap. 6.95 (0-86534-146-X) Sunstone Pr.
Page, Carole G. Bouquet of Good-Byes. 1992. pap. 4.99 (0-8024-8180-9) Moody.
—Change of Plans. 1992. pap. 4.99 (0-8024-8179-5) Moody.
—Hallie's Secret. 144p. 1987. pap. text ed. 4.99 (0-8024-3476-2) Moody.
—Heather's Choice. LC 82-3417. 128p. (gr. 7 up). 1982. pap. 4.99 (0-8024-8453-0) Moody.
—Neeley Never Said Good-By. (Orig.). (gr. 7 up). 1984. pap. 4.99 (0-8024-8454-9) Moody.
—A Song for Kasey. 1992. pap. 4.99 (0-8024-8176-0) Moody.
—Summer of a Stranger. 1992. pap. 4.99 (0-8024-8177-9) Moody.

—Taste of Fame. (gr. 2-6). 1992. pap. 4.99 (0-8024-8178-7) Moody.
Page, Dave. Ship Versus Shore: Civil War Engagements Between Land & Sea. (Illus.). 320p. (gr. 10 up). 1993. 19.95 (1-55853-267-6) Rutledge Hill Pr.
Page, David E. The Lemonade War. (Illus.). 64p. (gr. 1-3). 1993. pap. 2.50 (0-87406-648-4) Willowisp Pr.
Page, Jake. Forest. (Illus.). 176p. (gr. 7 up). 1983. 18.60 (0-8094-4344-9); lib. bdg. 24.60 (0-8094-4345-7) Time-Life.
Page, Jean R. From Hoof to Wheel. Page, Jean R., illus. 75p. (Orig.). (gr. 7-12). 1992. pap. 7.95 (0-9632755-0-X) Jean Page.
Page, P. K. A Flask of Sea Water. Gal, Laszio, illus. 34p. (gr. 2 up). 1989. bds. 17.00 laminated (0-19-540704-0) OUP.
Page, P. K., retold by. The Traveling Musicians of Bremen. Denton, Kady M., illus. 32p. (ps-3). 1992. 13.95 (0-316-68836-3, Joy St Bks) Little.
Page, Parker. Getting Along: A Set of Fun-Filled Stories, Songs, & Activities to Help Children Work & Play Together. Rose, Mitchell, illus. 64p. (Orig.). (ps-5). 1989. 12.95 (0-929831-00-4) Childrens TV Resource.
Page, Parker, et al. Getting Along Complete Kit. (gr. k-4). 1991. 107.95 (0-88671-407-9, 4670) Am Guidance.
—Getting Along Student Activities: Level 1. (Orig.). (gr. k-1). 1991. pap. 2.70 (0-88671-409-5, 4672) Am Guidance.
—Getting Along Student Activities: Level 2. (Orig.). (gr. 2-4). 1991. pap. 2.70 (0-88671-410-9, 4676) Am Guidance.
Page, Roberta. Horace Morris. (gr. 4 up). 1992. 7.95 (0-533-09733-9) Vantage.
Page, Roland. The Winner's Edge: What Every Young Person Should Know Before Experimenting with Life. Pickett, Christine, ed. Mills, Michael, illus. 176p. (Orig.). (gr. 6-12). 1990. pap. 10.00 (0-9626244-0-3) New Impres UT.
Pageler, Elaine. Numero Uno Gang Mysteries, 5 novels. (Illus.). 240p. (Orig.). (gr. 3-9). 1988. Set. pap. 15.00 (0-87879-550-2) High Noon Bks.
—Runaway Magic. Kratoville, Betty L., ed. (Illus.). 64p. (gr. 3-9). 1989. PLB 4.95 (0-87879-652-5) High Noon Bks.
Paget, Stephen. I Wonder: Essays for the Young People. facs. ed. LC 68-54365. (gr. 7 up). 1968. Repr. of 1911 ed. 14.00 (0-8369-0765-5) Ayer.
Pagliaro, Michael J. The Violin. (Illus.). 60p. (gr. 4-8). 1993. wkbk. 6.95 (1-884417-00-0) Ardsley Pr.
Pagliaro, Penny, ed. I Like Poems & Poems Like Me. Kim Chee, Wendy, illus. LC 76-50343. (gr. 1-6). 1977. PLB 8.95 (0-916630-03-X) Pr Pacifica.
Pagnol. Le Chateau de Ma Mere. (gr. 7-12). pap. 5.95 (0-88436-045-8, 40278) EMC.
Pagnucci, Franco. I Never Had a Pet. Pagnucci, Gian, ed. Pagnucci, Susan, illus. 32p. (gr. k-1). 1992. pap. 5.95 (0-929326-09-1) Bur Oak Pr Inc.
Pagnucci, Franco & Pagnucci, Susan. Paul Revere & Other Story Hours. (Illus.). 72p. (Orig.). (gr. k-6). 1988. pap. 7.95 (0-929326-00-8) Bur Oak Pr Inc.
—Story - Start Dinosaurs. (gr. 2-5). 1991. 8.95 (0-685-47917-X) Fearon Teach Aids.
—Story - Start Monsters. (gr. 2-5). 1991. 8.95 (0-86653-999-9) Fearon Teach Aids.
Pagnucci, Franco & Susan. Story Start Animals. (gr. 2-5). 1990. pap. 8.95 (0-8224-6398-9) Fearon Teach Aids.
Pagnucci, Gian, ed. see Pagnucci, Franco.
Pagnucci, Gianfranco, ed. Face the Poem. (Illus.). 32p. (Orig.). (gr. 2-8). 1979. Incl. animal poems with animal face masks for choral readings. 3.95 (0-929326-02-4) Bur Oak Pr Inc.
Pagnucci, Susan. Games to Cut. (Illus.). 20p. (Orig.). (gr. k-3). 1978. Incl. 5 reading & math games to make & use. 4.25 (0-929326-03-2) Bur Oak Pr Inc.
—Number Chomp. (Illus.). 48p. (Orig.). (gr. 1-2). 1984. Incl. reproducible math sheets with numbers 0-9 addition & subtraction. 4.50 (0-929326-04-0) Bur Oak Pr Inc.
Pagnucci, Susan, jt. auth. see Pagnucci, Franco.
Pagoan, Gianni. Break-Up. LC 90-46156. 1989. 10.95 (0-85953-310-7) Childs Play.
Paige, David. A Day in the Life of a Forest Ranger. Mauney, Michael, photos by. LC 78-68809. (Illus.). 32p. (gr. 4-8). 1980. PLB 11.79 (0-89375-227-4); pap. 2.95 (0-89375-231-2) Troll Assocs.
—A Day in the Life of a Librarian. Ruhlin, Roger, illus. LC 84-8552. 32p. (gr. 4-8). 1985. PLB 11.79 (0-8167-0101-6); pap. text ed. 2.95 (0-8167-0102-4) Troll Assocs.
—A Day in the Life of a Marine Biologist. Ruhlin, Roger, photos by. LC 80-54097. (Illus.). 32p. (gr. 4-8). 1981. PLB 11.79 (0-89375-446-3); pap. 2.95 (0-89375-447-1); cassette avail. Troll Assocs.
—A Day in the Life of a Police Detective. Ruhlin, Roger, photos by. LC 80-54102. (Illus.). 32p. (gr. 4-8). 1981. PLB 11.79 (0-89375-442-0); cassette avail. Troll Assocs.
—A Day in the Life of a Rock Musician. Ruhlin, Roger, photos by. LC 78-68808. (Illus.). 32p. (gr. 4-8). 1981. PLB 11.79 (0-89375-225-8); pap. 2.95 (0-89375-229-0) Troll Assocs.
—A Day in the Life of a School Basketball Coach. Smith, Bill, photos by. LC 80-54101. (Illus.). 32p. (gr. 4-8). 1981. PLB 11.79 (0-89375-452-8); cassettes avail. Troll Assocs.

—A Day in the Life of a Sports Therapist. Ruhlin, Roger, illus. LC 84-2433. 32p. (gr. 4-8). 1985. PLB 11.79 (*0-8167-0099-0*); pap. text ed. 2.95 (*0-8167-0100-8*) Troll Assocs.

—A Day in the Life of a Zoo Veterinarian. Mauney, Michael, illus. LC 84-6538. 32p. (gr. 4-8). 1985. PLB 11.79 (*0-8167-0095-8*); pap. text ed. 2.95 (*0-8167-0096-6*) Troll Assocs.

Paige, Rae. Sesame Street: The Whole Wide World. 1990. pap. write for info. (*0-307-15826-8*, Pub. by Golden Bks) Western Pub.

Paine, ed. see Stryker & Bingham.

Paine, Alan. Ode to Madonna & Other Poems. Mierzejewska, Anna, illus. 160p. (Orig.). (gr. 4 up). 1992. pap. 12.95 (*0-9632582-1-4*) Diogenes Pr.

Paine, Penelope, ed. see Rosentheil, Agnes.

Paine, Penelope, tr. see Rosentheil, Agnes.

Paine, Penelope C. Time for Horatio. Stryker, Sandy, ed. LC 89-18304. (Illus.). 48p. (ps-6). 1990. 14.95 (*0-911655-33-6*) Advocacy Pr.

Paine, Penelope C. & Bingham, Mindy. My Way Sally. Maeno, Itoko, illus. LC 88-2653. 48p. (ps-6). 1988. 14.95 (*0-911655-27-1*) Advocacy Pr.

Paine, Stephen W. Beginning Greek: A Functional Approach. (gr. 9 up). 1961. 22.00x (*0-19-501013-2*) OUP.

Paint, Box Books. Dinosaurs & Their Babies. 1989. pap. 0.71 (*0-394-82279-X*) Random Bks Yng Read.

Painter, Carol. Friends Helping Friends: A Manual for Peer Counselors. Sorenson, Don L., ed. 224p. (Illus.). (gr. 9-12). 1989. pap. text ed. 9.95x (*0-932796-28-1*) Ed Media Corp.

—Leading a Friends Helping Friends Program. Sorenson, Don L., ed. 160p. (Orig.). (gr. 9-12). 1989. pap. text ed. 8.95x (*0-932796-29-X*) Ed Media Corp.

Painter, Desmond. Columbus. Yapp, Malcolm, et al, eds. (Illus.). 32p. (gr. 6-11). 1980. pap. text ed. 3.45 (*0-89908-017-0*) Greenhaven.

—Mao Tse-Tung. Yapp, Malcolm & Killingray, Margaret, eds. (Illus.). (gr. 6-11). 1980. pap. 3.45 (*0-89908-102-9*) Greenhaven.

Painter, Desmond & Shepard, John. Religion. Yapp, Malcolm & Killinger, Margaret, eds. (Illus.). 32p. (gr. 6-11). 1980. pap. text ed. 3.45 (*0-89908-120-7*) Greenhaven.

Painter, Jacqueline B. The German Invasion of Western North Carolina: A Pictorial History. Bell, John L., frwd. by. LC 92-93524. (Illus.). 128p. (gr. 8 up). 1992. 28.00 (*0-9634256-0-9*) J B Painter.

Pajot-Smith, Jean. Li'l Tuffy & His ABC's. Smith, Jean P., illus. 64p. (ps-4). pap. 5.00 (*0-87485-063-0*) Johnson Chi.

Paker, Josephine. Beating the Drum. LC 92-5164. (Illus.). 48p. (gr. 2-6). 1992. PLB 13.90 (*1-56294-093-7*) Millbrook Pr.

—Music from Strings. LC 92-5162. (Illus.). 48p. (gr. 2-6). 1992. PLB 13.90 (*1-56294-283-2*) Millbrook Pr.

Palacios, Argentina. A Christmas Surprise for Chabelita. Lohstoeter, Lori, photos by. LC 93-22336. (Illus.). 32p. (gr. 5-9). 1993. PLB 14.95 (*0-8167-3131-4*); pap. write for info. (*0-8167-3132-2*) Brdgewater.

—The Hummingbird King: A Guatemalan Legend. Davalos, Felipe, illus. LC 92-21437. 32p. (gr. 2-5). 1993. lib. bdg. 11.89 (*0-8167-3051-2*); pap. text ed. 3.95 (*0-8167-3052-0*) Troll Assocs.

—Llama's Secret: A Peruvian Legend. Reasoner, Charles, illus. LC 92-21436. 32p. (gr. 2-5). 1993. lib. bdg. 11.89 (*0-8167-3049-0*); pap. text ed. 3.95 (*0-8167-3050-4*) Troll Assocs.

—Peanut Butter, Apple Butter, Cinnamon Toast: Food Riddles for You to Guess. Mahan, Ben, illus. 24p. (ps-2). 1990. PLB 14.60 (*0-8172-3584-1*); PLB 10.95 pkg. of 3 (*0-685-58553-0*) Raintree Steck-V.

—El Rey Colibri - the Hummingbird King: Una Leyenda Guatemalteca. (gr. 4-7). 1993. PLB 11.89 (*0-8167-3122-5*); pap. 3.95 (*0-8167-3071-7*) Troll Assocs.

—El Secreto de la Llama - the Llama's Secret: Una Leyenda Peruana. (gr. 4-7). 1993. PLB 11.89 (*0-8167-3123-3*); pap. 3.95 (*0-8167-3072-5*) Troll Assocs.

—Viva Mexico! The Story of Benito Juarez & Cinco de Mayo. Berelson, Howard, illus. LC 92-18071. 32p. (gr. 2-5). 1992. PLB 21.34 (*0-8114-7214-0*) Raintree Steck-V.

Palacios, Argentina, tr. see Aruego, Jose & Aruego, Ariane.

Palacios, Argentina, tr. see Bargar, Sherie & Johnson, Linda.

Palacios, Argentina, tr. see Bridwell, Norman.

Palacios, Argentina, tr. see Lindsay, Jeanne W.

Palacios, Argentina, tr. see Rowe, Erna.

Paladino, Catherine. Land, Sea, & Sky: Poems to Celebrate the Earth. (ps-3). 1993. 15.95 (*0-316-68892-4*, AMP) Little.

—Our Vanishing Farm Animals: Saving America's Rare Breeds. (ps-3). 1991. 15.95 (*0-316-68891-6*) Little.

—Pomona: The Birth of a Penguin. (Illus.). (gr. 2-4). 1991. 12.95 (*0-531-15212-X*); PLB 12.90 (*0-531-10988-7*) Watts.

—Spring Fleece: A Day of Sheepshearing. (ps-3). 1990. 14.95 (*0-316-68890-8*, Joy St Bks) Little.

Palangi, Paula. Last Straw. (ps-3). 1992. pap. 9.95 (*0-7814-0562-9*) Cook.

Palazzo, Janet. Our Friend the Sun. Hall, Susan, illus. LC 81-11460. 32p. (gr. k-2). 1982. PLB 11.59 (*0-89375-650-4*); pap. 2.95 (*0-89375-651-2*) Troll Assocs.

—Rainy Day Fun. Ulrich, George, illus. LC 87-10842. 32p. (gr. k-2). 1988. PLB 11.59 (*0-8167-1095-3*); pap. text ed. 2.95 (*0-8167-1096-1*) Troll Assocs.

—What Makes the Weather. Harvey, Paul, illus. LC 81-11383. 32p. (gr. k-2). 1982. PLB 11.59 (*0-89375-654-7*); pap. 2.95 (*0-89375-655-5*) Troll Assocs.

Palazzo, Tony. The Biggest & the Littlest Animals. Palazzo, Tony, illus. LC 77-112374. 40p. (gr. k-3). 1973. PLB 13.95 (*0-87460-225-4*) Lion Bks.

—Magic Crayon. Palazzo, Tony, illus. (gr. k-2). 1967. PLB 10.95 (*0-87460-089-8*) Lion Bks.

Palazzo-Craig, Janet. Case of the Missing Cat. Shire, Ellen, illus. LC 81-7635. 48p. (gr. 2-4). 1982. PLB 10.89 (*0-89375-594-X*); pap. text ed. 3.50 (*0-89375-595-8*) Troll Assocs.

—Mystery of the Missing Wigs. Harvey, Paul, illus. LC 81-7615. 48p. (gr. 2-4). 1982. PLB 10.89 (*0-89375-592-3*); pap. text ed. 3.50 (*0-89375-593-1*) Troll Assocs.

—The Upside-Down Boy. Burns, Ray, illus. LC 85-14067. 48p. (Orig.). (gr. 1-3). 1986. PLB 10.59 (*0-8167-0604-2*); pap. text ed. 3.50 (*0-8167-0605-0*) Troll Assocs.

—Who's Who at the Zoo! Burns, Ray, illus. LC 85-14123. 48p. (Orig.). (gr. 1-3). 1986. PLB 10.59 (*0-8167-0658-1*); pap. text ed. 3.50 (*0-8167-0659-X*) Troll Assocs.

Palder, Edward. Chemistry Magic. Mohrmann, gary, illus. 153p. (gr. 5 up). 1987. pap. 12.95 (*0-933149-25-5*) Woodbine House.

Paley, Alan L. Andrew Johnson: The President Impeached. Rahmas, D. Steve, ed. LC 74-190248. 32p. (gr. 7-12). 1972. lib. bdg. 4.95 incl. catalog cards (*0-87157-531-0*) SamHar Pr.

—Benito Mussolini: Fascist Dictator of Italy. Rahmas, D. Steve, ed. 32p. (Orig.). (gr. 7-12). 1975. lib. bdg. 4.95 incl. catalog cards (*0-87157-581-7*) SamHar Pr.

—Edgar Allan Poe: American Poet & Mystery Writer. Rahmas, D. Steve, ed. 32p. (gr. 7-12). 1975. lib. bdg. 4.95 incl. catalog cards (*0-87157-584-1*) SamHar Pr.

—H. G. Wells: Author of Famous Science Fiction Stories. Rahmas, D. Steve, ed. 32p. (Orig.). (gr. 7-12). 1972. lib. bdg. 4.95 incl. catalog cards (*0-87157-554-X*) SamHar Pr.

—Sinclair Lewis: Twentieth Century American Author & Nobel Prize Winner. Rahmas, D. Steve, ed. LC 73-87626. 32p. (Orig.). (gr. 7-12). 1974. lib. bdg. 4.95 incl. catalog cards (*0-87157-567-1*) SamHar Pr.

Palgrave, Francis T. & Press, John, eds. Golden Treasury of the Best Songs & Lyrical Poems in the English Language: From Shakespeare to Larkin. 5th ed. (gr. 5-9). 1987. 35.00 (*0-19-254156-0*); pap. 10.95 (*0-19-282035-4*) OUP.

Pallandt, Nicolas Van see Van Pallandt, Nicolas.

Pallotta, Jerry. The Bird Alphabet Book. Stewart, Edgar, illus. 32p. (ps-3). 1989. 14.95 (*0-88106-457-2*); pap. 6.95 (*0-88106-451-3*) Charlesbridge Pub.

—Cuenta los Insectos (The Icky Bug Counting Book) (Illus.). 32p. (ps-3). 1993. pap. 6.95 (*0-88106-419-X*) Charlesbridge Pub.

—The Dinosaur Alphabet Book. (Illus.). 32p. (Orig.). (ps-4). 1990. 14.95 (*0-88106-467-X*); pap. 6.95 (*0-88106-466-1*) Charlesbridge Pub.

—The Extinct Alphabet Book. Masiello, Ralph, illus. LC 93-1512. 1993. 14.95 (*0-88106-471-8*); PLB 15.00 (*0-88106-486-6*); pap. 6.95 (*0-88106-470-X*) Charlesbridge Pub.

—The Flower Alphabet Book. Evans, Leslie, illus. 32p. (ps-3). 1989. 14.95 (*0-88106-459-9*); pap. 6.95 (*0-88106-453-X*) Charlesbridge Pub.

—The Frog Alphabet Book. Masiello, Ralph, illus. 32p. (Orig.). (ps-4). 1990. 14.95 (*0-88106-463-7*); pap. 6.95 (*0-88106-462-9*) Charlesbridge Pub.

—The Furry Alphabet Book. Stuart, Edgar, illus. 32p. (Orig.). (ps-4). 1990. 14.95 (*0-88106-465-3*); pap. 6.95 (*0-88106-464-5*) Charlesbridge Pub.

—Going Lobstering. Bolster, Rob, illus. 32p. (Orig.). (ps-4). 1990. 15.95 (*0-88106-475-0*); pap. 7.95 (*0-88106-474-2*) Charlesbridge Pub.

—The Icky Bug Counting Book. (Illus.). 32p. (ps-8). 1991. 14.95 (*0-88106-497-1*); pap. 6.95 (*0-88106-496-3*) Charlesbridge Pub.

—The Ocean Alphabet Book. Mazzola, Frank, Jr., illus. 32p. (ps-3). 1989. 14.95 (*0-88106-458-0*); pap. 6.95 (*0-88106-452-1*) Charlesbridge Pub.

—The Underwater Alphabet Book. (Illus.). 32p. (ps-8). 1991. 14.95 (*0-88106-461-0*); pap. 6.95 (*0-88106-455-6*) Charlesbridge Pub.

—The Victory Garden Alphabet Book. (Illus.). 32p. (gr. 3-8). 1992. 14.95 (*0-88106-469-6*); pap. 6.95 (*0-88106-468-8*) Charlesbridge Pub.

—Yucky Reptile Alphabet Book. (ps-3). 1990. 14.95 (*0-88106-460-2*); pap. 6.95 (*0-88106-454-8*) Charlesbridge Pub.

Palmer, Bernard. Danny Orlis, No. 1: The Final Touchdown. 128p. 1989. pap. 4.99 (*0-8423-0562-9*) Tyndale.

—Danny Orlis, No. 2: The Last Minute Miracle. 128p. 1989. pap. 4.99 (*0-8423-0558-0*) Tyndale.

—Danny Orlis, No. 3: The Race Against Time. 128p. 1989. pap. 4.99 (*0-8423-0560-2*) Tyndale.

—Danny Orlis, No. 4: The Showdown. 128p. 1989. pap. 4.99 (*0-8423-0557-2*) Tyndale.

—Danny Orlis, No. 5: The Case of the Talking Rocks. 128p. 1989. pap. 4.99 (*0-8423-0559-9*) Tyndale.

—Danny Orlis, No. 6: The Sacred Ruins. 128p. 1989. pap. 4.99 (*0-8423-0561-0*) Tyndale.

Palmer, Bernard & Palmer, Marjorie. Who Helps. Webb, Gary A., illus. 32p. (Orig.). (ps-k). 1982. pap. 3.99 (*0-934998-08-6*) Bethel Pub.

—Who Shows. Webb, Gary A., illus. 32p. (Orig.). (ps-k). 1982. pap. 3.99 (*0-934998-09-4*) Bethel Pub.

Palmer, Bob, jt. auth. see Stone, Bob.

Palmer, Carole, jt. auth. see Arvetis, Chris.

Palmer, E. Lawrence. Fieldbook of Natural History. 2nd ed. Fowler, H. Seymour, rev. by. (Illus.). 1975. 42.95 (*0-07-048196-2*); text ed. 40.00 (*0-07-048425-2*) McGraw.

Palmer, Glenda. Blue Galoshes in Spring: God's Wonderful World of Seasons. LC 92-34716. (Illus.). 1993. write for info. (*0-7814-0710-9*, Chariot Bks) Cook.

—P Is for Pink Polliwogs: God's Wonderful World of Letters. LC 92-34715. (Illus.). 1993. write for info. (*0-7814-0708-7*, Chariot Bks) Cook.

—Sidewalk Squares & Triangle Birds: God's Wonderful World of Shapes. LC 92-34717. (Illus.). 1993. write for info. (*0-7814-0711-7*, Chariot Bks) Cook.

—Two Enormous Elephants: God's Wonderful World of Numbers. LC 92-34714. (Illus.). 1993. write for info. (*0-7814-0709-5*, Chariot Bks) Cook.

Palmer, Greg. The Falcon. (Orig.). 1993. pap. 4.50 playscript (*0-87602-319-7*) Anchorage.

Palmer, Hap. Hap Palmer: Songs to Enhance the Movement Vocabulary of Young Children. Schiff, Ronny, ed. 1987. pap. text ed. 18.95 (*0-88284-357-5*, 2072) Alfred Pub.

Palmer, Helen. A Fish Out of Water. LC 61-9579. (Illus.). 72p. (ps-3). 1961. 6.95 (*0-394-80023-0*); lib. bdg. 7.99 (*0-394-90023-5*) Beginner.

—A Fish Out of Water in English & Spanish. Rivera, Carlos, tr. (Illus.). (gr. k-3). 1967. lib. bdg. 5.99 (*0-394-91598-4*) Random Bks Yng Read.

Palmer, J. D. Biological Rhythms & Living Clocks. 2nd ed. Head, J. J., ed. LC 84-70786. (Illus.). 16p. (gr. 10 up). 1984. pap. 2.75 (*0-89278-192-0*, 45-9692) Carolina Biological.

—Human Biological Rhythms. Head, J. J., ed. Khoury, Diana, illus. LC 81-67983. 16p. (gr. 10 up). 1983. pap. 2.75 (*0-89278-304-4*, 45-9704) Carolina Biological.

Palmer, John M. Equipping for Ministry. LC 85-80220. 96p. (Orig.). (gr. k up). 1985. pap. 2.50 tchr's. bk. (*0-88243-802-6*, 02-0802) Gospel Pub.

Palmer, Joy. Deserts. LC 92-12406. (Illus.). 32p. (gr. 2-3). 1992. PLB 18.99 (*0-8114-3402-8*) Raintree Steck-V.

—Oceans. LC 92-12409. (Illus.). 32p. (gr. 2-3). 1992. PLB 18.99 (*0-8114-3401-X*) Raintree Steck-V.

—Polar Lands. LC 92-12405. (Illus.). 32p. (gr. 2-3). 1992. PLB 18.99 (*0-8114-3403-6*) Raintree Steck-V.

—Rain. LC 92-38554. (Illus.). 32p. (gr. 2-3). 1992. PLB 18.99 (*0-8114-3413-3*) Raintree Steck-V.

—Rain Forests. LC 92-10634. (Illus.). 32p. (gr. 2-3). 1992. PLB 18.99 (*0-8114-3400-1*) Raintree Steck-V.

—Rain Forests. (ps-3). 1993. pap. 3.95 (*0-8114-4911-4*) Raintree Steck-V.

—Recycling Metal. LC 90-32530. (Illus.). 32p. (gr. 9-12). 1991. PLB 12.40 (*0-531-14118-7*) Watts.

—Recycling Plastic. LC 90-32527. (Illus.). 32p. (gr. 9-12). 1991. PLB 12.40 (*0-531-14119-5*) Watts.

—Snow & Ice. LC 92-38438. (Illus.). 32p. (gr. 2-3). 1992. PLB 18.99 (*0-8114-3414-1*) Raintree Steck-V.

—Sunshine. LC 92-38437. (Illus.). 32p. (gr. 2-3). 1992. PLB 18.99 (*0-8114-3416-8*) Raintree Steck-V.

—Wind. LC 92-38439. (Illus.). 32p. (gr. 2-3). 1992. PLB 18.99 (*0-8114-3415-X*) Raintree Steck-V.

Palmer, Leslie. Lena Horne. King, Coretta Scott. (Illus.). 112p. (gr. 5 up). 1989. lib. bdg. 17.95x (*1-55546-594-3*) Chelsea Hse.

Palmer, Marilyn, jt. auth. see Evans, A. J.

Palmer, Marion, ed. see Harris, Joel C.

Palmer, Marjorie, jt. auth. see Palmer, Bernard.

Palmer, Martha. Advanced Multiplication & Division. Hoffman, Joan, ed. Cook, Chris, illus. 32p. (gr. 5-6). 1980. wkbk. 1.99 (*0-938256-36-X*) Sch Zone Pub Co.

—Beginning Addition & Subtraction. Hoffman, Joan, ed. Cook, Chris, illus. 32p. (gr. 1). 1980. wkbk. 1.99 (*0-938256-29-7*) Sch Zone Pub Co.

—Beginning Multiplication & Division. Hoffman, Joan, ed. Cook, Chris, illus. 32p. (gr. 3-4). 1980. wkbk. 1.99 (*0-938256-34-3*) Sch Zone Pub Co.

—Fractions. Hoffman, Joan, ed. Cook, Chris, illus. 32p. (gr. 5-6). 1981. wkbk. 1.99 (*0-938256-43-2*) Sch Zone Pub Co.

—Transition Math. Hoffman, Joan, ed. Cook, Chris, illus. 32p. (gr. k-1). 1979. wkbk. 1.99 (*0-938256-27-0*) Sch Zone Pub Co.

Palmer, Mary R. Clean As a Whistle. LC 90-70148. 48p. (gr. 1-4). 1990. pap. 5.95 (*0-932433-66-9*) Windswept Hse.

—Sharing Secrets. LC 91-65294. (Illus.). 60p. (ps-4). 1991. pap. 8.95 (*0-932433-82-0*) Windswept Hse.

Palmer, Michael. Elizabeth I. (Illus.). 64p. (gr. 6-9). 1989. 19.95 (*0-7134-5660-4*, Pub. by Batsford UK) Trafalgar.

Palmer, Michele. Zoup Soup. Gugler, Janine, illus. LC 78-66342. (ps-1). 1978. pap. 1.95 (*0-932306-00-4*) Rocking Horse.

Palmer, Michele, ed. A Mother Goose Feast: Rhymes & Recipes. LC 79-65819. (Illus.). (ps-12). 1979. pap. 1.95 (*0-932306-01-2*) Rocking Horse.

—Rainy Day Rhymes: A Collection of Chants, Forecasts & Tales. Guerin, Penny, illus. LC 84-60412. 24p. (Orig.). (gr. k up). 1984. pap. 2.95 (*0-932306-02-0*) Rocking Horse.

Palmer, Patricia. Liking Myself. Shank, Will, illus. LC 77-88185. 80p. (gr. k-4). 1977. pap. 4.95 (*0-915166-41-0*) Impact Pubs Cal.
—The Mouse, the Monster & Me. Shank, Will, illus. LC 77-88186. 80p. (Orig.). (gr. 3-6). 1977. pap. 4.95 (*0-915166-43-7*) Impact Pubs Cal.
Palmer, Pete & Thom, John, eds. The Baseball Record Book. (Illus.). 96p. (gr. 3 up). 1991. pap. 5.95 (*0-671-70444-3*, Little Simon) S&S Trade.
Palmer, S. Blue Whales. (Illus.). 24p. (gr. k-5). 1988. PLB 11.94 (*0-86592-480-5*) Rourke Corp.
—Delfines (Dolphins) 1991. 8.95s.p. (*0-86592-849-5*) Rourke Enter.
—Dolphins. (Illus.). (gr. k-5). 1989. lib. bdg. 11.94 (*0-86592-363-9*); 8.95s.p. (*0-685-58619-7*) Rourke Corp.
—Fin Whales. (Illus.). 24p. (gr. k-5). 1988. PLB 11.94 (*0-86592-479-1*); 8.95s.p. (*0-685-58331-7*) Rourke Corp.
—Gray Whales. (Illus.). 24p. (gr. k-5). 1988. PLB 11.94 (*0-86592-477-5*); 8.95s.p. (*0-685-58327-9*) Rourke Corp.
—Great White Sharks. (Illus.). 24p. (gr. k-5). 1988. PLB 11.94 (*0-86592-462-7*); 8.95s.p. (*0-685-58314-7*) Rourke Corp.
—Hammerhead Sharks. (Illus.). 24p. (gr. k-5). 1988. PLB 11.94 (*0-86592-461-9*); 8.95s.p. (*0-685-67680-3*) Rourke Corp.
—Humpback Whales. (Illus.). 24p. (gr. k-5). 1988. PLB 11.94 (*0-86592-478-3*); 8.95s.p. (*0-685-58329-5*) Rourke Corp.
—Killer Whales. (Illus.). 24p. (gr. k-5). 1988. PLB 11.94 (*0-86592-481-3*); 8.95s.p. (*0-685-58330-9*) Rourke Corp.
—Leones Marinos (Sea Lions) 1991. 8.95s.p. (*0-86592-674-3*) Rourke Enter.
—Mako Sharks. (Illus.). 24p. (gr. k-5). 1989. PLB 11.94 (*0-86592-458-9*); 8.95s.p. (*0-685-58310-4*) Rourke Corp.
—Manatees. (Illus.). 24p. (gr. k-5). 1989. lib. bdg. 11.94 (*0-86592-359-0*); 8.95s.p. (*0-685-58620-0*) Rourke Corp.
—Manaties (Manatees) 1991. 8.95s.p. (*0-86592-672-7*) Rourke Enter.
—Morsas (Walruses) 1991. 8.95s.p. (*0-86592-689-1*) Rourke Enter.
—Narwhals. (Illus.). 24p. (gr. k-5). 1988. PLB 11.94 (*0-86592-476-7*); 8.95s.p. (*0-685-58328-7*) Rourke Corp.
—Nurse Sharks. (Illus.). 24p. (gr. k-5). 1988. PLB 11.94 (*0-86592-459-7*); 8.95s.p. (*0-685-58311-2*) Rourke Corp.
—Nutrias de Mar (Sea Otters) 1991. 8.95s.p. (*0-86592-681-6*) Rourke Enter.
—Osos Polares (Polar Bears) 1991. 8.95s.p. (*0-86592-673-5*) Rourke Enter.
—Polar Bears. (Illus.). 24p. (gr. k-5). 1989. lib. bdg. 11.94 (*0-86592-360-4*) Rourke Corp.
—Sea Lions. (Illus.). 24p. (gr. k-5). 1989. lib. bdg. 11.94 (*0-86592-362-0*); lib. bdg. 8.95s.p. (*0-685-58622-7*) Rourke Corp.
—Sea Otters. (Illus.). 24p. (gr. k-5). 1989. lib. bdg. 11.94 (*0-86592-361-2*) Rourke Corp.
—Spanish Language Books, Set 4: Mamifero Marino (Sea Mammals, 6 bks. 1991. 53.70s.p. (*0-86592-835-5*) Rourke Enter.
—Thresher Sharks. (Illus.). 24p. (gr. k-5). 1988. PLB 11.94 (*0-86592-460-0*); PLB 8.95s.p. (*0-685-58313-9*) Rourke Corp.
—Walruses. (Illus.). 24p. (gr. k-5). 1989. lib. bdg. 11.94 (*0-86592-358-2*); lib. bdg. 8.95s.p. (*0-685-58621-9*) Rourke Corp.
—Whale Sharks. (Illus.). 24p. (gr. k-5). 1988. PLB 11.94 (*0-86592-463-5*); PLB 8.95s.p. (*0-685-58309-0*) Rourke Corp.
Palmer, Sarah. Sea Mammal Discovery Library, 6 bks, Reading Level 2. (Illus.). 144p. (gr. k-5). 1989. Set. PLB 71.60 (*0-86592-357-4*); PLB 53.70s.p. (*0-685-58759-2*) Rourke Corp.
—World of Sharks, 6 vols. 1990. 7.99 (*0-517-02747-X*) Outlet Bk Co.
—World of Whales, 6 vols. 1990. 7.99 (*0-517-02746-1*) Outlet Bk Co.
Palmer, Thelma, jt. auth. see Moss, Peter.
Palmer, William M. Poisonous Snakes of North Carolina. (Illus.). 22p. (gr. 6-12). 1974. pap. 2.00 (*0-917134-00-1*) NC Natl Sci.
Palotta, Jerry. The Icky Bug Alphabet Book. Masiello, Ralph, illus. 32p. (ps-3). 1989. 14.95 (*0-88106-456-4*); pap. 6.95 (*0-88106-450-5*) Charlesbridge Pub.
Paltro, Piera. Angel of God. Daughters of St. Paul Staff, tr. from ITA. Curti, Anna M., illus. 14p. (Orig.). (ps-1). 1981. pap. 2.50 (*0-8198-0739-7*, CH0031P) St Paul Bks.
—Eternal Rest: A Prayer for People Who Have Died. Daughters of St. Paul Staff, tr. from ITA. Curti, Anna M., illus. 15p. (Orig.). (gr. k-3). 1992. pap. 2.50 (*0-8198-2332-5*) St Paul Bks.
—Glory to the Father. Daughters of St. Paul Staff, tr. from ITA. Curti, Anna M., illus. 24p. (Orig.). (ps up). 1987. pap. 2.50 (*0-8198-3043-7*, CH0227) St Paul Bks.
—Hail, Holy Queen. Daughters of St. Paul Staff, tr. from ITA. Curti, Anna M., illus. 16p. (Orig.). (gr. k-3). 1992. pap. 2.50 (*0-8198-3365-7*) St Paul Bks.
—Hail Mary. Daughters of St. Paul Staff, tr. from ITA. Curti, Anna M., illus. 24p. (gr. k-3). 1992. pap. 2.50 (*0-8198-3316-9*) St Paul Bks.

—I Believe: The Profession of Faith or Creed. Daughters of St. Paul Staff, tr. from ITA. Curti, Anna M., illus. 29p. (Orig.). (gr. k-3). 1992. pap. 2.50 (*0-8198-3664-8*) St Paul Bks.
—My Mass. Daughters of St. Paul Staff, tr. from ITA. Curti, Anna M., illus. 31p. (Orig.). (gr. k-3). 1992. pap. 2.50 (*0-8198-4765-8*) St Paul Bks.
—Our Father. Daughters of St. Paul Staff, tr. from ITA. Curti, Anna M., illus. 24p. (Orig.). (ps-1). 1991. pap. 2.50 (*0-8198-5416-6*, CH0416P) St Paul Bks.
Paltrowitz, Donna & Paltrowitz, Stuart. Robotics. LC 83-13108. 64p. (gr. 7-11). 1983. (J Messner); PLB 9.29 (*0-671-44077-2*) S&S Trade.
Paltrowitz, Donna, jt. auth. see Paltrowitz, Stuart.
Paltrowitz, Stuart & Paltrowitz, Donna. Content Area Reading Skills-Competency Canada: Main Idea. (Illus.). (gr. 4). 1987. pap. text ed. 3.25 (*0-89525-853-6*) Ed Activities.
—Content Area Reading Skills-Competency Mexico: Locating Details. (Illus.). (gr. 4). 1987. pap. text ed. 3.25 (*0-89525-854-4*) Ed Activities.
—Content Area Reading Skills-Competency U. S. History: Detecting Sequence. (Illus.). (gr. 4). 1987. pap. text ed. 3.25 (*0-89525-856-0*) Ed Activities.
—Content Area Reading Skills U. S. Geography: Cause & Effect. (Illus.). (gr. 4). 1987. pap. text ed. 3.25 (*0-89525-855-2*) Ed Activities.
Paltrowitz, Stuart, jt. auth. see Paltrowitz, Donna.
Palumbo, Nancy. A Birthday Present for Ree-Ree: Un Cadeau d'Anniversaire Pour Ree-Ree. Weaver, Judith, illus. 32p. (Orig.). (ps-6). 1989. wkbk. 5.95 (*0-927024-15-2*) Crayons Pubns.
—A Birthday Present for Ree-Ree: Un Regalo Cumpleanos Para Ree-Ree. Weaver, Judith, illus. 32p. (Orig.). (gr. k-6). 1989. wkbk. 5.95 (*0-927024-14-4*) Crayons Pubns.
—Early Learning Shape Book: El Libro de Figuras Geometricas. Weaver, Judith, illus. 32p. (gr. k-6). 1989. wkbk. 5.95 (*0-927024-06-3*) Crayons Pubns.
—Early Learning Shape Book: Le Livre Des Formes. Weaver, Judith, illus. 32p. (gr. k-6). 1989. wkbk. 5.95 (*0-927024-07-1*) Crayons Pubns.
—J.J. Goes to School: J.J. Va a L E'cole. Weaver, Judith, illus. 32p. (gr. k-6). 1989. wkbk. 5.95 (*0-927024-13-6*) Crayons Pubns.
—J.J. Goes to School: J.J. Va a la Escuela. Weaver, Judith, illus. 32p. (gr. k-6). 1989. wkbk. 5.95 (*0-927024-12-8*) Crayons Pubns.
—Lets Color & Count: Colorions et Comptons. Weaver, Judith, illus. 32p. (gr. k-6). 1989. wkbk. 5.95 (*0-927024-09-8*) Crayons Pubns.
—Meet Penelope P'Nutt: Conoza Penelope P'Nutt. Weaver, Judith, illus. 32p. (gr. k-6). 1989. wkbk. 5.95 (*0-927024-04-7*) Crayons Pubns.
—Meet Penelope P'Nutt: Viens Recontrer Penelope P'Nutt. Weaver, Judith, illus. 32p. (gr. k-6). 1989. wkbk. 5.95 (*0-927024-05-5*) Crayons Pubns.
—Penelope P'Nutt & the Spirit of Christmas: Penelope P'Nutt et L'Ambiance De Noel. Weaver, Judith, illus. 16p. (gr. k-6). 1989. wkbk. 5.95 (*0-927024-03-9*) Crayons Pubns.
—Penelope P'Nutt & the Spirit of Christmas: Penelope P'Nutt y el Espiritu de la Navidad. Weaver, Judith, illus. 16p. (gr. k-6). 1989. wkbk. 5.95 (*0-927024-02-0*) Crayons Pubns.
—Penelope P'Nutt at Play: Los Juegos de Penelope P'Nutt. Weaver, Judith, illus. 32p. (gr. k-6). 1989. wkbk. 5.95 (*0-927024-16-0*) Crayons Pubns.
—Penelope P'Nutt at Play: Penelope P'Nutt au Jeu. Weaver, Judith, illus. 32p. (Orig.). (gr. k-6). 1989. wkbk. 5.95 (*0-927024-17-9*) Crayons Pubns.
—Rainy Days Are for Baking: Les Recettes Preferee de Penelope P'Nutt. Weaver, Judith, illus. 32p. (gr. k-6). 1989. wkbk. 5.95 (*0-927024-01-2*) Crayons Pubns.
Palumbo, Thomas. Language Arts Thinking Motivators. 96p. (gr. 2-7). 1988. wkbk. 9.95 (*0-86653-432-6*, GA1050) Good Apple.
Palumbo, Thomas J. Thursday Think Time. Hyndman, Kathryn, illus. 64p. (gr. 3-8). 1985. wkbk. 7.95 (*0-86653-311-7*, GA 650) Good Apple.
—Tuesday Timely Teasers. Hyndman, Kathryn, illus. 64p. (gr. 3-8). 1985. wkbk. 7.95 (*0-86653-309-5*, GA 648) Good Apple.
—Wednesday Midweek Winners. Hyndman, Kathryn, illus. 64p. (gr. 3-8). 1985. wkbk. 7.95 (*0-86653-310-9*, GA 649) Good Apple.
Palumbo, Tom. Measurement Motivators. 96p. (gr. 3-7). 1989. 9.95 (*0-86653-500-4*, GA1095) Good Apple.
Pamer, Nan M. Modesty. Agnew, Tim, illus. LC 90-30491. 50p. (Orig.). 1990. pap. 2.99 (*0-932581-62-5*) Word Aflame.
Pamplin, Laurel J. Masquerade on the Western Trail. Roberts, M., ed. (Illus.). 112p. (gr. 4-8). 1991. 9.95 (*0-89015-755-3*) Eakin-Sunbelt.
Panday, Daulat. The Tales of India, Vol. 1. 114p. (gr. 3-8). 1985. pap. 5.95 (*0-89071-330-8*, Pub. by Sri Aurobindo Ashram IA) Aurobindo Assn.
—The Tales of India, Vol. 2. 126p. (gr. 3-8). 1985. pap. 5.95 (*0-89071-331-6*, Pub. by Sri Aurobindo Ashram IA) Aurobindo Assn.
Pandell, Karen. By Day & by Night. Kramer, Linda, ed. Noble, Marty, illus. LC 90-52635. 32p. (ps-2). 1991. 14.95 (*0-915811-26-X*) H J Kramer Inc.
—Land of Dark, Land of Light: The Arctic National Wildlife Refuge. Bruemmer, Fred, photos by. LC 92-40405. (Illus.). 32p. (ps-3). 1993. 14.99 (*0-525-45094-7*, DCB) Dutton Child Bks.
Pangaea Pr. Staff, ed. see Wing, Ralph.

Pangaea Press Staff, ed. see Wing, Ralph.
Pangallo, Michelle. North American Forts & Fortifications. (Illus.). 48p. (gr. 4 up). 1986. 11.95 (*0-521-26642-4*); pap. 6.50 (*0-521-31982-X*) Cambridge U Pr.
Pangburn, Thelma I. Raoul Wallenberg: Hero of the Holocaust. Buchanan, John G., ed. (gr. 7-12). 1987. lib. bdg. 4.95 incl. catalog cards (*0-87157-597-3*) SamHar Pr.
Pang Guek Cheng. Canada. LC 93-11018. (gr. 5 up). 1993. 21.95 (*1-85435-579-1*) Marshall Cavendish.
Pangle, Mary Ann, jt. auth. see Forte, Imogene.
Pank, Rachel. Sonia & Barnie & the Noise in the Night. 1991. pap. 13.95 (*0-590-44657-6*) Scholastic Inc.
—Under the Blackberries. 1992. 13.95 (*0-590-45481-1*, Scholastic Hardcover) Scholastic Inc.
Pankow, Eleanor. Let's Talk about Jesus. (Illus.). (gr. k-6). 1963. 3.99 (*3-90117-015-4*) CEF Press.
Pannell, Gerard. MMXXVI - The Vision. Adams, Brian, illus. LC 93-84363. 12p. (Orig.). 1993. pap. 9.50 (*1-883588-00-6*) PAAS Pr.
Panova, V. On Faraway Street. Gabel, Rya, tr. White, Anne Terry, adapted by. LC 68-12891. (Illus.). 129p. (gr. 3-7). 1968. 3.95 (*0-8076-0445-3*) Braziller.
Pansini, Anna, ed. Best Jokes & Riddles. Loh, Carolyn, illus. LC 89-20324. 48p. (gr. 2-6). 1990. PLB 8.59 (*0-8167-1917-9*); pap. text ed. 2.50 (*0-8167-1918-7*) Troll Assocs.
—Great Answer Book. Kinnealy, Janice, illus. LC 90-44452. 48p. (gr. 3-6). 1991. PLB 10.89 (*0-8167-2308-7*); pap. text ed. 2.95 (*0-8167-2309-5*) Troll Assocs.
—Great Riddles, Giggles & Jokes. Loh, Carolyn, illus. LC 89-5200. 48p. (gr. 2-6). 1990. PLB 8.59 (*0-8167-1915-2*); pap. text ed. 2.50 (*0-8167-1916-0*) Troll Assocs.
—I Wonder Why. Barto, Renzo, illus. LC 90-44455. 48p. (gr. k-2). 1991. PLB 10.89 (*0-8167-2304-4*); pap. text ed. 2.95 (*0-8167-2305-2*) Troll Assocs.
—Kids' Question & Answer Book. Barto, Renzo, illus. LC 90-43969. 48p. (gr. 2-4). 1991. PLB 10.89 (*0-8167-2306-0*); pap. text ed. 2.95 (*0-8167-2307-9*) Troll Assocs.
Pantell, Dora, jt. auth. see MacGregor, Ellen.
Pantiel, Mindy & Petersen, Becky. Kids, Teachers, & Computers: A Guide to Computers in the Elementary School. (Illus.). 176p. 1984. pap. text ed. 25.00 (*0-13-515420-0*); pap. text ed. 16.95 (*0-13-515396-4*) P-H.
Panunzi, Paul. Love As Strong As Death. LC 66-30822. (gr. 3-7). 1966. 3.00 (*0-8198-0239-5*) St Paul Bks.
Panzer, Nora, ed. Celebrate America: In Poetry & Art. LC 93-32336. 1994. 18.95 (*1-56282-664-6*); PLB 18.89 (*1-56282-665-4*) Hyprn Child.
Paola, Tomie De see De Paola, Tomie.
Paola, Tomie de see De Paola, Tomie.
Paola, Tomie De see De Paola, Tomie.
Paola, Tomie de see De Paola, Tomie.
Paola, Tomie De see De Paola, Tomie.
Paola, Tomie de see De Paola, Tomie.
Paola, Tomie De see De Paola, Tomie.
Paola, Tomie de see De Paola, Tomie.
Paola, Tomie De see De Paola, Tomie.
Paola, Tomie de see De Paola, Tomie.
Paola, Tomie De see De Paola, Tomie.
Paola, Tomie de see De Paola, Tomie.
Paola, Tomie De see De Paola, Tomie.
Paola, Tomie de see De Paola, Tomie.
Paola, Tomie De see De Paola, Tomie.
Paolo, Tomie De see De Paola, Tomie.
Paolucci, Bridget. Beverly Sills: Opera Singer. Horner, Matina S., intro. by. LC 89-17324. (Illus.). 112p. (gr. 5 up). 1990. 17.95 (*1-55546-677-X*) Chelsea Hse.
Papa, Ethyl R. A Very Special Family: A Story Book to Color & Teach Your Child to Read. (Illus.). 32p. (ps-2). 1983. saddle stitch, double stapled binding 9.95 (*0-915925-00-1*) Innovative Educ Pub.
Papa, Iantorno. Turning Points Four. 128p. (gr. 7-12). 1989. pap. text ed. 10.48 (*0-201-06324-7*) Addison-Wesley.

Papagapitos, Karen. Jose's Basket. 1993. 6.95 (*0-9637328-1-1*) Kapa Hse Pr. JOSE's BASKET is a touching portrayal of a family forced to be always on the move. Luis & Socorro Vasquez are migrant farm workers, who follow whatever crops need to be harvested. This continuous change of surrounding is very difficult on their four children. The parents try to make the transitions easier by anticipating all the new & exciting things that are sure to be waiting for them at the next stop. At one particular town, in Arizona, eight-year-old Jose (an excellent student & gifted writer) finds a school he never wants to leave. Of course, there does come a time when he must leave this new place & his wonderful teacher, Mrs. Ortega. By learning to

piece together his adventures in every new place, much like his mother weaves reeds & grasses from the desert into her special basket (the grasses come from each place in which they pick crops), Jose is able to find the courage he needs to move on & stay in school. *Publisher Provided Annotation.*

—Socorro, Daughter of the Desert. Kleinman, Estelle, ed. Collete, Rondi, illus. 64p. (gr. 1-4). 1993. 6.95 (0-9637328-0-3) Kapa Hse Pr. SOCORRO, DAUGHTER OF THE DESERT is the story of a young girl, who knows the answer to a mystery that nobody else seems to see. It is through the eyes of Socorro Hernandez that we find out who the mysterious phantom of the desert road is, & why he wants to warn people of any danger that might lie in their path. Socorro's family is going through a difficult period at the same time, & through this young girl's hard work & perseverance they manage to weather the father's bout with malaria. This book profiles the resourcefulness, courage & hope women historically have exhibited in trying times. Young readers should enjoy the several appearances of the mysterious phantom & still come away from the conclusion with a strong respect for women & their strength in an often unsettled world. *Publisher Provided Annotation.*

Papajani, Janet. Museums. LC 82-23621. (Illus.). 48p. (gr. k-4). 1983. PLB 15.27 (0-516-01682-2); pap. 4.95 (0-516-41682-0) Childrens.
Papantoniou, D. The Greek Children. (GRE., Illus.). (gr. 2-3). text ed. 4.00 (0-686-79628-4); wkbk. 2.50 (0-686-79629-2) Divry.
—Greek Letters. (GRE.). 158p. (gr. 4-5). 4.00 (0-686-79634-9) Divry.
—Greek Stories. (GRE.). (gr. 3-4). 4.00 (0-686-79633-0) Divry.
Paparone, Pam. Who Built the Ark? LC 93-31383. 1994. write for info. (0-671-87129-3, S&S BFYR) S&S Trade.
Papastavrou, Vassili. Seals & Sea Lions. LC 91-9127. (Illus.). (gr. 2-5). 1992. PLB 12.40 (0-531-18455-2, Pub. by Bookwright Pr) Watts.
—Turtles & Tortoises. LC 91-20098. (Illus.). 32p. (gr. 2-5). 1992. PLB 12.40 (0-531-18453-6, Pub. by Bookwright Pr) Watts.
—Whales & Dolphins. LC 90-14400. (Illus.). 32p. (gr. k-4). 1991. 12.40 (0-531-18394-7, Pub. by Bookwright Pr) Watts.
Papastavrov, Vassili. Whale. Greenaway, Frank, illus. 64p. (gr. 5 up). 1993. 15.00 (0-679-83884-8); PLB 15.99 (0-679-93884-2) Knopf Bks Yng Read.
Pape, et al. Oddo Sound Series: 1968, 1974, 1978, 10 vols. (Illus.). (gr. 2-5). 1978. Set. PLB 109.50 (0-87783-165-3) Oddo.
Pape, D. L. King Robert, the Resting Ruler. LC 68-56823. (Illus.). 48p. (gr. 2-5). 1968. PLB 10.95 (0-87783-021-5) Oddo.
—Liz Dearly's Silly Glasses. LC 68-56824. (Illus.). 48p. (gr. 2-5). 1968. PLB 10.95 (0-87783-023-1) Oddo.
—Professor Fred & the Fid Fuddlephone. LC 68-56825. (Illus.). 48p. (gr. 2-5). 1968. PLB 10.95 (0-87783-032-0) Oddo.
—Scientist Sam. LC 68-56826. (Illus.). 48p. (gr. 2-5). 1968. PLB 10.95 (0-87783-034-7) Oddo.
—Shoemaker Fooze. Frank, Lola E., illus. LC 68-56827. 48p. (gr. 2-5). 1969. PLB 10.95 (0-87783-036-3) Oddo.
—Three Thinkers of Thay-Lee. LC 68-56828. (Illus.). 48p. (gr. 2-5). 1968. PLB 10.95 (0-87783-040-1) Oddo.
Pape, David S., ed. see Rosenfeld, Dina.
Pape, Donna L. The Book of Foolish Machinery. Winkowski, Frederic, illus. 32p. (gr. 2-5). 1988. pap. 2.50 (0-590-40907-7) Scholastic Inc.
—The Children's Arkansas Puzzle Book. Mueller, Virginia & Karle, Carol, illus. 28p. (gr. k up). 1984. pap. 2.00 (0-914546-55-4) Rose Pub.
Papi, Liza. Carnavalia! African-Brazilian Folklore & Crafts. LC 93-38451. 1994. write for info. (0-8478-1779-2) Rizzoli Intl.
Pappas, Lou S. Holiday Feasts: Festive Cooking for Family & Friends. 1993. 99.50 (0-8118-9162-3) Chronicle Bks.

Pappas, Michael G. Sweet Dreams for Little Ones. Wenz-Victor, Ilse, illus. 64p. (Orig.). 1985. pap. 10.00 (0-86683-641-1, AY8156) Harper SF.
Paquet, jt. auth. see Carr.
Parachute Press Staff. Over in the Meadow. 1987. pap. 2.95 (0-553-15573-3) Bantam.
—The Story of Davey Crockett. (Illus.). 1993. pap. 3.50 (0-440-40881-4) Dell.
—The Twelve Days of Christmas. 24p. 1988. pap. 2.50 (0-553-15638-1, Bantam Aud Pub) Bantam.
Parapan, S. M. A Mexican Legend: Quetzalcoat! The Bird-Serpent. Castillo, L., illus. 24p. (Orig.). (gr. k-3). 1989. pap. text ed. write for info.; write for info. tchr's. activity guide Parapan.
Paraquin, Charles. Optical Illusion Puzzles. Kuttner, Paul, tr. LC 83-18198. (Illus.). 96p. (Orig.). (gr. 7 up). 1984. 12.95 (0-8069-6868-0) Sterling.
Paraquin, Charles H. Eye Teasers: Optical Illusion Puzzles. Kuttner, Paul, tr. LC 76-21844. (Illus.). (gr. 3 up). 1976. 7.95 (0-8069-4538-9); PLB 9.99 (0-8069-4539-7) Sterling.
—World's Best Optical Illusions. Kuttner, Paul, tr. LC 87-13885. (Illus.). 96p. (Orig.). (gr. 4-12). 1987. pap. 4.95 (0-8069-6644-0) Sterling.
Paraskevas, Betty. Junior Kroll. Paraskevas, Michael, illus. LC 92-14207. (gr. k up). 1993. 13.95 (0-15-241497-5) HarBrace.
—Junior Kroll & Company. Paraskevas, Michael, illus. LC 93-9138. (ps-6). 1994. write for info. (0-15-292855-3) HarBrace.
—On the Edge of the Sea. Paraskevas, Michael, illus. LC 91-31489. 32p. 1992. 14.00 (0-8037-1130-1); PLB 13.89 (0-8037-1263-4) Dial Bks Young.
—Shamlanders. Paraskevas, Michael, illus. LC 92-32980. 1993. 13.95 (0-15-292854-5) HarBrace.
—The Strawberry Dog. Paraskevas, Michael, illus. LC 92-18216. (ps-3). 1993. 13.99 (0-8037-1367-3); PLB 13.89 (0-8037-1368-1) Dial Bks Young.
Pardee, Arthur B. & Veer Reddy, G. P. Cancer: Fundamental Ideas. 2nd ed. Head, J. J., ed. LC 86-72193. (Illus.). 32p. (gr. 10 up). 1986. pap. 3.00 (0-89278-128-9, 45-9728) Carolina Biological.
Pare, R. Circus Days. (Illus.). 24p. (ps-8). 1988. PLB 14.95 (1-55037-021-9, Pub. by Annick CN); pap. 4.95 (1-55037-020-0, Pub. by Annick CN) Firefly Bks Ltd.
—A Friend Like You. (Illus.). 24p. (ps-8). 1984. 12.95 (0-920303-04-8, Pub. by Annick CN); pap. 4.95 (0-920303-05-6, Pub. by Annick CN) Firefly Bks Ltd.
—Play Time. (Illus.). 24p. (ps-8). 1988. 12.95 (1-55037-087-1, Pub. by Annick CN); pap. 4.95 (1-55037-086-3, Pub. by Annick CN) Firefly Bks Ltd.
—Summer Days. (Illus.). 24p. (ps-8). 1988. 12.95 (1-55037-043-X, Pub. by Annick CN); pap. 4.95 (1-55037-044-8, Pub. by Annick CN) Firefly Bks Ltd.
Pare, Roger. A, B, C...Play with Me! 1988. Incl. one bk., one game, & two puzzles. pap. 5.00 (0-88166-121-X) Meadowbrook.
—L' Alphabet : A Child's Introduction to the Letters & Sounds of French. Pare, Roger, illus. 32p. 1990. 7.95 (0-8442-1395-0, Natl Textbk) NTC Pub Grp.
—Animal Capers. Pare, Roger, illus. 24p. 1992. PLB 14.95 (1-55037-243-2, Pub. by Annick Pr); pap. 4.95 (1-55037-244-0, Pub. by Annick Pr) Firefly Bks Ltd.
—The Annick ABC. Pare, Roger, illus. 24p. (ps-2). 1989. pap. 0.99 (0-920303-78-1, Pub. by Annick CN) Firefly Bks Ltd.
—A Friend Like You. Pare, Roger, illus. 24p. (ps-2). 1989. pap. 0.99 (0-920303-80-3, Pub. by Annick CN) Firefly Bks Ltd.
—Winter Games. Pare, Roger, illus. 24p. 1991. PLB 14.95 (1-55037-187-8, Pub. by Annick CN); pap. 4.95 (1-55037-184-3, Pub. by Annick CN) Firefly Bks Ltd.
Parent, Frederick, jt. auth. see Rundquist, Thomas J.
Parent, Laurence E. Capulin Volcano National Monument. Priehs, T. J. & Jorgen, Randolph, eds. Parent, Laurence E., photos by. LC 91-60463. 16p. (Orig.). 1991. pap. 2.95 (0-911408-94-0) SW Pks Mnmts.
—Gila Cliff Dwellings National Monument. Priehs, T. J. & Jorgen, Randolph, eds. Parent, Laurence E., photos by. LC 91-60461. 16p. (Orig.). 1992. pap. 2.95 (0-911408-96-7) SW Pks Mnmts.
—Lake Meredith National Recreation Area. Foreman, Ronald J. & Priehs, T. J., eds. 16p. (Orig.). 1992. pap. 2.95 (1-877856-16-9) SW Pks Mnmts.
Parenteau. One Hundred Plus Super Pig Jokes, Puns, & Riddles. 1993. pap. 1.95 (0-590-41656-1) Scholastic Inc.
Parents Nursery School Staff. Kids Are Natural Cooks. (Illus.). (ps-6). 1974. pap. 8.70 (0-395-18521-1, Sandpiper) HM.
Paretta, Joseph, ed. see Vollaro, Joseph.
Pargment, Lila, adapted by. How the Moolah Was Taught a Lesson & Other Tales from Russia. Titiev, Estelle, adapted by. LC 75-9200. (Illus.). 56p. 1985. (Dial); PLB 5.47 (0-8037-5746-8, Dial) Doubleday.
Parham, Vanessa R. The African-American Child's Heritage Cookbook. Rolle-Whatley, R., ed. LC 92-60006. (Illus.). 296p. (Orig.). 1992. pap. 19.95 (0-9627756-2-2) Sandcastle Pub.
Parietti, Jeff. One Hundred & One Wacky Sports Quotes. (gr. 4-7). 1991. pap. 1.95 (0-590-44146-9) Scholastic Inc.
Parin, Edgar P., jt. auth. see D'Aulaire, Ingri.
Paris, Nancy M. My Brother Is Different. (Illus.). (gr. 1-4). 1992. 6.95 (1-55523-512-3) Winston-Derek.
Paris, Pat. Old MacDonald Had a Farm. (Illus.). 12p. (ps-1). 1989. text ed. 10.95 (0-8120-6107-1) Barron.

—On a Rainy Day: A Playtime Pop-Up. (Illus.). 10p. (ps). 1992. pap. 4.95 casebound (0-671-74175-6, Little Simon) S&S Trade.
—On a Windy Day: A Playtime Pop-Up. (Illus.). 10p. (ps). 1992. pap. 4.95 casebound (0-671-74174-8, Little Simon) S&S Trade.
—On Christmas Day. (Illus.). 10p. (ps). 1991. pap. 4.95 casebound (0-671-74173-X, Little Simon) S&S Trade.
—Pop up Frog. 1989. 4.95 (0-671-67554-0) S&S Trade.
—This Old Man. (Illus.). 12p. (ps-1). 1989. text ed. 9.95 (0-8120-6109-8) Barron.
Paris, Pat, illus. Bear Cubs. 10p. (ps). 1989. 4.95 (0-8120-5987-5) Barron.
—Bunnies. 10p. (ps). 1989. 4.95 (0-8120-5990-5) Barron.
—Kittens. 10p. (ps). 1989. 4.95 (0-8120-5989-1) Barron.
—Puppies. 10p. (ps). 1989. 4.95 (0-8120-5988-3) Barron.
—Who's in the Box, Bobby? 28p. (ps). 1987. 9.95 (0-8431-1906-3) Price Stern.
Paris, Pat & All, Wendy, illus. Rose-Petal. 12p. (ps-3). 1984. cancelled 4.00 (0-910313-53-9) Parker Bros.
—Sunny Sunflower. 14p. (ps-3). 1984. cancelled 4.00 (0-910313-55-5) Parker Bros.
Paris, Pat & Lipking, Ron, illus. A Garden of Love to Share: A Panorama. (ps-3). 1984. 4.00 (0-910313-56-3) Parker Bros.
Paris, Susan. Mommy & Daddy Are Fighting: A Book for Children about Family Violence. Labinski, Gail, illus. LC 85-22193. 24p. (Orig.). (ps-4). 1986. pap. 8.95 (0-931188-33-4) Seal Pr Feminist.
Parish, Peggy. Amelia Bedelia. newly illus. ed. Siebel, Fritz, illus. LC 91-10163. 64p. (gr. k-3). 1992. 14.00 (0-06-020186-X); PLB 13.89 (0-06-020187-8) HarpC Child Bks.
—Amelia Bedelia. newly illus. ed. Siebel, Fritz, illus. LC 91-10164. 64p. (gr. k-3). 1992. pap. 3.50 (0-06-444155-5, Trophy) HarpC Child Bks.
—Amelia Bedelia & the Baby. Sweat, Lynn, illus. LC 80-22263. 64p. (gr. 1-3). 1981. 14.00 (0-688-00316-8); PLB 13.93 (0-688-00321-4) Greenwillow.
—Amelia Bedelia & the Baby. Sweat, Lynn, illus. 64p. (gr. k-3). 1982. pap. 3.99 (0-380-57067-X, Camelot) Avon.
—Amelia Bedelia & the Surprise Shower. Siebel, Fritz, illus. LC 66-18655. 64p. (gr. k-3). 1966. 14.00 (0-06-024642-1); PLB 13.89 (0-06-024643-X) HarpC Child Bks.
—Amelia Bedelia & the Surprise Shower. Siebel, Fritz, illus. LC 66-18655. 64p. (gr. k-3). 1979. pap. 3.50 (0-06-444019-2, Trophy) HarpC Child Bks.
—Amelia Bedelia & the Surprise Shower. Siebel, Fritz, illus. LC 66-18655. 64p. (gr. k-3). 1986. incl. cassette 5.98 (0-694-00161-9, Trophy) HarpC Child Bks.
—Amelia Bedelia & the Surprise Shower. unabr. ed. Tripp, Wallace, illus. (ps-3). 1990. pap. 6.95 incl. cassette (1-55994-216-9, Caedmon) HarperAudio.
—Amelia Bedelia Goes Camping. LC 84-7979. (Illus.). 56p. (gr. 1-3). 1985. 12.95 (0-688-04058-6); PLB 12.88 (0-688-04057-8) Greenwillow.
—Amelia Bedelia Helps Out. Sweat, Lynn, illus. LC 79-11729. 64p. (gr. 1-3). 1979. 14.00 (0-688-80231-1); PLB 13.93 (0-688-84231-3) Greenwillow.
—Amelia Bedelia Helps Out. Sweat, Lynn, illus. 64p. (gr. k-3). 1981. pap. 3.99 (0-380-53405-3, Camelot) Avon.
—Amelia Bedelia's Family Album. Sweat, Lynn, illus. LC 87-15641. 48p. (gr. 3-9). 1988. 13.95 (0-688-07676-9); lib. bdg. 11.88 (0-688-07677-7) Greenwillow.
—Amelia Bedelia's Family Album. 48p. 1989. pap. 5.95 (0-380-70760-8, Camelot) Avon.
—Amelia Bedelia's Family Album. 48p. 1991. pap. 3.50 (0-380-71698-4, Camelot) Avon.
—Be Ready at Eight. Kessler, Leonard, illus. LC 87-1040. 64p. (gr. 1-4). 1987. pap. 3.95 (0-689-71163-8, Aladdin) Macmillan Child Grp.
—The Cats' Burglar. Sweat, Lynn, illus. LC 82-11751. 64p. (gr. 1-3). 1983. 12.95 (0-688-01825-4); PLB 13.93 (0-688-01826-2) Greenwillow.
—The Cats' Burglar. (gr. k-6). 1988. pap. 2.75 (0-440-40054-6, YB) Dell.
—Clues in the Woods. 160p. (gr. k-6). 1980. pap. 3.50 (0-440-41461-X, YB) Dell.
—Come Back, Amelia Bedelia. Tripp, Wallace, illus. LC 73-121799. 64p. (ps-3). 1971. 14.00 (0-06-024667-7); PLB 13.89 (0-06-024668-5) HarpC Child Bks.
—Come Back, Amelia Bedelia. Tripp, Wallace, illus. LC 73-121799. 64p. (gr. k-3). 1986. incl. cassette 5.98 (0-694-00112-0, Trophy); pap. 3.50 (0-06-444016-8, Trophy) HarpC Child Bks.
—Come Back, Amelia Bedelia. unabr. ed. Tripp, Wallace, illus. (ps-3). 1990. pap. 6.95 incl. cassette (1-55994-225-8, Caedmon) HarperAudio.
—Dinosaur Time. Lobel, Arnold, illus. LC 73-14331. 32p. (gr. k-3). 1974. 14.00 (0-06-024653-7); PLB 13.89 (0-06-024654-5) HarpC Child Bks.
—Dinosaur Time. Lobel, Arnold, illus. LC 73-14331. 32p. (ps-2). 1983. pap. 3.50 (0-06-444037-0, Trophy) HarpC Child Bks.
—The Ghosts of Cougar Island. (Orig.). (gr. 2-4). 1986. pap. 3.50 (0-440-42872-6, YB) Dell.
—Good Hunting, Blue Sky. Watts, James, illus. LC 84-43143. 64p. (gr. k-3). 1988. 14.00 (0-06-024661-8); PLB 13.89 (0-06-024662-6) HarpC Child Bks.
—Good Hunting, Blue Sky. Watts, James, illus. LC 84-43143. 64p. (gr. k-3). 1991. pap. 3.50 (0-06-444148-2, Trophy) HarpC Child Bks.
—Good Work, Amelia Bedelia. Sweat, Lynn, illus. LC 75-20360. 56p. (gr. 1-4). 1976. 14.00 (0-688-80022-X); PLB 13.93 (0-688-84022-1) Greenwillow.

—Good Work, Amelia Bedelia. Sweat, Lynn, illus. 164p. (gr. k-5). 1980. pap. 3.99 (0-380-49171-0, Camelot) Avon.
—Haunted House. 160p. (gr. k-6). 1981. pap. 3.25 (0-440-43459-9, YB) Dell.
—Haunted House. (gr. 4-6). 1991. 16.25 (0-8446-6391-3) Peter Smith.
—Key to the Treasure. 160p. (gr. k-6). 1980. pap. 3.50 (0-440-44438-1, YB) Dell.
—Let's Be Early Settlers with Daniel Boone. LC 67-14068. (Illus.). 96p. (gr. 3-5). 1967. PLB 14.89 (0-06-024648-0) HarpC Child Bks.
—Merry Christmas, Amelia Bedelia. Sweat, Lynn, illus. LC 85-24919. 64p. (gr. 1-4). 1986. 13.00 (0-688-06101-X); PLB 12.93 (0-688-06102-8) Greenwillow.
—Merry Christmas, Amelia Bedelia. Sweat, Lynn, illus. 64p. 1987. pap. 3.99 (0-380-70325-4, Camelot) Avon.
—Mind Your Manners. Hafner, Marylin, illus. LC 77-19096. 56p. (gr. 1-3). 1978. PLB 13.88 (0-688-84157-0) Greenwillow.
—Mind Your Manners. Hafner, Marilyn, illus. 56p. (gr. 1 up). Date not set. pap. 3.95 (0-688-13109-3, Mulberry) Morrow.
—Mr. Adams's Mistake. Owens, Gail, illus. LC 81-17221. 64p. (gr. 1-4). 1982. SBE 11.95 (0-02-769800-9) Macmillan Child Grp.
—No More Monsters for Me. Simont, Marc, illus. LC 81-47111. 64p. (gr. k-3). 1981. 14.00 (0-06-024657-X); PLB 13.89 (0-06-024658-8) HarpC Child Bks.
—No More Monsters for Me! Simont, Marc, illus. LC 81-47111. 64p. (gr. k-3). 1987. pap. 3.50 (0-06-444109-1, Trophy) HarpC Child Bks.
—Pirate Island Adventure. 176p. (gr. k-6). 1981. pap. 3.50 (0-440-47394-2, YB) Dell.
—Pirate Island Adventure. (gr. 3-6). 1991. 17.00 (0-8446-6453-7) Peter Smith.
—Play Ball, Amelia Bedelia. Tripp, Wallace, illus. LC 71-85028. 64p. (gr. k-3). 1972. 14.00 (0-06-024655-3); PLB 13.89 (0-06-024656-1) HarpC Child Bks.
—Play Ball, Amelia Bedelia. Tripp, Wallace, illus. LC 71-85028. 64p. (ps-3). 1985. (Trophy). pap. 3.50 (0-06-444005-2, Trophy) HarpC Child Bks.
—Play Ball, Amelia Bedelia. unabr. ed. Tripp, Wallace, illus. (ps-3). 1990. pap. 6.95 incl. cassette (1-55994-241-X, Caedmon) HarperAudio.
—Scruffy. Oechsli, Kelly, illus. LC 87-45564. 64p. (gr. k-3). 1988. 14.00 (0-06-024659-6); PLB 13.89 (0-06-024660-X) HarpC Child Bks.
—Scruffy. Oechsli, Kelly, illus. LC 87-45564. 64p. (gr. k-3). 1990. pap. 3.50 (0-06-444137-7, Trophy) HarpC Child Bks.
—Teach Us, Amelia Bedelia. Sweat, Lynn, illus. LC 76-22663. 56p. (gr. 1-4). 1977. 12.95 (0-688-80069-6); PLB 12.88 (0-688-84069-8) Greenwillow.
—Teach Us, Amelia Bedelia. Sweat, Lynn, illus. 64p. (gr. k-3). 1987. pap. 2.95 (0-590-43345-8) Scholastic Inc.
—Thank You, Amelia Bedelia. Siebel, Fritz, illus. LC 64-11835. (gr. k-3). 1964. 13.00 (0-06-024665-0); PLB 12.89 (0-06-024652-9) HarpC Child Bks.
—Thank You, Amelia Bedelia. newly illus ed. Thomas, Barbara, illus. LC 92-5746. 64p. (gr. k-3). 1993. 14.00 (0-06-022979-9); PLB 13.89 (0-06-022980-2) HarpC Child Bks.
—Thank You, Amelia Bedelia. Siebel, Fritz, illus. LC 92-5746. 64p. (ps-3). 1993. pap. 3.50 (0-06-444171-7, Trophy) HarpC Child Bks.
—Too Many Rabbits. (ps-3). 1992. pap. 2.99 (0-440-40591-2) Dell.
—Willy Is My Brother. Rogers, Jacqueline, illus. (ps up). 1989. 12.95 (0-385-29723-8) Delacorte.
—Willy Is My Brother. 1989. pap. 12.95 (0-440-50221-7) Dell.
Parish, Peggy & Lobel, Arnold. Dinosaur Time. 32p. (ps-2). 1990. pap. 6.95 (1-55994-262-2, Caedmon) HarperAudio.
Parisi, L. The World: Lands & Peoples: Copy Masters. (Illus.). 236p. (gr. 6). 1992. 95.00 (0-87746-361-1) Graphic Learning.
Park, Barbara. Almost Starring Skinnybones. LC 87-28752. (gr. 3-7). 1988. lib. bdg. 11.99 (0-394-99831-6) Knopf Bks Yng Read.
—Beanpole. LC 83-111. 160p. (gr. 5 up). 1983. 13.00 (0-394-85811-5) Knopf Bks Yng Read.
—Beanpole. 160p. (gr. 5 up). 1984. pap. 2.95 (0-380-69840-4, Flare) Avon.
—Buddies. LC 84-12521. 144p. (gr. 5-9). 1985. lib. bdg. 9.99 (0-394-96934-0) Knopf Bks Yng Read.
—Buddies. (gr. 7 up). 1986. pap. 2.95 (0-380-69992-3, Flare) Avon.
—Dear God, Help! Love, Earl. LC 92-20909. 128p. (gr. 3-7). 1993. 15.00 (0-679-83431-1); 15.99 (0-679-93431-6) Knopf Bks Yng Read.
—Don't Make Me Smile. LC 81-4880. 128p. (gr. 4-7). 1981. PLB 10.99 (0-394-94978-1) Knopf Bks Yng Read.
—Don't Make Me Smile. 132p. (gr. 4-7). 1983. pap. 2.95 (0-380-61994-6, Camelot) Avon.
—Don't Make Me Smile. LC 81-4880. 128p. (gr. 3-7). 1990. pap. 3.25 (0-394-84745-8) Random Bks Yng Read.
—Junie B. Jones & a Little Monkey Business. Brunkus, Denise, illus. LC 92-56706. 80p. (Orig.). (gr. 1-4). 1993. PLB 9.99 (0-679-93886-9); pap. 2.99 (0-679-83886-4) Random Bks Yng Read.

—Junie B. Jones & Her Big Fat Mouth. Brunkus, Denise, illus. LC 92-50957. 80p. (Orig.). (gr. 1-4). 1993. PLB 9.99 (0-679-94407-9); pap. 2.99 (0-679-84407-4) Random Bks Yng Read.
—Junie B. Jones & Some Sneaky Peeky Spying. Brunkus, Denise, illus. LC 93-5557. 1994. write for info. (0-679-85101-1); PLB write for info. (0-679-95101-6) Random Bks Yng Read.
—Junie B. Jones & the Stupid Smelly Bus. Brunkus, Denise, illus. LC 91-51104. 80p. (Orig.). (gr. 1-4). 1992. PLB 9.99 (0-679-92642-9); pap. 2.99 (0-679-82642-4) Random Bks Yng Read.
—The Kid in the Red Jacket. LC 86-20113. 128p. (gr. 3-7). 1988. Repr. of 1987 ed. 3.25 (0-394-80571-2) Knopf Bks Yng Read.
—Maxie, Rosie, & Earl...Partners in Grime. Strogart, Alexander, illus. LC 89-28027. 128p. (gr. 3-7). 1990. 13.00 (0-679-80212-6); PLB 13.99 (0-679-90212-0) Random Bks Yng Read.
—My Mother Got Married: (And Other Disasters) LC 88-27257. 128p. (gr. 3-7). 1989. 13.00 (0-394-82149-1); lib. bdg. 13.99 (0-394-92149-6) Knopf Bks Yng Read.
—Operation: Dump the Chump. Sauber, Rob, illus. LC 81-8147. 128p. (gr. 3-6). 1982. lib. bdg. 10.99 (0-394-95179-4) Knopf Bks Yng Read.
—Operation: Dump the Chump. 112p. (gr. 3-7). 1983. pap. 2.75 (0-380-63974-2, Camelot) Avon.
—Operation: Dump the Chump. LC 81-8147. 128p. 1989. pap. 2.95 (0-394-82592-6) Knopf Bks Yng Read.
—Rosie Swanson: Fourth-Grade Geek for President. LC 91-8616. 114p. (gr. 3-6). 1991. 14.00 (0-679-82094-9); lib. bdg. 14.99 (0-679-92094-3) Knopf Bks Yng Read.
—Skinnybones. LC 81-20791. 128p. (gr. 3-6). 1982. PLB 10.99 (0-394-94988-9) Knopf Bks Yng Read.
—Skinnybones. LC 81-20791. 112p. (gr. 3-6). 1989. pap. 3.50 (0-394-82596-9) Knopf Bks Yng Read.
Park, Dave, jt. auth. see Anderson, Neil.
Park, Dave, jt. auth. see Anderson, Neil T.
Park, Jae S. Now What? Auto Accident Claims Guide. 100p. (Orig.). 1989. pap. text ed. 3.95 (0-685-28055-1) Park Pub Co.
Park, Margaret. Crab-Bags & Other Bean-Beings. Bluestone, Sara, illus. (gr. 5 up). 1979. pap. 2.95 (0-915556-05-7) Great Ocean.
Park, Margaret & Iosa, Ann. Harvey & Rosie...& Ralph. LC 91-43306. (Illus.). 64p. (gr. 2-5). 1992. 11.00 (0-525-44836-5, DCB) Dutton Child Bks.
Park, Ruth. My Sister Sif. 186p. (gr. 5 up). 1991. 14.00 (0-670-83924-8) Viking Child Bks.
—Playing Beatie Bow. LC 81-8097. 204p. (gr. 5-9). 1982. SBE 14.95 (0-689-30889-2, Atheneum Child Bk) Macmillan Child Grp.
—Playing Beatie Bow. 200p. (gr. 5-9). 1984. pap. 3.99 (0-14-031460-1, Puffin) Puffin Bks.
—Things in Corners. (gr. 5-9). 1991. 12.95 (0-670-82225-6) Viking Child Bks.
—Things in Corners. 208p. (gr. 5 up). 1993. pap. 3.99 (0-14-032713-4, Puffin) Puffin Bks.

Park, Y. H. & Leibowitz, Jeff.

Taekwondo for Children: The Ultimate Reference Guide for Children Interested in the World's Most Popular Martial Art. Bu Ho Choi, illus. 128p. (Orig.). (gr. 4-8). 1993. PLB 9.95 (0-9637151-0-0) YH Pk Taekwondo. This book (endorsed by The World Taekwondo Federation) explains the philosophy & basic techniques of the ancient Korean martial art & modern day sport of taekwondo in simple terms. Taekwondo is recognized as an official Olympic sport & the Co-Author was Coach of the 1988 USA Olympic Team. The book stresses how taekwondo's philosophy of strength tempered by gentleness can help a youngster in all aspects of his or her life. It describes how children can improve academic performance, boost self-esteem & confidence & learn to respect themselves & others. It dispels many myths that had previously made parents apprehensive about taekwondo. Taekwondo teaches highly effective self-defense, mainly with its devastating kicks. But it also teaches an individual how to be his or her very best-- physically & mentally. Its emphasis is on what attitudinal changes a child can & should strive toward as he undertakes the study of taekwondo. Negative outlets from reality such as drugs, alcohol & abusive language & behavior have no place in the life of a taekwondo practitioner. This book illustrates why & suggests that taekwondo practice can profoundly improve the life of any child. *Publisher Provided Annotation.*

Parke, Sara. No Fair Peeking. LC 90-85436. (Illus.). 32p. (gr. k-3). 1991. 5.95 (1-56282-037-0) Disney Pr.
Parker. I Love Spiders. 1993. pap. 28.67 (0-590-50153-4) Scholastic Inc.
—The Norfin Trolls from A to Z. 1993. pap. 2.50 (0-590-46957-6) Scholastic Inc.
—U. S. Paper Money Today. Date not set. 15.00 (0-06-023411-3, Festival); PLB 14.89 (0-06-023412-1, Festival) HarpC Child Bks.
Parker, A. E. The Case of the Invisible Cat. (gr. 4-7). 1992. pap. 2.95 (0-590-45632-6) Scholastic Inc.
—Mystery at the Masked Ball. (gr. 4-7). 1993. pap. 2.95 (0-590-45633-4) Scholastic Inc.
Parker, A. E., created by. Who Killed Mr. Boddy? 160p. (gr. 4 up). 1992. pap. 2.95 (0-590-46110-9, Apple Paperbacks) Scholastic Inc.
Parker, Andrew D. Keeping the Promise: A Guide for Mentors & Confirmands. (gr. 9-12). 1994. write for info. mentor's ed. (0-8192-4113-X); write for info. confirmand's wkbk. (0-8192-4114-8) Morehouse Pub.
Parker, Ann N. A Christmas Trilogy. Vickery, Diane, illus. (gr. k-4). 1988. pap. 3.95 (0-943487-14-5) Sevgo Pr.
—Home Is Where the Shade Tree Is. Vickery, Diane, illus. 18p. (gr. k-4). 1988. pap. 3.95 (0-943487-13-7) Sevgo Pr.
Parker, Beth. Thomas Knew There Were Pirates Living in the Bathroom. Mansfield, Renee, illus. 28p. (ps-3). 1990. 12.95 (0-88753-224-1, Pub. by Black Moss Pr CN); pap. 4.95 (0-88753-201-2, Pub. by Black Moss Pr CN) Firefly Bks Ltd.
Parker, Cam. Camp Off-the-Wall. 128p. (gr. 3-7). 1987. pap. 2.50 (0-380-75196-8, Camelot) Avon.
—A Horse in New York. 144p. (Orig.). (gr. 5 up). 1989. pap. 2.75 (0-380-75704-4, Camelot) Avon.
Parker, Carol. Why Do You Call Me Chocolate Boy? Barter, Nan, illus. LC 93-79098. 28p. (Orig.). (gr. 2-6). 1993. pap. 5.95 (0-9637267-0-6) Gull Crest.
Parker, Donald & Hewitt, David. Table Tennis. rev. ed. (Illus.). 80p. (gr. 10-12). 1993. pap. 7.95 (0-7063-7159-3, Pub. by Ward Lock UK) Sterling.
—Table Tennis. (Illus.). 80p. (gr. 10-12). 1993. pap. 7.95 (0-7137-2412-9, Pub. by Blandford Pr UK) Sterling.
Parker, Ed, illus. Jack & the Beanstalk. LC 78-18072. 32p. (gr. k-4). 1979. PLB 9.79 (0-89375-125-1); pap. 1.95 (0-89375-103-0) Troll Assocs.
—Three Billy Goats Gruff. LC 78-18068. 32p. (gr. k-3). 1979. PLB 9.79 (0-89375-121-9); pap. 1.95 (0-89375-099-9); cassette 9.95 (0-685-04953-1) Troll Assocs.
Parker, Eric. Colonel Hawker's Shooting Diaries. 2nd ed. Northcote, James, illus. 300p. (gr. 10 up). 1990. Repr. of 1931 ed. 35.00 (1-56416-000-9) Derrydale Pr.
Parker, Gary. Dry Bones & Other Fossils. Chong, Jonathon, illus. LC 79-51174. (gr. 2-4). 1979. pap. 5.95 (0-89051-118-7) Master Bks.
—Life Before Birth. (Orig.). (gr. 1-8). 1987. 10.95 (0-89051-117-9) Master Bks.
Parker, George C. The Night the Day Was Stolen. 1991. 7.95 (0-533-09461-5) Vantage.
Parker, Harvey C., jt. auth. see Parker, Roberta N.
Parker, Jackie. Love Letters to My Fans. 176p. (Orig.). (gr. 7-12). 1986. pap. 2.50 (0-553-25725-0, Starfire) Bantam.
Parker, James. Glossary of Terms Used in Heraldry. LC 77-94021. (Illus.). 692p. (gr. 9 up). 1970. 40.00 (0-8048-0715-9) C E Tuttle.
Parker, Jane, jt. auth. see Parker, Steve.
Parker, Julie F. Careers for Women As Clergy. Rosen, Ruth, ed. (gr. 7-12). 1993. PLB 13.95 (0-8239-1424-0); pap. 9.95 (0-8239-1727-4) Rosen Group.
Parker, Kristy. My Dad the Magnificent. Hoban, Lillian, illus. LC 86-24077. 32p. (ps-2). 1987. 10.95 (0-525-44314-2, DCB) Dutton Child Bks.
—My Dad the Magnificent. Hoban, Lillian, illus. LC 86-24077. 32p. (ps-2). 1990. pap. 3.95 (0-525-44607-9, DCB) Dutton Child Bks.
Parker, Liz, ed. see Bricker, Sandra D.
Parker, Liz, ed. see Brin, Susannah.
Parker, Liz, ed. see Buchanan, Paul.
Parker, Liz, ed. see Horton, Randy.
Parker, Liz, ed. see Press, Skip.
Parker, Liz, ed. see Schraff, Anne.
Parker, Liz, ed. see Steel, Richard.
Parker, Liz, ed. see Wells, Colin.
Parker, Liz, ed. see Woodson, Frank.
Parker, Lois. Return to Jerusalem. Wheeler, Gerald, ed. 160p. (Orig.). 1988. pap. 6.95 (0-8280-0426-9) Review & Herald.
Parker, Lois & McConnell, David. A Little Peoples' Beginning on Michigan. Deeter, Theresa, illus. 32p. (Orig.). (gr. 1-2). 1981. pap. 5.50 (0-910726-06-X) Hillsdale Educ.
Parker, Madeleine, jt. auth. see Paxford, Sandra.
Parker, Margot. What Is Columbus Day? Bates, Matt, illus. LC 85-12748. 48p. (ps-3). 1985. PLB 15.00 (0-516-03781-1) Childrens.

—What Is Martin Luther King, Jr. Day? Bates, Matt, illus. LC 89-29254. 48p. (ps-3). 1990. 15.00 (*0-516-03784-6*); pap. 4.95 (*0-516-43784-4*) Childrens.
—What Is Thanksgiving Day? Bates, Matt, illus. LC 88-11112. 48p. (ps-3). 1988. PLB 15.00 (*0-516-03783-8*); pap. 4.95 (*0-516-43783-6*) Childrens.
—What Is Veterans Day? Bates, Matt, illus. LC 86-11732. 48p. (ps-3). 1986. PLB 15.00 (*0-516-03782-X*) Childrens.
Parker, Marjorie H. Jellyfish Can't Swim, & Other Secrets from the Animal World. (gr. 4-7). 1992. pap. 4.99 (*1-55513-393-2*) Cook.
Parker, Nancy W. Frogs, Toads, Lizards & Salamanders. Wright, Joan R., illus. (gr. 1 up). 1990. 15.00 (*0-688-08680-2*); PLB 13.93 (*0-688-08681-0*) Greenwillow.
—The President's Cabinet & How It Grew. Parker, Nancy W., illus. LC 89-70851. 40p. (gr. 3-5). 1991. PLB 14.89 (*0-06-021618-2*) HarpC Child Bks.
—The President's Cabinet & How It Grew. LC 89-70851. (Illus.). 40p. (gr. 3-5). 1992. pap. 5.95 (*0-06-446131-9*, Trophy) HarpC Child Bks.
—Working Frog. LC 90-24173. 40p. (gr. k up). 1992. 14.00 (*0-688-09918-1*); PLB 13.93 (*0-688-09919-X*) Greenwillow.
Parker, Nancy W. & Wright, Joan R. Bugs. LC 86-29387. (Illus.). 40p. (gr. 1-4). 1987. 11.95 (*0-688-06623-2*); lib. bdg. 11.88 (*0-688-06624-0*) Greenwillow.
—Bugs. Parker, Nancy W., illus. LC 86-29387. (ps-3). 1988. pap. 4.95 (*0-688-08296-3*, Mulberry) Morrow.
Parker, Richard. The Old Powder Line. (gr. 4-7). 19.75 (*0-8446-6432-4*) Peter Smith.
Parker, Roberta N. & Parker, Harvey C. Making the Grade: An Adolescent's Struggle with ADD. DiMatteo, Richard, tr. (Illus.). 48p. (Orig.). (gr. 5-10). 1992. pap. 12.00 (*0-9621629-1-4*) Impact FL.
Parker, Roy, Jr. Cumberland County: A Brief History. (Illus.). xi, 158p. (Orig.). (gr. 8 up). 1990. pap. 8.00 (*0-86526-243-8*) NC Archives.
Parker, Steve. Alarming Animals. Savage, Ann, illus. LC 93-6651. 38p. (gr. 3-6). 1993. PLB 19.97 (*0-8114-0658-X*) Raintree Steck-V.
—Awesome Amphibians. Savage, Ann, illus. LC 92-43196. 38p. (gr. 3-6). 1993. PLB 19.97 (*0-8114-0661-X*) Raintree Steck-V.
—Be an Animal Detective. 40p. (gr. 2 up). 1989. 3.99 (*0-517-68023-8*) Outlet Bk Co.
—Beastly Bugs. Savage, Ann, illus. LC 92-43197. 38p. (gr. 3-6). 1993. PLB 19.97 (*0-8114-0689-X*) Raintree-Steck-V.
—The Body & How It Works. LC 91-58203. (Illus.). 64p. (gr. 3 up). 1992. 11.95 (*1-879431-95-5*); PLB 12.99 (*1-879431-96-3*) Dorling Kindersley.
—The Body Atlas. Fornari, Giuliano, illus. LC 92-54307. 64p. (gr. 3 up). 1993. 19.95 (*1-56458-224-8*) Dorling Kindersley.
—Brain & Nervous System. (ps-3). 1990. PLB 12.90 (*0-531-14026-1*) Watts.
—The Brain & Nervous System. rev. ed. (Illus.). 48p. (gr. 5 up). 1991. pap. 6.95 (*0-531-24600-0*) Watts.
—Camouflage. LC 91-10275. (Illus.). 32p. (gr. 5-8). 1991. PLB 12.40 (*0-531-17313-5*, Gloucester Pr) Watts.
—The Car. (Illus.). 32p. (gr. 5-8). 1993. PLB 12.40 (*0-531-17415-8*, Gloucester Pr) Watts.
—Catching a Cold: How You Get Ill, Suffer & Recover. (Illus.). 32p. (gr. k-4). 1992. PLB 11.40 (*0-531-14146-2*) Watts.
—Charles Darwin & Evolution. Parker, Steve, illus. LC 91-30272. 32p. (gr. 3-7). 1992. 14.00 (*0-06-020733-7*) HarpC Child Bks.
—Cunning Carnivores. Savage, Ann, illus. LC 93-27256. 1993. write for info. (*0-8114-2347-6*) Raintree Steck-V.
—Dime Como Funciona (How Things Work) (SPA., Illus.). 64p. (gr. 4 up). 1992. PLB 19.90 (*1-56294-179-8*) Millbrook Pr.
—Dinosaurs & How They Lived. LC 91-60143. (Illus.). 64p. (gr. 3 up). 1991. 11.95 (*1-879431-13-0*); PLB 12.99 (*1-879431-28-9*) Dorling Kindersley.
—Draw Partner: How to Draw Wild West Cartoons for Kids. Parker, Steve, illus. 32p. (gr. 1-6). 1990. pap. 2.95 (*0-929526-08-2*) Double B Pubns.
—Dreaming in the Night: How You Rest, Sleep & Dream. (Illus.). 32p. (gr. k-4). 1991. PLB 11.40 (*0-531-14099-7*) Watts.
—The Drug War. (Illus.). 32p. (gr. 5-8). 1990. PLB 12.40 (*0-531-17241-4*, Gloucester Pr) Watts.
—The Ear & Hearing. rev. ed. Mayron-Parker, Alan, contrib. by. (Illus.). 48p. (gr. 5-6). 1989. PLB 12.90 (*0-531-10712-4*) Watts.
—The Ear & Hearing. rev. ed. (Illus.). 48p. (gr. 5 up). 1991. pap. 5.95 (*0-531-24601-9*) Watts.
—The Earth & How It Works. Gornari, Giuliano & Corbella, Luciano, illus. LC 92-54317. 64p. (gr. 3-7). 1993. 12.95 (*1-56458-235-3*) Dorling Kindersley.
—Eating a Meal: How You Eat, Drink & Digest. (Illus.). 32p. (gr. k-4). 1991. PLB 11.40 (*0-531-14086-5*) Watts.
—Everyday Things & How They Work. Bull, Peter & Moores, Ian, illus. LC 91-1213. 40p. (gr. 2-5). 1991. pap. 3.99 (*0-679-80866-3*) Random Bks Yng Read.
—Eye & Seeing. 1989. PLB 12.90 (*0-531-10654-3*) Watts.
—The Eye & Seeing. rev. ed. (Illus.). 48p. (gr. 5 up). 1991. pap. 6.95 (*0-531-24602-7*) Watts.
—Fearsome Fish. Savage, Ann, illus. LC 93-28905. 1993. write for info. (*0-8114-2346-8*) Raintree Steck-V.

—Fish. King, Dave & Keates, Colin, photos by. LC 89-36445. (Illus.). 64p. (gr. 5 up). 1990. 15.00 (*0-679-80439-0*); PLB 15.99 (*0-679-90439-5*) Random Bks Yng Read.
—Flight & Flying Machines. Corbella, Luciano, illus. LC 92-54316. 64p. (gr. 3-7). 1993. 12.95 (*1-56458-236-1*) Dorling Kindersley.
—Food & Digestion. rev. ed. (Illus.). 48p. (gr. 5 up). 1991. pap. 5.95 (*0-531-24603-5*) Watts.
—Galileo & the Universe. Parker, Steve, illus. LC 91-28315. 32p. (gr. 3-7). 1992. 14.00 (*0-06-020735-3*) HarpC Child Bks.
—The Heart & Blood. rev. ed. Mayron-Parker, Alan, contrib. by. (Illus.). 48p. (gr. 5-6). 1989. PLB 12.90 (*0-531-10711-6*) Watts.
—The Heart & Blood. rev. ed. (Illus.). 48p. (gr. 5 up). 1991. pap. 5.95 (*0-531-24604-3*) Watts.
—The History of Medicine. LC 90-23744. (Illus.). 64p. (gr. 4-6). 1991. PLB 19.93 (*0-8368-0024-9*) Gareth Stevens Inc.
—How It Works. Pleasance, Geoff, illus. 48p. (gr. 3-6). 1992. pap. 2.95 (*1-56680-010-2*) Mad Hatter Pub.
—How Things Are Made. LC 92-21676. (Illus.). 128p. (ps-3). 1993. 10.00 (*0-679-83695-0*); PLB 11.99 (*0-679-93695-5*) Random Bks Yng Read.
—The Human Body. LC 93-7752. (Illus.). 64p. (gr. 3-6). 1993. 15.95 (*1-56458-325-2*) Dorling Kindersley.
—The Human Body. (Illus.). 32p. (gr. 5-7). 1993. PLB 12.40 (*0-531-17337-2*, Gloucester Pr) Watts.
—Human Body. LC 93-31076. 1994. write for info. (*1-56458-322-8*) Dorling Kindersley.
—Inside Dinosaurs & Other Prehistoric Creatures. Dewan, Ted, illus. LC 93-10045. (gr. 1-8). 1994. 16.95 (*0-385-31143-5*); pap. 10.95 (*0-385-31189-3*) Delacorte.
—Japan. Kossmann, Walter & Fink, Joanne, eds. (Illus.). 48p. (gr. 5 up). 1991. PLB 16.98 (*0-382-24246-7*) Silver Burdett Pr.
—Keeping Cool: How You Sweat, Shiver & Keep Warm. (Illus.). 32p. (gr. k-4). 1992. PLB 11.40 (*0-531-14147-0*) Watts.
—Learning a Lesson: How You See, Think & Remember. (Illus.). 32p. (gr. k-4). 1991. PLB 11.40 (*0-531-14087-3*) Watts.
—Living with Blindness. LC 89-9091. (Illus.). 32p. (gr. 5-8). 1989. PLB 12.40 (*0-531-10843-0*) Watts.
—Living with Heart Disease. LC 89-8979. (Illus.). 32p. (gr. 5-8). 1989. PLB 12.40 (*0-531-10845-7*) Watts.
—The Living World. Hull, Richard, illus. 48p. (gr. 3-6). 1992. pap. 2.95 (*1-56680-011-0*) Mad Hatter Pub.
—The Lungs & Breathing. rev. ed. Mayron-Parker, Alan, contrib. by. (Illus.). 48p. (gr. 5-6). 1989. PLB 12.90 (*0-531-10710-8*) Watts.
—The Lungs & Breathing. rev. ed. (Illus.). 48p. (gr. 5 up). 1991. pap. 5.95 (*0-531-24605-1*) Watts.
—Mammal. Burton, Jane & King, Dave, photos by. LC 88-22656. (Illus.). 64p. (gr. 5 up). 1989. 15.00 (*0-394-82258-7*); lib. bdg. 15.99 (*0-394-92258-1*) Knopf Bks Yng Read.
—Marie Curie & Radium. LC 92-3616. (Illus.). 32p. (gr. 3-7). 1992. 14.00 (*0-06-020847-3*); PLB 13.89 (*0-06-021472-4*) HarpC Child Bks.
—Marie Curie & Radium. Parker, Steve, illus. LC 92-3616. 32p. (gr. 3-7). 1992. pap. 5.95 (*0-06-446143-2*, Trophy) HarpC Child Bks.
—Mysterious Microbes. Orr, Chris, Illustration Staff & Savage, Ann, illus. LC 93-36476. 1994. write for info. (*0-8114-2344-1*) Raintree Steck-V.
—Nerves to Senses: Projects with Biology. (Illus.). 32p. (gr. 5-8). 1991. PLB 12.40 (*0-531-17295-3*, Gloucester Pr) Watts.
—Pond & River. Dowell, Philip, photos by. LC 88-1575. (Illus.). 64p. (gr. 5 up). 1988. 15.00 (*0-394-89615-7*); lib. bdg. 15.99 (*0-394-99615-1*) Knopf Bks Yng Read.
—Prehistoric Life. Sergio, illus. LC 92-54452. 64p. (gr. 3-7). 1993. 12.95 (*1-56458-238-8*) Dorling Kindersley.
—The Random House Book of How Nature Works. LC 92-14566. (Illus.). 128p. (gr. 3-7). 1993. PLB 19.99 (*0-679-93700-5*); pap. 15.00 (*0-679-83700-0*) Random Bks Yng Read.
—The Random House Book of How Things Work. LC 90-9137. (Illus.). 160p. (Orig.). (gr. 3-7). 1991. PLB 19.99 (*0-679-90908-7*); pap. 14.95 (*0-679-80908-2*) Random Bks Yng Read.
—Revolting Reptiles. Savage, Ann, illus. LC 92-43725. 38p. (gr. 3-6). 1992. PLB 19.97 (*0-8114-0692-X*) Raintree Steck-V.
—Rock & Minerals. LC 93-12643. (Illus.). 64p. (gr. 3-6). 1993. 9.95 (*1-56458-394-5*) Dorling Kindersley.
—Running a Race: How You Walk, Run & Jump. (Illus.). 32p. (gr. k-4). 1991. PLB 11.40 (*0-531-14096-2*) Watts.
—Scary Spiders. Savage, Ann, illus. LC 93-27876. 1993. write for info. (*0-8114-2345-X*) Raintree Steck-V.
—Seashore. King, Dave, illus. LC 88-27173. 64p. (gr. 5 up). 1989. 15.00 (*0-394-82254-4*); PLB 15.99 (*0-394-92254-9*) Knopf Bks Yng Read.
—Seashore. (Illus.). 48p. (gr. 7-9). 1992. 13.95 (*0-563-34410-5*, BBC-Parkwest); pap. 6.95 (*0-563-34411-3*, BBC-Parkwest) Parkwest Pubns.
—Singing a Song: How You Sing, Speak & Make Sounds. Kline, Marjory, ed. (Illus.). 32p. (gr. k-4). 1992. PLB 11.40 (*0-531-14212-4*) Watts.
—Skeleton. Dowell, Philip, photos by. LC 87-26314. (Illus.). 64p. (gr. 5 up). 1988. 15.00 (*0-394-89620-3*); lib. bdg. 15.99 (*0-394-99620-8*) Knopf Bks Yng Read.

—The Skeleton & Movement. rev. ed. LC 88-51608. (Illus.). 48p. (gr. 4-7). 1989. PLB 12.90 (*0-531-10709-4*) Watts.
—The Skeleton & Movement. rev. ed. (Illus.). 48p. (gr. 5 up). 1991. pap. 6.95 (*0-531-24606-X*) Watts.
—The Story of Dinosaurs. Forsey, Chris, illus. LC 91-39007. 32p. (gr. 1-4). 1993. PLB 11.89 (*0-8167-2707-4*); pap. text ed. 3.95 (*0-8167-2708-2*) Troll Assocs. Postponed.
—Thomas Edison & Electricity. LC 92-6805. (Illus.). 32p. (gr. 3-7). 1992. 14.00 (*0-06-020859-7*); PLB 13.89 (*0-06-021473-2*) HarpC Child Bks.
—Thomas Edison & Electricity. Parker, Steve, illus. LC 92-6805. 32p. (gr. 3-7). 1992. pap. 5.95 (*0-06-446144-0*, Trophy) HarpC Child Bks.
—Touch, Taste & Smell. rev. ed. Mayron-Parker, Alan, contrib. by. (Illus.). 48p. (gr. 5-6). 1989. PLB 12.90 (*0-531-10655-1*) Watts.
—Touch, Taste & Smell. rev. ed. (Illus.). 48p. (gr. 5 up). 1991. pap. 5.95 (*0-531-24607-8*) Watts.
—Touching a Nerve: How You Touch, Sense & Feel. (Illus.). 32p. (gr. k-4). 1992. PLB 11.40 (*0-531-14215-9*) Watts.
—Weather. Bull, Peter & Chen, Kuo K., illus. 40p. (gr. 5-8). 1990. PLB 12.90 (*0-531-19086-2*, Warwick) Watts.
Parker, Steve & Parker, Jane. Migration. LC 92-9831. 1992. 12.40 (*0-531-17311-9*, Gloucester Pr) Watts.
—Territories. LC 91-29820. (Illus.). 32p. (gr. 4-7). 1992. PLB 12.40 (*0-531-17310-0*, Gloucester Pr) Watts.
Parker, Violette & Mammen, Lori. TAAS Quick Review Reading: Grade 4. (Illus.). 96p. (gr. 3). 1992. pap. text ed. 12.95 (*0-944459-36-6*) ECS Lrn Systs.
Parkes, Brenda. Farmer Schnuck. Webb, Philip, illus. LC 92-31078. 1993. 4.25 (*0-383-03568-6*) SRA Schl Grp.
—One Foggy Night. Cullo, Ned, illus. LC 92-32514. 1993. 4.25 (*0-383-03588-0*) SRA Schl Grp.
Parkhurst, Carole. Visiting Tacoma. Hamer, Bonnie, illus. 24p. (Orig.). (gr. 1-4). 1983. pap. 2.75 (*0-933992-38-6*) Coffee Break.
Parkhurst, Christine, jt. auth. see Fellows, Marian.
Parkin, Rex. The Red Carpet. Parkin, Rex, illus. LC 92-19912. 48p. (gr. k-3). 1993. pap. 4.95 (*0-689-71678-8*, Aladdin) Macmillan Child Grp.
Parkin, Tom. Green Giants: Rainforests of the Pacific Northwest. (Illus.). 48p. (Orig.). (gr. 8-12). 1992. pap. 7.95 (*1-895565-07-3*) Firefly Bks Ltd.
Parkinson, Carolyn S. My Mommy Has Cancer. Verstraete, Elaine, illus. 20p. (ps-4). 1991. pap. 8.95 (*0-9630287-0-7*) Solace Pub.
Parkinson, Cornelia M. Alex Livingston, the Tomato Man. (Illus.). 20p. (gr. 4 up). 1985. pap. 1.50 (*0-938404-05-9*, AWL) Hist Tales.
Parkinson, Curtis. Tom Foolery. Bobak, Cathy, illus. LC 92-7852. 32p. (ps-2). 1993. RSBE 13.95 (*0-02-770025-9*, Bradbury Pr) Macmillan Child Grp.
Parkinson, Kathy, illus. The Enormous Turnip. LC 85-14432. 32p. (ps-1). 1985. 13.95 (*0-8075-2062-4*) A Whitman.
—The Farmer in the Dell. LC 87-25322. 32p. (ps-2). 1988. PLB 13.95 (*0-8075-2271-6*) A Whitman.
Parkinson, Robert W. Growing up on Purpose. 73p. 1989. Braille. Braille ed. 5.84 (*1-56956-248-2*) W A T Braille.
Parkis, Michael. Everything You Always Wanted to Know about Arithmetic. (gr. 4-8). 1987. 5.00 (*0-87879-804-8*, Ann Arbor Div) Acad Therapy.
Parkison, Jami. Pequena the Burro. Maeno, Itoko, illus. LC 93-30377. 32p. (gr. 1-4). 1994. 16.95 (*1-55942-055-3*, 7657); video, tchr's. guide & storybook 79.95 (*1-55942-058-8*, 9376) Marshfilm.
Parkison, Ralph F. Big Red & the Fence Post. Withrow, Marion O., ed. Bush, William, illus. 53p. (Orig.). (gr. 2-8). 1988. pap. write for info. Little Wood Bks.
—Days. Withrow, Marion O., ed. Bush, William, illus. 60p. (Orig.). (gr. 2-8). 1988. pap. write for info. Little Wood Bks.
—Eovl. Withrow, Marion O., ed. Bush, William, illus. 36p. (Orig.). (gr. 2-8). 1988. pap. write for info. Little Wood Bks.
—In the Middle of the Corn Patch. Withrow, Marion O., ed. Bush, William, illus. 55p. (Orig.). (gr. 2-8). 1988. pap. write for info. Little Wood Bks.
—The Little Flea. Withrow, Marion O., ed. Bush, William, illus. 21p. (Orig.). (gr. 2-8). 1988. pap. write for info. Little Wood Bks.
—The Little Girl & the Inchworm. Withrow, Marion O., ed. Bush, William, illus. 75p. (Orig.). (gr. 2-8). 1988. pap. write for info. Little Wood Bks.
—The Little Girl, the Lillipop, & the Green Bird, Bk. 1. Withrow, Marion O., ed. Bush, William, illus. 31p. (Orig.). (gr. 2-6). 1988. pap. 4.25 (*0-929949-00-5*) Little Wood Bks.
—The Old Goat. Withrow, Marion O., ed. Bush, William, illus. 112p. (Orig.). (gr. 2-8). 1988. pap. write for info. Little Wood Bks.
—The Pea in the Pod, Bk. 3. Withrow, Marion O., ed. Bush, William, illus. 10p. (Orig.). (gr. 2-6). 1988. pap. text ed. 3.00 (*0-929949-02-1*) Little Wood Bks.
—The Pencil. Withrow, Marion O., ed. Bush, William, illus. 47p. (Orig.). (gr. 2-8). 1988. pap. write for info. Little Wood Bks.
—Santa's Wheat Kernels. Withrow, Marion O., ed. Bush, William, illus. 60p. (Orig.). (gr. 2-8). 1988. pap. write for info. Little Wood Bks.
—Seeds & Seeds & Seeds. Withrow, Marion O., ed. Bush, William, illus. 65p. (Orig.). (gr. 2-8). 1988. pap. write for info. Little Wood Bks.

—The Soda Pop Can & the Road Sign, Bk. 4. Withrow, Marion O., ed. Bush, William, illus. 13p. (Orig.). (gr. 2-6). 1988. pap. text ed. 3.73 (0-929949-03-X) Little Wood Bks.
—The Spot on the Ground. Withrow, Marion O., ed. Bush, William, illus. 83p. (Orig.). (gr. 2-8). 1988. pap. write for info. Little Wood Bks.
—A This or a That. Withrow, Marion O., ed. Bush, William, illus. 53p. (Orig.). (gr. 2-8). 1988. pap. write for info. Little Wood Bks.
—The Twig & the Mouse, Bk. 2. Withrow, Marion O., ed. Bush, William, illus. 17p. (Orig.). (gr. 2-6). 1988. pap. 4.25 (0-929949-01-3) Little Wood Bks.
—Yodeling. Withrow, Marion O., ed. Bush, William, illus. 71p. (Orig.). (gr. 2-8). 1988. pap. write for info. Little Wood Bks.
Parkman, Francis. Oregon Trail. (gr. 6 up). 1964. pap. 1.50 (0-8049-0037-X, CL-37) Airmont.
—Oregon Trail. Guthrie, A. B., Jr., frwd. by. 288p. (RL 8). 1950. pap. 4.95 (0-451-52513-2, Sig Classics) NAL-Dutton.
Parks, Aileen W. Davy Crockett: Young Rifleman. Pearson, Justin, illus. LC 86-10781. 192p. (gr. 2-6). 1986. pap. 3.95 (0-02-041840-X, Aladdin) Macmillan Child Grp.
Parks, Barbara, jt. auth. see Catron, Carol.
Parks, Edd W. Teddy Roosevelt: Young Rough Rider. Morrow, Gray, illus. LC 89-37819. 192p. (gr. 2-6). 1989. pap. 3.95 (0-689-71349-5, Aladdin) Macmillan Child Grp.
Parks, James D. Robert S. Duncanson: Nineteenth Century Black Romantic Painter. 1990. 12.95 (0-87498-011-9) Assoc Pubs DC.
Parks, Joe E. Christmas Around the World. Date not set. 4.50 (0-685-68526-8, BCMC-45); cassette 9.98 (0-685-68527-6, BCTA-9034C) Lillenas.
—A Night to Remember. Date not set. 4.50 (0-685-68530-6, BCMC-249) Lillenas.
Parks, Rosa. Rosa Parks: Mother to a Movement. Haskins, Jim, contrib. by. LC 89-1124. (Illus.). 200p. 1992. 17.00 (0-8037-0673-1) Dial Bks Young.
Parks, Van D., ed. see Harris, Joel C.
Parlin, John. Amelia Earhart: Pioneer in the Sky. (Illus.). 80p. (gr. 2-6). 1992. Repr. of 1962 ed. lib. bdg. 12.95 (0-7910-1437-1) Chelsea Hse.
—Andrew Jackson: Pioneer & President. (Illus.). 80p. (gr. 2-6). 1991. Repr. of 1962 ed. lib. bdg. 12.95 (0-7910-1442-8) Chelsea Hse.
Parnall, Peter. Apple Tree. Parnall, Peter, illus. LC 86-23730. 32p. (gr. k-3). 1988. RSBE 14.95 (0-02-770160-3, Macmillan Child Bk) Macmillan Child Grp.
—Cats from Away. Parnall, Peter, illus. LC 88-30532. 32p. (ps up). 1989. RSBE 14.95 (0-02-770150-6, Macmillan Child Bk) Macmillan Child Grp.
—Feet! Parnall, Peter, illus. LC 88-5272. 32p. (ps-1). 1988. RSBE 14.95 (0-02-770110-7, Macmillan Child Bk) Macmillan Child Grp.
—Marsh Cat. Parnall, Peter, illus. LC 90-25733. 128p. (gr. 3 up). 1991. SBE 13.95 (0-02-770120-4, Macmillan Child Bk) Macmillan Child Grp.
—Quiet. Parnall, Peter, illus. LC 89-2847. 32p. 1989. 13.95 (0-688-08204-1); PLB 13.88 (0-688-08205-X, Morrow Jr Bks) Morrow Jr Bks.
—The Rock. Parnall, Peter, illus. LC 90-6021. 32p. (gr. k-3). 1991. RSBE 14.95 (0-02-770181-6, Macmillan Child Bk) Macmillan Child Grp.
—Spaces. LC 92-1712. (Illus.). 32p. (gr. k-3). 1993. PLB 14.90 (1-56294-336-7) Millbrook Pr.
—Stuffer. Parnall, Peter, illus. LC 90-26997. 32p. (gr. k-4). 1992. RSBE 14.95 (0-02-770152-2, Macmillan Child Bk) Macmillan Child Grp.
—Water Pup. Parnall, Peter, illus. LC 92-40850. 144p. (gr. 3 up). 1993. SBE 13.95 (0-02-770151-4, Macmillan Child Bk) Macmillan Child Grp.
—Woodpile. Parnall, Peter, illus. LC 89-29322. 32p. (gr. k-3). 1990. RSBE 14.95 (0-02-770155-7, Macmillan Child Bk) Macmillan Child Grp.
Parnell, Helga. Cooking the German Way. (Illus.). 48p. (gr. 5 up). 1988. PLB 14.95 (0-8225-0918-0) Lerner Pubns.
—Cooking the South American Way. (Illus.). 48p. (gr. 5 up). 1991. PLB 14.95 (0-8225-0925-3) Lerner Pubns.
Parolini, Stephen. Sermon on the Mount. (Illus.). 48p. (gr. 6-8). 1992. pap. 7.99 (1-55945-129-7) Group Pub.
—Today's Music: Good or Bad? 48p. (Orig.). (gr. 6-8). 1990. pap. 7.99 (1-55945-101-7) Group Pub.
Parolini, Stephen & Young, Christine. Peace & War. (Illus.). 48p. (gr. 6-8). 1991. pap. 7.99 (1-55945-123-8) Group Pub.
Parolini, Stephen, jt. auth. see Cabral, Brian.
Parolini, Stephen, ed. Peer Pressure. 48p. (Orig.). (gr. 6-8). 1990. pap. 7.99 (1-55945-103-3) Group Pub.
Parr, Frederique, ed. see Waggoner, Carmen.
Parr, John. Baby Animals. Parr, John, illus. LC 79-62943. (ps). 1979. 3.50 (0-394-84244-8) Random Bks Yng Read.
Parr, Letitia. A Man & His Hat. (Illus.). 32p. (ps-2). 1991. 13.95 (0-399-22255-3, Philomel Bks) Putnam Pub Group.
—When Sea & Sky Are Blue. Watts, John, illus. LC 78-151272. 32p. (ps-3). 7.95 (0-87592-059-4) Scroll Pr.
Parramon, J. M. Los Arboles Frutales. (ps-3). 1991. pap. 6.95 (0-8120-4714-1) Barron.
—El Bosque. (ps-3). 1991. pap. 6.95 (0-8120-4712-5) Barron.
—The Fascinating World of Ants. (Illus.). 48p. (gr. 3-7). 1991. pap. 7.95 (0-8120-4721-4) Barron.

—The Fascinating World of Bees. (Illus.). 48p. (gr. 3-7). 1991. pap. 6.95 (0-8120-4720-6) Barron.
—The Fascinating World of Butterflies. (Illus.). 48p. (gr. 3-7). 1991. pap. 7.95 (0-8120-4722-2) Barron.
—El Huerto. (ps-3). 1991. pap. 6.95 (0-8120-4716-8) Barron.
—El Jardin. (ps-3). 1991. pap. 6.95 (0-8120-4713-3) Barron.
—Mi Primera Vista a La Granja. 1990. pap. 5.95 (0-8120-4400-2) Barron.
—Mi Primera Vista al Aviario. 1990. pap. 5.95 (0-8120-4403-7) Barron.
—Mi Primera Vista al Zoo. 1990. pap. 5.95 (0-8120-4402-9) Barron.
—Mi Primeros Colores. (SPA.). (ps-3). 1991. pap. 6.95 (0-8120-4726-5) Barron.
—Mi Primeros Formas. (SPA.). (ps-3). 1991. pap. 6.95 (0-8120-4728-1) Barron.
—Mi Primeros Numeros. (SPA.). (ps-3). 1991. pap. 6.95 (0-8120-4727-3) Barron.
—My First Colors. (Illus.). 32p. (ps). 1991. pap. 5.95 (0-8120-4725-7) Barron.
—My First Numbers. (Illus.). 32p. (ps). 1991. pap. 5.95 (0-8120-4723-0) Barron.
—My First Series, 3 vols. (ps). 1991. Boxed set. pap. 17.95 (0-8120-7791-1) Barron.
—My First Shapes. (Illus.). 32p. (ps). 1991. pap. 5.95 (0-8120-4724-9) Barron.
—My First Visit to a Farm. 1990. pap. 5.95 (0-8120-4305-7) Barron.
—My First Visit to the Aquarium. Sales, G., illus. 32p. (ps). 1990. pap. 5.95 (0-8120-4304-9) Barron.
—My First Visit to the Aviary. Sales, G., illus. 32p. (ps). 1990. pap. 4.95 (0-8120-4303-0) Barron.
—My First Visit to the Zoo. Sales, G., illus. 32p. (ps). 1990. pap. 5.95 (0-8120-4302-2) Barron.
—Plants & Trees, 4 vols. (ps-3). 1991. Boxed set. pap. 23.95 (0-8120-7771-7) Barron.
Parramon, J. M. & Puig, J. J. Hearing. Rius, Maria, illus. 32p. (Orig.). (ps). 1985. pap. 5.95 ea.; pap. 6.95 (0-8120-3563-1) Span. ed (0-8120-3606-9) Barron.
—Sight. Rius, Maria, illus. 32p. (Orig.). (ps). 1985. pap. 5.95 (0-8120-3564-X); pap. 6.95 Spanish ed. (0-8120-3605-0) Barron.
—Smell. Rius, Maria, illus. 32p. (ps). 1985. pap. 5.95 (0-8120-3565-8); pap. 6.95 (0-8120-3607-7) Span. ed. Barron.
—Taste. Rius, Maria, illus. 32p. (ps). 1985. pap. 5.95 (0-8120-3566-6); Span. ed. pap. 6.95 (0-8120-3608-5) Barron.
—Touch. Rius, Maria, illus. 32p. (Orig.). (ps). 1985. pap. 5.95 (0-8120-3567-4); Span. ed. pap. 6.95 (0-8120-3609-3) Barron.
Parramon, J. M. & Rius, Maria. Life in the Air. 32p. (gr. 3-5). 1987. Eng. ed. pap. 5.95 (0-8120-3863-0); Span. ed.: La Vida en el Aire. pap. 6.95 (0-8120-3867-3) Barron.
—Life in the Sea. 32p. (gr. 3-5). 1987. Eng. ed. pap. 6.95 (0-8120-3865-7); Span. ed.: La Vida en el Mar. pap. 5.95 (0-8120-3869-X) Barron.
—Life on the Land. 32p. (gr. 3-5). 1987. Eng. ed. pap. 5.95 (0-8120-3864-9); Span. ed.: La Vida Sobre la Tierra. pap. 6.95 (0-8120-3868-1) Barron.
—Life Underground. 32p. (gr. 3-5). 1987. pap. 5.95 ea.; Eng. ed. pap. 5.95 (0-8120-3862-2); Span. ed.: La Vida Bajo la Tierra. pap. 6.95 (0-8120-3866-5) Barron.
Parramon, J. M. & Vendrell, C. S. El Fuego. (SPA.). 32p. (ps). 1985. pap. 6.95 (0-8120-3619-0) Barron.
Parramon, J. M., jt. auth. see Rius, Maria.
Parramon, J. M., et al. El Verano. (SPA.). (ps). 1986. pap. 6.95 (0-8120-3645-X) Barron.
—Five Senses, 5 bks. (ps). 1985. pap. 29.95 boxed set (0-8120-7365-7) Barron.
—El Agua. (SPA.). 32p. (ps). 1985. pap. 6.95 (0-8120-3621-2) Barron.
—Air. 32p. (ps). 1985. pap. 5.95 (0-8120-3597-6) Barron.
—El Aire. (SPA.). 32p. (ps). 1985. pap. 6.95 (0-8120-3620-4) Barron.
—Children. 32p. (gr. 3-5). 1987. pap. 6.95 ea.; Eng. ed. pap. 6.95 (0-8120-3850-9); Span. ed.: Los Ninos. pap. 5.95 (0-8120-3854-1) Barron.
—Earth. 32p. (ps). 1985. pap. 6.95 (0-8120-3596-8) Barron.
—The Four Elements, 4 Bks. (ps). 1985. boxed set 23.95 (0-8120-7367-3) Barron.
—Grandparents. 32p. (gr. 3-5). 1987. Eng. ed. pap. 4.95 (0-8120-3853-3); Span. ed.: Los Abuelos. pap. 6.95 (0-8120-3857-6) Barron.
—Parents. 32p. (gr. 3-5). 1987. Eng. ed. pap. 6.95 (0-8120-3852-5); Span. ed.: Los Padres. pap. 5.95 (0-8120-3856-8) Barron.
—La Primavera. (SPA.). (ps). 1986. pap. 6.95 (0-8120-3648-4) Barron.
—Teenagers. 32p. (gr. 3-5). 1987. Eng. ed. pap. 3.95 (0-8120-3851-7); Span. ed.: Los Jovenes. pap. 6.95 (0-8120-3855-X) Barron.
—La Tierra. (SPA.). 32p. (ps). 1985. pap. 6.95 (0-8120-3618-2) Barron.
—Water. 32p. (ps). 1985. pap. 6.95 (0-8120-3599-2) Barron.
Parramon, Josep M., jt. auth. see Rius, Maria.
Parramon, Merce. How Our Blood Circulates. (Illus.). 1994. 13.95 (0-7910-2127-0, Am Art Analog) Chelsea Hse.
Parramore, Barbara & Hopke, Bill. Activities for the Children's Dictionary of Occupations. rev. ed. Jones, Scott, illus. 20p. (gr. 3-4). 1992. wkbk. 12.95 (1-56191-191-7) Meridian Educ.

—Activities for the Children's Dictionary of Occupations. rev. ed. Jones, Scott, illus. 20p. (gr. 5-6). 1992. wkbk. 12.95 (1-56191-192-5) Meridian Educ.
—The Children's Dictionary of Occupations. rev. ed. Jones, Scott, illus. 130p. (gr. 3-8). 1992. pap. text ed. 12.95 (1-56191-190-9) Meridian Educ.
Parramore, Barbara & Hopke, William E. Career Exploration Activities Booklet: 25 Activities to Help Explore Occupations. 48p. (Orig.). (gr. 6 up). 1989. pap. text ed. 17.75 pkg. of 10 (0-685-31414-6) Careers Inc.
Parrett, Sherii & Brown, Sylvia. Slippy Cleans Up. (Illus.). 24p. (Orig.). (ps-6). 1992. pap. 5.99 (1-56722-002-9) Word Aflame.
Parris, Paula. Ruth: Woman of Courage. Cassell, Robert, illus. (gr. 1-6). 1977. bds. 5.95 (0-8054-4229-4, 4242-29) Broadman.
Parrish, Annette, ed. see Finley, Tom.
Parrish, Rhett. Puppy Dogs Polka at the Kitty Cat Carnival: A Music Gift Set with a Fun Approach to Learning. 48p. (ps-2). 1991. incl. 2 cass. 14.95 (0-9632433-0-6) RPM Record.
Parrot, Andrea. Coping with Date Rape & Acquaintance Rape. rev. ed. Rosen, Roger, ed. (gr. 7 up). 1993. PLB 13.95 (0-8239-1649-9); pap. 8.95 (0-8239-0808-9) Rosen Group.
Parry, Alan. Bruno Makes Friends. LC 91-70402. 16p. (ps-3). 1991. pap. 1.49 (0-8066-2530-9, 9-2530) Augsburg Fortress.
Parry, Alan & Parry, Linda. Baby Jesus. Parry, Alan, illus. 24p. (ps). 1990. pap. 0.99 (0-8066-2478-7, 9-2478) Augsburg Fortress.
—Baby Moses. Parry, Alan, illus. 24p. (ps). 1990. pap. 0.99 (0-8066-2477-9, 9-2477) Augsburg Fortress.
—The Beginning. (Illus.). 24p. (ps). 1990. pap. 0.99 (0-8066-2473-6, 9-2473) Augsburg Fortress.
—Bruno Helps Out. Parry, Alan & Parry, Linda, illus. LC 91-70401. 16p. (ps-k). 1991. bds. 1.49 (0-8066-2528-7, 9-2528, Augsburg) Augsburg Fortress.
—Bruno Is Sorry. Parry, Alan & Parry, Linda, illus. LC 91-70402. 16p. (ps-k). 1991. bds. 1.49 (0-8066-2529-5, 9-2529, Augsburg) Augsburg Fortress.
—Bruno Makes Friends. Parry, Alan & Parry, Linda, illus. LC 91-70402. 16p. (ps-k). 1991. bds. 1.49 (0-685-59565-X, 9-2530, Augsburg) Augsburg Fortress.
—Bruno Says Thanks. Parry, Alan & Parry, Linda, illus. LC 91-70404. 16p. (ps-k). 1991. bds. 1.49 (0-8066-2531-7, 9-2531, Augsburg) Augsburg Fortress.
—Caleb & Katie's Big Book of Bible Adventures. (Illus.). 64p. (gr. k-5). 1993. 12.99 (0-8499-0982-1) Word Inc.
—The Farmer & the Seed. Parry, Alan, illus. 24p. (ps). 1990. pap. 0.99 (0-8066-2474-4, 9-2474) Augsburg Fortress.
—Jesus is Alive! Parry, Alan, illus. 24p. (ps). 1990. pap. 0.99 (0-8066-2479-5, 9-2479) Augsburg Fortress.
—Joseph & His Coat. Parry, Alan, illus. 24p. (ps). 1990. pap. 0.99 (0-8066-2476-0, 9-2476) Augsburg Fortress.
—Noah & the Ark. Parry, Alan, illus. 24p. (ps). 1990. pap. 0.99 (0-8066-2475-2, 9-2475) Augsburg Fortress.
—Paul Meets Jesus. Parry, Alan, illus. 24p. (ps). 1990. pap. 0.99 (0-8066-2480-9, 9-2480) Augsburg Fortress.
Parry, Alan, jt. auth. see Parry, Linda.
Parry, Caroline, compiled by. Zoomerang a Boomerang: Poems to Make Your Belly Laugh. Martchenko, Michael, illus. LC 92-26589. 32p. (ps-3). 1993. pap. 4.99 (0-14-054869-6) Puffin Bks.
Parry, Cindy. Activities That Build Young Women, Vol. 2. 48p. 1993. pap. 6.98 (0-88290-457-4) Horizon Utah.
Parry, Linda & Parry, Alan. Jacob & Esau. Parry, Linda & Parry, Alan, illus. LC 90-80555. 24p. (Orig.). (ps-2). 1990. pap. 1.99 (0-8066-2490-6, 9-2490, Augsburg) Augsburg Fortress.
—Jesus & You. Parry, Linda & Parry, Alan, illus. LC 91-71033. 10p. (ps-k). 1991. 3.99 (0-8066-2557-0, 9-2557, Augsburg) Augsburg Fortress.
—Jesus Loves You. Parry, Linda & Parry, Alan, illus. LC 91-71034. 10p. 1991. 5.99 (0-8066-2558-9, 9-2558, Augsburg) Augsburg Fortress.
—Joseph & His Brothers. Parry, Linda & Parry, Alan, illus. LC 90-80557. 24p. (Orig.). (ps-2). 1990. pap. 1.99 (0-8066-2488-4, 9-2488, Augsburg) Augsburg Fortress.
—Martha & Mary. Parry, Linda & Parry, Alan, illus. LC 90-80558. 24p. (Orig.). (ps-2). 1990. pap. 1.99 (0-8066-2487-6, 9-2487, Augsburg) Augsburg Fortress.
—Miriam & Moses. Parry, Linda & Parry, Alan, illus. LC 90-80556. 24p. (Orig.). (ps-2). 1990. pap. 1.95 (0-8066-2489-2, 9-2489, Augsburg) Augsburg Fortress.
—Wonderful Jesus! A Pop-up Activity Book. (Illus.). 12p. 1993. 15.99 (0-7847-0045-1, 24-03643) Standard Pub.
—Wonderful You. LC 92-9872. (Illus.). 1992. 14.99 (0-8407-7720-5) Oliver-Nelson.
Parry, Linda, jt. auth. see Parry, Alan.
Parry, Marian, illus. City Mouse - Country Mouse & Two More Mouse Tales from Aesop. (gr. 2-3). 1989. big bk. 28.67 (0-590-65228-1) Scholastic Inc.
Parry-Jones, Jemima. Amazing Birds of Prey. Dunning, Mike, photos by. LC 92-909. (Illus.). 32p. (Orig.). (gr. 1-5). 1992. PLB 9.99 (0-679-92771-9); pap. 7.99 (0-679-82771-4) Knopf Bks Yng Read.
Parsley, Bonnie M. The Choice Is Yours: A Teenager's Guide to Self-Discovery, Relationships, Values, & Spiritual Growth. 160p. (Orig.). 1992. pap. 9.00 (0-671-75046-1, Fireside) S&S Trade.
Parsley, Reed. Sugar Ships. LC 91-16984. (Illus.). 1991. 12.95 (0-671-74956-0, Green Tiger) S&S Trade.

Parsons, Alexandra. Amazing Birds. (ps-3). 1990. PLB 9.99 (*0-679-90223-6*); pap. 7.99 (*0-679-80223-1*) Knopf Bks Yng Read.
—Amazing Cats. Young, Jerry, photos by. LC 90-31885. (Illus.). 32p. (Orig.). (gr. 1-5). 1990. lib. bdg. 9.99 (*0-679-90690-8*); pap. 7.99 (*0-679-80690-3*) Knopf Bks Yng Read.
—Amazing Mammals. Young, Jerry, photos by. LC 89-38831. (Illus.). 32p. (gr. 1-5). 1990. 6.95 (*0-679-90224-X*); PLB 9.99 (*0-679-90224-4*) Random Bks Yng Read.
—Amazing Poisonous Animals. Young, Jerry, photos by. LC 90-31883. 32p. (Orig.). (gr. 1-5). 1990. lib. bdg. 9.99 (*0-679-90699-1*); pap. 6.95 (*0-679-80699-7*) Knopf Bks Yng Read.
—Amazing Snakes. Young, Jerry, photos by. LC 89-38944. (Illus.). 32p. (gr. 1-5). 1990. 7.99 (*0-679-80225-8*); PLB 9.99 (*0-679-90225-2*) Random Bks Yng Read.
—Amazing Spiders. Young, Jerry, photos by. LC 89-38833. (Illus.). 32p. (gr. 1-5). 1990. 7.99 (*0-679-80226-6*); PLB 9.99 (*0-679-90226-0*) Random Bks Yng Read.
Parsons, Judith. Math-a-Draw, 6 vols. Incl. Vol. I. Math-a-Draw. (gr. k-2). pap. 8.95 (*0-8224-4569-7*); Vol. II. Math-a-Draw. (gr. 1-3). pap. 8.95 (*0-8224-4570-0*); Vol. III. Math-a-Draw. (gr. 2-4). pap. 8.95 (*0-8224-4571-9*); Vol. IV. Math-a-Draw. (gr. 3-5). pap. 8.95 (*0-8224-4572-7*); Vol. V. Math-a-Draw. (gr. 3-5). pap. 8.95 (*0-8224-4573-5*); Vol. VI. Math-a-Draw. pap. 8.95 (*0-8224-4574-3*). (gr. 1-6). 1983. pap. Fearon Teach Aids.
Parsons, Mary P. Farmer Brown's Friends. Geurts, Kelly, illus. LC 90-71980. 65p. (Orig.). 1992. pap. 8.00 (*1-56002-040-7*) Aegina Pr.
Partee, Phillip E. The Layman's Guide to Fasting & Losing Weight: Introduced by Dick Gregory. Levy, H. M., Jr., ed. Gregory, Dick, intro. by. LC 78-64863. (Illus., Orig.). (gr. 10-12). 1979. pap. text ed. 4.95 (*0-685-94383-6*) United Pr.
Partin, Charlotte C. Daydreams & Sunbeams: An Album of Framable Word Pictures. Partin, Robin C., illus. 18p. (Orig.). (gr. 7 up). 1987. pap. 4.00 (*0-9619816-0-1*) C C Partin.
Parton, Dolly. Coat of Many Colors. Sutton, Judith, illus. LC 93-3866. 1994. 14.00 (*0-06-023413-X*, HarpT); PLB 13.89 (*0-06-023414-8*) HarpC.
Parton, Mary F., ed. see Jones, Mother.
Pasachoff, Naomi. Basic Judaism for Young People, Vol. 1: Israel. 150p. (gr. 4-5). 1987. pap. text ed. 7.95 (*0-87441-423-7*); By Lesley Silverstone. student activity bk., 90pgs. 4.25x (*0-87441-440-7*) Behrman.
—Basic Judaism for Young People, Vol 2: Torah. 150p. (gr. 5-6). 1986. pap. text ed. 7.95 (*0-87441-424-5*); By Lois M. Cohn. student activity bk., 92pps. 4.25x (*0-87441-442-3*) Behrman.
—Basic Judaism for Young People, Vol. 3: God. (gr. 6-7). 7.95 (*0-317-70146-0*); tchr's guide & dupl. masters 12.50 (*0-317-70147-9*); student activity bk. 4.25 (*0-317-70148-7*) Behrman.
Pasamanick, Judith & Thoms, Judith J. Folk Tales Told Around the World. Hudson, Carol, illus. LC 92-47128. 48p. (gr. 4-6). 1993. PLB 13.98 (*0-382-24363-3*); 11.98 (*0-382-24372-2*) Silver Burdett Pr.
Pasca, Sue-Rhee. Your First Canary. (Illus.). 36p. (Orig.). 1991. pap. 1.95 (*0-86622-059-3*, YF-103) TFH Pubns.
Pascal, Francine. Against the Odds. large type ed. 151p. (gr. 5-8). 1989. Repr. of 1988 ed. PLB 10.50 (*1-55905-016-0*, Dist. by Gareth Stevens); 9.50 (*1-55905-006-3*, Dist. by Gareth Stevens) Grey Castle.
—Against the Rules. 1987. pap. 3.25 (*0-553-15676-4*) Bantam.
—All Night Long. large type ed. 134p. (gr. 5-8). 1989. Repr. of 1984 ed. PLB 10.50 (*1-55905-014-4*, Dist. by Gareth Stevens); 9.50 (*1-55905-004-7*) Grey Castle.
—Almost Married. (gr. 7 up). 1994. pap. 3.50 (*0-553-29859-3*) Bantam.
—Alone in the Crowd. 1986. pap. 2.99 (*0-553-28087-2*) Bantam.
—Amy Moves In. (gr. 4-7). 1991. pap. 3.25 (*0-553-15837-6*) Bantam.
—Amy's Pen Pal. 1990. pap. 3.25 (*0-553-15772-8*) Bantam.
—Amy's True Love. 1991. pap. 2.99 (*0-553-28963-2*) Bantam.
—Anything for Love. 1994. pap. 3.50 (*0-553-56311-4*) Bantam.
—April Fool! 1989. pap. 3.25 (*0-553-15688-8*) Bantam.
—Are We in Love. 1993. pap. 3.25 (*0-553-29851-8*) Bantam.
—The Arrest. 1993. pap. 3.50 (*0-553-29853-4*) Bantam.
—Best Friends. 112p. (Orig.). (gr. 7-12). 1986. pap. 3.25 (*0-553-15655-1*, Skylark) Bantam.
—The Best Thanksgiving Ever. (ps-3). 1992. pap. 2.99 (*0-553-48007-3*) Bantam.
—Beware the Babysitter. 1993. pap. 3.50 (*0-553-29856-9*) Bantam.
—The Big Party Weekend. (gr. 4-7). 1991. pap. 3.25 (*0-553-15952-6*) Bantam.
—The Big Race. (ps-3). 1993. pap. 2.99 (*0-553-48011-1*) Bantam.
—Booster Boycott. (gr. 4-7). 1991. pap. 2.99 (*0-553-15933-X*) Bantam.
—Bossy Steven. (ps-3). 1991. pap. 2.99 (*0-553-15881-3*) Bantam.
—Boy Trouble. 1990. pap. 2.95 (*0-553-28317-0*) Bantam.
—Boys Against Girls. 1988. pap. 3.25 (*0-553-15666-7*) Bantam.

—Brooke & Her Rock Star Mom. 1992. pap. 3.25 (*0-553-15965-8*) Bantam.
—Buried Treasure. 1987. pap. 3.25 (*0-553-15692-6*) Bantam.
—The Carnival Ghost. (gr. 3-7). 1990. pap. 3.50 (*0-553-15859-7*) Bantam.
—Caroline's Halloween Spell. (ps-3). 1992. pap. 2.99 (*0-553-48006-5*) Bantam.
—Carolyn's Mystery Dolls. (gr. 4-7). 1991. pap. 2.99 (*0-553-15870-8*) Bantam.
—The Case of the Christmas Thief. (ps-3). 1992. pap. 3.25 (*0-553-48063-4*) Bantam.
—Case of the Haunted Camp. (gr. 4-7). 1992. pap. 3.25 (*0-553-15894-5*) Bantam.
—The Case of the Hidden Treasure. (gr. 1-3). 1993. pap. 3.25 (*0-553-48064-2*) Bantam.
—The Case of the Magic Christmas Bell. (ps-3). 1991. pap. 2.99 (*0-553-15964-X*) Bantam.
—The Case of the Million-Dollar Diamonds. (ps-3). 1993. pap. 3.25 (*0-553-48115-0*) Bantam.
—The Case of the Secret Santa. (gr. k-3). 1990. pap. 3.25 (*0-553-15860-0*) Bantam.
—Center of Attention. 1988. pap. 2.50 (*0-553-15581-4*, Skylark) Bantam.
—The Charm School Mystery. (gr. 4-7). 1992. pap. 3.25 (*0-553-48050-2*) Bantam.
—Cheating to Win. 1991. pap. 2.99 (*0-553-29145-9*) Bantam.
—Choosing Sides. 1986. pap. 2.99 (*0-553-15658-6*) Bantam.
—Christmas Ghost. (gr. 7-12). 1990. pap. write for info. Bantam.
—A Christmas Without Elizabeth. (gr. 4-7). 1993. pap. 3.75 (*0-553-15947-X*) Bantam.
—Ciao, Sweet Valley! (gr. 4-7). 1992. pap. 3.25 (*0-553-15940-2*) Bantam.
—Claim to Fame. (gr. 7 up). 1988. pap. 2.75 (*0-553-15624-1*) Bantam.
—Class Trip. (Orig.). (gr. 7 up). 1988. pap. 3.50 (*0-553-15588-1*) Bantam.
—College Girls. (gr. 6 up). 1993. pap. 3.50 (*0-553-56308-4*) Bantam.
—Cousin Kelly's Family Secret. (ps-3). 1991. pap. 2.99 (*0-553-15920-8*) Bantam.
—Crybaby Lois. (gr. 4 up). 1990. pap. 2.99 (*0-553-15818-X*) Bantam.
—The Curse of the Ruby Necklace. (gr. 4-7). 1993. pap. 3.50 (*0-553-15949-6*) Bantam.
—Dangerous Love. (gr. 7 up). 1984. pap. 3.25 (*0-553-27741-3*) Bantam.
—Danny Means Trouble. (gr. 3-6). 1990. pap. 3.25 (*0-553-15806-6*) Bantam.
—Date with a Werewolf. 1994. pap. 3.50 (*0-553-56228-2*) Bantam.
—The Dating Game. 1991. pap. 2.99 (*0-553-29187-4*) Bantam.
—Deadly Summer. 1989. pap. 3.50 (*0-553-28010-4*) Bantam.
—Dear Sister. (gr. 7 up). 1984. pap. 3.25 (*0-553-27672-7*) Bantam.
—Deceptions. 1984. pap. 3.25 (*0-553-27939-4*) Bantam.
—Decisions. (gr. 6 up). 1988. pap. 2.99 (*0-553-27278-0*) Bantam.
—Don't Go Home with John. 1993. pap. 3.50 (*0-553-29236-6*) Bantam.
—Double Jeopardy. 214p. (Orig.). (gr. 7-12). 1987. pap. 3.50 (*0-553-26905-4*) Bantam.
—Double Love. large type ed. 186p. (gr. 5-8). 1989. Repr. of 1983 ed. PLB 10.50 (*1-55905-010-1*, Dist. by Gareth Stevens); 9.50 (*1-55905-000-4*) Grey Castle.
—Dreams of Forever. 208p. (gr. 7 up). 1988. pap. 2.95 (*0-553-26700-0*, Starfire) Bantam.
—Elizabeth & Jessica Run Away. 1992. pap. 2.99 (*0-553-48004-9*) Bantam.
—Elizabeth Betrayed. 1992. pap. 3.25 (*0-553-29235-8*) Bantam.
—Elizabeth the Hero. (gr. 4-7). 1993. pap. 3.25 (*0-553-48060-X*) Bantam.
—Elizabeth the Impossible. 144p. 1991. pap. 3.25 (*0-553-15927-5*) Bantam.
—Elizabeth's Broken Arm. (ps-3). 1993. pap. 2.99 (*0-553-48009-X*) Bantam.
—Elizabeth's First Kiss. (gr. 4-7). 1990. pap. 3.25 (*0-553-15835-X*) Bantam.
—Elizabeth's New Hero. 1989. pap. 3.25 (*0-553-15753-1*) Bantam.
—Elizabeth's Piano Lessons. (ps-3). 1994. pap. 2.99 (*0-553-48102-9*) Bantam.
—Elizabeth's Super-Selling Lemonade. 1990. pap. 2.99 (*0-553-15807-4*) Bantam.
—Elizabeth's Valentine, No. 4. 1990. pap. 2.99 (*0-553-15761-2*) Bantam.
—Elizabeth's Video Fever. (ps-3). 1993. pap. 2.99 (*0-553-48010-3*) Bantam.
—Ellen Is Home Alone. (ps-3). 1993. pap. 2.99 (*0-553-48013-8*) Bantam.
—Enid's Story. (gr. 7 up). 1990. pap. 3.50 (*0-553-28576-9*) Bantam.
—Family Secrets. 160p. (Orig.). (gr. 7 up). 1988. pap. 2.99 (*0-553-27176-8*) Bantam.
—Fearless Elizabeth. (gr. 4-7). 1991. pap. 2.99 (*0-553-15844-9*) Bantam.
—Forbidden Love. 1987. pap. 2.99 (*0-553-27521-6*) Bantam.
—Forever & Always. 176p. (gr. 6 up). 1988. pap. 2.95 (*0-553-26788-4*, Starfire) Bantam.
—Friend Against Friend. (gr. 9-12). 1990. pap. 3.50 (*0-553-28636-6*) Bantam.

—Get the Teacher! (ps-3). 1994. pap. 2.99 (*0-553-48106-1*) Bantam.
—Ghost in Bell Tower. (gr. 4-7). 1992. pap. 3.50 (*0-553-15893-7*) Bantam.
—The Ghost of Tricia Martin. 1990. pap. 3.25 (*0-553-28487-8*) Bantam.
—Ghosts in the Graveyard. (gr. 4-7). 1990. pap. 3.50 (*0-553-15801-5*) Bantam.
—Girl They Both Loved. 1991. pap. 3.25 (*0-553-29226-9*) Bantam.
—Good-bye, Eva? (ps-3). 1993. pap. 2.99 (*0-553-48012-X*) Bantam.
—The Great Boyfriend Switch. (gr. 4-7). 1993. pap. 3.25 (*0-553-48053-7*) Bantam.
—The Hand-Me-Down Kid. 176p. (gr. k-6). 1982. pap. 2.95 (*0-440-43449-1*, YB) Dell.
—The Hand-Me-Down Kid. LC 79-5462. (gr. 5-9). 1980. pap. 12.95 (*0-670-35969-6*) Viking Child Bks.
—The Hand-Me-Down Kid. 176p. (gr. 3-7). 1990. pap. 2.75 (*0-590-43391-1*) Scholastic Inc.
—Hangin' out with Cici. 160p. (gr. 5 up). 1985. pap. 2.95 (*0-440-93364-1*, LFL) Dell.
—Hangin' Out with Cici. (gr. 4-7). 1991. pap. 3.95 (*0-14-034885-9*, Puffin) Puffin Bks.
—Haunted House. 1986. pap. 3.25 (*0-553-15657-8*) Bantam.
—Head over Heels. (Orig.). (gr. 5). 1985. pap. 3.25 (*0-553-27444-9*) Bantam.
—Heartbreaker. 176p. (gr. 7 up). 1984. pap. 2.99 (*0-553-27569-0*) Bantam.
—Holiday Mischief. 144p. 1988. pap. 3.75 (*0-553-15641-1*, Skylark) Bantam.
—Hostage! 1986. pap. 3.25 (*0-553-27670-0*) Bantam.
—In Love Again. (gr. 7 up). 1989. pap. 2.99 (*0-553-28193-3*) Bantam.
—In Love with a Prince. 1993. pap. 3.25 (*0-553-29237-4*) Bantam.
—Jealous Lies. 144p. (Orig.). (gr. 7-12). 1986. pap. 2.75 (*0-553-25816-8*) Bantam.
—Jealous Lies. 1986. pap. 3.25 (*0-553-27558-5*) Bantam.
—Jessica Against Bruce. 1992. pap. 3.25 (*0-553-29232-3*) Bantam.
—Jessica & Jumbo. (ps-3). 1991. pap. 2.99 (*0-553-15936-4*) Bantam.
—Jessica & the Brat Attack. 1989. pap. 2.75 (*0-553-15695-0*) Bantam.
—Jessica & the Earthquake. (gr. 4-7). 1994. pap. 3.25 (*0-553-48061-8*) Bantam.
—Jessica & the Money Mix-Up. (gr. 4-7). 1990. pap. 3.25 (*0-553-15798-1*) Bantam.
—Jessica & the Secret Star. (gr. 4-7). 1991. pap. 3.25 (*0-553-15911-9*) Bantam.
—Jessica & the Spelling Bee Surprise. 80p. 1991. pap. 2.99 (*0-553-15917-8*) Bantam.
—Jessica Gets Spooked. (ps-3). 1993. pap. 2.99 (*0-553-48094-4*) Bantam.
—Jessica Saves the Trees. (gr. 4-7). 1993. pap. 3.25 (*0-553-15946-1*) Bantam.
—Jessica the Babysitter. (gr. 4-7). 1991. pap. 2.99 (*0-553-15838-4*) Bantam.
—Jessica the Nerd. 1992. pap. 3.25 (*0-553-15963-1*) Bantam.
—Jessica the Rock Star. (gr. 5 up). 1989. pap. 3.25 (*0-553-15766-3*) Bantam.
—Jessica the Thief. (gr. 4-7). 1993. pap. 3.25 (*0-553-48054-5*) Bantam.
—Jessica the TV Star. (ps-3). 1991. pap. 2.99 (*0-553-15850-3*) Bantam.
—Jessica's Big Mistake. (ps-3). 1990. pap. 2.99 (*0-553-15799-X*) Bantam.
—Jessica's Christmas Carol. (gr. 4-6). 1989. pap. 3.50 (*0-553-15767-1*) Bantam.
—Jessica's Monster Nightmare. (gr. 1-3). 1993. pap. 2.99 (*0-553-48008-1*) Bantam.
—Jessica's New Look. (gr. 4-7). 1991. pap. 3.25 (*0-553-15869-4*) Bantam.
—Jessica's Secret. (gr. 4-7). 1990. pap. 3.25 (*0-553-15824-4*) Bantam.
—Jessica's Snobby. 1992. pap. 2.99 (*0-553-15922-4*) Bantam.
—Jessica's Unburied Treasure. (ps-3). 1992. pap. 2.99 (*0-553-15926-7*) Bantam.
—Jessica's Zoo Adventure. (ps-3). 1990. pap. 2.99 (*0-553-15802-3*) Bantam.
—Keeping Secrets. 96p. (Orig.). 1987. pap. 3.25 (*0-553-15702-7*, Skylark) Bantam.
—Kidnapped! 160p. (Orig.). 1984. pap. 3.25 (*0-553-27877-0*) Bantam.
—Kidnapped by a Cult. 1992. pap. 3.25 (*0-553-29228-5*) Bantam.
—Last Chance. 1987. pap. 3.50 (*0-553-27662-X*) Bantam.
—Left Back. 1992. pap. 2.99 (*0-553-48005-7*) Bantam.
—Left Behind. 112p. (Orig.). 1988. pap. 3.25 (*0-553-15609-8*, Skylark) Bantam.
—Left-Out Elizabeth. (ps-3). 1992. pap. 2.99 (*0-553-15921-6*) Bantam.
—Lila's Haunted House Party. (gr. 4-7). 1991. pap. 2.99 (*0-553-15919-4*) Bantam.
—Lila's Music Video. (gr. 4-7). 1993. pap. 3.25 (*0-553-48059-6*) Bantam.
—Lila's Secret, No. 6. 1990. pap. 2.99 (*0-553-15773-6*) Bantam.
—Lila's Story. (gr. 7 up). 1989. pap. 3.50 (*0-553-28296-4*) Bantam.
—Lois Strikes Back. 1990. pap. 2.99 (*0-553-15789-2*) Bantam.
—The Long, Lost Brother. 1991. pap. 3.25 (*0-553-29214-5*) Bantam.

—Love & Betrayal & Hold the Mayo! (gr. 5-9). 1986. pap. 2.95 (*0-440-94735-9*, LFL) Dell.
—Love Letters. 160p. (gr. 6 up). 1985. pap. 2.75 (*0-553-26883-X*) Bantam.
—Love Letters. 1985. pap. 3.25 (*0-553-27931-9*) Bantam.
—Love Letters for Sale. (gr. 4-7). 1992. pap. 3.25 (*0-553-29234-X*) Bantam.
—Love, Lies & Jessica Wakefield. 1993. pap. 3.50 (*0-553-56306-8*) Bantam.
—The Love Potion. (gr. 4-6). 1993. pap. 3.25 (*0-553-48058-8*) Bantam.
—Lovestruck. 160p. (Orig.). (gr. 7-12). 1986. pap. 2.75 (*0-553-26750-7*) Bantam.
—Lovestruck. 1986. pap. 2.99 (*0-553-27885-1*) Bantam.
—Lucky Takes the Reins. (gr. 4-7). 1991. pap. 3.25 (*0-553-15843-0*) Bantam.
—Mademoiselle Jessica. (gr. 4-7). 1991. pap. 3.25 (*0-553-15849-X*) Bantam.
—The Magic Christmas. (gr. 4-7). 1992. pap. 3.75 (*0-553-48051-0*) Bantam.
—Malibu Summer. 208p. (Orig.). (gr. 4). 1986. pap. 3.50 (*0-553-26050-2*) Bantam.
—Mansy Miller Fights Back. (gr. 4-7). 1991. pap. 3.25 (*0-553-15880-5*) Bantam.
—Mary Is Missing. 1990. pap. 3.25 (*0-553-15778-7*) Bantam.
—Memories. 1985. pap. 2.99 (*0-553-27492-9*) Bantam.
—The Middle School Gets Married. (gr. 4-7). 1993. pap. 3.25 (*0-553-48055-3*) Bantam.
—Miss Teen Sweet Valley. 1991. pap. 3.25 (*0-553-29060-6*) Bantam.
—The Missing Tea Set. (gr. 1-3). 1993. pap. 2.99 (*0-553-48015-4*) Bantam.
—The Morning After. 1993. pap. 3.50 (*0-553-29852-6*) Bantam.
—Ms. Quarterback. (gr. 9-12). 1990. pap. 3.25 (*0-553-28767-2*) Bantam.
—Murder on the Line. 1992. pap. 3.50 (*0-553-29308-7*) Bantam.
—My Best Friend's Boyfriend. 1992. pap. 3.25 (*0-553-29233-1*) Bantam.
—My First Love & Other Disasters. 176p. (gr. 7 up). 1986. pap. 2.95 (*0-440-95447-9*, LFL) Dell.
—My First Love & Other Disasters. (gr. 4-7). 1991. pap. 3.95 (*0-14-034886-7*, Puffin) Puffin Bks.
—New Elizabeth. 1990. pap. 2.99 (*0-553-28385-5*) Bantam.
—The New Girl. 96p. (Orig.). (gr. 7-12). 1987. pap. 2.50 (*0-553-15475-3*, Skylark) Bantam.
—The New Girl. 1987. pap. 3.25 (*0-553-15660-8*) Bantam.
—New Jessica. 1986. pap. 2.99 (*0-553-27560-7*) Bantam.
—A Night to Remember. (gr. 4 up) 1993. pap. 3.99 (*0-553-29309-5*) Bantam.
—Nowhere to Run. 1986. pap. 2.99 (*0-553-27944-0*) Bantam.
—Olivia's Story. 1991. pap. 3.50 (*0-553-29359-1*)
—One of the Gang. 1987. pap. 3.25 (*0-553-15677-2*) Bantam.
—One of the Gang, No. 10. 1987. pap. 2.50 (*0-553-15531-8*, Skylark) Bantam.
—Operation Love. (gr. 7 up). 1994. pap. 3.50 (*0-553-29860-7*) Bantam.
—Out of Control. 1987. pap. 2.99 (*0-553-27666-2*) Bantam.
—Out of Place. (gr. 7 up). 1988. pap. 3.25 (*0-553-15628-4*) Bantam.
—Out of Reach. large type ed. 151p. (gr. 5-8). 1989. Repr. of 1988 ed. PLB 10.50 (*1-55905-015-2*, Dist. by Gareth Stevens); 9.50 (*1-55905-005-5*) Grey Castle.
—The Parent Plot. 1990. pap. 2.99 (*0-553-28611-0*) Bantam.
—Patty's Last Dance. (gr. 4-7). 1993. pap. 3.25 (*0-553-48052-9*) Bantam.
—The Perfect Girl. 1991. pap. 3.25 (*0-553-28901-2*) Bantam.
—Perfect Shot. 1989. pap. 2.95 (*0-553-27915-7*) Bantam.
—Perfect Summer. 256p. (Orig.). (gr. 6 up). 1985. pap. 3.50 (*0-553-25072-8*) Bantam.
—Playing for Keeps. (gr. 7 up). 1988. pap. 3.50 (*0-553-27477-5*) Bantam.
—Playing Hooky. (gr. 6 up). 1988. pap. 3.25 (*0-553-15606-3*) Bantam.
—Playing with Fire. large type ed. 149p. (gr. 5-8). 1989. Repr. of 1983 ed. PLB 10.50 (*1-55905-002-0*); PLB 10.50 (*0-685-26540-4*, Dist. by Gareth Stevens) Grey Castle.
—Poor Lila! (gr. 4-7). 1992. pap. 3.25 (*0-553-15962-3*) Bantam.
—Power Play. 176p. (Orig.). (gr. 7 up). 1985. pap. 2.99 (*0-553-27493-7*) Bantam.
—Power Play. large type ed. 150p. (gr. 5-8). 1989. Repr. of 1983 ed. PLB 10.50 (*1-55905-013-6*, Dist. by Gareth Stevens); 9.50 (*1-55905-003-9*) Grey Castle.
—Promises. 160p. (Orig.). (gr. 7-12). 1985. pap. 2.75 (*0-553-26765-5*) Bantam.
—Promises, No. 15. 1985. pap. 3.25 (*0-553-27940-8*) Bantam.
—Psychic Sisters. (gr. 4-6). 1993. pap. 3.25 (*0-553-48057-X*) Bantam.
—Racing Hearts. 1984. pap. 3.25 (*0-553-27878-9*) Bantam.
—Rags to Riches. 160p. (Orig.). (gr. 5 up). 1985. pap. 3.25 (*0-553-27431-7*) Bantam.
—Regina's Legacy. 1991. pap. 3.25 (*0-553-28863-6*) Bantam.

—Robin in the Middle. (gr. 1-3). 1993. pap. 2.99 (*0-553-48014-6*) Bantam.
—Rock Star's Girl. (gr. 9-12). 1991. pap. 3.25 (*0-553-28841-5*) Bantam.
—Rosa's Lie. 1992. pap. 2.99 (*0-553-29227-7*) Bantam.
—Rumors. 1987. pap. 3.25 (*0-553-27884-3*) Bantam.
—Runaway. 176p. (Orig.). (gr. 5 up). 1985. pap. 2.75 (*0-553-26682-9*) Bantam.
—Runaway. 1985. pap. 2.99 (*0-553-27566-6*) Bantam.
—Runaway Hamster. (ps-3). 1989. pap. 2.99 (*0-553-15759-0*, Skylark) Bantam.
—Sarah's Dad & Sophia's Mom. 1992. pap. 3.25 (*0-553-15944-5*) Bantam.
—Say Goodbye. 1985. pap. 2.99 (*0-553-27951-3*) Bantam.
—Second Best. 1988. pap. 2.75 (*0-553-15665-9*) Bantam.
—Second Chance. (ps-1). 1989. pap. 2.95 (*0-553-27771-5*) Bantam.
—Second Chance. large type ed. 133p. (gr. 5-8). 1989. Repr. of 1989 ed. PLB 10.50 (*1-55905-018-7*, Dist. by Gareth Stevens); 9.50 (*1-55905-008-X*) Grey Castle.
—Secrets. large type ed. 118p. (gr. 5-8). 1989. Repr. of 1983 ed. PLB 10.50 (*1-55905-011-X*, Dist. by Gareth Stevens); 9.50 (*1-55905-001-2*) Grey Castle.
—She's Not What She Seems. 1993. pap. 3.25 (*0-553-29849-6*) Bantam.
—Showdown. 160p. (gr. 6). 1985. pap. 3.25 (*0-553-27589-5*) Bantam.
—Slam Book. 1988. pap. 3.95 (*0-553-05496-1*) Bantam.
—The Slime That Ate Sweet Valley. (gr. 4-7). 1991. pap. 3.25 (*0-553-15935-6*) Bantam.
—Sneaking Out. 1987. pap. 3.25 (*0-553-15659-4*) Bantam.
—Spring Fever: Spring Super Edition, No. 2. 240p. (Orig.). (gr. 7-12). 1987. pap. 3.50 (*0-553-26420-6*) Bantam.
—Starring Jessica. (gr. 9-12). 1991. pap. 3.25 (*0-553-28796-6*) Bantam.
—Starring Winston. (gr. 4-7). 1990. pap. 2.99 (*0-553-15836-8*) Bantam.
—Starting Over. 1987. pap. 2.95 (*0-553-27491-0*) Bantam.
—Stepsisters. 1993. pap. 3.25 (*0-553-29850-X*) Bantam.
—Steven's Bride. 1992. pap. 3.25 (*0-553-29229-3*)
—Steven's in Love. 1992. pap. 3.25 (*0-553-15943-7*) Bantam.
—The Substitute Teacher. (gr. k-3). 1990. pap. 2.99 (*0-553-15760-4*, Skylark) Bantam.
—Surprise! Surprise! (ps-3). 1989. pap. 2.99 (*0-553-15758-2*, Skylark) Bantam.
—Sweet Valley. 1992. pap. 3.25 (*0-553-15945-3*) Bantam.
—Sweet Valley. 1992. pap. 3.25 (*0-553-29230-7*) Bantam.
—Sweet Valley. 1992. pap. 3.25 (*0-553-29231-5*) Bantam.
—Sweet Valley Clean-Up. 1992. pap. 2.99 (*0-553-15923-2*) Bantam.
—Sweet Valley High, No. 68. 1990. pap. 3.25 (*0-553-28618-8*) Bantam.
—Sweet Valley Kids. 1992. pap. 2.75 (*0-685-52277-6*) Bantam.
—Sweet Valley Kids. 1992. pap. 2.75 (*0-685-52278-4*) Bantam.
—Sweet Valley Kids, No. 28: Elizabeth Meets Her Hero. (ps-3). 1992. pap. 2.99 (*0-553-15924-0*) Bantam.
—Sweet Valley Kids, No. 29: Andy & the Alien. (ps-3). 1992. pap. 2.99 (*0-553-15925-9*) Bantam.
—Sweet Valley Slumber Party. (gr. 4-7). 1991. pap. 2.99 (*0-553-15934-8*) Bantam.
—Sweet Valley Trick or Treat. (gr. 4-7). 1990. pap. 2.75 (*0-553-15825-2*) Bantam.
—Sweet Valley Twins. 96p. (Orig.). (gr. 7-12). 1987. pap. 2.50 (*0-553-15474-5*) Bantam.
—Sweet Valley Twins. 1992. pap. 3.25 (*0-553-15953-4*) Bantam.
—Taking Sides. 1986. pap. 3.25 (*0-553-27490-2*) Bantam.
—Teamwork. (ps-1). 1989. pap. 3.25 (*0-553-15681-0*, SVT #27) Bantam.
—That Fatal Night. (gr. 7 up). 1989. pap. 3.25 (*0-553-28264-6*) Bantam.
—The Boyfriend War. 1994. pap. 3.50 (*0-553-29858-5*) Bantam.
—The Evil Twin. 1993. pap. 3.99 (*0-553-29857-7*) Bantam.
—Todd's Story. 1992. pap. 3.50 (*0-553-29207-2*) Bantam.
—Together Forever. 176p. (gr. 7 up). 1988. pap. 2.95 (*0-553-26863-5*, Pub. by J C B Mohr GW) Bantam.
—Too Good to Be True. 592p. (Orig.). (gr. 7 up). 1984. pap. 2.75 (*0-553-26824-4*) Bantam.
—Too Good to Be True. 1985. pap. 3.25 (*0-553-27941-6*) Bantam.
—Too Much In Love. 1985. pap. 2.99 (*0-553-27952-1*) Bantam.
—Trouble at Home. 1990. pap. 2.99 (*0-553-28518-1*) Bantam.
—The Twins & the Wild West. (gr. 3-6). 1990. pap. 2.99 (*0-553-15811-2*) Bantam.
—The Twin's Big Pow-Wow. (ps-3). 1993. pap. 2.99 (*0-553-48098-7*) Bantam.
—The Twins Get Caught. (gr. 4 up). 1990. pap. 3.25 (*0-553-15810-4*) Bantam.
—The Twins Go to the Hospital. (gr. 4-7). 1991. pap. 2.99 (*0-553-15912-7*) Bantam.
—The Twins' Little Sister. (gr. 4-7). 1991. pap. 3.25 (*0-553-15899-6*) Bantam.
—Two-Boy Weekend. 1989. pap. 2.99 (*0-553-27856-8*) Bantam.

—Two-Boy Weekend. large type ed. 150p. (gr. 5-8). 1989. Repr. of 1989 ed. PLB 10.50 (*1-55905-019-5*, Dist. by Gareth Stevens); 9.50 (*1-55905-009-8*) Grey Castle.
—The Unicorns Go Hawaiian. (gr. 4-7). 1991. pap. 3.75 (*0-553-15948-8*) Bantam.
—The Verdict. 1993. pap. 3.50 (*0-553-29854-2*) Bantam.
—The Wakefield Legacy: The Untold Story. (gr. 7 up). 1992. pap. 3.99 (*0-553-29794-5*, Starfire) Bantam.
—The Wakefields of Sweet Valley. 352p. 1991. pap. 3.99 (*0-553-29278-1*) Bantam.
—Wakefields Strike. 1992. pap. 3.25 (*0-553-15950-X*) Bantam.
—War Between the Twins. (gr. 4-7). 1990. pap. 3.25 (*0-553-15779-5*) Bantam.
—The Wedding. 1993. pap. 3.50 (*0-553-29855-0*) Bantam.
—What You Parent's Don't Know. 1994. pap. 3.50 (*0-553-56307-6*) Bantam.
—White Lies. large type ed. 137p. (gr. 5-8). 1989. Repr. of 1989 ed. PLB 10.50 (*1-55905-017-9*); 9.50 (*1-55905-007-1*, Dist. by Gareth Stevens) Grey Castle.
—Who's to Blame? 1990. pap. 3.25 (*0-553-28555-6*) Bantam.
—Who's Who. 1990. pap. 3.25 (*0-553-28352-9*) Bantam.
—Winter Carnival. (Orig.). (gr. 7-12). 1986. pap. 3.50 (*0-553-26159-2*) Bantam.
—Won't Someone Help Anna? (gr. 4-7). 1993. pap. 3.25 (*0-553-48056-1*) Bantam.
—Wrong Kind of Girl. (gr. 7 up). 1984. pap. 3.25 (*0-553-27668-9*) Bantam.
—Yours for a Day. (gr. 4-7). 1994. pap. 3.25 (*0-553-48096-0*) Bantam.

Pascal, Francine & Stewart, Molly M. Jessica's Cat Trick. (ps-3). 1990. pap. 2.99 (*0-553-15768-X*, Skylark) Bantam.

Pascal, Francine, created by. Against the Odds. 160p. 1989. pap. 2.95 (*0-553-27650-6*) Bantam.
—Against the Rules. 96p. (Orig.). (gr. 7-12). 1987. pap. 2.50 (*0-553-15518-0*) Bantam.
—Alone in the Crowd. 160p. (Orig.). (gr. 7-12). 1986. pap. 2.75 (*0-553-26825-2*) Bantam.
—Buried Treasure. (gr. 3-7). 1987. pap. 2.50 (*0-553-15533-4*, Skylark) Bantam.
—Choosing Sides. 96p. (Orig.). (gr. 7-12). 1986. pap. 2.50 (*0-553-15459-1*) Bantam.
—Jumping to Conclusions. 112p. (Orig.). 1988. pap. 2.75 (*0-553-15635-7*) Bantam.
—Leaving Home High. (Illus.). 144p. (gr. 7-12). 1987. pap. 2.95 (*0-553-27631-X*) Bantam.
—Loving. 208p. (Orig.). (gr. 7-12). 1991. pap. 3.50 (*0-553-24716-6*) Bantam.
—The New Jessica. 160p. (Orig.). (gr. 7-12). 1986. pap. 2.75 (*0-553-26113-4*) Bantam.
—The Older Boy. (gr. 3-7). 1988. pap. 3.25 (*0-553-15664-0*, Skylark) Bantam.
—On the Edge. 160p. (gr. 7 up). 1987. pap. 3.25 (*0-553-27692-1*) Bantam.
—Out of Reach. 160p. 1988. pap. 2.95 (*0-553-27596-8*) Bantam.
—Promises Broken. 176p. (gr. 7-12). 1986. pap. 2.95 (*0-553-26156-8*) Bantam.
—Secret Admirer. 160p. (gr. 7 up). 1987. pap. 2.99 (*0-553-27691-3*) Bantam.
—Standing Out. 112p. 1989. pap. 3.25 (*0-553-15653-5*) Bantam.
—Stretching the Truth. (gr. 3-7). 1987. pap. 3.25 (*0-553-15654-3*, Skylark) Bantam.
—Sweet Valley High. 160p. (Orig.). 1989. pap. 2.95 (*0-553-27720-0*) Bantam.
—Sweet Valley High Super Thriller, No. 3. 240p. (Orig.). 1988. pap. 3.50 (*0-553-27554-2*) Bantam.
—Taking Charge. 112p. (Orig.). 1989. pap. 3.25 (*0-553-15669-1*) Bantam.
—Taking Sides. 160p. (Orig.). (gr. 7-12). 1986. pap. 2.75 (*0-553-25886-9*) Bantam.
—Tender Promises. 176p. (Orig.). (gr. 7-12). 1986. pap. 2.95 (*0-553-25812-5*, Starfire) Bantam.
—Tug of War. 112p. (Orig.). (gr. 7-12). 1987. pap. 3.25 (*0-553-15663-2*, Skylark) Bantam.

Paschkis. Wide Awake So Sleepy. Date not set. write for info. (*0-8050-3174-X*) H Holt & Co.

Paschos, Jacqueline & Destang, Francoise. Come to School. (ps). 1986. pap. 0.35 (*0-8091-6505-8*) Paulist Pr.

Pascoe, Elaine. Freedom of Expression: The Right to Speak Out in America. LC 92-7150. (Illus.). 128p. (gr. 7 up). 1992. PLB 14.90 (*1-56294-255-7*) Millbrook Pr.
—Neighbors At Odds: U. S. Policy in Latin America. LC 89-36006. 1990. PLB 14.40 (*0-531-10903-8*) Watts.
—South Africa: Troubled Land. rev. ed. LC 92-13608. (Illus.). 128p. (gr. 9-12). 1992. PLB 13.90 (*0-531-11139-3*) Watts.

Pashuk, Lauren. Fun with Colors. Pashuk, Lauren, illus. 32p. (ps-k). 1985. pap. 2.95 (*0-88625-106-0*) Durkin Hayes Pub.

Pashuk, Lauren, jt. auth. see Winik, J. T.

Passen, Lisa. Fat, Fat Rose Marie. Passen, Lisa, illus. LC 90-21112. 32p. (ps-3). 1991. 14.95 (*0-8050-1653-8*, Bks Young Read) H Holt & Co.
—Uncle's New Suit. LC 91-27727. (Illus.). 32p. (gr. 1-3). 1992. 14.95 (*0-8050-1652-X*, Bks Young Read) H Holt & Co.

Passes, David. Dragons: Truth, Myth, & Legend. Anderson, Wayne, illus. LC 92-44745. (gr. 7 up). 1993. 14.95 (*0-307-17500-6*, Artsts & Writers Guild) Western Pub.

Passport Books Editors. Apredamos Ingles Diccionario Ilustado. (gr. 4-7). 1993. 9.95 (*0-8442-7489-5*, Passport Bks) NTC Pub Grp.
—Let's Learn Hebrew Picture Dictionary. (gr. 4-7). 1993. 11.95 (*0-8442-8490-4*, Passport Bks) NTC Pub Grp.
Passport Books Staff. Aprendamos Espanol Diccinario. (Illus.). (gr. 4-7). 1992. pap. 9.95 (*0-8442-7499-2*, Passport Bks) NTC Pub Grp.
—Let's Learn Japanese Picture Dictionary. (gr. 4-7). 1992. 9.95 (*0-8442-8494-7*, Passport Bks) NTC Pub Grp.
—Let's Learn Portuguese Picture Dictionary. (Illus.). (gr. 4-7). 1992. 9.95 (*0-8442-4699-9*, Passport Bks) NTC Pub Grp.
Passport Books Staff, ed. Let's Learn English: Picture Dictionary. Goodman, Marlene, illus. 72p. 1990. 9.95 (*0-8442-5453-3*, Natl Textbk) NTC Pub Grp.
—Let's Learn Italian: Picture Dictionary. Goodman, Marlene, illus. 72p. 1990. 9.95 (*0-8442-8065-8*, Natl Textbk) NTC Pub Grp.
—Let's Learn Spanish: Picture Dictionary. Goodman, Marlene, illus. 72p. 1990. 9.95 (*0-8442-7558-1*, Natl Textbk) NTC Pub Grp.
Pastis, Steven, jt. auth. see Levy, Nathan.
Pastore, Michael. Lark's Magic. Warde, Ann, illus. LC 89-51204. 113p. (gr. 4-12). 1990. pap. 10.00 (*0-927379-36-8*, ZP36) Zorba Pr.
Patacsil, Priscilla M. Actividades Educativas Para Preescolares. 172p. (ps). 1988. pap. 6.25 (*0-311-11049-5*) Casa Bautista.
Patchett, Lynne. Glaciers. Burns, Robert, illus. LC 91-45080. 32p. (gr. 4-6). 1993. PLB 11.59 (*0-8167-2751-1*); pap. text ed. 3.95 (*0-8167-2752-X*) Troll Assocs. Postponed.
Pate, J'Nell L. Ranald Slidell Mackenzie: Brave Cavalry Colonel. LC 93-21952. (gr. 4-8). 1994. 14.95 (*0-89015-901-7*) Eakin-Sunbelt.
Patella, Chris & Oddo, Eileen. Makin Music! Schoonover, Kevin, illus. 75p. (Orig.). (gr. k-2). 1989. write for info. tchrs. ed. (*0-944333-02-8*); LP or Cassette avail. Musical Munchkins.
Pateman, Robert. Egypt. LC 92-10209. 1992. 21.95 (*1-85435-535-X*) Marshall Cavendish.
—Kenya. LC 92-39263. 1993. 21.95 (*1-85435-572-4*) Marshall Cavendish.
Patent, Dorothy H. African Elephants: Giants of the Land. Douglas-Hamilton, Oria, illus. LC 91-55028. 40p. (gr. 3-7). 1991. reinforced 14.95 (*0-8234-0911-2*) Holiday.
—All about Whales. LC 86-27126. (Illus.). 48p. (ps-4). 1987. reinforced bdg. 13.95 (*0-8234-0644-X*) Holiday.
—Appaloosa Horses. Munoz, William, photos by. LC 88-4470. (Illus.). 80p. (gr. 3-7). 1988. reinforced bdg. 14.95 (*0-8234-0706-3*) Holiday.
—An Apple a Day: From Orchard to You. Munoz, William, photos by. LC 89-33504. (Illus.). 64p. (gr. 3-7). 1990. 13.95 (*0-525-65020-2*, Cobblehill Bks) Dutton Child Bks.
—Babies! LC 87-26663. (Illus.). 40p. (ps-3). 1988. reinforced bdg. 14.95 (*0-8234-0685-7*); pap. 5.95 (*0-8234-0701-2*) Holiday.
—Baby Horses. Munoz, William, photos by. 56p. (ps-1). 1991. PLB 17.50 (*0-87614-690-6*) Carolrhoda Bks.
—Cattle. Munoz, William, photos by. LC 92-32987. (Illus.). 1993. 19.95 (*0-87614-765-1*) Carolrhoda Bks.
—The Challenge of Extinction. Munoz, William, illus. 64p. (gr. 6 up). 1991. lib. bdg. 15.95 (*0-89490-268-7*) Enslow Pubs.
—Deer & Elk. Munoz, William, illus. LC 93-25894. 1994. write for info. (*0-395-52003-7*, Clarion Bks) HM.
—Dogs: The Wolf Within. Munoz, William, photos by. LC 92-12334. 1992. 19.95 (*0-87614-691-4*) Carolrhoda Bks.
—Dogs: The Wolf Within. (gr. 4-7). 1993. pap. 7.95 (*0-87614-604-3*) Carolrhoda Bks.
—Dolphins & Porpoises. LC 87-45332. (Illus.). 96p. (gr. 4 up). 1987. reinforced bdg. 15.95 (*0-8234-0663-6*) Holiday.
—A Family Goes Hunting. Munoz, William, photos by. (Illus.). 64p. (gr. 4-9). 1991. 14.45 (*0-395-52004-5*, Clarion Bks) HM.
—Family Goes Hunting. (gr. 4-7). 1993. pap. 6.95 (*0-395-66507-8*, Clarion Bks) HM.
—Feathers. Munoz, William, photos by. (Illus.). 64p. (gr. 5 up). 1992. 15.00 (*0-525-65081-4*, Cobblehill Bks) Dutton Child Bks.
—Flowers for Everyone. Munoz, William, photos by. LC 89-23937. (Illus.). 64p. (gr. 5 up). 1990. 14.95 (*0-525-65025-3*, Cobblehill Bks) Dutton Child Bks.
—Gray Wolf, Red Wolf. Munoz, William, photos by. (Illus.). 64p. (gr. 4 up). 1990. 15.95 (*0-89919-863-5*, Clarion Bks) HM.
—Habitats: Saving Wild Places. LC 92-28082. (Illus.). 112p. (gr. 6 up). 1993. lib. bdg. 17.95 (*0-89490-401-9*) Enslow Pubs.
—Horses. Munoz, William, photos by. LC 93-12329. 1993. 14.95 (*0-87614-766-X*) Carolrhoda Bks.
—Horses of America. LC 81-4165. (Illus.). 80p. (gr. 3-7). 1981. reinforced bdg. 15.95 (*0-8234-0399-8*) Holiday.
—Hugger to the Rescue. Munoz, William, photos by. LC 93-32031. 1994. write for info. (*0-525-65161-6*, Cobblehill Bks) Dutton Child Bks.
—Humpback Whales. Ferrari, Mark J. & Glockner-Ferrari, Deborah A., illus. LC 89-2026. 32p. (ps-3). 1989. reinforced 14.95 (*0-8234-0779-9*) Holiday.
—Killer Whales. Ford, John K., photos by. LC 92-23949. (Illus.). 32p. (gr. 3-7). 1993. reinforced bdg. 15.95 (*0-8234-0999-6*) Holiday.

—Looking at Ants. Patent, Dorothy H., illus. LC 89-1943. 48p. (gr-4). 1989. reinforced 12.95 (*0-8234-0771-3*) Holiday.
—Looking at Dolphins & Porpoises. LC 88-39985. (Illus.). 48p. (ps-4). 1989. reinforced bdg. 13.95 (*0-8234-0748-9*) Holiday.
—Looking at Penguins. Robertson, Graham, illus. LC 92-37673. 40p. (ps-4). 1993. reinforced bdg. 15.95 (*0-8234-1037-4*) Holiday.
—Miniature Horses. Munoz, William, photos by. LC 90-38641. (Illus.). 48p. (gr. 3-7). 1991. 14.95 (*0-525-65049-0*, Cobblehill Bks) Dutton Child Bks.
—Mosquitoes. LC 86-45387. (Illus.). 40p. (gr. 3-7). 1986. reinforced bdg. 12.95 (*0-8234-0627-X*) Holiday.
—Nutrition: What's in the Food We Eat. Munoz, William, illus. LC 92-3665. 40p. (gr. 3-7). 1992. reinforced bdg. 14.95 (*0-8234-0968-6*) Holiday.
—Osprey. Munoz, William, photos by. LC 92-30103. (Illus.). 64p. (gr. 4-9). 1993. 14.45 (*0-395-63391-5*, Clarion Bks) HM.
—Pelicans. Munoz, William, illus. 64p. (gr. 4-7). 1992. 14.45 (*0-395-57224-X*, Clarion Bks) HM.
—Places of Refuge: Our National Wildlife Refuge System. Munoz, William, illus. 80p. (gr. 4-9). 1992. 15.95 (*0-89919-846-5*, Clarion Bks) HM.
—Prairie Dogs. Munoz, William, photos by. LC 92-34724. (Illus.). 1993. 15.45 (*0-395-56572-3*, Clarion Bks) HM.
—Seals, Sea Lions & Walruses. LC 90-55101. (Illus.). 96p. (gr. 3-7). 1990. reinforced 14.95 (*0-8234-0834-5*) Holiday.
—Singing Birds & Flashing Fireflies: How Animals Talk to Each Other. Morgan, Mary, illus. LC 89-9081. 32p. (gr. 1-3). 1989. PLB 12.90 (*0-531-10717-5*) Watts.
—The Way of the Grizzly. Munoz, William, photos by. LC 86-17562. (Illus.). 64p. (gr. 4 up). 1993. 12.95 (*0-89919-383-8*, Clarion Bks); pap. 6.95 (*0-395-58112-5*, Clarion Bks) HM.
—Whales: Giants of the Deep. Patent, Dorothy H., illus. LC 84-729. 96p. (gr. 3-7). 1984. reinforced bdg. 15.95 (*0-8234-0530-3*) Holiday.
—What Good Is a Tail? Munoz, William, photos by. LC 92-45639. (Illus.). 32p. (gr. 1-5). 1994. 13.99 (*0-525-65148-9*, Cobblehill Bks) Dutton Child Bks.
—Where Food Comes From. Munoz, William, illus. LC 90-49833. 40p. (gr. 3-7). 1991. reinforced 14.95 (*0-8234-0877-9*) Holiday.
—Where the Bald Eagles Gather. Munoz, William, illus. LC 83-20852. 64p. (gr. 3-6). 1984. 15.45 (*0-89919-230-0*, Clarion Bks) HM.
—Where the Bald Eagles Gather. Munoz, William, photos by. (Illus.). 56p. (gr. 3-7). 1990. pap. 5.95 (*0-395-52598-5*) HM.
—Where the Wild Horses Roam. (gr. 4-7). 1993. pap. 6.95 (*0-395-66506-X*, Clarion Bks) HM.
—Whooping Crane. (gr. 4-7). 1993. pap. 6.95 (*0-395-66505-1*, Clarion Bks) HM.
—The Whooping Crane: A Comeback Story. Munoz, William, photos by. LC 88-2871. (Illus.). 96p. (gr. 4 up). 1988. 14.95 (*0-89919-455-9*, Clarion Bks) HM.
—Wild Turkey. Munoz, William, illus. LC 89-613. 64p. (gr. 3-6). 1989. 14.45 (*0-89919-704-3*, Clarion Bks) HM.
—Wild Turkey, Tame Turkey. (gr. 4-7). 1992. pap. 5.70 (*0-395-55275-3*, Clarion Bks) HM.
—Yellowstone Fires: Flames & Rebirth. Munoz, William, et al, illus. LC 89-24544. 40p. (gr. 3-7). 1990. reinforced bdg. 14.95 (*0-8234-0807-8*) Holiday.
Patent, Hinshaw Dorothy. How Smart Are Animals? 189p. (gr. 7 up). 1990. 17.95 (*0-15-236770-5*) HarBrace.
Paterra, Mary E. Cambridge Stratford Study Skills Course, 20 Hour Edition. (Illus.). 196p. (gr. 6-8). 1986. tchr's. ed. 64.95 (*0-935637-03-6*); wkbk. 12.95 (*0-935637-02-8*); transparency set 60.00 (*0-935637-00-1*); listening tape set 40.00 (*0-935637-01-X*) Cambridge Strat.
—Cambridge Stratford Study Skills Course, 30 Hour Edition. (Illus.). (gr. 9-11). 1986. tchr's. ed. 64.95 (*0-935637-07-9*); wkbk. 12.95 (*0-935637-06-0*); transparency set 120.00 (*0-935637-04-4*); listening tape set 40.00 (*0-935637-05-2*) Cambridge Strat.
Paterson. Consider the Lilies. PLB 13.89 (*0-690-04463-1*, Crowell Jr Bks) HarpC.
Paterson, A. B. The Man from Snowy River. Macarthur-Onslow, Annette, illus. 32p. (gr. k-3). 1991. pap. 7.95 (*0-7322-7234-3*, Pub. by Angus & Robertson AT) HarpC.
—Man from Snowy River. (ps-3). 1992. pap. 7.95 (*0-207-15708-1*, Pub. by Angus & Robertson AT) HarpC.
—Waltzing Matilda. Digby, Desmond, illus. 32p. (gr. k-3). 1991. pap. 7.95 (*0-207-17098-3*, Pub. by Angus & Robertson AT) HarpC.
Paterson, Alan J. How Glass Is Made. (Illus.). 32p. (gr. 7 up). 1986. 12.95x (*0-8160-0038-7*) Facts on File.
Paterson, Bettina. In My House. LC 91-71754. (Illus.). 10p. (ps). 1992. bds. 3.95 (*0-8050-1882-4*, Bks Young Read) H Holt & Co.
—In My Yard. LC 91-71755. (Illus.). 10p. (ps). 1992. bds. 3.95 (*0-8050-1881-6*, Bks Young Read) H Holt & Co.
—My Clothes. LC 91-71752. (Illus.). 10p. (ps). 1992. bds. 3.95 (*0-8050-1884-0*, Bks Young Read) H Holt & Co.
—My First Wild Animals. Paterson, Bettina, illus. LC 89-17305. 32p. (ps-k). 1991. 8.95 (*0-690-04771-1*, Crowell Jr Bks); (Crowell Jr Bks) HarpC Child Bks.

—My Toys. LC 91-71753. (Illus.). 10p. (ps). 1992. bds. 3.95 (*0-8050-1883-2*, Bks Young Read) H Holt & Co.
—Scaredy-Ghost. (Illus.). 12p. (ps). 1993. bds. 2.50 (*0-448-40574-1*, G&D) Putnam Pub Group.
Paterson, Bettina, illus. Baby's ABC. 18p. 1992. bds. 4.95 (*0-448-40130-4*, G&D) Putnam Pub Group.
—Baby's 1, 2, 3. 18p. (ps). 1992. bds. 4.95 (*0-448-40265-3*, G&D) Putnam Pub Group.
—Jolly Snowman. 12p. (ps). 1992. bds. 2.50 (*0-448-40575-X*, G&D) Putnam Pub Group.
—Merry ABC. 24p. (ps). 1993. bds. 2.95 (*0-448-40553-9*, G&D) Putnam Pub Group.
—Merry Christmas, Santa! 12p. (ps). 1992. bds. 2.50 (*0-448-40576-8*, G&D) Putnam Pub Group.
—Potty Time. 12p. (ps). 1993. bds. 4.95 (*0-448-40539-3*, G&D) Putnam Pub Group.
Paterson, Bettina, illus. Busy Witch. 12p. (ps). 1993. bds. 2.50 (*0-448-40573-3*, G&D) Putnam Pub Group.
Paterson, Brian, jt. auth. see Paterson, Cynthia.
Paterson, Cynthia. The Foxwood Kidnap. Paterson, Brian, illus. 32p. (ps-3). 1986. 6.95 (*0-8120-5771-6*) Barron.
Paterson, Cynthia & Paterson, Brian. The Foxwood Smugglers. (Illus.). 32p. (ps-3). 1988. incl. dust jacket 6.95 (*0-8120-5984-0*) Barron.
—The Foxwood Surprise. (Illus.). 32p. (ps-3). 1988. 6.95 (*0-8120-5986-7*) Barron.
—The Foxwood Treasure. (Illus.). 32p. (ps-3). 1985. 6.95 (*0-8120-5664-7*) Barron.
—Robbery at Foxwood. (Illus.). 32p. (ps-3). 1985. 6.95 (*0-8120-5665-5*) Barron.
Paterson, Debi, jt. auth. see Brown, Cathy J.
Paterson, Diane. Smile for Auntie. LC 76-2285. (Illus.). (gr. k-2). 1977. 7.95 (*0-8037-8066-4*); Pied Piper Bk. pap. 3.50 (*0-8037-7981-X*) Dial Bks Young.
—Someday. Paterson, Diane, illus. LC 92-11401. 40p. (gr. 1-3). 1993. SBE 12.95 (*0-02-770565-X*, Bradbury Pr) Macmillan Child Grp.
Paterson, Diane, illus. Stone Soup. LC 80-27947. 32p. (gr. 1-4). 1981. PLB 9.79 (*0-89375-478-1*); pap. text ed. 1.95 (*0-89375-479-X*) Troll Assocs.
Paterson, John & Paterson, Katherine. Consider the Lilies: Flowers of the Bible. Dowden, Anne O., illus. LC 85-43603. 48p. (gr. 7 up). 1986. 14.00 (*0-690-04461-5*, Crowell Jr Bks) HarpC Child Bks.
Paterson, John, ed. see Eliot, George.
Paterson, Katherine. Angels & Other Strangers: Family Christmas Stories. LC 79-63797. 128p. (gr. 7 up). 1979. 14.00 (*0-690-03992-1*, Crowell Jr Bks) HarpC Child Bks.
—Angels & Other Strangers: Family Christmas Stories. LC 79-63797. 128p. (gr. 7 up). 1988. pap. 3.95 (*0-06-440283-5*, Trophy) HarpC Child Bks.
—Angels & Other Strangers: Family Christmas Stories. LC 79-63797. 128p. (gr. 7 up). 1991. PLB 13.89 (*0-690-04911-0*, Crowell Jr Bks) HarpC Child Bks.
—Bridge to Terabithia. Diamond, Donna, illus. LC 77-2221. (gr. 5 up). 1977. 14.00 (*0-690-01359-0*, Crowell Jr Bks) HarpC Child Bks.
—Bridge to Terabithia. Diamond, Donna, illus. LC 77-2221. 144p. (gr. 5-9). 1987. pap. 3.95 (*0-06-440184-7*, Trophy) HarpC Child Bks.
—Bridge to Terabithia. Diamond, Donna, illus. LC 77-2221. 144p. (gr. 5 up). 1987. Repr. of 1977 ed. PLB 13.89 (*0-690-04635-9*, Crowell Jr Bks) HarpC Child Bks.
—Bridge to Terabithia. large type ed. Diamond, Donna, illus. 155p. (gr. 2-6). 1987. Repr. of 1977 ed. lib. bdg. 14.95 (*1-55736-010-3*, Crnrstn Bks) BDD LT Grp.
—Bridge to Terabithia. 182p. (gr. 5-8). 1977. 14.56 (*0-685-66376-0*, BR8361) W A T Braille.
—Bridge to Terabithia. 182p. 1992. text ed. 14.56 (*1-56956-199-0*) W A T Braille.
—Bridge to Terabithia: (Puente Hasta Terabithia) (SPA.). (gr. 1-6). 8.95 (*84-204-3633-X*) Santillana.
—Come Sing, Jimmy Jo. LC 84-21123. 208p. (gr. 5 up). 1985. 12.95 (*0-525-67167-6*, Lodestar Bks) Dutton Child Bks.
—Come Sing, Jimmy Jo. 192p. (gr. 5 up). 1986. pap. 3.99 (*0-380-70052-2*, Flare) Avon.
—Flip-Flop Girl. 128p. (gr. 3-7). 1994. 13.99 (*0-525-67480-2*, Lodestar Bks) Dutton Child Bks.
—Gates of Excellence. 1992. pap. 10.00 (*0-14-036225-8*) Viking Child Bks.
—The Great Gilly Hopkins. LC 77-27075. (gr. 5 up). 1978. 14.00i (*0-690-03837-2*, Crowell Jr Bks); PLB 13.89 (*0-690-03838-0*, Crowell Jr Bks) HarpC Child Bks.
—The Great Gilly Hopkins. LC 77-27075. 192p. (gr. 5-9). 1987. pap. 3.95 (*0-06-440201-0*, Trophy) HarpC Child Bks.
—The Great Gilly Hopkins. large type ed. 170p. (gr. 2-6). 1987. Repr. of 1978 ed. lib. bdg. 14.95 (*1-55736-011-1*, Crnrstn Bks) BDD LT Grp.
—The Great Gilly Hopkins. (La Gran Gilly Hopkins) (SPA.). (gr. 1-6). 8.95 (*84-204-3222-9*) Santillana.
—Jacob Have I Loved. (gr. 7 up). 1981. pap. 2.95 (*0-380-56499-8*, Flare) Avon.
—Jacob Have I Loved. LC 80-668. 228p. (gr. 7 up). 1980. 14.00 (*0-690-04078-4*, Crowell Jr Bks); PLB 13.89 (*0-690-04079-2*, Crowell Jr Bks) HarpC Child Bks.
—Jacob Have I Loved. LC 80-668. 256p. (gr. 5 up). 1990. pap. 3.95 (*0-06-440368-8*, Trophy) HarpC Child Bks.
—Jacob Have I Loved. large type ed. 251p. (gr. k-6). 1990. Repr. lib. bdg. 15.95 (*1-55736-167-3*, Crnrstn Bks) BDD LT Grp.

—The King's Equal. Vagin, Vladimir, illus. LC 90-30527. 64p. (gr. 2-5). 1992. 17.00 (0-06-022496-7); PLB 16. 89 (0-06-022497-5) HarpC Child Bks.
—Lyddie. 240p. (gr. 5-9). 1991. 15.00 (0-525-67338-5, Lodestar Bks) Dutton Child Bks.
—Lyddie. LC 92-20304. 192p. (gr. 7 up). 1992. pap. 3.99 (0-14-034981-2) Puffin Bks.
—Lyddie. large type ed. 277p. 1993. Repr. lib. bdg. 15.95 (1-56054-616-6) Thorndike Pr.
—The Master Puppeteer. Wells, Haru, illus. 180p. (gr. 5 up). 1981. pap. 2.95 (0-380-53322-7, Camelot) Avon.
—The Master Puppeteer. Wells, Haru, illus. LC 75-8614. 192p. (gr. 6 up). 1976. 15.00 (0-690-00913-5, Crowell Jr Bks) HarpC Child Bks.
—The Master Puppeteer. Wells, Haru, illus. LC 75-8614. 192p. (gr. 4 up). 1989. pap. 3.95 (0-06-440281-9, Trophy) HarpC Child Bks.
—The Master Puppeteer. LC 75-8614. 192p. (gr. 7 up). 1991. PLB 14.89 (0-690-04905-6, Crowell Jr Bks) HarpC Child Bks.
—Of Nightingales That Weep. LC 74-8294. (Illus.). (gr. 5 up). 1974. 14.00 (0-690-00485-0, Crowell Jr Bks) HarpC Child Bks.
—Of Nightingales That Weep. Wells, Haru, illus. LC 74-8294. 192p. (gr. 4 up). 1989. pap. 3.95 (0-06-440282-7, Trophy) HarpC Child Bks.
—Park's Quest. LC 87-32422. 160p. (gr. 5 up). 1988. 12. 95 (0-525-67258-3, Lodestar Bks) Dutton Child Bks.
—Park's Quest. 160p. (gr. 5 up). 1989. pap. 3.99 (0-14-034262-1, Puffin) Puffin Bks.
—Rebels of the Heavenly Kingdom. LC 83-1529. 224p. (gr. 12 up). 1983. 11.95 (0-525-66911-6, Lodestar Bks) Dutton Child Bks.
—Rebels of the Heavenly Kingdom. 240p. (gr. 7 up). 1984. pap. 2.95 (0-380-68304-0, Flare) Avon.
—The Sign of the Chrysanthemum. Landa, Peter, illus. LC 72-7553. 128p. (gr. 6 up). 1988. pap. 3.95 (0-06-440232-0, Trophy) HarpC Child Bks.
—Sign of the Chrysanthemum. LC 72-7553. 128p. (gr. 7 up). 1991. PLB 14.89 (0-690-04913-7, Crowell Jr Bks) HarpC Child Bks.
—The Smallest Cow in the World. new ed. Brown, Jane C., illus. LC 90-30521. 64p. (gr. k-3). 1991. 14.00 (0-06-024690-1); PLB 13.89 (0-06-024691-X) HarpC Child Bks.
—Smallest Cow in the World. new ed. Brown, Jane C., illus. LC 90-30521. 64p. (gr. k-3). 1993. pap. 3.50 (0-06-444164-4, Trophy) HarpC Child Bks.
—The Spying Heart: More Thoughts on Reading & Writing Books for Children. LC 88-17686. 208p. 1990. 15.95 (0-525-67267-2, Lodestar Bks); pap. 8.95 (0-525-67269-9, Lodestar Bks) Dutton Child Bks.
—The Tale of the Mandarin Ducks. Dillon, Leo & Dillon, Diane, illus. (gr. k-3). 1990. 15.00 (0-525-67283-4, Lodestar Bks) Dutton Child Bks.
—Who Am I? Milanowski, Stephanie, illus. 96p. (Orig.). 1992. pap. 8.99 (0-8028-5072-3) Eerdmans.
Paterson, Katherine, jt. auth. see Paterson, John.
Paterson, Katherine, tr. see Ishii, Momoko.
Paterson, Katherine, tr. see Yagawa, Sumiko.
Patience, J. The Land of Nursery Rhymes. (Illus.). (ps-1). 1985. 1.98 (0-517-43878-X) Outlet Bk Co.
Patience, John. Adventures in Fern Hollow. (Illus.). 64p. (ps-1). 1985. 2.98 (0-517-45856-X) Outlet Bk Co.
—Dragon Tales. (Illus.). 32p. (gr. k-6). 1991. 3.99 (0-517-02329-6) Outlet Bk Co.
—Hubble Bubble. (Illus.). 32p. (gr. k-6). 1991. 3.99 (0-517-02333-4) Outlet Bk Co.
—The Little People. (Illus.). 32p. (gr. k-6). 1991. 3.99 (0-517-02334-2) Outlet Bk Co.
—Roarasaurus. Patience, John, illus. 12p. (ps up). 1994. pop-up 14.95 (0-8431-3686-3) Price Stern.
—The Seasons in Fern Hollow. (Illus.). 64p. (ps-1). 2.98 (0-517-45857-8) Outlet Bk Co.
—Tall Stories. (Illus.). 32p. (gr. k-6). 1991. 3.99 (0-517-02327-X) Outlet Bk Co.
—Who's Afraid of Tigers. Patience, John, illus. 6p. (gr. k-4). 1993. 14.99 (0-8431-3542-5) Price Stern.
Patkau, Karen. In the Sea. Patkau, Karen, illus. 24p. (ps). 1990. 15.95 (1-55037-067-7, Pub. by Annick CN); pap. 5.95 (1-55037-066-9, Pub. by Annick CN) Firefly Bks Ltd.
Patneaude, David. Someone Was Watching. Mathews, Judith, ed. LC 92-39130. 240p. (gr. 6-9). 1993. PLB 13.95 (0-8075-7531-3) A Whitman.
Paton, A. Cry, the Beloved Country. abr. ed. 115p. 1991. pap. text ed. 5.95 (0-582-53009-1, 79129) Longman.
Paton, Alan. Cry, the Beloved Country, 2 vols. large type ed. (gr. 10 up). Repr. of 1948 ed. Set. write for info. NAVH.
Paton, Caroline, jt. auth. see Paton, Sandy.
Paton, John. The Kingfisher Children's Encyclopedia. LC 92-4785. (Illus.). 816p. (gr. 3-9). 1992. 29.95 (1-85697-800-1) Kingfisher Bks.
Paton, John, ed. Doubleday Children's Encyclopedia. 1990. PLB 149.99 (0-385-41211-8) Doubleday.
Paton, Jonathan. The Land & People of South Africa. LC 89-2477. (Illus.). 304p. (gr. 6 up). 1990. 18.00 (0-397-32361-1, Lipp Jr Bks); PLB 17.89 (0-397-32362-X, Lipp Jr Bks) HarpC Child Bks.
Paton, Kathleen, ed. Poems to Share. Van Wright, Cornelius & Ying-Hwa Hu, illus. 24p. (ps-3). 1990. 4.95 (1-56288-050-0) Checkerboard.
Paton, Sandy & Paton, Caroline. I've Got a Song! A Collection of Songs for Youngsters. 2nd ed. Paton, Sandy & Paton, David, illus. 40p. (Orig.). (gr. k-4). 1989. pap. 10.98 (0-938702-05-X) Folk-Legacy.

—When the Spirit Says Sing: A Read-along, Sing-along, Coloring Book. Richardson, Joyce, illus. Wood, Chip, intro. by. (Illus.). 40p. (Orig.). (gr. k-8). 1989. pap. 13. 98 (0-938702-06-8) Folk-Legacy.
Paton Walsh, Jill. A Chance Child. (Illus.). 192p. (gr. 5 up). 1991. pap. 3.95 (0-374-41174-3, Sunburst) FS&G.
Paton-Walsh, Jill. Fireweed. LC 73-109554. 144p. (gr. 6 up). 1970. 14.95 (0-374-32310-0) FS&G.
Paton Walsh, Jill. Gaffer Samson's Luck. Cole, Brock, illus. LC 84-10180. 112p. (gr. 5 up). 1984. 14.00 (0-374-32498-0) FS&G.
—Gaffer Samson's Luck. Cole, Brock, illus. 128p. (gr. 3-7). 1990. pap. 3.50 (0-374-42513-2, Sunburst) FS&G.
—Goldengrove. LC 72-81484. 130p. (gr. 6 up). 1985. pap. 3.50 (0-374-42587-6, Sunburst) FS&G.
—Grace. 256p. (gr. 7 up). 1992. 16.00 (0-374-32758-0) FS&G.
—The Green Book. Bloom, Lloyd, illus. LC 81-12620. 80p. (gr. 5 up). 1982. 13.00 (0-374-32778-5) FS&G.
—Green Book. LC 81-12620. (Illus.). 80p. (gr. 5 up). 1986. pap. 3.50 (0-374-42802-6) FS&G.
—Parcel of Patterns. 1992. pap. 3.95 (0-374-45743-3) FS&G.
—Torch. LC 87-45995. 176p. 1988. 15.00 (0-374-37684-0) FS&G.
Paton-Walsh, Jill P. Fireweed. (gr. 6 up). 1988. pap. 3.50 (0-374-42316-4, Sunburst) FS&G.
Patrick & Remy. Civics for Americans, 4 vols. large type ed. 960p. (gr. 7-9). 1982. Repr. of 1980 ed. Set. 223. 42 (0-317-01881-7, 4-03700-00) Am Printing Hse.
Patrick, Ann. Let's Make Piano Music with Marvin, Bk. 1. 40p. (gr. k-7). 1985. pap. text ed. 6.95 (0-931759-06-4) Centerstream Pub.
—Lets Make Piano Music with Marvin, Bk. 2. Armstrong, Tom, illus. 48p. (gr. k-7). 1986. pap. text ed. 6.95 (0-931759-13-7) Centerstream Pub.
—Let's Make Piano Music with Marvin, Bk. 3. 40p. (Orig.). (gr. k-7). 1987. pap. 6.95 (0-685-17364-X) Centerstream Pub.
—Let's Make Piano Music with Marvin: Primer. 40p. (gr. k-7). 1985. pap. text ed. 6.95 (0-931759-05-6) Centerstream Pub.
Patrick, Bill. The Food & Drug Administration. Schlesinger, Arthur M., Jr., intro. by. (Illus.). 96p. (gr. 5 up). 1989. lib. bdg. 14.95 (0-87754-822-6) Chelsea Hse.
Patrick, Denice. Look Inside a House. (Illus.). 16p. (ps-1). 1989. 11.95 (0-448-19351-5, G&D) Putnam Pub Group.
—Look Inside a Ship. (Illus.). 16p. (ps-1). 1989. 11.95 (0-448-19352-3, G&D) Putnam Pub Group.
—Look Inside Your Body. (Illus.). 16p. (ps-1). 1989. bds. 11.95 (0-448-21033-9, G&D) Putnam Pub Group.
Patrick, Denice, jt. auth. see Ingoglia, Gina.
Patrick, Denise L. The Car Washing Street. Ward, John, illus. LC 92-9229. 32p. (ps up). 1993. 14.00 (0-688-11452-0, Tambourine Bks); PLB 13.93 (0-688-11453-9, Tambourine Bks) Morrow.
—Disney's Peek-a-Boo Bambi. Pacheco, Dave & Wakeman, Diana, illus. 14p. (ps-k). 1992. write for info. (0-307-12392-8, 12392) Western Pub.
—Disney's The Little Mermaid: Ariel's Secret. DiCicco, Sue, illus. 14p. (ps-k). 1992. bds. write for info. (0-307-12393-6, 12393, Golden Pr) Western Pub.
—Ghostwriter: The Mini Book of Kid's Puzzles Sports Issue. (ps-3). 1992. pap. 0.99 (0-553-37073-1) Bantam.
—Good Night, Baby. Lanza, Barbara, illus. 24p. (ps). 1993. bds. 3.50 (0-307-06144-2, 6144, Golden Pr) Western Pub.
—Red Dancing Shoes. Ransome, James E., illus. LC 91-32666. 32p. (ps). 1993. 14.00 (0-688-10392-8, Tambourine Bks); PLB 13.93 (0-688-10393-6, Tambourine Bks) Morrow.
Patrick, Denise L., adapted by. Walt Disney's Bambi. Mones, illus. 28p. (ps). 1992. bds. write for info. (0-307-12535-1, 12535, Golden Pr) Western Pub.
—Walt Disney's Snow White & the Seven Dwarfs. Mones, illus. 28p. (ps). 1992. bds. write for info. (0-307-12531-9, 12531, Golden Pr) Western Pub.
Patrick, Diane. Coretta Scott King. LC 91-17032. (Illus.). 144p. (gr. 9-12). 1991. PLB 14.40 (0-531-13005-3) Watts.
—Family Celebrations. Bryant, Michael, illus. LC 93-18456. 64p. (ps-4). 1993. PLB 11.95 (1-881889-04-1) Silver Moon.
—Martin Luther King, Jr. LC 89-24800. (Illus.). 1990. PLB 12.90 (0-531-10892-9) Watts.
Patrick, John J. The Young Oxford Companion to the Supreme Court of the United States. LC 93-6467. (gr. 5 up). 1993. 35.00 (0-19-507877-2) OUP.
Patrick, Laurie & Hill, Janis. From Kids with Love. (ps-3). 1987. pap. 8.95 (0-8224-3166-1) Fearon Teach Aids.
Patrick, Lewis. Walt Disney's Snow White & the Seven Dwarfs Counting Book. (ps). 1993. 3.95 (0-307-12529-7, Golden Pr) Western Pub.
Patrick, Sally, et al. The Month by Month Treasure Box. LC 86-82599. (Illus.). 80p. (Orig.). (ps-1). 1988. 7.95 (0-86530-124-7, IP 130-1) Incentive Pubns.
Patrignani. A Manual of Practical Devotion to St. Joseph. LC 82-50594. 328p. 1982. pap. 13.50 (0-89555-175-6) TAN Bks Pubs.
Patron, Susan. Bobbin Dustdobbin. Shemom, Mike, illus. LC 92-25099. 32p. (ps-2). 1993. 14.95 (0-531-05468-3); PLB 14.99 (0-531-08618-6) Orchard Bks Watts.

—Burgoo Stew. Shenon, Mike, illus. LC 90-43791. 32p. (ps-1). 1991. 13.95 (0-531-05916-2); RLB 13.99 (0-531-08516-3) Orchard Bks Watts.
—Dark Cloud Strong Breeze. Catalanotto, Peter, illus. LC 93-4873. (gr. 5 up). 1994. write for info. (0-531-06815-3); PLB write for info. (0-531-08665-8) Orchard Bks Watts.
—Five Bad Boys, Billy Que, & the Dustdobbin. Shenon, Mike, illus. LC 91-736. 32p. (ps-1). 1992. 13.95 (0-531-05989-8); PLB 13.99 (0-531-08589-9) Orchard Bks Watts.
—Maybe Yes, Maybe No, Maybe Maybe. Donahue, Dorothy, illus. LC 92-34067. 96p. (gr. 3-5). 1993. 14. 95 (0-531-05482-9); PLB 14.99 (0-531-08632-1) Orchard Bks Watts.
Patten, Jim, jt. auth. see Ferguson, Donald L.
Patterson. Koko's Kitten. 1993. pap. 4.95 (0-590-44425-5) Scholastic Inc.
Patterson, Charles. Animal Rights. (Illus.). 104p. (gr. 6 up). 1993. lib. bdg. 17.95 (0-89490-468-X) Enslow Pubs.
—Anti-Semitism: The Road to the Holocaust & Beyond. 160p. (gr. 8). 1988. pap. 9.95 (0-8027-7318-4) Walker & Co.
—Hafez Al-Asad. (Illus.). 128p. (gr. 8 up). 1991. lib. bdg. 13.98 (0-671-69468-5, J Messner); lib. bdg. 7.95 (0-671-69469-3) S&S Trade.
—Marian Anderson. Rosoff, Iris, ed. LC 88-10695. (Illus.). 160p. (gr. 7 up). 1988. PLB 14.40 (0-531-10568-7) Watts.
Patterson, Claire. Let's Celebrate Math. Fales, Jim, illus. 82p. (gr. 4-9). 1991. pap. 8.95 (0-9623835-6-2) Pieces of Lrning.
Patterson, Don. A Child's Trip to Christmas in Santa Fe: A Photographic Documentary. LC 91-62868. (Illus.). 120p. (gr. k-3). 1991. 29.95 (0-9629093-2-7) MyndSeye.
—Ski Vacation. Patterson, Don, photos by. (Illus.). 40p. (gr. k-6). 1991. 13.95 (0-9629093-3-5) MyndSeye.
Patterson, Francine. Koko's Kitten. Cohn, Ronald H., photos by. 50p. (gr. k up). 1985. pap. 13.95 (0-590-40952-2) Scholastic Inc.
—Koko's Story. Cohn, Ronald H., photos by. (Illus.). 40p. 1988. pap. 5.95 (0-590-41364-3) Scholastic Inc.
Patterson, Geoffrey. Jonah & the Whale. 1992. 14. 00 (0-688-11238-2); PLB 13.93 (0-688-11239-0) Lothrop.
Patterson, John, jt. auth. see Bumann, Joan.
Patterson, Jose. Angels, Prophets, Rabbis & Kings: From the Stories of the Jewish People. Bushe, Claire & Ripley, Edward, illus. 132p. (gr. 6 up). 1991. 22.50 (0-87226-912-4) P Bedrick Bks.
—A Circus Child. (Illus.). 25p. (gr. 2-4). 1991. 12.95 (0-237-60132-X, Pub. by Evans Bros Ltd) Trafalgar.
—Mazal-Tov: A Jewish Wedding. (Illus.). 25p. (gr. 2-4). 1991. 12.95 (0-237-60140-0, Pub. by Evans Bros Ltd) Trafalgar.
—A Traveller Child. (Illus.). 25p. (gr. 2-4). 1991. 12.95 (0-237-60129-X, Pub. by Evans Bros Ltd) Trafalgar.
Patterson, Lillie. Francis Scott Key: Poet & Patriot. (Illus.). 80p. (gr. 2-6). 1991. Repr. of 1963 ed. lib. bdg. 12.95 (0-7910-1461-4) Chelsea Hse.
—Frederick Douglass: Freedom Fighter. (Illus.). 80p. (gr. 2-6). 1991. Repr. of 1965 ed. lib. bdg. 12.95 (0-7910-1410-X) Chelsea Hse.
—Martin Luther King, Jr. & the Freedom Movement. 1989. 16.95x (0-8160-1605-4) Facts On File.
Patterson, Lillie & Wright, Cornelia H. Oprah Winfrey: Talk Show Host & Actress. LC 89-17002. (Illus.). 128p. (gr. 6 up). 1990. lib. bdg. 17.95 (0-89490-289-X) Enslow Pubs.
Patterson, Lily, jt. auth. see Norman, Winifred L.
Patterson, Mary Ann, jt. auth. see Jackson, Sarah.
Patterson, Nancy R. The Christmas Cup. Bowman, Leslie, illus. LC 88-29112. 80p. (gr. 3-5). 1989. 13.95 (0-531-05821-2); PLB 13.99 (0-531-08421-3) Orchard Bks Watts.
—The Christmas Cup. 80p. 1991. pap. 2.95 (0-590-43870-0, Apple Paperbacks) Scholastic Inc.
—The Shiniest Rock of All. Jerome, Karen A., illus. 80p. (gr. 3 up). 1991. 11.95 (0-374-36805-8) FS&G.
Patterson, Wayne. Koreans in America. 1992. pap. 5.95 (0-8225-1045-6) Lerner Pubns.
Patterson, Yvonne. Doubting Thomas. (gr. k-4). 1981. pap. 1.89 (0-570-06144-X, 59-1261) Concordia.
Patteson, Nelda. Clara Driscoll: Savior of the Alamo: Her Life Story Presented Through the Clothes She Wore. (Illus.). 32p. (gr. 4-7). 1991. pap. 14.95 (0-9629001-0-9) Smiley Originals.
Patti, Joyce. The First Christmas. (Illus.). 18p. (ps up). 1990. 13.95 (0-525-44606-0, DCB) Dutton Child Bks.
Pattis, Anne-Francoise. The French Culture Coloring Book. (Illus.). 64p. 1993. pap. 4.95 (0-8442-1377-2, Passport Bks) NTC Pub Grp.
Pattison, Darcy. The River Dragon. Tseng, Jean & Tseng, Mou-Sien, illus. LC 90-49931. 32p. (gr. k up). 1991. 13.95 (0-688-10426-6); PLB 13.88 (0-688-10427-4) Lothrop.
Patton, Barbara. Introducing Frederic Chopin. (Illus., Orig.). (gr. 3-9). 1990. pap. 6.95x (1-878636-00-6) Soundboard Bks.
Patton, Barbara W. Introducing Johann Sebastian Bach. (Illus.). 48p. (Orig.). (gr. 3-9). 1992. pap. 6.95x (1-878636-01-4) Soundboard Bks.
—Introducing Wolfgang Amadeus Mozart. (Illus.). 48p. (Orig.). (gr. 3-9). 1991. pap. 6.95 (1-878636-03-0) Soundboard Bks.

Patton, Sally. Alphabetics: A History of Our Alphabet. rev. ed. 96p. (gr. 2-8). 1989. pap. text ed. 14.95 (*0-913705-40-3*) Zephyr Pr AZ.

—Musicians. new. ed. 145p. (gr. 2-6). 1992. pap. text ed. 14.95 (*0-913705-37-3*, ZS03) Zephyr Pr AZ.

Patton, Sally & Maletis, Margaret. Inventors. rev. ed. 72p. (gr. 2-6). 1989. pap. text ed. 14.95 (*0-913705-35-7*, ZS01) Zephyr Pr AZ.

Patton, Sally & Maxon, Dianne. Architexture: A Shelter Word. rev. ed. 54p. (gr. 2-6). 1989. pap. text ed. 14.95 (*0-913705-38-1*) Zephyr Pr AZ.

Patton, Sarah, ed. see Pysz, Stephen.

Pattou, E. Hero's Song. (gr. 3-7). 1991. 16.95 (*0-15-233807-1*, HB Juv Bks) HarBrace.

Patz, Nancy. Moses Supposes His Toeses Are Roses: And Seven Other Silly Old Rhymes. Patz, Nancy, illus. LC 82-3099. 32p. (ps-3). 1983. 13.95 (*0-15-255690-7*, HB Juv Bks) HarBrace.

—No Thumping No Bumping No Rumpus Tonight! Patz, Nancy, illus. LC 88-7717. 32p. (gr. k-3). 1990. RSBE 13.95 (*0-689-31510-4*, Atheneum Child Bk) Macmillan Child Grp.

—Sarah Bear & Sweet Sidney. Patz, Nancy, illus. LC 88-21300. 32p. (ps-2). 1989. RSBE 13.95 (*0-02-770270-7*, Four Winds) Macmillan Child Grp.

—To Annabella Pelican from Thomas Hippopotamus. Patz, Nancy, illus. LC 90-30038. 32p. (ps-3). 1991. RSBE 13.95 (*0-02-770280-4*, Four Winds) Macmillan Child Grp.

Patz, Naomi, jt. auth. see Borowitz, Eugene.

Paul, Aileen. Coloring Calendar Cookbook for Kids. Chew, Gary, illus. 24p. (Orig.). (gr. 5 up). 1982. pap. 2.95 (*0-913270-90-3*) Sunstone Pr.

—Kids' Cooking Without a Stove: A Cookbook for Young Children. rev. ed. Inouye, Carol, illus. LC 84-22230. 64p. 1985. pap. 7.95 (*0-86534-060-9*) Sunstone Pr.

Paul, Ann W. Eight Hands Round: A Patchwork Alphabet. Winter, Jeanette, illus. LC 88-745. 32p. (gr. 3 up). 1991. 15.00 (*0-06-024689-8*); PLB 14.89 (*0-06-024704-5*) HarpC Child Bks.

—Shadows are About. Graham, Mark, illus. 32p. 1992. 13.95 (*0-590-44842-0*, Scholastic Hardcover) Scholastic Inc.

Paul, Frank A. Sign Language Feelings. 32p. 1985. 4.50 (*0-915035-05-7*, 4165) Dawn Sign.

—Sign Language Fun. 32p. 1984. 4.50 (*0-915035-02-2*, 4163) Dawn Sign.

—Sign Language Opposites. 32p. 1985. 4.50 (*0-915035-04-9*, 4164) Dawn Sign.

Paul, Kathleen. Aries. 40p. (gr. 4). 1989. PLB 13.95s.p. (*0-88682-255-6*) Creative Ed.

—Taurus. 40p. (gr. 4). 1989. PLB 13.95s.p. (*0-88682-257-2*) Creative Ed.

Paul, Korky. Pop-up Book of Ghost Tales. 24p. (gr. 3 up). 1991. 14.95 (*0-15-200589-7*, HB Juv Bks) HarBrace.

Paul, Korky & Carter, Peter. Captain Teachum's Buried Treasure. (Illus.). 32p. (ps up). 1991. bds. 13.95 (*0-19-279869-3*, 12150) OUP.

Paul, Korky, jt. auth. see Long, Jonathan.

Paul, Nic. Soccer: Tactics of Success. (Illus.). 80p. (gr. 10-12). 1992. pap. 8.95 (*0-7063-7089-9*, Pub. by Ward Lock UK) Sterling.

Paul, Paula. Sarah, Sissy Weed, & the Ships of the Desert. (Illus.). 112p. (gr. 5-6). 1985. 9.95 (*0-89015-504-6*); pap. 5.95 (*0-89015-552-6*) Eakin-Sunbelt.

Paul, Richard. A Handbook to the Universe: Explorations of Matter, Energy, Space, & Time for Beginning Scientific Thinkers. LC 92-39670. (Illus.). 320p. (Orig.). (gr. 6 up). 1993. pap. 14.95 (*1-55652-172-3*) Chicago Review.

Paul, Sally. Creative Fabric Frames. Pfeiffer, Cyndi, illus. 32p. (gr. 7-12). 1981. pap. 6.00 (*0-932946-06-2*) Burdett Ca.

Paul, Sherry. Blossom Bird Falls in Love. Miller, Bob, illus. 32p. (Orig.). (ps-2). 1981. pap. 14.10 Bks. only (*0-685-01192-5*); pap. 16.20 bks & Skill Masters (*0-685-01193-3*) CPI Pub.

—Blossom Bird Finds a Family. Miller, Bob, illus. 32p. (Orig.). (ps-2). 1981. pap. 14.10 set (*0-686-31343-7*); Bks. & Skill Masters Set 16.20 (*0-685-01194-1*) CPI Pub.

—Blossom Bird Goes South. Miller, Bob, illus. 32p. (Orig.). (ps-2). 1981. pap. 14.10 set (*0-675-01080-2*); Bks. & Skillmasters set 16.20 (*0-685-01195-X*) CPI Pub.

—Finn the Foolish Fish: Trouble with Bubbles. Miller, Bob, illus. 32p. (Orig.). (ps-2). pap. 14.10 set (*0-675-01084-5*); Bks. & Skillmasters set 16.20 (*0-685-01196-8*) CPI Pub.

—Two-B & the Rock 'n' Roll Band. Murphy, Bob, illus. 32p. (Orig.). (ps-2). pap. 14.10 set (*0-675-01082-9*); Bks & Skillmasters set 16.20 (*0-685-01197-6*) CPI Pub.

—Two-B & the Space Visitor. Murphy, Bob, illus. 32p. (Orig.). (ps-2). pap. 14.10 bks. only (*0-685-01198-4*); pap. 16.20 Bks. & Skill Masters (*0-685-01199-2*) CPI Pub.

Paul, Ted. The Christmas Collie. Kummer, Mary, illus. LC 89-17994. 42p. (ps-7). 1989. 12.95 (*0-89802-548-6*) Beautiful Am.

Paulita, Mary. Half-Pint on Guadalcanal: A Saga of Heroism, Commitment & Love. Gehring, Frederick P., frwd. by. (Illus.). 144p. (Orig.). (gr. 8). 1993. pap. 10.00 (*0-9631198-1-8*) Marist Miss Sis.

Paull, Robert C., jt. auth. see Brooks, B. David.

Paul-Matos, Janice. How to Get into College: Step by Step, Vol. 1. 24p. (Orig.). (gr. 9-12). 1985. pap. 5.00 (*0-9615165-0-X*) Coll Acceptance.

Paulsen, Brendan P. The Luck of the Irish. Connelly, Gwen, illus. (gr. 2-4). 1988. 17.96 (*0-8172-2752-0*) Raintree Steck-V.

—The Luck of the Irish. (Illus.). 32p. (gr. 2-4). 1988. incl. audiocassette 29.28 (*0-8172-2467-X*) Raintree Steck-V.

Paulsen, Gary. Amos Gets Famous. (gr. 4-7). 1993. pap. 3.25 (*0-440-40749-4*) Dell.

—Amos's Last Stand. (gr. 4-7). 1993. pap. 3.25 (*0-440-40775-3*) Dell.

—The Boy Who Owned the School. LC 89-23048. 112p. (gr. 6-9). 1990. 12.95 (*0-531-05865-4*); PLB 12.99 (*0-531-08465-5*) Orchard Bks Watts.

—Boy Who Owned the School. (gr. 4-7). 1991. pap. 3.50 (*0-440-40524-6*, YB) Dell.

—The Boy Who Owned the School. 1991. pap. 3.50 (*0-440-70694-7*) Dell.

—Boy Who Owned the School. (gr. 4-7). 1993. pap. 1.99 (*0-440-21626-5*) Dell.

—Canyons. 1990. 14.95 (*0-385-30153-7*) Delacorte.

—Canyons. 1991. 3.50 (*0-440-21023-2*) Dell.

—Canyons. (gr. 4-8). 1992. 16.50 (*0-8446-6590-8*) Peter Smith.

—The Case of the Dirty Bird. 96p. (gr. 4-7). 1992. pap. 3.25 (*0-440-40598-X*, YB) Dell.

—A Christmas Sonata. Bowman, Leslie, illus. LC 90-46891. 80p. (gr. 3-7). 1992. 14.00 (*0-385-30441-2*) Delacorte.

—The Cookcamp. LC 90-7734. 128p. (gr. 5-7). 1991. 13.95 (*0-531-05927-8*); PLB 13.99 (*0-531-08527-9*) Orchard Bks Watts.

—The Cookcamp. 128p. (gr. 4-7). 1992. pap. 3.50 (*0-440-40704-4*, YB) Dell.

—Cowpokes & Desperadoes. (gr. 4-7). 1994. pap. 3.50 (*0-440-40902-0*) Dell.

—The Crossing. LC 87-7738. 128p. (gr. 6-8). 1987. 11.95 (*0-531-05709-7*); PLB 11.99 (*0-531-08309-8*) Orchard Bks Watts.

—The Crossing. (gr. k up). 1990. pap. 3.50 (*0-440-20582-4*, LFL) Dell.

—Culpepper's Cannon. 96p. (gr. 3-7). 1992. pap. 3.50 (*0-440-40617-X*, YB) Dell.

—Dancing Carl. LC 83-2663. 144p. (gr. 6-8). 1983. SBE 13.95 (*0-02-770210-3*, Bradbury Pr) Macmillan Child Grp.

—Dancing Carl. LC 86-30245. (gr. 5 up). 1987. pap. 3.95 (*0-685-19101-X*, Puffin) Puffin Bks.

—Dancing Carl. 1987. pap. 3.99 (*0-14-032241-8*, Puffin) Puffin Bks.

—Dogsong. LC 84-20443. 192p. (gr. 7 up). 1985. SBE 14.95 (*0-02-770180-8*, Bradbury Pr) Macmillan Child Grp.

—Dogsong. (gr. 5-9). 1987. pap. 4.50 (*0-14-032235-3*, Puffin) Puffin Bks.

—Dunc & Amos & the Red Tatoos, No. 12. (gr. 4-7). 1993. pap. 3.25 (*0-440-40790-7*) Dell.

—Dunc & Amos Hit the Big Top. (gr. 4-7). 1993. pap. 3.25 (*0-440-40756-7*) Dell.

—Dunc & the Flaming Ghost. 96p. (gr. 3-7). 1992. pap. 3.25 (*0-440-40686-2*, YB) Dell.

—Dunc & the Haunted House. 1993. pap. 3.50 (*0-440-40893-8*) Dell.

—Dunc Breaks the Record. 96p. (Orig.). (gr. 3-7). 1992. pap. 3.25 (*0-440-40678-1*, YB) Dell.

—Dunc Gets Tweaked. 96p. (Orig.). (gr. 3-5). 1992. pap. 3.25 (*0-440-40642-0*, YB) Dell.

—Dunc's Doll. 80p. (gr. 4-7). 1992. pap. 3.25 (*0-440-40601-3*, YB) Dell.

—Dunc's Dump. (gr. 4-7). 1993. pap. 3.25 (*0-440-40762-1*) Dell.

—Dunc's Halloween. 96p. (gr. 3-7). 1992. pap. 3.50 (*0-440-40659-5*, YB) Dell.

—Dunc's Undercover. 1993. pap. 3.50 (*0-440-40874-1*) Dell.

—The Foxman. 128p. (gr. 4 up). 1990. pap. 11.95 (*0-670-83360-6*) Viking Child Bks.

—The Foxman. 128p. (gr. 4 up). 1990. pap. 3.99 (*0-14-034311-3*, Puffin) Puffin Bks.

—Full of Hot Air: Launching, Floating High, & Landing. Heltshe, Mary A., photos by. LC 92-31327. (Illus.). 1993. 14.95 (*0-385-30887-6*) Delacorte.

—Hatchet. large type ed. 232p. 1989. Repr. of 1987 ed. lib. bdg. 15.95 (*1-55736-117-7*, Crnrstn Bks) BDD LT Grp.

—Hatchet. (gr. 5-9). 1988. pap. 3.99 (*0-14-032724-X*, Puffin) Puffin Bks.

—Hatchet. LC 87-6416. 208p. (gr. 6-8). 1987. SBE 14.95 (*0-02-770130-1*, Bradbury Pr) Macmillan Child Grp.

—Hatchet Rack Trim. (gr. 4-7). 1989. pap. 3.99 (*0-14-034371-7*, Puffin) Puffin Bks.

—The Haymeadow. (gr. 4-7). 1992. 15.00 (*0-385-30621-0*) Doubleday.

—The Island. LC 87-24761. 224p. (gr. 6-9). 1988. 13.95 (*0-531-05749-6*); PLB 13.99 (*0-531-08349-7*) Orchard Bks Watts.

—The Island. (gr. k up). 1990. pap. 3.50 (*0-440-20632-4*, LFL) Dell.

—Madonna Stories. (gr. 4-7). 1993. pap. 8.95 (*0-15-655116-0*, HB Juv Bks) HarBrace.

—Mr. Tucket. LC 93-31180. 1994. write for info. (*0-385-31169-9*) Delacorte.

—Monument. 1993. pap. 3.99 (*0-440-40782-6*) Dell.

—Night the White Deer Died. 1991. pap. 3.50 (*0-440-21092-5*, YB) Dell.

—Nightjohn. LC 92-1222. 1993. pap. 14.00 (*0-385-30838-8*) Doubleday.

—Popcorn Days & Buttermilk Nights. 112p. (gr. 5-9). 1989. pap. 3.99 (*0-14-034204-4*, Puffin) Puffin Bks.

—The River. 1991. 15.00 (*0-385-30388-2*) Doubleday.

—River. 1993. pap. 3.99 (*0-440-40753-2*) Dell.

—Sentries. LC 85-26978. 160p. (gr. 7 up). 1986. SBE 14.95 (*0-02-770100-X*, Bradbury Pr) Macmillan Child Grp.

—Sentries. (gr. 5-9). pap. 3.95 (*0-317-62279-X*, Puffin) Puffin Bks.

—Sisters Hermanas. 1993. 10.95 (*0-15-275323-0*, HB Juv Bks); pap. 3.95 (*0-15-275324-9*) HarBrace.

—Tiltawhirl John. 1990. pap. 3.95 (*0-14-034312-1*, Puffin) Puffin Bks.

—Tracker. LC 83-22447. 96p. (gr. 6-8). 1984. SBE 12.95 (*0-02-770220-0*, Bradbury Pr) Macmillan Child Grp.

—Tracker. (gr. 5-9). pap. 3.95 (*0-317-62280-3*, Puffin) Puffin Bks.

—The Voyage of the Frog. LC 88-15261. (Illus.). 160p. (gr. 6-8). 1989. 13.95 (*0-531-05805-0*); PLB 13.99 (*0-531-08405-1*) Orchard Bks Watts.

—The Voyage of the Frog. 1990. pap. 3.50 (*0-440-40364-2*, Pub. by Yearling Classics) Dell.

—The Voyage of the Frog. LC 93-30238. (gr. 9-12). 1993. 15.95 (*0-7862-0060-X*) Thorndike Pr.

—The Winter Room. LC 89-42541. 128p. (gr. 6-9). 1989. 13.95 (*0-531-05839-5*); PLB 13.99 (*0-531-08439-6*) Orchard Bks Watts.

—Winter Room. (gr. 4-7). 1991. pap. 3.50 (*0-440-40454-1*) Dell.

—Woodsong. Paulsen, Ruth W., illus. LC 89-70835. 160p. (gr. 7 up). 1990. SBE 14.95 (*0-02-770221-9*, Bradbury Pr) Macmillan Child Grp.

—Woodsong. 144p. (gr. 7 up). 1991. pap. 3.99 (*0-14-034905-7*, Puffin) Puffin Bks.

Paulsen, Gary & Paulsen, Ruth. Dogteam. 1993. pap. 15.95 (*0-385-30550-8*) Delacorte.

Paulsen, Ruth, jt. auth. see Paulsen, Gary.

Paulsen, Nancy. Preschool Program, Pt. 1: Loving God - Loving Others. (Illus.). 140p. (ps). 1992. pap. 29.99 (*1-55945-400-8*) Group Pub.

Paulson, Sean D., jt. auth. see Paulson, Terry L.

Paulson, Terry L. & Paulson, Sean D. Secrets of Life Every Teen Needs to Know. Gooseart Publications Staff, illus. LC 90-63405. 160p. (Orig.). (gr. 7-12). 1990. pap. 6.95 (*0-939513-42-0*) Joy Pub SJC.

Paulson, Tim. The Beanstalk Incident. Corcoran, Mark, illus. 1992. pap. 8.95 (*0-8065-1313-6*, Citadel Pr) Carol Pub Group.

—How to Fly a 747. Keating, Edward, illus. 48p. (Orig.). (gr. 3 up). 1992. pap. 9.95 (*1-56261-061-9*) John Muir.

—Jack & the Beanstalk & the Beanstalk Incident. Corcoran, Mark, illus. (ps-2). 1990. 12.95 (*0-685-38934-0*, Birch Ln Pr) Carol Pub Group.

Pausacker, Jenny. Fast Forward. Rawlins, Donna, illus. (gr. 4-7). 1991. 12.95 (*0-688-10195-X*) Lothrop.

Pauw, Linda G. De see De Pauw, Linda G.

Pavao, John. Understanding Book. Perle, Ruth L., ed. Abisch, Roz & Kaplan, Boche, illus. (gr. 1). 1977. pap. text ed. 1.75 (*0-89796-863-8*) New Dimens Educ.

Pavis, Jose, jt. auth. see Steele, Ross.

Pavlicko, Marie, jt. auth. see Farr, J. Michael.

Pavloff, George. The Man Who Was It. (Illus.). 72p. (gr. 1 up). 1990. 12.95 (*0-931474-39-6*) TBW Bks.

—A Rainbow for Suzanne. (Illus.). 72p. (gr. 1 up). 1991. 12.95 (*0-931474-40-X*) TBW Bks.

Pawczuk, Eugene. Robin Hood. Pronk, Mary, ed. Pawczuk, Eugene, illus. 32p. (Orig.). (gr. 1-6). 1992. PLB 15.55 (*0-88625-266-0*); pap. 5.95 (*0-88625-264-4*) Durkin Hayes Pub.

Pawczuk, Eugene, illus. Tattercoats: European Folk Tales. 24p. (ps-2). 1992. pap. 3.50 (*0-88625-285-7*) Durkin Hayes Pub.

Pawlor, Elizabeth P. Discover Nature Close to Home: Things to Know & Things to Do. Archer, Pat, illus. 224p. (Orig.). (gr. 8 up). 1993. pap. 14.95 (*0-8117-3077-8*) Stackpole.

Paxford, Sandra & Parker, Madeleine. Sandra & Syd. 32p. (gr. 7-10). 1986. pap. 22.00x (*0-7223-2067-1*, Pub. by A H Stockwell England) St Mut.

Paxton, Lenore & Siadi, Phillip. Christmas Time of Year: A Sing, Color, 'n Say Fun Book-Tape Package. Lindsay, Warren & Huntoon, Cathy, illus. 32p. (ps-3). 1992. pap. 6.95 (*1-880449-04-8*) Wrldkids Pr.

—Going to Grandma's: A Sing, Color 'n Say Coloring Book Package. Farago, Julius, illus. 32p. (ps-3). 1991. Includes cassette tape. pap. 6.95 (*1-880449-00-5*) Wrldkids Pr.

—Happy B-I-R-T-H-DAY: A Sing, Color, 'n Say Fun Book-Tape Package. Lindsay, Warren & Huntoon, Cathy, illus. 32p. (ps-3). 1992. pap. 6.95 incl. tape (*1-880449-02-1*) Wrldkids Pr.

—His Name Was David, Around the World: The Story of David & Goliath. Snavely, Linda W., illus. 32p. (ps-4). Date not set. pap. 7.95 coloring bk.-cassette pkg. (*1-880449-07-2*) Wrldkids Pr.

—Noah & the Ark: Around the World. (Illus.). 24p. (ps-4). 1993. pap. 7.95 coloring bk.-cassette pkg. (*1-880449-06-4*) Wrldkids Pr.

Paxton, Tom. The Animals' Lullaby. Ingraham, Erick, illus. LC 92-18841. 40p. (ps up). 1993. 15.00 (*0-688-10468-1*); PLB 14.93 (*0-688-10469-X*) Morrow Jr Bks.

—Belling the Cat: And Other Aesop's Fables. Rayevsky, Robert, illus. LC 89-39851. 40p. (gr. 1 up). 1990. 13.95 (*0-688-08158-4*); PLB 13.88 (*0-688-08159-2*, Morrow Jr Bks) Morrow Jr Bks.

—Birds of a Feather: And Other Aesop's Fables. Payevsky, Robert, illus. LC 92-2909. 40p. (ps up). 1993. 15.00 (0-688-10400-2); PLB 14.93 (0-688-10401-0) Morrow Jr Bks.
—Engelbert the Elephant. Kellogg, Steven, illus. LC 89-9376. 32p. (ps up). 1990. 14.95 (0-688-08935-6); PLB 14.88 (0-688-08936-4, Morrow Jr Bks) Morrow Jr Bks.
—Jennifer's Rabbit. Ayers, Donna, illus. LC 87-14113. 32p. (ps-1). 1988. 12.95 (0-688-07431-6); lib. bdg. 12.88 (0-688-07432-4, Morrow Jr Bks) Morrow Jr Bks.
—Where's the Baby? Graham, Mark, illus. LC 92-39875. 32p. (ps up). 1993. 15.00 (0-688-10692-7); PLB 14.93 (0-688-10693-5) Morrow Jr Bks.
Paxton, Tom & Scharrett, Darcy. A Car Full of Songs. Fairbend, Kerstin, illus. 84p. (Orig.). (ps-6). 1991. 14.95 (0-89524-632-5) Cherry Lane.
—Tom Paxton's Children's Songbook. Fairbend, Kerstin, illus. 68p. (Orig.). (ps-5). 1990. 12.95 (0-89524-563-9) Cherry Lane.
Paxton, Tom, retold by. Androcles & the Lion: And Other Aesop's Fables. Rayevsky, Robert, illus. LC 90-19173. 40p. (ps up). 1991. 13.95 (0-688-09682-4); PLB 13.88 (0-688-09683-2) Morrow Jr Bks.
Paxton, Tom, retold by see Aesop.
Payne, Bernal C., Jr. Experiment in Terror. 224p. (gr. 5-9). 1987. 13.45 (0-395-44260-5) HM.
—Experiment in Terror. (gr. 5-9). 1988. pap. 2.75 (0-671-67261-4, Archway) PB.
Payne, Elizabeth. Meet the North American Indians. (Illus.). (gr. 2-6). 1965. 6.95 (0-394-80060-5); (Random Juv) Random Bks Yng Read.
—The Pharaohs of Ancient Egypt. LC 80-21392. (Illus.). 192p. (gr. 5-9). 1981. 4.95 (0-394-84699-0) Knopf Bks Yng Read.
Payne, Emmy. Katy No-Pocket. (gr. 1-3). 1973. reinforced bdg. 13.95 (0-395-17104-0) HM.
—Katy No-Pocket. Rey, H. A., illus. 32p. (gr. k-3). 1973. pap. 5.70 (0-395-13717-9, Sandpiper) HM.
—Katy No-Pocket. Rey, H. A., illus. (ps-3). 1989. pap. 8.70 incl. cassette (0-395-52141-6) HM.
Payne, Fiona, ed. The Human Body. LC 92-54481. (Illus.). (gr. k-3). 1993. 12.95 (1-56458-249-3) Dorling Kindersley.
Payne, Katharine. Elephants Calling. Payne, Katharine, photos by. LC 91-34547. (Illus.). 36p. (gr. 2-6). 1992. 14.00 (0-517-58175-2); PLB 14.99 (0-517-58176-0) Crown Bks Yng Read.
Payne, Lauren M. Just Because I Am: A Child's Book of Affirmation. Rohling, Claudia, illus. LC 93-30609. 1994. write for info. (0-915793-60-1) Free Spirit Pub.
Payne, Marvin. Love & Oranges. 2nd ed. 64p. (gr. 9 up). 1988. pap. 3.95 (0-929985-08-7) Sonos.
Payne, Mary. Up & down the Blood Sugar Trail. Berry, Cathy, illus. Smith, Lendon H., intro. by. (Illus., Orig.). (gr. k-4). 1987. pap. 1.98 (0-9619326-0-0) MstrWorks Pub.
Payne, Mary A. Russell's Journal: Trust. (Illus.). 48p. (gr. k-4). 1993. 7.95 (0-8059-3334-4) Dorrance.
Payne, Peggy, ed. see Richardson, Arleta.
Payne, Richard A. Charlie the Shy Cowboy. Schilling, Mickey E., illus. 36p. (gr. 1-9). 1993. pap. 4.95 (0-9636186-2-8) Blue Sky Grap.
—Collin the Canada Goose. (gr. 1-5). 1993. pap. text ed. 4.95 (0-9636186-0-1) Blue Sky Grap.
Payson, Patricia. Science Fiction: A Zephyr Learning Packet. 79p. (gr. k-8). 1990. pap. 19.95 spiral bdg. (0-913705-18-7) Zephyr Pr AZ.
Paz, Myrna De La see De La Paz, Myrna J.
Peabody, Paul. Blackberry Hollow. Peabody, Paul, illus. LC 92-8968. 160p. (gr. 3-7). 1993. 15.95 (0-399-22500-5, Philomel Bks) Putnam Pub Group.
Peace, Mary. Fireflies. (Illus.). 130p. (Orig.). (gr. 4-12). 1986. pap. 4.95 (1-56087-012-5) Top Mtn Pub.
Peach, S. Running Skills. (Illus.). 48p. (gr. 6-10). 1988. pap. 5.95 (0-7460-0165-7) EDC.
—Technical Drawing. (Illus.). 48p. (gr. 6 up). 1987. PLB 14.96 (0-7460-0247-4); pap. 7.95 (0-7460-0094-4) EDC.
Peach, S. & Butterfield, M. Photography. (Illus.). 48p. (gr. 6 up). 1987. PLB 14.96 (0-88110-292-X); pap. 7.95 (0-7460-0107-X) EDC.
Peach, S., jt. auth. see Millard, A.
Peach, S., jt. auth. see Potter, T.
Peacock, Graham. Electricity. LC 93-3347. 32p. (gr. 3-6). 1993. 13.95 (1-56847-048-7) Thomson Lrning.
—Electricity. (Illus.). 32p. Date not set. 14.95 (1-56847-078-9) Thomson Lrning.
—Heat. LC 93-34613. (Illus.). 32p. (gr. 2-4). 1994. 14.95 (1-56847-075-4) Thomson Lrning.
—Light. LC 93-7522. (Illus.). 32p. (gr. 2-5). 1993. 14.95 (1-56847-073-8) Thomson Lrning.
—Sound. LC 93-7521. (Illus.). (gr. 2-5). 1993. 14.95 (1-56847-074-6) Thomson Lrning.
—Water. (Illus.). 32p. (gr. 2-4). 1994. 14.95 (1-56847-077-0) Thomson Lrning.
Peacock, Graham & Chambers, Cally. The Super Science Book of Materials. LC 93-30779. (Illus.). 32p. (gr. 4-8). 1993. 14.95 (1-56847-096-7) Thomson Lrning.
Peacock, Graham & Hudson, Terry. Exploring Habitats. Hughes, Jenny, illus. LC 92-29907. 48p. (gr. 4-8). 1992. PLB 19.92 (0-8114-2608-4) Raintree Steck-V.
—The Super Science Book of Our Bodies. LC 93-7519. (Illus.). 32p. (gr. 4-8). 1993. 14.95 (1-56847-023-1) Thomson Lrning.
Peacock, Graham, jt. auth. see Hudson, Terry.
Peacock, Jimmy, ed. see Speer, Bonnie.
Peacock, Judith, jt. auth. see Wheeler, Leslie.

Peacock, Lindsay. Pilots. Stefoff, Rebecca, ed. LC 91-39097. (Illus.). 32p. (gr. 5-9). 1992. PLB 17.26 (1-56074-040-X) Garrett Ed Corp.
Peak, Jan & Hennig, Anna. Trash to Treasure Crafts: From Recyclable Materials. Peak, Jan, illus. 80p. (gr. 3 up). 1992. wkbk. 8.99 (0-87403-890-1, 14-02146) Standard Pub.
Peale, Norman Vincent, ed. Youth Prints. LC 88-16786. 128p. (Orig.). 1988. pap. 7.99 (0-8066-2380-2, 10-7499, Augsburg) Augsburg Fortress.
Pearce, Carol A. Amelia Earhart. (Illus.). 176p. (gr. 5 up). 1988. 16.95x (0-8160-1520-1) Facts on File.
Pearce, Colin. The Monkey & the Crocodile. (Illus.). (ps-2). 1990. 12.99 (0-8423-4537-X) Tyndale.
Pearce, Elvina T. Four O'Clock Tunes. Clark, Frances & Goss, Louise, eds. (gr. 2 up). 1986. pap. text ed. 3.50 (0-913277-19-3) New Schl Mus Study.
—Solo Flight. Clark, Frances & Goss, Louise, eds. (gr. 2 up). 1986. pap. text ed. 3.50 (0-913277-18-5) New Schl Mus Study.
Pearce, Fred. The Big Green Book. Winton, Ian, illus. LC 90-84673. 32p. (gr. 2-5). 1991. 13.95 (0-448-40142-8, G&D) Putnam Pub Group.
Pearce, J. C. Tug of War. LC 93-15037. 144p. (gr. 3-7). 1993. pap. 2.99 (0-14-036663-6, Puffin) Puffin Bks.
Pearce, Jenny. Colombia: The Drug War. (Illus.). 40p. (gr. 5-8). 1990. PLB 12.90 (0-531-17237-6, Gloucester Pr) Watts.
Pearce, Molly. Big Cat the Proud. Pearce, Molly, illus. LC 91-65488. 32p. (gr. k-2). 1991. pap. 4.95 (0-9628129-7-8) Sagebrush Bks.
—Jimmy the Beet Truck. Pearce, Molly, illus. LC 91-65464. 32p. (gr. k-2). 1991. pap. 4.95 (0-9628129-9-4) Sagebrush Bks.
—Tale of Three Tractors. Pearce, Molly, illus. LC 91-65489. 32p. (gr. k-2). 1991. pap. 4.95 (0-9628129-8-6) Sagebrush Bks.
Pearce, Philippa. Emily's Own Elephant. Lawrence, John, illus. LC 87-14039. 32p. (gr. k-3). 1988. 11.95 (0-688-07678-5); lib. bdg. 11.88 (0-688-07679-3) Greenwillow.
—Here Comes Tod! Gon, Adriano, illus. LC 93-20026. 1994. write for info. (1-56402-328-1) Candlewick Pr.
—Tom's Midnight Garden. (gr. k-6). 1991. pap. write for info. (Pub. by Yearling Classics) Dell.
—Tom's Midnight Garden. reissued ed. LC 69-12008. 240p. (gr. 5-9). 1992. PLB 13.89 (0-397-30477-3, Lipp Jr Bks) HarpC Child Bks.
—Tom's Midnight Garden. Einzig, Susan, intro. by. LC 69-12008. (Illus.). 240p. (gr. 3-7). 1992. pap. 4.95 (0-06-440445-5, Trophy) HarpC Child Bks.
—The Way to Sattin Shore. LC 84-23729. 176p. (gr. 5-9). 1985. pap. 3.95 (0-14-031644-2, Puffin) Puffin Bks.
—What the Neighbours Did & Other Stories. large type ed. 308p. (gr. 1-7). 1991. 13.95 (0-7451-1246-3, Galaxy Child Lrg Print) Chivers N Amer.
—Who's Afraid? & Other Strange Stories. LC 86-14299. 160p. (gr. 5-9). 1987. 10.25 (0-688-06895-2) Greenwillow.
Pearce, Phillipa. Fresh. Zimdars, Berta, illus. 64p. 1987. PLB 13.95s.p. (0-88682-125-8) Creative Ed.
Pearce, Q. L. All about Dinosaurs. Boney, Leslie, illus. (gr. 2 up). 1989. pap. 7.95 (0-671-64517-X, Little Simon) S&S Trade.
—Amazing Science Series, 8 bks. (Illus.). 256p. (gr. 4-6). 1989. Set. PLB 103.84 (0-671-94111-9, J Messner); Set. pap. 47.60 (0-671-94112-7) S&S Trade.
—Animal Footnotes: A Nature's Footprints Guide. Bettoli, Delana, illus. 40p. (ps-3). 1990. PLB 12.98 (0-671-69116-3); pap. 8.95 (0-671-69117-1) Silver Pr.
—Armadillos & Other Unusual Animals. Steltenpohl, Jane, ed. Fraser, Mary A., illus. 64p. (gr. 4-6). 1989. lib. bdg. 12.98 (0-671-68528-7, J Messner); lib. bdg. 5.95 (0-671-68645-3) S&S Trade.
—Camouflagers. (gr. 4-7). 1991. 8.95 (0-8431-2828-3) Price Stern.
—The Checkerboard Press Kids' Science Dictionary. LC 88-71150. (Illus.). 124p. (gr. 4-6). 1991. Repr. of 1989 ed. 12. (1-56288-003-9) Checkerboard.
—The Earth. Mallout, Christine, illus. 48p. (ps-2). 1991. wkbk. 2.95 (0-8431-2913-1) Price Stern.
—First Science Words: The Ocean. (Illus.). 48p. 1991. wkbk. 2.95 (0-8431-2912-3) Price Stern.
—Giants of the Deep. Petruccio, Steven J., illus. 48p. (gr. 3-7). 1993. pap. 5.95 (1-56565-042-5) Lowell Hse.
—Giants of the Land. Bonforte, Lisa, illus. 48p. (gr. 3-7). 1993. pap. 5.95 (1-56565-041-7) Lowell Hse.
—Lightning & Other Wonders of the Sky. Steltenpohl, Jane, ed. Fraser, Mary A., illus. 64p. (gr. 4-6). 1989. lib. bdg. 12.98 (0-671-68534-1, J Messner); lib. bdg. 5.95 (0-671-68648-8) S&S Trade.
—My Favorite Dinosaur: Tyrannosaurus Rex. Fraser, Mary A., illus. 32p. 1993. pap. 11.95 (1-56565-014-X) Lowell Hse.
—Piranhas & Other Wonders of the Jungle. Fraser, Mary A., illus. 64p. (gr. 4-6). 1990. lib. bdg. 12.98 (0-671-70689-6, J Messner); pap. 5.95 (0-671-70690-X) S&S Trade.
—Quicksand & Other Earthly Wonders. Steltenpohl, Jane, ed. Fraser, Mary A., illus. 64p. (gr. 4-6). 1989. lib. bdg. 12.98 (0-671-68530-9, J Messner); lib. bdg. 5.95 (0-671-68646-1) S&S Trade.
—Saber-Toothed Cats - Prehistoric Worlds. (Illus.). 64p. (gr. 4-6). 1991. lib. bdg. 12.98 (0-671-70691-8, J Messner); pap. 5.95 (0-671-70692-6) S&S Trade.
—The Stargazer's Guide to the Galaxy. 1991. pap. 4.99 (0-8125-9423-1) Tor Bks.

—Still More Scary Stories for Sleepovers. LC 93-12822. (Illus.). 128p. (Orig.). (gr. 4-7). 1993. pap. 4.99 (0-8431-3588-3) Price Stern.
—Strange Science: Planet Earth. 64p. (Orig.). 1993. pap. 3.50 (0-8125-2365-2) Tor Bks.
—Tell Me About Nature Dictionary. 1990. 5.99 (0-517-03567-7) Outlet Bk Co.
—Tidal Waves & Other Ocean Wonders. Steltenpohl, Jane, ed. Fraser, Mary A., illus. 64p. (gr. 4-6). 1989. lib. bdg. 12.98 (0-671-68532-5, J Messner); lib. bdg. 5.95 (0-671-68647-X) S&S Trade.
—Tyrannosaurus Rex & Other Dinosaur Wonders. Fraser, Mary A., illus. 64p. (gr. 4-6). 1990. lib. bdg. 12.98 (0-671-70687-X, J Messner); pap. 5.95 (0-671-70688-8) S&S Trade.
—Whales & Other Wonders - Frozen Worlds. (Illus.). 64p. (gr. 4-6). 1991. lib. bdg. 12.98 (0-671-70693-4, J Messner); pap. 5.95 (0-671-70694-2) S&S Trade.
Pearce, Q. L. & Pearce, W. J. In the Barnyard. Brook, Bonnie, ed. Bettoli, Delana, illus. 24p. (ps-1). 1990. 5.95 (0-671-68828-6); PLB 9.98 (0-671-68824-3) Silver Pr.
—Nature's Footprints Series, 4 vols. Bettoli, Delana, illus. 96p. (ps-1). 1990. Set. 23.80 (0-671-94431-2); Set. 17.85s.p. (0-685-46999-9); Set. PLB 39.92 (0-671-94430-4); Set. PLB 29.94s.p. (0-685-47000-8) Silver Pr.
Pearce, Q. L. & Pearce, W. L. In the African Grasslands. Brook, Bonnie, ed. Bettoli, Delana, illus. 24p. (ps-1). 1990. 5.95 (0-671-68831-6); PLB 9.98 (0-671-68827-8) Silver Pr.
—In the Desert. Brook, Bonnie, ed. Bettoli, Delana, illus. 24p. (ps-1). 1990. 5.95 (0-671-68829-4); PLB 9.98 (0-671-68825-1) Silver Pr.
—In the Forest. Brook, Bonnie, ed. Bettoli, Delana, illus. 24p. (ps-1). 1990. 5.95 (0-671-68830-8); PLB 9.98 (0-671-68826-X) Silver Pr.
Pearce, R. H., ed. see James, Henry.
Pearce, W. J., jt. auth. see Pearce, Q. L.
Pearce, W. L., jt. auth. see Pearce, Q. L.
Peare, Catherine O. The Helen Keller Story. LC 59-10979. 192p. (gr. 4-6). 1990. PLB 13.89 (0-690-04793-2, Crowell Jr Bks) HarpC Child Bks.
—The Helen Keller Story. LC 90-49173. (Illus.). 176p. (gr. 6-10). 1991. PLB 13.95 (1-55905-084-5) Marshall Cavendish.
Pearl, Lauren & Kennedy, Doris F., eds. Lingua Latina Mortua Non Est! Latin Is Not Dead. 22p. (gr. 6-12). 1991. pap. text ed. 1.70 (0-939507-31-5, B5) Amer Classical.
Pearl, Lizzy. The Adventures of Pussycat Wizzy Willums. Thatcher, Fran, illus. LC 92-9475. 26p. (ps-3). 1992. 13.95 (1-56566-020-X) Thomasson-Grant.
—The Story of Flight. Bergin, Mark, illus. LC 91-33412. 32p. (gr. 1-4). 1993. PLB 11.89 (0-8167-2709-0); pap. text ed. 3.95 (0-8167-2710-4) Troll Assocs. Postponed.
Pearlman, Cari J. Take New York Home. (Illus.). (gr. 9-12). 1988. write for info. (0-929644-01-8) MultiMap.
Pearse, Patricia. See How You Grow. Riddell, Edwina, illus. LC 87-33268. 32p. (gr. 1-4). 1988. 13.95 (0-8120-5936-0) Barron.
Pearson. Uncle Alphonso & the Greedy Green Dinosuar. 1992. write for info. (1-55513-424-6, Chariot Bks) Cook.
—Uncle Alphonso & the Puffy Proud Dinosuar. 1992. write for info. (1-55513-562-5, Chariot Bks) Cook.
Pearson, Anne. Ancient Greece. Nicholls, Nick, photos by. LC 92-4713. (Illus.). 64p. (gr. 5 up). 1992. 15.00 (0-679-81682-8); PLB 16.99 (0-679-91682-2) Knopf Bks Yng Read.
—Everyday Life in Ancient Greece. LC 93-37519. 1994. write for info. (0-531-14310-4) Watts.
—What Do We Know about the Greeks? LC 92-9692. (Illus.). 40p. (gr. 3-6). 1992. PLB 16.95 (0-87226-356-8) P Bedrick Bks.
Pearson, Carol L. Don't Count Your Chickens until They Cry Wolf: Musical. 1979. 4.50 (0-87602-122-4) Anchorage.
—I Believe in Make Believe. (Orig.). (gr. k up). 1984. pap. 4.50 (0-87602-255-7) Anchorage.
—A Lasting Peace. LC 90-37361. 158p. (gr. 9-12). 1990. pap. 5.95 (0-87579-302-9) Deseret Bk.
Pearson, Craig. Make Your Own Games Workshop. (gr. 3-8). 1982. pap. 10.95 (0-8224-9782-4) Fearon Teach Aids.
Pearson, David. Gymnastics. (Illus.). 80p. (gr. 10-12). 1991. pap. 6.95 (0-7063-6972-6, Pub. by Ward Lock UK) Sterling.
Pearson, Eileen. Hitler's Reich. Yapp, Malcolm & Killingray, Margaret, eds. (Illus.). (gr. 6-11). 1980. pap. text ed. 3.45 (0-89908-208-4) Greenhaven.
Pearson, Gayle. The Fog Doggies & Me. LC 92-41069. 128p. (gr. 4-8). 1993. SBE 13.95 (0-689-31845-6, Atheneum Child Bk) Macmillan Child Grp.
—One Potato, Tu: Seven Stories. LC 91-22307. 128p. (gr. 5-9). 1992. SBE 12.95 (0-689-31706-9, Atheneum Child Bk) Macmillan Child Grp.
Pearson, Jack. Uncle Alphonso & the Frosty, Fibbing Dinosaurs. Julien, Terry, illus. LC 92-39373. 1993. write for info. (0-7814-0100-3, Chariot Bks) Cook.
Pearson, John R., ed. see Rudig, Doug.
Pearson, Kit. The Daring Game. (Illus.). 240p. (gr. 3-7). 1991. pap. 3.95 (0-14-031932-8, Puffin) Puffin Bks.
—A Handful of Time. (Illus.). 192p. (gr. 3-7). 1991. pap. 3.95 (0-14-032268-X, Puffin) Puffin Bks.
—Looking at the Moon. 224p. (gr. 5-9). 1992. 12.95 (0-670-84097-1) Viking Child Bks.

—The Sky Is Falling. 256p. (gr. 3-7). 1990. pap. 15.00 (0-670-82849-1) Viking Child Bks.
Pearson, Kit, retold by. The Singing Basket. Blades, Ann, illus. 32p. (ps-3). 1991. 13.95 (0-88899-104-5, Pub. by Groundwood-Douglas & McIntyre CN) Firefly Bks Ltd.
Pearson, Mary R. All about God. LC 93-7692. 1993. 8.99 (0-8423-1215-3) Tyndale.
Pearson, Mary Rose. Bible Object Lessons. (gr. 1-6). 1991. packet 4.95 (0-89636-303-1) Accent CO.
—More Children's Church Time. LC 82-70390. 220p. (Orig.). (gr. 1-6). 1982. 14.95 (0-89636-082-2) Accent CO.
—Three Cheers for Big Ears. Park, Julie, illus. 48p. (gr. 2). 1992. pap. 2.99 (0-8423-1043-6) Tyndale.
Pearson, Max. The Trouble with Midas. (Illus.). 30p. (gr. 3 up). 1976. pap. 2.50 (0-88680-195-8); royalty on application 25.00 (0-317-03618-1) I E Clark.
Pearson, Sue. The Haunted School. Pearson, Sue, illus. (gr. 3-6). 1992. pap. 7.95 (1-56680-509-0) Mad Hatter Pub.
Pearson, Susan. The Baby & the Bear. Carlson, Nancy, illus. (ps-k). 1987. pap. 3.95 (0-670-81299-4) Viking Child Bks.
—The Bogeyman Caper. Fiammenghi, Giola, illus. 80p. (gr. 1-3). 1990. pap. 11.95 (0-671-70565-2, S&S BFYR); pap. 2.95 (0-671-70569-5, S&S BFYR) S&S Trade.
—The Campfire Ghosts. Fiammenghi, Giola, illus. 96p. (gr. 1-3). 1990. pap. 11.95 (0-671-70567-9, S&S BFYR); pap. 2.95 (0-671-70571-7, S&S BFYR) S&S Trade.
—The Day Porkchop Climbed the Christmas Tree. Brown, Rick, illus. (gr. k-3). 9.95 (0-317-62031-2) P-H.
—The Day Porkchop Climbed the Christmas Tree. Brown, Rick, illus. (ps up). 1989. pap. 9.95 (0-671-66370-4, S&S BFYR); (S&S BFYR) S&S Trade.
—Eagle-Eye Ernie Comes to Town. Fiammenghi, Gioia, illus. 80p. (gr. 1-3). 1990. pap. 11.95 jacketed (0-671-70564-4, S&S BFYR); pap. 2.95 (0-671-70568-7, S&S BFYR) S&S Trade.
—The Green Magician Puzzle. Fiammenghi, Gioia, illus. LC 90-22436. 1991. pap. 11.95 (0-671-74054-7, S&S BFYR); pap. 2.95 (0-671-74053-9, S&S BFYR) S&S Trade.
—Happy Birthday Grampie. Dillon, Leo & Dillon, Diane, illus. LC 86-31105. 32p. (ps-3). 1987. PLB 10.89 (0-8037-3458-1) Dial Bks Young.
—Jack & the Beanstalk. (ps-6). 1993. pap. 5.95 (0-671-87172-2, S&S BFYR) S&S Trade.
—Karin's Christmas Walk. Noble, Trinka H., illus. LC 80-11739. 32p. (ps-3). 1980. Dial Bks Young.
—Karin's Christmas Walk. Noble, Trinka H., illus. LC 80-11739. 32p. (ps-3). 1983. pap. 4.95 (0-8037-0020-2) Dial Bks Young.
—Lenore's Big Break. Carlson, Nancy, illus. 32p. (gr. k up). 1992. PLB 14.00 (0-670-83474-2) Viking Child Bks.
—Lenore's Big Break. Carlson, Nancy, illus. 32p. (ps-3). 1994. pap. 4.99 (0-14-054294-9) Puffin Bks.
—Monnie Hates Lydia. Paterson, Diane, illus. LC 75-9198. 32p. (ps-3). 1985. Dial Bks Young.
—My Favorite Time of Year. Wallner, John, illus. LC 87-45296. 32p. (ps-3). 1988. PLB 12.89 (0-06-024682-0) HarpC Child Bks.
—The One-Two-Three Zoo Mystery. (gr. 2). 1991. pap. write for info. (0-663-56222-8) Silver Burdett Pr.
—Porkchop's Halloween. Brown, Rick, illus. LC 88-4427. 32p. (gr. k-3). 1988. pap. 13.00 jacketed (0-671-66732-7, S&S BFYR) S&S Trade.
—Porkchop's Halloween. Brown, Rick, illus. 32p. (ps up). 1989. pap. 4.00 (0-671-68872-3, S&S BFYR) S&S Trade.
—The Spooky Sleepover. Fiammenghi, Gioia, illus. 64p. (gr. 1-3). 1991. pap. 12.00 jacketed (0-671-74070-9, S&S BFYR); pap. 3.00 (0-671-74069-5, S&S BFYR) S&S Trade.
—The Spy Code Caper. Fiammenghi, Gioia, illus. 64p. (gr. 1-3). 1991. pap. 12.00 jacketed (0-671-74071-7, S&S BFYR); pap. 3.00 (0-671-74072-5, S&S BFYR) S&S Trade.
—The Tap Dance Mystery. Fiammenghi, Giola, illus. 96p. (gr. 1-3). 1990. (S&S BFYR); pap. 2.95 (0-671-70570-9, S&S BFYR) S&S Trade.
—Well, I Never! Warhola, James, illus. LC 89-48016. 40p. (ps-1). 1990. pap. 13.95 (0-671-69199-6, S&S BFYR) S&S Trade.
—Well, I Never! (gr. 3). 1991. pap. write for info. (0-663-56234-1) Silver Burdett Pr.
Pearson, Susan, retold by. Jack & the Beanstalk. Warhola, James, illus. (ps-3). 1989. pap. 13.95 (0-671-67196-0, S&S BFYR) S&S Trade.
Pearson, Susan, ed. see Clarke, Gus.
Pearson, Susan, ed. see Darling, Kathy.
Pearson, Susan, ed. see Edwards, Michelle.
Pearson, Susan, ed. see Fleetwood, Jenni.
Pearson, Susan, ed. see Harvey, Amanda.
Pearson, Susan, ed. see Hawkes, Kevin.
Pearson, Susan, ed. see Heide, Florence P.
Pearson, Susan, ed. see Hughes, Shirley.
Pearson, Susan, ed. see Lamb, Nancy.
Pearson, Susan, ed. see McKee, David.
Pearson, Susan, ed. see Magnus, Erica.
Pearson, Susan, ed. see Melmed, Laura.
Pearson, Susan, ed. see Monson, A. M.
Pearson, Susan, ed. see Morris, Ann.

Pearson, Susan, ed. see Newton, Jill.
Pearson, Susan, ed. see Ormerod, Jan.
Pearson, Susan, ed. see Pittau, Francisco.
Pearson, Susan, ed. see Sattler, Helen R.
Pearson, Susan, ed. see Spohn, David.
Pearson, Susan, ed. see Wunsch, Marjory.
Pearson, Tracey C. The Howling Dog. (Illus.). 32p. (ps up). 1991. 13.95 (0-374-33502-8) FS&G.
—Old MacDonald Had a Farm. Pearson, Tracey C., illus. LC 83-18815. 32p. (ps-2). 1986. pap. 4.95 (0-8037-0274-4) Dial Bks Young.
—Sing a Song of Sixpence. Pearson, Tracey C., illus. LC 84-14206. 32p. (ps-2). 1988. Dial Bks Young.
—Storekeeper. (ps-3). 1991. pap. 3.95 (0-8037-1052-6, Dial Pied Piper) Puffin Bks.
Pearson, Tracey C., illus. Old MacDonald Had a Farm. LC 83-18815. 32p. (ps-2). 1984. 11.95 (0-8037-0068-7) Dial Bks Young.
—We Wish You a Merry Christmas. LC 82-22224. 32p. (ps up). 1983. 8.95 (0-8037-9368-5); pap. 3.95 (0-8037-0310-4) Dial Bks Young.
Peart, Jane. Dreams of a Longing Heart. 192p. (Orig.). (gr. 10 up). 1990. pap. 7.99 (0-8007-5373-9) Revell.
—Homeward the Seeking Heart. 192p. (Orig.). (gr. 10 up). 1990. pap. 7.99 (0-8007-5374-7) Revell.
—Quest for Lasting Love. (Orig.). (gr. 10 up). 1990. pap. 7.99 (0-8007-5372-0) Revell.
Peaslee, Ann & De Witt, Sorena. Guess What Day It Is? Clayson, David N., illus. 216p. (gr. 3-6). 1988. pap. 14.50 (0-89346-305-1) Heian Intl.
Peaslee, Ann & Kille, Jullien. You Can Make It! You Can Do It! 101 E-Z Holiday Craft-Tivities for Children. Ball, Dave, illus. 120p. (Orig.). (gr. 3-6). 1991. pap. 9.95 (0-89346-337-X) Heian Intl.
Peavy, Linda. Allison's Grandfather. large type ed. 40p. (gr. 3-4). 1984. Repr. of 1981 ed. 9.50 (0-317-01866-3, J-00780-00) Am Printing Hse.
Peavy, Linda & Smith, Ursula. Dreams into Deeds: Nine Women Who Dared. LC 85-40295. 160p. (gr. 6-9). 1985. SBE 14.95 (0-684-18484-2, Scribners Young Read) Macmillan Child Grp.
—Food, Nutrition, & You. LC 82-5694. (Illus.). 192p. (gr. 6 up). 1982. SBE 14.95 (0-684-17461-8, Scribners Young Read) Macmillan Child Grp.
—Women Who Changed Things. LC 82-21612. (Illus.). 208p. (gr. 5 up). 1983. SBE 14.95 (0-684-17849-4, Scribners Young Read) Macmillan Child Grp.
Pechter, Alese. What's in the Deep: An Underwater Adventure for Children. rev. ed. 1991. 14.95 (0-87491-983-5) Acropolis.
Peck, Harry T. The Adventures of Mabel. Rountree, Harry, illus. Cabaniss, Anne M., intro. by. (Illus.). 236p. (gr. k-5). 1986. Repr. of 1896 ed. 19.95 (0-9616844-0-2) Greenhouse Pub.
Peck, Ira. The Life & Words of Martin Luther King Jr. (Illus.). 96p. (Orig.). (gr. 3-7). 1991. pap. 2.95 (0-590-43827-1) Scholastic Inc.
Peck, Kay. Folsom Boy. LC 88-51030. 174p. 1989. pap. 6.95 (1-55523-173-X) Winston-Derek.
Peck, Lee. Coping with Cliques. Rosen, Ruth, ed. LC 92-12380. (gr. 7-12). 1992. 13.95 (0-8239-1412-7) Rosen Group.
Peck, M. Scott. The Friendly Snowflake: A Fable of Faith, Love & Family. Peck, Christopher S., illus. 40p. (gr. 3 up). 1992. 14.95 (1-878685-28-7) Turner Pub GA.
Peck, Marshall H., III, illus. Heavy-Duty Trucks. 14p. (ps-k). 1992. bds. 3.99 (0-679-83244-0) Random Bks Yng Read.
Peck, Richard. Anonymously Yours. 1991. 12.95 (0-671-74162-4, J Messner) S&S Trade.
—Are You in the House Alone? (gr. 10 up). 1976. pap. 15.00 (0-670-13241-1) Viking Child Bks.
—Bel-Air Bambi & the Mall Rats. LC 92-29377. 1993. 14.95 (0-385-30823-X) Delacorte.
—Blossom Culp & the Sleep of Death. (gr. k-6). 1994. pap. 3.99 (0-440-40676-5, YB) Dell.
—Close Enough to Touch. LC 81-65498. 192p. (gr. 7 up). 1981. 15.00 (0-385-28145-5) Delacorte.
—Close Enough to Touch. 144p. (gr. 7 up). 1982. pap. 3.50 (0-440-91282-2, LFL) Dell.
—Don't Look & It Won't Hurt. 1992. pap. 3.50 (0-440-21213-8) Dell.
—The Dreadful Future of Blossom Culp. (gr. 7 up). 1983. 15.00 (0-385-29300-3) Delacorte.
—The Dreadful Future of Blossom Culp. 224p. (gr. 7-12). 1984. pap. 2.95 (0-440-92162-7, LFL) Dell.
—The Dreadful Future of Blossom Culp. (gr. k-6). 1994. pap. 3.99 (0-440-42154-3, YB) Dell.
—Dreamland Lake. 128p. (gr. 7 up). 1990. pap. 3.50 (0-440-92079-5, LFL) Dell.
—Father Figure. LC 78-7909. 208p. (gr. 7 up). 1978. pap. 15.00 (0-670-30930-3) Viking Child Bks.
—Father Figure. (gr. k-12). 1989. pap. 3.50 (0-440-20069-5, LFL) Dell.
—The Ghost Belonged to Me. LC 74-34218. 184p. (gr. 7 up). 1975. pap. 14.95 (0-670-33767-6) Viking Child Bks.
—The Ghost Belonged to Me. 192p. (gr. 5 up). 1983. pap. 3.50 (0-440-93075-8, LFL) Dell.
—The Ghost Belonged to Me. (gr. k-6). 1987. pap. 3.99 (0-440-42861-0, YB) Dell.
—The Ghost Belonged to Me. large type ed. 230p. 1989. Repr. of 1975 ed. lib. bdg. 15.95 (1-55736-116-9, Crnrstn Bks) BDD LT Grp.
—Ghosts I Have Been. 256p. (gr. 5 up). 1979. pap. 3.50 (0-440-92839-7, LFL) Dell.
—Ghosts I Have Been. LC 77-9469. 224p. (gr. 7 up). 1977. pap. 15.00 (0-670-33813-3) Viking Child Bks.

—Ghosts I Have Been. (gr. k-6). 1987. pap. 3.99 (0-440-42864-5, YB) Dell.
—Ghosts I Have Been. (gr. 5 up). 1992. 16.50 (0-8446-6580-0) Peter Smith.
—Princess Ashley. (gr. k-12). 1988. pap. 3.50 (0-440-20206-X, LFL) Dell.
—Remembering the Good Times. (gr. 5-12). 1986. pap. 3.50 (0-440-97339-2, LFL) Dell.
—Representing Super Doll. 192p. (gr. 7 up). 1989. pap. 2.95 (0-440-97362-7, LFL) Dell.
—Secrets of the Shopping Mall. 192p. (gr. k-6). 1989. pap. 3.50 (0-440-40270-0, LFL); pap. 3.50 (0-440-98099-2) Dell.
—Something for Joey. 1983. pap. 3.99 (0-553-27199-7) Bantam.
—Those Summer Girls I Never Met. (gr. k up). 1989. pap. 3.50 (0-440-20457-7, LFL) Dell.
—Through a Brief Darkness. 144p. (gr. 7 up). 1989. pap. 3.25 (0-440-98809-8, LFL) Dell.
—Unfinished Portrait. 1993. pap. 3.99 (0-440-21886-1) Dell.
—Unfinished Portrait of Jessica. 1991. 15.00 (0-385-30500-1) Delacorte.
—Voices after Midnight. (gr. 5-9). 1989. 14.95 (0-385-29779-3) Delacorte.
—Voices after Midnight. 1990. pap. 3.50 (0-440-40378-2, Pub. by Yearling Classics) Dell.
—Write a Tale of Terror. (Illus.). 32p. (gr. 5-10). 1987. pap. 4.95 (0-913839-60-4) Bk Lures.
Peck, Richard, jt. ed. see Hoopes, Ned E.
Peck, Robert. Jo Silver. LC 85-3720. 144p. (gr. 8-12). 1985. 9.95 (0-910923-20-5) Pineapple Pr.
Peck, Robert M. Headhunters & Hummingbirds: An Expedition into Ecuador. LC 86-15908. (Illus.). 128p. (gr. 11 up). 1987. 14.95 (0-8027-6645-5); PLB 14.85 (0-8027-6646-3) Walker & Co.
Peck, Robert N. Arly. 160p. (gr. 5 up). 1989. 16.95 (0-8027-6856-3) Walker & Co.
—Arly. 160p. 1991. pap. 2.95 (0-590-43469-1, Point) Scholastic Inc.
—Arly's Run. 160p. (gr. 5-9). 1991. 16.95 (0-8027-8120-9) Walker & Co.
—A Day No Pigs Would Die. 144p. (gr. 7 up). 1979. pap. 3.50 (0-440-92083-3, LFL) Dell.
—Day No Pigs Would Die. large type ed. 210p. (gr. 3-7). 1987. lib. bdg. 14.95 (1-55736-094-4, Crnrstn Bks); bk. & 3 audio cass. 35.95 (1-55736-095-2) BDD LT Grp.
—Dukes. LC 84-4272. 128p. (gr. 5-9). 1984. 9.95 (0-910923-06-X) Pineapple Pr.
—Higbee's Halloween. 101p. (gr. 5-7). 1990. 13.95 (0-8027-6968-3); lib. bdg. 14.85 (0-8027-6969-1) Walker & Co.
—Little Soup's Birthday. (ps-3). 1991. pap. 2.99 (0-440-40551-3, YB) Dell.
—Little Soup's Bunny. (ps-3). 1993. pap. 2.99 (0-440-40772-9) Dell.
—Little Soup's Hayride. (ps-3). 1991. pap. 2.99 (0-440-40383-9) Dell.
—Little Soup's Turkey. Robinson, Charles, illus. 80p. (Orig.). (gr. 1-4). 1992. pap. 2.99 (0-440-40724-9, YB) Dell.
—Soup. (gr. 3 up). 1979. pap. 3.50 (0-440-48186-4, YB) Dell.
—Soup. Gehm, Charles, illus. LC 73-15117. 104p. (gr. 3 up). 1974. PLB 9.99 (0-394-92700-1) Knopf Bks Yng Read.
—Soup Ahoy. Robinson, Charles, illus. LC 93-14097. 1994. write for info. (0-679-84978-5); PLB write for info. (0-679-94978-X) Knopf.
—Soup & Me. Lilly, Charles, illus. LC 75-9514. 112p. (gr. 3-6). 1975. PLB 10.99 (0-394-93157-2) Knopf Bks Yng Read.
—Soup & Me. large type ed. 139p. 1990. Repr. lib. bdg. 15.95 (1-55736-162-2, Crnrstn Bks) BDD LT Grp.
—Soup for President. Lewin, Ted, illus. LC 77-3548. (gr. 6 up). 1978. PLB 10.99 (0-394-93675-2) Knopf Bks Yng Read.
—Soup for President. (gr. 3-6). 1986. pap. 3.25 (0-440-48188-0, YB) Dell.
—Soup in Love. (gr. 4-7). 1992. 14.00 (0-385-30563-X) Delacorte.
—Soup in Love. (gr. 4-7). 1993. pap. 3.25 (0-440-40755-9) Dell.
—Soup in the Saddle. Robinson, Charles, illus. LC 82-14010. 96p. (gr. 3-6). 1983. PLB 11.99 (0-394-95294-4) Knopf Bks Yng Read.
—Soup on Fire. Robinson, Charles, illus. LC 87-5261. 112p. (gr. 4-7). 1987. pap. 13.95 (0-385-29580-4) Delacorte.
—Soup on Fire. 1987. pap. 13.95 (0-440-50226-8) Dell.
—Soup on Ice. Robinson, Charles, illus. LC 85-218. 128p. (gr. 3-7). 1985. PLB 10.99 (0-394-97613-4) Knopf Bks Yng Read.
—Soup on Wheels. Robinson, illus. LC 80-17661. 128p. (gr. 3 up). 1981. PLB 11.99 (0-394-94581-6) Knopf Bks Yng Read.
—Soup on Wheels. (gr. 3-7). 1986. pap. 3.25 (0-440-48190-2, YB) Dell.
—Soup's Drum. Robinson, Charles, illus. LC 79-17982. 128p. (gr. 3-6). 1980. PLB 10.99 (0-394-94251-5) Knopf Bks Yng Read.
—Soup's Drum. (gr. k-6). 1988. pap. 2.95 (0-440-40003-1) Dell.
—Soup's Goat. Robinson, Charles, illus. LC 83-16245. 112p. (gr. 4-6). 1984. lib. bdg. 12.99 (0-394-96322-9) Knopf Bks Yng Read.
—Soup's Hoop. (gr. 4-7). 1992. pap. 3.25 (0-440-40589-0, YB) Dell.

—Soup's Uncle. Robinson, Charles, illus. LC 87-37538. 112p. (gr. 4-7). 1988. 13.95 (*0-440-50062-1*) Delacorte.
—Soup's Uncle. 1990. pap. 2.95 (*0-440-40308-1*) Dell.
—Spanish Hoof. LC 84-21776. 192p. (gr. 5-9). 1985. lib. bdg. 9.99 (*0-394-97261-9*) Knopf Bks Yng Read.
—Trig. 64p. (gr. 4-6). 1979. pap. 1.25 (*0-440-49098-7*, YB) Dell.
Peck, Rodney. Drugs & Sports. Rosen, Ruth, ed. LC 92-12359. (gr. 7-12). 1992. 14.95 (*0-8239-1420-8*) Rosen Group.
Peck, Sylvia. Kelsey's Raven. 240p. (gr. 5 up). 1992. 14.00 (*0-688-09583-6*) Morrow Jr Bks.
—Seal Child. Parker, Robert A., illus. LC 89-33700. 208p. (gr. 4 up). 1989. 12.95 (*0-688-08682-9*) Morrow Jr Bks.
—Seal Child. (gr. 3-7). 1991. Repr. 3.50 (*0-553-15868-6*, Skylark) Bantam.
Peckham, Alexander. Changing Landscapes. (Illus.). 40p. (gr. 6-9). 1991. PLB 12.90 (*0-531-17289-9*, Gloucester Pr) Watts.
—Global Warming. LC 90-45654. (Illus.). 32p. (gr. 5-8). 1991. PLB 12.40 (*0-531-17274-0*, Gloucester Pr) Watts.
—Resources Control. (Illus.). 40p. (gr. 5-8). 1990. PLB 12.90 (*0-531-17234-1*, Gloucester Pr) Watts.
Peckham, Herbert, jt. auth. see Luehrmann, Arthur.
Peckinpah, Sandra L. Chester...the Imperfect All Star. Moore, Trisha, illus. LC 92-74057. (gr. 1-5). 1993. PLB 15.95 (*0-9627806-1-8*); pap. text ed. 8.95 (*0-9627806-2-6*) Dasan Prodns.
—Rosey...the Imperfect Angel. Moore, Trisha, illus. LC 90-63058. 32p. (ps-4). 1991. 15.95 (*0-9627806-0-X*) Dasan Prodns.
Pedersen, Anne. Kidding Around Atlanta: A Young Person's Guide to the City. (Illus.). 64p. (gr. 3-8). 1989. pap. 9.95 (*0-945465-35-1*) John Muir.
—Kidding Around Washington D.C. A Young Person's Guide. 2nd ed. Finnell, Jim, illus. 64p. (gr. 3 up). 1993. pap. 9.95 (*1-56261-093-7*) John Muir.
—The Kid's Environment Book: What's Awry & Why. (Illus.). 192p. (Orig.). (gr. 6 up) 1991. pap. 13.95 (*0-945465-74-2*) John Muir.
Pedersen, Judy. Out in the Country. Pedersen, Judy, illus. LC 90-40032. 40p. (ps-2). 1991. PLB 14.99 (*0-679-90630-4*) Knopf Bks Yng Read.
—The Tiny Patient. Pedersen, Judy, illus. LC 88-21806. 40p. (ps-2). 1989. PLB 13.99 (*0-394-90170-3*) Knopf Bks Yng Read.
Pedicini, John G. Slow Moe. Serino, John, ed. Marderosian, Mark, illus. 32p. (gr. k-2). 1991. 9.95 (*0-9627436-7-4*) Je Suis Derby.
Peduzzi, Kelli. Ralph Nader: Crusader for Safe Consumer Products. Tolan, Mary, adapted by. LC 90-9924. (Illus.). 64p. (gr. 3-4). 1991. PLB 18.60 (*0-8368-0455-4*) Gareth Stevens Inc.
—Ralph Nader: Crusader for Safe Consumer Products & Lawyer for Public Interest. LC 89-4282. (Illus.). 68p. (gr. 5-6). 1990. PLB 18.60 (*0-8368-0098-2*) Gareth Stevens Inc.
Peduzzi, Kelli & Cummins, Ronnie. Oscar Arias: Peacemaker & Leader among Nations. LC 90-39917. (Illus.). 64p. (gr. 5-6). 1991. PLB 18.60 (*0-8368-0102-4*) Gareth Stevens Inc.
Peebles, Catherine & Edge, Denzil. A Natural Curiosity: Taffy's Search for Self. LC 87-36882. (Illus., Orig.). 1988. pap. 6.95 (*0-939991-01-2*) Learning KY.
Peebles, J. Winston. My Funny Cloud. Beach, Bettye, illus. LC 81-50915. 36p. (ps-3). 1981. 4.95 (*0-938232-00-2*) Winston-Derek.
Peek, Merle. The Balancing Act. LC 86-17547. 32p. (ps-1). 1987. 12.95 (*0-89919-458-3*, Clarion Bks) HM.
—Mary Wore Her Red Dress, & Henry Wore His Green Sneakers. Peek, Merle, illus. LC 84-12733. 32p. (ps-2). 1985. 14.95 (*0-89919-324-2*, Clarion Bks) HM.
—Mary Wore Her Red Dress, & Henry Wore His Green Sneakers. 1988. pap. 4.95 (*0-89919-701-9*, Clarion Bks) HM.
—Mary Wore Her Red Dress & Henry Wore His Green Sneakers. Peek, Merle, illus. 1993. Incl. cassette. 7.70 (*0-395-61577-1*, Clarion Bks) HM.
—Roll Over! A Counting Song. Peek, Merle, illus. 32p. (ps-2). 1981. 14.95 (*0-395-29438-X*, Clarion Bks) HM.
—Roll Over! A Counting Song. Peek, Merle, illus. 32p. (ps). 1993. pap. 4.80 (*0-395-58105-2*, Clarion Bks); pap. 7.95 incl. cassette (*0-395-60117-7*, Clarion Bks) HM.
Peel, John. Alien Prey. Cherry, Eric, illus. 144p. (gr. 3-7). 1993. pap. 3.50 (*0-448-40529-6*, G&D) Putnam Pub Group.
—Blood Wolf. Cherry, Eric, illus. 144p. (gr. 3-7). 1993. pap. 2.95 (*0-448-40527-X*, G&D) Putnam Pub Group.
—Carmen Sandiego: Golden Mini Play Lights. (gr. 4-7). 1993. 14.95 (*0-307-75403-0*, Pub. by Golden Bks) Western Pub.
—Dinotek: Golden Mini Play Lights. (ps-3). 1993. 14.95 (*0-307-75402-2*, Pub. by Golden Bks) Western Pub.
—Foul Play: Simon Says. 144p. (gr. 3-7). 1993. pap. 2.99 (*0-14-036055-7*, Puffin) Puffin Bks.
—Grave Doubts. Cherry, Eric, illus. 144p. (gr. 3-7). 1993. pap. 2.95 (*0-448-40528-8*, G&D) Putnam Pub Group.
—Hangman. LC 92-19940. 128p. (gr. 3-7). 1992. pap. 2.99 (*0-14-036052-2*) Puffin Bks.
—Hide & Seek. LC 92-3757000005. 128p. (gr. 3-7). 1993. pap. 2.99 (*0-14-036054-9*) Puffin Bks.
—Night Wings. Cherry, Eric, illus. 144p. (gr. 3-7). 1993. pap. 2.95 (*0-448-40526-1*, G&D) Putnam Pub Group.

—Shattered. 224p. (Orig.). (gr. 7 up) 1993. pap. 3.50 (*0-671-79406-X*, Archway) PB.
—Tag: You're Dead! LC 92-19939. 128p. (gr. 3-7). 1992. pap. 2.99 (*0-14-036053-0*) Puffin Bks.
—Talons. 224p. (Orig.). 1993. pap. 3.50 (*0-671-79405-1*, Archway) PB.
—Uptime Downtime. LC 90-27570. 1992. pap. 14.00 jacketed, 3-pc. bdg. (*0-671-73274-9*, S&S BFYR) S&S Trade.
—Where in America Is Carmen Sandiego? (Illus.). 32p. (gr. 2-5). 1992. write for info. (*0-307-15859-4*, 15859) Western Pub.
—Where in America's Past Is Carmen Sandiego? Nez, John, illus. Vaccarello, Paul, contrib. by. (Illus.). 96p. (gr. 3-7). 1992. pap. 2.95 (*0-307-22205-5*, 22205, Golden Pr) Western Pub.
—Where in Space Is Carmen Sandiego? (gr. 4-7). 1993. pap. 3.25 (*0-307-22207-1*, Golden Pr) Western Pub.
—Where in Space Is Carmen Sandiego? A Mark & See Book with Marker. (gr. 4-7). 1993. pap. 3.95 (*0-307-22305-1*, Golden Pr) Western Pub.
—Where in the World Is Carmen San Diego? 48p. (gr. 4-7). 1991. pap. 3.95 (*0-307-22301-9*, 22301) Western Pub.
—Where in Time Is Carmen San Diego? 48p. (gr. 4-7). 1991. pap. 3.95 (*0-307-22302-7*, 22302) Western Pub.
—Where in Time Is Carmen Sandiego, Pt. II. Nez, John, illus. 96p. (gr. 3-7). 1993. pap. 3.25 (*0-307-22206-3*, 22206-00, Golden Pr) Western Pub.
Peel, William J., jt. auth. see Dwight, John A.
Peelen, Julie, ed. see Capes, Richard.
Peeples, Freda. C & C Music Factory. (Illus.). 48p. 1992. 1.49 (*0-440-21435-1*) Dell.
—D. J. Jazzy Jeff & the Fresh Prince. (Illus.). 48p. 1992. 1.49 (*0-440-21429-7*) Dell.
—Queen Latifah. (Illus.). 48p. 1992. 1.49 (*0-440-21428-9*) Dell.
Peeples, Jerome. Hammer: What's Hot. 48p. (gr. 4-7). 1992. pap. 1.49 (*0-440-21380-0*) Dell.
Peery, Meira, jt. auth. see Winter, Magda.
Peet, Bill. The Ant & the Elephant. Peet, Bill, illus. LC 74-179918. 48p. (gr. k-3). 1980. 13.95 (*0-395-16963-1*); pap. 7.95 (*0-395-29205-0*) HM.
—Big Bad Bruce. Peet, Bill, illus. LC 76-62502. (gr. k-3). 1982. 13.95 (*0-395-25150-8*); pap. 5.95 (*0-395-32922-1*) HM.
—Big Bad Bruce. (gr. 3 up) 1987. Incl. cass. pap. 7.70 (*0-395-45741-6*) HM.
—Bill Peet: An Autobiography. Peet, Bill, illus. (gr. 3 up). 1989. 16.45 (*0-395-50932-7*) HM.
—Buford, the Little Bighorn. (Illus.). 48p. (gr. k-3). 1983. 13.95 (*0-395-20337-6*); pap. 5.95 (*0-395-34067-5*) HM.
—Caboose Who Got Loose. Peet, Bill, illus. LC 79-155554. 48p. (gr. k-3). 1980. 13.95 (*0-395-14805-7*); pap. 4.80 (*0-395-28715-4*) HM.
—The Caboose Who Got Loose. (gr. 3 up). 1993. pap. 7.95 incl. cassette (*0-395-45740-8*) HM.
—Capyboppy. (Illus.). 62p. (gr. 2-4). 1985. 12.95 (*0-395-24378-5*); pap. 5.95 (*0-395-38368-4*) HM.
—Chester the Worldly Pig. (Illus.). 48p. (gr. k-3). 1980. 13.45 (*0-395-18470-3*) HM.
—Chester the Worldly Pig. Peet, Bill, illus. (gr. k-3). 1978. pap. 4.80 (*0-395-27271-8*) HM.
—Cock-a-Doodle Dudley. Peet, Bill, illus. 48p. (gr. k-3). 1990. 14.45 (*0-395-55331-8*) HM.
—Cock-A-Doodle Dudley. Peet, Bill, illus. 48p. (gr. k-3). 1993. pap. 4.80 (*0-395-65745-8*) HM.
—Countdown to Christmas. Peet, Bill, illus. LC 72-78394. 48p. (gr. k-8). 1972. (Golden Gate); PLB 15.93 (*0-516-08716-9*) Childrens.
—Cowardly Clyde. (Illus.). 48p. (gr. k-3). 1984. 13.45 (*0-395-27802-3*); pap. 5.95 (*0-395-36171-0*) HM.
—Cyrus the Unsinkable Sea Serpent. LC 74-20646. (Illus.). 48p. (gr. k-3). 1982. 13.45 (*0-395-20272-8*); pap. 4.80 (*0-395-31389-9*) HM.
—Eli. Peet, Bill, illus. LC 77-17500. 48p. (gr. k-3). 1978. 13.45 (*0-395-26454-5*) HM.
—Eli. Peet, Bill, illus. LC 77-17500. 48p. (gr. k-3). 1984. pap. 4.95 (*0-395-36611-9*) HM.
—Ella. (Illus.). 48p. (gr. k-3). 1964. 13.45 (*0-395-17577-1*) HM.
—Ella. Peet, Bill, illus. 48p. (gr. k-3). 1978. pap. 4.80 (*0-395-27269-6*) HM.
—Encore for Eleanor. Peet, Bill, illus. 48p. (gr. k-3). 1981. 13.45 (*0-395-29860-1*); pap. 3.95 (*0-317-18520-9*) HM.
—Encore for Eleanor Pa. (ps-3). 1985. pap. 4.80 (*0-395-38367-6*) HM.
—Farewell to Shady Glade. Peet, Bill, illus. 48p. (gr. k-3). 1981. 13.45 (*0-395-18975-6*); pap. 5.70 incl. cassette (*0-395-60166-5*) HM.
—Fly Homer Fly. Peet, Bill, illus. (gr. k-3). 1979. 13.45 (*0-395-24536-2*); pap. 4.80 (*0-395-28005-2*) HM.
—The Gnats of Knotty Pine. Peet, Bill, illus. LC 75-17024. 48p. (gr. k-3). 1984. 13.45 (*0-395-21405-X*); pap. 4.80 (*0-395-36612-7*) HM.
—How Droofus the Dragon Lost His Head. Peet, Bill, illus. LC 75-135136. 48p. (gr. k-3). 1983. 13.45 (*0-395-15085-X*); pap. 4.80 (*0-395-34066-7*) HM.
—Hubert's Hair-Raising Adventure. (Illus.). 36p. (gr. k-3). 1959. 13.45 (*0-395-15083-3*) HM.
—Hubert's Hair-Raising Adventure. (Illus.). (gr. k-3). 1979. pap. 4.80 (*0-395-28267-5*) HM.
—Huge Harold. (Illus.). 48p. (gr. k-3). 1974. 13.45 (*0-395-18449-5*) HM.
—Huge Harold. Peet, Bill, illus. (gr. k-3). 1982. pap. 4.80 (*0-395-32923-X*) HM.

—Jennifer & Josephine. Peet, Bill, illus. (gr. k-3). 1980. 13.95 (*0-395-18225-5*); pap. 4.80 (*0-395-29608-0*) HM.
—Jethro & Joel Were a Troll. LC 86-20879. (Illus.). 32p. (gr. k-3). 1990. 12.95 (*0-395-43081-X*); pap. 4.80 (*0-395-53968-4*) HM.
—Kermit the Hermit. (Illus.). (gr. k-3). 1980. 14.95 (*0-395-15084-1*); pap. 5.95 (*0-395-29607-2*) HM.
—The Kweeks of Kookatumdee. Peet, Bill, illus. LC 84-22379. 32p. (gr. k-3). 1985. 13.95 (*0-395-37902-4*) HM.
—The Kweeks of Kookatumdee. Peet, Bill, illus. 32p. (gr. k-3). 1988. pap. 4.80 (*0-395-48656-4*, Sandpiper) HM.
—The Luckiest One of All. Peet, Bill, illus. (gr. k-3). 1982. 14.95 (*0-395-31863-7*); pap. 4.80 (*0-395-39593-3*) HM.
—Merle the High Flying Squirrel. Peet, Bill, illus. LC 73-18371. 32p. (gr. k-3). 1974. reinforced bdg. 13.45 (*0-395-18452-5*) HM.
—Merle the High Flying Squirrel. Peet, Bill, illus. 30p. (gr. k-3). 1983. pap. 5.70 (*0-395-34923-0*) HM.
—No Such Things. Peet, Bill, illus. LC 82-23234. 32p. (gr. k-3). 1983. 13.95 (*0-395-33888-3*); pap. 4.80 (*0-395-39594-1*) HM.
—Pamela Camel. Peet, Bill, illus. LC 83-18594. 32p. (gr. k-3). 1984. 14.45 (*0-395-35975-9*, 5-93025) HM.
—Pamela Camel. (Illus.). (gr. 4-8). 1986. pap. 4.80 (*0-395-41670-1*, Sandpiper) HM.
—Pinkish, Purplish, Bluish Egg. (Illus.). (gr. k-3). 1984. 13.45 (*0-395-18472-X*); pap. 4.80 (*0-395-36172-9*) HM.
—Randy's Dandy Lions. (Illus.). (gr. k-3). 1979. 13.95 (*0-395-18507-6*); pap. 4.80 (*0-395-27498-2*) HM.
—Smokey. (Illus.). (gr. k-3). 1962. 14.45 (*0-395-15992-X*) HM.
—Smokey. Peet, Bill, illus. 48p. (gr. k-3). 1983. pap. 3.80 (*0-395-34924-9*) HM.
—The Spooky Tail of Prewitt Peacock. (Illus.). (gr. k-3). 1979. pap. 4.80 (*0-395-28159-8*) HM.
—The Spooky Tail of Prewitt Peacock. Peet, Bill, illus. LC 72-7930. 32p. (gr. k-3). 1973. 13.95 (*0-395-15494-4*) HM.
—Whingdingdilly. Peet, Bill, illus. LC 71-98521. (gr. k-3). 1977. 14.45 (*0-395-24729-2*); pap. 4.80 (*0-395-31381-3*) HM.
—Wump World. Peet, Bill, illus. LC 72-124999. (gr. 3-5). 1974. 14.95 (*0-395-19841-0*); pap. 4.80 (*0-395-31129-2*) HM.
—The Wump World. Peet, Bill, illus. 1991. incl. cass. 7.70 (*0-395-58412-4*) HM.
—Zella, Zack & Zodiac. (gr. k-3). 1985. 12.95 (*0-317-40567-5*) HM.
—Zella, Zack, & Zodiac. (Illus.). 32p. (gr. k-3). 1989. pap. 4.80 (*0-395-52207-2*) HM.
Peeters, Benoit. Tintin & the World of Herge: An Illustrated History. (Illus.). 160p. (gr. 5 up). 1992. 40.00 (*0-316-69752-4*, Joy St Bks) Little.
Pef. Belles Lisses Poires de France. (FRE.). 56p. (gr. 1-5). 1990. pap. 8.95 (*2-07-031216-X*) Schoenhof.
—Dictionnaires des Mots Tordus. (FRE.). 79p. (gr. 1-5). 1989. pap. 10.95 (*2-07-031192-9*) Schoenhof.
—Ivre de Francais. (FRE.). 48p. (gr. 1-5). 1986. pap. 7.95 (*2-07-031246-1*) Schoenhof.
—Ivre de Nattes. (FRE.). 78p. (gr. 1-5). 1990. pap. 7.95 (*2-07-031240-2*) Schoenhof.
Peifer, Charles, Jr. George Patton: Soldier of Destiny: A Biography of George Patton. LC 88-20265. (Illus.). 128p. (gr. 5 up). 1988. RSBE 13.95 (*0-87518-395-6*, Dillon) Macmillan Child Grp.
—Houston. LC 88-20197. (Illus.). 60p. (gr. 3 up). 1988. RSBE 13.95 (*0-87518-387-5*, Dillon) Macmillan Child Grp.
Peifer, Jane. The Biggest Popcorn Party Ever in Center County. Nolt, Marilyn P., illus. LC 86-27063. 32p. (Orig.). (ps-1). 1987. pap. 4.95 (*0-8361-3435-4*) Herald Pr.
Peifer, Jane & Nolt, Marilyn. Good Thoughts about Me. (Illus.). 24p. (Orig.). (ps-2). 1985. pap. 2.95 (*0-8361-3389-7*) Herald Pr.
—Good Thoughts at Bedtime. (Illus.). 24p. (Orig.). (ps-2). 1985. pap. 2.95 (*0-8361-3388-9*) Herald Pr.
Peinkowski, Jan. Road Hog. Peinkowski, Jan, illus. 5p. (gr. k-3). 1993. 13.99 (*0-8431-3586-7*) Price Stern.
Peissel, Michel. Dangerous Mammals. (gr. 4-7). 1992. pap. 9.95 (*0-7910-1935-7*, Am Art Analog) Chelsea Hse.
—Dangerous Reptilian Creatures. (gr. 4-7). 1992. pap. 9.95 (*0-7910-1934-9*, Am Art Analog) Chelsea Hse.
—Dangerous Water Creatures. (gr. 4-7). 1992. pap. 9.95 (*0-7910-1932-2*, Am Art Analog) Chelsea Hse.
Peissel, Michel & Allen, Missy. Dangerous Environments. (Illus.). 112p. (gr. 5 up). 1993. PLB 19.95 (*0-7910-1793-1*, Am Art Analog) Chelsea Hse.
—Dangerous Flora. (Illus.). 112p. (gr. 5 up). 1993. PLB 19.95 (*0-7910-1786-9*, Am Art Analog) Chelsea Hse.
—Dangerous Insects. (Illus.). 112p. (gr. 5 up). 1993. PLB 19.95 (*0-7910-1785-0*, Am Art Analog); pap. 9.95 (*0-7910-1933-0*, Am Art Analog) Chelsea Hse.
—Dangerous Mammals. (Illus.). 112p. (gr. 5 up). 1993. PLB 19.95 (*0-7910-1790-7*, Am Art Analog) Chelsea Hse.
—Dangerous Natural Phenomena. (Illus.). 112p. (gr. 5 up). 1993. PLB 19.95 (*0-7910-1794-X*, Am Art Analog) Chelsea Hse.
—Dangerous Plants & Mushrooms. (Illus.). 112p. (gr. 5 up). 1993. PLB 19.95 (*0-7910-1787-7*, Am Art Analog) Chelsea Hse.

—Dangerous Professions. (Illus.). 112p. (gr. 5 up). 1993. PLB 19.95 (0-7910-1792-3, Am Art Analog) Chelsea Hse.

—Dangerous Reptilian Creatures. (Illus.). 112p. (gr. 5 up). 1993. PLB 19.95 (0-7910-1789-3, Am Art Analog) Chelsea Hse.

—Dangerous Sports. (Illus.). 112p. (gr. 5 up). 1993. PLB 19.95 (0-7910-1791-5, Am Art Analog) Chelsea Hse.

—Dangerous Sports. LC 92-23546. 1993. pap. write for info. (0-7910-1942-X) Chelsea Hse.

—Dangerous Water Creatures. (Illus.). 112p. (gr. 5 up). 1993. PLB 19.95 (0-7910-1788-5, Am Art Analog) Chelsea Hse.

—The Encyclopedia of Danger, 10 vols. (Illus.). (gr. 5 up). 1993. Set. PLB 199.50 (0-7910-1784-2, Am Art Analog) Chelsea Hse.

Peitz, Mary. Romeo & Juliet - Study Guide. Friedland, Joyce & Kessler, Rikki, eds. (gr. 9-12). Date not set. pap. text ed. 14.95 (0-88122-127-9) Lrn Links.

Pekarik, Andrew. Painting. LC 92-52987. (Illus.). 64p. (gr. 3-7). 1992. 18.95 (1-56282-296-9); PLB 18.89 (1-56282-297-7) Hyprn Child.

—Sculpture. LC 92-52988. (Illus.). 64p. (gr. 3-7). 1992. 18.95 (1-56282-294-2); PLB 18.89 (1-56282-295-0) Hyprn Child.

Peleg, Dorith E., jt. auth. see Sweetgall, Robert.

Pelfrey, Wanda. Celebrate the Bible. 144p. (gr. 1-6). 1988. 11.95 (0-86653-453-9, SS847, Shining Star Pubns) Good Apple.

Pelham, David. A Is for Animals. (ps) 1991. pap. 15.95 casebound, pop-up (0-671-72495-9, S&S BFYR) S&S Trade.

—Sam's Sandwich. Pelham, David, illus. 22p. (ps-4). 1991. 8.99 (0-525-44751-2, DCB) Dutton Child Bks.

—Sam's Surprise. (Illus.). 22p. (ps-4). 1992. 9.95 (0-525-44947-7, DCB) Dutton Child Bks.

—Worms Wiggle. Foreman, Michael, illus. (ps-1). 1989. pap. 9.95 (0-671-67218-5, Little Simon) S&S Trade.

Pelham, David, ed. see Miller, Jonathan.

Pelham, Erra, jt. auth. see Axsom, Dora.

Pelkey, Eddie J. Gifts of the Heart. LC 91-68090. 113p. (gr. 6 up). 1992. 8.95 (1-55523-503-4) Winston-Derek.

Pelkowski, Robert, jt. auth. see Smith, Alias.

Pella, Judith. Frontier Lady. 400p. (Orig.). 1993. pap. 8.99 (1-55661-293-1) Bethany Hse.

Pella, Judith, jt. auth. see Phillips, Michael.

Pellant, Chris. Rocks & Minerals. (Illus.). 64p. 1990. 7.99 (0-517-05148-6) Outlet Bk Co.

Pellegreno, Ann H. Iowa Takes to the Air: 1845-1918, Vol. 1. LC 79-55458. (Illus.). 288p. (gr. 4 up). 1981. 17.95x (0-935092-01-3) Aerodrome Pr.

—Iowa Takes to the Air: 1919-1941, Vol. 2. LC 79-55458. (Illus.). 336p. (gr. 4 up). 1986. 24.95x (0-935092-02-1) Aerodrome Pr.

Pellegrini, Nina. Charlie Claus: Santa's Best Friend. LC 93-1495. (Illus.). (ps-6). 1993. 4.99 (0-517-09309-X, Pub. by Derrydale Bks) Outlet Bk Co.

—Families Are Different. Pellegrini, Nina, illus. LC 90-22876. 32p. (ps-3). 1991. reinforced 14.95 (0-8234-0887-6) Holiday.

Pellegrini, Nina, jt. auth. see Garcia, Edward.

Pellowski, Anne. Hidden Stories in Plants... Sweat, Lynn, illus. LC 89-37166. 112p. (ps up). 1990. SBE 15.95 (0-02-770611-7, Macmillan Child Bk) Macmillan Child Grp.

Pellowski, Anne, jt. auth. see Miller, Teresa.

Pellowski, Anne, ed. A World of Children's Stories. Ortiz, Gloria, illus. LC 93-13509. 192p. (Orig.). (gr. 3-6). 1993. pap. 19.95 (0-377-00259-3) Friendship Pr.

Pellowski, Michael. Clara Joins the Circus. Kelley, True, illus. LC 80-25602. 48p. (ps-3). 1981. 5.95 (0-8193-1057-3); PLB 5.95 (0-8193-1058-1) Parents.

—Good-bye Millions, No. 10. LC 91-58617. (Illus.). 128p. (Orig.). (gr. 4-8). 1992. pap. 2.99 (1-56282-191-1) Hyprn Child.

—Is That Arabella, No. 9. LC 91-58614. (Illus.). 128p. (Orig.). (gr. 4-8). 1992. pap. 2.99 (1-56282-190-3) Hyprn Child.

—One Hundred Two Cat & Dog Jokes. LC 91-42769. (Illus.). 64p. (gr. 2-6). 1992. pap. text ed. 2.95 (0-8167-2790-2) Troll Assocs.

—One Hundred Two Wacky Monster Jokes. LC 91-44702. (Illus.). 64p. (gr. 2-6). 1992. pap. text ed. 2.95 (0-8167-2746-5) Troll Assocs.

—One Hundred Two Wild & Wacky Jokes. LC 91-30783. (Illus.). 64p. (gr. 2-6). 1991. pap. text ed. 2.95 (0-8167-2612-4) Troll Assocs.

—Tour Troubles - Betty Cooper, Baseball Star. LC 91-58616. (Illus.). 256p. (Orig.). (gr. 4-8). 1992. pap. 3.99 (1-56282-192-X) Hyprn Child.

Pellowski, Michael J. Bad News Boyfriend, No. 2. LC 91-71805. (Illus.). 128p. (gr. 4-8). 1991. pap. 2.99 (1-56282-108-3) Hyprn Child.

—Benny's Bad Day. Cushman, Doug, illus. LC 85-14016. 48p. (Orig.). (gr. 1-3). 1986. PLB 10.59 (0-8167-0620-4); pap. text ed. 3.50 (0-8167-0621-2) Troll Assocs.

—The Big Breakup, No. 5. LC 91-73839. (Illus.). 128p. (gr. 4-8). 1992. pap. 2.99 (1-56282-147-4) Hyprn Child.

—Class Clown, No. 7. LC 91-74005. (Illus.). 128p. (Orig.). (gr. 4-8). 1992. pap. 2.99 (1-56282-113-X) Hyprn Child.

—Copycat Dog. LC 85-14128. (Illus.). 48p. (Orig.). (gr. 1-3). 1986. PLB 10.59 (0-8167-0652-2); pap. text ed. 3.50 (0-8167-0653-0) Troll Assocs.

—The Duck Who Loved Puddles. Paterson, Diane, illus. LC 85-14058. 48p. (Orig.). (gr. 1-3). 1986. PLB 10.59 (0-8167-0578-X); pap. text ed. 3.50 (0-8167-0579-8) Troll Assocs.

—Fire Fighter. Lawn, John, illus. LC 88-10353. 32p. (gr. 1-3). 1989. PLB 10.89 (0-8167-1428-2); pap. text ed. 2.95 (0-8167-1429-0) Troll Assocs.

—Forest Ranger. Ulrich, George, illus. LC 88-10355. 32p. (gr. 1-3). 1989. PLB 10.89 (0-8167-1422-3); pap. text ed. 2.95 (0-8167-1423-1) Troll Assocs.

—Ghost in the Library. Durham, Robert, illus. LC 88-1236. 48p. (Orig.). (gr. 1-4). 1989. PLB 10.59 (0-8167-1337-5); pap. text ed. 3.50 (0-8167-1338-3) Troll Assocs.

—It's First Love, Jughead Jones, No. 4. LC 91-71804. (Illus.). 128p. (gr. 4-8). 1991. pap. 2.99 (1-56282-110-5) Hyprn Child.

—Magic Broom. Garry-McCord, Kathi, illus. LC 85-14054. 48p. (Orig.). (gr. 1-3). 1986. PLB 10.59 (0-8167-0636-0); pap. text ed. 3.50 (0-8167-0637-9) Troll Assocs.

—Maxwell Finds a Friend. Kennedy, Anne, illus. LC 85-14085. 48p. (Orig.). (gr. 1-3). 1986. PLB 10.59 (0-8167-0586-0); pap. text ed. 3.50 (0-8167-0587-9) Troll Assocs.

—The Messy Monster. Paterson, Diane, illus. LC 85-14064. 48p. (Orig.). (gr. 1-3). 1986. PLB 10.59 (0-8167-0570-4); pap. text ed. 3.50 (0-8167-0571-2) Troll Assocs.

—Mixed-up Magic. Cushman, Doug, illus. LC 88-1312. 48p. (Orig.). (gr. 1-4). 1989. PLB 10.59 (0-8167-1327-8); pap. text ed. 3.50 (0-8167-1328-6) Troll Assocs.

—Moosey Saves Money. Harvey, Paul, illus. LC 85-14053. 48p. (Orig.). (gr. 1-3). 1986. PLB 10.59 (0-8167-0628-X); pap. text ed. 3.50 (0-8167-0629-8) Troll Assocs.

—My Father, the Enemy, No. 8. LC 91-58615. (Illus.). 128p. (gr. 4-8). 1992. pap. 2.99 (1-56282-189-X) Hyprn Child.

—No Fleas, Please! Jones, John, illus. LC 85-14066. 48p. (Orig.). (gr. 1-3). 1986. PLB 10.59 (0-8167-0608-5); pap. text ed. 3.50 (0-8167-0609-3) Troll Assocs.

—One Hundred Two School Jokes. Pellowski, Michael, illus. LC 91-20702. 64p. (gr. 2-6). 1991. pap. 2.95 (0-8167-2579-9) Troll Assocs.

—One Last Date with Archie, No. 3. LC 91-71807. (Illus.). 128p. (gr. 4-8). 1991. pap. 2.99 (1-56282-109-1) Hyprn Child.

—Professor Possum's Great Adventure. Durrell, Julie, illus. LC 88-1281. 48p. (Orig.). (gr. 1-4). 1988. PLB 10.59 (0-8167-1341-3); pap. text ed. 3.50 (0-8167-1342-1) Troll Assocs.

—The Puppy Nobody Wanted. Robison, Bill, illus. 24p. (ps-3). 1988. 1.95 (0-87406-338-8) Willowisp Pr.

—Rich Girls Don't Have to Worry, No. 6. LC 91-73840. (Illus.). 128p. (gr. 4-8). 1992. pap. 2.99 (1-56282-148-2) Hyprn Child.

—Teddy on Time. Epstein, Len, illus. LC 85-14127. 48p. (Orig.). (gr. 1-3). 1986. PLB 10.59 (0-8167-0582-8); pap. text ed. 3.50 (0-8167-0583-6) Troll Assocs.

—The Trouble with Candy, No. 1. LC 91-71806. (Illus.). 128p. (gr. 4-8). 1991. pap. 2.99 (1-56282-107-5) Hyprn Child.

—What's It Like to Be a Police Officer. Dolobowsky, Mena, illus. LC 89-34395. 32p. (gr. k-3). 1990. lib. bdg. 10.89 (0-8167-1811-3); pap. text ed. 2.95 (0-8167-1812-1) Troll Assocs.

—Who Can't Follow an Ant? Swan, Susan, illus. LC 85-14009. 48p. (Orig.). (gr. 1-3). 1986. PLB 10.59 (0-8167-0592-5); pap. text ed. 3.50 (0-8167-0593-3) Troll Assocs.

Pelnar, Tom & Weber, Valerie, eds. Tanzania. Nakamura, Haruko, photos by. LC 88-42890. (Illus.). 64p. (gr. 5-6). 1989. PLB 19.93 (1-55532-210-7) Gareth Stevens Inc.

Pelowich, Nadia, jt. ed. see Stewart, Janet.

Pelphrey, Jo Ann. Into the Think Tank with Literature. Keeling, Jan, ed. (Illus.). 160p. (Orig.). (gr. k-3). 1992. pap. text ed. 14.95 (0-86530-192-1, IP193-6) Incentive Pubns.

Pelt, Nancy L. Van see Van Pelt, Nancy L.

Pelta, Kathy. Alexander Graham Bell. (Illus.). 144p. (gr. 5-9). 1989. PLB 13.98 (0-382-09529-4) Silver Burdett Pr.

—Bridging the Golden Gate. (Illus.). 96p. (gr. 4-8). 1987. PLB 15.95 (0-8225-1707-8); pap. 5.95 (0-8225-9521-4) Lerner Pubns.

—California. LC 93-1497. (Illus.). 1993. lib. bdg. write for info. (0-8225-2738-3) Lerner Pubns.

—Discovering Christopher Columbus: How History Is Invented. 112p. (gr. 4-6). 1991. PLB 19.95 (0-8225-4899-2) Lerner Pubns.

—Texas. LC 93-33390. 1994. PLB write for info. (0-8225-2749-9) Lerner Pubns.

—The U. S. Navy. (Illus.). 88p. (gr. 5 up). 1990. PLB 22.95 (0-8225-1435-4) Lerner Pubns.

—Vermont. LC 93-33389. 1994. PLB write for info. (0-8225-2729-4) Lerner Pubns.

Pelton, Dan, ed. see Pelton, Jeanette.

Pelton, Dan, ed. see Pelton, Jeanette & Pelton, Fawn.

Pelton, Fawn, jt. auth. see Pelton, Jeanette.

Pelton, Jeanette. Don't Call Me Emmy! 94p. (gr. 5-8). 1991. pap. 3.50 (1-879564-02-5) Long Acre Pub.

—Folks I Wish I'd Known. Pelton, Dan, ed. Pelton, Fawn, illus. 75p. (gr. 5-8). 1993. pap. 4.00 (1-879564-05-X) Long Acre Pub.

—God Wanted to Write a Best Seller, So in the Beginning Was the Word. LC 91-90003. 52p. (gr. 6 up). 1991. pap. 5.95 (1-879564-00-9, GWBS101) Long Acre Pub.

—Kids Grow in My Garden. Pelton, Fawn, illus. LC 91-90004. 88p. (gr. 4-6). 1991. pap. 3.50 (1-879564-01-7, GWG1) Long Acre Pub.

—Natural Morning. Pelton, Dan, ed. Pelton, Fawn, illus. 100p. (Orig.). (gr. 5-7). 1993. pap. 6.00 (1-879564-06-8) Long Acre Pub.

Pelton, Jeanette & Pelton, Fawn. Crafts for a Long, Boring, What-Do-I-Do-Now Afternoon. Pelton, Dan, ed. (Illus.). 50p. (Orig.). (gr. 4-7). 1993. pap. 4.00 (1-879564-04-1) Long Acre Pub.

Pelzel, Vernise E. The Story of Orange. Monk, Lenore, ed. Pelzel, Kelly C., illus. 48p. (gr. 3-12). 1987. pap. 6.95 (0-944131-01-8) HPL Pub.

Pemberton, Judy. Let's Get Cooking. Anderson, Judith, illus. 103p. (Orig.). (gr. 3-12). 1984. text ed. 7.95 (0-317-02695-X) King Fisher Pr.

Pemberton, Nancy. Animal Habitats: The Best Home of All. Dunnington, Tom, illus. LC 90-30633. 32p. (ps-2). 1990. PLB 21.35 (0-89565-578-0); PLB 14.95s.p. (0-685-56194-1) Childs World.

Pemberton, Nancy & Riehecky, Janet. Responsibility. Hohag, Linda, illus. LC 87-37557. 32p. (gr. k-3). 1988. PLB 21.35 (0-89565-418-0); PLB 14.95s.p. (0-685-55933-5) Childs World.

Pemberton, William E. George Bush. LC 92-46768. 1993. 19.93 (0-86625-478-1); 14.95s.p. (0-685-66539-9) Rourke Pubns.

Pembleton, Seliesa. The Armadillo. LC 91-43731. (Illus.). 60p. (gr. 4 up). 1992. RSBE 13.95 (0-87518-507-X, Dillon) Macmillan Child Grp.

—The Pileated Woodpecker. LC 88-20220. (Illus.). 60p. (gr. 3 up). 1988. RSBE 13.95 (0-87518-392-1, Dillon) Macmillan Child Grp.

Pen Notes Staff. Italic Calligraphy Kit. (gr. 3 up). 1979. incl. chisel tip market, italic bklet. instrns., parchment paper, plastic reusable template guidelines 9.95 (0-939564-10-6) Pen Notes.

—Learn to Print Spanish: (Aprendiendo a Escribir las Letras. (ps up). 1989. Bilingual instrns. 10.95 (0-939564-17-3) Pen Notes.

—Learn to Tell Time. (gr. 1 up). 1982. 8.95 (0-939564-02-5) Pen Notes.

—Learning to Print. (ps up). 1984. 10.95 (0-939564-01-7) Pen Notes.

Pena, Alba dela see Dela Pena, Alba.

Pena, Flora, tr. see Fine, Anne.

Pena, Sylvia C., ed. Kikiriki: Stories & Poems in English & Spanish for Children. 2nd ed. LC 81-68072. (ENG & SPA., Illus.). 116p. (Orig.). (gr. k-6). 1989. pap. 8.50 (0-685-34571-8) Arte Publico.

—Tun-Ta-Ca-Tun: More Stories & Poems in English & Spanish for Children. LC 84-72297. (ENG & SPA.). 80p. (Orig.). (ps up). 1985. pap. 9.50 (0-934770-43-3) Arte Publico.

Pender, Gresilda. God's Little People. 1993. 7.95 (0-8062-4631-6) Carlton.

Pendergast, Kathleen. Say Another One about How I Feel. Tindal, Pauline, illus. LC 81-90678. 54p. (Orig.). (gr. k-6). 1982. pap. 6.95 (0-942178-00-9) Madison Park Pr.

—Say Another One about My Family. Tindal, Pauline, illus. LC 82-61139. 54p. (gr. k-6). 1982. pap. 6.95 (0-942178-01-7) Madison Park Pr.

—Say Another One about Playing. LC 83-62129. (Illus.). 54p. (gr. k-6). 1983. pap. 6.95 (0-942178-02-5) Madison Park Pr.

Pendergraft, Patricia. As Far as Mill Springs. (gr. 5 up). 1991. 15.95 (0-399-22102-6, Philomel) Putnam Pub Group.

—Brushy Mountain. (gr. 5 up). 1989. 14.95 (0-399-21610-3, Philomel Bks) Putnam Pub Group.

—Hear the Wind Blow. 208p. (gr. 5 up). 1988. 14.95 (0-399-21528-X, Philomel Bks) Putnam Pub Group.

—The Legend of Daisy Flowerdew. 192p. 1990. 14.95 (0-399-22176-X, Philomel Bks) Putnam Pub Group.

—Miracle at Clement's Pond. (gr. 5 up). 1987. 13.95 (0-399-21438-0, Philomel Bks) Putnam Pub Group.

Pendle, George. History of Latin America. (Orig.). (gr. 11 up). 1963. pap. 6.95 (0-14-020620-5) Viking Child Bks.

Pene Du Bois, William. Bear Circus. (Illus.). 1987. pap. 3.95 (0-14-050792-2, Puffin) Puffin Bks.

—Gentleman Bear. LC 84-48320. (Illus.). 80p. (gr. k up). 1985. 14.95 (0-374-32533-2) FS&G.

—Gentleman Bear. (Illus.). 80p. (ps up). 1988. pap. 5.95 (0-374-42536-1) FS&G.

—Peter Graves. (Illus.). 172p. (gr. 3-7). 1991. pap. 3.95 (0-14-034784-4, Puffin) Puffin Bks.

—Twenty-One Balloons. Pene Du Bois, William, illus. 192p. (gr. 4-8). 1982. pap. 2.75 (0-440-49183-5, YB) Dell.

—The Twenty-One Balloons. Pene Du Bois, William, illus. LC 85-9. (gr. 5-9). 1947. pap. 15.00 (0-670-73441-1) Viking Child Bks.

Pene du Bois, William see Newbery Library Award Staff.

Penisten, John. Honolulu. LC 89-11973. (Illus.). 60p. (gr. 3 up). 1990. RSBE 13.95 (0-87518-416-2, Dillon) Macmillan Child Grp.

Penland, Violet & Johnson, Diane. Arizona Alphabet. Johnson, Diane, illus. (Orig.). 1989. pap. text ed. write for info. Bellwether UT.

Penn, Audrey. The Kissing Hand. Harper, Ruth E. & Leak, Nancy M., illus. LC 93-36159. 1993. 14.95 (*0-87868-585-5*) Child Welfare.
—No Bones about Driftiss. Loving, Judy V., illus. LC 89-13326. viii, 146p. (gr. 2-6). 1989. lib. bdg. 14.95 (*0-939923-11-4*); pap. 7.95 (*0-939923-12-2*) M & W Pub Co.
Penn, Audrey & Ewing, C. S. Blue Out of Season. LC 84-13584. (Illus.). (gr. 3-6). 1985. 10.95 (*0-915556-14-6*) Great Ocean.
Penn, Linda. Young Scientists Explore: Insects, Bk. 1. 32p. (gr. k-3). 1982. 5.95 (*0-86653-070-3*, GA 403) Good Apple.
—Young Scientists Explore: Seasons. Scott, Elaine, illus. 32p. (gr. k-3). 1983. wkbk. 5.95 (*0-86653-123-8*, GA 453) Good Apple.
Pennanen, Judi. Heads or Tails. (ps-8). 1989. pap. 7.95 (*0-921254-11-3*, Pub. by Penumbra Pr CA) U of Toronto Pr.
Penner, Fred. Ebeneezer Sneezer. Hicks, Barbara, illus. 36p. (Orig.). (gr. 2-6). 1990. pap. 5.95 (*0-920534-37-6*, Pub. by Hyperion Pr Ltd CN) Sterling.
—Fred Penner's Sing along - Play Along. Hicks, Barbara, illus. 112p. (Orig.). (gr.-p4). 1991. 14.95 (*0-89524-625-2*) Cherry Lane.
—Rollerskating. Hicks, Barbara, illus. 32p. (Orig.). (gr. 2-6). 1990. pap. 5.95 (*0-920534-64-3*, Pub. by Hyperion Pr Ltd CN) Sterling.
Penner, Fred & Oberman, Sheldon. Julie Gerond & the Polka Dot Pony. Pakarnyk, Alan, illus. 32p. (gr. 2-6). 1990. pap. 5.95 (*0-920534-70-8*, Pub. by Hyperion Pr Ltd CN) Sterling.
Penner, Lucille R. Celebration: The Story of American Holidays. Ohlsson, Ib, illus. LC 92-25871. 80p. (gr. 1 up). 1993. SBE 15.95 (*0-02-770903-5*, Macmillan Child Bk) Macmillan Child Grp.
—Colonial Cookbook. (Illus.). 128p. (gr. 4 up). 1976. 14. 95 (*0-8038-1202-7*) Hastings.
—Dinosaur Babies: A Step One Book. Barrett, Peter, illus. LC 90-36045. 32p. (Orig.). (ps-1). 1991. lib. bdg. 7.99 (*0-679-91207-X*); pap. 2.95 (*0-679-81207-5*) Random Bks Yng Read.
—Eating the Plates: A Pilgrim Book of Food & Manners. LC 90-5918. (Illus.). 128p. (gr. 1-5). 1991. SBE 14.95 (*0-02-770901-9*, Macmillan Child Bk) Macmillan Child Grp.
—The Tea Party Book. Wheeler, Jody, illus. LC 91-52093. 48p. (gr.-p4). 1993. 10.00 (*0-679-82440-5*); PLB 10.99 (*0-679-92440-X*) Random Bks Yng Read.
—The Thanksgiving Book. Donnelly, Judy, ed. LC 84-518. (Illus.). (gr. 4 up). 1985. 14.95 (*0-8038-7228-3*) Hastings.
Pennie. Love Songs for Our Children. Szasz, Suzanne, photos by. Siegel, Bernie S., intro. by. (Illus.). 40p. (Orig.). (ps up). 1989. pap. 13.95 incl. cassette (*0-9624135-1-8*) Songs & Co.
Pennington, Celeste, ed. see Durham, Jackie.
Pennington, Dan. Itseselu: Cherokee Harvest Festival. (Illus.). 32p. (ps-4). 1994. 14.95 (*0-88106-852-7*); PLB 15.00 (*0-88106-852-7*); pap. 6.95 (*0-88106-850-0*) Charlesbridge Pub.
Pennington, Eunice. Perry, the Pet Pig. Pennington, Eunice, illus. (gr. 4-7). 1966. 3.00 (*0-685-19374-8*, 911120-06-8*); pap. 1.00 (*0-685-19375-6*) Pennington.
Pennington, Lillian B. Snafu: The Littlest Clown. Gardner, Earle, illus. LC 73-90113. 32p. (gr. 1-6). 1972. PLB 9.95 (*0-913532-00-2*); cassette 7.94x (*0-87783-225-0*) Oddo.
Pennock, Michael. The Catholic Church Story. LC 90-64153. (Illus.). 224p. (Orig.). (gr. 9-12). 1991. pap. text ed. 8.95 (*0-87793-447-9*); tchr's ed. 12.95 (*0-87793-448-7*) Ave Maria.
—Choosing: Cases in Moral Decision Making. LC 90-85155. 160p. (Orig.). (gr. 9-12). 1991. spiral bdg. 7.95 (*0-87793-446-0*) Ave Maria.
—Forming a Catholic Conscience. LC 90-84839. (Illus.). 208p. (Orig.). (gr. 9-12). 1991. pap. text ed. 8.95 (*0-87793-444-4*); tchr's ed., 168 pgs. 11.95 (*0-87793-445-2*) Ave Maria.
—Growing in the Catholic Faith. LC 89-82328. (Illus., Orig.). (gr. 9-12). 1990. Student text, 200p. pap. text ed. 7.95 (*0-87793-418-5*); tchr's. manual, 168p. 10.95 (*0-87793-419-3*) Ave Maria.
—Jesus: Friend & Savior. LC 89-82459. (Orig.). (gr. 9-12). 1990. pap. text ed. 7.95 student text, 208p. (*0-87793-420-7*); tchr's. manual, 176p. 10.95 (*0-87793-421-5*) Ave Maria.
—The Sacraments: Celebrating the Signs of God's Love. LC 92-75347. (Illus.). 240p. (Orig.). (gr. 9-12). 1993. pap. 9.95 (*0-87793-503-3*); 13.95 (*0-87793-504-1*) Ave Maria.
Pennock, Michael F. Discovering the Promise of the Old Testament. LC 91-76778. (Illus.). 224p. (Orig.). (gr. 9-12). 1992. pap. text ed. 8.95 student text (*0-87793-472-X*); tchr's. manual 12.95 (*0-87793-473-8*) Ave Maria.
—Living the Message of the New Testament. LC 91-77474. (Illus.). 216p. (Orig.). (gr. 9-12). 1992. pap. text ed. 8.95 student text (*0-87793-469-X*); tchr's. manual 12.95 (*0-87793-468-1*) Ave Maria.
Penny, Malcolm. Bears. LC 90-35063. (Illus.). 32p. (gr. 2-4). 1991. PLB 12.40 (*0-531-18368-8*, Pub. by Bookwright Pr) Watts.
—Exploiting the Sea. LC 90-38112. (Illus.). 32p. (gr. 4-7). 1991. PLB 12.40 (*0-531-18359-9*, Pub. by Bookwright Pr) Watts.
—Let's Look At Bears. (ps-3). 1990. PLB 11.40 (*0-531-18321-1*, Pub. by Bookwright Pr) Watts.

—Let's Look At Sharks. (ps-3). 1990. PLB 11.40 (*0-531-18308-4*, Pub. by Bookwright Pr) Watts.
—Let's Look at Whales. (Illus.). 32p. (gr. k-4). 1990. PLB 11.40 (*0-531-18331-9*, Pub. by Bookwright Pr) Watts.
—The Monkey & the Ape: Close Relatives. Stefoff, Rebecca, ed. LC 92-10243. (Illus.). 31p. (gr. 3-6). 1992. PLB 17.26 (*1-56074-051-5*) Garrett Ed Corp.
—Pollution & Conservation. Furstinger, Nancy, ed. (Illus.). 48p. (gr. 5-8). 1989. PLB 16.98 (*0-382-09792-0*) Silver Burdett Pr.
—Protecting Wildlife. LC 90-9925. (Illus.). 48p. (gr. 4-9). 1990. PLB 19.92 (*0-8114-2389-1*); pap. 5.95 (*0-8114-3455-9*) Raintree Steck-V.
—Rhinos. LC 90-21968. (Illus.). 32p. (gr. k-4). 1991. 12. 40 (*0-531-18396-3*, Pub. by Bookwright Pr) Watts.
Penny, Rob. Romance Rhythm & Revolution: New & Selected Poetry. 2nd ed. 100p. (gr. 9-12). 1993. pap. text ed. 9.95 (*0-685-60180-3*) Magnolia PA.
Pennywell, Sylvia C. The Gift of Hope. Dean, William R., illus. 21p. 1992. pap. 12.00 (*0-9637324-0-4*) Silver Grace Pubs.
—The Gift of Peace. Dean, William R., illus. 21p. (Orig.). 1993. pap. 12.00 (*0-9637324-1-2*) Silver Grace Pubs.
Penovich, Beatrice A., ed. see Witter, Evelyn, et al.
Penovich, Geraldine, ed. see Witter, Evelyn, et al.
Penrod, John S. Copper Country. (Orig.). (gr. 9 up). 1990. pap. 4.49 (*0-942618-23-8*) Penrod-Hiawatha.
—Indiana, a Pictorial Guide. rev. ed. (gr. 9 up). 1990. pap. 4.49 (*0-942618-21-1*) Penrod-Hiawatha.
—Straits of Mackinac & Mackinac Island. rev. ed. (gr. 7 up). 1989. pap. 4.49 (*0-942618-20-3*) Penrod-Hiawatha.
—Tahquamenon in Michigan's Upper Peninsula. (gr. 7 up). 1988. pap. 4.49 (*0-942618-12-2*) Penrod-Hiawatha.
—The Upper Peninsula of Michigan. rev. ed. (gr. 7 up). 1988. pap. 4.49 (*0-942618-11-4*) Penrod-Hiawatha.
Penrose, Gordon. Dr. Zed's Dazzling Book of Science Activities. Bucholtz-Ross, Linda, illus. 48p. 1993. pap. 7.95 (*0-919872-78-6*, Pub. by Greey dePencier CN) Firefly Bks Ltd.
—Dr. Zed's Science Surprises. 1990. pap. 11.95 (*0-671-70542-3*); pap. 6.95 (*0-671-70541-5*) PB.
—More Science Surprises from Dr. Zed. LC 91-38935. (Illus.). 32p. (gr. k-3). 1992. pap. 12.00 (*0-671-77810-2*, S&S BFYR); pap. 6.00 (*0-671-77811-0*, S&S BFYR) S&S Trade.
—Sensational Science Activities with Dr. Zed. LC 90-9724. (Illus.). 48p. (gr. 3-7). 1990. pap. 11.95 (*0-671-72552-1*, S&S BFYR); pap. 5.95 (*0-671-72553-X*, S&S BFYR) S&S Trade.
Penson, Mary. You're an Orphan, Mollie Brown: A Novel. Shaw, Charles, illus. LC 92-23407. 122p. (gr. 5-8). 1993. pap. 9.95 (*0-87565-111-9*) Tex Christian.
Penzler, Otto. Danger! White Water. LC 75-21844. (Illus.). 32p. (gr. 5-10). 1976. PLB 10.79 (*0-89375-004-2*) Troll Assocs.
—Hang Gliding: Riding the Wind. LC 75-21843. (Illus.). 32p. (gr. 5-10). 1976. PLB 10.79 (*0-89375-008-5*); pap. 2.95 (*0-89375-024-7*) Troll Assocs.
—Hunting the Killer Shark. LC 75-23409. (Illus.). 32p. (gr. 5-10). 1976. PLB 10.79 (*0-89375-009-3*); pap. 2.95 (*0-89375-025-5*) Troll Assocs.
People for the Ethical Treatment of Animals Staff. We're All Animals Coloring Book. (Illus.). 16p. (Orig.). (gr. k-5). Date not set. pap. text ed. 3.35 (*0-9622101-0-2*) Peta Pubns.
Pepin, Muriel. Brave Little Fox. Fichaux, Catherine, illus. LC 93-4238. (gr. 4 up). 1993. write for info. (*0-89577-541-7*, Readers Digest Kids) RD Assn.
—Little Bear's New Friend. Geneste, Marcelle, illus. LC 91-40652. 22p. (ps). 1992. 6.99 (*0-89577-417-8*, Readers Digest Kids) RD Assn.
—Little Puppy Saves the Day. Geneste, Marcelle, illus. LC 91-46499. 22p. (ps). 1992. 6.99 (*0-89577-426-7*, Readers Digest Kids) RD Assn.
Peplow, Evelyn, jt. auth. see Harper, Peter.
Peplow, Mary. England. LC 89-21786. (Illus.). 96p. (gr. 6-12). 1990. PLB 19.92 (*0-8114-2428-6*) Raintree Steck-V.
Peplow, Mary & Shipley, Debra. Ireland. LC 90-32821. (Illus.). 96p. (gr. 6-12). 1990. PLB 19.92 (*0-8114-2430-8*) Raintree Steck-V.
Peppe, Rodney. ABC Index. LC 90-41951. (Illus.). 28p. (gr. k-2). 1991. 9.95 (*0-87226-441-6*, Bedrick Blackie) P Bedrick Bks.
—The Animal Directory: A First Counting Book. LC 89-18000. (Illus.). 24p. (gr. k-2). 1990. bds. 9.95 (*0-87226-421-1*, Bedrick Blackie) P Bedrick Bks.
—Circus Numbers. Peppe, Rodney, illus. LC 75-86381. (ps-3). 1969. 5.95 (*0-440-01288-0*); pap. 3.69 (*0-440-01289-9*) Delacorte.
—Circus Numbers: A Counting Book. (Illus.). 32p. (ps-2). 1985. 11.95 (*0-385-29424-7*) Delacorte.
—The Color Catalog. Peppe, Rodney, illus. 24p. (gr. k-2). 1992. 9.95 (*0-87226-472-6*, Bedrick Blackie) P Bedrick Bks.
—Here Comes Huxley Pig. (ps-3). 1993. pap. 2.99 (*0-440-40794-X*) Dell.
—The House That Jack Built. Peppe, Rodney, illus. 32p. (ps-3). 1985. pap. 4.95 (*0-385-28430-6*) Delacorte.
—Huxley Pig the Clown. 1990. 8.95 (*0-385-29819-6*) Doubleday.
—Huxley Pig the Clown. (ps-3). 1993. pap. 2.99 (*0-440-40795-8*) Dell.
—Huxley Pig's Airplane. Peppe, Rodney, illus. (ps-2). 1990. 8.95 (*0-385-30038-7*) Doubleday.

—Huxley Pig's Model Car. (ps). 1991. pap. 8.95 (*0-385-30238-X*) Doubleday.
—Mice on the Moon. (gr. 4 up). 1993. pap. 13.95 (*0-385-30839-6*) Doubleday.
—Run Rabbit, Run! A Pop-Up Book. Peppe, Rodney, illus. LC 82-70307. 12p. (ps-3). 1982. pap. 8.95 (*0-385-28851-4*) Delacorte.
—The Shapes Finder. Peppe, Rodney, illus. 24p. (ps). 1991. bds. 9.95 (*0-87226-462-9*, Bedrick Blackie) P Bedrick Bks.
—Thumbprint Circus. Peppe, Rodney, illus. (ps-1). 1989. 12.95 (*0-440-50154-7*) Delacorte.
—Thumbprint Circus. Peppe, Rodney, illus. 32p. (ps-1). 1992. pap. 3.99 (*0-440-40692-7*, YB) Dell.
Pepper Bird Staff. Copasetic: Adventures of Bojangles Robinson. Rose, Ann C., illus. 48p. (Orig.). (gr. 4-7). 1993. pap. 3.95 (*1-56817-000-9*) Pepper Bird.
—Frozen Fury: Adventures of Matthew Henson. Rose, Ann C., illus. 48p. (Orig.). (gr. 4-7). 1993. pap. 4.95 (*1-56817-001-7*) Pepper Bird.
—Pea Island Rescue. Rose, Ann C., illus. 48p. (Orig.). (gr. 4-7). 1993. pap. 4.95 (*1-56817-002-5*) Pepper Bird.
—Wild Frontier: Adventures of Jean Baptiste Du Sable. Rose, Ann C., illus. 48p. (Orig.). (gr. 4-7). 1993. pap. 4.95 (*1-56817-003-3*) Pepper Bird.
Pepper, Bob. The Care Bears' Book of Favorite Bedtime Stories. Cooke, Tom, illus. 48p. (ps-3). 1984. 5.95 (*0-910313-20-2*) Parker Bros.
Pepper, Dennis. The Oxford Merry Christmas Storybook. (Illus.). 160p. (gr. 1 up). 1990. jacketed 16.95 (*0-19-278127-8*) OUP.
Pepper, Dennis, ed. An Oxford Book of Christmas Stories. Brown, Judy, illus. 224p. (gr. 3 up). 1988. 16. 95 (*0-19-278119-7*); pap. 10.95 1988 (*0-19-278124-3*) OUP.
—The Oxford Book of Scary Tales. (Illus.). 160p. 1992. 19.00 (*0-19-278131-6*) OUP.
Peppin. Story of Painting. (Illus.). 32p. 1980. PLB 13.96 (*0-88110-030-7*); pap. 6.95 (*0-86020-441-3*) EDC.
Peppin, Anthea. Nature in Art. LC 91-35014. (Illus.). 48p. (gr. 2-6). 1992. PLB 13.90 (*1-56294-173-9*) Millbrook Pr.
—Nature in Art. 1992. pap. 6.70 (*0-395-64555-7*) HM.
—People in Art. LC 91-34983. (Illus.). 48p. (gr. 2-6). 1992. PLB 13.90 (*1-56294-171-2*) Millbrook Pr.
—People in Art. (gr. 4-7). 1992. pap. 6.70 (*0-395-64556-5*) HM.
—Places in Art. LC 91-34978. (Illus.). 48p. (gr. 2-6). 1992. PLB 13.90 (*1-56294-172-0*) Millbrook Pr.
—Places in Art. (gr. 4-7). 1992. pap. 6.70 (*0-395-64557-3*) HM.
Peppin, Anthea, jt. auth. see Armstrong, Carole.
Perales, Andre P. Fanfou dans les Bayous: The Adventures of a Bilingual Elephant in Louisiana. Jarlov, Christian, illus. LC 82-15148. 40p. (gr. 1-7). 1982. pap. 5.95 (*0-88289-378-5*); cassette 11.95 (*0-88289-410-2*) Pelican.
Peraza, Michael, illus. An Under-the-Sea Christmas: A Holiday Songbook. 48p. 1993. 9.95 (*1-56282-504-6*) Disney Pr.
Percy, Graham. Christmas Sticker Book. (Illus.). (ps-1). 1992. 9.00 (*1-56021-187-3*) W J Fantasy.
—City Mouse & Country Mouse, Heron & the Fish, Crow & the Fox, Lion & the Mouse, 4 bks. Percy, Graham, illus. 32p. (ps-2). 1993. Set. PLB 19.95 (*0-8050-2563-4*, Bks Young Read) H Holt & Co.
—Cock, the Mouse, & the Little Red Hen. LC 91-71857. (ps-3). 1994. pap. 5.99 (*1-56402-268-4*) Candlewick Pr.
—Favorite Fable Special. 1993. write for info. (*0-8050-3083-2*) H Holt & Co.
—Max and the Orange Door. LC 92-45563. (Illus.). (gr. 3 up). 1993. write for info. (*1-56766-076-2*) Childs World.
—Max & the Very Rare Bird. (Illus.). 32p. 1991. 22.80 (*0-89565-786-4*); 15.95 s.p. (*0-685-55068-0*) Childs World.
—Meg & Her Circus Tricks. (Illus.). 32p. 1991. 22.80 (*0-89565-785-6*); 15.95 s.p. (*0-685-55069-9*) Childs World.
—Meg & the Great Race. Percy, Graham, illus. LC 92-44851. 1993. write for info. (*1-56766-077-0*) Childs World.
Percy, Graham, retold by. & illus. The Tortoise & the Hare: And Other Favorite Fables, 4 bks. (ps-2). 1993. Set, 32p. eac. bk. boxed 19.95 (*0-8050-2556-1*) H Holt & Co.
Percy, Graham, illus. The Cock, the Mouse, & the Little Red Hen. LC 91-71857. 32p. (ps up). 1992. 14.95 (*1-56402-008-8*) Candlewick Pr.
—Elephants Never Forget: Classic Nursery Rhymes. 48p. (ps-1). 1992. 12.95 (*0-8118-0239-6*) Chronicle Bks.
Percy, Rachel, jt. auth. see Ansell, Rod.
Percy, Walker. Lancelot. (gr. 7 up). 1978. pap. 4.50 (*0-380-01861-6*, Bard) Avon.
Perdrizet, Marie-Pierre. The Cathedral Builders. Raycraft, Mary B., tr. from FRE. Krahenbuhl, Eddy, illus. LC 91-24233. 64p. (gr. 4-6). 1992. PLB 14.90 (*1-56294-162-3*) Millbrook Pr.
Perdue, Charles L., Jr., ed. Outwitting the Devil: Jack Tales from Wise County, Virginia. LC 87-71657. (Illus.). 129p. (Orig.). (gr. 9-12). 1987. 19.95 (*0-941270-43-2*); pap. 9.95 (*0-941270-42-4*) Ancient City Pr.

—Pig's Foot Jelly & Persimmon Beer: Foodways from Virginia's Writer's Project. LC 92-9356. (Illus.). 130p. (Orig.). (gr. 9 up). 1992. pap. 11.95 (0-941270-74-2) Ancient City Pr.

Perdue, Peggy K., jt. auth. see Vaszily, Diane A.

Perdue, Thea. The Cherokee. Porter, Frank W., III, intro. by. (Illus.). 111p. (Orig.). (gr. 5 up). 1989. 17.95 (1-55546-695-8); pap. 9.95 (0-7910-0357-4) Chelsea Hse.

Perelman, Richard B., ed. American Athletics Annual: 1980 Edition. 694p. (Orig.). (gr. 12 up). 1980. pap. 15. 00 (0-686-29735-0) Athletics Cong.

Perenyi, Constance. Growing Wild: Inviting Wildlife into Your Yard. Perenyi, Constance, illus. 40p. (gr. 1-3). 1991. 14.95 (0-941831-60-4); pap. 9.95 (0-941831-63-9) Beyond Words Pub.

—Wild Wild West: Wildlife Habitats of Western North America. Pevenyi, Constance, illus. LC 92-46995. 32p. (gr. 1 up). 1993. text ed. 14.95 (0-912365-82-X); pap. 8.95 (0-912365-90-0) Sasquatch Bks.

Perera, Hilda. Cuentos de Apolo. 3rd ed. (SPA., Illus.). 103p. (gr. 6 up). 1975. pap. 5.00 (0-89729-438-6) Ediciones.

—Kiki: A Cuban Boy's Adventures in America. 120p. (gr. 5-8). 1992. pap. 12.95 (0-940495-24-4) Pickering Pr.

Perera, Victor, tr. see Montejo, Victor.

Peretti, Frank. The Tombs of Anak. LC 86-73183. 144p. (Orig.). (gr. 5-8). 1987. pap. 4.99 (0-89107-442-2, Crossway Bks) Good News.

Peretti, Frank E. Door in the Dragons Throat. (gr. 4-7). 1990. pap. 4.99 (0-89107-591-7) Good News.

—Escape from the Island of Aquarius. (gr. 4-7). 1990. pap. 4.99 (0-89107-592-5) Good News.

—Tombs of Anak. (gr. 4-7). 1990. pap. 4.99 (0-89107-593-3) Good News.

—Trapped at the Bottom of the Sea. (gr. 4-7). 1990. pap. 4.99 (0-89107-594-1) Good News.

Peretz, I. L. & Shulevitz, Uri. The Magician. LC 85-42955. (Illus.). 32p. (gr. k-6). 1985. SBE 12.95 (0-02-782770-4, Macmillan Child Bk) Macmillan Child Grp.

Perez, Carla, jt. auth. see Robison, Deborah.

Perez, Demetrio, Jr. Citizens Training Handbook-Manual de Formacion Ciudadana: Discipline-Moral-Covism-Urbanity. (SPA & ENG., Illus.). 315p. 1991. 25.00 (0-9628780-0-6) Ed Lncln-Mrt.

Perez, Ed. A Look Around Endangered Animals. (Illus.). 32p. (gr. 1-3). 1992. pap. 2.50 (0-87406-579-8) Willowisp Pr.

—A Look Around Rain Forests. (Illus.). 32p. (gr. 1-3). 1993. pap. 2.99 (0-87406-643-3) Willowisp Pr.

Perez, Louis G. The Dalai Lama. LC 92-38325. 1993. 19. 93 (0-86625-480-3); 14.95s.p. (0-685-67761-3) Rourke Pubns.

Perez, N. A. Breaker. LC 87-33891. 216p. (gr. 5-9). 1988. 13.45 (0-395-45537-5) HM.

—One Special Year. LC 84-25258. 200p. (gr. 6-9). 1985. 13.95 (0-395-36693-3) HM.

—The Slopes of War. (Illus.). 224p. (gr. 7 up). 1990. 14. 45 (0-395-35642-3, 5-93140); pap. 4.80 (0-395-54979-5) HM.

Perez, Rosanne. The Legend of Eek Iguana. LC 91-71997. 64p. (gr. 3-7). 1993. pap. 7.00 (1-56002-078-4, Univ Edtns) Aegina Pr.

Perez, Theresa, jt. auth. see Marquez, Nancy.

Perham, Molly. People at Work. LC 86-2014. (Illus.). 32p. (gr. 2 up). 1986. RSBE 10.95 (0-87518-333-6, Dillon) Macmillan Child Grp.

Perham, Molly & Steele, Philip. The Children's Illustrated World Atlas: A Young Person's Guide to the World. (Illus.). 56p. (gr. 1 up). 1993. 9.98 (1-56138-331-7) Courage Bks.

Perham, Molly, jt. auth. see Rowe, Julian.

Perham, Molly, jt. auth. see Rowe, Julina.

Perham, Molly, retold by. King Arthur & the Legends of Camelot. Heller, Julek, illus. 176p. (gr. 1 up). 1993. 22.00 (0-670-84990-1) Viking Child Bks.

Perinchief, Robert. Drug-Free Word Spree. 58p. (ps-12). 1993. 19.95 (1-882809-01-7) Perry Pubns.
DRUG-FREE WORD SPREE & its companion cassettes (100 minutes of tape on two cassettes) contain nearly sixty original poems, raps, & songs created by Robert Perinchief, & used in his drug-education programs titled TOWARDS DRUG-FREE SCHOOLS. DRUG-FREE WORD SPREE is NOT a curriculum; nor is it a complete program as such. Rather, it is a collection of his poems & songs, ranging from some which are appropriate for very young children (even pre-schoolers) to those which will hit hard among teenagers. They are often humorous (but never flippant), & just as often they are hard-hitting. They touch on all types of drug abuse, from smoking to chewing tobacco, to abuse of beer & alcohol, to drug addiction with the "hard" stuff. Some have happy endings; but as is so often the case with such drug abuse, the endings are frequently painful, sobering, tragic. Perinchief brings a deep sense of purpose to the American drug scene with such poems as "Street Kid, Don't Start," & "I'm High On Life." To order DRUG-FREE WORD SPREE: Send check to Perry Publications, P.O. Box 204, Whitewater, WI 53190; or call 1-800-527-2966. $19.95 plus $3.00 S&H. *Publisher Provided Annotation.*

—Hamel the Camel: A Different Mammal. Nordensten, Ellen H., illus. 21p. (ps-5). 1993. 12.95 (1-882809-00-9) Perry Pubns.
HAMEL THE CAMEL is unlike any other camel. Because he is different (on the outside) from his cousin-dromedaries, he is teased, laughed at & abused. At last he meets someone who looks past his different appearance, & sees something special. In the end, we discover that because of HAMEL'S special nature, he plays a very important role in a story told & retold for centuries. We are reminded throughout the book & song that..." THOSE WHO ARE DIFFERENT DON'T NEED OUR ABUSE... THOSE WHO ARE DIFFERENT CAN BE OF GOOD USE." HAMEL was first a poem, then a song, & finally a book-with-cassette. He is an irresistible, lovable character with an inner beauty & purpose which eventually allows people to look past his feature which for so long was the subject of jeering. HAMEL has proven to be especially meaningful to children & youths with special needs, & those with latent doubts about their own self-esteem. It deals profoundly with the issue of the worthiness of everyone. In an age of stressing diversity, this book is essential. To order: Send check to Perry Publications, P.O. Box 204, Whitewater, WI 53190; or call 1-800-527-2966. $12.95 plus $3.00 S&H. *Publisher Provided Annotation.*

Peris, Carme, jt. auth. see Sanchez, Isidro.

Perkins, Al. Diggingest Dog. Gurney, Eric, illus. LC 67-21920. 72p. (gr. k-3). 1967. 6.95 (0-394-80047-8); lib. bdg. 7.99 (0-394-90047-2) Beginner.

—Ear Book. O'Brian, Bill, illus. LC 68-28464. (ps-1). 1968. 6.95 (0-394-81199-2); lib. bdg. 7.99 (0-394-91199-7) Random Bks Yng Read.

—Hand, Hand, Fingers, Thumb. LC 76-77841. (Illus.). (ps-1). 1969. 6.95 (0-394-81076-7); lib. bdg. 7.99 (0-394-91076-1) Random Bks Yng Read.

—Hugh Lofting's Travels of Doctor Dolittle. reissued ed. LC 67-25853. (Illus.). 64p. (gr. ps-2). 1967. 6.95 (0-394-80048-6); PLB 7.99 (0-394-90048-0) Random Bks Yng Read.

—Nose Book. McKie, Roy, illus. LC 71-117540. (ps-1). 1970. 6.95 (0-394-80623-9); lib. bdg. 7.99 (0-394-90623-3) Random Bks Yng Read.

—Tubby & the Lantern. LC 70-158390. (Illus.). (gr. k-2). 1971. lib. bdg. 4.99 (0-394-92297-2) Beginner.

Perkins, Anne T. Turtles. Lomax, James, illus. 8p. (ps-k). 1993. 12.00 (1-884204-00-7) Teach Nxt Door.

Perkins, Charles D. Swinging on a Rainbow. Hamilton, Thomas, illus. LC 91-78393. 1992. write for info. (0-86543-286-4); pap. write for info. (0-86543-287-2) Africa World.

—Swinging on a Rainbow. Hamilton, Thomas A., illus. LC 91-78393. 32p. (gr. k-3). 1993. 14.95 (0-86543-386-0); pap. 6.95 (0-86543-385-2) Africa World.

Perkins, David N. Thinking Connections: Learning to Think & Thinking to Learn. (gr. 4-7). 1993. pap. 24.95 (0-201-81998-8) Addison-Wesley.

Perkins, Gary. Silly Goofy Jokes. Nevins, Dan, illus. LC 92-20779. 64p. (gr. 2-6). 1992. pap. text ed. 1.50 (0-8167-2965-4, Pub. by Watermill Pr) Troll Assocs.

—Silly Haunted Jokes. Nevins, Dan, illus. LC 92-20760. 64p. (gr. 2-6). 1992. pap. text ed. 1.50 (0-8167-2963-8, Pub. by Watermill Pr) Troll Assocs.

—Silly School Jokes. Nevins, Dan, illus. LC 92-20437. 64p. (gr. 2-6). 1992. pap. text ed. 1.50 (0-8167-2964-6, Pub. by Watermill Pr) Troll Assocs.

Perkins, Hal. Leadership Multiplication Books: Book D, Following Jesus. 30p. (Orig.). (gr. 7 up). 1983. pap. 2.50 (0-8341-0860-7) Beacon Hill.

—Leadership Multiplication Books: Book F, Making Leaders in Families. 48p. (Orig.). (gr. 7 up). 1983. pap. 2.50 (0-8341-0862-3) Beacon Hill.

—Leadership Multiplication Books: Book G, Making Leaders in the Church. 48p. (Orig.). (gr. 7 up). 1983. pap. 2.50 (0-8341-0866-6) Beacon Hill.

—Leadership Multiplication Books: Book H, Making Leaders in the World. 32p. (Orig.). (gr. 9 up). 1983. pap. 2.50 (0-8341-0867-4) Beacon Hill.

Perkins, Judy, jt. auth. see Brown, Alan.

Perkins, Mary. Growing into Peace: A Manual for Peace-Builders in the 1990s & Beyond. (gr. 9-12). 1991. pap. 10.95 (0-85398-323-2) G Ronald Pub.

—Percival the Piano. Thomas, Wendy, illus. (Orig.). (gr. k-4). 1990. pap. 5.75 (0-85398-287-2) G Ronald Pub.

Perkins, Mitali. The Sunita Experiment. LC 92-37267. (gr. 1-6). 1993. 14.95 (0-316-69943-8, Joy St Bks) Little.

—The Sunita Experiment. 185p. (gr. ps-2). 1994. pap. write for info. (1-56282-671-9) Hyprn Ppbks.

Perkins, Myrna. Bored Betty's Wish. Perkins, William C. & Perkins, Lani, illus. 32p. (Orig.). (gr. 2-5). 1986. pap. 5.95 (0-937729-02-7) Markins Enter.

—What Does A Spider Do? Perkins, William C. & Perkins, Lori L., illus. 20p. (Orig.). (ps-3). 1985. pap. 3.95 (0-937729-00-0) Markins Enter.

—What Is This? Perkins, William C. & Perkins, Lori L., illus. 36p. (Orig.). (ps-3). 1986. pap. 4.95 (0-937729-01-9) Markins Enter.

—What Makes Honey? Perkins, William C. & Perkins, Lori L., illus. 32p. (Orig.). (ps-3). 1985. pap. 3.95 (0-937729-03-5) Markins Enter.

Perkins, Stan. Arvilla & the Tattler. 500p. Date not set. write for info. (0-9614640-9-7); pap. write for info. Broadblade Pr.

Perkins, Thornton. Junior High Champs. Chappick, Joseph, illus. 49p. (Orig.). (gr. 6-9). 1989. pap. 3.00 (0-9623407-0-7) NVEM.

Perkins, Useni. The Black Fairy & Other Plays for Children. Hill, Patrick, illus. LC 92-60054. 200p. (Orig.). 1993. pap. 13.95 (0-88378-077-1) Third World.

Perkovich, George. Thinking about the Soviet Union. (Illus.). 256p. (Orig.). 1989. pap. text ed. 25.00 (0-942349-00-8) Eductrs Soc Respons.

Perl, Lila. Annabelle Starr, E.S.P. LC 83-2068. 160p. (gr. 4-7). 1983. 11.95 (0-89919-187-8, Clarion Bks) HM.

—Candles, Cakes, & Donkey Tails: Birthday Symbols & Celebrations. De Larrea, Victoria, illus. LC 84-5803. 80p. (gr. 3-6). 1984. (Clarion Bks) HM.

—Don't Sing Before Breakfast, Don't Sleep in the Moonlight: Everyday Superstitions & How They Began. LC 87-24295. (Illus.). 96p. (gr. 3-6). 1988. 13. 95 (0-89919-504-0, Clarion Bks) HM.

—Fat Glenda Turns Fourteen. Giblin, James, ed. 176p. (gr. 5-9). 1991. 13.45 (0-395-53341-4, Clarion Bks) HM.

—From Top Hats to Baseball Caps, from Bustles to Blue Jeans: Why We Dress the Way We Do. Evans, Leslie, illus. LC 89-77717. 118p. (gr. 5-8). 1990. 14.45 (0-89919-872-4, Clarion Bks) HM.

—The Great Ancestor Hunt. LC 88-36211. (Illus.). 112p. (gr. 4 up). 1989. 15.45 (0-89919-745-0, Clarion Bks) HM.

—Great Ancestor Hunt: The Fun of Finding Out Who You Are. (gr. 4-7). 1990. pap. 5.70 (0-395-54790-3, Clarion Bks) HM.

—Hey, Remember Fat Glenda? 192p. (gr. 3-6). 1981. 14. 45 (0-395-31023-7, Clarion Bks) HM.

—Hey, Remember Fat Glenda? (gr. 4-7). 1982. pap. 2.25 (0-671-44954-0) PB.

—Hunter's Stew & Hangtown Fry. Cuffari, Richard, illus. LC 77-5366. 176p. (gr. 6 up). 1979. 13.95 (0-395-28922-X, Clarion Bks) HM.

—It Happened in America: True Stories from the Fifty States. Ohlsson, Ib, illus. 302p. (gr. 4-6). 1992. 21.95 (0-8050-1719-4, Bks Young Read) H Holt & Co.

—Junk Food, Fast Food, Health Food: What America Eats & Why. 192p. (gr. 5 up). 1980. 14.45 (0-395-29108-9, Clarion Bks) HM.

—Molly Picon: A Gift of Laughter. Ruff, Donna, illus. 64p. (gr. 4-7). 1990. 12.95 (0-8276-0336-3) JPS Phila.

—Mummies, Tombs, & Treasure: Secrets of Ancient Egypt. Weihs, Erika, illus. LC 86-17646. 128p. (gr. 4 up). 1987. 15.45 (0-89919-407-9, Clarion Bks) HM.

—Mummies, Tombs, & Treasure: Secrets of Ancient Egypt. Weihs, Erika, illus. LC 86-17646. 128p. (gr. 2-5). 1990. pap. 5.70 (0-395-54796-2, Clarion Bks) HM.

—Slumps, Grunts, & Snickerdoodles: What Colonial America Ate & Why. Cuffari, Richard, illus. LC 75-4894. 128p. (gr. 6 up). 1979. 14.95 (0-395-28923-8, Clarion Bks) HM.

—Telltale Summer of Tina C. 1984. pap. 2.50 (0-590-41324-4) Scholastic Inc.

Perl, Lila & Ada, Alma F. Pinatas & Paper Flowers-Pinatas y Flores de Papel: Holidays of the Americas in English & Spanish. De Larrea, Victoria, illus. LC 82-12211. 91p. (gr. 3-6). 1983. 12.95 (0-89919-112-6, Clarion Bks); pap. 5.95 (0-89919-155-X, Clarion Bks) HM.

Perle, Ruth L. Seek & Solve: Addition No. 1 Series 1, Level 1. Hefter, Richard, illus. (gr. k-2). 1976. wkbk. 1.95 (0-89796-848-4, SSW 01) New Dimens Educ.
—Seek & Solve: Subtraction No. 1, Series 1, Level 1. Hefter, Richard, illus. (gr. k-2). 1976. wkbk. 1.95 (0-89796-849-2, SSW 02) New Dimens Educ.
—Teammates: Home Team Book. Bergstrom, Evelyn J., ed. Gusman, Annie, illus. (ps-k). 1977. pap. text ed. 3.95 (0-89796-862-X) New Dimens Educ.
—Teammates School Team Book. Bergstrom, Evelyn J., ed. Gusman, Annie, illus. (ps-k). 1977. pap. text ed. 3.95 (0-89796-861-1) New Dimens Educ.

Perle, Ruth L., jt. auth. see Lamport, Joan.
Perle, Ruth L., ed. see Abisch, Roz, et al.
Perle, Ruth L., ed. see Howard, Wayne.
Perle, Ruth L., ed. see Pavao, John.
Perlee, ed. see Baumann, Susan K. & Mandell, Steven L.

Perlin, D. E. Father Miguel Hidalgo: A Cry for Freedom. McClure, Herman, illus. LC 90-27375. (ENG & SPA.). 32p. (gr. k-4). 1991. pap. 5.95 (0-937460-67-2) Hendrick-Long.

Perlman, Janet. Cinderella Penguin. (Illus.). 32p. (ps-3). 1993. 13.00 (0-670-84753-4) Viking Child Bks.

Perlman, Marc. Movie Classics. LC 92-30909. 1993. 18.95 (0-8225-1641-1) Lerner Pubns.
—Youth Rebellion Movies. LC 92-5534. 1993. 18.95 (0-8225-1640-3) Lerner Pubns.

Perlman, Ruthy. Working It Out. LC 90-82185. (gr. 7 up). 1990. 13.95 (1-56062-033-1); pap. 9.95 (1-56062-035-8) CIS Comm.

Perlwitz, Ellen C. Charlie's Little Moon Trip. (Illus.). 32p. (gr. k-3). 1992. 7.95 (1-880851-01-6) Greene Bark Pr.

Perna, Debi. The Birthday Book: Stickers to Stick & Cards to Create for Every Month of the Year. Perna, Debi, illus. 36p. (ps up). 1992. 6.95 (0-920775-57-8, Pub. by Greey de Pencier CN) Firefly Bks Ltd.

Perna, Debi, ed. & illus. see Chickadee Magazine Editors.

Perrault, Charles. Cinderella. (Fr.). (gr. 3-8). 9.95 (0-685-23349-9) Fr & Eur.
—Cinderella. new ed. Smith, Phil, illus. LC 78-18067. 32p. (gr. k-3). 1979. PLB 9.79 (0-89375-120-0); pap. 1.95 (0-89375-098-0) Troll Assocs.
—Cinderella. Jeffers, Susan, illus. Ehrlich, Amy, retold by. LC 85-1685. (Illus.). 32p. (ps-3). 1985. 14.00 (0-8037-0205-1); PLB 12.89 (0-8037-0206-X) Dial Bks Young.
—Cinderella. Goode, Diane, tr. from FRE. & illus. Lange, Jessica, contrib. by. LC 87-16886. 48p. (ps up) 1989. incl. cassette 15.95 (0-394-89600-9) Knopf Bks Yng Read.
—Cinderella. Alchemy II, Inc. Staff, illus. 26p. (ps). 1988. incl. cassette 9.95 (1-55578-911-0) Worlds Wonder.
—Cinderella. 2nd ed. Brown, Marcia, tr. from FRE. & illus LC 87-34920. 32p. (ps-3). 1988. pap. 4.50 (0-689-71261-8, Aladdin) Macmillan Child Grp.
—Cinderella. (ps-3). 1990. pap. 4.95 (0-8037-0830-0, Dial Pied Piper) Puffin Bks.
—Cinderella: And Other Tales from Perrault. Hague, Michael, illus. 78p. (ps-2). 1989. 18.95 (0-8050-1004-1, Bks Young Read) H Holt & Co.
—Cinderella & the Prince: A Colorful Pictorial Recount of the Cinderella Story. Nyborg, Randy, illus. 27p. (gr. k-10). 1992. 12.95 (1-87776-766-2); PLB 19.95 (1-87776-767-0) Regal Pubns.
—Cinderella; or, The Little Glass Slipper. Le Cain, Errol, illus. (gr. 1 up). 1977. pap. 3.95 (0-14-050137-1, Puffin) Puffin Bks.
—Contes de Ma Mere l'Oye. Dore, Gustave, illus. (FRE.). 223p. (gr. 5-10). 1988. pap. 8.95 (2-07-033443-0) Schoenhof.
—El Gato Con Botas: (Puss in Boots) Marcellino, Fred, illus. Marcuse, Aida, tr. (SPA., Illus.). 32p. 1991. 16.00 (0-374-36158-4) FS&G.
—Little Red Riding Hood. Moon, Sarah, photos by. (Illus.). 32p. (gr. 9 up). 1983. PLB 13.95s.p. (0-87191-943-5) Creative Ed.
—Little Red Riding Hood: A Classic Tale. Jose, Eduard, ed. Moncure, Jane B., tr. Lavarello, Jose M., illus. LC 88-37088. 32p. (gr. 1-4). 1988. PLB 19.95 (0-89565-457-1); PLB 13.95s.p. (0-685-56027-9) Childs World.
—The Pancake That Ran Away & Toads & Diamonds. (Illus.). 48p. (ps-3). 1985. 5.95 (0-88110-254-7) EDC.
—Perrault's Fairy Tales. Dore, Gustave, illus. LC 72-79522. viii, 117p. (gr. 4-6). 1969. pap. 5.95 (0-486-22311-6) Dover.
—Puss in Boots. new ed. Da Riff, Andrea, illus. LC 78-18061. 32p. (gr. k-3). 1979. PLB 9.79 (0-89375-130-8); pap. 1.95 (0-89375-108-1) Troll Assocs.
—Puss in Boots. Arthur, Malcolm, tr. Marcellino, Fred, illus. 32p. 1990. 16.00 (0-374-36160-6) FS&G.
—Puss in Boots. (Illus.). 20p. (ps up). 1992. write for info. incl. long-life batteries (0-307-74705-0, 64705, Golden Pr) Western Pub.
—Puss in Boots: A Classic Tale. Jose, Eduard, adapted by. Suire, Diane D., tr. Asensio, Augusti, illus. LC 88-35316. 32p. (gr. 1-4). 1988. PLB 19.95 (0-89565-482-2); PLB 13.95s.p. (0-685-56028-7) Childs World.
—Ricky the Tuft: A Classic Tale. Jose, Eduard, adapted by. Moncure, Jane B., tr. from SPA. Lavarello, Jose M., illus. LC 88-36792. 32p. (gr. 1-4). 1988. PLB 19.95 (0-89565-473-3); PLB 13.95s.p. (0-685-56041-4) Childs World.
—Sleeping Beauty: A Classic Tale. Jose, Eduard, adapted by. Moncure, Jane B., tr. from SPA. Asensio, Agusti, illus. LC 88-35212. 32p. (gr. 1-4). 1988. PLB 19.95 (0-89565-478-4); PLB 13.95s.p. (0-685-56040-6) Childs World.
—Sleeping Beauty & Other Classic French Fairy Tales. 1991. 12.99 (0-517-03706-8) Outlet Bk Co.
—Sleeping Beauty & Other Stories. LC 88-43558. 96p. 1989. 4.95 (0-89471-721-9) Running Pr.
—Sleeping Beauty & The Soldier & the Six Giants. (Illus.). 48p. (ps-3). 1985. 5.95 (0-88110-255-5) EDC.
—The Sleeping Beauty in the Woods. Collier, John, illus. 32p. (gr. 6 up). 1984. PLB 13.95s.p. (0-87191-944-3) Creative Ed.
—Tales from Perrault. Lawrence, Ann, tr. Chance, Tony J., illus. 118p. (gr. 3-7). 1989. jacketed 18.95 (0-19-274533-6) OUP.
—Three Wishes. Lightbown, Meredith, illus. LC 78-18060. 32p. (gr. k-3). 1979. PLB 9.79 (0-89375-129-4); pap. 1.95 (0-89375-107-3) Troll Assocs.
—Tom Thumb: A Classic Tale. Jose, Eduard, adapted by. Riehecky, Janet, tr. from SPA. Rovira, Francesc, illus. LC 88-35211. 32p. (gr. 1-4). 1988. PLB 19.95 (0-89565-462-8); PLB 13.95s.p. (0-685-56036-8) Childs World.

Perrault, Charles & Kipling, Rudyard. Cinderella & How the Elephant Got Its Trunk. (Illus.). 48p. (gr. 1-4). 1985. 5.95 (0-88110-252-0) EDC.

Perrault, Charles, jt. auth. see Brown, Marcia.

Perret, Gene. Funny Comebacks to Rude Remarks. LC 90-37815. (Illus.). 96p. (gr. 3-9). 1990. pap. 3.95 (0-8069-7240-8) Sterling.
—Laugh-a-Minute Joke Book. Hoffman, Sanford, illus. LC 90-27674. 96p. (gr. 2-10). 1991. 12.95 (0-8069-7414-1) Sterling.
—Laugh-a-Minute Joke Book. Hoffman, Sanford, illus. 96p. (gr. 3-9). 1991. pap. 3.95 (0-8069-7415-X) Sterling.
—Super Funny School Jokes. (Illus.). 96p. (gr. 2-10). 1991. 12.95 (0-8069-8294-2) Sterling.
—Super Funny School Jokes. Hoffman, Sanford, illus. LC 91-22501. 96p. (gr. 1-7). 1992. pap. 3.95 (0-8069-8295-0) Sterling.

Perricone, Jack. I Like to Dream. (Illus.). 16p. (ps-2). 1993. PLB 10.95 (1-879567-16-4, Valeria Bks) Wonder Well.
—Me Gusta Sonar. (Illus.). 16p. (ps-2). 1993. PLB 10.95 (1-879567-17-2, Valeria Bks) Wonder Well.

Perrin, Janet & Howlett, Charles F. A Walk Through History: A Community Named Amityville. (Illus.). 125p. (gr. 7-9). 1993. pap. text ed. write for info. (1-55787-096-9) Heart of the Lakes.

Perrin, Linda. Coming to America: Immigrants from the Far East. LC 80-65840. 192p. (gr. 9-12). 1980. 9.95 (0-440-01072-1) Delacorte.
—Immigrants from the Far East. LC 80-65840. 192p. 1980. 12.95 (0-385-28115-3) Delacorte.

Perrin, Penelope. Russia. (Illus.). 32p. (gr. 5). 1994. PLB 13.95 RSBE (0-89686-775-7, Crestwood Hse) Macmillan Child Grp.

Perrin, Steve. Elfquest: The Official Roleplaying Game. 2nd ed. Chodak, Yurek, ed. Pini, Wendy & Schultz, Carolyn, illus. Pini, Richard, intro. by. 192p. (gr. 9 up). 1989. pap. 19.95 (0-933635-54-0, 2605) Chaosium.
—Voice of Doom. 32p. (Orig.). (gr. 10-12). 1987. pap. 6.00 (0-915795-80-9, 38) Iron Crown Ent Inc.

Perrin, Steve, jt. auth. see St. Andre, Ken.

Perrine, Mary. Nannabah's Friend. Weisgard, Leonard, illus. 32p. (gr. k-3). 1989. pap. 4.80 (0-395-52020-7) HM.

Perrins, Lesley. How Paper Is Made. (Illus.). 32p. (gr. 7 up). 1986. 12.95x (0-8160-0036-0) Facts on File.

Perrotta, Mary, ed. see Brown, Fern G.
Perrotta, Mary, ed. see Mango, Karin N.

Perry, Anne. Riders Ready! A Book about BMX...with Advice from the Experts. Paerry, Anna, illus. LC 85-50294. 130p. (Orig.). (gr. 5-8). pap. 8.95 (0-9615253-0-4); perma-bound 12.05 (0-8479-9930-0) Tadpole.

Perry, Cheryl & Faulkner, Hal. Holiday Mathemagic. (Illus.). (gr. 4-10). 1977. pap. text ed. 7.95 (0-918932-50-5) Activity Resources.

Perry, Cindy. Activities That Build Young Women, Vol. 1. 48p. 1993. pap. 6.98 (0-88290-456-8) Horizon Utah.

Perry, David J., jt. auth. see Lebet, Philip E.

Perry, Frances B., ed. Let's Sing Together: Favorite Primary Songs of Members of the Church of Jesus Christ of Latter-day Saints. Heaston, Claudia, illus. 96p. (ps-6). 1981. 10.98 (0-941518-00-0) Perry Enterprises.
—Let's Sing Together: Favorite Primary Songs. Heaston, Claudia, illus. 96p. (ps-6). 1984. hard cover music 12.98 (0-941518-02-7) Perry Enterprises.

Perry, George. Rupert: A Bear's Life. Bestall, Alfred, contrib. by. (Illus.). 169p. (gr. 5-8). 1992. pap. 19.95 (1-85145-149-8, Pub. by Pavilion UK) Trafalgar.

Perry, Josephine. Cookies from Many Lands. 160p. (gr. 6-12). 1972. pap. 4.95 (0-486-22832-0) Dover.

Perry, Katy. My Grandmother Wears Crazy Hats. Minor, Mary E., ed. (Illus.). 16p. (gr. k-5). 1993. pap. 4.95 (0-9626823-4-9) Perry ME.

Perry, Marion. Dishes. Walsh, Joy, ed. Michael, Linda, illus. 25p. 1988. pap. 5.00 (0-938838-29-6) Textile Bridge.

Perry, Marvin. Man's Unfinished Journey: A World History. 2nd ed. LC 79-84595. (Illus.). (gr. 10-12). 1980. text ed. 47.04 (0-395-27563-6); instr's. guide & key 25.12 (0-395-27557-1); activities bk. 11.24 (0-395-27562-8); Activities bk. instr's. annot. ed. 14.04 (0-395-27558-X) HM.

Perry, Patricia, jt. auth. see Lynch, Marietta.

Perry, Philip & Weiss, Ellen. Facts America: Birds. LC 92-9403. (Illus.). 64p. (gr. 2-6). 1993. 7.98 (0-8317-2315-7) Smithmark.

Perry, Robert. Focus on Nicotine & Caffeine. (Illus.). 64p. (gr. 2-4). 1990. PLB 14.95 (0-8050-2217-1) TFC Bks NY.

Perry, Robert L. Guide to Self-Employment. LC 89-31828. (Illus.). 127p. (gr. 7-12). 1989. PLB 13.40 (0-531-10774-4) Watts.

Perry, Rufus L. The Cushite: Or the Children of Ham (the Negro Race) Obaba, Al I., ed. 49p. (Orig.). 1991. pap. text ed. 4.00 (0-916157-32-6) African Islam Miss Pubns.

Perry, Shauneille & Jackson, Donald. Mio & Other Plays for Young People. LC 73-92790. (gr. 4 up). 1976. 5.95 (0-89388-154-6) Okpaku Communications.

Perry, Susan. The Body Bandits. (Illus.). (gr. 1-8). 1992. PLB 14.95 (0-89565-875-5); Resale. 21.35 (0-685-60982-0) Childs World.
—A Cold Is Nothing to Sneeze At. Mitchell, Anastasia, illus. (gr. 1-8). 1992. PLB 14.95 (0-89565-819-4); Resale. 21.35 (0-685-60979-0) Childs World.
—Ecology. Nolte, Larry, illus. 48p. (gr. 3-6). Date not set. PLB 12.95 (1-56065-117-2) Capstone Pr. Postponed.
—Getting in Step. (Illus.). (gr. 1-8). 1992. PLB 14.95 (0-89565-872-0); Resale. 21.35 (0-685-60980-4) Childs World.
—How Are You Feeling Today? (Illus.). (gr. 1-8). 1992. PLB 14.95 (0-89565-876-3); Resale. 21.35 (0-685-60983-9) Childs World.
—Scientists. (Illus.). 128p. (gr. 3-6). Date not set. 19.95 (1-56065-122-9) Capstone Pr. Postponed.
—Women. (Illus.). 128p. (gr. 3-6). Date not set. 19.95 (1-56065-123-7) Capstone Pr. Postponed.
—Zoology. Nolte, Larry, illus. 48p. (gr. 3-6). Date not set. PLB 12.95 (1-56065-111-3) Capstone Pr. Postponed.

Perryman, Andrew. Gabon. (Illus.). 96p. (gr. 5 up). 1988. 14.95 (0-7910-0122-9) Chelsea Hse.

Persall, Holli C. The Magic Corn. Haley, Laura M., illus. 24p. (gr. k-4). 1990. 10.95 (0-9628486-0-3) Rhyme Time.

Persaud, Nancy. Bible Children Puzzles. 48p. (gr. 3 up). 1990. 6.95 (0-86653-534-9, SS891, Shining Star Pubns) Good Apple.
—Bible Number Puzzles. 48p. (gr. 3 up). 1989. 6.95 (0-86653-491-1, SS889, Shining Star Pubns) Good Apple.

Pershall, Mary K. You Take the High Road. 1990. 14.95 (0-8037-0700-2) Dial Bks Young.

Perske, Robert. Don't Stop the Music. LC 86-17426. (gr. 12 up). 1986. pap. 9.95 (0-687-11060-2) Abingdon.
—Show Me No Mercy: A Compelling Story of Remarkable Courage. LC 83-21384. 144p. (Orig.). (gr. 12 up). 1984. pap. 9.95 (0-687-38435-4) Abingdon.

Perucci, Dorianne, jt. auth. see Connors, Patricia.

Perugini, Donna. Don't Hug a Grudge. (Orig.). (gr. k-3). 1987. 3.98 (0-89274-433-2) Harrison Hse.
—The Flight of Orville Wright Caterpillar. (Illus.). 32p. (Orig.). (gr. k-6). 1983. pap. 3.98 (0-89274-297-6) Harrison Hse.

Pervier, Evelyn. Horsemanship: Basics for Beginners. LC 83-10004. (Illus.). 96p. (Orig.). (gr. 6 up). 1985. pap. 8.95 (0-668-05935-4) P-H.

Pesetski, Loretta, jt. auth. see Konczal, Dee.

Pesiri, Evelyn. Learn to Hear. Pesiri, Evelyn, illus. 64p. (gr. k-3). 1986. wkbk. 7.95 (0-86653-337-0, GA 675) Good Apple.
—Learn to See. Pesiri, Evelyn, illus. 64p. (gr. k-3). 1985. wkbk. 7.95 (0-86653-286-2, GA 674) Good Apple.
—Learn to Think. Pesiri, Evelyn, illus. 64p. (gr. k-3). 1986. wkbk. 7.95 (0-86653-343-5, GA 676) Good Apple.

Pesiri, Evelyn, ed. & illus. Learn to Write. 64p. (gr. k-3). 1986. wkbk. 7.95 (0-86653-342-7, GA 791) Good Apple.

Pessin, Deborah. Aleph-Bet Story Book. (Illus.). (gr. 1-3). 1989. pap. 6.95 (0-8276-0337-1) JPS Phila.
—History of the Jews in America. (Illus.). (gr. 8-10). 1957. pap. 4.95x (0-8381-0189-5) United Syn Bk.
—Jewish People, 3 Vols. (Illus.). (gr. 5-8). 1951-53. pap. 4.25x ea. Vol. I (0-8381-0182-8) Vol. II (0-8381-0185-2) Vol. III (0-8381-0187-9) pap. 2.50x ea. pupils' activity bks. Vol. I Activity Bk (0-8381-0183-0) Vol. II Activity Bk (0-8381-0186-0) Vol. III Activity Bk (0-8381-0188-7) United Syn Bk.

Petach, Heidi. Jonah: The Inside Story. Petach, Heidi, illus. 32p. (gr. k-2). 1989. 2.50 (0-87403-594-5, 3854) Standard Pub.

Pete, Jacelen D. Just Another Busy Day. (Illus.). 32p. 1989. 8.95 (0-934601-93-3) Peachtree Pubs.

Peteraf, Nancy J. A Plant Called Spot. Hoban, Lillian, illus. LC 92-27474. 1994. 13.95 (0-385-30885-X) Doubleday.

Peterkin, Allan. What about Me? When Brothers & Sisters Get Sick. Middendorf, Frances, illus. LC 92-20035. 32p. 1992. 16.95 (*0-945354-48-7*); pap. 6.95 (*0-945354-49-5*) Magination Pr.

Peterkin, Julia. A Plantation Christmas. Hendrickson, David, illus. LC 72-4563. (gr. 7 up). Repr. of 1934 ed. 10.50 (*0-8369-9119-2*) Ayer.

—A Plantation Christmas. Hendrickson, David, illus. LC 78-22014. (gr. 6 up). 1978. pap. 2.95 (*0-89783-007-5*) Cherokee.

Peterkin, Mike, illus. Three Little Pigs: Pop-up Book. LC 93-70940. 10p. (ps-3). 1993. 11.95 (*1-56282-513-5*) Disney Pr.

Peternel, Carolyn R. & Ahern, James. The I Like to Go to School Book. (Illus.). 36p. (Orig.). (gr. k-2). 1983. pap. 2.95 (*0-9612060-0-4*) Primary Progs.

Peters. October Smiled Back. 1993. 14.95 (*0-8050-1776-3*) H Holt & Co.

Peters, Claude D., intro. by see Moses, Elbert R.

Peters, David. From the Beginning: The Story of Human Evolution. LC 90-19187. (Illus.). 128p. (gr. 3 up). 1991. 13.95 (*0-688-09476-7*) Morrow Jr Bks.

—Giants of Land, Sea & Air - Past & Present: A Sierra Club Book Series. Peters, David, illus. LC 86-2719. 64p. (gr. 3 up). 1986. PLB 15.99 (*0-394-97805-6*) Knopf Bks Yng Read.

—Strange Creatures. Peters, David, illus. LC 91-36205. 48p. (gr. 3 up). 1992. 16.00 (*0-688-10154-2*); PLB 15.93 (*0-688-10155-0*) Morrow Jr Bks.

Peters, Emilie. Muffin, a Palm Beach Pooch. 30p. (gr. 3-8). 1992. pap. write for info. (*0-9635568-0-0*) Muffin Pubns.

Peters, Julie A. Stinky Sneakers Contest. (ps-3). 1992. 12.95 (*0-316-70214-5*) Little.

Peters, Kathleen, ed. see Bingham, Mindy, et al.

Peters, L. This Way Home. (gr. 4 up). 1993. 14.95 (*0-8050-1368-7*) H Holt & Co.

Peters, Lauren. Problems at the North Pole. Thatch, Nancy R., ed. Melton, David, intro. by. LC 90-5929. (Illus.). 26p. (ps-2). 1990. PLB 14.95 (*0-933849-25-7*) Landmark Edns.

Peters, Lisa. Water's Way. Rand, Ted, illus. 32p. (ps-2). 1991. 14.95 (*1-55970-062-9*) Arcade Pub Inc.

Peters, Lisa W. Burgess Shale Book. 1994. write for info. (*0-8050-2419-0*) H Holt & Co.

—Evolution Book. 1994. write for info. (*0-8050-2418-2*) H Holt & Co.

—The Hayloft. Plum, K. D., illus. LC 93-18718. Date not set. write for info. (*0-8037-1490-4*); lib. bdg. write for info. (*0-8037-1491-2*) Dial Bks Young.

—Purple Delicious Blackberry Jam. McGregor, Barbara, illus. 32p. (ps-3). 1992. 14.95 (*1-55970-167-6*) Arcade Pub Inc.

—The Room. Sneed, Brad, illus. LC 92-39807. 1994. write for info. (*0-8037-1431-9*); PLB write for info. (*0-8037-1432-7*) Dial Bks Young.

—Serengeti. LC 89-77859. (Illus.). 48p. (gr. 4-5). 1989. RSBE 13.95 (*0-89686-433-2*, Crestwood Hse) Macmillan Child Grp.

—The Sun, the Wind & the Rain. Rand, Ted, illus. LC 87-23808. 48p. (ps-2). 1988. 13.95 (*0-8050-0699-0*, Bks Young Read) H Holt & Co.

—The Sun, the Wind & the Rain. Rand, Ted, illus. LC 87-23808. 48p. (ps-2). 1990. pap. 4.95 (*0-8050-1481-0*, Owlet BYR) H Holt & Co.

—Tania's Trolls. Wooding, Sharon, illus. 64p. (gr. 2-4). 1989. 10.95 (*1-55970-040-8*) Arcade Pub Inc.

—Tania's Trolls. 64p. (gr. 3). 1992. pap. 2.99 (*0-380-71444-2*, Camelot Young) Avon.

Peters, Margaret W. The Ebony Book of Black Achievement. rev. ed. Ferguson, Cecil L., illus. LC 79-128544. 128p. (gr. 4-8). 1974. Repr. 8.95 (*0-87485-040-1*) Johnson Chi.

Peters, Max & Shostak, Jerome. How to Prepare for Catholic High School Entrance Examinations - COOP & HSPT. 576p. 1992. pap. 11.95 (*0-8120-4955-1*) Barron.

Peters, Mike. The Portable Mother Goose & Grimm. (Orig.). (gr. k-12). 1987. pap. 5.95 (*0-440-55860-3*, LE) Dell.

Peters, Robert C., ed. see Prokop, Michael S.

Peters, Russell. Clambake: A Wampanoag Tradition. (gr. 4-7). 1992. pap. 6.95 (*0-8225-9621-0*) Lerner Pubns.

Peters, Russell M. Clambake: A Wampanoag Tradition. Madama, John, photos by. (Illus.). 48p. (gr. 3-6). 1992. PLB 19.95 (*0-8225-2651-4*) Lerner Pubns.

Peters, Sharon. Animals at Night. Harvey, Paul, illus. LC 82-19226. 32p. (gr. k-2). 1983. lib. bdg. 11.59 (*0-89375-903-1*); pap. 2.95 (*0-8167-1477-0*) Troll Assocs.

—Champ on Ice. Paterson, Diane, illus. LC 87-10908. 32p. (gr. k-2). 1988. PLB 11.59 (*0-8167-1093-7*); pap. text ed. 2.95 (*0-8167-1094-5*) Troll Assocs.

—Contento Juan. Harvey, Paul, illus. (SPA.). 32p. (gr. k-2). 1981. PLB 7.89 (*0-89375-952-X*); pap. 1.95 (*0-685-04945-0*) Troll Assocs.

—Feliz Cumpleanos. Harvey, Paul, illus. (SPA.). 32p. (gr. k-2). 1981. PLB 7.89 (*0-89375-553-2*); pap. 1.95 (*0-685-04948-5*) Troll Assocs.

—Five Little Kittens. Rosenberg, Amye, illus. LC 81-2317. 32p. (gr. k-2). 1981. PLB 11.59 (*0-89375-503-6*); pap. 2.95 (*0-89375-504-4*) Troll Assocs.

—Fun at Camp. Trivas, Irene, illus. 32p. (gr. k-2). 1980. PLB 7.89 (*0-89375-378-5*); pap. 1.95 (*0-89375-278-9*) Troll Assocs.

—Una Funcion De Titeres. Lee, Alana, illus. (SPA.). 32p. (gr. k-2). 1981. PLB 7.89 (*0-89375-551-6*); pap. 1.95 (*0-685-42387-5*) Troll Assocs.

—The Goofy Ghost. Garcia, Tom, illus. LC 81-2573. 32p. (gr. k-2). 1981. PLB 11.59 (*0-89375-533-8*); pap. 2.95 (*0-89375-534-6*) Troll Assocs.

—Happy Birthday. Harvey, Paul, illus. 32p. (gr. k-2). 1980. PLB 7.89 (*0-89375-379-3*); pap. 1.95 (*0-89375-279-7*) Troll Assocs.

—Happy Jack. Harvey, Paul, illus. 32p. (gr. k-2). 1980. PLB 7.89 (*0-89375-380-7*); pap. 1.95 (*0-89375-280-0*) Troll Assocs.

—Here Comes Jack Frost. Connor, Eulala, illus. LC 81-4093. 32p. (gr. k-2). 1981. PLB 11.59 (*0-89375-513-3*); pap. text ed. 2.95 (*0-89375-514-1*) Troll Assocs.

—Listos, En Sus Marcas, Adelante! Trivas, Irene, illus. (SPA.). 32p. (gr. k-2). 1981. PLB 7.89 (*0-89375-550-8*); pap. 1.95 (*0-89375-957-0*) Troll Assocs.

—The Marching Band Mystery. Trivas, Irene, illus. LC 84-8783. 48p. (gr. 2-4). 1985. PLB 10.89 (*0-8167-0406-6*); pap. text ed. 3.50 (*0-8167-0407-4*) Troll Assocs.

—Maxie the Mutt. Mahan, Ben, illus. LC 87-10914. 32p. (gr. k-2). 1988. PLB 11.59 (*0-8167-1087-2*); pap. text ed. 2.95 (*0-8167-1088-0*) Troll Assocs.

—Messy Mark. Trivas, Irene, illus. 32p. (gr. k-2). 1980. PLB 7.89 (*0-89375-381-5*); pap. 1.95 (*0-89375-281-9*) Troll Assocs.

—Puppet Show. Lee, Alan, illus. 32p. (gr. k-2). 1980. PLB 7.89 (*0-89375-385-8*); pap. 1.95 (*0-89375-286-X*) Troll Assocs.

—Pussycat Kite. Hall, Susan T., illus. LC 84-8632. 32p. (gr. k-2). 1985. PLB 11.59 (*0-8167-0358-2*); pap. text ed. 2.95 (*0-8167-0438-4*) Troll Assocs.

—Ready, Get Set, Go! Trivas, Irene, illus. 32p. (gr. k-2). 1980. PLB 7.89 (*0-89375-386-6*); pap. 1.95 (*0-89375-285-1*) Troll Assocs.

—The Rooster & the Weather Vane. Harvey, Paul, illus. LC 86-30838. 32p. (gr. k-2). 1988. PLB 7.89 (*0-8167-0980-7*); pap. text ed. 1.95 (*0-8167-0981-5*) Troll Assocs.

—Rub-a-Dub Suds. Carter, Penny, illus. LC 86-30856. 32p. (gr. k-2). 1988. PLB 7.89 (*0-8167-0984-X*); pap. text ed. 1.95 (*0-8167-0985-8*) Troll Assocs.

—Santa's New Sled. Dole, Bob, illus. LC 81-5028. 32p. (gr. k-2). 1981. PLB 11.59 (*0-89375-523-0*); pap. text ed. 2.95 (*0-89375-524-9*) Troll Assocs.

—Stop That Rabbit. Silverstein, Don, illus. 32p. (gr. k-2). 1980. PLB 7.89 (*0-89375-388-2*); pap. 1.95 (*0-89375-288-6*) Troll Assocs.

—The Tiny Christmas Elf. Durrell, Julie, illus. LC 86-30849. 32p. (gr. k-2). 1988. PLB 7.89 (*0-8167-0988-2*); pap. text ed. 1.95 (*0-8167-0989-0*) Troll Assocs.

—The Tooth Fairy. Sims, Deborah, illus. LC 81-5100. 32p. (gr. k-2). 1981. PLB 11.59 (*0-89375-519-2*); pap. 2.95 (*0-89375-520-6*) Troll Assocs.

—Trick or Treat Halloween. Hall, Susan T., illus. 32p. (gr. k-2). 1980. PLB 7.89 (*0-89375-392-0*); pap. 1.95 (*0-89375-292-4*) Troll Assocs.

Peters, Tim, ed. Little Hopper Catches a Cold. (Illus.). (ps-2). pap. 4.95 (*1-879874-27-X*) T Peters & Co.

—Toby Turtle Takes a Tumble. (Illus.). (ps-2). pap. 4.95 (*1-879874-29-6*) T Peters & Co.

Peterseil, Tamar. Aap It! A Microwave Cookbook Just for Kids. (gr. 4-7). 1993. 12.95 (*0-943706-13-0*) Yllw Brick Rd.

Peterseil, Tehila. Secret Files of Lisa Weiss. 1990. 11.95 (*0-87306-549-2*); pap. 9.95 (*0-87306-550-6*) Feldheim.

Petersen, Arona. Food & Folklore of the Virgin Islands. 300p. (Orig.). (gr. 9-12). 1990. 20.00 (*0-9626577-0-0*) A Petersen.

Petersen, Becky, jt. auth. see Pantiel, Mindy.

Petersen, Candyce A. Beauty the Butterfly. Stoffregen, Jill A., illus. 24p. (ps-3). Date not set. 11.95 (*1-56065-097-4*) Capstone Pr. Postponed.

—Eggbert the Robin. Stoffregen, Jill A., illus. LC 92-12894. 24p. (ps-3). Date not set. 11.95 (*1-56065-099-0*) Capstone Pr. Postponed.

—Lucky Becomes a Frog. Stoffregen, Jill, illus. LC 92-6417. Date not set. 11.95 (*1-56065-096-6*) Capstone Pr. Postponed.

—Silky the Spider. Stoffregen, Jill A., illus. 24p. (ps-3). Date not set. 11.95 (*1-56065-098-2*) Capstone Pr. Postponed.

Petersen, David. The Anasazi. LC 91-3036. 48p. (gr. k-4). 1991. PLB 15.27 (*0-516-01121-9*); pap. 4.95 (*0-516-41121-7*) Childrens.

—Apatosaurus. LC 88-37654. (Illus.). 48p. (gr. k-4). 1989. PLB 15.27 (*0-516-01159-6*); pap. 4.95 (*0-516-41159-4*) Childrens.

—Canyonlands National Park. LC 91-35274. (Illus.). 48p. (gr. k-4). 1992. PLB 15.27 (*0-516-01132-4*); pap. 4.95 (*0-516-41132-2*) Childrens.

—Carlsbad Caverns National Park. LC 93-36997. 1994. write for info. (*0-516-01051-4*) Childrens.

—Grand Canyon National Park. LC 92-11343. (Illus.). 48p. (gr. k-4). 1992. PLB 15.27 (*0-516-02197-4*) Childrens.

—Grand Canyon National Park. LC 92-11343. (Illus.). 48p. (gr. k-4). 1993. pap. 4.95 (*0-516-42197-2*) Childrens.

—Grand Teton National Park. LC 92-9209. (Illus.). 48p. (gr. k-4). 1992. PLB 15.27 (*0-516-01948-1*) Childrens.

—Grand Teton National Park. LC 92-9209. (Illus.). 48p. (gr. k-4). 1993. pap. 4.95 (*0-516-41948-X*) Childrens.

—Great Smoky Mountains National Park. LC 92-35049. (Illus.). 48p. (gr. k-4). 1993. PLB 15.27 (*0-516-01332-7*); pap. 4.95 (*0-516-41332-5*) Childrens.

—Helicopters. LC 82-23502. (Illus.). 48p. (gr. k-4). 1983. PLB 15.27 (*0-516-01680-6*) Childrens.

—Ishi: The Last of His People. LC 90-28887. (Illus.). 32p. (gr. 2-4). 1991. LC 14.60 (*0-516-04179-7*); pap. 3.95 (*0-516-44179-5*) Childrens.

—Mesa Verde National Park. LC 91-35275. (Illus.). 48p. (gr. k-4). 1992. PLB 15.27 (*0-516-01136-7*); pap. 4.95 (*0-516-41136-5*) Childrens.

—Newspapers. LC 83-10069. (Illus.). 48p. (gr. k-4). 1983. PLB 15.27 (*0-516-01702-0*) Childrens.

—Rocky Mountain National Park. LC 93-798. (Illus.). 48p. (gr. k-4). 1993. PLB 16.60 (*0-516-01196-0*) Childrens.

—Sequoyah: Father of the Cherokee Alphabet. LC 91-13313. 32p. (gr. 2-4). 1991. PLB 7.89 (*0-516-04180-0*); pap. 3.95 (*0-516-44180-9*) Childrens.

—Solar Energy at Work. LC 84-23208. (Illus.). 48p. (gr. k-4). 1985. PLB 15.27 (*0-516-01942-2*) Childrens.

—Submarines. LC 83-26253. (Illus.). 48p. (gr. k-4). 1984. PLB 15.27 (*0-516-01728-4*) Childrens.

—Tyrannosaurus Rex. LC 88-38054. (Illus.). 48p. (gr. k-4). 1989. PLB 15.27 (*0-516-01167-7*); pap. 4.95 (*0-516-41167-5*) Childrens.

—Waterton - Glacier International Peace Park. LC 92-9208. (Illus.). 48p. (gr. k-4). 1992. PLB 15.27 (*0-516-01946-5*) Childrens.

—Waterton-Glacier International Peace Park. LC 92-9208. (Illus.). 48p. (gr. k-4). 1993. pap. 4.95 (*0-516-41946-3*) Childrens.

—Yellowstone National Park. LC 91-37292. (Illus.). 48p. (gr. k-4). 1992. PLB 15.27 (*0-516-01148-0*); pap. 4.95 (*0-516-41148-9*) Childrens.

—Yosemite National Park. LC 92-39156. (Illus.). 48p. (gr. k-4). 1993. PLB 15.27 (*0-516-01335-1*); pap. 4.95 (*0-516-41335-X*) Childrens.

—Zion National Park. LC 92-35048. (Illus.). 48p. (gr. k-4). 1993. PLB 15.27 (*0-516-01336-X*); pap. 4.95 (*0-516-41336-8*) Childrens.

Petersen, David & Coburn, Mark. Meriwether Lewis & William Clark: Soldiers, Explorers, & Partners in History. LC 88-14040. (Illus.). 152p. (gr. 4 up). 1988. PLB 18.60 (*0-516-03264-X*) Childrens.

Petersen, Emma M. About Baptism. 6.95 (*0-88494-055-1*) Bookcraft Inc.

—Book of Mormon Stories for Young LDS. 9.95 (*0-88494-019-5*) Bookcraft Inc.

Petersen, Ken. Choice Adventures: Quarterback Sneak. 160p. (gr. 4-8). 1992. pap. 4.99 (*0-8423-5029-2*) Tyndale.

Petersen, P. J. The Boll Weevil Express. 92p. (gr. 6 up). 1984. pap. 2.95 (*0-440-91040-4*, LFL) Dell.

—Corky & the Brothers Cool. LC 84-15579. 192p. (gr. 7 up). 1985. 14.95 (*0-318-18244-0*) Delacorte.

—Corky & the Brothers Cool. (gr. 6 up). 1986. pap. 2.75 (*0-440-91624-0*, LFL) Dell.

—Fireplug Is First Base. LC 89-25724. (Illus.). 64p. (gr. 2-5). 1990. 10.95 (*0-525-44587-0*, DCB) Dutton Child Bks.

—The Fireplug Is First Base. James, Betsy, illus. LC 92-18956. 64p. (gr. 2-5). 1992. pap. 3.99 (*0-14-036165-0*) Puffin Bks.

—Going for the Big One. (gr. k-12). 1987. pap. 2.95 (*0-440-93158-4*, LFL) Dell.

—Good-Bye to Good Ol' Charlie. LC 86-2016. 168p. (gr. 7 up). 1987. pap. 14.95 (*0-385-29483-2*) Delacorte.

—Good-Bye to Good Ol' Charlie. (gr. k-12). 1988. pap. 2.95 (*0-440-20162-4*, LFL) Dell.

—Here's to the Sophomores. LC 83-14362. 192p. (gr. 7 up). 1984. pap. 13.95 (*0-385-29319-4*) Delacorte.

—Here's to the Sophomores. 192p. (gr. 6 up). 1986. pap. 2.50 (*0-440-93394-3*, LFL) Dell.

—How Can You Hijack a Cave? LC 88-7139. 160p. (gr. 5-9). 1988. pap. 14.95 (*0-440-50063-X*) Delacorte.

—How Can You Hijack a Cave? (gr. k up). 1990. pap. 3.25 (*0-440-20583-2*, LFL) Dell.

—I Hate Camping. Remkiewicz, Frank, illus. LC 90-39650. 80p. (gr. 4-7). 1991. 13.00 (*0-525-44673-7*, DCB) Dutton Child Bks.

—I Hate Camping. Remkiewicz, Frank, illus. 96p. (gr. 2-5). 1993. pap. 3.99 (*0-14-036446-3*, Puffin) Puffin Bks.

—I Want Answers & a Parachute. DiVito, Anna, illus. LC 92-38262. (gr. 6 up). 1993. pap. 13.00 (*0-671-86577-3*, S&S BFYR) S&S Trade.

—Liars. LC 91-28490. 176p. (gr. 5-9). 1992. pap. 14.00 jacketed, 3-pc. bdg. (*0-671-75035-6*, S&S BFYR) S&S Trade.

—Nobody Else Can Walk It for You. LC 81-69669. 224p. (gr. 7 up). 1982. 12.95 (*0-385-28730-5*) Delacorte.

—Nobody Else Can Walk It for You. 224p. (gr. 6 up). 1984. pap. 2.95 (*0-440-96733-3*, LFL) Dell.

—The Sub. Johnson, Meredith, illus. LC 92-22269. (gr. 2-5). 1993. 12.99 (*0-525-45059-9*, DCB) Dutton Child Bks.

—Would You Settle for Improbable? 160p. (gr. 5-9). 1983. pap. 3.25 (*0-440-99733-X*, LFL) Dell.

—Would You Settle for Improbable? A Novel. LC 80-69465. 192p. (gr. 5-9). 1981. 8.95 (*0-440-09601-4*); PLB 8.44 (*0-440-09672-3*) Delacorte.

Petersen, Palle. Inunguak: The Little Greenlander. LC 90-40472. (gr. 4-7). 1993. 14.00 (*0-688-09876-2*) Lothrop.

—Inunguak: The Little Greenlander. LC 90-40472. (ps-3). 1993. 13.95 (*0-688-09877-0*) Lothrop.

Petersen, Peter L. The Danes in America. (Illus.). 96p. (gr. 5 up). 1987. PLB 15.95 (0-8225-0233-X); pap. 5.95 (0-8225-1031-6) Lerner Pubns.

Petersen, Sandy, ed. see Hargrave, et al.

Petersen, Sandy, ed. see Love, Penelope & Morrison, Mark.

Petersen-Fleming, Judy & Fleming, Bill. Kitten Care & Critters, Too! Reingold-Reiss, Debra, photos by. LC 93-24200. (Illus.). 40p. 1994. 15.00 (0-688-12563-8, Tambourine Bks); PLB 14.93 (0-688-12564-6, Tambourine Bks) Morrow.

—Puppy Care & Critters, Too! Ringold-Reiss, Debra, photos by. LC 93-23129. (Illus.). 40p. 1993. 15.00 (0-688-12565-4, Tambourine Bks); PLB 14.93 (0-688-12566-2, Tambourine Bks) Morrow.

Petersham. Christ Child. 1985. pap. 12.95 (0-385-07260-0) Doubleday.

Petersham, Maud & Petersham, Miska. The Box with Red Wheels. 32p. (ps-2). 1978. pap. 4.95 (0-02-044760-4, Aladdin) Macmillan Child Grp.

—Circus Baby. Petersham, Maud & Petersham, Miska, illus. LC 50-9295. 32p. (ps-1). 1968. RSBE 13.95 (0-02-771670-8, Macmillan Child Bk) Macmillan Child Grp.

—The Circus Baby. Petersham, Maud & Petersham, Miska, illus. LC 88-7369. 32p. (ps-1). 1989. pap. 3.95 (0-689-71295-2, Aladdin) Macmillan Child Grp.

—The Rooster Crows: A Book of American Rhymes & Jingles. Petersham, Maud & Petersham, Miska, illus. LC 46-446. 64p. (ps-2). 1969. RSBE 13.95 (0-02-773100-6, Macmillan Child Bk) Macmillan Child Grp.

—The Rooster Crows: A Book of American Rhymes & Jingles. Petersham, Maud & Petersham, Miska, illus. LC 87-1138. 64p. (ps-3). 1987. pap. 4.95 (0-689-71153-0, Aladdin) Macmillan Child Grp.

Petersham, Miska, jt. auth. see Petersham, Maud.

Peterson. My Mama Sings. Date not set. 14.95 (0-06-023854-2, Festival); PLB 14.89 (0-06-023859-3, Festival) HarpC Child Bks.

Peterson, Anne, jt. auth. see Peterson, Cliff.

Peterson, Beth. Myrna Never Sleeps. LC 93-8301. 1995. text ed. 11.95 (0-689-31893-6, Atheneum) Macmillan.

Peterson, Carolyn S. Story Programs Activities for Older Children. Sterchele, Christina, illus. (Orig.). (gr. 3-6). 1987. 20.00 (0-913545-11-2) Moonlight FL.

Peterson, Carolyn S. & Fenton, Ann D. Christmas Story Programs. Sterchele, Christina L., illus. (ps-6). 1981. 10.00 (0-913545-01-5) Moonlight FL.

Peterson, Cliff & Peterson, Anne. The Adventures of Sir Wellington Boots. 1993. 7.95 (0-533-10328-2) Vantage.

Peterson, Cris. Extra Cheese, Please! Mozzarella's Journey from Cow to Pizza. Upitis, Alvis, illus. 32p. (ps-3). 1994. 13.95 (1-56397-177-1) Boyds Mills Pr.

Peterson, David. Airplanes. LC 81-7671. (Illus.). 48p. (gr. k-4). 1981. PLB 15.27 (0-516-01606-7); pap. 4.95 (0-516-41606-5) Childrens.

—Airports. LC 81-7736. (Illus.). 48p. (gr. k-4). 1981. PLB 15.27 (0-516-01607-5) Childrens.

Peterson, Donald I. Relief from Headache. 2nd ed. LC 83-71941. (Illus.). 226p. 1990. pap. 9.95 (0-913657-00-X) D E Donel.

Peterson, Elizabeth J. Beginning Math at Home. Dewagian, Jeanette, illus. 75p. (ps-1). 4 sets 10.95, (0-938911-01-5) Indiv Educ Syst.

—Beginning Reading at Home. Dewagian, Jeanette, illus. 136p. (ps-1). 1992. Repr. of 1986 ed. write for info. (0-938911-00-7) Indiv Educ Syst.

—Christina & the Little Red Bird. Mcknight, C. D., illus. 23p. (Orig.). (ps-1). pap. 5.95 (0-938911-02-3) Indiv Educ Syst.

Peterson, Elizabeth J., ed. see Skiff, Andrea.

Peterson, Esther A. A Child's Life of Christ. Lee, Nancy, illus. 44p. (gr. 3-8). 1987. 6.95 (1-55523-045-8) Winston-Derek.

Peterson, Francisca E., tr. see Rape & Abuse Crisis Center Staff.

Peterson, Franklynn, jt. auth. see Kesselman-Turkel, Judi.

Peterson, George C. Stuck in the Mud, Vol. 1. Peterson, George, illus. 208p. (Orig.). (gr. 9-12). 1988. pap. write for info. (0-9621320-0-4) G Peterson.

Peterson, James E. Otter Creek: The Indian Road. LC 90-82089. (Illus.). 176p. (Orig.). (gr. 5 up). 1990. pap. 15.00 (0-914960-83-0) Academy Bks.

Peterson, Jeanne W. I Have a Sister, My Sister Is Deaf. Ray, Deborah, illus. LC 76-24306. (gr. k-3). 1977. PLB 13.89 (0-06-024702-9) HarpC Child Bks.

—I Have a Sister, My Sister Is Deaf. Ray, Deborah, illus. LC 76-24306. 32p. (ps-3). 1984. pap. 4.95 (0-06-443059-6, Trophy) HarpC Child Bks.

Peterson, Jeanne W. see Peterson, Jeanne W.

Peterson, John. Littles. (gr. 4-7). 1993. pap. 2.75 (0-590-46225-5) Scholastic Inc.

—Littles & the Lost Children. (gr. 4-7). 1991. pap. 2.75 (0-590-43026-2) Scholastic Inc.

—The Littles & the Terrible Tiny Kid. (gr. 4-7). 1993. pap. 2.75 (0-590-45578-8) Scholastic Inc.

—Littles & the Trash Tinies. (gr. 4-7). 1993. pap. 2.75 (0-590-46595-3) Scholastic Inc.

—The Littles Give a Party. (gr. 4-7). 1993. pap. 2.75 (0-590-46597-X) Scholastic Inc.

—The Littles Go Exploring. (gr. 4-7). 1993. pap. 2.75 (0-590-46596-1) Scholastic Inc.

—The Littles Have a Wedding. (gr. 4-7). 1993. pap. 2.75 (0-590-46224-5) Scholastic Inc.

—The Littles Take a Trip. (gr. 2-5). 1988. 14.50 (0-8446-6351-4) Peter Smith.

—The Littles Take a Trip. 96p. (gr. 2-5). 1986. pap. 2.50 (0-590-42713-X) Scholastic Inc.

—Littles Take a Trip. (gr. 4-7). 1993. pap. 2.75 (0-590-46222-9) Scholastic Inc.

—The Littles to the Rescue. (gr. 4-7). 1993. pap. 2.75 (0-590-46223-7) Scholastic Inc.

Peterson, Jonathan, ed. see Wolfman, Marv.

Peterson, Julienne, retold by. Caterina the Clever Farm Girl: A Tuscan Tale. Giannini, Enzo, illus. LC 93-15161. 1994. write for info. (0-8037-1181-6); PLB write for info. (0-8037-1182-4) Dial Bks Young.

Peterson, Larry, jt. auth. see Gesme, Carole.

Peterson, Linda. Careers Without College: Emergencies. Hupping, Carol & Grimaldi, Alicia, eds. 96p. 1993. pap. 7.95 (1-56079-252-3) Petersons Guides.

Peterson, Liz. Wind in the Willows: (A Musical) (Orig.). 1993. pap. 4.50 playscript (0-87602-325-1) Anchorage.

Peterson, Lois C. The ABC's of Being a Teenager. LC 87-34664. (Orig.). (gr. 7-9). 1988. pap. 4.99 (0-8054-4705-9) Broadman.

Peterson, Lorraine. Anybody Can Be Cool, but Awesome Takes Practice. LC 88-19454. (Illus.). 160p. (gr. 9-12). 1988. pap. 7.99 (1-55661-040-8) Bethany Hse.

—Dying of Embarassment & Living to Tell about It. LC 87-35334. 224p. (Orig.). (gr. 9-12). 1988. pap. 7.99 (0-87123-967-1) Bethany Hse.

—Falling Off Cloud Nine & Other High Places. Dugan, LeRoy, illus. LC 81-38465. 159p. (Orig.). (gr. 8-12). 1981. pap. 7.99 (0-87123-167-0) Bethany Hse.

—If God Loves Me, Why Can't I Get My Locker Open? LC 80-27014. 141p. (Orig.). (gr. 6-12). 1980. pap. 7.99 (0-87123-251-0) Bethany Hse.

—If the Devil Made You Do It, You Blew It. 192p. (Orig.). (gr. 8 up). 1989. pap. 7.99 (1-55661-052-1) Bethany Hse.

—If You Really Trust Me, Why Can't I Stay Out Longer? 224p. (Orig.). 1991. pap. 7.99 (1-55661-212-5) Bethany Hse.

—Radical Advice from the Ultimate Wiseguy. 192p. (Orig.). (gr. 8-12). 1990. pap. 7.99 (1-55661-141-2) Bethany Hse.

—Trying to Get Toothpaste Back Into the Tube. 192p. (Orig.). (gr. 7-10). 1993. pap. 7.99 (1-55661-315-6) Bethany Hse.

—Why Isn't God Giving Cash Prizes? Dugan, LeRoy, illus. LC 82-17866. 160p. (gr. 8-12). 1982. pap. 6.99 (0-87123-626-5) Bethany Hse.

Peterson, Marge & Peterson, Rob. Argentina: A Wild West Heritage. LC 89-11707. (Illus.). 32p. (gr. 5 up). 1990. RSBE 14.95 (0-87518-413-8, Dillon) Macmillan Child Grp.

Peterson, Melvin N. David's Star Studded Adventures. (Illus.). 58p. (gr. 1-4). 1988. spiral binding 48.00 (0-938880-07-1) MNP Star.

Peterson, P. J. Some Days, Other Days. LC 93-3871. 1994. text ed. 14.95 (0-684-19595-X, Scribner) Macmillan.

Peterson, Patricia R. The Know It All: Resource Book for Kids. (Illus.). 112p. (gr. 2 up). 1989. pap. 15.95 (0-913705-45-4, ZB14-B) Zephyr Pr AZ.

Peterson, Pete, ed. see Douglis, Marjie.

Peterson, Pete, ed. see Oke, Janette.

Peterson, Pete, ed. see Springer, Jean.

Peterson, Richard A. see Pope, Liston.

Peterson, Rob, jt. auth. see Peterson, Marge.

Peterson, Sandy, ed. see Hargrave, et al.

Peterson, Sandy, ed. see Stafford, Greg.

Peterson, Scott K. Face the Music! Jokes about Music. Hanson, Joan, illus. 32p. (gr. 1-4). 1988. PLB 11.95 (0-8225-0995-4) Lerner Pubns.

—Out on a Limb: Riddles about Trees & Plants. Burke, Susan S., illus. 32p. (gr. 1-4). 1989. PLB 11.95 (0-8225-2328-0) Lerner Pubns.

—What's Your Name? Jokes about Names. Hanson, Joan, illus. 32p. (gr. 1-4). 1987. PLB 11.95 (0-8225-0994-6, First Ave Edns); pap. 3.95 (0-8225-9520-6, First Ave Edns) Lerner Pubns.

—Wing It! Riddles about Birds. (Illus.). 32p. (gr. 1-4). 1991. PLB 11.95 (0-8225-2333-7) Lerner Pubns.

—Wing It: Riddles about Birds. (ps-3). 1991. pap. 3.95 (0-8225-9591-5) Lerner Pubns.

Peterson, Sherrie. Help! for Substitutes. Schmid, Ross, illus. 80p. 1985. tchr's. wkbk. 5.95 (0-86653-277-3, GA 642) Good Apple.

Peterson, Steve & McDonald, George, eds. Enemies. Williams, Mark, illus. 24p. (gr. 10-12). 1986. pap. 6.00 (0-915795-51-5, 02) Iron Crown Ent Inc.

Peterson, Wayne, ed. see McAllister, Dawson & Altman, Tim.

Petit, Genevieve. The Seventh Walnut. Boucher, Joelle, illus. Aubertin, Marc, contrib. by. LC 92-10588. 1992. 13.95 (0-922984-10-7) Wellington IL.

Petralia, Joseph F. Gold! Gold! A Beginner's Handbook & Recreational Guide: How & Where to Prospect for Gold. 5th, rev. ed. Applegate, Jill, ed. Neri, Susan, illus. LC 81-126200. 144p. 1992. pap. 9.95 (0-9605890-5-8, AB92) Sierra Trading.

Petras, John W., jt. auth. see Aho, Jennifer J.

Petreshene, Susan S. More Mind Joggers! One Hundred Two Ready-to-Use Activities That Make Kids Think. 288p. (gr. 1-6). 1988. pap. 27.95x (0-87628-584-1) Ctr Appl Res.

—Research Pleasers. Sussman, Ellen, ed. Rundell, Wendi S., illus. (Orig.). (gr. 3-6). 1982. pap. text ed. 5.95 (0-933606-19-2, MS-618) E Sussman Educ.

Petrick, Thomas W., ed. see Powell, Mary.

Petrie, Catherine. Hot Rod Harry. Sharp, Paul, illus. LC 81-15549. 32p. (ps-2). 1982. PLB 11.93 (0-516-03493-6); pap. text ed. 2.95 (0-516-43493-4) Childrens.

—Hot Rod Harry Big Book. (Illus.). 32p. (ps-2). 1991. PLB 30.60 (0-516-49516-X) Childrens.

—Joshua James Likes Trucks. Warshaw, Jerry, illus. LC 81-17076. 32p. (ps-2). 1982. PLB 11.93 (0-516-03525-8); pap. text ed. 2.95 (0-516-43525-6) Childrens.

—Joshua James Likes Trucks Big Book. (Illus.). 32p. (ps-2). 1987. PLB 30.60 (0-516-49504-6) Childrens.

—A Pedro Perez le Gustan los Camiones (Joshua James Likes Trucks) Warshaw, Jerry, illus. LC 81-17076. (SPA.). 32p. (ps-2). 1988. PLB 11.93 (0-516-33525-1); pap. 2.95 (0-516-53525-0) Childrens.

—Sandbox Betty. Elzaurdia, Sharon, illus. LC 81-15547. 32p. (ps-2). 1982. PLB 11.93 (0-516-03578-9); pap. 2.95 (0-516-43578-7) Childrens.

Petrie, Chuck, ed. see Grange, Wallace B.

Petrie, Mildred M. Duck, Duck: The Different Duck. Errickson, Shirley V., illus. LC 87-80921. 40p. 1987. 12.95 (0-9618241-0-7) Enfield Pubs.

Petrillo, Daniel J. Robert F. Kennedy. Schlesinger, Arthur M., Jr., intro. by. (Illus.). 112p. (Orig.). (gr. 5 up). 1989. 17.95 (1-55546-840-3); pap. 9.95 (0-7910-0581-X) Chelsea Hse.

Petrochilos, Elizabeth A. Stone the Poet. 110p. (Orig.). 1991. pap. write for info. (0-9629730-0-9) E Petrochilos.

Petroske, Mimi. Boy My Very Special Friend. Caroland, Mary, ed. (Illus.). 44p. (gr. k-3). 1991. 5.95 (1-55523-381-3) Winston-Derek.

Petrovich, Janice, jt. auth. see Witt, Sandi.

Petrucelli. Cher, Reading Level 2. (Illus.). 24p. (gr. 1-4). 1989. PLB 14.60 (0-86592-432-5) Rourke Corp.

—Consideration, Reading Level 2. (Illus.). 32p. (gr. 1-4). 1989. PLB 15.94 (0-86592-443-0); lib. bdg. 11.95 (0-685-58778-9) Rourke Corp.

—Creativity, Reading Level 2. (Illus.). 32p. (gr. 1-4). 1989. PLB 15.94 (0-86592-444-9) Rourke Corp.

—Henry Cisneros, Reading Level 2. (Illus.). 24p. (gr. 1-4). 1989. PLB 14.60 (0-86592-431-7); 10.95s.p. (0-685-58799-1) Rourke Corp.

—Jim Henson, Reading Level 2. (Illus.). 24p. (gr. 1-4). 1989. PLB 14.60 (0-86592-426-0); 10.95s.p. (0-685-58800-9) Rourke Corp.

—Loyalty, Reading Level 2. (Illus.). 32p. (gr. 1-4). 1989. PLB 15.94 (0-86592-441-4); 11.95s.p. (0-685-58786-X) Rourke Corp.

—Michael Jordan, Reading Level 2. (Illus.). 24p. (gr. 1-4). 1989. PLB 14.60 (0-86592-428-7); 10.95 (0-685-58801-7) Rourke Corp.

Petry, Ann. The Drugstore Cat. Suba, Susanna, illus. LC 88-3303. 96p. (gr. k-3). 1988. PLB 15.00 (0-318-35207-9, NL3); pap. 6.95 (0-8070-8309-7, BP801) Beacon Pr.

—Harriet Tubman: Conductor on the Underground Railway. LC 55-9215. 247p. (gr. 7-11). 1955. 15.00 (0-690-37236-1, Crowell Jr Bks) HarpC Child Bks.

—Harriet Tubman: Conductor on the Underground Railroad. LC 90-48980. (Illus.). 176p. (gr. 6-10). 1991. PLB 13.95 (1-55905-097-7) Marshall Cavendish.

—Harriet Tubman: Conductor on the Underground Railroad. (gr. 7). 1991. pap. write for info. (0-663-56311-9) Silver Burdett Pr.

—Tituba of Salem Village. LC 64-20691. 254p. (gr. 7 up). 1988. PLB 14.89 (0-690-04766-5, Crowell Jr Bks) HarpC Child Bks.

—Tituba of Salem Village. LC 64-20691. 272p. (gr. 5 up). 1991. pap. 3.95 (0-06-440403-X, Trophy) HarpC Child Bks.

Petschek, Joyce. Silver Dreams: A Myth of the Sixth Sense. LC 90-82143. (Illus.). 208p. (gr. 8-12). 1990. 29.95 (0-89087-619-3); pap. 19.95 (0-89087-620-7) Celestial Arts.

Petterson, Jay, illus. Giants, Witches & Dragons Three-D Coloring Book. 32p. (Orig.). 1990. pap. 3.95 (0-942025-81-4) Kidsbks.

Pettersson, Bertil. In the Bears' Forest. Murray, Steven T., tr. Fuller, Kathryn S., intro. by. (Illus.). 38p. 1991. bds. 11.95 (91-29-59866-4, Pub. by R & S Bks) FS&G.

Pettigrew, Eileen. Night Time. Kimber, William, illus. 24p. (ps-1). 1992. PLB 14.95 (1-55037-235-1, Pub. by Annick Pr); pap. 4.95 (1-55037-242-4, Pub. by Annick Pr) Firefly Bks Ltd.

Pettigrew, Vera. Fionuala the Glendalough Goat. Myler, Terry, illus. 112p. (Orig.). (gr. 1-8). 1990. 10.95 (0-947962-42-5, Pub. by Anvil Bks Ltd Ireland); pap. 7.95 (0-947962-43-3, Pub. by Anvil Bks Ltd Ireland) Irish Bks Media.

Pettit, Jayne. My Name Is San Ho. 192p. 1992. 13.95 (0-590-44172-8, Scholastic Hardcover) Scholastic Inc.

—Place to Hide: True Stories of Holocaust Rescues. (gr. 4-7). 1993. pap. 2.95 (0-590-45353-X) Scholastic Inc.

Pettit, Ray. My Excellent Adventure: Achievement Activities for Young Latter-Day Saints. LC 90-37121. 141p. (gr. 3-6). 1990. pap. 6.95 (0-87579-358-4) Deseret Bk.

Petts, Ken. The Illustrated Children's Bible. (Illus.). 243p. (gr. k-3). 1985. pap. text ed. 15.95 (0-448-14494-8) Putnam Pub Group.

Petty, Kate. Baby Animals: Bears. (Illus.). 24p. (ps-3). 1992. pap. 3.95 (0-8120-4964-0) Barron.

—Baby Animals: Chimpanzees. (Illus.). 24p. (ps-3). 1992. pap. 3.95 (0-8120-4965-9) Barron.

—Baby Animals: Elephants. (Illus.). 24p. (ps-3). 1992. pap. 3.95 (0-8120-4966-7) Barron.
—Baby Animals: Kittens. (Illus.). 24p. (ps-3). 1992. pap. 3.95 (0-8120-4967-5) Barron.
—Baby Animals: Pandas. (Illus.). 24p. (ps-3). 1992. pap. 3.95 (0-8120-4968-3) Barron.
—Baby Animals: Puppies. (Illus.). 24p. (ps-3). 1992. pap. 3.95 (0-8120-4969-1) Barron.
—Baby Animals: Seals. (Illus.). 24p. (ps-3). 1992. pap. 3.95 (0-8120-4970-5) Barron.
—Baby Animals: Tigers. (Illus.). 24p. (ps-3). 1992. pap. 3.95 (0-8120-4971-3) Barron.
—Bears. LC 90-44447. (Illus.). 24p. (gr. k-3). 1991. PLB 10.90 (0-531-17286-4, Gloucester Pr) Watts.
—Being Bullied. Firmin, Charlotte, illus. 24p. (ps-2). 1991. pap. 4.95 (0-8120-4661-7) Barron.
—Cats. (Illus.). 24p. (ps-3). 1993. pap. 3.95 (0-8120-1485-5) Barron.
—Chimpanzees. (gr. 4-7). 1990. PLB 10.90 (0-531-17193-0, Gloucester Pr) Watts.
—Cobayos. Thompson, George, illus. LC 90-71412. (SPA.). 24p. (gr. k-4). 1991. PLB 10.90 (0-531-07914-7) Watts.
—Crocodiles & Alligators. Johnson, Karen, illus. 1990. pap. 3.95 (0-531-15153-0) Watts.
—Deserts. Wood, Jakki, illus. 32p. (gr. 2-4). 1993. pap. 5.95 (0-8120-1762-5) Barron.
—Dogs. (Illus.). 24p. (ps-3). 1993. pap. 3.95 (0-8120-1484-7) Barron.
—Ducklings. (Illus.). 24p. (gr. k-4). 1990. PLB 10.90 (0-531-17229-5, Gloucester Pr) Watts.
—Ducklings. 24p. (gr. k-3). 1993. pap. 3.95 (0-8120-1489-8) Barron.
—Earth. LC 90-31022. (Illus.). 32p. (gr. k-4). 1991. PLB 11.90 (0-531-14098-9) Watts.
—Elephants. LC 89-26037. (ps-3). 1990. PLB 10.90 (0-531-17194-9, Gloucester Pr) Watts.
—Feeling Left Out. Firmin, Charlotte, illus. 24p. (ps-2). 1991. pap. 4.95 (0-8120-4658-7) Barron.
—Fire. (Illus.). 32p. (gr. k-4). 1990. PLB 11.90 (0-531-14060-1) Watts.
—Frogs & Toads. Baker, Alan, illus. 32p. (gr. k-3). 1990. pap. 3.95 (0-531-15154-9) Watts.
—Gatos. Thompson, George, illus. LC 88-83087. (SPA.). 24p. (gr. k-4). 1991. PLB 10.90 (0-531-07916-3) Watts.
—The Ground Below Us. (Illus.). 32p. (gr. 2-4). 1993. pap. 5.95 (0-8120-1232-1) Barron.
—Hamsteres. Thompson, George, illus. LC 90-71413. (SPA.). 24p. (gr. k-4). 1991. PLB 10.90 (0-531-07913-9) Watts.
—Hamsters. Thompson, George, illus. LC 89-50455. 32p. (gr. k-2). 1989. PLB 10.90 (0-531-17159-0, Gloucester Pr) Watts.
—Hamsters. (Illus.). 24p. (ps-3). 1993. pap. 3.95 (0-8120-1472-3) Barron.
—Into Space. Wood, Jakki, illus. 32p. (gr. 2-4). 1993. pap. 5.95 (0-8120-1761-7) Barron.
—Kangaroos. (ps-3). 1990. PLB 10.90 (0-531-17195-7, Gloucester Pr) Watts.
—Kangaroos. (Illus.). (gr. k-3). 1993. pap. 3.95 (0-8120-1492-8) Barron.
—Kittens. (Illus.). 24p. (gr. k-4). 1990. PLB 10.90 (0-531-17231-7, Gloucester Pr) Watts.
—Lions. LC 89-26036. (ps-3). 1990. PLB 10.90 (0-531-17196-5, Gloucester Pr) Watts.
—Lions. 24p. (gr. k-3). 1993. pap. 3.95 (0-8120-1490-1) Barron.
—Making Friends. Firmin, Charlotte, illus. 24p. (ps-2). 1991. pap. 4.95 (0-8120-4660-9) Barron.
—Maps & Journals. (Illus.). 32p. (gr. 2-4). 1993. pap. 5.95 (0-8120-1235-6) Barron.
—Mr. Toad to the Rescue. Baker, Alan, illus. 24p. (ps-2). 1992. 8.95 (0-8120-6273-6) Barron.
—Mr. Toad's Narrow Escape. (ps-3). 1992. pap. 4.95 (0-8120-1475-8) Barron.
—Mr. Toad's Narrow Escapes. (ps-3). 1992. 8.95 (0-8120-6289-2) Barron.
—My First Atlas, Vol. 1. King, Colin, illus. (ps-8). 1991. 9.95 (1-55782-361-8, Pub. by Warner Juvenile Bks) Little.
—My First Book of Knowledge. 1990. 5.99 (0-517-05177-X) Outlet Bk Co.
—New Bike. Barber, Ed, photos by. (Illus.). 32p. (gr. 2 up). 1992. bds. 12.95 (0-7136-3482-0, Pub. by A&C Black UK) Talman.
—New Car. Barber, Ed, photos by. (Illus.). 32p. (gr. 2 up). 1992. bds. 12.95 (0-7136-3484-7, Pub. by A&C Black UK) Talman.
—New Shampoo. Barber, Ed, photos by. (Illus.). 32p. (gr. 2 up). 1992. bds. 12.95 (0-7136-3481-2, Pub. by A&C Black UK) Talman.
—New Shoes. Barber, Ed, photos by. (Illus.). 32p. (gr. 2 up). 1992. bds. 12.95 (0-7136-3483-9, Pub. by A&C Black UK) Talman.
—Our Globe, Our World. (Illus.). 32p. (gr. 2-4). 1993. pap. 5.95 (0-8120-1236-4) Barron.
—Pandas. LC 90-45005. (Illus.). 24p. (gr. k-3). 1991. PLB 10.90 (0-531-17287-2, Gloucester Pr) Watts.
—Perros. Thompson, George, illus. (SPA.). 24p. (gr. k-4). 1991. PLB 10.90 (0-531-07915-5) Watts.
—Playing the Game. Firmin, Charlotte, illus. 24p. (ps-2). 1991. pap. 4.95 (0-8120-4659-5) Barron.
—Ponies & Foals. Kline, M. LC 90-32381. (Illus.). 24p. (gr. k-4). 1990. PLB 10.90 (0-531-17230-9, Gloucester Pr) Watts.
—Ponies & Foals. 24p. (gr. k-3). 1993. pap. 3.95 (0-8120-1487-1) Barron.

—Puppies. (Illus.). 24p. (gr. k-4). 1990. PLB 10.90 (0-531-17232-5, Gloucester Pr) Watts.
—Rabbits. (Illus.). 24p. (ps-3). 1993. pap. 3.95 (0-8120-1473-1) Barron.
—Rainforests. Wood, Jakki, illus. 32p. (gr. 2-4). 1993. pap. 5.95 (0-8120-1760-9) Barron.
—Seals. (Illus.). 24p. (gr. k-3). 1991. PLB 10.90 (0-531-17285-6, Gloucester Pr) Watts.
—The Sky Above Us. (Illus.). 32p. (gr. 2-4). 1993. pap. 5.95 (0-8120-1234-8) Barron.
—Stop, Look & Listen, Mr. Toad. Baker, Alan, illus. 24p. (ps-2). 1991. 8.95 (0-8120-6230-2) Barron.
—Tigers. Kline, M., ed. LC 90-18361. (Illus.). 24p. (gr. k-3). 1991. PLB 10.90 (0-531-17284-8, Gloucester Pr) Watts.
—Under the Sea. Wood, Jakki, illus. 32p. (gr. 2-4). 1993. pap. 5.95 (0-8120-1759-5) Barron.
Petz, Rita K., ed. see Cannon, Frances A.
Pevear & Radunsky. Baron Munchausen. 1994. 14.95 (0-8050-1228-1) H Holt & Co.
Pevear, Richard. Our King Has Horns! Payevsky, Robert, illus. LC 86-23525. 32p. (gr. k-3). 1987. RSBE 14.95 (0-02-773920-1, Macmillan Child Bk) Macmillan Child Grp.
Pevear, Richard, tr. see Chekhov, Anton.
Pevear, Richard, tr. see Marshak, Samuel.
Pevsner, Stella. And You Give Me a Pain, Elaine. (gr. 7-9). 1989. pap. 2.99 (0-671-68838-3, Archway) PB.
—And You Give Me a Pain, Elaine. LC 78-5857. 192p. (gr. 6 up). 1979. 13.45 (0-395-28877-0, Clarion Bks) HM.
—And You Give Me A Pain, Elaine. (gr. 7). 1991. pap. write for info. (0-663-56255-4) Silver Burdett Pr.
—Cute Is a Four-Letter Word. 176p. (gr. 7 up). 1989. pap. 2.75 (0-671-68845-6, Archway) PB.
—How Could You Do It, Diane? LC 88-35923. 192p. (gr. 5-9). 1989. 13.45 (0-395-51041-4, Clarion Bks) HM.
—I'm Emma, I'm a Quint. LC 92-36952. 1993. 13.45 (0-395-64166-7, Clarion Bks) HM.
—Me, My Goat & My Sister's Wedding. (gr. 4-7). 1987. pap. 2.75 (0-671-66206-4, Minstrel Bks) PB.
—The Night the Whole Class Slept Over. 176p. (gr. 4-9). 1991. 13.95 (0-89919-983-6, Clarion Bks) HM.
—The Night the Whole Class Slept Over. McDonald, Pat, ed. 176p. (gr. 3-6). 1992. pap. 2.99 (0-671-78157-X, Minstrel Bks) PB.
—Sister of the Quints. LC 86-17565. 192p. (gr. 5-9). 1987. 13.95 (0-89919-498-2, Clarion Bks) HM.
—A Smart Kid Like You. LC 74-19320. 192p. (gr. 4-8). 1979. 14.45 (0-395-28876-2, Clarion Bks) HM.
Peyton, John L. Voices from the Ice. Peyton, John L., illus. 56p. (gr. k-4). 1990. pap. 7.95 (0-939923-15-7) M & W Pub Co.
Peyton, K. M. Darkling. 1990. 14.95 (0-385-30086-7) Doubleday.
—Darkling. 1992. pap. 3.50 (0-440-21211-1) Dell.
—The Edge of the Cloud. 192p. (gr. 7 up). 1989. pap. 3.99 (0-14-030905-5, Puffin) Puffin Bks.
—The Edge of the Cloud. (gr. 7 up). 1992. 16.50 (0-8446-6566-5) Peter Smith.
—Flambards. 224p. (gr. 7 up). 1989. pap. 3.95 (0-14-034153-6, Puffin) Puffin Bks.
—Flambards in Summer. (gr. 7 up). 1992. 16.50 (0-8446-6567-3) Peter Smith.
—A Midsummer's Night Death. 192p. (gr. 7 up). 1982. pap. 1.75 (0-440-95615-3, LE) Dell.
Pezzoli, F. & Mora, E. Farm Animals. (Illus.). 30p. (ps-1). 1986. 3.95 (0-8120-5723-6) Barron.
Pfanner, Louise. Louise Builds a Boat. LC 89-70929. (Illus.). 40p. (ps-1). 1990. 12.95 (0-531-05888-3); PLB 12.99 (0-531-08488-4) Orchard Bks Watts.
—Louise Builds a House. LC 88-23415. (Illus.). 32p. (ps-1). 1989. 12.95 (0-531-05796-8); PLB 12.99 (0-531-08396-9) Orchard Bks Watts.
Pfannes, Charles E. & Salamone, Victor A. The Great Commanders of World War II. (gr. 7 up). 1981. pap. 2.75 (0-89083-727-9) Zebra.
Pfannes, Charles E. & Salamone, Victor. The Great Commanders of World War II: Vol. II, the British. (gr. 7 up). 1981. pap. 2.75 (0-89083-786-4) Zebra.
Pfeffer. Kid Power Strikes Back. 1993. pap. 2.75 (0-590-44427-1) Scholastic Inc.
—Twin Troubles. 1994. pap. write for info. (0-8050-3272-X) H Holt & Co.
Pfeffer, Pierre. Bears, Big & Little. Bogard, Vicki, tr. from FRE. Stephan, Franck, illus. LC 89-8883. 38p. (gr. k-5). 1989. 4.95 (0-944589-23-5, 023) Young Discovery Lib.
—Elephants: Big, Strong & Wise. Matthews, Sarah, tr. from FRE. Mettler, Rene, illus. LC 87-33995. 38p. (gr. k-5). 1988. 4.95 (0-944589-04-9, 049) Young Discovery Lib.
Pfeffer, Susan B. About David. 176p. (gr. 7 up). 1982. pap. 3.50 (0-440-90022-0, LFL) Dell.
—About David: A Novel. LC 80-65837. 176p. (gr. 7 up). 1980. 11.95 (0-385-28013-0) Delacorte.
—April Upstairs. LC 90-44022. 144p. (gr. 4-6). 1990. 13.95 (0-8050-1306-7, Bks Young Read) H Holt & Co.
—April Upstairs. 1992. pap. 3.50 (0-553-15939-9) Bantam.
—Claire at Sixteen. 1989. 13.95 (0-553-05819-3, Starfire) Bantam.
—Claire at Sixteen. 1990. pap. 2.95 (0-553-28460-6) Bantam.
—Courage, Dana. 160p. (gr. k-6). 1984. pap. 2.75 (0-440-41541-1, YB) Dell.

—Darcy Downstairs. LC 90-44020. 144p. (gr. 4-6). 1990. 13.95 (0-8050-1307-5, Bks Young Read) H Holt & Co.
—Darcy Downstairs. (ps-3). 1993. pap. 3.50 (0-553-15942-9) Bantam.
—Dear Dad, Love Laurie. (gr. 4-6). 1990. pap. 2.75 (0-590-41682-0) Scholastic Inc.
—Family of Strangers. 1992. 16.00 (0-553-08364-3) Bantam.
—Family of Strangers. 1994. pap. 3.99 (0-440-21895-0) Dell.
—Future Forward. Glass, Andrew, illus. (gr. 5 up). 1989. 13.95 (0-385-29740-8) Delacorte.
—Future Forward. (gr. 4-7). 1991. pap. 3.25 (0-440-40475-4) Dell.
—Just Between Us. Tomei, Lorna, illus. LC 79-53606. 128p. (gr. 4-6). 1980. pap. 9.89 (0-385-28594-9) Delacorte.
—Just Between Us. 128p. (gr. k-6). 1981. pap. 2.25 (0-440-44194-3, YB) Dell.
—Kid Power. 121p. (gr. 3-7). 1988. pap. 2.95 (0-590-42607-9) Scholastic Inc.
—Make Believe. 160p. (gr. 4-7). 1993. PLB 14.95 (0-8050-1754-2, Bks Young Read) H Holt & Co.
—A Matter of Principle. LC 81-15288. 192p. (gr. 7 up). 1982. 11.95 (0-385-28649-X) Delacorte.
—Meg at Sixteen. 1990. 13.95 (0-553-05854-1) Bantam.
—Most Precious Blood. 1993. pap. 3.99 (0-553-56128-6) Bantam.
—Paperdolls. 160p. (Orig.). (gr. 7-12). 1984. pap. 2.25 (0-440-96777-5, LFL) Dell.
—Rewind to Yesterday. (gr. 4-7). 1991. pap. 3.25 (0-440-40474-6) Dell.
—The Riddle Streak. Chesworth, Michael, illus. 64p. (gr. 2-4). 1993. PLB 14.95 (0-8050-2147-7, Bks Young Read) H Holt & Co.
—The Ring of Truth. LC 92-25272. 1993. 15.95 (0-553-09224-3) Bantam.
—Sara Kate Super Kid1. 1994. write for info. (0-8050-3147-2) H Holt & Co.
—Sara Kate Super Kid2. 1995. write for info. (0-8050-3148-0) H Holt & Co.
—The Sebastian Sisters: Evvie at Sixteen. (gr. 5 up). 1988. 13.95 (0-553-05475-9, Starfire) Bantam.
—Sebastian Sisters: Meg at Sixteen. 1991. pap. 3.50 (0-553-28836-9) Bantam.
—Starring Peter & Leigh. LC 78-72855. 1978. 7.95 (0-440-08226-9) Delacorte.
—Sybil at Sixteen. (gr. 7 up). 1989. 13.95 (0-553-05842-8) Bantam.
—Sybil at Sixteen. (gr. 7 up). 1990. pap. 2.95 (0-553-28614-5, Starfire) Bantam.
—Turning Thirteen. LC 88-11347. 144p. (gr. 6-8). 1988. pap. 12.95 (0-590-40764-3, Scholastic Hardcover) Scholastic Inc.
—Turning Thirteen. (gr. 6-8). 1989. pap. 2.75 (0-590-40765-1, Apple Paperbacks) Scholastic Inc.
—Twin Surprises. Carter, Abby, illus. 64p. (gr. 2-4). 1991. 13.95 (0-8050-1850-6, Redfeather BYR) H Holt & Co.
—Twin Surprises. Carter, Abby, illus. LC 91-13968. 64p. (gr. 2-4). 1993. pap. 4.95 (0-8050-2626-6, Redfeather BYR) H Holt & Co.
—Twin Troubles. Carter, Abby, illus. LC 92-5773. 1992. write for info. (0-8050-2146-9, Redfeather BYR) H Holt & Co.
—What Do You Do When Your Mouth Won't Open? Tomei, Lorna, illus. LC 80-68731. 160p. (gr. 4-6). 1981. 8.95 (0-440-09471-2); pap. 9.89 (0-385-29140-X) Delacorte.
—What Do You Do When Your Mouth Won't Open? 128p. (gr. 4-8). 1982. pap. 2.75 (0-440-49320-X, YB) Dell.
—The Year without Michael. 176p. (gr. 7-12). 1987. 16.00 (0-553-05430-9, Starfire) Bantam.
—The Year without Michael. (gr. 7-12). 1988. pap. 3.50 (0-553-27373-6, Starfire) Bantam.
Pfeffer, Wendy. Frogs & Tadpoles. Keller, Holly, illus. LC 93-3135. (gr. 3 up). 1994. 14.00 (0-06-023044-4); PLB 13.89 (0-06-023117-3) HarpC Child Bks.
—Popcorn Park Zoo. Smith, J. Gerard, photos by. LC 91-3273. (Illus.). 64p. (gr. 2-5). 1992. 14.95 (0-671-74587-5, J Messner); lib. bdg. 16.98 (0-671-74589-1, J Messner) S&S Trade.
Pfeifer, Kathryn. Henry O. Flipper. (Illus.). 80p. (gr. 4-7). 1993. PLB 14.95 (0-8050-2351-8) TFC Bks NY.
—Seven Hundred Sixty-First Battalion. 1994. PLB write for info. (0-8050-3057-3) H Holt & Co.
Pfeiffer, Christine. Chicago. LC 88-20199. (Illus.). 60p. (gr. 3 up). 1988. RSBE 13.95 (0-87518-385-9, Dillon) Macmillan Child Grp.
—Germany: Two Nations, One Heritage. LC 86-32954. (Illus.). 176p. (gr. 5 up). 1987. RSBE 14.95 (0-87518-361-1, Dillon) Macmillan Child Grp.
—Poland: Land of Freedom Fighters. LC 90-26093. (Illus.). 144p. (gr. 5 up). 1991. RSBE 14.95 (0-87518-464-2, Dillon) Macmillan Child Grp.
Pfister, Marcus. The Christmas Star. Pfister, Marcus, illus. James, J. Alison, tr. from GER. (Illus.). 32p. (gr. k-3). 1993. 16.95 (1-55858-203-7); lib. bdg. 16.88 (1-55858-204-5) North-South Bks NYC.
—Hopper. Pfister, Marcus, illus. LC 90-47065. 32p. (ps-k). 1991. 14.95 (1-55858-106-5) North-South Bks NYC.
—Hopper Hunts for Spring. Pfister, Marcus, illus. Lanning, Rosemary, tr. from GER. LC 91-29671. (Illus.). 32p. (gr. k-3). 1992. 14.95 (1-55858-139-1); lib. bdg. 14.88 (1-55858-147-2) North-South Bks NYC.

—Les Nouveaux Amis De Pit. Pfister, Marcus, illus. (FRE.). 32p. (gr. k-3). 1992. 13.95 (3-85539-632-9) North-South Bks NYC.
—Penguin Pete. Pfister, Marcus, illus. LC 87-1627. 32p. (gr. k-3). 1987. 13.95 (1-55858-018-2) North-South Bks NYC.
—Penguin Pete, Ahoy! Lanning, Rosemary, tr. from GER. Pfister, Marcus, illus. LC 93-19921. 32p. (gr. k-3). 1993. 14.95 (1-55858-220-7); PLB 14.88 (1-55858-221-5) North-South Bks NYC.
—Penguin Pete & Pat. Pfister, Marcus, illus. Bell, Anthea, tr. from GER. LC 88-25296. (Illus.). 32p. (gr. k-3). 1989. 14.95 (1-55858-003-4) North-South Bks NYC.
—Penguin Pete's New Friends. Pfister, Marcus, illus. LC 87-72037. 32p. (gr. k-3). 1988. 13.95 (1-55858-025-5) North-South Bks NYC.
—Pinguin Pit. Pfister, Marcus, illus. (GER.). 32p. (gr. k-3). 1992. 13.95 (3-314-00297-1) North-South Bks NYC.
—Pit et Pat. Pfister, Marcus, illus. (FRE.). 32p. (gr. k-3). 1992. 13.95 (3-85539-657-4) North-South Bks NYC.
—Pit, le Petit Pingouin. Pfister, Marcus, illus. (FRE.). 32p. (gr. k-3). 1992. 13.95 (3-314-20627-5) North-South Bks NYC.
—Pit und Pat. Pfister, Marcus, illus. (GER.). 32p. (gr. k-3). 1992. 13.95 (3-314-00327-7) North-South Bks NYC.
—Pit's Neue Freunde. Pfister, Marcus, illus. (GER.). 32p. (gr. k-3). 1992. 13.95 (3-85825-301-4) North-South Bks NYC.
—Rainbow Fish. Pfister, Marcus, illus. James, J. Alison, tr. from GER. LC 91-42158. (Illus.). 32p. (gr. k-3). 1992. 16.95 (1-55858-009-3); PLB 16.88 (1-55858-010-7) North-South Bks NYC.
—Sun & Moon. (gr. 4-7). 1993. pap. 4.95 (0-590-44490-5) Scholastic Inc.
Pfister, Marcus, jt. auth. see Siegenthaler, Kathrin.
Pfister, Marcus, selected by. & illus. I See the Moon: Good-Night Poems & Lullabies. LC 91-10841. 32p. (ps-k). 1991. 14.95 (1-55858-119-7) North-South Bks NYC.
Pfister, Marcus, illus. My Penguin Pete Address Book. 1991. 7.95 (1-55858-126-X) North-South Bks NYC.
—My Penguin Pete Birthday Book. 1991. 7.95 (1-55858-127-8) North-South Bks NYC.
Pflaum, Rosalynd. Marie Curie & Her Daughter Irene. LC 92-2453. 1993. 21.50 (0-8225-4915-8) Lerner Pubns.
Pfleger, Deborah B., jt. auth. see Warren, Sandra.
Pfloog, Jan. Asi Son los Gatitos! (Kittens are Like That) Pfloog, Jan, illus. Saunders, Paola B., tr. LC 93-19920. (Illus.). 32p. (ps-3). 1993. pap. 2.25 (0-679-84719-7) Random Bks Yng Read.
—Asi Son los Perritos! Pfloog, Jan, illus. (SPA.). 32p. (ps-3). 1993. pap. 2.25 (0-394-85064-5) Random Bks Yng Read.
—Asi Son los Perritos. (SPA.). 1982. 2.25 (0-394-85604-X) Random Bks Yng Read.
—The Farm Book. (Illus.). 24p. (ps-k). 1989. pap. write for info. (0-307-58117-9, Pub. by Golden Bks) Western Pub.
—The Kitten Book. (Illus.). 24p. (ps-k). 1968. pap. write for info. (0-307-10079-0, Pub. by Golden Bks) Western Pub.
—Kittens Are Like That. Pfloog, Jan, illus. LC 75-36469. 32p. (ps-1). 1976. 2.25 (0-394-83243-4) Random Bks Yng Read.
—Puppies Are Like That. Pfloog, Jan, illus. LC 74-2542. 32p. (Orig.). (ps-1). 1975. pap. 2.25 (0-394-82923-9) Random Bks Yng Read.
—The Puppy Book. (Illus.). 24p. (ps-k). 1968. pap. write for info (0-307-10078-2, Pub. by Golden Bks) Western Pub.
—The Zoo Book. (Illus.). 24p. (ps-k). 1989. pap. write for info. (0-307-58118-7, Pub. by Golden Bks) Western Pub.
Pfluger, A. Karate: Basic Principles. Kuttner, Paul & Cunningham, Dale S., trs. LC 67-27760. (Illus.). (gr. 8 up). 1969. Repr. of 1967 ed. 6.95 (0-8069-4432-3); PLB 7.49 (0-8069-4433-1) Sterling.
Pfoutz, Sally. Missing Person. 176p. (gr. 7 up). 1993. 14.99 (0-670-84663-5) Viking Child Bks.
Pfrimmer, Mildred. Books to Learn & Live by, 5 bks. Incl. Bk. 1. The ABC's of Creation; Bk. 2. The ABC's of the Flood; Bk. 3. The Aardvark in the Art; Bk. 4. Elephant in Eden; Bk. 5. The Tale of the Whale. (gr. 3-9). 1977. Set. 17.50 (0-685-80546-8) Triumph Pub.
Phair, Charles. Atlantic Salmon Fishing. Plesissner, Ogden M. & Nisbet, Richard C., illus. Hunt, Richard C., intro. by. 193p. (gr. 10 up). 1993. Repr. of 1937 ed. 50.00 (1-56416-049-1) Derrydale Pr.
Phares, Ross. Cavalier in the Wilderness. Hastings, Jack, illus. LC 76-1409. 290p. (gr. 6-12). 1976. 16.95 (0-88289-128-6); pap. 11.95 (0-88289-127-8) Pelican.
Pharma Realm Buddhist University Faculty Staff, compiled by. Human Roots: Buddhist Stories for Young Readers, Vol. 1. (Illus.). 95p. (Orig.). (gr. 3 up). 1982. pap. 5.00 (0-88139-500-5) Buddhist Text.
Phears, William D. Ain't, but It Can Be: Persistence & Faith Overcoming Racist-Related Adversities. 321p. 1993. pap. 12.95 (1-878398-37-7) Blue Note Pubns.
Pheby, John A., ed. The Oxford-Duden Pictorial English Dictionary. (Illus.). 824p. (gr. 9 up). 1984. pap. 15.95 (0-19-864155-9) OUP.
Phelps, Ethel J. The Maid of the North: Feminist Folk Tales from Around the World. Bloom, Lloyd, illus. LC 80-21500. 196p. (gr. 4-6). 1981. (Bks Young Read); pap. 9.95 (0-8050-0679-6) H Holt & Co.

Phelps, Ethel J., ed. Tatterhood & Other Tales. Baldwin-Ford, Pamela, illus. Phelps, Ethel, intro. by. LC 78-9352. (Illus.). 192p. (Orig.). (gr. 1 up). 1978. o. p. 11.95 (0-912670-49-5); pap. 9.95 (0-912670-50-9) Feminist Pr.
Phelps, Lauren M. The News Is Love. 1992. pap. 2.99 (0-553-29459-8) Bantam.
Phifer, Kate G. Tall & Small: A Book about Height. Kendrick, Dennis, illus. LC 86-32401. 96p. (gr. 5 up). 1987. 11.95 (0-8027-6684-6); PLB 12.85 (0-8027-6685-4) Walker & Co.
Philabaum, Dabney M. Desert Buddies. Alegret, Nancy L., illus. 40p. (gr. k-4). 1994. pap. 8.95 (0-9639215-0-9) Earth Buddies.
Philadelphia Schools Students. From the Young at Heart: A Student Anthology. Goodman, Sharon L., ed. Saahaddin, Anwar, et al, illus. 20p. (Orig.). (gr. 1-8). 1989. pap. write for info. (0-935369-19-8) In Tradition Pub.
Philbrick, W. R. Freak the Mighty. LC 93-19913. 176p. (gr. 5-9). 1993. 13.95 (0-590-47412-X) Scholastic Inc.
Philip, Neil, compiled by. Fairy Tales from Eastern Europe. Wilkes, Larry, illus. Philip, Neil, retold by. (Illus.). 160p. (gr. 4 up). 1991. 19.45 (0-395-57456-0, Clarion Bks) HM.
—Poems for the Young. Lawrence, John, illus. LC 92-344. 96p. 1992. 19.95 (1-55670-262-0) Stewart Tabori & Chang.
Philip, Neil, as told by. The Tale of Sir Gawain. Keeping, Charles, illus. 112p. (gr. 5 up). 1987. 13.95 (0-399-21488-7, Philomel) Putnam Pub Group.
Philip, Neil, intro. by see Lang, Andrew.
Philip, Neil, selected by see Yeats, William Butler.
Philip, Neil, tr. see Andersen, Hans Christian.
Philip, Neil see Philip, Neil & Simborowski, Nicoletta.
Philip, Neil see Yeats, William Butler.
Philipp, Lillie H. Piano Technique: Tone, Touch, Phrasing & Dynamics. (Illus.). 90p. (gr. 7 up). 1982. pap. 5.95 (0-486-24272-2) Dover.
Philipps, Myra. Smooth As Silk. 2nd ed. Ramon, Estelle, illus. (gr. 3 up). 1979. 1.95 (0-686-10960-0) Basin Pub.
Philips, Barbara. Don't Call Me Fatso. Cogancherry, Helen, illus. Okun, Barbara, intro. by. LC 85-24341. (Illus.). 32p. (gr. k-6). 1980. PLB 17.96 (0-8172-1350-3) Raintree Steck-V.
Philips, Martha & Hadden, Mary. Behind Stone Walls & Barbed Wire. Lynn, Claire, ed. (Illus.). 176p. (Orig.). (gr. 5 up). 1991. pap. 2.25 (0-89323-057-X) Bible Memory.
Phillimore, J. Mansfield. (Illus.). 112p. (gr. 7 up). 1990. lib. bdg. 19.94 (0-86593-020-1); lib. bdg. 14.95s.p. (0-685-46451-2) Rourke Corp.
Phillips, Ana M., jt. auth. see Colonna, Phyllia.
Phillips, Angela. Discrimination. LC 92-39446. (Illus.). 48p. (gr. 6 up). 1993. RSBE 12.95 (0-02-786881-8, New Discovery) Macmillan Child Grp.
Phillips, Ann. A Haunted Year. Flavin, Teresa, illus. LC 92-45638. 144p. (gr. 4-7). 1994. SBE 14.95 (0-02-774605-4, Macmillan Child Bk) Macmillan Child Grp.
—The Multiplying Glass. Moyes, Liz, illus. 158p. 1987. 15.00 (0-19-271455-4) OUP.
—The Peace Child. (Illus.). 160p. (gr. 5 up). 1988. 15.00 (0-19-271560-7) OUP.
Phillips, Anne W. The Ocean. LC 90-36296. (Illus.). 48p. (gr. 5-6). 1990. RSBE 12.95 (0-89686-541-X, Crestwood Hse) Macmillan Child Grp.
Phillips, Barbara. Don't Call Me Fatso. (ps-3). 1993. pap. 3.95 (0-8114-5203-4) Raintree Steck-V.
Phillips, Betty L. Brush up Hair Care. Johnson, Lois, illus. LC 82-60643. 64p. (gr. 9-12). 1983. lib. bdg. 9.29 (0-671-43852-2, J Messner) S&S Trade.
—Go! Fight! Win! The NCA Guide for Cheerleaders. Herkimer, Lawrence R., illus. Shepherd, Francis, photos by. LC 79-53607. (Illus.). 160p. (gr. 7 up). 1981. PLB 11.80 (0-440-02957-0); pap. 9.95 (0-385-29336-4) Delacorte.
Phillips, Bob. Awesome Good Clean Jokes for Kids. LC 92-12109. 207p. 1992. pap. 3.99 (1-56507-062-3) Harvest Hse.
—The Best of the Good Clean Jokes. LC 89-32386. 192p. (gr. 5 up). 1989. pap. 4.99 (0-89081-769-3) Harvest Hse.
—Best of the Good Clean Jokes. LC 89-32386. 192p. (gr. 5 up). 1993. spiral bdg. 9.99 (1-56507-115-8) Harvest Hse.
—Good Clean Jokes for Kids. 1991. pap. 3.99 (0-89081-902-5) Harvest Hse.
—Loony Good Clean Jokes for Kids. LC 93-23529. 1994. write for info. (1-56507-178-6) Harvest Hse.
—Ultimate Good Clean Jokes for Kids. 1993. pap. 3.99 (1-56507-085-2) Harvest Hse.
—Wacky Good Clean Jokes for Kids. 1993. pap. 4.99 (1-56507-141-7) Harvest Hse.
Phillips, Cheryl & Harvey, Bonnie C., eds. My Jesus Pocketbook of God's Fruit. Fulton, Ginger A., illus. LC 83-50194. 32p. (ps-3). 1983. pap. 0.69 (0-937420-08-5) Stirrup Assoc.
Phillips, Cheryl M. & Harvey, Bonnie C., eds. My Jesus Pocketbook of the Lord's Prayer. Fulton, Ginger A., illus. LC 83-50193. 32p. (ps-3). 1983. pap. 0.69 (0-937420-07-7) Stirrup Assoc.
Phillips, Cheryl M., ed. see Stirrup Associates, Inc. Staff.
Phillips, Dave. Animal Mazes. (Illus.). 48p. 1991. pap. 2.95 (0-486-26707-5) Dover.
—Mother Goose Mazes. LC 92-17679. 1992. pap. write for info. (0-486-27319-9) Dover.

—Space Age Mazes. (gr. 2 up). 1988. pap. 2.95 (0-486-25659-6) Dover.
Phillips, Dave, illus. Hidden Treasure Maze Book. 48p. (Orig.). (gr. 2 up). 1984. pap. 2.95 (0-486-24566-7) Dover.
Phillips, Douglas A. & Levi, Steven C. The Pacific Rim Region: Emerging Giant. LC 88-3876. (Illus.). 160p. (gr. 6 up). 1988. lib. bdg. 18.95 (0-89490-191-5) Enslow Pubs.
Phillips, Eleanor. Chung, the China Gold, & Me. 150p. (Orig.). (gr. 6-10). 1990. pap. 7.95 (0-9624210-0-6) Laurelwood Pr.
Phillips, Eva. Nodley, the Duck Who Paddled Backwards. LC 91-65791. 44p. (gr. k-3). 1991. pap. 6.95 (1-55523-446-1) Winston-Derek.
Phillips, Gina. First Facts about Giant Sea Creatures. Persico, F. S., illus. 24p. 1991. 2.98 (1-56156-084-7) Kidsbks.
—First Facts about Giant Sea Creatures. Persico, F. S., illus. 24p. 1992. pap. 2.50 (1-56156-156-8) Kidsbks.
—First Facts about Prehistoric Animals. Persico, F. S., illus. 24p. 1991. 2.98 (1-56156-083-9) Kidsbks.
—First Facts about Prehistoric Animals. Persico, F. S., illus. 24p. 1992. pap. 2.50 (1-56156-157-6) Kidsbks.
—First Facts about Snakes & Reptiles. Persico, F. S., illus. 24p. (Orig.). 1991. pap. 2.50 (1-56156-037-5) Kidsbks.
—First Facts about Snakes & Reptiles. Persico, F. S., illus. 24p. 1991. write for info. (1-56156-060-X) Kidsbks.
—First Facts about Wild Animals. Persico, F. S., illus. 24p. (Orig.). 1991. pap. 2.50 (1-56156-038-3) Kidsbks.
—First Facts about Wild Animals. Persico, F. S., illus. 24p. 1991. write for info. (1-56156-061-8) Kidsbks.
Phillips, Gina, ed. Three Minute Aesop's Fables. Persico, F. S., illus. 24p. 1991. 2.98 (1-56156-088-X) Kidsbks.
—Three Minute Bedtime Stories. Persico, F. S., illus. 24p. 1991. 2.98 (1-56156-087-1) Kidsbks.
Phillips, Joan. Lucky Bear. Miller, J. P., illus. LC 85-14467. 32p. (ps-1). 1986. lib. bdg. 7.99 (0-394-97987-7); pap. 3.50 (0-394-87987-2) Random Bks Yng Read.
—Mickey Mouse & the Pet Show. (Illus.). 40p. (gr. k-2). 1989. write for info. (0-307-11684-0, Pub. by Golden Bks) Western Pub.
—My New Boy. Munsinger, Lynn, illus. LC 85-30129. 32p. (ps-1). 1986. lib. bdg. 7.99 (0-394-98277-0); 3.50 (0-394-88277-6) Random Bks Yng Read.
—Peek-a-Boo! I See You! Wilburn, Kathy, illus. 1983. 4.95 (0-448-03092-6, G&D) Putnam Pub Group.
—Tiger Is a Scaredy Cat: A Step One Book. Gorbaty, Norman, illus. LC 85-19673. 32p. (ps-1). 1986. lib. bdg. 7.99 (0-394-98056-5); pap. 3.50 (0-394-88056-0) Random Bks Yng Read.
—Walt Disney Bambi's Game. Langley, Bill & Wakeman, Diana, illus. 32p. (ps-1). 1992. pap. write for info. (0-307-15968-X, 15968) Western Pub.
—Walt Disney's Bambi's Game. Langley, Bill & Wakeman, Diana, illus. (ps-1). 1991. write for info. (0-307-11599-2, Golden Pr) Western Pub.
—Walt Disney's Winnie the Pooh & the Toy Airplane. (ps-3). 1990. write for info. (0-307-11586-0) Western Pub.
—Walt Disney's Winnie the Pooh & the Very Big Bear. (ps-3). 1990. write for info. (0-307-11593-3) Western Pub.
—Walt Disney's Winnie the Pooh & the Very Big Bear. Langley, Bill & Wakeman, Diana, illus. 32p. (ps-1). 1992. pap. write for info. (0-307-15969-8, 15969) Western Pub.
Phillips, JoAnn. The Run According to Hawkeye. Holden, Tim P., illus. Ogle, John C., intro. by. (Illus.). 24p. (Orig.). 1993. pap. write for info. (0-9638403-0-4) Cherokee Strip.
Phillips, Louis. Alligator Wrestling & You: An Impractical Guide to an Impossible Sport. 96p. (Orig.). (gr. 7-12). 1992. pap. 3.50 (0-380-76303-6, Camelot) Avon.
—Ask Me Anything about the Presidents. 144p. (Orig.). 1994. pap. 3.99 (0-380-76426-1, Camelot) Avon.
—Going Ape: Jokes from the Jungle. Shein, Bob, illus. 64p. (gr. 2-7). 1988. pap. 10.95 (0-670-81520-9) Viking Child Bks.
—Going Ape: Jokes from the Jungle. Shein, Bob, illus. 64p. (gr. 2 up). 1990. pap. 3.95 (0-14-032263-9, Puffin Bks) Puffin Bks.
—Haunted House Jokes. LC 87-8336. (Illus.). 64p. (gr. 2-6). 1987. pap. 11.95 (0-670-81050-9) Viking Child Bks.
—Haunted House Jokes. Marshall, James, illus. 64p. (gr. 2-5). 1988. pap. 3.95 (0-14-032062-8, Puffin) Puffin Bks.
—Hide-&-Seek Puzzle Book. (Illus.). 48p. 1991. pap. 2.95 (0-8431-2869-0) Price Stern.
—How Do You Get a Horse Out of the Bathtub? Profound Answers to Preposterous Questions. Stevenson, James, illus. 80p. (gr. 1 up). 1983. pap. 10.95 (0-670-38119-5) Viking Child Bks.
—How Do You Get a Horse Out of the Bathtub? Profound Answers to Preposterous Questions. Stevenson, James, illus. (gr. 4-6). 1983. pap. 4.95 (0-14-031618-3, Puffin Bks) Puffin Bks.
—How to Tell if Your Parents are Aliens. 80p. 1994. pap. 3.50 (0-380-77387-2, Camelot) Avon.
—Invisible Oink: Pig Jokes. Dubanevich, Arlene, illus. LC 92-24803. 64p. 1993. 11.99 (0-670-84387-3) Viking Child Bks.

—Louis Phillips's Loose Leaf: The Wackiest School Notebook Yet. Farris, Joseph, illus. LC 89-28082. 48p. (gr. 5 up). 1990. SBE 11.95 (0-689-31437-X, Atheneum Child Bk) Macmillan Child Grp.

—Riddlegrams. (Illus.). 48p. (Orig.). (gr. 3-6). 1989. pap. 2.95 (0-8431-2404-0) Price Stern.

—Two Hundred Sixty-Three Brain Busters: Just How Smart Are You, Anyway? Stevenson, James, illus. LC 85-40446. 87p. (gr. 4-7). 1985. pap. 3.99 (0-14-031875-5, Puffin) Puffin Bks.

—The Upside down Riddle Book. Gardner, Beau, illus. LC 82-73. 32p. (gr. k up). 1982. 14.95 (0-688-00931-X); PLB 14.88 (0-688-00932-8) Lothrop.

—Wachysaurus: Dinosaur Jokes. (gr. 4-7). 1991. 10.95 (0-670-83751-2) Viking Child Bks.

—Wackysaurus: Dinosaur Jokes. Barrett, Ron, illus. LC 93-15134. 64p. (gr. 2-5). 1993. pap. 3.99 (0-14-034687-2, Puffin) Puffin Bks.

—Way Out! Jokes from Outer Space. Dubanevich, Arlene, illus. LC 89-14700. 58p. (gr. 4-8). 1989. pap. 10.95 (0-670-82755-X) Viking Child Bks.

—Way Out! Jokes from Outer Space. (gr. 4-7). 1991. pap. 3.95 (0-14-034099-8, Puffin) Puffin Bks.

—Willie Shoemaker. LC 88-14966. (Illus.). 48p. (gr. 5-6). 1988. RSBE 11.95 (0-89686-381-6, Crestwood Hse) Macmillan Child Grp.

Phillips, Louis, jt. auth. see Braden, Vic.

Phillips, Louis, jt. auth. see Sweat, Lynn.

Phillips, Louise S. The First Snowflake of Winter. LC 87-62210. (Illus.). 40p. (gr. k-4). 1987. pap. 6.95 (0-932433-36-7) Windswept Hse.

Phillips, Margaret I. Governors of Tennessee. LC 77-26845. (Illus.). 193p. (gr. 6-12). 1978. 15.95 (0-88289-169-3) Pelican.

Phillips, Mark, et al, eds. America Takes Note: Official Menc Songbook: Piano - Vocal. (Illus.). 112p. (Orig.). 1988. pap. text ed. 14.95 (0-89524-369-5) Cherry Lane.

Phillips, Martin A. The Official National Table Hockey League Handbook, Vol. 1. Phillips, Zoe A., ed. Rullestad, Chris, illus. LC 89-91696. 66p. (Orig.). (gr. 12). 1989. write for info. (0-9623588-0-0); pap. write for info. (0-9623588-1-9) Gnu Wine Pr.

Phillips, Michael. Land of the Brave & the Free. 304p. (Orig.). 1993. pap. 8.99 (1-55661-308-3) Bethany Hse.

Phillips, Michael & Pella, Judith. A House Divided. 400p. (Orig.). 1992. pap. 9.99 (1-55661-173-0) Bethany Hse.

—Journals of Corrie Belle Hollister. (Orig., Set incls. My Father's World, Daughter of Grace, On the Trail of the Truth, A Place in the Sun & Sea to Shining Sea). 1992. Giftset. pap. 39.99 (1-55661-766-6) Bethany Hse.

—A Place in the Sun. 320p. (Orig.). (gr. 9 up). 1991. pap. 8.99 (1-55661-222-2) Bethany Hse.

—The Russians 1-3 Giftset. 1992. 29.99 (1-55661-770-4) Bethany Hse.

—Sea to Shining Sea. 304p. (Orig.). 1992. pap. 8.99 (1-55661-227-3) Bethany Hse.

—Treasure of Stonewycke. LC 88-7531. 352p. (Orig.). (gr. 11 up). 1988. pap. 8.99 (0-87123-902-7) Bethany Hse.

Phillips, Michael, ed. see MacDonald, George.

Phillips, Michael R., ed. see MacDonald, George.

Phillips, Michael R., ed. see Wright, Harold B.

Phillips, Mildred. The Sign in Mendel's Window. LC 85-5049. (Illus.). 32p. (gr. k-3). 1985. RSBE 13.95 (0-02-774600-3, Macmillan Child Bk) Macmillan Child Grp.

Phillips, Millie. What Color Will Bear Wear? 12p. 1989. 4.95 (0-8167-1602-1) Troll Assocs.

—What Will Rabbit Do? 12p. 1989. 4.95 (0-8167-1600-5) Troll Assocs.

—What's It for Anyhow? 12p. 1989. 4.95 (0-8167-1603-X) Troll Assocs.

—Where Does a Pig Live? 12p. 1989. 4.95 (0-8167-1601-3) Troll Assocs.

Phillips, Robert B. One of God's Children: In the Toe River Valley. LC 83-70886. (Illus.). 176p. (gr. 9-12). 1983. 7.00 (0-9620577-0-3) R B Phillips Pub.

—Through My Picture Window. Phillips, Bobby, photos by. LC 88-90639. (Illus.). 256p. (gr. 9-12). 1988. 9.95 (0-9620577-1-1) R B Phillips Pub.

Phillips, Tamara. Day Care ABC. Levine, Abby, ed. Leder, Dora, illus. LC 88-33911. 32p. (ps-2). 1989. PLB 13.95 (0-8075-1483-7) A Whitman.

Phillips, Tony. Turbo Cowboys: Jump Start, No. 1. (gr. 3 up). 1988. pap. 2.95 (0-345-35121-5) Ballantine.

Phillips, Wanda C. Daily Grams: Guided Review Aiding Mastery Skills for 4th & 5th. (gr. 4-5). 1987. pap. text ed. 14.50 (0-936981-06-7) ISHA Enterprises.

—Daily Grams: Guided Review Aiding Mastery Skills. (gr. 6 up). 1987. pap. text ed. 14.50 (0-936981-05-9) Isha Enterprises.

—Easy Grammar. 505p. (Orig.). (gr. 4 up). 1985. pap. 20.95 (0-936981-00-8) ISHA Enterprises.

—Easy Grammar: Adverbs. (gr. 4-12). 1987. pap. text ed. 11.50 (0-936981-04-0) ISHA Enterprises.

—Easy Grammar: Direct Objects & Indirect Objects. 33p. (gr. 4-12). 1986. pap. text ed. 5.50 (0-936981-02-4) ISHA Enterprises.

—Easy Grammar: Verbs. 130p. (gr. 4-12). 1986. pap. text ed. 12.50 (0-936981-03-2) ISHA Enterprises.

—Easy Grammar Workbook. 259p. (gr. 4 up). 1985. 8.95 (0-936981-01-6) ISHA Enterprises.

—My Mother Doesn't Like to Cook. Claycamp, Micah, illus. 28p. (Orig.). (ps-5). 1993. pap. 6.95 (0-936981-20-2) ISHA Enterprises.

Phillips, Zoe A., ed. see Phillips, Martin A.

Phillpotts, Beatrice. Germany. (Illus.). 48p. (gr. 4-8). 1989. lib. bdg. 14.98 (0-382-09794-7) Silver Burdett Pr.

Philpot, Graham. The Fabulous Fairy Tale Follies. LC 93-30479. 1994. write for info. (0-679-85316-2) Random Bks Yng Read.

Philpot, Graham, jt. auth. see Oivardi, Anne.

Philpott, V. & McNeil, M. J. Puppets: A Simple Guide to Making & Working Puppets. (Illus.). 32p. (gr. 3-6). 1977. pap. 5.95 (0-86020-003-5) EDC.

Phipson, Joan. Bianca. LC 88-13192. 192p. (gr. 7 up). 1988. SBE 14.95 (0-689-50448-9, M K McElderry) Macmillan Child Grp.

—Hit & Run. 132p. (gr. 7 up). 1989. pap. 3.95 (0-02-044665-9, Collier Young Ad) Macmillan Child Grp.

Phleger, Frederick B. Red Tag Comes Back. Lobel, Arnold, illus. LC 61-11452. 64p. (gr. k-3). 1961. PLB 13.89 (0-06-024706-1) HarpC Child Bks.

Phleger, Marjorie. Pilot Down, Presumed Dead. LC 63-16244. 224p. (gr. 5-9). 1975. pap. 3.95 (0-06-440067-0, Trophy) HarpC Child Bks.

Piasecki, Jerry. They're Torturing Teachers in Room 104. 1992. pap. 3.50 (0-553-48024-3) Bantam.

Piazza, Domenica Di see Di Piazza, Domenica.

Picard, Barbara. Tales of Ancient Persia. Ambrus, Victor G., illus. 176p. 1993. pap. 10.95 (0-19-274154-3) OUP.

Picard, Barbara L. French Legends, Tales & Fairy Stories. Kiddell-Monroe, Joan, illus. 216p. (gr. 4 up). 1992. pap. 10.95 (0-19-274149-7) OUP.

—The Iliad of Homer. Kiddell-Monroe, Joan, illus. 224p. (gr. 4 up). 1991. pap. 10.95 (0-19-274147-0) OUP.

—Odyssey by Homer. Kiddell-Monroe, Joan, illus. 288p. (gr. 4 up). 1991. pap. 10.95 (0-19-274146-2) OUP.

Pick, C. Undersea. (Illus.). 32p. 1976. PLB 13.96 (0-88110-437-X); pap. 6.95 (0-86020-092-2) EDC.

Pickart, Joan Elliott. Mixed Signals. 1990. pap. 2.50 (0-553-44018-7, Loveswept) Bantam.

Pickens, Kel, jt. auth. see Meyer, Carolyn.

Pickering, H. G. The Pickering Collection: Neighbors Have My Ducks, Merry Xmas, Mr. Williams Dog Days on Trout Waters & Angling of the Test. Timmins, Harry L. & Gardner, Donald, illus. 189p. (gr. 10 up). 1993. Repr. of 1933 ed. 40.00 (1-56416-047-5) Derrydale Pr.

Pickering, Ken. Beowulf: A Rock Musical. (Illus.). 42p. (Orig.). (gr. 7 up). 1986. pap. 4.00 (0-88680-248-2); piano score 15.00 (0-88680-249-0); royalty on application 60.00 (0-685-67506-8) I E Clark.

Pickering, Ken, et al. The Inside Story. 24p. (Orig.). 1992. pap. 4.00 (0-88680-371-3); royalty on application 35.00 (0-685-62712-8) I E Clark.

Pickering, Lucienne. Boy Talk. (Illus.). 96p. (gr. 5-9). pap. 7.95 (0-225-66674-X) Cassell.

—Girl Talk. (Illus.). 96p. (gr. 5-9). pap. 7.95 (0-225-66675-8) Cassell.

Pickering, R. I Can Be an Archaeologist. LC 87-14683. (Illus.). 32p. (gr. k-3). 1987. PLB 14.60 (0-516-01909-0); pap. 3.95 (0-516-41909-9) Childrens.

Pickett, Anola. Old Enough for Magic. Delaney, Ned, illus. LC 88-30320. 64p. (gr. k-3). 1989. PLB 13.89 (0-06-024732-0) HarpC Child Bks.

—Old Enough for Magic. Delaney, Ned, illus. LC 88-30320. 64p. (gr. k-3). 1993. pap. 3.50 (0-06-444161-X, Trophy) HarpC Child Bks.

Pickett, Cecil, adapted by see Shakespeare, William.

Pickett, Christine, ed. see Page, Roland.

Pickett, Margaret E. What's Keeping You, Santa? A Christmas Musical Program Package. Brown, Blanche M., illus. 74p. (gr. k-12). 1983. Incl Production Guide with choir arranged songs, cass of songs, thirty slides from bk. 49.95 (0-913939-01-3) TP Assocs.

—What's Keeping You, Santa? A Christmas Story Book. Brown, Blanche M., illus. LC 83-50122. 64p. (gr. k-5). 1983. PLB 24.95 (0-913939-00-5); read a long Cassette 4.95 (0-913939-03-X) TP Assocs.

Pickett, Sue. Little Dog Scooter. 21p. (gr. 4). 1992. pap. text ed. write for info. (0-9633197-0-1) Instant Heirloom.

Pickett, Timothy, ed. see Hober, David.

Pickford, Susan. Barron & Lyla. (Illus.). 38p. (Orig.). (gr. 3-7). 1991. pap. 2.50 (0-88680-356-X); royalty on application 25.00 (0-685-59143-3) I E Clark.

Pickford, Susan T. It's up to You, Griffin! Ramsey, Marcy D., illus. 32p. (gr. k-4). 1993. bds. 10.95 (0-87033-446-8) Tidewater.

Pickford, Ted. Bobby's Watching. 1993. pap. 3.50 (0-553-56089-1) Bantam.

Pickney, Gloria J. The Sunday Outing. Pickney, Jerry, illus. LC 93-25383. 1994. 14.99 (0-8037-1198-0); PLB 14.89 (0-8037-1199-9) Dial Bks Young.

Pico, Fernando & Izcoa, Carmen R. Puerto Rico, Tierra Adentro y Maratuera: Historia y Cultura de los Puertorriquenos. LC 91-71358. (SPA.). 304p. (gr. 7). 1991. text ed. 22.95 (0-929157-12-5) Ediciones Huracan.

Picott, J. Rupert. A Quarter Century of the Black Experience in Elementary & Secondary Education, 1950-1975. 1990. 9.95 (0-87498-087-9) Assoc Pubs DC.

Picott, J. Rupert, ed. Walter Washington. 1990. 5.95 (0-87498-094-1) Assoc Pubs DC.

Picott, R. & Ridley, W. N. History of the Restitution Fund Commission of the Episcopal Diocese of Pennsylvania, a Challenge. 1990. 15.95 (0-87498-091-7) Assoc Pubs DC.

Piemontes, Grayce. Classic Shirley Temple-Paperdolls. 1989. pap. 3.95 (0-486-25193-4) Dover.

Piening, Ekkehard, tr. see Streit, Jacob.

Piening, Jacob, tr. see Streit, Jacob.

Pienkowski, Jan. ABC. Pienkowski, Jan, illus. (ps). 1989. 2.95 (0-671-68133-8, Little Simon) S&S Trade.

—Casa Embrujada. (SPA., Illus.). 12p. (ps-6). 1992. 14.95 (0-525-45002-5, DCB) Dutton Child Bks.

—Colors. Pienkowski, Jan, illus. 14p. (ps). 1989. 2.95 (0-671-68134-6, Little Simon) S&S Trade.

—Dinnertime. (Illus.). 10p. 1991. 5.99 (0-8431-2963-8) Price Stern.

—Doorbell, With Ringer: Pop-Up. (ps-3). 1992. 13.99 (0-8431-3452-6) Price Stern.

—Faces. Pienkowski, Jan, illus. 24p. (ps-k). 1991. pap. 2.95 (0-671-72846-6, Little Simon) S&S Trade.

—Farm. (Illus.). 32p. (ps-1). 1985. 13.95 (0-434-95651-1, Pub. by W Heinemann Ltd) Trafalgar.

—Farm. 14p. 1990. pap. 2.95 (0-671-70476-1, S&S BFYR) S&S Trade.

—Ferme. (FRE.). 5.95 (2-07-056307-3) Schoenhof.

—Food. Pienkowski, Jan, illus. 24p. (ps-k). 1991. pap. 2.95 (0-671-72845-8, Little Simon) S&S Trade.

—The Haunted House. (Illus.). 12p. (ps up) 1979. 14.95 (0-525-31520-9, DCB) Dutton Child Bks.

—Homes. 14p. (ps). 1990. pap. 2.95 (0-671-70478-8, Little Simon) S&S Trade.

—Little Monsters. (Illus.). 10p. 1986. 9.95 (0-8431-1241-7) Price Stern.

—Little Monsters. (Illus.). 10p. 1991. 5.99 (0-8431-2964-6) Price Stern.

—Oh My, a Fly! Pienkowski, Jan, illus. 10p. (ps up) 1989. pop-up book 9.95 (0-8431-2765-1) Price Stern.

—Oh My a Fly. (Illus.). 10p. 1991. 5.99 (0-8431-2965-4) Price Stern.

—One Two Three. Pienkowski, Jan, illus. 14p. (ps). 1989. 2.95 (0-671-68136-2) S&S Trade.

—Pets. Pienkowski, Jan, illus. 24p. (ps). 1992. pap. 2.95 (0-671-74518-2, Little Simon) S&S Trade.

—Phone Book. (Illus.). 12p. 1991. 13.99 (0-8431-2967-0) Price Stern.

—Robot. Pienkowski, Jan, illus. 12p. (gr. 1 up). 1981. 9.95 (0-440-07459-2) Delacorte.

—Robot. 1992. 15.00 (0-440-40539-4, YB) Dell.

—Shapes. Pienkowski, Jan, illus. (ps). 1989. 2.95 (0-671-68135-4, Little Simon) S&S Trade.

—Sizes. Pienkowski, Jan, illus. 24p. (ps-k). 1991. pap. 2.95 (0-671-72844-X, Little Simon) S&S Trade.

—Small Talk. 12p. (ps-4). 1983. 9.95 (0-8431-0982-3) Price Stern.

—Small Talk. (Illus.). 10p. 1991. 5.00 (0-8431-2966-2) Price Stern.

—Stop Go. Pienkowski, Jan, illus. 24p. (ps). 1992. pap. 2.95 (0-671-74519-0, Little Simon) S&S Trade.

—Time. Pienkowski, Jan, illus. 24p. (ps-k). 1991. pap. 2.95 (0-671-72847-4, Little Simon) S&S Trade.

—Weather - Nursery Board Book. (ps). 1990. pap. 2.95 (0-671-70479-6, Little Simon) S&S Trade.

—Wheels. Pienkowski, Jan, illus. 24p. (ps). 1992. pap. 2.95 (0-671-74517-4, Little Simon) S&S Trade.

—Yes No. Pienkowski, Jan, illus. 24p. (ps). 1992. pap. 2.95 (0-671-74520-4, Little Simon) S&S Trade.

—Zoo. Pienkowski, Jan, illus. 32p. (ps-1). 1985. 13.95 (0-434-95652-X, Pub. by W Heinemann Ltd) Trafalgar.

—Zoo - Nursery Board Book. (ps). 1990. pap. 2.95 (0-671-70477-X, Little Simon) S&S Trade.

Pienkowski, Jan, jt. auth. see Nicoll, Helen.

Pienkowski, Jan, illus. ABC Dinosaurs: And Other Prehistoric Creatures. 10p. (ps-k). 1993. 18.99 (0-525-67468-3, Lodestar Bks) Dutton Child Bks.

—Christmas. LC 84-5719. 32p. (ps-8). 1989. 9.95 (0-394-82609-4) Knopf Bks Yng Read.

—Christmas. miniature ed. 32p. 1991. 6.95 (0-679-81442-6) Knopf Bks Yng Read.

—Easter. 32p. 1992. 6.99 (0-679-82670-X) Knopf Bks Yng Read.

Piequet, Miriam. Fingertip Phonics. Anyone Can Read Staff, ed. Ritchie, Fern, illus. Piequet, M., intro. by. (Illus.). 290p. (Orig.). (gr. 1-12). 1985. 19.95 (0-914275-05-4) Anyone Can Read Bks.

—The Flying Mule Car. Anyone Can Read Staff, ed. Blanton, Betty, illus. 149p. (Orig.). (gr. 4-6). 1988. pap. 15.00 (0-914275-11-9) Anyone Can Read Bks.

—My Furry Bear. Anyone Can Read Staff, ed. Gregory, Miriam, illus. 43p. (Orig.). (gr. 3-5). 1985. 15.00 (0-914275-02-X) Anyone Can Read Bks.

—Ting-Li's Tales Told on the Devil's Mountain. Anyone Can Read Staff, ed. Yin-Chwang, Wang Tsen-Zan. (Illus.). 60p. (Orig.). (gr. 3-7). 1987. pap. write for info. (0-914275-13-5) Anyone Can Read Bks.

Piequet, Miriam, jt. auth. see Herr, Selma.

Pierce, Anne M. So Many Gifts. Campbell, Donna P., illus. 30p. (ps up) 1989. 14.95 (0-685-44721-9); 7.50x (0-685-27188-9) Forword MN.

—So Many Gifts. Campbell, Donna P., illus. 32p. (gr. k-6). 1989. Repr. of 1990 ed. 14.95g (0-9623937-0-3) Forword MN.

Pierce, Brenda H. Creative Art Picture Starters: General Subjects - Level II. Pierce, Brenda H., illus. 32p. (gr. 4-6). 1988. tchr's. ed. 3.95 (0-922694-03-6) Moons Creat Prods.

Pierce, Catherine D. Christmas Thief. Gallagher, Jane, illus. (Illus.). (ps-k). 1988. pap. text ed. 4.50 (0-9621397-0-X) C D Pierce.

Pierce, David. Forever Yours. 1994. pap. 3.50 (0-06-106174-3, Harp PBks) HarpC.

Pierce, Glen, ed. see Hostetler, Paul.

Pierce, Glen A., ed. see Johns, Helen & Leadley, Robert.
Pierce, Meredith A. Dark Moon. 256p. (gr. 7 up). 1992. 15.95 (*0-685-59346-0*, Joy St Bks) Little.
—Dark Moon, Vol. II: Firebringer Trilogy. (Illus.). (gr. 7 up). 1992. 16.95 (*0-316-70744-9*, Joy St Bks) Little.
—A Gathering of Gargoyles. 272p. 1985. pap. 2.95 (*0-8125-4902-3*) Tor Bks.
—Pearl of the Soul of the World, Vol. 1. 1990. 15.95 (*0-316-70743-0*, Joy St Bks) Little.
Pierce, Pat. A Pop-Up Book of North American Cities. Jacobs, Phil & Field, James, illus. 20p. (gr. 2-6). 1991. 12.95 (*0-8249-8517-6*, Ideals Child) Hambleton-Hill.
Pierce, Q. L. Find the Mistakes Science: Fantastic Fish. (gr. 4-7). 1991. pap. 2.95 (*0-8431-2816-X*) Price Stern.
—More Scary Stories for Sleep-Overs. LC 92-21705. 128p. 1992. pap. 4.99 (*0-8431-3451-8*) Price Stern.
Pierce, Sharon. Making Whirligigs & Other Wind Toys. LC 84-26782. (Illus.). 132p. (Orig.). (gr. 10-12). 1985. pap. 9.95 (*0-8069-7980-1*) Sterling.
Pierce, Tamora. Alanna: The First Adventure Song of the Lioness, Bk. One. LC 83-2595. 252p. (gr. 6 up). 1983. SBE 15.95 (*0-689-30994-5*, Atheneum Child Bk) Macmillan Child Grp.
—In the Hand of the Goddess. LC 84-2946. 240p. (gr. 5 up). 1990. pap. 3.50 (*0-679-80111-1*) Random Bks Yng Read.
—In the Hand of the Goddess: Song of the Lioness, Bk. Two. LC 84-2946. 240p. (gr. 7 up). 1984. SBE 15.95 (*0-689-31054-4*, Atheneum Child Bk) Macmillan Child Grp.
—Lioness Rampant: Song of the Lioness, Bk. Four. LC 88-6213. 336p. (gr. 6 up). 1988. SBE 15.95 (*0-689-31116-8*, Atheneum Child Bk) Macmillan Child Grp.
—Wild Magic. large type ed. LC 93-8427. 1993. write for info. (*1-56054-796-0*) Thorndike Pr.
—Wild Magic: The Immortals. LC 91-43909. 272p. (gr. 5 up). 1992. SBE 16.95 (*0-689-31761-1*, Atheneum Child Bk) Macmillan Child Grp.
—Wolf-Speaker. LC 93-21909. 192p. (gr. 4-8). 1994. SBE 15.95 (*0-689-31833-2*, Atheneum Child Bk) Macmillan Child Grp.
—The Woman Who Rides Like a Man. LC 85-20054. 256p. (gr. 6 up). 1990. pap. 3.50 (*0-679-80112-X*) Knopf Bks Yng Read.
—The Woman Who Rides Like a Man: Song of the Lioness, Book Three. LC 85-20054. 276p. (gr. 7 up). 1986. SBE 15.95 (*0-689-31117-6*, Atheneum Child Bk) Macmillan Child Grp.
Piercy, Patricia A. The Great Encounter: A Special Meeting Before Columbus. Wilkerson, Napoleon, illus. 47p. (gr. 1-7). 1991. pap. 5.95 (*0-913543-26-8*) African Am Imag.
Pierre, Keith C. La see La Pierre, Keith C.
Pierre, Stephanie St. see St. Pierre, Stephanie.
Piers, Helen. Puppy's ABC. (Illus.). 32p. (ps-k). 1987. 9.95 (*0-19-520606-1*) OUP.
—Taking Care of Cat. (Illus.). 32p. 1992. pap. 4.95 (*0-8120-4873-3*) Barron.
—Taking Care of Your Dog. (Illus.). 32p. 1992. pap. 4.95 (*0-8120-4874-1*) Barron.
—Taking Care of Your Gerbils: Young Pet Owner's Guides Ser. Vriends, Matthew M., ed. LC 92-26959. 32p. 1993. pap. 4.95 (*0-8120-1369-7*) Barron.
—Taking Care of Your Goldfish. Vriends, Matthew M., ed. LC 92-32170. 32p. 1993. pap. 4.95 (*0-8120-1368-9*) Barron.
—Taking Care of Your Guinea Pig. 32p. (gr. 3 up). 1993. pap. 4.95 (*0-8120-1367-0*) Barron.
—Taking Care of Your Hamster. 32p. 1992. pap. 4.95 (*0-8120-4695-1*) Barron.
—Taking Care of Your Parakeet. 32p. (gr. 3 up). 1993. pap. 4.95 (*0-8120-1370-0*) Barron.
—Taking Care of Your Rabbit. 32p. 1992. pap. 4.95 (*0-8120-4697-8*) Barron.
Piersel. Photomath. (gr. 3-9). pap. 1.99x (*0-87783-076-2*); tchrs. guide 0.29x (*0-87783-201-3*) Oddo.
—Photophonics I. (Illus.). (gr. 1-5). 1968. pap. 1.99x (*0-87783-073-8*); tchr's guide 0.29x (*0-685-03702-9*) Oddo.
—Photophonics II. (Illus.). (gr. 1-5). 1968. pap. 2.39x (*0-87783-074-6*); tchr's guide 0.29x (*0-685-03703-7*) Oddo.
Pierson, Jim. Just Like Everybody Else. Parks, Kathy, illus. Tada, Joni E., intro. by. (Illus.). 32p. (ps-3). 1993. 10.99 (*0-87403-842-1*, 24-03661) Standard Pub.
Piette, Nadine, illus. Mi Primer ABC. (SPA.). 60p. (ps-k). 1993. Repr. of 1991 ed. 3.95 (*970-607-186-5*) CKG Pubs.
—Mis Primeras Palabras En Ingles. (SPA.). 60p. (ps-k). 1993. Repr. of 1991 ed. 3.95 (*970-607-187-3*) CKG Pubs.
—Mis Primeros Conocimentos. (SPA.). 60p. (ps-k). 1993. Repr. of 1993 ed. 3.95 (*970-607-188-1*) CKG Pubs.
Pifer, Joanne. EarthWise: Earth's Energy. (Illus.). 48p. (gr. 5-8). 1993. pap. text ed. 7.95 (*0-9633019-3-4*) WP Pr.
—EarthWise: Earth's Oceans. (Illus.). 48p. (gr. 5-8). 1992. pap. text ed. 7.95 (*0-9633019-2-6*) WP Pr.
—EarthWise: Environmental Learning Series, Vol. II. (Illus.). 192p. (gr. 5-8). Date not set. Incl., Earth's Atmosphere, Earth's Humans, Earth's Wildlife, Earth's Waste. 24.95 (*0-9633019-6-9*) WP Pr.
—EarthWise: Environmental Learning Series, Vol. 1. (Illus.). 216p. (gr. 5-8). 1993. Incl. Earth's Trees, Sunlight, Earth's Oceans, Earth's Energy, Earth's Food. pap. text ed. 24.95 (*0-9633019-5-0*) WP Pr.

Piggins, Carol A. A Multicultural Portrait of the Civil War. LC 93-10319. 1993. 18.95 (*1-85435-660-7*, Pub. by M Cavendish Bks UK) Marshall Cavendish.
Piggins, Carol A., jt. auth. see Johnson, Rolf E.
Pighetti, Toni. The Children's Organizer: A Calendar System of Daily Tasks for Children. Kiefer, Scott, illus. 32p. (Orig.). (gr. k-8). 1983. pap. 7.95 (*0-913005-03-7*) TAM Assoc.
Pihl, Marshall R. Korean Word Book. Roschana, illus. LC 93-73161. (KOR & ENG.). 112p. (gr. k-6). 1993. 15.95 (*1-880188-53-8*); pap. 11.95 (*1-880188-52-X*) Bess Pr.
Pijanowski, Kathy, ed. see Kehret, Peg.
Pijanowski, Kathy, ed. see Novelly, Maria C.
Pike, Christopher. The Ancient Evil. MacDonald, Patricia, ed. 240p. (Orig.). 1992. pap. 3.99 (*0-671-74506-9*, Archway) PB.
—Bury Me Deep. MacDonald, Patricia, ed. 224p. (Orig.). 1991. pap. 3.99 (*0-671-69057-4*, Archway) PB.
—Christopher Pike, 4 vols. 1990. pap. 11.80 boxed (*0-671-96377-5*) S&S Trade.
—Die Softly. MacDonald, Patricia, ed. 224p. (Orig.). 1991. pap. 3.99 (*0-671-69056-6*, Archway) PB.
—The Eternal Enemy. MacDonald, Pat, ed. 224p. (Orig.). 1993. pap. 3.99 (*0-671-74509-3*) PB.
—Fall into Darkness. 224p. 1991. pap. 3.99 (*0-671-73684-1*, Archway) PB.
—Gimme a Kiss. 160p. (gr. 8 up). 1991. pap. 3.99 (*0-671-73682-5*, Archway) PB.
—The Graduation. (Orig.). (gr. 9 up). 1991. pap. 3.99 (*0-671-73680-9*, Archway) PB.
—The Immortal. MacDonald, Pat, ed. 256p. (Orig.). 1993. 14.00 (*0-671-87039-4*, Archway); pap. 3.99 (*0-671-74510-7*, Archway) PB.
—The Immortal. LC 93-32608. (gr. 9-12). 1993. 15.95 (*0-7862-0011-5*) Thorndike Pr.
—Master of Murder. MacDonald, Pat, ed. (Orig.). 1992. pap. 3.99 (*0-671-69059-0*, Archway) PB.
—The Midnight Club. MacDonald, Pat, ed. LC 93-20917. 256p. (Orig.). 1994. 14.00 (*0-671-87255-9*, Archway); pap. 3.99 (*0-671-87263-X*, Archway) PB.
—Monster. MacDonald, Pat, ed. 256p. (Orig.). (gr. 7 up). 1992. pap. 3.99 (*0-671-74507-7*, Archway) PB.
—Road to Nowhere. MacDonald, Pat, ed. 224p. (Orig.). (gr. 9 up). 1993. pap. 3.99 (*0-671-74508-5*, Archway) PB.
—See You Later. MacDonald, Patricia, ed. 240p. (gr. 8 up). 1991. pap. 3.99 (*0-671-74390-2*, Archway) PB.
—Slumber Party. 1985. pap. 3.50 (*0-590-43014-9*) Scholastic Inc.
—Weekend. 1986. pap. 2.75 (*0-590-42968-X*) Scholastic Inc.
—Weekend. 230p. (Orig.). (gr. 9 up). 1986. pap. 3.50 (*0-590-44256-2*) Scholastic Inc.
—The Wicked Heart. MacDonald, Patricia, ed. 224p. (Orig.). 1993. 14.00 (*0-671-87314-8*, Archway); pap. 3.99 (*0-671-74511-5*, Archway) PB.
—Witch. MacDonald, Patricia, ed. 240p. (Orig.). (gr. 8 up). 1990. pap. 3.99 (*0-671-69055-8*, Archway) PB.
Pike, D., ed. see Ledbetter, H. & Lomax, John A.
Pike, Norman. The Peach Tree. DeWitt, Robin & DeWitt, Patricia, illus. 36p. (ps up). 1984. 10.95 (*0-8045-014-2*) Stemmer Hse.
Pike, Raffi, ed. see Ledbetter, H. & Lomax, John A.

Pike, Robert W. Winning Checkers for Kids of All Ages. Nelson, Scott, illus. 64p. (Orig.). (gr. 3-8). 1992. pap. 9.95 (*0-9635300-0-3*) C&M Pub MA. WINNING CHECKERS FOR KIDS OF ALL AGES is the ONLY available primer written for children on this subject. Well illustrated with cartoon characters & checkerboard graphics, WINNING CHECKERS FOR KIDS OF ALL AGES is a "straightforward" easily digested guide that explains the basic rules of the game & offers strategies for competitive play."--The Landmark Press, Holden, Massachusetts. Tactics that give the reader an edge are described & reinforced with clear annotated checkerboard illustrations. The player learns how to control the center of the board, protect the back row & spot enough double & triple opportunities to crown more than their fair share of Kings. Children can clip out a numbered checkerboard on the last page & use pennies & dimes as checkers pieces if they don't have their own game set. "With so many requests, the absence of any substantive material on this most popular of lifetime board games for children has always been frustrating. Well written & engagingly illustrated, WINNING CHECKERS FOR CHILDREN OF ALL AGES fills a definite void in a most enjoyable & easy to follow way - our kids love it."--Jane Dutton, Children's Librarian, Holden, Massachusetts. *Publisher Provided Annotation.*

Pilar, Arlene. Reading Books for Social Studies: A Study Guide. Friedland, Joyce & Kessler, Rikki, eds. (gr. 1-3). 1991. pap. text ed. 19.95 (*0-88122-692-0*) LRN Links.
Pilbeam, Mavis. Japan. (Illus.). 32p. (gr. 4-8). 1992. 17.95 (*0-237-60187-7*, Pub. by Evans Bros Ltd) Trafalgar.
Pile, Robert B. Top Entrepreneurs & Their Businesses. LC 92-38267. (Illus.). 160p. (gr. 5-12). 1993. PLB 14.95 (*1-881508-04-8*) Oliver Pr MN.
Pilger, Mary A. Holidays & Special Days Project Index for Young People. LC 92-12977. 160p. 1992. lib. bdg. 29.50 (*0-87287-998-4*) Libs Unl.
Pilgrim, Millie W. Jason's Adventures with the Tuskegee Airmen. rev. ed. Pilgrim, Millie W., illus. 54p. (gr. 3 up). 1992. pap. text ed. 8.00 (*0-685-60294-X*, 133-720); tchr's. guide 2.00 (*0-685-60293-1*) H&M Ent.
Pilipski, Mark. Les Belles Lettres, Ser. IV: Four Roles for Three Characters. LC 92-62380. 50p. (gr. k-8). 1993. pap. write for info. (*1-882965-03-5*) Markov Pr.
Pilkey, Dav. Dogzilla. LC 92-37906. (gr. 4 up). 1993. 10.95 (*0-15-223944-8*); pap. 5.95 (*0-15-223945-6*) HarBrace.
—Dragon Gets By. LC 90-46027. (Illus.). 48p. (gr. 1-3). 1991. 12.95 (*0-531-05935-9*); PLB 12.99 (*0-531-08535-X*) Orchard Bks Watts.
—Dragon's Fat Cat. LC 91-16369. (Illus.). 48p. (gr. 1-3). 1992. 12.95 (*0-531-05982-0*); lib. bdg. 12.99 (*0-531-08582-1*) Orchard Bks Watts.
—Dragon's Halloween. LC 91-21107. (Illus.). 48p. (gr. 1-3). 1993. 12.95 (*0-531-05990-1*); PLB 12.99 (*0-531-08590-2*) Orchard Bks Watts.
—Dragon's Merry Christmas. LC 91-1996. (Illus.). 48p. (gr. 1-3). 1991. 12.95 (*0-531-05957-X*); RLB 12.99 (*0-531-08557-0*) Orchard Bks Watts.
—A Friend for Dragon. LC 90-45219. (Illus.). 48p. (gr. 1-3). 1991. 12.95 (*0-531-05934-0*); PLB 12.99 (*0-531-08534-1*) Orchard Bks Watts.
—Kat Kong. LC 92-14483. (ps-3). 1993. 10.95 (*0-15-242036-3*); pap. 5.95 (*0-15-242037-1*) HarBrace.
—Twas the Night Before Thanksgiving. Pilkey, Dav, illus. LC 89-48941. 32p. (ps-2). 1990. 14.95 (*0-531-05905-7*); PLB 14.99 (*0-531-08505-8*) Orchard Bks Watts.
—When Cats Dream. LC 91-31355. (Illus.). 32p. (ps-2). 1992. 14.95 (*0-531-05997-9*); PLB 14.99 (*0-531-08597-X*) Orchard Bks Watts.
—World War Won. Pilkey, Dav, illus. LC 87-2711. 32p. (gr. 1 up). 1987. PLB 14.95 (*0-933849-22-2*) Landmark Edns.
Pilkington, Brian. Grandpa Claus. Pilkington, Brian, illus. 28p. (ps-3). 1990. PLB 19.95 (*0-87614-436-9*) Carolrhoda Bks.
Pillar, Marjorie. Join the Band! Pillar, Marjorie, illus. LC 90-23261. 32p. (gr. 1-3). 1992. 15.00 (*0-06-021834-7*); PLB 14.89 (*0-06-021829-0*) HarpC Child Bks.
Pilling, Ann. Before I Go to Sleep: A Collection of Bible Stories, Poems & Prayers for Children. Denton, Kady M., illus. LC 89-7816. 96p. 1990. PLB 15.99 (*0-517-58019-5*) Crown Bks Yng Read.
—The Big Pink. large type ed. 382p. 1989. lib. bdg. 18.95 (*0-7451-0959-4*, Lythway Large Print) Hall.
—Donkey's Day Out. (ps-3). 1990. 11.95 (*0-7459-1618-X*) Lion USA.
—Our Kid. large type ed. 368p. (gr. 3-7). 1991. 13.95 (*0-7451-1295-1*, Galaxy Child Lrg Print) Chivers N Amer.
—Realms of Gold: Myths & Legends from Around the World. Denton, Kady M., illus. LC 92-30858. 1993. 16.95 (*1-85697-913-X*) Kingfisher Bks.
Pilling, Ann, retold by. The Kingfisher Children's Bible. Denton, Kady M., illus. LC 92-42679. 1993. 18.95 (*1-85697-840-0*) Kingfisher Bks.
Pillion, jt. auth. see Pootler.
Pillsbury Co. Staff. Little Book for a Little Cook. 1992. incl. apron 14.95 (*1-55709-172-2*) Applewood.
Pillsbury Company Editors. The Pillsbury Doughboy's First Cookbook. (Illus.). 72p. (ps-3). 1992. 15.00 (*0-385-23871-1*) Doubleday.
Piltch, B. Stories about Workers. large type ed. 128p. (gr. 7-12). 1983. Repr. of 1975 ed. 22.45 (*0-317-01944-9*, 4-23280-00) Am Printing Hse.
Piltch, Benjamin. Real Jobs for Real People. (Illus.). 64p. (gr. 3). 1988. pap. text ed. 3.75 (*0-88323-246-4*, 208); tchr's. key 1.25 (*0-318-33408-9*, 263) Pendergrass Pub.
Piltch, Benjamin & Smergut, Peter. Class Trips. 64p. (gr. 4-8). 1983. 3.95 (*0-934618-00-3*) Learning Well.
—Money Matters. 64p. (gr. 7-12). 1983. 3.95 (*0-934618-03-8*) Learning Well.
Piltch, Benjamin, ed. see Funes, Marilyn & Lazarus, Alan.
Piltch, Benjamin, ed. see Kaufman, Tanya & Wishny, Judith.
Pilurs, David B. Sun & Storm: The Codex. Caruso, Lenore & Caruso, Sara, eds. (Illus.). 96p. (gr. 7 up). 1993. pap. 12.95 perfect bound (*0-9636551-1-6*) Storm Pr.

—Sun & Storm: The Enchiridion. Caruso, Lenore R. & Caruso, Sara L., eds. (Illus.). 96p. (gr. 7 up). 1993. pap. 12.95 perfect bound (*0-9636551-0-8*) Storm Pr.
—Sun & Storm: The Terminus. Caruso, Lenore R., ed. (Illus.). 16p. (gr. 7 up). 1993. 8.95 (*0-9636551-2-4*, 26635) Storm Pr.

Pilutik, Anastasia D., jt. auth. see Seco, Nina.

Pimlott, John. Middle East: A Background to the Conflicts. (Illus.). 40p. (gr. 5-8). 1991. PLB 12.90 (*0-531-17329-1*, Gloucester Pr) Watts.

Pinatti, Gloria J, ed. see Mozeleski, Peter A.

Pinatti, Gloria J., ed. see Mozeleski, Peter A.

Pinatti, Gloria J., ed. see Mozeleski, Peter A. & Mozelski, Paul M.

Pinchot, Jane. The Mexicans in America. rev. ed. LC 72-3587. (Illus.). 104p. (gr. 5 up). 1989. PLB 15.95 (*0-8225-0222-4*); pap. 5.95 (*0-8225-1016-2*) Lerner Pubns.

Pincus, Debbie. Feeling Good about Yourself. (Illus.). 96p. (gr. 3-8). 1990. 10.95 (*0-86653-516-0*, GA 1139) Good Apple.
—Interactions. 96p. (gr. 4-9). 1988. wkbk. 9.95 (*0-86653-448-2*, GA1057) Good Apple.
—Manners Matter. (Illus.). 112p. (gr. 3-7). 1992. wkbk. 9.95 (*0-86653-688-4*, 1422) Good Apple.
—Sharing. Lasky, Mark, illus. 80p. (gr. 4-8). 1983. wkbk. 8.95 (*0-86653-117-3*, GA 468) Good Apple.

Pincus, Debbie & Ward, Richard J. Citizenship. 112p. (gr. 4-9). 1991. 9.95 (*0-86653-608-6*, GA 1327) Good Apple.

Pinczes, Elinor J. One Hundred Hungry Ants. MacKain, Bonnie, illus. 32p. (gr. k-3). 1993. 13.95 (*0-395-63116-5*) HM.

Pinder, Polly. Polly Pinder's Chocolate Cookbook. Pinder, Polly, illus. Search Studios Staff, photos by. (Illus.). 144p. (gr. 7 up). 1988. 24.95 (*0-85532-603-4*, Pub. by Search Pr UK) Pathway Bk Serv.

Pine, A. DuGuay. Beyond the Secret Passage. (Illus.). 144p. (gr. 1-5). 1988. 9.95 (*0-8059-3106-6*) Dorrance.

Pine, Jonathan. Backyard Birds. Zickefoose, Julie, illus. LC 91-45184. 48p. (gr. 2-5). 1993. 12.00 (*0-06-021039-7*); PLB 11.89 (*0-06-021040-0*) HarpC Child Bks.
—Backyard Birds. Zickefoose, Julie, illus. LC 91-45184. 48p. (gr. 2-5). 1993. pap. 7.95 (*0-06-446150-5*, Trophy) HarpC Child Bks.
—Trees. Joudrey, Ken, illus. LC 93-3136. 1994. 13.00 (*0-06-021468-6*); PLB 12.89 (*0-06-021469-4*) HarpC Child Bks.

Pine, Nicholas. Night School. 192p. (Orig.). 1994. pap. 3.50 (*0-425-14151-9*) Berkley Pub.
—Terror Academy: The New Kid. 1993. pap. 3.50 (*0-425-13970-0*) Berkley Pub.

Pineda, Leonardo A., jt. auth. see Davidson, Alma.

Pineda, Sysy, tr. see Brown, J. Aaron.

Pinegar, Ed J. Preparing for Your Mission. 109p. (Orig.). (gr. 12 up). 1992. pap. 7.95 (*0-87579-646-X*) Deseret Bk.

Pines, Tonya, ed. Thirteen. 304p. 1991. pap. 3.50 (*0-590-45256-8*, Point) Scholastic Inc.

Pingry, Patricia. Story of Daniel & the Lions. Britt, Stephanie, illus. 24p. (Orig.). (ps-3). 1988. pap. 3.95 (*0-8249-8179-0*, Ideals Child) Hambleton-Hill.
—Story of David & the Slingshot. 24p. (gr. k-3). 1988. pap. 3.95 (*0-8249-8180-4*, Ideals Child) Hambleton-Hill.
—The Story of Esther. Harrison, Susan, illus. 24p. (ps-3). 1990. pap. 3.95 (*0-8249-8420-X*, Ideals Child) Hambleton-Hill.
—Story of Johan & the Big Fish. Venturi-Pickett, Stacy, illus. 24p. (Orig.). (ps-3). 1988. pap. 3.95 (*0-8249-8181-2*, Ideals Child) Hambleton-Hill.
—Story of Joseph & a Dream Come True. Spence, James, illus. 24p. (Orig.). (ps-3). 1988. pap. 3.95 (*0-8249-8182-0*, Ideals Child) Hambleton-Hill.
—Story of Joshua & the Bugles of Jericho. Spence, James, illus. 24p. (Orig.). (ps-3). 1988. pap. 3.95 (*0-8249-8178-2*, Ideals Child) Hambleton-Hill.
—The Story of Moses & the Ten Commandments. Britt, Stephanie, illus. (ps-3). 1990. pap. 3.95 (*0-8249-8418-8*, Ideals Child) Hambleton-Hill.
—Story of Noah & the Rainbow. 24p. (gr. k-3). 1988. pap. 3.95 (*0-8249-8176-6*, Ideals Child) Hambleton-Hill.

Pini, Richard, jt. auth. see Pini, Wendy.

Pini, Wendy & Pini, Richard. Elfquest: Captives of Blue Mountain. rev. ed. (Illus.). 192p. (gr. 4 up). 1988. pap. 17.95 (*0-936861-08-8*, Father Tree Pr) Warp Graphics.
—Elfquest: Fire & Flight. rev. ed. (Illus.). 192p. (gr. 4 up). 1993. 19.95 (*0-936861-16-9*, Father Tree Pr) Warp Graphics.
—Elfquest: Kings of the Broken Wheel. (Illus.). 160p. (gr. 4 up). 1992. 17.95 (*0-936861-24-X*, Father Tree Pr) Warp Graphics.
—Elfquest: Quest's End. rev. ed. (Illus.). 208p. (gr. 4 up). 1988. pap. 17.95 (*0-936861-09-6*, Father Tree Pr) Warp Graphics.
—Elfquest: Siege at Blue Mountain. (Illus.). 144p. (Orig.). (gr. 4 up). 1988. pap. 16.95 (*0-936861-10-X*, Father Tree Pr) Warp Graphics.
—Elfquest: The Cry from Beyond. (Illus.). 160p. (Orig.). (gr. 4 up). 1990. 19.95 (*0-936861-17-7*, Father Tree Pr) Warp Graphics.
—Elfquest: The Forbidden Grove. rev. ed. (Illus.). 208p. (gr. 4 up). 1988. pap. 17.95 (*0-936861-07-X*, Father Tree Pr) Warp Graphics.

—Elfquest: The Secret of Two-Edge. (Illus.). 144p. (Orig.). (gr. 4 up). 1988. pap. 16.95 (*0-936861-11-8*, Father Tree Pr) Warp Graphics.

Pinkney, Andrea D. Dear Benjamin Banneker. Pinkney, Brian, illus. LC 93-31162. 1994. write for info. (*0-15-200417-3*, Gulliver Bks) HarBrace.
—Seven Candles for Kwanzaa. Pinkney, Brian, illus. LC 92-3698. 32p. (gr. k up). 1993. 14.99 (*0-8037-1292-8*); lib. bdg. 14.89 (*0-8037-1293-6*) Dial Bks Young.

Pinkney, Brian. Max Found Two Sticks. LC 93-12525. 1994. pap. 15.00 (*0-671-78776-4*, S&S BFYR) S&S Trade.

Pinkney, Gloria J. Back Home. Pinkney, Jerry, illus. LC 91-22610. 40p. (gr. k-4). 1992. 15.00 (*0-8037-1168-9*); PLB 14.89 (*0-8037-1169-7*) Dial Bks Young.

Pinkney, Jerry, jt. auth. see Gibson, Barbara.

Pinkney, Nathaniel, illus. Conversation Games: Vol. I-People Times. 87p. (Orig.). (ps-6). 1978. pap. 15.00 (*0-939632-17-9*) ILM.
—Conversation Games: Vol. II-Experiences. 87p. (Orig.). (ps-6). 1978. pap. 15.00 (*0-939632-20-9*) ILM.

Pinkston, Joan & Tipton, Nancy. Songs of Our Heritage. (Illus.). 80p. (Orig.). 1991. pap. 7.95 (*0-89084-608-1*) Bob Jones Univ Pr.

Pinkston, William S., Jr. With Wings As Eagles. (Illus.). 127p. (gr. 2). 1983. pap. 6.94 (*0-89084-231-0*) Bob Jones Univ Pr.

Pinkus, Sue, jt. auth. see Robertson, Bruce.

Pinkus, Sue, jt. auth. see Robertson, Jane.

Pinkwater, D. Manus. Fat Men from Space. Pinkwater, D. Manus, illus. 64p. (gr. 4-6). 1980. pap. 3.25 (*0-440-44542-6*, YB) Dell.
—Hoboken Chicken Emergency. LC 76-41910. (Illus.). 94p. (gr. k-3). 1990. pap. 12.95 jacketed (*0-671-73980-8*, S&S BFYR); pap. 4.95 (*0-671-66447-6*, S&S BFYR) S&S Trade.
—The Hoboken Chicken Emergency. (gr. 4). 1992. pap. write for info. (*0-663-56237-6*) Silver Burdett Pr.

Pinkwater, Daniel. Aunt Lulu. Pinkwater, Daniel, illus. LC 88-1736. 32p. (gr. k-3). 1988. RSBE 12.95 (*0-02-774661-5*, Macmillan Child Bk) Macmillan Child Grp.
—Aunt Lulu. Pinkwater, Daniel, illus. LC 90-39981. 32p. (gr. k-3). 1991. pap. 3.95 (*0-689-71413-0*, Aladdin) Macmillan Child Grp.
—Author's Day. Pinkwater, Daniel, illus. LC 92-18154. 32p. (gr. k-3). 1993. RSBE 13.95 (*0-02-774642-9*, Macmillan Child Bk) Macmillan Child Grp.
—Big Orange Splot. (ps-3). 1993. pap. 3.95 (*0-590-44510-3*) Scholastic Inc.
—Borgel. LC 89-13421. 160p. (gr. 5 up). 1990. SBE 13.95 (*0-02-774671-2*, Macmillan Child Bk) Macmillan Child Grp.
—Borgel. LC 91-42914. 176p. (gr. 3-7). 1992. pap. 3.95 (*0-689-71620-6*, Aladdin) Macmillan Child Grp.
—Doodle Flute. Pinkwater, Daniel, illus. LC 90-6622. 32p. (gr. k-3). 1991. RSBE 13.95 (*0-02-774635-6*, Macmillan Child Bk) Macmillan Child Grp.
—Guys from Space. Pinkwater, Daniel, illus. LC 88-13485. 32p. (gr. k-3). 1989. RSBE 13.95 (*0-02-774672-0*, Macmillan Child Bk) Macmillan Child Grp.
—Guys from Space. Pinkwater, Daniel, illus. LC 91-20100. 32p. (gr. k-3). 1992. pap. 3.95 (*0-689-71590-0*, Aladdin) Macmillan Child Grp.
—I Was a Second Grade Werewolf. LC 82-17715. (Illus.). 32p. (ps-2). 1983. 12.95 (*0-525-44038-0*, DCB) Dutton Child Bks.
—I Was a Second Grade Werewolf. Pinkwater, Daniel, illus. (gr. 1-3). 1986. incl. cassette 19.95 (*0-87499-010-6*); pap. 12.95 incl. cassette (*0-87499-008-4*); incl. cassette, 4 paperbacks guide 27.95 (*0-87499-009-2*) Live Oak Media.
—I Was a Second Grade Werewolf. Pinkwater, Daniel, illus. LC 82-17715. 32p. (ps-2). 1985. pap. 3.95 (*0-525-44194-8*, DCB) Dutton Child Bks.
—Jolly Roger: A Dog of Hoboken. LC 84-12629. (Illus.). 64p. (gr. 4-8). 1984. 13.95 (*0-688-03898-0*) Lothrop.
—The Magic Moscow. LC 92-27150. (Illus.). 64p. (gr. 3-7). 1993. pap. 3.95 (*0-689-71710-5*, Aladdin) Macmillan Child Grp.
—The Muffin Fiend. LC 85-10944. (Illus.). 48p. (gr. 3-7). 1986. 12.95 (*0-688-04274-0*); PLB 12.88 (*0-688-04275-9*) Lothrop.
—The Phantom of the Lunch Wagon. LC 92-3051. (Illus.). 32p. (gr. k up). 1992. RSBE 13.95 (*0-02-774641-0*, Macmillan Child Bk) Macmillan Child Grp.
—Roger's Umbrella. Marshall, James, illus. LC 81-2294. 32p. (gr. 1-3). 1982. 11.95 (*0-525-38555-X*, DCB) Dutton Child Bks.
—Roger's Umbrella. Marshall, James, illus. LC 81-2294. 32p. (gr. 1-3). 1985. pap. 3.95 (*0-525-44223-5*, DCB) Dutton Child Bks.
—The Snarkout Boys & the Avocado of Death. LC 81-11737. 160p. (gr. 5 up). 1982. 12.95 (*0-688-00871-2*) Lothrop.
—The Snarkout Boys & the Avocado of Death. 160p. (gr. 9-12). 1983. pap. 3.50 (*0-451-16320-6*, Sig) NAL-Dutton.
—The Snarkout Boys & the Baconburg Horror. (Illus.). 160p. (gr. 9-12). 1985. pap. 3.50 (*0-451-16242-0*, Sig) NAL-Dutton.
—Spaceburger: A Kevin Spoon & Mason Mintz Story. Pinkwater, Daniel, illus. LC 93-6658. 32p. (gr. k-3). 1993. RSBE 13.95 (*0-02-774643-7*, Macmillan Child Bk) Macmillan Child Grp.

—Tooth-Gnasher Superflash. Pinkwater, Daniel, illus. LC 89-18207. 32p. (gr. k-3). 1990. Repr. of 1981 ed. RSBE 13.95 (*0-02-774655-0*, Macmillan Child Bk) Macmillan Child Grp.
—Tooth-Gnasher Superflash. LC 89-18207. (Illus.). 32p. (gr. k-3). 1990. pap. 3.95 (*0-689-71407-6*, Aladdin) Macmillan Child Grp.
—Wempires. Pinkwater, Daniel, illus. LC 90-46925. 32p. (gr. k-3). 1991. RSBE 13.95 (*0-02-774411-6*, Macmillan Child Bk) Macmillan Child Grp.
—The Wuggie Norple Story. De Paola, Tomie, illus. LC 88-878. 40p. (gr. k-4). 1988. pap. 4.50 (*0-689-71257-X*, Aladdin) Macmillan Child Grp.

Pinkwater, Daniel M. Big Orange Splot. (Illus.). 32p. 1992. Repr. of 1972 ed. 12.95 (*0-8038-9346-9*) Hastings.
—Blue Moose, & Return of the Moose. Pinkwater, Daniel M., illus. LC 93-22614. 112p. (Orig.). (gr. 2-7). 1993. pap. 3.99 (*0-679-84717-0*) Random Bks Yng Read.
—Fat Men from Space. (Illus.). 64p. (gr. 3-7). 1977. 13.95 (*0-399-21913-7*, Putnam) Putnam Pub Group.
—The Hoboken Chicken Emergency. LC 76-41910. (Illus.). (gr. 3-7). 1984. 10.95 (*0-13-392514-5*); pap. 4.95 (*0-13-392499-8*) P-H.
—The Snarkout Boys & the Baconburg Horror. 1985. pap. 2.50 (*0-451-13581-4*, Sig Vista) NAL-Dutton.

Pinkwater, Daniel M., jt. auth. see Pinkwater, Jill.

Pinkwater, Jill. Buffalo Brenda. LC 88-31929. 192p. (gr. 5-9). 1989. SBE 14.95 (*0-02-774631-3*, Macmillan Child Bk) Macmillan Child Grp.
—Buffalo Brenda. LC 91-14806. 208p. (gr. 3-7). 1992. pap. 3.95 (*0-689-71586-2*, Aladdin) Macmillan Child Grp.
—Tails of the Bronx: A Tale of the City. LC 90-48914. 176p. (gr. 3-7). 1991. SBE 14.95 (*0-02-774652-6*, Macmillan Child Bk) Macmillan Child Grp.
—Tails of the Bronx: A Tale of the Bronx. LC 92-20623. 208p. (gr. 3-7). 1993. pap. 3.95 (*0-689-71671-0*, Aladdin) Macmillan Child Grp.

Pinkwater, Jill & Pinkwater, Daniel M. Superpuppy: How to Choose, Raise & Train the Best Possible Dog for You. LC 76-8825. (Illus.). 208p. (gr. 6 up). 1979. (Clarion Bks); pap. 7.95 (*0-89919-084-7*, Clarion) HM.

Pinkwater, Manus. Blue Moose. (Illus.). 48p. (gr. k-3). 1975. 13.95 (*0-396-07151-1*, Putnam) Putnam Pub Group.

Pinola, Lanny, jt. auth. see London, Jonathan.

Pinsker, Judith. A Lot Like You. (gr. 5 up). 1989. pap. 2.95 (*0-553-27852-5*, Starfire) Bantam.
—A Lot Like You. 1988. 13.95 (*0-553-05445-7*) Bantam.

Pinson, William M., Jr., jt. auth. see Maston, T. B.

Pinta, Thanom, tr. see Kemvichanuvat, Cherdchai.

Pinta, Thanom, tr. see Rausiri, Supa.

Pinto, Richard W. Lo see Lo Pinto, Richard W.

Pinzon, Scott. Tales of Evermore. 90p. (Orig.). (gr. 7-12). 1991. pap. 4.95 (*0-8474-6621-3*) Back to Bible.

Pio, Adam. Magic Donkey. (Illus.). 32p. 1989. PLB 29.28 (*0-8172-2461-0*); pap. 17.96 (*0-8172-2777-6*) Raintree Steck-V.

Pioneer. Frederick Banting. 1992. PLB 13.95 (*0-8050-2335-6*) H Holt & Co.

Piontac, Nechemiah. The Arizal: The Life & Times of Rabbi Yitzchak Luria. Weinbach, Shaindel, tr. from HEB. Bardugo, Miriam, illus. 288p. (gr. 5-12). 1988. 12.95 (*0-89906-835-9*); pap. 9.95 (*0-89906-836-7*) Mesorah Pubns.

Pious, Richard M. The Presidency. (Illus.). 128p. (gr. 5 up). 1991. PLB 13.98 (*0-382-24316-1*); pap. 8.95 (*0-382-24322-6*) Silver Burdett Pr.
—Richard Nixon. (gr. 7 up). 1992. lib. bdg. 13.98 (*0-671-72852-0*, J Messner); pap. 7.95 (*0-671-72853-9*, J Messner) S&S Trade.
—The Young Oxford Companion to the Presidency of the United States. LC 93-19908. 1993. Alk. paper. 35.00 (*0-19-507799-7*) OUP.

Pipe, Rhona. Daniel & the Lions' Den. Spencely, Annabel, illus. LC 92-12073. 1993. 7.99 (*0-8407-3422-0*) Oliver-Nelson.
—The Easter Story. Spencely, Annabel, illus. LC 92-13325. 1993. 7.99 (*0-8407-3420-4*) Oliver-Nelson.
—Samson the Strong Man. Press, Jenny, illus. LC 92-13326. (gr. 1 up). 1993. 7.99 (*0-8407-3421-2*) Oliver-Nelson.
—When Time Began. Press, Jenny, illus. LC 92-13321. 1993. 7.99 (*0-8407-3419-0*) Oliver-Nelson.

Pipe, Rhona & Hunt. Where's Jesus? An Interactive Bible Storybook. (ps-3). 1993. 7.99 (*1-56507-146-8*) Harvest Hse.
—Where's Noah? An Interactive Bible Storybook. (ps-3). 1993. 7.99 (*1-56507-144-1*) Harvest Hse.

Piper, John. What's the Difference? Manhood & Womanhood According to the Bible. Elliot, Elisabeth, frwd. by. 64p. (Orig.). 1990. pap. 3.50 (*0-89107-562-3*, Crossway Bks) Good News.

Piper, Watty. The Easy-to-Read-Little Engine That Could. Retan, Walter, adapted by. Mateus, illus. 32p. (ps-2). 1986. pap. 2.25 (*0-448-19078-8*, G&D); incl. cassette 5.95 (*0-448-19088-5*) Putnam Pub Group.
—The Easy-to-Read Little Engine That Could. Mateu, illus. Retan, Walter, adapted by. (Illus.). (ps-2). 1990. pap. 4.95 (*0-448-34344-4*, Platt & Munk Pubs) Putnam Pub Group.
—The Fast Rolling Little Engine That Could. Super, Terri, illus. LC 85-70661. 12p. (ps). 1985. 6.95 (*0-448-09878-4*, G&D) Putnam Pub Group.
—The Little Engine That Could. 40p. 1981. Repr. PLB 15.95x (*0-89966-366-4*) Buccaneer Bks.

—The Little Engine That Could. 69p. 1981. Repr. PLB 10.95x (*0-89967-040-7*) Harmony Raine.
—The Little Engine That Could. Walz, Richard, illus. LC 99-44044. 12p. (ps-2). 1984. 8.95 (*0-448-18963-1*, Platt & Munk) Putnam Pub Group.
—Little Engine That Could. 1991. 5.95 (*0-448-40520-2*, Platt & Munk Pubs) Putnam Pub Group.
—The Little Engine That Could Board Book. (Illus.). 12p. (ps). 1991. bds. 4.95 (*0-448-40101-0*, G&D) Putnam Pub Group.
—The Little Engine That Could Let's Count 123. Ong, Cristina, illus. LC 90-83240. 24p. (ps). 1991. 9.95 (*0-448-40131-2*, G&D) Putnam Pub Group.
—The Little Engine That Could: Miniature Edition. Hauman, George & Hauman, Doris, illus. 48p. 1990. pap. 2.95 (*0-448-40071-5*, Platt & Munk Pubs) Putnam Pub Group.
—The Little Engine That Could: Sixtieth Anniversary Edition. Hauman, George & Hauman, Doris, illus. 48p. 1990. 12.95 (*0-448-40041-3*, Platt & Munk Pubs) Putnam Pub Group.
Piper, Watty, retold by. The Little Engine That Could. 16p. (ps-2). 1993. write for info. (*1-883366-15-1*) YES Ent.
Pippen, Christie. A Very Scraggly Christmas Tree. Beckes, Shirley V., illus. (gr. 2-4). 1988. 17.96 (*0-8172-2754-7*) Raintree Steck-V.
—A Very Scraggly Christmas Tree. (Illus.). 32p. (gr. 2-4). 1988. incl. audiocassette 29.28 (*0-8172-2469-6*) Raintree Steck-V.
Pippen, Christine. Very Scraggly Christmas Tree. (ps-3). 1993. pap. 3.95 (*0-8114-5214-X*) Raintree Steck-V.
Pirani, Felix. Rosalie, Sylvia & Melanie. (Illus.). (gr. 1-8). 1992. PLB 8.95 (*0-89565-888-7*); Resale. 12.75 (*0-685-60987-1*) Childs World.
Pirner, Connie. Even Little Kids Get Diabetes. Tucker, Kathy, ed. Westcott, Nadine B., illus. LC 90-12738. 24p. (ps-2). 1991. 10.95 (*0-8075-2158-2*) A Whitman.
Piron, Claude. Gerda malaperis! Vortlisto - Wordlist. 26p. 1993. pap. text ed. 3.75 (*1-882251-05-9*) Eldonejo Bero.
Pirotta, Saviour. Chloe on the Jungle Gym. (ps-3). 1992. 13.95 (*0-8120-6269-8*); pap. 5.95 (*0-8120-4829-6*) Barron.
—Follow That Cat! Melnyczuk, Peter, illus. LC 92-38287. 32p. (gr. k-3). 1993. 13.99 (*0-525-45125-0*, DCB) Dutton Child Bks.
—Hey Riddle Riddle! Hellen, Nancy, illus. LC 88-34356. 32p. (gr. 2 up). 1989. PLB 9.95 (*0-87226-408-4*, Bedrick Blackie) P Bedrick Bks.
—Jerusalem. LC 92-30130. (Illus.). 48p. (gr. 5 up). 1993. RSBE 13.95 (*0-87518-569-X*, Dillon) Macmillan Child Grp.
—Little Bird. Butler, Stephen, illus. LC 91-25413. 32p. (ps-3). 1992. 14.00 (*0-688-11289-7*, Tambourine Bks); PLB 13.93 (*0-688-11290-0*, Tambourine Bks) Morrow.
—Rome. LC 92-19685. (Illus.). 48p. (gr. 5 up). 1993. RSBE 13.95 (*0-87518-570-3*, Dillon) Macmillan Child Grp.
Pisano, Mary B. Going to New Orleans to Visit Weezie Anna. LC 93-34203. 1993. 8.95 (*0-937552-52-6*) Quail Ridge.
Pisarski, Cathryn, contrib. by. Robin Hood. Smith, Phil. (Illus.). 28p. (Orig.). (gr. 1 up). 1988. pap. 2.75 (*0-88680-308-X*); piano-vocal score 7.50 (*0-88680-309-8*); royalty on application 35.00 (*0-685-58411-9*) I E Clark.
Pistolesi, Roseanna. Let's Celebrate Christmas: A Book of Drawing Fun. Pistolesi, Roseanna, illus. LC 87-61376. 32p. (gr. 2-6). 1988. PLB 10.65 (*0-8167-1133-X*); pap. text ed. 1.95 (*0-8167-1134-8*) Troll Assocs.
—Let's Celebrate Halloween: A Book of Drawing Fun. Pistolesi, Roseanna, illus. LC 87-50426. 32p. (gr. 2-6). 1988. PLB 10.65 (*0-8167-1002-3*); pap. text ed. 1.95 (*0-8167-1003-1*) Troll Assocs.
Pitch, Anthony S., jt. auth. see Alvarez, Everett, Jr.
Pitcher, Diana. The Mischief Maker. Dove, Sally, illus. 64p. 1990. pap. 5.95 (*0-86486-106-0*, Pub. by D Philip South Africa) Interlink Pub.
—Tokoloshi: African Folktales Retold. Rutherford, Meg, illus. 64p. (gr. 5 up). 1993. pap. write for info. (*1-883672-03-1*) Tricycle Pr.
Pitcher, Valerie. Anya Astern, Come Down from the Sky. LC 90-71860. 44p. (gr. 6). 1991. 6.95 (*1-55523-412-7*) Winston-Derek.
Pitchford, Gene. Young Folks' Hawaiian Time. (Illus.). (ps). 1965. pap. 2.00 (*0-87505-275-4*) Borden.
Pitre, Felix, retold by. Juan Bobo & the Pig: A Puerto Rican Folktale. Hale, Christy, illus. LC 92-28063. 32p. (gr. k-3). 1993. 13.99 (*0-525-67429-2*, Lodestar Bks) Dutton Child Bks.
Pitre, Verne. Grandma Was a Sailmaker: Tales of the Cajun Wetlands. Ledet, Billy, illus. 160p. (Orig.). (gr. 9). 1991. pap. 12.95 (*0-9621724-5-6*) Blue Heron LA.
Pitt, Jane. Secret Hearts. (Orig.). (gr. 6 up). 1986. pap. 2.50 (*0-440-97722-3*, LFL) Dell.
Pitt, Valeria. Enciclopedia Juvenil de la Ciencia. (SPA.). 260p. 1975. 95.00 (*0-8288-5870-5*, S26475) Fr & Eur.
Pittau, Francisco. Tightrope Walker. LC 92-54429. (ps-3). 1993. 13.00 (*0-688-12379-1*) Lothrop.
—Voyage under the Stars. Pearson, Susan, ed. Packager, Belgian, tr. from FRE. Gervais, Bernadette, illus. LC 91-26075. 32p. (ps-3). 1992. 13.00 (*0-688-11328-1*); PLB 12.93 (*0-688-11329-X*) Lothrop.

Pittenger, Shari. Listen, Color & Learn: A Coloring Book for Family Devotions, Vol. I, Psalm 1-30. Pittenger, Shari, illus. Harris, Gregg, intro. by. 35p. (Orig.). (ps-6). 1989. pap. text ed. 4.95 (*0-923463-49-6*) Noble Pub Assocs.
—Listen, Color, & Learn, Vol. II: A Coloring Book for Family Devotions, Psalm 31-60. 40p. 1990. wkbk. 5.00 (*0-923463-75-5*) Noble Pub Assocs.
—Listen Color & Learn, Vol. III: A Coloring Book for Family Devotions, Psalm 61-90. 40p. 1991. wkbk. 5.00 (*0-923463-77-1*) Noble Pub Assocs.
Pittman, Helena C. A Dinosaur for Gerald. Pittman, Helena C., illus. 32p. (gr. k-3). 1990. PLB 18.95 (*0-87614-431-8*) Carolrhoda Bks.
—Gerald-Not-Practical. (Illus.). 32p. (gr. k-3). 1990. PLB 18.95 (*0-87614-430-X*) Carolrhoda Bks.
—The Gift of the Willows. Pittman, Helena C., illus. 32p. (gr. k-4). 1988. 18.95 (*0-87614-354-0*) Carolrhoda Bks.
—A Grain of Rice. LC 84-4670. (Illus.). (gr. k-4). 1986. lib. bdg. 12.95 (*0-8038-9289-6*) Hastings.
—A Grain of Rice. 1992. pap. 2.99 (*0-553-15986-0*) Bantam.
—Miss Hindy's Cats. Pittman, Helena C., illus. LC 89-22214. 32p. (ps-3). 1990. pap. 18.95 (*0-87614-368-0*) Carolrhoda Bks.
—Miss Hindy's Cats: Picture Book. (ps-3). 1991. pap. 6.95 (*0-87614-538-1*) Carolrhoda Bks.
—The Moon's Party. LC 92-40866. 1994. write for info. (*0-399-22541-2*, Putnam) Putnam Pub Group.
—Once When I Was Scared. Rand, Ted, illus. LC 88-3598. 32p. (gr. k-3). 1988. 14.00 (*0-525-44407-6*, DCB) Dutton Child Bks.
—Once When I Was Scared. Rand, Ted, illus. 36p. (ps-3). 1993. pap. 4.99 (*0-14-054932-3*, Puffin Unicorn) Puffin Bks.
Pittman, Rachel N. The Wedding of G. Washington Bear. Askew, Rebecca T., illus. 42p. (Orig.). (ps-5). 1986. pap. 6.95 (*0-9615382-1-X*) Pittman Pub.
Pitts, Paul. For a Good Time, Don't Call Claudia. LC 86-90772. 128p. (gr. 7 up). 1986. pap. 2.50 (*0-380-75117-8*, Flare) Avon.
—Racing the Sun. 160p. 1988. pap. 3.50 (*0-380-75496-7*, Camelot) Avon.
—The Shadowman's Way. 128p. (Orig.). (gr. 5). 1992. pap. 3.50 (*0-380-76210-2*, Camelot) Avon.
—Zwort's Nature Report: Forest Trail. Needham, James, illus. 36p. (ps-4). 1991. pap. 4.95 incl. audiocassette (*1-55999-152-6*) LinguiSystems.
—Zwort's Nature Report: Ocean Dive. Needham, James, illus. 36p. (ps-4). 1991. pap. 4.95 incl. audiocassette (*1-55999-153-4*) LinguiSystems.
—Zwort's Nature Report: Safari Adventure. Needham, James, illus. 36p. (ps-4). 1991. pap. 4.95 incl. audiocassette (*1-55999-154-2*) LinguiSystems.
Pitts, Teresa A. The Music of a Poet's Heart. Spangler, Melissa & Meyer, Lydia V., illus. 147p. (Orig.). (gr. 7 up). 1987. pap. 10.00 (*0-9618600-0-6*) T A Pitts.
—Where Freedom Begins. Meyer-Brauer, Lydia, illus. 27p. (Orig.). (gr. 5 up). 1990. pap. 10.00 (*0-9618600-1-4*) T A Pitts.
Pitts, V. Peter, ed. Children's Pictures of God. LC 79-56298. (Illus.). (gr. 1-4). 1979. pap. 3.95 (*0-915744-20-1*) Character Res.
Piumini, Roberto. The Saint & the Circus. Holmes, Olivia, tr. from ITA. Root, Barrett V., illus. LC 90-23481. 32p. (ps-3). 1991. 14.95 (*0-688-10377-4*, Tambourine Bks); PLB 14.88 (*0-688-10378-2*, Tambourine Bks) Morrow.
—Store. (ps). 1992. 4.50 (*1-56397-203-4*); Set of 3 bks. 13.50 (*1-56397-211-5*) Boyds Mills Pr.
Pizar, Kathleen, ed. see Dickens, Charles.
Pizer, Abigail. Charlie the Puppy. (Illus.). 32p. (ps-2). 1989. PLB 11.95 (*0-87614-363-X*) Carolrhoda Bks.
—Hattie the Goat. (Illus.). 32p. (ps-2). 1989. PLB 11.95 (*0-87614-364-8*) Carolrhoda Bks.
—It's a Perfect Day. Pizer, Abigail, illus. LC 89-37937. 32p. (ps-3). 1990. pap. 4.95 (*0-06-443302-1*, Trophy) HarpC Child Bks.
—Penelope Pig. (Illus.). 32p. (ps-2). 1989. PLB 11.95 (*0-87614-366-4*) Carolrhoda Bks.
—Percy the Duck. (Illus.). 32p. (ps-2). 1989. PLB 11.95 (*0-87614-365-6*) Carolrhoda Bks.
Pizzo, Joan. Pelican Bill. Geronimi, Clyde, illus. (gr. k-6). 1990. PLB 11.95 (*0-939126-10-9*) Back Bay.
Pizzo, Joan E. Amy Avocet. Geronimi, Clyde, illus. LC 83-70739. (gr. k-6). 1983. 8.95 (*0-939126-06-0*) Back Bay.
—Little Crumb Fun Book. (Illus.). 32p. (Orig.). (gr. k-6). 1983. pap. 3.95 (*0-939126-04-4*) Back Bay.
—Little Crumb: Tales of the Back Bay. Geronimi, Clyde, illus. 29p. (Orig.). (gr. k-6). 1980. PLB 10.95 (*0-939126-00-1*); pap. 7.95 (*0-939126-01-X*); tchr's manual, 35p 8.95 (*0-939126-03-6*) Back Bay.
Place, Irene. Opportunities in Business Management Careers. rev. ed. LC 90-50738. 160p. (gr. 7 up). 1991. 13.95 (*0-8442-8158-1*, VGM Career Bks); pap. 10.95 (*0-8442-8160-3*, VGM Career Bks) NTC Pub Grp.
Place, Robin. The Romans: Fact & Fiction. (Illus.). 32p. 1989. 11.95 (*0-521-33267-2*); pap. 7.50 (*0-521-33787-9*) Cambridge U Pr.
—The Vikings: Fact & Fiction: Adventures of Young Vikings in Jorvik. Ryley, Chris, illus. 52p. (gr. 2-8). 1987. pap. 7.50 (*0-521-31572-7*) Cambridge U Pr.
Planche, Bernard. Living on a Tropical Island. Matthews, Sarah, tr. from FRE. Broutin, Christian, illus. LC 87-34592. 38p. (gr. k-5). 1988. 4.95 (*0-944589-13-8*, 138) Young Discovery Lib.

—Living with the Eskimos. Matthews, Sarah, tr. from FRE. Grant, Donald, illus. LC 87-31805. 38p. (gr. k-5). 1988. 4.95 (*0-944589-12-X*, 12X) Young Discovery Lib.
Plant, Andrew. Drawing Is Easy. Plant, Andrew, illus. LC 93-16116. 1994. pap. write for info. (*0-383-03692-5*) SRA Schl Grp.
Plante, Edmund. Alone in the House. 176p. (Orig.). (gr. 5). 1991. pap. 3.50 (*0-380-76424-5*, Flare) Avon.
—Last Date. 176p. (Orig.). (gr. 5). 1993. pap. 3.50 (*0-380-77154-3*, Flare) Avon.
Plante, Patricia & Bergman, David. The Turtle & the Two Ducks: Animal Fables Retold from La Fontaine. Rockwell, Anne, illus. LC 81-47409. 32p. (ps-2). 1981. (Crowell Jr Bks) HarpC Child Bks.
Plantinga, Cornelius, Jr. A Sure Thing. LC 86-8280. (Illus.). 300p. (gr. 8-10). 1986. text ed. 14.95 (*0-930265-27-0*); tchr's manual 11.95 (*0-930265-28-9*) CRC Pubns.
Plantos, T. Heather Hits Her First Home Run. (Illus.). 24p. (ps-8). 1989. pap. 4.95 (*0-88753-185-7*, Pub. by Black Moss Pr CN) Firefly Bks Ltd.
Plas, Rob Van der see Van der Plas, Rob.
Plas, Robert Van Der see Van Der Plas, Robert.
Plass, Richard M., jt. auth. see Reep, Marianna L.
Plass, Richard M., ed. see Kranepool, Harry A.
Plastow, John R. Football, Pizza & Success! 130p. (Orig.). (gr. 7-12). 1987. pap. 5.95 (*0-937382-03-5*) Rhinos Pr.
Plath, Sylvia. The Bed Book. McCully, Emily A., illus. LC 76-3825. 40p. (ps-3). 1989. pap. 6.95 (*0-06-443184-3*, Trophy) HarpC Child Bks.
Plato. Plato Reader. Levinson, Ronald B., ed. (gr. 9 up). 1967. pap. 9.16 (*0-395-05197-5*, RivEd) HM.
—Plato's Republic. Jowett, Benjamin, tr. Gemme, F., intro. by. (gr. 11 up). 1968. pap. 2.75 (*0-8049-0172-4*, CL-172) Airmont.
—Republic. rev. ed. Lee, H. D., tr. (Orig.). (gr. 9 up). 1955. pap. 5.95 (*0-14-044048-8*, Penguin Classics) Viking Penguin.
Platt, Kin. Big Max. newly illus. ed. Lopshire, Robert, illus. LC 91-14743. (gr. k-3). 1978. pap. 3.50 (*0-06-444006-0*, Trophy) HarpC Child Bks.
—Big Max. newly illus. ed. Lopshire, Robert, illus. LC 91-14742. 64p. (gr. k-3). 1965. 13.00 (*0-06-024750-9*); PLB 12.89 (*0-06-024751-7*) HarpC Child Bks.
—Crocker. LC 82-48456. 128p. (gr. 7 up). 1983. (Lipp Jr Bks) HarpC Child Bks.
—Darwin & the Great Beasts. LC 90-39674. 64p. (gr. 2 up). 1992. 14.00 (*0-688-10030-9*) Greenwillow.
—Dracula, Go Home. Mayo, Frank, illus. 96p. (gr. 7 up). 1981. pap. 1.25 (*0-440-92022-1*, LE) Dell.
—The Ghost of Hellsfire Street. LC 80-10446. 256p. (gr. 4-6). 1980. 12.95 (*0-385-28317-2*) Delacorte.
—Run for Your Life. 96p. (gr. 7 up). 1979. pap. 1.95 (*0-440-97557-3*, LFL) Dell.
Platt, Kin, ed. see London, Jack.
Platt, Kin, ed. see Stevenson, Robert Louis.
Platt, Richard. Del Interior de las Cosas - Incredible Cross-Sections. Puncel, Maria & Vasquez, Juan J., eds. Bermejo, Ana & Aixela, Javier F., trs. Bietsy, Stephen, illus. (SPA.). 48p. (gr. 5-12). 1992. write for info. (*84-372-4524-9*) Santillana.
—Film. King, Dave, photos by. LC 91-53133. (Illus.). 64p. (gr. 5 up). 1992. 15.00 (*0-679-81679-8*); PLB 15.99 (*0-679-91679-2*) Knopf Bks Yng Read.
—Incredible Cross Sections. Biesty, Stephen, illus. LC 91-27439. 48p. 1992. 20.00 (*0-679-81411-6*) Knopf Bks Yng Read.
Platt, Richard, jt. auth. see Biesty, Stephen.
Plattner, Sandra S. Connecting Around the World. (ps-k). 1991. pap. 10.95 (*0-86653-978-6*) Fearon Teach Aids.
—Connecting with Holidays. (ps-k). 1991. pap. 10.95 (*0-8224-1634-4*) Fearon Teach Aids.
—Connecting with My Community. (ps-k). 1991. pap. 10.95 (*0-8224-3912-3*) Fearon Teach Aids.
—Connecting with Myself. (ps-k). 1991. pap. 10.95 (*0-86653-986-7*) Fearon Teach Aids.
—Connecting with Nature. (ps-k). 1991. pap. 10.95 (*0-86653-976-X*) Fearon Teach Aids.
—Connecting with the Seasons. (ps-k). 1991. pap. 10.95 (*0-86653-977-8*) Fearon Teach Aids.
Plaut, David. Start Collecting Baseball Cards. LC 89-43016. (Illus.). 96p. (Orig.). (gr. 4 up). 1989. pap. 9.95 (*0-89471-762-6*) Running Pr.
Plaut, W. Gunther, ed. Deluxe Torah Commentary. 1835p. 1988. deluxe ed. 55.00 (*0-8074-0333-4*, 381630) UAHC.
Plazy, Gilles. A Weekend with Rousseau. LC 93-12187. 1993. write for info. (*0-8478-1717-2*) Rizzoli Intl.
Pleasant Company Staff. My Trip to Felicity's Williamsburg: An American Girl's Journal. (Illus.). 14p. (gr. 2-5). 1991. 4.95 (*1-56247-028-0*); map, 2 sides & 6 panels 1.95 (*1-56247-029-9*) Pleasant Co.
Please Touch Museum Staff. Please Touch Cookbook. Brook, Bonnie, ed. (Illus.). 64p. (ps-2). 1990. pap. 6.95 spiral (*0-671-70558-X*, S&S BYR) S&S Trade.
Plemons, Marti. Brooke & the Guilty Secret. (Illus.). 128p. (gr. 3-6). 1992. pap. 4.99 (*0-87403-938-X*, 24-03768) Standard Pub.
—Erin & the Special Promise. (Illus.). 128p. (gr. 3-6). 1992. pap. 4.99 (*0-87403-935-5*, 24-03765) Standard Pub.
—Georgie & the New Kid. (Illus.). 128p. (gr. 3-6). 1992. pap. 4.99 (*0-87403-687-9*, 24-03727) Standard Pub.
—Josh & the Guinea Pig. (Illus.). 128p. (gr. 3-6). 1992. pap. 4.99 (*0-87403-686-0*, 24-03726) Standard Pub.

—Marty & the Mystery Gift. (Illus.). 128p. (gr. 3-6). 1992. pap. 4.99 (0-87403-937-1, 24-03767) Standard Pub.
—Megan & the Owl Tree. (Illus.). 128p. (gr. 3-6). 1992. pap. 4.99 (0-87403-685-2, 24-03725) Standard Pub.
—Michael & the Dark Cross. (Illus.). 128p. (gr. 3-6). 1992. pap. 4.99 (0-87403-936-3, 24-03766) Standard Pub.
—Scott & the Ogre. (Illus.). 128p. (gr. 3-6). 1992. pap. 4.99 (0-87403-688-7, 24-03728) Standard Pub.
Plenk, Dagmar. Sophie & the Incas. LC 90-71979. 72p. (Orig.). (gr. 3-7). 1991. pap. 9.00 (1-56002-039-3) Aegina Pr.
Pletcher, Jean E., et al. Memories of the Michigan City Lighthouse & Description of the United States Lighthouse Service. 24p. (Orig.). (gr. 6 up). 1991. pap. 2.00 (0-935549-15-3) MI City Hist.
Pliska, Greg, jt. auth. see Gill, Madelaine.
Pliskin, Jacqueline. The Jewish Holiday Game & Workbook. (Illus.). (gr. 8-12). 1989. pap. 5.95 (0-933503-85-7) Shapolsky Pubs.
—My Animated Haggadah & Story of Passover. (Illus.). 48p. (gr. 5-8). 1989. pap. 5.95 (0-933503-28-8) Shapolsky Pubs.
—My Very Own Animated Jewish Holiday Activity Book. (Illus.). 96p. (gr. 4-8). 1987. pap. 5.95 (0-933503-16-4) Shapolsky Pubs.
Pliskin, Jacqueline J. The Bible Game & Workbook. 96p. 1990. pap. 5.95 (0-944007-84-8) Shapolsky Pubs.
—The Bible Story Activity Book. Pliskin, Jacqueline J., illus. 96p. (gr. 1-4). 1990. pap. 5.95 (0-944007-67-8) Shapolsky Pubs.
Ploetz & Lebitritt. Kooken. (gr. 3 up). 14.95 (0-8050-2163-9) H Holt & Co.
Ploetz, Craig T. Milo's Friends in the Dark. Koslowski, Richard K., illus. 32p. (ps-4). 1992. PLB 11.95 (1-882172-00-0) Milo Prods.
Ploetz, Richard, jt. auth. see Lebentritt, Julia.
Ploss, Douglas A. The Tweens at Deep Lake: An Original American Fantasy. Ploss, Douglas A., illus. LC 79-90996. 88p. (gr. 3 up). 1979. PLB 13.50 (0-9603632-0-3); pap. 8.50 (0-9603632-1-1) OPC.
Plotkin, Gregory & Plotkin, Rita. Cooking the Russian Way. (Illus.). 48p. (gr. 5 up). 1986. PLB 14.95 (0-8225-0915-6) Lerner Pubns.
Plotkin, Rita, jt. auth. see Plotkin, Gregory.
Plott, Dave, ed. see Long, Evelyn.
Plott, Dave, et al, eds. see Long, Evelyn.
Plotz, Helen. Imagination's Other Place: Poems of Science & Mathematics. Reissue. ed. Leighton, Clare, illus. LC 55-9216. 200p. (gr. 7 up). 1987. PLB 12.89 (0-690-04700-2, Crowell Jr Bks) HarpC Child Bks.
—A Week of Lullabies. Russo, Marisabina, illus. LC 86-18458. 32p. (ps-3). 1988. 11.95 (0-688-06652-6); lib. bdg. 11.88 (0-688-06653-4) Greenwillow.
Plowden, Martha W. Famous Firsts of Black Women. Jones, Ronald, illus. 112p. (gr. 4-8). 1993. 11.95 (0-88289-973-2) Pelican.
Pluckrose, Henry. Book Craft. (Illus.). 48p. (gr. 5-8). 1992. PLB 12.40 (0-531-14169-1) Watts.
—Build It! Fairclough, Chris, photos by. (Illus.). 32p. (gr. k-4). 1990. PLB 10.90 (0-531-14062-8) Watts.
—Change It! Fairclough, Chris, photos by. LC 89-70746. (Illus.). 32p. (gr. k-4). 1990. PLB 10.90 (0-531-14064-4) Watts.
—Clean It! Fairclough, Chris, photos by. (Illus.). 32p. (gr. k-4). 1990. PLB 10.90 (0-531-14063-6) Watts.
—Cut It! Fairclough, Chris, photos by. LC 89-14759. (Illus.). 32p. (ps-k). 1989. PLB 10.90 (0-531-10849-X) Watts.
—Fingers & Feelers. (Illus.). 32p. (gr. k-4). 1990. PLB 10.90 (0-531-14050-4) Watts.
—Homes, Holes & Hives. (Illus.). 32p. (gr. k-4). 1990. PLB 10.90 (0-531-14046-6) Watts.
—Join It! (Illus.). 32p. (gr. k-4). 1989. PLB 10.90 (0-531-10730-2) Watts.
—Move It! 1990. PLB 10.90 (0-531-14020-2) Watts.
—Store It! 1990. PLB 10.90 (0-531-14021-0) Watts.
—Tongues & Tasters. (Illus.). 32p. (gr. k-4). 1990. PLB 10.90 (0-531-14049-0) Watts.
—Wear It! Fairclough, Chris, photos by. (Illus.). 32p. (gr. k-4). 1990. PLB 10.90 (0-531-14065-2) Watts.
—Whoops, Words & Whistles. (Illus.). 32p. (gr. k-4). 1990. PLB 10.90 (0-531-14047-4) Watts.
Plueddemann, Jim. Keeping Cool in a Crazy World. (Illus.). 32p. (gr. 4-6). 1988. saddle-stitched camper 1.50 (0-87788-454-4); saddle-stitched counselor 3.50 (0-87788-455-2) Shaw Pubs.
—Ready! Get Set! Grow! (Illus.). 48p. 1987. Camper Ed. saddle-stitched 1.50 (0-87788-715-2); Counselor Ed. saddle-stitched 3.50 (0-87788-716-0) Shaw Pubs.
Plum, jt. auth. see Wayman.
Plum, Carol T. The Butterfly Secret: I Am Special Childrens Story Books. 32p. (ps-3). 1989. lib. bdg. 9.95 (0-87973-017-X, 17); pap. text ed. 5.95 (0-87973-014-5, 14) Our Sunday Visitor.
—Pandy's Rainbow. Schneck, Susan, illus. 32p. (gr. k-3). 1991. 9.95 (0-87973-008-0, 8); pap. 5.95 (0-87973-009-9, 9) Our Sunday Visitor.
—Peter Can't Wait. Most, Andee, illus. 32p. (gr. k-3). 1991. 9.95 (0-87973-006-4, 6); pap. 5.95 (0-87973-007-2, 7) Our Sunday Visitor.
—Peter's Angry Toys: I Am Special Childrens Story Books. 32p. (ps-3). 1989. lib. bdg. 9.95 (0-87973-015-3, 15); pap. text ed. 5.95 (0-87973-012-9, 12) Our Sunday Visitor.

—The Swinging Tree: I Am Special Childrens Story Books. 32p. (gr. 3-8). 1989. lib. bdg. 9.95 (0-87973-016-1, 16); pap. text ed. 5.95 (0-87973-013-7, 13) Our Sunday Visitor.
—Where the Big River Runs. Most, Richard, illus. 32p. (gr. k-3). 1991. 9.95 (0-87973-011-0, 11); pap. 5.95 (0-87973-010-2, 10) Our Sunday Visitor.
Plum, Joan. I Am Special Fun Book. 32p. (Orig.). (ps-2). 1989. pap. 2.95 (0-685-26964-7, 55) Our Sunday Visitor.
Plume, Alice, tr. see Langton, Jane.
Plume, Ilse. The Bremen-Town Musicians. Plume, Ilse, illus. LC 86-42990. 32p. (ps-3). 1987. pap. 5.95 (0-06-443141-X, Trophy) HarpC Child Bks.
—The Christmas Witch. Plume, Ilse, illus. LC 91-71380. 32p. (gr. k-4). 1991. 13.95 (1-56282-077-X); PLB 13. 89 (1-56282-078-8) Hyprn Child.
—The Christmas Witch. Plume, Ilse, illus. LC 91-71380. 32p. (gr. k-3). 1993. pap. 4.95 (1-56282-524-0) Hyprn Ppbks.
—The Twelve Days of Christmas. Plume, Ilse, illus. LC 89-49063. 32p. (gr. 1 up). 1990. PLB 16.89 (0-06-024738-X) HarpC Child Bks.
Plume, Ise, ed. Lullaby Book. LC 93-4425. (Illus.). Date not set. 15.00 (0-06-023501-2); PLB 14.89 (0-06-023502-0) HarpC.
Plume, Llse. Shoemaker & the Elves. 32p. (ps-3). 1991. 14.95 (0-15-274050-3, HB Juv Bks) HarBrace.
Plumini, Roberto. The Knot in the Tracks. Fedorov, Mikhail, illus. Holmes, Olivia, tr. from ITA. LC 93-20343. (Illus.). 32p. 1993. 14.00 (0-685-67813-X, Tambourine Bks); PLB 13.93 (0-688-11167-X, Tambourine Bks) Morrow.
Plummer, Cameron, ed. see Walter, Eugene.
Plummer, Louise. My Name is Sus5an Smith: The Five Is Silent. 1991. 15.00 (0-385-30043-3) Delacorte.
—My Name Is Sus5an Smith, the 5 Is Silent. 1993. pap. 3.50 (0-440-21451-3) Dell.
—The Romantic Obsessions & Humiliations of Annie Sehlmeier. (gr. k up). 1989. pap. 2.95 (0-440-20315-5, LFL) Dell.
—A Walk to Grow On. Cook, Tom, illus. 40p. (ps-3). 1985. 5.95 (0-910313-85-7) Parker Bros.
Plumpp, Sterling. Ballad of Harriet Tubman. Burrowes, Adjoa J., illus. 1993. 18.95 (0-88378-062-3) Third World.
—Paul Robeson. Burrowes, Adjoa J., illus. 1992. pap. 5.95 (0-88378-065-8) Third World.
Plunkett, Mark W., ed. see Jackson, Carol.
Plunkett, Stephanie H., jt. ed. see Han, Oki S.
Pluta, Terry, jt. auth. see Ahbe, Dottie.
Plutarch. Plutarch's Lives. White, John S., ed. LC 66-28487. (Illus.). 468p. (gr. 7 up). 1900. 22.00 (0-8196-0174-8) Biblo.
Pochocki, Ethel. The Attic Mice. Catrow, David, illus. LC 90-32064. 128p. (gr. 2-4). 1990. 13.95 (0-8050-1298-2, Bks Young Read) H Holt & Co.
—Attic Mice. (ps-3). 1993. pap. 3.50 (0-440-40745-1) Dell.
—The Gypsies' Tale. Kelly, Laura, illus. LC 93-3320. (gr. 4 up). 1994. pap. 14.00 (0-671-79934-7, S&S BFYR) S&S Trade.
—Mushroom Man. 1993. 15.00 (0-671-75951-5, Green Tiger) S&S Trade.
—Rosebud & Red Flannel. Owens, Mary B., illus. LC 90-4933. 32p. (ps-2). 1991. 14.95 (0-8050-1213-3, Bks Young Read) H Holt & Co.
—Wildflower Tea. Essley, Roger, illus. LC 92-29872. 1993. 14.00 (0-671-78115-4, Green Tiger) S&S Trade.
Pochocki, Ethel F. The Fox Who Found Christmas. Bell, Thomas P., illus. LC 90-82095. 56p. (Orig.). 1990. pap. 5.95 (0-87793-431-2) Ave Maria.
Pocock, Rita. Annabelle & the Big Slide. 28p. (ps-k). 1989. 10.95 (0-15-200407-6, Gulliver Bks) HarBrace.
Podendorf, Illa. Animal Homes. LC 82-4466. (Illus.). 48p. (gr. k-4). 1982. PLB 15.27 (0-516-01666-0) Childrens.
—Animals of Sea & Shore. LC 81-38453. (Illus.). 48p. (gr. k-4). 1982. PLB 15.27 (0-516-01615-6); pap. 4.95 (0-516-41615-4) Childrens.
—Baby Animals. LC 81-9938. (Illus.). 48p. (gr. k-4). 1981. PLB 15.27 (0-516-01605-9); pap. 4.95 (0-516-41605-7) Childrens.
—Energy. LC 81-12309. (Illus.). 48p. (gr. k-4). 1982. PLB 15.27 (0-516-01625-3) Childrens.
—Insects. LC 81-7689. (Illus.). 48p. (gr. k-4). 1981. PLB 15.27 (0-516-01627-X); pap. 4.95 (0-516-41627-8) Childrens.
—Jungles. LC 82-4454. (gr. k-4). 1982. 15.27 (0-516-01631-8) Childrens.
—Pets. LC 81-7679. (Illus.). 48p. (gr. k-4). 1981. PLB 15. 27 (0-516-01641-5) Childrens.
—Rocks & Minerals. LC 81-38494. (Illus.). 48p. (gr. k-4). 1982. PLB 15.27 (0-516-01648-2); pap. 4.95 (0-516-41648-0) Childrens.
—Seasons. LC 81-7751. (Illus.). 48p. (gr. k-4). 1981. PLB 15.27 (0-516-01647-4); pap. 4.95 (0-516-41647-2) Childrens.
—Space. LC 82-4507. (gr. k-4). 1982. 15.27 (0-516-01650-4); pap. 4.95 (0-516-41650-2) Childrens.
—Spiders. LC 81-38444. (Illus.). 48p. (gr. k-4). 1982. PLB 15.27 (0-516-01653-9); pap. 4.95 (0-516-41653-7) Childrens.
—Trees. LC 81-12313. (Illus.). 48p. (gr. k-4). 1982. PLB 15.27 (0-516-01657-1) Childrens.
Podhaizer, Mary E. Following Christ: Activity Book. Puccetti, Patricia I., ed. 41p. (Orig.). (gr. 6). 1985. pap. 3.00 (0-89870-066-3) Ignatius Pr.

—Jesus Our Life: Activity Book. Puccetti, Patricia I., ed. 76p. (Orig.). (gr. 2). 1984. pap. 3.00 (0-89870-063-9) Ignatius Pr.
Podnecky-Spiegel, Janet, jt. auth. see Long, Lynellyn D.
Podolsky, Leo, ed. Guild Repertoire: Prepatory A. 48p. (Orig.). (gr. 6-12). 1960. pap. text ed. 7.95 (0-87487-645-1) Summy-Birchard.
Poe, Edgar Allan. The Best of Poe. new & abr. ed. Farr, Naunerle, ed. Taloac, G., et al, illus. (gr. 4-12). 1977. pap. text ed. 2.95 (0-88301-269-3) Pendulum Pr.
—The Black Cat. Redpath, Ann, ed. Delessert, Etienne, illus. 32p. (gr. 9 up). 1985. PLB 13.95s.p. (0-88682-001-4) Creative Ed.
—The Black Cat. rev. ed. (gr. 9-12). 1989. Repr. of 1902 ed. multi-media kit 35.00 (0-685-31130-9) Balance Pub.
—The Cask of Amontillado. LC 80-21466. (Illus.). 32p. (gr. 9 up). 1980. PLB 13.95s.p. (0-87191-773-4) Creative Ed.
—The Cask of Amontillado. Cutts, David E., adapted by. Toulmin-Rothe, Ann, illus. LC 81-15997. 32p. (gr. 5-10). 1982. PLB 10.79 (0-89375-622-9); pap. text ed. 2.95 (0-89375-623-7); cassettes avail. Troll Assocs.
—Edgar Allan Poe, Stories & Poems. (gr. 9 up). 1962. pap. 3.25 (0-8049-0008-6, CL-8) Airmont.
—Edgar Allan Poe's Tales of Terror. Martin, Les, adapted by. Chandler, Karen, illus. LC 90-52926. 96p. (Orig.). (gr. 2-7). 1991. lib. bdg. 5.99 (0-679-91046-8); pap. 2.95 (0-679-81046-3) Random Bks Yng Read.
—Eight Tales of Terror. 208p. (gr. 7-12). 1961. pap. 2.95 (0-590-41136-5) Scholastic Inc.
—The Fall of the House of Usher. Cutts, David E., adapted by. Crowell, James, illus. LC 81-15958. 32p. (gr. 5-10). 1982. PLB 10.79 (0-89375-624-5); pap. text ed. 2.95 (0-89375-625-3) Troll Assocs.
—Fall of the House of Usher & Other Tales. (gr. 7). 1960. pap. 2.95 (0-451-52174-9, Sig Classics) NAL-Dutton.
—Ghostly Tales & Eerie Poems of Edgar Allan Poe. Schwinger, Larry, illus. LC 92-30884. 256p. 1993. 13. 95 (0-448-40533-4, G&D) Putnam Pub Group.
—The Gold-Bug. 80p. (gr. 6). 1990. PLB 13.95s.p. (0-88682-303-X) Creative Ed.
—The Masque of the Red Death. Cutts, David E., adapted by. Lawn, John, illus. LC 81-15959. 32p. (gr. 5-10). 1982. PLB 10.79 (0-89375-620-2); pap. text ed. 2.95 (0-89375-621-0); cassettes avail. Troll Assocs.
—The Masque of the Red Death. 1991. PLB 13.95s.p. (0-88682-477-X) Creative Ed.
—The Pit & the Pendulum. (Illus.). 48p. (gr. 9 up). 1980. PLB 13.95s.p. (0-87191-771-8) Creative Ed.
—The Pit & the Pendulum. Cutts, David E., adapted by. Eisenberry, Monroe, illus. LC 81-16432. 32p. (gr. 5-10). 1982. PLB 10.79 (0-89375-626-1); pap. text ed. 2.95 (0-89375-627-X); cassettes avail. Troll Assocs.
—The Purloined Letter. LC 86-4156. 48p. (gr. 9 up). 1986. PLB 13.95s.p. (0-88682-061-8) Creative Ed.
—The Raven & Other Poems. 80p. (gr. 7 up). 1992. pap. 2.95 (0-590-45260-6, Apple Classics) Scholastic Inc.
—Reader's Digest Best Loved Books for Young Readers: Tales of Poe. Ogburn, Jackie, ed. Liebman, Oscar, illus. 152p. (gr. 4-12). 1989. 3.99 (0-945260-24-5) Choice Pub NY.
—Tales of Edgar Allan Poe. Shaw, Charlie, illus. Stewart, Diana, adapted by. LC 80-14064. (Illus.). 48p. (gr. 4 up). 1980. PLB 18.64 (0-8172-1662-6) Raintree Steck-V.
—Tales of Mystery & Imagination, Retold by Henniker-Major, Owen, C., illus. (gr. 3 up). 1975. pap. text ed. 4.95x (0-19-580511-9) OUP.
—Tales of Terror: Ten Short Stories. Waldman, Neil, illus. LC 84-22290. 208p. (gr. 5 up). 1985. 12.95 (0-13-884214-0) P-H.
—The Tell-Tale Heart. (Illus.). 32p. (gr. 9 up). 1980. PLB 13.95s.p. (0-87191-772-6) Creative Ed.
—The Tell-Tale Heart. rev. ed. (gr. 9-12). 1989. Repr. of 1902 ed. multi-media kit 35.00 (0-685-31131-7) Balance Pub.
Poe, Elizabeth. Focus on Sexuality. 225p. 1990. lib. bdg. 39.00 (0-87436-116-8) ABC-CLIO.
Poe, Margie. The No-Cooking Cookbook for Kids. (Illus.). (gr. k-6). 1985. pap. 4.95 (0-936985-75-5, 1096A) Kidsmart.
Poelker, Kathy. At the Firehouse. Judge, Matt, ed. Hedran, Susan, illus. 8p. (Orig.). (ps-3). 1988. pap. text ed. 15.00 (0-929842-00-6) Hawthorne Pubs.
—Look at the Holidays. Schiller, Juel K., illus. 64p. (ps-4). 1988. Repr. of 1980 ed. tchr's. ed. 7.95 (0-317-91200-3) LAM Co.
—One Little Drop of Sunshine. Judge, Matt, ed. Hedran, Susan, illus. 8p. (Orig.). (ps-3). 1988. pap. text ed. 15. 00 (0-929842-01-4) Hawthorne Pubs.
Poepoe, Karen, jt. auth. see Kahalewai, Marilyn.
Poesnecker, Gerald E. see Maeterlinck, Maurice.
Poet's Workshop Staff. Be Somebody Be Yourself Poetry, Bk. 1. 11p. (Orig.). (gr. 7-12). 1990. pap. 4.50 (0-913597-98-8, Pub. by Alpha Pyramis) Prosperity & Profit.
—Black American History: Rap & Rhyme. 8p. (gr. 6-12). 1989. pap. text ed. 2.50 (0-913597-53-8, Pub. by Alpha Pyramis) Prosperity & Profits.
Poffenberger, Nancy & Bane, Rosemary. Instant Recorder Package 2. Shaffer, Jim, illus. 32p. (Orig.). (gr. 3-6). 1989. pap. write for info. incl. recorder (0-938293-17-6) Fun Pub OH.
Poffenberger, Nancy. Instant Fun With Sacred Songs. 24p. (gr. k up). pap. 5.95 (0-938293-27-3) Fun Pub OH.

—Instant Piano Fun: Book One. 34p. (gr. 4). 1985. pap. 9.95 (*0-938293-25-7*) Fun Pub OH.
—Instant Recorder Fun: Book One. 32p. (gr. 4). 1986. pap. 4.95 (*0-938293-14-1*) Fun Pub OH.
—Instant Recorder Fun Package 1 (recorder & book) 32p. (ps-3). 1986. Repr. of 1983 ed. blister-pak pkg. 10.95 (*0-938293-15-X*) Fun Pub OH.
—Now! Instant Keyboard Fun I. 32p. (gr. 4 up). 1985. pap. 4.95 (*0-938293-39-7*) Fun Pub OH.
Poganski, Donald J. Fifty Object Lessons. (gr. 2-5). 1967. 5.99 (*0-570-03172-9*, 12-2282) Concordia.
Poggenpohl, Sharon H., ed. Graphic Design: A Career Guide & Educational Directory. Hightower, Caroline, intro. by. (Illus.). 160p. (Orig.). Date not set. pap. write for info. (*1-884081-00-2*) Am Inst Graphic Arts.
Pogorelsky, Antony. The Black Hen: or The Underground Inhabitants. Hamilton, Morse, retold by. Yuditskaya, Tatyana, illus. LC 92-28599. 32p. (gr. 2-5). 1994. 14.99 (*0-525-65133-0*, Cobblehill Bks) Dutton Child Bks.
Pogrund, Benjamin. Nelson Mandela. LC 91-50541. (Illus.). 68p. (gr. 3-4). 1992. PLB 18.60 (*0-8368-0621-2*) Gareth Stevens Inc.
—Nelson Mandela: Strength & Spirit of a Free South Africa. LC 90-24026. (Illus.). 68p. (gr. 5-6). 1992. PLB 18.60 (*0-8368-0357-4*) Gareth Stevens Inc.
Pohl, Constance & Harris, Kathleen K. Transracial Adoption: Children & Parents Speak. LC 92-10991. (Illus.). 144p. (gr. 9-12). 1992. PLB 14.40 (*0-531-11134-2*) Watts.
Pohl, Kathleen. Crabs. (Illus.). 32p. (gr. 3-7). 1986. PLB 17.96 (*0-8172-2716-4*) Raintree Steck-V.
—Crayfish. (Illus.). 32p. (gr. 3-7). 1986. pap. text ed. 17.96 (*0-8172-2718-0*) Raintree Steck-V.
—Dandelions. (Illus.). 32p. (gr. 3-7). 1986. pap. text ed. 17.96 (*0-8172-2708-3*) Raintree Steck-V.
—Giant Water Bugs. (Illus.). 32p. (gr. 3-7). 1986. pap. text ed. 17.96 (*0-8172-2714-8*) Raintree Steck-V.
—Gourds. (Illus.). 32p. (gr. 3-7). 1986. PLB 17.96 (*0-8172-2712-1*) Raintree Steck-V.
—Hermit Crabs. (Illus.). 32p. (gr. 3-7). 1986. PLB 17.96 (*0-8172-2721-0*) Raintree Steck-V.
—Killifish. (Illus.). 32p. (gr. 3-7). 1986. PLB 17.96 (*0-8172-2720-2*) Raintree Steck-V.
—Morning Glories. (Illus.). 32p. (gr. 3-7). 1986. PLB 17.96 (*0-8172-2711-3*) Raintree Steck-V.
—Potatoes. (Illus.). 32p. (gr. 3-7). 1986. PLB 17.96 (*0-8172-2723-7*) Raintree Steck-V.
—The Praying Mantis. (Illus.). 32p. (gr. 3-7). 1986. PLB 17.96 (*0-8172-2715-6*) Raintree Steck-V.
—Sparrows. (Illus.). 32p. (gr. 3-7). 1986. PLB 17.96 (*0-8172-2719-9*) Raintree Steck-V.
—Stickleback Fish. (Illus.). 32p. (gr. 3-7). 1986. PLB 17.96 (*0-8172-2722-9*) Raintree Steck-V.
—Sunflowers. (Illus.). 32p. (gr. 3-7). 1986. PLB 17.96 (*0-8172-2710-5*) Raintree Steck-V.
—Tulips. (Illus.). 32p. (gr. 3-7). 1986. PLB 17.96 (*0-8172-2709-1*) Raintree Steck-V.
Pohl, Kathleen, ed. see Oda, Hidetomo.
Pohl, Kathy, ed. see Endo, Kimio.
Pohl, Kathy, ed. see Hasegawa, Yo.
Pohl, Kathy, ed. see Nanao, Jun.
Pohl, Kathy, ed. see Oda, Hidetomo.
Pohl, Kathy, ed. see Ogawa, Hiroshi.
Pohl, Kathy, ed. see Otani, Takeshi.
Pohl, Kathy, ed. see Struble, Steve.
Pohl, Kathy, ed. see Takeuchi, Hiroshi.
Pohl, Kathy, ed. see Yajima, Minoru.
Pohl, Linda. The Ah-Chooo Book. Ostermayer, Sharon, illus. 20p. (ps-2). 1990. 3.95 (*0-9625453-0-9*) L P Pohl.
—The Wiggly Tooth Book. Kelley, Colleen M., illus. 16p. (ps-2). 1991. 3.95 (*0-9625453-1-7*) L P Pohl.
Points, Larry, jt. auth. see Jauck, Andrea.
Points, Maureen. The Adventures of Pepe the Poodle & Other Stories. Points, Maureen, illus. 1978. pap. 3.50 (*0-9601594-1-X*) Maureen Points.
Poirier-Brode, Karen. Adolescent Pregnancy & Prenatal Care. Head, J. J., ed. Steffen, Ann T., illus. LC 84-71144. 16p. (Orig.). (gr. 10 up). 1987. pap. text ed. 2.75 (*0-89278-348-6*, 45-9748) Carolina Biological.
Poix, Carol de see De Poix, Carol.
Pokeberry, P. J. The Secret of Hilhouse: An Adult Book for Teens. Mueller, Peggy, illus. Urie, Luanna, frwd. by. 96p. (Orig.). (gr. 5 up). 1993. pap. 6.50 (*0-943962-02-1*) Viewpoint Pr.
Polacco, Patricia. Appelemando's Dreams. Polacco, Patricia, illus. 32p. (ps-3). 1991. 14.95 (*0-399-21800-9*, Philomel Bks) Putnam Pub Group.
—Babushka's Doll. LC 89-6122. (Illus.). 40p. (ps-1). 1990. pap. 14.95 jacketed, 3-pc. bdg. (*0-671-68343-8*, S&S BFYR) S&S Trade.
—Babushka's Doll. (gr. 2). 1990. pap. write for info. (*0-663-56215-5*) Silver Burdett Pr.
—The Bee Tree. LC 92-8660. (Illus.). 32p. (ps up). 1993. PLB 14.95 (*0-399-21965-X*, Philomel Bks) Putnam Pub Group.
—Chicken Sunday. Polacco, Patricia, illus. 32p. (ps-3). 1992. PLB 14.95 (*0-399-22133-6*, Philomel Bks) Putnam Pub Group.
—Just Plain Fancy. Polacco, Patricia, illus. (ps-3). 1990. 14.95 (*0-553-05884-3*, Little Rooster); PLB 15.99 (*0-553-07062-2*, Little Rooster) Bantam.
—The Keeping Quilt. Polacco, Patricia, illus. 32p. (ps-3). 1988. pap. 14.95 3-pc. bdg. (*0-671-64963-9*, S&S BFYR) S&S Trade.
—The Keeping Quilt. (gr. 3). 1992. pap. write for info. (*0-663-56228-7*) Silver Burdett Pr.

—The Keeping Quilt. Polacco, Patricia, illus. (gr. k-4). 1993. 14.95 (*0-685-64811-7*); audiocassette 11.00 (*1-882869-82-6*) Read Advent.
—Meteor! Polacco, Patricia, illus. 32p. (gr. k-3). 1987. 14.95 (*0-399-21699-5*, Putnam) Putnam Pub Group.
—Meteor! (Illus.). 32p. (ps-3). 1992. pap. 5.95 (*0-399-22407-6*, Sandcastle Bks) Putnam Pub Group.
—Mrs. Katz & Tush. 1992. 15.00 (*0-553-08122-5*, Little Rooster) Bantam.
—My Rotten, Redheaded, Older Brother. Polacco, Patricia, illus. 1994. pap. 15.00 (*0-671-72751-6*, S&S BFYR) S&S Trade.
—Picnic at Mudsock Meadow. (Illus.). 32p. (ps-3). 1992. 14.95 (*0-399-21811-4*, Putnam) Putnam Pub Group.
—Rechenka's Eggs. Polacco, Patricia, illus. 32p. (ps-3). 1988. 14.95 (*0-399-21501-8*, Philomel Bks) Putnam Pub Group.
—Some Birthday! LC 90-10381. (Illus.). 40p. (ps-2). 1991. pap. 14.95 jacketed, 3-pc. bdg. (*0-671-72750-8*, S&S BFYR) S&S Trade.
—Some Birthday! (gr. 3). 1990. pap. write for info. (*0-663-56229-5*) Silver Burdett Pr.
—Some Birthday. (ps-6). 1993. pap. 5.95 (*0-671-87170-6*, S&S BFYR) S&S Trade.
—Thunder Cake. (Illus.). 32p. (ps-3). 1990. 14.95 (*0-399-22231-6*, Philomel Bks) Putnam Pub Group.
—Uncle Vova's Tree. Polacco, Patricia, illus. 32p. (ps-3). 1989. 14.95 (*0-399-21617-0*, Philomel Bks) Putnam Pub Group.
Polacco, Patricia & Polacco, Patricia. Babushka Baba Yaga. LC 92-30361. (Illus.). 32p. 1993. 14.95 (*0-399-22531-5*, Philomel Bks) Putnam Pub Group.
Polakiewicz, David M. & Mellen, Stephanie. The Teeny Tiny Voice. Mellen, Stephanie, illus. 52p. (Orig.). (gr. k-12). 1992. pap. 5.95 (*1-878040-08-1*) Personal Growth.
Poland, Marguerite. The Wood-Ash Stars. Altshuler, Shanne, illus. 64p. 1990. pap. 5.95 (*0-86486-089-7*, Pub. by D Philip South Africa) Interlink Pub.
Polansky, Leslie, jt. auth. see Torrence, Susan.
Polcovar, Jane. The Charming. 160p. (Orig.). (gr. 7-12). 1984. pap. 2.50 (*0-553-26691-8*) Bantam.
—Harriet Tubman. Bloch, Alex, illus. 48p. (gr. 2-4). 1988. pap. 2.50 (*0-681-40357-8*) Longmeadow Pr.
—Hey, Good Looking! 144p. (gr. 6 up). 1985. pap. 2.25 (*0-553-24383-7*) Bantam.
Polese, Carolyn. Promise Not to Tell. Barrett, Jennifer, illus. LC 84-19767. 66p. (gr. 3 up). 1985. 16.95 (*0-89885-239-0*) Human Sci Pr.
—Promise Not to Tell. Barrett, Jennifer, illus. LC 92-24599. 64p. (gr. 4 up). 1993. pap. 3.95 (*0-688-12026-1*, Pub. by Beech Tree Bks) Morrow.
Polesetsky, Matt, jt. ed. see Wekesser, Carol.
Polesetsky, Matthew & Cozic, Charles, eds. Energy Alternatives. LC 91-24387. 200p. (gr. 10 up). 1991. PLB 16.95 (*0-89908-577-6*); pap. text ed. 9.95 (*0-89908-583-0*) Greenhaven.
Polesetsky, Matthew & Dudley, William, eds. The New World Order: Opposing Viewpoints. LC 91-12374. (Illus.). 240p. (gr. 10 up). 1991. lib. bdg. 17.95 (*0-89908-183-5*); pap. 9.95 (*0-89908-158-4*) Greenhaven.
Polesetsky, Matthew, et al, eds. Global Resources: Opposing Viewpoints. LC 90-24088. (Illus.). 264p. (gr. 10 up). 1991. PLB 17.95 (*0-89908-177-0*); pap. 9.95 (*0-89908-152-5*) Greenhaven.
Polette, Keith. Read, Write, Now! Dillon, Paul, illus. 44p. (gr. 5-9). 1993. pap. text ed. 5.95 (*1-879287-20-X*) Bk Lures.
—The Winter Duckling. McKissack, Patricia & McKissack, Fredrick, eds. Martin, Clovis, illus. LC 88-60393. 32p. (Orig.). (gr. 1-3). 1990. text ed. 8.95 (*0-88335-777-1*); pap. text ed. 4.95 (*0-88335-789-5*) Milliken Pub Co.
Polette, Keith, jt. auth. see Polette, Nancy.
Polette, Nancy. The ABCs of Books & Thinking Skills. (Illus.). 144p. (gr. 1-8). 1987. pap. 14.95 (*0-913839-61-2*) Bk Lures.
—Amelia Bedelia Thinking Book. expanded ed. (Illus.). 48p. (gr. k-3). 1994. pap. 5.95 (*1-879287-10-2*) Bk Lures.
—Apple Trees to Zinnias. (Illus.). 48p. 1992. pap. 5.95 (*1-879287-14-5*) Bk Lures.
—Bartering with Books. (Illus.). 48p. (gr. 4-7). 1992. pap. 5.95 (*1-879287-16-1*) Bk Lures.
—The Best Ever Writing Models. (Illus.). 124p. (gr. 4-9). 1989. pap. 12.95 (*0-913839-78-7*) Bk Lures.
—Birds in Literature. (Illus.). 48p. (gr. k-3). 1990. pap. 5.95 (*0-913839-86-8*) Bk Lures.
—The Book Bag. (Illus.). 64p. 1986. pap. 7.95 (*0-913839-46-9*) Bk Lures.
—Concert Reading. expanded ed. (Illus.). 48p. (gr. k-3). 1992. pap. 5.95 (*1-879287-07-2*) Bk Lures.
—E Is for Everybody: A Manual for Bringing Fine Picture Books into the Hands & Hearts of Children. 2nd ed. LC 82-10508. 194p. (gr. 1-7). 1982. 20.00 (*0-8108-1579-6*) Scarecrow.
—Earthwatch. Dillon, Paul, illus. 48p. (gr. 3-6). 1993. pap. 5.95 (*1-879287-26-9*) Bk Lures.
—Enjoying Fairy Tales. (Illus.). 48p. (gr. 4-7). 1991. pap. 5.95 (*0-913839-94-9*) Bk Lures.
—Expanded First Research Projects. 2nd ed. (Illus.). 48p. (gr. 1-3). 1991. pap. 5.95 (*0-913839-92-2*) Bk Lures.
—Exploring Themes with Aesop's Fables & Picture Books. (Illus.). 48p. (gr. 2-6). 1992. pap. 5.95 (*1-879287-12-9*) Bk Lures.
—Favorite Novel Animals. (Illus.). 48p. (gr. 3-6). 1992. pap. 5.95 (*1-879287-15-3*) Bk Lures.

—Frog & Toad Thinking Book. expanded ed. (Illus.). 48p. (gr. k-3). 1992. pap. 5.95 (*1-879287-09-9*) Bk Lures.
—The Hole by the Apple Tree. Akgulian, Nishan, illus. LC 90-24646. 32p. 1992. 14.00 (*0-688-10557-2*); PLB 13.93 (*0-688-10558-0*) Greenwillow.
—Literature-Based Spelling & Writing Activities for Primary Grades. Dillon, Paul, illus. 48p. (Orig.). (gr. 1-4). 1993. pap. 5.95 (*1-879287-23-4*) Bk Lures.
—Little Old Woman & the Hungry Cat. LC 88-18788. (Illus.). 24p. (ps up). 1989. 12.95 (*0-688-08314-5*); PLB 12.88 (*0-688-08315-3*) Greenwillow.
—Mother Goose's Animals. (Illus.). 128p. (gr. 1-4). 1992. pap. 12.95 (*1-879287-13-7*) Bk Lures.
—Multi-Cultural Literature: Books & Activities. Dillon, Paul, illus. 48p. (Orig.). (gr. 3-6). 1993. pap. 5.95 (*1-879287-22-6*) Bk Lures.
—Novel Booktalks. 144p. (Orig.). (gr. 4-8). 1992. pap. 9.95 (*1-879287-18-8*) Bk Lures.
—Novel Thinking. (Illus.). 128p. (gr. 6-12). 1987. pap. 12.95 (*0-913839-47-7*) Bk Lures.
—Pick a Pattern. 4th, expanded ed. (Illus.). 48p. (gr. k-3). 1992. pap. 5.95 (*1-879287-05-6*) Bk Lures.
—Picture Booktalks. 144p. (gr. 1-3). 1992. pap. 9.95 (*1-879287-17-X*) Bk Lures.
—Reader's Almanac. (Illus.). 148p. (gr. 4-8). 1985. pap. 14.95 (*0-913839-44-2*) Bk Lures.
—Reading the World with Folktales. Dillon, Paul, illus. 124p. (Orig.). (gr. 2-4). 1993. pap. 12.95 (*1-879287-19-6*) Bk Lures.
—Reading with Music. expanded ed. (Illus.). 48p. (gr. 4-7). 1992. pap. 5.95 (*1-879287-04-8*) Bk Lures.
—Research Almanac. (Illus.). 172p. (gr. 4-9). 1986. pap. 14.95 (*0-913839-27-2*) Bk Lures.
—Research Book of the Fifty States. expanded ed. (Illus.). 48p. (gr. 4-7). 1991. pap. 5.95 (*1-879287-03-X*) Bk Lures.
—The Research Project Book. 2nd ed. (Illus.). 128p. (gr. 4-9). 1992. pap. 12.95 (*1-879287-06-4*) Bk Lures.
—Research Without Copying. 2nd, expanded ed. Dillon, Paul, illus. 48p. (gr. 4-9). 1991. pap. 5.95 (*0-913839-91-4*) Bk Lures.
—Survival. Dillon, Paul, illus. 48p. (Orig.). (gr. 4-8). 1991. pap. 5.95 (*0-913839-93-0*) Bk Lures.
—Teaching Critical Reading with Children's Literature. (Illus.). 128p. (gr. 4-9). 1988. pap. 12.95 (*0-913839-73-6*) Bk Lures.
—Ultimate Book Report Book. expanded ed. (Illus.). 48p. (gr. 5-9). 1991. pap. 5.95 (*0-913839-95-7*) Bk Lures.
—Unforgettable Characters. Dillon, Paul, illus. 48p. (Orig.). (gr. 3-6). 1991. pap. 5.95 (*0-913839-97-3*) Bk Lures.
—U. S. Historical Fiction: A Whole Language Approach. (Illus.). 48p. (gr. 5-8). 1990. pap. 5.95 (*0-913839-85-X*) Bk Lures.
—Write Your Own Fairy Tale. enl. ed. Dillon, Paul, illus. 48p. (Orig.). (gr. 3-7). 1993. pap. 5.95 (*1-879287-25-0*) Bk Lures.
—Young Heroines. Dillon, Paul, illus. 48p. (Orig.). (gr. 4-8). 1991. pap. 5.95 (*0-913839-96-5*) Bk Lures.
Polette, Nancy & Mealy, Virginia. Enjoying Tall Tales. Dillon, Paul, illus. 48p. (Orig.). (gr. 3-6). 1991. 5.95 (*0-913839-90-6*) Bk Lures.
Polette, Nancy & O'Neal, Kathleen. The Crosby Bonsall Thinking Book. (Illus.). 32p. 1987. pap. 4.95 (*0-913839-65-5*) Bk Lures.
—Easy Reader Thinking Book. expanded ed. (Illus.). 48p. (gr. k-3). 1994. pap. 5.95 (*1-879287-08-0*) Bk Lures.
Polette, Nancy & Polette, Keith. Readers Theatre. (Illus.). 48p. (gr. 4-8). 1986. pap. 5.95 (*0-913839-56-6*) Bk Lures.
Polette, Nancy, jt. auth. see Albert, Kristine.
Polette, Nancy, jt. auth. see Levine, Gloria.
Polhamus, Jean B. Dinosaur Do's & Don'ts. O'Neill, Steven, illus. LC 75-11743. (gr. 1-3). 1975. (Pub. by Treehouse); pap. 2.50 (*0-13-214668-1*) P-H.
Polick, Bill, jt. auth. see Bryce, James.
Policoff, Stephen P. & Skinner, Jeffrey. Real Toads in Imaginary Gardens: Suggestions & Starting Points for Young Creative Writers. Teschner, Amy, ed. LC 91-26524. 200p. (Orig.). (gr. 5 up). 1991. pap. 11.95 (*1-55652-137-5*) Chicago Review.
Polidori, John. The Vampire. Martin, Les, adapted by. Munching, Paul V., illus. LC 88-34078. 96p. (Orig.). (gr. 3-7). 1989. lib. bdg. 5.99 (*0-394-93844-5*); pap. 2.95 (*0-394-83844-0*) Random Bks Yng Read.
Polikof, Barbara G. Herbert C. Hoover: Thirty-First President of the United States. Young, Richard G., ed. LC 89-39946. (Illus.). 128p. (gr. 5-9). 1990. PLB 17.26 (*0-944483-58-5*) Garrett Ed Corp.
—James Madison: Fourth President of the United States. Young, Richard G., ed. LC 88-24537. (Illus.). (gr. 5-9). 1989. PLB 17.26 (*0-944483-22-4*) Garrett Ed Corp.
Polikoff, Barbara. Life's a Funny Proposition, Horatio. LC 91-28010. 144p. (gr. 4-7). 1992. 13.95 (*0-8050-1972-3*, Bks Young Read) H Holt & Co.
Polikoff, Barbara G. Life's a Funny Proposition, Horatio. 112p. (gr. 3-7). 1994. pap. 3.99 (*0-14-036644-X*) Puffin Bks.
Poling, Nancy W. Most Ministers Wear Sneakers. Ortiz, Gloria C., illus. LC 91-15116. 32p. (gr. 4-8). 1991. 6.95 (*0-8298-0907-4*, P-0907-4); pap. 6.95 (*0-8298-0901-5*, P-0901-5) Pilgrim OH.
Polisar, Barry L. Captured Live & in the Act. (gr. k-6). 1978. incl. audio cassette 9.95 (*0-9615696-9-7*) Rainbow Morn.

—Dinosaurs I Have Known. Stewart, Michael, illus. 48p. (Orig.). (gr. 2-6). 1988. 9.95 (*0-938663-00-3*); pap. 7.95 (*0-938663-05-4*) Rainbow Morn.
—Don't Do That: A Child's Guide to Bad Manners, Ridiculous Rules & Inadequate Etiquette. Young, Debby, illus. 64p. (Orig.). (gr. 3-6). 1989. 9.95 (*0-938663-01-1*); pap. 7.95 (*0-938663-10-0*) Rainbow Morn.
—Family Concert. (gr. k-6). 1990. incl. cassette 9.95 (*0-938663-12-7*) Rainbow Morn.
—The Haunted House Party: A Halloween Story. (Illus.). 40p. (gr. 3-6). 1987. 9.95 (*0-938663-02-X*); pap. 7.95 (*0-938663-11-9*) Rainbow Morn.
—I Eat Kids & Other Songs for Rebellious Children. (gr. k-6). 1987. Repr. of 1975 ed. incl. cassette 9.95 (*0-9615696-3-8*) Rainbow Morn.
—Juggling Babies. (ps-6). 1989. incl. cassette 9.95 (*0-9615696-2-X*) Rainbow Morn.
—My Brother Thinks He's a Banana & Other Provocative Songs for Children. (gr. k-6). 1987. Repr. of 1977 ed. incl. cassette 9.95 (*0-9615696-4-6*) Rainbow Morn.
—Naughty Songs for Boys & Girls. (gr. k-6). 1987. Repr. of 1978 ed. incl. cassette 9.95 (*0-9615696-5-4*) Rainbow Morn.
—Noises from under the Rug: The Barry Louis Polisar Songbook. Stewart, Michael, illus. 208p. (gr. k-6). 1985. 18.98 (*0-9615696-0-3*); pap. 13.95 (*0-9615696-1-1*) Rainbow Morn.
—Off Color Songs for Kids. (gr. k-6). 1983. incl. cassette 9.95 (*0-9615696-8-9*) Rainbow Morn.
—Peculiar Zoo. Clark, David, illus. 32p. (gr. k-6). 1993. 14.95 (*0-938663-14-3*) Rainbow Morn.
—The Snake Who Was Afraid of People. Clark, David, illus. 32p. (gr. k-4). 1993. Repr. of 1988 ed. 14.95 (*0-938663-16-X*) Rainbow Morn.
—Snakes & the Boy Who Was Afraid of Them. Clark, David, illus. 32p. (gr. 1-6). 1993. Repr. of 1988 ed. 14. 95 (*0-938663-15-1*) Rainbow Morn.
—Stanley Stole My Shoelace & Rubbed It in His Armpit & Other Songs My Parents Won't Let Me Sing. (gr. k-6). 1981. incl. cassette 9.95 (*0-9615696-7-0*) Rainbow Morn.
—The Trouble with Ben. Clark, David, illus. 32p. (gr. k-4). 1992. 14.95 (*0-938663-13-5*) Rainbow Morn.
Polish, Daniel F., et al. Drugs, Sex, & Integrity: What Does Judaism Say? Diaz, Jose, illus. LC 90-28763. (gr. 7-9). 1991. pap. 10.00 (*0-8074-0459-4*, 168505) UAHC.
Politi, Leo. Song of the Swallows. Politi, Leo, illus. 32p. (gr. k-3). 1987. pap. 4.95 (*0-689-71140-9*, Aladdin) Macmillan Child Grp.
—Song of the Swallows. reissue ed. LC 49-8215. (Illus.). 32p. (gr. 1-4). 1987. SBE 13.95 (*0-684-18831-7*, Scribners Young Read) Macmillan Child Grp.
—Three Stalks of Corn. reissue ed. Politi, Leo, illus. LC 75-35009. 32p. (gr. k-3). 1993. RSBE 14.95 (*0-684-19538-0*, Scribners Young Read) Macmillan Child Grp.
—Three Stalks of Corn. Politi, Leo, illus. LC 93-19737. 32p. (gr. k-3). 1994. pap. 4.95 (*0-689-71782-2*, Aladdin) Macmillan Child Grp.
Polk, Betty J., jt. auth. see Abbott, Marti.
Polk, Stella G. Glory Girl. 144p. (gr. 4-7). 1986. 9.95 (*0-89015-582-8*, Pub. by Panda Bks) Eakin-Sunbelt.
Polkinhorn, Harry. Bleeding. Winkler, Christ, ed. Watten, Barrett, intro. by. 38p. (Orig.). (gr. 10-12). 1989. pap. text ed. 4.00 (*0-929611-05-5*) Plutonium Pr.
Pollack, Cecilia. How Hip Are You, Bk. 2. (Illus.). (gr. 5-12). 1978. wkbk. 5.95 (*0-87594-162-1*) Book Lab.
—How Hip Are You, Bk 3. (Illus.). (gr. 5-12). 1978. wkbk. 5.95 (*0-87594-161-3*) Book-Lab.
—How Hip Are You, Bk. 4. (Illus.). (gr. 5-12). 1978. wkbk. 5.95 (*0-87594-163-X*) Book Lab.
Pollack, Eileen. Whisper Whisper Jesse, Whisper Whisper Josh: A Story about AIDS. Templeman, Kristine, ed. Gilfoy, Bruce, illus. LC 92-72471. (Illus.). 32p. (ps up). 1992. PLB 16.95 (*0-9624828-4-6*); pap. 5.95 (*0-9624828-3-8*) Advantage-Aurora.
Pollack, Jill S. Shirley Chisholm. LC 93-31175. 1994. write for info. (*0-531-20168-6*) Watts.
Pollack, Pamela, compiled by. The Random House Book of Humor for Children. Zelinsky, Paul O., illus. LC 86-31478. 320p. (gr. 2-6). 1988. 15.95 (*0-394-88049-8*); lib. bdg. 16.99 (*0-394-98049-2*) Random Bks Yng Read.
Pollack, Steve. Animal Life. LC 89-11367. (Illus.). 64p. (gr. 4-6). 1989. PLB 19.93 (*0-8368-0003-6*) Gareth Stevens Inc.
—Ecology. (Illus.). 64p. (gr. 3-6). 1993. 15.95 (*1-56458-326-0*) Dorling Kindersley.
Pollack, Steve, jt. auth. see Harrison, Virginia.
Pollak, Felix. The Castle & the Flaw. 1963. pap. 4.00 (*0-685-01010-4*) Elizabeth Pr.
Pollak, Richard A., ed. Explore Antarctica! (Illus.). 58p. (gr. 5-9). 1991. 3-ring binder/laserdisc 295.00 (*0-922649-14-6*) ETC MN.
—Explore Antarctica! Barcode Guide. 188p. (gr. 5-9). 1992. spiral bdg. 125.00 (*0-922649-15-4*) ETC MN.
Polland, Barbara K. Feelings: Inside You & Outloud Too. LC 74-25835. (Illus.). 64p. (ps-3). 1984. pap. 6.95 (*0-89087-006-3*) Celestial Arts.
—Grandma & Grandpa Are Special People. Reinertson, Barbara, illus. LC 80-66961. 80p. (gr. k-3). 1984. pap. 7.95 (*0-89087-343-7*) Celestial Arts.
—The Sensible Book: A Celebration of Your Five Senses. rev. ed. Hammid, Hella, illus. 64p. 1993. pap. write for info. (*0-89087-707-6*) Celestial Arts.

Pollard, H. B. & Barclay-Smith, Phyllis. British & American Game Birds. Rickman, Philip, illus. 48p. (gr. 10 up). Date not set. 50.00 (*1-56416-071-8*) Derrydale Pr.
Pollard, Jean A. The Ice Ladder. Weinberger, Jane, ed. Pollard, Jean A., illus. LC 87-62209. 58p. (Orig.). (gr. 4-8). 1988. pap. 5.00 (*0-932433-31-6*) Windswept Hse.
Pollard, Michael. Absolute Rulers. Stefoff, Rebecca, ed. LC 91-33297. (Illus.). 48p. (gr. 5-8). 1992. PLB 19.93 (*1-56074-034-5*) Garrett Ed Corp.
—Air, Water & Weather. (Illus.). 48p. (gr. 1-4). 1987. 12. 95x (*0-8160-1781-6*) Facts on File.
—Beliefs & Believers. Stefoff, Rebecca, ed. LC 91-36503. (Illus.). 48p. (gr. 5-9). 1992. PLB 19.93 (*1-56074-037-X*) Garrett Ed Corp.
—Empire Builders. Stefoff, Rebecca, ed. LC 91-36501. (Illus.). 48p. (gr. 5-8). 1992. PLB 19.93 (*1-56074-038-8*) Garrett Ed Corp.
—From Cycle to Spaceship: The Story of Transport. (Illus.). 48p. (gr. 1-4). 1987. 12.95x (*0-8160-1779-4*) Facts on File.
—The House That Science Built. (Illus.). 48p. (gr. 1-4). 1987. 12.95x (*0-8160-1780-8*) Facts on File.
—Maria Montessori. LC 89-49417. (Illus.). 68p. (Orig.). 1990. pap. 7.95 (*0-8192-1539-2*) Morehouse Pub.
—Maria Montessori. LC 89-49417. (Illus.). 64p. (gr. 5-6). 1990. PLB 18.60 (*0-8368-0217-9*) Gareth Stevens Inc.
—The Nineteenth Century. LC 92-19080. (Illus.). 80p. (gr. 2-6). 1993. 17.95x (*0-8160-2791-9*) Facts on File.
—People Who Care. Stefoff, Rebecca, ed. LC 91-36502. (Illus.). 48p. (gr. 5-8). 1992. PLB 19.93 (*1-56074-035-3*) Garrett Ed Corp.
—The Red Cross & the Red Crescent. LC 93-26383. 1994. write for info. (*0-02-774720-4*, New Discovery Bks) Macmillan Child Grp.
—Revolutionary Power. Stefoff, Rebecca, ed. LC 91-36504. (Illus.). 48p. (gr. 5-8). 1992. PLB 19.93 (*1-56074-039-6*) Garrett Ed Corp.
—Thinkers. Stefoff, Rebecca, ed. LC 91-33296. (Illus.). 48p. (gr. 5-8). 1992. PLB 19.93 (*1-56074-036-1*) Garrett Ed Corp.
—Train Technology. (Illus.). 48p. (gr. 5-8). 1990. PLB 12. 90 (*0-531-18338-6*, Pub. by Bookwright Pr) Watts.
Pollard, Michael, jt. auth. see Wilkinson, Philip.
Pollard, Nan. Friends Together. Pollard, Nan, illus. 32p. (ps-3). 1990. 4.95 (*1-56288-048-9*) Checkerboard.
Pollard, Rita, jt. auth. see Daniels, Lolee.
Pollen, Gerry, jt. auth. see Goodwin, Mary T.
Pollinger, Eileen. Building Christian Discipline. 96p. (Orig.). (gr. 8). 1986. pap. 6.99 (*0-87123-877-2*); tchr's. guide 7.99 (*0-87123-878-0*) Bethany Hse.
—Stacey. LC 87-71604. 176p. (Orig.). (gr. 9-12). 1987. pap. 3.99 (*0-87123-943-4*) Bethany Hse.
Pollock. Soccer for Juniors. 1980. 9.95 (*0-684-16487-6*, Scribner) Macmillan.
Pollock, Dean. Joseph: Chief of the Nez Perce. 5th ed. (Illus.). 64p. (gr. 5 up). 1990. pap. 7.95 (*0-8323-0482-4*) Binford Mort.
Pollock, Jean, jt. auth. see Pollock, Robert.
Pollock, Penny, retold by. The Turkey Girl: A Zuni Cinderella. Young, Ed, illus. LC 93-28947. 1995. 15. 95 (*0-316-71314-7*) Little.
Pollock, Robert & Pollock, Jean. Common Campground Critters of the West. (gr. 1-6). 1987. pap. 5.95 (*0-911797-77-7*) R Rinehart.
Pollock, Stephen. The Atlas of Endangered Animals. LC 92-20387. (Illus.). 64p. (gr. 6-9). 1993. 17.95 (*0-8160-2856-7*) Facts on File.
Pollock, Steve. The Atlas of Endangered Places. LC 92-20388. (Illus.). 64p. 1993. 17.95 (*0-8160-2857-5*) Facts on File.
—Dinosaurs. (Illus.). 48p. (gr. 7-9). 1992. 13.95 (*0-563-34753-8*, BBC-Parkwest); pap. 6.95 (*0-563-34607-8*, BBC-Parkwest) Parkwest Pubns.
—Wildlife Safari. (Illus.). 48p. (gr. 7-9). 1992. 13.95 (*0-563-34354-0*, BBC-Parkwest); pap. 6.95 (*0-563-34162-9*, BBC-Parkwest) Parkwest Pubns.
Pollotta, Nick & Foglio, Phil. Illegal Aliens. Foglio, Phil, illus. LC 88-51727. 320p. (Orig.). 1989. pap. 3.95 (*0-88038-715-7*) TSR Inc.
Polo, Marco. Travels of Marco Polo. (gr. 9 up). 1968. pap. 1.50 (*0-8049-0186-4*, CL-186) Airmont.
Polon, Linda. Paragraph Production. 48p. (gr. 4-6). 1981. 5.95 (*0-88160-039-3*, LW 224) Learning Wks.
—Stir up a Story. 48p. (gr. 3-6). 1981. 5.95 (*0-88160-037-7*, LW 222) Learning Wks.
Polonsky, Daniel L. The Letter Bandits. (Illus.). 72p. (gr. 3 up). 1991. 12.95 (*0-931474-41-8*) TBW Bks.
Polonsky, Stanford I. The Truth about Tubby & Slim. LC 92-60812. 50p. (gr. k-3). 1993. 7.95 (*1-55523-543-3*) Winston-Derek.
Polsky, Carol, ed. see Los Angeles Children's Museum Staff.
Polsky, Milton, et al. The King of Escapes. (Orig.). (gr. 3-12). 1985. pap. 6.00 play script (*0-88734-510-7*) Players Pr.
Poltarnees, Welleran. Amy & Nathaniel. Cline, Paul, illus. 32p. 1991. 11.95 (*0-88138-118-7*, Green Tiger) S&S Trade.
—Children from the Golden Age. (Illus.). 128p. 1991. pap. 14.95 (*0-88138-094-6*, Green Tiger) S&S Trade.
Poltarnees, Welleran, et al, eds. A. B. C. of Fashionable Animals. Neilson, Harry B., et al, illus. Rep. 4p. 1991. 12. 95 (*0-88138-122-5*, Green Tiger) S&S Trade.
Poltarness, Weller. Martin & Tommy. Krestjanoff, illus. LC 93-13609. (gr. 4 up). 1994. 14.00 (*0-671-88067-5*, Green Tiger Pr) S&S Trade.

Polushkin, Maria. Kitten in Trouble. Levin, Betsy, illus. LC 85-5753. 32p. (ps-k). 1988. RSBE 13.95 (*0-02-774740-9*, Bradbury Pr) Macmillan Child Grp.
—Mother, Mother, I Want Another. Dawson, Diane, illus. 32p. (ps-1). 1988. pap. 5.99 (*0-517-55947-1*) Crown Bks Yng Read.
—Who Said Meow? Weiss, Ellen, illus. LC 87-28073. 32p. (ps). 1988. RSBE 13.95 (*0-02-774770-0*, Bradbury Pr) Macmillan Child Grp.
Polyzoides, G. Ancient Greek History. (GRE., Illus.). (gr. 4-6). 4.00 (*0-686-79636-5*) Divry.
—History of Byzantine & Modern Greece. (GRE., Illus.). (gr. 4-6). 4.00 (*0-686-79635-7*) Divry.
—Stories from the Old Testament. (GRE., Illus.). 71p. (gr. 5 up). 4.00 (*0-686-80434-1*) Divry.
Pomaska, Anna. Cut & Assemble a Peter Rabbit. 1984. pap. 4.95 (*0-486-24713-9*) Dover.
—Easy Mazes Activity Book. (Illus.). (ps up). 1988. pap. 1.00 (*0-486-25531-X*) Dover.
—The Little Alphabet Follow-the-Dots Book. (ps up). 1988. pap. 1.00 (*0-486-25623-5*) Dover.
—The Little Christmas Activity Book. (ps up). 1988. pap. 1.00 (*0-486-25679-0*) Dover.
—The Little Dinosaur Activity Book. (ps up). 1987. pap. 1.00 (*0-486-25344-9*) Dover.
—The Little Follow the Dots Book. 1986. pap. 1.00 (*0-486-25157-8*) Dover.
—The Little Seashore Activity Book. (ps up). 1988. pap. 1.00 (*0-486-25608-1*) Dover.
—Peter Rabbit Bookmarks. (ps up). 1989. pap. 3.50 (*0-486-25444-5*) Dover.
Pomerantz, Barbara. Bubby, Me & Memories. Lurie, Leon, photos by. LC 83-191743. (Illus.). 32p. (ps up). 1983. 7.95 (*0-8074-0253-2*, 104025) UAHC.
—Who Will Lead Kiddush? Ruff, Donna, illus. 32p. (Orig.). (gr. 1-3). 1985. pap. 6.00 (*0-8074-0306-7*, 102000) UAHC.
Pomerantz, Charlotte. The Chalk Doll. Lessac, Frane, illus. LC 88-872. 32p. (gr. k-3). 1989. 15.00 (*0-397-32318-2*, Lipp Jr Bks); PLB 14.89 (*0-397-32319-0*) HarpC Child Bks.
—Chalk Doll. Lessac, Frane, illus. LC 88-872. 32p. (ps-3). 1993. pap. 4.95 (*0-06-443333-1*, Trophy) HarpC Child Bks.
—Flap Your Wings & Try. LC 88-18766. (Illus.). 24p. (ps up). 1989. 12.95 (*0-688-08019-7*); PLB 12.88 (*0-688-08020-0*) Greenwillow.
—The Half-Birthday Party. DeSalvo-Ryan, DyAnne, illus. LC 84-4963. 48p. (gr. 1-4). 1984. 13.95 (*0-89919-273-4*, Clarion Bks) HM.
—Halfway to Your House. Vincent, Gabrielle, illus. LC 92-30083. 32p. (ps up). 1993. 14.00 (*0-688-11804-6*); PLB 13.93 (*0-688-11805-4*) Greenwillow.
—Here Comes Henny. Parker, Nancy W., illus. LC 93-5480. 1994. write for info. (*0-688-12355-4*); PLB write for info. (*0-688-12356-2*) Greenwillow.
—How Many Trucks Can a Tow Truck Tow. Alley, R. W., illus. LC 89-3657. 24p. (ps-k). 1987. PLB 5.99 (*0-394-98775-6*); pap. 6.00 (*0-394-88775-1*) Random Bks Yng Read.
—If I Had a Paka. reissued ed. LC 81-6624. (Illus.). 32p. (ps). 1993. 14.00 (*0-688-11900-X*); PLB 13.93 (*0-688-11901-8*) Greenwillow.
—If I Had a Paka: Poems in Eleven Languages. Tafuri, Nancy, illus. 32p. 1982. 11.75 (*0-688-00836-4*); PLB 11.88 (*0-688-00837-2*) Greenwillow.
—If I Had a Paka: Poems in Eleven Languages. Tafuri, Nancy & Rice, Eve, illus. LC 92-33088. 32p. (ps up). 1993. pap. 4.95 (*0-688-12510-7*, Mulberry) Morrow.
—One Duck, Another Duck. Aruego, Jose & Dewey, Ariane, illus. LC 83-20767. 24p. (ps-1). 1984. 10.25 (*0-688-03744-5*); PLB 13.93 (*0-688-03745-3*) Greenwillow.
—The Outside Dog. Plecas, Jennifer, illus. LC 91-6351. 64p. (gr. k-3). 1993. 14.00 (*0-06-024782-7*); PLB 13. 89 (*0-06-024783-5*) HarpC Child Bks.
—The Piggy in the Puddle. Marshall, James, illus. LC 73-6047. 32p. (ps-1). 1974. RSBE 14.95 (*0-02-774900-2*, Macmillan Child Bk) Macmillan Child Grp.
—The Piggy in the Puddle. Marshall, James, illus. LC 88-8368. 32p. (ps-1). 1989. pap. 3.95 (*0-689-71293-6*, Aladdin) Macmillan Child Grp.
—Serena Katz. Alley, R. W., illus. LC 90-48672. 32p. (gr. k-3). 1992. RSBE 13.95 (*0-02-774901-0*, Macmillan Child Bk) Macmillan Child Grp.
—The Tamarindo Puppy. reissued ed. Barton, Byron, illus. LC 79-16584. 32p. (ps up). 1993. 14.00 (*0-688-11902-6*); PLB 13.93 (*0-688-11903-4*) Greenwillow.
—The Tamarindo Puppy & Other Poems. Barton, Byron, illus. 32p. (ps). 1993. pap. 4.95 (*0-688-11514-4*, Mulberry) Morrow.
—Timothy Tall Feather. Stock, Catherine, illus. LC 85-24819. 32p. (gr. k-3). 1986. 11.75 (*0-688-04246-5*); PLB 11.88 (*0-688-04247-3*) Greenwillow.
—Where's the Bear? Barton, Byron, illus. LC 83-1697. 32p. (ps-1). 1984. 15.00 (*0-688-01752-5*); PLB 14.93 (*0-688-01753-3*) Greenwillow.
—Where's the Bear. Barton, Byron, illus. LC 83-1697. 32p. (ps-3). 1991. pap. 3.95 (*0-688-10999-3*, Mulberry) Morrow.
—Whiff, Sniff, Nibble, & Chew: The Gingerbread Boy Retold. Incisa, Monica, illus. LC 83-14179. 24p. (gr. k-3). 1984. PLB 8.59 (*0-688-02552-8*) Greenwillow.
Pomeray, J. K. Ireland. (Illus.). 128p. (gr. 5 up). 1988. lib. bdg. 14.95x (*1-55546-794-6*) Chelsea Hse.

Pomeroy, Johanna P. Content Area Reading Skills Electricity & Magnetism. (Illus.). (gr. 4). 1987. pap. text ed. 3.25 (0-89525-859-5) Ed Activities.
—Content Area Reading Skills Geology: Detecting Sequence. (Illus.). (gr. 4). 1987. pap. text ed. 3.25 (1-55737-085-0) Ed Activities.
—Content Area Reading Skills Light: Main Idea. (Illus.). (gr. 3). 1989. pap. text ed. 3.25 (1-55737-687-5) Ed Activities.
—Content Area Reading Skills Machines: Detecting Sequence. (Illus.). (gr. 3). 1989. pap. text ed. 3.25 (1-55737-690-5) Ed Activities.
—Content Area Reading Skills Matter: Locating Details. (Illus.). (gr. 4). 1988. pap. text ed. 3.25 (1-55737-086-9) Ed Activities.
—Content Area Reading Skills Mechanics: Cause & Effect. (Illus.). (gr. 4). 1988. pap. text ed. 3.25 (1-55737-088-5) Ed Activities.
—Content Area Reading Skills Oceans: Main Idea. (Illus.). (gr. 4). 1987. pap. text ed. 3.25 (0-89525-857-9) Ed Activities.
—Content Area Reading Skills Our Earth: Locating Details. (Illus.). (gr. 3). 1989. pap. text ed. 3.25 (1-55737-688-3) Ed Activities.
—Content Area Reading skills Reproduction & Heredity: Main Idea. (Illus.). (gr. 4). 1988. pap. text ed. 3.25 (1-55737-087-7) Ed Activities.
—Content Area Reading Skills Solar System: Locating Details. (Illus.). (gr. 4). 1987. pap. text ed. 3.25 (0-89525-858-7) Ed Activities.
—Content Area Reading Skills Sound & Hearing: Detecting Sequence. (Illus.). (gr. 4). 1987. pap. text ed. 3.25 (0-89525-860-9) Ed Activities.
—Content Area Reading Skills Weather: Cause & Effect. (Illus.). (gr. 3). 1989. pap. text ed. 3.25 (1-55737-689-1) Ed Activities.
Pomeroy, Wardell B. Boys & Sex. rev. ed. 176p. (Orig.). (gr. 7 up). 1981. pap. 3.25 (0-440-90753-5, LE) Dell.
—Boys & Sex. 3rd ed. 1991. pap. 3.95 (0-440-20811-4) Dell.
—Girls & Sex. rev. ed. 176p. (Orig.). (gr. 7 up). 1981. pap. 3.25 (0-440-92904-0, LE) Dell.
—Girls & Sex. 3rd ed. 1991. pap. 3.95 (0-440-20812-2) Dell.
Ponce, Blanca N. de see De Ponce, Blanca N.
Ponce, Omar. Educate para una Mejor Condicion Fisica: Guia Basica para el Desarrollo de un Programa de Eficiencia Fisica. Figueroa, Ivelisse, illus. (SPA.). 75p. (Orig.). 1986. write for info. B Ponce.
Poncela, Enrique J. Noche de Primavera sin Sueno: Comedia Humoristica en Tres Actos. Lacosta, Francisco C., ed. LC 67-25113. (SPA.). (gr. 9 up). 1967. pap. text ed. 6.95x (0-89197-320-6) Irvington.
Pond, Joyce. Lost in the Corn. Koehn, Sara, illus. 31p. (Orig.). (gr. 6). 1992. pap. 6.95 (0-9635877-0-6) JBP Press.
Pond, Mildred M. Mother Teresa. (Illus.). 80p. (gr. 3-5). 1992. lib. bdg. 12.95 (0-7910-1755-9) Chelsea Hse.
Pondsmith, Michael. Cyberpunk. Liu, Sam, et al, illus. Fisk, Colin, contrib. by. 98p. (gr. 10-12). 1988. game bk. 10.00 (0-937279-05-6, CP 3001) R Talsorian.
—Mekton II. 2nd ed. Bryant, Linda, et al, eds. Dunn, Benn, et al, illus. 93p. (gr. 7-12). 1987. game bk. 12.00 (0-937279-04-8, MK 1002) R Talsorian.
Pontiero, Giovanni, tr. see Nunes, Lygia B.
Pool, James M. Among These Hills: A Child's History of Harrison County. Crowder, Beth, illus. 240p. 1985. 12.95 (0-9615566-0-9) Clarksburg-Harrison Bicent.
Poole, Gray, jt. auth. see Poole, Lynn.
Poole, Josephine, ed. see Grimm, Jacob & Grimm, Wilhelm K.
Poole, Lynn & Poole, Gray. Danger, Iceberg Ahead. (Illus.). (gr. 1-4). 1961. lib. bdg. 4.39 (0-394-90121-5) Random Bks Yng Read.
—Weird & Wonderful Ants. Petersen, R. F., illus. (gr. 5 up). 1961. 8.95 (0-8392-3041-9) Astor-Honor.
Poole, Susan D. Chester A. Arthur: The President Who Reformed. LC 76-40379. 112p. (gr. 7-9). 1977. text ed. 8.95 (0-87881-056-0, Pub. by M. Bloomfield & Co.) Mojave Bks.
Pooley, Sarah. A Night of Lullabies. (Illus.). 64p. (ps-1). 1992. 16.95 (0-370-31491-3, Pub. by Bodley Head UK) Trafalgar.
Pooley, Sarah, compiled by. & illus. It's Raining, It's Pouring: A Book for Rainy Days. LC 92-16859. (ps up). 1993. 18.00 (0-688-11803-8) Greenwillow.
Poore, Clara. Weaving with Wheat: A Manual for Beginning Wheat Weavers, No. 1. 2nd ed. Poore, Clara, illus. 16p. (gr. 2-6). 1984. pap. 4.00 (0-9613993-1-7) Wheat'N Flower.
—Weaving with Wheat: A Manual for Beginning Wheat Weavers, No. 1. 3rd ed. (Illus.). 16p. (gr. 6-12). 1987. pap. 4.00 (0-318-50006-X) Wheat'N Flower.
Poore, Luz, ed. see Thomas, Mary A.
Poorten, Carolyn T. Can We See God. LC 91-68355. 42p. (gr. k-3). 1992. 6.95 (1-55523-507-7) Winston-Derek.
Pootler & Pillion. Take a Ride. (Illus.). 32p. (ps-k). 1994. pap. 8.95 (0-9638479-3-7) Magnolia MA.
Pope, Elizabeth M. The Perilous Gard. Cuffari, Richard, illus. LC 73-21648. 272p. (gr. 6 up). 1974. 16.95 (0-395-18512-2) HM.
—The Perilous Gard. Cuffari, Richard, illus. 288p. (gr. 7 up). 1992. pap. 4.99 (0-14-034912-X) Puffin Bks.
—The Sherwood Ring. (gr. 6 up). 19.00 (0-8446-6416-2) Peter Smith.

—The Sherwood Ring. Ness, Evaline, illus. 272p. (gr. 7 up). 1992. pap. 3.99 (0-14-034911-1, Puffin) Puffin Bks.
Pope, Gregory. Camelot World: Hot Machines. 128p. (Orig.). 1990. pap. 2.95 (0-380-76039-8, Camelot) Avon.
Pope, Joyce. Animal Babies. Aloof, Andrew, illus. LC 91-45381. 32p. (gr. 3-6). 1993. PLB 11.59 (0-8167-2773-2); pap. text ed. 3.95 (0-8167-2774-0) Troll Assocs. Postponed.
—Animal Homes. Field, James, illus. LC 91-45380. 32p. (gr. 3-6). 1993. PLB 11.59 (0-8167-2775-9); pap. text ed. 3.95 (0-8167-2776-7) Troll Assocs. Postponed.
—Animal Journeys. Weare, Phil, illus. LC 91-45379. 32p. (gr. 3-6). 1993. PLB 11.59 (0-8167-2777-5); pap. text ed. 3.95 (0-8167-2778-3) Troll Assocs. Postponed.
—Do Animals Dream? Children's Questions about Animals Most Often Asked of the Natural History Museum. LC 86-40029. (Illus.). 96p. 1986. pap. 16.95 (0-670-81233-1) Viking Child Bks.
—The Duck. (Illus.). 24p. (gr. 3-6). 1991. 8.95 (0-237-60249-0, Pub. by Evans Bros Ltd) Trafalgar.
—Fossil Detective. Forsey, Chris, illus. LC 91-45170. 32p. (gr. 3-6). 1993. PLB 11.59 (0-8167-2781-3); pap. text ed. 3.95 (0-8167-2782-1) Troll Assocs. Postponed.
—Horses. (Illus.). 32p. (gr. 4-6). 1991. 13.95 (0-237-60173-7, Pub. by Evans Bros Ltd) Trafalgar.
—Kenneth Lilly's Animals. Lilly, Kenneth, illus. LC 87-31147. 96p. (gr. 3 up). 1988. 16.95 (0-688-07696-3) Lothrop.
—Life in the Dark. LC 91-18646. (Illus.). 48p. (gr. 4-8). 1992. PLB 19.92 (0-8114-3150-9); pap. 4.95 (0-8114-6252-8) Raintree Steck-V.
—Living Fossils. Stillwell, Stella & Ward, Helen, illus. LC 91-13998. 48p. (gr. 4-8). 1992. PLB 19.92 (0-8114-3151-7); pap. 4.95 (0-8114-6256-0) Raintree Steck-V.
—Mistaken Identity. LC 91-17136. (Illus.). 48p. (gr. 4-8). 1992. PLB 19.92 (0-8114-3152-5); pap. 4.95 (0-8114-6253-6) Raintree Steck-V.
—Night Creatures. Tamblin, Treave, illus. LC 91-45171. 32p. (gr. 3-6). 1993. PLB 11.59 (0-8167-2783-X); pap. text ed. 3.95 (0-8167-2784-8) Troll Assocs. Postponed.
—Plant Partnerships. LC 90-32395. (Illus.). 62p. (gr. 6 up). 1991. PLB 15.95 (0-8160-2422-7) Facts on File.
—Plants & Flowers. Pantry, Stuart, illus. LC 91-45378. 32p. (gr. 3-6). 1993. PLB 11.59 (0-8167-2779-1); pap. text ed. 3.95 (0-8167-2780-5) Troll Assocs. Postponed.
—Plants of the Tropics. 64p. 1990. 15.95x (0-8160-2423-5) Facts on File.
—Practical Plants. 64p. 1990. 15.95x (0-8160-2424-3) Facts on File.
—Reptiles. (Illus.). 32p. (gr. 4-6). 1991. 13.95 (0-237-60166-4, Pub. by Evans Bros Ltd) Trafalgar.
—Seashores. Weare, Phil, illus. LC 89-20318. 32p. (gr. 3-6). 1990. PLB 11.59 (0-8167-1965-9); pap. text ed. 3.95 (0-8167-1966-7) Troll Assocs.
—The Starling. (Illus.). 24p. (gr. 3-6). 1991. 8.95 (0-237-60251-2, Pub. by Evans Bros Ltd) Trafalgar.
—Taking Care of Your Cat. 1990. pap. 3.95 (0-531-15165-4) Watts.
—Taking Care of Your Dog. LC 85-51604. (Illus.). 32p. (gr. 4-8). 1990. PLB 11.40 (0-531-10160-6) Watts.
—Taking Care of Your Fish. Franklin Watts Ltd., ed. (Illus.). 32p. (gr. 7-9). 1990. Watts.
—Taking Care of Your Gerbil. 1990. pap. 3.95 (0-531-15168-9) Watts.
—Taking Care of Your Guinea Pig. (Illus.). 32p. (gr. 4-9). 1990. pap. 3.95 (0-531-15169-7) Watts.
—Two Lives. Stilwell, Stella & Ward, Helen, illus. LC 91-17460. 48p. (gr. 4-8). 1992. PLB 19.92 (0-8114-3153-3); pap. 4.95 (0-8114-6257-9) Raintree Steck-V.
Pope, Joyce, jt. auth. see Whitfield, Philip.
Pope, Lillie, et al. Special Needs: Special Answers. Fargo, Jerry, illus. (gr. k-6). 1979. 19.95 (0-87594-181-8) Book-Lab.
Pope, Liston. Millhands & Preachers: A Study of Gastonia. Peterson, Richard A. & Demerath, N. J., 3rdintro. by. (Illus.). 1965. pap. 18.00x (0-300-00182-7) Yale U Pr.
Pope, Saxton. Hunting with the Bow & Arrow. (Illus.). 257p. (gr. 10 up). 1993. Repr. of 1925 ed. 39.95 (1-56416-098-X) Derrydale Pr.
—A Study of Bows & Arrows. St. Charles, Glenn, frwd. by. (Illus.). 160p. (gr. 10 up). 1992. Repr. 39.95 (1-56416-088-2) Derrydale Pr.
Popescu, Julian. Bulgaria. (Illus.). 96p. (gr. 5 up). 1988. 14.95 (1-55546-177-8) Chelsea Hse.
—Hungary. (Illus.). 96p. (gr. 5 up). 1988. 14.95 (0-222-00945-4) Chelsea Hse.
Popkin, Arlene. My April Fool Book. (Illus.). (ps-1). 1974. PLB 6.89x (0-914844-04-0) J Alden.
Popkin, Michael H. Free the Horses: Storybook & Songbook. Greathead, Susan D. & Sardinas-Wyssling, Karen, eds. Bork, Beatrice, illus. 80p. (gr. 1-3). 1991. pap. 6.95 (0-9618020-7-3) Active Parenting.
Poploff, Michelle. Busy O'Brien & the Caterpillar Punch Bunch. (Illus.). 119p. (gr. 2-5). 1992. 13.95 (0-8027-8151-9) Walker & Co.
—Busy O'Brien & the Great Bubble Gum Blowout. Carter, Abby, illus. 96p. (gr. 2-5). 1990. 12.95 (0-8027-6983-7); lib. bdg. 13.85 (0-8027-6984-5) Walker & Co.
—Busy O'Brien & the Great Bubblegum Blowout. MacDonald, Pat, ed. Carter, Abby, illus. 96p. 1992. pap. 2.99 (0-671-74082-2, Minstrel Bks) PB.

Popov, Nicolai. Stravinsky. Gallaz, Christophe, illus. LC 92-40383. 1993. 14.95 (0-88682-605-5) Creative Ed.
Poppe, Carol A. & Van Matre, Nancy A. K-3 Science Activities Kit. 256p. (gr. k-3). 1988. pap. text ed. 24.95x (0-87628-477-2) Ctr Appl Res.
Poppel, George. Planet of Trash. Moyer, Barry S., illus. 32p. (ps-3). 1987. 9.95 (0-915765-42-X, Pub. by Panda Monium Bks.) Natl Pr Bks.
Poppel, Hans & Bodden, Ilona. When the Moon Shines Brightly on the House. 24p. (ps). 1985. 5.95 (0-8120-5669-8) Barron.
Popperwell, Jeral. Science Crossword Puzzles. (Illus.). 48p. (gr. 2-5). 1988. Dinosaurs. pap. 2.95 (0-8431-2290-0); Human Body. pap. 2.95 (0-8431-2291-9); Wild Animals. pap. 2.95 (0-8431-2293-5); Space. pap. 2.95 (0-8431-2292-7) Price Stern.
Popson, Martha. That We Might Have Life. LC 80-2080. 128p. (gr. 6 up). 1981. pap. 2.75 (0-385-17438-1, Im) Doubleday.
Porazinska, Janina. The Enchanted Book: A Tale from Krakow. Smith, Bozena, tr. Brett, Jan, photos by. LC 86-22918. 32p. (gr. k-4). 1987. 13.95 (0-15-225950-3) HarBrace.
Porch, Adelle. Your First Ferret. (Illus.). 34p. (Orig.). 1991. pap. 1.95 (0-86622-115-8, YF-105) TFH Pubns.
Porett, Jane. When I Was Little Like You. Lipczenko, Susan D., illus. LC 93-13974. 1993. 12.95 (0-87868-530-8) Child Welfare.
Porizkova, Paulina & Russell, Joanne. The Adventures of Ralphie the Roach. (Illus.). 48p. (gr. k-4). 1992. 15.00 (0-385-42402-7) Doubleday.
Porritt, Jonathon & Nadler, Ellis. Captain Eco & the Fate of the Earth. LC 91-60142. (Illus.). 48p. (gr. 3 up). 1991. 13.95 (1-879431-12-2); PLB 14.99 (1-879431-27-0) Dorling Kindersley.
Portch, Elizabeth, tr. see Jansson, Tove.
Porte, Barbara A. Fat Fanny, Beanpole Bertha, & the Boys. Chambliss, Maxie, illus. LC 90-7686. 112p. (gr. 3-5). 1991. 14.95 (0-531-05928-6); PLB 14.99 (0-531-08528-7) Orchard Bks Watts.
—Harry Gets an Uncle. Abolafia, Yossi, illus. LC 90-39562. 48p. (gr. k up). 1991. 13.95 (0-688-09389-2); PLB 13.88 (0-688-09390-6) Greenwillow.
—Harry in Trouble. Abolafia, Yossi, illus. LC 87-21253. 48p. (gr. 1 up). 1989. 15.00 (0-688-07633-5); PLB 14.93 (0-688-07722-6) Greenwillow.
—Harry in Trouble. 1990. pap. 2.95 (0-440-40370-7, YB) Dell.
—Harry's Birthday. Abolafia, Yossi, illus. LC 93-18189. 48p. (gr. k up). 1994. write for info. (0-688-12142-X); PLB write for info. (0-688-12143-8) Greenwillow.
—Harry's Dog. Abolafia, Yossi, illus. LC 84-14129. 48p. (gr. 1-3). 1983. 13.95 (0-688-02555-2); PLB 13.88 (0-688-02556-0) Greenwillow.
—Harry's Mom. Abolafia, Yossi, illus. LC 84-25955. 48p. (gr. 1-4). 1985. 10.25 (0-688-04817-X); lib. bdg. 10.88 (0-688-04818-8) Greenwillow.
—Harry's Mom. 1990. pap. 2.95 (0-440-40362-6, YB) Dell.
—Harry's Visit. (Orig.). (gr. k-6). 1990. pap. 2.95 (0-440-40331-6, YB) Dell.
—I Only Made up the Roses. LC 86-18307. 128p. (gr. 7 up). 1987. reinforced 12.95 (0-688-05216-9) Greenwillow.
—Jesse's Ghost & Other Stories. LC 83-1451. 128p. (gr. 7 up). 1983. reinforced 10.25 (0-688-02301-0) Greenwillow.
—Leave That Cricket Be, Alan Lee. Ruff, Donna, illus. LC 92-29401. 32p. (ps up). 1993. 14.00 (0-688-11793-7); PLB 13.93 (0-688-11794-5) Greenwillow.
—Ruthann & Her Pig. LC 88-31452. (Illus.). 96p. (gr. 2-5). 1989. 14.95 (0-531-05825-5); PLB 14.99 (0-531-08425-6) Orchard Bks Watts.
—The Take-Along Dog. McCully, Emily A., illus. LC 88-18775. 40p. (gr. 1 up). 1989. 11.95 (0-688-08053-7); PLB 11.88 (0-688-08054-5) Greenwillow.
—Taxicab Tales. Abolafia, Yossi, illus. LC 90-24609. 56p. 1992. 13.00 (0-688-09908-4) Greenwillow.
—A Turkey Drive & Other Tales. Abolafia, Yossi, illus. LC 91-48032. 64p. (gr. k up). 1993. 14.00 (0-688-11336-2) Greenwillow.
—When Aunt Lucy Rode A Mule & Other Stories. Chambliss, Maxie, illus. LC 93-4874. 1994. write for info. (0-531-06816-1); PLB write for info. (0-531-08666-6) Orchard Bks Watts.
—When Grandma Almost Fell off the Mountain & Other Stories. Chambliss, Maxie, illus. LC 91-41174. 32p. (ps-2). 1993. 14.95 (0-531-05965-0); PLB 14.99 (0-531-08565-1) Orchard Bks Watts.
Porter, A. P. Greg LeMond: Premier Cyclist. (Illus.). 56p. (gr. 4-9). 1990. PLB 13.50 (0-8225-0476-6) Lerner Pubns.
—Greg Lemond: Premier Cyclist. LC 89-13700. (gr. 4-7). 1991. pap. 4.95 (0-8225-9584-2) Lerner Pubns.
—Jump at de Sun: The Story of Zora Neale Hurston. 88p. (gr. 3-6). 1992. PLB 17.50 (0-87614-667-1) Carolrhoda Bks.
—Jump at de Sun: The Story of Zora Neale Hurston. (gr. 4-7). 1992. pap. 6.95 (0-87614-546-2) Carolrhoda Bks.
—Kwanzaa. Van Buren, Bobby, illus. 48p. (gr. k-4). 1991. PLB 14.95 (0-87614-668-X); pap. 5.95 (0-87614-545-4) Carolrhoda Bks.
—Minnesota. Lerner Geography Department Staff, ed. (Illus.). 72p. (gr. 4-7). 1992. PLB 17.50 (0-8225-2718-9) Lerner Pubns.

—Nebraska. (Illus.). 72p. (gr. 3-6). 1991. PLB 17.50 (0-8225-2708-1) Lerner Pubns.
—Zina Garrison. 56p. (gr. 4-9). 1991. PLB 13.50 (0-8225-0499-5) Lerner Pubns.
—Zina Garrison: Ace. (Illus.). 64p. (gr. 4-9). 1992. pap. 3.95 (0-8225-9596-6) Lerner Pubns.
Porter, Angela. The Story of Tommy Teacup & Family. (ps-6). 1993. 6.95 (0-8062-4396-1) Carlton.
Porter, Barbara. All Kinds of Answers. Marsh, Dilleen, illus. LC 92-6976. 29p. (gr. 1-3). 1992. 11.95 (0-87579-538-2) Deseret Bk.
Porter, Barbara J. Grandpa & Me & the Wishing Star. Marsh, Dilleen, illus. LC 90-81831. 32p. (ps) 1990. 10.95 (0-87579-269-3) Deseret Bk.
Porter, Bruce. Bill & the Burning Bush. Porter, Bruce, illus. 40p. (Orig.). (gr. up). 1987. pap. 3.95 (0-939925-12-5) R C Law & Co.
—Butch & the Bad Baloney. Porter, Bruce, illus. 40p. (Orig.). (gr. 1 up). 1987. pap. 3.95 (0-939925-15-X) R C Law & Co.
—Jonah Gets the Jitters. Porter, Bruce, illus. 40p. (Orig.). (gr. 3 up). 1987. pap. 3.95 (0-939925-14-1) R C Law & Co.
—The Parable of Pa Diggle's Son. Porter, Bruce, illus. 40p. (Orig.). (gr. 3 up). 1987. pap. 3.95 (0-939925-11-7) R C Law & Co.
—Samuel & the Strange Sound. Porter, Bruce, illus. 40p. (Orig.). (gr. 3 up). 1987. pap. 3.95 (0-939925-13-3) R C Law & Co.
—Squirt & the Super Soldier. Porter, Bruce, illus. 40p. (Orig.). (gr. 3 up). 1987. pap. 3.95 (0-939925-16-8) R C Law & Co.
Porter, Cathy. Women in Revolutionary Russia. (Illus.). 48p. (gr. 7-12). 1987. pap. 6.95 (0-521-31969-2) Cambridge U Pr.
Porter, Connie. Addy Learns a Lesson. Rosales, Melodye, illus. 70p. (Orig.). (gr. 2-5). 1993. PLB 12.95 (1-56247-078-7); pap. 5.95 (1-56247-077-9) Pleasant Co.
—Meet Addy. Rosales, Melodye, illus. 69p. (Orig.). (gr. 2-5). 1993. PLB 12.95 (1-56247-076-0); pap. 5.95 (1-56247-075-2) Pleasant Co.
Porter, Dorothy. The Witch Number. 1993. pap. 10.95 (0-7022-2460-X, Pub. by Univ Queensland Pr AT) Intl Spec Bk.
Porter, Eleanor. Pollyanna. (Illus.). (gr. k-9). 1987. pap. 2.95 (0-590-44769-6) Scholastic Inc.
Porter, Eleanor H. Pollyanna. (Orig.). (gr. k-6). 1987. pap. 4.95 (0-440-45985-0, Pub. by Yearling Classics) Dell.
—Pollyanna. 1988. pap. 2.25 (0-14-035023-3, Puffin) Puffin Bks.
—Pollyanna Grows Up. 308p. (gr. 4 up). 1980. Repr. of 1915 ed. lib. bdg. 20.95 (0-89968-193-X) Lightyear.
—Pollyanna Grows Up. 272p. (gr. 5 up). 1989. pap. 2.99 (0-14-035024-1, Puffin) Puffin Bks.
Porter, Frank W. The Bureau of Indian Affairs. Schlesinger, Arthur M., Jr., intro. by. (Illus.). 112p. (gr. 5 up). 1988. lib. bdg. 14.95 (0-87754-828-5) Chelsea Hse.
—The Coast Salish Peoples. (Illus.). 104p. (gr. 5 up). 1989. 17.95 (1-55546-701-6) Chelsea Hse.
Porter, Gene S. Freckles. George, Jean C., afterword by. (gr. 5 up). 1988. pap. 4.95 (0-317-68987-8, Pub. by Yearling Classics) Dell.
—Freckles. 272p. (gr. 5 up). 1992. pap. 2.99 (0-14-035144-2) Puffin Bks.
—A Girl of the Limberlost. (Orig.). (gr. 3-7). 1986. pap. 4.95 (0-440-43090-9, Pub. by Yearling Classics) Dell.
—Girl of the Limberlost. (Illus.). 496p. 1992. 8.99 (0-517-07235-1, Pub. by Gramercy) Outlet Bk Co.
—A Girl of the Limberlost. 432p. (gr. 5 up). 1992. pap. 3.99 (0-14-035143-4) Puffin Bks.
Porter, Jane. The Scottish Chiefs. reissued ed. Wyeth, N. C., illus. LC 91-8521. 528p. 1991. SBE 29.95 (0-684-19340-X, Scribners Young Read); deluxe ed. 75.00 limited ed. (0-684-19339-6, Scribners Young Read) Macmillan Child Grp.
Porter, John D., Jr., jt. auth. see Veazey, Steve.
Porter, Keith. Discovering Butterflies & Moths. LC 85-73664. (Illus.). 48p. (gr. 4-9). 1986. PLB 12.40 (0-531-18055-7, Pub. by Bookwright Pr) Watts.
—Discovering Butterflies & Moths. (Illus.). 48p. (gr. 2 up). 1990. pap. 4.95 (0-531-18364-5, Pub. by Bookwright Pr) Watts.
—How Animals Behave. (Illus.). 48p. (gr. 1-4). 1987. 12.95x (0-8160-1785-9) Facts on File.
—Looking at Animals. (Illus.). 48p. (gr. 1-4). 1987. 12.95x (0-8160-1784-0) Facts on File.
Porter, Malcolm, illus. The Dillon Press Children's Atlas. 96p. (gr. 5 up). 1993. lib. bdg. 17.95 RSBE (0-87518-606-8, Dillon) Macmillan Child Grp.
Porter, Mark. Wow, What a Week! Halverson, Lydia, illus. 24p. (Orig.). (gr. 1-3). 1991. pap. text ed. 29.95 big bk. (1-56334-051-8); pap. text ed. 6.00 small bk. (1-56334-057-7) Hampton-Brown.
Porter, Mark & Aymerich, Angela F. The Three Pups. Billin-Frye, Paige, illus. 16p. (Orig.). (gr. 1-3). 1991. pap. text ed. 29.95 big bk. (1-56334-049-6); pap. text ed. 4.15 small bk. (1-56334-055-0) Hampton-Brown.
Porter, Patrick K. Awaken the Genius: Mind Technology for the 21st Century. De Shazo, Jerry, ed. Sylvia, Dean, illus. 200p. (Orig.). 1994. pap. 14.98 (0-9637611-8-8) Pure Light.
Porter, Steven. The Prairie Man. LC 89-92532. 62p. (Orig.). 1990. pap. text ed. 6.00 (0-9625372-0-9) Phantom Pubns.

Porter, Stratton. Freckless. (Orig.). 1988. pap. 4.95 (0-440-40050-3, Pub by Yearning Classics) Dell.
Porter, Sue. Little Wolf & the Giant. (ps-1). 1990. pap. 13.95 jacketed (0-671-70363-3, S&S BFYR) S&S Trade.
—Little Wolf & the Giant. LC 89-21886. (Illus.). 32p. (ps-6). 1993. pap. 7.95 (0-671-79853-7, S&S BYR) S&S Trade.
—My Little Rabbit Tale. LC 93-29765. 1994. 9.95 (1-56458-339-2) Dorling Kindersley.
Porter, Wes. Garden Book & Greenhouse. LC 89-40372. (Illus.). 64p. (Orig.). (gr. k-5). 1992. Packaged in greenhouse with seed packets & peat pellets. pap. 10.95 (0-89480-346-8, 1346) Workman Pub.
Porter, William S. The Best of O. Henry. abr. ed. Fago, John N., ed. Caravana, Anton, illus. (gr. 4-12). 1977. pap. 2.95 (0-88301-268-5) Pendulum Pr.
Porter-Chase, Mary. The Return of Sinta Claus: A Family Winter Solstice Tale. Walsh, Lloyd, illus. (Orig.). (gr. 3-12). 1991. pap. 6.00 (0-9630798-0-8) Samary Pr.
Porterfield, Kay M. Coping with an Alcoholic Parent. rev. ed. (gr. 7-12). 1990. 13.95 (0-8239-1143-8) Rosen Group.
Porter-Gaylord, Laurel. I Love My Daddy Because... Wolff, Ashley, illus. LC 90-2865. 24p. (ps). 1991. 5.95 (0-525-44624-9, DCB) Dutton Child Bks.
—I Love My Mommy Because... Wolff, Ashley, illus. LC 90-2792. 24p. (ps). 1991. 5.95 (0-525-44625-7, DCB) Dutton Child Bks.
Porter-Lane, Esther. St. George & the Dragon. (Orig.). (gr. 4 up). 1985. pap. 4.50 (0-87602-249-2) Anchorage.
Portis, Charles. True Grit. (RL 8). 1969. pap. 3.95 (0-451-16022-3, Sig) NAL-Dutton.
Portlock, Rob. Buster the Biker Sheep. Portlock, Rob, illus. 32p. (Orig.). (ps-2). 1993. pap. 4.99 (0-8308-1904-5, 1904) InterVarsity.
—My Dad Ran over a Frog. Portlock, Rob, illus. LC 92-11584. 32p. (Orig.). (ps-1). 1992. pap. 4.99 (0-8308-1901-0, 1901) InterVarsity.
—Noon on the Moon. Portlock, Rob, illus. 32p. (Orig.). (ps-2). 1993. pap. 4.99 (0-8308-1903-7, 1903) InterVarsity.
—Someone's Trying to Cut off My Head. Portlock, Rob, illus. LC 92-12483. 32p. (Orig.). (ps-1). 1992. pap. 4.99 (0-8308-1902-9, 1902) InterVarsity.
Portnoy, Mindy A. Mommy Never Went to Hebrew School. Haas, Shelly O., illus. LC 89-30874. 32p. (gr. k-5). 1989. pap. 4.95 (0-930494-97-0) Kar Ben.
Portugal, Jan. ABC Sillies. Portugal, Jan, illus. LC 83-10291. 56p. (Orig.). (ps-1). 1983. pap. 3.00 (0-937148-13-X) Wild Horses.
Posell, Elsa. Cats. LC 82-23484. (Illus.). 48p. (gr. k-4). 1983. PLB 15.27 (0-516-01671-7) Childrens.
—Deserts. LC 81-15548. (Illus.). 48p. (gr. k-4). 1982. PLB 15.27 (0-516-01613-X); pap. 4.95 (0-516-41613-8) Childrens.
—Dogs. LC 81-7742. (Illus.). 48p. (gr. k-4). 1981. PLB 15.27 (0-516-01614-8); pap. 4.95 (0-516-41614-6) Childrens.
—Elephants. LC 81-38470. (Illus.). 48p. (gr. k-4). 1982. PLB 15.27 (0-516-01621-0) Childrens.
—Homecoming. 230p. (gr. 7 up). 1987. 14.95 (0-15-235160-4, HB Juv Bks) HarBrace.
—Horses. LC 81-7741. (Illus.). 48p. (gr. k-4). 1981. PLB 15.27 (0-516-01623-7); pap. 4.95 (0-516-41623-5) Childrens.
—Whales & Other Sea Mammals. LC 82-4451. (gr. k-4). 1982. 15.27 (0-516-01663-6); pap. 4.95 (0-516-41663-4) Childrens.
Posell, Elsa Z. This Is an Orchestra. rev. ed. (Illus.). 96p. (gr. 2-5). 1973. 13.45 (0-395-17712-X) HM.
Posey, jt. auth. see Arnold.
Posey, Pam, illus. Thomas the Tank Engine - Colors. Awdry, W., contrib. by. (Illus.). 12p. (ps). 1993. bds. 2.29 (0-679-81646-1) Random Bks Yng Read.
—Thomas the Tank Engine: Coming & Going -- A Book of Opposites. Awdry, W., contrib. by. (Illus.). 14p. (ps). 1991. pap. 2.29 (0-679-81645-3) McKay.
Poskanzer, Susan. Riddles about Hannukah. Brook, Bonnie, ed. Gray, Rob, illus. 32p. (ps-3). 1990. 6.95 (0-671-70555-5); PLB 10.98 (0-671-70553-9) Silver Pr.
—Riddles about Passover. Gray, Rob, photos by. (Illus.). 32p. (ps-3). 1991. 6.95 (0-671-72725-7); PLB 10.98 (0-671-72724-9) Silver Pr.
Poskanzer, Susan C. Dairy Farmer. Ulrich, George, illus. LC 88-10040. 32p. (gr. k-3). 1989. PLB 10.89 (0-8167-1426-6); pap. text ed. 2.95 (0-8167-1427-4) Troll Assocs.
—The Great Soap-Bubble Ride. Fiammenghi, Gioia, illus. LC 85-14022. 48p. (Orig.). (gr. 1-3). 1986. PLB 10.59 (0-8167-0622-0); pap. text ed. 3.50 (0-8167-0623-9) Troll Assocs.
—Little Raccoon Who Could. Hall, Susan, illus. LC 85-14020. 48p. (Orig.). (gr. 1-3). 1986. PLB 10.59 (0-8167-0624-7); pap. text ed. 3.50 (0-8167-0625-5) Troll Assocs.
—Puppeteer. Paterson, Diane, illus. LC 88-10042. 32p. (gr. 1-3). 1989. PLB 10.89 (0-8167-1432-0); pap. text ed. 2.95 (0-8167-1433-9) Troll Assocs.
—Sanitation Worker. Eitzen, Allan, illus. LC 88-10044. 32p. (gr. k-3). 1989. PLB 10.89 (0-8167-1436-3); pap. text ed. 2.95 (0-8167-1437-1) Troll Assocs.

—The Superduper Collector. Harvey, Paul, illus. LC 85-14051. 48p. (Orig.). (gr. 1-3). 1986. PLB 10.59 (0-8167-0606-9); pap. text ed. 3.50 (0-8167-0607-7) Troll Assocs.
—A Surprise for Baby Blueberry Muffin. Sustendal, Pat, illus. 40p. (ps-3). 1984. cancelled 5.95 (0-910313-23-7) Parker Bros.
—What's It Like to Be a Chef. Pellaton, Karen E., illus. LC 89-34390. 32p. (gr. k-3). 1990. lib. bdg. 10.89 (0-8167-1797-4); pap. text ed. 2.95 (0-8167-1798-2) Troll Assocs.
—What's It Like to Be an Astronaut. Eitzen, Allan, illus. LC 89-34393. 32p. (gr. k-3). 1990. PLB 10.89 (0-8167-1793-1); pap. text ed. 2.95 (0-8167-1794-X) Troll Assocs.
Poskanzer, Susan C., retold by. Aesop's Fables. Bettoli, Delana, illus. 64p. (gr. 2 up). 1992. 15.95 (0-671-74116-0); lib. bdg. 16.98 (0-671-74117-9) Silver Pr.
Posner, Richard. Goodnight, Cinderella. LC 89-17091. 242p. 1989. 13.95 (0-87131-587-4) M Evans.
—Sweet Sixteen & Never Been Killed. MacDonald, Pat, ed. 256p. (Orig.). (gr. 5 up). 1993. pap. 3.50 (0-671-86506-4, Archway) PB.
Post, Beverly & Eads, Sandra. Logic, Anyone? One Hundred Sixty-Five Brain-Stretching Problems. (gr. 5-12). 1982. pap. 12.95 (0-8224-4326-0); wkbk. 5.95 (0-8224-4327-9) Fearon Teach Aids.
Post, Beverly, jt. auth. see Eads, Sandra.
Post, Elizabeth. Emily Post Talks with Teens about Manners & Etiquette. 1991. pap. 9.00 (0-06-273163-7, Harp PBks) HarpC.
Post, Libby, ed. Through the Eyes of Children: Liberty & Justice for All. Wachtter, Sol, intros. by. (Illus.). 48p. (Orig.). 1989. pap. write for info. NY State Alliance.
Postell, Alice E. Where Did the Reindeer Come From? Alaska Experience the First Fifty Years. York, Susan P., ed. DeArmond, Robert N., frwd. by. LC 90-146. (Illus.). 144p. (gr. 9 up). 1990. write for info. (0-9626090-0-5) Amaknak Pr.
Postgate, Oliver & Linnell, Naomi. Columbus: The Triumphant Failure. Postgate, Oliver, illus. 44p. (gr. 5-8). 1992. 14.95 (0-531-15240-5) Watts.
Postma, Lidia. The Stolen Mirror. Postma, Lidia, illus. LC 75-43888. 32p. (ps-3). 1976. McGraw.
Potaracke, Rochelle. Nanny's Special Gift. Mitchell, Mark, illus. LC 93-26093. 1994. pap. 3.95 (0-8091-6615-1) Paulist Pr.
Potash, Dorothy. El Cuento de Ned y Su Nariz. Sperling, Thomas, illus. (SPA.). 24p. (ps-4). 1993. PLB 13.95 (1-879567-24-5, Valeria Bks) Wonder Well.
—The Tale of Ned & His Nose. Sperling, Thomas, illus. 24p. (gr. k-4). 1993. PLB 13.95 (1-879567-23-7, Valeria Bks) Wonder Well.
Potok, Chaim. The Tree of Here. Auth, Tony, illus. LC 92-28412. (gr. k-4). 1993. 13.00 (0-679-84010-9); PLB 13.99 (0-679-94010-3) Knopf Bks Yng Read.
Potter. Computer Controlled Robots. Gower, illus. 48p. (gr. 5-8). 1985. PLB 10.96 (0-88110-213-X, Pub. by Usborne) EDC.
Potter, Beatrix. Animal Homes. 12p. 1991. bds. 3.50 (0-7232-3782-4) Warne.
—Appley Dapply's Nursery Rhymes. 1987. 5.95 (0-7232-3481-7); pap. 2.25 (0-7232-3506-6) Warne.
—Beatrix Potter & Peter Rabbit Classic Treasury. 1988. 9.99 (0-517-67150-6) Outlet Bk Co.
—Beatrix Potter Collection, 3 vols. (ps-3). 1987. Set. write for info. (0-317-52263-9); Collection #1. 24.00 (0-7232-5163-0); Collection #2. 21.00 (0-7232-5164-9); Collection #3. 21.00 (0-7232-5165-7) Warne.
—Beatrix Potter Mask Book. (ps-3). 1990. pap. 9.95 (0-7232-3654-2) Warne.
—Beatrix Potter Tale of Baby Da. (gr. k up). 1979. 17.00 (0-8378-8011-4) Gibson.
—Beatrix Potter's Farmhouse Box. (Illus.). (ps-3). 1989. Set of 6. 28.95 (0-7232-5169-X) Warne.
—Beatrix Potter's Nursery Rhyme Book. 56p. (ps-4). 1984. 11.00 (0-7232-3254-7) Warne.
—Beatrix Potter's Peter Rabbit: A Lift-the-Flap Rebus Book. (ps-3). 1991. 11.95 (0-7232-3798-0) Warne.
—Benjamin Bunny: Beatrix Potter Deluxe Pop Up. (Illus.). 1992. 4.99 (0-517-07001-4) Outlet Bk Co.
—Benjamin Bunny's Colors. (Illus.). 24p. (ps). 1994. bds. 2.99 (0-7232-4118-X) Warne.
—Birthday Book of Peter Rabbit. (Illus.). 256p. (ps up) 1983. 5.99 (0-517-40303-X) Outlet Bk Co.
—Cecily Parsley's Nursery Rhymes. Atkinson, Allen, illus. 1983. pap. 2.25 (0-553-15229-7) Bantam.
—Cecily Parsley's Nursery Rhymes. 1987. 5.95 (0-7232-3482-5); pap. 2.25 (0-7232-3507-4) Warne.
—A Child's Treasury of Beatrix Potter. (Illus.). 80p. (gr. k-3). 1987. 6.98 (0-681-40281-4) Longmeadow Pr.
—The Complete Adventures of Peter Rabbit. 80p. (ps-3). 1984. pap. 6.95 (0-14-050444-3, Puffin) Puffin Bks.
—The Complete Adventures of Peter Rabbit. Potter, Beatrix, illus. 96p. (ps-3). 1987. 12.95 (0-7232-2951-1) Warne.
—The Complete Adventures of Tom Kitten. (ps-3). 1987. pap. 5.95 (0-14-050503-2, Puffin) Puffin Bks.
—Complete Adventures of Tom Kitten & His Friends. (Illus.). 80p. (ps-3). 1993. 13.00 (0-7232-3288-1) Warne.
—The Complete Tales of Beatrix Potter. Potter, Beatrix, illus. 384p. (ps-6). 1989. 35.00 (0-7232-3618-6) Viking Child Bks.

—Complete Tales of Peter Rabbit: And Other Favorite Stories. Santore, Charles, illus. LC 86-10116. 36p. (gr. k up). 1986. 9.98 (0-89471-460-0) Courage Bks.
—The Complete Tales of Peter Rabbit: And Other Favorite Stories. Santore, Charles, illus. LC 90-52736. 56p. (gr. 2 up). 1991. pap. 5.95 (0-89471-855-X) Running Pr.
—El Cuento de Juanito Raton de Ciudad. (SPA., Illus.). 64p. 1988. 5.95 (0-7232-3560-0) Warne.
—El Cuento de la Oca Carlota. (SPA., Illus.). 64p. 1988. 5.95 (0-7232-3557-0) Warne.
—El Cuento de los Dos Malvados Ratones. (SPA., Illus.). 64p. 1988. 5.95 (0-7232-3559-7) Warne.
—El Cuento de Pedrito Conejo. Marcuse, Aida, tr. from ENG. McPhail, David, illus. (SPA.). (gr. k-4). 1993. pap. 2.95 (0-590-46475-2) Scholastic Inc.
—El Cuento de Perico, el Conejo Travieso. (SPA., Illus.). 64p. 1988. 5.95 (0-7232-3556-2) Warne.
—El Cuento del Conejito Benjamin. (SPA., Illus.). 64p. 1988. 5.95 (0-7232-3558-9) Warne.
—El Cuento del Gato Tomas. (SPA., Illus.). 64p. 1988. 4.95 (0-7232-3565-1) Warne.
—Deux Vilaines Souris. (FRE.). 59p. 1990. 10.95 (2-07-056070-8) Schoenhof.
—Deux Vilaines Souris. (FRE.). 59p. 1990. 9.95 (0-7859-3625-4, 2070560708) Fr & Eur.
—Dinner Time. 12p. 1991. bds. 3.50 (0-7232-3781-6) Warne.
—Farmyard Noises. 12p. 1991. bds. 3.50 (0-7232-3784-0) Warne.
—Further Tales from Beatrix Potter. (Illus.). 112p. (ps-3). 1987. 7.95 (0-7232-3509-0) Warne.
—Giant Treasury of Beatrix Potter. (Illus.). 52p. (gr. k-6). 1985. 6.99 (0-517-43121-1) Outlet Bk Co.
—Giant Treasury of Peter Rabbit. Wilkins, C., intro. by. (Illus.). 92p. (gr. k-6). 1985. 6.99 (0-517-31687-0) Outlet Bk Co.
—Ginger & Pickles. LC 85-13641. (Illus.). 64p. (gr. 2 up). 1985. pap. 1.75 (0-486-24969-7) Dover.
—The Great Big Treasury of Beatrix Potter. LC 92-12165. 1992. 11.99 (0-517-07246-7, Pub. by Derrydale Bks) Outlet Bk Co.
—Happy Families. 12p. 1991. bds. 3.50 (0-7232-3783-2) Warne.
—Hill Top Tales. (Illus.). 128p. (ps up). 1989. 8.95 (0-7232-3548-1) Warne.
—Jeannot Lapin. (FRE.). 58p. 1990. 10.95 (2-07-056094-5) Schoenhof.
—Jeannot Lapin. (FRE., Illus.). 58p. 1990. 9.95 (0-7859-3631-9, 2070560945) Fr & Eur.
—Jemima Puddle-Duck Bath Book. (Illus.). 8p. (ps). 1988. pap. 3.99 waterproof (0-7232-3512-0) Warne.
—The Jemima Puddle-Duck Pop-up Book. (Illus.). 6p. (ps-3). 1993. 13.00 (0-7232-4122-8) Viking Child Bks.
—Jemima Puddle-Duck's Numbers. (Illus.). 24p. (ps). 1994. bds. 2.99 (0-7232-4091-4) Warne.
—Jemima Puddleduck. 1988. 2.99 (0-517-65275-7) Outlet Bk Co.
—Jemima Puddleduck. (Illus.). 24p. (ps-1). 1992. 3.99 (0-517-05077-3) Outlet Bk Co.
—Jemima Puddleduck: Beatrix Potter Deluxe Pop Up. (Illus.). 1992. 4.99 (0-517-06999-7) Outlet Bk Co.
—Jemima Puddleduck Pop-Up. 1988. 3.99 (0-517-67097-6) Outlet Bk Co.
—Jeremie Peche-a-la-Ligne. (FRE.). 58p. 1990. 10.95 (2-07-056074-0) Schoenhof.
—Jeremie Peche-a-la-Ligne. (FRE., Illus.). 58p. 1990. 9.95 (0-7859-3628-9, 2070560740) Fr & Eur.
—Jeremy Fisher. Twinn, Colin, illus. 10p. (ps-5). 1992. 5.99 (0-7232-3999-1) Warne.
—Jeremy Fisher Bath Book. (Illus.). 8p. (ps). 1989. 2.95 (0-7232-3513-9) Warne.
—Letters to Children. (Illus.). 48p. (gr. 2 up). 1986. pap. 5.95 (0-8027-7293-5) Warne.
—Little Treasury of Beatrix Potter Nursery Rhymes. LC 93-8697. (Illus.). 1994. 5.99 (0-517-10030-4, Pub. by Derrydale Bks) Outlet Bk Co.
—Madame Piquedru. (FRE.). 58p. 1990. 10.95 (2-07-056068-6) Schoenhof.
—Madame Piquedru. (FRE., Illus.). 58p. 1990. 9.95 (0-7859-3623-8, 2070560686) Fr & Eur.
—Madame Trotte-Menu. (FRE.). 59p. 1990. 10.95 (2-07-056105-4) Schoenhof.
—Madame Trotte-Menu. (FRE., Illus.). 58p. 1990. 9.95 (0-7859-3634-3, 2070561054) Fr & Eur.
—Mademoiselle Mitoufle. (FRE.). 37p. 1990. 10.95 (2-07-056104-6) Schoenhof.
—Mademoiselle Mitoufle. (FRE., Illus.). 58p. 1990. 9.95 (0-7859-3633-5, 2070561046) Fr & Eur.
—Mechant Petit Lapin. (FRE.). (gr. 5-10). 1990. 10.95 (2-07-056073-2) Schoenhof.
—Mechant Petit Lapin. (FRE., Illus.). 58p. 1990. 9.95 (0-7859-3627-0, 2070560732) Fr & Eur.
—Meet Benjamin Bunny. (Illus.). 12p. (ps). 1987. bds. 2.95 (0-7232-3451-5) Warne.
—Meet Hunca Munca. Potter, Beatrix, illus. 12p. (ps). 1986. bds. 2.95 (0-7232-3421-3) Warne.
—Meet Jemima Puddle-Duck. Potter, Beatrix, illus. 12p. (ps). 1986. bds. 3.50 (0-7232-3420-5) Warne.
—Meet Jeremy Fisher. (Illus.). 12p. (ps). 1987. bds. 2.95 (0-7232-3453-1) Warne.
—Meet Mrs. Tiggy-Winkle. (Illus.). 12p. (ps). 1987. bds. 2.95 (0-7232-3454-X) Warne.
—Meet Peter Rabbit. Potter, Beatrix, illus. 12p. (ps). 1986. bds. 3.50 (0-7232-3418-3) Warne.
—Meet Squirrel Nutkin. (Illus.). 12p. (ps). 1987. bds. 2.95 (0-7232-3452-3) Warne.

—Meet Tom Kitten. Potter, Beatrix, illus. 12p. (ps). 1986. bds. 3.50 (0-7232-3419-1) Warne.
—Mini Peter Rabbit Bookshop, 23 bks. (Illus.). (ps-3). 1993. Set. 35.00 (0-7232-3989-4) Warne.
—More Tales from Beatrix Potter. (ps-3). 1988. 8.95 (0-7232-3366-7) Warne.
—Mouse Tales. (Illus.). 128p. 1989. 8.95 (0-7232-3543-0) Warne.
—My First Peter Rabbit Book & Toy. (ps-3). 1991. 14.95 (0-7232-4014-0) Warne.
—My First Year: A Beatrix Potter Baby Book. (Illus.). 29p. 1989. 9.95 (0-7232-3157-5) Warne.
—My First Year: My Peter Rabbit Keepsake. (Illus.). boxed set 19.99 (0-7232-8921-2) Warne.
—My Peter Rabbit Learning Box: Peter Rabbit's 123 & Peter Rabbit's ABC. (ps-3). 1988. Boxed Set. 13.95 (0-7232-5168-1) Warne.
—My Peter Rabbit Play Box. 1991. bds. 14.95 incl. tape & toy (0-7232-3794-8) Warne.
—Noisette l'Ecureuil. (FRE.). 58p. 1990. 10.95 (2-07-056075-9) Schoenhof.
—Noisette l'Ecureuil. (FRE., Illus.). 58p. 1990. 9.95 (0-7859-3629-7, 2070560759) Fr & Eur.
—The One Hundredth Anniversary 1-12 Presentation Box: The World of Beatrix Potter, 12 bks. (Illus.). 1993. Set. 70.00 (0-7232-4113-9) Warne.
—The One Hundredth Anniversary 1-23 Presentation Box: The World of Beatrix Potter, 23 bks. (Illus.). 1993. Set. 135.00 (0-7232-4112-0) Warne.
—The One Hundredth Anniversary 13-23 Presentation Box: The World of Beatrix Potter, 11 bks. (Illus.). 1993. Set. 65.00 (0-7232-4114-7) Warne.
—Original Peter Rabbit Books: 13-23 Presentation Box. 1990. 65.00 (0-7232-5178-9) Warne.
—The Original Peter Rabbit Miniature Collection, No. I. Potter, Beatrix, illus. (ps-3). 1991. pap. 5.95 (0-7232-3982-7) Warne.
—The Original Peter Rabbit Miniature Collection, No. III. (Illus.). (ps-3). 1989. pap. 4.95 set of 4 in slipcase (0-7232-3984-3) Warne.
—Original Peter Rabbit Miniature Collection. (Illus.). 1989. Twelve-copy drawer. pap. 18.50 (0-7232-5173-8) Warne.
—Original Peter Rabbit Miniature Collection, No. IV. (ps-3). 1990. pap. 4.95 (0-7232-5076-6) Warne.
—Original Peter Rabbit Miniature Collection V. (ps-3). 1990. pap. 4.95 (0-7232-5078-2) Warne.
—Original Peter Rabbit Miniature Collection VI. (Illus.). (ps-3). 1991. pap. 4.95 (0-7232-3987-8) Warne.
—Panache Petitgris. (FRE.). 59p. 1990. 10.95 (2-07-056102-X) Schoenhof.
—Panache Petitgris. Potter, Beatrix, illus (FRE.). 60p. 1990. 9.95 (0-7859-3713-7) Fr & Eur.
—Peter Rabbit. LC 87-24226. (Illus.). 64p. (gr. k-5). 1989. 11.95 (0-916410-24-2) A D Bragdon.
—Peter Rabbit. (Illus.). 24p. (ps-1). 1992. 3.99 (0-517-05079-X) Outlet Bk Co.
—Peter Rabbit. Twinn, Colin, illus. 10p. (ps-5). 1992. 5.99 (0-7232-3997-5) Warne.
—Peter Rabbit & Benjamin Bunny Coloring Book. (Illus.). (gr. 1 up). 1987. pap. 1.49 (0-671-62987-5, Little Simon) S&S Trade.
—Peter Rabbit & Eleven Other Favorite Tales. Stewart, Pat, adapted by. Potter, Beatrix, illus. LC 93-14417. 96p. 1994. pap. 1.00t (0-486-27845-X) Dover.
—Peter Rabbit & Friends: Three Complete Tales, 3 vols. (Illus.). 178p. (gr. 2 up). 1985. Set. pap. 5.25 (0-486-24772-4) Dover.
—Peter Rabbit & His Friends. (Illus.). 24p. (ps). 1994. bds. 2.99 (0-7232-4093-0) Warne.
—Peter Rabbit & His Friends Word Book. 1989. 4.99 (0-517-64156-9) Outlet Bk Co.
—Peter Rabbit & Other Stories. 1993. 4.98 (0-89000-187-0) Bk Sales Inc.
—Peter Rabbit: Bath Book. 8p. (ps). 1989. 3.99 (0-7232-3584-8) Warne.
—Peter Rabbit: Beatrix Potter Deluxe Pop Up. (Illus.). 1992. 4.99 (0-517-07000-6) Outlet Bk Co.
—Peter Rabbit Comes Home. 1988. 2.99 (0-517-60596-1) Outlet Bk Co.
—Peter Rabbit Diary for Any Year. 1991. 6.95 (0-7232-3993-2) Warne.
—Peter Rabbit in Mr. McGregor's Garden. 1988. 2.99 (0-517-60597-X) Outlet Bk Co.
—The Peter Rabbit Make-a-Mobile Book. 20p. 1991. pap. 5.95 (0-7232-3764-6) Warne.
—The Peter Rabbit Nursery Frieze. (Illus.). (ps-k). 1989. shrink-wrapped 5.00 (0-7232-3583-X) Warne.
—The Peter Rabbit Pop-Up Book. 12p. 1983. 12.99 (0-7232-2950-3) Warne.
—The Peter Rabbit Stencil Book. (Illus.). 28p. (ps-3). 1994. pap. 6.99 (0-7232-4046-9) Warne.
—The Peter Rabbit Theatre. (Illus.). 16p. (gr. 1). 1992. 6.95 (0-7232-4006-X) Warne.
—Peter Rabbit with Many Other Beloved Beatrix Potter Characters Coloring Book. (Illus.). (gr. 1 up). 1987. pap. 1.49 (0-671-62984-0, Little Simon) S&S Trade.
—Peter Rabbit's ABC. Potter, Beatrix, illus. 48p. (ps-2). 1987. 6.95 (0-7232-3423-X) Warne.
—Peter Rabbit's ABC Frieze. 1987. 5.00 (0-7232-5637-3) Warne.
—Peter Rabbit's Christmas Book. (ps-3). 1990. pap. 5.95 (0-7232-3778-6) Warne.
—Peter Rabbit's Colors. 48p. (ps-k). 1988. 6.95 (0-7232-3612-7); frieze 5.00 (0-7232-3613-5) Warne.
—Peter Rabbit's One Two Three. (ps-k). 1988. 6.95 (0-7232-3424-8) Warne.

—Peter Rabbit's 1 2 3 Frieze. 1988. 5.00 (0-7232-5630-6) Warne.
—The Pie & the Patty-Pan. (Illus.). 46p. 1976. pap. 1.75 (0-486-23383-9) Dover.
—Pierre Lapin. (FRE.). 62p. 1980. 10.95 (2-07-056069-4) Schoenhof.
—Pierre Lapin. (FRE., Illus.). 62p. 1980. 9.95 (0-7859-3624-6, 2070560694) Fr & Eur.
—Pierre Lapin: Peter Rabbit. (FRE., Illus.). (gr. 3-7). 1973. 5.00 (0-7232-0650-3) Warne.
—The Rabbit's Christmas Party: A. Frieze. (Illus.). 1989. pap. 4.95 (0-7232-3566-X) Warne.
—The Roly-Poly Pudding. 64p. (Orig.). 1984. pap. 2.25 (0-553-15249-1) Bantam.
—The Roly-Poly Pudding. 80p. (gr. 1 up). 1986. pap. 2.75 (0-486-25099-7) Dover.
—Scenes from the Tale of Peter Rabbit. (Illus.). 1989. 6.95 (0-7232-3547-3) Warne.
—The Stories of Beatrix Potter, Vol. 1. Potter, Beatrix, illus. 96p. (ps-2). 1991. 4 bks. & 2 audio cassettes 16.98 (1-55886-063-0) Smarty Pants.
—The Stories of Beatrix Potter, Vol. 2. Potter, Beatrix, illus. 96p. (ps-2). 1992. 4 bks. & 2 audio cassettes 16.98 (1-55886-067-3) Smarty Pants.
—The Story of a Fierce Bad Rabbit. 1987. 5.95 (0-7232-3479-5); pap. 2.25 (0-7232-3504-X) Warne.
—The Story of Miss Moppet. 1987. 5.95 (0-7232-3480-9); pap. 2.25 (0-7232-3505-8) Warne.
—Tailleur de Gloucester. (FRE.). 58p. 1991. 10.95 (2-07-056076-7) Schoenhof.
—Tailleur de Gloucester. (FRE., Illus.). 58p. 1991. 9.95 (0-7859-3630-0, 2070560767) Fr & Eur.
—The Tailor of Gloucester. (Illus.). 57p. (gr. k-3). 1973. pap. 1.75 (0-486-20176-7) Dover.
—The Tailor of Gloucester. Atkinson, Allen, illus. 1984. pap. 2.25 (0-553-15220-3) Bantam.
—The Tailor of Gloucester. Jorgensen, David, illus. LC 88-11510. 44p. (ps up). 1991. pap. 14.95 (0-88708-080-4, Rabbit Ears); bk. & cass. pkg. 19.95 (0-88708-085-5, Rabbit Ears) Picture Bk Studio.
—The Tailor of Gloucester. 1987. 5.95 (0-7232-3462-0); pap. 2.25 (0-7232-3487-6) Warne.
—The Tailor of Gloucester. Horden, Michael, read by. (Illus.). (ps-3). 1989. pap. 6.95 bk. & tape (0-7232-3668-2) Warne.
—The Tailor of Gloucester. (Illus.). 60p. 1993. deluxe ed. 16.00 (0-7232-4094-9) Warne.
—Tailor of Gloucester. (Illus.). 36p. (ps-3). 1993. 4.99 (0-7232-4137-6) Warne.
—The Tailor of Gloucester Model Book. (Illus.). (ps-3). 1987. pap. 3.95 (0-7232-3455-8) Warne.
—The Tailor or Gloucester Christmas Activity Book. (Illus.). 36p. (ps-3). 1993. 4.99 (0-7232-4136-8) Warne.
—The Tale of Benjamin Bunny. Stewart, Pat, illus. LC 74-78812. 59p. (gr. 2 up). 1974. pap. 1.75 (0-486-21102-9) Dover.
—The Tale of Benjamin Bunny. Kirk, Tim, illus. LC 80-27468. 32p. (gr. k-3). 1981. PLB 9.79 (0-89375-484-6); pap. text ed. 1.95 (0-89375-485-4) Troll Assocs.
—The Tale of Benjamin Bunny. Atkinson, Allen, illus. 64p. 1984. pap. 2.25 (0-553-15203-3) Bantam.
—The Tale of Benjamin Bunny. (Illus.). 64p. (ps-3). 1986. 3.95 (0-671-62925-5, Little Simon) S&S Trade.
—The Tale of Benjamin Bunny. Leach, Rosemary, read by. Davis, Carl, contrib. by. (Illus.). 1989. pap. 6.95 incl. tape (0-7232-3628-3) Warne.
—The Tale of Benjamin Bunny. 1987. 5.95 (0-7232-3463-9); pap. 2.25 (0-7232-3488-4) Warne.
—Tale of Benjamin Bunny. 1988. 2.99 (0-517-65277-3) Outlet Bk Co.
—The Tale of Benjamin Bunny. 1992. 3.99 (0-517-07240-8) Outlet Bk Co.
—Tale of Benjamin Bunny Pop Up. 1988. 3.99 (0-517-67096-8) Outlet Bk Co.
—Tale of Benjamin Bunny-Sticker. 1990. pap. 2.95 (0-671-69254-2, Little Simon) S&S Trade.
—The Tale of Ginger & Pickles. 1987. 5.95 (0-7232-3477-9); pap. 2.25 (0-7232-3502-3) Warne.
—The Tale of Jemima Puddle-Duck. 64p. (Orig.). (ps). 1984. pap. 2.25 (0-553-15251-3) Bantam.
—The Tale of Jemima Puddle-duck. (Illus.). 64p. 1984. pap. 1.75 (0-486-24634-5) Dover.
—The Tale of Jemima Puddle-Duck. (Illus.). 64p. (ps-3). 1987. 3.95 (0-671-63236-1, Little Simon) S&S Trade.
—The Tale of Jemima Puddle-Duck. (ps-3). 1987. 5.95 (0-7232-3468-X); pap. 2.25 (0-7232-3493-0) Warne.
—The Tale of Jemima Puddle-Duck. West, Timothy, read by. Davis, Carl, contrib. by. (Illus.). (ps-3). 1989. pap. 6.95 incl. tape (0-7232-3630-5) Warne.
—The Tale of Jemima Puddle-Duck. Potter, Beatrix, illus. 24p. (ps-3). 1991. incl. cassette 5.98 (1-55886-057-6) Smarty Pants.
—The Tale of Jemima Puddle-Duck. (Illus.). 32p. (ps-3). 1992. pap. 3.99 (0-14-054498-4) Puffin Bks.
—The Tale of Jemima Puddle-Duck & Other Farmyard Tales. (Illus.). 80p. (ps-3). 1990. pap. 5.95 (0-14-050588-1, Puffin) Puffin Bks.
—The Tale of Jemima Puddle-Duck & Other Farmyard Tales. (Illus.). 80p. (ps-3). 1993. 13.00 (0-7232-3425-6) Warne.
—Tale of Jeremy Fisher-Coloring Book. 1985. pap. 2.50 (0-486-24964-6) Dover.
—The Tale of Johnny Town-Mouse. (ps-3). 1987. 5.95 (0-7232-3472-8); pap. 2.25 (0-7232-3497-3) Warne.

—The Tale of Little Pig Robinson. 1987. 5.95 (0-7232-3478-7); pap. 2.25 (0-7232-3503-1) Warne.
—The Tale of Mr. Jeremy Fischer. 1992. 3.99 (0-517-07238-6) Outlet Bk Co.
—The Tale of Mr. Jeremy Fisher. LC 74-75269. (Illus.). 59p. (gr. 2-4). 1974. pap. 1.75 (0-486-23066-X) Dover.
—The Tale of Mr. Jeremy Fisher. Atkinson, Allen, illus. 1983. pap. 2.25 (0-553-15221-1) Bantam.
—The Tale of Mr. Jeremy Fisher. 1987. 5.95 (0-7232-3466-3); pap. 2.25 (0-7232-3491-4) Warne.
—The Tale of Mr. Jeremy Fisher. Jorgensen, David, illus. LC 88-34668. 32p. (ps up). 1991. pap. 14.95 (0-88708-094-4, Rabbit Ears); incl. cassette 19.95 (0-88708-095-2, Rabbit Ears) Picture Bk Studio.
—The Tale of Mr. Jeremy Fisher. Horden, Michael, read by. (ps-3). 1989. pap. 6.95 bk. & tape (0-7232-3669-0) Warne.
—The Tale of Mr. Jeremy Fisher. Jorgensen, David, illus. LC 92-22584. 64p. 1992. Repr. of 1989 ed. 5.95 (0-88708-253-X, Rabbit Ears); Mini-bk. incl. cassette 9.95 (0-88708-252-1, Rabbit Ears) Picture Bk Studio.
—The Tale of Mr. Tod. 1987. 5.95 (0-7232-3473-6); pap. 2.25 (0-7232-3498-1) Warne.
—The Tale of Mrs. Tiggy-winkle. (Illus.). 57p. (gr. k-6). 1973. pap. 1.75 (0-486-20546-0) Dover.
—The Tale of Mrs. Tiggy-Winkle. Atkinson, Allen, illus. 1984. pap. 2.25 (0-553-15204-1) Bantam.
—The Tale of Mrs. Tiggy-Winkle. Routledge, Patricia, read by. Davis, Carl, contrib. by. (Illus.). (ps-3). 1989. pap. 6.95 incl. tape (0-7232-3629-1) Warne.
—The Tale of Mrs. Tiggy-Winkle. 1987. 5.95 (0-7232-3465-5); pap. 2.25 (0-7232-3490-6) Warne.
—The Tale of Mrs. Tiggy-Winkle. Potter, Beatrix, illus. 24p. (ps-2). 1991. incl. cassette 5.98 (1-55886-058-4) Smarty Pants.
—The Tale of Mrs. Tiggy-Winkle. 1992. 3.99 (0-517-07237-8) Outlet Bk Co.
—The Tale of Mrs. Tiggy-Winkle & Mr. Jeremy Fisher. (Illus.). 32p. (ps-3). 1994. pap. 4.99 (0-7232-4149-X) Warne.
—The Tale of Mrs. Tittlemouse. 1987. 5.95 (0-7232-3470-1); pap. 2.25 (0-7232-3495-7) Warne.
—The Tale of Mrs. Tittlemouse & Other Mouse Stories. LC 85-40386. (Illus.). 80p. (ps-3). 1985. 10.95 (0-7232-3324-1) Warne.
—The Tale of Peter Rabbit. (Illus.). 60p. (gr. 1-5). 1972. pap. 1.75 (0-486-22827-4) Dover.
—Tale of Peter Rabbit. new ed. Apple, Margot, illus. LC 78-18071. 32p. (gr. k-3). 1979. PLB 9.79 (0-89375-124-3); pap. 1.95 (0-89375-102-2) Troll Assocs.
—The Tale of Peter Rabbit. Atkinson, Allen, illus. 64p. (Orig.). 1984. pap. 2.50 (0-553-15470-2) Bantam.
—The Tale of Peter Rabbit. Graham, Florence, illus. LC 85-70809. 13p. (ps). 1986. 3.95 (0-448-10224-2, G&D) Putnam Pub Group.
—The Tale of Peter Rabbit. McPhail, David, illus. 32p. (Orig.). (gr. k-3). 1986. pap. 2.50 (0-590-41101-2); incl. cassette 5.95 (0-590-63091-1) Scholastic Inc.
—The Tale of Peter Rabbit. (Illus.). 64p. (ps-3). 1986. 3.95 (0-671-62924-7, Little Simon) S&S Trade.
—The Tale of Peter Rabbit. Frenck, Hal, illus. LC 87-40282. 24p. (ps up). 1990. incl. audio cassettes 6.95 (1-55782-015-5, Pub. by Warner Juvenile Bks) Little.
—The Tale of Peter Rabbit. Jorgensen, David, illus. LC 88-11509. 36p. (ps up). 1991. 14.95 (0-317-89758-6, Rabbit Ears); bk. & cass. pkg. 19.95 (0-88708-084-7, Rabbit Ears) Picture Bk Studio.
—The Tale of Peter Rabbit. Leach, Rosemary, read by. Davis, Carl, contrib. by. (Illus.). (ps-3). 1989. pap. 6.95 incl. tape (0-7232-3627-5) Warne.
—The Tale of Peter Rabbit. (ps-3). 1987. 5.95 (0-7232-3460-4); pap. 2.25 (0-7232-3485-X) Warne.
—The Tale of Peter Rabbit. Potter, Beatrix, illus. 24p. (ps-2). 1991. incl. cassette 5.98 (1-55886-055-X) Smarty Pants.
—Tale of Peter Rabbit. 1988. 2.99 (0-517-65276-5) Outlet Bk Co.
—Tale of Peter Rabbit. 1991. pap. 14.95 (0-88708-079-0, Rabbit Ears) Picture Bk Studio.
—The Tale of Peter Rabbit. Graham, Florence, illus. 32p. 1991. pap. 2.25 (0-448-40061-8, Platt & Munk Pubs) Putnam Pub Group.
—A Tale of Peter Rabbit. Officer, Robyn, illus. 1991. 6.95 (0-8362-4908-9) Andrews & McMeel.
—The Tale of Peter Rabbit. (Illus.). 32p. (ps-3). 1992. pap. 3.99 (0-14-054497-6, Puffin) Puffin Bks.
—The Tale of Peter Rabbit. 1992. 3.99 (0-517-07236-X) Outlet Bk Co.
—The Tale of Peter Rabbit. Streep, Meryl, read by. Jorgensen, David, illus. Mays, Lyle, contrib. by. (Illus.). 32p. (ps up). 1992. pap. write for info. slipcase pkg., incl. cassette (0-307-14328-7, 14328, Golden Pr) Western Pub.
—The Tale of Peter Rabbit. deluxe ed. (Illus.). 60p. 1993. 16.00 (0-7232-4026-4); Cased set. limited ed. 150.00x (0-7232-4045-0) Warne.
—The Tale of Peter Rabbit. Jorgensen, David, illus. LC 92-36655. 64p. 1993. Repr. of 1988 ed. 8.95 (0-88708-296-3, Rabbit Ears); incl. cassette 9.95 (0-88708-297-1) Picture Bk Studio.
—The Tale of Peter Rabbit. Szekeres, Cyndy, illus. 24p. (ps-3). 1993. 3.50 (0-307-12349-9, 12349, Golden Pr) Western Pub.
—The Tale of Peter Rabbit. (Illus.). 24p. (ps-3). 1993. pap. 17.99 (0-7232-4029-9) Warne.

—The Tale of Peter Rabbit: A Coloring Book in Signed English. Miller, Ralph R., illus. Roy, Howard L., et al. (Illus.). 64p. (ps-2). 1986. pap. 4.95 (0-930323-29-7, Pub. by K Green Pubns) Gallaudet Univ Pr.
—The Tale of Peter Rabbit & Benjamin Bunny. (Illus.). 32p. (ps-3). 1993. 4.99 (0-7232-4124-4) Warne.
—The Tale of Peter Rabbit & Other Favorite Stories, 7 vols. 447p. (gr. 2 up). Boxed Set. pap. 12.25 (0-486-23903-9) Dover.
—Tale of Peter Rabbit & Other Stories. 1983. pap. 2.25 (0-553-15202-5) Bantam.
—The Tale of Peter Rabbit: Die Geschichte Des Peterchen Hase. Werner, Meike, tr. (GER., Illus.). 64p. (Orig.). 1992. pap. 2.75t (0-486-27014-9) Dover.
—The Tale of Peter Rabbit: La Storia Del Coniglietto Pietro. Vettori, Alessandro, tr. (ITA., Illus.). 64p. (Orig.). 1992. pap. 2.75t (0-486-27015-7) Dover.
—Tale of Peter Rabbit Pop Up. 1988. 3.99 (0-517-67098-4) Outlet Bk Co.
—Tale of Peter Rabbit Sticker Book. 1990. pap. 2.95 (0-671-69255-0, Little Simon) S&S Trade.
—The Tale of Pigling Bland. 1987. 5.95 (0-7232-3474-4); pap. 2.25 (0-7232-3499-X) Warne.
—The Tale of Pigling Bland. (Illus.). (ps-3). 1993. pap. 4.99 (0-7232-4150-3) Warne.
—The Tale of Samuel Whiskers. 1987. 5.95 (0-7232-3475-2); pap. 2.25 (0-7232-3500-7) Warne.
—The Tale of Samuel Whiskers. (Illus.). 32p. (ps-3). 1993. pap. 4.99 (0-7232-4142-2) Warne.
—The Tale of Squirrel Nutkin. Atkinson, Allen, illus. 64p. 1984. pap. 2.25 (0-553-15205-X) Bantam.
—The Tale of Squirrel Nutkin. 1987. 5.95 (0-7232-3461-2); pap. 2.25 (0-7232-3486-8) Warne.
—The Tale of Squirrel Nutkin. Bond, Gary, read by. (Illus.). (ps-3). 1989. pap. 6.95 bk. & tape (0-7232-3671-2) Warne.
—The Tale of Squirrel Nutkin. (Illus.). 60p. (gr. 1-5). 1972. pap. 1.75 (0-486-22828-2) Dover.
—Tale of Squirrel Nutkin. 1992. 3.99 (0-517-07239-4) Outlet Bk Co.
—The Tale of the Flopsy Bunnies. 64p. (gr. 1 up). 1985. pap. 1.75 (0-486-24806-2) Dover.
—The Tale of the Flopsy Bunnies. (Illus.). 64p. (ps-3). 1987. 3.95 (0-671-63237-X, Little Simon) S&S Trade.
—The Tale of the Flopsy Bunnies. 1987. 5.95 (0-7232-3469-8); pap. 2.25 (0-7232-3494-9) Warne.
—The Tale of the Pie & the Patty-Pan. 1987. 5.95 (0-7232-3476-0); pap. 2.25 (0-7232-3501-5) Warne.
—The Tale of Timmy Tiptoes. (Illus.). 64p. (gr. 3 up). 1987. pap. 1.75 (0-486-25541-7) Dover.
—The Tale of Timmy Tiptoes. 1987. 5.95 (0-7232-3471-X); pap. 2.25 (0-7232-3496-5) Warne.
—The Tale of Tom Kitten. (Illus.). 58p. (gr. k up). 1983. pap. 1.75 (0-486-24502-0) Dover.
—The Tale of Tom Kitten. Atkinson, Allen, illus. 1983. pap. 2.25 (0-553-15224-6) Bantam.
—The Tale of Tom Kitten. (Illus.). 64p. (ps-3). 1986. 3.95 (0-671-62927-1, Little Simon) S&S Trade.
—The Tale of Tom Kitten. Frenck, Hal, illus. LC 87-40285. 24p. (ps up). 1990. incl. audio cassettes 6.95 (1-55782-018-X, Pub. by Warner Juvenile Bks) Little.
—The Tale of Tom Kitten. (Illus.). (ps-3). 1987. 5.95 (0-7232-3467-1); pap. 2.25 (0-7232-3492-2) Warne.
—The Tale of Tom Kitten. Routledge, Patricia, read by. (ps-3). 1992. pap. 6.95 bk. & tape (0-7232-3670-4) Warne.
—Tale of Tom Kitten. 1988. bds. 2.99 (0-517-65278-1) Outlet Bk Co.
—Tale of Tom Kitten. (Illus.). 24p. (ps-1). 1992. 3.99 (0-517-05076-5) Outlet Bk Co.
—Tale of Tom Kitten Pop-Up. 1988. 3.99 (0-517-67099-2) Outlet Bk Co.
—The Tale of Two Bad Mice. LC 74-75268. (Illus.). 59p. (gr. 2-4). 1974. pap. 1.75 (0-486-23065-1) Dover.
—The Tale of Two Bad Mice. 64p. (Orig.). 1984. pap. 2.25 (0-553-15219-X) Bantam.
—The Tale of Two Bad Mice. (Illus.). (ps-3). 1987. 5.95 (0-7232-3464-7); pap. 2.25 (0-7232-3489-2) Warne.
—The Tale of Two Bad Mice. 1992. 3.99 (0-517-07241-6) Outlet Bk Co.
—The Tale of Two Bad Mice. (Illus.). 32p. (gr. k-3). 1992. pap. 2.99 (0-87406-620-4) Willowisp Pr.
—Tales from Beatrix Potter. Potter, Beatrix, illus. 228p. (ps-3). 1986. 8.95 (0-7232-3971-1) Warne.
—Tales of Peter Rabbit. Santore, Charles, illus. LC 91-52695. 128p. 1991. 4.95 (1-56138-039-3) Running Pr.
—Tales of Peter Rabbit & His Friends, 2 vols. in 1. 1988. 7.99 (0-517-44901-3) Outlet Bk Co.
—A Tiny Tale of Peter Rabbit. Carlson, David, illus. 14p. (ps-k). 1982. bd 3.50 (0-671-44518-9, Little Simon) S&S Trade.
—Tom Chaton. (FRE.). 58p. 1980. 10.95 (2-07-056071-6) Schoenhof.
—Tom Chaton. (FRE., Illus.). 58p. 1980. 9.95 (0-7859-3626-2, 2070560715) Fr & Eur.
—Tom Kitten: Bath Book. 1989. 3.50 (0-7232-3585-6) Warne.
—Tom Kitten: Beatrix Potter Deluxe Pop Up. (Illus.). 1992. 4.99 (0-517-06998-9) Outlet Bk Co.
—Tom Kitten's Playtime. (Illus.). 24p. (ps-3). 1994. bds. 2.99 (0-7232-4092-2) Warne.
—A Treasury of Peter Rabbit & Other Stories. (Illus.). (gr. k up). 1985. 5.98 (0-517-23948-5) Outlet Bk Co.
—The Two Bad Mice Pop-Up Book. Potter, Beatrix, illus. (ps-3). 1986. 11.95 (0-7232-3360-8) Warne.
—What Time Is It, Peter Rabbit? (Illus.). (ps-k). 1989. 6.95 (0-7232-3586-4); pap. 5.00 (0-7232-3624-0) Warne.

—Where's Peter Rabbit? Twinn, Colin, illus. (ps-3). 1988. 6.95 (0-7232-3519-8) Warne.
—Where's Tom Kitten? 24p. (ps-3). 1990. 6.95 (0-7232-3597-X) Warne.
—The World of Peter Rabbit Postcard Book. (Illus.). 1990. pap. 6.95 (0-7232-3647-X) Warne.
—The World of Peter Rabbit Sticker Book. Twinn, Colin, illus. 32p. (ps-3). 1990. pap. 6.95 (0-7232-3645-3) Warne.
Potter, Beatrix, created by. Benjamin Bunny. Thiewes, Sam, et al, illus. 24p. (gr. 2-4). 1992. PLB 10.95 (1-56674-006-1, HTS Bks) Forest Hse.
—The Flopsy Bunnies. Schoonover, pat & Nelson, Anita, illus. 24p. (gr. 2-4). 1992. PLB 10.95 (1-56674-016-9, HTS Bks) Forest Hse.
—Ginger & Pickles. Thiewes, Sam & Nelson, Anita, illus. 24p. (gr. 2-4). 1992. PLB 10.95 (1-56674-017-7, HTS Bks) Forest Hse.
—Jemima Puddle-Duck. Schoonover, Pat & Nelson, Anita, illus. 24p. (gr. 2-4). 1992. PLB 10.95 (1-56674-018-5, HTS Bks) Forest Hse.
—Miss Moppet. Schoonover, Pat & Nelson, Anita, illus. 24p. (gr. 2-4). 1992. PLB 10.95 (1-56674-020-7, HTS Bks) Forest Hse.
—Mr. Jeremy Fisher. Schoonover, Pat & Nelson, Anita, illus. 24p. (gr. 2-4). 1992. PLB 10.95 (1-56674-019-3, HTS Bks) Forest Hse.
—Mrs. Tiggy-Winkle. Thiewes, Sam, et al, illus. 24p. (gr. 2-4). 1992. PLB 10.95 (1-56674-007-X, HTS Bks) Forest Hse.
—Peter Rabbit. Schoonover, Pat & Nelson, Anita, illus. 24p. (gr. 2-4). 1992. PLB 10.95 (1-56674-008-8, HTS Bks) Forest Hse.
—Pigling Bland. Thiewes, Sam & Nelson, Anita, illus. 24p. (gr. 2-4). 1992. PLB 10.95 (1-56674-021-5, HTS Bks) Forest Hse.
—Squirrel Nutkin. Schoonover, Pat & Nelson, Anita, illus. 24p. (gr. 2-4). 1992. PLB 10.95 (1-56674-009-6, HTS Bks) Forest Hse.
—Tom Kitten. Marsh, T. F., et al, illus. 24p. (gr. 2-4). 1992. PLB 10.95 (1-56674-010-X, HTS Bks) Forest Hse.
—Two Bad Mice. Marsh, T. F., et al, illus. 24p. (gr. 2-4). 1992. PLB 10.95 (1-56674-011-8, HTS Bks) Forest Hse.
Potter, Beatrix, illus. Baby's First Year: A Beatrix Potter Gift Set. 32p. 1990. 16.95 (0-7232-3763-8) Warne.
—My Peter Rabbit Keepsake: A Photograph Album. 32p. 1994. 9.99 (0-7232-4121-X) Warne.
—The Peter Rabbit Make-&-Play Book. 32p. (ps-5). 1992. pap. 6.99 (0-7232-3991-6) Warne.
—The Peter Rabbit Sticker Book. rev. ed. 20p. (ps-3). 1991. pap. 6.99 (0-7232-3979-7) Warne.
—Petit-Jean des Villes. (FRE., Illus.). 58p. 1990. 9.95 (0-7859-3632-7, 2070560953) Fr & Eur.
Potter, Betty M. The Just for Kids Cookbook. Linehan, Maxene M., illus. 180p. (Orig.). (gr. 1-6). 1985. pap. 9.95 comb. bdg. (0-913703-06-0) Branches.
Potter, Jamie & Powers, Janet. The Happy Garden. Potter, D. J., illus. 52p. (Orig.). (ps-4). 1985. pap. 5.95 (0-936511-00-1) Gopher.
Potter, Jean, jt. auth. see Kohl, MaryAnn.
Potter, Jerold C. Books of the Bible. Bowen & Bowen Type Setters Staff, ed. 36p. 1988. pap. text ed. 1.50 (0-925306-00-2) WOFPPM.
Potter, Joan & Clayton, Constance. African-American Firsts: Famous, Little-Known, & Unsung Triumphs of Blacks in America. Munoz, Alison, illus. LC 93-84716. 352p. (Orig.). (gr. 7 up). 1994. pap. 14.95 (0-9632476-1-1) Pinto Pr.
Potter, Katherine. Spike. LC 93-11476. 1994. write for info. (0-671-86733-4, S&S BFYR) S&S Trade.
Potter, Maureen. Theatre Cat. 64p. 1986. 11.95 (0-86278-085-3, Pub. by O'Brien Press Ltd Eire) Dufour.
Potter, Norris & Kasdon, Lawrence. The Hawaiian Monarchy. LC 82-74176. (Illus.). 256p. (gr. 5-8). 1983. 25.95 (0-935848-17-7); pap. 16.95 (0-935848-16-9); wkbk. 5.95 (0-935848-31-2); Tchr's manual 5.00 (1-880188-57-0) Bess Pr.
Potter, Robert R. Benjamin Franklin. (Illus.). 144p. (gr. 5-9). 1992. PLB 13.98 (0-382-24173-8); pap. 7.95 (0-382-24178-9) Silver Burdett Pr.
—Buckminster Fuller. Gallin, Richard, ed. (Illus.). 144p. (gr. 5-9). 1990. PLB 13.98 (0-382-09967-2); pap. 7.95 (0-382-09972-9) Silver Burdett Pr.
—Jefferson Davis. LC 92-16914. (Illus.). 128p. (gr. 7-10). 1992. PLB 22.80 (0-685-68786-4) Raintree Steck-V.
Potter, T. Car Travel Games. (Illus.). 32p. (gr. 2 up). 1986. pap. 4.95 (0-86020-926-1) EDC.
—Pottery. (Illus.). 48p. (gr. 6 up). 1986. PLB 14.96 (0-88110-319-5); pap. 6.95 (0-86020-944-X) EDC.
Potter, T. & Butterfield, M. Travel Games. (Illus.). 64p. (gr. 2 up). 1986. pap. 7.95 (0-86020-999-7, Usborne) EDC.
Potter, T. & Guild, I. Robotics. Priddy, R., illus. 48p. (gr. 6 up). 1983. PLB 13.96 (0-88110-152-4); pap. 6.95 (0-86020-724-2) EDC.
Potter, T. & Peach, S. Graphic Design. (Illus.). 96p. (gr. 6 up). 1993. pap. 12.95 (0-7460-0131-2) EDC.
Potter, Tessa. Cows. LC 89-26080. (Illus.). 32p. (gr. 1-4). 1990. PLB 15.96 (0-8114-2626-2); pap. 3.95 (0-8114-4610-7) Raintree Steck-V.
—Donkeys. LC 89-26079. (Illus.). 32p. (gr. 1-4). 1990. PLB 15.96 (0-8114-2631-9) Raintree Steck-V.
—Ducks & Geese. LC 89-22013. (Illus.). 32p. (gr. 1-4). 1990. PLB 15.96 (0-8114-2628-9) Raintree Steck-V.

—Goats. LC 89-22021. (Illus.). 32p. (gr. 1-4). 1990. PLB 15.96 (*0-8114-2629-7*); pap. 3.95 (*0-8114-4617-4*) Raintree Steck-V.
—Hens. LC 89-22020. (Illus.). 32p. (gr. 1-4). 1990. PLB 15.96 (*0-8114-2627-0*) Raintree Steck-V.
—Sheep. LC 89-22022. (Illus.). 32p. (gr. 1-4). 1990. PLB 15.96 (*0-8114-2630-0*) Raintree Steck-V.
Potter, Tony. How Television Works. (Illus.). 48p. (gr. 7-9). 1992. 13.95 (*0-563-34579-9*, BBC-Parkwest); pap. 6.95 (*0-563-34578-0*, BBC-Parkwest) Parkwest Pubns.
—See How It Works: Cars. Lawrie, Robin, illus. 28p. (ps-3). 1989. Repr. of 1989 ed. POB 7.95 (*0-689-71303-7*, Aladdin) Macmillan Child Grp.
—See How It Works: Earth Movers. Lawrie, Robin, illus. 28p. (ps-3). 1989. Repr. of 1989 ed. POB 7.95 (*0-689-71302-9*, Aladdin) Macmillan Child Grp.
—See How It Works: Planes. Lawrie, Robin, illus. 28p. (ps-3). 1989. Repr. of 1989 ed. POB 7.95 (*0-689-71304-5*, Aladdin) Macmillan Child Grp.
—See How It Works: Trucks. Lawrie, Robin, illus. 28p. (ps-3). 1989. Repr. of 1989 ed. POB 7.95 (*0-689-71301-0*, Aladdin) Macmillan Child Grp.
—Weather. (Illus.). 48p. (gr. 7-9). 1992. 13.95 (*0-563-21428-7*, BBC-Parkwest); pap. 6.95 (*0-563-21427-9*, BBC-Parkwest) Parkwest Pubns.
Potter, Tony & Wright, Nicola. The Macmillan First Atlas. LC 91-31257. (Illus.). 40p. (ps-2). 1992. SBE 12.95 (*0-02-774920-7*, Macmillan Child Bk) Macmillan Child Grp.
Potter, Velma M. God Flies Benny's Flag. Russell, Jervis F., ed. (Illus.). 235p. (gr. 4 up). 1989. pap. 12.95 (*0-939116-20-0*) Frontier OR.
Potts, Evangela, jt. auth. see Potts, Leanna K.
Potts, Jim. The House That Makes Shapes. LC 92-5847. (Illus.). 32p. (gr. k-3). 1992. 14.95 (*0-943173-74-4*) Harbinger AZ.
Potts, Leanna K. & Potts, Evangela. Thyme for Kids. Potts, Leanna K. & Potts, Evangela, illus. 84p. (ps-8). 1990. pap. 7.95 (*0-935069-24-0*) White Oak Pr.
Potts, Steve. All-Star Game. (gr. 5 up). 1992. PLB 14.95 (*0-88682-537-7*) Creative Ed.
—Buffalo Bills. (gr. 4 up). 1991. PLB 14.95s.p. (*0-88682-360-9*) Creative Ed.
—Denver Broncos. (gr. 4 up). 1991. PLB 14.95s.p. (*0-88682-365-X*) Creative Ed.
—Houston Oilers. (gr. 4 up). 1991. PLB 14.95s.p. (*0-88682-368-4*) Creative Ed.
—Minnesota Vikings. (gr. 4 up). 1991. PLB 14.95s.p. (*0-88682-374-9*) Creative Ed.
—New Orleans Saints. (gr. 4 up). 1991. PLB 14.95s.p. (*0-88682-376-5*) Creative Ed.
—San Francisco 49rs. (gr. 4 up). 1991. PLB 14.95s.p. (*0-88682-383-8*) Creative Ed.
—Track & Field Championship. (gr. 5 up). 1992. PLB 14. 95 (*0-88682-533-4*) Creative Ed.
Potulny, Janice C. Ribbons & Tadpoles. Credit, Alfred A., illus. 56p. (ps-4). 1990. 6.95 (*0-8059-3174-0*) Dorrance.
Poulet, Virginia. Azulin Visita a Mexico (Blue Bug Visits Mexico) Anderson, Peggy P., illus. LC 89-25420. (SPA.). 32p. (ps-3). 1990. PLB 15.00 (*0-516-33429-8*); pap. 3.95 (*0-516-53429-7*) Childrens.
—Blue Bug & the Bullies. Meighan, Don, illus. LC 79-159789. 32p. (ps-3). 1971. PLB 15.00 (*0-516-03418-9*) Childrens.
—Blue Bug Finds a Friend. Maloney, Mary & Fleming, Stan, illus. LC 76-30369. 32p. (ps-3). 1977. PLB 15.00 (*0-516-03426-X*) Childrens.
—Blue Bug Goes to Paris. Anderson, Peggy P., illus. LC 85-31390. 32p. (ps-3). 1986. pap. 3.95 (*0-516-43480-2*) Childrens.
—Blue Bug Goes to School. Anderson, Peggy P., illus. LC 84-23161. 32p. (ps-3). 1985. PLB 15.00 (*0-516-03416-0*); pap. 3.95 (*0-516-43416-0*) Childrens.
—Blue Bug Goes to the Library. Anderson, Peggy P., illus. LC 79-15219. 32p. (ps-3). 1979. PLB 15.00 (*0-516-03430-8*) Childrens.
—Blue Bug to the Rescue. LC 76-8547. (Illus.). 32p. (ps-3). 1976. PLB 15.00 (*0-516-03425-1*) Childrens.
—Blue Bug Visits Mexico. Anderson, Peggy P., illus. LC 89-25420. 32p. (ps-2). 1990. PLB 15.00 (*0-516-03429-4*); pap. 3.95 (*0-516-43429-2*) Childrens.
—Blue Bug's Beach Party. Fleming, Stan & Maloney, Mary, illus. LC 74-31224. 32p. (gr. k-3). 1975. PLB 15.00 (*0-516-03423-5*) Childrens.
—Blue Bug's Book of Colors. Anderson, Peggy P., illus. LC 80-23229. 32p. (ps-3). 1981. PLB 15.00 (*0-516-03442-1*); pap. 3.95 (*0-516-43442-X*) Childrens.
—Blue Bug's Christmas. LC 87-15793. (Illus.). 32p. (ps-3). 1987. PLB 15.00 (*0-516-03483-9*) Childrens.
—Blue Bug's Safety Book. Charles, Donald, illus. LC 72-8348. 32p. (gr. k-3). 1973. PLB 15.00 (*0-516-03419-7*) Childrens.
—Blue Bug's Surprise. Maloney, Mary & Fleming, Stan, illus. LC 76-50670. 32p. (gr. k-3). 1977. PLB 15.00 (*0-516-03427-8*) Childrens.
—Blue Bug's Vegetable Garden. Charles, Donald, illus. LC 73-8896. 32p. (gr. k-3). 1973. PLB 15.00 (*0-516-03421-9*) Childrens.
—El Libro de Colores de Azulin: Blue Bug's Book of Colors. 32p. (ps-3). 1989. PLB 15.00 (*0-516-33442-5*); pap. 3.95 (*0-516-53442-4*) Childrens.
—El Libro De Seguridad De Azulin: Blue Bug's Safety Book. LC 72-8348. (SPA., Illus.). 32p. (ps-3). 1992. PLB 15.00 (*0-516-33419-0*); pap. 3.95 (*0-516-53419-X*) Childrens.

—El Tesoro de Azulin (Blue Bug's Treasure) Maloney, M. & Fleming, S., illus. LC 75-40352. (SPA.). 32p. (ps-2). 1988. pap. 3.95 (*0-516-53424-6*) Childrens.
Poulin, Stephane. As-Tu Vu Josephine? Poulin, Stephane, illus. LC 86-51044. (FRE.). 24p. (gr. k-4). 1988. 12.95 (*0-88776-188-7*); pap. 6.95 (*0-88776-224-7*) Tundra Bks.
—Benjamin & the Pillow Saga. Poulin, Stephane, illus. 1990. 14.95 (*1-550370-69-3*, Pub. by Annick CN); pap. 5.95 (*1-550370-68-5*, Pub. by Annick CN) Firefly Bks Ltd.
—Can You Catch Josephine? Poulin, Stephane, illus. LC 87-50374. 24p. (gr. k-4). 1988. 12.95 (*0-88776-198-4*); pap. 6.95 (*0-88776-214-X*) Tundra Bks.
—Could You Stop Josephine? LC 88-50260. (Illus.). 24p. (ps-3). 1988. 12.95 (*0-88776-216-6*); pap. 6.95 (*0-88776-227-1*) Tundra Bks.
—Have You Seen Josephine? Poulin, Stephane, illus. LC 86-51043. 24p. (gr. k-4). 1988. 12.95 (*0-88776-180-1*); pap. 6.95 (*0-88776-215-8*) Tundra Bks.
—My Mother's Love. Poulin, Stephane, illus. 32p. (ps-1). 1990. 15.95 (*1-55037-149-5*, Pub. by Annick CN); pap. 5.95 (*1-55037-148-7*, Pub. by Annick CN) Firefly Bks Ltd.
—Peux-tu Attraper Josephine? LC 87-50375. (FRE., Illus.). 24p. (Orig.). (gr. k-4). 1988. 12.95 (*0-88776-199-2*); pap. 6.95 (*0-88776-225-5*) Tundra Bks.
—Pourrais-Tu Arreter Josephine? LC 88-50261. (FRE., Illus.). 24p. (ps-3). 1989. 12.95 (*0-88776-217-4*); pap. 6.95 (*0-88776-228-X*) Tundra Bks.
—Travels for Two: Stories & Lies from My Childhood. Poulin, Stephane, illus. 32p. (ps-2). 1991. PLB 15.95 (*1-55037-205-X*, Pub. by Annick CN); pap. 5.95 (*1-55037-204-1*, Pub. by Annick CN) Firefly Bks Ltd.
Poulson, Melodie. I Want to Be Somebody. 1992. 7.95 (*0-8062-4508-5*) Carlton.
Poulsson, Emilie. Finger Plays for Nursery & Kindergarten. Bridgman, L. T., illus. LC 74-165397. (ps-k). 1971. pap. 2.25 (*0-486-22588-7*) Dover.
Poulton, Michael. Augustus & the Ancient Romans. Molan, Christine, illus. LC 92-5824. 63p. (gr. 6-7). 1992. PLB 24.26 (*0-8114-3350-1*) Raintree Steck-V.
—Life in the Time of Pericles & the Ancient Greeks. James, John, illus. LC 92-5817. 63p. (gr. 6-7). 1992. PLB 24.26 (*0-8114-3352-8*) Raintree Steck-V.
Pouts-Lajus, Serge. Robots y Ordenadores (Robots & Computers) Villanueva, Marciano, tr. Davot, Francois, illus. (SPA.). 96p. (gr. 4 up). 1992. PLB 15.90 (*1-56294-178-X*) Millbrook Pr.
Pouyanne. Hare, Reading Level 3-4. (Illus.). 28p. (gr. 2-5). 1983. PLB 16.67 (*0-86592-853-3*); 12.50s.p. (*0-685-58818-1*) Rourke Corp.
—Hippo, Reading Level 3-4. (Illus.). 28p. (gr. 2-5). 1983. PLB 16.66 (*0-86592-855-X*); 12.50s.p. (*0-685-58819-X*) Rourke Corp.
—Ladybug, Reading Level 3-4. (Illus.). 28p. (gr. 2-5). 1983. PLB 16.67 (*0-86592-863-0*); 12.50 (*0-685-58821-1*) Rourke Corp.
Powell, Anton. Ancient Greece. (Illus.). 96p. 1989. 17.95 (*0-8160-1972-X*) Facts on File.
Powell, Darlene J. New Star: A Christmas Story. 1991. 7.95 (*0-533-09437-2*) Vantage.
Powell, Donalyn. A Reason to Live. 160p. (Orig.). (gr. 9 up). 1989. pap. 6.99 (*1-55661-076-9*) Bethany Hse.
Powell, E. S. Washington. LC 92-13366. 1993. PLB 17.50 (*0-8225-2726-X*) Lerner Pubns.
Powell, E. Sandy. Chance to Grow. (ps-3). 1992. pap. 4.95 (*0-87614-580-2*) Carolrhoda Bks.
—Chance to Grow. (ps-3). 1992. 13.50 (*0-87614-741-4*) Carolrhoda Bks.
—Daisy. Thornton, Peter, illus. 40p. (gr. 1-4). 1991. PLB 13.50 (*0-87614-449-0*) Carolrhoda Bks.
—Geranium Morning. Graef, Renee, illus. 40p. (gr. 1-4). 1990. PLB 13.50 (*0-87614-380-X*) Carolrhoda Bks.
—Geranium Morning: A Book about Grief. (ps-3). 1991. pap. 4.95 (*0-87614-542-X*) Carolrhoda Bks.
Powell, Harriet, compiled by. Game-Songs with Prof Dogg's Troupe. (Illus.). 64p. (ps-3). 1991. pap. 13.95 (*0-7136-2306-3*, Pub. by A&C Black UK) Talman.
Powell, Jillian. Climbers. (ps-3). 1992. 13.50 (*0-87614-700-7*) Carolrhoda Bks.
—Flyers. (ps-3). 1992. 13.50 (*0-87614-701-5*) Carolrhoda Bks.
—France. (Illus.). 32p. (gr. k-3). 1991. PLB 12.40 (*0-531-18372-6*, Pub. by Bookwright Pr) Watts.
—Italy. LC 91-59. (Illus.). 48p. (gr. 5-8). 1990. PLB 13.90 (*0-531-18337-8*, Pub. by Bookwright Pr) Watts.
—Italy. (Illus.). 32p. (gr. 2-4). 1992. PLB 12.40 (*0-531-18442-0*, Pub. by Bookwright Pr) Watts.
—Jumpers. (ps-3). 1992. 13.50 (*0-87614-702-3*) Carolrhoda Bks.
—Painting & Sculpture. LC 89-21863. (Illus.). 48p. (gr. 6-11). 1990. PLB 19.92 (*0-8114-2361-1*) Raintree Steck-V.
—Swimmers. (ps-3). 1992. 13.50 (*0-87614-703-1*) Carolrhoda Bks.
Powell, John. The Arts - Jack London. LC 92-46766. 1993. 19.93 (*0-86625-486-2*); 14.95s.p. (*0-685-66540-2*) Rourke Pubns.
Powell, Judith A., jt. auth. see Murray, Raymond L.
Powell, Leroy. Out of My Head. Warlick, Cal, illus. LC 89-28418. 240p. 1990. 15.95 (*0-934601-95-X*) Peachtree Pubs.
Powell, Mary. Katherine Stinson: Queen of the Air. Petrick, Thomas W., ed. (Illus.). 104p. (Orig.). (gr. 4-8). 1993. pap. text ed. 7.95 perfect bdg. (*1-880384-07-8*) Coldwater Pr.

Powell, Mary, ed. Wolf Tales: Native American Children's Stories. LC 92-29690. (Illus.). 70p. (Orig.). (gr. 3 up). 1993. pap. 8.95 (*0-941270-73-4*) Ancient City Pr.
Powell, Pamela. The Turtle Watchers. LC 92-5822. 160p. (gr. 3-7). 1992. 13.00 (*0-670-84294-X*) Viking Child Bks.
Powell, Patricia. Diddle Diddle Red Hot Fiddle. Metrejean, Nikki N., illus. 32p. (gr. 1-8). 1990. pap. text ed. 6.95 (*0-944512-01-1*) Radiant LA.
Powell, Patsy K. Dulac, Dat Cajun Cat: Dulac, Dat Cajun Party Animal. LC 87-91307. (Illus.). 32p. (gr. k up). 1988. pap. 6.95 (*0-944512-00-3*) Radiant LA.
Powell, Randy. Is Kissing a Girl Who Smokes Like Licking an Ashtray? 192p. 1992. 15.00 (*0-374-33632-6*) FS&G.
—My Underrated Year. 184p. (gr. 6 up). 1988. 15.00 (*0-374-35109-0*) FS&G.
—My Underrated Year. 184p. (gr. 6 up). 1991. pap. 3.95 (*0-374-45453-1*, Sunburst) FS&G.
Powell, Richard. How to Deal with Babies. Snow, Alan, illus. LC 91-3461. 24p. (gr. k-3). 1992. PLB 9.59 (*0-8167-2420-2*); pap. text ed. 2.95 (*0-8167-2421-0*) Troll Assocs.
—How to Deal with Friends. Snow, Alan, illus. LC 91-15164. 24p. (gr. k-3). 1992. PLB 9.59 (*0-8167-2422-9*); pap. text ed. 2.95 (*0-8167-2423-7*) Troll Assocs.
—How to Deal with Monsters. Snow, Alan, illus. LC 91-14975. 24p. (gr. k-3). 1992. PLB 9.59 (*0-8167-2424-5*); pap. text ed. 2.95 (*0-8167-2425-3*) Troll Assocs.
—How to Deal with Parents. Snow, Alan, illus. LC 91-14997. 24p. (gr. k-3). 1992. lib. bdg. 9.59 (*0-8167-2418-0*); pap. text ed. 2.95 (*0-8167-2419-9*) Troll Assocs.
Powell, Robert M. Recollections of a Texas Colonel at Gettysburg. Coco, Gregory A., ed. (Illus.). 62p. 1990. pap. text ed. 4.95 (*0-939631-26-1*) Thomas Publications.
Powell, Robin, jt. auth. see Herzfeld, Gerald.
Powell, Shirley S. Discovering the Magic of Museums: Especially Children's Museums. 32p. 1991. pap. write for info. (*0-9628995-0-X*) S Powell.
Powell, Suzanne. The Pueblos. LC 93-18368. (Illus.). 64p. (gr. 4-6). 1993. PLB 12.90 (*0-531-20068-X*) Watts.
Power, Vicki. Medicine & Health. (Illus.). 32p. (gr. 5-8). 1992. PLB 11.90 (*0-531-14198-5*) Watts.
Powers, Elizabeth. Nero. Schlesinger, Arthur M., Jr., intro. by. (Illus.). 112p. (gr. 5 up). 1988. lib. bdg. 17.95 (*0-87754-544-8*) Chelsea Hse.
Powers, Isaias. Father Ike's Stories for Children: Teaching Christian Values Through Animal Stories. LC 88-50332. (Illus.). 64p. (Orig.). 1988. pap. 4.95 (*0-89622-370-1*) Twenty-Third.
Powers, Janet, jt. auth. see Potter, Jamie.
Powers, Mary E. Our Teacher's in a Wheelchair. Tucker, Kathleen, ed. Powers, Mary E., illus. LC 86-1623. 32p. (ps-3). 1986. 11.95 (*0-8075-6240-8*) A Whitman.
Powers, Tom. Horror Movies. (Illus.). 80p. (gr. 5 up). 1989. 18.95 (*0-8225-1636-5*) Lerner Pubns.
—Horror Movies. (Illus.). 80p. (gr. 5 up). pap. 7.95 (*0-8225-9570-2*) Lerner Pubns.
—Movie Monsters. (Illus.). 80p. (gr. 5 up). 1989. 18.95 (*0-8225-1637-3*) Lerner Pubns.
—Movie Monsters. (Illus.). 80p. (gr. 5 up). Repr. of 1989 ed. 7.95 (*0-8225-9571-0*) Lerner Pubns.
—Special Effects in the Movies. LC 89-12703. (Illus.). 96p. (gr. 5-8). 1989. PLB 14.95 (*1-56006-102-2*) Lucent Bks.
Powhida, Elizabeth C. Anthony Mouse Goes Swimming. Peterson, Nancy M., illus. 40p. (ps-5). 1993. pap. write for info. (*0-9625842-1-5*, TXU538146) Kinderhook Pubs.
Powledge, Fred. So You're Adopted. LC 81-23278. 112p. (gr. 5 up). 1982. SBE 13.95 (*0-684-17347-6*, Scribners Young Read) Macmillan Child Grp.
—We Shall Overcome: Heroes of the Civil Rights Movement. LC 92-25184. (Illus.). 224p. (gr. 7 up). 1993. SBE 16.95 (*0-684-19362-0*, Scribners Young Read) Macmillan Child Grp.
—You'll Survive: Late Blooming, Early Blooming, Loneliness, Klutziness, & Other Problems of Adolescence, & How to Live Through Them. LC 85-43351. 144p. (gr. 6-8). 1986. SBE 13.95 (*0-684-18632-2*, Scribners Young Read) Macmillan Child Grp.
Pownall, Mark. Heroin. LC 91-27815. (Illus.). 64p. (gr. 6-12). 1991. PLB 19.92 (*0-8114-3201-7*) Raintree Steck-V.
Powzyk, Joyce. Animal Camouflage: A Closer Look. Powzyk, Joyce, illus. LC 89-9848. 40p. (gr. 2-9). 1990. SBE 15.95 (*0-02-774980-0*, Bradbury Pr) Macmillan Child Grp.
—Tasmania: A Wildlife Journey. Powzyk, Joyce, illus. LC 86-7288. 32p. (gr. 3-6). 1987. 12.95 (*0-688-06459-0*) Lothrop.
—Tracking Wild Chimpanzees. LC 87-16099. (Illus.). 32p. (gr. 1-4). 1988. 13.95 (*0-688-06733-6*); PLB 13.88 (*0-688-06734-4*) Lothrop.
—Wallaby Creek. LC 84-29757. (Illus.). 32p. (gr. 1-4). 1985. 12.95 (*0-688-05692-X*); PLB 12.88 (*0-688-05693-8*) Lothrop.
Poyner, Alice. East into Yesterday. 178p. (Orig.). (gr. 7-12). 1990. pap. 4.95 (*9971-972-94-8*) OMF Bks.
Poynor, Alice. East to the Shifting Sands. 190p. (Orig.). (gr. 6-9). 1992. pap. 4.95 (*981-3009-05-5*) OMF Bks.

Poynter, Margaret. Earthquakes: Looking for Answers. LC 89-36403. (Illus.). 64p. (gr. 6 up). 1990. lib. bdg. 15.95 (*0-89490-274-1*) Enslow Pubs.
—Marie Curie: Discoverer of Radium. LC 93-21224. 1994. write for info. (*0-89490-477-9*) Enslow Pubs.
—The Uncertain Journey: Stories of Illegal Aliens in El Norte. LC 91-8857. (Illus.). 176p. (gr. 5 up). 1992. SBE 14.95 (*0-689-31623-2*, Atheneum Child Bk) Macmillan Child Grp.
Prabhakar, Vishnu. Story of Swarajya: Part I. (Illus.). (gr. 1-10). 1979. pap. 2.50 (*0-89744-185-0*) Auromere.
Prado, Jan, ed. see McGuire, J. Victor.
Prady, Bill. Muppet Babies & the Time Machine. Brannon, Tom, illus. 26p. (ps up). 1987. 12.95 (*1-55578-605-7*) Worlds Wonder.
Prager, Annabelle. The Baseball Birthday Party. De Paola, Tomie, illus. LC 93-25258. 1994. write for info. (*0-679-84171-7*); PLB write for info. (*0-679-94171-1*) Random Bks Yng Read.
—The Spooky Halloween Party. De Paola, Tomie, illus. LC 81-1945. 48p. (gr. 1-4). 1981. 6.95 (*0-394-84370-3*); lib. bdg. 7.99 (*0-394-94370-8*) Pantheon.
—The Spooky Halloween Party. reissue ed. De Paola, Tomie, illus. 48p. (gr. k-4). 1992. pap. 6.99 incl. cass. (*0-679-83056-1*) Random Bks Yng Read.
—The Spooky Halloween Party: A Step 2 Book. De Paola, Tomie, illus. LC 88-37571. 48p. (gr. 1-3). 1989. lib. bdg. 7.99 (*0-394-94961-0*); pap. 2.95 (*0-394-84961-2*) Random Bks Yng Read.
—The Surprise Party. De Paola, Tomie, illus. LC 87-20649. 48p. (Orig.). (gr. 1-3). 1988. PLB 7.99 (*0-394-99596-1*); 3.50 (*0-394-89596-7*) Random Bks Yng Read.
Prager, Arthur & Prager, Emily. World War II Resistance Stories. Assel, Steven, illus. 96p. (gr. 7 up). 1980. pap. 2.25 (*0-440-99800-X*, LFL) Dell.
Prager, Emily, jt. auth. see Prager, Arthur.
Prager, Janice & LePoff, Arlene. Why Be Different: A Look into Judasim. 118p. (gr. 6-8). 1986. pap. text ed. 7.95 (*0-87441-427-X*) Behrman.
Pragoff, Fiona. Alphabet. LC 87-635. (Illus.). (ps-k). 1987. pap. 6.95 (*0-385-24171-2*) Doubleday.
—Autumn. Pragoff, Fiona, illus. 20p. (ps). 1993. spiral bdg. 5.95 (*0-689-71705-9*, Aladdin) Macmillan Child Grp.
—Clothes. (Illus.). 16p. (ps-k). 1989. 5.95 (*0-385-26388-0*, Zephyr-BFYR) Doubleday.
—Fiona Pragoff Board Books. (Illus.). (ps). 1988. pap. 4.95 (*0-318-32999-9*) Doubleday.
—Growing. LC 87-5239. (Illus.). 20p. (gr. k-3). 1987. 6.95 (*0-385-24174-7*) Doubleday.
—How Many? From Zero to Twenty. LC 87-5053. (Illus.). 28p. (gr. k-3). 1987. pap. 6.95 (*0-385-24172-0*) Doubleday.
—It's Fun to Be One. Pragoff, Fiona, illus. 24p. (ps). 1994. bds. 6.95 (*0-689-71813-6*, Aladdin) Macmillan Child Grp.
—It's Great to Be Two. Pragoff, Fiona, illus. 24p. (ps). 1994. bds. 6.95 (*0-689-71814-4*, Aladdin) Macmillan Child Grp.
—Let's Find Teddy. Pragoff, Fiona, illus. LC 92-2765. 32p. (ps). 1992. 10.00 (*0-679-83501-6*) Random Bks Yng Read.
—Odd One Out. (Illus.). 16p. (ps-k). 1989. 5.95 (*0-385-26410-0*, Zephyr-BFYR) Doubleday.
—Opposites. (Illus.). 16p. (ps-k). 1989. 5.95 (*0-385-26409-7*, Zephyr-BFYR) Doubleday.
—Shapes. (Illus.). 16p. (ps-k). 1989. 5.95 (*0-385-26408-9*, Zephyr-BFYR) Doubleday.
—Spring. (Illus.). 20p. (gr. k-3). 1993. pap. 5.95 spiralbound (*0-689-71707-5*, Aladdin) Macmillan Child Grp.
—Summer. (Illus.). 20p. (gr. k-3). 1993. pap. 5.95 spiralbound (*0-689-71706-7*, Aladdin) Macmillan Child Grp.
—What Color? LC 87-645. (Illus.). 20p. (gr. k-3). 1987. pap. 6.95 (*0-385-24173-9*) Doubleday.
—Winter. Pragoff, Fiona, illus. 20p. (ps). 1993. Repr. spiral bdg. 5.95 (*0-689-71704-0*, Aladdin) Macmillan Child Grp.
Prahlow, Lois, jt. auth. see Rathert, Donna.
Prairie-Plains Resource Institute Staff & Whitney, William S. Microcosm of the Platte: A Guide to Bader Memorial Park Natural Area. Whitney, Jan & Twedt, Curt, eds. Whitney, William S., illus. 140p. (Orig.). (gr. 10-12). 1988. pap. text ed. 10.00 (*0-945614-00-4*) Prairie Plains Res Inst.
Prakash, Sumangal. Story of Swarajya: Part II. Khemraj, P., illus. (gr. 1-10). 1979. pap. 2.50 (*0-89744-186-9*) Auromere.
Pranis, Eve, jt. auth. see Cohen, Joy.
Pranzo, Donard. Academic Sportfolio: Excuse Notes Are No Excuse. rev. ed. Gallup, Beth, ed. (Illus.). 1985. group of 40 lessons 249.00 (*0-924086-28-9*); Group 1, 400 photo masters incl. write for info. (*0-924086-29-7*); Group 2, 400 photo masters incl. write for info (*0-924086-30-0*) Acad Sportfolio.
Pranzo, Donard, ed. see Matovcik, Gerard.
Pranzo, Donard, ed. see Norberg, Jon.
Pratchett, Terry. Diggers. large type ed. 256p. 1992. 13.95 (*0-7451-1637-X*, Galaxy Child Lrg Print) Chivers N Amer.
—Truckers. large type ed. 320p. 1992. 13.95 (*0-7451-1469-5*, Galaxy Child Lrg Print) Chivers N Amer.

—Wings. large type ed. Kirby, C. Josh, contrib. by. 1993. 15.95 (*0-7451-1805-4*, Galaxy Child Lrg Print) Chivers N Amer.
Prater, John. The Gift. Prater, John, illus. 32p. (ps-3). 1986. pap. 9.95 (*0-670-80952-7*) Viking Child Bks.
—The Gift. LC 86-43071. (Illus.). 32p. (gr. 3-8). 1987. pap. 3.95 (*0-317-63653-7*, Puffin) Puffin Bks.
—No! Said Joe. Prater, John, illus. LC 91-71828. 32p. (ps up). 1992. 14.95 (*1-56402-037-1*) Candlewick Pr.
—Tim & the Blanket Thief: Timid Tim & the Cuggy Thief. Prater, John, illus. LC 93-6563. 32p. (ps-3). 1993. SBE 14.95 (*0-689-31881-2*, Atheneum Child Bk) Macmillan Child Grp.
Prater, John & French, Vivian, illus. Once upon a Time. LC 92-53139. 32p. (ps). 1993. 14.95 (*1-56402-177-7*) Candlewick Pr.
Prather, Alfred G., jt. auth. see Prather, Gloria A.
Prather, Alfred G., jt. auth. see Prather, Gloria M.
Prather, Arden C., ed. see Prather, Gloria A. & Prather, Alfred G.
Prather, Arden C., ed. see Prather, Gloria M. & Prather, Alfred G.
Prather, Gloria A. & Prather, Alfred G. My First Reader & Skills Book: One Hundred Words Plus. Prather, Arden C., ed. Hafer, Dick, illus. 36p. (Orig.). (gr. 1-3). 1988. pap. write for info. (*0-9619655-2-5*) Academic Packs Co.
Prather, Gloria M. & Prather, Alfred G. Especially for Special Children: The A-B-C's of Super Stars. Prather, Arden C., ed. Hafer, Dick, illus. 30p. (Orig.). 1988. Picture bk. PLB write for info. (*0-9619655-3-3*) Academic Packs Co.
—The Way to Go: Academic Travel Pack. Prather, Arden C. & Smith, Ellen, eds. Hafer, Dick & Daley, Natalie, illus. 48p. (gr. k-2). 1987. write for info. wkbk. (*0-9619655-0-9*) Academic Packs Co.
Prather, Hugh E., Jr. Circle of a Thought. 2nd, rev. ed. Helberg, Bob, ed. LC 87-73314. 80p. (gr. 9-12). 1987. pap. 7.95 (*0-944944-00-0*) Amethyst Aura.
Prather, Ray. Fish & Bones. LC 91-44227. 272p. (gr. 5-9). 1992. 14.00 (*0-06-025121-2*); PLB 13.89 (*0-06-025122-0*) HarpC Child Bks.
Pratt, Anne H. Junior Missionary Handbook. 64p. (Orig.). (gr. 3-6). 1987. pap. 5.95 (*0-88290-318-7*) Horizon Utah.
Pratt, Davis. Magic Animals of Japan. Kula, Elsa, illus. LC 67-17483. (gr. 1-4). 1967. (Pub. by Parnassus); PLB 5.88 (*0-87466-020-3*) HM.
Pratt, George. Enemy Ace: War Idyll. Helfer, Andrew, ed. Pratt, George, illus. Kubert, Joe, intro. (Illus.). 128p. (Orig.). 1991. pap. 14.95 (*0-930289-78-1*) DC Comics.
Pratt, Helen G. The Hawaiians: An Island People. Morgan, Rosamond S. & Fraser, Juliette M., illus. 210p. (gr. 6 up). 1991. pap. 9.95 (*0-8048-1709-X*) C E Tuttle.
Pratt, Kristen J. Walk in the Rainforest. (Illus.). 32p. 1992. 14.95 (*1-878265-99-7*); pap. 6.95 (*1-878265-53-9*) Dawn CA.
Pratt, Kristin. Un Paseo Por el Bosque Lluvioso: A Walk in the Rainforest. Pratt, Kristin J., illus. (SPA & ENG.). 32p. (ps-5). 1993. pap. 6.95 (*1-883220-02-5*) Dawn CA.
Pratt, Kristin J. A Swim Through the Sea. Pratt, Kristin J., illus. 44p. (Orig.). (ps-5). 1994. 14.95 (*1-883220-03-3*); pap. 6.95 (*1-883220-04-1*) Dawn CA.
Pratt, Pierre. Follow that Hat! Pratt, Pierre, illus. 32p. (ps-2). 1992. PLB 15.95 (*1-55037-261-0*, Pub. by Annick Pr); pap. 5.95 (*1-55037-259-9*, Pub. by Annick Pr) Firefly Bks Ltd.
—Leon sans Son Chapeau: Follow That Hat! Pratt, Pierre, illus. (FRE.). 32p. (ps-2). 1992. 15.95 (*1-55037-263-7*, Pub. by Annick Pr); pap. 6.95 (*1-55037-262-9*, Pub. by Annick Pr) Firefly Bks Ltd.
Pravda, Myra & Weiland, Jeanne. Off to Camp! Kiefhaber, Jan, illus. 72p. (Orig.). (gr. 2-7). 1989. pap. 4.95 perfect bdg. (*0-9622328-0-7*) JSP Pub.
Praytor, Phyllis, jt. auth. see Craig, Linda.
Prebenna, David, illus. A Car Trip for Mole & Mouse. 32p. (ps-3). 1991. pap. 3.50 (*0-14-054392-9*, Puffin) Puffin Bks.
Precek, Katharine W. Penny in the Road. Cullen-Clark, Patricia, illus. LC 88-13331. 32p. (gr. k-3). 1989. RSBE 14.95 (*0-02-774970-3*, Macmillan Child Bk) Macmillan Child Grp.
Precek, Katherine W. The Keepsake Chest. LC 91-14808. 160p. (gr. 3-7). 1992. SBE 13.95 (*0-02-775045-0*, Macmillan Child Bk) Macmillan Child Grp.
Prechtel, Martin. Grandmother Sweat Bath: A Story of the Tzutujil Mana. Prechtel, Martin, illus. Rodney, Janet, ed. (Illus.). 39p. (Orig.). (gr. 6 up). 1990. write for info. Weaselsleeves Pr.
Precilla, Maricell. Carribean Christmas. 1993. write for info. (*0-8050-2512-X*) H Holt & Co.
Pree, Bernice W. Quiet Time. Hyman, Mark, ed. 82p. (Orig.). Date not set. pap. write for info. (*0-915515-03-2*) Way Pub.
Preece, Alison & Cowden, Diane. Young Writers in the Making: Sharing the Process with Parents. LC 93-24636. 1993. pap. text ed. 15.00 (*0-435-08778-9*, 08778) Heinemann.
Preiss, Byron. Last of the Dinosaurs. (Illus.). 144p. (Orig.). (gr. 7-12). 1988. pap. 2.50 (*0-553-27007-9*) Bantam.
—Time Traveler. 80p. 1987. pap. 2.50 (*0-553-15483-4*, Skylark) Bantam.

—Vampire State Building. (gr. 4-7). 1992. pap. 3.50 (*0-553-15998-4*) Bantam.
—Where's Lulu? (ps-3). 1991. 9.99 (*0-553-07093-2*); pap. 3.50 (*0-553-35211-3*) Bantam.
Preiss, Byron & Bischoff, David. Search for Dinosaurs. Henderson, Doug & Nino, Alex, illus. 144p. (Orig.). 1984. pap. 2.25 (*0-553-25399-9*) Bantam.
Preiss, Byron & Gasperini, Jim. Secret of the Knights. Hescox, Richard, illus. 144p. (gr. 4 up). 1984. pap. 2.25 (*0-553-25368-9*) Bantam.
Preiss, Leah P. The Pig's Alphabet. LC 88-45808. (Illus.). 36p. 1989. 9.95 (*0-87923-781-3*) Godine.
Preller, James. How to Play Little League Baseball. (Illus.). 144p. 1991. pap. 2.95 (*1-56156-010-3*) Kidsbks.
—Wake Me in the Spring. Scherer, Jeffrey, illus. LC 93-16787. 1994. pap. 2.95 (*0-590-47500-2*, Cartwheel) Scholastic Inc.
Prelutsky, Jack. The Baby Uggs Are Hatching! Stevenson, James, illus. LC 81-7266. 32p. (gr. k-3). 1982. 13.95 (*0-688-00922-0*); PLB 13.88 (*0-688-00923-9*) Greenwillow.
—Baby Uggs Are Hatching! 1989. pap. 3.95 (*0-688-09239-X*, Mulberry) Morrow.
—Beneath a Blue Umbrella. Williams, Garth, illus. LC 86-19406. 64p. (ps up). 1990. 15.95 (*0-688-06429-9*) Greenwillow.
—Circus! Lobel, Arnold, illus. 32p. (ps-2). 1989. pap. 3.95 (*0-689-70806-8*, Aladdin) Macmillan Child Grp.
—The Dragons Are Singing Tonight. Sis, Peter, illus. LC 92-29013. 40p. (ps up). 1993. 15.00 (*0-688-09645-X*); PLB 14.93 (*0-688-12511-5*) Greenwillow.
—The Headless Horseman Rides Tonight. Lobel, Arnold, illus. LC 80-10372. 40p. (gr. 1-4). 1980. 13.95 (*0-688-80273-7*); PLB 13.88 (*0-688-84273-9*) Greenwillow.
—The Headless Horseman Rides Tonight. ALC Staff, ed. Lobel, Arnold, illus. LC 80-10372. 40p. (gr. 1 up). 1992. pap. 4.95 (*0-688-11705-8*, Mulberry) Morrow.
—It's Christmas. Hafner, Marilyn, illus. LC 81-1100. 48p. (gr. 1-3). 1981. 12.95 (*0-688-00439-3*); PLB 12.88 (*0-688-00440-7*) Greenwillow.
—It's Christmas. Hafner, Marylin, illus. 48p. (Orig.). (gr. k-3). 1986. 2.75 (*0-590-44048-9*); incl. cassette 5.95 (*0-590-63171-3*) Scholastic Inc.
—It's Halloween. Hafner, Marylin, illus. LC 77-2141. 56p. (gr. 1-4). 1977. 13.95 (*0-688-80102-1*); PLB 13.88 (*0-688-84102-3*) Greenwillow.
—It's Halloween. Hafner, Marylin, illus. 48p. (ps-3). 1987. pap. 2.50 (*0-590-41536-0*); Books & Cassette. 5.95 (*0-590-63252-3*) Scholastic Inc.
—It's Snowing! It's Snowing! Titherington, Jeanne, illus. LC 83-16583. 48p. (gr. 1-3). 1984. 12.95 (*0-688-01512-3*); PLB 14.93 (*0-688-01513-1*) Greenwillow.
—It's Thanksgiving. Hafner, Marilyn, illus. LC 81-1929. 48p. (gr. 1-3). 1982. 12.95 (*0-688-00441-5*); lib. bdg. 12.88 (*0-688-00442-3*) Greenwillow.
—It's Thanksgiving. Hafner, Marilyn, illus. 48p. (gr. k-3). 1989. Bk.-Cassette prepack. pap. 5.95 (*0-590-63169-1*); pap. 2.50 (*0-590-41571-9*) Scholastic Inc.
—It's Valentine's Day. Abolafia, Yossi, illus. LC 83-1449. 48p. (gr. 1-3). 1983. 14.95 (*0-688-02311-8*); PLB 14.88 (*0-688-02312-6*) Greenwillow.
—It's Valentine's Day. Abolafia, Yossi, illus. 48p. (gr. k-3). 1985. pap. 2.50 (*0-590-40979-4*) Scholastic Inc.
—It's Valentine's Day. Abolafia, Yossi, illus. 48p. (gr. k-3). 1988. pap. 5.95 bk & cassette (*0-590-63172-1*) Scholastic Inc.
—Kermit's Garden of Verses. McNally, Bruce, illus. LC 82-480. 64p. (gr. 4-6). 1982. lib. bdg. 5.99 (*0-394-95410-6*) Random Bks Yng Read.
—The Mean Old Mean Hyena. Lobel, Arnold, illus. LC 78-2300. 32p. (gr. k-3). 1978. PLB 11.88 (*0-688-84163-5*) Greenwillow.
—My Parents Think I'm Sleeping. Abolafia, Yossi, illus. LC 84-13640. 48p. (gr. 2-4). 1985. 13.95 (*0-688-04018-7*); lib. bdg. 13.88 (*0-688-04019-5*) Greenwillow.
—The New Kid on the Block. Stevenson, James, illus. LC 83-20621. 160p. (gr. 1 up). 1984. 15.00 (*0-688-02271-5*); PLB 14.88 (*0-688-02272-3*) Greenwillow.
—Nightmares: Poems to Trouble Your Sleep. Lobel, Arnold, illus. LC 76-4820. 40p. (gr. 3 up). 1976. 14.00 (*0-688-80053-X*); PLB 13.93 (*0-688-84053-1*) Greenwillow.
—Nightmares: Poems to Trouble Your Sleep. Lobel, Arnold, illus. 40p. 1993. pap. 4.95 (*0-688-04589-8*, Mulberry) Morrow.
—A Nonny Mouse Writes Again! Priceman, Marjorie, illus. LC 92-5214. 40p. (ps-5). 1993. 13.00 (*0-679-83715-9*); PLB 13.99 (*0-679-93715-3*) Knopf Bks Yng Read.
—The Queen of Eene. Chess, Victoria, illus. LC 77-17311. 32p. (gr. k-3). 1978. PLB 14.88 (*0-688-84144-9*) Greenwillow.
—Rainy, Rainy Saturday. Hafner, Marilyn, illus. LC 79-22217. 48p. (gr. 1-3). 1980. 13.95 (*0-688-80252-4*); PLB 13.88 (*0-688-84252-6*) Greenwillow.
—The Random House Book of Poetry for Children. Lobel, Arnold, illus. LC 81-85940. 248p. (gr. 1-5). 1983. 17.00 (*0-394-85010-6*); lib. bdg. 17.99 (*0-394-95010-0*) Random Bks Yng Read.
—Ride a Purple Pelican. Williams, Garth, illus. LC 84-6024. 64p. (ps up). 1986. 15.95 (*0-688-04031-4*) Greenwillow.

—Rolling Harvey Down the Hill. Chess, Victoria, illus. LC 79-18236. 32p. (gr. k-3). 1980. 14.95 (0-688-80258-3); PLB 12.88 (0-688-84258-5) Greenwillow.
—Rolling Harvey Down the Hill. Chess, Victoria, illus. LC 92-24606. 40p. (gr. 2 up). 1993. pap. 4.95 (0-688-12270-1, Mulberry) Morrow.
—The Sheriff of Rottenshot. Chess, Victoria, illus. LC 81-6420. 32p. (gr. k-3). 1982. 12.95 (0-688-00205-6); PLB 14.93 (0-688-00198-X) Greenwillow.
—The Snopp on the Sidewalk & Other Poems. Barton, Byron, illus. LC 76-46323. 32p. (gr. 3 up). 1977. PLB 15.93 (0-688-84084-1) Greenwillow.
—Something Big Has Been Here. Stevenson, James, illus. LC 89-34773. 160p. (gr. k up). 1990. 15.95 (0-688-06434-5) Greenwillow.
—Sweet & Silly Muppet Poems. 24p. (ps). 1992. 1.09 (0-307-10249-1, Golden Pr) Western Pub.
—The Terrible Tiger. Lobel, Arnold, illus. LC 88-7901. 32p. (ps-2). 1989. pap. 3.95 (0-689-71300-2, Aladdin) Macmillan Child Grp.
—Tyrannosaurus Was a Beast. LC 87-25131. (Illus.). 32p. (ps-6). 1988. 13.95 (0-688-06442-6); lib. bdg. 13.88 (0-688-06443-4) Greenwillow.
—Tyrannosaurus Was a Beast. Lobel, Arnold, illus. LC 87-25131. 32p. (ps up). 1992. pap. 4.95 (0-688-11569-1, Mulberry) Morrow.
—Tyrannosaurus Was a Beast. enl. ed. Lobel, Arnold, illus. 32p. (ps up). 1993. pap. 18.95 (0-688-12613-8, Mulberry) Morrow.
—What I Did Last Summer. Abolafia, Yossi, illus. LC 83-11561. 48p. (gr. 1-3). 1984. 13.95 (0-688-01754-1) Greenwillow.
—Zoo Doings: Animal Poems. Zelinsky, Paul O., illus. LC 82-11996. 80p. (gr. 1-3). 1983. 13.00 (0-688-01782-7); PLB 12.93 (0-688-01784-3) Greenwillow.
Prelutsky, Jack, compiled by. For Laughing Out Loud: Poems to Tickle Your Funnybone. Priceman, Marjorie, illus. LC 90-33010. 96p. (gr. 2-7). 1991. 14.95 (0-394-82144-0); PLB 15.99 (0-394-92144-5) Knopf Bks Yng Read.
Prelutsky, Jack, intro. by. Poems of A. Nonny Mouse. Drescher, Henrik, illus. LC 89-31672. 48p. (gr. 1-7). 1989. 12.95 (0-394-88711-5); lib. bdg. 14.99 (0-394-98711-X) Knopf Bks Yng Read.
Prelutsky, Jack, ed. Read-Aloud Rhymes for the Very Young. Brown, Marc, illus. Trelease, Jim, intro. by. LC 86-7147. (Illus.). 112p. (ps-3). 1988. bk. & cassette pkg. 19.95 (0-394-89833-8) Knopf Bks Yng Read.
—Read Aloud Rhymes for the Very Young. Brown, Marc, illus. Trelease, Jim, intro. by. LC 86-7147. (Illus.). 112p. (ps-3). 1986. 17.00 (0-394-87218-5); PLB 16.99 (0-394-97218-X) Knopf Bks Yng Read.
Prelutsky, Jack, tr. see Lindgren, Barbro.
Prentice, Diana, jt. auth. see Hensley, Dana.
Prentzas, G. S. The Hopi Indians. (Illus.). 1994. 13.95 (0-7910-1662-5, Am Art Analog) Chelsea Hse.
Prentzas, Scott. The Kwakiutl Indians. (Illus.). 80p. (gr. 2-5). 1993. PLB 12.95 (0-7910-1664-1) Chelsea Hse.
Prentzes, G. S. Thurgood Marshall: Champion of Justice. LC 92-34222. (Illus.). 1993. 13.95 (0-7910-1769-9, Am Art Analog); pap. 4.95 (0-7910-1969-1, Am Art Analog) Chelsea Hse.
Prenzlau, Sheryl. B. Y. Times: Running Away. Binyamini-Ariel, Liat, illus. Zakon, Miriam, contrib. by. (Illus.). 120p. (Orig.). (gr. 2-6). 1993. pap. 5.95 (1-56871-018-6) Targum Pr.
—By Times Kid Sisters, No. 6: Teacher's Pet. (Illus.). 115p. (Orig.). (gr. 3-7). 1993. pap. 6.95 (1-56871-025-9) Targum Pr.
Prenzlau, Sheryl, ed. Everything under the Sun: An Anthology for Young Teens. 448p. (gr. 5 up). 1993. 17.95 (1-56871-020-8); pap. 14.95 (1-56871-021-6) Targum Pr.
Pres, Francois Turenne Des see Turenne des Pres, Francois & California Afro-American Museum Foundation, Los Angeles Staff.
Preservation Society of Asheville & Buncombe County. Color Me Asheville. (Illus.). 40p. (gr. 4-8). 1987. pap. 4.00 (0-937481-01-7) Pres Soc Asheville.
Presnall, Judith. Animals That Glow. (Illus.). 64p. (gr. 5-8). 1993. pap. 5.95 (0-531-15672-9) Watts.
Presnall, Judith J. Animals That Glow. LC 92-25529. 1993. PLB 12.90 (0-531-20071-X) Watts.
Press, John, jt. ed. see Palgrave, Francis T.
Press, Skip. Cliffhanger. Parker, Liz, ed. Taylor, Marjorie, illus. (Orig.). (gr. 6-12). 1992. pap. text ed. 2.95 (1-56254-055-6) Saddleback Pubns.
Prest, Arthur. Illustrated History of the Nigerian People. LC 73-92798. (gr. 4 up). 1974. write for info. (0-89388-138-4) Okpaku Communications.
Prestine, Joan S. Someone Special Died, Picturebook. (ps-3). 1993. pap. 8.95 (0-86653-929-8) Fearon Teach Aids.
—Someone Special Died, Resource. (ps-3). 1993. pap. 8.95 (0-86653-928-X) Fearon Teach Aids.
—Sometimes I Feel Awful, Picturebook. (ps-3). 1993. pap. 8.95 (0-86653-927-1) Fearon Teach Aids.
—Sometimes I Feel Awful, Resource. (ps-3). 1993. pap. 8.95 (0-86653-926-3) Fearon Teach Aids.
Preston, Anthony. Aircraft Carriers. Gibbons, Tony, et al, illus. LC 84-9669. 48p. (gr. 5 up). 1985. PLB 13.50 (0-8225-1377-3, First Ave Edns); pap. 4.95 (0-8225-9504-4, First Ave Edns) Lerner Pubns.
Preston, Edna M. Squawk to the Moon, Little Goose. Cooney, Barbara, illus. LC 84-22296. 32p. (ps-1). 1985. pap. 3.95 (0-14-050546-6, Puffin) Puffin Bks.

Preston, Edna M. & Bennett, Rainey. The Temper Tantrum Book. (Illus.). (ps-3). 1976. pap. 4.95 (0-14-050181-9, Puffin) Puffin Bks.
Preston, Hap. Three Seas: A Christopher Columbus Counting Book. LC 92-80784. (Illus.). 44p. (ps-3). 1992. pap. 5.95 (1-55523-529-8) Winston-Derek.
Preston, Izola, jt. auth. see Morgan, Marian.
Preston, Judy J. The Outer Banks Story. Preston, Judy J., illus. (Orig.). (gr. 5 up). 1985. pap. 3.49 (0-9613824-0-6) Seabright.
Preston, Julia, jt. auth. see Byers, Patricia.
Preston, Kitty. Scott Joplin. King, Coretta Scott, intro. by. (Illus.). 112p. (Orig.). (gr. 5 up). 1988. 17.95 (1-55546-598-6); pap. 9.95 (0-7910-0205-5) Chelsea Hse.
Preston-Foster, Mary. Fun With Fiction. (gr. 2-5). 1988. pap. 8.95 (0-8224-3173-4) Fearon Teach Aids.
Preston Foster, Mary. Looking It Up. (gr. 2-5). 1988. pap. 8.95 (0-8224-4345-7) Fearon Teach Aids.
Preston-Mauks, Susan. Field Hockey Is for Me. Preston-Mauks, Susan & Sheehan-Burke, Julia, illus. LC 83-11268. 48p. (gr. 2-5). 1983. PLB 13.50 (0-8225-1141-X) Lerner Pubns.
—Synchronized Swimming Is For Me. Francetic, Karl D. & Sheehan-Burke, Julia, photos by. LC 82-17102. (Illus.). 48p. (gr. 2-5). 1983. PLB 13.50 (0-8225-1139-8) Lerner Pubns.
Preucil, Doris. Suzuki Viola School: Piano Accompaniments, Vol. 3. Suzuki, Shinichi, ed. 32p. (gr. k-12). 1983. pap. text ed. 6.50 (0-87487-246-4, Suzuki Method) Summy-Birchard.
—Suzuki Viola School, Viola Part, Vol. 1. Suzuki, Shinichi, ed. 32p. (gr. k-12). 1981. pap. text ed. 6.50 (0-87487-241-3) Summy-Birchard.
—Suzuki Viola School, Viola Part, Vol. 2. Suzuki, Shinichi, ed. 32p. (gr. k-12). 1982. pap. text ed. 6.50 (0-87487-242-1) Summy-Birchard.
Preucil, Doris & Suzuki, Shinichi, eds. Suzuki Viola School, Vol. A. 64p. (gr. k-12). 1982. pap. text ed. 10.95 (0-87487-245-6, Suzuki Method) Summy-Birchard.
Preucil, Doris, ed. see Suzuki, Shinichi.
Preussler, Otfried. The Satanic Mill. (gr. 5-9). 19.00 (0-8446-6196-1) Peter Smith.
—The Satanic Mill. 2nd ed. Bell, Anthea, tr. 256p. (gr. 7 up). 1991. pap. 3.95 (0-02-044775-2, Collier Young Ad) Macmillan Child Grp.
—The Tale of the Unicorn. Spirin, Gennady, illus. LC 88-7141. 32p. (ps up) 1989. 12.95 (0-8037-0583-2) Dial Bks Young.
—The Tale of the Unicorn. Spirin, Gennady, illus. 32p. (ps up). 1992. pap. 4.99 (0-14-054568-9, Puffin Pied Piper) Puffin Bks.
Prevedel, Michael, jt. auth. see Hursh, Heidi.
Prevert, Jacques. Contes pour Enfants pas Sages. (FRE.). 89p. (gr. 5-10). 1977. pap. 5.95 (2-07-033021-4) Schoenhof.
—Contes pour Enfants pas Sages. Henriquez, Elsa, illus. (FRE.). 88p. (gr. 1-5). 1990. pap. 10.95 (2-07-031181-3) Schoenhof.
Previtali, David R. The Life of Grace. (Illus., Orig.). (gr. 7). 1985. pap. 8.05, 176p. (0-89870-083-3); activity bk., 56p. 3.00 (0-89870-084-1); tchr's. manual by Mary C. Blanding, 157p. 9.95 (0-89870-124-4) Ignatius Pr.
Prevo, H. Work for Everyone Worktext. large type ed. 140p. (gr. 7-12). 1983. Repr. of 1971 ed. 25.91 (0-317-01970-8, 4-27810-00) Am Printing Hse.
Price, Betty G. & Caujolle, Claude. See Me Read. Ferguson, Elizabeth T., illus. (ps-k). 1985. pap. 19.95 (0-9614374-0-5) Prof Reading Serv.
Price, Brena. Giving, Christian Stewardship: Teaching Bks. Ressler, William, illus. 14p. (gr. 1-8). 1971. pap. text ed. 3.95 (0-86508-154-9) BCM Pubn.
—Our Bodies: Learning to Use Them to Please God. Wright, Meg, illus. 20p. (gr. 1-8). 1983. pap. 3.95 (0-86508-157-3) BCM Pubn.
Price, Cheryl. Bible Learning Centers. 96p. (gr. 2-6). 1989. 10.95 (0-86653-498-9, SS1817, Shining Star Pubns) Good Apple.
—Memory Verse Motivators. 96p. (ps-5). 1990. 10.95 (0-86653-550-0, SS1823, Shining Star Pubns) Good Apple.
Price, Donna. Greenberg's LGB Coloring Book. (Illus.). 32p. (Orig.). (gr. k-5). 1987. pap. 3.50 (0-89778-093-0, 10-7020) Greenberg Bks.
Price, Donna W. Greenberg's LGB Malbuch. (Illus.). 32p. (Orig.). (gr. k-5). 1988. text ed. 3.50 (0-89778-085-X, 10-7020G) Greenberg Bks.
Price, Gerry, illus. Fun Math Flip Book Series, 4 bks. (ps-3). 1994. No. 1: I Can Add! pap. 7.99 (0-553-09564-1); No. 2: I Can Subtract! pap. 7.99 (0-553-09565-X); No. 3: I Can Multiply! pap. 7.99 (0-553-09566-8); No. 4: I Can Divide! pap. 7.99 (0-553-09567-6) Bantam.
Price, Joan. Truth Is a Bright Star. LC 82-1345. 1982. pap. 8.95 (0-89087-333-X) Celestial Arts.
Price, Joyce. A Banged up Angel. Jones, M. L., ed. 192p. (Orig.). 1993. pap. text ed. 6.95 (1-882270-07-X) Old Rugged Cross.
Price, Leo. Hoover Wants to Help. LC 88-19188. (Illus.). 35p. (Orig.). (gr. 2-3). 1988. pap. 1.95 (0-8198-3313-4) St Paul Bks.
Price, M. & Le Cain, E. Have You Seen My Sister? (ps-2). 1991. 12.95 (0-15-200467-X, HB Juv Bks) HarBrace.
Price, Mathew. A la Cama (Bedtime) 1993. 4.99 (0-553-09562-5) Bantam.

—Amigos (Friends) (gr. 3 up). 1993. pap. 4.99 (0-553-09561-7) Bantam.
—Babies. (ps). 1992. 4.99 (0-440-40650-1, YB) Dell.
—Bebes (Babies) 1993. 4.99 (0-553-09563-3) Bantam.
—Bedtime. (ps). 1992. 4.99 (0-440-40655-2, YB) Dell.
—Clothes. (ps). 1992. 4.99 (0-440-40654-4, YB) Dell.
—Friends. (ps). 1992. 4.99 (0-440-40653-6, YB) Dell.
—Peekaboo! Claverie, Jean, illus. 24p. (ps). 1993. 5.99 (0-679-84031-1) Knopf Bks Yng Read.
—La Ropa (Clothes) Mlawer, Teresa, tr. Kemp, Moira, illus. 1993. 4.99 (0-553-09560-9) Bantam.
Price, Moe. Reindeer Christmas. (ps-3). 1993. 15.95 (0-15-266199-9, HB Juv Bks) HarBrace.
Price, Nelson L. Only the Beginning. LC 79-55662. (gr. 10 up). 1980. 7.95 (0-8054-5331-8, 4253-31) Broadman.
Price, Ray B. & Cox, Gale R. How to Acquire Wealth: One Man's Odyssey. LC 90-61189. 87p. (Orig.). 1990. pap. text ed. 8.95 (0-9626318-0-9) Price Pub SC.
Price, Roger. Kid Libs. 48p. 1990. pap. 2.95 (0-8431-2827-5) Price Stern.
Price, Roger & Stern, Leonard. Goofy Mad Libs, No. 5. (Orig.). 1968. pap. 2.95 (0-8431-0059-1) Price Stern.
—Vacation Fun Mad Libs. 48p. (gr. 4-10). pap. 2.95 (0-8431-1921-7) Price Stern.
Price, Roger, jt. auth. see Stern, Leonard.
Price, Shirley S. Deviner et Appendre. 77p. (gr. 9-12). 1991. text ed. 20.95 (0-88377-280-9, Newbury) Heinle & Heinle.
Price, Stern & Sloan Staff. Automobiles. (Illus.). 32p. (gr. 7-12). 1987. pap. 1.95 (0-8431-4288-X) Price Stern.
—Bare Bear's New Clothes. (Illus.). 22p. (gr. 3-6). 1986. 5.95 (0-8431-1824-5) Price Stern.
—Crazy Creatures. (Illus.). 22p. (gr. 3-6). 1986. 5.95 (0-8431-1822-9) Price Stern.
—Motorcycles. (Illus.). 32p. (gr. 7-12). 1987. pap. 1.95 (0-8431-4287-1) Price Stern.
—Ruth's Loose Tooth. (Illus.). 22p. (gr. 3-6). 1986. 5.95 (0-8431-1823-7) Price Stern.
Price Stern Editors. World's Worst Jokes. 1969. pap. 2.95 (0-8431-0068-0) Price Stern.
Price, Stern S. Sticker Atlas: Be Your Astronaut: Planets & Outer Space. (ps-3). 1992. pap. 3.95 (0-8431-3363-5) Price Stern.
—Sticker Atlas: Dinosaurs & Prehistoric Animals. (ps-3). 1992. pap. 3.95 (0-8431-3361-9) Price Stern.
—Sticker Atlas: Zoo Animals of the World. (ps-3). 1992. pap. 3.95 (0-8431-3362-7) Price Stern.
Price, Susan. The Ghost Drum. 176p. (gr. 3 up). 1989. pap. 3.50 (0-374-42547-7, Sunburst) FS&G.
—The Ghost Drum: A Cat's Tale. LC 86-46032. 176p. (gr. 5 up). 1987. 15.00 (0-374-32549-8) FS&G.
—Ghost Song. 1992. 15.00 (0-374-32544-8) FS&G.
Price, Susan, retold by. Jack & the Beanstalk & Other Stories. Maclean, Moira & Maclean, Colin, illus. LC 92-26442. 1993. 4.95 (1-85697-903-2) Kingfisher Bks.
—Little Red Riding Hood & Other Stories. Maclean, Moira & Maclean, Colin, illus. LC 92-26448. 1993. 5.95 (1-85697-904-0) Kingfisher Bks.
—The Three Bears & Other Stories. Maclean, Moira & Maclean, Colin, illus. LC 92-26450. 24p. (ps-1). 1993. 4.95 (1-85697-906-7) Kingfisher Bks.
Price, Susan, tr. see Slobodskoy, Seraphim.
Price, William S., Jr. There Ought to Be a Bill of Rights: North Carolina Enters a New Nation. (Illus.). 19p. (Orig.). (gr. 8-12). 1991. pap. 4.00 (0-86526-254-3) NC Archives.
Priceman, Marjorie. Friend or Frog. Priceman, Marjorie, illus. (ps-3). 1989. 13.45 (0-395-44523-X) HM.
—Friend or Frog. Priceman, Marjorie, illus. 32p. (gr. k-3). 1991. pap. 4.80 (0-395-60286-6, Sandpiper) HM.
—How to Make an Apple Pie & See The World. LC 93-12341. 1994. write for info. (0-679-83705-1); lib. bdg. write for info. (0-679-93705-6) Knopf.
Prichard, Mari, jt. auth. see Carpenter.
Pricken, Marie-Luise L., jt. auth. see Lemke, Stefan.
Pridmore, Saxby & McGrath, Mary. Julia, Mungo, & the Earthquake: A Story for Young People about Epilepsy. LC 91-7232. (Illus.). 48p. (gr. 3-6). 1992. pap. 7.95 (0-945354-31-2) Magination Pr.
Priebe, Vel. Wendy's Gift. Priebe, Vel, illus. 24p. (Orig.). (ps-2). 1988. pap. 1.50 (0-919797-67-9) Kindred Pr.
Priehs, T. J., ed. see Brugge, David.
Priehs, T. J., ed. see Gardner, Mark.
Priehs, T. J., ed. see Gnesios, Gregory.
Priehs, T. J., ed. see Houk, Rose.
Priehs, T. J., ed. see Lamb, Susan.
Priehs, T. J., ed. see Murphy, Daniel O.
Priehs, T. J., ed. see Parent, Laurence E.
Priehs, T. J., ed. see Torres, Luis.
Priehs, T. J., ed. see Udall, Stewart L. & Haury, Emil W.
Priehs, T. J., ed. see Utley, Robert.
Priest, Christine, jt. auth. see Rimm, Sylvia B.
Priest, James D. Kirins: The Flight of the Ain. Ranno, Jim & Johnson, Marc, illus. LC 91-91110. 336p. (Orig.). (gr. 6-12). 1992. pap. 11.95 (0-9626225-5-9) Yellow Pr MN.
—Kirins: The Spell of No'an. Round, Jim & Johnson, Marc, illus. LC 90-90174. 470p. (Orig.). 1990. pap. 11.95 (0-9626225-4-0) Yellow Pr MN.
Priest, Robert. The Town that Got Out of Town. LC 88-46108. (Illus.). 32p. 1989. 14.95 (0-87923-786-4) Godine.
Priestley, Dinah. Hector the Bully. Smith, Wendy, illus. 24p. (ps-3). 1989. PLB 17.50 (0-87614-356-7) Carolrhoda Bks.

Prieto. Pablo's Petunias. LC 72-190269. (Illus.). 32p. (gr. 3-5). 1972. PLB 9.95 (0-87783-058-4); pap. 3.94 deluxe ed. (0-87783-102-5) Oddo.

Primavera, Elise. Ralph's Frozen Tale. LC 90-35521. 32p. 1991. 14.95 (0-399-22252-9, Putnam) Putnam Pub Group.

—The Three Dots. Primavera, Elise, illus. LC 92-12979. 40p. (ps-3). 1993. 14.95 (0-399-22429-7, Putnam) Putnam Pub Group.

Prince, Amy, tr. see Winter, Jonah.

Prince, Michael. Oscar the Otter. 1992. 10.95 (0-533-10235-9) Vantage.

Prince, Pamela. The Best of Friends: Classic Illustrations of Children & Animals. (Illus.). 48p. 1991. 14.00 (0-517-57620-1, Harmony) Crown Pub Group.

—Once upon a Time. Smith, Jesse W., illus. LC 87-33359. 48p. (ps up). 1988. 12.95 (0-517-56832-2, Harmony) Crown Pub Group.

Prine, Mary, jt. auth. see Rosenbaum, Jean.

Pringle. Batman: Exploring the World of Bats. 1993. pap. 2.95 (0-590-46128-1) Scholastic Inc.

Pringle, Laurence. Animals at Play. LC 85-901. (Illus.). 70p. (gr. 3-7). 1985. 17.95 (0-15-203554-0, HB Juv Bks) HarBrace.

—Antarctica. 64p. 1992. pap. 15.00 jacketed (0-671-73850-X, S&S BFYR) S&S Trade.

—Batman: Exploring the World of Bats. Tuttle, Merlin D., illus. LC 90-8679. 48p. (gr. 4-6). 1991. SBE 14.95 (0-684-19232-2, Scribners Young Read) Macmillan Child Grp.

—Bearman: Exploring the World of Black Bears. Rogers, Lynn, illus. LC 89-5890. 48p. (gr. 5-7). 1989. 13.95 (0-684-19094-X, Scribners Young Read) Macmillan Child Grp.

—Death Is Natural. LC 90-46402. 64p. (gr. 1 up). 1991. pap. 5.95 (0-688-10528-9, Pub. by Beech Tree Bks) Morrow.

—Death Is Natural. LC 90-46402. (Illus.). 64p. (gr. 1 up). 1991. Repr. of 1977 ed. PLB 12.88 (0-688-10467-3) Morrow Jr Bks.

—The Earth Is Flat & Other Great Mistakes. LC 83-7966. (Illus.). 96p. (gr. 3-7). 1983. 12.95 (0-688-02466-1); lib. bdg. 12.88 (0-688-02467-X, Morrow Jr Bks) Morrow Jr Bks.

—Fire in the Forest. Marstall, Bob, illus. LC 92-32257. 32p. (gr. 2 up). 1993. 15.95 (0-02-775215-1, Macmillan Child Bk) Macmillan Child Grp.

—Global Warming: Assessing the Greenhouse Threat. 48p. (gr. 4-7). 1990. 15.95 (1-55970-012-2) Arcade Pub Inc.

—Golden Book of Insects & Spiders. (gr. 4-7). 1990. write for info. (0-307-15854-3, Pub. by Golden Bks) Western Pub.

—The Golden Book of Volcanoes, Earthquakes, & Powerful Storms. (Illus.). 48p. (gr. 3-7). 1992. write for info. (0-307-15952-3, 15952) Western Pub.

—Jackal Woman: Exploring the World of Jackals. Moehlman, Patricia D., photos by. LC 92-28207. (Illus.). 48p. (gr. 4-6). 1993. SBE 14.95 (0-684-19435-X, Scribners Young Read) Macmillan Child Grp.

—Jesse Builds a Road. Morrill, Leslie H., illus. LC 88-29297. 32p. (ps-1). 1989. RSBE 14.95 (0-02-775311-5, Macmillan Child Bk) Macmillan Child Grp.

—Living in a Risky World. LC 88-31686. (Illus.). 112p. (gr. 5 up). 1989. 12.95 (0-688-04326-7) Morrow Jr Bks.

—Living Treasure: Saving Earth's Threatened Biodiversity. LC 90-21463. 64p. (gr. 3 up). 1991. 12. 95 (0-688-07709-9); PLB 12.88 (0-688-07710-2, Morrow Jr Bks) Morrow Jr Bks.

—Nuclear Energy: Troubled Past, Uncertain Future. LC 88-28664. (Illus.). 144p. (gr. 7 up). 1989. SBE 14.95 (0-02-775391-3, Macmillan Child Bk) Macmillan Child Grp.

—Octopus Hug. Palmer, Kate S., illus. 32p. (ps-3). 1993. 14.95 (1-56397-034-1) Boyds Mills Pr.

—Oil Spills. LC 92-30348. (Illus.). 64p. (gr. 3 up). 1993. 14.00 (0-688-09860-6); PLB 13.93 (0-688-09861-4) Morrow Jr Bks.

—Rain of Troubles: The Science & Politics of Acid Rain. LC 87-34950. (Illus.). 128p. (gr. 7 up). 1988. SBE 14. 95 (0-02-775370-0, Macmillan Child Bk) Macmillan Child Grp.

—Restoring Our Earth. LC 87-615. (Illus.). 64p. (gr. 6 up). 1987. lib. bdg. 15.95 (0-89490-143-5) Enslow Pubs.

—Scorpion Man: Exploring the World of Scorpions. Polis, Gary A., photos by. LC 93-34936. 48p. (gr. 4 up). 1994. write for info. (0-684-19560-7, Scribner) MacMillan.

—Water: The Next Great Resource Battle. LC 81-23694. (Illus.). 64p. (gr. 6 up). 1982. SBE 14.95 (0-02-775400-6, Macmillan Child Bk) Macmillan Child Grp.

Pringle, Mary L. & Ellis, Joseph. Sis & Chris & the Knowbots in "We Don't Need Drugs to Be O. K." Educational Coloring Book. (gr. k-5). 1987. pap. 1.95 (0-935847-03-0) Inst Subs Abuse Res.

Prior, Katherine. Initiation Customs. LC 93-516. 32p. (gr. 4-8). 1993. 13.95 (1-56847-035-5) Thomson Lrning.

—Pilgrimages & Journeys. LC 93-16318. (Illus.). 32p. (gr. 4-8). 1993. 13.95 (1-56847-032-0) Thomson Lrning.

Prior, Natalie J. Amabel Abroad: More Amazing Adventures. Nicholson, John, illus. (Orig.). (gr. 6 up). 1993. pap. 7.95 (1-86373-130-X, Pub. by Allen & Unwin Aust Pty AT) IPG Chicago.

—The Amazing Adventures of Amabel. Nicholson, John, illus. 112p. (Orig.). (gr. 6 up). 1993. pap. 7.95 (0-04-442163-X, Pub. by Allen & Unwin Aust Pty AT) IPG Chicago.

Prior, R. W. The Great Monarch Butterfly Chase. Glick, Beth, illus. LC 92-7423. 32p. (ps-3). 1993. RSBE 14. 95 (0-02-775145-7, Bradbury Pr) Macmillan Child Grp.

Pritchett, V. S., ed. see Bronte, Emily.

Pritts, Kim D. The Mystery of Sadler Marsh. Archambault, Matthew, illus. 112p. (Orig.). (gr. 3-7). 1993. pap. 4.95 (0-8361-3618-7) Herald Pr.

Privensen, Alice. Shaker Lane. 1990. pap. 4.95 (0-14-050713-2, Puffin) Puffin Bks.

Prizzi, Elaine & Hoffman, Jeanne. Reading Around the World. (gr. 4-6). 1985. pap. 6.95 (0-8224-3182-3) Fearon Teach Aids.

—Reading Around Town. (gr. 4-6). 1985. pap. 6.95 (0-8224-3181-5) Fearon Teach Aids.

—Reading Everyday Stuff. (gr. 4-6). 1985. pap. 6.95 (0-8224-3180-7) Fearon Teach Aids.

—Teaching off the Wall. LC 80-81836. (gr. 2-5). 1981. pap. 10.95 (0-8224-6830-1) Fearon Teach Aids.

Prizzi, Elaine & Hoffmann, Jeanne. Beginning Book Reporting. LC 83-63175. (gr. 2-5). 1984. pap. 12.95 (0-8224-2175-5) Fearon Teach Aids.

—Interactive Bulletin Boards. LC 82-63176. (gr. 1-4). 1984. pap. 11.95 (0-8224-6256-7) Fearon Teach Aids.

Prizzi, Elaine, jt. auth. see Hoffman, Jeanne.

Probert, D. Cloze Clues. (gr. 4-6). 1988. 9.75 (0-88160-166-7, LW 276) Learning Wks.

Probosz, Kathilyn S. Alvin Ailey, Jr. (gr. 4-7). 1991. pap. 3.50 (0-553-15930-5) Bantam.

Prochazkova, Iva. The Season of Secret Wishes. Crawford, Elizabeth D., tr. from GER. LC 89-45291. 208p. (gr. 4-8). 1989. 12.95 (0-688-08735-3) Lothrop.

Prochnow, Dave & Prochnow, Kathy. How? More Experiments for the Young Scientist. (Illus.). 160p. 1992. 16.95 (0-8306-4024-X, 4177); pap. 9.95 (0-8306-4025-8, 4177) TAB Bks.

—Why? Experiments for the Young Scientist. (Illus.). 160p. (gr. 4-7). 1992. 16.95 (0-8306-4015-0, 4176); pap. 9.95 (0-8306-4023-1, 4176) TAB Bks.

Prochnow, Kathy, jt. auth. see Prochnow, Dave.

Proffitt, Bettina, tr. see Hutchinson, Hanna.

Profiles Corporation Staff. Inside the SAT. (Illus.). 80p. (gr. 11-12). 1992. wkbk. 15.95 (0-7836-1306-7, 2103) Profiles Corp.

Profilet, Cynthia. Kamal's Quest. Livingston, Francis, illus. 40p. (gr. 5-6). 1993. 15.95 (0-9637735-0-X) Sterling Pr MS.

Prohaska, Elizabeth. Trivial Pursuit - Science (Primary) (Illus.). 64p. (gr. 1-3). 1992. 12.95 (0-86653-647-7, GA1385) Good Apple.

Prokofieff, Sergei. Peter & the Wolf. Alchemy II, Inc. Staff, illus. 26p. (ps). 1988. incl. cassette 9.95 (0-317-89541-9) Worlds Wonder.

Prokofiev, Sergei. Peter & the Wolf. Carlson, Maria, tr. Mikolayack, Charles, illus. 32p. (ps-3). 1986. pap. 4.99 (0-14-050633-0, Puffin) Puffin Bks.

—Peter & the Wolf. Carlson, Maria, tr. Mikolaycak, Charles, illus. (gr. 2-5). 1987. incl. cassette 19.95 (0-87499-074-2); pap. 12.95 incl. cassette (0-87499-073-4); 4 paperbacks, cassette & guide 27.95 (0-87499-075-0) Live Oak Media.

—Peter & the Wolf. Crampton, Patricia, tr. Palecek, Josef, illus. LC 87-13915. (ps up). 1991. pap. 13.95 (0-88708-049-9) Picture Bk Studio.

—Peter & the Wolf. Voigt, Erna, illus. LC 79-92902. 32p. 1987. 15.95 (0-87923-331-1) Godine.

—Peter & the Wolf. Crampton, Patricia, tr. LC 91-40185. (Illus.). 28p. (gr. k up). 1992. pap. 4.95 (0-88708-226-2) Picture Bk Studio.

—Peter & the Wolf Pop-up-Book. Cooney, Barbara, illus. (gr. k-12). 1986. pap. 17.00 (0-670-80849-0) Viking Child Bks.

Prokofiev, Sergei & Chappell, Warren. Peter & the Wolf. (Illus.). (gr. 4 up). 1973. pap. 1.95 (0-394-82613-2) Knopf Bks Yng Read.

Prokop, Michael S. Divorce Happens to the Nicest Kids: A Self-Help Book For Kids (3-15) & Adults. Peters, Robert C., ed. Fogarty, Michelle D., illus. LC 85-72180. 224p. (Orig.). (gr. k up). 1986. 18.95 (0-933879-25-3); pap. 6.45 Kids' Divorce Wkbk. (0-933879-26-1); kids' Divorce wkbk. 6.45 (0-933879-27-X) Alegra Hse Pubs.

Prolman, Marilyn. The Story of the Capitol. Wiskur, Darrell, illus. LC 69-14681. 32p. (gr. 3-6). 1969. pap. 3.95 (0-516-44604-5) Childrens.

—The Story of the Constitution. Glaubke, Robert, illus. LC 69-14680. 32p. (gr. 3-6). 1969. PLB 13.27 (0-516-04605-5); pap. 3.95 (0-516-44605-3) Childrens.

Pronk, Mary, ed. see Pawczuk, Eugene.

Pronzini, Bill, ed. More Wild Westerns. 192p. 1989. 19. 95 (0-8027-4097-9) Walker & Co.

Prophet, Elizabeth C., jt. auth. see Prophet, Mark L.

Prophet, Mark L. & Prophet, Elizabeth C. Ascended Masters on Soul Mates & Twin Flames Bks I & II. 1985. 418p. 19.95, (0-916766-85-3); 404p. 19.95, (0-916766-86-1) Summit Univ.

Propp, Jim. Tuscanini. Weiss, Ellen, illus. LC 91-1240. 32p. (ps-1). 1992. RSBE 13.95 (0-02-774911-8, Bradbury Pr) Macmillan Child Grp.

Propper. Bear, Reading Level 3-4. (Illus.). 28p. (gr. 2-5). 1983. PLB 16.67 (0-86592-865-7) Rourke Corp.

—Dolphin, Reading Level 3-4. (Illus.). 28p. (gr. 2-5). 1983. PLB 16.67 (0-86592-861-4); 12.50s.p. (0-685-58815-7) Rourke Corp.

—Giraffe, Reading Level 3-4. (Illus.). 28p. (gr. 2-5). 1983. PLB 16.67 (0-86592-860-6); 12.50s.p. (0-685-58817-3) Rourke Corp.

—Panda, Reading Level 3-4. (Illus.). 28p. (gr. 2-5). 1983. PLB 16.67 (0-86592-851-7); 12.50 (0-685-58822-X) Rourke Corp.

—Turtle, Reading Level 3-4. (Illus.). 28p. (gr. 2-5). 1983. PLB 16.67 (0-86592-856-8); PLB 12.50s.p. (0-685-58828-9) Rourke Corp.

Propper, et al. World Animal Library, 17 bks, Reading Level 3-4. (Illus.). 476p. (gr. 2-5). 1983. Set. PLB 283. 39 (0-86592-850-9); PLB 212.50s.p. (0-685-58814-9) Rourke Corp.

Prose, Francine. Stories from Our Living Past. new ed. Harlow, Jules, ed. Weihs, Erika, illus. LC 74-8514. 128p. (gr. 3-4). 1974. 7.95 (0-87441-081-9); wkbk. 1 2.95 (0-87441-083-5); wkbk. 2 2.95 (0-87441-084-3); tchr's guide 14.95 (0-87441-082-7) Behrman.

Prosser, Jerry see Mayakovsky, Stanislaw, pseud.

Prosser, Robert. Disappearing Rainforest. (gr. 6 up). 1988. 19.95 (0-7134-9719-X, Pub. by Batsford UK) Trafalgar.

Prostano, Emanuel & Prostano, Joyce. Take Two Inventions & Two Patents. (Illus.). 130p. (Orig.). (gr. 8-12). 1991. pap. 19.95 (0-944397-14-X) In-Time Pubns.

Prostano, Joyce, jt. auth. see Prostano, Emanuel.

Prot, Viviane A. The Story of Birth. Bogard, Vicki, tr. from FRE. Gaudriault, Rozier, illus. LC 90-50777. 38p. (gr. k-5). 1991. 4.95 (0-944589-34-0, 340) Young Discovery Lib.

Protopopescu, Orel O. The Perilous Pit. Chwast, Jacqueline, illus. LC 92-290. 40p. (ps-1). 1993. JRT 14.00 (0-671-76910-3, Green Tiger) S&S Trade.

—Since Lulu Learned the Cancan. LC 90-85014. (Illus.). (ps). 1991. 13.95 (0-671-74791-6, Green Tiger) S&S Trade.

Provencher, Jean. Quebec. (Illus.). 144p. (gr. 4 up). 1992. PLB 26.60 (0-516-06617-X) Childrens.

Provensen, Alice. The Buck Stops Here: The Presidents of the United States. Provensen, Alice, illus. LC 88-35036. 56p. (gr. 2 up). 1990. 18.00 (0-06-024786-X); PLB 17.89 (0-06-024787-8) HarpC Child Bks.

—The Buck Stops Here: The Presidents of the United States. LC 88-35036. (Illus.). 56p. (gr. 2 up). 1992. pap. 7.95 (0-06-446132-7, Trophy) HarpC Child Bks.

—Punch in New York. 32p. (gr. 3). 1991. pap. 14.95 (0-670-82790-8) Viking Child Bks.

Provensen, Alice & Provensen, Martin. A Book of Seasons. Provensen, Alice & Provensen, Martin, illus. LC 75-36470. 32p. (ps-1). 1976. pap. 2.25 (0-394-83242-6) Random Bks Yng Read.

—The Glorious Flight. (gr. 4-6). 1987. pap. 4.99 (0-14-050729-9, Puffin) Puffin Bks.

—The Glorious Flight. (gr. 3-5). 1987. incl. bk. & cassette 19.95 (0-87499-062-9); pap. 27.95 incl. 4 bks. & cassette (0-87499-063-7); pap. 12.95 incl. bk. & cassette (0-87499-061-0) Live Oak Media.

—The Glorious Flight Across the Channel with Louis Bleriot. LC 82-7034. (Illus.). 40p. (gr. 5-8). 1983. pap. 14.95 (0-670-34259-9) Viking Child Bks.

—The Glorious Flight: Across the Channel with Louis Bleriot. (Illus.). 40p. (gr. 3-8). 1987. pap. 4.95 (0-317-63651-0, Puffin) Puffin Bks.

—Leonardo da Vinci: The Artist, Inventor, Scientist in Three-Dimensional Movable Pictures. LC 83-26005. (Illus.). 12p. 1984. pap. 17.95 (0-670-42384-X) Viking Child Bks.

—El Libro de las Estaciones. Cuenca, Pilar de & Alvarez, Ines, trs. LC 81-13821. (SPA., Illus.). 32p. (ps-3). 1982. lib. bdg. 5.99 (0-394-95143-3); pap. 2.25 (0-394-85143-9) Random Bks Yng Read.

—The Mother Goose Book. reissue ed. Provensen, Alice & Provensen, Martin, illus. LC 76-8548. 64p. (gr. 1 up). 1976. 10.00 (0-394-82122-X) Random Bks Yng Read.

—Old Mother Hubbard. Provensen, Alice & Provensen, Martin, illus. LC 76-24176. 32p. (ps-1). 1992. pap. 2.25 (0-394-83460-7) Random Bks Yng Read.

—Our Animal Friends at Maple Hill Farm. reissue ed. Provensen, Alice & Provensen, Martin, illus. LC 74-828. 64p. (ps-3). 1992. 10.00 (0-394-82123-8) Random Bks Yng Read.

—Shaker Lane. (ps up). 1987. 14.95 (0-670-81568-3) Viking Child Bks.

—The Year at Maple Hill Farm. Provensen, Alice & Provensen, Martin, illus. LC 88-10367. 32p. (ps-2). 1988. pap. 3.95 (0-689-71270-7, Aladdin) Macmillan Child Grp.

Provensen, Alice & Provensen, Martin, illus. A Peaceable Kingdom: The Shaker Abecedarius. Barsam, Richard M., afterword by. (gr. k-3). 1981. pap. 5.99 (0-14-050370-6, Puffin) Puffin Bks.

—A Peaceable Kingdom: The Shaker Abecedarius. Barsam, Richard M., afterword by. LC 78-125. 42p. (gr. k-2). 1978. pap. 16.00 (0-670-54500-7) Viking Child Bks.

Provensen, Martin, jt. auth. see Provensen, Alice.

Provost, C. Antonio. Modern Renaissance Poetry & Philosophy. Kroll, William, ed. Forster, Maria, frwd. by. LC 92-96848. (Illus.). 148p. (gr. 9-12). 1992. 14.00 (0-317-05253-5); pap. 10.00 (0-317-05254-7) Provost.

Provost, Gary. Good If It Goes. LC 89-18339. 160p. (gr. 4-7). 1990. pap. 3.95 (0-689-71381-9, Aladdin) Macmillan Child Grp.

Provost, Gary & Levine-Provost, Gail. David & Max. 196p. (gr. 5-9). 1991. pap. 8.95 (0-8276-0392-4) JPS Phila.

Prowense, Mary J. Pamela & the Revolution. Schatz, Molly, ed. Kear, Suzanne, illus. 130p. (gr. 7 up). 1993. 12.95 (0-9635107-2-X) Marc Anthony. Nominated for the Golden Kite Award for 1993, this book is highly recommended by teachers & parents for delightful reading while learning history 'firsthand.' Beautifully illustrated with 15 line drawings, this is how The Book Reader, Fall Issue described PAMELA & THE REVOLUTION. 'A time warp that uses some familiar historical figures to construct an engaging novel. A contemporary California teenager, Pamela visits Paris where she had lived as a youngster, excited at the memories of her family's long French ancestry. Her heritage would play a part more intimate than she could ever imagine, for upon leaving the ladies' room in her hotel, she hears strange voices. "The Americans will not be the only ones who will win their War of Independence! France will be next." It's not a movie set. Lafayette & Thomas Paine had not just come from wardrobe. Indeed, Pamela has been swooped back two centuries to the age of Marie Antoinette! She meets a mystic named Cazotte who relishes the chance acquaintance of a fellow-seer, & the chance to perhaps re-write history, & spare some of the bloodshed recounted in the Reign of Terror. He gives her a golden ring: "In my plan you will wear this ring. It will enable you to remember who you are." Pamela would become Marie Antoinette & move throughout the courts of her new time, adorned with new identity, & power & grace. She meets & puzzles Lafayette with her knowledge of future events, & she gets caught up in the gossip involving Madame DuBarry. And just when her hopes with Louis XVI seem the brightest, she twists her golden ring a special way, & returns to present time. A spell binding, delightful tale which enlivens history & does justice to the memory of Marie Antoinette.' PAMELA & THE REVOLUTION is destined to become a classic in children's literature. Be one of the first to get this charming way to learn about history while experiencing adventure. Marc Anthony Publications, P.O. Box 5610, Blue Jay, CA 92317. *Publisher Provided Annotation.*

Proysen, Alf. Little Old Mrs. Pepperpot. (gr. 1-4). 1960. 12.95 (0-8392-3021-4) Astor-Honor.
—Mrs. Pepperpot Again. Berg, Bjorn, illus. (gr. 1-4). 1961. 12.95 (0-8392-3023-0) Astor-Honor.
—Mrs. Pepperpot & the Moose. Fisher, Richard E., tr. Berg, Bjorn, illus. 28p. (ps up). 1991. bds. 13.95 (91-29-59924-5, Pub. by R & S Bks) FS&G.
—Mrs. Pepperpot in the Magic Wood. Berg, Bjorn, illus. 128p. (gr. 1-4). 1988. pap. 3.95 (0-14-030538-6, Puffin) Puffin Bks.
—Mrs. Pepperpot to the Rescue. (gr. k-6). 1987. pap. 16. 25 (0-440-45597-9, YB) Dell.
—Mrs. Pepperpot to the Rescue. Berg, Bjorn, photos by. (gr. 1-4). 1988. pap. 3.50 (0-317-69648-3, Puffin) Puffin Bks.
Prubhupada, A. C., tr. see Wilson, Karen.
Prudhomme, Frances & Sternberg, Susan T. The Gift of the Greeks: Art & Civilization of Ancient Greece. 24p. (Orig.). (gr. 4-7). 1982. pap. 8.95 (0-935213-04-X) A M Huntington Art.
Prue, Donald, jt. auth. see Orlandi, Mario.
Pruett, Robert H., ed. see Williams, Jane S.
Pruitt, A. B. Abstracts of Land Entries: Gates, Chowan, Perquimans, Pasquotank, Camden, & Currituck Cos, NC. (Illus.). 198p. (Orig.). (gr. 12). 1992. pap. 18.75 (0-944992-44-7) ABP Abstracts.

—Abstracts of Sales of Confiscated Land & Property in North Carolina. (Illus.). 249p. (Orig.). (gr. 12). 1990. pap. 23.00 (0-944992-26-9) ABP Abstracts.
—Colonial Petitions for Land Resurveys, Land Warrants, & Caveats. 142p. (gr. 12). 1993. pap. 14.50 (0-944992-47-1) ABP Abstracts.
—Petitions for Land Grant Suspensions in North Carolina. (Illus.). 402p. (Orig.). (gr. 12). 1993. pap. 39. 00 (0-944992-48-X) ABP Abstracts.
Pruitt, Pamela, jt. auth. see Johnston, Brenda A.
Pruitt, Pamela, et al. Henry Box Brown; Struggle for Freedom; Wildfire. 2nd ed. McCluskey, John A., ed. Howard, Cecelia, et al, illus. (Orig.). (gr. 4-7). 1993. pap. 3.00 (0-913678-25-2) New Day Pr.
Prunier, J. & Galeron, H., illus. Dinosaure. (FRE.). (ps-1). 1991. 17.95 (2-07-056642-0) Schoenhof.
Prunier, James. Livre des As et des Heros: Histoire de l'Aviation, No. 2. (FRE.). 77p. (gr. 4-9). 1988. 13.95 (2-07-039548-0) Schoenhof.
—Livre des Trains. (FRE.). 93p. (gr. 4-9). 1986. 15.95 (2-07-039527-8) Schoenhof.
Prunier, James, jt. auth. see Delafosse, Claude.
Prusski, Jeffrey. Bring Back the Deer. Waldman, Neil, illus. 32p. (ps-3). 1988. 13.95 (0-15-200418-1, Gulliver Bks) HarBrace.
Prust, Z. A. Photo-Offset Lithography. LC 77-21607. (Illus.). 160p. (gr. 9 up). 1977. text ed. 14.60 (0-87006-240-9); text ed. 10.95 s.p. (0-685-01933-0) Goodheart.
Pryde, Marion J., jt. auth. see Fleming, Beatrice J.
Pryor, Ainslie. The Baby Blue Cat & the Dirty Dog Brothers. (Illus.). (ps-3). 1987. 11.95 (0-670-81781-3) Viking Child Bks.
—Baby Blue Cat & the Smiley Worm Doll. (ps). 1990. 11.95 (0-670-83531-5) Viking Child Bks.
—The Baby Blue Cat & the Whole Batch of Cookies. (Illus.). 32p. (ps-1). 1989. 11.95 (0-670-81782-1) Viking Child Bks.
—The Baby Blue Cat & the Whole Batch of Cookies. (Illus.). 32p. (ps-1). 1991. pap. 3.95 (0-14-050770-1, Puffin) Puffin Bks.
—The Baby Blue Cat Who Said No. Pryor, Ainslie, illus. LC 87-21026. 32p. (ps-k). 1988. 11.95 (0-670-81780-5) Viking Child Bks.
—The Baby Blue Cat Who Said No. (Illus.). 32p. (ps-1). 1990. pap. 3.95 (0-14-050768-X, Puffin) Puffin Bks.
Pryor, Bonnie. Amanda & April. DeGroat, Diane, illus. LC 85-15308. 32p. (ps-1). 1986. 15.95 (0-688-05869-8); lib. bdg. 15.88 (0-688-05870-1) Morrow Jr Bks.
—The Beaver Boys. Baker, Karen, illus. LC 90-38515. 40p. (ps up). 1992. 15.00 (0-688-08702-7); lib. bdg. 14. 93 (0-688-08703-5) Morrow Jr Bks.
—Birthday Blizzard. Delaney, Molly, illus. LC 92-1713. 32p. (gr. k up). 1993. 15.00 (0-688-09423-6); PLB 14. 93 (0-688-09424-4) Morrow Jr Bks.
—Grandpa Bear. Degen, Bruce, illus. LC 84-25545. 32p. (ps-1). 1985. 12.95 (0-688-04551-0) Morrow Jr Bks.
—Grandpa Bear's Christmas. Degen, Bruce, illus. LC 85-29707. 32p. (ps-1). 1986. 12.95 (0-688-06063-3); lib. bdg. 12.88 (0-688-06064-1) Morrow Jr Bks.
—Greenbrook Farm. LC 89-11573. 40p. (gr. k-3). 1991. pap. 13.95 jacketed (0-671-69205-4, Little Simon) S&S Trade.
—Greenbrook Farm. Graham, Mark, illus. LC 89-11573. 40p. (ps-2). 1993. pap. 4.95 (0-671-79606-2, S&S BFYR) S&S Trade.
—Horses in the Garage. LC 92-7287. 160p. (gr. 4 up). 1992. 14.00 (0-688-10567-X) Morrow Jr Bks.
—The House on Maple Street. Peck, Beth, illus. LC 86-12648. 32p. (gr. k-3). 1987. 15.95 (0-688-06380-2); lib. bdg. 14.88 (0-688-06381-0) Morrow Jr Bks.
—The House on Maple Street. ALC Staff, ed. Peck, Beth, illus. LC 86-14628. 32p. (gr. k up). 1992. pap. 4.95 (0-688-12031-8, Mulberry) Morrow.
—Jumping Jenny. Riggio, Anita, illus. 192p. (gr. 2 up). 1992. 14.00 (0-688-09684-0) Morrow Jr Bks.
—Lottie's Dream. LC 91-3965. (ps-3). 1992. pap. 14.00 (0-671-74774-6, S&S BFYR) S&S Trade.
—Merry Christmas, Amanda & April. De Groat, Diane, illus. LC 89-39723. 32p. (ps up). 1990. 13.95 (0-688-07544-4); PLB 13.88 (0-688-07545-2, Morrow Jr Bks) Morrow Jr Bks.
—Mr. Munday & Space Creatures. (gr. k-3). 1991. pap. 4.95 (0-671-73620-5, S&S BFYR) S&S Trade.
—Mr. Munday & the Rustlers. Manyum, Wallop, illus. LC 87-17539. 32p. (ps-3). 1987. PLB 12.95 (0-13-604737-8) P-H.
—Mr. Munday & the Space Creatures. Lorenz, Lee, illus. (ps-3). 1989. pap. 13.95 (0-671-67114-6) S&S Trade.
—Mr. Munday & the Space Creatures. (gr. 2). 1991. pap. write for info. (0-663-56224-4) Silver Burdett Pr.
—The Plum Tree War. Leder, Dora, illus. LC 88-32426. 128p. (gr. 3-6). 1989. 11.95 (0-688-08142-8) Morrow Jr Bks.
—The Plum Tree War. Leder, Dora, illus. (gr. 4-7). 1992. pap. 3.25 (0-440-40619-6, Pub. by Yearling Classics) Dell.
—Poison Ivy & Eyebrow Wigs. Owens, Gail, illus. LC 92-38881. 176p. (gr. 3 up). 1993. 14.00 (0-688-11200-5) Morrow Jr Bks.
—The Porcupine Mouse. Begin, Maryjane, illus. LC 87-12305. 32p. (ps-2). 1988. 13.95 (0-688-07153-8); PLB 13.88 (0-688-07154-6, Morrow Jr Bks) Morrow Jr Bks.
—Rats, Spiders & Love. Higgenbottom, J. Winslow, illus. LC 85-25831. 128p. (gr. 4-6). 1986. 13.95 (0-688-05867-1) Morrow Jr Bks.

—Rats, Spiders, & Love. (gr. k-6). 1989. pap. 2.75 (0-440-40138-0, YB) Dell.
—Seth of the Lion People. LC 88-18747. 128p. (gr. 3-6). 1988. 11.95 (0-688-07327-1) Morrow Jr Bks.
—The Twenty-Four Hour Lipstick Mystery. Hamanaka, Sheila, illus. LC 89-34483. 128p. (gr. 3 up). 1989. 11. 95 (0-688-08198-3) Morrow Jr Bks.
—The Twenty-Four Hour Lipstick Mystery. Hamanaka, Sheila, illus. 144p. (gr. 4-7). 1992. pap. 3.50 (0-440-40736-2, YB) Dell.
—Vinegar Pancakes & Vanishing Cream. Owens, Gail, illus. LC 86-31085. 128p. (gr. 2-5). 1987. 12.95 (0-688-06728-X) Morrow Jr Bks.
—Vinegar Pancakes & Vanishing Cream. 128p. (gr. k-6). 1989. pap. 3.50 (0-440-40173-9, YB) Dell.
Pryor, Francis & Collison, David. Now Then: Digging up the Past. (Illus.). 48p. (gr. 7-10). 1994. 24.95 (0-7134-7290-1, Pub. by Batsford UK) Trafalgar.
Pryor, LaRita B. The African-American Writer's Survival Handbook: How & Where to Get Published. LC 90-20306. 250p. (gr. 9-12). 1991. text ed. 30.00 (0-89341-649-5, Longwood Academic); pap. text ed. 17.50 (0-89341-650-9) Hollowbrook.
Pryor, Nick & Bitmead, Michele. Putting on a Play. (Illus.). 48p. (gr. 2-5). 1994. 15.95 (1-56847-104-1) Thomson Lrning.
PSECC Staff. Hale'-Ta: Governing Guam: Before & After the Wars. 300p. (gr. 8). 1993. write for info. (1-883488-02-8) Polit Status ECC.
—Hale'-Ta: Hestorian Taotao Tano' History of the Chamorro People. 100p. (gr. 5). 1993. write for info. (1-883488-00-1) Polit Status ECC.
—Hale'-Ta: Issues in Guam's Political Development: The Chamorro Perspective. 100p. (gr. 9). 1993. write for info. (1-883488-03-6) Polit Status ECC.
—Hale'Ta: Insights: The Chamorro Identity. 200p. (gr. 12). 1993. write for info. (1-883488-01-X) Polit Status ECC.
Ptacek, Greg & Anderson, Lydia M. Champion for Children's Health: A Story about Dr. S. Josephine Baker. LC 93-10482. (Illus.). 1993. write for info. (0-87614-806-2) Carolrhoda Bks.
Ptacek, Greg, jt. auth. see Vare, Ethlie A.
Public Library Association, Job & Career Information Committee Staff. PLA Guide to Basic Resume Writing. LC 90-50722. 96p. (gr. 9 up). 1991. pap. 7.95 (0-8442-8123-9, VGM Career Bks) NTC Pub Grp.
Puccetti, Patricia I. Credo: I Believe: Activity Book. 46p. (Orig.). (gr. 5 up). 1985. pap. 3.00 (0-89870-082-5) Ignatius Pr.
Puccetti, Patricia I., ed. see Podhaizer, Mary E.
Puccetti, Patricia I., ed. see Sockey, Daria M.
Puckett, Christine S. & Barnes, Joe. A Panorama of Northeast Alabama & Etowah County: Lookout Mountain Meets the Coosa. 2nd ed. (Illus.). 136p. (Orig.). (gr. 4 up). 1992. 8.95 (0-9633116-0-3) Starr Pub AL.

Puckett, Kirby. Be the Best You Can Be. Houle, Tim, illus. 40p. 1993. 14.95 (0-931674-20-4) Waldman Hse Pr. Baseball superstar Kirby Puckett shares with kids his life story & the many values & lessons he has learned both on & off the field. Kirby tells about growing up in the south side of Chicago, his love & respect for his family, & his amazing baseball career. BE THE BEST YOU CAN BE inspires kids to reach for excellence in whatever they do. "...the book is a solid piece of inspirational biography that portrays both the man & the baseball player. It will be a useful purchase for school & public libraries."-- BOOKLIST. Filled with four-color illustrations & photographs. Hardcover, $14.95. 40pp. ISBN 0-931674-20-4. *Publisher Provided Annotation.*

Pucmer, Inka. Rampion. Pucmer, Inka, illus. 25p. (gr. 2-4). 1982. 19.95 (0-88010-064-8, Pub. by Walter Keller Pr) Anthroposophic.
Pudaite, Rochunga. Horizons Never End. Lombard, Lynette, illus. 20p. (gr. k-6). 1988. pap. text ed. 4.25 (1-55976-144-X) CEF Press.
Puebla, Luis M., tr. see LeLoeuff, Jean.
Puffer, Darrick J. I'm Not Your Angel. LC 92-60490. 241p. (gr. 7 up). 1993. pap. 8.95 (1-55523-533-6) Winston-Derek.
Puffer, Lela, jt. auth. see Fox, George.
Pugh, Ann. Across-the-Curriculum Guide, Diggy Armadillo Goes to Fort Worth Stock Show & Rodeo, Bk. 1: 140 Creative Activites. Hamptor, Cynthia V., illus. 60p. (Orig.). (gr. k-5). 1992. 10.00 (1-879465-01-9); Eng. & Spa. audiocassette 6.00 (0-685-60626-0) Diggy & Assocs.

Pugh, Ann & Anderson, Joan F. Diggy Armadillo Goes to the Stock Show & Rodeo. Morolez-de Anda, Martha, tr. Hampton, Cynthia V., illus. LC 90-93647. (SPA & ENG.). 62p. (Orig.). (gr. 2-5). 1992. pap. 7.95 (*1-879465-00-0*) Diggy & Assocs.

Pugh, Ann & Utter, Betty. Heidi. LC 79-53859. (Illus.). 68p. (gr. k up). 1962. pap. 4.00 (*0-88680-082-X*); Piano-Vocal Score, Music & Lyrics. pap. 15.00 (*0-88680-083-8*); royalty on application 60.00 (*0-317-03620-3*) I E Clark.
—It Happened in Hamelin. (Illus.). 56p. (gr. k up). 1973. pap. 4.00 (*0-88680-095-1*); Piano-Vocal Score, Music & Lyrics. pap. 15.00 (*0-88680-096-X*); royalty on application 60.00 (*0-317-03626-2*) I E Clark.

Pugh, Ann, et al. Diggy Armadillo Goes to Fort Worth Stock Show & Rodeo, Bk. 2: Further Adventures. Bold, Mary, ed. Van Way Hampton, Cindy, illus. 68p. (gr. 3-6). 1993. staple bdg. 7.95 (*1-879465-02-7*) Diggy & Assocs.

Pugh, Charles. The Griot. (ps-12). 1993. pap. 3.95 (*0-87067-697-0*) Holloway.

Pugh, Charles W., jt. auth. see Pugh, Doris.

Pugh, Doris & Pugh, Charles W. Country Woodcraft Patterns. LC 90-39880. (Illus.). 168p. (Orig.). (gr. 10-12). 1990. pap. 12.95 (*0-8069-7360-9*) Sterling.

Pugh, Lisa & Pugh, Virginia. Lisa's Story: A Young Girl's Life of Courage. LC 91-65722. 128p. (gr. 9-12). 1991. pap. 8.95 (*0-8358-0648-0*) Upper Room.

Pugh, Shirley. In One Basket. 1972. 4.50 (*0-87602-140-2*) Anchorage.

Pugh, Virginia, jt. auth. see Pugh, Lisa.

Puhalo, L. Lives of the Saints, Vols. 2. (gr. 4-6). 1977. pap. 2.50 ea.; Vol. 2. (*0-913026-75-1*); St Nectarios.

Puhalo, Lazar. Innokenty of Alaska. Novakshonoff, V., illus. 86p. (Orig.). (gr. 8 up). 1986. pap. 5.00 (*0-913026-86-7*) Synaxis Pr.

Puhalo, Lev. Lives of Saints for Young People, Vol. 1. (gr. 4-6). 1975. pap. 2.50 (*0-913026-11-5*) St Nectarios.

Puig, Enric. Lord, I Am One of Your Little Ones. Bayes, Pilarin, illus. 93p. (gr. 3-6). 1987. 8.95 (*0-8294-0545-3*) Loyola.

Puig, Evelyn. Chico the Street Boy. Johnson, W. Cameron, illus. 85p. (gr. 4-8). 1991. 3.95 (*0-901269-79-4*) Grosvenor USA.

Puig, J. J., jt. auth. see Parramon, J. M.

Pulaski High School Drama Club Staff & Mueller, Tobin J. I Want to Know! A Musical Time Line about the History of Science & Invention. Heller, Joe, et al, illus. 55p. (gr. 4-12). 1991. 14.95 (*1-56213-059-5*) Ctr Stage Prodns.

Pulham, Grace, jt. auth. see Eder, Enelle G.

Pullein-Thompson, Christine. The Long Search. LC 92-40349. 144p. (gr. 5-9). 1993. SBE 13.95 (*0-02-775445-6*, Bradbury Pr) Macmillan Child Grp.

Pullein-Thompson, Christine, compiled by. Horse Stories. Ambrus, Victor, illus. Fyfe, Charlotte, contrib. by. LC 93-29422. (Illus.). 1994. pap. 6.95 (*1-85697-966-0*) Kingfisher Bks.

Pulley, Patricia Wright. 1993. PLB 13.95 (*0-8050-2212-0*) H Holt & Co.

Pulley, Maxine. Acrobatics. Austin, Kent, photos by. (Illus.). (gr. 3-7). 1981. 8.95 (*0-13-003079-1*) P-H.

Pulley, Richard, jt. auth. see Mantin, Peter.

Pulleyn, Micah & Bracken, Sarah. Kids In The Kitchen: Delicious Fun, and Healthy Recipes to Cook and Bake. LC 93-39111. (gr. 4 up). 1993. Repr. of 1994 ed. write for info. (*0-8069-0447-X*, Sterling Pub) Sterling.

Pullman, Philip. The Broken Bridge. LC 91-15893. 256p. (gr. 7 up). 1992. 15.00 (*0-679-81972-X*); PLB 15.99 (*0-679-91972-4*) Knopf Bks Yng Read.
—The Ruby in the Smoke. Greenstein, Mina, designed by. LC 86-20983. 208p. (gr. 7 up). 1987. 11.95 (*0-394-88826-X*); lib. bdg. 11.99 (*0-394-98826-4*) Knopf Bks Yng Read.
—The Ruby in the Smoke. LC 86-20983. 240p. (gr. 7 up). 1988. pap. 3.99 (*0-394-89589-4*) Knopf Bks Yng Read.
—Shadow in the North. LC 87-29846. 320p. (gr. 7 up). 1988. PLB 13.99 (*0-394-99453-1*) Knopf Bks Yng Read.
—Spring-Heeled Jack. Mostyn, David, illus. LC 90-5151. 112p. (Orig.). (gr. 3-6). 1991. lib. bdg. 10.99 (*0-679-91057-3*); pap. 8.00 (*0-679-81057-9*) Knopf Bks Yng Read.
—The Tiger in the Well. LC 89-26677. 320p. (gr. 7 up). 1990. 15.95 (*0-679-80214-2*); lib. bdg. 16.99 (*0-679-90214-7*) Knopf Bks Yng Read.
—The Tin Princess. LC 93-38305. (gr. 9-12). 1994. lib. bdg. write for info. (*0-679-84757-X*); pap. write for info. (*0-679-84756-1*) Knopf Bks Yng Read.

Pullman, Phillip. White Mercedes. LC 92-11072. 160p. (gr. 7 up). 1993. 16.00 (*0-679-83198-3*) Knopf Bks Yng Read.

Pulver, Carol, jt. auth. see Haigh, Rosemary.

Pulver, Robin. The Holiday Handwriting School. Karas, G. Brian, illus. LC 89-77085. 32p. (gr. k-3). 1991. RSBE 12.95 (*0-02-775455-3*, Four Winds) Macmillan Child Grp.
—Homer & the House Next Door. Levin, Arnie, illus. LC 93-4377. Date not set. write for info. (*0-02-775457-X*, Four Winds) Macmillan Child Grp.
—Mrs. Toggle & the Dinosaur. Alley, R. W., illus. LC 90-35771. 32p. (ps-2). 1991. RSBE 12.95 (*0-02-775452-9*, Four Winds) Macmillan Child Grp.
—Mrs. Toggle's Beautiful Blue Shoe. Alley, R. W., illus. LC 92-40824. 32p. (ps-2). 1994. RSBE 14.95 (*0-02-775456-1*, Four Winds) Macmillan Child Grp.

—Mrs. Toggle's Zipper. LC 88-37251. (Illus.). 32p. (ps-2). 1990. RSBE 13.95 (*0-02-775451-0*, Four Winds Press) Macmillan Child Grp.
—Mrs. Toggle's Zipper. Alley, Robert W., illus. LC 92-39355. 32p. (ps-2). 1993. pap. 3.95 (*0-689-71689-3*, Aladdin) Macmillan Child Grp.
—Nobody's Mother Is in Second Grade. Karas, G. Brian, illus. LC 91-16395. 32p. (gr. k-3). 1992. 13.50 (*0-8037-1210-3*); PLB 13.89 (*0-8037-1211-1*) Dial Bks Young.

Puncel, Maria, ed. Animales - Animals. Del Carmen Blazquez, Maria, tr. (SPA., Illus.). 64p. (gr. 5-12). 1992. write for info. (*84-372-4525-5*) Santillana.
—Las Cosas de Cada Dia - Everyday Things. Aixela, Javier F., tr. (SPA., Illus.). 64p. (gr. 5-12). 1992. write for info. (*84-372-4527-3*) Santillana.

Puncel, Maria & Basquez, Juan J., eds. Cuerpo Humano - The Human Body. Secanell, Jose M., tr. (SPA., Illus.). 63p. (gr. 5-12). 1992. write for info. (*84-372-4528-1*) Santillana.

Puncel, Maria, ed. see Henrietta.

Puncel, Maria, ed. see Platt, Richard.

Puncel, Maria, tr. see Ahlberg, Janet & Ahlberg, Allan.

Puncel, Maria, tr. see Hayes, Sarah.

Puncel, Maria, tr. see Henrietta.

Punches, Laurie C. How to Simply Cut Hair. Martinez, Carla, et al, eds. Punches, Laurie C., illus. LC 88-92443. 109p. (Orig.). (gr. 11 up). 1989. pap. 8.95 (*0-929883-06-3*); VHS & Beta. video 29.95 (*0-929883-07-1*) Punches Prodns.
—How to Simply Cut Hair Even Better: Advanced Haircutting. Punches, Laurie C., illus. LC 88-92468. 129p. (Orig.). (gr. 11 up). 1989. pap. 9.95 (*0-929883-08-X*) Punches Prodns.
—How to Simply Highlight Hair. Punches, Laurie C., illus. LC 88-92469. 79p. (Orig.). (gr. 11 up). 1989. pap. 6.95 (*0-929883-02-0*); VHS & Beta. video 19.95 (*0-929883-03-9*) Punches Prodns.
—How to Simply Perm Hair. Punches, Laurie C., illus. LC 88-92467. 74p. (Orig.). (gr. 11 up). 1989. pap. 6.95 (*0-929883-04-7*); VHS & Beta. video 19.95 (*0-929883-05-5*) Punches Prodns.

Punkus, Sue, jt. auth. see Robertson, Sue.

Punnett, Dick. Does Anyone Have a Spare Bear? Endres, Helen, illus. LC 84-23009. 32p. (gr. k-3). 1985. PLB 19.95 (*0-89565-304-4*); PLB 13.95s.p. (*0-685-55732-4*) Childs World.
—Our Brat Cat. Rauh, Herb, illus. LC 84-23027. 32p. (gr. k-3). 1985. PLB 19.95 (*0-89565-303-6*); PLB 13.95s.p. (*0-685-55733-2*) Childs World.
—Talk-along-Help Dress Priscilla. Dunnington, Tom, illus. LC 84-23030. 32p. (ps). 1985. PLB 21.35 (*0-89565-217-X*); PLB 14.95s.p. (*0-685-55714-6*) Childs World.

Punnett, Dick & Dunnington, Tom. Peek-a-Boo Sue. LC 84-23003. (Illus.). 32p. (gr. k-3). 1985. PLB 19.95 (*0-89565-305-2*); PLB 13.95s.p. (*0-685-55734-0*) Childs World.

Punnett, Richard D. Count the Possums. Dunnington, Tom, illus. LC 81-21773. 32p. (ps-2). 1982. PLB 21.35 (*0-89565-215-3*); PLB 14.95s.p. (*0-685-57678-7*) Childs World.
—Help Jumbo Escape. Dunnington, Tom, illus. LC 81-21667. 32p. (ps-2). 1982. PLB 21.35 (*0-89565-214-5*); PLB 14.95s.p. (*0-685-55535-6*) Childs World.
—Name Lizzy's Colors. Dunnington, Tom, illus. LC 82-1172. 32p. (ps-2). 1982. PLB 21.35 (*0-89565-216-1*); PLB 14.95s.p. (*0-685-55533-X*) Childs World.
—Name Patty's Pets. Dunnington, Tom, illus. LC 81-18056. 32p. (ps-2). 1982. PLB 21.35 (*0-89565-213-7*); PLB 14.95s.p. (*0-685-55534-8*) Childs World.

Purcell, John W. African Animals. LC 82-9541. (Illus.). 48p. (gr. k-4). 1982. 15.27 (*0-516-01665-2*); pap. 4.95 (*0-516-41665-0*) Childrens.

Purdy, Carol. Iva Dunnit & the Big Wind. Kellogg, Steven, illus. LC 84-17441. 32p. (ps-3). 1985. 12.95 (*0-8037-0183-7*) Dial Bks Young.
—Iva Dunnit & the Big Wind. Kellogg, Steven, illus. LC 84-17441. 32p. (ps-3). 1988. pap. 4.99 (*0-8037-0493-3*) Dial Bks Young.
—Least of All. Arnold, Tim, illus. LC 86-12613. 32p. (gr. 1-4). 1987. SBE 12.95 (*0-689-50404-7*, M K McElderry) Macmillan Child Grp.
—Least of All. Arnold, Tim, illus. LC 92-19964. 32p. (gr. k-3). 1993. pap. 3.95 (*0-689-71681-8*, Aladdin) Macmillan Child Grp.
—Mrs. Merriwether's Musical Cat. Mathers, Petra, illus. LC 92-43934. 1994. write for info. (*0-399-22543-9*, Putnam) Putnam Pub Group.

Purdy, Linda, jt. auth. see Woodard, James.

Puricelli, Luigi, jt. auth. see Cristini, Ermanno.

Purnell. Rhyme Time Books: Humpty Dumpty. 1989. 1.98 (*0-671-09369-X*) S&S Trade.

Purrington, Sandra, et al. Music! Words! Opera, 4 vols, Level 1. Vogelsang, Johanna & Roth, Roger, illus. Fowler, Charles, frwd by. LC 90-19274. 264p. (gr. k-2). 1990. One vol., 264p. tchr's. manual 65.00 (*0-918812-65-8*, SE0694); Three vols., 24p. ea. wkbk. 3.50 (*0-918812-67-4*, SE0695, SE0696, SE0697) MMB Music.

Pursell, Carroll W., Jr., jt. ed. see Kranzberg, Melvin.

Purtell, April, et al. The Yellow Pages Guide to Educational Field Trips. Harris, Gregg, ed. 206p. 1993. pap. text ed. 18.00 (*0-923463-90-9*) Noble Pub Assocs.

Purtill, Richard. Enchantment at Delphi. LC 85-30556. (gr. 7 up). 1986. 14.95 (*0-15-200447-5*, Gulliver Bks) HarBrace.

Purves, Pamela. Decorating Eggs: In the Style of Faberge. Dace, Rosalind, ed. Search Press Studios Staff, illus. 96p. (Orig.). 1989. pap. 16.95 (*0-85532-644-1*, Pub. by Search Pr UK) A Schwartz & Co.

Pushker, Gloria T. Toby Belfer Never Had a Christmas Tree. Hierstein, Judith, illus. LC 91-14514. 32p. 1991. 14.95 (*0-88289-855-8*) Pelican.
—Toby Belfer's Seder: A Passover Story Retold. Hierstein, Judith, illus. LC 93-5585. 1994. write for info. (*0-88289-987-2*) Pelican.

Pushkin, Aleksandr. Golden Cockerel & Other Fairy Tales. Wood, Jessie, tr. Zvorykin, Boris, illus. Nureyev, Rudolf, intro. by. 1990. 24.95 (*0-385-26252-3*) Doubleday.
—The Snow Storm. Redpath, Ann, ed. 40p. (gr. 6 up). 1983. PLB 13.95s.p. (*0-87191-923-0*) Creative Ed.

Pusterla, Fred. My First Magnifier Book. Pusterla, Fred, illus. 12p. (ps-1). 1993. bds. 9.95 (*1-56293-140-7*) McClanahan Bk.

Puterbaugh, Donald L., jt. auth. see Fling, Paul N.

Putman, Bob, adapted by see Johnson, Gordon G.

Putman, Jeff. Hot Cars Poster Book. 32p. (gr. 3 up). 1992. pap. 3.99 (*0-87406-634-4*) Willowisp Pr.

Putnam, Jim. Mummy. LC 92-1591. 64p. (gr. 5 up). 1993. 15.00 (*0-679-83881-3*); PLB 16.99 (*0-679-93881-8*) Knopf Bks Yng Read.

Puzzle House Staff, ed. Picture Puzzles. (Illus.). 48p. (gr. 3-6). 1992. pap. 2.95 (*1-56680-007-2*) Mad Hatter Pub.
—Pocket Puzzler. (Illus.). 48p. (gr. 3-6). 1992. pap. 2.95 (*1-56680-006-4*) Mad Hatter Pub.

Pye, Ethel, ed. see Ceasor, Ebraska D.

Pye, Ethel, ed. see Durant, Charlotte T.

Pyke, Helen. Father Take Me Home. Wheeler, Gerald, ed. 160p. (Orig.). 1991. pap. 8.95 (*0-8280-0596-6*) Review & Herald.

Pyke, Magnus. Weird & Wonderful Science Facts. Burton, Terry, illus. LC 83-24288. 128p. (gr. 5 up). 1985. pap. 3.95 (*0-8069-6254-2*) Sterling.

Pyle, Howard. The Garden Behind the Moon. (Illus.). 192p. (gr. 6-8). 1988. Repr. of 1895 ed. 14.95 (*0-930407-06-7*) Parabola Bks.
—The Garden Behind the Moon: The Real Story of the Moon Angel. (Illus.). 176p. (gr. 6-8). 1991. pap. 10.95 (*0-930407-22-9*) Parabola Bks.
—King Arthur. Hinkle, Don, ed. Tirtitilli, Jerry, illus. LC 87-15461. 48p. (gr. 3-6). 1988. PLB 12.89 (*0-8167-1213-1*); pap. 3.95 (*0-8167-1214-X*) Troll Assocs.
—King Arthur & the Magic Sword. LC 89-27793. 21p. (gr. 2-7). 1990. 13.95 (*0-8037-0824-6*) Dial Bks Young.
—Men of Iron. Bennet, C. L., intro. by. (Illus.). (gr. 6 up). 1965. pap. 3.50 (*0-8049-0093-0*, CL-93) Airmont.
—Men of Iron. Hitchner, Earle, adapted by. Geehan, Wayne, illus. LC 89-33926. 48p. (gr. 3-6). 1990. PLB 12.89 (*0-8167-1871-7*); pap. text ed. 3.95 (*0-8167-1872-5*) Troll Assocs.
—The Merry Adventures of Robin Hood. Pyle, Howard, illus. LC 68-55820. xxii, 296p. (gr. 3-6). 1968. pap. 6.95 (*0-486-22043-5*) Dover.
—The Merry Adventures of Robin Hood. Pyle, Howard, illus. (gr. 4-8). 18.75 (*0-8446-2765-8*) Peter Smith.
—The Merry Adventures of Robin Hood. Mattern, Joanne, ed. Sauber, Robert, illus. LC 92-12702. 48p. (gr. 3-6). 1992. PLB 12.89 (*0-8167-2858-5*); pap. text ed. 3.95 (*0-8167-2859-3*) Troll Assocs.
—Otto of the Silver Hand. Pyle, Howard, illus. xv, 173p. (gr. 5-9). 1967. pap. 5.95 (*0-486-21784-1*) Dover.
—Otto of the Silver Hand. (gr. 5-9). 18.25 (*0-8446-6400-6*) Peter Smith.
—Reader's Digest Best Loved Books for Young Readers: The Merry Adventures of Robin Hood. Ogburn, Jackie, ed. Huens, Jean L., illus. 136p. (gr. 4-12). 1989. 3.99 (*0-945260-20-2*) Choice Pub NY.
—Reader's Digest Best Loved Books for Young Readers: The Story of King Arthur & His Knights. Ogburn, Jackie, ed. Sweet, Darrell, illus. 208p. (gr. 4-12). 1989. 3.99 (*0-945260-31-8*) Choice Pub NY.
—Robin Hood. abr. ed. Arneson, D. J., retold by. Clift, Eva, illus. 128p. 1991. pap. 2.95 (*1-56156-028-6*) Kidsbks.
—The Story of King Arthur & His Knights. Pyle, Howard, illus. xviii, 313p. (gr. 7 up). pap. 6.95 (*0-486-21445-1*) Dover.
—Story of King Arthur & His Knights. (gr. 6-12). 18.75 (*0-8446-2766-6*) Peter Smith.
—The Story of King Arthur & His Knights. (Illus.). (gr. 7 up). 1978. Repr. of 1903 ed. lib. bdg. 12.00 luxury ed. (*0-932106-01-3*, Pub by Marathon Pr) S J Durst.
—The Story of Sir Lancelot & His Companions. (Illus.). 360p. (gr. 5 up). 1985. SBE 18.95 (*0-684-18313-7*, Scribners Young Read) Macmillan Child Grp.
—The Story of the Champions of the Round Table. Pyle, Howard, illus. xviii, 329p. (gr. 5 up). 1968. pap. 7.95 (*0-486-21883-X*) Dover.
—The Story of the Champions of the Round Table. (Illus.). (gr. 6-12). 19.25 (*0-8446-0229-9*) Peter Smith.
—The Story of the Champions of the Round Table. LC 84-13881. (Illus.). 348p. (gr. 7 up). 1984. RSBE 19.95 (*0-684-18171-1*, Scribners Young Read) Macmillan Child Grp.
—The Story of the Grail & the Passing of Arthur. Pyle, Howard, illus. LC 85-40302. 340p. (gr. 7 up). 1985. SBE 19.95 (*0-684-18483-4*, Scribners Young Read) Macmillan Child Grp.

—The Story of the Grail & the Passing of Arthur. unabr. ed. LC 92-29058. (Illus.). 272p. 1992. pap. text ed. 7.95 (0-486-27361-X) Dover.
—Wonder Clock. (Illus.). (gr. 5 up). 19.25 (0-8446-2767-4) Peter Smith.
—The Wonder Clock or, Four & Twenty Marvelous Tales, Being One for Each Hour of the Day. (Illus.). xiv, 319p. (gr. 3-6). pap. 7.95 (0-486-21446-X) Dover.
Pyle, Howard, ed. see Mallory, Thomas.
Pyman, Kit, ed. Every Kind of Smocking. Messent, Jan, et al, illus. 126p. (Orig.). 1989. pap. 17.95 (0-85532-632-8, Pub. by Search Pr UK) A Schwartz & Co.
Pyne, K. D. All the Way to China. Whitten, Jessie, illus. 16p. (ps). 1993. saddle-stitch 4.95 (1-882185-06-4) Crnrstone Pub.
Pyrnelle, Louise-Clarke. Diddie, Dumps & Tot. (Illus.). 117p. (gr. 4-8). 1963. 14.95 (0-911116-17-6) Pelican.
Pysz, Stephen. Team Earth: Advanced ABC Environmental Coloring Book. America, Alexis & Marcil, Beth, illus. 56p. (gr. k-1). 1991. pap. text ed. 4.95 (0-9630186-7-1) Team Earth.
—Team Earth: Show You Care. Patton, Sarah, ed. America, Alexis, illus. 32p. (gr. 2-5). 1992. pap. text ed. 4.95 wkbk. (0-9630186-1-2) Team Earth.

Q

Qaderi, M. Taleem-Ul-Islam, 4. pap. 7.50 (0-933511-72-8) Kazi Pubns.
Qazi, M. A. ABC Islamic Reader. pap. 3.50 (0-935782-07-9) Kazi Pubns.
—Arabic Alphabet Coloring Book. 20p. (ps). 1984. pap. 3.50 (1-56744-220-X) Kazi Pubns.
Quackenbush, Hiroko C. The Grateful Crane. Ogawa & Tazawa, eds. (Illus.). 32p. 1993. pap. 7.00 (4-77001-761-8) Kodansha.
—Momotaro, the Peach Boy. Ogawa & Tazawa, eds. (Illus.). 32p. 1993. pap. 7.00 (4-77001-760-X) Kodansha.
—The Runaway Riceball. Ogawa & Tazawa, eds. (Illus.). 32p. 1993. pap. 7.00 (4-77001-762-6) Kodansha.
Quackenbush, Marcia & Sargent, Pamela. Teaching AIDS. rev. ed. 164p. 1988. pap. text ed. 19.95 (0-941816-41-9) ETR Assocs.
Quackenbush, Marcia & Villarreal, Sylvia. Does AIDS Hurt? Educating Young Children about AIDS. Nelson, Mary, ed. 148p. (Orig.). (ps-6). 1988. pap. 14.95 (0-941816-52-4) ETR Assocs.
Quackenbush, Marcia, illus. & see Gardner-Loulan, JoAnn, et al.
Quackenbush, Robert. Arthur Ashe & His Match with History. LC 93-14945. (gr. 5 up). 1994. pap. 14.00 (0-671-86597-8, S&S BFYR) S&S Trade.
—Arthur Ashe & His Match with History. (gr. 4-7). 1994. pap. 4.95 (0-671-88182-5, S&S BFYR) S&S Trade.
—The Beagle & Mr. Fly Catcher: A Story of Charles Darwin. LC 83-8721. (Illus.). 40p. (gr. 4-6). 1983. 8.95 (0-13-071290-6) P-H.
—Benjamin Franklin & His Friends. Quackenbush, Robert, illus. 32p. (gr. 2-5). 1991. 14.95 (0-945912-14-5) Pippin Pr.
—Bicycle to Treachery. Quackenbush, Robert, illus. 48p. (gr. 1-5). 1985. 10.95 (0-13-076258-X) P-H.
—Bicycle to Treachery. 48p. (gr. 1-5). 1991. pap. 2.95 (0-671-73346-X, S&S BFYR) S&S Trade.
—Cable Car to Catastrophe. Quackenbush, Robert, illus. 48p. (gr. 1-5). 1985. pap. 4.95 (0-13-110032-7) P-H.
—Clear the Cow Pasture: I'm Comin' In. LC 89-6164. 1990. pap. 11.95 (0-671-68548-1, S&S BFYR); pap. 3.95 (0-671-69218-6, S&S BFYR) S&S Trade.
—Danger in Tibet: A Miss Mallard Mystery. Quackenbush, Robert, illus. 32p. (gr. 1-4). 1989. 14.95 (0-945912-03-X) Pippin Pr.
—Detective Mole & Halloween Mystery. 1989. pap. 3.95 (0-671-67830-2, Little Simon) S&S Trade.
—Detective Mole & the Haunted Castle Mystery. LC 84-20141. (Illus.). 32p. (gr. k-3). 1985. lib. bdg. 12.88 (0-688-04641-X) Lothrop.
—Dig to Disaster: A Miss Mallard Mystery. (Illus.). 48p. (gr. 1-5). 1982. 9.95 (0-13-211870-X) P-H.
—Dogsled to Dread. LC 86-25394. (Illus.). 48p. (gr. 2-6). 1988. pap. 12.95 (0-671-66518-9, S&S BFYR) S&S Trade.
—Don't You Dare Shoot That Bear. LC 84-4693. 1990. pap. 11.95 (0-671-66295-3); pap. 3.95 (0-671-69440-5) S&S Trade.
—Evil Under the Sea: A Miss Mallard Mystery. Quackenbush, Robert, illus. 32p. (gr. 1-4). 1992. 14.95 (0-945912-16-1) Pippin Pr.
—Express Train to Trouble: A Miss Mallard Mystery. (Illus.). (gr. 1-4). 1981. 9.95 (0-13-298067-3) P-H.
—First Grade Jitters. Quackenbush, Robert, illus. LC 81-47757. 32p. (gr. k-2). 1982. PLB 11.89 (0-397-31981-9, Lipp Jr Bks) HarpC Child Bks.
—Gondola to Danger: A Miss Mallard Mystery. LC 83-9473. (Illus.). 48p. (gr. 2-4). 1983. 9.95 (0-13-360180-3) P-H.
—Henry Babysits. Quackenbush, Robert, illus. LC 83-2247. 48p. (ps-3). 1983. 5.95 (0-8193-1107-3); lib. bdg. 5.95 (0-8193-1108-1) Parents.

—Henry Babysits. Quackenbush, Robert, illus. 48p. (ps-2). 1990. pap. 2.95 (0-448-04338-6, G&D) Putnam Pub Group.
—Henry Babysits. LC 93-15472. 1993. PLB 13.27 (0-8368-0968-8) Gareth Stevens Inc.
—Henry Goes West. LC 82-7971. (Illus.). 48p. (ps-3). 1982. 5.95 (0-8193-1089-1); PLB 5.95 (0-8193-1090-5) Parents.
—Henry's Awful Mistake. Quackenbush, Robert, illus. LC 80-20327. 48p. (ps-3). 1981. 5.95 (0-8193-1039-5); PLB 5.95 (0-8193-1040-9) Parents.
—Henry's Important Date. Quackenbush, Robert, illus. LC 81-5026. 48p. (ps-3). 1982. 5.95 (0-8193-1067-0); PLB 5.95 (0-8193-1068-9) Parents.
—Henry's Important Date. LC 93-7772. 1993. PLB 13.27 (0-8368-0969-6) Gareth Stevens Inc.
—Henry's World Tour. Quackenbush, Robert, illus. LC 91-31257. 48p. (ps-3). 1992. pap. 14.00 (0-385-42010-2) Doubleday.
—I Did It with My Hatchet: A Story of George Washington. Quackenbush, Robert, illus. 32p. (gr. 2-6). 1989. 14.95 (0-945912-04-8) Pippin Pr.
—James Madison & Dolly Madison & Their Times. Quackenbush, Robert, illus. 40p. (gr. 2-5). 1992. 14.95 (0-945912-18-8) Pippin Pr.
—John Adams & Abigail Adams & Their Times. Quackenbush, Robert, illus. 40p. (gr. 2-5). 1994. 14.95 (0-945912-24-2) Pippin Pr.
—Lost in the Amazon: A Miss Mallard Mystery. Quackenbush, Robert, illus. 32p. (gr. 1-4). 1990. PLB 14.95 (0-945912-11-0) Pippin Pr.
—Mark Twain? What Kind of Name is That? A Story of Samuel Langhorn Clemens. LC 83-19086. (Illus.). 40p. (gr. 2-6). 1984. pap. 11.95 (0-671-66294-5, S&S BFYR) S&S Trade.
—Mark Twain? What Kind of Name is That? A Story of Samuel Langhorne Clemens. (gr. 4). 1990. pap. write for info. (0-663-56240-6) Silver Burdett Pr.
—Mouse Feathers. Quackenbush, Robert, illus. LC 87-15690. 40p. (gr. k-3). 1988. 12.95 (0-89919-527-X, Clarion Bks) HM.
—Oh, What an Awful Mess: The Story of Charles Goodyear. (Illus.). 40p. (gr. k-3). 1983. pap. 3.95 (0-13-633396-6, Pub. by Treehouse Bks) P-H.
—Old Silver Leg Takes Over: A Story of Peter Stuyvesant. Quackenbush, Robert, illus. 40p. (gr. 1-5). 1986. 10.95 (0-13-633934-4) P-H.
—Once upon a Time! A Story of the Brothers Grimm. LC 85-9410. (Illus.). 40p. (gr. 2-6). 1986. pap. 11.95 jacketed (0-671-66296-1, Little Simon) S&S Trade.
—Pass the Quill; I'll Write a Draft: A Story of Thomas Jefferson. Quackenbush, Robert, illus. 32p. (gr. 2-6). 1989. PLB 14.95 (0-945912-07-2) Pippin Pr.
—Quick, Annie, Give Me a Catchy Line! Quackenbush, Robert, illus. 32p. (gr. 3-7). 1983. 10.95 (0-13-749762-8) P-H.
—Rickshaw to Horror. LC 83-19083. (Illus.). 48p. 1984. 11.95 (0-13-781014-8) P-H.
—Sheriff Sally Gopher & the Thanksgiving Caper. Quackenbush, Robert, illus. LC 82-135. 32p. (gr. 1-3). 1982. PLB 13.88 (0-688-01293-0) Lothrop.
—Sherlock Chick & the Case of the Night Noises. Quackenbush, Robert, illus. LC 89-70984. 48p. (ps-3). 1990. 5.95 (0-8193-1194-4) Parents.
—Sherlock Chick & the Giant Egg Mystery. Quackenbush, Robert, illus. LC 88-4093. (ps-3). 1989. 5.95 (0-8193-1178-2) Parents.
—Sherlock Chick & the Peekaboo Mystery. Quackenbush, Robert, illus. LC 87-3591. 48p. (ps-3). 1987. 5.95 (0-8193-1149-9) Parents.
—Sherlock Chick & the Peekaboo Mystery. Quackenbush, Robert, illus. 48p. (gr. 3-7). 1990. pap. 2.95 (0-448-04334-3, G&D) Putnam Pub Group.
—Sherlock Chick's First Case. Quackenbush, Robert, illus. LC 86-9398. 48p. (ps-3). 1986. 5.95 (0-8193-1148-0) Parents.
—Stage Door to Terror. Quackenbush, Robert, illus. LC 84-22295. 48p. (gr. 1-5). 1985. 11.95 (0-13-840364-3) P-H.
—Stage Door to Terror. 48p. (gr. 1-5). 1991. pap. 2.95 (0-671-73347-8, S&S BFYR) S&S Trade.
—Stairway to Doom. LC 82-21484. (Illus.). 48p. (gr. 2-6). 1986. pap. 5.95 (0-671-67053-0, S&S BFYR) S&S Trade.
—Stairway to Doom: A Miss Mallard Mystery. LC 82-21484. (Illus.). 48p. (ps-5). 1983. PLB 9.95 (0-13-804595-X) P-H.
—Stairway to Down. Quackenbush, Robert, illus. 48p. (gr. 1-5). 1986. pap. 5.95 (0-13-840604-9) P-H.
—Stop the Presses, Nellie's Got a Scoop! A Story of Nellie Bly. LC 91-4408. (gr. 4-7). 1992. pap. 13.00 (0-671-76090-4, S&S BFYR); pap. 3.95 (0-671-76091-2, S&S BFYR) S&S Trade.
—Surfboard to Peril. LC 85-24430. (gr. 4-7). 1991. pap. 2.95 (0-671-73344-3, S&S BFYR) S&S Trade.
—Surfboard to Peril: A Miss Mallard Mystery. Quackenbush, Robert, illus. 48p. (gr. 1-5). 1986. 11.95 (0-13-877986-4) P-H.
—Taxi to Intrigue. Quackenbush, Robert, illus. LC 84-4691. 48p. (gr. 1-5). 1984. 10.95 (0-13-886813-1) P-H.
—Texas Trail to Calamity. Quackenbush, Robert, illus. 48p. (gr. 1-5). 1986. 11.95 (0-13-912544-2) P-H.
—Watt Got You Started, Mr. Fulton? Quackenbush, Robert, illus. 39p. (gr. 1-4). 1982. 7.95 (0-13-944397-5) P-H.
—What Has Wild Tom Done Now? A Story of Thomas Alva Edison. (gr. 1-4). 1981. 8.95 (0-13-952168-2) P-H.

—Who Let Muddy Boots into the White House? A Story of Andrew Jackson. LC 86-4989. (Illus.). 40p. (gr. 2-6). 1986. pap. 11.95 (0-671-66970-2, S&S BFYR) S&S Trade.
Quackenbush, Robert M. Henry's Awful Mistake. LC 92-32870. (Illus.). 42p. (ps-3). 1992. PLB 13.26 (0-8368-0882-7); PLB 13.26 s.p. (0-685-61513-8) Gareth Stevens Inc.
Quackenbush, Ross & Gastineau, Jerrel. Homework? My Locker Ate It! An Effective Method for Parents to Help Their Student Study at Home & Improve in School. Thiesies, Darlene, illus. 143p. (Orig.). (gr. 6-12). 1988. pap. 19.95 (0-9621701-0-0) CWP.
Quaglini, Juliana. The Night of the Shepherds: A Christmas Experience. Flanagan, Anne J., tr. from ITA. De Vico, Elvira, illus. LC 93-25027. 32p. (Orig.). (gr. 4 up). 1993. pap. 3.95 (0-8198-5128-0) St Paul Bks.
Qualey, Marsha. Everybody's Daughter. LC 90-46286. 208p. (gr. 7 up). 1991. 13.45 (0-395-55870-0) HM.
—Everybody's Daughter. 208p. (gr. 6 up). 1993. pap. 4.80 (0-395-65746-6) HM.
—Revolutions of the Heart. LC 92-24528. 192p. (gr. 6 up). 1993. 13.45 (0-395-64168-3) HM.
Quality Family Entertainment, Inc. Staff. Shining Time Station: Station House. 2p. (ps-2). 1993. write for info. (1-883366-10-0) YES Ent.
Quarton, Marjorie. The Cow Watched the Battle. 100p. (gr. 3-7). 1990. pap. 6.95 (1-85371-084-9, Pub. by Poolbeg Pr ER) Dufour.

Quatmann, Gail R. & Ewen, Patricia B. Building Blocks: An Infant Toddler Handbook. rev. ed. LC 92-93262. (Illus.). 85p. 1993. pap. write for info. (0-9631122-9-5) G R Quatmann. BUILDING BLOCKS (c) an INFANT TODDLER HANDBOOK presents a practical guide for the YOUNG MOM. It is easy reading & presents a clear understanding of growth & development during the first three years of an infant's life. Indexed tabs provide a quick reference into the developmental milestones of the infant-toddlers' thinking, communication, emotions, growth, feelings & physical development. Used as a supplementary text in Early Childhood Education courses, BUILDING BLOCKS uniquely outlines the major milestones. It applies developmentally appropriate activities & helpful hints for continued healthy growth & development. As all children progress at different growth rates the understanding of & interaction by PARENTS & CAREGIVERS is essential in maintaining a firm foundation by which all future learning is built. Written in first person, with personalized information pages, current immunization shots & sketches. BUILDING BLOCKS makes an excellent gift for new & expectant parents. "An excellent tool for caregivers of young children."--Virginia Barry, Ph.D., Professor of Education, Plymouth State. "A clear, fresh approach in understanding child development."--Rose Sullivan, R.N., Francis Scott Key Medical Center. For info. contact: Gail R. Quatmann, 8645 Black Oak Rd., Baltimore, MD 21234. Phone: 410-661-7938, FAX: 410-788-8280.
Publisher Provided Annotation.

Quattlebaum, Mary. Jackson Jones & the Puddle of Thorns. Rosales, Melodye, illus. LC 93-11433. (gr. 4-7). 1994. 13.95 (0-385-31165-6) Delacorte.
Quattrocki, Carolyn. Frosty's Snowy Day. Spellman, Susan & Graves, Linda, illus. 24p. (ps-4). 1992. PLB 10.95 (1-56674-022-3) Forest Hse.
—The Little Drummer Boy. Spellman, Susan & Graves, Linda, illus. 24p. (ps-4). 1992. PLB 10.95 (1-56674-023-1) Forest Hse.
—The Nutcracker. Spellman, Susan & Graves, Linda, illus. 24p. (ps-4). 1992. PLB 10.95 (1-56674-024-X) Forest Hse.

—Rudolph's Adventure. Spellman, Susan & Graves, Linda, illus. 24p. (ps-4). 1992. PLB 10.95 (*1-56674-025-8*) Forest Hse.
—Santa Claus Is Coming to Town. Spellman, Susan & Graves, Linda, illus. 24p. (ps-4). 1992. PLB 10.95 (*1-56674-026-6*) Forest Hse.
—Twas the Night Before Christmas. Spellman, Susan & Graves, Linda, illus. 24p. (ps-4). 1992. PLB 10.95 (*1-56674-027-4*) Forest Hse.
Quayle, Eric, retold by. The Shining Princess & Other Japanese Legends. Foreman, Michael, illus. 112p. (gr. k-5). 1989. 15.95 (*1-55970-039-4*) Arcade Pub Inc.
Quayle, Thomas E., ed. Jose' el Diablo: The World's Most Traveled Dog. Quayle, Greg, illus. 95p. (Orig.). 1985. pap. 3.00 (*0-9623144-0-4*) Vilate Pub.
Queen, J. Allen. Complete Karate. LC 93-24831. (Illus.). 192p. (gr. 10-12). 1993. 19.95 (*0-8069-8678-6*) Sterling.
—Fighting Karate. LC 88-22087. (Illus.). 128p. (gr. 5-9). 1989. 14.95 (*0-8069-6838-9*) Sterling.
—Fighting Karate. LC 88-22087. (Illus.). 128p. (gr. 3-10). 1990. pap. 6.95 (*0-8069-6839-7*) Sterling.
—Karate Basics. (Illus.). 128p. (gr. 3 up). 1993. pap. 7.95 (*0-8069-8677-8*) Sterling.
—Total Karate. LC 89-49313. (Illus.). 128p. 1990. 14.95 (*0-8069-6714-5*) Sterling.
—Total Karate. LC 89-49313. (Illus.). 128p. (gr. 4 up). 1991. pap. 7.95 (*0-8069-6715-3*) Sterling.
Queen, Margaret M. So You're off to Summer Camp: A Trunk Load of Tips for a Fun-Filled Camp Adventure. Matens, Margaret H., illus. 136p. (gr. 2-12). 1993. 14.95 (*1-882959-55-8*); perfect bdg. 6.95 (*1-882959-50-7*) Foxglove TN.
Querry, Ron. Native American Struggle for Equality. LC 92-7474. 1992. 22.60 (*0-86593-179-8*); 16.95s.p. (*0-685-59320-7*) Rourke Corp.
Quesenbury, Pat. What's a Girl to Do? Wright, Bobby J., ed. Bass, Jo Ann, illus. Haynes, Glenda, intro. by. (Illus.). 133p. (Orig.). (gr. 7 up). 1981. pap. 3.50 (*0-89114-108-1*) Baptist Pub Hse.
Quiggle, Kevin. COMAL Library of Functions & Procedures. (Illus.). 71p. (Orig.). (gr. 6 up). 1984. pap. 14.95 (*0-928411-03-6*) Comal Users.
Quigley, Betty. Our Master's Prayers: A Brief Story of Jesus' Life Based on His Prayers. Thurman, Nadine, pref. by. (Illus.). 160p. 1991. 12.50 (*0-9626735-1-X*); pap. 7.50 (*0-9626735-3-6*) Rabeth Pub Co.
Quigley, Elaine, jt. auth. see Buchter, Carol.
Quigley, Stacy. Do I Have To? Lexa, Susan, illus. Silverman, Manuel, intro. by. LC 85-24350. (Illus.). 32p. (gr. k-6). 1980. PLB 17.96 (*0-8172-1352-X*) Raintree Steck-V.
Quincannon, Alan, ed. Lifestyles of Colonial America. Lanawn-Shee Studios Staff, illus. 24p. (Orig.). (gr. k-6). 1992. pap. 3.95 (*1-878452-10-X*) Tory Corner Editions.
—More Soldiers of Colonial America. Lanawn-Shee Studios Staff, illus. 24p. (Orig.). (gr. k-6). 1992. pap. 3.95 (*1-878452-12-6*) Tory Corner Editions.
—People of Colonial America. Lanawn-Shee Studios Staff, illus. 20p. (Orig.). (gr. k-6). 1992. pap. 3.95 (*1-878452-09-6*) Tory Corner Editions.
—Soldiers of Colonial America. Lanawn-Shee Studios Staff, illus. 24p. (Orig.). (gr. k-6). 1992. pap. 3.95 (*1-878452-11-8*) Tory Corner Editions.
Quindlen, Anna. The Tree That Came to Stay. Carpenter, Nancy, illus. LC 91-31957. 32p. (ps-4). 1992. 13.00 (*0-517-58145-0*) Crown Bks Yng Read.
Quin-Harkin, Janet. Best Friends Forever, No. 6. 176p. (Orig.). (gr. 7-12). 1986. pap. 2.50 (*0-553-26111-8*) Bantam.
—Big Sister. 192p. (gr. 6 up). 1988. pap. 2.95 (*0-8041-0081-0*) Ivy Books.
—Billy & Ben: The Terrible Two. Newsom, Carol, illus. 1992. pap. 3.50 (*0-553-48022-7*) Bantam.
—Blind Date. 192p. (gr. 6 up). 1988. pap. 2.95 (*0-8041-0094-2*) Ivy Books.
—Boy Trouble for Tess & Ali. 1991. pap. 3.50 (*0-06-106065-8*, Harp PBks) HarpC.
—Campus Cousins. LC 88-91245. 186p. 1989. pap. 2.95 (*0-8041-0335-6*) Ivy Books.
—Dream Come True. (gr. 6 up). 1988. pap. 2.95 (*0-8041-0334-8*) Ivy Books.
—The Graduates. 176p. (Orig.). (gr. 7-12). 1986. 2.50 (*0-553-25723-4*) Bantam.
—Graduation Day. 1992. pap. 3.50 (*0-06-106096-8*, Harp PBks) HarpC.
—The Great Boy Chase. 192p. (gr. 7-12). 1985. pap. 2.50 (*0-553-25452-9*) Bantam.
—Growing Pains. 176p. (Orig.). (gr. 6 up). 1986. pap. 2.50 (*0-553-26034-0*) Bantam.
—Home Sweet Home. (gr. 6 up). 1988. pap. 2.95 (*0-8041-0333-X*) Ivy Books.
—Homecoming Dance. 1991. pap. 3.50 (*0-06-106093-3*, Harp PBks) HarpC.
—Magic Growing Powder. Cumings, Art, illus. LC 80-18019. 48p. (ps-3). 1981. 5.95 (*0-8193-1037-9*); PLB 5.95 (*0-8193-1038-7*) Parents.
—Magic Growing Powder. (Illus.). 48p. (ps-2). 1991. pap. 2.95 (*0-448-40104-5*, G&D) Putnam Pub Group.
—Make Me a Star. (gr. 6 up). 1988. pap. 2.95 (*0-8041-0075-6*) Ivy Books.
—My Phantom Love. (gr. 7 up). 1992. pap. 3.50 (*0-06-106770-9*, Harp PBks) HarpC.
—My Secret Love. 224p. (Orig.). (gr. 7-12). 1986. pap. 2.95 (*0-553-25884-2*) Bantam.
—New Year's Eve. 1991. pap. 3.50 (*0-06-106094-1*, Harp PBks) HarpC.
—Night of the Prom. (gr. 7 up). 1992. pap. 3.50 (*0-06-106095-X*, Harp PBks) HarpC.
—No Experience Required. 192p. 1990. pap. 3.50 (*0-449-14530-1*, Pub. by Girls Only) Fawcett.
—Old Friends, New Friends. 224p. (Orig.). (gr. 6 up). 1986. pap. 2.50 (*0-553-26186-X*) Bantam.
—On My Own. 1992. pap. 3.50 (*0-06-106722-9*, Harp PBks) HarpC.
—On Our Own. 176p. (Orig.). (gr. 6 up). 1986. pap. 2.50 (*0-685-13234-X*) Bantam.
—One Hundred One Ways to Meet Mr. Right. 176p. (Orig.). (gr. 6 up). 1985. pap. 2.25 (*0-553-24946-0*) Bantam.
—One Step Too Far. 192p. (Orig.). (gr. 9-11). 1989. pap. text ed. 2.95 (*0-8041-0337-2*) Ivy Books.
—Out In the Cold. 192p. (gr. 6 up). 1988. pap. 2.95 (*0-8041-0086-1*) Ivy Books.
—Out of Love. 208p. (Orig.). (gr. 6 up). 1986. pap. 2.50 (*0-553-25937-7*) Bantam.
—Roadtrip. (gr. 6 up). 1989. pap. 2.95 (*0-8041-0336-4*) Ivy Books.
—Septimus Bean & His Amazing Machine. Cumings, Art, illus. LC 79-163. 48p. (ps-3). 1980. 5.95 (*0-8193-0999-0*) Parents.
—Tess & Ali & the Teeny Bikini. 1991. pap. 3.50 (*0-06-106064-X*, Harp PBks) HarpC.
—The Trouble with Toni. 192p. (Orig.). (gr. 6 up). 1986. pap. 2.50 (*0-553-25724-2*) Bantam.
Quinlan, Hamid, ed. see Kishta, Leila.
Quinlan, Patricia. Anna's Red Sled. Grater, Lindsay, illus. 24p. (ps-2). 1989. 12.95 (*1-55037-073-1*, Pub. by Annick CN); pap. 4.95 (*1-55037-072-3*, Pub. by Annick CN) Firefly Bks Ltd.
—Brush Them Bright. Fernandes, Eugenie, illus. 24p. (ps-2). 1992. 8.95 (*1-56282-283-7*) Hyprn Child.
—Emma's Sea Journey. Marton, Jirina, illus. 24p. (ps-3). 1991. PLB 15.95 (*1-55037-179-7*, Pub. by Annick CN); pap. 5.95 (*1-55037-177-0*, Pub. by Annick CN) Firefly Bks Ltd.
—My Dad Takes Care of Me. Van Kampen, Vlasta, illus. 24p. (ps-3). 1987. PLB 14.95 (*0-920303-79-X*, Pub. by Annick CN); pap. 4.95 (*0-920303-76-5*, Pub. by Annick CN) Firefly Bks Ltd.
—Planting Seeds. Krykorka, Vladyana, illus. 24p. (ps-2). 1988. 12.95 (*1-55037-007-3*, Pub. by Annick CN); pap. 4.95 (*1-55037-006-5*, Pub. by Annick CN) Firefly Bks Ltd.
—Tiger Flowers. Wilson, Janet, illus. LC 93-15214. Date not set. write for info. (*0-8037-1407-6*); PLB write for info. (*0-8037-1408-4*) Dial Bks Young.
Quinn, Bridie & Cashman, S., eds. Wolfhound Book of Irish Poems for Young People. (Illus.). 192p. (ps-8). 1975. pap. 9.95 (*0-86327-002-6*, Pub. by Wolfhound Press Eire) Dufour.
Quinn, Dan & Davis, Larry. Multiplication Memorization Made Fun & Easy. 128p. (gr. 1-3). 1993. tchr's. ed. 9.95 (*0-9629746-1-7*) Texas Trends.
Quinn, David, jt. auth. see Boyd, Frances.
Quinn, John. The Gold Cross of Killadoo. 106p. (gr. 5 up). 1993. pap. 8.95 (*1-85371-220-5*, Pub. by Poolbeg Pr ER) Dufour.
—The Summer of Lily & Esme. 190p. (Orig.). (gr. 6 up). 1992. pap. 8.95 (*1-85371-208-6*, Pub. by Poolbeg Pr ER) Dufour.
Quinn, John & Kualter, Anne. Materials. (Illus.). 32p. (gr. 2-4). 1994. 14.95 (*1-56847-076-2*) Thomson Lrning.
Quinn, John R. The Kid's Fish Book: Setting up Your Own Native Fishes Aquarium. LC 93-31691. 1994. pap. 10.95 (*0-471-58601-3*) Wiley.
Quinn, Kay. Animals: Sixty Things I Can Draw. 1990. 4.99 (*0-517-03564-2*) Outlet Bk Co.
—Dinosaurs & Prehistoric Animals. Quinn, Kay, illus. 64p. (gr. 2-10). 1990. 4.99 (*0-517-03566-9*) Outlet Bk Co.
—Monsters: Sixty Things I Can Draw. 1990. 4.99 (*0-517-03565-0*) Outlet Bk Co.
Quinn, Kaye. Aquarium. (gr. 4-7). 1991. pap. 2.95 (*0-8431-2719-8*) Price Stern.
—Book of Bugs & Other Insects. (Illus.). 80p. (Orig.). (gr. 2-4). 1989. pap. 2.95 (*0-8431-2375-3*) Price Stern.
—Call of the Jungle. (Illus.). 48p. (Orig.). (gr. k-3). 1989. pap. 2.95 (*0-8431-2705-8*) Price Stern.
—Cars, Trucks, Trains, & Planes. (Illus.). 48p. (Orig.). (ps-2). 1989. pap. 2.95 (*0-8431-2727-9*) Price Stern.
—Creatures of the Deep. (Illus.). 48p. (Orig.). (ps-2). 1989. pap. 2.95 (*0-8431-2726-0*) Price Stern.
—Dolphin's Cave. (Illus.). 48p. (Orig.). (gr. k-3). 1989. pap. 2.95 (*0-8431-2707-4*) Price Stern.
—The Human Body. (Illus.). 80p. (Orig.). (gr. 2-4). 1989. pap. 2.95 (*0-8431-2378-8*) Price Stern.
—Inventive Inventions. Quinn, Kaye, illus. 40p. (gr. 2-6). 1986. pap. 2.95 (*0-8431-1893-8*) Price Stern.
—Mission: Space. Quinn, Kaye, illus. 40p. (gr. 2-6). 1986. pap. 2.95 (*0-8431-1894-6*) Price Stern.
—Reptiles. Quinn, Kaye, illus. 40p. (gr. 2-6). 1987. pap. 2.95 (*0-8431-1892-X*) Price Stern.
—Science Crosswords: Bizarre Bugs. 48p. 1990. pap. 2.95 (*0-8431-2374-5*) Price Stern.
—Science Crosswords: Freaky Fish. 48p. 1990. pap. 2.95 (*0-8431-2820-8*) Price Stern.
—Science Mysteries. (Illus.). 80p. (Orig.). (gr. 2-4). 1989. pap. 2.95 (*0-8431-2377-X*) Price Stern.
—Secret of Ghost Mountain. (Illus.). 48p. (Orig.). (gr. k-3). 1989. pap. 2.95 (*0-8431-2706-6*) Price Stern.
—Trip to the Lost Planet. (Illus.). 48p. (Orig.). (gr. k-3). 1989. pap. 2.95 (*0-8431-2708-2*) Price Stern.
—Under the Big Top. (Illus.). 48p. (Orig.). (ps-2). 1989. pap. 2.95 (*0-8431-2729-5*) Price Stern.
—Weird & Wacky Animals. (Illus.). 48p. (Orig.). (ps-2). 1989. pap. 2.95 (*0-8431-2728-7*) Price Stern.
—World of the Dinosaurs. Quinn, Kaye, illus. 40p. (gr. 2-4). 1987. pap. 2.95 (*0-8431-1890-3*) Price Stern.
—The World's Wierdest Plants. (Illus.). 80p. (Orig.). (gr. 2-4). 1989. pap. 2.95 (*0-8431-2379-6*) Price Stern.
—Zoo Animals. (gr. 4-7). 1991. pap. 2.95 (*0-8431-2720-1*) Price Stern.
Quinn, Kaye, illus. Cities. 48p. (ps-2). 1988. pap. 2.95 (*0-8431-2250-1*) Price Stern.
—Pets. 48p. (ps-2). 1988. pap. 2.95 (*0-8431-2252-8*) Price Stern.
—Playground. 48p. (ps-2). 1988. pap. 2.95 (*0-8431-2249-8*) Price Stern.
—Toys. 48p. (ps-2). 1988. pap. 2.95 (*0-8431-2251-X*) Price Stern.
Quinn, Nancy see Lamb, Wendy.
Quinn, Nancy D., jt. auth. see Quinn, Robert J.
Quinn, Patricia. Putting on the Brakes: A Child's Guide to Understanding & Gaining Control over Attention Deficit Hyperactivity Disorder. LC 91-20390. (gr. 4-7). 1991. pap. 8.95 (*0-945354-32-0*) Magination Pr.
Quinn, Patrick. Matthew Pinkowski's Special Summer. Quinn, Patrick, illus. LC 91-10982. 188p. (Orig.). (gr. 5-8). 1991. pap. 5.95 (*0-930323-82-3*, Pub. by K Green Pubns) Gallaudet Univ Pr.
Quinn, Robert J. & Quinn, Nancy D. Figure Skating Pins. LC 87-60429. (Illus.). 152p. (Orig.). (gr. 7-12). 1987. pap. 15.00 (*0-9618349-1-9*) Quin Tel Prodns.
Quinn, Tom, ed. Fish Tales: A Collection of Angling Stories. (Illus.). 189p. (gr. 8-12). 1992. 28.00 (*0-7509-0091-1*) A Sutton Pub.
Quinones, Wanda M., tr. see Fassler, David & McQueen, Kelly.
Quinsey, Mary Beth. Why Does That Man Have Such a Big Nose? Chan, Wilson, illus. LC 85-63760. 32p. (Orig.). (ps-1). 1986. lib. bdg. 16.95 (*0-943990-25-4*); pap. 5.95 (*0-943990-24-6*) Parenting Pr.
Quint, Artemis see Storr, Sherman, pseud.
Quintahlen, Patrique, ed. see Daves, Prentiss V.
Quintilone, Paul M. Brian Has a Winning Day. (gr. 3-5). 1988. pap. write for info. (*0-9616980-2-0*) Quintilone Ent.
—Michael Learns New Words. (Illus.). (gr. 3-5). 1988. pap. 2.98 (*0-9616980-1-2*) Quintilone Ent.
Quiri, Patricia R. Alexander Graham Bell. (Illus.). 64p. (gr. 3-5). 1991. PLB 12.90 (*0-531-20022-1*) Watts.
—The Algonquians. Rich, Mary P., ed. LC 91-29111. (Illus.). 64p. (gr. 3-5). 1992. PLB 12.90 (*0-531-20065-5*) Watts.
—The Algonquians. 64p. (gr. 5-8). 1992. pap. 5.95 (*0-531-15633-8*) Watts.
—Dating. Green, Anne C., illus. LC 89-5709. 95p. (gr. 5-10). 1989. PLB 13.40 (*0-531-10806-6*) Watts.
—Dolley Madison. LC 92-28300. 1993. 12.90 (*0-531-20097-3*) Watts.
—Metamorphosis. LC 91-3104. (Illus.). 64p. (gr. 5-8). 1991. PLB 12.90 (*0-531-20042-6*) Watts.
Quishenberry, Mary, jt. auth. see Linde, Lavaun.
Qunintilone, Paul M. Michael Learns to Trade. (Illus.). 27p. 1988. write for info. (*0-9616980-0-4*) Quintilone Ent.
Quon-Warner, Maryanna, jt. auth. see Rodecker, Stephen B.

R

Ra, Carol, jt. ed. see Smith, William J.
Ra, Carol F. Trot, Trot to Boston. Stock, Catherine, illus. LC 86-7354. 32p. (ps). 1987. 12.95 (*0-688-06190-7*); PLB 12.88 (*0-688-06191-5*) Lothrop.
Raab, Robert A. Coping with Death. rev. ed. Rosen, Ruth, ed. (gr. 7-12). 1989. PLB 13.95 (*0-8239-0960-3*) Rosen Group.
—Coping with Divorce. rev. ed. (gr. 7-12). 1984. PLB 13.95 (*0-8239-0428-8*) Rosen Group.
Rabazza, Gregory, tr. see Marquez, Gabriel G.
Rabbi Mindy Avra Portnoy. Ima on the Bima: My Mommy Is a Rabbi. Rubin, Steffi, illus. LC 86-3023. 32p. (ps-4). 1986. 10.95 (*0-930494-55-5*); pap. 4.95 (*0-930494-54-7*) Kar Ben.
Rabbitts, Muriel J. Thought of Childhood. 1991. 10.95 (*0-533-09371-6*) Vantage.
Rabe, Berniece. The Balancing Girl. Hoban, Lillian, illus. LC 80-22100. (ps-2). 1981. 12.95 (*0-525-26160-5*, 0995-300, DCB) Dutton Child Bks.
—The Balancing Girl. Hoban, Lillian, illus. LC 80-22100. 32p. (ps-2). 1988. pap. 4.99 (*0-525-44364-9*, 0382-120, DCB) Dutton Child Bks.
—Magic Comes in Its Time. Ben-Ami, Doron, illus. LC 92-19260. 1993. pap. 13.00 (*0-671-79454-X*, S&S BFYR) S&S Trade.
—A Smooth Move. Tucker, Kathleen, ed. Sims, Blanche, illus. LC 87-2099. (gr. 1-4). 1987. PLB 11.95 (*0-8075-7486-4*) A Whitman.
—Tall Enough to Own the World. LC 88-39139. 160p. (gr. 5-7). 1989. PLB 13.90 (*0-531-10681-0*) Watts.
—Where's Chimpy? Tucker, Kathleen, ed. Schmidt, Diane, photos by. LC 87-37259. (Illus.). 32p. (ps-2). 1988. PLB 13.95 (*0-8075-8928-4*); pap. 5.95 (*0-8075-8927-6*) A Whitman.

Rabe, Tish. My Name Is Ernie. Swanson, Maggie, illus. (ps-k). 1991. pap. write for info. (*0-307-11513-5*, Golden Pr) Western Pub.
—My Name Is Grover. Swanson, Maggie, illus. 24p. (ps-k). 1992. pap. write for info. (*0-307-11534-8*, 11534, Golden Pr) Western Pub.
Rabe, Tish S. Elmo Gets Homesick. (Illus.). 32p. (ps). 1990. write for info. (*0-307-12033-3*, Pub. by Golden Bks) Western Pub.
Rabell, Edda, ed. & tr. see Ronnholm, Ursula O.
Raber, Rom. Bo Jackson: Pro Sports Superstar. (Illus.). 64p. (gr. 4-9). 1991. PLB 13.50 (*0-8225-0487-1*); pap. 4.95 (*0-8225-9585-0*) Lerner Pubns.
Raber, Thomas R. Election Night. (Illus.). 88p. (gr. 4 up). 1988. lib. bdg. 14.95 (*0-8225-1751-5*) Lerner Pubns.
—Joe Montana: Comeback Quarterback. 1990. pap. 4.95 (*0-8225-9572-9*) Lerner Pubns.
—Michael Jordan: Basketball Skywalker. LC 92-8277. 1992. 13.50 (*0-8225-0549-5*) Lerner Pubns.
—Michael Jordan: Basketball Skywalker. (gr. 4-7). 1993. pap. 4.95 (*0-8225-9625-3*) Lerner Pubns.
—Presidential Campaign. (Illus.). 88p. (gr. 4 up). 1988. lib. bdg. 14.95 (*0-8225-1750-7*) Lerner Pubns.
Raber, Tom. Joe Montana: Comeback Quarterback. (Illus.). 64p. (gr. 4-9). 1989. PLB 13.50 (*0-8225-0486-3*) Lerner Pubns.
—Wayne Gretzky: Hockey Great. (Illus.). 64p. (gr. 4-9). 1991. PLB 13.50 (*0-8225-0539-8*) Lerner Pubns.
—Wayne Gretzky: Hockey Great. 1992. pap. 4.95 (*0-8225-9601-6*) Lerner Pubns.
Rabin, Arnold. The Outing. 53p. (Orig.). 1992. pap. 4.50 playscript (*0-87602-303-0*) Anchorage.
Rabin, Staton. Casey over There. Shed, Greg, illus. LC 92-30322. 1994. write for info. (*0-15-253186-6*) HarBrace.
—Monster Myths: The Truth about Water Monsters. Roxas, Reni, ed. (Illus.). 40p. (gr. 5-8). 1992. 15.95 (*0-531-15222-7*); PLB 15.90 (*0-531-11074-5*) Watts.
Rabinowich, Ellen. Underneath I'm Different. LC 82-14919. 192p. (gr. 7 up). 1983. 12.95 (*0-685-06447-6*) Delacorte.
Rabinowitz, Ann. Bethie. LC 88-22840. 208p. (gr. 7 up). 1989. SBE 14.95 (*0-02-775661-0*, Macmillan Child Bk) Macmillan Child Grp.
Rabinowitz, Jan. The Tzedakah Workbook. Golub, Jane & Grishaver, Joelrev. by. (Illus.). 32p. (Orig.). (gr. 4-5). 1986. pap. text ed. 3.95 (*0-933873-07-7*) Torah Aura.
Rabinowitz, Richard. What Is War? Fifty Questions & Answers for Kids. (gr. 4-7). 1991. pap. 2.95 (*0-380-76704-X*, Camelot) Avon.
Rabinowitz, Sandy. How I Trained My Colt. (ps). 1991. pap. 2.75 (*0-553-15848-1*) Bantam.
Rabkin, Sarah. My First Science Dictionary. Burke, Dianne O., illus. 64p. (gr. k-3). 1992. 10.95 (*1-56288-215-5*) Checkerboard.
Raboff, Ernest. Albrecht Durer. Durer, Albrecht, illus. LC 87-17702. 32p. (gr. 1 up). 1988. pap. 5.95 (*0-06-446071-1*, Trophy) HarpC Child Bks.
—Diego Rodriguez de Silva y Velasquez. LC 87-17697. (Illus.). 32p. (gr. 1 up). 1988. pap. 7.95 (*0-06-446073-8*, Trophy) HarpC Child Bks.
—Frederic Remington. Remington, Frederic, illus. LC 87-17698. 32p. (gr. 1 up). 1988. pap. 7.95 (*0-06-446079-7*, Trophy) HarpC Child Bks.
—Henri de Toulouse-Lautrec. De Toulouse-Lautrec, Henri, illus. LC 87-17703. 32p. (gr. 1 up). 1988. pap. 7.95 (*0-06-446070-3*, Trophy) Trophy HarpC Child Bks.
—Henri Matisse. Matisse, Henri, illus. LC 87-17701. 32p. (gr. 1 up). 1988. pap. 7.95 (*0-06-446080-0*, Trophy) HarpC Child Bks.
—Henri Rousseau. LC 87-17700. (Illus.). 32p. (gr. 1 up). 1988. pap. 7.95 (*0-06-446069-X*, Trophy) HarpC Child Bks.
—Leonardo da Vinci. Da Vinci, Leonardo, illus. LC 87-45146. 32p. (gr. 1 up). 1987. pap. 7.95 (*0-06-446076-2*, Trophy) HarpC Child Bks.
—Marc Chagall. LC 87-45297. (Illus.). 32p. (gr. 1 up). 1988. pap. 5.95 (*0-06-446066-5*, Trophy) HarpC Child Bks.
—Michelangelo Buonarroti. LC 87-45298. (Illus.). 32p. (gr. 1 up). 1988. pap. 7.95 (*0-06-446074-6*, Trophy) HarpC Child Bks.
—Pablo Picasso. 1987. pap. 7.95 (*0-06-446067-3*) HarpC Child Bks.
—Paul Gauguin. LC 87-17696. (Illus.). 32p. (gr. 1 up). 1988. pap. 5.95 (*0-06-446078-9*, Trophy) Trophy Child Bks.
—Paul Klee. LC 87-17699. (Illus.). 32p. (gr. 1 up). 1988. pap. 5.95 (*0-06-446065-7*, Trophy) HarpC Child Bks.
—Pierre Auguste Renoir. Picasso, Pablo, illus. LC 87-45147. 32p. (gr. 1 up). 1987. pap. 7.95 (*0-06-446068-1*, Trophy) HarpC Child Bks.
—Raphael Sanzio. Raboff, Ernest, illus. LC 87-45299. 32p. (gr. 1 up). 1988. pap. 7.95 (*0-06-446075-4*, Trophy) HarpC Child Bks.
—Rembrandt. Rembrandt, illus. LC 87-45148. 32p. (gr. 1 up). 1987. pap. 7.95 (*0-06-446072-X*, Trophy) HarpC Child Bks.
—Vincent Van Gogh. LC 87-45300. (Illus.). 32p. (gr. 1 up). 1988. pap. 7.95 (*0-06-446077-0*, Trophy) HarpC Child Bks.
Rabold, Ted & Fair, Phillip. New Jersey: Yesterday & Today. Ferguson, Laurie, illus. 110p. (Orig.). (gr. 4). 1982. 9.95 (*0-931992-41-9*); pap. text ed. 4.95 (*0-931992-43-5*) Penns Valley.

Raburn, Terry. Starting Blocks: Running the Race A-G Style. LC 88-80813. 128p. (Orig.). (gr. 7 up). 1988. pap. 2.95 (*0-88243-860-3*, 02-0860); tchr's. guide 4.50 (*0-88243-200-1*, 32-0200) Gospel Pub.
Race, Donna. Favorite Mother Goose Songs: A Musical Pop-up Book with Five Different Melodies. (Illus.). 12p. (ps-1). 1993. POB 12.95 (*0-689-71684-2*, Aladdin) Macmillan Child Grp.
—Jolly Old St. Nicholas: A Holiday Book with Lights & Music. LC 91-43087. (Illus.). 12p. (ps-1). 1992. POB 11.95 (*0-689-71622-2*, Aladdin) Macmillan Child Grp.
Rachlin, Ann. Bach. Hellard, Susan, illus. LC 92-9520. 1992. 5.95 (*0-8120-4991-8*) Barron.
—Brahms. Hellard, Susan, illus. 24p. (gr. k-3). 1993. pap. 5.95 (*0-8120-1542-8*) Barron.
—Chopin. Hellard, Susan, illus. 24p. (gr. k-3). 1993. pap. 5.95 (*0-8120-1543-6*) Barron.
—Handel. Hellard, Susan, illus. LC 92-11497. 1992. 5.95 (*0-8120-4992-6*) Barron.
—Haydn. Hellard, Susan, illus. LC 92-9521. 1992. 5.95 (*0-8120-4988-8*) Barron.
—Mozart. Hellard, Susan, illus. LC 92-10302. 1992. 5.95 (*0-8120-4989-6*) Barron.
—Schumann. Hellard, Susan, illus. LC 92-26965. 24p. (gr. k-3). 1993. pap. 5.95 (*0-8120-1544-4*) Barron.
—Tchaikovsky. Hellard, Susan, illus. 24p. (gr. k-3). 1993. pap. 5.95 (*0-8120-1545-2*) Barron.
Rachner, Mary J. Kerry's Thirteenth Birthday: Everything Your Parents & Their Friends Know about Sex but Are Too Polite to Talk About. rev. ed. LC 93-84599. 80p. (gr. 8 up). 1993. 1993. pap. text ed. 9.95 (*0-9623133-4-3*) Oxner Inst.
Rachner, Mary J., intro. by see Knot, Madonna.
Rackham, Arthur. Mother Goose, the Old Nursery Rhymes. (Illus.). (ps-6). 1978. Repr. of 1912 ed. lib. bdg. 12.00 luxury ed. (*0-932106-02-1*, Pub by Marathon Pr) S J Durst.
—Sleeping Beauty. Rackham, Arthur, illus. 110p. (gr. k-4). 1920. pap. 3.95 (*0-486-22756-1*) Dover.
Rackham, Arthur, illus. Aesop's Fables. (gr. 2-9). 1992. 7.99 (*0-517-17198-8*) Outlet Bk Co.
—The Arthur Rackham Fairy Book. 271p. (gr. 2-10). 1991. 3.99 (*0-517-24213-3*) Outlet Bk Co.
—Sixty Fairy Tales of the Brothers Grimm. (gr. 2-7). 8.98 (*0-517-28525-8*) Outlet Bk Co.
Radcliff, Sarah. Teen Esteem. 194p. 1992. 14.95 (*0-944070-80-9*) Targum Pr.
Radcliffe, Theresa. Shadow the Deer. Butler, John, illus. 32p. (ps-1). 1993. 13.99 (*0-670-83852-7*) Viking Child Bks.
Radencich, Marguerite, jt. auth. see Schumm, Jeanne S.
Rader, Laura. Mother Hubbard's Cupboard: A Mother Goose Surprise Book. Rader, Laura, illus. LC 92-45103. 48p. (ps up). 1993. 12.95 (*0-688-12562-X*, Tambourine Bks) Morrow.
Rader, Laura, illus. Goody New Shoes. 32p. (ps-3). 1991. pap. 3.50 (*0-14-054391-0*, Puffin) Puffin Bks.
—The Pudgy Where Is Your Nose? Book. 16p. 1989. bds. 2.95 (*0-448-02258-3*, G&D) Putnam Pub Group.
Radford, Derek. Bernie Drives a Truck. LC 91-58718. (Illus.). 32p. (gr. up). 1992. 9.95 (*1-56402-073-8*) Candlewick Pr.
—Building Machines & What They Do. Radford, Derek, illus. LC 91-71860. 32p. (gr. up). 1992. 8.95 (*1-56402-006-1*) Candlewick Pr.
—Cargo Machines & What They Do. Radford, Derek, illus. LC 91-71823. 32p. (gr. up). 1992. 8.95 (*1-56402-005-3*) Candlewick Pr.
—Harry at the Airport. Radford, Derek, illus. LC 91-16116. 32p. (gr. k-3). 1991. POB 10.95 (*0-689-71504-8*, Aladdin) Macmillan Child Grp.
—Let's Look Inside a Bus, Train, Ferry, & Plane. Radford, Derek, illus. LC 92-41487. 20p. (ps). 1993. 9.99 (*0-525-67459-4*, Lodestar Bks) Dutton Child Bks.
Radford, Don. Looking at Flight. (Illus.). 72p. (gr. 7-12). 1984. 18.95 (*0-7134-4257-3*, Pub. by Batsford UK) Trafalgar.
Radford, Elaine. A Step-by-Step Book about Parrots. (Illus.). 64p. (gr. 9-12). 1988. pap. 3.95 (*0-86622-484-X*, SK-031) TFH Pubns.
Radford, Ruby L. Prelude to Fame: Crawford Long's Discovery of Anaesthesia. LC 74-81776. (gr. 7 up). 1969. 4.95 (*0-87672-104-8*) Geron-X.
Radiguet, Raymond. Devil in the Flesh. Smith, A. M., tr. from FRE. 128p. 1993. pap. 10.95 (*0-7145-0193-X*, Dist. by Kampmann) M Boyars Pubs.
—Le Diable au Corps. (gr. 7-12). pap. 5.95 (*0-88436-059-8*, 40273) EMC.
Radin, Ruth Y. All Joseph Wanted. Ray, Deborah K., illus. LC 91-12643. 80p. (gr. 3-7). 1991. SBE 12.95 (*0-02-775641-6*, Macmillan Child Bk) Macmillan Child Grp.
—Carver. Swanson, Karl, illus. LC 89-13413. 80p. (gr. 3-7). 1990. SBE 12.95 (*0-02-775651-3*, Macmillan Child Bk) Macmillan Child Grp.
—High in the Mountains. Young, Ed, illus. LC 88-13395. 32p. (gr. k-4). 1989. RSBE 13.95 (*0-02-775650-5*, Macmillan Child Bk) Macmillan Child Grp.
—Tac's Island. 80p. (gr. 2-9). 1989. pap. 2.95 (*0-8167-1320-0*) Troll Assocs.
—Tac's Turn. 80p. (gr. 2-9). 1989. pap. 2.95 (*0-8167-1371-9*) Troll Assocs.
—A Winter Place. O'Kelley, Mattie L., illus. LC 82-15349. 32p. (gr. 3 up). 1982. 15.95 (*0-316-73218-4*, Joy St Bks) Little.
Radke, Martha E. The Cat Who Conducted with His Tail. Tootill, Ginger, illus. LC 81-90803. 28p. (Orig.). (ps-3). 1982. pap. 1.95 (*0-9607994-0-0*) G E Radke.

Radlauer, Ed. Bears, Bears & More Bears. Radlauer Productions Staff, illus. 32p. (ps-4). 1991. PLB 9.95 (*1-878363-34-4*) Forest Hse.
—Cats, Cats, & More Cats. Radlauer Productions Staff, illus. 32p. 1991. PLB 9.95 (*1-878363-35-2*) Forest Hse.
—Wheels, Wheels, & More Wheels. Radlauer Productions Staff, illus. 32p. 1991. PLB 9.95 (*1-878363-36-0*) Forest Hse.
Radlauer, Ed & Radlauer, Ruth. Earthquakes. LC 87-13772. (Illus.). 48p. (gr. 3 up). 1987. pap. 4.95 (*0-516-47841-9*) Childrens.
Radlauer, Edward. Shark Mania. 1986. pap. 3.95 (*0-516-47410-3*) Childrens.
Radlauer, Ruth. Acadia National Park. Radlauer, Ed & Radlauer, Ruth, illus. LC 77-18056. 48p. (gr. 3 up). 1978. PLB 17.27 (*0-516-07495-4*, Elk Grove Bks); pap. 4.95 (*0-516-47495-2*) Childrens.
—Bryce Canyon National Park. updated ed. Radlauer, Ed & Radlauer, Ruth, illus. LC 79-22722. 48p. (gr. 3 up). 1987. PLB 17.27 (*0-516-07484-9*, Elk Grove Bks.); pap. 4.95 (*0-516-47484-7*) Childrens.
—Carlsbad Caverns National Park. LC 81-4560. (Illus.). 48p. (gr. 3 up). 1981. PLB 17.27 (*0-516-07742-2*) Childrens.
—Everglades National Park. LC 75-11773. 48p. (gr. 3 up). 1976. pap. 4.95 (*0-516-47488-X*) Childrens.
—Great Smoky Mountains National Park. updated ed. Zillmer, Rolf, photos by. LC 76-9839. (Illus.). 48p. (gr. 3 up). 1985. pap. 4.95 (*0-516-47489-8*) Childrens.
—Haleakala National Park. updated ed. Zillmer, Rolf, illus. LC 79-10500. 48p. (gr. 3 up). 1987. PLB 17.27 (*0-516-07499-7*); pap. 4.95 (*0-516-47499-5*) Childrens.
—Hawaii Volcanoes National Park. updated ed. Radlauer, Ed & Radlauer, Ruth, illus. LC 78-19718. 48p. (gr. 3 up). 1987. PLB 17.27 (*0-516-07498-9*, Elk Grove Bks); pap. 4.95 (*0-516-47498-7*) Childrens.
—Mammoth Cave National Park. updated ed. Radlauer, Ed, illus. LC 77-26764. 48p. (gr. 3 up). 1987. (Elk Grove Bks); pap. 4.95 (*0-516-47496-0*) Childrens.
—Mesa Verde National Park. updated ed. Zillmer, Rolf, photos by. LC 76-27350. (Illus.). 48p. (gr. 3 up). 1984. pap. 4.95 (*0-516-47490-1*) Childrens.
—Volcanoes. LC 80-24564. (Illus.). 48p. (gr. 3 up). 1981. (Elk Grove Bks); pap. 4.95 (*0-516-47835-4*) Childrens.
Radlauer, Ruth & Gitkin, Lisa S. The Power of Ice. Gitkin, Lisa S., photos by. LC 85-5714. (Illus.). 48p. (gr. 3 up). 1985. pap. 4.95 (*0-516-47839-7*) Childrens.
Radlauer, Ruth & Stembridge, Charles. Planets. LC 83-21043. (Illus.). 48p. (gr. 3 up). 1984. pap. 4.95 (*0-516-47838-9*) Childrens.
Radlauer, Ruth, jt. auth. see Radlauer, Ed.
Radlauer, Ruth S. Breakfast by Molly. (gr. k-3). 1991. pap. 2.25 (*0-671-74021-0*, Little Simon) S&S Trade.
—Glacier National Park. updated ed. LC 76-48993. (Illus.). 48p. (gr. 3 up). 1977. pap. 4.95 (*0-516-47491-X*) Childrens.
—Honor the Flag: A Guide to Its Care & Display. Smith-Moore, J. J., illus. 48p. (gr. 2 up). 1992. PLB 12.95 (*1-878363-61-1*) Forest Hse.
—Molly. McCully, Emily A., illus. (ps-2). 1987. 10.95 (*0-13-599762-3*) P-H.
—Molly. (Illus.). (gr. k-3). 1991. pap. 2.50 (*0-671-74018-0*, Little Simon) S&S Trade.
—Molly at the Library. (Illus.). (gr. k-3). 1991. pap. 2.25 (*0-671-74019-9*, Little Simon) S&S Trade.
—Molly Goes Hiking. McCully, Emily A., illus. LC 86-18761. 32p. (ps-3). 1987. pap. 10.95 (*0-671-66860-9*) S&S Trade.
—Molly Goes Hiking. (Illus.). (gr. k-3). 1991. pap. 2.25 (*0-671-74022-9*, Little Simon) S&S Trade.
—Yosemite National Park. updated ed. Zillmer, Rolf, photos by. LC 75-2160. (Illus.). 48p. (gr. 3 up). 1984. PLB 17.27 (*0-516-07486-5*) Childrens.
Radley, Gail. The Golden Days. 160p. (gr. 3-7). 1991. SBE 13.95 (*0-02-775652-1*) Macmillan Child Grp.
—The Golden Days. LC 92-19526. 160p. (gr. 5 up). 1992. pap. 3.99 (*0-14-036002-6*) Puffin Bks.
—Special Strengths. Boddy, Joe, illus. 64p. (gr. 2-6). 1984. pap. 6.50 (*0-87743-702-5*, Pub. by Bellwood Pr) Bahai.
Radley, Gail, selected by. Rainy Day Rhymes. Kandoian, Ellen, illus. 48p. (gr. 2-5). 1992. 13.45 (*0-395-59967-9*) HM.
Radner, Barbara, ed. see Nero, Ann B.
Radunsky, Vladimir. Absent-Minded Fellow. 1993. 14.95 (*0-8050-1131-5*) H Holt & Co.
Radunsky, jt. auth. see Pevear.
Radunsky, Eugenia. Square, Triangle, Round, Skinny: Four Books in a Box. (ps). 1992. 18.95 (*0-8050-2205-8*, Bks Young Read) H Holt & Co.
Radvany, Ruth, et al. Intermediate Algebra Study Aid. 1974. pap. 2.50 (*0-87738-038-4*) Youth Ed.
Radzinski, Kandy, illus. The Twelve Cats of Christmas. 32p. 1992. 9.95 (*0-8118-0102-0*) Chronicle Bks.
Rae, Judy. Bye, Bye Boogieman. Rev. ed. Lalo, illus. Timm, Stephen A., intro. by. LC 83-70412. (Illus.). 42p. (Orig.). (ps-3). 1984. pap. 3.95 (*0-939728-09-5*) Steppingstone Ent.
Rae, Mary M. Over in the Meadow: A Counting-Out Rhyme. (Illus.). 32p. (ps-k). 1986. pap. 3.95 (*0-685-14199-3*, Penguin Bks) Viking Penguin.
Rae, Mary M., jt. auth. see Wadsworth, Olivia A.
Rae, Mary M., illus. The Farmer in the Dell: A Singing Game. 32p. (ps-1). 1990. pap. 3.95 (*0-14-050788-4*, Puffin) Puffin Bks.

Rae, Rusty. The World's Biggest Motorcycle Race: The Daytona 200. LC 77-92297. (Illus.). 56p. (gr. 4-9). 1978. PLB 14.95 (*0-8225-0422-7*) Lerner Pubns.

Rael, Elsa O. Marushka's Egg. Wezyk, Joanna, illus. LC 92-303. 40p. (gr. k-4). 1993. RSBE 14.95 (*0-02-775655-6*, Four Winds) Macmillan Child Grp.

Raemsch, Dorothy C. Spinning with Gold: Poems for Young & Old. Tosti, Selma, illus. 32p. 1991. pap. 7.50 (*0-9605398-2-4*) D C Raemsch.

Raferty, Kim G. & Raftery, Kevin. Kids Gardening: A Kid's Guide to Messing Around in the Dirt. M'Guinness, Jim, illus. 84p. (Orig.). 1989. pap. 12.95 incl. 15 varieties of seeds (*0-932592-25-2*) Klutz Pr.

Raffel, Burton. How to Read a Poem: Metrics. 260p. (gr. 9-12). 1989. pap. 8.95 (*0-452-00917-0*, Mer) NAL-Dutton.

Raffi. Baby Beluga. Wolff, Ashley, illus. LC 89-49367. 32p. (ps-2). 1990. 13.00 (*0-517-57839-5*); PLB 11.99 (*0-517-57840-9*) Crown Bks Yng Read.

—Baby Beluga. Wolff, Ashley, illus. LC 89-49367. 32p. (ps-2). 1992. pap. 3.99 (*0-517-58362-3*) Crown Bks Yng Read.

—Down by the Bay. Westcott, Nadine B., illus. 32p. (ps-2). 1988. PLB 14.00 (*0-517-56644-3*) Crown Bks Yng Read.

—Down by the Bay. Westcott, Nadine B., illus. LC 87-750291. 32p. (ps-2). 1988. pap. 3.99 (*0-517-56645-1*) Crown Bks Yng Read.

—Everything Grows. McMillan, Bruce, illus. LC 88-37162. 32p. (ps-2). 1989. 9.95 (*0-517-57387-3*) Crown Bks Yng Read.

—Everything Grows. McMillan, Bruce, illus. LC 88-37162. 32p. (ps-2). 1993. pap. 3.99 (*0-517-88098-9*) Crown Bks Yng Read.

—Five Little Ducks. 1988. 12.00 (*0-517-56945-0*) Crown Bks Yng Read.

—Five Little Ducks. Aruego, Jose & Dewey, Ariane, illus. LC 88-3752. 32p. (ps-2). 1992. pap. 3.99 (*0-517-58360-7*) Crown Bks Yng Read.

—Like Me & You. Hoban, Lillian, illus. LC 93-9840. 1994. 13.00 (*0-517-59587-7*, Crown); lib. bdg. 13.99 (*0-517-59588-5*, Crown) Crown Pub Group.

—One Light, One Sun. Fernandes, Eugenie, illus. LC 87-22256. 32p. (ps-2). 1990. pap. 3.99 (*0-517-57644-9*) Crown Bks Yng Read.

—The Raffi Everything Grows Songbook. (Illus.). 48p. (ps up) 1989. 13.95 (*0-517-57110-2*) Crown Bks Yng Read.

—The Raffi Singable Songbook. Yamamoto, Joyce, illus. 104p. (ps up) 1988. spiral bdg. 18.00 (*0-517-56638-9*) Crown Bks Yng Read.

—Shake My Sillies Out. Allender, David, illus. LC 87-750478. 32p. (ps-2). 1988. pap. 3.99 (*0-517-56647-8*) Crown Bks Yng Read.

—Tingalayo. Duke, Kate, illus. LC 88-3562. 32p. 1993. pap. 3.99 (*0-517-88099-7*) Crown Bks Yng Read.

—Wheels on the Bus. Wickstrom, Sylvie K., illus. LC 87-30126. 32p. (ps-2). 1990. pap. 3.99 (*0-517-57645-7*) Crown Bks Yng Read.

Raffi & Kelley, True, illus. The Spider on the Floor. LC 92-33442. 32p. (ps-3). 1993. 13.00 (*0-517-59381-5*); PLB 13.99 (*0-517-59464-1*) Crown Bks Yng Read.

Rafter, Rusalie & Alsia, Chero. RCT Writing: A Workbook. rev. ed. 204p. (gr. 9-12). 1990. 8.95 (*0-937820-60-1*) Westsea Pub.

Raftery, Kevin, jt. auth. see Raferty, Kim G.

Ragache, Claude-Catherine. Creation of the World. LC 90-25263. (Illus.). 48p. (gr. 4-8). 1991. PLB 13.95 (*0-685-52829-4*) Marshall Cavendish.

Ragache, Gilles. Dragons. LC 90-25902. (Illus.). 48p. (gr. 4-8). 1991. PLB 13.95 (*1-85435-265-2*) Marshall Cavendish.

Ragan, John D. Emiliano Zapata. Schlesinger, Arthur M., intro. by. (Illus.). 112p. (gr. 5 up). 1989. 17.95 (*1-55546-823-3*) Chelsea Hse.

—The Explorers of Alaska. (Illus.). 112p. (gr. 5 up). 1992. lib. bdg. 18.95 (*0-7910-1311-1*) Chelsea Hse.

Ragan, Lise B., ed. see Garcia, Mary H. & Gonzalez-Mena, Janet.

Ragan, Robert. Step-by-Step Bookkeeping: The Complete Handbook for the Small Business. rev. ed. LC 74-7814. (Illus.). 128p. (gr. 10-12). 1992. pap. 7.95 (*0-8069-8690-5*) Sterling.

Ragan-Reid, Gale. Divine. LC 93-60229. (Illus.). 44p. (gr. 1-4). 1994. 7.95 (*1-55523-606-5*) Winston-Derek.

Ragaway, Martin A. The World's Worst Golf Jokes. 48p. 1972. pap. 2.95 (*0-8431-0200-4*) Price Stern.

Ragland, Teresa B., illus. Cooking in the Kitchen with Santa. 24p. 1992. pap. 4.95 (*0-8249-3096-7*, Ideals Child) Hambleton-Hill.

—Cooking in the Kitchen with Santa. 32p. (ps up). 1992. PLB 11.95 (*1-56674-028-2*) Forest Hse.

Raglund, Teresa, illus. Baby Days & Lullabye Nights. 48p. 1993. 17.95 (*0-8249-8619-9*, Ideals Child); gift box incl. cass. 24.95 (*0-8249-7629-0*) Hambleton-Hill.

Ragsdale, Bruce A. The House of Representatives. Schlesinger, Arthur, Jr., intro. by. (Illus.). 96p. (gr. 5 up). 1989. lib. bdg. 14.95 (*1-55546-112-3*) Chelsea Hse.

Raguse, Dan. Prayer. 48p. (Orig.). (gr. 6-8). 1990. pap. 7.99 (*1-55945-104-1*) Group Pub.

Ragz, M. M. Eyeballs for Breakfast. MacDonald, Patricia, ed. 128p. (Orig.). (gr. 4-7). 1990. pap. 2.99 (*0-671-68567-8*, Minstrel Bks) PB.

Raham, R. Gary. Sillysaurs: Dinosaurs That Could Have Been. Raham, R. Gary, illus. 16p. (Orig.). (gr. k-4). 1990. write for info. saddle-stitched (*0-9626301-0-1*) Biostration.

Rahmas, D. Steve, ed. see Barger, James.
Rahmas, D. Steve, ed. see Buchanan, John G.
Rahmas, D. Steve, ed. see Finke, Blythe F.
Rahmas, D. Steve, ed. see Fleissner, Else M.
Rahmas, D. Steve, ed. see Fredman, Lionel E. & Kurland, Gerald.
Rahmas, D. Steve, ed. see Kurland, Gerald.
Rahmas, D. Steve, ed. see Laing, Martha.
Rahmas, D. Steve, ed. see Lichello, Robert.
Rahmas, D. Steve, ed. see Longo, Lucas.
Rahmas, D. Steve, ed. see Mushkat, Jerome.
Rahmas, D. Steve, ed. see Paley, Alan L.
Rahmas, D. Steve, ed. see Roucek, Joseph.
Rahmas, D. Steve, ed. see Roucek, Joseph S.
Rahmas, D. Steve, ed. see Salsini, Barbara.
Rahmas, D. Steve, ed. see Salsini, Paul.
Rahmas, D. Steve, ed. see Schoen, Celin V.
Rahmas, D. Steve, ed. see Shatraw, Harriett.
Rahmas, D. Steve, ed. see Shivanandan, Mary.
Rahmas, D. Steve, ed. see Victor, R. F.
Rahmas, D. Steve, ed. see Zierau, Lillee D.

Rahmas, Sigrid. Mother Sun & Her Planet Children. Rahmas, Sigrid, illus. 32p. (Orig.). (ps-3). 1991. 6.25 (*0-87157-099-8*); pap. 2.95 (*0-87157-599-X*) Story Hse Corp.

Rahmas, Sigurd C., ed. see Finke, Blythe F.
Rahmas, Sigurd C., ed. see Green, Bill.
Rahmas, Sigurd C., ed. see Kurland, Gerald.
Rahmas, Steve, ed. see Abbazia, Patrick.

Rahn, Joan E. Animals That Changed History. Rahn, Joan E., illus. LC 86-3635. 128p. (gr. 4-8). 1986. SBE 13.95 (*0-689-31137-0*, Atheneum Child Bk) Macmillan Child Grp.

—More Plants That Changed History. LC 84-21563. 136p. (gr. 5 up). 1985. SBE 13.95 (*0-689-31099-4*, Atheneum Child Bk) Macmillan Child Grp.

—Plants Up Close. (Illus.). (gr. 2-5). 1981. 13.45 (*0-395-31677-4*) HM.

Raichert, Lane. D.C. Hopper, the First Starbunny. Raichert, Lane, illus. LC 91-23055. 32p. (gr. 2-6). 1992. 15.95 (*1-880009-81-1*, DC-P1) Blue Zero Pub.

Raileanu, Lia, tr. see Segal, Bertha E.

Raimondo, Lois. The Little Lama of Tibet. LC 93-13627. (Illus.). 40p. (ps-4). 1994. 14.95 (*0-590-46167-2*) Scholastic Inc.

Raimondo, P. Domenico Di see Hart, Corinne.

Raimondo, P. Domenico Di see Shannon, Ellen & Hart, Corinne.

Rainboldt, Jo, jt. auth. see Gingras, Louie.

Rainbolt, Richard. Basketball's Big Men. LC 74-27471. (Illus.). 80p. (gr. 4 up). 1975. PLB 11.95 (*0-8225-1054-5*) Lerner Pubns.

—Football's Rugged Running Backs. LC 74-27469. (Illus.). 72p. (gr. 4 up). 1975. PLB 11.95 (*0-8225-1052-9*) Lerner Pubns.

—Hockey's Top Scorers. LC 74-27471. (Illus.). 72p. (gr. 4 up). 1981. PLB 11.95 (*0-8225-1056-1*) Lerner Pubns.

Rainey, Richard. The Monster Factory. LC 92-26191. (Illus.). 128p. (gr. 6 up). 1993. RSBE 13.95 (*0-02-775663-7*, New Discovery) Macmillan Child Grp.

Rainis, Kenneth G. Exploring with a Magnifying Glass. LC 91-18329. (Illus.). 144p. (gr. 9-12). 1991. PLB 13.90 (*0-531-12508-4*) Watts.

—Nature Projects for Young Scientists. 1989. pap. 6.95 (*0-531-15135-2*) Watts.

—Nature Projects for Young Scientists. Rainis, Kenneth G., illus. LC 89-5662. 142p. (gr. 6 up). 1989. PLB 13.90 (*0-531-10789-2*) Watts.

Raintree Publishers Inc. Volcanoes. LC 87-27785. (Illus.). 64p. (Orig.). (gr. 5-9). 1988. PLB 19.92 (*0-8172-3081-5*) Raintree Steck-V.

—Weather. LC 87-28715. (Illus.). 64p. (Orig.). (gr. 5-9). 1988. lib. bdg. 19.92 (*0-8172-3079-3*) Raintree Steck-V.

Raintree Publishers Inc. Staff. Dolphins. LC 87-28717. (Illus.). 64p. (Orig.). (gr. 5-9). 1988. PLB 19.92 (*0-8172-3085-8*) Raintree Steck-V.

—Energy. LC 87-28699. (Illus.). 64p. (Orig.). (gr. 5-9). 1988. PLB 19.92 (*0-8172-3076-9*) Raintree Steck-V.

—Prehistoric Animals. (Illus.). 64p. (Orig.). (gr. 5-9). 1988. PLB 19.92 (*0-8172-3082-3*) Raintree Steck-V.

Raintree Publishers Staff. Animals. LC 87-28712. (Illus.). 64p. (Orig.). (gr. 5-9). 1988. PLB 19.92 (*0-8172-3083-1*) Raintree Steck-V.

—Animals at the Water's Edge. LC 87-20687. (Illus.). 48p. (gr. k-6). 1987. PLB 17.28 (*0-8172-3115-3*) Raintree Steck-V.

—Animals in Cities & Parks. LC 87-20684. (gr. k-6). 1987. 17.28 (*0-8172-3116-1*) Raintree Steck-V.

—Animals in Houses & Gardens. LC 87-20775. (Illus.). (gr. k-6). 1987. PLB 17.28 (*0-8172-3114-5*) Raintree Steck-V.

—Animals in Rivers & Ponds. LC 87-20685. (Illus.). 48p. (gr. k-6). 1987. PLB 17.28 (*0-8172-3113-7*) Raintree Steck-V.

—Animals in the Forest. LC 87-20689. (Illus.). 48p. (gr. k-6). 1987. PLB 17.28 (*0-8172-3111-0*) Raintree Steck-V.

—Animals in the Mountains. LC 87-20688. (Illus.). 48p. (gr. k-6). 1987. PLB 17.28 (*0-8172-3112-9*) Raintree Steck-V.

—Archaeology. LC 87-28634. (Illus.). 64p. (Orig.). (gr. 5-9). 1988. PLB 19.92 (*0-8172-3077-7*) Raintree Steck-V.

—Astronomy. LC 87-28780. (Illus.). 64p. (Orig.). (gr. 5-9). 1988. PLB 19.92 (*0-8172-3080-7*) Raintree Steck-V.

—Birds. LC 87-28786. (Illus.). 64p. (Orig.). (gr. 5-9). 1988. PLB 19.92 (*0-8172-3084-X*) Raintree Steck-V.

Raintree Steck-Vaughn Staff. Atlas of the Environment. Coote, Roger, ed. LC 92-8196. (Illus.). 96p. (gr. 6-7). 1992. PLB 26.99 (*0-8114-7250-7*) Raintree Steck-V.

Rajaraman, Dharma. Computer: A Child's Play. 120p. 1989. pap. text ed. 12.95 (*0-9615336-9-2*) Silicon Pr.

Rajendra, Vijeya. Australia. LC 91-15864. (Illus.). 128p. (gr. 5-9). 1991. PLB 21.95 (*1-85435-400-0*) Marshall Cavendish.

Rajendra, Vijeya & Kaplan, Gisela. Iran. LC 92-10207. 1992. 21.95 (*1-85435-534-1*); Set. write for info. Marshall Cavendish.

Rakos, Jennie, ed. see Berger, Gilda.
Rakos, Jennie, ed. see Berke, Art.
Rakos, Jennie, ed. see Brimner, Larry D.
Rakos, Jennie, ed. see Dunnahoo, Terry.
Rakos, Jennie, ed. see Fisher, Maxine P.
Rakos, Jennie, ed. see Kleeberg, Irene C.
Rakos, Jennie, ed. see Smith, Beth.

Ralph, Margaret. Historias Que Jesus Conto. 28p. (gr. 4 up). 1979. 2.75 (*0-311-38537-0*, Edit Mundo) Casa Bautista.

—Jesus: Historias de su Vida. King, Gordon, illus. LaValle, Teresa, tr. (Illus.). 28p. (gr. 4). 1979. 2.75 (*0-311-38536-2*, Edit Mundo) Casa Bautista.

Ralston, Diane D. & Ralston, Henry J., III. The Nerve Cell. Head, J. J., ed. Imrick, Ann T., illus. LC 84-45836. 16p. (Orig.). (gr. 10 up). 1988. pap. text ed. 2.75 (*0-89278-357-5*, 45-9757) Carolina Biological.

Ralston, Henry J., III, jt. auth. see Ralston, Diane D.

Ram, Govinder. Rama & Sita: A Folk Tale from India. Ram, Govinder, illus. LC 87-14333. 32p. (gr. k-3). 1988. PLB 14.95 (*0-87226-171-9*, Bedrick Blackie) P Bedrick Bks.

Ramachander, Akumal. Little Pig. Eidregevicius, Stasys, illus. 32p. 1992. 15.00 (*0-670-84350-4*) Viking Child Bks.

Ramakrishna, Swami. Tales from Ramakrishna. Chakravarty, Biswarajan, illus. Ray, Irene R. & Gupta, Mallika C.retold by. (Illus.). 54p. (Orig.). (gr. 1-5). 1975. pap. 1.95 (*0-87481-152-X*) Vedanta Pr.

Ramakrishnan, Prema. King Kamel. Joshi, Jagdish, illus. 24p. (Orig.). (gr. k-3). 1980. pap. 2.50 (*0-89744-210-5*, Pub. by Childrens Bk Trust IA) Auromere.

Raman, Papri Sri, jt. auth. see Sen, Abhijit.

Ramas, D. Steve, ed. see Finke, Blythe F.

Rambaut, Paul. Space Medicine. Head, J. J., ed. LC 84-45837. (Illus.). 16p. (Orig.). (gr. 10 up). 1985. pap. text ed. 2.75 (*0-89278-366-4*, 45-9766) Carolina Biological.

Rambeck, Richard. Atlanta Falcons. (Illus.). 48p. (gr. 4 up). 1991. PLB 14.95s.p. (*0-88682-359-5*) Creative Ed.

—Atlanta Hawks. rev. ed. (Illus.). 32p. (gr. 4 up). 1993. PLB 14.95 (*0-88682-560-1*) Creative Ed.

—Baltimore Orioles. 48p. (gr. 4-10). 1992. PLB 14.95s.p. (*0-88682-451-6*) Creative Ed.

—Boston Red Sox. 48p. (gr. 4-10). 1992. PLB 14.95s.p. (*0-88682-450-8*) Creative Ed.

—California Angels. 48p. (gr. 4-10). 1992. PLB 14.95s.p. (*0-88682-449-4*) Creative Ed.

—Charlotte Hornets. (gr. 5 up). 1993. PLB 14.95 (*0-88682-559-8*) Creative Ed.

—Chicago White Sox. 48p. (gr. 4-10). 1992. PLB 14.95s.p. (*0-88682-448-6*) Creative Ed.

—Cincinnati Bengals. (gr. 4 up). 1991. PLB 14.95s.p. (*0-88682-362-5*) Creative Ed.

—Cleveland Browns. 48p. (gr. 4 up). 1991. PLB 14.95s.p. (*0-88682-363-3*) Creative Ed.

—Cleveland Cavaliers. rev. ed. (Illus.). 32p. (gr. 4 up). 1993. PLB 14.95 (*0-88682-527-X*) Creative Ed.

—Cleveland Indians. 48p. (gr. 4-10). 1992. PLB 14.95s.p. (*0-88682-439-7*) Creative Ed.

—Detroit Lions. 48p. (gr. 4 up). 1991. PLB 14.95s.p. (*0-88682-366-8*) Creative Ed.

—Detroit Pistons. rev. ed. (Illus.). 32p. (gr. 4 up). 1993. PLB 14.95 (*0-88682-521-0*) Creative Ed.

—Detroit Tigers. 48p. (gr. 4-10). 1991. PLB 14.95s.p. (*0-88682-447-8*) Creative Ed.

—Indiana Pacers. (Illus.). 32p. (gr. 4 up). 1993. PLB 14.95s.p. (*0-88682-522-9*) Creative Ed.

—The Indianapolis Colts. (gr. 4 up). 1991. PLB 14.95s.p. (*0-88682-369-2*) Creative Ed.

—Jim Abbott. LC 92-43044. 1993. write for info. (*1-56766-072-X*) Childs World.

—Kansas City Chiefs. (gr. 4 up). 1991. PLB 14.95s.p. (*0-88682-370-6*) Creative Ed.

—Kansas City Royals. 48p. (gr. 4-10). 1992. PLB 14.95s.p. (*0-88682-440-0*) Creative Ed.

—Kristi Yamaguchi. LC 92-43058. 1993. write for info. (*1-56766-071-1*) Childs World.

—Los Angeles Clippers. rev. ed. (Illus.). 32p. (gr. 4 up). 1993. PLB 14.95 (*0-88682-526-1*) Creative Ed.

—Los Angeles Rams. (gr. 4 up). 1991. PLB 14.95s.p. (*0-88682-372-2*) Creative Ed.

—Lou Gehrig. LC 92-40673. 1993. write for info. (*1-56766-073-8*) Childs World.

—Miami Heat. (gr. 5 up). 1993. PLB 14.95 (*0-88682-561-X*) Creative Ed.

—Milwaukee Brewers. 48p. (gr. 4-10). 1992. PLB 14.95s.p. (*0-88682-441-9*) Creative Ed.

—Minnesota Timberwolves. (gr. 5 up). 1993. PLB 14.95 (*0-88682-524-5*) Creative Ed.

—Minnesota Twins. 48p. (gr. 4-10). 1992. PLB 14.95s.p. (*0-88682-446-X*) Creative Ed.

—New England Patriots. 48p. (gr. 4 up). 1991. PLB 14.95s.p. (*0-88682-375-7*) Creative Ed.

—New York Yankees. 48p. (gr. 4-10). 1992. PLB 14.
95s.p. (*0-88682-445-1*) Creative Ed.
—Oakland A's. 48p. (gr. 4-10). 1992. PLB 14.95s.p.
(*0-88682-444-3*) Creative Ed.
—Orlando Magic. (gr. 5 up). 1993. PLB 14.95
(*0-88682-558-X*) Creative Ed.
—Philadelphia Eagles. 48p. (gr. 4 up). 1991. PLB 14.
95s.p. (*0-88682-379-X*) Creative Ed.
—Phoenix Cardinals. 48p. (gr. 4 up). 1991. PLB 14.95s.p.
(*0-88682-381-1*) Creative Ed.
—Phoenix Suns. rev. ed. (Illus.). 32p. (gr. 4 up). 1992.
PLB 14.95 (*0-88682-520-2*) Creative Ed.
—Portland Trailblazers. (Illus.). 38p. (gr. 4 up). 1993.
PLB 14.95 (*0-88682-518-0*) Creative Ed.
—San Antonio Spurs. (gr. 5 up). 1993. PLB 14.95
(*0-88682-519-9*) Creative Ed.
—San Diego Chargers. (gr. 4 up). 1991. PLB 14.95s.p.
(*0-88682-382-X*) Creative Ed.
—Seattle Seahawks. (gr. 4 up). 1991. PLB 14.95s.p.
(*0-88682-384-6*) Creative Ed.
—Tampa Bay Buccaneers. (Illus.). 48p. (gr. 4-12). 1991.
PLB 14.95s.p. (*0-88682-385-4*) Creative Ed.
—Texas Rangers. 48p. (gr. 4-10). 1992. PLB 14.95s.p.
(*0-88682-443-5*) Creative Ed.
—Toronto Blue Jays. 48p. (gr. 4-10). 1992. PLB 14.95s.p.
(*0-88682-442-7*) Creative Ed.
—Utah Jazz. 32p. (gr. 4). 1993. PLB 14.95
(*0-88682-525-3*) Creative Ed.
—Washington Redskins. (gr. 4 up). 1991. PLB 14.95s.p.
(*0-88682-386-2*) Creative Ed.
Ramboz, Ina W. Christmas Songs in Spanish. (SPA.).
32p. (gr. 6-9). 1985. pap. 7.95 (*0-8442-7097-0*,
Passport Bks) NTC Pub Grp.
Ramdin, Ron. West Indies. LC 91-7490. (Illus.). 96p. (gr.
6-12). 1991. PLB 19.92 (*0-8114-2442-1*) Raintree
Steck-V.
Ramey, Mary L., jt. auth. see Thomas, M. Angele.
Ramirez, Gloria, tr. see Mann, Peggy.
Ramos, Lindsey. Four Chinese Children's Stories. Troupe,
Connie, illus. 1991. 14.95 (*0-9628563-0-4*) Lttle Peop
Pr.
Ramos, Teresita V. & Clausen, Josie. Filipino Word
Book. Betco, Boboy, illus. (ENG & ILO & TAG.).
112p. (gr. k-6). 1993. pap. 11.95 (*1-880188-44-9*) Bess
Pr.
**Rampersad, Arnold see Bontemps, Arna & Hughes,
Langston.**
Rampo, Edogawa. Japanese Tales of Mystery &
Imagination. Harris, James B., tr. LC 56-6804. (Illus.).
232p. (gr. 9 up). 1956. pap. 12.95 (*0-8048-0319-6*) C
E Tuttle.
Ramsay, Jo, jt. auth. see Jordan, Louise.
Ramsay, Marjorie B. Nyra. Ramsay, Marjorie B., illus.
(gr. 4-7). 1979. 4.95 (*0-917182-10-3*) Triumph Pub.
Ramsay, Pamela. Early Childhood Planner: Year-Round
Activities & Planning Tips. 1992. pap. 18.70
(*0-201-81784-5*) Addison-Wesley.
Ramsey, Dan. Weather Forecasting: A Young
Meteorologist's Guide. (Illus.). 144p. 1990. 19.95
(*0-8306-8338-0*, 3338) pap. 10.95 (*0-8306-3338-3*)
TAB Bks.
Ramsey, James. Winter Watch. Dassow, Laura, illus.
154p. (Orig.). (gr. 10). 1989. pap. 9.95
(*0-88240-329-X*) Alaska Northwest.
Ramsey, Leola M. Beth, the Little Bethlehem Star: The
Christmas Story. 23p. 1991. 3.50 (*0-9629541-0-1*)
LMR Prodns.
—Chris: The Naughty Christmas Tree. 26p. 1992. 3.50
(*0-9629541-1-X*) LMR Prodns.
Ramsey, Marjorie E., ed. It's Music! LC 84-435. (Illus.).
56p. (ps-9). 1984. 7.50 (*0-87173-104-5*) ACEI.
Ramsey-Woodward, Maureen, ed. see Woodward, Dan.
Ramshaw, Gail. Sunday Morning. Jarrett, Judy, illus. 46p.
(gr. k-3). 1993. 15.95 (*1-56854-005-1*, SUN/AM)
Liturgy Tr Pubns.
Ramussen, Della M., jt. auth. see Colonna, Phyllis.
Rana, Indi. The Roller Birds of Rampur. 272p. (gr. 7 up).
1993. PLB 15.95 (*0-8050-2670-3*, Bks Young Read) H
Holt & Co.
Rancan, Janet. How to Draw Cats. Rancan, Janet, illus.
LC 81-52121. 32p. (gr. 2-6). 1982. PLB 10.65
(*0-89375-679-2*); pap. text ed. 1.95 (*0-89375-680-6*)
Troll Assocs.
Rand, Ann & Rand, Paul. Little One. (Illus.). 32p. 1991.
Repr. 16.95 (*0-8109-3558-9*) Abrams.
—Sparkle & Spin. (Illus.). 32p. 1991. Repr. 16.95
(*0-8109-3822-7*) Abrams.
Rand, Gloria. The Cabin Key. Rand, Ted, illus. LC 93-
10398. 1994. write for info. (*0-15-213884-6*)
HarBrace.
—Prince William. Rand, Ted, illus. LC 91-25180. 32p.
(gr. 1-3). 1992. 14.95 (*0-8050-1841-7*, Bks Young
Read) H Holt & Co.
—Salty Dog. Rand, Ted, illus. LC 88-13453. 32p. (ps-2).
1989. 13.95 (*0-8050-0837-3*, Bks Young Read) H Holt
& Co.
—Salty Dog. Rand, Ted, illus. LC 88-13453. 32p. (ps-2).
1991. pap. 4.95 (*0-8050-1847-6*, Bks Young Read) H
Holt & Co.
—Salty Sails North. Rand, Ted, illus. LC 89-39063. 32p.
(ps-2). 1990. 14.95 (*0-8050-1160-9*, Owlet BYR) H
Holt & Co.
—Salty Sails North. Rand, Ted, illus. LC 89-39063. 32p.
(ps-3). 1992. pap. 4.95 (*0-8050-2188-4*, Owlet BYR) H
Holt & Co.
—Salty Takes Off. Rand, Ted, illus. LC 90-46371. 32p.
(ps-2). 1991. PLB 14.95 (*0-8050-1159-5*, Bks Young
Read) H Holt & Co.

Rand, Jacki T. Wilma Mankiller. Still, Wayne A., illus.
LC 92-12813. 32p. (gr. 4-5). 1992. PLB 17.96
(*0-8114-6576-4*); pap. 4.95 (*0-8114-4097-4*) Raintree
Steck-V.
Rand McNally & Company Staff. Rand McNally
Children's Atlas of the World. rev. ed. LC 92-24028.
(Illus.). (gr. 4-7). 1992. pap. 7.95 (*0-528-83541-6*)
Rand McNally.
—Rand McNally Children's Atlas of the United States.
(Illus.). 112p. (gr. 3-6). 1991. Repr. of 1989 ed. PLB
18.95 (*1-878363-37-9*) Forest Hse.
Rand McNally Staff. Children's Atlas of Earth Through
Time. Fagan, Elizabeth, ed. (Illus.). 80p. 1990. 14.95
(*0-528-83415-0*) Rand McNally.
—Children's Atlas of the Environment. (gr. 4-7). 1991.
14.95 (*0-528-83438-X*) Rand McNally.
—Children's Atlas of the United States. (gr. 4-7). 1992.
pap. 27.95 (*0-528-83495-9*) Rand McNally.
—Children's Atlas of the Universe. (Illus.). (gr. 3-7).
1990. 14.95 (*0-528-83408-8*) Rand McNally.
—Children's Atlas of World Wildlife. Fagan, Elizabeth,
ed. Willis, Jan, illus. 96p. (gr. 3-7). 1990. 14.95
(*0-528-83409-6*) Rand McNally.
—First Atlas. Henley, Claire & Russell, Chris, illus. LC
93-37528. 1994. write for info. (*0-528-83679-X*) Rand
McNally.
—Picture Atlas of the World. 1991. 19.95
(*0-528-83437-1*) Rand McNally.
Rand McNally Staff & Reddy, Francis. Children's Atlas
of Native Americans Rand McNally: Native Cultures
of North & South America. Adelman, Elizabeth, ed.
Cunningham, David, illus. 78p. (gr. 3-12). Date not
set. 14.95 (*0-685-66563-1*); PLB write for info.
(*1-878363-99-9*) Forest Hse.
Rand, Paul, jt. auth. see Rand, Ann.
Rand, Suzanne. All American Girl. 208p. (Orig.). (gr. 7-
12). 1986. pap. 2.50 (*0-553-25427-8*) Bantam.
—The Boy She Left Behind. 192p. (Orig.). (gr. 6). 1985.
pap. 2.25 (*0-553-24890-1*) Bantam.
—The Good Luck Girl. 192p. (Orig.). (gr. 7-12). 1986.
pap. 2.50 (*0-553-25644-0*) Bantam.
Rand, T., jt. auth. see Bunting, E.
Randall, Bernice, tr. see Ada, Alma F.
Randall, Dudley. Cities Burning. LC 68-18623. (gr. 12
up). 1966. pap. 3.00 (*0-685-00860-6*) Broadside Pr.
—A Litany of Friends: New & Selected Poems. 2nd ed.
LC 83-82770. 103p. (gr. 9-12). 1983. pap. 6.00 perf.
bnd. (*0-916418-50-2*) Lotus.
Randall, Dudley, ed. Homage to Hoyt Fuller. LC 84-
72587. 356p. (gr. 12 up). 1984. 20.00 (*0-910296-22-7*);
pap. 15.00 (*0-910296-24-3*) Broadside Pr.
Randall, Dudley & Burroughs, Margaret G., eds. For
Malcolm: Poems on the Life & Death of Malcolm X.
2nd ed. LC 74-78642. (gr. 12 up). 1969. 7.00
(*0-910296-12-X*); pap. 7.00 (*0-685-00863-0*) Broadside
Pr.
Randall, E. T. Cosmic Kidnappers. Rogers, Jacqueline,
illus. LC 84-8579. 128p. (gr. 3-7). 1985. PLB 9.49
(*0-8167-0328-0*); pap. text ed. 2.95 (*0-8167-0329-9*)
Troll Assocs.
—Target: Earth. Rogers, Jacqueline, illus. LC 84-2740.
128p. (gr. 3-7). 1985. PLB 9.49 (*0-8167-0326-4*); pap.
text ed. 2.95 (*0-8167-0327-2*) Troll Assocs.
—Thieves from Space. Rogers, Jacqueline, illus. LC 84-
8538. 128p. (gr. 3-7). 1985. PLB 9.49
(*0-8167-0330-2*); pap. text ed. 2.95 (*0-8167-0331-0*)
Troll Assocs.
—Town in Terror. Rogers, Jacqueline, illus. LC 84-5617.
128p. (gr. 3-7). 1985. PLB 9.49 (*0-8167-0332-9*); pap.
2.95 (*0-8167-0333-7*) Troll Assocs.
Randall, Louise A. Bible Heroes: Stories for Children
Ages One to Six. Pardew, Louise, illus. LC 87-82112.
56p. (ps). 1988. pap. 4.95 (*0-88290-316-0*) Horizon
Utah.
—Scripture Stories for Tiny Tots: Read-Aloud Stories
from the Bible for Children 1 to 6. LC 83-83429. 38p.
(Orig.). (gr. k-3). 1983. pap. 4.95 (*0-88290-209-1*)
Horizon Utah.
Randall, Ronne. Gingerbread Man. 1988. text ed. 3.95
cased (*0-7214-5102-0*) Ladybird Bks.
Randall, Ronne P. Baby Forest Animals. Tourret, Gwen,
illus. 24p. (ps-k). 1987. pap. 1.25 (*0-7214-9546-X*,
S871-2) Ladybird Bks.
—Marcus & Lionel. 1989. cased 3.95 (*0-7214-5228-0*)
Ladybird Bks.
—One to Ten. Smallman, Steve, illus. 24p. (ps). 1987.
pap. 1.25 (*0-7214-9554-0*, S871-10) Ladybird Bks.
—Opposites. Smallman, Steve, illus. 24p. (ps). 1987. pap.
1.25 (*0-7214-9556-7*, S871) Ladybird Bks.
RanDelle, B. J. & Marshbum, Sandra. Lessons in Love.
Dodd, John & Taylor, Leigh, illus. LC 24-476. 64p.
(gr. k-4). 1982. text ed. 5.95 (*0-910445-00-1*) Randelle
Pubns.
Randle, Damian. Natural Resources. LC 93-25195.
(Illus.). 32p. (gr. 4-6). 1993. 14.95 (*1-56847-056-8*)
Thomson Lrning.
Randle, Kristen D. The Only Alien on the Planet. LC 93-
34594. 1994. 13.95 (*0-590-46309-8*) Scholastic Inc.
—Why Did Grandma Have to Die? pap. 5.95
(*0-88494-621-5*) Bookcraft Inc.
Randolph, Blythe. Amelia Earhart. LC 90-49175. (Illus.).
160p. (gr. 6-10). 1991. PLB 13.95 (*1-55905-078-0*)
Marshall Cavendish.
—Charles Lindbergh. LC 89-39713. (gr. 4-7). 1990. PLB
14.40 (*0-531-10918-6*) Watts.
Randolph, John. Backpacking Basics. (Illus.). 48p. (gr.
3-7). 1982. 9.95 (*0-13-055798-6*) P-H.

—Fishing Basics. Seiden, Art, illus. 48p. (gr. 3-7). 1985.
pap. 4.95 (*0-13-319732-8*) P-H.
Randolph, Sallie. Gerald R. Ford: President. LC 86-
16333. 128p. (gr. 5 up). 1987. 12.95 (*0-8027-6666-8*);
PLB 13.85 (*0-8027-6667-6*) Walker & Co.
—Richard M. Nixon, President. 128p. (gr. 5 up). 1989.
13.95 (*0-8027-6848-2*); PLB 14.85 (*0-8027-6849-0*)
Walker & Co.
—Woodrow Wilson. 128p. (gr. 6-9). 1992. 14.95
(*0-8027-8143-8*); PLB 15.85 (*0-8027-8144-6*) Walker
& Co.
Randolph, Sallie & Bolick, Nancy. Shaker Inventions.
(Illus.). (gr. 4-7). 1990. 12.95 (*0-8027-6933-0*); lib.
bdg. 13.85 (*0-8027-6934-9*) Walker & Co.
Randolph, Sallie G. Putting on Perfect Proms, Programs,
& Pageants. LC 91-18527. (Illus.). 144p. (gr. 9-12).
1991. PLB 13.90 (*0-531-11061-3*) Watts.
Randolph, Sallie G., jt. auth. see Bolick, Nancy O.
Random, Candice F. Jimmy Crack Corn. Haas, Shelly O.,
illus. LC 93-16657. 1993. 7.00 (*0-87614-786-4*)
Carolrhoda Bks.
Random House Staff. How to Get Better Test Scores on
Elementary School Standarized Tests. (Illus.). 152p.
(Orig.). (gr. 3-4). 1991. pap. 9.00 (*0-679-82108-2*)
Random Bks Yng Read.
—How to Get Better Test Scores on Elementary School
Standarized Tests. (Illus.). 152p. (Orig.). (gr. 5-6).
1991. pap. 9.00 (*0-679-82109-0*) Random Bks Yng
Read.
—How to Get Better Test Scores on Elementary School
Standarized Tests. (Illus.). 152p. (Orig.). (gr. 7-8).
1991. pap. 9.00 (*0-679-82110-4*) Random Bks Yng
Read.
Raney, Ken. It's Probably Good That Dinosaurs Are
Extinct. LC 92-33739. 1993. 14.00 (*0-671-86576-5*,
Green Tiger) S&S Trade.
—Stick Horse. (Illus.). 32p. (ps-1). 1991. 9.95
(*0-9625261-4-2*, Green Tiger) S&S Trade.
Raney, Nancy. The Big Bible Broadcast. (Illus.). 144p.
(gr. 1-6). 1989. 24.95 (*1-55513-870-5*, 68700) Cook.
Rangecroft, Derek. My First Garden Grows Nasturtiums.
(ps-3). 1993. pap. 4.99 (*0-440-40834-2*) Dell.
—My First Garden Grows Pumpkins. (ps-3). 1993. pap.
4.99 (*0-440-40831-8*) Dell.
—My First Garden Grows Sunflowers. (ps-3). 1993. pap.
4.99 (*0-440-40837-7*) Dell.
—My First Garden Grows Tomatoes. (ps-3). 1993. pap.
4.99 (*0-440-40828-8*) Dell.
Rankin, Chris, jt. auth. see Theiss, Nola.
Rankin, Laura. The Handmade Alphabet. 1991. 14.00
(*0-8037-0974-9*); PLB 13.89 (*0-8037-0975-7*) Dial Bks
Young.
Rankin, Louise. Daughter of the Mountains. Wiese, Kurt,
illus. LC 92-26793. 192p. (gr. 5 up). 1993. pap. 4.99
(*0-14-036335-1*) Puffin Bks.
Rankin, William. Come Hibernate with Me. Camphouse,
Marylyn J., frwd. by. (Illus.). 214p. (Orig.). (gr. 9 up).
1989. 30.00 (*0-9623948-0-7*) M Camphouse.
Ransford, Lynn. Creepy Crawlies for Curious Kids.
(Illus.). 48p. (gr. k-3). 1987. wkbk. 5.95
(*1-55734-217-2*) Tchr Create Mat.
—Happy Healthy Bodies. (Illus.). 48p. (gr. 1-4). 1987.
wkbk. 5.95 (*1-55734-223-7*) Tchr Create Mat.
Ransford, Lynn & Robinson, Phyllis. ABC Crafts &
Cooking. (Illus.). 64p. (ps-2). 1987. wkbk. 6.95
(*1-55734-090-0*) Tchr Create Mat.
Ransford, Sandy. Global Warming: A Pop-up Book of
Our Endangered Planet. (ps-3). 1992. pap. 15.00
(*0-671-77080-2*, S&S BFYR) S&S Trade.
Ransick, Gary, jt. auth. see Forsthoefel, John.
Ransom, Sabrina. 1993. pap. 2.75 (*0-685-66034-6*)
Scholastic Inc.
Ransom, Candice. The Big Green Pocketbook. Bond,
Felicia, illus. LC 92-29393. 32p. (ps-k). 1993. 14.00
(*0-06-020848-1*); PLB 13.89 (*0-06-020849-X*) HarpC
Child Bks.
—The Man on Stilts. Bowman, Leslie, illus. LC 92-39358.
1994. write for info. (*0-399-22537-4*, Philomel Bks)
Putnam Pub Group.
Ransom, Candice F. Emily, No. 11. 368p. (Orig.). (gr. 7
up). 1985. pap. 2.95 (*0-590-33410-7*) Scholastic Inc.
—Fourteen & Holding. 1990. pap. 2.95 (*0-590-43740-2*)
Scholastic Inc.
—Ladies & Jellybeans. LC 91-14710. 128p. (gr. 2-5).
1991. SBE 13.95 (*0-02-775665-3*, Bradbury Pr)
Macmillan Child Grp.
—Listening to Crickets: A Story about Rachel Carson.
Haas, Shelly O., illus. (gr. 3-6). 1993. 14.95
(*0-87614-727-9*) Carolrhoda Bks.
—Listening to Crickets: A Story about Rachel Carson.
(gr. 4-7). 1993. pap. 5.95 (*0-87614-615-9*) Carolrhoda
Bks.
—My Sister, the Traitor. 1990. pap. 2.75
(*0-590-41528-X*) Scholastic Inc.
—Nicole, No. 19. 224p. (Orig.). (gr. 7 up). 1986. pap.
2.25 (*0-590-40049-5*) Scholastic Inc.
—Shooting Star Summer. Milone, Karen, illus. 32p.
(ps-3). 1992. PLB 14.95 (*1-56397-005-8*) Boyds Mills
Pr.
—Sixth Grade High. 176p. (gr. 3-7). 1991. pap. 2.95
(*0-590-43891-3*, Apple Paperbacks) Scholastic Inc.
—So Young to Die: The Story of Hannah Senesh. (gr.
4-7). 1993. pap. 2.95 (*0-685-66520-9*) Scholastic Inc.
—Third Grade Stars: Tales from Third Grade. LC 93-
7868. (Illus.). 128p. (gr. 2-4). 1993. PLB 9.89
(*0-8167-2994-8*); pap. 2.95 (*0-8167-2995-6*) Troll
Assocs.

—Thirteen. 192p. (Orig.). (gr. 6-8). 1990. pap. 2.95 (0-590-43742-9) Scholastic Inc.
—We're Growing Together. Wright-Frierson, Virginia, illus. LC 92-7424. 32p. (ps-2). 1993. RSBE 14.95 (0-02-775666-1, Bradbury Pr) Macmillan Child Grp.
—Who Needs Third Grade? LC 92-30754. 128p. (gr. 2-4). 1992. PLB 9.89 (0-8167-2988-3); pap. text ed. 2.95 (0-8167-2989-1) Troll Assocs.
—Why Are Boys So Weird? LC 93-6222. (Illus.). 128p. (gr. 4-6). 1993. PLB 9.89 (0-8167-2990-5); pap. text ed. 2.95 (0-8167-2991-3) Troll Assocs.
Ransom, L. Children As Music Makers. 78p. (gr. k-3). 1979. pap. 8.00 (0-685-51018-2) High-Scope.
Ransome, Arthur. Coot Club. LC 88-46106. (Illus.). 352p. (gr. 4-6). 1989. pap. 10.95 (0-87923-787-2) Godine.
—The Fool of the World & the Flying Ship: A Russian Tale. Shulevitz, Uri, illus. (ps up). 1987. pap. 5.95 (0-374-42438-1) FS&G.
—The Fool of the World & the Flying Ship. Shulevitz, Uri, illus. LC 68-54105. 48p. (ps-3). 1968. 16.00 (0-374-32442-5) FS&G.
—Old Peter's Russian Tales. Jaques, Faith, illus. 256p. (gr. 5-9). 1975. pap. 3.50 (0-14-030696-X) Viking Child Bks.
—Pigeon Post. 372p. 1992. pap. 11.95 (0-87923-864-X) Godine.
—Tontimundo y el Barco Volador. Shulevitz, Uri, illus. Negroni, Maria, tr. (SPA., Illus.). 48p. (ps-3). 1991. 15.95 (0-374-32443-3) FS&G.
—Winter Holiday. LC 87-46246. (gr. 4-6). 1989. pap. 10. 95 (0-87923-661-2) Godine.
Ranucci, Ernest R. & Rollins, Wilma E. Brain Drain, 2 bks. Klassen, Grace & Nachtigall, Kelly, illus. 70p. (gr. 6-12). Bks. A & B. write for info. incl. tchr's. ed. (1-878669-09-5, 4301); wkbk., tchr's ed. 7.50 ea. Bk. A, 1975 (1-878669-10-9, 4301) Bk. B, 1978 (4420) Crea Tea Assocs.
Rao, Anthony. Cut & Make Animal Masks. 1989. pap. 4.95 (0-486-25199-3) Dover.
Rao, Anthony, illus. Halloween Masks. 24p. (ps-3). 1984. pap. 3.99 saddle-stitched (0-394-86126-4) Random Bks Yng Read.
—Nursery Rhymes. LC 90-85900. 32p. (ps-1). 1991. Repr. 8.95 (1-878093-24-X) Boyds Mills Pr.
Rap, Le. Bonjour, Mr. McGrue. 15p. (gr. k-2). 1991. pap. text ed. 23.00 big bk. (1-56843-040-X); pap. text ed. 4.50 (1-56843-087-6) BGR Pub.
—Little Betty Blue. 15p. (gr. k-2). 1991. pap. text ed. 23. 00 big bk. (1-56843-042-6); pap. text ed. 4.50 (1-56843-089-2) BGR Pub.
—A Lost Little Pig. 15p. (gr. k-2). 1991. pap. text ed. 23. 00 big bk. (1-56843-038-8); pap. text ed. 4.50 (1-56843-085-X) BGR Pub.
—The Secret of the Sheep. 15p. (gr. k-2). 1991. pap. text ed. 23.00 big bk. (1-56843-037-X); pap. text ed. 4.50 (1-56843-084-1) BGR Pub.
—Sherman Be Nimble. 15p. (gr. k-2). 1991. pap. text ed. 23.00 big bk. (1-56843-044-2); pap. text ed. 4.50 (1-56843-091-4) BGR Pub.
—Who's in the Shoe? 15p. (gr. k-2). 1991. pap. text ed. 23.00 big bk. (1-56843-041-8); pap. text ed. 4.50 (1-56843-088-4) BGR Pub.
Rape & Abuse Crisis Center Staff. Annie. rev. ed. Freed, Kecia S., illus. 21p. (ps up). 1985. pap. text ed. 2.50 (0-914633-03-1) Rape Abuse Crisis.
—Gente Bandera Roja y Gente Bandera Verde: Red Flag Green Flag People. rev. ed. Peterson, Francisca E., tr. from ENG. Freed, Kecia S., illus. (SPA.). 36p. (gr. k-5). 1987. wkbk. 4.00 (0-914633-13-9) Rape Abuse Crisis.
—Red Flag Green Flag People. Freed, Kecia S., illus. 28p. (gr. k up). 1985. pap. 4.00 wkbk. (0-914633-10-4) Rape Abuse Crisis.
Raphael, Antoine A. Fateful Encounters. 2nd ed. 142p. 1991. text ed. 11.95x (0-9631764-8-X); pap. text ed. 8. 00x (0-9631764-9-8); 9.05x (0-9631764-7-1) A A Raphael.
Raphael, Elaine & Bolognese, Don. Drawing History: Ancient Greece. Raphael, Elaine & Bolognese, Don, illus. 32p. (gr. 5-6). 1989. PLB 13.40 (0-531-10738-8) Watts.
Raphael, Elaine, jt. see Bolognese, Don.
Raphael, Lev, jt. auth. see Kaufman, Gershen.
Raphael, Morris. The Battle in the Bayou Country. Minville, Chestee H., illus. 199p. (gr. 5-12). 1976. 12. 95 (0-9608866-0-5) M Raphael.
—How Do You Know When You're in Acadiana. Hebert, Carrie, illus. 32p. (Orig.). (gr. 5 up). 1984. pap. 3.95 (0-9608866-3-X) M Raphael.
—The Loup-Garou of Cote Gelee. Rodrigue, George, illus. 48p. (gr. 3-9). 1990. 12.95 (0-9608866-7-2) M Raphael.
—Maria: Goddess of the Teche. Ferry, Kate, illus. 48p. (gr. 4-9). 1991. 13.95 (0-9608866-8-0) M Raphael.
—Weeks Hall: The Master of the Shadows. LC 81-90439. (Illus.). 207p. (gr. 5-12). 1981. 14.95 (0-9608866-1-3) M Raphael.
Raphael, Neil & Raphael, Ray. Comic Cops. 182p. (Orig.). (gr. 4-8). 1992. pap. 6.95 (1-881102-13-0) Real Bks.
Raphael, Ray, jt. auth. see Raphael, Neil.
Rapley, Janice, jt. auth. see Nash, Grace C.
Rapoport, Roger, ed. see Selberg, Ingrid.
Raposo, Joe. Bein' Green. Macari, Mario, illus. 24p. 1993. 12.95 (0-7935-1680-3, 00183008) H Leonard Pub Corp.

—C Is for Cookie. (Illus.). 16p. 1993. plastic clam shell 14.95 (0-7935-2155-6, 00824048) H Leonard Pub Corp.
—C Is for Cookie & Other Kids' Favorites. (Illus.). 1993. plastic clam shell 6.95 (0-7935-1954-3, 00823016) H Leonard Pub Corp.
—Sing. Backhaus, Kenn, illus. 24p. 1993. 12.95 (0-7935-1860-1, 00183012) H Leonard Pub Corp.
—Sing & Other Kids' Favorites. (Illus.). 1993. plastic clam shell 6.95 (0-7935-1955-1, 00823020) H Leonard Pub Corp.
Rapp, George, Jr. & Erickson, Laura L. Earth's Chemical Clues: The Story of Geochemistry. LC 89-7914. (Illus.). 64p. (gr. 6 up). 1990. lib. bdg. 15.95 (0-89490-153-2) Enslow Pubs.
Rapp, Joel. Let's Get Growing: Twenty-Five Quick & Easy Gardening Projects for Kids. 1992. pap. 7.00 (0-517-58880-3, Crown) Crown Pub Group.
Rappaport, Doreen. The Alger Hiss Trial. LC 92-46155. (Illus.). 192p. (gr. 5 up). 1993. 15.00 (0-06-025119-0); PLB 14.89 (0-06-025120-4) HarpC Child Bks.
—The Alger Hiss Trial. LC 92-46155. (Illus.). 192p. (gr. 5 up). 1993. pap. 4.95 (0-06-446115-7, Trophy) HarpC Child Bks.
—American Women: Their Lives in Their Words. LC 89-77621. (Illus.). 336p. (gr. 7 up). 1992. pap. 6.95 (0-06-446127-0, Trophy) HarpC Child Bks.
—The Boston Coffee Party. McCully, Emily A., illus. LC 87-45301. 64p. (gr. k-3). 1988. PLB 13.89 (0-06-024825-4) HarpC Child Bks.
—The Boston Coffee Party. McCully, Emily A., illus. LC 87-45301. 64p. (gr. k-3). 1990. pap. 3.50 (0-06-444141-5, Trophy) HarpC Child Bks.
—But She's Still My Grandma! Simmons, Bernadette, illus. LC 81-20236. 32p. (gr. 1-5). 1982. 16.95 (0-89885-072-X) Human Sci Pr.
—Escape from Slavery: Five Journeys to Freedom. Lilly, Charles, illus. LC 90-38170. 128p. (gr. 4-7). 1991. 13. 00 (0-06-021631-X); PLB 12.89 (0-06-021632-8) HarpC Child Bks.
—Friday Night with Grandpa. LC 93-34502. 1995. write for info. (0-399-22639-7, Putnam) Putnam Pub Group.
—Journey of Meng. (Illus.). 1991. 13.95 (0-8037-0895-5); PLB 13.89 (0-8037-0896-3) Dial Bks Young.
—Living Dangerously: American Women Who Risked Their Lives for Adventure. LC 90-28915. (Illus.). 128p. (gr. 4-7). 1991. 14.00 (0-06-025108-5); PLB 13. 89 (0-06-025109-3) HarpC Child Bks.
—The Lizzie Borden Trial. LC 91-23232. (Illus.). 176p. (gr. 5 up). 1992. 14.00 (0-06-025113-1); PLB 13.89 (0-06-025114-X) HarpC Child Bks.
—The Lizzie Borden Trial. LC 91-23232. (Illus.). 176p. (gr. 5 up). 1993. pap. 4.95 (0-06-446112-2, Trophy) HarpC Child Bks.
—Mrs. Santa's Christmas Present. LC 88-81465. (Illus.). 32p. (Orig.). (ps-2). 1988. pap. 8.95 (0-937124-19-2) Kimbo Educ.
—The Sacco-Vanzetti Trial. LC 91-47509. (Illus.). 176p. (gr. 5 up). 1992. 14.00 (0-06-025115-8); PLB 13.89 (0-06-025116-6) HarpC Child Bks.
—The Sacco-Vanzetti Trial. LC 91-47509. (Illus.). 176p. (gr. 5 up). 1994. pap. 4.95 (0-06-446113-0, Trophy) HarpC Child Bks.
—A Scary Day. (ps-1). 1988. 8.49 (0-87386-056-X); incl. cassette 16.99 (0-685-25200-0); pap. 1.95 (0-87386-052-7); pap. 9.95 incl. cassette (0-685-25201-9) Jan Prods.
—Tinker vs. Des Moines: Studen Rights on Trial. LC 92-25019. 160p. (gr. 5 up). 1994. pap. 4.95 (0-06-446114-9, Trophy) HarpC Child Bks.
—Tinker vs. Des Moines: Student Rights on Trial. Palencar, John, illus. LC 92-25019. 160p. (gr. 5 up). 1993. 15.00 (0-06-025117-4); PLB 14.89 (0-06-025118-2) HarpC Child Bks.
—Trouble at the Mines. Sandin, Joan, illus. LC 84-45339. 96p. (gr. 3-7). 1987. (Crowell Jr Bks) PLB 13.89 (0-690-04446-1, Crowell Jr Bks) HarpC Child Bks.
Rappaport, Doreen, ed. American Women: Their Lives in Their Words. LC 89-77621. (Illus.). 336p. (gr. 7 up). 1990. 18.00 (0-690-04819-X, Crowell Jr Bks); PLB 17. 89 (0-690-04817-3, Crowell Jr Bks) HarpC Child Bks.
Rappaport, Doreen, retold by. The Long-Haired Girl: A Chinese Legend. Yang Ming-Yi, illus. LC 93-28626. 1995. write for info. (0-8037-1411-4); PLB write for info. (0-8037-1412-2) Dial Bks Young.
Rappaport, Doreen, adapted by. The New King: A Madagascan Legend. Lewis, Earl B., illus. LC 93-28561. 1995. write for info. (0-8037-1460-2); PLB write for info. (0-8037-1461-0) Dial Bks Young.
Rappel, Yoel & Ben-Dov, Meir. Mosaics in the Holy Land: Christian, Moslem, & Jewish. (Illus.). 148p. (ps up). 1987. 15.95 (0-318-32655-8, Dist. by Watts) Modan-Adama Bks.
Rapp-Hunt, Tawney. The Boo Boo Zoo. 36p. 1993. text ed. 11.95 (0-9638882-0-X) Tawney Pubng.
Rappolt, Miriam. Queen Emma: A Woman of Vision. Rappolt, Miriam, prologue by. (Illus., Orig.). 1991. pap. 12.95 (0-916630-68-4) Pr Pacifica.
Rappoport, Doreen. The Night the Minute Hand Stopped. LC 88-81466. (Illus.). 32p. (Orig.). (ps-2). 1988. pap. 8.95 (0-937124-16-8) Kimbo Educ.
Rappoport, Ken. Bobby Bonilla. LC 92-34583. (Illus.). 144p. (gr. 5 up). 1993. 14.95 (0-8027-8255-8); PLB 15.85 (0-8027-8256-6) Walker & Co.
—Nolan Ryan: The Ryan Express. LC 92-3244. (Illus.). 64p. (gr. 3 up). 1992. RSBE 13.95 (0-87518-524-X, Dillon) Macmillan Child Grp.
Raquin, Michele, jt. auth. see Bookmaker.

Ras, Saphan, tr. see Ho, Minfong.
Rasbach, Hubert H. The Dinkywinkies & Snickity Snackety Snort. Ingram, Fred & Jennings, Elkay, illus. LC 79-89378. (ps-4). 1982. 6.95 (0-934822-05-0) Plus One Pub.
Raschka, Chris. Charlie Parker Played Be Bop. LC 91-38420. (Illus.). 32p. (ps-1). 1992. 13.95 (0-531-05999-5); PLB 13.99 (0-531-08599-6) Orchard Bks Watts.
—R & R: A Story about Two Alphabets. (Illus.). 1989. 7.95 (0-87178-731-8) Brethren.
—Yo! Yes? LC 92-25644. (Illus.). 32p. (ps-1). 1993. 14. 95 (0-531-05469-1); PLB 14.99 (0-531-08619-4) Orchard Bks Watts.
Rashad, Phylicia, read by see Chorao, Kay.
Rashbrook, F., jt. auth. see Civardi, Anne.
Rashkis, Harold A. & Tashjian, Levon D. Understanding Your Parents. LC 78-60444. (Illus.). 154p. (gr. 9-12). 1978. 6.95 (0-397-53067-6) Lippincott.
Raskin, Ellen. Figgs & Phantoms. Raskin, Ellen, illus. LC 73-17309. 160p. (gr. 4 up). 1977. pap. 15.95 (0-525-29680-8, 01063-320, DCB); (DCB) Dutton Child Bks.
—Figgs & Phantoms. (Illus.). 160p. (gr. 5-9). 1989. pap. 5.99 (0-14-032944-7, Puffin) Puffin Bks.
—The Mysterious Disappearance of Leon (I Mean Noel) (gr. 4-7). 1977. (DCB); (DCB) Dutton Child Bks.
—The Mysterious Disappearance of Leon (I Mean Noel) (Illus.). 160p. (gr. 5-9). 1989. pap. 4.95 (0-14-032945-5, Puffin) Puffin Bks.
—Nothing Ever Happens on My Block. Raskin, Ellen, illus. LC 89-31342. 32p. (gr. k-4). 1989. pap. 3.95 (0-689-71335-5, Aladdin) Macmillan Child Grp.
—Spectacles. 2nd ed. Raskin, Ellen, illus. LC 88-10363. 48p. (gr. k-4). 1988. pap. 4.50 (0-689-71271-5, Aladdin) Macmillan Child Grp.
—Tattooed Potato & Other Clues. (gr. 4-7). 1975. 15.95 (0-525-40805-3, 01451-440, DCB) Dutton Child Bks.
—Twenty-Two, Twenty-Three. LC 76-5475. (Illus.). 32p. (gr. k-3). 1976. SBE 12.95 (0-689-30529-X, Atheneum Childrens Bks) Macmillan Child Grp.
—The Westing Game. Raskin, Ellen, illus. 192p. (gr. 7 up). 1984. pap. 3.50 (0-380-67991-4, Flare) Avon.
—The Westing Game. (gr. 5-9). 1978. 15.95 (0-525-42320-6, DCB) Dutton Child Bks.
—Westing Game. large type ed. 300p. (gr. 5 up). 1988. Repr. of 1978 ed. lib. bdg. 15.95 (1-55736-031-6, Cnrrstn Bks) BDD LT Grp.
—The Westing Game. 192p. (gr. 5 up). 1992. pap. 3.99 (0-14-034991-X) Puffin Bks.
Raskin, Selma, jt. auth. see Cate, Jean M.
Rasmussen, David, jt. auth. see Rasmussen, Steven.
Rasmussen, Della M., jt. auth. see Colonna, Phyllis.
Rasmussen, Greta. The Great Unbored Blackboard Book. LC 85-51757. 56p. (Orig.). (gr. 2-6). 1985. pap. 4.95 (0-936110-05-8) Tin Man Pr.
—The Great Unbored Bulletin Board, Book II. LC 80-52305. (Illus.). (gr. 2-6). 1984. pap. 4.95 (0-936110-04-X) Tin Man Pr.
—The Great Unbored Bulletin Board Book. LC 80-52305. (Illus.). 56p. (Orig.). (gr. 2-6). 1984. pap. 4.95 (0-936110-01-5) Tin Man Pr.
—Is It Friday Already? Learning Centers That Work. LC 79-92710. (Illus.). 230p. (Orig.). (gr. 2-6). 1980. pap. 15.95 (0-936110-00-7) Tin Man Pr.
—OPQ: Offbeat Adventures with the Alphabet. LC 81-82798. (Illus.). 63p. (Orig.). (gr. 2-6). 1981. pap. 6.95 (0-936110-03-1) Tin Man Pr.
—Waiting for Lunch. LC 81-82797. (Illus.). 63p. (Orig.). (gr. 2-6). 1981. pap. 6.95 (0-936110-02-3) Tin Man Pr.
Rasmussen, Lore. Miquon Math Lab Series. rev. ed. Incl. Orange Book. pap. text ed. 4.95 (0-913684-50-3); Red Book. pap. text ed. 4.95 (0-913684-51-1); Blue Book. pap. text ed. 4.95 (0-913684-52-X); Green Book. pap. text ed. 4.95 (0-913684-53-8); Yellow Book. pap. text ed. 4.95 (0-913684-54-6); Purple Book. pap. text ed. 4.95 (0-913684-55-4); Notes to Teachers. 53p. 2.95 (0-913684-62-7); Lab Sheet Annotations. Rasmussen, Lore, et al. 372p. 12.95 (0-913684-64-3); First Grade Diary. Rasmussen, Lore & Hightower, Robert. 218p. 4.95 (0-685-02806-2) Key Curr Pr.
Rasmussen, Richard. Extraterrestrial Life. LC 91-15564. (Illus.). 112p. (gr. 5-8). 1991. PLB 14.95 (1-56006-126-X) Lucent Bks.
Rasmussen, Richard M. The UFO Challenge. LC 90-32962. (Illus.). 96p. (gr. 5-8). 1990. PLB 14.95 (1-56006-122-7) Lucent Bks.
Rasmussen, Steven & Rasmussen, David. Key to Percents: Answers & Notes for Books 1-3. 38p. (gr. 4-12). 1988. pap. text ed. 2.25 (0-913684-61-9) Key Curr Pr.
—Key to Percents, Bk. 1: Percent Concepts. 45p. (gr. 4-12). 1988. pap. text ed. 1.95 (0-913684-57-0) Key Curr Pr.
—Key to Percents, Bk. 2: Percents & Fractions. 45p. (gr. 4-12). 1988. pap. text ed. 1.95 (0-913684-58-9) Key Curr Pr.
—Key to Percents, Bk. 3: Percents & Decimals. 45p. (gr. 4-12). 1988. pap. text ed. 1.95 (0-913684-59-7) Key Curr Pr.
Raso, Anne M. Kris Kross Krazy. (gr. 4-7). 1992. pap. 3.50 (0-553-56179-0) Bantam.
Rasof, Henry, ed. see Abrams, Kathleen S.
Rasof, Henry, ed. see Beshore, George.
Rasof, Henry, ed. see Bleifeld, Maurice.
Rasof, Henry, ed. see Dolan, Edward F.
Rasof, Henry, ed. see Gardner, Robert.

Rasof, Henry, ed. see Gay, Kathlyn.
Rasof, Henry, ed. see Harris, Jacqueline L.
Rasof, Henry, ed. see Moss, Carol.
Rasof, Henry, ed. see Tannenbaum, Beulah &
   Tannenbaum, Harold E.
Rasof, Henry, ed. see Thomas, David A.
Rasof, Henry, ed. see Woods, Geraldine.
Rasovsky, Yuri, jt. auth. see Adorjan, Carol.
Rassmussen, Della M., jt. auth. see Colonna, Phyllis.
Raston, Emily, ed. see Dunnan, Nancy.
Ratcliffe, Dolores. Women Entrepreneurs, Networking &
   Sweet Potato Pie: Business Survival Guide. (gr. 10-12).
   1987. pap. 14.95 (0-933016-03-4) Corita Comm.
Rateliff, John D., jt. ed. see Weber, Valerie.
Ratera, Rosario K. A Gift. (Illus.). (gr. 1-3). 1972. 3.00
   (0-686-09524-3, Pub. by New Day Pub PI) Cellar.
Rathbone, R. Andrew. PC Secrets: Tips & Tricks to
   Make Your Computer More Effective. Lingham,
   Gretchen & Steward-Shahan, Leah, eds. 200p. (Orig.).
   1991. pap. text ed. 8.95 (0-945776-23-3) Comptr Pub
   Enterprises.
Rathbone, Tina. Hundreds of Fascinating Uses for Your
   Computer. Lingham, Gretchen & Steward-Shahan,
   Leah, eds. 200p. (Orig.). 1991. pap. text ed. 8.95
   (0-945776-22-5) Computer Pub Enterprises.
Rathbun, Carolyn R. Sara Bear's Surprise. Harvey,
   Chuck, illus. (Orig.). 1993. 12.95
   (0-9634808-0-4); pap. 4.50 (0-9634808-1-2) Endless
   Love.
Rathe, Gustave. The Wreck of the Barque Stefano off the
   North West Cape of Australia in 1875. (Illus.). 160p.
   1992. 17.00 (0-374-38585-8) FS&G.
Rathert, Donna. Advent Is for Waiting. (Illus.). 24p. (ps)
   1987. pap. 2.99 (0-570-04140-6, 56-1569) Concordia.
Rathert, Donna & Prahlow, Lois. Time for Church. 24p.
   (gr. 2-5). 1985. pap. 2.99 (0-570-04129-5, 56-1540)
   Concordia.
Rathert, Donna R. Job. (Illus.). 24p. (ps-2). 1989. pap.
   1.89 (0-570-09017-2, 59-1440) Concordia.
—Lent Is for Remembering. LC 56-1613. 24p. (Orig.).
   (ps-1). 1987. pap. 2.99 (0-570-04147-3, 56-1613)
   Concordia.
Rathjen, Carl H. Mystery at Smoke River. LC 68-23986.
   (gr. 6-10). 1968. PLB 7.19 (0-8313-0083-3) Lantern.
Rathman, Peggy. Ruby the Copycat. (ps-3). 1993. pap.
   4.95 (0-590-47423-5) Scholastic Inc.
Rathmann, Peggy. Goodnight, Gorilla. LC 92-29020.
   1993. write for info. (0-399-22445-9, Putnam) Putnam
   Pub Group.
—Ruby the Copycat. 32p. 1991. 13.95 (0-590-43747-X,
   Scholastic Hardcover) Scholastic Inc.
Ratliff, Gerald L. & Troth, Susan. Onstage, Producing
   Musical Theatre. (Illus.). 109p. (gr. 7-12). 1988. PLB
   14.95 (0-8239-0697-3) Rosen Group.
Ratner-Gantshar, Barbara. Philadelphia: The City &
   the Bell. Miller, Wynne, ed. LC 76-43573. (Illus.). (gr.
   4-8). 1976. 3.98 (0-686-16319-2); tchr's. & research
   guide 3.48 (0-686-16320-6) Artistic Endeavors.
Ratnett, Michael. Jenny's Bear. Goulding, June, illus.
   32p. (ps-3). 1992. 14.95 (0-399-22325-8, Putnam)
   Putnam Pub Group.
Rattenne, Ken. The Feather River Route, Pt. 1. LC 89-
   26861. (Illus.). 142p. (gr. 11). 1991. 42.95
   (0-87046-091-9, Pub. by Trans-Anglo) Interurban.
—The Feather River Route, Pt. 2. LC 89-26861. (Illus.).
   168p. (gr. 11). 1991. 47.95 (0-87046-103-6, Pub. by
   Trans-Anglo) Interurban.
Rattigan, Jama K. Dumpling Soup. Hsu-Flanders, Lillian,
   illus. (gr. 4-8). 1993. 15.95 (0-316-73445-4) Little.
—Truman's Aunt Farm. Karas, G. Brian, illus. LC 93-
   4860. 1994. write for info. (0-395-65661-3) HM.
Ratto, Linda L. Coping with a Physically Challenged
   Brother Or Sister. Rosen, Ruth, ed. (gr. 7-12). 1992.
   13.95 (0-8239-1492-5) Rosen Group.
—Coping with Being Physically Challenged. Rosen, Ruth,
   ed. (gr. 7-12). 1991. PLB 13.95 (0-8239-1344-9)
   Rosen Group.
Ratz de Tagyos, Paul. A Coney Tale. Ratz de Tagyos,
   Paul, illus. 32p. (gr. k-3). 1992. 14.45 (0-395-58834-0,
   Clarion Bks) HM.
—Showdown at Lonesome Pellet. LC 93-25733. 1994.
   write for info. (0-395-67645-2, Clarion Bks) HM.
Ratzlow, Helen. Edelmira Hernandez & the Kissing Dog.
   LC 92-25018. 24p. 1992. 8.95 (0-944957-38-2)
   Rivercross Pub.
Rau, Margaret. The Gray Kangaroo at Home. Hulsmann,
   Eva, illus. LC 77-14942. (gr. 5-8). 1978. lib. bdg. 6.99
   (0-394-93451-2) Knopf Bks Yng Read.
—The Snow Monkey at Home. Hulsmann, Eva, illus. LC
   78-31550. (gr. 4-7). 1979. lib. bdg. 6.99
   (0-394-93976-X) Knopf Bks Yng Read.
—Young Women in China. LC 88-31045. (Illus.). 160p.
   (gr. 6 up). 1989. lib. bdg. 18.95 (0-89490-170-2)
   Enslow Pubs.
Raub, Joyce. Cain & Abel. (Illus.). 24p. (gr. k-4). 1986.
   pap. 1.89 saddlestitched (0-570-06199-7, 59-1422)
   Concordia.
Rauch, Robert S. Smile: Be True to Your Teeth & They'll
   Never be False to You. rev. ed. Zuraw, Stephen, et al,
   illus. 105p. 1991. pap. text ed. 4.95 (0-9624076-0-7) R
   S Rauch.
Rausiri, Supa. The Beautiful Chick. Rodriguez, Gloria F.,
   ed. Chang, Phillip, illus. Pinta, Thanom, tr. (Illus.). (gr.
   k-2). 1979. pap. 3.00x (0-686-26620-X, Pub. by New
   Day Pub PI) Cellar.
Rauzon, Mark. Horns, Antlers, Fangs, & Tusks. LC 90-
   49726. (ps-3). 1993. 13.00 (0-688-10230-1); PLB 12.
   93 (0-688-10231-X) Lothrop.

—Skin, Scales, Feathers, & Fur. LC 90-409858. (ps-3).
   1993. 13.00 (0-688-10232-8); PLB 12.93
   (0-688-10233-6) Lothrop.
Rauzon, Mark & Bix, Cynthia O. Water, Water
   Everywhere. Rauzon, Mark, photos by. LC 92-34521.
   (Illus.). 1993. write for info. (0-87156-598-6) Sierra.
Rauzon, Mark J. Catch a Comet by the Tail. Rauzon,
   Mark J., illus. 48p. (gr. 5-10). 1985. pap. 6.95
   (0-935181-00-8) Marine Endeavors.
—Jungles. (gr. 4-7). 1992. pap. 13.00 (0-385-41412-9)
   Doubleday.
—The Last Condor. (Illus.). 24p. (Orig.). (gr. 5 up). 1986.
   pap. 3.95 (0-935181-02-4) Marine Endeavors.
Raven, Arlene, jt. auth. see Brown, Betty A.
Raven, James. The Best Enemy. 1993. pap. 3.25
   (0-553-29930-1) Bantam.
—Empty Hand, No. 6. 1993. pap. 3.25 (0-553-56301-7)
   Bantam.
—Entering the Way. 1993. pap. 3.25 (0-553-29929-8)
   Bantam.
—Sword of the Sensei. 1993. pap. 3.25 (0-553-56300-9)
   Bantam.
—Test of Wills. 1993. pap. 3.25 (0-553-56243-6) Bantam.
—The Ultimate Opponent. 1993. pap. 3.25
   (0-553-56133-2) Bantam.
Raven, John. Blues for Momma. (gr. 12 up). 1971. pap.
   0.50 (0-910296-54-5) Broadside Pr.
Raven, Pieter Van see Van Raven, Pieter.
Raven, Pieter van see Van Raven, Pieter.
Raven, Pieter Van see Van Raven, Pieter.
Ravenal, Earl C. Large-Scale Foreign Policy Change: The
   Nixon Doctrine as History & Portent. LC 89-84417.
   viii, 89p. 1989. pap. 8.50x (0-87725-535-0) U of Cal
   IAS.
Ravilious, Robin. Two in a Pocket. (ps-3). 1991. 14.95
   (0-316-73449-7) Little.
Rawcliffe, Michael. Finding out About: Life in
   Edwardian Britain. (Illus.). 48p. (gr. 7-10). 1989. 19.95
   (0-7134-5612-4, Pub. by Batsford UK) Trafalgar.
—Lenin. (Illus.). 64p. (gr. 6-9). 1989. 19.95
   (0-7134-5611-6, Pub. by Batsford UK) Trafalgar.
—Timeline: The Welfare State. (Illus.). 72p. (gr. 7 up).
   1990. 19.95 (0-7134-9806-4, Pub. by Batsford UK)
   Trafalgar.
—Victorian Town Life. (Illus.). 48p. (gr. 7-10). Date not
   set. 19.95 (0-7134-6355-4, Pub. by Batsford UK)
   Trafalgar.
Rawding, F. W. Gandhi. LC 79-11008. (Illus.). 48p. (gr. 7
   up). 1980. pap. 7.50 (0-521-20715-0) Cambridge U Pr.
—The Rebellion in India, 1857. (Illus.). 48p. (gr. 7 up).
   1977. pap. 7.50 (0-521-20683-9) Cambridge U Pr.
Rawles, Jess, ed. The House That Jack Built. Avery, Bob,
   illus. 32p. 1994. 3.95 (1-879384-24-8) Cypress Hse.
Rawlings, Marjorie K. The Secret River. 3rd, facsimile
   ed. Weisgard, Leonard, illus. Bigham, Julia S., intro.
   by. (Illus.). 57p. (gr. 3-6). 1987. Repr. of 1955 ed. PLB
   12.95 (0-935259-02-3) San Marco Bk.
—The Yearling. Wyeth, N. C., illus. LC 85-40301. 416p.
   1985. SBE 24.95 (0-684-18461-3, Scribners Young
   Read); deluxe, limited ed. o.s.i. 75.00 (0-684-18508-3,
   Scribners) Macmillan Child Grp.
—The Yearling. 2nd ed. Shenton, Edward, illus. LC 86-
   20743. 448p. (gr. 5 up). 1988. pap. 4.95
   (0-02-044931-3, Collier Young Ad) Macmillan Child
   Grp.
—The Yearling. 250p. 1991. Repr. lib. bdg. 19.95x
   (0-89966-841-0) Buccaneer Bks.
Rawlins, Donna. Digging to China. LC 89-42536. (Illus.).
   32p. (ps-2). 1989. 12.95 (0-531-05814-X); PLB 12.99
   (0-531-08414-0) Orchard Bks Watts.
Rawlinson, J. Cruisers. (Illus.). 48p. (gr. 3-8). 1989. lib.
   bdg. 18.60 (0-86625-085-9) Rourke Corp.
—Hunter-Killer Submarines. (Illus.). 48p. (gr. 3-8). 1989.
   lib. bdg. 18.60 (0-86625-086-7); 13.95s.p.
   (0-685-58644-8) Rourke Corp.
—Nuclear Carriers. (Illus.). 48p. (gr. 3-8). 1989. lib. bdg.
   18.60 (0-86625-084-0); 13.95s.p. (0-685-58646-4)
   Rourke Corp.
—Space to Seabed. (Illus.). 32p. (gr. 4 up). 1988. PLB 17.
   27 (0-86592-872-X); s.p. 12.95 (0-685-58292-2)
   Rourke Corp.
—Titanic. (Illus.). 32p. (gr. 4 up). 1988. PLB 17.27
   (0-86592-873-8); PLB 12.95s.p. (0-685-58290-6)
   Rourke Corp.
Rawlinson, Jon, jt. auth. see Walmer, Max.
Rawls, Bea O. & Johnson, Gwen. Drugs & Where to
   Turn. Rosen, Ruth, ed. (gr. 7-12). 1993. 14.95
   (0-8239-1466-6) Rosen Group.
Rawls, James J. Never Turn Back: Father Serra's
   Mission. Guzzi, George, illus. LC 92-12814. 52p. (gr.
   2-5). 1992. PLB 21.34 (0-8114-7221-3) Raintree
   Steck-V.
Rawls, Jim. Dame Shirley & the Gold Rush. Holder,
   John, illus. LC 92-18083. (gr. 2-5). 1992. PLB 21.34
   (0-8114-7222-1) Raintree Steck-V.
Rawls, Wilson. Summer of the Monkeys. LC 75-32295.
   1989. PLB (0-385-13004-X); pap. 14.95
   (0-385-11450-8) Doubleday.
—Summer of the Monkeys. large type ed. 358p. 1989.
   Repr. of 1976 ed. lib. bdg. 15.95 (1-55736-144-4,
   Crnrstn Bks) BDD LT Grp.
—Summer of the Monkeys. (gr. 4-7). 1992. pap. 3.99
   (0-553-29818-6) Bantam.
—Where the Red Fern Grows. 256p. (gr. 5-10). 1974.
   pap. 3.25 (0-553-25585-1) Bantam.
—Where the Red Fern Grows. 25th anniversary ed. LC
   61-9201. 216p. (gr. 5 up). 1961. pap. 11.95
   (0-385-05619-2) Doubleday.

—Where the Red Fern Grows. 1984. pap. 3.99
   (0-553-27429-5) Bantam.
—Where the Red Fern Grows. (gr. 7 up). 1992. 16.00
   (0-553-08900-5, Starfire) Bantam.
—Where the Red Fern Grows: The Story of Two Dogs &
   a Boy. large type ed. 280p. (gr. 5 up). 1987. Repr. of
   1961 ed. PLB 14.95 (1-55736-057-X, Crnrstn Bks)
   BDD LT Grp.
Rawson. Disguise & Make-Up. (gr. 2-5). 1979. (Usborne-
   Hayes); PLB 11.96 (0-88110-042-0); pap. 4.50
   (0-86020-166-X) EDC.
—Dragons, Giants & Witches. (Illus.). 96p. (gr. k-4).
   1979. 10.95 (0-86020-342-5, Usborne-Hayes) EDC.
—Giants. (gr. k-4). 1980. (Usborne-Hayes); PLB 4.50
   (0-88110-056-0); pap. 4.50 (0-86020-338-7) EDC.
—How Machines Work. (gr. 2-5). 1976. PLB 13.96
   (0-88110-115-X); pap. 6.95 (0-86020-197-X) EDC.
Rawson, jt. auth. see Cartwright.
Rawson, jt. auth. see Hindley.
Rawson, C. Stories for Young Children. Cartwright,
   Stephen, illus. 32p. (gr. 1-4). 1990. 12.95
   (0-7460-0800-7, Usborne) EDC.
Rawson, C. & Spector, J. Riding & Pony Care. 32p. (gr.
   2 up). 1987. PLB 14.96 (0-88110-297-0); pap. 8.95
   (0-7460-0111-8) EDC.
Rawson, Ruth. Acting. Matthau, W., intro. by. LC 68-
   21664. (Illus.). (gr. 7 up). 1970. PLB 14.95
   (0-8239-0151-3) Rosen Group.
Ray, David. Pumpkin Light. Ray, David, illus. LC 92-
   25118. 32p. (ps-3). 1993. 14.95 (0-399-22028-3,
   Philomel Bks) Putnam Pub Group.
Ray, Deborah K. My Daddy Was a Soldier: A World
   War Two Story. Ray, Deborah K., illus. LC 89-20056.
   40p. (ps-4). 1990. reinforced bdg. 12.95
   (0-8234-0795-0) Holiday.
—My Dog, Trip. Ray, Deborah K., illus. LC 87-401. 48p.
   (ps-4). 1987. reinforced bdg. 12.95 (0-8234-0662-8)
   Holiday.
—Stargazing Sky. Ray, Deborah K., illus. LC 90-36775.
   32p. (ps-2). 1991. 13.95 (0-517-57816-6); PLB 14.99
   (0-517-57838-7) Crown Bks Yng Read.
Ray, Delia. Behind the Blue & Gray: The Soldier's Life in
   the Civil War. (Illus.). 112p. (gr. 5-9). 1991. 16.00
   (0-525-67333-4, Lodestar Bks) Dutton Child Bks.
—Gold! the Klondike Adventure. (Illus.). (gr. 5-9). 1989.
   14.95 (0-525-67288-5, Lodestar Bks) Dutton Child
   Bks.
—A Nation Torn: The Story of How the Civil War
   Began. (Illus.). 128p. (gr. 5-9). 1990. 15.95
   (0-525-67308-3, Lodestar Bks) Dutton Child Bks.
Ray, Eric. Sofer: The Story of a Torah Scroll. LC 85-
   52420. (Illus.). 32p. (Orig.). (ps-4). 1986. pap. 4.95
   (0-933873-04-2) Torah Aura.
Ray, Frederic. Old Fort Niagara: An Illustrated History.
   rev. ed. (Illus.). 16p. 1988. pap. 1.25 (0-941967-06-9)
   Old Fort Niagara Assn.
Ray, Irene R. & Gupta, Mallika C. Story of
   Vivekananda. Banerjee, Ramananda, illus. (gr. 4-7).
   1971. pap. 1.95 (0-87481-125-2) Vedanta Pr.
Ray, Irene R. see Ramakrishna, Swami.
Ray, Jane. Noah's Ark. LC 90-32786. (Illus.). 32p. (ps
   up). 1990. 14.95 (0-525-44653-2, DCB) Dutton Child
   Bks.
Ray, Jane, illus. La Historia de Navidad. LC 91-578.
   (SPA.). 32p. (ps up). 1991. 16.00 (0-525-44830-6,
   DCB) Dutton Child Bks.
—The Story of Christmas: Words from the Gospels of
   Matthew & Luke. LC 91-11357. 32p. (ps up). 1991.
   15.95 (0-525-44768-7, DCB) Dutton Child Bks.
Ray, Jane, photos by. The Story of the Creation: Words
   from Genesis. LC 92-20862. (Illus.). 32p. (gr. 1 up).
   1993. 16.00 (0-525-44946-9, DCB); Spanish ed. 16.00
   (0-525-45055-6, DCB) Dutton Child Bks.
Ray, Karen. To Cross a Line. LC 93-11813. 160p. (gr. 7
   up). 1994. 14.95 (0-531-06831-5); lib. bdg. 14.99 RLB
   (0-531-08681-X) Orchard Bks Watts.
Ray, Lila, tr. see Ray, Satyajit.
Ray, Lou. The Burros of Mavrick Gulch. (Illus.). 44p.
   (Orig.). (gr. k-5). 1983. pap. 7.95 (0-9612346-0-1, 83-
   090410) Ray-Foster.
Ray, M. L. Pumpkins. Root, B., ed. 1992. 13.95
   (0-15-252252-2, Gulliver Bks) HarBrace.
Ray, Margret & Shalleck, Alan J. Curious George Goes
   to an Ice Cream Shop. (Illus.). 32p. (ps-2). 1989. 9.70
   (0-395-51943-8); pap. 2.80 (0-395-51937-3) HM.
Ray, Mary L. Alvah & Arvilla. Root, Barry, illus. LC 93-
   31874. 1994. 14.95 (0-15-202655-X) HarBrace.
—Angel Baskets: A Little Story about the Shakers.
   Colquhoun, Jean, illus. LC 87-50789. 32p. (Orig.).
   1987. pap. write for info. (0-9609384-3-5) M
   Wetherbee.
—A Rumbly Tumbly Glittery Gritty Place. Florian,
   Douglas, illus. LC 92-20084. 1993. 13.95
   (0-15-292861-8, HB Juv Bks) HarBrace.
—Shaker Boy. Winter, Jeanette, illus. LC 93-1333. 1994.
   write for info. (0-15-276921-8) HarBrace.
Ray, Sandy. The Lamb. Sytsma, Cheryle, ed. (Illus.). 15p.
   (Orig.). 1991. pap. write for info. (1-879068-10-9)
   Ray-Ma Natsal.
—The Little Seed. Sytsma, Cheryle, ed. LC 90-63623.
   (Illus.). 30p. (Orig.). (gr. k-5). 1991. pap. write for
   info. (1-879068-01-X) Ray-Ma Natsal.
—Sir Joshua, Himself. Sytsma, Cheryle, ed. LC 90-63622.
   (Illus.). 30p. (Orig.). (gr. k-5). 1991. pap. write for
   info. (1-879068-02-8) Ray-Ma Natsal.
Ray, Satyajit. Phatik Chand. Ray, Lila, tr. from BEN.
   108p. (gr. 6-8). 1984. 8.00 (0-86578-230-X) Ind-
   US Inc.

Ray, Stephen & Murdoch, Kathleen. The Ant Nest. Stewart, Chantal, illus. LC 92-34254. 1993. 4.25 (*0-383-03614-3*) SRA Schl Grp.

—Have You Ever Found a Beetle? Bruere, Julian, illus. LC 92-27265. 1993. 3.75 (*0-383-03627-5*) SRA Schl Grp.

—In the Forest. Ruth, Trevor, illus. LC 92-27266. 1993. 3.75 (*0-383-03635-6*) SRA Schl Grp.

—Just Right for the Night. Campbell, Caroline, illus. LC 92-21398. (gr. 4 up). 1993. 4.25 (*0-383-03580-5*) SRA Schl Grp.

—Snake. Campbell, Carolinee, illus. LC 92-21453. 1993. 4.25 (*0-383-03653-4*) SRA Schl Grp.

Rayburn, Cherie. Elizabeth's Castle Adventure: A Just Suppose(TM) Story. Gress, Jonna, ed. Beck, Connie & O'Toole, Tim, illus. 4p. (gr. 1-7). 1992. 18.80 (*0-944943-07-1*) Current Inc.

—Fee Fiddle Foo What Should We Do? Gress, Jonna, ed. Yalowitz, Paul, illus. LC 92-76154. 14p. (ps-3). 1993. pap. 11.40 (*0-944943-23-3*, 20588-8) Current Inc.

Rayburn, Cherie, ed. see Swaby, Barbara.

Rayburn, Richard. Elections. Buhler, Cheryl, et al, illus. 96p. (Orig.). (gr. 4-8). 1992. wkbk. 9.95 (*1-55734-069-2*) Tchr Create Mat.

Raycraft, Mary B., tr. see Perdrizet, Marie-Pierre.

Rayher, Ed. Alice's Flip Book. Rayher, Ed, illus. 38p. 1982. pap. 1.75 perfect bdg. (*0-934714-19-3*) Swamp Pr.

Raymo, Chet. Geologic & Topographic Profile of the United States along Interstate 80. Raymo, Chet, illus. 21p. (Orig.). (gr. 6-12). 1982. pap. text ed. 7.50 (*0-8331-1714-9*, 473) Hubbard Sci.

Raymond, Patrick. Daniel & Esther. LC 89-49588. 176p. (gr. 7 up). 1990. SBE 13.95 (*0-689-50504-3*, M K McElderry) Macmillan Child Grp.

Rayner, Claire. The Don't Spoil Your Body Book. King, Tony, tr. Lansdown, Richard, intro. by. (Illus.). 48p. (gr. 3 up). 1989. pap. 4.95 (*0-8120-6098-9*) Barron.

Rayner, Mary. Garth Pig & the IceCream Lady. LC 77-1647. (Illus.). 32p. (gr. k-3). 1978. SBE 13.95 (*0-689-30598-2*, Atheneum Child Bk) Macmillan Child Grp.

—Garth Pig Steals the Show. Rayner, Mary, illus. LC 92-24508. (ps-3). 1993. 13.99 (*0-525-45023-8*, DCB) Dutton Child Bks.

—Mr. & Mrs. Pig's Evening Out. Rayner, Mary, illus. LC 76-4476. 32p. (gr. k-3). 1976. SBE 13.95 (*0-689-30530-3*, Atheneum Child Bk) Macmillan Child Grp.

—Mrs. Pig Gets Cross & Other Stories. Rayner, Mary, illus. LC 86-13433. 64p. (ps-3). 1987. 11.95 (*0-525-44280-4*, DCB) Dutton Child Bks.

—Mrs. Pig Gets Cross & Other Stories. LC 86-13433. (Illus.). 64p. (ps-3). 1991. pap. 5.95 (*0-525-44705-9*, Puffin) Puffin Bks.

—Mrs. Pig's Bulk Buy. Rayner, Mary, illus. LC 80-19875. 32p. (gr. k-3). 1981. SBE 13.95 (*0-689-30831-0*, Atheneum Child Bk) Macmillan Child Grp.

—Oh, Paul! Rayner, Mary, illus. 42p. (gr. 2-4). 1989. 3.95 (*0-8120-6145-4*) Barron.

—Rug. rev. ed. Rayner, Mary, illus. 32p. (gr. k-2). 1989. Repr. of 1989 ed. lib. bdg. 10.50 (*1-878363-03-4*) Forest Hse.

Rayner, Ralph. Undersea Technology. (Illus.). 48p. (gr. 5-8). 1990. PLB 12.90 (*0-531-18347-5*) Watts.

Rayner, Shoo. Cat in a Flap. Rayner, Shoo, illus. 18p. 1992. 12.95 (*0-87226-501-3*, Bedrick Blackie) P Bedrick Bks.

—My First Picture Joke Book. (Illus.). 32p. (ps-1). 1990. pap. 11.95 (*0-670-82450-X*) Viking Child Bks.

—My First Picture Joke Book. (Illus.). 32p. (ps-1). 1993. pap. 3.99 (*0-14-050925-9*) Puffin Bks.

Raynor, Mary, illus. Thank You for the Tadpole. LC 87-474. (gr. k-2). 1988. pap. 2.50 (*0-317-69488-X*) Delacorte.

Raynor, Tom, jt. ed. see Cannastra, Lyn.

Rayson, Ann, jt. auth. see Wong, Helen.

Razvan. Two Little Shoes. Stupple, Deborah, tr. LC 92-40814. (Illus.). 32p. (ps-1). 1993. SBE 14.95 (*0-02-775667-X*, Bradbury Pr) Macmillan Child Grp.

Razzell, Mary. The Secret Code of DNA. Pennanen, Judi, illus. 36p. (ps-8). 1986. 7.95 (*0-920806-83-X*, Pub. by Penumbra Pr CN) U of Toronto Pr.

Razzi, Jim. Creature Feature: And Other Tales of Horror. Kretschmann, Karin, illus. 64p. 1990. (G&D); pap. 2.95 (*0-448-40066-9*, G&D) Putnam Pub Group.

—Custer & Crazy Horse. (gr. 3-7). 1989. pap. 2.95 (*0-590-41836-X*) Scholastic Inc.

—Disney. 1987. 4.95 (*0-553-05420-1*) Bantam.

—Disney. 1987. 4.95 (*0-553-05422-8*) Bantam.

—Dragons. 64p. (Orig.). (gr. 1-3). 1984. pap. text ed. 2.25 (*0-553-15465-6*, Skylark) Bantam.

—The Flying Carpet. 64p. (Orig.). (gr. 2). 1985. pap. 1.95 (*0-553-15306-4*) Bantam.

—The Fortune Teller & other Tales, No. 3. Holub, Joan, illus. LC 90-85300. 64p. (Orig.). (gr. 2-5). 1991. pap. 2.95 (*0-448-41082-6*, G&D) Putnam Pub Group.

—Fun with Unicorns. 48p. (gr. 1-3). 1987. pap. 1.95 (*0-590-40787-2*) Scholastic Inc.

—The Ghost in the Mirror: And Other Ghost Stories. Kretschmann, Karin, illus. 64p. 1990. (G&D); pap. 2.95 (*0-448-40058-8*, G&D) Putnam Pub Group.

—The Haunted Playground & Other Stories. LC 89-20281. 96p. (gr. 7 up). 1990. PLB 9.89 (*0-8167-1688-9*); pap. text ed. 2.95 (*0-8167-1689-7*) Troll Assocs.

—Jungle Book. LC 91-7135. 1992. 14.95 (*1-56282-057-5*) Disney Pr.

—Nightmare Island: And Other Real-Life Mysteries. Palencar, John J., illus. LC 92-32638. 96p. (gr. 3-7). 1993. pap. 3.95 (*0-06-440426-9*, Trophy) HarpC Child Bks.

—Paper Airplanes to Make & Fly. (gr. 5-7). 1990. pap. 2.25 (*0-590-42050-X*) Scholastic Inc.

—Pinocchio's Adventure. 1985. 4.95 (*0-553-05402-3*) Bantam.

—The Restless Dead: More Strange Real-Life Mysteries. Palencar, John J., illus. LC 93-34745. (gr. 6 up). 1994. pap. write for info. (*0-06-440427-7*, Trophy) HarpC Child Bks.

—The Scream Machine & other Scary Stories, No. 4. Rogers, Jacqueline & Holub, Joan, illus. LC 90-85301. (Orig.). (gr. 2-5). 1991. pap. 2.95 (*0-448-41084-2*, G&D) Putnam Pub Group.

—Sherluck Bones-Mystery Detective Book, No. 1. 48p. (Orig.). 1981. pap. 2.25 (*0-553-15382-X*) Bantam.

—Terror in the Mirror. LC 89-5230. 96p. (gr. 7 up). 1990. PLB 9.89 (*0-8167-1684-6*); pap. text ed. 2.95 (*0-8167-1685-4*) Troll Assocs.

—The Very Best Christmas Present. Fernandes, Henry, illus. LC 87-83045. 24p. (Orig.). (ps-3). 1988. pap. write for info. (*0-307-11711-1*) Western Pub.

—Walt Disney's Snow White & the Seven Dwarfs. Marvin, Fred, illus. LC 92-53430. 96p. 1993. 14.95 (*1-56282-362-0*); PLB 14.89 (*1-56282-363-9*) Disney Pr.

—Walt Disney's Snow White & the Seven Dwarfs. LC 92-5343. (Illus.). 64p. (gr. 2-6). 1993. pap. 2.95 (*1-56282-364-7*) Disney Pr.

Razzi, Jim & Razzi, Mary. The Search for King Pup's Tomb. 64p. (gr. 3). 1985. pap. 2.25 (*0-553-15312-9*) Bantam.

—Sherluck Bones Mystery, No. 3. (gr. 2-4). 1987. pap. 2.25 (*0-553-15440-0*, Skylark) Bantam.

—The Sherluck Bones Mystery-Detective Book, No. 5. (Orig.). (gr. 4-8). 1984. pap. 2.25 (*0-553-15425-7*, Skylark) Bantam.

—The Sherluck Bones Mystery-Detective Book, No. 6. 64p. (Orig.). (gr. 1-3). 1984. pap. text ed. 2.25 (*0-553-15412-5*, Skylark) Bantam.

Razzi, Jim, jt. auth. see Razzi, Mary.

Razzi, Jim, adapted by. Disney CYOA. 48p. (Orig.). 1986. pap. 4.95 (*0-553-05419-8*) Bantam.

—Disney's Mickey's Christmas Carol. LC 91-58970. (Illus.). 1992. 12.95 (*1-56282-238-1*); PLB 12.89 (*1-56282-236-5*) Disney Pr.

—Disney's Mickey's Christmas Carol. LC 92-58971. (Illus.). 1992. pap. 2.75 (*1-56282-239-X*) Disney Pr.

—The Jungle Book. 48p. (Orig.). (gr. 4). 1986. pap. 4.95 (*0-553-05409-0*) Bantam.

—Walt Disney's the Jungle Book. LC 91-58975. (Illus.). 64p. 1992. pap. 2.95 (*1-56282-243-8*) Disney Pr.

Razzi, Mary & Razzi, Jim. Sherluck Bones Mystery, No. 2. (gr. 2-4). 1987. pap. 1.95 (*0-685-19144-3*, Skylark) Dell.

Razzi, Mary, jt. auth. see Razzi, Jim.

Rea, Jesus Guerrero see Garcia, Richard.

Rea, Jesus Guerrero see Rohmer, Harriet & Guerrero Rea, Jesus.

REA Staff. High School Pre-Calculus Tutor. (gr. 9-12). 1993. 12.95 (*0-87891-910-4*) Res & Educ.

Read, Edward M. & Daley, Dennis C. You've Got the Power: A Recovery Guide for Young People with Drug & Alcohol Problems. Butler, Ralph, illus. Gondles, James A., Jr., frwd. by. (Illus.). 98p. (Orig.). 1993. pap. 10.00 (*0-929310-87-X*, 349) Am Correctional.

Read, James & Yapp, Malcolm. Law. Killingray, Margaret & O'Connor, Edmund, eds. (Illus.). (gr. 6-11). 1980. pap. text ed. 3.45 (*0-89908-119-3*) Greenhaven.

Read, Lorna. The Lies They Tell. 160p. (gr. 6-9). 1990. pap. 7.95 (*0-233-98444-5*, Pub. by A Deutsch England) Trafalgar.

Read, Thomas B. Sheridan's Ride. Parker, Nancy W., illus. LC 92-16225. 32p. (gr. k-3). 1993. 14.00 (*0-688-10873-3*); PLB 13.93 (*0-688-10874-1*) Greenwillow.

Reade, Eugene, ed. see Smith, Carl B.

Reade, Eugene W., ed. see Smith, Carl B.

Reader, Carl. The Twelfth Elf of Kindness. 53p. (gr. 4-6). 1990. pap. 7.00 (*0-9630560-0-X*) Reader.

Reader, Dennis. Butterfingers. Reader, Dennis, illus. LC 90-46124. 32p. (gr. k-3). 1991. 13.45 (*0-395-57581-8*) HM.

—I Want One! (ps-5). 1992. pap. 4.95 (*0-8249-8581-8*, Ideals Child) Hambleton-Hill.

Reader, Dennis J. Coming Back Alive. LC 79-5147. (Illus.). 256p. (gr. 7 up). 1981. 9.95 (*0-394-84359-2*) Random Bks Yng Read.

Reader's Digest Editors. The Reader's Digest Children's World Atlas. LC 90-28667. (Illus.). 128p. (gr. 3-7). 1991. 20.00 (*0-89577-388-0*) RD Assn.

Reader's Digest Editors, ed. The Reader's Digest Children's Songbook. (Illus.). 252p. (ps up). 1985. lie-flat spiral bdg. 29.95 (*0-89577-214-0*, Dist. by Random) RD Assn.

Reading, J. P. The Summer of Sassy Jo. LC 88-34130. (gr. 5 up). 1989. 13.45 (*0-395-48950-4*) HM.

—Summer of Sassy Jo. 1993. pap. 4.95 (*0-395-66956-1*) HM.

Reading, Susan. Desert Plants. 64p. 1990. 15.95x (*0-8160-2421-9*) Facts on File.

Ready, Anna. Mississippi. LC 92-31056. 1993. PLB 17.50 (*0-8225-2743-X*) Lerner Pubns.

Real, Maria E. Alvarez Del see Alvarez del Real, Maria E.

Real, Maria E. del see Editorial America, S. A., Staff.

Real, Maria E. del see Editorial America, S. A. Staff.

Real, Rory. A Baseball Dream. (Illus.). 32p. (ps-3). 1990. pap. 3.95 (*0-8120-4395-2*) Barron.

—The Fishing Derby. (Illus.). 32p. (ps-3). 1990. pap. 3.95 (*0-8120-4394-4*) Barron.

Reanult, Michael, ed. see Rolliet, D. G.

Reardon, Judy A. & Smock, Raymond W. The Western Civilization Slide Collection Master Guide. rev. ed. 253p. (Orig.). (gr. 7 up). 1988. 25.00 (*0-923805-01-X*) Instruc Resc MD.

—The Western Civilization Slide Collection. (Illus.). 253p. (Orig.). (gr. 7 up). 1988. incl. 2100 slides 895.00 (*0-923805-02-8*); pap. 25.00 (*0-685-24654-X*) Instruc Resc MD.

Reardon, Ruth & Rodegast, Roland. Listen to My Feelings. (Illus.). 1992. 8.95 (*0-8378-2499-0*) Gibson.

Reason, Sharon, ed. see Zakutinsky, Ruth.

Reasoner, Charles. Number Munch. Reasoner, Charles, illus. 36p. (ps). 1993. bds. 9.95 (*0-8431-3674-X*) Price Stern.

—Who, Who, Who Am I? (ps). 1993. 3.99 (*0-8431-3550-6*) Price Stern.

Reasoner, Charles, jt. auth. see Warren, Vic.

Reasoner, Charles, illus. First Words. 6p. (ps). 1992. bds. 3.95 (*1-56293-182-2*) McClanahan Bk.

—My First Calculator Book. 10p. (ps-2). 1991. bds. 10.95 (*1-56293-101-6*) McClanahan Bk.

—My First Musical Piggy Bank Book. 6p. (ps-2). 1992. bds. 9.95 (*1-56293-139-3*) McClanahan Bk.

—My First Phone Book. 10p. (ps-2). 1991. bds. 9.95 (*1-56293-100-8*) McClanahan Bk.

—My First Time Book. 10p. (ps-2). 1991. bds. 10.95 (*1-56293-102-4*) McClanahan Bk.

—Santa's Super Christmas, 22 bks. (ps-1). 1991. bds. 19.95 (*1-56293-138-5*, Set, mini-board bks. in a tray) McClanahan Bk.

Reasoner, Charles E. Alphabite. 32p. 1989. 9.95 (*0-8431-2361-3*) Price Stern.

Reasoner, Chuck. A Big Alphabet Book. Reasoner, Chuck, illus. 23p. (ps). 1993. bds. 9.99 (*0-8431-3552-2*) Price Stern.

—Big Busy Building. Lassen, Cary P., illus. 5p. (gr. k-3). 1993. bds. 9.95 (*0-8431-3659-6*) Price Stern.

—Chomp, Crunch, Chew! Reasoner, Chuck, illus. 6p. (ps). 1993. bds. 3.99 (*0-8431-3549-2*) Price Stern.

—One Big Counting Book. Reasoner, Chuck, illus. 23p. (ps). 1993. bds. 9.99 (*0-8431-3551-4*) Price Stern.

—Who's Peeking. Reasoner, Chuck, illus. 6p. (ps-1). 1993. text ed. 9.99 (*0-8431-3478-X*) Price Stern.

—Who's There. Reasoner, Chuck, illus. 6p. (ps-1). 1993. text ed. 9.99 (*0-8431-3479-8*) Price Stern.

Reasonover, Ila. Lottie Daughter of the Depression. Caroland, Mary, ed. LC 90-71004. 154p. (gr. 4-8). 1991. 7.95 (*1-55523-365-1*) Winston-Derek.

Reaver, Chap. Bill. 1994. write for info. (*0-385-31175-3*) Delacorte.

—A Little Bit Dead. LC 92-7185. 192p. (gr. 6 up). 1992. 15.00 (*0-385-30801-9*) Delacorte.

—Mote. 1992. pap. 3.50 (*0-440-21173-5*) Dell.

Reaves, Michael. Sword of the Samurai. Perry, Steve, illus. 144p. (gr. 4 up). 1984. pap. 2.75 (*0-553-26427-3*) Bantam.

Rebel Montgomery Temple Staff. Shadow of the Eagles. (Illus.). 157p. (Orig.). 1982. pap. 3.75x (*0-89279-045-8*, TXU 90-499) S&S Trade.

Rebellion, Boxer. The Invisible Man & The Butler. Abell, ed. & illus. (gr. 8 up). 1992. 24.00 (*1-56611-013-0*) Jones.

Reberg, Evelyne. A Devil in the Grog Garage. (Illus.). (gr. 1-8). 1992. PLB 8.95 (*0-89565-893-3*); Resale. 12.75 (*0-685-60991-X*) Childs World.

—The Old Woman & the Ghost. (Illus.). 48p. 1991. 12.75 (*0-89565-814-3*); 8.95s.p. (*0-685-57234-X*) Childs World.

Reboul, Antoine. Thou Shalt Not Kill. Craig, Stephanie, tr. LC 77-77312. (gr. 5-8). 1969. 21.95 (*0-87599-161-0*) S G Phillips.

Rebuck, Linda & Fettke, Tom. Gettin' Ready for the Miracle. Date not set. 4.50 (*0-685-68528-4*, BCMC-57); cassette 9.98 (*0-685-68529-2*, BCTA-9071C) Lillenas.

—To See a Miracle. Date not set. 4.50 (*0-685-68196-3*, BCMB-522); cassette 9.98 (*0-685-68197-1*, BCTA-9049C) Lillenas.

—To Tell the Truth. Date not set. 4.50 (*0-685-68203-X*, BCMB-546); cassette 9.98 (*0-685-68204-8*, BCTA-9065C) Lillenas.

Rebuck, Linda, jt. auth. see Fettke, Tom.

Rebuck, Linda, et al. Not a Creature Was Stirring. (gr. 2 up). Date not set. 4.50 (*0-685-68517-9*, BCMC-72); cassette 9.98 (*0-685-68518-7*, BCTA-9119C) Lillenas.

Rebuck, Linda, et al, eds. Twinkle & the All-star Angel Band. Date not set. singer's activity bk. 3.50 (*0-685-68510-1*, BCMC-78); director ed. bk. 9.98 (*0-685-68511-X*, BCMC-78A); cassette 9.98 (*0-685-68512-8*, BCTA-9142C) Lillenas.

Rector, Andy. Five Minutes 'til Bedtime: Twelve Quick-As-a-Wink Bible Stories. Patterson, Kathleen, illus. 32p. (Orig.). 1993. pap. 5.99 (*0-87401-110-8*, 24-03670) Standard Pub.

—Five Minutes 'til Bedtime: Twelve Quick-As-a-Wink Bible Stories. Patterson, Kathleen, illus. LC 93-7339. 1993. 5.99 (*0-7847-0110-5*) Standard Pub.

—Quick-As-a-Wink New Testament Bedtime Stories. Patterson, Kathleen, illus. 12p. (ps). 1993. bds. 4.99 (*0-7847-0112-1*, 24-03102) Standard Pub.

—Quick-As-a-Wink Old Testament Bedtime Bible Stories. Patterson, Kathleen, illus. 12p. (ps). 1993. bds. 4.99 (0-7847-0111-3, 24-03101) Standard Pub.
Rector, Andy, ed. see Tiner, John H.
Red Grammer Staff, narrated by see Cowcher, Helen.
Red Grammer Staff, narrated by see George, Lindsay B.
Red Grammer Staff, narrated by see George, William T.
Redding, Robert. One Man's Homestead. Clark, Marvin, ed. Hammer, Stanley, illus. 120p. (Orig.). 1990. pap. 10.95 (0-937708-23-2) Great Northwest.
Reddix, Valerie. Dragon Kite of the Autumn Moon. LC 91-1506. (ps-3). 1992. 14.00 (0-688-11030-4); PLB 14.93 (0-688-11031-2) Lothrop.
—Millie & the Mud Hole. Bodnar, Judit Z., ed. Wickstrom, Thor, illus. LC 90-21147. 32p. (ps-3). 1992. 14.00 (0-688-10212-3); PLB 13.93 (0-688-10213-1) Lothrop.
Reddy, Francis, jt. auth. see Rand McNally Staff.
Reddy, G. P. veer see Pardee, Arthur B. & Veer Reddy, G. P.
Redekopp, Elsa. Wish & Wonder: A Manitoba Village Child. Goulden, Veleda, illus. 59p. (Orig.). (gr. 3-6). 1982. pap. 3.95 (0-919797-21-0) Kindred Pr.
Redemptorist Pastoral Publication Staff. How You Live with Jesus: Catechism for Today's Young Catholic. LC 81-80097. 96p. (gr. 4-6). 1981. pap. 4.95 (0-89243-137-7) Liguori Pubns.
—Jesus Loves You: A Catholic Catechism for the Primary Grades. LC 82-8000658. 96p. (gr. 1-3). 1982. pap. 5.95 (0-89243-157-1) Liguori Pubns.
Redfield, Robert & Franz, Wanda K. AIDS & Young People. 32p. (gr. 9-12). 1987. pap. 4.00 (0-89526-774-8) Regnery Gateway.
Red Hawk, Richard. A,B,C's the American Indian Way. (Illus.). 55p. (Orig.). (ps-8). 1988. pap. 6.95 (0-940113-15-5) Sierra Oaks Pub.
Redhawk, Richard. Grandfather Origin Story: The Navajo Indian Begining. (Orig.). (gr. 3-6). 1988. pap. 6.95 (0-940113-07-4) Sierra Oaks Pub.
Red Hawk, Richard. Grandfather's Story of Navajo Monsters. Whitehorse, David, illus. (Orig.). (ps-7). 1988. pap. 6.95 (0-940113-11-2) Sierra Oaks Pub.
Redhawk, Richard. Grandmother's Christmas Story: A True Tale of the Quechan Indians. (Illus.). (ps-5). 1987. pap. 6.95 (0-940113-08-2) Sierra Oaks Pub.
Red Hawk, Richard. A Trip to a Pow Wow. Brook, Anne C., illus. 45p. (Orig.). (gr. k-3). 1988. pap. 6.95 (0-940113-14-7) Sierra Oaks Pub.
Redhead. The Big Block of Chocolate. 1993. pap. 28.67 (0-590-50157-7) Scholastic Inc.
Redhead, Janet S. Something Special for Miss Margery. Forss, Ian, illus. LC 93-6632. 1994. write for info (0-383-03673-9) SRA Schl Grp.
Redish, Jane. Promise Me Love. 176p. (Orig.). (gr. 7-12). 1986. pap. 2.50 (0-553-26158-4) Bantam.
Redjou, Pat C. No-Gluten Solution: Children's Cookbook. Rader, Marjie, illus. (gr. 4 up). 1991. pap. 22.00 (0-9626052-2-0) Rae Pub.
Redleaf, Rhoda. Busy Fingers, Growing Minds: Finger Plays, Verses & Activities for Whole Language Learning. Nelson, Eileen, ed. Kranz, Ellen, illus. Galle, Lynn, intro. by. LC 93-39636. (Illus.). 164p. (Orig.). (ps). 1993. pap. 18.95 (0-934140-79-0) Redleaf Pr.
Redmond, Barbara, jt. auth. see Thomas, Eberle.
Redmond, Ian. Elephant. LC 92-20855. 64p. (gr. 5 up). 1993. 15.00 (0-679-83880-5); PLB 16.99 (0-679-93880-X) Knopf Bks Yng Read.
—The Elephant in the Bush. Oxford Scientific Films Staff, photos by. LC 89-11297. (Illus.). 32p. (gr. 4-6). 1989. PLB 15.95 (0-8368-0116-4) Gareth Stevens Inc.
—Elephants. (Illus.). 32p. (gr. k-4). 1990. PLB 12.40 (0-531-18354-8, Pub. by Bookwright Pr) Watts.
—Gorillas. (Illus.). 32p. (gr. k-4). 1991. 12.40 (0-531-18395-5, Pub. by Bookwright Pr) Watts.
Redmond, Marilyn. Henry Hamilton, Graduate Ghost. Redmond, Marilyn, illus. LC 81-22693. 159p. (gr. 6 up). 1982. 11.95 (0-88289-303-3) Pelican.
—Henry Hamilton in Outer Space. LC 90-25176. (gr. 4-7). 1991. 11.95 (0-88289-820-5) Pelican.
Redpath, Ann. What Happens If You Become Homeless. (Illus.). 48p. (gr. 3-6). Date not set. PLB 12.95 (1-56065-132-6) Capstone Pr. Postponed.
—What Happens If You Go to Jail? (Illus.). 48p. (gr. 3-6). Date not set. PLB 12.95 (1-56065-135-0) Capstone Pr. Postponed.
—What Happens If You Have a Baby? (Illus.). 48p. (gr. 3-6). Date not set. PLB 12.95 (1-56065-138-5) Capstone Pr. Postponed.
—What Happens If You Join a Street Gang? (Illus.). 48p. (gr. 3-6). Date not set. PLB 12.95 (1-56065-139-3) Capstone Pr. Postponed.
—What Happens If You Quit School? (Illus.). 48p. (gr. 3-6). Date not set. PLB 12.95 (1-56065-136-9) Capstone Pr. Postponed.
—What Happens If You Run Away from Home? (Illus.). 48p. (gr. 3-6). Date not set. PLB 12.95 (1-56065-133-4) Capstone Pr. Postponed.
—What Happens If You Shoplift? (Illus.). 48p. (gr. 3-6). Date not set. PLB 12.95 (1-56065-137-7) Capstone Pr. Postponed.
—What Happens If You Use Drugs? (Illus.). 48p. (gr. 3-6). Date not set. PLB 12.95 (1-56065-134-2) Capstone Pr. Postponed.
Redpath, Ann, ed. see Asimov, Isaac.
Redpath, Ann, ed. see Broun, Heywood.
Redpath, Ann, ed. see Chekhov, Anton.
Redpath, Ann, ed. see De Maupassant, Guy.

Redpath, Ann, ed. see Einstein, Albert.
Redpath, Ann, ed. see Gallaz, Chrsitophe.
Redpath, Ann, ed. see Gandhi, Mahatma.
Redpath, Ann, ed. see Murtha, Philly.
Redpath, Ann, ed. see Poe, Edgar Allan.
Redpath, Ann, ed. see Pushkin, Aleksandr.
Redpath, Ann, ed. see Russell, Bertrand.
Redpath, Ann, ed. see Stevenson, Robert Louis.
Redwine, Mary F. Substitute Teacher's Handbook: Activities & Projects for Kindergarten Through Grade Six. (gr. k-6). 1970. pap. 6.95 (0-8224-6600-7) Fearon Teach Aids.
Reece, Colleen L. Escape from Fear. Wheeler, Penny E., ed. 96p. (Orig.). (gr. 6-9). 1988. pap. 4.95 (0-8280-0441-2) Review & Herald.
—Mi Primer Libro de el Dia de las Brujas: My First Halloween Book. Kratky, Lada, tr. Peltier, Pam, illus. LC 85-31396. (SPA.). 32p. (ps-3). 1986. PLB 15.00 (0-516-32902-2); pap. 3.95 (0-516-52902-1) Childrens.
—My First Christmas Book. Hohag, Linda, illus. LC 84-9431. 32p. (ps-2). 1984. PLB 15.00 (0-516-02901-0); pap. 3.95 (0-516-42901-9) Childrens.
—My First Halloween Book. Peltier, Pam, illus. LC 84-9431. 32p. (ps-2). 1984. pap. 3.95 (0-516-42902-7) Childrens.
—Saying Thank You. Connelly, Gwen, illus. LC 82-21992. 32p. (gr. 1-2). 1983. PLB 21.35 (0-89565-249-8); PLB 14.95s.p. (0-685-55662-X) Childs World.
—The Torchbearer. (gr. 7 up). 1988. pap. 12.00 (0-8309-0509-X) Herald Hse.
—What? Axeman, Lois, illus. LC 83-7308. 32p. (gr. k-2). 1983. pap. 3.95 (0-516-46591-0) Childrens.
—What Was It Before It Was Ice Cream? Axeman, Lois, illus. LC 85-13262. 32p. (ps-2). 1985. PLB 21.35 (0-89565-325-7); PLB 14.95s.p. (0-685-55776-6) Childs World.
Reece, June E. Jimmy & the Sun Drop. Reece, June E., intro. by. Richardson, Nichole, illus. 24p. (Orig.). (ps-3). 1992. pap. 3.50 (0-9631934-0-6) Sun Drop.
Reed, Amy. Oliver's Art Adventure. 1993. 7.95 (0-8062-4640-5) Carlton.
Reed, Barbara A., jt. auth. see Bauer, Lois M.
Reed, Bobbie. Life after Divorce. 196p. (Orig.). 1993. pap. 9.99 (0-570-04614-9) Concordia.
Reed, Catherine. Environment. LC 92-12423. 1992. 15.94 (0-86625-431-5); 11.95s.p. (0-685-59385-1) Rourke Pubns.
Reed, Crafton C., III. Thiu Soo-Pr Pum-Kn: The Super Pumpkin. (Illus.). (gr. 2-5). 1980. pap. text ed. 3.50 (0-87881-091-9) Mojave Bks.
Reed, Don C. The Dolphins & Me. Carroll, Pamela & Carroll, Walter, illus. 144p. (gr. 5 up). 1989. 14.95 (0-316-73659-7) Little.
—The Dolphins & Me. 1990. pap. 2.95 (0-590-43294-X) Scholastic Inc.
—Wild Lion of the Sea. Green, Norman, illus. (gr. 5 up). 1992. 14.95 (0-316-73661-9) Little.
Reed, Evelyn D. Coyote Tales from the Indian Pueblos. Strock, Glen, illus. LC 86-14544. 96p. (gr. 4 up). 1988. pap. 8.95 (0-86534-094-3) Sunstone Pr.
Reed, Gary. RDF Accelerated Training Program. Marciniszyn, Alex & Cartier, Randi, eds. Johnston, Dirk & Bright, Mark, illus. 56p. (Orig.). (gr. 8 up). 1988. pap. 7.95 (0-916211-32-0, 555) Palladium Bks.
Reed, Helen R. All about You: A Religious Physiology & Hygiene for Parents to Read to Their Children. 1992. 7.95 (0-533-10079-8) Vantage.
Reed, John M., ed. see Elementary School Children of California.
Reed, John M., ed. see Elementary School Children of Oregon.
Reed, John M., ed. see Elementary School Children of Washington State.
Reed, Joyce G. Take a Whistler's Walk. Reed, J., illus. 77p. (gr. 4-9). 1988. 12.95 (0-943487-08-0); pap. 4.95 (0-943487-07-2) Sevgo Pr.
Reed, Kevin. A Season for Dreams. Corrigan, Wendy O., illus. LC 89-90670. 152p. (gr. 5-7). 1989. pap. 5.95 (0-9614546-3-6) Chowder Pr.
Reed, Kevin J. The Saratoga Yearling. Herold, Meri G., ed. Corrigan, Wendy O., illus. 110p. (Orig.). (gr. 5-9). 1985. pap. 3.95 (0-9614546-0-1) Chowder Pr.
Reed, Louis. The Wicks & the Wacks. LC 85-70443. (ps-2). 1985. pap. 5.00 (0-916383-00-8, Univ Edtns) Aegina Pr.
Reed, Lynn R. Rattlesnake Stew. LC 90-55163. (Illus.). 32p. (gr. k-3). 1990. 13.95 (0-374-36190-8) FS&G.
Reed, Roland. The Miser. (gr. 4-12). 1973. 4.50 (0-87602-158-5) Anchorage.
Reed, Ronald, ed. I Wish That I Could Live Outdoors: Mohican Outdoor School Student Poetry Contest Winners & Others. (Illus.). 100p. (Orig.). (gr. 7-9). 1992. pap. 18.95 incl. cass. (0-685-53268-2) Mohican Schl.
Reed, Ronald F. Rebecca: A Novel for Children. Ham, Lisa K., illus. 37p. (Orig.). (ps-4). 1990. pap. 8.00 (0-924303-00-X) TX Wesleyan Coll.
Reed, Rose, adapted by. The Velveteen Rabbit. (Illus.). 24p. (ps up). 1990. write for info. (0-307-12105-4, Pub. by Golden Bks) Western Pub.
Reed, Willow. Succession: From Field to Forest. LC 90-3216. (Illus.). 64p. (gr. 6 up). 1991. lib. bdg. 15.95 (0-89490-271-7) Enslow Pubs.
Reeder, Carolyn. Grandpa's Mountain. LC 90-27126. 176p. (gr. 3-7). 1991. SBE 14.95 (0-02-775811-7, Macmillan Child Bk) Macmillan Child Grp.

—Grandpa's Mountain. 176p. 1993. pap. 3.50 (0-380-71914-2, Camelot) Avon.
—Moonshiner's Son. LC 92-39570. 208p. (gr. 3-7). 1993. SBE 14.95 (0-02-775805-2, Macmillan Child Bk) Macmillan Child Grp.
—Shades of Gray. LC 89-31976. 176p. (gr. 3-7). 1989. SBE 13.95 (0-02-775810-9, Macmillan Child Bk) Macmillan Child Grp.
—Shades of Gray. 160p. 1991. pap. 3.99 (0-380-71232-6, Camelot) Avon.
—Shades of Gray, 2 vols. 230p. (gr. 5 up). 1989. Set. 18.40 (0-685-63787-5, BR8548) W A T Braille.
Reed-King, Susan. Food & Farming. LC 93-3719. (Illus.). 32p. (gr. 4-6). 1993. 14.95 (1-56847-054-1) Thomson Lrning.
Reedstrom, E. Lisle. Apache Wars: An Illustrated Battle History. LC 90-38971. (Illus.). 272p. (gr. 10-12). 1992. pap. 16.95 (0-8069-7255-6) Sterling.
—Custer's Seventh Cavalry: From Fort Riley to the Little Big Horn. LC 92-26524. (Illus.). 176p. (gr. 10-12). 1992. pap. 14.95 (0-8069-8762-6) Sterling.
Reef, Catherine. Albert Einstein. LC 91-7560. (Illus.). 64p. (gr. 3 up). 1991. RSBE 13.95 (0-87518-462-6, Dillon) Macmillan Child Grp.
—Arlington National Cemetery. LC 91-17183. (Illus.). 72p. (gr. 4-6). 1991. RSBE 14.95 (0-87518-471-5, Dillon) Macmillan Child Grp.
—Baltimore. LC 89-25695. (Illus.). 60p. (gr. 3 up). 1990. 13.95 (0-87518-427-8, Dillon) (0-685-31388-3) Macmillan Child Grp.
—Benjamin Davis, Jr. (Illus.). 80p. (gr. 4-7). 1992. PLB 14.95 (0-8050-2137-X) TFC Bks NY.
—The Buffalo Soldiers. (Illus.). 80p. (gr. 4-7). 1993. PLB 14.95 (0-8050-2372-0) TFC Bks NY.
—Civil War Soldiers. (Illus.). 80p. (gr. 4-7). 1993. PLB 14.95 (0-8050-2371-2) TFC Bks NY.
—Colin Powell. (Illus.). 80p. (gr. 4-7). 1992. PLB 14.95 (0-8050-2136-1) TFC Bks NY.
—Collective Biography. 1994. PLB write for info. (0-8050-3106-5) H Holt & Co.
—Eat the Right Stuff: Food Facts. LC 93-1370. 64p. (gr. 4-7). 1993. PLB 15.95 (0-8050-2442-5) TFC Bks NY.
—Ellis Island. LC 91-18755. (Illus.). 72p. (gr. 4-6). 1991. RSBE 13.95 (0-87518-473-1, Dillon) Macmillan Child Grp.
—Gettysburg. LC 91-43653. (Illus.). 72p. (gr. 4 up). 1992. RSBE 13.95 (0-87518-503-7, Dillon) Macmillan Child Grp.
—Henry David Thoreau: A Neighbor to Nature. Raymond, Larry, illus. 72p. (gr. 4-7). 1992. PLB 14.95 (0-941477-39-8) TFC Bks NY.
—Jacques Cousteau: Champion of the Sea. Raymond, Larry, illus. 72p. (gr. 4-7). 1992. PLB 14.95 (0-8050-2114-0) TFC Bks NY.
—The Lincoln Memorial. LC 93-13708. (Illus.). 72p. (gr. 4). 1994. RSBE 14.95 (0-87518-624-6, Dillon) Macmillan Child Grp.
—Monticello. LC 91-15850. (Illus.). 72p. (gr. 4-6). 1991. RSBE 13.95 (0-87518-472-3, Dillon) Macmillan Child Grp.
—Mount Vernon. LC 91-33494. (Illus.). 72p. (gr. 4 up). 1992. RSBE 13.95 (0-87518-474-X, Dillon) Macmillan Child Grp.
—Rachel Carson: The Wonder of Nature. Raymond, Larry, illus. 68p. (gr. 4-7). 1992. PLB 14.95 (0-941477-38-X) TFC Bks NY.
—Stay Fit: Build a Strong Body. LC 93-19349. 64p. (gr. 4-7). 1993. 15.95 (0-8050-2441-7) TFC Bks NY.
—Think Positive: Cope with Stress. LC 93-3973. (gr. 4-7). 1993. 15.95 (0-8050-2443-3) TFC Bks NY.
—Washington, D. C. LC 89-12025. (Illus.). 60p. (gr. 3 up). 1990. RSBE 13.95 (0-87518-411-1, Dillon) Macmillan Child Grp.
Reef, Pat. Bernard Langlais, Sculptor. LC 84-81337. (Illus.). 48p. (gr. 3-7). 1985. pap. 9.95 (0-933858-06-X) Kennebec River.
Reef, Pat D. Dahlov Ipcar, Artist. (Illus.). 48p. (gr. 3-7). 1987. pap. 12.95 (0-933858-20-5) Kennebec River.
—William Thon, Painter. (Illus.). 56p. (gr. 4-7). 1991. pap. 12.95 (0-933858-28-0) Kennebec River.
Reep, Marianna L. & Plass, Richard M. New York State Regents Biology Laboratory Manual. (Illus.). 138p. (gr. 8-11). 1989. 5.95 (0-685-29317-3) Amer Scholastic.
Reepen, Ronald. Lefty Meets Hefty. Reepen, Ronald, illus. 40p. (gr. 2-7). 1987. 6.95 (0-930905-02-4) Platypus Bks.
Rees, Claudia. The Bird with the Word Talks about Self-Control. Rees, Claudia, illus. (gr. 1-3). 1987. pap. 0.98 (0-89274-451-0) Harrison Hse.
Rees, Ennis. Brer Rabbit & His Tricks. (ps-3). 1990. pap. 5.95 (0-929077-10-5) WaterMark Inc.
—Brer Rabbit & His Tricks. LC 88-50415. (Illus.). 56p. (gr. k-5). 1992. Repr. 12.95 (1-56282-215-2) Hyprn Child.
—Brer Rabbit & His Tricks. Gorey, Edward, illus. LC 88-50415. 56p. (gr. k-5). 1994. pap. 4.95 (1-56282-577-1) Hyprn Ppbks.
—Fast Freddie Frog: And Other Tongue-Twister Rhymes. (ps-3). 1993. 14.95 (1-56397-038-4) Boyds Mills Pr.
—More Brer Rabbit & His Tricks. 1990. pap. 5.95 (0-929077-11-3) WaterMark Inc.
—More of Brer Rabbit's Tricks. LC 88-50875. (Illus.). 56p. (gr. k-5). 1992. Repr. 13.95 (1-56282-217-9) Hyprn Child.

—More of Brer Rabbit's Tricks. Gorey, Edward, illus. LC 88-50878. 56p. (gr. k-5). 1994. pap. 4.95 (1-56282-578-X) Hyprn Ppbks.

Rees, Mary, adapted by. & illus. Ten in a Bed. (ps-1). 1988. 13.95 (0-316-73708-9, Joy St Bks) Little.

Rees, Yvonne. Cats. (Illus.). 64p. 1991. 4.99 (0-517-05153-2) Outlet Bk Co.

—Dogs. (Illus.). 64p. 1991. 4.99 (0-517-05152-4) Outlet Bk Co.

Reese, Bernnie, et al. Tahquitz Exchange. (Orig.). (gr. 12). 1993. pap. write for info. (0-9628802-3-X) DeChamp CA.

Reese, Bob. ABCs. Reese, Bob, illus. LC 92-12188. 24p. (ps-2). 1992. PLB 12.33 (0-516-05577-1) Childrens.

—Abert & Kaibab. Reese, Bob, illus. (gr. k-6). 1987. 7.95 (0-89868-226-6); pap. 2.95 (0-89868-227-4) ARO Pub.

—Abert & Kaibab. Reese, Bob, illus. (gr. k-6). 1987. pap. 20.00 (0-685-50872-2) ARO Pub.

—Ape Escape. Reese, Bob, illus. 1983. 7.95 (0-89868-147-2); pap. 2.95 (0-89868-146-4) ARO Pub.

—The Ape Team. Reese, Bob, illus. 1983. 7.95 (0-89868-145-6); pap. 2.95 (0-89868-144-8) ARO Pub.

—Apricot Ape. Reese, Bob, illus. 1983. 7.95 (0-89868-141-3); pap. 2.95 (0-89868-140-5) ARO Pub.

—Art. Reese, Bob, illus. LC 92-12187. 24p. (ps-2). 1992. PLB 12.33 (0-516-05578-X) Childrens.

—Bubba Bear. Reese, Bob, illus. (gr. k-6). 1986. 7.95 (0-89868-173-1); pap. 2.95 (0-89868-174-X) ARO Pub.

—Bubba Bear. Reese, Bob, illus. (gr. k-6). 1986. pap. 20.00 (0-685-50871-4) ARO Pub.

—Buffa Buffalo. Reese, Bob, illus. (gr. k-6). 1986. 7.95 (0-89868-175-8); pap. 2.95 (0-89868-176-6) ARO Pub.

—Bugle Elk & Little Toot. Reese, Bob, illus. (gr. k-6). 1986. 7.95 (0-89868-177-4); pap. 2.95 (0-89868-178-2) ARO Pub.

—Camper Critters. Reese, Bob, illus. (gr. k-6). 1986. 7.95 (0-89868-169-3); pap. 2.95 (0-89868-170-7) ARO Pub.

—Cocos Berry Party. Reese, Bob, illus. (gr. k-6). 1987. 7.95 (0-89868-193-6); pap. 2.95 (0-89868-194-4) ARO Pub.

—Coral Reef. LC 82-23610. (Illus.). 24p. (ps-2). 1983. pap. 2.95 (0-516-42312-6) Childrens.

—Crab Apple. Wasserman, Dan, ed. Reese, Dan, illus. (gr. k-1). 1979. 7.95 (0-89868-072-7); pap. 2.95 (0-89868-083-2) ARO Pub.

—The Critter Race. LC 81-3874. (Illus.). 24p. (ps-2). 1981. pap. 2.95 (0-516-42302-9) Childrens.

—Dale the Whale. LC 82-23588. (Illus.). 24p. (ps-2). 1983. pap. 2.95 (0-516-42313-4) Childrens.

—Field Trip. Reese, Bob, illus. LC 92-12186. 24p. (ps-2). 1992. PLB 12.33 (0-516-05579-8) Childrens.

—Forty Word Yellowstone Series, 6 bks. Reese, Bob, illus. (gr. k-6). 1986. Set. 47.70 (0-89868-239-8); Set. pap. 29.50 (0-89868-238-X) ARO Pub.

—Glasses. Reese, Bob, illus. LC 92-12185. 24p. (ps-2). 1992. PLB 12.33 (0-516-05580-1) Childrens.

—Going Bananas. Reese, Bob, illus. 1983. 7.95 (0-89868-143-X); pap. 2.95 (0-89868-142-1) ARO Pub.

—Honest Ape. Reese, Bob, illus. 1983. 7.95 (0-89868-149-9); pap. 2.95 (0-89868-148-0) ARO Pub.

—Huzzard Buzzard. LC 81-6118. (Illus.). 24p. (ps-2). 1981. pap. 2.95 (0-516-42303-7) Childrens.

—The Jungle Train. Reese, Bob, illus. 1983. 7.95 (0-89868-151-0); pap. 2.95 (0-89868-150-2) ARO Pub.

—Jungle Train. Reese, Bob, illus. (gr. k-3). 1983. pap. 20.00 (0-685-50868-4) ARO Pub.

—Lactus Cactus. LC 81-3866. (Illus.). 24p. (ps-2). 1981. pap. 2.95 (0-516-42304-5) Childrens.

—Little Dinosaur. Wasserman, Dan, ed. Reese, Bob, illus. (gr. k-1). 1979. 7.95 (0-89868-070-0); pap. 2.95 (0-89868-081-6) ARO Pub.

—Mickey Moose. Reese, Bob, illus. (gr. k-6). 1986. 7.95 (0-89868-171-5); pap. 2.95 (0-89868-172-3) ARO Pub.

—Ocean Fish School. LC 82-23572. (Illus.). 24p. (ps-2). 1983. pap. 2.95 (0-516-42314-2) Childrens.

—Old Faithful. Reese, Bob, illus. (gr. k-6). 1986. 7.95 (0-89868-167-7); pap. 2.95 (0-89868-168-5) ARO Pub.

—Oola Oyster. LC 82-23609. (Illus.). 24p. (ps-2). 1983. pap. 2.95 (0-516-42311-8) Childrens.

—Pamba & the Bink. Reese, Bob, illus. (gr. k-6). 1984. 11.95 (0-89868-152-9) ARO Pub.

—Rapid Robert Roadrunner. LC 81-6090. (Illus.). 24p. (ps-2). 1981. pap. 2.95 (0-516-42305-3) Childrens.

—Raven's Roost. Reese, Bob, illus. (gr. k-6). 1987. 7.95 (0-89868-195-2); pap. 2.95 (0-89868-196-0) ARO Pub.

—Ravens Roost. 1988. pap. 2.95 (0-516-42433-5) Childrens.

—Recess. Reese, Bob, illus. LC 92-12184. 24p. (ps-2). 1992. PLB 12.33 (0-516-05581-X) Childrens.

—Sack Lunch. Reese, Bob, illus. LC 92-12183. 24p. (ps-2). 1992. PLB 12.33 (0-516-05582-8) Childrens.

—Scary Larry the Very Very Hairy Tarantula. LC 81-3871. (Illus.). 24p. (ps-2). 1981. pap. 2.95 (0-516-42306-1) Childrens.

—Sixty Word Grand Canyon Series, 6 bks. Reese, Bob, illus. (gr. k-6). 1987. Set. 47.70 (0-89868-241-X); Set. pap. 29.50 (0-89868-240-1) ARO Pub.

—Slitherfoot Snake. Reese, Bob, illus. (gr. k-6). 1987. 7.95 (0-89868-191-X); pap. 2.95 (0-89868-192-8) ARO Pub.

—Spongee Sponge. LC 82-23608. (Illus.). 24p. (ps-2). 1983. pap. 2.95 (0-516-42315-0) Childrens.

—Sunshine. Wasserman, Dan, ed. Reese, Bob, illus. (gr. k-1). 1979. 7.95 (0-89868-073-5); pap. 2.95 (0-89868-084-0) ARO Pub.

—Surefoot Mule. Reese, Bob, illus. (gr. k-6). 1987. 7.95 (0-89868-197-9); pap. 2.95 (0-89868-198-7) ARO Pub.

—Ten Word Book Series, 10 bks. Wasserman, Dan, ed. Reese, Bob, illus. (gr. k-1). 1979. Set. write for info. (0-89868-077-8) ARO Pub.

—Tweedle-De-Dee Tumbleweed. LC 81-6155. (Illus.). 24p. (ps-2). 1981. pap. 2.95 (0-516-42307-X) Childrens.

—Wellington Pelican. LC 82-23587. (Illus.). 24p. (ps-2). 1983. pap. 2.95 (0-516-42316-9) Childrens.

—Wild Turkey Run. Reese, Bob, illus. (gr. k-6). 1987. 7.95 (0-89868-199-5); pap. 2.95 (0-89868-225-8) ARO Pub.

—Zero Word Going Ape Series, 6 bks. Reese, Bob, illus. 1983. Set. 47.70 (0-89868-139-1); Set. pap. 29.50 (0-89868-138-3) ARO Pub.

Reese, Bob, et al. Big Big Book Series, 7 bks. Reese, Bob, illus. (gr. k-6). 1987. pap. 140.00 (0-89868-244-4) ARO Pub.

Reese, Leslie A. Upside down Tapestry Mosaic History. LC 87-71058. 53p. (gr. 12 up). 1987. pap. 5.00 (0-940713-00-4) Broadside Pr.

Reese, Lyn. Spindle Stories, Bk. Two: Three Units on Women's World History. Dougherty, Mary A. & Wilkinson, Jean B., eds. Gorell, Nancy, illus. 118p. (gr. 6-10). 1991. pap. text ed. 15.00 (0-9625880-1-6) Women World CRP.

—Spindle Stories: World History Units for the Middle Grades, Bk. 1. Dougherty, Mary A. & Wilkinson, Jean B., eds. Gorell, Nancy, illus. 90p. (gr. 5-9). 1990. pap. text ed. 15.00g (0-9625880-0-8) Women World CRP.

Reese, Nancy, jt. auth. see Stadler, Bernice.

Reeser, Michael. Huan Ching & the Golden Fish. Sakahara, Dick, illus. 32p. (gr. 2-4). 1988. PLB 17.96 (0-8172-2751-2); pap. 3.95 (0-685-58496-8) Raintree Steck-V.

—Huan Ching & the Golden Fish. (ps-3). 1993. pap. 3.95 (0-8114-5213-1) Raintree Steck-V.

Reeve, Agnesa, compiled by. & intro. by. My Dear Mollie: Love Letters of a Texas Sheep Rancher. LC 90-41891. (Illus.). 192p. (gr. 5 up). 1990. 17.95 (0-937460-62-1) Hendrick-Long.

Reeve, John, et al. The Anglo-Saxons. (Illus.). (gr. 2-6). pap. 3.95 (0-7141-0537-6, Pub. by Brit Mus UK) Parkwest Pubns.

Reeve, Tim. Machines: A Book of Moving Pop-Ups. Andrew, Robert, illus. LC 92-5752. 22p. (gr. 1 up). 1993. 15.95 (0-399-21974-9, Philomel Bks) Putnam Pub Group.

Reeves, Adrienne E. Willie & the Number Three Door & Other Adventures. Hosack, Leona H., illus. 120p. (Orig.). (gr. 1-3). 1991. pap. 8.95 (0-87743-703-3) Bahai.

Reeves, Barbara. Bunnicula: A Study Guide. Friedland, Joyce & Kessler, Rikki, eds. (gr. 2-5). 1991. pap. text ed. 14.95 (0-88122-572-X) LRN Links.

—The Civil War: A Study Guide. (gr. 5-8). 1991. pap. text ed. 19.95 (0-88122-688-2) LRN Links.

—Farewell to Manzanar: A Study Guide. Friedland, Joyce & Kessler, Rikki, eds. (gr. 7-10). 1991. pap. text ed. 14.95 (0-88122-583-5) LRN Links.

—The Lillies of the Field: A Study Guide. Friedland, Joyce & Kessler, Rikki, eds. (gr. 8-12). 1991. pap. text ed. 14.95 (0-88122-585-1) LRN Links.

—Number the Stars: A Study Guide. Friedland, Joyce & Kessler, Rikki, eds. (gr. 5-8). 1991. pap. text ed. 14.95 (0-88122-579-7) LRN Links.

—The War Between the Classes: A Study Guide. Friedland, Joyce & Kessler, Rikki, eds. (gr. 7-10). 1991. pap. text ed. 14.95 (0-88122-586-X) LRN Links.

Reeves, Barbara, ed. see Friedland, Joyce & Kessler, Rikki.

Reeves, Eira. Story of Jesus. (ps). 1992. pap. 5.99 (0-7814-0975-6) Cook.

—Thank You God for Our Day in the Town. (Illus.). 24p. (Orig.). (ps). 1988. pap. 2.00 (0-8170-1136-6) Judson.

—Thank You God for Our Day Indoors. (Illus.). 24p. (Orig.). (ps). 1988. pap. 2.00 (0-8170-1137-4) Judson.

Reeves, Eira, illus. Doing Things. LC 91-76214. 12p. (ps). 1992. bds. 3.99 bds. (0-8066-2590-2, 9-2590, Augsburg) Augsburg Fortress.

—Going Places. LC 91-76215. 12p. (ps). 1992. 3.99 (0-8066-2589-9, 9-2589) Augsburg Fortress.

—Helping. LC 91-76216. 12p. (ps). 1992. bds. 3.99 (0-8066-2588-0, 9-2588, Augsburg) Augsburg Fortress.

—Playing. LC 91-76217. 12p. (ps). 1992. bds. 3.99 (0-8066-2587-2, 9-2587, Augsburg) Augsburg Fortress.

Reeves, Faye C. Howie Merton & the Magic Dust. Buller, Jon, illus. LC 90-38341. 64p. (Orig.). (gr. 2-4). 1991. lib. bdg. 6.99 (0-679-91527-3); pap. 2.50 (0-679-81527-9) Random Bks Yng Read.

Reeves, Greg. Judy Ford: World Champion Cowgirl. (Illus.). 46p. (gr. 4-8). 1992. pap. 5.95 (0-938349-88-0) State House Pr.

Reeves, James. Mr. Horrox & the Gratch. Blake, Quentin, illus. LC 91-13326. 32p. (gr. 1-6). 1991. 13.95 (0-922984-08-5) Wellington IL.

—Ragged Robin, Poems from A to Z. (ps-4). 1990. 16.95 (0-316-73829-8) Little.

Reeves, James, retold by. Exploits of Don Quixote. Ardizzone, Edward, illus. LC 85-11170. (gr. 5 up). 1985. 12.95 (0-87226-025-9, Bedrick Blackie); (Bedrick Blackie) P Bedrick Bks.

—Pilgrim's Progress. Troughton, Joanna, illus. LC 86-25902. 160p. (gr. 4 up). 1987. 12.95 (0-87226-147-6, Bedrick Blackie) P Bedrick Bks.

Reeves, Marjorie, ed. see Chamberlain, E. R.

Reeves, Marjorie, ed. see Sylvester, David W.

Reeves, Marjorie, ed. see Turner, Derek.

Reeves, Marjorie, ed. see Williams, Ann.

Reeves, Mona R. I Had a Cat. Downing, Julie, illus. LC 87-37608. 32p. (ps-1). 1989. RSBE 13.95 (0-02-775731-5, Bradbury Pr) Macmillan Child Grp.

—The Spooky Eerie Night Noise. Yalowitz, Paul, illus. LC 89-447. 32p. (ps-2). 1989. RSBE 12.95 (0-02-775732-3, Bradbury Pr) Macmillan Child Grp.

Reeves, Nicholas. Into the Mummy's Tomb: The Real-Life Discovery of Tutankhamun's Treasures. 1992. 16.95 (0-590-45752-7, Scholastic Hardcover) Scholastic Inc.

—Into the Mummy's Tomb: The Real-Life Discovery of Tutankhamun's Treasures. (gr. 4-7). 1993. pap. 6.95 (0-590-45753-5) Scholastic Inc.

Reeves, Randall, jt. auth. see Leatherwood, Stephen.

Reffin & Smith. Computer Programming. (gr. 5-9). 1982. (Usborne-Hayes); PLB 10.96 (0-88110-007-2) EDC.

Regan, Dana. At My School: Paint Box Fun. (ps-3). 1993. pap. 1.95 (0-590-46291-1) Scholastic Inc.

Regan, Dana, illus. Baby Boo! 12p. (ps). 1992. 5.99 (0-679-81544-9) Random Bks Yng Read.

Regan, Dennis, jt. auth. see Williams, Geoffrey.

Regan, Dian C. The Class with the Summer Birthdays. Guevara, Susan, illus. 80p. (gr. 2-4). 1991. 13.45 (0-8050-1657-0, Redfeather BYR) H Holt & Co.

—The Class with the Summer Birthdays. Guevara, Susan, illus. LC 90-19670. 80p. (gr. 2-4). 1992. pap. 4.95 (0-8050-2327-5, Redfeather BYR) H Holt & Co.

—The Curse of the Trouble Dolls. Chesworth, Michael, illus. LC 91-28572. 64p. (gr. 2-4). 1992. 14.95 (0-8050-1944-8, Bks Young Read) H Holt & Co.

—The Curse of the Trouble Dolls. Chesworth, Michael, illus. LC 91-28572. 64p. (gr. 2-4). 1993. pap. 4.95 (0-8050-2952-4, Bks Young Read) H Holt & Co.

—Game of Survival. 144p. (Orig.). 1989. pap. 2.75 (0-380-75585-8, Flare) Avon.

—The Initiation. 176p. (Orig.). (gr. 5). 1993. pap. 3.50 (0-380-76325-7, Flare) Avon.

—Liver Cookies. (gr. 4-7). 1991. pap. 2.75 (0-590-44337-2) Scholastic Inc.

—My Zombie Valentine. (gr. 4-7). 1993. pap. 2.95 (0-590-46038-2) Scholastic Inc.

—The Peppermint Race. 1994. write for info. (0-8050-2753-X) H Holt & Co.

—The Thirteen Hours of Halloween. Baeten, Lieve, illus. LC 92-41207. 1993. write for info. (0-8075-7876-2) A Whitman.

Regan, Mary. A Family in France. LC 84-19392. (Illus.). 32p. (gr. 2-5). 1985. PLB 13.50 (0-8225-1651-9) Lerner Pubns.

Regan, Peter. Touchstone. Leonard, Pamela, illus. 208p. (gr. 4-7). 1989. 13.95 (0-947962-44-1, Pub. by Childrens Pr) Irish Bks Media.

Regan, William. Keanu Reeves: What's Hot! 48p. (gr. 4-7). 1992. pap. 1.49 (0-440-21376-2) Dell.

Regehr, Lydia. Bible Riddles of Birds & Beasts & Creeping Things. (Illus.). 36p. (Orig.). (gr. 7-12). 1982. pap. 1.25 (0-89323-030-8) Bible Memory.

Regguinti, Gordon. The Sacred Harvest: Ojibway Wild Rice Gathering. Kakkak, Dale, photos by. (Illus.). 48p. (gr. 3-6). 1992. PLB 19.95 (0-8225-2650-6) Lerner Pubns.

—Sacred Harvest: Ojibway Wild Rice Gathering. (gr. 4-7). 1992. pap. 6.95 (0-8225-9620-2) Lerner Pubns.

Regier, Harold R. see Lehn, Cornelia.

Regina, Karen & Rhodes, Gregory L., eds. Cincinnati: An Urban History Sourcebook, Bk. 1. LC 87-72186. (Illus.). 88p. (Orig.). (gr. 4-6). 1988. pap. text ed. 6.95 (0-911497-01-3) Cinc Hist Soc.

—Cincinnati: An Urban History Sourcebook, Bk. II. LC 87-72186. (Illus.). 88p. (Orig.). (gr. 7-8). 1988. pap. text ed. 6.95 (0-911497-02-1) Cinc Hist Soc.

Reginald, R. & Menville, Douglas, eds. The Boyhood Days of Guy Fawkes: Or, the Conspirators of Old London. LC 75-46257. (Illus.). (gr. 7 up). 1976. Repr. of 1876 ed. lib. bdg. 18.00x (0-405-06118-2) Ayer.

Regniers, B Schenk De see Schenk de Regniers, Beatrice.

Regniers, Beatrice de see De Regniers, Beatrice S.

Regniers, Beatrice S. De see De Regniers, Beatrice S.

Regniers, Beatrice S. de see De Regniers, Beatrice S.

Regniers, Beatrice S. de see De Regniers, Beatrice S.

Regniers, Beatrice S. de see De Regniers, Beatrice S.

Regniers, Beatrice S. de see De Regniers, Beatrice S.

Regniers, Beatrice S. de see De Regniers, Beatrice S.

Regniers, Beatrice S. De see De Regniers, Beatrice S.

Regniers, Beatrice S. De see De Regniers, Beatrice S. & Haas, Irene.

Regniers, Beatrice S. de see Schenk de Regniers, Beatrice.

Regniers, Beatrice S. de see De Regniers, Beatrice S., et al.

Rego, Paul. Computer Encounters...of the First Kind: "What the Beginner Should Know Before Buying a Computer" (Illus.). 54p. (Orig.). (ps up). 1988. pap. 14.95 (0-945876-00-9) Insight Data.

—Computer Encounters...of the Fourth Kind: "What the Beginner Should Know When Exploring the Apple II" Rego, Paul, illus. 139p. (Orig.). (ps up). 1988. pap. 29.95 (0-945876-03-3) Insight Data.

—Computer Encounters...of the Second Kind: "What the Beginner Should Know After Buying a Computer" (Illus.). 84p. (Orig.). (ps up). 1988. pap. 32.95 (0-945876-01-7) Insight Data.

—Computer Encounters...of the Third Kind: "What the Beginner Should Know When Programming the Apple II" (Illus.). 126p. (Orig.). (ps up). 1988. pap. 29.95 (0-945876-02-5) Insight Data.

Rehm, Karl & Koike, Kay. Left or Right? (Illus.). 32p. (gr. k-2). 1991. 13.45 (0-395-58080-3, Clarion Bks) HM.

Rehnman, Mats. The Clay Flute. Bibb, Eric, tr. Rehnman, Mats, illus. (ps-4). 1989. 12.95 (91-29-59184-8, Pub. by R & S Bks) FS&G.

Rehwinkel, Alfred M. Flood. 2nd ed. (Orig.). (gr. 10-12). 1957. pap. 11.99 (0-570-03183-4, 12-2103) Concordia.

Reich, Janet. Gus & the Green Thing. LC 92-33845. 1993. 8.95 (0-8027-8252-3); PLB 9.85 (0-8027-8253-1) Walker & Co.

Reichart, Natalie, jt. auth. see Klopsteg, Paul E.

Reichel, Cara. A Stone Promise. Thatch, Nancy R., ed. Reichel, Cara, illus. Melton, David, intro. by. LC 91-15059. (Illus.). 26p. (gr. 5 up). 1991. PLB 14.95 (0-933849-35-4) Landmark Edns.

Reichert, Mickey Z. Godslayer. (gr. 9-12). 1990. pap. 2.95 (0-88677-207-9) DAW Bks.

Reichert, Richard. Making Moral Decisions. rev. ed. LC 83-60316. (Illus.). 191p. (gr. 11-12). 1983. pap. text ed. 8.00x (0-88489-150-X); tchrs. guide 9.00x (0-88489-151-8); Duplicating Masters. 15.95 (0-685-04741-5) St Marys.

Reichley, David. Jasper & Sam. Reichley, David, illus. (gr. 4-6). 1992. 14.95 (1-879260-04-2) Evanston Pub.

Reichman, Barry. The Pre-Calculus & Calculus Workbook & Videotape. 100p. (gr. 6-12). 1990. 225.00 (0-685-38398-9) Video Tutorial Serv.

Reichmeier, Betty, illus. Potty Time! Yellow Ladder Books for Toddlers Through 4 Years. 10p. 1988. vinyl 7.00 (0-394-89403-0) Random Bks Yng Read.

—Sing with Me Play-along & Counting Songs. (ps-1). 1987. incl. cassette 5.95 (0-394-88810-3) Random Bks Yng Read.

Reid. Sing a Song of Mother Goose. 1993. pap. 3.95 (0-590-41699-5) Scholastic Inc.

—Sing a Song of Mother Goose. 1993. pap. 28.67 (0-590-71380-9) Scholastic Inc.

Reid, Ace. Cowpokes Comin' Yore Way. 5th ed. Reid, Ace, illus. 64p. (gr. k up). 1985. pap. 5.95 (0-917207-05-X) Reid Ent.

—Cowpokes Cookbook & Cartoons. 12th ed. Reid, Ace, illus. 64p. (gr. 5 up). pap. 5.95 (0-917207-06-8) Reid Ent.

—Cowpokes Cow Country Cartoons. 14th ed. Reid, Ace, illus. Barker, S. Omar, intro. by. (Illus.). 56p. (gr. 5 up). pap. 5.95 (0-917207-00-9) Reid Ent.

—Cowpokes Home Remedies. 7th ed. Reid, Ace, illus. 56p. (gr. k-5). pap. 5.95 (0-917207-07-6) Reid Ent.

—Cowpokes Rarin' to Go. 2nd ed. Reid, Ace, illus. 74p. (gr. 5 up). pap. 5.95 (0-917207-09-2) Reid Ent.

—Cowpokes Ride Again. 4th ed. Reid, Ace, illus. 64p. (gr. k up). 1985. pap. 5.95 (0-917207-08-4) Reid Ent.

—Cowpokes Tales & Cartoons. 2nd ed. Reid, Ace, illus. Pickens, Slim, intro. by. (Illus.). 64p. (gr. 5 up). pap. 5.95 (0-917207-10-6) Reid Ent.

—Cowpokes Wanted. 12th ed. Reid, Ace, illus. Gipson, Fred, intro. by. (Illus.). 62p. (gr. 5 up). pap. 5.95 (0-917207-02-5) Reid Ent.

—Draggin' S Ranch Cowpokes. 14th ed. Reid, Ace, illus. 65p. (gr. 5 up). pap. 5.95 (0-917207-04-1) Reid Ent.

—More Cowpokes. 14th ed. Reid, Ace, illus. Robertson, FrankC., intro. by. (Illus.). 60p. (gr. 5 up). pap. 5.95 (0-917207-01-7) Reid Ent.

Reid, Alastair. Ounce Dice Trice. (Illus.). 64p. 1991. 14. 95 (0-8109-3655-0) Abrams.

Reid, Barbara. Two by Two. LC 92-9013. (Illus.). 32p. (gr. k-3). 1993. 14.95 (0-590-45869-8) Scholastic Inc.

—Zoe's Sunny Day. 12p. 1991. pap. 3.95 (0-590-44713-0) Scholastic Inc.

Reid, Carol, jt. auth. see Cochran, Belinda.

Reid, E., et al. Complete Set of Readers & Workbooks: Short Vowels, Long Vowels, & Digraphs, 30 vols. 440p. (ps-3). 1986. Set. pap. text ed. 49.95 (1-56422-045-1) Start Reading.

—Digraph Readers, 5 vols. 40p. (ps-3). 1986. Set. pap. text ed. 9.95 (1-56422-038-9) Start Reading.

—Digraph Readers & Workbooks, 10 vols. 144p. (ps-3). 1986. Set. pap. text ed. 18.95 (1-56422-044-3) Start Reading.

—Digraph Readers & Workbooks, 150 vols. 2160p. (ps-3). 1986. Set. pap. text ed. 269.95 (1-56422-048-6) Start Reading.

—Digraph Workbooks, 5 vols. 104p. (ps-3). 1986. Set. pap. text ed. 9.95 (1-56422-041-9) Start Reading.

—Long Vowel Readers, 5 vols. 40p. (ps-3). 1986. Set. pap. text ed. 9.95 (1-56422-037-0) Start Reading.

—Long Vowel Readers & Workbooks, 10 vols. 164p. (ps-3). 1986. Set. pap. text ed. 18.95 (1-56422-043-5) Start Reading.

—Long Vowel Readers & Workbooks, 150 vols. 2460p. (ps-3). 1986. Set. pap. text ed. 269.95 (1-56422-047-8) Start Reading.

—Long Vowel Workbooks, 5 vols. 124p. (ps-3). 1986. Set. pap. text ed. 9.95 (1-56422-040-0) Start Reading.

—Mastery Workbook for Ann: Short "a" Sound. 12p. (ps-3). 1986. pap. 1.99 wkbk. (1-56422-015-X) Start Reading.

—Mastery Workbook for Get Set: Short "e" Sound. 16p. (ps-3). 1986. pap. 1.99 wkbk. (1-56422-019-2) Start Reading.

—Mastery Workbook for the Blue Boat: Long "o" Sound. 28p. (ps-3). 1986. pap. 1.99 wkbk. (1-56422-023-0) Start Reading.

—Mastery Workbook for the Brown Mule: Long "u" Sound. 16p. (ps-3). 1986. pap. 1.99 wkbk. (1-56422-024-9) Start Reading.

—Mastery Workbook for the Chimp: Ch Sound. 20p. (ps-3). 1986. pap. 1.99 wkbk. (1-56422-027-3) Start Reading.

—Mastery Workbook for the Green Jeep: Long "e" Sound. 28p. (ps-3). 1986. pap. 1.99 wkbk. (1-56422-021-4) Start Reading.

—Mastery Workbook for the Queen: Qu Sound. 20p. (ps-3). 1986. pap. 1.99 wkbk. (1-56422-028-1) Start Reading.

—Mastery Workbook for the Red Plane: Long "a" Sound. 32p. (ps-3). 1986. pap. 1.99 wkbk. (1-56422-020-6) Start Reading.

—Mastery Workbook for the Shark: SH Sound. 20p. (ps-3). 1986. pap. 1.99 wkbk. (1-56422-026-5) Start Reading.

—Mastery Workbook for the Thing: Th Sound. 20p. (ps-3). 1986. pap. 1.99 wkbk. (1-56422-029-X) Start Reading.

—Mastery Workbook for the Whale: Wh Sound. 24p. (ps-3). 1986. pap. 1.99 wkbk. (1-56422-025-7) Start Reading.

—Mastery Workbook for the White Bike: Long "i" Sound. 20p. (ps-3). 1986. pap. 1.99 wkbk. (1-56422-022-2) Start Reading.

—Mastery Workbook for Top Dog: Short "o" Sound. 24p. (ps-3). 1986. pap. 1.99 wkbk. (1-56422-016-8) Start Reading.

—Mastery Workbook for up & Up: Short "u" Sound. 20p. (ps-3). 1986. pap. 1.99 wkbk. (1-56422-018-4) Start Reading.

—Mastery Worksheets. 72p. (ps-3). 1989. reproducible masters 39.95 (1-56422-032-X) Start Reading.

—Mastery Worksheets. 86p. (ps-3). 1989. reproducible masters 39.95 (1-56422-033-8) Start Reading.

—Mastery Worksheets. 73p. (ps-3). 1989. reproducible masters 39.95 (1-56422-034-6) Start Reading.

—Short Vowel, Long Vowel, Digraph Readers & Workbooks, 450 vols. 6600p. (ps-3). 1986. Set. pap. text ed. 649.95 (1-56422-049-4) Start Reading.

—Short Vowel Readers, 5 vols. 40p. (ps-3). 1986. Set. pap. text ed. 9.95 (1-56422-036-2) Start Reading.

—Short Vowel Readers & Workbooks, 10 vols. 132p. (ps-3). 1986. Set. pap. text ed. 18.95 (1-56422-042-7) Start Reading.

—Short Vowel Readers & Workbooks, 150 vols. 1980p. (ps-3). 1986. Set. pap. text ed. 269.95 (1-56422-046-X) Start Reading.

—Short Vowel Workbooks, 5 vols. 92p. (ps-3). 1986. Set. pap. text ed. 9.95 (1-56422-039-7) Start Reading.

—Start Reading with Ann: Short "A" Sound. 8p. (ps-3). 1986. pap. text ed. 1.99 (1-56422-000-1) Start Reading.

—Start Reading with Get Set: Short "e" Sound. 8p. (ps-3). 1986. pap. text ed. 1.99 (1-56422-004-4) Start Reading.

—Start Reading with Red Plane: Long "a" Sound. 8p. (ps-3). 1986. pap. text ed. 1.99 (1-56422-005-2) Start Reading.

—Start Reading with the Blue Boat: Long "o" Sound. 8p. (ps-3). 1986. pap. text ed. 1.99 (1-56422-006-0) Start Reading.

—Start Reading with the Brown Mule: Long "u" Sound. 8p. (ps-3). 1986. pap. text ed. 1.99 (1-56422-009-5) Start Reading.

—Start Reading with the Chimp: Ch Sound. 8p. (ps-3). 1986. pap. text ed. 1.99 (1-56422-012-5) Start Reading.

—Start Reading with the Green Jeep: Long "e" Sound. 8p. (ps-3). 1986. pap. text ed. 1.99 (1-56422-007-9) Start Reading.

—Start Reading with the Queen: Qu Sound. 8p. (ps-3). 1986. pap. text ed. 1.99 (1-56422-013-3) Start Reading.

—Start Reading with the Thing: Th Sound. 8p. (ps-3). 1986. pap. text ed. 1.99 (1-56422-010-9) Start Reading.

—Start Reading with the Whale: Wh Sound. 8p. (ps-3). 1986. pap. text ed. 1.99 (1-56422-014-1) Start Reading.

—Start Reading with the White Bike: Long "i" Sound. 8p. (ps-3). 1986. pap. text ed. 1.99 (1-56422-008-7) Start Reading.

—Start Reading with Tip: Short "i" Sound. 8p. (ps-3). 1986. pap. text ed. 1.99 (1-56422-001-X) Start Reading.

—Start Reading with Top Dog: Short "o" Sound. 8p. (ps-3). 1986. pap. text ed. 1.99 (1-56422-002-8) Start Reading.

—Start Reading with up & Up: Short "u" Sound. 8p. (ps-3). 1986. pap. text ed. 1.99 (1-56422-003-6) Start Reading.

Reid, Elizabeth. Bilingual ABC: Spanish & English. (SPA & ENG., Illus.). 64p. (gr. k-3). 1992. pap. text ed. 2.50 (0-9627080-6-2) In One EAR.

—Moms & Dads - Mamis y Papis: Bilingual Coloring Book. (SPA & ENG., Illus.). 64p. (gr. 1-4). 1992. pap. 1.95 (0-9627080-5-4) In One EAR.

Reid, George K. Pond Life. Zim, Herbert S., ed. Kaicher, Sally & Dolan, Tom, illus. (gr. 7 up). 1967. pap. write for info. (0-307-24017-7, Golden Pr) Western Pub.

Reid, John C. Bird Life in Wington: Practical Parables for Young People. Weidenaar, Reynold H., illus. 142p. (gr. 1-4). 1990. pap. 8.99 (0-8028-4062-0) Eerdmans.

—The First Rainbow: Favorite Bible Stories to Learn From. Riojas, Edward, illus. 248p. (Orig.). 1991. pap. 12.99 (0-8028-4056-6) Eerdmans.

—Parables from Nature: Earthly Stories with Heavenly Meanings. 2nd ed. Foley, Timothy, illus. 96p. (gr. k-4). 1991. pap. 8.99 (0-8028-4052-3) Eerdmans.

Reid, Kathryn G. & Fortune, Marie M. Preventing Child Sexual Abuse: A Curriculum for Children Ages 9-12. LC 89-33084. (Illus.). 96p. (Orig.). 1989. pap. 9.95 (0-8298-0810-8) Pilgrim OH.

Reid, Lynne. The Fairy Rebel. 146p. (gr. 3-6). 1985. 11. 68 (0-685-63794-8, BR7890) W A T Braille.

Reid, Margarette S. The Button Box. LC 89-38566. (Illus.). 24p. (ps-2). 1990. 13.99 (0-525-44590-0, DCB) Dutton Child Bks.

Reid, Martine. Indians of the Northwest. (gr. 1-9). 1992. pap. 3.95 (0-88388-112-8) Bellerophon Bks.

Reid, Mary. Anytime Parties for Children. Arthur, Lorraine, illus. 80p. (gr. 1-5). 1987. wkbk. 5.99 (0-87403-290-3, 2802) Standard Pub.

Reid, Mary C. Come to the Desert with Me. LC 91-71036. 32p. 1991. pap. 4.99 (0-8066-2552-X, 9-2552) Augsburg Fortress.

—Come to the Island With Me. LC 92-73012. 32p. 1992. pap. 4.99 (0-8066-2632-1, 9-2632) Augsburg Fortress.

—Come to the Mountain With Me. LC 92-73011. 32p. 1992. pap. 4.99 (0-8066-2631-3, 9-2631) Augsburg Fortress.

—Come to the Ocean with Me. LC 91-71035. 32p. 1991. pap. 4.99 (0-8066-2551-1) Augsburg Fortress.

Reid, Nancy G., ed. see Duncan, Shirley E.

Reid, Robert W. Science Experiments for the Primary Grades. (gr. 1-3). 1962. pap. 5.95 (0-8224-6300-8) Fearon Teach Aids.

Reid, S. Invention & Discovery. (Illus.). 128p. (gr. 6 up). 1987. PLB 15.96 (0-88110-231-8); pap. 9.95 (0-86020-956-3) EDC.

—Memory Skills. (Illus.). 48p. (gr. 6-10). 1988. PLB 12. 96 (0-88110-305-5); pap. 5.95 (0-7460-0162-2) EDC.

—Space Facts. (Illus.). 48p. (gr. 3-7). 1987. PLB 12.96 (0-88110-240-7); pap. 5.95 (0-7460-0024-3) EDC.

Reid, S. & Fara, P. Scientists. (Illus.). 48p. (gr. 4 up). 1993. PLB 14.96 (0-88110-587-2); pap. 7.95 (0-7460-1009-5) EDC.

Reid, Saralou L. Mommakitty's Surprise: "Skyler" LC 88-60613. (Illus.). (gr. k-3). write for info. (0-9620420-0-5); lib. bdg. write for info. (0-9620420-1-3); pap. write for info. (0-9620420-3-X) Surge Pub.

Reid, Struan. Bird World. (Illus.). (gr. 4-6). 1991. PLB 14.90 (1-56294-009-0) Millbrook Pr.

—Cultures & Civilizations. (Illus.). 48p. (gr. 6 up). 1994. PLB 15.95 RSBE (0-02-726315-0, New Discovery Bks) Macmillan Child Grp.

—Exploration by Sea. LC 93-14693. (Illus.). 48p. (gr. 6 up). 1994. RSBE 15.95 (0-02-775801-X, New Discovery Bks) Macmillan Child Grp.

—Inventions & Trade. (Illus.). 48p. (gr. 6 up). 1994. PLB 15.95 RSBE (0-02-726316-9, New Discovery Bks) Macmillan Child Grp.

Reidel, Marlene. From Egg to Bird. Reidel, Marlene, illus. 24p. (ps-3). 1981. PLB 10.95 (0-87614-159-9) Carolrhoda Bks.

—From Egg to Butterfly. Reidel, Marlene, illus. LC 81-204. 24p. (ps-3). 1981. PLB 10.95 (0-87614-153-X) Carolrhoda Bks.

—From Ice to Rain. Reidel, Marlene, illus. 24p. (ps-3). 1981. PLB 10.95 (0-87614-157-2) Carolrhoda Bks.

Reidelbach, Maria. MicroSoft Works for Windows Quick Reference Guide. Berkemeyer, Kathy, ed. (Illus.). 255p. (Orig.). (gr. 9-12). 1993. pap. text ed. 8.95 manual, spiral bdg. (1-56243-101-3, H-18) DDC Pub.

Reiff, Stephanie A. Secrets of Tut's Tomb & the Pyramids. LC 77-22770. (Illus.). (gr. 4 up). 1983. PLB 18.64 (0-8172-1051-2) Raintree Steck-V.

Reiff, Tana, retold by. Tales of Wonder: Reading Level 2-3. Dobbs, Holly J., illus. LC 93-16083. 1993. 4.00 (0-88336-459-X); read-along tape 10.00 (0-88336-524-3) New Readers.

Reigot, Betty P. A Book about Planets & Stars. (Illus.). 48p. (gr. 2-5). 1988. pap. 3.95 (0-590-40593-4) Scholastic Inc.

Reihecky, Janet. Carefulness. Hutton, Kathryn, illus. LC 89-71195. 32p. (gr. k-3). 1990. PLB 19.95 (0-89565-564-0); PLB 13.95s.p. (0-685-58727-4) Childs World.

—Cooperation. Hutton, Kathryn, illus. LC 89-48284. 32p. (gr. k-3). 1990. PLB 21.35 (0-89565-565-9); PLB 14. 95s.p. (0-685-56199-2) Childs World.

Reilly, Jim. Conrad. (Illus.). 112p. (gr. 7 up). 1990. lib. bdg. 19.94 (0-86593-021-X); lib. bdg. 14.95s.p. (0-685-36351-1) Rourke Corp.

—Eliot. (Illus.). 112p. (gr. 7 up). 1990. lib. bdg. 19.94 (0-86593-022-8); lib. bdg. 14.95s.p. (0-685-36353-8) Rourke Corp.

Reilly, Jim, et al. Life & Works, 6 bks, Set II. (Illus.). 672p. (gr. 7 up). 1990. Set. PLB 119.64 (0-86593-015-5); Set. PLB 89.70s.p. (0-685-36350-3) Rourke Corp.

Reilly, Mary J. Mexico. LC 90-22469. (Illus.). 128p. (gr. 5-9). 1991. PLB 21.95 (1-85435-385-3) Marshall Cavendish.

Reilly, Pat. Kidnap in San Juan. Roth, Harold, photos by. (Illus.). 96p. (Orig.). (gr. 7 up). 1984. pap. 2.50 (0-440-94460-0, LFL) Dell.

Reilly, Pauline. Echidna. Rolland, Will, illus. 32p. (Orig.). 1993. pap. 5.95 saddlestitched (0-86417-285-0, Pub. by Kangaroo Pr AT) Seven Hills Bk Dists.

—Emu That Walks Toward Rain. Rolland, Will, illus. 32p. (Orig.). 1993. pap. 5.95 saddlestitched (0-86417-059-9, Pub. by Kangaroo Pr AT) Seven Hills Bk Dists.
—Frillneck: An Australian Dragon. Rolland, Will, illus. 32p. (Orig.). 1993. pap. 5.95 saddlestitched (0-86417-414-4, Pub. by Kangaroo Pr AT) Seven Hills Bk Dists.
—Galah. Rolland, Will, illus. 32p. (Orig.). 1993. pap. 5.95 saddlestitched (0-86417-346-6, Pub. by Kangaroo Pr AT) Seven Hills Bk Dists.
—Kiwi. Rolland, Will, illus. 32p. (Orig.). 1993. pap. 5.95 saddlestitched (0-86417-488-8, Pub. by Kangaroo Pr AT) Seven Hills Bk Dists.
—Koala. Rolland, Will, illus. 32p. (Orig.). 1993. pap. 5.95 saddlestitched (0-86417-243-5, Pub. by Kangaroo Pr AT) Seven Hills Bk Dists.
—Kookabura That Helps at the Nest. Rolland, Will, illus. 32p. (Orig.). 1993. pap. 5.95 saddlestitched (0-86417-119-6, Pub. by Kangaroo Pr AT) Seven Hills Bk Dists.
—Lyrebird That Is Too Busy to Dance. Rolland, Will, illus. 32p. (Orig.). 1993. pap. 5.95 saddlestitched (0-86417-086-6, Pub. by Kangaroo Pr AT) Seven Hills Bk Dists.
—Mallefowl: The Incubator Bird. Rolland, Will, illus. 32p. (Orig.). 1993. pap. 5.95 saddlestitched (0-86417-317-2, Pub. by Kangaroo Pr AT) Seven Hills Bk Dists.
—The Penguin That Walks at Night. Rolland, Will, illus. 32p. (Orig.). 1993. pap. 5.95 saddlestitched (0-86417-034-3, Pub. by Kangaroo Pr AT) Seven Hills Bk Dists.
—Platypus. Rolland, Will, illus. 32p. (Orig.). 1993. pap. 5.95 saddlestitched (0-86417-391-1, Pub. by Kangaroo Pr AT) Seven Hills Bk Dists.
—Tasmanian Devil. Rolland, Will, illus. 32p. (Orig.). 1993. pap. 5.95 saddlestitched (0-86417-207-9, Pub. by Kangaroo Pr AT) Seven Hills Bk Dists.
—Wombat. Rolland, Will, illus. 32p. (Orig.). 1993. pap. 5.95 saddlestitched (0-86417-148-X, Pub. by Kangaroo Pr AT) Seven Hills Bk Dists.
Reimer, Luetta & Reimer, Wilbert. Mathematicians Are People, Too: Stories from the Lives of Great Mathematicians. (Illus.). 143p. (Orig.). (gr. 3-10). 1990. pap. 11.95 (0-86651-509-7, DS01032) Seymour Pubns.
Reimer, Luetta, jt. auth. see Reimer, Wilbert.
Reimer, Wilbert & Reimer, Luetta. Historical Connections in Mathematics: Resources for Using History of Mathematics in the Classroom. Howsepian, Brenda, illus. 103p. (Orig.). (gr. 4-9). 1992. pap. text ed. 14.95 (1-881431-35-5, 2002) AIMS Educ Fnd.
—Historical Connections in Mathematics: Resources for Using History of Mathematics in the Classroom, Vol. 2. (Illus.). 120p. (Orig.). (gr. 4-9). 1993. pap. 14.95 (1-881431-38-X, 2003) AIMS Educ Fnd.
Reimer, Wilbert, jt. auth. see Reimer, Luetta.
Reimers, David. The Immigrant Experience. Moynihan, Daniel P., intro. by. (Illus.). 112p. (gr. 5 up). 1989. 17. 95x (0-87754-881-1) Chelsea Hse.
Reimerth, Gudrun, tr. see Cohen, Donald.
Reinckens, Sunnhild. Making Dolls. Maclean, Donald, tr. (GER., Illus.). 56p. (ps-3). 1989. pap. 10.95 (0-86315-093-4, Pub. by Floris Bks UK) Gryphon Hse.
Reiner, Annie. The Potty Chronicles: A Story to Help Children Adjust to Toilet Training. LC 91-86. (Illus.). 32p. (ps-2). 1991. 16.95 (0-945354-36-3); pap. 6.95 (0-945354-35-5) Magination Pr.
—Visit to the Art Galaxy. LC 91-16989. (Illus.). (gr. 1 up). 1991. 15.95 (0-671-74957-9, Green Tiger) S&S Trade.
Reiners, Kenneth G. Addicted to the Addict: From Codependency to Recovery. LC 87-50843. 64p. (Orig.). (gr. 9-12). 1987. pap. 4.95 (0-934104-06-9) Woodland.
Rein-Hagen, Mark, et al. Vampire: The Masquerade. 2nd ed. Wieck, Stephen, ed. (Illus.). 264p. (gr. 10 up). 1993. pap. 25.00 (1-56504-029-5, 2002) White Wolf.
Reinhard, Dale W. Simply Celebrating Children: Parties As Unique & Special As a Child. 140p. 1991. 12.95 (0-9628888-0-X) Pressed Duck.
Reinhard, Margaret, jt. auth. see Forester, Anne.
Reinheimer, Joel. The Adventure of Squeek the Rabbit. 1990. 6.95 (0-533-08900-X) Vantage.
Reinholtd, Bill, jt. auth. see Anderson, Honey.
Reinman, Y. Y., ed. see Gold, Avner.
Reinman, Y. Y., ed. see Teichman, Avigail.
Reinsma, Carol. Friends Forever. Cori, Nathan, illus. 48p. (Orig.). (gr. 1-3). 1993. pap. 3.99 (0-7847-0096-6, 24-03944) Standard Pub.
—The Picnic Caper. Cori, Nathan, illus. LC 93-29567. 48p. (Orig.). (gr. k-3). 1994. pap. 3.99 (0-7847-0006-0, 24-03956) Standard Pub.
—A Place in the Palace. Cori, Nathan, illus. 48p. (Orig.). (gr. 1-3). 1993. pap. 3.99 (0-7847-0095-8, 24-03945) Standard Pub.
—The Secret of the Ring in the Offering. Schneider, Jennifer, illus. 48p. (Orig.). (gr. 1-3). 1993. pap. 3.99 (0-7847-0094-X, 24-03944) Standard Pub.
—The Shimmering Stone. Cori, Nathan, illus. 48p. (Orig.). (gr. k-3). 1994. pap. 3.99 (0-7847-0007-9, 24-03957) Standard Pub.
Reinstedt, Randall A. One-Eyed Charley: The California Whip. Bergez, John, ed. LC 90-81382. (Illus.). 84p. (gr. 3-6). 1990. casebound 11.95 (0-933818-23-8); pap. 7.95 (0-933818-77-7) Ghost Town.

—Otters, Octopuses, & Odd Creatures of the Deep. Bergez, John, ed. LC 87-82106. (Illus.). 64p. (gr. 3-6). 1987. casebound 11.95 (0-933818-21-1); pap. 7.95 (0-933818-76-9) Ghost Town.
—Stagecoach Santa. Bergez, John, ed. Macdonald, Judith L., illus. LC 86-81735. 48p. (gr. 3-6). 1986. case 11.95 (0-933818-20-3); pap. 7.95 (0-933818-75-0) Ghost Town.
—The Strange Case of the Ghosts of the Robert Louis Stevenson House. Bergez, John, ed. LC 88-81933. (Illus.). 70p. (gr. 3-6). 1988. case 11.95 (0-933818-22-X); pap. 7.95 (0-933818-78-5) Ghost Town.
—Tales & Treasures of California's Missions. Bergez, John, ed. LC 92-73253. (Illus.). 120p. (gr. 3-6). 1992. case 12.95 (0-933818-24-6); pap. 9.95 (0-685-62330-0) Ghost Town.
Reisberg. Baby Rattlesnake. 32p. (gr. 3-4). 1990. 19.92 (0-8172-6749-2) Raintree Steck-V.
Reische, Diana. Arafat & the Palestine Liberation Organization. (Illus.). 160p. (gr. 9-12). 1991. PLB 14. 40 (0-531-11000-1) Watts.
—Electing a U. S. President. Rich, Mary P., ed. LC 91-32330. (Illus.). 176p. (gr. 7-12). 1992. PLB 14.40 (0-531-11043-5) Watts.
Reisenauer, Cindy, illus. How to Draw Creepy Creatures. 32p. 1991. 3.98 (1-56156-019-7); pap. 2.95 (1-56156-064-2) Kidsbks.
Reiser, Howard. Barry Sanders: Lion with a Quiet Roar. LC 93-19780. 1993. write for info. (0-516-04377-3) Childrens.
—Jackie Robinson: Baseball Pioneer. Rich, Mary P., ed. LC 91-28617. (Illus.). 64p. (gr. 3-5). 1992. PLB 12.90 (0-531-20095-7) Watts.
—Jim Abbott (All-American Pitcher) 1993. write for info. (0-516-04376-5) Melmont.
—Ken Griffey, Jr. LC 93-41054. 1994. write for info. (0-516-04384-6) Childrens.
—Nolan Ryan: Strikeout King. LC 92-35741. (Illus.). 48p. (gr. 2-8). 1993. PLB 13.27 (0-516-04365-X); pap. 3.95 (0-516-44365-8) Childrens.
—Scottie Pippen: Prince of the Court. LC 92-42023. (Illus.). 48p. (gr. 2-8). 1993. PLB 13.27 (0-516-04366-8); pap. 3.95 (0-516-44366-6) Childrens.
Reiser, Lynn. Any Kind of Dog. LC 91-12771. 24p. (ps up). 1992. 14.00 (0-688-10914-4); PLB 13.93 (0-688-10915-2) Greenwillow.
—Bedtime Cat. LC 90-30751. (Illus.). 24p. (ps up). 1991. 13.95 (0-688-10025-2); PLB 13.88 (0-688-10026-0) Greenwillow.
—Christmas Counting. LC 91-32501. (Illus.). 32p. (ps-4). 1992. 14.00 (0-688-10676-5); PLB 13.93 (0-688-10677-3) Greenwillow.
—Dog & Cat. LC 90-3553. (Illus.). 24p. (ps up) 1991. 13.95 (0-688-09892-4); PLB 13.88 (0-688-09893-2) Greenwillow.
—Margaret & Margarita, Margarita y Margaret. LC 92-29012. 32p. (ps up). 1993. 14.00 (0-688-12239-6); lib. bdg. 13.93 (0-688-12240-X) Greenwillow.
—Night Thunder & the Queen of the Wild Horses. LC 93-25734. 1994. write for info. (0-688-11791-0); PLB write for info. (0-688-11792-9) Greenwillow.
—The Surprise Family. LC 93-16249. (Illus.). 32p. (ps up). 1994. write for info. (0-688-11671-X); PLB write for info. (0-688-11672-8) Greenwillow.
—Tomorrow on Rocky Pond. LC 91-45801. (Illus.). 32p. (ps up). 1993. 14.00 (0-688-10672-2); PLB 13.93 (0-688-10673-0) Greenwillow.
Reiser, Robert, jt. auth. see Balis, Andrea.
Reiser, Ronald J. Indiana Passport. (Illus.). 36p. (Orig.). (gr. 9-12). 1991. 3.95 (0-9625515-5-4) VJR Passports.
—Kentucky Passport. (Illus.). 36p. (Orig.). (gr. 9-12). 1991. 3.95 (0-9625515-9-7) VJR Passports.
—Michigan Passport. (Illus.). 36p. (Orig.). (gr. 9-12). 1991. 3.95 (0-9625515-7-0) VJR Passports.
—North Carolina Passport. (Illus.). 36p. (Orig.). (gr. 9-12). 1991. 3.95 (0-9625515-8-9) VJR Passports.
—Ohio Passport. (Illus.). 36p. (Orig.). (gr. 9-12). 1991. 3.95 (0-9625515-6-2) VJR Passports.
Reisfeld, Randi. Melrose Place: Meet the Stars of Today's Hottest New Show. Clancey, Lisa, ed. 192p. (gr. 5 up). 1992. pap. 4.50 (0-671-79781-6) PB.
—Nelson: Double Play. 1991. pap. 3.50 (0-553-29285-4) Bantam.
Reisgies, Teresa, jt. auth. see Salzman, Marian.
Reiss, Diana. Camelot World: The Secrets of the Dolphins. 144p. (Orig.). (gr. 7). 1991. pap. 2.95 (0-380-76046-0, Camelot) Avon.
Reiss, Elayne & Freidman, Rita. A-Choo. (Illus.). (gr. k-1). 1990. 10.50 (0-89796-864-6) New Dimens Educ.
Reiss, Elayne & Friedman, Rita. A Buttonmat for Beautiful Buttons. (gr. k-1). 1978. 10.50 (0-89796-865-4) New Dimens Educ.
—Exercise Expert. (gr. k-1). 10.50 (0-89796-866-2) New Dimens Educ.
—Fantastic Funny Feet. (gr. k-1). 10.50 (0-89796-867-0) New Dimens Educ.
—Hat Helpers Hullaballoo. (gr. k-1). 10.50 (0-89796-868-9) New Dimens Educ.
—The Tale of Tall Toothbrush. (gr. k-1). 1978. 10.50 (0-89796-869-7) New Dimens Educ.
Reiss, Johanna. The Journey Back. LC 76-12615. 224p. (gr. 7 up). 1987. pap. 3.95 (0-06-447042-3, Trophy) HarpC Child Bks.
—The Journey Back. LC 76-12615. 224p. (gr. 7 up). 1992. PLB 17.89 (0-06-021457-0) HarpC Child Bks.
—The Journey Back, 2 vols. 242p. (gr. 5-8). 1976. Set. 19.36 (0-685-63801-4, BR8398) W A T Braille.

—The Upstairs Room. LC 77-187940. 196p. (gr. 7 up). 1987. 15.00 (0-690-85127-8, Crowell Jr Bks); PLB 14. 89 (0-690-04702-9, Crowell Jr Bks) HarpC Child Bks.
—The Upstairs Room. LC 77-187940. 192p. (gr. 7 up). 1987. pap. 3.95 (0-06-447043-1, Trophy) HarpC Child Bks.
—The Upstairs Room. LC 77-187940. 208p. (gr. 7 up). 1990. pap. 3.95 (0-06-440370-X, Trophy) HarpC Child Bks.
—The Upstairs Room, 2 vols. 268p. (gr. 6 up). 1972. Set. 21.44 (0-685-63802-2, BR8399) W A T Braille.
Reiss, John J. Colors. Reiss, John J., illus. LC 69-13653. 32p. (ps-2). 1982. RSBE 13.95 (0-02-776130-4, Bradbury Pr) Macmillan Child Grp.
—Colors. Reiss, John J., illus. LC 86-22189. 32p. (ps-2). 1987. pap. 3.95 (0-689-71119-0, Aladdin) Macmillan Child Grp.
—Numbers. Reiss, John J., illus. LC 76-151313. 32p. (ps-2). 1982. RSBE 13.95 (0-02-776150-9, Bradbury Pr) Macmillan Child Grp.
—Numbers. Reiss, John J., illus. LC 86-22243. 32p. (ps-2). 1987. pap. 3.95 (0-689-71120-4, Aladdin) Macmillan Child Grp.
—Shapes. LC 73-76545. (Illus.). 32p. (ps-2). 1982. RSBE 13.95 (0-02-776190-8, Bradbury Pr) Macmillan Child Grp.
—Shapes. Reiss, John J., illus. LC 86-22164. 32p. (ps-2). 1987. pap. 3.95 (0-689-71121-2, Aladdin) Macmillan Child Grp.
Reiss, K. The Glass House People. 1992. 16.95 (0-15-231040-1, HB Juv Bks) HarBrace.
Reiss, Kathryn. Dreadful Sorry. LC 92-38780. (gr. 5-9). 1993. 16.95 (0-15-224213-9) HarBrace.
—Glass House People. (gr. 7 up). 1992. pap. 6.95 (0-15-231041-X, HB Juv Bks) HarBrace.
—Pale Phoenix. LC 93-32299. (gr. 5 up). 1994. write for info. (0-15-200030-5); pap. write for info. (0-15-200031-3) Harbrace.
—Time Windows. 260p. (gr. 5 up). 1991. 15.95 (0-15-288205-7, HB Juv Bks) HarBrace.
Reiss, Stephen. The Reiss Rules for Two-Hour Monopoly: Fun, Fast, Unofficial Way to Play America's Favorite Board Game. Johnson, Linda, illus. LC 93-85455. 64p. (Orig.). (gr. 1-12). 1994. pap. 6.95 (0-9637853-3-8) Prosprty Prtnrs.
Reist, Linnaeus L. The Colorful Landis Brothers: Founders of the Landis Valley Museum. Severs, Susan B., ed. & illus. LC 87-90447. 100p. (Orig.). (gr. 11-12). 1987. pap. write for info. (0-9618501-0-8) S R Severs.
Reit, Ann. The First Time. (Orig.). (gr. 5 up). 1986. pap. 2.50 (0-440-92560-6, LFL) Dell.
Reit, Seymour. Behind Rebel Lines: The Incredible Story of Emma Edmonds, Civil War Spy. LC 87-28079. 144p. (gr. 3-7). 1988. 12.95 (0-15-200416-5, Gulliver Bks) HarBrace.
—Behind Rebel Lines: The Incredible Story of Emma Edmonds, Civil War Spy. 114p. (gr. 3-7). 1991. pap. 4.95 (0-15-200424-6, Odyssey) HarBrace.
—Flying School Bus. 1990. pap. write for info. (0-307-10032-4, Golden Pr) Western Pub.
—Guns for General Washington: A Story of the American Revolution. (gr. 4-7). 1992. pap. 4.95 (0-15-232695-2) HarBrace.
—Guns for General Washington: The Impossible Journey. Ross, Richard, illus. 98p. (gr. 3-7). 1990. 15.95 (0-15-200466-1, Gulliver Bks) HarBrace.
—Rebus Bears-Bank Street. (ps-3). 1989. pap. 3.50 (0-553-34689-X) Bantam.
—Take a Ride with Mickey. Guell, Fernando, illus. LC 91-71336. 32p. (ps-1). 1991. 8.95 (1-56282-060-5) Disney Pr.
—Things That Go: A Traveling Alphabet. 1990. 9.99 (0-553-05856-8) Bantam.
—Trains. (ps-3). 1990. write for info. (0-307-17869-2, Pub. by Golden Bks) Western Pub.
Reit, Seymour V. The Rebus Bears: Level 1. Smith, Kenneth, illus. 1989. 9.99 (0-553-05822-3) Bantam.
Reit, Seymour V. & Navaroo, Jose G. Voyage with Columbus. 96p. (Orig.). 1986. pap. 2.50 (0-553-15431-1) Bantam.
Reitci, Rita, ed. see Tozuks, Takako.
Reiter, Edith, jt. auth. see Swerdlick, Harriet.
Reiter, John, ed. see Kolbisen, Irene M.
Rekela, George R. Hakeem Olajuwon: Tower of Power. LC 92-38905. 1993. lib. bdg. 13.50 (0-8225-0518-5); pap. 4.95 (0-8225-9637-7) Lerner Pubns.
Re'lem, Dyob & Melger, Boyd A. Hoge Bloeddruk, Myocardiale Infarct, Grafieken. (DUT., Illus.). 69p. (Orig.). (gr. 12 up). 1989. pap. write for info. (0-9622463-1-X) B Melger.
Relf, Pat. Hurry! Hurry! 24p. (ps up). 1992. write for info. (0-307-74802-2, 64802) Western Pub.
Relf, Pat & Hanavan, Louise. Barnyard Mystery. 24p. (ps up). 1992. write for info. (0-307-74801-4, 64801) Western Pub.
Relph, Ingeborg. Christmas Make & Bake. (Illus.). 48p. (gr. 1-5). 1993. pap. 12.95 (0-7459-2505-7) Lion USA.
Remarque, Erich M. All Quiet on the Western Front. (gr. 7 up). 1929. 19.95 (0-316-73992-8) Little.
Rembrandt, Elaine. Heroes, Heroines, & Holidays: Plays for Jewish Youth. Abrams, Sylvia, frwd. by. LC 81-67027. 148p. (Orig.). (gr. 5-12). 1981. pap. 6.50 (0-86705-002-0) A R E Pub.
Remkiewicz, Frank. GreedyAnna. LC 91-149230. (ps-3). 1992. 14.00 (0-688-10294-8); PLB 13.93 (0-688-10295-6) Lothrop.

—The Last Time I Saw Harris. LC 90-40263. (Illus.). 32p. (gr. k up). 1991. 13.95 (*0-688-10291-3*); PLB 13. 88 (*0-688-10292-1*) Lothrop.
—There's Only One Harris. LC 92-44163. (gr. 3-6). 1993. write for info. (*0-688-11827-5*); PLB write for info. (*0-688-11828-3*) Lothrop.
Remole, Mary J. Mary Jane's Cookbook: From the Heart of America. (Illus.). 144p. (gr. 9-12). 1986. text ed. 8.95 (*0-317-90470-1*) Mary Janes Cookbook.
Remy, jt. auth. see Patrick.
Remy, Bob. Louisiana Sports Encyclopedia. 358p. (gr. 4-10). 1977. pap. 9.95 (*0-88289-120-0*) Pelican.
Remy, Bob, jt. auth. see Mule, Marty.
Renard, Jules. Poil de Carotte. (gr. 7-12). pap. 4.95 (*0-88436-046-6*, 40264) EMC.
Renauld, Christiane. Journey in a Shell. (Illus.). 32p. (gr. 3-5). 1991. 18.50 (*0-89565-752-X*); 12.95s.p. (*0-685-55086-9*) Childs World.
—The Magic Shoes. (Illus.). 32p. (gr. 3-5). 1991. 18.50 (*0-89565-753-8*); 12.95s.p. (*0-685-55087-7*) Childs World.
—A Pal for Martin. (Illus.). 32p. (gr. 3-5). 1991. 18.50 (*0-89565-756-2*); 12.95s.p. (*0-685-55091-5*) Childs World.
—Tomorrow Will Be a Nice Day. (Illus.). 32p. (gr. k-2). 1991. 18.50 (*0-89565-763-5*); 12.95s.p. (*0-685-55080-X*) Childs World.
Renberg, Dalia. King Solomon & the Bee. Heller, Ruth, illus. LC 92-30411. 1994. 15.00 (*0-06-022899-7*); PLB 14.89 (*0-06-022902-0*) HarpC Child Bks.
Renberg, Dalia H. The Complete Family Guide to Jewish Holidays. LC 84-11008. (Illus.). (gr. 4 up). 1985. pap. 22.95 (*0-915361-09-4*) Modan-Adama Bks.
Rench, Janice. Understanding Sexual Identity. 1992. pap. 4.95 (*0-8225-9602-4*) Lerner Pubns.
Rench, Janice E. Family Violence: Coping with Modern Issues. 64p. (gr. 5 up). 1991. PLB 15.95 (*0-8225-0047-7*) Lerner Pubns.
—Teen Sexuality: Decisions & Choices. (Illus.). 72p. (gr. 6 up). 1988. lib. bdg. 15.95 (*0-8225-0041-8*) Lerner Pubns.
—Understanding Sexual Identity: A Book for Gay Teens & Their Friends. 72p. (gr. 5 up). 1990. PLB 15.95 (*0-8225-0044-2*) Lerner Pubns.
Rench, Janice E., jt. auth. see Terkel, Susan N.
Rendal, Justine. A Child of Their Own. 96p. (gr. 3-7). 1992. 13.00 (*0-670-84418-7*) Viking Child Bks.
—Dancing Cat. 40p. 1991. pap. 13.95 incl. jacket (*0-671-72637-4*, S&S BFYR) S&S Trade.
—The Girl Who Listened to Sinks. (ps-6). 1993. pap. 14. 00 (*0-671-77745-9*, S&S BFYR) S&S Trade.
Rendall, K. Norline. Just a Taste of Honey. 1975. pap. 3.99 (*0-8024-4494-6*) Moody.
Rendon, Marion B. & Kranz, Rachel. Straight Talk about Money. Ryan, Elizabeth A., ed. 128p. (gr. 7-12). 1992. lib. bdg. 16.95x (*0-8160-2612-2*) Facts on File.
Reneau, Jack, ed. Boone & Crockett Club's Twenty-First Big-Game Awards, 1989-1991. 500p. 1992. 39.95 ea. (*0-940864-19-3*) Boone & Crockett.
Reneau, Jack, jt. ed. see Nesbitt, W. H.
Reneaux, J. J. Cajun Folktales. 176p. (gr. 5 up). 1992. 19.95 (*0-87483-283-7*); pap. 9.95 (*0-87483-282-9*) August Hse.
Renfrew, Nita. Saddam Hussein. 218p. (gr. 5 up). 1993. 18.95 (*0-7910-1776-1*, Am Art Analog) Chelsea Hse.
Renfro, Nancy. Bags Are Big: A Paper Bag Craft Book. Cromack, Celeste, ed. (Illus.). 78p. (gr. 1-6). 1983. pap. 14.95 (*0-931044-10-3*) Renfro Studios.
—Puppet Shows Made Easy! Cromack, Celeste, ed. Renfro, Nancy, illus. 96p. (Orig.). (gr. 2-12). pap. 14. 95 (*0-931044-13-8*) Renfro Studios.
Renfro, Nancy & Armstrong, Beverly. Make Amazing Puppets. 32p. (gr. 1-6). 1979. 3.95 (*0-88160-007-5*, LW 109) Learning Wks.
Renfro, Nancy & Frazier, Nancy. Imagination: At Play with Puppets & Creative Drama. Schwalb, Ann W., ed. Sears, Lori, illus. 96p. (gr. 1-6). 1987. 16.95 (*0-931044-16-2*) Renfro Studios.
Renfro, Nancy & Sullivan, Debbie. Puppets U. S. A. - Texas: Exploring Folklore, Music & Crafts with Puppets. Schwalb, Ann W. & Marion, Craig A., eds. (Illus.). 96p. (Orig.). (gr. 1-6). 1985. pap. 15.95 (*0-931044-11-1*) Renfro Studios.
Renfro, Nancy, jt. auth. see Hunt, Tamara.
Renfro, Nancy, jt. auth. see Sullivan, Debbie.
Renineke, R. jt. ed. see Rothstein, Erica L.
Renna, Giani, jt. auth. see Crawford, Gail.
Renna, Giani, jt. auth. see Shore, Donna.
Renna, Giani, jt. auth. see Tyler, Laura.
Rennert, Maggie. I Love You. Frankel, Alona, illus. (ps up). 1987. 9.95 (*0-915361-71-X*) Modan-Adama Bks.
Rennert, Richard, ed. Book of Firsts: Leaders of America. King, Coretta Scott, intro. by. LC 93-25878. (Illus.). 1993. 13.95 (*0-7910-2065-7*, Am Art Analog); pap. write for info. (*0-7910-2066-5*, Am Art Analog) Chelsea Hse.
—Book of Firsts: Sports Heroes. LC 93-18437. (Illus.). 1993. 13.95 (*0-7910-2055-X*, Am Art Analog); pap. 5.95 (*0-7910-2056-8*, Am Art Analog) Chelsea Hse.
—Civil Rights Leaders. LC 92-37655. (Illus.). 1993. 13.95 (*0-7910-2051-7*, Am Art Analog); pap. 5.95 (*0-7910-2052-5*, Am Art Analog) Chelsea Hse.
—Female Writers. King, Coretta S., intro. by. LC 93-21673. (Illus.). (gr. 6 up). 1993. 13.95 (*0-7910-2063-0*, Am Art Analog); pap. write for info. (*0-7910-2064-9*) Chelsea Hse.

—Shapers of America. LC 92-39962. 1993. 13.95 (*0-7910-2053-3*, Am Art Analog); pap. 5.95 (*0-7910-2054-1*, Am Art Analog) Chelsea Hse.
Rennert, Richard S. Jesse Owens. (Illus.). 72p. (gr. 3-5). 1991. lib. bdg. 12.95 (*0-7910-1570-X*) Chelsea Hse.
—Julius Erving. (Illus.). (gr. 5 up). 1992. PLB 17.95 (*0-7910-1125-9*) Chelsea Hse.
Rennert, Rick. Jesse Owens: Junior World Biographies. (gr. 4-7). 1992. pap. 4.95 (*0-7910-1955-1*) Chelsea Hse.
Rennie, Ross. Boston Bruins. 32p. (gr. 4). 1990. PLB 14. 95s.p. (*0-88682-273-4*) Creative Ed.
—Buffalo Sabres. 32p. (gr. 4). 1990. PLB 14.95s.p. (*0-88682-274-2*) Creative Ed.
—Calgary Flames. 32p. (gr. 4). 1990. PLB 21.35 (*0-88682-275-0*); PLB 14.95s.p. (*0-685-28191-4*) Creative Ed.
—Chicago Blackhawks. 32p. (gr. 4). 1990. PLB 14.95s.p. (*0-88682-276-9*) Creative Ed.
—Detroit Red Wings. 32p. (gr. 4). 1990. PLB 14.95s.p. (*0-88682-277-7*) Creative Ed.
—Edmonton Oilers. 32p. (gr. 4). 1990. PLB 14.95s.p. (*0-88682-278-5*) Creative Ed.
—Hartford Whalers. 32p. (gr. 4). 1990. PLB 14.95s.p. (*0-88682-279-3*) Creative Ed.
—Los Angeles Kings. 32p. (gr. 4). 1990. PLB 14.95s.p. (*0-88682-280-7*) Creative Ed.
—Minnesota North Stars. 32p. (gr. 4). 1990. PLB 14. 95s.p. (*0-88682-281-5*) Creative Ed.
—Montreal Canadians. 32p. (gr. 4). 1990. PLB 14.95s.p. (*0-88682-282-3*) Creative Ed.
—New Jersey Devils. 32p. (gr. 4). 1990. PLB 14.95s.p. (*0-88682-283-1*) Creative Ed.
—New York Islanders. 32p. (gr. 4). 1990. PLB 14.95s.p. (*0-88682-284-X*) Creative Ed.
—New York Rangers. 32p. (gr. 4 up). PLB 14.95 (*0-88682-285-8*) Creative Ed.
—Philadelphia Flyers. 32p. (gr. 4). 1990. PLB 14.95s.p. (*0-88682-286-6*) Creative Ed.
—Pittsburgh Penguins. 32p. (gr. 4). 1990. PLB 14.95s.p. (*0-88682-287-4*) Creative Ed.
—Quebec Nordiques. 32p. (gr. 4). 1990. PLB 14.95s.p. (*0-88682-288-2*) Creative Ed.
—St. Louis Blues. 32p. (gr. 4). 1990. PLB 14.95s.p. (*0-88682-289-0*) Creative Ed.
—Toronto Maple Leafs. 32p. (gr. 4). 1990. PLB 14.95s.p. (*0-88682-290-4*) Creative Ed.
—Vancouver Canucks. 32p. (gr. 4). 1990. PLB 14.95s.p. (*0-88682-291-2*) Creative Ed.
—Washington Capitals. 32p. (gr. 4). 1990. PLB 14.95s.p. (*0-88682-292-0*) Creative Ed.
—Winnipeg Jets. 32p. (gr. 4). 1990. PLB 14.95s.p. (*0-88682-293-9*) Creative Ed.
Renshaw, Polly & Levens, Ann. Teacher's Guide for Uncle Noel's Fun Fables. Gray, Harrel, illus. 52p. (gr. 2-5). 1991. wkbk. 5.95 (*0-9630734-1-9*) Aesop Systs.
Rensselaer, Alexander Van see Van Rensselaer, Alexander.
Renton, Alice. Victoria: The Biography of a Pigeon. (gr. 7 up). 1988. pap. 3.50 (*0-8041-0395-X*) Ivy Books.
Repath, Ann, ed. see Schweitzer, Albert.
Repp, Gloria. His Best for God. (Illus.). 24p. (gr. k-6). 1989. pap. text ed. 4.25 (*1-55976-150-4*) CEF Press.
—A Man for God's Plan. (Illus.). 24p. (gr. k-6). 1991. 4.25 (*1-55976-155-5*) CEF Press.
—A Question of Yams: A Missionary Story Based on True Events. Daniels, Karen, ed. Bruckner, Roger, illus. 67p. (Orig.). (gr. 2-4). 1992. pap. 4.95 (*0-89084-614-6*) Bob Jones Univ Pr.
—Secret of the Golden Cowrie. (Illus.). 199p. (Orig.). (gr. 4-6). 1988. pap. 4.95 (*0-89084-459-3*) Bob Jones Univ Pr.
—The Stolen Years. 152p. (Orig.). (gr. 9-12). 1989. pap. 4.95 (*0-89084-481-X*) Bob Jones Univ Pr.
Repp, T. O. Main Streets of the Northwest. LC 89-15467. (Illus.). 160p. (gr. 11). 1989. 19.95 (*0-87046-085-4*, Pub. by Trans-Anglo) Interurban.
Resch, Barbara. A Place for Everyone. Resch, Barbara, illus. 28p. (ps-3). 1991. smythe sewn reinforced bdg. 9.95 (*1-56182-022-9*) Atomium Bks.
Resnick, A., et al. Every Day's a Holiday. (gr. 4-8). 1991. 21.95 (*0-8224-6372-5*) Fearon Teach Aids.
Resnick, Abraham. The Commonwealth of Independent States. (Illus.). 128p. (gr. 5-9). 1993. PLB 26.60 (*0-516-02613-5*) Childrens.
—The Holocaust. LC 91-441. (Illus.). 112p. (gr. 5-8). 1991. PLB 14.95 (*1-56006-124-3*) Lucent Bks.
—Russia: A History to 1917. LC 83-7369. (Illus.). 128p. (gr. 5-9). 1983. PLB 26.60 (*0-516-02785-9*) Childrens.
—The Union of Soviet Socialist Republics. LC 84-7602. (Illus.). 128p. (gr. 5-9). 1985. PLB 26.60 (*0-516-02789-1*) Childrens.
Resnick, Jane. Eyes on Nature: Fish. (Illus.). 32p. 1992. pap. 4.95 (*1-56156-150-9*) Kidsbks.
—Goldilocks & the Three Bears. 1986. 14.98 (*0-88705-151-0*) Joshua Morris.
—Original Fairy Tales from Brothers Grimm. 1991. 12.99 (*0-517-06577-0*) Outlet Bk Co.
Resnick, Jane P. The Ant & the Dove. Lindy, Heidi, illus. 1992. bds. 3.25 (*0-8378-2523-7*) Gibson.
—The Fox & the Crow. Lindy, Heidi, illus. 1992. bds. 3.25 (*0-8378-2525-3*) Gibson.
—The Lion & the Mouse. Lindy, Heidi, illus. 1992. bds. 3.25 (*0-8378-2526-1*) Gibson.
—The Tortoise & the Hare. Lindy, Heidi, illus. 1992. bds. 3.25 (*0-8378-2524-5*) Gibson.
Resnick, Kathleen. Kermit Learns Windows. 48p. (Orig.). (gr. 5 up). 1993. pap. 9.95 (*1-55958-366-5*) Prima Pub.

Resnik, Hank. Activities & Assignments: Student Workbook. rev. ed. Barr, Linda, ed. Robison, Don, illus. 178p. (gr. 6-8). 1988. wkbk. 4.85 (*0-933419-26-0*) Quest Intl.
Resnik, Hank, et al. Actividades y Asignaciones: Cuaderno del Estudiante. Callejas, Juan, et al, eds. Luobriel, Marta B., et al, trs. from ENG. Ordonez, Maria A., illus. (SPA., Orig.). (gr. 6-8). 1991. wkbk. 4.85 (*1-56095-022-6*) Quest Intl.
Respess, Kathryn. The Children of Israel: A Workbook Introduction to Ancient Israel. 124p. (gr. 9-12). 1984. student wkbk. 22.00 (*1-881678-08-3*) CRIS.
Ressler, Ralph. A World of Choice: Careers & You - Student Workbook. LC 77-4182. (Illus.). (gr. 9-12). 1978. pap. 14.95 (*0-88280-050-7*); tchr's. guide 19.95 (*0-88280-051-5*) ETC Pubns.
Ressmeyer, Roger. Astronaut to Zodiac: A Young Stargazer's Alphabet. LC 92-9615. (Illus.). 32p. (gr. k-6). 1992. 15.00 (*0-517-58805-6*); PLB 15.99 (*0-517-58806-4*) Crown Bks Yng Read.
Retan, Walter. Armies of Ants. Cassels, Jean, illus. LC 93-29782. 48p. (ps-4). 1994. pap. 3.50 (*0-590-47616-5*, Cartwheel) Scholastic Inc.
—The Big Book of Real Trains. Courtney, Richard, illus. 48p. (gr. 1-4). 1987. 7.95 (*0-448-19178-4*, G&D) Putnam Pub Group.
—One Hundred & One Facts about Snakes & Reptiles. (gr. 4-7). 1992. pap. 1.95 (*0-590-44891-9*) Scholastic Inc.
—Piggies Piggies Piggies. (gr. 3 up). 1993. pap. 15.00 (*0-671-75244-8*, S&S BFYR) S&S Trade.
—The Story of Daniel Boone. DeJohn, Marle, illus. 112p. (Orig.). (gr. 2-5). 1992. pap. 3.25 (*0-440-40711-7*, YB) Dell.
Retan, Walter, ed. Bunnies, Bunnies, Bunnies. Santoro, Christopher, et al, illus. LC 90-41486. 96p. (ps-2). 1991. pap. 14.95 (*0-671-73221-8*, S&S BYR); pap. 18. 98 (*0-671-73220-X*) S&S Trade.
Retan, Walter, compiled by. I Love Christmas: A Wonderful Collection of Christmas Stories, Poems, Carols, & More. Ewing, Carolyn, illus. 96p. (gr. k up). 1992. write for info. (*0-307-15875-6*, 15875, Golden Pr) Western Pub.
Retan, Walter, adapted by see Piper, Watty.
Retino, Ernie & Kerner Rettino, Debbie. Solomon, the Supersonic Salamander: Choosing Good Friends. 32p. (ps-2). 1992. 7.99 (*0-8499-1017-X*) Word Inc.
Rettino, Ernie & Kerner Rettino, Debbie. Solomon, the Supersonic Salamander: Telling the Truth. 32p. (ps-2). 1992. 7.99 (*0-8499-1018-8*) Word Inc.
Reuben, Gabriel. Electricity Experiments for Children. (Illus.). 88p. (gr. 5-9). pap. 2.95 (*0-486-22030-3*) Dover.
Reufenacht, Peter, jt. auth. see Bauer, Fred.
Reum, Earl. The Spirit of Student Council. Bruce, C., ed. (gr. 7-9). 1981. pap. 7.00 (*0-88210-117-X*) Natl Assn Principals.
Reuter, Bjarne. The Boys from St. Petri. 192p. (gr. 6 up). 1994. 14.99 (*0-525-45121-8*, DCB) Dutton Child Bks.
—Buster, the Sheikh of Hope Street. Bell, Anthea, illus. LC 91-19397. 144p. (gr. 4 up). 1991. 13.95 (*0-525-44772-5*, DCB) Dutton Child Bks.
—Buster's World. LC 89-11919. 160p. (gr. 4 up). 1989. 12.95 (*0-525-44475-0*, DCB) Dutton Child Bks.
—Buster's World. (Illus.). 154p. (gr. 5-9). 1991. pap. 3.95 (*0-14-034471-3*, Puffin) Puffin Bks.
Reuter, Eisabeth, jt. auth. see Becker, Antoinette.
Reuther, Ruth E. Meet at the Falls: The Story of the Pioneers. McCall, Jody, ed. (Illus.). 1989. pap. text ed. write for info. (*0-9622632-1-4*) Wee-Chee-Taw.
Revich, S. J. The Camel Boy. Hinlicky, Gregg, illus. 158p. (gr. 5-8). 1987. 9.95 (*0-935063-44-7*); pap. 7.95 (*0-935063-45-5*) CIS Comm.
—Ezra the Physician. Hinlicky, Gregg, illus. 126p. (gr. 5-7). 1988. 9.95 (*0-935063-63-3*); pap. 7.95 (*0-935063-64-1*) CIS Comm.
—Ibrahim the Magician. Hinlicky, Gregg, illus. 126p. (gr. 4-7). 1987. 9.95 (*0-935063-33-1*); pap. 7.95 (*0-935063-34-X*) CIS Comm.
—The Lion Tamer. 140p. (ps-8). 1990. 10.95 (*0-685-47680-4*); pap. 7.95 (*1-56062-054-4*) CIS Comm.
—The Poet & the Thief. Hinlicky, Gregg, illus. 158p. (gr. 5-7). 1989. 10.95 (*0-935063-71-4*); pap. 7.95 (*0-935063-72-2*) CIS Comm.
Reville, Julie D. The Many Voices of Paws: A Workbook for Young Stutterers. Metayer, Phil, illus. 64p. (ps-3). 1989. 25.00 (*0-937857-11-4*, 1568) Speech Bin.
Rew, Lois J. God's Green Liniment. Thomas, Avis T., illus. LC 81-84183. 208p. (Orig.). (gr. 3-8). 1981. pap. 7.50 (*0-938462-02-4*) Green Leaf CA.
Rex, Margery see Dunlea, Nancy.
Rex, Patricia. Bear Essentials. (ps-k). 1988. pap. 9.95 (*0-8224-0697-7*) Fearon Teach Aids.
Rey, H. A. Anybody at Home? (Illus.). 24p. (gr. k-3). 1942. pap. 2.10 (*0-395-07045-7*, Sandpiper) HM.
—Cecily G. & the Nine Monkeys. Rey, H. A., illus. 32p. (gr. 1-3). 1974. 14.45 (*0-395-18430-4*) HM.
—Cecily G. & the Nine Monkeys. Rey, H. A., illus. (ps-3). 1989. pap. 3.80 (*0-395-50651-4*, Sandpiper) HM.
—Curious George. (Illus.). 56p. (gr. k-3). 1973. 12.70 (*0-395-15993-8*) HM.
—Curious George. Rey, H. A., illus. 48p. (gr. k-3). 1973. pap. 4.80 (*0-395-15023-X*, Sandpiper) HM.
—Curious George Gets a Medal. (Illus.). 48p. (gr. k-3). 1957. 12.70 (*0-395-16973-9*) HM.

—Curious George Gets a Medal. Rey, H. A., illus. LC 57-7206. 48p. (gr. k-3). 1974. pap. 4.80 (0-395-18559-9, Sandpiper) HM.
—Curious George Learns the Alphabet. (Illus.). 72p. (gr. k-3). 1963. 12.70 (0-395-16031-6) HM.
—Curious George Learns the Alphabet. Rey, H. A., illus. LC 62-12261. 72p. (gr. k-3). 1973. pap. 4.80 (0-395-13718-7, Sandpiper) HM.
—Curious George Paper Doll. 1982. pap. 3.95 (0-486-24386-9) Dover.
—Curious George Rides a Bike. (Illus.). 48p. (gr. k-3). 1952. 12.95 (0-395-16964-X) HM.
—Curious George Rides a Bike. new ed. (Illus.). 48p. (gr. k-3). 1973. pap. 4.80 (0-395-17444-9, Sandpiper) HM.
—Curious George Takes a Job. (Illus.). 48p. (gr. k-3). 1973. 13.45 (0-395-15086-8) HM.
—Curious George Takes a Job. Rey, H. A., illus. 48p. (gr. k-3). 1974. pap. 4.80 (0-395-18649-8, Sandpiper) HM.
—Elizabite: Adventures of a Carnivorous Plant. Rey, H. A., illus. LC 90-4834. 32p. (ps-3). 1990. Repr. of 1942 ed. lib. bdg. 17.00 (0-208-02288-0, Linnet) Shoe String.
—Feed the Animals. (Illus.). 24p. (gr. k-3). 1944. pap. 2.10 (0-395-07063-5, Sandpiper) HM.
—Find the Constellations. rev. ed. (Illus.). 80p. (gr. 3-7). 1976. 16.45 (0-395-24509-5) HM.
—Find the Constellations. rev. ed. Rey, H. A., illus. 72p. (gr. 3-7). 1976. pap. 8.70 (0-395-24418-8, Sandpiper) HM.
—Jorge el Curioso. (SPA., Illus.). (gr. k-3). 1961. 13.95 (0-395-17075-3) HM.
—Jorge el Curioso. (SPA., Illus.). (ps-3). 1976. pap. 5.95 (0-395-24909-0, Sandpiper) HM.
—See the Circus. (Illus.). (gr. k-3). 1956. pap. 2.10 (0-395-07068-6, Sandpiper) HM.
—The Stars: A New Way to See Them. 3rd ed. (Illus.). (gr. 8 up). 1973. 16.45 (0-395-08121-1) HM.
—The Stars: A New Way to See Them. (gr. 4 up). 1976. pap. 9.70 (0-395-24830-2) HM.
—Where's My Baby? (Illus.). 24p. (ps-3). 1943. pap. 2.80 (0-395-07069-4, Sandpiper) HM.
Rey, H. A. & Rey, Margaret. Curious George Goes to the Hospital. (Illus.). 48p. (gr. 1-5). 1973. 12.95 (0-395-18158-5); pap. 4.80 (0-395-07062-7) HM.
Rey, H. A., jt. auth. see Rey, Margaret.
Rey, Margaret. Curious George & the Pizza. LC 85-2434. 32p. (ps-2). 1985. 8.70 (0-395-39039-7); pap. 3.80 (0-395-39033-8) HM.
Rey, Margaret & Rey, H. A. Curious George Flies a Kite. (Illus.). 80p. (gr. k-3). 1973. 12.70 (0-395-16965-8) HM.
—Curious George Flies a Kite. Rey, H. A., illus. (gr. k-3). 1977. pap. 4.80 (0-395-25937-1) HM.
Rey, Margaret & Shalleck, Alan J. Curious George & the Dinosaur. (Illus.). 32p. (ps-2). 1989. pap. 3.80 (0-395-51936-5) HM.
—Curious George at the Beach. (Illus.). 32p. (ps-2). 1988. HM.
—Curious George Bakes a Cake. (Illus.). 32p. (ps-2). 1990. HM.
—Curious George Goes Camping. (Illus.). 32p. (ps-2). 1990. HM.
—Curious George Goes to a Restaurant. (Illus.). 32p. (ps-2). 1988. HM.
—Curious George Goes to a Toy Store. (Illus.). 32p. (ps-2). 1990. HM.
—Curious George Goes to an Air Show. (Illus.). 32p. (ps-2). 1990. HM.
—Curious George Goes to School. (Illus.). 32p. (ps-2). 1989. 9.70 (0-395-51944-6); pap. 3.80 (0-395-51939-X) HM.
—Curious George Goes to School. (Illus.). (ps-3). 1990. Bk. & cass. pap. 7.95 (0-395-56483-2) HM.
—Curious George Goes to the Dentist. (Illus.). 32p. (ps-2). 1989. 9.95 (0-685-26499-8) HM.
Rey, Margaret & Shalleck, Allan J. Curious George & the Pizza. 1988. pap. 7.70 incl. cass. (0-395-48874-5) HM.
—Curious George at the Fire Station. 1988. pap. 7.70 incl. cass. (0-395-48875-3) HM.
—Curious George Visits the Zoo. 1988. pap. 7.70 incl. cass. (0-395-48876-1) HM.
Rey, Margaret, jt. auth. see Rey, H. A.
Rey, Margaret, ed. Curious George & the Dump Truck. (Illus.). 32p. (ps-2). 1984. pap. 3.80 (0-395-36629-1) HM.
—Curious George at the Fire Station. LC 85-2471. 32p. (ps-2). 1985. 9.70 (0-395-39037-0); pap. 3.80 (0-395-39031-1) HM.
—Curious George Goes to the Aquarium. (Illus.). 32p. (ps-2). 1984. 9.70 (0-395-36634-8); pap. 3.80 (0-395-36628-3) HM.
—Curious George Visits the Zoo. LC 85-2415. 32p. (ps-2). 1985. 8.70 (0-395-39036-2); pap. 3.80 (0-395-39030-3) HM.
Rey, Margaret & Shalleck, Allan J., eds. Curious George at the Airport. (Illus.). 32p. (ps-2). 1987. pap. 2.80 (0-395-45368-2) HM.
—Curious George Plays Baseball. LC 86-10609. (Illus.). 32p. (ps-2). 1986. 8.70 (0-395-39041-9); pap. 3.80 (0-395-39035-4) HM.
—Curious George Visits the Police Station. (Illus.). 32p. (ps-2). 1987. HM.
—Curious George Walks the Pets. LC 86-7470. (Illus.). 32p. (ps-2). 1986. HM.
Rey, Margret & Shalleck, Alan J. Curious George & the Dinosaur. (ps-3). 1989. 9.70 (0-395-51942-X) HM.

—Curious George & the Dinosaur. (Illus.). (ps-3). 1990. pap. 7.70 incl. cassette (0-395-56484-0, Clarion Bks) HM.
Reyero, Carlos. The Key to Art from Romanticism to Impressionism. (Illus.). 80p. (gr. 8 up). 1990. PLB 21.50 (0-8225-2058-3) Lerner Pubns.
Reyes, Gregg, jt. auth. see Hindley, Judy.
Reyher, Becky. My Mother Is the Most Beautiful Woman in the World. Gannett, Ruth, illus. 40p. (gr. k-3). 1945. PLB 14.88 (0-688-51251-8) Lothrop.
Reyhner, Jon, ed. see Holland, Royce Q., et al.
Reymond, Jean-Pierre. Metals: Born of Earth & Fire. Prunier, James, illus. LC 87-34596. 38p. (gr. k-5). 1988. 4.95 (0-944589-19-7, 197) Young Discovery Lib.
Reynolds, Alfred. Kiteman. 208p. (gr. 6 up). 1986. pap. 2.75 (0-553-26036-7, Spectra) Bantam.
Reynolds, Annette. The Christmas Baby. (Illus.). 12p. (ps-1). 1987. bds. 6.99 (0-7459-1368-7) Lion USA.
—The First Christmas Presents. (Illus.). 12p. (ps-1). 1987. bds. 6.99 (0-7459-1369-5) Lion USA.
Reynolds, Elizabeth. The Perfect Boy. 176p. (Orig.). (gr. 7-12). 1986. pap. 2.25 (0-553-25469-3) Bantam.
—Stolen Kisses. 144p. (Orig.). (gr. 7-12). 1986. pap. 2.50 (0-553-25726-9) Bantam.
Reynolds, Floria. Women at War. LC 93-4889. (Illus.). 48p. (gr. 5-9). 1993. 14.95 (1-56847-082-7) Thomson Lrning.
Reynolds, J. Down under: Vanishing Cultures. 1992. 16.95 (0-15-224182-5, HB Juv Bks); pap. 8.95 (0-15-224183-3, HB Juv Bks) HarBrace.
—Far North: Vanishing Cultures. 1992. 16.95 (0-15-227178-3, HB Juv Bks); pap. 8.95 (0-15-227179-1, HB Juv Bks) HarBrace.
Reynolds, James. Top Secret. 1987. pap. 3.50 (0-553-15733-7) Bantam.
Reynolds, James J., ed. Modern Poetry for Children, Bk. 8. LC 30-10164. (gr. 4). 1979. Repr. of 1928 ed. 15.00x (0-89609-167-8) Roth Pub Inc.
Reynolds, Jan. Amazon: Vanishing Cultures. LC 92-21089. (Illus.). 1993. 16.95 (0-15-202831-5, HB Juv Bks); pap. 8.95 (0-15-202832-3, HB Juv Bks) HarBrace.
—Frozen Land: Vanishing Cultures. LC 92-30324. 1993. write for info. (0-15-238787-0); pap. write for info. (0-15-238788-9) HarBrace.
—Himalaya Vanishing Cultures. 32p. (gr. 2 up). 1991. 16.95 (0-15-234465-9); pap. 8.95 (0-15-234466-7) HarBrace.
—Mongolia: Vanishing Cultures. LC 93-1351. (gr. 6 up). 1994. write for info. (0-15-255312-6); pap. write for info. (0-15-255313-4) HarBrace.
—Sahara Vanishing Cultures. 30p. (gr. 2 up). 1991. 16.95 (0-15-269959-7); pap. 8.95 (0-15-269958-9) HarBrace.
Reynolds, Jane L. Sing to the Earth. 84p. (gr. k-4). 1978. The Orange Book for First Chorus. 16p. write for info. (0-932320-01-5); The Yellow Book for Second Chorus. 20p. write for info. (0-932320-02-3); The Green Book for Third Chorus. 20p. write for info. (0-932320-03-1); The Blue Book for Fourth Chorus & Soloists. 24p. write for info. (0-932320-04-X); pap. write for info. (0-932320-00-7) Solar Studio.
Reynolds, Jean, ed. New Book of Knowledge. (gr. 3-8). 1989. write for info (0-7172-0520-7) Grolier Inc.
Reynolds, Jerry D., et al. What You Need to Know about Improving Basic English Skills. 256p. 1993. pap. text ed. 11.95 (0-685-62782-9, C5283-2, Natl Textbk); annotated tchr's. ed. 14.95 (0-685-62783-7, C5284-0, Natl Textbk) NTC Pub Grp.
Reynolds, Kathy, ed. Marco Polo. Woods, Dan, illus. LC 86-6678. 32p. (gr. 2-5). 1986. PLB 17.96 (0-8172-2627-3) Raintree Steck-V.
Reynolds, Lura S., jt. auth. see Naylor, Phyllis R.
Reynolds, Malvina. Magic Penny Big Book. Draper, Tani, illus. (ps-2). 1988. pap. text ed. 14.00 (0-922053-19-7) N Edge Res.
—Morningtown Ride. Leeman, Michael, illus. 20p. (ps-4). 1984. 10.95 (0-931793-00-9) Turn The Page.
—There's Music in the Air. Simmons, Elly, illus. LC 76-19261. 96p. (gr. 1-12). 1976. pap. 5.00 (0-915620-05-7) Schroder Music.
—Tweedles & Foodles for Young Noodles. Robbin, Jodi, illus. LC 73-80670. 42p. (gr. k-4). 1961. pap. 5.75 (0-915620-08-1) Schroder Music.
Reynolds, Moira. Coping with An Immigrant Parent. Rosen, Ruth, ed. (gr. 7-12). 1992. 13.95 (0-8239-1462-3) Rosen Group.
Reynolds, Moira, jt. auth. see Strazzabosco, Gina.
Reynolds, Patrick M. The Book of Silly Lists. LC 92-38660. 1993. 1.95 (0-89375-354-8, Pub. by Watermill Pr) Troll Assocs.
—Pennsylvania's Hectic Heritage. (Illus.). 56p. (gr. 7-12). 1982. pap. 3.50 (0-932514-06-5) Red Rose Studi.
—Texas Lore, Vols. 1, 2, 3, & 4. Reynolds, Patrick M., illus. 228p. (Orig.). (gr. 8-12). 1992. pap. 12.95 (0-932514-27-8) Red Rose Studio.
Reynolds, Phyllis. The Keeper. 192p. (gr. 6 up). 1987. pap. 2.95 (0-553-26882-1, Starfire) Bantam.
Reynolds, Quentin. Custer's Last Stand. LC 87-4650. (Illus.). 160p. (gr. 5-9). 1987. lib. bdg. 8.99 (0-394-90320-X) Random Bks Yng Read.
—The Wright Brothers. LC 50-11766. (Illus.). 160p. (gr. 5-9). 1981. pap. 4.99 (0-394-84700-8) Random Bks Yng Read.
Reynolds, Ralph V. The Cry of the Unborn: Understanding the Spiritual Birth Process. Jones, Jerry, frwd. by. 125p. (Orig.). Date not set. pap. 5.95 (1-877917-09-5) Alpha Bible Pubns.

—Dividing the Word of Truth. Sirstad, Raymond, frwd. by. 193p. (gr. 9). Date not set. pap. 14.95 (1-877917-08-7) Alpha Bible Pubns.
—Usando Bien la Palabra De Verdad. Geissler, Darry & Geissler, Kimberly, eds. Crossley, Darry, tr. Sirstad, Raymond, frwd. by. (SPA.). 220p. (Orig.). Date not set. pap. 14.95 (1-877917-12-5) Alpha Bible Pubns.
Reynolds, Susan L. Strandia. (Illus.). 240p. (gr. 9-12). 1991. 14.95 (0-374-37274-8) FS&G.
Reynolds, Tony. Cities in Crisis. (Illus.). 48p. (gr. 5 up). 1990. lib. bdg. 18.60 (0-86592-118-0); lib. bdg. 13.95s.p. (0-685-36376-7) Rourke Corp.
Reynolds, Tony, et al. World Issues, 2 bks. (Illus.). 336p. (gr. 5 up). 1990. Set. lib. bdg. 126.00 (0-86592-095-8); Set. lib. bdg. 94.50s.p. (0-685-36375-9) Rourke Corp.
Reynolds-Naylor, Phyllis. All Because I'm Older. (gr. k-6). 1989. pap. 2.99 (0-440-40131-3, YB) Dell.
—Beetles Lightly Toasted. (gr. k-6). 1989. pap. 3.25 (0-440-40143-7, YB) Dell.
—Night Cry. (gr. 4-7). 1993. pap. 3.50 (0-440-40017-1, YB) Dell.
—The Witch's Sister. (gr. k-6). 1993. pap. 3.50 (0-440-40028-7, B) Dell.
Reynoldson, Fiona. Conflict & Change, 1650-1800. LC 92-20460. (Illus.). 80p. (gr. 2-6). 1993. 17.95 (0-8160-2790-0) Facts on File.
Reynolds-Strauss, Karen & Gligor, Adrian. Romanian Fairy Tales. Reynolds-Strauss, Karen, illus. 85p. (Orig.). (ps-6). 1992. pap. text ed. 11.95 (0-9634797-0-9) K Strauss & A Gligor.
RGA Publishing Staff. Haunted Bronco Ranch. (Illus.). 48p. (gr. 1-4). 1993. pap. 2.95 (0-8431-3537-9) Price Stern.
—Horses & Ponies. (Illus.). 32p. (gr. 4-10). 1993. pap. 2.95 (0-8431-3538-7) Price Stern.
—Mystery of Pirate Island. 48p. (Orig.). (gr. 1-4). 1993. pap. 2.95 (0-8431-3536-0) Price Stern.
—Snakes & Lizards. (Illus.). (gr. 4-10). 1993. pap. 2.95 (0-8431-3539-5) Price Stern.
Rhea, Celeste. The Acorn Sprout & His Forest Friends. (Illus.). 23p. (Orig.). (gr. 1-4). 1978. pap. 1.00 (0-89323-010-3, 025) Bible Memory.
Rhea, John. The Department of the Air Force. (Illus.). 104p. (gr. 5 up). 1990. 14.95 (0-87754-834-X) Chelsea Hse.
Rhee, Nami. Magic Spring. (Illus.). 32p. (ps-3). 1993. PLB 14.95 (0-399-22420-3, Putnam) Putnam Pub Group.
Rhiannon, Thea, ed. see Chaney, Casey.
Rhie, Schi-Zhin. Soon-Hee in America. Rhie, Schi-Zhin, illus. LC 77-81780. 36p. (gr. k-3). 1977. PLB 6.50x (0-930878-00-0) Hollym Intl.
Rhijn, Patricia Van see Van Rhijn, Patricia.
Rhind, Mary. The Dark Shadow. (Illus.). 128p. (gr. 5-9). 1990. pap. 6.95 (0-86241-253-6, Pub. by Cnngt Pub Ltd) Trafalgar.
Rhoades, Jacqueline & McCabe, Margaret E. Simple Cooperation in the Classroom. Feingold, S. Norman. (Illus.). 165p. (Orig.). (ps up). 1985. pap. 15.95 (0-933935-07-2) ITA Pubns.
Rhoades, Jacqueline, jt. auth. see McCabe, Margaret E.
Rhoads, Dorothy. The Corn Grows Ripe. Charlot, Jean, illus. LC 92-24888. (gr. 8-12). 1993. 4.99 (0-14-036313-0, Puffin) Puffin Bks.
Rhoda, Michael D. Bible Favorites Acitvty Book. Gress, Jonna, ed. (Illus.). 6p. (ps-5). 1994. pap. 8.25 (0-944943-41-1, 22656-1) Current Inc.
Rhodes, Bennie. Christopher Columbus. Smith, A. G. & Smith, A. G., illus. LC 76-5788. (gr. 3-6). 1977. pap. 6.95 (0-915134-26-8) Mott Media.
Rhodes, Frank H., et al. Fossils. Perlman, Raymond, illus. (gr. 6 up). 1962. PLB write for info. (0-307-63515-5); pap. write for info. (0-307-24411-3, Golden Pr) Western Pub.
—Fossils: A Golden Guide. rev. ed. Perlman, Raymond, illus. 1990. pap. write for info. (Golden Pr) Western Pub.
Rhodes, Gregory L., jt. ed. see Regina, Karen.
Rhodes, Janis, jt. auth. see McClure, Nancee.
Rhodes, Judy C. The Hunter's Heart. LC 92-47025. 1993. write for info. (0-02-773935-X, Bradbury Pr) Macmillan Child Grp.
—The Hunter's Heart. LC 92-47025. 160p. (gr. 4-7). 1993. pap. 13.95 SBE (0-02-775935-0, Bradbury Pr) Macmillan Child Grp.
—The King Boy. LC 91-2159. 160p. (gr. 5-9). 1991. SBE 14.95 (0-02-776115-0, Bradbury Pr) Macmillan Child Grp.
Rhodes, Timothy, jt. auth. see Czernecki, Stefan.
Rhodes, Timothy, jt. auth. see Szernecki, Stefan.
Rhoton, Jessian L. The Magic Treble Tree. Erickson, Cindy R., illus. 48p. 1989. PLB write for info. Happy Music Pub.
—The Magic Treble Tree. Erickson, Cindy R., illus. 48p. 1990. write for info. (0-9624162-9-0) Happy Music Pub.
Rhue, Morton. The Wave. LC 81-70394. 144p. (gr. 7 up). 1981. 10.95 (0-440-09822-X) Delacorte.
—The Wave. 143p. (gr. 7 up). 1981. pap. 3.99 (0-440-99371-7, LFL); tchr's. guide by Lou Stanek 0.50 (0-685-01416-9) Dell.
Rhyne, Nancy. The South Carolina Lizard Man. Magellan, Mauro, illus. LC 92-17289. 128p. (gr. 5-9). 1992. pap. 7.95 (0-88289-907-4) Pelican.
Rhys, Ernest, jt. auth. see Daglish, Alice.
Ribaroff, Margaret, ed. see Rierden, Anne B.
Ricardo-Gil, Jose, ed. see Saloom, Barbara B.

Ricchiuti, Paul. Rocky & Me. (ps-3). 1990. pap. 5.95 (*0-8163-0898-5*) Pacific Pr Pub Assn.

Ricchiuti, Paul B. Ellen: Trial & Triumph on the American Frontier. LC 76-44051. 160p. (gr. 6 up). 1988. pap. 7.95 (*0-945460-03-1*) Upward Way.

—The End-of-the-World-Man & Other Stories. Woolsey, Raymond H., ed. 96p. (gr. 8). 1989. pap. 6.95 (*0-8280-0458-7*) Review & Herald.

Ricci, Ralph V. Multiple Choice Questions in Preparation for the AP Biology Examination. 2nd ed. 115p. (gr. 11-12). 1991. wkbk. 15.95 (*1-878621-12-2*); tchr's. manual, 71p. avail. (*1-878621-13-0*) D & S Mktg Syst.

Ricciuti, Edward. Amphibians. (Illus.). 64p. (gr. 4-8). 1993. PLB 16.95 (*1-56711-045-2*) Blackbirch.

—Birds. (Illus.). 64p. (gr. 4-8). 1993. PLB 16.95 (*1-56711-038-X*) Blackbirch.

—Birds. Simpson, Bill, illus. 64p. (gr. 4-8). 1993. jacketed 14.95 (*1-56711-053-3*) Blackbirch.

—Crustacea. (Illus.). 64p. (gr. 4-8). 1994. PLB 16.95 (*1-56711-046-0*) Blackbirch.

—Fish. (Illus.). 64p. (gr. 4-8). 1993. PLB 16.95 (*1-56711-041-X*) Blackbirch.

—Fish. Simpson, Bill, illus. 64p. (gr. 4-8). 1993. jacketed 14.95 (*1-56711-056-8*) Blackbirch.

—The Our Living World Resource Guide & Reference. (Illus.). 64p. (gr. 4-8). 1994. PLB 16.95 (*1-56711-057-6*) Blackbirch.

—Patterns in Nature. (Illus.). 64p. (gr. 4-8). 1994. PLB 16.95 (*1-56711-058-4*) Blackbirch.

—Reptiles. (Illus.). 64p. (gr. 4-8). 1993. PLB 16.95 (*1-56711-047-9*) Blackbirch.

—Reptiles. (Illus.). 64p. (gr. 3-7). 1993. 14.95 (*1-56711-063-0*) Blackbirch.

—The Unseen World. (Illus.). 64p. (gr. 4-8). 1994. PLB 16.95 (*1-56711-040-1*) Blackbirch.

Ricciuti, Edward & Tesar, Jenny. Our Living World, 14 vols. (Illus.). (gr. 4-8). Set. PLB 237.30 (*1-56711-036-3*) Blackbirch.

Ricciuti, Edward R. Somalia: A Crisis of Famine & War. LC 93-15094. (Illus.). 64p. (gr. 5-8). 1993. PLB 15.90 (*1-56294-376-6*) Millbrook Pr.

—War in Yugoslavia: The Breakup of a Nation. LC 92-32126. (Illus.). 64p. (gr. 5-8). 1993. PLB 15.90 (*1-56294-375-8*) Millbrook Pr.

Rice, jt. auth. see Bragger.

Rice, Alice H. Mrs. Wiggs of the Cabbage Patch. 1992. Repr. lib. bdg. 19.95x (*0-89968-273-1*) Lightyear.

Rice, Bebe F. Class Trip. 1993. pap. 3.50 (*0-06-106731-8*, Harp PBks) HarpC.

—My Sister, My Sorrow. 1992. pap. 3.50 (*0-440-21296-0*) Dell.

Rice, Cheryl F., jt. auth. see Cerbus, Deborah P.

Rice, Chris, jt. auth. see Rice, Melanie.

Rice, Eve. Aren't You Coming Too? Parker, Nancy W., illus. LC 86-33506. 32p. (ps-3). 1988. 11.95 (*0-688-06446-9*); lib. bdg. 11.88 (*0-688-06447-7*) Greenwillow.

—At Grammy's House. LC 89-34617. (Illus.). 32p. (ps up). 1990. 12.95 (*0-688-08874-0*); lib. bdg. 12.88 (*0-688-08875-9*) Greenwillow.

—Benny Bakes a Cake. LC 80-17313. (Illus.). 32p. (gr. k-3). 1981. write for info. (*0-688-80312-1*); PLB write for info. (*0-688-84312-3*) Greenwillow.

—Benny Bakes a Cake. LC 80-17313. (Illus.). 32p. (ps-3). 1993. pap. 4.95 (*0-688-07814-1*, Mulberry) Morrow.

—Benny Bakes a Cake. reissued ed. LC 80-17313. 32p. (ps-3). 1993. 14.00 (*0-688-11579-9*); PLB 13.93 (*0-688-11580-2*) Greenwillow.

—City Night. Sis, Peter, illus. 24p. (ps-1). 1987. 11.75 (*0-688-06856-1*); PLB 11.88 (*0-688-06857-X*) Greenwillow.

—Goodnight, Goodnight. LC 79-17253. (Illus.). (ps-1). 1980. 13.95 (*0-688-80254-0*); PLB 13.88 (*0-688-84254-2*) Greenwillow.

—Goodnight, Goodnight. ALC Staff, ed. LC 79-17253. (Illus.). 40p. (ps up) 1992. pap. 3.95 (*0-688-11707-4*, Mulberry) Morrow.

—Oh, Lewis! LC 73-19057. (Illus.). 32p. (ps-k). 1987. Repr. of 1974 ed. RSBE 12.95 (*0-02-775990-3*, Macmillan Child Bk) Macmillan Child Grp.

—Oh, Lewis! Rice, Eve, illus. LC 92-24584. 32p. 1993. pap. 4.95 (*0-688-11790-2*, Mulberry) Morrow.

—Once in a Wood. LC 78-16294. (Illus.). 64p. 1979. PLB 13.93 (*0-688-84191-0*) Greenwillow.

—Peter's Pockets. Parker, Nancy W., illus. LC 87-15640. 32p. (ps up). 1989. 16.95 (*0-688-07241-0*); PLB 14.88 (*0-688-07242-9*) Greenwillow.

—Sam Who Never Forgets. LC 76-30370. 32p. (ps-3). 1977. PLB 13.88 (*0-688-84088-4*) Greenwillow.

—Sam Who Never Forgets. LC 76-30370. (ps-3). 1987. pap. 3.95 (*0-688-07335-2*, Mulberry) Morrow.

—What Sadie Sang. (ps). 1983. 11.95 (*0-688-02179-4*) Greenwillow.

Rice, Eve, adapted by. & illus. Once in a Wood: Ten Tales from Aesop. LC 92-24605. 64p. (gr. 1 up). 1993. pap. 4.95 (*0-688-12268-X*, Mulberry) Morrow.

Rice, Helen S. The Story of the Christmas Guest. (Illus.). 34p. 1991. pap. 9.95x (*0-89966-842-9*) Buccaneer Bks.

Rice, James. Cajun Alphabet: Full-Color Edition. LC 90-39342. (Illus.). 32p. (ps-8). 1991. 16.95 (*0-88289-822-1*) Pelican.

—Cajun Night Before Christmas Coloring Book. 32p. (gr. k-4). 1976. pap. 2.75 (*0-88289-138-3*) Pelican.

—Cowboy Night Before Christmas. LC 90-7280. (Illus.). 32p. (ps-4). 1986. Repr. of 1986 ed. 12.95 (*0-88289-811-6*) Pelican.

—Cowboy Rodeo. Rice, James, illus. LC 91-34924. 32p. 1992. 14.95 (*0-88289-903-1*) Pelican.

—Gaston Drills an Offshore Oil Well. Rice, James, illus. LC 82-11240. 48p. (gr. 1-6). 1982. Pelican.

—Gaston Goes to Mardi Gras. LC 77-13302. (Illus.). 40p. (gr. 1-6). 1977. 12.95 (*0-88289-158-8*) Pelican.

—Gaston Goes to Nashville. Rice, James, illus. LC 85-6605. 32p. (gr. 1-6). 1985. 12.95 (*0-88289-477-3*) Pelican.

—Gaston Goes to Texas. Rice, James, illus. LC 78-12490. 32p. (gr. 1-6). 1978. 12.95 (*0-88289-204-5*) Pelican.

—Gaston Lays an Offshore Pipeline. LC 79-20335. (Illus.). (gr. 1-6). 1979. 12.95 (*0-88289-177-4*) Pelican.

—Gaston the Green-Nosed Alligator. (Illus.). 40p. (gr. 1-6). 1974. 12.95 (*0-88289-049-2*) Pelican.

—Gaston the Green-Nosed Alligator Coloring Book. Rice, James, illus. 32p. (gr. 1-6). 1976. pap. 2.75 (*0-88289-139-1*) Pelican.

—Lyn & the Fuzzy. Rice, James, illus. LC 75-19096. 40p. (gr. 2-6). 1975. 12.95 (*0-88289-087-5*) Pelican.

—La Nochebuena South of the Border. Smith, Ana, tr. Rice, James, illus. LC 93-13002. (ENG & SPA.). 32p. (gr. k-3). 1993. 14.95 (*0-88289-966-X*) Pelican.

—Texas Alphabet. Rice, James, illus. LC 87-31159. 132p. (gr. k-5). 1988. 12.95 (*0-88289-692-X*) Pelican.

—Texas Jack at the Alamo. Rice, James, illus. LC 88-31691. 40p. 1989. 12.95 (*0-88289-725-X*) Pelican.

—Texas Night Before Christmas. Rice, James, illus. LC 86-9445. 32p. (gr. 1-6). 1986. 12.95 (*0-88289-603-2*) Pelican.

—Texas Night Before Christmas: Coloring Book. Rice, James, illus. 1989. pap. 2.75 (*0-88289-727-6*) Pelican.

Rice, James, illus. Cowboy Alphabet. 40p. (gr. k-4). 1983. 10.95 (*0-88289-427-7*) Pelican.

Rice, James, illus. & retold by see Dickens, Charles.

Rice, Judith A. Those Mean Nasty Dirty Downright Disgusting but...Invisible Germs. Merrill, Reed, illus. Gwaltney, Jack M., Jr. LC 89-34409. (Illus.). 32p. (Orig.). (ps-3). 1989. pap. 7.95 (*0-934140-46-4*) Redleaf Pr.

Rice, Karen. Does Candy Grow on Trees? Cohen, Sharon, illus. LC 83-40407. 32p. (gr. 2-5). 1984. 9.95 (*0-8027-6555-6*) Walker & Co.

Rice, Mel C. All about Our World. 1989. 10.95 (*0-385-24819-9*); PLB 11.99 (*0-385-24820-2*) Doubleday.

Rice, Melanie. The Complete Book of Children's Activities. LC 92-30859. 1993. pap. 9.95 (*1-85697-907-5*) Kingfisher Bks.

Rice, Melanie & Rice, Chris. All About Me. Smith, Lesley, illus. LC 87-15498. 48p. (ps-3). 1988. PLB 11.99 (*0-385-24282-4*); pap. 10.95 (*0-385-24281-6*) Doubleday.

Rice, Peter L. Frost Death. Ippolito, Donna, ed. (Illus.). 272p. (Orig.). (gr. 7 up). 1991. pap. 7.95 (*1-55560-140-5*) FASA Corp.

Rice, Russell. Big Blue Machine: Kentucky Basketball. rev. ed. (Illus.). 492p. (gr. 6-12). 1988. 18.95 (*0-87397-306-2*) Strode.

Rice, Tim & Webber, Andrew L. Joseph & the Amazing Technicolor Dreamcoat. Blake, Quentin, illus. 32p. (gr. k-3). 1993. pap. 11.95 (*1-85793-119-X*, Pub. by Pavilion UK) Trafalgar.

Rice, Tony. Ocean World. (Illus.). 64p. (gr. 4-6). 1991. 14.90 (*1-56294-027-9*) Millbrook Pr.

Rice, Wayne. Great Ideas for Small Youth Groups. 256p. (Orig.). (gr. 7-12). 1986. pap. 9.99 (*0-310-34891-9*, 10823P) Zondervan.

Rice, Wayne & Yaconelli, Mike. Creative Activities for Small Youth Groups. Stamschror, Robert P., ed. Youth Specialities Clip Art Staff, illus. 101p. (gr. 7-12). 1991. pap. 12.95 (*0-88489-264-6*) St Marys.

—Creative Communication & Discussion Activities. Stamschror, Robert P., ed. Youth Specialties Clip Art Staff, illus. 96p. (gr. 7-12). 1991. pap. 12.95 (*0-88489-266-2*) St Marys.

—Creative Crowdbreakers, Mixers, & Games. Stamschror, Robert P., ed. Youth Specialties Clip Art Staff, illus. 96p. (gr. 7-12). 1991. pap. 12.95 (*0-88489-265-4*) St Marys.

—The Greatest Skits on Earth. 288p. (Orig.). (gr. 3-7). 1986. pap. 10.99 (*0-310-35141-3*, 10775P) Zondervan.

Rice, Wayne, ed. Ideas Combo Edition 33-36, 4 bks. in 1. (Illus.). 192p. (Orig.). 1988. pap. 19.95 (*0-910125-33-3*) Youth Special.

—One Hundred Ten Tips, Time-Savers & Tricks of the Trade for Youth Workers. Pagaard, Tim, illus. (Illus.). 72p. (Orig.). 1984. pap. 5.95 (*0-910125-04-X*) Youth Special.

Rice, Wayne & McLaughlin, Tim, eds. Ideas Combo Edition 41-44, 4 bks. in 1. Suggs, Robert, illus. 200p. (Orig.). 1988. pap. 19.95 (*0-910125-35-X*) Youth Special.

—Ideas Combo Edition 45-48, 4 bks. in 1. (Illus.). 208p. (Orig.). 1992. pap. 19.95 (*0-910125-36-8*) Youth Special.

—Ideas Combo Edition 49-52, 4 bks. in 1. (Illus.). 192p. (Orig.). 1992. pap. 19.95 (*0-910125-37-6*) Youth Special.

Rice, Wayne & Thigpen, Paul, eds. Ideas Combo Edition 37-40, 4 bks. in 1. Hillam, Corbin, illus. 200p. (Orig.). 1990. pap. 19.95 (*0-910125-34-1*) Youth Special.

Rice, Wayne & Yaconelli, Mike, eds. Ideas Combo Edition 1-4, 4 bks. in 1. (Illus.). 192p. (Orig.). 1979. pap. 19.95 (*0-910125-25-2*) Youth Special.

—Ideas Combo Edition 13-16, 4 bks. in 1. (Illus.). 208p. (Orig.). 1981. pap. 19.95 (*0-910125-28-7*) Youth Special.

—Ideas Combo Edition 17-20, 4 bks. in 1. (Illus.). 206p. (Orig.). 1981. pap. 19.95 (*0-910125-29-5*) Youth Special.

—Ideas Combo Edition 21-24, 4 bks. in 1. (Illus.). 200p. (Orig.). 1984. pap. 19.95 (*0-910125-30-9*) Youth Special.

—Ideas Combo Edition 25-28, 4 bks. in 1. (Illus.). 208p. (Orig.). 1985. pap. 19.95 (*0-910125-31-7*) Youth Special.

—Ideas Combo Edition 29-32, 4 bks. in 1. (Illus.). 200p. (Orig.). 1987. pap. 19.95 (*0-910125-32-5*) Youth Special.

—Ideas Combo Edition 5-8, 4 bks. in 1. (Illus.). 176p. (Orig.). 1984. pap. 19.95 (*0-910125-26-0*) Youth Special.

—Ideas Combo Edition 9-12, 4 bks. in 1. Pegoda, Dan & Wilson, Craig, illus. 180p. (Orig.). 1980. pap. 19.95 (*0-910125-27-9*) Youth Special.

Rich, Beatrice. ABCDEFGHIJKLMNOPQRSTUVWXYZ in English & French. LC 81-20838. (Illus.). 64p. (gr. k-2). 1983. PLB 14.95 (*0-87460-353-6*) Lion Bks.

Rich, Beverly. Louis Braille: Inventor of a Way to Read & Write That Has Helped Millions of Blind People Communicate with the World. LC 89-4275. (Illus.). 64p. (gr. 5-6). 1989. PLB 18.60 (*0-8368-0097-4*) Gareth Stevens Inc.

—Louis Pasteur: The Scientist Who Found the Cause of Infectious Disease & Invented Pasteurization. LC 88-24867. (Illus.). 64p. (gr. 5-6). 1989. PLB 18.60 (*1-55532-839-3*) Gareth Stevens Inc.

Rich, Chris. The Book of Papercutting: A Complete Guide to All the Techniques with More Than 100 Project Ideas. LC 92-21536. (Illus.). 128p. (gr. 10-12). 1993. 21.95 (*0-8069-0285-X*, Pub. by Lark Bks) Sterling.

Rich, George. Common Bible Questions of Our Day. (Orig.). 1991. pap. text ed. 1.75 study guide, 32p. (*0-87227-160-9*); leader's guide, 24p. 1.75 (*0-87227-164-1*) Reg Baptist.

—Famous Interviews with Jesus Christ. (gr. 6 up). 1991. pap. text ed. 1.75 study guide, 32p. (*0-87227-157-9*); leader's guide, 24p. 1.75 (*0-87227-165-X*) Reg Baptist.

Rich, Jason. Celebrity Teen Talk: Exclusive Celebrity Interviews, Video Game Tips & Reviews. (Illus.). 224p. (Orig.). (gr. 4-12). 1991. pap. 6.95 (*0-9625057-5-7*) DMS ID.

Rich, Mary P., ed. see Brown, Fern G.

Rich, Mary P., ed. see Mactire, Sean P.

Rich, Mary P., ed. see Myers, Arthur.

Rich, Mary P., ed. see Quiri, Patricia R.

Rich, Mary P., ed. see Reische, Diana.

Rich, Mary P., ed. see Reiser, Howard.

Rich, Mary P., ed. see Van Steenwyk, Elizabeth.

Rich, Mary P., ed. see Wolfe, Rinna E.

Rich, Ruth & D'Onofrio, Carol N. Decisions for Health. (Illus.). 488p. (gr. 9-12). 1993. text ed. 27.50 (*1-56269-053-1*); tchr's. manual, 520p. 39.25 (*1-56269-054-X*); Total tchr. support system. 208.75 (*1-56269-055-8*); write for info. audio pkg. (*1-56269-092-2*) Educ Assess Pub.

Rich, Sheila. Fun & Fitness: A Step-by-Step Guide. LC 89-27393. (Illus.). 64p. (gr. 4-8). 1990. PLB 9.79 (*0-8167-1949-7*); pap. text ed. 2.95 (*0-8167-1950-0*) Troll Assocs.

Richard, Christopher. Brazil. LC 90-22471. (Illus.). 128p. (gr. 5-9). 1991. PLB 21.95 (*1-85435-382-9*) Marshall Cavendish.

Richard, Francoise. On Cat Mountain. Levine, Arthur A., adapted by. Buguet, Anne, illus. LC 93-11408. 1994. write for info. (*0-399-22608-7*, Putnam) Putnam Pub Group.

Richard-Amato, Patricia A. Reading in the Content Areas: An Interactive Approach for Advanced Students. 1990. pap. text ed. 18.95 (*0-8013-0247-1*, 75902) Longman.

Richards, Arlene K. & Willis, Irene. How to Get It Together When Your Parents Are Coming Apart. 170p. (gr. 5-12). 1986. pap. 9.95x (*0-9615349-0-7*, HQ536.R48) Willard Pr.

—What to Do If You Or Someone You Know Is under 18 & Pregnant. LC 82-12698. (Illus.). 256p. 1983. pap. 8.95 (*0-688-01044-X*, Pub. by Beech Tree Bks) Morrow.

Richards, Dorothy F. Christopher Columbus, Who Sailed on! Nelson, John, illus. LC 78-7664. (gr. k-4). 1978. PLB 19.95 (*0-89565-032-0*); PLB 13.95s.p. (*0-685-55476-7*) Childs World.

—George Washington, a Talk with His Grandchildren. Nelson, John, illus. LC 78-8564. (gr. k-4). 1978. PLB 19.95 (*0-89565-034-7*); PLB 13.95s.p. (*0-685-55482-1*) Childs World.

—Marty Finds a Treasure. Karch, Paul, illus. LC 82-19906. 32p. (gr. 3-4). 1983. lib. bdg. 8.45 (*0-89565-251-X*) Childs World.

—Pocahontas, Child-Princess. Nelson, John, illus. LC 78-7719. (gr. k-4). 1978. PLB 19.95 (*0-89565-035-5*); PLB 13.95s.p. (*0-685-57685-X*) Childs World.

Richards, Dorothy S. The World of Cats. (Illus.). 64p. 1989. 7.99 (*0-517-69085-3*) Outlet Bk Co.

Richards, Elspeth & Fernyhough, Frances. Fun with Numbers. Kerr, Angela, illus. 64p. (gr. k-3). 1987. pap. 2.95 (*0-385-23844-4*, Zephyr-BFYR) Doubleday.

Richards, Ernie S., ed. see Weller, Robert F.

Richards, Gregory. Jim Thorpe: World's Greatest Athlete. LC 84-14240. (Illus.). 112p. (gr. 4 up). 1984. PLB 18.60 (*0-516-03207-0*) Childrens.

Richards, H. J. The Creed for Children. 28p. (Orig.). 1991. pap. 2.95 (*0-8146-2037-X*) Liturgical Pr.
—The Mass for Children. 28p. (Orig.). 1991. pap. 2.95 (*0-8146-2038-8*) Liturgical Pr.
Richards, Ivor A. Philosophy of Rhetoric. (gr. 9 up). 1965. pap. 7.95 (*0-19-500715-8*) OUP.
Richards, Ivor A., ed. see Coleridge, Samuel Taylor.
Richards, Jack & Richards, John. Piney the Tiny Christmas Tree. O'Neal, Marian, illus. 21p. (gr. k-5). 1993. 4.95 (*1-883025-00-1,* Piney Pubns); pap. 9.95 talking bk. cass. (*1-883025-01-X,* Piney Pubns); pap. 12.95 cass. & bk. (*1-883025-02-8*); pap. 14.95 video (*1-883025-03-6*); pap. 24.95 video, cass. & bk. (*1-883025-04-4*) Piney Prods.
Richards, Jean, retold by. God's Gift. Gorbaty, Norman, illus. LC 92-38265. 1993. pap. 15.95 (*0-385-31092-7,* Zephyr-BFYR) Doubleday.
Richards, Joanne & Standley, Marianne V. Dealing with Feelings. 72p. (gr. 3-7). 1982. 7.95 (*0-88160-015-6,* LW 118) Learning Wks.
Richards, Joanne & Standley, Marianne. One for the Books. (Illus.). 128p. (gr. 4-6). 1984. pap. text ed. 8.95 (*0-86530-023-2,* IP 23-2) Incentive Pubns.
—Write Here. (Illus.). 80p. (gr. 3-6). 1984. pap. text ed. 7.95 (*0-86530-013-5,* IP 13-5) Incentive Pubns.
Richards, Joanne, jt. auth. see Standley, Marianne.
Richards, John. Hidden Country: Nature on Your Doorstep. LC 72-12745. (Illus.). 144p. (gr. 5-8). 1973. PLB 21.95 (*0-87599-195-5*) S G Phillips.
Richards, John, jt. auth. see Richards, Jack.
Richards, Kelly F. Merry Christmas! Kopper, Lisa, illus. LC 90-83243. 24p. (ps-3). 1991. 2.50 (*0-448-40125-8,* G&D) Putnam Pub Group.
Richards, Kenneth G. The Gettysburg Address. LC 91-43371. (Illus.). 32p. (gr. 3-6). 1992. PLB 15.27 (*0-516-06654-4*) Childrens.
—The Gettysburg Address. LC 91-43371. (Illus.). 32p. (gr. 3-6). 1993. pap. 3.95 (*0-516-46654-2*) Childrens.
Richards, Larry. It Couldn't Just Happen. 191p. (gr. 2-7). 1989. write for info. (*0-8499-0715-2*) Word Inc.
Richards, Norman. Dreamers & Doers: Inventors Who Changed the World. LC 81-21029. (Illus.). 156p. (gr. 5 up). 1984. SBE 13.95 (*0-689-30914-7,* Atheneum Child Bk) Macmillan Child Grp.
—Story of Old Ironsides. Dunnington, Tom, illus. LC 67-20099. 32p. (gr. 3-6). 1967. pap. 3.95 (*0-516-44628-2*) Childrens.
—The Story of the Alamo. LC 70-100698. (Illus.). 32p. (gr. 3-6). 1970. 13.27 (*0-516-04601-2*); pap. 3.95 (*0-516-44601-0*) Childrens.
—The Story of the Declaration of Independence. LC 68-24379. (Illus.). 32p. (gr. 3-6). 1968. pap. 3.95 (*0-516-44606-1*) Childrens.
—The Story of the Mayflower Compact. Wiskur, Darrell, illus. LC 67-22901. 32p. (gr. 3-6). 1967. pap. 3.95 (*0-516-44625-8*) Childrens.
Richards, R. W. Brothers in Gray. Boart, Jeff, ed. (Illus.). 313p. 1993. pap. 12.95 (*0-9625502-1-3*) RoKarn Pubns.
—A Southern Yarn. Bogart, Jeffrey, ed. Willard-Chang, Nancy, illus. LC 89-92811. (Orig.). 1990. pap. write for info. (*0-9625502-0-5*) Rokarn Pubns.
Richards, Roy. One Hundred One Science Surprises: Exciting Experiments with Everyday Materials. Pang, Alex, illus. LC 92-32491. 104p. 1993. 14.95 (*0-8069-8822-3*) Sterling.
—One Hundred-One Science Tricks: Fun Experiments with Everyday Materials. LC 91-13263. (Illus.). 104p. (gr. 3-10). 1991. 14.95 (*0-8069-8388-4*) Sterling.
—One Hundred One Science Tricks: Fun Experiments with Everyday Materials. (Illus.). 104p. (gr. 4-10). 1993. pap. 9.95 (*0-8069-8389-2*) Sterling.
Richards, Selena. Rebecca Goes Out. Dubin, Jill, illus. 18p. (ps). 1992. 3.50 (*1-56288-269-4*) Checkerboard.
—Rebecca Goes to the Country. Dubin, Jill, illus. 18p. (ps). 1992. 3.50 (*1-56288-270-8*) Checkerboard.
—Rebecca Goes to the Park. Dubin, Jill, illus. 18p. (ps). 1992. 3.50 (*1-56288-271-6*) Checkerboard.
—Rebecca's Rainy Day. Dubin, Jill, illus. 18p. (ps). 1992. 3.50 (*1-56288-272-4*) Checkerboard.
Richardson, Allen F. Sports. Colton, Kitty, ed. Schmidt, Peggy, contrib. by. LC 93-4488. 96p. (gr. 10-12). 1993. pap. 7.95 (*1-56079-250-7*) Petersons Guides.
Richardson, Arleta. Andrew's Secret. Payne, Peggy & Yoder, Tamra, eds. Secaur, Emiline, illus. 30p. (Orig.). (gr. 1-3). 1989. pap. 3.00 (*0-89367-143-6*) Light & Life.
—At Home in North Branch. LC 88-9529. (gr. 3-7). 1988. pap. 3.99 (*1-55513-312-6,* Chariot Bks) Cook.
—Eighteen & on Her Own. LC 85-29050. 173p. (gr. 3-7). 1986. pap. 3.99 (*0-89191-512-5,* Chariot Bks) Cook.
—The Grandma's Attic Storybook. LC 92-33823. 1993. write for info. (*0-7814-0070-8*) Cook.
—A Heart for God in India. Payne, Peggy & Yoder, Tamra, eds. Ortega, Jennifer, illus. 52p. (Orig.). (gr. 4-6). 1989. pap. 4.00 (*0-89367-144-4*) Light & Life.
—In Grandma's Attic. LC 74-75541. 112p. (Orig.). (gr. 3-7). 1974. pap. 3.99 (*0-912692-32-4,* Chariot Bks) Cook.
—Looking for Home. LC 92-46259. 1993. write for info. (*0-7814-0921-7,* Chariot Bks) Cook.
—More Stories from Grandma's Attic. LC 78-73125. (Illus.). (gr. 3-7). 1979. pap. 3.99 (*0-89191-131-6,* Chariot Bks) Cook.
—New Faces, New Friends. (gr. 3-7). 1989. pap. 3.99 (*1-55513-985-X,* Chariot Bks) Cook.
—Sixteen & Away from Home. (gr. 3-7). 1985. pap. 3.99 (*0-89191-933-3,* 59337, Chariot Bks) Cook.

—Still More Stories from Grandma's Attic. (gr. 3-7). 1981. pap. 3.99 (*0-89191-252-5,* Chariot Bks) Cook.
—Stories from the Growing Years. (gr. 3-7). 1991. pap. 3.99 (*1-55513-819-5,* 38190, Chariot Bks) Cook.
—Treasures from Grandma's Attic. (gr. 3-7). 1984. pap. 3.99 (*0-89191-934-1,* 59345, Chariot Bks) Cook.
—Whistle-Stop West. LC 92-46260. 1993. write for info. (*0-7814-0922-5,* Chariot Bks) Cook.
Richardson, Ben & Foley, William A. Great Black Americans. LC 75-12841. (Illus.). 352p. (gr. 7 up). 1990. PLB 17.89 (*0-690-04791-6,* Crowell Jr Bks) HarpC Child Bks.
Richardson, Bob, jt. auth. see Richardson, Peter.
Richardson, Dawn. Smoke. 112p. (gr. 9-12). 1985. 7.95 (*0-920806-73-2,* Pub. by Penumbra Pr CN) U of Toronto Pr.
Richardson, Debbie, et al. Language Quicktionary Instruction Manual: A QuickDraw Game for Vocabulary Growth. (gr. 3-12). 1990. 29.95 (*1-55999-107-0*) LinguiSystems.
Richardson, Delores. Can You Dig It? Waldron, Sarah M., illus. 20p. (gr. 3-7). 1990. write for info. (*0-9619482-9-9*) Little Spirit.
Richardson, Frederick, illus. Great Children's Stories: Classic Volland Edition. Hunt, Irene, intro. by. LC 72-83891. (Illus.). 160p. (ps-3). 1938. 12.95 (*1-56288-040-3*) Checkerboard.
—Mother Goose. Classic Volland ed. Grover, Eulalie O., intro. by. LC 72-161577. (Illus.). 160p. (ps-4). 1915. 12.95 (*1-56288-254-6*) Checkerboard.
—Mother Goose: The Original Volland Edition. 128p. (gr. k up). 1985. 8.99 (*0-517-43619-1*) Outlet Bk Co.
Richardson, Freida. Madagascar's Miracle Story. Richardson, Jerry, intros. by. LC 89-32335. (Illus.). 156p. (Orig.). 1989. pap. 6.99 (*0-932581-47-1*) Word Aflame.
Richardson, Gale T. Serenity, Courage & Wisdom. 2p. (ps). 1989. 3.50 (*0-9614337-2-8*) Poetry Unltd.
—The Wings. (gr. 9-12). 1989. write for info. (*0-9614337-4-4*) Poetry Unltd.
Richardson, I. M. The Adventures of Eros & Psyche. Baxter, Robert, illus. LC 82-16057. 32p. (gr. 4-8). 1983. PLB 11.79 (*0-89375-861-2*); pap. text ed. 2.95 (*0-89375-862-0*) Troll Assocs.
—The Adventures of Hercules. Baxter, Robert, illus. LC 82-16557. 32p. (gr. 4-8). 1983. PLB 11.79 (*0-89375-865-5*); pap. text ed. 2.95 (*0-89375-866-3*) Troll Assocs.
—Demeter & Persephone: The Seasons of Time. Baxter, Robert, illus. LC 82-16023. 32p. (gr. 4-8). 1983. PLB 11.79 (*0-89375-863-9*); pap. text ed. 2.95 (*0-89375-864-7*) Troll Assocs.
—Prometheus & the Story of Fire. Baxter, Robert, illus. LC 82-15979. 32p. (gr. 4-8). 1983. PLB 11.79 (*0-89375-859-0*); pap. text ed. 2.95 (*0-89375-860-4*) Troll Assocs.
—Story of the Christmas Rose. De Kiefte, Kees, illus. LC 87-13817. 32p. (gr. k-4). 1988. PLB 9.79 (*0-8167-1069-4*); pap. text ed. 1.95 (*0-8167-1070-8*) Troll Assocs.
Richardson, I. M., ed. see Dickens, Charles.
Richardson, I. M., ed. see Grahame, Kenneth.
Richardson, I. M., ed. see Grimm, Jacob & Grimm, Wilhelm K.
Richardson, I. M., adapted by see Homer.
Richardson, Jack, jt. auth. see Richardson, Wendy.
Richardson, James. Science Dictionary of Animals. Quinn, Kaye, illus. LC 91-18826. 48p. (gr. 3-7). 1992. lib. bdg. 11.59 (*0-8167-2521-7*); pap. 3.95 (*0-8167-2440-7*) Troll Assocs.
—Science Dictionary of Dinosaurs. Quinn, Kaye, illus. LC 91-4110. 48p. (gr. 3-7). 1992. lib. bdg. 11.59 (*0-8167-2522-5*); pap. 3.95 (*0-8167-2441-5*) Troll Assocs.
—Science Dictionary of Space. Hunt, Joseph, illus. LC 91-16551. 48p. (gr. 3-7). 1992. lib. bdg. 11.59 (*0-8167-2524-1*); pap. 3.95 (*0-8167-2443-1*) Troll Assocs.
—Science Dictionary of the Human Body. Hung, Gil, illus. LC 91-19162. 48p. (gr. 3-7). 1992. lib. bdg. 11.59 (*0-8167-2523-3*); pap. 3.95 (*0-8167-2442-3*) Troll Assocs.

Richardson, Jean. The Courage Seed. Finney, Pat, illus. LC 93-20182. 76p. (gr. 3-6). 1993. 14.95 (*0-89015-902-5*) Eakin-Sunbelt.
Mary Manygoats is a Navajo girl orphaned by a tragedy. When she comes to live with her Aunt Betsy in Houston, she faces the daunting prospect of going to a strange school where she is different from everyone else. But as Mary meets her new classmates, she quickly learns how many distinct cultures can mingle & to be proud of her own heritage. THE COURAGE SEED was inspired by the author's experiences teaching on a Navajo reservation in New Mexico & the ethnic diversity of her Houston classes. Richardson weaves traditional

Navajo myths into Mary's story: the title comes from a Navajo belief that brave deeds nurture the seeds of courage planted in everyone's mind. The book includes a glossary of Navajo terms, several one-page essays on Navajo culture, & a list of books recommended for further reading. The story is illustrated by Pat Finney, a Houston artist & teacher. A good introduction to Native American culture for young readers. Ages 8-12. Order from: Eakin Press/Sunbelt Media, P.O. Box 90159, Austin, TX 78709-0159; 512-288-1771, FAX 512-288-1513.
Publisher Provided Annotation.

—Dino, the Ding Bat Cat. Peterson, Nancy G., illus. LC 92-17736. 48p. (gr. 1-3). 1992. 12.95 (*0-89015-869-X*) Eakin-Sunbelt.
—Out of Step: The Twins Were So Alike...but So Different. Holmes, Dawn, illus. LC 92-39666. 28p. (ps-3). 1993. 12.95 (*0-8120-5790-2*); pap. 5.95 (*0-8120-1553-3*) Barron.
—The Sleeping Beauty. Crespi, Francesca, illus. 32p. (ps-1). 1991. 14.95 (*1-55970-142-0*) Arcade Pub Inc.
—Stephen's Feast. Englander, Alice, illus. (ps-3). 1991. 15.95 (*0-316-74435-2*) Little.
—Tag-along Timothy Tours Alaska. Eakin, Edwin M., ed. Edington, Jo A., illus. 48p. (gr. 2-3). 1989. 12.95 (*0-89015-706-5,* Pub. by Panda Bks) Eakin-Sunbelt.
—Tag-along Timothy Tours Texas. (Illus.). 1992. 10.95 (*0-89015-817-7*) Eakin-Sunbelt.
—Thomas's Sitter. Holmes, Dawn, illus. LC 90-13799. 32p. (ps-1). 1991. SBE 13.95 (*0-02-776146-0,* Four Winds) Macmillan Child Grp.
Richardson, John. Bad Mood Bear. (ps). 1988. 6.95 (*0-8120-5871-2*) Barron.
—The Hiding Beast. Richardson, John, illus. (ps-3). 1989. 13.45 (*0-395-49213-0*) HM.
—Jack's Hat. (Illus.). 32p. (gr. k-3). 1992. 16.95 (*0-09-174524-1,* Pub. by Hutchinson UK) Trafalgar.
—Ten Bears in a Bed. Richardson, John, illus. LC 91-26501. 22p. (ps-k). 1992. 13.95 (*1-56282-157-1*) Hyprn Child.
—Where's Jack? A Christmas Pop-up Book. Richardson, John, illus. 24p. (ps-2). 1993. bds. 12.95 POB (*0-689-71713-X,* Aladdin) Macmillan Child Grp.
—The Wild Bears. (Illus.). 32p. (ps-2). 1992. 13.95 (*0-09-173800-8,* Pub. by Hutchinson UK) Trafalgar.
Richardson, Joy. Air. LC 91-42612. (Illus.). 30p. (gr. k-4). 1992. PLB 11.40 (*0-531-14201-9*) Watts.
—Birds. LC 93-18558. (Illus.). 32p. (gr. 2-4). 1993. PLB 11.90 (*0-531-14262-0*) Watts.
—Bridges. LC 93-30058. (Illus.). 1993. write for info. (*0-531-14289-2*) Watts.
—Day & Night. LC 92-31302. (Illus.). 30p. (gr. k-4). 1992. PLB 11.40 (*0-531-14139-X*) Watts.
—Fish. LC 92-32914. 1993. 11.40 (*0-531-14255-8*) Watts.
—Flowers. LC 93-18653. (Illus.). 32p. (gr. 2-4). 1993. PLB 11.40 (*0-531-14274-4*) Watts.
—Heat. LC 92-14419. (Illus.). (gr. k-4). 1993. 11.40 (*0-531-14239-6*) Watts.
—Insects. LC 92-32189. 1993. 11.40 (*0-531-14248-5*) Watts.
—Inside the Museum: A Children's Guide to the Metropolitan Museum of Art. (Illus.). 72p. 1993. pap. 12.95 (*0-8109-2561-3*) Abrams.
—Light. LC 92-14420. 1993. 11.40 (*0-531-14240-X*) Watts.
—Mammals. LC 92-32913. 1993. 11.40 (*0-531-14253-1*) Watts.
—Mollusks. LC 93-18542. (Illus.). 32p. (gr. 2-4). 1993. PLB 11.40 (*0-531-14263-9*) Watts.
—Reptiles. LC 92-32912. (Illus.). 32p. (gr. 2-4). 1993. PLB 11.40 (*0-531-14254-X*) Watts.
—Rocks & Soil. LC 91-42613. (Illus.). 30p. (gr. k-4). 1992. PLB 11.40 (*0-531-14206-X*) Watts.
—The Seasons. LC 91-29100. (Illus.). 30p. (gr. k-4). 1992. PLB 11.40 (*0-531-14158-6*) Watts.
—Trees. LC 93-18652. (Illus.). (gr. 4 up). 1994. write for info. (*0-531-14273-6*) Watts.
—Tunnels. LC 93-30057. (Illus.). 1994. write for info. (*0-531-14290-6*) Watts.
—The Water Cycle. LC 91-39572. (Illus.). 30p. (gr. k-4). 1992. PLB 11.40 (*0-531-14205-1*) Watts.
—The Weather. LC 91-43715. (Illus.). 30p. (gr. k-4). 1992. PLB 11.40 (*0-531-14164-0*) Watts.
Richardson, Judith B. Come to My Party. Mavor, Salley, illus. LC 91-16320. 32p. (ps-1). 1993. RSBE 13.95 (*0-02-776147-9,* Macmillan Child Bk) Macmillan Child Grp.
—David's Landing. Bang, Molly, illus. LC 84-22084. 150p. (gr. 3-7). 1984. write for info. (*0-9611374-1-X*) Woods Hole Hist.
—The Way Home. Mavor, Salley, illus. LC 88-35951. 32p. (ps-1). 1991. RSBE 13.95 (*0-02-776145-2,* Macmillan Child Bk) Macmillan Child Grp.
—The Way Home. Mavor, Sally, illus. (gr. k). 13.95 (*0-685-41406-X*) Macmillan.

—The Way Home. Mavor, Salley, illus. LC 93-25729. 32p. (gr. k-3). 1994. pap. 3.95 (0-689-71790-3, Aladdin) Macmillan Child Grp.

Richardson, Justine. The Great British Art Search. (Illus.). 9p. (Orig.). (gr. 2-6). 1993. pap. 2.50 wkbk. Yale Ctr Brit Art.

Richardson, Lee. Sophie's Surprise. 2nd ed. Holt, Shirley, illus. 28p. (gr. 3-8). 1984. 16.95 (0-9613476-0-0) Shirlee.

Richardson, Lee & Holt, Shirley, eds. Little Red Riding Hood. (Illus.). 28p. (gr. 3-8). 1985. 16.95 (0-9613476-1-9) Shirlee.

Richardson, Martha. Francisco Jose De Goya: Spanish Painter. LC 93-2326. (Illus.). (ps-3). 1994. PLB 18.95 (0-7910-1780-X, Am Art Analog); write for info. (0-7910-1799-0) Chelsea Hse.

Richardson, Martin J. Chess for Children. (gr. 4-7). 1991. 13.00 (0-08-041109-6, Pub. by CHES UK) Macmillan.

Richardson, Nigel. Edith Cavell. (Illus.). 64p. (gr. 5-9). 1991. 11.95 (0-237-60020-X, Pub. by Evans Bros Ltd) Trafalgar.

—J. F. Kennedy. (Illus.). 64p. (gr. 5-9). 1991. 11.95 (0-237-60029-3, Pub. by Evans Bros Ltd) Trafalgar.

—Martin Luther King. (Illus.). 64p. (gr. 5-9). 1991. 11.95 (0-237-60007-2, Pub. by Evans Bros Ltd) Trafalgar.

Richardson, Peter & Richardson, Bob. Great Careers for People Interested in How Things Work, 6 vols. LC 93-78076. (Illus.). 48p. (gr. 6-9). 1993. 16.95 (0-8103-9389-1, 102107, UXL) Gale.

—Great Careers for People Interested in Math & Computers, 6 vols. LC 93-78079. (Illus.). 48p. (gr. 6-9). 1993. 16.95 (0-8103-9385-9, 102103, UXL) Gale.

Richardson, Polly. Animal Poems. (ps-3). 1992. 12.95 (0-8120-6283-3) Barron.

Richardson, Samuel. Clarissa. Sherburn, George, ed. LC 62-52256. (gr. 9 up). 1962. pap. 9.16 (0-395-05164-9, RivEd) HM.

Richardson, Wendy & Richardson, Jack. Animals: Through the Eyes of Artists. LC 90-34276. (Illus.). 48p. (gr. 4 up). 1991. PLB 19.93 (0-516-09281-2); pap. 7.95 (0-516-49281-0) Childrens.

—Cities: Through the Eyes of Artists. LC 90-34277. 48p. (gr. 4 up). 1991. PLB 19.93 (0-516-09282-0); pap. 7.95 (0-516-49282-9) Childrens.

—Entertainers: Through the Eyes of Artists. LC 90-34278. 48p. (gr. 4 up). 1991. PLB 19.93 (0-516-09283-9); pap. 7.95 (0-516-49283-7) Childrens.

—Families: Through the Eyes of Artists. LC 90-34279. (Illus.). 48p. (gr. 4 up). 1991. PLB 19.93 (0-516-09284-7); pap. 7.95 (0-516-49284-5) Childrens.

—The Natural World: Through the Eyes of Artists. LC 90-34281. (Illus.). 48p. (gr. 4 up). 1991. PLB 19.93 (0-516-09285-5); pap. 7.95 (0-516-49285-3) Childrens.

—Water: Through the Eyes of Artists. LC 90-34280. 48p. (gr. 4 up). 1991. PLB 19.93 (0-516-09286-3); pap. 7.95 (0-516-49286-1) Childrens.

Richecky, Janet. Excuse Me. Connelly, Gwen, illus. 32p. (ps-2). 1989. PLB 18.50 (0-89565-539-X); PLB 12.95s.p. (0-685-25652-9) Childs World.

Richemont, Enid. The Glass Bird. Anstey, Carolina, illus. LC 92-54585. 112p. (gr. 3-6). 1993. 14.95 (1-56402-195-5) Candlewick Pr.

—The Magic Skateboard. Ormerod, Jan, illus. LC 92-53010. 80p. (gr. 3-6). 1993. 13.95 (1-56402-132-7) Candlewick Pr.

—The Time Tree. (gr. 3-7). 1990. 12.95 (0-316-74452-2) Little.

Riches, Judith. Giraffes Have More Fun. LC 91-21184. (Illus.). 32p. (ps-3). 1992. 14.00 (0-688-11042-8, Tambourine Bks); PLB 13.93 (0-688-11043-6, Tambourine Bks) Morrow.

Richie, Donald A. U. S. Constitution. Schlesinger, Arthur M., Jr., intro. by. (Illus.). 120p. (gr. 5 up). 1989. 14.95 (0-87754-894-3) Chelsea Hse.

—The Young Oxford Companion to the Congress of the United States. LC 93-6466. (gr. 5 up). 1993. 35.00 (0-19-507777-6) OUP.

Richler, Mordecai. Jacob Two-Two & the Dinosaur. Foster, Frances, ed. Eyolfson, Norman, illus. Rosenthal, Eileen, designed by. LC 86-20108. (Illus.). 96p. (gr. 1-5). 1987. 11.95 (0-394-88704-2); lib. bdg. 11.99 (0-394-98704-7) Knopf Bks Yng Read.

—Jacob Two-Two & the Dinosaur. 96p. (gr. 3-7). 1988. pap. 2.95 (0-553-15589-X) Bantam.

—Jacob Two-Two Hooded Fang. (gr. ps-7). 1987. pap. 2.50 (0-317-64199-9, Skylark) Bantam.

Richman. The Random House Book of Computer Literacy, 2 vols. large type ed. 396p. (gr. 6-12). 1984. Repr. of 1983 ed. 99.00 (0-317-01924-4, J-03920-00) Am Printing Hse.

Richman, Daniel A. James E. Carter: Thirty-Ninth President of the United States. Young, Richard G., ed. LC 88-24562. (Illus.). (gr. 5-9). 1989. PLB 17.26 (0-944483-24-0) Garrett Ed Corp.

Richman, Ellen. Spotlight on Computer Literacy. (gr. 6-8). 1984. pap. 14.00 (0-07-480653-X) McGraw.

Richmond, Gary. Backyard Safari. (ps-3). 1990. write for info. (0-8499-0741-1) Word Inc.

—Barnaby Goes Wild. (gr. 1-5). 1991. text ed. 6.99 (0-8499-0914-7) Word Inc.

—The Early Bird. 32p. 1992. 7.99 (0-8499-0924-4) Word Inc.

—The Forgotten Friend. (gr. 1-5). 1991. text ed. 6.99 (0-8499-0913-9) Word Inc.

—Henry & the Great Flood. 32p. 1990. write for info. (0-8499-0745-4) Word Inc.

—Howard the Horrible Gets Even. 32p. 1990. write for info. (0-8499-0744-6) Word Inc.

—Miss Otter Goes to the Movies. 1991. write for info. (0-8499-0743-8) Word Inc.

—Prodigal Wolf. 1990. 6.99 (0-8499-0746-2) Word Inc.

—A Scary Night at the Zoo. 1990. write for info. (0-8499-0742-X) Word Inc.

—Zookeeper Looks at Bears. (Illus.). (ps) 1991. PLB 3.99 (0-8499-0860-4) Word Inc.

—Zookeeper Looks at Big & Little Animals. (Illus.). (ps). 1991. PLB 3.99 (0-8499-0887-6) Word Inc.

—Zookeeper Looks at Big Cats. (Illus.). (ps). 1991. PLB 3.99 (0-8499-0862-0) Word Inc.

—Zookeeper Looks at Elephants. (Illus.). (ps). 1991. PLB 3.99 (0-8499-0888-4) Word Inc.

—Zookeeper Looks at Monkeys. 1991. pap. 3.99 (0-8499-0861-2) Word Inc.

—Zookeeper Looks at Mother & Baby Animals. 1991. pap. 3.99 (0-8499-0863-9) Word Inc.

Richmond, Merle. Phyllis Wheatley. Horner, Matina, intro. by. (Illus.). 112p. (Orig.). (gr. 5 up). 1988. 17.95 (1-55546-683-4); pap. 9.95 (0-7910-0218-7) Chelsea Hse.

Richmond, Robin. Animals in Art. Richmond, Robin, illus. 48p. (gr. 2-5). 1993. PLB 16.00 (0-8249-8626-1, Ideals Child); text ed. 15.95 (0-8249-8613-X) Hambleton-Hill.

—Children in Art: The Story in a Picture. Richmond, Robin, illus. 48p. (gr. 2-5). 1992. 15.95 (0-8249-8552-4, Ideals Child); PLB 16.00 (0-8249-8588-5) Hambleton-Hill.

—Introducing Michelangelo. (Illus.). 32p. (gr. 2-5). 1992. 14.95 (0-316-74440-9) Little.

Richmond, Sandra. Wheels for Walking. Kroupa, Melanie, ed. LC 85-70855. 196p. (gr. 6 up). 1985. 13.95 (0-316-74439-5, Joy St Bks) Little.

—Wheels for Walking. (Illus.). 176p. (gr. 9-12). 1988. pap. 2.50 (0-451-15235-2, Sig) NAL-Dutton.

Richtel, Anne, jt. auth. see Bedford, Viola.

Richter, Betts. Something Special Within. 2nd ed. Jacobsen, Alice, illus. 48p. (ps-5). 1982. pap. 6.95 (0-87516-488-9) DeVorss.

Richter, Betts & Jacobsen, Alice. Make It So! A Child's Book on Self-Direction Through Affirmations. 3rd ed. LC 79-84946. (Illus.). 55p. (gr. k-4). 1988. pap. 7.95 (0-87516-599-0) DeVorss.

Richter, Conrad. Light in the Forest. (gr. 5-12). 1990. pap. 3.99 (0-553-26878-3) Bantam.

Richter, Hans P. Friedrich. (gr. 5-9). 1987. pap. 4.99 (0-14-032205-1, Puffin) Puffin Bks.

—Friedrich. (gr. 6 up). 1992. 17.00 (0-8446-6573-8) Peter Smith.

—I Was There. (gr. 5-9). 1987. pap. 4.99 (0-14-032206-X, Puffin) Puffin Bks.

Richter, Konrad. Wipe Your Feet, Santa Claus. Wilkon, Jozef, illus. LC 85-7246. 24p. (gr. k-2). 1985. 14.95 (1-55858-016-6) North-South Bks NYC.

Rickard, G. Silver. (Illus.). 48p. (gr. 5 up). 1985. PLB 17.27 (0-86592-273-X); 12.95 (0-685-58323-6) Rourke Corp.

Rickard, Graham. Bioenergy. LC 91-9259. (Illus.). 32p. (gr. 4-6). 1991. PLB 17.27 (0-8368-0707-3) Gareth Stevens Inc.

—Bricks. LC 93-6833. (Illus.). 32p. (gr. 3-6). 1993. 13.95 (1-56847-046-0) Thomson Lrning.

—Building Homes. (Illus.). 32p. (gr. 2-5). 1989. 13.50 (0-8225-2129-6) Lerner Pubns.

—Geothermal Energy. (Illus.). 32p. (gr. 4-6). 1991. PLB 17.27 (0-8368-0708-1) Gareth Stevens Inc.

—Homes in Space. (Illus.). 32p. (gr. 2-5). 1989. 13.50 (0-8225-2125-3) Lerner Pubns.

—Mobile Homes. (Illus.). 32p. (gr. 2-5). 1989. 13.50 (0-8225-2130-X) Lerner Pubns.

—Oil. LC 93-18304. 32p. (gr. 3-5). 1993. 13.95 (1-56847-045-2) Thomson Lrning.

—Solar Energy. (Illus.). 32p. (gr. 4-6). 1991. PLB 17.27 (0-8368-0709-X) Gareth Stevens Inc.

—Water Energy. (Illus.). 32p. (gr. 4-6). 1991. PLB 17.27 (0-8368-0710-3) Gareth Stevens Inc.

—Wind Energy. (Illus.). 32p. (gr. 4-6). 1991. PLB 17.27 (0-8368-0711-1) Gareth Stevens Inc.

Rickard, Graham, jt. auth. see Houghton, Graham.

Ricken, Robert. Love Me When I'm Most Unlovable, Vol. II. 32p. (gr. 6-9). 1987. pap. 4.00 (0-88210-198-6) Natl Assn Principals.

Rickerby, Laura. Ulysses S. Grant & the Strategy of Victory. (Illus.). 160p. (gr. 5 up). 1990. lib. bdg. 18.98 (0-382-09944-3); pap. 8.95 (0-382-24053-7) Silver Burdett Pr.

Rickert, Jessica A. Exploring Careers in Dentistry. rev. ed. 154p. (gr. 7-12). 1992. PLB 13.95 (0-8239-1373-2) Rosen Group.

Ricketts, Marijane, et al, eds. see Writers' League of Washington Staff.

Ricketts, Marijane G. Is It the Onions Making Life Pungent? Cameron, Dana, ed. (Orig.). (gr. 7 up). 1987. pap. 7.50 (0-9618223-0-9) M G Ricketts.

Ricklen, Neil. Babys Big & Little. 1990. 4.95 (0-671-69542-8) S&S Trade.

—Baby's Colors. 1990. 4.95 (0-671-69539-8) S&S Trade.

—Baby's Good Morning: A Super Chubby Board Book. (ps). 1992. pap. 4.95 (0-671-76084-X, Little Simon) S&S Trade.

—Baby's Good Night: A Super Chubby Board Book. (ps). 1992. pap. 4.95 (0-671-76085-8, Little Simon) S&S Trade.

—Baby's School: A Super Chubby Board Book. (ps). 1992. pap. 4.95 (0-671-76086-6, Little Simon) S&S Trade.

—Baby's Zoo: A Super Chubby Board Book. (ps). 1992. pap. 4.95 (0-671-76087-4, Little Simon) S&S Trade.

—Baby's 1-2-3. 1990. 4.95 (0-671-69541-X) S&S Trade.

—First Word Books: Colors. (ps). 1994. pap. 5.95 (0-671-86726-1, Little Simon) S&S Trade.

—First Word Books: Opposites. (ps). 1994. pap. 5.95 (0-671-86728-8, Little Simon) S&S Trade.

—First Word Books: 1-2-3. (ps). 1994. pap. 5.95 (0-671-86727-X, Little Simon) S&S Trade.

Ricklen, Neil, illus. My Clothes: Mi Ropa. LC 93-27162. (ENG & SPA.). 14p. (ps-k). 1994. bds. 3.95 (0-689-71773-3, Aladdin) Macmillan Child Grp.

—My Colors: Mis Colores. LC 93-27195. (ENG & SPA.). 14p. (ps-k). 1994. bds. 3.95 (0-689-71772-5, Aladdin) Macmillan Child Grp.

—My Family: Mi Familia. LC 93-30661. (ENG & SPA.). 14p. (ps-k). 1994. bds. 3.95 (0-689-71771-7, Aladdin) Macmillan Child Grp.

—My Numbers: Mis Numeros. LC 93-27165. (ENG & SPA.). 14p. (ps-k). 1994. bds. 3.95 (0-689-71770-9, Aladdin) Macmillan Child Grp.

Ricklen, Neil, photos by. Baby Inside. (Illus.). 24p. (ps). 1991. pap. 4.95 casebound, padded cover (0-671-73878-X, Little Simon) S&S Trade.

—Baby Outside. (Illus.). 24p. (ps). 1991. pap. 4.95 casebound, padded cover (0-671-73879-8, Little Simon) S&S Trade.

—Baby's ABC. (Illus.). 24p. 1990. casebound, padded cover 4.95 (0-671-69540-1, Little Simon) S&S Trade.

—Baby's Birthday. (Illus.). 24p. (ps). 1991. pap. 4.95 casebound, padded cover (0-671-73880-1, Little Simon) S&S Trade.

—Baby's Christmas. (Illus.). 24p. (ps). 1991. pap. 4.95 casebound, padded cover (0-671-73881-X, Little Simon) S&S Trade.

Ricklen, Neil. Baby's Friends. 1986. 4.95 (0-671-62076-2) S&S Trade.

—Baby's Toys. 1986. 4.95 (0-671-62078-9) S&S Trade.

Ricklen, Neil, photos by. Daddy & Me. (Illus.). 28p. (ps). 1988. 4.95 (0-671-64537-4, Little Simon) S&S Trade.

—Grandma & Me. (Illus.). 28p. (ps-k). 1988. 4.95 (0-671-64540-4, S&S BFYR) S&S Trade.

—Grandpa & Me. (Illus.). 28p. (ps-k). 1988. 4.95 (0-671-64539-0, S&S BFYR) S&S Trade.

—Mommy & Me. (Illus.). 28p. (ps-k). 1988. 4.95 (0-671-64538-2, Little Simon) S&S Trade.

Rico, Armando B. Hay Roca en Tu Coca. Rico, Armando B., illus. (SPA.). 47p. (Orig.). 1992. pap. 2.75 (1-879219-05-0) Veracruz Pubs.

—Later with the Latex: AIDS. 44p. (Orig.). 1992. pap. 2.95 (1-879219-06-9) Veracruz Pubs.

—School Adventures: Aventuras Escolares. 27p. (Orig.). 1989. pap. text ed. 4.95 (1-879219-04-2) Veracruz Pubs.

—A Sound Mind in a Sound Body. 23p. (Orig.). 1990. pap. 16.00 (1-879219-03-4) Veracruz Pubs.

—There's a Rock in Your Coke. 47p. (Orig.). 1987. pap. 2.50 (1-879219-02-6) Veracruz Pubs.

Riddel, Frank S., jt. auth. see Coffey, William E.

Riddell, Chris. The Bear Dance. LC 90-9475. (Illus.). 32p. (ps-4). 1993. pap. 7.95 (0-671-79852-9, S&S BYR) S&S Trade.

—The Trouble with Elephants. Riddell, Chris, illus. LC 87-24963. 32p. (ps-2). 1990. pap. 5.95 (0-06-443170-3, Trophy) HarpC Child Bks.

—When the Walrus Comes: The Screenplay. Riddell, Chris, illus. LC 89-31718. 1990. 13.95 (0-385-29858-7) Doubleday.

Riddell, Edwina. My First Animal Word Book. (Illus.). 32p. (ps). 1989. 9.95 (0-8120-6127-6) Barron.

—My First Ballet Class. LC 92-24450. (Illus.). 32p. (ps-2). 1993. 10.95 (0-8120-6296-5); pap. 5.95 (0-8120-1674-2) Barron.

—My First Day at Preschool. (Illus.). 32p. (ps). 1992. 9.95 (0-8120-6261-2) Barron.

—One Hundred First Words. (Illus.). 32p. (ps). 1988. 8.95 (0-8120-5786-4) Barron.

—One Hundred First Words. 32p. (ps). 1992. pap. 4.95 (0-8120-4888-1) Barron.

Riddell, Edwina, jt. auth. see Smallman, Clare.

Riddell, Ruth. Ice Warrior. LC 91-29506. 144p. (gr. 4-7). 1992. SBE 13.95 (0-689-31710-7, Atheneum Child Bk) Macmillan Child Grp.

Riddle, Marilyn R. Unicorns for Everyone. large type ed. Ziese, Mark, illus. 24p. (Orig.). 1980. pap. 5.00 (0-9603748-1-7) Sandpiper OR.

Riddle, S., et al. Practice Exercises in Basic English. large type ed. (gr. 3-9). 1983. Repr. of 1976 ed. Grade 4, 18 pt. 34.00 (0-317-03357-3, J-21340-00); Grade 5, 18 pt. 34.00 (0-317-03358-1, J-21350-00); Grade 6, 18pt. 34.00 (0-317-03359-X, J-21360-00); Grade 7, 18pt. 26.54 (0-317-03360-3, 4-21370-00) Am Printing Hse.

Riddle, Tohby. Careful With That Ball, Eugene! LC 90-43015. (Illus.). 32p. (ps-1). 1991. 12.95 (0-531-05917-0); PLB 12.99 (0-531-08517-1) Orchard Bks Watts.

Riddlebaugh, Mary Jane. Millions & Illions. Hunter, Karen, illus. (gr. 4-8). 1990. pap. 11.95 (1-878347-16-0) NL Assocs.

Ride, Sally. Voyager: An Adventure to the Edge of the Solar System. NASA Staff, photos by. LC 91-32495. (Illus.). 36p. (gr. 2-6). 1992. 14.00 (0-517-58157-4); PLB 14.99 (0-517-58158-2) Crown Bks Yng Read.

Ride, Sally & Okie, Susan. To Space & Back. LC 85-23757. (Illus.). 96p. (gr. 1 up). 1989. Repr. of 1985 ed. 16.95 (*0-688-06159-1*) Lothrop.
—To Space & Back. LC 85-23757. (Illus.). 96p. (gr. 1 up). 1989. pap. 12.95 (*0-688-09112-1*, Pub. by Beech Tree Bks) Morrow.
Ride, Sally & O'Shaughnessy, Tam. The Third Planet. LC 92-40609. 1994. write for info.; PLB write for info. Crown Bks Yng Read.
Rideau, S. Noel. Uncle Noel's Fun Fables Program. Gray, Harrel, illus. 80p. (gr. 2-5). 1991. wkbk. 8.95 (*0-9630734-0-0*) Aesop Systs.
Ridenour, Fritz. How to Be a Christian Without Being Religious. 166p. 1991. 5.99 (*0-8307-1026-4*, S182104); leader's guide 14.99 (*0-8307-1511-8*, SH215) Regal.
Ridenour, Fritz, jt. auth. see Smith, Michael W.
Rider, Joanne. First Grade Valentines. Lewin, Betsy, illus. LC 91-35388. 32p. (gr. k-2). 1992. PLB 9.79 (*0-8167-3004-0*); pap. text ed. 2.95 (*0-8167-3005-9*) Troll Assocs.
Rider, Tracy, ed. see Bennett, Gerald M.
Rider, Tracy, ed. see Bennett, Geraldine M.
Rider Montgomery, Elizabeth. Alexander Graham Bell: Man of Sound. (Illus.). 80p. (gr. 2-6). 1993. Repr. of 1963 ed. lib. bdg. 12.95 (*0-7910-1423-1*) Chelsea Hse.
Ridett, Anthea, tr. see Chadefaud, Catherine & Coblence, Jean-Michel.
Ridett, Anthea, tr. see Sabbagh, Antoine.
Ridge, Delores F., ed. see Matanah.
Ridgeway, Frank. Bugs Bunny in the Little Surprise. (Illus.). 24p. (ps). 1990. pap. write for info. (*0-307-11668-9*, Pub. by Golden Bks) Western Pub.
Ridgewell, Jenny. A Taste of Japan. LC 93-14148. (Illus.). 48p. (gr. 3-5). 1993. 14.95 (*1-56847-097-5*) Thomson Lrning.
Ridgwell, Jenny. A Taste of Italy. LC 93-25200. (Illus.). 48p. 1993. 14.95 (*1-56847-098-3*) Thomson Lrning.
Ridington, Jillian & Ridington, Robin. People of the Longhouse: How the Iroquoian Tribes Lived. Bateson, Ian, illus. 48p. (gr. 3-7). 1992. pap. 7.95 (*1-55054-221-4*, Pub. by Groundwood-Douglas & McIntyre CN) Firefly Bks Ltd.
Ridington, Jillian, jt. auth. see Ridington, Robin.
Ridington, Robin & Ridington, Jillian. People of the Trail: How the Northern Forest Indians Lived. Bateson, Ian, illus. 40p. (gr. 3-7). 1992. pap. 7.95 (*0-88894-412-8*, Pub. by Groundwood-Douglas & McIntyre CN) Firefly Bks Ltd.
Ridington, Robin, jt. auth. see Ridington, Jillian.
Ridley, jt. auth. see Khanna.
Ridley, Alison & Garfield, Curtis F. As Ancient Is This Hostelry: The Story of the Wayside Inn. Evans, Robert R., illus. 335p. (Orig.). (gr. 7 up). 1989. pap. 14.00 (*0-9621976-0-2*) Porcupine Enter.
Ridley, Chas, ed. see Brooks, Jennifer.
Ridley, Philip. Krindlekrax: Or How Ruskin Splinter Battled a Horrible Monster & Saved His Entire Neighborhood. Hovland, Gary, illus. LC 91-23374. 144p. (gr. 3-7). 1992. 15.00 (*0-679-81764-6*); PLB 15.99 (*0-679-91764-0*) Knopf Bks Yng Read.
Ridley, W. N., jt. auth. see Picott, R.
Ridout, Ronald. Activity Picture Dictionary. Wingham, Peter, illus. 48p. (gr. 1 up). 1987. 9.95 (*0-8120-5844-5*) Barron.
Ridpath, Ian. Atlas of Stars & Planets. LC 92-32463. 80p. (gr. 5-10). 1993. 16.95 (*0-8160-2926-1*) Facts on File.
—Space. LC 91-7455. (Illus.). 48p. (gr. 5-8). 1991. PLB 13.90 (*0-531-19144-3*, Warwick) Watts.
—Space. LC 92-53096. (Illus.). 48p. (Orig.). (gr. 3-8). 1992. pap. 5.95 (*1-85697-814-1*) Kingfisher Bks.
Riebe, Ernest. Mister Block: IWW Comics. Rosemont, Franklin, ed. (Illus.). 36p. pap. 5.95 (*0-88286-062-3*) C H Kerr.
Rieck, Sondra & Rutledge, Carol. Move & Match Colors with Busy Bear. 22p. (ps-k). 1990. 9.95 (*0-9634376-0-7*) Woodville Pr.
Rieck, Sondra & Stippel, Lori. Learn Basic Concepts with Cuddles Clown. 24p. (ps-k). 1990. 9.95 (*0-9634082-0-8*) Woodville Pr.
Riecken, Nancy. Andrew's Own Place. Aubrey, Meg K., illus. LC 92-22953. 1993. 14.95 (*0-395-64723-1*) HM.
Ried, Glenda E., jt. auth. see Gaylord, Gloria L.
Riede, Anne M. Coach's Clipboards. (Illus.). 306p. (Orig.). (gr. 5-8). 1986. 10.95 (*0-931983-02-9*, BCLTXT-3) Basic Comp Lit.
Riedman, Sarah R. & Barish, Wendy. The Good Looks Skin Book. (Illus.). 144p. (gr. 10 up). 1983. 9.29 (*0-685-06727-0*) S&S Trade.
Riegel, Martin P. Ghost Ports of the Pacific, Vol. I: California. LC 89-90772. (Illus.). 52p. (Orig.). 1989. 11.00 (*0-944871-18-6*); pap. 4.95 (*0-944871-19-4*) Riegel Pub.
—Ghost Ports of the Pacific, Vol. II: Oregon. LC 89-90772. (Illus.). 52p. (Orig.). 1989. 11.00 (*0-944871-20-8*); pap. 4.95 (*0-944871-21-6*) Riegel Pub.
—Ghost Ports of the Pacific, Vol. III: Washington. LC 89-90772. (Illus.). 52p. (Orig.). 1989. 11.00 (*0-944871-22-4*); pap. 4.95 (*0-944871-23-2*) Riegel Pub.
—Historic Ships of Hawaii. LC 88-92776. (Illus.). 44p. (Orig.). 1988. 11.00 (*0-944871-12-7*); pap. 4.95 (*0-944871-13-5*) Riegel Pub.
—Historic Ships of Oregon. LC 88-92771. (Illus.). 48p. (Orig.). 1988. 11.00 (*0-944871-14-3*); pap. 4.95 (*0-944871-15-1*) Riegel Pub.

—Historic Ships of Washington. LC 88-63929. (Illus.). 52p. (Orig.). 1988. 11.00 (*0-944871-16-X*); pap. 4.95 (*0-944871-17-8*) Riegel Pub.
—The Ships of the California Gold Rush. LC 88-92421. (Illus.). 48p. (Orig.). 1988. 11.00 (*0-944871-11-9*); pap. 4.95 (*0-685-24979-4*) Riegel Pub.
—The Ships of the Orange Coast. Riegel, Martin P., illus. LC 88-92522. 40p. (Orig.). (gr. 9 up). 1988. PLB 11.00 (*0-944871-08-9*); pap. 4.75 (*0-944871-09-7*) Riegel Pub.
Riegert, Evelyn, ed. see Mohr-Stephens, Judy.
Riehecky, J. Jack & Jill's Adventure in Alphabet Town. Hohag, L., illus. LC 91-20541. 32p. (ps-2). 1992. PLB 14.60 (*0-516-05410-4*) Childrens.
—Little Lady's Adventure in Alphabet Town. McCallum, J., illus. LC 91-20542. 32p. (ps-2). 1992. PLB 14.60 (*0-516-05412-0*) Childrens.
Riehecky, Janet. After You. Connelly, Gwen, illus. 32p. (ps-2). 1989. PLB 18.50 (*0-89565-538-1*); PLB 12.95s.p. (*0-685-25650-2*) Childs World.
—Allosaurus. Hunter, Llyn, illus. LC 88-1693. 32p. (gr. k-4). 1988. PLB 21.35 (*0-89565-421-0*); PLB 14.95s.p. (*0-685-55918-1*) Childs World.
—Anatosaurus. Magnuson, Diana, illus. 32p. (gr. k-4). 1989. PLB 21.35 (*0-89565-545-4*); PLB 14.95s.p. (*0-685-56086-4*) Childs World.
—Ankylosaurus. Magnuson, Diana, illus. 32p. (gr. k-4). 1990. PLB 21.35 (*0-89565-621-3*); PLB 14.95s.p. (*0-685-58728-2*) Childs World.
—Apatosaurus. Halverson, Lydia, illus. LC 88-1694. 32p. (gr. k-4). 1988. PLB 21.35 (*0-89565-423-7*); PLB 14.95s.p. (*0-685-55919-X*) Childs World.
—Baryonyx. Conaway, Jim, illus. 32p. (gr. k-4). 1990. PLB 21.35 (*0-89565-622-1*); PLB 14.95s.p. (*0-685-56207-7*) Childs World.
—Brachiosaurus. Conaway, James, illus. LC 89-22069. 32p. 1989. PLB 21.35 (*0-89565-542-X*); PLB 14.95s.p. (*0-685-56084-8*) Childs World.
—Carolina Herrera: International Fashion Designer. LC 90-28886. (Illus.). 32p. (gr. 2-4). 1991. PLB 14.60 (*0-516-04178-9*); pap. 3.95 (*0-516-44178-7*) Childrens.
—Cinco de Mayo. Stasiak, Krystyna, illus. LC 93-13249. 1993. write for info. (*0-516-00681-9*) Childrens.
—Coelophysis. Halverson, Lydia, illus. 32p. (gr. k-4). 1990. PLB 21.35 (*0-89565-623-X*); PLB 14.95s.p. (*0-685-56208-5*) Childs World.
—Compsognathus. Lexa-Senning, Susan, illus. 32p. (gr. k-4). 1990. PLB 21.35 (*0-89565-624-8*); PLB 14.95s.p. (*0-685-58729-0*) Childs World.
—Deinonychus. Hunter, Llyn, illus. 32p. (gr. k-4). 1990. PLB 21.35 (*0-89565-625-6*); PLB 14.95s.p. (*0-685-56210-7*) Childs World.
—Dinosaur Relatives. Magnuson, Diana, illus. 32p. (gr. k-4). 1990. PLB 21.35 (*0-89565-626-4*); PLB 14.95s.p. (*0-685-56211-5*) Childs World.
—Diplodocus. Conaway, Jim, illus. 32p. (gr. k-4). 1990. PLB 21.35 (*0-89565-627-2*); PLB 14.95s.p. (*0-685-56212-3*) Childs World.
—Discovering Dinosaurs. Endres, Helen, illus. 32p. (gr. k-4). 1990. PLB 21.35 (*0-89565-620-5*); PLB 14.95s.p. (*0-685-56205-0*) Childs World.
—Good Sportsmanship. Rigo, Cristina, illus. LC 89-29663. 32p. (gr. k-3). 1990. PLB 21.35 (*0-89565-563-2*); PLB 14.95s.p. (*0-685-56197-6*) Childs World.
—Haunted Houses. Halverson, Lydia & Siculan, Dan, illus. LC 88-38780. 100p. (gr. 3-7). 1989. PLB 21.35 (*0-89565-454-7*); pap. 14.95 (*0-89565-534-9*) Childs World.
—Hypsilophodon. Ching, illus. 32p. (gr. k-4). 1990. PLB 21.35 (*0-89565-628-0*); PLB 14.95s.p. (*0-685-56213-1*) Childs World.
—Iguanodon. Magnuson, Diana, illus. LC 89-15850. 32p. (gr. k-4). 1989. PLB 21.35 (*0-89565-544-6*); PLB 14.95s.p. (*0-685-56087-2*) Childs World.
—I'm Sorry. (ps-2). 1989. PLB 18.50 (*0-89565-389-3*); PLB 12.95s.p. (*0-685-62606-7*) Childs World.
—Kwanzaa. Halverson, Lydia, illus. LC 93-17076. (gr. 4 up). 1993. write for info. (*0-516-00686-X*) Childrens.
—Maiasaura. Magnuson, Diana, illus. LC 89-22076. 32p. (gr. k-4). 1989. PLB 21.35 (*0-89565-543-8*); PLB 14.95s.p. (*0-685-56085-6*) Childs World.
—May I? Connelly, Gwen, illus. LC 88-16838. 32p. (ps-2). 1989. PLB 18.50 (*0-89565-388-5*); PLB 12.95s.p. (*0-685-55996-3*) Childs World.
—Oviraptor. Magnuson, Diana, illus. 32p. (gr. k-4). 1990. PLB 21.35 (*0-89565-631-0*); PLB 14.95s.p. (*0-685-56216-6*) Childs World.
—Pachycephalosaurus. Hunter, Llyn, illus. 32p. (gr. k-4). 1990. PLB 21.35 (*0-89565-632-9*); PLB 14.95s.p. (*0-685-56217-4*) Childs World.
—Parasaurolophus. LeBlanc, Andre, illus. 32p. (gr. k-4). 1990. PLB 21.35 (*0-89565-633-7*); PLB 14.95s.p. (*0-685-56218-2*) Childs World.
—Please. Connelly, Gwen, illus. LC 88-16841. 32p. 1989. PLB 18.50 (*0-89565-386-9*); PLB 12.95s.p. (*0-685-55998-X*) Childs World.
—Polka-Dot Puppy's Visitor: A Book about Opposites. Hohag, Linda, illus. LC 88-10935. 32p. (ps-2). 1988. PLB 21.35 (*0-89565-378-8*); PLB 14.95s.p. (*0-685-55929-7*) Childs World.
—Polka-Dot Puppy's Walk: A Book about Sequences. Hohag, Linda, illus. LC 88-10934. 32p. (ps-2). 1988. PLB 21.35 (*0-89565-379-6*); PLB 14.95s.p. (*0-685-55930-0*) Childs World.
—Protoceratops. Magnuson, Diana, illus. 32p. (gr. k-4). 1990. PLB 21.35 (*0-89565-634-5*); PLB 14.95s.p. (*0-685-56219-0*) Childs World.

—Robots: Here They Come! Hohag, Linda, illus. LC 90-30634. 32p. (ps-2). 1990. PLB 19.95 (*0-89565-577-2*); PLB 13.95s.p. (*0-685-56193-3*) Childs World.
—Saltasaurus. Raskin, Betty, illus. 32p. (gr. k-4). 1990. PLB 21.35 (*0-89565-635-3*); PLB 14.95s.p. (*0-685-58730-4*) Childs World.
—Saving the Forests: A Rabbit's Story. Hohag, Linda, illus. LC 89-28122. 32p. (ps-2). 1990. PLB 19.95 (*0-89565-561-6*); PLB 13.95s.p. (*0-685-56182-8*) Childs World.
—Sharing. Rigo, Christina, illus. LC 87-26811. 32p. (gr. k-3). 1988. PLB 21.35 (*0-89565-416-4*); PLB 14.95s.p. (*0-685-55934-3*) Childs World.
—Snow: When Will It Fall? Friedman, Joy, illus. LC 89-28084. 32p. (ps-2). 1990. PLB 19.95 (*0-89565-560-8*); PLB 13.95s.p. (*0-685-56181-X*) Childs World.
—Stegosaurus. Magnuson, Diana, illus. LC 88-15347. 32p. (gr. k-4). 1988. PLB 21.35 (*0-89565-385-0*); PLB 14.95s.p. (*0-685-67670-6*) Childs World.
—Thank-You. Connelly, Gwen, illus. LC 88-16840. 32p. (ps-2). 1989. PLB 18.50 (*0-89565-387-7*); PLB 12.95s.p. (*0-685-55997-1*) Childs World.
—Triceratops. Magnuson, Diana, illus. LC 88-508. 32p. (gr. k-4). 1988. PLB 21.35 (*0-89565-422-9*); PLB 14.95s.p. (*0-685-55938-6*) Childs World.
—Troodon. Conaway, James, illus. 32p. (gr. k-4). 1990. PLB 21.35 (*0-89565-636-1*); PLB 14.95s.p. (*0-685-58731-2*) Childs World.
—Tyrannosaurus. Magnuson, Diana L., illus. LC 88-1692. 32p. (gr. k-4). 1988. PLB 21.35 (*0-89565-424-5*); PLB 14.95s.p. (*0-685-55939-4*) Childs World.
—UFOs. Siculan, Dan, illus. LC 88-25730. 100p. (gr. 3-7). 1989. PLB 21.35 (*0-89565-453-9*); PLB 14.95s.p. (*0-685-55995-5*) Childs World.
—Walrus' Adventure in Alphabet Town. Magnuson, Diana, illus. LC 92-1330. 32p. (ps-2). 1992. PLB 14.60 (*0-516-05423-6*) Childrens.
—What Plants Give Us: The Gift of Life. Collette, Rondi, illus. LC 90-30374. 32p. (ps-2). 1990. PLB 19.95 (*0-89565-570-5*); PLB 13.95s.p. (*0-685-56186-0*) Childs World.
Riehecky, Janet, jt. auth. see Pemberton, Nancy.
Riehecky, Janet, tr. see Andersen, Hans Christian.
Riehecky, Janet, tr. see Carroll, Lewis.
Riehecky, Janet, tr. see Grimm, Jacob & Grimm, Wilhelm K.
Riehecky, Janet, tr. see Jose, Eduard.
Riehecky, Janet, tr. see Perrault, Charles.
Riehm, Sarah. Teenage Entrepreneur's Guide: 50 Money-Making Business Ideas. 2nd ed. LC 87-1904. (Illus., Orig.). (gr. 7-12). 1990. pap. 10.95 (*0-940625-17-2*) Surrey Bks.
Riekehof, Lottie. Talk to the Deaf: A Manual of Approximately 1,000 Signs Used by the Deaf of North America. LC 63-17975. (Illus.). 154p. (gr. k up). 1963. tchr's. bk 8.95 (*0-88243-612-0*, 02-0612) Gospel Pub.
Riekehof, Lottie L., jt. auth. see Hillebrand, Linda L.
Riekes, Linda & Ackerly, Salley M. Lawmaking. 2nd ed. (Illus.). 142p. (gr. 5-9). 1980. pap. text ed. 17.75 (*0-8299-1023-9*); tchr's. ed. 17.75 (*0-8299-1024-7*) West Pub.
—Young Consumers. 2nd ed. (Illus.). 124p. (gr. 5-9). 1980. pap. text ed. 17.75 (*0-8299-1021-2*); tchr's. ed. 17.75 (*0-8299-1022-0*) West Pub.
Rierden, Anne B. Reshaping the Supreme Court: New Justices, New Directions. Ribaroff, Margaret, ed. LC 87-25958. (Illus.). 128p. (gr. 7-12). 1988. PLB 13.40 (*0-531-10512-1*) Watts.
Rieu, Emil V., tr. see Homer.
Rifas, Leonard. Food First Comic. Goldenman, Gretta, ed. 24p. (Orig.). (gr. 7-12). 1982. pap. 1.00 (*0-935028-11-0*) Inst Food & Develop.
Riff, Andrea Da see Perrault, Charles.
Riffel, Paul. Reading Maps. LC 79-13628. (Illus.). (gr. 7 up). 1973. pap. 8.95 plastic comb bdg. (*0-8331-1300-3*) Hubbard Sci.
Rifkin, Mark. The Nez Perce Indians. LC 93-12221. (Illus.). 80p. (gr. 2-5). 1993. PLB 13.95 (*0-7910-1668-4*, Am Art Analog); pap. write for info. (*0-7910-1992-6*, Am Art Analog) Chelsea Hse.
Rifkin, Mark, jt. auth. see Braybrooks, Ann.
Rigby, Rodney. Hello, This Is Your Penguin Speaking. Rigby, Rodney, illus. LC 91-39501. 32p. (ps-2). 1992. 13.95 (*1-56282-231-4*); PLB 13.89 (*1-56282-232-2*) Hyprn Child.
—The Night the Moon Fell Asleep. Rigby, Rodney, illus. LC 92-45928. 32p. (ps-3). 1993. 13.95 (*1-56282-334-5*); PLB 13.89 (*1-56282-335-3*) Hyprn Child.
—There's a Building on Sixth Avenue. Rigby, Rodney, illus. LC 91-23097. 32p. (ps-3). 1992. 13.95 (*1-56282-155-5*); PLB 13.89 (*1-56282-156-3*) Hyprn Child.
Rigby, Susan. Caves. Burns, Robert, illus. LC 91-45082. 32p. (gr. 4-6). 1993. PLB 11.59 (*0-8167-2749-X*); pap. text ed. 3.95 (*0-8167-2750-3*) Troll Assocs. Postponed.
Rigg, Lucy. Baby's Christmas. 1990. 2.95 (*0-8378-1883-4*) Gibson.
—Little Christmas Treasure Books: Christmas Joys. (Illus.). (gr. 2 up). 1989. 2.95 (*0-8378-1870-2*) Gibson.
—Little Christmas Treasure Books: Christmas Cookies. (Illus.). (gr. 2 up). 1989. 2.95 (*0-8378-1871-0*) Gibson.
—Little Christmas Treasure Books: Silent Night. (Illus.). (ps up). 1989. 2.95 (*0-8378-1872-9*) Gibson.
—Little Christmas Treasure Books: The Night Before Christmas. (Illus.). (ps up). 1989. 2.95 (*0-8378-1869-9*) Gibson.
—Thank You, God. 1990. 2.95 (*0-8378-1884-2*) Gibson.

Riggio, Anita. A Moon in My Teacup. Riggio, Anita, illus. 32p. (ps-3). 1993. PLB 14.95 smythe sewn (*1-56397-008-2*) Boyds Mills Pr. Postponed.

Rights, Mollie. Beastly Neighbors: All About Wild Things in the City or Why Earwigs Make Good Mothers. (Illus.). 128p. (Orig.). (gr. 3 up). 1981. 14.95 (*0-316-74576-6*); pap. 9.95 (*0-316-74577-4*) Little.

Rigmaiden, Paul. God Loves Us All. (Illus.). 32p. (Orig.). (gr. k-4). 1988. pap. 5.00 (*0-9621598-0-8*) Dada Pubns.

Rigney, Francis J. A Beginner's Book of Magic. (Illus.). (gr. 6 up). 1963. 9.95 (*0-8159-5103-5*) Devin.

Rigney, Francis J., jt. auth. see Murray, William D.

Rigo, Christian, tr. see Stortz, Diane M.

Riha, Susanne. Animals in Winter. (Illus.). 32p. (gr. 1-5). 1989. PLB 19.95 (*0-87614-355-9*) Carolrhoda Bks.

Rikys, Bodel. Red Bear. LC 91-9039. (Illus.). 32p. (ps). 1992. 11.00 (*0-8037-1048-8*) Dial Bks Young.

—Red Bear's Fun with Shapes. LC 91-46997. (Illus.). 32p. (ps-k). 1993. 10.99 (*0-8037-1317-7*) Dial Bks Young.

Riley, Anne. Help Me. LC 90-82929. (Illus.). 10p. 1990. text ed. 3.99 (*0-8066-2495-7*, 9-2495) Augsburg Fortress.

—I'm Sorry. LC 90-82927. (Illus.). 10p. 1990. text ed. 3.99 (*0-8066-2494-9*, 9-2494) Augsburg Fortress.

—Please God. LC 90-82930. (Illus.). 10p. 1990. text ed. 3.99 (*0-8066-2496-5*, 9-2496) Augsburg Fortress.

—Thank You. LC 90-82928. (Illus.). 10p. 1990. text ed. 3.99 (*0-8066-2493-0*, 9-2493) Augsburg Fortress.

Riley, Dorothy W. The Blackburn Affair. 25p. (gr. 4-12). 1986. pap. write for info. (*1-880234-04-1*) Winbush Pub.

—Family Reunion. 25p. 1986. pap. write for info. (*1-880234-02-5*) Winbush Pub.

—It's up to You. 25p. (gr. 4-12). 1986. pap. write for info. (*1-880234-03-3*) Winbush Pub.

—My Soul Looks Back, 'Less I Forget. 332p. 1991. write for info. (*1-880234-06-8*); pap. write for info. (*1-880234-00-9*) Winbush Pub.

—My Soul Looks Back, 'Less I Forget, Vol. 2. 332p. 1992. pap. write for info. (*1-880234-01-7*) Winbush Pub.

Riley, Dorothy W. & Riley, Tiaudra. Dorothy Mae's Cornbread. 25p. 1992. pap. write for info. (*1-880234-05-X*) Winbush Pub.

Riley, Edward M. Starting America: The Story of Independence Hall. rev. ed. (Illus.). 64p. 1990. pap. text ed. 4.95 (*0-939631-23-7*) Thomas Publications.

Riley, Gail B. Miranda vs. Arizona: Rights of the Accused. LC 93-34380. 1994. write for info. (*0-89490-504-X*) Enslow Pubs.

Riley, Helen. The Bat in the Cave. Oxford Scientific Films Staff, photos by. LC 89-4469. (Illus.). 32p. (gr. 4-6). 1989. PLB 15.93 (*0-8368-0112-1*) Gareth Stevens Inc.

—Frogs & Toads. LC 92-41476. 32p. (gr. 2-5). 1993. 14.95 (*1-56847-007-X*) Thomson Lrning.

—Tigers. (Illus.). 32p. (gr. k-4). 1990. PLB 12.40 (*0-531-18355-6*, Pub. by Bookwright Pr) Watts.

Riley, Helen, jt. auth. see Harrison, Virginia.

Riley, James, et al. Helping Your Child with Mathematics. (Illus.). 144p. (Orig.). (ps-2). 1993. pap. 12.95 (*0-673-36061-X*) GdYrBks.

Riley, James A., ed. Black Baseball Journal, Vol. 1, No. 1. (Illus.). 64p. (Orig.). 1990. pap. 6.95 (*0-9614023-5-0*) TK Pubs.

Riley, James W. Riley Child Rhymes with Hoosier Pictures. (Illus.). 188p. Repr. 18.95 (*1-878208-17-9*) Guild Pr IN.

Riley, Jane & Carlson, Mary. Help for Parents of Gifted & Talented Children. Grossman, Dan, illus. 64p. (gr. k-6). 1984. wkbk. 5.95 (*0-86653-190-4*, GA 539) Good Apple.

Riley, Jocelyn. Crazy Quilt. 176p. (gr. 7-12). 1986. pap. 2.50 (*0-553-25640-8*) Bantam.

—Only My Mouth Is Smiling. LC 81-18688. 224p. (gr. 7-9). 1982. 12.95 (*0-688-01087-3*) Morrow Jr Bks.

Riley, Kelly. Celebrate Easter. Filkins, Vanessa, illus. 144p. (gr. k-6). 1987. pap. 11.95 (*0-86653-385-0*, SS 842, Shining Star Pubns) Good Apple.

Riley, Linda C. Aquarium: Bringing the Seas Inside. LC 93-16341. (Illus.). (ps-6). 1993. write for info. (*0-7167-6509-8*, Sci Am Yng Rdrs) W H Freeman.

Riley, Martin. Boggart's Sandwich. (Illus.). 95p. (gr. 7-9). 1992. pap. 3.95 (*0-563-20871-6*, BBC-Parkwest) Parkwest Pubns.

Riley, Peter. Looking at Microscopes. (Illus.). 48p. (gr. 5-8). 1985. 19.95 (*0-7134-4632-3*, Pub. by Batsford UK) Trafalgar.

Riley, Peter D. The Earth & Space. (Illus.). 48p. (gr. 4-6). 1986. 19.95 (*0-85219-598-2*, Pub. by Batsford UK) Trafalgar.

—Materials. (Illus.). 48p. (gr. 7-12). 1986. 17.95 (*0-85219-628-8*, Pub. by Batsford UK) Trafalgar.

Riley, Sue. Afraid. LC 77-15627. (Illus.). (gr. k-2). 1978. PLB 18.50 (*0-89565-011-8*); PLB 12.95s.p. (*0-685-55472-4*) Childs World.

—Angry. LC 77-16791. (Illus.). (ps-2). 1978. PLB 18.50 (*0-89565-014-2*); PLB 12.95s.p. (*0-685-55473-2*) Childs World.

—Help! LC 77-16030. (Illus.). (ps-2). 1978. PLB 18.50 (*0-89565-012-6*); PLB 12.95s.p. (*0-685-55484-8*) Childs World.

—Sharing. LC 77-16293. (Illus.). (ps-2). 1978. PLB 18.50 (*0-89565-015-0*); PLB 12.95s.p. (*0-685-55543-7*) Childs World.

—Sorry. LC 77-16811. (Illus.). (ps-2). 1978. PLB 18.50 (*0-89565-013-4*); PLB 12.95s.p. (*0-685-55550-X*) Childs World.

—Success. LC 77-20992. (Illus.). (ps-2). 1978. 18.50 (*0-89565-016-9*); PLB 12.95 (*0-685-58842-4*) Childs World.

Riley, T. The Amazing World of Dinosaurs. (Illus.). 80p. (gr. 2-6). 1991. 4.99 (*0-517-63993-9*) Outlet Bk Co.

Riley, Tiaudra, jt. auth. see Riley, Dorothy W.

Rimm, Sylvia B. & Priest, Christine. Gifted Kids Have Feelings Too: And Other Not-So-Fictitious Stories for & about Teenagers. Maas, Katherine, illus. LC 90-81442. 162p. (Orig.). (gr. 6-12). 1990. pap. text ed. 15.00 (*0-937891-06-1*); pap. text ed. 15.00 discussion book (*0-937891-07-X*) Apple Pub Wisc.

Rimner, I. Movies - FX. (Illus.). 48p. (gr. 3-8). 1989. PLB 18.60 (*0-86592-453-8*); 13.95 (*0-685-58294-9*) Rourke Corp.

Rimson, Ole, ed. see Blair, Carvel.

Rinaldi, Ann. A Break with Charity: A Story about the Salem Witch Trials. LC 92-8858. 1992. 16.95 (*0-15-200353-3*, Gulliver Bks) HarBrace.

—The Fifth of March. 1993. pap. 3.95 (*0-15-227517-7*, HB Juv Bks) HarBrace.

—Fifth of March: A Story of the Boston Massacre. 1993. 10.95 (*0-15-200343-6*) HarBrace.

—In My Father's House. LC 91-46839. 304p. (gr. 7 up). 1993. 13.95 (*0-590-44730-0*) Scholastic Inc.

—The Last Silk Dress. LC 87-25128. 368p. (gr. 5 up). 1988. 15.95 (*0-8234-0690-3*) Holiday.

—A Ride into Morning: The Story of Tempe Wick. Grove, Karen, ed. 289p. (gr. 7 up). 1991. 15.95 (*0-15-200573-0*, Gulliver Bks) HarBrace.

—A Stitch in Time. 304p. (gr. 7 up). 1994. 13.95 (*0-590-46055-2*, Scholastic Hardcover) Scholastic Inc.

—A Stitch in Time. LC 93-8964. 1994. 13.95 (*0-590-46056-0*) Scholastic Inc.

—Time Enough for Drums. LC 85-24869. 256p. (gr. 7 up). 1986. 15.95 (*0-8234-0603-2*) Holiday.

—Time Enough for Drums. 249p. 1989. pap. 2.50 (*0-8167-1269-7*) Troll Assocs.

—Wolf by the Ears. 1991. 13.95 (*0-590-43413-6*, Scholastic Hardcover) Scholastic Inc.

—Wolf by the Ears. 1993. pap. 3.50 (*0-590-43412-8*) Scholastic Inc.

Rinard, Judith E. Along a Rocky Shore. (Illus.). (gr. k-4). 1990. Set. 13.95 (*0-87044-822-6*); lib. bdg. 16.95 (*0-87044-823-4*) Natl Geog.

—Puppies. Crump, Donald J., ed. LC 82-47857. 32p. (ps-3). 1982. 13.95 (*0-87044-451-4*) Natl Geog.

—Zoos Without Cages. LC 79-3243. (Illus.). 104p. (gr. 3-8). 1981. 8.95 (*0-87044-335-6*); PLB 12.50 (*0-87044-340-2*) Natl Geog.

Rinard, Judith E. see National Geographic Society Staff.

Rinard, Judy. Amazing Animals of the Sea. Crump, Donald J., ed. LC 80-8796. (Illus.). 104p. (gr. 3-8). 1981. 8.95 (*0-87044-382-8*); PLB 12.50 (*0-87044-387-9*) Natl Geog.

Rinden, David, jt. auth. see Olsen, Warren.

Rinden, David, ed. see Foss, Allen J.

Rinden, David, intro. by see Foss, Allen J.

Rinden, David, jt. ed. see Olsen, Warren.

Rinehart, Kimberly R. The Greatest Gift of All. Rettmer, Georgia M., illus. 70p. 1987. 12.95 (*0-942865-02-2*) It Takes Two.

Rinehart, Paula. Never Too Small for God. 56p. (gr. 2-6). 1989. pap. 5.00 (*0-89109-270-6*) NavPress.

—One of a Kind. 64p. (gr. 2-6). 1989. pap. 5.00 (*0-89109-269-2*) NavPress.

—Stuck Like Glue. 48p. (gr. 2-6). 1988. pap. 5.00 (*0-89109-268-4*) NavPress.

Ring, Elizabeth. Assistance Dogs: In Special Service. LC 93-735. (Illus.). 32p. (gr. 2-4). 1993. PLB 12.90 (*1-56294-290-5*) Millbrook Pr.

—Companion Dogs: More Than Best Friends. (Illus.). 32p. (gr. 2-4). 1994. 12.90 (*1-56294-293-X*) Millbrook Pr.

—Detector Dogs: Hot on the Scent. LC 93-7275. (Illus.). 32p. (gr. 2-4). 1993. PLB 12.90 (*1-56294-289-1*) Millbrook Pr.

—Henry David Thoreau: In Step with Nature. LC 92-11559. (Illus.). 48p. (gr. 2-4). 1993. PLB 12.40 (*1-56294-258-1*) Millbrook Pr.

—Patrol Dogs: Keeping the Peace. (Illus.). 32p. (gr. 2-4). 1994. 12.90 (*1-56294-291-3*) Millbrook Pr.

—Rachel Carson: Caring for the Earth. LC 91-37644. (Illus.). 48p. (gr. 2-4). 1992. PLB 12.40 (*1-56294-056-2*) Millbrook Pr.

—Rachel Carson: Caring for the Earth. (gr. 4-7). 1992. pap. 4.95 (*0-395-64730-4*) HM.

—Sled Dogs: Arctic Athletes. (Illus.). 32p. (gr. 2-4). 1994. 12.90 (*1-56294-292-1*) Millbrook Pr.

—Tiger Lilies & Other Beastly Plants. Bash, Barbara, illus. LC 84-7499. 32p. (gr. 3 up). 1985. 9.95 (*0-8027-6540-8*) Walker & Co.

Ring, Kathryn M., jt. auth. see Steere, Susan.

Ringgold, Faith. Aunt Harriet's Underground in the Sky. Ringgold, Faith, illus. LC 92-20072. 32p. (ps-4). 1993. 16.00 (*0-517-58767-X*, Clarkson Potter); lib. bdg. 17.99 (*0-517-58768-8*, Clarkson Potter) Crown Bks Yng Read.

—Dinner at Aunt Connie's House. Ringgold, Faith, illus. LC 92-54871. 32p. (gr. 1-4). 1993. 14.95 (*1-56282-425-2*); PLB 14.89 (*1-56282-426-0*) Hyprn Child.

—Tar Beach. Ringgold, Faith, illus. LC 90-40410. 32p. (ps-3). 1991. 16.00 (*0-517-58030-6*); lib. bdg. 16.99 (*0-517-58031-4*) Crown Bks Yng Read.

Ringling Bros. & Barnum & Bailey Combined Shows, Inc. Staff. Animals of the Circus. Self, Kathy A., ed. LC 90-62395. (Orig.). 1990. pap. 3.50 (*1-878163-01-9*) Ringling Bros.

—Circus Days Cookbook. Self, Kathy A., ed. LC 90-62393. (Orig.). 1990. pap. 13.00 (*1-878163-00-0*) Ringling Bros.

Ringstad, M. Adventures on Library Shelves. Pearson, C., illus. LC 68-16398. 48p. (gr. 2 up). 1967. PLB 12.35 prebound (*0-87783-001-0*) Oddo.

Ringstad, Muriel. Eye of the Changer. Croly, Donald, illus. LC 83-7121. 96p. (Orig.). (gr. 4 up). 1984. pap. 9.95 (*0-88240-251-X*) Alaska Northwest.

Rinkoff, Barbara. The Remarkable Ramsey. Greenwald, Sheila, illus. (gr. 2-6). 15.25 (*0-8446-6195-3*) Peter Smith.

Riordan, James. Eastern Europe. (Illus.). 48p. (gr. 5 up). 1987. PLB 16.98 (*0-382-09468-9*) Silver Burdett Pr.

—Favorite Stories of the Ballet. Ambrus, Victor G., illus. Nureyev, Rudolf, frwd. by. LC 84-42778. (Illus.). 128p. (gr. 4 up). 14.95 (*1-56288-252-X*) Checkerboard.

—Pinocchio. Ambrus, Victor G., illus. 96p. (gr. 3 up). 1988. 18.95 (*0-19-279855-3*) OUP.

—Russia & the Commonwealth of Independent States. (Illus.). 48p. (gr. 5 up). 1992. PLB 16.98 (*0-382-24244-0*) Silver Burdett Pr.

—Tales from the Arabian Nights. Ambrus, Victor G., illus. LC 84-62456. 128p. (gr. 4 up). 1985. 14.95 (*1-56288-258-9*) Checkerboard.

—Tales of King Arthur. Ambrus, Victor G., illus. LC 81-86152. 128p. (gr. 4-7). 1982. 14.95 (*1-56288-251-1*) Checkerboard.

—Thumbelina. (Illus.). 32p. (ps-3). 1991. 15.95 (*0-399-21756-8*, Putnam) Putnam Pub Group.

—The Woman in the Moon & Other Tales of Forgotten Heroines. Barrett, Angela, illus. LC 84-20050. 96p. (ps up). 1985. 13.00 (*0-8037-0194-2*) Dial Bks Young.

Riordan, James & Lewis, Brenda R. An Illustrated Treasury of Myths & Legends. Ambrus, Victor, illus. 152p. (gr. 7 up). 1991. 12.95 (*0-87226-349-5*) P Bedrick Bks.

Riordan, James, retold by. Peter & the Wolf. Ambrus, Victor G., illus. 24p. (ps-6). 1987. 15.00 (*0-19-279824-3*) OUP.

—Peter & the Wolf. Ambrus, Victor G., illus. 24p. (gr. k up). 1989. pap. 5.95 (*0-19-272201-8*) OUP.

Riordan, James, retold by see Lambert, Stephen.

Riordan, James, ed. see Swift, Jonathan.

Riordan, James, tr. see Tolstoy, Leo.

Ripamonti, Aldo, jt. auth. see Marshall, Norman F.

Riper, Guernsey V., Jr. Knute Rockne: Young Athlete. Doremus, Robert, illus. LC 86-10791. 192p. (gr. 2-6). 1986. pap. 3.95 (*0-02-042110-9*, Aladdin) Macmillan Child Grp.

Riper, Guernsey Van see Van Riper, Guernsey, Jr.

Ripley, C. Peter. Richard Nixon. Schlesinger, Arthur M., Jr., intro. by. (Illus.). 112p. (gr. 5 up). 1988. lib. bdg. 17.95 (*0-87754-585-5*) Chelsea Hse.

Ripley, Catherine. Two Dozen Dinosaurs: A First Book of Dinosaur Facts & Mysteries, Games & Fun. Louie, Bo-Kim, illus. 32p. (gr. k up). 1992. pap. 7.95 (*0-920775-55-1*, Pub. by Greey dePencier CN) Firefly Bks Ltd.

Ripley, Dorothy. Winter Barn. Schories, Pat, illus. LC 93-32420. 1994. write for info. (*0-679-84472-4*) Random Bks Yng Read.

Ripley, Jill, ed. see Hunger, Bill.

Ripley, Robert L. Amazing Records. Stott, Carol, illus. 48p. (gr. 3-6). 1992. PLB 12.95 (*1-56065-124-5*) Capstone Pr.

—Clothing. Stott, Carol, illus. 48p. (gr. 3-6). Date not set. PLB 12.95 (*1-56065-131-8*) Capstone Pr. Postponed.

—Incredible Journeys. Stott, Carol, illus. 48p. (gr. 3-6). Date not set. PLB 12.95 (*1-56065-129-6*) Capstone Pr. Postponed.

—Inventions. Stott, Carol, illus. 48p. (gr. 3-6). Date not set. PLB 12.95 (*1-56065-125-3*) Capstone Pr. Postponed.

—Literature. Stott, Carol, illus. 48p. (gr. 3-6). 1992. PLB 12.95 (*1-56065-130-X*) Capstone Pr.

—Math & Science Facts. Stott, Carol, illus. 48p. (gr. 3-6). 1992. PLB 12.95 (*1-56065-128-8*) Capstone Pr.

—The Psychic & Supernatural. Stott, Carol, illus. 48p. (gr. 3-6). 1992. PLB 12.95 (*1-56065-127-X*) Capstone Pr.

—Puzzles. Stott, Carol, illus. 48p. (gr. 3-6). Date not set. PLB 12.95 (*1-56065-126-1*) Capstone Pr. Postponed.

Ripley Staff. Fun & Games. Stott, Carol, illus. 48p. (gr. 3-6). 1991. 11.95 (*1-56065-062-1*) Capstone Pr.

—Hours, Days & Years. (Illus.). 48p. (gr. 3-6). 1991. 11.95 (*1-56065-061-3*) Capstone Pr.

Ripoll, Jamie. How Our Senses Work. (Illus.). 1994. 13.95 (*0-7910-2128-9*, Am Art Analog) Chelsea Hse.

Ripslinger, Jon. Triangle. 1994. write for info. (*0-15-200048-8*); pap. write for info. (*0-15-200049-6*) HarBrace.

Riquier, Aline. The Cotton in Your T-Shirt. Bogard, Vicki, tr. from FRE. Riquier, Aline, illus. LC 91-45786. 38p. (gr. k-5). 1992. 4.95 (*0-944589-40-5*) Young Discovery Lib.

—The Cotton in Your T-Shirt. Riquier, Aline, illus. 40p. (gr. k-5). 1993. PLB 9.95 (*1-56674-058-4*, HTS Bks) Forest Hse.

Riskind, Mary. Apple Is My Sign. 160p. (gr. 5-8). 1981. 13.45 (*0-395-30852-6*) HM.

—Apple is My Sign. 160p. (gr. 5-9). 1993. pap. 3.80 (*0-395-65747-4*) HM.

—Follow That Mom. LC 86-20049. (gr. 4-6). 1987. 13.45 (0-395-41553-5) HM.

Risom, Ole. I Am a Kitten. Szekeres, Cyndy, illus. 26p. (ps). 1993. bds. 3.95 (0-307-12169-0), 12169, Golden Pr) Western Pub.

Risom, Ole, ed. see Zallinger, Peter.

Rispin, Karen. Anika's Mountain. LC 93-31345. (Illus.). 1994. pap. write for info. (0-8423-1219-6) Tyndale.

—Tianna, the Terrible. LC 92-19294. 1992. 4.99 (0-8423-2031-8) Tyndale.

Ristow, Kate S. & Comeaux, Maureen N. Harvest: A Faithful Approach to Life Issues for Junior High People. Titra, Stephen, illus. 167p. (gr. 6-8). 1984. pap. 24.50 (0-940634-20-1) Puissance Pubns.

Riswold, G., jt. auth. see Wilde, Oscar.

Ritch, Ronald. Bones of Molech. Graves, Helen, ed. LC 86-51078. 240p. 1987. pap. 9.95 (1-55523-061-X) Winston-Derek.

Ritchie, Alan. Erin McEwan, Your Days Are Numbered. (gr. 4-7). 1990. PLB 11.99 (0-679-90321-6) Knopf Bks Yng Read.

Ritchie, Donald A. The Senate. Schlesinger, Arthur M., Jr., intro. by. (Illus.). 96p. (gr. 5 up). 1988. lib. bdg. 14.95 (1-55546-121-2) Chelsea Hse.

Ritchie, Jo-An. Jonie Graduates. LC 78-27431. (gr. 6-12). 1979. pap. 4.50 (0-8127-0201-8) Review & Herald.

—Jonie in Alaska. Wheeler, Gerald, ed. 128p. (Orig.). (gr. 8 up). 1985. pap. 5.50 (0-8280-0250-9) Review & Herald.

Ritchie, Rita. Mountain Gorillas in Danger. Nichols, Michael, photos by. LC 91-10831. (Illus.). 32p. (gr. 2-3). 1991. PLB 15.93 (0-8368-0447-3) Gareth Stevens Inc.

Ritchie, Rita, adapted by. The Emperor's New Clothes. 20p. (ps up). 1992. write for info. (0-307-74704-2) Western Pub.

—The Princess & the Pea. 20p. (ps up). 1992. write for info. (0-307-74702-6, 64702) Western Pub.

Ritchie, Sheri & Lavranos, Destini. Goodnight Little Reindeer. (Illus.). 2p. (ps-k). 1993. 14.95 (0-9638393-1-4) Bedtime Bks.

Rithcie, Sheri, jt. auth. see Lavranos, Destini.

Ritthaler, Shelly. Dinosaurs for Lunch. 80p. (Orig.). (gr. 2). 1993. pap. 3.50 (0-380-76796-1, Camelot Young) Avon.

—Dinosaurs Wild! 96p. 1994. pap. 3.50 (0-380-77322-8, Camelot Young) Avon.

Ritvo, Edward, jt. auth. see Katz, Illana.

Ritz, David. Ray Charles: Musician. LC 93-30224. (Illus.). 1994. 18.95 (0-7910-2080-0, Am Art Analog); pap. write for info. (0-7910-2093-2, Am Art Analog) Chelsea Hse.

Rius, Maria & Parramon, J. M. The City. (ps). 1986. 6.95 (0-8120-5748-1); pap. 3.95 (0-8120-3700-6) Barron.

—The Countryside. (ps). 1986. 6.95 (0-8120-5749-X); pap. 3.95 (0-8120-3701-4) Barron.

—The Mountains. (ps). 1986. 6.95 (0-8120-5746-5); pap. 3.95 (0-8120-3698-0) Barron.

—The Seaside. (ps). 1986. 6.95 (0-8120-5747-3); pap. 5.95 (0-8120-3699-9) Barron.

Rius, Maria & Parramon, Josep M. El Campo (Countryside) (SPA., Illus.). 32p. (ps-1). 1986. pap. 6.95 (0-8120-3750-2) Barron.

—La Ciudad (City) (SPA.). 32p. (ps-1). 1986. pap. 6.95 (0-8120-3753-7) Barron.

—El Mar (Seaside) (SPA.). 32p. (ps). 1987. pap. 6.95 (0-8120-3751-0) Barron.

—La Montana (Mountains) (SPA.). 32p. (ps-1). 1987. pap. 6.95 (0-8120-3752-9) Barron.

Rius, Maria, jt. auth. see Parramon, J. M.

River, Chatham. Animal Antics ABC's. 48p. 1990. 4.99 (0-517-68881-6) Outlet Bk Co.

—Animal Fun: A-Z Activity Books. 32p. 1989. 3.50 (0-517-68796-8) Outlet Bk Co.

—Make a Pinocchio String Puppet. 1990. 4.99 (0-517-69513-8) Outlet Bk Co.

Rivera, Carlos & Eastman, P. D., trs. Are You My Mother? (SPA & ENG.). (gr. 2-4). 1967. 8.95 (0-394-81596-3) Random Bks Yng Read.

Rivera, Carlos, tr. see Dr. Seuss.

Rivera, Carlos, tr. see Palmer, Helen.

Rivers, Alice, jt. auth. see Jenness, Aylette.

Rivers, Glenn. Those Who Love the Game: Glenn "Doc" Rivers on Life in NBA & Elsewhere. (Illus.). 128p. (gr. 6 up). 1994. PLB 15.95 (0-8050-2822-6, Bks Young Read) H Holt & Co.

Rivers, Larry. Some American History: Slavery: The Black Man & the Man. Childs, Charles, intro. by. LC 72-153088. 50p. (Orig.). 1971. pap. text ed. 8.95 (0-318-42723-0, Dist. by U of TX Pr) Inst for the arts.

Rivers, W. Napoleon, et al, eds. see Dumas, Alexandre.

Rives, Elsie. Abraham: Man of Faith. (Illus.). (gr. 1-6). 1976. 5.99 (0-8054-4223-5, 4242-23) Broadman.

—The Shoemakers: God's Helpers. LC 86-4148. (gr. 4-6). 1986. pap. 5.95 (0-8054-4328-2) Broadman.

Rivinus, Edward F. Jim Thorpe. Viola, Herman, intro. by. (Illus.). 32p. (gr. 3-6). 1990. PLB 17.96 (0-8172-3403-9); pap. 4.95 (0-8114-4094-X) Raintree Steck-V.

Rivlin, Asher E. & Gimmestad, Nancy, eds. Poetry Unfolding Basic Kit. 450p. (gr. 4-12). 1983. pap. 200.00 (0-915291-05-3) Know Unltd.

Rizer, Arden, Jr. I Am the Power. Twins, Ahbleza, illus. 87p. (Orig.). (gr. 7-12). 1992. pap. 10.00x (0-939795-46-9) Amer Spirit.

Rizzo, Jeff, jt. auth. see Landes, William-Alan.

Rizzo, Kay D. Gospel in the Grocery Store. Wheeler, Penny E., ed. 96p. (gr. 7 up). 1989. pap. 4.95 (0-8280-0446-3) Review & Herald.

Rizzoto, Flora M., jt. auth. see Streiber, William R.

Rizzuto, James. How to Prepare for SAT II: Mathematics Level I. 6th ed. 1994. pap. 11.95 (0-8120-1814-1) Barron.

Roa, Annia. Peter Pelican-Pedro Pelicano. Henry, William, illus. LC 64-22715. (SPA & ENG.). (gr. k-4). 1974. 8.95 (0-87208-006-4) Island Pr Pubs.

Roach, Margaret J. I Love You, Charles Henry: Cats & Dogs in My Life. Moore, Susan & Craft, Page, eds. Moore, Susan J., illus. (gr. 1-6). 1994. pap. 13.50 (1-882666-02-X) M Roach & Assocs.
This book is actually about not only Charles Henry, her latest year old puppy. It is a collection of stories, true ones, about each of her dogs & cats in her lifetime. Laddie, the cat & Lindy, the dog belong to her 10 year old era; Charles Henry belongs with Caleb, Ebony & Tiger to her 70's era. In the years in between there have been purebreds & pets of questionable ancestry. The author has loved each with intensity & loyal possession, with much love. Cats have always come from friends with too many kittens, the humane society, or from friends moving from a house to a "NO PET" apartment. Each pet has added a new dimension into her life by their individual expressions of love. Her cats she never possessed; they possessed her. Her dogs have given & received enough love for all their lives & hers. Perhaps she has learned gentleness from her pets & how to love unconditionally. Order from: Margaret Jo Roach, 4515 NW Big Oak Place, #10, Corvallis, OR 97330, (503) 752-3396.
Publisher Provided Annotation.

—Mac & His Dog, Sir John. Moore, Susan J., illus. (Orig.). (gr. k-8). 1993. Spanish ed., Mac y Su Perro, Don Juan. pap. 13.50 (1-882666-01-1); English ed. pap. 13.50 (1-882666-00-3) M Roach & Assocs.
Sir John, the hero in the book, MAC & HIS DOG, SIR JOHN, was (in real life) CANIM HANIM which means in Turkish, "My dear Lady." I got her as a very young puppy when I was stationed in Okinawa with the USO... 1963-65. Mac, the sergeant of the USAF Sentry Dog School near Kadena Air Base, believed that no woman knew how to take care of a precious German shepherd. Much against his wishes, I got the shepherd. It was fun to prove him wrong. After Mac found out I did know how to take care of a German shepherd, Canim Hanim was invited to join the obedience training for sentry dogs. She proved to be an able student except for her fear of the dark, two-barrel tunnel. He had watched Sir John, the young lean German shepherd, go part way through the two-barrel tunnel & then stop. No urging commands could make the dog move through the tunnel. When all failed, Mac decided to take his willful pup off the training field for a walk around the Air Base on Okinawa. The ending is a delightful surprise, & proves there is really nothing to be afraid of in the dark. "Jo's story gives us characters we can admire: the kind & patient trainer, the beautiful courageous dog. Three cheers for Sir John!"--Anne Warren Smith, Writing teacher & author of young adult novels. Illustrated by Susan J. Moore. Volume discounts available from the publisher. Margaret Jo Roach, P.O. Box 213, Philomath, OR 97370. 503/752-4478.
Publisher Provided Annotation.

Roalf, Peggy. Cats. LC 91-73829. (Illus.). 48p. (gr. 3-7). 1992. PLB 14.89 (1-56282-092-3); pap. 6.95 (1-56282-091-5) Hyprn Child.

—Children. LC 92-52982. (Illus.). 48p. (Orig.). (gr. 3-7). 1993. PLB 14.89 (1-56282-308-6); pap. 6.95 (1-56282-309-4) Hyprn Child.

—Circus. LC 92-52983. (Illus.). 48p. (Orig.). (gr. 3-7). 1993. PLB 14.89 (1-56282-304-3); pap. 6.95 (1-56282-305-1) Hyprn Child.

—Dancers. LC 91-73827. (Illus.). 48p. (gr. 3-7). 1992. PLB 14.89 (1-56282-090-7); pap. 6.95 (1-56282-089-3) Hyprn Child.

—Dogs. (Illus.). 48p. (gr. 3-7). 1993. pap. 6.95 (1-56282-530-5) Hyprn Ppbks.

—Dogs. (Illus.). (gr. 3-7). 1993. PLB 14.89 (1-56282-531-3) Hyprn Child.

—Families. LC 91-73830. (Illus.). 48p. (gr. 3-7). 1992. PLB 14.89 (1-56282-088-5); pap. 6.95 (1-56282-087-7) Hyprn Child.

—Flowers. LC 92-72015. (Illus.). 48p. (gr. 3-7). 1993. PLB 14.89 (1-56282-359-0); pap. 6.95 (1-56282-358-2) Hyprn Child.

—Horses. LC 92-52979. (Illus.). 48p. (Orig.). (gr. 3-7). 1993. PLB 14.89 (1-56282-306-X); pap. 6.95 (1-56282-307-8) Hyprn Child.

—Landscapes. LC 92-52980. (Illus.). 48p. (Orig.). (gr. 3-6). 1992. PLB 14.89 (1-56282-302-7); pap. 6.95 (1-56282-303-5) Hyprn Child.

—Musicians. LC 93-15555. (Illus.). 48p. (gr. 3-7). 1993. PLB 14.89 (1-56282-533-X); pap. 6.95 (1-56282-532-1) Hyprn Ppbks.

—Seascapes. LC 91-73828. (Illus.). 48p. (gr. 3-7). 1992. PLB 14.89 (1-56282-094-X); pap. 6.95 (1-56282-093-1) Hyprn Child.

—Self-Portraits. LC 92-72042. (Illus.). 48p. (gr. 3-7). 1993. PLB 14.89 (1-56282-357-4); pap. 6.95 (1-56282-356-6) Hyprn Child.

Robart, Rose. The Cake That Mack Ate. Kovalski, Maryann, illus. LC 86-47709. (ps-3). 1987. 14.95 (0-316-74890-0) Little.

—The Cake That Mack Ate. Kovalski, Maryann, illus. (ps-3). 1991. pap. 4.95 (0-316-74891-9) Little.

Robb, Laura, compiled by. Music and Drum: Voices of War and Peace, Hope and Dreams. LC 92-39312. 1994. write for info. (0-399-22024-0, Philomel Bks) Putnam Pub Group.

Robb, Tom. First Steps in Paint: A New & Simple Way to Learn How to Paint. (Illus.). 64p. (ps up). 1992. 12.95 (0-87663-619-9) Universe.

Robbie, Dorothy & Hand, Desmond. Alice in Wonderland. (gr. k up). 1970. pap. 1.50x (0-912262-19-2) Proscenium.

Robbins. Air. 1994. write for info. (0-8050-2292-9) H Holt & Co.

—Earth. 1995. write for info. (0-8050-2294-5) H Holt & Co.

—Fire. 1995. write for info. (0-8050-2293-7) H Holt & Co.

—Water. 1994. write for info. (0-8050-2257-0) H Holt & Co.

Robbins, Alan. Heading for Trouble: A Soccer Sleuths Mystery. (Illus.). 20p. (gr. 5-7). 1992. bklt., incl. puzzle & pouch 12.95 (0-922242-34-8) Lombard Mktg.

Robbins, Albert. Immigrants from Northern Europe. LC 80-68741. 224p. 1982. 9.95 (0-385-28138-2) Delacorte.

Robbins, Barbara H. Just for Fun: Nature Stories in Sign Language. (Illus.). 112p. (Orig.). (gr. k-12). 1991. pap. 12.95 (0-9630060-0-2) Robbinspring.

Robbins, Bonnie N. Nap-Time Tales. 1992. 7.95 (0-533-10232-4) Vantage.

Robbins, Duffy. Have I Got News for You! 112p. 1993. pap. 6.99 (0-310-37461-8, Pub. by Youth Spec) Zondervan.

—It's How You Play the Game. 132p. 1991. pap. 4.99 (0-89693-856-5) SP Pubns.

Robbins, Ken. Boats. 1989. pap. 12.95 (0-590-41157-8) Scholastic Inc.

—Bridges. (Illus.). 1991. 13.95 (0-8037-0929-3); PLB 13.89 (0-8037-0930-7) Dial Bks Young.

—A Flower Grows. Robbins, Ken, illus. (gr. k up). 1990. 12.95 (0-8037-0764-9); PLB 12.89 (0-8037-0765-7) Dial Bks Young.

—Make Me a Peanut Butter Sandwich & a Glass of Milk. (Illus.). (ps up). 1992. 14.95 (0-590-43550-7, 023, Scholastic Hardcover) Scholastic Inc.

Robbins, Ken, photos by & text by. Power Machines. LC 92-30649. (Illus.). 32p. (gr. k-3). 1993. 15.95 (0-8050-1410-1, Bks Young Read) H Holt & Co.

Robbins, Mari L. Dragonwings. Vasconcelles, Keith, illus. 48p. 1993. wkbk. 5.95 (1-55734-429-9) Tchr Create Mat.

Robbins, Neal E. Ronald W. Reagan: Fortieth President of the United States. Young, Richard G., ed. LC 89-39955. (Illus.). 128p. (gr. 5-9). 1990. PLB 17.26 (0-944483-66-6) Garrett Ed Corp.
—Rutherford B. Hayes: Nineteenth President of the United States. Young, Richard G., ed. LC 88-24565. (Illus.). 128p. (gr. 5-9). 1989. PLB 17.26 (0-944483-23-2) Garrett Ed Corp.
Robbins, Phillip, jt. auth. see Beatty, Patricia.
Robbins, Robin. Looking at Nature. (Illus.). 48p. (gr. 7-9). 1992. 13.95 (0-563-34498-9, BBC-Parkwest); pap. 6.95 (0-563-34499-7, BBC-Parkwest) Parkwest Pubns.
Robbins, Ruth. Baboushka & the Three Kings. Sidjakov, Nicholas, illus. LC 60-15036. (ps up) 1960. 13.45 (0-395-27673-X, Pub. by Parnassus) HM.
—Baboushka & the Three Kings. Sidjakov, Nicholas, illus. LC 60-15036. 32p. (ps-3). 1986. pap. 5.95 (0-395-42647-2) HM.
Robbins, Sandra. Big Annie: An American Tall Tale. Oseki, Iku, illus. 32p. (gr. k-4). 1991. pap. text ed. 3.99 (1-882601-09-2); pap. text ed. 9.98 incl. cass. (1-882601-03-3) See-Mores Wrkshop.
—The Growing Rock: A Southwest Native American Tale. Oseki, Iku, illus. 32p. (Orig.). (ps-4). 1993. pap. 9.98 incl. cass. (1-882601-15-7) See-Mores Wrkshop.
—How the Turtle Got Its Shell: An African Tale. Oseki, Iku, illus. 32p. (gr. k-6). 1991. pap. text ed. 3.99 (1-882601-10-6); pap. text ed. 9.98 incl. cass. (1-882601-04-1) See-Mores Wrkshop.
—Lumpy Bumpy Pumpkin. rev. ed. Davis, Richard, illus. 32p. (ps-4). Date not set. pap. 9.98 incl. cass. (1-882601-18-1) See-Mores Wrkshop.
—Ring Around a Rainbow. Oseki, Iku, illus. 32p. (gr. k-6). 1991. pap. text ed. 3.99 (1-882601-08-4); pap. text ed. 9.98 incl. cass. (1-882601-05-X) See-Mores Wrkshop.
—Tobias Turkey. Robbins, Michael, illus. 32p. (ps-3). 1991. pap. text ed. 3.99 (1-882601-07-6); pap. text ed. 9.98 incl. cass. (1-882601-06-8) See-Mores Wrkshop.
Robbins, Trina. Catswalk: The Growing of a Girl. (Illus.). 83p. (Orig.). (gr. 3-6). 1990. pap. 17.95 (0-89087-608-8) Celestial Arts.
Robe, Rosebud Y. Tonweya & the Eagles. LC 78-72470. (Illus.). 118p. (gr. 2-6). 1992. 14.00 (0-8037-8973-4); PLB 13.89 (0-8037-8974-2) Dial Bks Young.
Roberson, John R. Transforming Russia, 1682-1991. LC 92-1377. (Illus.). 192p. (gr. 5 up). 1992. SBE 14.95 (0-689-31495-7, Atheneum Child Bk) Macmillan Child Grp.
Roberson, Kenneth see Kaczorek, Keith.
Roberson, Virginia L. Careers in Graphic Arts. rev. ed. (Illus.). (gr. 7-12). 1993. PLB 13.95 (0-8239-1349-X); pap. 9.95 (0-8239-1715-0) Rosen Group.
Robert, Adrian. The Awful Mess Mystery. Harvey, Paul, illus. LC 84-8724. 48p. (gr. 2-4). 1985. PLB 10.89 (0-8167-0402-3); pap. text ed. 3.50 (0-8167-0403-1) Troll Assocs.
—Ellen Ross, Private Detective. Garcia, T. R., illus. LC 84-8744. 48p. (gr. 2-4). 1985. PLB 10.89 (0-8167-0414-7); pap. text ed. 3.50 (0-8167-0415-5) Troll Assocs.
—My Grandma, the Witch. Fiammenghi, Gioia, illus. LC 84-8742. 48p. (gr. 2-4). 1985. PLB 10.89 (0-8167-0422-8); pap. text ed. 3.50 (0-8167-0423-6) Troll Assocs.
—Secret of the Haunted Chimney. Trivas, Irene, illus. LC 84-8763. 48p. (gr. 2-4). 1985. PLB 10.89 (0-8167-0408-2); pap. text ed. 3.50 (0-8167-0409-0) Troll Assocs.
—Secret of the Old Barn. Carter, Penny, illus. LC 84-8743. 48p. (gr. 2-4). 1985. PLB 10.89 (0-8167-0412-0); pap. text ed. 3.50 (0-8167-0413-9) Troll Assocs.
Robert, Harvey. George Washington Swept Here. 32p. (gr. 2 up). 1975. pap. 3.00 (0-88680-068-4); Director's Production Script. pap. 10.00 (0-88680-069-2); royalty on application 35.00 (0-317-03601-7) I E Clark.
Roberts. Fun with Sun Prints & Box Cameras. 1981. 8.95 (0-679-20629-9) McKay.
Roberts, Alison J. Fun with Fitness. Hayes, Dympna, ed. Mansfield, Renee & Pawczuk, Eugene, illus. 32p. (gr. 2). 1987. PLB 14.97 (0-88625-167-2); pap. 2.95 (0-88625-157-5) Durkin Hayes Pub.
Roberts, Allan. Fossils. LC 82-23521. (Illus.). 48p. (gr. k-4). 1983. PLB 15.27 (0-516-01678-4); pap. 4.95 (0-516-41678-2) Childrens.
Roberts, Allene. The Curiosity Club: Kids' Nature Activity Book. 1992. text ed. cancelled (0-471-55590-8); pap. text ed. 12.95 (0-471-55589-4) Wiley.
Roberts, Anne F., ed. see Burkett, Lucille F.
Roberts, Anne F., ed. see Findlay, Lois P.
Roberts, Bethany. Halloween Mice! Cushman, Doug, illus. LC 93-17192. 1994. write for info. (0-395-67064-0, Clarion Bks) HM.
—The Two O'Clock Secret. Grant, Christy, ed. Kramer, Robin, illus. LC 92-6405. 32p. (ps-2). 1993. 13.95g (0-8075-8159-3) A Whitman.
—Waiting-for-Christmas Stories. Stapler, Sarah, illus. LC 93-11480. Date not set. write for info. (0-395-67324-0) HM.
—Waiting-for-Spring Stories. Joyce, William, illus. LC 83-49486. 32p. (ps-3). 1984. PLB 14.89 (0-06-025062-3) HarpC Child Bks.
Roberts, Brenda C. Sticks & Stones, Bobbie Bones. (gr. 4-7). 1993. pap. 2.95 (0-590-46518-X) Scholastic Inc.
Roberts, Calvin, jt. auth. see Roberts, Susan.

Roberts, Donald. Grace: God's Special Gift. (gr. 1-4). 1982. pap. 3.99 (0-570-04060-4, 56-1363) Concordia.
Roberts, Elizabeth. Georgia, Armenia, & Azerbaijan. Akiner, Sharon, contrib. by. LC 92-2242. (Illus.). 32p. (gr. 4-6). 1992. PLB 13.90 (1-56294-309-X) Millbrook Pr.
—Glasnost: The Gorbachev Revolution. (Illus.). 94p. (gr. 9-12). 1991. 16.95 (0-237-60042-0, Pub. by Evans Bros Ltd) Trafalgar.
—The New Europe: Maastricht & Beyond - Update. LC 93-11187. (Illus.). 40p. (gr. 6-8). 1993. PLB 12.90 (0-531-17429-8, Gloucester Pr) Watts.
Roberts, Fulton, retold by see Chaucer, Geoffrey.
Roberts, Gail C. & Guttormson, Lorraine. You & School: A Survival Guide for Adolescence. Wallner, Rosemary, ed. 120p. (Orig.). (gr. 4-8). 1990. pap. 8.95 (0-915793-25-3) Free Spirit Pub.
—You & Stress: A Survival Guide for Adolescence. Wallner, Rosemary, ed. 128p. (Orig.). (gr. 4-8). 1990. pap. 8.95 (0-915793-26-1) Free Spirit Pub Co.
—You & Your Family: A Survival Guide for Adolescence. Espeland, Pamela, ed. 112p. (Orig.). (gr. 4-8). 1990. pap. 8.95 (0-915793-24-5) Free Spirit Pub.
Roberts, Helen H. see Harrington, John P.
Roberts, Howard W. Doc. LC 86-90702. (Illus.). 176p. (gr. 11 up). 1987. 11.95 (0-9617971-0-X) Circuit Writer.
Roberts, Jack L. Ruth Bader Ginsburg: Supreme Court Justice. LC 93-39015. Date not set. PLB write for info. (1-56294-497-5) Millbrook Pr.
Roberts, Jane. Emir's Education in the Proper Use of Magical Powers. Cherry, Lynne, illus. 138p. (gr. 3 up). 1984. pap. 8.95 (0-913299-08-1, Dist. by PGW) Stillpoint.
Roberts, Jenny. Samurai Warriors. 1990. PLB 12.40 (0-531-17202-3) Watts.
Roberts, Jim & Scheck, Joann. Bible Pop-O-Rama Books, 2 vols. Incl. The Brightest Star (0-8066-1601-6, 10-0915). (Illus.). 12p. (gr. 3 up). 1978. 5.99 ea., laminated (Augsburg) Augsburg Fortress.
Roberts, Jo-Anna. Alligator & the Toothfairy. Kinnell, Shannon, illus. 56p. (ps-2). 1991. 11.50g (1-879212-00-5) Desert Star Intl.
Roberts, John & Roberts, Nedra. Excellence in English. 1987. pap. text ed. 12.00 (0-8013-0134-3, 75798) Longman.
Roberts, L., et al. Action Library Four Program: Replacement Components. large type ed. Incl. The Break-In. 100p. 18.98 (0-317-02038-2, 4-00850-00); Crazy George. 100p. 18.98 (0-317-02039-0, 4-00860-00); The Day after Tomorrow. 100p. 18.98 (0-317-02040-4, 4-00870-00); Dead-Start Scramble. 100p. 18.98 (0-317-02041-2, 4-00880-00); The House on Willow Street. 100p. 18.98 (0-317-02042-0, 4-00890-00); Teacher's Guide. 24p. 1981. Am Printing Hse.
Roberts, M, ed. see Grimmer, Glenna.
Roberts, M., ed. see Kahrimanis, Leola.
Roberts, M., ed. see Kerr, Rita.
Roberts, M., ed. see Liles, Maurine W.
Roberts, M., ed. see Pamplin, Laurel J.
Roberts, M. L. World's Weirdest Reptiles. LC 93-8493. (Illus.). 32p. (gr. 2-9). 1993. PLB 11.89 (0-8167-3229-9, Pub. by Watermill Pr); pap. 2.95 (0-8167-3221-3, Pub. by Watermill Pr) Troll Assocs.
—World's Weirdest Underwater Creatures. LC 93-21053. 1993. PLB 11.89 (0-8167-3230-2, Pub. by Watermill Pr); pap. 2.95 (0-8167-3222-1, Pub. by Watermill Pr) Troll Assocs.
Roberts, Margaret. Pioneer California: Tales of Explorers, Indians, & Settlers. Mello, Marsha & Bancroft Library, illus. LC 81-22543. 296p. (gr. 6 up). 1982. 12.95 (0-914598-42-2); pap. text ed. cancelled (0-914598-43-0) Bear Flag Bks.
Roberts, Mary, ed. see Scherer, Bonnie L.
Roberts, Melissa, ed. see Baker, Charlotte.
Roberts, Melissa, ed. see Clendenin, Mary J.
Roberts, Melissa, ed. see Ebeling, Jean.
Roberts, Melissa, ed. see Gurasich, Marjorie A.
Roberts, Melissa, ed. see Harman, Betty & Meador, Nancy.
Roberts, Melissa, ed. see Hart, Jan S.
Roberts, Melissa, ed. see Kerr, Rita.
Roberts, Melissa, ed. see Matthews, Billie P. & Chichester, A. Lee.
Roberts, Melissa, ed. see Swendson, Patsy.
Roberts, Melissa, ed. see Townsend, Tom.
Roberts, Melissa, ed. see Wade, Mary D.
Roberts, Melissa, ed. see Westmoreland, Ronald P.
Roberts, Melissa, ed. see Wiggs, Susan.
Roberts, Nadine. Terror in Oak Grove High. 128p. (Orig.). 1991. pap. 3.50 (0-449-70382-7, Juniper) Fawcett.
Roberts, Nancy. America's Most Haunted Places. (Illus.). 95p. (gr. 5 up). 1987. pap. 7.95 (0-87844-074-7) Sandlapper Pub Co.
—Ghosts & Specters of the Old South. Roberts, Bruce, photos by. LC 73-20909. (Illus.). 93p. (gr. 4-12). 1984. pap. 7.95 (0-87844-058-5) Sandlapper Pub Co.
—Southern Ghosts. (Illus.). 72p. (gr. 5 up). 1987. pap. 6.95 (0-87844-075-5) Sandlapper Pub Co.
Roberts, Naurice. Andrew Young: Freedom Fighter. rev. ed. LC 83-7633. (Illus.). 32p. (gr. 2-5). 1990. PLB 14.60 (0-516-03450-2); pap. 3.95 (0-516-43450-0) Childrens.
—Barbara Jordan: The Great Lady from Texas. rev. ed. LC 83-23169. (Illus.). 32p. (gr. 2-5). 1990. PLB 14.60 (0-516-03511-8); pap. 3.95 (0-516-43511-6) Childrens.

—Cesar Chavez & La Causa. LC 85-27980. (Illus.). 32p. (gr. 2-4). 1986. PLB 14.60 (0-516-03484-7); pap. 3.95 (0-516-43484-5) Childrens.
—Cesar Chavez y la Causa: Cesar Chavez & La Causa. 32p. (gr. 2-5). 1986. PLB 13.27 (0-516-33484-0); pap. 3.95 (0-516-53484-X) Childrens.
—Harold Washington: Mayor with a Vision. LC 87-7247. (Illus.). 32p. (gr. 2-4). 1988. PLB 14.60 (0-516-03657-0); pap. 3.95 (0-516-43657-0) Childrens.
—Henry Cisneros: A Leader for the Future. rev. ed. LC 91-2330. 32p. (gr. 2-4). 1991. PLB 14.60 (0-516-04175-4); pap. 3.95 (0-516-44175-2) Childrens.
—Henry Cisneros: Alcalde Mexico-Americano. LC 85-29057. 32p. (gr. 2-5). 1987. PLB 13.27 (0-516-33485-9); pap. 3.95 (0-516-53485-8) Childrens.
Roberts, Nedra, jt. auth. see Roberts, John.
Roberts, Pamela J. The Real Texas Coloring Book: (For "Real" Texans) Neal, Jo A., illus. 38p. (ps-3). 1992. pap. 3.95 (1-881345-00-9) Penzance Co.
Roberts, Paul M. Review Text in United States History. 2nd ed. (gr. 7-9). 1989. pap. text ed. 13.33 (0-87720-857-3) AMSCO Sch.
Roberts, Paulette & Whaley, Jeanette. Seeds for Progress. LC 89-52122. (Illus.). 140p. 1990. pap. 12.95 (1-55523-309-0) Winston-Derek.
Roberts, Rachel S. Crisis at Pemberton Dike. Converse, James, illus. LC 83-18664. 152p. (gr. 7-10). 1984. pap. 4.95 (0-8361-3350-1) Herald Pr.
Roberts, Ray. Paper Airplanes from Around the World, Vol. I. 3rd, rev. & enl. ed. Roberts, Ken G., illus. 240p. (gr. 6 up). 1992. Repr. of 1988 ed. lib. bdg. 19.95 (0-929995-00-7) AIR Burbank.
Roberts, S., jt. auth. see Hawthorn, P.
Roberts, Sarah. The Adventures of Big Bird in Dinosaur Days. Mathieu, Joe, illus. LC 83-61891. 32p. (ps-3). 1984. pap. 1.50 (0-394-85926-X) Random Bks Yng Read.
—The Adventures of Grover in Outer Space. McPheeters, Neal, illus. LC 84-60188. 32p. (ps-3). 1984. pap. 1.25 (0-394-86300-3) Random Bks Yng Read.
—Bert & the Missing Mop Mix-Up. Mathieu, Joe, illus. LC 82-22971. 40p. (gr. k-2). 1983. 4.95 (0-394-85752-6) Random Bks Yng Read.
—Don't Cry, Big Bird. Leigh, Tom, illus. LC 81-4075. 40p. (gr. k-2). 1981. 4.95 (0-394-84868-3) Random Bks Yng Read.
—Don't Cry, Big Bird. Leigh, Tom, illus. LC 81-4075. 40p. (ps-3). 1993. pap. 2.99 (0-679-83950-X) Random Bks Yng Read.
—Ernie's Big Mess. Mathieu, Joe, illus. LC 81-2464. 40p. (ps-3). 1992. pap. 2.99 (0-679-82398-0) Random Bks Yng Read.
—I Want to Go Home. Mathieu, Joe, illus. LC 84-11725. 40p. (ps-3). 1985. 4.95 (0-394-87027-1) Random Bks Yng Read.
—Nobody Cares about Me! Mathieu, Joe, illus. LC 81-15913. 40p. (ps-3). 1992. pap. 2.99 (0-679-82399-9) Random Bks Yng Read.
Roberts, Sharon L. Friendship. Hohag, Linda, illus. LC 86-9641. 32p. (gr. k-3). 1986. PLB 21.35 (0-89565-350-8) Childs World.
—Somebody Lives Inside: The Holy Spirit. (Illus.). 24p. (Orig.). (gr. k-4). 1986. pap. 3.99 saddlestitched (0-570-08530-6, 56-1557) Concordia.
Roberts, Sheena, compiled by. Birds & Beasts. Price, David, illus. 80p. (gr. 1-6). 1992. 12.95 (0-7136-5653-0, Pub. by A&C Black UK) Talman.
Roberts, Susan & Roberts, Calvin. A History of New Mexico. rev. ed. (Illus.). 400p. (gr. 6-9). 1991. text ed. 45.00 (0-8263-1264-0) U of NM Pr.
Roberts, Thom. Atlantic Free Balloon Race. (gr. 3-7). 1986. pap. 2.50 (0-380-89868-3, Camelot) Avon.
—Summerdog. (Illus.). 128p. (Orig.). (gr. 1 up). 1978. pap. 2.25 (0-380-01950-7, Camelot) Avon.
Roberts, Tom. Goldilocks. Kubinyi, Laszlo, illus. LC 93-6679. (ps-6). 1993. Incl. cassette. 9.95 (0-88708-322-6, Dist. by S&S Trade) Picture Bk Studio.
—Goldilocks & the Three Bears. Kubinyi, Laszlo, illus. 32p. (gr. k up). 1991. pap. 14.95 (0-88708-146-0, Rabbit Ears); pap. 19.95 incl. cass. (0-88708-147-9, Rabbit Ears) Picture Bk Studio.
—Red Riding Hood. minibook ed. Kubinyi, Laszlo, illus. LC 93-12152. (ps-6). 1993. Incl. cassette. 9.95 (0-88708-320-X, Rabbit Ears) Picture Bk Studio.
—The Three Billy Goats Gruff. Jorgensen, David, illus. LC 89-32138. 32p. (gr. 1 up). 1991. pap. 14.95 (0-88708-117-7, Rabbit Ears); incl. cassette 19.95 (0-88708-118-5, Rabbit Ears) Picture Bk Studio.
—The Three Billy Goats Gruff. minibook ed. Jorgensen, David, illus. LC 93-6678. (ps-6). 1993. 9.95 (0-88708-319-6, Dist. by S&S Trade) Picture Bk Studio.
—The Three Little Pigs. Jorgensen, David, illus. LC 89-70097. 32p. (ps up). 1991. pap. 14.95 (0-88708-132-0, Rabbit Ears); pap. 19.95 incl. cass. (0-88708-133-9, Rabbit Ears) Picture Bk Studio.
—The Three Little Pigs. Jorgensen, David, illus. 64p. 1993. Repr. of 1990 ed. incl. cass. 9.95 (0-88708-299-8, Rabbit Ears) Picture Bk Studio.
Roberts, Tom, adapted by. Red Riding Hood. Kubinyi, Laszio, illus. LC 90-25377. 32p. (gr. k up). 1991. pap. 14.95 (0-88708-162-2, Rabbit Ears); pap. 19.95 incl. cassette (0-88708-163-0, Rabbit Ears) Picture Bk Studio.
—The Three Little Pigs. Jorgensen, David, illus. LC 92-36277. 1993. 4.95 (0-88708-298-X, Rabbit Ears) Picture Bk Studio.

Roberts, Tom & Hunter, Holly, eds. The Three Billy Goats Gruff. Jorgensen, David, illus. Lande, Art, contrib. by. (Illus.). 32p. (ps up) 1993. pap. write for info. slipcase pkg., incl. cassette (0-307-14329-5, 14329, Golden Pr) Western Pub.
—The Three Little Pigs. Jorgensen, David, illus. Lande, Art, contrib. by. (Illus.). 32p. (ps up). 1993. pap. write for info. (0-307-14327-9, 14327, Golden Pr) Western Pub.
Roberts, Tom & Ryan, Meg, eds. Goldilocks. Kubinyi, Laszlo, illus. Lande, Art, contrib. by. (Illus.). 32p. (ps up). 1992. pap. write for info. slipcase pkg., incl. cassette (0-307-14332-5, 14332, Golden Pr) Western Pub.
Roberts, Tom, adapted by see Andersen, Hans Christian.
Roberts, Willo D. Baby-Sitting Is a Dangerous Job. LC 84-20445. 192p. (gr. 4-6). 1985. SBE 13.95 (0-689-31100-1, Atheneum Child Bk) Macmillan Child Grp.
—Baby-Sitting Is a Dangerous Job. 144p. 1987. pap. 3.99 (0-449-70177-8, Juniper) Fawcett.
—Caroline, No. 7. 368p. (gr. 7 up). 1984. pap. 2.95 (0-590-33239-2) Scholastic Inc.
—Caught! LC 93-14422. 160p. (gr. 3-7). 1994. SBE 14.95 (0-689-31903-7, Atheneum Child Bk) Macmillan Child Grp.
—Caught! LC 93-14422. 1994. 14.95 (0-685-68835-6, Atheneum Child Bk) Macmillan Child Grp.
—Dark Secrets. 1991. pap. 3.50 (0-449-70395-9) Fawcett.
—Don't Hurt Laurie! Sanderson, Ruth, illus. LC 76-46569. 176p. (gr. 4-6). 1977. SBE 14.95 (0-689-30571-0, Atheneum Child Bk) Macmillan Child Grp.
—Don't Hurt Laurie! Sanderson, Ruth, illus. LC 87-21742. 176p. (gr. 3-7). 1988. pap. 3.95 (0-689-71206-5, Aladdin) Macmillan Child Grp.
—Eddie & the Fairy Godpuppy. Morrill, Leslie, illus. LC 83-15678. 136p. (gr. 3-5). 1984. SBE 12.95 (0-689-31021-8, Atheneum Child Bk) Macmillan Child Grp.
—Eddie & the Fairy Godpuppy. Morrill, Leslie, illus. LC 91-38003. 128p. (gr. 3-7). 1992. pap. 3.95 (0-689-71602-8, Aladdin) Macmillan Child Grp.
—The Girl with the Silver Eyes. LC 80-12391. 192p. (gr. 4-7). 1980. SBE 14.95 (0-689-30786-1, Atheneum Child Bk) Macmillan Child Grp.
—The Girl with the Silver Eyes. 208p. (gr. 3-7). 1991. pap. 2.95 (0-590-44248-1) Scholastic Inc.
—Jo & the Bandit. LC 91-4100. 192p. (gr. 4-7). 1992. SBE 14.95 (0-689-31745-X, Atheneum Child Bk) Macmillan Child Grp.
—The Magic Book. LC 85-20056. 156p. (gr. 3-7). 1986. SBE 13.95 (0-689-31120-6, Atheneum Child Bk) Macmillan Child Grp.
—The Magic Book. LC 88-19360. 160p. (gr. 2-6). 1988. pap. 3.95 (0-689-71284-7, Aladdin) Macmillan Child Grp.
—Megan's Island. LC 87-17505. 192p. (gr. 3-7). 1988. SBE 13.95 (0-689-31397-7, Atheneum Child Bk) Macmillan Child Grp.
—Megan's Island. LC 89-18457. 192p. (gr. 4-7). 1990. pap. 3.95 (0-689-71387-8, Aladdin) Macmillan Child Grp.
—The Minden Curse. LC 89-18336. 224p. (gr. 4-7). 1990. pap. 3.95 (0-689-71378-9, Aladdin) Macmillan Child Grp.
—More Minden Curses. LC 90-31674. 240p. (gr. 3-7). 1990. pap. 3.95 (0-689-71412-2, Aladdin) Macmillan Child Grp.
—Nightmare. LC 89-7038. 192p. (gr. 5-9). 1989. SBE 14.95 (0-689-31551-1, Atheneum Child Bk) Macmillan Child Grp.
—Nightmare. LC 91-26831. 224p. (gr. 7 up). 1992. pap. 3.95 (0-02-044938-0, Collier Young Ad) Macmillan Child Grp.
—No Monsters in the Closet. LC 91-46059. 128p. (gr. 3-7). 1992. pap. 3.95 (0-689-71577-3, Aladdin) Macmillan Child Grp.
—The Pet-Sitting Peril. LC 82-13757. 192p. (gr. 4-6). 1983. SBE 14.95 (0-689-30963-5, Atheneum Child Bk) Macmillan Child Grp.
—The Pet-Sitting Peril. 2nd ed. LC 89-77696. 176p. (gr. 3-7). 1990. pap. 3.95 (0-689-71427-0, Aladdin) Macmillan Child Grp.
—Scared Stiff. LC 90-37732. 192p. (gr. 3-7). 1991. SBE 14.95 (0-689-31692-5, Atheneum Child Bk) Macmillan Child Grp.
—Sugar Isn't Everything: A Support Book, in Fiction Form, for the Young Diabetic. LC 86-17275. 208p. (gr. 4 up) 1987. SBE 14.95 (0-689-31316-0, Atheneum Child Bk) Macmillan Child Grp.
—Sugar Isn't Everything: A Support Book, in Fiction Form, for the Young Diabetic. LC 88-3358. 192p. (gr. 3-7). 1988. pap. 3.95 (0-689-71225-1, Aladdin) Macmillan Child Grp.
—To Grandmother's House We Go. LC 89-34972. 192p. (gr. 3-7). 1990. SBE 14.95 (0-689-31594-5, Atheneum Child Bk) Macmillan Child Grp.
—The View from the Cherry Tree. LC 75-6759. 192p. (gr. 5 up). 1975. SBE 14.95 (0-689-30483-8, Atheneum Child Bk) Macmillan Child Grp.
—The View from the Cherry Tree. LC 86-22233. 192p. (gr. 4). 1987. pap. 3.95 (0-689-71131-X, Aladdin) Macmillan Child Grp.
—The View from the Cherry Tree. 3rd ed. LC 93-31170. 192p. (gr. 3-7). 1994. pap. 3.95 (0-689-71784-9, Aladdin) Macmillan Child Grp.

—What Are We Going to Do about David? LC 92-4726. 176p. (gr. 3-7). 1993. SBE 14.95 (0-689-31793-X, Atheneum Child Bk) Macmillan Child Grp.
—What Could Go Wrong? LC 88-27484. 176p. (gr. 3-7). 1989. SBE 13.95 (0-689-31438-8, Atheneum Child Bk) Macmillan Child Grp.
—What Could Go Wrong? LC 92-26177. 176p. (gr. 3-6). 1993. pap. 3.95 (0-689-71690-7, Aladdin) Macmillan Child Grp.
Roberts, Zack, jt. auth. see Joyer, Mike.
Robertson. Three Stuffed Owls, 2 vols. large type ed. (gr. 6-7). Repr. of 1965 ed. Set. write for info. NAVH.
Robertson, Brian. Brian Robertson's Favorite Texas Tales. Wilson, J. Kay, illus. LC 92-17115. 112p. (gr. 4-7). 1992. 12.95 (0-89015-862-2) Eakin-Sunbelt.
Robertson, Bruce & Pinkus, Sue. Let's All Draw Dinosaurs, Pterodactyls & Other Prehistoric Creatures. (Illus.). 144p. (gr. 3-7). 1991. pap. 9.95 (0-8230-2706-6, Watson-Guptill Bks) Watson-Guptill.
Robertson, Debbie. Blast off with Book Reports. Barry, Pat, illus. 64p. (gr. 3-8). 1985. wkbk. 7.95 (0-86653-327-3, GA 682) Good Apple.
Robertson, Everett, ed. Puppet Scripts for Use at Church, No. 2. LC 78-72843. (gr. k up). 1980. saddle-wire 7.95 (0-8054-7519-2) Broadman.
Robertson, James I., Jr. Civil War! America Becomes One Nation. LC 91-19177. (Illus.). 192p. (gr. 5-9). 1992. 14.00 (0-394-82996-4); PLB 16.99 (0-394-92996-9) Knopf Bks Yng Read.
Robertson, Jane & Pinkus, Sue. Let's All Draw Cats, Dogs & Other Animals. (Illus.). 144p. (gr. 3-7). 1991. pap. 9.95 (0-8230-2705-8, Watson-Guptill Bks) Watson-Guptill.
—Let's All Draw Monsters, Ghosts, Ghouls & Demons. (Illus.). 144p. (gr. 3-7). 1991. pap. 9.95 (0-8230-2707-4, Watson-Guptill Bks) Watson-Guptill.
Robertson, Janet. Oscar's Spots. LC 93-22199. (Illus.). 32p. (ps-2). 1993. PLB 13.95 (0-8167-3133-0); pap. write for info. (0-8167-3134-9) BrdgeWater.
Robertson, Jenny. Enciclopedia de Historias Biblicas. LaValle, Maria T., tr. King, Gordon, illus. (SPA.). 272p. (gr. 3-5). 1984. 17.00 (0-311-03671-6) Casa Bautista.
—Fear in the Glen. 128p. (gr. 5-8). 1990. pap. 4.99 (0-7459-1874-3) Lion USA.
Robertson, Jo, ed. see Benzel, David.
Robertson, Jo, ed. see Finn, Tony.
Robertson, Jo, ed. see Kjellander, Mike.
Robertson, Jo, ed. see Klarich, Tony.
Robertson, Jo, ed. see McMillan, Kent.
Robertson, Jo, ed. see Scarpa, Ron & Dorner, Terrence.
Robertson, Jo, ed. see Waterski Magazine Staff.
Robertson, Joanne. Sea Witches. (ps-3). 1991. 14.95 (0-8037-1070-4) Dial Bks Young.
Robertson, Keith. Henry Reed, Inc. McCloskey, Robert, illus. (gr. 4-6). 1958. pap. 14.95 (0-670-36796-6) Viking Child Bks.
—Henry Reed, Inc. McCloskey, Robert, illus. 240p. (gr. 4-6). 1989. pap. 4.99 (0-14-034144-7, Puffin) Puffin Bks.
—Henry Reed's Baby-Sitting Service. 206p. (gr. 2-5). 1974. pap. 3.25 (0-440-43565-X, YB) Dell.
—Henry Reed's Baby-Sitting Service. McCloskey, Robert, illus. (gr. 5-8). 1966. pap. 14.95 (0-670-36825-3) Viking Child Bks.
—Henry Reed's Baby-Sitting Service. McCloskey, Robert, illus. 208p. (gr. 4-6). 1989. pap. 3.99 (0-14-034146-3, Puffin) Puffin Bks.
—Henry Reed's Big Show. McCloskey, Robert, illus. (gr. 4-6). 1970. pap. 14.95 (0-670-36839-3) Viking Child Bks.
—Henry Reed's Big Show. McCloskey, Robert, illus. 208p. (gr. 4-7). 1978. pap. 2.50 (0-440-43570-6, YB) Dell.
—Henry Reed's Journey. LC 63-8522. 224p. (gr. 2-5). 1974. pap. 3.25 (0-440-43555-2, YB) Dell.
—Henry Reed's Journey. McCloskey, Robert, illus. 224p. (gr. 4-6). 1989. pap. 4.99 (0-14-034145-5, Puffin) Puffin Bks.
—Henry Reed's Think Tank. LC 86-4070. 176p. (gr. 3-7). 1986. pap. 12.95 (0-670-80968-3) Viking Child Bks.
Robertson, Sue & Punkus, Sue. Let's All Draw Cars, Trucks & Other Vehicles. (Illus.). 144p. (gr. 3-7). 1991. pap. 9.95 (0-8230-2704-X, Watson-Guptill Bks) Watson-Guptill.
Robertson-Boudreaux, Jane, ed. see Hughes, Deborah L.
Robertus, Polly. The Dog Who Had Kittens. Stevens, Janet, illus. LC 90-39174. 32p. (ps-3). 1991. reinforced bdg. 14.95 (0-8234-0860-4); pap. 5.95 (0-8234-0974-0) Holiday.
Robie, Joan H. Teenage Mutant Ninja Turtles Exposed. (gr. 3 up). 1991. pap. 5.95 (0-914984-31-4) Starburst.
Robinet, Harriette G. Children of the Fire. LC 91-9484. 144p. (gr. 3-7). 1991. SBE 13.95 (0-689-31655-0, Atheneum Child Bk) Macmillan Child Grp.
—Ride the Red Cycle. (Illus.). (gr. 1-5). 1980. 13.45 (0-395-29183-6) HM.
Robinette, Joseph. ABC (America Before Columbus) 40p. (gr. k-8). 1984. pap. 3.00 (0-88680-212-1); royalty on application (non-musical version) 50.00 (0-685-57918-2); (musical version) 60.00 (0-685-57919-0) I E Clark.
—Beanstalk! (Illus.). 44p. (Orig.). (gr. 2 up). 1985. pap. 3.50 (0-88680-236-9); piano & vocal score 10.00 (0-88680-237-7); royalty on application 60.00 (0-685-58014-8) I E Clark.

Robinette, Joseph & Shaw, James R. Penny & the Magic Medallion. (Illus.). 44p. (Orig.). (gr. k up). 1987. pap. 3.00 (0-88680-283-0); piano & vocal score 12.50 (0-88680-284-9); royalty on application 60.00 (0-685-58256-6) I E Clark.
Robins, Dave. Just Punishment. (Illus.). 64p. (gr. 5-8). 1990. PLB 12.40 (0-531-17252-X) Watts.
Robins, Deri. Making Prints. LC 92-40216. 40p. (gr. 3-7). 1993. 10.95 (1-85697-925-3); pap. 5.95 (1-85697-924-5) Kingfisher Bks.
—Papier Mache. LC 92-41102. (Illus.). 40p. (gr. 3-7). 1993. 10.95 (1-85697-927-X); pap. 5.95 (1-85697-926-1) Kingfisher Bks.
Robins, Deri & Buchanan, George. Santa's Sackful of Best Christmas Ideas. LC 92-41103. 32p. (gr. 2-6). 1993. pap. 5.95 (1-85697-919-9) Kingfisher Bks.
Robins, Deri, et al. The Kids Can Do It Book: Fun Things to Make and Do. Stowell, Charlotte, illus. LC 92-43345. 80p. (gr. k-4). 1993. pap. 9.95 (1-85697-860-5) Kingfisher Bks.
Robins, Dorothy. Katie's Birthday Wish. LC 88-81467. (Illus.). 32p. (Orig.). 1988. pap. 8.95 (0-937124-18-4) Kimbo Educ.
Robins, Eleanor. Meg Parker, 5 in each set, Sets 1 & 2. (Illus.). (gr. 2-7). 1984. Set. ea. 15.00 (0-685-61074-8) Set 1 (0-87879-439-5) Set 2 (0-87879-472-7) High Noon Bks.
Robins, Joan. Addie Meets Max. Truesdell, Sue, illus. LC 84-48329. 32p. (ps-3). 1985. PLB 13.89 (0-06-025064-X) HarpC Child Bks.
—Addie Meets Max. Truesdell, Sue, illus. LC 84-48329. 32p. (ps-2). 1988. pap. 3.50 (0-06-444116-4, Trophy) HarpC Child Bks.
—Addie Runs Away. Truesdell, Sue, illus. LC 88-24350. 32p. (ps-2). 1989. PLB 10.89 (0-06-025081-X) HarpC Child Bks.
—Addie Runs Away. Truesdell, Sue, illus. LC 88-24350. 32p. (ps-2). 1991. pap. 3.50 (0-06-444147-4, Trophy) HarpC Child Bks.
—Addie's Bad Day. Truesdell, Sue, illus. LC 92-13101. 32p. (ps-2). 1993. 14.00 (0-06-021297-7); PLB 13.89 (0-06-021298-5) HarpC Child Bks.
Robinson. Mom, You're Fired! 1992. pap. 2.75 (0-590-44903-6, Apple Paperbacks) Scholastic Inc.
Robinson, Amelia B. A Bridge over Jordan. 2nd & rev. ed. Huth, Christina & Wertz, Marianna, eds. LaRouche, Lyndon H., Jr., intros. by. LC 90-62730. (Illus.). 415p. (gr. 12 up). 1991. pap. 10.00 (0-9621095-4-1) Schiller Inst.
Robinson, Andrew. Wrath of the Seven Horsemen. MacDonald, George & Charlton, S. Coleman, eds. 32p. (Orig.). (gr. 10-12). 1987. pap. 6.00 (0-915795-86-8, 31) Iron Crown Ent Inc.
Robinson, Andrew M. The Gadgets! 48p. (gr. 10-12). 1986. pap. 8.00 (0-915795-64-7, 23) Iron Crown Ent Inc.
Robinson, Ann. Cappy Claus. Hall, Constance, illus. 16p. (ps-6). 1992. pap. 4.95 (0-9633373-0-0) Chameleon FL.
Robinson, Barbara. The Best Christmas Pageant Ever. Brown, Judith G., illus. LC 72-76501. 96p. (gr. 3 up). 1972. 14.00 (0-06-025043-7); PLB 13.89 (0-06-025044-5) HarpC Child Bks.
—The Best Christmas Pageant Ever. Brown, Judith G., illus. LC 72-76501. 96p. (gr. 3 up). 1988. pap. 28.00 (0-06-440278-9, Trophy); 3.95 (0-685-44099-0) HarpC Child Bks.
—The Herdmans, Back Again. 96p. (gr. 3 up). 1994. 14.00 (0-06-023039-8); PLB 13.89 (0-06-023043-6) HarpC Child Bks.
—My Brother Louis Measures Worms: And Other Louis Stories. LC 87-45302. 160p. (gr. 3-7). 1988. 13.00 (0-06-025082-8); PLB 12.89 (0-06-025083-6) HarpC Child Bks.
—My Brother Louis Measures Worms: and Other Louis Stories. LC 87-45302. 160p. (gr. 5 up). 1990. pap. 3.50 (0-06-440362-9, Trophy) HarpC Child Bks.
Robinson, Betty. A Guide to Arkansas Horse Trails. (Illus.). 82p. (Orig.). (gr. 8 up). 1991. pap. 8.95 (0-929183-03-7) Equestrian Unlimited.
Robinson, Betty & Gordon, Pat. The Horse Source: A Resource Guide for Mail Order Horse & Rider Supplies. 2nd ed. 60p. (gr. 8 up). 1991. pap. 6.95 (0-929183-02-9) Equestrian Unlimited.
Robinson, Clarie. Penguin. Hargreaves, Angela, illus. LC 91-44727. 32p. (gr. 4-6). 1993. text ed. 11.59 (0-8167-2771-6); tchr's. ed. 3.95 (0-8167-2772-4) Troll Assocs. Postponed.
Robinson, Colin. Sunrise. Robinson, Colin, illus. LC 91-40988. 32p. (ps-1). 1992. PLB 12.95 (0-87226-468-8, Bedrick Blackie) P Bedrick Bks.
Robinson, Dennis M, jt. auth. see Robinson, Jacqueline.
Robinson, Dorothy. The Legend of Africania. Temple, Herbert, illus. LC 74-4781. 32p. (gr. k-5). 1974. 10.95 (0-87485-037-1) Johnson Chi.
Robinson, Fay. A Frog Inside My Hat. Moore, Cyd, photos by. LC 93-22200. (Illus.). 64p. (ps-3). 1993. PLB 16.95 (0-8167-3129-2); pap. write for info. (0-8167-3130-6) BrdgeWater.
—A Ghost in the Toy Box. Iosa, Ann W., illus. LC 92-10758. 32p. (ps-2). 1993. PLB 15.00 (0-516-02371-3); pap. 3.95 (0-516-42371-1) Childrens.
—Old MacDonald Had a Farm. Iosa, Ann W., illus. LC 92-10757. 32p. (ps-2). 1993. PLB 15.00 (0-516-02372-1) Childrens. Postponed.
—Pizza Soup. Iosa, Ann W., illus. LC 92-10756. 32p. (ps-2). 1993. PLB 15.00 (0-516-02373-X); pap. 3.95 (0-516-42373-8) Childrens.

—Real Bears & Alligators. Iosa, Ann W., illus. LC 92-10755. 32p. (ps-2). 1992. PLB 15.00 (0-516-02374-8) Childrens.
—Real Bears & Alligators. Iosa, Ann, illus. LC 92-10755. 32p. (ps-2). 1993. pap. 3.95 (0-516-42374-6) Childrens.
—Rhymes We Like. Iosa, Ann W., illus. LC 92-10754. 32p. (ps-2). 1993. PLB 15.00 (0-516-02375-6) Childrens. Postponed.
—Space Probes to the Planets. Grant, Christy, ed. LC 92-10792. (Illus.). 32p. (gr. k-3). 1993. 14.95g (0-8075-7548-8) A Whitman.
—We Love Fruit! LC 92-13312. (Illus.). 32p. (ps-2). 1992. PLB 12.60 (0-516-06006-6); big bk. 30.60 (0-516-49633-6) Childrens.
—We Love Fruit. LC 92-13312. (Illus.). 32p. (ps-2). 1993. pap. 3.95 (0-516-46006-4) Childrens.
—When Nicki Went Away. Iosa, Ann W., illus. LC 92-13835. 32p. (ps-2). 1992. PLB 15.00 (0-516-02376-4) Childrens.
—When Nicki Went Away. Iosa, Ann, illus. LC 92-13835. 32p. (ps-2). 1993. pap. 3.95 (0-516-42376-2) Childrens.
Robinson, Fay, jt. auth. see Mathews, Judith.
Robinson, Fay, jt. auth. see Matthews, Judith.
Robinson, Glen. Fifty-Two Things to Do on Sabbath. Wheeler, Gerald, ed. Kinzer, Kaaren, illus. (Orig.). 1983. pap. 2.95 (0-8280-0199-5) Review & Herald.
Robinson, Heather. The Simply Wonderful Cookbook. (Illus.). 48p. (gr. 4-8). 1992. text ed. 12.95 (0-7459-2204-X) Lion USA.
Robinson, J. H. & Robinson, R. D. Involving Children in One Hundred Four Sunday School Openings. 72p. 1983. pap. 5.99 (0-570-03912-6, 12HH2851) Concordia.
Robinson, Jackie & Duckett, Alfred. Breakthrough to the Big League: The Story of Jackie Robinson. LC 90-48588. (Illus.). 160p. (gr. 6-10). 1991. PLB 13.95 (1-55905-094-2) Marshall Cavendish.
Robinson, Jacqueline & Robinson, Dennis M. How to take High School Entrance Exams: Fully Revised & Enlarged. rev. ed. 608p. (gr. 7-8). 1988. pap. 9.95 wkbk. (0-13-162264-1) P-H.
Robinson, Jacqueline S. I'm Ready for Reading. (ps-k). 1990. 19.95 (0-9624827-0-6) A Plus Lrn.
—More Ready for Reading. (gr. k-2). 1990. 19.95 (0-9624827-1-4) A Plus Lrn.
Robinson, Jan. The Story of Warple. Jewell, Jack, illus. 32p. (ps). 1990. 12.95 (0-89334-137-1) Humanics Ltd.
Robinson, Jane. The Whale in Lowell's Cove. Robinson, Jane, illus. LC 91-77670. 48p. (gr. 1-4). 1992. 14.95 (0-89272-308-4) Down East.
Robinson, Jeri. Activities for Anyone, Anytime, Anywhere. LC 82-15353. 96p. 1983. pap. 10.95 (0-316-75145-6) Little.
Robinson, Jerry W., et al. Applied Keyboarding. LC 93-7454. 1994. write for info. (0-538-62297-0); pap. write for info. (0-538-62298-9) S-W Pub.
Robinson, Jessie B., jt. auth. see Eisenberg, Azriel.
Robinson, Joan. WordBuilding. (gr. 4-8). 1989. pap. 9.95 (0-8224-7450-6) Fearon Teach Aids.
—WordStrength. (gr. 4-8). 1989. pap. 9.95 (0-8224-7451-4) Fearon Teach Aids.
—WordWise. (gr. 4-8). 1989. pap. 9.95 (0-8224-7452-2) Fearon Teach Aids.
Robinson, Lafayette. Penmanship from A to Z. Robinson, Lafayette, illus. 72p. (gr-4). 1988. wkbk. 7.95 (0-9621081-1-1) Educ Graphics.
—Rite Easy from A to Z. Gonzalez, Inez, tr. Wigglesworth, Sheila, illus. (SPA & ENG.). 48p. (gr. 1-3). 1993. lib. bdg. write for info. (0-9621081-0-3) Educ Graphics.
Robinson, Linton H. Mexican Slang: A Guide. 160p. (Orig.). 1992. pap. 6.95 (0-9627080-7-0) In One EAR.
Robinson, Marc. Cock-a-Doodle Doo! What Does It Sound Like to You? Jenkins, Steve, illus. LC 92-30961. 32p. 1993. 12.95 (1-55670-267-1) Stewart Tabori & Chang.
Robinson, Margaret A. A Woman of Her Tribe. LC 90-31534. 144p. (gr. 7 up). 1990. SBE 13.95 (0-684-19223-3, Scribners Young Read) Macmillan Child Grp.
—A Woman of Her Tribe. 1991. pap. 3.99 (0-449-70405-X, Juniper) Fawcett.
Robinson, Marileta. The Big Bicycle Race. Morrill, Leslie, illus. 1984. incl. cassette 7.95 (0-685-42663-7); 5.95 (0-910313-29-6) Parker Bros.
Robinson, Marlene. What Good Is a Tail? (gr. 4-7). 1994. pap. 7.95 (1-56171-086-5) Shapolsky Pubs.
—Who Knows This Nose? (gr. 4-7). 1994. pap. 7.95 (1-56171-085-7) Shapolsky Pubs.
Robinson, Mary. The Amazing Valvano & the Mystery of the Hooded Rat. LC 87-26179. 168p. (gr. 3-7). 1988. 13.95 (0-395-44314-8) HM.
—The Amazing Valvano & the Mystery of the Hooded Rat. 160p. (gr. 5). 1990. pap. 2.75 (0-380-70713-6, Camelot) Avon.
—Give It up, Mom. (gr. 5-9). 1989. 13.45 (0-395-49700-0) HM.
—Give It up, Mom. 144p. (gr. 4). 1992. pap. 2.99 (0-380-71126-5, Camelot) Avon.
Robinson, Matt. Gordon of Sesame Street Storybook. (Illus.). (gr. 7-9). 1972. lib. bdg. 5.99 (0-394-92406-1) Random Bks Yng Read.
Robinson, Nancy K. Angela & the Broken Heart. 1991. 12.95 (0-590-43212-5, Scholastic Hardcover) Scholastic Inc.

—Angela & the Broken Heart. 144p. 1992. pap. 2.95 (0-590-43211-7, Apple Paperbacks) Scholastic Inc.
—Angela, Private Citizen. LC 89-5918. 146p. (gr. 3-6). 1989. pap. 10.95 (0-590-41726-6) Scholastic Inc.
—Countess Veronica. 176p. (gr. 3-7). 1994. 13.95 (0-590-44485-9, Scholastic Hardcover) Scholastic Inc.
—The Ghost of Whispering Rock. Eagle, Ellen, illus. LC 92-58256. 64p. (gr. 2-6). 1992. 13.95 (0-8234-0944-9) Holiday.
—Just Plain Cat. LC 82-18258. 128p. (gr. 3-6). 1983. SBE 13.95 (0-02-777350-7, Four Winds) Macmillan Child Grp.
—Just Plain Cat. reissue ed. 1992. pap. 2.95 (0-590-45850-7, Apple Paperbacks) Scholastic Inc.
—Oh Honestly, Angela! 128p. (gr. 4-6). 1985. pap. 10.95 (0-590-41287-6) Scholastic Inc.
—Oh Honestly, Angela! Williams, Richard, illus. 128p. 1991. pap. 2.95 (0-590-44902-8, Apple Paperbacks) Scholastic Inc.
—Veronica Knows Best. 128p. (gr. 4-6). 1987. pap. 10.95 (0-590-40509-8) Scholastic Inc.
—Veronica Knows Best. 160p. 1992. pap. 2.95 (0-590-44900-1, Apple Paperbacks) Scholastic Inc.
—Veronica Meets Her Match. (gr. 3-7). 1990. 12.95 (0-590-41512-3, Scholastic Hardcover) Scholastic Inc.
—Veronica Meets Her Match. 128p. 1992. pap. 2.95 (0-590-45766-7, Apple Paperbacks) Scholastic Inc.
—Veronica the Show-Off. LC 85-44483. 128p. (gr. 3-6). 1984. SBE 13.95 (0-02-777360-4, Four Winds) Macmillan Child Grp.
—Wendy & the Bullies. (gr. 4-7). 1991. pap. 2.95 (0-590-44899-4) Scholastic Inc.
—Wendy on the Warpath. LC 93-32739. (gr. 3 up). 1994. 13.95 (0-590-45571-0) Scholastic Inc.
Robinson, Phyllis, jt. auth. see Ransford, Lynn.
Robinson, R. D., jt. auth. see Robinson, J. H.
Robinson, Ronald W. Stanley, the Talking Parrot. Todd, Thomas, illus. LC 89-60801. 22p. (Orig.). (gr. 3-4). 1989. Incl. cassette & filmstrip pkg. 12.95 (0-9622692-2-0); Incl. cassette pkg. 8.95 (0-9622692-1-2); pap. 4.95 (0-9622692-0-4) R W Robinson.
Robinson, Sandra C. The Everywhere Bear. (Illus.). 64p. (gr. 4-6). 1992. pap. 7.95 (1-879373-07-6) R Rinehart.
—Mountain Lion: Puma, Panther, Painter, Cougar. (Illus.). 64p. (gr. 4-6). 1991. pap. 7.95 (1-879373-00-9) R Rinehart.
—Sea Otters, River Otters: A Story & Activity Book. Opsahl, Gail K., illus. LC 92-62078. 64p. (Orig.). (gr. 1-6). 1993. pap. 7.95 (1-879373-41-6) R Rinehart.
—The Wonder of Wolves: A Story & Activity Book. Opsahl, Gail K., illus. (gr. 1-6). 1989. pap. 7.95 (0-911797-65-3) R Rinehart.
Robinson, Scott. Indy Cars. LC 87-30509. (Illus.). 48p. (gr. 5-6). 1988. RSBE 11.95 (0-89686-356-5, Crestwood Hse) Macmillan Child Grp.
Robinson, Terry, ed. see Axiom Information Resources Staff.
Robinson, Tom, jt. auth. see Heus, John.
Robinson, W. Heath. Adventures of Uncle Lubin. (ps-3). 1992. 15.95 (0-87923-884-4) Godine.
Robinson, W. Wright. Incredible Facts about the Ocean: The Land Below, the Life Within, Vol. 2. LC 85-25430. (Illus.). 120p. (gr. 4 up). 1987. RSBE 13.95 (0-87518-358-1, Dillon) Macmillan Child Grp.
—Incredible Facts about the Ocean, Vol. 3: How We Use It, How We Abuse It. (Illus.). 128p. (gr. 4 up). 1990. RSBE 13.95 (0-87518-435-9, Dillon) Macmillan Child Grp.
Robinsunne. Nannee. Robinsunne, illus. 36p. (ps). 1993. 15.95 (0-9636986-0-5) Robinsunne Pstcrd.
Robison, Deborah & Perez, Carla. Your Turn, Doctor. Robison, Deborah, illus. LC 81-68778. 32p. (ps-2). 1982. Dial Bks Young.
Robison, Nancy. Buffalo Bill. LC 90-47221. (Illus.). 64p. (gr. 3-5). 1991. PLB 12.90 (0-531-20007-8) Watts.
—Ten Tall Soldiers. Knight, Hilary, illus. LC 87-32090. 32p. (ps-2). 1991. 13.95 (0-8050-0768-7, Bks Young Read) H Holt & Co.
Robison, Phyllis, jt. auth. see Smith, Mary.
Robles, Harold. Albert Schweitzer: An Adventurer for Humanity. Miller, Rhena S., pref. by. (Illus.). 64p. (gr. 4-6). 1994. 14.90 (1-56294-352-9) Millbrook Pr.
Robson, Denny. Animal Homes. (ps). 1991. 5.95 (0-8120-6242-6) Barron.
—Butterflies & Moths. (Illus.). 32p. (gr. 4-6). 1991. 13.95 (0-237-60170-2, Pub. by Evans Bros Ltd) Trafalgar.
—Cooking: Hands-on Projects. LC 91-2738. (Illus.). 32p. (gr. k-4). 1991. PLB 11.90 (0-531-17344-5, Gloucester Pr) Watts.
—Grow It for Fun: Hands-on Projects. LC 91-2737. (Illus.). 32p. (gr. k-4). 1991. PLB 11.90 (0-531-17343-7, Gloucester Pr) Watts.
—Jewelry: Arts & Crafts. LC 93-4835. (Illus.). 32p. (gr. 3-5). 1993. PLB 11.90 (0-531-17427-1, Gloucester Pr) Watts.
—Kites & Flying Objects. LC 91-75995. (Illus.). 32p. (gr. 2-4). 1992. PLB 11.90 (0-531-17342-9, Gloucester Pr) Watts.
—Masks & Funny Faces. LC 91-75994. (Illus.). 32p. (gr. 2-4). 1992. PLB 11.90 (0-531-17345-3, Gloucester Pr) Watts.
—Paper Craft: Arts & Crafts. LC 93-8580. (Illus.). 32p. 1993. PLB 11.90 (0-531-17428-X, Gloucester Pr) Watts.
—The Planets. LC 91-10315. (Illus.). 32p. (gr. k-4). 1991. PLB 11.90 (0-531-17335-6, Gloucester Pr) Watts.

—Sharks. LC 91-34966. (Illus.). 32p. (gr. 1-4). 1992. PLB 11.90 (0-531-17354-2, Gloucester Pr) Watts.
—Snakes. (Illus.). 32p. (gr. 1-4). 1992. PLB 11.90 (0-531-17355-0, Gloucester Pr) Watts.
—The Sun. LC 91-10316. (Illus.). 32p. (gr. k-4). 1991. PLB 11.90 (0-531-17336-4, Gloucester Pr) Watts.
Robson, Denny A. Christmas. LC 92-3214. 1992. 11.90 (0-531-17333-X, Gloucester Pr) Watts.
—Having a Party. LC 92-9552. 1992. 11.90 (0-531-17340-2, Gloucester Pr) Watts.
—Racing Cars. LC 92-9551. 1992. 11.90 (0-531-17380-1, Gloucester Pr) Watts.
Robson, John, ed. Me & You. (Illus.). 48p. (Orig.). (gr. 6-9). 1982. pap. 2.50 (0-936098-33-3) Intl Marriage.
—You & Your Family. (Illus.). 30p. (Orig.). (gr. 2-4). 1981. pap. 2.50 (0-936098-30-9) Intl Marriage.
Robson, Pam. Clocks, Scales & Measurements. (Illus.). 32p. (gr. 5-7). 1993. PLB 12.40 (0-531-17419-0, Gloucester Pr) Watts.
—Electricity. LC 92-37099. (Illus.). 32p. (gr. 5-8). 1993. PLB 12.40 (0-531-17398-4, Gloucester Pr) Watts.
—Light, Color & Lens: Science Workshop. (gr. 4-7). 1993. 17.71 (0-531-71407-1) Watts.
—Light, Prisms & Optics. (Illus.). 32p. (gr. 4-7). 1993. PLB 17.71 (0-531-17407-7, Gloucester Pr) Watts.
—Magnetism. LC 92-37098. (Illus.). 32p. (gr. 5-8). 1993. PLB 12.40 (0-531-17399-2, Gloucester Pr) Watts.
—Water, Paddles, & Boats. LC 92-375. 1992. 12.40 (0-531-17376-3, Gloucester Pr) Watts.
Robson, Pam, jt. auth. see Chapman, Gillian.
Robson, Pat, illus. Oil. 32p. (gr. 3-5). 1985. 7.95x (0-86685-449-5) Intl Bk Ctr.
—Rain. 32p. (gr. 3-5). 1985. 7.95x (0-86685-451-7) Intl Bk Ctr.
Robson, Tom. Musical Wisdom: Songs & Drawings for the Child in Us All. James, Nancy V., illus. 88p. (Orig.). (gr. k-6). 1992. pap. 16.95 (0-9633332-0-8) Laughing Cat.
Robson, W. W., intro. by see Kipling, Rudyard.
Roby, Cynthia. Feeling Different, Feeling Fine: Kids Talk about Their Learning Problems. LC 93-6532. 1993. write for info. (0-8075-2334-8) A Whitman.
—When Learning Is Tough: Kids Talk about Learning Disabilities. (ps-3). 1993. 12.95 (0-8075-8892-X) A Whitman.
Roc, Margaret. Little Koala. (ps-3). 1993. pap. 7.00 (0-207-17039-8, Pub. by Angus & Robertson AT) HarpC.
Rocard, Ann. Cool Calvin. Rousset, Francoise, illus. (ps-4). 1991. 9.95 (1-56182-030-X) Atomium Bks.
—Hobee Scrogneenee. Degano, Marino, illus. 28p. (ps-4). 1991. smythe sewn reinforced bdg. 9.95 (1-56182-000-8) Atomium Bks.
—Hobee Scrogneenee at Joey's School. Degano, Marino, illus. 28p. (ps-4). 1991. smythe sewn reinforced bdg. 9.95 (1-56182-001-6) Atomium Bks.
—Kouk & the Ice Bear. Morgan, illus. 38p. (ps-1). 1991. smythe sewn reinforced bdg. 9.95 (1-56182-029-6) Atomium Bks.
Roche, Luane. The Proud Tree. 64p. (gr. 2-6). 1981. pap. 1.95 (0-89243-146-6) Liguori Pubns.
Roche, P. K. Webster & Arnold & the Giant Box. Roche, P. K., illus. LC 80-11595. 56p. (ps-3). 1980. Dial Bks Young.
—Webster & Arnold Go Camping. (Illus.). 32p. (ps-3). 1991. pap. 3.95 (0-14-050806-6, Puffin) Puffin Bks.
Roche, P. K., selected by. & illus. At Christmas Be Merry. 32p. (ps-1). 1989. pap. 3.95 (0-14-050680-2, Puffin) Puffin Bks.
Roche, Richard. The Call of the Wood Pigeon - Glaoch an Choluir Choille: A Day in the Life of a Monk in Pre-Viking Ireland. (Illus., Orig.). (gr. 1-8). 1990. pap. 9.95 (1-85390-047-8, Pub. by Veritas Pubns ER) Irish Bks Media.
Rochelle, Belinda. When Jo Louis Won the Title. Johnson, Larry, illus. LC 93-34317. (gr. 4 up). 1994. write for info. (0-395-66614-7) HM.
—Witnesses to Freedom: Young People Who Fought for Civil Rights. LC 93-16165. (Illus.). 112p. (gr. 3-7). 1993. 15.99 (0-525-67377-6, Lodestar Bks) Dutton Child Bks.
Rochester Folk Art Guild Staff. Little Shooter of Birds & the Great Sun. (ps-7). 1981. 9.50 (0-686-33125-7) Rochester Folk Art.
—Sunlight in the Morning: Songs from the Farm. (Illus.). 40p. (gr. k-6). 1983. 13.00 (0-686-40298-7); cassette tape 6.00 (0-317-00393-3) Rochester Folk Art.
Rochester, Lois & Mandell, Judy. The One Hour College Applicant. rev. ed. LC 90-52815. (Illus.). 112p. (gr. 10-12). 1990. pap. 8.95 (0-914457-38-1) Mustang Pub.
Rochevelle, David la see La Rochelle, David.
Rochman, H. Voices in the Dark. Date not set. 14.00 (0-06-025024-0, Festival); PLB 13.89 (0-06-025025-9, Festival) HarpC Child Bks.
Rochman, Hazel. Against Borders: Promoting Books for a Multicultural World. LC 93-17840. 288p. (Orig.). (gr. 7 up). 1993. pap. text ed. 16.95 (0-8389-0601-X) ALA.
—Who Do You Think You Are? Stories of Friends & Enemies. 1993. 15.95 (0-316-75355-6) Little.
Rochman, Hazel, ed. Somehow Tenderness Survives: Stories of Southern Africa. LC 88-916. 160p. (gr. 7 up). 1988. 12.95 (0-06-025022-4); PLB 12.89 (0-06-025023-2) HarpC Child Bks.
—Somehow Tenderness Survives: Stories of Southern Africa. LC 88-916. 208p. (gr. 7 up). 1990. pap. 3.95 (0-06-447063-6, Trophy) HarpC Child Bks.

Rock, Gail. Addie & the King of Hearts. (gr. 4-6). 1986. pap. 2.50 (0-440-40076-7, YB) Dell.
—A Dream for Addie. (gr. 4-6). 1986. pap. 2.50 (0-440-42151-9, YB) Dell.
—The House Without a Christmas Tree. Gehm, Charles, illus. LC 74-162. 96p. (gr. 2 up). 1974. lib. bdg. 9.99 (0-394-92833-4) Knopf Bks Yng Read.
—The House Without a Christmas Tree. (gr. 4-6). 1985. pap. 2.95 (0-440-43394-0, YB) Dell.
—The Thanksgiving Treasure. Gehm, Charles, illus. LC 74-163. 96p. (gr. 2 up). 1974. PLB 11.99 (0-394-92834-2) Knopf Bks Yng Read.
Rock, Lois. The Lord's Prayer for Children. (Illus.). 32p. (gr. k-2). 1993. 8.99 (0-7459-2542-1) Lion USA.
—Simply Wonderful Craftbook. (Illus.). 48p. (gr. 3-6). 1993. 13.95 (0-7459-2503-0) Lion USA.
Rock, Louise, ed. see Allen, Robert A.
Rock, Maxine. The Automobile & The Environment. (Illus.). (gr. 5 up). 1992. lib. bdg. 19.95 (0-7910-1592-0) Chelsea Hse.
Rockefeller, R. D. & Chen, Gerald H. World Famous Investors Advice for 1993-2000: The Greatest Investors of All Time & Their Favorite Stocks, Bonds, Mutual Funds, Income & New Strategies for 1993-2000. Folder, M. Michael, ed. LC 93-774404. 96p. (gr. 9 up). 1993. pap. 12.95 (0-9632572-2-6) MDMI Int Pubns.
Rockefeller, Ruth, frwd. by see Edmisten, Donald D.
Rocklin. Grandmaman Hockey. 1993. 15.95 (0-8050-2322-4) H Holt & Co.
Rocklin, Joanne. Discovering Martha. LC 91-18973. 144p. (gr. 3-7). 1991. SBE 13.95 (0-02-777444-9, Macmillan Child Bk) Macmillan Child Grp.
—Jace the Ace. De Groat, Diane, illus. LC 90-34095. 112p. (gr. 2-6). 1990. SBE 12.95 (0-02-777445-7, Macmillan Child Bk) Macmillan Child Grp.
—Musical Chairs & Dancing Bears. De Matharel, Laure, illus. LC 92-41078. 32p. (ps-2). 1993. PLB 14.95 (0-8050-2374-7, Bks Young Read) H Holt & Co.
—Sonia Begonia. Downing, Julie, illus. LC 85-23120. 96p. (gr. 3-7). 1986. SBE 12.95 (0-02-777310-8, Macmillan Child Bk) Macmillan Child Grp.
—Sonia Begonia. 112p. (gr. 3-7). 1987. pap. 2.50 (0-380-70307-6, Camelot) Avon.
—Three Smart Pals. Brunkus, Denise, illus. 48p. (ps-4). 1994. pap. 3.50 (0-590-47431-6, Cartwheel) Scholastic Inc.
Rocklin, Joanne, jt. auth. see Levinson, Nancy S.
Rockwell, Anne. Apples & Pumpkins. Rockwell, Lizzy, illus. LC 88-22628. 24p. (ps-1). 1989. RSBE 13.95 (0-02-777270-5, Macmillan Child Bk) Macmillan Child Grp.
—At the Beach. Rockwell, Harlow, illus. LC 86-2943. 24p. (ps-1). 1987. RSBE 13.95 (0-02-777940-8, Macmillan Child Bk) Macmillan Child Grp.
—At the Beach. Rockwell, Harlow, illus. LC 90-45620. 24p. (ps-1). 1991. pap. 3.95 (0-689-71494-7, Aladdin) Macmillan Child Grp.
—Bear Child's Book of Special Days. LC 89-1633. (Illus.). 32p. (ps-1). 1989. 12.95 (0-525-44508-0, DCB) Dutton Child Bks.
—Big Boss. (Illus.). 64p. (gr. 1-3). 1987. pap. 3.95 (0-689-71125-5, Aladdin) Macmillan Child Grp.
—Big Wheels. Rockwell, Anne, illus. LC 85-16248. 24p. (ps-1). 1986. 12.95 (0-525-44226-X, DCB) Dutton Child Bks.
—Bikes. Rockwell, Ann, illus. LC 86-19923. 24p. (ps-1). 1987. 11.95 (0-525-44287-1, DCB) Dutton Child Bks.
—Bikes. LC 86-19923. (Illus.). 24p. (ps-1). 1991. pap. 3.95 (0-525-44736-9, Puffin) Puffin Bks.
—Boats. Rockwell, Anne, illus. LC 82-2420. 24p. (ps). 1985. 12.95 (0-525-44004-6, DCB); (DCB) Dutton Child Bks.
—Boats. (Illus.). 24p. 1994. pap. 4.99 (0-14-054988-9, Puffin Unicorn) Puffin Bks.
—Cars. Rockwell, Anne, illus. LC 83-14080. 24p. (ps-1). 1984. 12.95 (0-525-44079-8, DCB) Dutton Child Bks.
—Cars. Rockwell, Anne, illus. LC 83-14080. 24p. (ps-1). 1986. pap. 3.95 (0-525-44241-3, DCB) Dutton Child Bks.
—Cars. 1994. pap. 4.50 (0-14-054741-X, Puffin Unicorn) Puffin Bks.
—Come to Town. Rockwell, Anne, illus. LC 86-6217. 32p. (ps-1). 1987. (Crowell Jr Bks) HarpC Child Bks.
—Ducklings & Polliwogs. Rockwell, Lizzy, illus. LC 93-16600. (gr. 3 up). 1994. write for info. (0-02-777452-X) Macmillan Child Grp.
—The Emergency Room. Rockwell, Harlow, illus. LC 84-20161. 24p. (ps-2). 1985. RSBE 13.95 (0-02-777300-0, Macmillan Child Bk) Macmillan Child Grp.
—Fire Engines. Rockwell, Anne, illus. LC 86-4464. 24p. (ps-1). 1986. 12.95 (0-525-44259-6, DCB) Dutton Child Bks.
—Fire Engines. (Illus.). 24p. (ps-1). 1993. pap. 4.50 (0-14-055250-2, Puffin Unicorn) Puffin Bks.
—First Comes Spring. LC 84-45331. (Illus.). 32p. (ps-1). 1985. 14.95 (0-694-00106-6, Crowell Jr Bks); PLB 12.89 (0-690-04455-0) HarpC Child Bks.
—First Comes Spring. Rockwell, Anne, illus. LC 84-45331. 32p. (ps-1). 1991. pap. 4.95 (0-06-107412-8) HarpC Child Bks.
—Hugo at the Park. Rockwell, Anne, illus. LC 89-2417. 32p. (ps-k). 1990. RSBE 13.95 (0-02-777301-9, Macmillan Child Bk) Macmillan Child Grp.
—Hugo at the Window. Rockwell, Anne, illus. LC 87-11058. 32p. (ps-k). 1988. SBE 13.95 (0-02-777330-2, Macmillan Child Bk) Macmillan Child Grp.

—In the Morning. Rockwell, Anne, illus. LC 85-47742. 15p. (ps). 1986. 2.50 (0-694-00078-7, Crowell Jr Bks) HarpC Child Bks.
—Mr. Panda's Painting. Rockwell, Anne, illus. LC 92-9220. 32p. (ps-3). 1993. RSBE 14.95 (0-02-777451-1, Macmillan Child Bk) Macmillan Child Grp.
—My Spring Robin. Rockwell, Harlow & Rockwell, Lizzy, illus. LC 88-13333. 24p. (ps-1). 1989. RSBE 13.95 (0-02-777611-5, Macmillan Child Bk) Macmillan Child Grp.
—On Our Vacation. Rockwell, Anne, illus. LC 88-29996. 32p. (ps-1). 1989. 12.95 (0-525-44487-4, DCB) Dutton Child Bks.
—Our Garage Sale. Rockwell, Harlow, illus. LC 80-16704. 24p. (ps-1). 1984. 10.25 (0-688-80278-8); PLB 10.88 (0-688-84278-X) Greenwillow.
—Our Yard Is Full of Birds. Rockwell, Lizzy, illus. LC 90-30436. 32p. (ps-2). 1992. RSBE 13.95 (0-02-777273-X, Macmillan Child Bk) Macmillan Child Grp.
—Planes. Rockwell, Anne, illus. LC 84-13732. 24p. (ps-1). 1985. 12.95 (0-525-44159-X, DCB) Dutton Child Bks.
—Planes. 1994. pap. 4.99 (0-14-054782-7, Puffin Unicorn) Puffin Bks.
—Pots & Pans. Rockwell, Lizzy, illus. LC 91-4976. 32p. (ps-1). 1993. RSBE 13.95 (0-02-777631-X, Macmillan Child Bk) Macmillan Child Grp.
—Root-a-Toot-Toot. LC 90-46747. (Illus.). 24p. (ps-1). 1991. RSBE 13.95 (0-02-777272-1) Macmillan Child Grp.
—Things That Go. Rockwell, Anne, illus. LC 86-6199. 24p. (ps-1). 1986. 10.95 (0-525-44266-9, DCB) Dutton Child Bks.
—Things That Go. LC 86-6199. (Illus.). 24p. (ps-1). 1991. pap. 3.95 (0-525-44703-2, Puffin) Puffin Bks.
—Things to Play With. Rockwell, Anne, illus. LC 87-33399. 24p. (ps-1). 1988. 11.95 (0-525-44409-2, DCB) Dutton Child Bks.
—Things to Play With. (Illus.). 24p. (ps-1). 1994. pap. 3.99 (0-14-050308-0, Puffin Unicorn) Puffin Bks.
—The Three Bears & Fifteen Other Stories. LC 74-5381. (Illus.). 128p. (gr. k-5). 1975. (Crowell Jr Bks); PLB 13.89 (0-690-00598-9) HarpC Child Bks.
—Three Sillies & Ten Other Stories. Rockwell, Anne, illus. LC 85-45404. 96p. (ps-3). 1986. pap. 8.95 flexibind (0-06-443093-6, Trophy) HarpC Child Bks.
—Toolbox. LC 89-34818. (Illus.). 24p. (ps-1). 1990. pap. 3.95 (0-689-71382-7, Aladdin) Macmillan Child Grp.
—Trains. Rockwell, Anne, illus. LC 87-22180. 24p. (ps-1). 1988. 13.00 (0-525-44377-0, 01063-320, DCB) Dutton Child Bks.
—Trains. 1994. pap. 4.50 (0-14-054979-X, Puffin Unicorn) Puffin Bks.
—Trucks. Rockwell, Anne, illus. LC 84-1556. 24p. (ps-1). 1984. 11.95 (0-525-44147-6, DCB) Dutton Child Bks.
—Trucks. Rockwell, Anne, illus. LC 84-1556. 24p. (ps-1). 1988. pap. 3.95 (0-525-44432-7, DCB) Dutton Child Bks.
—Trucks. 06/1992 ed. (ps-3). 1992. pap. 4.50 (0-14-054790-8) Viking Child Bks.
—The Way to Captain Yankee's. Rockwell, Anne, illus. LC 92-44644. 32p. (ps-2). 1994. RSBE 13.95 (0-02-777271-3, Macmillan Child Bk) Macmillan Child Grp.
—What We Like. Rockwell, Anne, illus. LC 91-4990. 24p. (ps-1). 1992. RSBE 13.95 (0-02-777274-8, Macmillan Child Bk) Macmillan Child Grp.
—When Hugo Went to School. LC 89-13211. (Illus.). 32p. (ps-1). 1991. RSBE 13.95 (0-02-777305-1, Macmillan Child Bk) Macmillan Child Grp.
—When We Grow Up. Rockwell, Anne, illus. LC 80-21768. (ps-1). 1981. 10.95 (0-525-42575-6, Dutton) NAL-Dutton.
—Willy Can Count. Rockwell, Anne, illus. 32p. (ps). 1989. 13.95 (1-55970-013-0) Arcade Pub Inc.
Rockwell, Anne & Rockwell, Harlow. The First Snowfall. LC 86-23712. (Illus.). 24p. (ps-1). 1987. RSBE 13.95 (0-02-777770-7) Macmillan Child Grp.
—The First Snowfall. Rockwell, Harlow, illus. LC 91-41247. 24p. (ps-1). 1992. pap. 3.95 (0-689-71614-1, Aladdin) Macmillan Child Grp.
—Happy Birthday to Me. Rockwell, Anne & Rockwell, Harlow, illus. LC 81-3738. 24p. (ps-k). 1981. RSBE 9.95 (0-02-777680-8, Macmillan Child Bk) Macmillan Child Grp.
—How My Garden Grew. LC 81-17145. (Illus.). 24p. (ps-k). 1982. RSBE 9.95 (0-02-777660-3, Macmillan Child Bk) Macmillan Child Grp.
—I Play in My Room. Rockwell, Anne & Rockwell, Harlow, illus. LC 81-2634. 24p. (ps-k). 1981. RSBE 9.95 (0-02-777670-0, Macmillan Child Bk) Macmillan Child Grp.
—Machines. LC 72-185149. (Illus.). 24p. (ps-2). 1972. RSBE 13.95 (0-02-777520-8, Macmillan Child Bk) Macmillan Child Grp.
—My Baby-Sitter. LC 85-5000. (Illus.). 24p. (ps-k). 1985. RSBE 9.95 (0-02-777780-4, Macmillan Child Bk) Macmillan Child Grp.
—Sick in Bed. Rockwell, Anne & Rockwell, Harlow, illus. LC 81-15637. 24p. (ps-k). 1982. RSBE 9.95 (0-02-777730-8, Macmillan Child Bk) Macmillan Child Grp.
—Toolbox. LC 72-119836. (Illus.). 24p. (ps-2). 1971. RSBE 13.95 (0-02-777540-2, Macmillan Child Bk) Macmillan Child Grp.

Rockwell, Anne, as told by. & illus. Puss in Boots & Other Stories. LC 87-14976. 96p. (gr. k-4). 1988. SBE 15.95 (0-02-777781-2, Macmillan Child Bk) Macmillan Child Grp.
Rockwell, Bart. The World's Strangest Baseball Stories. LC 92-10120. (Illus.). 96p. (gr. 3-7). 1992. PLB 9.89 (0-8167-2933-6); pap. text ed. 2.95 (0-8167-2850-X) Troll Assocs.
—World's Strangest Basketball Stories. LC 92-25676. 1992. lib. bdg. 9.89 (0-8167-2935-2, Pub. by Watermill Pr); pap. 2.95 (0-8167-2852-6, Pub. by Watermill Pr) Troll Assocs.
—The World's Strangest Football Stories. LC 92-10121. (Illus.). 96p. (gr. 3-7). 1992. PLB 9.89 (0-8167-2934-4); pap. text ed. 2.95 (0-8167-2851-8) Troll Assocs.
—World's Strangest Hockey Stories. LC 92-25992. (Illus.). 96p. (gr. 3-7). 1992. PLB 9.89 (0-8167-2936-0); pap. text ed. 2.95 (0-8167-2853-4) Troll Assocs.
Rockwell, Harlow. Look at This. Rockwell, Harlow, illus. LC 87-1033. 64p. (gr. 1-4). 1987. pap. 3.95 (0-689-71165-4, Aladdin) Macmillan Child Grp.
—My Dentist. LC 75-6974. (Illus.). 32p. (ps-3). 1975. 16.00 (0-688-80011-4); PLB 15.93 (0-688-84004-3) Greenwillow.
—My Dentist. (ps-3). 1987. pap. 3.95 (0-688-07040-X, Mulberry) Morrow.
—My Doctor. Rockwell, Harlow, illus. LC 72-92442. 24p. (ps-1). 1973. SBE 13.95 (0-02-777480-5, Macmillan Child Bk) Macmillan Child Grp.
—My Doctor. Rockwell, Harlow, illus. LC 91-27163. 24p. (ps-2). 1992. pap. 3.95 (0-689-71606-0, Aladdin) Macmillan Child Grp.
—My Kitchen. LC 79-15929. (Illus.). 24p. (ps-2). 1980. 13.95 (0-688-80236-2); PLB 15.88 (0-688-84236-4) Greenwillow.
—My Nursery School. 32p. (ps). 1984. pap. 3.95 (0-14-050478-8, Puffin) Puffin Bks.
—My Nursery School. LC 75-25871. (Illus.). 32p. (ps-3). 1990. pap. 3.95 (0-688-09351-5, Mulberry) Morrow.
Rockwell, Harlow, jt. auth. see Rockwell, Anne.
Rockwell, Jane. All about Ponds. Veno, Joseph, illus. LC 83-4835. 32p. (gr. 3-6). 1984. lib. bdg. 10.59 (0-89375-971-6); pap. text ed. 2.95 (0-89375-972-4) Troll Assocs.
Rockwell, Norman, illus. Home for Christmas: An Advent Book. 1993. 13.99 (0-525-44894-2, DCB) Dutton Child Bks.
Rockwell, Thomas. Hey, Lover Boy. LC 80-68739. 160p. (gr. 8-12). 1981. 8.95 (0-440-03583-X) Delacorte.
—How to Eat Fried Worms. 128p. 1953. pap. 3.99 (0-440-44545-0, YB) Dell.
—How to Eat Fried Worms. McCully, Emily, illus. LC 73-4262. (gr. 4-6). 1973. PLB 13.90 (0-531-02631-0) Watts.
—How to Eat Fried Worms. large type ed. 190p. (gr. 3-7). 1988. lib. bdg. 14.95 (1-55736-051-0, Crnrstn Bks); bk. & 2 audio cass. 29.95 (1-55736-091-X) BDD LT Grp.
—How to Eat Fried Worms. (gr. 4-7). 1992. pap. 1.99 (0-440-21367-3) Dell.
—How to Eat Fried Worms: And Other Plays. Schick, Joel, illus. LC 78-72854. (gr. 4-7). 1980. 9.95 (0-440-03498-1); PLB 9.89 (0-440-03499-X) Delacorte.
—How to Fight a Girl. 144p. (gr. k-6). 1988. pap. 2.95 (0-440-40111-9, YB) Dell.
—How to Fight a Girl. large type ed. (gr. 3-7). 1988. Repr. of 1987 ed. lib. bdg. 15.95 (1-55736-077-4, Crnrstn Bks) BDD LT Grp.
—How to Get Fabulously Rich. Frammenghi, Gioia, illus. 128p. (gr. 5-8). 1990. 13.95 (0-531-15180-8); PLB 13.90 (0-531-10877-5) Watts.
—How to Get Fabulously Rich. (gr. 4-7). 1991. pap. 3.50 (0-440-40546-7, YB) Dell.
Rodack, Jaine. As Cool As a Cucumber. Rolfes, Ellen, ed. 96p. (gr. k-6). 1993. spiral bdg. 5.95 (1-879958-19-8) Tradery Hse.
Rodanas, Kristina. Dance of the Sacred Circle. LC 93-19626. 1994. 14.95 (0-316-75358-0) Little.
—The Story of Wali Dad. Rodanas, Kristina, illus. LC 86-34423. 32p. (gr. k-3). 1988. 13.95 (0-688-07262-3); PLB 13.88 (0-688-07263-1) Lothrop.
Rodanas, Kristina, retold by. & illus. Dragonfly's Tale. 32p. (gr. k-3). 1992. 14.45 (0-395-57003-4, Clarion Bks) HM.
Rodda, Emily. The Best Kept Secret. Young, Noela, illus. 112p. (gr. 2-4). 1990. 14.95 (0-8050-0936-1, Bks Young Read) H Holt & Co.
—The Best-Kept Secret. 112p. (gr. 5). 1991. pap. 2.95 (0-380-75870-9, Camelot) Avon.
—Finders Keepers. LC 90-47850. (Illus.). (gr. 5 up). 1991. 13.95 (0-688-10516-5) Greenwillow.
—Finders Keepers. Young, Noela, illus. LC 92-43776. 192p. (gr. 5 up). 1993. pap. 3.95 (0-688-11846-1, Pub. by Beech Tree Bks) Morrow.
—The Pigs Are Flying! Young, Noela, illus. LC 88-2449. 160p. (gr. 4-6). 1988. Repr. of 1986 ed. 13.95 (0-688-08130-4) Greenwillow.
—The Pigs Are Flying! (Illus.). 144p. (gr. 2 up). 1989. pap. 2.95 (0-380-70555-9, Camelot) Avon.
—Something Special. Young, Noela, illus. 80p. (gr. 2-4). 1991. pap. 4.95 (0-8050-1641-4, Bks Young Read) H Holt & Co.
—The Timekeeper. Young, Noela, illus. LC 92-31512. 160p. (gr. 5 up). 1993. 14.00 (0-688-12448-8) Greenwillow.

Roddie, Shen. Animal Stew. Gallagher, Patrick J., illus. 32p. (ps). 1992. 13.45 (*0-395-57582-6*) HM.
—Chicken Pox. Cony, Frances, illus. LC 92-53851. 1993. 14.95 (*0-316-75347-5*, Joy St Bks) Little.
—Hatch, Egg, Hatch: Touch & Feel Action Flap Book. (ps). 1991. 13.95 (*0-316-75345-9*) Little.
—Mrs. Wolf: A Three-Dimensional Picture Book. Paul, Korky, illus. LC 92-1202. 24p. (gr. k-3). 1993. 13.99 (*0-8037-1300-2*) Dial Bks Young.
—The Terrible Itch. Roffey, Maureen, illus. 24p. (ps-1). 1993. pap. 13.00 casebound (*0-671-79169-9*, S&S BFYR) S&S Trade.
Roddis, Ingrid. Sudan. (Illus.). 96p. (gr. 5 up). 1988. 14. 95 (*0-222-00964-0*) Chelsea Hse.
Roddy, Lee. The City Bear's Adventures. 144p. (gr. 3-7). 1985. pap. 4.99 (*0-88207-496-2*, Victor Books) SP Pubns.
—Danger on Thunder Mountain. 176p. (Orig.). (gr. 3 up). 1989. pap. 5.99 (*1-55661-028-9*) Bethany Hse.
—The Dangerous Canoe Race. (Orig.). (gr. 3-6). 1990. pap. 4.99 (*0-929608-62-3*) Focus Family.
—Dooger, the Grasshopper Hound. 144p. (gr. 3-7). 1985. pap. 4.99 (*0-88207-497-0*, Victor Books) SP Pubns.
—The Flaming Trap. 176p. (Orig.). (gr. 4-8). 1990. pap. 5.99 (*1-55661-095-5*) Bethany Hse.
—The Ghost Dog of Stoney Ridge. 144p. (gr. 3-7). 1985. pap. 4.99 (*0-88207-498-9*, Victor Books) SP Pubns.
—Ghost of the Moaning Mansion. 132p. (gr. 3-7). 1987. pap. 4.99 (*0-89693-349-0*, Victor Books) SP Pubns.
—The Gold Train Bandits. 176p. (Orig.). (gr. 3-8). 1992. pap. 5.99 (*1-55661-211-7*) Bethany Hse.
—The Hair-Pulling Bear Dog. 144p. (gr. 3-7). 1985. pap. 4.99 (*0-88207-499-7*, Victor Books) SP Pubns.
—The Hermit of Mad River. 132p. (gr. 3-7). 1988. pap. 4.99 (*0-89693-475-6*, Victor Books) SP Pubns.
—High Country Ambush. 176p. (Orig.). (gr. 3-8). 1992. pap. 5.99 (*1-55661-287-7*) Bethany Hse.
—The Legend of Fire. rev. ed. 148p. (gr. 3-6). 1989. pap. 4.99 (*0-929608-17-8*) Focus Family.
—The Legend of the White Raccoon. 144p. (gr. 3-7). 1986. pap. 4.99 (*0-89693-500-0*, Victor Books) SP Pubns.
—The Mad Dog of Lobo Mountain. 132p. (gr. 8-12). 1986. pap. 4.99 (*0-89693-482-9*, Victor Books) SP Pubns.
—The Mystery of the Black Hole Mine. 132p. (gr. 3-7). 1987. pap. 4.99 (*0-89693-320-2*, Victor Books) SP Pubns.
—Mystery of the Island Jungle. 160p. (Orig.). (gr. 3-7). 1989. pap. 4.99 (*0-929608-19-4*) Focus Family.
—Mystery of the Phantom Gold. 176p. (Orig.). (gr. 3-8). 1991. pap. 5.99 (*1-55661-210-9*) Bethany Hse.
—Mystery of the Wild Surfer. 160p. (Orig.). (gr. 3-6). 1990. pap. 4.99 (*0-929608-64-X*) Focus Family.
—The Overland Escape. LC 88-63471. 160p. (gr. 2-6). 1989. pap. text ed. 5.99 (*1-55661-026-2*) Bethany Hse.
—Robert E. Lee: Gallant Christian Soldier. (Illus.). (gr. 3-6). 1977. pap. 6.95 (*0-915134-40-3*) Mott Media.
—The Secret of the Howling Cave. 192p. (Orig.). (gr. 4-10). 1990. pap. 5.99 (*1-55661-094-7*) Bethany Hse.
—Secret of the Shark Pit. 136p. (Orig.). (gr. 3-6). 1989. pap. 4.99 (*0-929608-14-3*) Focus Family.
—Secret of the Sunken Sub. 160p. (Orig.). (gr. 3-6). 1990. pap. 4.99 (*0-929608-63-1*) Focus Family.
—Terror at Forbidden Falls. LC 93-3379. 1993. write for info. (*1-56179-137-7*) Focus Family.
—Terror in the Sky. 176p. (Orig.). (ps-8). 1991. pap. 5.99 (*1-55661-096-3*) Bethany Hse.
Roddy, Patricia. Api & the Boy Stranger: A Village Creation Tale. Russell, Lynne, illus. LC 93-8359. Date not set. 14.99 (*0-8037-1221-9*); PLB 14.89 (*0-8037-1222-7*) Dial Bks Young.
Roddy, Ruth M. Kids' Stuff. 64p. (Orig.). (gr. 1-7). 1993. pap. 7.95 (*0-940669-23-4*, D30) Dramaline Pubns.
—Monologues for Kids. 64p. (Orig.). (gr. 1-3). 1987. pap. 6.95 (*0-940669-02-1*) Dramaline Pubns.
—More Monologues for Kids. 64p. (Orig.). (gr. 6-9). 1992. pap. 7.95 (*0-940669-18-8*) Dramaline Pubns.
—Scenes for Kids. 64p. (Orig.). (gr. 2-6). 1990. pap. 7.95 (*0-940669-14-5*) Dramaline Pubns.
Rodecker, Stephen B. & Quon-Warner, Maryanna. Las Ciencias Fisicas: Metodos, Investigaciones, Retos y Actividades - M.I.R.A. Appel, Sergio, tr. 342p. (gr. 7 up). 1993. lab manual 39.95 (*0-9638008-1-7*) Spectrum CA.
—Laboratory Experiments & Activities in Physical Science: L.E.A.P.S. 342p. (gr. 7 up). 1993. lab manual 39.95 (*0-9638008-0-9*) Spectrum CA.
Rodegast, Roland, jt. auth. see Reardon, Ruth.
Rodenas, Paula. The Random House Book of Horses & Horsemanship. Cassels, Jean, illus. Farley, Walter, frwd. by. LC 86-42934. (Illus.). 192p. (gr. 3-7). 1991. 17.95 (*0-394-88705-0*); PLB 18.99 (*0-394-98705-5*) Random Bks Yng Read.
Roders, Mary M., jt. auth. see Hoff, Mary.
Roderus, Frank. Duster. Conoly, Walle, illus. LC 85-14759. 266p. (gr. 4 up). 1987. 14.95 (*0-87565-055-4*); pap. 10.95 (*0-87565-095-3*) Tex Christian.
Rodger, Elizabeth. Boo to You, Too. LC 92-40023. 1993. write for info. (*0-671-86765-2*, S&S BFYR); pap. 2.95 (*0-671-86766-0*, S&S BFYR) S&S Trade.
—Ollie Solves a Messy Mystery. (Illus.). 32p. (ps-2). 1993. pap. 2.50 (*0-590-44885-4*) Scholastic Inc.
Rodger, Jude. Dragon Book. 1993. pap. 15.95 (*1-85756-042-6*, Pub. by Janus Pub UK) Intl Spec Bk.
Rodgers, A. Mary. A Billion for Boris. LC 74-3586. 192p. (gr. 5 up). 1974. PLB 13.89 (*0-06-025054-2*) HarpC Child Bks.

Rodgers, Elizabeth. Ollie Goes to School. (Illus.). 32p. (ps-2). 1992. pap. 2.50 (*0-590-44785-8*, Cartwheel) Scholastic Inc.
Rodgers, Frank. I Can't Get to Sleep. (Illus.). 32p. (ps). 1991. pap. 13.95 jacketed (*0-671-74129-2*, S&S BFYR) S&S Trade.
—I Can't Get to Sleep. LC 90-19607. (Illus.). 32p. (ps-1). 1993. pap. 7.95 (*0-671-79848-0*, S&S BYR) S&S Trade.
—Looking after Your First Monster. (ps-3). 1992. pap. 3.95 (*0-590-45695-4*) Scholastic Inc.
—Who's Afraid of the Ghost Train? Rodgers, Frank, illus. 23p. (ps-1). 1989. 12.95 (*0-15-200642-7*, Gulliver Bks) HarBrace.
Rodgers, G. Kryptic: The Little Space Guy. (Illus.). 32p. (gr. 2-6). 1989. 10.95 (*0-88625-246-6*) Durkin Hayes Pub.
Rodgers, Joann. Cancer. (Illus.). 112p. (gr. 6 up). 1990. 18.95 (*0-7910-0059-1*) Chelsea Hse.
—Drugs & Sexual Behavior. Mendelson, Jack H. & Mello, Nancyintro. by. (Illus.). 96p. (gr. 5 up). 1988. lib. bdg. 19.95 (*1-55546-215-4*) Chelsea Hse.
Rodgers, Judith. Winston Churchill. (Illus.). 112p. (gr. 5 up). 1986. lib. bdg. 17.95 (*0-87754-563-4*) Chelsea Hse.
Rodgers, Mary. A Billion for Boris. LC 74-3586. 192p. (gr. 5 up). 1976. pap. 3.50 (*0-06-440075-1*, Trophy) HarpC Child Bks.
—Freaky Friday. LC 74-183158. 156p. (gr. 5-8). 1972. 14.00 (*0-06-025048-8*); PLB 13.89 (*0-06-025049-6*) HarpC Child Bks.
—Freaky Friday. LC 74-183158. 156p. (gr. 5 up). 1973. pap. 3.95 (*0-06-440046-8*, Trophy) HarpC Child Bks.
—Freaky Friday. large type ed. 184p. (gr. 3-7). 1988. Repr. of 1972 ed. lib. bdg. 15.95 (*1-55736-027-8*, Crnrstn Bks) BDD LT Grp.
—Freaky Friday - Viernes Embrujado. McShane, Barbara & Alfaya, Javier, trs. (SPA). 118p. (gr. 5-8). 1987. pap. 5.95 (*84-204-3640-2*) Santillana.
—Summer Switch. LC 79-2690. 192p. (gr. 5 up). 1982. 14.00 (*0-06-025058-5*); PLB 12.89 (*0-06-025059-3*) HarpC Child Bks.
—Summer Switch. LC 79-2690. 192p. (gr. 5 up). 1984. pap. 3.50 (*0-06-440140-5*, Trophy) HarpC Child Bks.
Rodgers, Mary M. & Hoff, Mary. Our Endangered Planet: Oceans. (Illus.). 72p. (gr. 4-6). 1991. PLB 21. 50 (*0-8225-2505-4*) Lerner Pubns.
Rodgers, Mary M., jt. auth. see Hoff, Mary.
Rodgers, Mary M., jt. auth. see Winckler, Suzanne.
Rodgers, Raboo. Magnum Fault. 192p. (gr. 5 up). 1984. 11.95 (*0-685-07882-5*, 5-95260) HM.
Rodgers, Richard & Hammerstein, Oscar, II. A Real Nice Clambake. Westcott, Nadine B., illus. 32p. (ps-3). 1992. 14.95 (*0-316-75422-6*, Joy St Bks) Little.
Rodgers, Richard, jt. auth. see Hammerstein, Oscar, II.
Rodieck, Jorma. The Little Bitty Snake. Burnett, Yumiko M. & Contreras, Moyra, trs. LC 82-60393. (Illus.). 24p. (ps up). 1983. English-Japanese. pap. 4.95 (*0-940880-07-5*); English-Spanish. pap. 4.95 (*0-940880-03-2*); English-French. pap. 4.95 (*0-940880-05-9*) Open Hand.
Rodino, A. Music Master. LC 68-20526. (Illus.). (gr. 3-7). 1968. 3.00 (*0-8198-0105-4*) St Paul Bks.
Rodney, Janet, ed. see Prechtel, Martin.
Rodolph, Stormy. Quest for Courage. Lucero, Ruth, illus. 102p. (Orig.). (gr. 5-12). 1984. pap. 8.95 (*0-89992-092-6*) Coun India Ed.
—Quest for Courage. Lambert, Paulette L., illus. 112p. (gr. 4-6). 1993. pap. 8.95x (*1-879373-57-2*) R Rinehart.
Rodowsky, Colby. Dog Days. Howell, Kathleen C., illus. 96p. (gr. 2-6). 1990. 14.00 (*0-374-36342-0*) FS&G.
—Dog Days. (gr. 4-7). 1993. pap. 4.50 (*0-374-41818-7*, Sunburst) FS&G.
—Fitchett's Folly. LC 86-31859. 160p. (gr. 4 up). 1987. 15.00 (*0-374-32342-9*) FS&G.
—The Gathering Room. LC 81-5360. 186p. (gr. 5 up). 1981. 14.00 (*0-374-32520-0*) FS&G.
—H, My Name Is Henley. LC 82-12164. 184p. (gr. 5 up). 1982. 14.00 (*0-374-32831-5*) FS&G.
—Hannah in Between. (gr. 5 up). 1994. 15.00 (*0-374-32837-4*) FS&G.
—Jenny & the Grand Old Great-Aunts. Roman, Barbara, illus. LC 90-42563. 40p. (gr. 1-4). 1992. RSBE 12.95 (*0-02-777785-5*, Bradbury Pr) Macmillan Child Grp.
—Julie's Daughter. LC 85-47589. 231p. (gr. 7 up). 1985. 15.00 (*0-374-33963-5*) FS&G.
—Julie's Daughter. (gr. 7 up). 1992. pap. 3.95 (*0-374-43973-7*) FS&G.
—Keeping Time. LC 83-14122. 137p. (gr. 5-9). 1983. 14.00 (*0-374-34061-7*) FS&G.
—Lucy Peale. 208p. 1992. 15.00 (*0-374-36381-1*) FS&G.
—P. S. Write Soon. 158p. (gr. 5 up). 1987. pap. 3.50 (*0-374-46032-9*) FS&G.
—P.S. Write Soon. 160p. (gr. 5-7). 1980. pap. 1.50 (*0-440-97119-5*, LFL) Dell.
—Sydney, Herself. 176p. (gr. 7 up). 1989. 15.00 (*0-374-30649-4*) FS&G.
—Sydney, Herself. 1993. pap. 3.95 (*0-374-47390-0*) FS&G.
—What About Me? 144p. (gr. 3 up). 1989. pap. 3.50 (*0-374-48316-7*, Sunburst) FS&G.
Rodriguez, Agatha A. Catability. Medina, Mary L., illus. 20p. (Orig.). 1990. pap. text ed. 7.95g (*0-933196-04-0*) Bilingue Pubns.
—Paracaidas, Paracaidas. Medina, Mary L., illus. (SPA). 20p. (Orig.). 1992. pap. 5.00 (*0-933196-05-9*) Bilingue Pubns.

Rodriguez, Alejo. It's Tough Being a Kid These Days. LC 93-85309. 65p. (gr. 6-12). 1994. pap. 5.95 (*1-55523-638-3*) Winston-Derek.
—Simple Poems for Children: Hey What Kind of World Is This? LC 90-71368. 126p. (gr. 3-9). 1991. pap. 5.95 (*1-55523-393-7*) Winston-Derek.
Rodriguez, Anita. Aunt Martha & the Golden Coin. Rodrigues, Anita, illus. LC 92-7316. 32p. (ps-2). 1993. 14.00 (*0-517-59337-8*, Clarkson Potter); PLB 14.99 (*0-517-59338-6*, Clarkson Potter) Crown Bks Yng Read.
—Jamal & the Angel. Rodriguez, Anita, illus. LC 91-11636. 32p. (ps-2). 1992. 14.00 (*0-517-58601-0*); PLB 15.99 (*0-517-59115-4*) Crown Bks Yng Read.
Rodriguez, Consuelo. Cesar Chavez. (Illus.). 112p. (gr. 5 up). 1991. lib. bdg. 17.95 (*0-7910-1232-8*) Chelsea Hse.

Rodriguez, David & Rodriguez, Judy. Times Tables the Fun Way: A Picture Method of Learning the Multiplication Facts. Bagley, Val & Barwald, Diana, illus. 86p. (gr. 2-8). 1992. 19.95 (*1-883841-25-9*) Key Pubs UT. Times tables come alive with this revolutionary method of learning the multiplication facts. The facts are presented as part of a complete mini-story of colorful cartoon characters. Children easily visualize the animated scene, & then remember the characters which trigger the answer to the fact. Proven by numerous studies, visualization & association enhance retention of facts in long term memory. To teach six times six, the story tells of twin sixes who travel across the desert to visit cousins. The twin sixes get low on water becoming thirsty sixes, a word play on 36. The picture shows perspiring, hot & drooping sixes crossing the Sahara. A reminder under the illustration reads: When 6 is with 6, they are very thirsty sixes (36). The book covers the multiplication facts through the nines. Numerical tricks & association are used to teach the ones, twos, fives, & nines while the remaining facts have their own picture & story. Studies have shown a 33% increase in retention with the picture-story method versus conventional methods. Children are eager to learn the stories & parents & teachers enjoy the refreshing approach of the picture method. Also available are the TIMES TABLES THE FUN WAY Flash Cards, Student Workbook, & Teacher's Manual. *Publisher Provided Annotation.*

—Times Tables the Fun Way Book for Kids: A Picture Method of Learning the Multiplication Facts. 2nd, rev. ed. Bagley, Val & Barwald, Diana, illus. 86p. (gr. 2-8). 1993. 19.95 (*1-883841-26-7*); 54p. 7.95 (*1-883841-27-5*); tchr's. manual, 56p. 39.00 (*1-883841-28-3*); flash cards 4.95 (*1-883841-29-1*) Key Pubs UT.

Rodriguez, Gina M. Green Corn Tamales - Tamales de Elote. (SPA & ENG., Illus.). 36p. 1994. 14.95 Hispanic Bk Dist. GREEN CORN TAMLAES - TAMALES DE ELOTE narrates the experience of one small girl growing up in an Hispanic-American family which gathers every year at grandmother's ranch to make wonderful green corn tamales. In this bilingual tale, the young girl learns how families should work together as grandmother orchestrates the preparation of their holiday meal. The text is closely followed by bright, colorful illustrations. *Publisher Provided Annotation.*

Rodriguez, Gloria F., ed. see Kemvichanuvat, Cherdchai.
Rodriguez, Gloria F., ed. see Rausiri, Supa.
Rodriguez, Judy, jt. auth. see Rodriguez, David.
Rodriguez, Kathryn, jt. auth. see Vredevelt, Pamela.
Rodriguez, Luis J. Always Running: Gang Days in L. A.
   LC 92-39002. (Orig.). (gr. 9 up). 1993. 19.95
   (1-880684-06-3) Curbstone.
Rodriguez-Nieto, Alcides, ed. see Salinas-Norman,
   Bobbi.
Rodriguez-Nieto, Catherine, ed. see Salinas-Norman,
   Bobbi.
Rodriquez, Judy, tr. see Brinkley, Ginny & Sampson,
   Sherry.
Rodwell, Jenny. Beginner's Guides: Painting in Pastels.
   (Illus.). 96p. (gr. 10-12). 1993. pap. 17.95
   (0-289-80073-0, Pub. by Cassell UK) Sterling.
—Beginner's Guides: Painting in Watercolour. (Illus.).
   96p. (gr. 10-12). 1992. pap. 17.95 (0-289-80056-0,
   Pub. by Studio Vista UK) Sterling.
Rody, Lee. The Desperate Search. LC 88-63476. 160p.
   (gr. 2-6). 1989. pap. 5.99 (1-55661-027-0) Bethany
   Hse.
Rody, Martyn. The Breakup of Yugoslavia. (Illus.). 48p.
   (gr. 6 up). 1994. PLB 13.95 RSBE (0-02-792529-3,
   New Discovery Bks) Macmillan Child Grp.
Roe, Cheryl. Tym, the Turtle Boy. Hilliard, Peg, illus. LC
   89-51373. 40p. (Orig.). (gr. 2-5). 1990. pap. 9.95
   (0-9624183-1-5) Timeless Sales.
Roe, Cheryl A. Tym, the Turtle Boy. Hilliard, Peg, illus.
   52p. (Orig.). (ps-3). 1989. pap. write for info.
   (0-9624183-0-7) Timeless Sales.
Roe, Earl O., ed. see Stowell, Gordon.
Roe, Eileen. All I Am. LC 88-30510. (Illus.). 32p. (ps-1).
   1990. RSBE 13.95 (0-02-777372-8, Bradbury Pr)
   Macmillan Child Grp.
—Con Mi Hermano with My Brother. Casilla, Robert,
   illus. LC 90-33983. 32p. (ps-3). 1991. RSBE 12.95
   (0-02-777373-6, Bradbury Pr) Macmillan Child Grp.
Roe, JoAnn. Marco the Manx Series, 3 bks. Runestrand,
   Meredith & Mayo, Steve, illus. (gr. k-5). Set. write for
   info. (0-931551-06-4); Fisherman Cat, 1988. PLB 10.
   95 (0-931551-02-1); Alaska Cat. PLB 10.95
   (0-931551-05-6); Castaway Cat. pap. 5.95
   (0-931551-03-X); Fisherman Cat, 1988. pap. 6.95
   (0-931551-01-3); Alaska Cat. pap. 6.95
   (0-931551-04-8) Montevista Pr.

—Samurai Cat: Marco the Manx Ser.
(Illus.). 64p. (gr. k-5). 1993. PLB 11.95
(0-931551-08-0); pap. 6.95
(0-931551-07-2) Montevista Pr.
Now the big yellow cat, Marco the
Manx, is off to Japan. In SAMURAI
CAT, fourth in the series, Marco is
given to a Japanese fisherman by his
Alaskan family, when they move to
Anchorage. At sea, Marco is thrown
against the bulkhead during a storm &
breaks a leg. As Marco recovers in
Tateyama, Japan, nursed by the ship
captain's wife, he wanders over to
become friendly with the children of a
nearby kindergarten, especially shy,
Mieko, who suffers trauma from an
accident. Although there is no physical
reason for the problem, she cannot talk
or walk properly. Marco earns the
name SAMURAI CAT when he
defends the children against a large
dog, & a teacher explains to the
children about the samurai warriors. In
the telling, the author explores
Japanese lifestyle & culture, including
a comical story about Marco growing a
long, long nose after antagonizing a
TENGU, a popular legendary figure in
Japanese children's literature. As the
book closes, the large dog reappears &
chases Marco toward the street. In fear
for his life, Mieko runs & screams to
save him. Her love for the cat
overcame the mental trauma. ISBN 0-
931551-07-2 paper. ISBN 0-931551-
08-0 library.
Publisher Provided Annotation.

Roe, Richard. Baby Animals. Roe, Richard, illus. LC 85-
   2223. 24p. (ps-1). 1985. 3.95 (0-394-86956-7) Random
   Bks Yng Read.
Roebuck, Susan H. Alaska Wildlife: A Coloring Book.
   Holen, Anne M., ed. Heshiki, Kazumi, tr. from ENG.
   Arehart, Betsy H., illus. (JPN.). 48p. (Orig.). (gr. 3-8).
   1990. pap. 5.95 (0-922127-01-8) Paisley Pub.
Roed, Tom, ed. see Garson, Mike.

Roeda, Jack. Decisions. 2nd ed. Stoub, Paul, illus. Smith,
   Harvey A., intro. by. (Illus.). 80p. (gr. 9-12). 1992.
   pap. text ed. 6.50 (0-930265-96-3, 1240-4920); tchr's.
   manual 8.50 (1-56212-000-X, 1240-4940); session
   guides 4.95 (0-685-60757-7, 1240-4910) CRC Pubns.
Roehl, Harvey N. A Carousel of Limericks. Hyman, Pat,
   illus. LC 85-22538. 60p. (Orig.). (gr. 4-8). 1986. pap.
   7.95 (0-911572-47-3) Vestal.
Roehlkepartain, Jolene L. Surviving School Stress. 108p.
   (Orig.). (gr. 7-12). 1990. pap. 6.99 (0-931529-95-6)
   Group Pub.
Roehm, Michelle, ed. see Burke-Weiner, Kimberly.
Roehm, Michelle, ed. see Lewis, Paul O.
Roehm, Michelle, ed. see White Deer of Autumn Staff.
Roehrig, Catherine. Fun with Hieroglyphs: From the
   Metropolitan Museum of Art. 1990. 19.95
   (0-670-83576-5) Viking Child Bks.
Roennfeldt, Mary. What's That Noise? Roennfeldt,
   Robert, illus. LC 91-16215. 32p. (ps-1). 1992. 13.95
   (0-531-05972-3); lib. bdg. 13.99 (0-531-08572-4)
   Orchard Bks Watts.
Roes, Carol. Children's Christmas Hulas. (gr. k-1). 1965.
   pap. 35.00 incl. 4 records (0-930932-18-8) M Loke.
—Children's Hulas from Hawaii, Bk. 5. Kaiulani, illus.
   13p. (gr. 8). 1966. pap. 5.50 (0-930932-10-2); record
   incl. M Loke.
—Children's Songs from Hawaii. Stone, Lloyd, illus. LC
   81-670132. (ps-3). 1973. PLB 31.95 (0-930932-01-3,
   A875377) M Loke.
—Eight Children's Songs from Hawaii. Stone, Lloyd, illus.
   (gr. 3-4). 1958. pap. text ed. 5.50 (0-930932-06-4,
   EP126127) M Loke.
—Hulas from Hawaii. 15p. (gr. k-8). 1978. pap. 5.50
   (0-930932-03-X); record incl. M Loke.
—Introduction to the Hula. (Illus.). 12p. (gr. 1-3). 1961.
   pap. 2.50 (0-930932-07-2) M Loke.
—Keiki Songs of Hawaii. Stone, Lloyd, illus. 26p. (gr. 6).
   1966. pap. 5.50 (0-930932-16-1) M Loke.
—Santa's Hawaiian Party. (gr. 1-8). 1966. pap. 35.00 20
   minute program (0-930932-19-6); record incl. M Loke.
—Song Stories of Hawaii. Stone, Lloyd, illus. 24p. (gr.
   1-8). 1959. pap. 5.50 (0-930932-17-X) M Loke.
Roes, Carol & Kaiulani. Children's Hulas for Song
   Stories, Bk. 3. Stone, L., illus. 24p. (gr. 3-4). 1963.
   pap. 5.50 (0-930932-08-0); record incl. M Loke.
—Children's Hulas from Hawaii, Bk. 2. (gr. 4-5). 1962.
   pap. text ed. 5.50 (0-930932-04-8, A572149); record
   incl. M Loke.
—Hulas for 4 Songs. 18p. (gr. 8 up). 1963. pap. 5.50
   (0-930932-09-9); record incl. M Loke.
Roes, Carol & Tuulikki. Children's Hulas from Hawaii,
   Bk. 1. Stone, Lloyd, illus. (gr. k). 1961. pap. text ed.
   5.50 (0-930932-05-6, A516842); record incl. M Loke.
Roes, Mimi. Poems for Young Children. Fuhrman,
   James, illus. (ps-6). 1979. pap. 1.95x (0-89780-003-6)
   NAR Pubns.
Roes, Mon. Sitting on a Wall: Selected Writings of Mon
   Roes. 194p. 1993. 18.00 (0-685-67895-4) M M Fain.
Roes, Ruth, ed. & illus. see Johnson, Connie.
Roesler. Gansebraten. (gr. 7-12). pap. 4.95
   (0-88436-109-8, 45262) EMC.
Roessel, Monty. Kinaalda: A Navajo Girl Grows Up. (gr.
   4-7). 1993. pap. 3.95 (0-8225-9641-5) Lerner Pubns.
Roessel, Monty, photos by & text by. Kinaalda: A
   Navajo Girl Grows Up. LC 92-35204. (Illus.). 1993.
   19.95 (0-8225-2655-7) Lerner Pubns.
Roetger, Doris. Weather Watch. (gr. k-3). 1991. pap. 8.95
   (0-86653-969-7) Fearon Teach Aids.
Roets, Lois. Famous People. 48p. (gr. 3 up). 1988. tchr's.
   ed. 8.00 (0-911943-15-3) Leadership Pub.
—Philosophy & Philosophers. 48p. (gr. 5-12). 1987. pap.
   8.00 tchr's. manual & text in one volume
   (0-911943-12-9) Leadership Pub.
—Readers' Theater, Vol. 1: General Interest. 106p.
   (Orig.). (gr. 5-12). 1992. pap. text ed. 15.00
   (0-911943-29-3) Leadership Pub.
—Readers' Theater, Vol. 2: Famous People. 108p. (Orig.).
   (gr. 5-12). 1992. pap. text ed. 15.00 (0-911943-30-7)
   Leadership Pub.
—Readers' Theater, Vol. 3: Entrepreneurs. 96p. (Orig.).
   (gr. 5-12). 1992. pap. 15.00 (0-911943-31-5)
   Leadership Pub.
—Student Projects: Ideas & Plans. 272p. (gr. 3 up). 1987.
   pap. text ed. 30.00 (0-911943-11-0) Leadership Pub.
Roets, Lois F. Outline Wizard. 48p. (gr. 4-6). 1980. 5.95
   (0-88160-034-2, LW 219) Learning Wks.
—Survey & Public Opinion Research: Grades Five to
   Twelve. 2nd ed. 120p. (gr. 3 up). 1988. 14.00
   (0-911943-14-5) Leadership Pub.
Roets, Lois S. Understanding Success & Failure. 36p. (gr.
   5 up). 1985. 8.00 (0-911943-07-2) Leadership Pubs.
Roettger, Doris. The Environment. (gr. 4-6). 1993. pap.
   8.95 (0-86653-939-5) Fearon Teach Aids.
—Growing up Healthy. (gr. k-3). 1991. pap. 8.95
   (0-86653-970-0) Fearon Teach Aids.
—Our Ecosystem. (gr. 4-6). 1993. pap. 8.95
   (0-86653-936-0) Fearon Teach Aids.
Roever, Joan M. Snake Secrets. Roever, Joan M., illus.
   LC 78-4318. (gr. 5 up). 1979. PLB 11.85
   (0-8027-6333-2) Walker & Co.
Rofes, Eric, ed. The Kids' Book of Divorce: By, for &
   about Kids. LC 82-4004. (Illus.). 144p. (gr. 2 up).
   1982. pap. 9.00 (0-394-71018-5, Vin) Random.
Rofes, Eric E., ed. see Fayerweather Street School Staff.
Roff, Sue R., ed. see Eleanor Roosevelt Institute Staff.
Roffey, Maureen. Bathtime. Roffey, Maureen, illus. LC
   89-18413. 32p. (ps). 1990. pap. 4.95 (0-689-70808-4,
   Aladdin) Macmillan Child Grp.

—Here, Kitty Kitty! Roffey, Maureen, illus. 24p. (ps).
   1991. 6.70 (0-395-57584-2, Sandpiper) HM.
—I Spy at the Zoo. Roffey, Maureen, illus. LC 87-12116.
   32p. (ps-2). 1988. SBE 12.95 (0-02-777150-4, Four
   Winds) Macmillan Child Grp.
—I Spy at the Zoo. Roffey, Maureen, illus. LC 88-19360.
   32p. (ps-2). 1989. pap. 3.95 (0-689-71227-8, Aladdin)
   Macmillan Child Grp.
—Mealtime. Roffey, Maureen, illus. LC 89-48006. 32p.
   (ps). 1990. pap. 4.95 (0-689-70809-2, Aladdin)
   Macmillan Child Grp.
—Quick, Catch Dan! Roffey, Maureen, illus. 24p. (ps).
   1991. 6.70 (0-395-57583-4, Sandpiper) HM.
Roffey, Maureen, illus. The Grand Old Duke of York.
   rev. ed. Lodge, Bernard, contrib. by. LC 92-21339.
   (Illus.). 32p. (gr-12). 1993. 13.95 (1-879085-79-8)
   Whsprng Coyote Pr.
Rogak, Lisa. Steroids: Dangerous Game. 64p. (gr. 5-10).
   1992. PLB 15.95 (0-8225-0048-5) Lerner Pubns.
Rogasky, Barbara. Smoke & Ashes: The Story of the
   Holocaust. LC 87-28617. (Illus.). 192p. (gr. 5 up).
   1988. 18.95 (0-8234-0697-0); pap. 9.95
   (0-8234-0878-7) Holiday.
Rogasky, Barbara, retold by. The Water of Life. Hyman,
   Trina S., illus. LC 84-19226. 40p. (gr. k-3). 1986.
   reinforced bdg. 15.95 (0-8234-0552-4); pap. 5.95
   (0-8234-0907-4) Holiday.
Rogasky, Barbara, retold by see Grimm, Jacob &
   Grimm, Wilhelm K.
Roger, Alan. Blue Tortoise. Roger, Alan, illus. LC 90-
   9833. 16p. (ps-1). 1990. PLB 13.27 (0-8368-0404-X)
   Gareth Stevens Inc.
Roger, Cynthia A. Why Aren't There Any Dinosaurs
   Here at the Zoo? 1993. 7.95 (0-533-10582-X)
   Vantage.
Rogera, Emma, jt. auth. see Rogers, Paul.
Rogers. Josephine the Short Necked Giraffe. 1985. 3.95
   (0-8331-0036-X) Hubbard Sci.
—Speedy Delivery. 1985. 3.95 (0-8331-0037-8) Hubbard
   Sci.
Rogers, Alan. Green Bear. Rogers, Alan, illus. LC 90-
   9831. (ps). 1990. PLB 13.27 (0-8368-0406-6) Gareth
   Stevens Inc.
—Little Giants, 4 vols. Rogers, Alan, illus. 64p. (ps-1).
   1990. Set. PLB 53.08 (0-8368-0434-1) Gareth Stevens
   Inc.
—Red Rhino. Rogers, Alan, illus. LC 90-9830. 16p.
   (ps-1). 1990. PLB 13.27 (0-8368-0403-1) Gareth
   Stevens Inc.
—Yellow Hippo. Rogers, Alan, illus. LC 90-9834. 16p.
   (ps-1). 1990. PLB 13.27 (0-8368-0405-8) Gareth
   Stevens Inc.
Rogers, Alison. Luke Has Asthma, Too. Middleton,
   Michael, illus. Plaut, Thomas F., frwd. by. LC 87-
   40053. (Illus.). 32p. (Orig.). (ps-2). 1987. pap. 6.95
   (0-914525-06-9) Waterfront Bks.
Rogers, Barbara. God Rescues His People Activity Book.
   72p. (Orig.). (ps-1). 1983. pap. 3.00 (0-8361-3338-2)
   Herald Pr.
—God's Chosen King Activity Book. 88p. (Orig.). (ps-1).
   1984. pap. 3.00 (0-8361-3370-6) Herald Pr.
Rogers, Barbara R. South Africa. Rogers, Stillman, illus.
   LC 89-43188. 64p. (gr. 5-6). 1991. PLB 19.93
   (0-8368-0247-0) Gareth Stevens Inc.
—Zambia. Rogers, Stillman, photos by. LC 89-43178.
   (Illus.). 64p. (gr. 5-6). 1991. PLB 19.93
   (0-8368-0257-8) Gareth Stevens Inc.
Rogers, Betty. Will Rogers. Collins, Reba, frwd. by.
   (Illus.). 312p. (gr. 8 up). 1982. pap. 13.95
   (0-8061-1600-5) U of Okla Pr.
Rogers, Bettye. Prairie Dog Town. Komicar, Alexi,
   narrated by. Howland, Deborah, illus. (gr. k-3).
   1993. 11.95 (1-56899-005-7); incl. audiocassette 16.95
   (1-56899-004-9); incl. audiocassette, 11 in. plush toy
   39.95 (1-56899-002-2); incl. audiocassette, 8 in. plush
   toy 25.95 (1-56899-003-0) Soundprints.
Rogers, Bruce H. Tales & Declarations. 32p. (Orig.). (gr.
   10 up). 1991. pap. 4.00 (0-916155-13-7) Trout Creek.
Rogers, Carol A. Just Picture This: My Own Photo
   Album. 10p. 1993. vinyl 24.95 (0-9635899-0-3) New
   Vision VA.
Rogers, Daniel. Exploring the Sea. (Illus.). 32p. (gr. 5-8).
   1991. 12.40 (0-531-18389-0, Pub. by Bookwright Pr)
   Watts.
—Food from the Sea. (Illus.). 32p. (gr. 5-8). 1991. 12.40
   (0-531-18388-2, Pub. by Bookwright Pr) Watts.
—The Thames. Lilly, Isabel, illus. LC 92-44702. 48p. (gr.
   5-6). 1993. PLB 22.80 (0-8114-3104-5) Raintree
   Steck-V.
Rogers, Donald J. Banned! Censorship in the Schools.
   LC 87-7736. 128p. (gr. 5 up). 1987. lib. bdg. 12.98
   (0-671-63708-8, J Messner) S&S Trade.
Rogers, Elizabeth. The Children's Book of Talking
   Numbers. (Illus.). 16p. (gr. 1-3). 1994. saddlestitch
   bdg. 5.95 (0-8059-3470-7) Dorrance.
Rogers, Emma, jt. auth. see Rogers, Paul.
Rogers, Ethel T. Thanks, God! Date not set. 6.95
   (0-685-68222-6, BCMB-551) Lillenas.
Rogers, Fred. Going to Day Care. LC 84-24940. (Illus.).
   32p. (gr. k-2). 1985. 12.95 (0-399-21235-3, Putnam);
   (Putnam) Putnam Pub Group.
—Going to the Dentist. Judkis, Jim, photos by. (Illus.).
   32p. (Orig.). (ps-2). 1989. (Putnam); pap. 5.95
   (0-399-21634-0, Putnam) Putnam Pub Group.
—Going to the Doctor. Judkis, Jim, illus. 32p. (ps-2).
   1986. 12.95 (0-399-21298-1, Putnam); (Putnam)
   Putnam Pub Group.

—Going to the Hospital. Judkis, Jim, photos by. (Illus.). 32p. (ps-4). 1988. 14.95 (0-399-21503-4, Putnam); pap. 5.95 (0-399-21530-1, Putnam) Putnam Pub Group.
—Going to the Potty. Judkis, Jim, illus. 32p. (ps-2). 1986. 14.95 (0-399-21296-5, Putnam); pap. 5.95 (0-399-21297-3, Putnam) Putnam Pub Group.
—Making Friends. Judkis, Jim, photos by. (Illus.). (ps-1). 1987. 12.95 (0-399-21382-1, Putnam); pap. 5.95 (0-399-21385-6, Putnam) Putnam Pub Group.
—Moving. (Illus.). 32p. (ps-4). 1987. 12.95 (0-399-21383-X, Putnam); (Putnam) Putnam Pub Group.
—The New Baby. Judkis, Jim, photos by. LC 84-26210. (Illus.). 32p. (gr. k-2). 1985. 12.95 (0-399-21236-1, Putnam); pap. 5.95 (0-399-21238-8, Putnam) Putnam Pub Group.
—When a Pet Dies. Judkis, Jim, photos by. (Illus.). 32p. (ps-4). 1988. (Putnam); pap. 5.95 (0-399-21529-8, Putnam) Putnam Pub Group.
Rogers, George L. Mac & Zach from Hackensack. Eskander, Stefanie C., illus. 32p. (gr. k-6). 1992. PLB 12.95 (0-938399-07-1); pap. 4.95 (0-938399-06-3) Acorn Pub MN.
Rogers, Hal. Generals. LC 92-9478. 1992. PLB 17.26 (0-86593-154-2); 12.95s.p. (0-685-59323-1) Rourke Corp.
—Skiing. LC 93-23410. 1993. write for info. (0-86593-348-0) Rourke Corp.
Rogers, Jacqueline. Best Friends Sleep Over. LC 92-56895. 1993. write for info. (0-590-44793-9) Scholastic Inc.
—The Christmas Pageant. (Illus.). 32p. (ps-3). 1992. pap. 5.95 (0-448-40256-4, G&D) Putnam Pub Group.
Rogers, James T. The Secret War: Espionage in World War II. (Illus.). 128p. (gr. 7-10). 1991. lib. bdg. 16.95x (0-8160-2395-6) Facts on File.
Rogers, Jean. Dinosaurs Are Five Hundred Sixty-Eight. (gr. 4-7). 1991. pap. 2.99 (0-440-40434-7) Dell.
—Dinosaurs Are 568. Hafner, Marylin, illus. LC 88-5501. 96p. (gr. 3 up). 1988. 10.95 (0-688-07931-8) Greenwillow.
—Goodbye, My Island. Munoz, Rie, illus. LC 82-15816. 96p. (gr. 5-7). 1983. 12.95 (0-688-01964-1); PLB 12.88 (0-688-01965-X) Greenwillow.
—King Island Christmas. Munoz, Rie, illus. LC 84-25865. 32p. (gr. k-3). 1985. 13.00 (0-688-04236-8); lib. bdg. 12.93 (0-688-04237-6) Greenwillow.
—Raymond's Best Summer. Hafner, Marylin, illus. LC 89-34772. 80p. (gr. 1 up). 1990. 12.95 (0-688-09391-4) Greenwillow.
—Runaway Mittens. Munoz, Rie, illus. LC 87-12024. 24p. (ps-3). 1988. 15.00 (0-688-07053-1); lib. bdg. 14.93 (0-688-07054-X) Greenwillow.
—The Secret Moose. LC 84-12897. (Illus.). 64p. (gr. 3-5). 1985. 13.95 (0-688-04248-1); PLB 13.88 (0-688-04249-X) Greenwillow.
Rogers, June W. Heidi. 1969. pap. text ed. 3.75 (0-87129-200-9, H14) Dramatic Pub.
Rogers, Kathleen A. Writing to Explain. (gr. 3-6). 1987. pap. 8.95 (0-8224-7537-5) Fearon Teach Aids.
—Writing to Inform. (gr. 3-6). 1987. pap. 8.95 (0-8224-7536-7) Fearon Teach Aids.
—Writing to Persuade. (gr. 3-6). 1987. pap. 8.95 (0-8224-7538-3) Fearon Teach Aids.
Rogers, Marion. Caribbean ABC. Roger, Marion, illus. 26p. (Orig.). (ps-1). 1992. pap. 3.50 (0-935357-02-5) CRIC Prod.
Rogers, Mary. Baby Birds. 33p. (ps-k). 1992. pap. text ed. 23.00 big bk. (1-56843-003-5); pap. text ed. 4.50 (1-56843-053-1) BGR Pub.
—Big Brother. 19p. (gr. k). 1992. pap. text ed. 23.00 big bk. (1-56843-010-8); pap. text ed. 4.50 (1-56843-060-4) BGR Pub.
—Daniel's First Bus Ride. 30p. (gr. k). 1992. pap. text ed. 23.00 big bk. (1-56843-008-6); pap. text ed. 4.50 (1-56843-058-2) BGR Pub.
—The Ducks. 28p. (ps-k). 1992. pap. text ed. 23.00 big bk. (1-56843-000-0); pap. text ed. 4.50 (1-56843-050-7) BGR Pub.
—Funny Names. 35p. (gr. 1). 1992. pap. text ed. 23.00 big bk. (1-56843-016-7); pap. text ed. 4.50 (1-56843-066-3) BGR Pub.
—I Want to Play. 26p. (gr. 1). 1992. pap. text ed. 23.00 big bk. (1-56843-020-5); pap. text ed. 4.50 (1-56843-070-1) BGR Pub.
—Moving. 32p. (ps-k). 1992. pap. text ed. 23.00 big bk. (1-56843-001-9); pap. text ed. 4.50 (1-56843-051-5) BGR Pub.
—New Puppy. 35p. (gr. k). 1992. pap. text ed. 23.00 big bk. (1-56843-012-4); pap. text ed. 4.50 (1-56843-062-0) BGR Pub.
—Too Little. 30p. (ps-k). 1992. pap. text ed. 23.00 big bk. (1-56843-002-7); pap. text ed. 4.50 (1-56843-052-3) BGR Pub.
—The Torn Jacket. 30p. (gr. 1). 1992. pap. text ed. 23.00 big bk. (1-56843-018-3); pap. text ed. 4.50 (1-56843-068-X) BGR Pub.
—The Twins' First Bike. 34p. (gr. 1). 1992. pap. text ed. 23.00 big bk. (1-56843-019-1); pap. text ed. 4.50 (1-56843-069-8) BGR Pub.
Rogers, Mary & Rosario, Bernada D. New Glasses. 28p. (gr. 1). 1992. pap. text ed. 23.00 big bk. (1-56843-021-3); pap. text ed. 4.50 (1-56843-071-X) BGR Pub.

Rogers, Mary B. & Smith, Sherry A. We Can Fly: Stories of Katherine Stinson & Other Gutsy Texas Women. LC 82-80441. (Illus.). 184p. (Orig.). (gr. 7up). 1983. 14.95 (0-936650-02-8) E C Temple.
Rogers, Paul. Don't Blame Me! (Illus.). 32p. (gr. k-2). 1992. 15.95 (0-370-31204-X, Pub. by Bodley Head UK) Trafalgar.
—From Me to You. Johnson, Jane, illus. LC 87-7943. 32p. (ps-2). 1988. 12.95 (0-531-05732-1); PLB 12.99 (0-531-08332-2) Orchard Bks Watts.
—Funimals. Fuge, Charles, illus. 32p. (ps-1). 1991. 12.95 (0-8120-6216-7) Barron.
—The Shapes Game. Tucker, Sian, illus. LC 89-19957. 32p. (ps-2). 1990. 12.95 (0-8050-1280-X, Bks Young Read) H Holt & Co.
—What Will the Weather Be Like Today? LC 88-32736. (Illus.). (ps up). 1990. 13.95 (0-688-08950-X); lib. bdg. 13.88 (0-688-08951-8) Greenwillow.
Rogers, Paul & Rogera, Emma. Zoe's Tower. Corfield, Robin B., illus. LC 90-48291. 32p. (gr. 4-7). 1991. pap. 13.95 jacketed (0-671-73811-9, S&S BFYR) S&S Trade.
Rogers, Paul & Rogers, Emma. Bat Boy. Goffe, Toni, illus. 96p. (gr. 5-8). 1993. pap. 6.95 (0-460-88153-1, Pub. by J M Dent & Sons) Trafalgar.
—Our House. Lamont, Priscilla, illus. LC 92-53015. 40p. (gr. k-3). 1993. 14.95 (1-56402-134-3) Candlewick Pr.
—Zoe's Tower. (gr. 2). 1991. write for info. (0-663-56214-7) Silver Burdett Pr.
Rogers, Paul T. Forget-Me-Not. Berridge, Celia, illus. 32p. (ps-k). 1986. pap. 3.50 (0-685-43615-2, Puffin) Puffin Bks.
Rogers, Quint. The Guardian Coloring Book, Safety Tips for Children. (Illus.). 20p. (gr. k-4). 1993. pap. 1.50 (0-9637930-0-4) Creat Wrld.
Rogers, Rick. Earth Tales & Bird Song. Hayes, Suzanne, illus. Rogers, Rick, intro. by. (Illus.). 125p. (Orig.). (gr. k-9). 1991. pap. 7.50 (0-9631017-0-6) Timberdoodle.
Rogers, Teresa. George Washington Carver: Nature's Trailblazer. Raymond, Larry, illus. 72p. (gr. 4-7). 1992. PLB 14.95 (0-8050-2115-9) TFC Bks NY.
Rogers, Teresa, jt. auth. see Shulman, Jeffrey.
Rogerson, John. The Bible. Evans, Gillian, ed. (Illus.). 96p. (gr. 6-9). 1993. 17.95 (0-8160-2908-3) Facts on File.
—The Bible: Cultural Atlas for Young Children. LC 92-34670. 1993. write for info. (0-8160-2923-7) Facts on File.
Roggow, Linda & Owens, Carolyn. Handbook for Pregnant Teenagers. (Orig.). (gr. 9-12). 1984. pap. 8.99 (0-310-45821-8, 12734P) Zondervan.
Rogler, Ingrid. Small Folk Quilters. Moss, Pamela, ed. Cordoba, Liglia, illus. 68p. (gr. 3-10). 1989. pap. text ed. 9.95 (0-9622565-0-1) Chitra Pubns.
Rogoff, Mike. Israel. LC 90-10027. (Illus.). 96p. (gr. 6-12). 1990. PLB 19.92 (0-8114-2432-4) Raintree Steck-V.
Rogulic-Newsome, Lisa. Theme for a Day. 128p. (gr. 1-6). 1990. 11.95 (0-86653-545-4, GA1154) Good Apple.
Rohmann, Eric. Time Flies. LC 93-28200. 1994. write for info. (0-517-59598-2); lib. bdg. write for info. (0-517-59599-0) Crown Bks Yng Read.
Rohmer, Harriet & Anchondo, Mary. How We Came to the Fifth World (Como Vinimos al Quinto Mundo) Lopez, Graciela C., illus. LC 76-7240. (ENG & SPA.). 24p. (gr. 2-6). 1988. 13.95 (0-89239-024-7) Childrens Book Pr.
Rohmer, Harriet & Guerrero Rea, Jesus. Atariba & Niguayona. Castillo, Consuelo M., illus. LC 76-17495. (ENG & SPA.). 24p. (gr. 2-6). 1988. 13.95 (0-89239-026-3) Childrens Book Pr.
Rohmer, Harriet & Wilson, Dorminster. Mother Scorpion Country: La tierra de la madre escorpion. LC 86-32649. (SPA & ENG., Illus.). (gr. 2-7). 1987. 13.95 (0-89239-032-8) Childrens Book Pr.
Rohmer, Harriet, adapted by. The Legend of Food Mountain (La montana del alimento) Carrillo, Graciela, illus. LC 81-71634. 24p. (gr. k-8). 1982. 13.95 (0-89239-022-0) Childrens Book Pr.
—Uncle Nacho's Hat (El Sombrero de Tio Nacho) Flor Ada, Alma & Zubizarreta, Rosalma, trs. Reisberg, Veg, illus. LC 88-37090. (ENG & SPA.). 32p. (ps-5). 1989. 13.95 (0-89239-043-3) Childrens Book Pr.
—Uncle Nacho's Hat: El sombrero del Tio Nacho. Ada, Alma F. & Zubizarreta, Rosalma, trs. (ENG & SPA., Illus.). 32p. (ps-5). 1993. pap. 5.95 (0-89239-112-X) Childrens Book Pr.
Rohmer, Harriet & Gomez, Cruz, eds. Mr. Sugar Came to Town (La visita del Senor Azucar) Zubizarreta, Rosalma, tr. Chagoya, Enrique, illus. (SPA & ENG.). 32p. (ps-5). 1989. 13.95 (0-89239-045-X) Childrens Book Pr.
Rohmer, Harriet & Olivarez, Anna, eds. The Adventures of Connie & Diego Audiocassette. (SPA & ENG.). 1989. 8.95 (0-89239-051-4) Childrens Book Pr.
—Brother Anansi & the Cattle Ranch Read-Along. (SPA & ENG.). (gr. 3-7). 1989. incl. audiocassette 22.95 (0-89239-063-8) Childrens Book Pr.
—How We Came to the Fifth World Read-Along. (SPA & ENG.). (gr. 2-7). 1987. incl. audiocassette 22.95 (0-89239-038-7) Childrens Book Pr.
—Uncle Nacho's Hat Read-Along. (ENG & SPA.). (ps-7). 1990. incl. audiocassette 22.95 (0-89239-061-1) Childrens Book Pr.
Rohmer, Harriet, jt. ed. see Olivarez, Anna.

Rohmer, Harriet, et al, eds. The Invisible Hunters (Los cazadores invisibles) Sam, Joe, illus. LC 86-32658. (ENG & SPA.). (gr. 2-7). 1987. 13.95 (0-89239-031-X) Childrens Book Pr.
—Invisible Hunters: Los cazadores invisibles. (SPA & ENG., Illus.). 32p. (gr. 2-7). 1993. pap. 5.95 (0-89239-109-X) Childrens Book Pr.
Rohr, Janelle. Science & Religion: Opposing Viewpoints. LC 87-38066. (Illus.). (gr. 10 up). 1988. pap. text ed. 9.95 (0-89908-406-0) Greenhaven.
Rohr, Janelle, ed. Animal Rights: Opposing Viewpoints. LC 89-2227. (Illus.). 235p. (gr. 10 up). 1989. PLB 17.95 (0-89908-440-0); pap. 9.95 (0-89908-415-X) Greenhaven.
—Eastern Europe: Opposing Viewpoints. LC 90-44330. (Illus.). 240p. (gr. 10 up). 1990. PLB 17.95 (0-89908-480-X); pap. text ed. 9.95 (0-89908-455-9) Greenhaven.
—The Third World: Opposing Viewpoints. LC 89-36524. (Illus.). 264p. (gr. 10 up). 1989. PLB 17.95 (0-89908-447-8); pap. 9.95 (0-89908-422-2) Greenhaven.
—Violence in America: Opposing Viewpoints. LC 89-25943. (Illus.). 288p. (gr. 10 up). 1990. lib. bdg. 17.95 (0-89908-449-4); pap. text ed. 9.95 (0-89908-424-9) Greenhaven.
Rohr, Janelle & Anderson, Robert, eds. Israel: Opposing Viewpoints. LC 88-24432. (Illus.). 250p. (gr. 10 up). 1988. PLB 17.95 (0-89908-435-4); pap. text ed. 9.95 (0-89908-410-9) Greenhaven.
Rohrbacher, Richard W., jt. auth. see Westwood, Phoebe L.
Rohrer, Doug. More Thought Provokers. (gr. 9-12). 1993. 9.95 (1-55953-070-7) Key Curr Pr.
—Thought Provokers. 57p. (gr. 9-12). 1993. pap. 9.95 (1-55953-065-0) Key Curr Pr.
Rohrer, Josef, ed. see Hildebrand, Sigrid S. & Hildebrand, Eckart.
Rohrer, Josef, ed. see Winitz, Harris.
Rohrer, Josef, tr. see Winitz, Harris.
Rohwer, Lee O. What Is God Like? Muelken, Mary, illus. 64p. (Orig.). (gr. k-4). 1986. pap. 5.95 (0-9617788-0-6) Damon Pub.
—What Is God Like? 2nd, rev. ed. Muelken, Mary, illus. 68p. (Orig.). (gr. 8 up). 1989. pap. 7.95 (0-9617788-1-4) Damon Pub.
Rojankovsky, Feodor. Award Puzzles: Frog Went a-Courting. 1991. 5.95 (0-938971-69-7) JTG Nashville.
—Tall Book of Mother Goose. Rojankovsky, Feodor, illus. 120p. (ps up). 1942. 9.95 (0-06-025055-0) HarpC Child Bks.
—Tall Book of Nursery Tales. Rojankovsky, Feodor, illus. LC 44-3881. 120p. (ps-3). 1944. 9.95 (0-06-025065-8) HarpC Child Bks.
Rojankovsky, Feodor, jt. auth. see Langstaff, John.
Rojankovsky, Feodor, illus. Three Best-Loved Tales: The Three Bears; The Cow Went over the Mountain; Hop, Little Kangaroo! 80p. (ps-2). 1992. write for info. (0-307-15631-1, 15631, Golden Pr) Western Pub.
Rojany, Lisa. Hands-On Book of Big Machines. (ps-3). 1992. 11.95 (0-316-41904-4) Little.
—Jake & Jenny on the Town. Saltzberg, Barney, illus. 18p. (gr. k-3). 1993. 7.95 (0-8431-3584-0) Price Stern.
—Santa's New Suit. Lester, Mike, illus. 11p. (gr. 1-4). 1993. 7.95 (0-8431-3587-5) Price Stern.
—The Story of Hanukkah: A Lift-the-Flap Rebus Book. Jones, Holly, illus. 16p. (ps-3). 1993. 12.95 (1-56282-420-1) Hyprn Child.
—Things That Go Zoom! Wallner, John, illus. 18p. (gr. k-3). 1993. 6.95 (0-8431-3605-7) Price Stern.
—Where's That Pig? Wallner, John, illus. 24p. (gr. k-3). 1993. 6.95 (0-8431-3604-9) Price Stern.
Rojany, Lisa & Hargreaves, Adam. Mr. Bump. Hargreaves, Adam, illus. 5p. (gr. k-3). 1993. 5.00 (0-8431-3639-1) Price Stern.
—Mr. Funny. Hargreaves, Adam, illus. 5p. (gr. k-3). 1993. 5.00 (0-8431-3637-5) Price Stern.
—Mr. Silly. Hargreaves, Adam, illus. 5p. (gr. k-3). 1993. 5.00 (0-8431-3638-3) Price Stern.
Rojany, Lisa & Strong, Stacie. Exploring the Human Body. Griffith, Linda, illus. Haber, Jon Z. & Smith, Rodgerconcept by. LC 92-7514. (Illus.). (gr. 4-7). 1992. 13.95 (0-8120-6298-1) Barron.
Rojany, Lisa, adapted by. King Arthur's Camelot: A Pop-up Castle & Four Storybooks. Batki, Laszlo, illus. (ps up). 1993. Set, 12p. ea. 18.99 (0-525-45026-2, DCB) Dutton Child Bks.
Rojas, Hector. Origami Animals. LC 92-18266. (Illus.). 160p. (gr. 3-9). 1992. 24.95 (0-8069-8648-4) Sterling.
—Origami Animals. (Illus.). 160p. (gr. 7 up). 1993. pap. 12.95 (0-8069-8649-2) Sterling.
Rojas, Miriam M., tr. see Bartel, Nettie R., et al.
Rol, Ruud Van Der see Verhoeven, Rian & Van Der Rol, Ruud.

Roland, Donna. Grandfather's Stories. Oden, Ron, illus. (Orig.). (gr. k-3). 1993. pap. 4.95 (0-941996-00-X); Tchr's. ed. 5.50 (0-685-42442-1); Flannelboard set. 12.00; Video cass. 32.00; Audio cass., per culture. 5.95 Open My World.
This is a series which provides students with both cultural information as well as a strong sense of personal & social

values. The series portrays families living in the U.S., but through the eyes of Grandfather the grandchildren learn about their cultural heritage. Cultures presently available are: Cambodia, Germany, Mexico, the Philippines, & Viet Nam. Each culture is represented by two books: GRANDFATHER'S STORIES, which introduces the culture by means of sharing about its history & social customs. In the first book Grandfather also shares what values he would most want to pass on to his grandchildren. The second book of each culture, MORE OF GRANDFATHER'S STORIES continues to emphasize values. This time Grandfather actually tells a folktale which illustrates the values shared in the first book. The teacher's guide & activity book offers numerous suggestions & additional information which enhances & expands the storyline. Although written on a 2nd grade reading level the format & illustrations lend themselves to older grades as well, especially when the teaccher's guide is used in conjunction with the student books. The student books are available in both paperback as well as hardcover versions. Video cassette, flannelboard sets & cassettes also available. Published by Open My World Publishing, San Diego, CA. Distributed by: Paperback versions, Multicultural Publishing, 800 N. Grand Ave., Covina CA 91724, Weiser Educational, 30085 Comercio, Ranchos Santa Margarita, CA 92688, Shen's Books & Supplies, 821 S. First Ave., Arcadia, CA 91724, Yellow Book Road, 8315 La Mesa Blvd., La Mesa, CA 91941. Hardcover versions: Econo-Clad, 2101 N. Topeka Blvd., Topeka, KS 66608, Hertzberg-New Method (Perma Bound) 617 E. Vandalla Rd., Jacksonville, IL 62650-3599. Flannelboard Sets: Elfs, 22916 Styles St., Woodland Hills, CA 91367, Open My World Publishing, P.O. Box 15011, San Diego, CA 92175. *Publisher Provided Annotation.*

—Grandfather's Stories from Cambodia. (gr. k-3). 1984. pap. 4.95x (0-941996-05-0); tchr's ed. 5.50 (0-685-55724-3) Open My World.
—Grandfather's Stories from Germany. (gr. k-3). 1984. pap. 4.95x (0-941996-03-4); tchr's ed. 5.50 (0-941996-15-8) Open My World.
—Grandfather's Stories from Mexico. (gr. k-3). 1986. pap. 4.95 (0-941996-09-3); tchr's ed. 5.50 (0-941996-16-6) Open My World.
—More of Grandfather's Stories. Oden, Ron, illus. 25p. (Orig.). (gr. k-3). 1993. pap. 4.95 (0-941996-02-6); tchr's ed. 5.50 (0-941996-13-1) Open My World.
—More of Grandfather's Stories from Cambodia. (gr. 1-3). 1984. pap. 4.95x (0-941996-06-9); tchr's ed. 5.50 (0-941996-14-X) Open My World.
—More of Grandfather's Stories from Germany. (gr. 1-3). 1984. pap. 4.95x (0-941996-04-2); tchr's ed. 5.50 (0-685-55723-5) Open My World.
—More of Grandfather's Stories from Mexico. (gr. 1-3). 1986. pap. 4.95 (0-941996-10-7); tchr's ed. 5.50 (0-685-55812-6) Open My World.
—More of Grandfather's Stories from the Philippines. (gr. 1-3). 1985. pap. 4.95x (0-941996-08-5); tchr's ed. 5.50 (0-941996-17-4) Open My World.
—More of Grandfather's Stories from Vietnam. (gr. 1-3). 1985. pap. 4.95x (0-941996-12-3); tchr's ed. 5.50 (0-941996-18-2) Open My World.
Roland, Timothy. Detective Dan & the Flying Frog Mystery. 48p. (gr. 2-5). 1993. pap. 3.99 (0-310-38121-5, Pub. by Youth Spec) Zondervan.
—Detective Dan & the Gooey Gumdrop Mystery. 48p. (gr. 2-5). 1993. pap. 3.99 (0-310-38111-8, Pub. by Youth Spec) Zondervan.
—Detective Dan & the Missing Marble Mystery. 2nd, abr., & rev. ed. 48p. (gr. 2-5). 1993. pap. 3.99 (0-310-38091-X, Pub. by Youth Spec) Zondervan.

—Detective Dan & the Puzzling Pizza Mystery. 48p. (gr. 2-5). 1993. pap. 3.99 (0-310-38101-0, Pub. by Youth Spec) Zondervan.
Rolater. Japanese Americans. 1991. 13.95s.p. (0-86593-138-0); 18.60 (0-685-59186-7) Rourke Corp.
Rolde, Neil. Maine: A Narrative History. (Illus.). 368p. (Orig.). 1990. pap. 19.95 (0-88448-069-0) Tilbury Hse.
—So You Think You Know Maine. LC 84-47758. (Illus.). 216p. (Orig.). (gr. 6-12). 1984. pap. 13.95 (0-88448-025-9) Tilbury Hse.
Rolfe, John. Bo Jackson. (gr. 4-7). 1991. pap. 4.95 (0-316-75457-9, Spts Illus Kids) Little.
—Bo Jackson. (Illus.). 124p. (gr. 3-6). 1991. PLB 19.95 (0-8225-3109-7) Lerner Pubns.
—Curveballs Strikes Again: More Wacky Facts to Bat Around. Kopecky, Robert, illus. 32p. (gr. 3-7). 1992. pap. 4.95 (0-316-75460-9, Spts Illus Kids) Little.
—David Robinson. (Illus.). (gr. 3-7). 1991. pap. 4.95 (0-316-75461-7, Spts Illus Kids) Little.
—Jerry Rice. McGarry, Steve, illus. 1993. pap. 3.99 (0-553-48157-6) Bantam.
—Jim Abbott. 144p. (gr. 3-6). 1991. PLB 19.95 (0-8225-3108-9) Lerner Pubns.
—Jim Abbott: Sports Illustrated Kids. (gr. 4-7). 1991. pap. 4.95 (0-316-75459-5, Spts Illus Kids) Little.
Rolfes, Ellen, ed. see Neill, Robert H.
Rolfes, Ellen, ed. see Rodack, Jaine.
Rolfes, Ellen, ed. see Williams, Thelma.
Rolff, Ray, jt. auth. see Edgerton, Jean.
Rollerson, Michael, tr. see Helakisa, Kaarina.
Rolle-Whatley, R., ed. see Parham, Vanessa R.
Rolliet, D. G. Your Name & Colors: Secret Keys to Your Beauty, Personality, & Success, the Rolliett Letter-Color Theory. Reanult, Michael & Wolf, Jeannie, eds. Sherwood, Ed, illus. LC 89-91991. 192p. (Orig.). 1990. pap. text ed. 12.95 (0-9621693-0-7) Spectra Pubns Hse.
Rollings, Willard H. The Comanche. Porter, Frank W., III, intro. by. (Illus.). 112p. (gr. 5 up). 1989. 17.95 (1-55546-702-4); pap. 9.95 (0-7910-0359-0) Chelsea Hse.
Rollini, Art. When Will Summer Come? Balla, Laszlo, illus. LC 90-70904. 21p. (ps-6). 1991. pap. 5.95 (1-55523-354-6) Winston-Derek.
Rollins, Charlemae, ed. Christmas Gif' An Anthology of Christmas Poems, Songs, & Stories, Written by & about Black People. Bryan, Ashley, illus. Baker, Augusta, intro. by. LC 92-18976. (Illus.). 128p. 1993. lib. bdg. 13.93 (0-688-11668-X) Morrow.
Rollins, Charlemae H., ed. Christmas Gif' An Anthology of Christmas Poems, Songs, & Stories Written by & about African-Americans. Bryan, Ashley, illus. Baker, Augusta, intro. by. LC 92-18976. (Illus.). 128p. 1993. 15.00 (0-688-11667-1) Morrow Jr Bks.
Rollins, Jack, jt. auth. see Nelson, Steve.
Rollins, Wilma E., jt. auth. see Ranucci, Ernest R.
Rollo, Vera F. A Geography of Maryland: Ask Me! (About Maryland) 188p. (gr. k-6). 1983. casebound 14.95 (0-917882-10-5); tchrs. handbk. 8.00 (0-686-96786-0) MD Hist Pr.
Rollyson, Carl. The Arts - Pablo Picasso. LC 92-44757. 1992. 19.93 (0-86625-488-9); 14.95s.p. (0-685-67772-9) Rourke Pubns.
Rom, Christine S. Creepy Castles. LC 89-28986. (Illus.). 48p. (gr. 5 up). 1990. RSBE 11.95 (0-89686-505-3, Crestwood Hse) Macmillan Child Grp.
—Everglades. LC 88-18644. (Illus.). (gr. 4-8). 1988. RSBE 13.95 (0-89686-404-9, Crestwood Hse) Macmillan Child Grp.
Romack, Janice R. The Glass Jar. LC 93-85311. (Illus.). 40p. (gr. k-3). 1994. 6.95 (1-55523-643-X) Winston-Derek.
Romain, Trevor. The Big Cheese. (Illus.). 32p. (Orig.). (ps-3). 1991. pap. 5.95 (1-880092-00-X) Bright Bks TX.
Roman, Joseph. King Philip. (Illus.). 112p. (gr. 5 up). 1992. lib. bdg. 17.95 (0-7910-1704-4) Chelsea Hse.
—Octavio Paz: Mexican Poet & Critic. LC 92-47051. (Illus.). 1994. PLB 18.95 (0-7910-1249-2, Am Art Analog); pap. write for info. (0-7910-1276-X, Am Art Analog) Chelsea Hse.
—Pablo Neruda. (Illus.). (gr. 5 up). 1992. lib. bdg. 17.95 (0-7910-1248-4) Chelsea Hse.
Romano, Louis G., jt. auth. see Georgiady, Nicholas P.
Romanova, Natalia. Once There Was a Tree. Spirin, Gennady, illus. LC 85-6730. (ps up). 1989. pap. 4.99 (0-8037-0705-3) Dial Bks Young.
—Once There Was a Tree. 1985. 13.95 (0-8037-0235-3) Dial Bks Young.
Romanowich, Barbara, jt. auth. see Kemnitz, Thomas M.
Romatowski, Jane, jt. auth. see Lipson, Greta.
Romer, A. S. see Glut, D. F.
Romer, Ken. Dorothy & the Wooden Soldiers. (Illus.). 52p. (gr. 3-7). 1987. Colorina book with story. pap. 3.95 (0-932458-35-1) Star Rover.
Romo, Alberto, tr. see Marzollo, Jean.
Romo, Alberto, tr. see San Souci, Robert.
Ron, Van Der Meer see Van Der Meer, Ron.
Ronan, Christine, jt. auth. see Bartok, Mira.
Ronan, Colin A., ed. Science Explained: The World of Science in Everyday Life. LC 93-15439. (Illus.). 240p. (gr. 7 up). 1993. 45.00 (0-8050-2551-0, Bks Young Read) H Holt & Co.
Ronan, Margaret. All about Our Fifty States. rev. ed. Meyerriecks, William & Ronan, Frank, illus. LC 78-16658. (gr. 5-9). 1978. 11.00 (0-394-80244-6) Random Bks Yng Read.

Ronchi, Susanna, illus. Where in the World Is Geo? A Child's First Atlas. 12p. (ps-4). 1991. bds. 14.95 (0-8120-6251-5) Barron.
Rondthaler, Katharine B. Tell Me a Story. Holder, Elizabeth j., illus. 64p. (ps-5). pap. 4.00 (1-878422-06-5) Moravian Ch in Amer.
Ronen, Avraham. Stones & Bones! How Archaeologists Trace Human Origins. LC 93-2480. (gr. 6 up). 1993. lib. bdg. write for info. (0-8225-3207-7, Runestone Pr) Lerner Pubns.
Ronnholm, Paul, ed. see Ronnholm, Ursula O.
Ronnholm, Paul F., jt. auth. see Ronnholm, Ursula O.
Ronnholm, Paul F., ed. see Ronnholm, Ursula O.
Ronnholm, Ursula O. Aprende a Leer a Trave's de Musica, Juegos y Ritmos. rev. ed. Rabell, Edda, ed. & tr. Montero, Miguel, illus. (SPA.). 42p. (gr. k-2). 1989. pap. text ed. 20.00 incl. cass. (0-941911-07-1) Two Way Bilingual.
—Aprende a Leer a Traves de Musica, Juegos y Ritmos. Deliz, Osdila O., ed. Montero, Miguel, illus. (SPA.). 42p. (gr. k up). 1986. text ed. 20.00 incl. cassette (0-941911-01-2) Two Way Bilingual.
—Learning to Read Through Music, Games & Reading. Ronnholm, Paul F., ed. Montero, Miguel, tr. (Illus.). 60p. (gr. k up). 1985. pap. text ed. 20.00 (0-941911-00-4); cassette incl. Two Way Bilingual.
—Mi Libro de Escritura. Montero, Miguel, illus. (SPA.). 74p. (gr. k-3). 1986. 4.00 (0-941911-05-5) Two Way Bilingual.
—Mi Libro de Palabras, Oraciones y Cuentos. Deliz, Osdila O., ed. Montero, Miguel, illus. 100p. (gr. k-6). pap. text ed. 7.00 (0-941911-02-0) Two Way Bilingual.
—Mi Libro de Palabras: Oraciones y Cuentos. rev. ed. Rabell, Edda, ed. & tr. Montero, Miguel, illus. (SPA.). 100p. (gr. k-6). 1989. pap. 7.00 (0-941911-08-X) Two Way Bilingual.
—Two Way Bilingual Songs for Elementary School. Archo, Mayra, illus. 41p. (gr. k-12). 1987. pap. text ed. 8.00 (0-941911-06-3); cassettes incl. Two Way Bilingual.
—Writing Through Music. rev. ed. Ronnholm, Paul, ed. Montero, Miguel, tr. from SPA. (Illus.). 74p. (gr. k-3). 1989. pap. text ed. 4.00 (0-941911-09-8) Two Way Bilingual.
Ronnholm, Ursula O. & Ronnholm, Paul F. My Book of Words, Songs & Sentences. Enrique, Miguel M., illus. 91p. (gr. k-3). 1986. pap. text ed. 7.00 (0-941911-03-9) Two Way Bilingual.
Roocroft, Alan, jt. auth. see Tibbitts, Alison.
Rood, Ronald. How Do You Spank a Porcupine? LC 83-62565. (Illus.). 160p. (gr. 7 up). 1983. pap. 8.95 (0-933050-19-4) New Eng Pr VT.
—Tide Pools. Classen, Martin, illus. LC 92-2581. 48p. (gr. 2-5). 1993. 12.00 (0-06-027074-8); PLB 11.89 (0-06-027075-6) HarpC Child Bks.
—Tide Pools. Classen, Martin, illus. LC 92-2581. 48p. (gr. 2-5). 1993. pap. 7.95 (0-06-446151-3, Trophy) HarpC Child Bks.
—Wetlands. Donnelly, Marlene H., illus. LC 92-47140. (gr. 1-4). 1994. 14.00 (0-06-023010-X); PLB 13.89 (0-06-023011-8) HarpC Child Bks.
Roof, Christopher, ed. see Montague, William A.
Rook, E. C. & Rook, Lizzie J., eds. Young People's Speaker: Designed for Young People of Twelve Years. facsimile ed. LC 70-37019. (gr. 7 up). Repr. of 1892 ed. 14.00 (0-8369-6318-0) Ayer.
Rook, Lizzie & Goodfellow, E. J. Tiny Tot's Speaker. facsimile ed. LC 73-160907. (gr. 7 up). Repr. of 1895 ed. 14.00 (0-8369-6271-0) Ayer.
Rook, Lizzie J., jt. ed. see Rook, E. C.
Rooney, Lisa, jt. auth. see Bell, Alison.
Rooney, Robert & Lipuma, Anthony. Learn to Be the Master Student: How to Develop Self-Confidence & Effective Study Skills. De Silva, Jessica, illus. LC 92-80281. 248p. (Orig.). (gr. 9-12). 1992. pap. 14.95 (0-9632530-8-5) Maydale Pub.
Roop, Connie, jt. auth. see Roop, Peter.
Roop, Connie, ed. see Columbus, Christopher.
Roop, Connie, jt. ed. see Roop, Peter.
Roop, Peter. The Cry of the Conch. Patric, illus. LC 84-4232. (gr. 3-5). 1984. 8.95 (0-916630-39-0) Pr Pacifica.
—Go Hog Wild! (ps-3). 1990. pap. 2.95 (0-8225-9555-9) Lerner Pubns.
—Little Blaze & the Buffalo Jump. Wells, Jesse, illus. 28p. (Orig.). (gr. 3-8). 1984. pap. 2.45 (0-89992-089-6) Coun India Ed.
—Natosi: Strong Medicine. 32p. (gr. 3-8). 1984. pap. 2.45 (0-89992-090-X) Coun India Ed.
—Sik-Ki-Mi. 32p. (gr. 3-6). 1984. pap. 1.95 (0-89992-091-8) Coun India Ed.
Roop, Peter & Roop, Connie. Ahyoka & the Talking Leaves. Miyake, Yoshi, illus. LC 91-3036. (gr. 1 up). 1992. text ed. 12.00 (0-688-10697-8) Lothrop.
—Buttons for General Washington. Hanson, Peter E., illus. LC 86-6120. 48p. (gr. k-4). 1986. lib. bdg. 14.95 (0-87614-294-3); pap. 4.95 (0-87614-476-8) Carolrhoda Bks.
—Buttons for General Washington. Hanson, Peter E., illus. 48p. (gr. k-4). 1987. pap. 5.95 (0-685-18657-1, First Ave Edns) Lerner Pubns.
—Going Buggy! Jokes about Insects. (Illus.). 32p. (gr. 1-4). 1986. PLB 11.95 (0-8225-0988-1, First Ave Edns); pap. 2.95 (0-8225-9530-3, First Ave Edns) Lerner Pubns.

—Keep the Lights Burning, Abbie. Hanson, Peter E., illus. LC 84-27446. 40p. (gr. k-4). 1985. lib. bdg. 14.95 (0-87614-275-7); pap. 5.95 (0-87614-454-7) Carolrhoda Bks.
—Keep the Lights Burning, Abbie. Hanson, Peter E., illus. (gr. 2-4). 1989. incl. cass. 19.95 (0-87499-135-8); pap. 12.95 incl. cass. (0-87499-134-X); Set; incl. 4 bks., guide, & cass. pap. 27.95 (0-87499-136-6) Live Oak Media.
—Let's Celebrate! Jokes about Holidays. (Illus.). 32p. (gr. 1-4). 1986. PLB 11.95 (0-8225-0989-X, First Ave Edns); pap. 2.95 (0-8225-9529-X, First Ave Edns) Lerner Pubns.
—Off the Map: The Journals of Lewis & Clark. Tanner, Tim, illus. LC 92-18340. 48p. (gr. 3-7). 1993. 14.95 (0-8027-8207-8); PLB 15.85 (0-8027-8208-6) Walker & Co.
—One Earth, a Multitude of Creatures. Kells, Valerie A., illus. LC 92-14057. 32p. 1992. 14.95 (0-8027-8192-6); lib. bdg. 15.85 (0-8027-8193-4) Walker & Co.
—Out to Lunch: Jokes about Food. Hanson, Joan, illus. LC 84-4416. 32p. (gr. 1-4). 1984. PLB 11.95 (0-8225-0983-0, First Ave Edns); pap. 2.95 (0-8225-9552-4, First Ave Edns) Lerner Pubns.
—Poltergeists: Opposing Viewpoints. LC 87-7572. (Illus.). 96p. (gr. 5-8). 1988. lib. bdg. 14.95 (0-89908-052-9) Greenhaven.
—Seasons of the Cranes. (Illus.). 32p. (gr. 4-7). 1989. 14. 95 (0-8027-6859-8); PLB 15.85 (0-8027-6860-1) Walker & Co.
—Snips the Tinker. McKissack, Patricia & McKissack, Fredrick, eds. Brown, Craig M., illus. LC 88-60385. 32p. (Orig.). (gr. 1-3). 1990. text ed. 8.95 (0-88335-785-2); pap. text ed. 4.95 (0-88335-797-6) Milliken Pub Co.
—The Solar System: Opposing Viewpoints. LC 87-18347. (Illus.). 112p. (gr. 5-8). 1988. lib. bdg. 14.95 (0-89908-053-7) Greenhaven.
—Stick Out Your Tongue! Jokes about Doctors & Patients. (Illus.). 32p. (gr. 1-4). 1986. PLB 11.95 (0-8225-0990-3, First Ave Edns); pap. 2.95 (0-8225-9546-X, First Ave Edns) Lerner Pubns.
—Stonehenge: Opposing Viewpoints. (Illus.). 112p. (gr. 5-8). 1989. PLB 14.95 (0-89908-066-9) Greenhaven.
Roop, Peter & Roop, Connie, eds. Capturing Nature: The Writings & Art of John James Audubon. Farley, Rick, illus. LC 92-15662. 1993. 16.95 (0-8027-8204-3); PLB 17.85 (0-8027-8205-1) Walker & Co.
—I, Columbus: My Journal - 1492. Hanson, Peter, illus. 57p. (gr. 4-7). 1990. 13.95 (0-8027-6977-2); lib. bdg. 14.85 (0-8027-6978-0) Walker & Co.
Roop, Peter, ed. see Columbus, Christopher.
Roop, Peter, et al. Go Hog Wild: Jokes from down on the Farm. Hanson, Joan, illus. LC 84-5662. 32p. (gr. 1-4). 1984. PLB 11.95 (0-8225-0982-2) Lerner Pubns.
—Space Out: Jokes about Outer Space. Hanson, Joan, illus. LC 84-5650. 32p. (gr. 1-4). 1984. PLB 11.95 (0-8225-0984-9) Lerner Pubns.
Roos, Kelley & Roos, Stephen. The Incredible Cat Caper. (gr. 3-6). 1986. pap. 2.75 (0-440-44084-X, YB) Dell.
Roos, Rogers. Crocodile Christmas. 1993. pap. 3.50 (0-440-40872-5) Dell.
Roos, Stephen. And the Winner Is... DeRosa, Dee, illus. LC 86-27519. 128p. (gr. 3-7). 1989. SBE 13.95 (0-689-31300-4, Atheneum Child Bk) Macmillan Child Grp.
—Confessions of a Wayward Preppie. LC 85-16241. 144p. (gr. 7 up). 1986. 13.95 (0-385-29454-9) Delacorte.
—Confessions of a Wayward Preppie. (gr. k-12). 1987. pap. 2.75 (0-440-91586-4, LFL) Dell.
—Cottontail Caper: The Pet Lovers Club. (gr. 4-7). 1992. 14.00 (0-385-30549-4) Delacorte.
—Crocodile Christmas: The Pet Lovers Club. Rogers, Jacqueline, illus. LC 91-47079. 128p. (gr. 3-6). 1992. 14.00 (0-385-30681-4) Delacorte.
—Dear Santa, Make Me a Star. Premo, Steve, illus. 96p. (gr. 2-6). 1991. pap. 3.50 perfect bdg. (0-89486-764-4, T5174) Hazelden.
—The Fair-Weather Friends. DeRosa, Dee, illus. LC 86-17246. 128p. (gr. 3-6). 1987. SBE 13.95 (0-689-31297-0, Atheneum Child Bk) Macmillan Child Grp.
—Fair-Weather Friends. 128p. (gr. 2-9). 1988. pap. 2.95 (0-8167-1306-5) Troll Assocs.
—Leave It to Augie. Premo, Steve, illus. 96p. (gr. 2-6). 1991. pap. 3.50 perfect bdg. (0-89486-774-1, T5172) Hazelden.
—Love Me, Love My Werewolf. (gr. 4-7). 1993. pap. 3.50 (0-440-40812-1) Dell.
—My Blue Tongue. Premo, Steve, illus. 96p. (gr. 2-6). 1991. pap. 3.50 perfect bdg. (0-89486-784-9, T5173) Hazelden.
—My Favorite Ghost. DeRosa, Dee, illus. LC 85-15186. 128p. (gr. 3-7). 1988. SBE 13.95 (0-689-31301-2, Atheneum Child Bk) Macmillan Child Grp.
—My Horrible Secret. Newsom, Carol, illus. 128p. (Orig.). (gr. 4-7). 1991. pap. 3.25 (0-440-43956-6, YB) Dell.
—My Horrible Secret. Newsom, Carol, illus. LC 82-14954. 128p. (gr. 4-6). 1983. pap. 10.95 (0-385-29246-5) Delacorte.
—My Secret Admirer. Newsom, Carol, illus. LC 84-5010. 112p. (gr. 4-6). 1984. 14.95 (0-385-29342-9); PLB 13. 95 (0-385-29343-7) Delacorte.
—My Secret Admirer. (gr. k-12). 1991. pap. 3.25 (0-440-45950-8, YB) Dell.

—Never Trust a Sister over Twelve. De Groat, Diane, illus. LC 92-34406. 1993. 13.95 (0-385-31048-X) Delacorte.
—Silver Secrets: Maple Street Kids Ser. Premo, Steve, illus. 96p. (gr. 2-6). 1991. pap. 3.50 perfect bdg. (0-89486-777-6, T5171) Hazelden.
—The Terrible Truth: Secrets of a Sixth-Grader. Newsom, Carol, illus. LC 83-5253. 128p. (gr. 4-6). 1983. 12.95 (0-385-29306-2) Delacorte.
—The Terrible Truth: Secrets of a Sixth-Grader. Newsom, Carol, illus. 128p. (gr. 4-7). 1991. pap. 3.25 (0-440-48578-9, YB) Dell.
—Thirteenth Summer. 112p. (gr. 4-7). 1992. pap. 2.95 (0-8167-1840-7) Troll Assocs.
—Twelve-Year-Old Vows Revenge: After Being Dumped by Extraterrestrial on First Date. (gr. 4-7). 1991. pap. 3.25 (0-440-40465-7) Dell.
—You'll Miss Me When I'm Gone. (gr. k-12). 1989. pap. 2.95 (0-440-20485-2, LE) Dell.
Roos, Stephen, jt. auth. see Roos, Kelley.
Roosevelt, Franklin D., Jr. see Lash, Joseph P.
Root. Contrary Bear. Date not set. 15.00 (0-06-025085-2, Festival); PLB 14.89 (0-06-025086-0, Festival) HarpC Child Bks.
Root, B., ed. see Ray, M. L.
Root, Betty. Dictionary. LC 91-26178. (Illus.). 96p. (gr. 1-5). 1992. pap. 13.00 (0-671-76002-5, S&S BFYR); pap. 8.00 (0-671-76003-3, S&S BFYR) S&S Trade.
—Three Hundred First Words. Dann, Geoff, photos by. 156p. (ps). 9.95 (0-8120-6356-2) Barron.
—Three Hundred First Words - Palabras Primeras. Dann, Geoff, photos by. (ENG & SPA). 156p. (ps) 9.95 (0-8120-6358-9) Barron.
—Three Hundred First Words - Premiers Mots. Dann, Geoff, photos by. (ENG & FRE.). 156p. (ps) 1993. 9.95 (0-8120-6357-0) Barron.
Root, Betty, jt. auth. see Leyton, Lawrence.
Root, Clive. Bamboo Bears. (Illus.). 112p. (Orig.). (gr. 8-12). 1990. pap. 17.95 (0-920534-61-9, Pub. by Hyperion Pr Ltd CN) Sterling.
Root, Kimberly B., jt. auth. see Wolff, Patricia R.
Root, Loretta P. Outflowing Love: Auntie-Bai, Effie Southworth's Life. Benson, Mary C., ed. Benson, John, illus. 124p. (Orig.). 1989. pap. 5.95 (0-89367-142-8) Light & Life.
Root, Phyllis. Coyote & the Magic Words. LC 92-3893. (gr. 4-7). 1993. 14.00 (0-688-10308-1) Lothrop.
—Coyote & the Magic Words. LC 92-3893. (gr. ps-3). 1993. 13.93 (0-688-10309-X) Lothrop.
—Glacier. LC 88-18945. (Illus.). 48p. (gr. 4-5). 1988. 13. 95 (0-89686-408-1, Crestwood Hse) Macmillan Child Grp.
—The Listening Silence. McDermott, Dennis, illus. LC 90-37425. 128p. (gr. 3-7). 1992. 14.00 (0-06-025092-5); PLB 13.89 (0-06-025093-3) HarpC Child Bks.
—Moon Tiger. Young, Ed, illus. LC 85-7572. 32p. (ps-2). 1988. pap. 3.95 (0-8050-0803-9, Bks Young Read) H Holt & Co.
—The Old Red Rocking Chair. Sandford, John, illus. 32p. (ps-3). 1992. 14.95 (1-55970-063-7) Arcade Pub Inc.
—Sam, Who Was Swallowed by a Shark. Scheffler, Axel, illus. LC 93-2884. 1994. write for info. (1-56402-198-X) Candlewick Pr.
Root, Phyllis & McCormick, Maxine. Galapagos Islands. LC 89-7918. (Illus.). 48p. (gr. 4-5). 1989. RSBE 13.95 (0-89686-434-0, Crestwood Hse) Macmillan Child Grp.
—Great Basin. LC 88-18645. (Illus.). 48p. (gr. 4-5). 1988. RSBE 13.95 (0-89686-410-3, Crestwood Hse) Macmillan Child Grp.
Roper, Gail. Seventh Grade Soccer Star. LC 88-9496. 132p. (gr. 3-7). 1988. pap. 4.49 (1-55513-507-2, Chariot Bks) Cook.
Roper, Gayle. The Case of the Missing Melody. LC 92-39317. (Illus.). 1993. write for info. (1-55513-702-4, Chariot Bks) Cook.
—A Race to the Finish. 128p. (gr. 3-7). 1991. pap. 4.49 (1-55513-816-0, 38166, Chariot Bks) Cook.
Roper, Harlin J. In the Beginning God: Genesis - Exodus 18. 64p. 1989. Repr. wkbk. 4.50 (0-86606-350-1, 1) Roper Pr.
—In the Beginning God: Genesis - Exodus 18. 64p. (gr. 7-12). 1988. Repr. wkbk. 4.50 (0-86606-362-5, 1Y) Roper Pr.
—In the Beginning God: Genesis - Exodus 18. (Illus.). 64p. (gr. 4-6). 1989. Repr. of 1956 ed. wkbk. 4.50 (0-86606-374-9, 1J) Roper Pr.
Roper, Robert. In Caverns of Blue Ice. (gr. 4-7). 1991. 14.95 (0-316-75606-7) Little.
Roper, William. Sequoia & His Miracle. (gr. 5-12). 1972. 4.95 (0-89992-056-X) Coun India Ed.
Rosa, Don, jt. auth. see Barks, Carl.
Rosal, Lorenca. The Liberty Key: The Story of the N.H. Constitution. (Illus.). 300p. 1987. 12.95 (0-685-19456-6) Equity Pub NH.
Rosales, Melodye. Double Dutch & the Voodoo Shoes: An Urban Folktale. Rosales, Melodye, illus. LC 91-13153. 32p. (ps-3). 1991. PLB 16.93 (0-516-05133-4); pap. 5.95 (0-516-45133-2) Childrens.
Rosales, Michael & Sider, Eva. The Adventures of Panchito & Miguel: Panchito's Guide to Computers. Agustini, Michelle, illus. 24p. (Orig.). (gr. 1-4). 1988. pap. text ed. 4.95 (0-929297-00-8, 301-158 (005996642)) R & S Books.
Rosamond, Peggy J. Antique French Doll Paper Dolls: An Armenian-American Memoir. 8p. (gr. 8-12). 1976. pap. 4.00 (0-914510-07-X) Evergreen.

Rosario, Bernada D., jt. auth. see Rogers, Mary.
Rosario, Idalia. Idalia's Project ABC-Proyecto ABC: An Urban Alphabet Book in English & Spanish. Idalia, Rosario, illus. LC 80-21013. (ps-2). 1981. (Bks Young Read); pap. 5.95 (0-8050-0296-0) H Holt & Co.
Rosario Marquez, Nieves del see Del Rosario Marquez, Nieves.
Rosato, Amelia, jt. auth. see O'Neal, Debbie T.
Rose, Agatha. Hide-&-Seek in the Yellow House. Spohn, Kate, illus. 32p. (ps-1). 1992. PLB 14.00 (0-670-84383-0) Viking Child Bks.
Rose, Anne. The Triumphs of Fuzzy Fogtop. De Paola, Tomie, illus. LC 78-72204. (gr. k-3). 1979. Dial Bks Young.
Rose, David S. Maynard's Dreams. Rose, David S., illus. LC 92-43146. 32p. (ps-3). 1993. SBE 14.95 (0-689-31847-2, Atheneum Child Bk) Macmillan Child Grp.
Rose, Deborah L. Meredith's Mother Takes the Train. Levine, Abby, ed. Trivas, Irene, illus. LC 90-12756. 24p. (ps-k). 1991. 11.95 (0-8075-5061-2) A Whitman.
Rose, Dorothy. Baby Games: Follow Me. (ps). 1994. pap. 3.50 (0-671-88361-5, Little Simon) S&S Trade.
—Baby Games Peek A Boo. (ps). 1994. pap. 3.50 (0-671-88358-5, Little Simon) S&S Trade.
—Baby Games What do Lambs Say? (ps). 1994. pap. 3.50 (0-671-88359-3, Little Simon) S&S Trade.
—Baby Games: Where's Your Nose. (ps). 1994. pap. 3.50 (0-671-88360-7, Little Simon) S&S Trade.
Rose, Gerald. Grumps. (Illus.). 32p. (gr. k-2). 1993. 17.95 (0-370-31575-8, Pub. by Bodley Head UK) Trafalgar.
—Trouble in the Ark. LC 89-37270. (ps-1). 1989. 10.95 (0-8192-1511-2) Morehouse Pub.
Rose, Jennifer, ed. see Fleming, Red.
Rose, Joan E. The Princess on the Glass Mountain. (gr. k). 1993. 7.95 (0-8062-4609-X) Carlton.
Rose, John R. Keys to Success. 128p. 1992. pap. write for info. (1-881170-00-4) Rose Pub OR.
Rose, Jonathan. Otto von Bismarck. Schlesinger, Arthur M., Jr., intro. by. (Illus.). 112p. (gr. 5 up). 1987. lib. bdg. 17.95 (0-87754-510-3) Chelsea Hse.
Rose, Kenneth J. Classification of the Animal Kingdom. (gr. 7 up). 1980. 8.95 (0-679-20508-X) McKay.
Rose, Laura. Picture This: Teaching Reading Through Visualization. 176p. (Orig.). (gr. 4-8). 1988. pap. text ed. 17.95 (0-913705-32-2) Zephyr Pr AZ.
Rose, M. The Highest Form of Killing. 1992. 16.95 (0-15-234270-2, HB Juv Bks) HarBrace.
Rose, Marilyn S. My First Horse. 53p. (Orig.). (gr. 3-4). 1991. pap. 9.95 (0-9632117-0-6) AMI & Arabian Mktg.
Rose, Mary C. Clara Barton: Soldier of Mercy. Johnson, E. Harper, illus. 80p. (gr. 2-6). 1991. Repr. of 1960 ed. lib. bdg. 12.95 (0-7910-1403-7) Chelsea Hse.
Rose, Mary K. The Children's Tarot: The Road Is a River. Rose, Mary K., illus. 52p. (Orig.). (ps-8). 1993. pap. 18.95 incl. audio cass. & set of 24 cards (0-9636234-0-0) Wild Rose CO.
Rose, Phoebe E. You & the Cow. Skidmore, Joan L., illus. LC 91-60008. 20p. (Orig.). (gr. k-6). 1991. pap. 8.50 (0-9630050-0-6) Oregon Info.
Rose, Susanna Van see Van Rose, Susanna.
Rose, Walter. The Village Carpenter. LC 88-3. (Illus.). 146p. (gr. 10 up). 1988. pap. 9.95 (0-941533-18-2) New Amsterdam Bks.
Rose, Willi, jt. auth. see McMahan, Dean.
Roseman, Kenneth. All in My Jewish Family. Leipzig, Arthur, photos by. (Illus.). 32p. (gr. k-3). 1984. pap. 5.00 wkbk. (0-8074-0266-4, 103800) UAHC.
—The Cardinal's Snuffbox. Negron, Bill, illus. 128p. (gr. 4-6). 1982. pap. text ed. 7.95 (0-8074-0059-9, 140060) UAHC.
—Escape from the Holocaust. 192p. (Orig.). (gr. 4-6). 1985. pap. 7.95 (0-8074-0307-5, 140070) UAHC.
—The Melting Pot. (Illus.). 144p. (Orig.). (gr. 4-6). 1984. pap. 7.95 (0-8074-0269-9, 146065) UAHC.
Roseman, Kenneth D. The Other Side of the Hudson. (Orig.). (gr. 4-6). 1993. pap. 7.95 (0-8074-0506-X, 140061) UAHC.
—The Tenth of Av. 96p. (Orig.). (gr. 4-6). 1988. pap. text ed. 7.95 (0-8074-0359-8, 123928) UAHC.
Rosemond, Peggy De see DeRosemond, Peggy.
Rosemont, Franklin, ed. see Riebe, Ernest.
Rosen, Anne, et al. Family Passover. Salzmann, Laurence, photos by. LC 79-89298. 64p. (gr. 2 up). 1980. 8.95 (0-8276-0169-7) JPS Phila.
Rosen, Billi. Andi's War. (Illus.). 144p. (gr. 5 up). 1991. pap. 3.95 (0-14-034404-7, Puffin) Puffin Bks.
Rosen, C. Party Fun. (Illus.). 14p. (gr. 2-6). 1986. pap. 4.50 (0-7460-0124-X) EDC.
Rosen, C., jt. auth. see Wilkes, A.
Rosen, David. Henry's Tower. Feldman, Lynne, illus. LC 84-61581. 36p. (gr. k-5). 1984. 10.95 (0-930905-01-6); pap. 4.95 (0-930905-00-8) Platypus Bks.
Rosen, Dorothy, jt. auth. see Rosen, Sidney.
Rosen, Gary & Shontz, Bill. Quiet Time. Weller, Linda, illus. 24p. (ps-1). 1990. pap. 9.95 incl. cassette (0-679-80801-9) Random Bks Yng Read.
—Sing a Happy Song. Petach, Heidi, illus. 24p. (ps-1). 1990. pap. 9.95 incl. cassette (0-679-80805-1) Random Bks Yng Read.
Rosen, Joan M. Guessing: Reading As Prediction. (Illus.). 198p. 1986. pap. text ed. 11.95x (0-916224-0-7); 11. 95x (0-685-13952-2, Tchrs ed.) Innovative Lrn.
Rosen, Lillian. Just Like Everybody Else. LC 81-47534. 155p. (gr. 7 up). 1981. 12.95 (0-15-241652-8, HB Juv Bks) HarBrace.

Rosen, M. How the Animals Got Their Colors: Animal Myths from Around the World. Clementson, J., illus. 1992. 14.95 (*0-15-236783-7*, HB Juv Bks) HarBrace.
Rosen, Michael. The Deadman Tapes. 160p. (gr. 7-9). 1989. pap. 7.95 (*0-233-98443-7*, Pub. by A Deutsch England) Trafalgar.
—Down at the Doctor's: The Sick Book. Blake, Quentin, illus. 24p. (gr. k-4). 1988. 10.95 (*0-13-218942-9*, Little Simon) S&S Trade.
—Hard-Boiled Legs: The Breakfast Book. Blake, Quentin, illus. (gr. k-4). 1986. 10.95 (*0-13-383746-7*) P-H.
—Itsy-Bitsy Beasties: Poems from Around the World. (ps-3). 1992. 19.95 (*0-87614-747-3*) Carolrhoda Bks.
—Little Rabbit Foo Foo. LC 90-9598. (Illus.). 32p. (ps-1). 1990. pap. 12.95 jacketed (*0-671-70968-2*, S&S BFYR) S&S Trade.
—Little Rabbit Foo Foo. Robins, Arthur, illus. LC 90-9598. 32p. (ps-1). 1993. pap. 3.95 (*0-671-79604-6*, Little Simon) S&S Trade.
—Mind Your Own Business. Blake, Quentin, illus. LC 74-9969. 96p. (gr. 3 up). 1974. 21.95 (*0-87599-209-9*) S G Phillips.
—Moving. Williams, Sophy, illus. 32p. (ps-1). 1993. 12.99 (*0-670-84865-4*) Viking Child Bks.
—Off the Wall: A Very Silly Story Book. Brown, Mik, illus. LC 93-28643. 1994. pap. 2.95 (*1-85697-949-0*) Kingfisher Bks.
—Under the Bed. Blake, Quentin, illus. 32p. 1986. 10.95 (*0-13-935412-3*) P-H.
—We're Going on a Bear Hunt. Oxenbury, Helen, illus. LC 88-13338. 40p. (ps-4). 1989. SBE 15.95 (*0-689-50476-4*, M K McElderry) Macmillan Child Grp.
—We're Going on a Bear Hunt. LC 92-8836. (Illus.). 40p. (ps-1). 1992. POB 5.95 (*0-689-71653-2*, Aladdin) Macmillan Child Grp.
Rosen, Michael, compiled by. Funny Stories. Blundell, Tony, illus. LC 92-26447. 256p. (gr. 4-9). 1993. 6.95 (*1-85697-883-4*) Kingfisher Bks.
Rosen, Michael, retold by. How Giraffe Got Such a Long Neck--& Why Rhino Is So Grumpy: A Tale from East Africa. Clementson, John, illus. LC 92-46662. 32p. (ps-3). 1993. 13.99 (*0-8037-1621-4*) Dial Bks Young.
Rosen, Michael, selected by. The Kingfisher Book of Children's Poetry. LC 92-26444. (Illus.). 256p. (gr. 3-9). 1993. RLB 16.95 (*1-85697-910-5*); pap. 10.95 (*1-85697-909-1*) Kingfisher Bks.
Rosen, Michael, ed. Poems for the Very Young. Graham, Bob, illus. LC 92-45574. 80p. (gr. k-3). 1993. 15.95 (*1-85697-908-3*) Kingfisher Bks.
—South & North, East & West: The Oxfam Book of Children's Stories. Goldberg, Whoopi, intro. by. LC 91-58749. (Illus.). 96p. (ps up). 1992. 19.95 (*1-56402-117-3*) Candlewick Pr.
Rosen, Michael J. All Eyes on the Pond. (Illus.). 32p. (ps-2). 1994. 14.95 (*1-56282-475-9*); PLB 14.89 (*1-56282-476-7*) Hyprn Child.
—Bonesy & Isabel. Ransome, James, illus. LC 93-7892. 1994. write for info. (*0-15-209813-5*) HarBrace.
—Elijah's Angel. Robinson, A., illus. 1992. 13.95 (*0-15-225394-7*, HB Juv Bks) HarBrace.
—Goodnight Hands: A Bedtime Adventure. Hague, Scott, illus. LC 91-67933. 32p. (ps-3). 1992. pap. 14. 95 (*1-880444-01-1*) Times to Treas.
—I Love My Dog Best Dog Book & Neighborhood Field Guide. (gr. 4-7). 1993. pap. 12.95 (*1-56305-317-9*, 3317) Workman Pub.
—The Kids' Book of Fishing. Biedrzycki, David, illus. LC 90-50949. 96p. (Orig.). (gr. 2-6). 1991. pap. 12.95 (*0-89480-866-4*, 1866) Workman Pub.
—The Lullaby & Goodnight Sleepkit: The Gift of Sweet Dreams & Family Memories. Hague, Scott, illus. 32p. (ps-3). 1992. Boxed gift set incl. cass. & parents' guide. deluxe ed. 29.95 (*1-880444-00-3*); Mini ed. mini ed. cass & parents' guide, Aug. 1992 14.95 (*1-880444-02-X*) Times to Treas.
Rosen, Michael J., ed. Home: A Collaboration of Thirty Authors & Illustrators of Children's Books to Aid the Homeless. Williams, Vera, illus. LC 91-29125. 32p. (ps-3). 1992. 16.00 (*0-06-021788-X*); PLB 15.89 (*0-06-021789-8*) HarpC Child Bks.
—Speak! Children's Book Illustrators Brag about Their Favorite Dogs. LC 92-30325. 1993. 16.95 (*0-15-277848-9*) HarBrace.
Rosen, Mike. Autumn Festivals. (Illus.). 32p. (gr. k-4). 1990. PLB 11.90 (*0-531-18352-1*) Watts.
—Conquest of Everest. (ps-3). 1990. PLB 11.90 (*0-531-18319-X*, Pub. by Bookwright Pr) Watts.
—The First Transatlantic Flight. (Illus.). 32p. (gr. 5-6). 1989. PLB 11.90 (*0-531-18303-3*, Pub. by Bookwright Pr) Watts.
—The Journey to the North Pole. LC 89-48312. (Illus.). 32p. (gr. 5-8). 1990. PLB 11.90 (*0-531-18344-0*, Pub. by Bookwright Pr) Watts.
—The Journeys of Hannibal. (Illus.). 32p. (gr. 5-8). 1990. PLB 11.90 (*0-531-18334-3*, Pub. by Bookwright Pr) Watts.
—People at Work. LC 89-11328. (Illus.). 64p. (gr. 2-3). 1990. PLB 19.93 (*0-8368-0034-6*) Gareth Stevens Inc.
—Spring Festivals. (Illus.). 32p. (gr. 3-7). 1991. PLB 11. 90 (*0-531-18384-X*, Pub. by Bookwright Pr) Watts.
—Summer Festivals. (Illus.). 32p. (gr. 3-7). 1991. PLB 11. 90 (*0-531-18383-1*, Pub. by Bookwright Pr) Watts.
—The Travels of Marco Polo. Bull, Peter, illus. LC 88-23375. 32p. (gr. 4-6). 1989. PLB 11.90 (*0-531-18241-X*, Pub. by Bookwright Pr) Watts.

—Winter Festivals. LC 90-828. (Illus.). 32p. (gr. k-4). 1990. PLB 11.90 (*0-531-18353-X*, Pub. by Bookwright Pr) Watts.
—The World of Work. LC 89-11327. (Illus.). 64p. (gr. 4-6). 1990. PLB 19.93 (*0-8368-0009-5*) Gareth Stevens Inc.
Rosen, R., ed. see Cole, Barbara S.
Rosen, R., ed. see Cooney, Judith.
Rosen, R., ed. see Kurland, Morton L.
Rosen, R., ed. see Lee, Mary P. & Lee, Richard.
Rosen, R., ed. see Schauer, Donald D.
Rosen, Rochelle S. College in California, the Inside Track, 1994 Edition: The Comprehensive & Practical Guide for Students, Parents, & Educators. (Illus.). 592p. (gr. 8 up). 1993. pap. 24.95 (*1-880403-12-9*) Baywood.
Rosen, Roger, ed. see Allman, Paul.
Rosen, Roger, ed. see Beit-Hallahmi, Benjamin.
Rosen, Roger, ed. see Bergreen, Gary.
Rosen, Roger, ed. see Bleich, Alan R.
Rosen, Roger, ed. see Buckalew, Walker.
Rosen, Roger, ed. see Carter, Sharon.
Rosen, Roger, ed. see Dumond, Michael.
Rosen, Roger, ed. see Edwards, Gabrielle I.
Rosen, Roger, ed. see Epstein, Lawrence.
Rosen, Roger, ed. see Hughes, Tracy.
Rosen, Roger, ed. see McClaskey, Marilyn H.
Rosen, Roger, ed. see Macdonald, Robert.
Rosen, Roger, jt. ed. see McSharry, Patra.
Rosen, Roger, ed. see Mahoney, Ellen V.
Rosen, Roger, ed. see Parrot, Andrea.
Rosen, Roger, ed. see Rue, Nancy.
Rosen, Roger, ed. see Rue, Nancy N.
Rosen, Roger, ed. see Southworth, Scott.
Rosen, Roger, ed. see Webb, Margot.
Rosen, Ruth, ed. Jesus for Jews. Owens, Nate, illus. LC 87-20343. 336p. (Orig.). (gr. 12). 1987. 13.95 (*0-9616148-3-8*); pap. 7.95 (*0-9616148-4-6*); pap. 4.95 mass market (*0-9616148-2-X*) Purple Pomegranate.
Rosen, Ruth, ed. see Allman, Paul.
Rosen, Ruth, ed. see Ayer, Eleanor.
Rosen, Ruth, ed. see Beyer, Kay.
Rosen, Ruth, ed. see Black, Beryl.
Rosen, Ruth, ed. see Bowen-Woodward, Kathy.
Rosen, Ruth, ed. see Brown, Margaret F.
Rosen, Ruth, ed. see Buckalew, M. Walker.
Rosen, Ruth, ed. see Carlson, Linda.
Rosen, Ruth, ed. see Carter, Sharon.
Rosen, Ruth, ed. see Carter, Sharon & Monnig, Judith.
Rosen, Ruth, ed. see Clayton, Lawrence.
Rosen, Ruth, ed. see Clayton, Lawrence & Carter, Sharon.
Rosen, Ruth, ed. see Clayton, Lawrence & Morrison, Jaydene.
Rosen, Ruth, ed. see Cohen, Paul & Cohen, Shari.
Rosen, Ruth, ed. see Cohen, Shari.
Rosen, Ruth, ed. see Collins, Robert F.
Rosen, Ruth, ed. see Connors, Patricia & Perucci, Dorianne.
Rosen, Ruth, ed. see Cristall, Barbara.
Rosen, Ruth, ed. see Diskavich, Laura & Woods, Samuel, Jr.
Rosen, Ruth, ed. see Edwards, E. W.
Rosen, Ruth, ed. see Feller, Robyn M.
Rosen, Ruth, ed. see Field, Shelly.
Rosen, Ruth, ed. see Gartner, Bob.
Rosen, Ruth, ed. see Gooden, Kimberly W.
Rosen, Ruth, ed. see Grant, Edgar.
Rosen, Ruth, ed. see Greenwald, Dorothy.
Rosen, Ruth, ed. see Grosshandler, Janet.
Rosen, Ruth, ed. see Haddock, Patricia.
Rosen, Ruth, ed. see Heron, Jackie.
Rosen, Ruth, ed. see Hill, Margaret.
Rosen, Ruth, ed. see Hopkins, Del & Hopkins, Margaret.
Rosen, Ruth, ed. see Hurwitz, Ann R. & Hurwitz, Sue.
Rosen, Ruth, ed. see Hurwitz, Sue & Hurwitz, Jane.
Rosen, Ruth, ed. see Ignoffo, Matthew.
Rosen, Ruth, ed. see Johnson, Barbara L.
Rosen, Ruth, ed. see Kane, June K.
Rosen, Ruth, ed. see Keyishian, Elizabeth.
Rosen, Ruth, ed. see Koester, Pat.
Rosen, Ruth, ed. see Kurland, Adrienne.
Rosen, Ruth, ed. see Lee, Mary P.
Rosen, Ruth, ed. see Lee, Mary P. & Lee, Richard S.
Rosen, Ruth, ed. see Lee, Richard S. & Lee, Mary P.
Rosen, Ruth, ed. see Lobus, Catherine O.
Rosen, Ruth, ed. see Lytle, Elizabeth S.
Rosen, Ruth, ed. see Macdonald, Robert W.
Rosen, Ruth, ed. see McFarland, Rhoda.
Rosen, Ruth, ed. see McGlothin, Bruce.
Rosen, Ruth, ed. see Mahoney, Ellen V.
Rosen, Ruth, ed. see Mills, Rita.
Rosen, Ruth, ed. see Miller, Deborah.
Rosen, Ruth, ed. see Miller, Deborah A. & Waigandt, Alex.
Rosen, Ruth, ed. see Miller, Maryann.
Rosen, Ruth, ed. see Moe, Barbara.
Rosen, Ruth, ed. see Nelson, Cordner.
Rosen, Ruth, ed. see Neufld, Rose.
Rosen, Ruth, ed. see Osborn, Kevin.
Rosen, Ruth, ed. see Ottens, Allen & Myer, Rick.
Rosen, Ruth, ed. see Parker, Julie F.
Rosen, Ruth, ed. see Peck, Lee.
Rosen, Ruth, ed. see Peck, Rodney.
Rosen, Ruth, ed. see Raab, Robert A.
Rosen, Ruth, ed. see Ratto, Linda L.
Rosen, Ruth, ed. see Rawls, Bea O. & Johnson, Gwen.

Rosen, Ruth, ed. see Reynolds, Moira.
Rosen, Ruth, ed. see Rue, Nancy N.
Rosen, Ruth, ed. see St. Pierre, Stephanie.
Rosen, Ruth, ed. see Santamaria, Peggy.
Rosen, Ruth, ed. see Schleifer, Jay.
Rosen, Ruth, ed. see Septien, Al.
Rosen, Ruth, ed. see Shapiro, Stanley J.
Rosen, Ruth, ed. see Shniderman, Nancy & Hurwitz, Sue.
Rosen, Ruth, ed. see Shuker, Nancy.
Rosen, Ruth, ed. see Shuker-Haines, Frances.
Rosen, Ruth, ed. see Simpson, Carolyn.
Rosen, Ruth, ed. see Simpson, Carolyn & Simpson, Dwain.
Rosen, Ruth, ed. see Smith, Judie.
Rosen, Ruth, ed. see Smith, Sandra L.
Rosen, Ruth, ed. see Spencer, Jean.
Rosen, Ruth, ed. see Spies, Karen B.
Rosen, Ruth, ed. see Strauss, Linda.
Rosen, Ruth, ed. see Taylor, Barbara.
Rosen, Ruth, ed. see Vandenburg, Mary L.
Rosen, Ruth, ed. see Wagonseller, Bill, et al.
Rosen, Ruth, ed. see Webb, Margot.
Rosen, Ruth, ed. see White, Carl P.
Rosen, Ruth, ed. see Wilkinson, Beth.
Rosen, Ruth, ed. see Zeldis, Yona.
Rosen, Sidney. Can You Find a Planet? 40p. (gr. k-2). 1991. lib. bdg. 19.95 (*0-87614-683-3*) Carolrhoda Bks.
—Can You Hitch a Ride on a Comet? Lindberg, Dean, illus. LC 92-16808. 1993. 19.95 (*0-87614-719-8*) Carolrhoda Bks.
—How Far Is a Star? Lindberg, Dean, illus. 40p. (gr. k-2). 1992. 19.95 (*0-87614-684-1*) Carolrhoda Bks.
—Where Did the Moon Go? (Illus.). 40p. (gr. k-2). 1992. PLB 19.95 (*0-87614-685-X*) Carolrhoda Bks.
—Which Way to the Milky Way? (ps-3). 1992. 19.95 (*0-87614-709-0*) Carolrhoda Bks.
Rosen, Sidney & Rosen, Dorothy. The Magician's Apprentice. LC 93-10781. 1993. 19.95 (*0-87614-809-7*) Carolrhoda Bks.
Rosen, Suri. Water Ways: On the Go. (ps). 1992. 3.99 (*0-8431-3431-3*) Price Stern.
—Wheels to Go: On the Go. (ps). 1992. 3.99 (*0-8431-3430-5*) Price Stern.
Rosen, Teresa. The OTA Children's Coloring Book. (Illus.). 24p. (ps-8). 1989. pap. 3.95 (*0-685-27024-6*) Prac Psych Pr.
Rosenbaum, Cindy, et al. For the Love of Animals: Six Delightful Songs & a Story about How the Children Save the Animals. Feiza, Anne, illus. 24p. (Orig.). (ps-4). 1992. pap. text ed. 12.95 incl. audio tape (*1-881567-00-1*) Happy Kids Prods.
Rosenbaum, Eliza. Friends Afloat. Pidgeon, Jean, illus. LC 92-39029. 24p. (gr. 2-3). 1992. PLB 17.96 (*0-8114-3584-9*) Raintree Steck-V.
Rosenbaum, Jean & Prine, Mary. Opportunities in Fitness Careers. LC 90-50731. 160p. (gr. 7 up). 1991. 13.95 (*0-8442-8185-9*, VGM Career Bks); pap. 10.95 (*0-8442-8186-7*) NTC Pub Grp.
Rosenbaum, Robert. Aviators. (Illus.). 128p. (gr. 6-12). 1992. lib. bdg. 16.95x (*0-8160-2539-8*) Facts on File.
Rosenberg, Amye. Good Job, Jelly Bean! (Illus.). 24p. (ps-1). 1992. pap. 2.95 (*0-671-75512-9*, Little Simon) S&S Trade.
—Is It Christmas Yet? (ps). 1990. write for info. (*0-307-12168-2*) Western Pub.
—Jewels for Josephine. Rosenberg, Amye, illus. 28p. (ps-2). 1993. 12.95 (*0-448-40457-5*, G&D) Putnam Pub Group.
—Melly's Menorah. (Illus.). 24p. (ps-1). 1991. pap. 2.95 incl. stickers (*0-671-74495-X*, Little Simon) S&S Trade.
—Mitzvot. (Illus.). 30p. (gr. 1-5). pap. text ed. 4.25 (*0-87441-387-7*) Behrman.
—My Calendar. 66p. (gr. 1-2). 1984. pap. text ed. 4.25 (*0-87441-385-0*) Behrman.
—Sam the Detective's Reading Readiness Book. (Illus.). 63p. (ps). 1982. pap. text ed. 4.45x (*0-87441-361-3*) Behrman.
—Ten Treats for Ginger. (Illus.). 24p. (ps-1). 1992. pap. 2.95 (*0-671-75511-0*, Little Simon) S&S Trade.
—Tzedakah. (Illus.). (gr. k-1). 1979. pap. text ed. 4.25 (*0-87441-279-X*) Behrman.
Rosenberg, Amye & Mason, Patrice G. Sam the Detective & the Alef Bet Mystery. Rossel, Seymour, ed. Rosenberg, Amye, illus. 64p. (Orig.). (gr. 1-3). 1980. pap. text ed. 4.45 (*0-87441-328-1*) Behrman.
Rosenberg, Amye, illus. Nursery Rhymes. 24p. (ps-1). 1987. pap. 1.25 (*0-7214-9550-8*, S871-6) Ladybird Bks.
—The Pudgy Peek-a-Boo Book. 16p. (ps). 1983. pap. 2.95 (*0-448-10205-6*, G&D) Putnam Pub Group.
Rosenberg, Ellen. Growing up Feeling Good: A Growing up Handbook Especially for Kids. 1989. pap. 11.99 (*0-14-034264-8*, Puffin) Puffin Bks.
Rosenberg, Gary, jt. auth. see Gardner, Sandra.
Rosenberg, Gary B., jt. auth. see Gardner, Sandra.
Rosenberg, Harvey. Joey's Cabbage Patch. 32p. (gr. k-3). 1991. write for info. (*0-9629587-0-0*) Go Jolly Pubns.
Rosenberg, Jane. Dance Me a Story: Twelve Tales from the Classic Ballets. Ashley, Merrill, intro. by. LC 84-51701. (Illus.). (gr. 1-4). 1985. 19.95 (*0-500-01359-4*) Thames Hudson.
—Play Me a Story. LC 93-33490. (gr. 3 up). 1994. write for info. (*0-679-84391-4*) Knopf Bks Yng Read.
Rosenberg, Liz. Adelaide & the Night Train. Desimini, Lisa, illus. LC 88-39948. 32p. (ps-2). 1989. HarpC Child Bks.

—Grandmother & the Runaway Shadow. Peck, Beth, illus. LC 92-42349. 1994. write for info. (0-399-22545-5, Philomel Bks) Putnam Pub Group.
—Monster Mama. Gammell, Stephen, illus. 32p. (ps-3). 1993. PLB 14.95 (0-399-21989-7, Philomel Bks) Putnam Pub Group.
—The Scrap Doll. Ballard, Robin, illus. LC 90-35668. 32p. (ps-3). 1991. PLB 13.89 (0-06-024865-3) HarpC Child Bks.
—Window, Mirror, Moon. Richardson, Ruth, illus. LC 89-26971. 32p. (ps-3). 1990. HarpC Child Bks.
Rosenberg, Marjorie von see Von Rosenberg, Marjorie.
Rosenberg, Marjorie Von see Von Rosenberg, Marjorie.
Rosenberg, Maxine. Hiding to Survive: Fourteen Jewish Children & the Gentiles Who Rescued Them from the Holocaust. LC 93-28328. 1994. write for info. (0-395-65014-3, Clarion Bks) HM.
Rosenberg, Maxine B. Artists of Handcrafted Furniture at Work. Ancona, George, illus. LC 87-29342. 64p. (gr. 3 up). 1988. 14.95 (0-688-06875-8) Lothrop.
—Being a Twin, Having a Twin. Ancona, George, illus. LC 84-17159. 48p. (gr. 1-4). 1985. 11.95 (0-688-04328-3); lib. bdg. 11.88 (0-688-04329-1) Lothrop.
—Being Adopted. Ancona, George, photos by. LC 83-17522. (Illus.). 48p. (gr. 1-4). 1984. 13.95 (0-688-02672-9); lib. bdg. 13.88 (0-688-02673-7) Lothrop.
—Brothers & Sisters. Ancona, George, photos by. (Illus.). 32p. (gr. k-3). 1991. 14.45 (0-395-51121-6, Clarion Bks) HM.
—Finding a Way: Living with Exceptional Brothers & Sisters. Ancona, George, photos by. LC 88-6776. 48p. (gr. 1-4). 1988. 12.95 (0-688-06873-1); PLB 12.88 (0-688-06874-X) Lothrop.
—Growing up Adopted. LC 89-9899. 128p. (gr. 4 up). 1989. SBE 13.95 (0-02-777912-2, Bradbury Pr) Macmillan Child Grp.
—Living in Two Worlds. Ancona, George, illus. Spivey, Philip, afterword by. LC 85-23990. 48p. (ps-3). 1986. 11.95 (0-688-06278-4); PLB 11.88 (0-688-06279-2) Lothrop.
—Living with a Single Parent. LC 92-3883. (Illus.). 128p. (gr. 4 up). 1992. SBE 14.95 (0-02-777915-7, Bradbury Pr) Macmillan Child Grp.
—Making a New Home in America. Ancona, George, illus. LC 85-11642. 48p. (gr. 1-4). 1986. 11.95 (0-688-05824-8); PLB 11.88 (0-688-05825-6) Lothrop.
—My Friend Leslie: The Story of a Handicapped Child. Ancona, George, photos by. LC 82-12734. (Illus.). (gr. 1-3). 1983. 13.95 (0-688-01690-1); PLB 13.88 (0-688-01691-X) Lothrop.
—Not My Family: Sharing the Truth about Alcoholism. LC 88-10468. 112p. (gr. 4-7). 1988. SBE 14.95 (0-02-777911-4, Bradbury Pr) Macmillan Child Grp.
—On the Mend: Getting Away from Drugs. LC 91-11202. (Illus.). 128p. (gr. 4 up). 1991. SBE 14.95 (0-02-777914-9, Bradbury Pr) Macmillan Child Grp.
—Talking about Stepfamilies. Visher, Emily, afterword by. LC 90-33540. (Illus.). 160p. (gr. 4-7). 1990. SBE 14.95 (0-02-777913-0, Bradbury Pr) Macmillan Child Grp.
Rosenberg, Mona. Stick-tivity. (gr. k-1). 1991. write for info., incl. stickers (1-880056-07-0) Play-Media.
—Stick-tivity, Bk. 1: The Talking Drum & Trumpet. 16p. (gr. k-1). 1991. write for info., incl. stickers (1-880056-08-9) Play-Media.
—Stick-tivity, Bk. 2: Bob's Zoo. 16p. (gr. k-1). 1991. write for info., incl. stickers (1-880056-09-7) Play-Media.
—Stick-tivity, Bk. 3: On a Wet Day in Botswana. 16p. (gr. k-1). 1991. write for info., incl. stickers (1-880056-10-0) Play-Media.
—Stick-tivity, Bk. 4: Magical Thoughts on a Hot Day. 16p. (gr. k-1). 1991. write for info., incl. stickers (1-880056-11-9) Play-Media.
—Stick-tivity, Bk. 5: Planning to See the Whole World. 16p. (gr. k-1). 1991. write for info., incl. stickers (1-880056-12-7) Play-Media.
—Stick-tivity, Bk. 6: Mainly Math. 16p. (gr. k-1). 1991. write for info., incl. stickers (1-880056-13-5) Play-Media.
Rosenberg, R. Robert & Whitcraft, John E. Understanding Business & Consumer Law. 6th ed. (Illus.). (gr. 11-12). 1978. text ed. 25.12 (0-07-053631-7) McGraw.
Rosenberg, Robert. Bill Cosby: The Changing Black Image. (Illus.). 96p. (gr. 7 up). 1991. PLB 14.90 (1-878841-17-3) Millbrook Pr.
—Bill Cosby: The Changing Black Image. 1992. pap. 5.95 (0-395-63615-9) HM.
Rosenblatt, Aaron. Virginia Woolf for Beginners. Rosenblatt, Naomi, illus. (Orig.). (gr. 11 up). 1987. pap. 7.95 (0-86316-133-2) Writers & Readers.
Rosenblatt, Arthur. Keep on Caring. Cook, Tom, illus. 40p. (ps-3). 1985. 5.95 (0-910313-84-9) Parker Bros.
—The Magical Train. Yealdhall, Gary, illus. 32p. (ps-3). 1985. pap. 0.99 (0-87372-008-3) Parker Bros.
Rosenblatt, Arthur S. The Care Bears Battle the Freeze Machine. Ewers, Joe, illus. 40p. (ps-3). 1984. 5.95 (0-910313-15-6) Parker Bros.
—Runners to the Rescue. Ewers, Joe, illus. 40p. (ps-3). write for info (0-910313-76-8) Parker Bros.
—Strawberry Shortcake & the Deep, Dark Woods. Sustendal, Pat, illus. 40p. (ps-3). 1983. cancelled 5.95 (0-910313-07-5) Parker Bros.
Rosenblatt, Jeanette, jt. auth. see Schoenfield, Mark.
Rosenblatt, Ruth Y., jt. auth. see Beebe, Brooke M.

Rosenbloom, Joseph. Biggest Riddle Book in the World. Behr, Joyce, illus. LC 76-1165. (gr. 5 up). 1979. pap. 5.95 (0-8069-8884-3) Sterling.
—Deputy Dan & the Bank Robbers. Raglin, Tim, illus. LC 84-159969. 48p. (gr. 2-3). 1985. lib. bdg. 7.99 (0-394-97045-4); 3.50 (0-394-87045-X) Random Bks Yng Read.
—Deputy Dan Gets His Man. Raglin, Tim, illus. 48p. (gr. 2-3). 1985. pap. 2.95 (0-394-87250-9) Random Bks Yng Read.
—Doctor Knock-Knock's Official Knock-Knock Dictionary. Behr, Joyce, illus. LC 76-19796. 128p. (gr. 3 up). 1980. 12.95 (0-8069-4536-2); pap. 3.95 (0-8069-8936-X) Sterling.
—Funniest Dinosaur Book Ever. Wilhelm, Hans, illus. LC 87-7098. 24p. (gr. 1-6). 1987. 12.95 (0-8069-6624-6) Sterling.
—Funniest Haunted House Book Ever! Wilhelm, Hans, illus. LC 89-38605. 24p. (gr. 1-7). 1989. 12.95 (0-8069-6818-4); PLB 15.69 (0-8069-6819-2) Sterling.
—Funniest Joke Book Ever! Wilhelm, Hans, illus. LC 85-27859. 24p. (gr. k-6). 1986. 12.95 (0-8069-4724-1); PLB 15.69 (0-8069-4725-X) Sterling.
—The Funniest Riddle Book Ever! Wilhelm, Hans, illus. LC 84-16192. 24p. (ps up). 1985. 12.95 (0-8069-4698-9); lib. bdg. 15.69 (0-8069-4699-7) Sterling.
—Funny Insults & Snappy Put-Downs. Behr, Joyce, illus. LC 82-50547. 128p. (gr. 4 up). 1982. pap. 3.95 (0-8069-7644-6) Sterling.
—Gigantic Joke Book. Behr, Joyce, illus. LC 77-93310. 256p. (gr. 4-6). 1981. pap. 5.95 (0-8069-7514-8); 16.95 (0-8069-4590-9) Sterling.
—Giggles, Gags & Groaners. LC 86-30052. (Illus.). 128p. (gr. 2-8). 1988. pap. 3.95 (0-8069-6536-3) Sterling.
—Looniest Limerick Book in the World. 1991. 3.99 (0-517-07355-2) Outlet Bk Co.
—Monster Madness. 1991. 3.99 (0-517-07354-4) Outlet Bk Co.
—Nutty Knock Knocks! Hoffman, Sandy, illus. LC 85-27626. 128p. (Orig.). (gr. 2 up). 1986. pap. 3.95 (0-8069-6304-2) Sterling.
—Perfect Put-Downs & Instant Insults. LC 88-11710. (Illus.). 128p. (gr. 2-8). 1989. pap. 3.95 (0-8069-6940-7) Sterling.
—School's Out! Vacation Riddles & Jokes. LC 88-31868. (Illus.). 128p. (gr. 2-8). 1990. pap. 3.95 (0-8069-5760-3) Sterling.
—Six Hundred Ninety-Six Silly School Jokes & Riddles. Kendrick, Dennis, illus. 128p. (gr. 2 up). 1987. pap. 3.95 (0-8069-6392-1) Sterling.
—Spooky Riddles & Jokes. Hoffman, Sanford, illus. LC 87-17972. 128p. (gr. 4 up). 1988. pap. 3.95 (0-8069-6736-6) Sterling.
—Sports Riddles. Weissman, Sam Q., illus. LC 81-7232. 64p. (gr. 6 up). 1982. 8.95 (0-15-277994-9, HB Juv Bks) HarBrace.
—Super Sick Jokes & Riddles. Hoffman, Sanford, illus. 96p. (Orig.). (gr. 2-9). 1990. pap. 3.95 (0-8069-7458-3) Sterling.
—Twist These on Your Tongue. LC 78-16776. (Illus.). (gr. 4-8). 1978. 10.95 (0-525-66612-5, Lodestar Bks) Dutton Child Bks.
—World's Best Sports Riddles & Jokes. Hoffman, Sanford, illus. LC 87-30434. 128p. (gr. 3-9). 1989. pap. 3.95 (0-8069-6848-6) Sterling.
—World's Toughest Tongue Twisters. Kendrick, Dennis, illus. LC 86-5983. 128p. (gr. 2-8). 1987. pap. 3.95 (0-8069-6596-7) Sterling.
—The Zaniest Riddle Book in the World. Hoffman, Sanford, illus. LC 83-18102. 128p. (gr. 3 up). 1985. pap. 3.95 (0-8069-6252-6) Sterling.
Rosenblum, Joseph. Fun Two: Daffy Definitions. 1992. 3.99 (0-517-07776-0) Outlet Bk Co.
Rosenblum, Morris, jt. auth. see Nurnberg, Maxwell.
Rosenblum, Richard. Brooklyn Dodger Days. Rosenblum, Richard, illus. LC 90-36691. 32p. (gr. 1-5). 1991. SBE 12.95 (0-689-31512-0, Atheneum Child Bk) Macmillan Child Grp.
—Journey to the Golden Land. Rosenblum, Richard, illus. LC 91-44941. 32p. (gr. k-4). 1992. 14.95 (0-8276-0405-X) JPS Phila.
—The Old Synagogue. Rosenbloom, Roger, illus. 32p. (gr. k-3). 1989. 12.95 (0-8276-0322-3) JPS Phila.
Rosenbluth, Rosalyn. The Brave Little Mouse. Borgo, Deborah, illus. 24p. (ps-2). 1993. pap. text ed. 0.99 (1-56293-346-9) McClanahan Bk.
—The Land of Peek-A-Boo. Mahan, Ben, illus. 24p. (ps-2). 1993. pap. text ed. 0.99 (1-56293-344-2) McClanahan Bk.
—Rolf & Edgar. (Illus.). (gr. 1-4). 1991. 11.95 (0-88138-140-3, Green Tiger) S&S Trade.
—Scaredy-Cat Kitten. Borgo, Deborah, illus. 24p. (ps-2). 1993. pap. text ed. 0.99 (1-56293-352-3) McClanahan Bk.
Rosenfeld, Dina. All about Us. Zelcer, Amir, illus. 32p. (ps-1). 1989. 8.95 (0-922613-02-8); pap. 6.95 (0-922613-03-6) Hachai Pubns.
—A Chanukah Story for Night Number Three. Pape, David S., ed. Mandel, Harris, illus. 32p. (ps-1). 1989. 9.95 (0-922613-16-8); pap. 7.95 (0-922613-17-6) Hachai Pubns.
—Kind Little Rivka. Lederer, Ilene W., illus. 32p. (ps-1). 1991. 8.95 (0-922613-44-3); pap. 6.95 (0-922613-45-1) Hachai Pubns.
—Kind Little Rivka. Englin, A., tr. from ENG. Winn-Lederer, Ilene, illus. (RUS.). 32p. (ps-1). 1993. write for info. (0-922613-29-X) Hachai Pubns.

—Labels for Laibel. Nodel, Norman, illus. 32p. (ps-1). 1990. 8.95 (0-922613-35-4); pap. 6.95 (0-922613-36-2) Hachai Pubns.
—A Little Boy Named Avram. Lederer, Ilene W., illus. 32p. (ps-1). 1989. 8.95 (0-922613-08-7); pap. 6.95 (0-922613-09-5) Hachai Pubns.
—Why the Moon Only Glows. Holtzman, Yehudit, illus. 32p. (ps-1). 1992. 8.95 (0-922613-00-1); pap. 6.95 (0-922613-01-X) Hachai Pubns.
—Yossi & Laibel Hot on the Trail. Nodel, Norman, illus. 32p. (ps-1). 1991. 8.95 (0-922613-47-8); pap. 6.95 (0-922613-48-6) Hachai Pubns.
Rosenfeld, Dina, ed. see Jacobs, Chana R.
Rosenfeld, Dina, ed. see Sharfstein, Chana.
Rosenfield, Geraldine. The Heroes of Masada. Sugarman, S. Allan, illus. 38p. (gr. 6-10). pap. 1.50 (0-8381-0733-8, 10-732) United Syn Bk.
Rosenholtz, Stephen. Move Like the Animals. Yoshiko, Fujita, illus. LC 91-66970. 32p. (ps-3). 1992. incl. cassette 19.95 (0-9630979-1-1); pap. 14.95 incl. cassette (0-9630979-0-3) Rosewood Pub.
Rosenkrans, B., compiled by. My Book of Christmas Carols. Dyer, Jane, illus. 32p. (ps-2). 1986. pap. 1.95 (0-448-19079-6, G&D) Putnam Pub Group.
Rosenkranz, Shirley A., ed. Beyond the Doors. Rachford, Mary A., et al, illus. Konoske, Kathryn, intro. by. LC 88-72070. 240p. (gr. 5-12). 1988. pap. 5.95 (0-9620953-3-8) A Class Act.
Rosenstiehl, Agnes. Livre de la Langue Francaise. Gay, Pierre, illus. (FRE.). 93p. (gr. 4-9). 1985. 15.95 (2-07-039524-3) Schoenhof.
Rosenstock, D. Misfits & Miracles. 1994. pap. 3.99 (0-553-48046-4) Bantam.
Rosenstock, Harvey A., jt. auth. see Rosenstock, Judith D.
Rosenstock, Janet, jt. auth. see Adair, Dennis.
Rosenstock, Judith D. & Rosenstock, Harvey A. Your Hospital Stay...It'll Be Okay. Sorg, James M., illus. 36p. (Orig.). (gr. 1-5). 1988. pap. 4.95 (0-9622172-0-4) D Miller Fndtn.
Rosenthal, Alan, jt. auth. see Katz, Illana.
Rosenthal, Alan D., jt. auth. see Katz, Illana.
Rosenthal, Bert. Basketball. LC 82-19745. (Illus.). 48p. (gr. k-4). 1983. PLB 15.27 (0-516-01674-1); pap. 4.95 (0-516-41674-X) Childrens.
—Carl Lewis: The Second Jesse Owens. LC 83-23984. (Illus.). 48p. (gr. 2-8). 1984. PLB 13.27 (0-516-04336-6); pap. 3.95 (0-516-44336-4) Childrens.
—Dwight Gooden: King of the Ks. LC 85-11687. (Illus.). 48p. (gr. 2-8). 1985. PLB 13.27 (0-516-04348-X); pap. 3.95 (0-516-44348-8) Childrens.
—Isiah Thomas: Pocket Magic. LC 83-10080. (Illus.). 48p. (gr. 2-8). 1983. PLB 13.27 (0-516-04334-X); pap. 3.95 (0-516-44334-8) Childrens.
—Larry Bird: Cool Man on the Court. LC 80-27094. (Illus.). 48p. (gr. 2-8). 1981. PLB 13.27 (0-516-04312-9); pap. 3.95 (0-516-44312-7) Childrens.
—Lynette Woodard: The First Female Globetrotter. LC 86-9662. (Illus.). 48p. (gr. 2-8). 1986. pap. 3.95 (0-516-44360-7) Childrens.
—Soccer. LC 82-19753. (Illus.). 48p. (gr. k-4). 1983. PLB 15.27 (0-516-01658-X); pap. 4.95 (0-516-41658-8) Childrens.
—Sugar Ray Leonard: The Baby-faced Boxer. LC 82-4472. (Illus.). 48p. (gr. 2-8). 1982. PLB 13.27 (0-516-04326-9); pap. 3.95 (0-516-44326-7) Childrens.
Rosenthal, Burt. Track & Field. LC 93-23281. 1993. write for info. (0-8114-5778-8) Raintree Steck-V.
Rosenthal, Ellie. What Can I Do? Asked the Kangaroo. Rosenthal, David, illus. 1993. 7.95 (0-533-10358-4) Vantage.
Rosenthal, Gary. Soccer: The Game & How to Play It. rev. ed. Bolle, Frank, illus. LC 72-129116. 256p. (gr. 3-9). 1978. PLB 14.95 (0-87460-258-0) Lion Bks.
Rosenthal, Gilbert S. The Many Faces of Judaism: Orthodox, Conservative, Reconstructionist, & Reform. Rossel, Seymour, ed. LC 78-25898. (gr. 9-10). 1979. pap. 6.95x (0-87441-311-7); By Moshe Ben-Aharon. tchr's. guide 12.50x (0-87441-339-7); By Ellen Singer. student wkbk. 4.25 (0-87441-332-X) Behrman.
Rosenthal, Howard. Not with My Life I Don't: Preventing Your Suicide & That of Others. LC 88-70011. 266p. (gr. 9 up). 1988. pap. text ed. 18.95 (0-915202-77-8) Accel Devel.
Rosenthal, Lawrence. Exploring Careers in Accounting. rev. ed. (Illus.). 148p. (gr. 7-12). 1993. PLB 13.95 (0-8239-1501-8); pap. 9.95 (0-8239-1721-5) Rosen Group.
Rosenthal, Mark. Bears. LC 82-17910. (Illus.). 48p. (gr. k-4). 1983. PLB 15.27 (0-516-01675-X); pap. 4.95 (0-516-41675-8) Childrens.
Rosenthal, Paul. Where on Earth: A Geografunny Guide to the Globe. Rosenthal, Marc, illus. LC 92-1227. 112p. (Orig.). (gr. 3-7). 1992. PLB 15.99 (0-679-90833-1); pap. 11.00 (0-679-80833-7) Knopf Bks Yng Read.
Rosenthal, Steve, jt. auth. see Crosbie, Michael J.
Rosenthal, Yaffa. Mitzvos We Can Do. Kunda, Shmuel, illus. 32p. (gr. 1-8). 1982. 10.95 (0-89906-775-1); pap. 7.95 (0-89906-776-X) Mesorah Pubns.
—Thank You Hashem. Kunda, Shmuel, illus. 32p. (gr. 1-8). 1983. 10.95 (0-89906-777-8); pap. 7.95 (0-89906-778-6) Mesorah Pubns.
Rosentheil, Agnes. Mimi Makes a Splash. Stryker, Sandra & Paine, Penelope, eds. Paine, Penelope, tr. LC 91-11286. (Illus.). 48p. (Orig.). (gr-4). 1991. pap. 6.95 (0-911655-51-4) Advocacy Pr.

—Mimi Takes Charge. Stryker, Sandra & Paine, Penelope, eds. Paine, Penelope, tr. LC 91-11285. (Illus.). 48p. (Orig.). (ps-4). 1991. pap. 6.95 (0-911655-50-6) Advocacy Pr.
Roser, Bill, et al, eds. The Tale of the Frog Prince. 1979. pap. text ed. 3.75 (0-87129-199-1, T48) Dramatic Pub.
Rosholt, Malcolm & Rosholt, Margaret. The Child of Two Mothers. Larson, Lynn, illus. LC 83-63177. 108p. (gr. 4 up). 1983. PLB 9.95x (0-910417-03-2) Rosholt Hse.
—The Story of Old Abe Wisconsin's Civil War Hero. Mullen, Don, illus. 110p. (gr. 4-12). 1987. 14.95 (0-910417-09-1) Rosholt Hse.
Rosholt, Margaret, jt. auth. see Rosholt, Malcolm.
Rosicrucian Fellowship Staff. Children, Aquarian Age Stories For.., 7 vols, Vols. 1-7. 2nd ed. (Illus.). 1989. Set. pap. text ed. 15.00 (0-911274-94-4) Rosicrucian.
—Children, Sunday School Lessons For.., 6 vols, Vol. 1-6. 1985. Set. pap. text ed. 11.25 (0-911274-63-4) Rosicrucian.
Rosicrucian Fellowship Staff, ed. see Swainson, Esme.
Rosin, Arielle. Eclairs & Brown Bears. Czap, Daniel, photos by. Collomb, Etienne. LC 93-24971. (Illus.). Date not set. write for info. (0-395-68380-7) Ticknor & Fields.
—Pizzas & Punk Potatoes. Czap, Daniel, photos by. Collomb, Etienne, contrib. by. LC 93-24970. (Illus.). Date not set. 13.95 (0-395-68381-5) Ticknor & Fields.
Rosman, Steven M. Sidrah Stories: A Torah Companion. 120p. (gr. 4-6). 1989. pap. 7.95 (0-8074-0429-2, 121723) UAHC.
Rosman, Steven S. Deena the Damselfly. Carmi, Giora, illus. LC 91-43472. (gr. k-3). 1992. 10.95 (0-8074-0477-2, 101069) UAHC.
Rosmarin, Ike. South Africa. LC 92-38755. 1993. 21.95 (1-85435-575-9) Marshall Cavendish.
Rosner, Ruth. Arabba, Gah, Zee, Marissa & Me! Fay, Ann, ed. Rosner, Ruth, illus. LC 86-15904. 32p. (ps-3). 1987. PLB 13.95 (0-8075-0442-4) A Whitman.
Rosney, C., jt. auth. see Craig, A.
Rosoff, Barbara, tr. see Cornell, Donald.
Rosoff, Iris, ed. see Anderson, Madelyn K.
Rosoff, Iris, ed. see Corwin, Judith H.
Rosoff, Iris, ed. see Greene, Jacqueline D.
Rosoff, Iris, ed. see Landau, Elaine.
Rosoff, Iris, ed. see Mango, Karin N.
Rosoff, Iris, ed. see Markosian, Becky T. & Thayne, Emma L.
Rosoff, Iris, ed. see Newman, Shirlee P.
Rosoff, Iris, ed. see Patterson, Charles.
Rosoff, Iris, ed. see Shepherd, Donna A.
Rosoff, Iris, ed. see Terkel, Susan N.
Rosoff, Iris, ed. see Weishampel, David B.
Rosofsky, Iris. Miriam. LC 87-45859. 192p. (gr. 7 up). 1988. HarpC Child Bks.
—My Aunt Ruth. LC 90-4940. 224p. (gr. 7 up). 1991. 13. 95 (0-06-025087-9) HarpC Child Bks.
Ross, Alison, illus. Daytime Baby: Baby Books. 8p. (ps). 1992. bds. 3.50 (0-7214-1515-6, S9212-4) Ladybird Bks.
—Hello Baby: Baby Books. 8p. (ps). 1992. bds. 3.50 (0-7214-1497-4, S9212-3) Ladybird Bks.
—Noisy Baby: Baby Books. 8p. (ps). 1992. bds. 3.50 (0-7214-1496-6, S9212-1) Ladybird Bks.
—Playtime Baby: Baby Books. 8p. (ps). 1992. bds. 3.50 (0-7214-1514-8, S9212-2) Ladybird Bks.
Ross, Andrea. All about Turtles. LC 89-92455. 24p. (ps-3). 1990. incl. cass. 5.95x (0-943864-59-3) Davenport.

—Chester's Coloring Book. Ross, Andrea, illus. 70p. (Orig.). (gr. k-2). 1992. 7.00 (1-56002-016-4, Univ Edtns) Aegina Pr. CHESTER'S COLORING BOOK is a reading/coloring book. One page has the story/small picture...the next page has a larger version of small picture with coloring words but no text. 70 pages/$7 each. It is the story about Chester the little black earth ant. He lived in a beautiful valley, with grass & trees & sunlight & lots of other friendly ants. But Chester was so unhappy - none of the other ants were like him, & he did not like where he was. "STORY BOOK"...a children's television show created by Andrea Ross, won a P.A.L. Award for "BEST CHILDREN'S SHOW" on Paragon Cable in New York City. "CHESTER'S story is a real one & you've told it beautifully. He's unique & there should be other stories like: CHESTER Goes to Washington, CHESTER Goes to School..."--Andy Rooney/60 Minutes, CBS-TV. "CHESTER'S COLORING BOOK looks good. Thanks for passing it along. What a great little person Chester is. The children will adore him & all of his wonderful stories. My kids were thrilled."--Faith Daniels/NBC News Dept. "What a wonderful, happy book...CHESTER'S COLORING BOOK...You are a sensitive, courageous writer."--Dan Rather/CBS News Dept. "I am pleased about your success with CHESTER'S COLORING BOOK. It is a good learning tool. There's a magical, charismatic quality about Chester!"-- Bill Cosby/The Cosby Show. *Publisher Provided Annotation.*

—Oscar Crab & Rallo Car. LC 86-72872. 64p. (Orig.). (ps-2). 1987. pap. 5.00 (0-916383-18-0) Aegina Pr.
—Seymour. LC 81-71758. 24p. (gr. 2-3). 1992. pap. 3.50x (0-943864-64-X) Davenport.
Ross, Andrea see Davenport, May.
Ross, Angus, ed. see Defoe, Daniel.
Ross, Anna. Be My Friend. Gorbaty, Norman, illus. LC 89-24389. 24p. (ps). 1991. 3.95 (0-394-85496-9) Random Bks Yng Read.
—Big Bird's Big Bike. Cooke, Tom, illus. LC 92-60305. 22p. (ps). 1993. 3.25 (0-679-83271-8) Random Bks Yng Read.
—Elmo's Big Lift-&-Look Book. Mathieu, Joe, illus. 12p. (ps-k). 1994. 8.00 (0-679-84468-6) Random Bks Yng Read.
—Elmo's Little Playhouse. Cooke, Tom, illus. LC 91-68111. 22p. (ps). 1993. 3.25 (0-679-83270-X) Random Bks Yng Read.
—Grover's Ten Terrific Ways to Help Our Wonderful World. Leigh, Tom, illus. LC 91-11095. 32p. (Orig.). (ps-3). 1992. PLB 5.99 (0-679-91384-X); pap. 2.25 (0-679-81384-5) Random Bks Yng Read.
—I Did It! Gorbaty, Norman, illus. LC 89-34543. 24p. (ps). 1990. 3.95 (0-394-86019-5) Random Bks Yng Read.
—I Have to Go. Gorbaty, Norman, illus. LC 89-34542. 24p. (ps). 1990. 3.95 (0-394-86051-9) Random Bks Yng Read.
—Little Bert's Book of Numbers. Gorbaty, Norman, illus. LC 91-4921. 24p. (ps). 1992. 3.99 (0-679-82239-9) Random Bks Yng Read.
—Little Elmo's Book of Colors. Gorbaty, Norman, illus. LC 91-23979. 24p. (ps). 1992. 3.99 (0-679-82238-0) Random Bks Yng Read.
—Little Ernie's ABC's. Gorbaty, Norman, illus. LC 91-27823. 24p. (ps). 1992. 3.99 (0-679-82240-2) Random Bks Yng Read.
—Little Grover's Book of Shapes. Gorbaty, Norman, illus. LC 91-4920. 24p. (ps). 1992. 3.99 (0-679-82237-2) Random Bks Yng Read.
—Meet the Sesame Street Babies. LC 92-60973. 7p. (ps). 1993. bds. 3.95 (0-679-83486-9) Random Bks Yng Read.
—Naptime. Gorbaty, Norman, illus. LC 89-34545. 24p. (ps). 1990. 3.95 (0-394-85828-X) Random Bks Yng Read.
—Open Sesame. Chartier, Normand, illus. LC 91-67671. 14p. (ps-k). 1992. bds. 3.99 (0-679-83063-4) Random Bks Yng Read.
—Quiet Time. Gorbaty, Norman, illus. LC 89-24354. 24p. (ps). 1991. 3.95 (0-394-85495-0) Random Bks Yng Read.
—Say Bye-Bye. Gorbaty, Norman, illus. LC 90-52915. 24p. (ps). 1992. 3.95 (0-394-85485-3) Random Bks Yng Read.
—Say Good Night. Gorbaty, Norman, illus. LC 90-52914. 24p. (ps). 1992. 3.95 (0-394-85491-8) Random Bks Yng Read.
—Say the Magic Word, Please. Gorbaty, Norman, illus. LC 89-34544. 24p. (ps). 1990. 3.95 (0-394-85857-3) Random Bks Yng Read.
—Sesame Street Busy Little Neighborhood, 4 bks. Ewers, Joe, illus. (ps). 1991. Set, 12p. ea. bds. 8.00 (0-679-80252-5) Random Bks Yng Read.
Ross, Bill, illus. Crazy Christmas Characters. (Orig.). (ps-2). 1991. pap. 2.95 (0-8249-8522-2, Ideals Child) Hambleton-Hill.
—Easter Bunnyheads. 12p. (Orig.). (ps-2). 1992. pap. 2.95 (0-8249-8541-9, Ideals Child) Hambleton-Hill.
—Easter Eggheads. 12p. (Orig.). (ps-2). 1992. pap. 2.95 (0-8249-8540-0, Ideals Child) Hambleton-Hill.
Ross, Bob. Laugh, Lead & Profit: Building Productive Workplaces with Humor. 125p. (Orig.). 1989. pap. write for info. Arrowhead Pub.
Ross, Catherine. Amazing Milk Book. 1991. pap. 6.68 (0-201-57087-4) Addison-Wesley.
—Cognitive Challenge Cards. (gr. 4-8). 1976. pap. 12.00 (0-87879-188-4) Acad Therapy.
Ross, Catherine S. Circles: Fun Ideas for Getting A-Round in Math. Slavin, Bill, illus. LC 92-40159. (gr. 4-7). 1993. pap. 9.57 (0-201-62268-8) Addison-Wesley.
Ross, Christine. Lily & the Present. Ross, Christine, illus. LC 91-41134. 28p. (ps-3). 1992. 13.95 (0-395-61127-X) HM.
—The Whirlys & the West Wind. LC 92-39011. 1993. 13. 95 (0-395-65379-7) HM.

Ross, Cynthia. D'Aulaires Book of Greek Myths. Wright, Theresa M., illus. 48p. 1993. wkbk. 5.95 (1-55734-423-X) Tchr Create Mat.
Ross, Dana F. Call of the Wendigo. 1994. pap. 3.50 (0-553-29828-3) Bantam.
Ross, Dave. A Book of Hugs. Ross, Dave, illus. LC 79-7896. 32p. (gr. k up). 1991. pap. 3.95 (0-06-107418-7) HarpC Child Bks.
—How to Prevent Monster Attacks. LC 83-26536. (Illus.). 64p. (gr. 4 up). 1984. 7.00 (0-688-03790-9) Morrow Jr Bks.
—Little Mouse's Valentine. LC 85-15357. (Illus.). 32p. (ps-k). 1986. 11.95 (0-688-06224-5); (Morrow Jr Bks) Morrow Jr Bks.
—Tiny Turtle's Thanksgiving. Ross, Dave, illus. LC 86-5412. 32p. (ps-k). 1986. 12.95 (0-688-06440-X); lib. bdg. 12.88 (0-688-06441-8, Morrow Jr Bks) Morrow Jr Bks.
Ross, Dennis W. Blood. LC 87-70225. (Illus.). 16p. (Orig.). (gr. 10 up). 1988. pap. text ed. 2.75 (0-89278-184-X, 45-9784) Carolina Biological.
Ross, Edward S. Ants. LC 92-44257. (gr. 2 up). 1993. write for info. (1-56766-056-8) Childs World.
—Yellowjackets. LC 92-42934. 1993. write for info. (1-56766-017-7) Childs World.
Ross, Eileen. Lucinda the Late. Chapman, Wendy, illus. LC 92-14092. 32p. (ps-2). Date not set. 11.95 (1-56065-164-4) Capstone Pr. Postponed.
Ross, Elena & Champlin, Allen R., Sr. Ghost Riders in the Sky. Hartstrom, Noelle, ed. (Orig.). (gr. 12). Date not set. pap. write for info. (0-9628802-1-3) DeChamp CA.
Ross, Frank. Oracles Bones, Stars & the Wheelbarrows: Ancient Chinese Science & Technology. 1990. pap. 4.80 (0-395-54967-1) HM.
Ross, Frank, Jr. The Metric System: Measures for All Mankind. Galster, Robert, illus. LC 74-14503. 128p. (gr. 7-10). 1974. 27.95 (0-87599-198-X) S G Phillips.
Ross, Gayle. How Rabbit Tricked Otter & Other Cherokee Trickster Stories. Jacob, Murv, illus. LC 93-3637. 1994. 15.00 (0-06-021285-3, HarpT); PLB 14.89 (0-06-021286-1) HarpC.
Ross, Gwendolyn. A Child's Treasure for a Lifetime. 24p. (gr. 2-6). 1988. pap. 2.95 (0-88144-134-1) Christian Pub.
Ross, H. K. Black American Women, No. 3. (Illus.). 160p. (gr. 6-12). 1990. PLB 14.95 (0-87460-365-X) Lion Bks.
Ross, H. K., ed. Great Story Poems: Collection. 160p. (gr. 5-12). 1993. pap. 8.95 (0-87460-385-4) Lion Bks.
Ross, Harriet, ed. Great Horror Stories. Bolle, Frank, illus. 160p. (gr. 3-9). 1992. pap. 11.95 (0-87460-188-6) Lion Bks.
Ross, Harriet, compiled by. Great Mystery Stories. Bolle, Frank, illus. 160p. (gr. 3-9). 1993. pap. 8.95 (0-87460-194-0) Lion Bks.
—Great Stories about Horses. Bolle, Frank, illus. LC 63-18759. 160p. (gr. 3-9). 1992. PLB 10.95 (0-87460-202-5) Lion Bks.
Ross, Harriet, ed. Greek Myths: Tales of the Gods, Heroes & Heroines. 160p. (gr. 6-12). 1993. PLB 14.95 (0-87460-383-8) Lion Bks.
Ross, Harriet, compiled by. Heroes & Heroines of Many Lands. 160p. (gr. 3-9). 1992. Repr. of 1990 ed. PLB 14.95 (0-87460-214-9) Lion Bks.
Ross, Jane B. The George Medallion. 125p. (gr. 4-7). 1986. 9.95 (0-917949-07-2) Vimach Assocs.
Ross, Jean. The Martlet Box. 160p. (gr. 5-8). 1990. pap. 6.95 (0-86241-280-3, Pub. by Cnngt Pub Ltd) Trafalgar.
Ross, Josephine. Alexander Fleming. (Illus.). 64p. (gr. 5-9). 1991. 11.95 (0-237-60013-7, Pub. by Evans Bros Ltd) Trafalgar.
—Princess of Wales. (Illus.). 64p. (gr. 5-9). 1991. 11.95 (0-237-60023-4, Pub. by Evans Bros Ltd) Trafalgar.
Ross, K. K. Bert's Little Bedtime Story: A Sesame Street Book. Wenzel, Rick, illus. LC 89-64283. 28p. (ps). 1991. bds. 2.95 (0-679-80757-8) Random Bks Yng Read.
—Cozy in the Woods. Dyer, Jane, illus. LC 88-63931. 28p. (ps). 1990. 2.95 (0-394-85400-4) Random Bks Yng Read.
—The Little Red Car. Alley, R. W., illus. LC 88-63930. 28p. (ps). 1990. 2.95 (0-394-85376-8) Random Bks Yng Read.
Ross, Katharine. Fuzzy Kitten. McCue, Lisa, illus. LC 92-62262. 22p. (ps-3). 1993. 3.50 (0-679-84644-1) Random Bks Yng Read.
—Fuzzy Teddy. McCue, Lisa, illus. LC 92-62263. 22p. (ps). 1993. 3.50 (0-679-84643-3) Random Bks Yng Read.
—The Glow-in-the-Dark Zodiac Storybook. Marchesi, Stephen, illus. LC 92-61555. 24p. (gr. 3-7). 1993. 14. 00 (0-679-82470-7) Random Bks Yng Read.
—Grover, Grover, Come on Over: A Step 1 Book - Preschool-Grade 1. Cooke, Tom, illus. LC 90-33947. 32p. (Orig.). (ps-1). 1991. PLB 7.99 (0-679-91117-0); pap. 2.95 (0-679-81117-6) Random Bks Yng Read.
—The Little Ballerina. LC 92-42093. 1994. write for info. (0-679-84915-7) Random Bks Yng Read.
—The Little Noisy Book. Hirashima, Jean, illus. LC 88-62100. 28p. (ps). 1989. bds. 2.95 (0-394-82907-7) Random Bks Yng Read.
—The Little Pumpkin Book. Bratun, Katy, illus. LC 91-67669. 22p. (ps). 1992. bds. 2.95 (0-679-83384-6) Random Bks Yng Read.

—The Little Quiet Book. Hirashima, Jean, illus. LC 88-62101. 28p. (ps). 1989. bds. 2.95 (*0-394-82899-2*) Random Bks Yng Read.

—Open the Door, Little Dinosaur. Gorbaty, Norman, illus. LC 92-80950. 14p. (ps-k). 1993. bds. 3.99 (*0-679-83689-6*) Random Bks Yng Read.

—Rabbits' Carnival. Bratun, Katy, illus. LC 92-29930. 1994. write for info. (*0-679-93503-2*); lib. bdg. write for info. (*0-679-93503-7*) Random Bks Yng Read.

—Rainbow Babies. Petach, Heidi, illus. LC 91-66659. 28p. (ps). 1992. 2.95 (*0-679-83068-5*) Random Bks Yng Read.

—Teeny Tiny Farm. Flynn, Amy, illus. LC 91-50647. 22p. (ps). 1992. 2.95 (*0-679-83388-9*) Random Bks Yng Read.

—Twinkle, Twinkle, Little Bug: A Sesame Street Book. Cooke, Tom, illus. LC 90-61760. 24p. (Orig.). (ps-2). 1991. pap. 2.25 (*0-679-81372-1*) Random Bks Yng Read.

Ross, Katharine. The Fuzzytail Friends' Great Egg Hunt. McCue, Lisa, illus. LC 87-50812. 14p. (ps). 1988. bds. 2.95 (*0-394-89475-8*) Random Bks Yng Read.

Ross, Lillian. Getting Around in Jewish Miami. (Illus., Orig.). 1988. pap. 8.95 (*0-930029-03-8*) Central Agency.

Ross, Lillian H. Buba Leah & Her Paper Children. Morgan, Mary, illus. 32p. (gr. k-3). 1991. 16.95 (*0-8276-0375-4*) JPS Phila.

—Sarah, Also Known As Hannah. Cogancherry, Helen, illus. LC 93-29601. 1994. write for info. (*0-8075-7237-3*) A Whitman.

Ross, Michael E. Become a Bird & Fly! Parnall, Peter, illus. LC 91-36562. 32p. (gr. k up). 1992. PLB 14.90 (*1-56294-074-0*) Millbrook Pr.

—Cycles, Cycles, Cycles. (Illus.). 88p. (gr. 1-3). 1979. pap. 3.95 (*0-939666-01-4*) Yosemite Assn.

—What Makes Everything Go? 94p. (gr. k-2). 1979. pap. 3.95 (*0-939666-19-7*) Yosemite Assn.

—The World of Small: Nature Explorations with a Hand Lens. Medley, Steven P., ed. Trout, Cary M., illus. 64p. (gr. k-6). 1993. wire-o bdg., incl. magnification lens 15.95t (*0-939666-62-6*) Yosemite Assn.

—Yosemite Fun Book. 48p. (gr. 3-8). 1987. pap. 2.95 (*0-939666-45-6*) Yosemite Assn.

Ross, Monica L. Montana Molly & the Peppermint Kid: (Musical) 1989. Playscript. 4.50 (*0-87602-285-9*) Anchorage.

—Wilma's Revenge. 1989. Playscript. 4.50 (*0-87602-288-5*) Anchorage.

Ross, Pat. Hannah's Fancy Notions: A Story of Industrial New England. Dodson, Bert, illus. LC 92-20286. 64p. (gr. 2-6). 1992. pap. 3.99 (*0-14-032389-9*) Puffin Bks.

—M & M & the Bad News Babies. Hafner, Marylin, illus. 48p. (ps-3). 1985. pap. 3.95 (*0-14-031851-8*, Puffin) Puffin Bks.

—M & M & the Big Bag. 48p. (ps-3). 1985. pap. 3.99 (*0-14-031852-6*, Puffin) Puffin Bks.

—M & M & the Big Bag I Am Reading Book. Hafner, Marilyn, illus. LC 80-23299. 48p. (gr. 1-4). 1981. 6.95 (*0-394-84340-1*) Pantheon.

—M & M & the Halloween Monster. Hafner, Marylin, illus. LC 91-50294. 48p. (gr. 1-2). 1991. text ed. 10.95 (*0-670-83003-8*) Viking Child Bks.

—M & M & the Halloween Monster. Hafner, Marylin, illus. LC 93-15183. 64p. (gr. 2-5). 1993. pap. 3.99 (*0-14-034247-8*, Puffin) Puffin Bks.

—M & M & the Haunted House Game. Hafner, Marilyn, illus. 48p. (gr. 1-3). 1981. pap. 1.25 (*0-440-45544-8*, YB) Dell.

—M & M & the Haunted House Game. (gr. 4 up). 1990. pap. 4.50 (*0-14-034577-9*, Puffin) Puffin Bks.

—M & M & the Mummy Mess. Hafner, Marylin, illus. 48p. (gr. 1-4). 1986. pap. 3.95 (*0-14-032084-9*, Puffin) Puffin Bks.

—M & M & the Santa Secrets. Hafner, Marylin, illus. (gr. 1-4). pap. 2.95 (*0-317-62234-X*, Puffin) Puffin Bks.

—M & M & the Santa Secrets. (Illus.). 1987. pap. 3.99 (*0-14-032222-1*, Puffin) Puffin Bks.

—M & M & the Super Child Afternoon. Hafner, Marylin, illus. 48p. (gr. 1-4). 1989. pap. 3.95 (*0-14-032145-4*, Puffin) Puffin Bks.

—M & M & the Super Child Afternoon. 21p. (gr. 2-4). 1987. pap. 1.68 (*0-685-63783-2*, BR7953) W A T Braille.

—M & M & the Super Child Afternoon. 21p. 1992. Braille. 1.68 (*1-56956-277-6*) W A T Braille.

—M & M & the Superchild Afternoon. Hafner, Marylin, illus. LC 86-28128. (gr. 1-4). 1987. pap. 9.95 (*0-670-81208-0*) Viking Child Bks.

—Meet M & M. Hafner, Marylin, illus. 48p. (gr. 1-4). 1988. pap. 3.95 (*0-14-032651-0*, Puffin) Puffin Bks.

Ross, Ramon R. Harper & Moon. LC 92-17216. (Illus.). 192p. (gr. 4 up). 1993. SBE 14.95 (*0-689-31803-0*, Atheneum Child Bk) Macmillan Child Grp.

Ross, Rhea B. Bet's on, Lizzie Bingman! 1992. pap. 3.95 (*0-395-64375-9*) HM.

Ross, Sandra. The Nicelies at Home. (Illus.). 72p. (Orig.). (ps-3). 1992. pap. 4.95 (*1-881235-01-7*) Creat Opport.

Ross, Sandra J. Visiting the Nicelies. 58p. (Orig.). (ps-3). 1991. pap. 4.95 (*1-881235-00-9*) Creat Opport.

Ross, Shirley. ABCs Beginning Sounds. (ps). pap. 2.95 (*0-8431-2506-3*) Price Stern.

Ross, Shirley, jt. auth. see McCord, Cindy.

Ross, Stacey, jt. auth. see Argueta, Manlio.

Ross, Stewart. China since Nineteen Forty-Five. LC 87-3500. (Illus.). 64p. (gr. 7-12). 1989. PLB 13.40 (*0-531-18220-7*, Pub. by Bookwright Pr) Watts.

—Elizabethan Life. (Illus.). 72p. (gr. 7-11). 1991. 19.95 (*0-7134-6356-2*, Pub. by Batsford UK) Trafalgar.

—The Nineteen Eighties. (Illus.). 72p. (gr. 7-11). 1991. 19.95 (*0-7134-6361-9*, Pub. by Batsford UK) Trafalgar.

—Propaganda. LC 93-21730. 48p. (gr. 5-9). 1993. 14.95 (*1-56847-080-0*) Thomson Lrning.

—The Russian Revolution, Nineteen Fourteen to Nineteen Twenty-Four. (Illus.). 64p. (gr. 7-12). 1989. PLB 13.40 (*0-531-18221-5*, Pub. by Bookwright Pr) Watts.

—United Nations. 1990. PLB 13.40 (*0-531-18295-9*, Pub. by Bookwright Pr) Watts.

—The U. S. S. R. under Stalin. LC 90-24373. (Illus.). 64p. (gr. 9-12). 1991. 13.40 (*0-531-18409-9*, Pub. by Bookwright Pr) Watts.

—World Leaders. LC 93-20185. 48p. (gr. 5-9). 1993. 14.95 (*1-56847-079-7*) Thomson Lrning.

Ross, Suzanne. What's in the Rainforest? One Hundred Six Answers from A to Z. Ross, Suzanne, illus. LC 91-72682. 48p. (Orig.). (gr. 1-7). 1991. pap. 5.95 (*0-9629895-0-9*) Enchanted Rain Pr. In this book you will find 106 interesting & sometimes startling examples of the many creatures that dwell in the world's tropical rainforests. "A well known organized dictionary of the rainforest & its inhabitants. An extensive introduction provides some background information, followed by brief descriptions of a select list of plants & animals. A map outlining the world's rainforests is provided. The climate is discussed, as are the three layers that make up its unique structure...drawings of some of the plants & animals break up the text."-- School Library Journal. "For those working to raise rainforest awareness, a new tool for reaching 7 to 12 year-olds...106 examples of flora & fauna from the world's rainforests...familiar terms like gorilla & orchid are accompanied by unusual words such as. ..rafflesia (a three-foot-wide leafless parasite plant), & agouti (a rodent that can jump about 6 1/2 feet, straight up) - that may add to parents' knowledge of the rainforest as well."--World Monitor Magazine. "A book that teaches the importance of the rainforest in a fun & creative way."--Rainforest Action Network. $5.95 plus postage. Enchanted Rainforest Press, Box 29885, L.A., CA 90029. (213) 663-3405. FAX (818) 766-2905.
Publisher Provided Annotation.

Ross, Terry. Cults. (Illus.). 64p. (gr. 7 up). 1990. lib. bdg. 17.27 (*0-86593-070-8*); lib. bdg. 12.95s.p. (*0-685-36323-6*) Rourke Corp.

Ross, Tom, et al. Itzwibble & the Big Birthday Party. 32p. (Orig.). (ps-3). 1990. pap. 2.50 (*0-590-43861-1*) Scholastic Inc.

Ross, Tony. Don't Do That! Ross, Tony, illus. LC 91-9347. 32p. (ps-2). 1991. 12.00 (*0-517-58575-8*) Crown Bks Yng Read.

—A Fairy Tale. Ross, Tony, illus. 32p. (ps-3). 1992. cancelled 13.95 (*0-316-75750-0*) Little.

—Hansel & Gretel. (Illus.). 32p. (gr. k-3). 1990. 15.95 (*0-86264-210-8*, Pub. by Anderson Pr UK) Trafalgar.

—Happy Blanket. (Illus.). 32p. (ps-2). 1990. 12.95 (*0-374-32843-9*) FS&G.

—I Want a Cat. (Illus.). 26p. (ps up). 1989. 13.00 (*0-374-33621-0*) FS&G.

—I Want a Cat. (Illus.). 26p. (ps up). 1991. pap. 4.95 (*0-374-43544-8*) FS&G.

—I Want My Potty. LC 86-10568. (Illus.). 24p. (ps-k). 1986. 9.95 (*0-916291-08-1*, Cranky Nell Bk) Kane-Miller Bk.

—I Want My Potty. (Illus.). 24p. (ps-k). 1988. pap. 6.95 (*0-916291-14-6*) Kane-Miller Bk.

—I Want to Be. LC 92-41527. (Illus.). 32p. (ps-1). 1993. 11.95 (*0-916291-46-4*) Kane-Miller Bk.

—I'm Coming to Get You! LC 84-5831. (Illus.). 32p. (ps-2). 1987. pap. 4.95 (*0-8037-0434-8*) Dial Bks Young.

—Mrs. Goat & Her Seven Little Kids. Ross, Tony, illus. LC 89-17933. 32p. (gr. 1-3). 1990. 14.95 (*0-689-31624-0*, Atheneum Child Bk) Macmillan Child Grp.

—Stone Soup. (ps-3). 1990. pap. 3.95 (*0-8037-0890-4*, Dial Pied Piper) Puffin Bks.

—This Old Man. 12p. (ps-1). 1990. bds. 10.95 POB (*0-689-71386-X*, Aladdin) Macmillan Child Grp.

—Towser & the Haunted House. Ross, Tony, illus. 32p. (ps-1). 1987. 5.95 (*0-86264-079-2*, Pub. by Anderson Pr UK) Trafalgar.

—Towser & the Magic Apple. Ross, Tony, illus. 32p. (ps-1). 1987. 5.95 (*0-86264-078-4*, Pub. by Anderson Pr UK) Trafalgar.

—Treasure of Cozy Cove. (ps-3). 1990. 14.00 (*0-374-37744-8*) FS&G.

Ross, Tony, jt. auth. see Oram, Hiawyn.

Ross, Tony, jt. auth. see Thomson, Pat.

Ross, Tony, retold by. & illus. Goldilocks & the Three Bears. 26p. (ps-3). 1992. 13.95 (*0-87951-453-1*) Overlook Pr.

Ross, William M. The Ticket to Harmony. 94p. (Orig.). (gr. 4-9). 1993. pap. 4.95 (*1-883787-00-9*, Dist. by Baker & Taylor Bks.); incl. tchr's activities packet 7.95 (*1-883787-01-7*) Trolley Car.

Ross, Wilma. X-15 Rocket Plane. LC 93-1844. (Illus.). 48p. (gr. 5-6). 1994. RSBE 13.95 (*0-89686-831-1*, Crestwood Hse) Macmillan Child Grp.

Rossbach, Jean. Bernie, the Beagle Who Liked German Cooking. Bobak, Cathy, illus. LC 90-21782. 64p. (gr. 1-7). 1991. SBE 13.95 (*0-02-777787-1*, Bradbury Pr) Macmillan Child Grp.

Rossel, Karen T. & Mason, Patrice G. Hebrew Through Prayer, Vol. 1. 65p. (gr. 4-7). 1980. pap. text ed. 3.45x (*0-87441-313-3*); wkbk. 3.25 (*0-87441-284-6*); tchr's ed. 14.95 (*0-685-18651-2*) Behrman.

—Hebrew Through Prayer, Vol. 2. 65p. (gr. 4-7). 1980. pap. text ed. 3.45x (*0-87441-314-1*); wkbk. 3.25 (*0-87441-285-4*); tchr's ed. 14.95 (*0-317-60048-6*) Behrman.

Rossel, Seymour. Child's Bible: Lessons from the Writings & Prophets, Vol. 2. (gr. 3-5). 1989. pap. text ed. 8.50 (*0-318-42729-X*); tchr's. guide 14.95 (*0-87441-485-7*) Behrman.

—A Child's Bible: The Torah & Its Lessons. (gr. 1 up). 1988. text & activity bk., 160pps. 8.50 (*0-87441-466-0*); tchr's guide, 96pps. 14.95 (*0-87441-467-9*) Behrman.

—The Holocaust: The World & the Jews, 1933-1945. Altshuler, David, ed. 192p. (gr. 9-12). 1992. pap. text ed. write for info. (*0-87441-526-8*) Behrman.

—Introduction to Jewish History. Kozodoy, Neil, ed. Kahn, Katherine, illus. 128p. (gr. 4-5). 1981. pap. text ed. 6.95 (*0-87441-335-4*); By Lenore C. Kipper. tchr's guide 12.50x (*0-87441-378-8*); Malkah L. Avrami. student's activity bk. 4.25 (*0-87441-363-X*) Behrman.

—When a Jew Seeks Wisdom: The Sayings of the Fathers. LC 75-14119. (gr. 7). pap. 7.95 (*0-87441-089-4*); student's encounter bk. 3.95 (*0-685-00741-3*); tchr's guide 14.95 (*0-685-41999-1*) Behrman.

Rossel, Seymour, ed. see Kozodoy, Ruth.

Rossel, Seymour, ed. see Newman, Shirley.

Rossel, Seymour, ed. see Rosenberg, Amye & Mason, Patrice G.

Rossel, Seymour, ed. see Rosenthal, Gilbert S.

Rossell, Seymour. The Holocaust: The Fire That Raged. (Illus.). 128p. (gr. 10-12). 1990. 13.40 (*0-531-10674-8*) Watts.

Rosselson, Leon. Where's My Mom? Lamont, Priscilla, illus. LC 93-32383. 1994. write for info. (*1-56402-392-3*) Candlewick Pr.

Rosser, J. K. Teenage Mutant Ninja Turtles ABC's for a Better Planet. GEE Studio Staff, illus. LC 90-53247. 32p. (Orig.). (ps-3). 1991. PLB 5.99 (*0-679-91383-1*) Random Bks Yng Read.

Rosset, Lisa. James Baldwin. King, Coretta Scott, intro. by. (Illus.). 112p. (gr. 5 up). 1989. 17.95 (*1-55546-572-2*); pap. 9.95 (*0-7910-0230-6*) Chelsea Hse.

Rossetti, Christina. Color. Teichman, Mary, illus. LC 90-25588. 40p. (ps-1). 1992. 15.00 (*0-06-022626-9*); PLB 14.89 (*0-06-022650-1*) HarpC Child Bks.

—Fly Away, Fly Away over the Sea. Watts, Bernadette, illus. LC 90-42738. 32p. (ps-k). 1991. 14.95 (*1-55858-101-4*) North-South Bks NYC.

—Goblin Market. (Illus.). 48p. (gr. 4-7). 1989. pap. 9.95 (*0-575-04389-X*, Pub. by Gollancz England) Trafalgar.

—The Skylark. LC 91-13112. (Illus.). 24p. 1992. 4.95 (*0-8037-1143-3*) Dial Bks Young.

Rossetti, Christina G. Sing Song: A Nursery Rhyme Book. Hughes, Arthur, illus. LC 68-55822. x, 130p. (gr. 3-7). 1969. pap. 4.50 (*0-486-22107-5*) Dover.

Rossie, John P., pref. by. Handbook Two for Aerospace Education: A Guide to Projects & Applications. Walker, Charles, intro. by. LC 91-60903. (Illus.). 398p. (Orig.). 1991. pap. text ed. 19.50 (*0-911168-80-X*) Prakken.

Rossiter, Jane, jt. auth. see Mellett, Peter.

Rossiter, Phyllis. Moxie. LC 90-30027. 192p. (gr. 5 up). 1990. 14.95 (*0-02-777831-2*, Four Winds) Macmillan Child Grp.

Rossner, Richard. The Whole Story: Short Stories for Pleasure & Language Improvement. (gr. 9-12). 1988. pap. text ed. 14.95 (*0-582-79109-X*, 78326); cass. 22.95 (*0-582-01887-0*, 78325) Longman.

Rost, M. Strategies in Listening: Tasks for Listening Development. 80p. 1986. pap. text ed. 13.50 (*0-8013-0520-9*, 78366); tapescript & ans. key 9.95 (*0-8013-0521-7*, 78367); 3 cassettes 55.00 (*0-8013-0522-5*, 78368) Longman.

Rost, M. & Uruno, M. Basics in Listening: Short Tasks for Listening Development. 71p. 1985. pap. text ed. 13.50 (*0-8013-0517-9*, 78363); tapescript & ans. key 9.95 (*0-8013-0518-7*, 78364); 3 cassettes 55.00 (*0-8013-0519-5*, 78365) Longman.
Rostkowski, Margaret I. After the Dancing Days. LC 85-45810. 240p. (gr. 6-9). 1986. PLB 14.89 (*0-06-025078-X*) HarpC Child Bks.
—After the Dancing Days. LC 85-45810. 224p. (gr. 5-9). 1988. pap. 3.95 (*0-06-440248-7*, Trophy) HarpC Child Bks.
Rosy. Basil. (ps-3). 1993. 13.95 (*0-307-17502-2*, Artsts Writrs) Western Pub.
Rotenberg, Abie. The Place Where I Belong. Stern, Fruma, illus. (ps-1). 1988. 9.95 (*0-935063-43-9*) CIS Comm.
Roth, Alfred C. Small Gas Engines. rev. ed. (Illus.). 352p. (gr. 11-12). 1992. text ed. 26.60 (*0-87006-919-5*); text ed. 19.95s.p. (*0-685-49300-8*); wkbk. 7.96 (*0-87006-920-9*); 5.97s.p. (*0-685-49301-6*); instr's. guide 4.00 (*0-87006-921-7*); instr's. guide 3.00s.p. (*0-685-59021-6*) Goodheart.
Roth, Arlen. Arlen Roth's Heavy Metal Guitar. 186p. 1990. pap. 16.95 (*0-02-870010-4*) Schirmer Bks.
Roth, Arthur. Iceberg Hermit. 1989. pap. 2.95 (*0-590-44112-4*) Scholastic Inc.
Roth, Carol. Quiet As a Mouse. Schories, Pat, illus. 32p. (ps-3). 1991. 6.95 (*1-56288-121-3*) Checkerboard.
Roth, Charles E. The Amateur Naturalist: Explorations & Investigations. LC 93-13390. (Illus.). 144p. (gr. 6-9). 1993. PLB 12.90 (*0-531-11002-8*) Watts.
Roth, David & Maifair, Linda L. Colin Powell. 112p. (gr. 3-7). 1993. pap. 4.99 (*0-310-39851-7*, Pub. by Youth Spec) Zondervan.
Roth, Harold. A Day at the Races. LC 83-2345. (Illus.). 64p. (gr. 3-6). 1983. 10.95 (*0-394-85814-X*, Pant Bks Young) Pantheon.
Roth, Julee. Get Ready Get Set Go! An Advanced Sailing Manual. (Illus.). 208p. (Orig.). (gr. 7-12). 1993. pap. text ed. 15.95 (*0-9637423-0-2*) JRC Pubns.
Roth, Kevin. Lullabies for Little Dreamers. De Groat, Diane, illus. 24p. (ps-1). 1992. incl. cassette 9.95 (*0-679-82382-4*) Random Bks Yng Read.
—Songs for a Merry Christmas. Bollinger, Kristine, illus. 24p. (Orig.). (ps-1). 1992. pap. 9.95 incl. cass. (*0-679-83253-X*) Random Bks Yng Read.
Roth, Kevin, read by. Dinosaurs & Dragons. Byrd, Robert, illus. 24p. (ps-1). 1991. pap. 9.95 incls. cassette (*0-679-81744-1*) Random Bks Yng Read.
—Unbearable Bears. Hearn, Diane D., illus. 24p. (Orig.). (ps-1). 1991. pap. 9.95 incls. cassette (*0-679-81742-5*) Random Bks Yng Read.
Roth, Pamela K., jt. ed. see Nicol, Mary M.
Roth, Philip. The Conversion of the Jews. (gr. 5 up). 1992. PLB 13.95 (*0-88682-506-7*) Creative Ed.
Roth Publishing Editorial Board. Core Poetry Collection Index. 1127p. (Orig.). (gr. 9). 1993. pap. text ed. 75.00x (*0-89609-325-5*) Roth Pub Inc.
Roth, Roger. The Sign Painter's Dream. Roth, Roger, illus. LC 92-13041. 40p. (ps-3). 1993. 14.00 (*0-517-58920-6*); PLB 14.99 (*0-517-58921-4*) Crown Bks Yng Read.
Roth, Susan. Ishi's Tale of Lizard. (gr. 4-7). 1992. 14.00 (*0-374-33643-1*) FS&G.
—Princess. Roth, Susan, illus. LC 92-55042. 32p. (ps-3). 1993. 13.95 (*1-56282-465-1*); PLB 13.89 (*1-56282-466-X*) Hyprn Child.
Roth, Susan L. Another Christmas. Roth, Susan L., illus. LC 91-33148. 32p. (gr. k). 1992. 15.00 (*0-688-09942-4*); PLB 14.93 (*0-688-09943-2*) Morrow Jr Bks.
—Buddha. LC 93-8240. 1994. 15.95 (*0-385-31072-2*) Doubleday.
—Fire Came to the Earth People. (Illus.). 32p. (gr. 1 up). 1988. 9.95 (*0-312-01723-5*) St Martin.
—Gypsy Bird Song. (Illus.). 32p. (gr. 1 up). 1991. 14.95 (*0-374-32825-0*) FS&G.
—The Story of Light. LC 90-5654. (Illus.). 32p. (ps up). 1990. 12.95 (*0-688-08676-4*); PLB 12.88 (*0-688-08677-2*, Morrow Jr Bks) Morrow Jr Bks.
—We'll Ride Elephants Through Brooklyn. (ps up). 1989. 13.95 (*0-374-38258-1*) FS&G.
Rothaus, James R. Barry Sanders. 32p. 1991. 21.35 (*0-89565-737-6*); 14.95s.p. (*0-685-55134-2*) Childs World.
—Bo Jackson. 32p. 1991. 21.35 (*0-89565-731-7*); 14.95s.p. (*0-685-55138-5*) Childs World.
—David Robinson. 32p. 1991. 21.35 (*0-89565-784-8*); 14.95s.p. (*0-685-55140-7*) Childs World.
—Jennifer Capriati. 32p. 1991. 21.35 (*0-89565-738-4*); 14.95s.p. (*0-685-55139-3*) Childs World.
—Joe Montana. 32p. 1991. 21.35 (*0-89565-736-8*); 14.95s.p. (*0-685-55135-0*) Childs World.
—Jose Canseco. 32p. 1991. 21.35 (*0-89565-735-X*); 14.95s.p. (*0-685-55141-5*) Childs World.
—Ken Griffey, Jr. 32p. 1991. 21.35 (*0-89565-783-X*); 14.95s.p. (*0-685-55137-7*) Childs World.
—Magic Johnson. 32p. 1991. 21.35 (*0-89565-732-5*); 14.95s.p. (*0-685-55136-9*) Childs World.
—Michael Jordan. 32p. 1991. 21.35 (*0-89565-733-3*); 14.95s.p. (*0-685-55133-4*) Childs World.
—Steffi Graf. (Illus.). 32p. 1991. 21.35 (*0-89565-734-1*); 14.95s.p. (*0-685-57233-1*) Childs World.
Rothaus, Jim. Alligators & Crocodiles. 24p. (gr. 3). 1988. PLB 14.95s.p. (*0-88682-220-3*) Creative Ed.
—Animal Jokes. Woodworth, Viki, illus. (gr. 1-8). 1992. PLB 13.95 (*0-89565-861-5*); Resale. 19.95 (*0-685-60962-6*) Childs World.

—Babe Ruth. (gr. 1-8). 1992. PLB 14.95 (*0-89565-962-X*); Resale. 21.35 (*0-685-60966-9*) Childs World.
—Bears. 24p. (gr. 3). 1991. PLB 14.95s.p. (*0-88682-221-1*) Creative Ed.
—Bug Riddles. Woodworth, Viki, illus. (gr. 1-8). 1992. PLB 13.95 (*0-89565-864-X*); Resale. 19.95 (*0-685-60959-6*) Childs World.
—Cal Ripken. (gr. 1-8). 1992. PLB 14.95 (*0-89565-867-4*); Resale. 21.35 (*0-685-60965-0*) Childs World.
—Dinosaurs. 24p. (gr. 3). 1988. PLB 14.95s.p. (*0-88682-223-8*) Creative Ed.
—Ducks, Geese, & Swans. 24p. (gr. 3). 1988. PLB 14.95s.p. (*0-88682-224-6*) Creative Ed.
—Eagles. 24p. (gr. 3). 1988. PLB 14.95s.p. (*0-88682-225-4*) Creative Ed.
—Elephants. 24p. (gr. 3). 1988. PLB 14.95s.p. (*0-88682-226-2*) Creative Ed.
—Fairy Tale Jokes. Woodworth, Viki, illus. (gr. 1-8). 1992. PLB 13.95 (*0-89565-862-3*); Resale. 19.95 (*0-685-60961-8*) Childs World.
—Giant Pandas. 24p. (gr. 3). 1988. PLB 14.95s.p. (*0-88682-228-9*) Creative Ed.
—Karl Malone. (gr. 1-8). 1992. PLB 14.95 (*0-89565-961-1*); Resale. 21.35 (*0-685-60963-4*) Childs World.
—Kirby Puckett. (gr. 1-8). 1992. PLB 14.95 (*0-89565-960-3*); Resale. 21.35 (*0-685-60964-2*) Childs World.
—Koalas. 24p. (gr. 3). 1988. PLB 14.95s.p. (*0-88682-227-0*) Creative Ed.
—Monster Riddles. Woodworth, Viki, illus. (gr. 1-8). 1992. PLB 13.95 (*0-89565-863-1*); Resale. 19.95 (*0-685-60960-X*) Childs World.
—Sharks. 24p. (gr. 3). 1988. PLB 14.95s.p. (*0-88682-229-7*) Creative Ed.
Rothberg, Abraham, jt. auth. see Simon, Solomon.
Roth-Hano, Renee. Safe Harbors. 192p. (gr. 12 up). 1993. pap. 14.95 RSBE (*0-02-777795-2*, Four Winds) Macmillan Child Grp.
—Touch Wood: A Girlhood in Occupied France. LC 87-34326. 304p. (gr. 5-9). 1988. SBE 15.95 (*0-02-777340-X*, Four Winds) Macmillan Child Grp.
—Touch Wood: A Girlhood Occupied In France. 304p. (gr. 5 up). 1989. pap. 4.99 (*0-14-034085-8*, Puffin) Puffin Bks.
Rothlein, Liz & Wild, Terri C. Read it Again! Multicultural Books for the Primary Grades, Bk. 1. (Illus.). 144p. (Orig.). 1993. pap. 9.95 (*0-673-36064-4*) GdYrBks.
Rothlein, Liz, jt. auth. see Miller, Libby.
Rothman, Cynthia. Bread Around the World. 16p. (ps-2). 1994. pap. 14.95 (*1-56784-301-8*) Newbridge Comms.
—Think about the Weather. 16p. (ps-2). 1994. pap. 14.95 (*1-56784-300-X*) Newbridge Comms.
—Under the Sea. 16p. (ps-2). 1994. pap. 14.95 (*1-56784-302-6*) Newbridge Comms.
Rothman, Joel. The Antcyclopedia. Freshman, Shelley, illus. 4.95 (*0-685-86236-4*) Pubns Devl Co TX.
—A Moment in Time. Leake, Don, illus. LC 72-90693. 32p. (ps-2). 1973. 7.95 (*0-87592-034-9*) Scroll Pr.
—Once There Was a Stream. Roberts, Bruce, photos by. LC 72-90692. (Illus.). 32p. (gr. k-4). 1973. 8.95 (*0-87592-038-1*) Scroll Pr.
Rothman, Tony. Long Ago Is Far Away: Figuring Out How the Universe Began. LC 92-29745. 1993. write for info. (*0-7167-9000-9*) W H Freeman.
Roth-Nelson, Stephanie. S. E. E. K. (Self-Esteem Enhancement Kit) The Self-Esteem Enhancement Kit for Teen-Aged Girls. 158p. (Orig.). (gr. 7-12). 1993. pap. 14.95 (*0-942097-49-1*) Busn Plans Plus.
Rothstein, Chaya L. Mentchkins Make Friends. (gr. 4-8). 1988. pap. 4.95 (*0-87306-453-4*) Feldheim.
—The Mentchkins Make Shabbos. Perlstein, Rivky, illus. (ps-2). 1986. pap. 2.95 (*0-317-42728-8*) Feldheim.
Rothstein, Erica L. & Renineke, eds. Dell Book of Logic Problems, No. 3. (Orig.). 1988. pap. 10.95 (*0-440-50068-0*, Dell Trade Pbks) Dell.
Rothstein, Evelyn. Easy Writer Student Worksheets, 6 levels. Gess, Diane, ed. Schwartzfarb, Marilyn, illus. (Each level 35p.). (gr. 1-8). 1988. 14.95 ea. Level A Gr. 1-2 (*0-9606172-5-6*) Level B Gr. 2-3 (*0-9606172-1-3*) Level C Gr. 3-5 (*0-9606172-2-1*) Level D Gr. 4-6 (*0-9606172-3-X*) Level E Gr. 5-7 (*0-9606172-4-8*) Level F Gr. 6-8 (*0-9606172-6-4*) ERA-CCR.
Rothstein, Evelyn & Gess, Diane. EarlyWriter. Gompper, Gail, illus. 80p. (gr. k-1). 1989. pap. text ed. 7.95 (*0-913935-44-1*) ERA-CCR.
Rothstein, Evelyn, et al. Editing Writes, Blue Edition. Gompper, Gail, illus. (gr. 3-4). 1990. pap. 7.95 25 or more copies (*0-913935-46-8*) ERA-CCR.
—Editing Writes, Green Edition. Gompper, Gail, illus. (gr. 5-7). 1990. pap. 7.95 (*0-913935-47-6*) ERA-CCR.
—Editing Writes, Orange Edition. Gompper, Gail, illus. (gr. 2-8). 1990. pap. 7.95 25 or more copies (*0-913935-48-4*) ERA-CCR.
—Editing Writes, Red Edition. Gompper, Gail, illus. 110p. (gr. 4-6). 1989. pap. 7.95 (*0-913935-45-X*) ERA-CCR.
—Creative Writes, Bk. B. 34p. (gr. 5-12). 1984. pap. 14.95 (*0-913935-26-3*) ERA-CCR.
Rothsteis, Shmuel. Heir to the Throne. Hinlicky, Gregg, illus. LC 90-83945. 224p. (gr. 5-8). 1990. 13.95 (*1-56062-043-9*); pap. 10.95 (*1-56062-044-7*) CIS Comm.

Rotner, Shelley & Kreisler, Ken. Citybook. Rotner, Shelley, photos by. LC 93-6350. (Illus.). 32p. (ps-1). 1994. 14.95 (*0-531-06837-4*); lib. bdg. 14.99 RLB (*0-531-08687-9*) Orchard Bks Watts.
—Nature Spy. LC 91-38430. (Illus.). 32p. (ps-1). 1992. RSBE 14.95 (*0-02-777885-1*, Macmillan Child Bk) Macmillan Child Grp.
—Ocean Day. Rotner, Shelley, illus. LC 92-6114. 32p. (ps-1). 1993. RSBE 14.95 (*0-02-777886-X*, Macmillan Child Bk) Macmillan Child Grp.
Rotner, Shelley, jt. auth. see Allen, Marjorie N.
Rotsler, William. Plot-It-Yourself Adventure: Goonies Cavern of Horror. Arico, Diane, ed. 128p. (Orig.). (gr. 3-7). 1985. pap. 3.95 (*0-671-60135-0*) S&S Trade.
—The Star Trek II Gift Set, 3 vols. Boxed Set. pap. 9.50 (*0-317-12429-3*) S&S Trade.
—Star Trek III: Plot-It-Yourself Adventure Stories, the Vulcan Treasure. Barish, Wendy, ed. (Illus.). (gr. 3 up). 1984. pap. 3.85 (*0-671-50138-0*) S&S Trade.
—Star Trek III Short Stories. Barish, Wendy, ed. 160p. (Orig.). (gr. 3 up). 1984. pap. 3.85 (*0-671-50139-9*) S&S Trade.
Rott, Joanna R. & Groves, Seli. How on Earth Do We Recycle Glass? Seiden, Art, illus. LC 91-24241. 64p. (gr. 4-6). 1992. PLB 12.90 (*1-56294-141-0*) Millbrook Pr.
Rotter, Charles. Monarchs. (gr. 1-8). 1992. PLB 15.95 (*0-89565-840-2*); Resale. 22.75 (*0-685-66167-9*) Childs World.
—Seals & Sea Lions. 32p. 1991. 22.75 (*0-89565-714-7*); 15.95s.p. (*0-685-55062-1*) Childs World.
—Walruses. LC 92-8410. (gr. 1-8). 1992. PLB 15.95 (*0-89565-841-0*); Resale. 22.75 (*0-685-59391-6*) Childs World.
Rotter, Charles M. Fungi. LC 92-44441. (gr. 4 up). 1993. 18.95 (*0-88682-593-8*) Creative Ed.
—Hurricanes. LC 92-44442. (gr. 6 up). 1993. 18.95 (*0-88682-597-0*) Creative Ed.
—Mountains. LC 92-41340. 1993. 18.95 (*0-88682-596-2*) Creative Ed.
—The Prairie. LC 92-44822. (gr. 4 up). 1993. 18.95 (*0-88682-598-9*) Creative Ed.
Rotter, Charles M. & Taylor, Nicole. Wetlands. LC 92-41339. 1993. 18.95 (*0-88682-594-6*) Creative Ed.
Rotunno, Betsy, jt. auth. see Rotunno, Rocco.
Rotunno, Betsy, jt. auth. see Rotunno, Roccy.
Rotunno, Rocco & Rotunno, Betsy. How Snowshoe Saves Christmas. (Illus.). 12p. (Orig.). (gr. 2-6). 1993. mixed media pkg. incl. stamp pad, stamps, box of 4 crayons 7.00 (*1-881980-05-7*) Noteworthy.
—The Incredible Crash Dummies: The Dashboard Sandwich. (Illus.). 12p. (Orig.). (gr. 2-6). 1993. mixed media pkg. incl. stamp pad, stamps, box of 4 crayons 7.00 (*1-881980-06-5*) Noteworthy.
—Little Bear's Best Birthday. Rotunno, Betsy, illus. 12p. (gr. 2-6). 1992. Mixed Media Pkg. incl. stamp pad, stamps & box of 4 crayons. 7.00 (*1-881980-00-6*) Noteworthy.
—The Story of Christmas Tree Lane. (Illus.). 12p. (Orig.). (gr. 2-6). 1993. mixed media pkg. incl. stamp pad, stamps, box of 4 crayons 7.00 (*1-881980-04-9*) Noteworthy.
—Tessa Becomes a Ballerina. Rotunno, Betsy, illus. 12p. (gr. 2-6). 1992. Mixed Media Pkg. incls. stamp pad, stamps, box of 4 crayons. 7.00 (*1-881980-01-4*) Noteworthy.
—A Trick for Magic Bunny. Rotunno, Betsy, illus. 12p. (gr. 2-6). 1992. Mixed Media Pkg. incls. stamp pad, stamps & box of 4 crayons. 7.00 (*1-881980-02-2*) Noteworthy.
Rotunno, Roccy & Rotunno, Betsy. Dennis the Dinosaur Moves to Crystal Pond. Rotunno, Betsy, illus. 12p. (gr. 2-6). 1992. Mixed Media Pkg. incls. stamp pad, stamps & box of 4 crayons. 7.00 (*1-881980-03-0*) Noteworthy.
Roucek, Joseph. Tito: Modern Leader of Yugoslavia. Rahmas, D. Steve, ed. LC 73-87625. 32p. (Orig.). (gr. 7-12). 1973. lib. bdg. 4.95 incl. catalog cards (*0-87157-562-0*) SamHar Pr.
Roucek, Joseph S. Capital Punishment. new ed. Rahmas, D. Steve, ed. 32p. (gr. 7-12). 1975. lib. bdg. 4.95 incl. catalog cards (*0-87157-816-6*) SamHar Pr.
Round, G., jt. auth. see Tyler, J.
Round, Graham. God Creates. (ps). 1992. 5.99 (*0-8423-0994-2*) Tyndale.
—Jesus Saves. (ps). 1992. 5.99 (*0-8423-1873-9*) Tyndale.
Round, Graham, jt. auth. see Tyler, Jenny.
Round, Graham, jt. auth. see Waters, Gaby.
Rounds, David. Cannonball River Tales. Berenzy, Alix, illus. LC 92-11374. 136p. (gr. 4-7). 1992. 15.95 (*0-87156-577-3*) Sierra.
Rounds, Glen. Cowboys. Rounds, Glen, illus. LC 90-46501. 32p. (ps-3). 1991. reinforced 14.95 (*0-8234-0867-1*) Holiday.
—Cowboys. 1993. pap. 5.95 (*0-8234-1061-7*) Holiday.
—Ol' Paul, The Mighty Logger. LC 75-22163. (Illus.). 96p. (gr. 4-6). 1976. 15.95 (*0-8234-0269-X*); pap. 4.95 (*0-8234-0713-6*) Holiday.
—Old MacDonald Had a Farm. Rounds, Glen, illus. LC 88-24640. 32p. (ps-3). 1989. reinforced bdg. 14.95 (*0-8234-0739-X*); pap. 5.95 (*0-8234-0846-9*) Holiday.
—Wild Appaloosa. Rounds, Glen, illus. LC 82-48751. 96p. (gr. 3-7). 1983. 13.95 (*0-8234-0482-X*) Holiday.
—Wild Horses. Rounds, Glen, illus. 32p. (ps-3). 1993. reinforced bdg. 14.95 (*0-8234-1019-6*) Holiday.

Rounds, Glen, adapted by. & illus. The Blind Colt. LC 89-1779. 84p. (gr. 3-6). 1989. 15.95 (0-8234-0010-7); pap. 5.95 (0-8234-0758-6) Holiday.

Rounds, Glen, retold by. & illus. The Three Billy Goats Gruff. LC 92-23951. 32p. (ps-3). 1993. reinforced bdg. 14.95 (0-8234-1015-3) Holiday.

—Three Little Pigs & the Big Bad Wolf. LC 91-18173. 32p. (ps-3). 1992. reinforced bdg. 14.95 (0-8234-0923-6) Holiday.

Rounds, Glen, as told by. & illus. Washday on Noah's Ark: A Story of Noah's Ark. LC 91-4507. 32p. (ps-3). 1991. reinforced bdg. 14.95 (0-8234-0555-9); pap. 5.95 (0-8234-0880-9) Holiday.

Rounds, Glen, illus. I Know an Old Lady Who Swallowed a Fly. LC 89-46244. 32p. (ps-3). 1990. reinforced bdg. 14.95 (0-8234-0814-0) Holiday.

—I Know an Old Lady Who Swallowed a Fly. LC 89-46244. 32p. (ps-3). 1991. pap. 5.95 (0-8234-0908-2) Holiday.

Rourke, A. Decorating Your Room. (Illus.). 32p. (gr. 5 up). 1989. lib. bdg. 15.94 (0-86625-286-X) Rourke Corp.

Rourke, Arlene C. Los Manos y los Pies. LC 92-5661. (ENG & SPA.). 1992. 15.94 (0-86625-290-8); 11. 95s.p. (0-685-59319-3) Rourke Pubns.

Rouse & Cardoso, Ersillo. Dictionnaire Portugais. (SPA.). 1820p. (gr. 9-12). 1963. 49.95 (0-685-57714-7, M-6495) Fr & Eur.

Rouse, William H. Gods, Heroes & Men of Ancient Greece. 192p. (RL 5). 1957. pap. 4.50 (0-451-62669-9, Ment) NAL-Dutton.

Rouse, William H., tr. see Homer.

Rouss, Sylvia A. Fun with Jewish Holiday Rhymes. Steinberg, Lisa, illus. LC 91-40931. (ps). 1992. 10.95 (0-8074-0463-2, 101981) UAHC.

—Sammy Spider's First Hanukkah. Kahn, Katherine J., illus. LC 92-39639. 1993. 13.95 (0-929371-45-3); pap. 5.95 (0-929371-46-1) Kar Ben.

Rousseau, May. Everyone Is Dressing Up! (Illus.). 12p. (ps). 1991. bds. 4.95 (0-916291-38-3) Kane-Miller Bk.

Roussel, Mike. Clay. (Illus.). 32p. (gr. 2-6). 1990. lib. bdg. 15.94 (0-86592-485-6); lib. bdg. 11.95s.p. (0-685-36301-5) Rourke Corp.

—Scrap Materials. (Illus.). 32p. (gr. 2-6). 1990. lib. bdg. 15.94 (0-86592-487-2); 11.95s.p. (0-685-36305-8) Rourke Corp.

Roussel, Mike, et al. Craft Projects, 6 bks. (Illus.). 192p. (gr. 2-6). 1990. Set. lib. bdg. 95.64 (0-86592-482-1); Set. lib. bdg. 71.70s.p. (0-685-36300-7) Rourke Corp.

Roussy de Sales, R. de. Easy French Crossword Puzzles. (FRE., Illus.). 64p. (gr. 5 up). 1983. pap. 4.95 (0-8442-1330-6, Passport Bks) NTC Pub Grp.

—Jeux de Grammaire. (FRE., Illus.). 64p. (gr. 5 up). 1983. pap. 4.95 (0-8442-1380-2, Passport Bks) NTC Pub Grp.

Routledge, Patricia, read by see Potter, Beatrix.

Rovetch, Lissa. Trigwater Did It. Rovetch, Lissa, illus. LC 88-31791. 32p. (ps up). 1989. 12.95 (0-688-08057-X); PLB 12.88 (0-688-08058-8, Morrow Jr Bks) Morrow Jr Bks.

—Trigwater Did It. (Illus.). 32p. (ps-3). 1991. pap. 3.95 (0-14-054238-8, Puffin) Puffin Bks.

Rovin, Jeff. Five Hundred Hilarious Jokes for Kids. 144p. (Orig.). 1990. pap. 2.99 (0-451-16549-7, Sig) NAL-Dutton.

—Five Hundred More Hilarious Jokes for Kids. 1990. pap. 2.95 (0-451-16727-9, Sig) NAL-Dutton.

Rovira, Albert. Wax Crayon. Ballestar, Vincenc & Martinez, Francesc, illus. 48p. 1991. pap. 7.95 (0-8120-4718-4) Barron.

Rowan, Barbara. Denial of Rights. Powell, Michelle, illus. LC 90-84008. 153p. (Orig.). (gr. 8 up). 1991. pap. 8.00 (0-9622863-4-6) Bristlecone Pubns.

—Igor & Mom. Powell, Michelle, illus. LC 90-84009. 43p. (Orig.). (gr. k-4). 1991. pap. 7.50 (0-9622863-2-X) Bristlecone Pubns.

Rowan, Barbara C. Does That Goal Count? Manning, Janet, illus. LC 89-61850. 23p. (Orig.). (gr. 4-7). 1989. pap. 4.50 (0-9622863-1-1) Bristlecone Pubns.

Rowan, James P. Butterflies & Moths. LC 83-7216. (Illus.). 48p. (gr. k-4). 1983. PLB 15.27 (0-516-01692-X); pap. 4.95 (0-516-41692-8) Childrens.

—Prairies & Grasslands. LC 83-7310. (Illus.). 48p. (gr. k-4). 1983. PLB 15.27 (0-516-01706-3); pap. 4.95 (0-516-41706-1) Childrens.

Rowan, Jim. I Can Be a Zoo Keeper. LC 85-11327. 32p. (gr. k-3). 1985. pap. 3.95 (0-516-41889-0) Childrens.

Rowan, N. R. Women in the Marines: The Book Camp Challenge. Rowan, N. R., photos by. LC 93-9706. (Illus.). 1993. deluxe ed. 22.95 (0-8225-1430-3) Lerner Pubns.

Rowbotham, Judith. Good Girls Make Good Wives: Guidance for Girls in Victorian Fiction. (Illus.). 256p. (gr. 9-12). 1989. text ed. 45.00 (0-631-16345-6); pap. text ed. 15.95 (0-631-16396-4) Blackwell Pubs.

Rowe. Giant Dinosaurs. 1993. pap. 28.67 (0-590-73275-7) Scholastic Inc.

Rowe, Amy & Rowe, Philip. Ernest the Fierce Mouse. rev. ed. Norton, Andrea, illus. 32p. (gr. k-2). 1990. Repr. of 1985 ed. PLB 10.50 (1-878363-08-5) Forest Hse.

Rowe, Debi M. Introduction to the Siddur: The Brakhah System. Grishaver, Joel L., illus. 96p. (gr. 4-5). 1990. wkbk. 5.50 (0-933873-58-1) Torah Aura.

—Introduction to the Siddur: The Shema & Its Blessings. Grishaver, Joel L., illus. 164p. (gr. 5-6). 1991. wkbk. 5.95 (0-933873-60-3) Torah Aura.

Rowe, Erna. Los Dinosaurios Gigantes (Giant Dinosaurs) Palacios, Argentina, tr. Smith, Merle, illus. 32p. (ps-2). pap. 3.95 (0-590-40647-7) Scholastic Inc.

—Giant Dinosaurs. Smith, Merle, illus. (gr. k-3). 1975. pap. 2.95 (0-590-40262-5) Scholastic Inc.

Rowe, Frank. The Famous Airplanes of Kansas. Lickei, Elizabeth, ed. Rowe, Frank, illus. 64p. (Orig.). 1992. pap. 3.95 (1-880652-12-9) Wichita Eagle.

Rowe, Frederick J. AP Exam in Chemistry. 2nd ed. 208p. (gr. 9-12). 1990. pap. 15.95 (0-13-010448-5, Arco Test) P-H Gen Ref & Trav.

Rowe, Jeanine C. Eyes of Desire. Hannan, R., ed. 370p. 1991. pap. 5.99 (0-9626415-0-2) Intl Info NY.

Rowe, John. Jack the Dog. Rowe, John, illus. 28p. (gr. k up). 1993. 14.95 (0-88708-266-1) Picture Bk Studio.

—Rabbit Moon. Rowe, John, illus. LC 92-6047. 28p. 1992. pap. 14.95 (0-88708-246-7) Picture Bk Studio.

Rowe, John, ed. see Carpenter, Allan & Maginnis, Matthew.

Rowe, Julian & Perham, Molly. Colorful Light. LC 93-8217. (Illus.). 1993. write for info. (0-516-08131-4) Childrens.

—Feel & Touch! LC 93-8214. 1993. write for info. (0-516-08132-2) Childrens.

—Keeping Your Balance. LC 93-8215. 1993. write for info. (0-516-08133-0) Childrens.

—Make It Move! LC 93-13737. 1993. write for info. (0-516-08135-7) Childrens.

—Making Sounds. LC 92-13738. 1993. write for info. (0-516-08136-5) Childrens.

Rowe, Julian, jt. auth. see Lafferty, Peter.

Rowe, Julina & Perham, Molly. Keep it Afloat! LC 93-8213. 1993. write for info. (0-516-08134-9) Childrens.

Rowe, Philip, jt. auth. see Rowe, Amy.

Rowe, W. W. Amy & Gully in Rainbowland. Chow, Adam, illus. LC 92-9075. 84p. (Orig.). (gr. k-4). 1992. pap. 5.95 (1-55939-003-4) Snow Lion.

—Gully's Travels in Space-Time. LC 90-71370. 61p. (gr. k-3). 1991. pap. 5.95 (1-55523-385-6) Winston-Derek.

—Small Tall Tales. LC 88-51388. 78p. 1989. 5.95 (1-55523-200-0) Winston-Derek.

Rowell, Edmon L., Jr. Apostles: Jesus' Special Helpers. Padgett, James, illus. (gr. 1-6). 1979. 5.99 (0-8054-4246-4, 4242-46) Broadman.

Rowell, Trevor. The Scramble for Africa. (Illus.). 72p. (gr. 7-12). 1987. 19.95 (0-7134-5200-5, Pub. by Batsford UK) Trafalgar.

Rowen, Larry. Beyond Winning: Group Centered Games & Sports. (gr. 2-6). 1990. pap. 9.95 (0-8224-3380-X) Fearon Teach Aids.

Rowh, Mark. Opportunities in Metal Working Careers. LC 90-50730. 160p. (gr. 7 up). 1991. 13.95 (0-8442-8537-4, VGM Career Bks); pap. 10.95 (0-8442-8538-2, VGM Career Bks) NTC Pub Grp.

Rowinski, Kate. Ellie Bear & the Fly-Away Fly. Peterson, Dawn, illus. LC 93-25260. 32p. (gr. 1-4). 1993. 14.95 (0-89272-335-1) Down East.

—L. L. Bear's Island Adventure. Peterson, Dawn, illus. LC 92-71972. 32p. (ps-4). 1992. 14.95 (0-89272-320-3) Down East.

Rowland, Beth, ed. Lively Bible Lessons for Grades 1-2. LC 92-19504. 100p. 1992. pap. 11.99 (1-55945-098-3) Group Pub.

—Lively Bible Lessons for Kindergarten. LC 92-16301. 1992. 11.99 (1-55945-097-5) Group Pub.

Rowland, Della. Little Red Riding Hood & the Wolf's Tale. (ps-3). 1991. 13.95 (1-55972-072-7, Birch Ln Pr) Carol Pub Group.

—Martin Luther King, Jr. The Dream of Peaceful Revolution. Gallin, Richard, ed. Young, Andrew, intro. by. (Illus.). 128p. (gr. 5 up). 1990. lib. bdg. 16.98 (0-382-09924-9); pap. 7.95 (0-382-24062-6) Silver Burdett Pr.

—The Story of Sacajawea: Guide to Lewis & Clark. (gr. k-6). 1989. pap. 3.25 (0-440-40215-8, YB) Dell.

Rowland, Marcus L. Canal Priests of Mars. Harris, Dell, illus. 64p. (Orig.). 1990. pap. 8.00 (1-55878-039-4) Game Designers.

Rowland, Pleasant T. Our New Baby. Thieme, Jeanne, ed. Backes, Nick, illus. (ps). 1990. White Version. 19. 95 ea. (0-937295-64-7); African-American Version. 19. 95 (0-937295-65-5) Pleasant Co.

—Our New Baby - Asian Version. Backes, Nick, illus. 14p. (ps-k). 1991. 19.95 (1-56247-000-0) Pleasant Co.

Rowland-Entwistle, Theodore. The Pop-up Atlas of the World. Jacobs, Philip & Peterkin, Mike, illus. 18p. (gr. 3 up). 1988. pap. 12.95 (0-671-65898-0, S&S BFYR) S&S Trade.

—Prehistoric Life. LC 89-11373. (Illus.). 64p. (gr. 4-6). 1990. PLB 19.93 (0-8368-0006-0) Gareth Stevens Inc.

—Rivers & Lakes. (Illus.). 48p. (gr. 5-8). 1987. PLB 16.98 (0-382-09499-9) Silver Burdett Pr.

—Thomas Edison. (Illus.). 32p. (gr. 3-8). 1988. PLB 10. 95 (0-86307-928-8) Marshall Cavendish.

—Wilbur & Orville Wright. (Illus.). 32p. (gr. 3-8). 1988. PLB 10.95 (0-86307-927-X) Marshall Cavendish.

Rowland-Entwistle, Theodore & Cooke, Jean. Factfinder. LC 92-53118. (Illus.). 280p. (Orig.). (gr. 4-8). 1992. pap. 12.95 (1-85697-835-4); 16.95 (1-85697-803-6) Kingfisher Bks.

Rowland-Entwistle, Theodore, jt. auth. see Harrison, Virginia.

Rowland-Entwistle, Theodore. Jungles & Rainforests. (Illus.). 48p. (gr. 3-8). 1987. PLB 16.98 (0-382-09500-6) Silver Burdett Pr.

Rowland-Jones, A. Practice Book for the Treble Recorder. (gr. 9 up). 1962. pap. 15.95 (0-19-322340-6) OUP.

—Recorder Technique. (gr. 9 up). 1959. pap. 26.95 (0-19-322342-2) OUP.

Rowlands, Avril. Milk & Honey. 144p. (gr. 4 up). 1990. jacketed 14.95 (0-19-271627-1) OUP.

Rowland-Warne, L. Costume. McAulay, Liz, photos by. LC 91-53135. (Illus.). 64p. (gr. 5 up). 1992. 15.00 (0-679-81680-1); PLB 15.99 (0-679-91680-6) Knopf Bks Yng Read.

Rowley, Kay. Rock Concerts. LC 91-21367. (Illus.). 32p. (gr. 5-6). 1992. RSBE 13.95 (0-89686-715-3, Crestwood Hse) Macmillan Child Grp.

—Rock Music. LC 91-22085. (Illus.). 32p. (gr. 5-6). 1992. RSBE 13.95 (0-89686-714-5, Crestwood Hse) Macmillan Child Grp.

—Rock Stars. LC 91-15077. (Illus.). 32p. (gr. 5-6). 1992. RSBE 13.95 (0-89686-713-7, Crestwood Hse) Macmillan Child Grp.

—Rock Videos. LC 91-15073. (Illus.). 32p. (gr. 5-6). 1992. RSBE 13.95 (0-89686-712-9, Crestwood Hse) Macmillan Child Grp.

Rowley, Patric. Artists: A Kansas Collection. Harper, Steve, photos by. (Illus.). 108p. (gr. 7-12). 1989. 34.95 (0-9623079-0-4) Artists Registry.

Rowzee, Janet Z. & Watson, James A. The Song of the Shepherd Boy. 20p. (gr. 4-8). 1993. pap. 6.95 saddle bdg. (0-9638941-0-2) Eagles Three.

Rox, Lori M. Oodles of Riddles. Hoffman, Sanford, illus. LC 89-4549. 96p. (gr. 3-8). 1990. pap. 3.95 (0-8069-7202-5) Sterling.

Roxas, Reni, ed. see Adler, David A.

Roxas, Reni, ed. see Dolan, Edward F.

Roxas, Reni, ed. see Gay, Kathlyn.

Roxas, Reni, ed. see Goldman, Martin S.

Roxas, Reni, ed. see Hoobler, Dorothy & Hoobler, Thomas.

Roxas, Reni, ed. see Koch, Frances K.

Roxas, Reni, ed. see Rabin, Staton.

Roxbee-Cox, P. Atoms & Molecules. (Illus.). 32p. (gr. 6-9). 1993. PLB 13.96 (0-88110-589-9); pap. 6.95 (0-7460-0988-7) EDC.

Roy, Cal. Bubble, the Birds, & the Noise. Roy, Cal, illus. (gr. k-4). 1968. 8.95 (0-8392-3069-9) Astor-Honor.

—Friend Can Be. (Illus.). (gr. 2 up). 1969. 9.95 (0-8392-3075-3) Astor-Honor.

—Time Is Day. (Illus.). (gr. k-3). 1968. 9.95 (0-8392-3065-6) Astor-Honor.

—What Every Young Wizard Should Know. Roy, Cal, illus. (gr. 2 up). 1963. 8.95 (0-8392-3043-5) Astor-Honor.

Roy, Claude. Chat Qui Parlait Malgre Lui. Glaseur, Willi, illus. (FRE.). 87p. (gr. 5-10). 1982. pap. 6.95 (2-07-033194-6) Schoenhof.

—Enfantasques. (FRE.). (gr. 5-10). 1979. pap. 6.95 (2-07-033087-7) Schoenhof.

—Maison Qui S'Envole. Lemoine, Georges, illus. (FRE.). 90p. (gr. 5-10). 1977. pap. 6.95 (2-07-033001-X) Schoenhof.

Roy, J. Soul Daddy. 1992. 16.95 (0-15-277193-X, HB Juv Bks) HarBrace.

Roy, Jessie H. & Turner, Geneva C. Pioneers of Long Ago. Jones, Lois M., illus. 1990. 12.95 (0-87498-008-9) Assoc Pubs DC.

Roy, Ron. Move over, Wheelchairs Coming Through. Hausherr, Rosemarie, illus. LC 84-14314. 96p. (gr. 4-7). 1985. 15.45 (0-89919-249-1, Clarion Bks) HM.

—Whose Hat Is That? Hausherr, Rosemarie, photos by. (Illus.). 40p. (ps-3). 1990. pap. 5.70 (0-395-54778-4, Clarion Bks) HM.

—Whose Shoes Are These? LC 87-24279. (ps-3). 1988. 13.95 (0-89919-445-1, Clarion Bks) HM.

—Whose Shoes Are These? Hausherr, Rosmarie, illus. LC 87-24279. 40p. (ps-4). 1991. pap. 5.70 (0-395-55353-9, Clarion Bks) HM.

Roybal, Laura. Billy. LC 93-4837. 1994. write for info. (0-395-67649-5) HM.

Royds, Caroline, selected by. The Dragon, Giant & Monster Treasury. Spenceley, Annabel, illus. 96p. 1988. 13.95 (0-399-21587-5, Putnam) Putnam Pub Group.

Royer, Katherine. Nursery Happy Times Book. (Illus.). 48p. (ps). 1957. pap. 3.95x (0-8361-1277-6) Herald Pr.

—Nursery Stories of Jesus. (Illus.). 48p. (ps). 1957. pap. 3.95 (0-8361-1276-8) Herald Pr.

Royer, Katherine, ed. Nursery Songbook. (Illus.). 48p. (ps). 1957. pap. 3.95x (0-8361-1278-4) Herald Pr.

Royer, Mary P. Astrology: Opposing Viewpoints. LC 91-21657. (Illus.). 112p. (gr. 5-8). 1991. PLB 14.95 (0-89908-090-1) Greenhaven.

Royer, Ruth S. Sarah R. Royer - a Young Alzheimer's Patient: My Memory of Her. 1991. 8.95 (0-533-09187-X) Vantage.

Royster, Philip M. Songs & Dances. LC 80-85233. 61p. (gr. 9-12). 1981. pap. 3.50x perfect bd. (0-916418-28-6) Lotus.

Royston, Angela. The A to Z Book of Cars. (Illus.). (gr. k up). 1991. 12.95 (0-8120-6209-4) Barron.

—Big Machines. Pastor, Terry, illus. LC 93-16019. (gr. 3 up). 1994. 12.95 (0-316-76070-6) Little.

—Buildings, Bridges & Tunnels. Shone, Rob, illus. LC 90-13023. 40p. (gr. 4-5). 1991. PLB 12.40 (0-531-19108-7) Watts.

—Cars. LC 91-16122. (Illus.). 24p. (ps-k). 1991. POB 6.95 (0-689-71517-X, Aladdin) Macmillan Child Grp.

—Cow. LC 89-22536. (ps-3). 1990. PLB 10.90 (0-531-19077-3, Warwick) Watts.

—Flowers, Trees & Other Plants. LC 90-12994. (Illus.). 40p. (gr. 4-5). 1991. PLB 12.40 (0-531-19110-9) Watts.

—Goat. (ps-3). 1990. PLB 10.90 (*0-531-19078-1*, Warwick) Watts.
—Hen. (ps-3). 1990. PLB 10.90 (*0-531-19079-X*) Watts.
—The Human Body & How It Works. Shone, Rob, illus. 40p. (gr. 4-5). 1991. PLB 12.40 (*0-531-19102-8*, Warwick) Watts.
—The Human Body & How It Works. Stone, Rob, illus. LC 90-42978. 40p. (Orig.). (gr. 2-5). 1991. pap. 3.95 (*0-679-80860-4*) Random Bks Yng Read.
—My Lift the Flap Car Book. King, Colin, illus. LC 90-8615. 1991. 14.95 (*0-399-22006-2*, Putnam) Putnam Pub Group.
—My Lift-the-Flap Plane Book. King, Colin, illus. LC 92-38631. 18p. (ps-1). 1993. 14.95 (*0-399-22533-1*, Putnam) Putnam Pub Group.
—Pig. 1990. PLB 10.90 (*0-531-19080-3*, Warwick) Watts.
—Pony. 1990. PLB 10.90 (*0-531-19081-1*, Warwick) Watts.
—The Senses. Riddell, Edwina, illus. LC 92-25715. 24p. (ps-3). 1993. 13.95 (*0-8120-6272-8*) Barron.
—Sheep. 1990. PLB 10.90 (*0-531-19082-X*, Warwick) Watts.
—The Tiger. JV-Warwick Press Staff, ed. (Illus.). 24p. (gr. 1-3). 1988. 10.40 (*0-531-19043-9*, Warwick) Watts.
Royston, Angela & Thompson, Graham. Monster Building Machines. 24p. (ps-2). 1990. 9.95 (*0-8120-6174-8*) Barron.
—Monster Road Builders. (Illus.). 24p. (ps-2). 1989. 9.95 (*0-8120-6126-8*) Barron.
Royston, Robert. Cities Two Thousand. Asimov, Isaac, ed. (Illus.). 64p. (gr. 6 up). 1985. 14.95x (*0-8160-1154-0*) Facts on File.
Rozakis, Laurie. AP Exam in English Literature & Composition. 2nd ed. 384p. (gr. 9-12). 1990. pap. 13.00 (*0-13-011629-7*, Arco Test) P-H Gen Ref & Trav.
—Celebrate! Holidays Around the World. LC 92-81915. (gr. k-4). 1993. pap. 4.95 (*0-88160-217-5*, LW107) Learning Wks.
—Hanna & Barbera: Yabba-Dabba-Doo! (Illus.). 48p. (gr. 2-5). 1994. PLB 12.95 (*1-56711-065-7*) Blackbirch.
—Henson & Peary: The Race for the North Pole. (Illus.). 48p. (gr. 2-5). 1994. PLB 12.95 (*1-56711-066-5*) Blackbirch.
—Mary Kay. LC 92-45124. 1993. 15.93 (*0-86592-040-0*); 11.95s.p. (*0-685-66418-X*) Rourke Enter.
—Steven Jobs. LC 92-43268. (gr. 5 up). 1993. 15.93 (*0-86592-001-X*); 11.95s.p. (*0-685-66327-2*) Rourke Corp.
—Teen Pregnancy: Why Are Kids Having Babies? (Illus.). 64p. (gr. 5-8). 1993. PLB 14.95 (*0-8050-2569-3*) TFC Bks NY.
Rozell, O. B. Nathan the Nervous. (Illus.). 24p. (Orig.). (gr. 6-12). 1977. pap. 2.00 (*0-88680-136-2*); royalty on application 20.00 (*0-685-59271-5*) I E Clark.
Rozens. Floods. 1994. PLB write for info. (*0-8050-3097-2*) H Holt & Co.
Rozens, Aleksandrs. Wayne Gretzky. LC 93-18132. 1993. 15.93 (*0-86592-119-9*); 11.95s.p. (*0-685-66586-0*) Rourke Enter.
Roziere, Gael. Artist's Alphabet: A Child's Activity Book for Language, Movement & Painting. 28p. (ps-4). 1988. pap. 5.95 wkbk. (*0-9619004-2-3*) M Press NM.
Rozman, Deborah. The Crystal Lady. Royall, Sandy, illus. 72p. (gr. 1 up). 1991. 19.95 (*1-879052-01-6*, Planet Pubns) Planetary Pubns.
Rozman, Deborah, ed. see Childre, Doc L.
Ruane, J. Boats, Boats, Boats. (Illus.). 28p. (ps-2). 1990. 12.33 (*0-516-05351-5*); pap. 3.95 (*0-516-45351-3*) Childrens.
Rubalcaba, Jill, retold by. Uncegila's Seventh Spot: A Dakota Legend. Toddy, Irving, illus. LC 93-33350. 1995. write for info. (*0-395-68970-8*, Clarion Bks) HM.
Rubel, David. Elvis Presely: The Rise of Rock & Roll. 1992. pap. 5.95 (*0-395-63566-7*) HM.
—Elvis Presley: The Rise of Rock & Roll. (Illus.). 96p. (gr. 7 up). 1991. PLB 14.90 (*1-878841-18-1*) Millbrook Pr.
—Fannie Lou Hamer: From Sharecropping to Politics. Gallin, Richard, ed. Young, Andrew, intro. by. (Illus.). 128p. (gr. 4-8). 1990. lib. bdg. 16.98 (*0-382-09923-0*); pap. 7.95 (*0-382-24061-8*) Silver Burdett Pr.
—How to Drive an Indy Race Car. Keating, Edward, illus. 48p. (Orig.). (gr. 3 up). 1992. pap. 9.95 (*1-56261-062-7*) John Muir.
—The Scholastic Encyclopedia of the Presidents & Their Times. LC 93-11810. (Illus.). 224p. (gr. 4 up). 1994. 16.95 (*0-590-49366-3*, Scholastic Ref) Scholastic Inc.
Rubel, Nicole. Conga Crocodile. LC 92-31856. 1993. 14.95 (*0-395-58773-5*) HM.
—The Ghost Family Meets Its Match. Rubel, Nicole, illus. LC 91-10815. 32p. (ps-3). 1992. 14.00 (*0-8037-1093-3*); PLB 13.89 (*0-8037-1094-1*) Dial Bks Young.
—Goldie's Nap. Rubel, Nicole, illus. LC 90-4401. 32p. (ps-2). 1991. PLB 14.89 (*0-06-025107-7*) HarpC Child Bks.
—It Came from the Swamp. Rubel, Nicole, illus. LC 87-24653. 32p. (ps-3). 1988. 10.95 (*0-8037-0513-1*); PLB 10.89 (*0-8037-0515-8*) Dial Bks Young.
—It Came from the Swamp. Rubel, Nicole, illus. LC 87-24653. (Illus.). 32p. (ps-3). 1992. pap. 3.99 (*0-14-054541-7*, Puffin Pied Piper) Puffin Bks.
—Pete Apatosaurus. 48p. 1991. pap. 2.75 (*0-553-15957-7*) Bantam.
—Pirate Jupiter & the Moondogs. Rubel, Nicole, illus. LC 84-13815. 32p. (ps-3). 1985. Dial Bks Young.

Rubenstein, Gillian. Space Demons. MacDonald, Pat, ed. (gr. 6-9). 1989. pap. 2.95 (*0-671-67912-0*, Archway) PB.
Rubin, Audrey S., ed. see Liles, Parker, et al.
Rubin, Bob. Dan Marino: Wonder Boy Quarterback. LC 85-9724. (Illus.). 48p. (gr. 2-8). 1985. PLB 13.27 (*0-516-04347-1*); pap. 3.95 (*0-516-44347-X*) Childrens.
Rubin, Caroline, ed. see Barnes, Jill & Asuka, Ken.
Rubin, Caroline, ed. see Barnes, Jill & Ishinabe, Fusako.
Rubin, Caroline, ed. see Barnes, Jill & Kanabe, Junkichi.
Rubin, Caroline, ed. see Barnes, Jill & Sato, Wakiko.
Rubin, Caroline, ed. see Barnes, Jill & Sueyoshi, Akiko.
Rubin, Caroline, ed. see Barnes, Jill & Teramura, Terua.
Rubin, Caroline, ed. see Barnes, Jill & Tsurmi, Masao.
Rubin, Caroline, ed. see Bishop, Ann.
Rubin, Caroline, ed. see Goldman, Susan.
Rubin, Caroline, ed. see Litchfield, Ada B.
Rubin, Caroline, ed. see Simon, Norma.
Rubin, Caroline, ed. see Stanton, Elizabeth & Stanton, Henry.
Rubin, Chana S. A Time to Live. Hinlickey, Gregg, illus. 269p. (gr. 9-12). 1988. 14.95 (*0-935063-48-X*) CIS Comm.
Rubin, Cynthia E., selected by. ABC Americana from the National Gallery of Art. (Illus.). 26p. (ps up). 1989. 11.95 (*0-15-200660-5*, Gulliver Bks) HarBrace.
Rubin, Laurie. Food First Curriculum. (Illus.). 146p. (gr. 3-8). 1984. 12.00 (*0-935028-17-X*) Inst Food & Develop.
Rubin, Leigh. Notable Quotes. LC 81-69508. (Illus.). 80p. (Orig.). (gr. 4 up). 1981. pap. 5.95 (*0-943384-00-1*) Rubes Pubns.

Rubin, Mark. The Orchestra. Daniel, Alan, illus. 48p. (gr. k-3). 1992. pap. 7.95 (*0-920668-99-2*) Firefly Bks Ltd. THE ORCHESTRA, a non-fiction book for children, introduces musical instruments, basic musical concepts & the symphonic orchestra. The very straightforward text is accompanied by playful but accurate drawings. A number of musical concepts are explored, among them harmony, tempo & dynamics. The role of the composer & conductor are explored & each musical instrument described. A subplot, apparent only through the illustrations, shows two children who wend their way through the orchestra's rehearsal, visiting the instrument families, & culminates in a full-dress concert. Comprehensive but simple in its approach, the book combines solid information with an enjoyable format. Mark Rubin has produced a number of films & television shows for young children. Victor Feldbrill, conductor of the Toronto Symphony program for young children, has reviewed the text for accuracy. Alan Daniel has illustrated a number of books, among them FLYING & SWIMMING CREATURES & THE BAIT CHOPPER.
Publisher Provided Annotation.

Rubin, Susan G. Emily Good as Gold. 192p. (gr. 5-9). 1993. 10.95 (*0-15-276632-4*, Browndeer Pr); pap. 3.95 (*0-15-276633-2*, Browndeer Pr) HarBrace.
Rubin, Susan G., jt. auth. see Farrington, Liz.
Rubinstein. Galax Arena. Date not set. PLB 13.89 (*0-06-023450-4*, Festival) HarpC Child Bks.
Rubinstein, Gillian. Beyond the Labyrinth. LC 90-30627. 256p. (gr. 7 up). 1990. 14.95 (*0-531-05899-9*); PLB 14.99 (*0-531-08499-X*) Orchard Bks Watts.
—Dog in, Cat Out. James, Ann, illus. LC 92-39785. 1993. 13.45 (*0-395-66596-5*) Ticknor & Fields.
—Skymaze. LC 90-43796. 192p. (gr. 6-9). 1991. 14.95 (*0-531-05929-4*); PLB 14.99 (*0-531-08529-5*) Orchard Bks Watts.
—Skymaze. MacDonald, Pat, ed. 240p. (gr. 7 up). 1993. pap. 2.99 (*0-671-76988-X*, Archway) PB.
—Space Demons. LC 87-27542. 240p. (gr. 5-9). 1988. 13.95 (*0-8037-0534-4*) Dial Bks Young.
Rubinstein, Reva. We Are One Family. Zakutinsky, Ruth, ed. (Illus.). 24p. (gr. 1-3). 1992. PLB 9.95x (*0-911643-15-X*) Aura Bklyn.
Rubly-Burggraff, Roberta. Look Who's Drivin' the Bus. Robbins-Ptak, Elizabeth, illus. 150p. (Orig.). (gr. 9 up). 1993. pap. 29.95 (*0-937997-25-0*) Hi-Time Pub.
—Magnum Opus: An Affirmation Journal. Robbins-Ptak, Elizabeth, illus. 72p. (Orig.). (gr. 7-12). 1989. pap. 5.95 (*0-937997-14-5*) Hi-Time Pub.

Ruby, Jennifer. Costume in Context: Medieval Times. (Illus.). 64p. (gr. 7-11). 1990. 24.95 (*0-7134-6075-X*, Pub. by Batsford UK) Trafalgar.
—Costume in Context: The 1940s & 1950s. (Illus.). 64p. (gr. 7-11). 1990. 24.95 (*0-7134-6016-4*, Pub. by Batsford UK) Trafalgar.
—Costume in Context: The 1980s. (Illus.). 72p. (gr. 7-11). 1991. 24.95 (*0-7134-6539-5*, Pub. by Batsford UK) Trafalgar.
—The Edwardians & the First World War. (Illus.). 72p. (gr. 7-9). 1988. 24.95 (*0-7134-5605-1*, Pub. by Batsford UK) Trafalgar.
—The Eighteenth Century. (gr. 7 up). 1989. 24.95 (*0-7134-5772-4*, Pub. by Batsford UK) Trafalgar.
—The Nineteen Sixties & Nineteen Seventies. (Illus.). 64p. (gr. 6-9). 1989. 24.95 (*0-7134-6074-1*, Pub. by Batsford UK) Trafalgar.
—The Nineteen Twenties & Nineteen Thirties. (Illus.). 64p. (gr. 7-9). 1989. 24.95 (*0-7134-5773-2*, Pub. by Batsford UK) Trafalgar.
—The Regency. (Illus.). 64p. (gr. 6-9). 1989. 24.95 (*0-7134-5992-1*, Pub. by Batsford UK) Trafalgar.
—The Stuarts. (Illus.). 72p. (gr. 7-9). 1988. 24.95 (*0-7134-5604-3*, Pub. by Batsford UK) Trafalgar.
Ruby, Lois. Miriam's Well. LC 91-46301. 288p. (gr. 7 up). 1993. 13.95 (*0-590-44937-0*) Scholastic Inc.
—Pig-Out Inn. LC 86-21433. 180p. (gr. 5 up). 1987. 13.95 (*0-395-42714-2*) HM.
—Skin Deep. LC 93-13707. 1994. 14.95 (*0-590-47699-8*) Scholastic Inc.
Ruch, Sandi B. Junkyard Dog. Wunsch, Marjory, illus. LC 89-35652. 96p. (gr. 2-4). 1990. 14.95 (*0-531-05842-5*); PLB 14.99 (*0-531-08442-6*) Orchard Bks Watts.
Ruchlis, Hy. How Do You Know It's True? Discovering the Difference Between Science & Superstition. (Illus.). 100p. (Orig.). 1991. pap. 12.95 (*0-87975-657-8*) Prometheus Bks.
Rucker, Walt, jt. auth. see Ockenga, Earl.
Rucki, Ani. Turkey's Gift to the People. Rucki, Ani, illus. LC 92-10764. 32p. (ps-4). 1992. 14.95 (*0-87358-541-0*) Northland AZ.
Ruckman, Ivy. The Hunger Scream. LC 83-6522. 200p. (gr. 6 up). 1983. 14.95 (*0-8027-6514-9*) Walker & Co.
—Melba the Brain. (gr. 4-7). 1991. pap. 3.25 (*0-440-40423-1*) Dell.
—Melba the Mummy. (gr. 4-7). 1991. pap. 3.25 (*0-440-40437-1*) Dell.
—Night of the Twisters. LC 83-46168. 160p. (gr. 3-6). 1984. 14.00i (*0-690-04408-9*, Crowell Jr Bks); PLB 13.89 (*0-690-04409-7*, Crowell Jr Bks) HarpC Child Bks.
—Night of the Twisters. LC 83-46168. 160p. (gr. 3-6). 1986. pap. 3.95 (*0-06-440176-6*, Trophy) HarpC Child Bks.
—No Way Out. LC 87-47817. 224p. (gr. 6 up). 1988. (Crowell Jr Bks); PLB 12.89 (*0-690-04671-5*, Crowell Jr Bks) HarpC Child Bks.
—No Way Out. LC 87-47817. 224p. (gr. 7 up). 1989. pap. 3.95 (*0-06-447003-2*, Trophy) HarpC Child Bks.
—This Is Your Captain Speaking. (gr. 5 up). 1987. 14.95 (*0-8027-6734-6*) Walker & Co.
—What's an Average Kid Like Me Doing Way up Here? LC 82-72820. 144p. (gr. 4-6). 1983. PLB 11.89 (*0-440-08893-3*); pap. 11.95 (*0-385-29251-1*) Delacorte.
—What's an Average Kid Like Me Doing Way up Here? 144p. (gr. k-6). 1984. pap. 2.75 (*0-440-49448-6*, YB) Dell.
—Who Invited the Undertaker? LC 89-1865. 192p. (gr. 3-7). 1989. 14.00 (*0-690-04832-7*, Crowell Jr Bks); PLB 13.89 (*0-690-04834-3*, Crowell Jr Bks) HarpC Child Bks.
—Who Invited the Undertaker? LC 89-1865. 192p. (gr. 3-7). 1991. pap. 3.95 (*0-06-440352-1*, Trophy) HarpC Child Bks.
Rudd, Betty, ed. see Gluchowsky, Paul M.
Rudder Editors. Good Sailing: An Illustrated Course on Sailing. (Illus.). (gr. 7 up). 1976. pap. 5.95 (*0-679-50630-6*) McKay.
Ruddick, Bob, jt. auth. see Greer, Gary.
Ruddick, Bob, jt. auth. see Greer, Gery.
Ruddick, Robert, jt. auth. see Greer, Gery.
Ruddiman, Catherine, jt. auth. see Aird, Hazel B.
RuDenski, Kathy. Amazing Alphabet Animals. Brady, Steve, illus. LC 91-65792. 44p. (gr. k-3). 1992. 8.95 (*1-55523-447-X*) Winston-Derek.
Rudig, Doug. Big Bend Adventure Guide. Pearson, John R. & Deckert, Frank J., eds. (Illus.). 32p. (Orig.). (gr. k-6). 1983. pap. 2.00 (*0-912001-10-0*) Big Bend.
—Zion Adventure Guide. LC 77-78309. (Illus.). 32p. (gr. 2-7). 1978. pap. 1.95 (*0-915630-07-9*) Zion.
Rudin, Ellen, ed. Young Authors of America, Vol. 1. (Illus.). 102p. (gr. 5-8). 1988. pap. 0.60 (*0-440-84003-1*) Dell.
Rudin, Jacob. Haggadah for Children. (gr. 3 up). 1973. 2.95x (*0-8197-0032-0*) Bloch.
Rudman, Jack, ed. see Standish, Burt L.
Rudner, Barry. The Bumblebee & the Ram. Fahsbender, Thomas, illus. LC 89-81585. 32p. (Orig.). 1989. pap. 4.95 (*0-925928-03-8*) Tiny Thought.
—The Handstand. Fahsbender, Thomas, illus. 32p. 1991. pap. 4.95 (*0-925928-05-4*) Tiny Thought.
—The Littlest Tall Fellow. Carraro, J. M., ed. Fahsbender, Thomas, illus. 28p. (gr. k-6). 1989. pap. 4.95 (*0-925928-00-3*) Tiny Thought.
—Nonsense. Fahsbender, Thomas, illus. (gr. k-6). 1990. write for info. (*0-925928-04-6*) Tiny Thought.

—Will I Still Have to Make My Bed In The Morning? (Illus.). 32p. 1991. pap. 4.95 (*0-925928-10-0*) Tiny Thought.
Rudolph, John W. Las Olas. Henke, Teresa, illus. LC 87-80761. 101p. (Orig.). 1987. pap. 9.00 (*0-941611-09-4*) Shasta San Rafael.
Rudolph, Marguerita, adapted by see Mamin-Sibiryak, D. N.
Rudolph, Marguerita, adapted by see Ushinsky, Konstantin.
Rudolph, Marguerita, retold by see Zakhoder's, Boris.
Rudolph, Stormy. Many Horses (Sequel to Quest for Courage) (Illus.). (gr. 5-12). 1987. pap. 8.95 (*0-89992-112-4*) Coun India Ed.
Rudysmith, Christina. National Archives & Record Administration. Schlesinger, Arthur M., Jr., intro. by. (Illus.). 112p. (gr. 5 up). 1989. 14.95 (*1-55546-073-9*) Chelsea Hse.
Rue, Hazel M. Bomby the Bombardier Beetle. LC 82-71053. (Illus.). (gr. 2-4). 1984. pap. 4.95 (*0-89051-084-9*, Inst Creation) Master Bks.
Rue, Nancy. Home by Another Way. Griffin, Ted, ed. (gr. 9-12). 1991. pap. 8.95 (*0-89107-633-6*) Good News.
—Stop in the Name of Love. Rosen, Roger, ed. (gr. 7 up). 1988. PLB 12.95 (*0-8239-0794-5*) Rosen Group.
—The Value of Compassion. (gr. 7-12). 1991. PLB 15.95 (*0-8239-1240-X*) Rosen Group.
Rue, Nancy N. Coping with An Illiterate Parent. Rosen, Roger, ed. 64p. (gr. 7-12). 1990. PLB 13.95 (*0-8239-1070-9*) Rosen Group.
—Coping with Dating Violence. Rosen, Ruth, ed. (gr. 7-12). 1989. PLB 13.95 (*0-8239-0997-2*) Rosen Group.
Rue, T. S. The Attic. 1993. pap. 3.50 (*0-06-106157-3*, Harp PBks) HarpC.
—Nightmare Inn. (gr. 9-12). 1993. pap. 3.50 (*0-06-106740-7*, Harp PBks) HarpC.
—The Pool. 1993. pap. 3.50 (*0-06-106749-0*, Harp PBks) HarpC.
—Room Thirteen. (gr. 9-12). 1993. pap. 3.50 (*0-06-106746-6*, Harp PBks) HarpC.
Ruelle, Karen G. Seventy-Five Fun Things to Make & Do By Yourself. Haight, Sandy, illus. LC 93-5091. 80p. (gr. 2-10). 1993. 14.95 (*0-8069-0331-7*) Sterling.
Ruemmler, John D. Rangers of the North. (Illus.). 56p. (gr. 10-12). 1985. pap. 12.00 (*0-915795-22-1*, 3000) Iron Crown Ent Inc.
Ruemmler, John D., jt. auth. see Charlton, S. Coleman.
Ruemmler, John D., ed. see Kane, Thomas.
Ruemmler, John D., ed. see Kane, Tom.
Ruemmler, John D., ed. see Loback, Tom.
Ruemmler, John D., ed. see Taylor, Tim.
Ruemmler, John D., ed. see Taylor, Timothy.
Ruf, Mary. Peeka, Pooka, & the Dinosaur. (gr. 3 up). 1993. 7.95 (*0-8062-4737-1*) Carlton.
Ruffault, Charlotte. Animals Underground. Matthews, Sarah, tr. from FRE. Underhill, Graham, illus. LC 87-34616. 38p. (gr. k-5). 1988. 4.95 (*0-944589-03-0*, 030) Young Discovery Lib.
Ruffo, Dave. Football. LC 93-23274. 1993. write for info. (*0-8114-5780-X*) Raintree Steck-V.
Rugg, Frederick E. Rugg's Recommendations on the Colleges. 7th, rev. ed. LC 89-62896. 121p. (gr. 11-12). 1990. pap. 15.95 (*0-9608934-5-8*) Ruggs Recommend.
—Rugg's Recommendations on the Colleges. 10th ed. LC 89-62896. 136p. (gr. 11-12). 1993. pap. 17.95 (*0-9608934-8-2*) Ruggs Recommend.
—Rugg's Recommendations on the Colleges. 11th ed. LC 89-62896. 138p. (gr. 11-12). 1994. pap. 17.95 (*1-883062-01-2*) Ruggs Recommend.
—Rugg's Video on the Colleges. (gr. 11-12). 1993. incl. 59-min. video tape 20.00 (*1-883062-00-4*) Ruggs Recommend.
Ruggles, Grace, ed. see Harper-Deiters, Cyndi.
Ruggles, Robert, ed. see Harper-Deiters, Cyndi.
Ruiter, Barbara & Ruiter, Cindy. Pink Is Perfect for Pigs. (Illus.). 32p. (Orig.). Date not set. pap. 9.95 (*1-56883-019-X*) Colonial Pr AL.
Ruiter, Cindy, jt. auth. see Ruiter, Barbara.
Ruiz, Alberto de Larramendi see De Larramendi Ruis, Alberto.
Ruiz, Aristides. Cornballs: Cereal Box Joke Book. LC 92-60581. 400p. (gr. 4-7). 1993. pap. 2.99 (*0-679-83455-9*) Random Bks Yng Read.
Ruiz, Art, illus. The Weirdest Fun Book, Ever! 1992. 7.95 (*0-448-40503-2*, G&D) Putnam Pub Group.
Ruiz, Dana C. De see De Ruiz, Dana C.
Ruiz, Dana C. de see De Ruiz, Dana C. & Larios, Richard.
Ruiz de Larramendi, Alberto. Coral Reefs. LC 93-3438. (Illus.). 36p. (gr. 3 up). 1993. PLB 19.93 (*0-516-08384-8*) Childrens.
Rukstalis, Susan. How Many Steps Before the Queen? Rukstalis, Susan, illus. Kopen, Dan F., intro. by. LC 92-60664. (Illus.). 32p. (ps-4). 1992. 14.95 (*0-9628914-2-8*) Padakami Pr.
Rumalshah, Mano. Pakistan. (Illus.). 32p. (gr. 7-10). 1991. 17.95 (*0-237-60193-1*, Pub. by Evans Bros Ltd) Trafalgar.
Rumbaut, Hendle. Dove Dream. LC 93-26538. 1994. write for info. (*0-395-68393-9*) HM.
Rumbelow, jt. auth. see Hindley.
Rumble, Patricia B. The Archer & the Princess: A Comedy Based on a Russian Folk Tale. (Illus.). 48p. (Orig.). (gr. 4-10). 1990. pap. 3.00 (*0-88680-334-9*); royalty on application 40.00 (*0-685-58890-4*) I E Clark.

Rummel, Jack. Langston Hughes. King, Coretta Scott, intro. by. (Illus.). 112p. (Orig.). (gr. 5 up). 1989. 17.95 (*1-55546-595-1*); pap. 9.95 (*0-7910-0201-2*) Chelsea Hse.
—Malcolm X. King, Coretta Scott, intro. by. (Illus.). 112p. (gr. 5 up). 1989. lib. bdg. 17.95x (*1-55546-600-1*); pap. 9.95 (*0-7910-0227-6*) Chelsea Hse.
—Mexico. (Illus.). 128p. (gr. 5 up). 1990. 14.95 (*0-7910-1110-0*) Chelsea Hse.
—Muhammad Ali. King, Coretta Scott, intro. by. (Illus.). 112p. (Orig.). (gr. 5 up). 1988. 17.95 (*1-55546-569-2*); pap. 9.95 (*0-7910-0210-1*) Chelsea Hse.
—Robert Oppenheimer: Dark Prince. (Illus.). 144p. (gr. 7-12). 1992. lib. bdg. 16.95x (*0-8160-2598-3*) Facts on File.
—The U. S. Marine Corps. (Illus.). 128p. (gr. 5 up). 1990. 14.95 (*1-55546-110-7*) Chelsea Hse.
Rummel, Mary. God's Love for Happiness: A Return to Family Values. Dirks, Nathan & Brandt, Bill, illus. LC 92-91032. 64p. (Orig.). (gr. k up). 1992. pap. 9.95 (*0-9635091-0-1*) Olive Brnch.
Rumney, Donna. My Picture Book about Me. (Illus.). 20p. (ps). 1988. write for info. My Picture Bks.
Runcie, Jill. Cock a Doodle Doo. (Illus.). 40p. (ps). 1991. pap. 13.95 jacketed (*0-671-72602-1*, S&S BFYR) S&S Trade.
Rundquist, Thomas J. & Guild, Robert W., Jr. Drugs, Sex & Rock-n-Roll. (Illus.). 15p. (Orig.). (gr. 7-12). 1988. pap. text ed. 19.95 (*0-9618567-3-4*) Nova Media.
Rundquist, Thomas J. & Parent, Frederick. Horse Is Boss: Drug Culture Education & Prevention Game. 2nd ed. Randquist, Thomas J, illus. 42p. (Orig.). (gr. 7-12). 1988. pap. text ed. 30.50x (*0-9618567-1-8*) Nova Media.
Rungachary, Santha. Tales for All Times. Khemraj, P., illus. (gr. 1-9). 1979. pap. 2.50 (*0-89744-187-7*) Auromere.
Runk, Wesley T. Standing Up for Jesus. (gr. k-4). 1985. 4.50 (*0-89536-725-4*, 5809) CSS OH.
Runnels, Gayle S., jt. auth. see Lay, Artie K.
Running Press Staff. The Dinosaurs Postcard Book. (Illus.). 64p. (Orig.). (gr. k up). 1987. pap. 7.95 (*0-89471-553-4*) Running Pr.
—Unfolding World. (Illus.). (gr. 4-7). 1993. 5.95 (*1-56138-319-8*) Running Pr.
Running Press Staff, ed. KIDZ Family Car Songbook & Audiocassette. (Illus.). 128p. (Orig.). (gr. 1 up). 1991. incl. audiocassette 9.95 (*0-89471-996-3*) Running Pr.
—KIDZ Kids' Car Songbook & Audiocassette. (Illus.). 112p. (gr. 1 up). 1991. incl. audiocassette 9.95 (*1-56138-074-1*) Running Pr.
—KIDZ Laugh-Along Car Jokebook. (Illus.). 64p. (Orig.). 1992. incl. audiocass. 9.95 (*1-56138-178-0*) Running Pr.
—KIDZ Merry Christmas Car Songbook & Audiocassette. (Illus.). 80p. (gr. 1 up). 1991. incl. audiocassette 9.95 (*1-56138-051-2*) Running Pr.
—KIDZ Mother Goose Car Rhyme Book & Audiocassette. (Illus.). 96p. (Orig.). (gr. 1 up). 1991. incl. 60-min. audiocass. 9.95 (*1-56138-019-9*) Running Pr.
—KIDZ Sing along Car Songbook. (Illus.). 128p. 1992. incl. audiocass. 9.95 (*1-56138-177-2*) Running Pr.
—Miniature Mother Goose. Wright, Blanche F., illus. LC 91-50783. 128p. 1992. 4.95 (*1-56138-105-5*) Running Pr.
—Original Mother Goose. Wright, Blanche F., illus. LC 91-51057. 136p. 1992. 14.95 (*1-56138-113-6*) Running Pr.
Running-Crane, Jenny, jt. auth. see Boss-Ribs, Mary C.
Runyan, Cathy C. Knuckles Down! A Fun Guide to Marble Play. 2nd ed. (Illus.). 36p. (gr. 1-6). 1990. pap. 4.95 (*0-935295-01-1*) Right Brain.
Runyon, Linda. Wild Foods & Animals: Coloring Book. 2nd ed. Runyon, Linda, illus. 16p. (gr. 1 up). 1986. pap. 1.99 (*0-936699-01-9*) Wild Foods Co.
Ruoff, A. LaVonne. Literatures of the American Indian. (Illus.). 112p. (gr. 5 up). 1991. PLB 17.95 (*1-55546-688-5*) Chelsea Hse.
Rupert, Janet E. The African Mask. LC 93-7726. 1994. write for info. (*0-395-67295-3*, Clarion Bks) HM.
Rupert, Rona. Straw Sense. Dooling, Mike, illus. LC 92-8775. 1993. pap. 14.00 (*0-671-77047-0*, S&S BFYR) S&S Trade.
Ruppel, Maxine. Vostaas: The Story of Montana's Indian Nations. (gr. 3-11). 1970. 5.95 (*0-89992-001-2*) Coun India Ed.
Rupprecht, Maureen, illus. Cabbage Patch Kids Jumbo Activity & Coloring Book. 128p. 1984. pap. 2.50 (*0-910313-34-2*) Parker Bros.
Rupprecht, Siegfried P. The Tale of the Vanishing Rainbow. Wilkon, Jozef, illus. Lewis, Naomi, tr. from GER. LC 88-43120. (Illus.). 32p. (gr. k-3). 1989. 14.95 (*1-55858-001-8*) North-South Bks NYC.
Ruschak, Lynette. The Counting Zoo: A Pop-up Number Book. Rousseau, May, illus. LC 91-42462. 24p. (ps-2). 1992. POB 13.95 (*0-689-71619-2*, Aladdin) Macmillan Child Grp.
—Snack Attack: A Tasty Pop Up Book. Carter, David A., illus. 12p. (gr. 3-5). 1990. pap. 8.95 (*0-671-70448-6*, S&S BFYR) S&S Trade.
—Who's Hiding? (ps). 1991. pap. 8.95 (*0-671-73957-3*, S&S BFYR) S&S Trade.
Ruschak, Lynette & Norden, Beth B. Magnification. LC 92-19540. 10p. (gr. 2-5). 1993. 14.99 (*0-525-67417-9*, Lodestar Bks) Dutton Child Bks.

Ruse, Arnold, ed. see Gendusa, Sam.
Ruse, Christina & Hopton, Marilyn. Cassell Dictionary of Literary & Language Terms. (Illus.). 320p. (gr. 10-12). 1992. 17.95 (*0-304-31927-9*, Pub. by Cassell UK) Sterling.
Rush, Alison. The Last of Danu's Children. LC 82-2981. (gr. 7 up). 1982. write for info. HM.
Rush, Barbara, jt. auth. see Schwartz, Howard.
Rush, Barbara, jt. ed. see Schwartz, Howard.
Rush, Christopher. Venus Peter Saves the Whale. Hedderwick, Mairi, illus. LC 92-7808. 32p. (gr. 4-7). 1992. 14.95 (*0-88289-928-7*) Pelican.
Rush, Ken. The Seltzer Man. Rush, Ken, illus. LC 91-40905. 32p. (ps-3). 1993. RSBE 14.95 (*0-2-777917-3*, Macmillan Child Bk) Macmillan Child Grp.
Rushdie, Salman. Haroun & the Sea of Stories. large type ed. (gr. 1-8). 1991. 13.95 (*0-7451-1428-8*, Galaxy Child Lrg Print) Chivers N Amer.
Rushdoony, Haig. Exploring Our World With Maps. (gr. k-6). 1988. pap. 12.95 (*0-8224-4396-1*) Fearon Teach Aids.
Rushdoony, Haig A. Language of Maps: A Map Skills Program for Grades 4-6. (gr. 4-6). 1983. pap. 12.95 (*0-8224-4242-6*) Fearon Teach Aids.
Rushford, Patricia. Silent Witness. 1993. pap. 3.99 (*1-55661-332-6*) Bethany Hse.
—Too Many Secrets. 1993. pap. 3.99 (*1-55661-331-8*) Bethany Hse.
Rushton, Lucy. Birth Customs. LC 92-42174. (Illus.). 32p. (gr. 4-8). 1993. 13.95 (*1-56847-030-4*) Thomson Lrning.
—Death Customs. LC 92-42150. (Illus.). 32p. (gr. 4-8). 1993. 13.95 (*1-56847-031-2*) Thomson Lrning.
Ruskin, John. The King of the Golden River or the Black Brother. Doyle, Richard, illus. LC 74-82199. viii, 56p. (gr. 1 up). 1974. pap. 2.95 (*0-486-20066-3*) Dover.
Ruskin, Robert, ed. see Ruskin, Thelma.
Ruskin, Robert, illus. & intro. by see Ruskin, Thelma.
Ruskin, Thelma. Indians of the Tidewater Country: Of Maryland, Virginia, Delaware & North Carolina. Buchanan, Carol & Ruskin, Robert, eds. Ruskin, Robert, illus. & intro. by. LC 85-73263. 132p. (gr. 4-5). 1986. casebound 15.00 (*0-917882-20-2*) MD Hist Pr.
Rusling, Albert. The Mouse & Mrs. Proudfoot. Rusling, Albert, illus. LC 84-17871. 32p. (gr. k-3). 1985. 12.95 (*0-13-604265-1*) P-H.
Russell, A. E. Song & Its Fountains. Cash, Paul, intro. by. 110p. 1991. pap. 10.95 (*0-943914-52-3*) Larson Pubns.
Russell, Bertrand. Bertrand Russell. Redpath, Ann, ed. Delessert, Etienne, illus. 32p. (gr. 9 up). 1986. PLB 12.95s.p. (*0-88682-012-X*) Creative Ed.
Russell, Bob. Marriage by the Book: Biblical Models for Marriage Today. 112p. (Orig.). 1992. pap. 6.99 (*0-87403-906-1*, 29-03156) Standard Pub.
—When Life's a Zoo: God Still Loves You. Underwood, Jonathan, ed. 160p. (Orig.). 1993. pap. 5.99 (*0-7847-0078-8*, 11-39958) Standard Pub.
Russell, Bruce, jt. auth. see Magoldi, Mary.
Russell, Bruce, ed. see Magoldi, Mary.

Russell, Ching Y. A Day on a Shrimp Boat. Littlejohn, Beth, ed. Russell, Phillip K., illus. 57p. (gr. 3-6). 1993. 13.95 (*0-87844-120-4*) Sandlapper Pub Co.
This book is written by Ching Yeung Russell, who grew up in China & Hong Kong. The story, both educational & entertaining is told through the eyes of her 12-year old son Jeremy. Although eating shrimp & other delicacies of the sea is a favorite pastime of people who visit & live in the South Carolina low country, few of us know what goes into bringing the shrimp to the table. The Russell family decided to find out. They hitched a ride with Captain Bob Upton of St. Helena Island & spent a day on his trawler the "Abbie R." A DAY ON A SHRIMP BOAT allows the reader to share in their experience. This book is written for young readers, aged 9 & up, but is suitable for kids of all ages. The book's black & white photographs are provided by the author's husband Phillip K. Russell. *Publisher Provided Annotation.*

Russell, Dale A. & Acorn, John. The Thiny Perfect Dinosaur Book, Bones, Egg, & Poster: Presenting Tyrannosaurus Rex. Kish, Ely, illus. 1993. pap. 12.95 incl. poster & toy (*0-8362-4216-5*) Andrews & McMeel.
—The Tiny Perfect Dinosaur Book, Bones, Egg & Poster: Presenting Leptoceratops. Kish, Ely, illus. 32p. (Orig.). 1991. pap. 10.95 (*0-8362-4213-0*) Andrews & McMeel.

Russell, David A. Superbike. 180p. (gr. 4-7). 1993. 3.95 (*1-883174-00-7*) High Octane.
SUPERBIKE - Who wouldn't want a bike that flies! Bernard & his wise-cracking parrot take off for adventure in SUPERBIKE. Befriended by an older man with magical powers, Bernard overcomes adversity on the soccer field & off. SUPERBIKE is a grand tale in the tradition of E.T. with the homespun flavor of Mayberry R. F.D. Utilizing self-esteem, conflict-resolution & multi-cultural themes, author David Allen Russell vividly captures the challenges of childhood in the nineties in a thrill packed book that makes fantasy a reality. Ages 9-12. Soon to be a major motion picture. Join the SUPERBIKE CLUB. Read the SUPERBIKE JOURNAL. Call High Octane Press at 800-769-7620 for information. *Publisher Provided Annotation.*

Russell, George L. Map of American Indian Nations. 3rd ed. (gr. 6 up). 1993. pap. 15.00 (*1-881933-02-4*) Thundbird Ent.
Russell, Georgina. Christmas Bear. Press, Jenny, illus. 28p. (ps-2). 1991. 8.95 (*0-7214-5331-7*, S808) Ladybird Bks.
—Christmas Bear (Miniature) Press, Jenny, illus. 28p. (gr. 3-4). 1992. 2.95 (*0-7214-3506-8*) Ladybird Bks.
Russell, Hannah. Songs about the Sky. rev. ed. Hendrickson, June, illus. 18p. 1988. pap. 4.50 (*0-9614089-2-8*) Avitar Bks.
Russell, Helen D. Come in This House. 230p. (gr. 6-12). 1982. lib. bdg. 14.95 (*0-934188-07-6*) Evans Pubns.
Russell, Jervis F., ed. see Potter, Velma M.
Russell, Jim, illus. Moses of the Bullrushes: Retold by Catherine Storr. 32p. (gr. k-4). 1984. 14.65 (*0-8172-1990-0*, Raintree Children's Books Belitha Press Ltd. - London) Raintree Steck-V.
Russell, Joanne, jt. auth. see Porizkova, Paulina.
Russell, John J., intro. by. National Trade & Professional Associations of the U. S., 1994. 29th ed. LC 74-64774. 650p. 1994. pap. 75.00 (*1-880873-06-0*) Columbia Bks.
—State & Regional Associations of the U. S., 1994. 6th ed. 550p. 1994. pap. write for info. (*1-880873-07-9*) Columbia Bks.
Russell, Katherine B. Guiding Children Through Grief: A Resource Manual of Recommended Books to Help Young Children Cope with Death, Dying & Grief. Russell, Katherine B., illus. 48p. (Orig.). (ps up). 1989. pap. 5.25 (*1-56123-036-7*) Centering Corp.
Russell, Ken, jt. auth. see Carter, Philip J.
Russell, Ken, jt. ed. see Carter, Philip.
Russell, Ken A., jt. auth. see Carter, Philip J.
Russell, Kenneth L., ed. How in Parliamentary Procedure. 5th ed. (Illus.). 74p. (gr. 9-12). 1990. pap. text ed. 2.50 (*0-8134-2871-8*, 2171) Interstate.
Russell, Marjorie H., ed. & illus. see Fuller, Joy.
Russell, Naomi. The Stream. Russell, Naomi, illus. LC 90-47497. 32p. (ps-1). 1991. 9.95 (*0-525-44729-6*, DCB) Dutton Child Bks.
Russell, P. Craig. Fairy Tales of Oscar Wilde, Vol. 1. (Illus.). 48p. (gr. 3-7). 1992. 15.95x (*1-56163-056-X*) NBM.
—Fairy Tales of Oscar Wilde, Vol. 2. (gr. 3-7). 1994. 15.95x (*1-56163-085-3*) NBM.
Russell, Pamela & Stone, Beth. Do You Have a Secret? How to Get Help for Scary Secrets. McKee, Mary, illus. LC 85-27986. 36p. (Orig.). (ps-2). 1986. pap. 6.95 (*0-89638-098-X*) CompCare.
Russell, Robin. Soccer. LC 91-9556. (Illus.). 32p. (gr. 2-5). 1992. PLB 11.90 (*0-531-18462-5*, Pub. by Bookwright Pr) Watts.
Russell, Sharman. Frederick Douglass. King, Coretta Scott, intro. by. (Illus.). 112p. (Orig.). (gr. 5 up). 1988. 17.95 (*1-55546-580-3*); pap. 9.95 (*0-7910-0204-7*) Chelsea Hse.
Russell, Sharman A. The Humpbacked Fluteplayer. LC 92-44492. 1994. write for info. (*0-679-82408-1*); write for info. (*0-679-92408-6*) Knopf Bks Yng Read.
Russell, Willey. Our Day Out. 56p. 1988. pap. 7.95 (*0-413-54870-8*, A0201) Heinemann.
Russell, William F., ed. Animal Families of the Wild: A Read-Aloud Collection of Animal Literature. Butler, John, illus. LC 89-22226. 96p. (gr. 2 up). 1990. 12.95 (*0-517-57358-X*); PLB 13.99 (*0-517-57359-8*) Crown Bks Yng Read.
Russell, William F., selected by. Classics to Read Aloud to Your Children. LC 84-7033. 320p. (ps-5). 1984. 19.00 (*0-517-55404-6*, Crown) Crown Pub Group.

Russman, Penny & Wright, Sheila. Changing Bodies, Changing Goals & Other Youth Soccer Stories. Woog, Dan, ed. Wright, Curt, photos by. LC 84-71345. (Illus.). 96p. (Orig.). (gr. 5-9). 1984. pap. 5.95 (*0-9613538-0-5*) Ascot Pr.
Russo, Carol, illus. Three-D Hidden Pictures Activity Book. 16p. 1991. pap. write for info. (*1-56156-012-X*) Kidsbks.
Russo, David A. Go for It! Races, Rescues, Treasure Hunts & More. (gr. 4-7). 1992. pap. 12.00 (*0-671-73350-8*, S&S BFYR) S&S Trade.
Russo, Joe, et al. Planet of the Apes Revisited. Heston, Charlton, intro. by. (Illus.). 212p. (Orig.). (gr. 9-12). 1991. pap. 12.95 (*0-9627508-2-4*) Image NY.
Russo, Marisabina. Alex Is My Friend. LC 90-24643. 32p. 1992. 14.00 (*0-688-10418-5*); PLB 13.93 (*0-688-10419-3*) Greenwillow.
—I Don't Want to Go Back to School. LC 93-5479. 1994. write for info. (*0-688-04601-0*); PLB write for info. (*0-688-04602-9*) Greenwillow.
—The Line-up Book. Russo, Marisabina, illus. LC 85-24907. 24p. (Illus.). 1986. 11.75 (*0-688-06204-0*); PLB 11.88 (*0-688-06205-9*) Greenwillow.
—The Line Up Book. (Illus.). 24p. (ps-3). 1992. pap. 3.99 (*0-14-054471-2*) Puffin Bks.
—Only Six More Days. LC 86-19586. (Illus.). 32p. (ps-3). 1988. 11.95 (*0-688-07071-X*); lib. bdg. 11.88 (*0-688-07072-8*) Greenwillow.
—Only Six More Days. (Illus.). 32p. (ps-3). 1992. pap. 3.99 (*0-14-054473-9*) Puffin Bks.
—Time to Wake Up. LC 93-18185. (Illus.). 32p. (ps up). 1994. write for info. (*0-688-04599-5*); PLB write for info. (*0-688-04600-2*) Greenwillow.
—Trade-in Mother. LC 91-47681. (Illus.). 32p. (ps up). 1993. 14.00 (*0-688-11416-4*); PLB 13.93 (*0-688-11417-2*) Greenwillow.
—A Visit to Oma. LC 89-77716. (Illus.). 32p. (ps up). 1991. 13.95 (*0-688-09623-9*); PLB 13.88 (*0-688-09624-7*) Greenwillow.
—Waiting for Hannah. LC 87-37201. (Illus.). 32p. (ps up). 1989. 13.95 (*0-688-08015-4*); PLB 13.88 (*0-688-08016-2*) Greenwillow.
—Where Is Ben? LC 88-34916. (Illus.). 32p. (ps up). 1990. 12.95 (*0-688-08011-1*); PLB 12.88 (*0-688-08013-8*) Greenwillow.
—Where Is Ben? LC 92-8627. (gr. 4 up). 1992. Repr. of 1990 ed. 4.50 (*0-14-054474-7*) Puffin Bks.
—Why Do Grown-Ups Have All the Fun? Russo, Marisabina, illus. LC 86-4644. 24p. (ps-3). 1987. 11.75 (*0-688-06625-9*); PLB 11.88 (*0-688-06626-7*) Greenwillow.
Russo, Monica. Dinosaur Dots. (Illus.). 96p. 1991. pap. 4.95 (*0-8069-7388-9*) Sterling.
—Fantastic Creatures Dot-to-Dot: Connect the Dots & Color. (Illus.). 80p. (gr. 2-8). 1992. pap. 4.95 (*0-8069-8438-4*) Sterling.
—The Insect Almanac: A Year-Round Activity Guide. Byron, Kevin, photos by. LC 90-22438. (Illus.). 136p. (gr. 4-10). 1992. pap. 7.95 (*0-8069-7455-9*) Sterling.
—Prehistoric Animals Dot-to-Dot. (Illus.). 80p. (gr. 2-6). 1993. pap. 4.95 (*0-8069-8746-4*) Sterling.
—The Tree Almanac: A Year-Round Activity Guide. Byron, Kevin, photos by. LC 92-41347. (Illus.). (gr. 3 up). 1993. 14.95 (*0-8069-1252-9*) Sterling.
—Weird & Wonderful Dinosaur Facts. LC 92-45770. (Illus.). 96p. (gr. 6-12). 1992. 12.95 (*0-8069-8320-5*) Sterling.
—Weird & Wonderful Dinosaur Facts. LC 92-45770. (Illus.). 96p. (gr. 3-9). 1993. pap. 3.95 (*0-8069-8321-3*) Sterling.
Russo, Tom. Microchemistry: For High School Chemistry. rev. ed. Stone, Harry, ed. (Illus.). 90p. (gr. 9-12). 1990. lab manual 15.80 (*1-877960-05-5*, 4-400) Kemtec Educ.
Russomanno, Diane. Beneath the Deep Blue Sea. 32p. 1991. pap. text ed. write for info. (*1-880501-02-3*) Know Booster.
—The Journey Begins. 32p. 1991. pap. text ed. write for info. (*1-880501-03-1*) Know Booster.
—The Never Ending Journey of the Written Word. 32p. 1991. pap. text ed. write for info. (*1-880501-00-7*) Know Booster.
—The Story of the American Flag. 32p. 1991. pap. text ed. write for info. (*1-880501-01-5*) Know Booster.
Rust, Graham. Secret Garden Notebook. (gr. 4-7). 1991. 12.95 (*0-87923-890-9*) Godine.
Rutan, Debbie. Big Promises for Little People. 30p. 1991. pap. 3.95 (*0-685-39073-X*) Green & White Pub.
—Big Promises for Little People. Raber, Rhonda, illus. (gr. 1-3). 1991. pap. 3.95 (*0-9624777-2-9*) Green & White Pub.
Ruth, Eddie. How Do the Ducks Know? (Illus.). 28p. (Orig.). (gr. 1-4). 1981. pap. 2.50 saddle-stitched (*0-911826-18-1*, 5448) Am Atheist.
Ruth, Marianne & Locke, Raymond F. Cruel City. LC 90-52813. (Illus.). 240p. 1991. 19.95 (*0-915677-48-2*) Roundtable Pub.
Ruth, Susan, jt. auth. see Ruth, Trevor.
Ruth, Trevor & Ruth, Susan. Drawing My View. Ruth, Trevor & Ruth, Susan, illus. LC 93-11827. 1994. 4.95 (*0-383-03730-1*) SRA Schl Grp.
Rutherford, Erica. The Owl & the Pussycat. (Illus.). 24p. (gr. 1 up). 1986. text ed. 12.95 (*0-88776-181-X*, Dist. by Univ. of Toronto Pr) Tundra Bks.
Rutkovsky, Paul. Get. Rutkovsky, Paul, illus. 72p. (Orig.). (gr. 9-12). 1987. pap. 8.95 (*0-89822-048-3*) Visual Studies.

Rutland. Supercars. rev. ed. (gr. 4-6). 1984. (Usborne-Hayes); pap. 5.95 (*0-86020-181-3*) EDC.
—Supertrains. rev. ed. (gr. 4-6). 1984. (Usborne-Hayes); pap. 5.95 (*0-86020-180-5*) EDC.
Rutland, Jonathan. The Age of Steam. Atkinson, Mike, illus. LC 87-4788. 24p. (gr. 2-5). 1987. pap. 2.95 (*0-394-89216-X*, Random Juv) Random Bks Yng Read.
—Amazing Fact Book of Cars. (Illus.). 32p. (gr. 4-8). 1987. PLB 14.95s.p. (*0-87191-843-9*) Creative Ed.
—Amazing Fact Book of Ships. (Illus.). 32p. (gr. 4-8). 1987. PLB 14.95s.p. (*0-87191-849-8*) Creative Ed.
—Built to Speed. Atkinson, Mike, illus. LC 87-4790. 24p. (gr. 2-5). 1987. lib. bdg. 5.99 (*0-394-99215-6*); (Random Juv) Random Bks Yng Read.
Rutledge, Carol, jt. auth. see Rieck, Sondra.
Rutledge, Paul. The Vietnamese in America. (Illus.). 64p. (gr. 5 up). 1987. PLB 15.95 (*0-8225-0235-6*); pap. 5.95 (*0-8225-1033-2*) Lerner Pubns.
Rutman, Shereen. Cat Man. Jarka, Jeff, illus. 16p. (ps). 1993. wkbk. 2.25 (*1-56293-327-2*) McClanahan Bk.
—Hug a Cub. Silverstein, Cindy, illus. 16p. (ps). 1993. wkbk. 2.25 (*1-56293-323-X*) McClanahan Bk.
—My Wet Hen. Mahan, Ben, illus. 16p. (ps). 1993. wkbk. 2.25 (*1-56293-324-8*) McClanahan Bk.
—Snap the Clam. DeMarco, Susanne, illus. 16p. (ps). 1993. wkbk. 2.25 (*1-56293-326-4*) McClanahan Bk.
—The Thin Pig. Mahan, Ben, illus. 16p. (ps). 1993. wkbk. 2.25 (*1-56293-325-6*) McClanahan Bk.
—Top Hog. Neidigh, Sherry, illus. 16p. (ps). 1993. wkbk. 2.25 (*1-56293-322-1*) McClanahan Bk.
Rutman, Shereen G. All about Me. Jordan, Polly, illus. 32p. (ps). 1992. wkbk. 1.95 (*1-56293-174-1*) McClanahan Bk.
—My Book of Opposites. Loh, Carolyn, illus. 32p. (ps). 1992. wkbk. 1.95 (*1-56293-171-7*) McClanahan Bk.
—Numbers. Loh, Carolyn, illus. 16p. (ps). 1992. wkbk. 2.25 (*1-56293-191-1*) McClanahan Bk.
—Observing. Banta, Susan, illus. 16p. (ps). 1992. wkbk. 2.25 (*1-56293-189-X*) McClanahan Bk.
—Rhyming Words. Morgado, Richard, illus. 32p. (ps). 1992. wkbk. 1.95 (*1-56293-170-9*) McClanahan Bk.
—Shapes. Heck, Ed, illus. 16p. (ps). 1992. wkbk. 2.25 (*1-56293-188-1*) McClanahan Bk.
—Sorting. Banta, Susan, illus. 16p. (ps). 1992. wkbk. 2.25 (*1-56293-186-5*) McClanahan Bk.
—What Belongs? Morgado, Richard, illus. 32p. (ps). 1992. wkbk. 1.95 (*1-56293-175-X*) McClanahan Bk.
Ruuth, Marianne. Eddie: Eddie Murphy from A to Z. (Orig.). (ps-10). 1985. pap. 2.95 (*0-87067-717-9*) Holloway.
—The Supremes: Triumph & Tragedy. (ps-10). 1987. pap. 3.95 (*0-87067-725-X*, BH725) Holloway.
Ryan, Alizabeth A. Straight Talk about Drugs & Alcohol. 144p. (gr. 7 up). 1992. pap. 3.99 (*0-440-21392-4*, LFL) Dell.
Ryan, Betsy. Secret Love. LC 90-24058. 128p. (gr. 5-9). 1991. pap. text ed. 2.95 (*0-8167-1913-6*) Troll Assocs.
Ryan, Cary, ed. Louisa May Alcott: Her Girlhood Diary. Graham, Mark, illus. LC 93-22343. 56p. (gr. 5 up). 1993. PLB 14.95 (*0-8167-3139-X*); pap. write for info. (*0-8167-3150-0*) BrdgeWater.
Ryan, Cheli D. Hildilid's Night. reissued ed. Lobel, Arnold, illus. LC 86-5294. 32p. (ps-2). 1986. RSBE 13.95 (*0-02-777260-8*, Macmillan Child Bk) Macmillan Child Grp.
Ryan, Chris. The Eiffel Tower. 48p. (gr. 3-4). 1991. PLB 11.95 (*1-56065-026-5*) Capstone Pr.
Ryan, Deborah. Women's Basketball Drills: Conditioning Drills. (Orig.). (gr. 7 up). 1988. pap. 6.95 (*0-932741-58-4*) Championship Bks & Vid Prodns.
Ryan, Elizabeth. Hablemos Francamente de las Drogas y el Alcohol. Terrana, Alma, tr. from ENG. (SPA.). 160p. 1990. 16.95x (*0-8160-2496-0*) Facts on File.
—How to Be a Better Writer. LC 91-3135. 96p. (gr. 5-9). 1992. lib. bdg. 9.89 (*0-8167-2462-8*); pap. text ed. 3.95 (*0-8167-2463-6*) Troll Assocs.
—How to Build a Better Vocabulary. LC 91-3136. 112p. (gr. 5-9). 1992. lib. bdg. 9.89 (*0-8167-2460-1*); pap. text ed. 3.95 (*0-8167-2461-X*) Troll Assocs.
—How to Make Grammar Fun - & Easy! LC 91-12525. 112p. (gr. 5-9). 1992. lib. bdg. 9.89 (*0-8167-2456-3*); pap. text ed. 3.95 (*0-8167-2457-1*) Troll Assocs.
—How to Write Better Book Reports. LC 91-3134. 80p. (gr. 5-9). 1992. lib. bdg. 9.89 (*0-8167-2458-X*); pap. text ed. 3.95 (*0-8167-2459-8*) Troll Assocs.
Ryan, Elizabeth A. Straight Talk about Drugs & Alcohol. 160p. 1989. 16.95x (*0-8160-1525-2*) Facts on File.
—Straight Talk about Parents. 144p. 1989. 16.95x (*0-8160-1526-0*) Facts on File.
—Straight Talk about Parents. 132p. (gr. 7 up). 1992. pap. 3.99 (*0-440-21300-2*, LFL) Dell.
—Straight Talk about Prejudice. 128p. (gr. 5-12). 1992. lib. bdg. 16.95x (*0-8160-2488-X*) Facts on File.
—Student Thesaurus. O'Boyle, Rick, illus. LC 89-20305. 160p. (gr. 2-8). 1990. PLB 14.89 (*0-8167-1914-4*); pap. text ed. 6.95 (*0-8167-1856-3*) Troll Assocs.
Ryan, Elizabeth A., ed. see Dentemaro, Christine & Kranz, Rachel.
Ryan, Elizabeth A., ed. see Mufson, Susan & Kranz, Rachel.
Ryan, Elizabeth A., ed. see Rendon, Marion B. & Kranz, Rachel.
Ryan, John. Bad Year for Dragons. LC 89-37279. 28p. (gr. 1-4). 1989. 7.95 (*0-8192-1512-0*) Morehouse Pub.
—Jonah, a Whale of a Tale. Ryan, John, illus. 32p. (gr. 1-7). 1992. 11.95 (*0-7459-2150-7*) Lion USA.

—Mabel & the Tower of Babel. Ryan, John, illus. 32p. (gr. 4-8). 1990. 9.99 (0-7459-1742-9) Lion USA.
—Pugwash & the Buried Treasure. (Illus.). 32p. (gr. k-2). 1994. 19.95 (0-370-30338-5, Pub. by Bodley Head UK) Trafalgar.
—Pugwash & the Ghost Ship. Ryan, John, illus. LC 68-23218. (gr. k-3). 1968. 21.95 (0-87599-146-7) S G Phillips.
—Pugwash & the Sea Monster. (Illus.). 32p. (gr. k-2). 1994. 19.95 (0-370-10793-4, Pub. by Bodley Head UK) Trafalgar.
Ryan, Joseph. U. S. Employment Opportunities. 300p. (gr. 12). looseleaf (includes quarterly updates) 184.00 (0-937801-01-1) Wash Res Assocs.
Ryan, Margaret. How to Read & Write Poems. LC 91-12141. (Illus.). 64p. (gr. 5-8). 1991. PLB 12.90 (0-531-20043-4) Watts.
Ryan, Mary C. Frankie's Run. (gr. 3-7). 1987. 12.95 (0-316-76370-5) Little.
—Frankie's Run. 1988. pap. 2.50 (0-380-70537-0, Flare) Avon.
—Ghosts, Gadgets & Great Ideas. 96p. (Orig.). (gr. 3). 1993. pap. 3.50 (0-380-76537-3, Camelot Young) Avon.
—Me Two. (gr. 4-7). 1991. 15.95 (0-316-76376-4) Little.
—Me Two. 192p. 1993. pap. 3.50 (0-380-71826-X, Camelot) Avon.
—My Friend, O'Connell. 112p. (Orig.). (gr. 3-4). 1991. pap. 2.95 (0-380-76145-9, Camelot) Avon.
—The Voice from the Mendelsohns Maple. Roman, Irena, illus. LC 89-31569. 132p. (gr. 5-7). 1990. 13.95 (0-316-76360-8) Little.
—The Voice from the Mendelsohns' Maple. 144p. (gr. 5). 1992. pap. 3.50 (0-380-71140-0, Camelot) Avon.
—Who Says I Can't? 160p. (gr. 12 up). 1988. 12.95 (0-316-76374-8) Little.
—Who Says I Can't? 160p. (gr. 12 up). 1990. pap. 2.95 (0-380-70804-3, Flare) Avon.
Ryan, Mary E. Dance a Step Closer. 1988. pap. 2.95 (0-440-20127-6, LFL) Dell.
—I'd Rather Be Dancing. (gr. 7 up). 1989. 14.95 (0-440-50121-0) Delacorte.
—Me, My Sister, & I. LC 92-368. 1992. pap. 15.00 (0-671-73851-8, S&S BFYR) S&S Trade.
—My Sister Is Driving Me Crazy. LC 90-41263. 224p. (gr. 5-9). 1991. pap. 15.00 jacketed, 3-pc. bdg. (0-671-73203-X, S&S BFYR) S&S Trade.
—My Sister Is Driving Me Crazy. LC 90-41263. 224p. (gr. 5-9). 1993. pap. 3.95 (0-671-86694-X, Half Moon Bks) S&S Trade.
Ryan, Meg, jt. ed. see Roberts, Tom.
Ryan, Nan. Cloud Castle. (Orig.). (gr. 7 up). 1987. pap. 4.50 (0-440-11306-7) Dell.
Ryan, Pam M. One Hundred Is a Family. (Illus.). 32p. 1994. write for info. (1-56282-672-7); PLB write for info. (1-56282-673-5) Hyprn Child.
Ryan, Pat. The America's Cup. (gr. 5 up). 1992. PLB 14.95 (0-88682-532-6) Creative Ed.
—Chicago Bears. 48p. (gr. 4 up). 1991. 14.95 (0-88682-361-7) Creative Ed.
—Green Bay Packers. (gr. 4 up). 1991. PLB 14.95s.p. (0-88682-367-6) Creative Ed.
—The Heavyweight Championship. (gr. 5 up). 1992. PLB 14.95 (0-88682-554-7) Creative Ed.
—Los Angeles Raiders. (gr. 4 up). 1991. PLB 14.95s.p. (0-88682-371-4) Creative Ed.
—New York Giants. (gr. 4 up). 1991. PLB 14.95s.p. (0-88682-377-3) Creative Ed.
—New York Jets. (gr. 4 up). 1991. PLB 14.95s.p. (0-88682-378-1) Creative Ed.
—Pittsburgh Steelers. 1991. PLB 14.95s.p. (0-88682-380-3) Creative Ed.
Ryan, Perry T. The Criminal Justice System of Kentucky. (Illus.). 50p. (gr. 9). 1990. pap. 4.95 (0-9625504-1-8) P T Ryan.
Ryan, Peter. Explorers & Mapmakers. Molan, Chris, illus. LC 89-31824. 48p. (gr. 4-7). 1990. 14.95 (0-525-67285-0, Lodestar Bks) Dutton Child Bks.
Ryan, Roberta. The George Lozuks: Doers of the Word. LC 85-6615. (gr. 4-6). 1985. 5.95 (0-8054-4293-6, 4242-93) Broadman.
Ryan, Steve. Challenging Pencil Puzzlers. (Illus.). 96p. (gr. 6-10). 1992. pap. 4.95 (0-8069-8752-9) Sterling.
—Pencil Puzzlers. (Illus.). 96p. (gr. 7-12). 1992. pap. 4.95 (0-8069-8542-9) Sterling.
—Test Your Puzzle IQ. (Illus.). 96p. (gr. 10-12). 1993. pap. 4.95 (0-8069-0344-9) Sterling.
Ryan, Tom K. Let'er Rip Tumbleweeds. (Illus.). 128p. 1981. pap. 1.50 (0-449-13894-1, GM) Fawcett.
Ryan, Will. Grundo Beach Party. Becker, Mary, ed. High, David, et al, illus. 26p. (ps). 1986. 9.95 (0-934323-35-6); pre-programmed audio cass. tape incl. Alchemy Comms.
—Lost in Boggley Woods. Becker, Mary, ed. High, David, et al, illus. 26p. (ps). 1986. 9.95 (0-934323-38-0); pre-programmed audio cass. tape incl. Alchemy Comms.
Rybak, Bob. I Love a Mystery. (Illus.). 176p. (gr. 3-7). 1992. 12.95 (0-86653-655-8, GA1388) Good Apple.
—I Love an Adventure. (Illus.). 176p. (gr. 3-7). 1992. 12.95 (0-86653-656-6, GA1389) Good Apple.
Rybak, Sharon. ABC Clip & Copy. 208p. (ps-2). 1991. 14.95 (0-86653-586-1, GA1301) Good Apple.
—Good Apple Lesson Organizer. 128p. (gr. k-6). 1990. 19.95 (0-86653-563-2, GA1149) Good Apple.
—Launching a Great Year. 144p. (ps-2). 1989. 11.95 (0-86653-507-1, GA1093) Good Apple.

—Teach Smarter, Not Harder. 128p. (gr. k-6). 1991. 11.95 (0-86653-620-5, GA1339) Good Apple.
Rybakov, V., ed. see Sesemann, Dimitri.
Rybolt, Thomas R. & Mebane, Robert C. Environmental Experiments about Air. LC 92-26297. (Illus.). 96p. (gr. 4-9). 1993. lib. bdg. 16.95 (0-89490-409-4) Enslow Pubs.
—Environmental Experiments about Land. (Illus.). 96p. (gr. 4-9). 1993. lib. bdg. 16.95 (0-89490-411-6) Enslow Pubs.
—Environmental Experiments about Life. (Illus.). 96p. (gr. 4-9). 1993. lib. bdg. 16.95 (0-89490-412-4) Enslow Pubs.
—Environmental Experiments about Water. (Illus.). 96p. (gr. 4-9). 1993. lib. bdg. 16.95 (0-89490-410-8) Enslow Pubs.
—Science Experiments for Young People Series, 4 bks. (Illus.). 96p. (gr. 4-9). 1993. Set. lib. bdg. 67.80 (0-89490-448-5) Enslow Pubs.
Rybolt, Thomas R., jt. auth. see Mebane, Robert C.
Rydberg, Denny. How to Survive College. 160p. (Orig.). 1989. pap. 8.99 (0-310-35351-3) Zondervan.
Rydell, Wendy. All about Islands. Burns, Ray, illus. LC 83-4833. 32p. (gr. 3-6). 1984. lib. bdg. 10.59 (0-89375-975-9); pap. text ed. 2.95 (0-89375-976-7) Troll Assocs.
—Discovering Fossils. Burns, Ray, illus. LC 83-4832. 32p. (gr. 3-6). 1984. lib. bdg. 10.59 (0-89375-973-2); pap. text ed. 2.95 (0-89375-974-0) Troll Assocs.
Ryden, Hope. America's Bald Eagle. (Illus.). 64p. 1992. pap. 9.95 (1-55821-141-1) Lyons & Burford.
—The Beaver. (Illus.). 64p. 1992. pap. 9.95 (1-55821-142-X) Lyons & Burford.
—The Bobcat. (Illus.). 64p. 1992. pap. 9.95 (1-55821-143-8) Lyons & Burford.
—Joey: The Story of a Baby Kangaroo. Ryden, Hope, photos by. LC 93-15419. (Illus.). 40p. 1994. 15.00 (0-688-12744-4, Tambourine Bks); PLB 14.93 (0-688-12745-2, Tambourine Bks) Morrow.
—The Little Deer of the Florida Keys. rev. ed. (Illus.). 64p. (Orig.). (gr. 5 up). 1986. 13.95 (0-912451-13-0); pap. 8.95 (0-912451-14-9) Florida Classics.
—Wild Animals of Africa ABC. LC 89-2529. (Illus.). 32p. (ps-3). 1989. 12.95 (0-525-67290-7, Lodestar Bks) Dutton Child Bks.
—Wild Animals of America ABC. Ryden, Hope, photos by. LC 87-31127. (Illus.). (ps-3). 1988. 14.95 (0-525-67245-1, Lodestar Bks) Dutton Child Bks.
Ryden, Hope, photos by & text by. The Raggedy Red Squirrel. (Illus.). 48p. (gr. k-3). 1992. 16.00 (0-525-67400-4, Lodestar Bks) Dutton Child Bks.
—Your Cat's Wild Cousins. (Illus.). 48p. (gr. 2-5). 1992. 16.00 (0-525-67354-7, Lodestar Bks) Dutton Child Bks.
Ryden, Hope, photos by. Your Dog's Wild Cousins. LC 93-26855. 1994. write for info. (0-525-67482-9, Lodestar Bks) Dutton Child Bks.
Ryder, Donald G. The Inside Story: Living & Learning Through Life's Storms. Mullen, Don, illus. LC 85-27780. 56p. (gr. 7 up). 1985. 14.95 (0-935973-38-9) Ryder Pub Co.
Ryder, Joan. The Snail's Spell. Cherry, Lynn, illus. (gr. 3-8). 1988. pap. 4.99 (0-14-050891-0, Puffin) Puffin Bks.
Ryder, Joanne. The Bear on the Moon. Lacey, Carol, illus. LC 89-13133. 32p. (gr. 1 up). 1991. 14.95 (0-688-08109-6); PLB 14.88 (0-688-08110-X) Morrow Jr Bks.
—Catching the Wind. Rothman, Michael, illus. LC 88-23446. 32p. (gr. k up). 1989. 14.95 (0-688-07170-8); PLB 13.88 (0-688-07171-6, Morrow Jr Bks) Morrow Jr Bks.
—Chipmunk Song. Cherry, Lynne, illus. LC 86-19786. 32p. (ps-3). 1987. 13.95 (0-525-67191-9, Lodestar Bks); pap. 4.95 (0-525-67312-1, Lodestar Bks) Dutton Child Bks.
—Dancers in the Garden. Lopez, Judith, illus. LC 89-10555. 32p. (gr. k-4). 1992. 15.95 (0-87156-578-1) Sierra.
—Earthdance. 1994. write for info. (0-8050-2678-9) H Holt & Co.
—First Grade Elves. Lewin, Betsy, illus. LC 93-25543. 32p. (ps-2). 1993. PLB 9.89 (0-8167-3010-5); pap. text ed. 2.95 (0-8167-3011-3) Troll Assocs.
—First Grade Ladybugs. Lewin, Betsy, illus. LC 92-43528. 32p. (ps-2). 1993. PLB 9.79 (0-8167-3006-7); pap. text ed. 2.95 (0-8167-3007-5) Troll Assocs.
—The Goodbye Walk. Haeffele, Deborah, illus. LC 92-10325. 32p. (gr. k-3). 1993. 13.99 (0-525-67405-5, Lodestar Bks) Dutton Child Bks.
—Hello, First Grade. Lewin, Betsy, illus. LC 93-9041. 32p. (ps-2). 1993. PLB 9.89 (0-8167-3008-3); pap. text ed. 2.95 (0-8167-3009-1) Troll Assocs.
—Hello, Tree! Hays, Michael, illus. 32p. (gr. k-3). 1991. 13.95 (0-525-67310-5, Lodestar Bks) Dutton Child Bks.
—A House by the Sea. Sweet, Melissa, illus. LC 93-22149. 1994. write for info. (0-688-12675-8); PLB write for info. (0-688-12676-6) Morrow Jr Bks.
—Inside Turtle's Shell & Other Poems of the Field. Bonners, Susan, illus. LC 84-833. 64p. (gr. 2-5). 1985. RSBE 12.95 (0-02-778010-4, Macmillan Child Bk) Macmillan Child Grp.
—Lizard in the Sun. Rothman, Michael, illus. LC 89-33886. 32p. (gr. k up). 1990. 13.95 (0-688-07172-4); PLB 13.88 (0-688-07173-2, Morrow Jr Bks) Morrow Jr Bks.

—Mockingbird Morning. Nolan, Dennis, illus. LC 88-21305. 32p. (gr. k-3). 1989. RSBE 14.95 (0-02-777961-0, Four Winds) Macmillan Child Grp.
—My Father's Hands. Graham, Mark, illus. LC 93-27116. 1994. write for info. (0-688-09189-X); PLB write for info. (0-688-09190-3) Morrow Jr Bks.
—The Night Flight. Schwartz, Amy, illus. LC 85-4482. 32p. (gr. k-3). 1985. RSBE 13.95 (0-02-778020-1, Four Winds) Macmillan Child Grp.
—One Small Fish. Schwartz, Carol, illus. LC 92-21563. 32p. (gr. k up). 1993. 15.00 (0-688-07059-0); PLB 14.93 (0-688-07060-4) Morrow Jr Bks.
—The Snail's Spell. Cherry, Lynne, illus. 32p. (ps-3). 1992. PLB 14.00 (0-670-84385-7) Viking Child Bks.
—Step into the Night. Nolan, Dennis, illus. LC 87-37982. 32p. (gr. k-3). 1988. RSBE 14.95 (0-02-777951-3, Four Winds) Macmillan Child Grp.
—Under Your Feet. Nolan, Dennis, illus. LC 89-33897. 32p. (gr. k-3). 1990. RSBE 14.95 (0-02-777955-6, Four Winds) Macmillan Child Grp.
—Walt Disney's Bambi. Feldman, Thea, ed. LC 92-54875. (Illus.). 64p. (gr. 2-6). 1993. pap. 2.95 (1-56282-444-9) Disney Pr.
—When the Woods Hum. LC 90-37879. (Illus.). 32p. (gr. 1 up). 1991. 13.95 (0-688-07057-4); PLB 13.88 (0-688-07058-2, Morrow Jr Bks) Morrow Jr Bks.
—Where Butterflies Grow. Cherry, Lynne, illus. LC 88-37989. 32p. (ps-3). 1989. 14.00 (0-525-67284-2, Lodestar Bks) Dutton Child Bks.
—White Bear, Ice Bear. Rothman, Michael, illus. LC 87-36781. 32p. (gr. k-3). 1989. 13.95 (0-688-07174-0); PLB 13.88 (0-688-07175-9, Morrow Jr Bks) Morrow Jr Bks.
—Winter Whale. Rothman, Michael, illus. LC 90-19174. 32p. (gr. k up). 1991. 13.95 (0-688-07176-7); PLB 13.88 (0-688-07177-5) Morrow Jr Bks.
Ryder, Joanne, adapted by. Hardie Gramatky's Little Toot. Ross, Larry, illus. 32p. (ps-2). 1988. pap. 2.25 (0-448-34301-0, Platt & Munk Pubs) Putnam Pub Group.
Ryder, Joanne, ed. Sea Elf. Rothman, Michael, illus. LC 92-27608. 32p. (gr. k up). 1993. 15.00 (0-688-10060-0); PLB 14.93 (0-688-10061-9) Morrow Jr Bks.
Ryder, Joanne, adapted by. Walt Disney's Bambi. Pacheco, David & Clay, Jesse, illus. LC 92-54876. 96p. 1993. 14.95 (1-56282-442-2); PLB 14.89 (1-56282-443-0) Disney Pr.
Ryder, Marion C. Scuttle Watch. Raymond, Alex, illus. LC 79-91988. 286p. (gr. 4-12). 1979. pap. 4.95 (0-88492-034-8) W S Sullwold.
Ryder, Virginia P. Three Monkey Saves the Day. Kilgore, Julia, illus. 21p. (Orig.). (gr. k-12). 1991. pap. 8.95 (0-935098-04-6) Amigo Pr.
Rye, Jennifer. Look...What Do You See? Kerins, Tony, illus. LC 90-40231. 32p. (gr. k-3). 1991. lib. bdg. 11.59 (0-8167-2122-X); pap. text ed. 3.95 (0-8167-2123-8) Troll Assocs.
Rye, Jennifer, jt. auth. see Wood, Nicholas.
Ryen, Dag. Traces: The Story of Lexington's Past. Crow, James L. & Finkel, Becky, illus. 177p. (gr. 4 up). 1987. text ed. 13.95 (0-912839-08-2) Lexington-Fayette.
Ryland, Cynthia. Couple of Kooks: And Other Stories about Love. 1992. pap. 3.50 (0-440-21210-3) Dell.
—Soda Jerk. Calatanotto, Peter, illus. 48p. (gr. 7 up). 1993. pap. 3.95 (0-688-12654-5, Pub. by Beech Tree Bks) Morrow.
Rylant, Cynthia. All I See. Catalanotto, Peter, illus. LC 88-42547. 32p. (gr. k-2). 1988. 15.95 (0-531-05777-1); PLB 15.99 (0-531-08377-2) Orchard Bks Watts.
—All I See. Catalanotto, Peter, illus. LC 88-42547. 32p. (gr. k-2). 1994. pap. 5.95 (0-531-07048-4) Orchard Bks Watts.
—An Angel for Solomon Singer. Catalanotto, Peter, illus. LC 91-15957. 32p. 1992. 14.95 (0-531-05978-2); lib. bdg. 14.99 (0-531-08578-3) Orchard Bks Watts.
—Appalachia: The Voices of Sleeping Birds. (Illus.). 32p. (gr. k up). 1991. 14.95 (0-15-201605-8) HarBrace.
—Best Wishes. Ontal, Carlo, illus. 32p. (gr. 2-5). 1992. 12.95 (1-878450-20-4) R Owen Pubs.
—Birthday Presents. Stevenson, Sucie, illus. LC 87-5485. 32p. (ps-1). 1987. 13.95 (0-531-05705-4); PLB 13.99 (0-531-08305-5) Orchard Bks Watts.
—Birthday Presents. LC 87-5485. (Illus.). 32p. (ps-1). 1991. pap. 4.95 (0-531-07026-3) Orchard Bks Watts.
—A Blue-Eyed Daisy. LC 84-21554. 112p. (gr. 5-7). 1985. SBE 11.95 (0-02-777960-2, Bradbury Pr) Macmillan Child Grp.
—A Blue-Eyed Daisy. (gr. k-6). 1987. pap. 3.50 (0-440-40927-6, YB) Dell.
—But I'll Be Back Again. LC 93-16188. (Illus.). 64p. (gr. 7 up). 1993. pap. 3.95 (0-688-12653-7, Pub. by Beech Tree Bks) Morrow.
—But I'll Be Back Again: An Album. LC 88-17860. (Illus.). 80p. (gr. 5-7). 1989. 12.95 (0-531-05806-9); PLB 12.99 (0-531-08406-X) Orchard Bks Watts.
—Children of Christmas: Stories for the Season. Schindler, S. D., illus. LC 87-1690. 48p. (gr. 3 up). 1987. 13.95 (0-531-05706-2); PLB 13.99 (0-531-08306-3) Orchard Bks Watts.
—Children of Christmas: Stories for the Season. Schindler, S. D., illus. LC 87-1690. 48p. (gr. 3 up). 1993. pap. 5.95 (0-531-07042-5) Orchard Bks Watts.
—A Couple of Kooks: And Other Stories about Love. LC 90-30646. 112p. (gr. 7 up). 1990. 14.95 (0-531-05900-6); PLB 14.99 (0-531-08500-7) Orchard Bks Watts.

—The Dreamer. Moser, Barry, illus. LC 93-19915. 32p. (ps-6). 1993. 14.95 (0-590-47341-7) Scholastic Inc.
—Every Living Thing. Schindler, Stephen D., illus. LC 85-7701. 96p. (gr. 5-7). 1985. SBE 12.95 (0-02-777200-4, Bradbury Pr) Macmillan Child Grp.
—Every Living Thing. Schindler, S. D., illus. LC 88-19359. 96p. (gr. 5 up). 1988. pap. 3.50 (0-689-71263-4, Aladdin) Macmillan Child Grp.
—The Everyday Books: Everyday Children. Rylant, Cynthia, illus. LC 92-40932. 14p. (ps-k). 1993. bds. 4.95 with rounded corners (0-02-778022-8, Bradbury Pr) Macmillan Child Grp.
—The Everyday Books: Everyday Garden. Rylant, Cynthia, illus. LC 92-40542. 14p. (ps-k). 1993. bds. 4.95 with rounded corners (0-02-778023-6, Bradbury Pr) Macmillan Child Grp.
—The Everyday Books: Everyday House. Rylant, Cynthia, illus. LC 92-40943. 14p. (ps-k). 1993. bds. 4.95 with rounded corners (0-02-778024-4, Bradbury Pr) Macmillan Child Grp.
—The Everyday Books: Everyday Pets. Rylant, Cynthia, illus. LC 92-40934. 14p. (ps-k). 1993. bds. 4.95 with rounded corners (0-02-778025-2, Bradbury Pr) Macmillan Child Grp.
—The Everyday Books: Everyday Town. LC 92-40541. (Illus.). 14p. (ps-k). 1993. bds. 4.95 (0-02-788026-5, Bradbury Pr) Macmillan Child Grp.
—Everyday Town. Rylant, Cynthia, illus. LC 92-40541. 14p. (ps-k). 1993. bds. 4.95 with rounded corners (0-02-778026-0, Bradbury Pr) Macmillan Child Grp.
—A Fine White Dust. LC 86-1003. 120p. (gr. 6-8). 1986. SBE 13.95 (0-02-777240-3, Bradbury Pr) Macmillan Child Grp.
—A Fine White Dust. (gr. k-6). 1987. pap. 3.50 (0-440-42499-2, YB) Dell.
—Henry & Mudge & the Bedtime Thumps. Stevenson, Sucie, illus. LC 89-49529. 40p. (gr. 1-3). 1991. RSBE 12.95 (0-02-778006-6, Bradbury Pr) Macmillan Child Grp.
—Henry & Mudge & the Careful Cousin: The Thirteenth Book of Their Adventures. Stevenson, Sucie, illus. LC 92-12851. 48p. (gr. 1-3). 1994. RSBE 13.95 (0-02-778021-X, Bradbury Pr) Macmillan Child Grp.
—Henry & Mudge & the Forever Sea. Stevenson, Sucie, illus. LC 92-28646. 48p. (gr. 1-3). 1993. pap. 3.95 (0-689-71701-6, Aladdin) Macmillan Child Grp.
—Henry & Mudge & the Forever Sea: The Sixth Book of Their Adventures. Stevenson, Sucie, illus. LC 88-6130. 48p. (gr. 1-3). 1989. RSBE 12.95 (0-02-778007-4, Bradbury Pr) Macmillan Child Grp.
—Henry & Mudge & the Happy Cat. Stevenson, Sucie, illus. LC 88-18855. 48p. (gr. 1-3). 1990. RSBE 12.95 (0-02-778008-2, Bradbury Pr) Macmillan Child Grp.
—Henry & Mudge & the Happy Cat: The Eighth Book of Their Adventures. Stevenson, Sucie, illus. LC 93-10797. 48p. (gr. 1-3). 1994. pap. 3.95 (0-689-71791-1, Aladdin) Macmillan Child Grp.
—Henry & Mudge & the Long Weekend. Stevenson, Sucie, illus. LC 90-26799. 40p. (gr. 1-3). 1992. RSBE 12.95 (0-02-778013-9, Bradbury Pr) Macmillan Child Grp.
—Henry & Mudge & the Wild Wind. Stevenson, Sucie, illus. LC 91-12644. 40p. (gr. 1-3). 1993. RSBE 12.95 (0-02-778014-7, Bradbury Pr) Macmillan Child Grp.
—Henry & Mudge: Book & Toy. (Illus.). 48p. (ps-3). 1992. pap. 19.95 (0-689-71648-6, Aladdin) Macmillan Child Grp.
—Henry & Mudge Get the Cold Shivers: The Seventh Book of Their Adventures. Stevenson, Sucie, illus. LC 88-18854. 48p. (gr. 1-3). 1989. RSBE 12.95 (0-02-778011-2, Bradbury Pr) Macmillan Child Grp.
—Henry & Mudge in Puddle Trouble. LC 89-39810. (Illus.). 48p. (gr. 1-3). 1990. pap. 3.95 (0-689-71400-9, Aladdin) Macmillan Child Grp.
—Henry & Mudge in Puddle Trouble: The Second Book of Their Adventures. Stevenson, Sucie, illus. LC 86-13616. 48p. (gr. 1-3). 1987. RSBE 12.95 (0-02-778002-3, Bradbury Pr) Macmillan Child Grp.
—Henry & Mudge in the Green Time. Stevenson, Sucie, illus. LC 91-24942. 48p. (gr. 1-3). 1992. pap. 3.95 (0-689-71582-X, Aladdin) Macmillan Child Grp.
—Henry & Mudge in the Green Time: The Third Book of Their Adventures. Stevenson, Sucie, illus. LC 86-26386. 48p. (gr. 1-3). 1987. RSBE 12.95 (0-02-778003-1, Bradbury Pr) Macmillan Child Grp.
—Henry & Mudge in the Sparkle Days: The Fifth Book of Their Adventures. Stevenson, Sucie, illus. LC 86-23432. 40p. (gr. 1-3). 1988. RSBE 12.95 (0-02-778005-8, Bradbury Pr) Macmillan Child Grp.
—Henry & Mudge in the Sparkle Days: The Fifth Book of Their Adventures. Stevenson, Sucie, illus. LC 92-42535. 48p. (gr. 1-3). 1993. pap. 3.95 (0-689-71752-0, Aladdin) Macmillan Child Grp.
—Henry & Mudge Take the Big Test: The Tenth Book of Their Adventures. Stevenson, Sucie, illus. LC 90-35171. 40p. (gr. 1-3). 1991. RSBE 12.95 (0-02-778009-0, Bradbury Pr) Macmillan Child Grp.
—Henry & Mudge: The First Book. Stevenson, Sucie, illus. LC 89-39809. 48p. (gr. 1-3). 1990. pap. 3.95 (0-689-71399-1, Aladdin) Macmillan Child Grp.
—Henry & Mudge: The First Book of Their Adventures. Stevenson, Suzie, illus. LC 86-13615. 40p. (gr. 1-3). 1987. RSBE 12.95 (0-02-778001-5, Bradbury Pr) Macmillan Child Grp.
—Henry & Mudge under the Yellow Moon. Stevenson, Sucie, illus. LC 91-23135. 48p. (gr. 1-3). 1992. pap. 3.95 (0-689-71580-3, Aladdin) Macmillan Child Grp.
—Henry & Mudge under the Yellow Moon: The Fourth Book of Their Adventures. Stevenson, Sucie, illus. LC 86-26390. 48p. (gr. 1-3). 1987. RSBE 12.95 (0-02-778004-X, Bradbury Pr) Macmillan Child Grp.
—I Have Seen Castles. LC 92-42325. (gr. 5 up). 1993. 10. 95 (0-15-238003-5) HarBrace.
—A Kindness. LC 88-1454. 128p. (gr. 7 up). 1988. 13.95 (0-531-05767-4); PLB 13.99 (0-531-08367-5) Orchard Bks Watts.
—Miss Maggie. DiGrazia, Thomas, illus. LC 82-18206. 32p. (gr. k-3). 1983. 12.95 (0-525-44048-8, DCB) Dutton Child Bks.
—Missing May. LC 91-23303. 96p. (gr. 6 up). 1992. 13. 95 (0-531-05996-0); lib. bdg. 13.99 (0-531-08596-1) Orchard Bks Watts.
—Missing May. 1993. pap. 3.99 (0-440-40865-2) Dell.
—Mr. Griggs' Work. Downing, Julie, illus. LC 88-1484. 32p. (ps-2). 1989. 14.95 (0-531-05769-0); PLB 14.99 (0-531-08369-1) Orchard Bks Watts.
—Mr. Griggs' Work. Downing, Julie, illus. LC 88-1484. 32p. (ps-2). 1993. pap. 5.95 (0-531-07037-9) Orchard Bks Watts.
—Mr. Putter & Tabby Pour the Tea. Howard, Arthur, illus. LC 93-21470. (ps-6). 1994. write for info. (0-15-256255-9) HarBrace.
—Mr. Putter & Tabby Walk the Dog. Howard, Arthur, illus. LC 93-21467. (ps-6). 1994. write for info. (0-15-256259-1) HarBrace.
—Night in the Country. Szilagyi, Mary, illus. LC 85-70963. 32p. (ps-1). 1986. RSBE 14.95 (0-02-777210-1, Bradbury Pr) Macmillan Child Grp.
—Night in the Country. Szilagyi, Mary, illus. LC 90-1043. 32p. (ps-2). 1991. pap. 4.95 (0-689-71473-4, Aladdin) Macmillan Child Grp.
—The Relatives Came. Gammell, Stephen, illus. LC 85-10929. 32p. (ps-2). 1985. RSBE 14.95 (0-02-777220-9, Bradbury Pr) Macmillan Child Grp.
—The Relatives Came. Gammell, Stephen, illus. LC 92-41394. 32p. (ps-2). 1993. pap. 4.95 (0-689-71738-5, Aladdin) Macmillan Child Grp.
—Soda Jerk. Catalanotto, Peter, illus. LC 89-35654. 48p. (gr. 7 up). 1990. 14.95 (0-531-05864-6); PLB 14.99 (0-531-08464-7) Orchard Bks Watts.
—This Year's Garden. Szilagyi, Mary, illus. LC 84-10974. 32p. (gr. k-3). 1984. RSBE 13.95 (0-02-777970-X, Bradbury Pr) Macmillan Child Grp.
—This Year's Garden. Szilagyi, Mary, illus. LC 86-22224. 32p. (ps-3). 1987. pap. 4.95 (0-689-71122-0, Aladdin) Macmillan Child Grp.
—Waiting to Waltz: A Childhood. Gammell, Stephen, illus. LC 84-11030. 48p. (gr. 6-8). 1984. 12.95 (0-02-778000-7, Bradbury Pr) Macmillan Child Grp.
—When I Was Young in the Mountains. LC 81-5359. (Illus.). 32p. (ps-3). 1982. 14.00 (0-525-42525-X, 0966-290, DCB); pap. 3.99 (0-525-44198-0, DCB) Dutton Child Bks.

Rymer, Alta M. Beep-Bap-Zap-Jack. LC 74-20428. (Illus.). (gr. 4-6). 1974. 10.00 (0-9600792-0-3) Rymer Bks.
—Captain Zomo. Rymer, Alta M., illus. LC 79-67651. 48p. (Orig.). (gr. 4-6). 1985. pap. text ed. 12.50 (0-9600792-2-X) Rymer Bks.
—Hobart & Humbert Gruzzy. Rymer, Alta M., illus. LC 85-61860. 28p. (Orig.). (gr. 4-6). 1988. pap. 12.50 (0-9600792-6-2) Rymer Bks.
—Oopletrump's Odyssey, Bk. 4. Rymer, Alta M., illus. LC 85-61861. 38p. (Orig.). (gr. 4-6). 1987. pap. text ed. 12.50 (0-9600792-5-4) Rymer Bks.
—Stars of Obron: Chambo Returns. Rymer, Alta M., illus. 48p. (Orig.). (gr. 4-6). 1987. pap. text ed. 12.50 (0-9600792-3-8) Rymer Bks.
—Up from Uzam. Rymer, Alta M., illus. 28p. (Orig.). (gr. 2-4). 1987. pap. 11.50 (0-9600792-8-9) Rymer Bks.

Rynbach, Iris Van see Van Rynbach, Iris.

Rynerson, Fred. Exploring & Mining for Gems & Gold in the West. (Illus.). 204p. (gr. 4 up). 1970. 16.95 (0-911010-61-0); pap. 8.95 (0-911010-60-2) Naturegraph.

Rystrom, Zella R. Tales of a Nebraska Country Girl. Lawrence, Terry, illus. 48p. (Orig.). (gr. 6-12). 1988. pap. 4.95 (0-936015-18-7) Pocahontas Pr.

Ryuichi, Hirokawa. Children of the World: Jordan. LC 87-42618. (Illus.). 64p. (gr. 5-6). 1987. PLB 19.93 (1-55532-224-7) Gareth Stevens Inc.

S

Saal, Jocelyn & Burman, Margaret. On Thin Ice. 181p. (gr. 6 up). 1983. pap. 1.95 (0-553-17070-8) Bantam.

Saban, Vera. Jennie Barnes: Right Now Forever. Mills, Janie, illus. LC 90-39763. 130p. (Orig.). (gr. 4-6). 1990. pap. 6.95 (0-914565-34-6, Timbertrails) Capstan Pubns.
—Johnny Egan of the Paintrock. Saban, Sonja, illus. LC 85-30958. 130p. (Orig.). (gr. 4-8). 1986. pap. 6.95 (0-914565-13-3, Timbertrails) Capstan Pubns.
—Test of the Tenderfoot. Elliott, Tony, illus. LC 89-9729. 147p. (gr. 5-8). 1989. 6.95 (0-914565-35-4, Timbertrails) Capstan Pubns.

Sabatier, C. & Sabatier, R. Livre des Chansons de France: Deuxieme Livre. (FRE.). 163p. (gr. 4-9). 1990. 17.95 (2-07-039529-4) Schoenhof.
—Livre des Chansons de France: Troisieme Livre. (FRE.). 165p. (gr. 4-9). 1990. 17.95 (2-07-039535-9) Schoenhof.

Sabatier, R., jt. auth. see Sabatier, C.

Sabatier, Roland. Livre des Chansons de France. (FRE.). 157p. (gr. 4-9). 1991. 17.95 (2-07-039516-2) Schoenhof.

Sabato, Olive. An Easy Guide for Creating Computer Graphics in the Elementary Schools, Videocassette - Glenville School Computer Graphics. Tucker, Dorothy, ed. Dunlap, Susan, intro. by. (Illus.). 36p. (gr. 5-6). 1987. pap. 19.95 lesson plan (0-942475-06-2); videocassette 39.95, (0-942475-05-4) ArtsAmerica.

Sabbagh, Antoine. Europe in the Middle Ages. Ridett, Anthea, tr. from FRE. Morgan, illus. 77p. (gr. 7 up). 1988. 17.98 (0-382-09484-0) Silver Burdett Pr.

Sabia, Joe. The Modern Day Nursery Rhymes of Poppa Gander. (Illus., Orig.). 1993. pap. 7.95 (0-86534-196-6) Sunstone Pr.

Sabin, Fran & Sabin, Lou. The Great Easter Egg Mystery. Trivas, Irene, illus. LC 81-7610. 48p. (gr. 2-4). 1982. PLB 10.89 (0-89375-604-0); pap. text ed. 3.50 (0-89375-605-9) Troll Assocs.
—The Great Santa Claus Mystery. Trivas, Irene, illus. LC 81-7530. 48p. (gr. 2-4). 1982. PLB 10.89 (0-89375-602-4); pap. text ed. 3.50 (0-89375-603-2) Troll Assocs.
—Mystery at the Jellybean Factory. Trivas, Irene, illus. LC 81-10388. 48p. (gr. 2-4). 1982. PLB 10.89 (0-89375-600-8); pap. text ed. 3.50 (0-89375-601-6) Troll Assocs.
—Secret of the Haunted House. Trivas, Irene, illus. LC 81-8751. 48p. (gr. 2-4). 1982. PLB 10.89 (0-89375-598-2); pap. text ed. 3.50 (0-89375-599-0) Troll Assocs.

Sabin, Francene. Africa. Eitzen, Allan, illus. LC 84-10560. 32p. (gr. 3-6). 1985. PLB 9.49 (0-8167-0236-5); pap. text ed. 2.95 (0-8167-0237-3) Troll Assocs.
—Amazing World of Ants. Conner, Eulala, illus. LC 81-7492. 32p. (gr. 2-4). 1982. PLB 11.59 (0-89375-558-3); pap. text ed. 2.95 (0-89375-559-1) Troll Assocs.
—Amelia Earhart: Adventure in the Sky. Milone, Karen, illus. LC 82-15987. 48p. (gr. 4-6). 1983. PLB 10.79 (0-89375-839-6); pap. text ed. 3.50 (0-89375-840-X) Troll Assocs.
—American Revolution. Baxter, Robert, illus. LC 84-2582. 32p. (gr. 3-6). 1985. PLB 9.49 (0-8167-0136-9); pap. text ed. 2.95 (0-8167-0137-7) Troll Assocs.
—Arctic & Antarctic Regions. Eitzen, Allan, illus. LC 84-2730. 32p. (gr. 3-6). 1985. PLB 9.49 (0-8167-0234-9); pap. text ed. 2.95 (0-8167-0235-7) Troll Assocs.
—Computers. Veno, Joseph, illus. LC 84-2708. 32p. (gr. 3-6). 1985. PLB 9.49 (0-8167-0314-0); pap. text ed. 2.95 (0-8167-0315-9) Troll Assocs.
—Courage of Helen Keller. LC 81-23109. (Illus.). 48p. (gr. 4-6). 1982. PLB 10.79 (0-89375-754-3); pap. text ed. 3.50 (0-89375-755-1) Troll Assocs.
—Ecosystems & Food Chains. Cumings, Art, illus. LC 84-2707. 32p. (gr. 3-6). 1985. PLB 9.49 (0-8167-0282-9); pap. text ed. 2.95 (0-8167-0283-7) Troll Assocs.
—Elizabeth Blackwell: The First Woman Doctor. LC 81-23140. (Illus.). 48p. (gr. 4-6). 1982. PLB 10.79 (0-89375-756-X); pap. text ed. 3.50 (0-89375-757-8) Troll Assocs.
—Freedom Documents. Dole, Bob, illus. LC 84-8596. 32p. (gr. 3-6). 1985. PLB 9.49 (0-8167-0238-1); pap. text ed. 2.95 (0-8167-0239-X) Troll Assocs.
—Harriet Tubman. Frenck, Hal, illus. LC 84-2667. 32p. (gr. 3-6). 1985. PLB 9.49 (0-8167-0158-X); pap. text ed. 2.95 (0-8167-0159-8) Troll Assocs.
—Human Body. Sibley, Don, illus. LC 84-2591. 32p. (gr. 3-6). 1985. PLB 9.49 (0-8167-0170-9); pap. text ed. 2.95 (0-8167-0171-7) Troll Assocs.
—Jackie Robinson. Sheean, Michael, illus. LC 84-2603. 32p. (gr. 3-6). 1985. PLB 9.49 (0-8167-0164-4); pap. text ed. 2.95 (0-8167-0165-2) Troll Assocs.
—Jesse Owens, Olympic Hero. Frenck, Hal, illus. LC 85-1101. 48p. (gr. 4-6). 1986. lib. bdg. 10.79 (0-8167-0551-8); pap. text ed. 3.50 (0-8167-0552-6) Troll Assocs.
—Lewis & Clark. Lawn, John, illus. LC 84-2642. 32p. (gr. 3-6). 1985. PLB 9.49 (0-8167-0224-1); pap. text ed. 2.95 (0-8167-0225-X) Troll Assocs.
—Louis Pasteur: Young Scientist. Swan, Susan, illus. LC 82-15924. 48p. (gr. 4-6). 1983. PLB 10.79 (0-89375-853-1); pap. text ed. 3.50 (0-89375-854-X) Troll Assocs.
—The Magic String. Snyder, Joel, illus. LC 81-4076. 32p. (gr. k-2). 1981. PLB 11.59 (0-89375-547-8); pap. 2.95 (0-89375-548-6) Troll Assocs.
—Mammals. Veno, Joseph, illus. LC 84-2658. 32p. (gr. 3-6). 1985. PLB 9.49 (0-8167-0208-X); pap. text ed. 2.95 (0-8167-0209-8) Troll Assocs.
—Microbes & Bacteria. Acosta, Andres, illus. LC 84-2749. 32p. (gr. 3-6). 1985. PLB 9.49 (0-8167-0232-2); pap. text ed. 2.95 (0-8167-0233-0) Troll Assocs.
—Mozart, Young Music Genius. Miyake, Yoshi, illus. LC 89-33980. 48p. (gr. 4-6). 1990. lib. bdg. 10.79 (0-8167-1773-7); pap. text ed. 3.50 (0-8167-1774-5) Troll Assocs.
—Oceans. Goldsborough, June, illus. LC 84-8590. 32p. (gr. 3-6). 1985. PLB 9.49 (0-8167-0216-0); pap. text ed. 2.95 (0-8167-0217-9) Troll Assocs.
—Pioneers. Frenck, Hal, illus. LC 84-2580. 32p. (gr. 3-6). 1985. PLB 9.49 (0-8167-0120-2); pap. text ed. 2.95 (0-8167-0121-0) Troll Assocs.

—Rachel Carson: Friend of the Earth. Miyake, Yoshi, illus. LC 92-5825. 48p. (gr. 4-6). 1992. PLB 10.79 (*0-8167-2821-6*); pap. text ed. 3.50 (*0-8167-2822-4*) Troll Assocs.
—Renaissance. Frenck, Hal, illus. LC 84-2695. 32p. (gr. 3-6). 1985. PLB 9.49 (*0-8167-0246-2*); pap. text ed. 2.95 (*0-8167-0247-0*) Troll Assocs.
—Robert Louis Stevenson: Young Storyteller. Johnson, Pamela, illus. LC 91-3924. 48p. (gr. 4-6). 1992. PLB 10.79 (*0-8167-2507-1*); pap. text ed. 3.50 (*0-8167-2508-X*) Troll Assocs.
—Rockets & Satellites. Maccabe, Richard, illus. LC 84-2738. 32p. (gr. 3-6). 1985. PLB 9.49 (*0-8167-0288-8*); pap. text ed. 2.95 (*0-8167-0289-6*) Troll Assocs.
—Seasons. Burns, Raymond, illus. LC 84-2713. 32p. (gr. 3-6). 1985. PLB 9.49 (*0-8167-0308-6*); pap. text ed. 2.95 (*0-8167-0309-4*) Troll Assocs.
—South America. Eitzen, Allan, illus. LC 84-8586. 32p. (gr. 3-6). 1985. PLB 9.49 (*0-8167-0292-6*); pap. text ed. 2.95 (*0-8167-0293-4*) Troll Assocs.
—Swamps & Marshes. Flynn, Barbara, illus. LC 84-2717. 32p. (gr. 3-6). 1985. PLB 9.49 (*0-8167-0280-2*); pap. text ed. 2.95 (*0-8167-0281-0*) Troll Assocs.
—Whales & Dolphins. Johnson, Pamela, illus. LC 84-2709. 32p. (gr. 3-6). 1985. PLB 9.49 (*0-8167-0286-1*); pap. text ed. 2.95 (*0-8167-0287-X*) Troll Assocs.
—Women Who Win. 160p. (gr. 5 up). 1977. pap. 1.50 (*0-440-99643-0*, LFL) Dell.
—Wonders of the Forest. Willard, Michael, illus. LC 81-7401. 32p. (gr. 2-4). 1982. PLB 11.59 (*0-89375-572-9*); pap. text ed. 2.95 (*0-89375-573-7*) Troll Assocs.
—Wonders of the Pond. Grant, Leigh, illus. LC 81-7407. 32p. (gr. 2-4). 1982. PLB 11.59 (*0-89375-576-1*); pap. text ed. 2.95 (*0-89375-577-X*); cassette 9.95 (*0-685-04956-6*) Troll Assocs.
—Young Abigail Adams. Miyake, Yoshi, illus. LC 91-17112. 48p. (gr. 4-6). 1992. PLB 10.79 (*0-8167-2503-9*); pap. text ed. 3.50 (*0-8167-2504-7*) Troll Assocs.
—Young Eleanor Roosevelt. Ramsey, Marcy D., illus. LC 89-33939. 48p. (gr. 4-6). 1990. PLB 10.79 (*0-8167-1779-6*); pap. text ed. 3.50 (*0-8167-1780-X*) Troll Assocs.
—Young Queen Elizabeth. Lawn, John, illus. LC 89-33941. 48p. (gr. 4-6). 1990. PLB 10.79 (*0-8167-1785-0*); pap. text ed. 3.50 (*0-8167-1786-9*) Troll Assocs.
—Young Thomas Jefferson. Baxter, Robert, illus. LC 85-1093. 48p. (gr. 4-6). 1985. lib. bdg. 10.79 (*0-8167-0561-5*); pap. text ed. 3.50 (*0-8167-0562-3*) Troll Assocs.
Sabin, Lou. Teddy Roosevelt, Rough Rider. Baxter, Robert, illus. LC 85-1090. 48p. (gr. 4-6). 1986. lib. bdg. 10.79 (*0-8167-0555-0*); pap. text ed. 3.50 (*0-8167-0556-9*) Troll Assocs.
Sabin, Lou, jt. auth. see Sabin, Fran.
Sabin, Louis. Agriculture. Veno, Joseph, illus. LC 84-2710. 32p. (gr. 3-6). 1985. PLB 9.49 (*0-8167-0204-7*); pap. text ed. 2.95 (*0-8167-0205-5*) Troll Assocs.
—Amazing World of Butterflies & Moths. Helmer, Jean C., illus. LC 81-7504. 32p. (gr. 2-4). 1982. PLB 11.59 (*0-89375-560-5*); pap. text ed. 2.95 (*0-89375-561-3*); cassette 9.95 (*0-685-04943-4*) Troll Assocs.
—Ancient China. Frenck, Hal, illus. LC 84-2729. 32p. (gr. 3-6). 1985. PLB 9.49 (*0-8167-0316-7*); pap. text ed. 2.95 (*0-8167-0317-5*) Troll Assocs.
—Andrew Jackson, Frontier Patriot. Smolinski, Dick, illus. LC 85-1094. 48p. (gr. 4-6). 1986. lib. bdg. 10.79 (*0-8167-0547-X*); pap. text ed. 3.50 (*0-8167-0548-8*) Troll Assocs.
—Asia. Eitzen, Allan, illus. LC 84-10559. 32p. (gr. 3-6). 1985. PLB 9.49 (*0-8167-0274-8*); pap. text ed. 2.95 (*0-8167-0275-6*) Troll Assocs.
—Birthday Surprise. Magine, John, illus. LC 81-2632. 32p. (gr. k-2). 1981. PLB 11.59 (*0-89375-527-3*); pap. text ed. 2.95 (*0-89375-528-1*) Troll Assocs.
—Canada. Eitzen, Allan, illus. LC 84-40437. 32p. (gr. 3-6). 1985. PLB 9.49 (*0-8167-0302-7*); pap. text ed. 2.95 (*0-8167-0303-5*) Troll Assocs.
—Colonial Life in America. Frenck, Hal, illus. LC 84-2669. 32p. (gr. 3-6). 1985. PLB 9.49 (*0-8167-0138-5*); pap. text ed. 2.95 (*0-8167-0139-3*) Troll Assocs.
—Congressperson. Dole, Bob, illus. LC 84-2651. 32p. (gr. 3-6). 1985. PLB 9.49 (*0-8167-0266-7*); pap. text ed. 2.95 (*0-8167-0267-5*) Troll Assocs.
—Fish. Helmer, Jean C., illus. LC 84-2624. 32p. (gr. 3-6). 1985. PLB 9.49 (*0-8167-0178-4*); pap. text ed. 2.95 (*0-8167-0179-2*) Troll Assocs.
—Fossils. Maccabe, Richard, illus. LC 84-2716. 32p. (gr. 3-6). 1985. PLB 9.49 (*0-8167-0228-4*); pap. text ed. 2.95 (*0-8167-0229-2*) Troll Assocs.
—Grasslands. Watling, James, illus. LC 84-2661. 32p. (gr. 3-6). 1985. PLB 9.49 (*0-8167-0214-4*); pap. text ed. 2.95 (*0-8167-0215-2*) Troll Assocs.
—The Great Houdini, Daring Escape Artist. Eitzen, Allan, illus. LC 89-5170. 48p. (gr. 4-6). 1990. PLB 10.79 (*0-8167-1769-9*); pap. text ed. 3.50 (*0-8167-1770-2*) Troll Assocs.
—Jim Beckwourth: Adventures of a Mountain Man. Krupp, Marion, illus. LC 92-8717. 48p. (gr. 4-6). 1992. PLB 10.79 (*0-8167-2819-4*); pap. text ed. 3.50 (*0-8167-2820-8*) Troll Assocs.
—Johnny Appleseed. Smolinski, Dick, illus. LC 84-2732. 32p. (gr. 3-6). 1985. PLB 9.49 (*0-8167-0220-9*); pap. text ed. 2.95 (*0-8167-0221-7*) Troll Assocs.

—Ludwig Van Beethoven: Young Composer. Beier, Ellen, illus. LC 91-18616. 48p. (gr. 4-6). 1992. PLB 10.79 (*0-8167-2511-X*); pap. text ed. 3.50 (*0-8167-2512-8*) Troll Assocs.
—Marie Curie. Eitzen, Allan, illus. LC 84-2654. 32p. (gr. 3-6). 1985. PLB 9.49 (*0-8167-0162-8*); pap. text ed. 2.95 (*0-8167-0163-6*) Troll Assocs.
—Middle Ages. Frenck, Hal, illus. LC 84-2670. 32p. (gr. 3-6). 1985. PLB 9.49 (*0-8167-0174-1*); pap. text ed. 2.95 (*0-8167-0175-X*) Troll Assocs.
—Narcissa Whitman: Brave Pioneer. LC 81-23066. (Illus.). 48p. (gr. 4-6). 1982. PLB 10.79 (*0-89375-762-4*); pap. text ed. 3.50 (*0-89375-763-2*) Troll Assocs.
—North America. Eitzen, Allan, illus. LC 84-8625. 32p. (gr. 3-6). 1985. PLB 9.49 (*0-8167-0240-3*); pap. text ed. 2.95 (*0-8167-0241-1*) Troll Assocs.
—Patrick Henry: Voice of American Revolution. LC 81-23068. (Illus.). 48p. (gr. 4-6). 1982. PLB 10.79 (*0-89375-764-0*); pap. text ed. 3.50 (*0-89375-765-9*) Troll Assocs.
—Paul Bunyan. Smolinski, Dick, illus. LC 84-2747. 32p. (gr. 3-6). 1985. PLB 9.49 (*0-8167-0254-3*); pap. text ed. 2.95 (*0-8167-0255-1*) Troll Assocs.
—Plants, Seeds & Flowers. Moylan, Holly, illus. LC 84-2720. 32p. (gr. 3-6). 1985. PLB 9.49 (*0-8167-0226-8*); pap. text ed. 2.95 (*0-8167-0227-6*) Troll Assocs.
—Reptiles & Amphibians. Zink-White, Nancy, illus. LC 84-8445. 32p. (gr. 3-6). 1985. PLB 9.49 (*0-8167-0294-2*); pap. text ed. 2.95 (*0-8167-0295-0*) Troll Assocs.
—Roberto Clemente: Young Baseball Hero. DeJohn, Marie, illus. LC 91-17851. 48p. (gr. 4-6). 1992. PLB 10.79 (*0-8167-2509-8*); pap. text ed. 3.50 (*0-8167-2510-1*) Troll Assocs.
—Space Exploration & Travel. Moylan, Holly, illus. LC 84-2698. 32p. (gr. 3-6). 1985. PLB 9.49 (*0-8167-0258-6*); pap. text ed. 2.95 (*0-8167-0259-4*) Troll Assocs.
—Stars. Acosta, Andres, illus. LC 84-2605. 32p. (gr. 3-6). 1985. PLB 9.49 (*0-8167-0152-0*); pap. text ed. 2.95 (*0-8167-0153-9*) Troll Assocs.
—Television & Radio. Veno, Joseph, illus. LC 84-8446. 32p. (gr. 3-6). 1985. PLB 9.49 (*0-8167-0310-8*); pap. text ed. 2.95 (*0-8167-0311-6*) Troll Assocs.
—Thomas Alva Edison: Young Inventor. Ulrich, George, illus. LC 82-15889. 48p. (gr. 4-6). 1983. PLB 10.79 (*0-89375-841-8*); pap. text ed. 3.50 (*0-89375-842-6*) Troll Assocs.
—Weather. Veno, Joseph, illus. LC 84-2706. 32p. (gr. 3-6). 1985. PLB 9.49 (*0-8167-0200-4*); pap. text ed. 2.95 (*0-8167-0201-2*) Troll Assocs.
—Wilbur & Orville Wright: The Flight to Adventure. Lawn, John, illus. LC 82-15879. 48p. (gr. 4-6). 1983. PLB 10.79 (*0-89375-851-5*); pap. text ed. 3.50 (*0-89375-852-3*) Troll Assocs.
—Willie Mays, Young Superstar. Jones, John R., illus. LC 89-33979. 48p. (gr. 4-6). 1990. PLB 10.79 (*0-8167-1775-3*); pap. text ed. 3.50 (*0-8167-1776-1*) Troll Assocs.
—Wonders of the Desert. Baldwin-Ford, Pamela, illus. LC 81-7397. 32p. (gr. 2-4). 1982. PLB 11.59 (*0-89375-574-5*); pap. text ed. 2.95 (*0-89375-575-3*) Troll Assocs.
—Wonders of the Sea. Dodson, Bert, illus. LC 81-3334. 32p. (gr. 2-4). 1982. PLB 11.59 (*0-89375-578-8*); pap. text ed. 2.95 (*0-89375-579-6*) Troll Assocs.
—Young Mark Twain. Burns, Ray, illus. LC 89-33982. 48p. (gr. 4-6). 1990. PLB 10.79 (*0-8167-1783-4*); pap. text ed. 3.50 (*0-8167-1784-2*) Troll Assocs.
Sabin, Tracy. A Visit to the North Pole. (ps up). 1993. 15.95 (*0-8167-3137-3*) BrdgeWater.
Sabraw, John. I Wouldn't Be Scared. LC 88-23352. (Illus.). 32p. (ps-1). 1989. 13.95 (*0-531-05818-2*); PLB 13.99 (*0-531-08418-3*) Orchard Bks Watts.
Sabuda, Robert. Saint Valentine. Sabuda, Robert, illus. LC 91-25012. 32p. (gr. 1-4). 1992. SBE 14.95 (*0-689-31762-X*, Atheneum Child Bk) Macmillan Child Grp.
—Tutankhamen's Gift. Sabuda, Robert, illus. LC 93-5401. 32p. (gr. 1-4). 1994. SBE 14.95 (*0-689-31818-9*, Atheneum Child Bk) Macmillan Child Grp.
Saburi, Eugene, tr. see Miyazaki, Hayao.
Saccaro, Margherita, jt. auth. see Turin, Adela.
Sacco, William, et al. Dynamic Programming: An Elegant Problem Solver. (Illus.). 62p. (gr. 9 up). 1987. pap. text ed. 9.95 (*0-939765-05-5*, G102) Janson Pubns.
—Glyphs: Getting the Picture. (Illus.). 56p. (Orig.). (gr. 7 up). 1987. pap. text ed. 9.95 (*0-939765-07-1*, G104) Janson Pubns.
—Information Theory: Saving Bits. (Illus.). 64p. (Orig.). (gr. 9 up). 1988. pap. text ed. 9.95 (*0-939765-25-X*, G113) Janson Pubns.
—Mathematics & Medicine: How Serious Is the Injury? (Illus.). 61p. (Orig.). (gr. 9 up). 1987. pap. text ed. 9.95 (*0-939765-06-3*, G103) Janson Pubns.
Saccone, Vivian R. ABC's of What Is Black. Saccone, Vivian R., illus. LC 92-84105. 44p. (ps-3). Date not set. 5.95 (*1-55523-583-2*) Winston-Derek.
Sachan, Louis. Wayside School Is Falling Down. Schick, Joel, illus. LC 88-674. 192p. (gr. 3-7). 1989. 12.95 (*0-688-07868-0*) Lothrop.
Sachar, A. L. History of the Jews. rev. ed. (gr. 6 up). 1967. pap. text ed. 27.96 (*0-07-553559-9*); pap. text ed. 20.95 (*0-685-02836-4*) McGraw.

Sachar, Louis. The Boy Who Lost His Face. LC 88-22622. 192p. (gr. 5-9). 1989. 11.95 (*0-394-82863-1*); PLB 12.99 (*0-394-92863-6*) Knopf Bks Yng Read.
—Dogs Don't Tell Jokes. LC 91-2042. 176p. (gr. 5-9). 1991. 14.00 (*0-679-82017-5*); lib. bdg. 14.99 (*0-679-92017-X*) Knopf Bks Yng Read.
—Johnny's in the Basement. 128p. (Orig.). (gr. 4-7). 1983. pap. 2.99 (*0-380-83451-0*, Camelot) Avon.
—Johnny's in the Basement. 128p. (gr. 2-6). 1990. Repr. of 1981 ed. PLB 12.99 (*0-679-90411-5*) Random Bks Yng Read.
—Marvin Redpost: Alone in His Teacher's House. Sullivan, Barbara, illus. LC 93-19791. Date not set. write for info. (*0-679-81949-5*); PLB write for info. (*0-679-91949-X*) Random.
—Marvin Redpost: Is He a Girl? Sullivan, Barbara, illus. LC 92-40784. 1993. PLB 9.99 (*0-679-91948-1*); pap. 2.99 (*0-679-81948-7*) Random Bks Yng Read.
—Marvin Redpost: Kidnapped at Birth? Hughes, Neal, illus. LC 91-51105. 80p. (Orig.). (gr. 1-4). 1992. PLB 9.99 (*0-679-91946-5*); pap. 2.99 (*0-679-81946-0*) Random Bks Yng Read.
—Marvin Redpost: Why Pick on Me? Hughes, Neal, illus. LC 92-12858. 80p. (Orig.). (gr. 1-4). 1993. PLB 9.99 (*0-679-91947-3*); pap. 2.99 (*0-679-81947-9*) Random Bks Yng Read.
—Monkey Soup. Smith, Cat B., illus. LC 91-15858. 32p. (ps-3). 1992. 12.00 (*0-679-80297-5*); PLB 13.99 (*0-679-90297-X*) Knopf Bks Yng Read.
—Sideways Arithmetic from Wayside School. 96p. (gr. 4-8). 1992. pap. 2.95 (*0-590-45726-8*, Apple Paperbacks) Scholastic Inc.
—Sideways Stories from Wayside School. 128p. (gr. 2-6). 1990. Repr. of 1985 ed. PLB 12.99 (*0-679-90413-1*) Random Bks Yng Read.
—Sixth Grade Secrets. LC 86-4298. 208p. (gr. 4-6). 1987. pap. 12.95 (*0-590-40709-0*, Scholastic Hardcover) Scholastic Inc.
—Sixth Grade Secrets. 208p. (gr. 3-7). 1992. pap. 2.95 (*0-590-46075-7*, Apple Paperbacks) Scholastic Inc.
—Someday Angeline. Samuels, Barbara, illus. 160p. (Orig.). (gr. 3-7). 1983. pap. 3.50 (*0-380-83444-8*, Camelot) Avon.
—Someday Angeline. 160p. (gr. 2-6). 1990. Repr. of 1983 ed. PLB 12.99 (*0-679-90412-3*) Knopf Bks Yng Read.
—There's a Boy in the Girl's Bathroom. Greenstein, Mina, designed by. LC 86-20100. 224p. (gr. 5 up). 1987. lib. bdg. 13.99 (*0-394-98570-2*) Knopf Bks Yng Read.
—There's a Boy in the Girls' Bathroom. large type ed. 1990. Repr. lib. bdg. 15.95 (*1-55736-174-6*, Crnrstn Bks) BDD LT Grp.
—There's a Boy in the Girls' Bathroom. LC 86-20100. 208p. (gr. 3-7). 1988. Repr. of 1987 ed. 3.50 (*0-394-80572-0*) Knopf Bks Yng Read.
—Wayside School Is Falling Down. 192p. 1990. pap. 3.99 (*0-380-75484-3*, Camelot) Avon.
Sachner, Mark, ed. see Asimov, Isaac.
Sachs. Amy & Laura. 1993. pap. 2.95 (*0-590-44623-1*) Scholastic Inc.
—Hello... Wrong Number. 1993. pap. 2.95 (*0-590-44504-9*) Scholastic Inc.
Sachs, Albie see First, Ruth.
Sachs, Betsy. The Boy Who Ate Dog Biscuits. Apple, Margot, illus. LC 89-3905. 64p. (gr. 2-4). 1989. PLB 7.99 (*0-394-94778-9*); pap. 2.50 (*0-394-84778-4*) Random Bks Yng Read.
—Mountain Bike Madness. Dann, Penny, illus. LC 93-29929. 1994. PLB 7.99 (*0-679-93395-6*); pap. 2.99 (*0-679-83395-1*) Random Bks Yng Read.
—The Trouble with Santa. Apple, Margot, illus. LC 89-24257. 64p. (Orig.). (gr. 2-4). 1990. pap. 2.50 (*0-679-80410-2*) Random Bks Yng Read.
Sachs, Elizabeth A. Just Like Always. LC 89-18407. 176p. (gr. 4-7). 1990. pap. 3.95 (*0-689-71389-4*, Aladdin) Macmillan Child Grp.
Sachs, Elizabeth-Ann. I Love You, Janie Tannenbaum. LC 90-143. 160p. (gr. 3-7). 1990. pap. 3.95 (*0-689-71390-8*, Aladdin) Macmillan Child Grp.
—Kiss Me, Janie Tannenbaum. LC 91-28465. 144p. (gr. 5-9). 1992. SBE 13.95 (*0-689-31664-X*, Atheneum Child Bk) Macmillan Child Grp.
—A Special Kind of Friend. LC 90-40048. (Illus.). 112p. (gr. 3-7). 1991. pap. 3.95 (*0-689-71388-6*, Aladdin) Macmillan Child Grp.
Sachs, Leroy, ed. Projects to Enrich School Mathematics: Level 2. LC 88-5259. (Illus.). 96p. (Orig.). (gr. 7-9). 1988. pap. 8.00 (*0-87353-260-0*) NCTM.
—Projects to Enrich School Mathematics: Level 3. LC 88-5129. (Illus.). 128p. (Orig.). (gr. 10-12). 1988. pap. 11.00 (*0-87353-261-9*) NCTM.
Sachs, Marilyn. Almost Fifteen. LC 86-29209. (gr. 4-9). 1987. 12.95 (*0-525-44285-5*, DCB) Dutton Child Bks.
—At the Sound of the Beep. LC 89-25655. 128p. (gr. 4-7). 1990. 13.95 (*0-525-44571-4*, DCB) Dutton Child Bks.
—At the Sound of the Beep. 160p. (gr. 3-7). 1991. pap. 3.95 (*0-14-034681-3*, Puffin) Puffin Bks.
—Baby Sister. LC 85-16171. (gr. 7-11). 1986. 13.95 (*0-525-44213-8*, DCB) Dutton Child Bks.
—Baby Sister. 160p. 1987. pap. 3.50 (*0-380-70358-0*, Flare) Avon.
—The Bears' House. LC 86-29267. 80p. (gr. 4-7). 1987. 10.95 (*0-525-44286-3*, DCB) Dutton Child Bks.
—The Bears' House. 80p. (gr. 3-7). 1989. pap. 2.99 (*0-380-70582-6*, Camelot) Avon.
—Circles. LC 90-37516. 144p. (gr. 5-9). 1991. 14.95 (*0-525-44683-4*, DCB) Dutton Child Bks.

—Circles. LC 92-20287. 144p. (gr. 5 up). 1992. pap. 3.99 (0-14-034931-6) Puffin Bks.
—Class Pictures. 144p. (gr. 7 up). 1982. pap. 2.95 (0-380-61408-1, Flare) Avon.
—Class Pictures. 144p. (gr. 3-7). 1991. pap. 3.95 (0-14-034682-1, Puffin) Puffin Bks.
—Dorrie's Book. 144p. 1991. pap. 2.95 (0-380-76139-4, Camelot) Avon.
—The Fat Girl. LC 83-11697. 176p. (gr. 6 up). 1984. 13.95 (0-525-44076-3, DCB) Dutton Child Bks.
—The Fat Girl. (gr. 7 up). 1986. pap. 2.75 (0-440-92468-5, LFL) Dell.
—Fourteen. 128p. (gr. 7 up). 1985. pap. 2.95 (0-380-69842-0, Flare) Avon.
—Fran Ellen's House. 96p. 1989. pap. 2.75 (0-380-70583-4, Camelot) Avon.
—Just Like a Friend. LC 89-1168. 168p. (gr. 5-9). 1989. 14.95 (0-525-44524-2, DCB) Dutton Child Bks.
—Matt's Mitt & Fleet-Footed Florence. 80p. 1991. pap. 2.95 (0-380-70963-5, Camelot) Avon.
—A Pocket Full of Seeds. (Illus.). 144p. (gr. 5 up). 1994. pap. 3.99 (0-14-036593-1) Puffin Bks.
—A Secret Friend. 128p. (gr. 3-7). 1987. pap. 2.95 (0-590-40403-2, Apple Paperback) Scholastic Inc.
—A Summer's Lease. LC 78-12486. 128p. (gr. 5-9). 1979. 13.95 (0-525-40480-5, 0898-270, DCB) Dutton Child Bks.
—Thirteen Going on Seven. 112p. (gr. 5-9). 1993. 14.95 (0-525-45096-3, DCB) Dutton Child Bks.
—Thunderbird. Spence, Jim, illus. LC 84-21252. 88p. (gr. 7 up). 1985. 10.95 (0-525-44163-8, 01063-320, DCB) Dutton Child Bks.
—Underdog. LC 84-24676. 128p. (gr. 4-6). 1985. pap. 11.95 (0-385-17609-0) Doubleday.
—What My Sister Remembered. LC 91-32263. 120p. (gr. 5-9). 1992. 15.00 (0-525-44953-1, DCB) Dutton Child Bks.
Sachs, Marilyn, jt. ed. see Durell, Ann.
Sack, Steve. Professor Doodle's Just for Kids Corner. (gr. 4-7). 1991. pap. 4.95 (0-941263-32-0) Tribune FL.
Sack, Steve, jt. auth. see MacIntosh, Craig.
Sackett, Elisabeth. Danger on the African Grassland. (ps-3). 1991. 12.95 (0-316-76596-1) Little.
—Danger on the Arctic Ice. (ps-3). 1991. 12.95 (0-316-76598-8) Little.
Sackett, Pamela. Two Minutes to Shine, Bk. 3. 48p. (Orig.). 1993. pap. text ed. 8.95 (0-573-69384-6) French.
Sackett, Russell. Edge of the Sea. (Illus.). 176p. (gr. 7 up). 1983. 18.60 (0-8094-4334-1); lib. bdg. 24.60 (0-8094-4333-3) Time-Life.
Sacks, Margaret. Beyond Safe Boundaries. LC 88-27311. 160p. (gr. 7 up). 1989. 13.95 (0-525-67281-8, Lodestar Bks) Dutton Child Bks.
—Beyond Safe Boundaries. (gr. 4 up). 1990. pap. 3.95 (0-14-034407-1, Puffin) Puffin Bks.
—Themba. Clay, Wil, illus. LC 92-9754. 48p. (gr. 2-5). 1992. 12.00 (0-525-67414-4, Lodestar Bks) Dutton Child Bks.
Sader, Marion, ed. Reference Books for Young Readers: Authoritative Evaluations of Encyclopedias, Atlases, & Dictionaries. 627p. (ps up). 1988. 52.95 (0-8352-2366-3) Bowker.
Sadie Fields Productions Staff. Christmas Long Ago. (Illus.). 14p. 1992. 15.95 (0-399-21839-4, Putnam) Putnam Pub Group.
—On Christmas Eve. Ives, Penny, illus. 14p. 1992. 16.95 (0-399-22148-4, Putnam) Putnam Pub Group.
Sadiku, Matthew N. How to Discover God's Will for Your Life. Dunham, Steve, ed. (Illus.). 268p. (Orig.). 1991. 15.95 (1-879420-02-3); pap. 9.95 (1-879420-03-1) Covenant Pubs.
Sadler, Glenn E., ed. see MacDonald, George.
Sadler, Marilyn. Alistair & the Alien Invasion. Bollen, Roger, illus. LC 92-22828. 1994. pap. 14.00 (0-671-75957-4, S&S BFYR) S&S Trade.
—Alistair in Outer Space. LC 84-4896. 1989. pap. 13.95 jacketed (0-671-66678-9, S&S BFYR); pap. 5.95 (0-671-67938-4, S&S BFYR) S&S Trade.
—Alistair Underwater. 1990. pap. 13.95 jacketed (0-671-69406-5, S&S BFYR) S&S Trade.
—Alistair Underwater. LC 89-3658. (ps-3). 1992. pap. 5.95 (0-671-79246-6, S&S BFYR) S&S Trade.
—Alistair Underwater. (gr. 2). 1991. pap. write for info. (0-663-56212-0) Silver Burdett Pr.
—Alistair's Elephant. Bollen, Roger, illus. 44p. (Orig.). (gr. k-3). 1986. pap. 5.95 (0-13-022773-0) P-H.
—Alistair's Time Machine. Bollen, Roger, illus. 40p. (ps up). 1992. pap. 13.95 jacketed (0-671-66679-7, S&S BFYR); pap. 5.95 (0-671-68493-0, S&S BFYR) S&S Trade.
—Bedtime for Bunnies. Bollen, Roger, illus. 14p. (ps). 1994. bds. 3.99 (0-679-83868-6) Random Bks Yng Read.
—Bob 'n John's Cat & Mouse Joke Book. (ps-3). 1993. pap. 3.50 (0-307-11564-X, Golden Pr) Western Pub.
—Elizabeth & Larry. Bollen, Roger, illus. LC 89-11552. 1992. pap. 13.95 jacketed (0-671-69189-9, S&S BFYR); pap. 4.95 (0-671-77817-X, S&S BFYR) S&S Trade.
—Elizabeth, Larry & Ed. LC 91-341142. (ps-3). 1992. pap. 14.00 (0-671-75956-6, S&S BFYR) S&S Trade.
—It's Not Easy Being a Bunny. Bollen, Roger, illus. LC 83-2680. 48p. (gr. k-3). 1983. 6.95 (0-394-86102-7); lib. bdg. 7.99 (0-394-96102-1) Beginner.

—Knock, Knock, It's P. J. Funnybunny! Bollen, Roger, illus. 24p. (ps-1). 1992. 8.00 (0-679-81733-6) Random Bks Yng Read.
—Nanny Goat & the Lucky Kid. Bollen, Roger, illus. (ps-k). 1991. pap. write for info. (0-307-11514-3, Golden Pr) Western Pub.
—P.J. The Spoiled Bunny. Bollen, Roger, illus. LC 85-19650. 32p. (ps-3). 1986. lib. bdg. 5.99 (0-394-97245-7); pap. 2.25 (0-394-87245-2) Random Bks Yng Read.
—The Very Bad Bunny. LC 84-3319. (Illus.). 48p. (ps-3). 1984. 6.95 (0-394-86861-7); lib. bdg. 7.99 (0-394-96861-1) Beginner.
Sadler, Marilyn & Bollen, Roger. Alistair's Elephant. LC 82-23091. (Illus.). 48p. (gr. k-4). 1991. pap. 12.95 jacketed (0-671-66680-0, S&S BFYR); pap. 5.95 (0-671-66681-9) S&S Trade.
—Alistair's Time Machine. LC 85-28187. (Illus.). 40p. (gr. k-4). 1986. PLB 13.95 (0-13-022351-4) P-H.
Sadler, Norma. Mirabelle's Country Club for Cats & Other Poems. Gochnour, Luanne, illus. 48p. (gr. 2-7). 1986. pap. 9.95 (0-9617206-0-3) Riverstone Pr.
Sadler, T., jt. auth. see Morris, E.
Sadler, Tony. Forests & Their Environment. LC 93-25643. 1993. pap. write for info. (0-521-43786-5) Cambridge U Pr.
Saeed, Mahmud S. The Model of the Muslim Youth in the Story of Prophet Yusuf. Al-Johani, Maneh, intro. by. (ARA.). 32p. Date not set. pap. write for info. Wamy Intl.
Safran, Faigy. Uncle Moishy Visits Torah Island. Snowdone, Linda, illus. 32p. (gr. 2-8). 1987. incl. cassette 10.95 (0-318-32597-7); pap. 5.95 (0-89906-807-3) Mesorah Pubns.
Sagan, Miriam. Tracing Our Jewish Roots. Butler, Nate & Evans, Beth, illus. 48p. (gr. 4-7). 1993. text ed. 12.95 (1-56261-151-8) John Muir.
Sagarin, James & Sagarin, Lori. Oseh Shalom. (Illus.). (gr. 4-6). 1990. wkbk. 6.00x (0-8074-0351-2, 123703) UAHC.
Sagarin, Lori, jt. auth. see Sagarin, James.
Sagarna, Blanca. Medios de Transporte: Transportation - Spanish. Baker, Syd, illus. Winitz, Harris, intro. by. (SPA., Illus.). 50p. (gr. 7 up). 1989. pap. text ed. 22.00 incl. cass. (0-939990-75-X) Intl Linguistics.
Sagarna, Blanca, tr. see Winitz, Harris.
Sage, Alison. Play Beethoven. Gabby, Terry, illus. Bunting, Janet, contrib. by. (Illus.). 32p. (gr. 1-4). 1988. Incl. built-in 22-note electronic keyboard. 12.95 (0-8120-5978-6) Barron.
—Play Mozart. Gabby, Terry, illus. Bunting, Janet, contrib. by. (Illus.). 32p. (gr. 1-4). 1988. Incl. built-in 22-note electronic keyboard. 13.95 (0-8120-5924-7) Barron.
Sage, Alison, jt. auth. see Gretz, Susanna.
Sage, Alison, retold by see Grimm, Jacob & Grimm, Wilhelm K.
Sage, Chris. Happy Baby. LC 89-78045. (Illus.). 12p. (ps). 1990. Dial Bks Young.
Sage, Jacqueline I., illus. Many Furs: A Grimm's Fairy Tale. LC 81-947. 32p. (gr. 1-4). 1990. 9.95 (0-89742-041-1) Celestial Arts.
Sage, James. The Little Band. Narahashi, Keiko, illus. LC 90-40089. 32p. (ps-3). 1991. SBE 13.95 (0-689-50516-7, M K McElderry) Macmillan Child Grp.
—To Sleep. Hutton, Warwick, illus. LC 89-36931. 32p. (ps-3). 1990. SBE 13.95 (0-689-50497-7, M K McElderry) Macmillan Child Grp.
—Where the Great Bear Watches. Flather, Lisa, illus. 32p. (ps-3). 1993. 13.99 (0-670-84933-2) Viking Child Bks.
Sage, Kathleen A. Quakey Bear's Amazing Earthquake Adventure. 24p. (ps-3). 1992. pap. write for info. (0-9630089-5-1) Quakey Bear.
—Quakey Bear's Earthquake Lessons: A Gentle Earthquake Journey for Children. (ps-3). 1991. pap. write for info. (0-9630089-0-0) Quakey Bear.
Sage, Margaret A. Wee Taste & See: A Story Book - Cook Book - Coloring Book. Tusken, Dee, illus. 32p. (Orig.). (gr. 1-3). 1992. pap. 9.95 (0-9631988-1-5) Taste & See.
Sager, Linda C., ed. see Machamer, Gene.
Sahlin, Cliff. The Daligator. Sahlin, Cliff, illus. LC 88-83575. 28p. (Orig.). 1988. pap. text ed. 4.95 (0-9621714-0-9) Gamin Pr.
Said, Edward, ed. & intro. by see Kipling, Rudyard.
Saideman, Ellen, jt. auth. see Frankel, Marvin.
Saidman, Anne. Oprah Winfrey: Media Success Story. (Illus.). 56p. (gr. 4 up). 1990. PLB 13.50 (0-8225-0538-X) Lerner Pubns.
—Oprah Winfrey: Media Success Story. (gr. 4-7). 1993. pap. 4.95 (0-8225-9646-6) Lerner Pubns.
—Stephen King: Master of Horror. (Illus.). 64p. (gr. 4-12). 1992. PLB 13.50 (0-8225-0545-2) Lerner Pubns.
—Stephen King: Master of Horror. (gr. 4-7). 1992. pap. 4.95 (0-8225-9623-7) Lerner Pubns.
Sailer, John. A Vogt for the Environment. LC 93-15313. 1993. 6.95 (0-913990-34-5) Book Pub Co.
St. Andre, Ken & Perrin, Steve. Stormbringer: Fantasy Roleplaying in the World of Elric. 4th ed. Monroe, John B., ed. Whelan, Michael, et al, illus. 208p. (gr. 8 up). 1990. pap. 21.95 (0-933635-66-4, 2110) Chaosium.
St. Antoine, Sara. Ghostwriter: Dress Code Mess. (gr. 4-7). 1992. pap. 2.99 (0-553-48071-5) Bantam.
St. Aubyn, Giles. Art of Argument. LC 84-9739. (gr. 9 up). 1960. 12.95 (0-87523-133-0) Emerson.

St. Augustine. Confessions of Saint Augustine. (gr. 11 up). 1968. pap. 1.95 (0-8049-0190-2, CL-190) Airmont.
St. Clair, Barry & Jones, Bill. Dating: Going out in Style. 140p. (Orig.). 1993. pap. 5.99 (1-56476-189-4, Victor Books) SP Pubns.
—Love: Making It Last. 140p. (Orig.). 1993. pap. 5.99 (1-56476-188-6, Victor Books) SP Pubns.
—Sex: Desiring the Best. 140p. (Orig.). 1993. pap. 5.99 (1-56476-190-8, Victor Books) SP Pubns.
St. Clair, Barry & Naylor, Keith. Taking Your Campus for Christ. 112p. (Orig.). 1993. pap. 4.99 (1-56476-201-7, Victor Books) SP Pubns.
St. George, Judith. By George, Bloomers! Tomes, Margot, illus. LC 89-17898. 48p. (gr. 1-4). 1989. pap. 5.95 (1-55870-135-4) Shoe Tree Pr.
—Dear Dr. Bell - Your Friend, Helen Keller. 172p. (gr. 5-9). 1992. 15.95 (0-399-22337-1, Putnam) Putnam Pub Group.
—Dear Dr. Bell...Your Friend, Helen Keller. LC 93-9304. 96p. (gr. 6 up). 1993. pap. text ed. 4.95 (0-688-12814-9, Pub. by Beech Tree Bks) Morrow.
—Haunted. 160p. (gr. 6 up). 1986. pap. 2.50 (0-553-26047-2) Bantam.
—Mason & Dixon's Line of Fire. LC 90-21625. 128p. (gr. 3-7). 1991. 15.95 (0-399-22240-5, Putnam) Putnam Pub Group.
—The Mount Rushmore Story. LC 84-24963. (Illus.). 128p. (gr. 5 up). 1985. 13.95 (0-399-21117-9, Putnam) Putnam Pub Group.
—The Panama Canal: Gateway to the World. 144p. (gr. 5 up). 1989. 16.95 (0-399-21637-5, Putnam) Putnam Pub Group.
—What's Happening to My Junior Year? 160p. (gr. 5 up). 1986. 13.95 (0-399-21316-3, Putnam) Putnam Pub Group.
—The White House: Cornerstone of a Nation. (Illus.). 160p. (gr. 6-12). 1990. 16.95 (0-399-22186-7, Putnam) Putnam Pub Group.
St. George, Mark. Los Angeles: City of Dreams II. rev. ed. (Illus.). 160p. 1989. 16.95 (0-9620541-4-3); pap. 9.95 (0-9620541-5-1) Proteus LA.
—The Wolfpack. 210p. (Orig.). 1990. 14.95 (0-9620541-2-7); pap. 4.95 (0-9620541-3-5) Proteus LA.
St. George, Robert B., ed. Material Life in America, 1600-1860. 640p. 1988. text ed. 50.00x (1-55553-019-2); pap. text ed. 27.50x (1-55553-020-6) NE U Pr.
St. Germain, Sharon. The Terrible Fight. Zemke, Deborah, illus. 32p. (gr. k-3). 1990. 13.45 (0-395-50069-9) HM.
St. John, Charlotte. Red Hair Three. (gr. 7 up). 1992. pap. 3.99 (0-449-70406-8, Juniper) Fawcett.
—Red Hair, Too. 144p. (gr. 7 up). 1991. pap. 3.50 (0-449-70392-4, Juniper) Fawcett.
St. John, Chris. Golden Girl. (gr. 5 up). 1989. pap. 3.50 (0-449-13454-7) Fawcett.
—A Horse of Her Own. (gr. 5 up). 1989. pap. 2.95 (0-449-13451-2) Fawcett.
—Kate's Challenge. (gr. 5 up). 1989. pap. 2.95 (0-449-13453-9) Fawcett.
St. John, Jetty. A Family in Bolivia. LC 86-21034. (Illus.). 32p. (gr. 2-5). 1986. PLB 13.50 (0-8225-1670-5) Lerner Pubns.
—A Family in Chile. (Illus.). 32p. (gr. 2-5). 1986. lib. bdg. 13.50 (0-8225-1667-5) Lerner Pubns.
—A Family in England. (Illus.). 32p. (gr. 2-5). 1988. lib. bdg. 13.50 (0-8225-1679-9) Lerner Pubns.
—A Family in Hungary. (Illus.). 32p. (gr. 2-5). 1988. lib. bdg. 13.50 (0-8225-1683-7) Lerner Pubns.
—A Family in Norway. (Illus.). 32p. (gr. 2-5). 1988. lib. bdg. 13.50 (0-8225-1681-0) Lerner Pubns.
—A Family in Peru. (Illus.). 32p. (gr. 2-5). 1987. PLB 13.50 (0-8225-1669-1) Lerner Pubns.
—Monaco Grand Prix. (Illus.). 64p. (gr. 5 up). 1989. 17.50 (0-8225-0530-4) Lerner Pubns.
St. John, Maddie, et al. A Story from Widg. St. John, Maddie, illus. LC 90-71987. 64p. (Orig.). (gr. k-3). 1992. pap. 6.00 (1-56002-047-4) Aegina Pr.
St. John, Patricia. Friska, My Friend. 80p. (gr. 2-4). 1990. pap. 3.99 (1-55661-151-X) Bethany Hse.
—A King Is Risen. Scott, Richard, illus. (gr. 2-7). 8.99 (0-8024-4576-4) Moody.
—The Other Kitten. 80p. (gr. 2-4). 1990. pap. 3.99 (1-55661-152-8) Bethany Hse.
—Patricia St. John Books, 10 bks. (gr. 2-7). Set. 46.96 (0-8024-0726-9) Moody.
—The Secret at Pheasant Cottage. LC 78-24384. (gr. 6-8). 1979. pap. 4.50 (0-8024-7683-X) Moody.
—Secret of the Fourth Candle. LC 81-22400. 128p. 1981. pap. 4.50 (0-8024-7681-3) Moody.
—Star of Light. (gr. 5-8). 1953. pap. 4.99 (0-8024-0004-3) Moody.
—Three Go Searching. (Illus.). (gr. 9-12). 1977. pap. 4.50 (0-8024-8748-3) Moody.
—Treasures of the Snow. (gr. 5-8). 1950. pap. 4.50 (0-8024-0008-6) Moody.
—Where the River Begins. LC 80-12304. 128p. (Orig.). (gr. 5-8). pap. 4.50 (0-8024-0028-0) Moody.
St. John, Patricia M. Rainbow Garden. (gr. 2-5). pap. 4.99 (0-8024-0028-0) Moody.
—The Tanglewood's Secret. (gr. 5-8). 1951. pap. 4.99 (0-8024-0007-8) Moody.
St. Laurent, Fred. The Heavy House. Soule, Jean, et al, eds. (Illus.). 250p. (Orig.). (gr. 8 up). 1987. pap. 4.95 perfect bdg (0-938447-02-5) Rendezvous Pubns.

—I've Lost My Name. Soule, Jean C., ed. (Illus.). 40p. (gr. 1 up). 1987. text ed. 9.00 case bound, smyth sewn (0-938447-01-7) Rendezvous Pubns.
—The Jupiter Lighthouse Mystery. Soule, Jean C., et al, eds. (Illus.). 264p. (Orig.). (gr. 8 up). 1987. pap. 3.95 perfect bdg. (0-938447-00-9) Rendezvous Pubns.
—Towhead. Soule, Jean, et al, eds. (Illus.). 452p. (Orig.). (gr. 1 up). pap. 5.00 perfect bdg (0-938447-03-3) Rendezvous Pubns.
St. Onge, Susan, et al. Passerelles: Revision De Grammaire Francaise. Hausberger, Petra, ed. (FRE., Illus.). 372p. (gr. 10 up). 1991. pap. 28.95 (0-8384-1970-4); lab manual 23.95 (0-8384-2356-6) Heinle & Heinle.
St. Pierre, Stephanie. Dancing the Night Away. Duarte, Pamela, illus. 64p. (Orig.). (gr. 1-2). 1991. pap. 2.95 (0-8431-2906-9) Price Stern.
—Dinosaurs for Dessert: Book & Cookie Cutter Set. (Illus.). 16p. (gr. k-3). 1991. pap. 3.95 (0-590-68985-1) Scholastic Inc.
—Everything You Need to Know When a Parent Is in Jail. Rosen, Ruth, ed. (gr. 7-12). 1993. PLB 13.95 (0-8239-1526-3) Rosen Group.
—Gertrude Elion. LC 93-22315. (gr. 7-8). 1993. 15.93 (0-86592-130-X); 11.95s.p. (0-685-66593-3) Rourke Enter.
—Meet Shaquille O'Neal. Johnson, David, photos by. LC 93-1678. (Illus.). 112p. (gr. 3-5). 1993. pap. 2.99 (0-679-85444-4) Random Bks Yng Read.
—The Mysterious Dude of Ghost Ranch. Duarte, Pamela, illus. 64p. (Orig.). (gr. 1-2). 1991. pap. 2.95 (0-8431-2905-0) Price Stern.
—Our National Anthem. LC 91-38891. (Illus.). 48p. (gr. 2-4). 1992. PLB 12.90 (1-56294-106-2) Millbrook Pr.
—Project Boyfriend. 1991. pap. 2.95 (0-553-28900-4) Bantam.
—Soda Shop Surprise. Duarte, Pamela, illus. 64p. (Orig.). (gr. 1-2). 1991. pap. 2.95 (0-8431-2919-0) Price Stern.
—Story of Jim Henson. (gr. 4-7). 1991. pap. 2.95 (0-440-40453-3) Dell.
—Sun Kissed. 1990. pap. 2.75 (0-553-28517-3) Bantam.
—Valentine Kittens. 1990. pap. 3.95 (0-590-63481-X) Scholastic Inc.
—Where's That Turkey Lurking? Book & Cookie Cutter Pack. 16p. (Orig.). (gr. k-3). 1990. pap. 3.95 (0-590-68984-3) Scholastic Inc.
—Wildlife Rescue. Duarte, Pamela, illus. 64p. (Orig.). (gr. 1-2). 1991. pap. 2.95 (0-8431-2918-2) Price Stern.
St. Pierre, Stephanie & Lovak, Matt. Bunny Bakeshop: Book & Cookie Cutter Set. (gr. k-3). 1989. pap. 3.95 (0-590-63281-7) Scholastic Inc.
St. Tamara. Asian Crafts. St. Tamara, illus. LC 71-86983. (gr. 2-6). 1972. PLB 13.95 (0-87460-148-7) Lion Bks.
Saint-Exupery, Antoine de. Little Prince. Woods, Katherine, tr. Saint-Exupery, Antoine de, illus. LC 67-1144. 91p. (gr. 3-7). 1943. 13.95 (0-15-246503-0, HB Juv Bks) HarBrace.
—The Little Prince. Woods, Katherine, tr. LC 67-1144. (Illus.). 91p. (gr. 3-7). 1982. pap. 6.95 (0-15-646511-6, HB Juv Bks) HarBrace.
—The Little Prince. Woods, Katherine, tr. LC 67-1144. (Illus.). 111p. (gr. 3-7). 1968. pap. 3.95 (0-15-652820-7) HarBrace.
—Le Petit Prince. Saint-Exupery, Antoine de, illus. LC 43-5812. (FRE.). 91p. (gr. 3-7). 1943. 14.95 (0-15-243818-1, HB Juv Bks) HarBrace.
—Petit Prince. (FRE.). (gr. 3-8). write for info. Fr & Eur.
—El Principito - The Little Prince. (Illus.). 88p. (gr. 4 up). pap. 6.95 (0-8442-7622-7, Passport Bks) NTC Pub Grp.
Saint-Exupery, Antoine De see De Saint-Exupery, Antoine.
Saint-Exupery, Antoine de see De Saint-Exupery, Antoine.
Saint-Exupery, Antoine De see De Saint-Exupery, Antoine.
Saint-Exupery, Antoine de see Saint-Exupery, Antoine de.
St. John, Charlotte, ed. see Johnson, Kathryn T. & Balczon, Mary-Lynne J.
Saint Mars, Dominique de see De Saint Mars, Dominique.
Saintsing, David. The World of Butterflies. LC 86-5706. (Illus.). 32p. (gr. 2-3). 1986. 15.93 (1-55532-072-4) Gareth Stevens Inc.
—The World of Deer. Oxford Scientific Films Staff, illus. LC 87-6539. 32p. (gr. 2-3). 1987. PLB 15.93 (1-55532-302-2) Gareth Stevens Inc.
—The World of Owls. Oxford Scientific Films Staff, illus. LC 87-6537. 32p. (gr. 2-3). 1987. PLB 15.93 (1-55532-301-4) Gareth Stevens Inc.
—The World of Penguins. Oxford Scientific Films Staff, illus LC 87-6536. 32p. (gr. 2-3). 1987. PLB 15.93 (1-55532-274-3) Gareth Stevens Inc.
Saintsing, David & Allan, Douglas. The World of Seals. LC 87-6524. (Illus.). 32p. (gr. 2-3). 1987. PLB 15.93 (1-55532-300-6) Gareth Stevens Inc.
Sainz, Frances. La Caja de Botones. 23p. (ps-1). 1992. pap. text ed. 23.00 big bk. (1-56843-045-0); pap. text ed. 4.50 (1-56843-092-2) BGR Pub.
—Carino. 23p. (ps-1). 1992. pap. text ed. 23.00 big bk. (1-56843-047-7); pap. text ed. 4.50 (1-56843-094-9) BGR Pub.
—La Luna y las Olas. 24p. (ps-1). 1992. pap. text ed. 23. 00 big bk. (1-56843-049-3); pap. text ed. 4.50 (1-56843-096-5) BGR Pub.

—Nubecitas. 23p. (ps-1). 1992. pap. text ed. 23.00 big bk. (1-56843-046-9); pap. text ed. 4.50 (1-56843-093-0) BGR Pub.
—El Toro y el Becerrito. 11p. (ps-1). 1992. pap. text ed. 23.00 big bk. (1-56843-048-5); pap. text ed. 4.50 (1-56843-095-7) BGR Pub.
Sairigne, Catherine de see De Sairigne, Catherine.
Sakade, Florence. Japanese Children's Favorite Stories. Kurosaki, Yoshio, illus. LC 58-11620. 120p. (gr. 2-6). 1958. bds. 16.95 (0-8048-0284-X) C E Tuttle.
—Kintaro's Adventures & Other Japanese Children's Stories. Hayashi, Yoshio, illus. 60p. (gr. 1-5). 1958. pap. 8.95 (0-8048-0343-9) C E Tuttle.
—Little One-Inch & Other Japanese Children's Favorite Stories. (Illus.). 60p. (gr. 1-5). 1958. pap. 8.95 (0-8048-0384-6) C E Tuttle.
—Origami: Japanese Paper Folding, 3 Vols. LC 57-10685. (Illus., Orig.). (gr. 2 up). 1957. pap. 5.95 ea. Vol. 1 (0-8048-0454-0) Vol. 2 (0-8048-0455-9) Vol. 3 (0-8048-0456-7) C E Tuttle.
—Peach Boy & Other Japanese Children's Favorite Stories. Kurosaki, Yoshisuke, illus. 58p. (gr. 1-5). 1958. pap. 8.95 (0-8048-0469-9) C E Tuttle.
Sakade, Florence, ed. Urashima Taro & Other Japanese Children's Stories. (Illus.). 58p. (gr. 1-6). 1958. pap. 8.95 (0-8048-0609-8) C E Tuttle.
Sakai, Kimiko. Sachiko Means Happiness. Arai, Tomie, illus. LC 90-2248. 32p. (gr. k-5). 1990. 13.95 (0-89239-065-4) Childrens Book Pr.
Saki. The Story-Teller. 1991. PLB 13.95s.p. (0-88682-476-1) Creative Ed.
—Tobermory. 32p. (gr. 6). 1990. PLB 13.95s.p. (0-88682-305-6) Creative Ed.
Sakihara, Masako, jt. auth. see Sato, Esther M.
Sakkal, Joyce, jt. auth. see Bar-Lev, Geoffrey.
Sakson-Ford, Stephanie. Czech Americans. Moynihan, Daniel P., intro. by. (Illus.). 112p. (gr. 5 up). 1989. lib. bdg. 17.95 (0-87754-870-6) Chelsea Hse.
Sakurai, Jennifer. Rules of the Game: Basketball. 48p. 1990. pap. 3.95 (0-8431-2432-6) Price Stern.
—Rules of the Game: Football. 48p. 1990. pap. 3.95 (0-8431-2433-4) Price Stern.
—Rules of the Game: Soccer. 48p. 1990. pap. 3.95 (0-8431-2431-8) Price Stern.
Sakurai, Jennifer, ed. see Stein, Charlotte M.
Salak, John. Drugs in Society: Are They Our Suicide Pill? (Illus.). 64p. (gr. 5-8). 1993. PLB 14.95 (0-8050-2572-3) TFC Bks NY.
—The Los Angeles Riots: America's Cities in Crisis. LC 92-30572. (Illus.). 64p. (gr. 5-8). 1993. 15.90 (1-56294-373-1) Millbrook Pr.
Salaman, Maureen K. Foods That Heal. Scheer, James F., ed. Atkins, Robert, intro. by. 521p. (Orig.). 1989. pap. 19.95 (0-913087-02-5) Statford CA.
Salamone, Victor, jt. auth. see Pfannes, Charles E.
Salamone, Victor A., jt. auth. see Pfannes, Charles E.
Salant, Michael A. Arithmetic Is Fun: The Arithmetic Example Handbook of Grade-School Math. LC 91-90203. (Illus.). 128p. (Orig.). (gr. 1-6). 1992. 16.95x (0-9609288-5-5); pap. 10.95xt glow in the dark spiral bdg. (0-9609288-4-7) M A Salant.
—Our Industrious Robots: A Guide to What Robots Can Do & How They Work. LC 84-90027. (Illus.). 128p. (gr. 6 up). Date not set. 17.95 (0-9609288-3-9); pap. 12.95 (0-9609288-2-0) M A Salant.
Salariya, David, created by see Lambert, David.
Salassi, Otto. On the Ropes. LC 80-20399. 256p. (gr. 6 up). 1992. pap. 4.95 (0-688-11500-4, Pub. by Beech Tree Bks) Morrow.
Salassi, Otto R. Jimmy D. Sidewinder, & Me. (gr. 5 up). 1987. 11.75 (0-688-05237-1) Greenwillow.
Salat, Cristina. Alias Diamond Jones. Franke, Phil, illus. (gr. 4-7). 1993. pap. 2.99 (0-553-37216-5) Bantam.
—Living in Secret. LC 92-20889. 1993. 15.00 (0-553-08670-7, Skylark) Bantam.
Salaz, Ruben D. Cosmic Reader of the Southwest for Young People. Aragon, Loretta, illus. (gr. 4 up). 1976. pap. 6.95 (0-932492-00-2) Cosmic Hse NM.
—La Lectura Cosmica del Suroeste-para los Jovenes. Minkin, Rita, tr. from ENG. Aragon, Loretta, illus. (SPA.). (gr. 7 up). 1978. pap. 6.95 (0-932492-01-0) Cosmic Hse NM.
Salazar, Arturo, tr. see Tibo, Gilles.
Salazar, Yolanda L. The Beestys' Journey, 20 Vols, Vol. 1. Kelley, Midorie, illus. 36p. (gr. 3 up). 1989. write for info. ADAPT Pub Co.
—The Beestys' What Color Is... Kelley, Midorie, illus. 10p. (ps). 1989. 7.95 (0-317-94002-3) ADAPT Pub Co.
—The Beesty's What Shape Is... Kelley, Midorie, illus. 10p. (ps). 1989. 7.95 (0-317-94001-5) ADAPT Pub Co.
—The Beestys' What Time Is... Kelley, Midorie, illus. 10p. (ps). 1989. 7.95 (0-317-94003-1) ADAPT Pub Co.
Salazar-Alonso, Olvido, tr. see Blume, Judy.
Sale, William M., Jr., ed. see Bronte, Emily.
Saleem, M., tr. see Numani, Shibli.
Saleh, Umaru, ed. see Emekwulu, Paul C.
Salem, Lynn & Stewart, Josie. Aqui Esta Fido. (Illus.). 8p. (gr. 1). 1993. pap. 3.50 (1-880612-18-6) Seedling Pubns.
—The Cat Who Loved Red. (Illus.). 8p. (gr. 1). 1992. pap. 3.50 (1-880612-03-8) Seedling Pubns.
—Cuidando a Rosita. (Illus.). 8p. (gr. 1). 1993. 3.50 Seedling Pubns.
—Dia de Futbol. (Illus.). 8p. (gr. 1). 1993. pap. 3.50 (1-880612-27-5) Seedling Pubns.

—En Casa de Abuelita Norma. (Illus.). 16p. (gr. 1). 1993. pap. 3.50 (1-880612-19-4) Seedling Pubns.
—Espero Que No. (Illus.). 8p. (gr. 1). 1993. pap. 3.50 (1-880612-15-1) Seedling Pubns.
—Here's Skipper. (Illus.). 8p. (gr. 1). 1993. pap. 3.50 (1-880612-14-3) Seedling Pubns.
—Hope Not! (Illus.). 8p. (gr. 1). 1993. pap. 3.50 (1-880612-04-6) Seedling Pubns.
—I Suficiente. (Illus.). 12p. (gr. 1). 1993. 3.50 (1-880612-28-3) Seedling Pubns.
—It's Game Day! (Illus.). 8p. (gr. 1). 1992. pap. 3.50 (1-880612-02-X) Seedling Pubns.
—Just Enough. Graham, Jennifer, illus. 12p. (gr. 1). 1992. pap. 3.50 (1-880612-12-7) Seedling Pubns.
—Martian Goo. Tiefenthal, Colleen, illus. 8p. (gr. 1). 1993. pap. 3.50 (1-880612-13-5) Seedling Pubns.
—Mi Mascota. (Illus.). 8p. (gr. 1). 1993. pap. 3.50 (1-880612-24-0) Seedling Pubns.
—My Pet. Graham, Jennifer, illus. 8p. (gr. 1). 1992. pap. 3.50 (1-880612-11-9) Seedling Pubns.
—Never Be. (Illus.). 8p. (gr. 1). 1992. pap. 3.50 (1-880612-00-3) Seedling Pubns.
—No Luck. Collins, Tim, illus. 12p. (gr. 1). 1993. pap. 3.50 (1-880612-07-0) Seedling Pubns.
—Notes from Mom. (Illus.). 16p. (gr. 1). 1992. pap. 3.50 (1-880612-01-1) Seedling Pubns.
—Now He Knows. Poirier, Kathleen, illus. 12p. (gr. 1). 1993. pap. 3.50 (1-880612-06-2) Seedling Pubns.
—Nunca. (Illus.). 8p. (gr. 1). 1993. 3.50 (1-880612-25-9) Seedling Pubns.
—Que Escuela. (Illus.). 16p. (gr. 1). 1993. pap. 3.50 (1-880612-21-6) Seedling Pubns.
—Que Hay para Cenar. (Illus.). 12p. (gr. 1). 1993. pap. 3.50 (1-880612-20-8) Seedling Pubns.
—Recados de Mama. (Illus.). 16p. (gr. 1). 1993. pap. 3.50 (1-880612-23-2) Seedling Pubns.
—Sopa Marciana. (Illus.). 8p. (gr. 1). 1993. pap. 3.50 (1-880612-17-8) Seedling Pubns.
—Staying with Grandma Norma. Zala, Emma, illus. 16p. (gr. 1). 1993. pap. 3.50 (1-880612-08-9) Seedling Pubns.
—Taking Care of Rosie. Pendergast, Holly, illus. 8p. (gr. 1). 1992. pap. 3.50 (1-880612-05-4) Seedling Pubns.
—What a School. Hartman, David, illus. 16p. (gr. 1). 1992. pap. 3.50 (1-880612-10-0) Seedling Pubns.
—What's for Dinner? McDill, Layl, illus. 12p. (gr. 1). 1992. pap. 3.50 (1-880612-09-7) Seedling Pubns.
Salem Press Editors. The Twentieth Century: Great Athletes, 20 vols. (Illus.). 2924p. (gr. 6 up). 1992. lib. bdg. 400.00x (0-89356-775-2) Salem Pr.

Salem Press Editors, ed. The Twentieth Century: Great Scientific Achievements, 10 vols. (Illus.). 1800p. (gr. 6 up). 1994. Set. lib. bdg. 250.00 (0-89356-860-0) Salem Pr.
This third series in the Magill middle-school collection chronicles some 475 scientific achievements which occurred in this century. Astronomy, biology, chemistry, communications, earth science, medicine, physics & aviation are just some of the fields in which these important breakthroughs were made. Readers will discover exciting events such as Zeppelin's rigid airship or the first implantation of the human heart. Key-word, principal personages, type of science, & alphabetical title indexes assist the reader in locating the information. TWENTIETH CENTURY: GREAT ATHLETES 20 vol., Salem Press Editors, (Illus). 2924p. (gr. 6 up) 1992, Lib. bdg. $400. 00 (0-89356-775-2). The first in the collection, it provides interesting, informative biographical profiles of some 725 sports champions from around the world. Each profile is presented in an attractive, easy-to-read format with charts of statistical achievements & a photograph of the athlete. A glossary helps the reader understand the sports terminology used in the set. TWENTIETH CENTURY: GREAT EVENTS (ISBN 0-89356-796-5) 10 vol. illus. grade 6 up, 1992 $250.00, Lib. bdg. Second in the collection, it is designed in a format attractive to the young reader. Easy-to-read articles with photographs & illustrations bring to life 470 events that have shaped our world. Some of

the areas represented are Civil Rights, Civil War & Revolution, Economics, International Relations, Military Conflict & War, Politics & Government & Social Issues. There is a time line placing the events in chronological perspective. For more information call Salem Press at 800-221-1592 or FAX 201-871-8668. *Publisher Provided Annotation.*

Salerno, Dorsey P. Latin for Beginners. 121p. (gr. 6-12). 9.00 (*0-939507-09-9*, B13) Amer Classical.

Salerno, Tony, et al. Tony Salerno's Good News Express. Thompson, Del, et al, illus. 64p. (Orig.). (gr. k-6). Date not set. pap. write for info. (*1-881597-00-8*) Magination CA.

Sales, Francesc. Ibrahim. Simont, Marc, tr. from CAT. Sariola, Eulalia, illus. LC 87-29382. 32p. (gr. k-3). 1989. (Lipp Jr Bks) HarpC Child Bks.

Sales, R. de Roussy De see Roussy de Sales, R. de.

Saleska, Edward J., jt. ed. see Gockel, Herman W.

Salim, Ahmed I. People of the Coast: Swahili. (Illus.). 40p. (gr. 6-9). 1991. pap. 4.95 (*0-237-50894-X*, Pub. by Evans Bros Ltd) Trafalgar.

Salinas, Ana M., jt. auth. see Lubeck, Maria-Garza.

Salinas, Roger. Silly Ghost Riddles. Rodriguez, Carlos, illus. 32p. (Orig.). (gr. 3-5). 1987. pap. 2.95 (*0-942673-00-X*) Salinas Salinas & Matthews.

Salinas-Norman, Bobbi. Salinas-Norman's ABC's. Rodriguez-Nieto, Catherine & Rodriguez-Nieto, Alcides, eds. (Illus.). 80p. (ps-6). 1986. wkbk. 7.95 (*0-934925-02-X*); tchr's guide, 150 p. 13.95 (*0-934925-01-1*) Pinata Pubns.

Salinger, J. D. The Catcher in the Rye. 302p. 1951. 19.95 (*0-316-76953-3*) Little.

—The Catcher in the Rye, 2 vols. large type ed. Repr. of 1945 ed. Set. write for info. (*0-89064-019-X*) NAVH.

—The Catcher in the Rye. 224p. 1991. pap. 4.99 (*0-316-76948-7*) Little.

—Franny & Zooey. 208p. 1991. pap. 4.99 (*0-316-76949-5*) Little.

—Franny & Zooey: Two Novellas. 201p. 1961. 19.95 (*0-316-76954-1*) Little.

—Nine Stories. LC 52-12626. 302p. 1953. 19.95 (*0-316-76956-8*) Little.

—Raise High the Roof Beam, Carpenters & Seymour: An Introduction. Bd. with Seymour - An Introduction. 248p. 1963. 18.95 (*0-316-76957-6*) Little.

—Raise High the Roof Beam, Carpenters & Seymour: An Introduction. 224p. 1991. pap. 4.99 (*0-316-76951-7*) Little.

Salisbury, Graham. Blue Skin of the Sea: A Novel in Stories. (gr. 4-7). 1992. 15.00 (*0-385-30596-6*) Doubleday.

Salisbury-Willis, Barbara. Theatre Arts in the Elementary Classroom, Vol. 1. 272p. (gr. k-3). 1986. 32.00 (*0-87602-024-4*) Anchorage.

Salisbury-Wills, Barbara. Theatre Arts in the Elementary Classroom, Vol. 2. 304p. (gr. 4-6). 1986. 32.00 (*0-87602-025-2*) Anchorage.

Salk, Lee & Litvin, Jay. How to Be a Super Sitter. 128p. (gr. 9 up). 1990. pap. 7.95 (*0-8442-8547-1*, Natl Textbk) NTC Pub Grp.

Salkey, Andrew. Brother Anancy & Other Stories. LC 93-24266. 1993. write for info. (*0-582-22581-7*, Pub. by Longman UK) Longman.

Salladay, Susan. I Want a Puppy! (Illus.). 48p. (gr. 1-3). 1992. pap. 2.99 (*0-8423-1645-0*) Tyndale.

Saller, Carol. The Bridge Dancers. Talifero, Gerald, illus. 40p. (gr. 2-4). 1991. PLB 17.50 (*0-87614-653-1*) Carolrhoda Bks.

—The Bridge Dancers. Talifero, Gerald, illus. (gr. 2-4). 1993. pap. 5.95 (*0-87614-579-9*) Carolrhoda Bks.

—Pug, Slug, & Doug the Thug. Redenbaugh, Vicki J., illus. LC 92-44340. 1993. 13.95 (*0-87614-803-8*) Carolrhoda Bks.

Salmon, Otilia, tr. see Brinkley, Ginny & Sampson, Sherry.

Salmon-White, Shirley, jt. auth. see Tindall, Judith.

Salome, Richard, jt. auth. see Hobbs, Jack.

Saloom, Barbara B. Conversational Spanish: Quick & Easy. Cogger, Virginia & Ricardo-Gil, Jose, eds. Mrviein, Mark, illus. 120p. (Orig.). 1988. pap. text ed. 12.95 (*0-9627755-0-9*) B B Saloom.

Salop, Byrd. The Kiddush Cup Who Hated Wine. Goldstein, Lil, illus. 32p. (gr. 1 up). 1981. pap. 5.95 (*0-8246-0265-X*) Jonathan David.

Salsbury, Darrell L., jt. auth. see Simmons, Paula.

Salsini, Barbara. Elizabeth Stanton: A Leader of the Woman's Suffrage Movement. Rahmas, D. Steve, ed. LC 72-89214. 32p. (gr. 7 up). 1972. lib. bdg. 4.95 incl. catalog cards (*0-87157-547-7*) SamHar Pr.

Salsini, Paul. Cole Porter: Twentieth Century Composer of Popular Songs. Rahmas, D. Steve, ed. LC 72-89206. 32p. (Orig.). (gr. 7-12). 1972. lib. bdg. 4.95 incl. catalog cards (*0-87157-538-8*) SamHar Pr.

Salsitz, Rhondi V. The Twilight Gate. Clark, Alan M., illus. LC 92-22040. 192p. (gr. 7 up). 1993. 16.95 (*0-8027-8213-2*) Walker & Co.

Salt, Jane. First Words & Pictures. Hawksley, Gerald, illus. LC 92-53115. 96p. (ps-k). 1992. 9.95 (*1-85697-818-4*) Kingfisher Bks.

—First Words: For Babies & Toddlers. Hawksley, Gerald, illus. LC 90-8037. 192p. (ps-k). 1991. 9.95 (*0-679-80831-0*) Random Bks Yng Read.

—My Giant Word & Number Book. Pooley, Sarah, illus. LC 92-31508. 1993. 9.95 (*1-85697-861-3*) Kingfisher Bks.

Salten, Felix. Bambi. 134p. 1981. Repr. PLB 16.95x (*0-89966-358-3*) Buccaneer Bks.

—Bambi. 112p. 1981. Repr. PLB 16.95x (*0-89967-032-6*) Harmony Raine.

—Bambi. Cooney, Barbara, illus. (ps up). 1988. pap. 3.50 (*0-671-66607-X*, Minstrel Bks) PB.

—Bambi. Woods, Michael J., illus. LC 90-26533. 160p. (ps up). 1992. pap. 18.00 jacketed, three-piece bdg (*0-671-73937-9*, S&S BFYR) S&S Trade.

—Bambi's Children. (Illus.). 316p. 1992. Repr. PLB 21.95x (*0-89966-894-1*) Buccaneer Bks.

—Walt Disney's Bambi Comic Album. Crawford, Mel & Hultgren, Ken, illus. Blum, Geoffrey, intro. by. 48p. (Orig.). (ps up). 1988. pap. 5.95 (*0-944599-09-5*) Gladstone Pub.

Salter, Charles A. Food Risks & Controversies: Minimizing the Dangers in Your Diet. LC 92-37442. (Illus.). 144p. (gr. 7 up). 1993. PLB 15.40 (*1-56294-259-X*) Millbrook Pr.

—Looking Good, Eating Right: A Sensible Guide to Proper Nutrition & Weight Loss for Teens. (Illus.). 144p. (gr. 7 up). 1991. PLB 14.90 (*1-56294-047-3*) Millbrook Pr.

—The Nutrition-Fitness Link: How Diet Can Help Your Body & Mind. LC 92-35146. (Illus.). 144p. (gr. 7 up). 1993. PLB 15.40 (*1-56294-260-3*) Millbrook Pr.

—The Vegetarian Teen. (Illus.). 112p. (gr. 7 up). 1991. PLB 14.90 (*1-56294-048-1*) Millbrook Pr.

Salter, Heidi. Taddy McFinley & the Great Grey Grimly. Thatch, Nancy R., ed. Salter, Heidi, illus. Melton, David, intro. by. LC 89-31820. (Illus.). 26p. (gr. 3-8). 1989. PLB 14.95 (*0-933849-21-4*) Landmark Edns.

Salter, James L., jt. auth. see Nilsen, Frances S.

Salter, Mary J. The Moon Comes Home. Schuett, Stacey, illus. LC 88-31735. 40p. (ps-2). 1989. 12.95 (*0-394-89983-0*); lib. bdg. 13.99 (*0-394-99983-5*) Knopf Bks Yng Read.

Salter-Mathieson, Nigel. Little Chief Mischief. Gruen, Chuck, illus. (gr. 2-7). 1962. 10.95 (*0-8392-3020-6*) Astor-Honor.

Saltman, Judith. Goldie & the Sea. LaFave, Kim, illus. 32p. (ps-2). 1991. 4.95 (*0-88899-133-9*, Pub. by Groundwood-Douglas & McIntyre CN) Firefly Bks Ltd.

Saltoon, Diana. Four Hands: Green Gulch Poems. 25p. (Orig.). (gr. 7 up). 1988. pap. 2.95 (*0-931191-08-4*) Rob Briggs.

Salts, Bobbi. Beaches Are for Kids! An Activity Book for Kids. Parker, Steve, illus. 32p. (gr. 1-6). 1990. pap. 2.95 (*0-929526-09-0*) Double B Pubns.

—Color Sedona. Parker, Steve, illus. 32p. (Orig.). (ps-6). 1991. pap. 2.95 (*0-929526-10-4*) Double B Pubns.

—Death Valley Discovery! Parker, Steve, illus. 32p. (Orig.). (gr. k-6). 1991. pap. 3.95 (*1-878900-19-6*) DVNH Assn.

—Desert Discovery: An Activity Book for Kids. Parker, Steve, illus. 32p. (gr. 1-6). 1989. pap. text ed. 2.95 (*0-929526-01-5*) Double B Pubns.

—Discover Devils Tower National Monument. 32p. (gr. 3-5). 1992. 2.50 (*1-881667-00-6*) Devils Tower NHA.

—Discover Grand Teton National Park. NPS Staff, ed. Parker, Steve, illus. 32p. 1992. pap. 3.95 (*0-931895-22-7*) Grand Teton NHA.

—Discover the Oregon Trail. Parker, Steve, illus. 32p. (Orig.). (gr. 4-6). 1992. pap. 3.95 (*0-931056-06-3*) Jefferson Natl.

—Discover Westward Expansion. Parker, Steve, illus. 32p. (Orig.). (gr. 4-6). 1992. pap. text ed. 3.95 (*0-931056-03-9*) Jefferson Natl.

—Grand Canyon Discovery: An Activity Book. (Illus.). 32p. (Orig.). (gr. 1-6). 1989. pap. 2.95 (*0-929526-03-1*) Double B Pubns.

—New Mexico Is for Kids! An Activity Book. Parker, Steve, illus. 32p. (gr. 1-6). 1989. pap. 2.95 (*0-929526-02-3*) Double B Pubns.

—Sequoia & Kings Canyon Discovery. Parker, Steve, illus. 36p. (Orig.). (gr. 1-6). 1992. pap. 3.95 (*1-878441-05-1*) Sequoia Nat Hist Assn.

—Southwestern American Indian Discovery. Parker, Steve, illus. (gr. 2-8). 1991. pap. 3.95 (*0-929526-11-2*) Double B Pubns.

—Utah Is for Kids! Parker, Steve, illus. 32p. (Orig.). (gr. 1-6). 1991. pap. 3.95 (*0-929526-06-6*) Double B Pubns.

Salts, Bobbi, ed. California Is for Kids! An Activity Book. Parker, Steve, illus. 32p. (gr. 1-6). 1990. pap. 2.95 (*0-929526-04-X*) Double B Pubns.

Salts, Roberta. Arizona Is for Kids. Fischer, Bruce, illus. 32p. (gr. 1-4). 1988. pap. 2.95 (*0-685-21928-3*) Double B Pubns.

Saltzberg, Barney. Mrs. Morgan's Lawn. Saltzberg, Barney, illus. 32p. (ps-2). 1993. write for info. (*1-56282-423-6*); PLB write for info. (*1-56282-424-4*) Hyprn Child.

Saltzman, Mark. The Adventures of Milo & Otis. LC 88-33011. (Illus.). 96p. 1989. 14.95 (*0-688-08808-2*); lib. bdg. 14.88 (*0-688-08216-5*, Morrow Jr Bks) Morrow Jr Bks.

—Woodchuck Nation. Buller, Jon, illus. LC 93-4641. 1994. 15.00 (*0-679-85107-0*) Knopf Bks Yng Read.

Salvadori, Mario. The Art of Construction: Projects & Principles for Beginning Engineers & Architects. 3rd ed. Hooker, Saralinda & Ragus, Christopher, illus. LC 89-49406. 144p. (gr. 5 up). 1990. pap. 9.95 (*1-55652-080-8*) Chicago Review.

Salvner, Gary M., jt. ed. see Monseau, Virginia R.

Salzberg, Allen, jt. auth. see Baskin-Salzberg, Anita.

Salzman, Marian & Reisgies, Teresa. One Hundred Fifty Ways Teens Can Make a Difference. LC 91-2965. 156p. (Orig.). 1991. pap. 7.95 (*1-56079-093-8*) Petersons Guides.

Salzman, Yuri, retold by. & illus. The Three Little Pigs. LC 87-81773. 24p. (ps-k). 1988. pap. write for info. (*0-307-10099-5*, Pub. by Golden Bks) Western Pub.

Salzman, Yuri, illus. The Three Bears. 24p. (gr. 2-5). 1987. pap. write for info. (*0-307-10050-2*, Pub. by Golden Bks) Western Pub.

Samaha, MaryLou. Little Love's Color Corner: Color Me Book. Samaha, MaryLou, illus. 16p. (ps-2). 1988. write for info. (*0-9619988-0-6*) Ronmar Ent.

Samet, Peggy. The Secret on Volcano Hill. LC 89-51672. 44p. (ps). 1989. pap. 5.95 (*1-55523-269-8*) Winston-Derek.

Sammons, Sandra W. Henry Flagler, Builder of Florida. (gr. 4-7). 1993. pap. 9.95 (*0-9631241-3-7*) Tail Tours.

Sampson, Emma S. Billy & the Major. 300p. 1992. Repr. lib. bdg. 21.95x (*0-89966-921-2*) Buccaneer Bks.

—Miss Minerva & William Green Hill. 275p. 1992. Repr. lib. bdg. 21.95x (*0-89966-922-0*) Buccaneer Bks.

Sampson, Fay. Chris & the Dragon. Bennett, Jill, illus. 96p. (gr. 4-6). 1987. 14.95 (*0-575-03661-3*, Pub. by Gollancz England) Trafalgar.

—Finnglas & the Stones of Choosing. (Illus.). 128p. (gr. 4-8). 1989. pap. 4.99 (*0-7459-1124-2*) Lion USA.

—Finnglas of the Horses. (Illus.). 178p. (gr. 4-8). 1989. pap. 4.99 (*0-85648-899-2*) Lion USA.

—A Free Man on Sunday. 138p. (gr. 4-6). 1989. 17.95 (*0-575-04114-5*, Pub. by Gollancz England) Trafalgar.

—Josh's Panther. (Illus.). 96p. (gr. 3-5). 1988. 13.95 (*0-575-03914-0*, Pub. by Gollancz England) Trafalgar.

—Pangur Ban. (Illus.). 128p. (Orig.). (gr. 4-8). 1989. pap. 4.99 (*0-85648-580-2*) Lion USA.

—Serpent of Senargad. (Illus.). 128p. (gr. 4-8). 1989. pap. 4.99 (*0-7459-1520-5*) Lion USA.

—Shape-Shifter. (Illus.). 128p. (gr. 4-8). 1989. pap. 4.99 (*0-7459-1347-4*) Lion USA.

—White Horse Is Running. (gr. 4-7). 1990. pap. 4.99 (*0-7459-1915-4*) Lion USA.

Sampson, Jennifer, tr. see Joyce, Susan.

Sampson, Mary Y. The Golden Falcon. Bertschmann, Mary, ed. Bertschmann, Harry, illus. 120p. (Orig.). 1993. pap. 25.00 fine print, letter press ed. (*0-935505-08-3*) Bank St Pr.

Sampson, Mary Y. & Bertschmann, Harry. Crow. Bertschmann, Mary, ed. Bertschmann, Harry, illus. 48p. 1989. pap. 8.00x (*0-935505-05-9*) Bank St Pr.

Sampson, Rebecca, jt. auth. see McSweeney, Sean.

Sampson, Sherry, jt. auth. see Brinkley, Ginny.

Sampugna, Joe, jt. auth. see Martin, David.

Sams, Kenneth. Flying Toys. (Illus.). (gr. 9-12). 1992. pap. 6.95 (*1-86351-038-9*, Pub. by S Milner AT) Sterling.

Samson, Smadar. Ophir. (Illus.). 32p. (gr. k-2). 1993. 16.95 (*0-370-31740-8*, Pub. by Bodley Head UK) Trafalgar.

—Through the Glass Door. (Illus.). 32p. (ps-2). 1992. 16.95 (*0-370-31573-1*, Pub. by Bodley Head UK) Trafalgar.

Samstag, Nicholas. Kay Kay Comes Home. Shahn, Ben, illus. (gr. 5-7). 1962. 10.95 (*0-8392-3015-X*) Astor-Honor.

Samton, Sheila. Amazing Aunt Agatha. Bandk, Yvette, illus. 24p. (ps-2). 1990. PLB 14.60 (*0-8172-3575-2*); pap. 10.95 pkg. of 3 (*0-8114-2932-6*) Raintree Steck-V.

—Jenny's Journey. (Illus.). 32p. (ps-3). 1991. 13.95 (*0-670-83490-4*) Viking Child Bks.

—El Viaje de Jenny: Jenny's Journey. (Illus.). 32p. (ps-3). 1993. PLB 14.99 (*0-670-84843-3*) Viking Child Bks.

Samton, Sheila W. Jenny's Journey. LC 92-40724. (Illus.). 32p. (ps-3). 1993. pap. 4.99 (*0-14-054308-2*, Puffin) Puffin Bks.

—Moon to Sun: An Adding Book. Samton, Sheila W., illus. LC 90-85729. 24p. (ps-1). 1991. 9.95 (*1-878093-13-4*) Boyds Mills Pr.

—My Haunted House: A Lift-the-Flap Book. Samton, Sheila W., illus. 24p. (ps-k). 1992. bds. 12.95 (*1-56397-093-7*) Boyds Mills Pr.

—Oh No! A Naptime Adventure. Samton, Sheila W., illus. 32p. (ps-1). 1993. RB 13.99 (*0-670-84250-8*) Viking Child Bks.

—On the River: An Adding Book. Samton, Sheila W., illus. LC 90-85730. 24p. (ps-1). 1991. 9.95 (*1-878093-14-2*) Boyds Mills Pr.

—Tilly & the Rhinoceros. (Illus.). 32p. (ps-3). 1993. PLB 14.95 (*0-399-21973-0*, Philomel Bks) Putnam Pub Group.

—The World from My Window. Samton, Sheila W., illus. LC 90-85732. 28p. (ps-3). 1991. Repr. 14.95 (*1-878093-15-0*) Boyds Mills Pr.

Samuels, Barbara. Duncan & Dolores. Samuels, Barbara, illus. LC 85-17119. 32p. (ps-2). 1986. RSBE 13.95 (*0-02-778210-7*, Bradbury Pr) Macmillan Child Grp.

—Duncan & Dolores. Samuels, Barbara, illus. LC 85-17119. 32p. (ps-3). 1989. pap. 3.95 (*0-689-71294-4*, Aladdin) Macmillan Child Grp.

—Faye & Dolores. Samuels, Barbara, illus. LC 84-1612. 40p. (ps-2). 1985. RSBE 13.95 (*0-02-778120-8*, Bradbury Pr) Macmillan Child Grp.
—Faye & Dolores. Samuels, Barbara, illus. LC 87-1419. 40p. (ps-3). 1987. pap. 4.95 (*0-689-71154-9*, Aladdin) Macmillan Child Grp.
—Happy Birthday, Dolores. LC 88-15469. (Illus.). 32p. (ps-1). 1989. 13.95 (*0-531-05791-7*); PLB 13.99 (*0-531-08391-8*) Orchard Bks Watts.
—What's So Great about Cindy Snappleby? LC 91-17809. (Illus.). 32p. (ps-1). 1992. 13.95 (*0-531-05979-0*); lib. bdg. 13.99 (*0-531-08579-1*) Orchard Bks Watts.
Samuels, Cynthia K. It's a Free Country! A Young Person's Guide to Politics & Elections. LC 87-30857. (Illus.). 144p. (gr. 5 up). 1988. SBE 13.95 (*0-689-31416-7*, Atheneum Child Bk) Macmillan Child Grp.
Samuels, Gertrude. Run, Shelley, Run. (RL 7). 1975. pap. 2.50 (*0-451-13987-9*, AE2746, Sig) NAL-Dutton.
—Run, Shelley, Run. (Illus.). 160p. (gr. 9-12). 1975. pap. 3.99 (*0-451-15635-8*, Sig) NAL-Dutton.
Samuels, Steven. Jorge Luis Borges. (Illus.). (gr. 5 up). 1992. lib. bdg. 17.95 (*0-7910-1236-0*) Chelsea Hse.
—Paul Robeson. King, Coretta Scott, intro. by. (Illus.). 112p. (Orig.). (gr. 5 up). 1988. 17.95 (*1-55546-608-7*); pap. 9.95 (*0-7910-0206-3*) Chelsea Hse.
Samuels, Vyanne. Carry Go Bring Come. Northway, Jennifer, illus. LC 89-1528. 32p. (ps-2). 1989. SBE 13.95 (*0-02-778121-6*, Four Winds) Macmillan Child Grp.
Samuelson, Arnold, ed. see Meltabarger, P. J.
Samuelson, Billie, ed. see Meltabarger, P. J.
Samuelson, Mary L. & Schlaepfer, Gloria. The African Rhinoceros. LC 91-40953. (Illus.). 60p. (gr. 4 up). 1992. RSBE 13.95 (*0-87518-505-3*, Dillon) Macmillan Child Grp.
Samuelson, Mary L. & Schlaepfer, Gloria G. The Coyote. LC 92-44739. (Illus.). 64p. (gr. 5 up). 1993. RSBE 13.95 (*0-87518-560-6*, Dillon) Macmillan Child Grp.
Samuelson, Rita. Sound Strategist. 86p. (gr. k-12). 1989. pap. 35.00 (*0-930599-50-0*) Thinking Pubns.
—Super Speech Adventures. Madsen, Kris, illus. 96p. (gr. k-4). 1991. pap. text ed. 10.00 (*0-930599-65-9*) Thinking Pubns.
—Super Speech Adventures. (Illus.). 96p. (gr. k-4). 1991. pap. text ed. 10.00 (*0-930599-70-5*) Thinking Pubns.
Samz, Jane. Vision. (Illus.). 104p. (gr. 6-12). 1990. 18.95 (*0-7910-0031-1*) Chelsea Hse.
San Diego County School Children. San Diego County's Special Species: Nature Essays Written by & for Children. Moran, Barbara, ed. 44p. (gr. 1-12). 1993. pap. 4.95 (*0-9634474-1-6*) Ms B Bks.
—Special Species: An Anthology Written by & for the Children of San Diego County. Moran, Barbara, ed. (Illus.). 40p. (Orig.). (gr. 1-12). 1992. pap. 3.95 (*0-9634474-0-8*) Ms B Bks.
San Diego Museum of Art Staff, compiled by. Dr. Seuss from Then to Now. Dr. Seuss, illus. LC 87-4838. 96p. (ps up). 1987. 12.95 (*0-394-89268-2*) Random Bks Yng Read.
Sanborn, Jane, jt. auth. see Sanborn, Laura.
Sanborn, Laura & Eberhardt, Lorraine. Swim Free. Jones, Shari, illus. 32p. (gr. 6-12). 1982. pap. 6.95x (*0-910715-00-9*) Search Public.
Sanborn, Laura & Sanborn, Jane. The Mystery of Horseshoe Mountain. Wallace, Joan, illus. 108p. (Orig.). (gr. 4-12). 1983. pap. 4.95x (*0-910715-01-7*) Search Public.
Sance, Melvin M., jt. auth. see Martinello, Marian L.
Sancha, Sheila. Walter Dragun's Town: Crafts & Trade in the Middle Ages. Sancha, Shelia, illus. LC 88-34066. 64p. (gr. 4 up). 1989. (Crowell Jr Bks); PLB 15.89 (*0-690-04806-8*, Crowell Jr Bks) HarpC Child Bks.
Sanchez, Brenda L. Max Science & the Thunderstorm. Sanchez, J. A., ed. Beard, Derrick, illus. 26p. (gr. k-5). 1991. pap. 3.95 (*1-879350-02-5*) Max Sci Pub.
Sanchez, Brenda L., ed. see Edwards, Roger.
Sanchez, Brenda L., ed. see Sanchez, Jesus A.
Sanchez, Gail J. & Gerbino, Mary. Overeating: Let's Talk about It. Raap, Cynthia, illus. LC 85-25388. 120p. (gr. 4 up). 1987. RSBE 9.95 (*0-87518-371-9*, Dillon) Macmillan Child Grp.
Sanchez, Isidro. I Draw, I Paint: Drawing. 1992. pap. 7.95 (*0-8120-1374-3*) Barron.
—I Draw, I Paint: Tempera. (gr. 4-7). 1992. pap. 7.95 (*0-8120-1373-5*) Barron.
—Watercolor. Ferron, Miguel, et al, illus. 48p. 1991. pap. 7.95 (*0-8120-4717-6*) Barron.
Sanchez, Isidro & Peris, Carme. City Sports. 32p. (ps-1). 1992. pap. 5.95 (*0-8120-4866-0*) Barron.
—La Ciudad. 32p. (ps-1). 1992. pap. 6.95 (*0-8120-4871-7*) Barron.
—The Farm. (Illus.). 32p. (ps). 1991. pap. 5.95 (*0-8120-4711-7*) Barron.
—The Forest. (Illus.). 32p. (ps). 1991. pap. 5.95 (*0-8120-4709-5*) Barron.
—The Garden. (Illus.). 32p. (ps). 1991. pap. 5.95 (*0-8120-4708-7*) Barron.
—El Mar. 32p. (ps-1). 1992. pap. 6.95 (*0-8120-4869-5*) Barron.
—La Montana. 32p. (ps-1). 1992. pap. 6.95 (*0-8120-4872-5*) Barron.
—Mountain Sports. 32p. (ps-1). 1992. pap. 5.95 (*0-8120-4867-9*) Barron.
—La Nieve. 32p. (ps-1). 1992. pap. 6.95 (*0-8120-4870-9*) Barron.

—The Orchard. (Illus.). 32p. (ps). 1991. pap. 5.95 (*0-8120-4710-9*) Barron.
—Summer Sports. (Illus.). 32p. (ps-1). 1992. pap. 5.95 (*0-8120-4865-2*) Barron.
—Winter Sports. (Illus.). 32p. (ps-1). 1992. pap. 5.95 (*0-8120-4868-7*) Barron.
—The World of Sports Series, 4 bks. (Illus.). 32p. (ps-1). 1992. Boxed set. pap. 23.95 (*0-8120-7862-4*) Barron.
Sanchez, J. A., ed. see Sanchez, Brenda L.

Sanchez, J. L. & Pacheco, M. A. La Nina Invisible (The Invisible Girl) Wensell, Uliises, illus. (SPA.). 42p. (gr. k-2). 1988. write for info. (*84-372-1829-2*) Santillana.
An outstanding selection from the DERECHOS DEL NINO series (The Rights of Children). Each book portrays one of the rights of children declared by the United Nations General Assembly. In this selection, a young girl named Maria is friendless. She lives in an area between the Green City & the Blue City. The children from the two cities despise each other & Maria belongs to neither. Maria grows so lonely & miserable that one day she simply becomes invisible. But in this new state she is able to bring about amazing changes in the two cities. Young readers will enjoy this heartwarming story & its message. Simplistic illustrations by Ulises Wendell add to the charm. To order: Santillana, 901 West Walnut, Compton, CA 90220. Telephone 1-310-763-0455. *Publisher Provided Annotation.*

Sanchez, Jesus A. Max Science & the Burned Out Bulb. Sanchez, Brenda L., ed. Sanchez, Jesus A., illus. 24p. (gr. k-5). 1990. pap. 3.95 (*1-879350-00-9*) Max Sci Pub.

Sanchez, Jose R. El Reino de la Geometria. (SPA., Illus.). 24p. 1993. PLB 16.95x (*1-56492-109-3*) Laredo. In the Kingdom of Geometry, the triangles, squares, circles, & other geometrical forms all live in peaceful harmony until one day when the King decides that squares are superior. By means of this metaphor, the book is an effective & enjoyable learning tool to discuss with children the issues of discrimination. In Spanish. *Publisher Provided Annotation.*

Sanchez, Sharon S. About Ballet Performance. Bower, Adele, illus. 32p. (ps up). 1990. pap. 5.95 (*0-9626651-1-8*) Dance Data.
—About Jazz Dance. Roussan, Irina, illus. 32p. (Orig.). 1991. pap. text ed. 5.95 (*0-9626651-2-6*) Dance Data.
Sanchez, Sharon S., ed. About Ballet Class. Bower, Adele, illus. 32p. (Orig.). (ps up). 1990. pap. 5.95 (*0-9626651-0-X*) Dance Data.
Sanchez, Sonia. Adventures of Small Head, Square Head & Fat Head. new ed. Taiwo, illus. 32p. (gr. 2-6). 1973. 11.95 (*0-89388-094-9*) Okpaku Communications.
—Homecoming. LC 77-78640. (gr. 12 up). 1969. pap. 3.00 (*0-685-00866-5*) Broadside Pr.
—It's a New Day: Poems for Young Brothas & Sistuhs. Olugebefola, Ademola & Sherman, Ed, illus. LC 72-155311. (gr. 5 up). 1971. pap. 3.00 (*0-910296-60-X*) Broadside Pr.
Sand, Dee. The Amazing Floating Zoo, Bk. 2. LC 93-70743. (Illus.). 60p. (Orig.). (gr. 2-5). 1993. pap. 4.99 (*0-87509-530-5*) Chr Pubns.
Sand, George. Histoire du Veritable Gribouille. Sand, Maurice, illus. (FRE.). 122p. (gr. 5-10). 1978. pap. 7.95 (*2-07-033043-5*) Schoenhof.
—The Mysterious Tale of Gentle Jack & Lord Bumblebee. Spirin, Gennady, illus. LC 87-30490. 80p. (ps up). 1988. Dial Bks Young.
Sandak, Cass. Columbus Day. LC 89-25399. (Illus.). 48p. (gr. 5 up). 1990. RSBE 12.95 (*0-89686-498-7*, Crestwood Hse) Macmillan Child Grp.
—Easter. LC 89-28626. (Illus.). 48p. (gr. 5 up). 1990. RSBE 12.95 (*0-89686-499-5*, Crestwood Hse) Macmillan Child Grp.
—Halloween. LC 89-25396. (Illus.). 48p. (gr. 5 up). 1990. 12.95 (*0-89686-500-2*, Crestwood Hse) Macmillan Child Grp.

—Patriotic Holidays. LC 89-25380. (Illus.). 48p. (gr. 5 up). 1990. RSBE 12.95 (*0-89686-501-0*, Crestwood Hse) Macmillan Child Grp.
—Valentine's Day. (Illus.). 48p. (gr. 5 up). 1990. RSBE 12.95 (*0-89686-504-5*, Crestwood Hse) Macmillan Child Grp.
Sandak, Cass A. The Carters: First Families Ser. LC 93-3943. (Illus.). 48p. (gr. 5 up). 1993. RSBE 12.95 (*0-89686-652-1*, Crestwood Hse) Macmillan Child Grp.
Sandak, Cass R. The Bushes. LC 91-11153. (Illus.). 48p. (gr. 5-6). 1991. RSBE 12.95 (*0-89686-632-7*, Crestwood Hse) Macmillan Child Grp.
—The Eisenhowers. (Illus.). 48p. (gr. 5 up). 1993. lib. bdg. 12.95 RSBE (*0-89686-653-X*, Crestwood Hse) Macmillan Child Grp.
—The Franklin Roosevelts. LC 91-30256. (Illus.). 48p. (gr. 5 up). 1992. RSBE 11.95 (*0-89686-639-4*, Crestwood Hse) Macmillan Child Grp.
—The Jacksons. LC 91-30363. (Illus.). 48p. (gr. 5 up). 1992. RSBE 12.95 (*0-89686-636-X*, Crestwood Hse) Macmillan Child Grp.
—The Jeffersons. LC 91-33061. (Illus.). 48p. (gr. 5 up). 1992. RSBE 11.95 (*0-89686-637-8*, Crestwood Hse) Macmillan Child Grp.
—John Adamses. LC 92-9262. (Illus.). 48p. (gr. 6). 1992. RSBE 12.95 (*0-89686-640-8*, Crestwood Hse) Macmillan Child Grp.
—The Kennedys. LC 91-2911. (Illus.). 48p. (gr. 5-6). 1991. RSBE 12.95 (*0-89686-633-5*, Crestwood Hse) Macmillan Child Grp.
—The Lincolns. LC 92-6880. (Illus.). 48p. (gr. 5). 1992. RSBE 12.95 (*0-89686-641-6*, Crestwood Hse) Macmillan Child Grp.
—Living Fossils. Cohn, Tom, ed. LC 91-34423. (Illus.). 64p. (gr. 3-6). 1992. PLB 12.90 (*0-531-20048-5*) Watts.
—The Lyndon Johnsons. LC 92-33522. (Illus.). 48p. (gr. 6). 1993. RSBE 12.95 (*0-89686-644-0*, Crestwood Hse) Macmillan Child Grp.
—The Madisons. LC 92-14040. (Illus.). 48p. (gr. 5). 1992. RSBE 12.95 (*0-89686-642-4*, Crestwood Hse) Macmillan Child Grp.
—The Monroes. LC 92-34408. (Illus.). 48p. (gr. 6). 1993. RSBE 12.95 (*0-89686-645-9*, Crestwood Hse) Macmillan Child Grp.
—The Nixons. LC 91-40216. (Illus.). 48p. (gr. 5 up). 1992. RSBE 11.95 (*0-89686-638-6*, Crestwood Hse) Macmillan Child Grp.
—The Reagans. LC 92-37838. (Illus.). 48p. (gr. 6). 1993. RSBE 12.95 (*0-89686-646-7*, Crestwood Hse) Macmillan Child Grp.
—A Reference Guide to Clean Air. LC 89-25601. 128p. (gr. 6 up). 1990. lib. bdg. 17.95 (*0-89490-261-X*) Enslow Pubs.
—The Tafts. LC 92-37839. (Illus.). 48p. (gr. 6). 1993. RSBE 12.95 (*0-89686-647-5*, Crestwood Hse) Macmillan Child Grp.
—The Theodore Roosevelts. LC 91-7377. (Illus.). 48p. (gr. 5-6). 1991. RSBE 12.95 (*0-89686-634-3*, Crestwood Hse) Macmillan Child Grp.
—The Trumans. LC 92-6879. (Illus.). 48p. (gr. 5). 1992. RSBE 12.95 (*0-89686-643-2*, Crestwood Hse) Macmillan Child Grp.
—The United States. (Illus.). 32p. (gr. 5). 1994. PLB 13.95 RSBE (*0-89686-776-5*, Crestwood Hse) Macmillan Child Grp.
—The Washingtons. (Illus.). 48p. (gr. 5-6). 1991. RSBE 12.95 (*0-89686-635-1*, Crestwood Hse) Macmillan Child Grp.
—The Wilsons. LC 93-3503. (Illus.). 48p. (gr. 5 up). 1993. RSBE 12.95 (*0-89686-651-3*, Crestwood Hse) Macmillan Child Grp.
Sandberg, Inger. Dusty Wants to Borrow Everything. Sandberg, Lasse, illus. Maurer, Judy A., tr. (Illus.). 32p. (ps up). 1988. 6.95 (*91-29-58782-4*, R & S Bks) FS&G.
—Dusty Wants to Help. Mauver, Judy A., tr. from SWE. Sandberg, Lasse, illus. 32p. (ps up). 1987. 6.95 (*91-29-58336-5*, Pub. by R & S Bks) FS&G.
Sandberg, Peter L. Dwight D. Eisenhower. Schlesinger, Arthur M., Jr., intro. by. (Illus.). 112p. (gr. 5 up). 1986. lib. bdg. 16.95 (*0-87754-521-9*); pap. 9.95 (*0-7910-0566-6*) Chelsea Hse.
Sandberg, Phillip. Stereogram Book of Fossils. (gr. 7 up). plastic comb bdg. 9.90 (*0-8331-1702-5*) Hubbard Sci.
Sandburg, Carl. Abe Lincoln Grows Up. Daugherty, James, illus. LC 74-17180. 222p. (gr. 7 up). 1985. 19.95 (*0-15-201037-8*, HB Juv Bks); pap. 5.95 (*0-15-602615-5*) HarBrace.
—Arithmetic. LC 32-5291. (gr. 4-7). 1993. 15.95 (*0-15-203865-5*) HarBrace.
—Early Moon. Daugherty, James, illus. LC 77-16488. 136p. (gr. 5 up). 1978. pap. 1.95 (*0-15-627326-8*, Voyager Bks) HarBrace.
—More Rootabagas. Zelinsky, Paul, illus. LC 92-14930. 96p. (ps up). 1993. 18.00 (*0-679-80070-0*); PLB 18.99 (*0-679-90070-5*) Knopf Bks Yng Read.
—Prairie-Town Boy. Hague, Michael & Krush, Joe, illus. 228p. (gr. 3-7). 1990. pap. 4.95 (*0-15-263332-4*, Odyssey) HarBrace.
—Rootabaga Stories, Pt. 1. Hague, Michael, illus. 192p. (gr. 3-7). 1988. 19.95 (*0-15-269061-1*) HarBrace.
—Rootabaga Stories, Pt. 1. Hague, Michael, contrib. by. 85p. (gr. 3-7). 1990. pap. 4.95 (*0-15-269065-4*, Odyssey) HarBrace.
—Rootabaga Stories, Pt. 2. Hague, Michael, illus. 179p. (gr. 3-7). 1989. 19.95 (*0-15-269062-X*) HarBrace.

—Rootabaga Stories, Pt. 2. Hague, Michael, contrib. by. 158p. (gr. 3-7). 1990. pap. 4.95 (0-15-269063-8, Odyssey) HarBrace.
—Sandburg Treasury: Prose & Poetry for Young People. Bacon, Paul, illus. LC 79-120818. 480p. (gr. 7 up). 1970. 24.95 (0-15-270180-X, HB Juv Bks) HarBrace.
—The Wedding Procession of the Rag Doll & the Broom Handle & Who Was in It. Pincus, Harriet, illus. LC 67-10211. 32p. (ps-3). 1978. pap. 3.95 (0-15-695487-7, Voyager Bks) HarBrace.
Sandell, Elizabeth. Ankylosaurus: The Armored Dinosaur. Oelerich, Marjorie & Hansen, Harlan S., eds. Vista III Design Staff, illus. LC 88-39806. 32p. (gr. k-5). 1989. PLB 12.95 (0-944280-16-1); pap. text ed. 5.95 (0-944280-22-6) Bancroft-Sage.
—Apatosaurus: The Deceptive Dinosaur. Oelerich, Marjorie & Hansen, Harlan S., eds. Vista III Design Staff, illus. LC 88-39805. 32p. (gr. k-5). 1989. PLB 12.95 (0-944280-12-9); pap. text ed. 5.95 (0-944280-18-8) Bancroft-Sage.
—Archaeopteryx: The First Bird. Oelerich, Marjorie & Hansen, Harlan S., eds. Vista III Design Staff, illus. LC 88-39803. 32p. (gr. k-5). 1989. PLB 12.95 (0-944280-13-7); pap. text ed. 5.95 (0-944280-19-6) Bancroft-Sage.
—Compsognathus: The Smallest Dinosaur. Oelerich, Marjorie & Hansen, Harlan S., eds. Vista III Design Staff, illus. LC 88-39801. 32p. (gr. k-5). 1989. PLB 12.95 (0-944280-14-5); pap. text ed. 5.95 (0-944280-20-X) Bancroft-Sage.
—Dimetrodon: The Sail-Backed Dinosaur. Oelerich, Marjorie & Hansen, Harlan S., eds. Vista III Design Staff, illus. LC 88-39802. 32p. (gr. k-5). 1989. PLB 12.95 (0-944280-15-3); pap. text ed. 5.95 (0-944280-21-8) Bancroft-Sage.
—Maiasaura: The Good Mother Dinosaur. Oelerich, Marjorie & Hansen, Harlan S., eds. Vista III Design Staff, illus. LC 88-39799. 32p. (gr. k-5). 1989. lib. bdg. 12.95 (0-944280-17-X); pap. text ed. 5.95 (0-944280-23-4) Bancroft-Sage.
—Plesiosaurus: The Swimming Reptile. Oelerich, Marjorie & Schroeder, Howard, eds. Vista III Design, illus. LC 88-962. 32p. (gr. k-5). 1988. lib. bdg. 12.95 (0-944280-04-8); pap. 5.95 (0-944280-10-2) Bancroft-Sage.
—Pteranodon: The Flying Reptile. Oelerich, Marjorie & Schroeder, Howard, eds. Vista III Design, illus. LC 88-953. 32p. (gr. k-5). 1988. lib. bdg. 12.95 (0-944280-05-6); pap. 5.95 (0-944280-11-0) Bancroft-Sage.
—Seismosaurus: The Longest Dinosaur. Oelerich, Marjorie & Schroeder, Howard, eds. Vista III Design, illus. LC 88-963. 32p. (gr. k-5). 1988. lib. bdg. 12.95 (0-944280-03-X); pap. 5.95 (0-944280-09-9) Bancroft-Sage.
—Stegosaurus: The Dinosaur with the Smallest Brain. Oelerich, Marjorie & Schroeder, Howard, eds. Vista III Design, illus. LC 88-995. 32p. (gr. k-5). 1988. lib. bdg. 12.95 (0-944280-02-1); pap. 5.95 (0-944280-08-0) Bancroft-Sage.
—Triceratops: The Last Dinosaur. Oelerich, Marjorie & Schroeder, Howard, eds. Vista III Design, illus. LC 88-952. 32p. (gr. k-5). 1988. lib. bdg. 12.95 (0-944280-01-3); pap. 5.95 (0-944280-07-2) Bancroft-Sage.
—Tyrannsasaurus Rex: The Fierce Dinosaur. Oelerich, Marjorie & Schroeder, Howard, eds. Vista III Design, illus. LC 88-958. 32p. (gr. k-5). 1988. lib. bdg. 12.95 (0-944280-00-5); pap. 5.95 (0-944280-06-4) Bancroft-Sage.
Sandelson, Robert. Ball Sports. LC 91-21804. (Illus.). 48p. (gr. 5-6). 1991. RSBE 13.95 (0-89686-664-5, Crestwood Hse) Macmillan Child Grp.
—Combat Sports. LC 91-24685. (Illus.). 48p. (gr. 5-6). 1991. RSBE 13.95 (0-89686-668-8, Crestwood Hse) Macmillan Child Grp.
—Ice Sports. LC 91-3881. (Illus.). 48p. (gr. 5-6). 1991. RSBE 13.95 (0-89686-667-X, Crestwood Hse) Macmillan Child Grp.
—Swimming & Diving. LC 91-16117. (Illus.). 48p. (gr. 5-6). 1991. RSBE 13.95 (0-89686-670-X, Crestwood Hse) Macmillan Child Grp.
—Track Athletics. LC 90-27449. (Illus.). 48p. (gr. 5-6). 1991. RSBE 13.95 (0-89686-671-8, Crestwood Hse) Macmillan Child Grp.
Sandelson, Robert & Merrison, Tim. Olympic Sports, 8 Bks. (Illus.). (gr. 6). 1991. Set. RSBE 89.28 (0-89686-754-4, Crestwood Hse) Macmillan Child Grp.
Sandercock, Lois, jt. auth. see Kienlen, Helen.
Sanders, Addie M. Alligators, Monsters & Cool School Poems. Sanders, Dave, Jr., illus. 80p. (Orig.). (gr. 3-10). 1993. pap. 9.00 (0-911943-36-6) Leadership Pub.
Sanders, Andrew, ed. see Hughes, Thomas P.
Sanders, Bill. Almost Everything Teens Want Parents to Know: But Are Afraid to Tell Them. 160p. (Orig.). 1987. pap. 7.99 (0-8007-5245-7) Revell.
—Goalposts: Devotions for Girls. (Orig.). 1990. pap. 7.99 (0-8007-5353-4) Revell.
—Goalposts: Devotions for Guys. (Orig.). 1990. pap. 7.99 (0-8007-5354-2) Revell.
—Hot & Cool: A Daily Calendar. (Illus.). 380p. (Orig.). (gr. 9-12). 1993. spiral bdg. 9.99 (0-8007-7211-3) Revell.
—Life, Sex & Everything in Between: Straight on Answers to the Questions That Trouble You Most. 160p. (Orig.). 1991. pap. 7.99 (0-8007-5385-2) Revell.

—Outtakes: Devotions for Girls. 160p. (gr. 7-12). 1988. pap. 7.99 (0-8007-5284-8) Revell.
—Stand Tall: Learning to Really Love Yourself. LC 92-13985. 160p. (Orig.). 1992. pap. 7.99 (0-8007-5452-2) Revell.
—Stand Up: Making Peer Pressure Work for You. 200p. (Orig.). 1993. pap. 7.99 (0-8007-5458-1) Revell.
—Tough Turf: A Teen Survival Manual. (Orig.). Date not set. pap. 7.99 (0-8010-5212-2) Revell.
Sanders, Catharine. Odette Churchill. (Illus.). 64p. (gr. 6-10). 1991. 15.95 (0-237-60039-0, Pub. by Evans Bros Ltd) Trafalgar.
Sanders, Christopher, tr. see Helgadottir, Gudrun.
Sanders, Corine & Turner, Cynthia. Coping. Villalpando, Eleanor, illus. 64p. (gr. 2-8). 1983. wkbk. 7.95 (0-9607366-2-X, GA 494) Good Apple.
Sanders, Corine, jt. auth. see Bisignano, Judith.
Sanders, Corinne. Choosing. Tom, Darcy, illus. 64p. (gr. 3-8). 1985. wkbk. 7.95 (0-86653-333-8, GA 677) Good Apple.
Sanders, Corinne, jt. auth. see Kino Learning Center Staff.
Sanders, E., jt. auth. see Eichel, C.
Sanders, Franklin. Heiland. 276p. (Orig.). 1989. pap. text ed. 6.00 (0-685-26841-1) Footstool Pubns.
Sanders, George. The Mix & Match Book of Dinosaurs. Block, Alex, illus. 10p. (ps-6). 1992. pap. 7.95 (0-671-76911-1, Little Simon) S&S Trade.
Sanders, John. All about Animal Migrations. Burns, Ray, illus. LC 83-6630. 32p. (gr. 3-6). 1984. PLB 10.59 (0-89375-977-5); pap. text ed. 2.95 (0-89375-978-3) Troll Assocs.
—All about Deserts. Boyd, Patti, illus. LC 83-4857. 32p. (gr. 3-6). 1984. lib. bdg. 10.59 (0-89375-965-1); pap. text ed. 2.95 (0-89375-966-X) Troll Assocs.
Sanders, Lawrence. The Great Coaster Ride. Block, Lori, illus. Sargent, Dave, intro. by. (Illus.). 135p. (Orig.). (gr. k-8). 1993. text ed. 11.95 (1-56763-099-5); pap. text ed. 5.95 (1-56763-100-2) Ozark Pub.
Sanders, Louise. Knave of Hearts. 1993. 12.95 (0-89815-520-7) Ten Speed Pr.
Sanders, Nancy. Amazing Bible Puzzles: New Testament. (Illus.). 80p. (Orig.). (gr. 3-7). 1993. pap. 4.99 (0-570-04749-8) Concordia.
—Amazing Bible Puzzles: Old Testament. (Illus.). 80p. (Orig.). (gr. 3-7). 1993. pap. 4.99 (0-570-04748-X) Concordia.
Sanders, Pete. Food & Hygiene. LC 90-3246. (Illus.). 32p. (gr. 2-5). 1990. PLB 11.40 (0-531-17243-0) Watts.
—Why Do People Smoke? (Illus.). 32p. (gr. 2-5). 1989. PLB 11.40 (0-531-17192-2) Watts.
Sanders, Peter. Death & Dying. LC 90-43995. (Illus.). 32p. (gr. k-3). 1991. PLB 11.40 (0-531-17278-3, Gloucester Pr) Watts.
—Disabled People. LC 92-6682. (Illus.). 32p. (gr. k-4). 1992. PLB 11.40 (0-531-17371-2, Gloucester Pr) Watts.
—What It's Like to Be Old. LC 92-6683. (Illus.). 32p. (gr. k-4). 1992. PLB 11.40 (0-531-17372-0, Gloucester Pr) Watts.
Sanders, Renfield. El Salvador. (Illus.). 104p. (gr. 5 up). 1988. lib. bdg. 14.95 (1-55546-781-4) Chelsea Hse.
—Iran. (Illus.). 112p. (gr. 5 up). 1990. 14.95 (0-7910-1104-6) Chelsea Hse.
—Malawi. (Illus.). 104p. (gr. 5 up). 1988. lib. bdg. 14.95 (1-55546-193-X) Chelsea Hse.
Sanders, Richard S. Government in Oregon. LC 91-62149. (Orig.). (gr. 6 up). 1991. pap. 19.95 (1-880118-02-5) MESD Pr.
Sanders, Scott R. Aurora Means Dawn. Kastner, Jill, illus. LC 88-24127. 32p. (gr. 1-5). 1989. 13.95 (0-02-778270-0, Bradbury Pr) Macmillan Child Grp.
—Bad Man Ballad. LC 86-2695. 224p. (gr. 6-8). 1986. SBE 14.95 (0-02-778230-1, Bradbury Pr) Macmillan Child Grp.
—Hear the Wind Blow: American Folk Songs Retold. Goembel, Ponder, illus. LC 85-4160. 224p. (gr. 6 up). 1985. SBE 14.95 (0-02-778140-2, Bradbury Pr) Macmillan Child Grp.
—Here Comes the Mystery Man. Cogancherry, Helen, illus. LC 92-24572. 32p. (gr. k-5). 1993. RSBE 15.95 (0-02-778145-3, Bradbury Pr) Macmillan Child Grp.
—Warm As Wool. LC 91-34987. (Illus.). 32p. (gr. k-5). 1992. RSBE 14.95 (0-02-778139-9, Bradbury Pr) Macmillan Child Grp.
Sanders, Scott R; see Leguin, Ursula K.
Sanderson, Jeannette. Dog to the Rescue: Seventeen True Tales of Dog Heroism. (gr. 4-7). 1993. pap. 2.95 (0-590-47112-0) Scholastic Inc.
Sanderson, Ruth. The Enchanted Wood. (Illus.). (ps-3). 1991. 15.95 (0-316-77018-3) Little.
Sanderson, Ruth, retold by. The Twelve Dancing Princesses. (gr. 2-4). 1990. 14.95 (0-316-77017-5) Little.
—The Twelve Dancing Princesses. (Illus.). (gr. 4-8). 1993. pap. 5.95 (0-316-77062-0, Joy St Bks) Little.
Sanderson, Ruth, illus. The Pudgy Bunny Book. 16p. (gr. k). 1984. 2.95 (0-448-10210-2, G&D) Putnam Pub Group.
Sandford. N. Lous Do Pb, Vol. 1. (ps-3). 1993. 6.95 (0-316-77080-9) Little.
Sandford, John. The Gravity Company. Sanford, John, illus. LC 88-10549. (gr. 2 up). 1988. 1.50 (0-687-15686-6) Abingdon.
—Nellie Lou's Hairdos. Sandford, John, illus. 32p. 1990. pap. 9.95 (1-55782-098-8, Pub. by Warner Juvenile Bks) Little.

Sandifer, Helga M. Alice in Language Land. (SPA, FRE, GER & ENG.). 1992. Set. PLB 19.95 (1-56650-999-8) AIL Pub.
Sandifer, Shannon, ed. see Coltharp, Barbara.
Sandin, Joan. The Long Way to a New Land. Sandin, Joan, illus. LC 80-8942. 64p. (gr. k-3). 1981. PLB 13.89 (0-06-025194-8) HarpC Child Bks.
—The Long Way to a New Land. Sandin, Joan, illus. LC 80-8942. 64p. (gr. k-3). 1986. pap. 3.50 (0-06-444100-8, Trophy) HarpC Child Bks.
—The Long Way Westward. Sandin, Joan, illus. LC 89-2024. 64p. (gr. k-3). 1989. 14.00 (0-06-025206-5); PLB 13.89 (0-06-025207-3) HarpC Child Bks.
—The Long Way Westward. Sandin, Joan, illus. LC 89-2024. 64p. (gr. k-3). 1992. pap. 3.50 (0-06-444198-9, Trophy) HarpC Child Bks.
Sandin, Joan, tr. see Bergstrom, Gunilla.
Sandin, Joan, tr. see Bjork, Christina.
Sandlain-Buchanan, Deborah. The Chocolate Tree: An African Folktale. Sandlain-Buchanan, Deborah, illus. 16p. (Orig.). (gr. k-3). 1993. write for info. (0-9639057-2-4); lib. bdg. write for info. (0-9639057-3-2); pap. 3.99 (0-9639057-0-8); 5.00 (0-9639057-1-6) Chocolate Tree.
Sandler, Martin W. Cowboys. Billington, James, illus. LC 93-20386. 96p. (gr. 3 up). 1994. 19.95 (0-06-023318-4); PLB 20.89 (0-06-023319-2) HarpC Child Bks.
—Pioneers. Billington, James. LC 92-47495. (Illus.). 96p. (gr. 3 up). 1994. 19.95 (0-06-023023-1); PLB 20.89 (0-06-023024-X) HarpC Child Bks.
Sandlin, Joan, tr. see Bjork, Christina.

Sandling, R. Harris. What Do You Do with a Cardboard Box on a Day When the Rain's Pourin' Down? Carter, Mary C., ed. Venema, Jon R., illus. 50p. (gr. 3 up). 1993. write for info. (1-883194-00-8) Emerald Hummngbrd. "I'm Bored! There's nothing to do!" So begins a great adventure for Justin. He doesn't know it, yet, but the wonder of his imagination is about to be unleashed. From an impromptu parade to barn-storming planes that fight the Red Baron & fly to the moon, Justin begins his great adventure. His guides are none other than Dad, Grandmom & good old Grandad, "whose ideas are always rad!" From these three Justin learns about a valuable set of keys that open mysterious doors to great treasures. The trick is discovering the whereabouts of the keys & knowing how to unlock the doors. Does Justin do it? What about the barn-storming plane? How do Dad, Grandmom & good old Grandad know about these mysterious keys? Where will this adventure lead Justin? Here is a delightfully charming story that all children, be they nine or ninety, will have great fun with! Justin's story is the story of every child that has lived since the beginning of time. WHAT DO YOU DO WITH A CARDBOARD BOX ON A DAY WHEN THE RAIN'S POURIN' DOWN? is rich with warmth, silliness & pearls of love & wisdom. This reading is a must for every individual who has known & experienced the boredom of a rainy afternoon. For pre-publication order & general information: Write: Emerald Hummingbird Productions, P.O. Box 577438, Modesto, CA 95355-7438. USA. Phone: 209-527-1771. *Publisher Provided Annotation.*

Sandoval, Dolores. Be Patient, Abdul. Sandoval, Dolores, illus. LC 93-34224. 1994. write for info. (0-689-50607-4, M K McElderry) Macmillan Child Grp.
Sandoz, Mari. Cheyenne Autumn. 1964. pap. 4.95 (0-380-01094-1) Avon.
—The Horsecatcher. LC 86-4360. 192p. (gr. 5-8). 1986. pap. 6.95 (0-8032-9160-4, Bison) U of Nebr Pr.
—The Story Catcher. LC 85-31810. (Illus.). 175p. (gr. 7-10). 1986. pap. 5.95 (0-8032-9163-9, Bison Books) U of Nebr Pr.

—These Were the Sioux. Kills Two & Amos Bad Heart Bull, illus. LC 85-8914. 118p. (gr. 6-12). 1985. pap. 5.95 (0-8032-9151-5, Bison Books) U of Nebr Pr.
Sands, AnnaMaria. Annie Wilkins Mystery Series, 5 novels. Heidinger, Herbert, illus. 240p. (Orig.). (gr. 2-7). 1988. Set. pap. 15.00 (0-87879-571-5) High Noon Bks.
Sands, Catherine D. & Gorman, Michael J., eds. Award-Winning Community Service Programs in Independent Schools. 4th ed. 125p. (gr. k up). 1992. pap. 19.00 (1-881678-40-7) CRIS.
Sands, Iso, tr. see Hoover, Evalyn, et al.
Sands, Stella. Odisea. Wolff, Barbara M., illus. (SPA.). 32p. (gr. k-4). 1992. PLB 13.95 (1-879567-18-0, Valeria Bks) Wonder Well.
—Odyssea. Wolff, Barbara M., illus. 32p. (gr. k-4). 1991, PLB 13.95 (1-879567-04-0, Valeria Bks); pap. text ed. 7.95 (1-879567-03-2) Wonder Well.
Sanfield, Steve. The Adventures of High John the Conqueror. Ward, John, illus. LC 88-17946. 128p. (gr. 3 up). 1989. 12.95 (0-531-05807-7); PLB 12.99 (0-531-08407-8) Orchard Bks Watts.
—Adventures of High John the Conqueror. (gr. 4-7). 1992. pap. 3.50 (0-440-40556-4) Dell.
—The Feather Merchants: & Other Tales of the Fools of Chelm. Magaril, Mikhail, illus. LC 90-29273. 112p. (gr. 3 up). 1991. 15.95 (0-531-05958-8); RLB 15.99 (0-531-08558-9) Orchard Bks Watts.
—The Feather Merchants & Other Tales of the Fools of Chelm. Magaril, Mikhail, illus. LC 92-43767. 96p. (gr. 5 up). 1993. pap. 3.95 (0-688-12568-9, Pub. by Beech Tree Bks) Morrow.
—A Natural Man: The True Story of John Henry. Thornton, Peter, illus. LC 85-45965. 32p. (gr. 2-6). 1990. pap. 9.95 (0-87923-844-5) Godine.
San Fillipo, Patrick R. A Study Workout for Sixth, Seventh, Eighth Graders, Pt. One: A Workout for the Mind. 26p. (gr. 6-8). 1991. wkbk. incls. video 34.95 (0-9630443-1-1); wkbk. 11.95 (0-9630443-0-3) Educ Excell Via.
Sanford, Agnes. Melissa & the Little Red Book. Heinen, Sandy, illus. (gr. 1-6). pap. 2.25 (0-910924-81-3) Macalester.
Sanford, Bill & Green, Carl. American Pit Bull Terrier. LC 89-31072. (Illus.). 48p. (gr. 4-5). 1989. 12.95 (0-89686-447-2, Crestwood Hse) Macmillan Child Grp.
—Dalmatian. LC 89-31107. (Illus.). 48p. (gr. 4-5). 1989. 12.95 (0-89686-449-9, Crestwood Hse) Macmillan Child Grp.
—Doberman Pinscher. LC 89-31071. (Illus.). 48p. (gr. 4-5). 1989. RSBE 12.95 (0-89686-454-5, Crestwood Hse) Macmillan Child Grp.
—English Springer Spaniel. LC 89-31069. (Illus.). 48p. (gr. 4-5). 1989. 12.95 (0-89686-453-7, Crestwood Hse) Macmillan Child Grp.
—Greyhound. LC 89-31113. (Illus.). 48p. (gr. 4-5). 1989. 12.95 (0-89686-450-2, Crestwood Hse) Macmillan Child Grp.
—Old English Sheepdog. LC 89-31073. (Illus.). 48p. (gr. 4-5). 1989. RSBE 12.95 (0-89686-452-9, Crestwood Hse) Macmillan Child Grp.
—Samoyed. LC 89-31070. (Illus.). 48p. (gr. 4-5). 1989. RSBE 12.95 (0-89686-451-0, Crestwood Hse) Macmillan Child Grp.
—Shih Tzu. LC 89-31108. (Illus.). 48p. (gr. 4-5). 1989. RSBE 12.95 (0-89686-448-0, Crestwood Hse) Macmillan Child Grp.
Sanford, Bill, jt. auth. see Green, Carl.
Sanford, Doris. David Has AIDS. Evans, Graci, illus. LC 89-3162. 29p. (gr. k-4). 1989. 6.99 (0-88070-299-0, Gold & Honey) Questar Pubs.
—Don't Look at Me: A Child's Book about Feeling Different. Evans, Graci, illus. LC 86-185484. 27p. (gr. k-6). 1986. 7.99 (0-88070-150-1, Gold & Honey) Questar Pubs.
—Don't Make Me Go Back, Mommy. Evans, Graci, illus. (gr. k-6). 1990. 7.99 (0-88070-367-9, Gold & Honey) Questar Pubs.
—For Your Own Good. Evans, Graci, illus. 28p. (gr. k-6). 1993. 7.99 (0-88070-604-X, Gold & Honey) Questar Pubs.
—Help! Fire! Escaping with My Life. Heaney, Liz, ed. Evans, Gracie, illus. 1992. 9.99 (0-88070-520-5, Gold & Honey) Questar Pubs.
—I Can't Talk about It: A Child's Book about Sexual Abuse. Evans, Graci, illus. LC 86-831. 32p. (gr. k-6). 1986. 7.99 (0-88070-149-8, Gold & Honey) Questar Pubs.
—It Must Hurt a Lot: A Child's Book about Death. Evans, Graci, illus. LC 86-25009. 32p. (gr. k-6). 1985. 7.99 (0-88070-131-5, Gold & Honey) Questar Pubs.
—It Won't Last Forever. Evans, Graci, illus. 28p. (gr. k-6). 1993. 7.99 (0-88070-605-8, Gold & Honey) Questar Pubs.
—Lisa's Parents Fight. Davis, Deena, ed. Evans, Graci, illus. LC 89-31409. 28p. (gr. k-4). 1989. 6.99 (0-88070-301-6, Gold & Honey) Questar Pubs.
—Maria's Grandma Gets Mixed Up. Evans, Graci, illus. LC 89-3161. 31p. (gr. k-4). 1989. 6.99 (0-88070-298-2, Gold & Honey) Questar Pubs.
—My Friend, the Enemy: Surviving a Prison Camp. Evans, Gracie, illus. 1992. 9.99 (0-88070-518-3, Gold & Honey) Questar Pubs.
—My Real Family. Evans, Gracie, illus. 28p. (gr. k-6). 1993. 7.99 (0-88070-466-7, Gold & Honey) Questar Pubs.

—No Longer Afraid: Living with Cancer. Evans, Gracie, illus. 1992. 9.99 (0-88070-519-1, Gold & Honey) Questar Pubs.
—Please Come Home: A Child's Book about Divorce. Evans, Graci, illus. LC 86-106753. 32p. (ps-5). 1985. 7.99 (0-88070-138-2, Gold & Honey) Questar Pubs.
—Something Must Be Wrong with Me. 28p. (gr. k-6). Date not set. 7.99 (0-88070-469-1, Gold & Honey) Questar Pubs.
—Yes, I Can: Challenging Cerebral Palsy. Heaney, Liz, ed. Evans, Gracie, illus. 32p. 1992. 9.99 (0-88070-510-8, Gold & Honey) Questar Pubs.
Sanford, James, Jr. Nuclear War Diary. Alexander, Frank, ed. Sanford, James, Jr. & Bates, Dawn, illus. 186p. (gr. 7-12). 1989. pap. 6.95 (0-915256-28-2, 130) Front Row.
Sanford, Monard G. The Free Pigs. Bookless, George, ed. Skivington, Janice, illus. LC 86-63205. 21p. (ps-5). 1987. PLB 13.00 (0-940273-00-4) Mill Creek Ent.
Sanford, Willam R. & Green, Carl R. The Murders in the Rue Morgue. LC 86-24399. (Illus.). 48p. (gr. 3-5). 1987. RSBE 11.95 (0-89686-308-5, Crestwood Hse) Macmillan Child Grp.
Sanford, William & Green, Carl. The Beagle. LC 90-34211. (Illus.). 48p. (gr. 5-6). 1990. RSBE 12.95 (0-89686-529-0, Crestwood Hse) Macmillan Child Grp.
—The Cocker Spaniel. LC 90-34059. (Illus.). 48p. (gr. 5-6). 1990. RSBE 12.95 (0-89686-531-2, Crestwood Hse) Macmillan Child Grp.
—The Dachshund. LC 90-34058. (Illus.). 48p. (gr. 5-6). 1990. RSBE 12.95 (0-89686-530-4, Crestwood Hse) Macmillan Child Grp.
—Dracula's Daughter. LC 84-27462. (Illus.). 48p. (gr. 3-5). 1985. RSBE 10.95 (0-89686-260-7, Crestwood Hse) Macmillan Child Grp.
—The German Shepherd. LC 90-34212. (Illus.). 48p. (gr. 5-6). 1990. RSBE 12.95 (0-89686-527-4, Crestwood Hse) Macmillan Child Grp.
—Ghost of Frankenstein. LC 84-29231. (Illus.). 48p. (gr. 3-5). 1985. RSBE 10.95 (0-89686-261-5, Crestwood Hse) Macmillan Child Grp.
—The Mole People. LC 84-23913. (Illus.). 48p. (gr. 3-5). 1985. RSBE 10.95 (0-89686-262-3, Crestwood Hse) Macmillan Child Grp.
—The Poodle. LC 90-34199. (Illus.). 48p. (gr. 5-6). 1990. RSBE 12.95 (0-89686-528-2, Crestwood Hse) Macmillan Child Grp.
Sanford, William, jt. auth. see Green, Carl.
Sanford, William R. & Green, Carl R. Babe Didrikson Zaharias. LC 91-44870. (Illus.). 48p. (gr. 5). 1993. RSBE 11.95 (0-89686-736-6, Crestwood Hse) Macmillan Child Grp.
—Billie Jean King. LC 92-27458. (Illus.). 48p. (gr. 4 up). 1993. RSBE 11.95 (0-89686-781-1, Crestwood Hse) Macmillan Child Grp.
—The Black Cat. LC 86-24336. (Illus.). 48p. (gr. 3-5). 1987. RSBE 10.95 (0-89686-310-7, Crestwood Hse) Macmillan Child Grp.
—The Boa Constrictor. LC 86-32868. (Illus.). 48p. (gr. 5-6). 1987. RSBE 12.95 (0-89686-320-4, Crestwood Hse) Macmillan Child Grp.
—The Cape Buffalo. LC 86-32859. (Illus.). 48p. (gr. 4-5). 1987. RSBE 12.95 (0-89686-321-2, Crestwood Hse) Macmillan Child Grp.
—Dorothy Hamill. LC 92-21356. (Illus.). 48p. (gr. 4 up). 1993. RSBE 11.95 (0-89686-779-X, Crestwood Hse) Macmillan Child Grp.
Sanford, William R. & Green, Carl. R. House of Fear. LC 86-28768. (Illus.). 48p. (gr. 3-5). 1985. RSBE 10.95 (0-89686-311-5, Crestwood Hse) Macmillan Child Grp.
Sanford, William R. & Green, Carl R. The House of the Seven Gables. LC 86-16241. (Illus.). 48p. (gr. 3-5). 1987. RSBE 10.95 (0-89686-312-3, Crestwood Hse) Macmillan Child Grp.
—The Invisible Man. LC 86-24263. (Illus.). 48p. (gr. 3-5). 1987. RSBE 11.95 (0-89686-307-7, Crestwood Hse) Macmillan Child Grp.
—Joe DiMaggio. LC 91-42180. (Illus.). 48p. (gr. 5). 1993. RSBE 11.95 (0-89686-738-2, Crestwood Hse) Macmillan Child Grp.
—Joe Namath. LC 92-26324. (Illus.). 48p. (gr. 4 up). 1993. RSBE 11.95 (0-89686-782-X, Crestwood Hse) Macmillan Child Grp.
—Kangaroos. LC 86-32881. (Illus.). 48p. (gr. 4-5). 1987. RSBE 12.95 (0-89686-322-0, Crestwood Hse) Macmillan Child Grp.
—Kareem Abdul-Jabbar. LC 92-3592. (Illus.). 48p. (gr. 5). 1993. RSBE 11.95 (0-89686-737-4, Crestwood Hse) Macmillan Child Grp.
—Missouri. LC 89-35082. 144p. (gr. 4 up). 1989. PLB 26.60 (0-516-00471-9) Childrens.
—Missouri. 205p. 1993. text ed. 15.40 (1-56956-171-0) W A T Braille.
—Muhammad Ali. LC 91-42181. (Illus.). 48p. (gr. 5). 1993. RSBE 11.95 (0-89686-739-0, Crestwood Hse) Macmillan Child Grp.
—The Phantom of the Opera. LC 86-24272. (Illus.). 48p. (gr. 3-5). 1987. RSBE 10.95 (0-89686-309-3, Crestwood Hse) Macmillan Child Grp.
—The Revenge of the Creature. LC 86-24268. (Illus.). 48p. (gr. 3-5). 1987. RSBE 10.95 (0-89686-313-1, Crestwood Hse) Macmillan Child Grp.
—Sandy Koufax. LC 92-31249. (Illus.). 48p. (gr. 5). 1993. RSBE 11.95 (0-89686-780-3, Crestwood Hse) Macmillan Child Grp.
Sanford, William R., jt. auth. see Green, Carl R.

Sanger, David. North America's ENDANGERED Species. Lynch, Don, ed. Mathewson, Mel, illus. 97p. (Orig.). (ps-8). 1992. pap. text ed. 4.00 (0-913205-17-6); special price 2.40 Grace Dangberg.
This exciting book for young people contains 97 pages of 44 selected endangered wildlife representing nine categories. The 9" x 11 1/2" paperback book includes maps showing locations of the endangered wildlife, a summary of information about each selection, & a full-page black & white drawing of each wildlife which can be colored. Young people will enjoy the original art work by Mel Mathewson & learn of the endangered from it. Published by The Grace Dangberg Foundation, Inc. in 1992, the book is celebrated by a 20" x 30" color poster of the endangered wildlife represented in the book. The poster is now available from the Foundation.
Publisher Provided Annotation.

Sanhez, Isidro. Colored Pencils. Segu, Jordi & Sabat, Jordi, illus. 48p. 1991. pap. 7.95 (0-8120-4719-2) Barron.
San Jose, Christine, ed. see Dixon, Debra S. & Henry, Susan V.
Sankofa, jt. auth. see Anderson, David A.
Sanschagrin, Joceline. Lollypop's Baby Sister. (Illus.). 16p. (ps). 1993. bds. 5.95 (2-921198-45-2, Pub. by Les Edits Herit CN) Adams Inc MA.
—Lollypop's Potty. (Illus.). 16p. (ps). 1993. bds. 5.95 (2-921198-44-4, Pub. by Les Edits Herit CN) Adams Inc MA.
Sanseri, Gary & Sanseri, Wanda. The New England Primer of 1777. (Illus.). 115p. 1993. Repr. of 1777 ed. 14.95 (1-88004-510-9) Back Home Indust.
Sanseri, Wanda, jt. auth. see Sanseri, Gary.
Sansevere-Dreher, Diane. Benazir Bhutto. (gr. 4-7). 1991. pap. 3.50 (0-553-15857-0) Bantam.
—Stephen Biko. (gr. 4-7). 1991. pap. 3.50 (0-553-15931-3) Bantam.
Sansome, Constance J. Minnesota in Maps: A Trailblazer Atlas. Sansome, Constance J. & Jefferson, Lisa E., illus. 32p. (gr. 3 up). 1990. 17.95 (0-9626025-0-7); pap. 12.95 (0-9626025-1-5) Trailblazer Bks.
Sansom-Flood, Renee & Bernie, Shirley A. Remember Your Relatives, Vol. 1: Yankton Sioux Images, 1851 to 1904. Bruguier, Leonard R., ed. Flood, William J., et al, illus. Hoover, Herbert T., intro. by. 55p. (Orig.). (gr. 12). 1985. pap. 8.50 (0-9621936-0-7) Yankton Sioux Tribe.
Sansone, Barbara. Holidays in Bloom. (Illus.). 56p. (Orig.). (gr. 3-6). 1990. pap. 6.95 (0-933606-87-7, MS-691) E Sussman Educ.
—Special Days in Bloom. (Illus.). 56p. (Orig.). (gr. 3-6). 1990. pap. 6.95 (0-685-58699-5, MS-692) E Sussman Educ.
San Souci, Daniel. Country Road. LC 92-8379. 1993. pap. 14.95 (0-385-30867-1) Doubleday.
San Souci, Daniel, illus. The Bedtime Book. LC 85-12898. 48p. (gr. k-3). 1985. PLB 11.79 (0-685-42987-3, J Messner) S&S Trade.
—The Easter Treasures. Arico, Diane, compiled by. (ps-4). 1989. 8.95 (0-385-24401-0) Doubleday.
San Souci, Robert. The Boy & the Ghost. Pinkney, J. Brian, illus. (ps-3). 1989. pap. 13.95 jacketed (0-671-67176-6, S&S BFYR) S&S Trade.
—Cut from the Same Cloth. Pinkney, Brian, illus. 144p. (gr. 5 up). 1993. 16.95 (0-399-21987-0, Philomel Bks) Putnam Pub Group.
—Legend of Scarface. San Souci, Daniel, illus. LC 77-15170. 40p. (gr. k-3). 1987. pap. 7.00 (0-385-15874-2, Pub. by Zephyr-BFYR) Doubleday.
—Legend of Sleepy Hollow. San Souci, Daniel, illus. LC 86-2064. 32p. (ps-3). 1986. 11.95 (0-385-23396-5, Zephyr-BFYR); PLB 11.95 (0-385-23397-3, Zephyr-BFYR) Doubleday.
—The Loch Ness Monster: Opposing Viewpoints. LC 89-12026. (Illus.). 112p. (gr. 5-8). 1989. PLB 14.95 (0-89908-072-3) Greenhaven.
—N. C. Wyeth's Pilgrims. Wyeth, N. C., illus. 40p. (gr. 3-7). 1991. 13.95 (0-87701-806-5) Chronicle Bks.
—Los Peregrinos de N. C. Wyeth. Romo, Alberto, tr. (Illus.). 34p. (gr. 4-6). 1992. 14.95 (1-880507-03-X) Lectorum Pubns.
—Talking Eggs. 1989. PLB 14.89 (0-8037-0620-0) Dial Bks Young.
SanSouci, Robert. The Tsar's Promise. Mills, Lauren, illus. 32p. (ps up). 1992. 14.95 (0-399-21581-6, Philomel Bks) Putnam Pub Group.
San Souci, Robert D. Boy & the Ghost. LC 89-418. 40p. (ps-3). 1992. pap. 5.95 (0-671-79248-2, S&S BFYR) S&S Trade.

—The Boy & the Ghost. (gr. 3). 1990. write for info. (0-663-56233-3) Silver Burdett Pr.

—Christmas Ark. (gr. 4-7). 1991. 16.00 (0-385-24836-9) Doubleday.

—The Enchanted Tapestry. Gal, Laszlo, illus. LC 85-29283. 32p. (ps-3). 1987. 11.95 (0-8037-0304-X); PLB 11.89 (0-8037-0306-6) Dial Bks Young.

—The Enchanted Tapestry. Fogelman, Phyllis J., ed. Gal, Laszlo, illus. LC 85-29283. 32p. (ps-3). 1990. pap. 4.95 (0-8037-0862-9) Dial Bks Young.

—Feathertop: Based on the Tale by Nathaniel Hawthorne. San Souci, Daniel, illus. LC 91-10104. 32p. (gr. 1-5). 1992. pap. 16.00 (0-385-42044-7) Doubleday.

—The Firebird. LC 91-574. (Illus.). 32p. (ps-3). 1992. 14.00 (0-8037-0799-1); PLB 13.89 (0-8037-0800-9) Dial Bks Young.

—The Hobyahs. Natchev, Alexi, illus. LC 92-28655. 1994. 14.95 (0-385-30934-1) Doubleday.

—The House in the Sky. Clay, Wil, photos by. LC 92-39958. (Illus.). 1995. 13.99 (0-8037-1284-7); PLB 13.89 (0-8037-1285-5) Dial Bks Young.

—The Samurai's Daughter. Johnson, Stephen T., illus. LC 91-15585. 32p. (ps-3). 1992. 15.00 (0-8037-1135-2); PLB 14.89 (0-8037-1136-0) Dial Bks Young.

—Sukey & the Mermaid. Pinkney, Brian, illus. LC 90-24559. 32p. (gr. k-3). 1992. RSBE 14.95 (0-02-778141-0, Four Winds) Macmillan Child Grp.

—The Talking Eggs. Pinkney, Jerry, illus. (ps-3). 1989. 15.00 (0-8037-0619-7) Dial Bks Young.

—The White Cat. Spirin, Gennady, illus. LC 88-19698. 32p. (ps-3). 1990. 15.95 (0-531-05809-3); PLB 15.99 (0-531-08409-4) Orchard Bks Watts.

—Young Guinevere. LC 91-12499. (ps-3). 1993. 16.00 (0-385-41623-7) Doubleday.

San Souci, Robert D. & Coville, Katherine. Short & Shivery: Thirty Chilling Tales. LC 86-29067. 192p. (gr. 4-6). 1987. 14.95 (0-385-23886-X) Doubleday.

San Souci, Robert D. & Ginsburg, Max. Kate Shelley: Bound for Legend. LC 93-20438. (gr. 4-7). 1994. write for info. (0-8037-1289-8); write for info. (0-8037-1290-1) Dial Bks Young.

San Souci, Robert D., retold by. The Snow Wife. Johnson, Stephen T., illus. LC 92-28966. 32p. (ps-3). 1993. 14.99 (0-8037-1409-2); PLB 14.89 (0-8037-1410-6) Dial Bks Young.

San Suu Kyi Sung. Burma. (Illus.). 96p. (gr. 5 up). 1988. 14.95 (0-222-00979-9) Chelsea Hse.

—Nepal. (Illus.). 96p. (gr. 5 up). 1988. 14.95 (0-222-00981-0) Chelsea Hse.

Sant Bani School Children, illus. Book of Jonah. LC 84-50924. (gr. 1-6). 1984. pap. 6.95 (0-89142-044-4) Sant Bani Ash.

Sant, Thomas. The Amazing Adventures of Albert & His Flying Machine. De Rosa, Dee, illus. 160p. (gr. 4-7). 1990. 13.95 (0-525-67302-4, Lodestar Bks) Dutton Child Bks.

—Amazing Adventures of Albert & His Flying Machine. (gr. 4-7). 1993. pap. 3.50 (0-440-40814-8) Dell.

Santa Barbara Museum of Natural History. California's Chumash Indians. rev. ed. Powell, Ann, et al, illus. 72p. (ps-4). 1988. pap. 5.95 (0-945092-00-8) EZ Nature.

Santa, Beauel M. & Hardy, Lois L. How to Use the Library. 2nd ed. LC 55-6606. (Illus.). 128p. (gr. 7-12). 1966. pap. text ed. 6.95x (0-87015-145-2) Pacific Bks.

Santa Fe Writers Group. Bizarre & Beautiful Ears. (Illus.). 48p. (gr. 3 up). 1993. 14.95 (1-56261-122-4) John Muir.

—Bizarre & Beautiful Eyes. (Illus.). 48p. (gr. 3 up). 1993. 14.95 (1-56261-121-6) John Muir.

—Bizarre & Beautiful Feelers. Brigman, Chris, illus. LC 93-2034. 48p. 1993. text ed. 14.95 (1-56261-125-9) John Muir.

—Bizarre & Beautiful Noses. (Illus.). 48p. (gr. 3 up). 1993. 14.95 (1-56261-124-0) John Muir.

Santa Fe Writer's Group Staff. Bizarre & Beautiful Tongues. Brigman, Chris, illus. 48p. (gr. 4-7). 1993. text ed. 14.95 (1-56261-123-2) John Muir.

Santacruz, Daniel, tr. Dentro Fuera: Un Libro Disney de Opuestos. Duerrstein, Richard, illus. (SPA.). 12p. 1993. 5.95 (1-56282-458-9) Disney Pr.

—Mickey Esta Feliz: Un Libro Disney de Emociones. Duerrstein, Richard, illus. (SPA.). 12p. 1993. 5.95 (1-56282-459-7) Disney Pr.

—Un Raton Mickey: Un Libro Disney de Numeros. Duerrstein, Richard, illus. (SPA.). 12p. 1993. 5.95 (1-56282-460-0) Disney Pr.

Santacruz, Daniel M., tr. see Manushkin, Fran.

Santamaria, Peggy. Arrivals & Departures: How to Use All Kinds of Schedules. LC 93-29642. 1993. 12.95 (0-8239-1605-7) Rosen Group.

—Money Smarts. Rosen, Ruth, ed. (gr. 7-12). 1992. 12.95 (0-8239-1470-4) Rosen Group.

Santori, Helen. The Perfect Couple. (gr. 5 up). 1988. pap. 2.95 (0-8041-0238-4) Ivy Books.

Santoro, Chris, illus. Lift a Rock, Find a Bug. LC 91-62580. 22p. (ps-k). 1993. 3.50 (0-679-80904-X) Random Bks Yng Read.

—Lift the Hood, Find a Motor. LC 91-62581. 22p. (ps-k). 1993. 3.50 (0-679-80903-1) Random Bks Yng Read.

—Open the Barn Door, Find a Cow. LC 91-62579. 22p. (ps-k). 1993. 3.50 (0-679-80901-5) Random Bks Yng Read.

—Open the Box, Find a Prize. LC 91-62573. 22p. (ps-k). 1993. 3.50 (0-679-80902-3) Random Bks Yng Read.

Santoro, Christopher, jt. auth. see Johnson, Evelyne.

Santoro, Christopher, illus. Rudolph the Red-Nosed Reindeer. LC 86-62550. 14p. (ps-1). 1987. 5.95 (0-394-88923-1) Random Bks Yng Read.

Santos, Elsie S. The Frog in the Bog. Santos, Duarte, illus. 44p. (Orig.). (ps-2). 1986. pap. 3.95 (0-914151-04-5) Shawme Ent.

—The Master of Song. Santos, Duarte S., illus. 44p. (Orig.). (ps-1). 1984. pap. 3.95 (0-914151-02-9) Shawme Ent.

—The Mystery at Shawme Pond. Alvaro, Albert M., ed. Santos, Duarte, illus. 20p. (Orig.). (ps-1). 1983. pap. 3.95 (0-914151-01-0) Shawme Ent.

Santos, Harry G. Town Team: The Folklore of Town Team Baseball. (Illus.). 120p. (Orig.). 1988. pap. 12.95 (0-940151-09-X) Statesman Exam.

Santos, Nina D. Strangers on the Mountain. 128p. 1991. pap. 22.00x (0-85088-665-1, Pub. by Gomer Pr UK) St Mut.

Santrey, Laurence. Ancient Egypt. Frenck, Hal, illus. LC 84-2728. 32p. (gr. 3-6). 1985. PLB 9.49 (0-8167-0248-9); pap. text ed. 2.95 (0-8167-0249-7) Troll Assocs.

—Australia. Eitzen, Allan, illus. LC 84-2636. 32p. (gr. 3-6). 1985. PLB 9.49 (0-8167-0124-5); pap. text ed. 2.95 (0-8167-0125-3) Troll Assocs.

—Birds. Johnson, Pamela, illus. LC 84-2731. 32p. (gr. 3-6). 1985. PLB 9.49 (0-8167-0192-X); pap. text ed. 2.95 (0-8167-0193-8) Troll Assocs.

—Conservation & Pollution. Maccabe, Richard, illus. LC 84-2703. 32p. (gr. 3-6). 1985. PLB 9.49 (0-8167-0260-8); pap. text ed. 2.95 (0-8167-0261-6) Troll Assocs.

—Davy Crockett: Young Pioneer. Livingston, Francis, illus. LC 82-16040. 48p. (gr. 4-6). 1983. PLB 10.79 (0-89375-847-7); pap. text ed. 3.50 (0-89375-848-5) Troll Assocs.

—Discovering the Stars. Watling, James, illus. LC 81-7489. 32p. (gr. 2-4). 1982. PLB 11.59 (0-89375-568-0); pap. text ed. 2.95 (0-89375-569-9); cassette 9.95 (0-685-04946-9) Troll Assocs.

—Earthquakes & Volcanoes. Jones, John, illus. LC 84-2676. 32p. (gr. 3-6). 1985. PLB 9.49 (0-8167-0212-8); pap. text ed. 2.95 (0-8167-0213-6) Troll Assocs.

—Energy & Fuels. Burns, Raymond, illus. LC 84-2704. 32p. (gr. 3-6). 1985. PLB 9.49 (0-8167-0290-X); pap. text ed. 2.95 (0-8167-0291-8) Troll Assocs.

—George Washington: Young Leader. LC 81-23150. (Illus.). 48p. (gr. 4-6). 1982. PLB 10.79 (0-89375-758-6); pap. text ed. 3.50 (0-89375-759-4) Troll Assocs.

—Heat. Birmingham, Lloyd, illus. LC 84-2711. 32p. (gr. 3-6). 1985. PLB 9.49 (0-8167-0306-X); pap. text ed. 2.95 (0-8167-0307-8) Troll Assocs.

—Helen Keller. Frenck, Hal, illus. LC 84-2682. 32p. (gr. 3-6). 1985. PLB 9.49 (0-8167-0156-3); pap. text ed. 2.95 (0-8167-0157-1) Troll Assocs.

—Jim Thorpe: Young Athlete. Ulrich, George, illus. LC 82-15982. 48p. (gr. 4-6). 1983. PLB 10.79 (0-89375-845-0); pap. text ed. 3.50 (0-89375-846-9) Troll Assocs.

—John Adams, Brave Patriot. Smolinski, Dick, illus. LC 85-1095. 48p. (gr. 4-6). 1986. lib. bdg. 10.79 (0-8167-0559-3); pap. text ed. 3.50 (0-8167-0560-7) Troll Assocs.

—John Lennon, Young Rock Star. Beier, Ellen, illus. LC 89-33938. 48p. (gr. 4-6). 1990. lib. bdg. 10.79 (0-8167-1781-8); pap. text ed. 3.50 (0-8167-1782-6) Troll Assocs.

—Lakes & Ponds. Moylan, Holly, illus. LC 84-2653. 32p. (gr. 3-6). 1985. PLB 9.49 (0-8167-0206-3); pap. text ed. 2.95 (0-8167-0207-1) Troll Assocs.

—Louisa May Alcott, Young Writer. Speidel, Sandra, illus. LC 85-1086. 48p. (gr. 4-6). 1986. lib. bdg. 10.79 (0-8167-0563-1); pap. text ed. 3.50 (0-8167-0564-X) Troll Assocs.

—Magnets. Veno, Joseph, illus. LC 84-2597. 32p. (gr. 3-6). 1985. PLB 9.49 (0-8167-0140-7); pap. text ed. 2.95 (0-8167-0141-5) Troll Assocs.

—Moon. Schindler, S. D., illus. LC 84-8441. 32p. (gr. 3-6). 1985. PLB 9.49 (0-8167-0252-7); pap. text ed. 2.95 (0-8167-0253-5) Troll Assocs.

—Music. Croll, Carolyn, illus. LC 84-2648. 32p. (gr. 3-6). 1985. PLB 9.49 (0-8167-0218-7); pap. text ed. 2.95 (0-8167-0219-5) Troll Assocs.

—Oregon Trail. Livingston, Francis, illus. LC 84-2643. 32p. (gr. 3-6). 1985. PLB 9.49 (0-8167-0196-2); pap. text ed. 2.95 (0-8167-0197-0) Troll Assocs.

—Pocahontas. Wenzel, David, illus. LC 84-8443. 32p. (gr. 3-6). 1985. PLB 9.49 (0-8167-0276-4); pap. text ed. 2.95 (0-8167-0277-2) Troll Assocs.

—Prehistoric People. Smolinski, Dick, illus. LC 84-8464. 32p. (gr. 3-6). 1985. PLB 9.49 (0-8167-0242-X); pap. text ed. 2.95 (0-8167-0243-8) Troll Assocs.

—Rivers. Sweat, Lynn, illus. LC 84-8818. 32p. (gr. 3-6). 1985. lib. bdg. 9.49 (0-8167-0210-1); pap. text ed. 2.95 (0-8167-0211-X) Troll Assocs.

—Safety. Gold, Ethel, illus. LC 84-2700. 32p. (gr. 3-6). 1985. PLB 9.49 (0-8167-0230-6); pap. text ed. 2.95 (0-8167-0231-4) Troll Assocs.

—State & Local Government. Dole, Bob, illus. LC 84-8440. 32p. (gr. 3-6). 1985. PLB 9.49 (0-8167-0270-5); pap. text ed. 2.95 (0-8167-0271-3) Troll Assocs.

—Thomas Jefferson. Eitzen, Allan, illus. LC 84-2579. 32p. (gr. 3-6). 1985. PLB 9.49 (0-8167-0176-8); pap. text ed. 2.95 (0-8167-0177-6) Troll Assocs.

—Toussaint l'Ouverture, Lover of Liberty. Griffith, Gershom, illus. LC 93-18971. 48p. (gr. 4-6). 1993. PLB 10.79 (0-8167-2823-2); pap. text ed. 3.50 (0-8167-2824-0) Troll Assocs.

—Using the Library. Dole, Bob, illus. LC 84-2590. 32p. (gr. 3-6). 1985. PLB 9.49 (0-8167-0122-9); pap. text ed. 2.95 (0-8167-0123-7) Troll Assocs.

—What Makes the Wind? Dodson, Bert, illus. LC 81-7486. 32p. (gr. 2-4). 1982. PLB 11.59 (0-89375-584-2); pap. text ed. 2.95 (0-89375-585-0); cassette avail. Troll Assocs.

—Young Albert Einstein. Beier, Ellen, illus. LC 89-33940. 48p. (gr. 4-6). 1990. PLB 10.79 (0-8167-1777-X); pap. text ed. 3.50 (0-8167-1778-8) Troll Assocs.

—Young Ben Franklin. LC 81-23067. (Illus.). 48p. (gr. 4-6). 1982. PLB 10.79 (0-89375-768-3); pap. text ed. 3.50 (0-89375-769-1) Troll Assocs.

—Young Frederick Douglass: Fight for Freedom. Dodson, Bert, illus. LC 82-15993. 48p. (gr. 4-6). 1983. PLB 10.79 (0-89375-857-4); pap. text ed. 3.50 (0-89375-858-2) Troll Assocs.

Santrey, Louis. Autumn. Sabin, Francene, illus. LC 82-19396. 32p. (gr. 4-7). 1983. lib. bdg. 10.79 (0-89375-905-8); pap. text ed. 2.95 (0-89375-906-6) Troll Assocs.

—Spring. Sabin, Francene, illus. LC 82-19381. 32p. (gr. 4-7). 1983. lib. bdg. 10.79 (0-89375-909-0); pap. text ed. 2.95 (0-89375-910-4) Troll Assocs.

—Summer. LC 82-19384. (Illus.). 32p. (gr. 4-7). 1983. lib. bdg. 10.79 (0-89375-911-2); pap. text ed. 2.95 (0-89375-912-0) Troll Assocs.

—Winter. Sabin, Francene, illus. LC 82-19353. 32p. (gr. 4-7). 1983. lib. bdg. 10.79 (0-89375-907-4); pap. text ed. 2.95 (0-89375-908-2) Troll Assocs.

Santvoord, George Van see Harris, Joel C.

Sapaugh, Micah. Marlusk the Warrior. Sapaugh, Micah, illus. Sargent, Dave, intro. by. (Illus.). 48p. (Orig.). (gr. k-8). 1993. text ed. 11.95 (1-56763-092-8); pap. text ed. 5.95 (1-56763-093-6) Ozark Pub.

Saperstein, David, jt. auth. see Vorspan, Albert.

Saponaro, Sabina. The Ugly Duckling. (Illus.). 30p. (ps-1). 1986. 3.95 (0-8120-5725-2) Barron.

Saponaro, Sabrina. Puss-In-Boots. (Illus.). 30p. (ps-1). 1987. 3.95 (0-8120-5810-0) Barron.

Sapp, Kathy. I Am a Part of Something Big. (Illus.). 306p. (Orig.). (gr. 4-6). 1989. pap. text ed. 3.50 (0-936625-66-X, New Hope AL) Womans Mission Union.

Sappenfield, John R. Liza & Mother "Hug" Bear. 1993. 7.95 (0-8062-4842-4) Carlton.

Saqr, Abdul B. How to Call People to Islam. Ahmad, Shakil, tr. 154p. (Orig.). Date not set. pap. write for info. (1-882837-16-9) Wamy Intl.

Sara. Across Town. LC 90-7982. (Illus.). 32p. (ps-2). 1991. 13.95 (0-531-05932-4); PLB 13.99 (0-531-08532-5) Orchard Bks Watts.

—The Rabbit, the Fox, & the Wolf. LC 90-32443. (Illus.). 32p. (ps-2). 1991. 13.95 (0-531-05953-7); RLB 13.99 (0-531-08553-8) Orchard Bks Watts.

Saraga, Jessica. Tudor Monarchs. (Illus.). 72p. (gr. 7-11). 1991. 19.95 (0-7134-6350-3, Pub. by Batsford UK) Trafalgar.

Sarage, Jessica. Cromwell. (Illus.). 64p. (gr. 7-10). 1989. 19.95 (0-7134-6033-4, Pub. by Batsford UK) Trafalgar.

Sarasas, Claude. ABC's of Origami: Paper Folding for Children. Sarasas, Claude, illus. LC 64-17160. (gr. 3-8). 1964. bds. 12.95 (0-8048-0000-6) C E Tuttle.

Saraydarian, Torkom. The Psychology of Cooperation & Group Consciousness. LC 89-192444. 165p. 1989. pap. 12.00 (0-929874-11-0) TSG Pub Found.

Sardegna, Jill. K Is for Kiss Good Night. Hayes, Michael, illus. LC 92-34404. 1994. 13.95 (0-385-31044-7) Doubleday.

Sardin, Claudia. Dolly. (ps-12). 1987. pap. 2.95 (0-87067-723-3, BH723) Holloway.

Sardinas-Wyssling, Karen, ed. see Popkin, Michael H.

Sargeant, Frank. The Trout Book: A Complete Angler's Guide. LC 92-71318. (Illus.). 160p. (Orig.). 1992. pap. 9.95 (0-936513-21-7) Larsens Outdoor.

Sargent, Carl. London Sourcebook. Ippolito, Donna & Mulvihill, Sharon T., eds. Biske, Joel & Nielson, Mike, illus. 32p. (gr. 7 up). 1991. pap. 15.00 (1-55560-131-6, 7203) FASA Corp.

Sargent, Dave. Best Friends. Sapaugh, Blaine, illus. 48p. (Orig.). (gr. k-8). 1993. text ed. 11.95 (1-56763-056-1); pap. text ed. 5.95 (1-56763-057-X) Ozark Pub.

—Callie. 160p. 1992. pap. write for info. (1-56763-002-2) Ozark Pub.

—Raw Courage. 204p. 1992. pap. write for info. (1-56763-003-0) Ozark Pub.

—Spike. 199p. 1992. write for info. Ozark Pub.

—The Ties That Bind. 188p. 1992. write for info. Ozark Pub.

—An Uphill Climb. 344p. 1992. PLB write for info. (1-56763-000-6); pap. write for info. (1-56763-001-4) Ozark Pub.

Sargent, Dave & Sargent, Pat. Amy Armadillo. Sapaugh, Blaine, illus. 48p. (Orig.). (gr. k-8). 1993. text ed. 11.95 (1-56763-046-4); pap. text ed. 5.95 (1-56763-047-2) Ozark Pub.

—The Bandit. Sapaugh, Blaine, illus. 48p. (Orig.). (gr. k-8). 1993. text ed. 11.95 (1-56763-048-0); pap. text ed. 5.95 (1-56763-049-9) Ozark Pub.

—Big Jake. Sapaugh, Blaine, illus. 48p. (Orig.). (gr. k-8). 1993. text ed. 11.95 (1-56763-030-8); pap. text ed. 5.95 (1-56763-031-6) Ozark Pub.

—Billy Beaver. 64p. (gr. 2-6). 1992. pap. write for info. (1-56763-004-9) Ozark Pub.
—Bobby Bobcat. 64p. (gr. 2-6). 1992. pap. write for info. (1-56763-012-X) Ozark Pub.
—Brutus the Bear. 64p. (gr. 2-6). 1992. pap. write for info. (1-56763-006-5) Ozark Pub.
—Buddy Badger. Sapaugh, Blaine, illus. 48p. (Orig.). (gr. k-8). 1993. text ed. 11.95 (1-56763-036-7); pap. text ed. 5.95 (1-56763-037-5) Ozark Pub.
—Chrissy Cottontail. 64p. (gr. 2-6). 1992. pap. write for info. (1-56763-009-X) Ozark Pub.
—Dawn the Deer. 48p. (gr. 2-6). 1992. write for info. Ozark Pub.
—Dike the Wolf. 64p. (gr. 2-6). 1992. pap. write for info. (1-56763-008-1) Ozark Pub.
—Greta Groundhog. Sapaugh, Blaine, illus. 48p. (Orig.). (gr. k-8). 1993. text ed. 11.95 (1-56763-040-5); pap. text ed. 5.95 (1-56763-041-3) Ozark Pub.
—Mad Jack. Sapaugh, Blaine, illus. 48p. (Orig.). (gr. k-8). 1993. text ed. 11.95 (1-56763-034-0); pap. text ed. 5.95 (1-56763-035-9) Ozark Pub.
—Molly's Journey. Sapaugh, Blaine, illus. 48p. (Orig.). (gr. k-8). 1993. text ed. 11.95 (1-56763-038-3); pap. text ed. 5.95 (1-56763-039-1) Ozark Pub.
—Peggy Porcupine. Sapaugh, Blaine, illus. 48p. (Orig.). (gr. k-8). 1993. text ed. 11.95 (1-56763-044-8); pap. text ed. 5.95 (1-56763-045-6) Ozark Pub.
—Pokey Opossum. Sapaugh, Blaine, illus. 48p. (Orig.). (gr. k-8). 1993. text ed. 11.95 (1-56763-042-1); pap. text ed. 5.95 (1-56763-043-X) Ozark Pub.
—Redi Fox. 64p. (gr. 2-6). 1992. pap. write for info. (1-56763-010-3) Ozark Pub.
—Roy Raccoon. 64p. (gr. 2-6). 1992. pap. write for info. (1-56763-005-7) Ozark Pub.
—Sammy the Skunk. 64p. (gr. 2-6). 1992. pap. write for info. (1-56763-011-1) Ozark Pub.
—Tunnel King. Sapaugh, Blaine, illus. 48p. (Orig.). (gr. k-8). 1993. text ed. 11.95 (1-56763-032-4); pap. text ed. 5.95 (1-56763-033-2) Ozark Pub.
—White Thunder. 48p. (gr. 2-6). 1992. write for info. (1-56763-007-3) Ozark Pub.
Sargent, Lynne. My Peanut Butter Pond Think 'n' Do Book. Ducey, Beth, illus. 100p. (ps-1). 1990. wkbk. 3.95 (1-55999-125-9) LinguiSystems.
Sargent, Pamela. Alien Child. LC 87-45303. 256p. (gr. 7 up). 1988. HarpC Child Bks.
Sargent, Pamela, jt. auth. see **Quackenbush, Marcia.**
Sargent, Pat. Barney the Bear Killer. (Illus.). 120p. (Orig.). (gr. k-8). 1994. text ed. 18.95 (1-56763-054-5); pap. text ed. 8.95 (1-56763-055-3) Ozark Pub.
Sargent, Pat, jt. auth. see **Sargent, Dave.**
Sargent, Ruth. The Island Merry-Go-Round. Weinberger, Jane, ed. DeVito, Pamela, illus. LC 88-50277. 46p. (Orig.). (gr. 1-4). 1988. pap. 5.95 (0-932433-46-4) Windswept Hse.
—The Littlest Lighthouse. Litchfield, Marion, illus. LC 81-66268. 32p. (Orig.). (ps-1). 1981. pap. 4.50 (0-89272-119-7) Down East.
—The Nautical Alphabet. Carlson, Kathleen, illus. 32p. (ps-1). 1984. saddle-stitched 3.95 (0-89272-190-1) Down East.
—The Tunnel under the Sea. Weinberger, Jane, ed. Gorski, Paul & DeVito, Pam, illus. 120p. (gr. 3-6). 1993. pap. 9.95 (0-932433-11-1) Windswept Hse.
Sargent, Sara. Weird Henry Berg. 1986. pap. 2.50 (0-440-79346-7) Dell.
Sargent, Sarah. Between Two Worlds. LC 93-24533. 1994. 14.95 (0-395-66425-X, Ticknor & Flds Yng Read) HM.
—Jerry's Ghosts: The Mystery of the Blind Tower. LC 91-21971. 144p. (gr. 3-7). 1992. SBE 13.95 (0-02-778035-X, Bradbury Pr) Macmillan Child Grp.
—Jonas McFee, A. T. P. LC 91-42931. 128p. (gr. 3-7). 1992. pap. 3.95 (0-689-71579-X, Aladdin) Macmillan Child Grp.
—Weird Henry Berg. 160p. (gr. 5 up). 1981. pap. 2.25 (0-440-49346-3, YB) Dell.
Sargent, William. Night Reef: Dusk to Dawn on a Coral Reef. (Illus.). 40p. (gr. 5-8). 1991. 14.95 (0-531-15219-7); PLB 14.90 (0-531-11073-7) Watts.

Sarlas-Fontana, Jane. The Adventures of Spero the Orthodox Church Mouse: The Nativity of Our Lord Christ's Birth. Simic, Tim, illus. 20p. (ps-4). 1992. pap. 6.95 (0-937032-91-3) Light&Life Pub Co MN.

A delightful children's Christmas story & activity book. This book was designed for children ages 4 to 7 years old. Because children of these ages are active, curious, fun, joyful, mischievous, & full of energy...this book features some hands-on experiences & activities by which your children can grow...move...think...& learn! In this first ADVENTURES OF SPERO book, children will learn of the birth of Baby Jesus as seen through the eyes of Spero. Upon

completing the storybook part the children may then complete the activity pages at the back of the book, & then once completed, cut them out & place them on the refrigerator door. Look for other ADVENTURES OF SPERO, THE ORTHODOX CHURCH MOUSE! (EASTER, MAKING THE SIGN OF THE CROSS & many others.) 8.5 X 11 inches. Softbound, $6.95. "Many years ago my grandmother told me of Spero - a special mouse who lived in the basement of an Orthodox church. Spero had many adventures in church & when you meet him, you will learn of the many teachings of the Holy Orthodox Church. Look for other adventures of Spero in the near future." --Jane Sarlas-Fontana, Author. *Publisher Provided Annotation.*

—Spero Learns of Palm Sunday & Jesus' Love. 28p. (ps-4). 1993. pap. 5.95 (0-9638336-0-X) Spero & Me.
Sarna, Jonathan, ed. see **Leiman, Sondra.**
Sarndon, John. Eyewitness Question & Answer Book. LC 93-3523. (Illus.). 32p. (gr. 3-6). 1993. 16.95 (1-56458-347-3) Dorling Kindersley.
Sarnoff, Jane. Words: A Book about the Origins of Every Day Words & Phrases. Ruffins, Reynold, illus. LC 81-8943. 64p. (gr. 4-8). 1981. SBE 13.95 (0-684-16958-4, Scribners Young Read) Macmillan Child Grp.
Saro-Wiwa, Ken. A Forest of Flowers: Short Stories. 151p. (Orig.). (gr. 10 up). text ed. 15.00 (9-78246-003-6); pap. text ed. 8.50 (9-78246-004-4) Three Continents.
—Mr. B. Brimoh, Peregrino, illus. 154p. (Orig.). (gr. 6 up). pap. text ed. 8.50x (1-87071-601-9) Three Continents.
—Prisoners of Jebs. 182p. (Orig.). (gr. 10 up). pap. text ed. 11.00 (1-87071-602-7) Three Continents.
Saroyan, William. The Circus. Zimdars, Berta, illus. 32p. (gr. 4 up). 1986. PLB 13.95s.p. (0-88682-066-9) Creative Ed.
—The Parsley Garden. (gr. 4-12). Date not set. 13.95 (0-88682-355-2, 97221-098) Creative Ed.
Sarracino, William L., illus. Mother Spider & Her Little Ones. 16p. (Orig.). (ps-7). 1982. pap. 3.75 (0-915347-11-3) Pueblo Acoma Pr.
Sart, Jean de see De Sart, Jean.
Sasha, Mark. Hall of Beasts. LC 92-39520. 1994. pap. 14.00 (0-671-79893-6) S&S Trade.
Sass, Charles, ed. see **Walker, Tim & Thompson, Marcia.**
Sass, Karin. Mary Baker Eddy, a Special Friend. Kieffer, Christa, illus. LC 83-72002. 32p. (gr. k-3). 1983. 8.95 (0-87510-165-8) Christian Sci.
Sasse. Person to Person. (gr. 9-12). 1982. students guide 7.00 (0-02-665340-0); tchr's guide 16.60 (0-02-665330-3) Bennett IL.
Sasso, Sandy E. God's Paintbrush. Compton, Annette, illus. LC 92-15493. 32p. (gr. k-4). 1992. 15.95 (1-879045-22-2) Jewish Lights.
—In God's Name. (Illus.). 32p. (gr. k-6). 1994. 16.95 (1-879045-26-5) Jewish Lights.
Satchell, Jonathan. In the Wild: Fun.Fact.Flap. Guenier, Emma, illus. 16p. (gr. 2 up). 1993. 9.95 (0-87226-512-9, Bedrick Blackie) P Bedrick Bks.
—On the Farm: Fun.Flap.Flaps. Guenier, Emma, illus. 16p. (gr. 2 up). 1993. 9.95 (0-87226-513-7, Bedrick Blackie) P Bedrick Bks.
Sateren, Shelley S. Banff. LC 89-33152. (Illus.). 48p. (gr. 4-5). 1989. RSBE 13.95 (0-89686-431-6, Crestwood Hse) Macmillan Child Grp.
—Black Panther. LC 89-28267. (Illus.). 48p. (gr. 5). 1990. RSBE 12.95 (0-89686-519-3, Crestwood Hse) Macmillan Child Grp.
Sather, Edgar, et al. People at Work: Listening & Communicative Skills, Vocabulary Building. (Illus.). 112p. (gr. 8 up). 1990. student wkbk. only 13.95x (0-86647-037-9) Pro Lingua.
—People at Work: Student's Package. (Illus.). 112p. (gr. 8 up). 1990. incl. wkbk. & 3 cassettes 24.95x (0-86647-033-6) Pro Lingua.
Sathre, Vivian. Carnival Time. LC 91-4442. (ps-3). 1992. pap. 14.00 (0-671-76963-4, S&S BFYR) S&S Trade.
—J. B. Wigglebottom & the Parade of Pets. O'Neill, Catherine, illus. LC 92-17375. 96p. (gr. 2-6). 1993. SBE 12.95 (0-689-31811-1, Atheneum Child Bk) Macmillan Child Grp.
Sato, Esther M. & Sakihara, Masako. Japanese Now, Vol. 3. LC 81-23142. 304p. (gr. 9-12). 1987. text ed. 20.00x (0-8248-1042-2); tchr's ed. 20.00x (0-8248-1043-0); wkbk. 4.50x (0-8248-1044-9) UH Pr.
Sato, Satoru. I Wish I Had a Big, Big Tree. Murakami, Tsutomu, illus. LC 88-8080. 40p. (ps-2). 1989. 10.95 (0-688-07303-4); PLB 10.88 (0-688-07304-2) Lothrop.
Sato, Wakiko, jt. auth. see **Barnes, Jill.**
Satoh, Naomi, tr. see **Mahoney, Judy.**
Satoru Fujii, tr. see **Masaomi Kanzaki.**

Satsvarupa dasa Goswami. The Life Story of His Divine Grace A. C. Bhaktivedanta Swami Prabhupada. Ellwood, Robert S., pref. by. 32p. (gr. 4-7). 1984. saddlestitch 3.50 (0-89647-019-9) Bala Bks.
Satter, Leslie. Easter: Practical Activities for Teachers & Parents to Supplement Religious Instruction. Satter, Leslie, illus. 85p. (Orig.). (gr. k-3). 1991. pap. text ed. 9.95 (1-879599-00-7) L Ross Pubns.
—Easter: Practical Activities for Teachers & Parents to Supplement Religious Instruction. Satter, Leslie, illus. 86p. (Orig.). (gr. k-3). 1991. pap. text ed. 9.95 (1-879599-01-5) L Ross Pubns.
Sattgast. God Made Me Most Wonderfully. 1992. write for info. (1-55513-556-0, Chariot Bks) Cook.
Sattgast, L. J. My Very First Bible - New Testament. Flint, Russ, illus. (Orig.). (ps-3). 1989. 16.99 (0-89081-756-1) Harvest Hse.
—My Very First Bible - Old Testament. (Illus.). (ps-3). 1992. 16.99 (0-89081-941-6) Harvest Hse.
—Teach Me about God: Includes Special Tips to Help Parents Explain Big Truths to Small Children. (ps). 1993. 9.99 (0-945564-64-3, Gold & Honey) Questar Pubs.
Sattler, Helen R. Baby Dinosaurs. Zallinger, Jean D., illus. LC 83-25631. 40p. (ps-3). 1984. 12.95 (0-688-03817-4); PLB 12.88 (0-688-03818-2) Lothrop.
—The Book of Eagles. Zallinger, Jean D., illus. LC 88-38806. 64p. (gr. 3 up). 1989. 14.95 (0-688-07021-3); PLB 14.88 (0-688-07022-1) Lothrop.
—Dinosaurs of North America. Rao, Anthony, illus. Ostrom, John H., intro. by. LC 80-27411. (Illus.). 160p. (gr. 2 up). 1981. 17.95 (0-688-51952-0) Lothrop.
—The Earliest Americans. Zallinger, Jean D., illus. 128p. (gr. 4-7). 1993. 16.45 (0-395-54996-5, Clarion Bks) HM.
—Fish Facts & Bird Brains: Animal Intelligence. Maestro, Giulio, illus. LC 83-20805. 128p. (gr. 5-9). 1984. 13.95 (0-525-66915-9, Lodestar Bks) Dutton Child Bks.
—Giraffes: The Sentinels of the Savannas. Santoro, Christopher, illus. LC 89-2287. 80p. (gr. 3 up). 1990. 14.95 (0-688-08284-X); PLB 14.88 (0-688-08285-8) Lothrop.
—Hominids: A Look Back at Our Ancestors. Santoro, Christopher, illus. LC 86-10624. (gr. 3 up). 1988. PLB 15.95 (0-688-06061-7) Lothrop.
—The New Illustrated Dinosaur Dictionary. Powzyk, Joyce, illus. 1990. 24.95 (0-688-08462-1) Lothrop.
—The New Illustrated Dinosaur Dictionary. Powzyk, Joyce, illus. LC 90-3313. 352p. 1990. pap. 14.95 (0-688-10043-0, Pub. by Beech Tree Bks) Morrow.
—Pterosaurs: The Flying Reptiles. Santoro, Christopher, illus. LC 84-4428. 48p. (gr. 1-4). 1985. PLB 12.88 (0-688-03996-0) Lothrop.
—Recipes for Art & Craft Materials. rev. ed. Shohet, Marti, illus. LC 86-34271. 128p. (gr. 6 up). 1987. 13.95 (0-688-07374-3) Lothrop.
—Recipes for Art & Craft Materials. Shohet, Marti, illus. 144p. (gr. 5 up). 1994. pap. 3.95 (0-688-13199-9, Pub. by Beech Tree Bks) Morrow.
—Sharks, the Super Fish. Zallinger, Jean D., illus. LC 84-4381. 96p. (gr. 9 up). 1985. 15.95 (0-688-03993-6) Lothrop.
—Stegosaurs: The Solar-Powered Dinosaurs. Pearson, Susan, ed. MacCombie, Turi, illus. LC 90-49733. 32p. (gr. 1 up). 1992. 15.00 (0-688-10055-4); PLB 14.93 (0-688-10056-2) Lothrop.
—Train Whistles. rev. ed. LC 84-11279. (Illus.). 32p. (ps-2). 1985. 13.00 (0-688-03978-2) Lothrop.
—Tyrannosaurus Rex & Its Kin: The Mesozoic Monsters. Powzyk, Joyce, illus. LC 88-1577. 48p. (gr. 3 up). 1989. 14.95 (0-688-07747-1); PLB 13.88 (0-688-07748-X) Lothrop.
—Whales, the Nomads of the Sea. Zallinger, Jean D., illus. LC 86-10397. 128p. (gr. 3 up). 1987. 15.00 (0-688-05587-7) Lothrop.
Satullo, Jane, et al. It Happens to Boys Too... Bookless, Nan, illus. 156p. (ps-6). 1989. pap. 6.50 (0-9618618-0-0) RCC-Berkshires Pr.
Sauer, Julia. Fog Magic. Ward, Lynd, illus. 128p. (gr. 5-9). 1986. pap. 3.99 (0-14-032163-2, Puffin) Puffin Bks.
Sauer, Julia L. The Light at Tern Rock. Schrieber, Georges, illus. 64p. (gr. 3-7). 1994. pap. 3.99 (0-14-036857-4) Puffin Bks.
Sauer, Sue, et al. Stevie Has His Heart Examined. Goldstein, Nancy, ed. Albury, Mary, illus. (ps-7). 1983. pap. text ed. 4.25 (0-937423-00-9) U M H & C.
—Stevie Has His Heart Repaired. Goldstein, Nancy, ed. Albury, Mary, illus. (ps-7). 1979. pap. text ed. 4.25 (0-937423-01-7) U M H & C.
Sauerwein, Leigh. The Way Home. LC 93-10097. 1993. 14.00 (0-374-38247-6) FS&G.
Saul, Carol P. Peter's Song. De Groat, Diane, illus. LC 91-24674. 40p. (ps-1). 1992. pap. 14.00 jacketed (0-671-73812-7, S&S BFYR) S&S Trade.
—Someplace Else. Root, Barrett, illus. (gr. 4 up). 1995. pap. 14.00 (0-671-87283-4, S&S BFYR) S&S Trade.
Saul, John. Comes the Blind Fury. 384p. (Orig.). (gr. 9 up). 1990. pap. 5.99 (0-440-11475-6) Dell.
Saul, Judy. Bobby Bear & the Band. LC 85-61831. (Illus.). 32p. (ps-1). 1985. 6.95 (0-87783-203-X) Oddo.
Saules, Janet De see De Saules, Janet.
Saull, D. L. The Sunchildren. 1992. 7.95 (0-533-09619-7) Vantage.
Saulles, Janet De see Watson, Carol & De Saulles, Janet.
Saulnier, Karen, jt. auth. see **Bornstein, Harry.**
Saulnier, Karen L., jt. auth. see **Bornstein, Harry.**

Saunders, Dave & Saunders, Julie. Brave Jack. Saunders, Dave, illus. LC 92-23238. 32p. (ps-1). 1993. SBE 14.95 (*0-02-781073-9*, Bradbury Pr) Macmillan Child Grp.
—Dibble & Dabble. LC 88-24127. (Illus.). 32p. (ps-1). 1990. SBE 14.95 (*0-02-781071-2*, Bradbury Pr) Macmillan Child Grp.
—Snowtime. Saunders, Dave, illus. LC 90-42565. 32p. (ps-1). 1991. SBE 14.95 (*0-02-781075-5*, Bradbury Pr) Macmillan Child Grp.
Saunders, Dudley. Dracula's Treasure. 1975. 4.50 (*0-87602-123-2*) Anchorage.
Saunders, Graham. Shells. (Illus.). 64p. (gr. 8 up). 1993. pap. 4.50 (*0-86020-454-5*, Usborne) EDC.
Saunders, Julie, jt. auth. see Saunders, Dave.
Saunders, Kathleen. The Manmade Bear. Woon, Kay, illus. 33p. (gr. 2-5). 1980. pap. 2.95 (*0-939666-11-1*) Yosemite Assn.
Saunders, Kenneth. Hexagrams. (Illus.). 32p. (Orig.). (gr. 5 up). 1986. pap. 3.95 (*0-685-13310-9*, Pub. by Tarquin UK) Parkwest Pubns.
Saunders, Paola B., tr. see Elliott, Dan.
Saunders, Paola B., tr. see Hautzig, Deborah.
Saunders, Paola B., tr. see Pfloog, Jan.
Saunders, R. Balloon Voyager. (Illus.). 32p. (gr. 4 up). 1988. PLB 17.27 (*0-86592-870-3*); PLB 12.95s.p. (*0-685-58291-4*) Rourke Corp.
Saunders, Richard & Mackness, Brian. Horrorgami! LC 91-20005. (Illus.). 64p. (gr. 1-7). 1991. 14.95 (*0-8069-8480-5*) Sterling.
—Horrorgami: Spooky Paperfolding Just for Fun. LC 91-20005. (Illus.). 64p. (gr. 2-7). 1992. pap. 5.95 (*0-8069-8481-3*) Sterling.
Saunders, Rubie. Good Grooming for Boys. Green, Anne C., illus. 96p. (gr. 5-9). 1989. PLB 12.90 (*0-531-10768-X*) Watts.
—Good Grooming for Girls. Green, Anne C., illus. 96p. (gr. 5-9). 1989. PLB 12.90 (*0-531-10769-8*) Watts.
Saunders, Susan. Attack of the Monster Plants. 64p. (gr. 4). 1986. pap. 2.25 (*0-553-15399-4*) Bantam.
—Blizzard at Black Swan Inn. 64p. (Orig.). (gr. 4). 1986. pap. 2.25 (*0-553-15379-X*) Bantam.
—The Creature from Miller's Pond. (Illus.). (gr. 4-8). 1983. pap. 2.25 (*0-553-15424-9*) Bantam.
—The Daring Rescue of Marlon the Swimming Pig. Owens, Gail, illus. LC 87-4633. 64p. (gr. 2-4). 1987. lib. bdg. 6.99 (*0-394-98293-2*); pap. 1.95 (*0-394-88293-8*, Random Juv) Random Bks Yng Read.
—Dolly Parton: Country Goin' to Town. LC 85-40440. (Illus.). 56p. (gr. 2-6). 1985. pap. 10.95 (*0-670-80787-7*) Viking Child Bks.
—Dolly Parton: Country Goin' to Town. Pate, Rodney, illus. 64p. (gr. 2-6). 1986. pap. 3.95 (*0-14-032162-4*, Puffin) Puffin Bks.
—Dorothy & the Magic Belt. Rose, David, illus. LC 84-17946. 64p. (gr. 2-6). 1985. pap. 1.95 (*0-394-87067-0*) Random Bks Yng Read.
—The Golden Goose. Selzer, Isadore, illus. 32p. (gr. k-3). 1988. pap. 2.50 (*0-590-41715-0*) Scholastic Inc.
—The Green Slime. 64p. (gr. 1-8). 1982. pap. 2.25 (*0-553-15480-X*) Bantam.
—The Green Slime, No. 6. 1983. pap. 2.99 (*0-553-15680-2*) Bantam.
—Haunted Halloween Party. 64p. (Orig.). (gr. 4). 1986. pap. 2.99 (*0-553-15453-2*) Bantam.
—Jackrabbit & the Prairie Fire: Story of a Black-Tailed Jackrabbit. Thomas, Peter, narrated by. Bosson, Jo-Ellen, illus. LC 91-61144. 32p. (ps-3). 1991. 11.95 (*0-924483-29-6*); incl. audiocassette 16.95 (*0-924483-30-X*); incl. audiocassette & toy combination 39.95 (*0-924483-31-8*); incl. audiocassette & small toy combination 25.95 (*0-924483-38-5*); write for info audiocassette (*0-924483-32-6*) Soundprints.
—Kate the Boss. (gr. 4-7). 1990. pap. 2.50 (*0-590-43189-7*) Scholastic Inc.
—Kate the Winner! 128p. (gr. 3-7). 1991. pap. 2.75 (*0-590-43925-1*, Apple Paperbacks) Scholastic Inc.
—Kate's Camp-Out. 96p. (Orig.). (gr. 3-7). 1988. pap. 2.50 (*0-590-41337-6*, Apple Paperbacks) Scholastic Inc.
—Kate's Crush. 1989. pap. 2.50 (*0-590-42366-5*) Scholastic Inc.
—Kate's Sleepover Disaster. 1989. pap. 2.50 (*0-590-41846-7*) Scholastic Inc.
—Kate's Surprise. 96p. (Orig.). (gr. 4-6). 1987. pap. 2.50 (*0-590-40643-4*, Apple Paperbacks) Scholastic Inc.
—Kate's Surprise Visitor. (gr. 5-7). 1990. pap. 2.50 (*0-590-42819-5*) Scholastic Inc.
—Lauren I. 1990. pap. 2.50 (*0-590-42816-0*, SHLS) Scholastic Inc.
—Lauren Takes Charge. 1989. pap. 2.50 (*0-590-42300-2*) Scholastic Inc.
—Lauren's Afterschool Job. 128p. (gr. 3-7). 1990. pap. 2.75 (*0-590-43928-6*) Scholastic Inc.
—Lauren's Big Mix-Up. 80p. (gr. 3-7). 1988. pap. 2.50 (*0-590-41336-8*, Apple Paperbacks) Scholastic Inc.
—Lauren's Double Disaster. (gr. 4-7). 1991. pap. 2.75 (*0-590-43926-X*) Scholastic Inc.
—Lauren's New Address. 1990. pap. 2.50 (*0-590-43191-9*) Scholastic Inc.
—Lauren's New Friend. (gr. 5-7). 1990. pap. 2.50 (*0-590-43194-3*) Scholastic Inc.
—Lauren's Sleepover Exchange. 112p. (gr. 3-7). 1989. pap. 2.50 (*0-590-41697-9*, Apple Paperbacks) Scholastic Inc.
—Lauren's Treasure. 96p. (gr. 3-7). 1988. pap. 2.50 (*0-590-41695-2*) Scholastic Inc.

—Light on Burro Mountain. 64p. (Orig.). (gr. 4 up). 1987. pap. 2.25 (*0-553-15517-2*, Skylark) Bantam.
—Margaret Mead: The World Was Her Family. Lewin, Ted, illus. (Orig.). (gr. 2-6). 1988. pap. 3.99 (*0-14-032063-6*) Viking Child Bks.
—Miss Liberty Caper. (gr. 2-4). 1986. pap. 2.25 (*0-553-15416-8*, Skylark) Bantam.
—The Movie Mystery. (gr. 2-4). 1987. pap. 2.25 (*0-553-15509-1*, Skylark) Bantam.
—Mystery Cat, Bk. 1. (Orig.). (ps-3). 1986. pap. 2.25 (*0-553-15377-3*, Skylark) Bantam.
—Mystery Cat & the Chocolate Trap. 96p. (Orig.). 1986. pap. 2.25 (*0-553-15415-X*, Skylark) Bantam.
—Mystery Cat & the Monkey Business. 96p. (Orig.). 1986. pap. 2.25 (*0-553-15452-4*) Bantam.
—The Mystery of the Hard Luck Rodeo. Rosales, Melodye, illus. LC 88-37896. 64p. (Orig.). (gr. 2-4). 1989. PLB 6.99 (*0-394-92344-8*); pap. 1.95 (*0-394-82344-3*) Random Bks Yng Read.
—The New Kate. (gr. 5-7). 1990. pap. 2.50 (*0-590-44721-1*) Scholastic Inc.
—The New Stephanie. (gr. 4-7). 1991. pap. 2.75 (*0-590-43924-3*) Scholastic Inc.
—Patti's Last Sleepover, No. 9. 96p. (gr. 3-7). 1988. pap. 2.50 (*0-590-41696-0*) Scholastic Inc.
—Patti's Luck. 96p. (gr. 4-6). 1987. pap. 2.50 (*0-590-40641-8*) Scholastic Inc.
—Patti's New Look. 80p. (Orig.). (gr. 4-6). 1988. pap. 2.50 (*0-590-40644-2*, Apple Paperbacks) Scholastic Inc.
—Puss in Boots. 1989. pap. 2.50 (*0-590-41888-2*) Scholastic Inc.
—Runaway Spaceship. 64p. 1985. pap. 2.25 (*0-553-15463-X*) Bantam.
—Seasons of a Red Fox. Thomas, Peter, narrated by. Bosson, Jo-Ellen, illus. LC 91-61145. 32p. (ps-3). 1991. 11.95 (*0-924483-25-3*); incl. audiocassette 16.95 (*0-924483-26-1*); incl. audiocassette & toy combination 39.95 (*0-924483-27-X*); incl. audiocassette & small toy combination 25.95 (*0-924483-40-7*); write for info. audiocassette (*0-924483-28-8*) Soundprints.
—Starring Stephanie. (Illus.). 96p. (Orig.). (gr. 4-6). 1987. pap. 2.50 (*0-590-40642-6*) Scholastic Inc.
—Starstruck Stephanie. 1990. pap. 2.50 (*0-590-42817-9*) Scholastic Inc.
—Stephanie. 1989. pap. 2.50 (*0-590-42814-4*) Scholastic Inc.
—Stephanie & the Wedding. (gr. 5-7). 1990. pap. 2.50 (*0-590-43193-5*) Scholastic Inc.
—Stephanie Strikes Back. 96p. (gr. 3-7). 1988. pap. 2.50 (*0-590-41694-4*, Apple Paperbacks) Scholastic Inc.
—Stephanie's Big Story. 1989. pap. 2.50 (*0-590-42299-5*) Scholastic Inc.
—Stephanie's Family Secret. 1989. pap. 2.50 (*0-590-41845-9*) Scholastic Inc.
—The Tower of London. (gr. 2-4). 1984. pap. 2.25 (*0-553-15490-7*, Skylark) Bantam.
—Trouble with Patti. (gr. 5-7). 1990. pap. 2.50 (*0-590-42818-7*) Scholastic Inc.
—Tyrone Goes to School. (Illus.). 64p. (gr. 2-5). 1992. 11.99 (*0-525-44981-7*, DCB) Dutton Child Bks.
—A Valentine for Patti. (gr. 4-7). 1991. pap. 2.75 (*0-590-43927-8*) Scholastic Inc.
—You Are Invisible. 1989. pap. 2.99 (*0-553-15685-3*) Bantam.
Saunders, Susan & Packard, Edward. Ice Cave. (gr. 2-4). 1987. pap. 2.25 (*0-553-15467-2*, Skylark) Bantam.
Saunders, Susan, adapted by see Spyri, Johanna.
Saunderson, Jane. Heart & Lungs. Farmer, Andrew & Green, Robina, illus. LC 90-42881. 32p. (gr. 4-6). 1992. PLB 11.89 (*0-8167-2096-7*); pap. text ed. 3.95 (*0-8167-2097-5*) Troll Assocs.
—Muscles & Bones. Farmer, Andrew & Green, Robina, illus. LC 90-42882. 32p. (gr. 4-6). 1992. lib. bdg. 11.89 (*0-8167-2088-6*); pap. text ed. 3.95 (*0-8167-2089-4*) Troll Assocs.
Saunier. Tiger, Reading Level 3-4. (Illus.). 28p. (gr. 2-5). 1983. PLB 16.67 (*0-86592-866-5*); lib. bdg. 12.50 (*0-685-58827-0*) Rourke Corp.
Saurus, Alice. One Thousand & One Dinosaur Jokes for Kids. (Orig.). (ps-6). 1993. pap. 3.99 (*0-345-38496-2*) Ballantine.
Sauvain, Philip. Air. LC 91-27905. (Illus.). 48p. (gr. 6 up). 1992. RSBE 13.95 (*0-02-781076-3*, New Discovery) Macmillan Child Grp.
—Communications. LC 93-14869. (Illus.). 48p. (gr. 5-8). 1993. PLB 22.80 (*0-8114-2333-6*) Raintree Steck-V.
—El Alamein. LC 91-28378. (Illus.). 32p. (gr. 6 up). 1992. RSBE 13.95 (*0-02-781081-X*, New Discovery) Macmillan Child Grp.
—Hastings. LC 91-25369. (Illus.). 32p. (gr. 6 up). 1992. RSBE 13.95 (*0-02-781079-8*, New Discovery) Macmillan Child Grp.
—Midway. LC 92-29566. (Illus.). 32p. (gr. 6 up). 1993. RSBE 13.95 (*0-02-781090-9*, New Discovery) Macmillan Child Grp.
—Motion. LC 91-24480. (Illus.). 48p. (gr. 6 up). 1992. RSBE 13.95 (*0-02-781077-1*, New Discovery) Macmillan Child Grp.
—Over Four Hundred & Fifty Years Ago: In the New World. Rowe, Eric, illus. LC 93-2649. 32p. (gr. 6 up). 1993. RSBE 13.95 (*0-02-726327-4*, New Discovery Bks) Macmillan Child Grp.
—Over Sixteen Hundred Years Ago in the Roman Empire. LC 91-43328. (Illus.). 32p. (gr. 6 up). 1992. RSBE 13.95 (*0-02-781083-6*, New Discovery) Macmillan Child Grp.

—Over Three Thousand Years Ago: In Ancient Egypt. (Illus.). 32p. (gr. 6 up). 1993. RSBE 13.95 (*0-02-781084-4*, New Discovery) Macmillan Child Grp.
—Over Two Thousand Years Ago in Ancient Greece. LC 91-40072. (Illus.). 32p. (gr. 6 up). 1992. RSBE 13.95 (*0-02-781082-8*, New Discovery) Macmillan Child Grp.
—Roads. Stefoff, Rebecca, ed. LC 90-40359. (Illus.). 48p. (gr. 4-7). 1990. PLB 17.26 (*0-944483-77-1*) Garrett Ed Corp.
—Robert Scott in the Antarctic. LC 93-18209. (Illus.). 32p. (gr. 4-6). 1993. lib. bdg. 13.95 RSBE (*0-87518-532-0*, Dillon) Macmillan Child Grp.
—Skyscrapers. Stefoff, Rebecca, ed. LC 90-40358. (Illus.). 48p. (gr. 4-7). 1990. PLB 17.26 (*0-944483-78-X*) Garrett Ed Corp.
—Tunnels. Stefoff, Rebecca, ed. LC 90-40248. (Illus.). 48p. (gr. 4-7). 1990. PLB 17.26 (*0-944483-79-8*) Garrett Ed Corp.
—Water. LC 91-19145. (Illus.). 48p. (gr. 8-9). 1992. RSBE 13.95 (*0-02-781078-X*, New Discovery) Macmillan Child Grp.
—Waterloo. LC 92-29564. (Illus.). 32p. (gr. 6 up). 1993. RSBE 13.95 (*0-02-781096-8*, New Discovery) Macmillan Child Grp.
Saux, Alain Le see Le Saux, Alain.
Sauza, James de see De Sauza, James.
Savage, Candace. Eat Up! Clement, Gary, illus. 56p. 1993. pap. 9.95 (*1-895565-13-8*) Firefly Bks Ltd.
—Get Growing: How the Earth Feeds Us. Clement, Gary, illus. 56p. (gr. 3-7). 1991. pap. 9.95 (*0-920668-95-X*) Firefly Bks Ltd.
—Trash Attack: Garbage, & What We Can Do about It. Beinicke, Steve, illus. 56p. (gr. 3-7). 1991. pap. 9.95 (*0-920668-73-9*) Firefly Bks Ltd.
Savage, Cindy. Danger Down Under. 128p. (gr. 5-8). 1992. pap. 2.99 (*0-87406-589-5*) Willowisp Pr.
—My Sister, the Pig, & Me. (Illus.). 142p. (gr. 3-5). 1992. pap. 2.50 (*0-87406-638-7*) Willowisp Pr.
—The Popularity Secret. 112p. (gr. 5-8). 1988. 2.75 (*0-87406-315-9*, 37-16478-9) Willowisp Pr.
Savage, Deborah. The Flight of the Albatross. (gr. 7 up). 1989. 14.45 (*0-395-45711-4*) HM.
—A Rumor of Otters. (gr. 6 up). 1986. 13.45 (*0-395-41186-6*) HM.
—A Rumour of Otters. 160p. (gr. 6 up). 1993. pap. 3.80 (*0-395-65748-2*) HM.
—A Stranger Calls Me Home. 240p. (gr. 5-9). 1992. 14.45 (*0-395-59424-3*) HM.
Savage, Eileen. Winning over Asthma. (Illus.). 40p. (Orig.). (ps-3). pap. write for info. (*0-9622868-0-X*) Dolan Pr.
Savage, Eileen D. Winning over Asthma. Savage, Eileen D., illus. Plaut, Thomas F., intro. by. LC 89-50551. (Illus.). 32p. (gr. k-3). 1993. pap. 6.95 (*0-914625-09-8*) Pedipress.
Savage, Jeff. Karate. LC 93-27206. 1995. text ed. 13.95 (*0-89686-854-0*, Crestwood Hse) Macmillan.
—Kristi Yamaguchi. LC 92-42190. (Illus.). 64p. (gr. 3 up). 1993. RSBE 13.95 (*0-87518-583-5*, Dillon) Macmillan Child Grp.
—Running. LC 93-37943. Date not set. write for info. (*0-89686-855-9*, Crestwood Hse) Macmillan Child Grp.
—Sports Great Jim Abbott. LC 92-522. (Illus.). 64p. (gr. 4-10). 1993. lib. bdg. 15.95 (*0-89490-395-0*) Enslow Pubs.
—Thurman Thomas: Star Running Back. LC 93-2557. 1994. write for info. (*0-89490-445-0*) Enslow Pubs.
—Weight Lifting. LC 93-27211. (gr. 6 up). Date not set. write for info. (*0-89686-856-7*) MacMillan Child Grp.
Savage, John F. Dyslexia: Understanding Reading Problems. LC 85-8925. (Illus.). 96p. (gr. 4-8). 1985. lib. bdg. 10.98 (*0-671-54289-3*, J Messner) S&S Trade.
—Dyslexia: Understanding Reading Problems. (Illus.). 96p. (gr. 4-8). 1985. lib. bdg. 10.98 (*0-685-28823-4*, J Messner) S&S Trade.
Savage, Lon, ed. see Caldwell, Willie W.
Savage, Stephen. Ancient Greek Monuments to Make: The Parthenon & the Theatre of Dionysos. Savage, Stephen, illus. Moon, Warren G., intro. by. (Illus.). 48p. (Orig.). (gr. 7 up). 1990. pap. 7.95 (*0-88045-096-7*) Stemmer Hse.
—Animals Undercover. LC 92-30753. 1993. 12.95 (*0-525-67404-7*, Lodestar Bks) Dutton Child Bks.
—Making Tracks: A Slide-&-See Book. Savage, Stephen, illus. 10p. (gr. k-3). 1992. 10.00 (*0-525-67353-9*, Lodestar Bks) Dutton Child Bks.
Savage, Susan, jt. auth. see Hedrick, Basil.
Savage-Hubbard, Kathy & Speicher, Rose C. Paint Adventures! LC 92-45634. (Illus.). 48p. (ps). 1993. 11.95 (*0-89134-508-6*) North Light Bks.
Savan, Beth. Earthwatch: Earthcycles & Ecosystems. Cupples, Pat, illus. 96p. 1992. pap. 8.61 (*0-201-58148-5*) Addison-Wesley.
Savarin, Julian J. Lynx. 240p. 1986. 15.95 (*0-8027-0890-0*) Walker & Co.
Savary, Louis. The Life of Jesus. Goodwill, Rita, illus. 43p. (ps-4). 1989. 5.59 (*0-88271-099-0*) Regina Pr.
Savary, Louis & Frankhausen, Edward. The Bible As Narrated by Jesus, the Storyteller. 1989. 9.95 (*0-88271-198-9*) Regina Pr.
Savige, Katherine, ed. see Thompson, Denisse & Van Loy, Merrie.

Savigny, Francois. Il Etait Une Fois. (FRE., Illus.). 96p. 1991. pap. 9.95 incl. 60-min. cassette (0-8442-1440-X, Passport Bks); pap. 6.50 bk. only (0-685-41419-1, Passport Bks) NTC Pub Grp.

Savigny, Francoise. Il Etait Une Fois - Once Upon a Time. (FRE., Illus.). 96p. (gr. 4 up). pap. 6.95 (0-8442-1433-7, Passport Bks) NTC Pub Grp.

Saville, David. The Evolution of the World: A Revolving Picture Book. Martin, Josephine, illus. LC 91-71383. 12p. 1991. 13.95 (1-56282-095-8) Hyprn Child.

Savin, Marcia. The Moon Bridge. 1992. 13.95 (0-590-45873-6, Scholastic Hardcover) Scholastic Inc.
—Will Lithuania Comstock Please Come to the Courtesy Phone? LC 93-28441. (Illus.). 160p. (gr. 5-9). 1993. PLB 13.95 (0-8167-3324-4); pap. 3.95 (0-8167-3325-2) Troll Assocs.

Savitri. Savitri & Satyavan. Wheaton, Jaya, illus. (gr. 1-9). 1979. pap. 2.75 (0-89744-160-5) Auromere.
—Tales from Indian Classics, Bk. I. Biswas, Pulak, illus. (gr. 3-9). 1979. 4.50 (0-89744-167-2); pap. 3.00 (0-685-57665-5) Auromere.
—Tales from Indian Classics, Bk. II. Biswas, Pulak, illus. (gr. 3-9). 1979. 4.50 (0-89744-168-0); pap. 3.00 (0-685-57666-3) Auromere.
—Tales from Indian Classics, Bk. III. Chatterjee, Sukumar, illus. (gr. 3-9). 1979. 4.50 (0-89744-169-9); pap. 3.00 (0-685-57667-1) Auromere.

Savitt, Sam. Draw Horses with Sam Savitt. (Illus.). 96p. 1991. Repr. of 1981 ed. 20.95 (0-939481-23-5) Half Halt Pr.

Savitz, Harriet M. & Syring, K. Michael. The Pail of Nails. Shaw, Charles, illus. LC 88-7653. (gr. 3 up). 1990. 10.95 (0-687-29974-8) Abingdon.

Sawicki, Leo. Anytime Stories. Robinson, Michael, illus. 64p. (ps-8). 1988. 7.95 (0-920806-78-3, Pub. by Penumbra Pr CN) U of Toronto Pr.

Sawicki, Mary, adapted by see Hostetler, Jacob.

Sawicki, Norma J. The Little Red House. Goffe, Toni, illus. LC 88-2740. 24p. (ps). 1989. 9.95 (0-688-07891-5); PLB 9.88 (0-688-07892-3) Lothrop.
—Something for Mom. Weston, Martha, illus. LC 86-34421. 32p. (ps-1). 1987. PLB 12.88 (0-688-05590-7) Lothrop.

Sawin, Margaret M. I Didn't Want to Say Goodbye. (Illus.). 15p. (Orig.). (gr. k-2). 1989. pap. 3.50x (971-10-0277-9, Pub. by New Day Pub PI) Cellar.

Sawitz, Mike, jt. auth. see Ourth, John.

Saw Myat Yin. Burma. LC 89-25463. (Illus.). 128p. (gr. 5-9). 1991. PLB 21.95 (1-85435-299-7) Marshall Cavendish.

Sawyer, Kem K. Horace Mann. (Illus.). 112p. (gr. 5 up). 1993. PLB 17.95 (0-7910-1741-9) Chelsea Hse.
—Lucretia Mott: Friend of Justice. Carter, Rosalyn & Carter, Rosalynncontrib. by. LC 91-70822. (Illus.). 48p. (gr. 4-8). 1991. 14.95g (1-878668-04-8); pap. 7.95 (1-878668-08-0) Disc Enter Ltd.
—Marjory Stoneman Douglas: Guardian of the Everglades. Carow, Leslie, illus. 72p. (gr. 5-12). 1994. PLB 16.95 (1-878668-20-X); pap. 7.95 (1-878668-28-5) Disc Enter Ltd.
—National Foundation on the Arts & Humanities. (Illus.). 112p. (gr. 5 up). 1989. lib. bdg. 14.95 (1-55546-115-8) Chelsea Hse.
—U. S. Arms Control & Disarmament Agency. Schlesinger, Arthur M., Jr., intro. by. (Illus.). 112p. (gr. 5 up). 1990. lib. bdg. 14.95 (1-55546-125-5) Chelsea Hse.

Sawyer, Kieran. Sex & the Teenager: Choices & Decisions. LC 89-82512. (Orig.). (gr. 9-12). 1990. pap. text ed. 3.95 participant bk., 112p. (0-87793-423-1); spiral bdg., director's manual, 168p. 13.95 (0-87793-424-X) Ave Maria.

Sawyer, Ruth. Journey Cake, Ho! (ps-3). 1978. pap. 3.95 (0-14-050275-0) Puffin Bks.
—Roller Skates. Angelo, Valenti, illus. 192p. (gr. 4-7). 1969. pap. 1.50 (0-440-47499-X, YB) Dell.
—Roller Skates. Angelo, Valenti, illus. 184p. (gr. 5-9). 1986. pap. 3.99 (0-14-030358-8, Puffin) Puffin Bks.
—Roller Skates. (gr. 5-7). 1988. 16.50 (0-8446-6343-3) Peter Smith.

Saxby, Maurice. The Great Deeds of Heroic Women. Ingpen, Robert, illus. LC 91-11211. 152p. (gr. 4 up). 1992. 18.95 (0-87226-348-7) P Bedrick Bks.
—The Great Deeds of Superheroes. Ingpen, Robert, illus. 184p. (gr. 4 up). 1990. 24.95 (0-87226-342-8) P Bedrick Bks.
—The Great Deeds of Superheroes. Ingpen, Robert, illus. 184p. (gr. 4 up). 1993. pap. 14.95 sewn (0-87226-260-X) P Bedrick Bks.

Saxon, Ed, jt. auth. see Daizovi, Lonnie G.

Say, Allen. The Bicycle Man. Say, Allen, illus. 48p. (gr. k-3). 1982. 14.45 (0-395-32254-7); 11.95 (0-685-05704-6) HM.
—The Bicycle Man. Say, Allen, illus. (ps-3). 1989. pap. 5.70 (0-395-50652-2, Sandpiper) HM.
—El Chino. Say, Allen, illus. 32p. (gr. 2-8). 1990. 14.45 (0-395-52023-1) HM.
—Grandfather's Journey. LC 93-18836. 1993. 16.95 (0-395-57035-2) HM.
—Lost Lake. Say, Allen, illus. (gr. 1-4). 1989. 14.45 (0-395-50933-5) HM.
—The Lost Lake. Say, Allen, illus. 32p. (gr. k-3). 1992. pap. 4.80 (0-395-63036-3, Sandpiper) HM.
—A River Dream. Say, Allen, illus. 32p. (gr. k-3). 1988. 14.45 (0-395-48294-1) HM.
—A River Dream. Say, Allen, illus. 32p. (gr. k-3). 1993. pap. 4.95 (0-395-65749-0) HM.

—Tree of Cranes. Say, Allen, illus. 32p. (gr. k-3). 1991. 16.45 (0-395-52024-X, Sandpiper) HM.

Sayers, Dorothy L., tr. Song of Roland. (Orig.). (gr. 9 up). 1957. pap. 5.95 (0-14-044075-5, Penguin Classics) Viking Penguin.

Sayles, Rasheeda A. Rasheeda's Visitors. 1990. 6.95 (0-533-08920-4) Vantage.

Saylor, Melissa, illus. Mary Wore Her Red Dress Big Book. (ps-2). 1988. pap. text ed. 14.00 (0-922053-17-0) N Edge Res.
—My Aunt Came Back Big Book. (ps-2). 1988. pap. text ed. 14.00 (0-922053-12-X) N Edge Res.

Saylor-Marchant, Linda. Hammer: Two Legit Two Quit. LC 92-4412. (Illus.). 64p. (gr. 3 up). 1992. RSBE 13. 95 (0-87518-522-3, Dillon) Macmillan Child Grp.

Saypol, Judyth R. & Wikler, Madeline. Come Let Us Welcome Shabbat. LC 83-25638. (Illus.). 32p. (ps up). 1978. pap. 2.95 (0-930494-04-0) Kar Ben.
—My Very Own Haggadah. Rev. ed. Burstein, Chaya, illus. LC 83-6. 32p. (ps-3). 1983. pap. text ed. 2.95 (0-930494-23-7) Kar Ben.
—My Very Own Megillah. (Illus.). 32p. (gr. k-5). 1977. pap. 2.95 (0-930494-01-6) Kar Ben.
—My Very Own Rosh Hashanah. (Illus.). 32p. (gr. k-6). 1978. pap. 3.95 (0-930494-06-7) Kar Ben.
—My Very Own Shavuot Book. Wikler, Madeline & Fishman, Tamar, illus. 28p. (gr. k-6). 1982. pap. 2.95 (0-930494-15-6) Kar Ben.
—My Very Own Sukkot Book. Wikler, Madeline, illus. LC 83-26738. 40p. (gr. k-5). 1980. pap. 3.95 (0-930494-09-1) Kar Ben.
—My Very Own Yom Kippur Book. (Illus.). 32p. (gr. k-6). 1978. pap. 3.95 (0-930494-05-9) Kar Ben.
—The Purim Parade. Kahn, Katherine J., illus. LC 86-71816. 12p. (ps). 1986. bds. 4.95 (0-930494-60-1) Kar Ben.

Saypol, Judyth R. & Wikler, Madeline, illus. My Very Own Simchat Torah. 24p. (gr. k-5). 1981. pap. 3.95 (0-930494-11-3) Kar Ben.

Sayre, April P. Deserts. 1994. PLB write for info. (0-8050-2825-0) H Holt & Co.
—Prairie. 1994. PLB write for info. (0-8050-2827-7) H Holt & Co.
—Taiga. 1994. PLB write for info. (0-8050-2830-7) H Holt & Co.
—Temperate Forests. 1994. PLB write for info. (0-8050-2828-5) H Holt & Co.
—Tropical Rainforest. 1994. PLB write for info. (0-8050-2826-9) H Holt & Co.
—Tundra. 1994. PLB write for info. (0-8050-2829-3) H Holt & Co.

Scae, Bracha, tr. see Firer, Benzion.

Scalist, Paula, ed. see Eko, Paul M.

Scalist, Paula, ed. see Kamba, Polo.

Scallon, Cheryl V., ed. see Schneider, David C.

Scally, M. A. Walking Proud. 1990. 12.95 (0-87498-100-X) Assoc Pubs DC.

Scalzetto, Louis D. The Sky of Scattered Roads: Poems, Essays & Short Stories. LC 92-93371. 46p. (Orig.). (gr. 8-9). 1993. pap. 6.50 (1-879008-02-5) L D Scalzetto.

Scamell, Ragnhild. Buster's Echo. Webster, Genevieve, illus. LC 92-29868. 32p. (ps-2). 1993. 14.00 (0-06-022883-0); PLB 13.89 (0-06-022884-9) HarpC Child Bks.
—Solo Plus One. Martland, Elizabeth, illus. 32p. (ps-3). 1992. 13.95 (0-316-77242-9) Little.
—Three Bags Full. Hobson, Sally, illus. LC 92-50882. 32p. (ps-1). 1993. 14.95 (0-531-05486-1) Orchard Bks Watts.

Scamell, Rajnhild. Rooster Crows. Riches, Judith, illus. LC 93-31348. 1994. write for info. (0-688-13290-1, Tambourine Bks); PLB write for info. (0-688-13291-X, Tambourine Bks) Morrow.

Scandrett, Mary. Verbiage. (gr. 5-12). 1987. 39.00 (0-930599-12-8) Thinking Pubns.

Scandura, Alice M., jt. auth. see Lowerre, George F.

Scandure, Alice M., jt. auth. see Lowerre, George F.

Scannell, Vernon. Love Shouts & Whispers. (Illus.). 64p. (gr. k-3). 1992. 15.95 (0-09-174365-6, Pub. by Hutchinson UK) Trafalgar.

Scarboro, Elizabeth. The Secret Language of the SB. 128p. (gr. 3-7). 1992. pap. 3.99 (0-14-034310-5, Puffin) Puffin Bks.

Scarborough, M., et al. Target Spelling. large type ed. Incl. Target 180. 158p. 1983. 24.15 (0-317-04593-8, 4-25410-00); Target 360. 134p. 1983. 24.15 (0-317-04594-6, 4-25430-00); Target 540. 134p. 1983. 34.00 (0-317-04746-9, J-35450). (gr. 9-12). 24.15 (0-317-04592-X, 4-25410-00) Am Printing Hse.

Scarf, Maggi. Meet Benjamin Franklin. Fogarty, Pat, illus. LC 88-17657. 64p. (gr. 2-4). 1989. PLB 6.99 (0-394-91961-0); pap. text ed. 2.99 (0-394-81961-6) Random Bks Yng Read.

Scarffe, Bronwen. Alfred. Posey, Pam, illus. LC 92-21442. 1993. 3.75 (0-383-03612-7) SRA Schl Grp.
—Busy Bees. Costeloe, Brenda, illus. LC 92-31958. 1993. 3.75 (0-383-03558-9) SRA Schl Grp.
—Traffic Jam. Kelly, Geoff, illus. LC 92-31956. 1993. 3.75 (0-383-03599-6) SRA Schl Grp.
—Walter Hottle Bottle. Crossett, Warren, illus. LC 92-34271. 1993. 14.00 (0-383-03664-X) SRA Schl Grp.
—You're So Clever. Hunnam, Lucinda, illus. LC 92-34339. 1993. 3.75 (0-383-03669-0) SRA Schl Grp.

Scarffe, Bronwen, jt. auth. see Green, Robyn.

Scariano, Margaret. Summer Strike-Out. Kratoville, Betty L., ed. (Illus.). 64p. (gr. 3-9). 1989. PLB 4.95 (0-87879-617-7) High Noon Bks.

Scariano, Margaret & Cunningham, Marilyn. Nine to Five Series. (Illus.). (gr. 3-9). 1985. Set, 48p. ea. pap. 15.00 ea. (0-87879-502-2) High Noon Bks.

Scariano, Margaret M. Dr. Ruth Westheimer. LC 91-40923. (Illus.). 128p. (gr. 6 up). 1992. lib. bdg. 17.95 (0-89490-333-0) Enslow Pubs.

Scariano, Margaret M., jt. auth. see Dolan, Edward F.

Scarpa, Ron & Dorner, Terrence. Barefoot Water Skiing: An Illustrated Guide to Learning & Mastering the Sport. Robertson, Jo, ed. (Illus.). (gr. 7 up). 1988. pap. 11.95 (0-944406-01-7) World Pub FL.

Scarpino, Jane. Nellie, the Light House Dog. Weinberger, Jane, ed. Ensor, Robert, illus. 40p. (ps-3). 1993. pap. 9.95 (0-932433-23-5) Windswept Hse.

Scarry. Best Word Book. (FRE.). (gr. 3-8). 14.95 (0-685-28441-7) Fr & Eur.
—Dictionnaire Animaux. (FRE.). (gr. 3-8). 24.95 (0-685-28442-5) Fr & Eur.

Scarry, Huck. Aboard a Steam Locomotive. LC 86-16957. (Illus.). (gr. 4-12). 1987. 12.95 (0-13-000373-5) P-H.
—Balloon Trip: A Sketchbook. Scarry, Huck, illus. LC 82-23002. 68p. (gr. 3-7). 1983. 10.95 (0-13-055939-3) P-H.
—Life on a Barge: A Sketchbook. Scarry, Huck, illus. 72p. (gr. 3-7). 1982. 10.95 (0-13-535831-0) P-H.
—Life on a Fishing Boat: A Sketchbook. LC 83-9631. (Illus.). 72p. (gr. 3-5). 1983. 10.95 (0-13-535856-6) P-H.
—Things That Go. (ps-1). 1986. 3.98 (0-685-16834-4, 616556) Outlet Bk Co.
—Things That Sail. (ps-1). 1986. 3.98 (0-685-16828-X, 616564) Outlet Bk Co.

Scarry, Huck, illus. My First Picture Dictionary. LC 76-24174. (ps-2). 1978. lib. bdg. 5.99 (0-394-93486-5); pap. 2.25 (0-394-83486-0) Random Bks Yng Read.

Scarry, Patricia. Rags. Lanza, Barbara, illus. 32p. (ps-k). 1991. write for info. (0-307-15702-4, Golden Pr) Western Pub.

Scarry, Patricia M. Sweet Smell of Christmas. Miller, J. P., illus. 32p. (ps-2). 1970. write for info. (0-307-13527-6, Golden Bks) Western Pub.

Scarry, Patsy. My Puppy. reissued ed. Wilkin, Eloise, illus. 24p. (ps-k). 1992. write for info. (0-307-00147-4, 312-11, Golden Pr) Western Pub.
—Patsy Scarry's Big Bedtime Storybook. reissued ed. Saekeres, Cyndy, illus. LC 79-5450. 72p. (ps-1). 1990. 9.95 (0-679-80756-X) Random Bks Yng Read.

Scarry, Richard. Bananas Gorilla: Richard Scarry's Smallest Pop-up Book Ever! (Illus.). 10p. (ps-3). 1992. write for info. (0-307-12462-2, 12462, Golden Pr) Western Pub.
—Be Careful, Mr. Frumble! Scarry, Richard, illus. LC 89-43154. 24p. (Orig.). (ps-2). 1990. pap. 2.25 (0-679-80566-4) Random Bks Yng Read.
—The Best Mistake Ever! A Step Two Book. Scarry, Richard, illus. LC 84-2029. 48p. (ps-2). 1984. lib. bdg. 7.99 (0-394-96816-6); pap. 3.50 (0-394-86816-1) Random Bks Yng Read.
—Best Read It Yourself Book Ever. 1990. write for info. (0-307-16551-5, Golden Pr) Western Pub.
—The Bunny Book. (Illus.). 24p. (ps-k). 1987. pap. write for info (0-307-10048-0, Pub. by Golden Bks) Western Pub.
—Early Words. Scarry, Richard, illus. LC 75-36466. 14p. (ps-1). 1976. 3.95 (0-394-83238-8) Random Bks Yng Read.
—Fun with Numbers: Grade One. Scarry, Richard, illus. 32p. (ps-2). 1986. pap. 1.95 (0-394-87665-2) Random Bks Yng Read.
—The Funniest Storybook Ever. (Illus.). (ps-2). 1972. 10.00 (0-394-82432-6) Random Bks Yng Read.
—Getting Ready for Writing. Scarry, Richard, illus. 32p. (ps-k). 1987. pap. 1.95 (0-394-89038-8) Random Bks Yng Read.
—Huckle Cat's Busiest Day Ever. Scarry, Richard, illus. LC 92-64139. 48p. (ps-2). 1993. 10.00 (0-679-84188-1) Random Bks Yng Read.
—I Am a Bunny. Scarry, Richard, illus. 22p. (gr. k-2). 1967. write for info. (0-307-12125-9, Golden Bks) Western Pub.
—Mein Allerschonstes A B C. (Illus.). 19.95 Intl Lang.
—Mein Allerschonstes Buch Vom Backen Bauen und Flugzeugfliegen. (GER., Illus.). 1970. 12.95x (3-7735-4927-X) Intl Lang.
—Mi Diccionario Infantil. 3rd ed. (SPA.). 96p 1974. pap. 14.95 (0-8288-6073-4, S-27628) Fr & Eur.
—Mi Primer Gran Diccionario Infantil. 4th ed. (SPA.). 90p. 1978. 13.95 (0-8288-5253-7, S26637) Fr & Eur.
—Mr. Fix-It: Richard Scarry's Smallest Pop-up Book Ever! (Illus.). 10p. (ps-3). 1992. write for info. (0-307-12461-4, 12461, Golden Pr) Western Pub.
—Mr. Frumble: Richard Scarry's Smallest Pop-up Book Ever! (Illus.). 10p. (ps-3). 1992. write for info. (0-307-12463-0, 12463, Golden Pr) Western Pub.
—Mr. Frumble's Worst Day Ever! Scarry, Richard, illus. LC 91-62215. 48p. (ps-k). 1992. 10.00 (0-679-81616-X) Random Bks Yng Read.
—Richard Scarry Huckle's Book. Scarry, Richard, illus. (ps). 1979. 2.95 (0-394-84130-1) Random Bks Yng Read.
—Richard Scarry: Sergeant Murphy's Busiest Day Ever. (Illus.). 20p. (ps up). 1992. write for info. incl. long-life batteries (0-307-74710-7, 64710, Golden Pr) Western Pub.
—Richard Scarry's ABC Word Book. (Illus.). (ps-2). 1971. 11.00 (0-394-82339-7); lib. bdg. 5.99 (0-394-92339-1) Random Bks Yng Read.

—Richard Scarry's ABCs. Scarry, Richard, illus. (ps-k). 1991. pap. 1.25 (0-307-11515-1, Golden Pr) Western Pub.

—Richard Scarry's Animal Nursery Tales. (Illus.). (ps-1). 1975. write for info. (0-307-16810-7, Golden Bks) Western Pub.

—Richard Scarry's Bedtime Stories. reissue ed. LC 86-484. (Illus.). 32p. (ps-1). 1989. pap. 2.25 (0-394-88269-5) Random Bks Yng Read.

—Richard Scarry's Bedtime Stories. LC 86-484. (Illus.). 32p. (ps-1). 1990. pap. 5.95 incl. cassette (0-679-80803-5) Random Bks Yng Read.

—Richard Scarry's Best Busy Year Ever. Scarry, Richard, illus. (ps-1). 1991. 5.25 (0-307-15748-2, Golden Pr) Western Pub.

—Richard Scarry's Best Coloring Activity Book Ever. LC 74-6872. (Illus.). 176p. (ps-4). 1974. 6.95 (0-394-83018-0) Random Bks Yng Read.

—Richard Scarry's Best Counting Book Ever. Scarry, Richard, illus. LC 74-2544. 48p. (ps-2). 1975. 12.00 (0-394-82924-7); PLB 9.99 (0-394-92924-1) Random Bks Yng Read.

—Richard Scarry's Best First Book Ever. Scarry, Richard, illus. LC 79-3900. (ps-1). 1979. 11.95 (0-394-84250-2); lib. bdg. 11.99 (0-394-94250-7) Random Bks Yng Read.

—Richard Scarry's Best Friend Ever. (Illus.). 24p. (ps-k). 1989. pap. write for info. (0-307-11715-4, Pub. by Golden Bks) Western Pub.

—Richard Scarry's Best Little Word Book Ever! (Illus.). 24p. (ps-k). 1992. write for info. (0-307-00136-9, 312-01, Golden Pr) Western Pub.

—Richard Scarry's Best Make-It Book Ever. (Illus.). (gr. k-3). 1977. pap. 8.95 (0-394-83492-5) Random Bks Yng Read.

—Richard Scarry's Best Story Book Ever. Scarry, Richard, illus. (gr. 1-5). 1968. write for info. (0-307-16548-5, Golden Bks) Western Pub.

—Richard Scarry's Best Word Book Ever. Scarry, Richard, illus. (ps-3). 1963. write for info. (0-307-15510-2, Golden Bks) Western Pub.

—Richard Scarry's Biggest Make-It Book Ever! Scarry, Richard, illus. 256p. (Orig.). (ps-5). 1993. pap. 9.99 (0-679-84767-7) Random Bks Yng Read.

—Richard Scarry's Biggest Pop-up Book Ever! Scarry, Richard, illus. 6p. (ps-3). 1992. write for info. (0-307-12460-6, 12460, Golden Pr) Western Pub.

—Richard Scarry's Biggest Word Book Ever! Scarry, Richard, illus. 12p. (ps-1). 1985. bds. 29.95 (0-394-87374-2) Random Bks Yng Read.

—Richard Scarry's Boats. (Illus.). 24p. (ps-k). 1992. pap. write for info. (0-307-11537-2, 11537, Golden Pr) Western Pub.

—Richard Scarry's Busiest People Ever. LC 76-8123. (Illus.). (ps-2). 1976. lib. bdg. 9.99 (0-394-93293-5); PLB 9.95 (0-394-83293-0) Random Bks Yng Read.

—Richard Scarry's Busy Busy World. Scarry, Richard, illus. (gr. k-5). write for info. (0-307-15511-0, Golden Bks) Western Pub.

—Richard Scarry's Cars. (Illus.). 24p. (ps-k). 1992. pap. write for info. (0-307-11538-0, 11538, Golden Pr) Western Pub.

—Richard Scarry's Cars & Trucks & Things That Go. (Illus.). (ps-2). 1974. write for info. (0-307-15785-7, Golden Bks) Western Pub.

—Richard Scarry's Color Book. Scarry, Richard, illus. LC 75-36465. 14p. (ps-1). 1976. 3.95 (0-394-83237-X) Random Bks Yng Read.

—Richard Scarry's Counting Book. (Illus.). 24p. (ps). 1990. pap. write for info. (0-307-11659-X, Pub. by Golden Bks) Western Pub.

—Richard Scarry's Favorite Christmas Carols. 1991. 22.25 (1-55987-050-8) J B Comns.

—Richard Scarry's Find Your ABC's. (Illus.). (ps-1). 1973. pap. 2.25 (0-394-82683-3) Random Bks Yng Read.

—Richard Scarry's First Words. (Illus.). 24p. (ps-k). 1993. pap. 1.45 (0-307-11543-7, 11543, Golden Pr) Western Pub.

—Richard Scarry's Great Big Schoolhouse. Scarry, Richard, illus. (ps-2). 1969. 9.99 (0-394-80874-6) Random Bks Yng Read.

—Richard Scarry's Just Right Word Book: (Just Right for 2's & 3's) Scarry, Richard, illus. LC 89-42839. 24p. (ps). 1990. 6.00 (0-679-80073-5) Random Bks Yng Read.

—Richard Scarry's Little Red Riding Hood. (Illus.). 28p. (ps). 1993. bds. 3.25 (0-307-12522-X, 12522, Golden Pr) Western Pub.

—Richard Scarry's Lowly Worm Storybook. Scarry, Richard, illus. LC 77-79842. 32p. (Orig.). (ps-1). 1989. pap. 2.25 (0-394-88270-9) Random Bks Yng Read.

—Richard Scarry's Lowly Worm Word Book. Scarry, Richard, illus. LC 80-53103. 28p. (ps). 1981. pap. 2.95 board (0-394-84728-8) Random Bks Yng Read.

—Richard Scarry's Naughty Bunny. (Illus.). 24p. (ps-2). 1989. write for info. (0-307-12092-9, Pub. by Golden Bks) Western Pub.

—Richard Scarry's Pie Rats Ahoy! LC 92-50998. (gr. 1-8). 1994. write for info. (0-679-84760-X); lib. bdg. write for info. (0-679-94760-4) Random Bks Yng Read.

—Richard Scarry's Planes. (Illus.). 24p. (ps-k). 1992. pap. write for info. (0-307-11535-6, 11535, Golden Pr) Western Pub.

—Richard Scarry's Please & Thank You Book. LC 73-2441. (ps-2). 1973. 2.25 (0-394-82681-7); lib. bdg. 5.99 (0-394-92681-1) Random Bks Yng Read.

—Richard Scarry's Please & Thank You Book. LC 73-2441. (Illus.). 32p. (ps-1). 1990. pap. 5.95 incl. cassette (0-679-80799-3) Random Bks Yng Read.

—Richard Scarry's Postman Pig & His Busy Neighbors. LC 77-91646. (Illus.). (ps-2). 1978. lib. bdg. 5.99 (0-394-93898-4) Random Bks Yng Read.

—Richard Scarry's Storybook Dictionary. LC 99-901821. (Illus.). (gr. k-2). 1966. write for info. (0-307-15548-X, Golden Bks) Western Pub.

—Richard Scarry's the Cat Family Takes a Trip. (Illus.). 24p. (ps-3). 1992. write for info. (0-307-12760-5, 12760) Western Pub.

—Richard Scarry's the Cat Family's Busy Day. (Illus.). 24p. (ps-3). 1992. write for info. (0-307-12761-3, 12761) Western Pub.

—Richard Scarry's The Little Red Hen. (Illus.). 28p. (ps). 1993. bds. 3.25 (0-307-12523-8, 12523, Golden Pr) Western Pub.

—Richard Scarry's The Three Bears. (Illus.). 28p. (ps). 1993. bds. 3.25 (0-307-12524-6, 12524, Golden Pr) Western Pub.

—Richard Scarry's The Three Little Pigs. (Illus.). 28p. (ps). 1993. bds. 3.25 (0-307-12521-1, 12521, Golden Pr) Western Pub.

—Richard Scarry's Trains. (Illus.). 24p. (ps-k). 1992. pap. write for info. (0-307-11536-4, 11536, Golden Pr) Western Pub.

—Richard Scarry's What Do People Do All Day? (Illus.). (ps-3). 1968. 12.00 (0-394-81823-7) Random Bks Yng Read.

—Richard Scarry's Word Book with Huckle Cat & Lowly Worm. (Illus.). 24p. (ps-3). 1993. pap. 1.95 (0-307-12767-2, 12767, Golden Pr) Western Pub.

—Watch Your Step, Mr. Rabbit! Scarry, Richard, illus. LC 90-34336. 24p. (Orig.). (ps-2). 1991. pap. 2.25 (0-679-81072-2) Random Bks Yng Read.

Scarry, Richard, illus. Richard Scarry's Best Mother Goose Ever. (ps-1). 1970. write for info. (0-307-15578-1, Golden Bks) Western Pub.

—Richard Scarry's Cars & Trucks from A to Z. LC 89-64401. 22p. (ps). 1990. bds. 2.95 (0-679-80663-6) Random Bks Yng Read.

Scarsbrook, Ailsa & Scarsbrook, Alan. A Family in Pakistan. LC 85-6886. (Illus.). 32p. (gr. 2-5). 1985. PLB 13.50 (0-8225-1662-4) Lerner Pubns.

Scarsbrook, Alan, jt. auth. see Scarsbrook, Ailsa.

Scavone, Daniel. The Shroud of Turin: Opposing Viewpoints. LC 88-24355. (Illus.). 112p. (gr. 5-8). 1989. PLB 14.95 (0-89908-061-8) Greenhaven.

Scavone, Daniel C. Christopher Columbus. LC 92-29499. (Illus.). 112p. (gr. 5-8). 1992. PLB 14.95 (1-56006-034-4) Lucent Bks.

—Vampires: Opposing Viewpoints. LC 90-40131. (Illus.). 112p. (gr. 5-8). 1990. PLB 14.95 (0-89908-080-4) Greenhaven.

Scelsa, Greg & Millang, Steve. Dancin' Machine. Fritz, Ron, illus. 24p. (ps-1). 1992. incl. cassette 9.95 (0-679-82378-6) Random Bks Yng Read.

—Everybody Has Music Inside: Fun Songs & Activities for Kids. (Illus.). 32p. (Orig.). 1993. text ed. 9.95 incl. cass. (0-7935-2374-5, HL00330607) H Leonard Pub Corp.

—Everybody Has Music Inside: Fun Songs & Activities for Kids. (Illus.). 32p. (Orig.). 1993. pap. text ed. 12.95 incl. CD (0-7935-2373-7, HL00330606) H Leonard Pub Corp.

—The World Is a Rainbow. Holub, Joan, illus. 24p. (ps-1). 1992. incl. cassette 9.95 (0-679-81979-7) Random Bks Yng Read.

Scesney, Gladys. It's Your Constitution! rev. ed. Enrees, Michael B., illus. 32p. (gr. 1-6). 1987. pap. 1.50 (0-9618667-1-3) Scesney Pubns.

Schaaf, Fred. The Amateur Astronomer: Explorations & Investigations. LC 93-31788. 1994. write for info. (0-531-11138-5) Watts.

Schaap, James C. Intermission: Breaking Away with God. Treman, Terry, illus. Smith, Harvey A., intro. by. LC 85-4156. (Illus.). 221p. (Orig.). (gr. 9-12). 1987. pap. 11.50 (0-930265-06-8, 1701-5000) CRC Pubns.

Schaar, John E., illus. Portraits of Sedona. (Orig.). 1989. write for info. Canyon AZ.

Schachnowitz, Selig. Avrohom ben Avrohom: The Famous Historical Novel About the Ger Tzedek of Vilna. (gr. 7 up). 12.95 (0-87306-134-9); pap. 9.95 (0-685-01625-0) Feldheim.

Schackburg, Richard. Yankee Doodle. Emberley, Ed, contrib. by. LC 93-28633. 1994. write for info. (0-671-88559-6, S&S BFYR) S&S Trade.

Schad, Kathleen W. Run, Eunice: A Story of Childhood in the 1890s, Clarke County, Alabama. Brown, Mary W., intro. by. LC 90-82162. 144p. (Orig.). (gr. 5-12). 1990. pap. 8.95 (0-9618941-1-3) Ana Pubns.

Schade, Charlene. Move with Me One Two Three. Ziebarth, Pat, ed. Pileggi, Steve, illus. Senter, Sheri, intro. by. (Illus.). 58p. (Orig.). (ps-1). 1988. Includes audio cassette. 16.90 (0-924860-00-6) Exer Fun Pub.

Schade, Susan. Hello! Hello! LC 90-10081. 32p. (ps). 1991. pap. 12.95 jacketed (0-671-70848-1, S&S BFYR) S&S Trade.

—Hello! Hello! Buller, Jon, illus. 32p. (ps). 1993. pap. 2.25 (0-671-79608-9, Little Simon) S&S Trade.

Schade, Susan & Buller, Jon. Railroad Toad. Buller, Jon, illus. LC 92-23303. 32p. (ps-1). 1993. PLB 7.99 (0-679-93934-2); pap. 3.50 (0-679-83934-8) Random Bks Yng Read.

—Snug House, Bug House. LC 93-34058. (gr. 2 up). 1994. write for info. (0-679-85300-6); PLB write for info. (0-679-95300-0) Random Bks Yng Read.

Schade, Susan, jt. auth. see Buller, Jon.

Schade, Susan, ed. Space Rock. Buller, Jon, illus. LC 87-12762. 48p. (Orig.). (gr. k-2). 1988. lib. bdg. 7.99 (0-394-99384-5); pap. 2.95 (0-394-89384-0) Random Bks Yng Read.

Schadler, Reuben, jt. auth. see Laycock, Mary.

Schaefer, Carole L. In the Children's Garden. Pauley, Lynn, illus. LC 93-15980. 1994. write for info. (0-8050-1958-8) H Holt & Co.

Schaefer, Charles E. Cat's Got Your Tongue? A Story for Children Afraid to Speak. LC 91-42707. 32p. (ps-3). 1992. pap. 6.95 (0-945354-46-0); 16.95 (0-945354-45-2) Magination Pr.

—Cat's Got Your Tongue? A Story for Children Afraid to Speak. Friedman, Judith, illus. LC 92-56869. 1993. PLB 17.26 (0-8368-0930-0) Gareth Stevens Inc.

Schaefer, Jack. Shane. McCormick, J., illus. (gr. 7 up). 1954. 15.95 (0-395-07090-2) HM.

Schaefer, Margaret A. Let's Build a Car. McRae, Patrick, illus. 32p. (gr. k-5). 1992. pap. 4.95 (0-8249-8536-2, Ideals Child) Hambleton-Hill.

Schaefer, Susan E. Born to Shine. Weiner, Sally E., illus. 36p. 1993. 14.95 (0-9638908-4-0) Blink Bks.

Schaeffer, Brenda. Is It Love or Is It Addiction? 158p. (Orig.). 1989. pap. 10.00 (0-89486-413-0, 5022A) Hazelden.

Schaeffer, Jack. Old Ramon: Newbery Honor Book 1961. (gr. 4-7). 1993. pap. 6.95 (0-8027-7403-2) Walker & Co.

Schaeffer, Sue. Mine to Choose. LC 78-73144. (Illus.). 128p. (gr. 9-12). 1979. 2.50 (0-88243-553-1, 02-0553); leader's guide 2.50 (0-88243-337-7, 02-0337) Gospel Pub.

Schael, Hannelore, jt. auth. see Lohf, Sabine.

Schael, Hannelore, et al. Toys Made of Clay. LC 89-22253. 64p. 1989. pap. 8.95 (0-516-49256-X) Childrens.

Schafer, Louis S. Best of Gravestone Humor. LC 89-49402. (Illus.). 128p. (Orig.). (gr. 4 up). 1990. pap. 5.95 (0-8069-7274-2) Sterling.

Schafer, Susan. The Galapagos Tortoise. LC 92-7396. (Illus.). 64p. (gr. 4 up). 1992. RSBE 13.95 (0-87518-544-4, Dillon) Macmillan Child Grp.

—The Komodo Dragon. LC 91-34958. (Illus.). 60p. (gr. 4 up). 1992. RSBE 13.95 (0-87518-504-5, Dillon) Macmillan Child Grp.

Schaff, Joanne. Holidays & Celebrations: An Educational Activity Book. Schaff, Joanne, illus. 48p. (ps-3). 1993. pap. 5.95 (0-9619365-1-7) Tree City Pr.

—What Am I? Schaff, Joanne, illus. 38p. (Orig.). (ps-3). 1987. pap. 1.99 (0-9619365-0-9) Tree City Pr.

Schaffer, Frank, Publications Staff. Addition. (Illus.). 24p. (gr. 1-3). 1978. wkbk. 3.98 (0-86734-007-X, FS-3008) Schaffer Pubns.

—The Alphabet. (Illus.). 24p. (ps-2). 1978. wkbk. 3.98 (0-86734-001-0, FS-3002) Schaffer Pubns.

—Beginning Activities with Numbers. (Illus.). 24p. (ps-k). 1980. 3.98 (0-86734-014-2, FS-3027) Schaffer Pubns.

—Beginning Activities with Pencil & Paper. (Illus.). 24p. (ps-k). 1980. 3.98 (0-86734-017-7, FS-3030) Schaffer Pubns.

—Beginning Activities with Shapes. (Illus.). 24p. (ps-k). 1980. 3.98 (0-86734-013-4, FS-3026) Schaffer Pubns.

—Beginning Activities with the Alphabet. (Illus.). 24p. (ps-k). 1980. 3.98 (0-86734-015-0, FS-3028) Schaffer Pubns.

—Following Directions. (Illus.). 24p. (gr. 2-4). 1978. wkbk. 3.98 (0-86734-008-8, FS-3009) Schaffer Pubns.

—Getting Ready for Kindergarten. (Illus.). 24p. (ps-k). 1978. wkbk. 3.98 (0-86734-000-2, FS-3001) Schaffer Pubns.

—Getting Ready for Math. (Illus.). 24p. (ps-k). 1980. 3.98 (0-86734-020-7, FS-3033) Schaffer Pubns.

—Getting Ready for Phonics. (Illus.). 24p. (ps-k). 1980. wkbk. 3.98 (0-86734-018-5, FS-3031) Schaffer Pubns.

—Getting Ready for Reading. (Illus.). 24p. (ps-k). 1980. wkbk. 3.98 (0-86734-019-3, FS-3032) Schaffer Pubns.

—Getting Ready for Science. (Illus.). 24p. (ps-k). 1980. wkbk. 3.98 (0-86734-021-5, FS-3034) Schaffer Pubns.

—Getting Ready for Writing. (Illus.). 24p. (ps-k). 1980. wkbk. 3.98 (0-86734-016-9, FS-3029) Schaffer Pubns.

—Handwriting with Harvey Hippo. (Illus.). 24p. (gr. 2-4). 1978. wkbk. 3.98 (0-86734-009-6, FS-3010) Schaffer Pubns.

—Kindergarten, Bk. 1. (Illus.). 48p. (gr. k). 1983. wkbk. 4.98 (0-86734-024-X, FS-2653) Schaffer Pubns.

—Kindergarten, Bk. 2. (Illus.). 48p. (ps-k). 1983. wkbk. 4.98 (0-86734-025-8, FS-2654) Schaffer Pubns.

—Kindergarten Skills. (Illus.). 24p. (ps-k). 1980. wkbk. 3.98 (0-86734-012-6, FS-3025) Schaffer Pubns.

—Math: Addition & Subtraction 1-10. (Illus.). 48p. (gr. 1-2). 1983. wkbk. 4.98 (0-86734-041-X, FS-2670) Schaffer Pubns.

—Math: Addition & Subtraction 11-20. (Illus.). 48p. (gr. 1-2). 1983. 4.98 (0-86734-042-8, FS-2671) Schaffer Pubns.

—Math: Addition & Subtraction 2-3 Digits. (Illus.). 48p. (gr. 2-3). 1983. wkbk. 4.98 (0-86734-043-6, FS-2672) Schaffer Pubns.

—Math: Multiplication & Division. (Illus.). 48p. (gr. 3-4). 1983. wkbk. 4.98 (0-86734-044-4, FS-2673) Schaffer Pubns.

—Math: Time & Money. (Illus.). 48p. (gr. 2-3). 1983. wkbk. 4.98 (0-86734-045-2, FS-2674) Schaffer Pubns.

—Multiplication. (Illus.). 24p. (gr. 3-5). 1978. wkbk. 3.98 (0-86734-010-X, FS-3011) Schaffer Pubns.
—My First Words. (Illus.). 24p. (gr. 1-3). 1978. wkbk. 3.98 (0-86734-005-3, FS-3006) Schaffer Pubns.
—Numbers. (Illus.). 24p. (ps-2). 1978. wkbk. 3.98 (0-86734-002-9, FS-3003) Schaffer Pubns.
—Phonics: Blends & Digraphs. (Illus.). 48p. (gr. 1-3). 1983. wkbk. 4.98 (0-86734-027-4, FS-2656) Schaffer Pubns.
—Phonics: Consonants. (Illus.). 24p. (ps-2). 1978. wkbk. 3.98 (0-86734-003-7, FS-3004) Schaffer Pubns.
—Phonics-Consonants. (Illus.). 48p. (gr. 1-3). 1983. wkbk. 4.98 (0-86734-026-6, FS-2655) Schaffer Pubns.
—Phonics: Vowels. (Illus.). 24p. (gr. 1-3). 1978. wkbk. 3.98 (0-86734-004-5, FS-3005) Schaffer Pubns.
—Phonics: Vowels. (Illus.). 48p. (gr. 1-3). 1983. wkbk. 4.98 (0-86734-028-2, FS-2657) Schaffer Pubns.
—Pre-School, Bk. 1. (Illus.). 48p. (ps). 1983. wkbk. 4.98 (0-86734-022-3, FS-2651) Schaffer Pubns.
—Pre-School, Bk. 2. (Illus.). 48p. (ps). 1983. wkbk. 4.98 (0-86734-023-1, FS-2652) Schaffer Pubns.
—Printing with Peter Possum. (Illus.). 24p. (gr. k-2). 1978. wkbk. 3.98 (0-86734-006-1, FS-3007) Schaffer Pubns.
—Reading Comprehension. (Illus.). 24p. (gr. 3-5). 1978. wkbk. 3.98 (0-86734-011-8, FS-3012) Schaffer Pubns.
—Reading: Grade Four, Bk. 1. (Illus.). 48p. (gr. 4). 1983. wkbk. 4.98 (0-86734-038-X, FS-2667) Schaffer Pubns.
—Reading: Grade Four, Bk. 2. (Illus.). 48p. (gr. 4). 1983. wkbk. 4.98 (0-86734-039-8, FS-2668) Schaffer Pubns.
—Reading: Grade Four, Bk. 3. (Illus.). 48p. (gr. 4). 1983. wkbk. 4.98 (0-86734-040-1, FS-2669) Schaffer Pubns.
—Reading: Grade One, Bk. 1. (Illus.). 48p. (gr. 1). 1983. wkbk. 4.98 (0-86734-029-0, FS-2658) Schaffer Pubns.
—Reading: Grade One, Bk. 2. (Illus.). 48p. (gr. 1). 1983. wkbk. 4.98 (0-86734-030-4, FS-2659) Schaffer Pubns.
—Reading: Grade One, Bk. 3. (Illus.). 48p. (gr. 1). 1983. wkbk. 4.98 (0-86734-031-2, FS-2660) Schaffer Pubns.
—Reading: Grade Three, Bk. 1. (Illus.). 48p. (gr. 3). 1983. wkbk. 4.98 (0-86734-035-5, FS-2664) Schaffer Pubns.
—Reading: Grade Three, Bk. 2. (Illus.). 48p. (gr. 3). 1983. wkbk. 4.98 (0-86734-036-3, FS-2665) Schaffer Pubns.
—Reading: Grade Three, Bk. 3. (Illus.). 48p. (gr. 3). 1983. wkbk. 4.98 (0-86734-037-1, FS-2666) Schaffer Pubns.
—Reading: Grade Two, Bk. 1. (Illus.). 48p. (gr. 2). 1983. wkbk. 4.98 (0-86734-032-0, FS-2661) Schaffer Pubns.
—Reading: Grade Two, Bk. 2. (Illus.). 48p. (gr. 2). 1983. wkbk. 4.98 (0-86734-033-9, FS-2662) Schaffer Pubns.
—Reading: Grade Two, Bk. 3. (Illus.). 48p. (gr. 2). 1983. wkbk. 4.98 (0-86734-034-7, FS-2663) Schaffer Pubns.
Schaffer, Libor. Arthur Sets Sail. Mathieu, Agnes, illus. LC 87-1594. 32p. (gr. k-3). 1987. 14.95 (1-55858-059-X) North-South Bks NYC.
Schaffer, Patricia. Chag Sameach! A Jewish Holiday Book for Children. (Illus.). 28p. (Orig.). (ps-4). 1985. pap. 5.95 (0-935079-16-5) Tabor Sarah Bks.
—How Babies & Family Are Made-There Is More Than One Way! Corbett, Susanne, illus. LC 86-23087. 64p. (gr. k-4). 1988. pap. 6.95 (0-935079-17-3) Tabor Sarah Bks.
Schaffer, Rachel, ed. see Holland, Royce Q., et al.
Schaffer, Ulrich. Zilya's Secret Plan. Shoji, Takashi, illus. 32p. (ps-6). 1991. pap. 4.99 (0-7459-1957-X) Lion USA.
Schaffner, Betty. Designs to Color. (Illus.). (ps-3). 1991. pap. 2.95 (0-8431-1930-6) Price Stern.
Schal, Valda. Haiku for Children. (Illus.). 20p. 1991. write for info. (0-944231-14-4) Slvr Wings CA.
Schami, Rafik. A Hand Full of Stars. Lesser, Rika, tr. from GER. LC 89-25991. 224p. (gr. 7 up). 1990. 14.95 (0-525-44535-8, DCB) Dutton Child Bks.
—A Hand Full of Stars. Lesser, Rika, tr. from GER. 224p. (gr. 7 up). 1992. pap. 4.50 (0-14-036073-5, Puffin) Puffin Bks.
Schanback, Mindy. Does Third Grade Last Forever? Henry, Paul, illus. LC 89-20603. 96p. (gr. 2-4). 1990. PLB 9.89 (0-8167-1700-1); pap. text ed. 2.95 (0-8167-1701-X) Troll Assocs.
—What's New in Sixth Grade? LC 90-26792. 96p. (gr. 4-6). 1992. lib. bdg. 9.89 (0-8167-2388-5); pap. text ed. 2.95 (0-8167-2389-3) Troll Assocs.
Schanzer, Rosalyn. Ezra in Pursuit: A Book of Mazes. LC 92-25815. 1993. pap. 10.95 (0-385-30884-1) Doubleday.
—Ezra on a Quest: A Maze Chase Medieval. LC 93-19537. 1994. write for info. (0-385-32262-3) Doubleday.
Schanzer, Roz, illus. In the Synagogue. (ps). 1991. 4.95 (0-929371-60-7) Kar-Ben.
Schar, Grant. Hieroglyphic Coloring Book. Schar, Grant, illus. 48p. (gr. 1-12). 1992. pap. 4.95 (0-912057-57-2, 507440) AMORC.
Scharer, Niko. Emily's House. Fitzgerald, Joanne, illus. 24p. 1992. pap. 4.95 (0-88899-158-4, Pub. by Groundwood-Douglas & McIntyre CN) Firefly Bks Ltd.
Scharnhorst, Gary, ed. see Alger, Horatio.
Scharrett, Darcy, jt. auth. see Paxton, Tom.
Schartz, Sara, jt. auth. see Schwartz, Paula.
Schatell, Brian. Farmer Goff & His Turkey Sam. Schatell, Brian, illus. LC 81-47756. 32p. (gr. 1-3). 1982. PLB 13.89 (0-397-31983-5, Lipp Jr Bks) HarpC Child Bks.
Schatt, Paul see Higgins, Betty.

Schatz, Dennis. Astronomy Activity Book. (gr. 4-7). 1991. pap. 6.95 (0-671-70449-4, Little Simon) S&S Trade.
—Dinosaurs - A Journey Through Time: A Children's Activity Book. Quan, Daniel, designed by. 48p. (ps-6). 1987. pap. 9.95 (0-935051-01-5) Pacific Sci Ctr.
Schatz, Dennis & Osawa, Yasu. The Return of the Comet. Osawa, Yasu, illus. 42p. (gr. 4-9). 1985. pap. 7.95 (0-935051-00-7) Pacific Sci Ctr.
Schatz, Molly, ed. see Prowense, Mary J.
Schaub, Janine, jt. auth. see Kalman, Bobbie.
Schauer, Donald D. Careers in Trucking. rev. ed. Rosen, R., ed. (Illus.). 144p. (gr. 7-12). 1991. PLB 13.95 (0-8239-1348-1) Rosen Group.
Schaun, George & Schaun, Virginia. Everyday Life in Colonial Maryland. 130p. (gr. k-12). 1982. casebound 14.75 (0-917882-11-3) MD Hist Pr.
Schaun, Virginia, jt. auth. see Schaun, George.
Scheader, Catherine. Shirley Chisholm: Teacher & Congresswoman. LC 89-34451. (Illus.). 128p. (gr. 6 up). 1990. lib. bdg. 17.95 (0-89490-285-7) Enslow Pubs.
Scheck, Joann, jt. auth. see Roberts, Jim.
Schecter, Darrow. I Can Read About Magellan. LC 78-73713. (Illus.). (gr. 3-6). 1979. pap. 1.95 (0-89375-209-6) Troll Assocs.
—I Can Read About Planets. new ed. LC 78-66272. (Illus.). (gr. 3-6). 1979. pap. 1.95 (0-89375-215-0) Troll Assocs.
Schecter, Ellen. The Boy Who Cried Wolf. (ps-3). 1994. pap. 3.50 (0-553-37232-7) Bantam.
—Diamonds & Toads: A Classic Fairy Tale. Blackshear, Ami, illus. LC 93-14096. Date not set. write for info. (0-553-09046-1); pap. write for info. (0-553-37339-0) Bantam.
—Sim Chung & the River Dragon, Level Three: A Folktale from Korea. LC 92-7652. (ps-3). 1993. 9.99 (0-553-09117-4) Bantam.
—Sim Chung & the River Dragon, Level Three: A Folktale from Korea. LC 92-7652. (ps-3). 1993. pap. 3.50 (0-553-37109-6) Bantam.
—Warrior Maiden: A Hopi Legend. (ps-3). 1992. 9.99 (0-553-08949-8); pap. 3.50 (0-553-37022-7) Bantam.
Schecter, Ellen, jt. auth. see Orgel, Doris.
Schecter, Ellen, retold by. The Boy Who Cried Wolf! Chalk, Gary, illus. (gr. 4 up). 1994. 10.95 (0-553-09043-7) Bantam.
Schecter, Kate S. Boris Yeltsin. LC 92-37474. (Illus.). 1993. 18.95 (0-7910-1749-4, Am Art Analog); pap. write for info. (0-7910-1795-8, Am Art Analog) Chelsea Hse.
Schecter, Teri, jt. auth. see Garrity, Leslie.
Scheer, George F., intro. by. Cherokee Animal Tales. rev. ed. Frankenberg, Robert, illus. LC 91-73537. 79p. (gr. 3-6). 1991. pap. 7.95 (0-933031-60-2) Coun Oak Bks.
Scheer, James F., ed. see Salaman, Maureen K.
Scheer, Julian. Rain Makes Applesauce. Bileck, Marvin, illus. 36p. (ps-3). 1964. 15.95 (0-8234-0091-3) Holiday.
Scheets, Thomas M. The Bible Says: A Look at Opposing Claims. LC 88-62605. 64p. (Orig.). 1989. pap. 4.95 (1-55612-239-X) Sheed & Ward MO.
Scheffel, Vernon L. Flag Football: How to Play It. LC 87-51055. (Illus.). 90p. (gr. 7-12). 1987. pap. 6.95 (0-944450-00-8) La Sierra U Pr.
Scheffler, Ursel. The Giant Apple. Brix-Henker, Silke, illus. 32p. (gr. k-3). 1990. PLB 18.95 (0-87614-413-X) Carolrhoda Bks.
—The Return of Rinaldo the Sly Fox. Gider, Iskender, illus. James, J. Alison, tr. from GER. (Illus.). 32p. (gr. k-3). 1993. 12.95 (1-55858-227-4); lib. bdg. 12.88 (1-55858-228-2) North-South Bks NYC.
—Rinaldo, the Sly Fox. Gider, Iskender, illus. James, J. Alison, tr. from GER. LC 92-2376. (Illus.). 32p. (gr. 2-3). 1992. 13.95 (1-55858-181-2); PLB 13.88 (1-55858-182-0) North-South Bks NYC.
—Stop Your Crowing, Kasimir! Brix-Henker, Silke, illus. 32p. (gr. k-3). 1988. lib. bdg. 18.95 (0-87614-323-0) Carolrhoda Bks.
Scheffrin-Falk, Gladys. Another Celebrated Dancing Bear. Garrison, Barbara, illus. LC 89-13152. 32p. (gr. k-2). 1991. SBE 13.95 (0-684-19164-4, Scribners Young Read) Macmillan Child Grp.
Scheid, Margaret. Discovering Acadia: A Guide for Young Naturalists. Scheid, Margaret, illus. LC 86-71350. 80p. (gr-12). 1988. pap. 12.95 (0-934745-04-8) Acadia Pub Co.
Scheidl, Gerda M. Can We Help You, Saint Nicholas? Corderoc'h, Jean-Pierre, illus. Lanning, Rosemary, tr. from GER. LC 92-5231. (Illus.). 32p. (gr. k-3). 1992. 14.95 (1-55858-154-5); PLB 14.88 (1-55858-155-3) North-South Bks NYC.
—The Crystal Ball. Duroussy, Nathalie, illus. Lanning, Rosemary, tr. from GER. LC 92-44762. (Illus.). 32p. (gr. k-3). 1993. 14.95 (1-55858-197-9); PLB 14.88 (1-55858-198-7) North-South Bks NYC.
—Flowers for the Snowman. Lanning, Rosemary, tr. Wilkon, Jozef, illus. LC 88-42532. 32p. (gr. k-3). 1988. 13.95 (1-55858-068-9) North-South Bks NYC.
—Four Candles for Simon. Pfister, Marcus, illus. LC 86-33199. 32p. (gr. k-3). 1987. 13.95 (1-55858-065-4) North-South Bks NYC.
—The Little Donkey. Watts, Bernadette, illus. LC 87-73271. 32p. (gr. k-3). 1988. 13.95 (1-55858-026-3) North-South Bks NYC.

—Loretta & the Little Fairy. Unzner-Fischer, Christa, illus. James, J. Alison, tr. from GER. LC 92-33832. (Illus.). 32p. (gr. 2-3). 1993. 13.95 (1-55858-185-5); PLB 13.88 (1-55858-186-3) North-South Bks NYC.
Schein, Jonah. Forget-Me-Not. Schein, Jonah, illus. 24p. 1988. 12.95 (1-55037-001-4, Pub. by Annick CN); pap. 4.95 (1-55037-000-6, Pub. by Annick CN) Firefly Bks Ltd.
Scheiner, Mordecai, ed. see Silberman, Miriam.
Schell, Kent. How to Apply to College Step by Step. 1988. pap. 9.95 (0-87738-027-9) Youth Ed.
Schell, Mildred. Shoemaker's Dream. (ps-3). 1982. 10.00 (0-8170-0945-0) Judson.
Scheller, Melanie. My Grandfather's Hat. Narahashi, Keiko, illus. LC 91-12486. 32p. (ps-3). 1992. SBE 13.95 (0-689-50540-X, M K McElderry) Macmillan Child Grp.
Scheller, William. The World's Greatest Explorers. LC 92-18418. 160p. (gr. 5-12). 1992. PLB 14.95 (1-881508-03-X) Oliver Pr MN.
Schenk, Julie W. Julie Finds a Friend: Julie's Journey. Johnson, Sherry M., ed. Wyatt, Mildred, illus. 36p. (Orig.). (gr. 1-6). 1993. pap. write for info. (0-9635637-0-X) Amer Design.
Schenk De Regniers, B see Schenk de Regniers, Beatrice.
Schenk de Regniers, Beatrice. It Does Not Say Meow & Other Animal Riddle Rhymes. LC 72-75704. 40p. (gr. k-3). 1983. pap. 4.95 (0-89919-043-X, Clarion Bks) HM.
—The Way I Feel...Sometimes. Meddaugh, Susan, illus. (gr. 1-4). 1988. 13.95 (0-318-35052-1, Clarion Bks) HM.
Schenker, Dona. Fearsome. LC 93-8601. 1994. write for info. (0-679-85424-X) Knopf Bks Yng Read.
—Throw a Hungry Loop. LC 89-35496. 160p. (gr. 7 up). 1991. 12.95 (0-679-80332-7); PLB 13.99 (0-679-90332-1) Knopf Bks Yng Read.
Schenkerman, Rona D. Growing up in a Stepfamily. 16p. (gr. 3-8). 1993. 1.95 (1-56688-112-9) Bur For At-Risk.
—Growing up When Someone You Love Has Died. 16p. (gr. 3-8). 1993. 1.95 (1-56688-115-3) Bur For At-Risk.
—Growing up with a Single Parent. 16p. (gr. 3-8). 1993. 1.95 (1-56688-118-8) Bur For At-Risk.
—Growing up with an Alcoholic Parent. 16p. (gr. 3-8). 1993. 1.95 (1-56688-114-5) Bur For At-Risk.
—Growing up with Angry Feelings. 16p. (gr. 3-8). 1993. 1.95 (1-56688-113-7) Bur For At-Risk.
—Growing up with Divorce. 16p. (gr. 3-8). 1993. 1.95 (1-56688-110-2) Bur For At-Risk.
—Growing up with Drugs in Your Neighborhood. 16p. (gr. 3-8). 1993. 1.95 (1-56688-120-X) Bur For At-Risk.
—Growing up with Family Violence. 16p. (gr. 3-8). 1993. 1.95 (1-56688-111-0) Bur For At-Risk.
—Growing up with Peer Pressure. 16p. (gr. 3-8). 1993. 1.95 (1-56688-109-9) Bur For At-Risk.
—Growing up with Self-Esteem. 16p. (gr. 3-8). 1993. 1.95 (1-56688-119-6) Bur For At-Risk.
—Growing up with Sexual Abuse. 16p. (gr. 3-8). 1993. 1.95 (1-56688-117-X) Bur For At-Risk.
—Growing up with Stress. 16p. (gr. 3-8). 1993. 1.95 (1-56688-121-8) Bur For At-Risk.
Schenkman, Richard, ed. The Illustrated James Bond, 007. McLusky, John, illus. 90p. (Orig.). (gr. 5 up). 1981. pap. 6.95 (0-9605838-0-7) Bond Double-O Seven.
Schepige, Adele, jt. auth. see Field, Nancy.
Schepp, Brad, jt. auth. see Schepp, Debra.
Schepp, Debra & Schepp, Brad. Mac Club! Ellinger, Debra, illus. LC 93-8520. 1993. 19.60 (0-8306-4253-6) TAB Bks.
—Mac Party! Ellinger, Debra, illus. LC 93-8519. 1993. 19.60 (0-8306-4250-1) TAB Bks.
—Shareware for Kids: With Ready-to-Run Programs for the IBM for Ages 2 Through 5. LC 92-35447. (ps-k). 1993. write for info. (0-8306-4248-X) TAB Bks.
Schepp, Steven. All about Baby-Sitting: The Essential Guide for Concerned Parents & Baby-Sitters. Greene, Bruce, illus. Berner, Lorraine, contrib. by. LC 82-81281. (Illus.). 267p. (Orig.). 1982. pap. 7.95 (0-913279-00-5) Non Fiction Pubns.
Schepp, Steven, jt. auth. see Andry, Andrew C.
Scher, Anna. Desperate to Act: Anna Scher's All about Acting Book. 170p. 1991. pap. 6.95 (0-00-672852-9, 00689) Heinemann.
Scher, Linda. The Vote: Making Your Voice Heard. LC 92-14474. (Illus.). 48p. (gr. 5-6). 1992. PLB 21.34 (0-8114-7357-0) Raintree Steck-V.
Schera, Judith, et al. Biblical Performances for Vacation Bible School. 96p. (gr. 8). 1991. 10.95 (0-86653-578-0, Shining Star Pubns) Good Apple.
Scherer, Bonnie. Benjy's New Home. McCracken, Bill, illus. LC 89-60806. 7p. 1989. pap. 1.50 (0-9622421-0-1) B Scherer.
Scherer, Bonnie L. The Rescue of Rusty Rabbit. Roberts, Mary & Hendricks, Janie, eds. Thayer, Carolyn, illus. LC 90-63373. 12p. (Orig.). (gr. 1-6). 1991. pap. text ed. write for info. (0-9622421-1-X) B Scherer.
Scherer, Catharine D. Ladybug. Legman, Linda C., illus. LC 83-70738. 10p. (gr. 6-11). 1983. 2.95 (0-9611024-0-3) Drum Assocs.
Scherer, D. J., ed. see Hollman, Fred.
Scherer, Elise, tr. see Schnieper, Claudia.
Scherie, Strom. Stuffin' Muffin: Muffin Pan Cooking for Kids. Konefal, Norma, frwd. by. (Illus.). 100p. (Orig.). (gr. 4-7). 1982. pap. 13.95 (0-9606964-9-0) Yng Peoples Pr.

Scherling, Donald. Better All the Time: A Young Person's Recovery Workbook. 30p. (Orig.). 1989. pap. 7.95 wkbk. *(0-942421-12-4)* Parkside Pub.

Scherman, Nosson. Reb Yitzchak's Jewel: Rashi's Father Gets a Reward. Dershowitz, Yosef & Horen, Michael, illus. 32p. (gr. k-6). 1988. 6.95 *(0-89906-525-2)* Mesorah Pubns.

Scherman, Nosson & Gevirtz, Eliezer. The Story of the Chofetz Chaim. Dershowitz, Yosef, illus. 160p. (gr. 6-12). 1987. 11.95 *(0-89906-766-2)*; pap. 8.95 *(0-89906-767-0)* Mesorah Pubns.

Scherman, Nosson & Zlotowitz, Meir. The Artscroll Youth Megillah: Fully Illustrated with the Complete Text, Simplified Translation & Comments. Gold, Avie, ed. Horen, Michael, illus. 48p. (gr. 3-12). 1988. 15.95 *(0-89906-067-6)*; pap. 12.95 *(0-89906-068-4)* Mesorah Pubns.

Schermbrucker, Reviva. Charlie's House. (ps-3). 1991. 13.95 *(0-670-84024-6)* Viking Child Bks.

Scherra, J., et al. Biblical Puppet Performances. 96p. (ps-8). 1990. 10.95 *(0-86653-549-7*, SS1873, Shining Star Pubns) Good Apple.

Schertle, Alice. Gus Wanders Off. Edwards, Linda S., illus. LC 86-21311. 32p. (ps-2). 1988. 12.95 *(0-688-04984-2)*; PLB 12.88 *(0-688-04985-0)* Lothrop.
—Hob Goblin & the Skeleton. (ps-3). 1982. 10.25 *(0-685-05955-3)*; PLB 10.88 *(0-685-42443-X)* Lothrop.
—In My Treehouse. Dunham, Meredith, illus. LC 82-10016. 32p. (gr. k-3). 1983. 11.95 *(0-688-01638-3)* Lothrop.
—Jeremy Bean's St. Patrick's Day. Shute, Linda, illus. LC 86-7403. 32p. (ps-2). 1987. 12.95 *(0-688-04813-7)*; PLB 12.88 *(0-688-04814-5)* Lothrop.
—Little Frog's Song. Fisher, Leonard E., illus. LC 91-10405. 32p. (ps-2). 1992. 15.00 *(0-06-020059-6)*; PLB 14.89 *(0-06-020060-X)* HarpC Child Bks.
—That Olive! Wheeler, Cindy, illus. LC 84-10025. 32p. (ps-1). 1986. PLB 11.88 *(0-688-04091-8)* Lothrop.
—William & Grandpa. Stevenson, D., ed. Dabcovich, Lydia, illus. LC 88-666. 32p. (gr. k-3). 1988. 12.95 *(0-688-07580-0)*; PLB 12.88 *(0-688-07581-9)* Lothrop.
—Witch Hazel. Tomes, Margot, illus. LC 90-39630. 32p. (gr. k-4). 1991. 15.00 *(0-06-025140-9)*; PLB 14.89 *(0-06-025141-7)* HarpC Child Bks.

Schick, Alice, jt. auth. see Schick, Joel.
Schick, Alice, ed. see Shelley, Mary Wollstonecraft.
Schick, Alice, ed. see Stoker, Bram.

Schick, Eleanor. Art Lessons. LC 86-243. (Illus.). 48p. (gr. k-3). 1987. 11.75 *(0-688-05120-0)*; lib. bdg. 11.88 *(0-688-05121-9)* Greenwillow.
—I Have Another Language: The Language Is Dance. Schick, Eleanor, illus. LC 91-9485. 32p. (gr. k-6). 1992. RSBE 13.95 *(0-02-781209-X*, Macmillan Child Bk) Macmillan Child Grp.

Schick, Joel & Schick, Alice. Bram Stoker's Dracula. Schick, Joel & Schick, Alice, illus. LC 80-13619. 48p. (gr. 4-6). 1980. PLB 12.95 *(0-685-42954-7)*; pap. 6.95 *(0-385-28141-2)* Delacorte.
—Mary Shelley's Frankenstein. Schick, Joel & Schick, Alice, illus. LC 80-385. 48p. (gr. 4-6). 1981. PLB 11.95 *(0-385-28302-4)* Delacorte.
—Santaberry & the Snard. (gr. 4). 1976. 12.00 *(0-912846-23-2)* Bookstore Pr.

Schick, Joel, ed. see Shelley, Mary Wollstonecraft.
Schick, Joel, ed. see Stoker, Bram.

Schick, Lawrence. Heroic Worlds: A History & Guide to Role-Playing Games. (Illus.). 448p. (Orig.). (gr. 6 up). 1991. 34.95x *(0-87975-652-7)*; pap. 16.95 *(0-87975-653-5)* Prometheus Bks.

Schiff, Ronny, ed. see Palmer, Hap.
Schiff, Ronny S., ed. see Weissman, Julie, et al.
Schiffler, Don, jt. auth. see Duroska, Lud.

Schiffman, Roger. Golf Basics. Schoolcraft, Robert, illus. 48p. (gr. 3-7). 1986. 10.95 *(0-13-357955-7)* P-H.

Schiffman, Ruth. Josip Broz Tito. Schlesinger, Arthur M., Jr., intro. by. (Illus.). 112p. (gr. 5 up). 1987. lib. bdg. 17.95 *(0-87754-443-3)* Chelsea Hse.

Schilder, Rosalind. Dayenu - Enough! How Uncle Murray Saved the Seder. Kahn, Katherine J., photos by. LC 88-1238. (Illus., Orig.). (ps-3). 1988. pap. 4.95 *(0-930494-76-8)* Kar Ben.

Schiller, Alexandra. The Raisin Eater.
Martin, John J. & Schiller, Alexandra, eds. Schiller, Alexandra, illus. 44p. (gr. 3-4). 1984. 5.00 *(0-9618682-0-1)* A Schiller.
The dancing raisins illustrations created by the author for this publication were later adapted by the raisin industry for their animated caricature promotion of the tiny dried fruit. Although the text is at approximately a 3rd grade reading level, it is an enjoyable read-to story for younger children; & older readers may appreciate the subtle humor in the highly-imaginative & thoroughly amusing story about an 8 year old girl's fantasy adventure discovery of personified raisins. For all raisin lovers

young at heart. "A darling book...really well done."--Pat Holt, Book Review Editor, San Francisco Chronicle. *Publisher Provided Annotation.*

Schiller, Alexandra, ed. see Schiller, Alexandra.

Schiller, Barbara. Eric the Red & Leif the Lucky. LC 78-18055. (Illus.). 48p. (gr. 4-7). 1979. PLB 10.59 *(0-89375-174-X)*; pap. 3.50 *(0-89375-166-9)* Troll Assocs.

Schiller, David. My First Computer Book: Apple II Series. LC 90-50367. 64p. (ps-2). 1991. pap. 17.95 *(0-89480-368-9*, 1368) Workman Pub.
—My First Computer Book: IBM PC & Compatibles. LC 90-50367. 64p. (ps-2). 1991. pap. 17.95 *(0-89480-835-4*, 1835) Workman Pub.

Schiller, Lois G. Let's Laugh. LC 90-72114. 44p. 1991. 7.95 *(1-55523-422-4)* Winston-Derek.

Schimmel, Karen. Bolivia. (Illus.). 112p. (gr. 5 up). 1991. 14.95 *(0-7910-1109-7)* Chelsea Hse.

Schimminger, Lorraine, jt. auth. see Blansett, Mary L.

Schimpff, Jill W. Open Sesame Picture Dictionary: Featuring Jim Henson's Sesame Street Muppets, Children's Television Workshop. Cooke, Tom, illus. (gr. k-6). 1982. 12.75x *(0-19-503201-2)*; pap. 7.75x *(0-19-503035-4)*; activity book 4.95 *(0-19-434253-0)*; Picture Dictionary, English-Chinese. 7.75 *(0-19-583744-4)* OUP.

Schindel, John. I'll Meet You Halfway. Watts, James, illus. LC 91-44019. 32p. (ps-2). 1993. SBE 14.95 *(0-689-50564-7*, M K McElderry) Macmillan Child Grp.
—Something Fishy. Cocca-Leffler, Maryann, illus. LC 91-19223. 32p. (ps-1). 1993. pap. 13.00 JRT *(0-671-74777-0*, S&S BFYR) S&S Trade.
—Who Are You? Watts, James, illus. LC 90-39850. 32p. (ps-3). 1991. SBE 13.95 *(0-689-50523-X*, M K McElderry) Macmillan Child Grp.

Schindler, S. D., illus. The Twelve Days of Christmas. LC 90-22389. 24p. (ps up). 1991. 2.95 *(0-694-00363-8)* HarpC Child Bks.

Schlachter, Rita. Bear Needs Help! LC 81-14052. (Illus.). 48p. (Orig.). (gr. 1-3). 1986. PLB 10.59 *(0-8167-0600-X)*; pap. text ed. 3.50 *(0-8167-0601-8)* Troll Assocs.
—Good Luck, Bad Luck. Karas, G. Brian, illus. LC 85-14069. 48p. (Orig.). (gr. 1-3). 1986. PLB 10.59 *(0-8167-0572-0)*; pap. text ed. 3.50 *(0-8167-0573-9)* Troll Assocs.
—Winter Fun. Swan, Susan, illus. LC 85-14008. 48p. (Orig.). (gr. 1-3). 1986. PLB 10.59 *(0-8167-0584-4)*; pap. text ed. 3.50 *(0-8167-0585-2)* Troll Assocs.

Schlaepfer, Gloria, jt. auth. see Samuelson, Mary L.
Schlaepfer, Gloria G., jt. auth. see Samuelson, Mary L.

Schlank, Carol H. & Metzger, Barbara. Elizabeth Cady Stanton: A Biography for Young Children. Bond, Janice, illus. 32p. (ps-2). 1991. lib. bdg. 14.95 *(0-87659-177-2)*; pap. 6.95 *(0-87659-176-4)* Gryphon Hse.
—Martin Luther King, Jr. A Biography for Young Children. Kastner, John, illus. 24p. (ps-3). 1989. pap. 3.95 *(0-9613271-2-X)* RAEYC.
—Martin Luther King, Jr. A Biography for Young Children. rev. ed. Kastner, John, illus. 32p. (ps-k). 1990. PLB 14.95 *(0-87659-123-3)*; pap. 6.95 *(0-87659-122-5)* Gryphon Hse.

Schlee, Ann. The Vandal. LC 81-2859. (Illus.). 192p. (gr. 7 up). 1981. 8.95 *(0-517-54424-5)* Crown Bks Yng Read.
—The Vandal. large type ed. 296p. (gr. 5 up). 1988. 13.95 *(0-7451-0658-7*, Galaxy Child Lrg Print) Chivers N Amer.

Schlegl, William. Bible Christmas Puzzles. Van Kanegan, Jeff, illus. 48p. (gr. 3 up). 1987. pap. 6.95 *(0-86653-409-1*, SS 884, Shining Star Pubns) Good Apple.
—Bible Codes & Messages. (Illus.). 48p. (gr. 3 up). 1989. 6.95 *(0-86653-479-2*, SS887, Shining Star Pubns) Good Apple.
—Bible Trivia. Leedom, Valerie, illus. 48p. (gr. 3 up). 1986. wkbk. 6.95 *(0-86653-368-0*, SS 883, Shining Star Pubns) Good Apple.

Schleichert. Elizabeth Blackwell. 1991. 14.95 *(0-8050-2064-0)* H Holt & Co.

Schleichert, Elizabeth. The Life of Dorothea Dix. Castro, Antonio, illus. 80p. (gr. 4-7). 1991. PLB 13.95 *(0-941477-68-1)* TFC Bks NY.
—The Life of Elizabeth Blackwell. Castro, Antonio, illus. 80p. (gr. 4-7). 1991. PLB 13.95 *(0-941477-66-5)* TFC Bks NY.

Schleier, Curt. The Team Behind Your Airline Flight. LC 80-27174. 94p. (gr. 5-8). 1981. 10.00 *(0-664-32678-1*, Westminster) Westminster John Knox.

Schleifer, Jay. Bugatti. LC 93-15491. (Illus.). 48p. (gr. 5 up). 1994. RSBE 13.95 *(0-89686-813-3*, Crestwood Hse) Macmillan Child Grp.
—Camaro. LC 92-3809. (Illus.). 48p. (gr. 5). 1993. RSBE 13.95 *(0-89686-696-3*, Crestwood Hse) Macmillan Child Grp.
—Citizenship. (Illus.). 64p. (gr. 7-12,RL 4-6). 1990. PLB 13.95 *(0-8239-1113-6)* Rosen Group.
—Cobra. LC 92-14530. (Illus.). 48p. (gr. 5). 1993. RSBE 13.95 *(0-89686-701-3*, Crestwood Hse) Macmillan Child Grp.
—Corvette. LC 91-18096. (Illus.). 48p. (gr. 5). 1992. RSBE 13.95 *(0-89686-697-1*, Crestwood Hse) Macmillan Child Grp.
—Everything You Need to Know about Weapons in School & at Home. Rosen, Ruth, ed. (gr. 7-12). 1993. PLB 13.95 *(0-8239-1531-X)* Rosen Group.
—Ferrari. LC 91-21374. (Illus.). 48p. (gr. 5). 1992. RSBE 13.95 *(0-89686-700-5*, Crestwood Hse) Macmillan Child Grp.
—Firebird. LC 92-15069. (Illus.). 48p. (gr. 5). 1993. RSBE 13.95 *(0-89686-702-1*, Crestwood Hse) Macmillan Child Grp.
—Jaguar. LC 93-10529. (Illus.). 48p. (gr. 5 up). 1994. RSBE 13.95 *(0-89686-814-1*, Crestwood Hse) Macmillan Child Grp.
—Mercedes-Benz. LC 93-17505. (Illus.). 48p. (gr. 5 up). 1994. RSBE 13.95 *(0-89686-815-X*, Crestwood Hse) Macmillan Child Grp.
—Mustang. LC 91-27908. (Illus.). 48p. (gr. 5). 1992. RSBE 13.95 *(0-89686-699-8*, Crestwood Hse) Macmillan Child Grp.
—Our Declaration of Independence. LC 91-43229. (Illus.). 48p. (gr. 2-4). 1992. PLB 12.90 *(1-56294-205-0)* Millbrook Pr.
—Porsche. LC 91-31534. (Illus.). 48p. (gr. 5). 1992. RSBE 13.95 *(0-89686-703-X*, Crestwood Hse) Macmillan Child Grp.
—Thunderbird. LC 93-17241. (Illus.). 48p. (gr. 5 up). 1994. RSBE 13.95 *(0-89686-816-8*, Crestwood Hse) Macmillan Child Grp.

Schleifer, Jay, jt. auth. see Cruise, Beth.
Schleifer, Laura, jt. auth. see Cruise, Beth.

Schlein, Miriam. Big Talk. rev. ed. Auclair, Joan, illus. LC 89-35343. 32p. (ps-1). 1990. RSBE 13.95 *(0-02-781231-6*, Bradbury Pr) Macmillan Child Grp.
—The Dangerous Life of the Sea Horse. Cole, Gwen, illus. LC 85-26857. 40p. (gr. 3-6). 1986. SBE 13.95 *(0-689-31180-X*, Atheneum Child Bk) Macmillan Child Grp.
—Discovering Dinosaur Babies. Colbert, Margaret, illus. LC 89-23496. 40p. (gr. 1-5). 1991. RSBE 14.95 *(0-02-778091-0*, Four Winds) Macmillan Child Grp.
—I Sailed with Columbus. Newsom, Tom, illus. LC 90-24532. 144p. (gr. 3-6). 1991. 14.00 *(0-06-022513-0)*; PLB 13.89 *(0-06-022514-9)* HarpC Child Bks.
—I Sailed with Columbus. Newsom, Tom, illus. LC 90-24532. 144p. (gr. 3-6). 1992. pap. 3.95 *(0-06-440423-4*, Trophy) HarpC Child Bks.
—Jane Goodall's Animal World: Elephants. LC 89-38551. (Illus.). 32p. (gr. 3-7). 1990. SBE 11.95 *(0-689-31468-X*, Atheneum Child Bk) Macmillan Child Grp.
—Just Like Me. Janovitz, Marilyn, illus. LC 91-40019. 32p. (ps-2). 1993. 12.95 *(1-56282-233-0)*; PLB 12.89 *(1-56282-234-9)* Hyprn Child.
—Let's Go Dinosaur Tracking! Duke, Kate, illus. LC 90-39632. 48p. (gr. 2-5). 1991. PLB 14.89 *(0-06-025139-5)* HarpC Child Bks.
—Our Holidays. Kahn, Katherine, illus. 128p. (gr. k-3). 1983. pap. text ed. 7.95x *(0-87441-382-6)* Behrman.
—Project Panda Watch. Shetterly, Robert, illus. LC 84-2914. 96p. (gr. 4 up). 1984. SBE 13.95 *(0-689-31071-4*, Atheneum Child Bk) Macmillan Child Grp.
—Secret Land of the Past. (gr. 4-7). 1992. pap. 2.75 *(0-590-45701-2)* Scholastic Inc.
—Squirrel Watching. Pillar, Marjorie, illus. LC 91-6481. 64p. (gr. 2-6). 1992. 15.00 *(0-06-022753-2)*; PLB 14.89 *(0-06-022754-0)* HarpC Child Bks.
—Way Mothers Are. Lasker, Joe, illus. LC 63-13332. (ps-2). 1963. PLB 13.95 *(0-8075-8692-7)* A Whitman.
—The Way Mothers Are: Thirtieth Anniversary Edition. rev. ed. Tucker, Kathy, ed. Lasker, Joe, illus. LC 92-21516. 32p. (ps-k). 1993. PLB 13.95 *(0-8075-8691-9)* A Whitman.
—The Year of the Panda. Mak, Kam, illus. LC 89-71307. 96p. (gr. 3-7). 1990. (Crowell Jr Bks); PLB 13.89 *(0-690-04866-1*, Crowell Jr Bks) HarpC Child Bks.
—The Year of the Panda. Mak, Kam, illus. LC 89-71307. 96p. (gr. 2-5). 1992. pap. 3.95 *(0-06-440366-4*, Trophy) HarpC Child Bks.

Schlesinger, Arthur, Jr., intro. by. Franklin Roosevelt. (Illus.). 128p. (gr. 7-12). PLB 16.95 *(0-685-21876-7*, 087250) Know Unltd.

Schlesinger, Arthur M., Jr. see Lash, Joseph P.

Schliefer, Jay. Everything You Need to Know about Teen Suicide. rev. ed. (Illus.). 64p. (gr. 7 up). 1993. PLB 13.95 *(0-8239-1612-X)* Rosen Group.
—The Work Ethic. (gr. 7-12). 1991. PLB 13.95 *(0-8239-1227-2)* Rosen Group.

Schlink, Basilea. What Made Them So Brave? (Illus.). (gr. 3 up). 1978. gift edition 2.25 *(3-87209-655-9)* Evang Sisterhood Mary.

Schlitt, RaRa S. Robert Nathaniel's Tree.
Armstrong, Camilla B., illus. 36p. (gr. k up). 1993. 14.95 *(0-9630017-3-6)* Light-Bearer.
"This 36-page children's book was created by a young mother to help her oldest child better understand the death of his infant brother. As intended, ROBERT NATHANIEL'S TREE offers a source of inspiration for families facing loss; but this gentle, simple book is equally a celebration of life. The book addresses sensitive

subject matter & will help countless families better deal with the tragedy of a child's death. Upon the loss of a child, comfort is most commonly & understandably directed toward the parents; but brothers & sisters face a loss, as well. ROBERT NATHANIEL'S TREE will help bring some peace & comfort into the lives of grieving families."--Midwest Book Review, August 1993. Already in many school libraries, ROBERT NATHANIEL'S TREE meets a vital need. Beautiful picture-book format suitable for all ages. *Publisher Provided Annotation.*

Schloneger, Florence E. Sara's Trek. Quinn, Sidney, illus. 100p. (gr. 7 up). 1982. pap. 4.95 (0-87303-071-0) Faith & Life.

Schloredt, Valeri. Martin Luther King, Jr. America's Great Nonviolent Leader in the Struggle for Human Rights. Sherwood, Rhoda, ed. LC 88-2211. (Illus.). 68p. (gr. 5-6). 1988. PLB 18.60 (1-55532-817-2) Gareth Stevens Inc.

Schloredt, Valerie. Germany. (Illus.). 48p. (gr. 5 up). 1991. PLB 16.98 (0-382-24245-9) Silver Burdett Pr.

—Martin Luther King, Jr. LC 88-2211. (Illus.). 68p. (Orig.). 1990. pap. 7.95 (0-8192-1524-4) Morehouse Pub.

—Martin Luther King, Jr. Leader in the Struggle for Civil Rights. Birch, Beverley, adapted by. LC 89-77587. (Illus.). 64p. (gr. 3-4). 1990. PLB 18.60 (0-8368-0392-2) Gareth Stevens Inc.

—United States of America. rev. ed. LC 86-15565. (Illus.). 48p. (gr. 5 up). 1986. PLB 16.98 (0-382-09257-0) Silver Burdett Pr.

Schloss, Bevalee, ed. & illus. see Toomey, Marilyn M.

Schloss, Muriel. Mary Cleave, Astronaut. (gr. 5 up). 1990. 6.95 (0-9621820-2-8) Teachers Lab.

—Venus. LC 90-13101. (Illus.). 64p. (gr. 3-5). 1991. PLB 12.90 (0-531-20019-1) Watts.

Schlossberg, Dan. Pitching. (Illus.). 96p. (gr. 5 up). 1991. pap. 12.95 (0-671-73317-6, S&S BFYR); pap. 5.95 (0-671-70443-5, S&S BFYR) S&S Trade.

Schlossberg, Leon. The Johns Hopkins Human Anatomy Series. (Illus.). (gr. 8 up). 1986. markable ed. 36.95 (0-9603730-2-0) Anatomical Chart.

Schluep, J., jt. auth. see Westcott, Alvin.

Schmeltz, Susan A. Oh, So Silly! Cocca, Maryann, illus. LC 83-23754. 48p. (ps-3). 1984. 5.95 (0-8193-1122-7) Parents.

—Pets I Wouldn't Pick. Appleby, Ellen, illus. LC 81-11071. 48p. (ps-3). 1982. 5.95 (0-8193-1073-5); PLB 5.95 (0-8193-1074-3) Parents.

Schmeltz, Susan A., ed. This Book Is Just for You. Caudill-Paye, Judythe, illus. LC 81-11928. 100p. (gr. k-6). 1981. 11.95g (0-9606586-0-2) Quality MO.

Schmid, Eleonore. The Air Around Us. Schmid, Eleonore & James, J. Alison, illus. LC 92-9830. 32p. (gr. k-3). 1992. 14.95 (1-55858-165-0); PLB 14.88 (1-55858-166-9) North-South Bks NYC.

—Farm Animals. Schmid, Eleonore, illus. LC 85-63302. 12p. (ps-k). 1986. 3.95 (1-55858-045-X) North-South Bks NYC.

—Story of Christmas. Schmid, Eleanore, illus. LC 89-43724. 32p. (ps-3). 1990. 13.95 (1-55858-097-2) North-South Bks NYC.

—Wake up, Dormouse, Santa Claus Is Here. Schmid, Eleonore, illus. LC 89-42610. 32p. (gr. k-3). 1989. 14.95 (1-55858-020-4) North-South Bks NYC.

—Wake up, Dormouse, Santa Claus Is Here. (ps-3). 1991. pap. 2.95 (1-55858-077-8) North-South Bks NYC.

—The Water's Journey. Schmid, Eleonore, illus. LC 89-42872. 32p. (gr. k-3). 1990. 14.95 (1-55858-013-1) North-South Bks NYC.

Schmid, Eleonore, jt. auth. see Krenzer, Rolf.

Schmid-Belk, Donna D. The Arizona Alphabet Book. Belk, Gordon G., ed. Ives, Michael, illus. 32p. (Orig.). (ps-8). 1989. pap. text ed. 7.95 (0-685-28841-2) Donna Dee Bks.

Schmidt, Alex J. Our Federal & State Constitutions. rev. ed. 65p. (gr. 7-11). 1992. pap. text ed. 3.85 (0-931298-00-8) A J S Pubns.

Schmidt, Annemarie & Schmidt, Christian R. Apes. LC 92-10659. 1992. PLB 17.27 (0-8368-0840-1) Gareth Stevens Inc.

—Pigs & Peccaries. LC 93-13051. (gr. 3 up). 1993. write for info. (0-8368-1003-1) Gareth Stevens Inc.

Schmidt, Annie. Pink Lemonade. Ten Harmsel, Henrietta, tr. Foley, Timothy, illus. 64p. (ps-6). 1992. 14.99 (0-8028-4050-7) Eerdmans.

Schmidt, Bridget. Bayla & the SleepStone. (ps-3). 1992. pap. 14.99 (0-9634525-0-9) Bayla Prods.

Schmidt, Christian R., jt. auth. see Schmidt, Annemarie.

Schmidt, Cynthia. Colorado: Grassroots. (Illus.). 64p. (gr. 4-6). 1989. Repr. of 1983 ed. text ed. 11.95 (0-911981-12-8) Cloud Pub.

Schmidt, Diane. I Am a Jesse White Tumbler. Tucker, Kathy, ed. Schmidt, Diane, photos by. LC 89-16590. (Illus.). 40p. (gr. 2-8). 1990. 13.95 (0-8075-3444-7) A Whitman.

Schmidt, Elizabeth. Saint for the Young: The Story of St. John Bosco. Musio, Nino, illus. 34p. (Orig.). (gr. 4-8). 1987. 9.95 (0-89944-088-6, Don Bosco Pubns) Don Bosco Multimedia.

Schmidt, Fran & Friedman, Alice. Come in Spaceship Earth. Heyne, Chris, illus. 61p. (Orig.). (gr. 4-9). 1990. Incl. poster. pap. text ed. 21.95 (1-878227-06-8) Peace Educ. Students serve as crew members aboard Spaceship Earth. They learn to work cooperatively on a common mission - survival & improved quality of life for the human family. COME IN SPACESHIP EARTH is action-oriented as it guides students toward individual & social responsibility. The crew is challenged to tackle problems in their school, community, & world. They develop problem solving & critical thinking skills through role plays, brainstorming, & simulation games. As students plan & work together, they gain a new respect for individual differences & learn to handle conflict nonviolently. These experiences & skills help them to be responsible, capable & creative crew members now & in the future. "COME IN SPACESHIP EARTH started my students thinking about their roles as crew members in our classroom & in their world. It is wonderful to see my students begin to act as a cohesive team, creating a positive classroom environment."--Carol Bregman, Middle School, Miami, Florida. As students plan & work together, they are guided toward individual & social responsibility. *Publisher Provided Annotation.*

—Creative Conflict Solving for Kids: Grades 5-9. 2nd., rev. ed. Cranford, Kay K., et al, illus. 80p. (gr. 4-9). 1985. Incl. poster. pap. text ed. 21.95 (1-878227-00-9) Peace Educ. CREATIVE CONFLICT SOLVING FOR KIDS challenges your students to deal creatively & constructively with conflict. The activities can easily be incorporated into your social studies, science & language arts programs. The curriculum comes with 40 student pages & an extensive teacher's guide with many enjoyable extending activities. Your students will be actively involved in brainstorming, role playing, problem solving & decision making as they learn the skills of creative communication, active listening, fighting fair, critical thinking, & cooperation. Students will: develop positive interpersonal skills; respect human differences; understand the dynamics of conflict; practice conflict resolution strategies; learn ways to handle frustration & anger; explore conflict as a positive force of change. "My students just love CREATIVE CONFLICT SOLVING FOR KIDS. They enjoy all of the activities & I can honestly say that the program has made a significant difference in the way the children treat each other. Name calling & put downs are rarely heard & when they occur they are handled before they turn into a fight."--Joanne Sweeney, Fifth Grade, New York, New York. Students are involved

in problem solving, brainstorming, role playing, & responsible decision making. *Publisher Provided Annotation.*

—Creative Conflict Solving for Kids: Grades 3-4. 90p. (Orig.). (gr. 3-4). 1991. Incl. poster. 21.95 (1-878227-10-6); Set of 5, 24p. 11.95 (1-878227-11-4) Peace Educ.

—Creative Conflict Solving for Kids: Grades 3-4. 2nd ed. 90p. (gr. 3-4). 1993. Tchr's ed., incl. poster. 21.95 (1-878227-17-3); Wkbk. 11.95 (0-685-64734-X) Peace Educ. CREATIVE CONFLICT SOLVING FOR KIDS: GRADES 3-4 adds an exciting new dimension to your reading, language arts, social studies & science programs. The stories, fables, poetry, plays, cartoons, role plays, discussions, journal writing, & brainstorming will capture & hold the interest of your students as they learn to deal with conflict in a more positive manner. Students learn mediation by holding mock mediation sessions of the Pied Piper of Hamelin, Jack & the Beanstalk, & others. This interdisciplinary curriculum is designed especially to meet the needs of this age group. CREATIVE CONFLICT SOLVING FOR KIDS: GRADES 3-4 helps students: deal constructively with conflict; build positive self-esteem; make responsible decisions; develop sensitivity to all people; respect human differences. CREATIVE CONFLICT SOLVING FOR KIDS: GRADES 3-4 teaches communication, listening, critical thinking, problem solving, decision making, & mediation skills. CREATIVE CONFLICT SOLVING FOR KIDS: GRADES 3-4 includes reproducible student work sheets & an extensive teacher's guide written so that each activity can be implemented. It includes many suggestions on how to set up a nurturing classroom environment & how to prevent & deal with conflict. Ready-to-use student workbooks are also available. A new colorful poster of the Rules for Fighting Fair is included. *Publisher Provided Annotation.*

—Fighting Fair: Dr. Martin Luther King Jr. for Kids. Heyne, Chris, illus. 40p. (Orig.). (gr. 4-9). 1986. pap. text ed. 13.95 (1-878227-01-7) Peace Educ.

—Fighting Fair: Dr. Martin Luther King Jr. for Kids. rev. ed. Heyne, Chris, illus. (gr. 4-9). 1990. Set. pap. text ed. 74.95 69 p., incl. poster, video (1-878227-02-5); tchr's. ed., incl. poster 19.95 (1-878227-07-6); Set of 5. wkbk., 48p. 11.95 (1-878227-08-4) Peace Educ. Challenge your students to resolve conflicts with skills - not fists - within the framework of Dr. Martin Luther King Jr.'s philosophy of nonviolence. FIGHTING FAIR: DR. MARTIN LUTHER KING, JR. FOR KIDS provides many opportunities for students to apply the skills, strategies, & values of nonviolence to their daily lives & to explore nonviolence as a method of social change. The FIGHTING FAIR program includes: A provocative eighteen-minute, award winning video which shows a coach helping a group of angry kids resolve a conflict on the basketball court. Vivid scenes of the civil rights movement are used as backdrop to help the young people understand the dynamics of nonviolence. A comprehensive teacher's guide with 43 reproducible student pages. FIGHTING FAIR involves students in brainstorming, role playing, problem solving, responsible decision making, & mediation. A colorful poster of the Rules For Fighting Fair provides students with guidelines to "fight back effectively & nonviolently. "...a valuable acquisition for school libraries, for use in guidance & social studies classes & conflict resolution workshops."--School Library Journal. "The strong man is the man who can stand up for his rights & not hit back." --Dr. Martin Luther King, Jr. *Publisher Provided Annotation.*

—Peacemaking Skills for Little Kids. Le Shane, Phyllis, contrib. by. (Illus.). 76p. (Orig.). (gr. k-2). 1988. pap. text ed. 54.95 incl. poster, puppet, cassette (1-878227-03-3) Peace Educ.

—Peacemaking Skills for Little Kids. 2nd ed. (Illus.). 76p. (ps-2). 1993. Tchr's ed., incl. puppet, cass. & poster. 54.95 (1-878227-16-5); Wkbk. 11.95 (1-878227-15-7) Peace Educ. PEACEMAKING SKILLS FOR LITTLE KIDS, 2nd ed., affirms the preciousness of life, the uniqueness of each person, & the interdependence of all living things. Through puppetry, role playing, singing, body movement, storytelling, discussion, art, circle activities, & nature walks, children are actively involved in learning about themselves, others, & how they are connected to the world around them. Activities help children to develop positive self-esteem, sensitivity to the needs of others, respect for human differences, love for the natural environment & ways to handle conflict non-violently. Peacemaking skills become an integral part of everything children do in the primary classroom. PEACEMAKING SKILLS FOR LITTLE KIDS contains a curriculum complete with teacher's guide & children's activities, an excellent, annotated bibliography, "I-Care-Cat" puppet, audio cassette with "I-Care-Cat's" presentations & songs for children, & an "I-Care" classroom poster. "Invaluable! A MUST for every primary classroom. PEACEMAKING SKILLS FOR LITTLE KIDS is the best program that I've come across for children. The Introductions & Setting the Stage sections helped me create a nurturing classroom environment. The children just loved the visits by "I-Care-Cat". My students have become more caring, responsible & cooperative. "--Joan Watson, Kindergarten, Miami, Florida. Peacemaking skills become an integral part of everything the children do. *Publisher Provided Annotation.*

Schmidt, Fran, et al. Mediation for Kids. 2nd ed. (Illus.). 68p. (gr. 4-12). 1992. Incl. poster. 21.95 (1-878227-13-0); Set of 5, 28p. 11.95 (1-878227-14-9) Peace Educ. Kids arguing, pushing, name-calling, fighting. Sound familiar? Conflicts are a daily occurrence in all schools. Mediation offers the students the opportunity to take responsibility for their behavior. Start a student mediation program in your school. Mediation dissolves disputes with the help of a neutral third party. MEDIATION FOR KIDS contains easy to follow lessons which include active listening, paraphrasing, conflict clues, fighting fair, eight cases ready to mediate, a student mediator's certificate, & the Rules for Fighting Fair poster. MEDIATION FOR KIDS offers a step-by-step approach which includes: * Program goals & objectives * Why mediation? * Selection of students * When mediation is appropriate * Role of the school coordinator * Implementation models * Your school's commitment. "MEDIATION FOR KIDS is an excellent mediation training manual. I have used it successfully with hundreds of students, teachers & counselors. MEDIATION FOR KIDS makes it possible for schools to implement a student mediation program for a teacher to use it in the classroom."-- Jean Marvel, Conflict Resolution Specialist, Dade County Public Schools, Teacher Education Center. *Publisher Provided Annotation.*

Schmidt, Gary D. Hugh Lofting. LC 92-11256. 200p. 1992. text ed. 22.95 (0-8057-7023-2, Twayne) Macmillan.

Schmidt, J. David. Graffiti: Devotions for Girls. new ed. (Illus.). 128p. (Orig.). (gr. 8-12). 1983. pap. 7.99 (0-8007-5115-9) Revell.
—Graffiti: Devotions for Guys. new ed. (Illus.). 128p. (Orig.). (gr. 8-12). 1983. pap. 7.99 (0-8007-5114-0) Revell.
—More Graffiti: Devotions for Girls. (Illus.). 128p. (Orig.). (gr. 7-12). 1984. pap. 7.99 (0-8007-5143-4) Revell.
—More Graffiti: Devotions for Guys. (Illus.). 128p. (Orig.). (gr. 7-12). 1984. pap. 7.99 (0-8007-5142-6) Revell.

Schmidt, Jeremy. In the Village of the Elephants. Wood, Ted, photos by. LC 93-8545. (Illus.). 1994. 15.95 (0-8027-8226-4); PLB 16.85 (0-8027-8227-2) Walker & Co.

Schmidt, John J. Invitation to Friendship. Sorenson, Don L., ed. LC 87-82992. (Illus.). 104p. (Orig.). (gr. 6-8). 1988. pap. text ed. 6.95x (0-932796-23-0) Ed Media Corp.

Schmidt, Karen, jt. auth. see Leonard, Marcia.

Schmidt, Karen, illus. Down by the Station. 1987. pap. 6.99 incl. audiocassette (0-553-45902-3) Bantam.
—The Gingerbread Man. 32p. (gr. k-2). 1985. pap. 2.50 (0-590-41056-3) Scholastic Inc.

Schmidt, Karen L., illus. Chicken Little. 18p. (ps). 1986. 3.95 (0-448-10223-4, G&D) Putnam Pub Group.
—The Little Red Hen. 16p. (ps). 1984. 3.95 (0-448-10218-8, G&D) Putnam Pub Group.
—My First Book of Baby Animals. LC 85-62639. 12p. (ps). 1986. 3.95 (0-448-10826-7, Platt & Munk) Putnam Pub Group.

Schmidt, Mike & Ellis, Rob. The Mike Schmidt Hitting Study, Youth Version: Building a Foundation. Cheney, Paul & Bauer, Louise, illus. 80p. (Orig.). (gr. 4-10). 1993. pap. 8.95 (0-9634609-3-5) McGriff & Bell.

Schmidt, Norman. Discover Aerodynamics with Paper Airplanes. Schmidt, Norman, illus. 48p. (Orig.). (gr. 7-12). 1991. pap. 14.95 (0-920541-43-7) Peguis Pubs Ltd.

Schmitt, Lois. Smart Spending: A Consumer's Guide. LC 88-29524. 112p. (gr. 5-9). 1989. SBE 12.95 (0-684-19035-4, Scribners Young Read) Macmillan Child Grp.

Schmitt, Marshall L., jt. auth. see Buban, Peter.

Schmoker, Lisa, ed. see Gesme, Carole & Peterson, Larry.

Schnatz, Grace. A Child's Introduction to a Garden. Schnatz, Grace, illus. 33p. (gr. 4-8). 1984. PLB 4.75 (0-9614145-0-2) G Schnatz Pubns.

Schneck, Susan. Christian Clip & Copy Art. 96p. (ps-8). 1989. 10.95 (0-86653-503-9, SS1816, Shining Star Pubns) Good Apple.

Schneck, Susan & Strohl, Mary. Vacation Bible School Ideas & Summertime Fun. (Illus.). 96p. (ps-2). 1989. 10.95 (0-86653-477-6, SS1813, Shining Star Pubns) Good Apple.

Schneegans, Nicole. The Bird Fisherman. (Illus.). (gr. 1-8). 1992. PLB 8.95 (0-89565-896-8); Resale. 12.75 (0-685-60994-4) Childs World.

—The King's Twins. (Illus.). 48p. (gr. k-4). 1990. 12.75 (0-89565-813-5); 8.95s.p. (0-685-55100-8) Childs World.

Schneider, Amy, ed. see Howard, Lati, et al.

Schneider, Bill. The Flight of the Nez Perce. rev. ed. White, Dan, illus. LC 88-80227. 32p. 1993. pap. 5.95 (0-937959-39-1) Falcon Pr MT.

Schneider, D. Douglas. Symbolically Speaking. Holbrook, Clifford & LaMothe, Becky, illus. Michael, ed. 85p. (ps up). 1987. pap. 5.95 (0-939169-01-0) World Peace Univ.

Schneider, David C. A Visit to the People Zoo. Scallon, Cheryl V., ed. Hillman, Carole D., illus. LC 89-85637. 16p. (Orig.). (ps-1). 1989. pap. write for info. Early Childhood.

Schneider, Howie. Amos Camps Out: A Couch Adventure in the Woods. (ps-3). 1992. 14.95 (0-316-77402-2, Joy St Bks) Little.
—No Dogs Allowed. LC 93-10395. 1994. write for info. (0-399-22612-5, Putnam) Putnam Pub Group.
—Uncle Lester's Hat. Schneider, Howie, illus. LC 92-20750. 32p. (ps-3). 1993. 14.95 (0-399-22439-4, Putnam) Putnam Pub Group.

Schneider, Howie & Seligson, Susan. The Amazing Amos & the Greatest Couch on Earth. Schneider, Howie, illus. 32p. (ps-3). 1989. 13.95 (0-316-78033-2, Joy St Bks) Little.
—Amos: The Story of an Old Dog & His Couch. Schneider, Howie, illus. LC 87-2813. 32p. (ps-3). 1987. 14.95 (0-316-77404-9) Little.

Schneider, Jeff. My Friend the Manatee: An Ocean Magic Book. Spoon, Wilfred, illus. LC 90-61576. 12p. (ps). 1991. 4.95g (1-877779-08-3) Schneider Educational.
—My Friend the Penguin: An Ocean Magic Book. Spoon, Wilfred, illus. LC 90-61577. 12p. (ps). 1991. 4.95g (1-877779-09-1) Schneider Educational.
—My Friend the Polar Bear: An Ocean Magic Book. Spoon, Wilfred, illus. LC 90-61579. 12p. (ps). 1991. 4.95g (1-877779-12-1) Schneider Educational.
—My Friend the Porpoise: An Ocean Magic Book. Spoon, Wilfred, illus. LC 90-61572. 12p. (ps). 1991. 4.95g (1-877779-07-5) Schneider Educational.
—My Friend the Sea Otter: An Ocean Magic Book. Spoon, Wilfred, illus. LC 90-61578. 12p. (ps). 1991. 4.95g (1-877779-10-5) Schneider Educational.
—My Friend the Walrus: An Ocean Magic Book. Spoon, Wilfred, illus. LC 90-61581. 12p. (ps). 1991. 4.95g (1-877779-11-3) Schneider Educational.

Schneider, M. E. The Babysitter's Guide. (Orig.). (gr. 7-12). 1990. pap. 11.95 (0-685-30792-1) Marlin Pub.

Schneider, Mary J. The Hidatsa. Porter, Frank W., III, intro. by. (Illus.). 112p. (gr. 5 up). 1989. 17.95 (1-55546-707-5) Chelsea Hse.

Schneider, Maxine S. Science Projects for the Intermediate Grades. LC 70-132146. (gr. 4-6). 1971. pap. 7.95 (0-8224-6310-5) Fearon Teach Aids.

Schneider, Meg. I Wonder What College Is Like? Steltenpohl, Jane, ed. (Illus.). 160p. (gr. 7-9). 1989. lib. bdg. 13.98 (0-671-65847-6, J Messner; lib. bdg. 5.95 (0-671-67815-9) S&S Trade.
—Popularity Has Its Ups & Downs. LC 91-1447. (gr. 4-7). 1992. lib. bdg. 12.98 (0-671-72848-2, J Messner); pap. 5.95 (0-671-72849-0, J Messner) S&S Trade.

Schneider, Meg, ed. see Cahn, Julie.

Schneider, Meg, ed. see Keene, Carolyn.

Schneider, Meg, ed. see Tallarico, Tony.

Schneider, Meg F. The Practically Popular Crowd: Pretty Enough. 1992. 2.95 (0-590-44804-8, Apple Paperbacks) Scholastic Inc.
—The Practically Popular Crowd: Wanting More. 1992. pap. 2.95 (0-590-44803-X, Apple Paperbacks) Scholastic Inc.
—Romance! Can You Survive It? A Guide to Sticky Dating Situations. 160p. (Orig.). (gr. 7-12). 1984. pap. 2.25 (0-440-97478-X, LFL) Dell.

Schneider, Rex. That's Not All! Gregorich, Barbara, ed. (Illus.). 16p. (Orig.). (gr. k-2). 1985. pap. 2.25 (0-88743-019-8, 06019) Sch Zone Pub Co.
—That's Not All! Gregorich, Barbara, ed. (Illus.). 32p. (gr. k-2). 1992. pap. 3.95 (0-88743-417-7, 06069) Sch Zone Pub Co.
—The Wide-Mouthed Frog. LC 80-13449. (Illus.). 32p. (gr. k up). 1980. 13.95 (0-916144-58-5) Stemmer Hse.

Schneider, Terry & Fetterolf, Michele, eds. Study Abroad 1994: A Guide to Semester & Yearlong Academic Programs. 600p. 1993. pap. 18.95 (1-56079-327-9) Petersons Guides.

Schneider, Tom. Everybody's a Winner: A Kid's Guide to New Sports & Fitness. (Illus.). (gr. 3 up). 1976. 14.95 (0-316-77398-0, Brown Paper School) Little.

Schneidewind, Barbara F. Hi, I'm Cy. 1993. 7.95 (0-533-10555-2) Vantage.

Schnell, Louise. Seasonal Art. Evans, Carol, ed. Schnell, Louise, illus. 52p. (ps-3). 1988. wkbk. 5.95 (0-915505-01-0) Tchr Tested-Child.

Schnell, Robert W. Bonko. Wilkon, Jozef, illus. LC 77-99446. 28p. (ps-3). 8.95 (0-87592-008-X) Scroll Pr.

Schnieder, Bill. The Tree Giants. Dowden, D. D., illus. LC 88-80225. 32p. 1988. pap. 4.95 (0-937959-40-5) Falcon Pr MT.

Schnieper, Claudia. Amazing Spiders. Meier, Max, photos by. (Illus.). 48p. (gr. 2-5). 1989. 19.95 (0-87614-342-7); pap. 6.95 (0-87614-518-7) Carolrhoda Bks.

—An Apple Tree Through the Year. Baumli, Othmar, photos by. (Illus.). 48p. (gr. 2-5). 1987. PLB 19.95 *(0-87614-248-X)*; pap. 6.95 *(0-87614-483-0)* Carolrhoda Bks.
—Chameleons. Meier, Max, photos by. (Illus.). 48p. (gr. 2-5). 1989. 19.95 *(0-87614-341-9)*; pap. 6.95 *(0-87614-520-9)* Carolrhoda Bks.
—Lizards. Meirer, Max, illus. 48p. (gr. 2-6). 1990. PLB 19.95 *(0-87614-405-9)* Carolrhoda Bks.
—On the Trail of the Fox. Scherer, Elise, tr. (GER., Illus.). 48p. (gr. 2-5). 1986. lib. bdg. 19.95 *(0-87614-287-0)* Carolrhoda Bks.
—On the Trail of the Fox. (Illus.). 48p. (gr. 1-5). 1987. pap. 6.95 *(0-87614-480-6,* First Ave Edns) Lerner Pubns.
Schnitter, Jane. William Is My Brother. LC 90-21364. (Illus.). 32p. (ps-3). 1991. 10.95 *(0-944934-03-X)* Perspect Indiana.
Schnur, Steven. Hannah & Cyclops. (gr. 4-7). 1990. pap. 2.75 *(0-553-15796-5)* Bantam.
—The Narrowest Bar Mitzvah. Lazzaro, Victor, illus. 48p. (Orig.). (gr. 4-6). 1986. pap. text ed. 6.95 *(0-8074-0316-4,* 123923) UAHC.
—The Return of Morris Schumsky. Lazzaro, Victor, illus. 48p. (gr. 4-6). 1987. pap. 6.95 *(0-8074-0358-X,* 123927) UAHC.
Schnurr, Carl. The Pact of Pasaquine. McGlothlen, Ken, et al, eds. Miller, David, illus. 96p. (Orig.). (gr. 11 up). 1991. pap. 12.95 *(0-9627790-8-3)* White Wolf.
Schnurre. Die Tat - Ein Fall Fur Herrn Schmidt. pap. 5.95 *(0-88436-040-7,* 45272) EMC.
Schoberle, Cecile. Day Nights, Night Lights. Stevenson, Harvey, illus. LC 93-18680. (gr. 4 up). 1994. pap. 14.00 *(0-671-87439-X,* S&S BFYR) S&S Trade.
—Esmeralda & the Pet Parade. (gr. 2). 1991. write for info. *(0-663-56219-8)* Silver Burdett Pr.
Schoberle, Cecile & Stevenson, Harvey. Morning Sounds, Evening Sounds. LC 93-16786. (gr. 4 up). 1994. pap. 14.00 *(0-671-87437-3,* S&S BFYR) S&S Trade.
Schoch, Tim. Cat Attack. (gr. 3-7). 1988. pap. 2.75 *(0-380-75520-3,* Camelot) Avon.
—Flash Fry, Private Eye. 96p. (Orig.). (gr. 3-7). 1986. pap. 2.50 *(0-380-75108-9,* Camelot) Avon.
—Summer Camp Creeps. 160p. (Orig.). (gr. 3-7). 1987. pap. 2.95 *(0-380-75343-X,* Camelot) Avon.
Schoder, Judith & Shebar, Sharon S. The Bell Witch. Morril, Leslie, illus. LC 82-42873. 64p. (gr. 7 up). 1983. (J Messner); PLB 9.29 *(0-671-44005-5)* S&S Trade.
Schoder, Judy. Funny Bunny. Wasserman, Dan, ed. Reese, Bob, illus. (gr. k-1). 1979. 7.95 *(0-89868-069-7)*; pap. 2.95 *(0-89868-080-8)* ARO Pub.
Schodorf, Timothy, jt. auth. see Kennedy, Trish.
Schoen, Celin V. Pearl Buck: Famed American Author of Oriental Stories. Rahmas, D. Steve, ed. LC 70-190247. 32p. (Orig.). (gr. 7-12). 1972. lib. bdg. 4.95 incl. catalog cards *(0-87157-530-2)* SamHar Pr.
Schoen, Harold L., ed. Estimation & Mental Computation: 1986 Yearbook. LC 85-31947. (Illus.). 248p. (gr. k-12). 1986. 20.00 *(0-87353-226-0)* NCTM.
Schoen, Mark. Bellybuttons Are Navels. (Illus.). 40p. (ps-k). 1990. 12.95 *(0-8290-2409-3)* Irvington.
—Bellybuttons Are Navels. Quay, M. J., illus. Calderone, Mary, intro. by. (Illus.). 40p. (ps-3). 1990. Repr. 16.95 *(0-87975-585-7)* Prometheus Bks.
Schoenberg, Jane. My Bodyworks. Fritz, Ronald, illus. 32p. (ps-3). 1993. pap. 2.50 *(0-590-47231-3,* Cartwheel) Scholastic Inc.
Schoenfield, Mark & Rosenblatt, Jeanette. Adventures with Logic. (gr. 5-7). 1985. pap. 8.95 *(0-8224-0285-8)* Fearon Teach Aids.
—Discovering Logic. (gr. 4-6). 1985. pap. 8.95 *(0-8224-1915-7)* Fearon Teach Aids.
—Playing with Logic. (gr. 3-5). 1985. pap. 8.95 *(0-8224-5310-X)* Fearon Teach Aids.
Schoenherr, John. Bear. (Illus.). 32p. (ps-3). 1991. 14.95 *(0-399-22177-8,* Philomel Bks) Putnam Pub Group.
—Bear. Thomas, Peter, narrated by. Schoenherr, John, illus. 32p. (ps-4). 1991. incl. audiocassette tape & plush stuffed bear toy 44.95 *(0-924483-69-5)*; incl. audiocassette tape 17.95 *(0-924483-34-2)* Soundprints.
Schoepfer, G. R. River of Miracles. Schoepfer, Virginia B., ed. Brenes, Irma M., illus. (gr. 1-11). 1978. pap. text ed. 2.75x *(0-931436-01-X,* Children's Books) G R Schoepfer.
Schoepfer, Virginia B., ed. see Schoepfer, G. R.
Scholes, Katherine. The Landing: A Night of Birds. Wong, David, illus. 72p. (gr. 4 up). 1989. 12.95 *(0-385-26191-8,* Zephyr-BFYR) Doubleday.
—Peace Begins with You. Ingpen, Robert, illus. 40p. (gr. 1-5). 1990. 12.95 *(0-316-77436-7)* Sierra.
Scholey, Arthur. Baboushka. (ps-3). 1993. pap. 4.99 *(0-7459-2259-7)* Lion USA.
—Dickens Christmas Carol Show. 1979. 5.00 *(0-87602-119-4)* Anchorage.
Scholten, Dan, jt. auth. see Burns, Diane L.
Scholz, Jackson. Batter Up. LC 92-32796. 256p. (gr. 5 up). 1993. 13.00 *(0-688-12485-2)* Morrow Jr Bks.
—Batter Up. LC 92-32796. 1993. pap. 4.95 *(0-688-12158-6,* Pub. by Beech Tree Bks) Morrow.
—Fielder from Nowhere. 256p. (gr. 6 up). 1993. pap. 4.95 *(0-685-61565-0,* Pub. by Beech Tree Bks) Morrow.
—Fielder from Nowhere. LC 92-32797. 256p. (gr. 5 up). 1993. 13.00 *(0-688-12486-0)* Morrow Jr Bks.

—The Football Rebels. LC 92-43376. 256p. (gr. 5 up). 1993. Repr. of 1960 ed. 13.00 *(0-688-12523-9)* Morrow Jr Bks.
—Rookie Quarterback. LC 92-43375. 240p. (gr. 5 up). 1993. Repr. of 1965 ed. 13.00 *(0-688-12524-7)* Morrow Jr Bks.
Scholz, Jackson V. The Football Rebels. LC 92-43376. 224p. (gr. 6 up). 1993. pap. 4.95 *(0-688-12643-X,* Pub. by Beech Tree Bks) Morrow.
—Rookie Quarterback. LC 92-43375. 224p. (gr. 6 up). 1993. pap. 4.95 *(0-688-12644-8)* Morrow Jr Bks.
Schomp, Virginia. The Bottlenose Dolphin. LC 93-37927. (Illus.). 1994. write for info. *(0-87518-605-X,* Dillion) Macmillan Child Grp.
Schongut, Emanuel. Hush Kitten. Klimo, Kate, ed. Schongut, Emanuel, illus. 14p. 1983. 3.95 *(0-671-46386-1)* S&S Trade.
School Mathematics Projects Staff. Foundations. (Illus.). 141p. (gr. 9-12). 1993. pap. 7.95 *(0-521-38842-2)* Cambridge U Pr.
Schoolland, Marian M. Marian's Big Book of Bible Stories. (gr. k-4). 1947. 19.99 *(0-8028-5003-0)* Eerdmans.
Schoonmaker, David & Woods, Bruce. Whirligigs & Weathervanes: A Celebration of Wind Gadgets with Dozens of Creative Projects to Make. LC 91-12145. (Illus.). 128p. (gr. 10-12). 1992. pap. 12.95 *(0-8069-8365-5,* Pub. by Lark Bks) Sterling.
Schoonmaker, Peter K. The Living Forest. LC 89-33603. (Illus.). 64p. (gr. 6 up). 1990. lib. bdg. 15.95 *(0-89490-270-9)* Enslow Pubs.
Schoop, Janice. Boys Don't Knit. Beingessner, Laura, illus. 30p. (ps-3). 1988. pap. 4.95 *(0-86543-077-2)* Africa World.
Schorer, Mark, ed. see Austen, Jane.
Schories, Pat. He's Your Dog. (ps-3). 1993. 15.00 *(0-374-32906-0)* FS&G.
—Mouse Around. (ps-3). 1991. bds. 13.00 *(0-374-35080-9)* FS&G.
—Mouse Around. (ps-3). 1993. pap. 4.95 *(0-374-45414-0,* Sunburst) FS&G.
Schorsch, Kit. The Mouse's Christmas. Lynn, Patty, illus. 24p. (Orig.). (gr. k-1). 1990. pap. 0.99 *(1-878624-45-8)* McClanahan Bk.
Schorsch, Laurence. Mr. Boffin. Spier, Nancy, illus. 32p. (gr. k-3). 1993. 6.95 *(1-56288-353-4)* Checkerboard.
Schorsch, Laurence, retold by. David & Goliath. Schories, Pat, illus. 24p. (ps-3). 1992. 4.95 *(1-56288-221-X)* Checkerboard.
Schorsch, Laurence, ed. Evil Tales of Evil Things. Sperling, Thomas, illus. 128p. (gr. 3 up). 1993. pap. 3.50 *(1-56288-407-7)* Checkerboard.
Schorsch, Laurence, retold by. Noah's Ark. Schories, Pat, illus. 24p. (ps-3). 1992. 4.95 *(1-56288-223-6)* Checkerboard.
—The Story of Jonah. Hu, Ying-Hwa, illus. 24p. (ps-3). 1992. 4.95 *(1-56288-222-8)* Checkerboard.
—The Story of Joseph. Sperling, Tom, illus. 24p. (ps-3). 1992. 4.95 *(1-56288-224-4)* Checkerboard.
Schorsch, Laurence, ed. Tales of the Living Dead. Sperling, Thomas, illus. 128p. (gr. 3 up). 1993. pap. 3.50 *(1-56288-406-9)* Checkerboard.
Schorsch, Lawrence, compiled by. The Real Mother Goose Book of Christmas Carols. 1993. 9.95 *(1-56288-405-0)* Checkerboard.
Schorsch, Nancy. Saving the Condor. LC 90-47518. (Illus.). 64p. (gr. 3-6). 1991. PLB 12.90 *(0-531-20010-8)* Watts.
Schorsh, Laurence. Grandma's Visit. Pollard, Nan, illus. 32p. (ps-3). 1990. 4.95 *(1-56288-049-7)* Checkerboard.

Schott, Carolyn J. & Smith, Phillipa A. The Cracker Crumb Rescue. 40p. (gr. 3-6). 1992. PLB 16.95 *(0-9632461-0-0)* Harbour Duck.
"People are the problem, but people are the solution, too," I.P. said wisely. Children will learn, although humans create the problem of litter in the environment, they can be the solution as well. This book is the first of a proposed series that will explore environmental & preservation issues concerning the Chesapeake Bay. Cavu & Italian Princess, two mallards, are ready to explore the Bay, but are shocked to find that Cavu's mother is entrapped in a six-pack holder which could mean her death! She must be freed before they leave. Her rescue comes from a surprise source. The story underlines interdependence of humans & their fragile earth. Although the content is an upper elementary reading level, it is an enjoyable read-to story for younger children. Adults who have connections to the Bay also enjoy the antics of the ducks, & will quickly recognize the names of favorite anchorages. THE CRACKER CRUMB RESCUE provides diverse opportunities for interdisciplinary & theme units. "What a delightful demonstration of how real writers naturally integrate across the curriculum," writes Anna O'Toole, Language Arts Specialist of Chesterfield County, Virginia. Janet Keith, Language Arts Director, of Chesterfield adds, "This is wonderful! Let me know where I can purchase one -- it goes so well with our science program."
Publisher Provided Annotation.

Schott, Darlyne F. The Apple Tree, Vol. 9: Pasitos English Language Development Books. 16p. (gr. k-1). 1990. pap. text ed. 11.00 *(1-56537-068-6)* D F Schott Educ.
—Bono el Mono En la Escuela, Vol. 6: Pasitos Spanish Language Development Books. 25p. (gr. k-1). 1990. pap. text ed. 11.00 *(1-56537-055-4)* D F Schott Educ.
—Bono Goes to School, Vol. 6: Pasitos English Language Development Books. 25p. (gr. k-1). 1990. pap. text ed. 11.00 *(1-56537-065-1)* D F Schott Educ.
—Calabazas Opuestas, Vol. 5: Pasitos Spanish Language Development Books. 16p. (gr. k-1). 1990. pap. text ed. 11.00 *(1-56537-054-6)* D F Schott Educ.
—Cuatro Regalos, Vol. 2: Pasitos Spanish Language Development Books. 32p. (gr. k-1). 1990. pap. text ed. 11.00 *(1-56537-051-1)* D F Schott Educ.
—Cuento Del Manzano, Vol. 9: Pasitos Spanish Language Development Books. 16p. (gr. k-1). 1990. pap. text ed. 11.00 *(1-56537-058-9)* D F Schott Educ.
—Esta Nevando!, Vol. 10: Pasitos Spanish Language Development Books. 18p. (gr. k-1). 1990. pap. text ed. 11.00 *(1-56537-059-7)* D F Schott Educ.
—Four Pretty Presents, Vol. 2: Pasitos English Language Development Books. 31p. (gr. k-1). 1990. pap. text ed. 11.00 *(1-56537-061-9)* D F Schott Educ.
—It's Snowing!, Vol. 10: Pasitos English Language Development Books. 18p. (gr. k-1). 1991. pap. text ed. 11.00 *(1-56537-069-4)* D F Schott Educ.
—Mi Papalote Rojo, Vol. 8: Pasitos Spanish Language Development Books. 11p. (gr. k-1). 1990. pap. text ed. 11.00 *(1-56537-057-0)* D F Schott Educ.
—Mr. Opposite Pumpkin, Vol. 5: Pasitos English Language Development Books. 15p. (gr. k-1). 1990. pap. text ed. 11.00 *(1-56537-064-3)* D F Schott Educ.
—My Little Red Kite, Vol. 8: Pasitos English Language Development Books. 11p. (gr. k-1). 1990. pap. text ed. 11.00 *(1-56537-067-8)* D F Schott Educ.
—Oruga, Oruga, Vol. 3: Pasitos Spanish Language Development Books. 15p. (gr. k-1). 1990. pap. text ed. 11.00 *(1-56537-052-X)* D F Schott Educ.
—Pasitos English Language Development Books, 10 vols. (gr. k-1). 1991. Set. pap. text ed. 105.00 *(1-56537-091-0)* D F Schott Educ.
—Pasitos Reading Readiness Kit, A E I O U. (gr. k-1). 1984. Incl. 5 tchr's. manuals, 100 workbooks, copy masters, alphabet picture cards, 20 student alphabet cards. 330.00 *(1-56537-001-5)* D F Schott Educ.
—Pasitos Spanish Language Development Books. (gr. k-1). 1990. pap. text ed. 105.00 *(1-56537-090-2)* D F Schott Educ.
—Pasitos Student Workbook, Libro 1: Pasitos Reading Readiness Kit, A E I O U. 17p. (gr. k-1). 1984. 1.25 *(1-56537-021-X)* D F Schott Educ.
—Pasitos Student Workbook, Libro 10. Schott, Darlyne F., illus. (SPA.). 8p. (Orig.). (gr. k-1). 1991. pap. text ed. 1.25 *(1-56537-131-3,* 131) D F Schott Educ.
—Pasitos Student Workbook, Libro 2: Pasitos Reading Readiness Kit, A E I O U. 17p. (gr. k-1). 1984. 1.25 *(1-56537-022-8)* D F Schott Educ.
—Pasitos Student Workbook, Libro 3: Pasitos Reading Readiness Kit, A E I O U. 17p. (gr. k-1). 1985. 1.25 *(1-56537-023-6)* D F Schott Educ.
—Pasitos Student Workbook, Libro 4: Pasitos Reading Readiness Kit, A E I O U. 17p. (gr. k-1). 1985. 1.25 *(1-56537-024-4)* D F Schott Educ.
—Pasitos Student Workbook, Libro 5: Pasitos Reading Readiness Kit, A E I O U. 17p. (gr. k-1). 1985. 1.25 *(1-56537-025-2)* D F Schott Educ.
—Pasitos Student Workbook, Libro 6. Schott, Darlyne F., illus. (SPA.). 8p. (Orig.). (gr. k-1). 1991. pap. text ed. 1.25 *(1-56537-126-7,* 126) D F Schott Educ.
—Pasitos Student Workbook, Libro 7. Schott, Darlyne F., illus. (SPA.). 8p. (Orig.). (gr. k-1). 1991. pap. text ed. 1.25 *(1-56537-127-5,* 127) D F Schott Educ.
—Pasitos Student Workbook, Libro 8. Schott, Darlyne F., illus. (SPA.). 8p. (Orig.). (gr. k-1). 1991. pap. text ed. 1.25 *(1-56537-128-3,* 128) D F Schott Educ.
—Pasitos Student Workbook, Libro 9. Schott, Darlyne F., illus. (SPA.). 8p. (Orig.). (gr. k-1). 1991. pap. text ed. 1.25 *(1-56537-129-1,* 129) D F Schott Educ.
—Pasitos Supplementary Worksheets: Pasitos Reading Readiness Kit, A E I O U. 56p. (gr. k-1). 1985. tchr's. ed. 30.00 *(1-56537-030-9)* D F Schott Educ.

—Pasitos Teachers' Manual, Libro 1: Pasitos Reading Readiness Kit, A E I O U. 54p. (gr. k-1). 1985. 20.00 (*1-56537-011-2*) D F Schott Educ.
—Pasitos Teachers' Manual, Libro 2: Pasitos Reading Readiness Kit, A E I O U. 44p. (gr. k-1). 1985. 20.00 (*1-56537-012-0*) D F Schott Educ.
—Pasitos Teachers' Manual, Libro 3: Pasitos Reading Readiness Kit, A E I O U. 56p. (gr. k-1). 1985. 20.00 (*1-56537-013-9*) D F Schott Educ.
—Pasitos Teachers' Manual, Libro 4: Pasitos Reading Readiness Kit, A E I O U. 33p. (gr. k-1). 1985. 20.00 (*1-56537-014-7*) D F Schott Educ.
—Pasitos Teachers' Manual, Libro 5: Pasitos Reading Readiness Kit, A E I O U. 40p. (gr. k-1). 1985. 20.00 (*1-56537-015-5*) D F Schott Educ.
—Pretty Valentine, Vol. 7: Pasitos English Language Development Books. 19p. (gr. k-1). 1990. pap. text ed. 11.00 (*1-56537-066-X*) D F Schott Educ.
—El Puerco Raro, Vol. 1: Pasitos Spanish Language Development Books. 16p. (gr. k-1). 1990. pap. text ed. 11.00 (*1-56537-050-3*) D F Schott Educ.
—The Rare Pig, Vol. 1: Pasitos English Language Development Books. 15p. (gr. k-1). 1990. pap. text ed. 11.00 (*1-56537-060-0*) D F Schott Educ.
—Three Bears, Three Sizes, Vol. 4: Pasitos English Language Development Books. 24p. (gr. k-1). 1990. pap. text ed. 11.00 (*1-56537-063-5*) D F Schott Educ.
—Tres Osos, Tres Tamanos, Vol. 4: Pasitos Spanish Language Development Books. 25p. (gr. k-1). 1990. pap. text ed. 11.00 (*1-56537-053-8*) D F Schott Educ.
—Valentin Bonito, Vol. 7: Pasitos Spanish Language Development Books. 19p. (gr. k-1). 1990. pap. text ed. 11.00 (*1-56537-056-2*) D F Schott Educ.
—Where Are You Mrs. Caterpillar?, Vol. 3: Pasitos English Language Development Books. 14p. (gr. k-1). 1990. pap. text ed. 11.00 (*1-56537-062-7*) D F Schott Educ.

Schotter, Roni. Bunny's Night Out. Apple, Margot, illus. 32p. (ps-3). 1989. 13.95 (*0-316-77465-0*, Joy St Bks) Little.
—Captain Snap & the Children of Vinegar Lane. Sewall, Marcia, illus. LC 88-22489. 32p. (ps-3). 1989. 14.95 (*0-531-05797-6*); PLB 14.99 (*0-531-08397-7*) Orchard Bks Watts.
—Captain Snap & the Children of Vinegar Lane. Sewall, Marcia, illus. LC 88-22489. 32p. (ps-3). 1993. pap. 5.95 (*0-531-07038-7*) Orchard Bks Watts.
—Efan the Great. Pate, Rodney, illus. LC 84-25070. 32p. (gr. 2-5). 1986. 12.95 (*0-688-04986-9*); PLB 12.88 (*0-688-04987-7*) Lothrop.
—A Fruit & Vegetable Man. Winter, Jeanette, photos by. LC 92-17555. (Illus.). 1993. 15.95 (*0-316-77467-7*, Joy St Bks) Little.
—Hanukkah! Hafner, Marylin, illus. (ps-3). 1990. 14.95 (*0-316-77466-9*, Joy St Bks) Little.
—Hanukkah! (gr. 4-8). 1993. pap. 5.95 (*0-316-77469-3*, Joy St Bks) Little.
—Monsieur Cochon. Catalano, Dominic, illus. LC 92-26223. 1993. write for info. (*0-399-22023-2*, Philomel Bks) Putnam Pub Group.
—Passover Magic. Hafner, Marylin, illus. LC 93-20053. (gr. 1-8). 1994. 14.95 (*0-316-77468-5*) Little.
—Rhoda, Straight & True. LC 86-107. 192p. (gr. 6 up). 1986. 11.95 (*0-688-06157-5*) Lothrop.
—Warm at Home. Goldman, Dara, illus. LC 91-48145. 32p. (gr. k-3). 1993. RSBE 14.95 (*0-02-781295-2*, Macmillan Child Bk) Macmillan Child Grp.
—When Crocodiles Clean Up. Wickstrom, Thor, illus. LC 92-10808. 32p. (gr. 1-3). 1993. RSBE 14.95 (*0-02-781297-9*, Macmillan Child Bk) Macmillan Child Grp.

Schotz, Cheri, adapted by. Juke Box Puppet Band Station: I've Been Working on the Railroad. Allcroft, Britt, created by. 24p. (ps-3). 1993. pap. 3.99 (*1-884336-01-9*) Qual Family.
—Juke Box Puppet Band Station: This Old Band. Allcroft, Britt, created by. 24p. (ps-3). 1993. pap. 3.99 (*1-884336-00-0*) Qual Family.

Schouweiler, Thomas. The Devil: Opposing Viewpoints. LC 92-16424. (Illus.). 112p. (gr. 5-8). 1992. PLB 14.95 (*0-89908-091-X*) Greenhaven.
—Life after Death: Opposing Viewpoints. LC 90-39092. (Illus.). 112p. (gr. 5-8). 1990. PLB 14.95 (*0-89908-082-0*) Greenhaven.

Schouweiler, Tom. The Exxon-Valdez Oil Spill. LC 91-29499. (Illus.). 96p. (gr. 5-8). 1991. PLB 11.95 (*1-56006-016-6*) Lucent Bks.
—The Lost Colony of Roanoke: Opposing Viewpoints. LC 91-15188. (Illus.). 112p. (gr. 5-8). 1991. PLB 14.95 (*0-89908-093-6*) Greenhaven.

Schrade, Arlene O. Gabriel, the Happy Ghost. Incl. Gabriel en Mexico (Gabriel Learns About the Day of the Dead (*0-8442-7211-6*); Gabriel en Espana (Gabriel in Pampiona (*0-8442-7222-1*); Gabriel en Puerto Rico (Gabriel in the Caribbean (*0-8442-7224-8*) (ENG & SPA., Illus.). 32p. (gr. 4 up). 1983. pap. 6.60 ea. (Passport Bks) NTC Pub Grp.

Schrader, Ann. Healthy Yummies for Young Tummies. (Illus.). 192p. (Orig.). 1993. pap. 12.95 (*1-55853-174-2*) Rutledge Hill Pr.

Schrader, D. Take My Hands. (gr. k-8). 1981. 5.99 (*0-570-04035-3*, 61HH1019) Concordia.

Schrader, Richard A. Fungi: More Crucian Stories. Emanuel, Charles A., intro. by. LC 92-96921. (Illus.). 114p. 1993. pap. text ed. write for info. (*0-9622987-3-5*) R A Schrader.

Schraff, Anne. Nobody Lives in Apartment N-2. Parker, Liz, ed. Taylor, Marjorie, illus. 45p. (Orig.). (gr. 6-12). 1992. pap. text ed. 2.95 (*1-56254-057-2*) Saddleback Pubns.
—Swamp Furies. Parker, Liz, ed. Taylor, Marjorie, illus. 45p. (Orig.). (gr. 6-12). 1992. pap. text ed. 2.95 (*1-56254-056-4*) Saddleback Pubns.

Schraff, Anne E. The Great Depression & the New Deal: America's Economic Collapse & Recovery. (Illus.). 128p. (gr. 9-12). 1990. PLB 13.90 (*0-531-10964-X*) Watts.

Schrag, J. O. Nicholas. Ediger, Kristin, illus. 35p. (Orig.). (gr. k-3). 1991. pap. 7.95 (*0-945530-05-6*) Wordsworth KS.

Schramm, Mary. A Look at God's Book. (Illus.). 42p. (gr. k-6). 1973. pap. text ed. 14.99 (*1-55976-148-2*) CEF Press.

Schrank, Louise W. How to Choose the Right Career. LC 90-50727. (Illus.). 176p. (gr. 7 up). 1991. pap. 8.95 (*0-8442-8122-0*, VGM Career Bks) NTC Pub Grp.

Schreck, Peter. The Working Father's Survival Manual. (Orig.). (gr. 9-12). 1989. pap. write for info. (*0-9623787-0-4*) Working Father.

Schrecker, Judie. The Pet Shop Mouse. LC 93-60231. (Illus.). 44p. (ps-3). 1994. 7.95 (*1-55523-605-7*) Winston-Derek.

Schreckhise, Roseva. What Was It Before It Was My Chair? McLean, Mina G., illus. LC 85-13238. 32p. (ps-2). 1985. PLB 21.35 (*0-89565-326-5*); PLB 14. 95s.p. (*0-685-55777-4*) Childs World.
—What Was It Before It Was My Sweater? Endres, Helen, illus. LC 85-11401. 32p. (ps-2). 1985. PLB 21. 35 (*0-89565-324-9*); PLB 14.95s.p. (*0-685-55778-2*) Childs World.

Schreiber, Brad. Weird Wonders & Bizarre Blunders. LC 89-33911. 88p. 1989. pap. 4.95 (*0-88166-174-0*) Meadowbrook.

Schreiber, Jocelyn. How to Draw Zoo Animals. Schreiber, Jocelyn, illus. LC 87-50427. 32p. (gr. 2-6). 1988. PLB 10.65 (*0-8167-1004-X*, Pub. by Watermill Pr); pap. text ed. 1.95 (*0-8167-1005-8*, Pub. by Watermill Pr) Troll Assocs.

Schreiber, Suzanne L. Yoga for the Fun of It! Hatha Yoga for Preschool Children. 4th ed. Schreiber, Suzanne L., illus. Folan, Lilias, intro. by. (Illus.). 54p. (Orig.). (ps). 1991. pap. 9.00 (*0-9608320-0-9*) Sugar Marbel Pr.

Schreiber-Wicke, Edith. Cats' Carnival. Laimgruber, Monika, illus. LC 85-45964. 24p. 1986. 13.95 (*0-87923-627-2*) Godine.

Schreier, Joshua. Hank's Work. LC 92-15205. (ps-2). 1993. 13.50 (*0-525-44970-1*, DCB) Dutton Child Bks.

Schreiner, Davd, ed. see Schultz, Mark.
Schreiner, Dave, ed. see Schultz, Mark.
Schreiner, Elissa, et al. Let's Celebrate Passover! 16p. 1993. pap. 5.98 incl. 28 min. cassette (*0-943351-57-X*, XS2200) Astor Bks.

Schreiner, Nikki B., et al. The Whole World Kit: American Dream Activity Cards. Weathers, Susan, et al, illus. 60p. (gr. 4-8). 1990. pap. text ed. 215.00 (*1-879218-29-1*) Touch & See Educ.

Schreivogel, Paul A. More Prayers for Small Children: About Big & Little Things. Goldsborough, June, illus. LC 88-83018. 32p. (Orig.). (gr. 1 up). 1988. pap. 5.99 (*0-8066-2381-0*, 10-4547, Augsburg) Augsburg Fortress.
—Small Prayers for Small Children. Holmgren, George E., illus. LC 76-135226. 32p. (gr. k-4). 1980. pap. 5.99 (*0-8066-1804-3*, 10-5836, Augsburg) Augsburg Fortress.

Schrepfer, Margaret. Switzerland: The Summit of Europe. LC 88-35913. (Illus.). 144p. (gr. 5 up). 1989. RSBE 14.95 (*0-87518-405-7*, Dillon) Macmillan Child Grp.

Schrock, Sadie. Belize-Land by the Carib Sea. (gr. 3). 1991. 2.95 (*0-87813-539-1*) Christian Light.
—Nature Study of Belize. (gr. 3). 1991. pap. 2.95 (*0-87813-538-3*) Christian Light.

Schroeder, Alan. Booker T. Washington. King, Coretta Scott, intro. by. (Illus.). 144p. (gr. 5 up). 1992. 17.95 (*1-55546-616-8*) Chelsea Hse.
—Booker T. Washington: Leader of His People. (Illus.). 80p. (gr. 2-6). 1991. Repr. of 1962 ed. lib. bdg. 12.95 (*0-7910-1427-4*) Chelsea Hse.
—Jack London. (Illus.). 128p. (gr. 5 up). 1992. lib. bdg. 17.95 (*0-7910-1623-4*) Chelsea Hse.
—Josephine Baker. King, Coretta Scott, intro. by. (Illus.). 128p. (gr. 5 up). 1991. lib. bdg. 17.95 (*0-7910-1116-X*) Chelsea Hse.
—Ragtime Tumpie. Fuchs, Bernie, illus. (gr. k-4). 1989. 15.95 (*0-316-77497-9*, Joy St Bks) Little.
—Ragtime Tumpie. (ps-3). 1993. pap. 4.95 (*0-316-77504-5*, AMP) Little.
—The Stone Lion. Doney, Todd L., illus. LC 93-38257. 32p. (gr. 1-3). 1994. SBE 14.95 (*0-684-19578-X*, Scribners Young Read) Macmillan Child Grp.

Schroeder, Alan, adapted by. Lily & the Wooden Bowl: A Japanese Folktale. Ito, Yoriko, illus. LC 93-17900. Date not set. write for info. (*0-385-31073-0*) Dial Bks Young.

Schroeder, Bonnie, ed. see Anderson, Jill & Weinman, Susan.
Schroeder, Bonnie, ed. see Kennedy, Sandra.
Schroeder, Bonnie, ed. see Kennedy, Sandra & MacDonald, James.
Schroeder, Bonnie, ed. see Weinman, Susan.

Schroeder, Charles R. Boxing Skills for Fun and Fitness. (Illus.). 117p. (gr. 8 up). 1973. 10.95 (*0-914338-01-3*) Regmar Pub.
Schroeder, Howard, jt. auth. see Ahlstrom, Mark.
Schroeder, Howard, ed. see Sandell, Elizabeth.
Schroeder, Linda M. Becoming Excellent Students Today: Academic Organizer. 102p. (gr. 9-12). Date not set. pap. text ed. 6.95 (*1-883583-01-2*) Gratitude Pub.
—Becoming Excellent Students Today: Assignment Planner. 102p. (gr. 5-8). 1993. pap. text ed. 6.95 (*1-883583-00-4*) Gratitude Pub.
Schroeder, Mary. Extending U. S. History & Geography. West, James A., illus. 32p. (Orig.). (gr. 3-6). 1984. 6.50 (*0-88047-041-0*, 8404) DOK Pubs.
Schroeder, Mary A., jt. auth. see Burma-Washington, Marcay.
Schroeder, Ruth. The Adventure of Fifi's Honey Bee Bears & the Big Bee Hive. Dixon, David, illus. 28p. (gr. k-5). 1987. PLB 8.95 (*0-935087-24-9*) R & D Bks.
Schroeder, Ruth E. The Honey Bee Bears in Bluer Than Blueberries. Dixon, David, illus. 22p. (gr. k-5). 1989. 8.95 (*0-685-26760-1*); PLB 8.95 (*0-685-26761-X*) R & D Bks.

Schubert, Dieter. Where's My Monkey? LC 86-16578. (Illus.). 32p. (ps-2). 1992. pap. 3.99 (*0-8037-1071-2*, Dial Pied Piper) Puffin Bks.
Schubert, Dieter, jt. auth. see Schubert, Ingrid.
Schubert, Ingrid & Schubert, Dieter. Little Big Feet. Schubert, Ingrid & Schubert, Dieter, illus. 32p. (ps-3). 1990. PLB 18.95 (*0-87614-426-1*) Carolrhoda Bks.
—The Magic Bubble Trip. LC 84-25071. (Illus.). 32p. (ps-3). 1985. 9.95 (*0-916291-02-2*); pap. 6.95 (*0-916291-03-0*) Kane Miller Bk.
—Wild Will. LC 93-2484. 1993. 17.50 (*0-87614-816-X*) Carolrhoda Bks.

Schuchman, Joan. Two Places to Sleep. LaMarche, Jim, illus. LC 79-88201. 32p. (gr. 1-4). 1979. PLB 13.50 (*0-87614-108-4*) Carolrhoda Bks.

Schuett, Julie, jt. auth. see Burdick, Gerry.
Schuett, Virginia E., jt. auth. see Taylor, Margaret.
Schulke, Flip, ed. Martin Luther King, Jr. A Documentary...Montgomery to Memphis. King, Coretta Scott, intro. by. (Illus.). 224p. (gr. 8 up). 1976. limited ed. o.p. 100.00 (*0-685-62030-1*); pap. 15.95 (*0-393-07492-7*) Norton.

Schuller, Ahuva, jt. auth. see Strauss, Ruby G.
Schuller, Mary Ann. Wros-tonne & Other Stories of Science Fantasy. Judy, Ann F., illus. LC 87-90482. 134p. (Orig.). (gr. 3-8). 1987. pap. 4.95 (*0-9617889-0-9*) Sweet Koala Pr.

Schulman, Janet. The Big Hello. Hoban, Lillian, illus. 32p. (gr. 1-4). 1980. pap. 1.95 (*0-440-40484-3*, YB) Dell.
—The Big Hello. Hoban, Lillian, illus. LC 75-33672. (gr. 1-4). 1976. 13.95 (*0-688-80036-X*) Greenwillow.
—The Big Hello. LC 75-33672. (Illus.). 56p. (ps-3). pap. 3.95 (*0-688-08405-2*, Mulberry) Morrow.
—The Big Hello. 8p. (gr. 2-4). 1976. pap. 0.64 (*0-685-63792-1*, BR8409) W A T Braille.
—Big Hello. 8p. 1992. pap. text ed. 0.64 (*1-56956-194-X*) W A T Braille.
—The Great Big Dummy. Hoban, Lillian, illus. 32p. (gr. 1-3). 1961. pap. 2.50 (*0-440-43072-0*, YB) Dell.
—Jenny & The Tennis Nut. Hafner, Marilyn, illus. 64p. (gr. 1-4). 1981. pap. 2.50 (*0-440-44211-7*, YB) Dell.
Schulman, Janet, ed. see Bradman, Tony.
Schulman, Janet, ed. see Wood, John N.

Schulman, L. M., ed. The Random House Book of Sports Stories. Allen, Thomas B., illus. LC 89-12834. 256p. (gr. 5 up). 1990. lib. bdg. 16.99 (*0-394-92874-1*); pap. 16.00 (*0-394-82874-7*) Random Bks Yng Read.

Schulte, Elaine. Cara's Beach Party. 144p. (Orig.). 1993. pap. 4.99 (*1-55661-252-4*) Bethany Hse.
—Daniel Colton Kidnapped: Daniel Strikes a Bad Bargain - Now He Must Outsmart His Captors. (Illus.). 144p. (gr. 3-7). 1993. 4.99 (*0-310-57261-4*, Pub. by Youth Spec) Zondervan.
—Eternal Passage. 1989. pap. 5.99 (*1-55513-988-4*, 39883) Cook.
—Golden Dreams. 1991. pap. 5.95 (*1-55513-987-6*, 39875) Cook.
—Here Comes Ginger. LC 88-38763. (gr. 3-7). 1989. pap. 4.49 (*1-55513-770-9*, Chariot Bks) Cook.
—Here Comes Ginger. 1989. write for info. Prog Bapt Pub.
—Off to a New Start. (gr. 3-7). 1989. pap. 4.49 (*1-55513-771-7*, Chariot Bks) Cook.
—Twelve Candles, 4 vols, Vols. 1-4. 1993. Set. 19.96 (*1-55661-781-X*) Bethany Hse.
—With Wings As Eagles. 1990. pap. 8.99 (*1-55513-989-2*, 39891) Cook.

Schulte, Elaine L. Becky's Brainstorm. LC 92-15202. 144p. (Orig.). (gr. 3-7). 1992. pap. 4.99 (*1-55661-250-8*) Bethany Hse.
—A Colton Cousins Adventure: Susannah Strikes Gold. 144p. 1992. pap. 4.99 (*0-310-54611-7*, Youth Bks) Zondervan.
—Jess & the Fireplug. LC 92-15203. 128p. (Orig.). (gr. 3-7). 1992. pap. 4.99 (*1-55661-251-6*) Bethany Hse.
—Tricia's Got Trouble. (gr. 4-7). 1993. pap. 4.99 (*1-55661-253-2*) Bethany Hse.

Schulte, Karl, compiled by. Christmas Carols. Dolce, J. Ellen, illus. 1990. pap. write for info. (*0-307-02979-4*, Golden Pr) Western Pub.

Schultz, Anne, intro. by. Open Fist: An Anthology of Young Illinois Poets. 120p. (gr. 10 up). 1993. pap. 10. 95 (*1-882688-01-5*) Tia Chucha Pr.

　　　　　　　　　　　　　　　　　　　　　　　　　　　

Schultz, Betty K. Chooch. Becicka, Lori, illus. LC 90-91639. 64p. (gr. k-3). 1990. 14.95 (0-929568-00-1) Raspberry IL.
—Morn of Mystery. (Illus., Orig.). (gr. 3-5). 1991. pap. write for info. (0-929568-02-8) Raspberry IL.
—Purple Patches. Sperry, Angela, illus. 32p. (gr. k-3). 1991. write for info. (0-929568-01-X) Raspberry IL.
Schultz, Dave. Little Ditties. Ferrante, Len, intro. by. 64p. (Orig.). pap. 3.00 (0-937393-08-8) Fred Pr.
Schultz, Ellen. I Can Read About Birds. LC 78-73775. (Illus.). (gr. 2-4). 1979. pap. 1.95 (0-89375-204-5) Troll Assocs.
—I Can Read About Eskimos. LC 78-73735. (gr. 2-4). 1979. pap. 1.95 (0-89375-219-3) Troll Assocs.
—I Can Read About Frogs & Toads. LC 78-73714. (Illus.). (gr. 2-5). 1979. pap. 1.95 (0-89375-210-X) Troll Assocs.
—I Can Read About July Fourth, Seventeen Seventy-Six. LC 78-68470. (Illus.). (gr. 3-5). 1979. pap. 1.95 (0-89375-211-8) Troll Assocs.
—I Can Read About the Octopus. LC 78-73715. (gr. 2-4). 1979. pap. 1.95 (0-89375-213-4) Troll Assocs.
Schultz, Elva. Two Story Farmhouse. Tepley, Marilyn, illus. (ps-3). 1986. write for info. (0-9616431-0-2) E Schultz.
Schultz, Irene. The Woodland Gang & the Dark Old House. (Illus.). 128p. (gr. 3 up). 1984. pap. 4.95 (0-318-40971-2) Addison-Wesley.
—The Woodland Gang & the Dinosaur Bones. Cahoun, Cindy, illus. 128p. (gr. 3 up). 1988. pap. 4.95 (0-201-50056-6) Addison-Wesley.
—The Woodland Gang & the Ghost Cat. Kahoun, Cindy, illus. 128p. (gr. 3 up). 1988. pap. 4.95 (0-201-50054-X) Addison-Wesley.
—The Woodland Gang & the Hidden Jewels. (Illus.). 128p. (gr. 3 up). 1984. pap. 4.95 (0-685-25362-7) Addison-Wesley.
—The Woodland Gang & the Indian Cave. Kahoun, Cindy, illus. 128p. (gr. 3 up). 1988. pap. 4.95 (0-201-50055-8) Addison-Wesley.
—The Woodland Gang & the Missing Will. (Illus.). 128p. (gr. 3 up). 1984. pap. 4.95 (0-201-50073-6) Addison-Wesley.
—The Woodland Gang & the Museum Robbery. Kahoun, Cindy, illus. 128p. (Orig.). (gr. 3 up). 1988. pap. 4.95 (0-201-50053-1) Addison-Wesley.
—The Woodland Gang & the Mystery Quilt. Kahoun, Cindy, illus. 128p. (gr. 3 up). 1988. pap. 4.95 (0-201-50051-5) Addison-Wesley.
—The Woodland Gang & the Old Gold Coins. (Illus.). 128p. (gr. 3 up). 1984. pap. 4.95 (0-201-50075-2) Addison-Wesley.
—The Woodland Gang & the Secret Spy Code. Cahoun, Cindy, illus. 128p. (Orig.). (gr. 3 up). 1988. pap. 4.95 (0-201-50052-3) Addison-Wesley.
—The Woodland Gang & the Stolen Animals. (Illus.). 128p. (gr. 3 up). 1984. pap. 4.95 (0-201-50074-4) Addison-Wesley.
—The Woodland Gang & the Two Lost Boys. (Illus.). 128p. (gr. 3 up). 1984. pap. 4.95 (0-201-50072-8) Addison-Wesley.
Schultz, James W. The Loud Mouthed Gun. (gr. 4-8). 1984. pap. 4.95 (0-89992-095-0) Coun India Ed.
—Sinopah, the Indian Boy. LC 83-73494. (Illus.). 103p. (gr. 4-7). 1984. pap. 7.95 (0-8253-0320-6) Confluence Pr.
—Story of Running Eagle. (gr. 2-10). 1984. pap. 3.95 (0-89992-093-4) Coun India Ed.
Schultz, Janice. The First Frost. Caroland, Mary, ed. (Illus.). 44p. 1991. 5.95 (1-55523-370-8) Winston-Derek.
Schultz, Joani, jt. auth. see Schultz, Thom.
Schultz, John W. Famine Winter. (gr. 4-10). 1984. pap. 2.95 (0-89992-094-2) Coun India Ed.
Schultz, Mark. Cadillacs & Dinosaurs. Schreiner, Dave, ed. Jackson, Jack, et al. (Illus.). 392p. (gr. 3 up). 1993. Boxed set. pap. 39.95 (0-87816-259-3) Kitchen Sink.
—Cadillacs & Dinosaurs. Schreiner, Davd, ed. Schultz, Mark, illus. Williamson, Al, intro. by. (Illus.). 136p. (gr. 3 up). 1994. pap. 14.95 (0-87816-261-5) Kitchen Sink.
Schultz, Pamela & Schultz, Robert. Best of Schultz: Easy Piano. 64p. (Orig.). 1992. pap. text ed. 8.95 (0-89898-647-8) CPP Belwin.
Schultz, Robert, jt. auth. see Schultz, Pamela.
Schultz, Ron. Looking Inside Cartoon Animation. (Illus.). 48p. (Orig.). (gr. 3 up). 1992. pap. 9.95 (1-56261-066-X) John Muir.
—Looking Inside Caves & Caverns. Gadbois, Nick & Aschwanden, Peter, illus. (gr. 4-7). 1993. pap. 9.95 (1-56261-126-7) John Muir.
—Looking Inside Sports Aerodynamics. (Illus.). 48p. (Orig.). (gr. 3 up). 1992. pap. 9.95 (1-56261-065-1) John Muir.
—Looking Inside Sunken Treasure. (Illus.). 48p. (gr. 3 up). Date not set. pap. 9.95 (1-56261-074-0) John Muir.
—Looking Inside Telescopes & the Night Sky. (Illus.). 48p. (Orig.). (gr. 3 up). Date not set. pap. 9.95 (1-56261-072-4) John Muir.
—Looking Inside the Brain. (Illus.). 48p. (Orig.). (gr. 3 up). 1992. pap. 9.95 (1-56261-064-3) John Muir.
Schultz, Sam. One Hundred & One Animal Jokes. Hanson, Joan, illus. LC 81-20955. 48p. (gr. 1-4). 1982. PLB 11.95 (0-8225-0978-4) Lerner Pubns.
—One Hundred & One Family Jokes. Hanson, Joan, illus. LC 81-20861. 48p. (gr. 1-4). 1982. PLB 11.95 (0-8225-0981-4) Lerner Pubns.

—One Hundred & One Knock-Knock Jokes. Hanson, Joan, illus. LC 81-20954. 48p. (gr. 1-4). 1982. PLB 11.95 (0-8225-0976-8) Lerner Pubns.
—One Hundred & One Monster Jokes. Hanson, Joan, illus. LC 81-20953. 48p. (gr. 1-4). 1982. PLB 11.95 (0-8225-0977-6) Lerner Pubns.
—One Hundred & One School Jokes. Hanson, Joan, illus. LC 81-20912. 48p. (gr. 1-4). 1982. PLB 11.95 (0-8225-0979-2) Lerner Pubns.
—One Hundred & One Sports Jokes. Hanson, Joan, illus. LC 81-20913. 48p. (gr. 1-4). 1982. PLB 11.95 (0-8225-0980-6) Lerner Pubns.
Schultz, Thom & Schultz, Joani. Is Marriage in Your Future? 48p. (Orig.). (gr. 9-12). 1990. pap. 7.99 (1-55945-203-X) Group Pub.
Schulz, Beverly. The Adventures of Nelda Navajo & Her Forest Friends. 1993. 7.95 (0-8062-4818-1) Carlton.
Schulz, Charles. Los Amigos de Snoopy. (SPA.). 64p. 1971. 4.95 (0-8288-4507-7) Fr & Eur.
—Un Amour de Charlie Brown. (FRE.). 1985. 4.95 (0-8288-4514-X) Fr & Eur.
—Apuros Escolares. (SPA.). 64p. 1971. 4.95 (0-8288-4504-2) Fr & Eur.
—Le Beagle Est Revenu Sur Terre. (FRE.). 1985. 9.95 (0-8288-4532-8) Fr & Eur.
—Un Beagle Qui a Du Chien. (FRE.). 1985. 9.95 (0-8288-4531-X) Fr & Eur.
—Belle Mentalite, Snoopy. (FRE.). 1985. 4.95 (0-8288-4526-3) Fr & Eur.
—Bienvenue Snoopy. (FRE.). 45p. 1987. 19.95 (0-8288-4538-7) Fr & Eur.
—Du Calme, Charlie Brown. (FRE.). 1985. 4.95 (0-8288-4519-0) Fr & Eur.
—Carlitos y Snoopy. (SPA.). 64p. 1971. 4.95 (0-8288-4512-3) Fr & Eur.
—Le Chef des Briquets. (FRE.). 1985. 4.95 (0-8288-4518-2) Fr & Eur.
—Al Colegio. (SPA.). 64p. 1971. 4.95 (0-8288-4506-9) Fr & Eur.
—Deportes de Invierno. (SPA.). 64p. 1971. 4.95 (0-8288-4508-5) Fr & Eur.
—Les Dieux du Tennis Etaient Contre Moi. (FRE.). 1985. 9.95 (0-8288-4528-X) Fr & Eur.
—Dis Pas de Betises, Charlie Brown. (FRE.). 1985. 4.95 (0-8288-4520-4) Fr & Eur.
—Elementaire Mon Cher Snoopy. (FRE.). 48p. 1988. 18.95 (0-8288-4539-5) Fr & Eur.
—Fantastique Snoopy. (FRE.). 47p. 1988. 18.95 (0-8288-4540-9) Fr & Eur.
—Feu D'Artifice. (FRE.). 48p. 1989. 19.95 (0-8288-4541-7) Fr & Eur.
—Gente Menuda. (SPA.). 64p. 1971. 4.95 (0-8288-4502-6) Fr & Eur.
—Good Grief More Peanuts. (Illus.). 1994. pap. write for info. (0-8050-3312-2) H Holt & Co.
—El Gran Jefe. (SPA.). 64p. 1971. 4.95 (0-8288-4505-0) Fr & Eur.
—Le Grand Livre des Questions, No. 4. (FRE.). 160p. 1982. 29.95 (0-8288-4542-5) Fr & Eur.
—Le Grand Livre Des Questions, No. 5. (FRE.). 158p. 1983. 29.95 (0-8288-4543-3) Fr & Eur.
—Imbattable Snoopy. (FRE.). 48p. 1983. 18.95 (0-8288-4544-1) Fr & Eur.
—Inattaquable Snoopy. (FRE.). 48p. 1986. 18.95 (0-8288-4545-X) Fr & Eur.
—Incroyable Snoopy. (FRE.). 48p. 1982. 18.95 (0-8288-4546-8) Fr & Eur.
—Ineffable Snoopy. (FRE.). 48p. 1985. 18.95 (0-8288-4547-6) Fr & Eur.
—Inegalable Snoopy. (FRE.). 1985. 18.95 (0-8288-4536-0) Fr & Eur.
—Inenarrable Snoopy. (FRE.). 48p. 1987. 18.95 (0-8288-4548-4) Fr & Eur.
—Inepuisable Snoopy. (FRE.). 48p. 1987. 18.95 (0-8288-4549-2) Fr & Eur.
—L' Infaillible Snoopy. (FRE.). 47p. 1984. 18.95 (0-8288-4550-6) Fr & Eur.
—Intrepide Snoopy. (FRE.). 48p. 1983. 18.95 (0-8288-4551-4) Fr & Eur.
—Invincible Snoopy. (FRE.). 48p. 1985. 18.95 (0-8288-4552-2) Fr & Eur.
—Irresistible Snoopy. (FRE.). 48p. 1985. 18.95 (0-8288-4553-0) Fr & Eur.
—Je Ne T'Ai Jamais Promis un Verger. (FRE.). 1985. 9.95 (0-8288-4530-1) Fr & Eur.
—Joyeuses Paques. (FRE.). 1984. 14.95 (0-8288-4537-9) Fr & Eur.
—Meme Mes Critiques Ratent la Cible. (FRE.). 1985. 9.95 (0-8288-4533-6) Fr & Eur.
—Mi Pequeno Mundo. (SPA.). 64p. 1971. 4.95 (0-8288-4501-8) Fr & Eur.
—Misere! Charlie Brown. (FRE.). 1985. 4.95 (0-8288-4515-8) Fr & Eur.
—No Me Comprenden. (SPA.). 64p. 1971. 4.95 (0-8288-4511-5) Fr & Eur.
—El Pajarito Emilio. (SPA.). 64p. 1971. 4.95 (0-8288-4510-7) Fr & Eur.
—Peanuts Sunday. (Illus.). 1994. pap. write for info. (0-8050-3310-6) H Holt & Co.
—Regreso al Colegio. (SPA.). 64p. 1971. 4.95 (0-8288-4509-3) Fr & Eur.
—Reviens, Snoopy. (FRE.). 48p. 1982. 10.95 (0-8288-4554-9) Fr & Eur.
—Reviens, Snoopy: Presses Pocket. (FRE.). 124p. 1989. 10.95 (0-8288-4555-7) Fr & Eur.
—Snoopy Arbitre. (FRE.). 1984. 14.95 (0-8288-4559-X) Fr & Eur.

—Snoopy au Cirque. (FRE.). 50p. 1983. 14.95 (0-8288-4560-3) Fr & Eur.
—Snoopy Connait La Musique. (FRE.). 128p. 1974. 9.95 (0-8288-4561-1) Fr & Eur.
—Snoopy Delire. (FRE.). 50p. 1983. 14.95 (0-8288-4562-X) Fr & Eur.
—Snoopy Detective. (FRE.). 50p. 1983. 14.95 (0-8288-4563-8) Fr & Eur.
—Snoopy: Droles D'Oiseau. (FRE.). 128p. 1975. 9.95 (0-8288-4557-3) Fr & Eur.
—Snoopy Escritor. (SPA.). 64p. 1971. 4.95 (0-8288-4503-4) Fr & Eur.
—Snoopy et Compagnie. (FRE.). 156p. 1987. write for info. (0-8288-4564-6) Fr & Eur.
—Snoopy Et la Culture. (FRE.). 1975. 9.95 (0-8288-4565-4) Fr & Eur.
—Snoopy et la St-Valentin. (FRE.). 1984. 14.95 (0-8288-4566-2) Fr & Eur.
—Snoopy Et Ses Freres. (FRE.). 128p. 1974. 9.95 (0-8288-4567-0) Fr & Eur.
—Snoopy Et Son Copain Linus. (FRE.). 128p. 1975. 9.95 (0-8288-4568-9) Fr & Eur.
—Snoopy Grand Coeur. (FRE.). 1975. 9.95 (0-8288-4569-7) Fr & Eur.
—Snoopy: Joyeuses Paques. (FRE.). 1985. 14.95 (0-8288-4556-5) Fr & Eur.
—Snoopy, le Petit Receuil de Pensees. (FRE.). 1985. write for info. (0-8288-4558-1) Fr & Eur.
—Snoopy Patineur. (FRE.). 1984. 14.95 (0-8288-4570-0) Fr & Eur.
—Snoopy Prestidigitateur. (FRE.). 50p. 1983. 14.95 (0-8288-4571-9) Fr & Eur.
—Snoopy S'En Va-T-En Guerre. (FRE.). 128p. 1974. 9.95 (0-8288-4572-7) Fr & Eur.
—Sois Philosophe, Charlie Brown. (FRE.). 1985. 4.95 (0-8288-4517-4) Fr & Eur.
—T'As Pas de Veine, Charlie Brown. (FRE.). 1985. 4.95 (0-8288-4525-5) Fr & Eur.
—Te Fais Pas de Bile, Charlie Brown. (FRE.). 1985. 4.95 (0-8288-4523-9) Fr & Eur.
—T'Es le Meilleur, Charlie Brown. (FRE.). 1985. 4.95 (0-8288-4521-2) Fr & Eur.
—Tiens Bon, Charlie Brown. (FRE.). 1985. 4.95 (0-8288-4527-1) Fr & Eur.
—Tout Connaitre en S'Amusant: Bateaux. (FRE.). 34p. 1982. 10.95 (0-8288-4577-8) Fr & Eur.
—Tout Connaitre en S'Amusant: Camions. (FRE.). 32p. 1983. 10.95 (0-8288-4578-6) Fr & Eur.
—Tout Connaitre en S'Amusant: La Ferme. (FRE.). 34p. 1982. 10.95 (0-8288-4573-5) Fr & Eur.
—Tout Connaitre en S'Amusant: La Nature. (FRE.). 34p. 1983. 10.95 (0-8288-4574-3) Fr & Eur.
—Tout Connaitre en S'Amusant: La Plage. (FRE.). 34p. 1982. 10.95 (0-8288-4575-1) Fr & Eur.
—Tout Connaitre en S'Amusant: Les Avions. (FRE.). 34p. 1982. 10.95 (0-8288-4576-X) Fr & Eur.
—Tout Connaitre en S'Amusant: Maisons. (FRE.). 32p. 1983. 10.95 (0-8288-4579-4) Fr & Eur.
—Tout Connaitre en S'Amusant: Saisons. (FRE.). 32p. 1983. 10.95 (0-8288-4580-8) Fr & Eur.
—Tu Cours Apres l'Ete, et l'Hiver... (FRE.). 1985. 9.95 (0-8288-4535-2) Fr & Eur.
—Tu Te Crois Malin, Charlie Brown. (FRE.). 1985. 4.95 (0-8288-4522-0) Fr & Eur.
—Tu Veux Rire, Charlie Brown. (FRE.). 1985. 4.95 (0-8288-4524-7) Fr & Eur.
—Unsinkable Charlie Brown. (Illus.). 1994. pap. write for info. (0-8050-3311-4) H Holt & Co.
—Une Vie de Chien. (FRE.). 1985. 4.95 (0-8288-4513-1) Fr & Eur.
—Vois la Vie en Rose, Snoopy. (FRE.). 1985. 4.95 (0-8288-4516-6) Fr & Eur.
—Y'A Qu'Un Woodstock. (FRE.). 1985. 9.95 (0-8288-4529-8) Fr & Eur.
Schulz, Charles M. All This & Snoopy Too: Selected Cartoons from "You Can't Win, Charlie Brown, Vol. 2. (Illus.). (gr. 5 up). 1983. pap. 3.99 (0-449-20434-0, Crest) Fawcett.
—Apuros Escolares. (SPA., Illus.). (gr. 3-8). 1.50 (0-685-28419-0) Fr & Eur.
—A Charlie Brown Christmas. Namm, Diane, adapted by. Ellis, Kim, illus. LC 87-83488. 40p. (gr. 1 up). 1988. write for info. (0-307-13723-6) Western Pub.
—Charlie Brown Dictionary. (Illus.). (ps-3). 1973. text ed. 17.32 (0-13-084269-9) P-H.
—Don't Hassle Me with Your Sighs, Chuck. (gr. 4-6). 1976. 4.95 (0-03-018211-5, Bks Young Read) H Holt & Co.
—Guess Who, Charlie Brown. (Illus.). 1992. pap. 3.99 (0-449-22021-4) Fawcett.
—Have No Fear, Snoopy. 1988. pap. 3.99 (0-449-21490-7) Fawcett.
—Home Is on Top of a Doghouse. (Illus.). 1982. 6.95 (0-915696-52-5) Determined Prods.
—Love Is Walking Hand in Hand. (Illus.). 64p. (ps up). 1987. pap. 5.95 (0-345-34873-7, Pharos) F&W Inc NJ.
—Ne Me Casse Pas les Oreilles. (FRE.). 1984. 9.95 (0-8288-4534-4) Fr & Eur.
—Peanuts a Vendre. (FRE.). (gr. 3-8). 1985. pap. 1.95 (0-685-23404-5) Fr & Eur.
—Security Is a Thumb & a Blanket. LC 82-70029. (Illus.). 1982. 6.95 (0-915696-53-3) Determined Prods.
—Snoopy & the Twelve Days of Christmas. (gr. 1 up). 9.95 (0-317-13662-3) Determined Prods.
—Snoopy's Love Book. (gr. 1 up). 1994. write for info. (0-8050-3146-4) H Holt & Co.
—Summers Fly, Winters Walk. (Illus.). 128p. 1991. pap. 5.95 (0-8050-1692-9, Owl Bks) H Holt & Co.

—Talk Is Cheep, Charlie Brown. (Illus.). 128p. (Orig.). (gr. 2-6). 1988. pap. 5.95 (0-88687-379-7, Pharos) F&W Inc NJ.
—There's No One Like You, Snoopy: Selected Cartoons from "You're You, Charlie Brown, Vol. I. (Illus.). (gr. 1-5). 1985. pap. 2.95 (0-449-20776-5, Crest) Fawcett.
—What's Wrong with Being Crabby? 128p. (ps-2). 1992. pap. 6.95 (0-8050-2400-X, Owl Bks) H Holt & Co.
—Your Choice, Snoopy. 1987. pap. 2.95 (0-449-21327-7, Crest) Fawcett.
—You're on the Wrong Foot Again, Charlie Brown. (Illus.). 128p. (ps up). 1987. pap. 5.95 (0-88687-313-4, Pharos) F&W Inc NJ.
Schulz, Charles M., jt. auth. see Bayley, Monica.
Schulz, Charles M., jt. auth. see Dutton, June.
Schulz, Marjorie R. Community Services. (Illus.). 96p. (gr. 9-12). 1990. PLB 14.40 (0-531-10972-0) Watts.
—Hospitality & Recreation. LC 90-12240. (Illus.). 96p. (gr. 9-12). 1990. PLB 14.40 (0-531-10973-9) Watts.
—Transportation. LC 90-13024. (Illus.). 96p. (gr. 9-12). 1990. PLB 14.40 (0-531-10974-7) Watts.
—Travel & Tourism. LC 90-12235. (Illus.). 96p. (gr. 9-12). 1990. PLB 14.40 (0-531-10975-5) Watts.
Schulz, Walter A. Will & Orv. Schulz, Janet, illus. 48p. 1991. lib. bdg. 14.95 (0-87614-669-8) Carolrhoda Bks.
—Will & Orv. (ps-3). 1992. pap. 5.95 (0-87614-568-3) Carolrhoda Bks.
Schumacher, Claire. A Big Chair for Little Bear. Schumacher, Claire, illus. LC 89-10968. 32p. (Orig.). (ps-1). 1990. pap. 2.25 (0-679-80500-1) Random Bks Yng Read.
—Santa's Hat. (Illus.). 40p. (ps-3). 1987. PLB 10.95 (0-13-791187-4) P-H.
Schumacher, Claire W. Ghostly Tales of Lake Superior. Kopari, Catherine, illus. LC 87-91292. 94p. (Orig.). (gr. 9). 1987. PLB 6.95 (0-917378-06-7) Zenith City.
Schumacher, Philip, tr. see Knecht, F. J.
Schumacher, Philip, tr. see Schuster, Ignatius.
Schumake, John P., ed. see Giovanni.
Schumann, Peter. St. Francis Preaches to the Birds. Schumann, Peter, illus. LC 92-7383. 36p. (gr. 3-10). 1992. Repr. of 1978 ed. 8.95 (0-8118-0222-1) Chronicle Bks.
Schumm, Jeanne S. & Radencich, Marguerite. School Power: Strategies for Succeeding in School. Espeland, Pamela, ed. LC 92-10907. (Illus.). 130p. (Orig.). (gr. 5 up). 1992. pap. 11.95 (0-915793-42-3) Free Spirit Pub.
Schur, Maxine. Hannah Szenes: A Song of Light. LC 85-5794. (Illus.). 104p. (gr. 3-7). 1985. 10.95 (0-8276-0251-0) JPS Phila.
Schur, Maxine R. The Circlemaker. LC 93-17983. 1994. 13.99 (0-8037-1354-1) Dial Bks Young.
—Day of Delight: A Jewish Sabbath in Ethiopia. Pinkney, Brian, illus. LC 93-31451. 1994. write for info. (0-8037-1413-0); PLB write for info. (0-8037-1414-9) Dial Bks Young.
—Samantha's Surprise: A Christmas Story. Thieme, Jeanne, ed. Niles, Nancy & Lusk, Nancy N, illus. 72p. (gr. 2-5). 1986. 12.95 (0-937295-21-3); PLB 12.95 (0-937295-86-8); pap. 5.95 (0-937295-22-1) Pleasant Co.
Schurch, Maylan. Money, Sex, School & Other Obsessions. Woolsey, Raymond H., ed. 128p. (Orig.). (gr. 8-12). 1990. pap. 6.95 (0-8280-0577-X) Review & Herald.
—The Sword of Denis Anwyck. LC 92-22127. 1992. pap. 7.95 (0-8280-0658-X) Review & Herald.
Schurfranz, Julie. 1993. pap. 2.50 (0-590-42021-6) Scholastic Inc.
Schurfranz, Vivian. Danielle, No. 4. 368p. (gr. 7 up). 1984. pap. 2.95 (0-590-33156-6) Scholastic Inc.
—Josie. 224p. (Orig.). (gr. 6-10). 1988. pap. 2.75 (0-590-41207-8) Scholastic Inc.
—Megan, No. 16. 224p. (Orig.). (gr. 7 up). 1986. pap. 2.75 (0-590-41468-2) Scholastic Inc.
—Rachel, No. 21. 224p. (Orig.). (gr. 7 up). 1986. pap. 2.50 (0-590-40394-X) Scholastic Inc.
—Renee. 224p. (gr. 6-10). 1989. pap. 2.75 (0-590-42043-7) Scholastic Inc.
Schurr, Cathleen. The Shy Little Kitten. reissued ed. Tenggren, Gustaf, illus. 24p. (ps-k). 1992. write for info. (0-307-00145-8, 312-10, Golden Pr) Western Pub.
Schurr, Sandra, jt. auth. see Forte, Imogene.
Schuster, E. H. Words Are Important: Primary Level (Tan) Bk. (gr. 4). 1985. pap. 3.98 (0-8437-7983-7) Hammond Inc.
—Words Are Important Series. Incl. Level A (Blue) Bk. (gr. 5) (0-8437-7985-3); Level B (Red) Bk. (gr. 6) (0-8437-7991-8); Level C (Green) Bk. (gr. 7) (0-8437-7980-2); Level D (Orange) Bk. (gr. 8) (0-8437-7950-0); Level E (Purple) Bk. (gr. 9) (0-8437-7955-1); Level F (Brown) Bk. (gr. 10) (0-8437-7960-8); Level G (Pink) Bk. (gr. 11) (0-8437-7965-9); Level H (Grey) Bk. (gr. 12) (0-8437-7970-5). 1985. pap. 3.98 (0-685-02045-2) Hammond Inc.
Schuster, George N. Catholic Authors, Crown Edition. (Illus.). (gr. 11 up). 1952. pap. 5.95 (0-910334-23-4) Cath Authors.
Schuster, Helen H. The Yakima. (Illus.). 112p. (gr. 5 up). 1990. 17.95 (1-55546-735-0) Chelsea Hse.
Schuster, Ignatius. Bible History. Heck, H. J., ed. Schumacher, Philip, tr. (Illus.). (gr. 6-8). 1974. pap. 10.00 (0-89555-006-7) TAN Bks Pubs.
Schuster, Slade. The Slade Short Course. 2nd ed. 1982. pap. text ed. 8.25 (0-88334-161-1, 76128) Longman.

Schusterman, Neal. Speeding Bullet. (gr. 9-12). 1991. 14.95 (0-316-78905-4) Little.
Schutz, Mary E., jt. auth. see Woods, Tom.
Schutzer, Dena. Polka & Dot. Schutzer, Dena, illus. LC 93-29935. 1994. 8.99 (0-679-84192-X); PLB 9.99 (0-679-94192-4) Knopf Bks Yng Read.
Schutzsenberger, Anne A. Diccionario de la Tecnicas de Grupo. (SPA.). 260p. 1974. pap. 19.95 (0-8288-5983-3, S50365) Fr & Eur.
Schuyler, Royce. Boomerang: A One-Act Play for Grades 7-9. Kester, Ellen S., ed. Omoto, Larry, illus. 50p. (Orig.). 1989. pap. text ed. 6.95 (0-685-26284-7) Pickwick Pubs.
—Boomerang: Drama for Study & Performance. Kester, Ellen S., ed. Omoto, Larry, illus. 100p. (Orig.). 1989. pap. text ed. 35.00 (0-685-26285-5) Pickwick Pubs.
—Jessie J: Red Rock Ranch Detective: A Literary Adventure for Gifted Students. Kester, Ellen S., ed. Turner, Joseph R., III, illus. 190p. (Orig.). (gr. 3-6). 1989. pap. 6.95 (0-685-26280-4); tchr's. manual 35.00 (0-685-26281-2) Pickwick Pubs.
Schwabacher, Martin. Magic Johnson: Basketball Wizard. LC 93-16556. (Illus.). 1993. 13.95 (0-7910-2037-1, Am Art Analog); pap. write for info. (0-7910-2038-X, Am Art Analog) Chelsea Hse.
Schwager, Istar. Counting. Siede, George & Preis, Donna, photos by. (Illus.). 24p. (ps-3). 1993. PLB 12.95 (1-56674-067-3, HTS Bks) Forest Hse.
—Matching. Siede, George & Preis, Donna, photos by. (Illus.). 24p. (ps-3). 1993. PLB 12.95 (1-56674-068-1, HTS Bks) Forest Hse.
—Sorting. Siede, George & Preis, Donna, photos by. (Illus.). 24p. (ps-3). 1993. PLB 12.95 (1-56674-069-X, HTS Bks) Forest Hse.
—What's Different? Siede, George & Preis, Donna, photos by. (Illus.). 24p. (ps-3). 1993. PLB 12.95 (1-56674-070-3, HTS Bks) Forest Hse.
Schwalb, Ann, ed. see Hunt, Tamara & Renfro, Nancy.
Schwalb, Ann W., ed. see Hunt, Tamara & Renfro, Nancy.
Schwalb, Ann W., ed. see Renfro, Nancy & Frazier, Nancy.
Schwalb, Ann W., ed. see Renfro, Nancy & Sullivan, Debbie.
Schwaller, Catherine. Reading Sentences, Grade 1. Hoffman, Joan, ed. Cook, Chris, illus. 32p. (gr. 1). 1979. wkbk. 1.99 (0-938256-06-8) Sch Zone Pub Co.
—Reading Stories, Grade 1. Hoffman, Joan, ed. Cook, Chris, illus. 32p. (gr. 1). 1979. wkbk. 1.99 (0-938256-07-6) Sch Zone Pub Co.
Schwandt, Stephen. Holding Steady. 176p. 1990. pap. 2.95 (0-380-70754-3, Flare) Avon.
Schwandt, Stephen, jt. auth. see Coles, William E., Jr.
Schwartz. Wonderchild & Other Tales. Date not set. 16.00 (0-06-023517-9, Festival); PLB 15.89 (0-06-023518-7, Festival) HarpC Child Bks.
Schwartz, Alvin. All of Our Noses Are Here & Other Noodle Tales. Weinhaus, Karen A., illus. LC 84-48330. 64p. (gr. k-3). 1985. PLB 13.89 (0-06-025288-X) HarpC Child Bks.
—All of Our Noses Are Here & Other Noodle Tales. Weinhaus, Karen A., illus. LC 84-48330. 64p. (gr. k-3). 1987. pap. 3.50 (0-06-444108-3, Trophy) HarpC Child Bks.
—And the Green Grass Grew All Around: Folk Poetry from Everyone. Truesdell, Sue, illus. LC 89-26722. 208p. (gr. 1-7). 1992. 15.00 (0-06-022757-5); PLB 14.89 (0-06-022758-3) HarpC Child Bks.
—Busy Buzzing Bumblebees & Other Tongue Twisters. newly illus. ed. Meisel, Paul, illus. LC 91-4799. 64p. (gr. k-3). 1982. 13.00 (0-06-025268-5); PLB 12.89 (0-06-025269-3) HarpC Child Bks.
—Busy Buzzing Bumblebees & Other Tongue Twisters. newly illus. ed. Meisel, Paul, illus. LC 91-4800. 64p. (gr. k-3). 1982. pap. 3.50 (0-06-444036-2, Trophy) HarpC Child Bks.
—The Cat's Elbow: & Other Secret Languages. Zemach, Margot, illus. LC 81-5513. 96p. (gr. 3 up). 1982. 15.00 (0-374-31224-9) FS&G.
—Cross Your Fingers, Spit in Your Hat: Superstitions & Other Beliefs. Rounds, Glen, illus. LC 73-21912. 128p. (gr. 4-6). 1990. PLB 13.89 (0-397-32436-7, Lipp Jr Bks) HarpC Child Bks.
—Cross Your Fingers, Spit in Your Hat: Superstitions & Other Beliefs. LC 73-21912. (Illus.). 160p. (gr. 3 up). 1993. pap. 4.95 (0-06-446138-6, Trophy) HarpC Child Bks.
—Fat Man in a Fur Coat: And Other Bear Stories. Christiana, David, illus. LC 84-4161. 167p. (gr. 3 up). 1984. 14.00 (0-374-32291-0) FS&G.
—Fat Man in a Fur Coat: And Other Bear Stories. Christiana, David, illus. LC 84-4161. (gr. 5 up). 1987. pap. 3.50 (0-374-42273-7) FS&G.
—Flapdoodle: Pure Nonsense from American Folklore. O'Brien, John, illus. LC 79-9618. 128p. (gr. 5 up). 1980. PLB 13.89 (0-397-31920-7, Lipp Jr Bks) HarpC Child Bks.
—Ghosts! Ghostly Tales from Folklore. Chess, Victoria, illus. LC 90-21746. 64p. (gr. k-3). 1991. 14.00 (0-06-021796-0); PLB 13.89 (0-06-021797-9) HarpC Child Bks.
—Gold & Silver, Silver & Gold: Tales of Hidden Treasure. 1993. pap. 8.95 (0-374-42583-3, Sunburst) FS&G.
—I Saw You in the Bathtub & Other Folk Rhymes. Hoff, Syd, illus. LC 88-16111. 64p. (ps-2). 1991. pap. 3.50 (0-06-444151-2, Trophy) HarpC Child Bks.

—In a Dark, Dark Room. LC 83-47699. (Illus.). 64p. (gr. k-3). 1986. incl. cassette 5.98 (0-694-00163-5, Trophy); pap. 3.50 (0-06-444090-7, Trophy) HarpC Child Bks.
—In a Dark, Dark Room & Other Scary Stories. Zimmer, Dirk, illus. LC 83-47699. 64p. (gr. k-3). 1984. 14.00 (0-06-025271-5); PLB 13.89 (0-06-025274-X) HarpC Child Bks.
—Kickle Snifters & Other Fearsome Critters. Rounds, Glen, illus. LC 75-29048. (gr. 1-5). 1992. pap. 4.95 (0-06-446129-7, Trophy) HarpC Child Bks.
—More Scary Stories to Tell in the Dark: Collected & Retold from Folklore. Gammell, Stephen, illus. LC 83-49494. 128p. (gr. 4-7). 1984. 14.00 (0-397-32081-7, Lipp Jr Bks); PLB 13.89 (0-397-32082-5, Lipp Jr Bks) HarpC Child Bks.
—More Scary Stories to Tell in the Dark. Gammell, Stephen, illus. LC 83-49494. 112p. (gr. 4 up). 1986. pap. 3.95 (0-06-440177-4, Trophy) HarpC Child Bks.
—Scary Stories, Boxed set. Gammell, Stephen, illus. (gr. 4-7). 1992. pap. 11.85 (0-06-440465-X, Trophy) HarpC Child Bks.
—Scary Stories Fright Box. (gr. 8-12). 1993. 14.95 (0-694-00573-8, Festival) HarpC Child Bks.
—Scary Stories to Tell in the Dark. (Illus.). 128p. (gr. 4 up). 1986. pap. 3.95 (0-06-440170-7, Trophy) HarpC Child Bks.
—Scary Stories to Tell in the Dark: Collected from American folklore. Gammell, Stephen, illus. LC 80-8728. 128p. (gr. 5 up). 1981. 14.00 (0-397-31926-6, Lipp Jr Bks); PLB 13.89 (0-397-31927-4, Lipp Jr Bks) HarpC Child Bks.
—Scary Stories 3: More Tales to Chill Your Bones. Gammell, Stephen, illus. LC 90-47474. 128p. (gr. 4 up). 1991. 14.00 (0-06-021794-4); PLB 13.89 (0-06-021795-2) HarpC Child Bks.
—Scary Stories 3: More Tales to Chill Your Bones. Gammell, Stephen, illus. LC 90-47474. 128p. (gr. 4 up). 1991. pap. 3.95 (0-06-440418-8, Trophy) HarpC Child Bks.
—Stories to Tell a Cat. Huerta, Catherine, illus. LC 91-37257. 80p. (gr. 4 up). 1992. 15.00 (0-06-020850-3); PLB 14.89 (0-06-020851-1) HarpC Child Bks.
—Tales of Trickery from the Land of Spoof. Christiana, David, illus. 88p. (gr. 3 up). 1988. pap. 3.50 (0-374-47426-5) FS&G.
—Telling Fortunes: Love Magic, Dream Signs, & Other Ways to Learn the Future. Cameron, Tracey, illus. LC 85-45174. 128p. (gr. 4 up). 1987. 12.95 (0-397-32132-5, Lipp Jr Bks); PLB 12.89 (0-397-32133-3, Lipp Jr Bks) HarpC Child Bks.
—Telling Fortunes: Love Magic, Dream Signs, & Other Ways to Learn the Future. Cameron, Tracey, illus. LC 85-45174. 128p. (gr. 4 up). 1990. pap. 4.95 (0-06-446094-0, Trophy) HarpC Child Bks.
—Ten Copycats in a Boat & Other Riddles. Simont, Marc, illus. LC 79-2811. 64p. (gr. k-3). 1985. pap. 3.50 (0-06-444076-1, Trophy) HarpC Child Bks.
—There Is a Carrot in My Ear & Other Noodle Tales. Weinhaus, Karen A., illus. LC 80-8442. 64p. (gr. k-3). 1982. PLB 13.89 (0-06-025234-0) HarpC Child Bks.
—There Is a Carrot in My Ear & Other Noodle Tales. Weinhaus, Karen A., illus. LC 80-8442. 64p. (gr. k-3). 1986. pap. 3.50 (0-06-444103-2, Trophy) HarpC Child Bks.
—Tomfoolery: Trickery & Foolery with Words. Rounds, Glen, illus. LC 72-12900. 128p. (gr. 4-6). 1990. PLB 14.89 (0-397-32437-5, Lipp Jr Bks) HarpC Child Bks.
—A Twister of Twists, a Tangler of Tongues. Rounds, Glen, illus. LC 72-1434. 126p. (gr. 4 up). 1972. 14.00 (0-397-31387-X, Lipp Jr Bks) HarpC Child Bks.
—A Twister of Twists: A Tangler of Tongues. Rounds, Glen, illus. LC 85-45372. 128p. (gr. 5 up). 1991. PLB 13.89 (0-397-32501-0, Lipp Jr Bks) HarpC Child Bks.
—A Twister of Twists: Tangler of Tongues. LC 72-1434. (Illus.). 128p. (gr. 4 up). 1972. pap. 5.95 (0-06-446004-5, Trophy) HarpC Child Bks.
—Unriddling. Truesdell, Sue, illus. LC 82-48778. 128p. (gr. 4 up). 1983. PLB 13.89 (0-397-32030-2, Lipp Jr Bks) HarpC Child Bks.
—Unriddling: All Sorts of Riddles to Puzzle Your Guessary. Truesdell, Sue, illus. LC 82-48778. 128p. (gr. 4 up). 1987. pap. 4.95 (0-06-446057-6, Trophy) HarpC Child Bks.
—Whoppers: Tall Tales & Other Lies. LC 74-32024. (Illus.). 128p. (gr. 4 up). 1975. 14.00 (0-397-31575-9, Lipp Jr Bks) HarpC Child Bks.
—Witcracks: Jokes & Jests from American Folklore. (Illus.). 128p. (gr. 4 up). 1973. PLB 13.89 (0-397-31475-2, Lipp Jr Bks) HarpC Child Bks.
—Witcracks: Jokes & Jests from American Folklore. Rounds, Glen & Truesdell, Sue, illus. LC 73-7630. 128p. (gr. 5 up). 1993. 4.95 (0-06-446146-7, Trophy) HarpC Child Bks.
Schwartz, Alvin, jt. auth. see Finger, Bill.
Schwartz, Alvin, retold by. Ghosts! Ghostly Tales from Folklore. Chess, Victoria, illus. LC 90-21746. 64p. (gr. k-3). 1993. pap. 3.50 (0-06-444170-9, Trophy) HarpC Child Bks.
Schwartz, Alvin, ed. I Saw You in the Bathtub & Other Folk Rhymes. Hoff, Syd, illus. LC 88-16111. 64p. (gr. k-3). 1989. 14.00 (0-06-025298-7); PLB 13.89 (0-06-025299-5) HarpC Child Bks.
—Tales of Trickery from the Land of Spoof. Christiana, David, illus. LC 85-16004. 87p. (gr. 4 up). 1985. 14.00 (0-374-37378-7) FS&G.

—Whoppers: Tall Tales & Other Lies Collected from American Folklore. Rounds, Glen, illus. LC 74-32024. 128p. (gr. 4 up). 1990. pap. 3.95 (0-06-446091-6, Trophy) HarpC Child Bks.

Schwartz, Amy. Annabelle Swift, Kindergartner. Schwartz, Amy, illus. LC 87-15403. 32p. (ps-2). 1988. 14.95 (0-531-05737-2); PLB 14.99 (0-531-08337-3) Orchard Bks Watts.

—Annabelle Swift, Kindergartner. LC 87-15403. (Illus.). 32p. (ps-2). 1991. pap. 4.95 (0-531-07027-1) Orchard Bks Watts.

—Bea & Mr. Jones. Schwartz, Amy, illus. LC 81-18041. 32p. (ps-2). 1982. SBE 12.95 (0-02-781430-0, Bradbury Pr) Macmillan Child Grp.

—Bea & Mr. Jones. Schwartz, Amy, illus. 30p. (ps-3). 1983. pap. 3.95 (0-14-050439-7, Puffin) Puffin Bks.

—Bea & Mr. Jones. Schwartz, Amy, illus. LC 93-20572. 32p. (ps-3). 1994. pap. 3.95 (0-689-71796-2, Aladdin) Macmillan Child Grp.

—Begin at the Beginning. Schwartz, Amy, illus. LC 82-48257. 32p. (ps-3). 1983. PLB 12.89 (0-06-025228-6) HarpC Child Bks.

—Begin at the Beginning. Scwartz, Amy, illus. LC 82-48257. 32p. (gr. k-3). 1984. pap. 3.95 (0-06-443060-X, Trophy) HarpC Child Bks.

—Camper of the Week. LC 90-23033. (Illus.). 32p. (gr. k-2). 1991. 14.95 (0-531-05942-1); RLB 14.99 (0-531-08542-2) Orchard Bks Watts.

—Her Majesty, Aunt Essie. LC 84-11003. (Illus.). 32p. (gr. k-2). 1984. SBE 14.95 (0-02-781450-5, Bradbury Pr) Macmillan Child Grp.

—Mrs. Moskowitz & the Sabbath Candlesticks. Schwartz, Amy, illus. 32p. (gr. k-5). 1983. pap. 6.95t (0-8276-0231-6) JPS Phila.

—Oma & Bobo. LC 86-10665. (Illus.). 32p. (ps-2). 1987. RSBE 13.95 (0-02-781500-5, Bradbury Pr) Macmillan Child Grp.

—A Teeny, Tiny Baby. LC 93-4876. 1994. write for info. (0-531-06818-8); PLB write for info. (0-531-08668-2) Orchard Bks Watts.

—Yossel Zissel & the Wisdom of Chelm. Schwartz, Amy, illus. 32p. (gr. k-4). 9.95 (0-8276-0258-8) JPS Phila.

Schwartz, Amy & Marcus, Leonard S. Mother Goose's Little Misfortunes. Schwartz, Amy, illus. LC 89-77425. 32p. 1990. SBE 15.95 (0-02-781431-9, Bradbury Pr) Macmillan Child Grp.

Schwartz, Amy & Schwartz, Henry. Make a Face: A Book with a Mirror. (Illus.). 28p. (gr. 2 up). 1994. 9.95 (0-590-46301-2, Cartwheel) Scholastic Inc.

Schwartz, Amy, adapted by. & illu see Hale, Lucretia.

Schwartz, Anne, ed. see Keats, Ezra J.

Schwartz, Barbara. The Little Character That's Me, Vol. I. Burroughs, John, photos by. (Illus.). 65p. (Orig.). (ps-6). 1988. wkbk. 11.95 (0-685-22570-4); audio cassette 14.95 (0-685-22571-2) Little Prodns.

Schwartz, Barry L. Honi the Circlemaker: Eco-Fables from Ancient Israel. LC 92-33715. 1992. pap. 8.95 (0-377-00251-8) Friendship Pr.

Schwartz, Betty, ed. The Old-Fashioned Storybook. Howell, Troy, illus. 144p. (gr. k-6). 1985. 12.95 (0-685-10340-4) S&S Trade.

Schwartz, Betty, ed. see Dixon, Franklin W.

Schwartz, Betty, ed. see Milton, Hilary.

Schwartz, Carol. First Noel (Pop Up) 1991. 3.95 (0-8037-1015-1) Dial Bks Young.

—Friendly Beasts (Pop Up) 1991. 3.95 (0-8037-1018-6) Dial Bks Young.

—Little Juggler (Pop-Up) 1991. 3.95 (0-8037-1020-8) Dial Bks Young.

—Nutcracker (Pop Ups) 1991. 3.95 (0-8037-1014-3) Dial Bks Young.

—Twelve Days of Christmas (Pop Ups) 1991. 3.95 (0-8037-1017-8) Dial Bks Young.

—Visit from Saint Nicholas (Pop Up) 1991. 3.95 (0-8037-1019-4) Dial Bks Young.

Schwartz, David. Supergrandpa. (ps-3). 1991. 13.95 (0-688-09898-3) Lothrop.

—Supergrandpa. (ps-3). 1991. 13.88 (0-688-09899-1) Lothrop.

Schwartz, David A. If You Made a Million. (ps-3). 1989. 14.88 (0-688-07018-3) Lothrop.

Schwartz, David M. How Much Is a Million? Kellogg, Steven, illus. LC 84-5736. 40p. (gr. k-5). 1985. PLB 14.88 (0-688-04050-0); 15.00 (0-688-04049-7) Lothrop.

—How Much Is a Million? Kellogg, Steven, illus. 40p. (gr. k-3). 1987. Big Book. 28.67 (0-590-71767-7) Scholastic Inc.

—How Much Is a Million? Kellogg, Steven, illus. 40p. (gr. 1-4). 1986. pap. 3.95 (0-590-43614-7) Scholastic Inc.

—How Much Is a Million? Kellogg, Steven, illus. 40p. (gr. k up). 1993. pap. 4.95 (0-688-09933-5, Mulberry) Morrow.

—If You Made a Million. Kellogg, Steven, illus. LC 88-12819. 40p. (gr. 1-5). 1989. 14.95 (0-688-07017-5); PLB 14.88 (0-685-22780-4) Lothrop.

Schwartz, Frederick J. The Adventures of Rondy. Olson, Wayne, ed. Kuehn, Christopher, illus. 148p. (gr. k-7). 1985. 7.95 (0-9616638-0-4) Rondy Pubns.

Schwartz, Gary. Rembrandt. (Illus.). 92p. 1992. 19.95 (0-8109-3760-3) Abrams.

Schwartz, Harriet B. Backstage with Clawdio. Catrow, David A., illus. LC 92-21683. 40p. (ps-4). 1993. 15.00 (0-679-81763-8); PLB 15.99 (0-679-91763-2) Knopf Bks Yng Read.

Schwartz, Henry. Albert Goes Hollywood. Schwartz, Amy, illus. LC 91-18495. 32p. (ps-2). 1992. 14.95 (0-531-05980-4); lib. bdg. 14.99 (0-531-08580-5) Orchard Bks Watts.

—How I Captured a Dinosaur. Schwartz, Amy, illus. LC 88-1482. 32p. (ps-2). 1989. 14.95 (0-531-05770-4); PLB 14.99 (0-531-08370-5) Orchard Bks Watts.

—How I Captured a Dinosaur. Schwartz, Amy, illus. LC 88-1482. 32p. (ps-2). 1993. pap. 5.95 (0-531-07028-X) Orchard Bks Watts.

Schwartz, Henry, jt. auth. see Schwartz, Amy.

Schwartz, Howard & Rush, Barbara. The Diamond Tree: Jewish Tales from Around the World. Shulevitz, Uri, illus. LC 90-32420. 120p. (gr. 2-5). 1991. 17.00 (0-06-025239-1); PLB 16.89 (0-06-025243-X) HarpC Child Bks.

Schwartz, Howard & Rush, Barbara, eds. Sabbath Lion: A Jewish Folktale from Algeria. LC 91-35766. (Illus.). 32p. (gr. k-4). 1992. 14.00 (0-06-020853-8); PLB 13.89 (0-06-020854-6) HarpC Child Bks.

Schwartz, Howard, ed. see Freehof, Lillian S.

Schwartz, Jeanne. A Handful of Colors. Mansfield, Carol, illus. 32p. 1981. 4.25 (0-9604538-2-2) CBH Pub.

Schwartz, Joel L. Best Friends Don't Come in Threes. (Illus.). 126p. (Orig.). (gr. 4-6). 1985. pap. 2.75 (0-440-40603-X, YB) Dell.

—The Diary of a Teenage Health Freak. (gr. k-12). 1990. pap. text ed. 3.50 (0-440-20636-7, LFL) Dell.

—How to Get Rid of Your Older Brother. (gr. 4-7). 1992. pap. 3.25 (0-440-40623-4) Dell.

—Shrink. (Orig.). (gr. 3-6). 1986. pap. 2.75 (0-440-47687-9, YB) Dell.

—Upchuck Summer. Degen, Bruce, illus. 144p. (gr. 3-7). 1983. pap. 3.50 (0-440-49264-5, YB) Dell.

—Upchuck Summer. Degen, Bruce, illus. LC 81-65838. 144p. (gr. 4-6). 1982. 10.95 (0-385-29099-3); pap. 10.95 (0-385-29100-0) Delacorte.

—Upchuck Summer. Degen, Bruce, illus. LC 81-69670. 144p. (gr. 4-8). 9.95 (0-440-09264-7); PLB 9.89 (0-440-09269-8) Delacorte.

—Upchuck Summer's Revenge. 1990. 13.95 (0-385-29978-8) Doubleday.

—Upchuck Summer's Revenge. (gr. 4-7). 1991. pap. 3.50 (0-440-40471-1) Dell.

Schwartz, Karl. Microsoft Windows 3.0 Quick Reference Guide. (gr. 9-12). 1991. pap. 8.95 spiral bdg. (1-56243-032-7, N-17); transparencies 265.00 (1-56243-014-9, NT-19) DDC Pub.

Schwartz, L. Analogy Adventure. (gr. 4-8). 1989. 5.95 (0-88160-173-X, LW 280) Learning Wks.

—Creative Capers. (gr. 4-6). 1985. 5.95 (0-88160-117-9, LW 251) Learning Wks.

—Drug Questions & Answers. (gr. 6-9). 1989. 5.95 (0-88160-171-3, LW 282) Learning Wks.

—Feelings about Friends. (gr. 3-7). 1988. 4.95 (0-88160-168-3, LW 281) Learning Wks.

—Flip Kit. (gr. 1-6). 1989. 4.95 (0-88160-183-7, LW 146) Learning Wks.

—I Love Lists! 264p. (gr. 3-7). 1988. 19.95 (0-88160-157-8, LW 275) Learning Wks.

—Junior Question Collection. (gr. 1-6). 1988. 7.95 (0-88160-169-1, LW 279) Learning Wks.

—Pick a Picture. 40p. (gr. 3-6). 1993. 6.95 (0-88160-258-2, LW242) Learning Wks.

—Pick a Picture - Kit. 40p. (gr. 3-6). 1989. 9.95 (0-88160-179-9, LW 285) Learning Wks.

—Preschool Teacher's Pet. 192p. (ps). 1989. 14.95 (0-88160-185-3, LW 147) Learning Wks.

—Ride & Seek. (gr. 3 up). 1987. 5.95 (0-88160-159-4, LW 103) Learning Wks.

—Select a Story. 40p. (gr. 3-6). 1989. 9.95 (0-88160-182-9, LW 286) Learning Wks.

—Select a Story. 40p. (gr. 3-6). 1993. 6.95 (0-88160-259-0, LW249) Learning Wks.

—Sharpen Your Senses. (gr. 1-6). 1978. 3.95 (0-88160-056-3, LW 604) Learning Wks.

—Spelling Works. 48p. (gr. 3-8). 1993. 6.95 (0-88160-257-4, LW288) Learning Wks.

—The Travel Bug. LC 92-74104. 120p. (gr. 2-9). 1993. 9.95 (0-88160-256-6, LW203) Learning Wks.

—Trivia Trackdown - Animals & Science. (gr. 4-6). 1985. 3.95 (0-88160-119-5, LW 252) Learning Wks.

—Trivia Trackdown - Social Studies & Famous People. (gr. 4-6). 1985. 3.95 (0-88160-120-9, LW 253) Learning Wks.

—U. S. Geography Adventure Kit. (gr. 4-8). 1989. 24.95 (0-88160-174-8, LW 284) Learning Wks.

—U. S. Geography Journey. rev. ed. 48p. (gr. 4-8). 1992. Repr. of 1989 ed. 5.95 (0-88160-181-0, LW287) Learning Wks.

—What Do You Think? LC 92-74103. 184p. (gr. 3-7). 1993. 9.95 (0-88160-224-8, LW221) Learning Wks.

Schwartz, Linda. AIDS Answers for Teens. rev. ed. (Illus.). 32p. (Orig.). (gr. 7-12). 1993. pap. 4.95 (0-88160-155-1, LW273) Learning Wks.

—AIDS Questions & Answers for Kids. rev. ed. (Illus.). 24p. (gr. 4-6). 1993. 3.95 (0-88160-154-3, LW272) Learning Wks.

—All about My School. 32p. (gr. 1-6). 1994. 4.95 (0-88160-236-1, LW331) Learning Wks.

—Build a Doodle Kit. (gr. k-4). 1990. pap. 10.95 (0-88160-198-5) Learning Wks.

—Camp Mail from Me. 32p. (gr. 3-6). 1994. 5.95 (0-88160-225-6, LW320) Learning Wks.

—The Center Solution. 74p. (gr. 4-6). 1977. 7.95 (0-88160-025-3, LW 210) Learning Wks.

—Creative Writing Rocket. 48p. (gr. 1-4). 1976. 5.95 (0-88160-003-2, LW 104) Learning Wks.

—The Creative Writing Roundup. 48p. (gr. 4-7). 1976. 5.95 (0-88160-017-2, LW 201) Learning Wks.

—Dictionary Dig. 48p. (gr. 4-6). 1980. 5.95 (0-88160-033-4, LW 218) Learning Wks.

—Earth Book for Kids: Activities to Help Heal the Environment. Armstrong, Beverly, illus. LC 90-91737. 184p. (Orig.). (gr. 3-6). 1990. pap. 9.95x (0-88160-195-0, LW 289) Learning Wks.

—Fly & Find. (gr. 3 up). 1990. pap. 5.95 (0-88160-194-2, LW102) Learning Wks.

—From Me to You. 32p. (gr. 1-6). 1994. 4.95 (0-88160-237-X, LW332) Learning Wks.

—Fun With Proverbs. LC 91-77042. (Illus.). 40p. (gr. 2-6). 1991. 5.95 (0-88160-208-6, LW 298) Learning Wks.

—Gumball Grammar. 32p. (gr. 4-7). 1979. 3.95 (0-88160-068-7, LW 801) Learning Wks.

—Handwriting Hamburger. Armstrong, Bev, illus. 32p. (gr. 3-6). 1979. wkbk. 3.95 (0-88160-073-3, LW 806) Learning Wks.

—Handwriting Hot Dog. Armstrong, Bev, illus. 32p. (gr. k-3). 1979. wkbk. 3.95 (0-88160-078-4, LW 811) Learning Wks.

—Hannah the Hippo. LC 90-62596. (Illus.). 32p. (ps-3). 1991. 4.95 (0-88160-186-1, LW 1200) Learning Wks.

—Hot Fudge Fractions. (gr. 3-4). 1979. 3.95 (0-88160-065-2, LW 705) Learning Wks.

—How Can I Help? 184p. (gr. 4-8). 1994. 9.95 (0-88160-213-2, LW207) Learning Wks.

—I Am Special. 24p. (gr. 1-4). 1978. 3.95 (0-88160-053-9, LW 601) Learning Wks.

—The Jewish Question Collection. 176p. (gr. 1 up). 1994. 7.95 (0-88160-247-7, LW342) Learning Wks.

—Likeable Recyclables. LC 92-81436. 128p. (gr. 1-6). 1992. 9.95 (0-88160-210-8, LW256) Learning Wks.

—Long Vowel Voyage. 20p. (gr. 1-3). 1980. 3.95 (0-88160-058-X, LW 606) Learning Wks.

—Math Marathon. (gr. 5-7). 1979. pap. 3.95 (0-88160-066-0, LW 706) Learning Wks.

—Monkey See, Monkey Do. LC 90-62597. (ps-3). 1991. pap. 4.95 (0-88160-187-X, LW1201) Learning Wks.

—The Month-To-Month Me. 48p. (gr. 3-7). 1976. 5.95 (0-88160-021-0, LW 205) Learning Wks.

—My Book about Me. 32p. (gr. 1-6). 1994. 4.95 (0-88160-235-3, LW330) Learning Wks.

—My Camp Memories. 32p. (gr. 3-6). 1994. 5.95 (0-88160-226-4, LW321) Learning Wks.

—My Earth Book: Puzzles, Projects, Facts & Fun. Armstrong, Beverly, illus. LC 92-60123. 64p. (gr. 1-4). 1991. pap. 7.95 (0-88160-201-9, LW153) Learning Wks.

—My Polly & Paul Activity Book. 16p. (ps). 1991. wkbk. 3.95 (0-9631987-0-X) Put-Together Dev Toys.

—Plants. (Illus.). 48p. (gr. 2-5). 1990. 5.95 (0-88160-189-6, LW 148) Learning Wks.

—The Primary Teacher's Pet. 192p. (gr. 1-3). 1984. 14.95 (0-88160-110-1, LW 131) Learning Wks.

—Rain Forest Kit. 8p. (gr. 2-6). 1991. bklt., incl. poster 4.95 (0-88160-165-9, LW270) Learning Wks.

—The Reading Carnival. Williams, Tim, et al, illus. 150p. (gr. 1). 1993. tchr's. guide 29.95 (1-884126-01-4); software 49.95 (1-884126-00-6) Digital Theater.

—Responsible Rascal. LC 90-62595. (ps-3). 1991. pap. 4.95 (0-88160-188-8, LW1202) Learning Wks.

—Search & Research. 48p. (gr. 4-6). 1984. 5.95 (0-88160-116-0, LW 248) Learning Wks.

—Short Vowel Voyage. 20p. (gr. 1-3). 1980. 3.95 (0-88160-057-1, LW 605) Learning Wks.

—Study Skills Shortcake. 32p. (gr. 4-6). 1979. 3.95 (0-88160-071-7, LW 804) Learning Wks.

—The Teacher's Pet. 192p. (gr. 3-6). 1983. 14.95 (0-88160-097-0, LW 240) Learning Wks.

—Trivia Trackdown-Communication & Transportation. (Illus.). 32p. (gr. 4-6). 1986. 3.95 (0-88160-139-X, LW258) Learning Wks.

—Trivia Trackdown-Sports & Space. (Illus.). 32p. (gr. 4-6). 1986. 3.95 (0-88160-138-1, LW257) Learning Wks.

—The Usage Sleuth. 24p. (gr. 4-6). 1978. 3.95 (0-88160-055-5, LW 603) Learning Wks.

—What Would You Do? A Kid's Guide to Tricky & Sticky Situations. Armstrong, Beverly, illus. LC 90-63597. 184p. (gr. 3-7). 1991. pap. 9.95 (0-88160-196-9, LW294) Learning Wks.

—Your Body. (Illus.). 48p. (gr. 2-5). 1990. 5.95 (0-88160-191-8, LW 150) Learning Wks.

Schwartz, Linda & McKinley, Nancy L. Daily Communication: Strategies for the Language Disordered Adolescent. LC 84-50057. 300p. (Orig.). (gr. 5-12). 1984. pap. text ed. 33.00x (0-9610370-4-0) Thinking Pubns.

Schwartz, Linda, jt. auth. see McKinley, Nancy L.

Schwartz, Lynne S. The Four Questions. Sherman, Ori, illus. LC 88-18881. 40p. (gr. up). 1989. 15.95 (0-8037-0600-6); PLB 15.89 (0-8037-0601-4) Dial Bks Young.

Schwartz, Lynne S., jt. auth. see Sherman, Ori.

Schwartz, Mary A. Spiffen: A Tale of a Tidy Pig. Levine, Abby, ed. Munsinger, Lynn, illus. LC 88-15. 32p. (ps-3). 1988. PLB 13.95 (0-8075-7580-1) A Whitman.

Schwartz, Melissa. Cochise. (Illus.). 112p. (gr. 5 up). 1992. lib. bdg. 17.95 (0-7910-1706-0) Chelsea Hse.

—Geronimo. (Illus.). 128p. (gr. 5 up). 1992. lib. bdg. 17.95 (0-7910-1701-X) Chelsea Hse.

Schwartz, Meryl. The Environment & the Law. (Illus.). 112p. (gr. 5 up). 1993. PLB 19.95 (*0-7910-1595-5*) Chelsea Hse.
—The Environment & the Law. Train, Russell E., intro. by. LC 92-25542. 1993. write for info. (*0-7910-1596-3*); write for info. (*0-7910-1620-X*) Chelsea Hse.
Schwartz, Mimi. Writing for Many Roles. 230p. (Orig.). 1985. pap. text ed. 15.00x (*0-86709-097-9*) Boynton Cook Pubs.
Schwartz, Paula & Schartz, Sara. A Leaf Named Bud. (Illus.). 32p. (ps-1). 1993. 12.95 (*0-87663-795-0*) Universe.
Schwartz, Perry. How to Make Your Own Video. 1991. pap. 8.95 (*0-8225-9588-5*) Lerner Pubns.
—Make Your Own Video. Boe, David, illus. 64p. (gr. 5 up). 1991. PLB 19.95 (*0-8225-2301-9*) Lerner Pubns.
—Making Movies. (Illus.). 80p. (gr. 5 up). 1989. 18.95 (*0-8225-1635-7*) Lerner Pubns.
Schwartz, Roslyn. Rose & Dorothy. LC 90-43013. (Illus.). 32p. (ps-2). 1991. 13.95 (*0-531-05918-9*); PLB 13.99 (*0-531-08518-X*) Orchard Bks Watts.
Schwartz, Saryl Z. How to Find Money for College: The Disabled Student. (gr. 8 up). 1994. one add-on cassette 21.20 (*0-9629535-4-7*) Path-Coll Afford Prod.
—How to Find Money for College: The Minority Student. (gr. 8 up). 1993. one add-on cassette 21.20 (*0-9629535-3-9*) Path-Coll Afford Prod.
Schwartz, Sharon L., jt. auth. see Nichols, Eugene D.
Schwartz, Sheila. Bigger Is Better. (gr. 7 up). pap. 2.25 (*0-373-98009-4*) S&S Trade.
Schwartz, Stanley, epilogue by see Katz, Illana.
Schwartz, Yevgeny. Little Red Riding Hood. Shail, George, tr. from RUS. (gr. 4 up). Date not set. pap. text ed. 3.45 (*0-87129-196-7*, L25) Dramatic Pub.
Schwartzberg, Renee. Ronald Reagan. (Illus.). 136p. (gr. 5 up). 1991. 17.95 (*1-55546-849-7*) Chelsea Hse.
Schwartzentruber, Hubert see Lehn, Cornelia.
Schwartzman, Lee T. Crippled Detectives or the War of the Red Romer. Mandel, Gerry, ed. (Illus.). (gr. 3-8). 1978. 3.00 (*0-89409-009-7*) Childrens Art.
Schwarz, Ted. The Beginner's Guide to Stamp Collecting. 192p. (gr. 12 up). 1983. pap. 10.95 (*0-668-05551-0*) P-H Gen Ref & Trav.
Schwarzbauer, Heike, tr. see Ende, Michael.
Schwarzenegger, Arnold & Gaines, Charles. Arnold's Fitness for Kids: A Guide to Health, Exercise, & Nutrition. LC 92-28577. (gr. 1-5). 1993. 15.00 (*0-385-42267-9*) Doubleday.
—Arnold's Fitness for Kids Ages Birth to Five: A Guide to Health, Exercise, & Nutrition. LC 92-26209. (ps-k). 1993. 15.00 (*0-385-42266-0*) Doubleday.
—Arnold's Fitness for Kids Ages Eleven to Fourteen: A Guide to Health, Exercise, & Nutrition. LC 92-26786. (gr. 6-8). 1993. 15.00 (*0-385-42268-7*) Doubleday.
Schwatrz, L. Think on Your Feet. (gr. 4-8). 1989. 7.95 (*0-88160-172-1*, LW 283) Learning Wks.
Schweininger, Ann. Autumn Days. LC 93-16684. 32p. (ps-3). 1993. pap. 4.50 (*0-14-054055-5*, Puffin) Puffin Bks.
Schweitz, Rita. I Hate Lima Beans! Harrison, Marc, illus. LC 92-45561. (ps-3). 1993. 4.99 (*0-8499-0941-4*) Word Inc.
—The Incredible Bathtub Surprise. Harrison, Marc, illus. LC 92-45562. (ps-3). 1993. pap. 4.99 (*0-8499-0943-0*) Word Inc.
Schweitzer, Albert. Albert Schweitzer. Repath, Ann, ed. Winston, Richard & Winston, Clara, trs. Delessert, Etienne, illus. 32p. (gr. 9 up). 1986. PLB 12.95s.p. (*0-88682-013-8*) Creative Ed.
—J. S. Bach, 2 vols. Newman, Ernest, tr. Widor, C. M., pref. by. (Illus.). (gr. 7-12). pap. 9.95 ea.; Vol. 1. pap. (*0-486-21631-4*); Vol. 2. pap. (*0-486-21632-2*) Dover.
Schweizer, William H. Solemn Silence: The Complete Guide to Hood Canal, by Land, & Sea. Amundsen, Richard, illus. 304p. (Orig.). 1992. pap. write for info. (*0-925244-02-3*) EOS Pub.
Schwengel, Fred see Kennon, Donald R. & Strincer, Richard.
Schweninger, Ann. Autumn Days. (ps-3). 1991. 12.95 (*0-670-82758-4*) Viking Child Bks.
—Christmas Secrets. Schweninger, Ann, illus. 32p. (ps-1). 1986. pap. 4.99 (*0-14-050577-6*, Puffin) Puffin Bks.
—Halloween Surprises. Schweninger, Ann, illus. 32p. (ps-1). 1986. pap. 3.99 (*0-14-050634-9*, Puffin) Puffin Bks.
—Off to School! (Illus.). 32p. (ps-3). 1989. pap. 3.95 (*0-14-050661-6*, Puffin) Puffin Bks.
—Springtime. LC 92-22204. (Illus.). 32p. 1993. 13.50 (*0-670-82757-6*) Viking Child Bks.
—Summertime. Schweninger, Ann, illus. 32p. (ps-3). 1992. RB 13.50 (*0-670-83610-9*) Viking Child Bks.
—Valentine Friends. LC 87-22326. 32p. (ps-1). 1988. pap. 10.95 (*0-670-81448-2*) Viking Child Bks.
—Valentine Friends. (Illus.). 32p. (ps-1). 1990. pap. 3.95 (*0-14-050662-4*, Puffin) Puffin Bks.
—Wintertime. 1990. 11.95 (*0-670-83420-3*) Viking Child Bks.
—Wintertime. LC 93-16685. 32p. (ps-3). 1993. pap. 4.50 (*0-14-054286-8*, Puffin) Puffin Bks.
Schweninger, Ann, illus. Mary Had a Little Lamb. 24p. (ps). 1992. bds. write for info. (*0-307-06139-6*, 6139) Western Pub.
Schwerdtfeger, Don. America Does Not Have a Drug Problem. 131p. (Orig.). 1989. pap. 7.95 (*0-9624760-0-5*) Bding Better People.

Schwiebert, Ernest G. Luther & His Times: The Reformation from a New Perspective. (Illus.). (gr. 9 up). 1950. 26.95 (*0-570-03246-6*, 15-1164) Concordia.
Schwier, Karin M. Keith Edward's Different Day. Schwier, Karin M., illus. 36p. (Orig.). (gr. k-4). 1992. pap. 4.95 (*0-915166-74-7*) Impact Pubs Cal.
Schwinge, Joan. Sunny Sunflower. (Illus.). 28p. 1992. pap. 6.95 (*0-9632902-0-7*) Winston Bks.
Sciacca, Fran & Sciacca, Jill. Are Families Forever? Understanding Your Family. 64p. 1992. pap. 3.99 saddle stitch bdg. (*0-310-48071-X*) Zondervan.
—Burger, Fries & a Friend to Go. (gr. 7 up). 1987. pap. 3.95 (*0-89066-097-2*) World Wide Pubs.
—Burgers, Fries, & a Friend to Go: Making Friends. 64p. 1992. pap. 3.99 saddle stitch bdg. (*0-310-48041-8*) Zondervan.
—Caution: Contents under Pressure. 1990. pap. 3.95 (*0-89066-199-5*) World Wide Pubs.
—Cliques & Clones. (gr. 7 up). 1987. pap. 3.95 (*0-89066-100-6*) World Wide Pubs.
—Cliques & Clones: Facing Peer Pressure. 64p. 1992. pap. 3.99 saddle stitch bdg. (*0-310-48031-0*) Zondervan.
—Desperately Seeking Perfect Family. 1987. pap. 3.95 (*0-89066-098-0*) World Wide Pubs.
—Does Anyone Else Feel This Way? Conquering Loneliness & Depression. 64p. 1992. pap. 3.99 saddle stitch bdg. (*0-310-48021-3*) Zondervan.
—Does Anyone Else Feel This Way? Conquering Loneliness, Depression, & Thoughts of Suicide. 1990. pap. 3.95 (*0-89066-200-2*) World Wide Pubs.
—Does God Live Here Anymore? 1988. pap. 3.95 (*0-89066-113-8*) World Wide Pubs.
—Good News for a Bad News World. 1989. pap. 3.95 (*0-685-25653-7*) World Wide Pubs.
—Good News in a Bad News World: Understanding the Gospel. 64p. 1992. pap. 3.99 saddle stitch bdg. (*0-310-48061-2*) Zondervan.
—Is This the Real Thing? What Love Is & Isn't. 64p. 1992. pap. 3.99 saddle stitch bdg. (*0-310-48081-7*) Zondervan.
—Is This the Real Thing? What Love Is & What It Isn't. 1990. pap. 3.95 (*0-89066-201-0*) World Wide Pubs.
—Kick the Fear Habit. 1990. pap. 3.95 (*0-89066-198-7*) World Wide Pubs.
—Learning to Hope in a Wish-Filled World. 1988. pap. 3.95 (*0-89066-111-1*) World Wide Pubs.
—No Pain, No Gain. 1989. pap. 3.95 (*0-685-25654-5*) World Wide Pubs.
—Sex: When to Say Yes. 1987. pap. 3.95 (*0-89066-099-9*) World Wide Pubs.
—So What's Wrong with a Big Nose? 1988. pap. 3.95 (*0-89066-112-X*) World Wide Pubs.
—So What's Wrong with a Big Nose? Building Self-Esteem. 64p. 1992. pap. 3.99 saddle stitch bdg. (*0-310-48051-5*) Zondervan.
—Some Assembly Required. 1989. pap. 3.95 (*0-685-25748-7*) World Wide Pubs.
—Some Things Are Never Discounted. 1988. pap. 3.95 (*0-89066-114-6*) World Wide Pubs.
—Warning: This Christian Is Highly Explosive! 1989. pap. 3.95 (*0-685-25655-3*) World Wide Pubs.
—What Really Matters? Setting Priorities. 64p. 1992. pap. 3.99 saddle stitch bdg. (*0-310-48091-4*) Zondervan.
Sciacca, Jill, jt. auth. see Sciacca, Fran.
Scibor, Teresa. It's Fun to Speak French with Zozo. (Illus.). 32p. (ps-3). 1993. pap. 12.95 (*0-8120-8012-2*) Barron.
—It's Fun to Speak Spanish with ZoZo. Ollive, Richard, illus. 32p. (ps-3). 1993. pap. 12.95 incl. cassette (*0-8120-8107-2*) Barron.
Scieszka, Jon. The Frog Prince, Continued. Johnson, Steve, illus. 32p. (ps-3). 1991. 14.95 (*0-670-83421-1*) Viking Child Bks.
—The Good, the Bad, & the Goofy. Smith, Lane, illus. 64p. (gr. 3-7). 1992. 11.00 (*0-670-84380-6*) Viking Child Bks.
—The Good, the Bad, & the Goofy. Smith, Lane, illus. LC 93-15136. 80p. (gr. 2-5). 1993. pap. 3.50 (*0-14-036170-7*, Puffin) Puffin Bks.
—Knights of the Kitchen Table. Smith, Lane, illus. 64p. (gr. 3-7). 1991. 11.00 (*0-670-83622-2*) Viking Child Bks.
—Knights of the Kitchen Table. Smith, Lane, illus. 64p. (gr. 2-6). 1993. pap. 3.25 (*0-14-034603-1*, Puffin) Puffin Bks.
—The Not-So-Jolly-Roger. Smith, Lane, illus. 64p. (gr. 3-7). 1991. 11.00 (*0-670-83754-7*) Viking Child Bks.
—The Not-So-Jolly Roger. Smith, Lane, illus. 64p. (gr. 2-6). 1993. pap. 3.25 (*0-14-034684-8*, Puffin) Puffin Bks.
—The Stinky Cheese Man: And Other Fairly Stupid Tales. Smith, Lane, illus. 56p. (gr. 1). 1992. 16.00 (*0-670-84487-X*) Viking Child Bks.
—The True Story of the Three Little Pigs. Smith, Lane, illus. 32p. (ps-up). 1989. pap. 15.00 (*0-670-82759-2*) Viking Child Bks.
—Your Mother Was a Neanderthal. Smith, Lane, illus. 64p. (gr. 2-6). 1993. PLB 10.99 (*0-670-84481-0*) Viking Child Bks.
Scieszka, Jon, ed. see Wolf, A.
Scioscia, Mary. Bicycle Rider. Young, Ed, illus. LC 82-47702. 48p. (gr. 2-6). 1983. PLB 13.89 (*0-06-025223-5*) HarpC Child Bks.
—Bicycle Rider. Young, Ed, illus. LC 82-47702. 48p. (gr. 2-6). 1993. pap. 3.95 (*0-06-443295-5*, Trophy) HarpC Child Bks.

Sclavi, Tiziano. The Planet Putipoo. Lagana, Giuseppe, illus. 16p. 1989. 8.95 (*0-8120-5997-2*) Barron.
—What Animal Is It? Michelini, Carlo A., illus. 10p. (ps). 1994. prepub. 4.95 (*1-56397-345-6*) Boyds Mills Pr.
—What's on the Other Side? Michelini, Carlo A., illus. 10p. (ps). 1994. prepub. 4.95 (*1-56397-339-1*) Boyds Mills Pr.
Scobey, Joan. The Fannie Farmer Junior Cook Book. rev. ed. Brewster, Patience, illus. LC 92-42632. 1993. 19.95 (*0-316-77624-6*) Little.
Scoggan, Nita, ed. see Mason, Judy S.
Scoltock, Jack. Badger, Beano & the Magic Mushroom. Dunne, Jeanette, illus. 125p. (Orig.). (gr. 2-6). 1990. pap. 8.95 (*0-86327-263-0*, Pub. by Poolbeg Pr ER) Dufour.
—Jeremy's Adventure. (Illus.). 91p. (Orig.). (gr. 2-5). 1991. pap. 7.95 (*0-86327-305-X*, Pub. by Wolfhound Pr EIRE) Dufour.
Scoones, Simon. Jamaica. LC 91-39126. (Illus.). 32p. (gr. k-4). 1992. PLB 12.40 (*0-531-18419-6*, Pub. by Bookwright Pr) Watts.
—The Sahara & Its People. LC 93-16803. 48p. (gr. 5-8). 1993. 15.95 (*1-56847-088-6*) Thomson Lrning.
Scoppettone, Sandra. Happy Endings Are All Alike. 202p. (gr. 9-12). 1991. pap. 6.95 (*1-55583-177-X*) Alyson Pubns.
—Playing Murder. LC 83-47707. 224p. (gr. 7 up). 1987. pap. 2.75 (*0-06-447046-6*, Trophy) HarpC Child Bks.
—Trying Hard to Hear You. LC 91-28058. 264p. (gr. 7-12). 1991. pap. 7.95 (*1-55583-196-6*) Alyson Pubns.
Scordato, Ellen. The Creek Indians. LC 92-35972. (Illus.). 80p. (gr. 2-5). 1993. PLB 12.95 (*0-7910-1660-9*); pap. write for info. (*0-7910-1974-8*) Chelsea Hse.
—Sarah Winnemucca. (Illus.). 112p. (gr. 5 up). 1992. lib. bdg. 17.95 (*0-7910-1710-9*) Chelsea Hse.
—Sarah Winnemucca. (gr. 4-7). 1992. pap. 7.95 (*0-7910-1696-X*) Chelsea Hse.
Scoresby, A. Lynn. Knowledge Gain's Seven Effective Memory Processes. 70p. (gr. 9-12). 1993. pap. 9.95 (*1-884518-01-X*) Knowldge Gain.
—Knowledge Gain's Twelve Effective Study Strategies. 92p. (gr. 9-12). 1993. pap. 9.95 (*1-884518-00-1*) Knowldge Gain.
Scot, Reginald. Discoverie of Witchcraft. 1989. pap. 7.95 (*0-486-26030-5*) Dover.
Scott. Slave Ship Captain: John Newton. 1989. pap. 3.95 (*0-87508-623-5*) Chr Lit.
Scott, Alyson, jt. auth. see Turner, Margret.
Scott, Ann H. A Brand Is Forever. Himler, Ronald, illus. 48p. (gr. k-3). 1993. 12.95 (*0-395-60118-5*, Clarion Bks) HM.
—Cowboy Country. Lewin, Ted, photos by. LC 92-24499. 1993. 14.45 (*0-395-57561-3*, Clarion Bks) HM.
—Grandmother's Chair. Aubrey, Meg K., illus. 32p. (ps-1). 1990. 13.45 (*0-395-52001-0*, Clarion Bks) HM.
—On Mother's Lap. Coalson, Glo, illus. 32p. (ps-k). 1992. 14.45 (*0-395-58920-7*, Clarion Bks); pap. 5.70 (*0-395-62976-4*, Clarion Bks) HM.
—One Good Horse: A Cowpuncher's Counting Book. LC 89-1984. (Illus.). 32p. (ps-up). 1990. 12.95 (*0-688-09146-6*); lib. bdg. 12.88 (*0-688-09147-4*) Greenwillow.
—Sam. Shimin, Symeon, illus. 40p. (ps-8). 1992. PLB 14.95 (*0-399-22104-2*, Philomel Bks) Putnam Pub Group.
—Someday Rider. Himler, Ronald, illus. LC 88-35255. 32p. (ps-1). 1989. 13.45 (*0-89919-792-2*, Clarion Bks) HM.
—Someday Rider. Himler, Ronald, illus. 32p. (ps-3). 1991. pap. 4.95 (*0-395-58115-X*, Clarion Bks) HM.
Scott, Annie, jt. auth. see Dee, Abbie.
Scott, Arthur L., ed. Mark Twain: Selected Criticism. rev. ed. LC 66-29657. 318p. 1967. pap. 11.95x (*0-87074-105-5*) SMU Press.
Scott, Barbara A. Tug of War. LC 93-70369. 218p. (gr. 8-12). 1993. pap. 7.95x (*0-943864-70-4*) Davenport.
Scott, Beverly A. Santa's New Suit Funbook. (ps-6). 1973. pap. 3.00 (*0-686-11715-8*) B A Scott.
Scott, Bill. The Colt Who Had Never Been Ridden. LC 93-60919. (Illus.). 44p. 1994. 7.95 (*1-55523-648-0*) Winston-Derek.
—Many Kinds of Magic: Tales of Mystery, Myth & Enchantment. (gr. 4-7). 1990. 14.95 (*0-670-82971-4*) Viking Child Bks.
Scott, Blackie. It's Fun at Grandmother's House. LC 85-22021. (Illus.). 48p. (ps-3). 1992. 8.95 (*0-932419-01-1*) Peachtree Pubs.
Scott, Bob. The Backcountry. Arcade, Greg, illus. 24p. (gr. 4-12). 1989. cardstock cover 5.00 (*0-9621201-0-3*) B Scott Bks.
—The Ugly Christmas Tree. MacDonald, Hugh, illus. LC 92-93614. 24p. (Orig.). (gr. 3-8). 1993. 7.95 (*0-9621201-1-1*); pap. 4.95 (*0-9621201-2-X*) B Scott Bks.
Scott, Carlton. Grin's Message. Marcus, Laurie R., ed. Scott, Carlton, illus. 32p. (gr. k-4). 1993. 9.95 (*0-9636652-1-9*); pap. cancelled (*0-9636652-4-3*) C T Scott.
Scott, Carole. The Story of Astronomy. Forsey, Chris, illus. LC 91-36604. 32p. (gr. 1-4). 1993. PLB 11.89 (*0-8167-2703-1*); pap. text ed. 3.95 (*0-8167-2704-X*) Troll Assocs. Postponed.
Scott, Carolyn. Dr. Who Never Gave up, Ida Scudder. (gr. 5). 1979. pap. 3.95 (*0-87508-607-1*) Chr Lit.
Scott, Dennis. Sir Gawain & the Green Knight. (gr. k up). 1978. 5.50 (*0-87602-202-6*) Anchorage.
Scott, Dixon. A Fresh Wind in the Willows. (gr. k-6). 1987. pap. 2.50 (*0-440-42741-X*, YB) Dell.

Scott, Elaine. Choices. Thompson, Ellen, illus. LC 88-34537. 192p. (gr. 7 up). 1989. 12.95 (*0-688-07230-5*) Morrow Jr Bks.

—Funny Papers: Behind the Scenes of the Comics. Miller, Margaret, photos by. LC 92-46727. (Illus.). 96p. (gr. 3 up). 1993. 15.00 (*0-688-11575-6*); PLB 14.93 (*0-688-11576-4*) Morrow Jr Bks.

—Look Alive: Behind the Scenes of an Animated Film. Hewett, Richard, photos by. LC 91-36220. (Illus.). 80p. (gr. 3 up). 1992. 14.00 (*0-688-09936-X*); PLB 13.93 (*0-688-09937-8*) Morrow Jr Bks.

—The Making of Super Mario Brothers. (Illus.). 64p. (Orig.). (gr. 2-6). 1993. pap. write for info. (*1-56282-472-4*) Hyprn Child.

—Ramona: Behind the Scenes of a Television Show. Miller, Margaret, photos by. LC 87-33313. (Illus.). 96p. (gr. 3-7). 1988. 14.95 (*0-688-06818-9*); PLB 14.88 (*0-688-06819-7*, Morrow Jr Bks) Morrow Jr Bks.

—Safe in the Spotlight: The Dawn Animal Agency & the Sanctuary for Animals. Miller, Margaret, photos by. LC 90-49677. (Illus.). 80p. (gr. 3 up). 1991. 12.95 (*0-688-08177-0*); PLB 12.88 (*0-688-08178-9*, Morrow Jr Bks) Morrow Jr Bks.

Scott, Elaine, ed. The Times & Triumphs of American Woman. (Illus.). 79p. (gr. 4-9). 1986. pap. text ed. 8.00 book only (*0-9610622-1-5*) Natl Wmns Hall Fame.

Scott Foresman Co. Staff. Jr. Thesaurus. 1988. 11.95 (*0-673-12494-0*) Scott F.

Scott, Gavin, adapted by. Revolution! LC 91-51201. (Illus.). 136p. (Orig.). (gr. 4-8). 1992. pap. 3.50 (*0-679-83238-6*) Random Bks Yng Read.

Scott, Genio C. Fishing in American Waters. (Illus.). 484p. (gr. 10 up). 1993. Repr. of 1869 ed. 42.90 (*1-56416-118-8*) Derrydale Pr.

Scott, Geoffrey. Labor Day. Wyman, Cherie R., illus. LC 81-15485. 48p. (gr. k-4). 1982. PLB 14.95 (*0-87614-178-5*) Carolrhoda Bks.

—Memorial Day. Hanson, Peter E., illus. LC 83-1855. 48p. (gr. k-4). 1983. PLB 14.95 (*0-87614-219-6*) Carolrhoda Bks.

Scott, Heather, jt. auth. see Snape, Charles.

Scott, Jim. The Eagle in the Mountains. Shattil, Wendy & Rozinsky, Bob, photos by. LC 89-4461. (Illus.). 32p. (gr. 4-6). 1989. PLB 15.93 (*0-8368-0113-X*) Gareth Stevens Inc.

Scott, Jim, jt. auth. see Harrison, Virginia.

Scott, Johanna, ed. Science & Language Links: Classroom Implications. LC 92-44250. (Illus.). 91p. (gr. 4 up). 1993. pap. 13.50 (*0-435-08338-4*, 08338) Heinemann.

Scott, John A. Settlers on the Eastern Shore 1607-1750. (Illus.). 144p. 1990. 16.95x (*0-8160-2327-1*) Facts on File.

—The Story of America. Newhouse, Elizabeth L., ed. LC 84-2018. (Illus.). (gr. 4-8). 1984. 19.95 (*0-87044-508-1*) Natl Geog.

—The Story of America. rev. ed. Newhouse, Elizabeth L., ed. Cooke, Alistair, intro. by. LC 92-13800. (Illus.). 324p. 1992. pap. 21.95 (*0-87044-887-0*); PLB write for info. (*0-87044-888-9*) Natl Geog.

Scott, John A. & Scott, Robert A. John Brown of Harper's Ferry. (Illus.). 192p. (gr. 5 up). 1988. 16.95x (*0-8160-1347-0*) Facts on File.

Scott, John A., ed. see Miller, Douglas.

Scott, John M. Accept Yourself with Love & Confidence. LC 90-62654. 128p. (Orig.). 1991. pap. 5.95 (*0-87973-449-3*, 449) Our Sunday Visitor.

Scott, John W., et al. DeadBase Five: The Complete Guide to Grateful Dead Songlists. (Illus.). 480p. (Orig.). 1991. pap. 29.00 (*1-877657-07-7*) DeadBase.

—DeadBase Four: The Complete Guide to Grateful Dead Songlists. (Illus.). 480p. (Orig.). 1990. pap. 27.00 (*1-877657-05-0*) DeadBase.

—DeadBase '89: The Annual Edition of the Complete Guide to Grateful Dead Songlists. (Illus.). 192p. (Orig.). 1990. pap. 14.00 (*1-877657-04-2*) DeadBase.

—DeadBase '90: The Annual Edition of the Complete Guide to Grateful Dead Songlists. (Illus.). 224p. (Orig.). 1991. pap. 14.00 (*1-877657-06-9*) DeadBase.

Scott, Jonathan. The Leopard Family Book. Scott, Jonathan, photos by. LC 91-14578. (Illus.). 56p. (gr. k up). 1991. pap. 15.95 (*0-88708-186-X*) Picture Bk Studio.

Scott, Joseph & Scott, Lenore. Egyptian Hieroglyphs for Everyone: An Introduction to the Writing of Ancient Egypt. reissued ed. Scott, Joseph & Scott, Lenore, illus. LC 68-13080. 96p. (gr. 7 up). 1990. PLB 14.89 (*0-690-04753-3*, Crowell Jr Bks) HarpC Child Bks.

Scott, Judy, jt. auth. see Beck, Michael.

Scott, Kay & Shouse, Lucille. Help Me Bear Shows You How to Call 911. Semingson, Roberta, tr. Scott, Kay & Shouse, Lucille, illus. (ENG & SPA.). 16p. (Orig.). (gr. k-4). 1988. write for info. tchr's. ed. (*0-9620819-1-4*); write for info. color bk. (*0-9620819-0-6*) L Shouse.

Scott, Lenore, jt. auth. see Scott, Joseph.

Scott, Lesbia, text by. I Sing a Song of the Saints of God. Brown, Judith G., illus. LC 91-10393. 32p. (ps-5). 1991. Repr. 10.95 (*0-8192-1561-9*) Morehouse Pub.

Scott, Louise. Quiet Times. 66p. (ps). 1986. saddle stitched 9.95 (*0-513-01785-2*) Denison.

Scott, Louise B. Rhymes for Learning Times. LC 82-73392. 145p. (Orig.). (ps). 1984. pap. 15.95 (*0-513-01763-1*) Denison.

Scott, Lynn H. The Covered Wagon & Other Adventures. LC 87-5857. (Illus.). x, 135p. (gr. 4-7). 1993. 15.00x (*0-8032-4179-8*, Bison Books); pap. 7.95 (*0-8032-9222-8*, Bison) U of Nebr Pr.

Scott, Mary. A Picture Book of Farm Animals. Botto, Lisa, illus. LC 90-44888. 24p. (gr. 1-4). 1991. lib. bdg. 9.59 (*0-8167-2150-5*); pap. text ed. 2.50 (*0-8167-2151-3*) Troll Assocs.

—A Picture Book of Reptiles & Amphibians. Kinnelay, Janice, illus. LC 92-19054. 24p. (gr. 1-4). 1992. lib. bdg. 9.59 (*0-8167-2838-0*); pap. text ed. 2.50 (*0-8167-2839-9*) Troll Assocs.

—A Picture Book of Wild Cats. Pistolesi, Roseanna, illus. LC 91-16500. 24p. (gr. 1-4). 1992. PLB 9.59 (*0-8167-2430-X*); pap. 2.50 (*0-8167-2431-8*) Troll Assocs.

Scott, Mavis. Birdstone Summer. (ps-3). 1993. pap. 6.95 (*1-86373-231-4*, Pub. by Allen & Unwin Aust Pty AT) IPG Chicago.

—Little Ho & the Golden Kites. Reynolds, Pat, illus. 32p. (Orig.). (gr. k-2). 1993. pap. 6.95 (*0-04-442242-3*, Pub. by Allen & Unwin Aust Pty AT) IPG Chicago.

Scott, Michael. Celebrate the Season, Vol. 3: New Age Piano Stylings of Traditional Holiday Music. Tucker, Dale, ed. 24p. (Orig.). 1993. pap. text ed. 6.50 (*0-89898-650-8*) CPP Belwin.

—Irish Fairytales. Gervin, Joseph, illus. LC 89-50977. 142p. (gr. 2-5). 1989. pap. 11.95 (*0-85342-866-2*, Pub. by Mercier Press Ltd Eire) Dufour.

—The Last of the Fianna: An Irish Legend. (Illus.). 109p. (gr. 3-7). 1993. pap. 9.95 (*0-86278-308-9*, Pub. by OBrien Pr IE) Dufour.

—October Moon. LC 93-8693. 160p. (gr. 12 up). 1994. 14.95 (*0-8234-1110-9*) Holiday.

—The Piper's Ring. Deuchar, Ian, illus. 32p. (gr. 1-3). 1993. 17.95 (*0-460-88130-2*, Pub. by J M Dent & Sons) Trafalgar.

—The Seven Treasures: The Quest of the Sons of Tuireann. (Illus.). 158p. (gr. 3-7). 1993. pap. 9.95 (*0-86278-309-7*, Pub. by OBrien Pr IE) Dufour.

—WindLord: First of the De Dannan Tales. (Orig.). (gr. 3-9). 1991. pap. 8.95 (*0-86327-296-7*, Pub. by Wolfhound Pr EIRE) Dufour.

Scott, Michael, ed. Earthlord: Second of the De Danann Tales. (Illus.). 176p. (gr. 5-8). 1993. pap. 9.95 (*0-86327-343-2*, Pub. by Wolfhound Pr EIRE) Dufour.

Scott, Mike. Judith & the Traveller. 143p. (gr. 8-11). 1991. pap. 7.95 (*0-86327-299-1*, Pub. by Wolfhound Pr EIRE) Dufour.

Scott, R. C. Blood Sport. (gr. 7 up). 1984. pap. 2.25 (*0-553-23866-3*) Bantam.

Scott, Ricardo. Drive by Shootings: My Proverbial Mom. 75p. (Orig.). 1994. write for info. (*1-883427-22-3*) Crnerstone GA.

Scott, Ricardo A. Cornerstone Reggae Music Book of Light: Matshafa Berhan. (Illus.). 110p. (Orig.). Date not set. write for info. (*1-883427-18-5*) Crnerstone GA.

—For Jah Know: Truth & Rights for the Kids. (Illus.). 75p. (Orig.). 1994. write for info. (*1-883427-10-X*) Crnerstone GA.

—Ras Cardo Speaks on Reggae Issues, Vol. 1, No. 1: Reggae Spectrum. 200p. (Orig.). 1994. write for info. (*1-883427-20-7*) Crnerstone GA.

—Ras Cardo, the Man, the Legend & Reggae Music: Where Reggae Legends Trod. Cardo, Ras, illus. 150p. (Orig.). Date not set. write for info. (*1-883427-23-1*) Crnerstone GA.

—Reggae Legends Dance Steps: How Legends Skank. (Illus.). 50p. (Orig.). 1994. write for info. (*1-883427-12-6*) Crnerstone GA.

—Reggae Lyrics, Shangs, & Interpretations: Reggae Phraseology Explained. 85p. (Orig.). 1994. write for info. (*1-883427-14-2*) Crnerstone GA.

—Reggae Philosophy, Reggae Reality. (Illus.). 100p. (Orig.). Date not set. write for info. (*1-883427-19-3*) Crnerstone GA.

—Reggae's Healing Effects: A Reggae Education for a Healing of the Nations. (Illus.). 80p. (Orig.). 1994. write for info. (*1-883427-21-5*) Crnerstone GA.

Scott, Richard. Jackie Robinson. King, Coretta Scott, intro. by. (Illus.). 112p. (Orig.). (gr. 5 up). 1987. 17.95 (*1-55546-609-5*); pap. 9.95 (*0-7910-0200-4*) Chelsea Hse.

Scott, Robert A. Chief Joseph & the Nez Perces. (Illus.). 128p. (gr. 5 up). 1993. PLB 16.95x (*0-8160-2475-8*) Facts on File.

Scott, Robert A., jt. auth. see Scott, John A.

Scott, Sally. The Three Wonderful Beggars. LC 86-22825. (Illus.). 30p. (gr. k-3). 1988. Repr. of 1987 ed. 13.00 (*0-688-06656-9*); lib. bdg. 12.88 (*0-688-06657-7*) Greenwillow.

Scott, Sharon. How To Say No & Keep Your Friends. 112p. (gr. 6-12). 1986. pap. 7.95 (*0-87425-039-0*) Human Res Dev Pr.

—Too Smart for Trouble. Phillips, George, illus. 112p. (Orig.). (gr. k-5). 1990. pap. 7.95 (*0-87425-121-4*) Human Res Dev Pr.

—When to Say Yes & Make More Friends. 118p. (Orig.). (gr. 4-10). 1988. pap. text ed. 7.95 (*0-87425-066-8*) Human Res Dev Pr.

Scott, Sharon & Nicholas. Not Better... Not Worse... Just Different. Phillips, George, illus. 118p. (Orig.). (gr. k-5). 1992. pap. 7.95 (*0-87425-195-8*) Human Res Dev Pr.

When children are VERY young, they will usually make friends with anyone & everyone. This includes other children, adults of all ages, animals & even stuffed toys! They do not discriminate because of age, sex, race, intelligence, physical difference, or brand labels worn. Somewhere along the way, however, they learn that people are different & that society places higher value on certain physical traits. This can cause children to be unkind to one another, stare at differences, & tease unmercifully. NOT BETTER... NOT WORSE... JUST DIFFERENT is a beautifully illustrated, skills-based book that teaches children ages 5 to 10 to be kind to one another! Using his animal friends, Nicholas, the Cocker Spaniel co-author, presents specific steps for accepting all types of differences. Children will learn how to respect & accept one another regardless of learning or physical differences, race, or sex. To reinforce the learning, the last chapter contains real-life examples & practice sessions. This provides a safe environment for children to integrate these important skills that will further their development in becoming sensitive, kind individuals. *Publisher Provided Annotation.*

Scott, Timothy. You Can't Hurry Love: (A Guide to Christian Dating) 10p. (Orig.). (gr. 10-12). 1989. pap. write for info. (*1-877784-05-2*) T Scott Pub.

Scott, Victoria & Jones, Ernest. Sylvia Stark: A Pioneer. Lewis, Karen, illus. 64p. (Orig.). (gr. 4-12). 1992. PLB 12.95 (*0-940880-37-7*); pap. 6.95 (*0-940880-38-5*) Open Hand.

Scott, Virginia C. Dream Horse: A Girl with No Roots, a Boy with a Bad Reputation, a Horse Nobody Wants. 1993. pap. 3.50 (*0-06-106149-2*, Harp PBks) HarpC.

Scott, Virginia M. Belonging. Crowe, Patricia, illus. LC 85-31135. 176p. (gr. 7-12). 1987. pap. 2.95 (*0-930323-33-5*, Kendall Green Pubns) Gallaudet Univ Pr.

Scott, Walter. Ivanhoe. (gr. 9 up). 1964. pap. 2.95 (*0-8049-0034-5*, CL-34) Airmont.

—Kenilworth. new ed. (gr. 10 up). 1968. pap. 2.95 (*0-8049-0193-7*, CL-193) Airmont.

—Lady of the Lake & Other Poems. Bennet, C. L., intro. by. (gr. 9 up). 1967. pap. 1.75 (*0-8049-0137-6*, CL-137) Airmont.

—Quentin Durward. Bennet, C. L., intro. by. (gr. 9 up). 1967. pap. 2.50 (*0-8049-0132-5*, CL-132) Airmont.

Scott, Sir Walter. Ivanhoe. 512p. (RL 7). 1962. pap. 4.50 (*0-451-52194-3*, CE1876, Sig Classics) NAL-Dutton.

Scott, Whitney. In the Field. 24p. (Orig.). (gr. 7 up). 1989. pap. 7.50 (*0-9621039-1-8*) Outrider Pr.

Scott-Hughes, Brian, jt. auth. see Lambert, Alan.

Scotti, Juliet & Linksman, Ricki. Kirpal Singh: The Story of a Saint. 2nd ed. Tarrant, Valerie, illus. Zaffina, Bruno, intro. by. LC 77-79840. (Illus.). 96p. (gr. 1-7). 1982. pap. 12.95 (*0-918224-05-5*) Sawan Kirpal Pubns.

Scotti, Linda. Mr. Peek-a-Boo. 1993. 7.95 (*0-533-10353-3*) Vantage.

Scovel, Karen & Hunter, Ted. Joe's Earthday Birthday. Whitney, Jean, illus. 32p. (Orig.). (gr. 2-4). 1992. PLB 16.95 (*0-943990-85-8*); pap. 5.95 (*0-943990-84-X*) Parenting Pr.

Scribbins, Jim. The Four Hundred Story. (Illus.). 232p. (gr. 11). 1990. Repr. 49.95 (*0-937658-07-3*) Interurban.

Scribbles, R. J., pseud. Back to School. Scribbles, R. J., illus. 32p. (Orig.). (gr. 2-5). 1992. pap. 12.95 (*0-9632192-0-0*) R J Miller.

Scribner, Toni, illus. The Glo Friends' Good Night Book. LC 85-60757. 28p. (ps). 1986. 2.95 (*0-394-87797-7*) Random Bks Yng Read.

—Where's Baby? LC 86-43148. 14p. (ps). 1987. bds. 3.99 (*0-394-89071-X*) Random Bks Yng Read.

Scribner, Virginia. Gopher Takes Heart. Wilson, Janet, illus. LC 92-25939. 128p. (gr. 3-7). 1993. 13.99 (*0-670-84839-5*) Viking Child Bks.

Scruton, Clive. Mary's Pets. Scruton, Clive, illus. LC 88-12895. 32p. (ps-k). 1989. 10.95 (*0-688-08520-2*) Lothrop.

Sculfield, Byron. Hello! My Name Is Mr. ImGonChop. Omalade, Kip, illus. 1993. pap. 5.95 (*0-88378-097-6*) Third World.

Scullard, Sue. The Great Round-the-World Balloon Race. Scullard, Sue, illus. LC 90-40590. 32p. (gr. 2-5). 1991. 12.95 (*0-525-44692-3*, DCB) Dutton Child Bks.

—Miss Fanshawe & the Great Dragon Adventure. Scullard, Sue, illus. 32p. (ps-4). 1987. 9.95 (0-312-00510-5) St Martin.

Seablom, Seth H. The California Coloring Guide. (Illus.). 32p. (gr. 1-6). 1979. pap. 2.50 (0-918800-05-6) Seablom.
—China Coloring Guide. (Illus.). 32p. (gr. 1-6). 1979. pap. 2.50 (0-918800-06-4) Seablom.
—The Great Mukilteo to Friday Harbor Auto Race. Seablom, Seth H., illus. LC 75-38037. (gr. 1-3). 1976. pap. 2.00 (0-918800-00-5) Seablom.
—Seattle Coloring Guide. Seablom, Seth H., illus. (gr. 4-6). 1977. pap. 2.50 (0-918800-01-3) Seablom.
—Washington State Coloring Guide. (Illus.). 32p. (gr. 1-6). 1978. pap. 2.50 (0-918800-03-X) Seablom.

Seablom, Victoria, ed. see Swolgaard, Carole.

Seabrooke, Brenda. The Boy Who Saved the Town. Burns, Howard M., illus. LC 89-52027. 30p. (gr. 2-5). 1990. 7.95 (0-87033-405-0) Tidewater.
—The Bridges of Summer. LC 92-11642. 160p. (gr. 5 up). 1992. 14.00 (0-525-65094-6, Cobblehill Bks) Dutton Child Bks.
—The Chester Town Tea Party. Smith, Nancy, illus. 30p. (gr. k-5). 1991. 8.95 (0-87033-422-0) Tidewater.
—The Dragon That Ate Summer. 112p. (gr. 3-6). 1992. 14.95 (0-399-22115-8, Philomel Bks) Putnam Pub Group.
—The Dragon That Ate Summer. (gr. 4-7). 1993. pap. 2.95 (0-590-46986-X) Scholastic Inc.
—Jerry on the Line. LC 90-1745. 128p. (gr. 3-5). 1990. SBE 13.95 (0-02-781432-7, Bradbury Pr) Macmillan Child Grp.
—Jerry on the Line. 128p. (gr. 3-7). 1992. pap. 3.99 (0-14-034868-9) Puffin Bks.
—Judy Scuppernong. LC 90-31583. (Illus.). (gr. 4-7). 1990. 13.00 (0-525-65038-5, Cobblehill Bks) Dutton Child Bks.
—Judy Scuppernong. 1992. pap. 3.50 (0-553-29448-2) Bantam.

Seah, Audrey. Vietnam. LC 93-4380. 1993. 21.95 (1-85435-584-8) Marshall Cavendish.

Seal, Bernard. American Vocabulary Builder, 2 vols. 1990. pap. text ed. 13.95 ea. (78349) No. 1 (0-8013-0496-2, 78412) No. 2 (0-8013-0536-5) Longman.

Seale, Jan. Deaf Smith: The Eyes & Ears of the Texas Army. Seale, Carl, illus. 30p. (gr. k-3). 1987. pap. 2.95 (0-936927-20-8) Knowing Pr.
—Dilue Rose: The Girl Who Saw Texas Independence. Seale, Carl, illus. 30p. (gr. k-3). 1986. pap. 2.95 (0-936927-21-6) Knowing Pr.
—Juan Seguin: The Tejano Who Wouldn't Give Up. Seale, Carl, illus. 28p. (gr. k-3). 1987. pap. 2.95 (0-936927-19-4) Knowing Pr.
—Kian Long: The Slave Girl Who Helped Start Texas. Seale, Carl, illus. 30p. (gr. k-3). 1987. pap. 2.95 (0-936927-18-6) Knowing Pr.
—Madam Candelaria: The Nurse at the Alamo. Seale, Carl, illus. 27p. (gr. k-3). 1987. pap. 2.95 (0-936927-16-X) Knowing Pr.
—William Goyens: The Texan Who Said No to Failure. Seale, Carl, illus. 29p. (gr. k-3). 1987. pap. 2.95 (0-936927-17-8) Knowing Pr.

Seale, Jan E. The Ballad of the Men at Mier: The Black Bean Expedition. Coleman, Bernice, illus. 46p. (gr. 4-8). 1986. lib. bdg. 10.95 (0-936927-14-3); pap. 7.95 (0-936927-15-1) Knowing Pr.
—Texas History Classroom Plays, Vol. 1. (Illus.). 56p. (gr. 4-8). 1986. PLB 4.25 (0-317-89748-9) Knowing Pr.
—Texas History Plays Series. (Illus.). (ps-8). 1986. PLB 89.95 (0-317-89749-7) Knowing Pr.

Seale, Nancy. The Little Princess, Sara Crewe. (Orig.). 1982. playscript 5.00 (0-87602-231-X) Anchorage.

Seals, Angela D. D.U.D.LEY. 1992. 7.95 (0-533-09734-7) Vantage.

Sealy, Adrienne V. The Color Your Way into Black History Book. Abantu Industries, illus. 78p. (gr. 2-5). 1980. wkbk. 4.00 (0-9602670-6-9) Assn Family Living.
—Little Tommy & the Basketball. Walker, Walt, illus. (gr. 2-6). 1980. 3.50x (0-9602670-4-2) Assn Family Living.
—Mama, Watch Out - I'm Growing Up. (Illus.). (gr. 2-5). 1978. PLB 4.95x (0-9602670-1-8) Assn Family Living.
—No Hill Is Too High. Holder, Stanley, illus. (gr. 2-5). 1978. PLB 4.95 (0-9602670-0-X) Assn Family Living.

Sealy, Shirley. I, Jason. pap. 6.95 (1-55503-247-8, 29004721) Covenant Comms.

Seaman, Rosie. Discovering Our World. (ps-k). 1987. pap. 6.95 (0-8224-1926-2) Fearon Teach Aids.
—Discovering Ourselves. (ps-k). 1987. pap. 6.95 (0-8224-1927-0) Fearon Teach Aids.
—Discovering Plants & Animals. (ps-k). 1987. pap. 6.95 (0-8224-1928-9) Fearon Teach Aids.
—Fearon's Beginning Skills Worksheets. (ps-1). 1989. pap. 9.95 (0-8224-3057-6) Fearon Teach Aids.

Seamans, Andy. Who, What, When, Where, Why? In the World of Nature. (Illus.). 300p. (Orig.). (gr. 6 up). 1992. pap. 5.95 (0-8120-4699-4) Barron.

Sean, jt. auth. see Dante.

Searcy, Margaret Z. Alli Gator Gets a Bump on His Nose. Wise, Lu Celia, illus. LC 78-61369. (gr. 2-4). 1978. 7.50 (0-916620-20-4) Portals Pr.
—The Charm of the Bear Claw Necklace. Brough, Hazel, illus. LC 89-78044. 80p. (gr. 3-7). 1990. 12.95 (0-88289-821-3); pap. 6.95 (0-88289-777-2) Pelican.

—Ikwa of the Mound-Builder Indians. LC 89-3830. (Illus.). 80p. (gr. 3-7). 1989. 12.95 (0-88289-762-4); pap. 5.95 (0-88289-742-X) Pelican.
—Race of Flitty Hummingbird & Flappy Crane. (Illus.). (gr. 2-4). 1980. 7.50 (0-916620-21-2) Portals Pr.
—Tiny Bat & the Ball Game. Wise, Lu Celia, illus. LC 78-61367. (gr. 2-4). 1978. 7.50 (0-916620-19-0) Portals Pr.
—Wolf Dog of the Woodland Indians. Brough, Hazel, illus. LC 90-26215. 112p. (Orig.). 1991. pap. 5.95 (0-88289-778-0) Pelican.

Searl, Duncan. What Cat Is That? 32p. 1989. PLB 15.96 (0-8172-3502-7); pap. 3.95 (0-8114-6705-8) Raintree Steck-V.

Searle, Don L. Light in the Harbor. LC 91-17827. viii, 245p. (Orig.). 1991. pap. 8.95 (0-87579-528-5) Deseret Bk.

Searle-Barnes, Bonita. Air. (Illus.). 32p. (gr. k-3). 1993. 6.99 (0-7459-2694-0) Lion USA.
—Light. (Illus.). 32p. (gr. k-3). 1993. 6.99 (0-7459-2695-9) Lion USA.
—Sound. (Illus.). 32p. (gr. k-3). 1993. 6.99 (0-7459-2692-4) Lion USA.
—Water. (Illus.). 32p. (gr. k-3). 1993. 6.99 (0-7459-2693-2) Lion USA.
—The Wonder of God's World: Air. Smithson, Colin, illus. LC 92-44575. 1993. 6.99 (0-7459-2021-7) Lion USA.
—The Wonder of God's World: Light. Smithson, Colin, illus. LC 92-44275. 1993. 6.99 (0-7459-2022-5) Lion USA.
—The Wonder of God's World: Sound. Smithson, Colin, illus. LC 92-44284. 1993. 6.99 (0-7459-2023-3) Lion USA.
—The Wonder of God's World: Water. Smithson, Colin, illus. LC 92-44274. 1993. 6.99 (0-7459-2024-1) Lion USA.

Sears, David. Tales from Reb Nachman: Parables Told by Rabbi Nachman of Breslov. Sears, David, illus. 32p. (gr. k-6). 1987. 9.95 (0-89906-808-1); pap. 6.95 (0-89906-809-X) Mesorah Pubns.

Sears, Dovid. The Captured Tzaddik: A Tale of the Baalshem Tov Father. Sears, Dovid, illus. 71p. (gr. 7-10). 1990. 9.00 (0-940118-50-5) Moznaim.

Sears, Jeanne. Danger-Watch Out! Cohen, Dorothy P., illus. 12p. (ps-3). 1988. pap. 1.95 (0-9621086-0-X) J Sears.

Sears, Nancy, illus. Farm Animals. LC 77-70863. (ps-3). 1977. 8.99 (0-394-83541-7) Random Bks Yng Read.

Sears, Yvonne. Amber's Hallowe'en. Sears, Yvonne, illus. LC 87-90131. 36p. (gr. 2-5). 1988. 12.95 (0-9618803-0-9) Y-Knot.

Seaver, James E. A Narrative of the Life of Mrs. Mary Jemison. Abrams, George, intro. by. 196p. 1990. pap. text ed. 12.95x (0-8156-2491-3) Syracuse U Pr.

Sebarg, R. & Zakutinsky, Adina. Torah Shapes. Feld, Goldie, illus. 12p. (ps). 1987. 4.95 (0-911643-08-7) Aura Bklyn.

Sebastian, John. J.B.'s Harmonica. LC 91-35841. (ps-3). 1993. 13.95 (0-15-240091-5) HarBrace.

Sebesta, Judith L. The Etruscans. (Illus.). 94p. (Orig.). (gr. 9-12). 1992. pap. 13.20 spiral bdg. (0-939507-37-4, B422) Amer Classical.

Sebestyen, Ouida. Far from Home. 192p. (gr. 7 up). 1980. 15.95 (0-316-77932-6, Joy St Bks) Little.
—Far from Home. 208p. (gr. 7 up). 1983. pap. 2.95 (0-440-92640-8, LFL) Dell.
—The Girl in the Box: The Diary of Anne Frank. 160p. (gr. 7 up). 1988. 12.95 (0-316-77935-0, Joy St Bks) Little.
—IOU's. (gr. 7 up). 1986. pap. 2.75 (0-440-93986-0, LFL) Dell.
—On Fire. 208p. (gr. 6 up). 1985. 12.45 (0-87113-010-6, Joy St Bks) Little.
—On Fire. 192p. 1987. pap. 2.95 (0-553-26862-7, Starfire) Bantam.
—Out of Nowhere. (gr. 5 up). 1994. 14.95 (0-531-06839-0); lib. bdg. 14.99 RLB (0-531-08689-5) Orchard Bks Watts.
—Words by Heart. 144p. (gr. 4-8). 1983. pap. 3.99 (0-553-27179-2, Starfire) Bantam.
—Words by Heart. LC 78-27847. (gr. 5 up). 1979. 15.95 (0-316-77931-8, Joy St Bks) Little.

Sebranek & Kemper. Revising & Editing One: A Program of Revising & Editing & Strategies to Accompany Writers Inc. 92p. (Orig.). (gr. 9-10). 1991. pap. 3.95 wkbk. (0-939045-50-8); tchr's. ed. 3.95 (0-939045-55-9); reproducible set 39.95 (0-939045-58-3) Write Source.
—Revising & Editing Two: A Program of Revising & Editing Activities & Strategies to Accompany Writers Inc. 92p. (Orig.). (gr. 11-12). 1991. pap. 3.95 wkbk. (0-939045-51-6); tchr's. ed. 3.95 (0-939045-56-7); reproducible set 39.95 (0-939045-59-1) Write Source.

Sebranek, et al. Write Source Two Thousand: A Guide to Writing, Thinking, & Learning. Krenzke, Chris, illus. 400p. (Orig.). (gr. 4-9). 1990. text ed. 11.95 (0-939045-34-6); pap. text ed. 9.95 (0-939045-33-8); tchr's. ed., 116p. 9.95 (0-939045-52-4) Write Source.
—Writers Inc: A Guide to Writing, Thinking, & Learning. 2nd ed. Krenzke, Chris, illus. 360p. (gr. 9 up). 1990. text ed. 10.95 (0-939045-49-4); pap. text ed. 8.95 (0-939045-48-6); Inc Sights, 94p. tchr's. ed. 7.95 (0-939045-32-X) Write Source.

Sebranek, Patrick. Computer Folder. (Illus.). (gr. 7-12). 1984. pap. text ed. 0.95x (0-9605312-9-7) Write Source.

Sebranek, Patrick & Meyer, Verne. Basic English Revisited: A Student Handbook. 5th ed. LC 80-68894. (Illus.). (gr. 7-12). 1985. text ed. 8.95 (0-9605312-1-1); pap. text ed. 7.95 (0-9605312-0-3) Write Source.
—Punctuation Pockets: A Student Folder. (Illus.). (gr. 7-12). 1984. pap. text ed. 0.95x (0-9605312-8-9) Write Source.

Sebranek, Patrick, et al. The Write Source: A Student Handbook. Krenzke, Chris, illus. 304p. (gr. 4-8). 1987. 8.95 (0-939045-02-8); text ed. 8.95 (0-685-18820-5); pap. text ed. 5.95 (0-939045-03-6) Write Source.

Secanell, Jose M., tr. see Puncel, Maria & Basquez, Juan J.

Seco, Nina. The Life of St. Nina. Duckworth, Ruth, illus. (Orig.). (ps-1). 1991. pap. 6.00 (0-913026-28-X) St Nectarios.

Seco, Nina & Pilutik, Anastasia D. Saints Adrian & Natalie. Duckworth, Ruth, illus. (Orig.). (ps-1). 1991. pap. write for info. (0-913026-29-8) St Nectarios.

Seco, Nina, et al. A Cloud of Witnesses Series. Duckworth, Ruth, illus. (Orig.). (ps-1). 1991. pap. write for info. (0-913026-27-1) St Nectarios.

Seco, Nina S. The Life of St. Nicholas: A Cloud of Witnesses, Vol. 3. Duckworth, Ruch, illus. (Orig.). (gr. k-3). 1993. pap. 6.00 (0-913026-36-0) St Nectarios.

Seddon, Sue & Gilgallon, Barbara. Family Matters: Travel Games. (Illus.). 96p. (gr. 2-10). 1993. pap. 4.95 (0-7063-7093-7, Pub. by Ward Lock UK) Sterling.

Seddon, Sue, jt. auth. see Gilgallon, Barbara.

Seddon, Tony & Bailey, Jill. Living World. LC 86-16800. (Illus.). 160p. (gr. 3 up). 1987. pap. 12.95 (0-385-23754-5) Doubleday.
—Physical World. LC 87-6855. (Illus.). 160p. (gr. 3 up). 1987. 12.95 (0-385-24179-8) Doubleday.

Seddon, Tony, jt. auth. see Bailey, Jill.

Sedeen, Margaret, ed. see Gallant, Roy A.

Sedita, Joan. Landmark Study Skills Guide. LC 89-27870. (Orig.). (gr. 4-12). 1989. pap. text ed. 15.00 (0-9624119-0-6) Landmark Found.

Seebo, Donna D. God's Kiss: Mrs. Seebo's Fables. 32p. 1993. incl. cassette 19.95 (1-883164-01-X) Cassette (1-883164-02-8) Delphi Intl.

Seed, Deborah. Water Science. (Illus.). (gr. 2-7). 1992. pap. 8.61 (0-201-57778-X) Addison-Wesley.

Seed, Jenny. Ntombi's Song. Berry, Anno, illus. LC 88-39522. 48p. (gr. k-3). 1989. lib. bdg. 14.95 (0-8070-8318-6, NL6) Beacon Pr.

Seed, Suzanne. Saturday's Child. Seed, Suzanne, illus. LC 72-12599. (gr. 6-12). 1973. PLB 8.95 (0-87955-803-2); pap. 6.95 (0-87955-203-4) O'Hara.

Seeger, Pete. Abiyoyo. Hays, Michael, illus. LC 93-25730. 48p. 1994. pap. 4.95 (0-689-71810-1, Aladdin) Macmillan Child Grp.
—Abiyoyo: Based on a South African Lullaby & Folk Story. Hays, Michael, illus. LC 85-15341. 48p. (ps-4). 1985. RSBE 15.95 (0-02-781490-4, Macmillan Child Bk) Macmillan Child Grp.

Seeger, Ruth C. American Folk Songs for Children. Cooney, Barbara, illus. 192p. (gr. k-12). 1980. pap. 12.00 (0-385-15788-6, Zephyr-BFYR) Doubleday.
—Animal Folk Songs for Children. Cooney, Barbara, illus. LC 92-767692. 90p. (gr. 1-6). 1992. PLB 22.50 (0-208-02364-X, Pub. by Linnet); pap. 13.95 (0-208-02365-8, Pub. by Linnet) Shoe String.

Seek, Vesta. Danger for Old Ruff. Wilson, Deborah G., illus. 32p. (ps-2). 1991. pap. 4.49 (1-55513-360-6, 33605, Chariot Bks) Cook.
—Old Ruff & the Mother Bird. Wilson, Deborah G., illus. 32p. (ps-2). 1991. pap. 4.49 (1-55513-361-4, 33613, Chariot Bks) Cook.

Seeley, Laura L. The Book of Shadowboxes: A Story of the ABC's. Seeley, Laura L., illus. 64p. (ps-3). 1990. 16.95 (0-934601-65-8) Peachtree Pubs.
—The Magical Moonballs. LC 92-16698. 1992. 16.95 (1-56145-063-4) Peachtree Pubs.

Seeley, Mae. I am a Try-Frog, Vol. 4. Clarkson, Doris, illus. 32p. (ps-2). 1990. 4.95 (0-9624309-3-5) MYLAC Pub Co.
—I Am My Own Cheerleader. 32p. (ps-8). 1989. 4.95g (0-9624309-1-9) MYLAC Pub Co.
—I am Unique, Vol. 3. Clarkson, Doris, illus. 32p. (ps-2). 1990. 4.95 (0-9624309-2-7) MYLAC Pub Co.

Seelig, Tina L. Incredible Edible Science: The Amazing Things That Happen When You Cook. Brunelle, Lynn, illus. LC 93-33480. 1994. write for info. (0-7167-6501-2, Sci Am Yng Rdrs); pap. write for info. (0-7167-6507-1) W H Freeman.

Seevers, James. Space. rev. ed. LC 87-20801. (Illus.). 48p. (gr. 2-6). 1987. PLB 18.64 (0-8172-3260-5) Raintree Steck-V.

Sefkow, Paula & Berger, Helen. All Children Create: Levels Four to Six, an Elementary Art Curriculum, Vol. II. Gutek, Rob, illus. LC 80-82018. 204p. (Orig.). (gr. 4-6). 1981. pap. 24.95x (0-918452-25-2) Learning Pubns.
—All Children Create: Levels One to Three, an Elementary Art Curriculum, Vol. I. Gutek, Rob, illus. LC 80-82018. 204p. (gr. 1-3). 1981. pap. 24.95 (0-918452-24-4) Learning Pubns.

Sefton, Catherine. Along a Lonely Road. large type ed. 1993. 15.95 (0-7451-1909-3, Galaxy Child Lrg Print) Chivers N Amer.
—Island of the Strangers. LC 85-5437. 118p. (gr. 3-7). 1985. 12.95 (0-15-239100-2, HB Juv Bks) HarBrace.

Segal. Flying Moose. 1993. 14.95 (0-8050-1591-4) H Holt & Co.

Segal, Abraham. One People: A Study in Comparative Judaism. Zlotowitz, Bernard M., ed. 160p. (Orig.). (gr. 7-9). 1983. pap. text ed. 6.95 (0-8074-0169-2, 140025) UAHC.
Segal, Abraham, jt. auth. see Charry, Elias.
Segal, Bertha E. Aprendemos el Espanol por Medio de Accion. (SPA). 106p. (Orig.). (gr. 3-12). 1987. pap. text ed. 12.50 (0-938395-12-2) B Segal.
—Deutschunterricht Durch Handelh. 2nd ed. (GER.). 153p. (ps-12). 1984. Repr. of 1984 ed. tchr's. ed. 16.99 (0-938395-04-1) B Segal.
—L' Enseignement du Francais au Moyen de l'Action. Raileanu, Lia, tr. from ENG. (FRE.). 153p. (ps-12). 1983. tchr's. ed. 16.99 (0-938395-03-3) B Segal.
—Ensenando el Espanol por Medio de Accion. 3rd ed. Hatter, Mari, tr. from ENG. (SPA). 153p. (ps-12). 1982. tchr's. ed. 16.99 (0-938395-02-5) B Segal.
—Teaching English Through Action. 5th ed. 153p. (ps-12). 1987. tchr's. ed. 16.99 (0-938395-00-9) B Segal.
—We Learn English Through Action. 106p. (gr. 3-12). 1987. 12.50 (0-938395-11-4) B Segal.
Segal, Elizabeth, jt. auth. see Kimmel, Margaret M.
Segal, Jerry. The Place Where Nobody Stopped. Pilkey, Dav, illus. LC 90-43016. 160p. (gr. 6-8). 1991. 14.95 (0-531-05897-2); PLB 14.99 (0-531-08497-3) Orchard Bks Watts.
Segal, Lore. All the Way Home. Marshall, James, illus. 32p. (ps up). 1988. pap. 3.95 (0-374-40355-4) FS&G.
—The Book of Adam to Moses. Baskin, Leonard, illus. LC 87-2581. 144p. (gr. k up). 1987. lib. bdg. 14.99 (0-394-96757-7) Knopf Bks Yng Read.
—The Story of King Saul & King David. LC 90-52544. (Illus.). 144p. 1991. 19.50 (0-8052-4088-8) Pantheon.
—The Story of Mrs. Lovewright & Purrless Her Cat. reissued ed. Zelinsky, Paul, illus. LC 84-25011. 40p. (ps up). 1993. 14.00 (0-394-86817-X) Knopf Bks Yng Read.
—Tell Me a Mitzi. Pincus, Harriet, illus. LC 69-14980. 40p. (ps-3). 1982. 17.00 (0-374-37392-2) FS&G.
—Tell Me a Mitzi. LC 69-14980. (Illus.). 40p. (ps-3). 1991. pap. 5.95 (0-374-47502-4) FS&G.
—Tell Me a Trudy. Wells, Rosemary, illus. LC 77-24123. 40p. (ps-3). 1977. 15.00 (0-374-37395-7) FS&G.
—Tell Me a Trudy. Wells, Rosemary, illus. (ps up). 1989. pap. 4.95 (0-374-47504-0) FS&G.
Segal, Sheila F. Joshua's Dream: A Journey to the Land of Israel. Iskowitz, Joel, illus. LC 91-45513. (gr. k-3). 1992. 10.95 (0-8074-0476-4, 101062) UAHC.
Segal, Yocheved. Our Sages Showed me the Way, Vol. 4. (gr. 4-7). 1988. 11.95 (0-87306-452-6) Feldheim.
Segaloff, Nat & Erickson, Paul. Fish Tales. LC 89-26279. (Illus.). 32p. 1990. 12.95 (0-8069-7322-6); PLB 15.69 (0-8069-7323-4) Sterling.
—A Reef Comes to Life: Creating an Undersea Exhibit. (Illus.). 48p. (gr. 5-7). 1991. 14.95 (0-531-15216-2); PLB 14.90 (0-531-10994-1) Watts.
Segan, Eleanor. How to Write Right, No. 1: From Lists to Letters. (Illus.). 96p. (gr. 7-12). 1986. pap. 5.75 (0-941342-15-8, 2115) Entry Pub.
—How to Write Right, No. 2: Forms & More. (Illus.). 64p. (gr. 7-12). 1986. pap. 4.40 (0-941342-16-6, 2116) Entry Pub.
Segel, Elizabeth. Short Takes. (gr. 4-7). 1992. pap. 3.99 (0-440-40581-5) Dell.
—Short Takes: A Collection of Short Stories. Smith, Joseph A., illus. 160p. (gr. 9 up). 1986. 12.95 (0-688-06092-7) Lothrop.
Seger, Doris. Children of the Bible. Butcher, Sam & Geraldo, Esteban, illus. 64p. (gr. k-6). 1967. pap. text ed. 8.99 (1-55976-028-1) CEF Press.
Seger, Doris, jt. auth. see Mouillesseaux, Claire.
Seger, Doris L. Another Birthday. (Illus.). 18p. (gr. k-6). 1988. pap. text ed. 4.25 (1-55976-134-2) CEF Press.
Segnit, Clare & Segnit, Jack. The Ugly Duckling: A Classic Pop-up Storybook. Segnit, Clare & Segnit, Jack, illus. 12p. (ps-3). 1993. bds. 14.95 (0-689-71722-9, Aladdin) Macmillan Child Grp.
Segnit, Jack, jt. auth. see Segnit, Clare.
Segraves, Daniel. Hair Length in the Bible: A Study of First Corinthians 11: 2-16. LC 89-37912. 80p. (Orig.). 1989. pap. 5.99 (0-932581-57-9) Word Aflame.
Segraves, Judy. The Marriage-Go-Round: Practical Guidelines for a Successful Marriage. Agnew, Tim, illus. LC 90-30558. 138p. (Orig.). 1990. pap. 5.99 (0-932581-64-1) Word Aflame.
Seguin, Marilyn. Song of Courage, Song of Freedom: The Story of Mary Campbell. (Illus.). 120p. (Orig.). (gr. 4-9). 1993. pap. 12.95 (0-8283-1952-9) Branden Pub Co.
Segur, C. Les Malheurs de Sophie. Castelli, H., illus. (FRE.). 220p. (gr. 5-10). 1988. pap. 9.95 (2-07-033496-1) Schoenhof.
Segur, de see De Segur.
Sehlin, Gunhild. Mary's Little Donkey: A Christmas Story for Young Children. Latham, Hugh & Mackan, Donald, trs. Verheijn, Jan, illus. (SWE.). 157p. (gr. 3-6). 1992. pap. 10.95 (0-86315-064-0, Pub. by Floris Bks UK) Gryphon Hse.
Seib, Philip. Getting Elected. La Freniere, Annette, ed. Fuchs, Diane & Mohle, Flay, illus. LC 86-14999. 69p. (Orig.). (gr. 4 up). 1986. pap. 3.95 (0-937460-24-9) Hendrick-Long.
Seibert, Patricia. Mush! Across Alaska in the World's Longest Sled-Dog Race. Ellis, Jan D., illus. LC 91-38883. 32p. (gr. 2-4). 1992. PLB 14.90 (1-56294-053-8) Millbrook Pr.
—Mush! Across Alaska in the World's Longest Sled-dog Race! (gr. 4-7). 1992. pap. 4.95 (0-395-64537-9) HM.

Seibert, Roberta. The Leafing Page. 24p. (Orig.). 1992. pap. 5.95 (0-938911-04-X) Indiv Educ Syst.
Seibold, J. Otto, jt. auth. see Walsh, Vivian.
Seidel, Jennifer R. Jaeger Finds a Family. 40p. (gr. 3-4). 1992. 7.95 (1-880851-03-2) Greene Bark Pr.
Seidelin, Anna S. Danish Fairy Tales & Rhymes for Children & Adults: Folke Eventyr Og Remse. Zucker, William V., tr. from DAN. Brande, Marlie, illus. 147p. (Orig.). 1992. pap. 15.00 (0-9634440-1-8) Lester St Pub.
Seiden, Art. Michael Shows off Baltimore. Seiden, Art, illus. 32p. (gr. 1-5). 1982. 5.95 (0-942806-01-8) Outdoor Bks.
Seidenberg, Steven. Ecology & Conservation. LC 89-11281. (Illus.). 64p. (gr. 4-6). 1990. PLB 19.93 (0-8368-0005-2) Gareth Stevens Inc.
—Fuel & Energy. LC 90-23743. (Illus.). 64p. (gr. 4-6). 1991. PLB 19.93 (0-8368-0052-4) Gareth Stevens Inc.
Seidenberg, Steven, jt. auth. see Hogan, Paula.
Seidl, Herman. Mountain Bikes: Maintaining, Repairing & Upgrading. LC 92-18773. (Illus.). 128p. (gr. 4 up). 1992. 16.95 (0-8069-8764-2) Sterling.
—Mountain Bikes: Maintaining, Repairing & Upgrading. (Illus.). 128p. (gr. 10-12). 1993. pap. 10.95 (0-8069-8765-0) Sterling.
Seidler, Ann & Slepian, Jan. The Cat Who Wore a Pot on Her Head. Martin, Richard E., illus. 32p. (gr. k-3). 1987. pap. 3.95 (0-590-43708-9) Scholastic Inc.
Seidler, Ann, jt. auth. see Slepian, Jan.
Seidler, Babara. The Legend of King Piast. Kedron, Jane, tr. Rosinski, Grzegorz, illus. (gr. 2-8). 1977. pap. 1.00 (0-917004-08-6) Kosciuszko.
Seidler, Tor. A Rat's Tale. Marcellino, Fred, illus. 187p. (gr. 1-8). 1986. 16.00 (0-374-36185-1) FS&G.
—The Tar Pit. LC 87-74338. 160p. 1987. 14.00 (0-374-37383-3) FS&G.
—The Tar Pit. 160p. 1991. pap. 3.95 (0-374-47452-4) FS&G.
—Terpin. LC 82-11734. 96p. (gr. 7 up). 1982. 12.00 (0-374-37413-9) FS&G.
—The Wainscott Weasel. Marcellino, Fred, illus. LC 92-54526. 200p. (gr. 2 up). 1993. 20.00 (0-06-205032-X); PLB 19.89 (0-06-205033-8) HarpC Child Bks.
Seidler, Tor, retold by see Andersen, Hans Christian.
Seidletz, Marcia. Easy Spanish Word Power Games: Early Intermediate to Advanced. (SPA). 80p. 1993. pap. 4.95 (0-685-62805-1, F7246-9, Natl Textbk) NTC Pub Grp.
—Spanish Word Games for Beginners: Early Intermediate to Advanced. (SPA). 80p. 1993. pap. 11.95 (0-685-62804-3, F7191-8, Natl Textbk) NTC Pub Grp.
Seidman, Laurence I. Once in the Saddle: The Cowboy's Frontier 1866-1896. (Illus.). 160p. 1990. 16.95x (0-8160-2373-5) Facts on File.
Seif, Charles R. Making Birdhouses & Feeders. LC 85-8654. 128p. (Orig.). (gr. 10-12). 1985. pap. 9.95 (0-8069-6244-5) Sterling.
Seigel, Barbara & Seigel, Scott. Dark Fire. Greenberg, Ann, ed. 176p. (Orig.). 1992. pap. 2.99 (0-671-70906-2) PB.
Seigel, Scott, jt. auth. see Seigel, Barbara.
Seigel, Scott, jt. auth. see Seigel, Barbara.
Seiger, Barbara. Seeing Stars: A Book & Poster about the Constellations. Calsbeek, Craig, illus. LC 92-43199. 24p. (gr. 2-6). 1993. pap. 7.95 (0-448-40198-3, G&D) Putnam Pub Group.
Seignolle, Claude, jt. auth. see Kergueno, Jacqueline.
Seiji Horibuchi, ed. see Masaomi Kanzaki.
Seiler, Beth. Phonics Fun Crossword Puzzles. (Illus.). 48p. (gr. k-3). 1987. pap. 2.95 (0-8431-1920-9) Price Stern.
Seims, Tom. Miracles & Wonders. Arbuckle, Scott, illus. 32p. (Orig.). 1993. 7.99 (1-56476-046-4, Victor Books) SP Pubns.
—People & Places. Arbuckle, Scott, illus. 32p. (Orig.). 1993. 7.99 (1-56476-047-2, Victor Books) SP Pubns.
Seitz, Eileen. The Message of the White Unicorn. Seitz, Eileen, illus. LC 87-50260. 35p. (Orig.). (gr. 3-5). 1987. pap. 8.95 (1-55523-057-1) Winston-Derek.
Seixas, Judith. Allergies--What They Are, What They Do. Huffman, Tom, illus. LC 90-30753. 56p. (gr. 1 up). 1991. 12.95 (0-688-09638-7); PLB 12.88 (0-688-08877-5) Greenwillow.
—Tobacco: What It Is, What It Does. LC 81-837. 56p. (Orig.). (gr. 3-6). 1981. 13.95 (0-688-00769-4) Greenwillow.
Seixas, Judith S. Alcohol-What It Is, What It Does. Huffman, Tom, illus. LC 76-43344. 56p. (gr. 1-4). 1977. o.s.i 8.50 (0-688-80080-7, Mulberry); PLB 11.88 (0-688-84080-9, Mulberry) Morrow.
—Alcohol: What It Is, What It Does. (ps-3). 1981. pap. 6.95 (0-688-00462-8, Mulberry) Morrow.
—Drugs--What They Are, What They Do. Huffman, Tom, illus. LC 86-33624. 48p. (gr. 1-4). 1987. 12.95 (0-688-07399-9); lib. bdg. 12.88 (0-688-07400-6) Greenwillow.
—Drugs: What They Are, What They Do. Huffman, Tom, illus. LC 86-33624. 48p. 1991. pap. 4.95 (0-688-10487-8, Mulberry) Morrow.
—Junk Food--What It Is, What It Does. Huffman, Tom, illus. LC 83-14135. 48p. (gr. 1-3). 1984. 12.95 (0-688-02559-5); PLB 12.88 (0-688-02560-9) Greenwillow.
—Living with a Parent Who Drinks Too Much. LC 78-11108. 128p. (gr. 3-6). 1979. 12.95 (0-688-80196-X); PLB 11.88 (0-688-84196-1) Greenwillow.

—Living with a Parent Who Drinks Too Much. LC 78-11108. 112p. (gr. 4-6). 1991. pap. 3.95 (0-688-10493-2, Pub. by Beech Tree Bks) Morrow.
—Living with a Parent Who Takes Drugs. LC 89-1995. 96p. 1989. 13.95 (0-688-08627-6) Greenwillow.
—Tobacco: What It Is, What It Does. Huffman, Tom, illus. LC 81-837. 56p. (gr. 1-3). 1981. 12.95 (0-685-42145-7, Mulberry); (Mulberry) Morrow.
—Vitamins - What They Are, What They Do. Juffman, Tom, illus. LC 85-17761. 56p. (gr. 1-4). 1986. 12.95 (0-688-06065-X); PLB 12.93 (0-688-06066-8) Greenwillow.
—Water- What It Is, What It Does. Huffman, Tom, illus. LC 86-14926. 56p. (gr. 1-4). 1987. 12.95 (0-688-06607-0); lib. bdg. 12.88 (0-688-06608-9) Greenwillow.
Sekido, Isamu, photos by & text by. Fruit, Roots, & Fungi: Plants We Eat. LC 92-19958. (Illus.). 1993. 17. 50 (0-8225-2902-5) Lerner Pubns.
Selberg, Ingrid. Nature's Hidden World. Miller, Andrew, illus. 14p. (gr. k-2). 1984. 13.95 (0-399-20973-5, Philomel) Putnam Pub Group.
—Our Changing World: A Moving Parts Book. Miller, Andrew, illus. 12p. (ps-8). 1992. 12.95 (0-399-20869-0, Philomel Bks) Putnam Pub Group.
—Secrets of the Deep. Fogelman, Phyllis J., ed. McGuiness, Doreen, illus. 12p. (gr. 1-5). 1990. 14.95 (0-8037-0766-5) Dial Bks Young.
—Secrets of the Pond. Rapoport, Roger, ed. McGuinness, Doreen, illus. 12p. (gr. 1-6). 1993. text ed. 16.95g (0-9636161-0-2, Wetlands) RDR Bks.
Selberg, Ingrid, tr. see Svedberg, Ulf.
Selby, Anna. Spain. LC 93-28438. 1993. write for info. (0-8114-1848-0) Raintree Steck-V.
Selden, Bernice. The Story of Annie Sullivan, Helen Keller's Teacher. (Orig.). (gr. k-6). 1987. pap. 3.25 (0-440-48285-2, YB) Dell.
Selden, Bernice, adapted by see Melville, Herman.
Selden, George. Chester Cricket's New Home. Williams, Garth, illus. LC 82-24206. 144p. (gr. 4 up). 1983. 15. 00 (0-374-31240-0) FS&G.
—Chester Cricket's New Home. Williams, Garth, illus. 144p. (gr. 3 up). 1984. pap. 3.50 (0-440-41246-3, YB) Dell.
—Chester Cricket's Pigeon Ride. Williams, Garth, illus. 80p. (gr. 2-6). 1983. pap. 3.25 (0-440-41389-3, YB) Dell.
—Cricket in Times Square. Williams, Garth, illus. (gr. 2-7). 1970. pap. 3.99 (0-440-41563-2, YB) Dell.
—The Cricket in Times Square. Williams, Garth, illus. LC 60-12640. 160p. (gr. 4 up). 1960. 15.00 (0-374-31650-3) FS&G.
—Cricket in Times Square. (gr. 4-7). 1993. pap. 1.99 (0-440-21622-2) Dell.
—El Grillo en Times Square: The Cricket in Times Square. Longshaw, Robin, tr. Williams, Garth, illus. (SPA). 160p. (gr. 3-7). 1992. 15.00 (0-374-32790-4, Mirasol) FS&G.
—Harry Cat's Pet Puppy. 176p. (gr. 2-6). 1975. pap. 3.50 (0-440-45647-9, YB) Dell.
—Harry Cat's Pet Puppy. Williams, Garth, illus. LC 74-12436. 160p. (gr. 3 up). 1974. 15.00 (0-374-32856-0) FS&G.
—Harry Kitten & Tucker Mouse. Williams, Garth, illus. LC 83-16530. 64p. (gr. 2-5). 1986. 14.00 (0-374-32860-9) FS&G.
—Harry Kitten & Tucker Mouse. (gr. k-6). 1989. pap. 3.50 (0-440-40124-0, YB) Dell.
—The Old Meadow. Williams, Garth, illus. 192p. (gr. 3-7). 1987. 15.00 (0-374-35616-5) FS&G.
—Tucker's Countryside. Williams, Garth, illus. LC 69-14975. 176p. (gr. 3 up). 1969. 16.00 (0-374-37854-1) FS&G.
Selden, Kyoko, tr. see Honda, Maasaki.
Selden, Kyoko, tr. see Suzuki, Shinichi.
Selden, N., et al. Sprint Library Two: Replacement Components. large type ed. Incl. Flood. 68p. 1981. 12. 16 (0-317-04584-9, 4-23000-00); The Ghost of the Dutchman. 68p. 1981. 12.16 (0-317-02603-8, 4-23010-00); The Homesteaders. 68p. 1981. 12.16 (0-317-02604-6, 4-23020-00); Sam, Where Are You? 68p. 1981. 12.16 (0-317-02605-4, 4-23030-00); The Thirteenth Floor. 68p. 1981. 12.16 (0-317-02606-2, 4-23040-00); Teacher's Guide. 20p. 1981. 5.24 (0-317-02607-0, 4-24270-00). 1981. Repr. of 1974 ed. Am Printing Hse.
Seldon, George. The Cricket in Times Square. large type ed. 192p. 1990. Repr. PLB 15.95 (1-55736-170-3, Crnrstn Bks) BDD LT Grp.
—Tucker's Countryside. (gr. k-6). 1989. pap. 3.50 (0-440-40248-4, YB) Dell.
Selenick, Laurence. Cavalcade of Clowns. (gr. 1-9). 1992. pap. 3.95 (0-88388-042-3) Bellerophon Bks.
Self, Charles. One Hundred One Quick & Easy Woodworking Projects. LC 92-25310. (Illus.). 160p. (gr. 10-12). 1992. pap. 12.95 (0-8069-8298-5) Sterling.
Self, Kathy A., ed. see Ringling Bros. & Barnum & Bailey Combined Shows, Inc. Staff.
Self, Margaret, ed. One Hundred Fifty-Eight Things to Make. (Orig.). (gr. 1-6). 1971. pap. 4.99 (0-8307-0078-1, 5002605) Regal.
Self, Margaret, compiled by. Two Hundred Two Things to Do. LC 68-16267. (Illus., Orig.). (gr. k-2). 1968. pap. 4.99 (0-8307-0026-9, 5001102) Regal.
Selfridge, John W. Mikhail Gorbachev. (Illus.). 72p. (gr. 3-5). 1991. lib. bdg. 12.95 (0-7910-1567-X) Chelsea Hse.

—Pablo Picasso: Spanish Painter. LC 93-19205. (Illus.). (ps-3). 1993. PLB 18.95 (0-7910-1777-X, Am Art Analog); pap. write for info. (0-7910-1996-9) Chelsea Hse.

Selig, Syvie, jt. auth. see Turin, Adela.

Seligman, C. Dee. Texas Women: Legends in Their Own Time. LC 89-1731. (Illus.). 112p. (gr. 4 up) 1989. pap. 14.95 (0-937460-59-1) Hendrick-Long.

Seligson, Marcia. Dolphins at Grassy Key. Ancona, George, illus. LC 88-27143. 48p. (gr. 1 up) 1989. RSBE 15.95 (0-02-781800-4, Macmillan Child Bk) Macmillan Child Grp.

Seligson, Susan. Amos: The Story of an Old Dog & His Couch. Schneider, Howie, illus. (ps-3) 1992. pap. 4.95 (0-316-78034-0, Joy St Bks) Little.

Seligson, Susan, jt. auth. see Schneider, Howie.

Selleck, Jack. Contrast: A Design Principle. LC 75-21110. (Illus.). 80p. (gr. 7-12). 1975. 10.95 (0-87192-074-3) Davis Mass.

Selleck, Richelle R. Take-Home Stories. 96p. (ps-2). 1990. 9.95 (0-86653-567-5, GA1169) Good Apple.

Seller, Mick. Air, Wind, & Flight. LC 92-374. 1992. 12. 40 (0-531-17375-5, Gloucester Pr) Watts.
—Sound, Noise & Music. LC 92-33923. (Illus.). 32p. (gr. 5-8). 1993. PLB 12.40 (0-531-17408-5, Gloucester Pr) Watts.
—Wheels, Pulleys & Levers. (Illus.). 32p. (gr. 5-7). 1993. PLB 12.40 (0-531-17420-4, Gloucester Pr) Watts.

Sellon, Jeffrey, jt. auth. see DAvidson, Patricia.

Sellon, Jeffrey, jt. auth. see Dickens, Estelle.

Sells, Carole G. Rainbow Dragon: Lessons in Basic Values. Zellers, Toby, illus. Guese, Raymond F., intro. by. (Illus.). 34p. (Orig.). (ps-6). 1988. pap. 3.95 (0-926739-00-X) Sells Pub.

Sellwood, Colin. How to Have Fun & Play Better Soccer: PS-6 to PS-12. LC 90-84973. (Illus.). 112p. 1991. pap. 9.95 (0-932881-11-4) Greenpl Bks.

Selsam, Millicent. How to Be a Nature Detective. Donnelly, Marlene H., illus. LC 93-28523. 1995. write for info. (0-06-023447-4); PLB write for info. (0-06-023448-2) HarpC Child Bks.

Selsam, Millicent & Hunt, Joyce. Animal Mixups. Wallner, John, illus. LC 91-16114. 32p. (ps-2). 1992. RSBE 13.95 (0-02-778081-3, Macmillan Child Bk) Macmillan Child Grp.

Selsam, Millicent E. Backyard Insects. Goor, Ronald, photos by. 40p. (ps-3). 1988. pap. 2.95 (0-590-42256-1) Scholastic Inc.
—Cotton. Wexler, Jerome, illus. LC 82-6496. 48p. (gr. k-3). 1982. 12.95 (0-688-01499-2); lib. bdg. 14.88 (0-688-01500-X, Morrow Jr Bks) Morrow Jr Bks.
—Egg to Chick. rev. ed. Wolff, Barbara, illus. LC 74-85034. 64p. (ps-3). 1970. PLB 13.89 (0-06-025290-1) HarpC Child Bks.
—Egg to Chick. Wolff, Barbara, illus. LC 74-85034. 64p. (gr. k-3). 1987. pap. 3.50 (0-06-444113-X, Trophy) HarpC Child Bks.
—A First Look at Leaves. Selsam, Millicent E. & Hunt, Joyce, eds. Springer, Harriett, illus. LC 72-81376. 32p. (gr. 2-4). 1972. PLB 11.85 (0-8027-6118-6) Walker & Co.
—A First Look at Poisonous Snakes. 32p. (gr. 1-4). 1987. 11.95 (0-8027-6681-1); PLB 12.85 (0-8027-6683-8) Walker & Co.
—Greg's Microscope. Lobel, Arnold, illus. LC 63-8002. 64p. (gr. k-3). 1963. PLB 13.89 (0-06-025296-0) HarpC Child Bks.
—Greg's Microscope. Lobel, Arnold, illus. LC 63-8002. 64p. (gr. k-3). 1990. pap. 3.50 (0-06-444144-X, Trophy) HarpC Child Bks.
—How Kittens Grow. 1992. pap. 2.50 (0-590-44784-X) Scholastic Inc.
—How Puppies Grow. Johnson, Neil, photos by. (Illus.). 32p. (ps-3). 1990. pap. 2.50 (0-590-42736-9) Scholastic Inc.
—Is This a Baby Dinosaur? & Other Science Picture Puzzles. LC 72-76508. (Illus.). 32p. (ps-3). 1972. PLB 13.89 (0-06-025303-7) HarpC Child Bks.
—Is This a Baby Dinosaur? & Other Science Picture Puzzles. LC 72-76508. (Illus.). 32p. (gr. k-3). 1984. pap. 4.95 (0-06-443054-5, Trophy) HarpC Child Bks.
—Mushrooms. Wexler, Jerome, photos by. LC 85-18953. (Illus.). 48p. (gr. 2-5). 1986. 12.95 (0-688-06248-2); (Morrow Jr Bks) Morrow Jr Bks.
—Terry & the Caterpillars. Lobel, Arnold, illus. LC 62-13309. 64p. (gr. k-3). 1962. PLB 11.89 (0-06-025406-8) HarpC Child Bks.
—Tree Flowers. Lerner, Carol, illus. LC 83-17353. 32p. (gr. 4 up). 1984. PLB 12.88 (0-688-02769-5) Morrow Jr Bks.
—Tyrannosaurus Rex. LC 77-25677. (Illus.). (gr. 3-5). 1978. PLB 12.89 (0-06-025424-6) HarpC Child Bks.

Selsam, Millicent E. & Hunt, Joyce. A First Look at Animals That Eat Other Animals. Springer, Harriet, illus. 64p. (gr. 5 up). 1990. 11.95 (0-8027-6895-4); PLB 12.85 (0-8027-6896-2) Walker & Co.
—A First Look at Animals with Backbones. Springer, Harriet, illus. LC 78-4321. (gr. k-3). 1978. 6.95 (0-8027-6338-3); PLB 9.85 (0-8027-6339-1) Walker & Co.
—A First Look at Animals with Horns. Springer, Harriett, illus. (gr. 1-4). 1989. 10.95 (0-8027-6871-7); PLB 11.85 (0-8027-6872-5) Walker & Co.
—A First Look at Animals Without Backbones. Springer, Harriett, illus. LC 76-12056. (gr. 2-4). 1976. PLB 9.85 (0-8027-6269-7) Walker & Co.

—A First Look at Bats. 32p. (gr. 1-3). 1991. 11.95 (0-8027-8135-7); PLB 12.85 (0-8027-8136-5) Walker & Co.
—A First Look at Birds. Springer, Harriet, illus. LC 73-81404. 32p. (gr. 2-4). 1973. PLB 12.85 (0-8027-6164-X) Walker & Co.
—First Look at Cats. Springer, Harriett, illus. LC 80-7673. 32p. (gr. 1-4). 1981. 7.95 (0-8027-6398-7); PLB 9.85 (0-8027-6399-5) Walker & Co.
—A First Look at Dinosaurs. Springer, Harriett, illus. 32p. (gr. 1-4). 1982. 7.95 (0-8027-6454-1); PLB 12.85 (0-8027-6456-8) Walker & Co.
—A First Look at Dogs. Springer, Harriett, tr. 32p. (gr. 1-4). 1981. 7.95 (0-8027-6409-6); lib. bdg. 9.85 (0-8027-6421-5) Walker & Co.
—A First Look at Ducks, Geese & Swans. Springer, Harriet, illus. 32p. (gr. 1-4). 1990. 11.95 (0-8027-6975-6); lib. bdg. 12.85 (0-8027-6976-4) Walker & Co.
—A First Look at Fish. Springer, Harriet, illus. LC 72-81377. 32p. (gr. 2-4). 1972. 5.50 (0-8027-6119-4); PLB 9.85 (0-8027-6120-8) Walker & Co.
—A First Look at Frogs, Toads & Salamanders. Spunger, Harriett, illus. 32p. (gr. 2-4). 1976. PLB 12.85 (0-8027-6244-1) Walker & Co.
—A First Look at Insects. Springer, Harriett, illus. LC 73-92451. 32p. (gr. 2-4). 1974. PLB 12.85 (0-8027-6182-8) Walker & Co.
—A First Look at Kangaroos, Kaolas & Other Animals with Pouches. Springer, Harriet, illus. LC 85-3126. 32p. (gr. k-3). 1985. 9.95 (0-8027-6600-5); PLB 12.85 (0-8027-6579-3) Walker & Co.
—First Look at Mammals. PLB 9.85 (0-8027-6142-9) Walker & Co.
—A First Look at Monkeys & Apes. Springer, Harriett, illus. LC 78-74164. (gr. 1-4). 1979. 7.95 (0-8027-6358-8); lib. bdg. 9.85 (0-8027-6359-6) Walker & Co.
—A First Look at Owls, Eagles, & Other Hunters of the Sky. Springer, Harriet, illus. 32p. (gr. 6-9). 1986. 10.95 (0-8027-6625-0); PLB 10.85 (0-8027-6642-0) Walker & Co.
—A First Look at Rocks. LC 83-40394. 32p. (gr. 1-4). 1984. PLB 12.85 (0-8027-6531-9) Walker & Co.
—A First Look at Seals, Sea Lions, & Walruses. Springer, Harriett, illus. LC 87-29491. 36p. (ps-3). 1988. pap. 10.95 (0-8027-6787-7); pap. text ed. 11.85 (0-8027-6788-5) Walker & Co.
—A First Look at Seashells. Springer, Hariett, illus. LC 83-5876. 32p. (gr. 1-3). 1983. PLB 12.85 (0-8027-6503-3) Walker & Co.
—A First Look at Snakes, Lizards & Other Reptiles. Springer, Harriet, illus. LC 74-26315. 32p. (gr. 1-4). 1975. PLB 12.85 (0-8027-6211-5) Walker & Co.
—A First Look at the World of Plants. Springer, Harriett, illus. LC 77-78088. (gr. 1-4). 1978. PLB 9.85 (0-8027-6299-9) Walker & Co.
—A First Look at Whales. (gr. k-3). 1980. PLB 12.85 (0-8027-6388-X) Walker & Co.
—Keep Looking! Chartier, Normand, illus. LC 88-1416. 32p. (gr. k-3). 1989. RSBE 14.95 (0-02-781840-3, Macmillan Child Bk) Macmillan Child Grp.

Selsam, Millicent E., ed. see Asimov, Isaac.

Selsam, Millicent E., et al. A First Look at Birds' Nest. Springer, Harriett, illus. LC 84-15238. 32p. (gr. 1-4). 1984. lib. bdg. 9.85 (0-8027-6565-3) Walker & Co.
—A First Look at Sharks. Springer, Harriet, illus. (gr. k-3). 1979. PLB 12.85 (0-8027-6373-1) Walker & Co.

Seltzer, Doryle P., jt. auth. see Barris, Sara L.

Seltzer, Isadore. The House I Live In: At Home in America. Seltzer, Isadore, illus. LC 91-27469. 32p. (gr. 1-5). 1992. RSBE 14.95 (0-02-781801-2, Macmillan Child Bk) Macmillan Child Grp.

Seltzer, Joan. Go for It! 62p. (gr. 5-12). 1981. pap. 5.95 (0-9607732-1-5); write for info. tchr's ed.; write for info. wkbk. Jory Pubns.

Seltzer, Meyer. Here Comes the Recycling Truck! Mathews, Judith, ed. Seltzer, Meyer, photos by. LC 91-37927. (Illus.). 32p. (ps-2). 1992. PLB 13.95 (0-8075-3235-5) A Whitman.
—Hide-&-Go Shriek Monster Riddles. Levine, Abby, ed. Seltzer, Meyer, illus. LC 89-49379. 32p. (gr. 1-4). 1990. PLB 8.95 (0-8075-3273-8) A Whitman.
—Petcetera: The Pet Riddle Book. Fay, Ann, ed. LC 88-21. (Illus.). 32p. (gr. 1-5). 1988. PLB 8.95 (0-8075-6515-6) A Whitman.

Seltzer, Richard & Smith, Kathy. The Lizard of Oz Playscript. (gr. 4-9). 1977. 2.50 (0-915232-04-9) B & R Samizdat.

Seltzer, Richard W., Jr. The Lizard of Oz. Couture, Christin, illus. LC 74-20172. 128p. (Orig.). (gr. 7 up). 1974. pap. 4.50 (0-915232-01-4) B & R Samizdat.
—Now & Then & Other Tales from Ome. Seltzer, Richard W., Jr., illus. LC 76-12138. (gr. 5). 1976. 4.50 (0-915232-03-0); pap. 1.95 (0-915232-02-2) B & R Samizdat.

Selway, Martina. Don't Forget to Write. Selway, Martina, illus. 32p. (ps-2). 1992. 12.95 (0-8249-8543-5, Ideals Child) Hambleton-Hill.
—Greedyguts. (Illus.). 32p. (ps-2). 1992. 16.95 (0-09-174151-3, Pub. by Hutchinson UK) Trafalgar.
—I Hate Roland Roberts. LC 93-30916. 1994. 12.95 (0-8249-8660-1); pap. 4.95 (0-8249-8675-X) Ideals.

Selznick, Brian. The Houdini Box. Selznick, Brian, illus. LC 90-5387. 64p. (gr. 1-6). 1991. 13.00 (0-679-81429-9); PLB 13.99 (0-679-91429-3) Knopf Bks Yng Read.

Semel, Nava. Becoming Gershona. Simckes, Seymour, tr. 128p. (gr. 4 up). 1990. 12.95 (0-670-83105-0) Viking Child Bks.
—Becoming Gershona. Simckes, Seymour, tr. from HEB. LC 92-20306. 160p. (gr. 5 up). 1992. pap. 4.50 (0-14-036071-9) Puffin Bks.
—Flying Lessons. Halkin, Hillel, tr. LC 93-10811. 1994. 14.00 (0-06-021470-8); PLB 13.89 (0-06-021471-6) HarpC Child Bks.

Semingson, Roberta, tr. see Scott, Kay & Shouse, Lucille.

Sempe, J. J., jt. auth. see Modiano, Patrick.

Sempe, Jean-Jacques. Chronicles of Little Nicholas. 1993. 13.00 (0-374-31275-3) FS&G.
—Marcellin Caillou. (FRE.). 162p. (gr. 5-10). 1990. pap. 8.95 (2-07-033561-5) Schoenhof.

Sempe, Jean-Jacques & Goscinny, R. Joachim a des Ennuis. (FRE.). 190p. (gr. 5-10). 1987. pap. 9.95 (2-07-033444-9) Schoenhof.
—Petit Nicolas. (FRE.). 156p. 1991. pap. 8.95 (2-07-036423-2) Schoenhof.
—Petit Nicolas et les Copains. (FRE.). 184p. (gr. 5-10). 1988. pap. 9.95 (2-07-033475-9) Schoenhof.
—Recres du Petit Nicolas. (FRE.). 181p. (gr. 5-10). 1987. pap. 9.95 (2-07-033468-6) Schoenhof.
—Vacances du Petit Nicolas. (FRE.). 186p. (gr. 5-10). 1987. pap. 9.95 (2-07-033457-0) Schoenhof.

Sen, Abhijit & Raman, Papri Sri. Magic Bones. 264p. (gr. 9-10). 1992. 14.95 (0-932377-49-1) Facet Bks.

Sendak, Maurice. Alligators All Around. Sendak, Maurice, illus. 32p. (ps-3). 1962. PLB 12.89 (0-06-025530-7) HarpC Child Bks.
—Alligators All Around: An Alphabet. Sendak, Maurice, illus. LC 62-13315. 32p. (ps-3). 1991. pap. 3.95 (0-06-443254-8, Trophy) HarpC Child Bks.
—Chicken Soup with Rice. Sendak, Maurice, illus. 48p. (ps-3). 1962. PLB 12.89 (0-06-025535-8) HarpC Child Bks.
—Chicken Soup with Rice. Sendak, Maurice, illus. 32p. (gr. k-3). 1986. Big book. 19.95 (0-590-64645-1); pap. 2.50 (0-590-41033-4) Scholastic Inc.
—Chicken Soup with Rice. (ps-3). 1992. pap. 19.95 (0-590-71789-8) Scholastic Inc.
—Chicken Soup with Rice: A Book of Months. Sendak, Maurice, illus. LC 62-13315. 32p. (ps-3). 1991. pap. 3.95 (0-06-443253-X, Trophy) HarpC Child Bks.
—Hector Protector. 1965. 16.00 (0-06-025485-8); PLB 15.89 (0-06-025486-6) HarpC Child Bks.
—Hector Protector & As I Went over the Water: Two Nursery Rhymes. Sendak, Maurice, illus. LC 65-21388. 64p. (ps-1). 1990. pap. 5.95 (0-06-443237-8, Trophy) HarpC Child Bks.
—Higglety Pigglety Pop: Or, There Must Be More to Life. Sendak, Maurice, illus. LC 67-18553. 80p. (gr. k-3). 1967. 15.00 (0-06-025487-4) HarpC Child Bks.
—Higglety Pigglety Pop! Or There Must be More to Life. LC 67-18553. (Illus.). 80p. (gr. k-4). 1979. pap. 5.95 (0-06-443021-9, Trophy) HarpC Child Bks.
—Higglety Pigglety Pop! or There Must Be More to Life. (ps-3). 1967. PLB 14.89 (0-06-025488-2) HarpC Child Bks.
—In the Night Kitchen. Sendak, Maurice, illus. LC 70-105483. 48p. (ps-3). 1970. 16.00 (0-06-025489-0); PLB 15.89 (0-06-025490-4) HarpC Child Bks.
—In the Night Kitchen. Sendak, Maurice, illus. LC 70-105483. 48p. (ps-3). 1985. pap. 5.95 (0-06-443086-3, Trophy) HarpC Child Bks.
—Kenny's Window. LC 56-5148. (Illus.). 64p. (gr. k-3). 1956. 13.00 (0-06-025494-7); PLB 12.89 (0-06-025495-5) HarpC Child Bks.
—Kenny's Window. Sendak, Maurice, illus. LC 56-5148. 64p. (ps up). 1989. pap. 4.95 (0-06-443209-2, Trophy) HarpC Child Bks.
—Maurice Sendak Book & Poster Package: Where the Wild Things Are. Sendak, Maurice, illus. LC 63-21253. 48p. (gr. k-3). 1991. incl. poster 21.95 (0-06-025966-3) HarpC Child Bks.
—Maurice Sendak's Really Rosie. (Illus.). 48p. (gr. k-4). 1986. pap. 10.95 (0-06-443138-X, Trophy) HarpC Child Bks.
—The Night Kitchen: (La Cocina de Noche) Sendak, Maurice, illus. (SPA.). (gr. 1-6). 14.95 (84-204-4570-3) Santillana.
—Nutshell Library. Incl. Alligators All Around; Chicken Soup with Rice; One Was Johnny; Pierre. LC 62-13315. (ps-3). 1962. Set. 15.00i (0-06-025500-5) HarpC Child Bks.
—One Was Johnny: A Counting Book. Sendak, Maurice, illus. 32p. (ps-3). 1962. PLB 12.89 (0-06-025540-4) HarpC Child Bks.
—One Was Johnny: A Counting Book. Sendak, Maurice, illus. LC 62-13315. 48p. (ps-3). 1991. pap. 3.95 (0-06-443251-3, Trophy) HarpC Child Bks.
—Outside Over There. Sendak, Maurice, illus. LC 79-2682. 40p. (gr. k up). 1981. 20.00 (0-06-025523-4); PLB 19.89 (0-06-025524-2) HarpC Child Bks.
—Outside Over There. Sendak, Maurice, illus. LC 79-2682. 40p. (ps up). 1989. pap. 7.95 (0-06-443185-1, Trophy) HarpC Child Bks.
—Pierre: A Cautionary Tale. Sendak, Maurice, illus. LC 62-13315. 48p. (ps-3). 1991. pap. 3.95 (0-06-443252-1, Trophy) HarpC Child Bks.
—Pierre: A Cautionary Tale in Five Chapters & a Prologue. Sendak, Maurice, illus. 48p. (ps-3). 1962. PLB 12.89 (0-06-025965-5) HarpC Child Bks.
—Seven Little Monsters. Sendak, Maurice, illus. LC 76-18400. (gr. 1 up). 1977. PLB 13.89 (0-06-025478-5) HarpC Child Bks.

—Sign on Rosie's Door. Sendak, Maurice, illus. LC 60-9451. 48p. (gr. k-3). 1960. 14.00 (0-06-025505-6); PLB 13.89 (0-06-025506-4) HarpC Child Bks.
—Very Far Away. Sendak, Maurice, illus. LC 57-5356. (gr. k-3). 1962. 13.00 (0-06-025514-5); PLB 12.89 (0-06-025515-3) HarpC Child Bks.
—We Are All in the Dumps with Jack & Guy. Sendak, Maurice, illus. LC 93-77287. 56p. (ps up) 1993. 20.00 (0-06-205014-1); PLB 19.89 (0-06-205015-X) HarpC Child Bks.
—Where the Wild Things Are. 25th anniversary ed. Sendak, Maurice, illus. LC 63-21253. 48p. (ps up). 1988. 15.00 (0-06-025492-0); PLB 14.89 (0-06-025493-9) HarpC Child Bks.
—Where the Wild Things Are. new ed. Sendak, Maurice, illus. LC 63-21253. 48p. (ps up). 1988. pap. 4.95 (0-06-443178-9, Trophy) HarpC Child Bks.
—Where the Wild Things Are. LC 91-45366. (Illus.). 48p. (gr. k up). 1992. incl. mini Bernard doll 16.95 (0-694-00432-4, Festival); incl. mini Max doll 16.95 (0-694-00431-6, Festival) HarpC Child Bks.
—Where the Wild Things Are: (Donde Viven los Monstruos) Sendak, Maurice, illus. (SPA). (gr. 1-6). 22.95 (84-204-3022-6) Santillana.
Sendak, Maurice & Margolis, Matthew. Some Swell Pup or Are You Sure You Want a Dog? Sendak, Maurice, illus. 32p. (ps up). 1989. pap. 4.95 (0-374-46963-6) FS&G.
Sendak, Philip. In Grandpa's House. Barofsky, Semour, tr. from YID. Sendak, Maurice, illus. LC 85-42625. 48p. (ps up). 1985. 13.00 (0-06-025462-9); PLB 9.89 (0-06-025463-7) HarpC Child Bks.
Sender. Requiem por un Campesino. (gr. 7-12). 1972. pap. 5.95 (0-88436-055-5, 70273) EMC.
Sender, Ruth M. The Cage. LC 86-8562. 252p. (gr. 7 up). 1986. SBE 14.95 (0-02-781830-6, Macmillan Child Bk) Macmillan Child Grp.
—The Holocaust Lady. LC 92-13268. 192p. (gr. 7 up). 1992. SBE 14.95 (0-02-781832-2, Macmillan Child Bk) Macmillan Child Grp.
—To Life. LC 88-9312. 240p. (gr. 7 up). 1988. SBE 14.95 (0-02-781831-4, Macmillan Child Bk) Macmillan Child Grp.
—To Life. 240p. (gr. 6 up). 1990. pap. 4.95 (0-14-034367-9, Puffin) Puffin Bks.
Senderowicz, Ruth M. The Cage. (gr. 5 up). 1988. pap. 3.99 (0-553-27003-6, Starfire) Bantam.
Senelick, Laurence. Sleeping Beauty. (gr. 1-9). 1992. pap. 3.95 (0-88388-045-8) Bellerophon Bks.
Senger, Mary C. Let's Learn about the Church & Celebrate Its Message. (Illus.). 64p. (gr. 4-6). 1990. pap. 4.95 (0-8146-1888-X) Liturgical Pr.
Senior, Kathryn. Medicine: Doctors, Demons & Drugs. LC 93-10608. (gr. 5 up). 1993. 13.95 (0-531-14279-5) Watts.
—Medicine: Doctors, Demons & Drugs. (Illus.). 48p. (gr. 5-8). 1993. 13.95 (0-531-15263-4) Watts.
Senisi, Ellen. Brothers & Sisters. LC 92-42912. 1993. 12.95 (0-590-46419-1) Scholastic Inc.
Senn, Joyce. Jane Goodall: Naturalist. (Illus.). 64p. (gr. 3-7). 1993. PLB 14.95 (1-56711-010-X) Blackbirch.
Senn, Oscar S. Loonie Louie Meets the Space Fungus. 112p. 1991. pap. 2.95 (0-380-75894-6, Camelot) Avon.
Senn, Steve. The Double Disappearance of Walter Fozbek. new ed. 128p. (gr. 2-4). 1980. 9.95 (0-8038-1571-9) Hastings.
—The Double Disappearance of Walter Fozbek. Senn, Steve, illus. 128p. (gr. 3-5). 1983. pap. 2.50 (0-380-62737-X, 60064-1, Camelot) Avon.
—Sand Witch. 96p. (gr. 3-7). 1987. pap. 2.75 (0-380-75298-0, Camelot) Avon.
Senna, Carl. The Black Press & the Struggle for Civil Rights. (Illus.). 176p. (gr. 7-12). 1993. PLB 13.90 (0-531-11036-2) Watts.
—Colin Powell: A Man of War & Peace. LC 92-16099. 150p. 1992. 15.95 (0-8027-8180-2); PLB 16.85 (0-8027-8181-0) Walker & Co.
Sennet, Carole L. & Sennet, Edith. Power Words SAT Cartoon Flashcards. Monse, Keith, illus. (gr. 7 up). 1991. 301 2-sided cards plus thesaurus 21.95 (1-879871-01-7) Sennet & Sarnoff.
Sennet, Edith, jt. auth. see Sennet, Carole L.
Sensenig, Janet. Daryl Borrows a Brother. 166p. 1989. 6.70 (0-317-02911-8) Rod & Staff.
Senterfitt, Marilyn. Celebrate Jesus. 144p. (gr. 1-6). 1988. 11.95 (0-86653-425-3, SS845, Shining Star Pubns) Good Apple.
—Christian Crafts with Egg Cartons. 64p. (ps-5). 1991. 8.95 (0-86653-574-8, SS1882, Shining Star Pubns) Good Apple.
Senungetuk, Vivian & Tiulana, Paul. Place for Winter: Paul Tiulana's Story, (A) (Illus.). 120p. (gr. 10-12). 1989. Repr. of 1987 ed. 17.95 (0-938227-02-5) CIRI Found.
Septien, Al. Everything You Need to Know about Codependency. Rosen, Ruth, ed. (gr. 7-12). 1993. PLB 13.95 (0-8239-1527-1) Rosen Group.
Seraillier, Ian. The Silver Sword. large type ed. (gr. 1-8). 1991. 13.95 (0-7451-0339-1, Galaxy Child Lrg Print) Chivers N Amer.
Seredy, Kate. The Good Master. (Illus.). 196p. (gr. 5-9). 1986. pap. 4.95 (0-14-030133-X, Puffin) Puffin Bks.
—Singing Tree. (gr. 4 up). 1990. pap. 4.95 (0-14-034543-4, Puffin) Puffin Bks.
—The Singing Tree. (gr. 4 up). 1992. 17.25 (0-8446-6588-6) Peter Smith.
—The White Stag. LC 84-7. 1979. pap. 4.99 (0-14-031258-7, Puffin) Puffin Bks.

—White Stag. Seredy, Kate, illus. (gr. 7 up). 1937. pap. 13.00 (0-670-76375-6) Viking Child Bks.
Serenne, Jean-Pierre. Crazy Sunday. (Illus.). 48p. (gr. k-4). 1990. 12.75 (0-89565-811-9); 8.95s.p. (0-685-55097-4) Childs World.
Sereno, Paul C. How Tough Was a Tyrannosaurus? More Fascinating Facts about Dinosaurs. Coutney, Richard, illus. 32p. (ps-7). 1989. pap. 2.25 (0-448-19116-4, Platt & Munk Pubs) Putnam Pub Group.
Serfozo, Mary. Benjamin Bigfoot. Smith, Joseph A., illus. LC 92-321. 32p. (ps-3). 1993. SBE 14.95 (0-689-50570-1, M K McElderry) Macmillan Child Grp.
—Dirty Kurt. Poydar, Nancy, illus. LC 90-29065. 32p. (ps-3). 1992. SBE 13.95 (0-689-50537-X, M K McElderry) Macmillan Child Grp.
—Joe Joe. Montezinos, Nina, illus. LC 92-30133. 32p. (ps-k). 1993. SBE 15.95 (0-689-50578-7, M K McElderry) Macmillan Child Grp.
—Rain Talk. Narahashi, Keiko, illus. LC 89-12178. 32p. (ps-3). 1990. SBE 13.95 (0-689-50496-9, M K McElderry) Macmillan Child Grp.
—Rain Talk. Narahashi, Keiko, illus. LC 92-29562. 32p. (gr. k-3). 1993. pap. 4.95 (0-689-71699-0, Aladdin) Macmillan Child Grp.
—Who Said Red? Narahashi, Keiko, illus. LC 88-9345. 32p. (ps-1). 1988. RSBE 13.95 (0-689-50455-1, M K McElderry) Macmillan Child Grp.
—Who Said Red? Narahashi, Keiko, illus. LC 91-21160. 32p. (ps-1). 1992. pap. 4.95 (0-689-71592-7, Aladdin); pap. 18.95 big bk. (0-689-71651-6, Aladdin) Macmillan Child Grp.
—Who Wants One? Narahashi, Keiko, illus. LC 88-26614. 32p. (ps-1). 1989. SBE 13.95 (0-689-50474-8, M K McElderry) Macmillan Child Grp.
—Who Wants One? Narahashi, Keiko, illus. LC 92-4341. 32p. (ps-1). 1992. pap. 4.95 (0-689-71642-7, Aladdin); pap. 18.95 Big bk. (0-689-71652-4, Aladdin) Macmillan Child Grp.
Serino, John, ed. see Pedicini, John G.
Serman, Gina L., ed. see Fast, Suellen M.
Seros, Kathleen, adapted by. Sun & Moon: Fairy Tales from Korea. Sibley, Norman & Krause, Robert, illus. LC 82-82510. 61p. (gr. 3-9). 1982. PLB 16.50x (0-930878-25-6) Hollym Intl.
Serpico, Phil. Santa Fe Route to the Pacific. Serpico, Phil, illus. LC 87-46360. 150p. (gr. 6 up). 1988. 25.00 (0-88418-000-X) Omni Hawthorne.
Serra, Aurora M., tr. see Company, Merce.
Serra, Michael. Discovering Geometry: An Inductive Approach. 756p. (gr. 9-12). 1993. 32.29 (0-913684-08-2) Key Curr Pr.
—Patty Paper Geometry. (gr. 9-12). 1993. write for info. (1-55953-072-3) Key Curr Pr.
—Patty Paper Geometry Student Workbook. (gr. 9-12). 1993. write for info. (1-55953-074-X) Key Curr Pr.
—Patty Paper Geometry Teacher's Edition. (gr. 9-12). 1993. 18.95 (1-55953-073-1) Key Curr Pr.
Serraillier, Ian. Escape from Warsaw. 1990. pap. 2.95 (0-590-43715-1) Scholastic Inc.
—Silver Sword. Hodges, C. Walter, illus. LC 59-6556. (gr. 7-9). 1959. 25.95 (0-87599-104-1) S G Phillips.
Serratt, Mary L. Light Journey: Adventures in Personal Witnessing. Nelson, Becky, ed. 32p. (gr. 7-12). 1993. pap. text ed. 4.95 (1-56309-063-5) Womans Mission Union.
Serres, Alain. Du Commerce de la Souris. Lapointe, Claudine, illus. (FRE). 55p. (gr. 1-5). 1989. pap. 8.95 (2-07-031195-3) Schoenhof.
—Ogron. Deiss, Veronique, illus. (FRE). 104p. (gr. 3-7). 1991. pap. 10.95 (2-07-031218-6) Schoenhof.
Serrian, Michael. Now Hiring: Film. LC 93-2018. 1994. write for info. (0-89686-784-6, Crestwood Hse) Macmillan Child Grp.
Serventy, Vincent. Crocodile & Alligator. LC 84-15890. (Illus.). 24p. (gr. k-5). 1985. PLB 14.64 (0-8172-2404-1); pap. 3.95 (0-8114-6873-9) Raintree Steck-V.
—Crocodile & Alligator. Serventy, Vincent, et al, illus. 24p. (gr. k-3). 1986. pap. 2.50 (0-590-44722-X) Scholastic Inc.
—Kangaroo. LC 84-17994. (Illus.). 24p. (gr. k-5). 1985. PLB 14.64 (0-8172-2418-1); pap. 3.95 (0-8114-6878-X) Raintree Steck-V.
—Koala. LC 84-17995. (Illus.). 24p. (gr. k-5). 1985. PLB 14.64 (0-8172-2416-5); pap. 3.95 (0-8114-6879-8) Raintree Steck-V.
—Kookaburra. LC 84-17969. (Illus.). 24p. (gr. k-5). 1985. PLB 14.64 (0-8172-2417-3); pap. 3.95 (0-8114-6880-1) Raintree Steck-V.
—Lizard. (Illus.). 24p. (gr. k-5). 1986. PLB 14.64 (0-8172-2706-7); pap. 3.95 (0-8114-6882-8) Raintree Steck-V.
—Parrot. (Illus.). 24p. (gr. k-5). 1986. PLB 14.64 (0-8172-2705-9); pap. 3.95 (0-8114-6885-2) Raintree Steck-V.
—Penguin. LC 84-18045. (Illus.). 24p. (gr. k-5). 1985. PLB 14.64 (0-8172-2415-7); pap. 3.95 (0-8114-6886-0) Raintree Steck-V.
—Shark & Ray. LC 84-15097. (Illus.). 24p. (gr. k-5). 1984. PLB 14.64 (0-8172-2402-5); pap. 3.95 (0-8114-6888-7) Raintree Steck-V.
—Turtle & Tortoise. LC 84-15881. (Illus.). 24p. (gr. k-5). 1985. PLB 14.64 (0-8172-2403-3); pap. 3.95 (0-8114-6891-7) Raintree Steck-V.
—Turtle & Tortoise. (Illus.). 24p. (gr. 1-4). 1987. pap. 2.50 (0-590-42133-6) Scholastic Inc.

—Whale & Dolphin. LC 84-15118. (Illus.). 24p. (gr. k-5). 1985. PLB 14.64 (0-8172-2401-7); pap. 3.95 (0-8114-6892-5) Raintree Steck-V.
Server, Lee. Sharks. (Illus.). 128p. 1989. 14.99 (0-517-69091-8) Outlet Bk Co.
Service, Pamela F. Being of Two Minds. LC 90-24097. 176p. (gr. 3-7). 1991. SBE 13.95 (0-689-31524-4, Atheneum Child Bk) Macmillan Child Grp.
—Phantom Victory. 144p. (gr. 5-7). 1994. SBE 12.95 (0-684-19441-4, Scribners Young Read) Macmillan Child Grp.
—A Question of Destiny. LC 87-23926. 168p. (gr. 7 up). 1988. pap. 2.95 (0-02-044981-X, Collier Young Ad) Macmillan Child Grp.
—The Reluctant God. LC 87-16840. 224p. (gr. 5-8). 1988. SBE 14.95 (0-689-31404-3, Atheneum Child Bk) Macmillan Child Grp.
—Stinker from Space. LC 87-25266. 96p. (gr. 3-5). 1988. SBE 12.95 (0-684-18910-0, Scribners Young Read) Macmillan Child Grp.
—Stinker from Space. (gr. 6 up). 1989. pap. 3.99 (0-449-70330-4, Juniper) Fawcett.
—Stinker from Space. 105p. 1992. text ed. 8.40 (1-56956-122-2) W A T Braille.
—Stinker's Return. LC 92-21800. 96p. (gr. 4-6). 1993. SBE 12.95 (0-684-19542-9, Scribners Young Read) Macmillan Child Grp.
—Tomorrow's Magic. (gr. 5 up). 1988. pap. 3.95 (0-449-70305-3, Juniper) Fawcett.
—Under Alien Stars. LC 89-28025. 224p. (gr. 4-8). 1990. SBE 14.95 (0-689-31621-6, Atheneum Child Bk) Macmillan Child Grp.
—Under Alien Stars. 1991. pap. 3.99 (0-449-70404-1, Juniper) Fawcett.
—Weirdos of the Universe, Unite! LC 91-18438. 144p. (gr. 3-7). 1992. SBE 13.95 (0-689-31746-8, Atheneum Child Bk) Macmillan Child Grp.
—Weirdos of the Universe, Unite! 1993. pap. 3.99 (0-449-70429-7) Fawcett.
—Winter of Magic's Return. (gr. 5 up). 1986. pap. 3.95 (0-449-70202-2, Juniper) Fawcett.
Service, Robert. The Cremation of Sam McGee. Harrison, Ted, illus. LC 86-14971. 32p. (ps up). 1987. 15.95 (0-688-06903-7) Greenwillow.
—The Shooting of Dan McGrew. Harrison, Ted, illus. LC 88-6124. (gr. 3 up). 1988. 14.95 (0-87923-748-1) Godine.
Serwer-Bernstein, Blanche. Let's Steal the Moon. Hyman, Trina S., illus. 96p. (gr. 7 up). 1987. pap. 6.95 (0-933503-27-X) Shapolsky Pubs.
Sesame Street Editors. The Sesame Street ABC Book of Words. McNaught, Harry, illus. LC 86-62405. 48p. (ps-k). 1988. pap. 11.00 (0-394-88880-4) Random Bks Yng Read.
Sesame Street Staff. Big Bird's Farm. Barrett, John E., photos by. LC 81-50537. (Illus.). 14p. (ps). 1981. bds. 3.95 (0-394-84812-8) Random Bks Yng Read.
—Big Bird's Rhyming Book. Chartier, Norm, illus. LC 78-68790. (ps-3). 1979. 7.95 (0-394-84140-9) Random Bks Yng Read.
—Cookie Monster, Where Are You? Jones, Randy, illus. LC 75-39342. (ps-3). 1976. 8.99 (0-394-83257-4) Random Bks Yng Read.
—The Count's Counting Book. Cooke, Tom, illus. LC 79-56535. 16p. (ps-3). 1980. pap. 8.99 (0-394-84436-X) Random Bks Yng Read.
—Ernie & Bert Can...Can You. Smollin, Michael J., illus. LC 81-83696. 28p. (ps). 1982. 2.95 (0-394-85150-1) Random Bks Yng Read.
—Grover's New Kitten. Barrett, John E., photos by. LC 81-50538. (Illus.). 14p. (ps). 1981. bds. 3.95 (0-394-84872-1) Random Bks Yng Read.
—Grover's Super Surprise Book. Cooke, Tom, illus. LC 77-93776. (ps-3). 1978. 8.99 (0-394-83841-6) Random Bks Yng Read.
—In & Out, Up & Down. Smollin, Michael J., illus. LC 81-83697. 28p. (ps). 1982. bds. 2.95 (0-394-85151-X) Random Bks Yng Read.
—One Rubber Duckie. Barrett, John E., photos by. LC 81-86375. (Illus.). (ps). 1982. 3.95 (0-394-85309-1) Random Bks Yng Read.
—The Sesame Street Mother Goose. Jones, Randy, illus. LC 75-39341. (ps-3). 1976. 8.95 (0-394-83256-6) Random Bks Yng Read.
—Sesame Street Pop-up Riddle Book. Sutherland, David, illus. LC 77-70852. (ps-3). 1977. bds. 8.99 (0-394-83546-8) Random Bks Yng Read.
—Sesame Street Sign Language Fun. Cooke, Tom, illus. Selkirk, Neil, photos by. LC 79-5570. (Illus.). 72p. (ps-3). 1980. 10.00 (0-394-84212-X) Random Bks Yng Read.
—Sesame Street Storybook. (Illus.). (ps-4). 1971. 5.95 (0-394-82332-X); lib. bdg. 5.99 (0-394-92332-4) Random Bks Yng Read.
—Your Friends from Sesame Street. Smollin, Michael J., illus. (ps). 1979. 3.50 (0-394-84137-9) Random Bks Yng Read.
Sesame Street Staff & Hayward, Linda. The Sesame Street Dictionary. Mathieu, Joe, illus. LC 80-11644. 256p. (ps-3). 1980. bds. 15.95 (0-394-84007-0); PLB 17.99 (0-394-94007-5) Random Bks Yng Read.
Sesemann, Dimitri. V Moskve Vse Spokoino (All Is Calm in Moscow) Roman (A Novel) Jurovskii, A. & Rybakov, V., eds. LC 89-60955. (RUS). 222p. (Orig.). (gr. 9-12). 1990. pap. 12.50 (0-911971-47-5) Effect Pub.

Sesto, Cameron. Simply Great Cooking Instruction. (Illus.). 50p. (Orig.). 1989. pap. 18.00x *(0-916671-88-7)* Material Dev.

Seters, Virginia A. van see Van Seters, Virginia A.

Seters, Virginia A. van see Van Seters, Virginia A.

Seton, Ernest T. Animal Heroes. rev. ed. Seton, Ernest T., illus. LC 87-71143. 368p. (gr. 5 up). 1987. pap. 9.95 *(0-88739-055-2)* Creative Arts Bk.

—Lobo the Wolf: King of Currumpaw. rev. ed. Ryan, Donna, illus. 72p. (gr. 3-8). 1991. pap. 9.95 *(0-9623072-4-6)* S Ink WA.

—The Pacing Mustang. rev. ed. Ryan, Donna, illus. 72p. (gr. 3-8). 1991. pap. 9.95 *(0-9623072-5-4)* S Ink WA.

—Two Little Savages. (Illus.). 286p. (gr. 4-8). 1903. pap. 6.95 *(0-486-20985-7)* Dover.

—Wild Animals I Have Known. rev. ed. Seton, Ernest T., illus. LC 87-71147. 368p. (gr. 5 up). 1987. pap. 9.95 *(0-88739-053-6)* Creative Arts Bk.

Settel, Joanne & Baggett, Nancy. How Do Ants Know When You're Having A Picnic? (And Other Questions Kids Ask about Insects & Other Crawly Things) Tunney, Linda, illus. LC 86-3353. 112p. (gr. 3-7). 1986. SBE 13.95 *(0-689-31268-7,* Atheneum Childrens Bk) Macmillan Child Grp.

—Why Do Cats' Eyes Glow in the Dark? (And Other Questions Kids Ask about Animals) Tunney, Linda, illus. LC 87-13708. 112p. (gr. 3-7). 1988. SBE 13.95 *(0-689-31267-9,* Atheneum Child Bk) Macmillan Child Grp.

—Why Does My Nose Run? (And Other Questions Kids Ask about Their Bodies) Tunney, Linda, illus. LC 84-21549. 80p. (gr. 4-6). 1985. SBE 12.95 *(0-689-31078-1,* Atheneum Child Bk) Macmillan Child Grp.

Setterlund, Donna J. A Dream & a Promise: From a Child to a Woman with a Mother's Help along the Way. (Illus.). 240p. (gr. 8 up). 1990. write for info. *(0-9624342-2-1);* pap. write for info. Carriage Hse Studio Pubns.

—Elephant, Please Go Back to the Zoo. Setterlund, Donna J., illus. 30p. 1990. write for info. *(0-9624342-3-X)* Carriage Hse Studio Pubns.

—A Victorian Coloring Book, No. 1: Featuring Ferndale, California. (Illus.). 24p. (Orig.). 1990. pap. 4.95 *(0-9624342-1-3)* Carriage Hse Studio Pubns.

Seuling, Barbara. Abracadabra! Creating Your Own Magic Show from Beginning to End. (gr. 3-6). 1975. (Archway); pap. 1.25 *(0-671-29805-4)* PB.

—The Teeny Tiny Woman: An Old English Ghost Tale. Seuling, Barbara, illus. (gr. k-3). 1978. pap. 4.99 *(0-14-050266-1,* Puffin) Puffin Bks.

Seuss, Dr. see Dr. Seuss.

Sevaly, Karen. E-F Alphabook. Sevaly, Richard, et al, eds. Sevaly, Karen, illus. 128p. (Orig.). (gr. k-4). 1993. pap. 10.95 tchr's. ed. *(0-943263-23-9,* TF1803) Teachers Friend Pubns.

—G-H Alphabook. Sevaly, Richard, et al, eds. Sevaly, Karen, illus. 128p. (Orig.). (gr. k-4). 1993. pap. 10.95 *(0-943263-24-7,* TF1804) Teachers Friend Pubns.

Sevaly, Karen & Sevaly, Richard. The Instant Bulletin Board Book: December Holidays. Nazar, Steve, illus. 96p. (Orig.). (gr. 2-6). 1993. pap. 9.95 tchr's. ed. *(0-943263-36-0,* TF1904) Teachers Friend Pubns.

—The Instant Bulletin Board Book: Winter Playtime. Nazar, Steve, illus. 96p. (Orig.). (gr. 2-6). 1993. pap. 9.95 tchr's. ed. *(0-943263-37-9,* TF1905) Teachers Friend Pubns.

Sevaly, Richard, jt. auth. see Sevaly, Karen.

Sevaly, Richard, et al, eds. see Sevaly, Karen.

Sevcik, Otakar. School of Technic for Violin, Op. 1, Part 2. (FRE, GER & ENG.). 49p. 1900. pap. 8.00 *(0-8258-0035-8,* L 283) Fischer Inc NY.

—School of Technic for Violin: Op. 1 Part 1. (GER, FRE & ENG.). (gr. 6-12). 1900. pap. 8.95 *(0-8258-0034-X,* L 282) Fischer Inc NY.

Severance, Charles L. Tales of the Thumb. 2nd ed. LC 72-86863. (Illus.). (gr. 3-6). 1972. pap. 4.75 *(0-932411-00-2)* Pub Div JCS.

Severn, Bill. Bill Severn's Magic with Rope, Ribbon, & String. LC 93-17893. (Illus.). 224p. (gr. 4 up). 1994. 12.95 *(0-8117-2533-2)* Stackpole.

—Magic with Rope, Ribbon, & String. 224p. (gr. 6 up). 1981. 9.95 *(0-679-20813-5)* McKay.

Severn, Jeffrey. George & His Giant Shadow. Severn, Jeffrey, illus. 32p. (ps-1). 1990. 12.95 *(0-87701-634-8)* Chronicle Bks.

Severns, Karen. Hirohito. Schlesinger, Arthur M., intro. by. (Illus.). 112p. (gr. 5 up). 1988. 17.95 *(1-55546-837-3);* pap. 9.95 *(0-7910-0574-7)* Chelsea Hse.

Severs, Susan B., ed. & illus. see Reist, Linnaeus L.

Severson, Leigh. Native Americans - A Thematic Unit. Apodaca, Blanca, et al, illus. 80p. (Orig.). (gr. k-3). 1991. wkbk. 7.95 *(1-55734-276-8)* Tchr Create Mat.

Sevig, Mike, tr. see Egner, Thorbjorn.

Sewall, Marcia. Animal Song. Sewall, Marcia, illus. LC 87-4092. (ps-1). 1988. 14.95 *(0-316-78191-6,* Joy Street Bks) Little.

—People of the Breaking Day. Sewall, Marcia A., illus. LC 89-18194. 48p. (gr. 1 up). 1990. SBE 15.95 *(0-689-31407-8,* Atheneum Child Bk) Macmillan Child Grp.

—The Pilgrims of Plimoth. Sewall, Marcia, illus. LC 86-3362. 48p. (gr. 2 up). 1986. SBE 15.95 *(0-689-31250-4,* Atheneum Child Bk) Macmillan Child Grp.

Sewalson, Don. Street Self-Defense. Sewalson, Don, illus. 81p. (gr. 6-12). 1986. pap. 6.75 *(0-938419-01-3)* DM Pub.

—Street Self-Defense. Sewalson, Don, illus. 63p. (gr. 6-12). 1986. pap. 6.75 *(0-938419-03-X)* DM Pub.

—Street Self-Defense. Sewalson, Don, illus. 58p. (gr. 6-12). 1986. pap. 6.75 *(0-938419-02-1)* DM Pub.

—Street Self-Defense: Complete Edition. Sewalson, Don, illus. 193p. (gr. 6-12). 1986. 27.00 *(0-938419-04-8);* pap. 16.95 *(0-938419-00-5)* DM Pub.

Seward, Bernard. Writing American English. Olsen, Roger E., ed. (Illus.). 90p. (gr. 3-12). 1982. pap. text ed. 5.75 *(0-13-971102-3)* Alemany Pr.

Sewell, Anna. Black Beauty. (gr. 5 up). 1963. pap. 1.50 *(0-8049-0023-X,* CL-23) Airmont.

—Black Beauty. (Illus.). 320p. (gr. 4 up). 1945. 13.95 *(0-448-06007-8,* G&D); (G&D) Putnam Pub Group.

—Black Beauty. new ed. Farr, Naunerle, ed. Nebres, Rudy, illus. LC 59-12495. 64p. (Orig.). (gr. 5-10). 1973. pap. 2.95 *(0-88301-094-1)* Pendulum Pr.

—Black Beauty. LC 86-3353. 112p. (gr. 3-7). 1983. pap. 2.25 *(0-14-035006-3,* Puffin) Puffin Bks.

—Black Beauty. Vance, Eleanor G., ed. Jeffers, Susan, illus. LC 84-27575. 72p. (ps-5). 1986. 15.00 *(0-394-86575-8);* lib. bdg. 12.99 *(0-394-96575-2)* Random Bks Yng Read.

—Black Beauty. LC 59-12495. (gr. 4-6). 1989. pap. 3.25 *(0-590-42354-1)* Scholastic Inc.

—Black Beauty. (gr. 2-6). 1986. 7.98 *(0-685-16851-4)* Outlet Bk Co.

—Black Beauty. McKinley, Robin, adapted by. Jeffers, Susan, illus. Kingsley, Ben, contrib. by. (Illus.). 72p. (ps-5). 1987. incl. cass. 17.95 *(0-394-89228-3)* Random Bks Yng Read.

—Black Beauty, 2 vols. large type ed. (gr. 8 up). Repr. of 1946 ed. Set. write for info. NAVH.

—Black Beauty. reissued ed. Norby, Lisa, adapted by. D'Andrea, Domenick, illus. LC 89-62772. 96p. (Orig.). (gr. 2-6). 1993. lib. bdg. 5.99 *(0-679-90370-4);* pap. 2.99 *(0-679-80370-X)* Random Bks Yng Read.

—Black Beauty. (gr. 4 up). 1990. pap. 3.50 *(0-440-40355-3,* Pub. by Yearling Classics) Dell.

—Black Beauty. 75p. (ps-8). 1986. pap. 3.50 *(0-451-52295-8,* Sig Classics) NAL-Dutton.

—Black Beauty. Keeping, Charles, illus. 216p. (gr. 5 up). 1990. 19.95 *(0-374-30776-8)* FS&G.

—Black Beauty. (Illus.). 1992. write for info. *(0-89434-123-5)* Ferguson.

—Black Beauty. 256p. 1992. 9.49 *(0-8167-2548-9);* pap. 2.95 *(0-8167-2549-7)* Troll Assocs.

—Black Beauty. Needham, James, illus. 220p. 1992. 24.95 *(0-88363-200-4)* H L Levin.

—Black Beauty. Lindskoog, Kathryn, ed. (gr. 3 up). 1992. pap. 4.99 *(0-88070-498-5,* Gold & Honey) Questar Pubs.

—Black Beauty. Simpson, Anne, ed. La Padula, Tom, illus. LC 92-5805. 48p. (gr. 3-6). 1992. PLB 12.89 *(0-8167-2860-7);* pap. text ed. 3.95 *(0-8167-2861-5)* Troll Assocs.

—Black Beauty. Hollindale, Peter, ed. 240p. 1992. pap. 7.95 *(0-19-282812-6)* OUP.

—Black Beauty. Prittie, Edwin J., illus. 298p. 1993. Repr. 29.95 *(1-877767-86-7)* Regal Pubns.

—Black Beauty. abr. ed. Kliros, Thea, illus. LC 93-244. 96p. (gr. 1-9). 1993. pap. 1.00 *(0-486-27570-1)* Dover.

—Black Beauty. Ambrus, Victor, illus. LC 93-18939. 208p. (gr. 4-8). 1993. PLB 14.95 *(0-8050-2772-6,* Bks Young Read) H Holt & Co.

—Black Beauty. 1993. 13.95 *(0-679-42811-9,* Everymans Lib) Knopf.

Sewell, H., jt. auth. see Bulfinch, Thomas.

Sexias, Judith S. Living with a Parent Who Takes Drugs. LC 89-1995. 112p. (gr. 4-6). 1991. pap. 3.95 *(0-688-10492-4,* Pub. by Beech Tree Bks) Morrow.

Sexton, Nancy N., et al. My Days As a Youngling, John Jacob Niles. (Orig.). (gr. 4 up). 1982. playscript 5.50 *(0-87602-239-5)* Anchorage.

Seybolt, Peter J. Through Chinese Eyes: Revolution & Transformation. rev. ed. Clark, Leon E., ed. (Illus.). 280p. 1988. pap. text ed. 19.95x *(0-938960-29-6)* CITE.

Seymour, Dorothy Z. Toad Charts, Paper Faces, & Other Ideas for Visual Comprehension. (gr. k-3). 1987. pap. 7.95 *(0-673-18713-6)* Scott F.

Seymour, Flora W. Sacagawea: American Pathfinder. Doremus, Robert, illus. LC 90-23267. 192p. (gr. 3-7). 1991. pap. 3.95 *(0-689-71482-3,* Aladdin) Macmillan Child Grp.

Seymour, Peter. Discovering Our Past. Svensson, Borje, illus. 10p. (gr. 2-5). 1987. 8.95 *(0-02-782200-1,* Macmillan Child Bk) Macmillan Child Grp.

—Fire Fighters. Ingersoll, Norm, illus. 12p. (gr. k-3). 1990. 12.95 *(0-525-67295-8,* Lodestar Bks) Dutton Child Bks.

—The Happy Birthday Book: A Party-Time Book with Lights & Music. Ewing, Carolyn, illus. 12p. (ps-1). 1992. POB 10.95 *(0-689-71585-4,* Aladdin) Macmillan Child Grp.

—How the Weather Works. Springer, Sally, illus. 10p. (gr. 2-5). 1985. SBE 8.95 *(0-02-782110-2,* Macmillan Child Bk) Macmillan Child Grp.

—If Pigs Could Fly: A Pop-Up Book. (Illus.). 12p. 1989. 9.95 *(0-8431-2411-3)* Price Stern.

—Insects: A Close-Up Look. Helmer, Jean C., illus. 10p. (gr. 2-5). 1985. SBE 8.95 *(0-02-782120-X,* Macmillan Child Bk) Macmillan Child Grp.

—The Magic Toyshop. Welply, Michael, illus. (gr. 3 up). 1988. pap. 14.95 *(0-671-66907-9,* S&S BFYR) S&S Trade.

—Pilots. Ingersoll, Norm, illus. 12p. (gr. k-3). 1992. 13.00 *(0-525-67372-5,* Lodestar Bks) Dutton Child Bks.

—The Pop-up Book of Big Trucks. Murphy, Chuck, illus. (ps-3). 1989. 11.95 *(0-316-78197-5)* Little.

—What Lives in the Sea. (Illus.). 10p. (gr. 2-5). 1985. SBE 8.95 *(0-02-782170-6,* Macmillan Child Bk) Macmillan Child Grp.

—What's at the Beach? A Lift-the-Flap, Pop-up Book. Carter, David A., illus. LC 84-81819. 18p. (ps-2). 1993. PLB 11.95 *(0-8050-2869-2,* Bks Young Read) H Holt & Co.

—What's in the Cave? A Lift-the-Flap, Pop-up Book. Carter, David A., illus. LC 84-81820. 18p. (ps-2). 1993. PLB 11.95 *(0-8050-2868-4,* Bks Young Read) H Holt & Co.

—What's in the Deep Blue Sea? Carter, David A., illus. LC 90-80884. 18p. (ps-2). 1990. 10.95 *(0-8050-1449-7,* Bks Young Read) H Holt & Co.

—What's in the Jungle. Carter, David A., illus. LC 87-81818. 18p. (ps-2). 1988. 10.95 *(0-8050-0688-5,* Bks Young Read) H Holt & Co.

—What's in the Prehistoric Forest? Carter, David A., illus. LC 90-80885. 18p. (ps-2). 1990. 10.95 *(0-8050-1450-0,* Bks Young Read) H Holt & Co.

—You Can Be Anything. 22p. (ps-1). 1986. 5.95 *(0-8431-1462-2)* Price Stern.

Seymour, Peter, ed. see Ballard, Bob.

Seymour, Ruth G. & Grofe, Anne C. Sandy of Siam. 1992. 6.95 *(0-533-09667-7)* Vantage.

Seymour, Simon. Strange Creatures. LC 81-4433. (Illus.). 48p. (gr. 3-7). 1981. SBE 12.95 *(0-02-782860-3,* Four Winds) Macmillan Child Grp.

Seymour, Tres. Hunting the White Cow. Halperin, Wendy A., illus. LC 92-43757. 32p. (ps-2). 1993. 15.95 *(0-531-05496-9);* PLB 15.99 *(0-531-08646-1)* Orchard Bks Watts.

—I Love My Buzzard. Schindler, S. D., illus. LC 93-4877. 1994. write for info. *(0-531-06819-6);* lib. bdg. write for info. *(0-531-08669-0)* Orchard Bks Watts.

—Life in the Desert. LC 92-7945. 96p. (gr. 7-12). 1992. 12.95 *(0-531-05458-6);* PLB 12.99 *(0-531-08608-9)* Orchard Bks Watts.

—Pole Dog. Soman, David, photos by. LC 92-24174. (Illus.). (ps-1). 1993. 14.95 *(0-531-05470-5);* PLB 14.99 *(0-531-08620-8)* Orchard Bks Watts.

Seymour, Tryntje Van Ness see Van Ness Seymour, Tryntje.

Seymour-Jones, Carole. Homelessness. LC 92-39445. (Illus.). 48p. (gr. 6 up). 1993. RSBE 12.95 *(0-02-786882-6,* New Discovery) Macmillan Child Grp.

—Refugees. LC 92-14803. (Illus.). 48p. (gr. 6 up). 1992. RSBE 12.95 *(0-02-735402-4,* New Discovery) Macmillan Child Grp.

Sgarlata, Joseph. Law & Public Policy. 162p. (Orig.). (gr. 11-12). 1990. pap. text ed. 13.75x *(0-936826-34-7)* PS Assocs Croton.

Sgroi, Peter. The Living Constitution: Landmark Supreme Court Decisions. LC 86-23521. 128p. (gr. 5 up). 1987. lib. bdg. 12.98 *(0-671-61972-1,* J Messner) S&S Trade.

Shaaber, M. A., ed. see Shakespeare, William.

Shachtman, Tom. Driftwhistler: A Story of Daniel au Fond. (Illus.). 160p. (gr. 5 up). 1991. 14.95 *(0-8050-1285-0,* Bks Young Read) H Holt & Co.

—The President Builds a House: The Work of Habitat for Humanity. Carter, Jimmy, intro. by. (gr. 3 up). 1989. pap. 14.95 jacketed *(0-671-67705-5,* S&S BFYR) S&S Trade.

Shachtman, Tom & Shelare, Harriet. Video Power: A Complete Guide to Writing, Planning, & Shooting Videos. LC 87-23681. (Illus.). 96p. (gr. 6-9). 1988. (Bks Young Read); pap. 7.95 *(0-8050-0414-9)* H Holt & Co.

Shackelford, Bud. Draw Animals: Learn From Former Disney Artist Bud Shackelford. Shackelford, Bud, illus. LC 92-96937. 64p. (Orig.). (gr. k-6). 1993. pap. 9.50 *(0-9634693-0-4)* B Shackelford.

Shackelford, Robert D. Benefits of Righteousness. 73p. (Orig.). (gr. 9-12). 1988. pap. 3.95 *(0-9618308-2-4)* R Shackelford.

Shackell, John, jt. auth. see Claridge, Marit.

Shackleton, S. Paul. Opportunities in Electrical & Electronic Engineering. LC 76-42888. (Illus.). (gr. 8 up). 1982. 13.95 *(0-8442-6333-8,* VGM Career Bks); pap. 10.95 *(0-8442-6334-6,* VGM Career Bks) NTC Pub Grp.

Shad, A. R. Primer of Islam, Vol. 1. pap. 3.50 *(1-56744-192-0)* Kazi Pubns.

Shader, Laurel, jt. auth. see Zonderman, John.

Shadow Lawn Press Staff & Birnes, William J. Arco Computer Preparation for the SAT. (gr. 9 up). 1984. Boxed set incl. book, two computer diskettes & instr's. manual. 69.95 *(0-668-05996-6,* Arco Test) P-H Gen Ref & Trav.

Shaeffer, Claire B. Complete Book of Sewing Shortcuts. rev. ed. LC 81-8818. (Illus.). 256p. (gr. 6 up). 1992. pap. 14.95 *(0-8069-7564-4)* Sterling.

Shafe, James C. & Strickland, A. G. Career Direction: Facilitator's Guide. (Illus.). 100p. (gr. 11 up). 1987. tchr's. manual 25.00 *(0-685-26165-4)* Sales & Mgmt Trg.

Shafer, Robert, ed. see Bingham, Mindy & Stryker, Sandy.

Shaffer, Betty. Lisa. LC 82-72149. 141p. (Orig.). (gr. 8-12). 1982. pap. 3.99 (0-87123-316-9) Bethany Hse.
Shaffer, Dianna. The Man Who Loved Balloons. Shaffer, Dianna, illus. 32p. (ps-8). 1989. pap. text ed. 4.95 (1-877995-02-9) Koala Pub Co.
Shaffer, Dianna, jt. auth. see Case, Mary.
Shaffer, Elizabeth. Daughter of the Dawn. 1992. write for info. (0-936369-72-8) Son-Rise Pubns.
Shaffer, Paul R., jt. auth. see Zim, Herbert S.
Shaffer, Susan L., ed. Dine, the Navajo. Harper-Marinick & Kinzie, Mable B., illus. (gr. 6). 1987. incl. 30 student bklts. & 1 tchr's. resource binder which contains poster, lesson plans, overhead transparencies, 1 realia, color slides & audio-cassette 294.43 (0-934351-15-5); tchr's. resource binder only 197.95 (0-934351-26-0); student's bklt. only 4.95 (0-934351-31-7) Heard Mus.
—Inde, the Western Apache. Harper-Marinick, Maria & Kinzie, Mable B., illus. (gr. 5 up). 1987. incl. 30 student bklts. & 1 tchr's. resource binder which contains poster, lesson plans, overhead transparencies, 1 realia, color slides & audio-cassette 294.43 (0-934351-11-2); tchr's. resource binder only 197.95 (0-934351-22-8); student bklt. only 4.95 (0-934351-27-9) Heard Mus.
Shafir, Frol. Iz Ada v Nebesa: Pravdivye Istorii. LC 88-82530. (RUS.). 144p. 1988. 12.00 (0-911971-39-4) Effect Pub.
Shafner, R. L. & Weisberg, Eric J. Belly's Deli. LC 92-44636. 1993. 13.50 (0-8225-2101-6) Lerner Pubns.
—The Hearty Treatment. LC 92-43369. 1993. 13.50 (0-8225-2103-2) Lerner Pubns.
—Mrs. Bretsky's Bakery. LC 92-44338. 1993. 13.50 (0-8225-2102-4) Lerner Pubns.
Shah, Bharat S. A Programmed Text to Learn Gujarati, Set. Kapadia, Madhusudan, frwd. by. 300p. (Orig.). (gr. 6 up). 1990. pap. text ed. 18.00 (0-9623674-0-0) Setubandh Pubns.
Shahan, Leah S., ed. see Dunning, Jack.
Shahan, Sherry. Fifth Grade Crush. (Illus.). 128p. (gr. 3-5). 1992. 2.50 (0-87406-139-3) Willowisp Pr.
Shahani, Mohammad B., tr. from ARA. The Holy Qur'an & English Translation of Its Meaning, 30 vols, Vol. 1. LC 89-82570. (Illus.). 25p. (Orig.). 1989. pap. 1.25 (1-878534-00-9) Dawah Pubns.
—The Holy Qur'an & English Translation of Its Meaning, 30 vols, Vol. 2. LC 89-82570. (Illus.). 21p. (Orig.). 1989. pap. 1.25 (1-878534-01-7) Dawah Pubns.
—The Holy Qur'an & English Translation of Its Meaning, 30 vols, Vol. 3. LC 89-82570. (Illus.). 26p. (Orig.). 1990. pap. 1.25 (1-878534-02-5) Dawah Pubns.
Shahastra. From My Heart. (Illus.). 32p. (ps-7). 1982. coloring book 2.95 (0-911281-02-9) Magical Rainbow.
—Magical Rainbow Man. LC 81-90690. (Illus.). 64p. (ps-7). 1982. pap. 8.95 (0-911281-00-2) Magical Rainbow.
—Missing Magical Energy. LC 82-99874. (Illus.). 64p. (ps-7). 1982. pap. 8.95 (0-686-38241-2) Magical Rainbow.
Shail, George, tr. see Schwartz, Yevgeny.
Shaine, Frances. If Tiny Little Dinosaurs Played House... Bingham, Edith, illus. 30p. (Orig.). (ps-3). 1993. pap. 4.95 (1-884217-02-8) Wellford.
—My Doll Is Just Like Me. Bingham, Edith, illus. 30p. (Orig.). (ps-2). 1993. pap. 4.95 (1-884217-03-6) Wellford.
—A Walk in the Alphabet Zoo. Bingham, Edith, illus. 30p. (Orig.). (ps-2). 1993. pap. 4.95 (1-884217-00-1) Wellford.
—A Walk Through the Alphabet Garden. Bingham, Edith, illus. 30p. (Orig.). (ps-3). 1993. pap. 4.95 (1-884217-01-X) Wellford.
Shakelford, Jane D. My Happy Days. (Illus.). 1990. 7.95 (0-87049-004-6) Assoc Pubs DC.
Shakespeare, William. All's Well That Ends Well. Rowland, Beryl, intro. by. LC 85-4167. (gr. 9 up). 1968. pap. 0.60 (0-8049-1022-7, S22) Airmont.
—Antony & Cleopatra. Rudvik, O. H., intro. by. (gr. 10 up). 1966. pap. 0.60 (0-8049-1011-1, S-11) Airmont.
—As You Like It. Pitt, David G., intro. by. (gr. 10 up). 1965. pap. 1.25 (0-8049-1006-5, S-6) Airmont.
—As You Like It. Davidson, Diane, ed. LC 83-60731. (Illus.). 122p. (gr. 8-12). 1985. pap. 5.95x (0-934048-14-2) Swan Books.
—As You Like It. Gill, Roma, ed. (Illus.). 142p. 1987. pap. 7.50 (0-19-831934-7) OUP.
—Comedy of Errors. Rudzik, O. H., intro. by. (gr. 9 up). 1968. pap. 0.60 (0-8049-1023-5, S-23) Airmont.
—Complete Sonnets & Poems. Fisher, Neil H., intro. by. (gr. 9 up). 1966. pap. 0.60 (0-8049-1016-2, S-16) Airmont.
—Coriolanus. Rowland, Beryl, intro. by. (gr. 10 up). 1968. pap. 0.60 (0-8049-1021-9, S-21) Airmont.
—Falstaff & His Friends. (gr. 1-9). 1992. pap. 3.95 (0-88388-126-8) Bellerophon Bks.
—Hamlet. Mattea, Gino, intro. by. (gr. 11 up). pap. 1.95 (0-8049-1001-4, S1) Airmont.
—Hamlet. Farnham, Willard, ed. (gr. 9 up). 1957. pap. 3.50 (0-14-071405-7, Pelican Bks) Viking Penguin.
—Hamlet. Davidson, Diane, ed. LC 83-12310. (Illus.). 154p. (gr. 8-12). 1983. pap. 5.95 (0-934048-12-6) Swan Books.
—Hamlet. Mack, Maynard & Boynton, Robert W., eds. 180p. (gr. 9-12). 1990. pap. 4.50 (0-86709-019-7, 0019) Boynton Cook Pubs.
—Hamlet. Gill, Roma, ed. (Illus.). 160p. 1992. PLB 7.50 (0-19-831960-6) OUP.

—Hamlet for Young People. Davidson, Diane, ed. & illus. 64p. (gr. 5-8). 1993. pap. text ed. 4.95 (0-934048-24-X) Swan Books.
—Henry Fourth, Pt. 1. Shaaber, M. A., ed. (gr. 9 up). 1957. pap. 3.95 (0-14-071407-3, Pelican Bks) Viking Penguin.
—Henry IV, Pts. 1 & 2. Young, Archibald, intro. by. (gr. 10 up). pap. 1.25 ea Pt. 1 (0-8049-1018-9, S18) Pt. 2. pap. 0.60 (0-685-00150-4, S19) Airmont.
—Henry IV, Pt. I. Gill, Roma, ed. (Illus.). 176p. 1987. pap. 7.50 (0-19-831948-7) OUP.
—Henry the Fifth for Young People. Davidson, Diane, ed. & illus. LC 91-20093. 64p. (gr. 5-8). 1991. pap. text ed. 4.95 (0-934048-23-1) Swan Books.
—Julius Caesar. Rudzik, O. H., intro. by. (Illus.). (gr. 9 up). 1965. pap. 1.95 (0-8049-1004-9, S4) Airmont.
—Julius Caesar. Johnson, S. F., ed. (gr. 9 up). 1960. pap. 3.50 (0-14-071422-7, Pelican Bks) Viking Penguin.
—Julius Caesar. Shaw, Charlie, illus. Stewart, Diana, adapted by. LC 80-16406. (Illus.). 48p. (gr. 4 up). 1983. PLB 18.64 (0-8172-1664-2) Raintree Steck-V.
—Julius Caesar. Davidson, Diane, ed. LC 83-12307. (Illus.). 121p. (gr. 8-12). 1983. pap. 5.95 (0-934048-04-5) Swan Books.
—Julius Caesar. Mack, Maynard & Boynton, Robert W., eds. 148p. (gr. 9-12). 1990. pap. text ed. 4.50 (0-86709-023-5, 0023) Boynton Cook Pubs.
—Julius Caesar for Young People. Davidson, Diane, ed. LC 90-43038. (Illus.). 64p. (gr. 5-8). 1990. pap. text ed. 4.95 (0-934048-22-3) Swan Books.
—King Henry IV, Pt. II. Girling, Zoe. (gr. 10 up). 1967. pap. 0.60 (0-685-42963-6) Airmont.
—King Henry V. Thomas, Clara. (gr. 10 up). 1967. pap. 0.60 (0-8049-1017-0) Airmont.
—King John. Rowland, Beryl, intro. by. (gr. 9 up). 1968. pap. 1.95 (0-8049-1024-3, S24) Airmont.
—King Lear. Girling, H. K., intro. by. (gr. 11 up). 1966. pap. 1.75 (0-8049-1012-X, S12) Airmont.
—King Lear. Harbage, Alfred, ed. (gr. 9 up). 1958. pap. 3.50 (0-14-071414-6, Pelican Bks) Viking Penguin.
—Macbeth. Duffy, John D., intro. by. (gr. 11 up). 1965. pap. 1.75 (0-8049-1002-2, S2) Airmont.
—Macbeth. Harbage, Alfred, ed. (gr. 9 up). 1956. pap. 2.95 (0-14-071401-4, Pelican Bks) Viking Penguin.
—Macbeth. Stewart, Diana, adapted by. LC 81-19273. (Illus.). 48p. (gr. 4 up). 1983. PLB 18.64 (0-8172-1681-2); pap. 9.27 (0-8172-2014-3) Raintree Steck-V.
—Macbeth. Davidson, Diane, ed. LC 83-12312. (Illus.). 111p. (gr. 8-12). 1983. pap. 5.95 (0-934048-02-9) Swan Books.
—Macbeth. Gill, Roma, ed. (Illus.). 124p. 1987. pap. 7.50 (0-19-831933-9) OUP.
—Macbeth. Mack, Maynard & Boynton, Robert W., eds. 141p. (gr. 9-12). 1990. pap. text ed. 4.50 (0-86709-021-9, 0021) Boynton Cook Pubs.
—Macbeth: A Facing-Page Edition--The Original Text & a Translation into Modern English. Zuesse, Eric, tr. 192p. (Orig.). 1990. pap. 3.95 (0-9628103-0-4) Shakespeare VT.
—Macbeth for Young People. Davidson, Diane, ed. LC 86-5955. (Illus.). 64p. (gr. 5-8). 1986. pap. 4.95 (0-934048-21-5) Swan Books.
—Merchant of Venice. Redekop, Ernest, intro. by. (gr. 9 up). 1965. pap. 1.25 (0-8049-1003-0, S3) Airmont.
—Merchant of Venice. Stirling, Brents, ed. (gr. 9 up). 1960. pap. 3.95 (0-14-071421-9, Pelican Bks) Viking Penguin.
—Merchant of Venice. Davidson, Diane, ed. LC 83-12308. (Illus.). 112p. (gr. 8-12). 1983. pap. 5.95 (0-934048-08-8) Swan Books.
—The Merchant of Venice. King, Neil, ed. (Illus.). 90p. (gr. 9 up). 1993. pap. 14.95x (0-7487-1194-5) Dufour.
—Midsummer Night's Dream. Pitt, David G., intro. by. (gr. 10 up). 1965. pap. 1.95 (0-8049-1005-7, S5) Airmont.
—Midsummer Night's Dream. Doran, Madeleine, ed. (Orig.). (gr. 9 up). 1959. pap. 3.95 (0-14-071418-9, Pelican Bks) Viking Penguin.
—A Midsummer Night's Dream. Stewart, Diana, adapted by. LC 81-19272. (Illus.). 48p. (gr. 4 up). 1983. PLB 18.64 (0-8172-1680-4) Raintree Steck-V.
—A Midsummer Night's Dream. Pickett, Cecil, adapted by. (Illus.). 32p. (gr. 7 up). 1984. pap. 2.00 (0-88680-214-8); royalty on application 20.00 (0-685-57921-2) I E Clark.
—Midsummer Night's Dream. Davidson, Diane, ed. LC 83-12311. (Illus.). 99p. (gr. 8-12). 1983. pap. 5.95 (0-934048-10-X) Swan Books.
—A Midsummer Night's Dream. Gill, Roma, ed. (Illus.). 118p. 1987. pap. 7.50 (0-19-831938-X) OUP.
—Midsummer Night's Dream. Adams, Richard, ed. 1990. pap. text ed. 4.29 (0-582-01345-3, 78421) Longman.
—A Midsummer Night's Dream for Young People. Davidson, Diane, ed. LC 86-5957. (Illus.). 64p. (gr. 5-8). 1986. pap. text ed. 4.95 (0-934048-18-5) Swan Books.
—Much Ado about Nothing. Rowland, Beryl, intro. by. (gr. 10 up). 1967. pap. 0.60 (0-8049-1020-0, S20) Airmont.
—Narrative Poems. Wilbur, Richard & Harbage, Alfred, eds. (gr. 9 up). 1966. pap. 3.95 (0-14-071437-5, Pelican Bks) Viking Penguin.
—Othello. Rudvik, O. H., intro. by. (gr. 10 up). 1966. pap. 1.75 (0-8049-1013-8, S13) Airmont.
—Othello. Bentley, Gerald E., ed. (gr. 9 up). 1958. pap. 3.95 (0-14-071410-3, Pelican Bks) Viking Penguin.

—Othello. Gill, Roma, ed. (Illus.). 144p. (gr. 9 up). 1990. pap. 7.50 (0-19-831953-3) OUP.
—Othello, the Moor of Venice. Davidson, Diane, ed. LC 83-60730. (Illus.). 142p. (gr. 10-12). 1985. pap. 5.95x (0-934048-16-9) Swan Books.
—Richard Second. Young, Archibald M., intro. by. (gr. 9 up). 1966. pap. 0.60 (0-8049-1014-6, S14) Airmont.
—Richard Second. Black, Matthew W., ed. (gr. 9 up). 1957. pap. 3.50 (0-14-071406-5, Pelican Bks) Viking Penguin.
—Richard Third. Willoughby, John, intro. by. (gr. 9 up). 1966. pap. 0.60 (0-8049-1015-4, S15) Airmont.
—Romeo & Juliet. Thomas, Clara, intro. by. (gr. 8 up). 1966. pap. 1.75 (0-8049-1009-X, S9) Airmont.
—Romeo & Juliet. Shaw, Charles, illus. Stewart, Diana, adapted by. LC 79-24465. (Illus.). 48p. (gr. 4 up). 1983. PLB 18.64 (0-8172-1653-7) Raintree Steck-V.
—Romeo & Juliet. Davidson, Diane, ed. LC 83-12309. (Illus.). (gr. 8-12). 1983. pap. 5.95 (0-934048-06-1) Swan Books.
—Romeo & Juliet. Gill, Roma, ed. (Illus.). 164p. 1987. pap. 7.50 (0-19-831937-1) OUP.
—Romeo & Juliet. Mack, Maynard & Boynton, Robert W., eds. 159p. (gr. 9-12). 1990. pap. text ed. 4.50 (0-86709-035-9, 0035) Boynton Cook Pubs.
—Romeo & Juliet. Gibson, Rex, ed. (Illus.). 224p. 1992. pap. 5.95 (0-521-39574-7) Cambridge U Pr.
—Romeo & Juliet. rev. ed. Gill, Roma, ed. (Illus.). 168p. (gr. 9-11). 1993. pap. 7.50 (0-19-831972-X) OUP.
—Romeo & Juliet for Young People. Davidson, Diane, ed. LC 86-5958. (Illus.). 64p. (gr. 5-8). 1986. pap. 4.95 (0-934048-19-3) Swan Books.
—Shakespeare for Everyone: Hamlet, Macbeth, The Merchant of Venice, A Midsummer Night's Dream, Romeo & Juliet, Twelfth Night, 6 vols. Mulherin, Jennifer, retold by. (Illus.). 192p. (gr. 5-12). 1988. Set, 6 vols. PLB 65.76 (0-382-09811-0) Silver Burdett Pr.
—Sonnets. Bush, Douglas & Harbage, Alfred, eds. (gr. 9 up). 1963. pap. 3.95 (0-14-071423-5, Pelican Bks) Viking Penguin.
—Taming of the Shrew. Girling, Z. N., intro. by. (gr. 10 up). 1966. pap. 1.75 (0-8049-1010-3, S10) Airmont.
—The Taming of the Shrew. Fynes-Clinton, Michael & Mills, Perry, eds. (Illus.). 192p. (gr. 5 up). 1992. pap. 6.95 (0-521-42505-0) Cambridge U Pr.
—The Taming of the Shrew. rev. ed. Gill, Roma, ed. (Illus.). 144p. (gr. 9-11). 1993. pap. 7.50 (0-19-831976-2) OUP.
—The Taming of the Shrew for Young People. Davidson, Diane, ed. LC 86-5934. (Illus.). 64p. (gr. 5-8). 1986. pap. 4.95 (0-934048-20-7) Swan Books.
—Tempest. Pitt, D. G., intro. by. (gr. 11 up). pap. 1.25 (0-8049-1007-3, S7) Airmont.
—Three Great Plays of Shakespeare. (gr. 4-7). 1991. pap. 4.87 (0-582-03586-4, 79122) Longman.
—Twelfth Night. Pitt, David G., intro. by. (gr. 10 up). 1965. pap. 1.75 (0-8049-1008-1, S8) Airmont.
—Twelfth Night. abr. ed. Pickett, Cecil, adapted by. (Illus.). 36p. (gr. 7 up). 1984. pap. 2.00 (0-88680-213-X); royalty on application 20.00 (0-685-57924-7) I E Clark.
—Twelfth Night. Gill, Roma, ed. (Illus.). 136p. (ps-5). 1987. pap. 7.50 (0-19-831947-9) OUP.
—Twelfth Night. Adams, Richard, ed. 1989. pap. text ed. 4.29 (0-582-01346-1, 78433) Longman.
—Under the Greenwood Tree. Holdridge, Barbara, ed. DeWitt, Robin & DeWitt, Pat, illus. Rowse, A. L., pref. by. 80p. (gr. 4 up). 1986. 21.95 (0-88045-028-2); pap. 14.95 (0-88045-029-0); cass. & bk. 23.90 (0-88045-103-3); cassette only 8.95 (0-88045-100-9) Stemmer Hse.
Shakespeare, William, jt. auth. see Harris, Aurand.
Shalant, Phyllis. Look What We've Brought You from Mexico. (ps-3). 1992. lib. bdg. 11.98 (0-671-75256-1, J Messner); lib. bdg. 6.95 (0-671-75257-X, J Messner) S&S Trade.
—Look What We've Brought You from Vietnam: Crafts, Games, Recipes, Stories & Other Cultural Activities from New Americans. LC 87-20276. (Illus.). 48p. (gr. 2-6). 1988. lib. bdg. 9.98 (0-671-63919-6, J Messner); lib. bdg. 4.95 (0-671-65978-2) S&S Trade.
—The Rock Star, the Rooster, & Me, the Reporter. Robinson, Charles, illus. 169p. (gr. 3-7). 1991. pap. 3.95 (0-14-034596-5, Puffin) Puffin Bks.
—Shalom, Geneva Peace. 160p. (gr. 7 up). 1992. 15.00 (0-525-44868-3, DCB) Dutton Child Bks.
—Transformation of Faith Futterman. LC 89-27563. 144p. (gr. 4 up). 1990. 13.95 (0-525-44570-6, DCB) Dutton Child Bks.
—The Transformation of Faith Futterman. 144p. (gr. 3-7). 1992. pap. 3.99 (0-14-036026-3) Puffin Bks.
Shale, David & Coldrey, Jennifer. Man-of-War at Sea. LC 86-5703. (Illus.). 32p. (gr. 4-6). 1987. PLB 15.93 (1-55532-069-4) Gareth Stevens Inc.
—The World of a Jellyfish. LC 86-5704. (Illus.). 32p. (gr. 2-3). 1986. 15.93 (1-55532-073-2) Gareth Stevens Inc.
Shalit, Nathan. Science Magic Tricks: Over 50 Fun Tricks That Mystify & Dazzle. Ulan, Helen C., illus. LC 79-18645. 128p. (gr. 6 up). 1981. (Bks Young Read); pap. 5.95 (0-8050-0234-0) H Holt & Co.
Shalleck, Alan J., jt. auth. see Rey, Margret.
Shalleck, Alan J., jt. auth. see Rey, Margret.
Shalleck, Alan J., jt. auth. see Rey, Margret.
Shalleck, Allan J., jt. auth. see Rey, Margaret.
Shalleck, Allan J., jt. ed. see Rey, Margaret.
Shamir, Ilana, jt. auth. see Hoffman, Yair.

Shamir, Ilana & Shavit, Shlomo, eds. The Young Reader's Encyclopedia of Jewish History. LC 87-10599. (gr. 7 up). 1987. pap. 17.95 (0-670-81738-4) Viking Child Bks.

Shamir, Moshe. The Fifth Wheel. rev. ed. Hodes, Aubrey, tr. from HEB. Katz, Shmuel, illus. 115p. (gr. 8 up). 1986. pap. 8.95 (0-917883-02-0) Benmir Bks.

Shampton, Marianne J. One Hundred One More Talks for Children. 7.95 (0-88494-729-7) Bookcraft Inc.

—One Hundred One Talks for Children. 6.95 (0-88494-580-4) Bookcraft Inc.

Shanahan, Danny. Buckledown, the Workhound. LC 92-13433. 1993. 14.95 (0-316-78276-9) Little.

Shanahan, Timothy, ed. Reading & Writing Together: New Perspectives for the Classroom. Pearson, P. David, frwd. by. (Illus.). 296p. (gr. k-8). 1990. text ed. 34.95 (0-926842-04-8) CG Pubs Inc.

Shanahan, William F. College: Yes or No? The High School Student's Career Decision-Making Handbook. 2nd ed. LC 82-6775. 304p. (gr. 9 up). 1983. (Arco Test); pap. 7.95 (0-668-05590-1) P-H Gen Ref & Trav.

Shangold, Helen. Cloze Stories for Reading Success. (gr. k-3). 1981. 13.95x (0-8027-9124-7) Walker & Co.

Shanjar. Life with Grandfather. 9th ed. Shankar, illus. 54p. (Orig.). (gr. k-3). 1980. pap. 3.50 (0-89744-212-1, Pub. by Childrens Bk Trust IA) Auromere.

Shank, Charles C. Book of Wisdom for Children. 1993. pap. 7.95 (0-8059-3356-5) Dorrance.

Shank, Merna B. Happy Ways: Verses for Children. 1982. pap. 1.95 (0-87813-211-2) Christian Light.

—Thankful Days: Verses for Children. 1982. pap. 1.95 (0-87813-212-0) Christian Light.

Shankar. Treasury of Indian Tales: Book I. Mukerji, Debrabrata, illus. (gr. 8-12). 1979. 4.95 (0-89744-170-2) Auromere.

—Treasury of Indian Tales: Book II. Vyas, Anil, illus. (gr. 8-12). 1979. 4.95 (0-89744-171-0) Auromere.

Shankar, Alaka. The Seven Queens. Vyas, Anil, illus. 16p. (Orig.). (gr. k-3). 1980. pap. 2.50 (0-89744-217-2, Pub. by Childrens Bk Trust IA) Auromere.

—Sonali's Prayer. Joshi, Jagadish, illus. 16p. (Orig.). (gr. k-3). 1980. pap. 2.50 (0-89744-218-0, Pub. by Childrens Bk Trust IA) Auromere.

Shankar, R. Story of Gandhi. (Illus.). (gr. 3-10). 1979. 5.00 (0-89744-166-4) Auromere.

Shannon, Bill. The New York Mets. 1991. pap. 2.99 (0-517-05792-1) Outlet Bk Co.

Shannon, David. How Georgie Radbourn Saved Baseball. LC 93-2475. (Illus.). 32p. 1994. 14.95 (0-590-47410-3, Blue Sky Press); pap. write for info. (0-590-47411-1, Blue Sky Press) Scholastic Inc.

Shannon, Ellen & Hart, Corinne. Pedimos Perdon: Libro de Reconciliacion para Ninos. Silva, P. Fidencio & Di Raimondo, P. Domenico, trs. from ENG. Benner, Patti, illus. (SPA.). 32p. (ps-2). 1991. pap. 1.90 (1-55944-007-4) Franciscan Comns.

Shannon, Ellen, jt. auth. see Hart, Corinne.

Shannon, Foster H. The Green Leaf Bible Series, Year One. 174p. (gr. 3 up). 1982. pap. 15.00 (0-938462-06-7) Green Leaf CA.

—Green Leaf Bible Series, Year Four. 180p. (gr. 3 up). 1988. looseleaf 17.50 (0-938462-08-3) Green Leaf CA.

—Green Leaf Bible Series, Year Five. 180p. (gr. 3 up). 1989. looseleaf 17.50 (0-938462-09-1) Green Leaf CA.

—Green Leaf Bible Series: Year Six. 184p. (gr. 3 up). 1992. thermobound 17.50 (0-938462-10-5) Green Leaf Ca.

Shannon, George. Climbing Kansas Mountains. Allen, Thomas B., illus. 32p. (ps-2). 1993. RSBE 15.95 (0-02-782181-1, Bradbury Pr) Macmillan Child Grp.

—Dance Away! Aruego, Jose & Dewey, Ariane, illus. LC 81-6391. 32p. (gr. k-3). 1982. 13.95 (0-688-00838-0); PLB 13.88 (0-688-00839-9) Greenwillow.

—Dance Away. Aruego, Jose & Dewey, Ariane, illus. LC 81-6391. 32p. (gr. k-3). 1991. pap. 3.95 (0-688-10483-5, Mulberry) Morrow.

—Dancing the Breeze. Rogers, Jacqueline, illus. LC 88-37598. 32p. (ps-1). 1991. RSBE 13.95 (0-02-782190-0, Bradbury Pr) Macmillan Child Grp.

—Laughing All the Way. McLean, Meg, illus. LC 91-41135. 32p. (ps-3). 1992. 13.45 (0-395-62473-8) HM.

—Lizard's Song. Aruego, Jose & Dewey, Ariane, illus. LC 80-21432. 32p. (gr. k-3). 1981. 14.95 (0-688-80310-5); PLB 14.88 (0-688-84310-7) Greenwillow.

—Lizard's Song. Aruego, Jose & Dewey, Ariane, illus. LC 80-21432. 32p. (gr. k-3). 1992. pap. 3.95 (0-688-11516-0, Mulberry) Morrow.

—More Stories to Solve. Sis, Peter, illus. 64p. (gr. 4 up). 1994. pap. 3.95 (0-688-12947-1, Pub. by Beech Tree Bks) Morrow.

—More Stories to Solve: Fifteen Folktales from Around the World. Sis, Peter, illus. LC 89-7413. 64p. (gr. k up). 1991. 12.95 (0-688-09160-X) Greenwillow.

—The Piney Woods Peddler. Tafuri, Nancy, illus. LC 81-2219. 32p. (gr. k-3). 1981. PLB 14.88 (0-688-84304-2) Greenwillow.

—Sea Gifts. Azarian, illus. LC 88-45429. (gr. 2-4). 1989. 11.95 (0-87923-770-8) Godine.

—Seeds. Bjorkman, George, illus. LC 92-40738. 1994. write for info. (0-395-66990-1) HM.

—Stories to Solve: Folktales from Around the World. Sis, Peter, illus. LC 84-18656. 56p. (gr. 3-5). 1985. 14.00 (0-688-04303-8); PLB 13.93 (0-688-04304-6) Greenwillow.

—Stories to Solve: Folktales from Around the World. Sis, Peter, illus. LC 84-18656. 53p. (gr. 4-6). 1991. pap. 4.95 (0-688-10496-7, Pub. by Beech Tree Bks) Morrow.

—The Surprise. Aruego, Jose & Dewey, Ariane, illus. LC 83-1434. 32p. (gr. k-3). 1983. 13.95 (0-688-02313-4) Greenwillow.

Shannon, George, as told by. Still More Stories to Solve: Fifteen Folktales from Around the World. Sis, Peter, illus. LC 93-26529. 1994. write for info. reinforced bdg. (0-688-04619-3) Greenwillow.

Shannon, J. Michael. Riddles & More Riddles. Magnuson, Diana, illus. LC 82-19765. 48p. (gr. 1-5). 1983. PLB 13.27 (0-516-01873-6); pap. 3.95 (0-516-41873-4) Childrens.

—Still More Jokes. Magnuson, Diana, illus. LC 85-27971. 48p. (gr. 1-5). 1986. lib. bdg. 13.27 (0-516-01867-1); pap. 3.95 (0-516-41867-X) Childrens.

—Still More Riddles. Magnuson, Diana, illus. LC 85-29065. 48p. (gr. 1-5). 1986. pap. 3.95 (0-516-41869-6) Childrens.

Shannon, Jacqueline. Big Guy, Little Women. (gr. 6-8). 1989. pap. 2.75 (0-590-41685-5, Apple Paperbacks) Scholastic Inc.

—Faking It. 176p. (Orig.). 1989. pap. 2.95 (0-380-75601-3, Flare) Avon.

—I Hate My Hero. LC 92-890. (gr. 4-7). 1992. pap. 13.00 (0-671-75442-4, S&S BFYR) S&S Trade.

—Too Much T. J. (gr. k-12). 1988. pap. 2.95 (0-440-20222-1, LFL) Dell.

Shannon, Katherine, jt. auth. see White, Marjorie L.

Shannon, Margaret, text by. & illus. Elvira. LC 92-39784. 1993. 13.45 (0-395-66597-3) Ticknor & Fields.

Shannon, Mark. Gawain & the Green Knight. Shannon, David, illus. LC 93-13037. 1994. write for info. (0-399-22446-7, Putnam) Putnam Pub Group.

Shannon, Michael, compiled by. Space Jokes. Rigo, Russell, illus. LC 88-17488. 48p. (gr. 1-5). 1988. pap. 3.95 (0-516-41874-2) Childrens.

Shannon, Mike. Johnny Bench. (Illus.). 64p. (gr. 3 up). 1990. 14.95 (0-7910-1168-2) Chelsea Hse.

—Willie Stargell. (Illus.). 64p. (gr. 3 up). 1992. lib. bdg. 14.95 (0-7910-1192-5) Chelsea Hse.

Shannon, Monica. Dobry. Katchamakoff, Atanas, illus. LC 92-31442. 176p. (gr. 5 up). 1993. pap. 4.99 (0-14-036334-3) Puffin Bks.

Shannon, Robert L. Grandpap Remembers from the Book of Life. (Illus.). 40p. 1994. pap. 7.95 (0-8059-3476-6) Dorrance.

Shanower, Eric. Blue Witch of Oz. 1993. pap. 9.95 (1-878574-44-2) Dark Horse Comics.

—The Enchanted Apples of Oz. Oliver, Rick, ed. Ellison, Harlan, intro. by. (Illus.). 48p. (Orig.). 1986. pap. 7.95 (0-915419-04-1) First Pub IL.

—Enchanted Apples of Oz. 1993. pap. 7.95 (1-878574-66-3) Dark Horse Comics.

—The Forgotten Forest of Oz. Oliver, Rick, ed. Shanower, Eric, illus. 48p. (Orig.). 1991. pap. 8.95 (0-915419-44-0) First Pub IL.

—Forgotten Forest of Oz. 1993. pap. 8.95 (1-878574-64-7) Dark Horse Comics.

—The Giant Garden of Oz. Shunower, Eric, illus. (gr. 3 up). 1993. 39.95 (0-929605-23-3); pap. 11.95 (0-929605-22-5) Books Wonder.

—The Ice King of Oz. Oliver, Rick, ed. Shanower, Eric, illus. 48p. (Orig.). 1987. pap. 7.95 (0-915419-25-4) First Pub IL.

—Ice King of Oz. 1993. pap. 8.95 (1-878574-65-5) Dark Horse Comics.

—The Secret Island of Oz. Oliver, Rick, ed. Shanower, Eric, illus. 48p. (Orig.). 1988. pap. 7.95 (0-915419-08-4) First Pub IL.

—Secret Island of Oz. 1993. pap. 8.95 (1-878574-67-1) Dark Horse Comics.

Shanta. Nala Damayanti. Sonkaria, Gyan, illus. (gr. 1-9). 1979. pap. 3.00 (0-89744-158-3) Auromere.

Shapiro, Arnold. I Heard It from a Little Bird. Williams, Karin, illus. Dudley, Dick, designed by. (Illus.). 12p. (ps). 1991. 12.95 (0-8120-6204-3) Barron.

—The Neighbor Game: A Pop-up, Figure-It-Out Book. Billin-Frye, Paige, illus. LC 93-11199. Date not set. write for info. (0-8037-1239-1) Dial Bks Young.

—Shopping Trip. (ps-3). 1992. pap. 12.95 (0-8167-2747-3) Troll Assocs.

Shapiro, Arnold L. Who Says That? Wellington, Monica, illus. LC 90-3996. 32p. (ps). 1991. 13.95 (0-525-44698-2, DCB) Dutton Child Bks.

Shapiro, Ellen. The Croatian Americans. Moynihan, Daniel P. 112p. (gr. 5 up). 1989. 17.95x (0-87754-891-9) Chelsea Hse.

Shapiro, Ellen S. The Complete Mother Goose. Betts, Ethel F., et al, illus. 288p. (ps-1). 1988. 12.99 (0-517-63383-3) Outlet Bk Co.

Shapiro, Irwin. Joe Magarac & His U. S. A. Citizen Papers. Daugherty, James, illus. LC 78-66070. 58p. (gr. 1-8). 1979. pap. 5.95 (0-8229-5305-6) U of Pittsburgh Pr.

Shapiro, Irwin, ed. see Clemens, Samuel.

Shapiro, Irwin, ed. see Crane, Stephen.

Shapiro, Irwin, ed. see Melville, Herman.

Shapiro, Jane, jt. auth. see Appleman, Harlene.

Shapiro, Lawrence E. All Feelings Are Ok - It's What You Do with Them That Counts. Shose, Hennie M., ed. Mandel, Jille, illus. 100p. (Orig.). (gr. k-4). 1993. 14.95 (1-882732-04-9) Ctr Applied Psy.

—The Building Blocks of Self-Esteem. Laughlin, Christopher, illus. 108p. (Orig.). (gr. k-4). 1993. pap. 9.95 (1-882732-08-1) Ctr Applied Psy.

—Sometimes I Drive My Mom Crazy, but I Know She's Crazy about Me: A Self-Esteem Book for Overactive & Impulsive Children. Shore, Hennie M., ed. Parrotte, Timothy, illus. 80p. (gr. k-6). 1993. 9.95 (1-882732-03-0) Ctr Applied Psy.

Shapiro, Lawrence E., jt. auth. see Shelton, Laura S.

Shapiro, Lillian L. Teaching Yourself in Libraries: A Guide to the High School Media Center & Other Libraries. LC 78-16616. 180p. (gr. 7-12). 1978. 10.00 (0-8242-0628-2) Wilson.

Shapiro, Mary F. Learn-to-Read. Hinchberger, William D. & Hron, Debi, illus. 52p. (ps-k). 1986. 15.99 (0-934361-11-8) Kinder Read.

Shapiro, Mary S. My Playbook, One, Bk. 4. Hinchberger, William D., illus. 12p. (ps-k). 1985. wkbk. 3.95x (0-934361-04-5) Kinder Read.

—Play. Wisniewski, Dennis, photos by. (Illus.). 14p. (ps-k). 1985. 3.95 (0-934361-02-9); Set. write for info. Kinder Read.

—Red, Green, Yellow. Hron, Debi, illus. 12p. (ps-k). 1985. 3.95 (0-934361-01-0); Set. write for info. Kinder Read.

—Stop, Start. Hron, Debi, illus. 14p. (ps-k). 1985. 3.95 (0-934361-03-7); Set. write for info. (0-934361-00-2) Kinder Read.

Shapiro, Miles. Bill Russell. King, Coretta Scott, intro. by. (Illus.). 112p. (gr. 5 up). 1991. lib. bdg. 17.95 (0-7910-1136-4) Chelsea Hse.

—Maya Angelou, Author. King, Coretta Scott, intro. by. (Illus.). 112p. (gr. 5 up). 1994. PLB 18.95 (0-7910-1862-8, Am Art Analog); pap. write for info. (0-7910-1891-1, Am Art Analog) Chelsea Hse.

Shapiro, Nat & Hentoff, Nat, eds. Hear Me Talkin' to Ya: The Story of Jazz by the Men Who Made It. (gr. 7-12). 1966. pap. 7.95 (0-486-21726-4) Dover.

Shapiro, Sidney, tr. see Nai'an, Shi & Guanzhong, Luo.

Shapiro, Stanley J. Exploring Careers in Science. rev. ed. Rosen, Ruth, ed. (gr. 7-12). 1989. PLB 13.95 (0-8239-0969-7) Rosen Group.

Shapiro, William E., ed. The Young People's Encyclopedia of the United States, 10 vols. LC 91-4141. (Illus.). 800p. (gr. 4-8). 1992. Set. PLB 149.00 (1-56294-151-8) Millbrook Pr.

Shapiro, Zeva, tr. see Meir, Mira.

Shapley, R. Boomtowns. (Illus.). 32p. (gr. 3-8). 1990. lib. bdg. 18.00 (0-86625-370-X); 13.50s.p. (0-685-58647-2) Rourke Corp.

Shapley, R., et al. Wild West in American History, 14 bks, Set 2. (Illus.). 448p. (gr. 3-8). 1990. Set. lib. bdg. 252.00 (0-86625-367-X); Set. lib. bdg. 189.00s.p. (0-685-36328-7) Rourke Corp.

Shapolsky, Ian. The Jewish Trivia & Information Book. 400p. (gr. 6-12). 1985. pap. 5.95 (0-933503-08-3) Shapolsky Pubs.

Sharafuddin, Sadruddin. Ammar Yasir: The Distinguished Companion of the Holy Prophet. rev. ed. Haq, M. Fazal, tr. 264p. pap. 7.00x (0-941724-40-9) Islamic Seminary.

Sharfstein, Chana. The Little Leaf. Rosenfeld, Dina, ed. Blumenfeld, Rochelle, illus. 32p. (gr. k-4). 1989. 8.95 (0-922613-18-4); pap. 6.95 (0-922613-19-2) Hachai Pubns.

Sharma, Elizabeth. Brass. LC 93-20398. (Illus.). 32p. (gr. 4-6). 1993. 14.95 (1-56847-114-9) Thomson Lrning.

—Keyboards. LC 93-12819. (Illus.). 32p. (gr. 4-6). 1993. 14.95 (1-56847-117-3) Thomson Lrning.

—Percussion. LC 93-710. (Illus.). 32p. (gr. 4-6). 1993. 14.95 (1-56847-113-0) Thomson Lrning.

—Strings. LC 93-7249. (Illus.). 32p. (gr. 4-6). 1993. 14.95 (1-56847-112-2) Thomson Lrning.

—Voice. LC 93-1093. (Illus.). 32p. (gr. 4-6). 1993. 14.95 (1-56847-116-5) Thomson Lrning.

—Woodwinds. LC 93-709. (Illus.). 32p. (gr. 4-6). 1993. 14.95 (1-56847-115-7) Thomson Lrning.

Sharma, Rashmi. The Blue Jackal. (Illus.). 32p. (gr. 2 up). 1992. 14.95 (1-878099-50-7); pap. 6.95 (1-878099-51-5) Vidya Bks.

—A Brahmin's Castles in the Air. LC 92-61764. (Illus.). 32p. 1993. 14.95 (1-878099-56-6); pap. 6.95 (1-878099-57-4) Vidya Bks.

Sharma, Vijai P. Insane Jealousy: The Causes, Outcomes, & Solutions When Jealousy Gets Out of Hand: The Triangle of the Mind. Munro, Alistair, intro. by. 224p. (Orig.). (gr. 7-9). 1991. pap. text ed. 16.95 (0-9628382-6-8) Mind Pubns.

Sharman, Margaret. Nineteen Fifties. LC 92-25916. (Illus.). 47p. (gr. 6-7). 1992. PLB 22.80 (0-8114-3078-2) Raintree Steck-V.

—Nineteen Hundred Tens. LC 92-17521. (Illus.). 47p. (gr. 6-7). 1992. PLB 22.80 (0-8114-3074-X) Raintree Steck-V.

—Nineteen Hundreds. LC 93-12034. (Illus.). 47p. (gr. 6-7). 1993. PLB 22.80 (0-8114-3073-1) Raintree Steck-V.

—Nineteen Twenties. LC 92-17526. (Illus.). 47p. (gr. 6-7). 1992. PLB 22.80 (0-8114-3075-8) Raintree Steck-V.

Sharman, Tim. Rise of Solidarity. LC 86-20276. (Illus.). 78p. (gr. 7 up). 1987. 18.60 (0-86592-030-3); 13.95s.p. (0-685-58242-6) Rourke Corp.

Sharmat, Andrew, jt. auth. see Sharmat, Marjorie.

Sharmat, Craig, jt. auth. see Sharmat, Marjorie W.

Sharmat, Marjorie. The Field Day Mix-Up. (gr. 4-7). 1991. pap. 2.99 (0-06-106029-1, Harp PBks) HarpC.

—My Mother Never Listens to Me. Tucker, Kathleen, ed. Munsinger, Lynn, illus. LC 84-17201. 32p. (ps-3). 1984. 11.95 (0-8075-5347-6) A Whitman.

—Nate the Great & the Mushy Valentine. Simont, Marc, illus. LC 93-15488. 1994. 12.95 (*0-385-31166-4*) Delacorte.
—Pizza Monster. 1989. pap. 12.95 (*0-440-50086-9*) Dell.
Sharmat, Marjorie & Sharmat, Andrew. The Haunted Bus. (gr. 1-6). 1991. pap. 2.99 (*0-06-106030-5*, Harp PBks) HarpC.
Sharmat, Marjorie W. Attila the Angry. Hoban, Lillian, illus. LC 84-15860. 32p. (ps-3). 1985. reinforced bdg. 11.95 (*0-8234-0545-1*) Holiday.
—Best Valentine in the World. LC 81-13345. (Illus.). 32p. (ps-3). 1982. reinforced bdg. 14.95 (*0-8234-0440-4*) Holiday.
—A Big Fat Enormous Lie. McPhail, David, illus. LC 77-15645. (ps-2). 1978. 13.00 (*0-525-26510-4*, DCB) Dutton Child Bks.
—A Big Fat Enormous Lie. McPhail, David, illus. LC 77-15645. 32p. (ps-2). 1986. pap. 3.99 (*0-525-44242-1*, DCB) Dutton Child Bks.
—Chasing after Annie. Simont, Marc, illus. LC 80-7906. 80p. (gr. 2-5). 1991. pap. 3.50 (*0-06-440351-3*, Trophy) HarpC Child Bks.
—The Cooking Class. (gr. 4-7). 1991. pap. 2.99 (*0-06-106026-7*, PL) HarpC.
—Fighting over Me. (Orig.). (gr. 6 up). 1986. pap. 2.50 (*0-440-92530-4*, LFL) Dell.
—For Members Only. (Orig.). (gr. 5 up). 1986. pap. 2.50 (*0-440-92654-8*, LFL) Dell.
—Get Rich Mitch! Lustig, Loretta, illus. LC 85-8799. 160p. (gr. 3-7). 1985. 13.95 (*0-688-05790-X*) Morrow Jr Bks.
—Get Rich Mitch! 96p. (gr. 3-7). 1986. pap. 2.50 (*0-380-70170-7*, Camelot) Avon.
—Getting Closer. (Orig.). (gr. k-12). 1987. pap. 2.50 (*0-440-92828-1*, LFL) Dell.
—Getting Something on Maggie Marmelstein. Shecter, Ben, illus. LC 78-157895. 110p. (gr. 4-6). 1971. PLB 13.89 (*0-06-025552-8*) HarpC Child Bks.
—Gila Monsters Meet You at the Airport. Barton, Byron, illus. LC 80-12264. 32p. (gr. k-3). 1980. RSBE 14.95 (*0-02-782450-0*, Macmillan Child Bk) Macmillan Child Grp.
—Gila Monsters Meet You at the Airport. LC 89-38398. (Illus.). 32p. 1990. pap. 3.95 (*0-689-71383-5*, Aladdin) Macmillan Child Grp.
—Go to Sleep, Nicholas Joe. Himmelman, John, illus. LC 85-45689. 32p. (ps-3). 1988. PLB 11.89 (*0-06-025504-8*) HarpC Child Bks.
—The Great Genghis Khan Look-Alike Contest. Rigie, Mitch, illus. 80p. (Orig.). (gr. 1-4). 1993. PLB 9.99 (*0-679-95002-8*); pap. 2.99 (*0-679-85002-3*) Random Bks Yng Read.
—He Noticed I'm Alive & Other Hopeful Signs. (Orig.). (gr. k-12). 1989. pap. 2.95 (*0-440-93809-0*, LFL) Dell.
—Here Comes Mr. Right. (gr. 5 up). 1987. pap. 2.50 (*0-440-93841-4*) Dell.
—Hooray for Father's Day. Wallner, John, illus. LC 86-15037. 32p. (ps-3). 1987. reinforced bdg. 14.95 (*0-8234-0637-7*) Holiday.
—Hooray for Mother's Day! Wallner, John, illus. LC 85-14146. 32p. (ps-3). 1986. reinforced bdg. 14.95 (*0-8234-0588-5*) Holiday.
—How to Have a Gorgeous Wedding. 144p. (gr. k-12). 1989. pap. 2.95 (*0-440-93794-9*, LFL) Dell.
—How to Meet a Gorgeous Girl. 160p. (Orig.). (gr. k up). 1989. pap. 2.95 (*0-440-93808-2*, LFL) Dell.
—I Saw Him First. 192p. (gr. 7 up). 1989. pap. 2.95 (*0-440-94009-5*, LFL) Dell.
—I Saw Him First. LC 82-14839. 128p. (gr. 7 up). 1983. pap. 12.95 (*0-385-29243-0*) Delacorte.
—I Think I'm Falling in Love. (Orig.). (gr. 6 up). 1986. pap. 2.50 (*0-440-94011-7*, LFL) Dell.
—I'm Going to Get Your Boyfriend. (Orig.). (gr. k-12). 1987. pap. 2.50 (*0-440-94004-4*, LFL) Dell.
—I'm Santa Claus & I'm Famous. Hafner, Marylin, illus. LC 90-55106. 32p. (ps-4). 1990. reinforced 14.95 (*0-8234-0826-4*) Holiday.
—I'm Terrific. Chorao, Kay, illus. LC 76-9094. 32p. (ps-3). 1977. reinforced bdg. 13.95 (*0-8234-0282-7*) Holiday.
—I'm Terrific. Chorao, Kay, illus. LC 76-9094. 32p. (ps-3). 1992. pap. 4.95 (*0-8234-0955-4*) Holiday.
—I'm the Best. Hillenbrand, Will, illus. LC 90-39176. 32p. (ps-3). 1991. reinforced 14.95 (*0-8234-0859-0*) Holiday.
—Kids on the Bus, No. 3: Bully on the Bus. (gr. 4-7). 1991. pap. 2.95 (*0-06-106027-5*, Harp PBks) HarpC.
—Kids on the Bus, No. 4: The Secret Notebook. (gr. 4-7). 1991. pap. 2.95 (*0-06-106028-3*, Harp PBks) HarpC.
—Maggie Marmelstein for President. Shecter, Ben, illus. LC 75-6300. 128p. (gr. 4-6). 1975. PLB 13.89 (*0-06-025555-2*) HarpC Child Bks.
—Maggie Marmelstein for President. LC 75-6300. (Illus.). 128p. (gr. 3-7). 1976. pap. 3.95 (*0-06-440079-4*, Trophy) HarpC Child Bks.
—Mitchell Is Moving. Aruego, Jose & Dewey, Ariane, illus. LC 85-47782. 48p. (gr. 1-4). 1985. pap. 3.95 (*0-02-045260-8*, Aladdin) Macmillan Child Grp.
—Mitchell Is Moving. Aruego, Jose & Dewey, Ariane, illus. LC 78-6816. 48p. (gr. 1-4). 1978. RSBE 11.95 (*0-02-782410-1*, Macmillan Child Bk) Macmillan Child Grp.
—Mooch the Messy. Shecter, Ben, illus. LC 76-3842. 64p. (gr. k-3). 1976. PLB 13.89 (*0-06-025532-3*) HarpC Child Bks.
—Mysteriously Yours, Maggie Marmelstein. Shecter, Ben, illus. LC 81-48656. 160p. (gr. 3-6). 1984. pap. 3.95 (*0-06-440145-6*, Trophy) HarpC Child Bks.

—Nate the Great. 64p. (gr. 1-4). 1977. pap. 3.50 (*0-440-46126-X*, YB) Dell.
—Nate the Great. Simont, Marc, illus. 48p. (gr. 1-4). 1986. 12.95 (*0-698-20627-4*, Coward) Putnam Pub Group.
—Nate the Great & the Boring Beach Bag. Simont, Marc, illus. 48p. (gr. 1-4). 1987. 13.95 (*0-698-20631-2*, Coward) Putnam Pub Group.
—Nate the Great & the Boring Beach Bag. Simont, Marc, illus. 48p. (gr. 1-4). 1989. pap. 3.25 (*0-440-40168-2*, YB) Dell.
—Nate the Great & the Fishy Prize. (gr. k-6). 1988. pap. 3.25 (*0-440-40039-2*, YB) Dell.
—Nate the Great & the Halloween Hunt. (Illus.). 48p. (gr. 1-4). 1989. 12.95 (*0-698-20635-5*, Coward) Putnam Pub Group.
—Nate the Great & the Halloween Hunt. (gr. k-6). 1990. pap. 3.25 (*0-440-40341-3*, YB) Dell.
—Nate the Great & the Lost List. Simont, Marc, illus. 48p. 1981. pap. 3.25 (*0-440-46282-7*, YB) Dell.
—Nate the Great & the Lost List. (Illus.). 48p. (gr. 1-4). 1976. 11.95 (*0-698-20646-0*, Coward) Putnam Pub Group.
—Nate the Great & the Missing Key. Simont, Marc, illus. 48p. (gr. 1-4). 1982. pap. 3.25 (*0-440-46191-X*, YB) Dell.
—Nate the Great & the Missing Key. Simont, Marc, illus. 48p. (gr. 1-4). 1981. 11.95 (*0-698-20630-4*, Coward) Putnam Pub Group.
—Nate the Great & the Musical Note. (ps-3). 1991. pap. 3.25 (*0-440-40466-5*) Dell.
—Nate the Great & the Phony Clue. Simont, Marc, illus. 48p. (gr. k-6). 1981. pap. 3.25 (*0-440-46300-9*, YB) Dell.
—Nate the Great & The Snowy Trail. Simont, Marc, illus. 48p. (gr. 6-9). 1982. 11.95 (*0-698-20628-2*, Coward) Putnam Pub Group.
—Nate the Great & the Snowy Trail. Simont, Marc, illus. 48p. (gr. k-6). 1984. pap. 3.25 (*0-440-46276-2*, YB) Dell.
—Nate the Great & the Sticky Case. Simont, Marc, illus. (gr. k-6). 1981. pap. 3.25 (*0-440-46289-4*) Dell.
—Nate the Great & the Sticky Case. Simont, Marc, illus. (gr. 1-4). 1987. 11.95 (*0-698-20629-0*, Coward) Putnam Pub Group.
—Nate the Great: And the Stolen Base. Simont, Marc, illus. 48p. (gr. 1-4). 1992. 12.95 (*0-698-20708-4*, Coward) Putnam Pub Group.
—Nate the Great Goes Down. (ps-3). 1991. pap. 3.25 (*0-440-40438-X*) Dell.
—Nate the Great Goes Down in the Dumps. Simont, Marc, illus. 48p. (gr. 1-4). 1989. 13.95 (*0-698-20636-3*, Coward) Putnam Pub Group.
—Nate the Great Goes Undercover. 48p. 1978. pap. 3.25 (*0-440-46302-5*, YB) Dell.
—Nate the Great Goes Undercover. Simont, Marc, illus. 48p. (gr. 1-4). 1989. 13.95 (*0-698-20643-6*, Coward); (Coward) Putnam Pub Group.
—Nate the Great Stalks Stupidweed. Simont, Marc, illus. LC 85-30161. 48p. (gr. 1-4). 1986. 11.95 (*0-698-20626-6*, Coward) Putnam Pub Group.
—Nate the Great Stalks Stupidweed. Simont, Marc, illus. 48p. (gr. 9-12). 1989. pap. 3.25 (*0-440-40150-X*, YB) Dell.
—Nobody Knows How Scared I Am. (Orig.). (gr. k-12). 1987. pap. 2.50 (*0-440-96267-6*, LFL) Dell.
—One Terrific Thanksgiving. Obligado, Lilian, illus. LC 85-726. 32p. (ps-3). 1985. reinforced bdg. 14.95 (*0-8234-0569-9*) Holiday.
—The Princess of the Fillmore Street School. (gr. 4-7). 1991. pap. 2.75 (*0-440-40415-0*) Dell.
—Scarlet Monster Lives Here. Kendrick, Dennis, illus. LC 78-19484. 64p. (gr. k-3). 1979. PLB 11.89 (*0-06-025527-7*) HarpC Child Bks.
—Scarlet Monster Lives Here. Kendrick, Dennis, illus. LC 78-19484. 64p. (gr. k-3). 1986. pap. 3.50 (*0-06-444098-2*, Trophy) HarpC Child Bks.
—School Bus Cat. (gr. 4-7). 1990. pap. 2.99 (*0-06-106024-0*, PL) HarpC.
—Sly Spy: Olivia Sharp, Agent for Secrets. 1990. 12.95 (*0-385-29974-5*) Doubleday.
—Snobs Beware. (Orig.). (gr. 6 up). 1986. pap. 2.50 (*0-440-98092-5*, LFL) Dell.
—Spy in the Neighborhood. 1989. pap. 2.75 (*0-590-42633-8*) Scholastic Inc.
—The Story of Bentley Beaver. Hoban, Lillian, illus. LC 82-47715. 64p. (gr. k-3). 1984. HarpC Child Bks.
—The Three Hundred Twenty-Ninth Friend. 2nd ed. Szekeres, Cyndy, illus. LC 78-21770. 48p. (gr. k-3). 1992. RSBE 13.95 (*0-02-782259-1*, Four Winds) Macmillan Child Grp.
—Two Guys Noticed Me...& Other Miracles. (gr. k up). 1989. pap. 2.95 (*0-440-98846-2*, LFL) Dell.
—Walter the Wolf. LC 74-26659. (Illus.). 32p. (ps-3). 1975. pap. 5.95 (*0-8234-0778-0*) Holiday.
—What Are We Going to Do about Andrew? Cruz, Ray, illus. LC 88-3357. 32p. (gr. k-4). 1988. pap. 3.95 (*0-689-71264-2*, Aladdin) Macmillan Child Grp.
Sharmat, Marjorie W. & Sharmat, Craig. Nate the Great & the Musical Note. Simont, Marc, illus. 48p. (gr. 1-4). 1990. 13.95 (*0-698-20645-2*, Coward) Putnam Pub Group.
Sharmat, Marjorie W. & Sharmat, Mitchell. The Pizza Monster. Bruncus, Denise, illus. (ps up) 1989. 12.95 (*0-385-29722-X*) Delacorte.
—The Princess of the Fillmore Street School. Brunkus, Denise, illus. LC 89-1106. (gr. 2-4). 1989. 12.95 (*0-385-29811-0*) Delacorte.

Sharmat, Marjorie W. & Weinman, Rosalind. Nate the Great & the Pillowcase. Simont, Marc, illus. LC 92-34405. 1993. 12.95 (*0-385-31051-X*) Delacorte.
Sharmat, Mitchell. A Girl of Many Parts. (Orig.). (gr. k-12). 1988. pap. 2.95 (*0-440-20209-4*, LFL) Dell.
—Gregory, the Terrible Eater. Aruego, Jose & Dewey, Ariane, illus. LC 79-19172. 32p. (gr. k-3). 1980. RSBE 14.95 (*0-02-782250-8*, Four Winds) Macmillan Child Grp.
—Gregory, the Terrible Eater. Aruego, Jose & Dewey, Ariane, illus. 32p. (gr. k-3). 1984. pap. 3.95 (*0-590-43350-4*) Scholastic Inc.
Sharmat, Mitchell, jt. auth. see Sharmat, Marjorie W.
Sharon & Lois. Sharon, Lois & Bram Sing A to Z. LaFave, Kim, illus. LC 91-18990. 64p. (Orig.). (ps-4). 1992. 9.99 (*0-517-58723-8*) Crown Bks Yng Read.
Sharon, et al. Sharon, Lois & Bram's Mother Goose Songs, Finger Rhymes, Tickling Verses, Games & More. Kovalski, Mary A., illus. 96p. (gr. 2). 1986. 16.95i (*0-316-78281-5*, 782815); pap. 9.95i (*0-316-78282-3*) Little.
Sharp, Christopher. Bad Mouth Christopher. (gr. 1-4). 1980. pap. 4.99 (*0-570-03482-5*, 56-1703) Concordia.
Sharp, Donna. The Names Still Charlie. 1993. pap. 16.95 (*0-7022-2471-5*, Pub. by Univ Queensland Pr AT) Intl Spec Bk.
Sharp, Evelyn. Child's Christmas. 1991. 12.99 (*0-517-03369-0*) Outlet Bk Co.
Sharp, Floyd, jt. auth. see McAllister, Dawson.
Sharp, Harold E., jt. auth. see Kobayashi, Kiyoshi.
Sharp, Margery. Miss Bianca. Williams, Garth, illus. (gr. 2-4). 1923. 0.95 (*0-440-45761-0*, YB) Dell.
—Miss Bianca in the Salt Mines. 1978. pap. 1.25 (*0-440-45717-3*, YB) Dell.
—The Rescuers. (gr. 3-6). 17.00 (*0-8446-6412-X*) Peter Smith.
—The Turret. 144p. (gr. 3 up). 1974. pap. 1.25 (*0-440-48630-0*, YB) Dell.
Sharp, Mary. Bobbi Saves Christmas! Skar, Cynthia S., illus. 28p. (Orig.). (gr. 1-4). 1981. pap. 1.89 (*0-9603200-1-6*) Bobbi Ent.
Sharp, Mary & Niemi, Matt. Bobbi, Father of the Finnish White Tailed Deer. Shappell, Sherry, illus. LC 79-54100. (Orig.). (gr. 4-6). 1979. pap. 5.95 (*0-9603200-0-8*) Bobbi Ent.
Sharp, Melvin. The Vietnam War & Public Policy. (Illus.). 148p. (Orig.). (gr. 11-12). 1991. pap. text ed. 16.00x (*0-936826-37-1*) PS Assocs Croton.
Sharp, N. L. Today I'm Going Fishing with My Dad. Demarest, Chris L., illus. 32p. (ps-3). 1993. 14.95 (*1-56397-107-0*) Boyds Mills Pr.
Sharp, Olivia. Green Toenails Gang. (ps-3). 1991. 13.50 (*0-385-30248-7*) Delacorte.
Sharp, Paul. Paul the Pitcher. LC 84-7011. (Illus.). 32p. (ps-2). 1984. PLB 11.93 (*0-516-02064-1*); pap. 2.95 (*0-516-42064-X*) Childrens.
—Paul the Pitcher Big Book. (Illus.). 32p. (ps-2). 1991. PLB 30.60 (*0-516-49518-6*) Childrens.
—Ramon, el Lanzador (Paul the Pitcher) Sharp, Paul, illus. LC 84-7071. (SPA.). 32p. (ps-2). 1990. PLB 11.93 (*0-516-32064-5*); pap. 2.95 (*0-516-52064-4*) Childrens.
Sharp, Richard M. & Metzner, Seymour. The Sneaky Square & 113 Other Math Activities For Kids. (Illus.). 126p. (ps up) 1990. 15.95 (*0-8306-8474-3*, 3474); pap. 8.95 (*0-8306-3474-6*) TAB Bks.
Sharp, Vera. Little Princess' Musical Adventures: A Complete Audio-Visual Music Appreciation Course on the Instruments of the Symphony Orchestra for Preschool & Primary Grades. LC 93-2591. (Illus.). (ps-6). 1993. pap. 22.95 incl. 2 audios (*1-56087-060-5*) Top Mtn Pub.
—Little Princess' Symphony Adventures. Armstrong, M. J., illus. 76p. (ps-6). 1985. incl. 2 cassettes 49.00 (*0-9616987-0-5*) V Sharp.
Sharpe, Susan. Chicken Bucks. LC 92-5049. 144p. (gr. 5-8). 1992. SBE 13.95 (*0-02-782353-9*, Bradbury Pr) Macmillan Child Grp.
—Spirit Quest. Sharpe, Kate & Sharpe, Alison, illus. LC 91-4417. 128p. (gr. 4-6). 1991. SBE 13.95 (*0-02-782355-5*, Bradbury Pr) Macmillan Child Grp.
—Spirit Quest. 128p. (gr. 3-7). 1993. pap. 3.99 (*0-14-036282-7*) Puffin Bks.
—Trouble at Marsh Harbor. 172p. (gr. 3-7). 1991. pap. 3.95 (*0-14-034788-7*, Puffin) Puffin Bks.
—Waterman's Boy. LC 89-39332. 96p. (gr. 3-6). 1990. SBE 13.95 (*0-02-782351-2*, Bradbury Pr) Macmillan Child Grp.
Sharples, Joseph. The Flyaway Pantaloons. Scullard, Sue, illus. 32p. (gr. 4). 1990. PLB 18.95 (*0-87614-408-3*) Carolrhoda Bks.
Sharrar, Jack, jt. ed. see Slaight, Craig.
Sharrat, Nick. Mrs. Pirate. LC 93-878. (Illus.). Date not set. write for info. (*1-56402-249-8*) Candlewick Pr.
Sharratt, Nick. The Green Queen. Sharratt, Nick, illus. LC 91-58735. 24p. (ps up). 1992. 5.95 (*1-56402-093-2*) Candlewick Pr.
—I Look Like This. Sharratt, Nick, illus. LC 91-71846. 32p. (ps). 1992. 9.95 (*1-56402-016-9*) Candlewick Pr.
—Look What I Found! Sharratt, Nick, illus. LC 91-71833. 32p. (ps). 1992. 9.95 (*1-56402-017-7*) Candlewick Pr.
—Monday Run-Day. Sharratt, Nick, illus. LC 91-58745. 24p. (ps up). 1992. 5.95 (*1-56402-092-4*) Candlewick Pr.
—My Mom & Dad Make Me Laugh. LC 93-3558. (Illus.). 1994. write for info. (*1-56402-250-1*) Candlewick Pr.

—Smart Aunties. LC 92-47087. 1994. write for info. (1-56402-214-5) Candlewick Pr.

Shasha, Mark. Night of the Moonjellies. LC 91-4090. (gr. 4-8). 1992. pap. 14.00 (0-671-77565-0, S&S BFYR) S&S Trade.

Shatraw, Harriett. John Burroughs: The Famous Naturalist. Rahmas, D. Steve, ed. 32p. (Orig.). (gr. 7-12). 1972. lib. bdg. 4.95 incl. catalog cards (0-87157-543-4) SamHar Pr.

Shaver, Beth. In Friggleland...Safety Is No Accident! 1993. text ed. 12.95 personalized (1-883842-07-7); text ed. 7.95 (1-883842-06-9) Kids at Heart.

—Little Friggles...the Search for Christmas. 21p. 1992. Personalized. text ed. 12.95 (1-883842-03-4); text ed. 7.95 (1-883842-02-6) Kids at Heart.

—The Little Lost Friggle... Who Can Help? 21p. 1992. Personalized. text ed. 12.95 (1-883842-05-0); text ed. 7.95 (1-883842-04-2) Kids at Heart.

Shaver, Elizabeth, ed. Fifteen Years a Shakeress. Shaker Almanac, 1886, NYS Library Staff & Lee, Elizabeth, illus. 105p. 1990. Repr. of 1872 ed. perfect bdg. 5.95 (0-318-49991-6) Shaker Her Soc.

Shaver, James R. Understanding the U. S. Constitution. 1986. pap. 3.25 (0-87738-023-6) Youth Ed.

Shavit, Shlomo, jt. ed. see Shamir, Ilana.

Shaw, Alison. Beaufort Wind Scale. 1994. write for info. (0-8050-2770-X) H Holt & Co.

—Seashore Poems. 1994. write for info. (0-8050-2755-6) H Holt & Co.

Shaw, Charles. What's in the Dark? (Illus.). 32p. (gr. k-4). 1991. 11.95 (0-938349-66-X); pap. 5.95 (0-938349-67-8) State House Pr.

Shaw, Charles, et al. Texas Forever!! The Paintings. Shaw, Charles, illus. 100p. (gr. 9 up). 1991. 39.95 (0-9627589-0-6) Oak Creek Pr.

Shaw, Charles G. It Looked Like Spilt Milk. Shaw, Charles G., illus. LC 47-30767. 30p. (ps-2). 1947. 13. 00 (0-06-025566-8); PLB 12.89 (0-06-025565-X) HarpC Child Bks.

—It Looked Like Spilt Milk. Shaw, Charles G., illus. LC 47-30767. 32p. (ps-2). 1988. pap. 4.95 (0-06-443159-2, Trophy) HarpC Child Bks.

—It Looked Like Spilt Milk. Shaw, Charles G., illus. (ps-2). 1988. pap. 19.95 incl. cassette (0-87499-110-2); bk. & cassette 12.95 (0-87499-109-9); 4 cassettes & guide 27.95 (0-87499-111-0) Live Oak Media.

—It Looked Like Spilt Milk Big Book. Shaw, Charles G., illus. LC 47-30767. 32p. (ps-3). 1992. pap. 19.95 (0-06-443312-9, Trophy) HarpC Child Bks.

—It Looked Like Spilt Milk Board Book. Shaw, Charles G., illus. LC 47-30767. 24p. (ps-1). 1993. 4.95 (0-694-00491-X, Festival) HarpC Child Bks.

Shaw, Dena. Ronald McNair: Astronaut. (Illus.). 1993. 13.95 (0-7910-2110-6, Am Art Analog) Chelsea Hse.

Shaw, Denis. Pakistani Twins. Spence, Geraldine, illus. (gr. 6-9). 1965. 12.95 (0-8023-1094-X) Dufour.

Shaw, Diana. Gone Hollywood: A Carter Colborn Mystery. (gr. 7 up). 1988. 12.95 (0-316-78343-9, Joy St Bks) Little.

—Lessons in Fear. 176p. (gr. 7 up). 1988. pap. 2.50 (0-8167-1315-4) Troll Assocs.

—Lessons in Fear: A Carter Colborn Mystery. (gr. 7 up). 1987. 12.95 (0-316-78341-2, Joy St Bks) Little.

—Make the Most of a Good Thing: You! (gr. 5-9). 1986. (Joy St Bks) Little.

Shaw, Elizabeth. Little Black Sheep. 1985. 7.95 (0-86278-102-7, Pub. by O'Brien Press Ltd Eire) Dufour.

Shaw, George Bernard. Androcles & the Lion. (Orig.). (gr. 9 up). 1963. pap. 3.95 (0-14-048010-2, PL5) Viking Child Bks.

—Androcles & the Lion. Storr, Catherine, ed. Hood, Philip, illus. LC 86-6665. 32p. (gr. 7-). 1986. PLB 17. 96 (0-8172-2625-7) Raintree Steck-V.

—Arms & the Man. (gr. 9 up). 1950. pap. 4.95 (0-14-048012-8) Viking Child Bks.

—Caesar & Cleopatra. (gr. 11 up). pap. 0.95 (0-8049-0119-8, CL-119) Airmont.

—Major Barbara: Stage Version. (gr. 9 up). 1950. pap. 2.95 (0-14-048007-2, Penguin Bks) Viking Penguin.

—Man & Superman. Teitel, N. R., intro. by. (gr. 11 up). pap. 0.95 (0-8049-0096-5, CL-96) Airmont.

—Pygmalion. (gr. 9 up). 1950. pap. 2.95 (0-14-048003-X, Penguin Bks) Viking Penguin.

Shaw, George O. Vancouver's Discovery of Puget Sound. 28p. (gr. 9 up). pap. 1.95 (0-8466-0102-8, S102) Shorey.

Shaw, Gregory. How to Make Money Teaching Reading at Home: An Easy & Complete Program For Producing Wealth. Shaw, Sylvia, ed. 90p. (Orig.). (gr. 9-12). 1984. pap. 7.00 (0-933415-00-1); tchrs. e. 17.00 (0-933415-01-X) Mark Excell Pub.

Shaw, James R., jt. auth. see Robinette, Joseph.

Shaw, Janet. Changes for Kirsten: A Winter Story. Graef, Renee, illus. 65p. (Orig.). (gr. 2-5). 1988. 12.95 (0-937295-44-2); pap. 5.95 (0-937295-45-0) Pleasant Co.

—Changes for Kirsten: A Winter Story. Thieme, Jeanne, ed. Graef, Renee, illus. 72p. (gr. 2-5). 1988. PLB 12.95 (0-937295-94-9) Pleasant Co.

—Happy Birthday Kirsten! A Springtime Story. Thieme, Jeanne, ed. Graef, Renne, illus. 72p. (gr. 2-5). 1987. 12.95 (0-937295-32-9); PLB 12.95 (0-937295-88-4); pap. 5.95 (0-937295-33-7) Pleasant Co.

—Kirsten, 6 bks. Graef, Renee & Lackner, Paul, illus. 400p. (gr. 2-5). 1991. Boxed Set. 74.95 (1-56247-012-4); Boxed Set. lib. bdg. 74.95 (1-56247-049-3); Boxed Set. pap. 34.95 (0-937295-76-0) Pleasant Co.

—Kirsten Learns a Lesson: A School Story. Thieme, Jeanne, ed. Graef, Renee, illus. 72p. (gr. 2-5). 1986. 12.95 (0-937295-09-4); PLB 12.95 (0-937295-82-5); pap. 5.95 (0-937295-10-8) Pleasant Co.

—Kirsten Saves the Day: A Summer Story. Thieme, Jeanne, ed. Graef, Renee, illus. 72p. (gr. 2-5). 1988. 12.95 (0-937295-38-8); PLB 12.95 (0-937295-91-4); pap. 5.95 (0-937295-39-6) Pleasant Co.

—Kirsten's Surprise: A Christmas Story. Thieme, Jeanne, ed. Graef, Renee, illus. 72p. (gr. 2-5). 1986. 12.95 (0-937295-18-3); PLB 12.95 (0-937295-85-X); pap. 5.95 (0-937295-19-1) Pleasant Co.

Shaw, Janet, jt. auth. see Shaw, John R.

Shaw, Janet B. Meet Kirsten: An American Girl. Thieme, Jeanne, ed. Graef, Renee, illus. 72p. (gr. 2-5). 1986. 12.95 (0-937295-00-0); PLB 12.95 (0-937295-79-5); pap. 5.95 (0-937295-01-9) Pleasant Co.

Shaw, Janet M. Speech Sports: Games for Speech & Language Fun. (Illus.). 98p. (gr. k-8). 1991. 23.95 (0-937857-23-8, 1590) Speech Bin.

Shaw, Jean M. & Dyches, Richard W. First Science Dictionary. Sornat, Czeslaw, illus. LC 91-7528. 104p. (gr. k-4). 1991. 15.95 (0-531-15237-5); PLB 15.90 (0-531-11110-5) Watts.

—Primer Diccionario de Ciencia. Sornat, Czeslaw, illus. (SPA.). 104p. (gr. k-4). 1991. 15.95 (0-531-15235-9); PLB 15.90 (0-531-07925-2) Watts.

Shaw, Jean M., jt. auth. see Dyches, Richard W.

Shaw, Joan, jt. auth. see Bellamy, H. A.

Shaw, John R. & Shaw, Janet. The New Horizon Ladder Dictionary of the English Language. rev. & updated ed. 689p. (gr. 9-12). 1970. pap. 4.95 (0-451-16804-6, Sig) NAL-Dutton.

Shaw, Judy. Little Faith Builders. 30p. (Orig.). (gr. 1-3). 1983. pap. 0.98 (0-89274-290-9) Harrison Hse.

Shaw, Kathryn, jt. auth. see Shaw, Kiki.

Shaw, Kiki & Shaw, Kathryn. Maya & the Town that Loved a Tree. (Illus.). 32p. (ps-1). 1993. 14.95 (0-87663-796-9) Universe.

Shaw, Lee H., Jr. How to Live Forever in the New Jerusalem. 56p. (Orig.). (gr. 9-12). 1985. pap. 3.00x (0-9614311-0-5) Elijah-John.

Shaw, Marie. Basic Skills Spelling Tests Workbook, 2 bks. 64p. 1983. 1.98 ea. Grades 3-4 (0-8209-0566-6, STW-1) Grades 5-6 (0-8209-0567-4, STW-2) ESP.

Shaw, Marie-Jose. Jumbo Vocabulary Development Yearbook: Grade 3. 96p. (gr. 3). 1980. 18.00 (0-8209-0052-4, JVDY 3) ESP.

Shaw, Murray. Match Wits with Sherlock Holmes, Vol. 1. (gr. 4-7). 1991. pap. 4.95 (0-87614-528-4) Carolrhoda Bks.

—Match Wits with Sherlock Holmes, Vol. 2. (gr. 4-7). 1991. pap. 4.95 (0-87614-529-2) Carolrhoda Bks.

—Match Wits with Sherlock Holmes, Vol. 3. (gr. 4-7). 1991. pap. 4.95 (0-87614-530-6) Carolrhoda Bks.

—Match Wits with Sherlock Holmes, Vol. 4. (gr. 4-7). 1991. pap. 4.95 (0-87614-531-4) Carolrhoda Bks.

—Match Wits with Sherlock Holmes, Vol. 5: The Adventure of the Speckled Band, the Sussex Vampire. (gr. 4-7). 1992. pap. 4.95 (0-87614-549-7) Carolrhoda Bks.

—Match Wits with Sherlock Holmes, Vol. 6: The Adventure of the Abbey Grange, the Boscombe Valley. (gr. 4-7). 1992. pap. 4.95 (0-87614-550-0) Carolrhoda Bks.

—Match Wits with Sherlock Holmes, Vol. 8: The Hound of the Baskervilles. (gr. 4-7). 1993. pap. 4.95 (0-87614-556-X) Carolrhoda Bks.

Shaw, Murray, adapted by. The Adventure of the Dancing Men: The Three Garridebs. Overlie, George, illus. LC 92-21787. 1993. PLB 14.95 (0-87614-716-3); pap. 4.95 (0-87614-555-1) Carolrhoda Bks.

—The Adventures of Black Peter & The "Gloria Scott", Vol. I. Overlie, George, illus. (gr. 4-6). 1990. PLB 14. 95 (0-87614-385-0) Carolrhoda Bks.

—The Adventures of the Cardboard Box & Scandal in Bohemia, Vol. II. Overlie, George, illus. (gr. 4-6). 1990. PLB 14.95 (0-87614-386-9) Carolrhoda Bks.

—Adventures of the Copper Beeches & The Redheaded League, Vol. IV. Overlie, George, illus. (gr. 4-6). 1990. PLB 14.95 (0-87614-388-5) Carolrhoda Bks.

—Adventures of the Six Napoleons & the Blue Carbuncle, Vol. III. Overlie, George, illus. (gr. 4-6). 1990. PLB 14.95 (0-87614-387-7) Carolrhoda Bks.

—Match Wits with Sherlock Holmes, Vol. V: "The Adventure of the Speckled Bird" & "The Sussex Vampire" Overlie, George, illus. 64p. (gr. 4-6). 1991. PLB 14.95 (0-87614-665-5) Carolrhoda Bks.

—Match Wits with Sherlock Holmes, Vol. VI: "The Adventure of Abbey Grange" & "The Boscombe Valley Mystery" Overlie, George, illus. 64p. (gr. 4-6). 1991. PLB 14.95 (0-87614-666-3) Carolrhoda Bks.

Shaw, Nancy. Sheep in a Jeep. Apple, Margot, illus. LC 86-3101. 32p. (ps-k). 1986. 13.95 (0-395-41105-X) HM.

—Sheep in a Jeep. Apple, Margot, illus. 32p. (ps-k). 1991. pap. 3.80 (0-395-47030-7, Sandpiper); pap. 7.70 incl. cassette (0-395-60167-3, Sandpiper) HM.

—Sheep in a Shop. Apple, Margot, illus. LC 90-4139. 32p. (ps-k). 1991. 13.45 (0-395-53681-2) HM.

—Sheep on a Ship. Apple, Margot, illus. (ps). 1989. 13.45 (0-395-48160-0) HM.

—Sheep on a Ship. (ps-3). 1992. pap. 3.80 (0-395-64376-7) HM.

—Sheep Out to Eat. Apple, Margot, illus. LC 91-38425. 32p. (ps-1). 1992. 13.45 (0-395-61128-8) HM.

—Sheep Take a Hike. Apple, Margot, illus. LC 93-30725. 1994. write for info. (0-395-68394-7) HM.

Shaw, Naomi. Let the Hallelujahs Roll. LC 76-52280. 1977. pap. 1.95 (0-89221-028-1) New Leaf.

Shaw, Richard C. My Dad Sells Insurance. Snyder, Dan, illus. 40p. (ps-5). 1988. PLB write for info. (0-944900-00-3) Shaw & Co.

Shaw, Rick. Competition. (Illus.). 48p. (gr. 6-8). 1992. pap. 7.99 (1-55945-133-5) Group Pub.

Shaw, Sally. Composition Capers. 48p. (gr. 4-6). 1982. 5.95 (0-88160-044-X, LW 229) Learning Wks.

Shaw, Sheila. Kaleidometrics: The Art of Making Beautiful Patterns from Circles. (Illus.). 32p. (gr. 5-9). 1986. pap. 7.50 (0-906212-21-9, Pub. by Tarquin UK) Parkwest Pubns.

Shaw, Sylvia, ed. see Shaw, James.

Shaw DeVaney, Janet. ConverStations: The Go Anywhere Speech Book. DeVaney, Janet S., illus. 48p. (gr. 2-6). 1986. 16.95 (0-937857-00-9, 1551) Speech Bin.

Shawn, B. Foundations of Citizenship, 2 vols. in 1, Bks. 1 & 2. large type ed. 220p. (gr. 7-12). 1983. Repr. of 1980 ed. 50.56 (0-317-01888-4, 4-07020-00) Am Printing Hse.

Shay, Myrtle. Adventures of Ricky & Chub. Kennedy, Paul, illus. (gr. 4-8). PLB 7.19 (0-685-02937-9) Lantern.

Shay, Regan. Boyz II Men. (gr. 4-7). 1992. pap. 1.49 (0-440-21475-0) Dell.

Shaylen, C., ed. see Wood, A. & Wood, D.

Shaylen, J., ed. see Wood, A. & Wood, D.

Shazo, Jerry De see Porter, Patrick K.

Shea, George. Amazing Rescues. Peck, Marshall H., III, illus. LC 90-53221. 48p. (gr. 2-3). 1992. PLB 7.99 (0-679-91107-3); pap. 3.50 (0-679-81107-9) Random Bks Yng Read.

—On the Road: Fun Travel Games & Activities. Sinclair, Jeff, illus. 48p. (gr. 3-10). 1992. pap. 4.95 (0-8069-8228-4) Sterling.

—The Silent Hero. LC 93-5492. 1994. 9.99 (0-679-94361-2) Random.

Shea, Pegi D. Bungalow Fungalow. Sayles, Elizabeth, illus. 32p. (gr. k-3). 1991. 13.45 (0-395-55387-3, Clarion Bks) HM.

Shea, Regan. Brad Pitt. (gr. 4-7). 1992. pap. 1.49 (0-440-21474-2) Dell.

Shea, Richard. The Book of Success. 192p. (gr. 9 up). 1993. 12.95 (1-55853-254-4) Rutledge Hill Pr.

Sheafer, Silvia A. Women of the West. (Illus.). 152p. (gr. 12 up). 1978. 8.95 (0-201-06670-X, 920, Journal Pubns); pap. 5.95 (0-201-06671-8) Addison-Wesley.

Shealy, Daniel, ed. Louisa May Alcott's Fairy Tales & Fantasy Stories. LC 91-43144. (Illus.). 432p. (Orig.). 1992. text ed. 37.95x (0-87049-752-9); pap. 24.95 (0-87049-758-8) U of Tenn Pr.

Shearer, Aaron. Classic Guitar Technique. 82p. (Orig.). 1959. pap. text ed. 12.00 (0-89898-572-2) CPP Belwin.

—Classic Guitar Technique, Vol. 2. 160p. (Orig.). 1964. pap. 16.50 (0-89898-573-0) CPP Belwin.

Shearer, Cynthia A. The Greenleaf Guide to Ancient Egypt. 64p. (gr. 2-6). 1989. pap. 7.95 (1-882514-00-9) Greenleaf TN.

—The Greenleaf Guide to Famous Men of Greece. 62p. (gr. 4-8). 1989. pap. 7.95 (1-882514-02-5) Greenleaf TN.

—The Greenleaf Guide to Famous Men of Rome. 56p. (gr. 4-8). 1989. pap. 7.95 (1-882514-04-1) Greenleaf TN.

—The Greenleaf Guide to Famous Men of the Middle Ages. 106p. (gr. 4-8). 1992. pap. 9.95 (1-882514-06-8) Greenleaf TN.

Shearer, Cynthia A., jt. auth. see Hyde, Mary F.

Shearer, Marilyn J. The Adventures of Curious Eric: Learning Concepts. Roberts, Tom, illus. LC 90-60397. 16p. (ps-6). 1990. 19.95 (0-685-33064-8); pap. 10.95 (1-878389-01-7) L Ashley & Joshua.

—Annie's Birthday Party: Learning Colors & Shapes. Truax, Nancy, illus. 16p. (Orig.). (ps-6). 1989. 19.95 (0-685-30095-1); pap. 10.95 (0-685-30096-X) L Ashley & Joshua.

—Cinderella & the Glass Slipper: A Retelling. Edwards, Ron, illus. LC 90-60394. 16p. (ps-6). 1990. 19.95 (0-685-33063-X); pap. 10.95 (1-878389-02-5) L Ashley & Joshua.

—The Crown of Fools: Based on: The Tortoise & the Hare. 16p. (ps-6). 1989. 19.95 (0-685-30101-X); pap. 10.95 (0-685-30102-8) L Ashley & Joshua.

—I Like to Play. Roberts, Tom, illus. 16p. (Orig.). (ps-6). 1989. 19.95 (0-685-30097-8); pap. 10.95 (0-685-30098-6) L Ashley & Joshua.

—The Lonely Ten: A Book of Counting for Preschool & Above. Bostic, Alex, illus. 16p. (Orig.). (ps-6). 1989. pap. 19.95 (0-685-30094-3) L Ashley & Joshua.

—The Lonely Ten: A Book of Simple Addition for Preschool & Above. Bostic, Alex, illus. 16p. (Orig.). (ps-6). 1989. 19.95 (0-685-30093-5) L Ashley & Joshua.

—The Nubian Princess. Walker, Larry, illus. 16p. (Orig.). (ps-6). 1989. 19.95 (0-685-30091-9); pap. 10.95 (0-685-30092-7) L Ashley & Joshua.

—The Original Three Little Pigs Re-Told. Smith, Jonathan, illus. LC 90-60398. 16p. (ps-6). 1990. 19.95 (*0-685-33065-6*); pap. 10.95 (*1-878389-03-3*) L Ashley & Joshua.
—Sleeping Beauty. Walker, Larry, illus. 16p. (ps-6). 1989. 19.95 (*0-685-30099-4*); pap. 10.95 (*0-685-30100-1*) L Ashley & Joshua.
—Snow White. Moore, Daryl J., illus. LC 90-60396. 16p. (Orig.). (ps-6). 1990. 19.95 (*0-685-33066-4*); pap. 10. 95 (*1-878389-00-9*) L Ashley & Joshua.
Shearer, Robert G. Famous Men of the Renaissance & the Reformation. 160p. (gr. 4-8). 1994. pap. 15.95 (*1-882514-10-6*) Greenleaf TN.
Shearman, Deirdre. David Lloyd George. (Illus.). 112p. (gr. 5 up). 1988. lib. bdg. 17.95 (*0-87754-581-2*) Chelsea Hse.
—Queen Victoria. (Illus.). 112p. (gr. 5 up). 1987. lib. bdg. 17.95x (*0-87754-590-1*) Chelsea Hse.
Shebar, Judith & Shebar, Sharon S. The Cardiff Giant. Sullivan, Dave, illus. LC 83-13056. 64p. (gr. 7-11). 1983. lib. bdg. 9.29 (*0-671-43851-4*, J Messner) S&S Trade.
Shebar, Sharon. Franklin D. Roosevelt & the New Deal. (Illus.). 144p. (gr. 3-6). 1987. pap. 4.95 (*0-8120-3916-5*) Barron.
—Milk. Wasserman, Dan, ed. Reese, Bob, illus. (gr. k-1). 1979. 7.95 (*0-89868-067-0*); pap. 2.95 (*0-89868-078-6*) ARO Pub.
—Night Monsters. Reese, Bob, illus. (gr. k-3). 1979. pap. 20.00 (*0-685-50869-2*) ARO Pub.
—Nightmonsters. Wasserman, Dan, ed. Reese, Bob, illus. (gr. k-1). 1979. 7.95 (*0-89868-068-9*); pap. 2.95 (*0-89868-079-4*) ARO Pub.
Shebar, Sharon S. & Shebar, Susan E. Bats. (Illus.). 64p. (gr. 5-8). 1990. PLB 12.90 (*0-531-10863-5*) Watts.
Shebar, Sharon S., jt. auth. see Schoder, Judith.
Shebar, Sharon S., jt. auth. see Shebar, Judith.
Shebar, Susan, ed. see Barrie, J. M.
Shebar, Susan E., jt. auth. see Shebar, Sharon S.
Shecter, Ben. The Big Stew. Shecter, Ben, illus. LC 90-46271. 32p. (ps-2). 1991. PLB 14.89 (*0-06-025610-9*) HarpC Child Bks.
—When Will the Snow Trees Grow? Shecter, Ben, illus. LC 92-32557. 32p. (gr. k-3). 1993. 14.00 (*0-06-022897-0*); PLB 13.89 (*0-06-022898-9*) HarpC Child Bks.
Shedd, Alan, jt. auth. see Shedd, Edith S.
Shedd, Charlie W., ed. see Cosby, Bill, et al.
Shedd, Edith S. & Shedd, Alan. Do It with the Sun. Higginbotham, David, illus. LC 82-81309. 208p. (Orig.). (gr. 6-9). 1982. pap. 12.95 (*0-9608358-0-6*) Integ Energy.
Shedd, Warner. The Kids' Wildlife Book: Exploring Animal Worlds Through Indoor - Outdoor Experiences. (Illus.). 160p. (Orig.). (ps-5). 1994. pap. 12.95 (*0-913589-77-2*) Williamson Pub Co.
Shedenhelm, W. R. Discover Rocks & Minerals. (Illus.). 48p. (gr. 3-6). 1992. PLB 14.95 (*1-878363-70-0*, HTS Bks) Forest Hse.
Sheehan. Brontosaurus. (Illus.). 24p. 1981. PLB 14.00 (*0-86592-111-3*) Rourke Enter.
—Dinosaur Library, 4 bks, Set I. (Illus.). 96p. 1981. Set. PLB write for info. (*0-86592-110-5*) Rourke Enter.
—Stegosaurus. (Illus.). 24p. 1981. PLB 14.00 (*0-86592-112-1*) Rourke Enter.
—Triceratops. (Illus.). 24p. 1981. PLB 14.00 (*0-86592-113-X*) Rourke Enter.
—Tyrannosaurus. (Illus.). 24p. 1981. PLB 14.00 (*0-86592-114-8*) Rourke Enter.
Sheehan, Angela, ed. Encyclopedia of Health, 14 vols. LC 89-17336. (Illus.). 900p. (gr. 4-8). 1991. PLB 299. 95x (*1-85435-203-2*) Marshall Cavendish.
Sheehan, Canon P. My New Curate. LC 89-81657. 340p. (Orig.). (gr. 10-12). 1990. pap. 16.95 (*0-85342-877-8*, Pub. by Mercier Pr Eire) Dufour.
Sheehan, Cilla. The Colors That I Am. Elliot, Glen, photos by. LC 80-25351. (Illus.). 32p. (ps-5). 1981. 16. 95 (*0-89885-047-9*) Human Sci Pr.
Sheehan, Kathryn & Waidner, Mary. Earth Child. LC 91-70225. (Illus.). 327p. (ps-4). 1992. 24.95 (*0-933031-42-4*); pap. 16.95 (*0-933031-39-4*) Coun Oak Bks.
Sheehan, Nancy, illus. Families. 18p. (ps). 1993. bds. 4.95 (*0-448-40525-3*, G&D) Putnam Pub Group.
Sheehan, Nancy, photos by. What's That Sound? LC 90-83241. (Illus.). 24p. (ps). 1991. 2.50 (*0-448-40127-4*, G&D) Putnam Pub Group.
Sheehan, Patty. Gwendolyn's Gifts. Bumgarner-Kirby, Claudia, illus. LC 91-12335. 32p. 1991. 14.95 (*0-88289-845-0*) Pelican.
—Kylie's Concert. Maeno, Itoko, illus. 32p. 1993. 16.95 (*1-55942-046-4*, 7655); incl. video & tchr's. guide 79. 95 (*1-55942-049-9*, 9374) Marshfilm.
—Kylie's Song. LC 88-16779. (Illus.). 32p. (gr. k-6). 1988. 16.95 (*0-911655-19-0*) Advocacy Pr.
Sheehan, Pauline. God Hugs? Sheehan, Pauline, illus. 20p. (Orig.). 1986. pap. 3.95 (*0-9617018-0-3*) Sheehan Indus.
Sheehan, Sean. Jamaica. LC 93-11019. (Illus.). 128p. (gr. 5-9). 1993. 21.95 (*1-85435-581-3*, Pub by Cavenidsh Bks UK); write for info. (*1-85435-578-3*) Marshall Cavendish.
—Pakistan. LC 93-4379. (gr. 5 up). 1993. write for info. (*1-85435-583-X*) Marshall Cavendish.
—Turkey. LC 92-35930. 1993. Set. write for info.; 1 vol. 21.95 (*1-85435-576-7*) Marshall Cavendish.
—Zimbabwe. LC 92-38751. 1993. 21.95 (*1-85435-577-5*) Marshall Cavendish.

Sheehan, William. Nature's Wonderful World in Rhyme. Maeno, Itoko, illus. LC 93-15247. 1993. 14.95 (*0-911655-47-6*) Advocacy Pr.
Sheeley, Craig. Special Operations. Wiseman, Loren K., ed. 104p. (Orig.). 1992. pap. 12.00 (*1-55878-108-0*) Game Designers.
Sheely, Robert. Police Lab. (Illus.). 64p. (gr. 4-6). 1993. PLB 12.95 (*1-881889-40-8*) Silver Moon.
—Sports Lab. 64p. (gr. 4-6). 1994. PLB 12.95 (*1-881889-49-1*) Silver Moon.
Sheen, Jen, ed. see Brown, Eric.
Sheetz, Russ. The Man in the Blue Truck. Warren, Shirley, ed. Botwinick, Allan, illus. LC 93-15247. 1990. pap. 3.95 (*0-685-33385-X*) Still Waters.
Shefelman, Janice. A Mare for Young Wolf. Shefelman, Tom, illus. LC 91-42749. 48p. (Orig.). (gr. 2-3). 1993. PLB 7.99 (*0-679-93445-6*); pap. 3.50 (*0-679-83445-1*) Random Bks Yng Read.
—A Paradise Called Texas. (Illus.). 128p. (gr. 4-7). 1983. 10.95 (*0-89015-409-0*, Pub. by Panda Bks); pap. 5.95 (*0-89015-506-2*) Eakin-Sunbelt.
—A Peddler's Dream. Shefelman, Tom, illus. LC 91-35285. 32p. (gr. 2-5). 1992. 14.45 (*0-395-60904-6*) HM.
—Victoria House. Shefelman, Tom, illus. LC 86-33565. (ps-3). 1988. 12.95 (*0-15-200630-3*, Gulliver Bks) HarBrace.
—Willow Creek Home. Karl, Dan & Shefelman, Tom, illus. 128p. (gr. 5-7). 1985. 10.95 (*0-89015-535-6*, Pub. by Panda Bks) Eakin-Sunbelt.
Shefelman, Janice J. Spirit of Iron. Eakin, Edwin M., ed. Shefelman, Dan, et al, illus. 136p. (gr. 4-7). 1987. 10. 95 (*0-89015-636-0*, Pub. by Panda Bks); pap. 4.95 (*0-89015-624-7*) Eakin-Sunbelt.
Sheff, Alice. Be a Perfect Person in Just Three Days: A Study Guide. (gr. 1-3). 1989. tchr's. ed. & wkbk. 14.95 (*0-88122-044-2*) LRN Links.
—Freckle Juice: A Study Guide. (gr. 1-4). 1988. tchr's. ed. & wkbk. 14.95 (*0-88122-066-3*) LRN Links.
Sheffer, Susannah, ed. Earning Our Own Money: Homeschoolers 13 & under Describe How They Have Earned Money. Linn, Emily, tr. (Illus.). 28p. (Orig.). (gr. 1 up). 1991. pap. text ed. 3.95 (*0-913677-09-4*) Holt Assocs.
Sheffield, Anne & Frankel, Bruce, eds. When I Was Young I Loved School: Dropping Out & Hanging In. (gr. 7 up). 1989. 9.95 (*0-9621641-2-7*) CEF Inc.
Sheffield, Linda J., jt. auth. see Whitney, Julie.
Sheheen, Dennis, ed. A Child's Picture English-Hebrew Dictionary. Meshi, Ita, illus. (gr. 1-3). 1987. 9.95 (*0-915361-75-2*) Modan-Adama Bks.
Sheheen, Dennis, illus. Children's Picture Dictionary: English-Chinese. (gr. k up). 9.95 (*0-685-18873-6*) Modan-Adama Bks.
—A Child's Picture English-Arabic Dictionary. LC 85-15658. (gr. k-2). 1985. 9.95 (*0-915361-30-2*) Modan-Adama Bks.
—A Child's Picture English-Chinese Dictionary. (gr. k-6). 1987. Repr. 9.95 (*1-55774-001-1*) Modan-Adama Bks.
—A Child's Picture English-German Dictionary. LC 86-13987. (gr. k-2). 1986. 9.95 (*0-915361-41-8*) Modan-Adama Bks.
—A Child's Picture English-Italian Dictionary. LC 86-14052. (gr. k-2). 1986. 9.95 (*0-915361-57-4*) Modan-Adama Bks.
—A Child's Picture English-Japanese Dictionary. (gr. k-6). 1987. 9.95 (*1-55774-000-3*) Modan-Adama Bks.
—A Child's Picture English-Spanish Dictionary. LC 84-71801. (gr. k-2). 1984. 9.95 (*0-915361-11-6*, 09407-3) Modan-Adama Bks.
—A Child's Picture English-Yiddish Dictionary. LC 85-15659. (gr. k-2). 1985. 9.95 (*0-915361-29-9*) Modan-Adama Bks.
Sheil, Audrey, ed. see Bennett, Gerald M.
Sheil, Audrey, ed. see Bennett, Geraldine M.
Shelare, Harriet, jt. auth. see Shachtman, Tom.
Shelby, Anne. Potluck. Trivas, Irene, illus. LC 90-7757. 32p. (ps-1). 1991. 14.95 (*0-531-05919-7*); PLB 14.99 (*0-531-08519-8*) Orchard Bks Watts.
—Potluck. Trivas, Irene, illus. LC 90-7757. 32p. (ps-2). 1994. pap. 5.95 (*0-531-07045-X*) Orchard Bks Watts.
—We Keep a Store. Ward, John, illus. LC 89-35105. 32p. (ps-2). 1990. 14.95 (*0-531-05856-5*); PLB 14.99 (*0-531-08456-6*) Orchard Bks Watts.
—What to Do about Pollution. Trivas, Irene, illus. LC 92-24173. 32p. (ps-1). 1993. 14.95 (*0-531-05471-3*); PLB 14.99 (*0-531-08621-6*) Orchard Bks Watts.
Shelden, Bernice. Hello, Me! 192p. (Orig.). (gr. 6-9). 1986. pap. 2.50 (*0-553-25641-6*, Starfire) Bantam.
Sheldon, Ann. Linda Craig: Search for Scorpio. Barish, Wendy, ed. 166p. (Orig.). (gr. 3 up). 1984. pap. 3.95 (*0-671-53237-5*) S&S Trade.
—Linda Craig: The Clue on the Desert Trail. 192p. (gr. 3-7). 1981. S&S Trade.
—Linda Craig: The Haunted Valley. Barish, Wendy, ed. 192p. (gr. 3-7). 1982. 8.50 (*0-671-45551-6*) S&S Trade.
—Linda Craig: The Mystery in Mexico. rev. ed. 192p. (Orig.). (gr. 3-7). 1981. S&S Trade.
—Linda Craig: The Mystery of Horseshoe Canyon. 192p. (gr. 3-7). 1981. S&S Trade.
—Linda Craig: The Palomino Mystery. (gr. 3-7). 1981. pap. 3.50 (*0-671-42650-8*) S&S Trade.
—Linda Craig: The Secret of Rancho Del Sol. 192p. (gr. 3-7). 1981. S&S Trade.
—A Star in the Saddle. (Orig.). (gr. 3-6). 1989. pap. 2.75 (*0-318-41208-X*, Minstrel Bks) PB.

Sheldon, Bill, compiled by. & frwd. by. The Boy Scout Collector's Bibliography. 254p. (Orig.). (gr. 6-12). 1987. pap. 13.50 for info. (*0-9616668-0-3*) B Sheldon.
Sheldon, Charles. In His Steps. Larsen, Dan, adapted by. (gr. 3 up). 1992. 9.95 (*1-55748-275-6*) Barbour & Co.
Sheldon, Dyan. Harry & Chicken. Heap, Sue & Heap, Sue, illus. LC 91-71851. 80p. (gr. 3-6). 1992. 13.95 (*1-56402-012-6*) Candlewick Pr.
—Harry & Chicken. LC 91-71851. (gr. 4-7). 1994. pap. 3.99 (*1-56402-275-7*) Candlewick Pr.
—Harry on Vacation. Heap, Sue, illus. LC 92-52999. 144p. (gr. 3-6). 1993. 13.95 (*1-56402-127-0*) Candlewick Pr.
—Harry the Explorer. Heap, Sue & Heap, Sue, illus. LC 91-58734. 80p. (gr. 3-6). 1992. 13.95 (*1-56402-109-2*) Candlewick Pr.
—Love, Your Bear, Pete. Hurt-Newton, Tania, illus. LC 93-2883. 1994. write for info. (*1-56402-332-X*) Candlewick Pr.
—My Brother Is a Visitor from Another Planet. Brazell, Derek, illus. LC 92-53420. 96p. (gr. 3-6). 1993. 13.95 (*1-56402-141-6*) Candlewick Pr.
—Tall, Thin, & Blonde. LC 92-53021. (gr. 6-10). 1993. 14.95 (*1-56402-139-4*) Candlewick Pr.
—The Whales' Song. Blythe, Gary, illus. LC 90-46722. 32p. (ps-3). 1991. 15.99 (*0-8037-0972-2*) Dial Bks Young.
—When the Earth Was Large. Blythe, Gary, illus. LC 93-11711. 1994. write for info. (*0-8037-1670-2*) Dial Bks Young.
Sheldon, Dyan & De Lyman, Alicia G. Jack & Alice. (Illus.). 32p. (gr. k-2). 1992. 15.95 (*0-09-173638-2*, Pub. by Hutchinson UK) Trafalgar.
Sheldon, Harold P. Tranquility. 2nd ed. Boyer, Ralph, illus. 216p. (gr. 10 up). 1991. Repr. of 1936 ed. 35.00 (*1-56416-021-1*) Derrydale Pr.
Sheldon, Richard. Dag Hammarskjold. Schlesinger, Arthur M., Jr., intro. by. (Illus.). 112p. (gr. 5 up). 1987. lib. bdg. 17.95 (*0-87754-529-4*) Chelsea Hse.
Shellenberger, Robert. Wagons West: Trail Tales - 1848. LC 91-72903. (Illus.). 96p. (Orig.). 1991. pap. 9.95 (*0-9623048-3-2*) Heritage West.
Shellenberger, Susie. Straight Ahead: Twenty-Eight Devotionals for Teen Disciples. 32p. 1987. pap. 1.95 (*0-8341-1199-3*) Beacon Hill.
Shellenberger, Susie, jt. auth. see Johnson, Greg.
Shelley, Jeff, illus. Disney Babies Goodnight Lullabies. LC 91-71345. 32p. (ps). 1991. 7.95 (*1-56282-054-0*) Disney Pr.
Shelley, Mary V. Dr. Ed: The Story of General Edward Hand. Weatherlow, Regina, illus. LC 78-10331. 36p. (gr. 4-7). 1978. 5.75 (*0-915010-24-0*) Sutter House.
Shelley, Mary V. & Munro, Sandra H. Harriet Lane, First Lady of the White House. LC 80-20151. (Illus.). 48p. (gr. 4-6). 1980. 6.95 (*0-915010-29-1*) Sutter House.
Shelley, Mary Wollstonecraft. Frankenstein. (gr. 7 up). 1964. pap. 2.95 (*0-8049-0019-1*, CL-19) Airmont.
—Frankenstein. Schick, Alice & Schick, Joel, eds. LC 80-385. (Illus.). 48p. (gr. 3 up). 1980. PLB 10.89 (*0-440-02693-8*); pap. 4.95 (*0-440-02692-X*) Delacorte.
—Frankenstein. 224p. (gr. 7). 1965. pap. 1.95 (*0-451-52336-9*, Sig Classics) NAL-Dutton.
—Frankenstein. Binder, Otto, ed. Cruz, Nardo, illus. LC 73-57462. 64p. (Orig.). (gr. 5-10). 1973. pap. 2.95 (*0-88301-097-6*); student activity bk. 1.25 (*0-88301-177-8*) Pendulum Pr.
—Frankenstein. Kelley, Gary, illus. Stewart, Diana, adapted by. LC 81-5216. (Illus.). 48p. (gr. 4 up). 1983. PLB 18.64 (*0-8172-1674-X*) Raintree Steck-V.
—Frankenstein. Weinberg, Larry, adapted by. Barr, Ken, illus. LC 87-23543. 96p. (gr. 2-6). 1993. pap. 2.99 (*0-394-84827-6*) Random Bks Yng Read.
—Frankenstein. Kirn, Elaine, adapted by. (Illus.). 62p. (gr. 7-12). 1987. pap. text ed. 3.75 (*0-13-330515-5*, 20507) Prentice ESL.
—Frankenstein. 256p. (gr. 9-12). 1989. pap. 4.99 (*0-8125-0457-7*) Tor Bks.
—Frankenstein. Weinberg, Larry, adapted by. Barr, Ken, illus. 96p. (gr. 3-7). 1992. pap. 6.99 incl. cass. (*0-679-82443-X*) Random Bks Yng Read.
—Frankenstein. Arneson, D. J., retold by. Clift, Eva, illus. 128p. 1992. pap. 2.95 (*1-56156-142-8*) Kidsbks.
Shelley, Maynard, ed. see Clemmer Steiner, Susan.
Shelley, Percy Bysshe. Love's Philosophy. LC 91-602. (Illus.). 24p. 1992. 4.95 (*0-8037-1142-5*) Dial Bks Young.
Shelley, Rex. Japan. LC 89-23877. (Illus.). 128p. (gr. 5-9). 1991. PLB 21.95 (*1-85435-297-0*) Marshall Cavendish.
Shelly, Maynard, ed. see Harder, Geraldine & Harder, Milton.
Shelly, Maynard, ed. see Lehman, Paula D.
Shelly, Maynard, ed. see Unruh, Sophia.
Shelly, Walt & Stangl, Jean. Hats, Hats, & More Hats. (gr. 1-5). 1989. pap. 10.95 (*0-8224-3602-7*) Fearon Teach Aids.
Shelly, Walt, jt. auth. see Hart, Marj.
Shelton, Catherine. Puppets, Poems, & Songs. (ps-3). 1993. pap. 23.95 (*0-8224-5152-2*) Fearon Teach Aids.
Shelton, Helen, ed. Bibliography of Books for Children. 1988-89 ed. LC 89-345. 112p. (ps-6). 1989. 15.00 (*0-87173-118-5*) ACEI.
Shelton, Ingrid. Benji Bear's Adventure in the Thunderstorm. 31p. (ps-k). 1984. pap. 2.50 (*0-919797-09-1*) Kindred Pr.

—Benji Bear's Race. Block, Ruth W., illus. 35p. (Orig.). (ps-2). 1992. pap. 2.50 (*0-919797-74-1*) Kindred Pr.
—Benji Bear's Surprise Day. 30p. (ps-k). 1986. pap. 2.50 (*0-919797-54-7*) Kindred Pr.
—The Lord's Prayer. (gr. k-4). 1982. pap. 1.89 (*0-570-06161-X, 59-1308*) Concordia.
Shelton, Laura S. & Shapiro, Lawrence E. Take a Deep Breath: The Kids' Play-Away Stress Book. Beckett, Bob, illus. 100p. (Orig.). (gr. k-6). 1992. pap. 16.95 (*1-882732-02-2*) Ctr Applied Psy.
Shelton, Rick. Hoggle's Christmas. Gates, Donald, illus. LC 92-37861. 80p. (gr. 2-6). 1993. 12.99 (*0-525-65129-2*, Cobblehill Bks) Dutton Child Bks.
Shelton, Ricky Van see Van Shelton, Ricky.
Shely, Patricia. Los Animales Del Arca. Cranberry, Nola, tr. from ENG. Patterson, Ron, illus. (SPA.). 16p. (gr. 1-3). 1987. pap. 1.99 (*0-311-38561-3, X1982*) Casa Bautista.
—El Nino Jesus. Granberry, Nola, tr. Karch, Pat, illus. (SPA.). 16p. (gr. 1-3). 1987. pap. 1.40 (*0-311-38563-X*) Casa Bautista.
Shemie, Bonnie. Houses of Bark. (Illus.). 24p. (gr. 3-7). 1993. pap. 6.95 (*0-88776-306-5*) Tundra Bks.
—Houses of Bark: Tipi, Wigwam, & Longhouse. Shemie, Bonnie, illus. LC 90-70130. 24p. (gr. 3-7). 1990. 13.95 (*0-88776-246-8*) Tundra Bks.
—Houses of Hide & Earth. (Illus.). 24p. (gr. 3-7). 1993. pap. 6.95 (*0-88776-307-3*) Tundra Bks.
—Houses of Hide & Earth: Tipi & Earthlodges. LC 91-65369. (Illus.). 24p. (gr. 3-7). 1991. 13.95 (*0-88776-269-7*) Tundra Bks.
—Houses of Snow, Skin & Bones. (Illus.). 24p. (gr. 3-7). 1993. pap. 6.95 (*0-88776-305-7*) Tundra Bks.
—Houses of Snow, Skin & Bones: Native Dwellings: The Far North. LC 89-50778. (Illus.). 24p. (gr. 3-7). 1989. 13.95 (*0-88776-240-9*) Tundra Bks.
—Houses of Wood: The Northwest Coast. Shemie, Bonnie, illus. LC 92-80415. 24p. (gr. 3-6). 1992. 13.95 (*0-88776-284-0*) Tundra Bks.
—Maisons De Peau et Terre. (FRE., Illus.). 24p. (gr. 3-7). 1991. 13.95 (*0-88776-271-9*) Tundra Bks.
—Maisons D'Ecorce: Tipi, Wigwam et Longue Maison. Shemie, Bonnie, illus. 24p. (gr. 3-7). 1990. 13.95 (*0-88776-256-5*) Tundra Bks.
—Mounds of Earth & Shell: Native Sites: the Southeast. Shemie, Bonnie, illus. LC 93-60335. 24p. (gr. 3 up). 1993. 13.95 (*0-88776-318-9*) Tundra Bks.
Shemin, Margaretha. The Little Riders. Spier, Peter, illus. 80p. (gr. 3-7). 1988. 12.95 (*0-399-21462-3*, Putnam) Putnam Pub Group.
—The Little Riders. Spier, Peter, illus. 80p. (gr. 4 up). 1993. pap. 3.95 (*0-688-12499-2*, Pub. by Beech Tree Bks) Morrow.
Shennan, Christopher. Toymaker's Dream. (gr. 6-8). 1984. pap. 2.95 (*0-87508-767-1*) Chr Lit.
Shepard, jt. auth. see Milne, A. A.
Shepard, Aaron. The Baker's Dozen: A St. Nicholas Tale. Edelson, Wendy, photos by. LC 92-38261. (gr. 1-8). 1994. write for info. (*0-684-19577-1*, Scribner) Macmillan.
—The Legend of Lightning Larry. Goffe, Toni, illus. LC 91-43779. 32p. (gr. 1-3). 1993. SBE 14.95 (*0-684-19433-3*, Scribners Young Read) Macmillan Child Grp.
—Savitri: A Tale of Ancient India. Mathews, Judith, ed. Rosenberry, Vera, illus. LC 91-16591. 40p. (gr. 1-6). 1992. PLB 15.95 (*0-8075-7251-9*) A Whitman.
Shepard, Aaron, retold by. The Legend of Slappy Hooper. LC 92-18153. (Illus.). 32p. (gr. k-3). 1993. SBE 14.95 (*0-684-19535-6*, Scribners Young Read) Macmillan Child Grp.
Shepard, Alan B. see Baird, Anne.
Shepard, Ernest H., illus. Winnie-the-Pooh's Birthday Book. Milne, A. A., contrib. by. (Illus.). 128p. 1993. 11.99 (*0-525-45061-0*, DCB) Dutton Child Bks.
Shepard, Eva & Lehman, Celia. Nzuzi & the Spell. Hofstetter, Virginia, illus. LC 92-60935. 160p. (gr. 2-8). 1992. pap. 6.95 (*1-878893-22-X*) Telcraft Bks.
Shepard, John, jt. auth. see Painter, Desmond.
Shepard, Mary L. & Gaines, Edith. Forty Acres; Little Jess & the Circus; Jubilee Day. 2nd ed. McCluskey, John A., ed. Smith, Ron & Murchison, Leon, illus. (gr. 4-7). 1993. pap. 3.00 (*0-913678-26-0*) New Day Pr.
Shepard, Steve. Elvis Hornbill, International Business Bird. Shepard, Steve, illus. LC 90-44052. 32p. (ps-2). 1991. 14.95 (*0-8050-1617-1*, Bks Young Read) H Holt & Co.
Shepard, Steven. Fogbound. Thatch, Nancy R., ed. Shepard, Steven, illus. Melton, David, intro. by. LC 93-11422. (Illus.). 29p. (gr. 5-8). 1993. PLB 14.95 (*0-933849-43-5*) Landmark Edns.
Sheperd, Scott. What Do You Think of You? A Teen's Guide to Finding Self-Esteem. Hesse, Bonnie, ed. (Illus.). 100p. (Orig.). 1990. 6.95 (*0-89638-220-6*) CompCare.
Shephard, Esther. Paul Bunyan. Kent, Rockwell, illus. LC 85-5448. 233p. (gr. 7 up). 1985. 12.95 (*0-15-259749-2*, HB Juv Bks) HarBrace.
—Paul Bunyan. LC 85-5448. (Illus.). 233p. (gr. 7 up). 1985. pap. 6.95 (*0-15-259755-7*, Voyager Bks) HarBrace.
Shepheard, Patricia. South Korea. (Illus.). 96p. (gr. 5 up). 1988. 14.95 (*0-7910-0118-0*) Chelsea Hse.
Shepherd, C. A., et al. The Sly Fox. (Orig.). (gr. 3-12). 1985. pap. 8.00 play script (*0-88734-503-4*) Players Pr.
Shepherd, Donna A. The Aztecs. Rosoff, Iris, ed. LC 91-28397. (Illus.). 64p. (gr. 5-8). 1992. PLB 12.90 (*0-531-20064-7*) Watts.

Shepherd, Donna W. The Aztecs. (Illus.). 64p. (gr. 5-8). 1992. pap. 5.95 (*0-531-15634-6*) Watts.
Shepherd, Elizabeth. No Bones: A Key to Bugs & Slugs, Worms, & Ticks, Spiders & Centipedes, & Other Creepy Crawlies. Patterson, Ippy, illus. LC 87-1549. 96p. (gr. 2-5). 1988. SBE 13.95 (*0-02-782880-8*, Macmillan Child Bk) Macmillan Child Grp.
Shepherd, J. Canada. LC 87-14626. (Illus.). 128p. (gr. 5-9). 1987. PLB 26.60 (*0-516-02757-3*) Childrens.
Shepherd, John G. The Stream Team on Patrol. LC 93-15386. (gr. 4 up). 1993. 14.96 (*1-56239-207-7*) Abdo & Dghtrs.
Shepherd, Linda E. Ryan's Trials. LC 93-25995. (gr. 9-12). Date not set. pap. write for info. (*0-8407-9681-1*) Nelson.
Shepherd, Sarah & Shepherd, Thomas. AlphaBuddies Coloring & Reading Book, No. 1. 56p. (gr. 1-2). 1992. wkbk. 4.95 (*0-9634846-0-5*) AlphaBuddies.
Shepherd, Sue, et al. Color Me Special. Albury, Mary, illus. (ps-3). 1982. pap. text ed. 4.00 (*0-937423-02-5*) U M H & C.
Shepherd, Thomas, jt. auth. see Shepherd, Sarah.
Shepherd-Bartram, tr. see Gregorich, Barbara.

Sheppard, Jack G., jt. auth. see Sheppard, Dorothy M.
Sheppard, Jeff. I Know a Bridge. Sorensen, Henri, illus. LC 93-2656. 32p. (ps-k). 1993. RSBE 14.95 (*0-02-782457-8*, Macmillan Child Bk) Macmillan Child Grp.
—The Right Number of Elephants. Bond, Felicia, illus. LC 90-4148. 32p. (ps-3). 1990. 12.95 (*0-06-025615-X*); PLB 12.89 (*0-06-025616-8*) HarpC Child Bks.
—The Right Number of Elephants. Bond, Felicia, illus. LC 90-4148. 32p. (ps-3). 1992. pap. 4.95 (*0-06-443299-8*, Trophy) HarpC Child Bks.
—The Right Number of Elephants Big Book. Bond, Felicia, illus. 32p. (ps-3). 1993. pap. 19.95 (*0-06-443338-2*, Trophy) HarpC Child Bks.
—Splash, Splash. Panek, Dennis, illus. 32p. (ps-k). 1994. RSBE 14.95 (*0-02-782455-1*, Macmillan Child Bk) Macmillan Child Grp.
Sheppard, Nancy, adapted by. Alitji in Dreamland: Alitjinya Ngura Tjukurmankuntjala: An Aboriginal Version of Lewis Carroll's Alice's Adventures in Wonderland. Leslie, Donna, illus. LC 92-17640. 104p. (gr. 6 up). 1992. 16.95 (*0-89815-478-2*) Ten Speed Pr.
Sheppard, Nancy D. Jason & the Mischievous Mongoose. Powell, Terry, illus. LC 91-40480. 48p. (Orig.). 1991. pap. text ed. 3.95 (*0-87227-172-2*) Reg Baptist.
Shepperson, Bob. The Sandman. Shepperson, Bob, illus. 32p. (ps-3). 1989. 13.95 (*0-374-36405-2*) FS&G.
—The Sandman. Shepperson, Bob, illus. 32p. (ps-3). 1991. pap. 5.95 (*0-374-46450-2*) FS&G.
Sher, Barbara. Easy Going Games. Young, Janet, illus. LC 87-70022. 78p. (ps-6). 1987. pap. 8.00 (*0-930681-04-5*) Bright Baby.
—Moving Right Along. Stafslien, Barbara, illus. 84p. (ps-3). 1985. pap. text ed. 6.95 (*0-930681-03-7*) Bright Baby.
Sherbondy, Sharon, jt. auth. see Foling, Debra.
Sherburn, George, ed. see Richardson, Samuel.

Sherburne, Andrew. Memoirs of Andrew Sherburne: A Pensioneer of the Navy of the Revolution, Written by Himself. Zeinert, Karen, ed. LC 92-20542. (Illus.). 96p. (gr. 7-12). 1993. PLB 15.95 (*0-208-02354-2*, Pub. by Linnet) Shoe String.
Sherburne, Trudy R. As I Remember It: A Detailed Description of the North Family of the Watervliet, N. Y. Shaker Community. (Illus., Orig.). (gr. 5-10). 1987. pap. 4.95 (*0-944178-00-6*) World Shaker.
Shere, Irene & Friedman, Sharon. Cat's out of the Bag: Jokes about Cats. Hanson, Joan, illus. 32p. (gr. 1-4). 1986. 11.95 (*0-8225-0986-5*); pap. 2.95 (*0-8225-9527-3*) Lerner Pubns.
—Grin & Bear It! Jokes about Teddy Bears. (Illus.). 32p. (gr. 1-4). 1986. lib. bdg. 11.95 (*0-8225-0985-7*) Lerner Pubns.
—In the Doghouse! Jokes about Dogs. (Illus.). 32p. (gr. 1-4). 1986. lib. bdg. 11.95 (*0-8225-0987-3*, First Ave Edns); pap. 2.95 (*0-8225-9528-1*, First Ave Edns) Lerner Pubns.
Sheridan, Jeff. Nothing's Impossible: Stunts to Entertain & Amaze. Moore, Jim, photos by. LC 81-20780. (Illus.). 64p. (gr. 5 up). 1982. 12.95 (*0-688-01169-1*) Lothrop.
Sheridan, Terri, jt. auth. see Darling, Kathy.
Sheringham, Hugh & Moore, John C., eds. Book of the Fly Rod. Sheringham, George, illus. 174p. (gr. 10 up). 1993. Repr. of 1921 ed. 42.90 (*1-56416-116-1*) Derrydale Pr.
Sherlock, Patti. Four of a Kind. LC 91-55038. 196p. (gr. 3-7). 1991. 13.95 (*0-8234-0913-9*) Holiday.
—Some Fine Dog. LC 91-856. 160p. (gr. 3-7). 1992. 13.95 (*0-8234-0947-3*) Holiday.
Sherlock, Philip M. West Indian Folk Tales. Kiddell-Monroe, Joan, illus. 151p. (gr. 3 up). 1988. pap. 10.95 (*0-19-274127-6*) OUP.
Sherman, Cindy. Fitcher's Bird: Based on a Tale by the Brothers Grimm. (Illus.). 32p. (ps-3). 1992. 17.95 (*0-8478-1567-6*) Rizzoli Intl.
Sherman, Eileen. Victor's Place. Trexler, Richard, illus. 598p. (Orig.). (gr. 10-12). 1989. pap. write for info. (*0-9604382-2-X*) Cornerstone Pr.
Sherman, Eileen B. Independence Avenue. 164p. (gr. 5-8). 1990. 13.95 (*0-8276-0367-3*) JPS Phila.
—Monday in Odessa. (gr. 5-9). 1986. 11.95 (*0-8276-0262-6*) JPS Phila.
—The Odd Potato. Kahn, Katherine J., illus. LC 84-17186. 32p. (gr. k-5). 1984. pap. 4.95 (*0-930494-37-7*) Kar-Ben.
Sherman, Harold M. Interference, & Other Football Stories. facsimile ed. LC 70-178460. (gr. 7 up). Repr. of 1932 ed. 18.00 (*0-8369-4061-X*) Ayer.
Sherman, Josepha. Child of Faerie, Child of Earth. 144p. (gr. 7 up). 1992. 15.95 (*0-8027-8112-8*) Walker & Co.
—Gleaming Bright. LC 93-24156. 1994. 16.95 (*0-8027-8296-5*) Walker & Co.
—Rachel the Clever: And Other Jewish Folktales. 1993. 18.95 (*0-87483-306-X*); pap. 9.95 (*0-87483-307-8*) August Hse.
—Windleaf. LC 93-615. 1993. 14.95 (*0-8027-8259-0*); cancelled (*0-8027-8260-4*) Walker & Co.
Sherman, Josepha, adapted by. Vassilisa the Wise: A Tale of Medieval Russia. San Souci, Daniel, illus. LC 87-8563. 26p. (gr. k-3). 1988. 14.95 (*0-15-293240-2*) HarBrace.
Sherman, Ori & Schwartz, Lynne S. The Four Questions. (Illus.). 32p. 1994. pap. 5.99 (*0-14-055269-3*, Puffin Pied Piper) Puffin Bks.
Sherman, Paul, ed. see Thoreau, Henry David.
Sherman, Steven. Henry Stanley & the European Explorers of Africa. (Illus.). (gr. 5 up). 1993. PLB 19.95 (*0-7910-1315-4*, Am Art Analog); pap. write for info. (*0-7910-1544-0*, Am Art Analog) Chelsea Hse.
Sherrard, Raymond & Stumpf, George. Badges of the United States Marshals. Esquivel, Jim & Leaf, Richard, illus. LC 89-61859. (Orig.). 1991. 35.45 (*0-914503-02-2*); pap. 22.45 (*0-914503-03-0*) RHS Ent.
Sherrill, Lou. Jovita Galan: Unselfish Teacher. LC 86-6110. (gr. 4-6). 1986. 5.99 (*0-8054-4326-6*) Broadman.
Sherrow, Victoria. Amsterdam. LC 91-31627. (Illus.). 96p. (gr. 6 up). 1992. RSBE 14.95 (*0-02-782465-9*, New Discovery) Macmillan Child Grp.
—Bill Clinton. (Illus.). 72p. (gr. 4-6). 1993. lib. bdg. 13.95 RSBE (*0-87518-620-3*, Dillon) Macmillan Child Grp.
—Challenges in Education. 1990. lib. bdg. 13.98 (*0-671-70556-3*, J Messner) S&S Trade.
—Chipmunk at Hollow Tree Lane. Davis, Allen, illus. LC 93-27267. 1994. 14.95 (*1-56899-028-6*); pap. 4.95 (*1-56899-029-4*) Soundprints.
—Dream Rooms, Decorating with Flair. Magnuson, Diana, illus. LC 90-48241. 128p. (gr. 5-9). 1991. lib. bdg. 10.89 (*0-8167-2293-5*); pap. text ed. 2.95 (*0-8167-2294-3*) Troll Assocs.
—Endangered Mammals. 1995. PLB write for info. (*0-8050-3253-3*); pap. write for info. (*0-8050-3252-5*) H Holt & Co.
—Great Scientists. (Illus.). 160p. (gr. 7-12). 1992. lib. bdg. 16.95x (*0-8160-2540-1*) Facts on File.
—Hillary Rodham Clinton. (Illus.). 72p. (gr. 4-6). 1993. lib. bdg. 13.95 RSBE (*0-87518-621-1*, Dillon) Macmillan Child Grp.
—The Hopis: Pueblo People of the Southwest. LC 92-45055. (Illus.). 64p. (gr. 4-6). 1993. PLB 14.90 (*1-56294-314-6*) Millbrook Pr.

—Huskings, Quiltings, & Barn Raisings: Work-Play Parties in Early America. Loturco, Laura, illus. LC 92-8725. 78p. 1992. 13.95 (*0-8027-8186-1*); PLB 14.85 (*0-8027-8188-8*) Walker & Co.
—Image & Substance: The Media in U. S. Elections. LC 91-42067. (Illus.). 128p. (gr. 7 up). 1992. PLB 14.90 (*1-56294-075-9*) Millbrook Pr.
—Indians of the Plateau & Great Basin. (Illus.). 96p. (gr. 5-8). 1991. lib. bdg. 18.95x (*0-8160-2388-3*) Facts on File.
—Iroquois. (gr. 4-7). 1993. pap. 6.95 (*0-7910-2027-4*) Chelsea Hse.
—The Iroquois Indians. (Illus.). 80p. (gr. 2-5). 1993. PLB 12.95 (*0-7910-1655-2*) Chelsea Hse.
—Jonas Salk: Research for a Healthier World. LC 92-32302. (Illus.). 128p. (gr. 6-9). 1993. 16.95x (*0-8160-2805-2*) Facts on File.
—The Maya Indians. LC 93-21751. (Illus.). (gr. 2-5). 1993. PLB 13.95 (*0-7910-1666-8*, Am Art Analog); pap. write for info (*0-7910-1994-2*, Am Art Analog) Chelsea Hse.
—Mohandas Gandhi: The Power of the Spirit. (Illus.). 160p. (gr. 7 up). 1994. 16.90 (*1-56294-335-9*) Millbrook Pr.
—The Nez Perces: People of the Plateau. (Illus.). 64p. (gr. 4-6). 1994. 14.90 (*1-56294-315-4*) Millbrook Pr.
—Phillis Wheatley. (Illus.). 80p. (gr. 3-5). 1992. lib. bdg. 12.95 (*0-7910-1753-2*) Chelsea Hse.
—Phyllis Wheatley. (gr. 4-7). 1993. pap. 4.95 (*0-7910-2036-3*) Chelsea Hse.
—The Pigs Got Out. Eagle, Mike, illus. 24p. (Orig.). (ps). 1992. pap. text ed. 3.00x (*0-685-60664-3*) Dushkin Pub.
—Political Leaders & Peacemakers. LC 93-38383. 1994. write for info. (*0-8160-2943-1*) Facts on File.
—The Porcupine. LC 90-3278. (Illus.). 60p. (gr. 3 up). 1991. RSBE 13.95 (*0-87518-442-1*, Dillon) Macmillan Child Grp.
—Los Puerquitos Se Escaparon. Writer, C. C. & Nielsen, Lisa C., trs. Eagle, Mike, illus. (SPA.). 24p. (Orig.). (ps). 1992. pap. text ed. 3.00x (*1-56134-171-1*) Dushkin Pub.
—Seals, Sea Lions, & Walruses. LC 91-4663. (Illus.). 64p. (gr. 5-8). 1991. PLB 12.90 (*0-531-20028-0*) Watts.
—Seals, Sea Lions, & Walruses. updated ed. LC 91-4663. (Illus.). 64p. (gr. 3-4). 1991. PLB 11.90 (*0-685-52512-0*) Denison.
—Separation of Church & State. LC 91-39770. (Illus.). 144p. (gr. 7-12). 1992. PLB 13.90 (*0-531-13000-2*) Watts.
—Skunk at Hemlock Circle. Davis, Allen, illus. LC 93-35511. 1994. 14.95 (*1-56899-031-6*); pap. 4.95 (*1-56899-032-4*) Soundprints.
Sherry, Helen J. Splashes. Sherry, Helen J., illus. 36p. (Orig.). 1989. pap. 2.75 (*0-922273-00-6*) Chocho Bks.
Sherwin, Jane. Human Rights. (Illus.). 48p. (gr. 5 up). 1990. lib. bdg. 18.60 (*0-86592-099-0*); lib. bdg. 13.95s.p. (*0-685-36379-1*) Rourke Corp.
Sherwood, Jonathan. Red Poppies for a Little Bird. Farrington, Liz, created by. (Illus.). 40p. (gr. k-4). 1993. 14.95 (*1-56844-005-7*) Enchante Pub.
—Tanya & the Green-Eyed Monster. Farrington, Liz, created by. (Illus.). 40p. (gr. k-4). 1993. 14.95 (*1-56844-002-2*) Enchante Pub.
Sherwood, Jonathan, jt. auth. see Farrington, Liz.
Sherwood, Rhoda, ed. see Birch, Beverley.
Sherwood, Rhoda, ed. see Brown, Pam.
Sherwood, Rhoda, ed. see Dodd, Lynley.
Sherwood, Rhoda, ed. see Edwards, Hazel.
Sherwood, Rhoda, ed. see Gray, Charlotte.
Sherwood, Rhoda, ed. see Jensen, Kiersten.
Sherwood, Rhoda, ed. see Langoulant, Allan.
Sherwood, Rhoda, ed. see Nicholson, Michael.
Sherwood, Rhoda, ed. see Nicholson, Michael & Winner, David.
Sherwood, Rhoda, ed. see Schloredt, Valeri.
Sherwood, Rhoda, ed. see Smith, Miriam.
Sherwood, Rhoda, ed. see Winch, Gordon.
Sherwood, Rhoda, ed. see Winner, David.
Sherwood, Rhoda I., jt. ed. see Tolan, Sally.
Sherwood, Rhoda I., ed. see Tozuks, Takako.
Shery, Clifford J. Drugs & Eating Disorders. LC 93-35719. 1994. write for info. (*0-8239-1540-9*) Rosen Group.
Shetterly, Susan H. Dwarf-Wizard of Uxmal. Shetlly, Robert, illus. LC 89-32864. 32p. (gr. k-3). 1990. SBE 13.95 (*0-689-31455-8*, Atheneum Child Bk) Macmillan Child Grp.
—Muwin & the Magic Hare. Shetterly, Robert, illus. LC 91-2170. 32p. (gr. 1-5). 1993. SBE 14.95 (*0-689-31699-2*, Atheneum Child Bk) Macmillan Child Grp.
—Raven's Light: A Myth from the People of the Northwest Coast. Shetterly, Robert, illus. LC 89-78183. 32p. (gr. 1-5). 1991. SBE 13.95 (*0-689-31629-1*, Atheneum Child Bk) Macmillan Child Grp.
—The Tinker of Salt Cove. Beckman, Siri, contrib. by. (Illus.). 48p. 1990. 13.95 (*0-88448-080-1*) Tilbury Hse.
Shetterly, W. Elsewhere. (gr. 9 up). 1991. 16.95 (*0-15-200731-8*, HB Juv Bks) HarBrace.
Shetterly, Will. Nevernever. LC 93-238. 1993. 16.95 (*0-15-257022-5*, J Yolen Bks) HarBrace.
Shettle, Andrea. Flute Song Magic. (gr. 7 up). 1990. pap. 2.95 (*0-380-76225-0*, Flare) Avon.
Shevett, Anita & Shevett, Steve, photos by. Baby's ABC. LC 85-62427. (Illus.). 28p. (ps). 1986. bds. 2.95 (*0-394-87870-1*) Random Bks Yng Read.

Shevrin, Aliza, selected by. & tr. from YID. Around the Table: Family Stories of Sholom Aleichem. Gowing, Toby, illus. LC 90-49273. 96p. (gr. 5-8). 1991. SBE 12.95 (*0-684-19237-3*, Scribners Young Read) Macmillan Child Grp.
Shevrin, Aliza, tr. see Aleichem, Sholom.
Shibano, Tamizo. The Old Man Who Made the Trees Bloom. Ooka, D. T., tr. from JPN. Iguchi, Bunshu, illus. 32p. 1985. 11.95 (*0-89346-247-0*) Heian Intl.
Shibles, Warren. Good & Bad Are Funny Things: Ethics in Rhyme for Children. LC 77-93808. (gr. k up). 1978. pap. 6.50 (*0-912386-14-2*) Language Pr.
—Time: A Critical Analysis for Children. LC 77-93811. (gr. 4-12). 1978. pap. 6.50 (*0-912386-17-7*) Language Pr.
Shibley, David & Shibley, Naomi. Special Times with God. LC 81-14116. 160p. (ps). 1981. 6.99 (*0-8407-5780-8*) Nelson.
Shibley, Naomi, jt. auth. see Shibley, David.
Shiefman, Vicky. Good-Bye to the Trees. LC 92-22260. 176p. (gr. 4-8). 1993. SBE 14.95 (*0-689-31806-5*, Atheneum Child Bk) Macmillan Child Grp.
—Sunday Potatoes, Monday Potatoes. August, Louise, illus. LC 92-46112. (gr. 3 up). 1994. pap. 14.00 (*0-671-86596-X*, S&S BFYR) S&S Trade.
Shields, Allan. Tragedy of Tenaya. (gr. 6). 1974. 5.95 (*0-89992-043-8*) Coun India Ed.
Shields, Bill. Anatomy of a Male Slut: PO Box 61564. Winkler, Chris, illus. 16p. (Orig.). (gr. 10 up). 1988. pap. 2.00 saddle stapled (*0-929611-02-0*) Plutonium Pr.
Shields, Carol D. I Am Really a Princess. Meisel, Paul, illus. LC 92-37161. 32p. (ps-3). 1993. 13.99 (*0-525-45138-2*, DCB) Dutton Child Bks.

Shields, Mary. The Alaskan Happy Dog Trilogy: Can Dogs Talk?, Loving a Happy Dog, Secret Messages-Training a Happy Dog, 3 vols. Gates, Donna, illus. 32p. (ps-3). 1993. Set. pap. 30.00 (*0-9618348-2-X*) Pyrola Pub.
THE ALASKAN HAPPY DOG TRILOGY, $30.00, ISBN 0-9618348-2-X, CAN DOGS TALK?, $10.00, ISBN 0-9618348-1-1, with audio tape, $13.00, ISBN 0-9618348-4-6, LOVING A HAPPY DOG, $12.00, ISBN 0-9618348-3-8, SECRET MESSAGES-TRAINING A HAPPY DOG, $12.00, ISBN 0-9618348-6-2. In the first volume, CAN DOGS TALK? Rita & Ryan answer their own question with the help of an Alaskan dog musher, a book, a team of friendly huskies & a lost puppy. In the second volume, LOVING A HAPPY DOG, the kids ask Mary to give them the lost puppy, named Happy. Mary helps the kids understand the responsibilities of loving & caring for a Happy Dog, including the knowledge of a dog's life span. A pull-out puzzle is included in this book. The final volume, SECRET MESSAGES-TRAINING A HAPPY DOG unfolds as Rita, Ryan & Happy discover messages along the trail as they hike to Mary's cabin. By evening the kids have learned how to train their dog, & another important lesson-its okay to ask for help. Each volume stands on its own, but the complete trilogy gives the young reader a well-rounded introduction in enjoying the companionship of a dog. The author, Mary Shields lives in Alaska, where she raises sled dogs for companions & wilderness travelers. Donna Gates creates her fine art images of sled dogs & interior Alaskan wildlife at her home near Denali Park, Alaska. Pyrola Publishing, P.O. Box 80961, Fairbanks, AK 99708. 907-455-6469 (Alaskan time please).
Publisher Provided Annotation.

—Can Dogs Talk, Vol. 1. Gates, Donna, illus. 32p. (Orig.). (ps-3). 1991. pap. 10.00 (*0-9618348-1-1*); incl. tape 13.00 (*0-9618348-4-6*); write for info. Pyrola Pub.
—Loving a Happy Dog. Gates, Donna, illus. 32p. 1992. pap. 12.00 (*0-9618348-3-8*) Pyrola Pub.

Shiffer, Eric. Pumping Iron for Teenage Guys. (Orig.). 1987. pap. 6.95 (*0-449-90187-4*, Columbine) Fawcett.
Shifflett, Crandall A. Victorian America. Balkin, Rick, ed. (Illus.). 300p. (gr. 5-10). 1994. 35.00 (*0-8160-2531-2*) Facts on File.
Shiffman, Lena, illus. My First Book of Words. 64p. 1992. 10.95 (*0-590-45142-1*, Cartwheel) Scholastic Inc.
Shifrin, Adah. Meher Baba Is Love. 2nd ed. Sargent, Patricia, illus. 56p. (gr. 1-3). 1987. pap. 6.95 (*0-913078-59-X*) Sheriar Pr.
Shigekawa, Marlene. Bluejay in the Desert. Kikuchi, Isao, illus. LC 92-35424. 36p. (gr. k-4). 1993. 12.95 (*1-879965-04-6*) Polychrome Pub.

Shigezawa, Ruth. Celeste. Altman, Robin W., illus. 28p. (gr. 2 up). 1993. 16.95 (*0-9637101-0-9*); pap. 7.95 (*0-9637101-1-7*) Cndlelght Pr.
"Who will be our next leader?" Everyone asks that question around the assembly. The cloud clusters meet during their hundred-year reunion & eagerly await the news. When retiring leader, Great Great Grandfather Thundercloud, announces the name of their new leader, the assembly is in disbelief. The leader has always been a thundercloud of great rain-giving gifts. No one expects the chosen leader to be a female cloud named Celeste. So begins Celeste's initiation journey across the earth to learn about the creatures below. In the course of her odyssey, her already surprising life takes an even more astonishing turn. Against the advice of the Great Thundercloud, Celeste attempts to help a farming family who struggles to nurture the land they cultivate. Celeste rebels against ancient tradition & in an unusual way expresses her creative skills. She thus learns to give her special gifts in this modern fable about caring for nature, discovering a life's purpose, & listening to the true voice within. Order from Candlelight Press, P.O. Box 50187, Irvine, CA 92619-0187.
Publisher Provided Annotation.

Shigley, Gordon. COMAL Workbook. Hejndorf, Frank, illus. 69p. (Orig.). (gr. 6 up). 1985. pap. text ed. 6.95 (*0-928411-05-2*) Comal Users.
Shimano, Jimmei. Oriental Fortune Telling. LC 65-18960. (Illus.). 170p. (gr. 9 up). 1965. 9.95 (*0-8048-0448-6*) C E Tuttle.
Shine, Deborah. The Little Engine That Could Pudgy Word Book. Ong, Christina, illus. 18p. (ps). 1988. bds. 2.95 (*0-448-19054-0*, G&D) Putnam Pub Group.
—The Pudgy Noisy Book. McCord, Kathleen G., illus. 18p. (ps). 1988. bds. 2.95 (*0-448-19055-9*, G&D) Putnam Pub Group.
—The Race. 16p. (ps-2). 1992. pap. 14.95 (*1-56784-051-5*) Newbridge Comms.
—Where's the Puppy? 16p. (ps-2). 1992. pap. 14.95 (*1-56784-052-3*) Newbridge Comms.
Shine, Michael. Mama Llama's Pajamas. Villegas, Carene, illus. 45p. (Orig.). (ps-3). 1990. pap. 8.95 (*0-945265-32-8*) Accord Comm.
Shinhav, Chaya. Adios, Berry. Writer, C. C. & Nielsen, Lisa C., trs. Eagle, Mike, illus. (SPA.). 24p. (Orig.). (ps). 1992. pap. text ed. 3.00x (*1-56134-154-1*) Dushkin Pub.
—Cien Cuartos. Writer, C. C. & Nielsen, Lisa C., trs. Elchanan, illus. (SPA.). 24p. (Orig.). (ps). 1992. pap. text ed. 3.00x (*1-56134-169-X*) Dushkin Pub.
—Goodbye, Berry. Kriss, David, tr. from HEB. Eagle, Mike, illus. 24p. (Orig.). (ps). 1992. pap. text ed. 3.00x (*1-56134-144-4*) Dushkin Pub.
—A Hundred Rooms. Kriss, David, tr. from HEB. Elchanan, illus. 24p. (Orig.). (ps). 1992. pap. text ed. 3.00x (*1-56134-159-2*) Dushkin Pub.
Shinn, Florence S. The Writings of Florence Scovel Shinn. 368p. (Orig.). 1988. pap. 14.95 (*0-87516-610-5*) DeVorss.
Shipley, Debra, jt. auth. see Peplow, Mary.
Shipman, Gary, illus. Tinga Layo. 16p. (ps-2). 1992. pap. 14.95 (*1-55799-228-2*) Evan-Moor Corp.
Shipton, Alyn. Brass. LC 93-2895. (Illus.). 32p. (gr. 5-8). 1993. PLB 19.97 (*0-8114-2317-4*) Raintree Steck-V.
—Keyboards. LC 93-16637. (Illus.). 32p. (gr. 5-8). 1993. PLB 19.97 (*0-8114-2318-2*) Raintree Steck-V.
—Percussion. LC 93-20013. (Illus.). 32p. (gr. 5-8). 1993. PLB 19.97 (*0-8114-2316-6*) Raintree Steck-V.

—Singing. LC 93-20006. (Illus.). 32p. (gr. 1-8). 1993. PLB 19.97 (*0-8114-2315-8*) Raintree Steck-V.
—Strings. LC 93-15278. (Illus.). 32p. (gr. 5-8). 1993. PLB 19.97 (*0-8114-2320-4*) Raintree Steck-V.
—Woodwinds. LC 93-20224. (Illus.). 32p. 1993. PLB 19.97 (*0-8114-2319-0*) Raintree Steck-V.
Shipton, Jonathan. Busy! Busy! Busy! (ps-3). 1991. 14.00 (*0-385-30305-X*) Delacorte.
—In the Night. Scriven, Gill, illus. 32p. (ps-3). 1992. 14.95 (*0-316-78586-5*) Little.
Shipton, P. Science with Batteries. (Illus.). 24p. (gr. 1-4). 1993. PLB 12.96 (*0-88110-633-X*); pap. 4.50 (*0-7460-1423-6*) EDC.
Shipton, Paul, jt. auth. see Heddle, Rebecca.
Shire, Donald R. Apes & Monkeys. (gr. 4-7). 1991. 13.00 (*0-385-26608-1*) Doubleday.
Shires, H. Bess & March, Rita N. Adventures in Pennsylvania. (gr. 5-6). 1984. pap. 4.95 (*0-931992-12-5*) Penns Valley.
Shirk-Heath, Sandra J. Mom's Metric Cookbook. LC 86-90378. 150p. (gr. 1-6). 1986. PLB write for info. (*0-9615104-0-4*) Shirk-Heath.
Shirkus, Lorraine, jt. auth. see Colby, Sas.
Shirley, David. Alex Haley, Author. LC 93-16762. (Illus.). (gr. 4 up). 1994. PLB 18.95 (*0-7910-1979-9*, Am Art Analog); pap. write for info. (*0-7910-1980-2*, Am Art Analog) Chelsea Hse.
—Gloria Estefan: Entertainer. (Illus.). 1993. 13.95 (*0-7910-2111-4*, Am Art Analog) Chelsea Hse.
—Malcolm X: Racial Spokesman. LC 93-17700. (Illus.). 1993. 13.95 (*0-7910-2106-8*, Am Art Analog); pap. 4.95 (*0-7910-2112-2*, Am Art Analog) Chelsea Hse.
—The Pueblo Indians. (Illus.). 1994. 13.95 (*0-7910-1669-2*, Am Art Analog) Chelsea Hse.
—Satchel Paige. King, Coretta Scott, intro. by. (Illus.). 112p. (gr. 5 up). 1993. PLB 17.95 (*0-7910-1880-6*); pap. write for info. (*0-7910-1983-7*) Chelsea Hse.
Shirley, Gayle. A Is for Animals. Bergum, Connie, illus. 56p. (ps-3). 1991. pap. 8.95 (*1-56044-025-2*) Falcon Pr MT.
—C Is for Colorado. Bergum, Connie, illus. LC 89-83793. 40p. (Orig.). (gr. k-3). 1989. 12.95 (*0-937959-85-5*) Falcon Pr MT.
—M Is for Montana. Bergum, Constance, illus. LC 87-73310. 32p. (Orig.). 1988. pap. 7.95 (*0-937959-32-4*, ABC Press) Falcon Pr MT.
Shirley, Gayle C. Montana Wildlife: A Children's Field Guide to the State's Most Remarkable Animals. Allnock, Sandy, illus. 48p. (Orig.). 1993. pap. 6.95 (*1-56044-154-2*) Falcon Pr MT.
Shirley, Gayle C., jt. auth. see Tewell, Debbie.
Shirley, Glenn. Belle Starr & Her Times: The Literature, the Facts, & the Legends. LC 81-14683. (Illus.). 336p. (gr. 10 up). 1990. pap. 13.95 (*0-8061-1713-3*); pap. 12.95 (*0-8061-2276-5*) U of Okla Pr.
Shirley, Jean, jt. auth. see Carpenter, Angelica S.
Shirley, Joseph. The Very Special Place. Mosteller, Rosella, illus. 32p. (Orig.). (gr. k-4). 1992. pap. 10.95 incl. cass. (*0-9632816-0-7*) NISIS.
Shirley, Sam, ed. see Lockborn, Paul, et al.
Shirts, Morris A. Warm up for Little League Baseball. rev. ed. MacDonald, Pat, ed. (Illus.). (gr. 3-6). 1990. pap. 2.99 (*0-671-70119-3*, Archway) PB.
Shivanandan, Mary. Nasser: Modern Leader of Egypt. Rahmas, D. Steve, ed. LC 73-87627. 32p. (Orig.). (gr. 7-12). 1973. lib. bdg. 4.95 incl. catalog cards (*0-87157-564-7*) SamHar Pr.
Shivens, Frank. Heavy Stuff Student Workbook. Robinson, Robbie, illus. (Orig.). (gr. 7-12). 1991. 5.95 (*1-8781270-1-2*) F Shivers Evangelistic.
Shiver, Lee A. Going to the Gator Game! 32p. (gr. k-5). 1992. 19.95 (*1-882466-00-4*) Our Mascot.
Shivers, Frank R. Heavy Stuff: Clear & Common-Sense Insight into Problems Youth Face. Hill, Junior, intro. by. (Illus., Orig.). (gr. 7-12). 1991. pap. 8.95 (*1-878127-00-4*) F Shivers Evangelistic.
Shivkumar. Krishna & Sudama. Gupta, M. L. Dutta, illus. (gr. 1-8). 1979. pap. 2.00 (*0-89744-156-7*) Auromere.
—Stories from Panchatantra: Book I. Biswas, Pulak, illus. (gr. 1-9). 1979. 4.50 (*0-89744-162-1*); pap. 3.00 (*0-685-57661-2*) Auromere.
—Stories from Panchatantra: Book II. Bhusan, Reboti, illus. (gr. 1-9). 1979. 4.50 (*0-89744-163-X*); pap. 3.00 (*0-685-57662-0*) Auromere.
—Stories from Panchatantra: Book III. Mukerji, Debrabrata, illus. (gr. 1-9). 1979. 4.50 (*0-89744-164-8*); pap. 3.00 (*0-685-57663-9*) Auromere.
—Stories from Panchatantra: Book IV. Biswas, Pulak, illus. (gr. 1-9). 1979. 4.50 (*0-89744-165-6*); pap. 3.00 (*0-685-57664-7*) Auromere.
Shklar, Judith. Montesquieu. 144p. (gr. 5up). 1987. 24.95 (*0-19-287649-X*) OUP.

Shles, Larry. The Adventure of the Squib Owl: Squib Ser. Shles, Larry, illus. 1988. pap. 7.95 each (*0-915190-85-0*) Jalmar Pr.
Squib the Owl series, written & whimsically illustrated by Larry Shles, teaches self-esteem & personal & social responsibility as it entertains. The author uses the name Squib to personify the small vulnerable part of us all that struggles & at times feels

helpless in an enormous world filled with emotions. This Series, five volumes, traces the adventures of this tiny owl as he struggles with his feelings searching at least for understanding. Each of the five titles explores a different vulnerability. MOTHS & MOTHERS, FEATHERS & FATHERS (explores feelings); HOOTS & TOOTS & HAIRY BRUTES (explores disabilities); ALIENS IN MY NEST (explores adolescent behavior); HUGS & SHRUGS (explores inner peace). The latest volume DO I HAVE TO GO TO SCHOOL TODAY? is great for the young reader who needs encouragement from teachers who accept him "just as he is". Brilliantly simple, yet realistically complex, Squib personifies each & every one of us. He is a reflection of what we are, & what we can become. Every reader who has struggled with life's limitations will recognize his own struggles & triumphs in the microcosm of Squib's forest world - in Squib we find a parable for all ages from 8-80.
Publisher Provided Annotation.

—Aliens in My Nest: Squib Meets the Teen Creature. Winch, Bradley L., ed. Shles, Larry, illus. LC 88-80770. 80p. (Orig.). (gr. k up). 1988. 7.95 (*0-915190-49-4*, JP9049-4) Jalmar Pr.
—Do I have to Go to School Today? Squib Measures Up. Winch, Bradley L., ed. Shles, Larry, illus. 64p. (Orig.). (gr. k up). 1989. pap. 7.95 (*0-915190-62-1*, JP9062-1) Jalmar Pr.
—Hoots & Toots & Hairy Brutes, Vol. 2: The Continuing Adventures of Squib. 2nd ed. Shles, Larry, illus. LC 89-83466. 72p. (gr. k-8). 1989. pap. 7.95 (*0-915190-56-7*, JP9056-7) Jalmar Pr.
—Hugs & Shrugs: The Continuing Saga of Squib. Shles, Larry, illus. LC 87-82162. 72p. (gr. k up). 1987. pap. 7.95 (*0-915190-47-8*, JP9047-8) Jalmar Pr.
—Moths & Mothers, Feathers & Fathers, Vol. 1: A Story about a Tiny Owl Named Squib. 2nd ed. Winch, Bradley, ed. Shles, Larry, illus. LC 89-83467. 72p. (gr. k-8). 1989. pap. 7.95 (*0-915190-57-5*, JP9057-5) Jalmar Pr.
—Scooter's Tail of Terror: A Fable of Addiction & Hope. Ciconte, Marie, ed. (Illus.). 80p. (Orig.). (gr. 2 up). 1992. pap. 9.95 (*0-915190-89-3*, JP9089-3) Jalmar Pr.
Shles, Lawrence. Hoots & Toots & Hairy Brutes: Squib the Owl Saves the Day. Shles, Lawrence, illus. 70p. (gr. k-3). 1984. 10.95 (*0-685-42996-2*); pap. 4.95 (*0-685-42997-0*) HM.
Shlesinger, B. Edward, Jr. How to Invent: A Text for Teachers & Students. rev. ed. LC 87-18608. (Illus.). 140p. (gr. 9-12). 1987. pap. 10.00 (*0-306-65210-2*, IFI-Plenum); video 150.00 (*0-685-19356-X*) Plenum.
Shniderman, Jeffrey & Hurwitz, Sue. Applications: A Guide to Filling Out All Kinds of Forms. LC 93-7911. 1993. 12.95 (*0-8239-1609-X*) Rosen Group.
Shniderman, Nancy & Hurwitz, Sue. Drugs & Birth Defects. Rosen, Ruth, ed. (gr. 7-12). 1993. 14.95 (*0-8239-1419-4*) Rosen Group.
Shockley, Robert & Cutlip, Glen W. Careers in Teaching. rev. ed. 64p. (gr. 7-12). 1990. PLB 13.95 (*0-8239-1137-3*); pap. 9.95 (*0-8239-1718-5*) Rosen Group.
Shodel, Elly, intro. by. In the Service: Workers on the Grand Estates of Long Island, 1890s-1940s. Gilligan, Lorraine, pref. by. (Illus.). 66p. (Orig.). (gr. 9-12). 1991. pap. 14.95 (*0-9615059-2-3*) Pt WA Pub Lib.
Shodell, Elly, ed. Particles of the Past: Sandmining on Long Island 1870s-1980s. 2nd ed. Pope, Genoroso, pref. by. (Illus.). 43p. (gr. 9-12). pap. 8.95 (*0-9615059-0-7*) Pt WA Pub Lib.
Shoecraft, Paul J. Think Links: Fractions, Decimals, Percent. (Illus.). 61p. (gr. 1-6). 1992. incl. tchr's. ed. 12.95x (*0-941530-07-8*) Move It Math.
—Think Links: Math-Language Arts. (Illus.). 80p. (gr. 1-4). 1992. incl. tchr's. ed. 14.95x (*0-941530-05-1*) Move It Math.
—Think Links: Math-Reading Readiness. (Illus.). 88p. (gr. k-2). 1992. incl. tchr's. ed. 14.95x (*0-941530-04-3*) Move It Math.
—Think Links: Whole Number Arithmetic. 67p. (gr. 1-4). 1992. incl. tchr's. ed. 10.95x (*0-941530-06-X*) Move It Math.
Shoemaker, Mrs. J. W., compiled by. Young Folks Recitations: Designed for Young People of Fourteen Years; Containing Selections in Prose & Poetry; Together with Some Short Dialogues & Tableaux. LC 73-2839. (gr. 8-10). 1973. Repr. of 1884 ed. 14.00 (*0-8369-6413-6*) Ayer.

Shofner, Myra. Second Ark Book of Riddles. Walles, Dwight, illus. (gr. 3-7). 1981. pap. 3.99 (*0-89191-531-1*, 55319, Chariot Bks) Cook.
Shoker, Nancy. Substance Abuse. Koop, C. Everett, intro. by. (Illus.). 112p. (gr. 6-12). 1993. 18.95 (*0-7910-0078-8*) Chelsea Hse.
Shone, Venice. My Activity Box. Shone, Venice, illus. LC 93-3288. 20p. (ps). 1993. 2.99 (*0-525-67449-7*, Lodestar Bks) Dutton Child Bks.
—My Lunch Box. Shone, Venice, illus. LC 93-3287. 20p. (ps). 1993. 2.99 (*0-525-67451-9*, Lodestar Bks) Dutton Child Bks.
—My Play Box. Shone, Venice, illus. LC 93-3289. 20p. (ps). 1993. 2.99 (*0-525-67448-9*, Lodestar Bks) Dutton Child Bks.
—My Toy Box. Shone, Venice, illus. LC 93-18682. 20p. (ps). 1993. 2.99 (*0-525-67450-0*, Lodestar Bks) Dutton Child Bks.
—Tools. (ps). 1991. 9.95 (*0-590-44472-7*) Scholastic Inc.
Shontz, Bill, jt. auth. see Rosen, Gary.
Shope, Kimberly A. A Bear Named Song: The Gift of a Lifetime. (Illus.). 32p. 1992. 11.99 (*0-87403-865-0*, 24-03565) Standard Pub.
Shore, Carol. Official Florida Coloring Book, Vol. 1. rev. ed. (Illus.). 40p. (ps-5). 1986. pap. 1.98 (*0-9612136-1-2*) C Shore Pr.
—The Official Florida Natives: A Friendly Introduction. LC 84-91492. (Illus.). 56p. (ps-7). 1985. pap. 2.98 (*0-9612136-2-0*) C Shore Pr.
Shore, Donna & Renna, Giani. Florence Nightingale. (Illus.). 104p. (gr. 5-8). 1990. 16.98 (*0-382-09978-8*); pap. 8.95 (*0-382-24004-9*) Silver Burdett Pr.
Shore, Hennie M., ed. see Shapiro, Lawrence E.
Shore, Nancy. Amelia Earhart. Horner, Matina, intro. by. (Illus.). 112p. (Orig.). (gr. 5 up). 1987. 17.95 (*1-55546-651-6*); pap. 9.95 (*0-7910-0415-5*) Chelsea Hse.
Short, David & Short, Pat. Entice Their Imaginations. Breviek, Phil, illus. 64p. (gr. k-6). 1985. wkbk. 7.95 (*0-86653-324-9*, GA 658) Good Apple.
Short, Edward P. Checkpoint: A Science Project Survival Guide. (Illus.). 48p. (Orig.). (gr. 3-8). 1992. pap. 9.95 (*0-9636375-1-7*) E P Short.
Short, J. Rodney & Dickerson, Beverly. The Newspaper: An Alternative Textbook. 64p. (gr. 6-11). 1980. pap. 9.95 (*0-8224-4661-8*) Fearon Teach Aids.
Short, Pat, jt. auth. see Short, David.
Short, Sondra J. Unicorns & Rainbows. LC 92-60808. 223p. (gr. 3 up). 1993. 9.95 (*1-55523-537-9*) Winston-Derek.
Shortall, Leonard. One Way: A Trip with Traffic Signs. (ps-3). 1981. (Pub. by Treehouse) P-H.
Shortall, Leonard, illus. Old MacDonald Had a Farm. LC 84-60028. (ps up). 1984. 5.95 (*0-394-86797-1*) Random Bks Yng Read.
Shortelle, Dennis, jt. auth. see Gardner, Robert.
Shorto, Russell. Abraham Lincoln & the End of Slavery. (Illus.). 32p. (gr. 2-4). 1991. PLB 12.40 (*1-878841-12-2*) Millbrook Pr.
—Abraham Lincoln: To Preserve the Union. (Illus.). 160p. (gr. 5 up). 1990. lib. bdg. 18.98 (*0-382-09937-0*); pap. 8.95 (*0-382-24046-4*) Silver Burdett Pr.
—Careers for Animal Lovers. LC 91-27657. (Illus.). 64p. (gr. 7 up). 1992. PLB 13.90 (*1-56294-160-7*) Millbrook Pr.
—Careers for Animal Lovers. 1992. pap. 4.95 (*0-395-63571-3*) HM.
—Careers for Foreign Language Experts. LC 91-27661. (Illus.). 64p. (gr. 7 up). 1992. PLB 13.90 (*1-56294-159-3*) Millbrook Pr.
—Careers for Foreign Language Experts. 1992. pap. 4.95 (*0-395-63572-1*) HM.
—Careers for Hands-on Types. LC 91-47146. (Illus.). 64p. (gr. 7 up). 1992. PLB 13.90 (*1-56294-065-1*) Millbrook Pr.
—Careers for People Who Like People. LC 91-27662. (Illus.). 64p. (gr. 7 up). 1992. PLB 13.90 (*1-56294-157-7*) Millbrook Pr.
—Careers for People Who Like People. 1992. pap. 4.95 (*0-395-63573-X*) HM.
—Careers for People Who Like to Perform. LC 91-27660. (Illus.). 64p. (gr. 7 up). 1992. PLB 13.90 (*1-56294-158-5*) Millbrook Pr.
—Careers for People Who Like to Perform. 1992. pap. 4.95 (*0-395-63574-8*) HM.
—Careers for the Curious. LC 91-47145. (Illus.). 64p. (gr. 7 up). 1992. PLB 13.90 (*1-56294-064-3*) Millbrook Pr.
—Cinderella & Cinderella's Stepsister. Lewis, (Illus.). (ps-2). 1990. 12.95 (*0-685-38933-2*, Birch Ln Pr) Carol Pub Group.
—David Farragut & the Great Naval Blockade. (Illus.). 160p. (gr. 5 up). 1990. lib. bdg. 18.98 (*0-382-09941-9*); pap. 8.95 (*0-382-24050-2*) Silver Burdett Pr.
—Geronimo. (Illus.). 144p. (gr. 5-7). 1989. PLB 12.98 (*0-382-09571-5*); pap. 7.95 (*0-382-09760-2*) Silver Burdett Pr.
—How to Fly the Space Shuttle. Keating, Edward, photos by. (Illus.). 48p. (Orig.). (gr. 4-7). 1992. pap. 9.95 (*1-56261-063-5*) John Muir.
—Jackie Robinson & the Breaking of the Color Barrier. (Illus.). 32p. (gr. 2-4). 1991. PLB 12.40 (*1-878841-15-7*) Millbrook Pr.
—Jane Fonda: Political Activism. (Illus.). 104p. (gr. 7 up). 1991. PLB 14.90 (*1-56294-045-7*) Millbrook Pr.
—Jane Fonda: Political Activist. 1992. pap. 5.95 (*0-395-63564-0*) HM.

—Tecumseh. Furstinger, Nancy, ed. (Illus.). 136p. (gr. 5-7). 1989. PLB 12.98 (0-382-09569-3); pap. 7.95 (0-382-09758-0) Silver Burdett Pr.

—Thomas Jefferson & the American Ideal. (Illus.). 144p. (gr. 3-6). 1987. pap. 5.95 (0-8120-3918-1) Barron.

—The Untold Story of Cinderella. Lewis, T., illus. 1992. pap. 8.95 (0-8065-1298-9, Citadel Pr) Carol Pub Group.

Shortridge, Cleona, frwd. by see Hill, Charlotte M.

Shortridge, Cleona, intro. by see Hill, Charlotte M.

Shortridge, Cleona, ed. see Hill, Charlotte M.

Shortridge, Cleona, ed. see Hill, Charlotte M. & Hill, Fred D.

Shortsleeve, Brian F., ed. see Shortsleeve, Kevin.

Shortsleeve, Kevin. The Story of Cape Cod. Shortsleeve, Brian F., ed Iwanowski, Elka, illus. 64p. (gr. k-3). 1993. pap. 9.75 (0-9622782-1-1) Cape Cod Life Mag.

Shose, Hennie M., ed. see Shapiro, Lawrence E.

Shostak. Preparation for College Board Achievement Tests: HTP CBAT - English. 7th ed. 288p. (gr. 7 up). 1991. pap. 10.95 (0-8120-4686-2) Barron.

Shostak, Jerome, jt. auth. see Peters, Max.

Shostak, Myra. Rainbow Candles: A Chanukah Counting Book. Kahn, Katherine J., illus. LC 86-81718. 12p. (ps). 1986. bds. 4.95 (0-930494-59-8) Kar Ben.

Shott, James. The House Across the Street. LC 87-51498. 30p. (gr. 2-4). 1988. 6.95 (1-55523-129-2) Winston-Derek.

Shott, Stephen, photos by. Bathtime. LC 91-11121. (Illus.). 12p. (ps). 1991. bds. 4.95 (0-525-44754-7, DCB) Dutton Child Bks.

—Look at Me. LC 91-11162. (Illus.). 12p. (ps). 1991. bds. 4.95 (0-525-44755-5, DCB) Dutton Child Bks.

—Mealtime. LC 91-2600. (Illus.). 12p. (ps). 1991. bds. 4.95 (0-525-44756-3, DCB) Dutton Child Bks.

—El Mundo del Bebe. (SPA., Illus.). 48p. (ps). 1992. 14.95 (0-525-44846-2, DCB) Dutton Child Bks.

—Playtime. LC 91-2601. (Illus.). 12p. (ps). 1991. bds. 4.95 (0-525-44757-1, DCB) Dutton Child Bks.

Shott, Steven, photos by. Baby's World. LC 90-30587. (Illus.). 48p. (ps). 1990. 13.95 (0-525-44617-6, DCB) Dutton Child Bks.

Shouse, C., jt. auth. see Mainwaring, S.

Shouse, Lucille, jt. auth. see Scott, Kay.

Showalter, Elaine, intro. by see Alcott, Louisa May.

Showalter, Lester. Investigating God's Orderly World, Bk. 1. (gr. 7-8). 1970. write for info. (0-686-05588-8); tchr's. ed. avail. (0-686-05589-6) Rod & Staff.

—Investigating God's Orderly World, Bk 2. (gr. 9-10). 1975. write for info. (0-686-11144-3); tchr's ed. avail. (0-686-11145-1) Rod & Staff.

Showell, Ellen. The Trickster Ghost. 1992. 2.75 (0-590-45795-0, Little Apple) Scholastic Inc.

Showell, Ellen H. Our Mountain. Carpenter, Nancy, illus. LC 90-2392. 80p. (gr. 2-6). 1991. SBE 12.95 (0-02-782551-5, Bradbury Pr) Macmillan Child Grp.

Showers, Paul. Drop of Blood. Madden, Don, illus. LC 67-23672. (gr. k-3). 1967. PLB 12.89 (0-690-24526-2, Crowell Jr Bks) HarpC Child Bks.

—A Drop of Blood. rev. ed. Madden, Paul, illus. LC 85-43021. 32p. (gr. k-4). 1989. pap. 4.50 (0-06-445090-2, Trophy) HarpC Child Bks.

—A Drop of Blood. rev. ed. Madden, Don, illus. LC 88-3623. 32p. (gr. k-4). 1989. (Crowell Jr Bks); PLB 13.89 (0-690-04717-7, Crowell Jr Bks) HarpC Child Bks.

—Ears Are for Hearing. Keller, Holly, illus. LC 89-17479. 32p. (gr. k-4). 1990. (Crowell Jr Bks); PLB 14.89 (0-690-04720-7, Crowell Jr Bks) HarpC Child Bks.

—Ears Are for Hearing. Keller, Holly, illus. LC 89-17479. 32p. (gr. k-4). 1993. pap. 4.50 (0-06-445112-7, Trophy) HarpC Child Bks.

—Hear Your Heart. Low, Joseph, illus. LC 68-11067. 40p. (gr. k-3). 1968. PLB 13.89 (0-690-37379-1, Crowell Jr Bks) HarpC Child Bks.

—How Many Teeth? Galdone, Paul, illus. 40p. (gr. k-3). 1962. PLB 13.89 (0-690-40716-5, Crowell Jr Bks) HarpC Child Bks.

—How Many Teeth? LC 68-11004. (Illus.). 40p. (ps-3). 1984. pap. 4.50 (0-06-445008-2, Trophy) HarpC Child Bks.

—How Many Teeth? rev. ed. Kelley, True, illus. LC 89-71731. 32p. (ps-1). 1991. pap. 4.95 (0-06-445098-8, Trophy) HarpC Child Bks.

—How Many Teeth? rev. ed. Kelley, True, illus. LC 89-13995. 32p. (ps-1). 1991. 14.00 (0-06-021633-6); PLB 13.89 (0-06-021634-4) HarpC Child Bks.

—How You Talk. rev. ed. Lloyd, Megan, illus. LC 90-1484. 32p. (gr. k-4). 1992. 14.00 (0-06-022767-2); PLB 13.89 (0-06-022768-0) HarpC Child Bks.

—How You Talk. rev. ed. Lloyd, Megan, illus. LC 90-4056. 32p. (gr. k-4). 1992. pap. 4.50 (0-06-445099-6, Trophy) HarpC Child Bks.

—Listening Walk. Aliki, illus. LC 61-10495. 40p. (gr. k-3). 1961. PLB 13.89 (0-690-49663-X, Crowell Jr Bks) HarpC Child Bks.

—The Listening Walk. rev. ed. Aliki, illus. LC 90-30526. 32p. (ps-2). 1991. 14.00 (0-06-021637-9); PLB 13.89 (0-06-021638-7) HarpC Child Bks.

—The Listening Walk. Aliki, illus. LC 90-30526. 32p. (ps-2). 1993. pap. 4.95 (0-06-443322-6, Trophy) HarpC Child Bks.

—Look at Your Eyes. rev. ed. Kelley, True, illus. LC 91-10167. 32p. (ps-1). 1992. 14.00 (0-06-020188-6); PLB 13.89 (0-06-020189-4) HarpC Child Bks.

—Look at Your Eyes. rev. ed. Kelley, True, illus. LC 91-10168. 32p. (ps-1). 1992. pap. 4.50 (0-06-445108-9, Trophy) HarpC Child Bks.

—Sleep Is for Everyone. Watson, Wendy, illus. LC 72-83785. 40p. (ps-3). 1974. PLB 13.89 (0-690-01118-0, Crowell Jr Bks) HarpC Child Bks.

—What Happens to a Hamburger? rev. ed. Rockwell, Anne, illus. LC 84-45343. 32p. (ps-3). 1985. (Crowell Jr Bks); PLB 14.89 (0-690-04427-5, Crowell Jr Bks) HarpC Child Bks.

—What Happens to a Hamburger? rev. ed. Rockwell, Anne, illus. LC 84-48784. 32p. (gr. k-3). 1985. pap. 4.50 (0-06-445013-9, Trophy) HarpC Child Bks.

—Where Does the Garbage Go? rev. ed. Chewning, Randy, illus. LC 91-46115. 32p. (gr. k-2). 1994. 15.00 (0-06-021054-0); PLB 14.89 (0-06-021057-5) HarpC Child Bks.

—Where Does the Garbage Go? rev. ed. Chewning, Paul, illus. LC 91-46115. 32p. (gr. k-4). 1994. pap. 4.95 (0-06-445114-3, Trophy) HarpC Child Bks.

—Your Skin & Mine. rev. ed. Kuchera, Kathleen, illus. LC 90-37430. 32p. (gr. k-4). 1991. 13.95 (0-06-022522-X); PLB 13.89 (0-06-022523-8) HarpC Child Bks.

—Your Skin & Mine. rev. ed. Kuchera, Kathleen, illus. LC 90-37429. 32p. (gr. k-4). 1991. pap. 4.50 (0-06-445102-X, Trophy) HarpC Child Bks.

Shpakow, Tanya. On the Way to Christmas. Shpakow, Tanya, illus. LC 90-5373. 40p. (ps-2). 1991. 15.00 (0-679-81796-4); lib. bdg. 15.99 (0-679-91796-9) Knopf Bks Yng Read.

Shreve, Susan. Amy Dunn Quits School. De Groat, Diane, illus. LC 92-41772. 96p. (gr. 3 up). 1993. 13.00 (0-688-10320-0, Tambourine Bks) Morrow.

—The Flunking of Joshua T. Bates. De Groat, Diane, illus. LC 83-19636. 96p. (gr. 2-6). 1984. PLB 13.99 (0-394-96380-6) Knopf Bks Yng Read.

—The Gift of the Girl Who Couldn't Hear. LC 91-2247. 80p. (gr. 3 up). 1991. 12.95 (0-688-10318-9, Tambourine Bks) Morrow.

—The Gift of the Girl Who Couldn't Hear. LC 92-43763. 80p. (gr. 6 up). 1993. pap. 3.95 (0-688-11694-9, Pub. by Beech Tree Bks) Morrow.

—Joshua T. Bates Takes Charge. Andreasen, Dan, illus. LC 92-19708. 112p. (gr. 3-5). 1993. 15.00 (0-394-84362-2) Knopf Bks Yng Read.

—Lily & the Runaway Baby. Truesdell, Sue, illus. LC 87-4684. 64p. (gr. 2-4). 1987. 2.50 (0-394-89104-X, Random Juv) Random Bks Yng Read.

—Lucy Forever & Miss Rosetree, Shrinks. LC 86-29513. 128p. (gr. 3-7). 1988. pap. 2.95 (0-394-80570-4) Knopf Bks Yng Read.

—The Masquerade. 160p. (gr. 7 up). 1981. pap. 1.95 (0-440-95396-0, LE) Dell.

—The Masquerade. LC 79-20073. 224p. 1980. lib. bdg. 7.99 (0-394-94142-X) Knopf Bks Yng Read.

—Wait for Me. De Groat, Diane, illus. LC 91-30233. 112p. (gr. 3 up). 1992. 13.00 (0-688-11120-3, Tambourine Bks) Morrow.

Shreve, Susan R. The Bad Dreams of a Good Girl. DeGroat, Diane, illus. LC 92-24593. 96p. (gr. 4 up). 1993. pap. 3.95 (0-688-12113-6, Pub. by Beech Tree Bks) Morrow.

—Country of Strangers. 1990. pap. 8.95 (0-385-26775-4, Anchor Pr) Doubleday.

Shriver, Jean A. Mayflower Man. 1991. 14.95 (0-385-30295-9) Delacorte.

Shrode, Mary. Just Imagine, with Barney. White, Stephen, ed. Eubank, Mary G., illus. 32p. (ps-k). 1992. 7.95g (0-7829-0137-9) Lyons Group.

Shroyer, Susan, jt. auth. see Warren, Jean.

Shroyer, Susan P. & Kimmel, Joan G. ABC - Sign with Me. Kimmel, Joan G., illus. 32p. (Orig.). (ps-2). 1987. pap. 4.95 (0-939849-00-3) Sugar Sign Pr.

Shub, Elizabeth. Cutlass in the Snow. Isadora, Rachel, illus. LC 85-5442. 48p. (gr. 1-4). 1986. 11.95 (0-688-05927-9); PLB 11.88 (0-688-05928-7) Greenwillow.

—The White Stallion. Isadora, Rachel, illus. LC 81-20308. 56p. (gr. 1-3). 1982. 15.95 (0-688-01210-8); PLB 15.88 (0-688-01211-6) Greenwillow.

—The White Stallion. Isadora, Rachel, illus. 64p. (gr. 1-4). 1984. pap. 2.50 (0-553-15244-0, Skylark) Bantam.

—The White Stallion. 1984. pap. 2.99 (0-553-15615-2) Bantam.

Shub, Elizabeth, tr. see Aleichem, Sholem.

Shub, Elizabeth, tr. see Grimm, Jacob & Grimm, Wilhelm K.

Shub, Elizabeth, tr. see Singer, Isaac Bashevis.

Shubert, Adrian. The Land & People of Spain. LC 91-9971. (Illus.). 256p. (gr. 6 up). 1992. 18.00 (0-06-020217-3); PLB 17.89 (0-06-020218-1) HarpC Child Bks.

Shubert, J. Lansing. The Legacy of George Partridgeberry. Steele, Robert, ed. Shubert, Christiane, illus. 381p. (Orig.). (gr. 9-12). 1990. pap. 12.95 (0-9627015-0-5) J L Shubert.

Shubkagel, Judy F. Show Me How to Write an Experimental Science Fair Paper: A Fill-in-the-Blank Handbook. (gr. 4-8). 1993. wkbk. 9.95 (1-883484-00-6) Show Me How.

Shuey, Karen. Dinosaurs. (Illus.). 48p. (gr. k-4). 1987. wkbk. 5.95 (1-55734-218-0) Tchr Create Mat.

Shufflebotham, Anne. Baby Bear Cub's Busy Day. LC 91-12965. (gr. 3 up). 1991. 5.99 (0-85953-425-1) Childs Play.

—Old Macdonald's Tub. (gr. 3 up). 1990. 4.95 (0-85953-444-8) Childs Play.

—Round & Round the Garden. LC 91-12964. (gr. 4 up). 1991. 5.99 (0-85953-426-X) Childs Play.

—This Little Piggy. (gr. 4 up). 1991. 4.95 (0-85953-445-6) Childs Play.

Shuker, Nancy. Elizabeth Arden. Furstinger, Nancy, ed. (Illus.). 140p. (gr. 7-10). 1989. PLB 13.98 (0-382-09587-1) Silver Burdett Pr.

—Everything You Need to Know about an Alcoholic Parent. Rosen, Ruth, ed. (gr. 7-12). 1989. PLB 13.95 (0-8239-1614-6) Rosen Group.

—John D. Rockefeller. Furstinger, Nancy, ed. (Illus.). 140p. (gr. 7-10). 1989. PLB 13.98 (0-382-09583-9) Silver Burdett Pr.

—Maya Angelou. Easton, Emily, ed. (Illus.). 128p. (gr. 7-9). 1990. 14.95 (0-382-24036-7); PLB 17.98s.p. (0-382-09908-7) Silver Burdett Pr.

Shuker, Nancy F. Martin Luther King, Jr. Schlesinger, Arthur M., Jr., intro. by. (Illus.). 112p. (Orig.). (gr. 5 up). 1989. lib. bdg. 17.95 (0-87754-567-7); pap. 9.95 (0-7910-0219-5) Chelsea Hse.

Shuker-Haines, Frances. Everything You Need to Know about a Drug-Abusing Parent. Rosen, Ruth, ed. (gr. 7-12). 1993. PLB 13.95 (0-8239-1529-8) Rosen Group.

—Everything You Need to Know about Date Rape. rev. ed. Rosen, Ruth, ed. (gr. 7-12). 1992. PLB 13.95 (0-8239-1509-3) Rosen Group.

—Rights & Responsibilities: Using Your Freedom. LC 92-25732. (Illus.). 48p. (gr. 5-6). 1992. PLB 21.34 (0-8114-7355-4) Raintree Steck-V.

Shulevitz, Uri. Dawn. Shulevitz, Uri, illus. LC 74-9761. 32p. (ps up). 1974. 16.00 (0-374-31707-0) FS&G.

—Dawn. Shulevitz, Uri, illus. 32p. (ps up). 1988. 5.95 (0-374-41689-3) FS&G.

—One Monday Morning. Shulevitz, Uri, illus. LC 66-24483. 48p. (ps-4). 1974. SBE 14.95 (0-684-13195-1, Scribners Young Read) Macmillan Child Grp.

—One Monday Morning. LC 85-28583. (Illus.). 32p. (ps-3). 1986. pap. 4.95 (0-689-71062-3, Aladdin) Macmillan Child Grp.

—Rain Rain Rivers. Shulevitz, Uri, illus. LC 73-85370. 32p. (ps-3). 1969. 16.00 (0-374-36171-1) FS&G.

—Rain Rain Rivers. (Illus.). 32p. 1988. pap. 3.95 (0-374-46195-3) FS&G.

—Secret Room. 1993. 15.00 (0-374-34131-1) FS&G.

—Soldier & Tsar in the Forest: A Russian Tale. Lourie, Richard, tr. from RUS. Shulevitz, Uri, illus. LC 72-188254. 32p. (ps-3). 1972. 16.00 (0-374-37126-1) FS&G.

—The Strange & Exciting Adventures of Jeramiah Hush. (Illus.). 96p. (gr. 2-5). 1986. 14.00 (0-374-33656-3) FS&G.

—El Tesoro: The Treasure. Negroni, Maria, tr. (SPA., Illus.). 32p. (ps-3). 1992. 16.00 (0-374-37422-8, Mirasol) FS&G.

—Toddlecreek Post Office. (Illus.). 32p. 1990. 14.95 (0-374-37635-2) FS&G.

—The Treasure. Shulvitz, Uri, illus. LC 78-12952. 32p. (ps-3). 1979. 15.95 (0-374-37740-5) FS&G.

—The Treasure. (Illus.). 32p. (gr. k-3). 1986. pap. 5.95 (0-374-47955-0, Sunburst) FS&G.

Shulevitz, Uri, jt. auth. see Peretz, I. L.

Shulevitz, Uri, tr. see Aleichem, Sholem.

Shulman. Karen Strange. 1991. 0.85 (0-8050-2028-4) H Holt & Co.

Shulman, Dee. Dora's New Brother. (Illus.). 32p. (ps-1). 1994. 19.95 (0-370-31814-5, Pub. by Bodley Head UK) Trafalgar.

—Roaring Billy. (Illus.). 32p. (ps-k). 1992. 15.95 (0-370-31585-5, Pub. by Bodley Head UK) Trafalgar.

—The Visit. (Illus.). 32p. (ps-1). 1993. 15.95 (0-370-31584-7, Pub. by Bodley Head UK) Trafalgar.

Shulman, Dee, jt. auth. see Barton, Chris.

Shulman, Jeffrey. The Drug-Alert Dictionary & Resource Guide. (Illus.). 91p. (gr. 2-4). 1991. PLB 14.95 (0-941477-85-1) TFC Bks NY.

—Drugs & Crime. Raymond, Larry, illus. 88p. (gr. 5-8). 1991. PLB 14.95 (0-941477-60-6) TFC Bks NY.

—Focus on Cocaine & Crack. Neuhaus, David, illus. 56p. (gr. 2-4). 1990. PLB 14.95 (0-941477-98-3) TFC Bks NY.

—Focus on Hallucinogens. (Illus.). 56p. (gr. 2-4). 1991. PLB 14.95 (0-941477-92-4) TFC Bks NY.

—Karen Strange: Children's Theater Producer. Brown, Pamela & Adkins, Bill, photos by. (Illus.). 40p. (gr. 2-4). 1991. PLB 15.95 (0-941477-57-6) TFC Bks NY.

Shulman, Jeffrey & Rogers, Teresa. Gaylord Nelson: A Day for the Earth. Raymond, Larry, illus. 68p. (gr. 4-7). 1992. PLB 14.95 (0-941477-40-1) TFC Bks NY.

Shulman, Jeffrey, jt. auth. see Aiello, Barbara.

Shuman, R. Baird. The Arts - Georgia O'Keeffe. LC 92-44759. 1993. 19.93 (0-86625-487-0); 14.95s.p. (0-685-67773-7) Rourke Pubns.

Shumate, Jane. Sojourner Truth & the Voice of Freedom. (Illus.). 32p. (gr. 2-4). 1991. PLB 12.40 (1-56294-041-4) Millbrook Pr.

Shumate, Jane A. Sequoyah: Inventor of the Cherokee Alphabet. LC 93-18107. (Illus.). (gr. 5 up). 1994. PLB 18.95 (0-7910-1720-6, Am Art Analog); pap. write for info. (0-7910-1990-X, Am Art Analog) Chelsea Hse.

Shumate, Mark, adapted by see De Beaumont, Madame.

Shumsky, Abraham & Shumsky, Adaia. Ahavat Chesed - Love Mercy: Reader. (Illus.). (gr. 4-6). 1970. text ed. 6.00 (0-8074-0175-7, 405304); tchrs'. guide 3.50 (0-8074-0176-5, 205305); wkbk. 6.00 (0-8074-0177-3, 405303) UAHC.

—Alef-Bet: A Hebrew Primer. Bass, Marilyn & Goldman, Marvin, illus. (gr. k-3). 1979. pap. text ed. 7.00 (0-8074-0026-2, 405309) UAHC.

—Asot Mishpat. Plowitz, Kurt, illus. (gr. 4-6). 1969. text ed. 6.00 (*0-8074-0178-1*, 405301); tchrs'. guide 3.50 (*0-8074-0179-X*, 205302); wkbk. 6.00 (*0-8074-0180-3*, 405300) UAHC.
—Hatznea Lechet: Walk Humbly. Spiro, Jack D., ed. Maidoff, Jules, illus. (gr. 4). 1971. text ed. 6.00 (*0-8074-0181-1*, 405307); tchrs'. guide 3.50 (*0-8074-0182-X*, 205308); wkbk. 6.00 (*0-8074-0183-8*, 405306) UAHC.
Shumsky, Abraham, jt. auth. see Shumsky, Adaia.
Shumsky, Adaia & Shumsky, Abraham. The Alef-Bet Primer Reading Practice Book. Bass, Marilyn, illus. 80p. (gr. k-3). 1984. pap. text ed. 5.00 (*0-8074-0257-5*, 405315) UAHC.
Shumsky, Adaia, jt. auth. see Shumsky, Abraham.
Shura. Winter Dreams, Christmas Love. 1993. pap. 3.50 (*0-685-66037-0*) Scholastic Inc.
Shura, Mary F. Diana. 224p. (gr. 6-10). 1988. pap. 2.75 (*0-590-41416-X*) Scholastic Inc.
—Don't Call Me Toad. 128p. 1988. pap. 2.95 (*0-380-70496-X*, Camelot) Avon.
—Don't Call Me Toad! (Illus.). 128p. (ps-8). 1987. 14.95 (*0-399-21706-1*, Putnam) Putnam Pub Group.
—Gentle Annie. (gr. 4-7). 1991. 12.95 (*0-590-44367-4*) Scholastic Inc.
—Jessica, No. 6. 368p. (gr. 7 up). 1984. pap. 2.95 (*0-590-33242-2*) Scholastic Inc.
—The Josie Gambit. 128p. (gr. 3-7). 1988. pap. 2.50 (*0-380-70497-8*, Camelot) Avon.
—The Josie Gambit. 160p. (gr. 3-7). 1986. 13.95 (*0-399-21708-8*, Putnam) Putnam Pub Group.
—The Josie Gambit. 153p. (gr. 6-9). 1986. 12.24 (*0-685-63796-4*, BR7844) W A T Braille.
—Marilee, No. 9. 368p. (Orig.). (gr. 7 up). 1985. pap. 2.95 (*0-590-33433-6*) Scholastic Inc.
—Our Teacher is Missing. (gr. 4-7). 1993. pap. 2.95 (*0-590-44677-0*) Scholastic Inc.
—Our Teacher is Missing. 1993. pap. 2.95 (*0-590-44597-9*) Scholastic Inc.
—Polly Panic. 128p. (gr. 5-8). 1990. 14.95 (*0-399-22214-6*, Putnam) Putnam Pub Group.
—Polly Panic. 128p. (gr. 5 up). 1992. pap. 3.50 (*0-380-71334-9*, Camelot) Avon.
—The Search for Grissi. (gr. 3-7). 1986. 12.95 (*0-399-21705-3*, Putnam) Putnam Pub Group.
—Some Kind of Friend. 128p. 1992. pap. 3.50 (*0-380-71181-8*, Camelot) Avon.
Shurin, Yisroel. Morei Ha'Umah. (HEB.). 214p. 1992. text ed. 8.00 (*1-878895-02-8*, D451) Torah Umesorah.
Shuster, Albert, ed. see Tilton, Martha.
Shuster, Albert H. & Miller, Russell R. The Young Citizen Observes the Law. Cooper, William H., ed. Butrick, Lyn M., illus. LC 83-80867. 93p. (gr. 4-8). 1983. pap. text ed. 5.27 (*0-914127-03-9*); tchr's ed. 4.88 (*0-685-07834-5*) Univ Class.
Shuster, Albert H., ed. see Dana, Katherine.
Shuster, Albert H., et al. The Young Christian Observes the Law. Cooper, William H., ed. Butrick, Lyn M., illus. LC 83-80868. 106p. (gr. 4-8). 1983. pap. text ed. 5.27 (*0-914127-02-0*) Univ Class.
Shusterman, Neal. Darkness Creeping: Tales to Trouble Your Sleep. Coy, Michael, illus. LC 93-13792. 128p. 1993. pap. 4.95 (*1-56565-069-7*) Lowell Hse.
—Dissidents. 224p. (gr. 7 up). 1989. 13.95 (*0-316-78904-6*) Little.
—The Eyes of Kid Midas. LC 92-17897. 1992. 15.95 (*0-316-77542-8*) Little.
—The Eyes of Kid Midas. 1994. pap. 3.99 (*0-8125-3460-3*) Tor Bks.
—Kid Heroes: True Stories of Rescuers, Survivors & Achievers. 1991. 14.95 (*0-312-85081-6*) Tor Bks.
—The Scorpion Shard. 1994. 14.95 (*0-312-85506-0*) Forge NYC.
—The Shadow Club. LC 87-35369. 183p. (gr. 7-9). 1988. 12.95 (*0-316-77540-1*) Little.
—Speeding Bullet. 1992. 3.25 (*0-590-45424-2*, Point) Scholastic Inc.
—What Daddy Did. 1991. pap. 15.95 (*0-316-78906-2*) Little.
—What Daddy Did. 240p. (gr. 7 up). 1993. pap. 3.95 (*0-06-447094-6*, Trophy) HarpC Child Bks.
Shusterman, Neil. Dissidents. 192p. 1994. pap. 3.99 (*0-8125-3461-1*) Tor Bks.
Shute, K. H., ed. Land of Song: For Primary Grades, Bk. 1. LC 78-57863. (Illus.). (gr. 1-3). 1978. Repr. of 1898 ed. 19.25x (*0-89609-101-5*) Roth Pub Inc.
Shute, Linda. Clever Tom & the Leprechaun. Shute, Linda, illus. LC 87-29671. 32p. (gr. k-3). 1988. 12.95 (*0-688-07488-X*); PLB 12.88 (*0-688-07489-8*) Lothrop.
—Clever Tom & the Leprechaun. 1990. pap. 3.95 (*0-590-43170-6*) Scholastic Inc.
—Halloween Party. LC 93-25215. (gr. 1 up). 1994. write for info. (*0-688-11714-7*); PLB write for info. Lothrop.
—How I Named the Baby. Grant, Christy, ed. Shute, Linda, illus. LC 92-33292. 32p. (ps-3). 1993. PLB 13.95 (*0-8075-3417-X*) A Whitman.
—Momotaro the Peach Boy. LC 85-9997. (Illus.). 32p. (ps-3). 1986. 13.95 (*0-688-05863-9*); PLB 13.88 (*0-688-05864-7*) Lothrop.
Shwed, Joanne, ed. see Bishop, Kathleen.
Shyer, Marlene. Ruby, the Red-Hot Witch at Bloomingdale's. 160p. (gr. 3-7). 1991. 13.95 (*0-670-83473-4*) Viking Child Bks.
Shyer, Marlene F. Here I Am, an Only Child. Carrick, Donald, illus. LC 87-1112. 32p. (ps-3). 1987. pap. 3.95 (*0-689-71156-5*, Aladdin) Macmillan Child Grp.

—Ruby, the Red-Hot Witch at Bloomingdale's. 160p. (gr. 3-7). 1993. pap. 3.99 (*0-14-034510-8*, Puffin) Puffin Bks.
—Welcome Home, Jellybean. LC 87-19483. 160p. (gr. 3-7). 1988. pap. 3.95 (*0-689-71213-8*, Aladdin) Macmillan Child Grp.
Siadi, Phillip, jt. auth. see Paxton, Lenore.
Sibbald, Jean. Sea Creatures on the Move. LC 89-12027. (Illus.). 128p. (gr. 4 up). 1990. RSBE 13.95 (*0-87518-412-X*, Dillon) Macmillan Child Grp.
—Strange Eating Habits of Sea Creatures. LC 85-11621. (Illus.). 112p. (gr. 4 up). 1987. RSBE 13.95 (*0-87518-349-2*, Dillon) Macmillan Child Grp.
Sibbald, Jean H. The Manatee. LC 89-26048. (Illus.). 60p. (gr. 3 up). 1990. RSBE 13.95 (*0-87518-429-4*, Dillon) Macmillan Child Grp.
—Sea Mammals: The Warm-Blooded Ocean Explorers. LC 87-33291. (Illus.). 128p. (gr. 4 up). 1988. RSBE 13.95 (*0-87518-372-7*, Dillon) Macmillan Child Grp.
Sibbald, Linda, pref. by. The Polite Academy, Vol. 2: London, Seventeen Sixty-Five. 3rd ed. (Illus.). 181p. 1973. Repr. leather bdg. 55.80 (*0-685-48091-7*) P Lang Pubs.
Sibbett, Ed. American Indian Cut & Use Stencils. pap. 4.95 (*0-486-24183-1*) Dover.
—Cut & Use Christmas Decorations. 1985. pap. 3.95 (*0-486-24912-3*) Dover.
—Decorative Americana Cut & Use Stencils. 1985. pap. 4.95 (*0-486-24970-0*) Dover.
—Decorative Cut & Use Stencils. 1988. pap. 4.95 (*0-486-23880-6*) Dover.
—Holidays & Special Occasions, Cut & Use Stencils. 1986. pap. 4.95 (*0-486-25052-0*) Dover.
—Messages & Greetings Cut & Use Stencils. 1985. pap. 4.95 (*0-486-24965-4*) Dover.
Sibbett, Ed., Jr. Easy-to-Make Articulated Wooden Toys: Patterns & Instructions for 18 Playthings That Move. (Illus.). 48p. 1983. pap. 2.95 (*0-486-24411-3*) Dover.
Sibbett, Ed, Jr. Floral Stained Glass Pattern Book. (Illus.). 64p. 1982. pap. 4.95 (*0-486-24259-5*) Dover.
Sibbick, John, illus. Creatures of Long Ago: Dinosaurs, Vol. 1. (ps-3). 1993. 16.00 (*0-87044-723-8*) Natl Geog.
Siberell, Anne. Whale in the Sky. Siberell, Anne, illus. LC 82-2483. 32p. (ps-3). 1985. 13.95 (*0-525-44021-6*, DCB); pap. 3.95 (*0-525-44197-2*, DCB) Dutton Child Bks.
Sibley, Brian. Land of Narnia: Brian Sibley Explores the World of C. S. Lewis. Baynes, Pauline, illus. LC 90-4192. 96p. (gr. 5 up). 1990. 19.95 (*0-06-025625-7*); PLB 19.89 (*0-06-025626-5*) HarpC Child Bks.
Sibley, Brian, compiled by. The Pooh Book of Quotations. Shepard, Ernest H., illus. LC 91-2628. 128p. (ps up). 1991. 12.50 (*0-525-44824-1*, DCB) Dutton Child Bks.
Sibley, Kenneth E. A Spring Surprise. (Illus.). 19p. (Orig.). (gr. 7 up). 1989. pap. 6.95 (*0-9619934-1-3*) K E Sibley.
Sicard, Gene, et al. Rappin' Mother Goose: Nursery Rhymes. 24p. (ps-3). 1991. incl. cassette 11.45 (*1-879755-00-9*) Recorded Pubns.
Sicaro, Judith M. Juma's Goat. (gr. 1-8). 1993. pap. 6.95 (*1-85756-095-7*, Pub. by Janus Pub UK) Intl Spec Bk.
Sichen, Kali, ed. see Williams, Mary A.
Sickle, Carol S. Van see Van Sickle, Carol S.
Sickles, William. Herman the Termite. (Illus.). (gr. 3-5). 1968. 10.95 (*0-8392-3066-4*) Astor-Honor.
Siddiqui, A. A. Elementary Teachings of Islam. pap. 4.95 (*0-935782-89-3*) Kazi Pubns.
Siddiqui, Zeba, ed. see Hutchinson, Haji U.
Sideline. Mickey & Donald Pillow Book. 1990. pap. 19.95 (*1-55923-048-7*) Stoneway Ltd.
—Mickey & Minnie Pillow Book. 1990. pap. 19.95 (*1-55923-047-9*) Stoneway Ltd.
Sider, Eva, jt. auth. see Rosales, Michael.
Siderman, Sheila, jt. auth. see Silverman, Helene.
Sides, Elizabeth. Wildlife at Risk: A Nature & Craft Book, 2 bks. (Illus.). 32p. (Orig.). (gr. 1-5). 1991. Set. pap. 6.95 (*0-685-54745-0*); Bk. 1. pap. 6.95 (*0-86278-252-X*); Bk. 2. pap. 6.95 (*0-86278-253-8*) Dufour.
Sidi, Smadar S. Chanukah A-Z. Nover, Teri, illus. (ps-2). 1988. 9.95 (*1-55774-041-0*) Modan-Adama Bks.
—The Dreidle Champ & Other Holiday Stories. Evers, June V., illus. 120p. (gr. 3-9). 1987. 13.95 (*0-915361-89-2*) Modan-Adama Bks.
—Little Daniel & the Jewish Delicacies. Schaer, Miriam, illus. (ps-5). 1988. 9.95 (*1-55774-028-3*) Modan-Adama Bks.
Sidney, Margaret. Ben Pepper. 1992. Repr. PLB 25.95x (*0-89966-969-7*) Buccaneer Bks.
—Five Little Peppers Abroad. 1987. Repr. lib. bdg. 25.95x (*0-89966-551-9*) Buccaneer Bks.
—The Five Little Peppers & How They Grew. 302p. 1981. Repr. PLB 25.95x (*0-89966-340-0*) Buccaneer Bks.
—Five Little Peppers & How They Grew. LC 89-62372. 288p. (gr. 4 up). 1990. pap. 2.95 (*0-14-035127-2*, Puffin) Puffin Bks.
—Five Little Peppers & How They Grew. 1989. pap. 2.95 (*0-590-42520-X*) Scholastic Inc.
—Five Little Peppers & Their Friends. 1992. Repr. PLB 25.95x (*0-89966-970-0*) Buccaneer Bks.
—Five Little Peppers at School. 1987. Repr. lib. bdg. 25.95x (*0-89966-552-7*) Buccaneer Bks.
—Five Little Peppers at School. (Orig.). (gr. k-6). 1988. pap. 4.95 (*0-440-40035-X*, YB) Dell.

—Five Little Peppers Grown up. 334p. 1981. Repr. lib. bdg. 25.95x (*0-89966-341-9*) Buccaneer Bks.
—Five Little Peppers in the Little Brown House. 1992. Repr. PLB 25.95x (*0-89966-968-9*) Buccaneer Bks.
—Five Little Peppers Midway. (Orig.). (gr. k-6). 1987. pap. 4.95 (*0-440-42589-1*, Pub. by Yearling Classics) Dell.
—Five Little Peppers Midway. 1987. Repr. lib. bdg. 25.95 (*0-89966-550-0*) Buccaneer Bks.
—Phronsie Pepper. 250p. 1992. Repr. PLB 25.95x (*0-89966-967-0*) Buccaneer Bks.
Sidon, et al. The Animated Israel. 54p. 1987. 14.95 (*0-8246-0326-5*) Jonathan David.
Sidon, The Animated Megillah. 54p. (gr. 1-5). 1987. 14.95 (*0-8246-0324-9*) Jonathan David.
Sidwell, Mark, ed. Faith of Our Fathers: Scenes from Church History. 216p. (Orig.). (gr. 9 up). 1989. pap. 6.95 (*0-89084-492-5*) Bob Jones Univ Pr.
Sidwell, Mark, ed. see Watkins, Dawn L.
Sidy, Richard V. Rebellion with Purpose: A Young Adult's Guide to the Improvement of Self & Society. 192p. (gr. 10 up). 1993. pap. text ed. 9.95 (*0-9633744-1-9*) SNS Pr.
Siebert, Diane. Heartland. Minor, Wendell, illus. LC 87-29380. 32p. (ps-3). 1989. 16.00 (*0-690-04730-4*, Crowell Jr Bks); PLB 15.89 (*0-690-04732-0*) HarpC Child Bks.
—Heartland. Minor, Wendell, illus. LC 87-29380. 32p. (gr. 2 up). 1992. pap. 5.95 (*0-06-443287-4*, Trophy) HarpC Child Bks.
—Mojave. Minor, Wendell, illus. LC 86-24329. 32p. (ps up). 1988. 15.00 (*0-690-04567-0*, Crowell Jr Bks); PLB 14.89 (*0-690-04569-7*, Crowell Jr Bks) HarpC Child Bks.
—Mojave. Minor, Wendell, illus. LC 86-24329. 32p. (gr. k-3). 1992. pap. 4.95 (*0-06-443283-1*, Trophy) HarpC Child Bks.
—Plane Song. Nasta, Vincent, illus. LC 92-17359. 32p. (ps-3). 1993. 15.00 (*0-06-021464-3*); PLB 14.89 (*0-06-021467-8*) HarpC Child Bks.
—Sierra. Minor, Wendell, illus. LC 90-30522. 32p. (ps-3). 1991. 16.00 (*0-06-021639-5*); PLB 15.89 (*0-06-021640-9*) HarpC Child Bks.
—Train Song. Wimmer, Mike, illus. LC 88-389. 32p. (ps-3). 1990. 15.00 (*0-690-04726-6*, Crowell Jr Bks); PLB 14.89 (*0-690-04728-2*, Crowell Jr Bks) HarpC Child Bks.
—Train Song. Wimmer, Mike, illus. LC 88-389. 32p. (gr. k-3). 1993. pap. 5.95 (*0-06-443340-4*, Trophy) HarpC Child Bks.
—Truck Song. Barton, Byron, illus. LC 83-46173. 32p. (ps-3). 1984. (Crowell Jr Bks); PLB 14.89 (*0-690-04411-9*) HarpC Child Bks.
—Truck Song. LC 83-46173. (Illus.). 32p. (ps-3). 1987. pap. 4.95 (*0-06-443134-7*, Trophy) HarpC Child Bks.
—Truck Song. Barton, Byron, illus. (gr. k-3). 1988. bk. & cassette 19.95 (*0-87499-093-9*); bk. & cassette 12.95 (*0-87499-092-0*); 4 cassettes & guide 27.95 (*0-87499-094-7*) Live Oak Media.
Siede, George & Preis, Donna, photos by. Alphabet: Active Minds. Schwager, Istar, contrib. by. (Illus.). 24p. (ps-3). 1992. PLB 9.95 (*1-56674-000-2*) Forest Hse.
—Colors: Active Minds. Schwager, Istar, contrib. by. (Illus.). 24p. (ps-3). 1992. PLB 9.95 (*1-56674-001-0*) Forest Hse.
—My Day: Active Minds. Schwager, Istar, contrib. by. (Illus.). 24p. (ps-3). 1992. PLB 9.95 (*1-56674-002-9*) Forest Hse.
—Numbers: Active Minds. Schwager, Istar, contrib. by. (Illus.). 24p. (ps-3). 1992. PLB 9.95 (*1-56674-003-7*) Forest Hse.
—Opposites: Active Minds. Schwager, Istar, contrib. by. (Illus.). 24p. (ps-3). 1992. PLB 9.95 (*1-56674-004-5*) Forest Hse.
—Shapes: Active Minds. Schwager, Istar, contrib. by. (Illus.). 24p. (ps-3). 1992. PLB 9.95 (*1-56674-005-3*) Forest Hse.
Siedler, Ann, jt. auth. see Slepian, Jan.
Sieg, Theodore Le see Le Sieg, Theodore.
Siegal, Aranka. Grace in the Wilderness: After the Liberation, 1945-1948. LC 85-20415. 220p. (gr. 5 up). 1985. 15.00 (*0-374-32760-2*) FS&G.
—Grace in the Wilderness: After the Liberation, 1945-1948. (gr. 7 up). 2.50 (*0-317-52861-0*, Sig Vista) NAL-Dutton.
—Upon the Head of the Goat. (Illus.). 192p. (gr. 9-12). 1968. pap. 3.95 (*0-451-15535-1*, Sig) NAL-Dutton.
—Upon the Head of the Goat: A Childhood in Hungary, 1939-1944. LC 81-12642. 214p. (gr. 7 up). 1981. 16.00 (*0-374-38059-7*) FS&G.
Siegal, Barbara & Siegal, Scott. Beyond Terror. MacDonald, Patricia, ed. 160p. (Orig.). 1991. pap. 3.50 (*0-671-70904-6*, Archway) PB.
—Midnight Chill. MacDonald, Patricia, ed. 176p. (Orig.). 1991. pap. 2.99 (*0-671-70905-4*, Archway) PB.
Siegal, Helene. Barbie Party Cookbook. (gr. 4-7). 1991. 9.95 (*0-8431-2895-X*) Price Stern.
Siegal, Scott, jt. auth. see Siegal, Barbara.
Siegel, Adam, ed. see Hurwitz, Ann R. & Hurwitz, Sue.
Siegel, Alice. Kid Stuff: People, Places, & Things to Know. (gr. 4-7). 1991. pap. 3.99 (*0-553-15914-3*) Bantam.
Siegel, Alice & Basta, Margo M. The Information Please Kids' Almanac. (Illus.). 400p. (gr. 3-9). 1992. 16.45 (*0-395-64737-1*); pap. 7.70 (*0-395-58801-4*) HM.

Siegel, Alice & McLoone, Margo. Kids' World Almanac of Records & Facts. (gr. 3-7). 1986. pap. 7.95 (*0-88687-319-3*, World Almanac) F&W Inc NJ.
Siegel, Alice, jt. auth. see McLoone-Basta, Margo.
Siegel, Balky. Baker's Dozen, No. 2: Ghosthunters. 1993. pap. 7.95 (*0-685-65303-X*) Feldheim.
Siegel, Barbara & Siegel, Scott. Cold Dread. MacDonald, Pat, ed. 176p. (Orig.). 1992. pap. 2.99 (*0-671-75946-9*) PB.
Siegel, Barbara & Siegel, Scott. Fatal Fear. MacDonald, Pat, ed. 160p. (Orig.). (gr. 7 up). 1992. pap. 2.99 (*0-671-75947-7*, Archway) PB.
—Final Frenzy. MacDonald, Pat, ed. 160p. (Orig.). 1993. pap. 3.50 (*0-671-75948-5*, Archway) PB.
Siegel, Beatrice. The Basket Maker & the Spinner. 64p. (gr. 3 up). 1987. 10.95 (*0-8027-6694-3*); PLB 11.85 (*0-8027-6695-1*) Walker & Co.
—Faithful Friend: The Story of Florence Nightingale. 144p. (gr. 3-7). 1991. pap. 2.95 (*0-590-43210-9*) Scholastic Inc.
—Fur Trappers & Traders: The Indians, the Pilgrims, & the Beaver. Bock, William S., illus. LC 80-7671. 64p. (gr. 3-7). 1987. PLB 11.85 (*0-8027-6397-9*) Walker & Co.
—George & Martha Washington at Home in New York. Aloise, Frank, illus. LC 88-24534. 80p. (gr. 4-7). 1989. SBE 12.95 (*0-02-782721-6*, Four Winds) Macmillan Child Grp.
—Indians of the Northeast Woodlands Before & after the Pilgrims. 96p. 1992. 13.95 (*0-8027-8155-1*); lib. bdg. 14.85 (*0-8027-8157-8*) Walker & Co.
—Murder on the Highway: The Viola Liuzzo Story. Parks, Rosa, intro. by. (Illus.). 128p. (gr. 4-7). 1994. SBE 14.95 (*0-02-782632-5*, Four Winds) Macmillan Child Grp.
—A New Look at the Pilgrims: Why They Came to America. Morris, Douglas, illus. LC 76-57060. 82p. (gr. 3-7). 1987. Repr. of 1977 ed. 13.85 (*0-8027-6292-1*) Walker & Co.
—Sam Ellis's Island. DiSalvo-Ryan, DyAnne, illus. LC 85-42799. 128p. (gr. 3-7). 1985. SBE 13.95 (*0-02-782720-8*, Four Winds) Macmillan Child Grp.
—The Sewing Machine. LC 83-40397. 64p. (gr. 5 up). 1984. PLB 10.85 (*0-8027-6532-7*) Walker & Co.
—The Steam Engine. LC 83-5616. (Illus.). 64p. (gr. 5 up). 1986. 10.95 (*0-8027-6655-2*); PLB 10.85 (*0-8027-6656-0*) Walker & Co.
—The Year They Walked: Rosa Parks & the Montgomery Bus Boycott. LC 91-14078. (Illus.). 128p. (gr. 4-7). 1992. SBE 13.95 (*0-02-782631-7*, Four Winds) Macmillan Child Grp.
Siegel, Danny. Tell Me a Mitzvah: Little & Big Ways to Repair the World. Friedman, Judith, illus. 64p. (Orig.). (gr. 2-6). 1993. pap. 7.95 (*0-929371-78-X*) Kar Ben.
Siegel, Dorothy S. Dental Health. Garell, Dale C. & Snyder, Solomon H., eds. (Illus.). 112p. (gr. 5-12). 1994. 19.95 (*0-7910-0014-1*, Am Art Analog) Chelsea Hse.
—The Glory Road: The Story of Josh White. LC 91-17985. (Illus.). 160p. (gr. 6 up). 1991. pap. 7.95 (*1-55870-217-2*) Shoe Tree Pr.
Siegel, Eli. Children's Guide to Parents & Other Matters: Little Essays for Children & Others. LC 78-171393. (Illus.). (gr. 1-6). 1971. text ed. 7.50 (*0-910492-16-6*) Definition.
Siegel, Felicia S. Let's Stop Fighting...Let's Start Playing. 42p. (gr. 2-8). 1988. comb. bdg. 4.95 (*0-9631627-0-5*) Social Skills.
Siegel, Margot, jt. auth. see Cohen, Judith L.
Siegel, Mark. Abortion: A Serious Issue. 52p. 1991. pap. text ed. 11.95 (*1-878623-14-1*) Info Plus TX.
Siegel, Mark, et al, eds. Capital Punishment: An Effective Punishment? 56p. 1991. pap. text ed. 11.95 (*1-878623-18-4*) Info Plus TX.
—Gambling: Who Wins? 40p. 1992. pap. text ed. 11.95 (*1-878623-32-X*) Info Plus TX.
—Gun Control: An American Issue. 52p. 1991. pap. text ed. 11.95 (*1-878623-17-6*) Info Plus TX.
—Illegal Drugs & Alcohol: Hurting American Society. 60p. 1991. pap. text ed. 11.95 (*1-878623-15-X*) Info Plus TX.
—Immigration: Looking for a New Home. 52p. 1991. pap. text ed. 11.95 (*1-878623-16-8*) Info Plus TX.
—Minorities: America's Rich Culture. 72p. 1992. pap. text ed. 12.95 (*1-878623-33-8*) Info Plus TX.
Siegel, Mark A., et al. Transportation: Getting from One Place to Another. (Illus.). 64p. (Orig.). (gr. 6-9). 1993. pap. text ed. 12.95 (*1-878623-54-0*) Info Plus TX.
Siegel, Mark A., et al, eds. Space: New Frontiers. (Illus.). 48p. (gr. 6-9). 1992. pap. text ed. 11.95 (*1-878623-44-3*) Info Plus Tx.
Siegel, Peggy C. Changes in You for Boys: A Clearly Illustrated, Simply Worded Explanation of the Changes of Puberty for Boys. Cohen, Vivien, illus. LC 90-86238. 44p. (Orig.). (gr. 4-8). 1991. pap. 8.95 (*0-9628687-1-X*) Fam Life Ed.
—Changes in You for Girls: A Beautifully Illustrated, Simply Worded Explanation of the Changes of Puberty for Girls. Cohen, Vivien, illus. LC 90-86237. 52p. (Orig.). (gr. 4-8). 1991. pap. 8.95 (*0-9628687-0-1*) Fam Life Ed.
Siegel, Scott, jt. auth. see Siegel, Barbara.
Siegel, Seth M., jt. auth. see Karl, Linda.
Siegelman, Irwin, ed. see Williams, George A. & Barnes, Richard.

Siegenthaler, Kathrin. Santa Claus & the Woodcutter. Pfister, Marcus, illus. Crawford, Elizabeth, tr. LC 87-32203. (Illus.). 32p. (gr. k-3). 1988. 13.95 (*1-55858-027-1*) North-South Bks NYC.
—Santa Claus & the Woodcutter. Crawford, Elizabeth, tr. from GER. Pfister, Marcus, illus. 32p. (gr. k-3). 1989. pap. 2.95 (*1-55858-032-8*) North-South Bks NYC.
Siegenthaler, Kathrin & Pfister, Marcus. Hopper's Easter Surprise. Pfister, Marcus, illus. Lanning, Rosemary, tr. from GER. LC 92-29117. (Illus.). 32p. (gr. k-3). 1993. 14.95 (*1-55858-199-5*); PLB 14.88 (*1-55858-200-2*) North-South Bks NYC.
Siegman, Meryl. Volcano. 128p. (Orig.). (gr. 4). 1987. pap. 2.25 (*0-553-26197-5*) Bantam.
Siegrist, Rachel. Spelling by Sound & Structure. (gr. 2-7). 1979. write for info. (*0-686-25261-6*); tchr's. ed. avail. (*0-686-25262-4*) Rod & Staff.
Siekkinen, Raija. The Curious Fawn. Taina, Hannu, illus. 32p. (gr. k-4). 1990. PLB 18.95 (*0-87614-379-6*) Carolrhoda Bks.
—Mister King. Steffa, Tim, tr. Taina, Hannu, illus. 32p. (gr. k-4). 1987. lib. bdg. 18.95 (*0-87614-315-X*) Carolrhoda Bks.
Siembieba, Kevin. Zentraedi. Marciniszyn, Alex, ed. (Illus.). 48p. (Orig.). (gr. 8 up). 1987. pap. 7.95 (*0-916211-22-3*, 552) Palladium Bks.
Siembieda, Florence, ed. see McCall, Randy & Siembieda, Kevin.
Siembieda, Florence, ed. see Wujcik, Erick.
Siembieda, Kevin. Africa. Marciniszyn, Alex, et al, eds. Parkinson, Keith, et al, illus. 160p. (Orig.). (gr. 8 up). 1993. pap. 15.95 (*0-916211-58-4*, 808) Palladium Bks.
—Atlantis. Marciniszyn, Alex & Bartold, Thomas, eds. Long, Kevin & Parkinson, Keith, illus. 160p. (Orig.). (gr. 8 up). 1992. pap. 15.95 (*0-916211-54-1*, 804) Palladium Bks.
—England. Marciniszyn, Alex, et al, eds. Parkinson, Keith, et al, illus. 152p. (Orig.). (gr. 8 up). 1993. pap. 15.95 (*0-916211-57-6*, 807) Palladium Bks.
—Further Adventures in the Northern Wilderness. Marciniszyn, Alex, ed. MacDougall, Larry, illus. 48p. (Orig.). (gr. 8 up). 1990. pap. 7.95 (*0-916211-40-1*, 457) Palladium Bks.
—Heroes Unlimited. rev. ed. Marciniszyn, Alex, ed. Gustovich, Michael & Dee, Jeff, illus. 248p. (gr. 8 up). 1987. pap. 19.95 (*0-916211-05-3*, 500) Palladium Bks.
—Macross II: The Role-Playing Game. Marciniszyn, Alex, et al, illus. 112p. (Orig.). (gr. 8 up). 1993. pap. 11.95 (*0-916211-62-2*, 590) Palladium Bks.
—The Mechanoids. Marciniszyn, Alex, et al, eds. Long, Kevin, et al, illus. 112p. (Orig.). (gr. 8 up). 1992. pap. 11.95 (*0-916211-55-X*, 805) Palladium Bks.
—The Palladium Book of Monsters & Animals. Marciniszyn, Alex, ed. (Illus.). 166p. (Orig.). (gr. 8 up). 1985. pap. 14.95 (*0-916211-12-6*, 454) Palladium Bks.
—The Palladium Role-Playing Game. rev. ed. Leasure, Paula, ed. Kucharski, Micheal, illus. 274p. (gr. 8 up). 1983. pap. 19.95 (*0-916211-04-5*, 450) Palladium Bks.
—The Palladium RPG Book II: Old Ones. Marciniszyn, Alex, ed. Kucharski, Michael, illus. 210p. (Orig.). (gr. 8 up). 1984. pap. 14.95 (*0-916211-09-6*, 453) Palladium Bks.
—Palladium RPG Book III: Adventures on the High Seas. Marcinsizyn, Alex, ed. (Illus.). 208p. (Orig.). (gr. 8 up). 1987. pap. 14.95 (*0-916211-17-7*, 455) Palladium Bks.
—RECON: Modern Combat. Marciniszyn, Alex, et al, eds. Gustovich, Mike, et al, illus. 180p. (gr. 8 up). 1994. pap. 19.95 (*0-916211-64-9*, 614) Palladium Bks.
—The REF Field Guide. Marciniszyn, Alex, ed. Long, Kevin, illus. 144p. (Orig.). (gr. 8 up). 1989. pap. 15.95 (*0-916211-36-3*, 558) Palladium Bks.
—Rifts Conversion Book. Marciniszyn, Alex & Bartold, Thomas, eds. Long, Kevin, et al, illus. 224p. (Orig.). (gr. 8 up). 1991. pap. 19.95 (*0-916211-53-3*, 803) Palladium Bks.
—Rifts Role-Playing Game. Marciniszyn, Alex & Bartold, Thomas, eds. Long, Kevin & Parkinson, Keith, illus. 256p. (Orig.). (gr. 8 up). 1990. pap. 24.95 (*0-916211-50-9*, 800) Palladium Bks.
—Rifts Sourcebook. Marciniszyn, Alex & Bartold, Thomas, eds. Long, Kevin, illus. 120p. (Orig.). (gr. 8 up). 1991. pap. 11.95 (*0-916211-51-7*, 801) Palladium Bks.
—Robotech Role-Playing Game. Marciniszyn, Alex, ed. (Illus.). 110p. (Orig.). (gr. 8 up). 1986. pap. 11.95 (*0-916211-21-5*, 550) Palladium Bks.
—The Sentinels. Marciniszyn, Alex, ed. Long, Kevin & Gould, Thomas, illus. 160p. (Orig.). (gr. 8 up). 1987. pap. 15.95 (*0-916211-33-9*, 557) Palladium Bks.
—Southern Cross. Marciniszyn, Alex, ed. (Illus.). 112p. (Orig.). (gr. 8 up). 1987. pap. 11.95 (*0-916211-27-4*, 553) Palladium Bks.
—The U. N. Spacy. Marciniszyn, Alex, et al, eds. Long, Kevin, et al, illus. 64p. (Orig.). (gr. 8 up). 1993. pap. 9.95 (*0-916211-63-0*, 591) Palladium Bks.
—The Vampire Kingdoms. Marciniszyn, Alex & Bartold, Thomas, eds. Long, Kevin, illus. 176p. (Orig.). (gr. 8 up). 1991. pap. 15.95 (*0-916211-52-5*, 802) Palladium Bks.
Siembieda, Kevin & Bartold, Thomas. Island at the Edge of the World. Marciniszyn, Alex & Osten, James, eds. Caldwell, Clyde, et al, illus. 144p. (Orig.). (gr. 8 up). 1993. pap. 15.95 (*0-916211-61-4*, 458) Palladium Bks.

Siembieda, Kevin & Long, Kevin. Boxed Nightmares. Marcinszyn, Alex & Bartold, Thomas, eds. Long, Kevin & Beauvais, Denis, illus. 80p. (Orig.). (gr. 8 up). 1990. pap. 11.95 (*0-916211-41-X*, 701) Palladium Bks.
—Triax & the NGR. Marciniszyn, Alex, et al, eds. Long, Kevin & Siembieda, Kevin, illus. 176p. (Orig.). (gr. 8 up). 1994. pap. 19.95 (*0-916211-60-6*, 810) Palladium Bks.
—Villains Unlimited. Marciniszyn, Alex & Bartold, Thomas, eds. Gustovich, Mike & Steranko, James, illus. 200p. (Orig.). (gr. 8 up). 1992. pap. 19.95 (*0-916211-49-5*, 501) Palladium Bks.
Siembieda, Kevin & Siembieda, Maryann. Compendium of Contemporary Weapons. Marciniszyn, Alex, et al, eds. Zeleznik, et al, illus. 176p. (Orig.). (gr. 8 up). 1993. pap. 19.95 (*0-916211-65-7*, 415) Palladium Bks.
Siembieda, Kevin & Truman, Timothy. Wormwood. Marciniszyn, Alex, et al, eds. Fales, et al, illus. 152p. (Orig.). (gr. 8 up). 1993. pap. 15.95 (*0-916211-59-2*, 809) Palladium Bks.
Siembieda, Kevin, jt. auth. see Greenberg, Daniel.
Siembieda, Kevin, jt. auth. see McCall, Randy.
Siembieda, Kevin, jt. auth. see Wallis, James.
Siembieda, Kevin, jt. auth. see Wujcik, Erick.
Siembieda, Kevin, ed. see Wujcik, Erick & Balent, Matthew.
Siembieda, Kevin, et al. Adventures in the Northern Wilderness. Marciniszyn, Alex, ed. Talbot, Eric, et al, illus. 96p. (Orig.). (gr. 8 up). 1989. pap. 9.95 (*0-916211-39-8*, 456) Palladium Bks.
Siembieda, Maryann, jt. auth. see Siembieda, Kevin.
Siemon, Michael, jt. auth. see Green, Sharon W.
Sienbieda, Kevin, jt. auth. see Wallis, James.
Sienkiewicz, Henryk. Quo Vadis. (gr. 10 up). 1968. pap. 2.50 (*0-8049-0188-0*, CL-188) Airmont.
Sierra Club Bks Staff. Baby Animals: A Sierra Club Postcard Book for Kids, Vol. 1. 48p. 1989. 8.95 (*0-316-79024-9*) Sierra.
Sierra Club Books Editors. More Baby Animals: A Sierra Club Postcard Book for Kids. (Illus.). 40p. (ps up) 1992. 8.95 (*0-87156-595-1*) Sierra.
Sierra, Judy. The Elephant's Wrestling Match. Pinkney, Brian, illus. 32p. (gr. k-3). 1992. 14.00 (*0-525-67366-0*, Lodestar Bks) Dutton Child Bks.
—Fantastic Theater: Puppets & Plays for Young Performers & Young Audiences. 250p. (gr. 3-7). 1991. 38.00 (*0-8242-0809-9*) Wilson.
—The Flannel Board Storytelling Book. LC 87-6260. 216p. (ps-4). 1987. 40.00 (*0-8242-0747-5*) Wilson.
—Good Night, Dinosaurs. Chess, Victoria, illus. LC 93-8855. Date not set. write for info. (*0-395-65016-X*, Clarion Bks) HM.
Sierra, Judy, ed. Nursery Tales Around the World. Vitale, Stefano, illus. LC 93-2068. Date not set. write for info. (*0-395-67894-3*, Clarion Bks) HM.
Sierra, Patricia. A Boy I Never Knew. 128p. (gr. 7 up). 1988. pap. 2.50 (*0-380-75208-5*, Flare) Avon.
—One-Way Romance. LC 85-91538. 128p. (gr. 6-10). 1986. pap. 2.50 (*0-380-75107-0*, Flare) Avon.
Sieruta, Peter D. Heartbeats: And Other Stories. LC 88-21351. 224p. (gr. 7 up). 1991. pap. 3.50 (*0-06-447064-4*, Trophy) HarpC Child Bks.
Sieveking, Anthea. Mary Had a Little Lamb & Other Animal Rhymes. (ps-3). 1991. bds. 5.95 (*0-8120-6217-5*) Barron.
—What Color? (Illus.). 24p. (ps-k). 1991. 9.95 (*0-8037-0909-9*) Dial Bks Young.
—What's Inside? LC 89-11897. 1990. 9.95 (*0-8037-0719-3*) Dial Bks Young.
Sieveking, Anthea, jt. auth. see MacKinnon, Debbie.
Sieveking, Anthea, illus. Rub a Dub Dub & Other Water Rhymes. 12p. (ps-3). 1991. bds. 5.95 (*0-8120-6219-1*) Barron.
—Twinkle, Twinkle, Little Star & Other Bedtime Rhymes. 12p. (ps-3). 1991. bds. 5.95 (*0-8120-6220-5*) Barron.
Siff, Shoshana M. Guess Who's Coming for Shabbos? Backman, Aidel, illus. 14p. (Orig.). (ps-2). 1987. 4.95 (*0-685-67641-2*); PLB 5.95 (*0-685-55892-4*) Aura Bklyn.
Sigel, Lois S. New Careers in Hospitals. rev. ed. (Illus.). (gr. 7-12). 1990. PLB 13.95 (*0-8239-1172-1*) Rosen Group.
Sigerman, Harriet. Laborers for Liberty: American Women 1865-1890. (Illus.). 144p. 1994. PLB 20.00 (*0-19-508046-7*) OUP.
—An Unfinished Battle: American Women 1848-1865. (Illus.). 144p. 1994. PLB 20.00 (*0-19-508110-2*) OUP.
Sigerman, Harriett. Young Oxford History of Women in the United States Supplement & Index. (Illus.). 144p. 1994. PLB 20.00 (*0-19-508829-8*) OUP.
Sight & Sound Staff. Santa's Narrow Escape Christmas Sound Story. (ps). 1991. 30.50 (*0-88704-205-8*) Sight & Sound.
Signer, Billie T. Cry of the Eagle. Bliss, Bob, illus. 190p. (Orig.). (gr. 5-8). 1990. pap. 4.95 (*0-8198-1455-5*) St Paul Bks.
—Shetland Summer. Bliss, Bob, illus. LC 88-18480. 125p. (Orig.). (gr. 5-8). 1990. pap. 3.95 (*0-8198-6884-1*) St Paul Bks.
Signer, Billie T., pseud. Sonny. Christian, Raleta, illus. Ervis, K. Leroy, intro. by. LC 90-82038. (Illus.). 134p. (gr. 5-8). 1990. lib. bdg. 17.95 (*0-944419-28-3*) Everett Cos Pub.
Signol, Anne. Norris on Broadway. (Illus.). 32p. (gr. 4-6). 1992. pap. 7.95 (*0-8059-3303-4*) Dorrance.
Sikes, Johnie. From Feathers to a King. 40p. 1992. pap. text ed. 3.95 (*0-9633262-0-1*) Vitamemoria.

Sikes, Johnie B. BackWhen Ben Again. 40p. 1992. pap. text ed. 3.95 (*0-9633262-3-6*) Vitamemoria.
—Tales of BackWhen Ben. 40p. 1992. pap. text ed. 3.95 (*0-9633262-2-8*) Vitamemoria.
Sikirycki, Igor. The Best Cook. Knobbe, Czeslaw, ed. & tr. from POL. Thoenes, Michael, illus. 26p. (gr. 1-6). 1993. text ed. 9.95 (*0-9630328-2-8*) SDPI.
Sikora, Pat. Small Group Bible Studies: How to Lead Them. 224p. (Orig.). 1991. pap. 9.99 (*0-87403-858-8*, 18-03218) Standard Pub.
Siks, Geraldine B. The Sandalwood Box. (gr. 1-7). 1954. 4.50 (*0-87602-199-2*) Anchorage.
Silberdick, Barbara F. Words in the News: A Student's Dictionary of American Government & Politics. Huehnergarth, John, illus. LC 93-19373. 144p. 1993. PLB 13.40 (*0-531-11164-4*) Watts.
Silberg, Francis B. The Story of Passover for Children. Britt, Stephanie, illus. 24p. (ps-2). 1989. pap. 3.95 (*0-8249-8309-2*, Ideals Child) Hambleton-Hill.
Silberman, Miriam. Der Lichtiger Kuk Fin der Baal Shem. Scheiner, Mordecai, ed. Silberman, Miriam, illus. 80p. (Orig.). (gr. 4-8). 1985. pap. text ed. 4.50 (*0-9618441-0-8*) Beth Chana.
Silberman, Shoshana. The Whole Megillah. Kahn, Katherine, illus. LC 90-5137. 40p. (gr. k-6). 1991. pap. 3.95 (*0-929371-23-2*) Kar Ben.
Silbert, Alvin, jt. auth. see Silbert, Linda P.
Silbert, Alvin J., jt. auth. see Silbert, Linda P.
Silbert, Jerome, jt. auth. see Engelmann, Siegfried.
Silbert, Linda P. & Silbert, Alvin. My Own Book of Feelings. (Illus.). (gr. k-8). 1977. 4.98 (*0-89544-017-2*, 017) Silbert Bress.
Silbert, Linda P. & Silbert, Alvin J. Agnes' Cardboard Piano. (Illus.). (gr. k-4). 1978. pap. 4.98 (*0-89544-054-7*) Silbert Bress.
—Guess What I Am Thinking of... (Illus.). (gr. 2-6). 1977. wkbk. 4.98 (*0-89544-021-0*, 021) Silbert Bress.
—I'll Be Your Best Friend. (Illus.). (gr. k-4). 1978. pap. 4.98 (*0-89544-056-3*) Silbert Bress.
—Lost in the Cave. (Illus.). (gr. k-4). 1978. pap. 4.98 (*0-89544-057-1*) Silbert Bress.
—Make My Own Book Kit Alphabet. (ps-2). 1984. wkbk. 4.98 (*0-89544-319-8*) Silbert Bress.
—Make My Own Book Kit Animals. (ps-2). 1984. wkbk. 4.98 (*0-89544-316-3*) Silbert Bress.
—Make My Own Book Kit Numbers. (ps-2). 1984. wkbk. 4.98 (*0-89544-318-X*) Silbert Bress.
—Make My Own Book Kit Shapes. (ps-2). 1984. wkbk. 4.98 (*0-89544-317-1*) Silbert Bress.
—My Own Book of Special Things. (Illus.). (ps-4). 1977. wkbk. 4.98 (*0-89544-019-9*, 019) Silbert Bress.
—My Own Book of Wishes. (Illus.). (gr. k-6). 1976. wkbk. 4.98 (*0-89544-016-4*) Silbert Bress.
—Penelope's Pen Pal. (Illus.). (gr. k-4). 1978. pap. 4.98 (*0-89544-053-9*) Silbert Bress.
—This Is My Opinion about... (Illus.). (gr. 5-12). 1977. 4.98 (*0-89544-020-2*, 020) Silbert Bress.
—Tiger, Take off Your Hat. (Illus.). (gr. k-4). 1978. pap. 4.98 (*0-89544-051-2*) Silbert Bress.
—Tuffy's Bike Race. (Illus.). (gr. k-4). 1978. pap. 4.98 (*0-89544-058-X*) Silbert Bress.
—Tyrone Goes Camping. (Illus.). (gr. k-4). 1978. pap. 4.98 (*0-89544-055-5*) Silbert Bress.
—What Would Happen If... (Illus.). (gr. 3-9). 1976. wkbk. 4.98 (*0-89544-018-0*, 018) Silbert Bress.
—Whitney's New Glasses. (Illus.). (gr. k-4). 1978. pap. 4.98 (*0-89544-052-0*) Silbert Bress.
—The Wonderful World of Gift Giving. (gr. 3-7). 1983. wkbk. 4.98 (*0-89544-024-5*) Silbert Bress.
Silbey, Uma. Paul & Mary & their Magic Crystals. Chien-Erikson, Nancy, illus. 48p. (Orig.). (ps-3). 1988. pap. 9.95 (*0-938925-07-5*) U-Music.
Silk, Silvia. My Friendly Snowman. (Illus.). 53p. (Orig.). (gr. 1 up). pap. write for info. (*0-938861-04-2*); cassette avail. (*0-938861-05-0*) Jasmine Texts.
Silkwood, Chris & Levicki, Nancy. Awesome Teen. Schwarzenegger, Arnold, frwd. by. (Illus.). 140p. (Orig.). (gr. 8-12). 1991. pap. 11.95 (*0-9631318-0-X*) NJL Interests.
Sill, Cathryn. About Birds: A Guide for Children. Sill, John, illus. 40p. (gr. 4 up). 1991. 14.95 (*1-56145-028-6*) Peachtree Pubs.
Silliman, Emery & Jonson, Liz. Addition. Nayer, Judith E., ed. Mahan, Ben, illus. 32p. (gr. k-1). 1991. wkbk. 1.95 (*1-878624-57-1*) McClanahan Bk.
Silliman, Emery, jt. auth. see Jonson, Liz.
Sills, Leslie. Inspirations: Stories about Women Artists. Fay, Ann, ed. LC 88-80. (Illus.). 56p. (gr. 4 up). 1989. PLB 16.95 (*0-8075-3649-0*) A Whitman.
—Visions: Stories about Women Artists. Sills, Leslie & Levine, Abby, eds. LC 92-32909. (Illus.). 64p. (gr. 4 up). 1993. PLB 18.95 (*0-8075-8491-6*) A Whitman.
Silsbe, Brenda. The Bears We Know. Ritchie, Scot, illus. 24p. (Orig.). (ps-2). 1989. pap. 0.99 (*1-55037-048-0*, Pub. by Annick CN) Firefly Bks Ltd.
—Just One More Color. Steffler, Shawn, illus. 24p. (ps-3). 1991. PLB 14.95 (*1-55037-133-9*, Pub. by Annick CN); pap. 4.95 (*1-55037-136-3*, Pub. by Annick CN) Firefly Bks Ltd.
Silsbee, Peter. The Big Way Out. (gr. k-12). 1987. pap. 2.75 (*0-440-90499-4*, LFL) Dell.
—The Temptation of Kate. LC 90-1351. 160p. (gr. 6-9). 1990. SBE 13.95 (*0-02-782761-5*, Bradbury Pr) Macmillan Child Grp.
Silva, P. Fidencio, tr. see Hart, Corinne.
Silva, P. Fidencio, tr. see Shannon, Ellen & Hart, Corinne.

Silvani, Harold. Animal Number Puzzles. 50p. (gr. 2-4). 1971. wkbk. 6.95 (*1-878669-25-7*, 4015) Crea Tea Assocs.
—Baseball Card Grand Slam Curriculum Activities. Garcia, Joe, illus. 30p. (gr. 4-8). 1992. wkbk. 11.95 (*1-878669-52-4*) Crea Tea Assocs.
—Famous Athletes Number Puzzles. Sharpsteen, Linda, illus. 28p. (gr. 4-6). 1975. wkbk. 6.95 (*1-878669-23-0*, 4161) Crea Tea Assocs.
—Famous People - Men. 30p. (gr. 4-8). 1975. wkbk. 6.95 (*1-878669-24-9*, 4005) Crea Tea Assocs.
—Famous People - Women. Cruz, Harry H., illus. 52p. (gr. 4-8). 1975. wkbk. 6.95 (*1-878669-22-2*, 4345) Crea Tea Assocs.
—Famous Places & Events. 56p. (gr. 3-6). 1975. wkbk. 6.95 (*1-878669-21-4*, 4014) Crea Tea Assocs.
—Kitchen, Garage & Garbage Can Science, Bks. A-C. Garcia, Joe, illus. 35p. (gr. 1-8). 1992. wkbk. ea. 6.95 (*0-685-65023-5*) Bk. A (*1-878669-44-3*) Bk. B (*1-878669-45-1*) Bk. C (*1-878669-46-X*) Crea Tea Assocs.
—Language Skills Builder - Intermediate. 30p. (gr. 4-8). 1988. wkbk. 16.50 (*1-878669-39-7*, CTA-6026) Crea Tea Assocs.
—Language Skills Builder - Primary. 30p. (gr. 1-3). 1988. wkbk. 16.50 (*1-878669-38-9*, CTA-6025) Crea Tea Assocs.
—Math Skills Builder - Intermediate. 31p. (gr. 4-8). 1988. wkbk. 16.50 (*1-878669-37-0*, CTA-4216) Crea Tea Assocs.
—Math Skills Builder - Primary. 31p. (gr. 1-3). 1988. wkbk. 16.50 (*1-878669-36-2*, CTA-4215) Crea Tea Assocs.
—Mystery Code. Garcia, Joe, illus. 45p. (gr. 4-8). 1989. wkbk. 7.95 (*1-878669-35-4*, CTA-4330) Crea Tea Assocs.
—Presidents Number Puzzles, 2 bks. 46p. Bks. A & B. write for info. set (*1-878669-15-X*, 4158); wkbk. 6.95 ea. Bk. A, Grades 3-5, 1977 (4158) Bk. B, Grades 4-7, 1973 (4159) Crea Tea Assocs.
—States & Capitals, 2 bks. Creative Teaching Assocs. Staff, illus. (gr. 3-6). 1975. Bks. A & B. write for info. set (*1-878669-12-5*, 4348); wkbk. 6.95 ea. Bk. A, 28p (*1-878669-13-3*, 4348) Bk. B, 53p (4395) Crea Tea Assocs.
—Wonders of Water. Todd, Amy, illus. 43p. (gr. 4-12). 1988. wkbk. 6.95 (*1-878669-29-X*, CTA-6552) Crea Tea Assocs.
Silver, A. David. A Young Person's First Book of Wealth. (Illus.). 300p. (gr. 7-12). 1987. wkbk. 15.95x (*0-945214-00-6*) Silver Prescrip Pr.
—Your First Book of Wealth: The Beginner's Guide to Collecting Investing & Starting Your Own Business. 224p. (Orig.). (gr. 9 up). 1989. pap. 10.95 (*0-934829-47-0*) Career Pr Inc.
Silver Dollar City, Inc. Staff, ed. see Barrett, John.
Silver Dollar City, Inc. Staff, ed. see Wiskur, Darrell.
Silver, Donald. Extinction Is Forever. Wynne, Patricia J., illus. LC 93-32567. 1994. write for info. (*0-671-86769-5*, J Messner); pap. write for info. (*0-671-86770-9*, J Messner) S&S Trade.
—Why Save the Rain Forest? Wynne, Patricia, illus. LC 93-22313. 1993. lib. bdg. 12.98 (*0-671-86609-5*, Messner); lib. bdg. 6.95 (*0-671-86610-9*, Messner) S&S Trade.
Silver, Donald & Wynne, Patricia. Dinosaur Life Activity Book. 32p. (gr. 1-3). 1988. pap. 2.50 (*0-486-25809-2*) Dover.
Silver, Donald M. The Animal World: From Single-Cell Creatures to Giants of the Land & Sea. Wynne, Patricia, illus. LC 86-3894. 112p. (gr. 5 up). 1987. lib. bdg. 9.99 (*0-394-96650-3*); (BYR) Random Bks Yng Read.
—The Checkerboard Press Nature Encyclopedia. Wynne, Patricia J., illus. LC 89-48801. 128p. (gr. 3-7). 1990. 12.95 (*1-56288-001-2*) Checkerboard.
—Earth: The Ever-Changing Planet. Wynne, Patricia J., illus. LC 88-11331. 96p. (Orig.). (gr. 5 up). 1989. lib. bdg. 12.99 (*0-394-99195-8*) Random Bks Yng Read.
—Life on Earth: Biology Today. Wynne, Patricia, illus. 96p. (gr. 5 up). 1983. lib. bdg. 7.99 (*0-394-95971-X*) Random Bks Yng Read.
—One Small Square Backyard. Wynne, Patricia J., illus. LC 93-18353. (gr. 4 up). 1993. 14.95 (*0-7167-6510-1*, Sci Am Yng Rdrs) W H Freeman.
—One Small Square: Cave. LC 93-36570. (Illus.). 1994. write for info. (*0-7167-6514-4*) W H Freeman.
—Seashore. (gr. 7-12). 1993. 14.95 (*0-7167-6511-X*, Sci Am Yng Rdrs) W H Freeman.
Silver, Jeffery H. The Clay Babies & Other Puget Sound Stories. 32p. (Orig.). (gr. 5 up). 1982. pap. 4.00 (*0-910867-00-3*) Silver Seal Bks.
Silver, Jeffrey H. The Rainier Ice Caves & Other Northwest Stories. Topolski, Diane F., illus. 32p. (gr. 5 up). 1983. pap. 4.00 (*0-910867-01-1*) Silver Seal Bks.
Silver, Jody. Rupert, Polly & Daisy. Silver, Jody, illus. LC 83-24979. 48p. (ps-3). 1984. 5.95 (*0-8193-1124-3*) Parents.
Silver, Leda. Tracing Our German Roots. Butler, Nate & Evans, Beth, illus. 48p. (gr. 4-7). 1993. text ed. 12.95 (*1-56261-150-X*) John Muir.
Silver, Lynette. My Ballet Book. Smith, Kay, contrib. by. (Illus.). 64p. (gr. 5 up). 1993. pap. 6.95 (*1-875169-15-6*, Pub. by S Milner AT) Sterling.
Silver, Norman. An Eye for Color. (gr. 8 up). 1993. 14.99 (*0-525-44859-4*, DCB) Dutton Child Bks.

—No Tigers in Africa. LC 91-29121. (Illus.). 100p. (gr. 7 up). 1992. 15.00 (*0-525-44733-4*, DCB) Dutton Child Bks.
—Python Dance. 192p. (gr. 8 up). 1993. 14.99 (*0-525-45161-7*, DCB) Dutton Child Bks.
Silverberg, Robert. Letters from Atlantis. Gould, Robert, illus. LC 90-562. 144p. (gr. 7 up). 1990. SBE 14.95 (*0-689-31570-8*, Atheneum Child Bk) Macmillan Child Grp.
—The Moundbuilders. LC 85-25953. 276p. 1986. pap. 7.95 (*0-8214-0839-9*) Ohio U Pr.
—Project Pendulum. (gr. 8 up). 1987. 15.95 (*0-8027-6712-5*) Walker & Co.
Silverman, Read to Study. (gr. 7 up). 1988. 9.99 (*0-89824-172-3*) Trillium Pr.
Silverman, Erica. Big Pumpkin. Schindler, S. D., illus. LC 91-14053. 32p. (ps-3). 1992. RSBE 14.95 (*0-02-782683-X*, Macmillan Child Bk) Macmillan Child Grp.
—The Freeze-in-Place Contest. Schindler, S. D., illus. LC 93-8707. 1994. write for info. (*0-02-782685-6*) Macmillan.
—Mrs. Peachtree & the Eighth Avenue Cat. Beier, Ellen, illus. LC 92-16973. 32p. (ps-3). 1994. RSBE 14.95 (*0-02-782684-8*, Macmillan Child Bk) Macmillan Child Grp.
—On Grandma's Roof. Ray, Deborah K., illus. LC 89-31255. 32p. (ps-2). 1990. RSBE 13.95 (*0-02-782681-3*, Macmillan Child Bk) Macmillan Child Grp.
—Warm in Winter. Deraney, Michael J., illus. LC 88-22691. 32p. (gr. k-3). 1989. RSBE 13.95 (*0-02-782661-9*, Macmillan Child Bk) Macmillan Child Grp.
Silverman, Helene & Siderman, Sheila. Your Days Are Numbered in Calendar Math. 64p. (gr. 2-6). 1980. pap. text ed. 8.50 (*0-914040-84-7*) Cuisenaire.
Silverman, Hillel, jt. auth. see Silverman, Morris.
Silverman, Jerry. African Roots. Clark, Kenneth B., intro. by. (Illus.). 64p. (gr. 5 up). 1994. PLB 15.95 (*0-7910-1828-8*, Am Art Analog); pap. 7.95 (*0-7910-1844-X*, Am Art Analog) Chelsea Hse.
—Childrens' Songs. (Illus.). (gr. 5 up). 1992. PLB 15.95 (*0-7910-1831-8*, Am Art Analog); pap. 7.95 (*0-7910-1847-4*, Am Art Analog) Chelsea Hse.
—Christmas Songs. (Illus.). 64p. (gr. 5 up). 1992. PLB 15.95 (*0-7910-1832-6*, Am Art Analog); pap. 7.95 (*0-7910-1848-2*, Am Art Analog) Chelsea Hse.
—Slave Songs. Clark, Kenneth B., intro. by. (Illus.). 64p. (gr. 5 up). 1994. PLB 15.95 (*0-7910-1837-7*, Am Art Analog); pap. 7.95 (*0-7910-1853-9*, Am Art Analog) Chelsea Hse.
—Songs of Protest & Civil Rights. Clark, Kenneth B., intro. by. (Illus.). 64p. (gr. 5 up). 1992. 15.95 (*0-7910-1827-X*, Am Art Analog); pap. 7.95 (*0-7910-1843-1*, Am Art Analog) Chelsea Hse.
Silverman, Maida. Baby's Book of ABC. Gleeson, Kate, illus. 12p. (ps). 1993. pap. 1.95 (*0-307-06037-3*, 6037, Golden Pr) Western Pub.
—Baby's First Body Book. Kramer, Robin, illus. (ps-1). 1987. 3.95 (*0-448-10554-3*, G&D) Putnam Pub Group.
—Bunny's ABC Box. Blonder, Ellen, illus. 24p. (ps-1). 1986. pap. 3.95 (*0-448-01464-5*, G&D) Putnam Pub Group.
—Dinosaur Babies. Inouye, Carol, illus. LC 88-4690. 1990. pap. 4.95 (*0-671-69438-3*, Little Simon) S&S Trade.
—Festival of Esther: The Story of Purim. Ewing, Carolyn S., illus. (gr. 1-5). 1989. pap. 8.95 (*0-671-67200-2*, Little Simon) S&S Trade.
—Festival of Freedom: The Story of Passover. Ewing, Carolyn S., illus. (gr. 1-5). 1988. pap. 8.95 (*0-671-64567-6*, S&S BFYR); pap. 3.95 (*0-671-66340-2*, S&S BFYR) S&S Trade.
—Festival of Lights: The Story of Hanukkah. Ewing, Carolyn S., illus. LC 87-16076. (gr. 1-5). 1987. (Little Simon); pap. 2.95 (*0-671-64376-2*, Little Simon) S&S Trade.
—The Glass Menorah & Other Stories for Jewish Holidays. Levine, Marge, illus. LC 91-13890. 64p. (gr. 1-4). 1992. RSBE 14.95 (*0-02-782682-1*, Four Winds) Macmillan Child Grp.
—The Golden Book of Monkeys, Apes, & Other Primates. Spence, James, illus. 24p. (gr. 3-6). 1991. 6.95 (*0-307-15858-6*, Golden Pr) Western Pub.
—The Great Big Walt Disney Word Book. Baker, Darrell, illus. 48p. (ps-2). 1992. write for info. (*0-307-15604-4*, 15604, Golden Pr) Western Pub.
—Ladybug's Color Book. Duell, Nancy, illus. 24p. (ps-1). 1986. 3.95 (*0-448-01461-0*, G&D) Putnam Pub Group.
—My First Book of Jewish Holidays. Garrison, Barbara, illus. LC 93-20370. (ps-8). 1994. 13.99 (*0-8037-1427-0*); lib. bdg. 13.89 (*0-8037-1428-9*) Dial Bks Young.
Silverman, Martin. My Tooth Is Loose. Aitken, Amy, illus. 32p. (ps-3). 1992. 8.95 (*0-670-83862-4*) Viking Child Bks.
Silverman, Morris & Silverman, Hillel. Prayer Book for Summer Camps. (gr. 3-12). 8.95x (*0-87677-060-X*); pap. 6.95x (*0-87677-061-8*) Prayer Bk.
Silverman, Morris, jt. auth. see Greenberg, Sidney.
Silvers, Rath, ed. see Jenkins, Sheila.
Silvers, Ruth, jt. auth. see Goodwin, Irene.
Silvers, Vicki. Sing a Song of Sound. Ehlert, Lois, illus. LC 72-90695. 32p. (ps-2). 1973. 7.95 (*0-87592-046-2*) Scroll Pr.
Silverstein, Alvin. Circulatory System. 1994. write for info. (*0-8050-2833-1*) H Holt & Co.

—Digestive System. 1994. PLB write for info. (0-8050-2832-3) H Holt & Co.
—Excretory Systems. 1994. PLB write for info. (0-8050-2834-X) H Holt & Co.
—Life in a Tidal Pool, Vol. 1. (gr. 4-7). 1990. 14.95 (0-316-79120-2, Joy St Bks) Little.
—Muscular System. 1994. PLB write for info. (0-8050-2836-6) H Holt & Co.
—Nervous System. 1994. PLB write for info. (0-8050-2835-8) H Holt & Co.
—Reproductive System. 1994. PLB write for info. (0-8050-2838-2) H Holt & Co.
—Respiratory System. 1994. PLB write for info. (0-8050-2831-5) H Holt & Co.
—Skeletal System. Date not set. PLB write for info. (0-8050-2837-4) H Holt & Co.
Silverstein, Alvin & Silverstein, Virginia B. AIDS: Deadly Threat. rev. & expanded ed. LC 89-33145. (Illus.). 160p. (gr. 6 up). 1991. lib. bdg. 18.95 (0-89490-175-3) Enslow Pubs.
—Cancer: Can It Be Stopped? new, rev. ed. LC 86-45500. (Illus.). 128p. (gr. 7 up). 1987. 12.95 (0-397-32202-X, Lipp Jr Bks); (Lipp Jr Bks) HarpC Child Bks.
Silverstein, Alvin & Silverstein, Virginia. Dogs: All about Them. LC 84-29723. (Illus.). 256p. (gr. 6 up). 1986. 12.95 (0-688-04805-6) Lothrop.
Silverstein, Alvin & Silverstein, Virginia B. Epilepsy. LC 74-31382. (Illus.). 64p. (gr. 4-6). 1990. PLB 12.89 (0-397-32413-8, Lipp Jr Bks) HarpC Child Bks.
—Futurelife: The Biotechnology Revolution. (Illus.). 96p. (gr. 7 up). 1982. 10.95 (0-13-345884-9) P-H.
—Genes, Medicine, & You. LC 88-37353. (Illus.). 160p. (gr. 6 up). 1989. lib. bdg. 18.95 (0-89490-154-0) Enslow Pubs.
—Glasses & Contact Lenses: Your Guide to Eyes, Eyewear, & Eye Care. LC 88-13026. (Illus.). 144p. (gr. 7 up). 1989. (Lipp Jr Bks); PLB 13.89 (0-397-32185-6, Lipp Jr Bks) HarpC Child Bks.
Silverstein, Alvin & Silverstein, Virginia. Hamsters: All About Them. LC 74-8863. (Illus.). 128p. (gr. 3-6). 1974. PLB 13.88 (0-688-50056-0) Lothrop.
Silverstein, Alvin & Silverstein, Virginia B. Heart Disease: America's Number One Killer. rev. ed. LC 83-49495. (Illus.). 160p. (gr. 7 up). 1985. (Lipp Jr Bks); (Lipp Jr Bks) HarpC Child Bks.
Silverstein, Alvin & Silverstein, Virginia. The Mystery of Sleep. Davis, Nelle, illus. 48p. (gr. 2-5). 1987. 12.95 (0-316-79117-2) Little.
Silverstein, Alvin & Silverstein, Virginia B. Respiratory System: How Living Creatures Breathe. Bakacs, George, illus. (gr. 3-7). 1969. 10.95 (0-13-774547-8) P-H.
—So You're Getting Braces: A Guide to Orthodontics. LC 77-16488. (Illus.). 128p. (gr. 5 up). 1978. (Lipp Jr Bks); pap. 3.95 (0-397-31787-5, Lipp Jr Bks) HarpC Child Bks.
Silverstein, Alvin & Silverstein, Virginia. Wonders of Speech. LC 87-31370. (Illus.). 160p. (gr. 7 up). 1988. 12.95 (0-688-06534-1) Morrow Jr Bks.
Silverstein, Alvin & Silverstein, Virginia B. The World of the Brain. LC 86-31007. (Illus.). 192p. (gr. 7up). 1986. 12.95 (0-688-05777-2) Morrow Jr Bks.
Silverstein, Alvin, et al. Overcoming Acne: The How & Why of Healthy Skin Care. Papa, Christopher M., pref. by. LC 89-13748. (Illus.). 112p. (gr. 7 up). 1990. 12.95 (0-688-08344-7) Morrow Jr Bks.
—So You Think You're Fat? LC 90-40761. 224p. (gr. 7 up). 1991. 14.00 (0-06-021641-7); PLB 13.89 (0-06-021642-5) HarpC Child Bks.
—The Addictions Handbook. LC 90-14093. 192p. (gr. 6 up). 1991. lib. bdg. 18.95 (0-89490-205-9) Enslow Pubs.
—Carbohydrates. Green, Anne C., illus. LC 91-41245. 48p. (gr. 3-6). 1992. PLB 13.90 (1-56294-207-7) Millbrook Pr.
—Common Cold & Flu. LC 93-4685. (gr. 9 up). 1994. write for info. (0-89490-463-9) Enslow Pubs.
—Diabetes. LC 93-41199. Date not set. write for info. (0-89490-464-7) Enslow Pubs.
—Fats. Green, Anne C., illus. LC 91-42169. 48p. (gr. 3-6). 1992. PLB 13.90 (1-56294-208-5) Millbrook Pr.
—Lyme Disease, the Great Imitator: How to Prevent & Cure It. Sigal, Leonard H., pref. by. LC 90-81250. (Illus.). 126p. (gr. 5 up). 1990. pap. 5.95 (0-9623653-9-4) Avstar Pub.
—Michael: Fun & Facts about a Popular Name & the People Who Made It Great. LC 90-80673. (Illus.). 64p. (gr. 5 up). 1990. 11.95 (0-9623653-6-X); pap. 4.95 (0-9623653-7-8) Avstar Pub.
—Proteins. Green, Anne C., illus. LC 91-41230. 48p. (gr. 3-6). 1992. PLB 13.90 (1-56294-209-3) Millbrook Pr.
—Recycling: Meeting the Challenge of the Trash Crisis. (Illus.). 128p. (gr. 5-9). 1992. 15.95 (0-399-22190-5, Putnam) Putnam Pub Group.
—Saving Endangered Animals. LC 92-1765. (Illus.). 128p. (gr. 6 up). 1993. lib. bdg. 17.95 (0-89490-402-7) Enslow Pubs.
—Smell, the Subtle Sense. Neumann, Ann, illus. LC 91-21745. 96p. (gr. 4 up). 1992. 14.00 (0-688-09396-5); PLB 13.93 (0-688-09397-3) Morrow Jr Bks.
—Some Ants are Farmers. LC 93-8753. Date not set. write for info. (0-688-12529-8); PLB write for info. (0-688-12530-1) Lothrop.
—Steroids: Big Muscles, Big Problems. LC 91-876. (Illus.). 112p. (gr. 6 up). 1992. lib. bdg. 17.95 (0-89490-318-7) Enslow Pubs.

—Vitamins & Minerals. Green, Anne C., illus. LC 91-41231. 48p. (gr. 3-6). 1992. PLB 13.90 (1-56294-206-9) Millbrook Pr.
Silverstein, Cindy, illus. Happy Birthday Books. (ps-k). 1993. Set, 8 mini-board bks., 6p. ea. bds. 12.95 (1-56293-214-4) McClanahan Bk.
Silverstein, Herma. The Alamo. LC 91-42461. (Illus.). 72p. (gr. 4 up). 1992. RSBE 14.95 (0-87518-502-9, Dillon) Macmillan Child Grp.
—Alcoholism. LC 90-12578. (Illus.). 96p. (gr. 9-12). 1990. PLB 13.40 (0-531-10879-1) Watts.
—Mad, Mad Monday. (gr. 7-9). 1989. pap. 2.50 (0-671-67403-X, Archway) PB.
—Scream Machines. 112p. 1991. pap. 2.95 (0-380-71461-2, Camelot) Avon.
—Scream Machines: Roller Coasters Past, Present & Future. (Illus.). 128p. (gr. 3 up). 1986. 13.95 (0-8027-6618-8); lib. bdg. 13.85 (0-8027-6619-6) Walker & Co.
—Teen Guide to Single Parenting. LC 88-51486. (Illus.). 62p. (gr. 7-12). 1989. PLB 13.40 (0-531-10669-1) Watts.
—Teenage & Pregnant: What You Can Do. (Illus.). (gr. 7 up). 1989. lib. bdg. 13.98 (0-671-65221-4, J Messner); lib. bdg. 5.95 (0-671-65222-2) S&S Trade.
—Teenage Depression. (Illus.). 128p. (gr. 9-12). 1990. 13.45 (0-531-15183-2); PLB 13.40 (0-531-10960-7) Watts.
Silverstein, Herma & Dunnahoo, Terry J. The Baseball Hall of Fame. LC 93-6915. (Illus.). 48p. (gr. 5-6). 1994. RSBE 13.95 (0-89686-849-4, Crestwood Hse) Macmillan Child Grp.
—Basketball. LC 93-448. (Illus.). 48p. (gr. 5-6). 1994. RSBE 13.95 (0-89686-850-8, Crestwood Hse) Macmillan Child Grp.
—Pro Football. LC 93-954. (Illus.). 48p. (gr. 5-6). 1994. RSBE 13.95 (0-89686-851-6, Crestwood Hse) Macmillan Child Grp.
Silverstein, Herma, et al. Messner Teen Interest Collection, 21 vols. (Illus.). (gr. 7 up). 1990. Set. lib. bdg. write for info. (0-671-31252-9, J Messner); lib. bdg. write for info. (0-671-31253-7); Set. PLB 212. 69s.p. (0-685-47104-7) S&S Trade.
Silverstein, Robert, jt. auth. see Alvin, Virginia.
Silverstein, Shel. Giraffe & a Half. Silverstein, Shel, illus. LC 64-19709. 48p. (gr. k-3). 1964. 15.00 (0-06-025655-9); PLB 14.89 (0-06-025656-7) HarpC Child Bks.
—Lafcadio, the Lion Who Shot Back. Silverstein, Shel, illus. LC 62-13320. 112p. (gr. 3-6). 1963. 15.00 (0-06-025675-3); PLB 14.89 (0-06-025676-1) HarpC Child Bks.
—A Light in the Attic. Silverstein, Shel, illus. LC 80-8453. 176p. 1981. 15.95 (0-06-025673-7); PLB 15.89 (0-06-025674-5) HarpC Child Bks.
—Where the Sidewalk Ends. (Illus.). 1986. pap. 7.95 (0-440-85056-8) Dell.
—Where the Sidewalk Ends: Poems & Drawings. Silverstein, Shel, illus. LC 70-105486. 176p. (gr. 4 up). 1974. 15.95 (0-06-025667-2); PLB 15.89 (0-06-025668-0) HarpC Child Bks.
—Who Wants a Cheap Rhinoceros? rev. ed. LC 82-23945. (Illus.). 56p. (ps-3). 1983. RSBE 12.95 (0-02-782690-2, Macmillan Child Bk) Macmillan Child Grp.
Silverstein, Virginia, jt. auth. see Silverstein, Alvin.
Silverstein, Virginia B., jt. auth. see Silverstein, Alvin.
Silverstre, Ruth. Stranger Who Lived in a Merry-Go-Round. (gr. 4-7). 1993. pap. 2.75 (0-590-45573-7) Scholastic Inc.
Silverthorne, Elizabeth. Fiesta: Mexico's Great Celebrations. LC 91-37178. (Illus.). 64p. (gr. 3-6). 1992. PLB 13.90 (1-56294-055-4) Millbrook Pr.
Silverthorne, Sandy. All-Time Awesome Bible Search. Silverthorne, Sandy, illus. 32p. (Orig.). (ps up). 1991. 11.99 (0-89081-920-3) Harvest Hse.
—The Great Bible Adventure. Silverthorne, Sandy, illus. LC 90-36385. 32p. (Orig.). (ps-8). 1990. 11.99 (0-89081-842-8) Harvest Hse.
Silvester, Susan B., ed. see Smith, Mary P.
Silvestro, Frank Di see Di Silvestro, Frank.
Sima, Patricia, et al. Immigration: A Thematic Unit. Welch, Sandy, illus. 80p. (gr. 3-5). 1993. wkbk. 7.95 (1-55734-234-2) Tchr Create Mat.
Sima, Patricia M., jt. auth. see Goldfluss, Karen J.
Sima, Patricia M., ed. see King, Jeanne.
Simak, Clifford D. All Flesh Is Grass. 256p. (gr. 7 up). 1978. pap. 3.50 (0-380-39933-4, 39933) Avon.
Simbal, Joanne. Gifts from the Heart, No. 146. 176p. (Orig.). 1988. pap. 2.50 (0-553-27228-4, Sweet Dreams) Bantam.
—Long Shot. 134p. 1988. pap. 2.50 (0-553-27594-1) Bantam.
Simborowski, Nicoletta, jt. tr. see Philip, Neil.
Simckes, Seymour, tr. see Semel, Nava.
Simcox, Helen E. My Book of Gray. Weinberger, Jane, ed. LC 89-50682. (Illus.). 44p. (ps-4). 1989. pap. 5.95 (0-932433-61-8) Windswept Hse.
Simcox, Helen E., ed. Dear Dark Faces: Portraits of a People. LC 79-92240. (Illus.). 104p. (gr. 7-12). 1980. pap. 6.00 perf. bound (0-916418-23-5) Lotus.
Simenon. Les Enigmes. (gr. 7-12). pap. 5.95 (0-38436-058-X, 40269) EMC.
Simenon, Georges. Maigret et le Clochard. pap. 5.95 (0-88436-047-4, 40270) EMC.

Simko, Carole B. Ear Gear: A Student Workbook on Hearing & Hearing Aids. Skrobisz, Jan, illus. 128p. (gr. 3-6). 1986. 7.95 (0-930323-15-7, Clerc Bks) Gallaudet Univ Pr.
—Wired for Sound: An Advanced Student Workbook on Hearing & Hearing Aids. Skrobisz, Jan, illus. 149p. (gr. 8-12). 1986. wkbk. 7.95x (0-930323-16-5, Clerc Bks) Gallaudet Univ Pr.
Simmonds, Posy. The Chocolate Wedding. Simmonds, Posy, illus. LC 90-4932. 32p. (gr. k-5). 1991. 12.95 (0-679-81447-7) Knopf Bks Yng Read.
Simmons, Aaron. Surface Thoughts. Thornton, Don, intro. by. Soto, Zachary & Bostick, Matthew, illus. 48p. (Orig.). (gr. 6-12). 1993. pap. 7.50 (1-882913-01-9) Thornton LA.
Simmons, Albert D. Wing Shots. 2nd ed. (Illus.). 83p. (gr. 10 up). 1990. Repr. of 1936 ed. 35.00 (1-56416-012-2) Derrydale Pr.
Simmons, Alex. Grounded for Life? Tiegreen, Alan, illus. DeMasco, Steve, created by. LC 93-22061. (Illus.). 64p. (gr. 1-4). 1993. PLB 9.59t (0-8167-3102-0); pap. 2.50 (0-8167-3103-9) Troll Assocs.
Simmons, Alex, jt. auth. see De Masco, Steve.
Simmons, Cassandra W. Becoming Myself: True Stories about Learning from Life. Espeland, Pamela, ed. (Orig.). (gr. 5 up). 1994. pap. 4.95 (0-915793-69-5) Free Spirit Pub.
Simmons, Dawn L. The Great White Owl of Sissinghurst. Schindler, S. D., illus. LC 91-17490. 32p. (ps-3). 1993. SBE 14.95g (0-689-50522-1, M K McElderry) Macmillan Child Grp.
Simmons, Herbert R. & Boyice, Lester L. Star Patrol: The Adventures Begin. Peck, Bill, illus. 56p. (ps-7). 1987. lib. bdg. 8.95 (0-930355-05-9) ELRAMCO Enter.
Simmons, Marc. New Mexico. (Illus.). 328p. (gr. 4). 1983. text ed. 17.25x (0-87905-135-3, Peregrine Smith) Gibbs Smith Pub.
—New Mexico! rev. ed. (Illus.). 313p. (gr. 4). 1991. text ed. 45.00 (0-8263-1265-9) U of NM Pr.
Simmons, Patricia M., jt. auth. see Hillery, Mable.
Simmons, Paul, jt. auth. see Crawford, Kenneth.
Simmons, Paula & Salsbury, Darrell L. Your Sheep: A Kid's Guide to Raising & Showing. Steege, Gwen, ed. LC 91-57947. (Illus.). 128p. 1992. (Garden Way Pub); pap. 12.95 (0-88266-769-6, Garden Way Pub) Storey Comm Inc.
Simmons, William S. The Narragansett. Porter, Frank W., III, intro. by. (Illus.). 112p. (gr. 5 up). 1989. 17.95 (1-55546-718-0) Chelsea Hse.
Simmons-Henry, Linda, et al. The Heritage of Blacks in North Carolina. (gr. 6-12). 1990. 60.00 (0-912081-12-0) Delmar Co.
Simms, George O. Brendan the Navigator: Exploring the Ancient World. LC 89-82004. (Illus.). 96p. (gr. 7-12). 1989. 13.95 (0-86278-202-3, Pub. by OBrien Pr IE) Dufour.
—St. Patrick: The Real Story of Patrick Who Became Ireland's Patron Saint. (Illus.). 93p. (gr. 5 up). 1993. pap. 9.95 (0-86278-347-X, Pub. by OBrien Pr ER) Dufour.
Simms, Laura & Kozodoy, Ruth. Exploring Our Living Past. Harlow, Jules, ed. Rosenberg, Amye & Weihs, Erika, illus. (gr. k-2). 1978. pap. 7.95 (0-87441-309-5); tchr's guide 19.95x (0-87441-276-5) Behrman.
Simms, Susan R. Rhyme Time with the Rymons: A Better Way Than Throw Away. Dallgas-Frey, Paul, illus. 36p. (ps-4). 1991. pap. 4.95 incl. audiocassette (1-55999-151-8) LinguiSystems.
—Rhyme Time with the Rymons: Birds, Frogs, & Puppydogs. Dallgas-Frey, Paul, illus. 36p. (ps-4). 1991. pap. 4.95 incl. audiocassette (1-55999-150-X) LinguiSystems.
—Rhyme Time with the Rymons: Kitchen Magician. Dallgas-Frey, Paul, illus. 36p. (ps-3). 1990. pap. 4.95 incl. audiocassette (1-55999-136-4) LinguiSystems.
—Rhyme Time with the Rymons: My Think-Along Funbook. Basso, Bill, illus. Dallgas-Frey, Paul, contrib. by. (Illus.). 100p. (ps-4). 1991. wkbk. 3.95 (1-55999-158-5) LinguiSystems.
—Rhyme Time with the Rymons: My Think 'n' Do Book. Basso, Bill, illus. 100p. (ps-3). 1990. pap. 3.95 spiral bdg., wkbk. (1-55999-139-9) LinguiSystems.
—Rhyme Time with the Rymons: Remedy for Emily. Dallgas-Frey, Paul, illus. 36p. (ps-3). 1991. pap. 4.95 incl. audiocassette (1-55999-149-6) LinguiSystems.
—Rhyme Time with the Rymons: Squeeze for the Keys. Dallgas-Frey, Paul, illus. 36p. (ps-3). 1990. pap. 4.95 incl. audiocassette (1-55999-138-0) LinguiSystems.
—Rhyme Time with the Rymons: Wakin' to the Bacon. Dallgas-Frey, Paul, illus. 36p. (ps-3). 1990. pap. 4.95 incl. audiocassette (1-55999-137-2) LinguiSystems.

Simms, Thomas E. Otokahekagapi (First Beginnings) Sioux Creation Story. (Illus.). 36p. (Orig.). 1987. pap. 3.50 (1-877976-06-7, 406-0005) Tipi Pr. The first in a series of Lakota legends, is written & illustrated to foster greater respect for a proud people's tradition. This account in English & Lakota presents the profundity of the creation mystery. The pictures are Indian pictures, because this is the beginning of the Sioux Creation account. But it is for all children everywhere, because everyone asks about how things got started & how the World began. "So this picture book is like a little ball game. We shall learn that the book is a ball. Wakantanka will throw this ball to us, which is this book, & we shall catch it. Then we shall understand it. And we shall enjoy ourselves. Bring the ball -- this book -- to the Center, which is your Heart, then you will receive a present. The present is invisible, like a little secret. Good. That's all. Now I shall throw the ball to you. Catch it!" *Publisher Provided Annotation.*

Simon. Gorillas. (gr. 4 up). Date not set. 16.00 *(0-06-023033-9,* Festival); PLB 15.89 *(0-06-023034-7,* Festival) HarpC Child Bks.
—Science Dictionary. Date not set. 22.00 *(0-06-025629-X,* Festival); PLB 21.89 *(0-06-025630-3,* Festival) HarpC Child Bks.
—Sharks. Date not set. 16.00 *(0-06-023029-0,* Festival); PLB 15.89 *(0-685-68958-1,* Festival) HarpC Child Bks.
Simon & Schuster Staff. Amazing Mazes. (Illus.). 64p. (gr. 2-5). 1990. pap. 1.79 *(0-671-72333-2,* Little Simon) S&S Trade.
—How Things Work: A Guide to How Human-Made & Living Things Function. (Illus.). 128p. (gr. 3-7). 1988. pap. 9.95 *(0-671-67032-8,* S&S BFYR) S&S Trade.
—In My Own Words Book, No. 5. 1992. 12.95 *(0-671-74168-3,* J Messner) S&S Trade.
—In My Own Words Book, No. 6. 1992. 12.95 *(0-671-74171-3,* S&S BFYR) S&S Trade.
—Where Is It? Questions & Answers. 1989. pap. 7.95 *(0-671-68468-X,* S&S BFYR) S&S Trade.
—Why Things Are: A Guide to Understanding the World Around Us. (Illus.). 128p. (gr. 3-7). 1988. pap. 9.95 *(0-671-67031-X,* S&S BFYR) S&S Trade.
Simon, Carly. Amy the Dancing Bear. Datz, Margot, illus. (ps-3). 1989. 12.95 *(0-385-26637-5)* Doubleday.
—Boy of the Bells. Datz, Margot, illus. 1990. 14.95 *(0-385-41587-7);* PLB 15.99 *(0-385-41736-5)* Doubleday.
—Fisherman's Song: A Romantic Story for All Ages. LC 91-6653. 1991. 15.00 *(0-385-41955-4)* Doubleday.
—The Nightime Chauffeur. Datz, Margot, illus. LC 92-44934. 1993. pap. 16.00 *(0-385-47009-6)* Doubleday.
Simon, Charnan. Chester A. Arthur. LC 89-35386. 100p. (gr. 3 up). 1989. PLB 17.27 *(0-516-01369-6)* Childrens.
—Christmas Eve. 10p. 1989. bds. 2.95 *(0-8167-1884-9)* Troll Assocs.
—Evelyn Cisneros: Prima Ballerina. LC 90-40104. (Illus.). 32p. (gr. 2-4). 1990. PLB 14.60 *(0-516-04276-9);* pap. 3.95 *(0-516-44276-7)* Childrens.
—Explorers of the Ancient World. LC 89-25431. (Illus.). 128p. (gr. 3 up). 1990. PLB 26.60 *(0-516-03053-1)* Childrens.
—Franklin Pierce. LC 88-10883. (Illus.). 100p. (gr. 3 up). 1988. PLB 17.27 *(0-516-01357-2)* Childrens.
—Henry the Navigator: Master Teacher of Explorers. LC 92-37048. (Illus.). 128p. (gr. 3 up). 1993. PLB 26.60 *(0-516-03071-X)* Childrens.
—Leif Eriksson & the Vikings: The Norse Discovery of America. LC 90-20804. (Illus.). 128p. (gr. 3 up). 1991. PLB 26.60 *(0-516-03060-4)* Childrens.
—Little Angel. 1989. 2.95 *(0-8167-1883-0)* Troll Assocs.
—Midori: Brilliant Violinist. LC 92-40674. (Illus.). 32p. (gr. 2-4). 1993. PLB 15.27 *(0-516-04187-8)* Childrens.
—Richard Burton: Explorer of Arabia & Africa. LC 90-20814. (Illus.). 128p. (gr. 3 up). 1991. PLB 26.60 *(0-516-03062-0)* Childrens.
—Santa's Helper. 10p. 1989. bds. 2.95 *(0-8167-1885-7)* Troll Assocs.
—Seiji Ozawa: Symphony Conductor. LC 91-36741. (Illus.). 32p. (gr. 2-5). 1992. PLB 14.60 *(0-516-04182-7);* 3.95 *(0-516-44182-5)* Childrens.
—Snow for Christmas. 1989. bds. 2.95 *(0-8167-1882-2)* Troll Assocs.
—The Story of the Haymarket Riot. LC 88-22803. (Illus.). 32p. (gr. 3-6). 1988. PLB 13.27 *(0-516-04740-X);* pap. 3.95 *(0-516-44740-8)* Childrens.
—Wilma P. Mankiller: Chief of the Cherokee. LC 91-4334. 32p. (gr. 2-4). 1991. PLB 14.60 *(0-516-04181-9);* pap. 3.95 *(0-516-44181-7)* Childrens.
Simon, Dominique, jt. auth. see Simon, Serge.
Simon, Hilda. The Magic of Color. Simon, Hilda, illus. LC 81-5044. 56p. (gr. 3 up). 1981. 12.95 *(0-688-00619-1)* Lothrop.
Simon, Jo A. Star. Helmer, Jean, illus. LC 88-38292. 64p. (Orig.). (gr. 2-4). 1989. PLB 6.99 *(0-394-92933-0);* pap. 1.95 *(0-394-82933-6)* Random Bks Yng Read.
Simon, Martin P., jt. auth. see Jahsmann, Allan H.
Simon, Mary M. Come to Jesus: Jesus Blesses the Children. Jones, Dennis, illus. 24p. (Orig.). (ps-1). 1992. pap. 2.39 *(0-570-04707-2)* Concordia.

—Daniel & the Tattletales: Daniel 6: Daniel in the Lions' Den. Jones, Dennis, illus. LC 92-31887. 32p. (Orig.). (gr. 1-3). 1993. pap. 3.99 *(0-570-04733-1)* Concordia.
—The First Christmas: Luke 2: 1-20: The Birth of Jesus. Jones, Dennis, illus. LC 92-21372. 32p. (Orig.). (gr. 1-3). 1993. pap. 3.99 *(0-570-04741-2)* Concordia.
—Follow That Star. Jones, Dennis, illus. 24p. (ps-1). 1990. pap. 2.39 *(0-570-04177-5)* Concordia.
—God's Children Pray. 1989. 5.99 *(0-570-04173-2,* 56-1633) Concordia.
—The Hide-&-Seek Prince: Second Kings 11-12: 16: Joash. Jones, Dennis, illus. LC 93-35606. 1994. write for info. *(0-570-04740-4)* Concordia.
—Hide the Baby: The Birth of Moses. Jones, Dennis, illus. 24p. (Orig.). (ps-1). 1991. pap. 2.39 *(0-570-04702-1)* Concordia.
—Hurray for the Lord's Army! Judges 6: 11 - 7: 22 (Gideon) Jones, Dennis, illus. LC 93-35604. 1994. write for info. *(0-570-04739-0)* Concordia.
—Jibber-Jabber: The Tower of Babel. Jones, Dennis, illus. 24p. (Orig.). (ps-1). 1992. pap. 2.39 *(0-570-04705-6)* Concordia.
—Little Visits on the Go. (Illus.). (ps-7). 1992. wire coated o's bdg., incl. cass. 13.99 *(0-570-03084-6)* Concordia.
—Little Visits with Jesus. (Illus.). 256p. (ps-3). 1987. 12. 99 *(0-570-03076-5,* 6-1191); pap. 9.99 *(0-570-03075-7,* 06-1190) Concordia.
—More Little Visits with Jesus. (Illus.). 304p. (ps-2). 1989. 12.99 *(0-570-03080-3,* 06-1195); pap. 9.99 *(0-570-03079-X,* 06-1194) Concordia.
—My First Diary. Dorenkamp, Michelle, illus. 80p. (Orig.). (gr. 2-5). 1992. pap. 4.99 *(0-570-04721-8)* Concordia.
—The No-Go King: Exodus 5-15: The Exodus. Jones, Dennis, illus. LC 92-31888. 32p. (Orig.). (gr. 1-3). 1993. pap. 3.99 *(0-570-04732-3)* Concordia.
—Row the Boat. Jones, Dennis, illus. 24p. (ps-1). 1990. pap. 2.39 *(0-570-04186-4,* 56-1645) Concordia.
—Send a Baby: Birth of John the Baptist. Jones, Dennis, illus. 24p. (Orig.). (ps-1). 1992. pap. 2.39 *(0-570-04706-4)* Concordia.
—A Silent Night: Hear Me Read Bible Stories Ser. (Illus.). 24p. (ps-1). 1991. pap. 2.39 *(0-570-04700-5,* 56-1659) Concordia.
—Sit Down! Mary & Martha. Jones, Dennis, illus. 24p. (Orig.). (ps-1). 1991. pap. 2.39 *(0-570-04701-3)* Concordia.
—Thank you, Jesus: Luke 17: 11-19; Jesus Heals Ten Men with Leprosy. Jones, Dennis, illus. LC 93-36192. 1994. write for info. *(0-570-04762-5)* Concordia.
—Through the Roof. Jones, Dennis, illus. LC 93-36193. 1994. write for info. *(0-570-04734-X)* Concordia.
—Too Tall, Too Small. Jones, Dennis, illus. 24p. (ps-1). 1990. pap. 2.39 *(0-570-04185-6)* Concordia.
—Toot! Toot! Jones, Dennis, illus. 24p. (ps-1). 1990. pap. 2.39 *(0-570-04184-8)* Concordia.
—A Walk on the Waves: Matthew 14: 13-32: Jesus Walks on the Water. Jones, Dennis, illus. LC 92-21374. 32p. (Orig.). (gr. 1-3). 1993. pap. 3.99 *(0-570-04735-8)* Concordia.
—Where Is Jesus? Easter. Jones, Dennis, illus. 24p. (Orig.). (ps-1). 1991. pap. 2.39 *(0-570-04703-X)* Concordia.
—Whoops! Jonah. Jones, Dennis, illus. 24p. (Orig.). (ps-1). 1992. pap. 2.39 *(0-570-04704-8)* Concordia.
Simon, Neil. Brighton Beach Memoirs. (Illus.). 144p. (gr. 9-12). 1986. pap. 4.99 *(0-451-16344-3,* Sig) NAL-Dutton.
—Broadway Bound. 132p. (gr. 9-12). 1988. pap. 8.00 *(0-452-26148-1,* Plume) NAL-Dutton.
Simon, Nissa. Don't Worry, You're Normal. LC 81-43324. 192p. (gr. 7 up). 1982. 10.10 *(0-690-04138-1,* Crowell Jr Bks); (Crowell Jr Bks) HarpC Child Bks.
—Good Sports: Plain Talk about Health & Fitness for Teens. Tobin, Patricia, illus. LC 89-78556. 128p. (gr. 7 up). 1990. 13.95 *(0-690-04902-1,* Crowell Jr Bks); PLB 13.89 *(0-690-04904-8,* Crowell Jr Bks) HarpC Child Bks.
Simon, Noel, tr. see Buholzer, Theres.
Simon, Noel, tr. see Fischer-Nagel, Heiderose & Fischer-Nagel, Andreas.
Simon, Norma. All Kinds of Families. Rubin, Caroline, ed. Lasker, Joe, illus. LC 75-42283. 40p. (gr. k-2). 1976. PLB 13.95 *(0-8075-0282-0)* A Whitman.
—Cats Do, Dogs Don't. Levine, Abby, ed. LC 86-5618. (Illus.). 32p. (ps-2). 1986. 13.95 *(0-8075-1102-1)* A Whitman.
—Children Do, Grownups Don't. Tucker, Kathleen, ed. Cogancherry, Helen, illus. LC 87-2205. (ps-3). 1987. PLB 13.95 *(0-8075-1144-7)* A Whitman.
—Every Friday Night. Weiss, Harvey, illus. (ps-k). plastic cover 4.50 *(0-8381-0708-7)* United Syn Bk.
—Fire Fighters. Paparone, Pam, illus. LC 93-4439. 1994. pap. 14.00 *(0-671-87282-6)* S&S Trade.
—Hanukah in My House. Gordon, Ayala, illus. (ps-k). 1960. plastic cover 4.50 *(0-8381-0705-2)* United Syn Bk.
—Happy Purim Night. Gordon, Ayala, illus. (ps-k). plastic cover 4.50 *(0-8381-0706-0,* 10-706) United Syn Bk.
—How Do I Feel? Lasker, Joe, illus. LC 77-126430. (ps-2). 1970. PLB 13.95 *(0-8075-3414-5)* A Whitman.
—I Am Not a Crybaby! Tucker, Kathleen, ed. Cogancherry, Helen, illus. LC 88-21698. 40p. (gr. k-4). 1989. 13.95 *(0-8075-3447-1)* A Whitman.

—I Am Not a Crybaby. Cogancherry, Helen, illus. 32p. (ps-3). 1991. pap. 3.95 *(0-14-054216-7,* Puffin) Puffin Bks.
—I Know What I Like. Leder, Dora, illus. LC 76-165822. (ps-2). 1971. PLB 11.95 *(0-8075-3507-9)* A Whitman.
—I Was So Mad! LC 73-22425. (Illus.). 40p. (gr. k-2). 1974. PLB 11.95 *(0-8075-3520-6);* pap. 4.95 *(0-8075-3519-2)* A Whitman.
—I Wish I Had My Father. Tucker, Kathleen, ed. LC 83-1287. (Illus.). 32p. (gr. 1-4). 1983. PLB 11.95 *(0-8075-3522-2)* A Whitman.
—I'm Busy, Too. Tucker, Kathleen, ed. Leder, Dora, illus. LC 79-18374. (ps-1). 1980. PLB 11.95 *(0-8075-3464-1)* A Whitman.
—Mama Cat's Year. Tucker, Kathleen, ed. Leder, Dora, illus. LC 90-26825. 32p. (ps-3). 1991. 14.95 *(0-8075-4958-4)* A Whitman.
—My Family Seder. Weiss, Harvey, illus. (ps-k). 1961. plastic cover 4.50 *(0-8381-0710-9,* 10-710) United Syn Bk.
—Nobody's Perfect, Not Even My Mother. Tucker, Kathleen, ed. Leder, Dora, illus. LC 81-520. 32p. (gr. k-3). 1981. PLB 11.95 *(0-8075-5707-2)* A Whitman.
—Oh, That Cat! Leder, Dora, illus. LC 85-15546. 32p. (ps-4). 1986. 11.95 *(0-8075-5919-9)* A Whitman.
—Our First Sukkah. Gordon, Ayala, illus. (ps-k). 1959. plastic cover 4.50 *(0-8381-0703-6)* United Syn Bk.
—Purim Party. Gordon, Ayala, illus. (ps-k). 1959. plastic cover 4.50 *(0-8381-0707-9)* United Syn Bk.
—Rosh Hashanah. Gordon, Ayala, illus. (ps-k). 1961. plastic cover 4.50 *(0-8381-0700-1)* United Syn Bk.
—The Saddest Time. (Illus.). 40p. (gr. 1-4). 1986. 11.95 *(0-8075-7203-9);* pap. 4.95 *(0-8075-7204-7)* A Whitman.
—Simhat Torah. Gordon, Ayala, illus. (ps-k). 1960. bds. 4.50 lam. *(0-8381-0704-4)* United Syn Bk.
—Tu Bishvat. Weiss, Harvey, illus. (ps-k). 1961. plastic cover 4.50 *(0-8381-0709-5)* United Syn Bk.
—Wedding Days. Tucker, Kathleen, ed. (Illus.). 32p. (ps-4). 1988. PLB 13.95 *(0-8075-8703-6)* A Whitman.
—What Do I Do: English - Spanish Edition. Lasker, Joe, illus. LC 74-79544. 40p. (ps-2). 1969. PLB 13.95 *(0-8075-8823-7)* A Whitman.
—What Do I Say. Lasker, Joe, illus. LC 67-17420. (ENG & SPA.). (ps-2). 1967. 13.95 *(0-8075-8828-8);* PLB 13. 95 *(0-8075-8826-1)* A Whitman.
—Why Am I Different? Rubin, Caroline, ed. Leder, Dora, illus. LC 76-41172. 32p. (gr. k-2). 1976. PLB 11.95 *(0-8075-9074-6)* A Whitman.
—Why Am I Different? (ps-3). 1993. pap. 4.95 *(0-8075-9076-2)* A Whitman.
—Yom Kippur. Gordon, Ayala, illus. (ps-k). 1959. plastic cover 4.50 *(0-8381-0702-8)* United Syn Bk.
Simon, Paul. At the Zoo. (ps up). 1991. 15.00 *(0-385-41771-3);* PLB 15.99 *(0-385-41906-6)* Doubleday.
Simon, Serge & Simon, Dominique. The Deer. (Illus.). 28p. (ps-4). 1993. pap. 6.95 *(0-88106-429-7)* Charlesbridge Pub.
Simon, Seymour. Animal Fact - Animal Fable. reissued ed. De Groat, Diane, illus. LC 78-14866. 48p. (gr. 1-5). 1992. PLB 12.99 *(0-517-58846-3)* Crown Bks Yng Read.
—Animal Fact: Animal Fable. De Groat, Diane, illus. LC 78-14866. (gr. k-3). 1986. pap. 7.00 *(0-517-53794-X)* Crown Bks Yng Read.
—Autumn Across America. Simon, Seymour, illus. LC 92-55043. 32p. (gr. 1-5). 1993. 14.95 *(1-56282-467-8);* PLB 14.89 *(1-56282-468-6)* Hyprn Child.
—The BASIC Book. Emberley, Barbara & Emberley, Ed E., illus. LC 85-42736. 32p. (gr. k-4). 1985. pap. 4.50 *(0-06-445015-5,* Trophy) HarpC Child Bks.
—Big Cats. Simon, Seymour, illus. LC 90-36374. 40p. (gr. k-3). 1991. 17.00 *(0-06-021646-8);* PLB 16.89 *(0-06-021647-6)* HarpC Child Bks.
—Big Cats. LC 90-36374. 40p. (gr. k-3). Date not set. pap. 5.95 *(0-06-446119-X,* Trophy) HarpC Child Bks.
—Deserts. LC 89-39738. (Illus.). 32p. (gr. k up). 1990. 13.95 *(0-688-07415-4);* PLB 13.88 *(0-688-07416-2,* Morrow Jr Bks) Morrow Jr Bks.
—The Dinosaur Is the Biggest Animal That Ever Lived & Other Wrong Ideas You Thought Were True. Maestro, Giulio, illus. LC 83-48960. 64p. (gr. 2-5). 1984. (Lipp Jr Bks); PLB 12.89 *(0-397-32076-0,* Lipp Jr Bks) HarpC Child Bks.
—The Dinosaur Is the Biggest Animal That Ever Lived, & Other Wrong Ideas You Thought Were True. Maestro, Giulio, illus. LC 83-48960. 64p. (gr. 2-5). 1986. pap. 4.95 *(0-06-446053-3,* Trophy) HarpC Child Bks.
—Earth: Our Planet in Space. LC 84-28754. (Illus.). 32p. (gr. k-3). 1984. RSBE 14.95 *(0-02-782830-1,* Four Winds) Macmillan Child Grp.
—Earth Words: A Dictionary of Ecology & Pollution. Kaplan, Mark, illus. LC 92-34005. 48p. (gr. 2-5). 1994. 15.00 *(0-06-020233-5);* PLB 14.89 *(0-06-020234-3)* HarpC Child Bks.
—Earthquakes. LC 90-19328. (Illus.). 32p. (gr. k up). 1991. 14.95 *(0-688-09633-6);* PLB 14.88 *(0-688-09634-4)* Morrow Jr Bks.
—Einstein Anderson Goes to Bat. Winkowski, Fred, illus. (gr. 3-7). 1987. pap. 3.99 *(0-14-032303-1,* Puffin) Puffin Bks.
—Einstein Anderson Lights up the Sky. Winkowski, Fred, illus. (gr. 3-7). pap. 3.95 *(0-317-62300-1,* Puffin) Puffin Bks.

—Einstein Anderson Makes Up for Lost Time. Winkowski, Fred, illus. 80p. (gr. 3-7). 1986. pap. 3.95 (0-14-032100-4, Puffin) Puffin Bks.
—Einstein Anderson, Science Sleuth. Winkowski, Fred, illus. 80p. (gr. 3-7). 1986. pap. 3.99 (0-14-032098-9, Puffin) Puffin Bks.
—Einstein Anderson Sees Through the Invisible Man. Winkowski, Fred, illus. (gr. 3-7). 1987. pap. 3.95 (0-14-032306-6, Puffin) Puffin Bks.
—Einstein Anderson Shocks His Friends. Winkowski, Fred, illus. 80p. (gr. 3-7). 1986. pap. 3.95 (0-14-032099-7, Puffin) Puffin Bks.
—Einstein Anderson Tells a Comet's Tale. Winkowski, Fred, illus. (gr. 3-7). 1987. pap. 3.95 (0-14-032302-3, Puffin) Puffin Bks.
—Galaxies. LC 87-23967. (Illus.). 32p. (ps-3). 1988. 14.95 (0-688-08002-2); PLB 14.88 (0-688-08004-9, Morrow Jr Bks) Morrow Jr Bks.
—Galaxies. LC 87-23967. (Illus.). 32p. (ps-3). 1991. pap. 5.95 (0-688-10992-6, Mulberry) Morrow.
—Hidden Worlds: Pictures of the Invisible. LC 83-5407. (Illus.). 48p. (gr. 3up). 1983. 13.95 (0-688-02464-5); lib. bdg. 13.88 (0-688-02465-3, Morrow Jr Bks) Morrow Jr Bks.
—How to Be a Space Scientist in Your Own Home. Morrison, Bill, illus. LC 81-47759. (gr. 4-7). 1982. (Lipp Jr Bks); (Lipp Jr Bks) HarpC Child Bks.
—How to Be an Ocean Scientist in Your Own Home. Carter, David A., illus. LC 87-45988. 144p. (gr. 5-9). 1988. (Lipp Jr Bks); PLB 13.89 (0-397-32292-5, Lipp Jr Bks) HarpC Child Bks.
—Icebergs & Glaciers. LC 86-18142. (Illus.). 32p. (ps-3). 1987. 14.95 (0-688-06186-9); lib. bdg. 14.88 (0-688-06187-7, Morrow Jr Bks) Morrow Jr Bks.
—The Largest Dinosaurs. Carroll, Pamela, illus. LC 85-24088. 32p. (gr. k-3). 1986. RSBE 13.95 (0-02-782910-3, Macmillan Child Bk) Macmillan Child Grp.
—Little Giants. Carroll, Pamela, illus. LC 82-14139. 48p. (gr. k-5). 1983. PLB 14.88 (0-688-01731-2) Morrow Jr Bks.
—The Long View into Space. LC 78-11388. (Illus.). (gr. 2-4). 1987. 13.95 (0-517-53659-5) Crown Bks Yng Read.
—Look to the Night Sky: An Introduction to Star Watching. (Illus.). (gr. 5-12). 1979. pap. 6.99 (0-14-049185-6, Puffin) Puffin Bks.
—Mars. LC 86-31106. (Illus.). 32p. (ps-3). 1987. 13.00 (0-688-06584-8); lib. bdg. 12.88 (0-688-06585-6, Morrow Jr Bks) Morrow Jr Bks.
—Mars. LC 86-31106. (Illus.). 32p. (ps-2). 1990. pap. 5.95 (0-688-09928-9, Mulberry) Morrow.
—Mercury. LC 91-17404. (Illus.). 24p. (gr. k up). 1992. 14.00 (0-688-10544-0); PLB 13.93 (0-688-10545-9) Morrow Jr Bks.
—Mirror Magic. Matsick, Anni, illus. LC 90-85921. 32p. (gr. 2-5). 1991. Repr. 9.95 (1-878093-07-X) Boyds Mills Pr.
—The Moon. LC 84-28753. (Illus.). 32p. (gr. k-3). 1984. RSBE 14.95 (0-02-782840-9, Four Winds) Macmillan Child Grp.
—Mountains. LC 93-11398. (gr. 6 up). 1994. write for info. (0-688-11040-1); PLB write for info. (0-688-11041-X) Morrow.
—Neptune. LC 90-13213. (Illus.). 32p. (gr. k up). 1991. 13.95 (0-688-09631-X); PLB 13.88 (0-688-09632-8, Morrow Jr Bks) Morrow Jr Bks.
—New Questions & Answers about Dinosaurs. Dewey, Jennifer, illus. LC 88-36226. 48p. (gr. k up). 1990. 13.95 (0-688-08195-9); PLB 13.88 (0-688-08196-7, Morrow Jr Bks) Morrow Jr Bks.
—New Questions & Answers about Dinosaurs. Dewey, Jennifer, illus. LC 92-25546. 48p. (gr. 2 up). 1993. pap. 4.95 (0-688-12271-X, Mulberry) Morrow.
—Oceans. LC 89-28452. (Illus.). 32p. (gr. k up). 1990. 13.95 (0-688-09453-8); PLB 13.88 (0-688-09454-6, Morrow Jr Bks) Morrow Jr Bks.
—One Hundred & One Questions & Answers about Dangerous Animals. Friedman, Ellen, illus. LC 84-42975. 96p. (gr. 3-7). 1985. SBE 14.95 (0-02-782710-0, Macmillan Child Bk) Macmillan Child Grp.
—Our Solar System. LC 91-36665. (Illus.). 72p. (gr. k). 1992. 20.00 (0-688-09992-0); PLB 19.93 (0-688-09993-9) Morrow Jr Bks.
—The Paper Airplane Book. (gr. 4-6). 1976. pap. 3.99 (0-14-030925-X, Puffin) Puffin Bks.
—The Paper Airplane Book. Byron, Barton, illus. (gr. 4-6). 1971. pap. 12.95 (0-670-53797-7) Viking Child Bks.
—Pets in a Jar: Collecting & Caring for Small Animals. Fraser, Betty, illus. (gr. 4-7). 1979. pap. 5.99 (0-14-049186-4, Puffin) Puffin Bks.
—Poisonous Snakes. Downey, William R., illus. LC 85-24202. 80p. (gr. 3-7). 1984. SBE 14.95 (0-02-782850-6, Four Winds) Macmillan Child Grp.
—Professor I. Q. Explores the Brain. 48p. (gr. 4-7). 1993. 13.95 (1-878093-27-4) Boyds Mills Pr.
—Professor I. Q. Explores the Senses. 48p. (gr. 4-7). 1993. 13.95 (1-878093-28-2) Boyds Mills Pr.
—Shadow Magic. Ormai, Stella, illus. LC 84-4433. 48p. (ps-3). 1985. PLB 13.88 (0-688-02682-6) Lothrop.
—The Smallest Dinosaurs. Rao, Anthony, illus. (gr. k-3). 1988. 4.95 (0-517-56550-1) Crown Bks Yng Read.
—Snakes. Simon, Seymour, illus. LC 91-15948. 32p. (gr. k-3). 1992. 16.00 (0-06-022529-7); PLB 15.89 (0-06-022530-0) HarpC Child Bks.

—Soap Bubble Magic. Ormai, Stella, illus. LC 84-4432. 48p. (ps-3). 1985. PLB 13.88 (0-688-02685-0) Lothrop.
—Space Words: A Dictionary. Chewning, Randy, illus. LC 90-37402. 48p. (gr. 2-5). 1991. 15.00 (0-06-022532-7); PLB 14.89 (0-06-022533-5) HarpC Child Bks.
—Storms. LC 88-22045. (Illus.). 32p. (gr. k-3). 1989. 12.95 (0-688-07413-8); PLB 12.88 (0-688-07414-6, Morrow Jr Bks) Morrow Jr Bks.
—Storms. ALC Staff, ed. LC 88-22045. (Illus.). 32p. (gr. 1 up). 1992. pap. 4.95 (0-688-11708-2, Mulberry) Morrow.
—Turtle Talk: A Beginner's Book of Logo. Emberley, Barbara & Emberley, Ed E., illus. LC 85-47890. 32p. (gr. 1-4). 1986. (Crowell Jr Bks); PLB 13.89 (0-690-04522-0, Crowell Jr Bks) HarpC Child Bks.
—Turtle Talk: A Beginner's Book of Logo. Emberley, Barbara & Emberley, Ed E., illus. LC 85-47890. 32p. (gr. 1-4). 1986. pap. 4.50 (0-06-445051-1, Trophy) HarpC Child Bks.
—Uranus. LC 86-31223. (Illus.). 32p. (ps-3). 1987. 13.00 (0-688-06582-1); lib. bdg. 12.88 (0-688-06583-X, Morrow Jr Bks) Morrow Jr Bks.
—Uranus. LC 86-31223. (Illus.). 32p. (ps-2). 1990. pap. 5.95 (0-688-09929-7, Mulberry) Morrow.
—Venus. LC 91-12171. (Illus.). 32p. (gr. k up). 1992. 15.00 (0-688-10542-4); PLB 14.93 (0-688-10543-2) Morrow Jr Bks.
—Volcanoes. LC 87-33316. (Illus.). 32p. (gr. k-3). 1988. 12.95 (0-688-07411-1); PLB 12.88 (0-688-07412-X, Morrow Jr Bks) Morrow Jr Bks.
—Weather. LC 92-31069. (Illus.). 40p. (gr. k up). 1993. 15.00 (0-688-10546-7); PLB 14.93 (0-688-10547-5) Morrow Jr Bks.
—Weather & Climate. (gr. 4-6). 1969. lib. bdg. 4.99 (0-394-90804-X) Random Bks Yng Read.
—Whales. LC 87-45285. (Illus.). 40p. (gr. k-3). 1989. 17.00 (0-690-04756-8, Crowell Jr Bks); PLB 16.89 (0-690-04758-4, Crowell Jr Bks) HarpC Child Bks.
—Whales. LC 87-45285. (Illus.). 40p. (gr. k-3). 1992. pap. 5.95 (0-06-446095-9, Trophy) HarpC Child Bks.
—Wolves. Simon, Seymour, illus. LC 92-25924. 32p. (gr. k-3). 1993. 16.00 (0-06-022531-9); PLB 15.89 (0-06-022534-3) HarpC Child Bks.
Simon, Sheridan. Stephen Hawking: Unlocking the Universe. (Illus.). 112p. (gr. 5 up). 1991. 13.95 (0-87518-455-3, Dillon) Macmillan Child Grp.
Simon, Shirley. Benny's Baby Brother. Gregorich, Barbara, ed. (Illus.). 16p. (Orig.). (gr. k-2). 1985. pap. 2.25 (0-88743-016-3, 06016) Sch Zone Pub Co.
—Foolish Goose. Gregorich, Barbara, ed. (Illus.). 16p. (Orig.). (gr. k-2). 1985. pap. 2.25 (0-88743-015-5, 06015) Sch Zone Pub Co.
—Foolish Goose. Gregorich, Barbara, ed. (Illus.). 32p. (gr. k-2). 1992. pap. 3.95 (0-88743-413-4, 06065) Sch Zone Pub Co.
—Get Lost, Becka! Gregorich, Barbara, ed. (Illus.). 16p. (Orig.). (gr. k-2). 1985. pap. 2.25 (0-88743-013-9, 06013) Sch Zone Pub Co.
—Get Lost, Becka! Gregorich, Barbara, ed. (Illus.). 32p. (gr. k-2). 1992. pap. 3.95 (0-88743-411-8, 06063) Sch Zone Pub Co.
Simon, Solomon. Adventures of Simple Shmerel. Fischel, Lillian, illus. (gr. 3-7). 1942. 4.95 (0-87441-127-0) Behrman.
—Wise Men of Helm. (gr. 3-7). 1942. pap. 6.50 (0-87441-125-4) Behrman.
Simon, Solomon & Bial, Morrison D. The Rabbis' Bible, Vol. 1: Torah, 2 pts. (gr. 5-6). 6.95 (0-317-70149-5); tchr's guide 12.50 (0-317-70150-9); tchr's resource bk. 14.95 (0-317-70151-7); student activity bk. 3.50 (0-317-70152-5) Behrman.
—The Rabbis' Bible, Vol. 2: Early Prophets. (gr. 6-7). 6.95 (0-317-70153-3); tchr's guide 12.50 (0-317-70154-1); tchr's resource bk. 14.95 (0-317-70155-X) Behrman.
Simon, Solomon & Rothberg, Abraham. The Rabbis' Bible, Vol. 3: Later Prophets. (gr. 7-8). 6.95 (0-317-70159-2); tchr's guide 12.50 (0-317-70160-6); tchr's resource bk. 14.95 (0-317-70161-4) Behrman.
Simonds, Christopher. The Model T Ford. (Illus.). 64p. (gr. 5 up). 1991. PLB 16.98 (0-382-24122-3); pap. 8.95 (0-382-24117-7) Silver Burdett Pr.
—Samuel Slater's Mill & the Industrial Revolution. (Illus.). 64p. (gr. 5 up). 1990. PLB 16.98 (0-382-09951-6); pap. 8.95 (0-382-09947-8) Silver Burdett Pr.
Simonelic, Ken. Effy & the Little Glass Soldier. LC 91-16066. (Orig.). (gr. 5-9). 1991. pap. 3.00 (0-915541-83-1) Star Bks Inc.
Simonelli, Susan B. Rose Kennedy. (Illus.). 112p. (gr. 5 up). 1992. lib. bdg. 17.95 (0-7910-1622-6) Chelsea Hse.
Simons, Donald L. I Refuse: Memories of a Vietnam War Objector. List, David, intro. by. LC 91-70992. 184p. (Orig.). (gr. 12 up). 1992. 27.50 (0-9620024-2-9); pap. 13.95 (0-9620024-3-7) Broken Rifle Pr.
Simons, Evelyn, jt. auth. see Simons, Scott.
Simons, Frank D. You Don't Cry for Heroes. Ferrell, Robert, intro. by. 197p. (Orig.). (gr. 12 up). 1989. pap. 7.95 (0-685-26939-6) CFFC POWs MIAs.
Simons, Jamie & Simons, Scott. Why Dolphins Call: A Story of Dionysus. (gr. 3). 1991. write for info. (0-663-56230-9) Silver Burdett Pr.
Simons, Jamie, jt. auth. see Simons, Scott.

Simons, John & Ward, Kay. Noah & His Great Ark. Ward, Kay, ed. (Illus.). 16p. (Orig.). (gr. 3-7). 1987. pap. text ed. 2.50 (0-937039-00-4) Sun Pr FL.
Simons, Scott & Simons, Evelyn. Opening a Can of Words. 1994. pap. 3.50 (0-8125-2948-0) Tor Bks.
—Opening a Can of Words. 1994. pap. 3.50 Tor Bks.
Simons, Scott & Simons, Jamie. The Gods of Olympus Series, 4 vols. Winograd, Deborah, illus. (gr. 2-5). 1992. Set, 32p. ea. incl. jacket 51.80 (0-671-31229-4); Set, 32p. ea. lib. bdg. 59.92 (0-671-31228-6) Silver Pr.
—Why Dolphins Call: A Story of Dionysus. Winograd, Deborah, illus. 32p. (gr. 2-5). 1992. 13.95 (0-671-69125-2); PLB 14.98 (0-671-69121-X) Silver Pr.
—Why Seashells Sing. Winograd, Deborah, illus. 32p. (gr. 2-5). 1992. incl. jacket 13.95 (0-382-69122-9); PLB 14.98 (0-382-69118-0) Silver.
—Why Spiders Spin: A Story of Arachne. Winograd, Deborah, illus. 32p. (gr. 2-5). 1992. 13.95 (0-671-69124-4); PLB 14.98 (0-671-69120-1) Silver Pr.
—Why Winter Comes. Wingrad, Deborah, illus. 32p. (gr. 2-5). 1992. incl. jacket 13.95 (0-671-69123-6); lib. bdg. 14.98 (0-671-69119-8) Silver Pr.
Simons, Scott, jt. auth. see Simons, Jamie.
Simons-Ailes, Sandra. Roundup. (Illus.). 34p. (Orig.). (ps-7). 1981. pap. 3.75 (0-915347-04-0) Pueblo Acoma Pr.
Simons-Ailes, Sandra, illus. Mrs. Ortiz Makes Fry Bread. 30p. (Orig.). (ps-7). 1979. pap. 3.00 (0-915347-06-7) Pueblo Acoma Pr.
Simont, Marc. The Lovely Summer. 1992. pap. 15.00 (0-553-07716-3, Little Rooster) Bantam.
Simont, Marc, tr. see Sales, Francesc.
Simpkins, Mark A. Rames Two. (gr. 4-7). 1986. pap. 5.95 (0-916095-10-X) Pubs Pr UT.
Simpson. Gretchens 123. Date not set. 16.00 (0-06-024305-8, Festival); PLB 15.89 (0-06-024306-6, Festival) HarpC Child Bks.
Simpson, Amos, jt. auth. see Cassidy, Vincent.
Simpson, Andrew L. The Library of Congress. (Illus.). 112p. (gr. 5 up). 1989. 14.95 (1-55546-109-3) Chelsea Hse.
Simpson, Ann M., jt. auth. see Meister, Teddy.
Simpson, Anne. How to Draw Wild Animals. Botto, Lisa C., illus. LC 91-26928. 32p. (gr. 2-6). 1991. text ed. 10.65 (0-8167-2481-4); pap. text ed. 1.95 (0-8167-2482-2) Troll Assocs.
—My Secret Diary. LC 92-20177. (Illus.). 64p. (gr. 4-6). 1992. pap. 2.95 (0-8167-2941-7) Troll Assocs.
Simpson, Anne, ed. see Sewell, Anna.
Simpson, Bert & Simpson, Bonnie. Shake My Sillies Out. Allender, David, illus. 32p. (ps-2). 1988. PLB 11.00 (0-517-56646-X) Crown Bks Yng Read.
Simpson, Bonnie, jt. auth. see Simpson, Bert.
Simpson, Carol. Daily Journals. (Illus.). 120p. (Orig.). (gr. k-3). 1993. pap. 9.95 (0-673-36062-8) GdYrBks.
Simpson, Carolyn. Coping with An Unplanned Pregnancy. rev. ed. Rosen, Ruth, ed. (gr. 7-12). 1993. PLB 13.95 (0-8239-1145-4) Rosen Group.
—Coping with Teenage Motherhood. Rosen, Ruth, ed. LC 92-8168. (gr. 7-12). 1992. 13.95 (0-8239-1458-5) Rosen Group.
Simpson, Carolyn & Simpson, Dwain. Exploring Careers in Social Work. rev. ed. Rosen, Ruth, ed. (gr. 7-12). 1993. PLB 13.95 (0-8239-1407-0); pap. 9.95 (0-8239-1817-3) Rosen Group.
Simpson, Catherine. My Little Book of Nursery Rhymes. Simpson, Catherine, illus. 32p. 1992. 5.95 (0-87226-502-1, Bedrick Blackie) P Bedrick Bks.
Simpson, Claude, ed. see Dreiser, Theodore.
Simpson, Dorothy. Island in the Bay. 16mo. (Orig.). (gr. 7-12). 1993. 9.95 (0-942396-62-6) Blackberry ME.
Simpson, Dwain, jt. auth. see Simpson, Carolyn.
Simpson, Gretchen D. Gretchen's Abc. Simpson, Gretchen D., illus. LC 90-19332. 32p. (ps up). 1991. 16.95 (0-06-025645-1); PLB 16.89 (0-06-025646-X) HarpC Child Bks.
Simpson, Holly. One Step Away. (gr. 6 up). 1989. pap. 2.95 (0-449-14593-X) Fawcett.
Simpson, Juwairah J. The Four Daughters of Yusuf the Dairy Farmer. Middendorf, Nancy, illus. 40p. (Orig.). (gr. 1-4). 1894. pap. 3.75 (0-89259-056-4) Am Trust Pubns.
—A Wicked Wazir. Sakkal, Ma'moun, illus. 48p. (Orig.). (gr. 3-6). 1990. pap. 6.50 (0-89259-084-X) Am Trust Pubns.
Simpson, Juwairiah J. L. The Princess Who Wanted to Be Poor. American Trust Publications, ed. (Illus.). 52p. 1987. pap. 4.75 (0-89259-104-8) Am Trust Pubns.
Simpson, Lesley. The Hug. Simpson, Lesley, illus. 24p. (ps-1). 1987. pap. 0.99 (0-920303-23-4, Pub. by Annick CN) Firefly Bks Ltd.
Simpson, Lesley B. Many Mexicos. 4th, rev. ed. (gr. 9 up). 1966. 45.00x (0-520-01179-1); pap. 15.00 (0-520-01180-5) U CA Pr.
Simpson, Lesley B., tr. The Poem of the Cid. (gr. 9 up). 1957. pap. 9.00x (0-520-01176-7) U CA Pr.
Simpson, Louis. Wei Wei & Other Friends. White, Robert, illus. 24p. 1990. pap. 25.00x (0-930126-30-0) Typographeum.
Simpson, Winifred R. Hello, World, You're Mine? (Illus.). (gr. 4-7). 1987. pap. 3.99 (0-570-03643-7, 39-1127) Concordia.
—I Can Help Mommy. (Illus.). (ps). 1987. pap. 2.50 (0-570-09112-8, 56-1587) Concordia.

Sims, Alicia M. Am I Still a Sister? 3th ed. Maus, Jim, illus. Sims, Darcie D., intro. by. LC 87-71613. (Illus.). 48p. (gr. k-9). 1993. pap. 5.00 (*0-9618995-0-6*) Big A NM.

Sims, Blanche, jt. auth. see Giff, Patricia R.

Sims, Claudette E. The Rainbow People. Williams, Mauri, illus. (Orig.). (ps-5). 1992. pap. 6.95x (*0-9616121-1-8*) Impressions TX.

Sims, Donald. Union Pacific's West. LC 91-2894. (Illus.). (gr. 11). 1991. 42.95 (*0-87046-098-6*) Interurban.

Sims, J. Puppets for Dreaming & Scheming. (gr. 1-6). 1988. 15.95 (*0-88160-167-5*, LW 277) Learning Wks.

Sims, Larry K. Little Spotted Moo. Antolik, Jerry, illus. 24p. (Orig.). 1991. pap. text ed. 3.95 (*1-880706-00-8*) Goldrock Bks.

Sims, Lesley. Exploring Space. LC 93-28858. 1994. write for info. (*0-8114-5507-6*) Raintree Steck-V.

—The Moon. LC 93-28659. 1994. write for info. (*0-8114-5504-1*) Raintree Steck-V.

—The Planets. LC 93-28660. 1994. write for info. (*0-8114-5506-8*) Raintree Steck-V.

—The Sun & Stars. LC 93-28280. 1994. write for info. (*0-8114-5505-X*) Raintree Steck-V.

Sims, Virginia, ed. see Morgan, Lael.

Sinberg, Janet & Daley, Dennis. I Can Talk about What Hurts: A Book for Kids in Homes Where There's Chemical Dependency. Hartman, Tim, illus. 48p. (Orig.). (gr. k-5). 1991. pap. 7.00 (*0-89486-641-9*, FDO911031 A) Hazelden.

Sinclair, Dorothy T. Tales of the Texians. Milam, Harris, illus. LC 85-90411. 104p. (Orig.). (gr. 4-7). 1986. 12.95 (*0-9615311-0-X*); pap. 7.95 (*0-9615311-1-8*) Sinclair Ent.

Sinclair, Iain. Downriver - Or the Vessels of Wrath: A Narrative in Twelve Tales. LC 92-36509. 448p. 1993. 23.00 (*0-679-42062-2*) Random Bks Yng Read.

Sinclair, Sandra. Extraordinary Eyes: How Animals See the World. LC 89-39618. (Illus.). 48p. (gr. 4-7). 1992. 15.00 (*0-8037-0803-3*); PLB 14.89 (*0-8037-0806-8*) Dial Bks Young.

Sinclair, Upton. The Jungle. (gr. 11 up). 1965. pap. 2.95 (*0-8049-0086-8*, CL-86) Airmont.

Sinclair-House, Elizabeth & Muir, Alison. Adulthood. LC 90-28921. (Illus.). 64p. (gr. 5-9). 1991. PLB 19.92 (*0-8114-7806-8*) Raintree Steck-V.

—Advanced Years. LC 90-28922. (Illus.). 64p. (gr. 5-9). 1991. PLB 19.92 (*0-8114-7807-6*) Raintree Steck-V.

Sincro Communications Staff, jt. auth. see Family of the America's Staff.

Sine, Megan & Sine, Willam H. Max Is Back. (Illus.). 80p. (gr. 4 up). 1989. pap. 3.95 (*0-449-90415-6*, Columbine) Fawcett.

Sine, Willam H., jt. auth. see Sine, Megan.

Sinetar, Marsha. Why Can't Grownups Believe in Angels? LC 93-12906. (Illus.). 48p. 1993. text ed. 14.95 (*0-89243-551-8*, Triumph Books) Liguori Pubns.

Singer. Ghost Host. 1993. pap. 2.95 (*0-590-44505-7*) Scholastic Inc.

Singer, A. L. Davy Crockett & the King of the River. Wepplo, Mike, illus. LC 91-71356. 80p. (gr. 1-4). 1991. PLB 12.89 (*1-56282-006-0*); pap. 2.95 (*1-56282-007-9*) Disney Pr.

—Davy Crockett & the Pirates at Cave-in Rock. Wepplo, Mike, illus. LC 91-71355. 80p. (gr. 1-4). 1991. PLB 12.89 (*1-56282-002-8*); pap. 2.95 (*1-56282-003-6*) Disney Pr.

—Home Alone Two: Lost in New York Mass Market Novelization. 1992. 3.25 (*0-590-45718-7*) Scholastic Inc.

—Surf Ninjas. (gr. 4-7). 1993. pap. 3.50 (*0-553-56361-0*) Bantam.

—Surf Warriors. (gr. 4-7). 1993. pap. 3.50 (*0-440-40799-0*) Dell.

Singer, A. L., adapted by. Disney's Aladdin. LC 91-58972. (Illus.). 64p. (gr. 1-4). 1992. pap. 2.95 (*1-56282-241-1*) Disney Pr.

—Disney's Aladdin. LC 91-58973. (Illus.). 96p. 1992. 14.95 (*1-56282-240-3*); PLB 14.89 (*1-56282-275-6*) Disney Pr.

—Disney's Beauty & the Beast. LC 91-71338. 64p. (gr. 2-6). 1991. pap. 2.95 (*1-56282-051-6*) Disney Pr.

—Disney's Beauty & the Beast. Dias, Ron, illus. LC 91-71340. 96p. 1991. 14.95 (*1-56282-049-4*); PLB 14.89 (*1-56282-050-8*) Disney Pr.

—Disney's Robin Hood. LC 91-73806. (Illus.). 64p. (Orig.). (gr. 2-6). 1992. pap. 2.95 (*1-56282-138-5*) Disney Pr.

—Disney's the Little Mermaid: Illustrated Classic. Dias, Ron, illus. LC 92-74259. 96p. 1993. 14.95 (*1-56282-429-5*); PLB 14.89 (*1-56282-430-9*) Disney Pr.

—Disney's the Little Mermaid: Junior Novelization. Dias, Ron, illus. LC 92-74260. 64p. (gr. 2-6). 1993. pap. 2.95 (*1-56282-436-8*) Disney Pr.

—Walt Disney's Sleeping Beauty. Gonzalez, Ric & Durrell, Dennis, illus. LC 92-56158. 96p. 1993. 14.95 (*1-56282-366-3*); PLB 14.89 (*1-56282-367-1*) Disney Pr.

—Walt Disney's Sleeping Beauty. LC 92-56157. (Illus.). 64p. (gr. 2-6). 1993. pap. 2.95 (*1-56282-368-X*) Disney Pr.

Singer, Arthur & Singer, Alan, illus. State Birds. Buckley, Virginia, text by. LC 86-2209. 64p. (gr. 4 up). 1986. 16.95 (*0-525-67177-3*, Lodestar Bks); pap. 5.95 (*0-525-67314-8*, Lodestar Bks) Dutton Child Bks.

Singer, Beverly R., jt. auth. see Hirschfelder, Arlene.

Singer, Beverly R., jt. ed. see Hirschfelder, Arlene B.

Singer, Bill. The Fox with Cold Feet. Kendrick, Dennis, illus. LC 80-10288. 48p. (ps-3). 1980. 5.95 (*0-8193-1021-2*); PLB 5.95 (*0-8193-1022-0*) Parents.

Singer, C. Gospel Prayers. (Illus.). 64p. (gr. 3-7). 1993. pap. 8.95 (*0-915531-12-7*) OR Catholic.

Singer, Edmund, ed. see Kreutzer, Rudolph.

Singer, Ellen. Our Sacred Texts: Discovering the Jewish Classics. Zlotowitz, Bernard M., contrib. by. LC 92-16438. (gr. 4-6). 1992. pap. 8.00 (*0-8074-0479-9*, 123936); tchr's. guide 5.00 (*0-8074-0481-0*, 208031) UAHC.

Singer, Howard. With Mind & Heart. (gr. 8 up). 3.95x (*0-8381-0203-4*, 10-203) United Syn Bk.

Singer, Isaac Bashevis. A Day of Pleasure: Stories of a Boy Growing up in Warsaw. Vishniac, Roman, photos by. LC 70-95461. (Illus.). 160p. (gr. 3 up). 1986. pap. 5.95 (*0-374-41696-6*, Sunburst) FS&G.

—Elijah the Slave. Frasconi, Antonio, illus. LC 70-124146. 32p. (ps-3). 1970. 16.00 (*0-374-32084-5*) FS&G.

—Elijah the Slave. Frasconi, Antonio, illus. 32p. (ps up). 1988. pap. 4.95 (*0-374-42047-5*) FS&G.

—The Fools of Chelm & Their History. Shub, Elizabeth, tr. from YID. Shulevitz, Uri, illus. LC 73-81500. 64p. (gr. 3 up). 1973. 14.00 (*0-374-32444-1*) FS&G.

—Naftali, the Storyteller & His Horse, Sus. Zemach, Margot, illus. (gr. 3 up). 1987. pap. 3.50 (*0-374-45487-6*) FS&G.

—Por Que Noe Eligio la Paloma: Why Noah Chose the Dove. Marcuse, Aida, tr. Carle, Eric, illus. (SPA.). 32p. (ps up). 1992. 16.00 (*0-374-36085-5*, Mirasol) FS&G.

—The Power of Light. 80p. (gr. 4 up). 1982. pap. 2.50 (*0-380-60103-6*, Camelot) Avon.

—Power of Light. 1990. pap. 6.95 (*0-374-45984-3*, Sunburst) FS&G.

—Short Friday & Other Stories. large type ed. (gr. 10-12). Repr. of 1961 ed. write for info. (*0-89064-057-2*) NAVH.

—Stories for Children. LC 84-13612. 338p. (gr. k up). 1984. 22.95 (*0-374-37266-7*); ltd. ed. o.s.i. 30.00 (*0-374-37267-5*) FS&G.

—Stories for Children. LC 84-13612. 338p. (gr. k up). 1985. pap. 12.95 (*0-374-46489-8*, Sunburst) FS&G.

—When Shlemiel Went to Warsaw & Other Stories. Zemach, Margot, illus. 161p. (gr. 3-7). 1986. pap. 4.95 (*0-374-48365-5*) FS&G.

—Zlateh the Goat & Other Stories. Sendak, Maurice, illus. LC 66-8114. (gr. 1-6). 1966. 16.00 (*0-06-025698-2*) HarpC Child Bks.

—Zlateh the Goat & Other Stories. Shub, Elizabeth, tr. Sendak, Maurice, illus. LC 66-8114. 96p. (gr. 3-7). 1984. pap. 4.95 (*0-06-440147-2*, Trophy) HarpC Child Bks.

Singer, Marcia. Crystal Kids: PLAYBook. Rendal, Camille, illus. LC 89-90988. 64p. (Orig.). 1989. pap. 9.95 (*0-9622543-0-4*) PLAY House.

—Eating for a Fresh Start: A P.L.A.Y. Book. Rendal, Camille, illus. LC 90-91969. 64p. (Orig.). (gr. 1-7). 1990. pap. write for info. (*0-9622543-1-2*) PLAY House.

—Love Me, Love My Planet P.L.A.Y. Book: An Environmental Guide. Rendal, Camille, illus. LC 91-91308. 64p. (Orig.). (gr. 1-7). 1991. pap. 7.95 (*0-9622543-2-0*) PLAY House. LOVE ME, LOVE MY PLANET: P. L.A.Y. BOOK. Teacher's/Family's environmental awareness guide, stressing interconnectedness of all living things & value of everyone's contributions. Scientific facts, terms, planet-saving 'do' ideas, edu-P.L.A.Y.-tional activities. Adorable, colorable illustrations. "An engaging educational tool for our most important budding environmentalists - our children."-- Daphne Loysham, Editor, Greenpeace Magazine. "A really good book,"-- Melissa Poe, KidsF.A.C.E. Also recommended by Whole Life Times, Mother-to-Mother Newsletter, LA Outdoor Science School. CRYSTAL KIDS: P.L.A.Y. BOOK. (ISBN 0-9622543-0-4) Metaphysics, meditations, healing arts, crystal fun for beginners. Feast of enchanting, colorable illustraP.L.A.Ytions, storyline, songs. Stimulates imagination, creativity. Recommended by Psychic Research Institute (Marsel Vogel) newsletter, Whole Life Times, & authors Dael Walker, Katrina Raphaell, Frank Alper, Terry Cole-Whittaker, Wabun Wind, & Hay House's Laura Wilson.

EATING FOR A FRESH START: P. L.A.Y.BOOK (ISBN 0-9622543-1-2). Teacher's/Family's guide to beginning vegetarianism & ecologically sound eating habits. Easy instructions for sprouting, food combining, good digestion practices. Yummy, simple recipes. Features scientific definitions, charmer, illustrations, activities, "rap" style verse. Promotes physical, emotional, mental health. "Balances sound nutritional principles with games & activities."--Marilyn Diamond, Fit For Life. "Helps children be more aware & healthy." John Robbins, Diet for A New America. Also recommended by Garbage Magazine, L.A. Weekly, L.A. County Office of Education, Vegetarian Society, author Gabriel Cousens, Earth Save & Earthtrust Foundations. *Publisher Provided Annotation.*

Singer, Marilyn. Big Wheel. 160p. (gr. 5-9). 1993. 14.95 (*1-56282-583-6*); PLB 14.89 (*1-56282-584-4*) Hyprn Child.

—California Demon. LC 92-52981. 160p. (gr. 5-9). 1992. 14.95 (*1-56282-298-5*); PLB 14.89 (*1-56282-299-3*) Hyprn Child.

—The Case of the Sabotaged School Play: A Sam & Dave Mystery. Glasser, Judy, illus. LC 83-48437. 64p. (gr. 3-7). 1987. pap. 3.95 (*0-06-440207-X*, Trophy) HarpC Child Bks.

—Charmed. LC 90-518. 224p. (gr. 5-9). 1990. SBE 14.95 (*0-689-31619-4*, Atheneum Child Bk) Macmillan Child Grp.

—Chester the Out-of-Work Dog. Smith, Cat B., illus. LC 92-1141. 32p. (ps-3). 1992. 14.95 (*0-8050-1828-X*, Bks Young Read) H Holt & Co.

—Family Reunion. Alley, R. W., illus. LC 92-40336. 32p. (gr. 4 up). 1994. RSBE 14.95 (*0-02-782883-2*, Macmillan Child Bk) Macmillan Child Grp.

—The Golden Heart of Winter. Rayevsky, Robert, illus. LC 90-35346. 40p. (gr. 1 up). 1991. 13.95 (*0-688-07717-X*); PLB 13.88 (*0-688-07718-8*) Morrow Jr Bks.

—In My Tent. McCully, Emily A., illus. LC 91-16115. 32p. (gr. k-3). 1992. RSBE 14.95 (*0-02-782701-1*, Macmillan Child Bk) Macmillan Child Grp.

—It's Hard to Read a Map with a Beagle on Your Lap. Oubrerie, Clement, photos by. LC 92-26166. (Illus.). 32p. (gr. 1-4). 1993. PLB 15.95 (*0-8050-2201-5*, Bks Young Read) H Holt & Co.

—Nine O'Clock Lullaby. Lessac, Frane, illus. LC 90-32116. 32p. (ps-3). 1991. PLB 14.89 (*0-06-025648-6*) HarpC Child Bks.

—Nine O'Clock Lullaby. Lessac, Frane, illus. LC 90-32116. 32p. (ps-3). 1993. pap. 4.95 (*0-06-443319-6*, Trophy) HarpC Child Bks.

—The Painted Fan. Ma, Wenhai, illus. LC 92-29796. 1994. write for info. (*0-688-11742-2*); lib. bdg. write for info. (*0-688-11743-0*) Morrow Jr Bks.

—Please Don't Squeeze. 1995. write for info. (*0-8050-3277-0*) H Holt & Co.

—Sky Words. Ray, Deborah K., illus. LC 92-3765. 32p. (gr. k-3). 1994. RSBE 14.95 (*0-02-782882-4*, Macmillan Child Bk) Macmillan Child Grp.

—Storm Rising. 1989. pap. 12.95 (*0-590-42173-5*) Scholastic Inc.

—Storm Rising. 224p. 1992. pap. 3.25 (*0-590-42174-3*, Point) Scholastic Inc.

—Thriteen Dreams. 1994. write for info. (*0-8050-3004-2*) H Holt & Co.

—Turtle in July. Pinkney, Jerry, illus. LC 89-2745. 32p. (gr. k-3). 1989. RSBE 14.95 (*0-02-782881-6*, Macmillan Child Bk) Macmillan Child Grp.

—Turtle in July. Pinkey, Jerry, illus. LC 93-14430. 32p. (gr. 3-7). 1994. pap. 4.95 (*0-689-71805-5*, Aladdin) Macmillan Child Grp.

—Twenty Ways to Lose Your Best Friend. Lindberg, Jeffrey, illus. LC 89-36576. 32p. (gr. 2-5). 1990. PLB 14.89 (*0-06-025643-5*) HarpC Child Bks.

—Twenty Ways to Lose Your Best Friend. Lindberg, Jeffrey, illus. LC 89-36576. 32p. (gr. 2-5). 1993. pap. 3.95 (*0-06-440353-X*, Trophy) HarpC Child Bks.

—Wasp Is Not a Bee. 1994. write for info. (*0-8050-2820-X*) H Holt & Co.

Singer, Muff. Animal Rhyme & Scramble Puzzles. 48p. 1990. pap. 2.95 (*0-8431-2834-8*) Price Stern.

Singer, Muff, jt. auth. see Lamb, Nancy.

Singer, S. B. Naftali the Storyteller & His Horse, Sus. (gr. 4 up). 1979. pap. 1.50 (*0-440-46642-3*) Dell.

Singerman, Ellen. Stephen's Bag. McKissack, Patricia & McKissack, Fredrick, eds. Kirchhoff, Art, illus. LC 87-61642. 32p. (Orig.). (gr. 1-3). 1987. pap. 8.95 (*0-88335-729-1*); pap. text ed. 4.95 (*0-88335-749-6*) Milliken Pub Co.

Singh, Anne. Living in India. Matthews, Sarah, tr. from FRE. Riquier, Aline, illus. LC 87-31803. 38p. (gr. k-5). 1988. 4.95 (0-944589-14-6, 146) Young Discovery Lib.

Singh, Bhagat. The Story of Krishna. (Illus.). 20p. (Orig.). (ps-5). 1976. pap. 2.50 (0-89744-135-4, Pub. by Hemkunt India) Auromere.

Singh, Mala. Kashmir. Sharma, P. N., photos by. (Illus.). (gr. 1-10). 1979. pap. 2.50 (0-89744-177-X) Auromere.

—The Story of Guru Nanak. (Illus.). (gr. 2-9). 1979. 7.25 (0-89744-138-9) Auromere.

Singh, Maria E. Carry on, My Friends. LC 88-71123. 64p. (Orig.). 1989. pap. 5.00 (0-916383-61-X) Aegina Pr.

Singh, Nikkyh-Guninder. Sikhism. (Illus.). 128p. (gr. 7-12). 1992. bds. 17.95x (0-8160-2446-4) Facts on File.

Singh, Vir & Bawa, Ujagar S. Cherished Events of Sri Guru Gobind Singh, the Tenth Sikh Guru. 130p. (Orig.). (gr. 8-12). 1988. pap. 5.00x (0-942245-01-6) Wash Sikh Ctr.

—Cherished Events of the Life of Sri Guru Nanak Dev Ji, Founder of the Sikh Religion. 129p. (Orig.). (gr. 8-12). 1989. pap. 5.00x (0-942245-04-0) Wash Sikh Ctr.

Singh, Vir S. & Bawa, Ujagar S. Satwant Kaur: A Fictional Account of an Abducted Sikh Girl. 224p. (gr. 8-12). 1987. pap. 10.00x (0-942245-00-8) Wash Sikh Ctr.

Singletary, Carol, jt. auth. see Stanish, Bob.

Singletary, Helen P. & Glover, Zebrena M. Computers & Children, Bk. I. Thrall, Sidney, illus. 81p. (Orig.). 1991. pap. text ed. 20.00 (1-880850-01-X) Comp Trng Clinic.

—Understanding Colors, Shapes, & Direction. Glover, Zebrena M., illus. 31p. (Orig.). (ps-6). 1991. pap. text ed. 20.00 (1-880850-02-8) Comp Trng Clinic.

—Understanding the Alphabets. Matthews, Sam, illus. 59p. (Orig.). (ps-6). 1991. pap. text ed. 20.00 (1-880850-03-6) Comp Trng Clinic.

Singletary, Helen P., et al. Understanding Numbers. Butler, Synovia, illus. 47p. (Orig.). (ps-6). 1991. pap. text ed. 20.00 (1-880850-04-4) Comp Trng Clinic.

Singleton, L. The World: Lands & People: Teacher's Guide. (Illus.). 247p. (gr. 6). 1992. 50.00 (0-87746-360-3) Graphic Learning.

Singleton, Linda J. Love to Spare. 1993. pap. 2.99 (0-553-29979-4) Bantam.

—Opposites Attract. 1991. pap. 2.99 (0-553-29021-5) Bantam.

Singleton, Skip. The Junior Tennis Handbook. LC 90-21927. (Illus.). 176p. (Orig.). (gr. 5 up). 1991. pap. 12.95 (1-55870-192-5) Shoe Tree Pr.

Sinnett, Kate. My Five Disguises. Lewis, Anthony, illus. LC 90-44374. 28p. (gr. 4-8). 1991. PLB 16.95 (0-87226-444-0, Bedrick Blackie) P Bedrick Bks.

Sinnott, Susan. Extraordinary Asian-Pacific Americans. LC 93-12678. (Illus.). 260p. (gr. 4 up). 1993. PLB 31.93 (0-516-03152-X) Childrens.

—Extraordinary Hispanic Americans. LC 91-13909. 260p. (gr. 4 up). 1991. PLB 30.60 (0-516-00582-0) Childrens.

—Jacques-Yves Cousteau: Undersea Adventurer. LC 91-32960. (Illus.). 128p. (gr. 3 up). 1992. PLB 26.60 (0-516-03069-8) Childrens.

—Zebulon Pike: Up the Mississippi & Out to the Rockies. LC 90-2221. (Illus.). 128p. (gr. 3 up). 1990. PLB 26.60 (0-516-03058-2) Childrens.

Sinnott, Trip. President Clinton Visits Hyde Park: Story & Coloring Book. Glass, Eric, illus. 52p. (Orig.). (gr. k-5). 1993. pap. 4.95 (1-883551-00-5) Attic Studio.

Sinykin, Sheri C. Apart at the Seams. LC 89-2076. (ps). 1990. 12.95 (0-688-09181-4); PLB 12.88 (0-688-09182-2) Greenwillow.

—The Buddy Trap. LC 90-49994. 144p. (gr. 3-7). 1991. SBE 12.95 (0-689-31674-7, Atheneum Child Bk) Macmillan Child Grp.

—Come out, Come out Wherever You Are! Graef, Renee, illus. 32p. (Orig.). (gr. k-5). 1990. pap. 5.00 (0-89486-694-X) Hazelden.

—Next Thing to Strangers. LC 90-25991. 176p. (gr. 5 up). 1991. text ed. 12.95 (0-688-10694-3) Lothrop.

—Sirens. LC 93-77099. 1993. write for info. (0-688-12309-0) Lothrop.

Sioles, Anna M. An Ethics Primer for Children, Honesty - Kindness - Respect: A Catalyst to Discussion. Sioles, Anna M. & Boethner, Sandra, illus. 83p. (Orig.). (gr. 1-7). 1989. pap. text ed. 7.95x (0-9620893-0-3) Agatha Pub Co.

Sipe, Daniel. Kickboxing. 48p. (gr. 3-10). 1994. PLB 17.27 (1-56065-203-9) Capstone Pr.

Sipherd, Ray. When Is My Birthday? Cooke, Tom, illus. LC 88-80284. 32p. (ps-1). 1988. write for info. (0-307-12028-7) Western Pub.

Sipiera, Paul. Gerald Ford. LC 89-33745. 100p. (gr. 3 up). 1989. PLB 17.27 (0-516-01371-8) Childrens.

—Globes. LC 91-15869. 48p. (gr. k-4). 1991. PLB 15.27 (0-516-01124-3); pap. 4.95 (0-516-41124-1) Childrens.

—I Can Be a Chemist. LC 92-5807. (Illus.). 32p. (gr. k-3). 1992. PLB 14.60 (0-516-01965-1) Childrens.

—I Can Be a Chemist. LC 92-5807. (Illus.). 32p. (gr. k-3). 1993. pap. 3.95 (0-516-41965-X) Childrens.

—I Can Be a Geographer. LC 90-2198. (Illus.). 32p. (gr. k-3). 1990. PLB 14.60 (0-516-01961-9); pap. 3.95 (0-516-41961-7) Childrens.

—I Can Be a Geologist. LC 86-9598. (Illus.). 32p. (gr. k-3). 1986. PLB 14.60 (0-516-01897-3); pap. 3.95 (0-516-41897-1) Childrens.

—I Can Be a Physicist. LC 90-20886. (Illus.). 32p. (gr. k-3). 1991. PLB 14.60 (0-516-01964-3); pap. 3.95 (0-516-41964-1) Childrens.

—I Can Be an Astronomer. LC 86-9629. (Illus.). 32p. (gr. k-3). 1986. PLB 14.60 (0-516-01883-3) Childrens.

—I Can Be an Oceanographer. LC 86-31006. (Illus.). 32p. (gr. k-3). 1987. PLB 14.60 (0-516-01905-8); pap. 3.95 (0-516-41905-6) Childrens.

—Roald Amundsen & Robert Scott: Race for the South Pole. LC 90-2178. (Illus.). 128p. (gr. 3 up). 1990. PLB 26.60 (0-516-03056-6) Childrens.

Sipiera, Paul P. I Can Be a Biologist. LC 91-39243. (Illus.). 32p. (gr. k-3). 1992. PLB 14.60 (0-516-01966-X); pap. 3.95 (0-516-41966-8) Childrens.

Siracusa, Catherine. Bingo, the Best Dog in the World. Levitt, Sidney, illus. LC 90-4400. 64p. (gr. k-3). 1991. 11.95 (0-06-025812-8); PLB 11.89 (0-06-025813-6) HarpC Child Bks.

—The Giant Zucchini. Siracusa, Catherine, illus. LC 92-72018. 48p. (gr. k-3). 1993. 10.95 (1-56282-286-1); PLB 10.89 (1-56282-287-X) Hyprn Child.

—No Mail for Mitchell: A Step 1 Book - Preschool-Gr. 1. Siracusa, Catherine, illus. LC 89-70010. 32p. (Orig.). (ps-1). 1990. lib. bdg. 7.99 (0-679-90476-X); pap. 2.95 (0-679-80476-5) Random Bks Yng Read.

—The Parrot Problem. (Illus.). 48p. 1994. write for info. (1-56282-626-3); PLB write for info. (1-56282-627-1) Hyprn Child.

Sirimarco. Health. 1991. 12.95s.p. (0-86593-122-4); PLB 17.27 (0-685-59200-6) Rourke Corp.

—Illiteracy. 1991. 12.95s.p. (0-86593-115-1); PLB 17.26 (0-685-59206-5) Rourke Corp.

Sirimarco, Elizabeth. AIDS. LC 93-24967. (gr. 4 up). 1993. write for info. (1-85435-609-7, Cavendish Schl Llb UK); 14.95 (1-85435-610-0) Marshall Cavendish.

—Motherhood. LC 91-11169. 64p. (gr. 6-12). 1991. 12.95s.p. (0-86593-121-6); lib. bdg. 17.27 (0-685-59204-9) Rourke Corp.

—War & the Environment. LC 93-1194. 1993. write for info. (0-8368-1014-7) Gareth Stevens Inc.

Sirimarko, Elizabeth. Tennis. LC 93-27152. 1993. write for info. (0-86593-343-X) Rourke Corp.

Sirken, Michael L. Mr. Fine Goes to the Eye Doctor. 28p. (ps-4). 1993. pap. 1.25 (0-9635483-0-1) Sirken Pubns.

Sirof, Harriet. Because She's My Friend. LC 92-46426. (Illus.). 192p. (gr. 5-9). 1993. text ed. 14.95 (0-689-31844-8, Atheneum Child Bk) Macmillan Child Grp.

—The Road Back: Living with a Physical Disability. LC 92-43581. 144p. (gr. 6 up). 1993. RSBE 13.95 (0-02-782885-9, New Discovery Bks) Macmillan Child Grp.

Sirois, Allen. Dinosaur Dress Up Street, Janet, illus. LC 91-10583. 32p. (ps-3). 1992. 15.00 (0-688-10459-2, Tambourine Bks); PLB 14.93 (0-688-10460-6, Tambourine Bks) Morrow.

Sirota, Mike. Journey to Mesharra. (Orig.). (gr. 7 up). 1981. pap. 2.25 (0-89083-726-0) Zebra.

Sirvaitis, Karen. Florida. LC 93-25402. (gr. 5 up). 1994. lib. bdg. write for info. (0-8225-2728-6) Lerner Pubns.

—Michigan. LC 92-44847. 1993. PLB 17.50 (0-8225-2722-7) Lerner Pubns.

—Tennessee. 72p. (gr. 3-6). 1991. PLB 17.50 (0-8225-2711-1) Lerner Pubns.

—Utah. (Illus.). 72p. (gr. 3-6). 1991. PLB 17.50 (0-8225-2707-3) Lerner Pubns.

—Virginia. (Illus.). 72p. (gr. 3-6). 1991. PLB 17.50 (0-8225-2702-2) Lerner Pubns.

Sis, Peter. Beach Ball. Sis, Peter, illus. LC 89-2076. 24p. (ps). 1990. 12.95 (0-688-09181-4); PLB 12.88 (0-688-09182-2) Greenwillow.

—Follow the Dream. Sis, Peter, illus. LC 90-5392. 40p. (gr. k-5). 1991. 15.00 (0-679-80628-8); lib. bdg. 15.99 (0-679-90628-2) Knopf Bks Yng Read.

—Going Up! A Color Counting Book. LC 87-37203. (Illus.). 24p. (ps up). 1989. 12.95 (0-688-08125-8); PLB 12.88 (0-688-08126-6) Greenwillow.

—Komodo! LC 92-25811. (Illus.). 32p. (ps up). 1993. 15.00 (0-688-11583-7); PLB 14.93 (0-688-11584-5) Greenwillow.

—An Ocean World. LC 89-11692. (Illus.). 24p. (ps-3). 1992. 14.00 (0-688-09067-2); PLB 13.93 (0-688-09068-0) Greenwillow.

—Rainbow Rhino. reissued ed. Sis, Peter, illus. LC 87-2679. 40p. (ps-2). 1993. pap. 4.99 (0-679-85005-8) Knopf Bks Yng Read.

—A Small, Tall Tale from the Far, Far North. Sis, Peter, illus. LC 92-75906. 40p. (gr. k-5). 1993. 15.00 (0-679-84345-0); PLB 15.99 (0-679-94345-5) Knopf Bks Yng Read.

—Waving. LC 86-25762. (Illus.). 24p. (ps-1). 1988. 11.95 (0-688-07159-7); lib. bdg. 11.88 (0-688-07160-0) Greenwillow.

Siska, Heather S. People of the Ice: How the Inuit Lived. Bateson, Ian, illus. 48p. (gr. 4-7). 1992. pap. 7.95 (0-88894-404-7, Pub. by Groundwood-Douglas & McIntyre CN) Firefly Bks Ltd.

Siskind, Leda. Hopscotch Tree. (gr. 4-7). 1992. 15.00 (0-553-08715-0) Bantam.

Sisson, James E., ed. see London, Jack.

Sisson, Joan. Marigold. Sisson, Joan, illus. 24p. (Orig.). (ps-5). 1988. pap. 4.00 (0-317-93622-0) J Sisson.

Sisson, Pamla A. Kasandra's Mystery in Mazatlan. 64p. 1993. pap. 5.99 (0-9638328-0-8) P A Sisson.

Sister, Fatimatu. The Do's & Dont's of a Happy Marriage. 16p. (Orig.). 1987. pap. 0.50 (0-916157-10-5) African Islam Miss Pubns.

Sisulu, Walter see Kumalo, Alf.

Sita, Lisa. The Rattle & the Drum. LC 93-27209. (gr. 3 up). Date not set. PLB write for info. (1-56294-420-7) Millbrook Pr.

Sitarz, Paula G. The Curtain Rises, Vol. II: A History of European Theater from the Eighteenth Century to the Present. LC 92-39007. (Illus.). 144p. (Orig.). (gr. 7 up). 1993. pap. 12.95 (1-55870-293-8) Betterway Bks.

Sitarz, Paula Gaj. The Curtain Rises, Vol. 1: Early Origins & Eastern Theater. LC 90-21953. (Illus.). 144p. (gr. 5-9). 1991. 14.95 (1-55870-198-2) Shoe Tree Pr.

Sitomer, Harry, jt. auth. see Sitomer, Mindel.

Sitomer, Mindel & Sitomer, Harry. How Did Numbers Begin? LC 75-11756. (Illus.). 40p. (gr. k-3). 1976. PLB 12.89 (0-690-00794-9, Crowell Jr Bks) HarpC Child Bks.

Sitton, Thad & King, Lincoln. The Loblolly Book II. LC 86-5935. (Illus.). (gr. 3-6). 1986. pap. 12.95 (0-87719-017-8, Lone Star Bks) Gulf Pub.

Sitvaitis, Karen. Nevada. Lerner Geography Department Staff, ed. (Illus.). 72p. (gr. 4-7). 1992. 17.50 (0-8225-2719-7) Lerner Pubns.

Siy, Alexandra. The Amazon Rainforest. LC 91-37640. (Illus.). 80p. (gr. 5 up). 1992. RSBE 14.95 (0-87518-470-7, Dillon) Macmillan Child Grp.

—Ancient Forests. LC 91-15422. (Illus.). 72p. (gr. 5 up). 1991. RSBE 14.95 (0-87518-466-9, Dillon) Macmillan Child Grp.

—Arctic National Wildlife Refuge. LC 91-3882. (Illus.). 80p. (gr. 5 up). 1991. RSBE 14.95 (0-87518-468-5, Dillon) Macmillan Child Grp.

—The Eeyou: People of Eastern James Bay. LC 92-34887. (Illus.). 80p. (gr. 5 up). 1993. RSBE 14.95 (0-87518-549-5, Dillon) Macmillan Child Grp.

—The Efe: People of the Ituri Rain Forest. (Illus.). 72p. (gr. 5 up). 1993. RSBE 14.95 (0-87518-551-7, Dillon) Macmillan Child Grp.

—The Great Astrolabe Reef. LC 91-37267. (Illus.). 80p. (gr. 5 up). 1992. RSBE 14.95 (0-87518-499-5, Dillon) Macmillan Child Grp.

—Hawaiian Islands. LC 91-14185. (Illus.). 80p. (gr. 5 up). 1991. RSBE 14.95 (0-87518-467-7, Dillon) Macmillan Child Grp.

—Native Grasslands. LC 91-18412. (Illus.). 72p. (gr. 5 up). 1991. RSBE 13.95 (0-87518-469-3, Dillon) Macmillan Child Grp.

—The Penan: People of the Borneo Jungle. LC 93-10007. (Illus.). 72p. (gr. 5 up). 1993. RSBE 14.95 (0-87518-552-5, Dillon) Macmillan Child Grp.

—The Waorani: People of the Ecuadoran Rain Forest. LC 92-36985. (Illus.). 80p. (gr. 5 up). 1993. RSBE 14.95 (0-87518-550-9, Dillon) Macmillan Child Grp.

Sizemore, Deborah L. The LH7 Ranch in Houston's Shadow: From Longhorns to the Salt Grass Trail. LC 91-20920. (Illus.). 249p. 1991. 22.50 (0-929398-28-9) UNTX Pr.

Sizemore, Denver. Thirteen Lessons in Christian Doctrine: Youth Edition. Hunter, John, ed. 112p. (gr. 4-6). 1991. pap. text ed. 5.95 (0-89900-397-4); cancelled (0-89900-398-2) College Pr Pub.

Sjogren, Birgitta, tr. see Widerberg, Siv.

Skaggs, Calvin, ed. The American Short Story, Vol. I. 400p. (gr. 7 up). 1979. pap. 5.99 (0-440-30294-3, LE) Dell.

Skaggs, Keith A., ed. see Menken, Dan.

Skaist, Solomon. Targilon Shmuel Aleph. 53p. (gr. 5-6). pap. 2.50 (0-318-13639-2) Board Jewish Educ.

Skeem, Kenneth A. Genesis Fossil Booklet. Skeem, Jeanette, illus. (gr. 3-12). 1992. pap. text ed. 2.00 (0-9606782-1-2) Behemoth Pub.

Skeen, David L., designed by see Skeen, Nina B.

Skeen, Nina B. You Can Have Lasting Joy. Skeen, David L., designed by. Tyson, Tommy, frwd. by. (Illus.). 336p. (Orig.). 1990. 17.95 (0-9626994-0-3); pap. 14.95 (0-9626994-1-1); boxed cassettes 26.95 (0-685-47240-X) Joy Pubs.

Skelly, Maryan, jt. auth. see Dasso, Margaret.

Skelton, Mindy. Graphics Primer. Schmidt, Wayne, illus. 84p. (Orig.). (gr. 6 up). 1984. pap. 14.95 (0-928411-04-4) Comal Users.

Skelton, Renee. Charles Darwin. LC 87-19564. (Illus.). 144p. (gr. 3-6). 1987. pap. 5.95 (0-8120-3923-8) Barron.

Skidd, David R. The Gladstone Lakes Mystery. Skidd, David R., illus. 130p. (Orig.). (gr. 4-7). 1993. pap. write for info. (0-9636214-0-8) Midnight Ink.

—The Great Inukin Mystery. Skidd, David R., illus. 142p. (Orig.). (gr. 4-7). 1993. pap. write for info. (0-9636214-1-6) Midnight Ink.

Skidmore, Steve. Poison! Beware! Be an Expert Poison Spotter. (Illus.). 40p. (gr. 2-6). 1991. PLB 12.90 (1-878841-29-7) Millbrook Pr.

—What a Load of Trash! Rescue Your Household Waste. (Illus.). 40p. (gr. 2-6). 1991. PLB 12.90 (1-878841-27-0) Millbrook Pr.

Skidmore, Thomas E. Politics in Brazil, Nineteen Thirty - Nineteen Sixty-Four: An Experiment in Democracy. LC 67-20406. (Illus.). 464p. (gr. 9 up). 1986. pap. 19.95 (0-19-500784-0) OUP.

Skiff, Andrea. Blueberry & the Victorian House. Peterson, Elizabeth J., ed. (Illus.). 27p. (Orig.). (gr. 2-5). 1992. pap. 5.95 (0-938911-03-1) Indiv Educ Syst.

Skillings, Otis, jt. auth. see Nielson, Johnj M.

Skilton, Christine. The Magic Gourd. 1991. 7.954 (0-86685-568-8) Intl Bk Ctr.

Skinner, Ada M. Little Child's Book of Stories. 1988. 12.99 (0-517-65959-X) Outlet Bk Co.

Skinner, Ada M. & Skinner, Eleanor. Very Little Child's Book of Stories. 1990. 12.99 (0-517-69332-1) Outlet Bk Co.

Skinner, Ada M. & Skinner, Eleanor L. A Child's Book of Country Stories. Smith, Jessie W., illus. 224p. (gr. 1-7). 1992. 12.99 (0-517-69333-X, Child Classics) Outlet Bk Co.

Skinner, Cornelia Otis. Madam Sarah, 2 vols. large type ed. (gr. 10 up). Repr. of 1966 ed. Set. write for info. NAVH.

Skinner, Daphne, adapted by. Tim Burton's Nightmare Before Christmas. (Illus.). 96p. (gr. 2-6). 1993. pap. 2.95 (1-56282-592-5) Hyprn Ppbks.

Skinner, David. You Must Kiss a Whale. LC 91-30352. 104p. (gr. 6 up). 1992. pap. 14.00 3-pc. bdg. (0-671-74781-9, S&S BFYR) S&S Trade.

—You Must Kiss a Whale. LC 90-24079. 176p. (gr. 5-9). 1993. pap. 4.95 (0-671-86697-4, Half Moon Bks) S&S Trade.

Skinner, Eleanor, jt. auth. see Skinner, Ada M.
Skinner, Eleanor L., jt. auth. see Skinner, Ada M.
Skinner, Eliott, jt. auth. see Chu, Daniel.
Skinner, Elliott P., jt. auth. see Jefferson, Margo.
Skinner, Jeffrey, jt. auth. see Policoff, Stephen P.
Skipp, David, jt. auth. see Lawson, Michael.

Skipper, G. C. Pearl Harbor. LC 83-6569. (Illus.). 48p. (gr. 4-8). 1983. PLB 15.00 (0-516-04774-4) Childrens.

Skipper, Myr. The Big Sigh. 32p. 1992. pap. 6.95 (0-8059-3298-4) Dorrance.

Skira-Venturi, Rosabianca. A Weekend with Degas. LC 91-38364. (Illus.). 64p. (gr. 1-6). 1992. 19.95 (0-8478-1439-4) Rizzoli Intl.

—Weekend with Leonardo Da Vinci. (Illus.). 64p. (gr. 4-7). 1993. 19.95 (0-8478-1440-8) Rizzoli Intl.

Skivington, Janice. How Anansi Obtained the Sky God's Stories. Livington, Janice, illus. LC 91-7581. 48p. (ps-3). 1991. PLB 19.00 (0-516-05134-2); pap. 6.95 (0-516-45134-0) Childrens.

Skivington, Janice, illus. The Girl from the Sky: An Inca Folktale from South America. LC 91-42163. 24p. (ps-3). 1992. PLB 16.93 (0-516-05138-5); pap. 5.95 (0-516-45138-3) Childrens.

Sklansky, Jeff. James Farmer. (Illus.). 112p. (gr. 5 up). 1992. lib. bdg. 17.95 (0-7910-1126-7) Chelsea Hse.

Sklenitzka, Franz S. The Red Sports Car. (Illus.). 96p. (gr. 1-3). 1988. pap. 2.95 (0-8120-3937-8) Barron.

Skochko, Stephen, jt. auth. see Skochko, Sydney.

Skochko, Sydney & Skochko, Stephen. Dinosaurs Don't Do Drugs: Say NO to Drugs with C, D, & E. LC 92-85568. (Illus.). 47p. (ps-3). 1992. 13.95 (1-880125-26-9) Newmark CA.

Skofield, James. Crow Moon, Worm Moon. Powzyk, Joyce, illus. LC 89-1370. 32p. (gr. k-3). 1990. RSBE 13.95 (0-02-782915-4, Four Winds) Macmillan Child Grp.

—Round & Round. Hale, James G., illus. LC 90-32831. 32p. (ps-2). 1993. 15.00 (0-06-025746-6); PLB 14.89 (0-06-025747-4) HarpC Child Bks.

Skofield, James, tr. see Korschunow, Irina.

Skoglund, Elizabeth. Harold's Dog Horace Is Scared of the Dark. Bjorkman, Dale, illus. 48p. (gr. 2). 1992. pap. 2.99 (0-8423-1047-9) Tyndale.

Skoglund, Elizabeth R. Alfred MacDuff Is Afraid of War. Johnson, Meredith, illus. 48p. (ps-2). 1991. pap. 3.99 (0-8423-0032-5) Tyndale.

Skold, Betty W. Lord, I Have a Question: Story Devotions for Girls. LC 79-50079. 112p. (gr. 3-6). 1979. pap. 5.99 (0-8066-1718-7, 10-4096, Augsburg) Augsburg Fortress.

—Lord, I Need An Answer: Story Devotions for Girls. LC 81-52279. 112p. (gr. 3-8). 1985. pap. 5.99 (0-8066-1911-2, 10-4099, Augsburg) Augsburg Fortress.

Skolnick, Georgette B. To Be a Doctor: A Health Education Workbook. Barr, Charlotte & Cook, Tonya, illus. 215p. (Orig.). (gr. 6-9). 1982. student's wkbk. 8.00 (0-913855-00-6) GBS CA.

Skolout, Patricia F. Colorado Springs: History A to Z. rev. ed. (Illus.). 69p. (gr. k-6). 1991. pap. text ed. 4.95 (0-9625712-3-7) P F Skolout.

—Colorado Springs History A to Z: For Children. Rasmusseu-Frerichs, Cyndy, illus. 37p. (gr. k-6). 1990. Repr. of 1989 ed. activity bk. 3.95 (0-9625712-0-2) P F Skolout.

Skowronski, Deborah. The Non-Reader's Telephone Directory. Jacobson, Julie, illus. LC 82-61510. 36p. 1982. pap. text ed. 2.25 (0-9609618-0-1) Sunburst.

Skramstad, Jill. Wildlife Southwest. Richard, Ellis, intro. by. (Illus.). 64p. (gr. 3-7). 1991. 9.95 (0-8118-0126-8) Chronicle Bks.

Skulan, Tom, ed. see Barker, Clive & Niles, Steve.

Skulavik, Mary A. Bert. Kostrko, Zofia, illus. 32p. (ps-3). 1990. 13.95 (0-8027-6962-4); lib. bdg. 14.85 (0-8027-6963-2) Walker & Co.

Skurzynski, Glona. Lost in the Devil's Desert. Scrofani, Joseph M., illus. LC 92-45656. 96p. (gr. 5 up). 1993. pap. 3.95 (0-688-04593-6, Pub. by Beech Tree Bks) Morrow.

Skurzynski, Gloria. Almost the Real Thing: Simulation in Your High-Tech World. (Illus.). 64p. (gr. 9 up). 1991. SBE 16.95 (0-02-778072-4, Bradbury Pr) Macmillan Child Grp.

—Dangerous Ground. LC 88-31394. 128p. (gr. 3-7). 1989. SBE 13.95 (0-02-782731-3, Bradbury Pr) Macmillan Child Grp.

—Get the Message: Telecommunications in Your High-Tech World. LC 92-14892. (Illus.). 64p. (gr. 4 up). 1993. SBE 16.95 (0-02-778071-6, Bradbury Pr) Macmillan Child Grp.

—Good Bye, Billy Radish. LC 92-7577. (Illus.). 144p. (gr. 5 up). 1992. SBE 14.95 (0-02-782921-9, Bradbury Pr) Macmillan Child Grp.

—Here Comes the Mail. LC 91-40454. (Illus.). 32p. (ps-3). 1992. RSBE 13.95 (0-02-782916-2, Bradbury Pr) Macmillan Child Grp.

—Know the Score: Video Games in Your High-Tech World. LC 93-19470. 1994. write for info. (0-02-782352-0, Bradbury Pr) Macmillan Child Grp.

—Know the Score: Video Games in Your High-Tech World. Skurzynski, Gloria, illus. LC 93-19470. 64p. (gr. 4 up). 1994. RSBE 16.95 (0-02-782922-7, Bradbury Pr) Macmillan Child Grp.

—Lost in the Moving Mountains. (Illus.). 144p. (gr. 5 up). 1994. pap. 3.95 (0-688-12945-5, Pub. by Beech Tree Bks) Morrow.

—The Minstrel in the Tower. Heller, Julek, illus. LC 87-26614. 64p. (Orig.). (gr. 2-4). 1988. lib. bdg. 6.99 (0-394-99598-8); pap. 1.95 (0-394-89598-3) Random Bks Yng Read.

—Robots: Your High-Tech World. LC 89-70805. (Illus.). 64p. (gr. 4 up). 1990. SBE 15.95 (0-02-782917-0, Bradbury Pr) Macmillan Child Grp.

—Trapped in Slickrock Canyon. Soucie, Daniel S., illus. LC 83-14988. 128p. (gr. 4-6). 1984. 13.95 (0-688-02688-5) Lothrop.

—What Happened in Hamelin. LC 79-12814. (Illus.). 192p. (Orig.). (gr. 5-9). 1993. pap. 3.99 (0-679-83645-4) Random Bks Yng Read.

Skutina, Vladimir. Nobody Has Time for Me. Klein, Zanvel, ed. Herrmann, Dagmar, tr. from CZE. Sacre, Marie-Jose, illus. LC 91-4457. 32p. (gr. k-3). 1991. 14.95 (0-922984-07-7) Wellington IL.

Skwarek, Skip. The Horrors of Howling Hall. Compass Productions Staff, illus. LC 91-46526. 10p. (gr. k-4). 1992. 4.95 (0-8037-1185-9) Dial Bks Young.

—In the Deep Dark Dungeon. Compass Productions Staff, illus. LC 91-45515. 10p. (gr. k-4). 1992. 4.95 (0-8037-1187-5) Dial Bks Young.

—The Mystery of Maggoty Mill. Compass Productions Staff, illus. LC 91-47021. 10p. (gr. k-4). 1992. 4.95 (0-8037-1186-7) Dial Bks Young.

—The Weirdies of Wailing Wood. Compass Productions Staff, illus. LC 91-46916. 10p. (gr. k-4). 1992. 4.95 (0-8037-1188-3) Dial Bks Young.

Sky Rivers, ed. see Ferguson, Joe.

Slaby, Zdenck K. Book of Bedtime Stories. 1991. pap. 14.95 (0-671-08105-5) S&S Trade.

Slack, Anne, et al. French for Communication, One. LC 77-87429. (Illus.). (gr. 9). 1979. write for info. complete program HM.

Slack, Gordy. Ferdinand Marcos. Schlesinger, Arthur M. (Illus.). 112p. (gr. 5 up). 1988. 17.95 (1-55546-842-X) Chelsea Hse.

Slack, Thomas, ed. The Pleasing Instructor. Graham, Joanne, et al. 368p. 1973. Repr. of 1785 ed. 66.75 (3-261-01008-8) P Lang Pubs.

Slade, John, ed. see Felder, Pamela T.

Slade, Michael. The Horses of Central Park. 96p. 1992. 12.95 (0-590-44659-2, Scholastic Hardcover) Scholastic Inc.

Slade, Richard. Your Book of Modelling. (gr. 4 up). 1968. 7.95 (0-571-08387-0) Transatl Arts.

Slagle, Robert W. Tales of Joshua. 2nd ed. Slagle, Robert W., illus. 230p. (gr. 3). 1992. 14.95 (0-9614218-2-7); pap. 9.95 (0-9614218-1-9) Family Relat.

Slaight, Craig, ed. New Plays from ACT's Young Conservatory. 255p. 1992. pap. 14.95 (1-880399-25-3) Smith & Kraus.

Slaight, Craig & Sharrar, Jack, eds. Great Scenes & Monologues for Children. 1993. pap. 11.95 (1-880399-15-6) Smith & Kraus.

Slane, Kathleen M. Adventures in Time. (gr. 5 up). 1993. 7.95 (0-8062-4637-5) Carlton.

Slappey, Mary M. The Constitution of the United States. 17p. (gr. 1 up). 1987. pap. 5.00 (0-930061-20-9) Interspace Bks.

—Democracies in Crisis. (Illus.). 150p. 1992. pap. 10.95 (0-930061-27-6) Interspace Bks.

—Exploring Military Service for Women. rev. ed. (Illus.). 168p. (gr. 9-12). 1989. PLB 14.95 (0-8239-0996-4) Rosen Group.

Slate. Who Is Coming to Our House? Wolff, illus. 32p. 1991. pap. 5.95 (0-399-21790-8, Sandcastle Bks) Putnam Pub Group.

Slate, Barbara, et al. Barbie. 96p. 1992. pap. 8.95 (0-87135-878-6) Marvel Entmnt.

Slate, Joseph. Who Is Coming to Our House? Wolff, Ashley, illus. LC 87-7319. 32p. (ps-1). 1988. PLB 14.95 (0-399-21537-9, Putnam) Putnam Pub Group.

Slater, Barbara & Slater, Ron. Tracking Down Trivia. 48p. (gr. 5-12). 1982. 6.95 (0-86653-078-9, GA 423) Good Apple.

Slater, Barbara R., jt. auth. see Boehm, Ann E.

Slater, Helen. Doctor. Mitchell, Lyn, illus. 24p. 1992. 2.98 (0-8317-9508-5) Smithmark.

—Fuzzy Friends: Cuddle the Kitten. (Illus.). 10p. 1993. 3.95 (0-681-41812-5) Longmeadow Pr.

—Fuzzy Friends: Hug the Duck. (Illus.). 10p. 1993. 3.95 (0-681-41810-9) Longmeadow Pr.

—Fuzzy Friends: Pet the Puppy. (Illus.). 10p. 1993. 3.95 (0-681-41811-7) Longmeadow Pr.

—Fuzzy Friends: Snuggle the Bunny. (Illus.). 10p. 1993. 3.95 (0-681-41809-5) Longmeadow Pr.

Slater, Jack. Malcolm X. LC 93-12687. (Illus.). 32p. (gr. 3-6). 1993. PLB 15.93 (0-516-06669-2) Childrens.

Slater, Jim. Big Snowy. Slater, Christopher, illus. LC 80-53066. (ps-3). 1981. pap. 1.25 (0-394-84736-9) Random Bks Yng Read.

Slater, Robert. The Jewish Child's Book of Sports Heroes. LC 92-40087. 1993. 14.95 (0-8246-0360-5) Jonathan David.

Slater, Ron, jt. auth. see Slater, Barbara.

Slater, Teddy. Alice Meets the Aliens. Wallner, Alexandra, illus. 24p. (ps-1). 1992. 5.95 (0-671-72980-2); lib. bdg. 9.98 (0-671-72979-9) Silver Pr.

—All Aboard Fire Trucks. (Illus.). 32p. (ps-2). 1991. pap. 1.95 (0-448-34360-6, G&D) Putnam Pub Group.

—The Big Book of Real Fire Trucks. Mones, illus. 48p. (gr. 1-4). 1987. 7.95 (0-448-19176-8, G&D) Putnam Pub Group.

—The Bunny Hop. Difiori, Larry, illus. 32p. 1992. pap. 2.95 (0-590-45354-8, Cartwheel) Scholastic Inc.

—The Cow That Could Tap Dance. Forest, Sandra, illus. 24p. (ps-1). 1991. 5.95 (0-671-70412-5); PLB 9.98 (0-671-70408-7) Silver Pr.

—Dining with Prunella. Hearn, Diane D., illus. 24p. (ps-1). 1991. 5.95 (0-671-72982-9); PLB 9.98 (0-671-72981-0) Silver Pr.

—Disney's the Prince & the Pauper. Wilson, Phil, illus. LC 92-56165. 48p. 1993. 12.95 (1-56282-511-9); PLB 12.89 (1-56282-512-7) Disney Pr.

—Eloise Wilkin's Babies: A Book of Poems. (ps-3). 1993. 8.95 (0-307-15864-0, Golden Pr) Western Pub.

—The Fabulous Fish from Lake Wiggawalla. Rankin, Laura, illus. 24p. (ps-1). 1991. 5.95 (0-671-70413-3); PLB 9.98 (0-671-70409-5) Silver Pr.

—Henry & the Haunted House. Wallner, John, illus. 24p. (ps-1). 1992. 5.95 (0-671-72978-0); lib. bdg. 9.98 (0-671-72977-2) Silver Pr.

—Is That So? Series, 4 vols. Forest, Sandra & Rankin, Laura, illus. (ps-1). 1991. Set, 24p. ea. 23.80 (0-671-31251-0); Set, 24p. ea. lib. bdg. 39.92 (0-671-31249-9) Silver Pr.

—Jan & Dan & the Super Dads. Forest, Sandra, illus. 24p. (ps-1). 1991. 5.95 (0-671-70414-1); PLB 9.98 (0-671-70410-9) Silver Pr.

—Listening with Zachary. Alley, Robert, illus. 24p. (ps-1). 1991. 5.95 (0-671-72986-1); PLB 9.98 (0-671-72985-3) Silver Pr.

—Looking for Lewis. Alley, Robert, illus. 24p. (ps-1). 1991. 5.95 (0-671-72988-8); PLB 9.98 (0-671-72987-X) Silver Pr.

—Molly's Monsters. Morgan, Mary, illus. 32p. (ps-2). 1988. pap. 2.25 (0-448-19099-0, Platt & Munk Pubs) Putnam Pub Group.

—N-O Spells No! Johnson, Meredith, illus. LC 92-21422. 32p. (ps-2). 1993. pap. 2.95 (0-590-44186-8) Scholastic Inc.

—Shopping with Samantha. Hearn, Diane D., illus. 24p. (ps-1). 1991. 5.95 (0-671-72984-5); PLB 9.98 (0-671-72983-7) Silver Pr.

—What Rhymes? Series. Alley, Robert & Hearn, Diane D., illus. (ps-1). 1991. Set, 24p. ea. 23.80 (0-671-31245-6); Set, 24p. ea. lib. bdg. 39.92 (0-671-31244-8) Silver Pr.

—Why Buster Beasley Was Late for Lunch. Rankin, Laura, illus. 24p. (ps-1). 1991. 5.95 (0-671-70415-X); PLB 9.98 (0-671-70411-7) Silver Pr.

—Winnie the Pooh & the Blustery Day. Langley, Bill & Wakeman, Diana, illus. LC 92-55130. 48p. (ps-k). 1993. 12.95 (1-56282-488-0) Disney Pr.

—The Wrong-Way Rabbit. De Groat, Diane, illus. LC 92-14334. 32p. (ps-2). 1993. pap. 2.95 (0-590-45359-9) Scholastic Inc.

Slater, Teddy, adapted by. Walt Disney's Alice in Wonderland. Maten, Franc, illus. (ps-2). 1991. write for info. (0-307-12341-3, Golden Pr) Western Pub.

—Walt Disney's Dumbo. Dias, Ron, illus. LC 88-80740. 24p. (ps-1). 1988. write for info. (0-307-11994-7) Western Pub.

—Walt Disney's Lady & the Tramp. Langley, Bill & Dias, Ron, illus. 24p. (ps-3). 1993. 3.50 (0-307-12367-7, 12367, Golden Pr) Western Pub.

—Walt Disney's Mickey & the Beanstalk. Wilson, Phil, illus. 48p. 1993. 12.95 (1-56282-385-X); PLB 12.89 (1-56282-386-8) Disney Pr.

Slater, Teddy, retold by see Andersen, Hans Christian.

Slater, Teddy, retold by see Friedhoffer, Bob.

Slaton, Lana. Horses in History Color & Story Album. (Illus.). 32p. (gr. 2-6). 1987. pap. 4.50 (0-8431-1766-4) Price Stern.

Slattery, Anastasia S., jt. auth. see Hannon, Robert J.

Slattery, Britt E. WOW! The Wonders of Wetlands: An Educator's Guide. 3rd ed. (Illus.). 164p. (gr. k-12). 1993. tchr's. guide 12.00 (1-883226-01-5) Environ Concern.

—WOW! The Wonders of Wetlands: An Educator's Guide. 2nd, rev. ed. 160p. (gr. k-12). 1992. pap. text ed. write for info. (1-883226-00-7) Environ Concern.

Slattery, Kathryn. Grandma, I'll Miss You: A Child's Story about Death & New Life. LC 92-18984. 1993. write for info. (0-7814-0937-3, Chariot Bks) Cook.

Slaughter, Hope. A Cozy Place. Torrence, Susan, illus. LC 90-49715. 32p. (ps-2). 1990. 15.95 (0-931093-13-9) Red Hen Pr.

—The Deeeeelicious Dragon. Heaney, Rhonda K., illus. LC 86-652. 32p. (ps-3). 1986. pap. 4.95 (0-931093-05-8) Red Hen Pr.

—Plato's Fine Feathers. Shearer, Hope, illus. LC 84-4830. 32p. (ps-3). 1984. PLB 7.95 (*0-931093-00-7*); pap. 3.95 (*0-685-15364-9*) Red Hen Pr.
—Windmill Hill. Frascino, Edward, illus. 64p. (gr. 2-5). 1993. 14.95 (*0-945912-21-8*) Pippin Pr.
Slavin, Bill & Tucker, Kathleen, eds. The Cat Came Back. Slavin, Bill, illus. 32p. (gr. 1-6). 1992. 13.95g (*0-8075-1097-1*) A Whitman.
Slavin, Ed. Jimmy Carter. Schlesinger, Arthur M., intro. by. (Illus.). 112p. (gr. 5 up). 1989. 17.95 (*1-55546-828-4*) Chelsea Hse.
Slawson, Michele B. Apple Picking Time. Ray, Deborah K., illus. LC 92-23400. 1994. write for info.; PLB write for info. (*0-517-58976-1*) Crown Bks Yng Read.
Sleator, William. Among the Dolls. Hyman, Trina S., illus. (gr. 2-5). 1975. 12.50 (*0-525-25563-X*, DCB) Dutton Child Bks.
—The Boy Who Reversed Himself. LC 86-19700. 176p. (gr. 5-11). 1986. 13.95 (*0-525-44276-6*, DCB) Dutton Child Bks.
—The Duplicate. LC 87-30562. 160p. (gr. 5-11). 1988. 13.95 (*0-525-44390-8*, 01258-370, DCB) Dutton Child Bks.
—The Duplicate. (gr. 5 up). 1990. pap. 3.25 (*0-553-28634-X*, Starfire) Bantam.
—Fingers. 208p. (Orig.). (gr. 7). 1990. pap. 3.50 (*0-553-25004-3*, Starfire) Bantam.
—The Green Futures of Tycho. 144p. (gr. 7 up). 1991. pap. 3.95 (*0-14-034581-7*, Puffin) Puffin Bks.
—House of Stairs. LC 73-17417. 176p. (gr. 7 up). 1985. 14.95 (*0-525-32335-X*, DCB) Dutton Child Bks.
—House of Stairs. (Illus.). 172p. (gr. 7 up). 1991. pap. 3.95 (*0-14-034580-9*, Puffin) Puffin Bks.
—Interstellar Pig. 224p. (gr. 6 up). 1986. pap. 3.50 (*0-553-25564-9*, Starfire) Bantam.
—Into the Dream. Sanderson, Ruth, illus. LC 78-11825. 144p. (gr. 4-7). 1979. 13.95 (*0-525-32583-2*, DCB) Dutton Child Bks.
—Oddballs. LC 92-27666. (gr. 7 up). 1993. 14.99 (*0-525-45057-2*, DCB) Dutton Child Bks.
—Others See Us. (Illus.). 144p. (gr. 5-11). 1993. 14.99 (*0-525-45104-8*, DCB) Dutton Child Bks.
—Singularity. LC 84-26075. 192p. (gr. 7 up). 1985. 12.95 (*0-525-44161-1*, DCB) Dutton Child Bks.
—Singularity. 208p. 1986. pap. 3.50 (*0-553-25627-0*, Starfire) Bantam.
—Spirit House. LC 91-2131. 144p. (gr. 5-11). 1991. 13.95 (*0-525-44814-4*, DCB) Dutton Child Bks.
—The Spirit House. LC 93-7485. 144p. (gr. 7 up). 1993. pap. 3.99 (*0-14-036483-8*, Puffin) Puffin Bks.
—Strange Attractors. LC 89-33840. 176p. (gr. 5-11). 1990. 13.95 (*0-525-44530-7*, DCB) Dutton Child Bks.
—Strange Attractors. (Illus.). 144p. (gr. 7 up). 1991. pap. 3.99 (*0-14-034582-5*, Puffin) Puffin Bks.
Sledge, Sharlene. Guess What I Made!?! Recipes for Children from Around the World. Dillard, Karen, illus. 64p. (Orig.). (gr. 1-6). 1988. pap. 4.95 (*0-936625-39-2*, New Hope AL) Womans Mission Union.
—With My Whole Heart: Knowing God Through Prayer. Gross, Karen, ed. 64p. (gr. 4-6). 1993. pap. text ed. 4.95 (*1-56309-078-3*, New Hope) Womans Mission Union.
Slegers, Guusje. Toys. (ps). 1987. 1.95 (*0-8120-5802-X*) Barron.
Slepian, Jan. The Alfred Summer. LC 79-24097. 132p. (gr. 6 up). 1980. SBE 13.95 (*0-02-782920-0*, Macmillan Child Bk) Macmillan Child Grp.
—Back to Before. LC 92-10103. 192p. (gr. 5-9). 1993. 14. 95 (*0-399-22011-9*, Philomel Bks) Putnam Pub Group.
—The Broccoli Tapes. (gr. 3-7). 1989. 14.95 (*0-399-21712-6*, Philomel Bks) Putnam Pub Group.
—The Broccoli Tapes. (gr. 4-7). 1990. pap. 2.95 (*0-590-43473-X*) Scholastic Inc.
—The Broccoli Tapes. 225p. (gr. 6-9). 1988. 18.00 (*0-685-66380-9*, BR8145) W A T Braille.
—Broccoli Tapes. 225p. 1992. text ed. 18.00 (*1-56956-201-6*) W A T Braille.
—Broccoli Tapes. (gr. 4-7). 1990. pap. 2.95 (*0-590-44263-5*) Scholastic Inc.
—Hungry Thing Goes to a Restaurant. (ps-3). 1993. pap. 4.95 (*0-590-45525-7*) Scholastic Inc.
—Hungry Thing Returns. (ps-3). 1993. pap. 3.95 (*0-590-42891-8*) Scholastic Inc.
—Risk n' Roses. 176p. (gr. 6 up). 1990. 14.95 (*0-399-22219-7*, Philomel Bks) Putnam Pub Group.
—Risk N' Roses. 160p. (gr. 3-7). 1992. pap. 2.95 (*0-590-45361-0*, Apple Paperbacks) Scholastic Inc.
Slepian, Jan & Seidler, Ann. The Hungry Thing Returns. Martin, Richard E., illus. LC 89-6350. (ps-3). 1990. pap. 11.95 (*0-590-42890-X*) Scholastic Inc.
Slepian, Jan & Siedler, Ann. The Hungry Thing. Martin, Richard E., illus. 32p. (ps-3). 1988. pap. 3.95 (*0-590-42292-8*) Scholastic Inc.
Slepian, Jan, jt. auth. see Seidler, Ann.
Slier, Debby. Baby's Places. 12p. (ps) 1989. 2.95 (*1-56288-149-3*) Checkerboard.
—Brothers & Sisters. 12p. (ps) 1989. 2.95 (*1-56288-146-9*) Checkerboard.
—A First Book of Sign Language: Animal Signs. 16p. (ps). 1993. 4.95 (*1-56288-385-2*) Checkerboard.
—A First Book of Sign Language: Word Signs. 16p. (ps). 1993. 4.95 (*1-56288-386-0*) Checkerboard.
—Little Animals. 12p. (ps) 1989. 2.95 (*1-56288-147-7*) Checkerboard.
—Little Babies. 12p. (ps) 1989. 2.95 (*1-56288-148-5*) Checkerboard.

—More Baby Animals. (Illus.). 18p. (ps) 1992. bds. 4.50 (*1-56288-308-9*) Checkerboard.
—My First ABC. Bates, Louise, illus. 24p. (Orig.). (gr. k-1). 1990. pap. 0.99 (*1-878624-36-9*) McClanahan Bk.
—Teddy Beddy Bear's Bedtime Adventure. Reichmeier, Betty, illus. LC 85-60215. 28p. (ps) 1985. bds. 2.95 (*0-394-87535-4*) Random Bks Yng Read.
—Words I Know. 12p. (ps) 1989. 2.95 (*1-56288-145-0*) Checkerboard.
Slier, Debby, ed. Baby's Words. 12p. (ps) 1988. bds. 2.95 (*1-56288-085-3*) Checkerboard.
—Busy Baby. 12p. (ps) 1988. bds. 2.95 (*1-56288-086-1*) Checkerboard.
—Hello Baby. (Illus.). 12p. (ps) 1988. bds. 2.95 (*1-56288-087-X*) Checkerboard.
—Hello School. Dwight, Laura, illus. 28p. (ps) 1990. 2.95 (*0-02-689483-1*) Checkerboard.
—I Can Do It. (Illus.). 28p. (ps) 1990. 2.95 (*1-56288-378-X*) Checkerboard.
—Me & My Dad. Dwight, Laura, illus. 28p. (ps) 1990. 2.95 (*1-56288-380-1*) Checkerboard.
—Me & My Grandma. Dwight, Laura, photos by. (Illus.). 28p. (ps) 1992. bds. 2.95 (*1-56288-183-3*) Checkerboard.
—Me & My Grandpa. Dwight, Laura, photos by. (Illus.). 28p. (ps) 1992. bds. 2.95 (*1-56288-182-5*) Checkerboard.
—Me & My Mom. Dwight, Laura, illus. 28p. (ps) 1990. 2.95 (*1-56288-379-8*) Checkerboard.
—The Real Mother Goose: Book of American Rhymes. McCloskey, Patty, et al, illus. 128p. (ps-5). 1993. 12. 95 (*1-56288-399-2*) Checkerboard.
Slier, Deborah, ed. Farm Animals. (Illus.). 12p. (ps). 1988. 2.95 (*1-56288-084-5*) Checkerboard.
Sloan, Carolyn. Helen Keller. (Illus.). 64p. (gr. 5-9). 1991. 11.95 (*0-237-60016-1*, Pub. by Evans Bros Ltd) Trafalgar.
Sloan, Claudia, jt. auth. see Stern, Kati.
Sloan, Frank. Bismarck! LC 90-47858. (Illus.). 64p. (gr. 3-5). 1991. PLB 12.90 (*0-531-20002-7*) Watts.
—Titanic. LC 87-6214. (Illus.). 96p. (gr. 4-9). 1987. PLB 10.90 (*0-531-10396-X*) Watts.
Sloan, Phyllis J. Postcard from Heaven. Knight, Ginny, illus. 1990. 3.00 (*0-940248-81-6*) Guild Pr.
Sloan, Phyllis J., et al. Trembling with Wonder. Knight, Ginny, illus. (gr. 4 up). 1990. 3.00 (*0-940248-80-8*) Guild Pr.
Sloan, Stephen, ed. see Manry, Douglas.
Sloane, Eric. ABC Book of Early Americana. LC 89-24603. (Illus.). 64p. 1990. 16.95 (*0-8050-1294-X*) H Holt & Co.
Sloane, Paul & MacHale, Des. Challenging Lateral Thinking Puzzles. Miller, Myron, illus. 96p. (gr. 10-12). 1993. pap. 4.95 (*0-8069-8671-9*) Sterling.
—Logical Thinking Puzzles. Miller, Myron, illus. LC 92-19095. 96p. (gr. 5 up). 1992. 12.95 (*0-8069-8670-0*) Sterling.
Sloat, Teri. From Letter to Letter. Sloat, Teri, illus. LC 89-1135. 32p. (ps-3). 1989. 13.95 (*0-525-44518-8*, DCB) Dutton Child Bks.
—From One to One Hundred. Sloat, Teri, illus. LC 91-21948. 32p. 1991. 13.95 (*0-525-44764-4*, DCB) Dutton Child Bks.
Sloat, Teri, as told by. & illus. The Eye of the Needle. 32p. (ps-3). 1993. pap. 4.99 (*0-14-054933-1*, Puffin Unicorn) Puffin Bks.
Sloat, Teri, retold by. & illus. The Eye of the Needle: Based on a Yupik Tale Told by Betty Huffman. LC 89-49476. 32p. (ps-3). 1990. 13.95 (*0-525-44623-0*, DCB) Dutton Child Bks.
—The Hungry Giant of the Tundra. LC 93-12166. 32p. (ps-3). 1993. 14.99 (*0-525-45126-9*, DCB) Dutton Child Bks.
Sloate, Susan. Looking Good. Richey, Donald, illus. LC 89-28019. 128p. (gr. 5-9). 1991. lib. bdg. 10.89 (*0-8167-1999-3*); pap. text ed. 2.95 (*0-8167-2000-2*) Troll Assocs.
—Racing Hearts. (gr. 7 up). 1991. pap. 2.99 (*0-553-28962-4*) Bantam.
Slobodkin, Louis. The Space Ship Returns to the Apple Tree. Slobodkin, Louis, illus. LC 93-10747. 128p. (gr. 3-7). 1994. pap. 3.95 (*0-689-71768-7*, Aladdin) Macmillan Child Grp.
—The Space Ship under the Apple Tree. 2nd ed. Slobodkin, Louis, illus. LC 92-42712. 128p. (gr. 3-7). 1993. pap. 3.95 (*0-689-71741-5*, Aladdin) Macmillan Child Grp.
Slobodkina, Esphyr. Caps for Sale. Slobodkina, Esphyr, illus. LC 84-43122. 1947. 13.00 (*0-201-09147-X*); PLB 12.89 (*0-06-025778-4*) HarpC Child Bks.
—Caps for Sale. Slobodkina, Esphyr, illus. LC 84-43122. 48p. (ps-2). 1987. pap. 3.95 (*0-06-443143-6*, Trophy) HarpC Child Bks.
—Caps for Sale. Slobodkina, Esphyr, illus. (gr. k-3). 1987. incl. cassette 19.95 (*0-87499-059-9*); pap. 12.95 incl. cassette (*0-87499-058-0*); 4 paperbacks, cassette & guide 27.95 (*0-87499-060-2*) Live Oak Media.
—Caps for Sale. (gr. k-3). 1989. Big Book. 28.67 (*0-590-64643-5*); pap. 2.95 (*0-590-71775-8*) Scholastic Inc.
—The Wonderful Feast. LC 92-23416. (Illus.). 24p. 1993. 14.00 (*0-688-12348-1*); PLB 13.93 (*0-688-12349-X*) Greenwillow.
Slobodskoy, Seraphim, compiled by. The Law of God, for Study at Home & School. Price, Susan, tr. from RUS. (Illus.). 650p. (gr. 1-7). 1993. 50.00 (*0-88465-044-8*) Holy Trinity.

Slocombe, Lorna. Sailing Basics. Seiden, Art, illus. 48p. (gr. 3-7). 1982. 8.95 (*0-13-786053-6*) P-H.
Sloss, Lesley. Anthony & the Aardvark. Clarke, Gus, illus. LC 90-6528. 32p. (ps up). 1991. 13.95 (*0-688-10302-2*); PLB 13.88 (*0-688-10303-0*) Lothrop.
Slote, Alfred. Finding Buck McHenry. LC 90-39190. 256p. (gr. 3-7). 1991. 14.00 (*0-06-021652-2*); PLB 13. 89 (*0-06-021653-0*) HarpC Child Bks.
—Finding Buck McHenry. LC 90-39190. 256p. (gr. 3-7). 1993. pap. 3.95 (*0-06-440469-2*, Trophy) HarpC Child Bks.
—A Friend Like That. LC 87-35053. 160p. (gr. 3-7). 1990. pap. 3.50 (*0-06-440266-5*, Trophy) HarpC Child Bks.
—Hang Tough, Paul Mather. LC 72-11531. 160p. (gr. 3-7). 1992. PLB 14.89 (*0-397-32509-6*, Lipp Jr Bks) HarpC Child Bks.
—Hang Tough, Paul Mather. reissue ed. LC 72-11531. 160p. (gr. 3-7). 1985. pap. 3.95 (*0-06-440153-7*, Trophy) HarpC Child Bks.
—Make-Believe Ball Player. Newsom, Tom, illus. LC 89-30598. 112p. (gr. 2-5). 1989. 13.00 (*0-397-32285-2*, Lipp Jr Bks); PLB 12.89 (*0-397-32286-0*, Lipp Jr Bks) HarpC Child Bks.
—Make-Believe Ball Player. LC 89-30598. 112p. (gr. 2-5). 1992. pap. 3.95 (*0-06-440425-0*, Trophy) HarpC Child Bks.
—Matt Gargan's Boy. LC 74-26669. 160p. (gr. 3-7). 1985. pap. 3.95 (*0-06-440154-5*, Trophy) HarpC Child Bks.
—My Robot Buddy. LC 85-45393. (Illus.). 96p. (gr. 2-5). 1986. pap. 3.95 (*0-06-440165-0*, Trophy) HarpC Child Bks.
—My Robot Buddy. reissued ed. Schick, Joel, illus. LC 75-9922. 80p. (gr. 2-5). 1991. PLB 13.89 (*0-397-32505-3*, Lipp Jr Bks) HarpC Child Bks.
—My Trip to Alpha I. Berson, Harold, illus. LC 78-6463. 96p. (gr. 2-5). 1992. (Lipp Jr Bks); PLB 13.89 (*0-397-32510-X*, Lipp Jr Bks) HarpC Child Bks.
—My Trip to Alpha I. Berson, Harold, illus. LC 85-45394. 96p. (gr. 2-5). 1986. pap. 3.95 (*0-06-440166-9*, Trophy) HarpC Child Bks.
—Omega Station. Kramer, Anthony, illus. LC 85-45395. 160p. (gr. 2-5). 1986. pap. 3.95 (*0-06-440167-7*, Trophy) HarpC Child Bks.
—Rabbit Ears. LC 81-47760. 128p. (gr. 4-7). 1983. pap. 3.95 (*0-06-440134-0*, Trophy) HarpC Child Bks.
—The Trading Game. LC 89-12851. 208p. (gr. 3-7). 1990. 15.00 (*0-397-32397-2*, Lipp Jr Bks); PLB 14.89 (*0-397-32398-0*, Lipp Jr Bks) HarpC Child Bks.
—The Trading Game. LC 89-12851. 208p. (gr. 3-7). 1992. pap. 3.95 (*0-06-440438-2*, Trophy) HarpC Child Bks.
—The Trouble on Janus. Watts, James, illus. LC 85-40099. 192p. (gr. 3-6). 1985. PLB 13.89 (*0-397-32159-7*, Lipp Jr Bks) HarpC Child Bks.
—The Trouble on Janus. Watts, James, illus. LC 85-40099. 192p. (gr. 3-6). 1988. pap. 3.50 (*0-06-440216-9*, Trophy) HarpC Child Bks.
Slote, Elizabeth. Nelly's Garden. Slote, Elizabeth, illus. LC 90-33382. 32p. (ps-1). 1991. 13.95 (*0-688-10013-9*, Tambourine Bks); PLB 13.88 (*0-688-10014-7*, Tambourine Bks) Morrow.
—Nelly's Grannies. Slote, Elizabeth, illus. LC 91-32600. 32p. (ps up). 1993. 14.00 (*0-688-11314-1*, Tambourine Bks); PLB 13.93 (*0-688-11315-X*, Tambourine Bks) Morrow.
Slovenz-Low, Madeline, jt. auth. see Waters, Kate.
Sloyer, Cliff. Fantastiks of Mathematiks: Applications of Secondary Mathematics. LC 86-21326. (Illus.). 160p. (Orig.). (gr. 7-12). 1987. pap. 13.95 (*0-939765-00-4*, G101) Janson Pubns.
Sloyer, Clifford, et al. Queues: Will This Wait Never End! (Illus.). 42p. (Orig.). (gr. 9 up). 1987. pap. text ed. 9.95 (*0-939765-08-X*, G105) Janson Pubns.
Smagorinsky, Peter. Expressions: Multiple Intelligences in the English Class. 77p. (gr. 7-12). 1991. pap. 10.50 (*0-8141-1664-7*) NCTE.
Smajda, Michael J. A Deer Love Story. (Illus.). 39p. 1988. text ed. 9.50 (*0-533-07680-3*) Vantage.
Small, Carol B. Art Concepts for Children. Small, Carol B., illus. LC 89-14917. 112p. (Orig.). (gr. 6 up). 1989. pap. 8.95 (*0-938267-04-3*) Bold Prodns.
Small, David. Imogene's Antlers. Small, David, illus. LC 84-12085. 32p. (ps-2). 1988. PLB 13.95 (*0-517-55564-6*); pap. 3.95 (*0-517-56242-1*) Crown Bks Yng Read.
—Paper John. LC 86-45261. (Illus.). 32p. (ps-3). 1987. 15.00 (*0-374-35738-2*) FS&G.
—Paper John. (ps up) 1989. pap. 3.95 (*0-374-45725-5*, Sunburst) FS&G.
—Ruby Mae Has Something to Say. Small, David, illus. LC 91-33785. 40p. (ps-4). 1992. 12.00 (*0-517-58248-1*); PLB 12.99 (*0-517-58249-X*) Crown Bks Yng Read.
Small, Ernest & Lent, Blair. Baba Yaga. (Illus.). 48p. (gr. k-3). 1966. 14.45 (*0-395-16975-5*) HM.
—Baba Yaga. Lent, Blair, illus. 48p. (gr. k-3). 1992. pap. 5.70 (*0-395-63037-1*, Sandpiper) HM.
Small, Howard I. Monty's Pal. Hengen, Nona, illus. LC 78-73621. viii, 120p. (gr. 3-8). 1979. 6.95 (*0-931474-08-6*) TBW Bks.
Small, Terry. Legend of John Henry. (gr. 4-7). 1994. 14. 95 (*0-385-31168-0*) Doubleday.
—Legend of Pecos Bill. (ps-3). 1992. 16.00 (*0-553-07583-7*) Bantam.
—Legend of William Tell. (ps-3). 1991. 14.95 (*0-553-07031-2*) Bantam.

—Tails, Claws, Fangs & Paws: An Alpha Beast Caper. Small, Terry, illus. 32p. (ps-3). 1990. 13.95 (0-553-05852-5) Bantam.
Smalley, Donald, ed. see Browning, Robert.
Smalley, Guy, illus. My Very Own Book of ABCs. 32p. (ps-2). 1989. 9.95 (0-929793-02-1) Camex Bks Inc.
—My Very Own Book of Mother Goose Animals. 24p. (ps-2). 1989. 9.95 (0-929793-01-3) Camex Bks Inc.
—My Very Own Book of Numbers. 28p. (ps-2). 1989. 9.95 (0-929793-00-5) Camex Bks Inc.
—My Very Own Book of Sizes. 24p. (ps-2). 1989. 9.95 (0-929793-04-8) Camex Bks Inc.
—My Very Own Book of Toys. 24p. (ps-2). 1989. 9.95 (0-929793-03-X) Camex Bks Inc.
—My Very Own Book of What's for Lunch. 24p. (ps-2). 1989. 9.95 (0-929793-05-6) Camex Bks Inc.
Smalley, Mark. The Rhine. Cumming, David, illus. LC 92-24041. 48p. (gr. 5-6). 1993. PLB 22.80 (0-8114-3102-9) Raintree Steck-V.
Smallman, Clare & Riddell, Edwina. Outside In. (Illus.). 32p. (ps-2). 1986. 13.95 (0-8120-5760-0) Barron.
Smalls, Hector I. Irene & the Big, Fine Nickel, Vol. 1. (ps-3). 1991. 14.95 (0-316-79871-1) Little.
Smalls-Hector, Irene. Dawn & the Round-to-It. Geter, Tyrone, illus. LC 93-19731. 1994. pap. 14.00 (0-671-87166-8, S&S BFYR) S&S Trade.
—Irene Jennie & the Christmas Masquerade: The Johnkankus. Goodnight, Paul, illus. LC 93-7037. 1994. 15.95 (0-316-79878-9) Little.
—Jonathan & His Mommy. (ps-3). 1992. 14.95 (0-316-79870-3) Little.
Smallwood, Joyce C. Golden Chips for Junior Snacking. 1993. 7.95 (0-8062-4602-2) Carlton.
Smallwood, William L. The Air Force Academy Candidate Book. (Illus.). 200p. (Orig.). (gr. 10-12). 1988. pap. write for info. Beacon Bks.
Smarananananda. Story of Sarada Devi. Chakravarty, Biswaranjan, illus. 36p. (Orig.). (gr. k-4). 1987. pap. 1.95 (0-87481-229-1, Pub. by Advaita Ashram IA) Vedanta Pr.
Smarananananda, Swami. The Story of Ramakrishna. Chakravarty, Biswaranjan, illus. (Orig.). (gr. k-5). 1976. pap. 1.95 (0-87481-168-6) Vedanta Pr.
Smarandache, Florentin. Fugit... Jurnal de Lagar din Turcia. Stroe, Gheorghe, ed. Rotaro, Ion, intro. by. (RUM.). 350p. (Orig.). 1991. write for info. (1-879585-26-X) Erhus Univ Pr.
—Povesti de Adormit Copiii. Xiquan Publishing House Staff, ed. (RUM.). 70p. (Orig.). 1992. pap. 5.99 (1-879585-19-7) Erhus Univ Pr.
—Profesor in Africa: Jurnal Marocan. Xiquan Publishing House Staff, ed. (RUM.). 100p. (Orig.). 1991. pap. 9.99 (1-879585-24-3) Erhus Univ Pr.
Smart, Christopher. The Poetical Works of Christopher Smart, Vol. IV: Miscellaneous Poems, English & Latin. Williamson, Karina, ed. (Illus.). 496p. (gr. 5 up). 1987. 115.00 (0-19-812768-5) OUP.
Smart, Janette & Camsey, Terry. Get on Board, Children. Skillings, Otis, contrib. by. Date not set. 4.50 (0-685-68198-X, BCMB-410); song charts 29.95 (0-685-68199-8, BCMU-710); cassette 9.98 (0-685-68200-5, BCTA-7137C) Lillenas.
Smart, M., et al. Building Understanding (Middle) (gr. 4-8). 1990. 8.95 (0-918932-97-1) Activity Resources.
Smart, Margaret. Focus on Decimals, 2 vols. (Illus.). (gr. 7-9). 1977. pap. text ed. 7.50 ea.; Vol. 1. (0-918932-12-2); Vol. 2. (0-918932-13-0) Activity Resources.
—Focus on Percent. Laycock, Mary, ed. (Illus.). (gr. 5-9). 1978. pap. text ed. 7.95 (0-918932-54-8) Activity Resources.
Smart, Margaret & Tuel, Patricia. Focus on Fractions, 3 vols. Laycock, Mary, intro. by. (Illus.). (gr. 6-9). 1977. pap. text ed. 7.50 ea.; Set. 16.50 (0-918932-69-6) Vol. 1 (0-918932-14-9) Vol. 2 (0-918932-15-7) Vol. 3 (0-918932-16-5) Activity Resources.
Smart, Margaret, jt. auth. see Laycock, Mary.
Smart, Margaret, jt. auth. see Lund, Charles.
Smart, Margaret A. Focus on Pre-Algebra. Laycock, Mark, intro. by. (Illus.). 48p. (Orig.). (gr. 6-9). 1983. pap. text ed. 7.95 (0-918932-81-5) Activity Resources.
Smart, Margaret A. & Laycock, Mary. Create a Cube. Kyzer, Walter & Kyzer, Martha, illus. 64p. (Orig.). (gr. 4-12). 1985. pap. text ed. 7.95 (0-918932-84-X) Activity Resources.
Smart, Terry L., jt. auth. see Kownslar, Allan O.
Smart Elephant Peter. Wondering of Little Zero. 1991. write for info. (1-879789-76-0) AdRem.
Smath, Jerry. But No Elephants. Smath, Jerry, illus. LC 79-16136. 48p. (ps-3). 1979. 5.95 (0-8193-1007-7); PLB 5.95 (0-8193-1008-5) Parents.
—But No Elephants. Smath, Jerry, illus. 48p. (ps-2). 1991. pap. 2.95 (0-448-41078-8, G&D) Putnam Pub Group.
—Elephant Goes to School. Smath, Jerry, illus. LC 83-23823. 48p. (ps-3). 1984. 5.95 (0-8193-1126-X) Parents.
—Elephant Goes to School. LC 93-7769. 1993. PLB 13.27 (0-8368-0967-X) Gareth Stevens Inc.
—A Hat so Simple. LC 93-22205. (Illus.). 32p. (ps-3). 1993. PLB 13.95 (0-8167-3016-4); pap. write for info. (0-8167-3017-2) BrdgeWater.
—The Housekeeper's Dog. Smath, Jerry, illus. LC 80-10580. 48p. (ps-3). 1980. 5.95 (0-8193-1023-9); PLB 5.95 (0-8193-1024-7) Parents.
—Leon's Prize. LC 87-25800. (Illus.). 40p. (ps-3). 1987. 5.95 (0-8193-1169-3) Parents.

—Leon's Prize. (ps-2). 1990. pap. 2.95 (0-448-04339-4, G&D) Putnam Pub Group.
—Pretzel & Pop's Closetful of Stories. Smath, Jerry, illus. 64p. (gr. 1-3). 1991. 13.95 (0-671-72232-8); PLB 14.98 (0-671-72231-X) Silver Pr.
—Up Goes Mr. Downs. LC 84-1199. (Illus.). 48p. (ps-3). 1985. 5.95 (0-8193-1137-5) Parents.
—Up Goes Mr. Downs. LC 93-13041. 1993. PLB 13.27 (0-8368-0979-3) Gareth Stevens Inc.
Smath, Jerry, illus. Helicopters. 12p. (ps) 1992. bds. 3.95 (0-448-41093-1, G&D) Putnam Pub Group.
—Jumbo Jet. 12p. (ps). 1992. bds. 3.95 (0-448-41094-X, G&D) Putnam Pub Group.
—Peek-a-Bug. LC 89-61381. 14p. (ps). 1990. pap. 3.99 (0-679-80139-1) Random Bks Yng Read.
—Space Shuttle. 12p. (ps). 1992. bds. 3.95 (0-448-41095-8, G&D) Putnam Pub Group.
Smax, Willy. Big Pig's Hat. Ludlow, Keren, illus. LC 92-19442. (ps-3). 1993. 13.99 (0-8037-1476-9) Dial Bks Young.
Smead, Howard. The Afro-Americans. Moynihan, Daniel P., intro. by. (Illus.). (gr. 5 up). 1989. lib. bdg. 17.95 (0-87754-854-4); pap. 9.95 (0-7910-0256-X) Chelsea Hse.
Smee, Doug. Acting Up! Date not set. 7.95 (0-685-68690-6, BCMP-661) Lillenas.
Smee, Nicola. Down in the Woods. rev. ed. Smee, Nicola, illus. 32p. (gr. k-2). 1989. Repr. of 1985 ed. lib. bdg. 10.50 (1-878363-00-X) Forest Hse.
—Finish the Story, Dad. LC 90-28602. (Illus.). 32p. (ps-1). 1991. pap. 13.95 jacketed (0-671-74478-X, S&S BFYR) S&S Trade.
—Finish the Story, Dad. LC 90-28602. (Illus.). 32p. (ps-1). 1993. pap. 7.95 (0-671-79845-6, S&S BYR) S&S Trade.
—Noah's Ark Board Books, 6 vols. (ps). 1993. Boxed set. 14.95 (0-316-79895-9) Little.
—Three Little Bunnies. (Illus.). 10p. (ps). 1994. bds. 6.95 (0-590-48078-2, Cartwheel) Scholastic Inc.
—Three Little Chicks. (Illus.). 10p. (ps). 1994. bds. 6.95 (0-590-48079-0, Cartwheel) Scholastic Inc.
—The Tusk Fairy. Smee, Nicola, illus. LC 93-28444. 32p. (ps-2). 1993. PLB 14.95 (0-8167-3311-2); pap. 3.95 (0-8167-3312-0) Troll Assocs.
Smelcer, John E., ed. A Cycle of Myths: Native Legends from Southeast Alaska. Vienneau, Larry, illus. 116p. (Orig.). (gr. 7 up). 1993. pap. 12.95 (0-9634000-2-9) Salmon Run.
Smelser, Georgia & Westberg, Barbara. Fifty-Two Visualized Talks for Children's Church. (Illus., Orig.). (gr. 3-6). 1981. pap. 5.99 tchr's ed. (0-912315-13-X) Word Aflame.
Smelser, Georgia, jt. auth. see Urshan, Benjamin D.
Smergut, Peter, jt. auth. see Piltch, Benjamin.
Smetzer, Mary B., ed. see Yarber, Yvonne & Choy, Carol R.
SMI Staff. Adventures in Growth. 18th ed. (Illus.). (gr. 3-7). 1988. text ed. 120.00 (0-924121-00-9) LMI TX.
Smidt, Inez, tr. see Vos, Ida.
Smith. Changing Places. 1993. pap. 2.95 (0-590-44723-8) Scholastic Inc.
—Help! There's a Cat Washing Here. (ps-7). 1987. pap. 2.50 (0-553-15374-9, Skylark) Bantam.
Smith, jt. auth. see Reffin.
Smith, A. How to Draw People. (Illus.). 32p. (gr. 4 up). 1993. PLB 12.96 (0-88110-626-7); pap. 4.95 (0-7460-0998-4) EDC.
Smith, A. G. Civil War Paper Soldiers in Full Color. 1985. pap. 4.95 (0-486-24987-5) Dover.
—A Coloring Book of Stained Glass Windows from the Cathedral of St. John the Divine. Smith, A. G., illus. (gr. 1-6). 1983. pap. 2.95 (0-915075-00-8) Cathedral Shop.
—Cut & Assemble a Medieval Castle. 1984. pap. 5.95 (0-486-24663-9) Dover.
—Cut & Assemble an Early American Seaport. 1984. pap. 5.95 (0-486-24754-6) Dover.
—Cut & Assemble an Old Fashioned Carousel in Full Color. 1985. pap. 5.95 (0-486-24992-1) Dover.
—Cut & Assemble an Old-Fashioned Train. 1989. pap. 5.95 (0-486-25324-4) Dover.
—Cut & Assemble Circus Parade. 1985. pap. 5.95 (0-486-24861-5) Dover.
—Cut & Assemble New York Harbor. 1986. pap. 4.95 (0-486-25026-1) Dover.
—Cut & Assemble 3-D Geometric Shapes. 1986. plastic comb bdg. 5.95 (0-486-25093-8) Dover.
—Dinosaur Punch out Stencils. 1989. pap. 3.50 (0-486-25305-8) Dover.
—Easy to Make Periscope. 1990. pap. 3.95 (0-486-26426-2) Dover.
—Easy to Make Pinwheels. 1990. pap. 2.95 (0-486-26435-1) Dover.
—Easy-to-Make Playtime Castle. 1989. pap. 2.95 (0-486-25469-0) Dover.
—Easy-to-Make Playtime Farm. 1989. pap. 2.95 (0-486-25585-9) Dover.
—Easy-to-Make Playtime Village. 1989. pap. 2.95 (0-486-25478-X) Dover.
—Fun with Dinosaur Stencils. 1989. pap. 1.00 (0-486-25450-X) Dover.
—Fun with Favorite Pets Stencils. 1989. pap. 1.00 (0-486-25451-8) Dover.
Smith, A. M., tr. see Radiguet, Raymond.
Smith, Agnes. The Bluegreen Tree. Sharkey, J. Thomas, illus. LC 76-50105. 180p. (Orig.). 1977. 9.00 (0-87012-271-1) Westwind Pr.

—An Edge of the Forest. Sharkey, J. Thomas, illus. 207p. (gr. 7 up). 1974. 9.00 (0-87012-171-5) Westwind Pr.
Smith, Alan & Dwyer, Christopher. Key Chemistry: Investigating Chemistry in the Contemporary World, Bk. 2: Energy, Matter & the Market Place. 712p. (gr. 9-12). 1992. pap. text ed. 29.95 (0-522-84461-8, Pub. by Melbourne U Pr A) Intl Spec Bk.
Smith, Alastair, jt. auth. see Beasant, Pam.
Smith, Alias & Pelkowski, Robert. Basketball: Rodney Rebound & Willie Dribble & DeeDee Dribble in The Runaway Basketball. 32p. (ps-3). 1989. pap. 3.95 (0-8120-4241-7) Barron.
—Football: Frankie Fumble in Football Friends. 32p. (ps-3). 1989. pap. 3.95 (0-8120-4242-5) Barron.
—Hockey: Freddie Face-off & Fanny Falls in Ice Monster. 32p. (ps-3). 1989. pap. 3.95 (0-8120-4243-3) Barron.
—Skiing: Speedy Slopes & Fluffy Snow in Ski School. 32p. (ps-3). 1989. pap. 3.95 (0-8120-4244-1) Barron.
Smith, Alice. Sir Francis Drake & the Struggle for an Ocean Empire. Goetzmann, William H., ed. Collins, Michael, intro. by. (Illus.). 112p. (gr. 6-12). 1993. PLB 19.95 (0-7910-1302-2, Am Art Analog); pap. write for info. (0-7910-1525-4, Am Art Analog) Chelsea Hse.
Smith, Alison. Come Away Home. Haeffele, Deborah, illus. LC 90-41534. 112p. (gr. 3-5). 1991. SBE 12.95 (0-684-19283-7, Scribners Young Read) Macmillan Child Grp.
Smith, Allan H., ed. How to Make School Fun. Trachsler, Don, illus. LC 84-90227. 200p. (Orig.). (gr. 6-12). 1984. pap. 10.00 (0-931113-03-2) Success Publ.
—Teenage Money Making Guide. Trachsler, Don, illus. LC 84-90126. 281p. (Orig.). (gr-12). 1984. pap. 10.00 (0-931113-00-8) Success Publ.
Smith, Ana, tr. see Rice, James.
Smith, Anne. Get into the Action: An Activity Book for Children on Mission Action. 31p. (Orig.). (gr. 1-6). 1990. pap. text ed. 2.95 (0-936625-84-8) Womans Mission Union.
—Thank You, God. 24p. (Orig.). (ps). 1988. pap. text ed. 1.75 (0-936625-44-9) Womans Mission Union.
Smith, Anne, ed. see Watkins, Dawn L.
Smith, Anne W. Blue Denim Blues. 128p. (gr. 6 up). 1988. pap. 2.75 (0-380-70379-3, Flare) Avon.
—Sister in the Shadow. 176p. (gr. 7-12). 1988. pap. 2.75 (0-380-70378-5, Flare) Avon.
Smith, Audrey. Memories of the Past. Al-Sunaidi, Julie, ed. (Illus.). 125p. (gr. 12). 1993. 12.95 (1-882935-04-7) Rolla Fine Arts.
Smith, Barbara A. Historic Denver for Kids. rev. ed. Taylor, Alice, illus. 90p. (Orig.). (gr. k up). 1982. pap. 5.00 (0-943804-25-6) U of Denver Teach.
—Somewhere Just Beyond. 96p. (gr. 3-7). 1993. SBE 12.95 (0-689-31877-4, Atheneum Child Bk) Macmillan Child Grp.
Smith, Barry. A Child's Guide to Bad Behavior. Smith, Barry, illus. 32p. (ps). 1991. 9.70 (0-395-57435-8, Sandpiper) HM.
—Cumberland Road. Smith, Barry, illus. 32p. (gr. k-3). 1989. 9.70 (0-395-51739-7) HM.
—The First Voyage of Christopher Columbus. Smith, Barry, illus. 32p. (ps-3). 1992. 12.95 (0-670-84051-3) Viking Child Bks.
—Minnie & Ginger: A Twentieth-Century Romance. Smith, Barry, illus. LC 90-40330. 32p. (ps-3). 1991. 13.95 (0-517-58253-8, Clarkson Potter) Crown Bks Yng Read.
Smith, Beatrice S. The Road to Galveston. LC 72-7657. (Illus.). 132p. (gr. 4 up). 1973. PLB 10.95 (0-8225-0755-2) Lerner Pubns.
Smith, Beatrice S., jt. auth. see Wergin, Joseph P.
Smith, Beth. Castles. Green, Ann C., illus. Rakos, Jennie, ed. LC 87-25181. (Illus.). 96p. (gr. 7-9). 1988. PLB 10.90 (0-531-10511-3) Watts.
Smith, Beth C. Mystery Tour: A Student Guide to North Carolina Ghosts & Legends. (Illus.). 135p. (gr. 4 up). 1992. 12.95 (0-916107-94-9) Broadfoot.
Smith, Betsy. A Day in the Life of a Firefighter. Noren, Catherine, photos by. LC 80-54099. (Illus.). 32p. (gr. 4-8). 1981. PLB 11.79 (0-89375-444-7); cassettes avail. Troll Assocs.
Smith, Betsy C. A Day in the Life of an Actress. Buckley, F. Reid, Jr., illus. LC 84-8678. 32p. (gr. 4-8). 1985. PLB 11.79 (0-8167-0105-9); pap. text ed. 2.95 (0-8167-0106-7); cassettes avail. Troll Assocs.
—Jimmy Carter, President. LC 86-5589. (Illus.). 128p. (gr. 10 up). 1986. 12.95 (0-8027-6650-1); PLB 13.85 (0-8027-6652-8) Walker & Co.
—Women Win the Vote. (Illus.). 64p. (gr. 5 up). 1989. PLB 16.98 (0-382-09837-4); pap. 8.95 (0-382-09854-4) Silver Burdett Pr.
Smith, Betty N., ed. see Theo Carus Harter, Kaboblin.
Smith, Bob. Old African Tales Told Again. (Illus.). 78p. 1993. pap. 6.95 (0-89733-395-0) Academy Chi Pubs.
—Stunt Flying with Paper Airplanes. (Illus.). 32p. (gr. 3 up). 1992. pap. 2.50 (0-87406-625-5) Willowisp Pr.
Smith, Bozena, tr. see Porazinska, Janina.
Smith, Brad, jt. auth. see Smith, Mary D.
Smith, Brad R. Country Antiques: A Child's Guide. Sagendorf, Kit, illus. 64p. (Orig.). (gr. 1-3). 1987. pap. 11.95 (0-9618645-0-8) Sanford Hse Pr.
Smith, Bruce. Geology Projects for Young Scientists. (gr. 4-7). 1992. pap. 6.95 (0-531-15651-6) Watts.
Smith, Bruce & McKay, David. Geology Projects for Young Scientists. LC 91-43705. (Illus.). 144p. (gr. 9-12). 1992. PLB 13.90 (0-531-11012-5) Watts.
Smith, Bruce G., jt. auth. see McKay, David W.

Smith, C., et al, eds. Macmillan Spelling. large type ed. Incl. No. 2, 2 vols. 392p. (gr. 2). 1983. 99.88 (*0-317-02411-6*, 4-13320-00); No. 5, 2 vols. 400p. (gr. 5). 1984. 99.88 (*0-317-02414-0*, 4-13350-00); No. 6, 2 vols. 424p. (gr. 6). 1984. 111.20 (*0-317-02415-9*, 4-13360-00); No. 7, 2 vols. 424p. (gr. 7). 1984. 111.20 (*0-317-02416-7*, 4-13370-00); No. 8, 2 vols. 400p. (gr. 8). 1984. 111.20 (*0-317-02417-5*, 4-13380-00). (gr. 2-8). 99.88 (*0-317-04891-0*, 4-13320-00) Am Printing Hse.

Smith, Candace. The Sunday Activity Book. pap. 5.95 (*0-88494-511-1*) Bookcraft Inc.

Smith, Cara L. Twenty-Six Rabbits Run Riot. (ps-4). 1990. 12.95 (*0-316-80185-2*) Little.

Smith, Carl B. Elementary Grammar: A Child's Resource Book. Reade, Eugene W., ed. 280p. (Orig.). (gr. 1-4). 1991. pap. 13.95 (*0-9628556-2-6*) Grayson Bernard Pubs.

—Grammar Handbook for Home & School. Reade, Eugene W., ed. LC 92-19371. 96p. (Orig.). (gr. 5 up). 1992. pap. 8.95 (*0-9628556-7-7*) Grayson Bernard Pubs.

—Intermediate Grammar: A Student's Resource Book. Reade, Eugene, ed. LC 92-3659. 320p. (Orig.). (gr. 5 up). 1992. pap. 16.95 (*0-9628556-3-4*) Grayson Bernard Pubs.

Smith, Carter. A Day in the Life of an FBI Agent-in-Training. Jantzen, Franz, illus. LC 90-11150. 32p. (gr. 4-8). 1991. PLB 11.79 (*0-8167-2210-2*); pap. text ed. 2.95 (*0-8167-2211-0*) Troll Assocs.

—The Jamestown Colony. (Illus.). 64p. (gr. 5 up). 1991. PLB 16.98 (*0-382-24121-5*); pap. 8.95 (*0-382-24116-9*) Silver Burdett Pr.

—The Korean War. (Illus.). 64p. (gr. 5 up). 1990. PLB 16.98 (*0-382-09953-2*); pap. 8.95 (*0-382-09949-4*) Silver Burdett Pr.

—The Pyramid Builders. (Illus.). 64p. (gr. 7 up). 1991. PLB 16.98 (*0-382-24131-2*); pap. 8.95 (*0-382-24137-1*) Silver Burdett Pr.

Smith, Carter, ed. Arts & Sciences: A Sourcebook on Colonial America. (Illus.). 96p. (gr. 5-8). 1991. PLB 18.90 (*1-56294-037-6*) Millbrook Pr.

—Battles in a New Land: A Sourcebook on Colonial America. LC 91-13940. (Illus.). 96p. (gr. 5-8). 1991. PLB 18.90 (*1-56294-034-1*) Millbrook Pr.

—Behind the Lines: A Sourcebook on the Civil War. LC 92-16662. (Illus.). 96p. (gr. 5-8). 1993. PLB 18.90 (*1-56294-265-4*) Millbrook Pr.

—Bridging the Continent: A Sourcebook on the American West. LC 91-31129. (Illus.). 96p. (gr. 5-8). 1992. PLB 18.90 (*1-56294-130-5*) Millbrook Pr.

—The Conquest of the West: A Sourcebook on the American West. LC 91-31130. (Illus.). 96p. (gr. 5-8). 1992. PLB 18.90 (*1-56294-129-1*) Millbrook Pr.

—Daily Life: A Sourcebook on Colonial America. LC 91-13941. (Illus.). 96p. (gr. 5-8). 1991. PLB 18.90 (*1-56294-038-4*) Millbrook Pr.

—Eighteen Sixty-Three: The Crucial Year: A Sourcebook on the Civil War. LC 92-16547. (Illus.). 96p. (gr. 5-8). 1993. PLB 18.90 (*1-56294-263-8*) Millbrook Pr.

—Explorers & Settlers: A Sourcebook on Colonial America. (Illus.). 96p. (gr. 5-8). 1991. PLB 18.90 (*1-56294-035-X*) Millbrook Pr.

—Exploring the Frontier: A Sourcebook on the American West. LC 91-31131. (Illus.). 96p. (gr. 5-8). 1992. PLB 18.90 (*1-56294-128-3*) Millbrook Pr.

—The First Battles: A Sourcebook on the Civil War. LC 92-16544. (Illus.). 96p. (gr. 5-8). 1993. PLB 18.90 (*1-56294-262-X*) Millbrook Pr.

—The Founding Presidents: A Sourcebook on the U. S. Presidency. LC 93-12751. (Illus.). 96p. (gr. 5-8). 1993. PLB 18.90 (*1-56294-357-X*) Millbrook Pr.

—Governing & Teaching: A Sourcebook on Colonial America. (Illus.). 96p. (gr. 5-8). 1991. PLB 18.90 (*1-56294-036-8*) Millbrook Pr.

—The Legendary Wild West: A Sourcebook on the American West. LC 91-31126. (Illus.). 96p. (gr. 5-8). 1992. PLB 18.90 (*1-56294-133-X*) Millbrook Pr.

—Native Americans of the West: A Sourcebook on the American West. LC 91-31128. (Illus.). 96p. (gr. 5-8). 1992. PLB 18.90 (*1-56294-131-3*) Millbrook Pr.

—One Nation Again: A Sourcebook on the Civil War. LC 92-16661. (Illus.). 96p. (gr. 5-8). 1993. PLB 18.90 (*1-56294-266-2*) Millbrook Pr.

—Prelude to War: A Sourcebook on the Civil War. LC 92-16545. (Illus.). 96p. (gr. 5-8). 1993. PLB 18.90 (*1-56294-261-1*) Millbrook Pr.

—Presidents in a Time of Change: A Sourcebook on the U. S. Presidency. LC 93-15092. (Illus.). 96p. (gr. 5-8). 1993. 18.90 (*1-56294-362-6*) Millbrook Pr.

—Presidents of a Growing Country: A Sourcebook on the U. S. Presidency. LC 93-15090. (Illus.). 96p. (gr. 5-8). 1993. 18.90 (*1-56294-358-8*) Millbrook Pr.

—Presidents of a World Power: A Sourcebook on the U. S. Presidency. LC 93-15091. (Illus.). 96p. (gr. 5-8). 1993. 18.90 (*1-56294-361-8*) Millbrook Pr.

—Presidents of a Young Republic: A Sourcebook on the U. S. Presidency. LC 93-12752. (Illus.). 96p. (gr. 5-8). 1993. 18.90 (*1-56294-359-6*) Millbrook Pr.

—The Revolutionary War: A Sourcebook on Colonial America. LC 91-13938. (Illus.). 96p. (gr. 5-8). 1991. PLB 18.90 (*1-56294-039-2*) Millbrook Pr.

—The Riches of the West: A Sourcebook on the American West. LC 91-31127. (Illus.). 96p. (gr. 5-8). 1992. PLB 18.90 (*1-56294-132-1*) Millbrook Pr.

—The Road to Appomattox: A Sourcebook on the Civil War. LC 92-16546. (Illus.). 96p. (gr. 5-8). 1993. PLB 18.90 (*1-56294-264-6*) Millbrook Pr.

Smith, Carter, III. One Giant Leap for Mankind. rev. ed. (Illus.). 64p. (gr. 5 up). 1989. PLB 16.98 (*0-382-09909-5*); pap. 8.95 (*0-382-09910-9*) Silver Burdett Pr.

Smith, Carter, III, jt. auth. see Avakian, Monique.

Smith, Charlotte B., jt. auth. see Herman, Charlotte.

Smith, Chris. Conflict in Southern Africa. LC 92-23331. (Illus.). 48p. (gr. 6 up). 1993. RSBE 13.95 (*0-02-785956-8*, New Discovery) Macmillan Child Grp.

Smith, Chris & Harbor, Bernard. Military Technology. (Illus.). 48p. (gr. 5-8). 1991. 12.90 (*0-531-18456-0*, Pub. by Bookwright Pr) Watts.

Smith, Chuck. New Testament Study Guide. 224p. 1982. pap. 2.95 (*0-936728-33-7*) Word For Today.

Smith, Cindy. Amazing Stories from Genesis. 96p. 1992. pap. 12.99 (*1-55945-094-0*) Group Pub.

Smith, Curtis W. Spirits of London: A Psychobiography for Travelers. LC 87-91611. 108p. (Orig.). (gr. 11 up). 1988. pap. 4.95 (*0-944208-00-2*) Seventh Wing Pubns.

—Spirits of London: A Psychobiography for Travelers. LC 87-91611. 110p. (Orig.). (gr. 10 up). 1989. 11.95 (*0-944208-05-3*) Seventh Wing Pubns.

Smith, D. The Waitress. 144p. 1992. pap. 2.95 (*0-590-45063-8*, Point) Scholastic Inc.

Smith, Dan & Whyte, Malcolm. Zoo Action Set, No. 2. (Illus.). 24p. 1990. pap. 5.95 (*0-8431-2831-3*) Price Stern.

Smith, David. The Food Cycle. LC 93-24391. (Illus.). 32p. (gr. 2-5). 1993. 12.95 (*1-56847-093-2*) Thomson Lrning.

—Golf: Tactics of Success. (Illus.). 80p. (gr. 10-12). 1992. pap. 8.95 (*0-7063-7091-0*, Pub. by Ward Lock UK) Sterling.

—The Water Cycle. LC 93-976. 32p. (gr. 2-5). 1993. 12.95 (*1-56847-092-4*) Thomson Lrning.

Smith, David & Newton, Derek. Troll Young People's Dictionary. Goldsmith, Evelyn, rev. by. Bayly, Clifford, illus. LC 89-27331. 128p. (gr. 1-4). 1991. PLB 14.89 (*0-8167-2255-2*); pap. 9.95 (*0-8167-2256-0*) Troll Assocs.

Smith, David B. Bad News in Bangkok. Wheeler, Gerald, ed. LC 92-19353. 1993. pap. 4.95 (*0-8280-0697-0*) Review & Herald.

—Making Waves at Hampton Beach High. Wheeler, Gerald, ed. 128p. (Orig.). (gr. 7-12). 1990. pap. 4.95 (*0-8280-0580-X*) Review & Herald.

Smith, Dennis. Little Fire Engine That Saved the City. 1990. 9.95 (*0-385-26257-4*) Doubleday.

Smith, Derek. Glory Yards: A Game-by-Game History of the South's Most Legendary Pigskin Bloodletting. (Illus.). 320p. (gr. 10 up). 1993. 19.95 (*1-55853-244-7*) Rutledge Hill Pr.

—Hard Cash. 184p. (gr. 5 up). 1992. 15.95 (*0-571-16174-X*) Faber & Faber.

Smith, Dian G. Happy Birthday to Me! A Four-Year Record Book for Birthday Boys & Girls. Franc-Nohain, Marie M., illus. 48p. (gr. 2-5). 1989. pap. 9.95 (*0-684-19046-X*, Scribners Young Read) Macmillan Child Grp.

Smith, Diane, jt. auth. see Smith, Tom.

Smith, Dick & Bernard, Felix. Winter Wonderland. Rogers, Jacqueline, illus. 32p. (ps-1). 1993. pap. 2.50 (*0-590-46657-7*, Cartwheel) Scholastic Inc.

Smith, Dodie. The Hundred & One Dalmatians. Grahame-Johnstone, Janet & Grahame-Johnstone, Anne, illus. 208p. (gr. 1 up). 1976. pap. 2.50 (*0-380-00628-6*, Camelot) Avon.

—The Hundred & One Dalmatians. (Illus.). 208p. 1989. pap. 14.95 (*0-670-82660-X*) Viking Child Bks.

—The Hundred & One Dalmatians. Dooling, Michael, illus. (gr. 4 up). 1989. pap. 3.95 (*0-318-41739-1*, Puffin) Puffin Bks.

—The One Hundred & One Dalmatians. Dooling, Michael, illus. (gr. 5-9). 1989. pap. 3.99 (*0-14-034034-3*, Puffin) Puffin Bks.

Smith, Don. The Baja Run: Racing Fury. LC 75-23412. (Illus.). 32p. (gr. 5-10). 1976. PLB 10.79 (*0-89375-000-X*) Troll Assocs.

—The Grand Canyon: Journey Through Time. new ed. LC 75-23413. (Illus.). 32p. (gr. 5-10). 1976. PLB 10.79 (*0-89375-007-7*); pap. 2.95 (*0-89375-023-9*) Troll Assocs.

—Surfing, the Big Wave. new ed. LC 75-21847. (Illus.). 32p. (gr. 5-10). 1976. PLB 10.79 (*0-89375-011-5*) Troll Assocs.

Smith, Dona. Shock Shots: Ghosts. (gr. 4-7). 1993. pap. 1.25 (*0-590-47568-1*) Scholastic Inc.

—Shock Shots: Monsters. (gr. 4-7). 1993. pap. 1.25 (*0-590-47566-5*) Scholastic Inc.

—Shock Shots: Mummies. (gr. 4-7). 1993. pap. 1.25 (*0-590-47571-1*) Scholastic Inc.

—Shock Shots: Vampires. (gr. 4-7). 1993. pap. 1.25 (*0-590-47569-X*) Scholastic Inc.

—Shock Shots: Werewolves. (gr. 4-7). 1993. pap. 1.25 (*0-590-47570-3*) Scholastic Inc.

—Shock Shots: Zombies. (gr. 4-7). 1993. pap. 1.25 (*0-590-47567-3*) Scholastic Inc.

Smith, Donald. Tiny Mermaid's Hide & Seek Adventure. (Illus.). 16p. (ps-2). 1993. 12.95 (*0-590-46673-9*) Scholastic Inc.

Smith, Donna G., ed. see Garlits, Don & Yates, Brock.

Smith, Doris B. Best Girl. LC 92-25931. 144p. (gr. 3-7). 1993. 13.99 (*0-670-83752-0*) Viking Child Bks.

—The First Hard Times. 144p. (gr. 5-9). 1984. pap. 2.50 (*0-440-42532-8*, YB) Dell.

—The First Hard Times. (gr. 4 up). 1990. pap. 3.95 (*0-14-034538-8*, Puffin) Puffin Bks.

—Karate Dancer. 208p. (gr. 6-9). 1987. 14.95 (*0-399-21464-X*, Putnam) Putnam Pub Group.

—Kelly's Creek. Tiegreen, Alan, illus. LC 75-6761. 80p. (gr. 4-6). 1989. PLB 13.89 (*0-690-04774-6*, Crowell Jr Bks) HarpC Child Bks.

—Last Was Lloyd. 144p. (gr. 3-7). 1981. pap. 12.95 (*0-670-41921-4*) Viking Child Bks.

—Last Was Lloyd. 128p. (gr. 3 up). 1990. pap. 3.95 (*0-14-034444-6*, Puffin) Puffin Bks.

—The Pennywhistle Tree. Bowman, Leslie, illus. LC 90-23119. 144p. (gr. 5-9). 1991. 14.95 (*0-399-21840-8*, Putnam) Putnam Pub Group.

—Remember the Red-Shouldered Hawk. LC 93-14405. 1994. write for info. (*0-399-22443-2*, Putnam) Putnam Pub Group.

—Return to Bitter Creek. LC 85-40838. 180p. (gr. 3-7). 1986. pap. 12.95 (*0-670-80783-4*) Viking Child Bks.

—Return to Bitter Creek. 176p. (gr. 3-7). 1988. pap. 3.95 (*0-14-032223-X*, Puffin) Puffin Bks.

—A Taste of Blackberries. Robinson, Charles, illus. LC 72-7558. 64p. (gr. 3-6). 1973. PLB 12.89 (*0-690-80512-8*, Crowell Jr Bks) HarpC Child Bks.

—A Taste of Blackberries. Wimmer, Mike, illus. LC 88-45077. 64p. (gr. 3-6). 1988. pap. 3.95 (*0-06-440238-X*, Trophy) HarpC Child Bks.

—Voyages. 176p. (gr. 5-9). 1991. pap. 3.95 (*0-14-032224-8*, Puffin) Puffin Bks.

Smith, Doris M. Benjie's Fun Time with Numbers. (Illus.). 16p. (ps-k). pap. 5.95 (*0-8059-3341-7*) Dorrance.

Smith, Dorothy. Saint Joan: The Girl in Armour. Broomfield, Robert, illus. 1990. 2.95 (*0-8091-6594-5*) Paulist Pr.

—Thomas More: The King's Good Servant. Broomfield, Robert, illus. 1990. 2.95 (*0-8091-6595-3*) Paulist Pr.

Smith, Dorothy L. Pete's Lesson. 1993. 8.95 (*0-8062-4425-9*) Carlton.

Smith, Douglas W. Schizophrenia. LC 92-21140. (Illus.). (gr. 7-12). 1993. PLB 13.40 (*0-531-12514-9*) Watts.

Smith, Douglas W., jt. auth. see Smith, Norman F.

Smith, Duncan. Fred & the Rocket. (Illus.). 32p. 1993. 10.95 (*0-237-51145-2*, Pub. by Evans Bros Ltd) Trafalgar.

—Fred Goes Fishing. (Illus.). 25p. (gr. k-2). 1991. 11.95 (*0-237-51126-6*, Pub. by Evans Bros Ltd) Trafalgar.

—Fred Goes to France. (Illus.). 25p. (gr. k-2). 1991. 11.95 (*0-237-51125-8*, Pub. by Evans Bros Ltd) Trafalgar.

—Fred the Pirate. (Illus.). 25p. (gr. k-2). 1991. 11.95 (*0-237-51144-4*, Pub. by Evans Bros Ltd) Trafalgar.

—Fred the Ted. (Illus.). 25p. (gr. k-2). 1991. 11.95 (*0-237-51101-0*, Pub. by Evans Bros Ltd) Trafalgar.

—Fred under the Bed. (Illus.). 25p. (gr. k-2). 1991. 11.95 (*0-237-51112-6*, Pub. by Evans Bros Ltd) Trafalgar.

Smith, E. Boyd. The Farm Book. Smith, E. Boyd, illus. 64p. (gr. 3-5). 1982. 15.45 (*0-395-32951-5*) HM.

—The Farm Book. Smith, E. Boyd, illus. 64p. (ps up). 1990. pap. 6.70 (*0-395-54951-5*) HM.

—The Railroad Book. Smith, E. Boyd, illus. 56p. (gr. 3-5). 1983. 16.45 (*0-395-34832-3*) HM.

—The Seashore Book. Smith, E. Boyd, illus. LC 84-22483. 56p. (gr. k-12). 1985. Repr. of 1912 ed. 13.45 (*0-395-38015-4*) HM.

Smith, Edmund W. One Eyed Poacher of Privilege. 2nd ed. Lassell, A., illus. 187p. (gr. 10 up). 1991. Repr. of 1941 ed. 35.00 (*1-56416-019-X*) Derrydale Pr.

—Tall Tales & Short. 2nd ed. Weiler, Milton, illus. 187p. (gr. 10 up). 1991. Repr. of 1938 ed. 35.00 (*1-56416-020-3*) Derrydale Pr.

—A Tomato Can Chronicle. 2nd ed. Boyer, Ralph, illus. 189p. (gr. 10 up). 1991. Repr. of 1937 ed. 35.00 (*1-56416-018-1*) Derrydale Pr.

Smith, Elizabeth S. Cloth: Inventions That Changed Our Lives. LC 84-25768. (Illus.). 60p. (gr. 4-7). 1985. PLB 10.85 (*0-8027-6577-7*) Walker & Co.

—Coming Out Right: The Story of Jackie Cochran, the First Woman Aviator to Break the Sound Barrier. (Illus.). 128p. (gr. 5 up). 1991. 14.95 (*0-8027-6988-8*); PLB 15.85 (*0-8027-6989-6*) Walker & Co.

—A Dolphin Goes to School: The Story of Squirt, a Trained Dolphin. LC 85-28407. (Illus.). 96p. (gr. 2-5). 1986. 12.95 (*0-688-04815-3*); lib. bdg. 12.88 (*0-688-04816-1*, Morrow Jr Bks) Morrow Jr Bks.

—Five First Ladies. (Illus.). 122p. (gr. 10 up). 1986. 12.95 (*0-8027-6640-4*); lib. bdg. 14.85 (*0-8027-6641-2*) Walker & Co.

—A Guide Dog Goes to School: The Story of a Dog Trained to Lead the Blind. Dodson, Bert, illus. LC 87-11056. 64p. (gr. 1-4). 1987. 12.95 (*0-688-06844-8*); lib. bdg. 12.88 (*0-688-06846-4*, Morrow Jr Bks) Morrow Jr Bks.

—Paper. LC 84-7271. (Illus.). 64p. (gr. 4 up). 1984. PLB 10.85 (*0-8027-6569-6*) Walker & Co.

—A Service Dog Goes to School: The Story of a Dog Trained to Help the Disabled. Petruccio, Steven, illus. LC 88-17598. 64p. (gr. 1-4). 1988. 12.95 (*0-688-07648-3*); PLB 12.88 (*0-688-07649-1*, Morrow Jr Bks) Morrow Jr Bks.

Smith, Ellen, ed. see Prather, Gloria M. & Prather, Alfred J.

Smith, Elva S., compiled by. Christmas in Legend & Story: A Book for Boys & Girls Illustrated from Famous Paintings. Hazeltine, Alice I., compiled by. LC 72-39390. (gr. 7 up). Repr. of 1915 ed. 18.00 (*0-8369-6353-9*) Ayer.

Smith, Emma. Emily the Traveling Guinea Pig. (gr. 1-5). 1960. 10.95 (*0-8392-3007-9*) Astor-Honor.

Smith, Frances. The Little Girl Who Grew up to be Governor: Stories from the Life of Martha Layne Collins. Pullen, Pip, illus. LC 91-73725. 64p. (gr. 2-4). 1991. 13.95 (*0-9630135-0-5*) Denham Pub.

Smith, Frank C. How to Draw Cats and Kittens. (ps-3). 1988. pap. 1.95 (*0-590-44000-4*) Scholastic Inc.

—How to Draw Dinosaurs. (ps-3). 1989. pap. 1.95 (*0-590-43799-2*) Scholastic Inc.

—How to Draw Horses & Ponies. (ps-3). 1990. pap. 1.95 (*0-590-42462-9*) Scholastic Inc.

—How to Draw Silly Monsters. (Illus.). 32p. (gr. 1-6). 1989. pap. 1.95 (*0-590-43914-6*) Scholastic Inc.

—I Can Draw Comics & Cartoons. Smith, Frank C., illus. 64p. (Orig.). (gr. 3 up). 1982. pap. 3.95 (*0-671-44490-5*, Little Simon) S&S Trade.

Smith, Gene. Lee & Grant. 448p. (gr. 9-12). 1985. pap. 12.95 (*0-452-01000-4*, Mer) NAL-Dutton.

Smith, George S. The Christmas Eve Cattle Drive. Bacon, Eliza, illus. 32p. (gr. 1-4). 1991. pap. 3.95 (*0-89015-820-7*) Eakin-Sunbelt.

Smith, Gina H. Blooming Mother Nature: Fun Language Activities to Unfold the Wonders of Nature Based on Bloom's Taxonomy. (Illus.). 80p. (ps-4). 1990. pap. 14.95 perfect bdg. (*1-55999-119-4*) LinguiSystems.

Smith, Glen, jt. ed. see Smith, Louisa.

Smith, Glenna C. The Little Mouse Was a Grouch. Jordan, Alton, ed. (Illus.). (gr. k-3). 1981. (Read Res); pap. text ed. 20.00 (*0-89868-106-5*) ARO Pub.

Smith, H. N., ed. see Twain, Mark.

Smith, Harry W. The ABC's of Maine. LC 79-67415. (Illus.). 60p. (ps up) 1980. pap. 6.95 (*0-89272-070-0*) Down East.

Smith, Helene & Swetnam, George. Hannah's Town. LC 73-84564. (Illus.). 113p. 1973. 7.95 (*0-685-27129-3*) MacDonald-Sward.

Smith, Henry. Amazing Air. Firth, Barbara, et al, illus. LC 82-80991. 48p. (gr. 3-6). 1983. PLB 11.88 (*0-688-00973-5*) Lothrop.

—Amazing Air. Firth, Barbara, et al, illus. LC 82-80991. 48p. (gr. 3-6). 1983. pap. 7.95 (*0-688-00977-8*, Pub. by Beech Tree Bks) Morrow.

Smith, Howard E. Reptiles & Amphibians. Bonforte, Lisa, illus. LC 89-29384. 1991. write for info. (*0-385-41177-4*); PLB write for info. (*0-385-41178-2*) Doubleday.

Smith, Howard E., Jr. All about Arrowheads & Spear Points. Dewey, Jennifer O., illus. LC 88-39089. 80p. (gr. 4-6). 1989. 14.95 (*0-8050-0892-6*, Bks Young Read) H Holt & Co.

—Daring the Unknown: A History of N. A. S. A. LC 86-33617. (Illus.). 128p. (gr. 3-7). 1987. 16.95 (*0-15-200435-1*, Gulliver Bks) HarBrace.

Smith, Iris. Little Witch. Church, Caroline, illus. LC 92-39671. 28p. (ps-2). 1993. 12.95 (*0-8120-5791-0*); pap. 5.95 (*0-8120-1552-5*) Barron.

Smith, James C., ed. see Atwood, Marjorie, Jr.

Smith, James C., Jr., ed. see Yoder, Walter D.

Smith, Jane D. The Tabernacle. Butcher, Sam, illus. 38p. (gr. k-6). 1972. pap. text ed. 9.45 (*1-55976-022-2*) CEF Press.

Smith, Janet A., ed. The Faber Book of Children's Verse. 412p. (gr. 4 up). 1953. pap. 10.95 (*0-571-05457-9*) Faber & Faber.

Smith, Janice L. The Baby Blues: An Adam Joshua Story. Gackenbach, Dick, illus. LC 93-14492. 1994. write for info. (*0-06-023642-6*, HarpT); PLB write for info. (*0-06-023643-4*, HarpT) HarpC.

—It's Not Easy Being George: Stories about Adam Joshua (& His Dog) Gackenbach, Dick, illus. LC 88-33075. 128p. (gr. 1-4). 1989. 10.95 (*0-06-025852-7*); PLB 10.89 (*0-06-025853-5*) HarpC Child Bks.

—It's Not Easy Being George: Stories about Adam Joshua (& His Dog) Gackenbach, Dick, illus. LC 88-33075. 128p. (gr. 1-4). 1991. pap. 3.50 (*0-06-440338-6*, Trophy) HarpC Child Bks.

—The Kid Next Door & Other Headaches: More Stories about Adam Joshua. Gackenbach, Dick, illus. LC 83-47689. 160p. (gr. 1-4). 1986. pap. 3.95 (*0-06-440182-0*, Trophy) HarpC Child Bks.

—The Kid Next Door & Other Headaches: Stories about Adam Joshua. Gackenbach, Dick, illus. LC 83-47689. 160p. (gr. 1-4). 1984. PLB 12.89 (*0-06-025793-8*) HarpC Child Bks.

—The Monster in the Third Dresser Drawer. Gackenbach, Dick, illus. LC 81-47109. 96p. (gr. 1-4). 1981. 13.00 (*0-06-025734-2*); PLB 12.89 (*0-06-025739-3*) HarpC Child Bks.

—The Monster in the Third Dresser Drawer: And Other Stories about Adam Joshua. Gackenbach, Dick, illus. LC 81-47109. 96p. (gr. 1-4). 1988. pap. 3.95 (*0-06-440223-1*, Trophy) HarpC Child Bks.

—Nelson in Love: An Adam Joshua Valentine's Day Story. Gackenbach, Dick, illus. LC 91-14667. 80p. (gr. 1-4). 1992. 13.00 (*0-06-020292-0*); PLB 12.89 (*0-06-020293-9*) HarpC Child Bks.

—Serious Science: An Adam Joshua Story. Gackenbach, Dick, illus. LC 91-30824. 80p. (gr. 1-4). 1993. 12.00 (*0-06-020779-5*); PLB 11.89 (*0-06-020782-5*) HarpC Child Bks.

—The Show-&-Tell War: And Other Stories about Adam Joshua. Gackenbach, Dick, illus. LC 85-45842. 176p. (gr. 1-4). 1988. PLB 11.89 (*0-06-025815-2*) HarpC Child Bks.

—The Show-&-Tell War: And Other Stories about Adam Joshua. Gackenbach, Dick, illus. LC 85-45842. 176p. (gr. 1-4). 1990. pap. 3.95 (*0-06-440312-2*, J312, Trophy) HarpC Child Bks.

—There's a Ghost in the Coatroom: Adam Joshua's Christmas. Gackenbach, Dick, illus. LC 90-23068. 96p. (gr. 1-4). 1991. 12.95 (*0-06-022863-6*); PLB 12.89 (*0-06-022864-4*) HarpC Child Bks.

—The Turkeys' Side of It. Gackenbach, Dick, illus. LC 89-78419. 64p. (gr. 1-4). 1992. pap. 3.95 (*0-06-440452-8*, Trophy) HarpC Child Bks.

—The Turkeys' Side of It: Adam Joshua's Thanksgiving. Gackenbach, Dick, illus. LC 89-78419. 64p. (gr. 1-4). 1990. 12.00 (*0-06-025857-8*); PLB 11.89 (*0-06-025859-4*) HarpC Child Bks.

—Wizard & Wart. Meisel, Paul, illus. LC 92-41170. 1994. 13.00 (*0-06-022960-8*, HarpT); PLB 12.89 (*0-06-022961-6*, HarpT) HarpC.

Smith, Jean B. The Tartan Tiger. (Illus., Orig.). (gr. 7 up). 1986. pap. 8.00 (*0-935827-00-5*) Tartan Tiger.

Smith, Jennifer. Grover & the New Kid. Cooke, Tom, illus. LC 86-42965. 40p. (ps-3). 1987. 4.95 (*0-394-88519-8*) Random Bks Yng Read.

Smith, Jerry, jt. auth. see Hammond, Vicky L.

Smith, Jessie. Sesame Street: Going Places. Ewers, Joseph, illus. LC 87-81768. 24p. (ps-k). 1988. pap. write for info. (*0-307-10057-X*, Pub. by Golden Bks) Western Pub.

Smith, Jo R., jt. auth. see Black, Ann N.

Smith, John, jt. auth. see Lopez, Arcadia.

Smith, John F. The Song of the Whango-Whee. Colon, Odette E., illus. Hannaford, Joey, contrib. by. (Illus.). 24p. (ps-5). 1993. 13.95 (*1-884375-00-6*) Chinky-Po Tree.

Smith, Josephine A. Being Cool, Going to School. Wilkins, Natalie, ed. Dowley, May, illus. LC 92-74244. 64p. (Orig.). 1994. pap. text ed. 2.99 (*1-881958-02-7*) Hickle Pickle.

—Off the Vine, Doin' Fine. Dowley, May, illus. LC 92-96865. 48p. (Orig.). 1992. pap. 2.99 (*1-881958-01-9*, TXU328879) Hickle Pickle.

Smith, Josie, tr. from ENG. El Joven y las Misiones - Missions Bible Study for Youth. (SPA., Illus.). 62p. (Orig.). (gr. 10 up). 1991. pap. 3.10 (*0-311-11068-1*) Casa Bautista.

Smith, Joyce M. Demons, Doubters & Dead Men. 64p. (Orig.). (gr. 4-7). 1986. 2.95 (*0-8423-0542-4*) Tyndale.

Smith, Judie. Coping with Suicide. rev. ed. LC 86-10076. 128p. (gr. 7-12). 1990. PLB 13.95 (*0-8239-1052-0*) Rosen Group.

—Drugs & Suicide. Rosen, Ruth, ed. (gr. 7-12). 1992. 14.95 (*0-8239-1421-6*) Rosen Group.

Smith, Judy G. Teaching Children about Prayer. 25p. (Orig.). (gr. 4-6). 1988. pap. 6.95 (*0-940754-56-8*) Ed Ministries.

Smith, K. Skeeter. (gr. 6 up). 1989. 14.95 (*0-395-49603-9*) HM.

—Skeeter. (gr. 4-7). 1992. pap. 4.80 (*0-395-61621-2*) HM.

Smith, K. T. Beverly Hills, 90210: Fantasies. 1992. pap. 3.99 (*0-06-106727-X*, Harp PBks) HarpC.

Smith, Kaitlin. Funny Things Happen. Smith, Kaitlin, illus. 15p. (gr. k-3). 1993. pap. 12.95 (*1-56606-020-6*) Bradley Mann.

—Take a Walk with Me. Smith, Kaitlin, illus. 12p. (gr. k-3). 1993. pap. 10.95 (*1-56606-019-2*) Bradley Mann.

Smith, Kaitlin M. Arizona Is Hot. Smith, Kaitlin M., illus. 14p. (gr. k-3). 1992. pap. 10.95 (*1-895583-18-7*) MAYA Pubs.

—Big Monster Learns about Manners. Smith, Kaitlin M., illus. 18p. (gr. 1-5). 1992. pap. 10.95 (*1-56606-006-0*) Bradley Mann.

—Counting with Buster Bear. Smith, Kaitlin M., illus. 15p. (gr. k-3). 1992. pap. 12.95 (*1-895583-15-2*) MAYA Pubs.

—Going to the Hospital. Smith, Kaitlin M., illus. 18p. (gr. k-3). 1992. pap. 13.95 (*1-895583-17-9*) MAYA Pubs.

—It's Time, Dad. Smith, Kaitlin M., illus. 15p. (gr. k-3). 1992. pap. 15.95 (*1-895583-16-0*) MAYA Pubs.

—Sally Writes a Letter to Santa Claus. Smith, Kaitlin M., illus. 15p. (gr. 1-4). 1992. pap. 10.95 (*1-56606-005-2*) Bradley Mann.

—Skating with Katie. Smith, Kaitlin M., illus. 15p. (gr. k-3). 1992. pap. 17.95 (*1-895583-19-5*) MAYA Pubs.

Smith, Kaitlin M., jt. auth. see Kontoyiannaki, Kosta.

Smith, Karen M. New Paths to Power: American Women 1890-1920. (Illus.). 144p. 1994. lib. bdg. 20.00 (*0-19-508111-0*) OUP.

Smith, Kathie B. Abraham Lincoln. Seward, James, illus. LC 86-28060. 24p. (gr. 4-6). 1987. PLB 7.98 (*0-671-64148-4*, J Messner); PLB 5.99s.p. (*0-685-18829-9*) S&S Trade.

—Albert Einstein. Steltenpohl, Jane, ed. Seward, James, illus. 24p. (gr. 4-6). 1989. lib. bdg. 7.98 (*0-671-67514-1*, J Messner); PLB 5.99s.p. (*0-685-25426-7*) S&S Trade.

—Dinosaurs. 1987. pap. 2.95 (*0-671-63238-8*, Little Simon) S&S Trade.

—Enchanted Unicorn. 1987. pap. 2.95 incl. stickers (*0-671-63239-6*, Little Simon) S&S Trade.

—George Washington. Seward, James, illus. 24p. (gr. 4-6). 1987. (J Messner); PLB 5.99s.p. (*0-685-47101-2*) S&S Trade.

—The Great Americans Series, 9 vols. Seward, James, illus. 216p. (gr. 4-6). 1989. Set. PLB 71.82 (*0-671-93118-0*, J Messner); Set. PLB 53.91s.p. (*0-685-54168-1*) S&S Trade.

—Harriet Tubman. Steltenpohl, Jane, ed. Seward, James, illus. 24p. (gr. 4-6). 1989. lib. bdg. 7.98 (*0-671-67513-3*, J Messner); PLB 5.99s.p. (*0-685-25427-5*) S&S Trade.

—John F. Kennedy. Seward, James, illus. LC 86-33863. 24p. (gr. 4-6). 1987. lib. bdg. 7.98 (*0-671-64602-8*, J Messner); PLB 5.99s.p. (*0-685-18831-0*) S&S Trade.

—John F. Kennedy. (gr. k-5). 1987. pap. 2.25 (*0-671-64025-9*, Little Simon) S&S Trade.

—Martin Luther King, Jr. Seward, James, illus. LC 86-28059. 24p. (gr. 4-6). 1987. lib. bdg. 7.98 (0-671-64149-2, J Messner); PLB 5.99s.p. (0-685-18830-2) S&S Trade.
—Men of the Constitution. (Illus.). 32p. (gr. k-5). 1987. pap. 2.25 (0-671-64028-3, Little Simon) S&S Trade.
—Sitting Bull. (Illus.). 32p. (gr. k-5). 1987. pap. 2.25 (0-671-64027-5, Little Simon) S&S Trade.
—Sitting Bull. Seward, James, illus. LC 86-33888. 24p. (gr. 4-6). 1987. lib. bdg. 7.98 (0-671-64603-6, J Messner); PLB 5.99s.p. (0-685-47297-3) S&S Trade.
—Thomas Jefferson. Steltenpohl, Jane, ed. Seward, James, illus. 24p. (gr. 4-6). 1989. lib. bdg. 7.98 (0-671-67512-5, J Messner); PLB 5.99s.p. (0-685-25428-3) S&S Trade.
—United States Atlas for Young People. LC 90-675059. (Illus.). 128p. (gr. 3-7). 1991. lib. bdg. 14.89 (0-8167-2195-5); pap. text ed. 9.95 (0-8167-2196-3) Troll Assocs.

Smith, Kathie B. & Bradbury, Pamela. Men of the Constitution. Seward, James, illus. 24p. (gr. 4-6). 1987. (J Messner); PLB 5.99s.p. (0-685-54169-X) S&S Trade.

Smith, Kathie B. & Bradbury, Pamela Z. Albert Einstein. (Illus.). 24p. (ps up). 1989. pap. 2.25 (0-671-64767-9, Little Simon) S&S Trade.
—Harriet Tubman. (Illus.). 24p. (ps up). 1989. pap. 2.25 (0-671-64026-7, Little Simon) S&S Trade.
—Thomas Jefferson. (Illus.). 32p. (ps up). 1989. pap. 2.25 (0-671-64768-7, Little Simon) S&S Trade.

Smith, Kathie B. & Crenson, Victoria. Hearing. Storms, Robert S., illus. LC 87-5854. 24p. (gr. k-3). 1988. PLB 10.59 (0-8167-1006-6); pap. text ed. 2.50 (0-8167-1007-4) Troll Assocs.
—Seeing. Storms, Robert S., illus. LC 87-5862. 24p. (gr. k-3). 1988. PLB 10.59 (0-8167-1008-2); pap. text ed. 2.50 (0-8167-1009-0) Troll Assocs.
—Smelling. Storms, Robert S., illus. LC 87-5887. 24p. (gr. k-3). 1988. PLB 10.59 (0-8167-1010-4); pap. text ed. 2.50 (0-8167-1011-2) Troll Assocs.
—Tasting. LC 87-5884. (Illus.). 24p. (gr. k-3). 1988. PLB 10.59 (0-8167-1014-7); pap. text ed. 2.50 (0-8167-1015-5) Troll Assocs.
—Thinking. Storms, Robert S., illus. LC 87-5886. 24p. (gr. k-3). 1988. PLB 10.59 (0-8167-1016-3); pap. text ed. 2.50 (0-8167-1017-1) Troll Assocs.
—Touching. Storms, Robert S., illus. LC 87-5885. 24p. (gr. k-3). 1988. PLB 10.59 (0-8167-1012-0); pap. text ed. 2.50 (0-8167-1013-9) Troll Assocs.

Smith, Kathy, jt. auth. see Seltzer, Richard.

Smith, L. How to Draw, Vol. III. (Illus.). 32p. (gr. 4 up). 1993. pap. 9.95 (0-7460-1501-1) EDC.
—How to Draw Horses. (Illus.). 32p. (gr. 4 up). 1993. PLB 12.96 (0-88110-631-3); pap. 4.95 (0-7460-1000-1) EDC.
—Learn to Play Guitar. (Illus.). 64p. (gr. 6-12). 1988. PLB 14.96 (0-88110-384-5); pap. 8.95 (0-7460-0193-2) EDC.
—Survival Skills. (Illus.). 48p. (gr. 6-10). 1987. pap. 5.95 (0-7460-0169-X) EDC.

Smith, L., jt. auth. see Bessant, P.

Smith, L. J. The Awakening. 1991. pap. 3.99 (0-06-106097-6, Harp PBks) HarpC.
—The Captive. 1992. pap. 3.99 (0-06-106715-6, Harp PBks) HarpC.
—Dark Reunion. 1992. pap. 3.99 (0-06-106775-X, Harp PBks) HarpC.
—The Fury. 1991. pap. 3.99 (0-06-106099-2, Harp PBks) HarpC.
—Heart of Valor. LC 90-5827. 224p. (gr. 5 up). 1990. SBE 14.95 (0-02-785861-8, Macmillan Child Bk) Macmillan Child Grp.
—The Night of the Solstice. LC 87-11068. 240p. (gr. 5 up). 1987. SBE 14.95 (0-02-785840-5, Macmillan Child Bk) Macmillan Child Grp.
—Night of the Solstice. 1993. pap. 3.99 (0-06-106172-7, Harp PBks) HarpC.
—The Power. 1992. pap. 3.99 (0-06-106719-9, Harp PBks) HarpC.
—Secret Circle: The Initiation, Vol. 1. 1992. pap. 3.99 (0-06-106712-1, Harp PBks) HarpC.
—The Struggle. 1991. pap. 3.99 (0-06-106098-4, Harp PBks) HarpC.

Smith, Lane. The Big Pets. Smith, Lane, illus. 32p. (ps-3). 1991. 14.95 (0-670-83378-9) Viking Child Bks.
—The Big Pets. LC 93-18608. (Illus.). 32p. (ps-3). 1993. pap. 4.99 (0-14-054265-5, Puffin) Puffin Bks.
—Flying Jake. Smith, Lane, illus. LC 87-25976. 32p. (ps-3). 1988. RSBE 14.95 (0-02-785830-8, Macmillan Child Bk) Macmillan Child Grp.
—Glasses: Who Needs 'em? (ps-3). 1991. 13.95 (0-670-84160-9) Viking Child Bks.
—The Happy Hocky Family. Smith, Lane, illus. 64p. (ps-3). 1993. reinforced bdg. 13.99 (0-670-85206-6) Viking Child Bks.

Smith, Lani. Ziggy's Christmas Book Level 1. Wilson, Tom, illus. 32p. (Orig.). 1991. pap. 5.95 (0-89328-112-3) Lorenz Corp.
—Ziggy's Christmas Book Level 2. Wilson, Tom, illus. 32p. (Orig.). 1991. pap. 5.95 (0-89328-113-1) Lorenz Corp.

Smith, Laura L. Sophisticated Josephine: The East African Bush Elephant. (Illus.). 32p. (gr. 3-5). 1993. pap. 6.95 (0-8059-3311-5) Dorrance.

Smith, Laure, jt. auth. see McEvoy, Seth.

Smith, Lester. Dark Conspiracy. 336p. (Orig.). 1991. pap. 22.00 (1-55878-076-9) Game Designers.

—Dark Races, Vol. 1. 104p. (Orig.). 1992. pap. 12.00 (1-55878-105-6) Game Designers.
—Proto-Dimensions, Vol. 1. 104p. (Orig.). 1992. pap. 12.00 (1-55878-114-5) Game Designers.

Smith, Lester, jt. auth. see Gygax, Gary.

Smith, Lester, jt. auth. see Nystul, Mike.

Smith, Lester, ed. see Gygax, Gary.

Smith, Lester W. Beastman of Mars. Aulisio, Janet, illus. 64p. (Orig.). 1989. pap. 8.00 (1-55878-022-X) Game Designers.
—Deathwatch Program. Aulisio, Janet, illus. 64p. (Orig.). 1990. pap. 8.00 (1-55878-051-3) Game Designers.

Smith, Linda J. Cat's Wedding. (Illus.). 32p. 1989. 12.95 (0-8249-8402-1, Ideals Child) Hambleton-Hill.
—Three Little Kittens. Smith, Linda J., illus. LC 90-5102. 32p. (ps-1). 1991. 13.95 (0-8249-8490-0, Ideals Child) Hambleton-Hill.

Smith, Louisa & Smith, Glen, eds. The Not Like Any Other Children's Book, Book. Smith, Glen, illus. 40p. (Orig.). (gr. 2 up). 1982. pap. 8.95 (0-9609230-0-4) Smith & Smith Pub.

Smith, Louise. Mary Baker Eddy. Horner, Matina S., intro. by. 112p. (gr. 5 up). 1991. 17.95 (1-55546-652-4) Chelsea Hse.

Smith, Lucinda I. Growing up Female: New Challenges, New Choices. LC 86-31261. 160p. (gr. 7 up). 1987. lib. bdg. 12.98 (0-671-63445-3, J Messner) S&S Trade.
—Women Who Write: From the Past & the Present to the Future. Steltenpohl, Jane, ed. (Illus.). 192p. (gr. 7 up). 1989. lib. bdg. 14.98 (0-671-65668-6, J Messner); lib. bdg. 9.95 (0-671-65669-4) S&S Trade.

Smith, M. L., ed. Diary of Ruth Anna Hatch, Woods Hole, 1881. Tappan, Eva M., illus. 1992. text ed. write for info. (0-9611374-3-6) Woods Hole Hist.

Smith, M. Sherry & Cendejas, Deena L. Holiday Potpourri. (Illus.). (gr. k-8). 1992. 16.95 (0-937857-36-X, 1520) Speech Bin.
—Potpourri: Bouquet of Language Activities. (gr. 2-5). 1991. wkbk. 16.95 (0-937857-25-4, 1587) Speech Bin.

Smith, Maggie. My Grandma's Chair. LC 90-2278. (ps-3). 1992. 14.00 (0-688-10663-3); PLB 13.93 (0-688-10664-1) Lothrop.
—Noly Poly Rabbit Tail & Me. 1990. 13.95 (0-688-09570-4); PLB 13.88 (0-688-09571-2) Lothrop.
—There's a Witch Under the Stairs. (ps-3). 1991. 13.95 (0-688-09884-3) Lothrop.
—There's a Witch Under the Stairs. (ps-3). 1991. PLB 13.88 (0-688-09885-1) Lothrop.

Smith, Marcella, et al. Careers in Agribusiness & Industry. 4th ed. LC 76-106341. (Illus.). 395p. (gr. 9-12). 1991. 34.60 (0-8134-2898-X); text ed. 25.95 (0-685-54235-1); tchr's. manual 6.95 (0-8134-2899-8) Interstate.

Smith, Margaret D. Mississippi High School Students & the Law, Vol. II. LC 89-3745. 206p. (gr. 8-12). 1990. pap. 9.95 (0-937552-36-4) Quail Ridge.

Smith, Marjorie. I Like My Teacher: You Know Why? Gross, Karen, ed. 24p. (Orig.). (ps). 1992. pap. text ed. 3.95 (1-56309-055-4, New Hope) Womans Mission Union.

Smith, Mark, jt. auth. see Kennedy, Christine.

Smith, Martha. Arabella the Itchy Witch. Graves, Helen, ed. Smith, Martha, illus. LC 85-40893. 86p. (gr. 3 up). 1986. 6.95 (1-55523-007-5) Winston-Derek.

Smith, Mary & Robison, Phyllis. Easy Art. Astrom, Lena, illus. 48p. (gr. k-3). 1982. wkbk. 5.95 (1-55734-004-8) Tchr Create Mat.

Smith, Mary D. & Smith, Brad. Creative Writing Patterns. Tom, Tiana, illus. 48p. (gr. k-4). 1983. wkbk. 5.95 (1-55734-130-3) Tchr Create Mat.

Smith, Mary D., jt. auth. see Cracchiolo, Rachelle.

Smith, Mary M. Orla's Upside Down Day. rev. ed. Lewis, Jan, illus. 32p. (gr. k-2). 1990. Repr. of 1989 ed. PLB 10.50 (1-878363-05-0) Forest Hse.

Smith, Mary P. Boy Captive of Old Deerfield. (Illus.). (gr. 5-6). Repr. of 1904 ed. lib. bdg. 19.95x (0-89190-961-3, Pub. by River City Pr) Amereon Ltd.
—Boys & Girls of Seventy-Seven. 2nd ed. Silvester, Susan B., ed. Grunwald, C., illus. LC 86-30607. 333p. (gr. 5 up). 1987. Repr. of 1909 ed. 17.00 (0-913993-08-5) Paideia MA.

Smith, Mary P. Wells see Smith, Mary P.

Smith, Marya. Winter-Broken. 114p. (gr. 6 up). 1990. 13.95 (1-55970-064-5) Arcade Pub Inc.

Smith, MaryLou M. Grandmother's Adobe Dollhouse. Blackstone, Ann, illus. 32p. (gr. k-6). 1988. PLB 12.95 (0-937206-03-2); pap. 6.95 (0-937206-07-5) New Mexico Mag.

Smith, Matthew V. Billy Jean. Smith, Matthew V., illus. 14p. (gr. k-3). 1993. pap. 9.95 (1-895583-57-8) MAYA Pubs.
—Clowns Are People Too. Smith, Matthew V., illus. 12p. (gr. 1-3). 1992. pap. 11.95 (1-56606-010-9) Bradley Mann.
—Flip the Cat. Smith, Matthew V., illus. 10p. (gr. k-3). 1993. pap. 10.95 (1-56606-013-3) Bradley Mann.
—Fun Time with Bonzo. Smith, Matthew V., illus. 12p. (gr. k-3). 1992. pap. 11.95 (1-895583-32-2) MAYA Pubs.
—Harold Gets a New Bike. Smith, Matthew V., illus. 12p. (gr. k-3). 1993. pap. 11.95 (1-56606-014-1) Bradley Mann.
—Harvey Takes a Ride to the Park. Smith, Matthew V., illus. 15p. (gr. k-3). 1992. pap. 10.95 (1-895583-05-5) MAYA Pubs.
—An Invitation to Sally's. Smith, Matthew V., illus. 18p. (gr. k-3). 1992. pap. 12.95 (1-895583-07-1) MAYA Pubs.

—Jennie Learns to Drive. Smith, Matthew V., illus. 15p. (gr. k-3). 1992. pap. 12.95 (1-895583-30-6) MAYA Pubs.
—A Penny for the Gum Machine. Smith, Matthew V., illus. 12p. (gr. k-3). 1992. pap. 9.95 (1-895583-09-8) MAYA Pubs.
—Ralph's Funtime. Smith, Matthew V., illus. 17p. (gr. k-3). 1992. pap. 19.95 (1-895583-08-X) MAYA Pubs.
—Shapes & Colours. Smith, Matthew V., illus. 12p. 1992. pap. 4.95 (1-895583-03-9) MAYA Pubs.
—Time for Learning Colors. Smith, Matthew V., illus. 12p. (gr. k-3). 1993. pap. 10.95 (1-895583-55-1) MAYA Pubs.
—Wake Up, Mommy. Smith, Matthew V., illus. 15p. (gr. 1-3). 1992. pap. 10.95 (1-56606-009-5) Bradley Mann.
—What's a Right Turn. Smith, Matthew V., illus. 13p. (gr. k-3). 1993. pap. 12.95 (1-895583-56-X) MAYA Pubs.
—When Not to Say Help. Smith, Matthew V., illus. 16p. (gr. k-3). 1992. pap. 11.95 (1-895583-34-9) MAYA Pubs.
—When to Say Help. Smith, Matthew V., illus. 18p. (gr. k-3). 1992. pap. 12.95 (1-895583-33-0) MAYA Pubs.
—Where Are All the Children. Smith, Matthew V., illus. 10p. (gr. 1-2). 1992. pap. 12.95 (1-56606-002-8) Bradley Mann.
—Where Do We Go from Here? Smith, Matthew V., illus. 15p. (gr. k-3). 1992. pap. 11.95 (1-895583-35-7) MAYA Pubs.
—Where Is All the Honey? Smith, Matthew V., illus. 17p. (gr. k-3). 1992. pap. 13.95 (1-895583-31-4) MAYA Pubs.
—Why Do Clowns Smile? Smith, Matthew V., illus. 14p. (gr. k-3). 1992. pap. 14.95 (1-895583-06-3) MAYA Pubs.

Smith, Mavis. Circles. (ps-8). 1991. 3.95 (1-55782-366-9, Pub. by Warner Juvenile Bks) Little.
—Crescents. (ps-8). 1991. 3.95 (1-55782-367-7, Pub. by Warner Juvenile Bks) Little.
—Fred, Is That You? A Lift-the-Flap Book. (Illus.). (ps-1). 1992. 7.95 (0-316-80241-7) Little.
—I'm Going to Get You! (ps-3). 1991. pap. 5.95 (0-14-054435-6, Puffin) Puffin Bks.
—Look Out! (ps-3). 1991. pap. 5.95 (0-14-054433-X, Puffin) Puffin Bks.
—A Snake Mistake. Smith, Mavis, illus. LC 90-43152. 32p. (gr. k-3). 1991. PLB 11.89 (0-06-026909-X); pap. 3.95 (0-06-107426-8) HarpC Child Bks.
—Squares. (ps-8). 1991. 3.95 (1-55782-364-2, Pub. by Warner Juvenile Bks) Little.
—Triangles. (ps-8). 1991. 3.95 (1-55782-365-0, Pub. by Warner Juvenile Bks) Little.

Smith, Mavis, jt. auth. see Ziefert, Harriet.

Smith, Mavis, illus. Harry Gets Ready for School. 32p. (ps-3). 1991. pap. 3.50 (0-14-054388-0, Puffin) Puffin Bks.

Smith, Melanie. Master-Minded: Ten Stories of Contemporary Servants. Nelson, Becky, ed. 91p. (Orig.). (gr. 7-12). 1992. pap. text ed. 4.95 (1-56309-046-5, New Hope) Womans Mission Union.

Smith, Michael W. & Ridenour, Fritz. Old Enough to Know. 111p. 1989. 6.99 (0-8499-3162-2) Word Inc.
—Old Enough to Know. large type ed. 111p. (gr. 7 up). 1989. pap. 12.99 (0-8499-3163-0) Word Inc.

Smith, Mildred S. Where Is Jeffrey's Yo-Yo? (Illus.). 56p. (ps-12). 1988. 8.50 (0-9612296-5-9) Williams SC.

Smith, Miriam. Annie & Moon. Sherwood, Rhoda, ed. Mahuika, A. T., tr. Moyes, Lesley, illus. LC 88-42909. 32p. (gr. 3-4). 1988. PLB 18.60 (1-55532-928-4) Gareth Stevens Inc.

Smith, Miriam F., jt. auth. see Hazouri, Sandra P.

Smith, Monte, ed. see Overstreet, Charles.

Smith, Monte, ed. see Tykal, Jack B.

Smith, Nancy & Milligan, Lynda. Sewing Machine Fun. Holmes, Sharon, ed. Robinson, Marilyn, illus. 72p. (gr. 1-12). 1993. pap. 15.95 GBC bdg. (1-880972-04-2, DreamSpinners) Pssblts Denver.
—Sewing Machine Fun: Activity Kit. Holmes, Sharon, ed. Robinson, Marilyn, illus. 72p. (gr. 1-12). 1993. pap. 29.95 (1-880972-10-7, DreamSpinners) Pssblts Denver.
—Step Into Patchwork. Holmes, Sharon, ed. Robinson, Marilyn, illus. 72p. (gr. 1-12). 1994. pap. 15.95 plastic comb bdg. (1-880972-09-3, DreamSpinners) Pssblts Denver.

Smith, Nancy J. & Milligan, Lynda. More Sewing Machine Fun. Holmes, Sharon, ed. Robinson, Marilyn, illus. 72p. (gr. 2-8). 1993. pap. 15.95 plastic comb. (1-880972-05-0) Pssblts Denver.

Smith, Neraida. Let's Sing & Learn in French. (FRE.). 64p. 1991. pap. 4.95 (0-8442-1455-8, Passport Bks); pap. 9.95 incl. audiocassette (0-8442-1454-X, Passport Bks) NTC Pub Grp.
—Let's Sing & Learn in Spanish. (SPA & ENG., Illus.). 64p. 1991. pap. text ed. 9.95 incl. audiocassette (0-8442-7075-X, Passport Bks) NTC Pub Grp.

Smith, Nora A., jt. ed. see Wiggin, Kate D.

Smith, Norman F. How Fast Do Your Oysters Grow: Investigate & Discover Through Science Project. LC 82-60649. (Illus.). 128p. (gr. 7 up). 1982. lib. bdg. 10.98 (0-671-42629-X, J Messner) S&S Trade.
—How to Do Successful Science Projects. rev. ed. Steltenpohl, Jane, ed. (Illus.). 128p. (gr. 6-9). 1990. lib. bdg. 11.98 (0-671-70685-3, J Messner); pap. 5.95 (0-671-70686-1) S&S Trade.
—Millions & Billions of Years Ago: Dating Our Earth & Its Life. LC 92-42744. (Illus.). 128p. (gr. 7-12). 1993. PLB 13.40 (0-531-12533-5) Watts. Postponed.

Smith, Norman F. & Smith, Douglas W. Simulators. Leyden, Richard, illus. LC 89-9083. 126p. (gr. 6-9). 1989. PLB 12.90 (*0-531-10812-0*) Watts.
Smith, Pamela, jt. auth. see Coats, Carolyn.
Smith, Parker. Universal Monsters: The Mummy. Ruiz, Art, illus. 96p. (gr. 3-7). 1992. pap. 2.95 (*0-307-22332-9*, 22332, Golden Pr) Western Pub.
—The Young Indiana Jones Chronicles: The Mummy's Curse. Mones, illus. 24p. (ps-3). 1992. pap. write for info. (*0-307-12689-7*, 12689, Golden Pr) Western Pub.
Smith, Pat, jt. auth. see Fulton, Eleanor.
Smith, Patricia. Snakes! Moffatt, Judith, illus. LC 92-24466. 48p. (gr. 1-3). 1993. lib. bdg. 7.99 (*0-448-40514-8*, G&D); pap. 3.50 (*0-448-40513-X*, G&D) Putnam Pub Group.
Smith, Patricia, jt. auth. see Kadra, Sheila.
Smith, Patty. Mango Days: A Teen-Ager Facing Eternity Reflects on the Beauty of Life. Smith, Patty, illus. Smith, Kit, intro. by. LC 92-10039. (Illus.). 135p. (Orig.). (gr. 9-12). 1992. lib. bdg. 17.95 (*0-932727-59-X*); pap. 11.95 (*0-932727-58-1*) Hope Pub Hse.
Smith, Peter. Your First Hamster. (Illus.). 36p. (Orig.). 1991. pap. 1.95 (*0-86622-067-4*, YF-110) TFH Pubns.
Smith, Philip, ed. Aladdin & Other Favorite Arabian Nights Stories. Kliros, Thea, illus. LC 93-22073. 96p. (gr. 3 up). 1993. pap. 1.00 (*0-486-27571-X*) Dover.
—Favorite Poems of Childhood. (Illus.). 96p. (Orig.). 1992. pap. 1.00t (*0-486-27089-0*) Dover.
—Irish Fairy Tales. Kliros, Thea, illus. LC 93-243. 96p. 1993. pap. 1.00 (*0-486-27572-8*) Dover.
—Japanese Fairy Tales. Fujiyama, Kakuzo, illus. LC 92-17648. 96p. 1992. pap. 1.00 (*0-486-27300-8*) Dover.
Smith, Phillipa A., jt. auth. see Schott, Carolyn J.
Smith, Robert. Waco Cult Inferno. LC 93-5154. 1993. 11.96 (*1-56239-260-3*) Abdo & Dghtrs.
Smith, Robert. Squeaky Wheel. (gr. 3-7). 1990. 13.95 (*0-385-30155-3*) Delacorte.
Smith, Robert D. Tommy's Father. 32p. (gr. 2). 1991. pap. 8.95 (*1-880404-03-6*) Bkwrights.
Smith, Robert E. Mammalian Homeostasis. Head, J. J., ed. Steffen, Ann T., illus. LC 84-71146. 16p. (gr. 10 up). 1987. pap. text ed. 2.75 (*0-89278-349-4*, 45-9749) Carolina Biological.
Smith, Robert K. Bobby Baseball. Tiegreen, Alan, illus. (gr. 3-7). 1989. 13.95 (*0-385-29807-2*) Delacorte.
—Bobby Baseball. (gr. 4-7). 1991. pap. 3.50 (*0-440-40417-7*) Dell.
—Bobby Baseball. (gr. 4-7). 1991. pap. 3.25 (*0-440-80212-1*) Dell.
—Chocolate Fever. 96p. (gr. 2-6). 1978. pap. 3.50 (*0-440-41369-9*, YB) Dell.
—Chocolate Fever. (gr. 4-7). 1992. pap. 1.99 (*0-440-21371-1*) Dell.
—Jelly Belly. 160p. (gr. 4-9). 1982. pap. 3.50 (*0-440-44207-9*, YB) Dell.
—Jelly Belly. Jones, Bob, illus. LC 80-23898. 160p. (gr. 4-6). 1981. pap. 13.95 (*0-385-28477-2*) Delacorte.
—Mostly Michael. Coville, Katherine, illus. LC 86-19618. 192p. (gr. 4-6). 1987. pap. 13.95 (*0-385-29545-6*) Delacorte.
—Mostly Michael. 192p. (gr. k-6). 1988. pap. 3.50 (*0-440-40097-X*, YB) Dell.
—The Squeaky Wheel. (gr. 3-7). 1992. 3.50 (*0-440-40631-5*, YB) Dell.
—The War with Grandpa. Lauter, Richard, illus. LC 83-14366. 128p. (gr. 4-8). 1984. pap. 12.95 (*0-385-29314-3*) Delacorte.
—The War with Grandpa. Lauter, Richard, illus. 128p. (gr. 5-9). 1984. pap. 3.99 (*0-440-49276-9*, YB) Dell.
Smith, Rodger see Rojany, Lisa & Strong, Stacie.
Smith, Roger. The Empty Island. LC 90-45497. (Illus.). 32p. (ps-5). 1991. 13.95 (*0-940793-69-5*, Crocodile Bks) Interlink Pub.
Smith, Roland. Inside the Zoo Nursery. Munoz, William, illus. LC 92-3344. 64p. (gr. 5 up). 1993. 15.00 (*0-525-65084-9*, Cobblehill Bks) Dutton Child Bks.
—Primates in the Zoo. Munoz, William, illus. LC 91-46968. 64p. (gr. 3-6). 1992. PLB 13.90 (*1-56294-210-7*) Millbrook Pr.
—Sea Otter Rescue, the Aftermath of an Oil Spill. LC 89-49446. (Illus.). (gr. 4-7). 1990. 13.95 (*0-525-65041-5*, Cobblehill Bks) Dutton Child Bks.
—Snakes in the Zoo. Munoz, William, illus. LC 91-45588. 64p. (gr. 3-6). 1992. PLB 13.90 (*1-56294-211-5*) Millbrook Pr.
—Whales, Dolphins, & Porpoises in the Zoo. Munoz, William, photos by. LC 93-35425. (Illus.). 1994. lib. bdg. write for info. (*1-56294-318-9*) Millbrook Pr.
Smith, Ruffin B. Computers. 32p. (gr. 5-9). 1981. (Usborne-Hayes); PLB 10.96 (*0-88110-002-1*); pap. 3.95 (*0-86020-542-8*) EDC.
Smith, Sally Ann. Candle, a Story of Love & Faith. Luther, Luana, ed. Jung, Mary, illus. LC 91-72745. 32p. (gr. 3-6). 1991. pap. 9.95 (*0-944875-22-X*) Doral Pub.
Smith, Samantha. Journey to the Soviet Union. (Illus.). 1985. 19.45i (*0-316-80175-5*); pap. 14.95i (*0-316-80176-3*) Little.
Smith, Samuel P. Kiddie Patter & Little Feats: Entertaining Pre-Schoolers with Magic & Funny Stuff. (Illus.). 200p. 1993. text ed. 25.00 (*1-881099-02-4*) SPS Pubns.
Smith, Sanderson M. & Griffin, Frank W. AP Exam in Mathematics: Calculus AB & Calculus BC. 2nd ed. 320p. (gr. 9-12). 1990. pap. 12.95 (*0-13-019050-0*, Arco Test) P-H Gen Ref & Trav.

Smith, Sandra L. Coping with Changing Schools. LC 93-20433. 1993. 13.95 (*0-8239-1602-2*) Rosen Group.
—Coping with Decision Making. rev. ed. Rosen, Ruth, ed. (gr. 7 up). 1993. PLB 13.95 (*0-8239-1000-8*) Rosen Group.
—Discovering Your Own Space. (gr. 7-12). 1992. PLB 14.95 (*0-8239-1279-5*) Rosen Group.
—Drugs & Your Friends. rev. ed. (Illus.). 64p. (gr. 7-12). 1993. PLB 14.95 (*0-8239-1657-X*) Rosen Group.
—Drugs & Your Parents. rev. ed. (Illus.). 64p. (gr. 7-12). 1993. lib. bdg. 14.95 (*0-8239-1684-7*) Rosen Group.
—Great Grooming for Girls. Rosen, Ruth, ed. (gr. 7-12). 1993. 12.95 (*0-8239-1469-0*) Rosen Group.
—Heroin. rev. ed. (gr. 7-12). 1993. PLB 14.95 (*0-8239-1685-5*) Rosen Group.
—Setting Goals. Rosen, Ruth, ed. LC 92-15262. (gr. 7-12). 1992. 12.95 (*0-8239-1451-8*) Rosen Group.
—The Value of Self-Control. (gr. 7-12). 1991. PLB 15.95 (*0-8239-1270-1*) Rosen Group.
Smith, Sherri C. Wrong-Way Romance. (gr. 9-12). 1991. pap. 2.95 (*0-553-28840-7*) Bantam.
Smith, Sherry A., jt. auth. see Rogers, Mary B.
Smith, Sherwood. Wren to the Rescue. 216p. (gr. 7 up). 1990. 15.95 (*0-15-200975-2*, J Yolen Bks) HarBrace.
—Wren to the Rescue. (gr. 4-7). 1993. pap. 3.50 (*0-440-40773-7*) Dell.
—Wren's Quest. LC 92-18988. 1993. write for info. (*0-15-200976-0*, J Yolen Bks) HarBrace.
Smith, Simpson E. Bear Bryant: Football's Winning Coach. LC 83-40404. (Illus.). 128p. (gr. 7 up). 1984. 11.95 (*0-8027-6526-2*) Walker & Co.
Smith, Sinclair. Dream Date. 1993. pap. 3.25 (*0-590-46126-5*) Scholastic Inc.
Smith, Stan & Valentine, Tom. Inside Tennis. new ed. LC 73-20692. (Illus.). 96p. (gr. 5-8). 1974. 7.95 (*0-8092-8887-7*) Contemp Bks.
Smith, Susan. Angela & the King-Size Crusade. (gr. 3-7). 1988. pap. 2.50 (*0-317-69592-4*) PB.
Smith, Susan M. The Booford Summer. Glass, Andrew, illus. LC 93-27925. 1994. write for info. (*0-395-66590-6*, Clarion Bks) HM.
Smith, Sybil C. Twin Cities Fishing Guide. LC 81-65635. 161p. (Orig.). (gr. 6 up). 1982. pap. 8.95 (*0-9615221-0-0*) Fins Pubns.
Smith, T. H. Cry to the Night Wind. (gr. 5-9). 1988. pap. 4.95 (*0-14-031931-X*, Puffin) Puffin Bks.
Smith, T. L. Word Search Puzzles. 34p. (gr. k-6). 1991. saddle stitch bdg. 1.69 (*1-880825-02-3*) Tracey Smith.
Smith, Timothy, ed. see Brunton, Paul.
Smith, Tom & Smith, Diane. Northwest Indian Coloring Book. Smith, Tom, illus. 32p. (gr. 1-4). 1993. pap. 3.99 (*0-8431-3491-7*) Troubador Pr.
Smith, Tony, illus. The Great Pyramids & the Sphinx. 48p. (gr. 3-5). 1987. 7.95x (*0-86685-454-1*) Intl Bk Ctr.
—The Treasures of Tutankhamen. 48p. (gr. 3-5). 1987. 7.95x (*0-86685-453-3*) Intl Bk Ctr.
Smith, Trevor. Amazing Lizards. Young, Jerry, photos by. LC 90-31884. (Illus.). 32p. (Orig.). (gr. 1-5). 1990. lib. bdg. 9.99 (*0-679-90819-6*); pap. 7.99 (*0-679-80819-1*) Knopf Bks Yng Read.
Smith, Ursula, jt. auth. see Peavy, Linda.
Smith, Vanessa. I Like Me. Kelly, George, illus. 32p. (Orig.). (gr. 1-2). Date not set. pap. write for info. (*0-9634122-4-8*) Feather Fables.
Smith, Verena. The Life of St. Martin. Probst, Emile, illus. (gr. 2-5). 1993. pap. write for info. (*0-913026-43-3*) St Nectarios.
Smith, Vicki, jt. auth. see Olden, Diana J.
Smith, Viola B. Touch of Spring. Michel, Sandra S., ed. Keane, Marie, illus. (gr. k up). 1976. pap. 4.00 (*0-917178-02-5*) Lenape Pub.
Smith, W. Hovey. Guide to the Geology of Bartow County, Georgia. (Illus.). 46p. (Orig.). (gr. 8-12). 1985. pap. text ed. 5.00 (*0-916565-07-6*) Whitehall Pr.
Smith, W. Hovey, jt. auth. see Farnagle, A. E.
Smith, Walter M., ed. see Arban, Jean B.
Smith, Wendell. The Roots of Character. (Illus.). 1987. tchr's. ed. 37.95 (*0-914936-90-5*); student wkbk., 176p. 9.95 (*0-914936-89-1*) Bible Temple.
Smith, Wendy. The Lonely, Only Mouse. (Illus.). 32p. 1988. pap. 3.50 (*0-14-050651-9*, Puffin) Puffin Bks.
—Say Hello, Tilly. (ps-3). 1991. 13.95 (*0-553-07160-2*) Bantam.
—Think Hippo! (Illus.). 28p. (ps-2). 1989. PLB 17.50 (*0-87614-372-9*) Carolrhoda Bks.
—Twice Mice. (Illus.). 28p. (ps-2). 1989. PLB 17.50 (*0-87614-371-0*) Carolrhoda Bks.
—The Witch Baby. (ps-3). 1988. pap. 3.95 (*0-14-050590-3*, Puffin) Puffin Bks.
Smith, Whitney. American Flags from Washington to Lincoln. (Illus.). (gr. 7). 1977. pap. 1.50 (*0-88388-048-2*) Bellerophon Bks.
—Civil War Flags. (gr. 1-9). 1992. pap. 2.50 (*0-88388-094-6*) Bellerophon Bks.
—Flags of the American Revolution. (gr. 1-9). 1992. pap. 1.50 (*0-88388-032-6*) Bellerophon Bks.
Smith, William. Smith's Bible Dictionary. (gr. 7-12). 1984. pap. 5.95 (*0-515-08507-3*) Jove Pubns.
Smith, William J. Big & Little. Bolognese, Don, illus. LC 91-66057. 32p. (gr. 5 up). 1992. 15.95 (*1-56397-023-6*, Wordsong) Boyds Mills Pr.
—Birds & Beasts. Hnizdovsky, Jacques, illus. (gr. k up). 1990. 18.95 (*0-87923-865-8*) Godine.
—Ho for a Hat! Munsinger, Lynn, illus. LC 88-39864. (ps-1). 1989. 14.95 (*0-316-80120-8*, Joy St Bks) Little.
—Ho for a Hat! (gr. 3 up). 1993. pap. 4.95 (*0-316-80126-7*) Little.

—Laughing Time: Collected Nonsense. 176p. (gr. 4-8). 1990. 14.00 (*0-374-34366-7*); pap. 3.50 (*0-374-44315-7*, Sunburst) FS&G.
Smith, William J. & Ra, Carol, eds. Behind the King's Kitchen Door. Hnizdovsky, Jacques, illus. LC 91-66056. 56p. (gr. 5 up). 1992. 18.95 (*1-56397-024-4*, Wordsong) Boyds Mills Pr.
Smith-Brindle, Reginald. Serial Composition. (gr. 9 up). 1968. 26.95x (*0-19-311906-4*) OUP.
Smith Jessie, Willcox see Willcox Smith, Jessie.
Smithmark Staff. Where's Columbus? 1992. 4.98 (*0-8317-9284-1*) Smithmark.
Smith-Owens, Lois, jt. auth. see Gordon, Vivian V.
Smithsen, Richard. Freshwater Fishing: A Step-by-Step Guide. LC 89-20453. (Illus.). 64p. (gr. 4-8). 1990. lib. bdg. 9.79 (*0-8167-1941-1*); pap. text ed. 2.95 (*0-8167-1942-X*) Troll Assocs.
Smithson, Colin. Blunty. (Illus.). 32p. (ps-1). 1994. 15.95 (*1-85681-025-9*, Pub. by J MacRae UK) Trafalgar.
Smith-Trafzer, Lee A., jt. auth. see Trafzer, Clifford E.
Smock, Jerri. The Swan: A Storybook for Adults & Other Children. Poppler, Susan, illus. 21p. (gr. 7 up). 1989. incl. cassette 13.95g (*0-944586-00-7*) WIN Pub.
Smock, Raymond W., jt. auth. see Reardon, Judy A.
Smock, Raymond W., et al. The American History Slide Collection. 265p. (Orig.). (gr. 7 up). 1977. incl. 2100 slides 895.00 (*0-923805-06-0*) Instruc Resc MD.
—Master Guide to the American History Slide Collection. 265p. (gr. 7 up). 1977. pap. text ed. 25.00 (*0-923805-00-1*) Instruc Resc MD.
Smoke, Richard. Think about Nuclear Arms Control: Understanding the Arms Race. (Illus.). 178p. 1988. PLB 14.85 (*0-8027-6761-3*); pap. 5.95 (*0-8027-6762-1*) Walker & Co.
Smolinsky, Jill. Super Models. 32p. (Orig.). (gr. 3-7). 1993. pap. 2.95 (*1-56565-055-7*) Lowell Hse.
Smollin, Michael. Ernie's Bath Book. (ps-3). 1982. 3.95 (*0-394-85402-0*) Random Bks Yng Read.
Smollin, Michael, illus. Laugh-Along Songs. 32p. (Orig.). (ps-2). 1990. pap. 6.95 incl. cass. (*0-679-80305-X*) Random Bks Yng Read.
Smoothey, Marion. Angles. Evans, Ted, illus. LC 92-36222. 1993. 15.95 (*1-85435-466-3*) Marshall Cavendish.
—Area & Volume. Evans, Ted, illus. LC 92-10579. 1992. 15.95 (*1-85435-460-4*) Marshall Cavendish.
—Circles. Evans, Ted, illus. 64p. (gr. 4-8). 1992. text ed. 16.95 (*1-85435-456-6*) Marshall Cavendish.
—Let's Investigate Series, 6 vols. Evans, Ted, illus. 64p. (gr. 4-8). 1993. Set, Group 1. PLB 101.70 (*1-85435-455-8*); Set, Group 2. PLB write for info. (*1-85435-463-9*) Marshall Cavendish.
—Number Patterns. Evans, Ted, illus. 64p. (gr. 4-8). 1992. text ed. 16.95 (*1-85435-458-2*) Marshall Cavendish.
—Numbers. Evans, Ted, illus. 64p. (gr. 4-8). 1992. text ed. 16.95 (*1-85435-457-4*) Marshall Cavendish.
—Quadrilaterals. Evans, Ted, illus. LC 92-10436. 1992. 15.95 (*1-85435-459-0*) Marshall-Cavendish.
—Shape Patterns. Evans, Ted, illus. LC 92-36223. 1993. 15.95 (*1-85435-465-5*) Marshall Cavendish.
—Shapes. Evans, Ted, illus. LC 92-36224. 1993. 15.95 (*1-85435-464-7*) Marshall Cavendish.
—Solids. Evans, Ted, illus. LC 92-36220. 1993. 15.95 (*1-85435-469-8*) Marshall Cavendish.
—Statistics. Evans, Ted, illus. LC 92-35574. 1993. 15.95 (*0-685-62557-5*) Marshall Cavendish.
—Statistics. Evans, Ted, illus. 64p. (gr. 4-8). 1993. text ed. 16.95 (*1-85435-468-X*) Marshall Cavendish.
—Time, Distance, & Speed. Evans, Ted, illus. LC 92-36225. 1993. 15.95 (*1-85435-467-1*) Marshall Cavendish.
—Triangles. Evans, Ted, illus. LC 92-12156. 1992. 15.95 ea. (*1-85435-461-2*) Marshall-Cavendish.
Smothers, Ethel F. Down in the Piney Woods. LC 91-328. 144p. (gr. 5-9). 1992. 14.00 (*0-679-80360-2*); PLB 14.99 (*0-679-90360-7*) Knopf Bks Yng Read.
—Down in the Piney Woods. 156p. (gr. 3-7). 1994. pap. 3.99 (*0-679-84714-6*) Random Bks Yng Read.
Smucker, Anna E. No Star Nights. Johnson, Steve, illus. LC 88-2782. 48p. (ps-3). 1989. 12.95 (*0-394-89925-3*); lib. bdg. 13.99 (*0-394-99925-8*) Knopf Bks Yng Read.
—Outside the Window. Schuett, Stacey, illus. LC 92-33452. 1994. 15.00 (*0-679-84023-0*); PLB 15.99 (*0-679-94023-5*) Knopf Bks Yng Read.
Smucker, Barbara. Amish Adventure. Price, Caroline, illus. LC 83-80892. 144p. (Orig.). (gr. 6-9). 1983. pap. 6.95 (*0-8361-3339-0*) Herald Pr.
—Incredible Jumbo. 1991. 12.95 (*0-670-82970-6*) Viking Child Bks.
—Runaway to Freedom. Lilly, Charles, illus. LC 77-11834. 160p. (gr. 4-8). 1979. pap. 3.95 (*0-06-440106-5*, Trophy) HarpC Child Bks.
—Runaway to Freedom. (gr. 4-8). 1992. 16.75 (*0-8446-6585-1*) Peter Smith.
Smucker, Barbara C. Henry's Red Sea. LC 55-7810. (Illus.). 108p. (gr. 4-9). 1955. 4.50 (*0-8361-1372-1*) Herald Pr.
Smuin, Stephen K. Turn-Ons! One Hundred Eighty-Five Strategies for the Secondary Classroom. LC 77-92903. (gr. 7-12). 1978. pap. 12.95 (*0-8224-7051-9*) Fearon Teach Aids.
Smyers, Jacquelyn. The Time a Cloud Came into the Cabin (A Mountain Tale for Boys) Smyers, Carrie M., illus. LC 86-50627. 12p. (Orig.). (ps-6). 1986. pap. 3.98 (*0-9615130-3-9*) Very Idea.

—The Time a Cloud Came into the Cabin (A Mountain Tale for Girls) Smyers, Carrie M., illus. LC 86-50626. 12p. (Orig.). (ps-6). 1986. pap. 3.98 (0-9615130-4-7) Very Idea.

Smyrl, Frank H. Poley Morgan, Son of a Texas Scalawag: (A Historical Novel) Van Horn, Donald, illus. vi, 63p. 1990. 2.00 (0-910779-00-7) Tex St Hist Assn.

Smyth, Karen. Crystal: The Story of a Real Baby Whale. LC 85-52440. (Illus.). 96p. (gr. 2 up). 1986. pap. 8.95 (0-89272-327-0) Down East.

Smyth, Virginia S. Trippy. Walker, Erika D., ed. Smyth, Dale, illus. (Orig.). (gr. 1-3). 1989. pap. 5.00 (0-9624060-0-7) Mount Falcon.

Smythe, Reginald. Watch Your Step, Andy Capp. (Illus.). (gr. 4 up). 1979. pap. 1.25 (0-449-13562-4, P3562, GM) Fawcett.

Snape, Charles & Scott, Heather. How Amazing. (Illus.). 48p. 1993. pap. 9.95 (0-521-35672-5) Cambridge U Pr.

Snape, Charles, jt. auth. see Snape, Juliet.

Snape, Juliet. Boy with the Square Eyes. LC 87-1293. (gr. 4-7). 1990. pap. 5.95 (0-671-69445-6, S&S BFYR) S&S Trade.

Snape, Juliet & Snape, Charles. Frog Friends. (Illus.). 32p. (ps-1). 1994. 17.95 (1-85681-082-8, Pub. by J MacRae UK) Trafalgar.

—Frog Odyssey. LC 91-4201. (Illus.). 32p. (ps-2). 1992. pap. 14.00 (0-671-74741-X, S&S BFYR) S&S Trade.

—I'm Not Frightened of Ghosts. (Illus.). 32p. (gr. 2-5). 1987. 11.95 (0-13-451246-4) P-H.

Snazaroo. Five Minute Faces: Fantastic Face-Painting Ideas. LC 91-26669. (Illus.). 48p. (Orig.). 1992. PLB 10.99 (0-679-92810-3); 7.99 (0-679-82810-9) Random Bks Yng Read.

Snedden, Genevra S. Mountain Cattle & Frontier People. 2nd ed. (Illus.). 160p. (gr. 6). 1989. pap. 16.00 (0-685-32946-1) Intervale Pub Co.

Snedden, Robert. What Is a Bird? Oxford Scientific Films, photos by. (Illus.). 32p. (gr. 2-5). 1993. 13.95 (0-87156-539-0) Sierra.

—What Is a Fish? Lascom, Adrian, illus. Oxford Scientific Films Staff, photos by. LC 93-6495. (Illus.). 1993. write for info. (0-87156-545-5) Sierra.

—What Is an Amphibian? Lascom, Adrian, illus. Oxford Scientific Films Staff, photos by. LC 93-11619. (Illus.). 1994. write for info. (0-87156-469-6) Sierra.

—What Is an Insect? Oxford Scientific Films, photos by. LC 92-35060. (Illus.). 32p. (gr. 2-5). 1993. 13.95 (0-87156-540-4) Sierra.

Sneed, Brad. Lucky Russell. (Illus.). 32p. (ps-3). 1992. 14.95 (0-399-22329-0, Putnam) Putnam Pub Group.

Sneider, Cary & Gould, Alan. Height-O-Meters. Bergman, Lincoln & Fairwell, Kay, eds. Klofkorn, Lisa, illus. Hoyt, Richard. (Illus.). 60p. (gr. 6-10). 1989. pap. 8.50 (0-912511-22-2) Lawrence Science.

Sneider, Cary I. Earth, Moon, & Stars. Bergman, Lincoln & Fairwell, Kay, eds. Baker, Lisa H. & Bevilacqua, Carol, illus. Sneider, Cary I., photos by. 50p. (Orig.). (gr. 5-9). 1986. pap. 10.00 (0-912511-18-4) Lawrence Science.

—More Than Magnifiers. Bergman, Lincoln & Fairwell, Kay, eds. Bevilacqua, Carol, illus. Hoyt, Richard, photos by. (Illus.). 47p. (Orig.). (gr. 6-9). 1988. pap. 8.50 (0-912511-62-1) Lawrence Science.

—Oobleck: What Do Scientists Do? rev. ed. Bergman, Lincoln & Fairwell, Kay, eds. Baker, Lisa H. & Peterson, Adria, illus. Sneider, Cary I., photos by. 28p. (gr. 4-8). 1988. pap. 8.50 (0-912511-64-8) Lawrence Science.

Sneider, Cary I. & Barber, Jacqueline. Paper Towel Testing. Bergman, Lincoln & Fairwell, Kay, eds. Bevilacqua, Carol, illus. Hoyt, Richard, photos by. (Illus.). 29p. (Orig.). (gr. 5-9). 1987. pap. 8.50 (0-912511-65-6) Lawrence Science.

Sneider, Cary I. & Gould, Alan. The Wizard's Lab. Bergman, Lincoln & Fairwell, Kay, eds. Bevilacqua, Carol & Klofkorn, Lisa, illus. Hoyt, Richard, photos by. 72p. 1989. pap. 20.00 (0-912511-71-0) Lawrence Science.

Sneider, Cary I., et al. The Magic of Electricity. Bergman, Lincoln & Fairwell, Kay, eds. Sneider, Cary I. & Baker, Lisa H., illus. Sneider, Cary I., photos by. 50p. (Orig.). (gr. 3-6). 1985. pap. 10.00 (0-912511-52-4) Lawrence Science.

Sneigoski, Stephen J. Department of Education. Schlesinger, Arthur M., Jr., intro. by. (Illus.). 96p. (gr. 5 up). 1988. lib. bdg. 14.95 (0-87754-838-2) Chelsea Hse.

Snell, Gordon. Cruncher Sparrow's Flying School. O'Cleary, Michael, illus. 76p. (Orig.). (gr. 2-6). 1991. pap. 6.95 (1-85371-163-2, Pub. by Poolbeg Pr ER) Dufour.

—Tom's Amazing Machine Takes a Trip. 186p. (ps-2). 1992. 15.95 (0-09-176345-2, Pub. by Hutchinson UK) Trafalgar.

—Tom's Amazing Machine Zaps Back! (Illus.). 144p. (gr. 4-6). 1992. 15.95 (0-09-173888-1, Pub. by Hutchinson UK) Trafalgar.

Snell, Nigel. A Bird in the Hand. reissue ed. (Illus.). 32p. (ps-1). 1992. 11.95 (0-237-60295-4, Pub. by Evans Bros Ltd) Trafalgar.

—Hearing. (Illus.). 32p. (gr. k-2). 1991. 10.95 (0-237-60256-3, Pub. by Evans Bros Ltd) Trafalgar.

—Seeing. (Illus.). 32p. (gr. k-2). 1991. 10.95 (0-237-60257-1, Pub. by Evans Bros Ltd) Trafalgar.

—Tasting & Smelling. (Illus.). 32p. (gr. k-2). 1991. 10.95 (0-237-60258-X, Pub. by Evans Bros Ltd) Trafalgar.

—Touching. (Illus.). 32p. (gr. k-2). 1991. 10.95 (0-237-60259-8, Pub. by Evans Bros Ltd) Trafalgar.

—What Do You Say? A Child's Guide to Manners. (Illus.). 25p. (gr. k-2). 1991. 13.95 (0-237-60294-6, Pub. by Evans Bros Ltd) Trafalgar.

Snellenberger, Bonita, jt. auth. see Snellenberger, Earl.

Snellenberger, Earl & Snellenberger, Bonita. God Created Birds of the World. Snellenberger, Earl & Snellenberger, Bonita, illus. 36p. (Orig.). (ps-6). 1989. pap. 4.95 (0-89051-152-7) Master Bks.

—God Created Sea Life of the World. Snellenberger, Earl & Snellenberger, Bonita, illus. 36p. (Orig.). (ps-6). 1989. pap. 4.95 (0-89051-151-9) Master Bks.

—God Created the Dinosaurs of the World. Snellenberger, Earl & Snellenberger, Bonita, illus. 36p. (Orig.). (ps-6). 1993. pap. 4.95 (0-89051-153-5) Master Bks.

—God Created the World & the Universe. Snellenberger, Earl & Snellenberger, Bonita, illus. 36p. (Orig.). (ps-6). 1989. pap. 4.95 (0-89051-149-7) Master Bks.

Snellgrove, L. E. Early Modern Age. (Illus.). 256p. (Orig.). (gr. 7-12). 1980. 19.92 (0-582-31784-3, 78447) Longman.

Snellgrove, L. E., jt. auth. see Cootes, R. J.

Snelling, et al. Holidays & Festivals, 7 bks, Set I, Reading Level 4. (Illus.). 288p. (gr. 3-8). 1987. Set. PLB 111.58 (0-86592-975-0); Set. 83.65s.p. (0-86592-982-3) Rourke Corp.

Snelling, John. Buddhist Festivals. (Illus.). 48p. (gr. 3-8). 1987. PLB 15.94 (0-86592-980-7); 11.95s.p. (0-685-67596-3) Rourke Corp.

Snelling, Lauraine. Call for Courage. LC 92-16240. 160p. (Orig.). (gr. 7-10). 1992. pap. 5.99 (1-55661-260-5) Bethany Hse.

—Eagles' Wings. 160p. (Orig.). (gr. 7-10). 1991. pap. 5.99 (1-55661-203-6) Bethany Hse.

—Go for the Glory. 160p. (Orig.). (gr. 7-10). 1991. pap. 5.99 (1-55661-218-4) Bethany Hse.

—Kentucky Dreamer. 160p. (Orig.). (gr. 7-10). 1992. pap. 5.99 (1-55661-234-6) Bethany Hse.

—Out of the Mist. 1993. pap. 5.99 (1-55661-338-5) Bethany Hse.

—The Race. 176p. (Orig.). (gr. 7-9). 1991. pap. 5.99 (1-55661-161-7) Bethany Hse.

—Shadow over San Mateo. 160p. (Orig.). (gr. 7-10). 1993. pap. 5.99 (1-55661-292-3) Bethany Hse.

Snellings, M. L. Jessie Strikes Louisiana Gold. (gr. 3-7). 1969. 3.95 (0-87511-116-5) Claitors.

Snelson, Karin. Seattle. LC 91-38232. (Illus.). 64p. (gr. 4 up). 1992. RSBE 13.95 (0-87518-509-6, Dillon) Macmillan Child Grp.

Sneve, Virginia D. The Chichi Hoohoo Bogeyman. Agard-Smith, Nadema, illus. LC 93-15909. 64p. (ps-6). 1993. pap. 6.95 (0-8032-9219-8, Bison Books) U of Nebr Pr.

—The Seminoles. Himler, Ronald, illus. LC 93-14316. 32p. (gr. 7-11). 1994. 15.95 (0-8234-1112-5) Holiday.

—The Sioux: A First American's Book. Himler, Ronald, illus. LC 92-23946. 32p. (gr. 2-6). 1993. reinforced bdg. 15.95 (0-8234-1017-X) Holiday.

—When Thunders Spoke. Lyons, Oren, illus. LC 93-10953. 96p. (gr. 5 up). 1993. pap. 7.95 (0-8032-9220-1, Bison Books) U of Nebr Pr.

Sneve, Virginia Driving Hawk. The Navajos: A First Americans Book. Himler, Ronald, illus. LC 92-40330. 32p. (gr. 2-6). 1993. reinforced bdg. 15.95 (0-8234-1039-0) Holiday.

Sneve, Virginia H., ed. Dancing Teepees: Poems of American Indian Youth. Gammell, Stephen, illus. LC 88-11075. 32p. (ps-4). 1989. reinforced bdg. 15.95 (0-8234-0724-1) Holiday.

Sneve, Virginia H., selected by. Dancing Teepees: Poems of American Indian Youth. Gammell, Stephen, illus. LC 88-11075. 32p. (ps-4). 1991. pap. 5.95 (0-8234-0879-5) Holiday.

Snider, Catherine. Mommy Loves Jesus. Arnsteen, Katy K., illus. LC 93-13354. 24p. (Orig.). (ps-6). 1993. pap. 3.95 (0-8198-4731-3) St Paul Bks.

Snider, Chrystle L., jt. ed. see Allen, Linda.

Snider, Dee & Bashe, Philip. Dee Snider's Teenage Survival Guide. LC 86-32963. (gr. 6-12). 1987. (Dolp); pap. 8.95 (0-385-23900-9, Dolp) Doubleday.

Snodden, Ruth V., jt. auth. see Hall, Nancy M.

Snodgrass, Jameward. Making the Most of School. (Illus.). 48p. (gr. 6-8). 1991. pap. 7.99 (1-55945-113-0) Group Pub.

Snodgrass, M. E. Environmental Awareness: Acid Rain. James, Jody, ed. Vista Three Design Staff, illus. LC 90-26255. 48p. (gr. 4 up). 1991. lib. bdg. 14.95 (0-944280-30-7) Bancroft-Sage.

—Environmental Awareness: Air Pollution. James, Jody, ed. Vista Three Design Staff, illus. LC 90-25726. 48p. (gr. 4 up). 1991. lib. bdg. 14.95 (0-944280-31-5) Bancroft-Sage.

—Environmental Awareness: Land Pollution. James, Jody, ed. Vista Three Design Staff, illus. LC 91-8303. 48p. (gr. 4 up). 1991. lib. bdg. 14.95 (0-944280-29-3) Bancroft-Sage.

—Environmental Awareness: Solid Waste. James, Jody, ed. Vista Three Design Staff, illus. LC 90-20950. 48p. (gr. 4 up). 1991. PLB 14.95 (0-944280-28-5) Bancroft-Sage.

—Environmental Awareness: Toxic Waste. James, Jody, ed. Vista Three Design Staff, illus. LC 91-7427. 48p. (gr. 4 up). 1991. lib. bdg. 14.95 (0-944280-27-7) Bancroft-Sage.

—Environmental Awareness: Water Pollution. James, Jody, ed. Vista Three Design Staff, illus. LC 90-20949. 48p. (gr. 4 up). 1991. PLB 14.95 (0-944280-26-9) Bancroft-Sage.

Snodgrass, Mary E. Japan & the United States: Economic Competitors. LC 92-33017. (Illus.). 64p. (gr. 5-8). 1993. 15.90 (1-56294-374-X) Millbrook Pr.

—Silver: A Study Guide. Friedland, Joyce & Kessler, Rikki, eds. (gr. 2-5). 1991. pap. text ed. 14.95 (0-88122-571-1) LRN Links.

Snodgrass, Mary E., ed. see National Curriculum Editors.

Snodgrass, Mary E., ed. see National Curriculum Publishing Editors.

Snolo, Allen. Baby Bear Learns Colors. 1988. 3.99 (0-517-65509-8) Outlet Bk Co.

Snow, Alan. How Dogs Really Work! LC 92-54651. 1993. 14.95 (0-316-80261-1) Little.

—The Monster Book of ABC Sounds. Snow, Alan, illus. LC 90-39384. 32p. (ps-2). 1991. 12.95 (0-8037-0935-8) Dial Bks Young.

—My First Atlas. 1992. 5.98 (0-8317-0226-5) Smithmark.

—My First Atlas. LC 91-24303. (Illus.). 32p. (gr. k-3). 1992. lib. bdg. 12.79 (0-8167-2517-9); pap. text ed. 4.95 (0-8167-2518-7) Troll Assocs.

—My First Dictionary. Snow, Alan, illus. LC 91-23485. 32p. (gr. k-3). 1992. PLB 12.79 (0-8167-2515-2); pap. text ed. 4.95 (0-8167-2516-0) Troll Assocs.

—My First Encyclopedia. 1991. 5.98 (0-8317-0227-3) Smithmark.

—My First Encyclopedia. Snow, Alan, illus. LC 91-24320. 32p. (gr. k-3). 1992. PLB 12.79 (0-8167-2519-5); pap. 4.95 (0-8167-2520-9) Troll Assocs.

Snow, Dean R. The Archaeology of North America. Porter, Frank W., III, intro. by. (Illus.). 144p. (gr. 5 up). 1989. 17.95 (1-55546-691-5) Chelsea Hse.

Snow, Frances, et al. Thunder Waters: Experiences of Growing up in Different Indian Tribes. (gr. 3-8). 1975. pap. 1.50 (0-89992-072-1) Coun India Ed.

Snow, Jack. The Magical Mimics in Oz. Kramer, Frank, illus. 240p. (gr. 3 up). 1991. 24.95 (0-929605-08-X); pap. 11.95 (0-929605-09-8) Books Wonder.

—The Shaggy Man of Oz. Kramer, Frank, illus. 256p. (gr. 3 up). 1991. 24.95 (0-929605-10-1); pap. 11.95 (0-929605-11-X) Books Wonder.

Snow, John. Secrets of Ponds & Lakes. Jack, Susan, ed. Dowling, Jak, intro. by. (Illus.). 96p. (Orig.). (gr. 4-10). 1982. pap. 3.95 (0-930096-30-4) G Gannett.

Snow, Misti. Take Time to Play Checkers: Wise Words from Kids on Their Parents & Friends, Their Worries & Hopes & the Wonderful & Hard Years of Growing Up. LC 92-54079. 1992. 16.00 (0-670-84061-0) Viking Child Bks.

Snow, Pegeen. Atlanta. LC 88-20243. (Illus.). 60p. (gr. 3 up). 1989. RSBE 13.95 (0-87518-389-1, Dillon) Macmillan Child Grp.

—Come los Guisantes, Cuanto Antes: (Eat Your Peas, Louise!) Venezia, Mike, illus. LC 84-27445. (ENG & SPA.). 32p. (ps-2). 1989. PLB 11.93 (0-516-32067-X); pap. 2.95 (0-516-52067-9) Childrens.

—Eat Your Peas, Louise! Venezia, Mike, illus. LC 84-27445. 32p. (ps-2). 1985. PLB 11.93 (0-516-02067-6); pap. 2.95 (0-516-42067-4); pap. 30.60 big bk. (0-516-49452-X) Childrens.

—A Pet for Pat. Dunnington, Tom, illus. LC 83-23159. 32p. (ps-2). 1984. PLB 11.93 (0-516-02049-8); pap. 2.95 (0-516-42049-6) Childrens.

Snow, Reed C., jt. auth. see Gordon, Patricia.

Snow, Suzanne see Douillard, Jeanne.

Snow, Ted. Global Change. LC 90-37680. (Illus.). 48p. (gr. k-4). 1990. PLB 15.27 (0-516-01105-7); pap. 4.95 (0-516-41105-5) Childrens.

Snowball, Marilyn. Preschool Packrat. 112p. (ps). 1982. 9.95 (0-88160-011-3, LW 113) Learning Wks.

—Preschool Pelican. 112p. (ps). 1982. 9.95 (0-88160-085-7, LW 114) Learning Wks.

Snowden, S. The Young Astronomer. (Illus.). 32p. (gr. 5-10). 1983. PLB 13.96 (0-88110-028-5); pap. 6.95 (0-86020-651-3) EDC.

Snyder, Anne. Kids & Drinking. Harlan, Susan, illus. 47p. (gr. 3-7). 1977. pap. 4.95 (0-89638-010-6) CompCare.

—My Name Is Davy-I'm an Alcoholic. (RL 5). 1986. pap. 3.50 (0-451-16181-5, Sig) NAL-Dutton.

—The Truth about Alex. (Illus.). 176p. (gr. 9-12). 1987. pap. 2.75 (0-451-14996-3, Sig) NAL-Dutton.

Snyder, Barbara. Entre Culturas: Intermediate Through Advanced. (SPA.). 144p. 1993. pap. 8.95 (0-685-62801-9, F7655-3, Natl Textbk); tchr's. manual 7.95 (0-685-62802-7, F7669-3, Natl Textbk) NTC Pub Grp.

Snyder, Bernadette. One Hundred-Fifteen Saintly Fun Facts. (Illus.). 144p. (Orig.). 1993. pap. 5.95 (0-89243-562-3) Liguori Pubns.

Snyder, Bernadette M. The Fun Facts Dictionary: A World of Weird & Wonderful Words. Sharp, Chris, illus. 144p. (Orig.). (gr. 5-12). 1991. pap. text ed. 5.95 (0-89243-348-5) Liguori Pubns.

—One Hundred Fifty Fun Facts Found in the Bible: For Kids of All Ages. Sharp, Chris, illus. LC 90-70802. 144p. (gr. 1-6). 1990. pap. 5.95 (0-89243-330-2) Liguori Pubns.

—Three Hundred Sixty-Five Fun Facts for Catholic Kids. LC 89-84983. 144p. (Orig.). (gr. 4-12). 1989. pap. 5.95 (0-89243-309-4) Liguori Pubns.

Snyder, Carol. Dear Mom & Dad, Don't Worry. (gr. 7 up). 1989. 13.95 (0-553-05801-0, Starfire) Bantam.

—Dear Mom & Dad, Don't Worry. 1993. pap. 3.50 (0-553-29646-9) Bantam.
—God Must Like Cookies, Too. Glick, Beth, illus. LC 92-26886. 32p. (ps-3). 1993. 16.95 (0-8276-0423-8) JPS Phila.
—The Great Condominium Rebellion. Kramer, Anthony, illus. LC 81-65491. 128p. (gr. 4-6). 1981. PLB 11.95 (0-385-28352-0) Delacorte.
—Ike & Mama & the Once-a-Year Suit. Robinson, Charles, illus. LC 92-9201. 48p. (gr. 2-5). 1992. pap. 9.95 (0-8276-0418-1) JPS Phila.
—One Up, One Down. Chambliss, Maxie, illus. LC 93-36282. 1994. 15.95 (0-689-31828-6, Atheneum) Macmillan.

Snyder, Carrie A. How to Draw Dogs. Snyder, Carrrie A., illus. LC 81-52120. 32p. (gr. 2-6). 1982. PLB 10.65 (0-89375-686-5); pap. text ed. 1.95 (0-89375-687-3) Troll Assocs.
—How to Draw Horses. Snyder, Carrie A., illus. LC 84-51871. 32p. (gr. 2-6). 1985. PLB 10.65 (0-8167-0381-7, Pub. by Watermill Pr); pap. text ed. 1.95 (0-8167-0382-5) Troll Assocs.
—You Can Draw Funny Animals. Snyder, Carrie A., illus. LC 81-69659. 32p. (gr. 2-6). 1981. PLB 10.65 (0-89375-689-X); pap. text ed. 1.95 (0-89375-409-9) Troll Assocs.

Snyder, Diane, retold by. The Boy of the Three-Year Nap. Say, Allen, illus. LC 87-30674. 32p. (ps-3). 1988. 15.45 (0-395-44090-4) HM.

Snyder, Dianne. Boy of the Three-Year Nap. (ps-3). 1993. pap. 4.95 (0-395-66957-X) HM.
—George & the Dragon Word. Lies, Brian, illus. 56p. (gr. 2-4). 1991. 13.45 (0-395-55129-3, Sandpiper) HM.
—George & the Dragon Word. 1994. pap. 2.99 (0-671-79393-4, Minstrel Bks) PB.

Snyder, Frank V., intro. by. Tales of the Sea: An Illustrated Collection of Adventure Stories. Neill, Peter, pref. by. LC 92-2841. (Illus.). 144p. (gr. 4-7). 1992. 24.95 (0-8478-1578-1) Rizzoli Intl.

Snyder, Henry D., jt. auth. see Dalton, LeRoy C.

Snyder, J. L. What Christmas Means to Me. Powell, Terry, illus. 43p. (gr. 8-12). 1989. pap. text ed. 2.50 (0-87227-134-X) Reg Baptist.

Snyder, James R. What's (Bad) Good about Divorce? 1977. 1st ed. LC 77-84446. (Illus.). 23p. 1977. 6.95 (0-9601452-1-4) FIG Ltd.

Snyder, Jerry. Basic Instructor Guitar. (Illus.). 96p. (Orig.). 1993. pap. text ed. 9.95 (0-89898-570-6) CPP Belwin.

Snyder, Lee, jt. auth. see Cocetti, Robert A.

Snyder, Linda. Guys & Girls: Understanding Each Other. (Illus.). 48p. (gr. 6-8). 1991. pap. 7.99 (1-55945-110-6) Group Pub.
—School Struggles. 48p. (Orig.). (gr. 9-12). 1990. pap. 7.99 (1-55945-201-3) Group Pub.

Snyder, Margaret, adapted by. The Trolls & the Shoemaker. Kong, Emilie, illus. 24p. (ps-4). 1992. 20.00 (0-307-74027-7, 64027, Golden Pr) Western Pub.

Snyder, P. B., jt. auth. see Boyer, Robert E.

Snyder, Patricia. Spanish Holiday Activity Workbook. (Illus.). 100p. (Orig.). (gr. 9-12). 1986. 16.95 (0-9617764-0-4) PS Enterprises.

Snyder, Phillip C. Pa Pong: A Siamese Kitty. Mohrman, Janet S., illus. 28p. (ps-1). 1981. pap. text ed. 3.95 (0-940560-03-8) Custom Hse.
—Poochie. Mohrman, Janet S., illus. 28p. (Orig.). (ps). 1982. pap. 3.95 (0-940560-04-6) Custom Hse.

Snyder, Ruth M. Forts & Ports. LC 90-72116. 44p. (gr. 2-4). 1991. pap. 5.95 (1-55523-418-6) Winston-Derek.

Snyder, Solomon H., ed. see Carson-Finnerty, LaVonne.

Snyder, Solomon H., ed. see Feinberg, Brian.

Snyder, Solomon H., jt. ed. see Garell, Dale C.

Snyder, Solomon H., ed. see Murphy, Wendy & Murphy, Jack.

Snyder, Solomon H., ed. see Siegel, Dorothy S.

Snyder, Solomon H., ed. see Wax, Nina.

Snyder, Thomas F. Archeology Search Book. O'Neill, Martha, ed. Cullinan, Dorothy K. & Podgorski, Mary E., illus. 32p. (gr. 4-12). 1982. pap. text ed. 8.08 (0-07-059467-8) McGraw.
—Energy Searchbook. Cullinan, Dorothy K., illus. Snyder, Thomas F., intro. by. 56p. (gr. 4-12). 1982. pap. text ed. 8.08 (0-07-059472-4) McGraw.

Snyder, Thomas F. & O'Neill, Martha. Community Search Apple Set. Cullinan, Dorothy K. & Podgorski, Mary E., illus. (gr. 4-12). 1982. Set. 219.76 (0-07-079006-X) McGraw.
—Community Searchbook. Cullinan, Dorothy K. & Podgorski, Mary E., illus. 32p. (gr. 4 up). 1982. pap. text ed. 8.08 reorders (0-07-059463-5) McGraw.

Snyder, Vern W. For the Lov'va Winkie. 135p. 1988. write for info.; pap. write for info. V W Snyder.
—For the Lov'va Winkie. 90p. (gr. 3 up). 1989. pap. 8.95 (0-926366-00-9) V W Snyder.

Snyder, Zilpha K. And All Between. 224p. (gr. 5 up). 1992. pap. 3.50 (0-440-21265-0, LFL) Dell.
—And Condors Danced. LC 87-5364. 216p. (gr. 4-6). 1987. 14.95 (0-385-29575-8) Delacorte.
—And Condors Danced. 224p. (gr. k-6). 1989. pap. 3.50 (0-440-40153-4, YB) Dell.
—Below the Root. 244p. (gr. 5 up). 1992. pap. 3.50 (0-440-21266-9, LFL) Dell.
—Black & Blue Magic. Holtan, Gene, illus. LC 66-12850. 192p. (gr. 3-7). 1972. Spartan ed. 5.95 (0-689-30075-1, Atheneum) Macmillan Child Grp.
—Black & Blue Magic. (gr. k-6). 1994. pap. 3.99 (0-440-40053-8, YB) Dell.

—Blair's Nightmare. LC 83-15677. 204p. (gr. 4-6). 1984. SBE 13.95 (0-689-31022-6, Atheneum Child Bk) Macmillan Child Grp.
—The Changing Maze. Mikolaycak, Charles, illus. LC 91-45323. 32p. (gr. k-3). 1992. pap. 4.95 (0-689-71618-4, Aladdin) Macmillan Child Grp.
—The Egypt Game. Raible, Alton, illus. LC 67-10467. 224p. (gr. 4-6). 1967. SBE 14.95 (0-689-30006-9, Atheneum Child Bk) Macmillan Child Grp.
—The Egypt Game. LC 67-2717. (gr. 4-6). 1986. pap. 3.99 (0-440-42225-6, YB) Dell.
—The Famous Stanley Kidnapping Case. (gr. 4-6). 1985. pap. 3.50 (0-440-42485-2, YB) Dell.
—The Headless Cupid. Raible, Alton, illus. LC 78-154763. 208p. (gr. 4-6). 1971. SBE 14.95 (0-689-20687-9, Atheneum Child Bk) Macmillan Child Grp.
—The Headless Cupid. Raible, Alton, illus. (gr. 3-7). 1985. pap. 3.50 (0-440-43507-2, YB) Dell.
—Janie's Private Eyes. (gr. 5-7). 1989. 14.95 (0-440-50123-7) Delacorte.
—Janie's Private Eyes. (gr. 3-5). 1989. 14.95 (0-385-30146-4) Doubleday.
—Libby on Wednesday. 1990. 14.95 (0-385-29979-6) Delacorte.
—Libby on Wednesday. (gr. 4-7). 1991. pap. 3.50 (0-440-40498-3) Dell.
—A Season of Ponies. (gr. k-6). 1988. pap. 2.95 (0-440-40006-6) Dell.
—Song of the Gargoyle. 1991. 14.95 (0-385-30301-7) Delacorte.
—Song of the Gargoyle. (gr. 4-7). 1994. pap. 3.99 (0-440-40898-9) Dell.
—Squeak Saves the Day. (ps-3). 1992. pap. 3.25 (0-440-40585-8, YB) Dell.
—Squeak Saves the Day & Other Tooley Tales. Morrill, Leslie, illus. LC 87-31010. 192p. (gr. 2-5). 1988. pap. 14.95 (0-385-29661-4) Delacorte.
—The Tooleys, the New. 1988. write for info. Delacorte.
—The Truth About Stone Hollow. (gr. k-6). 1986. pap. 3.25 (0-440-48846-X, YB) Dell.
—Until the Celebration. 208p. (gr. 5 up). 1992. pap. 3.50 (0-440-21348-7, LFL) Dell.
—The Velvet Room. (gr. k-6). 1988. pap. 3.50 (0-440-40042-2, YB) Dell.
—The Velvet Room. (gr. 4-6). 16.25 (0-8446-6419-7) Peter Smith.
—The Witches of Worm. Raible, Alton, illus. LC 72-75283. 192p. (gr. 4-8). 1972. SBE 14.95 (0-689-30066-2, Atheneum Child Bk) Macmillan Child Grp.
—The Witches of Worm. (gr. k-6). 1986. pap. 3.25 (0-440-49727-2, YB) Dell.

Snypp, Wilbur & Hunter, Bob. Buckeyes: Ohio State Football. (Illus.). 352p. (gr. 6-12). 1988. 16.95 (0-87397-307-0) Strode.

So, Meilo. The Emperor & the Nightingale. Meilo So, illus. LC 91-40693. 32p. (ps-2). 1992. SBE 13.95 (0-02-786045-0, Bradbury Pr) Macmillan Child Grp.

Soaries, Buster. My Family Is Driving Me Crazy. 132p. 1991. pap. 4.99 (0-89693-939-1) SP Pubns.

Sobel, Barbara. Great-Grandma, Heroine! LC 87-1235. (gr. 3-6). 1987. 7.59 (0-87386-049-7); bk. & cassette 16.99 (0-317-55324-0); pap. 1.95 (0-87386-048-9) Jan Prods.
—Jake Finds a Penny. Ziffer, Louise, illus. LC 86-81370. 32p. (gr. k-2). 1986. PLB 7.59 (0-87386-019-5); pap. 1.95 (0-87386-015-2) Jan Prods.
—The Jewels from the Sea. LC 87-81237. (gr. 3-6). 1987. 7.59 (0-87386-043-8); bk. & cassette 16.99 (0-317-55335-6); pap. 1.95 (0-87386-042-X) Jan Prods.
—The Little Bird. Neulinger, Karen, illus. LC 86-81462. 32p. (gr. k-2). 1986. PLB 7.59 (0-87386-018-7); pap. 1.95 (0-87386-014-4) Jan Prods.
—Papa, Molly & the Great Prairie. LC 87-81236. (gr. 3-6). 1987. 7.59 (0-87386-045-4); bk. & cassette 16.99 (0-317-55334-8); pap. 1.95 (0-87386-044-6) Jan Prods.
—To Catch a Thief! LC 87-81234. (gr. 3-6). 1987. 7.59 (0-87386-047-0); bk. & cassette 16.99 (0-317-55326-7); pap. 1.95 (0-87386-046-2) Jan Prods.

Sobel, Max, ed. see Glatzer, David & Glatzer, Joyce.

Sober, Nancy H. The Intruders: The Illegal Residents of the Cherokee Nation, 1866-1907. 2nd ed. LC 90-84850. (Illus.). 222p. (gr. 12). 1991. PLB 24.95 (0-9628188-0-1) Cherokee Bks.

Sobol. Encyclopedia Brown Gets His Man. large type ed. (gr. 4-6). Repr. of 1967 ed. write for info. NAVH.

Sobol, David J. Encyclopedia Brown's Book of Strange but True Facts. (gr. 4-7). 1991. 12.95 (0-590-44147-7) Scholastic Inc.

Sobol, Donald. Finds The Clues. (gr. 4-7). 1987. pap. 2.50 (0-553-15570-9) Bantam.

Sobol, Donald J. The Amazing Power of Ashur Fine. (gr. 4-8). 1987. pap. 2.95 (0-8167-1049-X) Troll Assocs.
—Encyclopedia Brown. 1982. pap. 3.25 (0-553-15722-1) Bantam.
—Encyclopedia Brown - Pitches. 1982. pap. 3.25 (0-553-15736-1) Bantam.
—Encyclopedia Brown - Saves. 1982. pap. 2.95 (0-553-15734-5) Bantam.
—Encyclopedia Brown - Tracks. 1982. pap. 2.95 (0-553-15721-3) Bantam.
—Encyclopedia Brown & the Case of the Dead Eagles. Shortall, Leonard & Brandi, Lillian, illus. LC 75-15911. 96p. (gr. 3-5). 1979. 12.50 (0-525-67220-6, Lodestar Bks) Dutton Child Bks.

—Encyclopedia Brown & the Case of the Disgusting Sneakers. Owens, Gail, illus. LC 89-13939. 96p. (gr. 3 up). 1990. 12.95g (0-688-09012-5) Morrow Jr Bks.
—Encyclopedia Brown & the Case of the Mysterious Handprints. Owens, Gail, illus. LC 85-8798. 96p. (gr. 3-7). 1985. 12.95 (0-688-04626-6) Morrow Jr Bks.
—Encyclopedia Brown & the Case of the Mysterious Handprints, No. 16. 128p. 1986. pap. 2.95 (0-553-15739-6, Skylark) Bantam.
—Encyclopedia Brown & the Case of the Midnight Visitor. Brandi, Lillian & Shortall, Leonard, illus. LC 77-22159. 96p. (gr. 3-5). 1979. 12.50 (0-525-67221-4, Lodestar Bks) Dutton Child Bks.
—Encyclopedia Brown & the Case of the Midnight Visitor, No. 13. 96p. 1982. pap. 2.95 (0-553-15738-8) Bantam.
—Encyclopedia Brown & the Case of the Secret Pitch. (gr. 4-8). 1978. pap. 2.25 (0-553-15587-3, Skylark Bks) Bantam.
—Encyclopedia Brown & the Case of the Secret Pitch. Shortall, Leonard & Brandi, Lillian, illus. LC 65-199640. 96p. (gr. 3-5). 1979. 12.50 (0-525-67202-8, Lodestar Bks) Dutton Child Bks.
—Encyclopedia Brown & the Case of the Treasure Hunt. Owens, Gail, illus. LC 87-22048. 96p. (gr. 3-7). 1988. 12.95 (0-688-06955-X) Morrow Jr Bks.
—Encyclopedia Brown Boy Detective. (gr. 4-8). 1985. pap. 3.25 (0-553-15724-8) Bantam.
—Encyclopedia Brown, Boy Detective. Shortall, Leonard & Brandi, Lillian, illus. LC 63-9632. 96p. (gr. 3-5). 1979. 12.95 (0-525-67200-1, Lodestar Bks) Dutton Child Bks.
—Encyclopedia Brown Carries On. Ohlsson, Ib, illus. LC 79-6340. 80p. (gr. 3-7). 1984. SBE 12.95 (0-02-786190-2, Four Winds) Macmillan Child Grp.
—Encyclopedia Brown Finds the Clues. (gr. 4-8). 1982. pap. 3.25 (0-553-15725-6) Bantam.
—Encyclopedia Brown Finds the Clues. Shortall, Leonard & Brandi, Lillian, illus. LC 66-10230. 96p. (gr. 3-5). 1979. 12.95 (0-525-67204-4, Lodestar Bks) Dutton Child Bks.
—Encyclopedia Brown Gets His Man. Shortall, Leonard & Brandi, Lillian, illus. LC 67-24666. 96p. (gr. 3-5). 1979. 12.50 (0-525-67206-0, Lodestar Bks) Dutton Child Bks.
—Encyclopedia Brown Gets His Man, No. 4. LC 67-24666. (gr. 4-8). 1982. pap. 2.50 (0-553-15526-1, Skylark Bks) Bantam.
—Encyclopedia Brown Keeps the Peace. Shortall, Leonard & Brandi, Lillian, illus. LC 73-82912. 96p. (gr. 3-5). 1979. 12.50 (0-525-67208-7, Lodestar Bks) Dutton Child Bks.
—Encyclopedia Brown Keeps the Peace, No. 6. 1982. pap. 3.25 (0-553-15735-3, Skylark Bks) Bantam.
—Encyclopedia Brown Lends a Hand. Shortall, Leonard & Brandi, Lillian, illus. LC 74-10281. 96p. (gr. 3-5). 1979. 13.00 (0-525-67218-4, Lodestar Bks) Dutton Child Bks.
—Encyclopedia Brown Lends a Hand. (gr. 4-6). 1993. pap. 3.25 (0-553-48133-9) Bantam.
—Encyclopedia Brown Saves the Day. Shortall, Leonard & Brandi, Lillian, illus. LC 71-117149. 96p. (gr. 3-5). 1979. 12.50 (0-525-67210-9, Lodestar Bks) Dutton Child Bks.
—Encyclopedia Brown Saves the Day, No. 7. (gr. 4-8). 1982. pap. 2.50 (0-553-15539-3, Skylark Bks) Bantam.
—Encyclopedia Brown Sets the Pace. Ohlsson, Ib, illus. LC 81-69511. 96p. (gr. 3-7). 1984. SBE 12.95 (0-02-786200-3, Four Winds) Macmillan Child Grp.
—Encyclopedia Brown Sets the Pace. 96p. (gr. 3-7). 1991. pap. 2.95 (0-590-44577-4, Apple Paperbacks) Scholastic Inc.
—Encyclopedia Brown Shows the Way. Shortall, Leonard & Brandi, Shortall, illus. LC 72-2911. 96p. (gr. 3-5). 1979. 12.50 (0-525-67216-8, Lodestar Bks) Dutton Child Bks.
—Encyclopedia Brown Shows the Way, No. 9. 96p. (gr. 3-6). 1982. pap. 3.25 (0-553-15737-X) Bantam.
—Encyclopedia Brown Solves Them All. Shortall, Leonard & Brandi, Lillian, illus. LC 68-22746. 96p. (gr. 3-5). 1979. 12.50 (0-525-67212-5, Lodestar Bks) Dutton Child Bks.
—Encyclopedia Brown Solves Them All. (gr. 4-7). 1993. pap. 3.25 (0-553-48080-4) Bantam.
—Encyclopedia Brown Takes a Case. 1982. pap. 2.95 (0-553-15723-X) Bantam.
—Encyclopedia Brown Takes the Cake. (gr. 4-7). 1991. pap. 2.95 (0-590-44576-6) Scholastic Inc.
—Encyclopedia Brown Takes the Case. Shortall, Leonard & Brandi, Leonard, illus. LC 73-6443. 96p. (gr. 3-5). 1979. 12.50 (0-525-66318-5, Lodestar Bks) Dutton Child Bks.
—Encyclopedia Brown Takes the Case, No. 10. (gr. 8-12). 1982. pap. 2.50 (0-553-15528-8) Bantam.
—Encyclopedia Brown Tracks Them Down. Shortall, Leonard & Brandi, Lillian, illus. LC 77-160147. 96p. (gr. 3-5). 1979. 12.95 (0-525-67214-1, Lodestar Bks) Dutton Child Bks.
—Encyclopedia Brown Tracks Them Down, No. 8. 96p. (gr. 3-6). 1982. pap. 2.50 (0-553-15525-3) Bantam.
—Encyclopedia Brown's Book of the Wacky Outdoors. Enik, Ted, illus. LC 87-7851. 112p. (gr. 3-7). 1987. 12.95 (0-688-06635-6) Morrow Jr Bks.
—Encyclopedia Brown's Book of the Wacky Outdoors. (Orig.). (gr. 5 up). 1988. pap. 2.50 (0-553-15598-9) Bantam.

—Encyclopedia Brown's Book of Wacky Animals. Enik, Ted, illus. LC 84-22608. 128p. (gr. 3-7). 1985. 11.95 (*0-688-04152-3*) Morrow Jr Bks.
—Encyclopedia Brown's Book of Wacky Animals. 128p. (Orig.). 1985. pap. 2.25 (*0-553-15346-3*, Skylark) Bantam.
—Encyclopedia Brown's Book of Wacky Cars. Enik, Ted, illus. LC 86-23556. 128p. (gr. 3-7). 1987. 11.95 (*0-688-06222-9*) Morrow Jr Bks.
—Encyclopedia Brown's Book of Wacky Cars. Enik, Ted, illus. 128p. (gr. 3-7). 1987. pap. 2.75 (*0-553-15512-1*, Skylark) Bantam.
—Encyclopedia Brown's Book of Wacky Crimes. Enik, Ted, illus. LC 82-9683. 128p. (gr. 3-5). 1982. 12.95 (*0-525-66786-5*, Lodestar Bks) Dutton Child Bks.
—Encyclopedia Brown's Book of Wacky Crimes. Enik, Ted, illus. 1983. pap. 2.25 (*0-553-15358-7*) Bantam.
—Encyclopedia Brown's Book of Wacky Spies. Enik, Ted, illus. LC 83-17179. 128p. (gr. 3-7). 1984. 13.95 (*0-688-02744-X*) Morrow Jr Bks.
—Encyclopedia Brown's Book of Wacky Spies. Enik, Ted, illus. 112p. (gr. 4-6). 1984. pap. 2.25 (*0-553-15369-2*, Skylark) Bantam.
—Encyclopedia Brown's Book of Wacky Sports. Enik, Ted, illus. LC 82-84250. 128p. (gr. 3-7). 1984. 11.95 (*0-688-03884-0*) Morrow Jr Bks.
—Encyclopedia Brown's Book of Wacky Sports. Enik, Ted, illus. 128p. (Orig.). (gr. 3-7). 1984. pap. 2.50 (*0-553-15497-4*, Skylark) Bantam.
—Encyclopedia Brown's Record Book of Weird & Wonderful Facts. Murdocca, Sal, illus. LC 78-72857. (gr. 3 up). 1979. PLB 9.89 (*0-440-02330-0*) Delacorte.
—Encyclopedia Brown's Record Book of Weird & Wonderful Facts. Degen, Bruce, illus. (gr. 3-7). 1981. pap. 1.75 (*0-440-42361-9*, YB) Dell.
—Encyclopedia Brown's Second Record Book of Weird & Wonderful Facts. Degen, Bruce, illus. LC 81-790. 160p. (gr. 4-6). 1981. 10.95 (*0-385-28243-5*); PLB 10.95 (*0-685-01395-2*) Delacorte.
—Encyclopedia Brown's Third Record Book of Weird & Wonderful Facts. Murdocca, Sal, illus. LC 85-11613. 144p. (gr. 3-7). 1985. 11.95 (*0-688-05705-5*) Morrow Jr Bks.
—Encyclopedia Brown's Third Record Book of Weird & Wonderful Facts. 144p. 1985. pap. 2.50 (*0-553-15372-2*, Skylark) Bantam.
—The Secret Case of the Disgusting Sneakers. (gr. 4-7). 1991. pap. 3.25 (*0-553-15851-1*) Bantam.
—Still More Two-Minute Mysteries. 1993. pap. 2.75 (*0-590-44786-6*) Scholastic Inc.
—Two-Minute Mysteries. 160p. (Orig.). (gr. 5-8). 1986. pap. 2.50 (*0-590-41292-2*, Apple Paperbacks) Scholastic Inc.
—Two-Minute Mysteries. 160p. 1991. pap. 2.95 (*0-590-44787-4*, Apple Paperbacks) Scholastic Inc.
—The Wright Brothers at Kitty Hawk. 128p. (Orig.). (gr. 3-7). 1987. pap. 2.95 (*0-590-42904-3*) Scholastic Inc.
Sobol, Donald J. & Andrews, Glenn. Encyclopedia Brown Takes the Cake! A Cook & Case Book. Ohlsson, Ib, illus. LC 82-84250. 128p. (gr. 3-7). 1983. SBE 12.95 (*0-02-786210-0*, Four Winds) Macmillan Child Grp.
Sobol, Donald J. & Sobol, Rose. Encyclopedia Brown's Book of Strange But True Crimes. 128p. 1992. pap. 2.95 (*0-590-44148-5*, Apple Paperbacks) Scholastic Inc.
Sobol, Donald J. & Velasquez, Eric. Encyclopedia Brown & the Case of the Two Spies. LC 93-14350. 1994. 13.95 (*0-385-32036-1*) Delacorte.
Sobol, Harriet L. My Brother Steven Is Retarded. Agre, Patricia, illus. LC 76-46996. 32p. (gr. 3-6). 1977. RSBE 13.95 (*0-02-785990-8*, Macmillan Child Bk) Macmillan Child Grp.
Sobol, Jonah, jt. auth. see Sobol, Richard.
Sobol, Richard & Sobol, Jonah. Seal Journey. Sobol, Richard, photos by. LC 92-25974. (Illus.). 32p. (gr. 1-5). 1993. 14.99 (*0-525-65126-8*, Cobblehill Bks) Dutton Child Bks.
Sobol, Rose. Woman Chief. 112p. (gr. 5-9). 1979. pap. 1.25 (*0-440-99657-0*, LFL) Dell.
Sobol, Rose, jt. auth. see Sobol, Donald J.
Socarras-Roufagalas, Gilda, tr. see Fugate, Clara T.
Sochard, Ruth. Dagorlad & the Dead Marshes. (Illus.). 36p. (gr. 10-12). 1984. pap. 7.00 (*0-915795-20-5*, 8020) Iron Crown Ent Inc.
—Pirates of Pelargir. Fenlon, Peter, ed. McBride, Angus, illus. 32p. (Orig.). (gr. 10-12). 1987. pap. 6.00 (*0-915795-44-2*, 8104) Iron Crown Ent Inc.
—Weathertop, the Tower of the Wind. Fenlon, Peter C., Jr., ed. Martin, David & Martin, Elissa, illus. 32p. (Orig.). (gr. 10-12). 1987. pap. 6.00 (*0-915795-89-2*, 8201) Iron Crown Ent Inc.
Society of Brothers Staff, ed. Behold That Star: A Christmas Anthology: A Collection of Fifteen Christmas Stories. 3rd ed. Maendel, Maria A., illus. LC 67-25968. 368p. (gr. 4 up). 1966. 17.00 (*0-87486-003-2*) Plough.
Society of Brothers Staff, ed. see Swinger, Marlys.
Sockey, Daria M. Credo: I Believe. Puccetti, Patricia I., ed. (Illus.). 132p. (gr. 5 up). 1985. pap. 6.80 (*0-89870-081-7*) Ignatius Pr.
—Jesus Our Life. Puccetti, Patricia I., ed. (Illus.). 151p. (Orig.). (gr. 2). 1984. pap. 5.55 (*0-89870-061-2*) Ignatius Pr.

—Our Heavenly Father. (Illus.). 127p. (gr. 1). 1987. pap. text ed. 5.55 (*0-89870-091-4*); activity bk., 63p. by Barbara Nacelewicz 3.00 (*0-89870-092-2*); tchr's. manual by Mary T. Wynne, 104p. 9.95 (*0-89870-127-9*) Ignatius Pr.
Sodano, Dominick, et al. Computer Literacy & Use. (gr. 4-12). 1983. pap. text ed. 3.25 (*0-9611246-0-1*) Ed Activities.
Sodaro, Craig, jt. auth. see Adams, Randy L.
Sodeika, Zita. Caged-In. Kezys, Algimantas, photos by. 94p. (Orig.). 1992. pap. 15.00 (*0-685-59569-2*) Galerija.
Soderstrom, Mary. Maybe Tomorrow I'll Have a Good Time. Wein, Charlotte E., illus. LC 80-25357. 32p. (ps-3). 1981. 16.95 (*0-89885-012-6*) Human Sci Pr.
Soentpiet, Chris K. Around Town. LC 93-23519. 1994. write for info. (*0-688-04572-3*); PLB write for info. (*0-688-04573-1*) Lothrop.
Sofer, G. A Story a Day, Vol. I: Tishrei-Cheshvan. Weinbach, Shaindel, tr. from HEB. Bardugo, Miriam, illus. 206p. (gr. 7-12). 1989. 12.95 (*0-89906-950-9*); pap. 9.95 (*0-89906-951-7*) Mesorah Pubns.
—A Story a Day, Vol. II: Kislev-Teves. Weinbach, Shaindel, tr. from HEB. Bardugo, Miriam, illus. 232p. (gr. 7-12). 1988. 14.95 (*0-89906-952-5*); pap. 10.95 (*0-89906-953-3*) Mesorah Pubns.
—A Story a Day, Vol. III: Shevat-Adar. Weinbach, Shaindel, tr. from HEB. Bardugo, Miriam, illus. 224p. (gr. 7-12). 1989. 14.95 (*0-89906-954-1*); pap. 10.95 (*0-89906-955-X*) Mesorah Pubns.
—A Story a Day, Vol. IV: Nissan-Iyar. Weinbach, Shaindel, tr. from HEB. Bardugo, Miriam, illus. 210p. (gr. 7-12). 1989. 14.95 (*0-89906-956-8*); pap. 10.95 (*0-89906-957-6*) Mesorah Pubns.
—A Story a Day, Vol. V: Sivan-Tammuz. Weinbach, Shaindel, tr. from HEB. Bardugo, Miriam, illus. 210p. (gr. 7-12). 1989. 14.95 (*0-89906-958-4*); pap. 10.95 (*0-89906-959-2*) Mesorah Pubns.
—A Story a Day, Vol. VI: Ev-Elul. Weinbach, Shaindel, tr. from HEB. Bardugo, Miriam, illus. 210p. (gr. 7-12). 1989. 14.95 (*0-89906-960-6*); pap. 10.95 (*0-89906-961-4*) Mesorah Pubns.
Sohi, Morteza E. Look What I Did with a Leaf. LC 92-35142. 32p. (gr. 4-8). 1993. 14.95 (*0-8027-8215-9*); PLB 15.85 (*0-8027-8216-7*) Walker & Co.
Sohl, Marcia & Dackerman, Gerald. Black Beauty Student Activity Book. (Illus.). 16p. (gr. 4-10). 1976. pap. 1.25 (*0-88301-183-2*) Pendulum Pr.
—The Call of the Wild Student Activity Book. (Illus.). 16p. (gr. 4-10). 1976. pap. 1.25 (*0-88301-182-4*) Pendulum Pr.
—The Great Adventures of Sherlock Holmes: Student Activity Book. Cruz, E. R., illus. (gr. 4-10). 1976. wkbk 1.25 (*0-88301-187-5*) Pendulum Pr.
—Gulliver's Travels: Student Activity Book. Cruz, E. R., illus. (gr. 4-10). 1976. wkbk 1.25 (*0-88301-188-3*) Pendulum Pr.
—Hunchback of Notre Dame: Student Activity Book. (Illus.). (gr. 4-10). 1976. wkbk 1.25 (*0-88301-189-1*) Pendulum Pr.
—The Invisible Man: Student Activity Book. Nino, Alex, illus. (gr. 4-10). 1976. wkbk 1.25 (*0-88301-190-5*) Pendulum Pr.
—Journey to the Center of the Earth: Student Activity Book. Colaquian, Val, illus. (gr. 4-10). 1976. 1.25 (*0-88301-191-3*) Pendulum Pr.
—Kidnapped: Student Activity Book. Redondo, Frank, illus. (gr. 4-10). 1976. wkbk. 1.25 (*0-88301-192-1*) Pendulum Pr.
—Moby Dick Student Activity Book. Nino, Alex, illus. (gr. 4-10). 1976. pap. 1.25 (*0-88301-181-6*) Pendulum Pr.
—Mysterious Island: Student Activity Book. Cruz, E. R., illus. (gr. 4-10). 1976. wkbk. 1.25 (*0-88301-193-X*) Pendulum Pr.
—The Red Badge of Courage: Student Activity Book. Cruz, E. R., illus. 16p. (gr. 4-10). 1976. pap. 1.25 (*0-88301-184-0*) Pendulum Pr.
—The Scarlet Letter: Student Activity Book. Redondo, Virgilio, illus. (gr. 4-10). 1976. wkbk 1.25 (*0-88301-194-8*) Pendulum Pr.
—The Story of My Life: Student Activity Book. Zuniga, A. de, illus. (gr. 4-10). 1976. wkbk 1.25 (*0-88301-195-6*) Pendulum Pr.
—A Tale of Two Cities: Student Activity Book. Alcola, Alfredo P., illus. (gr. 4-10). 1976. pap. 1.25 (*0-88301-196-4*) Pendulum Pr.
—The Three Musketeers: Student Activity Book. Nino, Alex, illus. (gr. 4-10). 1976. wkbk 1.25 (*0-88301-197-2*) Pendulum Pr.
—Me Time Machine: Student Activity Book. (Illus.). 16p. (gr. 4-10). 1976. pap. 1.25 (*0-88301-186-7*) Pendulum Pr.
—Treasure Island. 16p. (gr. 4-10). 1976. pap. 2.95 (*0-88301-106-9*); pap. 1.25 student activity bk. (*0-88301-185-9*) Pendulum Pr.
—The War of the Worlds: Student Activity Book. Nino, Alex, illus. (gr. 4-10). 1976. wkbk 1.25 (*0-88301-198-0*) Pendulum Pr.
Sohn, David A., ed. Ten Top Stories. Bd. with Flowers for Algernon. Keyes; So Much Unfairness of Things. Bryan; Backward Boy. Coghlan; Denton's Daughter. Lowenberg; Words I Have Known. Spatt; Planet of the Condemned. Murphy; Test. Thomas; See How They Run. Coxe; Polar Night. Burke; The Turtle. Vukelich. (Orig.). (gr. 6-12). 1985. pap. 3.95 (*0-553-25326-3*) Bantam.

Soike, Thomas E. Harriet's Chariot. LC 91-91311. 30p. (gr. 4-6). 1991. write for info. (*0-9631201-0-7*) T E Soike.
Sokolinsky, Martin, tr. see Gallaz, Christophe.
Sokoloff, David. Classic Jewish Tales. (ps-3). 1993. pap. 8.95 (*1-56171-112-8*) Shapolsky Pubs.
—Jewish Stories of Fun & Adventure. (Illus.). 96p. (gr. 1-3). 1990. pap. 5.95 (*0-685-35727-9*) Shapolsky Pubs.
—The New Jewish Holiday Activity & Coloring Book. 96p. (ps-8). 1990. pap. 5.95 (*0-944007-92-9*) Shapolsky Pubs.
Sokoloff, Myka-Lynne, jt. auth. see Wise, Beth A.
Sokolow, Fred. Complete Rock & Metal Guitar. Stang, Aaron, ed. 80p. (Orig.). 1982. pap. text ed. 16.95 (*0-89898-576-5*) CPP Belwin.
Solarino, Claudio, jt. auth. see Morgan, Lee.
Solberg, S. E. The Land & People of Korea. LC 90-5952. (Illus.). 240p. (gr. 6 up). 1991. 17.95 (*0-06-021648-4*); PLB 17.89 (*0-06-021649-2*) HarpC Child Bks.
Solecki, John. Hosni Mubarak. (Illus.). (gr. 5 up). 1991. 17.95 (*1-55546-844-6*) Chelsea Hse.
Solensten, Lori, ed. see Hunig, Klaus.
Solga, Kim. Draw! (Illus.). 48p. (gr. 1-6). 1991. 11.95 (*0-89134-385-7*) North Light Bks.
—Make Cards! (Illus.). 48p. (gr. 4-7). 1992. 11.95 (*0-89134-481-0*) North Light Bks.
—Make Clothes Fun! (Illus.). 48p. (gr. 1-6). 1992. 11.95 (*0-89134-421-7*) North Light Bks.
—Make Crafts! LC 92-44905. (Illus.). 48p. (ps). 1993. 11.95 (*0-89134-493-4*) North Light Bks.
—Make Gifts! (Illus.). 48p. (gr. 1-6). 1991. 11.95 (*0-89134-386-5*) North Light Bks.
—Make Prints! (Illus.). 48p. (gr. 1-6). 1991. 11.95 (*0-89134-384-9*) North Light Bks.
—Make Sculptures! (Illus.). 48p. (gr. 1-6). 1992. 11.95 (*0-89134-420-9*) North Light Bks.
—Paint! (Illus.). 48p. (gr. 1-6). 1991. 11.95 (*0-89134-383-0*) North Light Bks.
Solimini, Cheryl, ed. see Stine, Megan, et al.
Soliven, Marivi. Pillow Tales. 1991. 6.95 (*0-533-09188-8*) Vantage.
Soller, Joelle. The Seal. (Illus.). 28p. (gr. 3-8). 1992. pap. 6.95 (*0-88106-428-9*) Charlesbridge Pub.
Sollie, Eddie C. Wolf Stories: Myths & True Life Tales from Around the World. Livingston, Julie, ed. Lund, Gary, illus. 48p. (Orig.). (gr. 1-6). 1993. 11.95 (*0-941831-84-1*); pap. 7.95 (*0-941831-83-3*) Beyond Words Pub.
Sollisch, James. Coming up for Air. LC 86-72866. 144p. (Orig.). (gr. 7 up). 1987. pap. 6.00 (*0-916383-15-6*) Aegina Pr.
Sollitt, Kenneth. Our Changing Lives. 182p. 1986. pap. 6.95 (*0-940652-04-8*) Sunrise Bks.
Soloff-Levy, B. Summer Fun Dot-To-Dot Activity Book. 1989. pap. 1.25 (*0-89375-831-0*) Troll Assocs.
Soloff-Levy, Barbara. Circus Time Dot-To-Dot Activity Book. 32p. 1989. pap. 1.25 (*0-8167-0000-1*) Troll Assocs.
—How to Draw Birds. LC 86-50550. (Illus.). 32p. (gr. 2-6). 1987. PLB 10.65 (*0-8167-0876-2*, Pub. by Watermill Pr); pap. text ed. 1.95 (*0-8167-0877-0*, Pub. by Watermill Pr) Troll Assocs.
—How to Draw Fairy-Tale Characters. LC 90-26789. (Illus.). 32p. (gr. 2-6). 1991. lib. bdg. 10.65 (*0-8167-2378-8*); pap. text ed. 1.95 (*0-8167-2379-6*) Troll Assocs.
—How to Draw Farm Animals. LC 84-51872. (Illus.). 32p. (gr. 2-6). 1985. PLB 10.65 (*0-89375-797-7*, Pub. by Watermill Pr); pap. 1.95 (*0-89375-798-5*) Troll Assocs.
—How to Draw Forest Animals. Soloff-Levy, Barbara, illus. LC 84-51873. 32p. (gr. 2-6). 1985. PLB 10.65 (*0-8167-0334-5*, Pub. by Watermill Pr); pap. text ed. 1.95 (*0-8167-0335-3*) Troll Assocs.
—How to Draw Ghosts, Goblins & Witches: And Other Spooky Characters. Soloff-Levy, Barbara, illus. LC 81-52124. 32p. (gr. 2-6). 1982. PLB 10.65 (*0-89375-678-4*); pap. text ed. 1.95 (*0-89375-557-5*) Troll Assocs.
—How to Draw Sea Creatures. LC 86-50469. (Illus.). 32p. (gr. 2-6). 1987. PLB 10.65 (*0-8167-0844-4*, Pub. by Watermill Pr); pap. text ed. 1.95 (*0-8167-0845-2*, Pub. by Watermill Pr) Troll Assocs.
Solomakos, Linda. Cosmic Coloring: Gingerbread Moonman. (Illus.). 20p. (gr. 1-12). 1987. pap. 2.95 (*0-317-93488-0*) Cosmic Color Bks.
—Cosmic Coloring: Star People. (Illus.). 20p. (gr. 1-12). 1987. pap. 2.95 (*0-9622288-0-X*) Cosmic Color Bks.
—Cosmic Coloring: The Magic Robe. (Illus., Orig.). (gr. 1-5). 1987. pap. 2.95 (*0-9622288-1-8*) Cosmic Color Bks.
Solomon, Abbot N. Secrets of the Super Athletes: Tip for Fans & Players-Football. (Illus., Orig.). (gr. 7 up). 1982. pap. 1.95 (*0-440-97979-X*, LFL) Dell.
Solomon, Chuck. Major-League Batboy. Solomon, Chuck, photos by. LC 90-43275. (Illus.). 32p. (gr. 2-5). 1991. 11.95 (*0-517-58244-9*); PLB 12.99 (*0-517-58245-7*) Crown Bks Yng Read.
—Our Soccer League. (Illus.). 40p. (ps-2). 1988. PLB 11.95 (*0-517-56956-6*) Crown Bks Yng Read.
Solomon, Dorothy E. Color Bright. Solomon, Dorothy E., illus. 32p. (gr. 3-7). 1990. 12.95 (*0-933813-02-3*); pap. 7.95 (*0-933813-04-X*) Mdsn Pub Assocs.
Solomon, Joan. Bobbi's New Year. (Illus.). 32p. (gr. 3-5). 1993. 12.95 (*0-237-60114-1*, Pub. by Evans Bros Ltd) Trafalgar.
—Chopsticks & Chips. (Illus.). 25p. (gr. 2-4). 1991. 12.95 (*0-237-60142-7*, Pub. by Evans Bros Ltd) Trafalgar.

—A Day by the Sea. (Illus.). 25p. (gr. 2-4). 1991. 12.95 (0-237-60152-4, Pub. by Evans Bros Ltd) Trafalgar.
—News from Dad. (Illus.). 25p. (gr. 2-4). 1991. 12.95 (0-237-60115-X, Pub. by Evans Bros Ltd) Trafalgar.
—Spiky Sunday. (Illus.). 25p. (gr. 2-4). 1991. 12.95 (0-237-60141-9, Pub. by Evans Bros Ltd) Trafalgar.
Solomon, L. Ursa. The Friendship of Hesper & Rani. Mello, Marsha, illus. 60p. (gr. 1 up). 1985. spiral bdg. 7.95 (0-9615756-1-1) Henchanted Bks.
—The Rotten Chicken: A Modern Fable. rev., 2nd ed. Cummings, B. Martin, illus. Lewis, Benjamin G., frwd. by. (Illus.). 34p. 1989. Repr. of 1984 ed. wire 7.95 (0-9615756-3-8) Henchanted Bks.
—There Must Be More to Life Than This. Hemmings, Tamra, illus. 30p. (gr. k up). 1989. spiral 6.95 (0-9615756-2-X) Henchanted Bks.
Solomon, Marti. StudiAct: Queen. Butler, Cathy, ed. 31p. (Orig.). 1991. pap. text ed. 2.25 (1-56309-006-6) Womans Mission Union.
—StudiAct: Queen Regent. Turrentine, Jan, ed. 32p. (Orig.). (gr. 7-12). 1991. pap. text ed. 2.25 (1-56309-003-1) Womans Mission Union.
—StudiAct: Queen Regent in Service. Turrentine, Jan, ed. 31p. (Orig.). (gr. 7-12). 1991. pap. text ed. 2.25 (1-56309-004-X) Womans Mission Union.
—StudiAct: Queen with Scepter. Turrentine, Jan, ed. 31p. (Orig.). (gr. 7-12). Date not set. pap. text ed. 2.25 (1-56309-005-8) Womans Mission Union.
—StudiAct: Service Aide. Turrentine, Jan, ed. 16p. (Orig.). (gr. 7-12). 1991. pap. text ed. 2.25 (1-56309-002-3) Womans Mission Union.
Solomon, Maury. An Album of Voyager. (Illus.). 64p. (gr. 5-8). 1990. PLB 13.90 (0-531-10876-7) Watts.
Solomon, Maury, ed. see Berke, Art.
Solomon, Maury, ed. see Frommer, Harvey.
Solomon, Maury, ed. see Greene, Laura & Dicker, Eva B.
Solomon, Maury, ed. see Lee, Sally.
Solomon, Susan, jt. auth. see Lipson, Greta.
Solotareff, Gregoire. Never Trust an Ogre! LC 87-30239. (Illus.). 32p. (ps-2). 1988. Repr. of 1986 ed. 11.95 (0-688-07740-4); lib. bdg. 11.88 (0-688-07741-2) Greenwillow.
—Noel's Christmas Secret. 1989. 13.95 (0-374-35544-4) FS&G.
—The Ogre & the Frog King. LC 87-8531. (FRE., Illus.). 32p. (ps-1). 1988. 11.95 (0-688-07078-7); lib. bdg. 11. 88 (0-688-07079-5) Greenwillow.
Solotaroff, Gregoire. Don't Call Me Little Bunny. LC 88-45430. (Illus.). 32p. (ps up). 1988. 13.95 (0-374-35012-4) FS&G.
Soloukhin, Vladimir. Laughter over the Left Shoulder. Martin, David, tr. 160p. 1990. 36.00 (0-7206-0798-1, Pub. by Peter Owen Ltd., UK) Dufour.
Solzhenitsyn, Aleksandr. One Day in the Life of Ivan Denisovich. (gr. 10-12). 1984. pap. 4.99 (0-553-24777-8) Bantam.
Somers, Adele. Learn from Everyone! Practical Guidelines to Living. Somers, Stanley E., illus. 192p. (Orig.). (gr. 8 up). 1985. pap. 7.95 (0-9615032-0-3) World Relations Pr.
Somerville, L. First Book of America. (Illus.). 32p. 1990. PLB 13.96 (0-88110-440-X); pap. 6.95 (0-7460-0338-2) EDC.
—First Book of France. (Illus.). 32p. 1989. PLB 13.96 (0-88110-391-8); pap. 6.95 (0-7460-0322-6) EDC.
—How to Do Origami. (Illus.). 32p. (gr. 3-7). 1991. PLB 12.96 (0-88110-628-3, Usborne); pap. 5.95 (0-7460-1489-9, Usborne) EDC.
—How to Make Kites. (Illus.). 32p. (gr. 3-7). 1992. PLB 12.96 (0-88110-543-0, Usborne); pap. 5.95 (0-7460-0708-6, Usborne) EDC.
—How to Make Superplanes. (Illus.). 32p. (gr. 3-7). 1992. PLB 12.96 (0-88110-542-2, Usborne); pap. 5.95 (0-7460-0667-5, Usborne) EDC.
Somerville, L. & Gibson, R. How to Make Pop-Ups. (Illus.). 32p. (gr. 3-7). 1991. lib. bdg. 12.96 (0-88110-541-4, Usborne); pap. 5.95 (0-7460-1273-X, Usborne) EDC.
Somerville, Sheila, illus. Five Little Pumpkins Big Book. (ps-2). 1988. pap. text ed. 14.00 (0-922053-18-9) N Edge Res.
—Over in the Meadow Big Book. (ps-2). 1988. pap. text ed. 14.00 (0-922053-09-X) N Edge Res.
Somerville, Sheila & Muren, Nancy L., illus. Finger Plays & Action Rhymes Big Book. (ps-2). 1988. pap. text ed. 15.00 (0-922053-01-4) N Edge Res.
Somme, Lauritz & Kalas, Sybille. The Penguin Family Book. LC 87-32830. (Illus.). (ps-12). 1991. pap. 15.95 (0-88708-057-X) Picture Bk Studio.
Sommer, Ann. Youngest Shepherd. (ps-2). 1989. 12.99 (1-55513-602-8, Chariot Bks) Cook.
Sommer, Elyse. I Read You Loud & Clear: A Kid's Thesaurus of Colorful Phrases. Kirschbaum, John, illus. 128p. 1990. text ed. 10.95 (0-88687-575-7, World Almanac) F&W Inc NJ.
—The Kids' World Almanac of Music: From Rock to Bach & Back Again. Lane, John, illus. 288p. (Orig.). 1992. 14.95 (0-88687-522-6, World Almanac); pap. 7.95 (0-88687-521-8, World Almanac) F&W Inc NJ.
Sommer, Karen. New Kid on the Block. LC 86-24323. (gr. 3-7). 1987. pap. 4.49 (0-89191-746-2, Chariot Bks) Cook.
—Satch & the Motormouth. (gr. 3-7). 1987. pap. 4.49 (1-55513-063-1, Chariot Bks) Cook.
Sommer, Robin L. Nien Cheng: Prisoner in China. (Illus.). 64p. (gr. 3-7). 1992. PLB 14.95 (1-56711-011-8) Blackbirch.

Sommer, Robin L. & MacDonald, Patricia. Pablo Picasso. (Illus.). 128p. (gr. 7-9). 1990. 14.95 (0-382-24031-6); lib. bdg. 17.98 (0-382-09903-6) Silver Burdett Pr.
Sommer, Susan. And I'm Stuck with Joseph. Moon, Ivan, illus. LC 84-611. 120p. (gr. 7-9). 1984. pap. 3.95 (0-8361-3356-0) Herald Pr.
Sommer-Bodenburg, Angela. If You Want to Scare Yourself. Cafiero, Renee V., tr. from GER. Spiess, Helga, illus. LC 87-45316. 112p. (gr. 2-5). 1989. (Lipp Jr Bks); PLB 12.89 (0-397-32210-0, Lipp Jr Bks) HarpC Child Bks.
—My Friend the Vampire. Glienke, Amelie, illus. LC 83-23930. 160p. (gr. 3-5). 1984. PLB 9.89 (0-8037-0046-6) Dial Bks Young.
—The Vampire in Love. Glienke, Amelie, illus. 128p. (gr. 2-6). 1991. 13.00 (0-8037-0905-6); lib. bdg. 12.89 (0-8037-0906-4) Dial Bks Young.
—The Vampire Moves In. Glienke, Amelie, illus. (gr. 2-6). 1990. pap. 2.95 (0-671-73698-1, Minstrel Bks) PB.
—The Vampire Takes a Trip. Glienke, Amelie, illus. LC 84-22995. 160p. (gr. 2-6). 1985. PLB 9.89 (0-8037-0201-9) Dial Bks Young.
Sommer-Bodengery, Angela. The Vampire in Love. 144p. (gr. 3-6). 1993. pap. 2.99 (0-671-75877-2, Minstrel Bks) PB.
Sommerfield, Elissa B. A Beginner's Guide to the SATs. 85p. (Orig.). (gr. 7-10). 1987. pap. text ed. 10.95 (0-9604058-2-8) Ed Skills Dallas.
—Junior SAT Exercises: SAT Exercises for the Ninth & Tenth Grades. 94p. (Orig.). (gr. 9-10). 1987. pap. text ed. 10.95 (0-9604058-1-X) Ed Skills Dallas.
Sommers, Beverly. The Meaning of Sisterhood. (Orig.). (gr. 9-12). 1993. pap. 3.99 (0-449-70420-3, Juniper) Fawcett.
Sommers, Maxine. The Magical Powers of "Frank" the World Famous Texas Cool Cat! large type ed. Birchum, Donald, illus. 10p. (gr. k-2). 1991. pap. 1.95 (0-943991-23-4) Pound Sterling Pub.
Sommers, Maxine S. A Children's Texas Cool Cat Cookbook. large type ed. Birchum, Donald, illus. 10p. (Orig.). (gr. 1-9). 1991. pap. 3.25 (0-943991-22-6) Pound Sterling Pub.
—Encouraging the Creative Talents in the Young Writer. Kennedy, Suzanne, ed. 32p. (gr. 4-6). 1993. pap. 5.00 wkbk. (0-943991-37-4) Pound Sterling Pub.
—Learn to Count & Color with Spot the Cat. Kennedy, Suzanne, ed. (Illus.). 10p. (Orig.). (gr. k-1). 1993. pap. 2.50 (0-685-65603-9) Pound Sterling Pub.
—Texas Cool Cat Coloring Book. Birchum, Don, illus. 10p. (Orig.). (gr. k-1). 1991. pap. 1.95 size: 8 1/2" x 11" (0-943991-20-X) Pound Sterling Pub.
Sommers, Tish. Big Bird Goes to the Doctor. Cooke, Tom, illus. LC 85-81562. 32p. (ps-k). 1986. write for info. (0-307-12019-8, Pub. by Golden Bks) Western Pub.
—A Bird's Best Friend. Swanson, Maggie, illus. 32p. (ps-k). 1986. write for info. (0-307-12018-X, Pub. by Golden Bks) Western Pub.
Somper, J. Pyramid Plot. (Illus.). 48p. (gr. 3-8). 1993. PLB 11.96 (0-88110-403-5); pap. 4.95 (0-7460-0506-7) EDC.
Somtow, S. P. The Wizard's Apprentice. Jainschigg, Nicholas, illus. 144p. (gr. 7 up). 1993. SBE 14.95 (0-689-31576-7, Atheneum Child Bk) Macmillan Child Grp.
Sonberg, Lynn. The Bigfoot Mystery. (gr. 4-9). 1983. pap. 2.25 (0-553-15436-2) Bantam.
—A Horse Named Paris. Robbins, Ken, illus. LC 86-6886. 48p. (gr. 2-4). 1986. SBE 15.95 (0-02-786260-7, Bradbury Pr) Macmillan Child Grp.
—Wild Horse Country. 64p. (gr. 2-4). 1984. pap. 2.25 (0-553-15489-3, Skylark) Bantam.
Sonder, Ben. Eating Disorders: When Food Turns Against You. LC 92-37547. (Illus.). 96p. (gr. 9-12). 1993. PLB 13.40 (0-531-11175-X) Watts.
—The Tenement Writer: An Immigrant's Story. Rosner, Meryl, illus. LC 92-14400. 72p. (gr. 2-5). 1992. PLB 21.34 (0-8114-7235-3) Raintree Steck-V.
Sonder, Ben, jt. auth. see Jumper, Moses.
Sondheimer, Ilse. The Boy Who Could Make His Mother Stop Yelling. DeRosa, Dee, illus. 32p. (ps-6). 1982. lib. bdg. 9.95 (0-943156-00-9); pap. 2.95 (0-943156-01-7) Rainbow Pr NY.
—The Magic of Pomme. DeRosa, Dee, illus. LC 86-62731. (gr. k-4). 1990. PLB 13.95 (0-943156-02-5); pap. 4.95 (0-943156-03-3) Rainbow Pr NY.
Song, Cathy, jt. ed. see Kono, Juliet S.
Songhurst, Hazel. Glass. LC 92-45670. (Illus.). 32p. (gr. 3-6). 1993. 13.95 (1-56847-042-8) Thomson Lrning.
Song Nan Zhang. A Little Tiger in the Chinese Night. Song Nan Zhang, illus. LC 93-60336. 48p. (gr. 6-9). 1993. 19.95 (0-88776-320-0) Tundra Bks.
Sonkin, Susan. How to Draw Baby Animals. Sonkin, Susan, illus. LC 81-52119. 32p. (gr. 2-6). 1982. PLB 10.65 (0-89375-684-9); pap. text ed. 1.95 (0-89375-685-7) Troll Assocs.
Sonneborn, Elizabeth. Will Rogers: Cherokee Entertainer. (Illus.). 112p. (gr. 4-9). 1994. PLB 18.95 (0-7910-1719-2, Am Art Analog); pap. write for info. (0-7910-1988-8, Am Art Analog) Chelsea Hse.
Sonneborn, Liz. The Cheyenne Indians. (Illus.). 80p. (gr. 2-5). 1992. lib. bdg. 12.95 (0-7910-1654-4) Chelsea Hse.
—Clara Barton. (Illus.). 72p. (gr. 3-5). 1991. lib. bdg. 12. 95 (0-7910-1565-3) Chelsea Hse.

Sonneborn, Ruth. Friday Night Is Papa Night. McCully, Emily A., illus. 32p. (ps-2). 1987. pap. 4.99 (0-14-050754-X, Puffin) Puffin Bks.
Sonnenblick, Carol, jt. auth. see Friedman, Judith.
Sonnenfeld, Shlomo Z. Jerusalem Gems: Great Tales about Everyday People In Old Jerusalem. Dershowitz, Y., illus. 160p. 1987. 12.95 (0-89906-839-1); pap. 9.95 (0-89906-840-5) Mesorah Pubns.
Sonnenmark, Laura. The Lie. 176p. 1992. 13.95 (0-590-44740-8, Scholastic Hardcover) Scholastic Inc.
Sonnenmark, Laura A. Something's Rotten in the State of Maryland. 1990. pap. 12.95 (0-590-42876-4) Scholastic Inc.
—Something's Rotten in the State of Maryland. 1993. pap. 2.95 (0-590-42877-2) Scholastic Inc.
Sonnenschein, Harriet. Harold's Hideaway Thumb. Obrist, Jurg, illus. 32p. (ps-k). 1993. pap. 2.25 (0-671-79602-X, Little Simon) S&S Trade.
—Harold's Hideway Thumb. Obrist, Jurg, illus. LC 91-6486. 40p. (ps-k). 1991. pap. 12.95 jacketed (0-671-73568-3, S&S BFYR) S&S Trade.
—Harold's Runaway Nose. Obrist, Jurg, illus. LC 91-6486. 40p. (ps). 1989. pap. 12.95 jacketed (0-671-66912-5, Little Simon) S&S Trade.
—Harold's Runaway Nose. 40p. (ps). 1991. pap. 2.25 (0-671-74075-X, S&S BFYR) S&S Trade.
Sonnleitner, A. T. Cave Children. Bell, Anthea, tr. from GER. LC 70-120785. (Illus.). (gr. 8 up). 1971. 21.95 (0-87599-169-6) S G Phillips.
Sonntag, Linda, ed. The Ghost Story Treasury. Spenceley, Annabel, illus. 96p. (gr. 7 up). 1987. 12.95 (0-399-21477-1, Putnam) Putnam Pub Group.
Sonstegard, Jeff, ed. see Mosse, Richard.
Sook Nyul Choi. Year of Impossible Goodbyes. 176p. (gr. 5 up). 1991. 13.45 (0-395-57419-6, Sandpiper) HM.
Sookram, Brian. France. (Illus.). 128p. (gr. 5 up). 1990. 14.95 (0-7910-1111-9) Chelsea Hse.
Sophocles. Electra & Other Plays. Watling, E. F., tr. Incl. Women of Trachis; Philoctetes. (gr. 9 up). 1953. pap. 4.95 (0-14-044028-3, Penguin Classics) Viking Penguin.
—Theban Plays. Watling, E. F., tr. Incl. King Oedipus; Oedipus at Colonus; Antigone. (Orig.). (gr. 9 up). 1950. pap. 6.95 (0-14-044003-8, Penguin Classics) Viking Penguin.
Sophocles see Lind, Levi R.
Sopko, Eugen. The White Raven & the Black Sheep. Sopko, Eugen, illus. Graves, Helen, tr. from GER. LC 91-7254. (Illus.). 32p. (gr. k-3). 1991. 14.95 (1-55858-118-9) North-South Bks NYC.
Sorensen, David A. The Friendship Olympics: A Young Christian Book for Boys. LC 86-32259. 112p. (gr. 3-7). 1987. pap. 5.99 (0-8066-2248-2, 10-2430, Augsburg) Augsburg Fortress.
—It's a Mystery to Me, Lord: Bible Devotions for Boys. LC 85-22993. 112p. (Orig.). (gr. 3-7). 1985. pap. 5.99 (0-8066-2183-4, 10-3445, Augsburg) Augsburg Fortress.
—Me, Myself, & God. LC 89-49096. 112p. (Orig.). (gr. 3-7). 1990. pap. 5.99 (0-8066-2442-6, 9-2442) Augsburg Fortress.
Sorensen, LaDawn. Magical Mr. E. (Illus.). 44p. (gr. k-2). 1991. pap. 5.95 (1-55523-360-0) Winston-Derek.
Sorensen, Lynda. Comets & Meteors. LC 93-15690. (gr. 5 up). 1993. write for info. (0-86593-277-8) Rourke Corp.
—The Earth. LC 93-17007. 1993. 12.67 (0-86593-275-1); 9.50s.p. (0-685-66579-8) Rourke Corp.
—Moon. LC 93-14875. (ps-6). 1993. 12.67 (0-86593-273-5); 9.50s.p. (0-685-66589-5) Rourke Corp.
—Planets. LC 93-14874. (ps-6). 1993. 12.67 (0-86593-274-3); 9.50s.p. (0-685-66588-7) Rourke Corp.
—Stars. LC 93-10475. 1993. write for info. (0-86593-276-X) Rourke Corp.
—Sun. LC 93-14872. (ps-6). 1993. 12.67 (0-86593-272-7); 9.50s.p. (0-685-66587-9) Rourke Corp.
Sorensen, Virginia. Miracles on Maple Hill. Davis, Lambert, contrib. by. 232p. (gr. 3-7). 1990. pap. 3.95 (0-15-254561-1, Odyssey) HarBrace.
—Plain Girl. Krush, Beth & Krush, joe, illus. 151p. (gr. 3-7). 1988. pap. 5.95 (0-15-262437-6, Voyager Bks) HarBrace.
—Plain Girl. (gr. 3-7). 17.75 (0-8446-6398-0) Peter Smith.
Sorenson, Don L. Conflict Resolution & Mediation for Peer Helpers. Sorenson, Reid, illus. LC 92-70818. 128p. (Orig.). (gr. 8-12). 1992. pap. text ed. 8.95x (0-932796-42-7) Ed Media Corp.
Sorenson, Don L., jt. auth. see Myrick, Robert D.
Sorenson, Don L., ed. see Painter, Carol.
Sorenson, Don L., ed. see Schmidt, John J.
Sorenson, Jody. The Secret Letters of Mama Cat. LC 87-25333. 122p. (gr. 5-8). 1988. 12.95 (0-8027-6779-6); PLB 13.85 (0-8027-6791-5) Walker & Co.
Sorenson, Richard. Focus on Texas History & Geography. (Illus.). 56p. (gr. 6 up). 1987. pap. 12.95 (0-937460-29-X) Hendrick-Long.
Sorenson, Stephen. Growing up Is an Adventure, Lord. LC 92-27056. 112p. (gr. 3-7). 1992. pap. 5.99 (0-8066-2647-X, 9-2647) Augsburg Fortress.
—Growing up Isn't Easy, Lord: Story Devotions for Boys. LC 79-50080. 112p. (gr. 3-6). 1979. pap. 5.99 (0-8066-1713-6, 10-2904, Augsburg) Augsburg Fortress.

Sorenson, Stephen W. Lord, I Want to Know You Better: Story Devotions for Boys. LC 81-52280. 112p. (Orig.). (gr. 3-7). 1982. pap. 5.99 (*0-8066-1912-0*), 10-4103, Augsburg Fortress.

Sorine, Stephanie R. Our Ballet Class. Sorine, Daniel S., illus. LC 80-28927. 48p. (gr. k-3). 1981. lib. bdg. 8.99 (*0-394-94821-1*) Knopf Bks Yng Read.

Sorrentino, Joanna, jt. auth. see Kirschner, Frances.

Sortor, Toni, ed. see Hurlbut, Jesse L.

Sosa, Maria. Dragsters. LC 87-15568. (Illus.). 48p. (gr. 5-6). 1987. RSBE 11.95 (*0-89686-350-6*, Crestwood Hse) Macmillan Child Grp.

Sose, Bonnie. Designed by God, So I Must Be Special. 22p. 1988. pap. 3.50 (*0-9615279-8-6*) Character Builders.

—Designed by God So I Must Be Special. Sose, Bonnie, illus. 24p. (ps-2). 1991. 10.95 (*0-9615279-6-X*); Afro-American version available. 10.95 (*0-9615279-4-3*) Character Builders.

—Little Artist. (ps-3). 1993. Afro American Version. 11. 00 (*0-9615279-1-9*); White Version. 11.00 (*0-9615279-2-7*) Character Builders.

—Little Artist: A Child's Art Book. 32p. (gr. 3 up). 11.00 (*0-685-65933-X*) Character Builders.

Sosin, Donald, jt. ed. see Okun, Milton.

Sotnak, Lewann. Haunted Houses. LC 89-70792. (Illus.). 48p. (gr. 5 up). 1990. RSBE 11.95 (*0-89686-508-8*, Crestwood Hse) Macmillan Child Grp.

—Hawaii Volcanoes. LC 89-33550. (Illus.). 48p. (gr. 4-5). 1989. RSBE 13.95 (*0-89686-432-4*, Crestwood Hse) Macmillan Child Grp.

Soto, G. Neighborhood Odes. Diaz, D., illus. 1992. 15.95 (*0-15-256879-4*, HB Juv Bks) HarBrace.

—Taking Sides. 138p. (gr. 3-7). 1991. 15.95 (*0-15-284076-1*, HB Juv Bks) HarBrace.

Soto, Gary. Baseball in April: And Other Stories. 111p. (gr. 7 up). 1990. 14.95 (*0-15-205720-X*) HarBrace.

—Baseball in April & Other Stories. 137p. (gr. 3-7). 1991. pap. 4.95 (*0-15-205721-8*, Odyssey) HarBrace.

—The Cat's Meow. Soto, Caroline, illus. LC 87-17982. 64p. (Orig.). 1987. pap. 4.95 (*0-89407-087-8*) Strawberry Hill.

—Crazy Weekend. LC 93-13967. 144p. (gr. 3-7). 1994. 13.95 (*0-590-47814-1*) Scholastic Inc.

—Fire in My Hands. 64p. 1991. 11.95 (*0-590-45021-2*, Scholastic Hardcover) Scholastic Inc.

—Fire in My Hands: A Book of Poems. 1992. pap. 2.95 (*0-590-44579-0*) Scholastic Inc.

—Living up the Street: Narrative Recollections. 1992. pap. 3.50 (*0-440-21170-0*) Dell.

—Local News. LC 92-37905. 1993. 13.95 (*0-15-248117-6*) HarBrace.

—Pacific Crossing. 1992. write for info. (*0-15-259187-7*, HB Juv Bks) HarBrace.

—Pacific Crossing. LC 91-4690. (gr. 4-7). 1992. pap. write for info. (*0-15-259188-5*) HarBrace.

—The Pool Party. Casilla, Robert, illus. LC 92-34407. 1993. 13.95 (*0-385-30890-6*) Delacorte.

—The Shirt. Velasquez, Eric, illus. LC 91-26145. 64p. (gr. 2-5). 1992. 14.00 (*0-385-30665-2*) Delacorte.

—Small Faces. (gr. 4-7). 1993. 3.50 (*0-440-21553-6*) Dell.

—Summer Life. 1991. pap. 3.50 (*0-440-21024-0*) Dell.

—Taking Sides. 1992. pap. 6.95 (*0-15-284077-X*) HarBrace.

—Too Many Tamales. Martinez, Ed, illus. 32p. (ps-3). 1993. 14.95 (*0-399-22146-8*, Putnam) Putnam Pub Group.

Soto, Gary see Kennedy, Dorothy M., et al.

Sottong, Mary L. The Aunt Rocker: Songs of Sottong, Vol. 8. Bowman, Joyce & Guest, Mary J., illus. LC 89-92205. 64p. (Orig.). (ps-3). 1989. pap. 5.98 (*0-9624136-1-5*) Songs Sottong.

Souci, Daniel San see San Souci, Daniel.

Souci, Robert D. San see San Souci, Robert D.

Souci, Robert San see San Souci, Robert.

Soule, Gardner. Christopher Columbus: Green Sea of Darkness. LC 90-48975. (Illus.). 112p. (gr. 6-10). 1991. PLB 13.95 (*1-55905-076-4*) Marshall Cavendish.

Soule, Jean, et al, eds. see St. Laurent, Fred.

Soule, Jean C., ed. see St. Laurent, Fred.

Soule, Jean C., et al, eds. see St. Laurent, Fred.

Souter, Gillian. Card Crafting: Over Forty-Five Ideas for Making Greeting Cards & Stationery. LC 92-11414. (Illus.). 128p. (gr. 2-10). 1992. 19.95 (*0-8069-8682-4*) Sterling.

—Card Crafting: Over Forty-Five Ideas for Making Greeting Cards & Stationery. (Illus.). 128p. (gr. 6 up). 1993. pap. 9.95 (*0-8069-8683-2*) Sterling.

Souter, John. Choice Adventures: Abandoned Gold Mine. 160p. (gr. 4-8). 1992. pap. 4.99 (*0-8423-5031-4*) Tyndale.

Souter, John C. Date. (gr. 7 up) 1981. pap. 5.99 (*0-8423-0636-6*) Tyndale.

—Survive! (Orig.). (gr. 9-12). 1983. pap. 4.95 (*0-8423-6694-6*) Tyndale.

—Trivia. 96p. (gr. 8-12). 1984. 4.95 (*0-8423-7338-1*) Tyndale.

South, Sheri C. The Cinderella Game. 1992. pap. 2.99 (*0-553-29454-7*) Bantam.

—The Terrorist Group. (gr. 4-7). 1991. pap. 3.25 (*0-553-29289-7*) Bantam.

—That Certain Feeling. 1991. pap. 2.99 (*0-553-29354-0*) Bantam.

Southall, Ivan. Let the Balloon Go. reissue ed. Weiman, Jon, illus. LC 84-5984. 144p. (gr. 4-6). 1985. SBE 12. 95 (*0-02-786220-8*, Bradbury Pr) Macmillan Child Grp.

—The Long Night Watch. LC 83-48702. 160p. (gr. 7 up). 1984. 14.00 (*0-374-34644-5*) FS&G.

—Rachel. LC 86-45509. 147p. (gr. 5 up). 1986. 14.00 (*0-374-36163-0*) FS&G.

Souther, Shelia, jt. auth. see Call, Betty.

Southey, Robert. Cataract of Lodore. (ps-3). 1991. 13.95 (*0-8037-1025-9*); PLB 13.89 (*0-8037-1026-7*) Dial Bks Young.

—The Cataract of Lodore. Catrow, David, illus. LC 91-29748. 32p. (gr. 1-3). 1992. 15.95 (*0-8050-1945-6*, Bks Young Read) H Holt & Co.

Southgate, Mark. The Fisherman & His Wife. (Illus.). 32p. (gr. k-3). 1988. 13.95 (*0-86264-160-8*, Pub. by Anderson Pr UK) Trafalgar.

—Muddy Milford. LC 90-41953. (Illus.). 28p. (gr. 2-5). 1991. PLB 10.95 (*0-87226-442-4*, Bedrick Blackie) P Bedrick Bks.

Southgate, Vera. Rapunzel. 1987. text ed. 3.50 cased (*0-7214-0947-4*) Ladybird Bks.

—Rumpelstiltskin. 1987. pap. 3.50 cased (*0-7214-0948-2*) Ladybird Bks.

Southworth, John V. American History in Verse: Special Bicentennial Edition. Reams, Ron, illus. LC 76-590. 120p. (gr. 7 up). 1976. pap. 10.00 (*0-912760-20-6*) Valkyrie Pub Hse.

Southworth, Mary C. Wordworks. 1986. pap. text ed. 13. 50 (*0-88334-192-1*, 76157) Longman.

Southworth, Scott. Exploring High-Tech Careers. rev. ed. Rosen, Roger, ed. 118p. (gr. 7-12). 1993. 13.95 (*0-8239-1502-6*); pap. 9.95 (*0-8239-1717-7*) Rosen Group.

Souza, Chris de see De Souza, Chris.

Souza, D. M. Catch Me If You Can. (ps-3). 1992. 17.50 (*0-87614-713-9*) Carolrhoda Bks.

—Powerful Waves. (ps-3). 1992. 17.50 (*0-87614-661-2*) Carolrhoda Bks.

—Roaring Reptiles. (ps-3). 1992. 17.50 (*0-87614-710-4*) Carolrhoda Bks.

—Slinky Snakes. (ps-3). 1992. 17.50 (*0-87614-711-2*) Carolrhoda Bks.

—Space Sailing. LC 92-45176. 1993. 19.95 (*0-8225-2850-9*) Lerner Pubns.

—What's under that Shell? (Illus.). 40p. (gr. 1-4). 1992. 17.50 (*0-87614-712-0*) Carolrhoda Bks.

Souza, Dorothy. Eight Legs. (Illus.). 40p. (gr. 1-4). 1991. PLB 17.50 (*0-87614-441-5*) Carolrhoda Bks.

—Insects Around the House. (Illus.). 40p. (gr. 1-4). 1991. PLB 17.50 (*0-87614-438-5*) Carolrhoda Bks.

—Insects in the Garden. (Illus.). 40p. (gr. 1-4). 1991. PLB 17.50 (*0-87614-439-3*) Carolrhoda Bks.

—What Bit Me? (Illus.). 40p. (gr. 1-4). 1991. PLB 17.50 (*0-87614-440-7*) Carolrhoda Bks.

Souza, Dorothy M. Northern Lights: Nature in Action Ser. LC 93-3027. 1993. 17.50 (*0-87614-799-6*) Carolrhoda Bks.

Sowerby, Lynda. A Very Special Christmas Present. Cannizzo, John, illus. 1991. 6.95 (*0-533-09198-5*) Vantage.

Sowers, Jacquelyn G., et al. Understanding Sexuality: A Teaching Module for High Schools. (gr. 9-12). 1987. tchr's. ed. 60.00 (*0-944584-04-7*) Sopris.

Sowler, Sandie. Amazing Animal Disguises. Young, Jerry, photos by. LC 91-53141. (Illus.). 32p. (Orig.). (gr. 1-5). 1992. PLB 9.99 (*0-679-92768-9*); pap. 6.95 (*0-679-82768-4*) Knopf Bks Yng Read.

—Amazing Armored Animals. Young, Jerry, photos by. LC 91-53140. (Illus.). 32p. (Orig.). (gr. 1-5). 1992. PLB 9.99 (*0-679-92767-0*); pap. 6.95 (*0-679-82767-6*) Knopf Bks Yng Read.

Space, Peggy. A Trip on a Jet Plane: Photos & Fun for Boys & Girls. Space, Peggy & Scarpace, Frank, illus. 32p. (gr. 3-7). 1981. pap. 2.50 (*0-942772-00-8*) Image Pubns.

Spacone, Carl. No Monkey Too Big. Hoffman, John, ed. Brophy, Paul, illus. 224p. (Orig.). (gr. 9 up). 1987. 8.95 (*0-944712-00-2*); pap. text ed. 8.95 (*0-318-23727-X*) Spacone Pub.

Spagnoli, Cathy, jt. ed. see Mao Wall, Lina.

Spagnoli, Cathy, jt. ed. see Xiong, Blia.

Spain, Valerie. Meet Hillary Rodham Clinton. LC 93-29194. 1994. write for info. (*0-679-85089-9*); PLB write for info. (*0-679-95089-3*) Random Bks Yng Read.

Spainhower, Steven D. School Smart: Behaviors & Skills for Student Success, 93-94. Wilson, Dana & Brown, Steven J., eds. (Illus.). 205p. (Orig.). (gr. 7-12). 1993. pap. text ed. 18.95 (*0-9637573-0-X*) Education Res.

Spancer, Cookie. Gifted & Talented Math Workbook. Whitten, Leesa, illus. 96p. (ps-3). 1992. pap. 3.95 (*0-929923-82-0*) Lowell Hse.

Spangenberg, Ray & Moser, Diane. Living & Working in Space. (Illus.). 136p. 1989. 22.95x (*0-8160-1849-9*) Facts on File.

—Opening the Space Frontier. (Illus.). 136p. 1989. 22. 95x (*0-8160-1848-0*) Facts on File.

Spangenburg, Ray & Moser, Diane. Exploring the Reaches of the Solar System. 1990. 22.95x (*0-8160-1850-2*) Facts on File.

—Space People from A to Z. 136p. 1990. 22.95x (*0-8160-1851-0*) Facts on File.

—The Story of Air Transport in America. (Illus.). 96p. (gr. 6-12). 1992. bds. 18.95x (*0-8160-2260-7*) Facts on File.

—The Story of America's Bridges. (Illus.). 96p. (gr. 6-9). 1991. lib. bdg. 18.95x (*0-8160-2259-3*) Facts on File.

—The Story of America's Canals. (Illus.). 96p. (gr. 6-12). 1992. bds. 18.95x (*0-8160-2256-9*) Facts on File.

—The Story of America's Railroads. (Illus.). 96p. (gr. 6-9). 1991. lib. bdg. 18.95x (*0-8160-2257-7*) Facts on File.

—The Story of America's Roads. (Illus.). 96p. (gr. 6-9). 1991. lib. bdg. 18.95x (*0-8160-2255-0*) Facts on File.

Spangenburg, Ray & Moser, Diane K. The History of Science from the Ancient Greeks to the Scientific Revolution. LC 92-33180. (Illus.). 192p. (gr. 6-9). 1993. 17.95x (*0-8160-2739-0*) Facts on File.

—The History of Science from 1895-1945. LC 93-26820. 1994. write for info. (*0-8160-2742-0*) Facts on File.

—The History of Science in the Eighteenth Century. LC 92-41500. (Illus.). 176p. (gr. 6-9). 1993. 17.95x (*0-8160-2740-4*) Facts on File.

—The History of Science in the 19th Century. LC 93-10576. 1993. write for info. (*0-8160-2741-2*) Facts on File.

—The Story of America's Tunnels. 96p. (gr. 5 up). 1990. PLB 19.00 (*0-8160-2258-5*) Facts on File.

Spangler, Carol S., jt. auth. see Collins, Linda B.

Spanjian, Beth. Baby Colt. (ps-1). 1990. write for info. (*0-307-12603-X*) Western Pub.

—Baby Lamb. (ps-1). 1990. write for info. (*0-307-12604-8*) Western Pub.

Spanner, Helmut. Getting Dressed Is Fun. LC 91-61576. (Illus.). 4p. 1991. bds. 3.95 (*0-8431-2930-1*) Price Stern.

—Meow Meow. LC 91-61574. (Illus.). 4p. (ps). 1991. bds. 3.95 (*0-8431-2929-8*) Price Stern.

—Teddy Bear's Day. (Illus.). 4p. 1991. bds. 3.95 (*0-8431-0946-7*) Price Stern.

—What's Teddy Bear Doing? (Illus.). 4p. 1991. bds. 3.95 (*0-8431-0945-9*) Price Stern.

Spanogla, Howard, ed. see Glenbard East Echo Staff.

Spanogle, Howard, jt. ed. see Glenard East Echo Staff.

Spar, J. Willy, a Story of Water. LC 68-56819. (Illus.). 32p. (gr. 2-3). 1968. PLB 9.95 (*0-87783-051-7*); pap. 3.94 deluxe ed (*0-87783-117-3*) Oddo.

Sparger, Rex. The Doll. (ps-7). 1987. pap. 2.50 (*0-553-26759-0*) Bantam.

Spargo, Edward. The College Student. 4th ed. 251p. (gr. 12). 1994. pap. 12.00 (*0-89061-757-0*) Jamestown Pubs.

Sparks, Judy, ed. Yes! Jesus Loves Me. Woggon, Bill, illus. 24p. (ps-2). 1985. 2.50 (*0-87239-882-X*, 3682) Standard Pub.

Sparks, Richard W. A Candle Opera. Acheson, Robert B., illus. 54p. (gr. 1-10). 1983. pap. 5.95 (*0-9614185-0-8*) S J F Co.

Spataro, Lucian. Ride Across America: An Environmental Commitment. Baird, Tate, ed. Goodall, Jane, frwd. by. LC 90-72061. (Illus.). 183p. (gr. 9 up). 1991. 15.95 (*0-914127-44-6*, 1R-1) Univ Class.

Spate, Wolfgang. Top Secret Bird: The Luftwaffe's ME-163 Comet. Machat, Mike, illus. LC 88-90967. 276p. (Orig.). (gr. 8-12). 1989. pap. text ed. 11.95 (*0-929521-08-0*) Pictorial Hist.

Spatt see Sohn, David A.

Spaulding, Janet. Creative Child Care: You Can Make a Difference. Majesty, Paul, illus. 140p. (Orig.). 1992. pap. 18. 00 spiral bdg. (*0-9634214-0-9*) MARV Pubns.
CREATIVE CHILD CARE: YOU CAN MAKE A DIFFERENCE was written for moms who are home with their young children & for people with home child-care businesses. This book was created to give ideas about various activities to help keep children away from the television. At the same time it offers over 150 activities with step-by-step instructions to stimulate young minds. There are guidelines for discipline, social skills, coping with children's fears & lies, potty training, safety precautions, how to make homemade baby food, ways to deal with infant colic, giving children choices, & dealing with various age levels. The book has sample certificates, a health chart, behavior chart, curriculum, & contracts. The author has included suggestions on how to use the newest terminology in order to replace phrases such as, 'Good Boy', 'Be Careful' etc. The new terminology helps instill positive self-esteem & promotes higher level thinking skills. To order contact: MARV Publications, 402A West Taylor Ave. Ste. 183, Round Rock, TX 78664.
Publisher Provided Annotation.

Spaulding, Robert K. How Spanish Grew. (gr. 9-12). 1943. pap. 10.00x (*0-520-01193-7*) U CA Pr.
Speaker-Yuan, Margaret. Agnes De Mille. Horner, Matina, intro. by. (Illus.). 112p. (gr. 5 up). 1990. lib. bdg. 17.95 (*1-55546-648-6*) Chelsea Hse.
Spear. Life Science: All Creatures Great & Small. (gr. 7-9). 1991. text ed. 10.00 (*0-89824-534-6*); manual 5.00 (*0-89824-535-4*) Trillium Pr.
Spear, Cindy G., ed. see Osborn, Marvin.
Spear, Laurinda. Fisherman & His Wife: Based on a Tale by the Brothers Grimm. LC 90-26315. (ps-3). 1992. 17.95 (*0-8478-1370-3*) Rizzoli Intl.
Speare, Elizabert G. Sign of the Beaver. (gr. 4-7). 1993. pap. 1.99 (*0-440-21623-0*) Dell.
Speare, Elizabeth see Newbery Library Award Staff.
Speare, Elizabeth G. Bronze Bow. 256p. (gr. 6 up). 1961. 13.45 (*0-395-07113-5*) HM.
—The Bronze Bow. LC 61-10640. (Illus.). 272p. (gr. 6 up). 1973. pap. 7.70 (*0-395-13719-5*, Sandpiper) HM.
—Calico Captive. Mars, Witold T., illus. 288p. (gr. 7-9). 1957. 13.45 (*0-395-07112-7*) HM.
—Calico Captive. (gr. k-6). 1973. pap. 3.99 (*0-440-41156-4*, YB) Dell.
—The Sign of the Beaver. 144p. (gr. 5 up). 1983. 13.45 (*0-395-33890-5*) HM.
—The Sign of the Beaver. 144p. (gr. 5-9). 1984. pap. 3.50 (*0-440-47900-2*, YB) Dell.
—The Witch of Blackbird Pond. 256p. (gr. k-6). 1972. pap. 3.99 (*0-440-49596-2*, YB) Dell.
—Witch of Blackbird Pond. (Illus.). 256p. (gr. 7 up). 1958. 14.95 (*0-395-07114-3*) HM.
—The Witch of Blackbird Pond. 256p. (gr. 5 up). 1978. pap. 3.99 (*0-440-99577-9*, LFL) Dell.
—The Witch of Blackbird Pond. large type ed. 280p. 1989. Repr. of 1958 ed. PLB 15.95 (*1-55736-138-X*, Crnrstn Bks) BDD LT Grp.
Speare, Jean. A Candle for Christmas. Blades, Ann, illus. LC 86-61560. 32p. (gr. k-4). 1987. SBE 13.95 (*0-689-50417-9*, M K McElderry) Macmillan Child Grp.
Spears-Stewart, Reta. Toby's Big Truck Adventure. LC 92-35750. 1993. 7.95 (*0-8163-1141-2*) Pacific Pr Pub Assn.
Specht, Robert. Tisha: The Story of a Young Teacher in the Alaska Wilderness. (gr. 4-8). 1984. pap. 4.95 (*0-553-26596-2*) Bantam.
Speck, Greg. Living for Jesus When the Party's Over. 1991. pap. 7.99 (*0-8024-4791-0*) Moody.
—Sex: It's Worth Waiting For. Hillam, Corbin A., illus. (Orig.). 1989. pap. 6.99 (*0-8024-7692-9*) Moody.
Specter, B. J. Beetlejuice, No. 6: Trial by Ghost. Ashby, Ruth, ed. 96p. (Orig.). 1992. pap. 2.99 (*0-671-75561-7*, Minstrel Bks) PB.
—Camp Fright. MacDonald, Pat, ed. 96p. (Orig.). 1992. pap. 2.99 (*0-671-75559-5*, Minstrel Bks) PB.
—Twisted Tours. Ashby, Ruth, ed. 128p. (Orig.). 1992. pap. 2.99 (*0-671-75558-7*, Minstrel Bks) PB.
Spector, Debra. Secret Admirer. 160p. (gr. 6 up). 1985. pap. 2.25 (*0-553-24688-7*) Bantam.
Spector, J., jt. auth. see Rawson, C.
Spector, Joanna. Horses & Ponies. (Illus.). 64p. (gr. 3 up). 1993. pap. 4.50 (*0-86020-255-0*, Usborne) EDC.
Speed, Peter. Harald Hardrada & the Vikings. Hook, Richard, illus. LC 92-5818. 63p. (gr. 6-7). 1992. PLB 24.26 (*0-8114-3353-6*) Raintree Steck-V.
Speed, Toby. One Leaf Fell. 1993. 14.95 (*1-55670-271-X*) Stewart Tabori & Chang.
—Two Cool Cows. Root, Barry, illus. LC 93-34258. 1995. write for info. (*0-399-22647-8*, Putnam) Putnam Pub Group.
Speer, Bonnie. Hillback to Boggy: A Family Struggles for Survival During the Great Depression, in a Tent in the Hills of Oklahoma. Speer, Jess W. & Peacock, Jimmy, eds. LC 89-64193. (Illus.). 200p. (gr. 6-12). 1992. PLB 19.95x (*0-9619639-7-2*); pap. write for info. (*0-9619639-5-6*) Reliance Pr.
—Sons of Thunder: A Search for Identity. Speer, Jess W. & Peacock, Jimmy, eds. LC 92-8061. (Illus.). 200p. (Orig.). (gr. 6-12). 1992. pap. 9.95x (*0-9619639-8-0*) Reliance Pr.
Speer, Jess W., ed. see Speer, Bonnie.
Speer, Mildred C. Bootsteps: Poems of the West-Then & Now. (Illus.). 84p. (gr. 5 up). 1978. pap. 3.00 (*0-317-13142-7*) Paramount TX.
Speicher, Helen R., jt. auth. see Borland, Kathryn K.
Speicher, Rose C., jt. auth. see Savage-Hubbard, Kathy.
Speirs, Gill. I Can Draw Sharks & Whales. 64p. 1986. pap. 3.95 (*0-671-60477-5*, Little Simon) S&S Trade.
Speirs, John. Ghostly Games. LC 91-22407. (Illus.). 32p. (gr. k-6). 1991. 9.95 (*0-89577-393-7*, Reader's Digest Kids) RD Assn.
—The Great Carnival Caper. LC 92-38171. 1993. 9.95 (*0-89577-453-4*, Readers Digest Kids) RD Assn.
—The Quest for the Golden Mane. Speirs, John, illus. LC 91-33894. 32p. 1991. 9.95 (*0-89577-394-5*, Reader's Digest Kids) RD Assn.
—Safari for the Tigrus. LC 92-11328. (Illus.). 32p. (gr. k up). 1992. 9.95 (*0-89577-452-6*, Readers Digest Kids) RD Assn.
Speirs, John, illus. The Twelve Days of Christmas. 24p. (Orig.). (ps-3). 1992. pap. 4.99 (*0-679-82730-7*) Random Bks Yng Read.
Speiser, E., ed. Math Skills by Objectives. 288p. (gr. 7-9). 1988. pap. text ed. 6.00 (*0-8428-0200-2*) Cambridge Bk.
Speiser, E. & Weiser, M., eds. Math Skills by Objectives. 352p. (gr. 7-9). 1988. pap. text ed. 6.00 (*0-8428-0202-9*) Cambridge Bk.

Spektor, Zev. Shadows in the Night. (Illus.). 150p. (gr. 5-6). 1991. 11.95 (*1-56062-100-1*); pap. 8.95 (*0-685-52958-4*) CIS Comm.
Spellerberg, Ian & McKerchar, Marit. Reptile World. Quinn, David, illus. 32p. (gr. 4-7). 1985. PLB 13.96 (*0-88110-174-5*, Pub. by Usborne); pap. 5.95 (*0-86020-845-1*) EDC.
Spellman, L. Codes. 40p. (gr. 4-8). 1992. 6.95 (*0-88160-253-1*, LW1402) Learning Wks.
Spellman, Linda. Book Report Backpack. 48p. (gr. 4-6). 1980. 5.95 (*0-88160-035-0*, LW 220) Learning Wks.
—Castles, Codes, Calligraphy. 112p. (gr. 4-6). 1984. 9.95 (*0-88160-103-9*, LW 904) Learning Wks.
—Creative Investigations. 48p. (gr. 4-8). 1982. 5.95 (*0-88160-045-8*, LW 230) Learning Wks.
—Monsters, Mysteries, UFOs. 112p. (gr. 4-6). 1984. 9.95 (*0-88160-095-4*, LW 903) Learning Wks.
—More Creative Investigations. 48p. (gr. 4-8). 1984. 5.95 (*0-88160-114-4*, LW 246) Learning Wks.
—Poetry Party. 48p. (gr. 4-6). 1981. 5.95 (*0-88160-038-5*, LW 223) Learning Wks.
Speltz, Bob. A Real Runabouts Review of Canoes. 72p. (Orig.). 1991. pap. 12.95 (*0-932299-08-3*) R G Speltz.
Spence, Lora T., et al. There Once Was a Cook. Baker, Gary G., illus. (gr. k up). 1985. pap. 12.95 (*0-9614501-0-X*) Wesley Inst.
Spence, Lundie, ed. see Dixon, Debra S. & Henry, Susan V.
Spence, Margaret. Fossil Fuels. LC 92-33919. (Illus.). (gr. k-4). 1993. PLB 11.90 (*0-531-17394-1*, Gloucester Pr) Watts.
—Solar Power. LC 92-33920. (Illus.). 32p. (gr. k-4). 1993. PLB 11.90 (*0-531-17378-X*, Gloucester Pr) Watts.
—Toxic Waste. (Illus.). 32p. (gr. 2-4). 1992. PLB 11.90 (*0-531-17297-X*, Gloucester Pr) Watts.
Spenceley, Annabel, jt. auth. see Van DeWeyer, Robert.
Spencer, Anne. Molly's Pilgrim: A Study Guide. Friedland, J. & Kessler, R., eds. 19p. (gr. 2-4). 1992. pap. text ed. 14.95 (*0-88122-700-5*) Lrn Links.
—The Trumpet of the Swan: A Study Guide. Friedland, J. & Kessler, R., eds. 24p. (gr. 4-6). 1992. pap. text ed. 14.95 (*0-88122-710-2*) Lrn Links.
Spencer, Donald D. BASIC Programming. LC 82-17689. 224p. (gr. 8 up). 1983. 7.95 (*0-89218-062-5*, NO. 1133) Camelot Pub.
—BASIC Workbook for Microcomputers. (Illus.). 128p. (gr. 8 up). 1983. pap. 3.95 (*0-89218-069-2*, NO. 1100) Camelot Pub.
—Computer Mathematics with BASIC Programming. LC 89-7323. 304p. (gr. 9 up). 1990. pap. 25.95 (*0-89218-135-4*, NO. 3064); tchr's. manual 15.95 (*0-89218-136-2*, NO. 3065); test bank 12.95 (*0-89218-137-0*, NO. 3066); diskette for IBM PC 18. 00 (*0-89218-138-9*, NO. 3067); diskette for Apple II 18.00 (*0-89218-139-7*, NO. 3068) Camelot Pub.
—Computer Mathematics with Pascal Programming. LC 90-31380. 336p. 1990. pap. 24.95 (*0-89218-130-3*, NO. 3077); tchr's. manual 15.95 (*0-89218-131-1*, NO. 3078); test bank 12.95 (*0-89218-132-X*, NO. 3079); diskette for IBM PC 18.00 (*0-89218-133-8*, NO. 3080); diskette for Apple II 18.00 (*0-89218-134-6*, NO. 3081) Camelot Pub.
—Discover Computers. LC 88-6044. 240p. (gr. 6-9). 1988. pap. 14.95 (*0-89218-121-4*, NO. 3083); tchr. resource bk. 19.95 (*0-89218-123-0*, NO. 3084); student wkbk. 6.95 (*0-89218-122-2*, NO. 3085) Camelot Pub.
—Exploring the World of Computers. LC 82-4116. 102p. (gr. 4-6). 1982. 6.95 (*0-89218-055-2*, NO. 1110); pap. 2.95 (*0-89218-054-4*, NO. 1134) Camelot Pub.
—Microcomputer Coloring Book. 32p. (gr. 2-4). 1982. pap. 3.25 (*0-317-65455-1*, NO. 1126) Camelot Pub.
—Problem Solving with BASIC. LC 82-17875. 160p. (gr. 8 up). 1983. pap. 3.95x (*0-89218-075-7*, NO. 1135) Camelot Pub.
—Understanding Computers. 2nd ed. LC 87-27738. 272p. (gr. 7 up). 1988. pap. 16.95 (*0-89218-092-7*, NO. 3025); tchr's. manual 15.95x (*0-89218-118-4*, NO. 3031); student wkbk. 6.95 (*0-89218-119-2*, NO. 3034); test bank 12.95 (*0-89218-120-6*, NO. 3035) Camelot Pub.
—What Computers Can Do. 2nd ed. LC 81-21664. 256p. (gr. 9 up). 1982. 6.95x (*0-89218-043-9*, 1003) Camelot Pub.
Spencer, Eve. Animal Babies One Two Three. David, Susan, illus. 24p. (ps-2). 1990. PLB 14.60 (*0-8172-3581-7*); pap. 10.95 pkg. of 3 (*0-8114-2930-X*) Raintree Steck-V.
—A Flag for Our Country. Eagle, Mike, illus. LC 92-14414. 32p. (gr. 2-5). 1992. PLB 21.34 (*0-8114-7211-6*) Raintree Steck-V.
—Three Ships for Columbus. Sperling, Tom, illus. LC 92-14401. 32p. (gr. 2-5). 1992. PLB 21.34 (*0-8114-7212-4*) Raintree Steck-V.
Spencer, Guy. An Ancient Forest. Staub, Frank J., illus. LC 87-3487. 32p. (gr. 3-6). 1988. PLB 10.79 (*0-8167-1167-4*); pap. text ed. 2.95 (*0-8167-1168-2*) Troll Assocs.
—A Living Desert. Fuller, Tim, illus. LC 87-3488. 32p. (gr. 3-6). 1988. PLB 10.79 (*0-8167-1169-0*); pap. text ed. 2.95 (*0-8167-1170-4*) Troll Assocs.
Spencer, Jean. Careers in Word Processing & Desktop Publishing. Rosen, Ruth, ed. (gr. 7-12). 1989. PLB 13.95 (*0-8239-0967-0*) Rosen Group.
—Exploring Careers As a Computer Technician. rev. ed. Rosen, Ruth, ed. (gr. 7-12). 1989. PLB 13.95 (*0-8239-0994-8*) Rosen Group.

—Exploring Careers in the Electronic Office. rev. ed. Rosen, Ruth, ed. (gr. 7-12). 1989. PLB 13.95 (*0-8239-1009-1*) Rosen Group.
Spencer, Kathleen, jt. auth. see Beach, Judy.
Spencer, Ladonna, ed. Happy the Kings Clown. 30p. 1985. pap. 3.50 (*0-88144-057-4*) Christian Pub.
Spencer, Pat. Bulletin Boards Through the Year. Spencer, Pat, illus. 96p. (gr. k-4). 1988. wkbk. 9.95 (*1-55734-062-5*) Tchr Create Mat.
Spencer, Sara. Little Women. 1940. 4.50 (*0-87602-150-X*) Anchorage.
—Tom Sawyer. (gr. 1-9). 1935. 4.50 (*0-87602-211-5*) Anchorage.
Spencer, Steven L., jt. auth. see White, Laurie A.
Spencer, William. The Challenge of World Hunger. LC 90-49430. (Illus.). 64p. (gr. 6 up). 1991. lib. bdg. 15.95 (*0-89490-283-0*) Enslow Pubs.
—The Land & People of Turkey. LC 89-2421. (Illus.). 224p. (gr. 6 up). 1990. 14.95 (*0-397-32363-8*, Lipp Jr Bks); PLB 14.89 (*0-397-32364-6*, Lipp Jr Bks) HarpC Child Bks.
Spencer, Zane. One Hundred & Fifty Plus! Games & Activities for Early Childhood. LC 75-32842. (ps-k). 1976. pap. 10.95 (*0-8224-5068-2*) Fearon Teach Aids.
Speregen, Devra. Arielle & the Hanukkah Surprise. 1992. pap. 2.50 (*0-590-46125-7*, Cartwheel) Scholastic Inc.
Speregen, Devra. Blossom's Family Album. (gr. 4-7). 1993. pap. 4.95 (*0-590-47234-8*) Scholastic Inc.
Sperling, A. More Funny Faces Tracing Fun. (gr. 5-7). 1990. pap. 1.95 (*0-590-43489-6*) Scholastic Inc.
—Silly Monsters Tracing Fun Book. 1990. pap. 1.95 (*0-590-43531-0*) Scholastic Inc.
Sperling, Anita. Funny Animals Tracing Fun. 1989. pap. 1.95 (*0-590-42197-2*) Scholastic Inc.
—Sports Tracing Fun Book. (gr. 3-7). 1990. pap. 1.95 (*0-590-42492-0*) Scholastic Inc.
Sperling, Anita, et al. Funny Faces Tracing Fun. Wildman, George, illus. 24p. (gr. k-3). 1987. pap. 1.95 (*0-590-40889-5*) Scholastic Inc.
Sperling, Jerry. The Little Menorah Who Forgot Chanukah. Carmi, Giora, illus. (Orig.). 1993. pap. 12. 95 incl. cassette (*0-8074-0508-6*, 101971) UAHC.
Sperry, Armstrong. Call It Courage. reissued ed. Sperry, Armstrong, illus. LC 40-4229. 96p. (gr. 5-7). 1968. SBE 13.95 (*0-02-786030-2*, Macmillan Child Bk) Macmillan Child Grp.
—Call It Courage. LC 40-4229. (gr. 5-7). 1973. pap. 3.95 (*0-02-045270-5*, Collier Young Ad) Macmillan Child Grp.
—Call It Courage. large type ed. 1989. Repr. of 1940 ed. 15.95 (*1-55736-147-9*, Crnrstn Bks) BDD LT Grp.
—Call It Courage. 2nd ed. LC 89-18456. 96p. (gr. 4-7). 1990. pap. 3.95 (*0-689-71391-6*, Aladdin) Macmillan Child Grp.
Spethman, Martin J. How to Get into & Graduate from College in Four Years with Good Grades, a Useful Major, a Lot of Knowledge, a Little Debt, Great Friends, Happy Parents, Maximum Party Attendance, Minimal Weight Gain, Decent Habits, Fewer Hassles, a Career Goal, & a Super Attitude All While Remaining Extremely Cool. Cabrera, Ralph, illus. 192p. (Orig.). (gr. 11-12). 1993. pap. 10.95 (*0-9633598-0-0*) Westgate Pub & Ent.
Spicer, Dorothy. Humming Top. LC 68-31176. (gr. 7-11). 1968. 21.95 (*0-87599-147-5*) S G Phillips.
Spicer, Robert, jt. auth. see Goodman, Robert.
Spicer, Venetia. The Adventures of Chatrat. (Illus.). 48p. 1981. 9.95 (*0-7043-2269-2*, Pub. by Quartet England) Charles River Bks.
Spiegel, Richard. BiblioMania, Vol. 2. Fisher, Barbara, ed. (Illus.). 52p. (Orig.). (gr. 7-12). 1991. pap. 3.00 (*0-934830-49-5*) Ten Penny.
Spiegel, Richard & Fisher, Barbara, eds. BiblioMania, Vol. 1. (Illus.). 36p. (Orig.). (gr. 2-6). 1991. pap. 3.00 (*0-934830-48-7*) Ten Penny.
—Streams VI. (Illus.). 152p. (Orig.). (gr. 7-12). 1992. pap. 5.00 (*0-934830-50-9*) Ten Penny.
Spiegel, Richard, ed. see Day, Adrienne.
Spiegel, Richard, jt. ed. see Fisher, Barbara.
Spiegel, Richard, ed. see Mennella, Roxanna.
Spiegel, Richard, ed. see New York Book Fair Staff.
Spiegel, Richard A. & Fisher, Barbara, eds. Streams, No. V. (Illus.). 150p. (Orig.). (gr. 8-12). 1991. pap. 5.00 (*0-934830-47-9*) Ten Penny.
Spieler, Benjamin D. The Student Clarinetist: A Method for Class Instruction, 3 bks. rev. ed. (Illus.). (gr. 4-9). 1989. pap. 2.80 ea. Bk. I, 56p. Bk. II, 64p. Bk. III, 36 p. Player Pr.
Spielman, Patrick. Making Wood Signs. LC 80-54342. (Illus.). 144p. (gr. 10-12). 1981. pap. 9.95 (*0-8069-8984-X*) Sterling.
Spier, Peter. And So My Garden Grows. Spier, Peter, illus. 48p. (ps-3). 1992. pap. 3.99 (*0-440-40714-1*, YB) Dell.
—Award Puzzles: Noah's Ark. 1990. 5.95 (*0-938971-62-X*) JTG Nashville.
—Book of Jonah. 1985. 14.00 (*0-385-19334-3*); PLB 12. 99 (*0-385-19335-1*) Doubleday.
—Bored, Nothing to Do. Spier, Peter, illus. LC 77-20726. 48p. (gr. 1-3). 1978. 11.95 (*0-385-13177-1*) Doubleday.
—Bored, Nothing to Do. LC 77-20726. (Illus.). 48p. (gr. k-3). 1987. pap. 5.95 (*0-385-24104-6*, Pub. by Zephyr-BFYR) Doubleday.
—Crash! Bang! Boom! (ps-1). 1990. 5.95 (*0-385-26569-7*) Doubleday.
—Dreams. Spier, Peter, illus. LC 85-13130. 32p. (ps-3). 1986. Doubleday.

—The Erie Canal. Spier, Peter, illus. LC 70-102055. 36p. (gr. 1-3). 1990. pap. 10.95 (0-385-06777-1); pap. 5.95 (0-385-05234-0) Doubleday.
—Fast-Slow High-Low. Spier, Peter, illus. LC 72-76207. 24p. (ps-k). 1988. 5.95 (0-385-24093-7) Doubleday.
—Fast-Slow High-Low: A Book of Opposites. Spier, Peter, illus. LC 72-76207. 48p. (gr. k-3). 1972. pap. 10.95 (0-385-06781-X); pap. 10.95 (0-385-02876-8); pap. 2.95 (0-685-01490-8) Doubleday.
—Father, May I Come? LC 92-31328. 1993. 13.95 (0-385-30935-X) Doubleday.
—Fox Went Out on a Chilly Night. Spier, Peter, illus. LC 60-7139. 42p. (gr. k-3). 1961. pap. 11.95 (0-385-07990-7) Doubleday.
—Fox Went Out on a Chilly Night. LC 60-7139. (Illus.). (gr. 1-3). 1989. pap. 5.95 (0-385-01065-6, Zephyr) Doubleday.
—Fox Went Out On a Chilly Night: An Old Song. (ps-3). 1993. 4.99 (0-440-40829-6) Dell.
—Gobble, Growl, Grunt. Spier, Peter, illus. LC 79-14430. 24p. (ps-1). 1988. 8.00 (0-385-24094-5) Doubleday.
—Hurrah, We're Outward Bound! Spier, Peter, illus. 48p. (ps-3). 1992. pap. 3.99 (0-440-40715-X, YB) Dell.
—London Bridge Is Falling Down. Spier, Peter, illus. LC 67-17695. (ps). 1985. pap. 10.95 (0-385-08717-9) Doubleday.
—London Bridge Is Falling Down. Spier, Peter, illus. 48p. (ps-3). 1992. pap. 3.99 (0-440-40710-9, YB) Dell.
—Noah's Ark. Spier, Peter, illus. LC 76-43630. 44p. (gr. k-3). 1977. PLB 15.95 (0-385-09473-6) Doubleday.
—Noah's Ark. 1989. incl. audiocassette 17.95 (0-525-44525-0, DCB) Dutton Child Bks.
—Noah's Ark. Spier, Peter, illus. 48p. (ps-1). 1992. pap. 4.99 (0-440-40693-5, YB) Dell.
—Oh, Were They Ever Happy. Spier, Peter, illus. LC 77-78144. 48p. (gr. k-3). 1978. 12.95 (0-385-13175-5); pap. 10.95 (0-385-13176-3) Doubleday.
—Oh, Were They Ever Happy! LC 77-78144. (Illus.). 48p. (ps-3). 1988. pap. 6.95 (0-385-24477-0, Zephyr-BFYR) Doubleday.
—People. Spier, Peter, illus. LC 78-19832. 48p. (gr. 1-3). 1980. PLB 15.00 (0-385-13181-X) Doubleday.
—People. LC 78-19832. (Illus.). 48p. (ps up). 1988. pap. 9.00 (0-385-24469-X, Zephyr-BFYR) Doubleday.
—Peter Spier's Christmas! Spier, Peter, illus. LC 80-2875. 40p. (ps up). 1983. PLB 13.95 (0-385-13184-4); pap. 14.95 (0-385-13183-6) Doubleday.
—Peter Spier's Christmas! Spier, Peter, illus. 48p. (ps-5). 1992. 4.99 (0-440-40730-3, YB) Dell.
—Peter Spier's Circus! Spier, Peter, illus. LC 90-23282. 48p. (ps-3). 1992. pap. 16.00 (0-385-41969-4) Doubleday.
—Peter Spier's Dogs. 1984. pap. 2.50 (0-385-18196-5) Doubleday.
—Peter Spier's Ducks. 1984. pap. 2.50 (0-385-18199-X) Doubleday.
—Peter Spier's Little Animal Books, 4 bks. Spier, Peter, illus. (ps). 1987. Boxed Set. bds. 10.00 laminated (0-385-19715-2) Doubleday.
—Peter Spier's Little Cats. LC 82-45494. (Illus.). 14p. (ps-1). 1984. 2.50 (0-385-18197-3) Doubleday.
—Peter Spier's Rabbits. 1984. pap. 2.50 (0-385-18198-1) Doubleday.
—Peter Spier's Rain. Spier, Peter, illus. LC 81-43506. 40p. (ps-3). 1982. PLB 12.95 (0-385-15485-2, Zephyr-BFYR) Doubleday.
—Peter Spier's Rain. LC 81-43506. (Illus.). (gr. k-3). 1987. pap. 7.00 (0-385-24105-4, Pub. by Zephyr-BFYR) Doubleday.
—Peter Spier's Rain. LC 81-43056. (ps-3). 1982. 14.00 (0-385-15484-4) Doubleday.
—Pop-up Peter Spier's Birthday Cake. 1990. 15.95 (0-385-26370-8) Doubleday.
—The Star-Spangled Banner. Spier, Peter, illus. LC 73-79112. 48p. (gr. 1 up). 1973. 15.00 (0-385-09458-2); pap. 11.95 (0-385-07746-7) Doubleday.
—Star-Spangled Banner. Spier, Peter, illus. LC 73-79112. 48p. (gr. 1 up). 1986. pap. 8.00 (0-385-23401-5, Pub. by Zephyr-BFYR) Doubleday.
—Star-Spangled Banner. (ps-3). 1992. pap. 3.99 (0-440-40697-8, YB) Dell.
—Tin Lizzie. Spier, Peter, illus. LC 74-1510. 48p. (gr. 3-5). 1990. 5.95 (0-385-13342-1); pap. 8.95 (0-385-09470-1) Doubleday.
—To Market, to Market. Spier, Peter, illus. LC 67-18664. 52p. (gr. 1-3). 1967. 8.95a (0-385-08755-1); pap. 5.95 (0-385-09081-1) Doubleday.
—To Market! To Market! Spier, Peter, illus. 48p. (ps-3). 1992. pap. 3.99 (0-440-40713-3, YB) Dell.
—We the People: The Constitution of the United States of America. (ps). 1991. pap. 8.00 (0-385-41903-1) Doubleday.
—We the People: The Story of the U. S. Constitution. Spier, Peter, illus. LC 86-24205. 48p. (gr. k-3). 1987. PLB 16.00 (0-385-23589-5) Doubleday.

Spiers, Gill. I Can Draw Faces. 64p. 1984. pap. 3.95 (0-671-49664-6, Little Simon) S&S Trade.
—I Can Draw People. 1985. pap. 3.95 (0-671-55343-7, SSJ) S&S Trade.

Spies. Earthquakes. 1994. PLB write for info. (0-8050-3096-4) H Holt & Co.

Spies, Karen. Denver. LC 88-20246. (Illus.). 60p. (gr. 3 up). 1988. RSBE 13.95 (0-87518-386-7, Dillon) Macmillan Child Grp.
—Everything You Need to Know about Incest. (gr. 7-12). 1992. PLB 13.95 (0-8239-1325-2) Rosen Group.
—Our Folk Heroes. (Illus.). 48p. (gr. 2-4). 1994. 12.90 (1-56294-440-1) Millbrook Pr.

—Our National Holidays. LC 91-38894. (Illus.). 48p. (gr. 2-4). 1992. PLB 12.90 (1-56294-109-7) Millbrook Pr.

Spies, Karen B. The American Family: Can It Survive? (Illus.). 64p. (gr. 5-8). 1993. PLB 14.95 (0-8050-2568-5) TFC Bks NY.
—Barbara Bush: Helping America Read. LC 91-17725. (Illus.). 72p. (gr. 4-6). 1991. RSBE 13.95 (0-87518-488-X, Dillon) Macmillan Child Grp.
—Everything You Need to Know about Diet Fads. Rosen, Ruth, ed. (gr. 7-12). 1993. PLB 13.95 (0-8239-1533-6) Rosen Group.
—George Bush: Power of the President. LC 91-15862. (Illus.). 72p. (gr. 4-6). 1991. RSBE 13.95 (0-87518-487-1, Dillon) Macmillan Child Grp.
—Our Money. LC 91-43231. (Illus.). 48p. (gr. 2-4). 1992. PLB 12.90 (1-56294-212-3) Millbrook Pr.

Spiesman, Harriet. Debbi Fields: The Cookie Lady. Young, Richard G., ed. LC 91-32783. (Illus.). 64p. (gr. 4-8). 1992. PLB 17.26 (1-56074-015-9) Garrett Ed Corp.
—John Scully: Building the Apple Dream. Young, Richard G., ed. LC 91-28542. (Illus.). 64p. (gr. 4-8). 1992. PLB 17.26 (1-56074-023-X) Garrett Ed Corp.

Spilka, Arnold. Monkeys Write Terrible Letters: And Other Poems. (Illus.). 32p. (gr. k-5). 1994. 14.95 (1-56397-132-1, Wordsong) Boyds Mills Pr.

Spiller, Burton L. Grouse Feathers. 2nd ed. Hunt, Lynn B., illus. 207p. (gr. 10 up). 1989. Repr. 35.00 (1-56416-008-4) Derrydale Pr.
—More Grouse Feathers. 2nd ed. Hunt, Lynn B., illus. 238p. (gr. 10 up). 1990. Repr. of 1938 ed. 35.00 (1-56416-009-2) Derrydale Pr.
—Thoroughbred. 2nd ed. Hunt, Lynn B., illus. 200p. (gr. 10 up). 1989. Repr. of 1936 ed. 35.00 (1-56416-010-6) Derrydale Pr.

Spina, Russell, illus. Disney Babies Wake up & Play. LC 91-71344. 32p. (ps). 1991. 7.95 (1-56282-055-9) Disney Pr.
—Disney's Haunted Mansion Pop-up Book. 5p. 1993. 13. 95 (1-56282-499-6) Disney Pr.

Spinal-Robinson, Phyllis & Easton-Wickham, Randi. Cartwheels: A Workbook for Children Who Have Been Sexually Abused (Ages 10-13) (Illus.). 95p. (Orig.). (gr. 5-7). 1993. pap. 12.95 (0-9627375-1-8); therapist's guide 2.00 (0-9627375-2-6) Jalice Pubs.

Spinelli. Deep Snow. Date not set. 15.00 (0-06-023370-2, Festival) PLB 14.89 (0-06-023371-0, Festival) HarpC Child Bks.

Spinelli, Eileen. Baby Animals. (Illus.). 64p. (gr. k-4). 1992. PLB 12.95 (1-878363-80-8, HTS Bks) Forest Hse.
—Boy, Can He Dance! Yalowitz, Paul, illus. LC 92-12929. 32p. (ps-2). 1993. RSBE 14.95 (0-02-786350-6, Four Winds) Macmillan Child Grp.
—Cats. (Illus.). 64p. (gr. k-4). 1992. PLB 12.95 (1-878363-82-4, HTS Bks) Forest Hse.
—Farm Animals. (Illus.). 64p. (gr. k-4). 1992. PLB 12.95 (1-878363-84-0, HTS Bks) Forest Hse.
—Horses. (Illus.). 64p. (gr. k-4). 1992. PLB 12.95 (1-878363-85-9, HTS Bks) Forest Hse.
—If You Want to Find Golden. Shuett, Stacey, illus. LC 93-12000. (gr. 1-3). 1993. 14.95 (0-8075-3585-0) A Whitman.
—Kittens. (Illus.). 64p. (gr. k-4). 1992. PLB 12.95 (1-878363-86-7, HTS Bks) Forest Hse.
—Lizzie Logan Wears Purple Sunglasses. Durrell, Julie, illus. LC 93-29104. 1994. write for info. (0-671-74685-5, S&S BFYR) S&S Trade.
—Puppies. (Illus.). 64p. (gr. k-4). 1992. PLB 12.95 (1-878363-87-5, HTS Bks) Forest Hse.
—Reptiles. (Illus.). 64p. (gr. k-4). 1992. PLB 12.95 (1-878363-88-3, HTS Bks) Forest Hse.
—Sharks. (Illus.). 64p. (gr. k-4). 1992. PLB 12.95 (1-878363-89-1, HTS Bks) Forest Hse.
—Somebody Loves You, Mr. Hatch. Yalowitz, Paul, illus. LC 90-33016. 32p. (ps-2). 1992. RSBE 13.95 (0-02-786015-9, Bradbury Pr) Macmillan Child Grp.
—Thanksgiving at the Tappletons' Cocca-Leffler, Maryann, illus. LC 84-40793. 32p. (gr. k-3). 1984. 11. 95 (0-201-15892-2, Lipp Jr Bks) HarpC Child Bks.
—Thanksgiving at the Tappletons' newly illustrated ed. Cocca-Leffler, Maryann, illus. LC 91-33250. 32p. (gr. k-3). 1989. pap. 4.95 (0-06-443204-1, Trophy) HarpC Child Bks.
—Thanksgiving at the Tappletons' newly illus. ed. Cocca-Leffler, Maryann, illus. LC 91-33250. 32p. (gr. k-3). 1992. 15.00 (0-06-020871-6); PLB 14.89 (0-06-020872-4) HarpC Child Bks.
—Whales. (Illus.). 64p. (gr. k-4). 1992. PLB 12.95 (1-878363-90-5, HTS Bks) Forest Hse.
—Zoo Animals. (Illus.). 64p. (gr. k-4). 1992. PLB 12.95 (1-878363-91-3, HTS Bks) Forest Hse.

Spinelli, Jerry. Bathwater Gang. (gr. 4-7). 1990. 10.95 (0-316-80720-6) Little.
—The Bathwater Gang. Johnson, Meredith, illus. 64p. (gr. 2-4). 1992. pap. 3.95 (0-316-80779-6) Little.
—Bathwater Gang Gets down to Business. (ps-3). 1992. 12.95 (0-316-80808-3) Little.
—Do the Funky Pickle. 1992. 2.95 (0-590-45448-X, Apple Paperbacks) Scholastic Inc.
—Dump Days. (gr. 4-7). 1991. pap. 3.25 (0-440-40421-5) Dell.
—Fourth Grade Rats. (ps-3). 1991. 13.95 (0-590-44243-0, Scholastic Hardcover) Scholastic Inc.
—Fourth Grade Rats. (gr. 4-7). 1993. pap. 2.95 (0-590-44244-9, Apple Classics) Scholastic Inc.
—Jason & Marceline. (gr. k-12). 1988. pap. 3.50 (0-440-20166-7, LFL) Dell.

—Maniac Magee. (gr. 4-7). 1990. 14.95 (0-316-80722-2, Joy St Bks) Little.
—Maniac Magee. LC 89-27144. 192p. (gr. 3-7). 1992. pap. 3.95 (0-06-440424-2, Trophy) HarpC Child Bks.
—Night of the Whale. (gr. k-12). 1988. pap. 3.50 (0-440-20071-7, LFL) Dell.
—Picklemania. (gr. 8-12). 1993. pap. 2.95 (0-590-45447-1) Scholastic Inc.
—Report to the Principal's Office! 1992. 2.95 (0-590-46277-6, Apple Paperbacks) Scholastic Inc.
—Space Station Seventh Grade. LC 82-47915. 192p. (gr. 7 up). 1982. 14.95 (0-316-80709-5) Little.
—Space Station Seventh Grade. (gr. 7-12). 1984. pap. 2.95 (0-440-96165-3, LFL) Dell.
—Space Station Seventh Grade. (gr. 3-7). 1991. write for info.. Little.
—There's a Girl in My Hammerlock. LC 91-8765. 208p. (gr. 5-9). 1991. pap. 13.00 jacketed, 3-pc. bdg. (0-671-74684-7, S&S BFYR) S&S Trade.
—There's a Girl in My Hammerlock. LC 91-8765. 208p. (gr. 5-9). 1993. pap. 3.95 (0-671-86695-8, Half Moon Bks) S&S Trade.
—There's a Girl in My Hammerlock. (gr. 8). 1990. write for info. (0-663-56261-9) Silver Burdett Pr.
—Who Put That Hair in My Toothbrush? LC 83-20716. (gr. 5-9). 1984. 15.95 (0-316-80712-5) Little.
—Who Put That Hair in My Toothbrush? (gr. 5-9). 1986. pap. 3.50 (0-440-99485-3, LFL) Dell.
—Who Ran My Underwear up the Flagpole? 1992. 2.95 (0-590-46278-4, Apple Paperbacks) Scholastic Inc.

Spingarn, Lawrence P. Journey to the Interior & Other Stories. Fortin, David, illus. Hansen, Joseph, intro. by. LC 92-50241. (Illus.). 103p. (Orig.). (gr. 4 up). 1992. pap. 9.95 (0-912288-30-2) Perivale Pr.

Spink, Reginald, tr. see Andersen, Hans Christian.

Spinka, Penina K. Mother's Blessing. LC 91-31342. 224p. (gr. 5-9). 1992. SBE 14.95 (0-689-31758-1, Atheneum Child Bk) Macmillan Child Grp.
—White Hare's Horses. LC 90-42777. 160p. (gr. 5-9). 1991. SBE 13.95 (0-689-31654-2, Atheneum Child Bk) Macmillan Child Grp.

Spinner, Stephanie. Little Sure Shot: The Story of Annie Oakley. Miralles, Jose, illus. LC 92-17014. 48p. (Orig.). (gr. 2-3). 1993. PLB 7.99 (0-679-93432-4); pap. 3.50 (0-679-83432-X) Random Bks Yng Read.
—The Mummy's Tomb. 64p. (gr. 2 up). 1985. pap. 2.25 (0-553-15439-7) Bantam.

Spinner, Stephanie, jt. auth. see Etra, Jon.
Spinner, Stephanie, jt. auth. see Etra, Jonathan.
Spinner, Stephanie, ed. see Kanao, Keiko.
Spinner, Stephanie, adapted by see Stoker, Bram.

Spirack, Doris. Creative Writing Carousel. 48p. (gr. 4-6). 1982. 7.95 (0-88160-086-5, LW 239) Learning Wks.

Spires, Elizabeth. The Falling Star. Michelini, Carlo A., illus. LC 84-80288. 24p. (ps-k). 1989. 9.95 (0-448-21026-6, G&D) Putnam Pub Group.

Spirit, Bonnie. It's Fun to Read Coloring, Vol. 1. Lightfoot, Patricia, illus. 10p. (Orig.). (ps up). 1988. pap. text ed. 3.95 (0-9614089-1-X) Avitar Bks.
—Pink Rose Bush. Lightfoot, Patricia, illus. 64p. (ps up). 1985. text ed. 9.95 (0-9614089-0-1) Avitar Bks.

Spirn, Michele. The Cat Who Couldn't Meow. (ps-1). 1988. 8.49 (0-87386-054-3); incl. cassette 16.99 (0-685-25195-0); pap. 1.95 (0-87386-050-0); pap. 9.95 incl. cassette (0-685-25196-9) Jan Prods.
—The Kite Race. (ps-1). 1988. 8.49 (0-685-44566-6); incl. cassette 16.99 (0-685-25198-5); pap. 1.95 (0-87386-051-9); pap. 9.95 incl. cassette (0-685-25199-3) Jan Prods.
—What's in the Trunk? (ps-1). 1988. 8.49 (0-87386-057-8); incl. cassette 16.99 (0-685-25202-7); pap. 1.95 (0-87386-053-5); pap. 9.95 incl. cassette (0-685-25203-5) Jan Prods.

Spiro, Jack D., ed. see Shumsky, Abraham & Shumsky, Adaia.

Spitzer, Lena. My Rock & My Redeemer: A Novel of Gibraltar. 205p. (gr. 9-12). 1993. 11.95 (1-56871-023-2) Targum Pr.

Spitzer, Lewis F. Nice Girls Don't Finish Last. (Illus.). 64p. (gr. 7-12). 1983. pap. 3.00 (0-88680-138-9); royalty on application 35.00 (0-685-57859-3) I E Clark.

Spivak, Darlene. Crossword Puzzles, Wordsearches & Codes. Spivak, Darlene, illus. 48p. (gr. 2-5). 1986. wkbk. 5.95 (1-55734-067-6) Tchr Create Mat.
—Hidden Pictures. Smythe, Linda, illus. 32p. (gr. k-2). 1988. wkbk. 4.95 (1-55734-120-6) Tchr Create Mat.
—My Favorite Things. Olsen, Shirley, illus. 48p. (gr. k-2). 1988. wkbk. 5.95 (1-55734-375-6) Tchr Create Mat.
—Sequence Fun. Wright, Theresa, illus. 32p. (gr. k-2). 1988. wkbk. 4.95 (1-55734-121-4) Tchr Create Mat.

Spivak, Darlene & Sterling, Mary E. Valentine's Day Activities. Wright, Theresa & Spence, Paula, illus. 48p. (gr. 1-4). 1989. wkbk. 5.95 (1-55734-009-9) Tchr Create Mat.

Spivak, Darlene, ed. see Carratello, John & Carratello, Patty.

Spivak, Darlene, ed. see Carratello, Patty.

Spivak, Darlene E. Graph Art Puzzles. Wright, Theresa N., illus. 48p. (gr. 2-5). 1987. wkbk. 5.95 (1-55734-068-4) Tchr Create Mat.
—Scrambled Word Puzzles. Spivak, Darlene E., illus. 48p. (gr. 2-5). 1987. wkbk. 5.95 (1-55734-066-8) Tchr Create Mat.

Spizman, Robyn. All Aboard with Bulletin Boards. Pesiri, Evelyn, illus. 96p. (gr. k-8). 1983. wkbk. 9.95 (0-86653-105-X, GA 467) Good Apple.

—Bulletin Boards: For Reading, Spelling & Language
Skills. Pesiri, Evelyn, illus. 64p. (gr. k-6). 1984. wkbk.
7.95 (0-86653-210-2, GA 574) Good Apple.
—Bulletin Boards: Ideas for Holidays & Special Days.
Pesiri, Evelyn, illus. 64p. (gr. k-6). 1984. wkbk. 7.95
(0-86653-211-0, GA 567) Good Apple.
—Bulletin Boards Plus. 112p. (gr. k-6). 1989. 9.95
(0-86653-510-1, GA1080) Good Apple.
—Bulletin Boards: Seasonal Ideas & Activities. Pesiri,
Evelyn, illus. 64p. (gr. k-6). 1984. wkbk. 7.95
(0-86653-218-8, GA 568) Good Apple.
—Bulletin Boards to Promote Good Study Skills &
Positive Self-Concept. Pesiri, Evelyn, illus. 48p. (gr.
k-6). 1984. wkbk. 6.95 (0-86653-261-7, GA 575)
Good Apple.
—Bulletin Boards: To Reinforce Basic Math Skills. Pesiri,
Evelyn, illus. 64p. (gr. k-6). 1984. wkbk. 7.95
(0-86653-208-0, GA 573) Good Apple.
—Good Apple & Bulletin Board Bonanzas. 144p. (gr.
3-7). 1981. 11.95 (0-86653-049-5, GA 281) Good
Apple.
Spizman, Robyn F. Lollipop Grapes & Clothespin
Critters: Quick, On-the-Spot Remedies for Restless of
Children 2-10. LC 84-24548. 160p. (ps-5). 1985. pap.
8.61 (0-201-06497-9) Addison-Wesley.
Spizman, Robyn F. & Garber, Marianne D. Air
(Intermediate) (Illus.). 48p. (gr. 4-7). 1992. wkbk. 7.95
(0-86653-632-9, 1408) Good Apple.
—Land (Intermediate) (Illus.). 48p. (gr. 4-7). 1992. wkbk.
7.95 (0-86653-675-2, 1409) Good Apple.
—Water (Intermediate) (Illus.). 48p. (gr. 4-7). 1992.
wkbk. 7.95 (0-86653-676-0, 1410) Good Apple.
Spizzirri, Linda, ed. see Spizzirri Publishing Co. Staff.
Spizzirri, Linda, ed. see Spizzirri Publishing Co. Staff.
**Spizzirri, Linda, jt. auth. see Spizzirri Publishing Co.
Staff.**
Spizzirri, Linda, ed. Prehistoric Fish: Educational
Coloring Book. (Illus.). 32p. (gr. 1-8). 1981. pap. 1.75
(0-86545-021-8) Spizzirri.
—Prehistoric Mammals: An Educational Coloring Book.
(Illus.). 32p. (gr. 1-8). 1981. pap. 1.75 (0-86545-022-6)
Spizzirri.
Spizzirri, Linda, ed. see Spizzirri, Peter M.
Spizzirri, Linda, ed. see Spizzirri Publishing Co. Staff.
Spizzirri, Linda, ed. see Spizzirri Publishing Inc Staff
Spizzirri, Linda, ed. see Spizzirri Publishing, Inc. Staff.
Spizzirri, Peter M. Bird Mazes: Educational Activity-
Coloring Book. Spizzirri, Linda, ed. (Illus.). 32p. (gr.
k-5). 1984. pap. 1.00 (0-86545-060-9) Spizzirri.
—Colonies: An Educational Coloring Book. Spizzirri,
Linda, ed. (Illus.). 32p. (gr. 1-8). 1989. pap. 1.75
(0-86545-137-0) Spizzirri.
—Dinosaur Mazes: Educational Activity-Coloring Book.
Spizzirri, Linda, ed. (Illus.). 32p. (gr. k-5). 1984. pap.
1.00 (0-86545-057-9) Spizzirri.
—Farm Maze: Educational Activity-Coloring Book.
Spizzirri, Linda, ed. (Illus.). 32p. (gr. k-3). 1992. pap.
1.00 (0-86545-205-9) Spizzirri.
—Fish Dot to Dot: Educational Activity-Coloring Book.
Spizzirri, Linda, ed. (Illus.). 32p. (gr. k-3). 1992. pap.
1.25 (0-86545-206-7) Spizzirri.
—Fish Mazes: Educational Activity-Coloring Book.
Spizzirri, Linda, ed. (Illus.). 32p. (gr. k-5). 1984. pap.
1.00 (0-86545-061-7) Spizzirri.
—Flower Mazes: Educational Activity-Coloring Book.
Spizzirri, Linda, ed. (Illus.). 32p. (gr. k-5). 1984. pap.
1.00 (0-86545-058-7) Spizzirri.
—Pets: Alphabet Dot to Dot: Educational Activity-
Coloring Book. Spizzirri, Linda, ed. (Illus.). 32p. (gr.
k-3). 1992. pap. 1.00 (0-86545-209-1) Spizzirri.
—Reptiles Dot to Dot: Educational Activity-Coloring
Book. Spizzirri, Linda, ed. (Illus.). 32p. (gr. k-3). 1992.
pap. 1.00 (0-86545-207-5) Spizzirri.
—Shark Mazes: Educational Activity-Coloring Book.
Spizzirri, Linda, ed. (Illus.). 32p. (gr. k-5). 1984. pap.
1.00 (0-86545-056-0) Spizzirri.
—Turtle Mazes: Educational Activity-Coloring Book.
Spizzirri, Linda, ed. (Illus.). 32p. (gr. k-5). 1984. pap.
1.00 (0-86545-059-5) Spizzirri.
—Zoo Animals: Alphabet Dot to Dot: Educational
Activity-Coloring Book. Spizzirri, Linda, ed. (Illus.).
32p. (gr. k-3). 1992. pap. 1.00 (0-86545-208-3)
Spizzirri.
—Zoo Maze: Educational Activity-Coloring Book.
Spizzirri, Linda, ed. (Illus.). 32p. (gr. k-3). 1992. pap.
1.00 (0-86545-204-0) Spizzirri.
Spizzirri Publishing Co. Staff. Aircraft: An Educational
Coloring Book. Spizzirri, Linda, ed. Fuller, Glenn &
Spizzirri, Peter M., illus. 32p. (gr. 1-8). 1981. pap.
1.75 (0-86545-033-1) Spizzirri.
—Animal Alphabet: An Educational Coloring Book.
Spizzirri, Linda, ed. (Illus.). 32p. (gr. 1-8). 1982. pap.
1.75 (0-86545-042-0) Spizzirri.
—Automobiles: An Educational Coloring Book. Spizzirri,
Linda, ed. Fuller, Glenn, et al, illus. 32p. (gr. 1-8).
1981. pap. 1.75 (0-86545-032-3) Spizzirri.
—Birds: Educational Coloring Book. Spizzirri, Linda, ed.
Goodman, Marlene, et al, illus. 32p. (gr. 1-8). 1981.
pap. 1.75 (0-86545-026-9) Spizzirri.
—California Indians: An Educational Coloring Book.
Spizzirri, Linda, ed. (Illus.). 32p. (gr. 1-8). 1986. pap.
1.75 (0-86545-080-3) Spizzirri.
—Cats of the Wild: An Educational Coloring Book.
Spizzirri, Linda, ed. (Illus.). 32p. (gr. 1-8). 1982. pap.
1.75 (0-86545-045-5) Spizzirri.
—Cave Man (Cro-Magnon) Educational Coloring Book.
Spizzirri, Linda, ed. (Illus.). 32p. (gr. 1-8). 1984. pap.
1.75 (0-86545-055-2) Spizzirri.

—Comets: An Educational Coloring Book. Spizzirri,
Linda, ed. (Illus.). 32p. (gr. k-5). 1982. pap. 1.75
(0-86545-071-4) Spizzirri.
—Counting & Coloring Dinosaurs: An Educational
Coloring Book. Spizzirri, Linda, ed. (Illus.). 32p. (gr.
1-8). 1982. pap. 1.75 (0-86545-044-7) Spizzirri.
—Dinosaurs: An Educational Coloring Book. Spizzirri,
Linda, ed. Kohn, Arnie, illus. 32p. (gr. 1-8). 1981. pap.
1.75 (0-86545-019-6) Spizzirri.
—Dinosaurs of Prey: An Educational Coloring Book.
Spizzirri, Linda, ed. (Illus.). 32p. (gr. k-5). 1985. pap.
1.75 (0-86545-063-3) Spizzirri.
—Dogs: An Educational Coloring Book. Spizzirri, Linda,
ed. (Illus.). 32p. (gr. 1-8). 1986. pap. 1.75
(0-86545-076-5) Spizzirri.
—Dolls: An Educational Coloring Book. Spizzirri, Linda,
ed. Goodman, Marlene & Spizzirri, Peter M., illus.
32p. (gr. 1-8). 1981. pap. 1.75 (0-86545-034-X)
Spizzirri.
—Dolphins: An Educational Coloring Book. Spizzirri,
Linda, ed. (Illus.). 32p. (gr. 1-8). 1986. pap. 1.75
(0-86545-073-0) Spizzirri.
—Dot-to-Dot Dinosaurs: An Educational Activity-
Coloring Book. Spizzirri, Linda, ed. (Illus.). 32p. (gr.
1-8). 1986. pap. 1.00 (0-86545-078-1) Spizzirri.
—Dot-to-Dot Whales: An Educational Activity-Coloring
Book. Spizzirri, Linda, ed. (Illus.). 32p. (gr. 1-8). 1986.
pap. 1.00 (0-86545-079-X) Spizzirri.
—Eagles: An Educational Coloring Book. Spizzirri,
Linda, ed. (Illus.). 32p. (gr. k-5). 1985. pap. 1.75
(0-86545-067-6) Spizzirri.
—Endangered Species: An Educational Coloring Book.
Spizzirri, Linda, ed. (Illus.). 32p. (gr. 1-8). 1982. pap.
1.75 (0-86545-041-2) Spizzirri.
—Fish: An Educational Coloring Book. Spizzirri, Linda,
ed. (Illus.). 32p. (gr. k-5). 1982. pap. 1.75
(0-86545-028-5) Spizzirri.
—Horses: An Educational Coloring Book. Spizzirri,
Linda, ed. (Illus.). 32p. (gr. k-5). 1985. pap. 1.75
(0-86545-068-4) Spizzirri.
—Kachina Dolls: An Educational Coloring Book.
Spizzirri, Linda, ed. (Illus.). 32p. (gr. 1-8). 1982. pap.
1.75 (0-86545-046-3) Spizzirri.
—Lautrec Posters: Educational Coloring Book. Spizzirr,
Linda, ed. (Illus.). 32p. (gr. 1-8). 1983. pap. 1.75
(0-86545-052-8) Spizzirri.
—Mammals: An Educational Coloring Book. Spizzirri,
Linda, ed. Spizzirri, Peter M., et al, illus. 32p. (gr.
1-8). 1981. pap. 1.75 (0-86545-027-7) Spizzirri.
—Northeast Indians: An Educational Coloring Book.
Spizzirri, Linda, ed. (Illus.). 32p. (gr. 1-8). 1982. pap.
1.75 (0-86545-040-4) Spizzirri.
—Northwest Indians: An Educational Coloring Book.
Spizzirri, Linda, ed. (Illus.). 32p. (gr. 1-8). 1983. pap.
1.75 (0-86545-047-1) Spizzirri.
—Paleozoic Life: An Educational Coloring Book.
Spizzirri, Linda, ed. Spizzirri, Peter M., illus. 32p. (gr.
1-8). 1981. pap. 1.75 (0-86545-024-2) Spizzirri.
—Picture Crosswords: An Educational Activity-Coloring
Book. Spizzirri, Linda, ed. (Illus.). 32p. (gr. 1-8). 1986.
pap. 1.75 (0-86545-081-1) Spizzirri.
—Picture Dictionary: An Educational Coloring Book.
Spizzirri, Linda, ed. (Illus.). 32p. (gr. 1-8). 1982. pap.
1.75 (0-86545-049-8) Spizzirri.
—Plains Indians: An Educational Coloring Book.
Spizzirri, Linda, ed. Spizzirri, Peter M., illus. 32p. (gr.
1-8). 1981. pap. 1.75 (0-86545-025-0) Spizzirri.
—Planets: An Educational Coloring Book. Spizzirri,
Linda, ed. (Illus.). 32p. (gr. 1-8). 1982. pap. 1.75
(0-86545-043-9) Spizzirri.
—Poisonous Snakes: An Educational Coloring Book.
Spizzirri, Linda, ed. (Illus.). 32p. (gr. 1-8). 1984. pap.
1.75 (0-86545-054-4) Spizzirri.
—Prehistoric Birds: An Educational Coloring Book.
Spizzirri, Linda, ed. Spizzirri, Peter M., illus. 32p. (gr.
1-8). 1981. pap. 1.75 (0-86545-023-4) Spizzirri.
—Prehistoric Sea Life: An Educational Coloring Book.
Spizzirri, Linda, ed. Kohn, Arnie, illus. 32p. (gr. 1-8).
1981. pap. 1.75 (0-86545-020-X) Spizzirri.
—Primates: An Educational Coloring Book. Spizzirri,
Linda, ed. Fuller, Glenn, et al, illus. 32p. (gr. 1-8).
1981. pap. 1.75 (0-86545-030-7) Spizzirri.
—Reptiles: An Educational Coloring Book. Spizzirri,
Linda, ed. Fuller, Glenn, et al, illus. 32p. (gr. 1-8).
1981. pap. 1.75 (0-86545-031-5) Spizzirri.
—Rockets: An Educational Coloring Book. Spizzirri,
Linda, ed. (Illus.). 32p. (gr. 1-8). 1986. pap. 1.75
(0-86545-072-2) Spizzirri.
—Satellites: An Educational Coloring Book. Spizzirri,
Linda, ed. (Illus.). 32p. (gr. 1-8). 1986. pap. 1.75
(0-86545-074-9) Spizzirri.
—Sharks: An Educational Coloring Book. Spizzirri,
Linda, ed. Fuller, Glenn, et al, illus. 32p. (gr. 1-8).
1981. pap. 1.75 (0-86545-029-3) Spizzirri.
—Ships: An Educational Coloring Book. Spizzirri, Linda,
ed. Fuller, Glenn & Spizzirri, Peter M., illus. 32p. (gr.
1-8). 1981. pap. 1.75 (0-86545-035-8) Spizzirri.
—Shuttle Craft: An Educational Coloring Book. Spizzirri,
Linda, ed. (Illus.). 32p. (gr. 1-8). 1986. pap. 1.75
(0-86545-077-3) Spizzirri.
—Southeast Indians: An Educational Coloring Book.
Spizzirri, Linda, ed. (Illus.). 32p. (gr. k-5). 1985. pap.
1.75 (0-86545-065-X) Spizzirri.
—Southwest Indians: An Educational Coloring Book.
Spizzirri, Linda, ed. (Illus.). 32p. (gr. 1-8). 1986. pap.
1.75 (0-86545-075-7) Spizzirri.

—Space Craft: An Educational Coloring Book. Spizzirri,
Linda, ed. Spizzirri, Peter M., illus. 32p. (gr. 1-8).
1981. pap. 1.75 (0-86545-036-6) Spizzirri.
—Space Explorers: An Educational Coloring Book.
Spizzirri, Linda, ed. Spizzirri, Peter M., illus. 32p. (gr.
1-8). 1981. pap. 1.75 (0-86545-037-4) Spizzirri.
—State Birds: An Educational Coloring Book. Spizzirri,
Linda, ed. (Illus.). 32p. (gr. 1-8). 1983. pap. 1.75
(0-86545-050-1) Spizzirri.
—Texas: An Educational Coloring Book. Spizzirri, Linda,
ed. (Illus.). 32p. (gr. 1-8). 1985. pap. 1.75
(0-86545-070-6) Spizzirri.
—Transportation: Educational Coloring Book. Spizzirri,
Linda, ed. Spizzirri, Peter M., illus. 32p. (gr. 1-8).
1981. pap. 1.75 (0-86545-038-2) Spizzirri.
—Trucks: An Educational Coloring Book. Spizzirri,
Linda, ed. (Illus.). 32p. 1979. pap. 1.75
(0-86545-051-X) Spizzirri.
—Whales: An Educational Coloring Book. Spizzirri,
Linda, ed. (Illus.). 32p. (gr. 1-8). 1982. pap. 1.75
(0-86545-039-0) Spizzirri.
Spizzirri Publishing Co. Staff & Spizzirri, Linda. Animal
Family Calendar: An Educational Coloring Book.
(Illus.). 32p. (gr. k-5). 1983. pap. 2.25
(0-86545-048-X) Spizzirri.
—Animal Giants: An Educational Coloring Book. (Illus.).
32p. (gr. k-5). 1985. pap. 1.75 (0-86545-066-8)
Spizzirri.
—California Missions: An Educational Coloring Book.
(Illus.). 32p. (gr. k-5). 1985. pap. 1.75 (0-86545-062-5)
Spizzirri.
—Cats: An Educational Coloring Book. (Illus.). 32p. (gr.
k-5). 1985. pap. 1.75 (0-86545-069-2) Spizzirri.
—Deep-Sea Fish: An Educational Coloring Book. (Illus.).
32p. (gr. k-5). 1985. pap. 1.75 (0-86545-064-1)
Spizzirri.
Spizzirri Publishing Inc Staff. Atlantic Fish: An
Educational Coloring Book. Spizzirri, Linda, ed.
(Illus.). 32p. (gr. 1-8). 1989. pap. 1.75 (0-86545-135-4)
Spizzirri.
—Butterfly Mazes: An Educational-Activity Coloring
Book. Spizzirri, Linda, ed. (Illus.). 32p. (gr. 1-8). 1989.
pap. 1.00 (0-86545-146-X) Spizzirri.
—Cowboys: An Educational Coloring Book. Spizzirri,
Linda, ed. (Illus.). 32p. (gr. 1-8). 1989. pap. 1.75
(0-86545-139-7) Spizzirri.
Spizzirri Publishing, Inc. Staff. Endangered Birds: An
Educational Coloring Book. Spizzirri, Linda, ed.
(Illus.). 32p. (gr. k-5). 1992. pap. 1.75 (0-86545-171-0)
Spizzirri.
Spizzirri Publishing Inc Staff. Eskimos: An Educational
Coloring Book. Spizzirri, Linda, ed. (Illus.). 32p. (gr.
1-8). 1989. pap. 1.75 (0-86545-140-0) Spizzirri.
—Farm Animals: An Educational Coloring Book.
Spizzirri, Linda, ed. (Illus.). 32p. (gr. 1-8). 1989. pap.
1.75 (0-86545-141-9) Spizzirri.
—Mammal Mazes: An Educational-Activity Coloring
Book. Spizzirri, Linda, ed. (Illus.). 32p. (gr. 1-8). 1989.
pap. 1.00 (0-86545-144-3) Spizzirri.
—Pacific Fish: An Educational Coloring Book. Spizzirri,
Linda, ed. (Illus.). 32p. (gr. 1-8). 1989. pap. 1.75
(0-86545-136-2) Spizzirri.
—Penguins: An Educational Coloring Book. Spizzirri,
Linda, ed. (Illus.). 32p. (gr. 1-8). 1989. pap. 1.75
(0-86545-134-6) Spizzirri.
—Pioneers: An Educational Coloring Book. Spizzirri,
Linda, ed. (Illus.). 32p. (gr. 1-8). 1989. pap. 1.75
(0-86545-138-9) Spizzirri.
—Shell Mazes: An Educational-Activity Coloring Book.
Spizzirri, Linda, ed. (Illus.). 32p. (gr. 1-8). 1989. pap.
1.00 (0-86545-145-1) Spizzirri.
—State Flowers: An Educational Coloring Book.
Spizzirri, Linda, ed. (Illus.). 32p. (gr. 1-8). 1989. pap.
1.75 (0-86545-142-7) Spizzirri.
—Tree Mazes: An Educational-Activity Coloring Book.
Spizzirri, Linda, ed. (Illus.). 32p. (gr. 1-8). 1989. pap.
1.00 (0-86545-143-5) Spizzirri.
Splendor, Meg. Dream Catcher: A Starlight Journey with
Meg Splendor. LC 93-1015. 77p. (Orig.). (ps up).
1993. pap. 12.95 incl. audio tape (1-882979-17-6)
What the Heck.
Spohn, David. Home Field. LC 92-5459. 1993. write for
info. (0-688-11172-6); lib. bdg. write for info.
(0-688-11173-4) Lothrop.
—Nate's Treasure. (ps-3). 1991. 9.88 (0-688-10091-0)
Lothrop.
—Nate's Treasure. (ps-3). 1991. 9.95 (0-688-10092-9)
Lothrop.
—Starry Night. Pearson, Susan, ed. LC 91-33802. (Illus.).
32p. (gr. k up). 1992. 10.00 (0-688-11170-X); PLB
9.93 (0-688-11171-8) Lothrop.
—Winter Wood. LC 90-49944. (Illus.). 32p. (gr. k up).
1991. 13.95 (0-688-10093-7); PLB 13.88
(0-688-10094-5) Lothrop.
Spohn, Kate. Christmas at Anna's. Spohn, Kate, illus.
32p. (ps-3). 1993. 13.99 (0-670-84895-6) Viking Child
Bks.
—Clementine's Winter Wardrobe. LC 89-42531. (Illus.).
32p. (ps-1). 1989. 13.95 (0-531-05841-7); PLB 13.99
(0-531-08441-8) Orchard Bks Watts.
—Fanny & Margarita: Five Stories about Two Best
Friends. LC 92-22208. (Illus.). 32p. (gr. 3-8). 1993. 13.
99 (0-670-84692-X) Viking Child Bks.
—Introducing Fanny. Spohn, Kate, illus. LC 90-7736.
32p. (ps-2). 1991. 14.95 (0-531-05920-0); PLB 14.99
(0-531-08520-1) Orchard Bks Watts.

—Ruth's Bake Shop. Spohn, Kate, illus. LC 89-70930. 32p. (ps-2). 1990. 13.95 (*0-531-05889-1*); PLB 13.99 (*0-531-08489-2*) Orchard Bks Watts.

Spoon, Wilfred. Ocean Magic Book of Masks. Spoon, Wilfred, illus. LC 90-62142. (ps-1). 1991. incl. 6 punch-out hand-held face masks - manatee 5.95, penguin, polar bear, porpoise, sea otter, walrus (*1-877779-13-X*) Schneider Educational.

Spoon, Wilfred, illus. Ocean Magic "Press 'n Peel" Game Board. LC 90-62146. (ps-1). 1991. incl. laminated ocean playboard, 18 vinyl stickers & storage guard for stickers 7.95 (*1-877779-14-8*) Schneider Educational.

Spooner, Alan, jt. ed. see Weston, John.

Spooner, Michael. Legend of Snowshoes. 1995. write for info. (*0-8050-3137-5*) H Holt & Co.

—A Moon in Your Lunch Box: Poems. Ohlsson, Ib, illus. LC 92-32662. 64p. (gr. 2-6). 1993. PLB 14.95 (*0-8050-2209-0*, Bks Young Read) H Holt & Co.

Sprague, Gary. My Parents Got a Divorce. 1992. pap. 7.99 (*0-7814-0486-X*) Cook.

Sprague, Gilbert M. The Nome King's Shadow in Oz. Abbott, Donald, illus. 120p. (gr. 3 up). 1992. 39.95 (*0-929605-19-5*); pap. 9.95 (*0-929605-18-7*) Books Wonder.

—Patchwork Bride of Oz. (Illus.). 40p. (gr. 1 up). 1993. 19.95 (*0-929605-28-4*); pap. 6.95 (*0-929605-27-6*) Books Wonder.

Sprague, Jane, jt. auth. see Asmann, Lynn.

Sprague, Sydney, ed. see Brown, Charlene & Davis, Carolyn.

Sprang, Marie E. Jeannie & Her Patches. 1993. 9.50 (*0-8062-4714-2*) Carlton.

Spray, Carole. The Mare's Egg. La Fave, Kim, illus. Atwood, Margaret, afterword by. (Illus.). 56p. (Orig.). (gr. k-7). 1981. (Pub. by Camden Hse CN); pap. 9.95 (*0-920656-07-2*, Pub. by Camden Hse CN) Firefly Bks Ltd.

Spremich, Andrew. Flight of the Dragon. Kratoville, Betty L., ed. (Illus.). 64p. (gr. 3-9). 1989. PLB 4.95 (*0-87879-619-3*) High Noon Bks.

Spring, Grace J. The Fabulous House of Marcella Mouse. Spring, Grace J., illus. LC 85-7518. 24p. (gr. 1-6). 1985. pap. 3.95 (*0-317-39846-6*) Andrew Mtn Pr.

Springate, Kay W. Let's Learn about Good Health. 64p. (ps-2). 1988. wkbk. 7.95 (*0-86653-438-5*, GA1041) Good Apple.

Springer, Eintou P. The Caribbean. rev ed. (Illus.). 48p. (gr. 5 up). 1987. PLB 16.98 (*0-382-09469-7*) Silver Burdett Pr.

Springer, Harriett, tr. see Selsam, Millicent E. & Hunt, Joyce.

Springer, Jean. The Great Forest. Peterson, Pete, ed. French, Ed, illus. 169p. (gr. 3-6). 1986. pap. 3.99 (*0-934998-25-6*) Bethel Pub.

Springer, Margaret. A Royal Ball. O'Sullivan, Tom, illus. 32p. (gr. k-3). 1992. bds. 9.95 (*1-878093-64-9*) Boyds Mills Pr.

Springer, Nancy. The Boy on a Black Horse. LC 92-27158. 160p. (gr. 5-9). 1994. SBE 14.95 (*0-689-31840-5*, Atheneum Child Bk) Macmillan Child Grp.

—Colt. (gr. 4-7). 1991. 13.95 (*0-8037-1022-4*) Dial Bks Young.

—Colt. 128p. (gr. 5 up). 1994. pap. 3.99 (*0-14-036480-3*) Puffin Bks.

—The Friendship Song. LC 91-9483. 144p. (gr. 4 up). 1992. SBE 13.95 (*0-689-31727-1*, Atheneum Child Bk) Macmillan Child Grp.

—The Great Pony Hassle. Duffy, Daniel M., illus. LC 92-34781. (gr. 3-7). 1993. 12.99 (*0-8037-1306-1*); PLB 13.89 (*0-8037-1308-8*) Dial Bks Young.

—Horse to Love. LC 86-45487. 192p. (gr. 3-7). 1987. HarpC Child Bks.

—Not on a White Horse. LC 87-3477. 192p. (gr. 5 up). 1988. SBE 13.95 (*0-689-31366-7*, Atheneum Child Bk) Macmillan Child Grp.

—The Red Wizard. LC 88-29376. 144p. (gr. 4 up). 1990. SBE 13.95 (*0-689-31485-X*, Atheneum Child Bk) Macmillan Child Grp.

—They're All Named Wildfire. LC 88-27497. 112p. (gr. 4 up). 1989. SBE 12.95 (*0-689-31450-7*, Atheneum Child Bk) Macmillan Child Grp.

Springer, Sally, illus. High Holiday Fun for Little Hands. 32p. (ps). 1993. wkbk. 3.95 (*0-929371-76-3*) Kar Ben.

—Let's Make Latkes. LC 91-60403. 12p. (ps). 1991. bds. 4.95 (*0-929371-58-5*) Kar Ben.

—Sukkot & Simchat Torah Fun for Little Hands. 32p. (ps). 1993. wkbk. 3.95 (*0-929371-77-1*) Kar Ben.

Springstubb, Tricia. Pet-Sitters Plus Five. (gr. 4-7). 1993. pap. 2.75 (*0-590-46127-3*) Scholastic Inc.

—Two Plus One Makes Trouble. (ps-3). 1991. pap. 2.50 (*0-590-44648-7*) Scholastic Inc.

—Which Way to the Nearest Wilderness? (gr. k-12). 1987. pap. 2.75 (*0-440-99554-X*, LFL) Dell.

—Which Way to the Nearest Wilderness? (gr. k-6). 1987. pap. 2.75 (*0-440-49554-7*, YB) Dell.

—Which Way to the Wilderness? (gr. 4-7). 1984. 14.95 (*0-316-80787-7*) Little.

—With a Name Like Lulu, Who Needs More Trouble? Kastner, Jill, illus. (gr. 5-9). 1989. 14.95 (*0-385-29823-4*) Delacorte.

Sprock, Inge & Biser, Len. The Land of Flop-Eared Piggies. Sprock, Inge, illus. 32p. (ps-3). 1992. write for info. (*1-880015-30-7*) Petra Pub Co.

Sprott, Maxine. Malik: The History the Legend the Myth (the Story of Malcolm X) Allen, James R., intro. by. (Illus.). 66p. (Orig.). (gr. 5). 1991. pap. 8.00 (*0-9629982-9-X*) Vital Edits.

Sproule, Anna. Abraham Lincoln. LC 91-50540. (Illus.). 68p. (gr. 3-4). 1992. PLB 18.60 (*0-8368-0620-4*) Gareth Stevens Inc.

—Abraham Lincoln: Leader of a Nation in Crisis. LC 90-10374. (Illus.). 68p. (gr. 5-6). 1992. PLB 18.60 (*0-8368-0216-0*) Gareth Stevens Inc.

—Body Watch: Know Your Insides. (Illus.). 48p. (gr. 1-4). 1987. 12.95x (*0-8160-1782-4*) Facts on File.

—Food for the World. (Illus.). 48p. (gr. 1-4). 1987. 12.95x (*0-8160-1783-2*) Facts on File.

—Great Britain: The Land & Its People. LC 86-17674. (Illus.). 48p. (gr. 5 up). 1991. PLB 16.98 (*0-382-24243-2*) Silver Burdett Pr.

—Italy. (Illus.). 48p. (gr. 5 up). 1987. PLB 16.98 (*0-382-09473-5*) Silver Burdett Pr.

—Mikhail Gorbachev. LC 91-50542. 68p. (gr. 3-4). 1992. PLB 18.60 (*0-8368-0619-0*) Gareth Stevens Inc.

Sproule, Anna, jt. auth. see Bailey, Donna.

Sproxton, Mildred. Children's Treasure House of Poetry. (gr. 7-10). 1986. 22.00x (*0-7223-2073-6*, Pub. by A H Stockwell England) St Mut.

Sproyle, Anna. Mikhail Gorbachev: Revolutionary for Democracy. LC 90-10010. (Illus.). 64p. (gr. 5-6). 1991. PLB 18.60 (*0-8368-0401-5*) Gareth Stevens Inc.

Spryi, Johanna. Heidi. (Illus.). 1992. write for info. (*0-89434-124-3*) Ferguson.

Spuler, Frances B., jt. auth. see Harrison, Ann S.

Spurgeon, R. Energy & Power. (Illus.). 48p. 1990. PLB 13.96 (*0-88110-418-3*); pap. 7.95 (*0-7460-0422-2*) EDC.

Spurr, Elizabeth. The Biggest Birthday Cake in the World. Grove, Karen, ed. Litzinger, Rosanne, illus. LC 89-19901. 32p. (ps-3). 1991. 14.95 (*0-15-207150-4*) HarBrace.

—Mrs. Minetta's Car Pool. Sims, Blanche, illus. LC 84-20483. 32p. (ps-3). 1985. SBE 12.95 (*0-689-31103-6*, Atheneum Child Bk) Macmillan Child Grp.

—Mrs. Minetta's Car Pool. Sims, Blanche, illus. LC 90-35. 32p. (gr. k-3). 1990. pap. 3.95 (*0-689-71430-0*, Aladdin) Macmillan Child Grp.

Spyri, Johanna. Heidi. LC 85-13292. (gr. 5 up). 1964. pap. 1.95 (*0-8049-0018-3*, CL-18) Airmont.

—Heidi. LC 85-13292. (Illus.). (gr. 4-6). 1988. pap. 3.25 (*0-590-42046-1*) Scholastic Inc.

—Heidi. LC 85-13292. 240p. (gr. 3-7). 1983. pap. 2.25 (*0-14-035002-0*, Puffin) Puffin Bks.

—Heidi. LC 85-13292. (Illus.). (ps-3). 1985. 1.98 (*0-517-30779-0*) Outlet Bk Co.

—Heidi. (gr. k-1). 1986. 8.98 (*0-685-16841-7*, 618141) Outlet Bk Co.

—Heidi. Saunders, Susan, adapted by. Rowland, Jada, illus. LC 87-15466. 48p. (gr. 2-5). 1988. PLB 12.89 (*0-8167-1215-8*); pap. 3.95 (*0-8167-1216-6*) Troll Assocs.

—Heidi. 1988. 12.99 (*0-517-61814-1*) Outlet Bk Co.

—Heidi. (gr. 4 up). 1990. pap. 3.50 (*0-440-40357-X*) Dell.

—Heidi. rev. & abr. ed. De Graaf, Anne, ed. Molan, Chris, illus. 96p. (gr. 1-5). 1991. 8.95 (*0-89107-600-X*) Good News.

—Heidi. 352p. 1992. 9.49 (*0-8167-2550-0*); pap. 2.95 (*0-8167-2551-9*) Troll Assocs.

—Moni, the Goat Boy: And Other Stories. (Illus.). 218p. 1993. pap. 5.95 (*1-883453-00-3*) Deutsche Buchhandlung.

—Tomi Ingerer's Heidi: The Classic Novel. Dole, Helen B., tr. Ungerer, Tomi, illus. Githens, John, contrib. by. (gr. 3-6). 1990. 19.95 (*0-385-30244-4*) Delacorte.

Spyropulos, Diana. Greece: A Spirited Independence. LC 85-25412. (Illus.). 128p. (gr. 5 up). 1990. RSBE 14.95 (*0-87518-311-5*, Dillon) Macmillan Child Grp.

Squier, Karl. Leapin Lizzie. Love, Judith D., illus. LC 84-27784. 32p. (gr. k-5). 1985. pap. 12.95 incl. cassette (*0-931905-00-1*); pap. 7.95 (*0-931905-01-X*); cassette 7.95 (*0-931905-02-8*) Lady Lake Learn.

Squire, Ann. One Hundred & One Questions & Answers about Pets & People. Karas, Brian, illus. LC 87-36457. 96p. (gr. 3-7). 1988. SBE 13.95 (*0-02-786580-0*, Macmillan Child Bk) Macmillan Child Grp.

—Understanding Man's Best Friend: Why Dogs Look & Act the Way They Do. LC 90-30631. (Illus.). 128p. (gr. 3-7). 1991. SBE 14.95 (*0-02-786590-8*, Macmillan Child Bk) Macmillan Child Grp.

Squire, Ann, jt. auth. see Gravelle, Karen.

Squire, David. Wheels. LC 79-5064. (Illus.). 36p. (gr. 3-6). 1980. PLB 13.50 (*0-8225-1186-X*) Lerner Pubns.

Squire-Buresh, Anne L. To Touch the Sky. LC 89-50050. 44p. (gr. k-3). 1989. 5.95 (*1-55523-224-8*) Winston-Derek.

Srinivasan, A. V. A Hindu Primer: Yaksha Prashna. Satchidananda, Swami, frwd by. (Illus.). 8p. (gr. 6-12). 1984. pap. 7.70 (*0-86578-249-0*, 6203) Ind-US Inc.

Srinivasan, Rodbika. India. LC 89-25466. (Illus.). 128p. (gr. 5-9). 1991. PLB 21.95 (*1-85435-298-9*) Marshall Cavendish.

Srivastava, Jane J. Statistics. Reiss, John, illus. LC 72-7559. (gr. 1-5). 1973. PLB 12.89 (*0-690-77300-5*, Crowell Jr Bks) HarpC Child Bks.

Sr. Mary Anne. He Did Something Special. (gr. 1 up). 1988. 2.00 (*0-8198-3335-5*, CH0272) St Paul Bks.

Sroda, George. Life Story of TV Star & Celebrity Herman the Worm. Hughes, Janet, illus. 189p. (gr. k-7). 1979. 4.95 (*0-9604486-2-4*); pap. 3.95 (*0-685-01814-8*) G Sroda.

—No Angle Left Unturned: Facts About Nightcrawlers. Hughes, Janet, illus. 111p. (gr. 10 up). 1975. pap. 4.95 (*0-9604486-0-8*) G Sroda.

Sroka, Stephen R. Guia Para Educadores Sobre el SIDA y Otras ETS. Urizar, Hugo, tr. from ENG. (SPA., Illus.). 105p. (gr. 5-12). 1991. tchr's. ed. 25.00 (*0-9622034-1-6*) Hlth Educ Consults.

Stabell, B. B. Little Chefs Cook Book. 70p. (gr. 7 up). 1982. pap. 4.75 (*0-9610872-0-X*) B B Stabell.

Stabile, Angela C. The Miracle of My Dog King. 1991. 6.95 (*0-533-09038-5*) Vantage.

Stacey, Tom. Airplanes: The Lure of Flight. LC 90-6471. (Illus.). 96p. (gr. 5-8). 1990. PLB 15.95 (*1-56006-203-7*) Lucent Bks.

—The Hindenburg. McGovern, Brian, illus. LC 90-6256. 64p. (gr. 5-8). 1990. PLB 11.95 (*1-56006-010-7*) Lucent Bks.

—The Titanic. LC 89-33553. (Illus.). 64p. (gr. 5-8). 1989. PLB 11.95 (*1-56006-006-9*) Lucent Bks.

Stack, Mary E. San Diego, California: The Travel Guide for Kids. Koch, Richard L., illus. 32p. (gr. k-4). 1991. pap. 4.95 (*0-945600-06-2*) Colormore Inc.

Stack, Richard L. Doggonest Puppy Love. 1992. pap. 14. 95 (*0-9628262-1-9*) Windmill MD.

—The Doggonest Vacation. Mowrer, Sheri L., illus. 1991. write for info. (*0-9628262-0-0*) Windmill MD.

Stackpole, Michael A. Evil Ascending. 320p. (Orig.). 1991. pap. 4.95 (*1-55878-099-8*) Game Designers.

—Evil Triumphant. 352p. (Orig.). 1992. pap. 4.95 (*1-55878-119-6*) Game Designers.

—A Gathering Evil. 328p. (Orig.). 1992. pap. 4.95 (*1-55878-092-0*) Game Designers.

Stacy, Darryl. Arizona: Gobierno y Ciudadania. (SPA., Illus.). 144p. (Orig.). (gr. 7-9). 1983. pap. text ed. 17. 95 (*0-911981-24-1*) Cloud Pub.

—Arizona: Government & Citizenship. rev. ed. (Illus.). 160p. (gr. 7-9). 1993. Repr. of 1990 ed. text ed. 17.95 (*0-911981-56-X*) Cloud Pub.

—Arizona: Government & Citizenship. rev. ed. (Illus.). 48p. (gr. 7-9). 1990. wkbk. 5.45 (*0-911981-57-8*) Cloud Pub.

—Missouri: Studies. Stacy, Darryl, illus. 56p. (gr. 7-9). 1988. wkbk. 5.25 (*0-911981-51-9*) Cloud Pub.

—United States: Government & Citizenship. (Illus.). 176p. (gr. 7-9). 1992. text ed. 19.45 (*0-911981-67-5*) Cloud Pub.

—United States: Government & Citizenship. 48p. (gr. 7-9). 1992. wkbk. 5.45 (*0-911981-71-3*) Cloud Pub.

—United States: Government & Citizenship. 24p. (gr. 7-9). 1992. tchr's ed. 8.45 (*0-911981-70-5*) Cloud Pub.

Stacy, Darryl & Bimes, James D. Missouri: Studies: Government & Constitution. Stacy, Darryl, illus. 120p. (gr. 7-9). 1989. Repr. of 1988 ed. text ed. 15.95 (*0-911981-50-0*) Cloud Pub.

Stacy, Darryl & McCabe, Michael. Arizona: Studies: Map Skills Program. (Illus.). 59p. (gr. 4-6). 1990. binder 42.95 (*0-911981-53-5*) Cloud Pub.

Stacy, Dennis. Nifty (& Thrifty) Science Activities. (gr. 2-6). 1988. pap. 6.95 (*0-8224-4777-0*) Fearon Teach Aids.

Stacy, Don. Drawing & Painting from Imagination. LC 79-27795. (Illus.). 224p. (gr. 9-12). 1980. 14.95 (*0-87396-083-1*) Stravon.

Stacy, Selmarie. Ganbatte: (How to Read Japanese) (Illus.). 58p. (Orig.). (gr. 7 up). 1990. pap. 6.95 wkbk. (*0-935984-09-7*) Spheric Hse.

Stacy, Tom. Earth, Sea & Sky. Vestal, J., ed. Forsey, Chris, illus. LC 90-12974. 40p. (gr. 4-5). 1991. PLB 12.40 (*0-531-19106-0*) Watts.

—Earth, Sea & Sky. Forsey, Chris, illus. LC 90-42976. 40p. (Orig.). (gr. 2-5). 1991. pap. 3.95 (*0-679-80861-2*) Random Bks Yng Read.

—The Fifties. LC 89-21662. (Illus.). 48p. (gr. 5-9). 1990. PLB 19.92 (*0-8114-4212-8*) Raintree Steck-V.

—The Sun, Stars & Planets. Bull, Peter & Quigley, Sebastian, illus. 40p. (gr. 4-5). 1991. PLB 12.40 (*0-531-19107-9*, Pub. by Bookwright Pr) Watts.

—Sun, Stars & Planets. Bull, Peter, illus. LC 90-42979. 40p. (Orig.). (gr. 2-5). 1991. pap. 3.95 (*0-679-80862-0*) Random Bks Yng Read.

—Wings, Wheels & Sails. (Illus.). 40p. (gr. 4-5). 1991. PLB 12.40 (*0-531-19105-2*) Watts.

—Wings, Wheels & Sails. Bull, Peter, illus. LC 90-42977. 40p. (Orig.). (gr. 2-5). 1991. pap. 3.95 (*0-679-80863-9*) Random Bks Yng Read.

—The World of Animals. Robson, Eric, illus. 40p. (gr. 4-5). 1991. PLB 12.40 (*0-531-19103-6*) Watts.

—The World of Animals. Robson, Eric, illus. LC 90-42619. 40p. (Orig.). (gr. 2-5). 1991. pap. 3.95 (*0-679-80864-7*) Random Bks Yng Read.

Stadler, Bernice & Reese, Nancy. Celebrations of the Word for Children: Cycle C. LC 88-90102. 104p. (Orig.). (gr. 3-8). 1988. pap. text ed. 9.95 (*0-89622-362-0*) Twenty-Third.

Stadler, John. The Adventures of Snail at School. Stadler, John, illus. LC 91-45403. 64p. (gr. k-3). 1993. 14.00 (*0-06-021041-9*); PLB 13.89 (*0-06-021042-7*) HarpC Child Bks.

—Animal Cafe. LC 85-26789. (Illus.). 32p. (ps-2). 1986. pap. 3.95 (*0-689-71063-1*, Aladdin) Macmillan Child Grp.

—Cat at Bat. Stadler, John, illus. LC 87-36400. 32p. (ps-2). 1988. 9.95 (*0-525-44416-5*, DCB) Dutton Child Bks.

—Cat is Back at Bat. Stadler, John, illus. LC 90-24831. 32p. (ps-2). 1991. 10.95 (*0-525-44762-8*, DCB) Dutton Child Bks.

—Hector the Accordion-Nosed Dog. LC 81-7713. (Illus.). 32p. 1985. pap. 4.50 (*0-02-045250-0*, Aladdin) Macmillan Child Grp.

—Hooray for Snail! LC 83-46164. (Illus.). 32p. (ps-2). 1984. PLB 14.89 (0-690-04413-5, Crowell Jr Bks) HarpC Child Bks.
—Hooray for Snail! Stadler, John, illus. LC 83-46164. 32p. (ps-2). 1985. pap. 5.95 (0-06-443075-8, Trophy) HarpC Child Bks.
—Three Cheers for Hippo! Stadler, John, illus. LC 87-497. 32p. (gr. k-3). 1990. pap. 3.95 (0-06-443220-3, Trophy) HarpC Child Bks.

Stadler, Richard H. Living As a Winner. Fischer, William E., ed. Woodfin, James, illus. 64p. (gr. 9-12). 1985. pap. 2.95 leaders guide (0-938272-23-3); pap. 2.95 students guide (0-938272-22-5) WELS Board.

Stadtler, Bea. The Adventures of Gluckel of Hameln. LC 67-18814. (gr. 6-10). 3.75 (0-8381-0731-1, 10-731) United Syn Bk.
—The Holocaust: A History of Courage & Resistance. Bial, Morrison D., ed. Martin, David S., illus. Bauer, Yehuda, intro. by. LC 74-11469. (Illus.). 210p. (gr. 5-7). 1975. pap. text ed. 5.95x (0-87441-231-5); Discussion Guide: By Nancy Karkowsky. pap. text ed. 6.95 (0-87441-257-9) Behrman.
—Story of Dona Gracia Mendes. Shevo, Aharon, illus. LC 70-83166. (gr. 6-9). 1969. 4.50 (0-8381-0734-6) United Syn Bk.

Stadtler, Christa. The United Kingdom. LC 91-6521. (Illus.). 32p. (gr. 2-4). 1992. PLB 12.40 (0-531-18444-7, Pub. by Bookwright Pr) Watts.
—West Germany. LC 90-996. (Illus.). 32p. (gr. k-3). 1991. PLB 12.40 (0-531-18371-8, Pub. by Bookwright Pr) Watts.

Stafford, Greg. Prince Valiant: The Storytelling Game. Dunn, Bill & Willis, Lynn, eds. Foster, Hal, illus. 128p. (Orig.). (gr. 6 up). 1989. pap. 19.95 (0-933635-50-8, 2801) Chaosium.
—Runequest: Deluxe. Peterson, Sandy, ed. (Illus.). 96p. (gr. 8 up). 1989. 29.95 (0-911605-51-7) Avalon Hill.

Stafford, Greg & Dunn, Bill. Pendragon: Roleplaying in King Arthur's Britain. 3rd ed. Krinard, Sue, et al, illus. 208p. (gr. 9 up). 1990. pap. 21.95 (0-933635-59-1, 2) Chaosium.

Stafford, Jean. The Scarlet Letter. LC 92-44056. 1994. write for info. (0-88682-588-1) Creative Ed.

Stafford, Kim R. We Got Here Together. Frasier, Debra, illus. LC 93-9814. (gr. 5 up). 1994. write for info. (0-15-294891-0) HarBrace.

Stafford, Marilyn. Modeling: How to Make It in Modeling Without Having to Go to Modeling School. rev. ed. Terschluse, Ann, ed. Crane, Charles, illus. Lee, Sharon, intro. by. (Illus.). 150p. (gr. 7 up). 1990. Set. incl. video 55.90 (0-685-36259-0); video avail. MidCoast Comns.

Stafford, Mark. W. E. B. Dubois. King, Coretta Scott, intro. by. LC 89-9705. (Illus.). 128p. (Orig.). (gr. 5 up). 1989. lib. bdg. 17.95 (1-55546-582-X); pap. 9.95 (0-7910-0238-1) Chelsea Hse.

Stafford, Patricia. Your Two Brains. Tunney, Linda, illus. LC 85-28575. 96p. (gr. 3-7). 1986. SBE 13.95 (0-689-31142-7, Atheneum Child Bk) Macmillan Child Grp.

Stafford, Patricia A. Dreaming & Dreams. LC 91-22898. (Illus.). 64p. (gr. 3-7). 1992. 12.95 (0-689-31658-5, Atheneum Child Bk) Macmillan Child Grp.

Stafford, Shirley, jt. auth. see Packard, Ann.

Stafford, Tim. Do You Sometimes Feel Like a Nobody? 144p. 1991. pap. 7.99 (0-310-71131-2, Campus Life) Zondervan.
—John Porter in Big Trouble. (Illus.). 32p. (gr. 2-8). 1990. 11.95 (0-7459-1807-7) Lion USA.
—Love, Sex & the Whole Person: Everything You Want to Know. 280p. 1991. pap. 9.99 (0-310-71181-9, Campus Life) Zondervan.

Stafford, Tim, jt. auth. see Dravecky, Dave.

Stafford, Tim, jt. auth. see Kesler, Jay.

Stafford, W. The Animal that Drank up Sound. Frasier, D., illus. 1992. 13.95 (0-15-203563-X, HB Juv Bks) HarBrace.

Stafford, William, jt. auth. see Dunning, Stephen.

Stagg, Mildred A. & Lamb, Cecile. Song of the Seed. Faltico, Mary L., illus. 28p. (ps). 1992. 2.50 (0-87403-956-8, 24-03596) Standard Pub.

Stahl, Dean. Dolphins. 32p. 1991. 22.75 (0-89565-718-X); 15.95s.p. (0-685-55051-6) Childs World.

Stahl, Hilda. Big Trouble for Roxie. Griffin, Ted, ed. 160p. (gr. 4-7). 1992. pap. 3.99 (0-89107-658-1) Good News.
—The Case of the Missing Money. LC 86-72124. 128p. (gr. 3-6). 1987. pap. 3.95 (0-89636-227-2, Chariot Bks) Cook.
—Chelsea & the Alien Invasion. LC 93-8294. 160p. (Orig.). (gr. 6-9). 1993. pap. 3.99 (0-89107-749-9, Crossway Bks) Good News.
—Chelsea & the Outrageous Phone Bill. Griffin, Ted, ed. 160p. (gr. 4-7). 1992. pap. 3.99 (0-89107-657-3) Good News.
—Chelsea's Special Gift. LC 92-37203. 160p. (gr. 4-7). 1993. 3.99 (0-89107-712-X, Crossway Bks) Good News.
—Daisy Punkin. Bishop, Lila, ed. 128p. (gr. 2-5). 1991. pap. 4.99 (0-89107-617-4) Good News.
—Daisy Punkin: The Bratty Brother. Bishop, Lila, ed. 128p. (gr. 2-5). 1992. pap. 4.99 (0-89107-662-X) Good News.
—Elizabeth Gail & Double Trouble, No. 11. 128p. 1989. pap. 4.99 (0-8423-0801-6) Tyndale.
—Elizabeth Gail & the Dangerous Double, No. 4. 128p. (gr. 5 up). 1988. 4.99 (0-8423-0742-7) Tyndale.

—Elizabeth Gail & the Great Canoe Conspiracy. 1991. PLB 4.99 (0-8423-0815-6) Tyndale.
—Elizabeth Gail & the Handsome Stranger, No. 15. 128p. pap. 4.99 (0-8423-0806-7) Tyndale.
—Elizabeth Gail & the Holiday Mystery. 128p. 1989. pap. 4.99 (0-8423-0802-4) Tyndale.
—Elizabeth Gail & the Missing Love Letters, No. 13. 128p. 1989. pap. 4.99 (0-8423-0807-5) Tyndale.
—Elizabeth Gail & the Music Camp Romance. 128p. 1989. pap. 4.99 (0-8423-0808-3) Tyndale.
—Elizabeth Gail & the Mystery at the Johnson Farm, No. 1. 128p. (gr. 5 up). 1988. 4.99 (0-8423-0739-7) Tyndale.
—Elizabeth Gail & the Mystery of the Hidden Key, No. 20. (gr. 4-7). 1992. pap. 4.99 (0-8423-0816-4) Tyndale.
—Elizabeth Gail & the Secret Box, No. 2. 128p. (gr. 5 up). 1988. 4.99 (0-8423-0740-0) Tyndale.
—Elizabeth Gail & the Secret Love, No. 16. 128p. pap. 4.99 (0-8423-0809-1) Tyndale.
—Elizabeth Gail & the Secret of the Gold Charm, No. 21. (gr. 4-7). 1992. pap. 4.99 (0-8423-0817-2) Tyndale.
—Elizabeth Gail & the Silent Piano, No. 10. 128p. (gr. 3-9). 1989. pap. 4.99 (0-8423-0810-5) Tyndale.
—Elizabeth Gail & the Strange Birthday Party. 128p. 1989. pap. 4.99 (0-8423-0803-2) Tyndale.
—Elizabeth Gail & the Teddy Bear Mystery. (gr. 3-9). 1979. pap. 4.99 (0-8423-0722-2) Tyndale.
—Elizabeth Gail & the Teddy Bear Mystery, No. 3. 128p. (gr. 5 up). 1988. 4.99 (0-8423-0811-3) Tyndale.
—Elizabeth Gail & the Terrifying News. 128p. 1989. pap. 4.99 (0-8423-0812-1) Tyndale.
—Elizabeth Gail & Time for Love. 128p. 1989. pap. 4.99 (0-8423-0813-X) Tyndale.
—Elizabeth Gail & Trouble at Sandhill Ranch. 128p. 1989. pap. 4.99 (0-8423-0814-8) Tyndale.
—Elizabeth Gail & Trouble from the Past. 128p. 1989. pap. 4.99 (0-8423-0804-0) Tyndale.
—Hannah & the Snowy Hideaway. LC 93-8295. 160p. (Orig.). (gr. 6-9). 1993. pap. 3.99 (0-89107-748-0, Crossway Bks) Good News.
—Hannah & the Special 4th of July. Griffin, Ted, ed. 160p. (gr. 4-7). 1992. pap. 3.99 (0-89107-660-3) Good News.
—Hannah's Dangerous Mystery. LC 92-43994. 160p. (gr. 4-7). 1993. pap. 3.99 (0-89107-714-6, Crossway Bks) Good News.
—Kathy's Baby-Sitting Hassle. Griffin, Ted, ed. 160p. (gr. 4-7). 1992. pap. 3.99 (0-89107-659-X) Good News.
—Kathy's New Brother. LC 92-9135. 160p. (gr. 4-7). 1992. pap. 3.99 (0-89107-682-4, Crossway Bks) Good News.
—Kayla O'Brian & the Dangerous Journey. LC 90-80618. 128p. (Orig.). (gr. 4-7). 1990. pap. 4.95 (0-89107-577-1, Crossway Bks) Good News.
—Kayla O'Brian & the Runaway Orphans. Griffin, Ted, ed. 128p. (gr. 4-7). 1991. pap. 4.95 (0-89107-631-X) Good News.
—Kayla O'Brian: Trouble at Bitter Creek Ranch. 128p. (Orig.). (gr. 4-7). 1991. pap. 4.95 (0-89107-611-5) Good News.
—A Made-over Chelsea. 160p. (gr. 4-7). 1992. pap. 3.99 (0-89107-683-2, Crossway Bks) Good News.
—The Missing Newspaper Caper. LC 86-71178. 128p. (gr. 4-6). 1987. pap. 3.95 (0-89636-221-3, Chariot Bks) Cook.
—Mystery at Bellwood Estate. LC 92-41738. 160p. (gr. 4-7). 1993. pap. 3.99 (0-89107-713-8, Crossway Bks) Good News.
—The Mystery at the Wheeler Place. LC 85-73456. 128p. (Orig.). (gr. 4-6). 1986. pap. 3.95 (0-89636-203-5, Chariot Bks) Cook.
—No Friends for Hannah. LC 92-13272. 160p. (gr. 4-7). 1992. pap. 3.99 (0-89107-684-0, Crossway Bks) Good News.
—Roxie & the Red Rose Mystery. LC 92-4851. 160p. (gr. 4-7). 1992. pap. 3.99 (0-89107-681-6, Crossway Bks) Good News.
—Roxie's Mall Madness. LC 93-22575. 160p. (Orig.). (gr. 6-9). 1993. pap. 3.99 (0-89107-753-7, Crossway Bks) Good News.
—Sadie Rose & the Champion Sharpshooter. Griffin, Ted, ed. 128p. (gr. 4-7). 1991. pap. 4.99 (0-89107-630-1) Good News.
—Sadie Rose & the Cottonwood Creek Orphan. LC 88-71808. 128p. (gr. 4-7). 1989. pap. 4.99 (0-89107-513-5, Crossway Bks) Good News.
—Sadie Rose & the Daring Escape. LC 88-70496. 144p. (gr. 4-7). 1988. pap. 4.99 (0-89107-492-9, Crossway Bks) Good News.
—Sadie Rose & the Double Secret. LC 89-25423. 124p. (gr. 4-7). 1990. pap. 4.99 (0-89107-546-1) Good News.
—Sadie Rose & the Impossible Birthday Wish. 128p. 1992. pap. write for info. (0-89107-685-9, Crossway Bks) Good News.
—Sadie Rose & the Mad Fortune Hunters. LC 90-80619. 128p. (Orig.). (gr. 4-7). 1990. pap. 4.99 (0-89107-578-X, Crossway Bks) Good News.
—Sadie Rose & the Mysterious Stranger. 128p. (Orig.). (gr. 6-9). 1993. pap. 4.99 (0-89107-747-2, Crossway Bks) Good News.
—Sadie Rose & the Outlaw Rustlers. LC 89-50331. 128p. (gr. 4-7). 1989. pap. 4.99 (0-89107-528-3, Crossway Bks) Good News.
—Sadie Rose & the Phantom Warrior. 128p. (Orig.). (gr. 4-7). 1991. pap. 4.95 (0-89107-612-3) Good News.

—Sadie Rose & the Secret Romance. Nahrstadt, Jennifer, ed. 128p. (gr. 4-7). 1992. pap. 4.99 (0-89107-661-1) Good News.
—Sendi Lee Mason & the Big Mistake. 128p. (Orig.). (gr. 1-4). 1991. pap. 4.95 (0-89107-613-1) Good News.
—Sendi Lee Mason & the Great Crusade. Bishop, Lila, ed. 128p. (gr. 2-5). 1991. pap. 4.99 (0-89107-632-8) Good News.
—Sendi Lee Mason & the Milk Carton Kids. LC 89-81253. 126p. (gr. 2-5). 1990. pap. 4.95 (0-89107-547-X) Good News.
—Sendi Lee Mason & the Stray Striped Cat. LC 90-80621. 128p. (Orig.). (gr. 2-5). 1990. pap. 4.95 (0-89107-580-1, Crossway Bks) Good News.
—Tim Avery's Secret. LC 85-70271. 128p. (gr. 4-6). 1986. pap. 3.95 (0-89636-213-2, Chariot Bks) Cook.
—Tough Choices for Roxie. LC 92-37055. 160p. (gr. 4 up). 1993. pap. 3.99 (0-89107-711-1, Crossway Bks) Good News.
—The Tyler Twins: Latchkey Kids. 128p. (Orig.). (gr. 6-8). 1988. 3.50 (0-8423-7628-3) Tyndale.
—The Tyler Twins, No. 3: Pet Show Panic. 144p. (gr. 4-7). 1990. pap. 4.99 (0-8423-7633-X) Tyndale.
—The Tyler Twins, No. 5: Tree House Hideaway. 128p. (gr. 4-7). 1990. pap. 4.99 (0-8423-7635-6) Tyndale.

Stahl, Robert J. Cooperative Learing in Social Studies: Making it Work in the Social Studies Classroom. (gr. 9-12). 1992. pap. 32.00 (0-201-81786-1) Addison-Wesley.

Stahler, Charles, jt. ed. see Wasserman, Debra.

Stain, Dan. Teddy Bears' Halloween Party. (gr. 1-7). 1989. pap. 2.50 (0-89954-962-4) Antioch Pub Co.

Stainer, Tom & Sutton, Harry. Cathedrals. McEwan, Joseph, illus. 32p. (gr. 4-6). 1992. pap. 4.95 (0-563-34161-0, BBC-Parkwest) Parkwest Pubns.
—The Greeks. McEwan, Joseph, illus. 25p. (gr. 4-6). 1992. pap. 4.95 (0-563-21174-1, BBC-Parkwest) Parkwest Pubns.
—The Vikings. Kesteven, Peter, illus. 32p. (gr. 4-6). 1992. pap. 4.95 (0-563-21356-6, BBC-Parkwest) Parkwest Pubns.

Staines, Bill. All God's Critters Got a Place in the Choir. Zemach, Margot, illus. LC 88-31696. 32p. (ps-2). 1989. 13.95 (0-525-44469-6, DCB) Dutton Child Bks.
—All God's Critters Got a Place in the Choir. Zemach, Margot, illus. 32p. (ps-2). 1993. pap. 4.99 (0-14-054838-6) Puffin Bks.
—River. Spohn, Kate, illus. LC 93-27864. 1994. 13.99 (0-670-85353-4) Viking Child Bks.

Staines, Shirley. Early Learning Games. (Illus.). 96p. (gr. 1-6). 1991. pap. 4.95 (0-7063-6771-5, Pub. by Ward Lock UK) Sterling.

Stair, Lila B. Careers in Marketing. LC 90-50728. 160p. (gr. 9 up). 1991. 16.95 (0-8442-8142-5, VGM Career Bks); pap. 12.95 (0-8442-8143-3, VGM Career Bks) NTC Pub Grp.

Stake, Fran. The Animals Talk to One Another: A Christmas Folktale Retold & Illustrated by Fran Stake. STake, Fran, illus. 20p. (ps). 1993. Set with painting. 1100.00 (0-9619075-0-9) Stake Studio.

Staley, Gregory A., ed. Ancient Elections & Politics: Mini-Lessons. 17p. (Orig.). (gr. 9-12). 1991. 1.40 (0-939507-02-1, B316) Amer Classical.

Stallings, Pat. Puzzling Your Way into Algebra. new ed. Stallings, Pat, illus. (gr. 7-10). 1978. pap. text ed. 7.95 (0-918932-58-0) Activity Resources.
—Puzzling Your Way into Geometry. new ed. (Illus.). (gr. 9-12). 1978. pap. text ed. 7.95 (0-918932-52-1) Activity Resources.

Stallman, Birdie. Learning about Dragons. Halverson, Lydia, illus. LC 81-4746. 48p. (gr. 2-6). 1981. pap. 4.95 (0-516-46531-7) Childrens.

Stallone, Linda. The Flood That Came to Grandma's House. Schooley, Joan, illus. LC 91-33955. 21p. (ps-3). 1992. 9.95 (0-912975-02-4) Upshur Pr. Newsclips of hurricane disasters never tell the whole story. This year, more than ever, kids need to know about hurricanes & the entire process of recovery from destruction that forces thousands to flee their homes. THE FLOOD THAT CAME TO GRANDMA'S HOUSE has been reviewed enthusiastically by newspapers from Corning, New York down to St. Petersburg, Florida. "Teachers & parents find in its pages a way to explain to children what happens during a natural disaster." (Bloomsburg, PA Press Enterprise.) Used in hundreds of schools & loved by children or anyone who has experienced a flood, the book helps young children think through what could be traumatic or confusing. The story begins with the first days of rain from Hurricane Agnes & pulls the

reader through the drama as the citizens attempt to sandbag the river, but are finally forced to evacuate. Humorous yet realistic illustrations show children exactly what happens inside a house that is filled with water & the mess left in its wake. A true story, simply told & lovingly illustrated. Captures a slice of history, while it helps young children understand why a flood isn't "fun" water. "Reassures how natural disasters are handled." "Satisfies curiosity of young readers." Order from: Upshur Press, P.O. Box 609, Dallas, PA 18612; or call 1-(800)-777-1461 or (717) -675-8835.
Publisher Provided Annotation.

Stallones, Jared. Zebulon Pike & the Explorers of the American West. Goetzmann, William H., ed. Collins, Michael, intro. by. (Illus.). 112p. (gr. 5 up). 1992. lib. bdg. 18.95 (0-7910-1317-0) Chelsea Hse.
Stamler, Suzanne. Three Wise Birds. Nolan, Gary, illus. (gr. 1-6). 1976. pap. 7.95 (0-913546-68-2) Dharma Pub.
Stamm, Claus. Three Strong Women. Tseng, Jean & Tseng, Mou-sien, illus. 32p. (gr. 2-5). 1990. pap. 12.95 (0-670-83323-1) Viking Child Bks.
Stamm, Claus & Mizumura, Kazue. Three Strong Women. Tseng, Jean & Tseng, Mou-sien, illus. LC 92-25331. 1993. pap. 4.99 (0-14-054530-1) Puffin Bks.
Stamper. More Night Frights. 1993. pap. 2.95 (0-590-46045-5) Scholastic Inc.
Stamper, J. B. Even More Tales for the Midnight Hour. 112p. (gr. 4 up). 1992. pap. 2.75 (0-590-44143-4, Point) Scholastic Inc.
—More Tales for the Midnight Hour. 1992. pap. 2.95 (0-590-45344-0, Point) Scholastic Inc.
—Night Frights: Thirteen Scary Stories. (gr. 4-7). 1993. pap. 2.95 (0-590-46046-3) Scholastic Inc.
—Still More Tales for the Midnight Hour. 1992. pap. 2.95 (0-685-53518-5, Point) Scholastic Inc.
—Tales for the Midnight Hour. 128p. 1992. pap. 2.95 (0-590-45343-2, Point) Scholastic Inc.
Stamper, Jamie. Kitty the Raccoon. 2nd ed. Heinonen, Susan, illus. 50p. (gr. k-10). 1989. pap. 8.95 (0-9623072-0-3) S Ink WA.
Stamper, Judith. Christmas Holiday Grab Bag. Regan, Dana, illus. LC 92-13226. 48p. (gr. 2-5). 1992. PLB 11.89 (0-8167-2908-5); pap. text ed. 3.95 (0-8167-2909-3) Troll Assocs.
—Easter Holiday Grab Bag. Durrell, Julie, illus. LC 92-10132. 48p. (gr. 2-5). 1992. PLB 11.89 (0-8167-2912-3); pap. text ed. 3.95 (0-8167-2913-1) Troll Assocs.
—Five Funny Frights. Raglin, Tim, illus. LC 92-44538. (gr. 4 up). 1993. pap. 2.95 (0-590-46416-7) Scholastic Inc.
—Halloween Holiday Grab Bag. Girouard, Patrick, illus. LC 92-13224. 48p. (gr. 2-5). 1992. PLB 11.89 (0-8167-2904-2); pap. text ed. 3.95 (0-8167-2905-0) Troll Assocs.
—Thanksgiving Holiday Grab Bag. Iosa, Ann, illus. LC 92-13420. 48p. (gr. 2-5). 1992. PLB 11.89 (0-8167-2906-9); pap. text ed. 3.95 (0-8167-2907-7) Troll Assocs.
—Valentine Holiday Grab Bag. Weissman, Bari & Garcia, T. R., illus. LC 92-13225. 48p. (gr. 2-5). 1992. PLB 11.89 (0-8167-2910-7); pap. text ed. 3.95 (0-8167-2911-5) Troll Assocs.
—What's It Like to Be a Bus Driver. Garcia, T. R., illus. LC 89-34388. 32p. (gr. k-3). 1990. lib. bdg. 10.89 (0-8167-1795-8); pap. text ed. 2.95 (0-8167-1796-6) Troll Assocs.
—What's It Like to Be a Dentist. Gustafson, Dana, illus. LC 89-34392. 32p. (gr. k-3). 1989. lib. bdg. 10.89 (0-8167-1799-0); pap. text ed. 2.95 (0-8167-1800-8) Troll Assocs.
—What's It Like to Be a Veterinarian. Ramsey, Marcy D., illus. LC 89-34391. 32p. (gr. k-3). 1990. lib. bdg. 10.89 (0-8167-1817-2); pap. text ed. 2.95 (0-8167-1818-0) Troll Assocs.
Stamper, Judith B. New Friends in a New Land: A Thanksgiving Story. Jezierski, Chet, illus. LC 92-18072. 32p. (gr. 2-5). 1992. PLB 21.34 (0-8114-7213-2) Raintree Steck-V.
—Save the Everglades! Davis, Allen, illus. LC 92-18085. 56p. (gr. 2-5). 1992. PLB 21.34 (0-8114-7219-1) Raintree Steck-V.
—Totally Terrific Valentine Party Book. 1990. pap. 1.95 (0-590-41713-4) Scholastic Inc.
—Truck Driver. Ulrich, George, illus. LC 88-10039. 32p. (gr. k-3). 1989. PLB 10.89 (0-8167-1424-X); pap. text ed. 2.95 (0-8167-1425-8) Troll Assocs.
—Zoo Worker. Garry-McCord, Kathleen, illus. LC 88-10046. 32p. (gr. k-3). 1989. PLB 10.89 (0-8167-1440-1); pap. text ed. 2.95 (0-8167-1441-X) Troll Assocs.
Stamper, Laura. Getting Help, Gaining Hope: The Second & Third Steps for Teens. 20p. 1990. pap. 1.75 (0-925190-10-1, F911021 C) Deaconess Pr.

—Searching & Sharing: The Fourth & Fifth Steps for Teens. 30p. 1991. pap. 1.75 (0-925190-19-5, F911124 C) Deaconess Pr.
—Taking the First Step: Being Honest with Yourself. 14p. pap. 1.75 (0-925190-03-9, F911007 C) Deaconess Pr.
Stamschror, Robert, ed. see Doolittle, Robert.
Stamschror, Robert P., ed. see Doolittle, Robert.
Stamschror, Robert P., ed. see Hakowski, Maryann.
Stamschror, Robert P., ed. see O'Connell, Frances H.
Stamschror, Robert P., ed. see Rice, Wayne & Yaconelli, Mike.
Stamschror, Robert P., ed. see Zanzig, Thomas.
Stan, S. The Navajo. (Illus.). 32p. (gr. 5-8). 1989. lib. bdg. 15.94 (0-86625-380-7); lib. bdg. 11.95s.p. (0-685-58580-8) Rourke Corp.
—The Ojibwe. (Illus.). 32p. (gr. 5-8). 1989. lib. bdg. 15.94 (0-86625-381-5); 11.95 (0-685-58581-6) Rourke Corp.
Stanchfield, Jo M. Patterns, Level 3, Bk. B. LC 77-83336. (Illus.). (gr. 9). 1979. pap. 20.08 (0-395-25230-X); tchr's. guides 16.72 (0-395-25231-8); skillbook 5.08 (0-685-02303-6); tchr's. annotated skillbk 11.40 (0-395-25248-2) HM.
Stanchfield, Jo M., et al. Horizons, Level 1, Bk. A. LC 77-83336. (Illus.). (gr. 7). 1979. pap. 20.08 (0-395-25225-3); ancillaries avail. HM.
—Networks, Level 3, Bk. A. LC 77-83336. (Illus.). (gr. 9). 1979. pap. 20.08 (0-395-25235-0); tchr's. guide 16.72 (0-395-25235-0); skillbk 11.08 (0-395-25241-5); tchr's. annot ed. skillbk 11.40 (0-395-25247-4) HM.
—Paces, Level 2, Bk. B. LC 77-83336. (Illus.). (gr. 8). 1979. pap. 20.08 (0-395-25228-8); tchr's. guide 16.72 (0-395-25234-2); tchr's. annot ed. skillbk 11.40 (0-395-25246-6); skillbk 11.08 (0-395-25240-7) HM.
—Summits, Level 1, Bk. B. LC 77-83336. (Illus.). (gr. 7). 1979. pap. 20.08 (0-395-25226-1); tchr's. guide 16.72 (0-395-25232-6); tchr's. annot ed. skillbk 11.40 (0-395-25244-X) HM.
—Tempos, Level 2, Bk. A. LC 77-83336. (Illus.). (gr. 8). 1979. pap. 20.08 (0-395-25227-X); tchr's. guide 16.72 (0-395-25233-4); skillbk 11.08 (0-395-25239-3); tchr's. annotated ed. ski 11.40 (0-395-25245-8) HM.
Stancil, Eva. Kids on Camera: A Comprehensive Guide to Child Modeling & Acting. LC 90-38486. (Illus.). 160p. 1990. pap. 14.95 (1-56145-003-0) Peachtree Pubs.
Stancil, Rosemary D. & Wilkins, Lorela N. Kids' Simply Scrumptious Microwaving. 1987. pap. 7.95 (0-449-90226-9, Columbine) Fawcett.
—Kids' Simply Scrumptious Microwaving. (Illus.). 99p. (Orig.). (gr. k-8). 1985. pap. 6.95 (0-9615522-0-4) Kitchen Classics.
Standard Educational Corporation Staff. New Standard Encyclopedia, 20 vols. Downey, Douglas W., et al, eds. LC 92-5529. (gr. 6-12). 1993. Set. write for info. (0-87392-198-4) Standard Ed.
—New Standard Encyclopedia. Downey, Douglas W., et al, eds. LC 93-7724. (Illus.). (gr. 6-12). 1994. Set. write for info. (0-87392-199-2) Standard Ed.
Standard Publishing Staff. First Christmas: A Picture Window Book. (ps). 1992. 6.99 (0-87403-883-9) Standard Pub.
—Jonah & the Big Fish: A Picture Window Book. (ps). 1992. 6.99 (0-87403-882-0) Standard Pub.
—Noah's Ark Picture Window Book. (ps). 1992. 6.99 (0-87403-884-7) Standard Pub.
—Story of Creation: A Picture Window Book. (ps). 1992. 6.99 (0-87403-881-2, 24-03791) Standard Pub.
Standiford, Natalie. The Best Little Monkeys in the World. Knight, Hilary, illus. LC 86-15425. 48p. (gr. 1-3). 1987. lib. bdg. 7.99 (0-394-98616-4); 3.50 (0-394-88616-X) Random Bks Yng Read.
—The Bravest Dog Ever: The True Story of Balto. Cook, Donald, tr. LC 89-3465. (Illus.). 47p. (Orig.). (gr. 1-3). 1989. PLB 7.99 (0-394-99695-X); pap. 3.50 (0-394-89695-5) Random Bks Yng Read.
—Space Dog & Roy. 80p. 1990. pap. 2.95 (0-380-75953-5, Camelot) Avon.
—Space Dog & the Pet Show. 80p. 1990. pap. 2.95 (0-380-75954-3, Camelot) Avon.
Standiford, Natalie, retold by. The Headless Horseman. Cook, Donald, illus. LC 90-53228. 48p. (Orig.). (ps-2). 1992. PLB 7.99 (0-679-91241-X); pap. 3.50 (0-679-81241-5) Random Bks Yng Read.
Standing, E. M. Maria Montessori: Her Life & Work. McDermott, John J., intro. by. (Illus.). 382p. (gr. 9-12). 1989. pap. 9.95 (0-452-26090-6, Plume) NAL-Dutton.
Standish, Burt L. Frank Merriwell Down South. Rudman, Jack, ed. (gr. 9 up). Date not set. 9.95 (0-8373-9305-1); pap. 3.95 (0-8373-9005-2) F Merriwell. Postponed.
—Frank Merriwell in Europe. Rudman, Jack, ed. (gr. 9 up). Date not set. 9.95 (0-8373-9308-6); pap. 3.95 (0-8373-9008-7) F Merriwell. Postponed.
—Frank Merriwell's Bravery. Rudman, Jack, ed. (gr. 9 up). Date not set. 9.95 (0-8373-9306-X); pap. 3.95 (0-8373-9006-0) F Merriwell. Postponed.
—Frank Merriwell's Chums. Rudman, Jack, ed. (gr. 9 up). 1970. 9.95 (0-8373-9302-7); pap. 3.95 (0-8373-9002-8) F Merriwell.
—Frank Merriwell's Foes. Rudman, Jack, ed. (gr. 9 up). 1970. 9.95 (0-8373-9303-5); pap. 3.95 (0-8373-9003-6) F Merriwell.
—Frank Merriwell's Hunting Tour. Rudman, Jack, ed. (gr. 9 up). Date not set. 9.95 (0-8373-9307-8); pap. 3.95 (0-8373-9007-9) F Merriwell. Postponed.

—Frank Merriwell's Schooldays. Rudman, Jack, ed. (gr. 9 up). 1970. 9.95 (0-8373-9309-4); pap. 3.95 (0-8373-9009-5) F Merriwell.
—Frank Merriwell's Sports Afield. Rudman, Jack, ed. (gr. 9 up). Date not set. 9.95 (0-8373-9310-8); pap. 3.95 (0-8373-9010-9) F Merriwell. Postponed.
—Frank Merriwell's Trip West. Rudman, Jack, ed. (gr. 9 up). Date not set. 9.95 (0-8373-9304-3); pap. 3.95 (0-8373-9004-4) F Merriwell. Postponed.
Standish, Marilyn, jt. auth. see Landes, William-Alan.
Standley, Marianne & Richards, Joanne. School Spirit & Self-Esteem Bulletin Boards. (Illus.). 64p. (gr. k-6). 1986. pap. text ed. 6.95 (0-86530-135-2, IP-112-4) Incentive Pubns.
Standley, Marianne, jt. auth. see Richards, Joanne.
Standley, Marianne V., jt. auth. see Richards, Joanne.
Standring, Gillian. Pandas. (Illus.). 32p. (gr. k-4). 1991. 12.40 (0-531-18397-1, Pub. by Bookwright Pr) Watts.
—Wolves. (Illus.). 32p. (gr. 2-5). 1992. PLB 12.40 (0-531-18452-8, Pub. by Bookwright Pr) Watts.
Stanek, Lou W. Katy Did. 256p. (Orig.). (gr. 6 up). 1992. pap. 2.99 (0-380-76170-X, Flare) Avon.
Stanek, Muriel. All Alone after School. Fay, Ann, ed. Owens, Gay, illus. LC 84-17243. 32p. (gr. 1-4). 1985. PLB 11.95 (0-8075-0278-2) A Whitman.
—Don't Hurt Me, Mama. Fay, Ann, ed. LC 83-16771. (Illus.). 32p. (gr. 1-3). 1983. PLB 11.95 (0-8075-1689-9) A Whitman.
—I Speak English for My Mom. Tucker, Kathleen, ed. Friedman, Judith, illus. LC 88-20546. 32p. (gr. 2-5). 1989. 11.95 (0-8075-3659-8) A Whitman.
—I Won't Go Without a Father. Mill, Eleanor, illus. LC 78-188435. 32p. (gr. 1-3). 1972. PLB 11.95 (0-8075-3524-9) A Whitman.
—My Mom Can't Read. Levine, Abby, ed. Rogers, Jacqueline, illus. LC 86-1637. 32p. (gr. 1-4). 1986. 11.95 (0-8075-5343-3) A Whitman.
—Starting School. Fay, Ann, ed. De Luna, Tony & De Luna, Betty, illus. LC 81-297. 32p. (ps-1). 1981. PLB 10.95 (0-8075-7617-4) A Whitman.
—We Came from Vietnam. Fay, Ann, ed. McMahon, W. Franklin, illus. LC 84-29927. 48p. (gr. 1-6). 1985. PLB 10.50 (0-8075-8699-4) A Whitman.
Stanford, Gene. McGraw-Hill Vocabulary, Bk. 3. 2nd ed. (Illus.). 128p. 1981. pap. text ed. 6.80 (0-07-060773-7) McGraw.
Stanford, Sylvia. I'm Growing. (Illus.). (ps). 1986. 4.95 (0-8054-4167-0) Broadman.
Stang, Aaron, ed. Rock Deference Library: Hot Metal Guitar. 96p. (Orig.). 1993. pap. text ed. 19.95 (0-89898-566-8) CPP Belwin.
—Rock Reference Library: Classic Blues - Rock Guitar. 128p. (Orig.). 1993. pap. text ed. 12.95 (0-89898-569-2) CPP Belwin.
—Rock Reference Library: Hot Rock Guitar Hits. 128p. (Orig.). 1993. pap. text ed. 12.95 (0-89898-567-6) CPP Belwin.
—The Yuletide Guitar Songbook. 48p. (Orig.). 1993. pap. text ed. 8.95 (0-89898-640-0) CPP Belwin.
Stang, Aaron, ed. see Berle, Arnie.
Stang, Aaron, ed. see Brooks, Garth.
Stang, Aaron, ed. see Elden, Lucky.
Stang, Aaron, ed. see Gluklikh, Alexander.
Stang, Aaron, ed. see Griggs, John & Barbosa-Lima, Carlos.
Stang, Aaron, ed. see Morgen, Howard.
Stang, Aaron, ed. see Sokolow, Fred.
Stang, Aaron, ed. see ZZ Top Staff.
Stang, Jean. Crystals & Crystal Gardens You Can Grow. (Illus.). (ps-3). 1990. PLB 12.90 (0-531-10889-9) Watts.
Stangl, Jean. Fingerlings: Finger Puppet Fun. (ps-3). 1986. pap. 8.95 (0-8224-3061-4) Fearon Teach Aids.
—Flannel Graphs: Flannel Board Fun. (ps-3). 1986. pap. 9.95 (0-8224-3060-6) Fearon Teach Aids.
—Gardening Fun. (gr. k-3). 1991. pap. 10.95 (0-8224-3381-8) Fearon Teach Aids.
—H20 Science. (gr. 3-6). 1990. pap. 10.95 (0-8224-3604-3) Fearon Teach Aids.
—Is Your Storytale Dragging? (ps-3). 1988. pap. 9.95 (0-8224-3904-2) Fearon Teach Aids.
—Magic Mixtures. (ps-3). 1986. pap. 8.95 (0-8224-4377-5) Fearon Teach Aids.
—Paper Stories. LC 84-60238. (ps-3). 1984. pap. 10.95 (0-8224-5402-5) Fearon Teach Aids.
—Recycling Activities for the Primary Grades. (ps-3). 1993. pap. 10.95 (0-86653-938-7) Fearon Teach Aids.
—Science Toolbox: Making & Using the Tools of Science. LC 93-29389. (ps-3). 1993. 17.95 (0-8306-4605-1); pap. 9.95 (0-8306-4352-4) TAB Bks.
—The Tools of Science: Ideas & Activities for Guiding Young Scientists. rev. ed. (Illus.). 160p. 1989. 16.95 (0-8306-9216-9); pap. 8.95 (0-8306-3216-6) TAB Bks.
Stangl, Jean, jt. auth. see Shelly, Walt.
Staniforth, Maxwell, tr. see Marcus Aurelius.
Stanish, Bob. Accents & Ascendings. 144p. (gr. 3-8). 1990. 11.95 (0-86653-566-7, GA1155) Good Apple.
—The Ambidextrous Mind Book. 144p. (gr. 2-8). 1989. 11.95 (0-86653-502-0, GA1092) Good Apple.
—Connecting Rainbows. 96p. (gr. 3-12). 1982. 9.95 (0-86653-081-9, GA 426) Good Apple.
—Creative Activity Cards. 96p. (gr. 3-8). 1991. 10.95 (0-86653-613-2, GA1332) Good Apple.
—Creativity for Kids Through Writing. (Illus.). 64p. (gr. 1 up). 1983. wkbk. 7.95 (0-86653-118-1, GA 486) Good Apple.
—The Giving Book. 112p. (gr. 3-8). 1988. 9.95 (0-86653-459-8, GA1065) Good Apple.

—Hippogriff Feathers. (gr. 3-12). 1981. 10.95 (0-86653-009-6, GA 237) Good Apple.

—I Believe in Unicorns. (gr. 3-8). 1979. 9.95 (0-916456-51-X, GA107) Good Apple.

—Lessons from the Hearthstone Traveler. 136p. (gr. 3-12). 1988. wkbk. 11.95 (0-86653-433-4, GA1043) Good Apple.

—Mindanderings. (Illus.). 112p. (gr. 4-9). 1990. 9.95 (0-86653-526-8, GA1140) Good Apple.

—Mindglow. Stanish, Jon, illus. 96p. (gr. 3-12). 1986. wkbk. 9.95 (0-86653-346-X, GA 693) Good Apple.

—A Monster's Shoe & the Cat. Stanish, Bob, illus. 44p. (gr. 1-4). 1983. pap. 9.95 tchr's. enrichment bk. (0-88047-018-6, 8303) DOK Pubs.

—Sunflowering. 92p. (gr. 4-12). 1977. 9.95 (0-916456-12-9, GA69) Good Apple.

—The Unconventional Invention Book. (gr. 3-12). 1981. 11.95 (0-86653-035-5, GA 263) Good Apple.

Stanish, Bob & Singletary, Carol. Inventioneering. Skiles, Janet, illus. 64p. (gr. 3-9). 1987. pap. 7.95 (0-86653-402-4, GA 1019) Good Apple.

Stanislaw, Mary Anne. Kalagas: The Wall Hangings of Southeast Asia. Stedman, Robert, photos by. 64p. (Orig.). (gr. 7 up). 1987. pap. 12.50 (0-9618445-0-7) Ainslies.

Stankowich, Mimi. A Child's Guide to Computers, 4 vols. Taylor, Karen & Arkle, Dave, illus. (ps-3). 1984. 3.95 ea. Bk. 1 (0-916881-00-8, ALP701) Bk. 2 (0-916881-01-6, ALP702) Bk. 3 (0-916881-02-4, ALP703) Bk. 4 (0-916881-03-2, ALP704) Advan Learning.

Stanley, Carol. Dog Walkers Club. (gr. 4 up). 1990. pap. 2.95 (0-380-75916-0, Camelot) Avon.

—The Last Great Summer. 1992. pap. 3.25 (0-590-45705-5, Point) Scholastic Inc.

Stanley, Diane. Birdsong Lullaby. Stanley, Diane, illus. LC 85-5654. 32p. (ps-2). 1985. 12.95 (0-688-05804-3) Morrow Jr Bks.

—Captain Whiz-Bang. Stanley, Diane, illus. LC 86-16432. 32p. (ps-2). 1987. 12.95 (0-688-06226-1); lib. bdg. 12.88 (0-688-06227-X, Morrow Jr Bks) Morrow Jr Bks.

—The Conversation Club. Stanley, Diane, illus. LC 83-739. 32p. (ps-2). 1983. RSBE 12.95 (0-02-786740-4, Macmillan Child Bk) Macmillan Child Grp.

—The Conversation Club. Stanley, Diane, illus. LC 89-18665. 32p. (gr. k-2). 1990. pap. 3.95 (0-689-71401-7, Aladdin) Macmillan Child Grp.

—A Country Tale. Stanley, Diane, illus. LC 84-14399. 32p. (gr. k-3). 1985. RSBE 12.95 (0-02-786780-3, Four Winds) Macmillan Child Grp.

—Fortune. Stanley, Diane, illus. LC 88-13204. 32p. (ps-4). 1990. 12.95 (0-688-07210-0); PLB 12.88 (0-688-07211-9, Morrow Jr Bks) Morrow Jr Bks.

—The Gentleman & the Kitchen Maid. Nolan, Dennis, illus. LC 93-157. 1994. 13.99 (0-8037-1320-7); lib. bdg. 13.89 (0-8037-1321-5) Dial Bks Young.

—The Good-Luck Pencil. Degen, Bruce, illus. LC 85-13122. 32p. (gr. k-2). 1986. RSBE 12.95 (0-02-786800-1, Four Winds) Macmillan Child Grp.

—Moe the Dog in Tropical Paradise. Primavera, Elise, illus. 32p. (ps-3). 1992. 14.95 (0-399-22127-1, Putnam) Putnam Pub Group.

—Peter the Great. Stanley, Diane, illus. LC 85-13060. 32p. (gr. k-3). 1986. RSBE 14.95 (0-02-786790-0, Four Winds) Macmillan Child Grp.

—Peter the Great. Stanley, Diane, illus. LC 91-20089. 32p. (gr. 1-4). 1992. pap. 4.95 (0-689-71548-X, Aladdin) Macmillan Child Grp.

—Siegfried. (ps-3). 1991. 15.00 (0-553-07022-3) Bantam.

Stanley, Diane & Vennema, Peter. The Bard of Avon: The Story of William Shakespeare. Stanley, Diane, illus. LC 90-46564. 48p. (gr. 2 up). 1992. 15.00 (0-688-09108-3); PLB 14.93 (0-688-09109-1) Morrow Jr Bks.

—Charles Dickens: The Man Who Had Great Expectations. Stanley, Diane, illus. LC 91-41552. 48p. (gr. 2 up). 1993. 15.00 (0-688-09110-5); PLB 14.93 (0-688-09111-3) Morrow Jr Bks.

—Good Queen Bess: The Story of Queen Elizabeth I of England. Stanley, Diane, illus. LC 88-37501. 40p. (gr. 1-4). 1990. RSBE 15.95 (0-02-786810-9, Four Winds) Macmillan Child Grp.

—Shaka, King of the Zulus. Stanley, Stanley, illus. LC 87-27376. 40p. (gr. 1-4). 1988. 14.95 (0-688-07342-5); PLB 14.88 (0-688-07343-3, Morrow Jr Bks) Morrow Jr Bks.

—Shaka: King of the Zulus. Stanley, Diane, illus. LC 93-11730. 32p. (gr. k up). 1994. pap. 4.95 (0-688-13114-X, Mulberry) Morrow.

Stanley, Diane, illus. Cleopatra. Vennema, Peter. LC 93-27032. (Illus.). (gr. 4 up). 1994. pap. write for info. (0-688-10413-4); PLB write for info. (0-688-10414-2) Morrow Jr Bks.

Stanley, Fay. The Last Princess: The Story of Princess Ka'iulani of Hawai'i. Stanley, Diane, illus. LC 89-71445. 40p. (gr. 1-4). 1991. RSBE 15.95 (0-02-786785-4, Four Winds) Macmillan Child Grp.

Stanley, George E. Codebreaker Kids. 112p. (gr. 3-7). 1987. pap. 2.95 (0-380-75228-X, Camelot) Avon.

—The Codebreaker Kids Return. 128p. (gr. 3-7). 1989. pap. 2.50 (0-380-75608-0, Camelot) Avon.

—The Italian Spaghetti Mystery. 112p. (gr. 3 up). 1987. pap. 2.50 (0-380-75166-6, Camelot) Avon.

Stanley, Jerry. Children of the Dust Bowl: The True Story of the School at Weedpatch Camp. LC 92-323. (Illus.). 96p. (gr. 4 up). 1993. pap. 6.99 (0-517-88094-6) Crown Bks Yng Read.

—Children of the Dustbowl: The True Story of the School at Weedpatch Camp. LC 92-393. (Illus.). 96p. (gr. 4 up). 1992. 15.00 (0-517-58781-5); PLB 15.99 (0-517-58782-3) Crown Bks Yng Read.

Stanley, Jerry W. The Basketball Player's Training Diary. (gr. 7-12). 1988. plastic bdg. 7.95 (0-685-21918-6) Sports Diary Pub.

—The Football Player's Training Diary. 120p. (gr. 7-12). 1988. plastic bdg. 7.95 (0-685-24024-X) Sports Diary Pub.

—The Track & Field Training Diary: Your Personal Workout Record. (gr. 7-12). 1988. plastic bdg. 7.95 (0-685-44186-5) Sports Diary Pub.

—The Wrestler's Training Diary. 120p. (gr. 7-12). 1988. plastic bdg. 7.95 (0-685-21917-8) Sports Diary Pub.

Stanley, Lynn. Change of Heart. LC 90-61781. 168p. (gr. 4-7). 1990. pap. 6.00 (0-89109-298-6) NavPress.

—Reason For Living. LC 90-61782. 204p. (gr. 4-7). 1990. pap. 6.00 (0-89109-297-8) NavPress.

Stanley, Monty M. They Call Me a Delinquent. 91p. (Orig.). (gr. 5-12). 1989. 8.95 (0-9622667-1-X) Illini Pubns.

Stanley, Samuel & Oberg, Pearl. The Hunt. 32p. (gr. 5-9). 1976. pap. 1.50 (0-89992-047-0) Coun India Ed.

Stanley, Sandra C. Women in the Military. LC 93-22312. 1993. lib. bdg. 14.98 (0-671-75549-8, Messner); lib. bdg. 8.95 (0-671-75550-1, Messner) S&S Trade.

Stanley, Sanna. The Rains Are Coming. LC 92-1347. (Illus.). 24p. (ps up). 1993. 14.00 (0-688-10948-9); PLB 13.93 (0-688-10949-7) Greenwillow.

Stanley, Steven M. Earth & Life Through Time. 2nd ed. LC 88-16454. (Illus.). 704p. 1988. text ed. 45.95 (0-7167-1975-4) W H Freeman.

Stanley-Baker, Penny. Australia: On the Other Side of the World. Valat, Pierre-Marie, illus. LC 87-34523. 38p. (gr. k-5). 1988. 4.95 (0-944589-15-4, 154) Young Discovery Lib.

Stannard, Russell. The Time & Space of Uncle Albert. large type ed. Levers, John, illus. 176p. 1993. 13.95 (0-7451-1660-4, Galaxy Child Lrg Print) Chivers N Amer.

Stan-Padilla, Viento. Dream Feather. Stan-Padilla, Viento, illus. LC 87-17823. 60p. (Orig.). (gr. 7 up). 1987. pap. 10.95 (0-913990-57-4) Book Pub Co.

Stanphill, Ira F. Happiness Is the Lord. (Illus.). (gr. k-6). 1987. visualized song 5.99 (3-90117-011-1) CEF Press.

Stanton, Elizabeth & Stanton, Henry. Sometimes I Like to Cry. Rubin, Caroline, ed. Leyden, Richard, illus. LC 77-19131. 32p. (ps-2). 1978. PLB 13.95 (0-8075-7537-2) A Whitman.

Stanton, Henry, jt. auth. see Stanton, Elizabeth.

Stanton, P. The Yellow Star Sticker. Moser, Jeanie W., illus. (gr. k-3). Bk. & cassette 4.95 (0-932715-08-7) Evans FL.

Stanush, Barbara E. Texans: A Story of Texan Cultures for Young People. Grades 4-7. tchr's. guide 4.95 (0-86701-045-2) U of Tex Inst Tex Culture.

—Texans: The Story of Texan Cultures for Young People. Cosgrove, Jim, illus. LC 88-50983. 122p. (gr. 4-7). 1988. 19.95 (0-86701-040-1) U of Tex Inst Tex Culture.

Staple, Michele & Gamlin, Linda. The Random House Book of One Thousand One Questions & Answers about Animals. LC 90-30716. (Illus.). 160p. (Orig.). (gr. 3-7). 1990. lib. bdg. 13.00 (0-679-80731-4); pap. 12.99 (0-679-90731-9) Random Bks Yng Read.

Staplehurst, Graham. Gates of Mordor. Fenlon, Peter C., Jr., ed. McBride, Angus, illus. 32p. (Orig.). (gr. 10-12). 1987. pap. 6.00 (0-915795-81-7, 8105, Dist. by Berkley Pub Group) Iron Crown Ent Inc.

—Minas Tirith. Fenlon, Peter C., Jr., ed. McBride, Angus, illus. 192p. (gr. 10-12). 1988. 18.00 (1-55806-001-4, 8301) Iron Crown Ent Inc.

—Mouths of the Entwash. Fenlon, Peter C., Jr., ed. Sharp, Shawn & McBride, Angus, illus. 40p. (Orig.). (gr. 12). 1988. pap. 7.00 (1-55806-010-3, 8011) Iron Crown Ent Inc.

—The Phantom of the Northern Marches. Fenlon, Peter, ed. Horne, Daniel, illus. 32p. (Orig.). (gr. 10-12). 1986. pap. 6.00 (0-915795-47-7, 8102) Iron Crown Ent Inc.

—Robin Hood. Fenlon, Peter & Charlton, S. Coleman, eds. McBride, Angus, illus. 160p. (Orig.). (gr. 10-12). 1987. pap. 15.00 (0-915795-28-0, 1010) Iron Crown Ent Inc.

Stapler, Harry. Pioneers of Forest & City. Price, Susan & Nelson, Kelly, illus. Blanchard, James J. & Austin, Richard H.intro. by. LC 85-62817. 227p. (gr. 4-8). 1985. 12.00 (0-935719-00-8) MI Dept Hist.

Stapler, Sarah. Cordellia, Dance! LC 89-39352. (Illus.). 32p. (ps-3). 1990. 10.95 (0-8037-0792-4); PLB 10.89 (0-8037-0793-2) Dial Bks Young.

—Spruce the Moose Cuts Loose. (Illus.). 32p. (ps-3). 1992. 14.95 (0-399-21861-0, Putnam) Putnam Pub Group.

Staples, Danny & Mahoney, Carole. Flutes, Reeds, & Trumpets. LC 92-5165. (Illus.). 48p. (gr. 2-6). 1992. PLB 13.90 (1-56294-092-9) Millbrook Pr.

Staples, Donna. Arena Beach. LC 92-36302. 1993. 14.95 (0-395-65366-5) HM.

Staples, Suzanne F. Haveli. LC 92-29054. 1993. write for info. (0-06-798443-6) Knopf.

—Haveli. LC 92-29054. (Illus.). 272p. (gr. 7 up). 1993. 18.00 (0-679-84157-1) Knopf Bks Yng Read.

—Shabanu: Daughter of the Wind. LC 89-2714. (Illus.). 256p. (gr. 7 up). 1989. 18.00 (0-394-84815-2); lib. bdg. 18.99 (0-394-94815-7) Knopf Bks Yng Read.

Stapleton, John T. The Littlest Mermaid. Flanigan, Ruth J., illus. 24p. (ps-2). 1992. pap. 0.99 (1-56293-109-1) McClanahan Bk.

Star, Robin R. We Can, 2 vols. (gr. 4 up). 1980. Set. PLB 4.95 (0-685-00153-9) Vol. 1 88 pgs (0-88200-135-3, C2670) Vol. 2 98 pgs (0-88200-136-1, C2786) Alexander Graham.

Star Wars. The Adventures of Teebo: A Tale of Magic & Suspense. Johnston, Joe, illus. 48p. (gr. 2-7). 1984. lib. bdg. 5.99 (0-394-96568-X) Random Bks Yng Read.

Starboard Cove Publishing Staff, ed. see Davis, Marion M.

Starbuck, Marnie. The Gladimals Learn about Friendship. 16p. (ps-3). 1991. pap. text ed. 0.75 (1-56456-229-8) W Gladden Found.

—The Gladimals Learn about Grief. 16p. (ps-3). 1991. pap. text ed. 0.75 (1-56456-226-3) W Gladden Found.

—The Gladimals Learn about Responsibility. 1991. pap. text ed. 0.75 (1-56456-228-X) W Gladden Found.

—The Gladimals Learn Healthy Habits. 16p. (ps-3). 1991. pap. text ed. 0.75 (1-56456-227-1) W Gladden Found.

—The Gladimals Talk about Feelings. 16p. (ps-3). 1991. pap. text ed. 0.75 (1-56456-225-5) W Gladden Found.

Stark, Al. Australia: A Lucky Land. LC 87-13424. (Illus.). 152p. (gr. 5 up). 1988. RSBE 14.95 (0-87518-365-4, Dillon) Macmillan Child Grp.

—Zimbabwe: A Treasure of Africa. LC 85-6944. (Illus.). 160p. (gr. 5 up). 1986. RSBE 14.95 (0-87518-308-5, Dillon) Macmillan Child Grp.

Stark, Elizabeth, ed. see Moore, April.

Stark, Evan. Everything You Need to Know about Family Violence. rev. ed. (Illus.). 64p. (gr. 7-12). 1993. 13.95 (0-8239-1755-X) Rosen Group.

—Everything You Need to Know about Sexual Abuse. rev. ed. (Illus.). 64p. (gr. 7-12). 1993. 13.95 (0-8239-1611-1) Rosen Group.

—Everything You Need to Know about Street Gangs. (gr. 7-12). 1992. PLB 13.95 (0-8239-1319-8) Rosen Group.

Stark, Fred. Start Exploring Gray's Anatomy: A Fact-Filled Coloring Book. (Illus.). 128p. (Orig.). (gr. 2 up). 1991. pap. 8.95 (0-89471-863-0) Running Pr.

Stark, John. Haunted House Stories. (Illus.). 96p. (Orig.). 1988. pap. 1.95 (0-942025-17-2) Kidsbks.

Starkie, Walter, tr. see De Cervantes, Miguel.

Starkman, Neal. The Apple. Yasuki, Meredith, illus. LC 91-16800. 44p. (Orig.). (gr. 7-9). 1991. pap. 7.00 (0-935529-29-2) Comprehen Health Educ.

—The Boy & the Hat. LC 91-16798. 32p. (Orig.). (gr. 3). 1991. pap. text ed. 8.00 (0-935529-27-6) Comprehen Health Educ.

—Face to Face. Dinkelman, Craig, illus. (Orig.). (gr. 6-9). 1988. pap. 5.00 (0-935529-09-8) Comprehen Health Educ.

—The Forever Secret. Karas, G. Brian, illus. LC 91-16799. 50p. (Orig.). (gr. 5). 1991. pap. 9.00 (0-935529-28-4) Comprehen Health Educ.

—Personal Views. Gellos, Nancy, illus. LC 89-22302. 43p. (Orig.). (gr. 6-12). 1989. pap. 7.00 (0-935529-12-8) Comprehen Health Educ.

—The Quitters. Combs, Jonathan, illus. LC 91-16797. 28p. (Orig.). (gr. 4). 1991. pap. 7.00 (0-935529-26-8) Comprehen Health Educ.

—The Riddle. Sasaki, Ellen J., illus. LC 89-25405. 50p. (Orig.). (gr. 2). 1989. pap. 11.00 (0-935529-13-6) Comprehen Health Educ.

—Your Decision. Gellos, Nancy, illus. LC 88-71482. 118p. (Orig.). (gr. 9-12). 1988. pap. 13.00 (0-935529-10-1) Comprehen Health Educ.

—Z's Gift. Ellen, G. & Sasaki, Joy, illus. LC 88-71483. 52p. (Orig.). (gr. 4-6). 1988. pap. 7.00 (0-935529-08-X) Comprehen Health Educ.

Starlin, Jim. Batman: The Cult. Thorsland, Dan & O'Neil, Dennis, eds. Wrightson, Bernie, illus. Starlin, Jim, intro. by. (Illus.). 208p. (Orig.). 1991. pap. 14.95 (0-930289-85-4) DC Comics.

Starosta, Paul. The Bee. (Illus.). 28p. (ps-4). 1993. pap. 6.95 (0-88106-430-0) Charlesbridge Pub.

Starowitz, Anne M. The Day We Met Cindy. LC 88-8979. (Illus.). 16p. (gr. k-3). 1988. pap. 9.50 (0-930323-43-2, Kendall Green Pubns) Gallaudet Univ Pr.

Starr, Aloa. I Want to Know. Tyree, Michael, illus. (Orig.). (ps-6). 1990. pap. 7.00 (0-929686-02-0, Dist. by Aloa Starr) Temple Golden Pubns.

Starr, Constance. The Music Road, Bk. 3. 96p. 1985. pap. 7.95 (0-914425-02-1) Kingston Ellis.

Starr, Jerold M., ed. see Hass, Marv E.

Starr, Joyce R. Medal of Drought. 1994. write for info. (0-8050-3019-0) H Holt & Co.

Starr, Ringo, narrated by see Awdry, W.

Starr, Susan B. I Was Good to the Earth Today. Sterling, Terry S., illus. 32p. (ps-k). 1992. PLB 12.95 (0-9619556-0-0); pap. 5.95 (0-9619556-1-9) Starhse Pub.

Starry, Paul & Cleave, Andrew. Nature Search: Rain Forest. (gr. 4-7). 1992. 14.00 (0-89577-448-8) RD Assn.

—Nature Search: Underwater. Holmes, David, et al, illus. 32p. (gr. 4-7). 1992. 14.00 (0-89577-449-6) RD Assn.

Starwatcher Graphics Staff, tr. see Charlier, J. M.

Staskowski, Andrea. Movie Musicals. (Illus.). 80p. (gr. 5-12). 1992. PLB 18.95 (0-8225-1639-X) Lerner Pubns.

—Science Fiction Movies. (Illus.). 80p. (gr. 5 up). 1991. PLB 18.95 (0-8225-1638-1) Lerner Pubns.

Stassun, Peter G., jt. auth. see Feild, William B., Jr.

State of Being Staff. Some States of Being. State of Being Staff, illus. 22p. (Orig.). (gr. 7 up) 1988. pap. 2.00 (*0-929611-03-9*) Plutonium Pr.

Staton, Hilarie N. Think & Write: Activities for Grades 4-6. (Illus.). 120p. (Orig.). (gr. 4-6). 1984. pap. 12.95 (*0-673-18028-X*) GdYrBks.

Staub, Frank. America's Prairies. LC 93-7841. 1993. 19.95 (*0-87614-781-3*) Carolrhoda Bks.

—A Day in the Life of a Ski Patroller. Staub, Frank, photos by. LC 90-37382. (Illus.). 32p. (gr. 4-8). 1991. lib. bdg. 11.79 (*0-8167-2220-X*); pap. text ed. 2.95 (*0-8167-2221-8*) Troll Assocs.

—The Yellowstone Fires. LC 92-29631. 1993. 19.95 (*0-87614-778-3*) Carolrhoda Bks.

—Yellowstone Park. Staub, Frank, illus. LC 89-34371. 32p. (gr. 3-6). 1990. lib. bdg. 10.79 (*0-8167-1737-0*); pap. text ed. 2.95 (*0-8167-1738-9*) Troll Assocs.

Staub, Wendy C. Summer Lightning. 1993. pap. 3.50 (*0-06-106778-4*, Harp PBks) HarpC.

Stauffacher, Sue. S'gana, the Black Whale. LC 92-17573. 224p. (gr. 2-7). 1992. 15.95 (*0-88240-396-6*) Alaska Northwest.

Stauffer, Brooke. Fruit Blasterz from Outer Space. 96p. (Orig.). 1993. pap. 3.50 (*0-380-76404-0*, Camelot Young) Avon.

Stauffer, Darlene. Grace Comes Home. LC 83-83119. 128p. (Orig.). (gr. 7-11). 1984. pap. 2.50 (*0-88243-804-2*, 02-0804) Gospel Pub.

Stauffer, P. Wayne. The Crystal Dragon. Tunmore, Gary, ed. Stauffer, P. Wayne, illus. 47p. (gr. 3-5). 1991. 12.95 (*0-924649-04-6*); PLB 15.95 (*0-924649-05-4*); pap. 7.95 (*0-924649-06-2*) Scribblers Pub.

Stauffer, Patricia I. Farming Is OK. Mattingly, Jennie, ed. Taylor, Neil, illus. LC 87-50262. 44p. (gr. 1-3). 1987. 6.95 (*1-55523-077-6*) Winston-Derek.

Stauffer, Russell G. & Berg, Jean H. Super Reading. 295p. (gr. 10-12). 1981. pap. text ed. 49.95 (*1-55678-036-2*); audiocassettes incl. Learn Inc.

—Super Reading Junior. 256p. 1981. pap. text ed. 49.95 (*1-55678-039-7*); audiocassettes incl. Learn Inc.

Steadman, Barbara, jt. auth. see Cirker, Hayward.

Steadman, Ralph. The Jelly Book. Steadman, Ralph, illus. LC 73-99918. 32p. (ps-3). 7.95 (*0-685-04570-6*) Scroll Pr.

—No Room to Swing a Cat. (Illus.). 32p. (gr. k-2). 1990. 15.95 (*0-86264-241-8*, Pub. by Anderson Pr UK) Trafalgar.

Stearman, G. G., ed. see Church, J. R.

Stearns, Michael, ed. A Wizard's Dozen. LC 93-22150. 1993. 16.95 (*0-15-200965-5*, J Yolen Bks); pap. write for info. (*0-15-200966-3*, J Yolen Bks) HarBrace.

Steber, Rick. Children's Stories. Gray, Don, illus. 60p. (Orig.). 1989. pap. 4.95 (*0-945134-06-1*); cassette 9.95 (*0-945134-56-8*) Bonanza Pub.

—Cowboys. Gray, Don, illus. 60p. (Orig.). 1988. pap. 4.95 (*0-945134-04-5*); cassette 9.95 (*0-945134-54-1*) Bonanza Pub.

—Grandpa's Stories. Gray, Don, illus. 60p. (Orig.). 1991. pap. 4.95 (*0-945134-10-X*); cassette 9.95 (*0-945134-60-6*) Bonanza Pub.

—Indians. Gray, Don, illus. 60p. (Orig.). 1987. pap. 4.95 (*0-945134-03-7*); cassette 9.95 (*0-945134-53-3*) Bonanza Pub.

—Loggers. Gray, Don, illus. 60p. (Orig.). 1989. pap. 4.95 (*0-945134-07-X*); cassette 9.95 (*0-945134-57-6*) Bonanza Pub.

—Miners. Gray, Don, illus. 60p. (Orig.). 1990. pap. 4.95 (*0-945134-09-6*); cassette 9.95 (*0-945134-59-2*) Bonanza Pub.

—Mountain Men. Gray, Don, illus. 60p. (Orig.). 1990. pap. 4.95 (*0-945134-08-8*); cassette 9.95 (*0-945134-58-4*) Bonanza Pub.

—Oregon Trail. Gray, Don, illus. 60p. (Orig.). 1986. pap. 4.95 (*0-945134-01-0*); 9.95 (*0-945134-51-7*) Bonanza Pub.

—Pacific Coast. Gray, Don, illus. 60p. (Orig.). 1987. pap. 4.95 (*0-945134-02-9*); cassette 9.95 (*0-945134-52-5*) Bonanza Pub.

—Women of the West. Gray, Don, illus. 60p. (Orig.). 1988. pap. 4.95 (*0-945134-05-3*); cassette 9.95 (*0-945134-55-X*) Bonanza Pub.

Stebner, Karey H. Travel Wonderful Wyoming with Jesse Jackalope. 28p. (gr-4). 1992. pap. 3.00 (*0-9632746-3-5*) Karey Kreations.

Steck-Vaughn Company Staff. Voices from America's Past. LC 90-44955. (Illus.). 128p. (gr. 5-9). 1990. PLB 19.92 (*0-8114-2770-6*) Raintree Steck-V.

—Voices from Around the World. LC 90-10133. (Illus.). 128p. (gr. 5-9). 1990. PLB 19.92 (*0-8114-2772-2*) Raintree Steck-V.

—Voices from Distant Lands. LC 90-44912. (Illus.). 128p. (gr. 5-9). 1990. PLB 19.92 (*0-8114-2773-0*) Raintree Steck-V.

—Voices from Our Nation. LC 90-41623. (Illus.). 128p. (gr. 5-9). 1990. PLB 19.92 (*0-8114-2771-4*) Raintree Steck-V.

Steckler, Arthur. One Hundred & One Words & How They Began. LC 78-1012. (Illus.). 96p. 1979. pap. 6.95 (*0-385-14074-6*) Doubleday.

Stedman, Nancy. The Common Cold & Influenza. Reingold, Michael, illus. LC 86-8387. 72p. (gr. 4-8). 1986. lib. bdg. 11.98 (*0-671-60022-2*, J Messner) S&S Trade.

Steed, Alice. I Am Three - I Am Four. Trapani, Iza, illus. 32p. (ps-k). 1993. bds. 3.95 (*1-879085-78-X*) Whsprng Coyote Pr.

Steed, Miriam. Ancient Egypt. (Illus.). 40p. (gr. 3-7). 1992. 13.95 (*0-237-60165-6*, Pub. by Evans Bros Ltd) Trafalgar.

Steedman, Scott. Amazing Monkeys. Young, Jerry, photos by. LC 90-19238. (Illus.). 32p. (Orig.). (gr. 1-5). 1991. PLB 9.99 (*0-679-91517-6*); pap. 6.95 (*0-679-81517-1*) Knopf Bks Yng Read.

Steege, Gwen, ed. see Gillis, Jennifer S.

Steege, Gwen, ed. see Simmons, Paula & Salsbury, Darrell L.

Steel, Danielle. Freddie & the Doctor. Rogers, Jacqueline, illus. 32p. (Orig.). (gr. 1-3). 1992. pap. 2.99 (*0-440-40575-0*, YB) Dell.

—Freddie's Accident. Rogers, Jacqueline, illus. 32p. (Orig.). (gr. 1-3). 1992. pap. 2.99 (*0-440-40576-9*, YB) Dell.

—Freddie's First Night Away. (ps-3). 1992. pap. 2.99 (*0-440-40574-2*) Dell.

—Freddie's Trip. (ps-3). 1992. pap. 2.99 (*0-440-40573-4*) Dell.

—Martha & Hillary & the Stranger. (ps-3). 1991. 9.95 (*0-385-30212-6*) Delacorte.

—Martha's Best Friend. Rogers, Jacqueline, illus. (ps-2). 1989. 8.95 (*0-385-29801-3*) Delacorte.

—Martha's New Daddy. Rogers, Jacqueline, illus. (ps-2). 1989. 8.95 (*0-385-29799-8*) Delacorte.

—Martha's New Puppy. 1990. 9.95 (*0-385-30166-9*) Delacorte.

—Martha's New School. Rogers, Jacqueline, illus. (ps-2). 1989. 8.95 (*0-385-29800-5*) Delacorte.

—Max & Grandma & Grandpa Winky. (ps-3). 1991. 9.95 (*0-385-30165-0*) Delacorte.

—Max & the Baby-Sitter. Rogers, Jacqueline, illus. (ps-2). 1989. 8.95 (*0-385-29796-3*) Delacorte.

—Max Runs Away. 1990. 9.95 (*0-385-30213-4*) Delacorte.

—Max's Daddy Goes to the Hospital. Rogers, Jacqueline, illus. (ps-2). 1989. 8.95 (*0-385-29797-1*) Delacorte.

—Max's New Baby. Rogers, Jacqueline, illus. (ps-2). 1989. 8.95 (*0-385-29798-X*) Delacorte.

Steel, Richard. Touchdown. Parker, Liz, ed. Taylor, Marjorie, illus. 45p. (Orig.). (gr. 6-12). 1992. pap. text ed. 2.95 (*1-56254-054-8*) Saddleback Pubns.

Steele, B., ed. Cues & Signals 1: A Self-Instruction Workbook for Visual Accuracy. reusable ed. (gr. 3). 1971. wkbk. 9.00 (*0-87879-752-1*, Ann Arbor Div) Acad Therapy.

Steele, B. & Wehrli, K., eds. Cues & Signals 2: A Self-Instruction Workbook for Visual Accuracy. reusable ed. (gr. 3). 1971. wkbk. 9.00 (*0-87879-753-X*, Ann Arbor Div) Acad Therapy.

—Cues & Signals 3: A Self-Instruction Workbook for Visual Accuracy. reusable ed. (gr. 3). 1971. wkbk. 9.00 (*0-87879-754-8*, Ann Arbor Div) Acad Therapy.

—Cues & Signals 4: A Self-Instruction Workbook for Visual Accuracy. reusable ed. (gr. 3). 1971. wkbk. 9.00 (*0-87879-755-6*, Ann Arbor Div) Acad Therapy.

Steele, Christine, ed. see Muhaiyaddeen, M. R.

Steele, David H. The Pebble Searcher. 16p. (gr. 7-10). 1986. 22.00x (*0-317-52595-6*, Pub. by A H Stockwell England) St Mut.

Steele, Jason. Shadow over Loch Ness. 128p. (gr. 5-8). 1993. pap. 2.99 (*0-87406-498-8*) Willowisp Pr.

Steele, Lawrence, tr. see Groth, Lynn.

Steele, Mary Q. Anna's Garden Songs. Anderson, Lena, illus. LC 88-5660. 32p. (gr. k up) 1989. 11.95 (*0-688-08217-3*); PLB 11.88 (*0-688-08218-1*) Greenwillow.

—Anna's Summer Songs. Anderson, Lena, illus. LC 86-27109. (SWE.). 32p. (gr. k-3). 1988. 11.95 (*0-688-07180-5*); lib. bdg. 11.88 (*0-688-07181-3*) Greenwillow.

—Because of the Sand Witches There. Galdone, Paul, illus. LC 75-5932. 192p. (gr. 3-7). 1975. 11.75 (*0-688-80001-7*); PLB 11.88 (*0-688-84001-9*) Greenwillow.

—Journey Outside. Negri, Rocco, illus. (gr. 3-7). 1979. pap. 3.95 (*0-14-030588-2*, Puffin Bks) Puffin Bks.

—Journey Outside. (gr. 5-9). 1984. 17.00 (*0-8446-6169-4*) Peter Smith.

Steele, Mary Q. see Gage, Wilson, pseud.

Steele, Philip. Astronomy. LC 90-20633. (Illus.). 32p. (gr. 5-6). 1991. RSBE 11.95 (*0-89686-586-X*, Crestwood Hse) Macmillan Child Grp.

—Birds. LC 90-42015. (Illus.). 32p. (gr. 5-6). 1991. RSBE 11.95 (*0-89686-583-5*, Crestwood Hse) Macmillan Child Grp.

—Birds. (gr. 4-7). 1991. lib. bdg. 4.95 (*0-671-72244-1*, J Messner) S&S Trade.

—Boats. LC 90-41177. (Illus.). 32p. (gr. 5-6). 1991. RSBE 11.95 (*0-89686-522-3*, Crestwood Hse) Macmillan Child Grp.

—Cars & Trucks. LC 90-41180. (Illus.). 32p. (gr. 5-6). 1991. RSBE 11.95 (*0-89686-521-5*, Crestwood Hse) Macmillan Child Grp.

—Castles Had Moats & Other Questions about Long Ago. LC 93-31303. 1994. 8.95 (*1-85697-879-6*) Kingfisher Bks.

—Censorship. LC 91-40235. (Illus.). 48p. (gr. 6 up). 1992. RSBE 12.95 (*0-02-735404-0*, New Discovery) Macmillan Child Grp.

—China. LC 89-21655. (Illus.). 96p. (gr. 6-12). 1990. 19.92 (*0-8114-2426-X*) Raintree Steck-V.

—China. LC 93-25237. (Illus.). 32p. (gr. 5). 1994. RSBE 13.95 (*0-89686-771-4*, Crestwood Hse) Macmillan Child Grp.

—City Through the Ages. Lapper, Ivan, et al, illus. LC 91-37350. 32p. (gr. 3-6). 1993. PLB 11.89 (*0-8167-2727-9*); pap. text ed. 3.95 (*0-8167-2728-7*) Troll Assocs. Postponed.

—Collage. LC 92-42678. 40p. (gr. 3-7). 1993. 10.95 (*1-85697-921-0*); pap. 5.95 (*1-85697-920-2*) Kingfisher Bks.

—Deserts. LC 90-20759. (Illus.). 32p. (gr. 5-6). 1991. RSBE 11.95 (*0-89686-588-6*, Crestwood Hse) Macmillan Child Grp.

—The Egyptians & the Valley of the Kings. (Illus.). 32p. (gr. 5). 1994. PLB 13.95 RSBE (*0-87518-539-8*, Dillon) Macmillan Child Grp.

—Extinct Amphibians: And Those in Danger of Extinction. Kline, Marjory, ed. LC 91-9886. (Illus.). 32p. (gr. 4-7). 1992. PLB 11.90 (*0-531-11031-1*) Watts.

—Extinct Birds: And Those in Danger of Extinction. Kline, Marjory, ed. (Illus.). 32p. (gr. 5-8). 1991. PLB 11.90 (*0-531-11027-3*) Watts.

—Extinct Insects: And Those in Danger of Extinction. Kline, Marjory, ed. (Illus.). 32p. (gr. 4-7). 1992. PLB 11.90 (*0-531-11032-X*) Watts.

—Extinct Land Mammals: And Those in Danger of Extinction. Kline, Marjory, ed. (Illus.). 32p. (gr. 4-7). 1992. PLB 11.90 (*0-531-11028-1*) Watts.

—Extinct Reptiles: And Those in Danger of Extinction. Kline, Marjory, ed. (Illus.). 32p. (gr. 5-8). 1991. PLB 11.90 (*0-531-11030-3*) Watts.

—Extinct Underwater Creatures: And Those in Danger of Extinction. Kline, Marjory, ed. (Illus.). 32p. (gr. 4-7). 1992. PLB 11.90 (*0-531-11029-X*) Watts.

—Factory Through the Ages. Lapper, Ivan, et al, illus. LC 91-33262. 32p. (gr. 3-6). 1993. PLB 11.89 (*0-8167-2729-5*); pap. text ed. 3.95 (*0-8167-2730-9*) Troll Assocs. Postponed.

—Farm Through the Ages. Howett, Andrew & Davidson, Gordon, illus. LC 92-37819. 32p. (gr. 3-6). 1993. PLB 11.89 (*0-8167-2731-7*); pap. text ed. 3.95 (*0-8167-2732-5*) Troll Assocs. Postponed.

—Fish. (gr. 4-7). 1991. lib. bdg. 4.95 (*0-671-72240-9*, J Messner) S&S Trade.

—Food & Feasts in Ancient Rome. LC 93-28384. (Illus.). 32p. (gr. 6 up) 1994. RSBE 14.95 (*0-02-726321-5*, New Discovery Bks) Macmillan Child Grp.

—Frost: Causes & Effects. LC 90-44596. (Illus.). 32p. (gr. 5-8). 1991. PLB 12.40 (*0-531-11025-7*) Watts.

—Great Britain. LC 93-4365. (Illus.). 32p. (gr. 5). 1994. RSBE 13.95 (*0-89686-774-9*, Crestwood Hse) Macmillan Child Grp.

—Heatwave: Causes & Effects. (Illus.). 32p. (gr. 5-8). 1991. PLB 12.40 (*0-531-11023-0*) Watts.

—House Through the Ages. Howett, Andrew & Davidson, Gordon, illus. LC 91-36481. 32p. (gr. 3-6). 1993. PLB 11.89 (*0-8167-2733-3*); pap. text ed. 3.95 (*0-8167-2734-1*) Troll Assocs. Postponed.

—The Incas & Machu Picchu. LC 92-42283. (Illus.). 32p. (gr. 6-8). 1993. RSBE 13.95 (*0-87518-536-3*, Dillon) Macmillan Child Grp.

—Insects. LC 90-42016. (Illus.). 32p. (gr. 5-6). 1991. RSBE 11.95 (*0-89686-581-9*, Crestwood Hse) Macmillan Child Grp.

—Insects. 32p. (gr. 3-5). 1991. lib. bdg. 9.98 (*0-671-72235-2*, J Messner); pap. 4.95 (*0-671-72236-0*) S&S Trade.

—Journey Through China. Camm, Martin, et al, illus. LC 90-10943. 32p. (gr. 3-5). 1991. PLB 11.89 (*0-8167-2112-2*); pap. text ed. 3.95 (*0-8167-2113-0*) Troll Assocs.

—Kidnapping. LC 91-42691. (Illus.). 48p. (gr. 6 up). 1992. RSBE 12.95 (*0-02-735403-2*, New Discovery) Macmillan Child Grp.

—Little Bighorn. LC 91-24065. (Illus.). 32p. (gr. 6 up). 1992. RSBE 13.95 (*0-02-786885-0*, New Discovery) Macmillan Child Grp.

—Mammals. 32p. (gr. 3-5). 1991. (J Messner); pap. 4.95 (*0-671-72234-4*) S&S Trade.

—Mountains. LC 90-20741. (Illus.). 32p. (gr. 5-6). 1991. RSBE 11.95 (*0-89686-587-8*, Crestwood Hse) Macmillan Child Grp.

—Over Fifty Years Ago: In Europe During World War II. (Illus.). 32p. (gr. 6 up). 1993. RSBE 13.95 (*0-02-786886-9*, New Discovery) Macmillan Child Grp.

—The People Atlas. (Illus.). 64p. 1991. 16.95 (*0-19-520846-3*, 3395) OUP.

—Planes. LC 90-41181. (Illus.). 32p. (gr. 5-6). 1991. RSBE 11.95 (*0-89686-524-X*, Crestwood Hse) Macmillan Child Grp.

—Prehistoric Animals. (gr. 4-7). 1991. lib. bdg. 4.95 (*0-671-72242-5*, J Messner) S&S Trade.

—Rain: Causes & Effects. (Illus.). 32p. (gr. 5-8). 1991. PLB 12.40 (*0-531-10989-5*) Watts.

—Reptiles. LC 90-42017. (Illus.). 32p. (gr. 5-6). 1991. RSBE 11.95 (*0-89686-582-7*, Crestwood Hse) Macmillan Child Grp.

—Reptiles & Amphibians. (gr. 4-7). 1991. lib. bdg. 4.95 (*0-671-72238-7*, J Messner) S&S Trade.

—Reptiles & Amphibians. 32p. (gr. 4-7). 1991. lib. bdg. 9.98 (*0-671-72237-9*, J Messner) S&S Trade.

—Riots. LC 92-24195. (Illus.). 48p. (gr. 6 up). 1993. RSBE 12.95 (*0-02-786883-4*, New Discovery) Macmillan Child Grp.

—River Through the Ages. Ingpen, Robert, illus. LC 91-33279. 32p. (gr. 3-6). 1993. PLB 11.89 (*0-8167-2735-X*); pap. text ed. 3.95 (*0-8167-2736-8*) Troll Assocs. Postponed.

—Road Through the Ages. Howett, Andrew & Davidson, Gordon, illus. LC 91-35878. 32p. (gr. 3-6). 1993. PLB 11.89 (*0-8167-2737-6*); pap. text ed. 3.95 (*0-8167-2738-4*) Troll Assocs. Postponed.

—The Romans & Pompeii. (Illus.). 32p. (gr. 5). 1994. PLB 13.95 RSBE (*0-87518-538-X*, Dillon) Macmillan Child Grp.

—Sharks & Other Creatures of the Deep. LC 91-72484. (Illus.). 64p. (gr. 3 up). 1991. 11.95 (*1-879431-16-5*); PLB 12.99 (*1-879431-31-9*) Dorling Kindersley.

—Smuggling. LC 92-13611. (Illus.). 48p. (gr. 6 up). 1993. RSBE 12.95 (*0-02-786884-2*, New Discovery) Macmillan Child Grp.

—Snow: Causes & Effects. (Illus.). 32p. (gr. 5-8). 1991. PLB 12.40 (*0-531-10990-9*) Watts.

—Space Travel. LC 90-20735. (Illus.). 32p. (gr. 5-6). 1991. RSBE 11.95 (*0-89686-585-1*, Crestwood Hse) Macmillan Child Grp.

—Storms: Causes & Effects. (Illus.). 32p. (gr. 5-8). 1991. PLB 12.40 (*0-531-11026-5*) Watts.

—Terrorism. LC 91-39803. (Illus.). 48p. (gr. 6 up). 1992. RSBE 12.95 (*0-02-735401-6*, New Discovery) Macmillan Child Grp.

—Thermopylae. LC 93-2645. (Illus.). 32p. (gr. 6 up). 1993. RSBE 13.95 (*0-02-786887-7*, New Discovery Bks) Macmillan Child Grp.

—Thor Heyerdahl & the Kon-Tiki Voyage. LC 93-9335. (Illus.). 32p. (gr. 4-6). 1993. lib. bdg. 13.95 RSBE (*0-87518-533-9*, Dillon) Macmillan Child Grp.

—Trains. LC 90-41179. (Illus.). 32p. (gr. 5-6). 1991. RSBE 11.95 (*0-89686-523-1*, Crestwood Hse) Macmillan Child Grp.

—Wild Animals. LC 90-42014. (Illus.). 32p. (gr. 5-6). 1991. RSBE 11.95 (*0-89686-584-3*, Crestwood Hse) Macmillan Child Grp.

—Wind: Causes & Effects. (Illus.). 32p. (gr. 5-8). 1991. PLB 12.40 (*0-531-11024-9*) Watts.

Steele, Philip, jt. auth. see Perham, Molly.

Steele, Phillip. Germany. LC 92-39685. (Illus.). 32p. (gr. 4 up). 1993. RSBE 13.95 (*0-89686-777-3*, Crestwood Hse) Macmillan Child Grp.

—The Last Cherokee Warriors. 2nd ed. LC 86-25348. (Illus.). 111p. (gr. 6-12). 1978. pap. 7.95 (*0-88289-203-7*) Pelican.

Steele, Phillip W. Ozark Tales & Superstitions. Chapman, Donna & Doege, Erwin, illus. LC 82-22425. 96p. (gr. 6 up). 1983. pap. 5.95 (*0-88289-404-8*) Pelican.

Steele, Robert, ed. see Shubert, J. Lansing.

Steele, Ross & Pavis, Jose. L' Express: Aujourd'hui la France: Advanced. (FRE.). 160p. pap. text ed. 15.95 (*0-685-66254-3*, F1276-8, Natl Textbk); tchr's. manual 3.95 (*0-685-66255-1*, F1277-6, Natl Textbk); 3 60-min. audiocassettes 34.95 (*0-685-66256-X*, F1278-X, Natl Textbk) NTC Pub Grp.

Steele, Ruth M. Ambrose. 1991. 6.95 (*0-533-09080-6*) Vantage.

Steele, Susanna & Styles, Morag, eds. Mother Gave a Shout: Poems by Women & Girls. Ray, Jane, illus. LC 90-12938. 128p. (gr. 3-8). 1991. 14.95 (*0-912078-90-1*) Volcano Pr.

Steele, William O. Buffalo Knife. 123p. (gr. 3-7). 1990. pap. 3.95 (*0-15-213212-0*, Odyssey) HarBrace.

—Flaming Arrows. 41p. (gr. 3-7). 1990. pap. 3.95 (*0-15-228427-3*, Odyssey) HarBrace.

—Perilous Road. 156p. (gr. 3-7). 1990. pap. 3.95 (*0-15-260647-5*, Odyssey) HarBrace.

—Winter Danger. LC 54-5157. (Illus.). 131p. (gr. 3-7). 1990. pap. 3.95 (*0-685-51103-0*, HB Juv Bks) HarBrace.

Steelsmith, Shari. Elizabeth Blackwell: The Story of the First Woman Doctor. Kerstetter, Judy, illus. LC 86-62434. 32p. (Orig.). (ps-4). 1987. lib. bdg. 16.95 (*0-943990-31-9*); pap. 5.95 (*0-943990-30-0*) Parenting Pr.

—Juliette Gordon Low: Founder of the Girl Scouts. Pope, Connie J., illus. LC 89-62673. 32p. (Orig.). (ps-4). 1990. lib. bdg. 16.95 (*0-943990-37-8*); pap. 5.95 (*0-943990-36-X*) Parenting Pr.

Steelsmith, Shari, ed. see Hendrickson, Karen.

Steen, Sandra & Steen, Susan. Colonial Williamsburg. LC 92-26192. (Illus.). 72p. (gr. 4 up). 1993. RSBE 14.95 (*0-87518-546-0*, Dillon) Macmillan Child Grp.

Steen, Shirley & Edwards, Anne. A Child's Bible: Old Testament & New Testament. (gr. 1-8). 1986. 11.95 (*0-8091-2867-5*) Paulist Pr.

Steen, Susan. Independence Hall. Steen, Susan, illus. LC 93-5365. 72p. (gr. 4). 1994. RSBE 14.95 (*0-87518-603-3*, Dillon) Macmillan Child Grp.

Steen, Susan, jt. auth. see Steen, Sandra.

Steenstra, Virginia G. Best Cat. 1993. 7.95 (*0-8062-4608-1*) Carlton.

Steenwyk, Elizabeth Van see Van Steenwyk, Elizabeth.

Steenwyk, Elizabeth Van see Van Steenwyk, Elizabeth.

Steere, D'Ann. Choice Adventures, No. 4: The Rain Forest Mission. (gr. 3-7). 1991. PLB 4.99 (*0-8423-5028-4*) Tyndale.

Steere, Susan & Ring, Kathryn M. The Reef & the Wrasse. Steere, Susan, illus. LC 88-24528. 32p. (Orig.). (gr. 4-6). 1988. pap. 6.95 (*0-943173-24-8*) Harbinger AZ.

Steeves, Margo, ed. see Tomei, Joseph A.

Stefanik, Alfred. Copycat Sam: Developing Ties with a Special Child. Huff, Laura, illus. LC 81-20212. 32p. (gr. k-5). 1982. 16.95 (*0-89885-058-4*) Human Sci Pr.

Steffa, Tim, tr. see Siekkinen, Raija.

Steffens, Bradley. Animal Rights: Distinguishing Between Fact & Opinion. LC 89-2200. (Illus.). 32p. (gr. 3-6). 1990. PLB 10.95 (*0-89908-635-7*) Greenhaven.

—The Children's Crusade. LC 91-29498. (Illus.). 96p. (gr. 5-8). 1991. PLB 11.95 (*1-56006-019-0*) Lucent Bks.

—The Fall of the Roman Empire: Opposing Viewpoints. LC 93-11025. 1994. 14.95 (*1-56510-098-0*) Greenhaven.

—Free Speech: Identifying Propaganda Techniques. LC 92-23594. (Illus.). 32p. (gr. 4-7). 1992. PLB 10.95 (*0-89908-098-7*) Greenhaven.

—Phonograph: Sound on Disk. LC 92-27850. (Illus.). 96p. (gr. 5-8). 1992. PLB 15.95 (*1-56006-222-3*) Lucent Bks.

—Photography: Preserving the Past. LC 91-15570. (Illus.). 96p. (gr. 5-8). 1991. PLB 15.95 (*1-56006-212-6*) Lucent Bks.

—The Printing Press: Ideas into Type. LC 90-6619. (Illus.). 96p. (gr. 5-8). 1990. PLB 15.95 (*1-56006-205-3*) Lucent Bks.

—Working Mothers: Understanding Words in Context. LC 89-35434. (Illus.). 32p. (gr. 3-6). 1990. PLB 10.95 (*0-89908-644-6*) Greenhaven.

Steffens, Bradley, jt. auth. see House, James.

Steffens, J. & Carr, J. Action & Adventure. (gr. 7-12). 1983. 9.95 (*0-88160-101-2*, LW 1007) Learning Wks.

—Mystery & Suspense. (gr. 7-12). 1983. 9.95 (*0-88160-096-2*, LW 1006) Learning Wks.

—Myths & Fables. (gr. 7-12). 1984. 9.95 (*0-88160-113-6*, LW 1008) Learning Wks.

Steffy, Jan. The School Picnic. Bond, Denny, illus. LC 87-14867. 32p. (ps-3). 1987. 12.95 (*0-934672-52-0*) Good Bks PA.

Stefoff, Rebecca. Abraham Lincoln: Sixteenth President of the United States. Young, Richard G., ed. LC 88-28488. (Illus.). (gr. 5-9). 1989. PLB 17.26 (*0-944483-14-3*) Garrett Ed Corp.

—The Accidental Explorers. (Illus.). 152p. 1992. PLB 20.00 (*0-19-507685-0*) OUP.

—Adolescence. (Illus.). 104p. (gr. 6-12). 1990. 18.95 (*0-7910-0033-8*) Chelsea Hse.

—Al Gore: Vice President. (Illus.). 48p. (gr. 2-4). 1994. 12.40 (*1-56294-433-9*) Millbrook Pr.

—Andrew Jackson: 7th President of the United States. Young, Richard G., ed. LC 87-32878. (Illus.). (gr. 5-9). 1988. PLB 17.26 (*0-944483-08-9*) Garrett Ed Corp.

—The Drug Enforcement Administration. (Illus.). 104p. (gr. 5 up). 1990. 14.95 (*0-87754-849-8*) Chelsea Hse.

—Environmental Disasters. Train, Russell E., intro. by. LC 93-8183. 1994. write for info. (*0-7910-1584-X*) Chelsea Hse.

—Extinction. (Illus.). 128p. (gr. 5 up). 1992. lib. bdg. 19.95 (*0-7910-1578-5*) Chelsea Hse.

—Faisal. (Illus.). 112p. (gr. 5 up). 1989. 17.95 (*1-55546-833-0*) Chelsea Hse.

—Ferdinand Magellan & the Discovery of the World Ocean. Goetzmann, William H., ed. Collins, Michael, intro. by. (Illus.). 128p. (gr. 5 up). 1990. lib. bdg. 18.95 (*0-7910-1291-3*) Chelsea Hse.

—Friendship & Love. (Illus.). 104p. (gr. 6-12). 1989. 18.95 (*0-7910-0039-7*) Chelsea Hse.

—George H. W. Bush: Forty-First President of the United States. Iraq War. Young, Richard G., ed. LC 91-30666. (Illus.). 140p. (gr. 5-9). 1992. PLB 17.26 (*1-56074-033-7*) Garrett Ed Corp.

—Gloria Estefan. (Illus.). 104p. (gr. 5 up). 1991. lib. bdg. 17.95 (*0-7910-1244-1*) Chelsea Hse.

—Herman Melville. LC 93-11751. 1994. PLB write for info. (*0-671-86771-7*, J Messner); pap. write for info. (*0-671-86772-5*, J Messner) S&S Trade.

—Independence & Revolution in Mexico, 1810-1940. (Illus.). 128p. (gr. 6-9). 1993. 16.95x (*0-8160-2841-9*) Facts on File.

—James Monroe: 5th President of the United States. Young, Richard G., ed. LC 87-32845. (Illus.). (gr. 5-9). 1988. PLB 17.26 (*0-944483-11-9*) Garrett Ed Corp.

—Japan. (Illus.). 112p. (gr. 5 up). 1988. lib. bdg. 14.95 (*1-55546-199-9*) Chelsea Hse.

—John Adams: 2nd President of the United States. Young, Richard G., ed. LC 87-32757. (Illus.). (gr. 5-9). 1988. PLB 17.26 (*0-944483-10-0*) Garrett Ed Corp.

—Lewis & Clark. (Illus.). 80p. (gr. 3-5). 1992. lib. bdg. 12.95 (*0-7910-1750-8*) Chelsea Hse.

—Marco Polo & the Medieval Explorers. (Illus.). 112p. (gr. 5 up). 1992. lib. bdg. 18.95 (*0-7910-1294-8*) Chelsea Hse.

—Mary Kay Ash: Mary Kay, a Beautiful Business. Young, Richard G., ed. LC 91-32055. (Illus.). 64p. (gr. 4-8). 1992. PLB 17.26 (*1-56074-012-4*) Garrett Ed Corp.

—Norman Schwarzkopf. (Illus.). 112p. (gr. 5 up). 1992. lib. bdg. 17.95 (*0-7910-1725-7*) Chelsea Hse.

—Overpopulation. (Illus.). (gr. 5 up). 1992. lib. bdg. 19.95 (*0-7910-1581-5*); pap. write for info. (*0-7910-1606-4*) Chelsea Hse.

—Placido Domingo. (Illus.). (gr. 5 up). 1992. PLB 17.95 (*0-7910-1563-7*) Chelsea Hse.

—Pol Pot. (Illus.). 112p. (gr. 5 up). 1990. 17.95 (*1-55546-848-9*) Chelsea Hse.

—Raul Julia: Puerto Rican Actor. (Illus.). (gr. 5 up). 1994. PLB 18.95 (*0-7910-1556-4*, Am Art Analog) Chelsea Hse.

—Recycling. (Illus.). 128p. (gr. 5 up). 1991. lib. bdg. 19.95 (*0-7910-1573-4*) Chelsea Hse.

—Richard M. Nixon: Thirty-Seventh President of the United States. Young, Richard G., ed. LC 89-39944. (Illus.). 128p. (gr. 5-9). 1990. PLB 17.26 (*0-944483-59-3*) Garrett Ed Corp.

—Scientific Explorers. (Illus.). 144p. 1992. PLB 20.00 (*0-19-507689-3*) OUP.

—Ted Turner: Television's Triumphant Tiger. Young, Richard G., ed. LC 91-32774. (Illus.). 64p. (gr. 4-8). 1992. PLB 17.26 (*1-56074-024-8*) Garrett Ed Corp.

—Theodore Roosevelt: 26th President of the United States. Young, Richard G., ed. LC 87-35953. (Illus.). (gr. 5-9). 1988. PLB 17.26 (*0-944483-09-7*) Garrett Ed Corp.

—Thomas Jefferson: 3rd President of the United States. Young, Richard G., ed. LC 87-32818. (Illus.). (gr. 5-9). 1988. PLB 17.26 (*0-944483-07-0*) Garrett Ed Corp.

—Vasco da Gama & the Portuguese Explorers. Goetzmann, William H., ed. Collins, Michael, intro. by. (Illus.). 112p. (gr. 6-12). 1993. PLB 18.95 (*0-7910-1303-0*); pap. write for info. (*0-7910-1526-2*) Chelsea Hse.

—The Viking Explorers. Goetzmann, William H., ed. Collins, Michael, intro. by. (Illus.). 112p. (gr. 6-12). 1993. PLB 19.95 (*0-7910-1295-6*, Am Art Analog); pap. write for info. (*0-7910-1520-3*, Am Art Analog) Chelsea Hse.

—West Bank-Gaza Strip. (Illus.). 104p. (gr. 5 up). 1988. lib. bdg. 14.95 (*1-55546-782-2*) Chelsea Hse.

—William Henry Harrison: Ninth President of the United States. Young, Richard G., ed. LC 89-25652. (Illus.). 128p. (gr. 5-9). 1990. PLB 17.26 (*0-944483-54-2*) Garrett Ed Corp.

—Women of the World. (Illus.). 144p. 1992. PLB 20.00 (*0-19-507687-7*) OUP.

—Yasir Arafat. Schlesinger, Arthur M., intro. by. (Illus.). 112p. (gr. 5 up). 1989. 17.95 (*1-55546-826-8*); pap. 9.95 (*0-7910-0554-2*) Chelsea Hse.

Stefoff, Rebecca, ed. see Ardley, Neil.

Stefoff, Rebecca, ed. see Baskerville, Judith.

Stefoff, Rebecca, ed. see Bradshaw, Jeremy.

Stefoff, Rebecca, ed. see Brett, Caroline.

Stefoff, Rebecca, ed. see Burch, Jonathan.

Stefoff, Rebecca, ed. see Cash, Terry.

Stefoff, Rebecca, ed. see Chandler, Jane.

Stefoff, Rebecca, ed. see Dixon, Annabelle.

Stefoff, Rebecca, ed. see Geser, Ingrid.

Stefoff, Rebecca, ed. see Gipson, Morrell & Frank, Herta.

Stefoff, Rebecca, ed. see Gipson, Morrell & Hansson, Peter.

Stefoff, Rebecca, ed. see Gipson, Morrell & Mangold, Paul.

Stefoff, Rebecca, ed. see Gipson, Morrell & Mann, Marek.

Stefoff, Rebecca, ed. see Gipson, Morrell & Mayer, Lene.

Stefoff, Rebecca, ed. see Haycock, Kate.

Stefoff, Rebecca, ed. see Jennings, Terry J.

Stefoff, Rebecca, ed. see Linley, Mike.

Stefoff, Rebecca, ed. see McDonald, Kendall.

Stefoff, Rebecca, ed. see Merrison, Tim.

Stefoff, Rebecca, ed. see Moss, Miriam.

Stefoff, Rebecca, ed. see Peacock, Lindsay.

Stefoff, Rebecca, ed. see Penny, Malcolm.

Stefoff, Rebecca, ed. see Pollard, Michael.

Stefoff, Rebecca, ed. see Sauvain, Philip.

Stefoff, Rebecca, ed. see Thomson, Ruth.

Stefoff, Rebecca, ed. see Wake, Susan.

Stefoff, Rebecca, ed. see Wallington, Neil.

Stefoff, Rebecca, ed. see Walpole, Brenda.

Stefoff, Rebecca, ed. see Ware, Derek.

Stefoff, Rebecca, ed. see Wood, Tim.

Stegenga, Susan J. Christian Crafts - Paper Bag Puppets. 64p. (ps-5). 1990. 8.95 (*0-86653-552-7*, SS1881, Shining Star Pubns) Good Apple.

Stegenga, Susan J., jt. auth. see Daniel, Rebecca.

Stegeren, Theo van see Van Stegeren, Theo.

Stegeren, Frederic. Quack-Quack. Stehr, Frederic, illus. 28p. (ps up). 1988. pap. 3.95 (*0-374-46141-4*) FS&G.

Stehr, Tamara. The Pappenheimers: An Animation & Vocabulary Guide. Garbers, Fred, illus. (gr. k-6). 1983. text ed. 12.95 (*3-468-96795-0*) Langenscheidt.

Steiber, Ellen. Eighth Grade Changes Everything. LC 91-2495. 128p. (gr. 6-9). 1992. lib. bdg. 9.89 (*0-8167-2390-7*); pap. text ed. 2.95 (*0-8167-2391-5*) Troll Assocs.

Steidl, Kim S. Portraits of Asian-Pacific Americans. 96p. (gr. 4-8). 1991. 9.95 (*0-86653-598-5*, GA1323) Good Apple.

Steig, Jeanne. Alpha Beta Chowder. Steig, William, illus. LC 92-52641. 48p. (gr. k up). 1992. 15.00 (*0-06-205006-0*); PLB 14.89 (*0-06-205007-9*) HarpC Child Bks.

Steig, William. Abel's Island. Steig, William, illus. LC 75-35916. 128p. (gr. 1 up). 1976. 14.00 (*0-374-30010-0*) FS&G.

—Abel's Island. LC 75-35916. (Illus.). 128p. (gr. 1 up). 1985. pap. 3.95 (*0-374-40016-4*, Sunburst Bks) FS&G.

—The Amazing Bone. Steig, William, illus. LC 76-26479. 32p. (ps-3). 1983. 17.00 (*0-374-30248-0*) FS&G.

—The Amazing Bone. Steig, William, illus. 32p. (gr. 1-3). 1977. pap. 3.95 (*0-14-050247-5*, Puffin) Puffin Bks.

—Amazing Bone. (ps-3). 1993. pap. 4.95 (*0-374-40358-9*, Sunburst) FS&G.

—Amos y Boris: Amos & Boris. (ps-3). 1992. 17.00 (*0-374-30279-0*) FS&G.

—Award Puzzles: Sylvester & the Magic Pebble. 1990. 5.95 (*0-938971-60-3*) JTG Nashville.
—Brave Irene. LC 86-80957. (Illus.). 32p. (ps-4). 1986. 17.00 (*0-374-30947-7*) FS&G.
—C D C? (Illus.). 64p. (gr. 3 up). 1986. pap. 3.95 (*0-374-41024-0*, Sunburst) FS&G.
—Caleb & Katie. Steig, William, illus. LC 77-4947. 32p. (ps-3). 1977. 16.00 (*0-374-31016-5*) FS&G.
—Caleb & Katie. Steig, William, illus. 32p. (ps up). 1986. pap. 4.95 (*0-374-41038-0*) FS&G.
—CDB! LC 80-12376. (Illus.). 48p. (gr. 1-4). 1987. pap. 3.95 (*0-671-66689-4*, S&S BFYR) S&S Trade.
—Doctor de Soto. LC 82-15701. (ps-3). 1982. 16.00 (*0-374-31803-4*) FS&G.
—Doctor De Soto Goes to Africa. Steig, William, illus. LC 91-76414. 32p. (ps up). 1992. 15.00 (*0-06-205002-8*); PLB 14.89 (*0-06-205003-6*) HarpC Child Bks.
—Dominic. LC 70-188272. (Illus.). 160p. (gr. 2 up). 1984. pap. 3.95 (*0-374-41826-8*, Sunburst) FS&G.
—Farmer Palmer's Wagon Ride. (gr. k-5). 1992. pap. 4.95 (*0-374-42268-0*, Sunburst) FS&G.
—Gorky Rises. (Illus.). 32p. (ps up). 1986. pap. 4.95 (*0-374-42784-4*) FS&G.
—El Hueso Prodigioso: The Amazing Bone. (ps-3). 1993. 17.00 (*0-374-33504-4*, Mirasol) FS&G.
—Ile d'Abel. (FRE.). 144p. (gr. 5-10). 1982. pap. 8.95 (*2-07-033156-3*) Schoenhof.
—Irene, la Valiente: Brave Irene. Mlawer, Teresa, tr. (SPA., Illus.). 32p. (ps-3). 1991. 14.95 (*0-374-30948-5*) FS&G.
—Irene, la Valiente: Brave Irene. (gr. 4-7). 1993. pap. 4.95 (*0-374-43620-7*) FS&G.
—La Isla de Abel: Abel's Island. (ps-3). 1992. 14.00 (*0-374-34286-5*) FS&G.
—The Real Thief. Steig, William, illus. LC 73-77910. 64p. (ps up). 1976. 12.95 (*0-374-36217-3*) FS&G.
—Real Thief. LC 73-77910. (Illus.). 64p. (ps up). 1984. pap. 3.50 (*0-374-46208-9*, Sunburst) FS&G.
—Roland the Minstrel Pig. (Illus.). (gr. k-3). 1968. 12.95 (*0-06-025761-X*) HarpC Child Bks.
—Shrek! (gr. 4-7). 1993. pap. 4.95 (*0-374-46623-8*) FS&G.
—Silvestre y la Piedrecita Magica. Mlawer, Teresa, tr. from ENG. Steig, William, illus. 40p. (gr. 3). 1990. PLB 12.95 (*0-9625162-0-1*); pap. 5.95 (*0-9625162-7-9*) Lectorum Pubns.
—Solomon the Rusty Nail. Steig, William, illus. 32p. (ps up). 1985. 16.00 (*0-374-37131-8*) FS&G.
—Solomon the Rusty Nail. (Illus.). 32p. (ps up). 1987. pap. 4.95 (*0-374-46903-2*) FS&G.
—Spinky Sulks. LC 88-81292. (Illus.). 32p. (ps up). 1988. 15.00 (*0-374-38321-9*) FS&G.
—Spinky Sulks. (gr. 4-8). 1991. pap. 4.95 (*0-374-46990-3*) FS&G.
—Sylvester & the Magic Pebble. (Illus.). 32p. (ps-3). 1988. (Little Simon); (S&S BFYR) S&S Trade.
—Sylvester & the Magic Pebble. Steig, William, illus. 32p. (ps-1). 1988. Bk. & cassette. pap. 8.95 (*0-671-67144-8*, S&S BFYR) S&S Trade.
—Sylvester & the Magic Pebble. LC 80-12314. (Illus.). 32p. (gr. k-4). 1988. pap. 14.00 (*0-671-66154-X*, S&S BFYR); pap. 5.95 (*0-671-66269-4*, S&S BFYR) S&S Trade.
—Sylvester & the Magic Pebble. (gr. 2). 1992. write for info. (*0-663-56220-1*) Silver Burdett Pr.
—Tiffky Doofky. (Illus.). (ps up). 1987. pap. 3.95 (*0-374-47748-5*) FS&G.
—El Verdadero Ladron: The Real Thief. (ps-3). 1993. 15.00 (*0-374-30458-0*, Mirasol) FS&G.
—Yellow & Pink. Steig, William, illus. LC 84-80503. 32p. (ps up). 1984. 12.00 (*0-374-38670-6*) FS&G.
—Yellow & Pink. LC 84-80503. 32p. (ps up). 1988. pap. 3.95 (*0-374-48735-9*) FS&G.
—The Zabajaba Jungle. Steig, William, illus. LC 87-17690. (ps-4). 1987. 15.00 (*0-374-38790-7*) FS&G.
—The Zabajaba Jungle. LC 87-17690. (Illus.). (ps-4). 1991. pap. 4.95 (*0-374-49594-7*) FS&G.

Steiger, Brad. Beyond Belief: Strange, True Mysteries of the Unknown. 176p. (gr. 5 up). 1992. pap. 2.95 (*0-590-44252-X*) Scholastic Inc.

Steiger, Brad & Steiger, Sherry H. The Mystery of Animal Intelligence. (Orig.). 1994. pap. 3.99 (*0-8125-3367-4*) Tor Bks.

Steiger, Sherry H., jt. auth. see Steiger, Brad.

Stein. Johnstown Flood. 1989. pap. 3.95 (*0-516-44680-0*) Childrens.
—Monitor & Merrimac. 1989. pap. 3.95 (*0-516-44662-2*) Childrens.

Stein, Aidel. Baker's Dozen, No. 3: And the Winner Is... 1993. pap. 7.95 (*0-685-65304-8*) Feldheim.
—Baker's Dozen, No. 4: Stars in Their Eyes. 1993. pap. 7.95 (*0-685-65305-6*) Feldheim.
—Baker's Dozen: Stars in Their Eyes, No. 4. 1992. pap. 7.95 (*0-944070-85-X*) Targum Pr.

Stein, Barbara. Kids' World Almanac of Transportation: Rockets, Planes, Trains, Cars, Boars & Other Ways to Travel. 1991. 14.95 (*0-88687-491-2*, World Almanac); pap. 6.95 (*0-88687-490-4*, World Almanac) F&W Inc NJ.

Stein, Charlotte M. The Stained Glass Window. Sakurai, Jennifer, ed. Stein, Michele P., illus. LC 88-70883. 150p. (Orig.). 1993. pap. 11.95 incl. wkbk. (*0-916634-12-4*) Double M Pr.

Stein, Conrad R. Walter Payton: Record-Breaking Runner. LC 87-13241. (Illus.). 48p. (gr. 2-8). 1987. PLB 13.27 (*0-516-04363-3*); pap. 3.95 (*0-516-44363-1*) Childrens.

Stein, Ellie. Squeeze. (Illus.). 55p. (Orig.). (gr. 7-12). 1989. pap. 4.00 (*0-88680-319-5*); royalty on application 35.00 (*0-685-67715-X*) I E Clark.

Stein, Gertrude. The World Is Round. limited ed. Hurd, Clement, illus. Hurd, Margaret T., intro. by. (Illus.). (gr. 3 up). 1985. 200.00 (*0-910457-16-6*) Arion Pr.
—The World Is Round. Arenson, Roberta, illus. LC 93-562. 160p. 1993. Repr. of 1939 ed. 6.00 (*1-56957-905-9*) Shambhala Pubns.

Stein, Jovial B. Son of Fury. (ps). 1991. pap. 2.75 (*0-553-15854-6*) Bantam.

Stein, Kevin. Brothers Majere. LC 88-51720. (Illus.). 352p. (Orig.). 1990. pap. 4.95 (*0-88038-776-9*) TSR Inc.

Stein, R. C. The Story of the Monitor & the Merrimac. LC 82-23503. (Illus.). 32p. (gr. 3-6). 1983. PLB 13.27 (*0-516-04662-4*) Childrens.
—Washington. LC 91-13509. 144p. (gr. 4 up). 1991. PLB 26.60 (*0-516-00493-X*) Childrens.

Stein, R. Conrad. Apollo Eleven. 2nd ed. LC 91-33220. 32p. (gr. 3-6). 1992. PLB 15.27 (*0-516-06651-X*) Childrens.
—The Assassination of John F. Kennedy. LC 91-44546. (Illus.). 32p. (gr. 3-6). 1992. PLB 15.27 (*0-516-06652-8*) Childrens.
—The Assassination of John F. Kennedy. LC 91-44546. (Illus.). 32p. (gr. 3-6). 1993. pap. 3.95 (*0-516-46652-6*) Childrens.
—The Bill of Rights. LC 91-41541. (Illus.). 32p. (gr. 3-6). PLB 15.27, Apr. 1992 (*0-516-04853-8*); pap. 3.95, Jul. 1992 (*0-516-44853-6*) Childrens.
—California. LC 87-37948. (Illus.). 144p. (gr. 4 up). 1988. PLB 26.60 (*0-516-00451-4*) Childrens.
—California. 209p. 1993. text ed. 15.40 (*1-56956-174-5*) W A T Braille.
—Christopher Columbus. LC 91-34744. (Illus.). 32p. (gr. 3-6). PLB 15.27, Apr. 1992 (*0-516-04851-1*); pap. 3. 95, Jul. 1992 (*0-516-44851-X*) Childrens.
—D-Day. LC 92-36809. (Illus.). 32p. (gr. 3-6). 1993. PLB 15.27 (*0-516-06661-7*); pap. 3.95 (*0-516-46661-5*) Childrens.
—David Robinson, the Admiral. LC 93-38039. 1994. write for info. (*0-516-04382-X*) Childrens.
—Ellis Island. 2nd ed. LC 91-33222. (Illus.). 32p. (gr. 3-6). PLB 15.27, Apr. 1992 (*0-516-06653-6*); pap. 3. 95, Jul. 1992 (*0-516-46653-4*) Childrens.
—Francisco de Coronado: Explorer of the American Southwest. LC 91-32207. 128p. (gr. 3 up). 1992. PLB 26.60 (*0-516-03068-X*) Childrens.
—Greece. LC 87-13225. (Illus.). 128p. (gr. 5-9). 1987. PLB 26.60 (*0-516-02759-X*) Childrens.
—Hernando Cortes: Conqueror of Mexico. LC 90-20655. (Illus.). 128p. (gr. 3 up). 1991. PLB 26.60 (*0-516-03059-0*) Childrens.
—Hindenburg Disaster. LC 92-34520. (Illus.). 32p. (gr. 3-6). 1993. PLB 15.27 (*0-516-06663-3*); pap. 3.95 (*0-516-46663-1*) Childrens.
—The Holocaust. LC 85-31415. (Illus.). 48p. (gr. 4-8). 1986. PLB 15.00 (*0-516-04767-1*) Childrens.
—Hong Kong. LC 84-23199. (Illus.). 128p. (gr. 5-9). 1985. PLB 26.60 (*0-516-02765-4*) Childrens.
—Illinois. (Illus.). 144p. (gr. 4 up). 1987. 26.60 (*0-516-00459-X*) Childrens.
—Illinois. 202p. 1993. text ed. 15.40 (*1-56956-169-9*) W A T Braille.
—Indiana. LC 89-25281. (Illus.). 144p. (gr. 4 up). 1990. PLB 26.60 (*0-516-00460-3*) Childrens.
—Indiana. 194p. 1993. text ed. 15.40 (*1-56956-161-3*) W A T Braille.
—Italy. LC 83-14259. (Illus.). 128p. (gr. 5-9). 1984. PLB 26.60 (*0-516-02768-9*) Childrens.
—Kenya. LC 85-14949. (Illus.). 127p. (gr. 5-9). 1985. PLB 26.60 (*0-516-02770-0*) Childrens.
—The Mexican Revolution, 1910-1920. LC 93-17259. (Illus.). 144p. (gr. 6 up). 1994. SBE 14.95 (*0-02-786950-4*, New Discovery Bks) Macmillan Child Grp.
—Mexico. LC 83-21049. (Illus.). 128p. (gr. 5-9). 1984. PLB 26.60 (*0-516-02772-7*) Childrens.
—Michigan. LC 87-9383. (Illus.). 144p. (gr. 4 up). 1987. PLB 26.60 (*0-516-00468-9*) Childrens.
—Michigan. 188p. 1993. text ed. 15.40 (*1-56956-175-3*) W A T Braille.
—Minnesota. LC 90-35384. (Illus.). 144p. (gr. 4 up). 1990. PLB 26.60 (*0-516-00469-7*) Childrens.
—New Mexico. LC 87-34113. (Illus.). 144p. (gr. 4 up). 1988. PLB 26.60 (*0-516-00477-8*) Childrens.
—New Mexico. 199p. 1993. text ed. 15.40 (*1-56956-129-X*) W A T Braille.
—New York. LC 88-11748. (Illus.). 144p. (gr. 4 up). 1988. PLB 26.60 (*0-516-00478-6*) Childrens.
—New York. 202p. 1993. text ed. 15.40 (*1-56956-158-3*) W A T Braille.
—North Carolina. LC 89-17298. 144p. (gr. 4 up). 1989. PLB 26.60 (*0-516-00479-4*) Childrens.
—North Carolina. 190p. 1993. text ed. 15.40 (*1-56956-168-0*) W A T Braille.
—Oregon. LC 88-38528. (Illus.). 144p. (gr. 4 up). 1989. PLB 26.60 (*0-516-00483-2*) Childrens.
—Oregon. 189p. 1993. text ed. 15.40 (*1-56956-128-1*) W A T Braille.
—The Oregon Trail. LC 93-36994. 1994. write for info. (*0-516-06674-9*) Childrens.
—Prisoners of War. (Illus.). 48p. (gr. 4-8). 1987. 15.00 (*0-516-04799-X*) Childrens.
—The Roaring Twenties. LC 93-37029. 1994. write for info. (*0-516-06675-7*) Childrens.

—South Africa. LC 86-9651. (Illus.). 128p. (gr. 5-9). 1986. PLB 26.60 (*0-516-02784-0*) Childrens.
—The Story of D-Day. Dunnington, Tom, illus. LC 77-5089. 32p. (gr. 3-6). 1977. pap. 3.95 (*0-516-44609-6*) Childrens.
—The Story of Lexington & Concord. LC 82-23518. (Illus.). 32p. (gr. 3-6). 1983. PLB 13.27 (*0-516-04661-6*); pap. 3.95 (*0-516-44661-4*) Childrens.
—The Story of Little Bighorn. LC 83-6594. (Illus.). 32p. (gr. 3-6). 1983. pap. 3.95 (*0-516-44663-0*) Childrens.
—The Story of Mississippi Steamboats. Dunnington, Tom, illus. 32p. (gr. 3-6). 1987. pap. 3.95 (*0-516-44726-2*) Childrens.
—The Story of the Boston Tea Party. LC 83-27319. (Illus.). (gr. 3-6). 1984. PLB 13.27 (*0-516-04666-7*); pap. 3.95 (*0-516-44666-5*) Childrens.
—The Story of the Chicago Fire. Wahl, Richard, illus. LC 81-15543. 32p. (gr. 3-6). 1982. pap. 3.95 (*0-516-44633-9*) Childrens.
—The Story of the Erie Canal. Neely, Keith, illus. LC 84-28525. 32p. (gr. 3-6). 1985. PLB 13.27 (*0-516-04682-9*); pap. 3.95 (*0-516-44682-7*) Childrens.
—The Story of the Great Depression. Greene, Nathan, illus. LC 85-11039. 32p. (gr. 3-6). 1985. PLB 13.27 (*0-516-04694-2*) Childrens.
—The Story of the Lewis & Clark Expedition. Aronson, Lou, illus. LC 78-4648. 32p. (gr. 3-6). 1978. pap. 3.95 (*0-516-44620-7*) Childrens.
—The Story of the Lone Star Republic. LC 87-35467. (Illus.). 32p. (gr. 3-6). 1988. pap. 3.95 (*0-516-44735-1*) Childrens.
—The Story of the Montgomery Bus Boycott. Greene, Nathan, illus. LC 85-31349. 32p. (gr. 3-6). 1986. PLB 13.27 (*0-516-04697-7*); pap. 3.95 (*0-516-44697-5*) Childrens.
—The Story of the Nineteenth Amendment. LC 82-44419. (Illus.). 32p. (gr. 3-6). 1982. PLB 13.27 (*0-516-04639-X*); pap. 3.95 (*0-516-44639-8*) Childrens.
—The Story of the Powers of Congress. Neely, Keith, illus. LC 85-10943. 32p. (gr. 3-6). 1985. PLB 13.27 (*0-516-04695-0*); pap. 3.95 (*0-516-44695-9*) Childrens.
—The Story of the Powers of the Supreme Court. LC 89-15885. 32p. (gr. 3-6). 1989. PLB 13.27 (*0-516-04721-3*) Childrens.
—The Story of the San Francisco Earthquake. LC 83-10135. (Illus.). 32p. (gr. 3-6). 1983. PLB 13.27 (*0-516-04664-0*); pap. 3.95 (*0-516-44664-9*) Childrens.
—The Story of the Spirit of St. Louis. Meents, Len W., illus. LC 83-23174. 32p. (gr. 3-6). 1984. pap. 3.95 (*0-516-44667-3*) Childrens.
—The Story of the Trail of Tears. Catrow, David, III, illus. LC 84-28507. 32p. (gr. 3-6). 1985. PLB 13.27 (*0-516-04683-7*); pap. 3.95 (*0-516-44683-5*) Childrens.
—The Story of the Underground Railroad. LC 82-3801. (Illus.). 32p. (gr. 3-6). 1981. PLB 13.27 (*0-516-04643-8*); pap. 3.95 (*0-516-44643-6*) Childrens.
—The Story of the United Nations. Canaday, Ralph, illus. LC 85-31356. 32p. (gr. 3-6). 1986. pap. 3.95 (*0-516-44698-3*) Childrens.
—The Story of Valley Forge. Eads, Nancy, illus. LC 84-23203. 32p. (gr. 3-6). 1985. PLB 13.27 (*0-516-04681-0*) Childrens.
—The Story of Wounded Knee. LC 83-6584. (Illus.). 32p. (gr. 3-6). 1983. pap. 3.95 (*0-516-44665-7*) Childrens.
—Texas. LC 88-38400. (Illus.). 144p. (gr. 4 up). 1989. PLB 26.60 (*0-516-00489-1*) Childrens.
—Texas. 193p. 1993. text ed. 15.40 (*1-56956-151-6*) W A T Braille.
—The Trail of Tears. LC 92-33422. (Illus.). 32p. (gr. 3-6). 1993. PLB 15.27 (*0-516-06666-8*); pap. 3.95 (*0-516-46666-6*) Childrens.
—The United States of America. LC 93-35492. 1994. write for info. (*0-516-02623-2*) Childrens.
—The USS Arizona. LC 91-44646. (Illus.). 32p. (gr. 3-6). 1992. PLB 15.27 (*0-516-06656-0*) Childrens.
—The USS Arizona. LC 91-44646. (Illus.). 32p. (gr. 3-6). 1993. pap. 3.95 (*0-516-46656-9*) Childrens.
—Washington. 208p. 1993. text ed. 15.40 (*1-56956-146-X*) W A T Braille.
—West Virginia. LC 90-33848. (Illus.). 144p. (gr. 4 up). 1990. PLB 26.60 (*0-516-00494-8*) Childrens.
—West Virginia. 195p. 1993. text ed. 15.40 (*1-56956-144-3*) W A T Braille.
—Wisconsin. LC 87-9376. (Illus.). 144p. (gr. 4 up). 1987. PLB 26.60 (*0-516-00495-6*) Childrens.
—Wisconsin. 210p. 1993. text ed. 15.40 (*1-56956-173-7*) W A T Braille.

Stein, R. Conrad, III. The Story of the Oregon Trail. LC 83-23997. (Illus.). 31p. (gr. 3-5). 1984. 13.27 (*0-516-04668-3*); pap. 3.95 (*0-516-44668-1*) Childrens.

Stein, Richard C. The Great Depression. LC 93-752. (Illus.). 32p. (gr. 3-6). 1993. PLB 15.93 (*0-516-06668-4*) Childrens.
—The Manhattan Project. LC 93-12686. (Illus.). 32p. (gr. 3-6). 1993. PLB 15.93 (*0-516-06670-6*) Childrens.
—The Montgomery Bus Boycott. LC 93-16854. (Illus.). 32p. (gr. 3-6). 1993. PLB 15.93 (*0-516-06671-4*) Childrens.

Stein, Sara. The Body Book. LC 91-50957. (Illus.). (gr. 4-7). 1992. 19.95 (*1-56305-298-9*, 3298); pap. 11.95 (*0-89480-805-2*, 1805) Workman Pub.
—The Evolution Book. Stein, Sara, illus. LC 84-40682. 400p. (Orig.). (gr. 5-9). 1986. pap. 12.95 (*0-89480-927-X*, 927) Workman Pub.
—Oh Baby. (ps-3). 1993. 14.95 (*0-8027-8261-2*); PLB 15.85 (*0-8027-8262-0*) Walker & Co.

—The Science Book. LC 79-64786. (Illus.). 288p. (gr. 4-7). 1980. pap. 9.95 (0-89480-120-1, 291) Workman Pub.

Stein, Sara B. About Dying. LC 73-15268. (Illus.). 48p. (ps-8). 1984. pap. 8.95 (0-8027-7223-4) Walker & Co.
—About Dying. LC 73-15268. (Illus.). 48p. (gr. 1 up). 1974. 10.95 (0-8027-6172-0) Walker & Co.
—About Handicaps. LC 73-15270. (Illus.). 48p. (ps-8). 1984. pap. 8.95 (0-8027-7225-0) Walker & Co.
—About Handicaps. LC 73-15270. (Illus.). 48p. (gr. 1 up). 1974. 12.95 (0-8027-6174-7) Walker & Co.
—About Phobias. LC 78-65615. (Illus.). 48p. (ps-8). 1984. pap. text ed. 8.95 (0-8027-7219-6) Walker & Co.
—About Phobias. Stone, Erika, illus. (ps-8). 1979. 10.95 (0-8027-6348-0) Walker & Co.
—The Adopted One. Stone, Erika, illus. (gr. k-6). 1979. 12.95 (0-8027-6346-4); pap. 7.95 (0-8027-7224-2) Walker & Co.
—A Hospital Story. LC 73-15269. (Illus.). 48p. (ps-8). 1984. pap. 8.95 (0-8027-7222-6) Walker & Co.
—A Hospital Story. LC 73-15269. (Illus.). 48p. (gr. 1 up). 1974. 10.95 (0-8027-6173-9) Walker & Co.
—Making Babies. LC 73-15267. (Illus.). 48p. (gr. 1 up). 1974. 10.95 (0-8027-6171-2) Walker & Co.
—Making Babies. LC 73-15267. (Illus.). 48p. (ps-8). 1984. pap. 7.95 (0-8027-7221-8) Walker & Co.
—On Divorce. LC 78-15687. (Illus.). 48p. (ps-8). 1984. pap. 4.95 (0-8027-7226-9) Walker & Co.
—On Divorce. Stone, Erika, illus. 48p. 1979. 10.95 (0-8027-6344-8) Walker & Co.
—That New Baby. LC 73-15271. (Illus.). 48p. 1984. pap. 8.95 (0-8027-7227-7) Walker & Co.
—That New Baby. LC 73-15271. (Illus.). 48p. (gr. 1 up). 1974. 12.95 (0-8027-6175-5) Walker & Co.

Stein, Stephanie. Lucy's Feet. Imler, Kathryn A., illus. LC 92-4602. 32p. (ps-3). 1992. 12.95 (0-944934-05-6) Perspect Indiana.

Stein, Wendy. Ancient Ireland. Swanberg, Nancy & Anderson, L., illus. (gr. k). 1978. pap. text ed. 3.95 (0-88388-060-1) Bellerophon Bks.
—Atlantis: Opposing Viewpoints. LC 88-24470. (Illus.). 112p. (gr. 5-8). 1989. PLB 14.95 (0-89908-056-1) Greenhaven.
—Shamans: Opposing Viewpoints. LC 91-14498. (Illus.). 112p. (gr. 5-8). 1991. PLB 14.95 (0-89908-088-X) Greenhaven.

Steinbauer, Janine. Katherine Mansfield. LC 93-10634. (gr. 6 up). 1994. write for info. (0-88682-623-3) Creative Ed.
—Willa Cather. LC 93-10628. (gr. 5 up). 1994. write for info. (0-88682-622-5) Creative Ed.

Steinbaum, Michael & Cohen, Diana. Simon & His Shrinking Socks. Balkovek, James, illus. 64p. (ps-4). 1993. pap. 9.95 (0-8449-4253-7); FRE Translation Tool, "Trans-it" 4.95 (0-8449-4293-6); CHI Translation Tool, "Trans-it" 4.95 (0-8449-4295-2); GER Translation Tool, "Trans-it" 4.95 (0-8449-4294-4); SPA Translation Tool, "Trans-it" 4.95 (0-8449-4292-8) Good Morn Tchr.

Steinbaum, Michael & Warmbold, Jean. The Tumble-Down Tower. Balkovek, James, illus. (ps-4). 1993. pap. 9.95 (0-8449-4254-5); FRE Translation Tool, "Trans-it" 4.95 (0-8449-4297-9); CHI Translation Tool, "Trans-it" 4.95 (0-8449-4299-5); GER Translation Tool, "Trans-it" 4.95 (0-8449-4298-7); SPA Translation Tool, "Trans-it" 4.95 (0-8449-4296-0) Good Morn Tchr.

Steinbeck, John. The Gift. (gr. 5 up). 1992. PLB 13.95 (0-88682-507-5) Creative Ed.
—Of Mice & Men. (gr. 9-12). 1970. pap. 2.75 (0-553-26675-6) Bantam.
—The Red Pony. reissue ed. Dennis, Wesley, illus. (gr. 7 up). 1986. pap. 15.95 (0-670-59184-X) Viking Child Bks.

Steinberg, Barbara, jt. auth. see Tabs, Judy.

Steinberg, Michael. Our Wilderness: How the People of New York Found, Changed & Preserved the Adirondacks. LC 91-16550. (Illus.). 112p. (gr. 4 up). 1993. 18.95 (0-935272-56-9); pap. 11.95 (0-935272-57-7) ADK Mtn Club.
A history of the 6-million-acre Adirondack Park of New York State, which includes towns & farms, businesses & timberlands as well as 1.2 million acres of wilderness. Written for ages 10 & up (Gr. 4 plus). Described by KIRKUS REVIEWS as "a cultural history full of charming, quirky people, plus both funny & sobering anecdotes... Gracefully written with lessons that go far beyond regional interest." APPALACHIA noted that "there is probably no other book available that can provide as thorough an introduction to Adirondack history, particularly with anything close to the brevity & efficiency of this book." Author received award from

Adirondack Park Centennial Committee for his contribution to education via OUR WILDERNESS. Historic photographs by Stoddard & Apperson. Publication coincided with the 1992 Centennial of the Adirondack Park. Book carries conservationist message. "The entertaining & informative 'young people's history'... contains plenty of interest the mature mind."--New York's Rochester DEMOCRAT & CHRONICLE. *Publisher Provided Annotation.*

Steinberg, Sari. And Then There Were Dinosaurs. (ps-3). 1993. 14.95 (0-943706-19-X) Yllw Brick Rd.
Steinberg, Shalom D. The Third Beis Hamikdash: The Third Temple. Miller, Moshe L., tr. from HEB. Margolis, Ezrachi, illus. 240p. (gr. 11-12). 1993. 15.95 (0-940118-80-7) Moznaim.
Steinbock, Steven E. Torah: The Growing Gift. (Illus., Orig.). (gr. 4-6). 1994. pap. 8.00 (0-8074-0502-7, 123939); tchr's. guide 6.00 (0-8074-0503-5, 208035) UAHC.
Steindam, Harold. Growing Together: Sermons for Children. Heck, J. Parker, illus. LC 88-28718. 136p. (Orig.). 1989. pap. 9.95 (0-8298-0800-0) Pilgrim OH.
Steiner, Barbara. Deathline. 176p. (Orig.). (gr. 5). 1993. pap. 3.50 (0-380-77066-0, Flare) Avon.
—Dolby & the Woof-Off. LC 90-21464. (Illus.). 128p. (gr. 2 up). 1991. 12.95 (0-688-08435-4) Morrow Jr Bks.
—Dreamstalker. 160p. (Orig.). (gr. 4 up). 1992. pap. 3.50 (0-380-76611-6, Flare) Avon.
—Foghorn Flattery & the Dancing Horses. 112p. (Orig.). (gr. 5). 1991. pap. 2.95 (0-380-76147-5, Camelot) Avon.
—Ghost Cave. 135p. (gr. 3-7). 1990. 13.95 (0-15-230752-4) HarBrace.
—Ghost Cave. Ashby, Ruth, ed. 144p. (gr. 3-6). 1993. pap. 2.99 (0-671-74785-1, Minstrel Bks) PB.
—Night Cries. 144p. (Orig.). (gr. 4). 1993. pap. 3.50 (0-380-76990-5, Flare) Avon.
—Oliver Dibbs & the Dinosaur Cause. Christelow, Eileen, illus. LC 86-9941. 128p. (gr. 3-7). 1986. SBE 13.95 (0-02-787880-5, Four Winds) Macmillan Child Grp.
—Oliver Dibbs & the Dinosaur Cause. 160p. 1988. pap. 2.95 (0-380-70466-8, Camelot) Avon.
—Oliver Dibbs to the Rescue! Christelow, Eileen, illus. LC 85-42801. 96p. (gr. 3-5). 1985. SBE 12.95 (0-02-787890-2, Four Winds) Macmillan Child Grp.
—Oliver Dibbs to the Rescue! Christelow, Eileen, illus. 128p. 1988. pap. 2.50 (0-380-70465-X, Camelot) Avon.
—Phantom. 1993. pap. 3.50 (0-590-46425-6) Scholastic Inc.
—The Photographer. 144p. 1989. pap. 3.50 (0-380-75758-3, Flare) Avon.
—The Photographer Two: The Dark Room. 176p. (Orig.). 1993. pap. 3.50 (0-380-77064-4, Flare) Avon.
—Tessa. LC 87-31524. 224p. (gr. 7 up). 1988. 12.95 (0-688-07232-1) Morrow Jr Bks.
—Whale Brother. Mayo, Gretchen W., illus. (ps-3). 1988. 12.95 (0-8027-6804-0); PLB 13.85 (0-8027-6805-9) Walker & Co.
Steiner, Claude. A Warm Fuzzy Tale. Dick, Joann, illus. Freed, Alvyn M., intro. by. LC 77-77981. (Illus., Orig.). (gr. k up). 1977. 8.95 (0-915190-08-7, JP9008-7) Jalmar Pr.
Steiner, Connie. Paul's New Ears. Steiner, Connie, illus. 24p. (Orig.). (gr. k-3). 1991. pap. 9.95 (0-920541-44-5) Peguis Pubs Ltd.
Steiner, Connie C. On Eagles Wings & Other Things. 32p. (gr. k-4). 1987. 12.95 (0-8276-0274-X) JPS Phila.
Steiner, Frank, tr. see Keckeis, M. B., et al.
Steiner, Frank, tr. see Keckeis, M. B. & Beaubeau, Anne.
Steiner, Frank, et al, trs. see Keckeis, M. B.
Steiner, Jorge. The Animals' Rebellion. Muller, Jorg, illus. 32p. 1991. smythe sewn reinforced bdg. 15.95 (1-56182-025-3) Atomium Bks.
Steiner, Michael P., Sr. Not a Wicked Stepmother. rev. ed. (Illus.). 42p. (Orig.). (gr. 4 up). 1991. pap. text ed. 12.95 (1-879417-00-6) Stern & Stern.
Steiner, Robert A. The Truth Shall Make You Free: An Inquiry into the Legend of God. Dugger, Kim, illus. Patterson, John W., intro. by. LC 80-80646. (Illus.). 47p. (Orig.). (gr. 6 up). 1980. pap. 4.95 (0-9604044-0-6) Wide-Awake Bks.
Steiner, Rudolf. And It Came to Pass: An Old Testament, Reader for Children. 1973. lib. bdg. 79.95 (0-87968-556-5) Krishna Pr.
Steinkamp, Anja J. Your First Guinea Pig. (Illus.). 36p. (Orig.). 1991. pap. 1.95 (0-86622-066-6, YF-109) TFH Pubns.
Steinke, Ann. Marie Curie. (Illus.). 144p. (gr. 3-6). 1987. pap. 5.95 (0-8120-3924-6) Barron.
—My Cheating Heart. 1993. pap. 3.50 (0-06-106733-4, Harp PBks) HarpC.
Steinmetz, Shirley A. Silly Scribbles: A Complete Readiness Program for Young Children. 272p. (ps-k). 1988. pap. 24.95x (0-87628-776-3) Ctr Appl Res.

Steins. Allies Against Axis. 1993. write for info. (0-8050-3165-0) H Holt & Co.
Steins, Richard. The Allies Against the Axis: World War II (1940-1950) (Illus.). 64p. (gr. 5-8). 1993. PLB 14.95 (0-8050-2586-3) TFC Bks NY.
—Berlin. (Illus.). 64p. (gr. 3-7). PLB 14.95 (1-56711-019-3) Blackbirch.
—The Death Penalty: Is It Justice? (Illus.). 64p. (gr. 5-8). 1993. PLB 14.95 (0-8050-2571-5) TFC Bks NY.
—Leontyne Price: Opera Star. (Illus.). 64p. (gr. 3-7). 1993. PLB 14.95 (1-56711-009-6) Blackbirch.
—The Mideast after the Gulf War. LC 91-29944. (Illus.). 64p. (gr. 5-8). 1992. PLB 15.90 (1-56294-156-9) Millbrook Pr.
—Mideast after the Gulf War. 1992. pap. 4.95 (0-395-62471-1) HM.
—The Nation Divides: The Civil War, 1820-1880. LC 93-24993. (Illus.). 64p. (gr. 5-8). 1993. PLB 14.95 (0-8050-2583-9) TFC Bks Ny.
—A Nation Is Born: Rebellion & Independence in America, 1700-1820. LC 93-24994. (Illus.). 64p. (gr. 5-8). 1993. PLB 14.95 (0-8050-2582-0) TFC Bks Ny.
—Our National Capital. (Illus.). 48p. (gr. 2-4). 1994. 12.90 (1-56294-439-8) Millbrook Pr.
—Post War Years: The Cold War & the Atomic Age (1950-1959) (Illus.). 64p. (gr. 5-8). 1993. PLB 14.95 (0-8050-2587-1) TFC Bks NY.
Steinwachs, Robert. Brain Bafflers. Miller, Myron, illus. 128p. (gr. 10-12). 1993. pap. 4.95 (0-8069-8787-1) Sterling.
Stelling, Bill. Simply Spiritual: A Sharing. (Illus.). 64p. (Orig.). (gr. 9-12). 1992. pap. 9.95 (0-940829-07-X) Eagle Wing Bks.
—Simply Spiritual Exercise Workbook. 38p. (Orig.). (gr. 10 up). 1992. pap. 6.00 (0-940829-08-8) Eagle Wing Bks.
Stelson, Caren B. Safari. Stelson, Kim A., illus. 40p. (gr. k-4). 1988. PLB 19.95 (0-87614-324-9) Carolrhoda Bks.
—Safari. Stelson, Kim A., illus. 40p. (gr. k-4). 1989. pap. 5.95 (0-87614-512-8, First Ave Edns) Lerner Pubns.
Steltenpohl, Jane, ed. see Beard, Charles A. & Vagts, Detlev.
Steltenpohl, Jane, ed. see Bornstein, Sandy.
Steltenpohl, Jane, ed. see Chirinian, Alain.
Steltenpohl, Jane, ed. see Cleeve, Roger.
Steltenpohl, Jane, ed. see Coil, Suzanne M.
Steltenpohl, Jane, ed. see Cook, Fred J.
Steltenpohl, Jane, ed. see DuPrau, Jeanne.
Steltenpohl, Jane, ed. see Farley, Karin C.
Steltenpohl, Jane, ed. see Gardner, Robert.
Steltenpohl, Jane, ed. see Gardner, Robert & Shortelle, Dennis.
Steltenpohl, Jane, ed. see Gravelle, Karen & Haskins, Charles.
Steltenpohl, Jane, ed. see Imershein, Betsy.
Steltenpohl, Jane, ed. see Kelch, Joseph W.
Steltenpohl, Jane, ed. see Kronenwetter, Michael.
Steltenpohl, Jane, ed. see Landau, Elaine.
Steltenpohl, Jane, ed. see MacMillan, Dianne & Freeman, Dorothy.
Steltenpohl, Jane, ed. see Madison, Arnold.
Steltenpohl, Jane, ed. see Pearce, Q. L.
Steltenpohl, Jane, ed. see Schneider, Meg.
Steltenpohl, Jane, ed. see Smith, Kathie B.
Steltenpohl, Jane, ed. see Smith, Lucinda I.
Steltenpohl, Jane, ed. see Smith, Norman F.
Steltenpohl, Jane, ed. see Sullivan, George.
Steltenpohl, Jane, ed. see Webster, David.
Steltenpohl, Jane, ed. see Wyler, Rose.
Steltenpohl, Jane, ed. see Zipko, Stephen J.
Steltzer, Ulli. Building an Igloo. Steltzer, Ulli, illus. 32p. (ps-2). 1991. pap. 4.95 (0-88899-118-5, Pub. by Groundwood-Douglas & McIntyre CN) Firefly Bks Ltd.
—The New Americans. Marin, Peter, intro. by. (Illus.). 176p. (gr. 6 up). 1988. pap. 24.95x (0-939165-07-4) NewSage Press.
Stembridge, Charles, jt. auth. see Radlauer, Ruth.
Stenbock, Evelyn, compiled by. Children's Day Program Builder, No. 6. 32p. Date not set. 3.95 (0-685-68749-X, BCMP-106) Lillenas.
—Children's Day Program Builder, No. 7. 32p. Date not set. 3.95 (0-685-68748-1, BCMP-107) Lillenas.
—Children's Day Program Builder, No. 8. 32p. Date not set. 3.95 (0-685-68747-3, BCMP-108) Lillenas.
—Children's Day Program Builder, No. 9. 32p. Date not set. 3.95 (0-685-68746-5, BCMP-109) Lillenas.
Stenbock, Evelyn, ed. Twenty for Teens. Date not set. 3.95 (0-685-68740-6, BCMP-611) Lillenas.
Stenson, Elizabeth. Early Settler Activity Guide. (Illus.). 128p. (gr. 4-5). 1983. pap. 15.95 (0-86505-036-8) Crabtree Pub Co.
Stenstrup, Allen. Hazardous Waste. LC 91-25864. 128p. (gr. 4-8). 1991. PLB 26.60 (0-516-05506-2) Childrens.
Stepanchuk, Carol. Celebrating Chinese Festivals. 32p. (gr. 3-8). 1993. 15.95 (1-881896-08-0) Pacific View Pr.
Stepanek, Sally. Martin Luther. Schlesinger, Arthur M., Jr., intro. by. (Illus.). 112p. (gr. 5 up). 1986. lib. bdg. 17.95 (0-87754-538-3) Chelsea Hse.
—Mary, Queen of Scots. Schlesinger, Arthur M., Jr., intro. by. (Illus.). 112p. (gr. 5 up). 1987. lib. bdg. 17.95 (0-87754-540-5) Chelsea Hse.
Stepanoff, N. C. & Flier, Michael S. Say It in Russian. 256p. (gr. 6 up). pap. 3.95 (0-486-20810-9) Dover.
Stephanides Brothers Staff. Greek Mythology, 6 vols. (gr. 5-10). Set. 60.00x (0-916634-25-6) Double M Pr.

—Greek Mythology, 6 Vols. (gr. 5-10). Set. 60.00 (*0-916634-26-4*) Double M Pr.

Stephen, R. J. Picture World of Aircraft Carriers. (Illus.). 1990. PLB 12.40 (*0-531-14008-3*) Watts.

—The Picture World of Airliners. (Illus.). 32p. (gr. k-4). 1989. PLB 12.40 (*0-531-10724-8*) Watts.

—Picture World of Combat Aircraft. (Illus.). 1990. PLB 12.40 (*0-531-14009-1*) Watts.

—The Picture World of Helicopters. (Illus.). 32p. (gr. k-4). 1989. PLB 12.40 (*0-531-10726-4*) Watts.

—Picture World of Military Helicopters. (Illus.). 1990. PLB 12.40 (*0-531-14010-5*) Watts.

—Picture World of Submarines. (Illus.). 1990. PLB 12.40 (*0-531-14011-3*) Watts.

—The Picture World of Trucks. (Illus.). 32p. (gr. k-4). 1989. PLB 12.40 (*0-531-10729-9*) Watts.

—Picture World of Warships. (Illus.). 1990. PLB 12.40 (*0-531-14013-X*) Watts.

Stephen, Richard. Deserts. McLean, Dee, et al, illus. LC 89-20300. 32p. (gr. 4-6). 1990. PLB 11.59 (*0-8167-1969-1*); pap. text ed. 3.95 (*0-8167-1970-5*) Troll Assocs.

—Rivers. Bowring, Isabel, et al, illus. LC 89-20303. 32p. (gr. 4-6). 1990. PLB 11.59 (*0-8167-1975-6*); pap. text ed. 3.95 (*0-8167-1976-4*) Troll Assocs.

Stephens, Amanda. Peter Cottontail. Santoro, Christopher, illus. 32p. (ps-3). 1994. pap. 2.50 (*0-590-47761-7*, Cartwheel) Scholastic Inc.

Stephens, Andrea. Stressed-Out but Hangin' Tough. 160p. (Orig.). (gr. 8-12). 1989. pap. 6.99 (*0-8007-5326-7*) Revell.

Stephens, Andrea & Stephens, Bill. Prime Time: Devotions for Girls. (Orig.). 1992. pap. 7.99 (*0-8007-5390-9*) Revell.

—Prime Time: Devotions for Guys. (Orig.). 1992. pap. 7.99 (*0-8007-5391-7*) Revell.

—Ready for Prime Time: Devotions for Girls. LC 92-31717. 176p. (Orig.). 1993. pap. 7.99 (*0-8007-5459-X*) Revell.

—Ready for Prime Time: Devotions for Guys. LC 92-31721. 176p. (Orig.). 1993. pap. 7.99 (*0-8007-5460-3*) Revell.

Stephens, Bill, jt. auth. see Stephens, Andrea.

Stephens, Fran. Baking Projects for Children. (Illus.). 128p. (ps-4). PLB 16.95 (*1-878363-62-X*) Forest Hse.

—Baking Projects for Children: Fun Foods to Make with Children from 4 to 10. Macdonald, Roland B. & Gray, Dan, illus. 128p. (gr. k-5). 1991. pap. 9.95 (*1-878767-10-0*) Murdoch Bks.

Stephens, Jane. Katie's Too Big Coat. (ps-6). 1993. pap. 14.00 (*0-671-77774-2*, S&S BFYR) S&S Trade.

Stephens, Mary. Adventures of the Frog Family. (Illus.). 53p. (gr. k-4). 1994. pap. write for info. (*0-9639088-0-4*) Half Moon Pubng.

Stephens, Michael. Matinee. (Orig.). (gr. 6 up). 1993. pap. 10.95 (*0-04-442194-X*, Pub. by Allen & Unwin Aust Pty AT) IPG Chicago.

—Titans. (Illus.). 1993. pap. 6.95 (*1-86373-133-4*, Pub. by Allen & Unwin Aust Pty AT) IPG Chicago.

Stephens, Nancy. Horse Tails: A Look at Life with Horses. (Illus.). 220p. (Orig.). (gr. 7-12). 1990. pap. 9.95 (*0-685-29151-0*) Squared Away.

Stephenson, Ginny. Star Message. (Illus.). 30p. (Orig.). (gr. 5-12). 1979. pap. 2.00 (*0-88680-185-0*); royalty on application 15.00 (*0-685-59243-X*) I E Clark.

Stephenson, Jean. Dogwood Stew & Catnip Tea. LC 92-40804. (Illus.). 160p. (Orig.). (gr. 4-7). 1993. pap. 4.99 (*0-89107-717-0*, Crossway Bks) Good News.

Stephenson, R. Rex. The Jack Tales. (Illus.). 66p. (Orig.). (gr. k up). 1991. pap. 4.00 (*0-88680-361-6*); royalty on application 60.00 (*0-685-59137-9*) I E Clark.

Stephenson, Robert & Browne, Roger. Exploring Earth in Space. Hughes, Jenny, illus. LC 91-44198. 48p. (gr. 4-8). 1992. PLB 19.92 (*0-8114-2603-3*) Raintree Steck-V.

—Exploring Variety of Life. Clay, Marilyn, illus. LC 92-34357. 48p. (gr. 4-8). 1992. PLB 19.92 (*0-8114-2606-8*) Raintree Steck-V.

Stephenson, Ruth M. Abigail. (Illus.). 32p. (Orig.). (ps-5). 1988. pap. 7.95 (*0-945705-00-X*) Young Life Pub.

Stephenson, Sallie. Autocross Racing. LC 91-13635. (Illus.). 48p. (gr. 5-6). 1991. RSBE 12.95 (*0-89686-692-0*, Crestwood Hse) Macmillan Child Grp.

—Circle Track Racing. (Illus.). 48p. (gr. 5-6). 1991. RSBE 12.95 (*0-89686-693-9*, Crestwood Hse) Macmillan Child Grp.

—Race Cars. 48p. (gr. 3-4). 1991. PLB 11.95 (*1-56065-068-0*) Capstone Pr.

—Rally Racing. LC 91-13641. (Illus.). 48p. (gr. 5-6). 1991. RSBE 12.95 (*0-89686-694-7*, Crestwood Hse) Macmillan Child Grp.

—Sports Cars. 48p. (gr. 3-4). 1991. PLB 11.95 (*1-56065-078-8*) Capstone Pr.

—Winston Cup Racing. (Illus.). 48p. (gr. 5-6). 1991. RSBE 12.95 (*0-89686-695-5*, Crestwood Hse) Macmillan Child Grp.

Stephenson, T. S. The Cosmos Kids. 1992. pap. 8.95 (*0-533-10206-5*) Vantage.

Stepien, William, et al. Discovering Illinois. (Illus.). 184p. (gr. 4). 1986. 20.00 (*0-685-24528-4*, Peregrine Smith) Gibbs Smith Pub.

Stepto, Michele. Snuggle Piggy & the Magic Blanket. Himmelman, John, illus. LC 86-23943. 24p. (ps-k). 1990. pap. 3.95 (*0-525-44609-5*, DCB) Dutton Child Bks.

Stepto, Michele, ed. Our Song, Our Toil: The Story of American Slavery As Told by Slaves. LC 93-8323. (Illus.). 96p. (gr. 4-6). 1994. PLB 15.90 (*1-56294-401-0*) Millbrook Pr.

Steptoe, John. Award Puzzles: Mufaro's Beautiful Daughters. 1991. 5.95 (*0-938971-67-0*) JTG Nashville.

—Baby Says. Steptoe, John, illus. LC 87-17296. 32p. (ps). 1988. 13.95 (*0-688-07423-5*); lib. bdg. 13.88 (*0-688-07424-3*) Lothrop.

—Baby Says. ALC Staff, ed. LC 87-17296. (Illus.). 28p. (ps up). 1992. pap. 3.95 (*0-688-11855-0*, Mulberry) Morrow.

—Birthday. Steptoe, John, illus. LC 72-182782. 32p. (ps-2). 1991. 14.95 (*0-8050-1849-2*, Bks Young Read) H Holt & Co.

—Daddy Is a Monster...Sometimes. Steptoe, John, illus. LC 77-4464. 32p. (gr. k-3). 1980. PLB 13.89 (*0-397-31893-6*, Lipp Jr Bks) HarpC Child Bks.

—Daddy Is a Monster...Sometimes. LC 77-4464. (Illus.). 32p. (gr. k-3). 1983. pap. 6.95 (*0-06-443042-1*, Trophy) HarpC Child Bks.

—Marcia. (Illus.). 80p. (gr. 7 up). 1991. pap. 3.99 (*0-14-034669-4*, Puffin) Puffin Bks.

—Mufaro's Beautiful Daughters: An African Tale. Steptoe, John, illus. LC 84-7158. 32p. (gr. k-3). 1987. 14.95 (*0-688-04045-4*); PLB 14.88 (*0-688-04046-2*) Lothrop.

—Mufaro's Beautiful Daughters: Big Book Edition. (ps-3). 1993. pap. 18.95 (*0-688-12935-8*, Mulberry) Morrow.

—Stevie. Steptoe, John L., illus. LC 69-16700. 32p. (ps-3). 1969. PLB 12.89 (*0-06-025764-4*) HarpC Child Bks.

—Stevie. LC 69-16700. (Illus.). 32p. (ps-3). 1986. pap. 4.95 (*0-06-443122-3*, Trophy) HarpC Child Bks.

—Stevie. Steptoe, John, illus. (gr. 1-4). 1987. incl. cassette 19.95 (*0-87499-050-5*); pap. 12.95 incl. cassette (*0-87499-049-1*); 4 paperbacks, cassette & guide 27.95 (*0-87499-051-3*) Live Oak Media.

—The Story of Jumping Mouse. Steptoe, John, illus. LC 82-14848. 40p. (gr. k-3). 1984. 13.95 (*0-688-01902-1*); PLB 13.88 (*0-688-01903-X*) Lothrop.

—The Story of the Jumping Mouse. LC 82-14848. (Illus.). (gr. 1 up). 1989. pap. 4.95 (*0-688-08740-X*, Mulberry) Morrow.

Steptoe, Lamont B. Crimson River. 3rd ed. 24p. (gr. 11 up). 1991. pap. text ed. 7.00 (*0-922827-07-9*) Whirlwind Pr.

Sterbenz, Carol E. The Dog Album: A Pet Owner's Memory Book. Sterbenz, Carol E., et al, illus. 32p. (ps up). 1987. 11.95 (*0-399-21460-7*, Putnam) Putnam Pub Group.

Sterchele, Christina L., illus. A Hole in the Bottom of the Sea. (Orig.). (gr. k-6). 1984. pap. 3.50 (*0-913545-09-0*) Moonlight Fl.

—Twelve Days of Christmas. (ps-6). 1981. 3.50 (*0-913545-07-4*) Moonlight Fl.

Sterchele, Norman. Beginning at the Beginning with Your MS-DOS Microcomputer: An Introduction to: The Machine, DOS & Procedures. (Illus.). 96p. (Orig.). (gr. 10). 1989. pap. 11.95 (*0-9624107-0-5*) Compu-Aid.

Sterling, Dorothy. Freedom Train: The Story of Harriet Tubman. 192p. (gr. 4-6). 1987. pap. 2.95 (*0-590-43628-7*); tchr's. guide o.p. 1.25 (*0-590-40988-3*) Scholastic Inc.

Sterling, Mary E. Clothespin Games. Vasconcelles, Keith, illus. 28p. (ps-k). 1989. wkbk 7.95 (*1-55734-172-9*) Tchr Create Mat.

—Explorers: A Thematic Unit. Buhler, Cheryl, illus. 80p. (Orig.). (gr. 5-8). 1992. pap. 7.95 wkbk. (*1-55734-288-1*) Tchr Create Mat.

—File Folder Games. Vasconcelles, Keith, illus. 28p. (ps-k). 1989. wkbk 7.95 (*1-55734-171-0*) Tchr Create Mat.

—Holidays on Parade. Olsen, Shirley, illus. 64p. (gr. k-2). 1988. wkbk. 6.95 (*1-55734-377-2*) Tchr Create Mat.

—Making Big & Little Books. Apodaca, Blanca & Vasconcelles, Keith, illus. 80p. (Orig.). (gr. k-3). 1991. wkbk. 7.95 (*1-55734-133-8*) Tchr Create Mat.

—Patterns for Big Books. Vasconcelles, Keith, illus. 80p. (ps-3). 1991. wkbk. 7.95 (*1-55734-132-X*) Tchr Create Mat.

—Synonym-Antonym-Homonym Word Games. Spence, Paula, illus. 48p. (gr. 2-5). 1988. wkbk. 5.95 (*1-55734-368-3*) Tchr Create Mat.

—Transcontinental Railroad: A Thematic Unit. Vasconcelles, Keith, illus. 80p. (gr. 5-8). 1993. wkbk. 7.95 (*1-55734-295-4*) Tchr Create Mat.

—Wheel Games. Vasconcelles, Keith, illus. 28p. (ps-k). 1989. wkbk 7.95 (*1-55734-170-2*) Tchr Create Mat.

Sterling, Mary E. & Nowlin, Susan S. Crossword Puzzles. Spence, Paula & Wright, Terry, illus. 48p. (gr. 2-5). 1988. wkbk. 5.95 (*1-55734-365-9*) Tchr Create Mat.

—December Monthly Activities. Spence, Paula, et al, illus. 80p. (gr. 1-5). 1989. wkbk. 7.95 (*1-55734-154-0*) Tchr Create Mat.

—November Monthly Activities. Spence, Paula, et al, illus. 80p. (gr. 1-5). 1989. wkbk. 7.95 (*1-55734-153-2*) Tchr Create Mat.

—October Monthly Activities. Spence, Paula, et al, illus. 80p. (gr. 1-5). 1989. wkbk. 7.95 (*1-55734-152-4*) Tchr Create Mat.

—Patriotic Wordsearches, Codes & Crossword Puzzles. Spence, Paula, illus. 48p. (gr. 2-5). 1988. wkbk. 5.95 (*1-55734-367-5*) Tchr Create Mat.

—September Monthly Activities. Spence, Paula, et al, illus. 80p. (gr. 1-5). 1989. wkbk. 7.95 (*1-55734-151-6*) Tchr Create Mat.

Sterling, Mary E., jt. auth. see Levin, Ina M.

Sterling, Mary E., jt. auth. see Nowlin, Susan.

Sterling, Mary E., jt. auth. see Spivak, Darlene.

Sterman, Betsy & Sterman, Samuel. Backyard Dragon. Wenzel, David, illus. LC 92-26292. 192p. (gr. 3-7). 1993. 14.00 (*0-06-020783-3*); PLB 13.89 (*0-06-020784-1*) HarpC Child Bks.

—Too Much Magic. Glasser, Judy, illus. LC 85-45861. 160p. (gr. 3-7). 1994. pap. 3.95 (*0-06-440404-8*, Trophy) HarpC Child Bks.

Sterman, Samuel, jt. auth. see Sterman, Betsy.

Stermer, Dugald, jt. auth. see Kortum, Jeanie.

Stern, Benjamin J. Opportunities in Machines Shop Trades. (gr. 8 up). 1986. 13.95 (*0-8442-6147-5*, VGM Career Bks); pap. 10.95 (*0-8442-6148-3*, VGM Career Bks) NTC Pub Grp.

Stern, Charles. My Big Book of Animals. 1991. 5.99 (*0-517-05182-6*) Outlet Bk Co.

Stern, Gary M. The Congress: America's Lawmakers. LC 92-27030. (Illus.). 48p. (gr. 5-6). 1992. PLB 21.34 (*0-8114-7351-1*); pap. write for info. (*0-8114-5579-3*) Raintree Steck-V.

Stern, Jennifer. The Filipino Americans. Moynihan, Daniel P., intro. by. (Illus.). 112p. (gr. 5 up). 1990. lib. bdg. 17.95 (*0-87754-877-3*) Chelsea Hse.

Stern, Kati & Sloan, Claudia. The World's Worst Knock Knock Jokes. 1974. 2.95 (*0-8431-0204-7*) Price Stern.

Stern, Leonard. Dino Mad Libs. 48p. (gr. 1-12). 1993. pap. 2.95 (*0-8431-3528-X*) Price Stern.

Stern, Leonard & Price, Roger. Mad Libs from Outer Space. (Illus.). 48p. (Orig.). (gr. 3 up). 1989. pap. 2.95 (*0-8431-2443-1*) Price Stern.

—Spooky Silly Mad Libs. (Illus.). 48p. (Orig.). 1989. pap. 2.95 (*0-8431-2758-9*) Price Stern.

Stern, Leonard, jt. auth. see Price, Roger.

Stern, Madeline B., ed. see Alcott, Louisa May.

Stern, Peter. Max the Dragon. LC 89-48310. (Illus.). 32p. (ps-2). 1990. 12.95 (*0-517-57587-6*); PLB 13.99 (*0-517-57588-4*) Crown Bks Yng Read.

Stern, Robert A. The House That Bob Built. LC 90-26901. (Illus.). 32p. 1991. 17.95 (*0-8478-1369-X*) Rizzoli Intl.

Stern, Steve. Hershel & the Beast. Gills, K. King, illus. LC 86-27789. 64p. (Orig.). (gr. 1-5). 1987. text ed. 13.95 (*0-938507-05-2*) Ion Books.

Stern, Susan, created by. Keep on Looking. LC 92-52986. (Illus.). 64p. (Orig.). (gr. 2-6). 1992. pap. 9.95 (*1-56282-289-6*) Hyprn Child.

Sternberg, Betty. Attribute Acrobatics. (Illus., Orig.). (gr. 1-9). 1974. pap. 8.95 (*0-918932-01-7*) Activity Resources.

—Colored Cubes Activity Cards. (Illus., Orig.). (gr. 2-8). 1973. pap. 6.50 (*0-918932-06-8*) Activity Resources.

Sternberg, Betty, jt. auth. see McLean, Peggy.

Sternberg, Betty J., jt. auth. see Clark, Clara E.

Sternberg, Pat & Beechman, Dolly. Sojourner. 46p. 1989. Playscript. 4.50 (*0-87602-283-2*) Anchorage.

Sternberg, Patricia. On Stage: How to Put on a Play. LC 82-60651. (Illus.). 160p. (gr. 7 up). 1983. (J Messner); PLB 9.29 (*0-671-45246-0*) S&S Trade.

—Speak Up: A Guide to Public Speaking. LC 84-10829. 144p. (gr. 7 up). 1984. lib. bdg. 8.79 (*0-671-47371-9*, J Messner) S&S Trade.

Sternberg, Robert J. How to Prepare for the MAT: Miller Analogies Test. 6th ed. 1994. pap. 11.95 (*0-8120-1776-5*) Barron.

Sternberg, Susan T., jt. auth. see Prudhomme, Frances.

Sternburg, Sharon. Suzie Q. Mouse Adventures. Coyne, John P., illus. 39p. (Orig.). (ps-1). 1993. pap. 5.99 (*0-9633513-1-1*) S M Resar Pub.

—Suzie Q. Mouse Adventures: Coloring Book. Coyne, John P., illus. 39p. (Orig.). (ps-1). Date not set. pap. 1.99x (*0-9633513-0-3*) S M Resar Pub.

Sterne, Emma G. The Slave Ship. 1988. 2.95 (*0-590-44360-7*) Scholastic Inc.

Sterne, Laurence. Tristram Shandy. (gr. 11 up). 1967. pap. 1.95 (*0-8049-0152-X*, CL-152) Airmont.

Sterne, Noelle. Tyrannosaurus Wrecks. Chess, Victoria, illus. LC 78-22499. 32p. (gr. 1-4). 1983. pap. 4.95 (*0-06-443043-X*, Trophy) HarpC Child Bks.

—Tyrannosaurus Wrecks: A Book of Dinosaur Riddles. Chess, Victoria, illus. LC 78-22499. 32p. (gr. 1-4). 1979. PLB 13.89 (*0-690-03960-3*, Crowell Jr Bks) HarpC Child Bks.

Sterrett, Cliff. The Complete Color Polly & Her Pals, Vol. I: The Surrealist Period, 1926-1927. Marschall, Richard, intros. by. Spiegelman, Art, intro. by. 96p. 1990. 34.95 (*0-924359-14-5*) Remco Wrldserv Bks.

Sterry, Paul. Nature Watching Kit. (Illus.). (gr. 2 up). 1993. 19.95 (*1-56138-213-2*) Running Pr.

Stevens, Bernardine S. Colonial American Craftspeople. (Illus.). 112p. (gr. 5-8). 1993. PLB 12.90 (*0-531-12536-X*) Watts.

Stevens, Biddy. Toto in France. (gr. 4-7). 1992. 12.95 (*0-8442-9180-3*, Passport Bks) NTC Pub Grp.

—Toto in Italy. (gr. 4-7). 1992. 12.95 (*0-8442-9289-3*, Passport Bks) NTC Pub Grp.

Stevens, Bryna. Ben Franklin's Glass Armonica. (ps-3). 1992. pap. 3.25 (*0-440-40584-X*) Dell.

—Deborah Sampson Goes to War. (ps-3). 1991. pap. 2.99 (*0-440-40552-1*, YB) Dell.

—Frank Thompson: Her Civil War Story. LC 91-45382. (Illus.). 144p. (gr. 5-9). 1992. SBE 13.95 (*0-02-788185-7*, Macmillan Child Bk) Macmillan Child Grp.

—Handel: And the Famous Sword Swallower of Halle.
Councell, Ruth T., illus. 32p. (ps-3). 1990. 14.95
(0-399-21548-4, Philomel Bks) Putnam Pub Group.
—Witches: Opposing Viewpoints. LC 87-18346. (Illus.).
112p. (gr. 3-10). 1988. lib. bdg. 14.95 (0-89908-054-5)
Greenhaven.
Stevens, Carla. Anna, Grandpa & the Big Storm. Tomes,
Margot, illus. 48p. (gr. 6-9). 1982. 13.45
(0-89919-066-9, Clarion Bks) HM.
—Anna, Grandpa, & the Big Storm. Tomes, Margot, illus.
64p. (gr. 1-4). 1986. (Puffin); pap. 3.99
(0-14-031705-8, Puffin) Puffin Bks.
—A Book of Your Own: Keeping a Diary or Journal. LC
92-33818. 1993. 14.95 (0-89919-256-4, Clarion Bks)
HM.
—Book of Your Own: Keeping a Diary or Journal. (gr.
4-7). 1993. pap. 7.95 (0-395-67887-0, Clarion Bks)
HM.
—Lily & Miss Liberty. 80p. 1992. 12.95 (0-590-44919-2,
Scholastic Hardcover) Scholastic Inc.
—Lily & Miss Liberty. (gr. 4-7). 1993. pap. 2.75
(0-590-44920-6) Scholastic Inc.
—Trouble for Lucy. Himler, Ronald, illus. LC 79-10445.
80p. (gr. 3-6). 1987. pap. 3.95 (0-89919-523-7, Clarion
Bks) HM.
Stevens, Edward E. What Happened in 70 A. D.? A
Study in Bible Prophecy. rev. ed. (Illus.). 38p. 1988.
pap. 2.95 (0-9621311-0-5) E E Stevens Pub.
Stevens, Florence & Lamont-Clarke, Ginette. Et Si
L'Autobus Nous Oublie? Ouellet, Odile, illus. LC 90-
70136. 24p. (ps-2). 1990. 12.95 (0-88776-252-2); pap.
6.95 (0-88776-260-3) Tundra Bks.
—What If Dad Gets Lost at the Zoo? Langevin, Isabelle,
illus. LC 91-65365. 24p. (ps-2). 1991. 12.95
(0-88776-265-4); pap. 6.95 (0-685-48807-1) Tundra
Bks.
—What If the Bus Doesn't Come? Ouellet, Odile, illus.
LC 90-70135. 24p. (ps-2). 1990. 12.95
(0-88776-251-4); pap. 6.95 (0-88776-259-X) Tundra
Bks.
Stevens, Florence, jt. auth. see Lamont-Clarke, Ginette.
Stevens, Jan R. Carlos & the Squash Plant: Carlos y la
Planta Calabaza. Arnold, Jeanne, illus. LC 92-82137.
(SPA & ENG). 32p. (gr. k). 1993. 14.95
(0-87358-559-3) Northland AZ.
Stevens, Janet. Androcles & the Lion. Stevens, Janet,
illus. LC 89-1953. 32p. (ps-3). 1989. reinforced bdg.
14.95 (0-8234-0768-3); pap. 5.95 (0-8234-0906-6)
Holiday.
—How the Manx Cat Lost Its Tail. (ps-8). 1992. pap.
4.95 (0-15-236766-7) HarBrace.
—The Three Billy Goats Gruff. Stevens, Janet, illus. LC
86-33512. 40p. (ps-3). 1987. 12.95 (0-15-286396-6,
HB Juv Bks) HarBrace.
—Three Billy Goats Gruff. 32p. (ps-3). 1990. pap. 4.95
(0-15-286397-4, Voyager Bks) HarBrace.
—The Tortoise & the Hare: An Aesop Fable. Steven,
Janet, illus. LC 83-18668. 32p. (ps-3). 1984. reinforced
bdg. 14.95 (0-8234-0510-9); pap. 5.95 (0-8234-0564-8)
Holiday.
Stevens, Janet, retold by. & illus. Coyote Steals the
Blanket: A Ute Tale. LC 92-54415. 32p. (ps-3). 1993.
reinforced bdg. 15.95 (0-8234-0996-1) Holiday.
Stevens, Janet, retold by. Goldilocks & the Three Bears.
LC 85-27312. (Illus.). 32p. (ps-3). 1986. reinforced
bdg. 14.95 (0-8234-0608-3) Holiday.
Stevens, Janet, adapted by. & illus. Tops & Bottoms. LC
93-19154. (ps-6). 1994. write for info. (0-15-292851-0)
HarBrace.
—The Town Mouse & the Country Mouse. LC 86-14276.
32p. (ps-3). 1987. reinforced bdg. 14.95
(0-8234-0633-4); pap. 5.95 (0-8234-0733-0) Holiday.
**Stevens, Janet, adapted by see Andersen, Hans
Christian.**
**Stevens, Janet, retold by. & illu see Grimm, Jacob &
Grimm, Wilhelm K.**
Stevens, Janet, illus. The Emperor's New Clothes:
Adapted from Hans Christian Andersen. LC 85-728.
32p. (ps-3). 1985. reinforced 14.95 (0-8234-0566-4)
Holiday.
—The House That Jack Built: A Mother Goose Nursery
Rhyme. LC 84-15832. 32p. (ps-3). 1985. reinforced
bdg. 14.95 (0-8234-0548-6) Holiday.
Stevens, Jared & Michaels, Judy. How to Write for
Everyday Living. (Illus.). (gr. 7 up). 1981. wkbk. 4.95
(0-89525-132-9) Ed Activities.
Stevens, Jill. A Happy Life Songbook: Imagination Songs
for Children. Boldway, John & Stevens, Jill, illus.
Sacks, Jonathan, contrib. by. 63p. (Orig.). (ps-5). 1988.
pap. 10.95 spiral bound (1-877614-02-5) Two Wings.
—We Are Free! Songbook: Children's Songs of America.
Boldway, John, illus. Sacks, Jonathan, contrib. by.
(Illus.). 72p. (Orig.). (ps-5). 1989. pap. 10.95 spiral
bound (1-877614-04-1) Two Wings.
Stevens, Jill & Gaskill, Rebecca. Believing in Yourself:
Songbook for Children. Boldway, John, illus. Sacks,
Jonathan. (Illus.). 70p. (Orig.). (ps up) 1987. pap. 10.
95 spiral bound (1-877614-00-9) Two Wings.
Stevens, John, ed. Sharks. (Illus.). 240p. 1987. 35.00
(0-8160-1800-6) Facts on File.
Stevens, Kathleen. The Beast & the Babysitter. Bowler,
Ray, illus. LC 88-42917. 32p. (gr. 2-3). 1989. PLB 18.
60 (1-55532-929-2) Gareth Stevens Inc.
—The Beast in the Bathtub. Bowler, Ray, illus. LC 86-
45074. 32p. (ps-3). 1987. pap. 5.95 (0-06-443121-5,
Trophy) HarpC Child Bks.

—The Beast in the Bathtub. Bowler, Ray, illus. LC 85-
12691. 32p. (gr. 2-3). 1985. PLB 18.60
(0-918831-15-6) Gareth Stevens Inc.
—Bully for the Beast! Bowler, Ray, illus. LC 88-33090.
32p. (gr. 2-3). 1990. PLB 18.60 (0-8368-0020-6)
Gareth Stevens Inc.
—Eddie's Luck. LC 91-11922. 176p. (gr. 3-7). 1992. SBE
13.95 (0-689-31682-8, Atheneum Child Bk)
Macmillan Child Grp.
Stevens, LaVerne. Look & See H O T V or Letter E.
Stevens, LaVerne, illus. LC 91-75641. 32p. (ps-k).
1991. CIS cover 15 pt. with plastic comb binding 8.00
(0-9630441-0-9) B&B Pr.
Stevens, Lawrence. Alexander & the Greeks: Mini-Play
& Activities. (gr. 7 up). 1981. 6.50 (0-89550-339-5)
Stevens & Shea.
—Black Death: Mini-Play & Activities. (gr. 7 up). 1981.
6.50 (0-89550-342-5) Stevens & Shea.
—Christopher Columbus: Mini-Play & Activities. (gr. 7
up). 1981. 6.50 (0-89550-344-1) Stevens & Shea.
—Computer Graphics Basics. Seiden, Art, illus. LC 84-
6826. 48p. (gr. 3-7). 1984. 9.95 (0-13-164054-2) P-H.
—Computer Programming Basics: An Introduction for
Young People. Seiden, Art, illus. 48p. 1984. 9.95
(0-13-164260-X) P-H.
—Ecology Basics. D'Amato, Janet, illus. 48p. (gr. 3-7).
1986. 10.95 (0-13-223215-4) P-H.
—French Revolution: Mini-Play & Activities. (gr. 7 up).
1981. 6.50 (0-89550-341-7) Stevens & Shea.
—Giuseppe Garibaldi: Mini-Play & Activities. (gr. 7 up).
1981. 6.50 (0-89550-345-X) Stevens & Shea.
—Hitler & Fascism: Mini-Play & Activities. (gr. 7 up).
1981. 6.50 (0-89550-348-4) Stevens & Shea.
—Laser Basics. Seiden, Art, illus. 48p. (gr. 3-7). 1985. 10.
95 (0-13-523606-1) P-H.
—Lenin & Trotsky: Mini-Play & Activities. (gr. 7 up).
1981. 6.50 (0-89550-347-6) Stevens & Shea.
—Napoleon & the French Empire: Mini-Play &
Activities. (gr. 7 up). 1981. 6.50 (0-89550-340-9)
Stevens & Shea.
—Robert Clive & Imperialism: Mini-Play & Activities.
(gr. 7 up). 1981. 6.50 (0-89550-343-3) Stevens & Shea.
—Winston Churchill: Mini-Play & Activities. (gr. 7 up).
1981. 6.50 (0-89550-346-8) Stevens & Shea.
Stevens, Lawrence A. Thinking Tools. Radrigan, Roberto,
illus. 73p. (Orig.). (gr. 5-10). 1984. pap. text ed. 6.50
(0-89550-223-2) Stevens & Shea.
Stevens, Mallory. Can't Buy Me Love. 1992. pap. 3.50
(0-06-106710-5, Harp PBks) HarpC.
—Christmas Colt. (gr. 4-7). 1992. pap. 3.50
(0-06-106721-0, Harp PBks) HarpC.
Stevens, Margaret M. Stepping Stones for Boys & Girls.
Stevens, David S., illus. (gr. 5 up). 1977. pap. 4.50
(0-87516-248-7) DeVorss.
—Stepping Stones for Little Feet. Stevens, David S., illus.
31p. (gr. 4-6). 1975. pap. 4.50 (0-87516-202-9)
DeVorss.
—Stepping Stones Three. Stevens, David, illus. 32p. (gr.
1-8). 1983. pap. 4.50 (0-87516-518-4) DeVorss.
Stevens, Paul. Ferdinand & Isabella. Schlesinger, Arthur
M., Jr., intro. by. (Illus.). 112p. (gr. 5 up). 1988. lib.
bdg. 17.95 (0-87754-523-5) Chelsea Hse.
Stevens, Philippa J. Bonk! Goes the Ball. Martin, Clovis,
illus. LC 89-48561. 32p. (ps-2). 1990. PLB 11.93
(0-516-02061-7); pap. 2.95 (0-516-42061-5) Childrens.
Stevens, Ray. Everything Is Beautiful. Karpinski, John E.,
illus. 24p. 1993. 12.95 (0-7935-1856-3, 00183011) H
Leonard Pub Corp.
Stevens, Rita. Andrew Johnson: Seventeenth President of
the United States. Young, Richard G., ed. LC 88-
28487. (Illus.). (gr. 5-9). 1989. PLB 17.26
(0-944483-16-X) Garrett Ed Corp.
—Benjamin Harrison: Twenty-Third President of the
United States. Young, Richard G., ed. LC 88-24747.
(Illus.). (gr. 5-9). 1989. PLB 17.26 (0-944483-15-1)
Garrett Ed Corp.
—Calvin Coolidge: Thirtieth President of the United
States. Young, Richard G., ed. LC 89-39949. (Illus.).
128p. (gr. 5-9). 1990. PLB 17.26 (0-944483-57-7)
Garrett Ed Corp.
—Chester A. Arthur: 21st President of the United States.
Young, Richard G., ed. LC 87-36120. (Illus.). (gr.
5-9). 1989. PLB 17.26 (0-944483-05-4) Garrett Ed
Corp.
—Madagascar. (Illus.). 112p. (gr. 5 up). 1988. lib. bdg. 14.
95 (1-55546-195-6) Chelsea Hse.
—Venda. (Illus.). 96p. (gr. 5 up). 1989. lib. bdg. 14.95
(1-55546-788-1) Chelsea Hse.
Stevens, S. K., ed. see Wallower, Lucille.
Stevens, Sarah. Cults. LC 91-17774. (Illus.). 48p. (gr.
5-6). 1992. RSBE 11.95 (0-89686-723-4, Crestwood
Hse) Macmillan Child Grp.
—Steroids. LC 90-48050. (Illus.). 48p. (gr. 5-6). 1991.
RSBE 12.95 (0-89686-606-8, Crestwood Hse)
Macmillan Child Grp.
Stevens, Susanna, tr. see Claesson, Stig.
Stevens, Susanna, tr. see Lagerlof, Selma.
Stevens, Tim. North Carolina High School Record Book.
96p. (gr. 9 up). 1991. pap. 3.00 (0-935400-17-6) News
& Observer.
Stevens, Wendelle C. UFO Calendar 1990. (Illus.). 26p.
(gr. 9-12). 1989. wkbk. 9.95 (0-934269-19-X) UFO
Photo.
—UFO...Contact from Reticulum, Update. Stevens,
Wendelle C., et al, illus. 444p. (gr. 9-12). 1989. PLB
18.95 (0-934269-15-7) UFO Photo.

—UFO...Contact from the Pleiades: A Supplementary
Investigation Report. Stevens, Wendelle C., illus.
552p. (gr. 9-12). 1989. PLB 29.95 (0-9608558-4-X)
UFO Photo.
**Stevens, Wendelle C., ed. see Butts, Donna R. & Corder,
S. Scott.**
Stevens, Wendelle C., ed. see Crum, Wesley S.
Stevenson. Sword of Caesar. (ps-7). 1987. pap. 2.50
(0-553-26531-8) Bantam.
Stevenson, Amy. The Super Bowl. 32p. (gr. 4). 1990. PLB
14.95s.p. (0-88682-315-3) Creative Ed.
Stevenson, Augusta. Abraham Lincoln: The Great
Emancipator. Robinson, Jerry, illus. 192p. (gr. 2-6).
1986. pap. 3.95 (0-02-042030-7, Aladdin) Macmillan
Child Grp.
—Benjamin Franklin: Young Printer. Quigley, Ray, illus.
LC 86-10786. 192p. (gr. 2-6). 1986. pap. 3.95
(0-02-041920-1, Aladdin) Macmillan Child Grp.
—Buffalo Bill: Frontier Daredevil. Dreany, F. Joseph,
illus. LC 90-23767. 192p. (gr. 3-7). 1991. pap. 3.95
(0-689-71479-3, Aladdin) Macmillan Child Grp.
—Clara Barton: Founder of the American Red Cross.
Giacoia, Frank, illus. LC 86-10750. 192p. (gr. 2-6).
1986. pap. 3.95 (0-02-041820-5, Aladdin) Macmillan
Child Grp.
—Daniel Boone: Young Hunter & Tracker. Doremus,
Robert, illus. LC 86-10795. 192p. (gr. 2-6). 1986. pap.
3.95 (0-02-041830-2, Aladdin) Macmillan Child Grp.
—George Washington: Young Leader. Dreany, E. J., illus.
LC 86-10914. 192p. (gr. 2-6). 1986. pap. 3.95
(0-02-042150-8, Aladdin) Macmillan Child Grp.
—Molly Pitcher: Young Patriot. Garriott, Gene, illus. LC
86-10744. 192p. (gr. 2-6). 1986. pap. 3.95
(0-02-042040-4, Aladdin) Macmillan Child Grp.
—Paul Revere: Boston Patriot. Nicholas, Frank, illus. LC
86-10743. 192p. (gr. 2-6). 1986. pap. 3.95
(0-02-042090-0, Aladdin) Macmillan Child Grp.
—Wilbur & Orville Wright: Young Fliers. Doremus,
Robert, illus. LC 86-10747. 192p. (gr. 2-6). 1986. pap.
3.95 (0-02-042170-2, Aladdin) Macmillan Child Grp.
Stevenson, D., ed. see Schertle, Alice.
Stevenson, Dinah, ed. see Carlson, Natalie S.
Stevenson, Dinah, ed. see Joseph, Lynn.
Stevenson, Dinah, ed. see Terban, Marvin.
Stevenson, Drew. One Ghost Too Many: A Sarah
Capshaw Mystery. Kelly, Kathleen M., illus. LC 90-
47361. 128p. (gr. 4-6). 1991. 13.95 (0-525-65052-0,
Cobblehill Bks) Dutton Child Bks.
—Toying with Danger: A Sarah Capshaw Mystery.
Ramsey, Marcy D., illus. LC 92-19325. (gr. 4-6).
1993. 14.00 (0-525-65115-2, Cobblehill Bks) Dutton
Child Bks.
Stevenson, Frederick W. Exploratory Problems in
Mathematics. LC 91-34782. (Illus.). 168p. (Orig.). (gr.
7-12). 1992. pap. 16.00 (0-87353-338-0) NCTM.
Stevenson, Harvey. Grandpa's House. (Illus.). 32p. (ps-3).
1994. 14.95 (1-56282-588-7); PLB 14.89
(1-56282-589-5) Hyprn Child.
Stevenson, Harvey, jt. auth. see Schoberle, Cecile.
Stevenson, James. Brrr! LC 89-34615. (Illus.). 32p. (ps
up). 1991. 13.95 (0-688-09210-1); PLB 13.88
(0-688-09211-X) Greenwillow.
—Could Be Worse! Stevenson, James, illus. LC 76-28534.
32p. (gr. k-3). 1977. 13.95 (0-688-80075-0); PLB 13.
88 (0-688-84075-2) Greenwillow.
—Could Be Worse! LC 76-28534. (Illus.). 32p. (ps-3).
1987. pap. 3.95 (0-688-07035-3, Mulberry) Morrow.
—Don't You Know There's a War On? LC 91-31461.
(Illus.). 32p. (gr. k-8). 1992. 14.00 (0-688-11383-4);
PLB 13.93 (0-688-11384-2) Greenwillow.
—Emma. Stevenson, James, illus. LC 84-4141. 32p. (gr.
k-3). 1985. 11.75 (0-688-04020-9); PLB 11.88
(0-688-04021-7) Greenwillow.
—Emma. LC 84-4141. (gr. k-3). 1987. pap. 3.95
(0-688-07336-0, Mulberry) Morrow.
—Emma at the Beach. LC 88-3491. (Illus.). (gr. k up).
1990. 12.95 (0-688-08806-6); lib. bdg. 12.88
(0-688-08807-4) Greenwillow.
—The Flying Acorns. LC 91-45678. (Illus.). 32p. (gr. k
up). 1993. 14.00 (0-688-11418-0); PLB 13.93
(0-688-11419-9) Greenwillow.
—Fried Feathers for Thanksgiving. Stevenson, James,
illus. LC 86-3100. 32p. (gr. k-3). 1986. 13.95
(0-688-06675-5); PLB 13.88 (0-688-06676-3)
Greenwillow.
—Fun - No Fun. LC 93-18187. (Illus.). 32p. (gr. k up).
1994. write for info. (0-688-11673-6); PLB write for
info. (0-688-11674-4) Greenwillow.
—Grandpa's Great City Tour: An Alphabet Book.
Stevenson, James, illus. LC 83-1459. 48p. (gr. k-3).
1983. PLB 12.95 (0-688-02324-X); 12.88
(0-688-02323-1) Greenwillow.
—Grandpas Too-Good Garden. LC 88-18786. (Illus.).
32p. (gr. k up). 1989. 12.95 (0-688-08485-0); PLB 12.
88 (0-688-08486-9) Greenwillow.
—The Great Big Especially Beautiful Easter Egg.
Stevenson, James, illus. LC 82-11731. 32p. (gr. k-3).
1983. 15.88 (0-688-01789-4); PLB 13.88
(0-688-01791-6) Greenwillow.
—The Great Big Especially Beautiful Easter Egg. LC 82-
11731. (ps-3). 1990. 4.95 (0-688-09355-8, Mulberry)
Morrow.
—Happy Valentine's Day, Emma! LC 87-13. (Illus.). 32p.
(gr. k-3). 1987. 11.75 (0-688-07357-3); lib. bdg. 12.88
(0-688-07358-1) Greenwillow.
—Higher on the Door. LC 86-14925. (Illus.). 32p. (gr.
k-3). 1987. 11.75 (0-688-06636-4); PLB 11.88
(0-688-06637-2) Greenwillow.

—July. Stevenson, James, illus. LC 88-37584. (gr. k up). 1990. 12.95 (0-688-08822-8); PLB 12.88 (0-688-08823-6) Greenwillow.
—Mr. Hacker. Modell, Frank, illus. LC 89-30479. 32p. (gr. k up). 1990. 12.95 (0-688-09216-0); PLB 12.88 (0-688-09217-9) Greenwillow.
—Monty. LC 91-20657. 32p. (ps up). 1992. 14.00 (0-688-11241-2) Greenwillow.
—Monty. Stevenson, James, illus. LC 78-11409. 32p. (ps up). 1992. pap. 4.95 (0-688-11288-9, Mulberry) Morrow.
—The Mud Flat Olympics. LC 93-28118. 1994. write for info. (0-688-12923-4); PLB write for info. (0-688-12924-7) Greenwillow.
—National Worm Day. LC 88-34915. (Illus.). 40p. (gr. k up). 1990. 12.95 (0-688-08771-X); lib. bdg. 12.88 (0-688-08772-8) Greenwillow.
—The Night after Christmas. LC 81-1022. (Illus.). 32p. (gr. k-3). 1981. 13.95 (0-688-00547-0); PLB 13.88 (0-688-00548-9) Greenwillow.
—The Night after Christmas. (Illus.). 32p. (ps up). 1993. pap. 4.95 (0-688-04590-1, Mulberry) Morrow.
—No Friends. Stevenson, James, illus. LC 85-27247. 32p. (gr. k-3). 1986. 11.75 (0-688-06506-6); PLB 11.88 (0-688-06507-4) Greenwillow.
—No Need for Monty. Stevenson, James, illus. LC 86-22818. 32p. (gr. k-3). 1987. 11.75 (0-688-07083-3); lib. bdg. 11.88 (0-688-07084-1) Greenwillow.
—Oh No, It's Waylon's Birthday! LC 88-4574. (Illus.). 48p. (gr. 1 up). 1989. 11.95 (0-688-08235-1); PLB 11.88 (0-688-08236-X) Greenwillow.
—The Pattaconk Brook. LC 92-29404. 32p. (ps up). 1993. 14.00 (0-688-11954-9); lib. bdg. 13.93 (0-688-11955-7) Greenwillow.
—Quick! Turn the Page! LC 89-34616. (Illus.). 32p. (ps up). 1990. 12.95 (0-688-09308-6); PLB 12.88 (0-688-09309-4) Greenwillow.
—Rolling Rose. LC 90-24169. 24p. (ps up). 1992. 14.00 (0-688-10674-9); PLB 13.93 (0-688-10675-7) Greenwillow.
—The Stowaway. LC 89-25861. (Illus.). 32p. (ps up). 1990. 12.95 (0-688-08619-5); PLB 12.88 (0-688-08620-9) Greenwillow.
—The Supreme Souvenir Factory. LC 87-33390. (Illus.). 56p. (gr. 1-4). 1988. 13.95 (0-688-07782-X) Greenwillow.
—That Dreadful Day. Stevenson, James, illus. LC 84-4164. 32p. (gr. k-3). 1985. 15.00 (0-688-04035-7); lib. bdg. 14.93 (0-688-04036-5) Greenwillow.
—That Terrible Halloween Night. LC 79-27775. (Illus.). 32p. (ps). 1980. PLB 14.93 (0-688-84281-X) Greenwillow.
—That Terrible Halloween Night. LC 79-27775. (Illus.). 32p. (ps-2). 1990. pap. 3.95 (0-688-09932-7, Mulberry) Morrow.
—That's Exactly the Way It Wasn't. LC 90-30749. (Illus.). 30p. (ps up). 1991. 13.95 (0-688-09868-1); PLB 13.88 (0-688-09869-X) Greenwillow.
—There's Nothing to Do! Stevenson, James, illus. LC 85-8104. 32p. (gr. k-3). 1986. 11.75 (0-688-04698-3); PLB 11.88 (0-688-04699-1) Greenwillow.
—Un-Happy New Year, Emma! LC 88-18802. (Illus.). 32p. (ps up). 1989. 12.95 (0-688-08342-0); PLB 12.88 (0-688-08343-9) Greenwillow.
—We Can't Sleep. LC 81-20307. (Illus.). 32p. (gr. k-3). 1982. 13.95 (0-688-01213-2); PLB 13.88 (0-688-01214-0) Greenwillow.
—We Hate Rain! LC 87-21204. (Illus.). 32p. (gr. k-3). 1988. 11.95 (0-688-07786-2); lib. bdg. 11.88 (0-688-07787-0) Greenwillow.
—What's under My Bed? Stevenson, James, illus. LC 83-1454. 32p. (gr. k-3). 1983. 13.95 (0-688-02325-8); PLB 13.88 (0-688-02327-4) Greenwillow.
—What's under My Bed. LC 83-1454. (Illus.). 32p. (ps-3). 1990. pap. 3.95 (0-688-09350-7, Mulberry) Morrow.
—When I Was Nine. Stevenson, James, illus. LC 85-9777. 32p. (gr. k-3). 1986. 14.00 (0-688-05942-2); PLB 13.93 (0-688-05943-0) Greenwillow.
—Which One Is Whitney? LC 89-34614. (Illus.). 40p. (gr. k up). 1990. 12.95 (0-688-09061-3); lib. bdg. 12.88 (0-688-09062-1) Greenwillow.
—Will You Please Feed Our Cat? Stevenson, James, illus. LC 86-11927. 32p. (gr. k-3). 1987. 11.75 (0-688-06847-2); lib. bdg. 11.88 (0-688-06848-0) Greenwillow.
—The Wish Card Ran Out! Stevenson, James, illus. LC 80-22139. 32p. (gr. k-4). 1981. 11.75 (0-688-80305-9) Greenwillow.
—Worse Than the Worst. LC 93-239. (Illus.). 32p. (gr. k up). 1994. write for info. (0-688-12249-3); PLB write for info. (0-688-12250-7) Greenwillow.
—Worse Than Willy! Stevenson, James, illus. LC 83-14201. 32p. (gr. k-3). 1984. 10.25 (0-688-02596-X); PLB 10.88 (0-688-02597-8) Greenwillow.
—The Worst Person in the World. LC 77-22141. (Illus.). 32p. (gr. k-3). 1978. PLB 13.88 (0-688-84127-9) Greenwillow.
—The Worst Person in the World at Crab Beach. LC 86-31931. (Illus.). 32p. (gr. k-3). 1988. 13.95 (0-688-07298-4); lib. bdg. 13.88 (0-688-07299-2) Greenwillow.
—The Worst Person's Christmas. LC 90-39716. (Illus.). 32p. (ps up). 1991. 14.00 (0-688-10210-7); PLB 13.88 (0-688-10211-5) Greenwillow.
—Yuck! Stevenson, James, illus. LC 83-25421. 32p. (gr. k-3). 1984. 11.75 (0-688-03829-8); PLB 11.88 (0-688-03830-1) Greenwillow.

—Yuck! LC 83-25421. (Illus.). (ps-3). 1986. 3.95 (0-688-06524-4, Mulberry) Morrow.
Stevenson, James, jt. auth. see Zolotow, Charlotte.
Stevenson, James W. If I Owned a Candy Factory. Stevenson, James, illus. LC 87-37581. 32p. (ps up). 1989. 11.95 (0-688-08106-1); PLB 11.88 (0-688-08107-X) Greenwillow.
Stevenson, Jocelyn. Bert's New Collection: A Story about What Belongs Together. Winborn, Marsha, illus. LC 87-83489. 32p. (ps-1). 1988. write for info. (0-307-13109-2) Western Pub.
—The Great Muppet Caper. LC 81-4583. (Illus.). 64p. (gr. 4-7). 1981. lib. bdg. 6.99 (0-394-94874-2) Random Bks Yng Read.
—O'Diddy. Truesdell, Sue, illus. LC 87-22676. 64p. (Orig.). (gr. 2-4). 1988. lib. bdg. 6.99 (0-394-99609-7); pap. 1.95 (0-394-89609-2) Random Bks Yng Read.
Stevenson, Jocelyn, compiled by. The Bear Brigade. (Illus.). 64p. (gr. 3-5). 1992. pap. 11.95 (1-85158-400-5, Pub. by Mnstream UK) Trafalgar.
Stevenson, Laura. Happily after All. 256p. (gr. 5-9). 1990. 14.95 (0-395-50216-0) HM.
Stevenson, Laura C. Happily after All. 240p. 1993. pap. 3.50 (0-380-71549-X, Camelot) Avon.
—The Island & the Ring. 304p. (gr. 5-9). 1991. 15.45 (0-395-56401-8, Sandpiper) HM.
Stevenson, Lisbeth G. African-American History: Heroes in Hardship. (Illus.). 352p. (Orig.). (gr. 8-9). 1991. pap. text ed. 12.50 (0-944348-01-7) Cambdgport Pr.
Stevenson, Peter. Play Mask Book - Cinderella. 12p. (ps-3). 1991. pap. 5.95 (0-8167-2371-0) Troll Assocs.
—Play Mask Book - Goldilocks & the Three Bears. 12p. (ps-3). 1991. pap. 5.95 (0-8167-2372-9) Troll Assocs.
—Play Mask Book: Little Red Riding Hood. 12p. (ps-3). 1991. pap. 5.95 (0-8167-2370-2) Troll Assocs.
Stevenson, Peter, illus. Picture Word Book Three. 28p. (ps). 1991. 3.50 (0-7214-1436-2, 916-3) Ladybird Bks.
—Picture Word Book Two. 28p. (ps). 1991. 3.50 (0-7214-1435-4, 916-2) Ladybird Bks.
Stevenson, Ralph L., Jr. Sam's Stamp Store. Wolgamott, Elizabeth, illus. O'Neil, Greg, intro. by. (Illus.). 28p. (Orig.). (ps-2). 1983. pap. 3.50 (0-9610762-0-8) Sirius Leag.
Stevenson, Robert Louis. Black Arrow. (gr. 6 up). 1964. pap. 2.95 (0-8049-0020-5, CL-20) Airmont.
—Black Arrow. (gr. 4 up). 1990. pap. 3.50 (0-440-40359-6) Dell.
—Block City. Wolff, Ashley, illus. LC 87-33397. 32p. (ps-2). 1988. 12.95 (0-525-44399-1, DCB) Dutton Child Bks.
—Block City. Wolff, Ashley, illus. 32p. (ps-2). 1992. pap. 3.99 (0-14-054551-4, Puffin Unicorn) Puffin Bks.
—A Child's Garden of Verses. Gregori, Lee, illus. LC 85-12766. (gr. 3 up). 1969. pap. 2.25 (0-8049-0195-3, CL-195) Airmont.
—A Child's Garden of Verses. Eulalie, illus. LC 85-12766. 86p. (ps-3). 1957. 15.95 (0-448-40510-5, G&D); (G&D) Putnam Pub Group.
—A Child's Garden of Verses. LC 85-12766. (Illus.). (gr. 3-5). 1950. pap. 2.95 (0-14-030022-8, Puffin) Puffin Bks.
—A Child's Garden of Verses. Tudor, Tasha, illus. LC 85-12766. 72p. (ps up). 1988. SBE 13.95 (0-02-788365-5) Macmillan Child Grp.
—A Child's Garden of Verses. Smith, Jessie W., illus. LC 85-12766. 120p. (ps-4). 1905. 17.95 (0-684-20949-7, Scribners Young Read) Macmillan Child Grp.
—A Child's Garden of Verses. Robinson, Charles, illus. (gr. 1 up). 1976. pap. 9.95 (0-85967-313-8, Pub. by Scolar Pr UK) Ashgate Pub Co.
—A Child's Garden of Verses. Wildsmith, Brian, illus. 96p. (gr. 1-4). 16.00 (0-19-276032-7); pap. 10.95 (0-19-276065-3) OUP.
—A Child's Garden of Verses. LC 85-12766. (gr. 5-6). 14.95 (0-89190-739-4, Pub. by Am Repr) Amereon Ltd.
—A Child's Garden of Verses. Foreman, Michael, illus. LC 85-12766. 128p. (ps-3). 1985. 14.95 (0-385-29430-1) Delacorte.
—A Child's Garden of Verses. LC 88-43564. 144p. 1989. 4.95 (0-89471-715-4) Running Pr.
—A Child's Garden of Verses. (Illus.). 128p. 1989. 15.95 (0-87701-608-9) Chronicle Bks.
—Child's Garden of Verses. 1984. 4.98 (0-671-06537-8) S&S Trade.
—Child's Garden of Verses. (Illus.). 112p. (gr. k up). 1991. 15.95 (0-399-21818-1, Philomel Bks) Putnam Pub Group.
—Child's Garden of Verses. Messenger, Jannat, illus. 12p. (ps-6). 1992. 13.95 (0-525-44997-3, DCB) Dutton Child Bks.
—A Child's Garden of Verses. Robinson, Charles, illus. LC 92-53175. 128p. 1992. 12.95 (0-679-41799-0, Evrymans Lib Childs Class) Knopf.
—A Child's Garden of Verses. unabr. ed. Kliros, Thea, illus. LC 92-25818. 96p. 1992. pap. 1.00 (0-486-27301-6) Dover.
—A Child's Garden of Verses. Dorr, Mary A., illus. 24p. (ps-2). 1993. pap. text ed. 0.99 (1-56293-351-5) McClanahan Bk.
—A Child's Garden of Verses. Robinson, Charles, illus. LC 93-41101. 1994. 6.00 (1-56957-926-1) Barefoot Bks.
—Child's Garden of Verses-Coloring Book. 1950. pap. 2.75 (0-486-23481-9) Dover.
—Complete Stories. (gr. 5 up). 1994. write for info. (0-8050-3204-5) H Holt & Co.

—Dr. Jekyll & Mr. Hyde. (gr. 8 up). 1964. pap. 2.25 (0-8049-0042-6, CL-42) Airmont.
—Dr. Jekyll & Mr. Hyde. new ed. Platt, Kin, ed. Redondo, Nestor, illus. LC 73-75457. 64p. (Orig.). (gr. 5-10). 1973. pap. 2.95 (0-88301-096-8); student activity bk. 1.25 (0-88301-176-X) Pendulum Pr.
—Dr. Jekyll & Mr. Hyde. McMullan, Kate, ed. Van Munching, Paul, illus. LC 83-15972. 96p. (gr. 3-7). 1988. pap. 2.95 (0-394-86365-8) Random Bks Yng Read.
—Dr. Jekyll & Mr. Hyde. 1990. pap. 2.50 (0-8125-0448-8) Tor Bks.
—Dr. Jekyll & Mr. Hyde. 208p. 1991. pap. 3.25 (0-590-45169-3) Scholastic Inc.
—From a Railway Carriage. Thomas, Llewellyn, illus. 32p. (ps-3). 1993. 14.99 (0-670-84894-8) Viking Child Bks.
—Ile au Tresor. (FRE.). 284p. (gr. 5-10). 1987. pap. 9.95 (2-07-033441-4) Schoenhof.
—Kidnapped. (gr. 8 up). 1964. pap. 1.95 (0-8049-0010-8, CL-10) Airmont.
—Kidnapped. 240p. (RL 6). 1959. pap. 2.50 (0-451-52333-4, CW1754, Sig Classics) NAL-Dutton.
—Kidnapped. 232p. (gr. 3-7). 1983. pap. 2.99 (0-14-035012-8, Puffin) Puffin Bks.
—Kidnapped. Wyeth, N. C., illus. 304p. 1989. 12.99 (0-517-68783-6) Outlet Bk Co.
—Kidnapped. 1991. pap. 2.50 (0-8125-0473-9) Tor Bks.
—Kidnapped. Mattern, Joanne, retold by. Parton, Steve, illus. LC 92-5803. 48p. (gr. 3-6). 1992. PLB 12.89 (0-8167-2862-3); pap. text ed. 3.95 (0-8167-2863-1) Troll Assocs.
—Kidnapped. Wyeth, N. C., illus. LC 89-43033. 290p. (gr. 6 up). 1993. Repr. of 1989 ed. 16.95 (1-56138-262-0) Running Pr.
—Kidnapped. (gr. 4-7). 1993. pap. 3.50 (0-440-40836-9) Dell.
—Kidnapped. Norby, Lisa, adapted by. LC 93-4609. 1994. pap. 2.99 (0-679-85091-0) Random Bks Yng Read.
—Kidnapped & Treasure Island. 464p. (gr. 9-12). 1981. pap. 3.50 (0-451-52206-0, Sig Classics) NAL-Dutton.
—Kidnapped: Being Memoirs of the Adventures of David Balfour in the Year 1751. (Illus.). 326p. 1992. Repr. PLB 29.95 (0-685-59599-4) Regal Pubns.
—The Land of Nod & Other Poems for Children. Hague, Michael, illus. LC 87-26533. 64p. (ps-2). 1988. 16.95 (0-8050-0746-6, Bks Young Read) H Holt & Co.
—Master of Ballantrae. (gr. 8 up). 1964. pap. 1.95 (0-8049-0047-7, CL-47) Airmont.
—The Moon. Saldutti, Denise, illus. LC 83-47704. 32p. (ps-3). 1986. pap. 4.95 (0-06-443098-7, Trophy) HarpC Child Bks.
—My Shadow. LC 88-46107. (Illus.). 32p. (gr. 1 up). 1989. 14.95 (0-87923-788-0) Godine.
—My Shadow. Rand, Ted, illus. 32p. 1990. 14.95 (0-399-22216-2, Putnam) Putnam Pub Group.
—Reader's Digest Best Loved Books for Young Readers: Kidnapped - The Adventures of David Balfour. Ogburn, Jackie, ed. Wyeth, N. C., illus. 136p. (gr. 4-12). 1989. 3.99 (0-945260-32-6) Choice Pub NY.
—Reader's Digest Best Loved Books for Young Readers: Treasure Island. Ogburn, Jackie, ed. Glanzman, Louis S., illus. 144p. (gr. 4-12). 1989. 3.99 (0-945260-23-7) Choice Pub NY.
—The Sire de Maletroit's Door. Redpath, Ann, ed. Delessert, Etienne, illus. 58p. (gr. 6 up). 1985. PLB 13.95s.p. (0-87191-967-2) Creative Ed.
—Strange Case of Dr. Jekyll & Mr. Hyde & the Suicide Club. 176p. (gr. 5 up). 1986. pap. 2.95 (0-14-035047-0, Puffin) Puffin Bks.
—Treasure Island. (gr. 7 up). 1962. pap. 2.95 (0-8049-0002-7, CL-2) Airmont.
—Treasure Island. (Illus.). (gr. 1-9). 1947. deluxe ed. 13.95 (0-448-06025-6, G&D) Putnam Pub Group.
—Treasure Island. (RL 6). 1965. pap. 1.95 (0-451-52189-7, Sig Classics) NAL-Dutton.
—Treasure Island. 224p. (gr. 2-5). 1984. pap. 2.95 (0-14-035016-0, Puffin) Puffin Bks.
—Treasure Island. Craft, Kinuko Y., illus. Edwards, Jane, adapted by. LC 79-24100. (Illus.). (gr. 4-12). 1983. PLB 18.64 (0-8172-1655-3) Raintree Steck-V.
—Treasure Island. Wyeth, N. C., illus. LC 81-8788. 273p. (gr. 3 up). 1981. SBE 24.95 (0-684-17160-0, Scribners Young Read) Macmillan Child Grp.
—Treasure Island. write for info. S&S Trade.
—Treasure Island. Letley, Emma, ed. (gr. 7-12). 1985. pap. 3.95 (0-19-281681-0) OUP.
—Treasure Island. (gr. 5-6). 19.95 (0-89190-236-8, Pub. by Am Repr) Amereon Ltd.
—Treasure Island. (gr. 7 up). 1965. pap. 1.75 (0-451-51917-5, Sig Classics) NAL-Dutton.
—Treasure Island. (gr. k-6). 1986. 7.98 (0-685-16845-X, 618168) Outlet Bk Co.
—Treasure Island. Hitchner, Earle, ed. De John, Marie, illus. LC 89-20561. 48p. (gr. 3-6). 1990. lib. bdg. 12.89 (0-8167-1877-6); pap. text ed. 3.95 (0-8167-1878-4) Troll Assocs.
—Treasure Island. reissued ed. Norby, Lisa, adapted by. Fernandez, Fernando, illus. LC 89-70039. 96p. (Orig.). (gr. 2-6). 1993. PLB 5.99 (0-679-90402-6); pap. 2.99 (0-679-80402-1) Random Bks Yng Read.
—Treasure Island. 224p. (gr. 6 up). 1988. pap. 2.95 (0-590-44501-4) Scholastic Inc.
—Treasure Island. (Illus.). (gr. 3-5). 3.50 (0-7214-0597-5) Ladybird Bks.
—Treasure Island. 272p. 1990. pap. 2.50 (0-8125-0508-5) Tor Bks.

—Treasure Island. (Illus.). 1992. write for info. (*0-89434-128-6*) Ferguson.
—Treasure Island. Wyeth, N. C., illus. 274p. (gr. 5 up). 1992. Repr. of 1911 ed. 24.95 (*1-879329-07-7*) Time Warner Libraries.
—Treasure Island. 304p. 1992. 9.49 (*0-8167-2560-8*); pap. 2.95 (*0-8167-2561-6*) Troll Assocs.
—Treasure Island. Ingpen, Robert, illus. 176p. 1992. 20.00 (*0-670-84685-6*) Viking Child Bks.
—Treasure Island. Peake, Mervyn, illus. LC 92-53174. 240p. 1992. 12.95 (*0-679-41800-8*, Evrymans Lib Childs Class) Knopf.
—Treasure Island. LC 92-29791. 160p. 1993. pap. 1.00 (*0-486-27559-0*) Dover.
—Treasure Island. Wyeth, N. C., illus. LC 89-43034. 274p. (gr. 5 up). 1993. Repr. of 1989 ed. 16.95 (*1-56138-264-7*) Running Pr.
—Treasure Island. (gr. 7). 1990. pap. write for info. (*0-382-09996-6*) Silver Burdett Pr.
—Treasure Island. McNaughton, Colin, illus. LC 93-18941. 272p. (gr. 4-8). 1993. PLB 15.95 (*0-8050-2773-4*, Bks Young Read) H Holt & Co.
—Treasure Island. (gr. 4-7). 1993. pap. 4.95 (*0-8114-6844-5*) Raintree Steck-V.
Stevenson, Sucie. Christmas Eve. Stevenson, Sucie, illus. 32p. (ps-2). 1992. pap. 3.99 (*0-440-40729-X*, YB) Dell.
—Do I Have to Take Violet? Stevenson, Sucie, illus. 32p. (ps-3). 1992. pap. 3.99 (*0-440-40682-X*, YB) Dell.
Stevenson, Sucie, retold by. & illu see Andersen, Hans Christian.
Stevenson, William. The Bushbabies. Ambrus, Victor, illus. (gr. 5-9). 1984. 16.00 (*0-8446-6167-8*) Peter Smith.
Stevermer, C. River Rats. 1992. 16.95 (*0-15-200895-0*, HB Juv Bks) HarBrace.
Steves, Rick. Kidding Around Seattle: A Young Person's Guide to the City. Meier, Melissa, illus. 64p. (Orig.). (gr. 3 up). 1991. pap. 9.95 (*0-945465-84-X*) John Muir.
Steward-Shahan, Leah, ed. see Dunning, Jack.
Steward-Shahan, Leah, ed. see Rathbone, R. Andrew.
Steward-Shahan, Leah, ed. see Rathbone, Tina.
Stewart & Champanier. The Door in the Wall: A Study Guide. (gr. 9-12). 1990. pap. text ed. 14.95 (*0-88122-410-3*) Lrn Links.
Stewart, A. C. Dark Dove. LC 74-14814. 192p. (gr. 6-9). 1974. 21.95 (*0-87599-203-X*) S G Phillips.
—Elizabeth's Tower. LC 72-4063. 220p. (gr. 6-9). 1972. 21.95 (*0-87599-193-9*) S G Phillips.
—Ossian House. LC 76-9645. (gr. 6 up). 1976. PLB 21.95 (*0-87599-219-6*) S G Phillips.
Stewart, Bonnie. L Is for Liberty. Elder, John, illus. 32p. (gr. 1 up). 1993. 15.95g (*1-879244-00-4*) Windom Bks.
Stewart, Celeste. Merry Berry. Weinberger, Jane & Black, Albert, eds. DeVito, Pamela, illus. LC 88-51280. 88p. (gr. 4-8). 1990. pap. 5.00 (*0-932433-53-7*) Windswept Hse.
Stewart, Charles, III. Disney's Columbus Sails to America. Wilson, Phil, illus. LC 91-73815. (gr. k-4). 1992. 16.95 (*1-56282-132-6*) Disney Pr.
Stewart, Charles P., jt. auth. see Stewart, Frances T.
Stewart, Charles P., III, jt. auth. see Stewart, Frances T.
Stewart, Dana. Friends from Galilee: A Bible-Times Visit with Micah & Hannah. Couri, Kathy, illus. 28p. (ps). 1994. 4.99 (*0-7847-0003-6*, 24-03869) Standard Pub.
—God Feeds the Animals. Garris, Norma, illus. 12p. (ps). 1992. deluxe ed. 4.99 (*0-87403-998-3*, 24-03118) Standard Pub.
—The Happy Times Players Present - The Story of Creation. McCallum, Jodie, illus. 12p. (ps). 1993. 4.99 (*0-7847-0127-X*, 23-02219) Standard Pub.
—The Happy Times Players Present - The Story of Noah's Ark. McCallum, Jodie, illus. 12p. (ps). 1993. 4.99 (*0-7847-0128-8*, 23-02220) Standard Pub.
Stewart, David. Fathering & Career: Keeping a Healthy Balance. 2nd ed. LC 87-63156. 16p. (gr. 7 up). 1987. pap. 1.95 (*0-934426-16-3*) NAPSAC Reprods.
Stewart, Diana, adapted by see Homer.
Stewart, Diana, adapted by see James, Henry.
Stewart, Diana, adapted by see Shakespeare, William.
Stewart, Diana, adapted by see Twain, Mark.
Stewart, Dianne. The Dove. Daly, Jude, illus. LC 91-45798. 32p. (ps up). 1993. 14.00 (*0-688-11264-1*); PLB 13.93 (*0-688-11265-X*) Greenwillow.
Stewart, Frances T. & Stewart, Charles P. Birds & Their Environments. Barrett, Rob, illus. 32p. (ps up). 1988. sticker bk. 7.95 (*0-694-00257-7*) HarpC Child Bks.
—The Birth of Jesus. (Orig.). (gr. 3 up). 1985. pap. 7.95 (*0-8054-4171-9*) Broadman.
Stewart, Frances T. & Stewart, Charles P., III. When Jesus Was a Boy. (Orig.). (gr. k-3). 1987. pap. 7.95 (*0-8054-4188-3*) Broadman.
Stewart, G. Chicago. (Illus.). 48p. (gr. 5 up). 1989. lib. bdg. 15.94 (*0-86592-538-0*); lib. bdg. 11.95s.p. (*0-685-58587-5*) Rourke Corp.
—Houston. (Illus.). 48p. (gr. 5 up). 1989. lib. bdg. 15.74 (*0-86592-539-9*); 11.95s.p. (*0-685-58588-3*) Rourke Corp.
—In Space. (Illus.). 32p. (gr. 3-8). 1989. lib. bdg. 11.95s.p. (*0-86592-116-4*); PLB 15.74 (*0-685-58599-9*) Rourke Corp.
—In the Desert. (Illus.). 32p. (gr. 3-8). 1989. lib. bdg. 15.74 (*0-86592-106-7*); 11.95s.p. (*0-685-58594-8*) Rourke Corp.

—In the Future. (Illus.). 32p. (gr. 3-8). 1989. lib. bdg. 15.74 (*0-86592-115-6*); 11.95s.p. (*0-685-58595-6*) Rourke Corp.
—In the Mountains. (Illus.). 32p. (gr. 3-8). 1989. lib. bdg. 15.74 (*0-86592-107-5*); 11.95s.p. (*0-685-58598-0*) Rourke Corp.
—In the Polar Regions. (Illus.). 32p. (gr. 3-8). 1989. lib. bdg. 15.74 (*0-86592-108-3*); 11.95s.p. (*0-685-58596-4*) Rourke Corp.
—Los Angeles. (Illus.). 48p. (gr. 5 up). 1989. lib. bdg. 15.94 (*0-86592-540-2*); 11.95 (*0-685-58589-1*) Rourke Corp.
—New York. (Illus.). 48p. (gr. 5 up). 1989. lib. bdg. 15.94 (*0-86592-541-0*); 11.95s.p. (*0-685-58586-7*) Rourke Corp.
—On the Water. (Illus.). 32p. (gr. 3-8). 1989. lib. bdg. 15.94 (*0-86592-109-1*); 11.95s.p. (*0-685-58597-2*) Rourke Corp.
Stewart, Gail. Acid Rain. LC 90-5854. (Illus.). 112p. (gr. 5-8). 1990. PLB 14.95 (*1-56006-111-1*) Lucent Bks.
—Child Abuse. LC 89-1386. (Illus.). 48p. (gr. 4 up). 1989. RSBE 12.95 (*0-89686-442-1*, Crestwood Hse) Macmillan Child Grp.
—Coal Miners. LC 88-11860. (Illus.). 48p. (gr. 5-6). 1988. RSBE 11.95 (*0-89686-395-6*, Crestwood Hse) Macmillan Child Grp.
—Death. LC 89-31257. (Illus.). 48p. (gr. 4-5). 1989. RSBE 12.95 (*0-89686-446-4*, Crestwood Hse) Macmillan Child Grp.
—Discrimination. LC 89-31259. (Illus.). 48p. (gr. 4-5). 1989. RSBE 12.95 (*0-89686-445-6*, Crestwood Hse) Macmillan Child Grp.
—Drug Trafficking. LC 90-6196. (Illus.). 96p. (gr. 5-8). 1990. PLB 14.95 (*1-56006-116-2*) Lucent Bks.
—Frontiersmen. (Illus.). 32p. (gr. 3-8). 1990. PLB 18.00 (*0-86625-406-4*); 13.50s.p. (*0-685-34709-5*) Rourke Corp.
—Living Spaces, 6 bks, Reading Level 4. (Illus.). 192p. (gr. 3-8). 1990. Set. PLB 95.64 (*0-86592-105-9*); 71.70s.p. (*0-685-58770-3*) Rourke Corp.
—Lumberman. (Illus.). 32p. (gr. 3-8). 1990. lib. bdg. 18.00 (*0-86625-407-2*); 13.50s.p. (*0-685-58649-9*) Rourke Corp.
—Motorcycle Racing. LC 87-33198. (Illus.). 48p. (gr. 5-6). 1988. RSBE 11.95 (*0-89686-360-3*, Crestwood Hse) Macmillan Child Grp.
—Nineteen Hundreds. LC 89-9936. (Illus.). 48p. (gr. 4-5). 1989. RSBE 11.95 (*0-89686-471-5*, Crestwood Hse) Macmillan Child Grp.
—Nineteen Tens. LC 89-9946. (Illus.). 48p. (gr. 4-5). 1989. RSBE 11.95 (*0-89686-472-3*, Crestwood Hse) Macmillan Child Grp.
—Nineteen Thirties. LC 89-34405. (Illus.). 48p. (gr. 4 up). 1989. RSBE 11.95 (*0-89686-474-X*, Crestwood Hse) Macmillan Child Grp.
—Nineteen Twenties. (Illus.). 48p. (gr. 4-5). 1989. RSBE 11.95 (*0-89686-473-1*, Crestwood Hse) Macmillan Child Grp.
—Off-Shore Oil Rig Workers. LC 88-12006. (Illus.). 48p. (gr. 5-6). 1988. RSBE 11.95 (*0-89686-397-2*, Crestwood Hse) Macmillan Child Grp.
—Peer Pressure. LC 89-31258. (Illus.). 48p. (gr. 4 up). 1989. RSBE 12.95 (*0-89686-444-8*, Crestwood Hse) Macmillan Child Grp.
—The Revolutionary War. LC 91-29889. (Illus.). 112p. (gr. 5-8). 1991. PLB 17.95 (*1-56006-400-5*) Lucent Bks.
—Rivermen. (Illus.). 32p. (gr. 3-8). 1990. PLB 18.00 (*0-86625-409-9*); 13.50 (*0-685-58652-9*) Rourke Corp.
—Scouts. (Illus.). 32p. (gr. 3-8). 1990. PLB 18.00 (*0-86625-404-8*); 13.50 (*0-685-58651-0*) Rourke Corp.
—Smokejumpers & Forest Firefighters. LC 88-12008. (Illus.). 48p. (gr. 5-6). 1988. RSBE 11.95 (*0-89686-398-0*, Crestwood Hse) Macmillan Child Grp.
—Stuntpeople. LC 88-14946. (Illus.). 48p. (gr. 5-6). 1988. RSBE 11.95 (*0-89686-396-4*, Crestwood Hse) Macmillan Child Grp.
—Teen Suicide. LC 88-20281. (Illus.). 48p. (gr. 5-6). 1988. RSBE 12.95 (*0-89686-413-8*, Crestwood Hse) Macmillan Child Grp.
—Texans. (Illus.). 32p. (gr. 3-8). 1990. PLB 18.00 (*0-86625-408-0*); PLB 13.50s.p. (*0-685-58650-2*) Rourke Corp.
—Trappers & Traders. (Illus.). 32p. (gr. 3-8). 1990. PLB 18.00 (*0-86625-401-3*); PLB 13.50s.p. (*0-685-58655-3*) Rourke Corp.
—The Trojan War: Opposing Viewpoints. LC 89-11616. (Illus.). 112p. (gr. 5-8). 1989. PLB 14.95 (*0-89908-065-0*) Greenhaven.
—World War One. LC 91-16729. (Illus.). 112p. (gr. 5-8). 1991. PLB 17.95 (*1-56006-406-4*) Lucent Bks.
Stewart, Gail, jt. auth. see Loewen, Nancy.
Stewart, Gail B. Adoption. LC 89-1525. (Illus.). 47p. (gr. 4 up). 1989. RSBE 12.95 (*0-89686-443-X*, Crestwood Hse) Macmillan Child Grp.
—Alternative Healing: Opposing Viewpoints. LC 90-3807. (Illus.). 112p. (gr. 5-8). 1990. PLB 14.95 (*0-89908-083-9*) Greenhaven.
—Antarctica. LC 91-8523. (Illus.). 48p. (gr. 5-6). 1991. RSBE 12.95 (*0-89686-656-4*, Crestwood Hse) Macmillan Child Grp.
—Benjamin Franklin. LC 92-23315. (Illus.). 112p. (gr. 5-8). 1992. PLB 14.95 (*1-56006-026-3*) Lucent Bks.
—China. LC 90-35497. (Illus.). 48p. (gr. 5-6). 1990. RSBE 12.95 (*0-89686-538-X*, Crestwood Hse) Macmillan Child Grp.

—Colombia. LC 90-47694. (Illus.). 48p. (gr. 5-6). 1991. RSBE 12.95 (*0-89686-603-3*, Crestwood Hse) Macmillan Child Grp.
—Cuba. LC 91-12352. (Illus.). 48p. (gr. 5-6). 1991. RSBE 12.95 (*0-89686-658-0*, Crestwood Hse) Macmillan Child Grp.
—Drought. LC 90-36293. (Illus.). 48p. (gr. 5-6). 1990. RSBE 12.95 (*0-89686-544-4*, Crestwood Hse) Macmillan Child Grp.
—Egypt. LC 91-33485. (Illus.). 48p. (gr. 5-6). 1992. RSBE 11.95 (*0-89686-744-7*, Crestwood Hse) Macmillan Child Grp.
—El Salvador. LC 90-47691. (Illus.). 48p. (gr. 5-6). 1991. RSBE 12.95 (*0-89686-602-5*, Crestwood Hse) Macmillan Child Grp.
—Ethiopia. LC 90-49795. (Illus.). 48p. (gr. 5-6). 1991. RSBE 12.95 (*0-89686-601-7*, Crestwood Hse) Macmillan Child Grp.
—Famous Hoaxes. LC 89-25422. (Illus.). 48p. (gr. 5 up). 1990. RSBE 11.95 (*0-89686-507-X*, Crestwood Hse) Macmillan Child Grp.
—Germany. LC 90-2244. (Illus.). 48p. (gr. 5-6). 1990. RSBE 12.95 (*0-89686-548-7*, Crestwood Hse) Macmillan Child Grp.
—India. LC 91-34399. (Illus.). 48p. (gr. 5-6). 1992. RSBE 11.95 (*0-89686-745-5*, Crestwood Hse) Macmillan Child Grp.
—Iraq. LC 91-11893. (Illus.). 48p. (gr. 5-6). 1991. RSBE 12.95 (*0-89686-657-2*, Crestwood Hse) Macmillan Child Grp.
—Lebanon. LC 90-35499. (Illus.). 48p. (gr. 5-6). 1990. RSBE 12.95 (*0-89686-550-9*, Crestwood Hse) Macmillan Child Grp.
—Liberia. LC 91-31532. (Illus.). 48p. (gr. 5-6). 1992. RSBE 11.95 (*0-89686-746-3*, Crestwood Hse) Macmillan Child Grp.
—Microscopes: Bringing the Unseen World into Focus. LC 92-17316. (Illus.). 96p. (gr. 5-8). 1992. PLB 15.95 (*1-56006-211-8*) Lucent Bks.
—The New Deal. LC 92-41264. (Illus.). 96p. (gr. 6 up). 1993. RSBE 14.95 (*0-02-788369-8*, New Discovery Bks) Macmillan Child Grp.
—Northern Ireland. LC 90-36291. (Illus.). 48p. (gr. 5-6). 1990. RSBE 12.95 (*0-89686-551-7*, Crestwood Hse) Macmillan Child Grp.
—Panama. LC 90-36249. (Illus.). 48p. (gr. 5-6). 1990. RSBE 12.95 (*0-89686-536-3*, Crestwood Hse) Macmillan Child Grp.
—The Philippines. LC 91-11143. (Illus.). 48p. (gr. 5-6). 1991. RSBE 12.95 (*0-89686-659-9*, Crestwood Hse) Macmillan Child Grp.
—Poland. LC 90-35498. (Illus.). 48p. (gr. 5-6). 1990. RSBE 12.95 (*0-89686-549-5*, Crestwood Hse) Macmillan Child Grp.
—Romania. LC 90-24946. (Illus.). 48p. (gr. 5-6). 1991. RSBE 12.95 (*0-89686-600-9*, Crestwood Hse) Macmillan Child Grp.
—South Africa. LC 90-36292. (Illus.). 48p. (gr. 5-6). 1990. RSBE 12.95 (*0-89686-539-8*, Crestwood Hse) Macmillan Child Grp.
—The Soviet Union. LC 90-38408. (Illus.). 48p. (gr. 5-6). 1990. RSBE 12.95 (*0-89686-537-1*, Crestwood Hse) Macmillan Child Grp.
—The Soviet Union. LC 92-40. (Illus.). 48p. (gr. 5-6). 1992. RSBE 12.95 (*0-89686-747-1*, Crestwood Hse) Macmillan Child Grp.
—What Happened to Judge Crater? LC 91-16554. (Illus.). 48p. (gr. 5 up). 1992. RSBE 11.95 (*0-89686-617-3*, Crestwood Hse) Macmillan Child Grp.
—Where Lies Butch Cassidy? LC 91-25368. (Illus.). 48p. (gr. 5 up). 1992. RSBE 11.95 (*0-89686-618-1*, Crestwood Hse) Macmillan Child Grp.
—Why Buy Quantrill's Bones? LC 91-23120. (Illus.). 48p. (gr. 5 up). 1992. RSBE 11.95 (*0-89686-614-9*, Crestwood Hse) Macmillan Child Grp.
Stewart, Gail B., jt. auth. see Duden, Jane.
Stewart, George R. The Pioneers Go West. LC 87-4568. 160p. (gr. 5-9). 1964. pap. 2.95 (*0-394-89180-5*, Random Juv) Random Bks Yng Read.
Stewart, J. Dinosaurs: A New Discovery. (Illus.). 32p. (gr. 1-6). 1989. 10.95 (*0-88625-234-2*) Durkin Hayes Pub.
—Kids' Cuisine. (Illus.). 48p. (gr. 2-6). 1988. pap. 5.95 (*0-88625-153-2*) Durkin Hayes Pub.
Stewart, J. & Hamilton, N. Great Escapes. (Illus.). 48p. (gr. 5-9). 1988. PLB 14.97 (*0-88625-208-3*); pap. 5.95 (*0-88625-207-5*) Durkin Hayes Pub.
Stewart, Janet, ed. Kid's Party Cookbook. Rowden, Rick, et al, illus. 32p. (gr. 2-6). 1988. PLB 14.65 (*0-88625-201-6*); pap. 5.95 (*0-88625-200-8*) Durkin Hayes Pub.
Stewart, Janet & Pelowich, Nadia, eds. Amazing Rescues. (Illus.). 48p. (gr. 4). 1987. PLB 14.65 (*0-88625-172-9*); pap. 5.95 (*0-88625-151-6*) Durkin Hayes Pub.
Stewart, Jeffrey E. Community Sign Reading. (Illus.). 82p. (Orig.). 1977. pap. 32.50 (*1-877866-06-7*) J E Stewart.
—Food! A Reading Program. (Illus.). 116p. (Orig.). (gr. 4 up). 1987. pap. 32.50 (*1-877866-00-8*) J E Stewart.
—More Food! A Reading Program. (Illus.). 116p. (Orig.). (gr. 4 up). 1988. pap. 32.50 (*1-877866-01-6*) J E Stewart.
—Work! A Reading Program. (Illus.). 116p. (Orig.). 1988. pap. 32.50 (*1-877866-02-4*) J E Stewart.
Stewart, Josie, jt. auth. see Salem, Lynn.

Stewart, Judi & Weit, Kathryn. Around Portland with Kids. rev. ed. (Illus.). 205p. (ps-7). 1987. pap. 9.95 (0-9614261-2-8) Discovery Pr.

Stewart, Judy. A Family in Morocco. (Illus.). 32p. (gr. 2-5). 1986. lib. bdg. 13.50 (0-8225-1664-0) Lerner Pubns.

—A Family in Sudan. (Illus.). 32p. (gr. 2-5). 1988. lib. bdg. 13.50 (0-8225-1682-9) Lerner Pubns.

Stewart, K. K. God Made Me Special. LC 82-62731. (Illus.). 24p. (ps-2). 1983. 2.50 (0-87239-635-5, 3555) Standard Pub.

Stewart, Linda. Sam the Cat Detective. (gr. 4-7). 1993. pap. 2.95 (0-590-46145-1) Scholastic Inc.

Stewart, lyn, ed. see Norman, Floyd.

Stewart, Lyn, ed. see Norman, Floyd E.

Stewart, Lyn, ed. see Norman, Floyd & Sullivan, Leo.

Stewart, Lyn, ed. see Sullivan, Leo.

Stewart, Lyn, ed. see Sullivan, Leo & Norman, Floyd.

Stewart, Margaret A. The Best Book a Mother Ever Had. Imholte, Max, illus. 146p. (ps-3). 1985. pap. 12. 95 spiral bdg. (0-931047-00-5) KinderPr.

Stewart, Marjabelle Y. & Buchwald, Ann. Stand Up, Shake Hands, Say "How Do You Do" What Boys Need to Know about Today's Manners News. rev. ed. LC 77-8159. (gr. 7 up). 1988. 12.95 (0-88331-100-3) Luce.

Stewart, Mollie D. Noah's Land. 1991. 12.95 (0-533-09336-8) Vantage.

Stewart, Molly M., jt. auth. see Pascal, Francine.

Stewart, Pat, adapted by see Potter, Beatrix.

Stewart, Pat, illus. Jesus' Bethlehem Birthday. (ps-1). 1989. 9.99 (1-55513-814-4, Chariot Bks) Cook.

Stewart, Rachel. Margot Fonteyn. (Illus.). 64p. (gr. 5-9). 1991. 11.95 (0-237-60033-1, Pub. by Evans Bros Ltd) Trafalgar.

Stewart, Robert. Leadership for Agricultural Industry. Amberson, Max L., ed. (Illus.). (gr. 9-10). 1978. text ed. 17.96 (0-07-000847-7) McGraw.

Stewart, Sarah. The Money Tree. Small, David, illus. 32p. (gr. k up). 1991. 14.95 (0-374-35014-0) FS&G.

Stewart, Susan, jt. auth. see Helwig, Barbara.

Stewart, Whitney. To the Lion Throne. (Illus.). 60p. (Orig.). (gr. 3 up). 1990. PLB 8.95 (0-937938-75-0) Snow Lion.

Stewig, John W. Moon's Choice. (ps-6). 1993. pap. 15.00 (0-671-76962-6, S&S BFYR) S&S Trade.

Stewig, John W., retold by. The Fisherman & His Wife. Tomes, Margot, illus. LC 88-1698. 32p. (ps-3). 1988. reinforced bdg. 13.95 (0-8234-0714-4) Holiday.

—Stone Soup. Tomes, Margot, illus. LC 90-46502. 32p. (ps-3). 1991. reinforced 14.95 (0-8234-0863-9) Holiday.

Steyn. The Bushman of the Kalahari, Reading Level 5. (Illus.). 48p. (gr. 4-8). 1989. PLB 16.67 (0-86625-267-3); 12.50 (0-685-58810-6) Rourke Corp.

Stich, Paul, ed. see Osborne, John, et al.

Stich, Paul, et al. United States History & Government: A Competency Review Text. 2nd ed. Gamsey, Wayne, ed. Fairbanks, Eugene B., illus. 384p. (gr. 7-12). 1992. pap. text ed. 8.33 (0-935487-20-4) N & N Pub Co.

—United States History & Government: A Regents Review Text. 6th ed. Gamsey, Wayne, ed. Fairbanks, Eugene B., illus. 416p. (gr. 7-12). 1992. pap. text ed. 6.22 (0-935487-21-2) N & N Pub Co.

—United States History & Government: Ten Day Competency. rev. ed. Gamsey, Wayne, ed. Fairbanks, Eugene B., illus. 128p. (gr. 7-12). 1992. pap. text ed. 4.95 (0-935487-54-9) N & N Pub Co.

—United States History & Government: Ten Day Regents Review. rev. ed. Gamsey, Wayne, ed. Fairbanks, Eugene B., illus. 128p. (gr. 7-12). 1992. pap. text ed. 4.95 (0-935487-49-2) N & N Pub Co.

Stickland, Henrietta. The Christmas Bear. Stickland, Paul, illus. LC 93-10157. 32p. (ps-3). 1993. 15.99 (0-525-45062-9, DCB) Dutton Child Bks.

Stickland, Paul. A Child's Book of Things. LC 90-30647. (Illus.). 32p. (ps-1). 1990. 13.95 (0-531-05906-5); PLB 13.99 (0-531-08506-6) Orchard Bks Watts.

—Machines As Big As Monsters. LC 88-26511. (Illus.). 32p. (gr. k-3). 1989. lib. bdg. 10.99 (0-394-93913-1) Random Bks Yng Read.

—Machines As Tall As Giants. Stickland, Paul, illus. LC 88-34695. (gr. k-3). 1989. PLB 10.99 (0-394-95375-4) Random Bks Yng Read.

Stickland, Paul, illus. Working Wheels. 14p. (ps). 1993. 3.50 (0-525-67457-8, Lodestar Bks) Dutton Child Bks.

Stickler, Kristine R. Guide to Analysis of Language Transcripts. LC 86-51417. 252p. (ps-4). 1987. wire spiral bdg. 27.00 (0-930599-11-X) Thinking Pubns.

Stickler, Ruth, ed. see Cake, J. C.

Stickles, Frances. A Crown for Henrietta Maria. LC 88-61639. (Illus.). 100p. (gr. 2-6). 1988. 16.75 (0-917882-27-X) MD Hist Pr.

Stidworthy, John. Environmentalist. (Illus.). 32p. (gr. 4-7). 1992. PLB 12.40 (0-531-17268-6, Gloucester Pr) Watts.

—Flowers, Trees & Other Plants. Pepperell, Liz, et al, illus. LC 91-215. 40p. (Orig.). (gr. 2-5). 1991. pap. 3.99 (0-679-80867-1) Random Bks Yng Read.

—Hibernation. LC 91-2674. (Illus.). 32p. (gr. 5-8). 1991. PLB 12.40 (0-531-17309-7, Gloucester Pr) Watts.

—Insects. (Illus.). 32p. (gr. 5-6). 1989. PLB 12.40 (0-531-17184-1, Gloucester Pr) Watts.

—Naturalist. LC 91-2660. (Illus.). 32p. (gr. 5-8). 1991. PLB 12.40 (0-531-17356-9, Gloucester Pr) Watts.

—Plants & Seeds. 1990. PLB 12.40 (0-531-17220-1, Gloucester Pr) Watts.

—Ponds & Streams. Loates, Mick & Male, Alan, illus. LC 89-20331. 32p. (gr. 3-6). 1990. PLB 11.59 (0-8167-1963-2); pap. text ed. 3.95 (0-8167-1964-0) Troll Assocs.

Stidworthy, John, jt. auth. see O'Toole, Christopher.

Stidworthy, John, et al. Mammals: Large Plant-Eaters. (Illus.). 96p. 1988. 17.95x (0-8160-1960-6) Facts on File.

Stieg, William. Rotten Island. (gr. 2 up). 1992. pap. 7.95 (0-87923-960-3) Godine.

Stieglitz, Cliff, ed. see Edwards, Don.

Stieglitz, Maria. Career Education For Physically Disabled Students: Career Awareness Curriculum. LC 80-83986. (Illus.). 100p. (gr. k-8). 1981. 2.00 (0-686-38797-X) Human Res Ctr.

—Career Education For Physically Disabled Students: Self-Concept Curriculum. LC 80-82643. (Illus.). 96p. (gr. k-3). 1981. 2.00 (0-686-38800-3) Human Res Ctr.

Stifle, J. M., jt. auth. see Haskins, James S.

Stiles, Barbara J. Cheeky Rubs. Arthur, John, illus. LC 89-164732. 20p. (ps-5). 1989. text ed. 12.95 (0-9622057-1-0); pap. text ed. 7.95 (0-9622057-0-2) Manzanita Canyon.

—Trinkets & Toads & Other Treasures. LC 91-60705. 48p. 1991. 12.95 (0-9622057-3-7); pap. 8.95 (0-9622057-2-9) Manzanita Canyon.

Stiles, Louise. Little Tree. Torvik, Brian, illus. 32p. (gr. 3 up). 1987. pap. 5.95 (0-88144-051-5) Christian Pub.

Stiles, Martha B. James the Vinepuller. (ps-3). 1992. 14. 95 (0-87614-047-9) Carolrhoda Bks.

—Kate of Still Waters. LC 90-5546. 256p. (gr. 3-7). 1990. SBE 14.95 (0-02-788395-7, Macmillan Child Bk) Macmillan Child Grp.

—Sarah the Dragon Lady. 96p. (gr. 3-7). 1988. pap. 2.75 (0-380-70471-4, Camelot) Avon.

Stiles, Norman. Sesame Street, the Ernie & Bert Book. Mathieu, Joe, illus. 24p. (ps-k). 1977. pap. write for info. (0-307-10072-3, Pub. by Golden Bks) Western Pub.

Stiles, Norman & Wilcox, Daniel. Grover & the Everything in the Whole Wide World Museum. Mathieo, Joe, illus. LC 73-18736. 32p. (ps-k). 1974. pap. 2.25 (0-394-82707-4) Random Bks Yng Read.

Stiles, T. J. Jesse James. LC 92-45210. (Illus.). 1993. 18. 95 (0-7910-1737-0, Am Art Analog); pap. write for info. (0-7910-1738-9, Am Art Analog) Chelsea Hse.

Still, James. The King of the Golden River. (Orig.). 1992. pap. 4.50 playscript (0-685-61713-0) Anchorage.

Still, James, adapted by. The Velveteen Rabbit. 33p. (Orig.). 1989. playscript 4.50 (0-87602-289-1) Anchorage.

Still, James, tr. see Thomas, Mary A.

Still, John. Amazing Beetles. Young, Jerry, illus. LC 91-6516. 32p. (Orig.). (gr. 1-5). 1991. lib. bdg. 9.99 (0-679-91519-2); pap. 6.95 (0-679-81519-8) Knopf Bks Yng Read.

—Amazing Butterflies & Moths. Young, Jerry, photos by. LC 90-19234. (Illus.). 32p. (Orig.). (gr. 1-5). 1991. PLB 9.99 (0-679-91515-X); pap. 6.95 (0-679-81515-5) Knopf Bks Yng Read.

Still, Judith A. Little David Had No Fear. Phillips, Ted, Jr., illus. (Orig.). (gr. 6-8). 1990. write for info. (1-877873-03-9); pap. write for info. Master-Player Lib.

Stille, Darlene. Air Pollution. LC 89-25348. (Illus.). 48p. (gr. k-4). 1990. PLB 15.27 (0-516-01181-2); pap. 4.95 (0-516-41181-0) Childrens.

—The Greenhouse Effect. LC 90-2147. (Illus.). 48p. (gr. k-4). 1990. PLB 15.27 (0-516-01106-5); pap. 4.95 (0-516-41106-3) Childrens.

—Oil Spills. LC 90-21455. (Illus.). 48p. (gr. k-4). 1991. PLB 15.27 (0-516-01116-2); pap. 4.95 (0-516-41116-0) Childrens.

—The Ozone Hole. LC 90-20843. (Illus.). 48p. (gr. k-4). 1991. PLB 15.27 (0-516-01117-0); pap. 4.95 (0-516-41117-9) Childrens.

—Soil Erosion & Pollution. LC 89-25360. (Illus.). 48p. (gr. k-4). 1990. 15.27 (0-516-01188-X); pap. 4.95 (0-516-41188-8) Childrens.

—Spacecraft. LC 90-19992. (Illus.). 48p. (gr. k-4). 1991. PLB 15.27 (0-516-01120-0); pap. 4.95 (0-516-41120-9) Childrens.

—Water Pollution. LC 89-25344. (Illus.). 48p. (gr. k-4). 1990. PLB 15.27 (0-516-01190-1); pap. 4.95 (0-516-41190-X) Childrens.

Stille, Darlene R. Ice Age. LC 90-37681. (Illus.). 48p. (gr. k-4). 1990. PLB 15.27 (0-516-01107-3); pap. 4.95 (0-516-41107-1) Childrens.

Stillinger, Scott, jt. auth. see Cassidy, John.

Stillman, Karen. The First Apartment Houses. LC 92-75994. (gr. 1-6). 1993. 9.95 (0-383-03817-0) CPI.

Stillwater, Maitreya. Windows of Nature: A Story-Coloring Book. Stillwater, Maitreya, illus. 40p. (Orig.). (ps-3). 1987. pap. 6.95 (0-87516-580-X) DeVorss.

Stillwell, Jim. The Perceptual-Motor Activities Book. Gimlin, Rick & Kamiya, Artie, illus. 96p. (Orig.). (gr. k-6). 1990. pap. 10.00 (0-945872-05-4) Great Activities Pub Co.

Stilwell, Alison. Chin Ling, the Chinese Cricket. Stilwell, Alison, illus. LC 81-90045. 48p. (gr. 1-4). 1981. Repr. of 1947 ed. 12.95 (0-9605862-0-2) Stilwell Studio.

Stimson, Joan. Animals: Stories for under Fives. Maclean, Colin & Maclean, Moira, illus. 44p. (ps-k). 1992. 3.50 (0-7214-1484-2) Ladybird Bks.

—Bedtime: Stories for under Fives. Round, Graham, illus. 44p. (ps-k). 1992. 3.50 (0-7214-1487-7) Ladybird Bks.

—Big Panda, Little Panda. Rutherford, Meg, illus. LC 93-36235. 32p. (ps-2). 1994. 12.95 (0-8120-6404-6); pap. 4.95 (0-8120-1691-2) Barron.

—Farmyard: Stories for under Fives. Archer, Rebecca, illus. 44p. (ps-k). 1992. 3.50 (0-7214-1506-7) Ladybird Bks.

—Kim Meets Santa Claus. Matthews, Anne, illus. 28p. (ps-1). 1991. 3.95 (0-7214-9615-6, S808-24 SER.) Ladybird Bks.

—Monster: Stories for under Fives. Hawksley, Gerald, illus. 44p. (ps-k). 1992. 3.50 (0-7214-1505-9) Ladybird Bks.

—Storytime for One Year Olds. Strop, John & Strop, Caroline, illus. 28p. (ps). 1991. 3.50 (0-7214-1419-2, 887-7) Ladybird Bks.

Stinchecum, Amanda M., tr. see Gomi, Taro.

Stinchecum, Amanda M., tr. see Hidaka, Masako.

Stinchecum, Amanda M., tr. see Nomura, Takaaki.

Stinchecum, Amanda M., tr. see Yagyu, Genichiro.

Stine. Be Careful What You Wish For. 1993. pap. 2.95 (0-590-49447-3) Scholastic Inc.

Stine, Bob. One Hundred & One Silly Monster Jokes. Taylor, B. K., illus. 96p. (Orig.). (gr. 4-7). 1986. pap. 1.95 (0-590-33889-7) Scholastic Inc.

—One Hundred & One Wacky Kid Jokes. Orehek, Don, illus. 96p. 1988. pap. 1.95 (0-590-41399-6) Scholastic Inc.

—One Hundred One More Monster Jokes. 96p. (Orig.). (gr. 4-7). 1990. pap. 1.95 (0-590-43171-4) Scholastic Inc.

—One Hundred One School Cafeteria Jokes. 96p. (Orig.). (gr. 3-7). 1990. pap. 1.95 (0-590-43759-3) Scholastic Inc.

—The Pigs' Book of World Records. Lippman, Peter, illus. LC 79-5239. 96p. (gr. 3 up). 1980. pap. 4.99 (0-394-94402-X) Random Bks Yng Read.

Stine, H. William, jt. auth. see Stine, Megan.

Stine, H. William, jt. ed. see Stine, Megan.

Stine, Jane & Stine, Jovial B. Everything You Need to Survive: Money Problems. Murdocca, Sal, illus. LC 82-23117. 96p. (gr. 5-9). 1983. pap. 1.95 (0-394-85247-8) Random Bks Yng Read.

Stine, Jovial B. The Amazing Adventures of Me, Myself, & I. (gr. 2-5). 1991. pap. 2.75 (0-553-15834-1, Skylark) Bantam.

—One Hundred & One Vacation Jokes. 1990. pap. 1.95 (0-590-43610-4) Scholastic Inc.

Stine, Jovial B., jt. auth. see Stine, Jane.

Stine, Jovial Bob. Pork & Beans: Play Date. Aruego, Jose & Dewey, Ariane, illus. (ps-2). 1989. pap. 12.95 (0-590-41579-4) Scholastic Inc.

Stine, Megan. Dylan's Secret. 112p. (Orig.). (gr. 4-9). 1992. pap. 2.95 (0-448-40493-1, G&D) Putnam Pub Group.

—The Hanukkah Miracles. (Illus.). (ps-3). 1993. pap. 3.99 (0-553-37294-7) Bantam.

—The Story of Laura Ingalls Wilder. Ramsey, Marcy D., illus. 112p. (Orig.). (gr. 2-5). 1992. pap. 3.50 (0-440-40578-5, YB) Dell.

—Story of Malcolm X, Civil Rights Leader. (gr. 4-7). 1994. pap. 3.50 (0-440-40900-4) Dell.

—Tattoo Mania: The Newest Craze in Wearable Art. (gr. 1-3). 1993. pap. 5.99 (0-553-48144-4) Bantam.

—They Survived Mount St. Helens. LC 93-5505. 1994. 2.99 (0-679-84362-0); lib. bdg. 9.99 (0-679-94362-5) Random Bks Yng Read.

Stine, Megan & Stine, H. William. Fifth Grade Flop. Henry, Paul, illus. LC 89-20624. 96p. (gr. 4-6). 1990. lib. bdg. 9.89 (0-8167-1704-4); pap. text ed. 2.95 (0-8167-1705-2) Troll Assocs.

—Haunted Halloween. (Illus.). 80p. 1988. pap. 2.95 (0-449-90327-3, Columbine) Fawcett.

—How I Survived Fifth Grade. LC 90-26790. 96p. (gr. 4-6). 1992. lib. bdg. 9.89 (0-8167-2386-9); pap. text ed. 2.95 (0-8167-2387-7) Troll Assocs.

—Long Shot, Bk. 10. LC 89-24355. 144p. (gr. 5 up). 1990. lib. bdg. 7.99 (0-679-90526-X) Random Bks Yng Read.

—Murder to Go. LC 88-14693. 144p. (gr. 5 up). 1989. PLB 6.99 (0-394-99980-0) Random Bks Yng Read.

—Murder to Go. LC 88-14693. 144p. (Orig.). (gr. 5 up). 1989. pap. 2.95 (0-394-89980-6) Knopf Bks Yng Read.

—Mysterious Max. (Illus.). 80p. 1988. pap. 2.95 (0-449-90326-5, Columbine) Fawcett.

—Thriller Diller. LC 88-45881. (Illus.). 144p. (Orig.). (gr. 5 up). 1989. pap. 2.95 (0-394-82936-0) Knopf Bks Yng Read.

—Thriller Diller. 1989. lib. bdg. 6.99 (0-394-92936-5) Random Bks Yng Read.

—Young Indiana Jones & the Lost Gold of Durango. 132p. (Orig.). (gr. 3-7). 1993. pap. 2.99 (0-679-84926-2) Random Bks Yng Read.

Stine, Megan & Stine, William H. Baseball Card Fever. (Illus.). 80p. (gr. 4 up). 1989. pap. 3.95 (0-449-90416-4, Columbine) Fawcett.

—Max's Secret Formula. (Illus.). 80p. (gr. 4 up). 1989. pap. 3.95 (0-449-90417-2, Columbine) Fawcett.

Stine, Megan & Stine, H. William, eds. The Mummy's Curse. LC 91-53167. (Illus.). 136p. (Orig.). (gr. 4-8). 1992. PLB cancelled (0-679-92774-3); pap. 3.50 (0-679-82774-9) Random Bks Yng Read.

Stine, Megan, et al. Hands-On Science: Color & Light. Taback, Simms, illus. LC 92-56889. 1993. PLB 18.60 (0-8368-0954-8) Gareth Stevens Inc.

—Hands-On Science: Food & the Kitchen. Taback, Simms, illus. LC 92-56890. 1993. PLB 18.60 (0-8368-0955-6) Gareth Stevens Inc.

—Hands-On Science: Fun Machines. Taback, Simms, illus. LC 92-56891. 1993. PLB 18.60 (0-8368-0956-4) Gareth Stevens Inc.

—Hands-On Science: Games, Puzzles, & Toys. Taback, Simms, illus. LC 92-56892. 1993. PLB 18.60 (0-8368-0957-2) Gareth Stevens Inc.

—Hands-On Science: Mystery & Magic. Taback, Simms, illus. LC 92-56893. 1993. PLB 18.60 (0-8368-0958-0) Gareth Stevens Inc.

—Hands-On Science: Things That Grow. Taback, Simms, illus. LC 92-56894. 1993. PLB 18.60 (0-8368-0959-9) Gareth Stevens Inc.

—More Science Activities. Solimini, Cheryl, ed. (Illus.). 100p. (gr. 2-6). 1988. pap. text ed. 8.95 (0-939456-16-8) Galison.

—Smithsonian Science Activity Book. Solimini, Cheryl, ed. (Illus.). 100p. (gr. 2-6). 1987. pap. text ed. 8.95 (0-939456-51-6) Galison.

—Still More Science Activities. 3rd ed. Taback, Simms, illus. Falk, John, intro. by. (Illus.). 100p. (gr. 2-6). 1989. pap. text ed. 8.95 (0-929648-01-3) Galison.

Stine, R. L. The Baby-Sitter. 176p. (Orig.). (gr. 7 up). 1989. pap. 3.50 (0-590-44236-8, Point) Scholastic Inc.

—Baby-Sitter II. 176p. 1991. pap. 3.50 (0-590-44332-1, Point) Scholastic Inc.

—Baby-Sitter III. 1993. pap. 3.50 (0-590-46099-4) Scholastic Inc.

—Beach House. 224p. (gr. 7 up). 1992. pap. 3.25 (0-590-45386-6, Point) Scholastic Inc.

—Beach Party. 1990. pap. 3.50 (0-590-43278-8, Point) Scholastic Inc.

—The Best Friend. McDonald, Pat, ed. 160p. (Orig.). (gr. 7 up). 1992. pap. 3.99 (0-671-73866-6, Archway) PB.

—The Betrayal. 176p. (Orig.). (gr. 6-9). 1993. pap. 3.99 (0-671-86831-4, Archway) PB.

—Blind Date. 1986. pap. 3.50 (0-590-43125-0, Point) Scholastic Inc.

—The Boyfriend. 176p. (gr. 7 up). 1990. pap. 3.50 (0-590-43279-6, Point) Scholastic Inc.

—Bozos on Patrol. 160p. 1992. pap. 2.75 (0-590-44747-5, Apple Paperbacks) Scholastic Inc.

—Broken Date. (gr. 6 up). 1988. write for info. (0-373-98021-3) S&S Trade.

—Broken Date. MacDonald, Patricia, ed. 224p. 1991. pap. 3.50 (0-671-69322-0, Archway) PB.

—Curtains. MacDonald, Patricia, ed. 160p. (Orig.). (gr. 7 up). 1990. pap. 3.50 (0-671-69498-7, Archway) PB.

—Dead Girlfriend. (gr. 9-12). 1993. pap. 3.50 (0-590-45387-4) Scholastic Inc.

—Double Date. 1994. pap. 3.99 (0-671-78570-2, Archway) PB.

—Fear Street Saga, No. 3: The Burning. 176p. (Orig.). (gr. 6-9). 1993. pap. 3.99 (0-671-86833-0, Archway) PB.

—First Date. MacDonald, Pat, ed. 176p. (Orig.). 1992. pap. 3.99 (0-671-73865-8) PB.

—The First Evil. MacDonald, Pat, ed. 176p. (Orig.). 1992. pap. 3.99 (0-671-75117-4, Archway) PB.

—The Girl Who Cried Monster. (gr. 4-7). 1993. pap. 2.95 (0-590-46618-6) Scholastic Inc.

—The Girlfriend. 176p. 1991. pap. 3.50 (0-590-44333-X, Point) Scholastic Inc.

—Goodnight Kiss. MacDonald, Pat, ed. 224p. (Orig.). 1992. pap. 3.99 (0-671-73823-2, Archway) PB.

—Goosebumps: Say Cheese & Die! 1992. pap. 2.95 (0-590-45368-8, Apple Paperbacks) Scholastic Inc.

—Goosebumps: The Ghost Next Door. (gr. 4-7). 1993. pap. 2.95 (0-590-49445-7) Scholastic Inc.

—Goosebumps: The Haunted Mask. (gr. 4-7). 1993. pap. 2.95 (0-590-49446-5) Scholastic Inc.

—Halloween Night. (gr. 9-12). 1993. pap. 3.50 (0-590-46098-6) Scholastic Inc.

—Halloween Party. McDonald, Patricia, ed. 160p. (Orig.). (gr. 9-12). 1990. pap. 3.99 (0-671-70243-2, Archway) PB.

—Haunted. MacDonald, Patricia, ed. 176p. (Orig.). (gr. 6-9). 1992. pap. 3.99 (0-671-74651-0, Archway) PB.

—Hit & Run. 1992. pap. 3.25 (0-590-45385-8, Point) Scholastic Inc.

—Hitchiker. 1993. pap. 3.50 (0-590-46100-1) Scholastic Inc.

—The Knife. 176p. (Orig.). 1992. pap. 3.99 (0-671-72484-3, Archway) PB.

—Lights Out. MacDonald, Patricia, ed. 176p. (Orig.). 1991. pap. 3.99 (0-671-72482-7, Archway) PB.

—Losers in Space. 144p. 1991. pap. 2.75 (0-590-44746-7, Apple Paperbacks) Scholastic Inc.

—Missing. 224p. (gr. 6-9). 1990. pap. 3.99 (0-671-69410-3, Archway) PB.

—The New Girl. (Orig.). (gr. 6-9). 1991. pap. 3.99 (0-671-74649-9, Archway) PB.

—Night of the Living Dummy. (gr. 3-7). 1993. pap. 2.95 (0-590-46617-8) Scholastic Inc.

—Party Summer. MacDonald, Patricia, ed. 176p. (Orig.). 1991. pap. 3.99 (0-671-72920-9, Archway) PB.

—Phone Calls. 160p. (Orig.). (gr. 7 up). 1990. pap. 3.50 (0-671-69497-9, Archway) PB.

—Piano Lessons Can Be Murder. (gr. 4-7). 1993. pap. 2.95 (0-590-49448-1) Scholastic Inc.

—The Secret. MacDonald, Pat, ed. 176p. (Orig.). (gr. 5 up). 1993. pap. 3.99 (0-671-86832-2, Archway) PB.

—The Secret Bedroom. MacDonald, Patricia, ed. 176p. (Orig.). 1991. pap. 3.99 (0-671-72483-5, Archway) PB.

—Silent Night. MacDonald, Patricia, ed. 224p. (Orig.). 1991. pap. 3.99 (0-671-73822-4, Archway) PB.

—Ski Weekend. MacDonald, Patricia, ed. 160p. 1991. pap. 3.99 (0-671-72480-0, Archway) PB.

—The Sleepwalker. 160p. (Orig.). (gr. 6-9). 1991. pap. 3.99 (0-671-74652-9, Archway) PB.

—Snowman. 1991. pap. 3.50 (0-590-43280-X) Scholastic Inc.

—Stay Out of the Basement: Goose Bumps Ser. 128p. 1992. pap. 2.95 (0-590-45366-1, Apple Paperbacks) Scholastic Inc.

—The Stepsister. MacDonald, Patricia, ed. 176p. (Orig.). (gr. 7 up). 1990. pap. 3.99 (0-671-70244-0, Archway) PB.

—The Surprise Party. (Orig.). (gr. 6-9). 1990. pap. 3.99 (0-671-73561-6, Archway) PB.

—The Third Evil: Fear Street. MacDonald, Pat, ed. 176p. (Orig.). 1992. pap. 3.99 (0-671-75119-0, Archway) PB.

—Twisted. 1987. pap. 3.50 (0-590-43139-0) Scholastic Inc.

—Welcome to Camp Nightmare. (gr. 3-7). 1993. pap. 2.95 (0-590-46619-4) Scholastic Inc.

—Welcome to Dead House. 128p. 1992. pap. 2.95 (0-590-45365-3, Apple Paperbacks) Scholastic Inc.

—The Werewolf of Fever Swamp. (gr. 8-12). 1993. pap. 23.95 (0-590-49449-X) Scholastic Inc.

Stine, William H., jt. auth. see Stine, Megan.

Stinnett, Leia. Color Me One. Stinnett, Leia, illus. 36p. (gr. 3 up). 1993. pap. text ed. 4.95 (1-880737-13-2) Crystal Jrns.

—The Twelve Universal Laws, Principles & Applications: A Workbook for Children of All Ages. Stinnett, Leia, illus. 138p. 1993. wkbk. 18.95 (1-880737-14-0) Crystal Jrns.

Stinson, Douglas. C Is for Coyote. Goggin, Lewisa, illus. 40p. (gr. 1 up). 1993. 15.95 (1-879244-04-7) Windom Bks.

Stinson, K. The Dressed up Book. (Illus.). 32p. (ps-8). 1990. PLB 14.95 (1-55037-103-7, Pub. by Annick CN); pap. 4.95 (1-55037-104-5, Pub. by Annick CN) Firefly Bks Ltd.

Stinson, Kathy. Bare Naked Book. Collins, Heather, illus. 32p. (gr. k-2). 1986. PLB 14.95 (0-920303-52-8, Pub. by Annick CN); pap. 4.95 (0-920303-53-6, Pub. by Annick CN) Firefly Bks Ltd.

—Big Or Little. Baird Lewis, Robin, illus. 32p. (gr. k-2). 1983. PLB 14.95 (0-920236-30-8, Pub. by Annick CN); pap. 4.95 (0-920236-32-4, Pub. by Annick CN) Firefly Bks Ltd.

—Big or Little. Lewis, Robin B., illus. 24p. (ps-1). 1987. pap. 0.99 (0-920303-19-6, Pub. by Annick CN) Firefly Bks Ltd.

—Mom & Dad Don't Live Together Anymore. Reynolds, Nancy L., illus. 32p. (gr. k-3). 1984. PLB 14.95 (0-920236-92-8, Pub. by Annick CN); pap. 4.95 (0-920236-87-1, Pub. by Annick CN) Firefly Bks Ltd.

—Red Is Best. Baird, Robin L., illus. 32p. (gr. k-3). 1982. PLB 14.95 (0-920236-24-3, Pub. by Annick CN); pap. 4.95 (0-920236-26-X, Pub. by Annick CN) Firefly Bks Ltd.

—Red Is Best. Lewis, Robin B., illus. (ps-1). 1992. 0.99 (1-55037-252-1, Pub. by Annick Pr) Firefly Bks Ltd.

—Steven's Baseball Mitt: A Book about Being Adopted. Lewis, Robin B., illus. 32p. (ps-4). 1992. PLB 14.95 (1-55037-233-5, Pub. by Annick CN); pap. 4.95 (1-55037-232-7, Pub. by Annick CN) Firefly Bks Ltd.

—Teddy Rabbit. Poulin, Stephane, illus. 32p. (gr. k-3). 1988. 12.95 (1-550370-17-0, Pub. by Annick CN); pap. 4.95 (1-550370-16-2, Pub. by Annick CN) Firefly Bks Ltd.

—Those Green Things. McLoughlin, Mary, illus. 24p. (gr. k-3). 1985. 12.95 (0-920303-40-4, Pub. by Annick CN); pap. 4.95 (0-920303-41-2, Pub. by Annick CN) Firefly Bks Ltd.

Stippel, Lori, jt. auth. see Rieck, Sondra.

Stirling, Brents, ed. see Shakespeare, William.

Stirling, Ian. Bears. Lang, Aubrey, photos by. (Illus.). 64p. (gr. 3-6). 1992. 14.95 (0-87156-574-9) Sierra.

Stirrup Associates, Inc. Staff. Beautiful Attitudes Matthew 5: 3-12. Phillips, Cheryl M. & Harvey, Bonnie C., eds. Fulton, Ginger A., illus. LC 84-50914. 32p. (ps). 1984. pap. 1.49 (0-937420-17-4) Stirrup Assoc.

—My Jesus Pocketbook of a Very Special Birth Day. Harvey, Bonnie C. & Phillips, Cheryl M., eds. Burnett, Lindy, illus. LC 84-50919. 32p. (ps). 1984. pap. 0.69 (0-937420-15-8) Stirrup Assoc.

—My Jesus Pocketbook of Daniel in the Lion's Den. Harvey, Bonnie C. & Phillips, Cheryl M., eds. Fulton, Ginger A., illus. LC 84-50916. 32p. (Orig.). (ps-3). 1984. pap. text ed. 0.69 (0-937420-12-3) Stirrup Assoc.

—My Jesus Pocketbook of Jonah & the Big Fish. Harvey, Bonnie C. & Phillips, Cheryl M., eds. Fulton, Ginger A., illus. LC 83-51679. 32p. (ps-3). 1984. pap. 0.69 (0-937420-09-3) Stirrup Assoc.

—My Jesus Pocketbook of Li'l Critters. Phillips, Cheryl M., ed. Sherman, Erin, illus. LC 82-63139. 32p. (Orig.). (ps-3). 1983. pap. text ed. 17.50 spiral bdg. (0-937420-05-0) Stirrup Assoc.

—My Jesus Pocketbook of Manners. Phillips, Cheryl M., ed. Sherman, Erin, illus. LC 82-63141. 32p. (ps-3). 1983. pap. 0.69 (0-937420-06-9) Stirrup Assoc.

—My Jesus Pocketbook of Noah & the Floating Zoo. Harvey, Bonnie C. & Phillips, Cheryl M., eds. Fulton, Ginger A., illus. LC 83-51680. 32p. (ps-3). 1984. pap. 0.69 (0-937420-10-7) Stirrup Assoc.

—My Jesus Pocketbook of Scripture Pictures. Sherman, Erin, illus. LC 82-80351. 32p. (Orig.). (ps-3). 1982. pap. 0.69 (0-937420-02-6) Stirrup Assoc.

—My Jesus Pocketbook of the Beginning. Harvey, Bonnie C. & Phillips, Cheryl M., eds. Burnett, Lindy, illus. LC 84-50918. 32p. (Orig.). (ps-3). 1984. pap. 0.69 (0-937420-14-X) Stirrup Assoc.

—My Jesus Pocketbook of the Big Little Person: The Story of Zacchaeus. Phillips, Cheryl M. & Harvey, Bonnie C., eds. Fulton, Ginger A., illus. LC 84-50917. 32p. (ps). 1984. pap. 0.69 (0-937420-13-1) Stirrup Assoc.

—My Jesus Pocketbook of the 23rd Psalm. Phillips, Cheryl M., ed. LC 82-63140. (Illus.). 32p. (Orig.). (ps-3). 1983. pap. text ed. 0.69 (0-937420-04-2) Stirrup Assoc.

Stith, Bari O. Lake County, Ohio: One Hundred Fifty Years of Tradition: An Illustrated History. (Illus.). 128p. (gr. 7 up). 1988. 25.95 (0-89781-249-2) Windsor Pubns Inc.

Stitt, S., jt. auth. see Tyler, J.

Stobbs, William. Gregory's Dog. (Illus.). 16p. 1987. pap. 2.95 (0-19-272141-0) OUP.

—Gregory's Garden. (Illus.). 16p. 1987. pap. 2.95 (0-19-272140-2) OUP.

—Little Red Hen. (Illus.). 32p. 1989. pap. 7.50 (0-19-272199-2) OUP.

—Old MacDonald Had a Farm. (Illus.). 36p. 1987. 12.95 (0-19-279817-0) OUP.

—There's a Hole in My Bucket. (Illus.). 28p. 1987. 10.00 (0-19-279755-7) OUP.

—Who Killed Cock Robin? (Illus.). 28p. (ps up). 1990. bds. 12.95 (0-19-279862-6) OUP.

Stochl, Susan, ed. Easter People, Grade 5: Gather. (Illus.). (gr. 5). 1980. pap. text ed. 5.65 (0-03-050761-8); wkbk. 3.90 (0-03-050776-6) Harper SF.

Stochl, Susan, et al, eds. Easter People, Grade 4: Remember. (Illus.). (gr. 4). 1980. activity pack 3.90 (0-03-042911-0) Harper SF.

—Easter People, Grade 1: Welcome. (gr. 1). 1979. activity pack 3.90 (0-03-020371-6, 162) Harper SF.

—Easter People, Grade 2: Belong. (gr. 2). 1979. activity pack 3.90 (0-03-020391-0, 166); parent bk. 2.25 (0-03-020381-3, 168) Harper SF.

—Easter People, Grade 3: Journey. (Illus.). (gr. 3). 1979. parent wkbk. 2.25 (0-03-020411-9, 172); activity pack 3.90 (0-03-020411-9, 170) Harper SF.

Stock, Catherine. Alexander's Midnight Snack: A Little Elephant's ABC. Stock, Catherine, illus. LC 88-2608. 40p. (ps-1). 1988. 13.95 (0-89919-512-1, Clarion Bks) HM.

—Armien's Fishing Trip. Stock, Catherine & Stock, Catherine, illus. LC 89-3266. 40p. (gr. 1 up). 1990. 13. 95 (0-688-08395-1); PLB 13.88 (0-688-08396-X, Morrow Jr Bks) Morrow Jr Bks.

—The Birthday Present. Stock, Catherine, illus. LC 90-1914. 32p. (ps-1). 1991. SBE 11.95 (0-02-788401-5, Bradbury Pr) Macmillan Child Grp.

—A Christmas Angel Collection. Stock, Catherine, illus. 32p. (gr. k up). 1988. pap. 3.95 (0-394-80266-7) Random Bks Yng Read.

—Christmas Time. Stock, Catherine, illus. LC 89-71249. 32p. (ps-1). 1990. SBE 11.95 (0-02-788403-1, Bradbury Pr) Macmillan Child Grp.

—Christmas Time. Stock, Catherine, illus. LC 92-42225. 32p. (ps-1). 1993. pap. 3.95 (0-689-71725-3, Aladdin) Macmillan Child Grp.

—Easter Surprise. Stock, Catherine, illus. LC 90-1915. 32p. (ps-1). 1991. SBE 11.95 (0-02-788371-X, Bradbury Pr) Macmillan Child Grp.

—Emma's Dragon Hunt. Stock, Catherine, illus. LC 83-25109. 32p. (gr. k up). 1984. 11.95 (0-688-02696-6); PLB 9.55 (0-688-02698-2) Lothrop.

—Halloween Monster. Stock, Catherine, illus. LC 89-49530. 32p. (ps-1). 1990. SBE 11.95 (0-02-788404-X, Bradbury Pr) Macmillan Child Grp.

—Halloween Monster. Stock, Catherine, illus. LC 92-42987. 32p. (ps-1). 1993. pap. 3.95 (0-689-71727-X, Aladdin) Macmillan Child Grp.

—Secret Valentine. Stock, Catherine, illus. LC 90-1916. 32p. (ps-1). 1991. SBE 11.95 (0-02-788372-8, Bradbury Pr) Macmillan Child Grp.

—Sophie's Bucket. 1994. write for info. (0-15-277162-X) HarBrace.

—Sophie's Knapsack. LC 87-3103. (Illus.). (ps-2). 1988. 12.95 (0-688-06457-4); 12.88 (0-688-06458-2) Lothrop.

—Thanksgiving Treat. Stock, Catherine, illus. LC 89-49528. 32p. (ps-1). 1990. SBE 11.95 (0-02-788402-3, Bradbury Pr) Macmillan Child Grp.

—Thanksgiving Treat. Stock, Catherine, illus. LC 92-43690. (Illus.). 32p. (ps-1). 1993. pap. 3.95 (0-689-71726-1, Aladdin) Macmillan Child Grp.

—Where Are You Going, Manyoni? Stock, Catherine, illus. LC 92-29793. 48p. (ps up). 1993. 15.00 (0-688-10352-9); PLB 14.93 (0-688-10353-7) Morrow Jr Bks.

Stock, Gregory. Kids' Book of Questions. LC 88-40230. (gr. 4-7). 1988. pap. 4.95 (0-89480-631-9, 1631) Workman Pub.

Stockbridge-Munsee Historical Committee Staff. The History of the Stockbridge-Munsee Band of Mohican Indians. 2nd ed. (Illus.). 36p. (gr. 4 up). 1993. pap. text ed. 4.00 (0-935790-02-0) Muh-He-Con-Neew.

Stockdale, Marina. William's Window: An Introduction to Shakespeare's Plays for Young People. 36p. (gr. 3-8). 1983. pap. 3.00 (0-88680-209-1); royalty on application 25.00 (0-685-57865-8) I E Clark.

Stocker, Fern N. Billy Sunday: Baseball Preacher. (Orig.). (gr. 2-7). 1985. pap. text ed. 4.50 (*0-8024-0442-1*) Moody.

Stocker, Fern N., et al. Preteen Biography Series, 6 bks. (gr. 2-7). Set. pap. 27.00 (*0-8024-6668-0*) Moody.

Stockham, Leslie C. Divirtamonos Con el Abecedario. Stockham, Leslie C., illus. 96p. (gr. k-2). 1993. wkbk. 8.95 (*0-9624096-2-6*) Bilingual Lang Mat.

—Divirtamonos Con Letras y Sonidos. (Illus.). 56p. (Orig.). (gr. k-2). 1993. pap. 5.98 (*0-9624096-1-8*) Bilingual Lang Mat.

—Poemas Tradicionales. (SPA., Illus.). 52p. (Orig.). (ps-2). 1991. pap. 5.98 (*0-9624096-0-X*) Bilingual Lang Mat.

Stockham, Peter, ed. The Mother's Picture Alphabet. Anelay, Henry, illus. 64p. (ps-3). 1975. pap. 4.50 (*0-486-23089-9*) Dover.

Stockley, C. Animal Behavior. (Illus.). 64p. (gr. 4-12). 1992. PLB 13.96 (*0-88110-513-9*, Usborne); pap. 7.95 (*0-7460-0639-X*, Usborne) EDC.

—Dictionary of Biology. (Illus.). 128p. (gr. 6 up). 1987. PLB 15.96 (*0-88110-229-6*); pap. 9.95 (*0-86020-819-2*) EDC.

—Dictionary of Physics. (Illus.). 128p. (gr. 6 up). 1988. PLB 15.96 (*0-88110-308-X*); pap. 9.95 (*0-86020-987-3*) EDC.

Stockley, C. & Colvin, L. Living World Encyclopedia. (Illus.). 128p. (gr. 5-7). 1992. PLB 16.96 (*0-88110-434-5*, Usborne); pap. 12.95 (*0-7460-0766-3*, Usborne) EDC.

Stockley, C. & Watts, L. Computer Jargon. Newton, Martin, illus. 48p. (gr. 6 up). 1983. lib. bdg. 10.96 (*0-88110-141-9*); pap. 3.95 (*0-86020-737-4*) EDC.

Stockley, C., jt. auth. see Oxlade, C.

Stockley, C., et al. Ornithology. (Illus.). 48p. (gr. 4-12). 1993. PLB 13.96 (*0-88110-514-7*, Usborne); pap. 7.95 (*0-7460-0685-3*, Usborne) EDC.

Stockton, Frank. The Bee-Man of Orn. Delessert, Etienne, illus. LC 85-23272. 40p. (gr. 4 up). 1986. PLB 13.95s.p. (*0-88682-055-3*) Creative Ed.

—The Lady or the Tiger? LC 83-71950. 32p. (gr. 4 up). 1983. PLB 13.95s.p. (*0-87191-968-0*) Creative Ed.

—Lady or the Tiger & Other Stories. Gennie, F. R., intro. by. (gr. 5 up). 1968. pap. 1.95 (*0-8049-0163-5*, CL-163) Airmont.

—Old Pipes & the Dryad. 1991. PLB 13.95s.p. (*0-88682-473-7*) Creative Ed.

Stockton, Frank R. The Bee-Man of Orn. Sendak, Maurice, illus. LC 85-45813. 48p. (ps up). 1987. Repr. of 1963 ed. 13.95 (*0-06-025818-7*); PLB 13.89 (*0-06-025819-5*) HarpC Child Bks.

—The Bee-Man of Orn. Sendak, Maurice, illus. LC 85-45813. 48p. (gr. 2 up). 1987. pap. 4.95 (*0-06-443125-8*, Trophy) HarpC Child Bks.

—The Griffin & the Minor Canon. Sendak, Maurice, illus. LC 85-45827. 56p. (ps up). 1986. Repr. of 1964 ed. 13.95 (*0-06-025816-0*); PLB 13.89 (*0-06-025817-9*) HarpC Child Bks.

—The Griffin & the Minor Canon. Sendak, Maurice, illus. LC 85-45827. 56p. (gr. 2 up). 1987. pap. 4.95 (*0-06-443126-6*, Trophy) HarpC Child Bks.

—The Lady or the Tiger. Carlson, Claudia & DeNieff, Jacqueline S., illus. Horowitz, Paul J., frwd. by. Bd. with The Discourager of Hesitancy. Repr. of 1885 ed. (Orig.). (gr. 1-8). pap. 4.95 (*0-934254-11-7*) Claymont Comm.

Stockwell, John. Daniel Ortega. Schlesinger, Arthur M., Jr., intro. by. (Illus.). 112p. (gr. 5 up). 1991. 17.95 (*1-55546-846-2*) Chelsea Hse.

Stodart, Eleanor. Australian Echidna. LC 90-33538. (Illus.). 40p. (gr. 3-7). 1991. 14.45 (*0-395-55992-8*) HM.

Stoddard, Edward. The First Book of Magic. (Illus.). 80p. (gr. 4-7). 1980. pap. 2.95 (*0-380-49221-0*, Camelot) Avon.

Stoddard, Sandol. Bedtime for Bear. Munsinger, Lynn, illus. LC 85-5259. 32p. (gr. k-3). 1985. pap. 4.80 (*0-395-47949-5*) HM.

—Bedtime Mouse. (ps-3). 1993. pap. 4.95 (*0-395-67436-0*) HM.

—A Child's First Bible. Chen, Tony, illus. 96p. (ps-3). 1991. 15.99 (*0-8037-0941-2*) Dial Bks Young.

—Doubleday Illustrated Children's Bible. Chen, Tony, illus. LC 82-45340. 384p. (gr. 4-6). 1983. 25.00 (*0-385-18521-9*) Doubleday.

—God's Little House. 32p. 1984. pap. 1.95 (*0-8091-6553-8*) Paulist Pr.

Stoddard, Sandol, compiled by. Prayers, Praises, & Thanksgivings. Isadora, Rachel, illus. LC 86-32822. 160p. 1992. 18.50 (*0-8037-0421-6*) Dial Bks Young.

Stodden, Norma J. & McCormick, Linda. The All Gone Book. Levy, Gail, ed. Loui, Jill, illus. 18p. (ps). 1988. bds. 3.95 (*0-943693-05-5*) TRI Pubns.

—The Love Book. Levy, Gail, ed. Loui, Jill, illus. 18p. (ps). 1988. bds. 3.95 (*0-943693-04-7*) TRI Pubns.

—The More Book. Levy, Gail, ed. Loui, Jill, illus. 18p. (ps). 1988. bds. 3.95 (*0-943693-03-9*) TRI Pubns.

Stoeke, Janet M. Minerva Louise. Stoeke, Janet M., illus. LC 87-24458. 24p. (ps-1). 1988. 12.00 (*0-525-44374-6*, 01063-320, DCB) Dutton Child Bks.

—Minerva Louise. LC 87-24458. (Illus.). 24p. (ps-1). 1992. pap. 3.99 (*0-14-054544-1*, Puffin Unicorn) Puffin Bks.

Stoff, Joshua. From Airship to Spaceship: Long Island Aviation & Spaceflight. LC 90-47647. (Illus.). 96p. (gr. 4-10). 1991. 15.00 (*1-55787-074-8*, NY71060, Empire State Bks); pap. 7.95 (*1-55787-075-6*, NY71059, Empire State Bks) Heart of the Lakes.

Stohl, Anita. Christian Crafts Yarn Art. (Illus.). 64p. (ps-5). 1992. 8.95 (*0-86653-701-5*, SS2831, Shining Star Pubns) Good Apple.

Stohs, Anita R. Animals of the Bible Activity Book. Koehler, Ed, illus. 32p. (Orig.). (ps-2). 1992. pap. 2.99 (*0-570-04712-9*) Concordia.

—Children of the Bible Activity Book. (Illus.). 32p. (Orig.). 1993. pap. 2.99 (*0-570-04750-1*) Concordia.

—Everyday Fun with Jesus Activity Book. (Illus.). 48p. (Orig.). 1994. pap. 4.99 (*0-570-04751-X*) Concordia.

Stoker, Bram. Dracula. Lowndes, R. A., intro. by. LC 83-5471. (gr. 7 up). 1965. pap. 2.25 (*0-8049-0072-8*, CL-72) Airmont.

—Dracula. Schick, Alice & Schick, Joel, eds. LC 83-5471. (Illus.). 48p. (gr. 3 up). 1980. PLB 10.89 (*0-440-01349-6*); pap. 6.95 (*0-440-01348-8*) Delacorte.

—Dracula. LC 83-5471. (RL 10). 1986. pap. 2.95 (*0-451-52337-7*, Sig Classics) NAL-Dutton.

—Dracula. Farr, Naunerle, ed. Redondo, Nestor, illus. LC 83-5471. 64p. (Orig.). (gr. 5-10). 1973. pap. 2.95 (*0-88301-100-X*); student activity bk. 1.25 (*0-88301-175-1*) Pendulum Pr.

—Dracula. Spinner, Stephanie, adapted by. Spence, Jim, illus. LC 87-235417. 96p. (gr. 2-5). 1988. lib. bdg. 4.99 (*0-394-94828-9*); pap. 2.95 (*0-394-84828-4*) Random Bks Yng Read.

—Dracula. (gr. 4-6). 1986. pap. 3.50 (*0-14-035048-9*, Puffin) Puffin Bks.

—Dracula. reissued ed. Spinner, Stephanie, adapted by. Spence, Jim, illus. 96p. (gr. 3-7). 1992. pap. 6.99 incl. cass. (*0-679-82445-6*) Random Bks Yng Read.

—Dracula. 1992. 3.50 (*0-590-46029-3*, 067, Apple Classics) Scholastic Inc.

Stoker, Bram, et al. Dracula, Frankenstein, Dr. Jekyll & Mr. Hyde. King, Stephen, intro. by. 672p. (RL 7). 1992. pap. 5.95 (*0-451-52363-6*, Sig Classics) NAL-Dutton.

Stoker, Richard G. & Gaydos, Janine. Hearing Aids for You & the Zoo. (Illus.). 32p. (gr. k-3). 1984. pap. 4.95 (*0-317-13888-X*) Alexander Graham.

Stoker, Wayne, jt. auth. see Lillegard, Dee.

Stokes. The Photography Book. 1992. 5.95 (*0-590-45257-6*) Scholastic Inc.

Stokes, Bill, ed. see Stonerod, David.

Stokes, Chris, jt. ed. see Dilts, Susan.

Stolarik, Mark. The Slovak Americans. Moynihan, Daniel P., intro. by. (Illus.). 112p. (gr. 5 up). 1988. lib. bdg. 17.95 (*1-55546-134-4*) Chelsea Hse.

Stoller, Nettie. The Little Beaver Who Had No Tail. 1993. pap. 7.95 (*0-533-10516-1*) Vantage.

Stolp, Hans. Golden Bird. (gr. 4-7). 1992. pap. 3.50 (*0-440-40611-0*) Dell.

Stolpe, Norman. Coming Attractions. (Illus.). 116p. (Orig.). (gr. 9-12). 1991. pap. text ed. 8.35 (*0-930265-94-7*); tchr's ed. 10.45 (*0-930265-95-5*) CRC Pubns.

Stolpe, Norman D. Genesis: The Beginnings. (Illus.). 48p. (gr. 6-8). 1991. pap. 7.99 (*1-55945-111-4*) Group Pub.

Stoltz, Donald R. Bunk One. Costa, Gwen, ed. LC 90-22976. 100p. (Orig.). 1991. pap. 13.95 (*0-87949-346-1*) Ashley Bks.

Stolz. Coco Grimes. Date not set. 14.00 (*0-06-024232-9*, Festival); PLB 13.89 (*0-06-024233-7*, Festival) HarpC Child Bks.

Stolz, Mary. Bartholomew Fair. LC 89-27230. 160p. (gr. 5 up). 1990. 12.95 (*0-688-09522-4*) Greenwillow.

—Bartholomew Fair. LC 89-27230. 160p. (gr. 6 up). 1992. pap. 3.95 (*0-688-11501-2*, Pub. by Beech Tree Bks) Morrow.

—Belling the Tiger. Montresor, Beni, illus. LC 61-5776. 64p. (gr. 2-5). 1990. PLB 12.89 (*0-06-025863-2*) HarpC Child Bks.

—Bully of Barkham Street. Shortall, Leonard, illus. LC 68-2661. 224p. (gr. 3-6). 1963. PLB 14.89 (*0-06-025821-7*) HarpC Child Bks.

—The Bully of Barkham Street. Shortall, Leonard, illus. LC 68-2661. 224p. (gr. 3-7). 1985. pap. 3.95 (*0-06-440159-6*, Trophy) HarpC Child Bks.

—Cat in the Mirror. 176p. (gr. 7 up). 1978. pap. 1.25 (*0-440-91123-0*, LFL) Dell.

—Cat Walk. Blegvad, Erik, illus. LC 82-47576. 128p. (gr. 3-7). 1983. HarpC Child Bks.

—Cat Walk. Blegvad, Erik, illus. LC 82-47576. 128p. (gr. 3-7). 1985. pap. 3.95 (*0-06-440155-3*, Trophy) HarpC Child Bks.

—Cezanne Pinto. LC 92-46765. 256p. (gr. 7 up). 1994. 15.00 (*0-679-84917-3*) Knopf Bks Yng Read.

—Cuckoo Clock. Johnson, Pamela, illus. LC 86-45538. 112p. 1986. 13.95 (*0-87923-653-1*) Godine.

—Cuckoo Clock. 1993. pap. 10.95 (*0-87923-938-7*) Godine.

—Deputy Shep. Johnson, Pamela, illus. LC 90-38664. 96p. (gr. 2-5). 1991. 12.95 (*0-06-026039-4*) HarpC Child Bks.

—Dog on Barkham Street. Shortall, Leonard, illus. LC 60-5787. 176p. (gr. 3-6). 1960. PLB 14.89 (*0-06-025841-1*) HarpC Child Bks.

—A Dog on Barkham Street. Shortall, Leonard, illus. LC 60-5787. 176p. (gr. 3-7). 1985. pap. 3.95 (*0-06-440160-X*, Trophy) HarpC Child Bks.

—Emmett's Pig. Williams, Garth, illus. LC 58-7763. 64p. (gr. k-3). 1959. PLB 13.89 (*0-06-025856-X*) HarpC Child Bks.

—The Explorer of Barkham Street. McCully, Emily A., illus. LC 84-48339. 192p. (gr. 4-6). 1985. 15.00 (*0-06-025976-0*); PLB 14.89 (*0-06-025977-9*) HarpC Child Bks.

—The Explorer of Barkham Street. McCully, Emily A., illus. LC 84-48339. 192p. (gr. 3-7). 1987. pap. 3.95 (*0-06-440210-X*, Trophy) HarpC Child Bks.

—Go & Catch a Flying Fish. LC 78-21785. 224p. (gr. 5 up). 1992. pap. 3.95 (*0-06-447090-3*, Trophy) HarpC Child Bks.

—Go Fish. Cummings, Pat, illus. LC 90-4860. 80p. (gr. 2-6). 1991. 13.00 (*0-06-025820-9*); PLB 12.89 (*0-06-025822-5*) HarpC Child Bks.

—Go Fish. Cummings, Pat, illus. LC 90-4860. 80p. (gr. 2-6). 1993. pap. 3.95 (*0-06-440466-8*, Trophy) HarpC Child Bks.

—Ivy Larkin. LC 86-4819. 226p. (gr. 7 up). 1986. 13.95 (*0-15-239366-8*, HB Juv Bks) HarBrace.

—Ivy Larkin. (gr. k-6). 1989. pap. 3.25 (*0-440-40175-5*, YB) Dell.

—King Emmett the Second. Williams, Garth, illus. LC 89-77506. 56p. (gr. 2 up). 1991. 12.95 (*0-688-09520-8*) Greenwillow.

—King Emmett the Second. (gr. 4-7). 1993. pap. 3.25 (*0-440-40777-X*) Dell.

—Night of Ghosts & Hermits: Nocturnal Life on the Seashore. Gallagher, Susan, illus. LC 84-15665. 48p. (gr. 3-7). 1985. 12.95 (*0-15-257333-X*, HB Juv Bks) HarBrace.

—Noonday Friends. Glanzman, Louis S., illus. LC 65-20257. 192p. (gr. 3-7). 1965. PLB 14.89 (*0-06-025946-9*) HarpC Child Bks.

—Noonday Friends. LC 65-20257. (Illus.). 192p. (gr. 4-7). 1971. pap. 3.95 (*0-06-440009-3*, Trophy) HarpC Child Bks.

—Pangur Ban. Johnson, Pamela, illus. LC 87-35049. 196p. (gr. 7 up). 1988. PLB 13.89 (*0-06-025862-4*) HarpC Child Bks.

—Quentin Corn. Johnson, Pamela, illus. LC 84-48321. 128p. (gr. 1-7). 1985. 14.95 (*0-87923-553-5*) Godine.

—Say Something. rev. & newly illus. ed. Koshkin, Alexander, illus. LC 92-8317. 32p. (ps-3). 1993. 15.00 (*0-06-021158-X*); PLB 14.89 (*0-06-021159-8*) HarpC Child Bks.

—Stealing Home. LC 92-5226. 160p. (gr. 3-6). 1992. 14.00 (*0-06-021154-7*); PLB 13.89 (*0-06-021157-1*) HarpC Child Bks.

—Storm in the Night. Cummings, Pat, illus. LC 85-45838. 32p. (gr. k-3). 1988. 15.00 (*0-06-025912-4*); PLB 14.89 (*0-06-025913-2*) HarpC Child Bks.

—Storm in the Night. Cummings, Pat, illus. LC 85-45838. 32p. (gr. k-3). 1990. pap. 4.95 (*0-06-443256-4*, Trophy) HarpC Child Bks.

—Tales at the Mousehole. Johnson, Pamela, illus. LC 88-46130. 96p. (gr. 2-4). 1992. 15.95 (*0-87923-789-9*) Godine.

—The Weeds & the Weather. Watson, N. Cameron, illus. LC 93-240. 40p. (gr. k up). 1994. write for info. (*0-688-12289-2*); PLB write for info. (*0-688-12290-6*) Greenwillow.

—What Time of Night Is It? LC 80-7917. 224p. (gr. 6 up). 1993. pap. 3.95 (*0-06-447093-8*, Trophy) HarpC Child Bks.

—Zekmet the Stone Carver: A Tale of Ancient Egypt. Lattimore, Deborah N., illus. LC 86-22931. 32p. (gr. 2-5). 1988. 14.95 (*0-15-299961-2*) HarBrace.

Stolzenberg, Mark. Be a Clown. LC 89-33783. (Illus.). 160p. (gr. 4-12). 1989. pap. 10.95 (*0-8069-5804-9*) Sterling.

—Be a Mime! Moore, Jim, photos by. LC 91-18171. (Illus.). 128p. (gr. 4-12). 1991. pap. 10.95 (*0-8069-8394-9*) Sterling.

Stone, et al. Multilink: Activities for the Intermediate Classroom. 48p. (gr. 3-5). 1993. wkbk. 7.95 (*1-884461-04-2*) NES Arnold.

—Multilink: Activities for the Primary Classroom. 48p. (gr. k-5). 1993. wkbk. 7.95 (*1-884461-03-4*) NES Arnold.

—Multilink: Patterns & Relationships. 40p. (gr. k-5). 1993. wkbk. 7.95 (*1-884461-00-X*) NES Arnold.

—Multilink: Problem Solving: Games, Puzzles & Investigations. 48p. (gr. 1-5). 1993. wkbk. 7.95 (*1-884461-02-6*) NES Arnold.

—Multilink: Spatial Awareness & Geometry. 48p. (gr. 1-5). 1993. wkbk. 7.95 (*1-884461-01-8*) NES Arnold.

Stone, Audrey. Dinni, the Dinosaur. Weinberger, Jane, ed. DeVito, Pamela, illus. LC 87-51330. 64p. (Orig.). (gr. 2-6). 1988. pap. 4.95 (*0-932433-41-3*) Windswept Hse.

Stone, Bernard. Quasimodo Mouse. Steadman, Ralph, illus. 32p. (gr. 1-4). 1987. 15.95 (*0-86264-072-5*, Pub. by Anderson Pr UK) Trafalgar.

Stone, Beth, jt. auth. see Russell, Pamela.

Stone, Bev. Santa Plus Martha. Stone, Gary, illus. 62p. (gr. k-6). 1992. pap. 12.95 (*0-9619791-1-9*) Stone Studios.

—The Secret of Santa Claus: Flower Blue & Snowie Elves Help Santa Meet His Brothers. Stone, Gary, illus. 64p. (gr. k-6). 1987. pap. 12.95 (*0-9619791-0-0*) Stone Studios.

Stone, Bob & Palmer, Bob. The Dating Dilemma: Handling Sexual Pressures. 160p. (Orig.). 1990. pap. 9.99 (*0-8010-8314-1*) Baker Bk.

Stone, Bruce. Half Nelson, Full Nelson. LC 85-42623. 224p. (gr. 7 up). 1987. pap. 2.95 (*0-06-447047-4*, Trophy) HarpC Child Bks.

Stone, Eddie. Donald Writes No More. (ps-12). 1988. pap. 2.95 (*0-87067-733-0*, BH733) Holloway.

—Jesse Jackson. rev. ed. (ps-10). 1988. pap. 3.95 (*0-87067-840-X*) Holloway.

Stone, Elaine M. Christopher Columbus. (Illus.). (gr. 3-7). 1991. 12.99 (*0-8423-0468-1*) Tyndale.

—Elizabeth Bayley Seton: An American Saint. Mitchell, Mark, illus. LC 92-42020. 96p. 1993. pap. 4.95 *(0-8091-6609-7)* Paulist Pr.
—Tekla & the Lion. LC 90-71366. (Illus.). 44p. (gr. 3-6). 1991. pap. 7.95 *(1-55523-388-0)* Winston-Derek.
Stone, Erika, illus. Baby Talk. 18p. (ps). 1992. bds. 2.95 *(0-448-40312-9,* G&D) Putnam Pub Group.
Stone, G. H. Fatal Error. LC 90-52580. 144p. (gr. 5 up). 1991. lib. bdg. 7.99 *(0-679-90587-1)* Random Bks Yng Read.
—Rough Stuff. LC 88-26689. 144p. (gr. 5 up). 1989. PLB 6.99 *(0-394-90178-9)* Random Bks Yng Read.
—Rough Stuff. LC 88-11904. 144p. (Orig.). (gr. 5 up). 1989. pap. 2.95 *(0-394-80178-4)* Knopf Bks Yng Read.
Stone, George K. More Science Projects You Can Do. Hunter, Mel, illus. (gr. 5 up). 1981. pap. 3.95 *(0-13-600916-6,* Pub. by Treehouse) P-H.
—Science Projects You Can Do. Peck, Stephen R., illus. 101p. (gr. 7-9). 1963. (Pub. by Treehouse); pap. 4.95 *(0-13-795328-3)* P-H.
Stone, Harris see Clark, John G.
Stone, Harry, ed. see Russo, Tom.
Stone, Irving. President's Lady: Biographcal Novel of Rachel & Andrew Jackson. LC 51-6885. 1951. 24.95 *(0-385-04362-7)* Doubleday.
Stone, J. David & Keefauver, Larry. Friend to Friend: Helping Your Friends Through Problems. rev. ed. LC 90-81968. 74p. (gr. 8-12). 1990. pap. 6.95x *(0-932796-31-1)* Ed Media Corp.
Stone, Jane. Challenge! The Big Thunderboats. new ed. LC 75-23408. (Illus.). 32p. (gr. 5-10). 1976. PLB 10.79 *(0-89375-003-4)*; pap. 2.95 *(0-89375-019-0)* Troll Assocs.
Stone, Jeanne. The Julian Messner Illustrated Dictionary of Science. (Illus.). 192p. (gr. 5 up). 1985. lib. bdg. 9.79 *(0-671-54548-5,* J Messner) S&S Trade.
Stone, Jon. Big Bird in China. (Illus.). (gr. 4-8). 1983. lib. bdg. 7.99 *(0-394-95645-1)* Random Bks Yng Read.
—Lovable Furry Old Grover's Resting Places. Smollin, Michael J., illus. LC 83-21087. 32p. (ps-3). 1984. pap. 2.25 *(0-394-86056-X)* Random Bks Yng Read.
—Would You Like to Play Hide & Seek in This Book with Lovable, Furry Old Grover? Smollin, Michael J., illus. LC 76-8120. (ps-1). 1976. pap. 2.25 *(0-394-83292-2)* Random Bks Yng Read.
Stone, Jon & Bailey, Joe. Christmas Eve on Sesame Street. Mathieu, Joe, illus. LC 81-50247. 64p. (ps-2). 1981. 7.95 *(0-394-84733-4)*; lib. bdg. 6.99 *(0-394-94733-9,* Random Juv) Random Bks Yng Read.
Stone, Kazuko. Aligay Saves the Stars. 32p. 1991. 13.95 *(0-590-44382-8,* Scholastic Hardcover) Scholastic Inc.
Stone, L. Arctic Tundra. (Illus.). 48p. (gr. 4-8). 1988. lib. bdg. 15.94 *(0-86592-436-8)*; PLB 11.95s.p. *(0-685-58568-9)* Rourke Corp.
—Caballos (Horses) 1991. 8.95s.p. *(0-86592-987-4)* Rourke Enter.
—Castores (Beavers) 1991. 8.95s.p. *(0-86592-832-0)* Rourke Enter.
—Cerdos (Pigs) 1991. 8.95s.p. *(0-86592-989-0)* Rourke Enter.
—Cheetahs. (Illus.). 24p. (gr. k-5). 1989. lib. bdg. 11.94 *(0-86592-503-8)* Rourke Corp.
—Cougars. (Illus.). 24p. (gr. k-5). 1989. lib. bdg. 11.94 *(0-86592-505-4)* Rourke Corp.
—Deserts. (Illus.). 48p. (gr. 4-8). 1989. lib. bdg. 15.94 *(0-86592-438-4)*; 11.95s.p. *(0-685-67722-2)* Rourke Corp.
—Jaguars. (Illus.). 24p. (gr. k-5). 1989. lib. bdg. 11.94 *(0-86592-506-2)*; 8.95s.p. *(0-685-58631-6)* Rourke Corp.
—Leopards. (Illus.). 24p. (gr. k-5). 1989. lib. bdg. 11.94 *(0-86592-502-X)*; 8.95s.p. *(0-685-58630-8)* Rourke Corp.
—Lions. (Illus.). 24p. (gr. k-5). 1989. lib. bdg. 11.94 *(0-86592-501-1)*; 8.95s.p. *(0-685-58629-4)* Rourke Corp.
—Lobos (Wolves) 1991. 8.95s.p. *(0-86592-834-7)* Rourke Enter.
—Mapaches (Raccoons) 1991. 8.95s.p. *(0-86592-798-7)* Rourke Enter.
—Mountains. (Illus.). 48p. (gr. 4-8). 1989. lib. bdg. 15.94 *(0-86592-448-1)*; 11.95s.p. *(0-685-67721-4)* Rourke Corp.
—Osos (Bears) 1991. 8.95s.p. *(0-86592-833-9)* Rourke Enter.
—Ostriches. (Illus.). 24p. (gr. k-5). 1989. lib. bdg. 11.94 *(0-86592-323-X)* Rourke Corp.
—Ovejas (Sheep) 1991. 8.95s.p. *(0-86592-915-7)* Rourke Enter.
—Owls. (Illus.). 24p. (gr. k-5). 1989. lib. bdg. 11.94 *(0-86592-326-4)* Rourke Corp.
—Patos (Ducks) 1991. 8.95s.p. *(0-86592-953-X)* Rourke Enter.
—Pollos (Chickens) 1991. 8.95s.p. *(0-86592-949-1)* Rourke Enter.
—Prairies. (Illus.). 48p. (gr. 4-8). 1989. lib. bdg. 15.94 *(0-86592-446-5)*; 11.95 *(0-685-58573-5)* Rourke Corp.
—Rain Forests. (Illus.). 48p. (gr. 4-8). 1989. lib. bdg. 15.94 *(0-86592-437-6)*; 11.95s.p. *(0-685-67720-6)* Rourke Corp.
—Seashores. (Illus.). 48p. (gr. 4-8). 1989. lib. bdg. 15.94 *(0-86592-435-X)*; 11.95s.p. *(0-685-58575-1)* Rourke Corp.
—Spanish Language Books, Set 1: Animales de Granja (Farm Animals, 6 bks. 1991. 53.70s.p. *(0-86592-948-3)* Rourke Enter.

—Spanish Language Books, Set 2: Animales Norteamericanos (North American Animals, 6 bks. 1991. 53.70s.p. *(0-86592-786-3)* Rourke Enter.
—Temperate Forests. (Illus.). 48p. (gr. 4-8). 1989. lib. bdg. 15.94 *(0-86592-439-2)*; 11.95 *(0-685-58574-3)* Rourke Corp.
—Tigers. (Illus.). 24p. (gr. k-5). 1989. lib. bdg. 11.94 *(0-86592-504-6)*; lib. bdg. 8.95s.p. *(0-685-58632-4)* Rourke Corp.
—Vacas (Cows) 1991. 8.95s.p. *(0-86592-952-1)* Rourke Enter.
—Venados (Deer) 1991. 8.95s.p. *(0-86592-831-2)* Rourke Enter.
—Wetlands. (Illus.). 48p. (gr. 4-8). 1989. lib. bdg. 15.94 *(0-86592-447-3)*; 11.95 *(0-685-58569-7)* Rourke Corp.
—Zorrillos (Skunks) 1991. 8.95s.p. *(0-86592-799-5)* Rourke Enter.
Stone, Lynn. African Animals Discovery Library, 6 bks. (Illus.). 144p. (gr. k-5). 1990. Set. lib. bdg. 71.64 *(0-86593-047-3)*; Set. lib. bdg. 53.70s.p. *(0-685-36343-0)* Rourke Corp.
—African Buffalo. (Illus.). 24p. (gr. k-5). 1990. lib. bdg. 11.94 *(0-86593-052-X)*; lib. bdg. 8.95s.p. *(0-685-36344-9)* Rourke Corp.
—Antelopes. (Illus.). 24p. (gr. k-5). 1990. lib. bdg. 11.94 *(0-86593-053-8)*; lib. bdg. 8.95s.p. *(0-685-36345-7)* Rourke Corp.
—Australian Animals Discovery Library, 6 bks. (Illus.). 144p. (gr. k-5). 1990. Set. lib. bdg. 71.64 *(0-86593-054-6)*; Set. lib. bdg. 53.70s.p. *(0-685-36368-6)* Rourke Corp.
—Baboons. (Illus.). 24p. (gr. k-5). 1990. lib. bdg. 11.94 *(0-86593-067-8)*; lib. bdg. 8.95s.p. *(0-685-36315-5)* Rourke Corp.
—Bears. (Illus.). 24p. (gr. k-5). 1990. lib. bdg. 11.94 *(0-86593-042-2)*; lib. bdg. 8.95s.p. *(0-685-46449-0)* Rourke Corp.
—Bears. LC 92-34487. 1993. 12.67 *(0-86625-438-2)*; 9. 50s.p. *(0-685-66262-4)* Rourke Pubns.
—Beavers. (Illus.). 24p. (gr. k-5). 1990. lib. bdg. 11.94 *(0-86593-041-4)*; lib. bdg. 8.95s.p. *(0-685-36338-4)* Rourke Corp.
—Big Cat Discover Library, 6 bks, Reading Level 2. (Illus.). (gr. k-5). 1990. Set. PLB 71.64 *(0-86592-500-3)* Rourke Corp.
—Bird Discovery Library, 6 bks, Reading Level 2. (Illus.). 144p. (gr. k-5). 1989. Set. PLB 71.64 *(0-86592-320-5)* Rourke Corp.
—Birds. LC 92-34485. 1993. 12.67 *(0-86625-440-4)*; 9. 50s.p. *(0-685-66270-5)* Rourke Pubns.
—Canids. LC 92-34486. 1993. 12.67 *(0-86625-439-0)*; 9. 50s.p. *(0-685-66271-3)* Rourke Pubns.
—Chickens. (Illus.). 24p. (gr. k-5). 1990. lib. bdg. 11.94 *(0-86593-034-1)*; lib. bdg. 8.95s.p. *(0-685-36308-2)* Rourke Corp.
—Chimpanzees. (Illus.). 24p. (gr. k-5). 1990. lib. bdg. 11. 94 *(0-86593-064-3)*; lib. bdg. 8.95s.p. *(0-685-36316-3)* Rourke Corp.
—Cows. (Illus.). 24p. (gr. k-5). 1990. lib. bdg. 11.94 *(0-86593-039-2)*; lib. bdg. 8.95s.p. *(0-685-36309-0)* Rourke Corp.
—Crocodiles. (Illus.). 24p. (gr. k-5). 1990. lib. bdg. 11.94 *(0-86593-060-0)*; lib. bdg. 8.95s.p. *(0-685-36369-4)* Rourke Corp.
—Deer. (Illus.). 24p. (gr. k-5). 1990. lib. bdg. 11.94 *(0-86593-043-0)*; lib. bdg. 8.95s.p. *(0-685-36339-2)* Rourke Corp.
—Dingoes. (Illus.). 24p. (gr. k-5). 1990. lib. bdg. 11.94 *(0-86593-057-0)*; lib. bdg. 8.95s.p. *(0-685-36370-8)* Rourke Corp.
—Ducks. (Illus.). 24p. (gr. k-5). 1990. lib. bdg. 11.94 *(0-86593-036-8)*; lib. bdg. 8.95s.p. *(0-685-36310-4)* Rourke Corp.
—Ecozones, 8 bks, Reading Level 6. (Illus.). 384p. (gr. 4-8). 1988. Set. PLB 127.52 *(0-86592-434-1)*; 95.60s.p. *(0-685-58766-5)* Rourke Corp.
—Farm Animals Discovery Library, 6 bks. (Illus.). 144p. (gr. k-5). 1990. Set. lib. bdg. 71.64 *(0-86593-033-3)*; Set. lib. bdg. 53.70s.p. *(0-685-36307-4)* Rourke Corp.
—Fish. LC 92-34489. 1993. 12.67 *(0-86625-436-6)*; 9. 50s.p. *(0-685-66264-0)* Rourke Pubns.
—Forts. LC 93-142. 1993. write for info. *(0-86625-447-1)* Rourke Pubns.
—Ghost Towns. LC 93-143. 1993. 15.93 *(0-86625-449-8)*; 11.95s.p. *(0-685-66533-X)* Rourke Pubns.
—Gibbons. (Illus.). 24p. (gr. k-5). 1990. lib. bdg. 11.94 *(0-86593-062-7)*; lib. bdg. 8.95s.p. *(0-685-36317-1)* Rourke Corp.
—Giraffes. (Illus.). 24p. (gr. k-5). 1990. lib. bdg. 11.94 *(0-86593-050-3)*; lib. bdg. 8.95s.p. *(0-685-36346-5)* Rourke Corp.
—Gorillas. (Illus.). 24p. (gr. k-5). 1990. lib. bdg. 8.95s.p. *(0-86593-063-5)*; 11.94 *(0-685-36318-X)* Rourke Corp.
—Hippopotamus. (Illus.). 24p. (gr. k-5). 1990. lib. bdg. 11.94 *(0-86593-051-1)*; 8.95s.p. *(0-685-36347-3)* Rourke Corp.
—Horses. (Illus.). 24p. (gr. k-5). 1990. lib. bdg. 11.94 *(0-86593-035-X)*; lib. bdg. 8.95s.p. *(0-685-36311-2)* Rourke Corp.
—Hyenas. (Illus.). 24p. (gr. k-5). 1990. lib. bdg. 11.94 *(0-86593-049-X)*; lib. bdg. 8.95s.p. *(0-685-36348-1)* Rourke Corp.
—Kangaroos. (Illus.). 24p. (gr. k-5). 1990. lib. bdg. 11.94 *(0-86593-058-9)*; lib. bdg. 8.95s.p. *(0-685-36371-6)* Rourke Corp.

—Koalas. (Illus.). 24p. (gr. k-5). 1990. lib. bdg. 11.94 *(0-86593-055-4)*; lib. bdg. 8.95s.p. *(0-685-36372-4)* Rourke Corp.
—Monkey Discovery Library, 6 bks. (Illus.). 144p. (gr. k-5). 1990. Set. lib. bdg. 71.60 *(0-86593-061-9)*; Set. lib. bdg. 53.70s.p. *(0-685-36314-7)* Rourke Corp.
—North American Animal Discovery Library, 6 bks. (Illus.). 144p. (gr. k-5). 1990. Set. lib. bdg. 71.64 *(0-86593-040-6)*; Set. lib. bdg. 53.70s.p. *(0-685-36336-8)* Rourke Corp.
—Orangutans. (Illus.). 24p. (gr. k-5). 1990. lib. bdg. 11.94 *(0-86593-065-1)*; lib. bdg. 8.95s.p. *(0-685-36319-8)* Rourke Corp.
—The Pelican. LC 89-26049. (Illus.). 60p. (gr. 3 up). 1990. RSBE 13.95 *(0-87518-430-8,* Dillon) Macmillan Child Grp.
—Pigs. (Illus.). 24p. (gr. k-5). 1990. lib. bdg. 11.94 *(0-86593-037-6)*; lib. bdg. 8.95s.p. *(0-685-36312-0)* Rourke Corp.
—Plantations. LC 93-771. (ps-6). 1993. 15.93 *(0-86625-446-3)*; 11.95s.p. *(0-685-66594-1)* Rourke Pubns.
—Raccoons. (Illus.). 24p. (gr. k-5). 1990. lib. bdg. 11.94 *(0-86593-045-7)*; lib. bdg. 8.95s.p. *(0-685-46450-4)* Rourke Corp.
—Reptiles. LC 92-34488. 1993. 12.67 *(0-86625-437-4)*; 9. 50s.p. *(0-685-66263-2)* Rourke Pubns.
—Sheep. (Illus.). 24p. (gr. k-5). 1990. lib. bdg. 11.94 *(0-86593-038-4)*; lib. bdg. 8.95s.p. *(0-685-36313-9)* Rourke Corp.
—Skunks. (Illus.). 24p. (gr. k-5). 1990. lib. bdg. 11.94 *(0-86593-046-5)*; lib. bdg. 8.95s.p. *(0-685-36341-4)* Rourke Corp.
—Snow Monkeys. (Illus.). 24p. (gr. k-5). 1990. lib. bdg. 11.94 *(0-86593-066-X)*; lib. bdg. 8.95s.p. *(0-685-36320-1)* Rourke Corp.
—Tasmanian Devils. (Illus.). 24p. (gr. k-5). 1990. lib. bdg. 11.94 *(0-86593-056-2)*; lib. bdg. 8.95s.p. *(0-685-36373-2)* Rourke Corp.
—Villages. LC 93-16152. 1993. write for info. *(0-86625-448-X)* Rourke Pubns.
—Wild Cats. LC 92-34499. 1993. 12.67 *(0-86625-441-2)*; 9.50s.p. *(0-685-66272-1)* Rourke Pubns.
—Wolves. (Illus.). 24p. (gr. k-5). 1990. lib. bdg. 11.94 *(0-86593-044-9)*; lib. bdg. 8.95s.p. *(0-685-36342-2)* Rourke Corp.
—Wombats. (Illus.). 24p. (gr. k-5). 1990. lib. bdg. 11.94 *(0-86593-059-7)*; lib. bdg. 8.95s.p. *(0-685-36374-0)* Rourke Corp.
—Zebras. (Illus.). 24p. (gr. k-5). 1990. lib. bdg. 11.94 *(0-86593-048-1)*; lib. bdg. 8.95s.p. *(0-685-36349-X)* Rourke Corp.
Stone, Lynn M. Alligators & Crocodiles. LC 89-9985. 48p. (gr. k-4). 1989. PLB 15.27 *(0-516-01170-7)*; pap. 4.95 *(0-516-41170-5)* Childrens.
—Antarctica. 48p. (gr. k-4). 1985. PLB 15.27 *(0-516-01265-7)* Childrens.
—The Arctic. LC 84-23248. (Illus.). 48p. (gr. k-4). 1985. PLB 15.27 *(0-516-01935-X)* Childrens.
—Back from the Edge: The American Bison. LC 90-38385. (Illus.). 48p. (gr. 4-6). 1991. PLB 16.67 *(0-86593-101-1)*; PLB 12.50s.p. *(0-685-59353-3)* Rourke Corp.
—Bats. LC 93-1535. 1993. write for info. *(0-86593-293-X)* Rourke Corp.
—Birds of Prey. LC 82-17909. (Illus.). 48p. (gr. k-4). 1983. PLB 15.27 *(0-516-01676-8)*; pap. 4.95 *(0-516-41676-6)* Childrens.
—Bluegrass Country. LC 93-23002. 1993. write for info. *(0-86593-306-5)* Rourke Corp.
—The Changing Earth. LC 93-41103. 1994. write for info. *(1-55916-017-9)* Rourke Bk Co.
—Dairy Country. LC 93-13503. 1993. write for info. *(0-86593-302-2)* Rourke Corp.
—Eagles. LC 88-26427. (Illus.). 24p. (gr. 2-4). 1989. PLB 11.94 *(0-86592-321-3)*; 8.95s.p. *(0-685-58505-0)* Rourke Corp.
—Endangered Animals. LC 83-26323. (Illus.). 48p. (gr. k-4). 1984. PLB 15.27 *(0-516-01724-1)*; pap. 4.95 *(0-516-41724-X)* Childrens.
—Fall. LC 93-39057. 1994. write for info. *(1-55916-019-5)* Rourke Bk Co.
—Florida. LC 87-9391. (Illus.). 144p. (gr. 4 up). 1987. PLB 26.60 *(0-516-00455-7)* Childrens.
—Florida. 216p. 1993. text ed. 15.40 *(1-56956-153-2)* W A T Braille.
—Flying Squirrels. LC 93-4146. 1993. write for info. *(0-86593-298-0)* Rourke Corp.
—The Great Horned Owl. LC 87-570. (Illus.). 48p. (gr. 5-6). 1987. RSBE 12.95 *(0-89686-325-5,* Crestwood Hse) Macmillan Child Grp.
—Grizzlies. LC 93-22074. 1993. 19.95 *(0-87614-800-3)* Carolrhoda Bks.
—Jellyfish. LC 93-19462. 1993. write for info. *(0-86593-284-0)* Rourke Corp.
—The Killer Whale. LC 86-32884. (Illus.). 48p. (gr. 5-6). 1987. RSBE 12.95 *(0-89686-323-9,* Crestwood Hse) Macmillan Child Grp.
—Marshes & Swamps. LC 82-17861. (Illus.). 48p. (gr. k-4). 1983. PLB 15.27 *(0-516-01681-4)*; pap. 4.95 *(0-516-41681-2)* Childrens.
—Missions. LC 93-18638. (Illus.). (gr. 3-7). 1993. 15.93 *(0-86625-445-5)*; 11.95s.p. *(0-685-66595-X)* Rourke Pubns.
—Moths. LC 93-15695. (gr. 4 up). 1993. 12.67 *(0-86593-297-2)*; 9.50s.p. *(0-685-66590-9)* Rourke Corp.

—Mountains. LC 83-7276. (Illus.). 48p. (gr. k-4). 1983. PLB 15.27 (*0-516-01698-9*); pap. 4.95 (*0-516-41698-7*) Childrens.
—Old New England. LC 93-22881. 1993. write for info. (*0-86593-303-0*) Rourke Corp.
—Opossums. LC 93-10724. 1993. write for info. (*0-86593-295-6*) Rourke Corp.
—Parrots. LC 93-7461. 1993. 12.67 (*0-86593-280-8*); 9. 50s.p. (*0-685-66584-4*) Rourke Corp.
—Pelicans. LC 88-26428. (Illus.). (gr. 2-4). 1989. PLB 11. 94 (*0-86592-322-1*) Rourke Corp.
—Penguin. (Illus.). 48p. (gr. 5-6). 1987. RSBE 12.95 (*0-89686-326-3*, Crestwood Hse) Macmillan Child Grp.
—Penguins. LC 88-31606. (Illus.). (gr. 2-4). 1989. PLB 11.94 (*0-86592-325-6*) Rourke Corp.
—Pennsylvania Dutch Country. LC 93-13976. 1993. write for info. (*0-86593-301-4*) Rourke Corp.
—Pond Life. LC 83-7311. (Illus.). 48p. (gr. k-4). 1983. PLB 15.27 (*0-516-01705-5*); pap. 4.95 (*0-516-41705-3*) Childrens.
—Prairie Dogs. LC 93-19463. 1993. write for info. (*0-86593-282-4*) Rourke Corp.
—Sea Turtles. LC 93-15691. 1993. write for info. (*0-86593-296-4*) Rourke Corp.
—Summer. LC 93-39058. 1994. write for info. (*1-55916-020-9*) Rourke Bk Co.
—Timber Country. LC 93-4522. (Illus.). 1993. write for info. (*0-86593-305-7*) Rourke Corp.
—Toads. LC 93-15696. (gr. 4 up). 1993. write for info. (*0-86593-294-8*) Rourke Corp.
—Vultures. LC 88-30196. (Illus.). 24p. (gr. 2-4). 1989. PLB 11.94 (*0-86592-324-8*); PLB 8.95s.p. (*0-685-58506-9*) Rourke Corp.
—Vultures. LC 92-26721. 1993. 19.95 (*0-87614-768-6*) Carolrhoda Bks.
—The Wildebeest's Great Migration. LC 90-38384. (Illus.). 48p. (gr. 4-6). 1991. PLB 16.67 (*0-86593-103-8*); lib. bdg. 12.50s.p. (*0-685-59354-1*) Rourke Corp.
—Winter. LC 93-39059. 1994. write for info. (*1-55916-021-7*) Rourke Bk Co.
Stone, Lynne M. Spring. LC 93-41104. 1994. write for info. (*1-55916-018-7*) Rourke Bk Co.
Stone, Maggie R. The Portrait, Bk. I. Schatz, Bud, intro. by. 161p. (Orig.). (gr. 5-12). 1990. pap. 5.95 (*0-685-38818-2*) M R Stone Minst.
Stone, Marti. The Singing Fir Tree. Root, Barry, illus. 32p. (ps-3). 1992. 14.95 (*0-399-22207-3*, Putnam) Putnam Pub Group.
Stone, Rosetta. Because a Little Bug Went Ka-Choo! Frith, Michael, illus. LC 75-1605. 48p. (gr. k-3). 1975. 6.95 (*0-394-83130-6*) Beginner.
Stone, S. C., jt. auth. see Tallarico, Beatrice.
Stone, S. Callis, jt. auth. see Tallarico, Beatrice.
Stone, Sandra J. Playing: A Kid's Curriculum. (Illus.). 240p. (Orig.). (ps-1). 1992. pap. 12.95 (*0-673-36041-5*) GdYrBks.
Stone, Susheila. Nadeem Makes Samosas. (Illus.). 25p. (gr. 1-4). 1991. 15.95 (*0-237-60155-9*, Pub. by Evans Bros Ltd) Trafalgar.
—Where Is Batool? (Illus.). 25p. (gr. 2-4). 1991. 15.95 (*0-237-60157-5*, Pub. by Evans Bros Ltd) Trafalgar.
Stone, Sylvia & Bye, Holly. Whole Language Units for the Alphabet. Apodaca-LaBounty, Blanca & Wright, Theresa M., illus. 144p. (ps-1). 1993. wkbk. 12.95 (*1-55734-202-4*) Tchr Create Mat.
Stoneback, Jean C. Pup Pup & Murray Find a New Home. Weisbecker, Gene, illus. 45p. (Orig.). (ps). 1984. pap. 4.00 (*0-931440-09-2*) Stoneback Pub.
Stonecipher, A. D. The Ocean's Call. Moore, Daniel, illus. LC 91-62027. 16p. (ps-4). 1992. lib. bdg. 9.95 (*0-9621759-2-7*) Rochester Pub Lib Dist.
Stonehouse, Bernard. Snow, Ice, & Cold. LC 92-26298. (Illus.). 48p. (gr. 6 up). 1992. RSBE 13.95 (*0-02-788530-5*, New Discovery) Macmillan Child Grp.
Stoneking, Robin, jt. auth. see Johnson, Anne A.
Stone-Peterson, Helen. Abigail Adams: Dear Partner. Fraser, Betty, illus. 80p. (gr. 2-6). 1991. Repr. of 1967 ed. lib. bdg. 12.95 (*0-7910-1402-9*) Chelsea Hse.
—Henry Clay: Leader in Congress. Dowd, Vic, illus. 80p. (gr. 2-6). 1991. Repr. of 1964 ed. lib. bdg. 12.95 (*0-7910-1457-6*) Chelsea Hse.
Stoner, Laura M. Acts - a Story Color Book. Huskey, Freeda, ed. Stoner, Laura M., illus. 80p. (Orig.). (gr. k-6). 1992. wkbk. 5.95 (*0-934426-46-5*) NAPSAC Reprods.
—Exodus: A Story Color Book. Stoner, Laura M., illus. 90p. (Orig.). (gr. k-6). 1986. pap. 3.95 (*0-934426-11-2*) Napsac Reprods.
—Jesus: A Story Color Book. (Illus.). 80p. (Orig.). (gr. 1-8). 1985. pap. 3.95 wkbk. (*0-934426-07-4*) Napsac Reprods.
Stonerod, David. Puzzles in Space. Laycock, Mary & Stokes, Bill, eds. (Illus.). (gr. 4-10). 1982. pap. 7.50 (*0-918932-80-7*) Activity Resources.
Stones, Anthony. Bill & the Maze at Grimley Grange. (Illus.). 32p. (Orig.). (gr. k-2). 1990. 10.95 (*0-86327-249-5*, Pub. by Wolfhound Pr EIRE) Dufour.
Stoneway Books Staff. How Does Monster Count to Nine? (ps-3). 1990. pap. 5.95 (*1-55923-038-X*) Stoneway Ltd.
Stong, Susan see Dumelle, Grace.
Stoops, Erik D. & Wright, Annette T. Snakes. LC 92-18995. (Illus.). 80p. (gr. 10-12). 1992. 14.95 (*0-8069-8482-1*) Sterling.

Stopple, Libby. A Box of Peppermints. Dromgoole, Dick, ed. Bell, Martha, illus. LC 75-20957. 96p. (gr. 2-10). 1975. 12.95 (*0-913632-08-2*); pap. 7.95 (*0-913632-07-4*) Am Univ Artforms.
Stoppleman, Monica. School Day. (Illus.). 32p. (gr. 3-6). 1992. 12.95 (*0-7136-3185-6*, Pub. by A&C Black UK) Talman.
Stops, Sue. Dulcie Dando, Soccer Star. Gliori, Debi, illus. LC 92-2259. (ps-2). 1992. 14.95 (*0-8050-2413-1*, Bks Young Read) H Holt & Co.
Stopsky, Fred. Bartolome De las Casas: Champion of Indian Rights. 64p. (Orig.). (gr. 5-9). 1992. pap. 4.95 (*1-878668-12-9*) Disc Enter Ltd.
Storer, Ronald, ed. Sleeping Beauty & Bluebeard. (gr. k-6). 1972. pap. 3.25x (*0-19-421746-9*) OUP.
Storey, Margaret. Timothy & the Two Witches. 92p. (gr. 2-5). 1974. pap. 0.75 (*0-440-48864-8*, YB) Dell.
Storey, T. R., jt. auth. see Weiner, Eric.
Storm, Betsy. I Can Be an Interior Designer. LC 89-15758. 32p. (gr. k-3). 1989. PLB 14.60 (*0-516-01958-9*); pap. 3.95 (*0-516-41958-7*) Childrens.
Storm, Derek. Vampire Island. LC 93-71550. 175p. 1993. pap. 3.95 (*1-56969-350-1*) FamilyVision.
Storms, John. Buddy the Beaver. Storms, Robert, illus. 24p. (Orig.). (gr. k-4). 1993. pap. 4.95 (*0-89346-529-1*) Heian Intl.
—Cory the Crocodile. Storms, Robert, illus. 24p. (Orig.). (gr. k-4). 1993. pap. 4.95 (*0-89346-530-5*) Heian Intl.
—Sammy the Sea Otter. Storms, Robert, illus. 24p. (gr. k-4). 1993. 4.95 (*0-89346-528-3*) Heian Intl.
—Tony the Tokay Gecko. Storms, Robert, illus. 24p. (Orig.). (gr. k-4). 1993. pap. 4.95 (*0-89346-531-3*) Heian Intl.
Storms, Laura, jt. auth. see Thomas, Art.
Storr, Catherine. Abraham & Isaac. Rowe, Gavin, illus. LC 84-18076. 32p. (gr. k-4). 1985. PLB 14.65 (*0-8172-1994-3*) Raintree Steck-V.
—Clever Polly & the Stupid Wolf. large type ed. Watts, Marjorie-Ann, illus. 117p. 1992. 13.95 (*0-7451-1623-X*, Galaxy Child Lrg Print) Chivers N Amer.
—Hansel & Gretel. Humperdinck, Engelbert, contrib. by. (Illus.). 32p. (ps up). 1988. pap. 9.95 (*0-571-10083-X*) Faber & Faber.
—Joan of Arc. Taylor, Robert, illus. LC 84-18346. 32p. (gr. 2-5). 1985. PLB 17.96 (*0-8172-2111-5*) Raintree Steck-V.
—King Midas. Codd, Mike, illus. LC 84-18307. 32p. (gr. 2-5). 1985. PLB 17.96 (*0-8172-2112-3*) Raintree Steck-V.
—King Midas. (ps-3). 1993. pap. 3.95 (*0-8114-7148-9*) Raintree Steck-V.
—The Nutcracker. Tchaikovsky, contrib. by. (Illus.). 32p. (ps up). 1988. pap. 9.95 (*0-571-10080-5*) Faber & Faber.
—Pied Piper of Hamelin. (ps-3). 1993. pap. 3.95 (*0-8114-8353-3*) Raintree Steck-V.
—Sword & the Stone. (ps-3). 1993. pap. 3.95 (*0-8114-7147-0*) Raintree Steck-V.
—The Sword in the Stone. Hunter, Susan, illus. LC 84-18293. 32p. (gr. 2-5). 1985. PLB 17.96 (*0-8172-2113-1*) Raintree Steck-V.
—The Trojan Horse. Codd, Mike, illus. LC 84-18292. 32p. (gr. 2-5). 1985. PLB 17.96 (*0-8172-2114-X*) Raintree Steck-V.
Storr, Catherine, retold by. Adam & Eve. Russell, Jim, illus. LC 82-23060. 32p. (gr. k-4). 1983. PLB 14.65 (*0-8172-1981-1*) Raintree Steck-V.
—The Birth of Jesus. Rowe, Gavin, illus. LC 82-9048. 32p. (gr. k-4). 1982. PLB 14.65 (*0-8172-1977-3*) Raintree Steck-V.
Storr, Catherine, as told by. Dick Whittington. LC 85-16904. (Illus.). 32p. (gr. 2-5). 1985. PLB 17.96 (*0-8172-2507-2*) Raintree Steck-V.
—The Flying Dutchman. LC 85-16711. (Illus.). 32p. (gr. k-5). 1985. PLB 17.96 (*0-8172-2501-3*) Raintree Steck-V.
Storr, Catherine, retold by. Miracles by the Sea. Molan, Christine, illus. LC 82-23022. 32p. (gr. k-4). 1983. PLB 14.65 (*0-8172-1983-8*) Raintree Steck-V.
Storr, Catherine, ed. Odysseus & the Enchanters. (Illus.). 32p. (gr. k-5). 1985. PLB 17.96 (*0-8172-2502-1*) Raintree Steck-V.
Storr, Catherine, retold by. The Pied Piper of Hamelin. LC 84-26971. (Illus.). 32p. (gr. k-5). 1984. PLB 17.96 (*0-8172-2107-7*); PLB 29.28 incl. cassette (*0-8172-2238-3*) Raintree Steck-V.
—The Prodigal Son. Rowe, Gavin, illus. LC 82-23011. 32p. (gr. k-4). 1983. PLB 14.65 (*0-8172-1982-X*) Raintree Steck-V.
—Rip Van Winkle. LC 83-26996. (Illus.). 32p. (gr. k-5). 1984. PLB 17.96 (*0-8172-2108-5*); PLB 29.28 incl. cassette (*0-8172-2236-7*) Raintree Steck-V.
—Robin Hood. LC 83-24417. (Illus.). 32p. (gr. k-5). 1984. PLB 17.96 (*0-8172-2109-3*); PLB 29.28 incl. cassette (*0-8172-2235-9*) Raintree Steck-V.
Storr, Catherine, as told by. Theseus & the Minotaur. (Illus.). 32p. (gr. k-5). 1985. PLB 17.96 (*0-8172-2506-4*) Raintree Steck-V.
—The Three Musketeers. (Illus.). 32p. (gr. k-5). 1985. PLB 17.96 (*0-8172-2500-5*) Raintree Steck-V.
Storr, Catherine, ed. see Shaw, George Bernard.
Storr, Sherman, pseud. The Ipswich Itinerants. Wiegand, Betty, ed. Storr, Sherman, illus. Kern, W. C., intro. by. (Illus.). 258p. (Orig.). (gr. 9-12). 1988. pap. 8.00 (*0-9621380-0-2*) Alacran Pr Inc.

Storry, Richard. History of Modern Japan. (Orig.). (gr. 9 up). 1960. pap. 6.95 (*0-14-020475-X*) Viking Child Bks.
Stortz, Diane. Alexander's Praise Time Band. Garris, Norma, illus. LC 92-32817. 28p. (ps-k). 1993. 4.99 (*0-7847-0036-2*, 24-03826) Standard Pub.
—Barnaby Mouse, Detective, & the Mystery of the Big Book. Girouard, Patrick, illus. LC 93-14425. 28p. (ps). 1994. 4.99 (*0-7847-0004-4*, 24-03870) Standard Pub.
—Five Small Loaves & Two Small Fish. Stites, Joe, illus. 28p. (ps). 1992. 2.50 (*0-87403-953-3*, 24-03593) Standard Pub.
—God Cares for Me. Garris, Norma, illus. 12p. (ps) 1992. deluxe ed. 4.99 (*0-87403-992-4*, 24-03112) Standard Pub.
—No Problem! Stuart, Don, illus. 28p. (ps). 1992. 2.50 (*0-87403-954-1*, 24-03594) Standard Pub.
—A One-Two-Three Christmas. Munger, Nancy, illus. 28p. (ps-k). 1993. 4.99 (*0-7847-0064-8*, 24-03844) Standard Pub.
—Zaccheus Meets Jesus. Fagan, Todd, illus. 28p. (ps). 1992. 2.50 (*0-87403-958-4*, 24-03598) Standard Pub.
Stortz, Diane, jt. auth. see Bennett, Marian.
Stortz, Diane M. Where Does the Puppy Live? Hackney, richard, illus. LC 87-62602. (ps). 1988. 1.59 (*0-87403-389-6*, 24-02019) Standard Pub.
—Who Tells the Wind? Rigo, Christian, tr. LC 87-62603. 20p. (ps). 1988. 1.59 (*0-87403-390-X*, 24-02020) Standard Pub.
Story, Bettie Wilson see Wilson Story, Bettie.
Story Rhyme Staff. Entrepreneural Kids: Story Rhymes, Ideas, How to Etc. Notebook. 60p. (gr. 8-12). 1993. 47.95 (*1-56820-094-3*) Story Time.
—Fish Convention Plus Twenty-Five Stories, Story Rhyme Coloring & Activity Book. rev. ed. Doyle, A. C., illus. 12p. (Orig.). (gr. 4-8). 1993. notebk. 19.95 (*0-913597-48-1*, Pub. by Alpha Pyramis) Prosperity & Profits.
—Recipe Story Rhyme Cookbook. Story Rhyme Staff, illus. 60p. (gr. 7-10). 1993. binder 21.95 (*1-56820-103-6*) Story Time.
—Recipe Story Rhyme: Greetings to Duplicate & Use. Story Rhyme Staff, illus. 60p. (gr. 7-10). 1993. binder 29.95 (*1-56820-104-4*) Story Time.
—Self Esteem: Stories & Poetry. Story Rhyme Staff, illus. 28p. (gr. 4-9). 1993. 8.95 (*1-56820-107-9*) Story Time.
—Story Rhyme Greetings: Directory of Story Letters for Birthdays, Celebrations, Holidays, Etcetera. Story Rhyme Staff, illus. 60p. (gr. 7-9). 1993. notebk. 39.95 (*1-56820-106-0*) Story Time.
Story Time Collection Staff. Tennis Shoes: A Story Rhyme. (Illus.). 20p. (Orig.). (ps-6). 1992. pap. text ed. 6.95 (*0-939476-75-4*, Pub. by Biblio Pr) Prosperity & Profits.
Story Time Staff. Home Schooling with Educational Story Rhymes. Story Time Staff, illus. 8p. (gr. 6-9). 1993. binder 21.95 (*1-56820-108-7*) Story Time.
—Stories That Educate, Inform, Entertain & Rhyme: Kids Workshop Workbook I. Story Time Staff, illus. 52p. 1992. GBC bdg. 29.95 (*1-56820-040-4*) Story Time.
—Stories That Educate, Inform, Entertain & Rhyme: Kids Workshop Workbook II. Story Time Staff, illus. 52p. 1992. GBC bdg. 29.95 (*1-56820-041-2*) Story Time.
Story Time Stories That Rhyme Staff. Bean Sprouts - a How to Story Rhyme & Activity Workbook. Doyle, A., illus. 30p. (Orig.). (gr. 4-7). 1992. pap. text ed. 17. 95 (*0-939476-82-7*, Pub. by Biblio Pr) Prosperity & Profits.
—Bean Sprouts: A How to Story Sample & Activity Pages. Story Time Stories That Rhyme Staff, illus. 28p. (gr. 4-7). 1992. GBC bdg. 9.95 (*1-56820-009-9*) Story Time.
—Christmas Stories That Rhyme. Story Time Stories That Rhyme Staff, illus. 39p. (gr. 4-7). 1992. binder 19.95 (*1-56820-015-3*) Story Time.
—Cowboy Boots: A Story Sample & Activity Pages. Story Time Stories That Rhyme Staff, illus. 16p. (gr. 4-7). 1992. GBC bdg. 9.95 (*1-56820-008-0*) Story Time.
—Fables, Tales, & Stories That Rhyme. Story Time Stories That Rhyme Staff, illus. 50p. (Orig.). (gr. 4-7). 1992. GBC bdg. 19.95 (*1-56820-016-1*) Story Time.
—Fish Convention: A Story Sample & Activity Pages. Story Time Stories That Rhyme Staff, illus. 37p. (gr. 4-7). 1992. GBC bdg. 9.95 (*1-56820-011-0*) Story Time.
—Greetings of Story Rhyme Letters to Duplicate & Use. (Illus.). 1992. binder 25.95 (*1-56820-003-X*) Story Time.
—Halloween Stories That Rhyme. Story Time Stories That Rhyme Staff, illus. 38p. (gr. 4-7). 1992. GBC bdg. 15.95 (*1-56820-013-7*) Story Time.
—Holiday Gift Giving with Story Rhyme Greeting Letters: 25 Story Rhyme Greeting Letters to Duplicate & Use. (Illus.). (gr. 3-6). 1992. binder 22.95 (*1-56820-001-3*) Story Time.
—Holiday Storytelling: Christmas, Easter, Halloween. (Illus.). 1992. binder 21.95 (*1-56820-002-1*) Story Time.
—Math in Stories That Rhyme. Story Time Stories That Rhyme Staff, illus. 50p. (Orig.). (gr. 4-7). 1992. GBC bdg. 19.95 (*1-56820-017-X*) Story Time.
—Mushrooms: A Story Sample & Activity Pages. Story Time Stories That Rhyme Staff, illus. 20p. (gr. 4-7). 1992. GBC bdg. 9.95 (*1-56820-010-2*) Story Time.

—Seaweeds: A Story Sample & Activity Pages. Story Time Stories That Rhyme Staff, illus. 17p. (gr. 4-7). 1992. GBC bdg. 9.95 (*1-56820-007-2*) Story Time.

—Stories with Activities That Educate & Inform: Sea Shell Edition. (Illus., Orig.). 1992. GBC bdg. 19.95 (*1-56820-006-4*) Story Time.

—Story Fest: Story Rhymes for Schools, Camps, & Storytime. (Illus.). 1992. binder 19.95 (*1-56820-004-8*) Story Time.

—Story Habitat: Plant & Animal Stories. Story Time Stories That Rhyme Staff, illus. 40p. (Orig.). (gr. 4-7). 1992. GBC bdg. 19.95 (*1-56820-014-5*) Story Time.

—Story Menus for Schools & Educational Locations to Duplicate & Use. (Illus.). 1992. binder 29.95 (*1-56820-000-5*) Story Time.

—Story Village: Recycling Stories That Rhyme. (Illus.). 1992. binder 19.95 (*1-56820-005-6*) Story Time.

—Tennis Shoes: A Story Sample & Activity Pages. Story Time Stories That Rhyme Staff, illus. 21p. (gr. 4-7). 1992. GBC bdg. 9.95 (*1-56820-012-9*) Story Time.

—Water World Convention: Stories & Word Mapping Activity Workbook. Story Time Stories That Rhyme Staff, illus. 50p. (Orig.). (gr. 4-7). 1992. binder 25.95 (*1-56820-018-8*) Story Time.

Storybook Heirlooms Staff. A Visit to Storybook Ranch. (Illus.). 10p. (Orig.). 1993. 9.00 (*0-9638614-0-9*) Strybook Heirlooms.

Storytime Stories That Rhyme Staff. Cowboy Boots - a Story Rhyme Plus Twenty Other Stories. (Illus.). 60p. (Orig.). (gr. 6-9). 1992. binder 19.95 (*0-317-04687-X*, Pub. by Alpha Pyramis) Prosperity & Profits.

Stott, Carole. Into the Unknown. (Illus.). 48p. (gr. 5-7). 1989. PLB 12.90 (*0-531-19513-9*) Watts.

—Night Sky. LC 93-644. (Illus.). 64p. (gr. 3-8). 1993. 9.95 (*1-56458-393-7*) Dorling Kindersley.

—Observing the Sky. LC 90-11018. (Illus.). 32p. (gr. 4-6). 1991. lib. bdg. 11.89 (*0-8167-2132-7*); pap. text ed. 3.95 (*0-8167-2133-5*) Troll Assocs.

Stott, Dorothy. Kitty & Me. (gr. 4 up). 1993. 9.99 (*0-525-45075-0*, DCB) Dutton Child Bks.

—Little Duck's Bicycle Ride. Stott, Dorothy, illus. LC 90-19425. 32p. (ps-k). 1991. 10.95 (*0-525-44728-8*, DCB) Dutton Child Bks.

—Puppy & Me. (gr. 3 up). 1993. 9.99 (*0-525-45080-7*, DCB) Dutton Child Bks.

—Too Much. LC 89-12078. (Illus.). 32p. (ps-k). 1990. 10. 95 (*0-525-44569-2*, DCB) Dutton Child Bks.

Stotz, Carl E. A Promise Kept: The Story of the Founding of Little League Baseball. Loss, Kenneth D. & Zebrowski, Stephanie R., eds. 208p. (gr. 7-12). 1992. 16.95 (*1-880484-05-6*) Zebrowski Hist.

Stout, Harry S., jt. auth. see DeFord, Deborah H.

Stout, Robert T. Children's Favorite Story of Santa Claus. Stout, Robert T., illus. 32p. (ps-6). 1982. 5.95 (*0-911049-08-8*); pap. 3.95 (*0-911049-04-5*) Yuletide Intl.

—The Noorps Are Coming. Stout, Robert T., illus. 32p. (ps-6). 1982. pap. 3.95 (*0-911049-05-3*) Yuletide Intl.

—The Original Story of Santa Claus. Stout, Robert T., illus. 56p. (ps-8). 1981. 6.95 (*0-911049-00-2*) Yuletide Intl.

—The Secret of Halloween. Stout, Robert T., illus. 24p. (Orig.). (ps-6). 1982. pap. 3.50 (*0-911049-02-9*) Yuletide Intl.

Stoutenburg, Adrien. American Tall Tales. Powers, Richard M., illus. (gr. 3-7). 1976. pap. 3.99 (*0-14-030928-4*, Puffin) Puffin Bks.

Stoutzenberger, Joseph. Celebrating Sacraments. rev. ed. Allaire, Barbara, ed. McCormick, Keith & Abrahamson, Evy, illus. 304p. (gr. 10). 1993. pap. text ed. 13.70 (*0-88489-279-4*); tchr's. ed., 290p. 18.95 (*0-88489-280-8*) St Marys.

Stover. When the Dolls Woke. 1993. pap. 2.95 (*0-590-44624-X*) Scholastic Inc.

Stover, Jill. Alamo Across Texas. LC 91-47572. 32p. (ps up). 1993. 13.00 (*0-688-11712-0*) Lothrop.

—Alamo Across Texas. LC 91-47572. (ps-3). 1993. 12.93 (*0-688-11713-9*) Lothrop.

Stover, Jo A. They Didn't Use Their Heads. Stover, Jo A., illus. 45p. (ps). 1990. pap. 4.95 (*0-89084-546-8*) Bob Jones Univ Pr.

Stover, Jo Ann. If Everybody Did. Stover, Jo Ann, illus. 48p. (Orig.). (gr. k-1). 1989. pap. 3.95 (*0-89084-487-9*) Bob Jones Univ Pr.

Stover, Marjorie. Midnight in the Dollhouse. Levine, Abby, ed. Loccisano, Karen, illus. LC 89-37904. 160p. (gr. 3-6). 1990. 11.95 (*0-8075-5124-4*) A Whitman.

—When the Dolls Woke. Levine, Abby, ed. Loccisano, Karen, illus. LC 85-3154. 128p. (gr. 3-6). 1985. PLB 10.95 (*0-8075-8882-2*) A Whitman.

Stover, Marjorie F. Midnight in the Dollhouse. (gr. 4-7). 1992. pap. 2.95 (*0-590-44924-9*) Scholastic Inc.

Stovicek, Vratislav. Book of Goodnight Stories. 1983. 5.98 (*0-671-05963-7*) S&S Trade.

Stow, Jenny, illus. The House That Jack Built. LC 91-23850. 32p. (ps-2). 1992. 14.00 (*0-8037-1090-9*) Dial Bks Young.

—The House That Jack Built. 32p. (ps-2). 1993. pap. 4.99 (*0-14-054590-5*, Puffin Pied Piper) Puffin Bks.

Stowe, Aurelia, ed. Love Will Come: Stories of Romance. 1963. lib. bdg. 4.99 (*0-394-91363-9*) Random Bks Yng Read.

Stowe, Cynthia. Dear Mom, in Ohio for a Year. 1992. 13.95 (*0-590-45060-3*, 024, Scholastic Hardcover) Scholastic Inc.

Stowe, Cynthia M. Home Sweet Home, Good-Bye. (gr. 4-7). 1993. pap. 2.95 (*0-590-42759-8*) Scholastic Inc.

Stowe, Harriet Beecher. Uncle Tom's Cabin. Corrigan, R. A., intro. by. (gr. 9 up). 1967. pap. 3.50 (*0-8049-0143-0*, CL-143) Airmont.

—Uncle Tom's Cabin. 496p. (RL 7). 1966. pap. 3.95 (*0-451-52302-4*, Sig Classics) NAL-Dutton.

Stowe, Lynn M. Grasshoppers. LC 93-7586. 1993. write for info. (*0-86593-286-7*) Rourke Corp.

Stowell, Gordon. Abraham. Lerin, S. D., tr. from ENG. (Illus.). 24p. (gr. 1). 1981. pap. 0.75 (*0-311-38511-7*, Edit Mundo) Casa Bautista.

—Ana. Lerin, S. D., tr. from ENG. (Illus.). 24p. (gr. 1). 1981. pap. 0.75 (*0-311-38512-5*, Edit Mundo) Casa Bautista.

—Dorcas. Lerin, S. D. de, tr. from ENG. (Illus.). 24p. (gr. 1). 1978. pap. 0.75 (*0-311-38517-6*, Edit Mundo) Casa Bautista.

—God Knows. 14p. (gr. 1-5). 1984. mini-bk. 0.79 (*0-8307-0959-2*, 5608425) Regal.

—Help Me. 14p. (gr. 1-5). 1984. mini-bk. 0.79 (*0-8307-0961-4*, 5608444) Regal.

—I Like. 14p. (ps-2). 1984. mini-bk. 0.79 (*0-8307-0962-2*, 5608579) Regal.

—I'm Sorry. 14p. (gr. 1-5). 1984. mini-bk. 0.79 (*0-8307-0957-6*, 5608400) Regal.

—It's Fun. (gr. 1-5). 1984. mini-bk. 0.79 (*0-8307-0956-8*, 5608392) Regal.

—Jesus Alimenta. Stowell, Gordon, illus. De Martinez, Violeta S., tr. from SPA. (Illus.). 24p. (ps). 1988. pap. 0.75 (*0-311-38614-8*) Casa Bautista.

—Jesus Ama. Stowell, Gordon, illus. De Martinez, Violeta S., tr. from SPA. (Illus.). 24p. (ps). 1984. pap. 0.75 (*0-311-38611-3*) Casa Bautista.

—Jesus & the Fisherman. (Illus.). 14p. (gr. 1-5). 1982. pap. 0.79 (*0-8307-0831-6*, 5608150) Regal.

—Jesus Cuenta. Stowell, Gordon, illus. De Martinez, Violeta S., tr. from SPA. (Illus.). 24p. (ps). 1984. pap. 0.75 (*0-311-38613-X*) Casa Bautista.

—Jesus Ensena. Stowell, Gordon, illus. De Martinez, Violeta S., tr. from SPA. (Illus.). 24p. (ps). 1984. pap. 0.75 (*0-311-38609-1*) Casa Bautista.

—Jesus Feeds the People. (Illus.). 14p. (gr. 1-5). 1982. pap. 0.79 (*0-8307-0832-4*, 5608167) Regal.

—Jesus Heals. (Illus.). 14p. (gr. 1-5). 1982. pap. 0.79 (*0-8307-0828-6*, 5608122) Regal.

—Jesus Llama. Stowell, Gordon, illus. De Martinez, Violeta S., tr. from SPA. (Illus.). 24p. (ps). 1984. pap. 0.75 (*0-311-38612-1*) Casa Bautista.

—Jesus Loves. 14p. (gr. 1-5). 1982. pap. 0.79 (*0-8307-0830-8*, 5608145) Regal.

—Jesus Nace. De Martinez, Violeta S., tr. from SPA. (Illus.). 24p. (ps). 1984. pap. 0.75 (*0-311-38608-3*) Casa Bautista.

—Jesus Sana. Stowell, Gordon, illus. De Martinez, Violeta S., tr. from ENG. (Illus.). 24p. (ps-1). 1984. pap. 0.75 (*0-311-38610-5*) Casa Bautista.

—Jesus Teaches. (Illus.). 14p. 1982. pap. 0.79 (*0-8307-0829-4*, 5608138) Regal.

—Jesus Tells Some Stories. (Illus.). 14p. (gr. 1-5). 1982. pap. 0.79 (*0-8307-0833-2*, 5608176) Regal.

—Jesus Vive. Stowell, Gordon, illus. De Martinez, Violeta S., tr. from SPA. (Illus.). 24p. (ps-1). 1984. pap. 0.75 (*0-311-38615-6*) Casa Bautista.

—Jonas. Lerin, S. D., tr. from ENG. (Illus.). 24p. (gr. 1). 1978. pap. 0.75 (*0-311-38514-1*, Edit Mundo) Casa Bautista.

—Juan el Bautista. Lerin, S. D., tr. from ENG. (Illus.). 24p. (gr. 1). 1981. pap. 0.75 (*0-311-38515-X*, Edit Mundo) Casa Bautista.

—Little Fish Surprise Picture Books. Roe, Earl O., ed. Incl. Noah's Big Boat. pap. 0.89 (*0-8307-1129-5*, 5608701); Joseph & His Dreams (*0-8307-1130-9*, 5608702); David the Shepherd Boy (*0-8307-1131-7*, 5608703); Christmas in Bethlehem. pap. 0.89 (*0-8307-1132-5*, 5608704); The Wise Men Find Jesus. pap. 0.89 (*0-8307-1133-3*, 5608705); The Little Man's Happy Day. pap. 0.89 (*0-8307-1134-1*, 5608706); The Great Big Picnic (*0-8307-1136-8*, 5608707); The First Easter (*0-8307-1137-6*, 5608708). (Illus.). 16p. (Orig.). (gr. 1 up). 1986. (*0-685-14585-9*) Regal.

—Pablo. Lerin, S. D., tr. from ENG. (Illus.). 24p. (gr. 1). 1981. pap. 0.75 (*0-311-38518-4*, Edit Mundo) Casa Bautista.

—Pedro. Lerin, S. D., tr. from ENG. (Illus.). 24p. (gr. 1). 1981. pap. 0.75 (*0-311-38516-8*, Edit Mundo) Casa Bautista.

—Please God. 14p. (gr. 1-5). 1984. mini-bk. 0.79 (*0-8307-0954-1*, 5608381) Regal.

—Rut. Lerin, S. D., tr. from ENG. (Illus.). 24p. (gr. 1). 1981. pap. 0.75 (*0-311-38513-3*, Edit Mundo) Casa Bautista.

—Thank You God. 14p. (gr. 1-7). 1984. mini-bk. 0.79 (*0-8307-0960-6*, 5608436) Regal.

Straalen, Alice van see Van Straalen, Alice.

Strachan. Whales & Dolphins. (Illus.). 32p. (gr. 4-6). 1991. 13.95 (*0-237-60168-0*, Pub. by Evans Bros Ltd) Trafalgar.

Strachan, Ian. Flawed Glass. (gr. 9-12). 1990. 14.95 (*0-316-81813-5*) Little.

Strahinich, Helen. Guns in America. 160p. (gr. 7 up). 1992. PLB 15.85 (*0-8027-8104-7*); pap. 9.95 (*0-8027-7356-7*) Walker & Co.

Strain, Jim. Bingo. (gr. 9). 1991. 14.95 (*1-55868-077-2*) Gr Arts Ctr Pub.

Straker, Joan A. see National Geographic Society Staff.

Strand, Julie & Boggs, Juanita. Sing a Song of Halloween: With Communication, Arts & Nutrition Activities. McBride, Molly J., illus. 133p. 1982. pap. text ed. 10.95 (*0-910817-00-6*) Collaborative Learn.

Strand, Mark. Rembrandt Takes a Walk. Grooms, Red, illus. (gr. 3 up). 1987. 14.95 (*0-517-56293-6*) Crown Bks Yng Read.

Strange, Florence. Rock-a-Bye Whale. LC 77-83196. (Illus.). (gr. k-4). 1977. 11.95 (*0-931644-00-3*) Manzanita Pr.

Strange, Johanna, jt. auth. see Thompson, Merita L.

Strangelo, Judy M. What Do Bunnies Do All Day? (Illus.). 32p. (ps-k). 1991. pap. 4.95 (*0-8249-8509-5*, Ideals Child) Hambleton-Hill.

Strangis, Joel. Grandfather's Rock. Recht, Ruth, illus. LC 92-26525. 1993. 14.95 (*0-395-65367-3*) HM.

Strasheim, Lorraine A. Oro Vos Faciatis... an Election Unit. 7p. (gr. 9-12). 1991. spiral bdg. 1.00 (*0-939507-32-3*, B11) Amer Classical.

Strasser, Todd. The Accident. (gr. k up). 1990. pap. 3.50 (*0-440-20635-9*, LFL) Dell.

—Angel Dust Blues. 208p. (gr. 9 up). 1981. pap. 2.95 (*0-440-90956-2*, LE); tchr's guide by Lou Stanek 0.50 (*0-685-01408-8*) Dell.

—Beyond the Reef. 1991. pap. 3.50 (*0-440-20881-5*) Dell.

—Complete Computer Popularity Contest. (gr. 4-7). 1991. pap. 3.25 (*0-440-40436-3*) Dell.

—The Diving Bell. 192p. 1992. 13.95 (*0-590-44620-7*, Scholastic Hardcover) Scholastic Inc.

—Freaked. (gr. 4-7). 1993. pap. 4.50 (*0-440-40908-X*) Dell.

—Free Willy: Digest Novelization. (gr. 4-7). 1993. pap. 3.25 (*0-590-46756-5*) Scholastic Inc.

—Hocus Pocus. (Illus.). 128p. (gr. 4-7). 1993. pap. 2.95 (*1-56282-373-6*) Disney Pr.

—Home Alone Movie Tie-In. 1991. pap. 2.95 (*0-590-44668-1*) Scholastic Inc.

—Home Alone Two: Lost in New York Digest Novelization. 1992. 3.25 (*0-590-45717-9*) Scholastic Inc.

—Rock It to the Top. 1987. write for info. Delacorte.

—Rock 'n Roll Nights. LC 81-12618. 224p. (gr. 7 up). 1982. pap. 10.95 (*0-385-28855-7*) Delacorte.

—Rock 'n Roll Nights. 224p. (gr. 7 up). 1983. pap. 2.95 (*0-440-97318-X*, LFL) Dell.

—Rookie of the Year. 1993. pap. 3.99 (*0-440-40910-1*) Dell.

—Super Mario Brothers Junior Novelization. (Illus.). 128p. (Orig.). (gr. 2-6). 1993. pap. write for info. (*1-56282-471-6*) Hyprn Child.

—Turn It Up! (gr. 6-12). 1985. pap. 2.50 (*0-440-99059-9*, LFL) Dell.

—A Very Touchy Subject. (gr. 6 up). 1986. pap. 2.95 (*0-440-98851-9*, LFL) Dell.

—The Villains Collection: Stories from the Films. DiCicco, Gil, illus. Rifkin, Mark, contrib. by. LC 93-70882. (Illus.). 80p. 1993. 14.95 (*1-56282-500-3*); PLB 14.89 (*1-56282-501-1*) Disney Pr.

—Wildlife. LC 86-19861. 224p. (gr. 7 up). 1987. pap. 14. 95 (*0-385-29560-X*) Delacorte.

—Wildlife. (gr. k-12). 1988. pap. 2.95 (*0-440-20151-9*, LE) Dell.

—Workin' for Peanuts. LC 82-14070. 192p. (gr. 7 up). 1983. pap. 12.95 (*0-385-29236-8*) Delacorte.

—Workin' for Peanuts. 208p. (Orig.). (gr. 7-12). 1984. pap. 2.95 (*0-440-99682-1*, LFL) Dell.

Strasser, Todd, adapted by. Honey, I Blew up the Kid. LC 91-58789. (Illus.). 224p. (gr. 6 up). 1992. pap. 3.50 (*1-56282-204-7*) Disney Pr.

—Lady & the Tramp: Illustrated Classic. Mateu, Franc, illus. LC 93-71378. 96p. 1994. 14.95 (*1-56282-613-1*); PLB 14.89 (*1-56282-615-8*) Disney Pr.

—Lady & the Tramp: Junior Novelization. LC 93-71379. (Illus.). 64p. (gr. 2-6). 1994. pap. 3.50 (*1-56282-614-X*) Disney Pr.

Strathern, Paul. Exploration by Land. LC 93-7147. (Illus.). 48p. (gr. 6 up). 1994. RSBE 15.95 (*0-02-788375-2*, New Discovery Bks) Macmillan Child Grp.

Stratton, Barbara R. What Is a Fish? (Illus.). 32p. (gr. k-4). 1991. 12.95 (*0-531-15223-5*); PLB 12.90 (*0-531-11020-6*) Watts.

Stratton, Mark, jt. auth. see Becker, Lois.

Stratton, Mark, ed. see Grimm, Jacob & Grimm, Wilhelm K.

Stratton-Porter, Gene. Freckles. 254p. 1980. Repr. PLB 21.95 (*0-89966-224-2*) Buccaneer Bks.

—The Harvester. 560p. 1977. PLB 24.95 (*0-89966-225-0*) Buccaneer Bks.

Straub, Cindie & Straub, Matthew. Mime: Basic for Beginners. (Illus., Orig.). (gr. 7-12). 1984. pap. 13.95 (*0-8238-0263-9*) Plays.

Straub, Matthew, jt. auth. see Straub, Cindie.

Strauch, Eileen W. Hey You, Sister Rose. LC 92-12170. 160p. (gr. 3 up). 1993. 13.00 (*0-688-11829-1*, Tambourine Bks) Morrow.

Strauss, Barbara & Friedland, Helen. See You Later Alligator. D'Elgin, Tershia, illus. 28p. 1986. 6.95 (*0-8431-1554-8*) Price Stern.

Strauss, Gwen. The Night Shimmy. Browne, Anthony, illus. LC 91-11294. 32p. (ps-2). 1992. 15.00 (*0-679-82384-0*); PLB 15.99 (*0-679-92384-5*) Knopf Bks Yng Read.

—Trail of Stones. Browne, Anthony, illus. LC 89-38358. 40p. 1990. 6.95 (*0-679-80582-6*); PLB 9.99 (*0-679-90582-0*) Knopf Bks Yng Read.

Strauss, Joyce. Imagine That!!! Exploring Make-Believe. Barrett, Jennifer, illus. LC 82-1089. 32p. (ps-3). 1983. 16.95 (*0-89885-128-9*); pap. 9.95 (*0-89885-306-0*) Human Sci Pr.

Strauss, Karen, jt. auth. see Gligor, Adrian.

Strauss, Larry. How to Reach Your Favorite Sports Star. (gr. 4-7). 1993. pap. 2.95 (0-307-22551-8, Golden Pr) Western Pub.
—Magic Man. 80p. (gr. 4-7). 1992. pap. 3.95 (0-929923-98-7) Lowell Hse.
Strauss, Linda. Coping When a Parent Has Cancer. Rosen, Ruth, ed. LC 88-18539. (gr. 7 up). 1988. PLB 13.95 (0-8239-0785-6) Rosen Group.
Strauss, Linda L. Alice Elizabeth Loved Surprises. (Illus.). 32p. (gr. k-3). 1993. pap. 2.99 (0-87406-653-0) Willowisp Pr.
Strauss, Lucy. The Story of Shoes. (Illus.). 32p. (gr. 1-4). 1989. PLB 15.96 (0-8172-3534-5); pap. 3.95 (0-8114-6732-5) Raintree Steck-V.
Strauss, Ruby, et al. The Hebrew Primer. Brison-Stack, Guy, illus. 128p. (Orig.). (gr. 1-6). 1985. pap. 4.95 (0-87441-392-3); tchr's guide 12.50x (0-87441-396-6) Behrman.
Strauss, Ruby G. Let's Learn the Alef Bet: Reading Readiness Book for the Hebrew Primer. Stack-Brison, Guy, illus. 94p. (gr. 4-7). 1987. pap. text ed. 4.45x (0-87441-439-3); tchr's pamphlet avail. Behrman.
Strauss, Ruby G. & Schuller, Ahuva. I Can Read Hebrew. Paiss, Jana, illus. 64p. (gr. k-2). 1982. pap. text ed. 4.25x (0-87441-358-3) Behrman.
Strauss, Ruby G., ed. see Hurwitz, Ann R. & Hurwitz, Sue.
Strauss, Susan. Coyote Stories for Children. Norman, Howard, ed. Lund, Gary, illus. 50p. (gr. 1-6). 1991. 10.95 (0-941831-61-2); pap. 6.95 (0-941831-62-0) Beyond Words Pub.
—Wolf Stories: Myths & True Life Tales from Around the World. (gr. 4-7). 1993. pap. 7.95 (0-941831-88-4) Beyond Words Pub.
Strawn, Kathy. Help! They Don't Read Yet. Gross, Karen, ed. 32p. (Orig.). (ps). 1992. pap. text ed. 3.95 (1-56309-056-2) Womans Mission Union.
—Matthew's Dad Is a Missionary. Sealy, Kathy, illus. 32p. (Orig.). (gr. 1-3). 1988. pap. 2.95 (0-936625-38-4) Womans Mission Union.
Strawn, Susan, jt. auth. see Donahue, Michael.
Strawn, Susan, jt. auth. see Opler, Paul.
Strazzabosco, Gina & Reynolds, Moira. The Telephone: Uses & Abuses. LC 93-25717. (gr. 5 up). 1993. 12.95 (0-8239-1608-1) Rosen Group.
Streatfeild, Noel. Ballet Shoes. reissue ed. Goode, Diane, illus. LC 89-24390. 288p. (gr. 4-9). 1991. gift ed. 15.00 (0-679-80105-7); lib. bdg. 16.99 gift ed. (0-679-90105-1) Random Bks Yng Read.
—Ballet Shoes. Goode, Diane, illus. LC 89-24390. 288p. (gr. 4-9). 1993. pap. 3.99 (0-679-84759-6) Random Bks Yng Read.
—Dancing Shoes. 288p. (gr. k-6). 1980. pap. 3.25 (0-440-42289-2, YB) Dell.
—Family Shoes. 224p. (gr. 5 up). 1985. pap. 3.50 (0-440-42479-8, YB) Dell.
—Gemma Alone. (Orig.). (gr. k-6). 1987. pap. 3.25 (0-440-42865-3, Yearling) Dell.
—Gemma & Sisters. (Orig.). (gr. k-6). 1987. pap. 3.25 (0-440-42862-9, YB) Dell.
—Good-Bye Gemma. (Orig.). (gr. k-6). 1987. pap. 3.25 (0-440-42871-8, YB) Dell.
—The Magic Summer. (Orig.). (gr. k-6). 1987. pap. 3.25 (0-440-45459-X, YB) Dell.
—Movie Shoes. 288p. (Orig.). (gr. 4-7). 1986. pap. 3.25 (0-440-45815-3, YB) Dell.
—Skating Shoes. (Orig.). (gr. 5 up). 1982. pap. 2.75 (0-440-47731-X, YB) Dell.
—Theater Shoes. 208p. (gr. k-6). 1983. pap. 2.95 (0-440-48791-9, YB) Dell.
—Thursday's Child. (Orig.). (gr. 5 up). 1986. pap. 3.50 (0-440-48687-4, YB) Dell.
—Traveling Shoes. 256p. (gr. 4-7). 1984. pap. 2.95 (0-440-48732-3, YB) Dell.
Streep, Meryl, read by see Potter, Beatrix.
Strege, Maxine G., jt. auth. see Loomer, Bradley M.
Streib, Sally. Treasures by the Sea. 159p. (gr. 4 up). 1991. pap. 7.95 (0-8163-0933-7) Pacific Pr Pub Assn.
Streiber, William R. & Rizzoto, Flora M. Popo: The Adventures of a Mexican Donkey. Ely, Gladys, illus. LC 70-146604. (gr. 1-4). 1971. 3.75 (0-8356-0420-9, Quest) Theos Pub Hse.
Streissguth, Thomas. Hoaxers & Hustlers. LC 93-23156. (Illus.). 160p. (gr. 5-12). 1994. PLB 14.95 (1-881508-13-7) Oliver Pr MN.
—International Terrorists. LC 92-45139. (Illus.). 160p. (gr. 5-12). 1993. PLB 14.95 (1-881508-07-2) Oliver Pr MN.
—Soviet Leaders from Lenin to Gorbachev. LC 92-19903. 160p. (gr. 5-12). 1992. PLB 14.95 (1-881508-02-1) Oliver Pr MN.
Streissguth, Tom. Say It with Music: A Story about Irving Berlin. Hagerman, Jennifer, illus. LC 93-4376. (gr. 4 up). 1993. 14.95 (0-87614-810-0) Carolrhoda Bks.
Streit, Jacob. And There Was Light. Piening, Ekkehard, tr. from GER. Turgenieff, Assja, illus. 112p. (gr. 3-4). 1976. pap. 13.00 (0-88010-034-6, Pub. by Verlag Walter Keller Switzerland) Anthroposophic.
—Animal Stories. Piening, Jacob, tr. from GER. 36p. (gr. 3-5). 1974. pap. 10.95 (0-88010-035-4, Pub. by Verlag Walter Keller Switzerland) Anthroposophic.
Streit, Robert, jt. auth. see Wirszup, Izaak.
Strejan, John. I Love to Eat Bugs: Pop-up Book. (ps). 1992. 9.95 (0-8431-3392-9) Price Stern.

Strelkoff, Tatiana. The Changer. (Illus.). 64p. (gr. 4-6). 1994. pap. 8.95

(0-945522-03-7) Rebecca Hse. THE CHANGER is about an old Choctaw, this Indian has a gift - the ability to become animals. The last of his tribe, his choice falls on Jeremy, a boy of ten who is part Choctaw to pass on this skill before Woodman's death. Jeremy meets Woodman with an open mind. As Jeremy learns how to be a changer he passes through many stages, from the initial excitement to a final realization of how great a gift he has been given - to great to ever belittle with showmanship. His life is enriched with the personal & intimate contact with the natural realm.
Publisher Provided Annotation.

Stren, P. For Sale: One Brother. Stren, P., illus. LC 91-73821. 32p. (gr. 1-4). 1993. 13.95 (1-56282-126-1); PLB 13.89 (1-56282-127-X) Hyprn Child.
Stren, Patti, jt. auth. see Wirths, Bowman-Kruhm Staff.
Strete, Craig K. Big Thunder Magic. Brown, Craig, illus. LC 89-34613. 32p. (ps up). 1990. 12.95 (0-688-08853-8); PLB 12.88 (0-688-08854-6) Greenwillow.
Stretton, Barbara. You Never Lose. 256p. (gr. 5-9). 1982. lib. bdg. 9.99 (0-394-95230-8) Knopf Bks Yng Read.
Strevens, Biddy. Toto in France. (FRE.). 32p. 1993. 12. 95 (0-685-62824-8, F9180-3, Natl Textbk) NTC Pub Grp.
Strichartz, Naomi. The Wise Woman. Moore, Ella, illus. 43p. (Orig.). (gr. 2-6). 1986. pap. 3.50 (0-9618182-0-4) Cranehill Pr.
—The Wise Woman's Sacred Wheel of the Year. Moore, Ella, illus. (Orig.). (gr. 2-6). 1988. pap. 3.50 (0-9618182-1-2) Cranehill Pr.
Strickland, A. G., jt. auth. see Shafe, James C.
Strickland, Brad. Dragon's Plunder. McCaig, Iaian, illus. LC 91-45664. 160p. (gr. 7 up). 1992. SBE 14.95 (0-689-31573-2, Atheneum Child Bk) Macmillan Child Grp.
—Stowaways. 1994. pap. 3.50 (0-671-88000-4, Minstrel Bks) PB.
Strickland, Dorothy S., ed. Listen Children, an Anthology of Black Literature. 1992. 16.50 (0-8446-6582-7) Peter Smith.
Strickland, Michael, ed. Poems That Sing to You. Leiner, Alan, illus. 64p. (gr. 5 up). 1993. 13.95 (1-56397-178-X, Wordsong) Boyds Mills Pr.
Strickland, Paul. Diggers. LC 93-12533. (Illus.). 14p. (ps). 1993. Repr. of 1986 ed. 3.50 (0-525-67453-5, Lodestar Bks) Dutton Child Bks.
—Tractors. LC 93-12540. (Illus.). 14p. (ps). 1993. Repr. of 1986 ed. 3.50 (0-525-67455-1, Lodestar Bks) Dutton Child Bks.
—Trucks. LC 93-12593. (Illus.). 14p. (ps). 1993. Repr. of 1986 ed. 3.50 (0-525-67454-3, Lodestar Bks) Dutton Child Bks.
Stricklard, Dorothy S. Listen Children. 176p. (Orig.). 1986. pap. 3.99 (0-553-27092-3) Bantam.
Stridh, Kicki. The Horrible Spookhouse. Eriksson, Eva, illus. LC 93-22076. 1993. write for info. (0-87614-811-9) Carolrhoda Bks.
Strieber, Whitley. Wolf of Shadows. LC 84-20133. (Illus.). 128p. (gr. 7-12). 1985. PLB 9.99 (0-394-97224-4) Knopf Bks Yng Read.
Striker, Susan. Anti-Coloring Book of Masterpieces. (Illus.). 96p. (Orig.). (gr. 2 up). 1982. pap. 6.95 (0-03-057874-4, Bks Young Read) H Holt & Co.
—Fourth Anti-Coloring Book. (gr. 2 up). 1981. pap. 6.95 (0-8050-2000-4, Owl) H Holt & Co.
—The Mystery-Anti-Coloring Book. (Illus.). 64p. (Orig.). (gr. 1 up). 1991. pap. 5.95 (0-8050-1600-7, Owl) H Holt & Co.
—The Newspaper Anti-Coloring Book. (Illus.). 64p. (gr. 2 up). 1992. pap. 6.95 (0-8050-1599-X, Owl) H Holt & Co.
—Third Anti-Coloring Book. 96p. (gr. 2 up). 1980. pap. 6.95 (0-8050-1447-0, Owl) H Holt & Co.
Strincer, Richard, jt. auth. see Kennon, Donald R.
Stroble, Bill. Frisky Kitties: My Book of What God Made. (ps). 1992. bds. 6.99 (1-55513-732-6) Cook.
—Hello Yellow! My Book of God's Colors. (ps). 1992. bds. 6.99 (1-55513-731-8) Cook.
Strode, William, photos by. Notre Dame: A Sense of Place. (Illus.). (gr. 9 up). 1992. pap. text ed. 21.95 (0-268-01475-2) U of Notre Dame Pr.
Stroe, Gheorghe, ed. see Smarandache, Florentin.
Stroh, R. W. Adventure in the Lost World. Mulkey, Kim, illus. LC 85-2530. 96p. (gr. 3-6). 1985. lib. bdg. 9.49 (0-8167-0535-6); pap. text ed. 2.95 (0-8167-0536-4) Troll Assocs.
Strohl, Mary, jt. auth. see Schneck, Susan.
Strom, Kay M. John Newton: The Angry Sailor. (Orig.). (gr. 2-7). 1984. pap. 4.50 (0-8024-0335-2) Moody.
Strom, Yale. A Tree Still Stands: Jewish Youth in Eastern Europe Today. Levitin, Sonia, intro. by. (Illus.). 112p. (gr. 3 up). 1990. 16.95 (0-399-22154-9, Philomel Bks) Putnam Pub Group.

—Uncertain Roads: Searching for the Gypsies. Strom, Yale, illus. LC 93-21962. 112p. (gr. 4-7). 1993. pap. 19.95 SBE (0-02-788531-3, Four Winds) Macmillan Child Grp.
Strombeck, Janet A. & Strombeck, Richard H. Making Timeless Toys in Wood: Quality Strom Toys & Plans. (Illus.). 96p. (Orig.). (gr. 10-12). 1986. pap. 9.95 (0-912355-05-0) Sun Designs.
Strombeck, Richard H., jt. auth. see Strombeck, Janet A.
Strommen, Judith B. Champ Hobarth. 160p. (gr. 4-6). 1993. PLB 14.95 (0-8050-2414-X, Bks Young Read) H Holt & Co.
—Grady the Great. 160p. (gr. 4-6). 1990. 13.95 (0-8050-1405-5, Bks Young Read) H Holt & Co.
—Johnson Falls Story. 1994. write for info. (0-8050-2415-8) H Holt & Co.
Stronck, David. Alcohol-The Real Story. Nelson, Mary & Clark, Kay, eds. Ransom, Robert D., illus. 30p. (gr. 5-8). 1987. pap. text ed. 2.95 (0-941816-35-4) ETR Assocs.
—Marijuana - The Real Story. Nelson, Mary & Clark, Kay, eds. Ransom, Robert D., illus. 30p. (gr. 5-8). 1987. pap. text ed. 2.95 (0-941816-36-2) ETR Assocs.
—Tobacco - The Real Story. Nelson, Mary & Clark, Kay, eds. Ransom, Robert D., illus. 30p. (gr. 5-8). 1987. pap. text ed. 2.95 (0-941816-34-6) ETR Assocs.
Strong & Guastella. Wandering Through the Wild Nature Mazes. 1992. pap. 2.50 (0-590-45016-6) Scholastic Inc.
Strong, Bryan & DeVault, Christine. Christy's Chance. Nelson, Mary, ed. Ransom, Robert D., illus. 72p. (gr. 5-8). 1987. pap. text ed. 3.95 (0-941816-33-8) ETR Assocs.
—Danny's Dilemma. Nelson, Mary, ed. Ransom, Robert D., illus. (gr. 5-8). 1987. pap. 3.95 (0-941816-31-1) ETR Assocs.
—Serena's Secret. Nelson, Mary, ed. Ransom, Robert, illus. (gr. 5-8). 1987. pap. 3.95 (0-941816-32-X) ETR Assocs.
Strong, Mary, jt. auth. see Neamen, Mimi.
Strong, Polly. African Tales: Folklore of the Central African Republic. Strong, Polly, tr. from SAG. Wimer, Rodney, illus. LC 91-66693. 96p. (gr. 2 up). 1992. 10. 95 (1-878893-15-7); pap. 6.95 (1-878893-14-9) Telcraft Bks.
Strong, Sarah M., tr. see Kenji, Miyazawa.
Strong, Stacie. Barbie Rockin' Rappin' Dancin' World Tour Pop-up Book. Duarte, Pamela, illus. 12p. (ps-2). 1992. write for info. (0-307-16560-4, 16560, Golden Pr) Western Pub.
—Who Makes This? Etow, Carole, illus. 8p. (ps). 1992. 5.95 (0-8431-2997-2) Price Stern.
Strong, Stacie & Butler, John. Animal Families of the Forest. Butler, John, illus. 6p. (gr. 1-6). 1993. 14.99 (0-8431-3391-0) Price Stern.
Strong, Stacie, jt. auth. see Rojany, Lisa.
Strong, W. M., tr. see Lecomte, Eva.
Strother, Deborah B., ed. see Christen, William & Murphy, Thomas.
Strother, William C., ed. see Christen, William & Murphy, Thomas.
Stroud, Virginia A. Doesn't Fall off His Horse. (Illus.). 1994. write for info. (0-8037-1634-6); PLB write for info. (0-8037-1635-4) Dial Bks Young.
Stroyer, Paul. It's a Deal. (Illus.). (gr. k-3). 1960. 10.95 (0-8392-3013-3) Astor-Honor.
—Second Treasure Chest of Tales. (Illus.). (gr. 3 up). 1960. 12.95 (0-8392-3032-X) Astor-Honor.
—Treasure Chest of Tales. (Illus.). (gr. 3 up). 1959. 12.95 (0-8392-3039-7) Astor-Honor.
Strub, Susanne. My Cat & I. Strub, Susanne, illus. LC 92-21839. 32p. (ps up). 1993. 14.00 (0-688-12008-3, Tambourine Bks); PLB 13.93 (0-688-12009-1, Tambourine Bks) Morrow.
—My Dog, My Sister, & I (Mon Chien, Ma Soeur, et Moi) Strub, Susanne, illus. LC 92-22063. (ENG & FRE.). 32p. (ps up). 1993. 14.00 (0-688-12010-5, Tambourine Bks); PLB 13.93 (0-688-12011-3, Tambourine Bks) Morrow.
Struble, Steve. To See or Not to See. Pohl, Kathy, ed. Garcia, Tom, illus. LC 85-15487. 32p. (gr. 2-4). 1986. PLB 17.96 (0-8172-2700-8) Raintree Steck-V.
Struik, Dirk J. Concise History of Mathematics. 4th, rev. ed. (Illus.). (gr. 7-12). 1987. pap. text ed. 7.95 (0-486-60255-9) Dover.
Strydesky, Rebecca, jt. auth. see Moffett, Carol G.
Stryker & Bingham. Mother Nature Nursery Rhymes. Paine, ed. Itoko Maeno, illus. 32p. (ps-6). 1990. 14.95 (0-911655-01-8) Advocacy Pr.
Stryker, Sandra, ed. see Rosentheil, Agnes.
Stryker, Sandy. Tonia the Tree. LC 88-16769. (Illus.). 32p. (gr. k-8). 1988. 14.95 (0-911655-16-6) Advocacy Pr.
Stryker, Sandy, jt. auth. see Bingham, Mindy.
Stryker, Sandy, ed. see Paine, Penelope C.
Stuart, Alexander & Vendrell, Carme S. Joe, Jo-Jo & the Monkey Masks. (Illus.). 32p. (gr. 1-4). 1989. 13.95 (0-86264-199-3, Pub. by Anderson Pr UK) Trafalgar.
Stuart, David. Calligraphy, A to Z. LC 84-16380. (Illus.). 208p. (gr. 9-12). 1985. 17.95 (0-87396-088-2) Stravon.
Stuart, Dee. The Astonishing Armadillo. LC 92-25970. 1993. 19.95 (0-87614-769-4) Carolrhoda Bks.
Stuart, Doris. All Aboard! Bracken, Carolyn, illus. LC 87-81766. 22p. (ps). 1988. write for info. (0-307-12117-8, Pub. by Golden Bks) Western Pub.

Stuart, Gene S. Animal Families. (Illus.). (gr. k-4). 1990. Set. 13.95 (*0-87044-819-6*); lib. bdg. 16.95 (*0-87044-824-2*) Natl Geog.
—Secrets from the Past. Crump, Donald J., ed. LC 79-1790. (Illus.). (gr. 3-8). 1979. 8.95 (*0-87044-316-X*); PLB 12.50 (*0-87044-321-6*) Natl Geog.
—Wildlife Alert. LC 79-1792. (Illus.). 104p. (gr. 3-8). 1980. 8.95 (*0-87044-318-6*); PLB 12.50 (*0-87044-323-2*) Natl Geog.
Stuart, Jesse. Andy Finds a Way. rev. ed. Herndon, Jerry A., ed. & intro. by. LC 91-41495. (Illus.). 96p. (gr. 3-6). 1992. 12.00 (*0-945084-25-0*); pap. 6.00 (*0-945084-26-9*) J Stuart Found.
—The Beatinest Boy. Miller, Jim W., et al, eds. Henneberger, Robert, illus. Zornes, Rocky, contrib. by. (Illus.). 80p. (gr. 3-6). 1989. 10.00 (*0-945084-12-9*); pap. 5.00 (*0-945084-13-7*) J Stuart Found.
—Hie to the Hunters. 5th ed. Herndon, Jerry A. & Zornes, Rockyintro. by. LC 93-20063. 270p. (gr. 8 up). 1988. 20.00 (*0-945084-06-4*) J Stuart Found.
—A Jesse Stuart Reader. 4th ed. Bogart, Max & DeMers, Ellafrwd. by. 344p. (gr. 8 up). 1988. Repr. of 1963 ed. text ed. 20.00 (*0-945084-05-6*) J Stuart Found.
—Kentucky Is My Land. Miller, Jim W., afterword by. LC 92-779. 107p. (gr. 10 up). 1987. Repr. of 1952 ed. 10.95 (*0-945084-01-3*) J Stuart Found.
—Old Ben. rev. ed. Gifford, James M. & Charles, Chuck D., eds. Cuffari, Richard, illus. LC 91-35578. 64p. (gr. 3-6). 1992. 10.00 (*0-945084-22-6*); pap. 3.00 (*0-945084-23-4*) J Stuart Found.
—A Penny's Worth of Character. Miller, Jim W., et al, eds. Zornes, Rocky, illus. 62p. (gr. 3-6). 1988. 10.00 (*0-945084-03-X*) J Stuart Found.
—A Penny's Worth of Character. 3rd ed. Miller, Jim W. & Herndon, Jerry A., eds. Zornes, Rocky, illus. LC 92-31438. 62p. (gr. 3-6). 1993. pap. 3.00 (*0-945084-32-3*) J Stuart Found.
—Plowshare in Heaven. 2nd ed. Herndon, Jerry A., et al, eds. LC 90-62718. (Illus.). 268p. (gr. 7 up). 1991. Repr. of 1958 ed. 20.00 (*0-945084-21-8*) J Stuart Found.
—Red Mule. 2nd ed. Herndon, Jerry A., ed. LC 92-31439. (Illus.). 96p. (gr. 3-6). 1993. 12.00 (*0-945084-34-X*); pap. text ed. 6.00 (*0-945084-33-1*) J Stuart Found.
—A Ride with Huey the Engineer. 3rd ed. Zornes, Rocky, illus. Gifford, James M., intro. by. (Illus.). 112p. (gr. 3 up). 1988. 12.00 (*0-945084-11-0*); pap. 6.00 (*0-945084-10-2*) J Stuart Found.
—The Rightful Owner. 2nd ed. Miller, Jim W., et al, eds. Henneberger, Robert, illus. Zornes, Rocky, contrib. by. (Illus.). 95p. (gr. 3-6). 1989. 12.00 (*0-945084-14-5*); pap. 6.00 (*0-945084-15-3*) J Stuart Found.
—Split Cherry Tree. rev. ed. Gifford, James M., et al, eds. Wise, Pamela, designed by. LC 90-62198. 56p. (gr. 7 up). 1990. pap. 3.00 (*0-945084-20-X*) J Stuart Found.
—Strength from the Hills: The Story of Mick Stuart, My Father. rev. ed. Gifford, James M., intro. by. LC 92-3995. (Illus.). 175p. (gr. 3 up). 1992. Repr. of 1968 ed. 12.00 (*0-945084-29-3*) J Stuart Found.
—To Teach, To Love. LeMaster, J. R., intro. by. LC 92-808. 317p. (gr. 10 up). 1987. Repr. of 1970 ed. 20.00 (*0-945084-02-1*) J Stuart Found.
—The Year of My Rebirth. 2nd ed. Gifford, James M. & Cunningham, Donald H., eds. Foster, Ruel E., intro. by. LC 90-62357. 392p. (gr. 7 up). 1991. 24.00 (*0-945084-17-X*) J Stuart Found.
Stuart, Marion W. Subtraction Wrap-ups: Individual Sets. (gr. 1-3). Date not set. text ed. write for info. learning aid (*0-943343-02-X*) Lrn Wrap-Ups.
Stuart, Nik, jt. auth. see Murdock, Tony.
Stuart, Pamela B. The Federal Trade Commission. (Illus.). 112p. (gr. 5 up). 1991. 14.95 (*1-55546-114-X*) Chelsea Hse.
Stuart, Sally E. & Young, Woody. One-Hundred Plus Party Games. Dongarra, Kathryn, ed. White, Craig, illus. 96p. (Orig.). 1988. pap. text ed. 7.95 (*0-939513-61-7*) Joy Pub SJC.
Stuart, Sally E. & Young, Woody C. One Hundred Plus Craft & Gift Ideas: Fun & Easy Ideas for Any Occasion. White, Craig, illus. 96p. (Orig.). (gr. 1 up). 1990. pap. 9.95 (*0-939513-62-5*) Joy Pub SJC.
Stuart, Sandra L. Why Do I Have to Wear Glasses? Robins, Arthur, illus. 48p. 1989. 12.00 (*0-8184-0477-9*) Carol Pub Group.
Stuart, W. J. Forbidden Planet. 212p. (gr. 5 up). 1990. pap. 3.95 (*0-374-42445-4*, Sunburst) FS&G.
Stuart-Clark, Christopher, jt. auth. see Harrison, Michael.
Stuart-Clark, Christopher, jt. ed. see Harrison, Michael.
Stubblefield, Fern. Tim & His Lamp. 52p. (gr. k-6). pap. 0.40 (*0-686-29170-0*); pap. 1.00 3 copies (*0-686-29171-9*) Faith Pub Hse.
Stubbs, Harriett, jt. auth. see Hessler, Edward W.
Stubbs, Harriett, et al. Acid Rain Curriculum. Flor, Dick, illus. (Orig.). (gr. 4-8). 1985. tchrs' ed. 19.95 (*0-935577-00-9*) Acid Rain Found.
Stubbs, Harriett S., et al. Acid Rain Reader. Eclov, Homer, illus. 20p. (Orig.). (gr. 4-8). 1989. pap. 5.95 (*0-935577-12-2*); pap. 2.50 (*0-685-17881-1*) Acid Rain Found.
Stuchbury, Dianne. Listen! Stuchbury, Dianne, illus. 24p. (ps-1). 1991. 4.99 (*0-7459-2001-2*) Lion USA.
—Look! Stuchbury, Dianne, illus. 24p. (ps-1). 1991. 4.99 (*0-7459-2000-4*) Lion USA.

—Taste & Smell! Stuchbury, Dianne, illus. 24p. (ps-1). 1991. 4.99 (*0-7459-2003-9*) Lion USA.
—Touch! Stuchbury, Dianne, illus. 24p. (ps-1). 1991. 4.99 (*0-7459-2002-0*) Lion USA.
Stuckey, Liz. One Hundred One Traditional Christmas Gifts. (Illus.). 144p. (gr. 6 up). 1992. 24.95 (*0-7153-9943-8*, Pub. by David & Charles Pub UK) Sterling.
Stucky, Naomi R. Sara's Summer. 144p. (Orig.). (gr. 6-12). 1990. pap. 5.95 (*0-8361-3534-2*) Herald Pr.
Studies & Research Unit of Wamy Staff. Principles of Dialogue. Al-Johani, Maneh, intro. by. (ARA.). 79p. Date not set. pap. write for info. (*1-882837-00-2*) Wamy Intl.
Studio D Staff. Fantastic Book of Picture Puzzles. LC 88-38022. (Illus.). 128p. (gr. 3-10). 1989. pap. 4.95 (*0-8069-6961-X*) Sterling.
Stufgis, Matthew. Tosca's Surprise. Mortimer, Anne, illus. 32p. (ps-3). 1994. pap. 4.50 (*0-14-055270-7*, Puffin Pied Piper) Puffin Bks.
Stuhlman, Daniel D. My Own Hanukah Story. Kuppersmith-Krause, Molly B., illus. (Orig.). (ps-5). 1980. pap. 3.95 personalized version (*0-934402-07-8*); decorations 1.00 (*0-934402-08-6*); trade version 2.50 (*0-934402-12-4*) BYLS Pr.
—My Own Pesah Story. Klugman, Micha, illus. (Orig.). (gr. 1-6). 1981. Personalized Version. pap. 3.95x (*0-934402-09-4*); Trade Version. pap. 3.00 (*0-934402-10-8*); Seder cards 1.50 (*0-934402-11-6*) BYLS Pr.
Stuhring, Celeste. Kid Sitter Basics: A Handbook for Babysitters. (Illus.). 88p. 1994. pap. 9.95 (*0-933701-62-4*) Westport Pubs.
Stull, Donald D., ed. On the Banks of the Grasshopper: Oral Traditions of the Kansas Kickapoo. Thomas, Fred, frwd. by. (Illus.). 82p. (Orig.). (gr. 7-12). 1984. pap. text ed. 7.95 (*0-317-13553-8*) Kickapoo Tribal.
Stull, Elizabeth C. Children's Books Activities Kit. 256p. (gr. 1-3). 1988. pap. 24.95x (*0-87628-014-9*) Ctr Appl Res.
Stump, Gladys S. Elisha's Room. (Illus.). (gr. 1). 1978. pap. 1.95 (*0-8127-0162-3*) Review & Herald.
—Paul. (Illus.). (gr. 1). 1978. pap. 1.95 (*0-8127-0165-8*) Review & Herald.
Stumpf, George, jt. auth. see Sherrard, Raymond.
Stupple, Deborah, tr. see Razvan.
Sturgeon, Theodore, jt. auth. see Asimov, Isaac.
Sturges, Jo. France. LC 92-35182. (Illus.). 32p. (gr. 4 up). 1993. RSBE 13.95 (*0-89686-778-1*, Crestwood Hse) Macmillan Child Grp.
Sturgis, Alexander. Introducing Rembrandt. LC 93-11418. (gr. 4 up). 1994. 15.95 (*0-316-82022-9*) Little.
Sturgis, Kent. Four Generations on the Yukon. LC 87-83743. (Illus.). 80p. (Orig.). (gr. 9-12). 1988. pap. 15.95 (*0-945397-01-1*) Epicenter Pr.
Sturgis, Matthew. Tosca's Christmas. Mortimer, Anne, illus. 1989. 11.95 (*0-8037-0722-3*) Dial Bks Young.
—Tosca's Christmas. Mortimer, Anne, illus. 32p. (ps-3). 1992. pap. 3.99 (*0-14-054840-8*, Puffin Pied Piper) Puffin Bks.
—Tosca's Surprise. Mortimer, Anne, illus. LC 90-38731. 32p. (ps-3). 1991. 11.95 (*0-8037-0946-3*) Dial Bks Young.
Sturkie, Joan. Listening with Love: True Stories from Peer Counseling. rev. ed. Edwards, Sarah, ed. LC 89-38311. 264p. (gr. 9-12). 1989. 17.95 (*0-89390-151-2*); pap. 11.95 (*0-89390-150-4*) Resource Pubns.
Sturkie, Joan & Cassady, Marsh. Acting It Out Junior. LC 92-29698. 264p. 1992. 15.95 (*0-89390-240-3*) Resource Pubns.
Sturman, Susan. Kansas City. LC 90-25614. (Illus.). 60p. (gr. 3 up). 1990. RSBE 13.95 (*0-87518-432-4*, Dillon) Macmillan Child Grp.
Sturrock, Walt, illus. Aesop's Fables. 48p. (ps-3). 1992. 5.95 (*0-88101-262-9*) Unicorn Pub.
—Ghosts. 160p. 1990. 14.95 (*0-88101-269-6*) Unicorn Pub.
Stutchner, Joan B. A Peanut Butter Waltz. Durrand, Diana, illus. 24p. (Orig.). (ps-2). 1990. pap. 0.99 (*1-55037-126-6*, Pub. by Annick CN) Firefly Bks Ltd.
Stutson, Caroline. On the River ABC. Crum, Anna M., illus. LC 92-61907. 32p. (gr. k-3). 1993. lib. bdg. 12.95 (*1-879373-46-7*) R Rinehart.
Stwertka, Albert. Superconductors: The Irresistible Future. LC 90-19309. (Illus.). 96p. (gr. 7-9). 1991. PLB 12.90 (*0-531-12526-2*) Watts.
Stwertka, Albert, jt. auth. see Stwertka, Eve.
Stwertka, Eve. Drip Drop Waters Journey. (gr. 4-7). 1990. lib. bdg. 5.95 (*0-671-69462-6*, J Messner) S&S Trade.
—Duke Ellington: A Life of Music. LC 93-21267. 1994. write for info. (*0-531-13035-5*) Watts.
—Heat Lights & Action. 1991. lib. bdg. 5.95 (*0-671-69464-2*, J Messner) S&S Trade.
—Hello Hello. 1991. lib. bdg. 5.95 (*0-671-69465-0*, J Messner) S&S Trade.
—Psychoanalysis: From Freud to the Age of Therapy. Kline, M., ed. LC 87-7357. (Illus.). 96p. (gr. 7-9). 1988. PLB 10.90 (*0-531-10481-8*) Watts.
—Rachel Carson. LC 90-13092. (Illus.). 64p. (gr. 3-6). 1991. PLB 12.90 (*0-531-20020-5*) Watts.
Stwertka, Eve & Stwertka, Albert. Cleaning Up: How Trash Becomes Treasure. Dolobowsky, Mena, illus. LC 91-28777. 40p. (gr. 2-5). 1993. lib. bdg. 10.98 (*0-671-69461-8*, J Messner); pap. 5.95 (*0-671-69467-7*, J Messner) S&S Trade.

—Genetic Engineering. rev. ed. LC 89-5808. (Illus.). 144p. (gr. 10 up). 1989. PLB 13.90 (*0-531-10775-2*) Watts.
—Make It Graphic: Drawing Graphs for Science & Social Studies Projects. 64p. (gr. 4 up). 1985. lib. bdg. 9.29 (*0-671-54288-5*, J Messner) S&S Trade.
—Microscope: How to Use It & Enjoy It. LC 88-23127. (Illus.). (gr. 4-7). 1988. lib. bdg. 9.98 (*0-671-63705-3*, J Messner); pap. 4.95 (*0-671-67060-3*) S&S Trade.
—Tuning in the Sounds of the Radio: The Sounds of the Radio. Dolobowsky, Mena, illus. LC 91-16058. 40p. (gr. 2-5). 1993. lib. bdg. 10.98 (*0-671-69460-X*, J Messner); pap. 5.95 (*0-671-69466-9*, J Messner) S&S Trade.
Styles, Morag, jt. ed. see Steele, Susanna.
Styx, Sherrie A. Genealogy Just for Kids! (Illus.). 28p. (gr. k-4). 1989. wkbk. 2.50 (*1-882121-25-2*) Styx Enter.
—Our Colorful Family Tree. (Illus.). 10p. (ps-2). 1989. write for info. (*1-882121-00-7*) Styx Enter.
Su, Lucy. Jinzi & Minzi Are Friends. Su, Lucy, illus. LC 91-58733. 24p. (ps up). 1992. 5.95 (*1-56402-051-7*) Candlewick Pr.
—Jinzi & Minzi at the Playground. Su, Lucy, illus. LC 91-58740. 24p. (ps up). 1992. 5.95 (*1-56402-052-5*) Candlewick Pr.
—Ten Little Teddies. LC 93-24148. 1994. write for info. (*1-56402-251-X*) Candlewick Pr.
Suarez, Diana. Color & Discover: A Children's Guide to the North Carolina Museum of Art. Fender, Susan, illus. LC 87-62986. 40p. (Orig.). (ps-6). 1987. pap. 3.50 (*0-88259-956-9*) NCMA.
Suarez, Maribel. La Letras: The Letters. (Illus.). 14p. (ps-1). 1990. 10.75 (*970-05-0094-2*) Hispanic Bk Dist.
Succot, Eliyah, tr. see Nachman of Breslov.
Succot, Miriam, tr. see Nachman of Breslov.
Suetake, Kunihiro, jt. auth. see Cassedy, Sylvia.
Sueur, Meridel Le see Le Sueur, Meridel.
Sueyoshi, Akiko, jt. auth. see Barnes, Jill.
Sufrin, Mark. F. Scott Fitzgerald. LC 93-17767. 160p. (gr. 6 up). 1994. SBE 14.95 (*0-689-31810-3*, Atheneum Child Bk) Macmillan Child Grp.
—George Bush: The Story of the Forty-First President of the United States. (gr. 5 up). 1989. 12.95 (*0-440-50158-X*) Delacorte.
—George Catlin: Painter of the Indian West. Catlin, George, illus. LC 90-19813. 160p. (gr. 5). 1991. SBE 14.95 (*0-689-31608-9*, Atheneum Child Bk) Macmillan Child Grp.
—Payton. LC 88-15751. (Illus.). 160p. (gr. 7 up). 1988. SBE 13.95 (*0-684-18940-2*, Scribners Young Read) Macmillan Child Grp.
—Stephen Crane. LC 91-47896. (Illus.). 160p. (gr. 7 up). 1992. SBE 13.95 (*0-689-31669-0*, Atheneum Child Bk) Macmillan Child Grp.
Sugarman, Joan, jt. auth. see Freeman, Grace.
Sugimoto, Etsu I. Daughter of the Samurai. LC 66-15849. (gr. 9 up). 1966. pap. 14.95 (*0-8048-1655-7*) C E Tuttle.
Sugimura, et al. American-Japanese Coloring & Talking Books, Bks. 6-10. (gr. k-4). pap. 1.95 ea.; Bk. 6, Customs. (*0-8048-0012-X*); Bk. 7, Dressing. (*0-8048-0013-8*); Bk. 8, Riding. (*0-8048-0017-0*) Vk. 9, Houses. (*0-8048-0016-2*); Bk. 10, Story Book Heroes. (*0-8048-0019-7*) C E Tuttle.
Sugita, Yutaka. Goodnight, One, Two, Three. Sugita, Yutaka, illus. LC 76-149045. 32p. (ps-2). 9.95 (*0-87592-022-5*) Scroll Pr.
Suhl, Yuri. Uncle Misha's Partisans: The Story of Young Freedom Fighters in Nazi-Occupied Europe. LC 88-63666. 211p. (gr. 2-10). 1988. pap. 7.95 (*0-933503-23-7*) Shapolsky Pubs.
Suhr, Mandy. How I Breathe. (ps-3). 1992. 13.50 (*0-87614-736-8*) Carolrhoda Bks.
—How I Breathe. (ps-3). Date not set. pap. 5.95 (*0-87614-593-4*) Carolrhoda Bks. Postponed.
—I am Growing. (ps-3). 1992. 13.50 (*0-87614-734-1*) Carolrhoda Bks.
—I Am Growing. (ps-3). Date not set. pap. 5.95 (*0-87614-594-2*) Carolrhoda Bks. Postponed.
—I Can Move. (ps-3). 1992. 13.50 (*0-87614-735-X*) Carolrhoda Bks.
—I Can Move. (ps-3). Date not set. pap. 5.95 (*0-87614-595-0*) Carolrhoda Bks. Postponed.
—When I Eat. (ps-3). 1992. 13.50 (*0-87614-737-6*) Carolrhoda Bks.
—When I Eat. (ps-3). Date not set. pap. 5.95 (*0-87614-596-9*) Carolrhoda Bks. Postponed.
Suib, Leonard & Broadman, Muriel. Marionettes: How to Make & Perform with Them. (gr. 5 up). 17.75 (*0-8446-6409-X*) Peter Smith.
Suid, Anna. Holiday Crafts. 64p. (gr. k-2). 1985. 6.95 (*0-912107-31-6*) Monday Morning Bks.
Suid, Annalisa. Learn to Recycle. (Illus.). 48p. (ps-6). 1993. pap. 9.95 (*1-878279-49-1*) Monday Morning Bks.
—Love the Earth. (Illus.). 48p. (gr. 1-3). 1993. pap. 9.95 (*1-878279-48-3*) Monday Morning Bks.
—Save the Animals. (Illus.). 48p. (gr. 1-3). 1993. pap. 9.95 (*1-878279-46-7*) Monday Morning Bks.
Suid, Murray. Cooperative Language Arts. 128p. (gr. 2-6). 1993. 12.95 (*1-878279-51-3*) Monday Morning Bks.
—Cooperative Research & Reports. 128p. (gr. 2-6). 1993. 12.95 (*1-878279-50-5*) Monday Morning Bks.
—Demonic Mnemonics. LC 80-82982. (gr. 5-12). 1981. pap. 9.95 (*0-8224-6464-0*) Fearon Teach Aids.

—For the Love of Research. (Illus.). 64p. (gr. 4-6). 1986. pap. 6.95 (*0-912107-50-2*) Monday Morning Bks.
—For the Love of Sentences. 64p. (gr. 4-6). 1986. 6.95 (*0-912107-51-0*) Monday Morning Bks.
—For the Love of Stories. 64p. (gr. 4-6). 1986. 6.95 (*0-912107-49-9*) Monday Morning Bks.
—For the Love of Words. 112p. (gr. 2-6). 1983. 9.95 (*0-912107-02-2*) Monday Morning Bks.
—Greeting Cards. 64p. (gr. 2-6). 1988. 6.95 (*0-912107-74-X*, MM981) Monday Morning Bks.
—How to Be President of the U. S. A. Barr, Marilynn G., illus. 80p. (Orig.). (gr. 3-8). 1992. pap. text ed. 9.95 (*1-878279-47-5*, MM1963) Monday Morning Bks.
—The Teacher-Friendly Computer Book. (Illus.). 96p. (gr. 2-6). 1984. pap. 8.95 (*0-912107-19-7*) Monday Morning Bks.
—Writing Hangups. 64p. (gr. 2-6). 1988. 6.95 (*0-912107-73-1*, MM980) Monday Morning Bks.
Suid, Murray & Lincoln, Wanda. Book Factory. Levine, Lisa, illus. 64p. (gr. 2-6). 1988. pap. 6.95 (*0-912107-72-3*) Monday Morning Bks.
—Ten-Minute Language Warm-ups. (Illus.). 128p. (gr. 2-6). 1992. pap. 11.95 (*1-878279-38-6*) Monday Morning Bks.
—Ten-Minute Thinking Tie-Ins. (Illus.). 128p. (gr. 2-6). 1992. pap. 11.95 (*1-878279-39-4*) Monday Morning Bks.
Suid, Murray, jt. auth. see Lincoln, Wanda.
Suid, Murray, et al. For the Love of Editing. (Illus.). 112p. (gr. 2-6). 1983. pap. 9.95 (*0-912107-00-6*) Monday Morning Bks.
Suire, Diane, compiled by. Monster Jokes. Hunter, Llyn, illus. LC 88-17487. 48p. (gr. 1-5). 1988. pap. 3.95 (*0-516-41866-1*) Childrens.
Suire, Diane D. Polka-Dot Puppy's Birthday: A Book about Colors. Hohag, Linda, illus. LC 88-10937. 32p. (ps-2). 1988. PLB 21.35 (*0-89565-381-8*); PLB 14.95s.p. (*0-685-55927-0*) Childs World.
—Seasons. Connelly, Gwen, illus. LC 89-773. 32p. (gr. k-3). 1989. PLB 21.35 (*0-89565-503-9*); PLB 14.95s.p. (*0-685-56083-X*) Childs World.
Suire, Diane D., ed. Family. Hohag, Linda, illus. LC 89-772. 32p. (gr. k-3). 1989. PLB 21.35 (*0-89565-504-7*); PLB 14.95s.p. (*0-685-56015-5*) Childs World.
Suire, Diane D., tr. see Andersen, Hans Christian.
Suire, Diane D., tr. see Browning, Robert.
Suire, Diane D., tr. see Jose, Eduard.
Suire, Diane D., tr. see Perrault, Charles.
Sullivan. Mr. President: A Book of U. S. Presidents. 1993. pap. 2.95 (*0-590-46540-6*) Scholastic Inc.
Sullivan, Ann. Molly Maguire: Wide Receiver. 112p. (Orig.). 1992. pap. 2.99 (*0-380-76114-9*, Camelot) Avon.
Sullivan Associates Staff. I Can Read, 8 bks. (gr. k-1). 1992. Set. pap. 36.00 (*0-8449-2998-0*) Good Morn Tchr.
Sullivan, Charles. Alphabet Animals. 1991. 15.95 (*0-8478-1377-0*) Rizzoli Intl.
—Circus. LC 92-19430. (Illus.). 48p. 1992. 15.95 (*0-8478-1604-4*) Rizzoli Intl.
—Cowboys. LC 92-42980. (Illus.). 48p. 1993. 17.95 (*0-8478-1680-X*) Rizzoli Intl.
—Numbers at Play: A Counting Book. LC 91-33154. (Illus.). 48p. (ps-2). 1992. 15.95 (*0-8478-1501-3*) Rizzoli Intl.
Sullivan, Charles, ed. Children of Promise: African-American Literature & Art for Young People. Campbell, Mary S., frwd. by. (Illus.). 128p. 1991. 24. 95 (*0-8109-3170-2*) Abrams.
—Imaginary Gardens: American Poetry & Art for Young People. (Illus.). 112p. 1989. 19.95 (*0-8109-1130-2*) Abrams.
Sullivan, Debbie & Renfro, Nancy. Pocketful of Puppets: Activities for the Special Child. (Illus.). 48p. (Orig.). (ps-4). 1982. pap. 9.95 (*0-931044-07-3*) Renfro Studios.
Sullivan, Debbie, jt. auth. see Renfro, Nancy.
Sullivan, Dianna. Christmas Activities from Around the World. Walhood, Darlene, illus. 48p. (gr. 1-4). 1985. wkbk. 5.95 (*1-55734-008-0*) Tchr Create Mat.
—Literature Activities for Young Children. Pence, Nedra, illus. 96p. (ps-1). 1989. wkbk. 9.95 (*1-55734-300-4*) Tchr Create Mat.
—Literature Activities for Young Children. Pence, Nedra, illus. 96p. (ps-1). 1989. wkbk. 9.95 (*1-55734-301-2*) Tchr Create Mat.
—Literature Activities for Young Children. Pence, Nedra, illus. 96p. (ps-1). 1989. wkbk. 9.95 (*1-55734-302-0*) Tchr Create Mat.
—Literature Activities for Young Children. Pence, Nedra, illus. 96p. (ps-1). 1989. wkbk. 9.95 (*1-55734-303-9*) Tchr Create Mat.
—Literature Activities for Young Children. Spears, Diane S., illus. 96p. (ps-1). 1990. wkbk. 9.95 (*1-55734-304-7*) Tchr Create Mat.
—Literature Activities for Young Children. Pence, Nedra L., illus. 96p. (ps-1). 1990. wkbk. 9.95 (*1-55734-305-5*) Tchr Create Mat.
—Literature Activities for Young Children. Pence, Nedra L., illus. 96p. (ps-1). 1990. wkbk. 9.95 (*1-55734-306-3*) Tchr Create Mat.
—Literature Activities for Young Children. Pence, Nedra L., illus. 96p. (ps-1). 1990. wkbk. 9.95 (*1-55734-307-1*) Tchr Create Mat.
—Make Your Own Adventure Books. Ecker, Beverly, illus. 48p. (gr. 1-4). 1988. wkbk. 5.95 (*1-55734-395-0*) Tchr Create Mat.

—Make Your Own Fable & Fairy Tale Books. Ecker, Beverly, illus. 48p. (gr. 1-4). 1988. wkbk. 5.95 (*1-55734-392-6*) Tchr Create Mat.
—Make Your Own Happy Times Books. Ecker, Beverly, illus. 48p. (gr. 1-4). 1988. wkbk. 5.95 (*1-55734-394-2*) Tchr Create Mat.
—Make Your Own Holiday Books. Ecker, Beverly, illus. 48p. (gr. 1-4). 1988. wkbk. 5.95 (*1-55734-393-4*) Tchr Create Mat.
Sullivan, Dianna J. Big & Easy Art for Fall. Ecker, Beverly, illus. 48p. (ps-2). 1987. wkbk. 5.95 (*1-55734-082-X*) Tchr Create Mat.
—Big & Easy Art for Patriotic Holidays. Adkins, Lynda, illus. 48p. (ps-2). 1987. wkbk. 5.95 (*1-55734-085-4*) Tchr Create Mat.
—Big & Easy Art for Spring & Summer. Ecker, Beverly, illus. 64p. (ps-2). 1987. wkbk 6.95 (*1-55734-084-6*) Tchr Create Mat.
—Big & Easy Art for Winter. Ecker, Beverly, illus. 48p. (ps-2). 1987. wkbk. 5.95 (*1-55734-083-8*) Tchr Create Mat.
—Big & Easy Community Helpers. Adkins, Lynda, illus. 48p. (ps-2). 1988. wkbk. 5.95 (*1-55734-106-0*) Tchr Create Mat.
—Big & Easy Dinosaurs. Adkins, Lynda, illus. 48p. (ps-2). 1988. wkbk. 5.95 (*1-55734-103-6*) Tchr Create Mat.
—Big & Easy Health. Adkins, Lynda, illus. 48p. (ps-2). 1988. wkbk. 5.95 (*1-55734-104-4*) Tchr Create Mat.
—Big & Easy Science. Adkins, Lynda, illus. 48p. (ps-2). 1988. wkbk. 5.95 (*1-55734-105-2*) Tchr Create Mat.
—Decorations & Clip Art for Holidays & Everyday. Ecker, Beverly, illus. 96p. (gr. k-4). 1987. wkbk. 9.95 (*1-55734-092-7*) Tchr Create Mat.
—Gifts for Holidays & Everyday. Adkins, Lynda, illus. 96p. (gr. k-4). 1987. wkbk. 9.95 (*1-55734-091-9*) Tchr Create Mat.
—Holiday Art. Sullivan, Dianna J., illus. 48p. (gr. k-3). 1985. wkbk. 5.95 (*1-55734-007-2*) Tchr Create Mat.
—Milk Carton Art Projects. Adkins, Lynda, illus. 32p. (gr. 1-4). 1988. wkbk. 4.95 (*1-55734-099-4*) Tchr Create Mat.
—Paper Bag Art Projects. Adkins, Lynda, illus. 32p. (gr. 1-4). 1988. wkbk. 4.95 (*1-55734-100-1*) Tchr Create Mat.
—Paper Plate Art Projects. Adkins, Lynda, illus. 32p. (gr. 1-4). 1988. wkbk. 4.95 (*1-55734-101-X*) Tchr Create Mat.
—Patriotic Holidays. Walhood, Darlene, illus. 48p. (gr. 1-5). 1986. wkbk. 5.95 (*1-55734-115-X*) Tchr Create Mat.
Sullivan, Eleanor & Manson, Cynthia, eds. Tales from Ellery Queen's Mystery Magazine: Short Stories for Young Adults. Nixon, Joan L., intro. by. LC 86-7634. 256p. (gr. 7 up). 1986. 13.95 (*0-15-284205-5*, HB Juv Bks) HarBrace.
Sullivan, George. All about Baseball. (Illus.). 128p. (gr. 3 up). 1989. (Putnam); pap. 6.95 (*0-399-21734-7*, Putnam) Putnam Pub Group.
—All about Basketball. LC 91-10141. (Illus.). 1991. pap. 7.95 (*0-399-21793-2*) Putnam Pub Group.
—All about Football. (Illus.). 128p. (gr. 3-7). 1990. (Putnam); pap. 7.95 (*0-399-21907-2*, Putnam) Putnam Pub Group.
—Any Number Can Play. Caldwell, John, illus. LC 89-35501. 128p. (gr. 3-7). 1990. (Crowell Jr Bks); (Crowell Jr Bks) HarpC Child Bks.
—Baseball Kids. LC 89-29102. (Illus.). 64p. (gr. 5 up). 1990. 13.95 (*0-525-65023-7*, Cobblehill Bks) Dutton Child Bks.
—Campaigns & Elections. (Illus.). 128p. (gr. 5 up). 1991. PLB 13.98 (*0-382-24315-3*); pap. 8.95 (*0-382-24321-8*) Silver Burdett Pr.
—Center. Madden, Don, illus. LC 85-48245. 64p. (gr. 3-7). 1988. (Crowell Jr Bks); (Crowell Jr Bks) HarpC Child Bks.
—Choosing the Candidates. (Illus.). 128p. (gr. 5 up). 1991. PLB 13.98 (*0-382-24314-5*); pap. 8.95 (*0-382-24319-6*) Silver Burdett Pr.
—Complete Sports Dictionary. (gr. 4-7). 1993. pap. 3.25 (*0-590-40411-3*) Scholastic Inc.
—The Day Pearl Harbor Was Bombed. 96p. 1991. pap. 5.95 (*0-590-43449-7*) Scholastic Inc.
—The Day We Walked on the Moon. 1990. 5.95 (*0-590-45587-7*, 064) Scholastic Inc.
—Day We Walked On the Moon: A Photo History of Space Exploration. (Illus.). (gr. 3-9). 1990. 14.95 (*0-590-43632-5*); pap. 4.95 (*0-685-58532-8*) Scholastic Inc.
—Disaster! The Destruction of Our Planet. (gr. 4-7). 1992. pap. 3.25 (*0-590-44331-3*) Scholastic Inc.
—Facts & Fun about the Presidents. 96p. (Orig.). (gr. 3-7). 1987. pap. 2.50 (*0-590-44428-X*) Scholastic Inc.
—Football Kids. LC 90-33096. (Illus.). (gr. 4-7). 1990. 13. 95 (*0-525-65040-7*, Cobblehill Bks) Dutton Child Bks.
—George Bush. Steltenpohl, Jane, ed. (Illus.). 128p. (gr. 6-10). 1989. lib. bdg. 12.98 (*0-671-64599-4*, J Messner); pap. 5.95 (*0-671-67814-0*) S&S Trade.
—Great Lives: Sports. LC 88-15673. (Illus.). 288p. (gr. 4-6). 1988. SBE 22.95 (*0-684-18510-5*, Scribners Young Read) Macmillan Child Grp.
—Here Come the Monster Trucks. LC 88-38464. (Illus.). (ps-8). 1989. 15.00 (*0-525-65005-9*, Cobblehill Bks) Dutton Child Bks.
—Here Come the Monster Trucks. (Illus.). 64p. (gr. 2-6). 1992. pap. 4.99 (*0-525-65085-7*, Dutton Unicorn) Puffin Bks.

—How an Airport Really Works. LC 92-20154. 128p. (gr. 5-9). 1993. 15.99 (*0-525-67378-4*, Lodestar Bks) Dutton Child Bks.
—How Do They Package It? LC 76-18089. (Illus.). 144p. (gr. 7-9). 1976. 8.00 (*0-664-32601-3*, Westminster) Westminster John Knox.
—How the White House Really Works. 1990. pap. 3.95 (*0-590-43403-9*) Scholastic Inc.
—In-Line Skating: A Complete Guide for Beginners. LC 92-25896. (Illus.). 48p. (gr. 4 up). 1993. 13.99 (*0-525-65124-1*, Cobblehill Bks) Dutton Child Bks.
—In-Line Skating: A Complete Guide for Beginners. 48p. (gr. 4 up). 1993. pap. 4.99 (*0-14-054987-0*, Puffin Unicorn) Puffin Bks.
—Mary Lou Retton. Arico, Diane, ed. (Illus.). 64p. (Orig.). 1985. pap. 2.95 (*0-671-55472-7*) S&S Trade.
—Mathew Brady: His Life & Photographs. LC 93-28354. (Illus.). 1994. write for info. (*0-525-65186-1*, Cobblehill Bks) Dutton Child Bks.
—Mikhail Gorbachev. LC 87-20273. (Illus.). 128p. (gr. 7 up). 1988. lib. bdg. 10.98 (*0-671-63263-9*, J Messner); lib. bdg. 5.95 (*0-671-66937-0*) S&S Trade.
—Mikhail Gorbachev. rev. ed. (Illus.). 128p. (gr. 7 up). 1990. lib. bdg. 13.98 (*0-671-72913-6*, J Messner); lib. bdg. 7.95 (*0-671-72914-4*) S&S Trade.
—Modern Bombers & Attack Planes. (Illus.). 128p. (gr. 7 up). 1992. PLB 17.95x (*0-8160-2354-9*) Facts on File.
—Modern Combat Helicopters. LC 92-31492. (Illus.). 128p. (gr. 6-9). 1993. 17.95x (*0-8160-2353-0*) Facts on File.
—Modern Fighter Planes. 128p. (gr. 6-10). 1991. lib. bdg. 17.95x (*0-8160-2352-2*) Facts on File.
—Pitchers: Twenty-Seven of the Greatest Pitchers. LC 93-3007. (Illus.). 80p. (gr. 1-4). 1994. SBE 17.95 (*0-689-31825-1*, Atheneum Child Bk) Macmillan Child Grp.
—Pope John Paul II: The People's Pope. LC 83-40395. (Illus.). 120p. (gr. 7 up). 1984. 11.95 (*0-8027-6523-8*) Walker & Co.
—Racing Indy Cars. LC 91-19439. (Illus.). 64p. (gr. 4 up). 1992. 15.00 (*0-525-65082-2*, Cobblehill Bks) Dutton Child Bks.
—Ronald Reagan. LC 85-13688. (Illus.). 128p. (gr. 5 up). 1985. lib. bdg. 10.98 (*0-671-60168-7*, J Messner) S&S Trade.
—Sadat: The Man Who Changed Mid-East History. LC 81-50739. (Illus.). 99p. (gr. 6 up). 1981. reinforced bdg 9.85 (*0-8027-6435-5*) Walker & Co.
—Sluggers! Twenty-Seven of Baseball's Greatest. LC 90-45817. (Illus.). 80p. (gr. 3 up). 1991. SBE 16.95 (*0-689-31566-X*, Atheneum Child Bk) Macmillan Child Grp.
—Strange But True Stories of World War II. 128p. (gr. 5 up). 1983. 14.95 (*0-8027-6489-4*) Walker & Co.
—They Shot the President: Ten True Stories. (gr. 4-7). 1993. pap. 3.25 (*0-590-46101-X*) Scholastic Inc.
—Treasure Hunt: The Sixteen-Year Search for the Lost Treasure Ship Atocha. LC 87-8791. (Illus.). 128p. (gr. 4-6). 1987. 13.95 (*0-8050-0569-2*, Bks Young Read) H Holt & Co.
—Unsolved! 1992. pap. 2.75 (*0-590-42990-6*, Point) Scholastic Inc.
Sullivan, Jem & Dixon, Jim. Flooty Hobbs & the Giggling Jolly Gollywobber. Sullivan, Jem, illus. 36p. (gr. k-2). 1991. 12.95 (*1-880453-00-2*) J Hefty Pub.
Sullivan, Kathryn D. see McPhee, Penelope & McPhee, Raymond.
Sullivan, Leo. Afro-Classic Folk Tales, Bk. 2: Anancy & the Tiger. Stewart, Lyn, ed. Norman, Floyd, illus. 28p. (Orig.). (gr. 4-7). 1992. pap. 9.95 (*1-881368-19-X*) Vignette.
Sullivan, Leo & Norman, Floyd. Afro-Classic Folk Tales, Bk. 3: Bro Rabbit. Stewart, Lyn, ed. Sullivan, Leo, illus. 28p. (Orig.). (gr. 4-7). 1992. pap. 9.95 (*1-881368-20-3*) Vignette.
—Afro-Classic Folk Tales, Bk. 5: Anancy's Riding Horse. Stewart, Lyn, ed. Sullivan, Leo, illus. 28p. (Orig.). (gr. 4-7). 1992. pap. 9.95 (*1-881368-22-X*) Vignette.
Sullivan, Leo, jt. auth. see Norman, Floyd.
Sullivan, Leo, illus. & intro. by see Norman, Floyd.
Sullivan, Margaret. The Philippines: Pacific Crossroads. LC 92-37093. (Illus.). 128p. (gr. 4 up). 1993. RSBE 14.95 (*0-87518-548-7*, Dillon) Macmillan Child Grp.
Sullivan, Mary B. & Bourke, Linda. A Show of Hands: Say It in Sign Language. LC 84-48782. (Illus.). 96p. (gr. 2-6). 1992. PLB 13.89 (*0-06-020860-0*) HarpC Child Bks.
Sullivan, Mary B., et al. A Show of Hands: Say It in Sign Language. Bourke, Linda, illus. LC 84-48782. 96p. (gr. 2-6). 1985. pap. 4.95 (*0-06-446007-X*, Trophy) HarpC Child Bks.
Sullivan, Michael J. Chris Mullin, Star Forward. LC 93-32727. 1994. write for info. (*0-89490-486-8*) Enslow Pubs.
Sullivan, Michael J., jt. auth. see Torres, John A.
Sullivan, Mick. Spare Time Cash: Every Student's Guide to Making Money on the Side. Moe, Mary, ed. 114p. (Orig.). (gr. 10 up). 1989. pap. 12.95 (*1-878330-00-4*) Sullivan MT.
Sullivan, Norman. Brain Power. (Illus.). 128p. (gr. 10-12). 1993. pap. 4.95 (*0-7063-7130-5*, Pub. by Ward Lock UK) Sterling.
—Brain Twisters. (Illus.). 128p. (gr. 10-12). 1992. pap. 4.95 (*0-7063-7086-4*, Pub. by Ward Lock UK) Sterling.
Sullivan, S. Adams. Bats, Butterflies, & Bugs, Vol. 1. (ps-3). 1990. 14.95 (*0-316-82185-3*, Joy St Bks) Little.

Sullivan, Scott. Tough Mazes. (Illus.). 48p. (Orig.). (gr. 6 up). 1989. pap. 3.50 (*0-8431-2332-X*) Price Stern.

Sullivan, Timothy J. What Can We Learn about Radon? (Illus., Orig.). (gr. 8-9). Date not set. pap. text ed. write for info. (*1-880062-22-4*) E&S Geog & Info Servs.

Sully, Nina. Looking at Food. (Illus.). 72p. (gr. 7-12). 1984. 18.95 (*0-7134-3536-4*, Pub. by Batsford UK) Trafalgar.

—Looking at Medicine. (Illus.). 72p. (gr. 7-12). 1984. 19.95 (*0-7134-3847-9*, Pub. by Batsford UK) Trafalgar.

Sumichrast, Michael J. & Christ, Dean. Opportunities in Financial Careers. rev. ed. LC 90-50736. 160p. (gr. 7 up). 1991. 13.95 (*0-8442-8166-2*, VGM Career Bks); pap. 10.95 (*0-8442-8167-0*, VGM Career Bks) NTC Pub Grp.

Sumiko. My Summer Vacation. Sumiko, illus. LC 89-43164. 32p. (Orig.). (ps-1). 1993. pap. 2.25 (*0-679-80525-7*) Random Bks Yng Read.

Sumile, Caridad, illus. & intro. by see Guard, David.

Sumio, Uchiyama. Children of the World: India. LC 87-42577. (Illus.). 64p. (gr. 5-6). 1988. PLB 19.93 (*1-55532-208-5*) Gareth Stevens Inc.

Summer, Lila & Woods, Samuel G. The Judiciary: Laws We Live By. LC 92-15199. (Illus.). 48p. (gr. 5-6). 1992. PLB 21.34 (*0-8114-7350-3*) Raintree Steck-V.

Summerfield, C. J., ed. Career Discovery Encyclopedia, 6 vols. (Illus.). (gr. 3 up). 1993. 129.95 (*0-89434-144-8*) Ferguson.

Summers, Jack L. The Christmas People. LC 88-51480. 180p. 1988. 7.95 (*1-55523-208-6*) Winston-Derek.

Summers, Jester. Joseph: the Forgiver. (Illus.). (gr. 1-6). 1976. bds. 5.99 (*0-8054-4224-3*, 4242-24) Broadman.

—The Two Nichols: Spent for Missions. LC 81-70910. (gr. 4-6). 1982. 5.95 (*0-8054-4279-0*, 4242-79) Broadman.

Summers, Joan. God's Little Animals: Easy Illustrations & Bible Parallels. (Illus.). 32p. (gr. k-4). 1969. pap. 1.95 (*0-8243-718-6*, 02-0718) Gospel Pub.

Summers-Dawes, Kate, jt. auth. see Jackson, Daniel.

Summit Group Staff. Kids on Cooking: Favorite Original Recipes, by Kids for Kids. (ps-3). 1993. pap. 6.95 (*1-56530-099-8*) Summit TX.

—You Can Illustrate Jack & the Beanstalk. (gr. 4-7). 1993. pap. 5.95 (*1-56530-057-2*) Summit TX.

—You Can Illustrate Johnny Appleseed. (gr. 4-7). 1993. pap. 5.95 (*1-56530-055-6*) Summit TX.

—You Can Illustrate Paul Bunyan. (gr. 4-7). 1993. pap. 5.95 (*1-56530-056-4*) Summit TX.

—You Can Illustrate Rumpelstiltskin. (gr. 4-7). 1993. pap. 5.95 (*1-56530-058-0*) Summit TX.

Summitt, Pat. Women's Basketball Drills: Offensive Drills. (Orig.). (gr. 7 up). 1988. pap. 6.95 (*0-932741-57-6*) Championship Bks & Vid Prodns.

Sumner, M. C. Deadly Stranger. (gr. 9-12). 1993. pap. 3.50 (*0-06-106742-3*, Harp PBks) HarpC.

Sumner, Patricia H., jt. auth. see Bernholz, Jean F.

Sumner, Robert, ed. see Whitman, Ken & Wilkey, Chris.

Sumners, Carolyn. Toys in Space: Exploring Science with the Astronauts. LC 93-21036. 1993. 17.95 (*0-8306-4533-0*); pap. 9.70 (*0-8306-4534-9*) TAB Bks.

Sumption, Christine & Thompson, Kathleen. Carlos Finlay. De Varona, Frank, intro. by. Didier, Les, illus. (SPA & ENG.). 32p. (gr. 3-6). 1990. PLB 15.96 (*0-8172-3378-4*) Raintree Steck-V.

Sumrall, Lester. Adventuring with Christ. 2nd ed. 161p. 1988. Repr. of 1938 ed. text ed. 11.95 (*0-937580-13-9*) LeSEA Pub Co.

Sun, Chyng F. Square Beak. Chen, Chih-hsien, illus. LC 92-19093. 40p. (gr. k-3). 1993. 13.95 (*0-395-64567-0*) HM.

Sun, Ming-Ju. Japanese Kimono-Paper Dolls. 1986. pap. 3.95 (*0-486-25094-6*) Dover.

Sun-Sentinel Staff. Andrew: Savagery from the Sea. 1992. pap. 9.99 (*0-941263-71-1*) Tribune FL.

Sun Star Publications Staff, ed. see Higgins, Betty.

Sunanda. Stories & Plays for Children. 91p. (gr. 3-8). 1984. pap. 3.00 (*0-89071-329-4*, Pub. by Sri Aurobindo Ashram IA) Aurobindo Assn.

Sun Bear. At Home in the Wilderness. Rev. ed. (Illus.). 90p. (gr. 4 up). 1973. pap. 5.95 (*0-87961-004-2*) Naturegraph.

Sund, R., et al. Accent on Science. large type ed. Incl. Grade II. 176p. 45.41 (*0-317-02033-1*, 4-00720-00); Grade III. 252p. 1982. 61.07 (*0-317-02034-X*, 4-00730-00); Grade IV, 2 vols. 348p. 1982. Set. 80.07 (*0-317-02035-8*, 4-00740-00); Grade V, 2 vols. 500p. 1982. Set. 122.16 (*0-317-02036-6*, 4-00750-00); Grade VI, 3 vols. 548p. 1982. Set. 136.21 (*0-317-02037-4*, 4-00760-00). (gr. 2-6). 1981. Am Printing Hse.

Sunday, Jane. Canada. LC 92-10767. 96p. 1992. lib. bdg. 19.92 (*0-8114-2455-3*) Raintree Steck-V.

Sundeen, Ann, ed. see Evans, Nate.

Sundeen, Poppy. Rosie, the Rosedown Rabbit: A Storybook to Color. West, Joanne, ed. & illus. 26p. (Orig.). 1988. pap. text ed. 5.95 (*0-929317-00-9*) Rosedown Plantation.

Sundgaard, Arnold. The Bear Who Loved Puccini. Catalano, Dominic, illus. 32p. (ps-3). 1992. PLB 14.95 (*0-399-22135-2*) Philomel Bks) Putnam Pub Group.

—The Lamb & the Butterfly. Carle, Eric, illus. LC 88-60092. 32p. (ps-2). 1988. 14.95 (*0-531-05779-8*); PLB 14.99 (*0-531-08379-9*) Orchard Bks Watts.

Sundquist, Nancy & Brin, Susannah. Fifty Magic Tricks I Can Do. (Illus.). 48p. (gr. 1-5). 1988. pap. 2.95 (*0-8431-1868-7*) Price Stern.

—Fifty Science Experiments I Can Do. (Illus.). 48p. (gr. 1-5). 1988. pap. 2.95 (*0-8431-1867-9*) Price Stern.

Sundquist, Nancy & Sundquist, Susannah. Fifty Mysteries I Can Solve. (Illus.). 48p. (gr. 1-5). 1988. pap. 2.95 (*0-8431-1869-5*) Price Stern.

Sundquist, Susannah, jt. auth. see Sundquist, Nancy.

Sundt, Wilbur A. Naval Science Four: An Illustrated Text for the NJROTC Student. 2nd, rev. & updated ed. Hobbs, Richard R., rev. by. LC 87-7957. (Illus.). 352p. (gr. 10-12). 1990. 16.95 (*0-87021-611-2*) Naval Inst Pr.

Sundvall, Viveca. Mimi & the Biscuit Factory. Eriksson, Eva, illus. Bibb, Eric, tr. (Illus.). 32p. (ps up). 1989. 12.95 (*91-29-59142-2*, Pub. by R & S Bks) FS&G.

—Mimi Gets a Grandpa. Eriksson, Eva, illus. Fisher, Richard E., tr. (Illus.). 32p. (ps up). 1991. bds. 13.95 (*91-29-59864-8*, Pub. by R&S Bks) FS&G.

Sunio, Delicia & Zorc, R. David. Hiligaynon Newspaper Reader. LC 91-75538. 1992. 45.00 (*0-931745-70-5*) Dunwoody Pr.

Sunset Editors. Best Kids Cook Book. 112p. (gr. 1-9). 1992. comb bdg. 9.99 (*0-376-02083-0*) Sunset Pub.

—Best Kids Garden Book. (Illus.). 96p. (gr. 1-9). 1992. 9.99 (*0-376-03076-3*) Sunset Pub.

Sunset Editors, ed. Best Kids Cookie Book. 112p. (gr. 4-7). 1993. pap. 11.99 (*0-376-02388-0*) Sunset Pub.

Sunshine, Catherine A. & Menkart, Deborah, eds. Caribbean Connections: Jamaica. LC 90-63270. (Illus., Orig.). (gr. 7-12). 1991. pap. text ed. 12.00 (*1-878554-05-0*) NECA.

Sunshine, Catherine A., jt. ed. see Menkart, Deborah.

Sunshine, Catherine H. & Menkart, Deborah, eds. Caribbean Connections: Overview of Regional History. (Illus., Orig.). (gr. 7-12). 1991. pap. text ed. 16.00 (*1-878554-06-9*) NECA.

Sunshine, Tina. An X-Rated Romance. 142p. (gr. 7 up). 1982. pap. 2.50 (*0-380-79905-7*, Flare) Avon.

Suntree, Susan. Rita Moreno. (Illus.). 112p. (gr. 5 up). 1992. lib. bdg. 17.95 (*0-7910-1247-6*) Chelsea Hse.

—Rita Moreno: Hispanics of Achievement. (gr. 4-7). 1992. pap. 7.95 (*0-7910-1274-3*) Chelsea Hse.

Supancich, Jo, illus. Second Story Window. 16p. (ps-2). 1992. pap. 14.95 (*1-55799-227-4*) Evan-Moor Corp.

—Skip to My Lou. 16p. (ps-2). 1992. pap. 14.95 (*1-55799-229-0*) Evan-Moor Corp.

Super, Gretchen. Drugs & Our World. (Illus.). 48p. (gr. k-3). 1990. PLB 14.95 (*0-8050-2888-9*) TFC Bks NY.

—Drugs & Our World. 48p. (ps-3). 1990. pap. 3.95 (*0-8167-2365-6*) Troll Assocs.

—Family Traditions. De Kiefte, Kees, illus. 48p. (gr. k-3). 1992. PLB 15.95 (*0-8050-2218-X*) TFC Bks NY.

—Sisters & Brothers. De Kiefte, Kees, illus. 48p. (gr. k-3). 1992. PLB 15.95 (*0-8050-2219-8*) TFC Bks NY.

—Tu Puedes Decirles "No" A las Drogas! You Can Say "No" to Drugs! Sims, Blanche, illus. (SPA). 48p. (gr. k-4). 1991. PLB 21.27 (*0-516-37372-2*) Childrens.

—What Are Drugs? (Illus.). 48p. (gr. k-3). 1990. PLB 14.95 (*0-8050-2549-9*) TFC Bks NY.

—What Are Drugs. 48p. (ps-3). 1990. pap. 3.95 (*0-8167-2364-8*) Troll Assocs.

—What Is a Family? De Keefte, Kees, illus. 56p. (gr. k-3). 1991. PLB 15.95 (*0-941477-63-0*) TFC Bks NY.

—What Kind of Family Do You Have? De Keefte, Kees, illus. 56p. (gr. k-3). 1991. PLB 15.95 (*0-941477-64-9*) TFC Bks NY.

—You Can Say "No" to Drugs! (Illus.). 48p. (gr. k-3). 1990. PLB 14.95 (*0-8050-2628-2*) TFC Bks NY.

—You Can Say No to Drugs. 48p. (ps-3). 1990. pap. 3.95 (*0-8167-2366-4*) Troll Assocs.

Super, Neil. Daniel "Chappie" James. (Illus.). 80p. (gr. 4-7). 1992. PLB 14.95 (*0-8050-2138-8*) TFC Bks NY.

—Vietnam War Soldiers. (Illus.). 64p. (gr. 4-7). 1993. PLB 14.95 (*0-8050-2307-0*) TFC Bks NY.

Super, Terri, illus. Animal Babies. LC 86-72426. 12p. (ps). 1988. pap. write for info. (*0-307-06056-X*, Pub. by Golden Bks) Western Pub.

—The Pudgy Pat-a-Cake. 16p. (ps). 1983. pap. 2.95 (*0-448-10204-8*, G&D) Putnam Pub Group.

—The Three Little Pigs. 16p. (ps-1). 1984. 3.95 (*0-448-10214-5*, G&D) Putnam Pub Group.

Superlove. Sunstar: Sun of Superlove. LC 80-53694. (Illus.). 200p. (Orig.). (gr. 7 up). 1980. pap. 7.00 (*0-9602334-1-5*); 20.00 (*0-685-04821-7*) Superlove.

Supervielle, Jules. Le Voleur D'enfants. pap. 4.95 (*0-88436-111-X*, 40265) EMC.

Supraner, Lauren, jt. auth. see Supraner, Robyn.

Supraner, Robyn. Amazing Mark. Levy, Pam, illus. LC 85-14070. 48p. (Orig.). (gr. 1-3). 1986. PLB 10.59 (*0-8167-0644-1*); pap. text ed. 3.50 (*0-8167-0645-X*) Troll Assocs.

—Case of the Missing Canary. new ed. Stillerman, Robbie, illus. LC 78-60122. 48p. (gr. 2-4). 1979. PLB 10.89 (*0-89375-087-5*); pap. 3.50 (*0-89375-075-1*) Troll Assocs.

—Case of the Missing Rattles. Goodman, Joan E., illus. LC 81-10378. 48p. (gr. 2-4). 1982. PLB 10.89 (*0-89375-590-7*); pap. text ed. 3.50 (*0-89375-591-5*) Troll Assocs.

—The Cat Who Wanted to Fly. Goodman, Joan E., illus. LC 85-14119. 48p. (Orig.). (gr. 1-3). 1986. PLB 10.59 (*0-8167-0612-3*); pap. text ed. 3.50 (*0-8167-0613-1*) Troll Assocs.

—Fun with Paper. Barto, Renzo, illus. LC 80-19859. 48p. (gr. 1-5). 1981. PLB 11.89 (*0-89375-430-7*); pap. 3.50 (*0-89375-431-5*) Troll Assocs.

—The Ghost in the Attic. LC 78-18039. (Illus.). 48p. (gr. 2-4). 1979. PLB 10.89 (*0-89375-095-6*); pap. 3.50 (*0-89375-083-2*) Troll Assocs.

—Great Masks to Make. Barto, Renzo, illus. LC 80-24077. 48p. (gr. 1-5). 1981. PLB 11.89 (*0-89375-436-6*); pap. 3.50 (*0-89375-437-4*) Troll Assocs.

—Happy Halloween: Things to Make & Do. Barto, Renzo, illus. LC 80-23889. 48p. (gr. 1-5). 1981. lib. bdg. 11.89 (*0-89375-420-X*); pap. 3.50 (*0-89375-421-8*) Troll Assocs.

—I Can Read About Baseball. LC 74-24926. (Illus.). (gr. 2-4). 1975. pap. 1.95 (*0-89375-062-X*) Troll Assocs.

—I Can Read About Homonyms. Snyder, Joel, illus. LC 76-54442. (gr. 2-5). 1977. pap. 1.95 (*0-89375-036-0*) Troll Assocs.

—I Can Read About Seasons. LC 74-24990. (Illus.). (gr. 2-4). 1975. pap. 1.95 (*0-89375-068-9*) Troll Assocs.

—I Can Read About Synonyms & Antonyms. McKeown, Gloria, illus. LC 76-54441. (gr. 2-5). 1977. pap. 1.95 (*0-89375-035-2*) Troll Assocs.

—I Can Read About Weather. LC 74-24992. (Illus.). (gr. 2-4). 1975. pap. 1.95 (*0-89375-070-0*) Troll Assocs.

—I Can Read About Witches. LC 74-24965. (Illus.). (gr. 2-4). 1975. pap. 1.95 (*0-89375-066-2*) Troll Assocs.

—Kitty: A Cat's Diary. Paterson, Diane, illus. LC 85-14023. 48p. (Orig.). (gr. 1-3). 1986. PLB 10.59 (*0-8167-0574-7*); pap. text ed. 3.50 (*0-8167-0575-5*) Troll Assocs.

—Magic Tricks You Can Do! Barto, Renzo, illus. LC 80-19780. 48p. (gr. 1-5). 1981. PLB 11.89 (*0-89375-418-8*); pap. text ed. 3.50 (*0-89375-419-6*) Troll Assocs.

—Merry Christmas: Things to Make & Do. Barto, Renzo, illus. LC 80-23884. 48p. (gr. 1-5). 1981. PLB 11.89 (*0-89375-422-6*); pap. 3.50 (*0-89375-423-4*) Troll Assocs.

—Molly's Special Wish. Rocklen, Margot, illus. LC 85-14087. 48p. (Orig.). (gr. 1-3). 1986. PLB 10.59 (*0-8167-0660-3*); pap. text ed. 3.50 (*0-8167-0661-1*) Troll Assocs.

—Mrs. Wigglesworth's Secret. Harvey, Paul, illus. LC 78-18041. 48p. (gr. 2-4). 1979. 10.89 (*0-89375-097-2*); pap. 3.50 (*0-89375-085-9*) Troll Assocs.

—Mystery at the Zoo. new ed. Dodson, Bert, illus. LC 78-60126. (gr. 2-4). 1979. PLB 10.89 (*0-89375-091-3*); pap. 3.50 (*0-89375-079-4*) Troll Assocs.

—Mystery of the Lost Ring (with Two Hearts) Winborn, Marsha, illus. LC 81-7520. 48p. (gr. 2-4). 1982. PLB 10.89 (*0-89375-596-6*); pap. text ed. 3.50 (*0-89375-597-4*); cassette 9.95 (*0-685-04951-5*) Troll Assocs.

—Mystery of the Witch's Shoes. new ed. Apple, Margot, illus. LC 78-60125. 48p. (gr. 2-4). 1979. PLB 10.89 (*0-89375-090-5*); pap. 3.50 (*0-89375-078-6*) Troll Assocs.

—No Room for a Sneeze! Trivas, Irene, illus. LC 85-14164. 48p. (Orig.). (gr. 1-3). 1986. PLB 10.59 (*0-8167-0656-5*); pap. text ed. 3.50 (*0-8167-0657-3*) Troll Assocs.

—Quick & Easy Cookbook. Barto, Renzo, illus. LC 80-24021. 48p. (gr. 1-5). 1981. PLB 11.89 (*0-89375-438-2*); pap. 3.50 (*0-89375-439-0*) Troll Assocs.

—Rainy Day Surprises You Can Make. LC 80-19858. (Illus.). 48p. (gr. 1-5). 1981. PLB 11.89 (*0-89375-428-5*); pap. 3.50 (*0-89375-429-3*) Troll Assocs.

—Science Secrets. Barto, Renzo, illus. LC 80-23794. 48p. (gr. 1-5). 1981. PLB 11.89 (*0-89375-426-9*); pap. 3.50 (*0-89375-427-7*) Troll Assocs.

—Stop & Look! Illusions. Barto, Renzo, illus. LC 80-23799. 48p. (gr. 1-5). 1981. PLB 11.89 (*0-89375-434-X*); pap. 3.50 (*0-89375-435-8*) Troll Assocs.

—Valentine's Day: Things to Make & Do. Barto, Renzo, illus. LC 80-23780. 48p. (gr. 1-5). 1981. PLB 11.89 (*0-89375-424-2*); pap. 3.50 (*0-89375-425-0*) Troll Assocs.

Supraner, Robyn & Supraner, Lauren. Plenty of Puppets to Make. Barto, Renzo, illus. LC 80-23785. 48p. (gr. 1-5). 1981. PLB 11.89 (*0-89375-432-3*); pap. 3.50 (*0-89375-433-1*) Troll Assocs.

Supree, Burton, jt. auth. see Charlip, Remy.

Surat, Michele M. Angel Child, Dragon Child. Vo-Dinh Mai, illus. LC 83-8606. 32p. (gr. 3-6). 1983. PLB 12.96 (*0-940742-12-8*) Raintree Steck-V.

—Angel Child, Dragon Child. (gr. 3-6). 1989. pap. 3.95 (*0-590-42271-5*) Scholastic Inc.

Surbeck, Jean-Jacques, tr. see Jacobs, Edgar P.

Surbeck, Jean-Jacques, tr. see Leloup, Roger.

Surcouf, Elizabeth G. Grace Kelly, American Princess. LC 92-9626. 1992. 17.50 (*0-8225-0548-7*) Lerner Pubns.

Surface, Mary H. Prodigy: Wolfgang Amadeus Mozart: (Musical) 50p. 1988. Playscript. 4.50 (*0-87602-281-6*) Anchorage.

—The Sorcerer's Apprentice. (Orig.). 1993. pap. 4.50 playscript (*0-87602-323-5*) Anchorage.

Surowiecki, Sandra L. Joshua's Day. 2nd ed. LC 77-20479. (Illus.). 27p. (ps-1). 1977. pap. 5.00 (*0-914996-18-5*) Lollipop Power.

Suschitsky, Anya. More Easy Piano Tunes. (Illus.). 64p. (gr. 3 up). 1993. pap. 8.95 (*0-7460-1390-6*, Usborne) EDC.

Suschitzky, A. More Easy Recorder Tunes. (Illus.). 64p. (gr. 2 up). 1993. pap. 8.95 (*0-7460-1392-2*) EDC.

—More Easy Recorder Tunes. (gr. 4-7). 1993. pap. 8.95 (*0-7460-1393-0*, Usborne) EDC.

Susen, Phyllis B., ed. Sound All Around. ps-4 ed. Blake, Amy, illus. 40p. (Orig.). 1992. pap. 8.50 (0-9635667-0-9) Phila Orchestra.

Sushiela. The Ant & the Grasshopper: A Love Story. Sushiela, illus. LC 89-92067. 129p. (Orig.). (gr. 5 up). 1990. pap. 15.95 (0-9623363-1-9) Running Water.

Sussman, Ellen. Creative Reading Resources. (Illus.). 56p. (gr. 2-5). 1993. text ed. 6.95 (0-933606-92-3) E Sussman Educ.

Sussman, Ellen & Maifair, Linda. Exciting Writing. (Illus.). 56p. (gr. 2-5). 1993. text ed. 6.95 (0-933606-91-5) E Sussman Educ.

Sussman, Ellen, ed. see Petreshene, Susan S.

Sussman, Ellen, intro. by see Thorne, Randy.

Sussman, Linda. A Raisin in the Sun - Study Guide. Friedland, Joyce & Kessler, Rikki, eds. (gr. 8-12). Date not set. pap. text ed. 14.95 (0-88122-124-4) Lrn Links.

Sussman, Susan. Hanukkah: Eight Lights Around the World. Levine, Abby, ed. LC 87-25346. (Illus.). 40p. (gr. 2 up). 1988. PLB 11.95 (0-8075-3145-6) A Whitman.

—There's No Such Thing As a Chanukah Bush, Sandy Goldstein. Tucker, Kathleen, ed. LC 83-1291. (Illus.). 48p. (gr. 3-7). 1983. PLB 8.95 (0-8075-7862-2) A Whitman.

—There's No Such Thing As a Chanukah Bush, Sandy Goldstein. (gr. 4-7). 1993. pap. 3.50 (0-8075-7863-0) A Whitman.

Sussman, Susan & James, Robert. Big Friend, Little Friend: A Book about Symbiosis. (Illus.). 32p. (gr. 2-5). 1989. 13.95 (0-395-49701-9) HM.

—Lies (People Believe) about Animals. Tucker, Kathleen, ed. Leavitt, Fred, illus. LC 86-15949. 48p. (gr. 2-7). 1987. PLB 11.95 (0-8075-4530-9) A Whitman.

Sustendal, Pat, illus. Sesame Street Farm Friends. 12p. (ps). 1985. 4.99 (0-394-87466-8) Random Bks Yng Read.

Susteren, Margery Van see Van Susteren, Margery.

Sutcliff, Rosemary. Beowulf. Keeping, Charles, illus. (gr. 5-9). 1984. 22.00 (0-8446-6165-1) Peter Smith.

—Black Ships Before Troy. Lee, Alan, illus. LC 92-38782. (gr. 4 up). 1993. 19.95 (0-385-31069-2) Delacorte.

—Blue Remembered Hills: A Recollection. (Illus.). 144p. 1992. pap. 8.95 (0-374-40714-2, Sunburst) FS&G.

—Bonnie Dundee. (gr. 7 up). 21.00 (0-8446-6363-8) Peter Smith.

—Chess-Dream in a Garden. Thompson, Ralph, illus. LC 92-54595. 48p. (ps up). 1993. 16.95 (1-56402-192-0) Candlewick Pr.

—Dragon Slayer. (gr. 4-6). 1976. pap. 3.99 (0-14-030254-9, Puffin) Puffin Bks.

—Eagle of the Ninth. 1993. pap. 3.95 (0-374-41930-2) FS&G.

—Flame-Colored Taffeta. 120p. (gr. 5 up). 1986. 14.00 (0-374-32344-5) FS&G.

—Flame-Colored Taffeta. 144p. (gr. 3 up). 1989. pap. 3.50 (0-374-42341-5, Sunburst) FS&G.

—The Minstrel & the Dragon Pup. Clark, Emma Chichester, illus. LC 92-53012. 48p. (ps-3). 1993. 16. 95 (1-56402-098-3) Candlewick Pr.

—Shining Company. 1992. pap. 4.95 (0-374-46616-5) FS&G.

—The Silver Branch. LC 93-7950. 1993. 3.95 (0-374-46648-3) FS&G.

—The Sword & the Circle. 256p. (gr. 4-7). 1981. 14.95 (0-525-40585-2, DCB) Dutton Child Bks.

—Tristan & Iseult. 150p. (gr. 5 up). 1991. pap. 3.95 (0-374-47982-8, Sunburst) FS&G.

Suteyev, V., tr. see Ginsburg, Mirra.

Sutherland, Bob & Sutherland, Mary. Fun with Fingerplays. 50p. 1992. pap. 9.95 (0-938293-03-6) Fun Pub OH.

Sutherland, Colleen. Jason Goes to Show & Tell. Weller, Linda, illus. 32p. (ps-k). 1992. bds. 9.95 (1-878093-89-4) Boyds Mills Pr.

Sutherland, Dorothy B. Scotland. LC 84-23227. (Illus.). 128p. (gr. 5-9). 1985. PLB 26.60 (0-516-02787-5) Childrens.

—Wales. LC 86-29954. (Illus.). 128p. (gr. 5-9). 1987. PLB 26.60 (0-516-02794-8) Childrens.

Sutherland, E. A. Studies in Christian Education: Christ's Education Was Gained from Heaven-Appointed Sources, from Useful Work, from the Study of the Scriptures, from Nature, & from the Experiences of Life - God's Lesson Books. 160p. (gr. 9 up). 1989. pap. 6.95 (0-945460-04-X) Upward Way.

Sutherland, Harry A. Dad's Car Wash. Chambliss, Maxie, illus. LC 87-15183. 32p. (ps-1). 1988. RSBE 13.95 (0-689-31335-7, Atheneum Child Bk) Macmillan Child Grp.

—Dad's Car Wash. Chambliss, Maxie, illus. LC 93-28734. 32p. (gr. k-3). 1994. pap. 4.95 (0-689-71807-1, Aladdin) Macmillan Child Grp.

Sutherland, James, ed. see Defoe, Daniel.

Sutherland, Mary, jt. auth. see Sutherland, Bob.

Sutherland, Robert D. Sticklewort & Feverfew. LC 79-92898. (Illus.). 360p. (gr. 2 up). 1980. 16.00 (0-936044-00-4); pap. 9.00 (0-936044-01-2) Pikestaff Pr.

Sutherland, Zena, ed. The Best in Children's Books: The University of Chicago Guide to Children's Literature, 1973-1978. LC 79-24331. (gr. 12 up). 1980. lib. bdg. 25.00x (0-226-78059-7) U Ch Pr.

Sutherland, Zena, selected by. The Orchard Book of Nursery Rhymes. Jaques, Faith, illus. LC 89-71002. 96p. 1990. 21.95 (0-531-05903-0) Orchard Bks Watts.

Sutphen, Dick. The Nasty Dragon Who Became a Nice Puppy: Reincarnation for Young People. (Illus.). 32p. (Orig.). (ps-3). 1992. pap. 10.98 incl. tape (0-87554-528-9) Valley Sun.

Suttner, Mindy. Winning Is Self-Control. LC 88-90932. (gr. 7-10). PLB write for info. (0-938762-26-5) Eagle Mktg Corp.

Sutton. Me & the Weirdos. (ps-7). 1987. pap. 2.25 (0-553-15395-1, Skylark) Bantam.

Sutton, Charyn, ed. Grio "The Praise Singer" The 1987 Chronicle of Afro-American Heritage, Vol. III. Massey, Cal, et al, illus. 80p. (gr. k-12). 1988. pap. text ed. 9.95 (0-936509-00-7); 183.25 (0-936509-01-5) Enteracom Inc.

Sutton, Elizabeth H. The Pony Champions. LC 92-10518. 48p. (gr. 1-4). 1992. 13.95 (1-56566-019-6) Thomasson-Grant.

—A Pony for Keeps. Gamma, M. B., photos by. LC 90-24435. (Illus.). 32p. (gr. k-3). 1991. 9.95 (0-934738-77-7) Thomasson-Grant.

Sutton, Harry, jt. auth. see Stainer, Tom.

Sutton, Jan. One Giant Step: Putting Feet to Missions. 80p. (Orig.). (gr. 7-12). 1990. pap. text ed. 3.95 (0-936625-85-6) Womans Mission Union.

Sutton, Jan, et al. Rainbows & Candles. Nelson, Becky, ed. 27p. (Orig.). (gr. 7-12). 1992. pap. text ed. 3.95 (1-56309-049-X) Womans Mission Union.

Sutton, Jane. Definitely Not Sexy. LC 88-18127. 160p. (gr. 7 up). 1988. 12.95 (0-316-82325-2) Little.

Sutton, Larry. Taildraggers High. LC 85-47592. 161p. (gr. 5 up). 1985. 14.00 (0-374-37372-8) FS&G.

Sutton, Rosalind, jt. auth. see Ife, Elaine.

Sutton, Scott E. The Family of Ree. Sutton, Scott E., illus. 45p. (gr. 2-4). 1986. 13.95x (0-9617199-1-5) Sutton Pubns.

—The Legend of Snow Pookas. Sutton, Scott E., illus. (gr. 2-4). 13.95x (0-9617199-6-6) Sutton Pubns.

—Look at the Size of That Long-Legged Ploot! Sutton, Scott E., illus. 48p. (gr. 2-4). 1990. 13.95x (0-9617199-5-8) Sutton Pubns.

—More Altitude, Quick! (Illus.). 51p. (gr. 2-4). 1988. 13. 95x (0-9617199-4-X) Sutton Pubns.

—Oh No! More Wizard Lessons! Sutton, Scott E., illus. 35p. (gr. 2-4). 1986. 13.95x (0-9617199-2-3) Sutton Pubns.

—The Secret of GorBee Grotto. (Illus.). 60p. (gr. 2-4). 1987. 13.95x (0-9617199-3-1) Sutton Pubns.

Suwa, Naomi, tr. see La Fonatine, Jean de.

Suzanne, Jamie. Against the Rules. large type ed. Pascal, Francine, created by. 104p. (gr. 7-12). 1991. Repr. of 1987 ed. 9.95 (1-55905-072-1) Grey Castle.

—Best Friends. large type ed. Pascal, Francine, created by. 104p. (gr. 7-12). 1990. Repr. of 1986 ed. 9.95 (1-55905-064-0) Grey Castle.

—Choosing Sides. large type ed. Pascal, Francine, created by. 104p. (gr. 7-12). 1990. Repr. of 1986 ed. 9.95 (1-55905-067-5) Grey Castle.

—First Place. large type ed. Pascal, Francine, created by. 106p. (gr. 7-12). 1991. Repr. of 1987 ed. 9.95 (1-55905-071-3) Grey Castle.

—The Haunted House. large type ed. Pascal, Francine, created by. 106p. (gr. 7-12). 1990. Repr. of 1986 ed. 9.95 (1-55905-066-7) Grey Castle.

—The New Girl. large type ed. Pascal, Francine, created by. 105p. (gr. 7-12). 1990. Repr. of 1987 ed. 9.95 (1-55905-069-1) Grey Castle.

—One of the Gang. large type ed. Pascal, Francine, created by. 104p. (gr. 7-12). 1991. Repr. of 1987 ed. 9.95 (1-55905-073-X) Grey Castle.

—Sneaking Out. large type ed. Pascal, Francine, created by. 106p. (gr. 7-12). 1990. Repr. of 1987 ed. 9.95 (1-55905-068-3) Grey Castle.

—Sweet Valley Twins, 10 bks. large type ed. Pascal, Francine, created by. (gr. 7-12). 1990. Repr. Set. 99.50 (1-55905-074-8) Grey Castle.

—Teacher's Pet. large type ed. Pascal, Francine, created by. 103p. (gr. 7-12). 1990. Repr. of 1986 ed. 9.95 (1-55905-065-9) Grey Castle.

—Three's a Crowd. large type ed. Pascal, Francine, created by. 105p. (gr. 7-12). 1990. Repr. of 1987 ed. 9.95 (1-55905-070-5) Grey Castle.

Suzuki, David. Looking at Insects. (Illus.). 96p. 1992. text ed. 22.95 (0-471-54747-6); pap. text ed. 9.95 (0-471-54050-1) Wiley.

—Looking at Plants. (Illus.). 96p. 1992. text ed. 22.95 (0-471-54748-4); pap. text ed. 9.95 (0-471-54049-8) Wiley.

—Looking at the Body. (Illus.). 96p. 1991. text ed. 22.95 (0-471-54752-2); pap. text ed. 9.95 (0-471-54052-8) Wiley.

—Looking at the Environment. (Illus.). 96p. 1992. text ed. 22.95 (0-471-54749-2); pap. text ed. 9.95 (0-471-54051-X) Wiley.

—Looking at Weather. (Illus.). 96p. 1991. text ed. 22.95 (0-471-54753-0); pap. text ed. 9.95 (0-471-54047-1) Wiley.

Suzuki, David & Hehner, Barbara. Looking at Senses. LC 9-110772. (Illus.). 96p. 1991. text ed. 22.95 (0-471-54751-4); pap. text ed. 9.95 (0-471-54048-X) Wiley.

Suzuki, Shinichi. Note Reading for Violin. Selden, Kyoko, tr. from JPN. 112p. (gr. 1-6). 1985. pap. text ed. 14.95 (0-87487-213-8, Suzuki Method) Summy-Birchard.

—Suzuki Cello School, Cello Part, Vol. 7. 24p. (gr. k-12). 1987. pap. text ed. 6.50 (0-87487-360-6, Suzuki Method) Summy-Birchard.

—Suzuki Cello School: Piano Accompaniment, Vol. 5. 24p. (gr. k-12). 1983. pap. text ed. 6.50 (0-87487-270-7, Suzuki Method) Summy-Birchard.

—Suzuki Cello School, Vol. 4: Cello Part. 16p. (gr. k-12). 1983. pap. text ed. 6.50 (0-87487-266-9, Suzuki Method) Summy-Birchard.

—Suzuki Cello School, Vol. 4: Piano Accompaniment. 24p. (gr. k-12). 1983. pap. text ed. 6.50 (0-87487-269-3, Suzuki Method) Summy-Birchard.

—Suzuki Cello School, Vol. 5: Cello Part. 24p. (gr. k-12). 1983. pap. text ed. 6.50 (0-87487-267-7, Suzuki Method) Summy-Birchard.

—Suzuki Cello School, Vol 6: Cello Part. 16p. (gr. k-12). 1984. pap. text ed. 6.50 (0-87487-268-5, Suzuki Method) Summy-Birchard.

—Suzuki Cello School, Vol. 6: Piano Accompaniments. 24p. (Orig.). (gr. 6-12). 1984. pap. text ed. 6.50 (0-87487-271-5, Suzuki Method) Summy-Birchard.

—Suzuki Cello School, Vol. 7: Piano Accompaniments. 32p. (gr. k-12). 1987. pap. text ed. 6.50 (0-87487-362-2, Suzuki Method) Summy-Birchard.

—Suzuki Viola School, Piano Accompaniments, Vol. 5. 52p. (gr. k-12). 1986. pap. text ed. 8.95 (0-87487-250-2, Suzuki Method) Summy-Birchard.

—Suzuki Viola School: Piano Accompaniments, Vol. 4. Preucil, Doris, ed. 64p. (gr. k-12). 1983. pap. text ed. 10.95 (0-87487-275-8, Suzuki Method) Summy-Birchard.

—Suzuki Viola School: Viola Part, Vol. 3. Preucil, Doris, ed. 24p. (gr. k-12). 1983. pap. text ed. 6.50 (0-87487-243-X, Suzuki Method) Summy-Birchard.

—Suzuki Viola School: Viola Part, Vol. 4. Preucil, Doris, ed. 32p. (gr. k-12). 1983. pap. text ed. 6.50 (0-87487-244-8, Suzuki Method) Summy-Birchard.

Suzuki, Shinichi, ed. Suzuki Piano School, Vol. 1. 32p. (Orig.). (gr. k-3). 1978. pap. text ed. 6.50 (0-87487-160-3, Suzuki Method) Summy-Birchard.

Suzuki, Shinichi, jt. ed. see Preucil, Doris.

Suzuki, Shinichi, ed. see Preucil, Doris.

Svaren, Jacqueline. Lojor's Letters: A Space-Age Story about a Boy & a Gnome & Learning Italic Handwriting. Kisvet, Fran, illus. Reynolds, Lloyd J., intro. by. LC 78-60185. (Illus.). 72p. (Orig.). (gr. 1 up). 1981. pap. 10.00 (0-931474-04-3) TBW Bks.

Svedberg, Ulf. Nicky the Nature Detective. Anderson, Lena, illus. Selberg, Ingrid, tr. (Illus.). 52p. (gr. 5 up). 1988. 12.95 (91-29-58786-7, R & S Bks) FS&G.

Svensson, Borje. Great Miracles of Jesus. Mitchell, Vic, illus. 10p. (ps-2). 1985. 9.99 (0-89191-940-6, 59402, Chariot Bks) Cook.

—Great Stories from the Bible. Mitchell, Vic, illus. 10p. (ps-2). 1985. 9.99 (0-89191-939-2, 59394, Chariot Bks) Cook.

Swaby, Barbara. I Like Colors. Rayburn, Cherie, ed. Phelps, Cheryl, illus. LC 93-72094. 19p. (gr. k-3). 1994. pap. text ed. 16.20 (0-944943-35-7, 91677-1) Current Inc.

—Love Is... Rayburn, Cherie, ed. Luedecke, Bev, illus. LC 93-72093. 16p. (gr. k-1). 1994. pap. text ed. 16.20 (0-944943-34-9) Current Inc.

—My Grandpa Henry. Rayburn, Cherie, ed. Martin, Bob, illus. LC 93-72092. 16p. (gr. k-3). 1994. pap. text ed. 16.20 (0-944943-28-4, 91675-3) Current Inc.

Swafford, Mrs. Z. W. Knowing God. rev. ed. 32p. (gr. k-2). 1980. tchr's. ed. 1.00 (0-89114-090-5); coloring bk. 0.50 (0-89114-091-3) Baptist Pub Hse.

Swafford, Z. W. Worshiping God. 32p. (gr. k-2). 1983. pap. 1.00 (0-89114-103-0); coloring bk. 0.50 (0-89114-104-9) Baptist Pub Hse.

Swain, Gwenyth. Indiana. Lerner Geography Department Staff, ed. (Illus.). 72p. (gr. 3-6). 1992. PLB 17.50 (0-8225-2721-9) Lerner Pubns.

—Pennsylvania. LC 93-12333. 1993. write for info. (0-8225-2727-8) Lerner Pubns.

Swainson, Esme. Children: The Adventures of Rex & Zendah in the Zodiac. Rosicrucian Fellowship Staff, ed. (Illus.). 112p. (ps-8). 1981. pap. text ed. 4.95 (0-911274-61-8) Rosicrucian.

Swajeski, Donna M. The Revolution Machine. rev. ed. (gr. 3-12). 1985. pap. 6.00 play script (0-88734-511-5) Players Pr.

Swalin, Benjamin. Hard Circus Road: The Odyssey of the North Carolina Symphony. McVaugh, Julia A., ed. (Illus.). 158p. Date not set. 24.95 (0-9618952-0-9) NC Symphony.

Swallow, Pamela C. Leave It to Christy. 160p. (gr. 5-8). 1987. 14.95 (0-399-21482-8, Putnam) Putnam Pub Group.

—Melvil & Dewey in the Chips. Brown, Judith, illus. LC 86-61092. 48p. (Orig.). (gr. 1-3). 1986. o. p. 9.95 (0-936915-02-1); pap. 4.95 (0-936915-03-X) Shoe Tree Pr.

—Melvil & Dewey in the Fast Lane. Brown, Judith, illus. LC 89-17926. 48p. (gr. k-3). 1989. pap. 4.95 (1-55870-134-6) Shoe Tree Pr.

—No Promises. 1990. pap. 2.95 (0-590-43209-5) Scholastic Inc.

—Wading Through Peanut Butter. (gr. 4-7). 1993. pap. 2.95 (0-590-45793-4) Scholastic Inc.

Swallow, Su. Air. LC 90-31033. (Illus.). 32p. (gr. k-4). 1991. PLB 11.90 (0-531-14097-0) Watts.

—Food for the World. LC 90-44954. (Illus.). 48p. (gr. 5-8). 1991. PLB 19.92 (0-8114-2800-1) Raintree Steck-V.

—Water. (Illus.). 32p. (gr. k-4). 1990. PLB 11.90 (0-531-14061-X) Watts.

Swami Raghaveshananda. Ramayana for Children. Padmavasan, illus. 44p. (Orig.). (gr. 3-6). 1989. pap. 3.95 (*81-7120-102-4*, Pub. by Ramakrishna Math Madras India) Vedanta Pr.
—Story of Sri Krishna for Children, Pt. I. Padmavasan, illus. 60p. (gr. 4). 1990. 3.95 (*81-7120-140-7*, Pub. by Ramakrishna Math Madras India) Vedanta Pr.
Swan, Deloris, ed. see Swan, Walter.
Swan, Dorothy, jt. auth. see Burns, Julie.
Swan, Frances M. Once upon a Rhyme. Criscuolo, Edna, illus. 48p. 1984. pap. 2.00 (*0-9602126-2-0*) F M Swan.
Swan, Robert. Destination: Antarctica. Mear, Roger & Ward, Rebecca, photos by. (Illus.). 48p. (gr. 2-7). 1989. pap. 5.95 (*0-590-41286-8*) Scholastic Inc.
Swan, Susan E., illus. The Twelve Days of Christmas. LC 80-28097. 32p. (gr. k-4). 1981. PLB 9.79 (*0-89375-474-9*); pap. text ed. 1.95 (*0-89375-475-7*) Troll Assocs.
Swan, Walter. Adventure Stories. Swan, Deloris, ed. Asch, Connie, et al, illus. 252p. (gr. k-5). 1991. 19.95 (*0-927176-08-4*) Swan Enterp.
—Brenda the Cow & the Little White Hen. Swan, Deloris, ed. Asch, Connie, illus. 16p. (Orig.). (gr. 2-3). 1989. pap. 1.50 (*0-927176-02-5*) Swan Enterp.
—The Little Green Tractor. Swan, Deloris, ed. Asch, Connie, illus. 16p. (Orig.). (gr. 2-4). 1989. pap. 1.50 (*0-927176-04-1*) Swan Enterp.
—Stick 'em up! I've Got You Covered! Swan, Deloris, ed. Asch, Connie, illus. 16p. (Orig.). (ps-8). 1989. pap. 1.50 (*0-927176-03-3*) Swan Enterp.
—Teeny Weeny. Swan, Deloris, ed. Asch, Connie, illus. 16p. (Orig.). (ps) 1989. pap. 1.50 (*0-927176-01-7*) Swan Enterp.
Swanberg, Nancie. American Dolls Coloring & Story Album. 32p. (ps up). 1985. pap. 4.50 (*0-8431-1753-2*) Price Stern.
Swann. Albertosaurus. (Illus.). 24p. 1984. PLB 14.00 (*0-86592-527-5*) Rourke Enter.
—Oviraptor. (Illus.). 24p. 1984. PLB 14.00 (*0-86592-528-3*) Rourke Enter.
—Struthiomimus. (Illus.). 24p. 1984. PLB 14.00 (*0-86592-525-9*) Rourke Enter.
Swann, jt. auth. see White.
Swann, Brian. A Basket Full of White Eggs: Riddle-Poems. Goembel, Ponder, illus. LC 87-11220. 32p. (gr. k-3). 1988. 14.95 (*0-531-05734-8*); PLB 14.99 (*0-531-08334-9*) Orchard Bks Watts.
—Tongue Dancing. Dodge, Katherine, illus. 56p. (gr. 7-12). 1984. 12.95g (*0-937672-12-2*) Rowan Tree.
Swann, Carinda. Bootnanny's Trip to Town. LC 62-63255. (Illus.). 44p. (gr. 2-5). 1993. PLB 12.95 (*1-55523-589-1*); pap. 7.95 (*1-55523-657-X*) Winston-Derek.
Swann, Donald, jt. auth. see Flanders, Michael.
Swann, F. Corythosaurus. (Illus.). 24p. (gr. 3 up). 1989. PLB 14.60 (*0-86592-521-6*); lib. bdg. 10.95s.p. (*0-685-58283-3*) Rourke Corp.
—Psittacosaurus. (Illus.). 24p. (gr. 3 up). 1989. PLB 14.60 (*0-86592-518-6*); 10.95s.p. (*0-685-58285-X*) Rourke Corp.
Swann, Jivan. Tantra: A Handbook for Spiritual Lovers. Westley, Christine, ed. (Illus.). 32p. 1989. pap. 6.00 (*0-9622052-1-4*) Turtle Prints.
Swann, L. Marie. The Sacred Lake, 3 bks. Swann, L. Marie, illus. (gr. 3-4). 1992. Set. pap. text ed. 25.00 (*1-882156-05-6*) Eye Of The Eagle.
—The Sacred Lake: A History of the Washo Tribe (Native American) Prior to the Coming of the Europeans. 65p. (gr. 3-4). 1992. PLB 14.00 (*1-882156-01-3*); pap. text ed. 12.00 (*1-882156-00-5*) Eye Of The Eagle.
Swann, Marie L. The Sacred Lake Activity Book: Activities to Accompany Reading "The Sacred Lake" 51p. (gr. 3-4). 1992. Repr. of 1991 ed. wkbk. 8.00 (*1-882156-04-8*) Eye Of The Eagle.
Swanson, Harry. Christmas Fortune. (Illus.). 24p. (Orig.). (gr. 9-12). 1989. pap. 4.00 (*1-878200-08-9*) Swanmark Bks.
—Easter Is Not for Bears. Swanson, Harry, illus. 56p. (Orig.). (ps-6). 1989. pap. 5.00 (*1-878200-04-6*) SwanMark Bks.
—Eli Eagle Builds a Nest. Swanson, Harry, illus. 52p. (Orig.). (ps-6). 1990. pap. 5.00 (*1-878200-09-7*) SwanMark Bks.
—Isn't There Room for Us All in Prince William Sound? (Illus.). 36p. (Orig.). (ps-6). 1989. pap. 5.00 (*1-878200-01-1*) Swanmark Bks.
—Oscar Otter Meets the Mayor. Swanson, Harry, illus. 48p. (Orig.). (ps-6). 1989. pap. 5.00 (*1-878200-02-X*) SwanMark Bks.
—Pets & Pathos. rev. ed. Swanson, Harry, illus. 52p. (gr. 9-12). 1989. pap. 5.00 (*1-878200-03-8*) SwanMark Bks.
—Seagraham Seal's Perfect Gift. Swanson, Harry, illus. 48p. (Orig.). (ps-6). 1989. pap. 5.00 (*1-878200-05-4*) Swanmark Bks.
Swanson, Helen M. Angel of Rainbow Gulch. 128p. (Orig.). (gr. 3-6). 1992. pap. 4.95 (*1-880188-08-2*) Bess PR.
Swanson, June. David Bushnell & His Turtle: The Story of America's First Submarine. Eagle, Mike, illus. LC 90-628. 40p. (gr. 2-5). 1991. SBE 13.95 (*0-689-31628-3*, Atheneum Child Bk) Macmillan Child Grp.
—Hot Stuff: Riddles about Deserts. Burke, Susan S., illus. LC 93-26294. 1994. 11.00 (*0-8225-2343-4*) Lerner Pubns.

—I Pledge Allegiance. Hanson, Rick, illus. 40p. (gr. k-4). 1990. PLB 14.95 (*0-87614-393-1*) Carolrhoda Bks.
—I Pledge Allegiance. LC 89-35414. (ps-3). 1991. pap. 5.95 (*0-87614-526-8*) Carolrhoda Bks.
—Summit Up: Riddles about Mountains. Burke, Susan S., illus. LC 93-19157. 1994. PLB 11.95 (*0-8225-2342-6*) Lerner Pubns.
—That's for Shore: Riddles from the Beach. Burke, Susan S., illus. 32p. (gr. 1-4). 1991. PLB 11.95 (*0-8225-2332-9*) Lerner Pubns.
—That's for Shore: Riddles from the Beach. (ps-3). 1991. pap. 3.95 (*0-8225-9592-3*) Lerner Pubns.
Swanson, Karl, jt. auth. see McDonald, Joyce.
Swanson, Leslie C. Riverboat Gamblers of History, Vol. I. (Illus.). 56p. (Orig.). 1990. pap. 4.00x perfect bdg. (*0-911466-09-6*) Swanson.
Swanson, Maggie, jt. auth. see Wetzel, Rick.
Swanson, Maria M. Hola, Amigos! Incl. Maria (*0-8442-7218-3*); Teresa (*0-8442-7219-1*). (ENG & SPA., Illus.). 32p. (gr. 4 up). 1983. 6.60 ea. (Passport Bks) NTC Pub Grp.
Swanson, Norma F. Horizons Plus: A Student's Progress Profile. 1988. write for info. Window World NY.
Swanson, Steve. Faith Journeys: Youth Devotions by Nine Youth Writers. LC 91-19369. 152p. (gr. 4 up). 1991. pap. 8.99 (*0-8066-2562-7*) Augsburg Fortress.
—Is There Life after High School? Making Decisions about Your Future. LC 90-15499. 112p. (Orig.). (gr. 9 up). 1991. pap. 5.99 (*0-8066-2500-7*, 9-2500, Augsburg) Augsburg Fortress.
Swanson, Steve, et al. Faith Prints: Youth Devotions for Every Day of the Year. LC 85-13466. 224p. (Orig.). (gr. 8 up). 1985. pap. 7.99 (*0-8066-2178-8*, 10-2189, Augsburg) Augsburg Fortress.
Swarthout, Glendon & Swarthout, Kathryn. The Ghost & the Magic Saber. (Illus.). (gr. 4-7). 1963. lib. bdg. 4.99 (*0-394-91194-6*) Random Bks Yng Read.
Swarthout, Kathryn, jt. auth. see Swarthout, Glendon.
Swartley, David W. My Friend, My Brother. Converse, James, illus. LC 79-26273. 104p. (gr. 6 up). 1980. pap. 3.95 (*0-8361-1916-9*) Herald Pr.
Swartz, Leslie. First Passover. (ps-3). 1994. pap. 4.95 (*0-671-88025-X*, Half Moon Bks.) S&S Trade.
Swartz, Susan S. Where & Why. Reeder, Bill, illus. 24p. (Orig.). (ps-6). 1987. pap. 4.50 wkbk. (*0-943901-00-6*) Creare Pubns.
Swartzentruber. God Made Me in a Good Way. 1976. 2.50 (*0-686-18183-2*) Rod & Staff.
—God Made the Animals. (gr. 1 up). 1976. 2.50 (*0-686-18185-9*) Rod & Staff.
—God Made the Firefly. 1976. 2.50 (*0-686-18186-7*) Rod & Staff.
—God Made Us in a Wonderful Way. 1976. 2.50 (*0-686-18184-0*) Rod & Staff.
—God Makes Seeds That Grow. 1976. 2.50 (*0-686-18182-4*) Rod & Staff.
—We Should Be Thankful. 1976. 2.50 (*0-686-18188-3*) Rod & Staff.
Swartzentruber, Mrs. James. God Made the Opossum. 1976. 2.50 (*0-686-18187-5*) Rod & Staff.
Swayne, Sam & Swayne, Zoa. Great-Grandfather in the Honey Tree. LC 81-90738. (Illus.). 53p. (gr. 3-5). 1982. pap. 4.95 perfect bdg. (*0-9608008-0-8*) Legacy Hse.
Swayne, Zoa, jt. auth. see Swayne, Sam.
Sweat, Lynn & Phillips, Louis. The Smallest Stegosaurus. Sweat, Lynn, illus. 32p. (ps-k). 1993. PLB 13.99 (*0-670-83865-9*) Viking Child Bks.
Sweatman, Glenn R. Poems of the Fantastic. LC 89-82518. 84p. (Orig.). 1993. pap. 9.95 (*0-938991-07-8*) Colonial Pr AL.
Sweeney. Disaster. 1980. 8.95 (*0-679-20954-9*) McKay.
Sweeney, Catherine, jt. auth. see Moriarty, Mary.
Sweeney, Jacqueline. Katie & the Night Noises. Johnson, Arden, illus. LC 93-22198. 32p. (ps-2). 1993. PLB 14.95 (*0-8167-3014-8*); pap. text ed. write for info. (*0-8167-3015-6*) BrdgeWater.
Sweeney, John. A Vegetable Catch Story. 32p. 1984. pap. write for info. (*0-9607946-2-X*) Bks of Our Times.
Sweeney, Joyce. The Dream Collector. (gr. 7 up). 1989. 14.95 (*0-385-29813-7*) Delacorte.
—Dream Collector. 1991. pap. 3.50 (*0-440-21131-X*, YB) Dell.
—Face the Dragon. 1990. 14.95 (*0-385-30164-2*) Delacorte.
—Face the Dragon. 1992. pap. 3.50 (*0-440-21246-4*) Dell.
—Right Behind the Rain. LC 86-19953. 192p. (gr. 7 up). 1987. pap. 14.95 (*0-385-29551-0*) Delacorte.
—Right Behind the Rain. 1991. pap. 3.25 (*0-440-20678-2*) Dell.
—The Tiger Orchard. 1993. 15.00 (*0-385-30841-8*) Doubleday.
Sweeney, Toni. Spacedog's Best Friend. Sweeney, Toni, illus. (Orig.). (gr. 5-12). 1989. pap. 6.95 (*0-933025-13-0*) Blue Bird Pub.
Sweeny, Joyce. Center Line. 256p. (gr. k-12). 1985. pap. 2.95 (*0-440-91127-3*, LFL) Dell.
Sweet, Dovie D. Red Light, Green Light: The Life of Garrett Morgan & His Invention of the Stop Light. 4th ed. (Orig.). (gr. 1-6). 1988. pap. 5.00 (*0-682-49088-1*) Kitwardo Pubs.
Sweet, Melissa, jt. auth. see Howe, James.
Sweet, Melissa, adapted by. & illus. Fiddle-I-Fee: A Farmyard Song for the Very Young. 32p. (ps-1). 1992. 14.95 (*0-316-82516-6*, Joy St Bks) Little.
Sweet, Melissa, illus. Hippity-Hop. 18p. (ps). 1992. bds. 2.95 (*0-448-40314-5*) Putnam Pub Group.

—Little Chick. 24p. (ps). 1994. bds. 2.95 (*0-448-40555-5*, G&D) Putnam Pub Group.
Sweet, Muriel. Common Edible & Useful Plants of the West. rev. ed. LC 76-58. (Illus.). 64p. (gr. 4 up). 1976. 12.95 (*0-87961-047-6*); pap. 4.95 (*0-87961-046-8*) Naturegraph.
Sweet, Phyllis. Something Happened to Me. Lindquist, Barbara, illus. LC 81-83422. (gr. 2-5). 1985. pap. 4.95 (*0-941300-00-5*) Mother Courage.
Sweeten, Sami. Wolf. LC 93-34493. 1994. write for info. (*0-8075-9160-2*) A Whitman.
Sweetgall, Rob. The Walking Wellness Student Workbook. Neeves, Robert, ed. (Illus.). 80p. (gr. 4-8). 1986. wkbk. 5.00 (*0-939041-00-6*); tchr's. curriculum guidebk. 12.95 (*0-939041-01-4*) Creative Walking.
Sweetgall, Robert & Peleg, Dorith E. Road Scholars: The Story of Twenty-Eight Kids Who Decided to Take a Hike for Their Health. (Illus.). 64p. (Orig.). 1989. pap. 20.00 (*0-939041-07-3*) Creative Walking.
Sweetman, Jack. American Naval History: An Illustrated Chronology of the U. S. Navy & Marine Corps, 1775-Prese t. 2nd ed. LC 90-29872. (Illus.). 384p. (gr. 7-12). 1991. 36.95 (*1-55750-785-6*) Naval Inst Pr.
Sweezy, Paul M., jt. auth. see Huberman, Leo.
Swendson, Patsy. The Potluck Adventures of Mrs. Marmalade: A Children's Cookbook. Roberts, Melissa, ed. Little, Debbie, illus. 32p. (gr. k-3). 1989. 10.95 (*0-89015-718-9*, Pub. by Panda Bks) Eakin-Sunbelt.
Swenson, Allan. Secrets of a Seashore. (Illus.). 80p. (gr. 4-10). 1981. pap. 3.95 (*0-930096-28-2*) G Gannett.
Swenson, May. The Centaur. Moser, Barry, illus. LC 92-14897. 32p. (gr. k-3). 1994. RSBE 14.95 (*0-02-788726-X*, Macmillan Child Bk) Macmillan Child Grp.
—The Complete Poems to Solve. Hale, Christy, illus. LC 92-26183. 128p. (gr. 3 up). 1993. SBE 13.95 (*0-02-788725-1*, Macmillan Child Bk) Macmillan Child Grp.
Swenson, May, jt. ed. see Knudson, R. R.
Swenson, Peter J. Secrets of Rivers & Streams. Jack, Susan, ed. Sabaka, Donna, illus. 90p. (gr. 4-10). 1982. pap. 3.95 (*0-930096-31-2*) G Gannett.
Swenson, Virginia. The Power of Industry. LC 81-50662. (gr. k-7). lib. bdg. write for info. (*0-911712-88-7*) Eagle Mktg Corp.
Swentzell, Rina. Children of Clay: A Family of Pueblo Potters. Steen, Bill, photos by. Dorris, Michael, frwd. by. LC 92-8680. 1992. 19.95 (*0-8225-2654-9*) Lerner Pubns.
—Children of Clay: A Family of Pueblo Potters: We Are Still Here. (gr. 4-7). 1993. pap. 6.95 (*0-8225-9627-X*) Lerner Pubns.
Swerdlick, Harriet & Reiter, Edith. President Games: Puzzles, Quizzes, & Mind Teasers for Every George, Abe, & Lyndon! 48p. (Orig.). (gr. 3 up). 1988. pap. 2.95 incl. chipboard (*0-8431-2240-4*) Price Stern.
Swerdlove, Larry, jt. auth. see McKay, Sindy.
Swetnam, George, jt. auth. see Smith, Helene.
Swiader, John M., et al. Producing Vegetable Crops. 4th ed. (Illus.). 626p. (gr. 9-12). 1992. 50.60 (*0-8134-2903-X*); text ed. 35.95 (*0-685-50796-3*); tchr's. manual 9.95 (*0-8134-2904-8*) Interstate.
Swiderska, Barbara. The Fisherman's Bride. Swiderska, Barbara, illus. LC 78-148051. 32p. (ps-3). 8.95 (*0-87592-018-7*) Scroll Pr.
Swiecki, Mark, jt. auth. see Marston, Bernice.
Swift, Carolyn. Bugsy Goes to Limerick. 170p. 1990. pap. 6.95 (*1-85371-014-8*, Pub. by Poolbeg Pr ER) Dufour.
—European Myths & Tales. 116p. (gr. 5 up). 1993. pap. 8.95 (*1-85371-203-5*, Pub. by Poolbeg Pr ER) Dufour.
—Irish Myths & Tales for Young People. 107p. (Orig.). (gr. 3-7). 1990. pap. 6.95 (*1-85371-103-9*, Pub. by Poolbeg Pr ER) Dufour.
—Robbers on TV. 160p. (ps-8). 1989. pap. 5.95 (*1-85371-033-4*, Pub. by Poolbeg Press Ltd Eire) Dufour.
Swift, Catherine. Eric Liddell. 176p. (gr. 8 up). 1990. 4.99 (*1-55661-150-1*) Bethany Hse.
—Gladys Aylward. LC 89-61792. 128p. 1989. pap. 4.99 (*1-55661-090-4*) Bethany Hse.
Swift, Hildegarde H. & Ward, Lynd. Little Red Lighthouse & the Great Gray Bridge. Ward, Lynd, illus. LC 42-36286. (ps-3). 1942. 15.95 (*0-15-247040-9*, HB Juv Bks) HarBrace.
—The Little Red Lighthouse & the Great Gray Bridge. LC 73-12861. (Illus.). 52p. (ps-3). 1974. pap. 4.95 (*0-15-652840-1*, Voyager Bks) HarBrace.
Swift, Jonathan. Gulliver's Adventures in Lilliput. Beneduce, Ann K., retold by. Spirin, Gennady, illus. LC 92-26200. 32p. (ps). 1993. 15.95 (*0-399-22021-6*, Philomel Bks) Putnam Pub Group.
—Gulliver's Stories. 1989. pap. 2.95 (*0-590-41842-4*) Scholastic Inc.
—Gulliver's Travels. LC 47-31082. (gr. 8 up). 1964. pap. 2.95 (*0-8049-0015-9*, CL-15) Airmont.
—Gulliver's Travels. (gr. 5-6). Repr. lib. bdg. 23.95x (*0-89190-845-5*, Pub. by River City Pr) Amereon Ltd.
—Gulliver's Travels. Watson, Aldren, illus. LC 47-31082. 352p. (gr. 4-6). 1947. 13.95 (*0-448-05461-2*, G&D) Putnam Pub Group.
—Gulliver's Travels. Cunliffe, M., frwd. by. LC 47-31082. 320p. (RL 9). 1960. pap. 2.95 (*0-451-52219-2*, Sig Classics) NAL-Dutton.
—Gulliver's Travels. Rackham, Arthur, illus. LC 47-31082. 3.98 (*0-517-46611-2*) Outlet Bk Co.

—Gulliver's Travels. James, Raymond, ed. Schindler, S.
D., illus. LC 89-33943. 48p. (gr. 3-6). 1990. PLB 12.
89 (0-8167-1865-2); pap. text ed. 3.95 (0-8167-1866-0)
Troll Assocs.
—Gulliver's Travels. Riordan, James, ed. Ambrus, Victor,
illus. 96p. 1992. 18.00 (0-19-279897-9) OUP.
—Gulliver's Travels. LC 92-53687. 220p. 1992. 5.98
(1-56138-169-1) Courage Bks.
—Gulliver's Travels. Arneson, D. J., retold by. Clift, Eva,
illus. 128p. 1992. pap. 1.95 (1-56156-143-6) Kidsbks.
Swinburne, Irene, jt. auth. see Swinburne, Laurence.
Swinburne, Laurence & Swinburne, Irene. The Deadly
Diamonds. LC 77-10764. (Illus.). 48p. (gr. 4 up).
1983. PLB 18.64 (0-8172-1064-4) Raintree Steck-V.
Swindells, Robert. Fallout. ALC Staff, ed. LC 84-22362.
160p. (gr. 7-12). 1992. pap. 3.95 (0-688-11778-3, Pub.
by Beech Tree Bks) Morrow.
—Room Thirteen. 192p. 1991. text ed. 15.95x
(0-7451-1371-0, Pub. by Chivers Pr UK) Hall.
Swindells, Robert, tr. see Bergstrom, Gunilla.
Swinford, Betty. Mystery at Pier Fourteen. LC 87-82753.
(Illus.). 144p. (gr. 7-11). 1988. 3.50 (0-88243-654-6,
02-0654) Gospel Pub.
Swinger, Marlys. Sing Through the Day: Ninety Songs
for Younger Children. 3rd ed. Society of Brothers
Staff, ed. Jeanie And Joanie And Judy, photos by. LC
68-9673. (Illus.). 144p. (gr. 5 up). 1968. 17.00
(0-87486-005-9); cassette 7.00 (0-87486-047-4)
Plough.
Swinger, Marlys, jt. auth. see Gick, Georg J.
Swinwood, Laurie. Farmer Boy. Wright, Theresa M.,
illus. 48p. 1993. wkbk. 5.95 (1-55734-428-0) Tchr
Create Mat.
Swirsky, Michael, tr. see Bergman, Tamar.
Swisher, Clarice. The Beginning of Language: Opposing
Viewpoints. LC 89-7940. (Illus.). 112p. (gr. 5-8). 1989.
PLB 14.95 (0-89908-064-2) Greenhaven.
—Relativity: Opposing Viewpoints. LC 90-3910. (Illus.).
112p. (gr. 5-8). 1990. PLB 14.95 (0-89908-076-6)
Greenhaven.
Swisher, Karin, ed. Drug Trafficking. LC 91-22022. 200p.
(gr. 10 up). 1991. PLB 16.95 (0-89908-576-8); pap.
text ed. 9.95 (0-89908-582-2) Greenhaven.
Swisher, Karin & Deal, Tara, eds. The Elderly: Opposing
Viewpoints. LC 89-25950. (Illus.). 264p. (gr. 10 up).
1990. lib. bdg. 17.95 (0-89908-475-3); pap. text ed.
9.95 (0-89908-450-8) Greenhaven.
Swisher, Karin, jt. ed. see Cozic, Charles.
Swisher, Karin, jt. ed. see Dudley, William.
Swisher, Karin, jt. ed. see O'Neill, Terry.
Swisher, Karin, jt. ed. see Wekesser, Carol.
Swisher, Karin L., jt. ed. see Biskup, Michael D.
Swisher, Karin L., jt. ed. see Cozic, Charles P.
Swisher, Karin L., jt. ed. see Wagner, Viqi.
Switzer, Ellen. Anyplace but Here: Young, Alone &
Homeless: What to Do. LC 92-15. 176p. (gr. 5 up).
1992. SBE 13.95 (0-689-31694-1, Atheneum Child
Bk) Macmillan Child Grp.
—The Nutcracker: A Story & A Ballet. Cara, Costas &
Cara, Stephen, photos by. LC 85-7463. (Illus.). 112p.
(gr. 4-6). 1985. SBE 16.95 (0-689-31061-7, Atheneum
Child Bk) Macmillan Child Grp.
Switzer, Ellen & Costas. Greek Myths: Gods, Heroes &
Monsters - Their Sources, Their Stories & Their
Meanings. LC 87-22690. (Illus.). 224p. (gr. 6 up).
1988. PLB 16.95 SBE (0-689-31253-9, Atheneum
Child Bk) Macmillan Child Grp.
Switzer, R., compiled by. Follett Vest-Pocket Dictionary:
French-English, English-French, 2 vols. large type ed.
(gr. 9 up). 1967. Repr. of 1962 ed. Set. 116.00
(0-317-01886-8, J-0693000-00) Am Printing Hse.
Swoboda, Dana. Mr. Man in the Skies. LC 88-35619.
(Orig.). (gr. 5-9). 1991. pap. 4.00 (0-915541-89-0) Star
Bks Inc.
Swolgaard, Carole. Sailboat Coloring Guide: A Great
Five Star Super Deluxe Coloring Book. Seablom,
Victoria, ed. Seablom, Seth H., illus. 32p. (Orig.). (gr.
1-6). 1979. pap. 2.50 saddle stitched (0-918800-07-2)
Seablom.
Swope, Sam. The Araboolies of Liberty Street. Root,
Barry, illus. LC 88-12687. 32p. (ps-3). 1989. 15.00
(0-517-56960-4, Clarkson Potter); PLB 15.99
(0-517-57411-X) Crown Bks Yng Read.
—The Krazees. Rocco, John, photos by. LC 92-24435.
(Illus.). 32p. (ps-1). Date not set. 15.00
(0-06-021541-0); PLB 14.89 (0-06-021542-9) HarpC
Child Bks.
Swortzell, Lowell. Gulliver's Travels. 84p. (Orig.). 1992.
pap. 5.00 playscript (0-87602-304-9) Anchorage.
—The Little Humpback Horse. (Orig.). (gr. 1 up). 1984.
pap. 5.00 (0-87602-244-1) Anchorage.
**Swoszowski, Sarah M., jt. auth. see Van House, Charles
L., Sr.**
Sylvester, D. Inventions. 40p. (gr. 4-8). 1992. 6.95
(0-88160-252-3, LW1401) Learning Wks.
Sylvester, D., jt. auth. see Dick, K.
Sylvester, David W. Captain Cook & the Pacific. Reeves,
Marjorie, ed. (Illus.). 92p. (gr. 7-12). 1971. pap. text
ed. 4.75x (0-582-20462-3) Longman.
Sylvester, Diane. Advertising, Communication,
Economics. 112p. (gr. 4-6). 1986. 9.95
(0-88160-129-2, LW907) Learning Wks.
—Inventions, Robots, Future. 112p. (gr. 4-6). 1984. 9.95
(0-88160-108-X, LW 905) Learning Wks.
Sylvester, Diane & Wiemann, Mary. Mythology,
Archeology, Architecture. 112p. (gr. 4-6). 1982. 9.95
(0-88160-081-4, LW 901) Learning Wks.

Sylvester, Sandra. Living with Stress - Middle School.
64p. (gr. 5-9). 1991. 7.95 (0-86653-594-2, GA1313)
Good Apple.
—Living with Stress - Primary. 64p. (gr. 1-4). 1991. 7.95
(0-86653-593-4, GA1312) Good Apple.
Syme, Daniel & Bogot, Howard. I'm Growing. Compere,
Janet, illus. 32p. (ps-1). 1982. pap. 4.00
(0-8074-0167-6, 101095) UAHC.
Syme, Daniel, jt. auth. see Bogot, Howard.
Syme, Daniel B. Jewish Mourning. 1989. pap. 3.00
(0-8074-0332-6, 388494) UAHC.
Syme, Daniel B., jt. auth. see Bogot, Howard.
**Syme, Daniel B., ed. see Marcus, Audrey F. & Zwerin,
Raymond A.**
Syme, Deborah S. Jewish Home Detectives. Ruthen,
Marlene L., illus. 32p. (gr. k-3). 1982. 4.00
(0-8074-0158-7, 101500) UAHC.
Syme, Ronald. Henry Hudson. LC 90-49174. (Illus.).
152p. (gr. 6-10). 1991. PLB 13.95 (1-55905-081-0)
Marshall Cavendish.
Symes, R. F. & Harding, Roger. Crystal & Gem. Keates,
Colin, photos by. LC 90-4930. (Illus.). 64p. (gr. 5 up).
1991. 15.00 (0-679-80781-0); PLB 15.99
(0-679-90781-5) Knopf Bks Yng Read.
Symonds, M. Think Bigger. 112p. (gr. 4-6). 1993. 8.95
(0-88160-260-4, LW255) Learning Wks.
Symonds, Martha. Think Big. 76p. (gr. 4-6). 1977. 7.95
(0-88160-024-5, LW 209) Learning Wks.
Symons & Westcott, Alvin. Dips 'n' Doodles. LC 74-
108726. (Illus.). 48p. (gr. 3-5). 1970. PLB 10.95
(0-87783-011-8); pap. 3.94 deluxe ed. (0-87783-090-8)
Oddo.
Symons, C., jt. auth. see Westcott, A.
Synge, Ursula. The People & the Promise. LC 74-10661.
192p. (gr. 7-10). 1974. 21.95 (0-87599-208-0) S G
Phillips.
—Weland: Smith of the Gods. Keeping, Charles, illus. LC
73-5945. 94p. (gr. 7 up). 1973. 21.95 (0-87599-200-5)
S G Phillips.
Sypher, Lucy J. Cousins & Circuses. Abel, Ray, illus.
250p. (gr. 3-7). 1991. pap. 3.95 (0-14-034551-5,
Puffin) Puffin Bks.
—The Edge of Nowhere. Abel, Ray, illus. 211p. (gr. 3-7).
1991. pap. 3.95 (0-14-034550-7, Puffin) Puffin Bks.
—The Spell of the Northern Lights. Abel, Ray, illus.
256p. (gr. 3-7). 1991. pap. 4.95 (0-14-034552-3,
Puffin) Puffin Bks.
—The Turnabout Year. Abel, Ray, illus. 224p. (gr. 3-7).
1991. pap. 4.95 (0-14-034553-1, Puffin) Puffin Bks.
Syring, K. Michael, jt. auth. see Savitz, Harriet M.
Syswerda, Jean. Reading Sentences, Grades 3-4.
Hoffman, Joan, ed. Cook, Chris, illus. 32p. (gr. 3-4).
1980. wkbk. 1.99 (0-938256-11-4) Sch Zone Pub Co.
—Spelling Puzzles: Grade 1. Hoffman, Joan, ed. Cook,
Chris, illus. 32p. (gr. 1). 1980. wkbk. 1.99
(0-938256-16-5) Sch Zone Pub Co.
—Spelling Puzzles: Grade 2. Hoffman, Joan, ed. Cook,
Chris, illus. 32p. (gr. 2). 1979. wkbk. 1.99
(0-938256-17-3) Sch Zone Pub Co.
—Spelling Puzzles: Grade 3. Hoffman, Joan, ed. Cook,
Chris, illus. 32p. (gr. 3). 1979. wkbk. 1.99
(0-938256-18-1) Sch Zone Pub Co.
—Spelling Puzzles: Grade 4. Hoffman, Joan, ed. Cook,
Chris, illus. 32p. (gr. 4). 1979. wkbk. 1.99
(0-938256-19-X) Sch Zone Pub Co.
Sytsma, Cheryle, ed. see Ray, Sandy.
Sytsma, Cheryle, ed. see Wilson, Ginger.
Sytsma, Cheryle, ed. see Woody, Sandra.
Szabos, Janice. Reading - A Novel Approach. Filkins,
Vanessa, illus. 112p. (gr. 4-8). 1984. wkbk. 11.95
(0-86653-186-6, GA 529) Good Apple.
Szekely, Edmond B. Brother Tree. Matinez, Antonielena
C., illus. 32p. 1977. pap. 3.50 (0-89564-074-0) IBS
Intl.
Szekely, Edmond B. & Bordeaux, Norma N. Messengers
from Ancient Civilizations. (Illus.). 44p. (gr. 5 up).
1974. pap. 3.50 (0-89564-068-6) IBS Intl.
Szeker, Cyndy. Cyndy Szekere's Kisses. (ps). 1993. 2.25
(0-307-06121-3, Golden Pr) Western Pub.
Szekeres, Cyndy. ABC. Szekeres, Cyndy, illus. LC 82-
839989. 22p. (ps-up). 1983. write for info.
(0-307-12120-8, 12120, Golden Bks) Western Pub.
—Cyndy Szekeres' Colors. Szekeres, Cyndy, illus. 24p.
(ps-k). 1992. bds. write for info. (0-307-12167-4,
12167, Golden Pr) Western Pub.
—Cyndy Szekeres' Favorite Mother Goose Rhymes.
(Illus.). 24p. (ps-2). 1992. write for info.
(0-307-12347-2, 12347) Western Pub.
—Cyndy Szekeres' Hugs. 1990. pap. write for info.
(0-307-06108-6, Golden Pr) Western Pub.
—Cyndy Szekeres' Nice Animals. 1990. pap. write for
info. (0-307-06109-4, Golden Pr) Western Pub.
—Cyndy Szekeres' Teeny Mouse Counts Herself.
Szekeres, Cyndy, illus. 12p. (ps). 1992. bds. write for
info. (0-307-06118-3, 6118, Golden Pr) Western Pub.
—Fluffy Duckling. (Illus.). 14p. (ps-k). 1992. write for
info. (0-307-12390-1, 12390) Western Pub.
—Good Night, Sweet Mouse. Szekeres, Cyndy, illus. LC
87-81789. 20p. (ps). 1988. write for info.
(0-307-12159-3) Western Pub.
—Moving Day. (Illus.). 24p. (ps-k). 1989. pap. write for
info. (0-307-11997-1, Pub. by Golden Bks) Western
Pub.
—The New Baby. (Illus.). (ps-k). 1989. pap. write for
info. (0-307-11998-X) Western Pub.
—Puppy Too Small. Szekeres, Cyndy, illus. LC 83-83353.
18p. (ps-k). 1992. bds. write for info. (0-307-12201-8,
12231, Golden Pr) Western Pub.

—Sammy's Special Day. Szekeres, Cyndy, illus. LC 85-
81986. 18p. (ps-k). 1992. bds. write for info.
(0-307-12288-3, 12296, Golden Pr) Western Pub.
—Things Bunny Sees. (ps-3). 1990. write for info.
(0-307-11591-7) Western Pub.
—Thumpity Thump Gets Dressed. Szekeres, Cyndy, illus.
LC 83-83284. 16p. (ps-k). 1991. 4.95 (0-307-12203-4,
12233, Golden Bks) Western Pub.
—What Bunny Loves. (ps-3). 1990. write for info.
(0-307-11590-9) Western Pub.
—What Bunny Loves. Szekeres, Cyndy, illus. (ps-1).
1990. write for info. (Golden Pr) Western Pub.
—What Bunny Loves. (Illus.). (ps-1). 1992. pap.
write for info. (0-307-15966-3, 15966) Western Pub.
Szernecki, Stefan & Rhodes, Timothy. Time Before
Dreams. (Illus.). 80p. (gr. 6-10). 1990. 14.95
(0-920534-49-X, Pub. by Hyperion Pr Ltd CN)
Sterling.
Szilagyi, Mary. Thunderstorm. Szilagyi, Mary, illus. LC
84-24570. 32p. (ps-2). 1985. RSBE 13.95
(0-02-788580-1, Bradbury Pr) Macmillan Child Grp.
Szumski, Bonnie. Christopher Columbus: Recognizing
Stereotypes. LC 92-19873. (Illus.). 32p. (gr. 4-7).
1992. PLB 10.95 (0-89908-069-3) Greenhaven.
—Immigration: Identifying Propaganda Techniques. LC
89-7508. (Illus.). 32p. (gr. 3-6). 1990. PLB 10.95
(0-89908-639-X) Greenhaven.
—Patriotism: Recognizing Stereotypes. LC 89-37555.
(Illus.). 32p. (gr. 3-6). 1990. PLB 10.95
(0-89908-640-3) Greenhaven.
—Smoking: Distinguishing Between Fact & Opinion. LC
89-2153. (Illus.). 32p. (gr. 3-6). 1990. PLB 10.95
(0-89908-642-X) Greenhaven.
—Toxic Wastes: Examining Cause & Effect Relationships.
LC 89-16906. (Illus.). 32p. (gr. 3-6). 1990. PLB 10.95
(0-89908-643-8) Greenhaven.
Szumski, Bonnie, jt. auth. see Bernards, Neal.
Szumski, Bonnie, ed. The Health Crisis: Opposing
Viewpoints. LC 88-24317. (Illus.). 250p. (gr. 10 up).
1988. PLB 17.95 (0-89908-438-9); pap. text ed. 9.95
(0-89908-413-3) Greenhaven.
—Latin America & U. S. Foreign Policy: Opposing
Viewpoints. LC 87-21088. (Illus.). (gr. 10 up). 1987.
lib. bdg. 17.95 (0-89908-399-4); pap. 9.95
(0-89908-374-9) Greenhaven.
Szumski, Bonnie, jt. ed. see Dudley, William.
Szymanski, Lois. Patches. 96p. (Orig.). 1993. pap. 3.50
(0-380-76841-0, Camelot Young) Avon.

T

Tab, Joan & Jon. Etruscans: Valentine's Day. rev. ed.
Abel, J., illus. 20p. (gr. 5-8). 1992. pap. 15.00
(1-56611-007-6) Jones.
—The House That Played Ball. rev. ed. Abel, J., illus.
50p. (gr. k-2). 1992. pap. 18.00 (1-56611-006-8) Jones.
Tabb, Doug, ed. see Johnson, Larry.
Taber, Anthony. The Boy Who Stopped Time. Taber,
Anthony, illus. LC 92-398. 32p. (ps-3). 1993. SBE 13.
95 (0-689-50460-8, M K McElderry) Macmillan Child
Grp.
Tabesh, Delight, ed. & illus. see Walters-Lucy, Jean.
Tabibian, Ina. Fearon's Refrigerator Display Rewards.
(ps-1). 1989. pap. 6.95 (0-8224-3152-1) Fearon Teach
Aids.
Tabor, Nancy. Albertina Anda Arriba: El Abecedario:
Albertina Goes Up: An Alphabet Book. (Illus.). 32p.
(ps-3). 1993. pap. 6.95 (0-88106-418-1) Charlesbridge
Pub.
Tabrah, Ruth M. Emily's Hawaii. Hall, Pat, illus. 191p.
(gr. 4-6). 1986. pap. 6.95 (0-916630-45-5) Pr PaCifica.
—The Red Shark. 2nd ed. Hall, Pat, illus. 224p. (gr. 5-
10). 1991. pap. 7.95 (0-916630-67-6) Pr Pacifica.
Tabs, Judy & Steinberg, Barbara. Matzah Meals: A
Passover Cookbook for Kids. McLean, Chari P., illus.
LC 85-40. 72p. (ps up). 1985. pap. 6.95 spiral bd.
(0-930494-44-X) Kar-Ben.
Tachau, Frank. Kemal Ataturk. Schlesinger, Arthur M.,
Jr., intro. by. (Illus.). 112p. (gr. 5 up). 1988. lib. bdg.
17.95 (0-87754-507-3) Chelsea Hse.
Tacitus. Complete Works. Hadas, Moses, ed. 1964. pap.
text ed. 9.30 (0-07-553639-0, T53) McGraw.
Tackach, James. Hank Aaron. Murray, Jim, intro. by.
(Illus.). 64p. (gr. 3 up). 1991. PLB 14.95
(0-7910-1165-8) Chelsea Hse.
—Roy Campanella. Murray, Jim, intro. by. (Illus.). 64p.
(gr. 3 up). 1991. lib. bdg. 14.95 (0-7910-1170-4)
Chelsea Hse.
Tackett, Eric, jt. auth. see Whitfield, Karen.
Tada, Joni E. Darcy. LC 87-35712. (gr. 3-7). 1988. pap.
4.49 (1-55513-809-8, Chariot Bks) Cook.
—Jeremy, Barnabas & the Wonderful Dream. LC 87-
18338. (ps-2). 1987. 8.99 (1-55513-802-0, Chariot
Bks) Cook.
—Joni's Story. Musser, Joe & Maifair, Linda L.contrib.
by. 112p. (gr. 3-9). 1992. pap. 4.99 (0-310-58661-5,
Pub. by Youth Spec) Zondervan.
—Meet My Friends. LC 87-22344. (gr. 3-7). 1987. pap.
4.49 (1-55513-808-X, Chariot Bks) Cook.
—Ryan & the Circus Wheels. LC 87-26912. (ps-1). 1988.
8.99 (1-55513-154-9, Chariot Bks) Cook.
Tada, Joni E. & Jensen, Steve. Darcy & the Meanest
Teacher in the World. LC 92-33075. (gr. 1-6). 1993.
write for info. (0-7814-0885-7, Chariot Bks) Cook.

—Darcy's Dog Dilemma. LC 93-36330. 1994. write for info. (0-7814-0167-4, Chariot Bks) Cook.

Tada, Joni E., jt. auth. see Jensen, Steven.

Tadjo, Veronique. Lord of the Dance: An African Retelling. Tadjo, Veronique, illus. LC 89-2785. 32p. (gr. 1-4). 1989. (Lipp Jr Bks); PLB 12.89 (0-397-32352-2, Lipp Jr Bks) HarpC Child Bks.

Taetzsch, Lyn, jt. auth. see Taetzsch, Sandra.

Taetzsch, Sandra & Taetzsch, Lyn. Preschool Games & Activities. (ps-k). 1974. pap. 9.95 (0-8224-5605-2) Fearon Teach Aids.

Tafuri, Nancy. All Year Long. Tafuri, Nancy, illus. LC 82-9275. 32p. (gr. k-2). 1983. PLB 13.88 (0-688-01416-X) Greenwillow.

—The Ball Bounced. LC 87-37582. (Illus.). 24p. (ps up). 1989. 11.95 (0-688-07871-0) Greenwillow.

—Do Not Disturb. LC 86-357. (Illus.). 24p. (ps-3). 1987. 11.75 (0-688-06541-4); PLB 11.88 (0-688-06542-2) Greenwillow.

—Early Morning in the Barn. Tafuri, Nancy, illus. LC 83-1436. 24p. (ps-1). 1983. 14.95 (0-688-02328-2); PLB 14.88 (0-688-02329-0) Greenwillow.

—Early Morning in the Barn. ALC Staff, ed. LC 83-1436. (Illus.). 24p. (ps up). 1992. pap. 3.95 (0-688-11710-4, Mulberry) Morrow.

—Follow Me! LC 89-23259. (Illus.). 24p. (ps up). 1990. 13.95 (0-688-08773-6); lib. bdg. 13.88 (0-688-08774-4) Greenwillow.

—Have You Seen My Duckling? Tafuri, Nancy, illus. LC 83-17196. 24p. (ps-1). 1984. 15.95 (0-688-02797-0); PLB 15.88 (0-688-02798-9) Greenwillow.

—Have you Seen My Duckling? 1986. pap. 3.99 (0-14-050585-7, Puffin) Puffin Bks.

—Have You Seen My Duckling? Tafuri, Nancy, illus. 32p. (ps-k). 1986. pap. 3.95 (0-14-050532-6) Viking Child Bks.

—Have You Seen My Duckling? LC 83-17196. (Illus.). 24p. (ps). 1991. pap. 3.95 (0-688-10994-2, Mulberry) Morrow.

—In a Red House. Tafuri, Nancy, illus. LC 86-27114. (ps). 1987. Board book. pap. 3.95 (0-688-07185-6) Greenwillow.

—Junglewalk. LC 87-8558. (Illus.). 32p. (ps-3). 1988. 14.95 (0-688-07182-1); lib. bdg. 14.88 (0-688-07183-X) Greenwillow.

—My Friends. Tafuri, Nancy, illus. LC 86-29388. 12p. (ps). 1987. Board book. 3.95 (0-688-07187-2) Greenwillow.

—One Wet Jacket. LC 87-8439. (Illus.). 12p. (ps). 1988. Board Book. pap. 3.95 (0-688-07465-0) Greenwillow.

—Rabbit's Morning. Tafuri, Nancy, illus. LC 84-10229. 24p. (ps-1). 1985. 13.95 (0-688-04063-2); PLB 13.88 (0-688-04064-0) Greenwillow.

—Spots, Feathers, & Curly Tails. LC 87-15638. (Illus.). 32p. (ps-1). 1988. 15.00 (0-688-07536-3); lib. bdg. 14. 93 (0-688-07537-1) Greenwillow.

—This Is the Farmer. LC 92-30082. (Illus.). 24p. (ps up). 1994. write for info. (0-688-09468-6); PLB write for info. (0-688-09469-4) Greenwillow.

—Two New Sneakers. LC 87-8418. (Illus.). 12p. (ps). 1988. bds. 3.95 (0-688-07462-6) Greenwillow.

—Where We Sleep. LC 86-27115. (Illus.). (ps). 1987. pap. 3.95 (0-688-07189-9) Greenwillow.

—Who's Counting? Tafuri, Nancy, illus. LC 85-17702. 24p. (ps-1). 1986. 14.95 (0-688-06130-3); PLB 14.88 (0-688-06131-1) Greenwillow.

—Who's Counting? LC 92-24587. (Illus.). 32p. (ps). 1993. pap. 4.95 (0-688-12266-3, Mulberry) Morrow.

Tagel, Peggy. Pop-up Baby Bunny. (Illus.). 14p. (ps-1). 1991. 3.95 (0-448-40054-5, G&D) Putnam Pub Group.

—Pop-up Little Duck. (Illus.). 14p. 1991. 3.95 (0-448-40056-1, G&D) Putnam Pub Group.

—Pop-up Tiny Chick. (Illus.). 14p. 1991. 3.95 (0-448-40055-3, G&D) Putnam Pub Group.

Tager, Miriam. Macaulay Culkin. (Illus.). 48p. 1992. 1.49 (0-440-21427-0) Dell.

—Paula Abdul. (Illus.). 48p. 1992. 1.49 (0-440-21434-3) Dell.

Taggart, George. Bible Promises for Tiny Tots, II. Coffen, Richard W., ed. 32p. (Orig.). (ps). 1985. pap. 4.50 (0-8280-0246-0) Review & Herald.

—Bible Promises for Tiny Tots, III. Coffen, Richard W., ed. 32p. (Orig.). (ps). 1987. pap. 4.50 (0-8280-0375-0) Review & Herald.

Tagore, Rabindranath. The Cheese Doll. Mukherjee, Meenakshi, tr. from BEN. (Illus.). (gr. 3-11). 1979. 6.25 (0-89744-143-5) Auromere.

—Paper Boats. Bochak, Grayce, illus. LC 91-72987. 32p. (ps-3). 1992. 14.95 (1-878093-12-6) Boyds Mills Pr.

Tagore, Rabindranath, jt. ed. see Gajadin, Chitra.

Tagyos, Paul Ratz De see Ratz de Tagyos, Paul.

Taha, Karen T. Gift for Tia Rosa. (gr. 4-7). 1991. pap. 2.99 (0-553-15978-X) Bantam.

—Marshmallow Muscles, Banana Brainstorms. 114p. (gr. 3-7). 1988. 13.95 (0-15-200525-0, Gulliver Bks) HarBrace.

—Marshmallow Muscles, Banana Brainstorms. (gr. 5-7). 1990. pap. 2.75 (0-590-43394-6) Scholastic Inc.

Tahta, S., jt. auth. see Meredith, S.

Tailor, Z. Little Red Riding Hood "Puzzle 'n Book" Belli, Fred, illus. 8p. (gr. k up). 1989. PLB write for info. ABC Child Bks.

Taitt, Henry A. Advanced Projects for Junior High. 51p. (Prog. Bk.). (gr. 7-9). 1984. pap. text ed. 11.95 (0-88193-115-2) Create Learn.

—Beginning Projects for Adults. 45p. (Prog. Bk.). (gr. 10 up). 1983. pap. text ed. 11.95 (0-88193-121-7) Create Learn.

—Beginning Projects for Junior High. 46p. (gr. 7-9). 1983. pap. text ed. 11.95 (0-88193-111-X) Create Learn.

—Intermediate Projects for Adults. 52p. (Prog. Bk.). (gr. 10 up). 1983. pap. text ed. 11.95 (0-88193-123-3) Create Learn.

—Intermediate Projects for Junior High. 46p. (gr. 7-9). 1983. pap. text ed. 11.95 (0-88193-113-6) Create Learn.

Taitt, Henry A. & Taitt, Jennifer. Atari, Vol. 3. 47p. (gr. 5-12). 1983. pap. text ed. 11.95 (0-88193-073-3) Create Learn.

—Atari, Vol. 4. 51p. (gr. 5-12). 1983. pap. text ed. 11.95 (0-88193-074-1) Create Learn.

—TRS-80, Vol. 3. 53p. (gr. 5-12). 1983. pap. text ed. 11. 95 (0-88193-013-X) Create Learn.

—TRS-80, Vol. 4. 54p. (gr. 5-12). 1983. pap. text ed. 11. 95 (0-88193-014-8) Create Learn.

—TRS-80, Vol. 5. 57p. (gr. 6-12). 1983. pap. text ed. 11. 95 (0-88193-015-6) Create Learn.

—TRS-80, Vol. 6. 54p. (gr. 6-12). 1984. pap. text ed. 11. 95 (0-88193-016-4) Create Learn.

Taitt, Henry A. & Taitt, Kathy. TRS-80, Vol. 1. 53p. (gr. 4-12). 1983. pap. text ed. 11.95 (0-88193-011-3) Create Learn.

—TRS-80, Vol. 2. 56p. (gr. 4-12). 1983. pap. text ed. 11. 95 (0-88193-012-1) Create Learn.

Taitt, Jennifer. IBM, Vol. 1. 55p. (gr. 4-12). 1983. pap. text ed. 11.95 (0-88193-031-8) Create Learn.

—IBM, Vol. 2. 54p. (gr. 4-12). 1983. pap. text ed. 11.95 (0-88193-032-6) Create Learn.

—IBM, Vol. 3. 51p. (gr. 5-12). 1983. pap. text ed. 11.95 (0-88193-033-4) Create Learn.

—IBM, Vol. 4. 66p. (gr. 5-12). 1983. pap. text ed. 11.95 (0-88193-034-2) Create Learn.

—IBM, Vol. 5. 53p. (gr. 6-12). 1984. pap. text ed. 11.95 (0-88193-035-0) Create Learn.

—IBM, Vol. 6. 65p. (gr. 6-12). 1984. pap. text ed. 11.95 (0-88193-036-9) Create Learn.

Taitt, Jennifer, jt. auth. see Taitt, Henry A.

Taitt, Kathy. Apple, Vol. 1. 59p. (gr. 4-12). 1983. pap. text ed. 11.95 (0-88193-001-6) Create Learn.

—Apple, Vol. 2. 61p. (gr. 4-12). 1983. pap. text ed. 11.95 (0-88193-002-4) Create Learn.

—Apple, Vol. 3. 55p. (gr. 5-12). 1983. pap. text ed. 11.95 (0-88193-003-2) Create Learn.

—Apple, Vol. 4. 57p. (gr. 5-12). 1983. pap. text ed. 11.95 (0-88193-004-0) Create Learn.

—Apple, Vol. 5. 57p. (gr. 6-12). 1983. pap. text ed. 11.95 (0-88193-005-9) Create Learn.

—Apple, Vol. 6. 68p. (gr. 6-12). 1984. pap. text ed. 11.95 (0-88193-006-7) Create Learn.

Taitt, Kathy, jt. auth. see Taitt, Henry A.

Taitt, Nancy. Atari, Vol. 1. 55p. (gr. 4-12). 1983. pap. text ed. 11.95 (0-88193-071-7) Create Learn.

—Atari, Vol. 2. 64p. (Prog. Bk.). (gr. 4-12). 1984. pap. text ed. 11.95 (0-88193-072-5) Create Learn.

Taitz, Emily & Henry, Sondra. Israel: A Sacred Land. LC 87-13449. (Illus.). 160p. (gr. 5 up). 1988. RSBE 14.95 (0-87518-364-6, Dillon) Macmillan Child Grp.

Taitz, Emily, jt. auth. see Henry, Sondra.

Takabatake, Jun. Rub-a-Dub-Dub: Who's in the Tub? LC 93-1805. (gr. 3 up). 1993. 10.95 (0-8118-0518-2) Chronicle Bks.

Takada, Noriko, jt. auth. see Kato, Horoshi.

Takahama, Toshie. Happy Origami. (Illus.). 60p. (Orig.). 1989. pap. 19.00 boxed set incl. 96 sheets origami paper (0-87040-830-5) Japan Pubns USA.

—Joy of Origami: Ten Basic Folds Which Create Many Forms. (Illus.). 128p. (Orig.). 1985. pap. 12.00 (0-87040-603-5) Japan Pubns USA.

Takai, Ronald T. Journey to Gold Mountain: The Chinese in Nineteenth-Century America. LC 93-4649. (Illus.). 1994. 18.95 (0-7910-2177-7, Am Art Analog); pap. write for info. (0-7910-2277-3, Am Art Analog) Chelsea Hse.

Takaki, Ronald. Spacious Dreams: The First Wave of Asian Immigration. (Illus.). 1994. 18.95 (0-7910-2176-9, Am Art Analog) Chelsea Hse.

Takashima, Shizuye. A Child in Prison Camp. (Illus.). 100p. (gr. 4 up). 1991. pap. 7.95 (0-88776-241-7) Tundra Bks.

Takeshita, Fumiko. The Park Bench. Kanagy, Ruth A., tr. from JPN. Suzuki, Mamoru, illus. 40p. (ps-3). 1988. 13.95 (0-916291-15-4) Kane-Miller Bk.

—The Park Bench. Kanagy, Ruth A., tr. from JPN. Suzuki, Mamoru, illus. 40p. (gr. 3-8). 1989. pap. 6.95 (0-916291-21-9) Kane-Miller Bk.

Takeshita, Jiro. Food in Japan. LC 88-31465. (Illus.). 32p. (gr. 3-6). 1989. lib. bdg. 15.94 (0-86625-340-8); 11.95s.p. (0-685-58501-8) Rourke Corp.

Takeuchi, Hiroshi. The World of Fishes. Pohl, Kathy, ed. LC 85-28212. (Illus.). 32p. (gr. 3-7). 1986. PLB 17.96 (0-8172-2548-X) Raintree Steck-V.

Takihara, Koji. Rolli. LC 87-29262. (Illus.). (ps-12). 1991. pap. 14.95 (0-88708-058-8) Picture Bk Studio.

Takvorian, Rick, tr. see Ende, Michael.

**Talbert, Stations of the Cross. Date not set. 15.00 (0-06-023383-4, Festival); PLB 14.89 (0-06-023384-2, Festival) HarpC Child Bks.

Talbert, Marc. Dead Birds Singing. LC 85-147. 224p. (gr. 6 up). 1985. 13.95 (0-316-83125-5) Little.

—Dead Birds Singing. (gr. 7 up). 1988. pap. 2.95 (0-440-20036-9, LFL) Dell.

—Double Or Nothing. (gr. 3-7). 1990. 15.00 (0-8037-0832-7) Dial Bks Young.

—Pillow of Clouds. LC 90-34264. 208p. (gr. 5-9). 1991. 15.00 (0-8037-0901-3) Dial Bks Young.

—The Purple Heart. LC 91-23084. 144p. (gr. 4-8). 1992. 14.00 (0-06-020428-1); PLB 13.89 (0-06-020429-X) HarpC Child Bks.

—The Purple Heart. 128p. (gr. 6). 1993. pap. 3.50 (0-380-71985-1, Camelot) Avon.

Talbot, Charlene J. An Orphan for Nebraska. Brown, Judith G., illus. LC 78-12179. 216p. (gr. 4-6). 1979. SBE 14.95 (0-689-30698-9, Atheneum Childrens Bks) Macmillan Child Grp.

Talbot, Daniel, ed. Film: An Anthology. 2nd ed. LC 59-11203. (gr. 9 up). 1966. pap. 13.00x (0-520-01251-8) U CA Pr.

Talbot, John. Hasn't He Grown! (Illus.). 32p. (ps-2). 1989. 13.95 (0-86264-232-9, Pub. by Anderson Pr UK) Trafalgar.

—Pins & Needles. LC 91-13317. (Illus.). 32p. (ps-2). 1992. 12.00 (0-8037-0942-0) Dial Bks Young.

—The Raries. (Illus.). 32p. (gr. k-3). 1989. 13.95 (0-86264-144-6, Pub. by Anderson Pr UK) Trafalgar.

Talbot, Marilyn. Shy Roland. (Illus.). 32p. (ps-k). 1994. 14.95 (0-86264-405-4, Pub. by Andersen Pr UK) Trafalgar.

Talbot, Mary. The Senses. (Illus.). 112p. (gr. 6-12). 1990. 18.95 (0-7910-0027-3) Chelsea Hse.

Talbott, Hudson. Going Hollywood! A Dinosaur's Dream. Talbott, Hudson, illus. LC 89-1190. 32p. (ps-3). 1989. 12.95 (0-517-57354-7) Crown Bks Yng Read.

—Going Hollywood: A Dinosaur's Dream. Talbott, Hudson, illus. LC 89-1190. 32p. (ps-2). 1993. pap. 4.99 (0-517-58983-4) Crown Bks Yng Read.

—King Arthur: The Sword in the Stone. LC 90-28104. (Illus.). 56p. (gr. 5 up). 1991. 14.95 (0-688-09403-1); PLB 14.88 (0-688-09404-X) Morrow Jr Bks.

—The Lady at Liberty. 32p. (Orig.). 1991. pap. 9.95 (0-380-76427-X) Avon.

—We're Back: A Dinosaur's Story. 32p. (ps-2). 1988. PLB 15.00 (0-517-56599-4) Crown Bks Yng Read.

—We're Back! A Dinosaur's Story. Talbott, Hudson, illus. LC 87-5355. 32p. (ps-2). 1993. pap. 4.99 (0-517-58985-0) Crown Bks Yng Read.

—Your Pet Dinosaur: An Owner's Manual. Talbott, Hudson, illus. LC 91-39762. 40p. (gr. 2 up). 1992. 15. 00 (0-688-11337-0); PLB 14.93 (0-688-11338-9) Morrow Jr Bks.

Talen, Maria. Ocean Pollution. LC 91-15567. (Illus.). 112p. (gr. 5-8). 1991. PLB 14.95 (1-56006-104-9) Lucent Bks.

Taliaferro, Margaret. Do You Ever Have Questions Like These? 2nd, rev. ed. (Illus.). 199p. (gr. k-6). 1991. pap. 6.95 (0-9618730-1-9) FEA Pub.

—The Real Reason for Christmas: Letters to Children for the Twelve Nights of Christmas. (Illus.). 118p. (gr. 1-7). pap. 6.95 (0-9618730-0-0) FEA Pub.

Taliercio, Carmela & Acocella, Christine. Tocca a Te. (ITA., Illus.). 160p. (Orig.). (gr. 7-9). 1990. wkbk. 14. 95 (1-879279-03-7, TX 3-018-189) Proficiency Pr.

Taliercio, Carmela, et al. The Foreign Language Teacher's Handbook: Aiming for Proficiency in Italian. (ITA., Illus.). 200p. (Orig.). (gr. 7-9). 1991. tchr's. ed. 28.95 (1-879279-05-3) Proficiency Pr.

Talkington, Bruce. Disney's Winnie the Pooh's Christmas. LC 91-71353. (Illus.). 48p. 1991. 12.95 (1-56282-068-0) Disney Pr.

—Disney's Winnie the Pooh's Easter. Langley, Bill & Wakeman, Diana, illus. LC 92-53441. 32p. (ps-4). 1993. 10.95 (1-56282-377-9) Disney Pr.

—Winnie the Pooh's Halloween. Vaccaro Associates Staff, illus. LC 93-70934. 32p. (ps-4). 1993. 11.95 (1-56282-540-2) Disney Pr.

Tallach, Isobel. Life of Jesus. (Orig.). (ps-3). 1984. pap. 1.75 (0-85151-345-X) Banner of Truth.

Tallach, John. They Shall Be Mine. 128p. (gr. 9-12). 1981. pap. 7.95 (0-85151-320-4) Banner of Truth.

Tallant, Robert. The Pirate Lafitte & the Battle of New Orleans. Chase, John, illus. 192p. (gr. 5 up). 1992. pap. 7.95 (0-88289-931-7) Pelican.

Tallarico, A. Stop & Find Maze Madness. (Illus.). 14p. 1991. pap. 1.95 (1-56156-108-8) Kidsbks.

—Stop & Find: Space Race Mazes. (Illus.). 12p. (Orig.). 1991. pap. 1.95 (1-56156-030-8) Kidsbks.

Tallarico, Anthony. Detect Donald. (Illus.). 24p. (Orig.). 1991. pap. 2.95 (0-942025-79-2) Kidsbks.

—Detect Donald. (Illus.). 24p. 1990. 9.95 (0-942025-99-7) Kidsbks.

—Endangered Animals Activity Book. (Illus.). 64p. (Orig.). 1990. pap. 1.95 (0-942025-12-1) Kidsbks.

—Find Frankie. (Illus., Orig.). 1991. pap. 2.95 (0-942025-76-8) Kidsbks.

—Find Frankie. (Illus.). 24p. 1990. 9.95 (0-942025-82-2) Kidsbks.

—Find Freddie. Tallarico, Anthony, illus. 24p. (gr. 2-6). 1990. lib. bdg. 10.59 (0-8167-1955-1); pap. 2.95 (0-685-44996-3) Troll Assocs.

—Find Freddie. (Illus.). 24p. (Orig.). 1988. pap. 2.95 (0-942025-65-2) Kidsbks.

—Find Freddie. (Illus.). 24p. 1990. 9.95 (0-942025-13-X) Kidsbks.

—Hunt for Hector. Tallarico, Anthony, illus. 24p. (gr. 2-6). 1990. lib. bdg. 10.59 (0-8167-1956-X); pap. 2.95 (0-685-44993-9) Troll Assocs.

—Hunt for Hector. (Illus.). 24p. (Orig.). 1988. pap. 2.95 (0-942025-68-7) Kidsbks.

—Hunt for Hector. (Illus.). 24p. 1990. 9.95 (0-942025-27-X) Kidsbks.

—I Can Draw Animals. 64p. (Orig.). (gr. 3 up). 1980. pap. 3.95 (0-671-41375-9, Little Simon) S&S Trade.

—Look for Laura. (Illus.). 24p. (Orig.). 1991. pap. 2.95 (*0-942025-77-6*) Kidsbks.
—Look for Laura. (Illus.). 24p. 1990. 9.95 (*0-942025-89-X*) Kidsbks.
—Look for Lisa. Tallarico, Anthony, illus. 24p. (gr. 2-6). 1990. lib. bdg. 10.59 (*0-8167-1957-8*); pap. 2.95 (*0-685-44994-7*) Troll Assocs.
—Look for Lisa. (Illus.). 24p. (Orig.). 1988. pap. 2.95 (*0-942025-66-0*) Kidsbks.
—Look for Lisa. (Illus.). 24p. 1990. 9.95 (*0-942025-61-X*) Kidsbks.
—Mystery Pictures to Draw. (Illus.). 64p. (Orig.). 1990. pap. 1.95 (*0-942025-19-9*) Kidsbks.
—Search for Sam. Tallarico, Anthony, illus. 24p. (gr. 2-6). 1990. lib. bdg. 10.59 (*0-8167-1958-6*); pap. 2.95 (*0-685-44995-5*) Troll Assocs.
—Search for Sam. (Illus.). 24p. (Orig.). 1988. pap. 2.95 (*0-942025-67-9*) Kidsbks.
—Search for Sam. (Illus.). 24p. 1990. 9.95 (*0-942025-58-X*) Kidsbks.
—Search for Santa. (Illus.). 32p. (Orig.). 1990. 10.95 (*0-942025-71-7*); pap. 3.95 (*0-942025-72-5*) Kidsbks.
—Search for Susie. (Illus.). 24p. (Orig.). 1991. pap. 2.95 (*0-942025-78-4*) Kidsbks.
—Search for Susie. (Illus.). 24p. 1990. 9.95 (*0-942025-97-0*) Kidsbks.
—Stop & Find Maze Madness. Tallarico, Anthony, illus. 12p. (Orig.). (gr. 4-7). 1990. pap. 1.95 (*1-878890-00-X*) Palisades Prodns.
—What's Wrong Here, No. 2. (Illus.). 64p. (Orig.). 1990. pap. 1.95 (*0-942025-92-X*) Kidsbks.
Tallarico, Beatrice & Stone, S. C. Tindel's Blue Door. 2nd ed. (Illus.). 19p. (gr. 2-8). 1986. pap. 2.95 (*0-936191-14-7*) Tallstone Pub.
Tallarico, Beatrice & Stone, S. Callis. The Weeuns Journey of Two Cousins. Stone, S. Callis, illus. 39p. (gr. 2-8). 1984. 12.95 (*0-936191-13-9*) Tallstone Pub.
Tallarico, Tony. Animals. (Illus.). 12p. (ps-1). 1982. bds. 3.95 (*0-448-40337-4*, Tuffy) Putnam Pub Group.
—Bunny Honey Springtime Search. (Illus.). 24p. 1992. pap. 3.95 (*1-56156-099-5*) Kidsbks.
—Colors. Tallarico, Tony, illus. 12p. (ps-1). 1982. bds. 3.95 (*0-89828-304-3*, Tuffy) Putnam Pub Group.
—Drawing & Cartooning Dinosaurs: A Step-by-Step Guide for the Aspiring Prehistoric Artist. LC 93-16278. (Illus.). 96p. (Orig.). 1993. pap. 7.95 (*0-399-51814-2*, Perigee Bks) Putnam Pub Group.
—Drawing & Cartooning Monsters: A Step-by-Step Guide for the Aspiring Monster-Maker. (Illus.). 128p. (Orig.). 1992. pap. 7.95 (*0-399-51785-5*, Perigee Bks) Putnam Pub Group.
—Famous People & Places. (Illus.). 24p. 1992. 4.98 (*0-8317-4982-2*) Smithmark.
—Find Frankie & His Monster Friends. (Illus.). 24p. 1992. pap. 2.95 (*1-56156-149-5*) Kidsbks.
—Find Freddie & Lisa in the Haunted House. (Illus.). 32p. 1991. 10.95 (*1-56156-016-2*) Kidsbks.
—Find Freddie & Lisa in the Haunted House. (Illus.). 32p. 1991. pap. 3.95 (*1-56156-041-3*) Kidsbks.
—Find Freddie Around the World. (Illus.). 24p. 1992. 9.95 (*1-56156-066-9*) Kidsbks.
—Freddie's Picture Puzzle Book. (Illus.). 24p. 1991. 3.98 (*1-56156-006-5*) Kidsbks.
—The Giant I Can Draw Everything. Schneider, Meg, ed. (Illus.). 192p. (Orig.). (gr. 3-7). 1982. pap. 4.95 (*0-671-44459-X*, Little Simon) S&S Trade.
—Hector's Picture Puzzle Books. (Illus.). 24p. 1991. 3.98 (*1-56156-008-1*) Kidsbks.
—Hidden Pictures: Crazy Classroom. (Illus.). 32p. 1992. pap. 2.95 (*1-56156-141-X*) Kidsbks.
—Hidden Pictures: Creepy Castles. (Illus.). 24p. 1992. 9.95 (*1-56156-120-7*) Kidsbks.
—Hidden Pictures: Monster Madness. (Illus.). 24p. 1992. 9.95 (*1-56156-121-5*) Kidsbks.
—Hidden Pictures: Santa's Super Surprises. (Illus.). 24p. 1992. 9.95 (*1-56156-118-5*) Kidsbks.
—Hidden Pictures: Twelve Days of Christmas. (Illus.). 24p. 1992. 9.95 (*1-56156-119-3*) Kidsbks.
—I Can Draw Cars, Trucks, Trains & Other Wheels. Tallarico, Tony, illus. 64p. (Orig.). (gr. 3 up). 1981. pap. 3.95 (*0-671-42535-8*, Little Simon) S&S Trade.
—I Can Draw Christmas. (Illus.). 64p. (gr. 4 up). 1990. pap. 3.95 perfect bdg. (*0-671-70446-X*, Little Simon) S&S Trade.
—I Can Draw Halloween. (ps). 1992. pap. 3.95 (*0-671-78376-9*, Little Simon) S&S Trade.
—I Can Draw Monsters. 69p. (gr. 3 up). 1980. pap. 3.95 (*0-671-41374-0*, Little Simon) S&S Trade.
—I Can Draw Pets. 64p. 1989. pap. 3.95 (*0-671-67803-5*, Little Simon) S&S Trade.
—I Can Draw Sports. (Illus.). 40p. (gr. 4 up). 1990. pap. 3.95 (*0-671-70447-8*, Little Simon) S&S Trade.
—I Didn't Know That! about Famous People & Places. (Illus.). 1992. pap. 2.95 (*1-56156-106-1*) Kidsbks.
—I Didn't Know That about Famous People & Places. (Illus.). 32p. 1992. 9.95 (*1-56156-114-2*) Kidsbks.
—I Didn't Know That about How Things Work. (Illus.). 32p. 1992. 9.95 (*1-56156-116-9*); pap. 2.95 (*1-56156-172-X*) Kidsbks.
—I Didn't Know That about Sports. (Illus.). 32p. 1992. pap. 2.95 (*1-56156-163-0*) Kidsbks.
—I Didn't Know That about Sports. (Illus.). 32p. 1992. 9.95 (*1-56156-115-0*); pap. 2.95 (*1-56156-111-8*) Kidsbks.
—I Didn't Know That about Strange but True Mysteries. (Illus.). 32p. 1992. 9.95 (*1-56156-117-7*); pap. 2.95 (*1-56156-177-0*) Kidsbks.

—Let's Take a Trip. Tallarico, Tony, illus. 12p. (ps-1). 1982. bds. 3.95 (*0-89828-305-1*, Tuffy) Putnam Pub Group.
—Lisa's Picture Puzzle Books. (Illus.). 24p. 1991. 3.98 (*1-56156-007-3*) Kidsbks.
—Look for Lisa: Time Traveller. (Illus.). 24p. 1992. 9.95 (*1-56156-067-7*) Kidsbks.
—Mr. Merlin's Puzzle & Game Book. Klimo, Kate, ed. Tallarico, Tony, illus. 64p. (Orig.). (gr. 3-6). 1981. pap. 2.95 (*0-671-44492-1*) S&S Trade.
—More Preschool Can You Find Picture Book. Tallarico, Tony, illus. (ps). 1991. 3.95 (*0-448-48801-9*, Tuffy) Putnam Pub Group.
—My First All about Cats Jigsaw Puzzle Book. Tallarico, Tony, illus. (ps). 1991. 4.95 (*0-448-48804-3*, Tuffy) Putnam Pub Group.
—My First All about Circus Jigsaw Puzzle Book. Tallarico, Tony, illus. (ps). 1991. 4.95 (*0-448-48805-1*, Tuffy) Putnam Pub Group.
—My First All about Dinosaurs Jigsaw Puzzle Book. Tallarico, Tony, illus. (ps). 1991. 4.95 (*0-448-48802-7*, Tuffy) Putnam Pub Group.
—My First All about Dogs Jigsaw Puzzle Book. Tallarico, Tony, illus. (ps). 1991. 4.95 (*0-448-48803-5*, Tuffy) Putnam Pub Group.
—Numbers. (Illus.). 12p. (ps-1). 1982. bds. 3.95 (*0-89828-303-5*, Tuffy) Putnam Pub Group.
—Preschool Can You Find ABC Picture Book. (Illus.). 12p. (ps). 1992. 3.95 (*0-448-40426-5*, G&D) Putnam Pub Group.
—Preschool Can You Find Counting Picture Book. (Illus.). 12p. (ps). 1992. 3.95 (*0-448-40425-7*, G&D) Putnam Pub Group.
—Preschool Can You Find Picture Book. Tallarico, Tony, illus. (ps). 1991. 3.95 (*0-448-48800-0*, Tuffy) Putnam Pub Group.
—Sam's Picture Puzzle Books. (Illus.). 24p. 1991. 3.98 (*1-56156-009-X*) Kidsbks.
—Search for Santa's Helpers. (Illus.). 32p. 1991. 10.95 (*1-56156-015-4*); pap. 3.95 (*1-56156-031-6*) Kidsbks.
—Search for Santa's Helpers. (Illus.). 32p. (Orig.). 1991. pap. 3.95 (*1-56156-042-1*) Kidsbks.
—Search for Sylvester. (Illus.). 24p. 1992. 9.95 (*1-56156-068-5*) Kidsbks.
—Seasons. (Illus.). 12p. (ps-1). 1982. bds. 3.95 (*0-89828-301-9*, Tuffy) Putnam Pub Group.
—Sounds. (Illus.). 28p. (ps). 1992. 2.95 (*0-448-40428-1*, G&D) Putnam Pub Group.
—Sports. (Illus.). 24p. 1992. 4.98 (*0-8317-4979-2*) Smithmark.
—Strange but True Mysteries. (Illus.). 24p. 1992. 4.98 (*0-8317-4980-6*) Smithmark.
—Things You Always Wanted to Know about Monsters: But Were Afraid to Ask. (Illus.). 64p. (Orig.). 1988. pap. 1.95 (*0-942025-59-8*) Kidsbks.
—What Can You Find. (Illus.). 28p. (ps). 1992. 2.95 (*0-448-40429-X*, G&D) Putnam Pub Group.
—What Time Is It? (Illus.). 12p. (ps-1). 1982. bds. 3.95 (*0-89828-302-7*, Tuffy) Putnam Pub Group.
—What's In. (Illus.). 28p. (ps). 1992. 2.95 (*0-448-40427-3*, G&D) Putnam Pub Group.
—What's Wrong Here? At School. (Illus.). 24p. 1991. pap. 2.95 (*1-56156-034-0*) Kidsbks.
—What's Wrong Here? At School. (Illus.). 24p. 1991. 9.95 (*1-56156-005-7*) Kidsbks.
—What's Wrong Here? At the Amusement Park. (Illus.). 32p. 1991. pap. 2.95 (*1-56156-032-4*) Kidsbks.
—What's Wrong Here? At the Amusement Park. (Illus.). 24p. 1991. 9.95 (*1-56156-003-0*) Kidsbks.
—What's Wrong Here? At the Movies. (Illus.). 24p. 1991. pap. 2.95 (*1-56156-035-9*) Kidsbks.
—What's Wrong Here? At the Movies. (Illus.). 24p. 1991. 9.95 (*1-56156-004-9*) Kidsbks.
—What's Wrong Here? In the Haunted House. (Illus.). 24p. 1991. pap. 2.95 (*1-56156-033-2*) Kidsbks.
—What's Wrong Here? In the Haunted House. (Illus.). 24p. 1991. 9.95 (*1-56156-002-2*) Kidsbks.
—Where Are They? (Illus.). 96p. 1992. 14.95 (*1-56156-139-8*) Kidsbks.
—Where's Columbus? (Illus.). 24p. 1992. 9.95 (*1-56156-098-7*) Kidsbks.
—Where's Columbus? (Illus.). 24p. 1992. pap. 2.95 (*1-56156-097-9*) Kidsbks.
—Where's Cupid? (Illus.). 32p. 1991. pap. 3.95 (*1-56156-043-X*) Kidsbks.
—Where's Cupid? (Illus.). 32p. 1991. 10.95 (*1-56156-048-0*) Kidsbks.
—Where's the Bunny? (Illus.). 32p. (Orig.). 1991. pap. 3.95 (*1-56156-011-1*) Kidsbks.
—Where's the Bunny? (Illus.). 28p. 1991. pap. 2.95 (*1-56156-096-0*) Kidsbks.
—Where's the Bunny? (Illus.). 24p. 1992. 10.95 (*1-56156-010-3*) Kidsbks.
—Where's Wendy? (Illus.). 24p. (Orig.). 1991. pap. 2.95 (*1-56156-040-5*) Kidsbks.
—Where's Wendy? (Illus.). 24p. 1992. 9.95 (*1-56156-069-3*) Kidsbks.
Tallarico, Tony, illus. A B C. 28p. (ps-1). 1988. bds. 2.95 (*0-448-48817-5*, Tuffy) Putnam Pub Group.
—Alphabet. 12p. (ps-1). 1987. bds. 3.95 (*0-89828-317-5*, Tuffy) Putnam Pub Group.
—At Home. 28p. (ps-1). 1984. bds. 2.95 (*0-448-48818-3*, Tuffy) Putnam Pub Group.
—Colors. 28p. (ps-1). 1988. bds. 2.95 (*0-448-48819-1*, Tuffy) Putnam Pub Group.
—Dinosaurs. 12p. (ps-1). 1988. bds. 3.95 (*0-89828-318-3*, Tuffy) Putnam Pub Group.

—Disney's Five Board Games to Go. 12p. (ps-5). 1990. bds. 16.95 (*0-448-48815-9*, Tuffy) Putnam Pub Group.
—Dolls, Dolls, Dolls. 12p. (ps-1). 1990. bds. 3.95 (*0-89828-405-8*, Tuffy) Putnam Pub Group.
—Finger Counting. 28p. (ps-1). 1984. bds. 2.95 (*0-448-48820-5*, Tuffy) Putnam Pub Group.
—Fire Engines. 12p. (ps-1). 1990. bds. 3.95 (*0-448-40333-1*, Tuffy) Putnam Pub Group.
—Five Wacky Games to Go. 12p. (ps-3). 1991. bds. 16.95 (*0-448-48816-7*, Tuffy) Putnam Pub Group.
—Happy Birthday. 12p. (ps-1). 1985. bds. 3.95 (*0-89828-313-2*, Tuffy) Putnam Pub Group.
—Haunted House. 12p. (ps-1). 1990. 3.95 (*0-89828-402-3*, Tuffy) Putnam Pub Group.
—Here We Go. 28p. (ps-1). 1988. bds. 2.95 (*0-448-48821-3*, Tuffy) Putnam Pub Group.
—How Many? 28p. (ps-1). 1984. bds. 2.95 (*0-448-48822-1*, Tuffy) Putnam Pub Group.
—I Love My Family. 12p. (ps-1). 1985. bds. 3.95 (*0-89828-314-0*, Tuffy) Putnam Pub Group.
—Little Engine That Could. 12p. (ps-1). 1990. bds. 3.95 (*0-448-40334-X*, Tuffy) Putnam Pub Group.
—Meet Peter Rabbit. 12p. (ps-1). 1988. bds. 3.95 (*0-89828-321-3*, Tuffy) Putnam Pub Group.
—Nursery Rhymes. 12p. (ps-1). 1988. bds. 3.95 (*0-89828-320-5*, Tuffy) Putnam Pub Group.
—Opposites. 12p. (ps-1). 1988. bds. 3.95 (*0-89828-319-1*, Tuffy) Putnam Pub Group.
—Peter Rabbit's Big Adventure. 12p. (ps-1). 1988. bds. 3.95 (*0-89828-324-8*, Tuffy) Putnam Pub Group.
—Peter Rabbit's Family. 12p. (ps-1). 1988. bds. 3.95 (*0-89828-312-4*, Tuffy) Putnam Pub Group.
—Pets. 12p. (ps-1). 1990. bds. 3.95 (*0-89828-400-7*, Tuffy) Putnam Pub Group.
—Shapes. 12p. (ps-1). 1985. bds. 3.95 (*0-89828-315-9*, Tuffy) Putnam Pub Group.
—Snowboy & Snowgirl. 12p. (ps-1). 1990. bds. 3.95 (*0-448-40336-6*, Tuffy) Putnam Pub Group.
—A Tale of Peter Rabbit. 12p. (ps-1). 1988. bds. 3.95 (*0-89828-322-1*, Tuffy) Putnam Pub Group.
—Time To... 28p. (ps-1). 1984. bds. 2.95 (*0-448-48823-X*, Tuffy) Putnam Pub Group.
—What's Opposite? 28p. (ps-1). 1984. bds. 2.95 (*0-448-48824-8*, Tuffy) Putnam Pub Group.
—Who Am I? 28p. (ps-1). 1984. bds. 2.95 (*0-448-48825-6*, Tuffy) Putnam Pub Group.
Tall Bull, Henry & Weist, Tom. Northern Cheyenne Fire Fighters: Modern Indians Fighting Forest Fires. (gr. 4 up). 1973. pap. 5.95 (*0-89992-016-0*) Coun India Ed.
Tallent, Mary M. The Secret at Robert's Roost. 168p. (Orig.). (gr. 4-8). 1988. pap. 3.95 (*0-941711-05-6*) Wyrick & Co.
Talley, Carol. Clarissa. Maeno, Itoko, illus. LC 91-29958. 32p. (gr. 1-4). 1992. 16.95 (*1-55942-014-6*, 7650) Marshfilm.
—Gumbo Goes Downtown. Maeno, Itoko, illus. LC 93-3551. 32p. (gr. 1-4). 1993. 16.95 (*1-55942-042-1*, 7654) Marshfilm.
—Hana's Year. Maeno, Itoko, illus. LC 92-19290. 32p. (gr. 1-4). 1992. 16.95 (*1-55942-034-0*, 7652); incl. video & tchr's. guide 79.95 (*1-55942-037-5*, 9371) Marshfilm.
—Papa Piccolo. Maeno, Itoko, illus. LC 92-4319. 32p. (gr. 1-4). 1992. 16.95 (*1-55942-028-6*, 7651) Marshfilm.
Talley, Gene W. How to Learn a Foreign Language: Easy-to-Use, Diagrammed Study Techniques That Will Help You Learn a New Language. LC 89-91138. 52p. (Orig.). (gr. 11-12). 1989. pap. 6.75 (*0-9622222-0-8*) G Talley.
Tallis, Robyn. Fire in the Sky. (gr. 6 up). 1989. pap. 2.95 (*0-8041-0463-8*) Ivy Books.
—Horrorvid. (gr. 6 up). 1989. pap. 2.95 (*0-8041-0461-1*) Ivy Books.
—Mountain of Stolen Dreams. (gr. 6 up). 1988. pap. 2.95 (*0-8041-0201-5*) Ivy Books.
—Night of Two New Moons. (gr. 6 up). 1989. pap. 2.95 (*0-8041-0209-0*) Ivy Books.
—Visions from the Sea. (gr. 6 up). 1989. pap. 2.95 (*0-8041-0206-6*) Ivy Books.
—Zero-Sum Games. (gr. 6 up). 1989. pap. 2.95 (*0-8041-0207-4*) Ivy Books.
Tallman, Edward. Garth Brooks: Straight from the Heart. LC 93-10214. (Illus.). 72p. (gr. 3 up). 1993. lib. bdg. 13.95 RSBE (*0-87518-595-9*, Dillon) Macmillan Child Grp.
TallMountain, Mary. Green March Moons. Senungetuk, Joseph E., illus. LC 87-6018. 32p. (Orig.). (gr. 6 up). 1987. pap. 7.95 (*0-938678-10-8*) New Seed.
Tallon, Robert, illus. ABCDEFGHIJKLMNOPQRSTUVWXYZ. LC 76-86987. (ENG & SPA.). 64p. (gr. k-2). 1969. PLB 14.95 (*0-87460-131-2*) Lion Bks.
Talmadge, Katherine S. Drugs & Sports. Raymond, Larry, illus. 88p. (gr. 5-8). 1991. PLB 14.95 (*0-941477-59-2*) TFC Bks NY.
—Focus on Steroids. (Illus.). 64p. (gr. 2-4). 1991. PLB 14.95 (*0-8050-2216-3*) TFC Bks NY.
—John Muir: At Home in the Wild. Castro, Antonio, illus. LC 92-36292. 80p. (gr. 4-7). 1993. PLB 14.95 (*0-8050-2123-X*) TFC Bks NY.
—The Life of Charles Drew. Castro, Antonio, illus. 80p. (gr. 4-7). 1991. PLB 13.95 (*0-941477-65-7*) TFC Bks NY.
Talwalker, Gopinath. Some Indian Saints. Jomra, J., illus. 64p. (Orig.). (gr. 5 up). 1980. pap. 2.50 (*0-89744-208-3*, Pub. by Natl Bk Trust IA) Auromere.

Tamar, Erika. Fair Game. 1993. pap. 3.95 (0-685-65843-0, HB Juv Bks) HarBrace.
—Fair Game. 1993. pap. 3.95 (0-15-227065-5) HarBrace.
—Good-Bye, Glamour Girl. LC 83-49493. 224p. (gr. 5 up). 1984. (Lipp Jr Bks); (Lipp Jr Bks) HarpC Child Bks.
—High Cheekbones. 240p. (gr. 7 up). 1990. pap. 12.95 (0-670-82843-2) Viking Child Bks.
—It Happened at Cecilia's. LC 88-28502. 144p. (gr. 6-9). 1989. SBE 13.95 (0-689-31478-7, Atheneum Child Bk) Macmillan Child Grp.
—It Happened at Cecilia's. LC 91-8171. 144p. (gr. 7 up). 1991. pap. 3.95 (0-02-045395-7, Collier Young Ad) Macmillan Child Grp.
—No Defense. LC 93-3248. (gr. 9-12). 1993. write for info. (0-15-278537-X) HarBrace.
—Out of Control. LC 91-4973. 208p. (gr. 7 up). 1991. SBE 14.95 (0-689-31689-5, Atheneum Child Bk) Macmillan Child Grp.
—Soccer Mania! 64p. (Orig.). (gr. 2-4). 1993. PLB 6.99 (0-679-93396-4); pap. 2.50 (0-679-83396-X) Random Bks Yng Read.
—The Truth about Kim O'Hara. LC 92-3943. 192p. (gr. 6-9). 1992. SBE 14.95 (0-689-31789-1, Atheneum Child Bk) Macmillan Child Grp.
Tamarin, Alfred, jt. auth. see Glubok, Shirley.
Tamarri, Kathie T., jt. auth. see Ourth, John.
Tamboise, Pierre. A Trip by Torpedo. (Illus.). (gr. 1-8). 1992. PLB 8.95 (0-89565-894-1); Resale. 12.75 (0-685-60992-8) Childs World.
Tambourine Books Staff, tr. see Leonard, Alain.
Tames, Richard. Alexander Fleming. (Illus.). 32p. (gr. 5-8). 1990. PLB 12.40 (0-531-14005-9) Watts.
—Alexander Graham Bell. (Illus.). 32p. (gr. 5-8). 1990. PLB 12.40 (0-531-14003-2) Watts.
—Amelia Earhart. (ps-3). 1990. PLB 12.40 (0-531-10851-1) Watts.
—Amelia Earhart. (Illus.). 32p. (gr. 5 up). 1991. pap. 5.95 (0-531-24610-8) Watts.
—The American West. (Illus.). 64p. (gr. 7-9). 1988. 19.95 (0-7134-5731-7, Pub. by Batsford UK) Trafalgar.
—Anne Frank. (Illus.). 32p. (gr. 5 up). 1991. pap. 4.95 (0-531-24608-6) Watts.
—Anne Frank. (Illus.). 32p. (gr. 7-9). 1990. 12.40 (0-531-10763-9) Watts.
—Cities. Yapp, Malcolm, et al, eds. (Illus.). 32p. (gr. 6-11). 1980. pap. text ed. 3.45 (0-89908-115-0) Greenhaven.
—Exploring Other Civilizations. 52p. (gr. 11 up). 1987. pap. 7.95 (0-685-19629-1, Pub. by S Thornes UK) Dufour.
—The First Day of the Somme. (Illus.). 64p. (gr. 7-11). 1990. 19.95 (0-85219-829-9, Pub. by Batsford UK) Trafalgar.
—Florence Nightingale. (Illus.). 32p. (gr. 5 up). 1991. pap. 5.95 (0-531-24611-6) Watts.
—Frederic Chopin. 1991. 12.40 (0-531-14179-9) Watts.
—The French Revolution. Killingray, Margaret, et al, eds. (Illus.). 32p. (gr. 6-11). 1980. pap. text ed. 3.45 (0-89908-111-8) Greenhaven.
—Giuseppe Verdi. (Illus.). 32p. 1991. PLB 12.40 (0-531-14109-8) Watts.
—Guglielmo Marconi. LC 89-29277. (Illus.). 32p. (gr. 5-8). 1990. PLB 12.40 (0-531-14024-5) Watts.
—Helen Keller. (Illus.). 32p. (gr. 5-6). 1989. PLB 12.40 (0-531-10764-7) Watts.
—Helen Keller. (Illus.). 32p. (gr. 5 up). 1991. pap. 4.95 (0-531-24609-4) Watts.
—Japan since Nineteen Forty-Five. (Illus.). 72p. (gr. 7-10). 1989. 19.95 (0-7134-5930-1, Pub. by Batsford UK) Trafalgar.
—The Japanese. (Illus.). 72p. (gr. 7-10). 1982. 19.95 (0-7134-4453-3, Pub. by Batsford UK) Trafalgar.
—Journey Through Canada. Camm, Martin, et al, illus. LC 90-10934. 32p. (gr. 3-5). 1991. lib. bdg. 11.89 (0-8167-2110-6); pap. text ed. 3.95 (0-8167-2111-4) Troll Assocs.
—Journey Through Japan. Camm, Martin, et al, illus. LC 90-10944. 32p. (gr. 3-5). 1991. PLB 11.89 (0-8167-2114-9); pap. text ed. 3.95 (0-8167-2115-7) Troll Assocs.
—Life in Wartime Britain. (Illus.). (gr. 7-10). 1993. 19.95 (0-7134-6543-3, Pub. by Batsford UK) Trafalgar.
—Louis Pasteur. (Illus.). 32p. (gr. 5-8). 1990. PLB 12.40 (0-531-14025-3) Watts.
—Ludwig Van Beethoven. LC 90-32377. (Illus.). 32p. 1991. PLB 12.40 (0-531-14106-3) Watts.
—Marie Curie. (Illus.). 32p. (gr. 7-9). 1990. PLB 12.40 (0-531-10850-3) Watts.
—Marie Curie. (Illus.). 32p. (gr. 5 up). 1991. pap. 4.95 (0-531-24612-4) Watts.
—Mother Teresa. (Illus.). 32p. (gr. 5 up). 1991. pap. 5.95 (0-531-24613-2) Watts.
—Napoleon. Yapp, Malcolm & Killingray, Margaret, eds. (Illus.). (gr. 6-11). 1980. pap. text ed. 3.45 (0-89908-019-7) Greenhaven.
—Nelson Mandela. (Illus.). 32p. 1991. PLB 12.40 (0-531-14124-1) Watts.
—The Nineteen Eighties. (Illus.). 48p. (gr. 5-8). 1990. PLB 13.40 (0-531-14079-2) Watts.
—Nineteen Fifties. (Illus.). 1990. PLB 13.40 (0-531-14034-2) Watts.
—Nineteen Hundred to Nineteen Nineteen. (Illus.). 48p. (gr. 5-8). 1991. PLB 13.40 (0-531-14181-0) Watts.
—Nineteen Thirties. LC 90-32322. (Illus.). 48p. 1991. PLB 13.40 (0-531-14059-8) Watts.
—The Nineteen Twenties. (Illus.). 48p. (gr. 5-8). 1991. PLB 13.40 (0-531-14182-9) Watts.

—Peter Ilyich Tchaikovsky. (Illus.). 32p. (gr. 5-8). 1991. PLB 12.40 (0-531-14108-X) Watts.
—Planters, Pilgrims & Puritans. 64p. (gr. 6-8). 1987. 19.95 (0-7134-5477-6, Pub. by Batsford UK) Trafalgar.
—Radicals, Reformers & Railways 1815-1851. (Illus.). 72p. (gr. 7-12). 1987. 19.95 (0-7134-5264-1, Pub. by Batsford UK) Trafalgar.
—Richard Wagner. (Illus.). 32p. (gr. 5-8). 1991. PLB 12.40 (0-531-14178-0) Watts.
—Thomas Edison. (Illus.). 32p. (gr. 5-8). 1990. PLB 12.40 (0-531-14004-0) Watts.
—Wolfgang Amadeus Mozart. LC 90-32378. (Illus.). 32p. 1991. PLB 12.40 (0-531-14107-1) Watts.
—The Wright Brothers. (Illus.). 32p. (gr. 5-8). 1990. PLB 12.40 (0-531-14002-4) Watts.
Tan, Amy. The Chinese Siamese Cat. Schields, Gretchen, illus. LC 93-24008. 1994. write for info. (0-02-788835-5, Macmillan Child Bk) Macmillan Child Grp.
—The Moon Lady. Schields, Gretchen, illus. LC 91-22321. 32p. (gr. 1 up). 1992. RSBE 16.95 (0-02-788830-4, Macmillan Child Bk) Macmillan Child Grp.
Tan, Jennifer. Food in China. LC 88-31644. (Illus.). 32p. (gr. 3-6). 1989. lib. bdg. 15.94 (0-86625-338-6); 11. 95s.p. (0-685-58502-6) Rourke Corp.
Tan, Jennifer, et al. International Foods, 6 bks, Reading Level 4. (Illus.). 192p. (gr. 3-6). 1989. Set. PLB 95.64 (0-86625-337-8); 71.70 (0-685-58769-X) Rourke Corp.
Tan, Pamela. Women in Society: China. LC 92-33354. 1993. 22.95 (1-85435-556-2) Marshall Cavendish.
Tanaka, Beatrice. The Chase: A Kutenai Indian Tale. Gay, Michael, illus. LC 91-10790. 32p. (ps-2). 1991. 14.00 (0-517-58623-1); lib. bdg. 14.99 (0-517-58624-X) Crown Bks Yng Read.
Tanaka, Rita K., ed. see Vincent, Richard J.
Tanaka, Shelley. The Cat Lover's Diary. Fanelli, Jenny, ed. Baron, Elaine, photos by. Reynolds, Nancy L. & Macpherson, Elaine, illus. 176p. (gr. 5 up). 1984. pap. 8.95 (0-394-86613-4) Random Bks Yng Read.
—The Disaster of the Hindenburg: The Last Flight of the Greatest Airship Ever Built. LC 92-39434. 1993. 16. 95 (0-590-45750-0) Scholastic Inc.
Tanaka, Shelly. The Heat Is On: Facing Our Energy Problem. Beinicke, Steve, illus. 56p. (gr. 3-7). 1991. pap. 9.95 (0-920668-94-1) Firefly Bks Ltd.
Tanenhaus, Sam. Louis Armstrong. King, Coretta Scott, intro. by. (Illus.). 112p. (gr. 5 up). 1989. text ed. 17.95 (1-55546-571-4); pap. 9.95 (0-7910-0221-7) Chelsea Hse.
Tangborn, Wendell V. Glaciers. rev. ed. Simont, Marc, illus. LC 87-45306. 32p. (ps-3). 1988. pap. 4.50 (0-06-445076-7, Trophy) HarpC Child Bks.
—Glaciers. rev. ed. Simont, Marc, illus. LC 87-47696. 32p. (ps-3). 1988. (Crowell Jr Bks); (Crowell Jr Bks) HarpC Child Bks.
Tangley, Laura. The Rainforest. (Illus.). (gr. 5 up). 1992. lib. bdg. 19.95 (0-7910-1579-3) Chelsea Hse.
Tangvald, Christine. Good for Me! LC 86-72319. (ps). 1987. bds. 5.88 (1-55513-162-X, Chariot Bks) Cook.
—Guess What? We're Moving. LC 87-34107. 24p. (ps-2). 1988. 7.99 (1-55513-481-5, Chariot Bks) Cook.
—I Can Talk to God. Goldsborough, June, illus. LC 85-70217. 20p. (ps). 1985. 5.88 (0-89191-907-4, 59071, Chariot Bks) Cook.
—Jesus Is for Me. 24p. (ps-1). 1989. pap. 3.49 (1-55513-740-7, Chariot Bks) Cook.
—Mom & Dad Don't Live Together Anymore. LC 87-34211. 24p. (ps-2). 1988. 7.99 (1-55513-502-1, Chariot Bks) Cook.
—My Family Is Special. LC 86-71797. (ps). 1987. bds. 5.88 (1-55513-169-7, Chariot Bks) Cook.
—My Friends Are Special. LC 86-71795. (ps). 1987. bds. 5.88 (1-55513-170-0, Chariot Bks) Cook.
—Oh Yes! Oh No! (ps). 1987. bds. 5.88 (1-55513-168-9, Chariot Bks) Cook.
—Someone I Love Died. 24p. (ps-2). 1988. 7.99 (1-55513-490-4, Chariot Bks) Cook.
—We Have a New Baby. LC 87-35457. 24p. (ps-2). 1988. 7.99 (1-55513-503-X, Chariot Bks) Cook.
Tangvald, Christine H. The Best Thing about Easter. Couri, Kathy, illus. 28p. (ps). 1993. PLB 4.99 (0-7847-0035-4, 24-03825) Standard Pub.
—The Bible Is for Me. Nelson, Donna, illus. 24p. (ps-1). 1988. pap. 3.49 (1-55513-706-7, Chariot Bks) Cook.
—Christmas Is for Me. Nelson, Donna, illus. 24p. (ps-1). 1988. pap. 3.49 (1-55513-705-9, Chariot Bks) Cook.
—Easter Is for Me. LC 88-70663. 24p. (ps-1). 1990. 3.49 (1-55513-741-5, Chariot Bks) Cook.
—Yea, Hooray! The Son Came Home Today, & Other Bible Stories about Wisdom. Sasaki, Ellen J., illus. LC 93-9244. 1993. write for info. (0-7814-0927-6, Chariot Bks) Cook.
Tangvald, Christine H., jt. auth. see Osborn, Susan T.
Tanis, Joel E. & Grooters, Jeff. The Dragon Pack Snack Attack. Tanis, Joel E., illus. LC 92-18433. 32p. (ps-2). 1993. RSBE 14.95 (0-02-788840-1, Four Winds) Macmillan Child Grp.
Tankersley-Cusick, Richie. The Locker. Date not set. pap. 3.99 (0-671-79404-3, Archway) PB.
Tannen, Mary, jt. auth. see Dahl, Roald.
Tannenbaum, Beulah & Tannenbaum, Harold E. Science of the Early American Indians. Rasof, Henry, ed. LC 87-25313. (Illus.). 96p. (gr. 5-8). 1988. PLB 10.90 (0-531-10488-5) Watts.
Tannenbaum, D. Leb. Getting Ready for Baby. Bahr, Amy C., ed. Rao, Tony, illus. 64p. 1982. pap. 3.95 (0-671-45324-6) S&S Trade.

Tannenbaum, Harold E., jt. auth. see Tannenbaum, Beulah.
Tanner, Fran A. Basic Drama Projects. 5th ed. (Illus.). 286p. (gr. 10-12). 1987. pap. text ed. 14.33 (0-931054-16-8) Clark Pub.
—Readers Theatre Fundamentals. 2nd ed. (Illus.). 280p. (gr. 10-12). 1993. pap. text ed. 19.33 (0-931054-30-3) Clark Pub.
Tanner, Helen H. Ojibwa. (gr. 4-7). 1992. pap. 7.95 (0-7910-0392-2) Chelsea Hse.
Tanner, Joey. Futuristics: A Time to Come. rev. ed. 73p. (gr. k-8). 1992. pap. 19.95 spiral bdg. (0-913705-16-0) Zephyr Pr AZ.
Tanner, Suzy-Jane. Bunnies & Bear Nature Box. (Illus.). 32p. (ps). 1992. 17.50 (0-525-44924-8, DCB) Dutton Child Bks.
—Bunnies & Bears Learning Box Set. (Illus.). 32p. (ps-6). 1993. 17.50 (0-525-44916-7, DCB) Dutton Child Bks.
—Twelve Days of Christmas. Tanner, Suzy-Jane, illus. 31p. (ps). 1993. Repr. 4.95 (1-882607-11-2) Merrybooks VA.
Tanobe, Miyuki. Quebec, I Love You: Je t'Aime. Tanobe, Miyuki, illus. 48p. (gr. 5 up). 1971. pap. 6.95 (0-88776-156-9) Tundra Bks.
Tant, Carl. Science Fair Spelled W-I-N. Crask, Tammy & Setzer, Debra, illus. 112p. (Orig.). (gr. 7-12). 1992. pap. 14.95 (1-880319-02-0) Biotech.
—Seeds, etc... Crask, Tammy & Setzer, Debra, illus. LC 91-76151. 166p. (gr. 6-9). 1992. pap. 13.95 (1-880319-01-2) Biotech.
Tanvald, Christine H. The Big Big Big Boat, & Other Bible Stories about Obedience. Girouard, Patrick, illus. LC 93-9234. 1993. write for info. (0-7814-0926-8, Chariot Bks) Cook.
Tanyi, Enoch N. The Covenant for Young People. (Illus.). 40p. (Orig.). (gr. k-4). 1991. pap. 7.95 (0-85398-337-2) G Ronald Pub.
Tapp, Kathy K. The Ghostmobile. 160p. (gr. 3-7). 1988. pap. 2.75 (0-590-43441-1) Scholastic Inc.
—The Sacred Circle of the Hula Hoop. LC 88-27369. 208p. (gr. 6-9). 1989. SBE 14.95 (0-689-50461-6, M K McElderry) Macmillan Child Grp.
—Smoke from the Chimney. LC 89-6816. 176p. (gr. 4-7). 1989. pap. 3.95 (0-689-71323-1, Aladdin) Macmillan Child Grp.
Tapp, Sandra. Missions Day Camp: Language Missions. McClain, Cindy, ed. 23p. (Orig.). (gr. 4-6). 1990. pap. text ed. 1.95 (0-936625-99-6) Womans Mission Union.
Tarcov, Edith H., retold by. The Frog Prince. Marshall, James, illus. 32p. (Orig.). (ps-2). 1987. pap. 2.50 (0-590-43132-3) Scholastic Inc.
—The Frog Prince. Marshall, James, illus. LC 92-25167. 32p. (ps-2). 1993. pap. 2.95 (0-590-46571-6) Scholastic Inc.
Tardi, Jacques, illus. The Enchanted Pig: Rumanian Fairy Tale. 32p. (gr. 6 up). 1984. PLB 13.95s.p. (0-87191-953-2) Creative Ed.
Tardy, Gene & Jackson, Al. Motorcycle: Cross-Country Racing. (Illus.). (gr. 3-7). 1974. PLB 6.89x (0-914844-00-8) J Alden.
—Motorcycle: Grand Prix Racing. (Illus.). (gr. 3-7). 1974. PLB 6.89x (0-914844-01-6) J Alden.
Tardy, Gene, jt. auth. see Jackson, Al.
Tarendash, Albert S. Let's Review: Chemistry. (gr. 9 up). 1993. pap. 9.95 (0-8120-1494-4) Barron.
Targ, Harry R., jt. auth. see Brill, Marlene T.
Tarling, D. H. Plate Tectonics & Biological Evolution. 2nd ed. Head, J. J., ed. (Illus.). 16p. (gr. 10 up). 1991. pap. 2.75 (0-89278-113-0) Carolina Biological.
Tarlow, Nora. An Easter Alphabet. (Illus.). 32p. 1991. 15.95 (0-399-22194-8, Putnam) Putnam Pub Group.
Tarlton. Going to Grandma's. 1993. pap. 28.67 (0-590-50159-3) Scholastic Inc.
Tarr, Bill. One Hundred One Easy-to-Do Magic Tricks. unabr., unaltered ed. Daniel, Frank, illus. LC 92-22895. 224p. 1992. pap. text ed. 7.95t (0-486-27367-9) Dover.
Tarr, Judith. His Majesty's Elephant. 1993. 16.95 (0-15-200737-7, HB Juv Bks) HarBrace.
Tarrant. Nursery Rhymes & Fairy Tales. 1984. 5.98 (0-671-06535-1) S&S Trade.
Taruffi, Piero. Technique of Motor Racing. Fangio, Juan M., frwd. by. LC 60-1662. 168p. (gr. 9 up). 1989. 25. 00 (0-8376-0228-9) Bentley.
Tashjian, Levon D., jt. auth. see Rashkis, Harold A.
Tashlik, Phyllis, jt. auth. see Moffett, James.
Tashlin, Frank. Bear That Wasn't. (Illus.). v, 51p. (gr. 4 up). 1946. pap. 2.50 (0-486-20939-3) Dover.
Tatchell. Computer Graphics. Round, illus. 48p. (gr. 6up). 1984. PLB 9.96 (0-88110-163-X); pap. 3.95 (0-86020-739-0) EDC.
Tatchell & Cutter, N. Practical Things to Do with a Microcomputer. Round, Graham, illus. 48p. (gr. 6 up). 1983. pap. 3.95 (0-86020-731-5); PLB 10.96 (0-88110-140-0) EDC.
Tatchell, J. How to Draw, Vol. I. (Illus.). 32p. (gr. 4 up). 1993. pap. 9.95 (0-7460-0295-5) EDC.
—How to Draw Animals. 32p. (gr. 2 up). 1988. PLB 12. 96 (0-88110-315-2); pap. 4.95 (0-7460-0177-0) EDC.
—How to Draw Cartoons & Caricatures. 40p. (gr. 2 up). 1987. PLB 12.96 (0-88110-273-3); pap. 4.95 (0-7460-0067-7) EDC.
—How to Draw Lettering. 32p. (gr. 4 up). 1991. PLB 12.96 (0-88110-537-6, Usborne); pap. 4.95 (0-7460-0635-7, Usborne) EDC.
—Understanding Music. 32p. (gr. 4 up). 1990. lib. bdg. 13.96 (0-88110-382-9, Usborne); pap. 7.95 (0-7460-0302-1, Usborne) EDC.

Tatchell, J. & Evans, C. Young Cartoonist. 72p. (gr. 5 up). 1987. pap. 7.95 (0-7460-0083-9) EDC.

Tatchell, J. & Fraser, K. Food Fitness & Health. (Illus.). 96p. (gr. 6-10). 1987. 11.95 (0-7460-0079-0) EDC.

Tatchell, J. & Wells, D. You & Your Food. (Illus.). 48p. (gr. 6-10). 1986. PLB 13.96 (0-88110-222-9); pap. 6.95 (0-86020-939-3) EDC.

Tatchell, J., jt. auth. see Fraser, K.

Tatchell, Judy, jt. auth. see Bennett, Bill.

Tate, Albert J., III. Dad: Are People Using Alcohol & Drugs As an Alternative to Problem Solving? Design in Demand Staff, illus. 68p. (Orig.). (gr. 10). 1992. pap. 12.95 (0-9622996-9-3) Unique Memphis.

Tate, Baird, ed. see Butrick, Lyn M.

Tate, Carole. Pancakes & Pies: A Russian Folk Tale. LC 88-38111. 32p. (gr. k-3). 1989. PLB 14.95 (0-87226-407-6, Bedrick Blackie) P Bedrick Bks.

—Rhymes & Ballads of London. LC 72-90691. (Illus.). 32p. (gr. k-4). 1973. 6.95 (0-87592-042-X) Scroll Pr.

—The Tale of the Spiteful Spirits: A Kampuchean Folk Tale. Tate, Carole, illus. LC 90-41949. 32p. (gr. k-3). 1991. PLB 14.95 (0-87226-445-9, Bedrick Blackie) P Bedrick Bks.

Tate, Eleanor E. Front Porch Stories: At the One-Room School. (gr. 4-7). 1994. pap. 3.50 (0-440-40901-2) Dell.

Tate, Eleanora. Front Porch Stories at the One-Room School. 1992. 15.00 (0-553-08384-8) Bantam.

—Thank You, Dr. Martin Luther King, Jr. (gr. 4-7). 1992. pap. 3.99 (0-553-15886-4) Bantam.

Tate, Eleanora E. The Secret of Gumbo Grove. (Orig.). (gr. 7 up). 1988. pap. 3.50 (0-553-27226-8, Pub. by Starfire) Bantam.

—Thank You, Dr. Martin Luther King, Jr. 1990. PLB 14.90 (0-531-10904-6) Watts.

Tate, Joan. Ling & the Little Devils. Otto, Svend, illus. (ps-3). 9.95 (0-317-61896-2) Viking Child Bks.

Tate, Joan, tr. see Beckman, Gunnel.

Tate, Joan, tr. see Lindgren, Astrid.

Tate, Lindsey. Claire & the Friendly Snakes. (ps-3). 1993. 15.00 (0-374-31337-7) FS&G.

Tate, Mimi. The Belly Button Brigade. 1974. pap. 1.95 (0-685-47446-1, BBB01) Quality Pubns.

Tate, Susan. Benny Bear Believes for A Healing. Henjum, Marian, illus. (Orig.). (gr. k-3). 1993. pap. 3.99 (1-884395-00-7) Clear Blue Sky.

—Blessings of Abraham Coloring Book. Henium, Marian, illus. 12p. (Orig.). (gr. k-3). 1993. pap. 0.39 (1-884395-06-6) Clear Blue Sky.

—Bonnie Bunnie's Bicycle. Henium, Marian, illus. 40p. (gr. k-3). 1993. pap. 3.99 (1-884395-01-5) Clear Blue Sky.

—Faith Coloring Book. Henium, Marian, illus. 12p. (Orig.). (gr. k-3). 1993. pap. 0.39 (1-884395-04-X) Clear Blue Sky.

—George Goat's Guardian Angel. Henium, Marian, illus. 40p. (Orig.). (gr. k-3). 1993. pap. 3.99 (1-884395-02-3) Clear Blue Sky.

—Larry Lion Learns To Fear Not. Henium, Marian, illus. 40p. (gr. k-3). 1993. pap. 3.99 (1-884395-03-1) Clear Blue Sky.

—Ninety First Psalm Coloring Book. Henium, Marian, illus. 12p. (Orig.). (gr. k-3). 1993. pap. 0.39 (1-884395-05-8) Clear Blue Sky.

— Petal Pals Children's Stories, 4 bks. (gr. k-3). 1993. pap. 15.96 Clear Blue Sky.

This new series was written to prepare children to face the challenges of growing up in the 1990s. The books were designed to teach Bible principles & help children to develop their faith & confidence in God's promises. The Petal Pals face situations familiar to children everywhere, entertaining & teaching as they resolve their problems with the word of God. Each book contains 20 charming, full-color illustrations. Major teaching points are highlighted with scripture references. Benny Bear Believes For A Healing, 1-884395-00-7; Bonnie Bunnie's Bicycle, 1-884395-01-5; George Goat's Guardian Angel, 1-884395-02-3; Larry Lion Learns To Fear Not, 1-884395-03-1. Stories are complemented by a three-part series of coloring books. 1-884395-08-2. $0.39 retail; 40% discount. 12 pg., 8 1/2 X 5 1/2. Faith, 1-884395-04-X; 91st Psalm, 1-884395-05-8; Blessings of Abraham, 1-884395-06-6. Clear Blue Sky Publishing, 4320 S. Louise, Sioux Falls, SD 57106. 605-361-4151.
Publisher Provided Annotation.

—Petal Pals Coloring Books, 3 bks. Henium, Marian, illus. (gr. k-3). 1993. Set. pap. 1.17 (1-884395-08-2) Clear Blue Sky.

Tate, Suzanne. Billy Bluefish: A Tale of Big Blues. Melvin, James, illus. LC 88-92517. 28p. (gr. k-3). 1988. pap. 3.95 (0-9616344-4-8) Nags Head Art.

—Crabby & Nabby: A Tale of Two Blue Crabs. Melvin, James, illus. LC 88-61096. 28p. (gr. k-3). 1988. pap. 3.95 (0-9616344-3-X) Nags Head Art.

—Crabby's Water Wish: A Tale of Saving Sea Life. Melvin, James, illus. LC 91-60262. 28p. (Orig.). (gr. k-3). 1991. pap. 3.95 (1-878405-04-7) Nags Head Art.

—Danny & Daisy: A Tale of a Dolphin Duo. Melvin, James, illus. LC 92-93915. 28p. (Orig.). (gr. k-3). 1992. pap. 3.95 (1-878405-07-1) Nags Head Art.

—Flossie Flounder: A Tale of Flat Fish. Melvin, James, illus. LC 88-92679. 28p. (Orig.). (gr. k-3). 1989. pap. 3.95 (0-9616344-5-6) Nags Head Art.

—Flossie Flounder: Un Cuento Del Pez Chato. LC 90-61962. (Illus.). 28p. (Orig.). (gr. k-3). 1990. pap. 4.95 (1-878405-01-2) Nags Head Art.

—Harry Horseshoe Crab: A Tale of Crawly Creatures. Melvin, James, illus. LC 91-61375. 28p. (Orig.). (gr. k-9). 1991. pap. 3.95 (1-878405-03-9) Nags Head Art.

—Lucky Lookdown: A Tale of a Funny Fish. Melvin, James, illus. LC 89-92221. 28p. (Orig.). (gr. k-3). 1989. pap. 3.95 (0-9616344-8-0) Nags Head Art.

—Mary Manatee: A Tale of Sea Cows. Melvin, James, illus. LC 90-60102. 28p. (gr. k-3). 1990. pap. 3.95 (0-9616344-9-9) Nags Head Art.

—Old Reddy Drum: A Tale of Redfish. Melvin, James, illus. LC 93-83435. 28p. (Orig.). (gr. k-3). 1993. pap. 3.95 (1-878405-08-X) Nags Head Art.

—Pearlie Oyster: A Tale of an Amazing Oyster. Melvin, James, illus. LC 89-92226. 28p. (Orig.). (gr. k-3). 1989. pap. 3.95 (0-9616344-7-2) Nags Head Art.

—Salty Seagull: A Tale of an Old Salt. Melvin, James, illus. LC 92-60375. 28p. (Orig.). (gr. k-3). 1992. pap. 3.95 (1-878405-06-3) Nags Head Art.

—Sammy Shrimp: A Tale of a Little Shrimp. Melvin, James, illus. LC 90-61002. 28p. (Orig.). (gr. k-3). 1990. pap. 3.95 (1-878405-00-4) Nags Head Art.

—Spunky Spot: A Tale of One Smart Fish. Melvin, James, illus. LC 88-63784. 28p. (Orig.). (gr. k-3). 1989. pap. 3.95 (0-9616344-6-4) Nags Head Art.

—Spunky Spot: Un Cuento De Un Pez Inteligente. LC 90-61966. (Illus.). 28p. (Orig.). (gr. k-3). 1990. pap. 4.95 (1-878405-02-0) Nags Head Art.

—Stevie B. Sea Horse: A Tale of a Proud Papa. Melvin, James, illus. 28p. (Orig.). (gr. k-3). 1993. pap. 3.95 (1-878405-09-8) Nags Head Art.

—Tammy Turtle: A Tale of Saving Sea Turtles. Melvin, James, illus. LC 91-67275. 28p. (Orig.). (gr. k-3). 1991. PLB 3.95 (1-878405-05-5) Nags Head Art.

Tatihara, Erika. Picture Purrfect Kitten. Mizobuti, Masaru, illus. 32p. (ps-2). 1993. 12.95 (0-8120-6359-7); pap. 5.95 (0-8120-1712-9) Barron.

Tauben, Carol & Abrahams, Edith, eds. Integrating Arts & Crafts in the Jewish School, Vol. I. Tauben, Carol, illus. LC 79-15506. (gr. k-2). 1979. text ed. 14.95x (0-87441-288-9) Behrman.

Tauber, Debra. I Don't Care. Wibright, Betsy, illus. 16p. (Orig.). (gr. 1). 1993. pap. write for info. (1-882225-14-7) Tott Pubns.

Tauber, Gerald E. Relativity: From Einstein to Black Holes. Kline, M., ed. LC 87-25964. (Illus.). 128p. (gr. 6-12). 1988. PLB 13.40 (0-531-10482-6) Watts.

Taubes, Hella. Bible Speaks, 3 vols. Bloch, Lolla, tr. (Illus.). (gr. 4-6). 1974. 14.95x ea. (0-686-76831-0) Set. Bloch.

—The Bible Speaks By, 3 Vols. (gr. k-4). 1965. Set. 14.95 (0-900689-35-8) Soncino Pr.

Taulbee, Annette. Alphabet. (Illus.). 24p. (ps-k). 1986. 3.98 (0-86734-059-2, FS-3051) Schaffer Pubns.

—Alphabet Dot-to-Dot. (Illus.). 24p. (ps-k). 1986. 3.98 (0-86734-062-2, FS-3054) Schaffer Pubns.

—Colors. (Illus.). 24p. (ps-k). 1986. 3.98 (0-86734-060-6, FS-3052) Schaffer Pubns.

—Kindergarten Activities. (Illus.). 24p. (ps-k). 1986. 3.98 (0-86734-065-7, FS-3057) Schaffer Pubns.

—Kindergarten Math. (Illus.). 24p. (ps-k). 1986. 3.98 (0-86734-070-3, FS-3062) Schaffer Pubns.

—Kindergarten Thinking Skills. (Illus.). 24p. (ps-k). 1986. 3.98 (0-86734-067-3, FS-3060) Schaffer Pubns.

—Numbers. (Illus.). 24p. (ps-k). 1986. 3.98 (0-86734-061-4, FS-3053) Schaffer Pubns.

—Phonics. (Illus.). 24p. (ps-k). 1986. 3.98 (0-86734-066-5, FS-3058) Schaffer Pubns.

—Shapes & Colors. (Illus.). 24p. (ps-k). 1986. 3.98 (0-86734-068-1, FS-3061) Schaffer Pubns.

Taunton, Martha, jt. auth. see Colbert, Cynthia.

Tavzel, Carolyn. Blooming Holidays. (ps-5). 1989. pap. 14.95 (1-55999-025-2) LinguiSystems.

—Blooming Mother Goose: Fun Nursery Rhymes for Serious Language Enrichment Based on Bloom's Taxonomy. (ps-3). 1990. pap. 14.95 incl. worksheets (1-55999-102-X) LinguiSystems.

Tax, Meredith. Families. Hafner, Marilyn, illus. 32p. (ps-3). 1981. 15.95 (0-316-83240-5, Pub. by Atlantic) Little.

Taylor, Alice K. My Very Own Stories. Keitz, Roderick, illus. 16p. (gr. 2-8). 1993. PLB 11.95 (0-9638873-0-0) J Taylor Ltd.

Taylor, Allegra. A Kibbutz in Israel. (Illus.). 32p. (gr. 2-5). 1987. 13.50 (0-8225-1678-0) Lerner Pubns.

Taylor, Andrew. The Coal House. large type ed. (gr. 1-8). 1991. 13.95 (0-7451-0761-3, Galaxy Child Lrg Print) Chivers N Amer.

—The Private Nose. Schongut, Emanuel, illus. LC 92-53016. 96p. (gr. k-4). 1993. 13.95 (1-56402-135-1) Candlewick Pr.

Taylor, Anelise. Lights Off, Lights On. (Illus.). 32p. (ps-k). 1989. pap. 4.95 (0-19-272193-3) OUP.

Taylor, Ann. Chamber Music Primer: Four Piano Trio Pieces. Bryant, Larkin, illus. (Orig.). (gr. 1-6). 1983. pap. 6.75 (0-943644-01-1); cassette 5.98 (0-685-06794-7) Ivory Pal.

Taylor, Anne. Math in Art. Taylor, Anne, illus. (Orig.). (gr. 1-9). 1974. pap. 7.95 (0-918932-28-9) Activity Resources.

Taylor, Audilee Boyd. Where Did My Feather Pillow Come From? Dillon, Sharon Saseen, illus. LC 81-71027. 32p. (ps-3). 1982. 10.00 (0-942250-00-1) Castlemarsh.

Taylor, B., ed. American Short Stories. (Illus.). 119p. 1964. pap. text ed. 5.95 (0-582-53026-1) Longman.

Taylor, Barbara. Air & Flight. (Illus.). 40p. (gr. k-4). 1991. PLB 12.90 (0-531-19129-X, Warwick) Watts.

—Air & Flying. (Illus.). 32p. (gr. 5-8). 1991. PLB 12.40 (0-531-14183-7) Watts.

—The Animal Atlas. Lilly, Kenneth, illus. LC 91-53142. 64p. (gr. 3-7). 1992. 20.00 (0-679-80501-X); PLB 21.99 (0-679-90501-4) Knopf Bks Yng Read.

—Batteries & Magnets. LC 91-2558. (Illus.). 40p. (gr. k-4). 1991. PLB 12.90 (0-531-19130-3, Warwick) Watts.

—Be an Inventor. Weekly Reader Staff, illus. 74p. (gr. 3-7). 1987. 11.95 (0-15-205950-4, Voyager Bks); pap. 7.95 (0-15-205951-2, Voyager Bks) HarBrace.

—Be Your Own Map Expert. LC 93-31692. 1994. write for info. (0-8069-0664-2) Sterling.

—Bouncing & Bending Light. (ps-3). 1990. PLB 12.40 (0-531-14014-8) Watts.

—Charles Ginsburg. LC 93-494. (gr. 7-8). 1993. 15.93 (0-86592-159-8); 11.95s.p. (0-685-66582-8) Rourke Enter.

—Color & Light. (ps-3). 1990. PLB 12.40 (0-531-14015-6) Watts.

—Color & Light. LC 91-9571. (Illus.). 40p. (gr. k-4). 1991. PLB 12.90 (0-531-19127-3, Warwick) Watts.

—Coral Reef. LC 91-58198. (Illus.). 32p. (gr. 1-4). 1992. 9.95 (1-879431-92-0) Dorling Kindersley.

—Create Your Own Magazine. LC 92-46352. (Illus.). 46p. (gr. 2-10). 1993. 12.95 (0-8069-0425-9) Sterling.

—Desert Life. LC 91-58195. (Illus.). 32p. (gr. 1-4). 1992. 9.95 (1-879431-93-9) Dorling Kindersley.

—Electricity & Magnets. LC 90-31021. (Illus.). 32p. (gr. 5-8). 1990. PLB 12.40 (0-531-14083-0) Watts.

—Energy & Power. LC 90-31032. (Illus.). 32p. (gr. 5-8). 1990. PLB 12.40 (0-531-14080-6) Watts.

—Everything You Need to Know about AIDS. rev. ed. Rosen, Ruth, ed. (Illus.). 64p. (gr. 7 up). 1992. PLB 13.95 (0-8239-1401-1) Rosen Group.

—Everything You Need to Know about Alcohol. rev. ed. Glassman, Richard, photos by. (Illus.). 64p. (gr. 7-12). 1993. 13.95 (0-8239-1613-8) Rosen Group.

—Force & Movement. LC 89-21505. (Illus.). 32p. (gr. 5-8). 1990. PLB 12.40 (0-531-14081-4) Watts.

—Forest Life. Taylor, Kim, photos by. LC 92-53488. (Illus.). 32p. (gr. 2-5). 1993. 9.95 (1-56458-210-8) Dorling Kindersley.

—Get It in Gear! The Science of Movement. Bull, Peter, et al, illus. LC 90-42617. 40p. (Orig.). (gr. 2-5). 1991. pap. 4.95 (0-679-80812-4) Random Bks Yng Read.

—Green Thumbs Up! The Science of Growing Plants. Bull, Peter, et al, illus. LC 91-4290. 40p. (Orig.). (gr. 2-5). 1992. pap. 4.95 (0-679-82042-6) Random Bks Yng Read.

—Growing Plants. LC 91-2568. (Illus.). 40p. (gr. k-4). 1991. PLB 12.90 (0-531-19128-1, Warwick) Watts.

—Hear! Hear! The Science of Sound. Bull, Peter, et al, illus. LC 90-42617. 40p. (Orig.). (gr. 2-5). 1991. pap. 4.95 (0-679-80813-2) Random Bks Yng Read.

—Light. LC 92-7500. 1992. 12.40 (0-531-17381-X, Gloucester Pr) Watts.

—Liquid & Buoyancy. LC 89-78240. (Illus.). 40p. (gr. k-4). 1990. PLB 12.90 (0-531-19087-0, Warwick) Watts.

—Living with Deafness. LC 89-8895. (Illus.). 32p. (gr. 5-8). 1989. PLB 12.40 (0-531-10842-2) Watts.

—Living with Diabetes. LC 89-8935. (Illus.). 32p. (gr. 5-8). 1989. PLB 12.40 (0-531-10844-9) Watts.

—Machines & Movement. LC 89-78421. (Illus.). 40p. (gr. k-4). 1990. PLB 12.90 (0-531-19088-9, Warwick) Watts.

—Maps & Mapping: Geography Facts & Experiments. LC 92-23373. (Illus.). 32p. (ps-3). 1993. 10.95 (1-85697-863-X); pap. 5.95 (1-85697-936-9) Kingfisher Bks.

—Meadow. Taylor, Kim & Burton, Jane, photos by. LC 92-52821. (Illus.). 32p. (gr. 2-5). 1992. 9.95 (1-56458-129-2) Dorling Kindersley.

—More Power to You! The Science of Batteries & Magnets. Bull, Peter, et al, illus. LC 91-4293. 40p. (Orig.). (gr. 2-5). 1992. pap. 4.95 (0-679-82040-X) Random Bks Yng Read.

—Mountains & Volcanoes. LC 92-23374. (Illus.). 32p. (gr. 1-4). 1993. 10.95 (1-85697-874-5); pap. 5.95 (1-85697-938-5) Kingfisher Bks.

—Over the Rainbow! The Science of Color & Light. Bull, Peter, et al, illus. LC 91-4291. 40p. (Orig.). (gr. 2-5). 1992. pap. 4.95 (0-679-82041-8) Random Bks Yng Read.

—Pond Life. LC 91-58196. (Illus.). 32p. (gr. 1-4). 1992. 9.95 (1-879431-94-7) Dorling Kindersley.

—Rain Forest. LC 91-58197. (Illus.). 32p. (gr. 1-4). 1992. 9.95 (*1-879431-91-2*) Dorling Kindersley.
—River Life. Greenaway, Frank, photos by. LC 92-52822. (Illus.). 32p. (gr. 2-5). 1992. 9.95 (*1-56458-130-6*) Dorling Kindersley.
—Rivers & Oceans: Geography Facts & Experiments. LC 92-28421. (Illus.). 32p. (gr. 1-4). 1993. 10.95 (*1-85697-876-1*); pap. 5.95 (*1-85697-939-3*) Kingfisher Bks.
—Seeing Is NOT Believing! The Science of Shadow & Light. Bull, Peter, et al, illus. LC 90-42974. 40p. (Orig.). (gr. 2-5). 1991. pap. 4.95 (*0-679-80814-0*) Random Bks Yng Read.
—Shadows & Reflections. (Illus.). 40p. (gr. k-4). 1990. PLB 12.90 (*0-531-19089-7*, Warwick) Watts.
—Shoreline. Greenaway, Frank, photos by. LC 92-53491. (Illus.). 32p. (gr. 2-5). 1993. 9.95 (*1-56458-213-2*) Dorling Kindersley.
—Sink or Swim! The Science of Water. Bull, Peter, et al, illus. LC 90-42618. 40p. (Orig.). (gr. 2-5). 1991. pap. 4.95 (*0-679-80815-9*) Random Bks Yng Read.
—Sound. 92-348. 1992. 12.40 (*0-531-17382-8*, Gloucester Pr) Watts.
—Sound & Music. LC 89-78359. (Illus.). 40p. (gr. k-4). 1990. PLB 12.90 (*0-531-19090-0*, Warwick) Watts.
—Sound & Music. (Illus.). 32p. (gr. 5-8). 1991. PLB 12. 40 (*0-531-14185-3*) Watts.
—Structures & Materials. (Illus.). 32p. (gr. 5-8). 1991. PLB 12.40 (*0-531-14186-1*) Watts.
—Up, Up & Away! The Science of Flight. Bull, Peter, et al, illus. LC 91-4292. 40p. (Orig.). (gr. 2-5). 1992. pap. 4.95 (*0-679-82039-6*) Random Bks Yng Read.
—Water & Life. LC 90-32523. (Illus.). 32p. (gr. 5-8). 1991. PLB 12.40 (*0-531-14116-0*) Watts.
—Water at Work. LC 90-32525. (Illus.). 32p. (gr. 5-8). 1991. PLB 12.40 (*0-531-14117-9*) Watts.
—Weather & Climate: Geography Facts & Experiments. LC 92-28420. 32p. (gr. 1-4). 1993. 10.95 (*1-85697-878-8*); pap. 5.95 (*1-85697-940-7*) Kingfisher Bks.
—Weight & Balance. (Illus.). 32p. (gr. 5-8). 1990. PLB 12.40 (*0-531-14082-2*) Watts.
—Wind & Weather. (Illus.). 32p. (gr. 5-8). 1991. PLB 12. 40 (*0-531-14184-5*) Watts.
Taylor, Barbara, jt. auth. see Casn, Terry.
Taylor, Beth, jt. auth. see Heath, Lou.
Taylor, Binah B. Buyer Beware: Safeguarding Consumer Rights. LC 92-5493. 1992. 22.60 (*0-86593-172-0*); 16. 95s.p. (*0-685-59286-3*) Rourke Corp.
Taylor, C. J. Deux Plumes et la Solitude Disparue. Taylor, C. J., illus. 24p. (gr. 1-5). 1990. 13.95 (*0-88776-255-7*) Tundra Bks.
—Geurrier-Solitaire et le Fantome: Native. Boileau, Michele, tr. Taylor, C. J., illus. (FRE.). 24p. (gr. 1-5). 1991. 13.95 (*0-88776-264-6*) Tundra Bks.
—The Ghost & Lone Warrior. LC 91-65368. (Illus.). 24p. (gr. 1-5). 1991. 13.95 (*0-88776-263-8*) Tundra Bks.
—How Two-Feather Was Saved from Loneliness. Taylor, C. J., illus. LC 90-70138. 24p. (gr. 1-5). 1990. 13.95 (*0-88776-254-9*) Tundra Bks.
—How We Saw the World: Nine Native Stories of Beginnings. Taylor, C. J., illus. 32p. (gr. 1-5). 1993. 17.95 (*0-88776-302-5*) Tundra Bks.
—Little Water & the Gift of the Animals. Taylor, C. J., illus. LC 92-8413. 24p. (gr. 1-5). 1992. PLB 13.95 (*0-88776-285-9*) Tundra Bks.
—Le Secret Du Bison Blanc. Boileau, Michele, tr. from ENG. Taylor, C. J., illus. LC 93-60552. (FRE.). 24p. (gr. 3 up). 1993. 13.95 (*0-88776-322-7*) Tundra Bks.
—The Secret of the White Buffalo. Taylor, C. J., illus. LC 93-60551. 24p. (gr. 3 up). 1993. 13.95 (*0-88776-321-9*) Tundra Bks.
Taylor, C. L., jt. auth. see Taylor, L. B., Jr.
Taylor, C. W., retold by see Hsiung, S. I.
Taylor, Carol. Burger Time. Culic, Ned, illus. LC 93-9281. 1994. pap. write for info. (*0-383-03678-X*) SRA Schl Grp.
—Christmas Naturals: Ornaments, Wreaths & Decorations. LC 91-17552. (Illus.). 128p. (gr. 8 up). 1992. pap. 14.95 (*0-8069-8361-2*) Sterling.
—The Great T-Shirt Book & Kit: Make Your Own Spectacular, One-of-a-Kind Designs. LC 92-17643. (Illus.). 112p. (gr. 10-12). 1992. pap. 12.95 (*0-8069-8748-0*, Pub. by Lark Bks); pap. 35.00 incl. kit (*0-8069-5697-6*) Sterling.
—Marbling Paper & Fabric Book & Kit: Projects, Patterns, Instructions. (Illus.). 128p. (gr. 8 up). 1992. pap. 12.95 (*0-8069-8323-X*, Pub. by Lark Bks); pap. 40.00 incl. kit (*0-8069-5649-6*, Pub. by Lark Bks) Sterling.
—Toothless Albert. Moroney, Tracey, illus. LC 93-28937. 1994. 4.25 (*0-383-03780-8*) SRA Schl Grp.
Taylor, Clark. The House That Crack Built. Pritchard, Michael, afterword by. (Illus.). 40p. 1992. 11.95 (*0-8118-0133-0*); pap. 5.95 (*0-8118-0123-3*) Chronicle Bks.
Taylor, Colin. What Do We Know about the Plains Indians? (Illus.). 40p. (gr. 3 up). 1993. PLB 16.95 (*0-87226-368-1*); pap. 6.95 sewn (*0-87226-261-8*) P Bedrick Bks.
Taylor, Connie R. Before Birth, Beyond Death. LC 87-82117. 64p. (gr. 4-6). 1987. pap. 6.95 (*0-88290-315-2*) Horizon Utah.
Taylor, Dave. The Alligator & the Everglades. (Illus.). 32p. (gr. 3-4). 1990. PLB 15.95 (*0-86505-367-7*); pap. 7.95 (*0-86505-397-9*) Crabtree Pub Co.

—The Bison & the Great Plains. (Illus.). 32p. (gr. 3-4). 1990. PLB 15.95 (*0-86505-366-9*); pap. 7.95 (*0-86505-396-0*) Crabtree Pub Co.
—The Elephant & the Scrub Forest. (Illus.). 32p. (gr. 3-4). 1990. PLB 15.95 (*0-86505-365-0*); pap. 7.95 (*0-86505-395-2*) Crabtree Pub Co.
—Endangered Desert Animals. Kalman, Bobbie, ed. (Illus.). 32p. (gr. 3-6). 1992. PLB 15.95 (*0-86505-534-3*); pap. 7.95 (*0-86505-544-0*) Crabtree Pub Co.
—Endangered Forest Animals. (Illus.). (gr. 3-8). 1992. PLB 15.95 (*0-86505-529-7*); pap. 7.95 (*0-86505-539-4*) Crabtree Pub Co.
—Endangered Island Animals. Kalman, Bobbie, ed. (Illus.). 32p. (Orig.). (gr. 3-6). 1992. PLB 15.95 (*0-86505-532-7*); pap. 7.95 (*0-86505-542-4*) Crabtree Pub Co.
—Endangered Mountain Animals. (Illus.). 32p. (gr. 3-8). 1992. PLB 15.95 (*0-86505-531-9*); pap. 7.95 (*0-86505-541-6*) Crabtree Pub Co.
—Endangered Ocean Animals. Kalman, Bobbie, ed. (Illus.). 32p. (gr. 3-6). 1992. PLB 15.95 (*0-86505-533-5*); pap. 7.95 (*0-86505-543-2*) Crabtree Pub Co.
—Endangered Savannah Animals. Kalman, Bobbie, ed. (Illus.). 32p. (Orig.). (gr. 3-6). 1992. PLB 15.95 (*0-86505-535-1*); pap. 7.95 (*0-86505-545-9*) Crabtree Pub Co.
—Endangered Wetland Animals. (Illus.). 32p. (gr. 3-8). 1992. PLB 15.95 (*0-86505-530-0*); pap. 7.95 (*0-86505-540-8*) Crabtree Pub Co.
—The Lion & the Savannah. (Illus.). 32p. (gr. 3-4). 1990. PLB 15.95 (*0-86505-364-2*); pap. 7.95 (*0-86505-394-4*) Crabtree Pub Co.
Taylor, David. Animal Attackers. (Illus.). 48p. (gr. 4 up). 1990. 17.50 (*0-8225-2178-4*) Lerner Pubns.
—Animal Magicians. (Illus.). 48p. (gr. 4 up). 1989. 17.50 (*0-8225-2175-X*) Lerner Pubns.
—Animal Monsters. (Illus.). 48p. (gr. 4 up). 1989. 17.50 (*0-8225-2176-8*) Lerner Pubns.
—Animal Monsters: Fantasies & Facts of the Animal World. (Illus.). 48p. (gr. 4 up). Repr. of 1989 ed. 5.95g (*0-8225-9575-3*) Lerner Pubns.
—Animal Olympians. (Illus.). 48p. (gr. 4 up). 1989. 17.50 (*0-8225-2177-6*) Lerner Pubns.
—Animal Olympians: Sporting Champions of the Animal World. (Illus.). 48p. (gr. 4 up). Repr. of 1989 ed. 5.95g (*0-8225-9576-1*) Lerner Pubns.
—Endangered Grassland Animals. (Illus.). 32p. (gr. 3-8). 1992. PLB 15.95 (*0-86505-528-9*); pap. 7.95 (*0-86505-538-6*) Crabtree Pub Co.
—Nature's Creatures of the Dark: A Pop-up Glow-in-the-Dark Exploration. (Illus.). 14p. (gr. 1-5). 1993. 15.99 (*0-8037-1631-1*) Dial Bks Young.
Taylor, Donald G. Story Picture Poem & Coloring Book for Children. (Illus.). 30p. (ps-1). 1993. pap. 6.95 (*0-9638002-0-5*) D G Taylor.
Taylor, Doreen. Scotland. LC 90-10028. (Illus.). 96p. (gr. 6-11). 1990. PLB 19.92 (*0-8114-2431-6*) Raintree Steck-V.
Taylor, Dorothy L. Abigail's New Home. Schimmel, Beth, illus. LC 82-238196. 20p. (gr. k-3). 7.50 (*0-9610640-0-5*) D L Taylor.
Taylor, E. J. Goose Eggs. LC 91-58809. (Illus.). (ps up). 1992. 12.95 (*1-56402-123-8*) Candlewick Pr.
—Ivy Cottage. LC 91-58810. (Illus.). (ps up). 1992. 12.95 (*1-56402-124-6*) Candlewick Pr.
—Rag Doll Press. (ps up). 1992. 12.95 (*1-56402-150-5*) Candlewick Pr.
—Thorn Witch. (ps up). 1992. 12.95 (*1-56402-151-3*) Candlewick Pr.
Taylor, Edgar, tr. see Grimm, Jacob & Grimm, Wilhelm K.
Taylor, Elizabeth A., jt. auth. see Armbruster, Ann.
Taylor, Elizabeth B., tr. see Nickl, Peter.
Taylor, Gary. The Federal Reserve System. (Illus.). 104p. (gr. 5 up). 1989. 14.95 (*1-55546-136-0*) Chelsea Hse.
Taylor, Harriet P., retold by. & illus. Coyote Places the Stars. LC 92-46431. 32p. (ps-2). 1993. RSBE 14.95 (*0-02-788845-2*, Bradbury Pr) Macmillan Child Grp.
Taylor, Helen L. Little Pilgrim's Progress. (gr. 2-7). pap. 6.99 (*0-8024-4926-3*) Moody.
Taylor, Henry T. Know Your Wheels. Bylenok, Marsha, contrib. by. Greenough, Jackie & Taylor, Pamela, illus. 51p. (gr. 4-6). 1981. pap. write for info. (*0-938956-00-0*) H T Taylor.
Taylor, J. W., jt. auth. see French, P. M.
Taylor, Jane. Twinkle, Twinkle, Little Star. 1992. 10.95 (*0-590-45566-4*, Cartwheel) Scholastic Inc.
—Twinkle, Twinkle, Little Star. LC 92-421. (ps-3). 1992. 14.93 (*0-688-11169-6*) Morrow Jr Bks.
—Twinkle, Twinkle, Little Star. Noonan, Julia, illus. (ps-3). 1993. pap. 4.95 (*0-590-45928-7*, Cartwheel) Scholastic Inc.
Taylor, Jerry, jt. auth. see Griesbach, Ellen.
Taylor, Jody, ed. Mazes, Mazes, Mazes. 64p. (gr. 2-7). 1994. pap. 6.95 (*1-56397-334-0*) Boyds Mills Pr.
—Sports Hidden Pictures. (Illus.). 32p. (Orig.). (ps-5). 1993. pap. 3.95 (*1-56397-255-7*) Boyds Mills Pr.
Taylor, John. How Cars Are Made. LC 86-32878. (Illus.). 32p. (gr. 5-12). 1987. 12.95x (*0-8160-1689-5*) Facts on File.
—Volcano in Our Yard. (Illus.). (gr. 2-5). 1975. 4.95 (*0-686-11663-1*) Thompson's.
Taylor, Judith, et al. Beatrix Potter, 1866-1943: The Artist & Her World. 244p. (gr. 9 up). 1988. pap. 19.95 (*0-7232-3561-9*) Warne.

Taylor, Judy. The Adventures of Dudley Dormouse. Cross, Peter, illus. & created by. LC 91-58717. 80p. (ps up). 1992. 9.95 (*1-56402-043-6*) Candlewick Pr.
—Beatrix Potter: Artist, Storyteller & Countrywoman. (Illus.). 224p. (gr. 9 up). 1987. 24.95 (*0-7232-3314-4*) Warne.
—My Cat. Cartwright, Reg, illus. LC 88-22127. 32p. (ps-2). 1989. pap. 3.95 (*0-689-71209-X*, Aladdin) Macmillan Child Grp.
—My Dog. Cartwright, Reg, illus. LC 88-19441. 32p. (ps-2). 1989. pap. 3.95 (*0-689-71210-3*, Aladdin) Macmillan Child Grp.
—That Naughty Rabbit. 96p. (ps up). 1987. 15.95 (*0-7232-3442-6*) Warne.
Taylor, Judy, ed. So I Shall Tell You a Story: The Magic World of Beatrix Potter. Potter, Beatrix, illus. Sendak, Maurice, et al. (Illus.). 224p. 1993. 24.95 (*0-7232-4025-6*) Warne.
Taylor, Kate. Colors Shapes & Numbers. Taylor, Kate, illus. 14p. (gr. k-2). 1993. 7.95 (*0-87226-505-6*, Bedrick Blackie) P Bedrick Bks.
—What Do I Eat? Taylor, Kate, illus. 16p. 1993. 6.95 (*0-87226-506-4*, Bedrick Blackie) P Bedrick Bks.
Taylor, Ken. Good News for Little People. (ps-2). 1991. 10.99 (*0-8423-6628-8*) Tyndale.
Taylor, Kenneth. The Book for Children. 640p. 1985. 12. 99 (*0-8423-2145-4*) Tyndale.
—Devotions for the Children's Hour. 2nd ed. (gr. 1-8). 1987. pap. 6.99 (*0-8024-2226-8*) Moody.
—New Testament in Pictures for Little Eyes. (Illus.). 155p. (Orig.). 1989. pap. 6.99 (*0-8024-0682-3*) Moody.
—Stories for the Children's Hour. 2nd ed. (gr. 1-8). 1987. pap. 6.99 (*0-8024-2227-6*) Moody.
Taylor, Kenneth N. Bible in Pictures for Little Eyes. (Illus.). (ps-2). 1956. 14.99 (*0-8024-0595-9*) Moody.
—Big Thoughts for Little People. (ps-3). 1983. 10.99 (*0-8423-0164-X*) Tyndale.
—Catholic Family-Time Bible Stories in Pictures. (Illus.). 307p. (gr. 1-4). 1993. 14.95 (*0-87973-882-0*, 882) Our Sunday Visitor.
—Giant Steps for Little People. 64p. (ps-1). 1985. 10.99 (*0-8423-1023-1*) Tyndale.
—The Good Samaritan. (Illus.). 1989. bds. 3.99 (*0-8423-1127-0*) Tyndale.
—Jesus Feeds a Crowd. (Illus.). 1989. bds. 3.99 (*0-8423-1859-3*) Tyndale.
—The Lost Sheep. (Illus.). 1989. bds. 3.99 (*0-8423-3841-1*, 753841-1) Tyndale.
—McGee's Favorite Bible Stories. Hook, Richard & Hook, Frances, illus. LC 92-20265. 1992. 15.99 (*0-8423-4142-0*) Tyndale.
—My First Bible for Tots: Creation. (Illus.). 12p. (ps). 1992. bds. 3.99 (*0-8423-1696-5*) Tyndale.
—My First Bible for Tots: David & Goliath. (Illus.). 12p. (ps). 1992. bds. 3.99 (*0-8423-1697-3*) Tyndale.
—El Nuevo Testamento en Cuadros Para Ninos. (SPA.). 72p. 1991. 7.99 (*0-8254-1708-2*) Kregel.
—The Old Testament in Pictures for Little Eyes. 240p. 1993. pap. 7.99 (*0-8024-0683-1*) Moody.
—The Prodigal Son. (Illus.). 1989. bds. 3.99 (*0-8423-5040-3*, 755040-3) Tyndale.
—What High School Students Should Know about Creation. (gr. 9-12). 1983. pap. 2.95 (*0-8423-7872-3*) Tyndale.
—What High School Students Should Know about Evolution. 70p. (gr. 9-12). 1983. pap. 3.99 (*0-8423-7873-1*) Tyndale.
—Wise Words for Little People. 64p. (ps-2). 1987. 10.99 (*0-8423-8232-1*) Tyndale.
Taylor, Kenneth N., ed. My First Bible Stories in Pictures. Hook, Robert & Hook, Frances, illus. Lockwood, Robert P., intro. by. 272p. (gr. k-5). 1990. 14.95 (*0-87973-245-8*, 245); 10.95 (*0-87973-246-6*, 246) Our Sunday Visitor.
Taylor, Kent. Bible in Pictures for Little Eyes. Date not set. (*0-8024-0685-8*) Moody.
Taylor, Kim. Flying Start Science. 32p. (gr. 4-7). 1992. 12.95 (*0-471-57983-1*) Wiley.
—Flying Start Science: Pattern. 32p. (gr. 4-7). 1992. 12. 95 (*0-471-57982-3*) Wiley.
—Hidden by Darkness. (gr. 4-7). 1990. 9.95 (*0-385-30178-2*) Delacorte.
—Hidden Inside. (gr. 4-7). 1990. 9.95 (*0-385-30182-0*) Delacorte.
—Hidden under Water. (gr. 4-7). 1990. 9.95 (*0-385-30184-7*) Delacorte.
—Hidden Underneath. (gr. 4-7). 1990. 9.95 (*0-385-30180-4*) Delacorte.
—Secret Worlds. (gr. 4-8). 1991. 9.95 (*0-385-30218-5*) Delacorte.
—Too Clever to See. (gr. 2-5). 1991. 9.95 (*0-385-30216-9*) Delacorte.
—Too Slow to See. (gr. 2-5). 1991. 9.95 (*0-385-30214-2*) Delacorte.
—Too Small to See. (ps-7). 1991. 9.95 (*0-385-30220-7*) Delacorte.
Taylor, Kim & Burton, Jane, photos by. See How They Grow: Frog. (Illus.). 24p. (gr. k-3). 1991. 6.95 (*0-525-67345-8*, Lodestar Bks) Dutton Child Bks.
Taylor, L. B., Jr. & Taylor, C. L. Chemical & Biological Warfare. rev. ed. LC 92-17083. (Illus.). (gr. 9-12). 1992. 14.40 (*0-531-13029-0*) Watts.
Taylor, Laurie. How Could This Happen? Dealing with Crisis Pregnancy. Nelson, Becky, ed. 20p. (Orig.). (gr. 7-12). 1992. pap. text ed. 1.95 (*1-56309-034-1*, Wrld Changers Res) Womans Mission Union.
Taylor, LaVonne, ed. see Chambers, Vickie.

Taylor, Linda. The Lettuce Leaf Birthday Letter. Durrell, Julie, illus. LC 93-16906. 1994. 13.99 (*0-8037-1454-8*); PLB 13.89 (*0-8037-1455-6*) Dial Bks Young.

Taylor, Lisa. Beryl's Box. Dann, Penny, illus. LC 92-44990. 32p. (ps-2). 1993. 12.95 (*0-8120-6355-4*); pap. 5.95 (*0-8120-1673-4*) Barron.

Taylor, Livingston & Taylor, Maggie. Can I Be Good? Rand, Ted, illus. LC 92-23193. 1993. 14.95 (*0-15-200436-X*) HarBrace.

—Pajamas. Bowers, Tim, illus. 32p. (ps-3). 1988. 13.95 (*0-15-200564-1*, Gulliver Bks) HarBrace.

Taylor, Louis, ed. see Griesbach, Ellen & Taylor, Jerry.

Taylor, Lucinda. Mitchell D. Fardle. Young, Karen, illus. LC 93-28987. 1994. 4.25 (*0-383-03761-1*) SRA Schl Grp.

Taylor, Maggie, jt. auth. see Taylor, Livingston.

Taylor, Margaret & Schuett, Virginia E. You & PKU. (Illus.). 43p. 1988. pap. text ed. 5.00 (*0-299-97065-5*) U of Wis Pr.

Taylor, Marian W. Madame C. J. Walker: Pioneer Businesswoman. LC 93-14653. (Illus.). 1993. 13.95 (*0-7910-2039-8*, Am Art Analog); pap. write for info. (*0-7910-2040-1*, Am Art Analog) Chelsea Hse.

Taylor, Mark. The Best Prize of All. Ewers, Joe, illus. 40p. (ps-3). 1985. 5.95 (*0-910313-86-5*) Parker Bros.

—The Great Rescue. Brett, Jan, illus. LC 83-25113. 40p. (gr. 1-5). 1984. 6.95 (*0-910313-28-8*); incl. cassette 7.95 (*0-910313-61-X*) Parker Bros.

—Henry the Explorer. Booth, Graham, illus. 48p. (ps-3). 1988. pap. 5.95 (*0-316-83384-3*) Little.

Taylor, Mark A. Breakfast with Jesus. Stiles, Andy, illus. 28p. (ps). 1993. PLB 4.99 (*0-7847-0037-0*, 24-03827) Standard Pub.

—Leader's Guide for Come to the Party! 64p. (Orig.). 1994. pap. text ed. 4.49 (*0-7847-0145-8*) Standard Pub.

—One Tiny Baby. Hutton, Kathryn, illus. 32p. (gr. k-2). 1989. 2.50 (*0-87403-599-6*, 3859) Standard Pub.

Taylor, Maureen. Without Warning. LC 91-12470. 144p. 1991. pap. 4.99 (*0-8066-2538-4*, 9-2538) Augsburg Fortress.

Taylor, Maurie. Easy French Vocabulary Games. (FRE., Illus.). 64p. (gr. 4 up). 1988. pap. 4.95 (*0-8442-1323-3*, Passport Bks) NTC Pub Grp.

—Easy French Word Games & Puzzles. (FRE., Illus.). 64p. (gr. 4 up). 1983. pap. 4.95 (*0-8442-1321-7*, Passport Bks) NTC Pub Grp.

—Jeux Culturels. (FRE., Illus.). 64p. (gr. 5 up). 1983. pap. 4.95 (*0-8442-1398-5*, Passport Bks) NTC Pub Grp.

Taylor, Maurie, jt. auth. see Padilla, Jaime.

Taylor, Michael. Aircraft Carriers. 1989. pap. 3.95 (*0-590-41997-8*) Scholastic Inc.

Taylor, Mildred. Song of the Trees. Pinkney, Jeny, illus. LC 74-18598. 56p. (gr. 2-5). 1975. 13.50 (*0-8037-5452-3*); PLB 11.89 (*0-8037-5453-1*) Dial Bks Young.

Taylor, Mildred D. The Friendship. Ginsburg, Max, illus. LC 86-29309. 56p. (gr. 2-6). 1987. 13.95 (*0-8037-0417-8*); PLB 13.89 (*0-8037-0418-6*) Dial Bks Young.

—The Friendship & the Gold Cadillac. (gr. 2-6). 1989. pap. 3.50 (*0-553-15765-5*, Skylark) Bantam.

—The Gold Cadillac. Hays, Michael, illus. LC 86-11526. 48p. (gr. 2-6). 1987. 12.95 (*0-8037-0342-2*); PLB 12.89 (*0-8037-0343-0*) Dial Bks Young.

—Let the Circle Be Unbroken. LC 81-65854. 432p. (gr. 7 up). 1981. 15.95 (*0-8037-4748-9*) Dial Bks Young.

—Let the Circle Be Unbroken. (gr. 7-12). 1983. pap. 3.50 (*0-553-23436-6*) Bantam.

—Let the Circle Be Unbroken. (gr. 4-7). 1991. pap. 3.99 (*0-14-034892-1*, Puffin) Puffin Bks.

—Mississippi Bridge. LC 89-27898. (Illus.). 64p. 1990. 14.00 (*0-8037-0426-7*); PLB 13.89 (*0-8037-0427-5*) Dial Bks Young.

—Mississippi Bridge. Ginsberg, Max, illus. (gr. 4-7). 1992. pap. 3.50 (*0-553-15992-5*, Skylark) Bantam.

—The Road to Memphis. Fogelman, Phyllis J., ed. LC 88-33654. (Illus.). 240p. (gr. 7 up). 1990. 14.95 (*0-8037-0340-6*) Dial Bks Young.

—The Road to Memphis. 304p. (gr. 5-9). 1992. pap. 3.99 (*0-14-036077-8*, Puffin) Puffin Bks.

—Roll of Thunder, Hear My Cry. Pinkney, Jerry, illus. LC 76-2287. (Illus.). 210p. (gr. 6 up). 1976. 15.00 (*0-8037-7473-7*) Dial Bks Young.

—Roll of Thunder, Hear My Cry. large type ed. 304p. 1989. Repr. of 1976 ed. lib. bdg. 15.95 (*1-55736-140-1*, Crnrstn Bks) BDD LT Grp.

—Roll of Thunder, Hear My Cry. 276p. (gr. 5-9). 1991. pap. 3.99 (*0-14-034893-X*) Puffin Bks.

Taylor, Mildred G. How to Write a Research Paper. LC 71-180899. (Illus.). 55p. (Orig.). (gr. 7-12). 1974. pap. 1.75 (*0-87015-206-8*) Pacific Bks.

Taylor, Morris. Top of the Hill. 64p. 1988. pap. 4.95 (*0-87961-183-9*) Naturegraph.

Taylor, Nancy R. The Write to Read Method "Jotter" 27p. (Orig.). (gr. k-2). 1992. pap. 10.00 wkbk. (*0-9634324-2-7*) Progress Educ.

Taylor, Nick. Great Trains. (gr. 1-9). 1992. pap. 3.95 (*0-88388-070-9*) Bellerophon Bks.

—Modern Fighter Planes. (gr. 1-9). 1992. pap. 3.95 (*0-88388-095-4*) Bellerophon Bks.

Taylor, Nicole. Baby. LC 92-41338. 1993. 18.95 (*0-88682-595-4*) Creative Ed.

Taylor, Nicole, jt. auth. see Rotter, Charles M.

Taylor, Nigel. Going Live! Pet Book. (Illus.). 112p. 1992. pap. 3.95 (*0-563-20733-7*, BBC-Parkwest) Parkwest Pubns.

Taylor, Norra. My Mom, the Sailor. Laur, Calvin, illus. 1992. 12.95 (*0-533-10302-9*) Vantage.

Taylor, Paul. Fossil. Keates, Colin, photos by. LC 89-36444. (Illus.). 64p. (gr. 5 up). 1990. 15.00 (*0-679-80440-4*); PLB 15.99 (*0-679-90440-9*) Random Bks Yng Read.

Taylor, Paul S. The Great Dinosaur Mystery & the Bible. LC 89-81581. 63p. (gr. 4-8). 1990. 10.95 (*0-89636-264-7*, AC 215, Chariot Bks) Cook.

Taylor, Paula. Cancer. 40p. (gr. 4). 1989. PLB 13.95s.p. (*0-88682-261-0*) Creative Ed.

—Capricorn. 40p. (gr. 4). 1989. PLB 13.95s.p. (*0-88682-256-4*) Creative Ed.

—Gemini. 40p. (gr. 4). 1989. PLB 13.95s.p. (*0-88682-252-1*) Creative Ed.

—The Kids' Whole Future Catalog. LC 82-5279. (Illus.). 256p. (gr. 4-7). 1982. pap. 6.95 (*0-394-85090-4*) Random Bks Yng Read.

—Leo. 40p. (gr. 4). 1989. PLB 13.95s.p. (*0-88682-253-X*) Creative Ed.

—Sagittarius. 40p. (gr. 4). 1989. PLB 13.95s.p. (*0-88682-251-3*) Creative Ed.

Taylor, Phoebe, ed. Thoughts for the Free Life: Lao Tsu to the Present. 2nd ed. Buckley, Cicely, illus. 110p. (Orig.). (gr. 8 up). 1989. pap. 10.00 (*0-9617481-5-X*) Oyster River Pr.

Taylor, R. Craig. Napoleon's Battle, Napoleonic Miniatures Rules. (Illus.). 96p. (gr. 9 up). 1989. 25.00 (*1-56038-008-X*) Avalon Hill.

Taylor, Randy M. Dino Valentino. Taylor, Nancy S., illus. 33p. (gr. k-5). 1988. write for info. (*0-937745-05-7*) Traditions Pr.

Taylor, Richard L. The First Flight Across the United States: The Story of Calbraith Perry Rodgers & His Airplane, the Vin Fiz. LC 93-6881. (Illus.). 64p. (gr. 4-6). 1993. PLB 12.90 (*0-531-20159-7*) Watts.

Taylor, Richard, L. First Flight: The Story of the Wright Brothers. (Illus.). (ps-3). 1990. PLB 12.90 (*0-531-10891-0*) Watts.

Taylor, Richard L. The First Solo Flight Around the World: The Story of Wiley Post & His Airplane, the Winnie Mae. LC 93-6880. (Illus.). 64p. (gr. 4-6). 1993. PLB 12.90 (*0-531-20160-0*) Watts.

Taylor, Ron. Health Two Thousand. (Illus.). 64p. (gr. 7 up). 1986. 14.95x (*0-8160-1156-7*) Facts on File.

—The Invisible World. (Illus.). 64p. (gr. 7 up). 1986. 15.95x (*0-8160-1069-2*) Facts on File.

—Projects. (Illus.). 64p. (gr. 4-7). 1985. 15.95x (*0-8160-1076-5*) Facts on File.

—Through the Microscope. (Illus.). 64p. (gr. 4-7). 1985. 15.95x (*0-8160-1075-7*) Facts on File.

Taylor, Scott. Dinosaur James. LC 89-27268. (Illus.). 32p. (gr. k up). 1990. 13.95 (*0-688-08576-8*); PLB 13.88 (*0-688-08577-6*, Morrow Jr Bks) Morrow Jr Bks.

Taylor, Sydney. All-of-a-Kind Family. John, Helen, illus. 192p. (gr. k-6). 1980. pap. 3.50 (*0-440-40059-7*, YB) Dell.

—All-of-a-Kind Family. John, Helen, illus. 189p. (gr. 3-6). 1988. Repr. of 1951 ed. 11.95 (*0-929093-00-3*) Taylor Prodns.

—All-of-a-Kind Family Downtown. 188p. (gr. k-6). 1973. pap. 3.50 (*0-440-42032-6*, YB) Dell.

—All-of-a-Kind Family Downtown. Krush, Beth & Krush, Joe, illus. 187p. 1988. Repr. of 1972 ed. 11.95 (*0-929093-01-1*) Taylor Prodns.

—All-of-a-Kind Family Uptown. Stevens, Mary, illus. 160p. 1988. Repr. of 1958 ed. 11.95 (*0-929093-03-8*) Taylor Prodns.

—All-of-a-Kind Family Uptown. 166p. 1992. text ed. 13.28 (*1-56956-106-0*) W A T Braille.

—Ella All-of-a-Kind Family. 174p. 1992. text ed. 13.92 (*1-56956-111-7*) W A T Braille.

—Ella of All-of-a-Kind Family. Rosner, Meryl, illus. 133p. (gr. 4-8). 1988. Repr. of 1978 ed. 11.95 (*0-929093-04-6*) Taylor Prodns.

—More All-of-a-Kind Family. Stevens, Mary, illus. 160p. (gr. 3-6). 1988. Repr. of 1954 ed. 11.95 (*0-929093-02-X*) Taylor Prodns.

—More All-of-a-Kind Family. 166p. 1992. text ed. 13.28 (*1-56956-120-6*) W A T Braille.

—A Papa Like Everyone Else. (gr. k-6). 1989. pap. 2.95 (*0-440-40129-1*, YB) Dell.

Taylor, T. Maria: A Christmas Story. 1992. 13.95 (*0-15-217763-9*, HB Juv Bks) HarBrace.

—The Weirdo. 224p. (gr. 7 up). 1991. 15.95 (*0-15-294952-6*, HB Juv Bks) HarBrace.

Taylor, Theodore. Air Raid: Pearl Harbor. 179p. (gr. 3-7). 1991. pap. 4.95 (*0-15-201655-4*, Odyssey) HarBrace.

—The Battle in the English Channel. 144p. (Orig.). (gr. 7 up). 1983. pap. 3.50 (*0-380-85225-X*, Flare) Avon.

—The Battle off Midway Island. 144p. (Orig.). (gr. 7 up). 1981. pap. 3.95 (*0-380-78790-3*, Flare) Avon.

—Cay. LC 69-15161. 160p. (gr. 6-9). 1987. pap. 13.95 (*0-385-07906-0*) Doubleday.

—The Cay. large type ed. 154p. (gr. k-6). 1990. Repr. lib. bdg. 15.95 (*1-55736-163-0*, Crnrstn Bks) BDD LT Grp.

—The Cay. reissued ed. 144p. (gr. 6). 1977. pap. 3.99 (*0-380-00142-X*, Camelot) Avon.

—Maria. 80p. (gr. 4). 1993. pap. 3.50 (*0-380-72120-1*, Camelot) Avon.

—The Odyssey of Ben O'Neal. 224p. 1991. pap. 3.50 (*0-380-71026-9*, Camelot) Avon.

—Sniper. LC 89-7415. 227p. (gr. 7 up). 1989. 15.95 (*0-15-276420-8*) HarBrace.

—Sniper. 240p. 1991. pap. 3.99 (*0-380-71193-1*, Flare) Avon.

—Teetoncey. Cuffari, Richard, illus. (gr. 3-7). 1991. pap. 3.50 (*0-380-71024-2*, Camelot) Avon.

—Teetoncey & Ben O'Neal. Cuffari, Richard, illus. 192p. (gr. 5-7). 1991. pap. 3.50 (*0-380-71025-0*, Camelot) Avon.

—Timothy of the Cay. (gr. 4-7). 1993. 13.95 (*0-15-288358-4*, HB Juv Bks) HarBrace.

—Trouble with Tuck. LC 81-43139. 96p. (gr. 4-6). 1989. 13.95 (*0-385-17774-7*); pap. 10.95 (*0-385-17775-5*) Doubleday.

—The Trouble with Tuck. 120p. (gr. 5 up). 1983. pap. 3.50 (*0-380-62711-6*, Camelot) Avon.

—Tuck Triumphant. (gr. 5-7). 1991. 14.95 (*0-385-41480-3*) Doubleday.

—Tuck Triumphant. (gr. 4-7). 1992. pap. 3.50 (*0-380-71323-3*, Camelot) Avon.

—Waking up a Rainbow. LC 85-16239. 224p. (gr. 7 up). 1986. pap. 14.95 (*0-385-29435-2*) Delacorte.

—Walking up a Rainbow. (gr. k-12). 1988. pap. 2.95 (*0-440-99326-1*, LFL); pap. 2.95 (*0-440-20039-3*) Dell.

—The Weirdo. 240p. 1993. pap. 3.50 (*0-380-72017-5*, Flare) Avon.

Taylor, Theodore, jt. auth. see Hedren, Tippi.

Taylor, Tim. Cyclops Vale & Other Tales. Ruemmler, John D., ed. Roberts, Tony & Jaquays, Paul, illus. 32p. (Orig.). (gr. 12). 1989. pap. 6.00 (*1-55806-042-1*, 6009) Iron Crown Ent Inc.

Taylor, Timothy. The Orgillion Horror. Ruemmler, John D., ed. Martin, David & Jaquays, Paul, illus. 32p. (Orig.). (gr. 12). 1989. pap. 6.00 (*1-55806-029-4*, 6006) Iron Crown Ent Inc.

Taylor, Valerie. Til Death Did Us Part. 67p. (gr. 12). 1985. pap. 6.95 (*0-917117-01-8*) Creat Concern.

Taylor, Wendell H., jt. auth. see Barzun, Jacques.

Taylor, William. Agnes the Sheep. 176p. (gr. 5 up). 1991. 13.95 (*0-590-43365-2*, Scholastic Hardcover) Scholastic Inc.

—Knitwits. 1992. 13.95 (*0-590-45778-0*, 022, Scholastic Hardcover) Scholastic Inc.

—Paradise Lane. 176p. (gr. 7 up). 1989. pap. 2.75 (*0-590-41014-8*) Scholastic Inc.

Taylor-Boyd, Susan. Betty Friedan. LC 90-9691. (Illus.). 64p. (gr. 5-6). 1990. PLB 18.60 (*0-8368-0104-0*) Gareth Stevens Inc.

—Sojourner Truth. LC 89-4345. (Illus.). 68p. (Orig.). 1990. pap. 7.95 (*0-8192-1541-4*) Morehouse Pub.

—Sojourner Truth: The Courageous Former Slave Whose Eloquence Helped Promote Human Equality. LC 89-4345. (Illus.). 68p. (gr. 5-6). 1990. PLB 18.60 (*0-8368-0101-6*) Gareth Stevens Inc.

—Sojourner Truth: The Courageous Former Slave Who Led Others to Freedom. Tolan, Mary, adapted by. LC 90-37992. (Illus.). 64p. (gr. 3-4). 1991. PLB 18.60 (*0-8368-0458-9*) Gareth Stevens Inc.

Taylor-Boyd, Susan & Brown, Julie, eds. U. S. S. R. Miyajina, Yasuhiko, photos by. LC 88-42891. (Illus.). 64p. (gr. 5-6). 1989. PLB 19.93 (*1-55532-215-8*) Gareth Stevens Inc.

Taylor-Boyd, Susan, jt. auth. see O'Brien, John.

Taylor-Cork, Barbara. Weather Forecaster. LC 91-30539. (Illus.). 32p. (gr. 4-7). 1992. PLB 12.40 (*0-531-17267-8*, Gloucester Pr) Watts.

Taylor-McMillan, Birah, ed. see Borba, Michele.

Tazawa, ed. see Quackenbuch, Hiroko C.

Tazawa, ed. see Quackenbush, Hiroko C.

Tazewell. Littlest Angel. new ed. 32p. 1991. 21.27 (*0-516-09218-9*) Childrens.

Tazewell, Charles. Littlest Angel. Leone, S., illus. 32p. (gr. 1 up). 1946. PLB 15.00 (*0-516-03533-9*) Childrens.

—The Littlest Angel. 32p. (gr. k-6). 1985. pap. 6.95 (*0-89542-923-3*, Ideals Child) Hambleton-Hill.

—The Littlest Angel. Micich, Paul, illus. LC 91-2442. 32p. (ps). 1991. 15.95 (*0-8249-8516-8*, Ideals Child) Hambleton-Hill.

Tchudi, Stephen. The Burg-O-Rama Man. LC 82-14075. 192p. (gr. 7 up). 1983. pap. 13.95 (*0-385-29239-2*) Delacorte.

—Lock & Key: The Secrets of Locking Things up, in, & Out. LC 92-43252. (Illus.). 128p. (gr. 5 up). 1993. SBE 14.95 (*0-684-19363-9*, Scribners Young Read) Macmillan Child Grp.

—Probing the Unknown: From Myth to Science. LC 89-35938. (Illus.). 160p. (gr. 7 up). 1990. SBE 14.95 (*0-684-19086-9*, Scribners Young Read) Macmillan Child Grp.

—Soda Poppery: The History of Soft Drinks in America. LC 85-40289. 160p. (gr. 7 up). 1986. SBE 14.95 (*0-684-18488-5*, Scribners Young Read) Macmillan Child Grp.

—The Young Learner's Handbook. LC 87-4523. 208p. (gr. 7 up). 1987. SBE 14.95 (*0-684-18676-4*, Scribners Young Read) Macmillan Child Grp.

Tchudi, Stephen, jt. auth. see Tchudi, Susan.

Tchudi, Susan & Tchudi, Stephen. The Young Writer's Handbook. LC 84-5312. 160p. (gr. 5 up). 1984. SBE 14.95 (*0-684-18090-1*, Scribners Young Read) Macmillan Child Grp.

—The Young Writer's Handbook: A Practical Guide for the Beginner Who Is Serious about Writing. LC 87-1463. (Illus.). 176p. (gr. 7 up). 1987. pap. 4.95 (*0-689-71170-0*, Aladdin) Macmillan Child Grp.

Teachers of the School District of Independence, Missouri Staff & Melton, David. Independence, the Queen City of the Trails. Henley, Robert L., pref. by. LC 86-21046. (Illus.). (gr. 2 up). 1986. 19.95 (*0-933849-04-4*) Landmark Edns.

Teague, Ken. Growing up in Ancient China. Hook, Richard, illus. LC 91-14879. 32p. (gr. 3-5). 1993. PLB 11.89 (*0-8167-2715-5*); pap. text ed. 3.95 (*0-8167-2716-3*) Troll Assocs. Postponed.

Teague, Mark. The Field Beyond the Outfield. 32p. 1992. 14.95 (*0-590-45173-1*, Scholastic Hardcover) Scholastic Inc.

—Frog Medicine. 1991. 13.95 (*0-590-44177-9*, Scholastic Hardcover) Scholastic Inc.

—Moog-Moog, Space Barber. (gr. 4-7). 1990. 12.95 (*0-590-43332-6*) Scholastic Inc.

—Moog-Moog, Space Barber. 32p. 1991. pap. 4.95 (*0-590-43331-8*) Scholastic Inc.

—Pigsty. LC 93-21179. 1994. write for info. (*0-590-45915-5*) Scholastic Inc.

—The Trouble with the Johnsons. (Illus.). (gr. k-3). 1989. pap. 12.95 (*0-590-42394-0*) Scholastic Inc.

Teague, Sam. The King of Hearts' Heart. 192p. (gr. 3-7). 1987. 13.95 (*0-316-83427-0*) Little.

Teague, Wells. Theo, the Indian Fighter. Eakin, Edwin M., ed. (Illus.). 112p. (gr. 4-7). 1987. 8.95 (*0-89015-614-X*, Pub. by Panda Bks) Eakin-Sunbelt.

Teal, R. Success at Work. large type ed. 166p. (gr. 7-12). 1983. Repr. of 1979 ed. 29.36 (*0-317-01946-5*, 4-23950-00) Am Printing Hse.

Teasdale, Sara. Christmas Carol. Gottlieb, Dale, illus. 32p. (ps-2). 1993. PLB 14.95 (*0-8050-2695-9*, Bks Young Read) H Holt & Co.

Teasley, Jamie, ed. see Benander, Carl D.

Teasley, Jamie, ed. see DeMaio, Toni.

Teasley, Jamie, ed. see Walter, Dean S.

Techner, David & Hirt-Manheimer, Judith. A Candle for Grandpa: A Guide to the Jewish Funeral for Children & Parents. Iskowitz, Joel, illus. (gr. k-3). 1993. 10.95 (*0-8074-0507-8*, 123070) UAHC.

Techter, D. see Glut, D. F.

Tedards, Anne. Marian Anderson. Horner, Matina, intro. by. (Illus.). 112p. (Orig.). (gr. 5 up). 1988. 17.95 (*1-55546-638-9*); pap. 9.95 (*0-7910-0216-0*) Chelsea Hse.

Tedesco, Donna. Do You Know How Much I Love You? Tedesco, Donna, illus. LC 92-7856. 32p. (ps-1). 1994. SBE 13.95 (*0-02-789120-8*, Bradbury Pr) Macmillan Child Grp.

Tedorw, T. L. Mountain Miracle. LC 92-19927. 1992. 4.99 (*0-8407-7733-7*) Nelson.

Tedrow, Carla. Trouble at the Cave. LC 93-71558. 150p. 1993. pap. 3.95 (*1-56969-175-4*) FamilyVision.

Tedrow, T. L. Days of Laura Ingalls Wilder, Vol. 2: Children of Promise. LC 92-1041. 1992. pap. 4.99 (*0-8407-3398-4*) Oliver-Nelson.

—Days of Laura Ingalls Wilder, Vol. 3: Good Neighbors. 1992. pap. 4.99 (*0-8407-3399-2*) Oliver-Nelson.

—Days of Laura Ingalls Wilder, Vol. 4: Home to the Prairie. 1992. pap. 4.99 (*0-8407-3401-8*) Oliver-Nelson.

—The Great Debate. LC 92-23716. 1992. pap. 4.99 (*0-8407-7734-5*) Nelson.

—Land of Promise. LC 92-28222. 1992. 4.99 (*0-8407-7735-3*) Nelson.

Tedrow, Thomas L. The World's Fair. LC 92-22727. 1992. pap. 4.99 (*0-8407-7732-9*) Nelson.

Teeny Books Staff. Patterns. Davies, Kate, illus. 10p. (ps). 1993. 4.95 (*0-448-40534-2*, G&D) Putnam Pub Group.

—Pictures. Davies, Kate, illus. 10p. (ps). 1993. 4.95 (*0-448-40535-0*, G&D) Putnam Pub Group.

Teeter, Barbara G. Hemingway for Teachers: Research & Creative Writing Projects & Activities for High School Youth. 96p. (gr. 9-12). 1992. pap. text ed. 13.95 (*0-944459-50-1*) ECS Lrn Systs.

Teeters, Peggy. Jules Verne: The Man Who Invented Tomorrow. 128p. 1993. 13.95 (*0-8027-8189-6*); PLB 14.85 (*0-8027-8191-8*) Walker & Co.

Tee-Van, Helen D. Small Mammals Are Where You Find Them. (Illus.). (gr. 3-7). 1967. lib. bdg. 5.99 (*0-394-91643-3*) Knopf Bks Yng Read.

Tegeler, Dorothy. Hello Arizona: The Arizona Activity Book. Hicks, Mark, illus. 32p. (Orig.). 1987. pap. 3.50 (*0-943169-07-0*) Fiesta Bks Inc.

Teich, Shmuel. The Rishonim: Biographical Sketches of the Prominent Early Rabbinic Sages & Leaders from the Tenth-Fifteenth Centuries. Goldwurm, Hersh, ed. & intro. by. (Illus.). 224p. (gr. 7-8). 1982. 16.95 (*0-89906-452-3*); pap. 13.95 (*0-89906-453-1*) Mesorah Pubns.

Teichman, Avigail. The Captive Sultan. Reinman, Y. Y., ed. Hinklicky, G., illus. LC 85-72403. 128p. (gr. 7-11). 1985. 7.95 (*0-935063-12-9*); pap. 5.95 (*0-935063-04-8*) CIS Comm.

Teichman, Mary, illus. Merry Christmas: A Victorian Verse. LC 92-29870. 32p. (gr. up). 1993. 10.00 (*0-06-022889-X*); PLB 9.89 (*0-06-022892-X*) HarpC Child Bks.

Teirstein, Mark A. Baseball. LC 93-23271. 1993. write for info. (*0-8114-5776-1*) Raintree Steck-V.

Teitelbaum, Chaya S. & Lederman, Raizel. Ich Lern Aleph-Beis. (YID., Illus.). 72p. (Orig.). 1991. pap. write for info wkbk.. (*0-9630821-0-8*) Ich Lern A-B.

Teitelbaum, Eli. A Basic Guide to the Mishkan. rev. ed. Malowicky, Sinai, ed. & illus. 16p. (gr. 7-12). 1992. pap. text ed. write for info. (*1-878895-01-X*, A320) Torah Umesorah.

Teitelbaum, M. Michael & Magic Poster Book. (Illus.). 1991. pap. 2.95 (*1-56156-062-6*) Kidsbks.

Teitelbaum, Michael. Alvin & the Chipmunks: Alvin's Daydreams. YES! Entertainment Corporation Staff, ed. 16p. (ps-2). 1993. write for info. (*1-883366-18-6*) YES Ent.

—Batman Returns. (Illus.). 24p. (ps-3). 1992. pap. write for info. (*0-307-12687-0*, 12687, Golden Pr) Western Pub.

—Beverly Hills 90210: Unauthorized Biography. (Illus.). 64p. 1992. pap. 2.95 (*1-56156-105-3*) Kidsbks.

—Did You Hear Something? (Illus.). 1992. 2.98 (*0-685-60663-5*) Kidsbks.

—Disney's Duck Tales: Journey to Magic Island. (Illus.). 24p. (ps-k). 1989. pap. write for info. (*0-307-11754-5*, Pub. by Golden Bks) Western Pub.

—Don't Be Afraid of the Dark. (Illus.). 1992. 2.98 (*1-56156-090-1*) Kidsbks.

—Dream Team Poster Book. (Illus.). 1992. pap. 2.95 (*1-56156-100-2*) Kidsbks.

—Family Matters: Behind the Scenes. LC 92-33899. 1992. pap. 2.95 (*0-8167-3038-5*) Troll Assocs.

—First Facts about Flying Machines. Persico, F. S., illus. 24p. 1991. 2.98 (*1-56156-086-3*) Kidsbks.

—First Facts about the Solar System. Friedman, Jon, illus. 24p. 1991. 2.98 (*1-56156-085-5*) Kidsbks.

—Full House Poster Book. (Illus.). 1992. pap. 2.95 (*1-56156-104-5*) Kidsbks.

—Ghastly Giggles & Ghoulish Guffaws. Billin-Frye, Paige, illus. LC 91-60998. 96p. (Orig.). (gr. 1-6). 1992. pap. 2.99 (*0-679-81787-5*) Random Bks Yng Read.

—Jack & the Beanstalk. (ps). 1990. pap. write for info. (*0-307-11681-6*) Western Pub.

—Jr. Karate, A Photo-Fact Book. (Illus.). 24p. (Orig.). 1988. pap. 1.95 (*0-942025-47-4*) Kidsbks.

—Playbook! Football: You're the Quarterback, You Call the Shots. (gr. 9-12). 1990. pap. 4.95 (*0-316-83623-0*, Spts Illus Kids) Little.

—Sonic the Hedgehog. Teitelbaum, Michael, illus. LC 93-14029. (gr. 2-4). 1993. pap. 2.50 (*0-8167-3199-3*) Troll Assocs.

—Stanley Cup Heroes. (Illus.). 1992. pap. 2.95 (*1-56156-102-9*) Kidsbks.

—Tae Kwon Do. (Illus.). 24p. (Orig.). 1990. pap. 2.50 (*0-942025-88-1*) Kidsbks.

—There's No Such Thing as a Ghost. (Illus.). 1992. 2.98 (*1-56156-091-X*) Kidsbks.

—There's Something Weird in That Cave! (Illus.). 1992. 2.98 (*1-56156-092-8*) Kidsbks.

—Universal Monsters: The Bride of Frankenstein. (gr. 4-7). 1993. pap. 3.25 (*0-307-22333-7*, Golden Pr) Western Pub.

—Welcome to Jurassic Park. (ps-3). 1993. pap. 2.25 (*0-307-12796-6*, Golden Pr) Western Pub.

—Why Did the Vampire Cross the Road? And Other Horrific Howlers. Billin-Frye, Paige, illus. LC 91-61001. 96p. (Orig.). (gr. 1-6). 1992. pap. 2.99 (*0-679-81788-3*) Random Bks Yng Read.

Teitelbaum, Michael, jt. auth. see Codor, Dick.

Teitelbaum, Michael, retold by. Little Bunny's Magic Nose. Macombi, Turi, illus. (ps-2). 1991. 5.25 (*0-307-15701-6*, Golden Pr) Western Pub.

Teitelbaum, Mike. Family Matters Poster Book. (Illus.). 1992. pap. 2.95 (*1-56156-140-1*) Kidsbks.

—History of the NHL: First 75 Years. (Illus.). 24p. 1992. pap. 2.95 (*1-56156-158-4*) Kidsbks.

—History of the Stanley Cup: First 100 Years. (Illus.). 24p. 1992. pap. 2.95 (*1-56156-155-X*) Kidsbks.

—Hockey Record Keeper. (Illus.). 16p. 1992. pap. 2.50 (*1-56156-159-2*) Kidsbks.

—Kris Kross Poster Book. (Illus.). 6p. 1992. pap. 2.95 (*1-56156-165-7*) Kidsbks.

—Paula Abdul Poster Book. (Illus.). 1991. pap. 2.95 (*1-56156-013-8*) Kidsbks.

—Story of the Toronto Blue Jays. (Illus.). 32p. 1993. pap. 4.25 (*1-56156-173-8*) Kidsbks.

—Universal Monsters: Dracula. Ruiz, Art, illus. 96p. (gr. 3-7). 1992. pap. 2.95 (*0-307-22331-0*, 22331, Golden Pr) Western Pub.

—Universal Monsters: Frankenstein. Ruiz, Art, illus. 96p. (gr. 3-7). 1992. pap. 2.95 (*0-307-22335-3*, 22335, Golden Pr) Western Pub.

—Vanilla Ice Poster Book. (Illus.). 1991. pap. 2.95 (*1-56156-014-6*) Kidsbks.

Teitlbaum, Michael. Little Mermaid. (ps-3). 1991. 3.50 (*0-307-12335-9*, Golden Pr) Western Pub.

Teitelbaum, Michael, retold by. The Fuzzy Duckling. Borgo, Deborah, illus. (ps-2). 1991. 5.25 (*0-307-15700-8*, Golden Pr) Western Pub.

Tejima, Keizaburo. The Bears' Autumn. Matsui, Susan, tr. from JPN. Tejima, Keizaburo, illus. LC 91-17118. 42p. (gr. 1-4). 1991. 12.95 (*0-671-74981-1*, Green Tiger) S&S Trade.

—Fox's Dream. Tejima, Keizaburo, illus. (ps-1). 1987. 14.95 (*0-399-21455-0*, Philomel Bks) Putnam Pub Group.

—Fox's Dream. (Illus.). 48p. (gr. 5 up). 1990. pap. 6.95 (*0-399-22017-8*, Sandcastle Bks) Putnam Pub Group.

—Ho-Limlim: A Rabbit Tale from Japan. (Illus.). 40p. (ps-3). 1990. 14.95 (*0-399-22156-5*, Philomel Bks) Putnam Pub Group.

Tekerian, Irisa & Watrous, Merrill. Art & Writing Throughout the Year. (gr. 1-6). 1988. pap. 15.95 (*0-8224-0499-0*) Fearon Teach Aids.

Telemaque, Eleanor W. Haiti Through Its Holidays. Hill, Earl, illus. LC 79-52858. 64p. (gr. 4-6). 1980. 8.50x (*0-685-00779-0*) Blyden Pr.

Telfer, Judy, ed. see Warner, Jerry S.

Tell, Bill & Tell, Sue. Well-Versed Kids. 224p. 1988. incl. parent-teacher manual 7.00 (*990-073-320-7*) NavPress.

Tell, Paul. Adventures of Blaze. Wimer, Rodney, illus. LC 92-80452. 64p. (gr. 2-6). 1992. PLB 12.95 (*1-878893-19-X*); pap. 5.95 (*1-878893-18-1*) Telcraft Bks.

—Fun with Aesop, Vol. I. Ross, Connie, illus. 32p. (gr. 2-6). 1991. pap. 2.25 (*1-878893-06-8*) Telcraft Bks.

—Fun with Aesop, Vol. II. Ross, Connie, illus. 32p. (gr. 2-6). 1991. pap. 2.25 (*1-878893-07-6*) Telcraft Bks.

—Fun with Aesop, Vol. III. Ross, Connie, illus. 32p. (gr. 2-6). 1991. pap. 2.25 (*1-878893-08-4*) Telcraft Bks.

—Fun with Aesop, 3 vols. Ross, Connie, illus. 32p. (gr. 2-6). 1991. Set. pap. 6.75 (*1-878893-09-2*) Telcraft Bks.

—Fun with Aesop Reader. Ross, Connie, illus. LC 91-90956. 96p. (gr. 2-6). 1991. 9.95 (*1-878893-05-X*); lib. bdg. 14.95 (*1-878893-10-6*); pap. 5.95 (*1-878893-04-1*) Telcraft Bks.

Tell, Sue, jt. auth. see Tell, Bill.

Teller, jt. auth. see Jillette, Penn.

Teller, Hanoch. Above the Bottom Line: Stories & Advice on Integrity. 416p. (gr. 8 up). 1988. write for info. (*0-9614772-5-3*) NYC Pub Co.

—Best of Storylines: Story for the Whole Family. Sifen, Debra, illus. 224p. (gr. 2-12). 1991. 14.95 (*0-9614772-9-6*) NYC Pub Co.

—Courtrooms of the Mind: Stories & Advice on Judging Others Favorably. 2nd ed. 288p. (gr. 12). 1988. Repr. 11.95 (*0-9614772-4-5*) NYC Pub Co.

—Once upon a Soul. 2nd ed. 224p. (gr. 12). 1988. Repr. of 1984 ed. 9.95 (*0-9614772-3-7*) NYC Pub Co.

—Sunset. 2nd ed. (Illus.). 288p. (gr. 12). 1988. Repr. of 1987 ed. 9.95 (*0-317-68545-7*) NYC Pub Co.

Telles, Cecilia R. Dinosaurs Galore. (Illus.). 32p. (ps-2). 1993. pap. 3.50 (*0-87406-652-2*) Willowisp Pr.

Temes, Roberta. The Empty Place: A Child's Guide Through Grief. Carlisle, Kim, illus. LC 92-60613. 48p. (Orig.). (gr. k-5). 1992. pap. 6.95 (*0-88282-118-0*) New Horizon NJ.

—The Empty Place: A Story for Children. (Illus.). 50p. (gr. 1-6). 1989. 12.95 (*0-8290-1345-8*) Irvington.

Temko, Florence. Jewish Origami. (Illus.). 12p. (Orig.). (gr. 1-9). 1991. pap. 5.95 (*0-89346-335-3*) Heian Intl.

—Jewish Origami II. (Illus.). 16p. (Orig.). (gr. 1-9). 1992. pap. 5.95 (*0-89346-375-2*) Heian Intl.

—Origami Magic. (gr. 4-7). 1993. pap. 7.95 (*0-590-47124-4*) Scholastic Inc.

—Paper Pandas & Jumping Frogs. Jackson, Paul, illus. Petersen, Richard, et al, photos by. LC 86-70960. (Illus.). 135p. (gr. 3-6). 1986. pap. 11.95 (*0-8351-1770-7*) China Bks.

Temple, Charles. On the Riverbank. Hall, Melanie, illus. LC 91-43942. 32p. (ps-3). 1992. 14.45 (*0-395-61591-7*) HM.

—Shanty Boat. Hall, Melanie, illus. LC 92-46025. 1994. write for info. (*0-395-66163-3*) HM.

Temple, Charles & Collins, Patrick, eds. Stories & Readers: New Perspectives on Literature in the Elementary Classroom. 296p. (gr. k-8). 1992. pap. 14.95 (*0-926842-10-2*) CG Pubs Inc.

Temple, Frances. Grab Hands & Run. LC 92-34063. 176p. (gr. 5 up). 1993. 14.95 (*0-531-05480-2*); PLB 14.99 (*0-531-08630-5*) Orchard Bks Watts.

—The Ramsay Scallop. LC 93-29697. 352p. (gr. 6-9). 1994. 15.95 (*0-531-06836-6*); lib. bdg. 15.99 RLB (*0-531-08686-0*) Orchard Bks Watts.

—Taste of Salt: A Story of Modern Haiti. LC 92-6716. 192p. (gr. 7-12). 1992. 14.95 (*0-531-05459-4*); PLB 14.99 (*0-531-08609-7*) Orchard Bks Watts.

Temple, Lannis. Dear World: How Children Around the World Feel about Our Environment. LC 92-29929. (Illus.). 152p. (gr. k up). 1993. pap. 15.00 (*0-679-84403-1*) Random Bks Yng Read.

Temple, Nancy M. & Aronson, Rande. Juggling Is for Me. (Illus.). 48p. (gr. 2-5). 1986. lib. bdg. 13.50 (*0-8225-1146-0*) Lerner Pubns.

Temple, Todd. Answers to Everything: Actually, 259 Answers to Questions about Life, Death, Love, Sex, Money, God, & the Future. LC 92-22917. 1992. 9.99 (*0-8407-9568-8*) Nelson.

Templeman, Kristine, ed. see Pollack, Eileen.

Templeton, Larry D. The Stars of Childsland. Templeton, Larry D., illus. 22p. (gr. k-3). 1982. pap. 1.98 (*0-9608914-0-4*) Templeton.

Templeton, Lee. Albert Geronimo. 104p. (gr. 4-7). 1986. 8.95 (*0-89015-561-5*) Eakin-Sunbelt.

Tempski, Armine von. Born in Paradise. LC 84-27345. 342p. 1985. 27.50 (*0-918024-65-X*); pap. 14.95 (*0-918024-34-X*) Ox Bow.

Tempski, Armine Von see Von Tempski, Armine.

Tenaille, Marie. The Day the Dragon Came to School. 9p. 1992. text ed. 0.72 (*1-56956-109-5*) W A T Braille.

Tengbom, Mildred. Does Anyone Care How I Feel? LC 81-3808. 122p. (gr. 4 up). 1981. pap. 6.99 (*0-87123-142-5*) Bethany Hse.

—Talking Together about Love & Sexuality. LC 85-22837. 160p. (gr. 4-8). 1985. pap. 7.99 (*0-87123-804-7*) Bethany Hse.

Tenggren, Gustaf, illus. Three Best-Loved Tales: Thumbelina; Tawny Scrawny Lion; The Poky Little Puppy. 80p. (ps-2). 1992. write for info. (*0-307-15630-3*, 15630, Golden Pr) Western Pub.

Ten Harmsel, Henrietta, tr. see Schmidt, Annie.

Tenniel, Sir John, jt. auth. see Carroll, Lewis.

Tennis, Rose H. The School That Was: A School Marm's Tale. Von Strohe, Patricia, illus. LC 90-70254. 80p. (Orig.). 1990. pap. text ed. 6.95 (0-923568-08-5) Wilderness Adventure Bks.

Tennyson, Alfred. Idylls of the King. (gr. 10 up). 1968. pap. 2.75 (0-8049-0180-5, CL-180) Airmont.

—The Lady of Shalott. Keeping, Charles, illus. 36p. 1987. 16.00 (0-19-276057-2) OUP.

—The Lady of Shalott. Keeping, Charles, illus. 32p. (gr. 1 up). 1990. pap. 7.50 (0-19-272211-5) OUP.

Tennyson, Noel. The Lady's Chair & the Ottoman. Tennyson, Noel, illus. LC 84-11196. 32p. (gr. k-3). 1987. PLB 12.88 (0-688-04098-5) Lothrop.

Tennyson, Noel, illus. Christmas Carols: A Treasury of Holiday Favorites with Words & Pictures. LC 83-60412. 24p. (gr. 1-5). 1983. 2.95 (0-394-86125-6) Random Bks Yng Read.

Teramura, Terua, jt. auth. see Barnes, Jill.

Terban, Marvin. The Dove Dove: Funny Homograph Riddles. Huffman, Tom, illus. LC 88-2611. 64p. (gr. 4-7). 1988. 12.95 (0-89919-723-X, Clarion Bks); pap. 6.95 (0-89919-810-4, Clarion Bks) HM.

—Eight Ate: A Feast of Homonym Riddles. Maestro, Giulio, illus. LC 81-12203. 64p. (gr. 1-3). 1982. 13.45 (0-89919-067-7, Clarion Bks); pap. 5.95 (0-89919-086-3, Clarion Bks) HM.

—Funny You Should Ask: How to Make up Jokes & Riddles with Wordplay. O'Brien, John, illus. 64p. (gr. 4-7). 1992. 13.95 (0-395-60556-3, Clarion Bks); pap. 5.95 (0-395-58113-3, Clarion Bks) HM.

—Guppies in Tuxedos: Funny Eponyms. Maestro, Giulio, illus. LC 87-32630. 64p. (gr. 4-7). 1988. (Clarion Bks); pap. 5.95 (0-89919-770-1, Clarion Bks) HM.

—Hey, Hay! A Wagonful of Funny Homonym Riddles. Stevenson, Dinah, ed. Hawkes, Kevin, illus. 64p. (gr. 3-7). 1991. 14.95 (0-395-54431-9, Clarion Bks); pap. 5.70 (0-395-56183-3, Clarion Bks) HM.

—I Think I Thought & Other Tricky Verbs. Maestro, Giulio, illus. LC 83-19034. 64p. (Orig.). (ps-4). 1984. (Clarion Bks); pap. 5.70 (0-89919-290-4, Clarion Bks) HM.

—In a Pickle & other Funny Idioms. Maestro, Giulio, illus. LC 82-9585. 64p. (gr. 1-4). 1983. (Clarion Bks); pap. 4.95 (0-89919-164-9, Clarion Bks) HM.

—It Figures. (gr. 4-7). 1993. pap. 5.95 (0-395-66591-4, Clarion Bks) HM.

—It Figures! Fun Figures of Speech. Maestro, Guilio, illus. LC 92-35529. 1993. 13.95 (0-395-61584-4, Clarion Bks) HM.

—Mad As a Wet Hen & Other Funny Idioms. Maestro, Giulio, illus. LC 86-17575. (gr. 3-6). 1987. (Clarion Bks); pap. 4.95 (0-89919-479-6, Clarion Bks) HM.

—Punching the Clock: Funny Action Idioms. Huffman, Tom, illus. 64p. (gr. 3-7). 1990. pap. 4.80 (0-89919-865-1) HM.

—Superdupers: Really Funny Real Words. Maestro, Giulio, illus. LC 88-38325. 63p. (gr. 4-8). 1989. 13.45 (0-89919-804-X, Clarion Bks); pap. 4.80 (0-395-51123-2, Clarion Bks) HM.

—Too Hot to Hoot: Funny Palindrome Riddles. Maestro, Giulio, illus. LC 84-14942. 64p. (gr. 2-5). 1985. 13.95 (0-89919-319-6, Clarion Bks); pap. 6.95 (0-89919-320-X, Clarion Bks) HM.

—Your Foot's on My Feet. 34p. 1992. text ed. 2.72 (1-56956-124-9) W A T Braille.

—Your Foot's on My Feet: And Other Tricky Nouns. Maestro, Giulio, illus. LC 85-19561. (gr. 2-5). 1986. pap. 11.95 (0-89919-411-7, Clarion Bks); pap. 4.95 (0-89919-413-3, Clarion Bks) HM.

Terborgh, John. Tropical Deforestation. Head, J. J., ed. (Illus.). 16p. (Orig.). (gr. 10 up). 1992. pap. text ed. 2.75 (0-89278-161-0, 45-9761) Carolina Biological.

Terdy, Dennis. Content Area ESL: Social Studies. Mrowicki, Linda, ed. (Illus.). 169p. (gr. 5-12). 1986. pap. 8.95 (0-916591-06-9) Linmore Pub.

Terhune, Albert P. Caleb Conover: Railroader. 111p. 1981. Repr. PLB 12.95x (0-89966-349-4) Buccaneer Bks.

—Caleb Conover, Railroader. 189p. 1981. Repr. PLB 12.95x (0-89967-023-7) Harmony Raine.

—A Dog Named Chips. 1992. Repr. lib. bdg. 24.95x (0-89966-985-9) Buccaneer Bks.

—Further Adventures of Lad. 1992. Repr. lib. bdg. 24.95x (0-89966-983-2) Buccaneer Bks.

—The Heart of a Dog. 1992. Repr. lib. bdg. 24.95x (0-89966-984-0) Buccaneer Bks.

—Lad: A Dog. 1981. Repr. PLB 24.95 (0-89966-348-6) Buccaneer Bks.

—Lad: A Dog. 189p. 1981. Repr. PLB 24.95 (0-89967-022-9) Harmony Raine.

—Lad: A Dog. (RL 6). 1978. pap. 2.50 (0-451-14626-3, AE1036, Sig) NAL-Dutton.

—Lad: A Dog. 256p. 1978. pap. 3.50 (0-451-16417-2, Sig) NAL-Dutton.

—Lad: A Dog. Savitt, Sam, illus. LC 93-9365. 288p. (gr. 5 up). 1993. pap. 3.99 (0-14-036474-9, Puffin) Puffin Bks.

—Treve. 1992. Repr. lib. bdg. 24.95x (0-89966-996-4) Buccaneer Bks.

—The Way of a Dog. 1992. Repr. lib. bdg. 24.95x (0-89966-986-7) Buccaneer Bks.

Terkel, Studs. Giants of Jazz. 2nd ed. LC 75-20024. (Illus.). 192p. (gr. 7 up). 1992. PLB 16.89 (0-690-04917-X, Crowell Jr Bks) HarpC Child Bks.

Terkel, Susan N. Abortion: Facing the Issues. Rosoff, Iris, ed. LC 88-14288. (Illus.). 160p. (gr. 7 up). 1988. PLB 13.40 (0-531-10565-2) Watts.

—All about Allergies. Harvey, Paul, illus. LC 92-17770. 64p. (gr. 2-5). 1993. 13.99 (0-525-67410-1, Lodestar Bks) Dutton Child Bks.

—Colonial American Medicine. LC 92-43988. 1993. 12.90 (0-531-12539-4) Watts.

—Ethics. 144p. (gr. 5 up). 1992. 15.00 (0-525-67371-7, Lodestar Bks) Dutton Child Bks.

—Should Drugs Be Legalized? (Illus.). 160p. (gr. 9-12). 1990. 14.45 (0-531-15182-4); PLB 14.40 (0-531-10944-5) Watts.

—Understanding Child Custody. Rosoff, Iris, ed. 128p. (gr. 7-12). 1991. PLB 13.40 (0-531-12521-1) Watts.

—Yoga Is for Me. Klein, Arthur, illus. LC 81-18623. 48p. (gr. 2-5). 1982. PLB 13.50 (0-8225-1098-7) Lerner Pubns.

Terkel, Susan N. & Brazz, Marlene L. Understanding Cancer. Shaw, Annette, illus. 64p. (gr. k-4). 1993. PLB 12.40 (0-531-11085-0) Watts.

Terkel, Susan N. & Rench, Janice E. Feeling Safe, Feeling Strong: How to Avoid Sexual Abuse & What to Do If It Happens to You. LC 84-9664. (Illus.). 72p. (gr. 4-8). 1984. PLB 15.95 (0-8225-0021-3) Lerner Pubns.

Terman, Douglas. By Balloon to the Sahara. (gr. 4). 1989. pap. 2.99 (0-553-26593-8) Bantam.

Terrana, Alma, tr. see Ryan, Elizabeth.

Terrell, Ruth H. A Kid's Guide to How to Stop the Violence. Genzo, John P., illus. 144p. (Orig.). 1992. pap. 2.99 (0-380-76652-3, Camelot) Avon.

Terrell, Sandy. Journey to Fairy Tale Castle. (Illus.). 224p. (gr. k-3). 1992. 16.95 (0-86653-657-4, GA1346) Good Apple.

Terrell, Sandy & White, Frank. Teacher's Choice. (Illus.). 192p. (gr. 4-9). 1992. wkbk. 13.95 (0-86653-691-4, 1425) Good Apple.

Terris, Daniel, jt. auth. see Harrison, Barbara.

Terris, Susan. Baby-Snatcher. 192p. (gr. 5 up). 1985. 14.00 (0-374-30473-4) FS&G.

—The Latchkey Kids. 167p. (gr. 5 up). 1986. 15.00 (0-374-34363-2) FS&G.

—Nell's Quilt. 176p. (gr. 7 up). 1988. pap. 2.50 (0-590-41914-5) Scholastic Inc.

—No Scarlet Ribbons. LC 80-28501. 154p. (gr. 5 up). 1981. 14.00 (0-374-35532-0) FS&G.

—Octopus Pie. LC 83-11517. 166p. (gr. 5 up). 1983. 14.00 (0-374-35571-1) FS&G.

Terry, Ellen & Anderson, Lynne. Makeup & Masks. rev. ed. LC 78-139744. 112p. (gr. 7 up). 1982. PLB 14.95 (0-8239-0232-3) Rosen Group.

Terry, Hilda. Does God Eat Us? A Contemporary Response to Old Questions. Terry, Hilda, illus. 271p. (Orig.). 1991. pap. 8.88 (0-685-54234-3) Art Ltd.

Terry, Jim & Terry, Mary. Soaring to the Top: The Success Manual for Young Adults. 300p. 1988. pap. 8.95 (0-931731-07-0) Jimar Prodns.

Terry, John. Pigs in the Playground. Brewis, Henry, illus. 208p. 1986. pap. 7.95 (0-85236-158-0, Pub by Farming Pr UK); pap. text ed. 6.95 (0-317-47058-2, Pub. by Farming Pr UK) Diamond Farm Bk.

Terry, Mary, jt. auth. see Terry, Jim.

Terry, Phyllis D., jt. auth. see Nolan, Virginia J.

Terschluse, Ann, ed. see Stafford, Marilyn.

Terushi, Jimbo. Children of the World: West Germany. LC 88-21052. (Illus.). 64p. (gr. 5-6). 1988. PLB 19.93 (1-55532-213-1) Gareth Stevens Inc.

Terzi, Marinella. Ancient Greece. LC 92-7508. (Illus.). 36p. (gr. 3 up). 1992. PLB 19.93 (0-516-08376-7) Childrens.

—Ancient Greece. LC 92-7508. (Illus.). 36p. (gr. 3 up). 1993. pap. 6.95 (0-516-48376-5) Childrens.

—The Chinese Empire. LC 92-7509. (Illus.). 36p. (gr. 3 up). 1992. PLB 19.93 (0-516-08377-5) Childrens.

—The Chinese Empire. LC 92-7509. 36p. (gr. 3 up). 1993. pap. 6.95 (0-516-48377-3) Childrens.

—The Land of the Pharaohs. LC 92-7510. (Illus.). 36p. (gr. 3 up). 1992. PLB 19.93 (0-516-08378-3) Childrens.

—Land of the Pharaohs. LC 92-7510. 36p. (gr. 3 up). 1993. pap. 6.95 (0-516-48378-1) Childrens.

—Prehistoric Rock Art. LC 92-7504. (Illus.). 36p. (gr. 3 up). 1992. PLB 19.93 (0-516-08379-1) Childrens.

—Prehistoric Rock Art. LC 92-7504. (Illus.). 36p. (gr. 3 up). 1993. pap. 6.95 (0-516-48379-X) Childrens.

Terzian, Alexandra. The Kids' Multicultural Art Book: Art & Craft Experiences from Around the World. Trezzo-Braren Studio Staff, illus. 160p. (Orig.). (ps-4). 1993. pap. 12.95 (0-913589-72-1) Williamson Pub Co.

Tesar, Jenny. Endangered Habitats. (Illus.). 128p. (gr. 7-12). 1991. lib. bdg. 18.95x (0-8160-2493-6) Facts on File.

—Food & Water: Threats, Shortages & Solutions. (Illus.). 128p. (gr. 7-12). 1992. lib. bdg. 18.95x (0-8160-2495-2) Facts on File.

—Fungi. (Illus.). 64p. (gr. 4-8). 1994. PLB 16.95 (1-56711-044-4) Blackbirch.

—Green Plants. (Illus.). 64p. (gr. 4-8). 1993. PLB 16.95 (1-56711-039-8) Blackbirch.

—Humans. (Illus.). 64p. (gr. 4-8). 1994. PLB 16.95 (1-56711-048-7) Blackbirch.

—Insects. (Illus.). 64p. (gr. 4-8). 1993. PLB 16.95 (1-56711-037-1) Blackbirch.

—Insects. Felber, Michael, illus. 64p. (gr. 4-8). 1993. jacketed 14.95 (1-56711-054-1) Blackbirch.

—Mammals. (Illus.). 64p. (gr. 4-8). 1993. PLB 16.95 (1-56711-042-8) Blackbirch.

—Mammals. Kray, Robert, illus. 64p. (gr. 4-8). 1993. jacketed 14.95 (1-56711-055-X) Blackbirch.

—Scientific Crime Investigation. LC 91-16368. (Illus.). 96p. (gr. 9-12). 1991. PLB 12.90 (0-531-12500-9) Watts.

—Spiders. (Illus.). 64p. (gr. 4-8). 1993. PLB 16.95 (1-56711-043-6) Blackbirch.

—Spiders. (Illus.). 64p. (gr. 3-7). 1993. 14.95 (1-56711-062-2) Blackbirch.

—Threatened Oceans. (Illus.). 128p. (gr. 7-12). 1992. lib. bdg. 18.95x (0-8160-2494-4) Facts on File.

Tesar, Jenny, jt. auth. see Ricciuti, Edward.

Tesar, Jenny E. Global Warming. (Illus.). 128p. (gr. 7-12). 1991. 18.95x (0-8160-2490-1) Facts on File.

—Shrinking Forests. (Illus.). 128p. (gr. 7-12). 1991. 18.95x (0-8160-2492-8) Facts on File.

—Waste Crisis. (Illus.). 128p. (gr. 9-12). 1991. 18.95x (0-8160-2491-X) Facts on File.

Teschner, Amy, ed. see Policoff, Stephen P. & Skinner, Jeffrey.

Tessendorf, K. C. Along the Road to Soweto: A Racial History of South Africa. LC 88-30535. (Illus.). 160p. (gr. 6 up). 1989. SBE 14.95 (0-689-31401-9, Atheneum Child Bk) Macmillan Child Grp.

—Barnstormers & Daredevils. LC 87-15194. (Illus.). 96p. (gr. 4 up). 1988. SBE 14.95 (0-689-31346-2, Atheneum Child Bk) Macmillan Child Grp.

—Uncle Sam in Nicaragua: A History. LC 86-17340. 144p. (gr. 7 up). 1987. SBE 14.95 (0-689-31286-5, Atheneum Child Bk) Macmillan Child Grp.

—Wings around the World: The American World Flight of 1924. LC 90-977. (Illus.). 112p. (gr. 4 up). 1991. SBE 14.95 (0-689-31550-3, Atheneum Child Bk) Macmillan Child Grp.

Tessler, Stephanie G., jt. auth. see Enderle, Judith R.

Testa, Fulvio. If You Look Around You. LC 83-5310. (Illus.). 32p. (ps-2). 1987. pap. 3.95 (0-8037-0432-1) Dial Bks Young.

—If You Take a Paintbrush: A Book of Colors. Testa, Fulvio, illus. LC 82-45512. 32p. (ps-2). 1986. pap. 4.95 (0-8037-0282-5) Dial Bks Young.

—If You Take a Pencil. LC 82-1505. 32p. (ps-2). 1985. pap. 4.95 (0-8037-0165-9) Dial Bks Young.

—The Paper Airplane. LC 81-8358. (Illus.). 32p. (gr. k-3). 1988. 14.95 (1-55858-060-3) North-South Bks NYC.

—Time to Get Out. Testa, Fulvio, illus. LC 93-60218. 32p. (ps up). 1993. 14.00 (0-688-12907-2, Tambourine Bks); PLB 13.93 (0-688-12908-0, Tambourine Bks) Morrow.

—Wolf's Favor. Testa, Fulvio, illus. LC 85-15934. 32p. (ps-3). 1986. 11.95 (0-8037-0244-2) Dial Bks Young.

—Wolf's Flavor. (ps-3). 1990. 3.95 (0-8037-0744-4, Dial) Doubleday.

Testa, Fulvio, illus. Aesop's Fables. 48p. (gr. 2 up). 1989. incl. dust jacket 12.95 (0-8120-5958-1) Barron.

Testa, Maria. Thumbs Up, Rico! Paterson, Diane, illus. 1994. write for info. (0-8075-7906-8) A Whitman.

Tester, Bronwyn, jt. auth. see Marshall, Val.

Tester, Sylvia. Jesus & the Children. Pistone, Nancy, illus. 12p. (ps). 1992. deluxe ed. 4.99 (0-87403-993-2, 24-03113) Standard Pub.

—Where Are We Going Today? Chase, Andra, illus. 12p. (ps). 1992. deluxe ed. 4.99 (0-87403-996-7, 24-03116) Standard Pub.

Tester, Sylvia R. A Day of Surprises. Hook, Frances, illus. LC 78-23263. (ps-3). 1979. PLB 21.35 (0-89565-022-3); PLB 14.95s.p. (0-685-55479-1) Childs World.

—Frustrated. Indereiden, Nancy, illus. LC 79-23804. (ps-2). 1980. PLB 18.50 (0-89565-110-6); PLB 12.95s.p. (0-685-55481-3) Childs World.

—Jealous. Indereiden, Nancy, illus. LC 79-24042. (ps-2). 1980. PLB 18.50 (0-89565-111-4); PLB 12.95s.p. (0-685-55490-2) Childs World.

—Magic Monsters Around the Year. LC 78-23800. (Illus.). (ps-3). 1979. PLB 21.35 (0-89565-059-2); PLB 14.95s.p. (0-685-55494-5) Childs World.

—Magic Monsters Halloween. Bowman, Patricia, illus. LC 79-25183. (gr. k-3). 1980. PLB 21.35 (0-89565-121-1); PLB 13.95s.p. (0-685-55496-1) Childs World.

—Magic Monsters Learn about Safety. Magine, John, illus. LC 78-24365. (ps-3). 1979. PLB 21.35 (0-89565-060-6); PLB 14.95s.p. (0-685-57683-3) Childs World.

—Magic Monsters Learn about Weather. Bowman, Patricia, illus. LC 79-24826. (gr. k-3). 1980. PLB 21.35 (0-89565-120-3); PLB 14.95s.p. (0-685-55501-1) Childs World.

—Sad. Indereiden, Nancy, illus. LC 79-26252. (ps-2). 1980. PLB 18.50 (0-89565-112-2); PLB 12.95s.p. (0-685-55541-0) Childs World.

—Sometimes I'm Afraid. Hook, Frances, illus. LC 78-23262. (ps-3). 1979. PLB 21.35 (0-89565-021-5); PLB 14.95s.p. (0-685-55549-6) Childs World.

—A Visit to the Zoo. Pilot Productions Staff, et al, photos by. LC 84-12697. (Illus.). 32p. (ps-3). 1987. PLB 15.00 (0-516-01494-3) Childrens.

—We Laughed a Lot, My First Day of School. Hook, Frances, illus. LC 78-10900. (ps-3). 1979. PLB 21.35 (0-89565-020-7); PLB 14.95s.p. (0-685-55556-9) Childs World.

—What Is a Monster? Magnuson, Diana, illus. LC 78-23642. (ps-3). 1979. PLB 21.35 (0-89565-055-X); PLB 14.95s.p. (0-685-55558-5) Childs World.

Tetz, Resanne. Andrew Can. 32p. 1992. pap. 5.95 (0-8163-1063-7) Pacific Pr Pub Assn.

Tetz, Rosanne. Nina Can. 32p. 1993. pap. 5.95 (0-8163-1111-0) Pacific Pr Pub Assn.

Teutsch, Betsy. One Little Goat: Had Gadya. LC 89-18298. (Illus.). 32p. 1990. 20.00 (0-87668-824-5) Aronson.

Tewell, Debbie & Shirley, Gayle C. Where Dinosaurs Still Rule: A Guide to Dinosaur Areas of the West. Mooney, David, illus. 48p. (Orig.). 1993. pap. 6.95 (1-56044-177-1) Falcon Pr MT.

Tewell, V. M., jt. auth. see Baggiani, J. M.

Tews, Susan. Gingerbread Doll. (ps-3). 1993. 14.95 (0-395-56438-7, Clarion Bks) HM.
—Nettie's Gift. Sayles, Elizabeth, illus. 32p. (gr. k-3). 1993. 14.95 (0-395-59027-2, Clarion Bks) HM.

Thacker, Nola. All on a Winter's Day. 144p. (gr. 7 up). 1990. pap. 2.95 (0-590-43416-0) Scholastic Inc.
—Summer Stories. Low, William, illus. LC 87-45880. 160p. (gr. 3-7). 1988. (Lipp Jr Bks); (Lipp Jr Bks) HarpC Child Bks.
—Summer Stories. Low, William, illus. (gr. 3-7). 1989. pap. 2.75 (0-590-42191-3, Apple Paperbacks) Scholastic Inc.
—Till's Christmas. 144p. 1991. 13.95 (0-590-43542-6, Scholastic Hardcover) Scholastic Inc.
—Till's Christmas. 1992. 2.95 (0-590-43543-4, Apple Paperbacks) Scholastic Inc.

Thackeray, William Makepeace. Vanity Fair. Threapleton, M. M., intro. by. (gr. 11 up). 1967. pap. 2.50 (0-8049-0138-4, CL-138) Airmont.

Thackray, Patricia. Fanny McFancy: A Passion for Fashion. Forrest, Sandra, illus. LC 91-16447. 40p. 1991. 12.95 (0-671-74980-3, Green Tiger) S&S Trade.

Thaler, Mike. The Bully Brothers: Gobblin' Halloween. Lee, Jared, illus. LC 92-34197. 32p. (ps-3). 1993. pap. 2.25 (0-448-40158-4, G&D) Putnam Pub Group.
—The Bully Brothers Trick the Tooth Fairy. Lee, Jared, illus. LC 92-72834. 32p. (ps-3). 1993. pap. 2.25 (0-448-40519-9, G&D) Putnam Pub Group.
—Camp Rottentime. Lee, Jared, illus. LC 92-3231. 32p. (ps-3). 1993. PLB 9.79 (0-8167-3024-5); pap. 2.95 (0-8167-3025-3) Troll Assocs.
—Cannon the Librarian. Lee, Jared, illus. 32p. (Orig.). 1993. pap. 3.50 (0-380-76964-6, Camelot Young) Avon.
—Catzilla. (gr. 4-7). 1991. pap. 2.95 (0-671-73297-8) S&S Trade.
—Come & Play, Hippo. Chambliss, Maxie, illus. LC 87-33489. 64p. (gr. k-3). 1991. 14.00 (0-06-026176-5); PLB 13.89 (0-06-026177-3) HarpC Child Bks.
—Come & Play, Hippo. Chambliss, Maxie, illus. LC 87-33489. 64p. (ps-3). 1993. pap. 3.50 (0-06-444165-2, Trophy) HarpC Child Bks.
—Fang the Dentist. Lee, Jared, illus. LC 92-18594. 32p. (ps-3). 1993. PLB 9.79 (0-8167-3020-2); pap. 2.95 (0-8167-3021-0) Troll Assocs.
—A Hippopotamus Ate the Teacher. Lee, Jared, illus. 32p. 1981. pap. 2.95 (0-380-78048-8, Camelot) Avon.
—How Far Will a Rubber Band Stretch. 1990. pap. 13.95 (0-671-69361-1, S&S BFYR) S&S Trade.
—In the Middle of the Puddle. Degen, Bruce, illus. LC 85-45830. 32p. (ps-1). 1988. HarpC Child Bks.
—In the Middle of the Puddle. Degen, Bruce, illus. LC 85-45830. 32p. (ps-1). 1992. pap. 4.95 (0-06-443288-2, Trophy) HarpC Child Bks.
—King Kong's Underwear. 96p. (Orig.). (gr. 7 up). 1986. pap. 2.50 (0-380-89823-3, Camelot) Avon.
—My Cat Is Going to the Dogs. Lee, Jared, illus. LC 92-18596. 32p. (ps-3). 1993. PLB 9.79 (0-8167-3022-9); pap. 2.95 (0-8167-3023-7) Troll Assocs.
—Never Mail an Elephant. Smath, Jerry, illus. LC 93-14395. 32p. (ps-3). 1993. PLB 9.89 (0-8167-3303-1); pap. text ed. 2.95 (0-8167-3304-X) Troll Assocs.
—Oinkers Away! Pig Riddles, Cartoons & Jokes. (gr. 3-6). 1989. pap. 2.50 (0-671-67456-0, Minstrel Bks) PB.
—Pack 109. Chartier, Normand, illus. LC 87-30493. 48p. (ps-2). 1988. 9.95 (0-525-44393-2, 0966-290, DCB) Dutton Child Bks.
—Pack 109. Chartier, Normand, illus. (gr. k-3). 1993. pap. 3.25 (0-14-036548-6, Puffin) Puffin Bks.
—Principal from the Black Lagoon. (ps-3). 1993. pap. 2.50 (0-590-45782-9) Scholastic Inc.
—The Riddle King's Camp Riddles. Harvey, Paul, illus. LC 88-63193. 32p. (gr. 1-5). 1989. pap. 1.25 (0-394-83995-1) Random Bks Yng Read.
—The Riddle King's Food Riddles. Harvey, Paul, illus. LC 88-63190. 32p. (gr. 1-5). 1989. pap. 1.25 (0-394-84041-0) Random Bks Yng Read.
—The Riddle King's Pet Riddles. Harvey, Paul, illus. LC 88-63191. 32p. (gr. 1-5). 1989. pap. 1.25 (0-394-83977-3) Random Bks Yng Read.
—The Riddle King's School Riddles. Harvey, Paul, illus. LC 88-63192. 32p. (gr. 1-5). 1989. pap. 1.25 (0-394-84004-6) Random Bks Yng Read.
—Teacher from the Black Lagoon. (gr. 1-4). 1989. pap. 2.50 (0-590-41962-5) Scholastic Inc.
—There's a Hippopotamus under My Bed. (Illus.). 32p. (gr. k-3). 1978. pap. 2.95 (0-380-40238-6, Camelot) Avon.
—Upside down Day. 32p. (gr. k-3). 1986. pap. 2.95 (0-380-89999-X, Camelot) Avon.
—Uses for Mooses & Other Popular Pets. Smath, Jerry, illus. LC 93-25542. 32p. (ps-3). 1993. PLB 9.89 (0-8167-3301-5); pap. text ed. 2.95 (0-8167-3302-3) Troll Assocs.
—What Could a Hippopotamus Be? Grossman, Robert, illus. LC 89-77080. 40p. (ps-2). 1990. pap. 13.95 (0-671-70847-3, S&S BFYR) S&S Trade.

Thaler, Shmuel, jt. auth. see Morgan, Terri.

Thane, Adele. Plays from Famous Stories & Fairy Tales. (gr. 4-7). 1989. pap. 15.00 (0-8238-0060-1) Plays.
—The Wizard of Oz. (gr. 1-7). 1957. 4.50 (0-87602-221-2) Anchorage.

Tharlet, Eve. Archibald the Great. Clements, Andrew, tr. from FRE. Tharlet, Eve, illus. 28p. (gr. k up). 1993. 14.95 (0-88708-267-X) Picture Bk Studio.
—Christmas Won't Wait. Clements, Andrew, tr. from FRE. (Illus.). (gr. k up). 1991. pap. 14.95 (0-88708-151-7) Picture Bk Studio.
—Little Pig, Big Trouble. Clements, Andrew, tr. Tharlet, Eve, illus. LC 89-31369. (ps up). 1991. pap. 14.95 (0-88708-073-1) Picture Bk Studio.
—Little Pig, Big Trouble. Clements, Andrew, tr. Tharlet, Eve, illus. LC 91-40637. 28p. (gr. k up). 1992. pap. 4.95 (0-88708-227-0) Picture Bk Studio.
—Little Pig, Bigger Trouble. Clements, Andrew, tr. Tharlet, Eve, illus. LC 91-40637. 28p. (gr. k up). 1992. pap. 14.95 (0-88708-237-8) Picture Bk Studio.
—Simon & the Holy Night. Clements, Andrew, tr. (Illus.). 28p. (gr. k up). 1992. pap. 14.95 (0-88708-185-1) Picture Bk Studio.
—Simon & the Holy Night. Clements, Andrew, adapted by. Tharlet, Eve, illus. LC 93-306. 1993. 4.95 (0-88708-324-2) Picture Bk Studio.

Tharp, Louise H. Tory Hole. (Illus.). (gr. 4up). 1976. pap. 7.50 (0-686-16261-7) DCA.

Thatch, Nan, ed. see Kerber, Karen M.

Thatch, Nancy R., ed. see Aushenker, Michael.

Thatch, Nancy R., ed. see Brady, Jennifer.

Thatch, Nancy R., ed. see Butenhoff, Lisa K.

Thatch, Nancy R., ed. see Cain, Michael.

Thatch, Nancy R., ed. see Chandrasekhar, Aruna.

Thatch, Nancy R., ed. see Gaige, Amity.

Thatch, Nancy R., ed. see Haidle, Elizabeth.

Thatch, Nancy R., ed. see Jones, Amy.

Thatch, Nancy R., ed. see Kahn, Jonathan.

Thatch, Nancy R., ed. see Kendall, Benjamin.

Thatch, Nancy R., ed. see Kolanovic, Dubravka.

Thatch, Nancy R., ed. see Leggat, Bonnie-Alise.

Thatch, Nancy R., ed. see MacKeen, Leslie A.

Thatch, Nancy R., ed. see Miller, Jayne.

Thatch, Nancy R., ed. see Moore, Adam.

Thatch, Nancy R., ed. see Moser, Adolph.

Thatch, Nancy R., ed. see Peters, Lauren.

Thatch, Nancy R., ed. see Reichel, Cara.

Thatch, Nancy R., ed. see Salter, Heidi.

Thatch, Nancy R., ed. see Shepard, Steven.

Thatch, Nancy R., ed. see Thomas, Anika D.

Thatch, Nancy R., ed. see Williams, Travis.

Thatcher, Barbara B. Assailing the Seven C's. York, Sheryl, ed. LC 87-40261. 91p. (Orig.). 1987. pap. 8.95 (1-55523-101-2) Winston-Derek.

Thatcher, Kevin & Brannon, Brian. Thrasher: The Radical Skateboard Book. LC 91-52544. (Illus.). 72p. (Orig.). (gr. 3 up). 1992. PLB 11.99 (0-679-92207-5); pap. 7.99 (0-679-82207-0) Random Bks Yng Read.

Thaxter, Celia. Celia's Island Journal. (ps-3). 1992. 15.95 (0-316-83921-3) Little.

Thayer, Bonita E. Emily Dickinson. LC 88-31376. (Illus.). 144p. (gr. 10-12). 1990. 14.40 (0-531-10658-6) Watts.

Thayer, Ernest L. Casey at the Bat. Hull, Jim, illus. Gardner, Martin, intro. by. (Illus.). 17.25 (0-8446-5613-5) Peter Smith.
—Casey at the Bat. LC 84-9891. (Illus.). (gr. 2-5). 1984. PLB 29.28 incl. cassette (0-8172-2243-X); PLB 17.96 (0-8172-2121-2) Raintree Steck-V.
—Casey at the Bat. Tripp, Wallace, illus. 32p. (Orig.). (ps-2). 1989. pap. 1.95 (0-448-19112-1, Platt & Munk Pubs) Putnam Pub Group.
—Casey at the Bat. Polacco, Patricia, illus. 32p. (ps-3). 1992. pap. 5.95 (0-399-21884-X, Sandcastle Bks) Putnam Pub Group.
—Casey at the Bat. (ps-3). 1993. pap. 3.95 (0-8114-8357-6) Raintree Steck-V.
—Casey at the Bat: A Ballad of the Republic, Sung in the Year 1888. Tripp, Wallace, illus. LC 77-21199. (gr. k-5). 1980. 14.95 (0-399-21585-9, Putnam); pap. 1.95 (0-698-20486-7, Putnam) Putnam Pub Group.
—Casey at the Bat: A Centennial Edition. Moser, Barry, illus. Hall, Donald, afterword by. LC 88-45285. (Illus.). 32p. (gr. 1 up). 1988. 14.95 (0-87923-722-8) Godine.

Thayer, Eva. Adventures in the Land of Me. (Illus.). 65p. (Orig.). (gr. 4-8). 1989. pap. 5.95 wkbk. (0-9616432-4-2) TES Pub.
—Me Esteem Creates We Esteem. (Illus.). 70p. (Orig.). (gr. 7-12). 1990. pap. 5.95 wkbk. (0-9616432-3-4) TES Pub.

Thayer, Jane. Gus Loved His Happy Home. Fleishman, Seymour, illus. LC 88-36962. 32p. (ps-2). 1989. PLB 15.00 (0-208-02249-X, Linnet) Shoe String.
—Popcorn Dragon. McCue, Lisa, illus. LC 88-39855. 32p. (ps up) 1989. 12.95 (0-688-08340-4); PLB 12.88 (0-688-08876-7, Morrow Jr Bks) Morrow Jr Bks.
—The Puppy Who Wanted a Boy. rev. ed. McCue, Lisa, illus. LC 85-15465. 48p. (ps-1). 1986. 12.95 (0-688-05944-9); PLB 12.88 (0-688-05945-7, Morrow Jr Bks); pap. 4.95 (0-685-43017-0, Mulberry Bks) Morrow Jr Bks.
—The Puppy Who Wanted a Boy. McCue, Lisa, illus. LC 85-15465. (ps-3). 1988. pap. 4.95 (0-688-08293-9, Mulberry) Morrow.

Thayne. The Day That Arnold J. Crumpet Did Just Disappear. LC 93-61295. (Illus.). 44p. (gr. k-3). 1994. 7.95 (1-55523-663-4) Winston-Derek.

Thayne, Emma L., jt. auth. see Markosian, Becky T.

The Elves. The Story of Santa Claus. 96p. (ps-3). 1993. 19.95 (1-878685-45-7) Turner Pub GA.

The Langauge School of the American Cultural Exchange, jt. auth. see Criminale, Ulrike.

The Language School of the American Cultural Exchange Staff, jt. auth. see Criminale, Ulrike.

The Doors. The Doors Complete. 232p. (Orig.). 1983. pap. text ed. 18.95 (0-89898-637-0) CPP Belwin.

Theisen, John A. Steppelords of Mars. Harris, Dell, illus. 64p. (Orig.). 1989. pap. 8.00 (1-55878-025-4) Game Designers.

Theiss, Nola. The Complete Guide to Remodeling & Expanding Your Dollhouse. LC 92-44443. (Illus.). 128p. 1993. pap. 12.95 (0-8069-8369-8, Pub. by Lark Bks) Sterling.

Theiss, Nola & Rankin, Chris. Floral Knits: More than Forty Beautiful, Timeless Sweaters to Make. LC 92-17563. (Illus.). 144p. (gr. 10-12). 1992. pap. 14.95 (0-8069-8367-1, Pub. by Lark Bks) Sterling.

Theobalds, Prue. For Teddy & Me. Theobalds, Prue, illus. 30p. (gr. k-3). 1992. 14.95 (0-87226-470-X, Bedrick Blackie) P Bedrick Bks.
—The Miniature Old MacDonald Had a Farm. Theobalds, Prue, illus. 28p. 1993. 5.95 (0-87226-503-X, Bedrick Blackie) P Bedrick Bks.
—The Miniature Teddy & Me. Theobalds, Prue, illus. 30p. (gr. 4 up). 1993. 5.95 (0-87226-514-5, Bedrick Blackie) P Bedrick Bks.
—Noah & the Animals. Theobalds, Prue, illus. LC 92-45630. 34p. (gr. 4 up). 1993. 12.95 (0-87226-507-2, Bedrick Blackie) P Bedrick Bks.
—Old MacDonald Had a Farm. Theobalds, Prue, illus. 32p. (ps-3). 1991. PLB 14.95 (0-87226-452-1, Bedrick Blackie) P Bedrick Bks.
—The Teddy Bears' Great Expedition. Theobalds, Prue, illus. LC 89-77039. 32p. (gr. k-3). 1990. PLB 12.95 (0-87226-425-4, Bedrick Blackie) P Bedrick Bks.
—Ten Tired Teddies. Theobalds, Prue, illus. 10p. 1992. 5.95 (0-87226-471-8, Bedrick Blackie) P Bedrick Bks.

Theo Carus Harter, Kaboblin. Turnabout Songs Program Complete Set: A Shortcut to Knowledge. Smith, Betty N. & Anderson, Catherine, eds. Gunder Heimer, Jocelyn C., illus. 262p. 1993. 2 in. 3-hole ring binder, incl. 9 cass. & cass. locator guide 150.00 (0-944528-41-4) Child Mus Wkshop.

Theodore, Alan. Origins & Sources of Drugs. Mendelson, Jack & Mello, Nancyintro. by. (Illus.). 128p. (gr. 5 up). 1988. lib. bdg. 19.95 (1-55546-234-0) Chelsea Hse.

Theodorou, Rod. Triceratops Had Horns & Other Questions about Dinosaurs. LC 93-29796. 1994. 8.95 (1-85697-880-X) Kingfisher Bks.

Theresa of Avila. Majestic Is Your Name. rev. ed. Hazard, David, ed. 144p. 1993. pap. 6.99 (1-55661-336-9) Bethany Hse.

Therio, Adrien & Burks, James F., eds. Temoins du Monde Francais. LC 68-12127. (FRE., Illus., Orig.). (gr. 9 up). 1968. pap. text ed. 9.95x (0-89197-446-6) Irvington.

Theriot, David. Leola et la pirogue. Easterling, Mae L., illus. (FRE.). 39p. (gr. 3). 1979. pap. text ed. 1.25 (0-911409-03-3) Natl Mat Dev.
—Les Trois Petits Amis et la Decouverte du Gumbo. Easterling, Mae L., illus. (FRE.). 41p. (gr. 3). 1979. pap. 1.25 (0-911409-04-1) Natl Mat Dev.

Theroux, Alexander. The Primary Colors. (gr. 3 up). 1994. write for info. (0-8050-3105-7) H Holt & Co.

Thesman, Jean. Appointment with a Stranger. (gr. 5-9). 1989. 13.45 (0-395-49215-7) HM.
—The Birthday Girls: I'm Not Telling. 128p. (Orig.). (gr. 4-8). 1992. pap. 2.99 (0-380-76523-3, Camelot) Avon.
—The Birthday Girls: Mirror, Mirror. 128p. (Orig.). (gr. 4-8). 1992. pap. 2.99 (0-380-76271-4, Camelot) Avon.
—The Birthday Girls: Who Am I, Anyway? 128p. (Orig.). (gr. 4-8). 1992. pap. 2.99 (0-380-76524-1, Camelot) Avon.
—Cattail Moon. LC 93-6814. (gr. 4-7). 1994. write for info. (0-395-67409-3) HM.
—Couldn't I Start Over? 176p. (Orig.). (gr. 7 up). 1989. pap. 2.95 (0-380-75717-6, Flare) Avon.
—The Last April Dancers. 224p. (gr. 7 up). 1987. 13.45 (0-395-43024-0) HM.
—The Last April Dancers. 224p. (gr. 7 up). 1989. pap. 2.75 (0-380-70614-8, Flare) Avon.
—Molly Donnelly. LC 92-10644. 192p. (gr. 5-9). 1993. 13.45 (0-395-64348-1) HM.
—Rachel Chance. 180p. (gr. 5-9). 1990. 13.45 (0-395-50934-3) HM.
—Rachel Chance. 192p. 1992. pap. 3.50 (0-380-71378-0, Flare) Avon.
—The Rain Catchers. LC 90-39343. 192p. (gr. 7 up). 1991. 13.45 (0-395-55333-4) HM.
—The Rain Catchers. 192p. 1992. pap. 3.50 (0-380-71711-5, Flare) Avon.
—When Does the Fun Start? 160p. (Orig.). 1991. pap. 3.50 (0-380-76129-7, Flare) Avon.
—When the Road Ends. 192p. (gr. 5-9). 1992. 13.45 (0-395-59507-X) HM.
—When the Road Ends. 192p. 1993. pap. 3.50 (0-380-72011-6, Camelot) Avon.
—The Whitney Cousins: Amelia. 144p. (gr. 4-5). 1990. pap. 2.95 (0-380-75874-1, Flare) Avon.
—The Whitney Cousins: Erin. 144p. (gr. 4-5). 1990. pap. 2.95 (0-380-75875-X, Flare) Avon.
—The Whitney Cousins: Heather. 160p. (gr. 4-5). 1990. pap. 2.95 (0-380-75869-5, Flare) Avon.
—The Whitney Cousins: Triple Trouble. 160p. (Orig.). 1992. pap. 3.50 (0-380-76464-4, Flare) Avon.

Thibault, Dominique. Long Ago in a Castle. Farre, Marie, illus. 40p. (gr. k-5). 1993. PLB 9.95 (*1-56674-071-1*, HTS Bks) Forest Hse.

Thibault, Frank, jt. auth. see Landin, Les.

Thiel, Elizabeth. The Polka Dot Horse. Milne, Terry, illus. LC 92-10221. 1993. pap. 14.00 (*0-671-79419-1*, S&S BYR) S&S Trade.

Thiele, Bob, jt. auth. see Weiss, George D.

Thiele, Colin. Jodie's Journey. LC 90-4072. 176p. (gr. 5 up). 1990. PLB 13.89 (*0-06-026133-1*) HarpC Child Bks.

—Shadow Shark. LC 87-45566. 224p. (gr. 5-7). 1988. PLB 13.89 (*0-06-026179-X*) HarpC Child Bks.

Thieme, Jeanne. The American Girls Album: A Picture Frame & Memory Book to Record Your Family History. (Illus.). 48p. (Orig.). (gr. 2-5). 1989. pap. 12.95 (*0-937295-57-4*) Pleasant Co.

—The American Girls Cookbook: A Peek at Dining in the Past with Meals You Can Cook Today. (Illus.). 64p. (Orig.). (gr. 2-5). 1989. pap. 9.95 (*0-937295-59-0*) Pleasant Co.

—The American Girls Diary: A Journal for Writing Your Secrets - An American Girls' Tradition. Backes, Nick, et al, illus. 96p. (Orig.). (gr. 2-5). 1989. pap. 9.95 (*0-937295-56-6*) Pleasant Co.

—American Girls PaperDolls: Kirsten, Samantha & Molly Paperdolls with All of Their Lovely Old-Fashioned Clothes. (Illus.). 32p. (Orig.). (gr. 2-5). 1989. pap. 6.95 (*0-937295-60-4*) Pleasant CO.

Thieme, Jeanne & Hansen, Robyn. The American Girls Games: Three Antique American Games That Kirsten, Samantha, & Molly Played. (Illus.). 32p. (Orig.). (gr. 2-5). 1989. pap. 17.95 (*0-937295-61-2*) Pleasant Co.

Thieme, Jeanne, jt. auth. see Tripp, Valerie.

Thieme, Jeanne, ed. see Adler, Susan S.

Thieme, Jeanne, ed. see Rowland, Pleasant T.

Thieme, Jeanne, ed. see Schur, Maxine R.

Thieme, Jeanne, ed. see Shaw, Janet.

Thieme, Jeanne, ed. see Shaw, Janet B.

Thieme, Jeanne, ed. see Tripp, Valerie.

Thies, James. The Little Island. 1992. 6.95 (*0-533-09296-5*) Vantage.

Thiesen, Charles & King, Deanna. Wordplay. rev. ed. LC 86-16178. (Illus.). 118p. (gr. 3-8). 1987. pap. 5.95 (*0-88166-088-4*) Meadowbrook.

Thiesing, Lisa, jt. auth. see Apablasa, Bill.

Thigpen, Paul, jt. auth. see Rice, Wayne.

Thigpen, Thomas P. Come Sing God's Song. John, Joyce, illus. LC 86-24197. (ps-1). 1987. 8.99 (*1-55513-052-6*, Chariot Bks) Cook.

Thill, Larry. The Adventures of Alice in Nutritionland: A Nutritional Storybook for Children. Thill, Michael, illus. 31p. (Orig.). (gr. k-6). 1989. pap. 8.00 (*0-317-93500-3*) Impressive Pubns.

Thiry, Joan. Discovering the Whole You. Sititra, illus. 64p. (Orig.). (gr. 5-6). 1991. pap. text ed. 6.00 (*0-935046-05-4*); tchr's. edition 14.00 (*0-935046-06-2*) Chateau Thierry.

—How to Cope with an Artichoke & other Mannerly Mishaps. Walsh, Karen J., illus. 40p. (gr. 7-12). 1982. pap. 4.95 (*0-935046-04-6*) Chateau Thierry.

—How to Entertain a Gnu & Not Disturb Your Family. Walsh, Karen J., illus. 40p. (gr. k-3). 1982. pap. 4.95 (*0-935046-02-X*) Chateau Thierry.

—How to Make a Courtesy Butter Sandwich & Serve it Properly. Walsh, Karen J., illus. 40p. (gr. 4-6). 1982. pap. 4.95 (*0-935046-03-8*) Chateau Thierry.

Thoburn, T., et al. Macmillan Mathematics. large type ed. Incl. Grade I, 2 vols. 350p. Set. 95.50 (*0-317-02386-1*, J-13210-00); Grade II, 2 vols. 348p. Set. 112.50 (*0-317-02387-X*, J-13220-00); Grade III, 4 vols. 828p. Set. 202.21 (*0-317-02388-8*, 4-13230-00); Grade IV, 4 vols. 900p. Set. 223.42 (*0-317-02389-6*, 4-13240-00); Grade V, 4 vols. 940p. Set. 232.00 (*0-317-02390-X*, J-13250-00); Grade VI, 4 vols. 890p. Set. 223.42 (*0-317-02391-8*, 4-13260-00). (gr. 1-6). 1982. Am Printing Hse.

Thoburn, Tina, jt. auth. see Ogle, Lucille.

Thoburn, Tina, compiled by. My First Golden Dictionary. Chandler, Jean, illus. LC 87-81750. 24p. 1988. write for info. (*0-307-11992-0*, Pub. by Golden Bks) Western Pub.

Thoelke, Shay, jt. auth. see Neilson, Stefan.

Thoene, Bodie. In My Father's House. 400p. (Orig.). 1992. pap. 11.99 (*1-55661-189-7*) Bethany Hse.

—The Key to Zion. LC 88-7439. 352p. (Orig.). (gr. 11 up). 1988. pap. 9.99 (*1-55661-034-3*) Bethany Hse.

—Light in Zion. LC 88-4578. 352p. (Orig.). (gr. 11-12). 1988. pap. 9.99 (*0-87123-990-6*) Bethany Hse.

—Say to This Mountain. 400p. (Orig.). 1993. pap. text ed. 11.99 (*1-55661-191-9*) Bethany Hse.

—Zion Covenant, 3 bks, Bks. 1-3. 1993. Set. 32.97 (*1-55661-779-8*) Bethany Hse.

—Zion Covenant, 3 bks, Bks. 4-6. 1993. Set. 32.97 (*1-55661-780-1*) Bethany Hse.

Thoene, Bodie, jt. auth. see Thoene, Brock.

Thoene, Brock & Thoene, Bodie. Cannons of the Comstock. 224p. 1992. pap. 7.99 (*1-55661-166-8*) Bethany Hse.

—Gold Rush Prodigal. 224p. (Orig.). (gr. 9-12). 1991. pap. 7.99 (*1-55661-162-5*) Bethany Hse.

—Shooting Star. LC 93-16175. 224p. (Orig.). 1993. pap. 7.99 (*1-55661-320-2*) Bethany Hse.

Thoenen, Eugenia G., ed. see Coffey, William E., et al.

Thom, John, jt. auth. see Palmer, Pete.

Thomas. Alex Haley Boyhood Years. Date not set. 15.00 (*0-06-023417-2*, Festival); PLB 14.89 (*0-06-023418-0*, Festival) HarpC Child Bks.

—Comeback Dog. (ps-7). 1983. pap. 3.25 (*0-553-15521-0*, Skylark) Bantam.

—Nana's Rocking Chair. 1993. 15.95 (*0-8050-2265-1*) H Holt & Co.

—Ten Amazing Women. Date not set. 15.00 (*0-06-023469-5*, Festival); PLB 14.89 (*0-06-023472-5*, Festival) HarpC Child Bks.

—Twelve Dark Riders. Date not set. 15.00 (*0-06-023477-6*, Festival); PLB 14.89 (*0-06-023478-4*, Festival) HarpC Child Bks.

Thomas see Sohn, David A.

Thomas, A. Ballet. (Illus.). 48p. (gr. 5 up). 1987. PLB 14.96 (*0-88110-244-X*); pap. 7.95 (*0-7460-0085-5*) EDC.

—First Book of the Piano. (Illus.). 64p. (gr. 2-6). 1988. PLB 14.96 (*0-88110-332-2*); pap. 8.95 (*0-7460-0197-5*) EDC.

—Things That Float. (Illus.). 24p. (gr. 2-4). 1987. pap. 3.95 (*0-7460-0102-9*) EDC.

Thomas, A., jt. auth. see Little, Karen E.

Thomas, A., et al. Ballet & Dance. (Illus.). 96p. (gr. 5 up). 1987. pap. 12.95 (*0-7460-0201-7*) EDC.

Thomas, Abagail. Lily. Low, William, illus. LC 93-14199. (gr. 5 up). 1994. write for info. (*0-8050-2690-8*) H Holt & Co.

Thomas, Abigail. Pearl Paints. 1994. write for info. (*0-8050-2976-1*) H Holt & Co.

—Wake up, Wilson Street. Low, William, illus. LC 92-10873. 32p. (gr. 5 up). 1993. 15.95 (*0-8050-2006-3*, Bks Young Read) H Holt & Co.

Thomas, Alicia. Self-Esteem. (gr. 7-12). 1991. PLB 13.95 (*0-8239-1225-6*) Rosen Group.

Thomas, Anika D. Life in the Ghetto. Thatch, Nancy R., ed. Thomas, Anika D., illus. Melton, David, intro. by. LC 91-13944. (Illus.). 26p. (gr. 5 up). 1991. PLB 14.95 (*0-933849-34-6*) Landmark Edns.

Thomas, Art. Fencing Is for Me. Sheehan-Burke, Julia, illus. LC 81-20716. 48p. (gr. 2-5). 1982. PLB 13.50 (*0-8225-1129-0*) Lerner Pubns.

—Merry-Go-Rounds. Overlie, George, illus. LC 81-3825. 48p. (gr. k-4). 1981. PLB 14.95 (*0-87614-168-8*) Carolrhoda Bks.

Thomas, Art & Storms, Laura. Boxing Is for Me. Thomas, Art, photos by. LC 80-20086. (Illus.). 48p. (gr. 2-5). 1982. PLB 13.50 (*0-8225-1133-9*) Lerner Pubns.

Thomas, Benjamin E., ed. Africa. rev. ed. LC 85-81418. (Illus.). (gr. 5 up). 1986. text ed. 11.95 (*0-88296-144-6*); tchr's. guide 8.95 (*0-88296-363-5*); unit tests 6.95 (*0-934291-51-9*) Gateway Pr MI.

Thomas, Carol. When the Nightingale Sings. Lilly, Charles, illus. LC 92-6045. 160p. (gr. 7 up). 1994. pap. 3.95 (*0-06-440524-9*, Trophy) HarpC Child Bks.

Thomas, Carolyn S. Kenta Comes to Colorado: A Bilingual Educational Activity Book. Holdorf, Kurt, illus. Romer, Roy, intro. by. (ENG & JPN., Illus.). 64p. (gr. k-4). 1990. pap. 6.95 (*0-913730-41-6*) Robinson Pr.

Thomas, Charles B. Water Gardens for Plants & Fish. (Illus.). 189p. (gr. 7 up). 1988. PLB 19.95 (*0-86622-942-6*, TS-102) TFH Pubns.

Thomas, Charlotte E. Our Little Flower Girl: A Child Has Her First Experience Participating in a Wedding. Jonsson, Deborah, illus. LC 92-72538. 32p. (ps-3). 1992. PLB 16.95 singer-sewn (*0-9633607-0-1*) Golden Rings. Finally, the first storybook written specifically to help little girls selected to be a flower girl in a wedding ceremony. While informing them of what their role will entail, it also entertains them with a delightful story. The tale begins with her invitation to join the bridal party & proceeds through the many preparations & customs leading up to THE BIG DAY. Her finery is chosen & she discovers it must be ordered, which is a new experience for her. She solicits her friends & their toys to help her practice for her exciting role. The meanings of rehearsal & reception are also made known to her. A very apprehensive child in the beginning of the story, she ends up eagerly anticipating becoming a bride herself someday. This must have book is beautifully illustrated in full color & contains a page for signatures of the wedding party & special friends making it a true KEEPSAKE. *Publisher Provided Annotation.*

Thomas, Claire & Thomas, Thornton. Naming Game: Storybook to Color. Jones, S. Max, illus. 22p. (Orig.). (gr. k-3). 1988. pap. 3.95 (*0-317-92517-2*) Sparky Star Pr.

Thomas, Claire & Thomas, Thornton, eds. Naming Game: Storybook to Color by Grandpa T. Jones, S. Max, illus. 18p. (Orig.). (gr. k-3). 1988. 2.95x (*0-9621616-0-8*) Sparky Star Pr.

Thomas, David A. How Ships Are Made. LC 89-31328. (Illus.). 32p. (gr. 4-8). 1989. 12.95x (*0-8160-2040-X*) Facts on File.

—Math Projects for Young Scientists. Rasof, Henry, ed. LC 87-21064. (Illus.). 128p. (gr. 7-12). 1988. PLB 13.90 (*0-531-10523-7*) Watts.

Thomas, Dean S., jt. auth. see Coates, Earl J.

Thomas, Dylan. A Child's Christmas in Wales. Ardizzone, Edward, illus. LC 80-66216. 48p. 1980. 14.95 (*0-87923-339-7*); pap. 9.95 (*0-87923-529-2*) Godine.

—A Child's Christmas in Wales. Hyman, Trina S., illus. LC 85-766. 48p. (gr. 4-6). 1985. reinforced bdg. 14.95 (*0-8234-0565-6*) Holiday.

—A Conversation about Christmas. 1991. PLB 13.95s.p. (*0-88682-468-0*) Creative Ed.

Thomas, Earl. Unusual Events, 5 novels. (Illus.). 48p. (gr. 2-9). 1986. Set. pap. 15.00 (*0-87879-530-8*) High Noon Bks.

Thomas, Eberle & Redmond, Barbara. Six Canterbury Tales. (Orig.). 1993. pap. 5.50 playscript (*0-87602-305-7*) Anchorage.

Thomas, Elizabeth. Green Beans. (ps-3). 1992. 19.95 (*0-87614-708-2*) Carolrhoda Bks.

Thomas, Frances. The Prince & the Cave. 1992. pap. 23.00x (*0-86383-768-9*, Pub. by Gomer Pr UK) St Mut.

—Zak. large type ed. 200p. (gr. 5 up). 1988. 13.95 (*0-7451-0727-3*, Galaxy Child Lrg Print) Chivers N Amer.

Thomas, Frank, jt. auth. see Johnston, Ollie.

Thomas, Glenn. A Guided Journey Through the World of Entertainment: Songs-Films-Television-Sports & Birthdays Every Day of the Year. LC 90-86204. (Illus.). 32p. (Orig.). 1991. pap. 12.95 (*0-9623944-3-2*) Art & Entertainment.

Thomas, Graham. Timeline: People's Republic of China. (Illus.). 72p. (gr. 7 up). 1990. 19.95 (*0-85219-791-8*, Pub. by Batsford UK) Trafalgar.

Thomas, Heather S. A Week in the Woods. Woolsey, Raymond H., ed. 64p. (gr. 2-4). 1988. pap. 4.95 (*0-8280-0435-8*) Review & Herald.

Thomas, Iolette. Mermaid Janine. (ps-3). 1993. pap. 4.95 (*0-590-46594-5*) Scholastic Inc.

Thomas J. Safe at Home, Safe Alone. (Illus.). 64p. (Orig.). (gr. 3-5). 1985. pap. 4.95 (*0-917917-01-4*) Miles River.

Thomas, J. P. The Cricket Angel. 1992. 7.95 (*0-533-09713-4*) Vantage.

Thomas, Jane R. The Comeback Dog. Howell, Troy, illus. 64p. (gr. 2-6). 1981. 13.45 (*0-395-29432-0*, Clarion Bks) HM.

—Courage at Indian Deep. LC 83-14404. (Illus.). 128p. (gr. 3-7). 1984. 13.95 (*0-89919-181-9*, Clarion Bks) HM.

—Courage at Indian Deep. (gr. 4-7). 1990. pap. 4.95 (*0-395-55699-6*, Clarion Bks) HM.

—Fox in a Trap. Howell, Troy, illus. LC 86-17412. 96p. (gr. 3-6). 1987. 13.95 (*0-89919-473-7*, Clarion Bks) HM.

—Fox in a Trap. Howell, Troy, illus. LC 86-17412. 96p. (gr. 2-5). 1990. pap. 3.95 (*0-395-54426-2*, Clarion Bks) HM.

—Lights on the River. Dooling, Michael, illus. LC 93-33636. Date not set. 14.95; PLB 14.89 Hyprn Child.

—The Princess in the Pigpen. LC 89-856. 128p. (gr. 3-7). 1989. 13.95 (*0-395-51587-4*, Clarion Bks) HM.

—The Princess in the Pigpen. 144p. 1993. pap. 3.50 (*0-380-71194-X*, Camelot) Avon.

—Saying Good-bye to Grandma. Sewall, Marcia, illus. LC 87-20826. 40p. (gr. 1-4). 1988. 15.45 (*0-89919-645-4*, Clarion Bks) HM.

—Saying Good-Bye to Grandma. LC 87-20826. 40p. (ps-3). 1990. pap. 5.70 (*0-395-54779-2*, Clarion Bks) HM.

—Wheels. LC 85-18404. (ps-3). 1986. 12.95 (*0-317-39001-5*) HM.

—Wheels. McCully, Emily A., illus. LC 85-13291. 32p. (ps-3). 1986. 14.95 (*0-89919-410-9*, Clarion Bks) HM.

Thomas, Janet. Newcomer. 33p. (Orig.). (gr. k-3). 1987. pap. 4.50 playscript (*0-87602-268-9*) Anchorage.

Thomas, Janis & Thomas, Lenerd. Sir Lacksalot & the Two Headed Dragon Meet the Savage Sea Serpent. Yakovetic, illus. LC 91-61114. 48p. (gr. k-5). 1991. 16.95 (*1-879480-01-8*) L T Pub.

Thomas, Janis, jt. auth. see Thomas, Lenerd.

Thomas, Jennifer. Masterpiece of the Month. Apodaca, Blanqui & Wright, Theresa, illus. (gr. k-5). 1990. wkbk. 9.95 (*1-55734-018-8*) Tchr Create Mat.

Thomas, Jerry D. Detective Zack & the Red Hat Mystery. LC 93-4322. 1993. write for info. (*0-8163-1169-2*) Pacific Pr Pub Assn.

—Detective Zack & the Secret of Noah's Flood: Starburst. LC 92-5730. 128p. 1992. pap. 7.95 (*0-8163-1107-2*) Pacific Pr Pub Assn.

—Detective Zack & the Secrets in the Sand. LC 92-29931. 1993. 7.95 (*0-8163-1129-3*) Pacific Pr Pub Assn.

Thomas, Jesse L. The Three Missing Rabbits. 1993. 7.75 (*0-8062-4682-0*) Carlton.

Thomas, Joan G. The Christmas Angel. Thomas, Joan G., illus. 20p. (gr. 1-5). 1988. pap. 3.95 (0-8192-1429-9) Morehouse Pub.

—If Jesus Came to My House. Thomas, Joan G., illus. 24p. (gr. k-3). 1951. 12.95 (0-688-40981-4) Lothrop.

Thomas, John W. Making Changes: A Guide to Future Oriented Education. (Illus.). (gr. 6-12). 1981. pap. text ed. 14.95 (0-88280-081-7); tchrs' ed. 19.95 (0-88280-082-5) ETC Pubns.

Thomas, Joyce C. Brown Honey in Broomwheat Tea. Cooper, Floyd, illus. LC 91-46043. 32p. (gr. k up). 1993. 15.00 (0-06-021087-7); PLB 14.89 (0-06-021088-5) HarpC Child Bks.

—A Gathering of Flowers. LC 90-4043. 256p. (gr. 7 up). 1992. pap. 3.95 (0-06-447082-2, Trophy) HarpC Child Bks.

—Journey. (gr. 7 up). 1988. pap. 12.95 (0-590-40627-2, Scholastic Hardcover) Scholastic Inc.

—Marked by Fire. 160p. (gr. 7 up). 1982. pap. 3.99 (0-380-79327-X, Flare) Avon.

—When the Nightingale Sings. LC 92-6045. 160p. (gr. 7 up). 1992. 14.00 (0-06-020294-7); PLB 13.89 (0-06-020295-5) HarpC Child Bks.

Thomas, Joyce C., ed. A Gathering of Flowers: Stories about Being Young in America. LC 90-4043. 256p. (gr. 7 up). 1990. PLB 14.89 (0-06-026174-9) HarpC Child Bks.

Thomas, Kathy. The Angel's Quest. Seitz, Jacqueline, illus. 32p. (gr. 2-6). 1983. casebound 9.95 (0-914544-99-3) Living Flame Pr.

Thomas, Lenerd & Thomas, Janis. Sir Lacksalot & the Two Headed Dragon. Yakovetic, illus. (gr. k-6). 1990. 16.95 (1-879480-00-X) L T Pub.

Thomas, Lenerd, jt. auth. see Thomas, Janis.

Thomas, M. Embroidery Book. 320p. (gr. 5-8). 32.50 (0-87559-110-8) Shalom.

Thomas, M. Angele & Ramey, Mary L. Many Children Coloring Book. (Illus.). 24p. 1988. pap. 1.50 (0-9619293-1-6) M A Thomas.

—Many Children: Religions Around the World. Lucas, Patti L., illus. LC 87-91771. 70p. (Orig.). (gr. 2-6). 1987. pap. text ed. 6.95 (0-9619293-0-8) M A Thomas.

Thomas, Mack. Bible Tells Me So: The Beginner's Guide to Loving & Understanding God's Word. (gr. 5-10). 1992. 14.99 (0-945564-20-1, Gold & Honey) Questar Pubs.

—From God with Love. 64p. (ps-2). 1993. 13.99 (0-945564-78-3, Gold & Honey) Questar Pubs.

—In His Hands; What Would Jesus Do? The Continuing Story. (ps-3). 1993. 12.99 (0-945564-44-9, Gold & Honey) Questar Pubs.

—Lets Make Jesus Happy. 256p. (ps-2). 1993. 12.99 (0-945564-76-7, Gold & Honey) Questar Pubs.

—My First Step Bible: Blue for Boys. (ps). 1992. 6.99 (0-945564-48-1, Gold & Honey) Questar Pubs.

—My First Step Bible: Pink for Girls. (ps). 1992. 6.99 (0-945564-49-X, Gold & Honey) Questar Pubs.

—A Tale of Two Princes - Eckart Zur Nieden. 32p. (ps-2). 1993. 12.99 (0-88070-598-1, Gold & Honey) Questar Pubs.

—What Would Jesus Do? Mortenson, Denis, illus. 253p. (ps-2). 1991. 12.99 (0-945564-05-8, Gold & Honey) Questar Pubs.
Almost a century ago, a new novel revolutionized the concept of Christian discipleship. The book was Charles M. Sheldon's In His Steps. Conservative estimates place the book's sales at more than 25 million copies--ranking it behind only the Bible in popularity among Christian readers in this century. And now, In His Steps has been retold for children, with its timeless message as clear & powerful as ever. As both a book & audio cassette, WHAT WOULD JESUS DO? presents the stirring call of following Christ in a way that young children can easily understand & embrace. The delightful text is written in short, simple sentences, & is set in a clear typeface especially recommended for early readers. Each short chapter focuses in a fresh way on the book's core concept--learning to ask throughout the day, What would Jesus do? Discussion questions for each chapter help parents & teachers highlight this truth for children. Enhancing the text are full-color illustrations on more than 200 pages. Detailed & charming, they capture the book's flavor as a work that transcends

time & cultures. Order from Questar Publications, P.O. Box 1720, Sisters, OR 97759, 503-549-1144.
Publisher Provided Annotation.

Thomas, Mack & Alex, Ben. Beginners Bible Questions & Answer Book. (Illus.). 384p. (Orig.). (gr. 7-12). 1992. 14.99 (0-945564-21-X, Gold & Honey) Questar Pubs.

Thomas, Mack, ed. The Wonder Bible. 512p. (gr. 2-5). 1993. 16.99 (0-945564-59-7, Gold & Honey) Questar Pubs.
The perfect transition between Bible storybooks & an adult Bible, THE WONDER BIBLE highlights sections of every book in God's Word for children ages 7-10, focusing on passages that have the greatest meaning for young readers. This concentrated introduction to the Scriptures includes colorful illustrations, key memory verses, book overviews, background information, index to Bible characters & much more! Easy-to-understand text selected from the popular INTERNATIONAL CHILDREN'S BIBLE. Order from QUESTAR Publishers/Gold 'n' Honey Books, P.O. Box 1720, Sisters, OR 97759. 503-549-1144.
Publisher Provided Annotation.

Thomas, Margaret. Volcano! LC 90-45372. (Illus.). 48p. (gr. 5-6). 1991. RSBE 12.95 (0-89686-595-9, Crestwood Hse) Macmillan Child Grp.

Thomas, Margaret, jt. auth. see Facklam, Margery.

Thomas, Marlo. Free to Be... You & Me. (gr. 1 up). 1992. 21.00 (0-8446-6602-5) Peter Smith.

—Free to Be...You & Me. Hart, Carole, ed. 1987. pap. 9.95 (0-317-62189-0) McGraw.

—Free to Be...You & Me. Steinem, Gloria, intro. by. (gr. 1 up). 1987. pap. 12.95 (0-553-34544-3) Bantam.

Thomas, Mary. Mary Thomas's Knitting Book. (Illus.). 269p. (gr. 6-12). 1972. pap. 5.95 (0-486-22817-7) Dover.

Thomas, Mary A. Jump with Jeremy: What Hoosiers Do on the Way to the Zoo. Hodge, Ellen & Poore, Luz, eds. Still, James & Escabar, URias, trs. from ENG. Graham-Rice, Kathy, illus. (SPA.). 47p. (Orig.). 1988. pap. 9.95 (0-944326-00-5) Childrens Corner.

Thomas, Mary L., jt. auth. see Bowlby, Linda A.

Thomas, Meredith. Paper Shapes. Thomas, Meredith, illus. LC 93-27994. 1994. 4.25 (0-383-03767-0) SRA Schl Grp.

Thomas Nelson Publishers Staff. Bible Stories, Bk. 3. (gr. 2 up). 1993. 6.99 (0-8407-4911-2) Nelson.

—David & Goliath. LC 93-24836. (gr. 2 up). 1993. 6.99 (0-8407-4913-9) Nelson.

Thomas, Patricia. One & Only Super-Duper, Golly-Whopper, Jim-Dandy, Really-Handy Clock-Tock Stopper. 32p. 1990. 13.95 (0-688-09340-X); PLB 13.88 (0-688-09341-8) Lothrop.

—Stand Back, Said the Elephant, I'm Going to Sneeze! Tripp, Wallace, illus. LC 89-43215. 32p. (ps-2). 1990. 13.95 (0-688-09338-8); lib. bdg. 13.88 (0-688-09339-6) Lothrop.

Thomas, Paul. The Central Asian States. Channon, John, contrib. by. LC 92-2239. (Illus.). 32p. (gr. 4-6). 1992. PLB 13.90 (1-56294-307-3) Millbrook Pr.

Thomas, Peter, narrated by see Bailer, Darice.

Thomas, Peter, jt. ed. see Boyle, Doe.

Thomas, Peter, narrated by see Boyle, Doe.

Thomas, Peter, narrated by see Cowcher, Helen.

Thomas, Peter, narrated by see Limpert, Dana.

Thomas, Peter, narrated by see Saunders, Susan.

Thomas, Peter, narrated by see Schoenherr, John.

Thomas, Peter, narrated by see Thompson-Hoffman, Susan.

Thomas, Peter, narrated by see Viola, Herman J.

Thomas, Piri. Stories from el Barrio. LC 78-328. (gr. 5-9). 1992. 15.00 (0-394-83568-9) Knopf Bks Yng Read.

Thomas, Robert. How to Talk Midwestern. Carlson, Bruce, ed. Thomas, Tony & Carlson, Bruce, illus. 109p. (gr. 9 up). 1990. pap. 7.95 (1-878488-21-X) Quixote Pr IA.

Thomas, Scott. Dinosaurs for Christmas. 1993. 8.75 (0-8062-4764-9) Carlton.

Thomas, Sue & Dinges, Susan. Curtain I: A Guide to Creative Drama for Children 5-8 Years Old. (gr. k-3). 1985. 15.00 (0-89824-148-0) Trillium Pr.

Thomas, Sue, jt. auth. see Dinges, Susan.

Thomas, Thornton, jt. auth. see Thomas, Claire.

Thomas, Thornton, jt. ed. see Thomas, Claire.

Thomas, Valerie. Winnie the Witch. Paul, Korky, illus. 32p. (ps-3). 1987. 13.95 (0-916291-13-8) Kane-Miller Bk.

—Winnie the Witch. Paul, Korky, illus. 32p. (ps-3). 1990. pap. 6.95 (0-916291-32-4) Kane-Miller Bk.

Thomas, Vernon. Aesop's Fables. Bhushan, Reboti, illus. 135p. (gr. 1-7). 1981. 7.50 (0-89744-231-8, Pub. by Hemkunt IA) Auromere.

—More Stories from the Arabian Nights. Bose, R. K., illus. 135p. (gr. 1 up). 1981. 7.50 (0-89744-232-6, Pub. by Hemkunt India) Auromere.

—Stories from the Arabian Nights. Basu, R. K., illus. (gr. 8-12). 1979. 7.50 (0-89744-142-7) Auromere.

Thomas, Vernon, ed. Fairy Tales from India. (Illus.). (gr. 1-9). 1979. 7.50 (0-89744-137-0) Auromere.

—Folk Tales from India. Ghosh, R. B., illus. (gr. 3-10). 1979. 7.95 (0-89744-141-9) Auromere.

Thomasma, Kenneth. Amazing Indian Children. (gr. 3-8). 1991. 9.95 (1-880114-12-7); pap. 6.95 (0-685-49336-9) Grandview.
AMAZING INDIAN CHILDREN is a series of five books, historic fiction written for a third grade read-ability. They are packed with Indian lore, history, geography & high adventure. Each book has a child as the central character who lives during a key time in that tribe's history. Through the Indian child's eyes the reader relives dramatic historic events. These books are accurately researched & are in use in over 1000 schools. They have been translated into Danish, Dutch, Eskimo & Spanish. Over 300,000 have been sold. NAYA NUKI: GIRL WHO RAN-ISBN 1-880114-01-1 cloth; 1-880114-00-3 pbk. With her friend, Sacagewea, a Shoshoni Indian Girl is taken prisoner, escapes & makes a 1000 mile wilderness journey back to her people. SOUN TETOKEN: NEZ PERCE BOY-ISBN 1-880114-08-9 cloth; 1-880114-07-0 pbk. Although mute since the death of his parents in a forest fire a young boy in Chief Joseph's band lives a happy adventurous life until the War of 1877 changes his life forever. OM-KAS-TOE OF THE BLACKFEET-ISBN 1-880114-06-2 cloth; 1-800114-05-4 pbk. Life changes dramatically for the Blackfeet people in the early 1700s when a twin brother & sister discover a strange animal & succeed in capturing it & returning it to their tribe. KUNU: ESCAPE ON THE MISSOURI-ISBN 1-880114-04-6 cloth; 1-880114-03-8 pbk. Following the forced removal of his people from Minnesota to South Dakota, a Winnebago Indian boy & his dying grandfather embark on a dangerous river journey back to their homeland. PATHKI NANA: KOOTENAI GIRL-ISBN 1-800114-10-0 cloth; 1-800114-09-7 pbk. A 9 year-old Kootenai girl with a very poor self-image leaves her village to seek her guardian spirit & finds herself in a life & death struggle with an evil man who seeks to end her life before she can return to her people. To order call 1-800-525-7344.
Publisher Provided Annotation.

—Kunu: Winnebago Boy Escapes. Fleuter, Craig, illus. LC 89-15074. 183p. (ps-8). 1992. 10.99 (0-8010-8891-7); pap. 6.99 (0-8010-8892-5) Baker Bk.

—Naya Nuki: Shoshoni Girl Who Ran. 2nd ed. Hundley, Eunice, illus. LC 89-143272. 175p. (Orig.). 1992. 10.99 (0-8010-8869-0); pap. 6.99 (0-8010-8868-2) Baker Bk.

—Om-Kas-Toe of the Blackfeet: Blackfeet Twin Captures an Elkdog. Poindexter, Cathlene & Brouwer, Jack, illus. LC 89-14879. 215p. (gr. 4-8). 1992. 10.99 (0-8010-8883-6); pap. 6.99 (0-8010-8884-4) Baker Bk.

—Pathki Nana: Kootenai Girl. (gr. 3-8). 1991. 9.95 (1-880114-10-0); pap. 6.95 (1-880114-09-7) Grandview.

Thomason, Kendra. My Family Plays & Prays: Mission Activity Book for Preschoolers. Gross, Karen, ed. 32p. (Orig.). (ps). 1992. pap. text ed. 3.95 (1-56309-050-3, New Hope) Womans Mission Union.

Thomassie, Tynia. Feliciana Feydra LeRoux. Smith, Cat B., illus. LC 93-30347. 1994. 14.95 (0-316-84125-0) Little.

Thomason, Merry. Hey Look at Me! Baby Days. LC 90-61135. 20p. (ps). 1990. 9.95 (0-9615407-5-3) Merrybooks VA.

—Hey Look at Me-Boys. (ps). 1990. 9.95 (0-9615407-3-7) Merrybooks VA.

—Hey Look at Me! Here We Go. Havens, Greg, illus. LC 85-62576. 20p. (ps-2). 1987. 9.95 (0-9615407-0-2) Thomasson-Grant.

—Hey Look at Me! I Can Be. Poole, Valerie, illus. LC 87-90455. 20p. (ps-2). 1987. 9.95 (0-9615407-1-0) Thomasson-Grant.

—Hey Look at Me! I Can Help. LC 91-91301. 20p. (ps-2). 1992. 9.95 (0-685-62733-0) Thomasson-Grant.

—Hey Look at Me! I Like to Dream. Poole, Valerie, illus. LC 87-90547. 20p. (ps-2). 1987. 9.95 (0-9615407-2-9) Thomasson-Grant.

—Hey Look at Me! I Like to Play Book for Girls. (ps-2). 1990. 9.95 (0-9615407-4-5) Merrybooks VA.

Thomasson, Merry F. Hey, Look at Me! Merry Manners: Merry Manors. Pound, Garry, illus. Date not set. write for info. (1-882607-06-6) Merrybooks VA.

—I Can Draw. (ps). 1992. 9.95 (0-9615407-6-1) Merrybooks VA.

—I Can Help. (ps). 1992. 9.95 (0-9615407-7-X) Merrybooks VA.

—Wee Babies. (ps). 1992. 9.95 (0-9615407-8-8) Merrybooks VA.

Thompson. Trees. (gr. 2-5). 1980. (Usborne-Hayes); PLB 11.96 (0-88110-071-4); pap. 3.95 (0-86020-473-1) EDC.

Thompson, Annie. Oakey the Ostrich. 1993. 7.95 (0-8062-4633-2) Carlton.

Thompson, Brenda & Giesen, Rosemary. Bones & Skeletons. Viner, Carole & Giesen, Rosemary, illus. LC 76-22420. (gr. k-3). 1977. PLB 7.95 (0-8225-1352-8) Lerner Pubns.

Thompson, Brenda & Overbeck, Cynthia. The Great Wall of China. Austin, Caroline, illus. LC 76-22443. 24p. (gr. k-3). 1977. PLB 7.95 (0-8225-1357-9) Lerner Pubns.

—Under the Sea. Beisner, Monica, illus. LC 76-22470. 24p. (gr. k-3). 1977. PLB 7.95 (0-8225-1363-3) Lerner Pubns.

Thompson, Brian. Puffin First Picture Dictionary. Berridge, Celia, illus. 38p. (ps-3). 1989. pap. 3.95 (0-14-050777-9, Puffin) Puffin Bks.

Thompson, C. E. Dinosaur Bones! Billin-Frye, Paige, illus. 32p. (ps-3). 1992. 6.95 (0-448-41087-7, G&D) Putnam Pub Group.

—Glow-in-the-Dark Constellations: A Field Guide for Young Stargazers. Chewning, Randy, illus. 32p. (gr. 1-5). 1989. 11.95 (0-448-09070-8, G&D) Putnam Pub Group.

Thompson, Cameron V. Master Secrets of Prayer. 112p. (Orig.). (gr. 8 up). 1990. pap. 5.95 (0-9627630-0-4) Light & Living.

Thompson, Carol. Alphaboo: A Hidden Letter ABC Book. Hartelius, Margaret A., illus. LC 93-26925. (gr. 1 up). 1994. pap. write for info. (0-448-40213-0, G&D) Putnam Pub Group.

—Baby Days. Thompson, Carol, illus. LC 90-28298. 48p. (ps). 1991. SBE 15.95 (0-02-789325-1, Macmillan Child Bk); pap. 4.95 counting frieze (0-02-789195-X) Macmillan Child Grp.

—In My Bedroom. 1990. 8.95 (0-385-29857-9) Doubleday.

Thompson, Cliff. Charles Chesnutt. King, Coretta Scott, intro. by. (Illus.). 112p. (gr. 5 up). 1993. PLB 17.95 (1-55546-578-1) Chelsea Hse.

Thompson, Colin. Looking for Atlantis. LC 93-24068. 1994. 15.00 (0-679-85648-X) Knopf Bks Yng Read.

—The Paper Bag Prince. Thompson, Colin, illus. LC 91-27453. 32p. (gr. 2-7). 1992. 15.00 (0-679-83048-0); PLB 15.99 (0-679-93048-5) Knopf Bks Yng Read.

—Pictures of Home. LC 92-11359. 32p. (ps-2). 1993. JRT 14.00 (0-671-79584-8, Green Tiger) S&S Trade.

Thompson, David. Nevada: A History of Changes. Dickerson, Donald, ed. Barker, Bill, illus. Thompson, David, intro. by. LC 86-82332. (Illus.). 232p. (Orig.). (ps-6). 1986. pap. text ed. 17.50 (0-913205-09-5); special price 10.50 Grace Dangberg.

Thompson, David, jt. auth. see Lynch, Don.

Thompson, Denisse & Van Loy, Merrie. Fundamental Skills of Mathematics. Howland, Joe & Savige, Katherine, eds. Howland, Thomas, illus. LC 87-50098. 536p. (gr. 9-12). 1987. text ed. 19.95 (0-943202-16-7) H & H Pub.

Thompson, Don. Captain Noah. Meyer, Rita, illus. 32p. (gr. 3-5). 1991. 9p. 1.19 (0-87123-696-6) Bethany Hse.

—General Joshua. (Illus.). 32p. (gr. 3-5). 1989. 9p. 1.19 (0-87123-697-4) Bethany Hse.

Thompson, Dorothea M. The Sokokis: Native Americans of New Hampshire. Thompson, Brownlow L., illus. 150p. (Orig.). (gr. 4). 1986. pap. 9.95x (0-931947-50-2) Thompson Pr.

—Will Stark & Boobear: Ranger Scouts, Vol. 2. 2nd ed. Thompson, Brownlow L., illus. 150p. (gr. 5-10). pap. text ed. 9.95 (0-931947-52-9) Thompson Pr.

Thompson, Dorothy. Out of Bed & Back Again. (ps). 1992. pap. 9.95 (0-671-78377-7, Little Simon) S&S Trade.

Thompson, Elizabeth, jt. auth. see Ziner, Feenie.

Thompson, Emily. Imagine: A Million Kittens for Elmo. (ps-3). 1993. pap. 2.25 (0-307-13122-X, Golden Pr) Western Pub.

—Just Like Ernie. Cooke, Tom, illus. LC 87-81762. 32p. (ps-k). 1988. write for info. (0-307-12025-2, Pub. by Golden Bks) Western Pub.

Thompson, Frances. Monterey Bay Aquarium Coloring Book. Monterey Bay Aquarium Education Department Staff, ed. Thompson, Frances, illus. 16p. (Orig.). (gr. k-6). 1988. pap. 3.95 (0-9604542-1-7) Inkstone Books.

Thompson, Frances M. Five-Minute Challenges for Secondary School. (gr. 7-12). 1988. pap. 7.95 (0-918932-94-7) Activity Resources.

—Miss Circo Comes Apart at the Seams. Holt, Cather C., illus. 18p. (Orig.). (gr. k-3). 1986. pap. 3.95 (0-9616207-0-6) Bks By Brooks.

—More Five Minute Challenges: Mini-Problem Solving Activities. (Illus.). 64p. (Orig.). (gr. 8-12). 1992. pap. text ed. 7.95 (0-918932-98-X, A-2224) Activity Resources.

Thompson, Frederick. Dickon Dicky & Mr. Wheelspoke. 1991. 7.95 (0-533-09384-8) Vantage.

Thompson, Graham, jt. auth. see Royston, Angela.

Thompson, Gregory. Step by Step Theatre. (gr. 1-4). 1989. pap. 10.95 (0-8224-6348-2) Fearon Teach Aids.

Thompson, Gunnar. American Discovery: The Real Story. Thompson, Gunnar, illus. 350p. (Orig.). (gr. 11). 1992. pap. 15.00 (0-9621990-4-4) Argonauts OTMI.

Thompson, Hildegard, ed. & tr. see Morgan, William.

Thompson, Jean. Don't Forget Michael. Apple, Margot, illus. LC 79-16637. 64p. (gr. k-3). 1979. 11.95 (0-688-22196-3); (Morrow Jr Bks) Morrow Jr Bks.

Thompson, Joan. The Mudpack & Me. MacDonald, Pat, ed. 160p. (Orig.). 1993. pap. 3.50 (0-671-72862-8, Minstrel Bks) PB.

Thompson, Jonathon J., Jr. ABC Limericks. (Illus.). 40p. (gr. 3-6). 1992. 3.95 (0-933479-04-2) Thompson.

—Air Raiders. (Illus.). 75p. (gr. 6-12). 1992. 4.50 (0-933479-02-6) Thompson.

—Air Raiders Five. 50p. (gr. 7-12). 1992. 5.00 (0-933479-09-3) Thompson.

—Air Raiders Four. (Illus.). 65p. (gr. 7-12). 1992. 4.35 (0-933479-07-7) Thompson.

—Air Raiders Six. (Illus.). (gr. 7-12). 1992. write for info. (0-933479-17-4) Thompson.

—Air Raiders Three. (Illus.). 85p. (gr. 7-12). 1992. 5.25 (0-933479-06-9) Thompson.

—Air Raiders Two. (Illus.). 70p. (gr. 7-12). 1987. 4.60 (0-933479-10-7) Thompson.

—Away at Camp. 20p. (gr. 1-6). 1992. 3.00 (0-933479-11-5) Thompson.

—Haunted House Hoax. 10p. (gr. 3-6). 1992. 2.50 (0-933479-12-3) Thompson.

—Semantography. (Illus.). 60p. (gr. 7-12). 1992. write for info. (0-933479-13-1) Thompson.

—Superflyer: Captain John Champion Flyer. 40p. (gr. 3-6). 1992. 3.95 (0-933479-08-5) Thompson.

—Witch Hazel's Crazy Adventures. (Illus.). 80p. (gr. 3-6). 1985. 4.50 (0-933479-05-0) Thompson.

—Witch Hazel's Whackey Adventures. Thompson, Jonathon, illus. 104p. (gr. 3-6). 1985. 5.50 (0-933479-01-8) Thompson.

—Witch Hazel's Whackola Adventures. (Illus.). 143p. (gr. 4-8). 1986. 6.50 (0-933479-03-4) Thompson.

Thompson, Julian. Gypsyworld. LC 93-15451. 240p. (gr. 7 up). 1993. pap. 3.99 (0-14-036531-1, Puffin) Puffin Bks.

Thompson, Julian F. Discontinued. 304p. (gr. 7 up). 1986. 12.95 (0-590-33321-6); pap. 3.50 (0-590-42464-5) Scholastic Inc.

—Facing It. 240p. (gr. 7 up). 1983. pap. 2.95 (0-380-84491-5, Flare) Avon.

—Goofbang Value Daze. (gr. 7 up). 1989. pap. 12.95 (0-590-41946-3) Scholastic Inc.

—Goofbang Value Daze. 1990. pap. 2.95 (0-590-41945-5) Scholastic Inc.

—Gypsyworld. 172p. (gr. 7 up). 1992. 15.95 (0-8050-1907-3, Bks Young Read) H Holt & Co.

—Herb Seasoning. 1990. pap. 12.95 (0-590-43023-8) Scholastic Inc.

—Herb Seasoning. (gr. 7 up). 1990. pap. 3.25 (0-590-43024-6) Scholastic Inc.

—A Question of Survival. 320p. (gr. 8 up). 1984. pap. 2.50 (0-380-87775-9, Flare) Avon.

—Shepherd. 176p. (gr. 8 up). 1993. PLB 15.95 (0-8050-2106-X, Bks Young Read) H Holt & Co.

—Simon Pure. 336p. (gr. 10-12). 1987. pap. 12.95x (0-590-40507-1, Scholastic Hardcover) Scholastic Inc.

—Simon Pure. 336p. (gr. 7 up). 1988. pap. 3.50 (0-590-41823-8, Point) Scholastic Inc.

—The Taking of Mariasburg. 288p. (gr. 7 up). 1988. pap. 12.95 (0-590-41247-7, Scholastic Hardcover) Scholastic Inc.

—The Taking of Mariasburg. (gr. 8 up). 1989. pap. 2.95 (0-590-41246-9) Scholastic Inc.

Thompson, Kathleen. Alabama. LC 87-26486. 48p. (gr. 3 up). 1988. 18.64 (0-8174-4613-3) Raintree Steck-V.

—Alaska. LC 87-26487. 48p. (gr. 3 up). 1988. 18.64 (0-8174-4710-5) Raintree Steck-V.

—Arkansas. LC 87-16372. 48p. (gr. 3 up). 1987. 18.64 (0-8174-4494-7) Raintree Steck-V.

—California. LC 87-16395. 48p. 1987. 18.64 (0-8174-4621-4) cancelled 3/4" video (0-86514-237-8) Raintree Steck-V.

—Colorado. LC 87-16374. 48p. (gr. 3 up). 1987. 18.64 (0-86514-463-X) Raintree Steck-V.

—Delaware. 48p. (gr. 3 up). 1986. pap. text ed. 18.64 (0-8174-4508-0) Raintree Steck-V.

—Kansas. LC 87-16406. 48p. (gr. 4 up). 1987. 18.64 (0-8174-4648-6) (0-86514-091-X) cancelled 3/4" video (0-86514-241-6) Raintree Steck-V.

—Michigan. LC 87-16373. 48p. (gr. 3 up). 1987. 18.64 (0-86514-465-6) Raintree Steck-V.

—Minnesota. LC 87-16405. 48p. (gr. 3 up). 1988. 18.64 (0-86514-466-4) Raintree Steck-V.

—Mississippi. LC 87-16440. 48p. (gr. 3 up). 1987. 18.64 (0-86514-467-2) Raintree Steck-V.

—Montana. LC 87-26465. 48p. (gr. 3 up). 1988. 18.64 (0-86514-468-0) Raintree Steck-V.

—Nebraska. LC 87-264855. 48p. (gr. 3 up). 1988. 18.64 (0-86514-473-7) Raintree Steck-V.

—New Hampshire. LC 87-26480. 48p. (gr. 3 up). 1988. 18.64 (0-86514-469-9) Raintree Steck-V.

—New York. LC 87-26481. 48p. (gr. 3 up). 1988. 18.64 (0-86514-474-5) Raintree Steck-V.

—Ohio. LC 87-26482. 48p. (gr. 3 up). 1988. 18.64 (0-86514-455-9) Raintree Steck-V.

—West Virginia. LC 87-26483. 48p. (gr. 3 up). 1988. 18.64 (0-86514-476-1) Raintree Steck-V.

—Wyoming. LC 87-16442. 48p. (gr. 3 up). 1987. 18.64 (0-86514-460-5) Raintree Steck-V.

Thompson, Kathleen, jt. auth. see Geitler, Jan.

Thompson, Kathleen, jt. auth. see Gleiter, Jan.

Thompson, Kathleen, jt. auth. see Sumption, Christine.

Thompson, Kay. Eloise. Knight, Hilary, illus. LC 55-11039. (gr. k-6). 1969. pap. 15.95 jacketed (0-671-22350-X, S&S BFYR) S&S Trade.

—Eloise. (Illus.). 66p. 1991. Repr. PLB 21.95x (0-89966-833-X) Buccaneer Bks.

—Eloise. (FRE.). 116p. (gr. 5-10). 1982. pap. 9.95 (2-07-033223-3) Schoenhof.

—Eloise in Paris. (Illus.). 66p. 1991. Repr. PLB 21.95x (0-89966-834-8) Buccaneer Bks.

—Eloise in Paris. (ps-3). 1992. pap. 16.00 (0-671-79253-9, S&S BFYR) S&S Trade.

Thompson, Kim, jt. auth. see Hilderbrand, Karen.

Thompson, Kim M. & Hilderbrand, Karen M. Addition. Kuzjak, Goran, illus. 24p. (gr. 1-4). 1993. wkbk. 9.98 (1-882331-20-6, TWIN 402) Twin Sisters.

—Addition: Twinset. Kuzjak, Goran, illus. 48p. (gr. 1-4). 1993. wkbk. 14.99 (1-882331-04-4, TWIN 300) Twin Sisters.

—Division. Kuzjak, Goran, illus. 24p. (gr. 3-6). 1993. wkbk. 9.98 (1-882331-22-2, TWIN 404) Twin Sisters.

—Division: Twinset. Kuzjak, Goran, illus. 48p. 1993. wkbk. 14.99 (1-882331-06-0, TWIN 304) Twin Sisters.

—A Little Rhythm, Rhyme & Read: Colors & Shapes. Kozjak, Goran, illus. 28p. (ps-1). 1993. Wkbk., incl. audio cass. 9.98 (1-882331-16-8) Twin Sisters. Twin Sisters Productions, Inc. is introducing the second title in their Early Childhood Education Series: A LITTLE "RHYTHM, RHYME & READ" COLORS & SHAPES. A LITTLE "RHYTHM, RHYME & READ" COLORS & SHAPES is a deluxe 28 page activity book filled with easy-to-read sheet music & lyrics for sing-along fun. The book contains developmentally appropriate activities, creative art projects, simple coloring pages, & easy-to-follow lesson plans. Children are encouraged to learn about their strengths & individuality as they complete an "I Am Special Activity." Animated characters help children remember concepts as they sing about "Sammy Sue," a friendly shark with triangular teeth & circular eyes, who loves to eat square lunch boxes! Vivid sound effects enhance the many musical genres from the jazzy "Betty Bunny" to the multicultural "All The Children Of The World." All products are teacher written & classroom tested. Call 1-800-248-TWIN to place an order or to find out about the many other fine quality Twin Sisters Productions' products. Twin Sisters Productions, Inc., 488 Graham Rd., Cuyahoga Falls, OH 44221.
Publisher Provided Annotation.

—A Little Rhythm, Rhyme & Read: Letters & Numbers. Kozjak, Goran, illus. 28p. (ps-1). 1993. Wkbk., incl. audio cass. 9.98 (*1-882331-15-X*) Twin Sisters.

Twin Sisters Productions, Inc. is introducing the first title in their Early Childhood Educational Series: A LITTLE "RHYTHM, RHYME & READ" LETTERS & NUMBERS. A LITTLE "RHYTHM, RHYME & READ" LETTERS & NUMBERS is a deluxe 28 page activity book filled with easy-to-read sheet music & lyrics for sing-along fun. The book contains developmentally appropriate activities, creative art projects, simple coloring pages, & easy-to-follow lesson plans. Children are encouraged to make letters out of pretzel dough, take an alphabet hike & learn basic addition with jelly beans. Vivid sound effects & easy-to-sing melodies make learning numerical sequences, letter names & basic addition fun. A variety of original & familiar melodies combines fun & educational learning. All products are teacher written & clasroom tested. Call 1-800-248-TWIN to place an order to find out about the many other fine quality Twin Sisters Productions' products. Twin Sisters Productions, Inc., 488 Graham Rd., Cuyahoga Falls, OH 44221.
Publisher Provided Annotation.

—Multiplication. Kuzjak, Goran, illus. 24p. (gr. 2-6). 1993. wkbk. 9.98 (*1-882331-19-2*, TWIN 401) Twin Sisters.

—Multiplication: Twinset. Kuzjak, Goran, illus. 48p. (gr. 2-6). 1993. wkbk. 14.99 (*1-882331-03-6*, TWIN 301) Twin Sisters.

—Phonics. Kuzjak, Goran, illus. 24p. (gr. k-3). 1993. wkbk. 9.98 (*1-882331-23-0*, TWIN 405) Twin Sisters.

—Phonics: Twinset. Kuzjak, Goran, illus. 64p. (gr. k-3). 1993. wkbk. 14.99 (*1-882331-07-9*, TWIN 305) Twin Sisters.

—Rhythm, Rhyme & Read: States & Capitals. Kocjak, Gordon, illus. 48p. (gr. 3-6). 1992. 6.99 (*0-9632249-5-6*); audio cass. 8.39 (*0-9632249-6-4*) Twin Sisters.

—States & Capitals. Kuzjak, Goran, illus. (gr. 2-6). 1993. wkbk. 9.98 (*1-882331-24-9*, TWIN 406) Twin Sisters.

—States & Capitals: Twinset. Kuzjak, Goran, illus. 48p. (gr. 2-6). 1993. wkbk. 14.99 (*1-882331-08-7*, TWIN 306) Twin Sisters.

—Subtraction. Kuzjak, Goran, illus. 24p. 1993. wkbk. 9.98 (*1-882331-21-4*, TWIN 403) Twin Sisters.

—Subtraction: Twinset. Kuzjak, Goran, illus. 48p. (gr. 1-4). 1993. wkbk. 14.99 (*1-882331-05-2*, TWIN 303) Twin Sisters.

Thompson, Kim M., jt. auth. see Hilderbrand, Karen M.

Thompson, Marcia, jt. auth. see Walker, Tim.

Thompson, Margurite. Martin Luther King Jr. A Story For Children. 24p. (gr. k-3). 1983. 3.00 (*0-912444-25-8*) DARE Bks.

Thompson, Mary. My Brother, Matthew. Thompson, Mary, illus. LC 92-9858. 28p. (gr. k-6). 1992. 14.95 (*0-933149-47-6*) Woodbine House.

Thompson, Mary, jt. auth. see Campbell, Richard.

Thompson, Maurice. The Witchery of Archery. Elmer, Robert, ed. St. Charles, Glenn, frwd. by. (Illus.). 258p. (gr. 10 up). 1992. Repr. of 1878 ed. 39.95 (*1-56416-089-0*) Derrydale Pr.

Thompson, Merita L. & Strange, Johanna. Discover: Skills for Life, Level K: Pupil Edition. (Illus.). 48p. (gr. k). 1991. text ed. 10.60 (*0-942277-00-7*) Educ Assess Pub.

—Discover: Skills for Life, Level K: Spanish Home Worksheets. (SPA., Illus.). 7p. (gr. k). 1991. text ed. 7.55 (*0-942277-56-2*) Educ Assess Pub.

—Discover: Skills for Life, Level K: Student Edition Big Book. (Illus.). 48p. (gr. k). 1991. text ed. 76.95 (*0-942277-88-0*) Educ Assess Pub.

—Discover: Skills for Life, Level 1: Pupil Book. (Illus.). 48p. (gr. 1). 1991. text ed. 10.60 (*0-942277-04-X*) Educ Assess Pub.

—Discover: Skills for Life, Level 1: Spanish Home Worksheets. (SPA., Illus.). 7p. (gr. 1). 1991. text ed. 7.55 (*0-942277-81-3*) Educ Assess Pub.

—Discover: Skills for Life, Level 1: Student Edition Big Book. (Illus.). 64p. (gr. 1). 1991. text ed. 76.95 (*0-942277-43-0*) Educ Assess Pub.

—Discover: Skills for Life, Level 2: Spanish Home Worksheet. (SPA., Illus.). 7p. (gr. 2). 1991. text ed. 7.55 (*0-942277-82-1*) Educ Assess Pub.

—Discover: Skills for Life, Level 2: Student Book. (Illus.). 64p. (gr. 2). 1991. text ed. 10.60 (*0-942277-08-2*) Educ Assess Pub.

—Discover: Skills for Life, Level 3: Spanish Home Worksheet. (SPA., Illus.). 7p. (gr. 3). 1991. text ed. 7.55 (*0-942277-83-X*) Educ Assess Pub.

—Discover: Skills for Life, Level 3: Student Book. (Illus.). 80p. (gr. 3). 1991. text ed. 11.45 (*0-942277-12-0*) Educ Assess Pub.

—Discover: Skills for Life, Level 4: Spanish Home Worksheets. (SPA., Illus.). 7p. (gr. 4). 1991. text ed. 7.55 (*0-942277-84-8*) Educ Assess Pub.

—Discover: Skills for Life, Level 4: Student Book. (Illus.). 80p. (gr. 4). 1991. text ed. 11.45 (*0-942277-16-3*) Educ Assess Pub.

—Discover: Skills for Life, Level 5: Spanish Home Worksheets. (SPA., Illus.). 7p. (gr. 5). 1991. text ed. 7.55 (*0-942277-85-6*) Educ Assess Pub.

—Discover: Skills for Life, Level 5: Student Book. (Illus.). 128p. (gr. 5). 1991. text ed. 12.65 (*0-942277-20-1*) Educ Assess Pub.

—Discover: Skills for Life, Level 6: Spanish Home Worksheets. (SPA., Illus.). 7p. (gr. 6). 1991. text ed. 7.55 (*0-942277-86-4*) Educ Assess Pub.

—Discover: Skills for Life, Level 6: Student Book. (Illus.). 144p. (gr. 6). 1991. text ed. 13.65 (*0-942277-24-4*) Educ Assess Pub.

—Discover: Skills for Life, Level 7: Student Book. (Illus.). 240p. (gr. 7). 1991. text ed. 16.60 (*0-942277-28-7*) Educ Assess Pub.

—Skills for Life. (Illus.). 168p. (gr. 6). 1991. tchr's. ed. 34.18 (*0-942277-25-2*) Educ Assess Pub.

Thompson, Pat. My Friend Mr. Morris. (gr. k-6). 1988. pap. 2.50 (*0-440-40061-9*) Dell.

Thompson, Paul B. & Carter, Tonya R. Darkness & Light. LC 88-51718. (Illus.). 352p. (Orig.). 1989. pap. 4.95 (*0-88038-722-X*) TSR Inc.

Thompson, R. Draw - & - Tell. Thompson, Richard, illus. 88p. 1988. 19.95 (*1-55037-032-4*, Pub. by Annick CN) Firefly Bks Ltd.

—Foo. (Illus.). 24p. (ps-8). 1988. 12.95 (*1-55037-005-7*, Pub. by Annick CN); pap. 4.95 (*1-55037-004-9*, Pub. by Annick CN) Firefly Bks Ltd.

—Gurgle Bubble Splash. (Illus.). 24p. (ps-8). 1989. 12.95 (*1-55037-029-4*, Pub. by Annick CN); pap. 4.95 (*1-55037-028-6*, Pub. by Annick CN) Firefly Bks Ltd.

—I Have to See This! (Illus.). 24p. (ps-8). 1988. 12.95 (*1-55037-015-4*, Pub. by Annick CN); pap. 4.95 (*1-55037-014-6*, Pub. by Annick CN) Firefly Bks Ltd.

—Jenny's Neighbours. (Illus.). 24p. (ps-8). 1987. 12.95 (*0-920303-73-0*, Pub. by Annick CN); pap. 4.95 (*0-920303-70-6*, Pub. by Annick CN) Firefly Bks Ltd.

—Sky Full of Babies. (Illus.). 24p. (ps-8). 1987. 12.95 (*0-920303-93-5*, Pub. by Annick CN); pap. 4.95 (*0-920303-92-7*, Pub. by Annick CN) Firefly Bks Ltd.

—Zoe & the Mysterious X. (Illus.). 24p. (ps-8). 1989. 14.95 (*1-55037-081-2*, Pub. by Annick CN); pap. 5.95 (*1-55037-080-4*, Pub. by Annick CN) Firefly Bks Ltd.

Thompson, R. W., Jr. The Christmas Eve Tradition. Keitz, Roderick K., illus. 16p. (ps-3). 1993. PLB 8.95 (*0-9636442-1-1*) N Pole Chron.

Thompson, Richard. Don't Be Scared, Eleven. Fernandes, Eugenie, illus. 24p. 1993. lib. bdg. 14.95 (*1-55037-286-6*, Pub. by Annick CN); pap. 4.95 (*1-55037-287-4*, Pub. by Annick CN) Firefly Bks Ltd.

—Effie's Bath. Fernandes, Eugenie, illus. 1990. 14.95 (*1-550370-55-3*, Pub. by Annick CN); pap. 5.95 (*1-550370-52-9*, Pub. by Annick CN) Firefly Bks Ltd.

—Frog's Riddle: And Other Draw-&-Tell Stories. Thompson, Richard, illus. 96p. 1990. 19.95 (*1-55037-138-X*, Pub. by Annick CN) Firefly Bks Ltd.

—Jesse on the Night Train. Fernandes, Eugenie, illus. 32p. (ps-2). 1990. 12.95 (*1-55037-093-6*, Pub. by Annick CN); pap. 4.95 (*1-55037-094-4*, Pub. by Annick CN) Firefly Bks Ltd.

—Jill & the Jogero. Durham-Moulin, Francoise, illus. 24p. (ps-2). 1992. PLB 14.95 (*1-55037-245-9*, Pub. by Annick Pr); pap. 4.95 (*1-55037-246-7*, Pub. by Annick Pr) Firefly Bks Ltd.

—Maggee & the Lake Minder. Fernandes, Eugenie, illus. 32p. (gr. k-3). 1991. PLB 14.95 (*1-55037-154-1*, Pub. by Annick CN); pap. 4.95 (*1-55037-152-5*, Pub. by Annick CN) Firefly Bks Ltd.

—Tell Me One Good Thing: Bedtime Stories. Fernandes, Eugenie, illus. 48p. (ps-3). 1992. PLB 15.95 (*1-55037-215-7*, Pub. by Annick CN); pap. 7.95 (*1-55037-212-2*, Pub. by Annick CN) Firefly Bks Ltd.

Thompson, Richard W. The First Star: The Pearl Harbor Attack Comes Alive. 80p. (gr. 10-12). 1991. pap. text ed. 9.95 (*0-9631097-0-7*) Barriclyn.

Thompson, Roy J. C. Wings of the Canadian Armed Forces 1913-1992. rev. ed. Thompson, Roy J. C., ed. Braham, Bob, intro. by. (Illus.). 200p. 1992. pap. text ed. 17.95 (*1-878973-04-5*) Hse History.

Thompson, Sharon E. The Greenhouse Effect. LC 92-27848. (Illus.). 112p. (gr. 5-8). 1992. PLB 14.95 (*1-56006-133-2*) Lucent Bks.

Thompson, Stith, ed. One Hundred Favorite Folktales. LC 68-27355. (Illus.). 456p. 1968. 29.95 (*0-253-15940-7*); pap. 12.95x (*0-253-20172-1*, MB-172) Ind U Pr.

Thompson, Susan C. Natural Materials: Creative Activities for Children. (Illus.). 200p. (Orig.). (ps-5). 1992. pap. 13.95 (*0-673-36033-4*) GdYrBks.

Thompson, Terri. Biz Kids Guide to Success: Money-Making Ideas for Young Entrepreneurs. (Illus.). 96p. (gr. 3 up). 1992. pap. 4.95 (*0-8120-4831-8*) Barron.

Thompson, Timothy J. Figs & Nuts. Thompson, Timothy J., illus. LC 80-83134. 15p. (Orig.). (ps-1). 1980. pap. text ed. 3.50 (*0-915676-03-6*) Ed Sys Pub.

—Ten Red Rods. Thompson, Timothy J., illus. LC 80-83135. 16p. (Orig.). (ps-1). 1980. pap. text ed. 3.50 (*0-915676-02-8*) Ed Sys Pub.

Thompson, Valerie, jt. auth. see Cohen, Judith L.

Thompson, Vivian L. Aukele the Fearless. Tepper, Elly, illus. LC 92-6126. 80p. (Orig.). (gr. k-5). 1992. pap. 9.95 (*0-8248-1445-2*) UH Pr.

—Hawaiian Legends of Tricksters & Riddlers. Wozniak, Patricia A., illus. LC 90-44432. 112p. (Orig.). (gr. 4-8). 1990. pap. 8.50 (*0-8248-1302-2*, Kolowalu Bk) UH Pr.

—Hawaiian Myths of Earth, Sea, & Sky. Kahalewai, Marilyn, illus. LC 88-1325. 88p. (gr. 3-8). 1988. pap. 8.50 (*0-8248-1171-2*, Kolowalu Bk) UH Pr.

—Kawelo, Roving Chief. Wozniak, Patricia A., illus. LC 91-13651. 96p. (gr. 4-6). 1991. 14.95 (*0-8248-1339-1*, Kolowalu Bk) UH Pr.

Thompson, Wendy. Claude Debussy. (Illus.). 48p. (gr. 5 up). 1993. 17.99 (*0-670-84482-9*) Viking Child Bks.

—Franz Schubert. 1991. pap. 17.95 (*0-670-84172-2*) Viking Child Bks.

—Joseph Haydn. 1991. 17.95 (*0-670-84171-4*) Viking Child Bks.

—Ludwig Van Beethoven. (Illus.). 48p. (gr. 7up). 1991. 17.95 (*0-670-83678-8*) Viking Child Bks.

—Pyotr Ilyich Tchaikovsky. (Illus.). 48p. (gr. 5 up). 1993. 17.99 (*0-670-84476-4*) Viking Child Bks.

—Wolfgang Amadeus Mozart. (Illus.). 48p. (gr. 7up). 1991. 17.95 (*0-670-83679-6*) Viking Child Bks.

Thompson-Hoffman, Susan. Delver's Danger. Chapin, Tom, narrated by. Buzzanco, Eileen M., illus. LC 88-64152. 32p. (gr. k-4). 1989. 11.95 (*0-924483-02-4*); incl. audiocassette 16.95 (*0-924483-05-9*); incl. audiocassette & toy combination 39.95 (*0-924483-08-3*); audiocassette and small toy combination 25.95_incl. (*0-924483-36-9*); write for info. audiocassette (*0-924483-11-3*) Soundprints.

—Little Porcupine's Winter Den. Thomas, Peter, narrated by. Haberstock, Jennifer, illus. 32p. (ps-3). 1992. 11.95 (*0-924483-64-4*); incl. audiocass. tape 16.95 (*0-924483-63-6*); incl. audiocass. tape & 9" stuffed porcupine toy 39.95 (*0-924483-62-8*); incl. audiocass. tape & 7 inch stuffed porcupine toy 25.95 (*0-924483-71-7*); pap. 5.95 (*0-924483-76-8*); write for info. audiocass. tape (*0-924483-73-3*) Soundprints.

—Tassel's Mission. Chapin, Tom, narrated by. Buzzanco, Eileen M., illus. LC 88-64151. 32p. (gr. k-4). 1989. 11.95 (*0-924483-00-8*); incl. audiocassette 16.95 (*0-924483-03-2*); incl. audiocassette & toy combination 39.95 (*0-924483-06-7*); incl. audiocassette & small toy combination 25.95 (*0-924483-41-5*); write for info. audiocassette (*0-924483-09-1*) Soundprints.

Thompson-Peters, Flossie E. Daniel Hale Williams: Surgeon. Wilson, Lillian, illus. 32p. (Orig.). (gr. 3-9). 1988. pap. 4.70 (*1-880784-05-X*) Atlas Pr.

—Dynamic Black Americans. Green, Kenneth L., illus. 32p. (gr. 1-8). 1988. pap. 4.70 (*1-880784-07-6*) Atlas Pr. DYNAMIC BLACK AMERICANS, a biographical series, is written by Flossie E. Thompson-Peters in lilting, rhythmic verse. Young readers find these books exciting as well as informative. Ideal as core literature, choral reading, dramatizations & read aloud books. JAN, THE SHOEMAN, Jan Matzeliger (inventor), BENJAMIN BANNEKER, 3rd ed. (1994) (pioneer urban planner), JEAN BAPTISTE DuSABLE (founder of Chicago), New Spanish edition available 2/94, MALCOLM X, HARRIET TUBMAN (freedom fighter & Civil War heroine), & DANIEL HALE WILLIAMS (first successful open heart surgeon). Ages 7-14, Appropriate for elementary grades & selected secondary & ESL students. DYNAMIC BLACK AMERICAN SERIES. ISBN 1-880784-07-6. $4.70 per copy. $23.50 for series (5 books). Paperback. THE SHEPHERD, A BIOGRAPHY of Dr. Arthur A. Peters, by Flossie Thompson-Peters, is about a community activist, civil rights leader & Los Angeles minister who started a church in 1943 & became a great influence in the civic, spiritual & political life of the African-American community of Los Angeles. "The book is of historical significance & is of more than local interest."--L.A. Times

Book Review. Photographs. General interest. Hardcover, 251 pages. $10.00. ISBN 1-880784-00-9. MARTIN LUTHER KING, JR. is a biography by Flossie Thompson-Peters in poetic, rhythmic style. Thhe life of Dr. King is chronicled from childhood, through trials & triumphs, to his tragic end, with emphasis upon his lasting influence. Ages 8 to adult. 94 pages. $7.50 ISBN 1-880784-06-8. Atlas Press, P.O. Box 56282. Jesse J. Peters, President. Los Angeles, CA 90008. (213) 295-3036.
Publisher Provided Annotation.

—El-Hajj Malik El-Shabazz: The Biography of Malcolm X. Behrens, Debra J. & Jeffery, Lisa E., eds. Green, Kenneth L., illus. 65p. (Orig.). (gr. 4-12). 1994. pap. 8.00 (*1-880784-08-4*) Atlas Pr.
—Harriet Tubman: Freedom Fighter. Wilson, Lillian M., illus. 32p. (Orig.). (gr. 3-9). 1988. pap. 4.70 (*1-880784-04-1*) Atlas Pr.
—La Historia De Jean Baptiste DuSable: El Padre De Chicago. Nolasco-Carrandi, Guadalupe, tr. from ENG. Clo, Kathy, illus. (SPA.). 32p. (gr. 3-8). 1994. pap. 4.70 (*1-880784-09-2*) Atlas Pr.
—Jan, the Shoeman: The Story of Jan Matzeliger. Clo, Kathy, illus. 32p. (Orig.). (gr. 3-9). 1985. pap. text ed. 4.70 (*1-880784-01-7*) Atlas Pr.
—Martin Luther King, Jr. Green, Ken, illus. Behrens, Debra J. & Jeffery, Lisa E., eds. (Illus.). 94p. (Orig.). (gr. 3-9). 1992. pap. 7.50 (*1-880784-06-8*) Atlas Pr.
—The Story of Benjamin Banneker. Clo, Kathy, illus. 32p. (Orig.). (gr. 1-6). 1986. pap. text ed. 4.70 (*1-880784-02-5*) Atlas Pr.
—The Story of Jean Baptiste DuSable: Father of Chicago. Clo, Kathy, illus. 32p. (Orig.). (gr. 3-9). 1986. pap. text ed. 4.70 (*1-880784-03-3*) Atlas Pr.
Thoms, Judith J., jt. auth. see Pasamanick, Judith.
Thomsen, Steve. The Great Pyramid of Cheops. 48p. (gr. 3-4). 1991. PLB 11.95 (*1-56065-024-9*) Capstone Pr.
—The White House. 48p. (gr. 3-4). 1991. PLB 11.95 (*1-56065-025-7*) Capstone Pr.
Thomson, Andy. Renegade in the Hills. Moore, Rebecca, ed. True, Stephanie, illus. 135p. (Orig.). (gr. 5-8). 1989. pap. 4.95 (*0-89084-494-1*) Bob Jones Univ Pr.
—Sheriff at Waterstop. (Illus.). 133p. (Orig.). (gr. 4-6). 1987. pap. 4.95 (*0-89084-371-6*) Bob Jones Univ Pr.
Thomson, Arthur. Handbook of Anatomy for Art Students. 5th ed. (Illus.). (gr. 9-12). 1929. pap. text ed. 9.95 (*0-486-21163-0*) Dover.
Thomson, Clarence. The Little Pine Tree's Christmas Dream. Laughlin, Denise D., illus. LC 93-5301. 32p. (Orig.). (gr. 1-6). 1993. pap. 4.95 (*0-8091-6614-3*) Paulist Pr.
Thomson, H. E. The Tour of the Forest Bike Race: A Guide to Bicycle Racing & the Tour de France. LC 90-80062. (Illus.). 64p. (Orig.). (gr. 5 up). 1990. 9.95 (*0-933201-35-4*) Bicycle Books.
Thomson, Neil, jt. auth. see Thomson, Ruth.
Thomson, Pat. Best Pest. (Illus.). 28p. (gr. 1-4). 1990. 13.95 (*0-575-04573-6*, Pub. by Gollancz UK) Trafalgar.
—Best Pest. Firmin, Peter, illus. 32p. (ps-1). 1993. pap. 6.95 (*0-575-05156-6*, Pub. by Gollancz UK) Trafalgar.
—Best Thing of All. Chamberlain, Margaret, illus. 32p. (gr. 1-4). 1990. 13.95 (*0-575-04578-7*, Pub. by Gollancz UK) Trafalgar.
—The Best Thing of All. Chamberlain, Margaret, illus. 32p. (ps-1). 1993. pap. 6.95 (*0-575-05159-0*, Pub. by Gollancz UK) Trafalgar.
—Beware of the Aunts! Clark, Emma C., illus. LC 90-28928. 32p. (gr. k-3). 1992. SBE 14.95 (*0-689-50538-8*, M K McElderry) Macmillan Child Grp.
—Can You Hear Me, Grandad? Alborough, Jez, illus. 32p. (gr. k-2). 1988. pap. 8.95 (*0-385-29599-5*) Delacorte.
—Can You Hear Me, Grandad? (gr. k-2). 1988. pap. 2.50 (*0-440-40025-2*, YB) Dell.
—Dial D for Disaster. Demeyer, Paul, illus. 32p. (gr. 1-4). 1990. 13.95 (*0-575-04572-8*, Pub. by Gollancz UK) Trafalgar.
—Good Girl Granny. (gr. k-6). 1988. pap. 2.50 (*0-440-40026-0*, YB) Dell.
—No Trouble at All. Wild, Jocelyn, illus. 28p. (gr. 1-4). 1990. 13.95 (*0-575-04577-9*, Pub. by Gollancz UK) Trafalgar.
—One of Those Days. (gr. k-6). 1987. pap. 2.50 (*0-440-46646-6*, YB) Dell.
—Thank You for the Tadpole. (gr. k-6). 1988. pap. 2.50 (*0-440-40027-9*, YB) Dell.
Thomson, Pat & Ross, Tony. The Treasure Sock. (Orig.). (gr. k-6). 1987. pap. 2.50 (*0-440-48814-1*, YB) Dell.
Thomson, Peggy. Auks, Rocks & the Odd Dinosaur: Inside Stories from the Smithsonian's Museum of Natural History. LC 85-47744. (Illus.). 128p. (gr. 3-7). 1985. PLB 14.89 (*0-690-04492-5*, Crowell Jr Bks) HarpC Child Bks.
—City Kids in China. Conklin, Paul, illus. LC 90-1993. 128p. (gr. 3-7). 1991. 14.95 (*0-06-021654-9*) HarpC Child Bks.

—Keepers & Creatures at the National Zoo. Conklin, Paul S., photos by. LC 87-47697. (Illus.). (gr. 3-7). 1988. 13.95 (*0-690-04710-X*, Crowell Jr Bks); PLB 13.89 (*0-690-04712-6*, Crowell Jr Bks) HarpC Child Bks.
—The King Has Horse's Ears. Small, David, illus. (gr. 2 up). 1988. pap. 12.95 (*0-671-64953-1*, S&S BFYR) S&S Trade.
—Siggy's Spaghetti Works. Kamen, Gloria, illus. LC 92-13186. 32p. (gr. 1 up). 1993. 14.00 (*0-688-11373-7*, Tambourine Bks); PLB 13.93 (*0-688-11374-5*, Tambourine Bks) Morrow.
Thomson, Peggy, retold by. The Brave Little Tailor. Warhola, James, illus. LC 91-20982. 48p. (ps-3). 1992. pap. 15.00 jacketed, 3-pc. bdg. (*0-671-73736-8*, S&S BFYR) S&S Trade.
Thomson, Ruth. Autumn. LC 89-5841. (Illus.). 32p. (gr. k-4). 1989. PLB 11.90 (*0-531-10732-9*) Watts.
—Aztecs. LC 92-14747. 1993. 11.90 (*0-531-14245-0*) Watts.
—Creepy Crawlies. Mansell, Dom, illus. LC 91-7482. 32p. (gr. k-3). 1991. pap. 5.95 (*0-689-71489-0*, Aladdin) Macmillan Child Grp.
—Eyes. FS Smart, ed. Galletly, Mike, illus. 32p. (gr. 1-3). 1988. PLB 10.90 (*0-531-10549-0*) Watts.
—In the Post. (Illus.). 32p. (gr. 3-6). 1992. 12.95 (*0-7136-3184-8*, Pub. by A&C Black UK) Talman.
—Indians of the Plains. (Illus.). 32p. (gr. k-4). 1991. PLB 11.90 (*0-531-14157-8*) Watts.
—Our Arctic Project. (Illus.). 25p. (gr. 2-4). 1991. 13.95 (*0-237-60150-8*, Pub. by Evans Bros Ltd) Trafalgar.
—Rice. Stefoff, Rebecca, ed. Das, Prodeepta, photos by. LC 90-40367. 32p. (gr. 3-5). 1990. PLB 15.93 (*0-944483-71-2*) Garrett Ed Corp.
—Spring. 1990. PLB 11.90 (*0-531-14018-0*) Watts.
—Summer. 1990. PLB 11.90 (*0-531-14019-9*) Watts.
—Washday. (Illus.). 32p. (gr. 3-6). 1992. 12.95 (*0-7136-3183-X*, Pub. by A&C Black UK) Talman.
—Winter. LC 89-5830. (Illus.). 32p. (gr. k-4). 1989. PLB 11.90 (*0-531-10733-7*) Watts.
Thomson, Ruth & Thomson, Neil. A Family in Thailand. (Illus.). 32p. (gr. 2-5). 1988. lib. bdg. 13.50 (*0-8225-1684-5*) Lerner Pubns.
Thorburn, James W. Murder at Sun Valley. Witte, Sue, illus. LC 86-50305. 304p. (Orig.). (gr. 6). 1986. 8.99 (*0-938191-00-4*) Woodside Pr ID.
Thoreau, Henry David. Walden. Langmack, F., intro. by. Bd. with On Civil Disobedience. (gr. 10 up). pap. 1.50 (*0-8049-0083-3*, CL-83) Airmont.
—Walden. Sherman, Paul, ed. Bd. with Civil Disobedience. LC 60-16148. (gr. 9 up). 1960. pap. 9.16 (*0-395-05113-4*, RivEd) HM.
—Walden. Lowe, Steve, ed. Sabuda, Robert, illus. 32p. 1990. 14.95 (*0-399-22153-0*, Philomel Bks) Putnam Pub Group.
Thorliefson, Alex. Ethel Barrymore. Horner, Matina, intro. by. (Illus.). 112p. (gr. 5 up). 1991. lib. bdg. 17.95 (*1-55546-640-0*) Chelsea Hse.
Thorn, Ian. Frankenstein Meets Wolfman. LC 81-9902. (Illus.). 48p. (gr. 3 up). 1981. RSBE 11.95 (*0-89686-188-0*, Crestwood Hse) Macmillan Child Grp.
Thorndike & Barnhart. Scott, Foresman Beginning Dictionary, 5 vols. large type ed. 1500p. (gr. 3-6). 1979. 349.00 (*0-317-01932-5*, J-22690-00) Am Printing Hse.
Thorne, Ian. The Blob. LC 81-19633. (Illus.). 48p. (gr. 4-8). 1982. RSBE 11.95 (*0-89686-212-7*, Crestwood Hse) Macmillan Child Grp.
—Creature from the Black Lagoon. LC 81-12468. (Illus.). 48p. (Orig.). (gr. 3-5). 1981. RSBE 11.95 (*0-89686-187-2*, Crestwood Hse) Macmillan Child Grp.
—The Deadly Mantis. LC 81-22074. (Illus.). 48p. (gr. 3 up). 1982. RSBE 11.95 (*0-89686-214-3*, Crestwood Hse) Macmillan Child Grp.
—Dracula. LC 76-51145. (Illus.). 48p. (gr. 3 up). 1977. RSBE 11.95 (*0-913940-67-4*, Crestwood Hse) Macmillan Child Grp.
—Frankenstein. LC 76-51144. (Illus.). 48p. (gr. 3 up). 1977. RSBE 11.95 (*0-913940-66-6*, Crestwood Hse); cass. 7.95 (*0-685-01269-7*) Macmillan Child Grp.
—Godzilla. LC 76-51148. (Illus.). 48p. (gr. 3 up). 1989. RSBE 11.95 (*0-913940-68-2*, Crestwood Hse); cass. 7.95 (*0-89686-486-3*) Macmillan Child Grp.
—It Came from Outer Space. LC 81-1419. (Illus.). 48p. (gr. 3 up). 1982. RSBE 11.95 (*0-89686-213-5*, Crestwood Hse) Macmillan Child Grp.
—King Kong. LC 76-51147. (Illus.). 48p. (gr. 3 up). 1977. RSBE 10.95 (*0-913940-69-0*, Crestwood Hse) Macmillan Child Grp.
—Mad Scientists. LC 76-51149. (Illus.). 48p. (gr. 3 up). 1989. RSBE 11.95 (*0-913940-70-4*, Crestwood Hse) Macmillan Child Grp.
—The Mummy. LC 81-12481. (Illus.). 48p. (gr. 3 up). 1981. RSBE 11.95 (*0-89686-186-4*, Crestwood Hse) Macmillan Child Grp.
—The Wolf Man. LC 76-51146. (Illus.). 48p. (gr. 3 up). 1989. RSBE 10.95 (*0-913940-71-2*, Crestwood Hse); cass. 7.95 (*0-89686-488-X*) Macmillan Child Grp.
Thorne, Kate, ed. see Walley, Deborah.
Thorne, Patrice, tr. see Georgiady, Nicholas P. & Romano, Louis G.
Thorne, Randy. Book Report Poster Pack. (Illus.). 15p. (gr. 2-5). 1993. text ed. 8.95 (*0-933606-90-7*) E Sussman Educ.

—Book Report Poster Party. Cathleen, Mella, illus. Sussman, Ellen, intro. by. (Illus.). 12p. (Orig.). (gr. 3-6). 1989. text ed. 6.95 (*0-933606-73-7*) E Sussman Educ.
—Quick & Short Book Reports. Sussman, Ellen, intro. by. (Illus.). 56p. (gr. 3-5). 1990. pap. 6.95 (*0-933606-86-9*, MS-690) E Sussman Educ.
Thorne-Thomsen, Kathleen. Frank Lloyd Wright for Kids. 1994. 14.95 (*1-55652-207-X*) Chicago Review.
Thornhill, Jan. A Tree in a Forest. LC 91-25857. (Illus.). 40p. (ps-3). 1992. pap. 15.00 (*0-671-75901-9*, S&S BFYR) S&S Trade.
—Wild Life ABC: A Natural Alphabet Book. LC 89-19711. (ps-3). 1994. pap. 5.95 (*0-671-88614-2*, Half Moon Bks) S&S Trade.
—Wild Life 123: A Nature Counting Book. LC 89-5970. (ps-3). 1994. pap. 5.95 (*0-671-88613-4*, Half Moon BKs) S&S Trade.
—Wildlife ABC: A Nature Alphabet Book. LC 89-19711. (ps-3). 1990. pap. 14.95 (*0-671-67925-2*, S&S BFYR) S&S Trade.
—The Wildlife 1-2-3: A Nature Counting Book. LC 89-5970. (Illus.). (ps-2). 1989. pap. 14.95 (*0-671-67926-0*, S&S BFYR) S&S Trade.
Thornhill, Jan, retold by. & illus. Animal Legends. LC 93-20205. (gr. 1-3). 1993. pap. 15.00 (*0-671-87428-4*, S&S BFYR) S&S Trade.
Thornley, G. C., ed. Stories from Many Lands. (Illus.). 133p. (Orig.). 1964. pap. text ed. 4.46 (*0-582-53025-3*) Longman.
Thornley, Stew. Cal Ripken, Jr: Oriole Ironman. (gr. 4-7). 1992. pap. 4.95 (*0-8225-9624-5*) Lerner Pubns.
—Cal Ripken, Jr. Oriole Ironman. (gr. 4-7). 1992. 13.50 (*0-8225-0547-9*) Lerner Pubns.
—Deion Sanders: Prime Time Player. LC 92-45686. 1993. 13.50 (*0-8225-0523-1*) Lerner Pubns.
—Deion Sanders: Prime Time Player. (gr. 4-7). 1993. pap. 4.95 (*0-8225-9648-2*) Lerner Pubns.
Thornton, Christine. Crosswords for Spelling. (gr. 4-6). 1985. pap. 8.95 (*0-8224-2354-5*) Fearon Teach Aids.
Thornton, Don, ed. & intro. by. Whiffle. (Illus.). 52p. (gr. 4-8). 1986. pap. write for info. (*0-933727-02-X*) Cajun Pubs.
Thornton, Don, intro. by see Louisiana School Students.
Thornton, Don, intro. by see Simmons, Aaron.
Thornton, Don, intro. by see Zeringue, Dona.
Thorp, Kate, jt. auth. see Chippindale, Jenny.
Thorpe, Jean J. Kirtpatrick's Kritters. Thorpe, Jean J., illus. 50p. (gr. k-6). 1988. pap. 7.95 (*0-317-93347-7*) Art & Earth.
Thorsland, Dan, ed. see Starlin, Jim.
Thrash, Jacquelyn R. Big Precious Patty Pride. 1992. pap. 12.95 (*0-9635247-6-3*) Three Pines.
—Brody Bates' Choice. 298p. 1992. 21.95 (*0-9635247-0-4*); pap. write for info. (*0-9635247-1-2*) Three Pines.
—The Chubby Cheek Dilemma. 1992. pap. 14.95 (*0-9635247-5-5*) Three Pines.
—Echoes in Detention. 1992. write for info. (*0-9635247-8-X*) Three Pines.
—Final Battleground. 1992. 22.95 (*0-9635247-9-8*) Three Pines.
—For Better, for Worse. 1992. 22.95 (*0-9635247-3-9*) Three Pines.
—Heart o' Desire. 1992. write for info. (*0-9635247-2-0*) Three Pines.
—Love Goes Round. 1992. pap. 14.95 (*0-9635247-4-7*) Three Pines.
Threadgall, Colin. Dinosaur Fright. Threadgall, Colin, illus. LC 91-40049. 32p. (ps up). 1993. 15.00 (*0-688-11733-3*, Tambourine Bks); PLB 14.93 (*0-688-11734-1*, Tambourine Bks) Morrow.
—Proud Rooster & the Fox. LC 91-15004. (Illus.). 32p. (ps-3). 1992. 14.00 (*0-688-11123-8*, Tambourine Bks); PLB 13.93 (*0-688-11124-6*, Tambourine Bks) Morrow.
Thro, Ellen. Genetic Engineering. (Illus.). 128p. (gr. 7 up). 1993. PLB 17.95x (*0-8160-2629-7*) Facts on File.
—Robotics. (Illus.). 128p. (gr. 7 up). 1993. PLB 17.95x (*0-8160-2628-9*) Facts on File.
—Taking a Stand Against Nuclear War. LC 89-24979. 1990. PLB 14.40 (*0-531-10922-4*) Watts.
—Volcanoes of the United States. LC 91-36002. (Illus.). 112p. (gr. 9-12). 1992. PLB 13.90 (*0-531-12522-X*) Watts.
Throssel, Richard. Blue Thunder. 32p. (gr. 6-12). 1976. 1.75 (*0-89992-046-2*) Coun India Ed.
Thrush, Robin A., ed. The Gray Whales Are Missing. De Groat, Diane, illus. LC 87-17822. 113p. (gr. 3-7). 1987. 14.95 (*0-15-200455-6*, Gulliver Bks) HarBrace.
Thum, Robert & Dworski, Susan. My Jewish World. (Illus., Orig.). (gr. 3-4). 1989. pap. text ed. 7.95 (*0-87441-478-4*); tchr's guide 14.95 (*0-87441-489-X*) Behrman.
Thumhart, Suzanne. Colorado Wonders. Ayer, Eleanor H., ed. Kline, Jane, illus. 48p. (gr. 4-7). 1986. pap. 6.95x (*0-939650-16-9*) R H Pub.
Thumhart, Suzanne, compiled by. Colorado Businesses. Kline, Jane, illus. 48p. (gr. 4-7). 1984. 11.95x (*0-939650-21-5*) R H Pub.
Thunander, Rudolf, ed. Deutsches Allerlei: Advanced Beginning Through Intermediate. 96p. 1994. pap. 4.95 (*0-685-62829-9*, F2291-7, Natl Textbk) NTC Pub Grp.
Thurber, Donald N. D'Nealian Handwriting ABC Book: Manuscript. (Illus.). 64p. (Orig.). (gr. k-2). 1992. pap. 6.95 (*0-673-36020-2*) GdYrBks.
—D'Nealian Handwriting Big Book of Letters. (Illus.). 32p. (Orig.). (ps-2). 1992. pap. 21.95 (*0-673-36021-0*) GdYrBks.

—D'Nealian Handwriting Cursive ABC Book. (Illus.). 64p. (Orig.). (gr. 2-4). 1993. pap. 6.95 (0-673-36022-9) GdYrBks.
Thurber, James. Many Moons. Slobodkin, Louis, illus. LC 43-51250. (gr. 3-7). 1943. 14.95 (0-15-251873-8, HB Juv Bks) HarBrace.
—Many Moons. Slobodkin, Louis, illus. LC 43-51250. 46p. (gr. 3-7). 1973. pap. 5.95 (0-15-656980-9, Voyager Bks) HarBrace.
—Many Moons. Simont, Marac, illus. LC 89-36465. 48p. (gr. 3-7). 1990. (0-15-251872-X) HarBrace.
—The Secret Life of Walter Mitty. LC 83-71786. 32p. (gr. 4 up). 1983. PLB 13.95s.p. (0-87191-961-3) Creative Ed.
—Thirteen Clocks. (gr. 4-7). 1992. pap. 3.50 (0-440-40582-3, YB) Dell.
—Wonderful O. (gr. 4-7). 1992. pap. 3.50 (0-440-40579-3, Pub. by Yearling Classics) Dell.
Thurber, James G. The Night the Ghost Got In. LC 83-71785. 32p. (gr. 4 up). 1983. PLB 13.95s.p. (0-87191-960-5) Creative Ed.
Thureen, Faythe D. Jenna's Big Jump. Sandeen, Eileen, illus. 112p. (gr. 2-5). 1993. SBE 12.95 (0-689-31834-0, Atheneum Child Bk) Macmillan Child Grp.
Thurman, Jim, jt. auth. see Connell, David D.
Thurman, Joann M., ed. Sixth Grade Was a Nightmare, & Seventh Is Worse. Costner, Howard, illus. Gangwer, Timothy, intro. by. (Illus.). 128p. (gr. 3-9). 1993. 11.95 (0-89896-335-4); pap. 7.95 (0-89896-336-2) Larksdale.
Thurman, Wallace. Blacker the Berry. Larson, Charles R., ed. O'Daniel, Thurman B., illus. (gr. 11 up). 1970. pap. 7.00 (0-02-054750-1, Collier Young Ad) Macmillan Child Grp.
Thuro, Barbara. A Bilingual Dictionary of School Terminology: English-Spanish. rev. ed. LC 85-70097. 110p. (Orig.). (ps-12). 1985. pap. 14.95 (0-932825-00-1) Ammie Enter.
—Reporting to Parents in English & Spanish. LC 89-86000. 150p. (Orig.). (ps-12). 1990. pap. 14.95 (0-932825-03-6) Ammie Enter.
—Spanish for the School Nurse's Office: English-Spanish. LC 85-70256. (Orig.). (ps-12). 1991. pap. 14.95 (0-932825-02-8) Ammie Enter.
Thurston, Cheryl M. Cottonwood Composition Book. 62p. (Orig.). (gr. 5-12). 1986. pap. text ed. 14.95 (1-877673-00-5) Cottonwood Pr.
—Cottonwood Game Book. 58p. (Orig.). (gr. 5-12). 1986. pap. text ed. 14.95 (1-877673-01-3) Cottonwood Pr.
—Extra Book, Level One. Blackstone, Ann, illus. 46p. (Orig.). (gr. 5-12). 1988. pap. text ed. 12.95 (1-877673-05-6) Cottonwood Pr.
—A Frog King's Daughter Is Nothing to Sneeze At. LC 88-93068. (Orig.). (gr. k-12). 1990. pap. 10.00 play script (0-88734-513-1) Players Pr.
—Ideas That Really Work! The Best of the Cottonwood Monthly, 1987-1991. (Illus.). 158p. (Orig.). (gr. 6-9). 1991. pap. text ed. 21.95 (1-877673-13-7) Cottonwood Pr.
—Melanie & the Trash Can Troll: A Modern-Day Fairy Tale. 67p. (Orig.). (gr. 6-9). 1991. pap. text ed. 5.95 (1-877673-11-0) Cottonwood Pr.
—Mystery of the Suffocated Seventh Grader. 23p. (Orig.). (gr. 5-9). 1988. pap. text ed. 8.95 (1-877673-03-X) Cottonwood Pr.
—What's in a Name? rev. ed. Blackstone, Ann, illus. 24p. (Orig.). (gr. 5-12). 1993. pap. text ed. 8.95 (1-877673-04-8) Cottonwood Pr.
Tibbetts, Cristopher, jt. auth. see May, Bob.
Tibbitts, Alison & Roocroft, Alan. African Elephant. (Illus.). 32p. (ps-2). 1992. PLB 12.95 (1-56065-100-8) Capstone Pr.
—California Condor. (Illus.). 32p. (ps-2). 1992. PLB 12.95 (1-56065-107-5) Capstone Pr.
—Crocodile. (Illus.). 24p. (ps-2). 1992. PLB 12.95 (1-56065-102-4) Capstone Pr.
—Koala. (Illus.). 24p. (ps-2). 1992. PLB 12.95 (1-56065-103-2) Capstone Pr.
—Polar Bears. (Illus.). 24p. (ps-2). 1992. PLB 12.95 (1-56065-104-0) Capstone Pr.
—Rhinoceros. (Illus.). 24p. (ps-2). 1992. PLB 12.95 (1-56065-101-6) Capstone Pr.
—Snow Leopard. (Illus.). 24p. (ps-2). 1992. PLB 12.95 (1-56065-106-7) Capstone Pr.
—Sumatran Tiger. (Illus.). 24p. (ps-2). 1992. PLB 12.95 (1-56065-105-9) Capstone Pr.
Tibo, Gilles. Paper Nights. Tibo, Gilles, illus. 32p. 1992. PLB 15.95 (1-55037-225-4, Pub. by Annick CN); pap. 5.95 (1-55037-224-6, Pub. by Annick CN) Firefly Bks Ltd.
—Pikolo: Le Secret du Garde-Robe (Paper Nights in French) Tibo, Gilles, illus. (FRE.). 32p. (Orig.). (ps-6). 1992. PLB 15.95 (1-55037-227-0, Pub. by Annick CN); pap. 5.95 (1-55037-226-2, Pub. by Annick CN) Firefly Bks Ltd.
—Simon & the Boxes. Tibo, Gilles, illus. LC 92-80416. 24p. (gr. k-4). 1992. PLB 10.95 (0-88776-287-5) Tundra Bks.
—Simon & the Snowflakes. Tibo, Gilles, illus. LC 88-50259. 24p. (ps-4). 1991. pap. 4.95 (0-88776-274-3) Tundra Bks.
—Simon & the Wind. Tibo, Gilles, illus. LC 89-50777. 24p. (gr. k-4). 1989. 10.95 (0-88776-234-4) Tundra Bks.
—Simon & the Wind. Tibo, Gilles, illus. LC 89-50776. 24p. (ps-4). 1991. pap. 4.95 (0-88776-276-X) Tundra Bks.
—Simon Au Clair De Lune. Tibo, Gilles, illus. LC 93-60333. 24p. (gr. k up). 1993. 10.95 (0-88776-317-0) Tundra Bks.
—Simon Celebra la Primavera (Simon Welcomes Spring) Salazar, Arturo, tr. from ENG. Tibo, Gilles, illus. LC 92-85471. (SPA.). 24p. (Orig.). (gr. k-3). 1993. pap. 5.95 (0-88776-297-2) Tundra Bks.
—Simon en Verano. Salazar, Arturo, tr. from ENG. Tibo, Gilles, illus. LC 92-85470. (SPA.). 24p. (Orig.). (gr. k-3). Date not set. pap. 5.95 (0-88776-298-0) Tundra Bks.
—Simon et le Soleil D'Ete. LC 90-72049. (FRE., Illus.). 24p. (ps). 1991. 10.95 (0-88776-262-X) Tundra Bks.
—Simon et le Vent d'Automne. Tibo, Gilles, illus. LC 89-50776. (FRE.). 24p. (gr. k-4). 1989. 10.95 (0-88776-235-2) Tundra Bks.
—Simon in Summer. LC 90-72048. (Illus.). 24p. (ps) 1991. 10.95 (0-88776-261-1) Tundra Bks.
—Simon in the Moonlight. Tibo, Gilles, illus. LC 93-60334. 24p. (gr. k up). 1993. 10.95 (0-88776-316-2) Tundra Bks.
—Simon Welcomes Spring. Tibo, Gilles, illus. LC 90-70132. 24p. (ps-4). 1990. 10.95 (0-88776-247-6) Tundra Bks.
—Simon Welcomes Spring. (Illus.). 24p. (gr. k-3). 1993. pap. 4.95 (0-88776-279-4) Tundra Bks.
Tichenor, Kay. Ballet Color & Story Album. (Illus.). 32p. 1976. pap. 4.50 (0-8431-1718-4) Price Stern.
Tickle, Phyllis, jt. auth. see Gilow, Betty.
Tidy, Bill. Incredible Bed. (Illus.). 32p. (ps-1). 1991. 13. 95 (0-86264-268-X, Pub. by Andersen Pr UK) Trafalgar.
Tiedt, Iris. Catching the Writing Express. (gr. 2-4). 1987. pap. 10.95 (0-8224-1307-8) Fearon Teach Aids.
—Enjoying the Written Word. (gr. 4-6). 1987. pap. 10.95 (0-8224-2703-6) Fearon Teach Aids.
—Learning to Use Written Language. (gr. 1-3). 1987. pap. 10.95 (0-8224-4267-1) Fearon Teach Aids.
Tierney, Robert J., et al. Portfolio Assessment in Reading - Writing Classrooms. 216p. (gr. k-12). 1991. pap. 18.95 (0-926842-08-0) CG Pubs Inc.
Tierney, Terence. Should You Become a Priest? 64p. (Orig.). (gr. 9 up). 1975. pap. 3.95 (0-89243-586-0, 29530) Liguori Pubns.
Tierney, Tom. Abraham Lincoln & His Family - Paper Dolls. 1989. pap. 3.95 (0-486-26024-0) Dover.
—American Family of the Civil War Era Paper Dolls in Full Color. 1985. pap. 3.95 (0-486-24833-X) Dover.
—American Family of the Colonial Era Paper Dolls in Full Color. 1982. pap. 3.95 (0-486-24394-X) Dover.
—Carmen Miranda Paper Dolls in Full Color. 1982. pap. 3.95 (0-486-24285-4) Dover.
—Chanel Fashions: Review Paper Dolls in Full Color. 1986. pap. 3.95 (0-486-25105-5) Dover.
—Diana & Prince Charles Fashion Paper Dolls in Full Color. 1985. pap. 3.95 (0-486-24961-1) Dover.
—Great Black Entertainers Paper Dolls. 1984. pap. 3.95 (0-486-24748-1) Dover.
—Great Empresses & Queen Paper Dolls. 1982. pap. 3.95 (0-486-24268-4) Dover.
—Great Fashion Design of the Fifties, Paper Dolls in Full Color. 1985. pap. 3.95 (0-486-24960-3) Dover.
—Great Fashion Designs of the Belle Epoque, Paper Dolls in Full Color. 1983. pap. 3.95 (0-486-24425-3) Dover.
—Great Fashion Designs of the 30s Paper Dolls. 1989. pap. 3.95 (0-486-24724-4) Dover.
—Greta Garbo Paper Dolls in Full Color. 1985. pap. 3.95 (0-486-24802-X) Dover.
—Joan Crawford Paper Dolls in Full Color. 1983. pap. 3.95 (0-486-24569-1) Dover.
—Legendary Baseball Stars Paper Dolls. 1985. pap. 3.95 (0-486-24846-1) Dover.
—Little Cupid Dolls-Paper Dolls. 1986. pap. 2.50 (0-486-25028-8) Dover.
—Marilyn Monroe-Paper Dolls. 1980. pap. 3.95 (0-486-23769-9) Dover.
—More Erte Fashion Paper Dolls in Full Color. 1984. pap. 3.95 (0-486-24630-2) Dover.
—Notable American Women Paper Dolls in Full Color. (Illus.). 32p. 1989. pap. 3.95 (0-486-26011-9) Dover.
—Paper Doll-Gibson Girl. 1985. pap. 3.95 (0-486-24980-8) Dover.
—Paper Doll-Judy Garland. 1982. pap. 3.95 (0-486-24404-0) Dover.
—Poiret Fashion Design Paper Dolls in Full Color. 1985. pap. 3.95 (0-486-24952-2) Dover.
—Ronald Reagan-Paper Dolls in Full Color. 1984. pap. 3.95 (0-486-24628-0) Dover.
—Santa Claus-Paper Dolls in Full Color. 1983. pap. 3.95 (0-486-24546-2) Dover.
—Three Little Kittens Paper Dolls in Full Color. 1986. pap. 3.50 (0-486-25065-2) Dover.
—Vivien Leigh Paper Dolls in Full Color. pap. 3.95 (0-486-24207-2) Dover.
Tiffault, Benette W. A Quilt for Elizabeth. McConnell, Mary, illus. 32p. (Orig.). (gr. 2-5). 1992. pap. 8.95x (1-56123-034-0) Centering Corp.
Tift, Tom. Santa & the Captain: A Mystic Christmas Tale. Clover, Barbara, illus. LC 89-81337. 24p. (Orig.). (gr. 2-4). 1989. pap. 6.95 (0-9624607-0-2) Hickory Ridge Pr.
Tiger, Steven. Arthritis. LC 85-8947. (Illus.). 72p. 1986. lib. bdg. 11.98 (0-671-55566-9, J Messner) S&S Trade.
—Diabetes. Reingold, Michael, illus. LC 86-23498. 72p. (gr. 4-8). 1987. lib. bdg. 13.98 (0-671-63273-6, J Messner) S&S Trade.
—Heart Disease. LC 85-8949. (Illus.). 72p. (gr. 4-8). 1986. lib. bdg. 11.98 (0-671-60021-4, J Messner) S&S Trade.
Tigerman, Stanley, et al. Dorothy in Dreamland. LC 91-7728. 32p. (gr. 5 up). 1991. 17.95 (0-8478-1393-2) Rizzoli Intl.
Tighe, Mike. I Was Afraid I'd Lose My Soul to a Chocolate Malt... And Other Stories of Everyday Spirituality. LC 89-63837. (Illus.). 96p. (Orig.). 1990. pap. 2.95 (0-89243-316-7) Liguori Pubns.
Tigwell, Tony. A Family in India. LC 84-19446. (Illus.). 32p. (gr. 2-5). 1985. PLB 13.50 (0-8225-1654-3) Lerner Pubns.
Tilden, Ruth. Cat Tricks: Pop-up Kittycats. (ps-3). 1994. pap. 7.95 (0-671-88305-4, Little Simon) S&S Trade.
—Dog Tricks. (ps-6). 1993. pap. 7.95 (0-671-87127-7, S&S BFYR) S&S Trade.
Tilgner, Linda. Let's Grow! Seventy-Two Gardening Adventures with Children. Burns, Deborah, ed. Kuykendall, John M., photos by. LC 87-45581. (Illus.). 216p. (Orig.). (ps up). 1988. 21.95 (0-88266-471-9, Garden Way Pub); pap. 10.95 (0-88266-470-0, Garden Way Pub) Storey Comm Inc.
Tilkin, Sheldon. Paragraph & Topic Sentence. Pape, Richard, illus. 24p. (gr. 3-4). 1980. wkbk. 2.95 (0-89403-606-8) EDC.
—Quotation Marks & Underlining. Pape, Richard, illus. 24p. (gr. 3-4). 1980. 2.95 (0-89403-594-0) EDC.
—Synonyms, Antonyms, Homonyms. Pape, Richard, illus. 24p. (gr. 3-4). 1980. wkbk. 2.95 (0-89403-603-3) EDC.
—Verbs. Pape, Richard, illus. 24p. (gr. 3-4). 1980. wkbk. 2.95 (0-89403-598-3) EDC.
Tilkin, Sheldon L. Establishing Sequence. Conoway, Judith, illus. 24p. (gr. 3-4). 1980. wkbk. 2.95 (0-89403-570-3) EDC.
—Finding the Main Idea. Conoway, Judith, illus. 24p. (gr. 3-4). 1980. wkbk. 2.95 (0-89403-569-X) EDC.
—Following Directions. Conoway, Judith, illus. 24p. (gr. 3-4). 1980. wkbk. 2.95 (0-89403-571-1) EDC.
—Nouns & Pronouns. Pape, Richard, illus. 24p. (gr. 3-4). 1980. wkbk. 2.95 (0-89403-599-1) EDC.
—Recalling Details. Conoway, Judith, illus. 24p. (gr. 4-5). 1980. wkbk. 2.95 (0-89403-568-1) EDC.
—Recognizing Cause & Effect. (Illus.). 24p. (gr. 3-4). 1980. 2.95 (0-89403-574-6) EDC.
Tilkin, Sheldon L. & Conoway, Judith. Distinquishing Between Fact & Opinion. (Illus.). 24p. (gr. 4-5). 1980. wkbk. 2.95 (0-89403-582-7) EDC.
—Drawing Conclusions. (Illus.). 24p. (gr. 3-4). 1980. wkbk. 2.95 (0-89403-573-8) EDC.
—Drawing Conclusions. (Illus.). 24p. (gr. 4-5). 1980. wkbk. 2.95 (0-89403-583-5) EDC.
—Establishing Sequence. (Illus.). 24p. (gr. 4-5). 1980. wkbk. 2.95 (0-89403-580-0) EDC.
—Finding the Main Idea. (Illus.). 24p. (gr. 4-5). 1980. wkbk. 2.95 (0-89403-579-7) EDC.
—Following Directions. (Illus.). 24p. (gr. 4-5). 1980. wkbk. 2.95 (0-89403-581-9) EDC.
—Making Judgments. (Illus.). 24p. (gr. 3-4). 1980. wkbk. 2.95 (0-89403-577-0) EDC.
—Making Judgments. (Illus.). 24p. (gr. 4-5). 1980. wkbk. 2.95 (0-89403-587-8) EDC.
—Predicting Outcomes. (Illus.). 24p. (gr. 3-4). 1980. wkbk. 2.95 (0-89403-575-4) EDC.
—Predicting Outcomes. (Illus.). 24p. (gr. 4-5). 1980. wkbk. 2.95 (0-89403-585-1) EDC.
—Recalling Details. (Illus.). 24p. (gr. 4-5). 1980. wkbk. 2.95 (0-89403-578-9) EDC.
—Recognizing Cause & Effect. (Illus.). 24p. (gr. 4-5). 1980. wkbk. 2.95 (0-89403-584-3) EDC.
—Recognizing Mood, Character & Plot. (Illus.). 24p. (gr. 4-5). 1980. wkbk. 2.95 (0-89403-586-X) EDC.
—Recognizing Mood, Character & Plot. (Illus.). 24p. (gr. 3-4). 1980. wkbk. 2.95 (0-89403-576-2) EDC.
Tiller, David. Wanna Be Number One? Stevens, Bill, illus. 40p. (Orig.). (gr. 4-6). pap. 2.00 (0-937170-32-1) Home Mission.
Tiller, Ruth. Cinnamon, Mint, & Mothballs: A Visit to Grandmother's House. Sogabe, Aki, illus. LC 92-32981. 1993. write for info. (0-15-276617-0) HarBrace.
Tilling, Robert I. Born of Fire: Volcanoes & Igneous Rocks. LC 89-25781. (Illus.). 64p. (gr. 6 up). 1991. lib. bdg. 15.95 (0-89490-151-6) Enslow Pubs.
Tilly, Jim. Puffin: A Journey Home. Sagan, Alexander, illus. 32p. 1993. 14.95 (0-9635083-3-4) Misty Mtn.
Tilly, Lois. The Survival Kit to Quick Learning. 22p. 1994. pap. 6.95 (0-8059-3452-9) Dorrance.
Tilly, Nancy. The Golden Girl. (gr. k-12). 1988. pap. 2.95 (0-440-20095-4, LFL) Dell.
Tilton, Martha. I Am a Library Book. Shuster, Albert, ed. (Illus.). 14p. (ps). 1993. pap. 0.89 (0-914127-22-5) Univ Class.
Time-Life Bks. Editors. Alice in Numberland: Fantasy Math. Mark, Sara, et al, eds. LC 93-9136. (Illus.). 64p. (ps-4). 1993. write for info. (0-8094-9978-9); lib. bdg. write for info. (0-8094-9979-7) Time-Life.
Time Life Book Editors. What Is a Bellybutton? First Questions & Answers about the Human Body. Kagan, Neil, ed. (Illus.). 48p. (ps). 1993. write for info. (0-7835-0854-9); lib. bdg. write for info. (0-7835-0855-7) Time-Life.
Time-Life Books Editors. Barnyard Babies: Oink, Baa, Moo, Meow, Neigh, Peep. Marshall, Blaine, ed. Time-Life Books Staff, illus. 6p. (ps). 1993. 16.95 (0-8094-6692-9) Time-Life.

—The Bumbletown Detectives: A Critical-Thinking Book. Kagan, Neil, ed. (Illus.). 64p. (gr. 3-7). 1991. write for info. (0-8094-9270-9); PLB write for info. (0-8094-9271-7) Time-Life.
—The Great ABC Treasure Hunt: A Hidden Picture Alphabet Book. (Illus.). 56p. (ps-2). 1991. write for info. (0-8094-9254-7); lib. bdg. write for info. (0-8094-9255-5) Time-Life.
—Guess Who? A Lift-the-Flap Animal Book. (Illus.). 20p. (ps). 1990. write for info. (0-8094-9250-4); lib. bdg. write for info. (0-8094-9251-2) Time-Life.
—How Many Hippos? A Mix-&-Match Counting Book. (Illus.). 40p. (ps-2). 1990. write for info. (0-8094-9258-X); lib. bdg. write for info. (0-8094-9259-8) Time-Life.
—The Human Body. 128p. (gr. 7 up). 1989. 14.99 (0-8094-6062-9); lib. bdg. 23.93 (0-8094-6063-7) Time-Life.
—Lands & Rivers. LC 92-34976. 176p. 1993. 18.60 (0-8094-9691-7); lib. bdg. 24.60 (0-8094-9692-5) Time-Life.
—The Secret Forest: A Lift-the-Flap Nature Book. Kagan, Neil, ed. (Illus.). 20p. (gr. 3-7). 1991. write for info. (0-8094-9275-X); PLB write for info. (0-8094-9276-8) Time-Life.
—Southeast Asia. (Illus.). 160p. (gr. 7 up). 1987. lib. bdg. 25.93 (0-8094-5318-5) Time-Life.
—Super Firm: Tough Workouts. (Illus.). 144p. 1989. 17. 27 (0-8094-6134-X); lib. bdg. 23.27 (0-8094-6135-8) Time-Life.
—Walking & Running. (Illus.). 144p. 1989. 17.27 (0-8094-6130-7); lib. bdg. 23.27 (0-8094-6131-5) Time-Life.
Time-Life Books Inc. Editors, tr. see Gakken Co. Ltd. Editors.
Time-Life Books Inc Editors, tr. see Gakken Co. Ltd. Editors.
Time-Life Books Inc. Editors, tr. see Gakken Co. Ltd. Staff.
Time-Life Books Inc., Staff, tr. see Gakken Co. Ltd., Staff.
Time Life Books Staff. Physical Forces. 1992. 18.95 (0-8094-9675-5) Time-Life.
—Planet Earth. 1992. 18.95 (0-8094-9666-6) Time-Life.
—Structure of Matter. 1992. 18.95 (0-8094-9662-3) Time-Life.
—Weather & Climate. 1992. 18.95 (0-8094-9683-6) Time-Life.
Time-Life Books Staff, ed. Animal Behavior. 144p. 1992. write for info. (0-8094-9658-5); lib. bdg. write for info. (0-8094-9659-3) Time-Life.
—Space & Planets. 144p. 1991. write for info. (0-8094-9650-X); lib. bdg. write for info. (0-8094-9651-8) Time-Life.
Time Life Inc. Editors. The Case of the Missing Zebra Stripes: Zoo Math. Crawford, Jean B., et al, eds. LC 92-16838. (Illus.). 64p. (gr. k-4). 1992. write for info. (0-8094-9954-1); lib. bdg. write for info. (0-8094-9955-X) Time-Life.
—CB: A Book about Time. Ward, Elizabeth & Kagan, Neil, eds. (Illus.). 30p. (ps-2). 1992. write for info. (0-8094-9303-9); lib. bdg. write for info. (0-8094-9304-7) Time-Life.
Time-Life Inc. Editors. Do Fish Drink? First Questions & Answers about Water. Kagan, Neil, ed. LC 92-40301. (Illus.). 48p. (ps). 1993. write for info. (0-7835-0850-6); PLB write for info. (0-7835-0851-4) Time-Life.
Time Life Inc. Editors. The Family Tree: A Familiy History Book. Ward, Elizabeth & Kagan, Neil, eds. (Illus.). 56p. (ps-2). 1993. write for info.; lib. bdg. write for info. Time-Life.
—From Head to Toe: Body Math. Crawford, Jean B. & Daniels, Patricia, eds. LC 92-34974. (Illus.). 64p. (gr. k-2). 1993. write for info. (0-8094-9966-5); PLB write for info. (0-8094-9967-3) Time-Life.
—Hound Bee! A Mix-&-Match Imagination Book. Kagan, Neil, ed. (Illus.). 40p. (ps-2). 1991. write for info. Time-Life.
—How Do Octopi Eat Pizza Pie? Pizza Math. Crawford, Jean B., et al, eds. (Illus.). 64p. (gr. k-4). 1992. write for info. (0-8094-9950-9); lib. bdg. write for info. (0-8094-9951-7) Time-Life.
—Look Both Ways: City Math. Crawford, Jean B., et al, eds. (Illus.). 64p. (gr. k-2). 1992. write for info. (0-8094-9958-4); lib. bdg. write for info. (0-8094-9959-2) Time-Life.
—Mr. Boggle's Peculiar Day: A Visual-Perception Book. Kagan, Neil & Ward, Elizabeth, eds. (Illus.). 56p. (ps-2). 1992. write for info. (0-8094-9311-X); lib. bdg. write for info. (0-8094-9312-8) Time-Life.
Time-Life Inc. Editors. On Top of Spaghetti: A Lift-the-Flap Poetry Book. (Illus.). 20p. (ps-2). 1992. write for info. (0-8094-9292-X); PLB write for info. (0-8094-9292-X) Time-Life.
—Play Ball: Sports Math. Mark, Sara, et al, eds. (Illus.). 64p. (gr. k-4). 1993. write for info. (0-8094-9970-3); lib. bdg. write for info. (0-8094-9971-1) Time-Life.
Time Life Inc. Editors. The Search for the Mystery Planet: Space Math. Crawford, Jean B., ed. (Illus.). 64p. (gr. k-2). 1993. write for info. (0-8094-9982-7); lib. bdg. write for info. (0-8094-9983-5) Time-Life.
—The Search for the Seven Sisters: A Hidden-Picture Geography Book. (Illus.). 56p. (ps-2). 1991. write for info. (0-8094-9287-3); PLB write for info. (0-8094-9288-1) Time-Life.

Time-Life Inc. Editors. See You Later Escalator: Mall Math. Crawford, Jean B., et al, eds. LC 93-6494. (Illus.). 64p. (gr. k-2). 1993. write for info. (0-8094-9974-6); PLB write for info. (0-8094-9975-4) Time-Life.
Time Life Inc. Editors. Tales for a Stormy Day: A Book about Good Behavior. Kagan, Neil & Ward, Elizabeth, eds. (Illus.). (ps-2). 1992. write for info. (0-8094-9307-1); lib. bdg. write for info. (0-8094-9308-X) Time-Life.
—The Three Storytellers of Or: A Flexible-Thinking Book. Kagan, Neil & Ward, Elizabeth, eds. (Illus.). 64p. (ps-2). 1991. write for info. (0-8094-9283-0); PLB write for info. (0-8094-9284-9) Time-Life.
—Voyage of the Micronauts: A Book about the Human Body. Fallow, Allan, ed. Cooke, Tom, illus. 64p. (ps-2). 1992. write for info. (0-8094-9295-4); PLB write for info. (0-8094-9296-2) Time-Life.
—Where Does the Sun Sleep? First Questions & Answers about Bedtime. Kagan, Neil, ed. (Illus.). 48p. (ps). 1993. write for info. (0-7835-0866-2); lib. bdg. write for info. (0-7835-0867-0) Time-Life.
—Why Is the Grass Green? First Questions & Answers about Nature. Kagan, Neil, ed. (Illus.). 48p. (ps). 1993. write for info. (0-7835-0858-1); lib. bdg. write for info. (0-7835-0859-X) Time-Life.
Time Life Inc., Staff. Balderdash the Brilliant: A Hole-in-the-Page Color Book. Kagan, Neil, ed. (Illus.). 56p. (ps-2). 1991. write for info. (0-8094-9266-0); lib. bdg. write for info. (0-8094-9267-9) Time-Life.
—Purple Parrots Eating Carrots: A Rebus Reader. Kagan, Neil, ed. 64p. (ps-2). 1991. write for info. (0-8094-9262-8); lib. bdg. write for info. (0-8094-9263-6) Time-Life.
Time Life Inc Staff. Right in Your Own Backyard: Nature Math. Ward, Elizabeth, et al, eds. LC 92-27222. (Illus.). 64p. (gr. k-4). 1992. write for info. (0-8094-9962-2); PLB write for info. (0-8094-9963-0) Time-Life.

Timlin, William M. The Ship That Sailed to Mars. (Illus.). 104p. (gr. 4-5). 1992. Repr. of 1923 ed. 25.00 (0-9633212-6-9) Stonewall Pubns.
Hailed as "the most beautiful & valuable science story book published this century," THE SHIP THAT SAILED TO MARS is now available to readers & collectors for the first time in seventy years. First published in 1923, this amusing, whimsical tale was created by British artist/author William M. Timlin. Weaving together 48 glorious illustrations with delightful prose, Timlin takes readers out of this world as his characters journey to Mars. The crew encounters strange, scary, & wondrous things on their voyage: a terrifying meteor, a jewel-eyed serpent, a planet full of pirates, & finally, Mars with its Shining City & bewildering beauty. Just as in the original book, the exquisite illustrations make this new edition of THE SHIP THAT SAILED TO MARS irresistible. The original 48 illustrations are printed along with the calligraphic text on heavyweight matte stock. The book is clothbound with a total of 104 pages. Every volume is protected by a full-color, glossy book jacket to maintain its keepsake quality. This beautiful volume is only $25.00. Please send check or money order payable to: Stonewall Publications, 4851 Aurora Drive, Ventura, CA 93003 or call (805) 650-9654 to place your order right away.
Publisher Provided Annotation.

Timm, Stephen A. The Dragon & the Mouse: The Dream. Lalo, illus. 45p. 1982. 12.95 (0-939728-05-2); pap. 4.95 (0-939728-06-0) Steppingstone Ent.
—The Dragon & the Mouse: Together Again. Lalo, illus. LC 81-90230. 46p. (ps-8). 1981. 12.95 (0-939728-03-6); pap. 4.95 (0-939728-04-4) Steppingstone Ent.
—The Floor That Said "No More" Neidigh, Sherry, illus. LC 86-60276. 48p. 1986. pap. 5.95 (0-939728-12-5) Steppingstone Ent.
Timm, Stephen A., intro. by see Rae, Judy.
Timmer, John. Once upon a Time: Story Sermons for Children. 144p. 1992. pap. 8.99 (0-310-58621-6, Pub. by Minister Res Lib) Zondervan.

Timmons, Dayle M. A Is Amazing. (ps-1). 1991. pap. 25. 95 (0-8224-0253-X) Fearon Teach Aids.
Timms, Diann. Hare & Bear Draw a Boat. (ps-3). 1993. 3.50 (0-89577-534-4, Readers Digest Kids) RD Assn.
—Hare & Bear Draw a Dinosaur. (ps-3). 1993. 3.50 (0-89577-533-6, Readers Digest Kids) RD Assn.
—Hare & Bear Draw a Horse. (ps-3). 1993. 3.50 (0-89577-532-8, Readers Digest Kids) RD Assn.
—Hare & Bear Draw a Tree. (ps-3). 1993. 3.50 (0-89577-530-1, Readers Digest Kids) RD Assn.
—Hare & Bear Draw an Airplane. (ps-3). 1993. 3.50 (0-89577-531-X, Readers Digest Kids) RD Assn.
Timms, Howard. Measuring & Computing. (Illus.). 40p. (gr. 5-9). 1989. PLB 12.40 (0-531-17188-4, Gloucester Pr) Watts.
Timothy, Kevin. The H. O. Scale Slot Car Collectors Price Reference Handbook, 1993. Collison, Joanne, ed. 96p. (Orig.). 1993. pap. text ed. 17.95 (1-883796-02-4) What It Is.
Timyan, Janis, illus. A Happy Day for Ramona & Other Missionary Stories for Children. LC 87-71018. (Orig.). (gr. 1-5). 1987. pap. 3.99 (0-87509-392-2) Chr Pubns.
—The Pink & Green Church & Other Missionary Stories for Children. LC 87-71019. (gr. 1-5). 1988. pap. 3.99 (0-87509-393-0) Chr Pubns.
Tinbergen, Niko. Kleew. (Illus.). 48p. (gr. 4 up). 1991. 10. 95 (1-55821-122-5) Lyons & Burford.
Tindall, Judith & Salmon-White, Shirley. Peers Helping Peers Program for the Preadolescent: Student Workbook. LC 90-80478. 230p. (Orig.). (gr. 4-7). 1990. 14.95 (1-55959-010-6) Accel Devel.
Tindall, Judith A. Peer Power, Bk. 1: Strategies Manual. 3rd ed. 200p. (Orig.). (gr. 7 up). 1993. pap. text ed. 16.95 (1-55959-058-0) Accel Devel.
—Peer Power, Bk. 1: Workbook. 3rd ed. 330p. (gr. 7 up). 1993. pap. 16.95 (1-55959-057-2) Accel Devel.
—Peer Programs. 300p. (gr. 4-6). 1993. pap. text ed. 24. 95 (1-55959-056-4) Accel Devel.
Tindimwebwa, Issy, jt. auth. see McKinzie, Harry.
Tiner, John H. Acts Word Puzzles. (Illus.). 48p. 1986. pap. 2.95 (1-56794-040-4, C2300) Star Bible.
—Find-the-Word Puzzles: Wisdom & Praise. Rector, Andy, ed. 48p. (Orig.). (gr. 5 up). 1993. pap. 3.99 (0-7847-0061-3, 28-02797) Standard Pub.
—Isaac Newton: The True Story of His Life. Biel, Bill & Biel, Bill, illus. LC 75-32562. (gr. 3-6). 1976. pap. 6.95 (0-915134-95-0) Mott Media.
—Johannes Kepler: Giant of Faith & Science. Burke, Rod, illus. LC 77-558. (gr. 3-6). 1977. pap. 6.95 (0-915134-11-X) Mott Media.
—Louis Pasteur. (gr. 3-6). 1991. pap. 6.95 (0-88062-159-1) Mott Media.
—Robert Boyle: Trailblazer of Science. (Illus.). (gr. 3-6). 1989. pap. 6.95 (0-88062-155-9) Mott Media.
—Samuel F. B. Morse: Artist with a Message. (Illus.). (gr. 3-6). 1987. pap. 6.95 (0-88062-137-0) Mott Media.
Tingay, G. & Marks, A. The Romans. (Illus.). 96p. 1990. PLB 16.96 (0-88110-439-6); pap. 10.95 (0-7460-0340-4) EDC.
Tingay, G. I. & Badcock, J. These Were the Romans. 1985. pap. 25.00 (0-7175-0591-X) Dufour.
Tingay, Graham, jt. auth. see Badcock, John.
Tingay, Graham I. & Badcock, John. These Were the Romans. LC 86-11654. (Illus.). 196p. (gr. 10-12). 1987. pap. 14.95 (0-8023-1280-2) Dufour.
Tingle, Dolli. Going to Be a Bride. (Illus.). 32p. 1987. 5.95 (0-8378-5080-0) Gibson.
Tinkham, Trudy, jt. auth. see Ogilvy, Carol.
Tinkle, Lon. The Alamo: Thirteen Days to Glory. (RL 7). 1960. pap. 2.95 (0-451-14943-2, AE2418, Sig) NAL-Dutton.
Tipp, Stacey. America's Prisons. rev. ed. (Illus.). 264p. (gr. 10 up). 1991. lib. bdg. 17.95 (0-89908-178-9); pap. text ed. 9.95 (0-89908-153-3) Greenhaven.
—Causes of Crime: Distinguishing Between Fact & Opinion. LC 91-22123. (Illus.). 32p. (gr. 4-7). 1991. PLB 10.95 (0-89908-615-2) Greenhaven.
—Child Abuse: Detecting Bias. LC 91-22101. (Illus.). 32p. (gr. 4-7). 1991. PLB 10.95 (0-89908-611-X) Greenhaven.
Tipp, Stacey, jt. ed. see Cozic, Charles P.
Tipp, Stacey, jt. ed. see Dudley, William.
Tippett, Steve. Listen to the Voices. Date not set. 4.50 (0-685-68519-5, BCMC-35); cassette 9.98 (0-685-68520-9, BCTA-231C) Lillenas.
Tippins, Sherill. Donna Karan: Designing an American Dream. Young, Richard G., ed. LC 91-32784. (Illus.). 64p. (gr. 4-8). 1992. PLB 17.26 (1-56074-019-1) Garrett Ed Corp.
—Michael Eisner: Fun for Everyone. Young, Richard G., ed. LC 91-28544. (Illus.). 64p. (gr. 4-8). 1992. PLB 17. 26 (1-56074-014-0) Garrett Ed Corp.
Tipps, E. Cooking Without Looking. large type ed. 208p. (gr. 6 up). 1959. 57.22 (0-317-01882-5, 4-04060-00) Am Printing Hse.
Tipton, Nancy. The Singer: Perspective in Music for Christian Schools. (Illus.). 113p. (Orig.). (gr. 7-12). 1991. pap. text ed. 10.60 (0-89084-564-6) Bob Jones Univ Pr.
Tipton, Nancy, jt. auth. see Pinkston, Joan.
Tipton, Nancy, et al. Songs of Our Faith. (Illus.). 51p. 1990. pap. 7.95 (0-89084-532-8) Bob Jones Univ Pr.
Tirabassi, Becky. Live It. 1991. pap. 7.99 (0-310-53751-7) Zondervan.
—Live It! A Daily Devotional for Students. 192p. 1990. pap. 7.95 (0-685-38929-4, Youth Bks) Zondervan.

—Quietimes Student Prayer: Notebook. 264p. (gr. 10 up). 1991. 3-ring binder 17.99 (0-8407-9121-6); pap. 7.99 filler (0-8407-9122-4) Oliver-Nelson.

Tison & Woodside. The Ultimate Collection of Computer Facts & Fun: A Kid's Guide to Computers. (Illus.). 100p. (Orig.). (gr. 3 up). 1991. pap. 12.95 (0-672-30093-1) Sams.

Tison, Annette. Look out for Ghosts! Taylor, Talus, illus. LC 92-60790. 32p. (ps-3). 1992. 12.00 (0-89577-438-0) RD Assn.

—You Can't Scare Me! Glow in the Dark. (ps-3). 1992. 12.00 (0-89577-437-2) RD Assn.

Tissot, John & Carlin, Matthew. The Auntiques & the Valentine Card. 16p. (Orig.). (gr. 2 up). 1991. pap. 2.50 (0-88680-357-8); royalty on application 25.00 (0-685-59142-5) I E Clark.

Tissot, Olivier. Livre de Tous les Francais. Blachon, Roger, illus. (FRE.). 92p. (gr. 4-9). 1989. 14.95 (2-07-039526-X) Schoenhof.

Titchenell, Elsa-Brita. Once Round the Sun. Gruelle, Justin C. & Russell, Elizabeth A., illus. LC 81-52615. iv, 57p. (gr. 1 up). 1981. Repr. of 1950 ed. 9.50 (0-911500-61-8) Theos U Pr.

Tite, Paola. First Two Hundred Words in Italian. Sleight, Katy, illus. LC 93-29560. 1994. write for info. (1-85697-956-3) Kingfisher Bks.

Titherington, Jeanne. Baby's Boat. LC 91-10359. 24p. (ps up). 1992. 14.00 (0-688-08555-5); PLB 13.93 (0-688-08556-3) Greenwillow.

—Big World, Small World. Titherington, Jeanne, illus. LC 84-4140. 24p. (ps-1). 1985. 11.75 (0-688-04022-5); PLB 11.88 (0-688-04023-3) GreenWillow.

—Child's Prayer. Titherington, Jeanne, illus. LC 88-16566. 24p. (ps up). 1989. 13.95 (0-688-08317-X); PLB 13.88 (0-688-08318-8) Greenwillow.

—A Child's Prayer: Miniature Edition. (Illus.). 32p. (ps up). 1993. 4.95 (0-688-12751-7, Tupelo Bks) Morrow.

—A Place for Ben. Titherington, Jeanne, illus. LC 86-7656. 24p. (ps-3). 1987. 11.95 (0-688-06493-0); PLB 11.88 (0-688-06494-9) Greenwillow.

—Pumpkin, Pumpkin. Titherington, Jeanne, illus. LC 84-25334. 24p. (ps-1). 1986. 13.95 (0-688-05695-4); PLB 13.88 (0-688-05696-2) Greenwillow.

—Pumpkin Pumpkin. LC 84-25334. (Illus.). 24p. (ps-2). 1990. pap. 3.95 (0-688-09930-0, Mulberry) Morrow.

—Where Are You Going, Emma? (Illus.). 24p. (ps-1). 1988. 11.95 (0-688-07081-7); lib. bdg. 11.88 (0-688-07082-5) Greenwillow.

Titus, Eve. Anatole. 1990. pap. 4.95 (0-553-34870-1) Bantam.

—Anatole & the Cat. (ps-3). 1990. pap. 4.95 (0-553-34871-X) Bantam.

—Anatole & the Piano. (ps-3). 1990. pap. 4.95 (0-553-34888-4) Bantam.

—Anatole & the Thirty Thieves. (ps-3). 1990. pap. 4.95 (0-553-34889-2) Bantam.

—Anatole & the Toy Shop. Galdone, Paul, illus. (ps-8). 1991. pap. 4.99 (0-553-35239-3) Bantam.

—Anatole over Paris. Galdone, Paul, illus. (ps-8). 1991. pap. 4.99 (0-553-35240-7) Bantam.

—Basil & the Pygmy Cats: A Basil of Baker Street Mystery. (Illus.). (gr. 3-6). 1989. pap. 2.75 (0-671-64119-0, Minstrel Bks) PB.

—Basil in Mexico: A Basil of Baker Street Mystery. Galdone, Paul, illus. 96p. (gr. 3-6). 1990. pap. 2.75 (0-671-64117-4, Minstrel Bks) PB.

—The Kitten Who Couldn't Purr. Fechner, Amrei, illus. LC 90-13418. 32p. (ps up). 1991. Repr. 12.95 (0-688-09363-9); PLB 12.88 (0-688-09364-7, Morrow Jr Bks) Morrow Jr Bks.

Titus, Eve & Galdone, Paul. Basil of Baker Street. (gr. 3-6). 1958. PLB 8.95 (0-07-064907-3) McGraw.

Tiulana, Paul, jt. auth. see Senungetuk, Vivian.

Tivers, Jacqueline & Day, Michael. The Viking Children's World Atlas. (Illus.). (ps-7). 1985. pap. 5.99 (0-14-031874-7, Puffin) Puffin Bks.

—The Viking Children's World Atlas: An Introductory Atlas for Young People. LC 83-675053. (Illus.). 48p. (gr. 4-6). 1983. pap. 9.95 (0-670-21791-3) Viking Child Bks.

Tjepkema, Edith R. Alaskan Paradise. 115p. (Orig.). (gr. 8 up). 1989. pap. 4.50 (0-9620280-1-0) Northland Pr.

—Lost in Paradise. 125p. (Orig.). (gr. 8-12). 1991. pap. 4.95 (0-9620280-3-7) Northland Pr.

—The Mountains of Paradise. 120p. (Orig.). (gr. 8-12). 1993. pap. 4.95 (0-9620280-5-3) Northland Pr.

—North to Paradise. 103p. (Orig.). (gr. 8-12). 1987. pap. 4.50 (0-9620280-0-2) Northland Pr.

—Return from Paradise. 100p. (Orig.). (gr. 8-12). 1992. pap. 4.95x (0-9620280-4-5) Northland Pr.

—Yukon Paradise. 126p. (Orig.). (gr. 8-12). 1990. pap. 4.50 (0-9620280-2-9) Northland Pr.

Tlkin, Sheldon L. & Conoway, Judith. Distinguishing Between Fact & Opinion. (Illus.). 24p. (gr. 3-4). 1980. wkbk. 2.95 (0-89403-572-X) EDC.

Toan, Debbie, jt. auth. see Fago, John N.

Tobias, Ann. Pot: What It Is, What It Does. Huffman, Tom, illus. LC 78-10817. 48p. (gr. 3-4). 1979. PLB 12.88 (0-688-84200-3) Greenwillow.

—Pot: What It Is, What It Does. Huffman, Tom, illus. LC 78-10817. 48p. (ps-3). 1991. pap. 4.95 (0-688-00463-6, Mulberry) Morrow.

Tobias, Jerry J. Imma Drug. Tobias, Jerry J., illus. 70p. (ps-6). Date not set. pap. write for info. (1-880017-12-1) Teddy Bear Pr.

—Imma Fish: And Other Related Poems. Tobias, Jerry J., illus. (Orig.). (ps-6). 1993. pap. 5.95 (1-880017-13-X) Teddy Bear Pr.

—Imma Insect, No. 8. rev. ed. (Illus.). 90p. (ps-6). 1992. pap. 5.95 (1-880017-07-5) Teddy Bear Pr.

Tobias, Tobi. The Dawdlewalk. Swofford, Jeanette, illus. LC 81-21666. 32p. (ps-2). 1983. PLB 13.50 (0-87614-190-4) Carolrhoda Bks.

—Pot Luck. Malone, Nola L., illus. LC 92-27678. 1993. write for info. (0-688-09824-X) Lothrop.

—Pot Luck. LC 92-27678. (ps-3). 1993. 14.93 (0-688-09825-8) Lothrop.

Tocci, Salvatore. Biology Projects for Young Scientists. 1989. pap. 6.95 (0-531-15127-1) Watts.

—Biology Projects for Young Scientists. LC 87-10432. (Illus.). 128p. (gr. 7-12). 1987. PLB 13.90 (0-531-10429-X) Watts.

—How to Do a Science Fair Project. (Illus.). 128p. (gr. 7-12). 1989. PLB 13.90 (0-531-10245-9); pap. 5.95 (0-531-15123-9) Watts.

Toda, Koshiro. A Tale of Six Colors. (Illus.). 44p. (ps-1). 1992. 11.95 (1-881267-01-6) Intercultural.

—What Color Would You Choose? (Illus.). 44p. (k-3). 1992. 11.95 (1-881267-00-8) Intercultural.

Todd, Anne O. From Flower to Fruit. LC 93-24972. (gr. 5 up). 1994. 13.95 (0-395-68376-9) Ticknor & Fields.

Todd, Armor. The Marin Mountain Bike Guide. 2nd ed. Todd, Linda, illus. 80p. (gr. 9-12). 1989. pap. 8.95t (0-9623537-0-1) A Todd.

Todd, Cynthia & Ziemann, Debbie. David David. Woessner, Circe, illus. 23p. (gr. k-6). 1990. PLB 7.95 (1-879056-01-1) Alpenhorn Pr.

—Heidelberg Castle. Woessner, Circe, illus. 28p. (gr. k-6). 1990. PLB 9.95 (1-879056-00-3) Alpenhorn Pr.

—Mother Earth. Woessner, Circe, illus. 24p. Date not set. pap. 9.95 (1-879056-03-8) Alpenhorn Pr.

—Nessie. 2nd ed. Woessner, Circe, illus. 9p. (gr. k-6). 1990. PLB 9.95 (1-879056-02-X) Alpenhorn Pr.

—People from Outer Space. Woessner, Circe, illus. 9p. 1991. PLB 9.95 (0-685-51627-X) Alpenhorn Pr.

—Take One Hand. Woessner, Circe, illus. 25p. (gr. k-6). 1990. PLB 9.95 (1-879056-05-4) Alpenhorn Pr.

Todd, Frank S. Sea World Book of Penguins. LC 86-25588. (Illus.). 96p. (gr. 4-7). 1981. 12.95 (0-15-271949-0, HB Juv Bks) HarBrace.

—The Sea World Book of Penguins. Todd, Frank S., photos by. LC 80-25588. (Illus.). 96p. (gr. 4-7). 1984. pap. 9.95 (0-15-271951-2, Voyager Bks) HarBrace.

Todd, H. E. The Silly Silly Ghost. Biro, Val, illus. 32p. (gr. k-3). 1989. 13.95 (0-340-41155-4, Pub. by Hodder & Stoughton UK) Trafalgar.

Todd, H. E. & Biro, Val. The Sleeping Policeman. (Illus.). 32p. (ps-1). 1989. 13.95 (0-340-41299-2, Pub. by Hodder & Stoughton UK) Trafalgar.

Todd, Justin, jt. auth. see Matthews, Andrew.

Todd, Leonard. Squaring Off. (gr. 7 up). 1990. 13.95 (0-670-83377-0) Viking Child Bks.

Todd, Richard E. Baptism. rev. ed. Miller, Alma E. & Kellner, Ron, illus. 26p. (gr. 2-6). 1993. wkbk. 2.45 (0-9605324-1-2) Crosswalk Res.

—Church. Miller, Alma E. & Kellner, Ron, illus. 26p. (gr. 2-6). 1993. wkbk. 2.45 (0-9605324-4-7) Crosswalk Res.

—Communion. rev. ed. Miller, Alma E. & Kellner, Ron, illus. 26p. (gr. 2-6). 1993. wkbk. 2.45 (0-9605324-3-9) Crosswalk Res.

—Salvation. rev. ed. Miller, Alma E. & Kellner, Ron, illus. 26p. (gr. 2-6). 1993. wkbk. 2.45 (0-9605324-6-3) Crosswalk Res.

Todd, Richard E., ed. Baptism. Kellner, Ron, illus. 16p. (Orig.). (gr. 1-6). 1980. pap. 0.50 (0-9605324-0-4) Crosswalk Res.

Todd, Sharon, ed. see Hembree, Mike, et al.

Todhunter, Jean M. Cipher in the Snow. 2nd ed. 6p. (gr. 8-12). 1988. pap. 1.95 stiched with dustcover (0-929985-07-9) Sonos.

Toepperwein, Emilie & Toepperwein, Fritz. Chinto, The Chaparral Cock. (gr. 4-7). 2.95 (0-910722-04-8) Highland Pr.

Toepperwein, Emilie & Toepperwein, Fritz A. Jose & the Mexican Jumping Bean. (Illus.). (gr. 4-7). 1965. PLB 2.95 (0-910722-05-6) Highland Pr.

Toepperwein, Fritz, jt. auth. see Toepperwein, Emilie.

Toepperwein, Fritz A., jt. auth. see Toepperwein, Emilie.

Tofts, Hannah. Paint Book. (gr. 1 up). 1990. pap. 11.95 (0-671-70364-1, S&S BFYR); pap. 4.95 (0-671-70365-X, S&S BFYR) S&S Trade.

—Paper Book. 1990. pap. 11.95 (0-671-70366-8); pap. 4.95 (0-671-70367-6) S&S Trade.

—Print Book. (ps-3). 1990. pap. 11.95 (0-671-70368-4, S&S BFYR); pap. 4.95 (0-671-70369-2, S&S BFYR) S&S Trade.

—Three-D. LC 89-27416. (ps-3). 1990. pap. 11.95 (0-671-70370-6, S&S BFYR); pap. 4.95 (0-671-70371-4, S&S BFYR) S&S Trade.

Tohtsonie, Clara, tr. see Crowder, Jack L. & Hill, Faith.

Tokuda, Wendy & Hall, Richard. Humphrey: The Lost Whale. Wakiyama, Hanako, illus. (gr. k-4). 1986. 11.95 (0-89346-270-5) Heian Intl.

—Humphrey, the Lost Whale: A True Story. Wakiyama, Hanako, illus. 32p. (gr. k-6). 1992. pap. 5.95 (0-89346-346-9) Heian Intl.

—Shiro in Love. Sasaki, Karen, illus. 32p. (gr. 1-3). 1989. 11.95 (0-89346-306-X) Heian Intl.

Tolan, Mary, adapted by see Brown, Pam.

Tolan, Mary, adapted by see Peduzzi, Kelli.

Tolan, Mary, adapted by see Taylor-Boyd, Susan.

Tolan, Sally. John Muir. LC 89-4367. (Illus.). 68p. (Orig.). 1990. pap. 7.95 (0-8192-1540-6) Morehouse Pub.

—John Muir: Naturalist, Writer & Guardian of the North American Wilderness. LC 89-4367. (Illus.). 64p. (gr. 5-6). 1989. PLB 18.60 (0-8368-0099-0) Gareth Stevens Inc.

Tolan, Sally & Sherwood, Rhoda I., eds. France. Pierre, Philippe, photos by. LC 88-42889. (Illus.). 64p. (gr. 5-6). 1990. PLB 19.93 (1-55532-212-3) Gareth Stevens Inc.

Tolan, Stephanie. A Time to Fly Free. LC 90-31676. 176p. (gr. 3-7). 1990. pap. 3.95 (0-689-71420-3, Aladdin) Macmillan Child Grp.

Tolan, Stephanie S. A Good Courage. LC 87-31306. 240p. (gr. 7 up). 1988. 12.95 (0-688-07446-4) Morrow Jr Bks.

—A Good Courage. (gr. 7 up). 1989. pap. 2.95 (0-449-70329-0, Juniper) Fawcett.

—The Great Skinner Enterprise. (gr. 5-9). 1988. pap. 3.95 (0-317-69630-0, Puffin) Puffin Bks.

—The Great Skinner Getaway. LC 86-22874. 204p. (gr. 7 up). 1987. SBE 13.95 (0-02-789361-8, Four Winds) Macmillan Child Grp.

—The Great Skinner Homestead. LC 88-3970. 160p. (gr. 7 up). 1988. SBE 13.95 (0-02-789362-6, Four Winds) Macmillan Child Grp.

—Marcy Hooper & the Greatest Treasure in the World. Milone, Karen, illus. LC 91-12176. 64p. (gr. 2 up). 1991. 12.95 (0-688-10078-3) Morrow Jr Bks.

—Plague Year. LC 89-13605. (Illus.). 208p. (gr. 7 up). 1990. 12.95 (0-688-08801-5) Morrow Jr Bks.

—Plague Year. 1991. pap. 3.99 (0-449-70403-3, Juniper) Fawcett.

—Save Halloween! LC 93-10635. 176p. (gr. 4 up). 1993. 14.00 (0-688-12168-3) Morrow Jr Bks.

—Sophie & the Sidewalk Man. Avishai, Susan, illus. LC 91-17317. 80p. (gr. 2-4). 1992. SBE 12.95 (0-02-789365-0, Four Winds) Macmillan Child Grp.

—The Witch of Maple Park. LC 92-7277. 160p. (gr. 4 up). 1992. 14.00 (0-688-10581-5) Morrow Jr Bks.

Tolbert-Rouchaleau, Jane. James Weldon Johnson. King, Coretta Scott, intro. by. (Illus.). 112p. (Orig.). (gr. 5 up). 1988. 17.95 (1-55546-596-X); pap. 9.95 (0-7910-0211-X) Chelsea Hse.

Tolhurst, Marilyn. China. (Illus.). 48p. (gr. 4-8). 1987. PLB 14.98 (0-382-09510-3) Silver Burdett Pr.

—Israel. (Illus.). 48p. (gr. 4-8). 1989. lib. bdg. 14.98 (0-382-09830-7) Silver Burdett Pr.

—Somebody & the Three Blairs. Abel, Simone, illus. LC 90-7747. 32p. (ps-1). 1991. 14.95 (0-531-05878-6); PLB 14.99 (0-531-08478-7) Orchard Bks Watts.

—U. S. S. R. (Illus.). 48p. (gr. 4-8). 1987. PLB 14.98 (0-382-09507-3) Silver Burdett Pr.

Toliusis, Juozas, ed. Ausra, Jubiliejine Stovykla. (LIT., Illus.). 72p. (gr. 1 up). 1983. pap. write for info. (0-9611488-1-0) Lith Scouts.

Tolkien, J. R. R. Bilbo's Last Song. Baynes, Pauline, illus. 32p. 1990. 14.45 (0-395-53810-6) HM.

—Bilbo's Last Song. Baynes, Pauline, illus. LC 89-48659. 32p. 1992. pap. 6.99 (0-679-82710-2) Knopf Bks Yng Read.

—The Father Christmas Letters. (Illus.). 48p. 1991. pap. 10.70 (0-395-59698-X) HM.

—The Hobbit. Hague, Michael, illus. 320p. (gr. 7 up). 1984. 24.45 (0-395-36290-3) HM.

—The Hobbit. Hague, Michael, illus. 300p. (ps up). 1989. pap. 16.45 (0-395-52021-5, Sandpiper) HM.

—The Shaping of Middle-Earth. LC 86-10338. (Illus.). 380p. 1986. 18.95 (0-395-42501-8) HM.

Toll, Nelly. Behind the Secret Window: A Memoir of a Hidden Childhood. (Illus.). 160p. (gr. 5 up). 1993. 17.00 (0-8037-1362-2) Dial Bks Young.

Tolles, Martha. Secret Sister. (gr. 4-7). 1992. pap. 2.95 (0-590-45245-2) Scholastic Inc.

Tollhurst, Marilyn. Spain. (Illus.). 48p. (gr. 4-8). 1989. lib. bdg. 14.98 (0-382-09821-8) Silver Burdett Pr.

Tollison, Hal. Cartoon Fun. (Illus.). 64p. (Orig.). (gr. k up). 1989. pap. 5.95 (1-56010-033-8, BA07) W Foster Pub.

Tolliver, Ruby C. Blind Bess, Buddy, & Me. Welch, Karen, ed. Miller, Lyle L., illus. 104p. (gr. 4 up). 1990. lib. bdg. 12.95 (0-937460-63-X) Hendrick-Long.

—Boomer's Kids. Miller, Lyle, illus. 134p. (gr. 4 up). 1992. 14.95 (0-937460-69-9) Hendrick-Long.

—Have Gun - Need Bullets. Washington, Burl, illus. LC 90-49350. 120p. (gr. 4 up). 1991. 15.95 (0-87565-085-6); pap. 10.95 (0-87565-089-9) Tex Christian.

—Muddy Banks. LC 85-20851. (Illus.). 154p. (gr. 4up). 1987. 14.95 (0-87565-062-7); pap. 6.95 (0-87565-049-X) Tex Christian.

—Santa Anna: Patriot or Scoundrel. (Illus.). 112p. (gr. 4 up). 1993. 12.95 (0-937460-82-6) Hendrick-Long.

Tolman, Newton F. Quick Tunes & Good Times. (gr. 7 up). 1972. 10.95 (0-87233-018-4) Bauhan.

Tolstoy, Leo. Chozjain I Rabotnik. (gr. 7-12). pap. 5.95 (0-88436-054-7, 65252) EMC.

—The Death of Ivan Ilych. 112p. (gr. 6). 1990. PLB 13.95s.p. (0-88682-298-X) Creative Ed.

—God Sees the Truth, but Waits. LC 85-29920. 32p. (gr. 4 up). 1986. PLB 13.95s.p. (0-88682-071-5) Creative Ed.

—The Lion & the Puppy. Sievert, Claus, illus. Riordan, James, tr. from RUS. LC 87-28653. (Illus.). 80p. (gr. 1 up). 1988. 15.95 (0-8050-0735-0, Bks Young Read) H Holt & Co.

—Papa Panov's Special Day. 2nd ed. Molder, Mig, retold by. Morris, Tony, illus. 32p. 1988. 11.95 (0-7459-1358-X) Lion USA.

—Shoemaker Martin. Watts, Bernadette, illus. Hanhart, Brigitte, adapted by. LC 86-60489. (Illus.). 32p. (gr. k-3). 1986. 14.95 (*1-55858-044-1*) North-South Bks NYC.

—The Three Questions. LC 83-71787. 32p. (gr. 4 up). 1983. PLB 13.95s.p. (*0-87191-962-1*) Creative Ed.

—Varya & Her Greenfinch. Klein, Erika, illus. (ps-2). 1988. 7.95 (*0-86315-043-8*, 20238) Gryphon Hse.

Tolstoy, Leo & Andersen, Hans Christian. The Three Bears & the Little Match Girl. (Illus.). 48p. (ps-3). 1985. 5.95 (*0-88110-250-4*) EDC.

Tom, Mister. Are You a Critter? Neely, David, ed. Van Sciver, Ethan, illus. 77p. (gr. 4-6). 1993. pap. 6.95 spiral bdg. (*0-925237-10-8*) Ten Pubns.

Tomalin, Ruth. A Summer Ghost. 112p. (gr. 3-7). 1992. pap. 4.95 (*0-571-16221-5*) Faber & Faber.

Toman, James A. The Shaker Heights Rapid Transit. LC 90-23221. (Illus.). 144p. (gr. 11). 1991. 36.95 (*0-916374-95-5*) Interurban.

Tomaselli, Cecilia. Noah's Family Carousel. (ps). 1993. 14.95 (*0-943706-10-6*) Yllw Brick Rd.

Tomb, Eric. American Composers. (gr. 1-9). 1992. pap. 3.95 (*0-88388-158-6*) Bellerophon Bks.

—Early Composers. Conkle, Nancy, illus. 48p. (Orig.). (gr. 7). 1988. pap. 3.95 (*0-88388-124-1*) Bellerophon Bks.

—Great Dogs. (gr. 1-9). 1992. pap. 2.95 (*0-88388-108-X*) Bellerophon Bks.

—Great Explorers. (gr. 1-9). 1992. pap. 3.95 (*0-88388-120-9*) Bellerophon Bks.

—Mozart. (gr. 1-9). 1992. pap. 2.95 (*0-88388-125-X*) Bellerophon Bks.

—New England Authors. Conkle, Nancy, illus. 64p. (gr. 8). 1991. pap. text ed. 3.95 (*0-88388-149-7*) Bellerophon Bks.

Tomb, Eric & Knill, Henry. California Authors. Conkle, Nancy, illus. 68p. (gr. 1-9). pap. 3.95 (*0-88388-178-0*) Bellerophon Bks.

Tomb, Howard. Living Monsters: The World's Most Dangerous Animals. Marchesi, Stephen, illus. 48p. (gr. 3-7). 1990. pap. 9.95 (*0-671-69017-5*, S&S BFYR) S&S Trade.

—Microaliens: Dazzling Journeys with an Electron Microscope. (gr. 4-7). 1993. 15.00 (*0-374-34960-6*) FS&G.

Tomb, Ubet. Cowboys. (Illus.). 48p. (gr. 6). 1984. pap. 3.95 (*0-88388-114-4*) Bellerophon Bks.

—Cowgirls. (gr. 1-9). 1992. pap. 3.95 (*0-88388-118-7*) Bellerophon Bks.

Tomblin, Gill. Small & Furry Animals: A Watercolor Sketchbook of Mammals in the Wild. Tomblin, Gill, illus. 64p. (gr. 2-5). 1992. 14.95 (*0-399-22122-0*, Putnam) Putnam Pub Group.

Tomblin, Gill, illus. Make Your Own Rain Forest. Johnston, Damian, concept by. & contrib. by. (Illus.). 18p. (gr. 3-7). 1993. incl. kit 12.95 (*0-525-67409-8*, Lodestar Bks) Dutton Child Bks.

Tomchek, Ann. The Hopi. LC 87-8037. (Illus.). 48p. (gr. k-4). 1987. PLB 15.27 (*0-516-01234-7*); pap. 4.95 (*0-516-41234-5*) Childrens.

—I Can Be a Chef. LC 85-11016. 32p. (gr. k-3). 1985. PLB 14.60 (*0-516-01886-8*) Childrens.

—Puedo Ser Cocinero: (I Can Be a Chef) LC 85-11016. (SPA., Illus.). 32p. (gr. k-3). 1988. PLB 13.93 (*0-516-31886-1*); pap. 3.95 (*0-516-51886-0*) Childrens.

Tomei, Jeri, ed. see Tomei, Joseph A.

Tomei, Joseph A. Music Notation - How to Read & Write: Learning to Read Notes Step by Step. Tomei, Jeri & Steeves, Margo, eds. 80p. (Orig.). 1994. pap. text ed. 12.95 (*0-9629973-1-5*) Minich Pubns.

Tomey, Ingrid. Grandfather's Day. McKay, Robert, illus. 64p. (gr. 3-7). 1992. PLB 12.95 (*1-56397-022-8*) Boyds Mills Pr.

—Neptune Princess. LC 91-30502. 144p. (gr. 3-6). 1992. SBE 13.95 (*0-02-789403-7*, Bradbury Pr) Macmillan Child Grp.

—Savage Carrot. 192p. (gr. 4-7). 1993. SBE 14.95 (*0-684-19633-6*, Scribners Young Read) Macmillan Child Grp.

Tomie, Paola De see De Paola, Tomie.

Tomioka, Chiyoko. Rise & Shine, Mariko-Chan! Tsuchida, Yoshiharu, illus. 32p. (ps-1). 1992. pap. 3.95 (*0-590-45507-9*) Scholastic Inc.

Tomkins, Jasper. Bear Sleep Soup. (ps-3). 1991. pap. 7.95 (*0-671-75278-2*, Green Tiger) S&S Trade.

—The Catalog. (Illus.). 56p. (gr. k up). 1991. pap. 5.95 (*0-671-74972-2*, Green Tiger) S&S Trade.

—The Hole in the Ocean. (Illus.). 60p. 1991. pap. 7.95 (*0-671-74974-9*, Green Tiger) S&S Trade.

—The Mountains Crack Up! (Illus.). 60p. (gr. k-6). 1991. pap. 5.95 (*0-671-75273-1*, Green Tiger) S&S Trade.

—My Cousin Has Eight Legs. Tomkins, Jasper, illus. 40p. (Orig.). (ps up) 1992. pap. 9.95 (*0-912365-68-4*) Sasquatch Bks.

—My Secret Sunrise. LC 91-22274. (Illus.). 60p. 1991. 11.95 (*0-671-74975-7*, Green Tiger); pap. 7.95 (*0-671-74978-1*, Green Tiger) S&S Trade.

—Nimby. (Illus.). 60p. 1991. pap. 7.95 (*0-671-74973-0*, Green Tiger) S&S Trade.

—The Sky Jumps Into Your Shoes at Night. (Illus.). 60p. 1991. pap. 7.95 (*0-671-74971-4*, Green Tiger) S&S Trade.

—When a Bear Bakes a Cake. (Illus.). 60p. (Orig.). (ps-2). 1991. pap. 7.95 (*0-88138-082-2*, Green Tiger) S&S Trade.

—When a Bear Bakes a Cake. (ps-3). 1991. pap. 7.95 (*0-671-75277-4*, Green Tiger) S&S Trade.

Tomlinson, Michael. Jonas Salk. LC 92-46284. 1993. 19.93 (*0-86625-495-1*); 14.95s.p. (*0-685-66537-2*) Rourke Pubns.

Tomlinson, Theresa. Riding the Waves. LC 92-3942. (Illus.). 144p. (gr. 4-8). 1993. SBE 13.95 (*0-02-789207-7*, Macmillan Child Bk) Macmillan Child Grp.

—Summer Witches. LC 90-38162. 96p. (gr. 2-7). 1991. SBE 11.95 (*0-02-789206-9*, Macmillan Child Bk) Macmillan Child Grp.

Tompert, Ann. Bamboo Hats & a Rice Cake: A Tale Adapted from Japanese Folklore. Demi, illus. LC 92-26849. 32p. (ps-3). 1993. 13.00 (*0-517-59272-X*); PLB 13.99 (*0-517-59273-8*) Crown Bks Yng Read.

—Grandfather Tang's Story. Parker, Robert A., illus. LC 89-22205. 32p. (ps-2). 1990. 15.00 (*0-517-57487-X*); PLB 15.99 (*0-517-57272-9*) Crown Bks Yng Read.

—Just a Little Bit. Munsinger, Lynn, illus. LC 92-31857. 1993. 14.95 (*0-395-51527-0*) HM.

—Nothing Sticks Like a Shadow. Munsinger, Lynn, illus. LC 83-18554. 32p. (gr. k-3). 1988. 14.45 (*0-395-35391-2*, 5-97100); pap. 4.80 (*0-395-47950-9*) HM.

—P. T. Barnum: The Greatest Showman on Earth: A Biography of P. T. Barnum. LC 87-13600. (Illus.). 120p. (gr. 6 up). 1988. RSBE 13.95 (*0-87518-370-0*, Dillon) Macmillan Child Grp.

—Savina, the Gypsy Dancer. Nolan, Dennis, illus. LC 90-5902. 32p. (gr. k-3). 1991. RSBE 13.95 (*0-02-789205-0*, Macmillan Child Bk) Macmillan Child Grp.

—The Silver Whistle. Peck, Beth, illus. LC 88-1446. 32p. (gr. k-3). 1988. RSBE 14.95 (*0-02-789160-7*, Macmillan Child Bk) Macmillan Child Grp.

—Sue Patch & the Crazy Clocks. LC 88-25720. (Illus.). 48p. (ps-3). 1992. pap. 3.99 (*0-8037-1061-5*, Dial Easy to Read) Puffin Bks.

—The Tzar's Bird. Rayevsky, Robert, illus. LC 89-31376. 32p. (gr. k-3). 1990. RSBE 14.95 (*0-02-789401-0*, Macmillan Child Bk) Macmillan Child Grp.

—Will You Come Back for Me? Tucker, Kathleen, ed. LC 87-37258. (Illus.). 32p. (ps-k). 1988. PLB 13.95 (*0-8075-9112-2*); pap. 5.95 (*0-8075-9113-0*) A Whitman.

Tompkins, Nancy. Grandma Moses. Horner, Matina, intro. by. (Illus.). 112p. (gr. 5 up). 1989. PLB 17.95x (*1-55546-670-2*) Chelsea Hse.

Tompkins, Susie P. Cotton-Patch Schoolhouse. LC 91-23331. 224p. (Orig.). 1992. pap. 19.95t (*0-8173-0563-7*) U of Ala Pr.

Tompkins, Terence. Ravaged Temperate Forests. LC 93-13048. 1993. write for info. (*0-8368-0728-6*) Gareth Stevens Inc.

Tompson, Cliff. The Meteor Man. (gr. 7 up). 1993. pap. 3.25 (*0-590-47300-X*) Scholastic Inc.

Tomscha, Terry. American Customs & Traditions. (Illus.). 31p. (Orig.). 1990. pap. text ed. 5.25 (*0-582-03641-0*, 78662) Longman.

Tonner, Leslie. My Mom, Your Dad. 128p. 1989. 14.95 (*0-89015-720-0*, Pub. by Panda Bks) Eakin-Sunbelt.

Tonsing-Carter, Betty. Lesotho. (Illus.). 96p. (gr. 5 up). 1988. 14.95 (*0-7910-0097-4*) Chelsea Hse.

Toomey, Marilyn M. Before & After: Simple Concepts of Time. Woods, Julie N., ed. (Illus.). 62p. 1989. wkbk. & cards 16.95 (*0-923573-10-0*) Circuit Pubns.

—Concepterms. Schloss, Bevalee, ed. & illus. 125p. (ps-5). 1986. vinyl binder 19.95 (*0-923573-02-X*) Circuit Pubns.

—Explanations: Level I. Schloss, Bevalee, illus. (gr. 2-6). 1988. cards & worksheets 27.50 (*0-923573-05-4*) Circuit Pubns.

—Explanations: Level II. Schloss, Bevalee, illus. (gr. 7-12). 1988. cards & worksheets 27.50 (*0-923573-06-2*) Circuit Pubns.

—Explanations: Primary. Schloss, Bevalee, illus. (ps-8). 1989. cards & worksheets 27.50 (*0-923573-04-6*) Circuit Pubns.

—Morph-Aid: A Source of Roots, Prefixes & Suffixes. 2nd ed. Schloss, Bevalee, illus. 124p. (gr. 4-10). 1989. pap. 15.95 (*0-923573-03-8*) Circuit Pubns.

—One Hundred One Categories. Schloss, Bevalee, illus. 106p. (ps-5). 1985. spiral bdg. 21.95 (*0-923573-01-1*) Circuit Pubns.

—Please Put Me: Simple Spatial Concepts. Palto, Susan C. & Hennessy, Jim, illus. 48p. (ps-8). 1989. 16 cards & 32 worksheets 17.95 (*0-923573-12-7*) Circuit Pubns.

—Sounds All Around: Initial & Final Consonants. Schloss, Bevalee, illus. 384p. 1989. pap. 19.95 (*0-923573-11-9*) Circuit Pubns.

—Verbs Past & Present. Christy-Pallo, Susan, illus. 77p. 1989. wkbk. & cards 17.95 (*0-923573-09-7*) Circuit Pubns.

—Where Does It Belong? Interactive Language Activities Featuring Vocabulary & Question Forms. Christen-Pallo, Susan & Hennessy, Jim, illus. (ps-8). 1989. cards & worksheets 16.95 (*0-923573-13-5*) Circuit Pubns.

Toomey, Marilyn M. & Carmel, Paula. R Complete. (Illus.). 204p. (gr. k-6). 1988. vinyl binder 28.00 (*0-923573-07-0*) Circuit Pubns.

—S Complete. (Illus.). 217p. (gr. k-6). 1988. vinyl binder 28.00 (*0-923573-08-9*) Circuit Pubns.

Toomey, Mary R. Jamari. (Illus.). 1991. 6.95 (*0-533-09132-2*) Vantage.

Toor, Rachel. Eleanor Roosevelt. Horner, Matina S., intro. by. (Illus.). 112p. (gr. 5 up). 1989. 17.95 (*1-55546-674-5*) Chelsea Hse.

—The Polish Americans. Moynihan, Daniel P., intro. by. 112p. (Orig.). (gr. 5 up). 1988. 17.95 (*0-87754-895-1*); pap. 9.95 (*0-7910-0274-8*) Chelsea Hse.

Tope, Lily R. Philippines. LC 91-15855. (Illus.). 128p. (gr. 5-9). 1991. PLB 21.95 (*1-85435-403-5*) Marshall Cavendish.

Topek, Susan R. A Holiday for Noah. Springer, Sally, illus. LC 89-48189. 24p. (ps). 1990. 10.95 (*0-929371-07-0*); pap. 4.95 (*0-929371-08-9*) Kar Ben.

—Israel Is... Kahn, Katherine J., illus. LC 88-83569. 12p. (ps). 1989. bds. 4.95 (*0-930494-92-X*) Kar Ben.

—Ten Good Rules. Schanzer, Rosalyn, illus. LC 91-32109. 24p. (ps-1). 1992. 12.95 (*0-929371-30-5*); pap. 5.95 (*0-929371-28-3*) Kar Ben.

—A Turn for Noah: A Hanukkah Story. Springer, Sally, illus. LC 92-22958. 1992. 12.95 (*0-929371-37-2*); pap. 4.95 (*0-929371-38-0*) Kar Ben.

Topek, Susan Remick. A Taste for Noah. Springer, Sally, illus. LC 92-39384. (gr. k up). 1993. 12.95 (*0-929371-39-9*); pap. 4.95 (*0-929371-40-2*) Kar Ben.

Topooco, Eusebio. Waira's First Journey. LC 92-44158. (gr. 4 up). 1993. write for info. (*0-688-12054-7*); write for info. (*0-688-12055-5*) Lothrop.

Topper, Frank. Mystery at the Bike Race. Rogers, Jackie, illus. LC 84-16452. 128p. (gr. 3-7). 1985. lib. bdg. 9.49 (*0-8167-0454-6*); pap. text ed. 2.95 (*0-8167-0455-4*) Troll Assocs.

Torbit, Stephen C. Large Mammals of the Central Rockies: A Guide to Their Locations & Ecology. Torbit, Stephen C., illus. 72p. (gr. 12). 1987. pap. 7.95 (*0-9618450-0-7*) Bennet Creek.

Tord, Bijou Le see Le Tord, Bijou.

Tord, Bijou le see Le Tord, Bijou.

Tord, Bijou Le see Le Tord, Bijou.

Tordjman, Nathalie. The Living Pond. Bogard, Vicki, tr. from FRE. Bour, Laura, illus. LC 90-50780. 38p. (gr. k-5). 1991. 4.95 (*0-944589-38-3*, 383) Young Discovery Lib.

Toretta-Fuentes, June. Maria's Secret. Machlin, Mikki, illus. LC 92-9866. 32p. 1992. pap. 3.95 (*0-8091-6606-2*) Paulist Pr.

Torgerson, Shirley R., et al. LOGO in the Classroom. 202p. (gr. k-5). 1984. tchr's. guide 15.95 (*0-924667-12-5*) Intl Society Tech Educ.

Toriseva, Jonelle. Rodeo Day. Casilla, Robert, illus. LC 92-39475. 32p. (ps-2). 1994. RSBE 14.95 (*0-02-789405-3*, Bradbury Pr) Macmillan Child Grp.

Torjman, Nathalie. History & Geography of Climates. (gr. 6 up). 1988. 4.95 (*0-8120-3838-X*) Barron.

Tornqvist, Rita. The Christmas Carp. Kilburn, Greta, tr. Tornqvist, Marit, illus. 32p. (gr. k-3). 1990. 13.95 (*91-29-59784-6*, Pub. by R & S Bks) FS&G.

—The Old Musician. Tornqvist, Marit, illus. LC 93-664. 1993. Repr. 13.00 (*91-29-62244-1*, Pub. by R & S Bks) FS&G.

Torre, Betty L., retold by. The Luminous Pearl: A Chinese Folktale. Inouye, Carol, illus. LC 89-70999. 32p. (ps-3). 1990. 14.95 (*0-531-05890-5*); PLB 14.99 (*0-531-08490-6*) Orchard Bks Watts.

Torrence, Charles, ed. see Torrence, Susan.

Torrence, Susan. The California Alphabet Book. Torrence, Charles, ed. Torrence, Susan, illus. LC 86-51505. 32p. (gr. k-3). 1987. pap. 6.95 (*0-914281-48-8*) Torrence Pubns.

Torrence, Susan & Polansky, Leslie. The Oregon Alphabet Book. 2nd ed. Torrence, Susan, illus. 32p. (ps-6). 1983. 5.95 (*0-914281-00-3*) Torrence Pubns.

Torres, John A. & Sullivan, Michael J. Sports Great Darryl Strawberry. LC 89-28918. (Illus.). 64p. (gr. 4-10). 1990. lib. bdg. 15.95 (*0-89490-291-1*) Enslow Pubs.

Torres, Leyla. Gorrion Del Metro: Subway Sparrow. (ps-3). 1993. esp. 16.00 (*0-374-32756-4*) FS&G.

—Subway Sparrow. LC 92-55104. (ENG, SPA & POL.). 1993. 15.00 (*0-374-37285-3*) FS&G.

Torres, Luis. San Antonio Missions National Historical Park. Priehs, T. J. & Foreman, Ronald J., eds. LC 92-62159. 16p. (Orig.). 1992. pap. 2.95 (*1-877856-17-7*) SW Pks Mnmts.

Torres-Ortiz, Rafael A. Biologia: Estudio de la Vida Texto Programado. (SPA., Illus.). 466p. (gr. 10-12). 1985. pap. 23.50 (*0-939081-00-8*); pap. text ed. 18.75 (*0-685-17446-8*); tchr's. ed. 9.95 (*0-939081-01-6*); manual 10.95 (*0-939081-02-4*) Edit Roche.

Torrie, Margaret, jt. auth. see Arehart, Lynda L.

Torumasu, Kimiaki, jt. auth. see Zimmerman, Julie.

Tostado, Rocio G., tr. see Cutburth, Ronald W.

Tott Publications Staff. I Can Hear. 8p. (gr. 1). 1988. pap. text ed. 2.50 (*1-882225-11-2*) Tott Pubns.

—Lost. 8p. (gr. 1). 1988. pap. text ed. 2.50 (*1-882225-10-4*) Tott Pubns.

—My School. 8p. (gr. 1). 1990. pap. text ed. 2.50 (*1-882225-03-1*) Tott Pubns.

Totten, Samuel & Kleg, Milton. Human Rights. LC 88-4257. (Illus.). 256p. (gr. 6 up). 1989. lib. bdg. 18.95 (*0-89490-156-7*) Enslow Pubs.

Tottle, Edward L. War in the Woods: The Day the United States Began July 9, 1755. (Illus.). gr. 8). 1992. text ed. 29.00 (*937117-05-6*) Educ Materials.

Tott-Rizzuti, Kim. Mommy, What Does Dying Mean? (Illus., Orig.). (gr. k-4). 1992. pap. 6.95 (*0-8059-3292-5*) Dorrance.

Touchstone, Samuel J. How to Build: Mud Chimney, Water Grist Mill, Brush Arbor, Charcoal-Tar Kiln, Wooden Rake, Lard Squeezer, No. 1. Touchstone, Samuel J., illus. LC 87-80814. 60p. (Orig.). (gr. 6 up). 1987. pap. 3.95 (*0-914917-01-3*) Folk-Life.

—Jessie Jackson Touchstone Clan & Parallel Touchstones. LC 90-81215. (Illus.). 80p. (Orig.). (gr. 6-12). 1990. pap. text ed. 14.95 (0-914917-06-4) Folk-Life.

Touger, Malka. Sefer Hamitzvot for Youth, Vols. 1 & 2. (gr. 7-10). 1988. 18.00 (0-940118-26-2) Vol. 1, 248 Positive Commandments, 95p. Vol. 2, 365 Negative Commandments, 144p. Moznaim.

Touger, Malke. Meam Loez for Youth: Ruth. Shlomo, Bat, illus. 47p. (gr. 6-9). 1988. 9.00 (0-940118-27-0) Moznaim.

Toure, Masee. Mariamah's Good Fortune & Other Stories. (Illus.). (gr. 6-9). 1993. 10.95 (0-533-10292-8) Vantage.

Toure, Nkenge, jt. auth. see Ozer, Elizabeth M.

Tournier, Michel. Barbedor. Lemoine, Georges, illus. (FRE.). 48p. (gr. 3-7). 1990. pap. 8.95 (2-07-031172-4) Schoenhof.

—Pierrot ou les Secrets de la Nuit. Bour, Daniele, illus. (FRE.). 56p. (gr. 3-7). 1989. pap. 8.95 (2-07-031205-4) Schoenhof.

—Rois Mages. Charrier, Michel, illus. (FRE.). 160p. (gr. 5-10). 1978. pap. 7.95 (2-07-033280-2) Schoenhof.

—Sept Contes. Hezard, Pierre, illus. (FRE.). 161p. (gr. 5-10). 1990. pap. 8.95 (2-07-033497-X) Schoenhof.

—Vendredi ou la Vie Sauvage. Lemoine, Georges, illus. (FRE.). 191p. (gr. 5-10). 1987. pap. 7.95 (2-07-033445-7) Schoenhof.

Toussaint, Michael E. The Playland Kids, Featuring Marcus Toussaint, the Recycler. Hamburg, Cary, illus. 24p. (Orig.). (gr. k-6). 1992. pap. 2.95 (0-9630905-0-X) Michael T Enter.

Toussaint, Eliza. Brave Little Blackfoot. Douglas, Cal, illus. 32p. (Orig.). (gr. 1 up). 1993. pap. text ed. write for info. (0-9630583-3-9) E Toussant.

—The Cootie Dragons. Douglas, Cal, illus. 120p. (gr. 4 up). 1993. pap. text ed. write for info. (0-9630583-2-0) E Toussant.
THE COOTIE DRAGONS was written to help children to better understand HIV & AIDS. The AIDS virus is a health problem that has been identified as "Public Enemy Number One." Children hear about AIDS, just as we all do. But the real question is, just how much do they understand? Before printing THE COOTIE DRAGONS, I gathered twenty students & asked them one by one to tell me what they knew about AIDS. Just as I expected they knew very little & were very confused about the subject. I gave each of the students a rough draft of THE COOTIE DRAGONS to take home with them & read. Three days later I met with the same group of children & asked them again what they knew about AIDS. Their knowledge level had improved one hundred percent. Basic health education should be started as early as possible, in keeping with parental & community standards. It is very important that middle school students (those entering their teens) learn to protect themselves from the AIDS virus. Children must also be taught values & responsibilty, as well as skills to help them resist peer pressure that might lead to risky behavior. These skills can be reinforced by religious & community groups. However, final responsibility rests with the parents. As a parent, I encourage you to read THE COOTIE DRAGONS, & discuss the book with your children.
Publisher Provided Annotation.

—Soddy Bear: The Persian Gulf War. Rasher, Steven, illus. 76p. (Orig.). (gr. 4 up). 1991. pap. 17.95 (0-9630583-0-4) E Toussant.
Eliza Toussant has put a new twist in the Persian Gulf War. Devastated by the war herself & seeing the fear & concerns of children, she decided to write the Bear facts about the DESERT STORM WAR from August 2, 1990 to February 27, 1991. It's not your average story by any means. The names have been changed, as has the natural resource. This story was written to help children understand the war, adding a little humor to take away some of the hostility felt during & after the war. The characters are as follows: 1) President Bush is portrayed as---President Tush. 2) Sadam Hussein is portrayed as---Soddy Bear. 3) General Norman Schwarzkopf as---Stormy Duke Bear. In her well illustrated book, Eliza Toussant placed killer bees in scud missiles & planted deadly scorpions across the fields of Kuwait. She spilled millions of gallons of honey into the Persian Gulf, she used bears as soldiers. This book is a learning tool for educators, parents, community workers, as well as children. Although SODDY BEAR, THE PERSIAN GULF WAR is listed as fiction, it is also non fiction, there was a Gulf War & the true facts are there. SODDY BEAR, THE PERSIAN GULF WAR is history.
Publisher Provided Annotation.

Towe, Kenneth M., jt. auth. see Hubley, Faith.

Towle, Wendy. The Real McCoy: The Life of an African-American Inventor. Clay, Wil, illus. LC 91-38895. 32p. (gr. k-4). 1993. 14.95 (0-590-43596-5) Scholastic Inc.

Towne, Mary. Boxed In. LC 81-43875. 160p. (gr. 4-6). 1982. PLB 11.89 (0-690-04239-6, Crowell Jr Bks) HarpC Child Bks.

—Paul's Game. LC 82-72750. 192p. (gr. 7 up). 1983. 13.95 (0-385-29248-1) Delacorte.

—Steve the Sure. LC 90-584. 144p. (gr. 4-7). 1990. SBE 13.95 (0-689-31646-1, Atheneum Child Bk) Macmillan Child Grp.

Townley, Roderick, tr. see Escudie, Rene.

Towns, Saundra. Lillian Hellman. Horner, Matina S., intro. by. (Illus.). 112p. (gr. 5 up). 1989. 17.95 (1-55546-657-5) Chelsea Hse.

Townsend. Dark Ships. 112p. (gr. 6-8). 1988. 10.95 (0-89015-579-8); pap. 5.95 (0-89015-590-9) Eakin-Sunbelt.

Townsend, Alecia C. Mikhail Baryshnikov. LC 92-42547. (gr. 1-8). 1993. 19.93 (0-86625-484-6); 14.95s.p. (0-685-66287-X) Rourke Pubns.

Townsend, Anne. Marvelous Me: All about the Human Body. (Illus.). 48p. (ps-1). 1985. 13.95 (0-85648-577-2) Lion USA.

Townsend, Betsy B., jt. auth. see Cochrane, Shirley G.

Townsend, Charles B. World's Best Magic Tricks. LC 91-41310. (Illus.). 128p. (gr. 6-12). 1992. 12.95 (0-8069-8582-8) Sterling.

—World's Best Magic Tricks. LC 91-41310. (Illus.). 128p. (gr. 3-9). 1993. pap. 4.95 (0-8069-8583-6) Sterling.

—The World's Best Puzzles. LC 85-30284. (Illus.). 128p. (Orig.). (gr. 6-10). 1986. pap. 4.95 (0-8069-4734-9) Sterling.

—World's Greatest Puzzles. LC 92-17484. (Illus.). 128p. (gr. 5 up). 1992. 12.95 (0-8069-8664-6) Sterling.

—World's Greatest Puzzles. (Illus.). 128p. (gr. 5-10). 1993. pap. 4.95 (0-8069-8665-4) Sterling.

—World's Hardest Puzzles. LC 91-41544. (Illus.). 128p. (gr. 10-12). 1992. 12.95 (0-8069-8516-X) Sterling.

—World's Hardest Puzzles. (Illus.). 128p. (gr. 5 up). 1993. pap. 4.95 (0-8069-8517-8) Sterling.

—World's Most Baffling Puzzles. LC 91-21324. (Illus.). 128p. (gr. 4-11). 1991. 12.95 (0-8069-5832-4) Sterling.

—World's Most Baffling Puzzles. LC 91-21324. (Illus.). 128p. (gr. 8 up). 1992. pap. 4.95 (0-8069-5833-2) Sterling.

—The World's Most Challenging Puzzles. LC 88-19729. (Illus.). 128p. (gr. 3-9). 1989. pap. 4.95 (0-8069-6731-5) Sterling.

—World's Toughest Puzzles. LC 89-49131. (Illus.). 96p. 1990. 12.95 (0-8069-6962-8) Sterling.

—World's Toughest Puzzles. LC 89-49131. 96p. (gr. 6-12). 1991. pap. 4.95 (0-8069-6963-6) Sterling.

Townsend, Charles B., compiled by. Great Victorian Puzzle Book. LC 93-22700. (Illus.). 128p. (gr. 10-12). 1993. pap. 4.95 (0-8069-0388-0) Sterling.

Townsend, Charles D. Index to the Gazetteer of Bennington County Vermont, 1880 Hamilton Child. 41p. (Orig.). (gr. 9 up). 1989. pap. 7.50 (0-685-45065-1) ACETO Bookmen.

Townsend, Jace, jt. auth. see Metil, Luana.

Townsend, John R. Rob's Place. LC 86-27373. (gr. 4-9). 1988. PLB 12.95 (0-688-07258-5) Lothrop.

Townsend, Sandra S. The Old Jail Remembers Tuscaloosa. (Illus.). 44p. (Orig.). (gr. 5-12). 1987. pap. 4.50 (0-943487-03-X) Sevgo Pr.

Townsend, Sue. The Secret Diary of Adrian Mole, Aged 13 3-4. 208p. (gr. 8 up). 1984. pap. 4.99 (0-380-86876-8, Flare) Avon.

Townsend, Tom. The Battle of Galveston. Eakin, Edwin M., ed. Little, Debbie, illus. 80p. (gr. 9-11). 1989. 10.95 (0-89015-685-9, Pub. by Panda Bks); pap. 5.95 (0-89015-713-8) Eakin-Sunbelt.

—Bubba's Truck. 128p. (gr. 6-12). 1992. 14.95 (0-89015-857-6) Eakin-Sunbelt.

—Davy Crockett: An American Hero. Eakin, Edwin M., ed. LC 87-16545. (Illus.). 72p. (gr. 4-7). 1987. 10.95 (0-89015-643-3); pap. 5.95 (0-89015-627-1) Eakin-Sunbelt.

—Ghost Flyers. LC 93-19906. 1993. 11.95 (0-89015-897-5) Eakin-Sunbelt.

—Powderhorn Passage: Sequel to Where the Pirates Are, Vol. 3. Roberts, Melissa, ed. (gr. 4-7). 1988. 10.95 (0-89015-642-5, Pub. by Panda Bks) Eakin-Sunbelt.

—Queen of the Wind. Roberts, Melissa, ed. (Illus.). 144p. (gr. 8-10). 1989. 12.95 (0-89015-715-4, Pub. by Panda Bks) Eakin-Sunbelt.

—Trader Wooly & the Ghost in the Colonel's Jeep. (Illus.). 110p. (gr. 6-8). 1991. 10.95 (0-89015-807-X) Eakin-Sunbelt.

—Trader Wooly & the Secret of the Lost Nazi Treasure. Roberts, Melissa, ed. (Illus.). 120p. (gr. 4-7). 1987. 10.95 (0-89015-602-6, Pub. by Panda Bks); pap. 5.95 (0-89015-634-4) Eakin-Sunbelt.

Townson, Duncan. Alexander. Killingray, Margaret, et al, eds. (Illus.). 32p. (gr. 6-11). 1980. pap. text ed. 3.45 (0-89908-014-6) Greenhaven.

—Spices & Civilizations. Yapp, Malcolm, et al, eds. (Illus.). (gr. 6-11). 1980. pap. text ed. 3.45 (0-89908-004-9) Greenhaven.

Townson, Hazel. What on Earth...? (ps-3). 1991. 13.95 (0-316-85138-8) Little.

Toye, William, retold by see Cleaver, Elizabeth.

Toynton, Evelyn. Frederick Douglass & the War Against Slavery. LC 92-36930. (Illus.). 32p. (gr. 2-4). 1993. PLB 12.40 (1-56294-341-3) Millbrook Pr.

Tozer, A. W. Let My People Go: The Life of Robert A. Jaffray. rev. ed. LC 90-80076. 128p. 1990. pap. 7.99 (0-87509-427-9) Chr Pubns.

Tozuka, Takako. Children of the World: Indonesia. LC 86-42807. (Illus.). 64p. (gr. 5-6). 1987. PLB 19.93 (1-55532-165-8) Gareth Stevens Inc.

Tozuks, Takako. Children of the World: Turkey. Reitci, Rita & Sherwood, Rhoda I., eds. Tozuka, Takako, photos by. LC 88-32745. (Illus.). 64p. (gr. 5-6). 1989. PLB 19.93 (1-55532-851-2) Gareth Stevens Inc.

Tracey, Patrick. Military Leaders of the Civil War. LC 92-34346. (Illus.). 128p. (gr. 6-9). 1993. 16.95x (0-8160-2671-8) Facts on File.

Tracqui, Valerie. Polar Bear: Master of the Ice. (Illus.). 28p. (gr. 3-8). 1994. pap. 6.95 (0-88106-432-7) Charlesbridge Pub.

Tracqui, Valerie, jt. auth. see Dupont, Philippe.

Tracqui, Valerie, jt. auth. see Fontanel, Beatrice.

Tracy, Brian S., jt. auth. see Youngs, Bettie B.

Tracy, Kristin. English Words Grow from Latin & Greek Roots. 27p. (Orig.). (gr. 1-4). 1992. spiral bdg. 3.80 (0-939507-40-4, B120) Amer Classical.

Tracy, Kristin K. Quinque Sensus: The Five Senses. 24p. (Orig.). (gr. k-3). 1991. 2.10 (0-939507-01-3, B15) Amer Classical.

Tracy, Michael S. My Favorite Things to Do. 31p. (ps-k). 1992. pap. text ed. 23.00 big bk. (1-56843-005-1); pap. text ed. 4.50 (1-56843-055-8) BGR Pub.

Tracy, Wesley D. What's a Nice God Like You Doing in a Place Like This? 120p. 1990. pap. 5.95 (0-8341-1371-6) Beacon Hill.

Traetta, John & Traetta, MaryJean. Gymnastics Basics. Gow, Bill, illus. 64p. (gr. 3-7). 1983. pap. 3.95 (0-13-371740-2, Pub. by Treehouse) P-H.

Traetta, MaryJean, jt. auth. see Traetta, John.

Trafzer, Cliff. American Indians as Cowboys. (Illus.). 70p. (Orig.). (gr. 4-6). 1992. 10.95 (0-940113-23-6) Sierra Oaks Pub.

Trafzer, Clifford E. California's Indians & the Gold Rush. LC 89-64434. (Illus.). 61p. (Orig.). (gr. 4-7). 1990. pap. 10.95 (0-940113-21-X) Sierra Oaks Pub.

—Chief Joseph: Nez Perce Leader. (Illus.). 112p. (gr. 5 up). 1994. PLB 18.95 (0-7910-1708-7, Am Art Analog); pap. write for info. (0-7910-1972-1, Am Art Analog) Chelsea Hse.

—The Chinook. Porter, Frank W., III, intro. by. (Illus.). 112p. (gr. 5 up). 1990. 17.95 (1-55546-698-2) Chelsea Hse.

—The Nez Perce: Northwest. (Illus.). (gr. 5 up). 1994. 18.95 (1-55546-720-2, Am Art Analog); pap. 7.95 (0-7910-0391-4, Am Art Analog) Chelsea Hse.

Trafzer, Clifford E. & Smith-Trafzer, Lee A. Creation of a California Tribe: Grandfather's Maidu Indian Tale. Coates, Ross, illus. LC 88-61007. 45p. (Orig.). (gr. 3-6). 1988. pap. 6.95 (0-940113-18-X) Sierra Oaks Pub.

Trager, Oliver, ed. The Arts & Media in America: Freedom or Censorship? 224p. 1991. 29.95x (0-8160-2578-9) Facts on File.

—Communism: The Final Crisis? 224p. 1990. lib. bdg. 29.95x (0-8160-2507-X) Facts on File.

—Gorbachev's Glasnost: Red Star Rising. 224p. (gr. 7-12). 1989. 29.95x (0-8160-2220-8) Facts on File.

—Sports in America: Paradise Lost? 224p. 1990. 29.95x (0-8160-2412-X) Facts on File.

Trahey, Jerome. Building Self-Esteem: A Workbook for Teens. Guelzow, Diane, illus. 176p. (Orig.). (gr. 7-12). 1992. pap. 14.95 (0-89390-231-4) Resource Pubns.

Train, Russell E., intro. by. Earth at Risk, 24 vols. (gr. 5 up). 1991. PLB 478.80 (*0-7910-1571-8*) Chelsea Hse.

Trainer, David. A Day in the Life of a TV News Reporter. Sanacore, Stephen, photos by. LC 78-68810. (Illus.). 32p. (gr. 4-8). 1980. PLB 11.79 (*0-89375-228-2*); pap. 2.95 (*0-89375-232-0*); cassettes avail. Troll Assocs.

Trainor, Timothy N. & Krasnewich, Diane. Computer Concepts & Applications. 2nd ed. LC 86-62012. (Illus.). 350p. (gr. 7-8). 1987. pap. text ed. 26.50 (*0-394-39052-0*) Mitchell Pub.

Traisman, Enid S. Fire in My Heart - Ice in My Veins: A Journal for Teenager Experiencing a Loss. Sieff, Ben, illus. 64p. (Orig.). (gr. 7-12). 1992. wkbk. 8.95 (*1-56123-056-1*) Centering Corp.

Traketellas, Demetrios. Growing in the Knowledge of Christ. 18p. (gr. 12). 1987. pap. 1.25 (*0-917651-43-X*) Holy Cross Orthodox.

Trammell, Larry. The Highest Calling of All: God's Ultimate Purpose for Each of Us. Kerby, Rob, ed. 176p. (Orig.). (gr. 7 up). 1990. pap. 7.95 (*0-9624370-0-X*) Ablaze Pub.

Tran, Kim-Lan. Tet: The New Year. Vo-Dinh, Mai, illus. 32p. (gr. 2-5). 1993. pap. 4.95 (*0-671-79843-X*, S&S BYR) S&S Trade.

Tran Khan Tuyet. Children of Viet-Nam. (gr. k-2). 1973. 2.50 (*0-686-10278-9*) Asia Resource.

Tran-Khan-Tuyet. The Little Weaver of Thai-Yen Village. Hom, Nancy, illus. LC 86-17186. (ENG & VIE.). 24p. (gr. 2-9). 1987. 13.95 (*0-89239-030-1*) Childrens Book Pr.

Trapani, Iza. What Am I? An Animal Guessing Game. Trapani, Iza, illus. LC 92-15029. 32p. (ps-8). 1992. smythe sewn reinforced 13.95 (*1-879085-76-3*) Whsprng Coyote Pr.

Trapani, Iza, retold by. & illus. The Itsy-Bitsy Spider. LC 92-25150. 32p. (ps-12). 1993. smythe sewn reinforced 14.95 (*1-879085-77-1*) Whsprng Coyote Pr.

Traub, James. The Billion Dollar Connection: The International Drug Trade. LC 82-14212. (Illus.). 160p. (gr. 7 up). 1983. lib. bdg. write for info. (*0-671-49495-3*, J Messner); PLB 9.79 (*0-671-45247-9*) S&S Trade.

Traugh, Steven. All about Colors. (Illus.). 32p. (Orig.). 1993. pap. text ed. 8.95 (*0-7935-2384-2*, HL00330501) H Leonard Pub Corp.

—All about the Alphabet: Fun with Letters A-Z. (Illus.). 32p. (Orig.). 1993. pap. 8.95 incl. cass. (*0-7935-2260-9*, 00330500) H Leonard Pub Corp.

Trautman, Neal E. & Wilder, Lon. Fifty Things Teens Can Do to Fight Drugs. 96p. (Orig.). (gr. 9-12). 1991. pap. 5.95 (*0-9627536-2-9*) Standards & Trg.

Travers, Pamela L. Friend Monkey. Keeping, Charles, illus. LC 70-161389. (ps up). 1971. 6.95 (*0-15-229555-0*, HB Juv Bks) HarBrace.

—Friend Monkey. (Orig.). (gr. k-6). 1987. pap. 4.95 (*0-440-42817-3*, Pub. by Yearling Classics) Dell.

—Mary Poppins. rev. ed. (gr. 4-7). 1991. pap. 3.99 (*0-440-40406-1*) Dell.

—Mary Poppins & the House Next Door. Shepard, Mary, illus. (gr. 4 up). 1989. 12.95 (*0-385-29749-1*) Delacorte.

—Mary Poppins & the House Next Door. Shepard, Mary, illus. 96p. (gr. 4-7). 1992. pap. 3.50 (*0-440-40656-0*, YB) Dell.

—Mary Poppins Comes Back. (gr. 4-7). 1991. pap. 3.50 (*0-440-40418-5*) Dell.

—Mary Poppins from A to Z. Shepard, Mary, illus. LC 62-15629. (gr. 1-4). 1962. 10.95 (*0-15-252590-4*, HB Juv Bks) HarBrace.

—Mary Poppins from A to Z. (gr. 4-7). 1991. pap. 3.50 (*0-440-40526-2*, YB) Dell.

—Mary Poppins in Cherry Tree Lane. (gr. 3-7). 1992. 3.50 (*0-440-40637-4*, YB) Dell.

—Mary Poppins in the Kitchen. (gr. 4-7). 1991. pap. 3.50 (*0-440-40527-0*, YB) Dell.

Travers, Pamela L. & Moore-Betty, Maurice. Mary Poppins in the Kitchen: A Cookery Book with a Story. Shepard, Mary, illus. LC 75-10131. 128p. (gr. k up). 1975. 6.95 (*0-15-252898-9*, HB Juv Bks) HarBrace.

Travis, David. The Land & People of Italy. LC 91-9771. (Illus.). 256p. (gr. 6 up). 1992. 18.00 (*0-06-022778-8*); PLB 17.89 (*0-06-022784-2*) HarpC Child Bks.

Travis, Dempsey J. I Refuse to Learn to Fail. (Illus.). 75p. (gr. 3-6). 1991. 15.00 (*0-941484-12-2*) Urban Res Pr.

Travis, F. & Hindley, J. Spycraft. (Illus.). 32p. (gr. 3-6). 1977. pap. 5.95 (*0-86020-005-1*) EDC.

Travis, F., et al. Spy's Guidebook (B - U) (Illus.). 192p. (gr. 2-6). 1993. pap. 8.95 (*0-86020-169-4*) EDC.

Travis, Falcon. Great Book of Whodunit Puzzles: Mini-Mysteries for You to Solve. LC 92-43853. (Illus.). 128p. (gr. 5 up). 1993. pap. 4.95 (*0-8069-0348-1*) Sterling.

—Super Sleuth: Mini-Mysteries for You to Solve. LC 84-26814. (Illus.). 128p. (gr. 5 up). 1985. 12.95 (*0-8069-4700-4*) Sterling.

Travis, Lucille. Tirzah. Garber, S. David, ed. LC 90-23580. 160p. (gr. 3-7). 1991. pap. 5.95 (*0-8361-3546-6*) Herald Pr.

Traxler, Mary A. Elementary Language Arts Flipper, No. I. 39p. (gr. 3-6). 1989. trade edition 5.95 (*1-878383-15-9*) C Lee Pubns.

Traynor, Pete. Cigarettes, Cigarettes. Traynor, Pete, illus. Reynolds, Patrick, frwd. by. LC 92-31033. (Illus.). 24p.

1993. 14.95 (*0-9629978-7-0*) Sights Prods.

This landmark children's book, with a foreword by Patrick Reynolds, tells a cautionary story that casts cigarette smoking in a most unfavorable light. The tale follows the afternoon adventure of four children, one of whom is a smoker & the object of unfortunate circumstances. As the book unfolds, the reader sees the danger of cigarettes themselves as well as the advertising tactics practiced by tobacco companies to market cigarettes to children. Through an allegorical narrative, the long-term danger of smoking takes on an immediacy that makes it easy to understand, & the advertising images that are so attractive to youth are strongly satirized. The book also features an illustrated section of factual information about smoking & health & an expose of the tobacco industry. Additionally, there is an interactive question & answer section to allow adults & children to discuss the book & reinforce its anti-smoking message. CIGARETTES, CIGARETTES paves the way for its coming companion volume, CRACK, CRACK which similarly warns children about the dangers of crack-cocaine. Volume discounts available from the publisher. ISBN 0-9629978-7-0, $14.95. SIGHTS PRODUCTIONS, P.O. Box, Mt. Airy, MD 21771, (410) 795-4582; FAX (301) 829-2585.
Publisher Provided Annotation.

Traynor, Shauwn. Little Man in England. 112p. 1989. pap. 5.95 (*1-85371-032-6*, Pub. by Poolbeg Press Ltd Eire) Dufour.

Trease, Geoffrey. A Flight of Angels. 120p. (gr. 4-8). 1989. PLB 14.95 (*0-8225-0731-5*) Lerner Pubns.

Treat, Lawrence. You're the Detective! Twenty-Four Solve-Them-Yourself Picture Mysteries. Borowik, Kathleen, illus. LC 82-49346. 80p. (Orig.). (gr. 3-6). 1983. pap. 7.95 (*0-87923-478-4*) Godine.

Treays, R. Essential Biology. (Illus.). 64p. 1992. PLB 12.96 (*0-88110-585-6*); pap. 5.95 (*0-7460-0743-4*) EDC.

Treece, Henry. Further Adventures of Robinson Crusoe. Nickless, Will, illus. LC 58-9623. (gr. 7-11). 1958. 21.95 (*0-87599-116-5*) S G Phillips.

—The Magic Wood. Moser, Barry, illus. LC 91-29547. 32p. (gr. 1 up). 1992. 16.00 (*0-06-020802-3*); PLB 15.89 (*0-06-020803-1*) HarpC Child Bks.

—Men of the Hills. Price, Christine, illus. LC 58-5448. (gr. 6-9). 1958. 21.95 (*0-87599-115-7*) S G Phillips.

—Ride into Danger. Price, Christine, illus. LC 59-12203. (gr. 7-10). 1959. 21.95 (*0-87599-113-0*) S G Phillips.

—Road to Miklagard. Price, Christine, illus. LC 57-12280. (gr. 6-10). 1957. 21.95 (*0-87599-118-1*) S G Phillips.

—Viking's Dawn. Price, C., illus. LC 56-9962. (gr. 7-9). 1956. 21.95 (*0-87599-117-3*) S G Phillips.

—Westward to Vinland. Stobbs, William, illus. (gr. 8 up). 1967. 21.95 (*0-87599-136-X*) S G Phillips.

Treece, Patricia. Soldier of God. Chatton, Ray, illus. 32p. (gr. 1-8). 1982. pap. 1.00 (*0-913382-22-1*, 111-1) Prow Bks-Franciscan.

Treese, James B. Van see Burbank, Linda.

Treese, James B. Van see Goodin, Evelyn.

Treese, James B. Van see Kohler, Jan.

Treese, James B. Van see Merfield, LeAnn.

Treese, James B. Van see Olson, Michelle.

Tregaskis, Richard. Guadalcanal Diary. LC 83-17662. (Illus.). 176p. (gr. 5-9). 1984. pap. 4.95 (*0-394-86268-6*) Random Bks Yng Read.

Tregebov, Rhea. The Big Storm. Kovalski, Maryann, illus. LC 92-55040. 32p. (ps-3). 1993. 13.95 (*1-56282-461-9*); PLB 13.89 (*1-56282-462-7*) Hyprn Child.

—The Extraordinary Ordinary Everything Room. Desputeaux, Helene, illus. (gr. k-2). 1991. pap. 5.95 (*0-929005-24-4*, Pub. by Second Story Pr CN) InBook.

Tregeebov, Rhea. Sasha & the Wiggly Tooth. Desputeaux, Helene, illus. 24p. 1993. 12.95 (*0-317-05541-0*, Pub. by Second Story Pr CN); pap. 5.95 (*0-929005-50-3*, Second Story Pr CN) InBook.

Treherne, Katie T., adapted by. & illu see Andersen, Hans Christian.

Trelease, Jim, ed. Hey! Listen to This: Stories to Read-Aloud. 240p. (Orig.). (gr. k-4). 1992. 22.00 (*0-670-83691-5*, Viking); pap. 11.00 (*0-14-014653-9*) Viking Child Bks.

—Read All About It! Great Stories, Poems, & Newspaper Pieces for Reading Aloud for Preteens & Teens. LC 93-21781. 416p. (Orig.). 1993. pap. 11.00 (*0-14-014655-5*, Penguin Bks) Viking Penguin.

Trella, Phyllis. Butterflies Have Grandparents, Too. Trella, Phyllis, illus. LC 82-73691. 48p. (gr. 2-6). write for info. (*0-914201-02-6*) Cheeruppet.

—Les Duit at the Olympics...& Be a Strong. Trella, Phyllis, illus. 48p. (gr. 2-6). write for info. (*0-914201-01-8*) Cheeruppet.

—Jodee's Closet. Trella, Phyllis, illus. LC 82-73689. 48p. (gr. 2-6). write for info. (*0-914201-04-2*) Cheeruppet.

—A Peek at Occupations. Trella, Phyllis, illus. LC 82-73692. 48p. (gr. 2-6). write for info. (*0-914201-03-4*) Cheeruppet.

Trenary, Jill. The Day I Skated for the Gold. 1989. pap. 14.95 (*0-671-68315-2*, S&S BFYR) S&S Trade.

Trenc, Milan. A Night in the Museum. (Illus.). 32p. (ps-3). 1993. 12.95 (*0-8120-6400-3*); pap. 5.95 (*0-8120-1523-1*) Barron.

Trenholm, Virginia C. Omen of the Hawks. LC 89-63585. (Illus.). 312p. (gr. 9-12). 1989. 18.95 (*0-943255-26-0*); pap. 9.95 (*0-943255-35-X*) Portfolio Pub.

Trent, John, et al. The Treasure Tree. 128p. (gr. k-3). 1992. 14.99 (*0-8499-0936-8*) Word Inc.

Trent, John T. There's a Duck in My Closet. Love, Judy, illus. LC 93-15707. (gr. k-5). 1993. 12.99 (*0-8499-1037-4*) Word Pub.

Trent, Linda M. Games That Make Homework Fun! 80p. (Orig.). (gr. 2-8). 1991. pap. 9.95 (*0-9630470-2-7*) For-Kids.

Trent, Robbie. The First Christmas. rev. ed. Simont, Marc, illus. LC 89-29729. 32p. (ps-2). 1990. pap. 3.50 (*0-06-443249-1*, Trophy) HarpC Child Bks.

—First Christmas Board Book. Simont, Marc, illus. LC 89-29729. 26p. (ps). 1992. 4.95 (*0-694-00423-5*, Festival) HarpC Child Bks.

Trepp, Leo. A History of the Jewish Experience: Eternal Faith, Eternal People. (gr. 9 up). 12.95 (*0-317-70167-3*) Behrman.

Treseder, Terry W. Hear O Israel: A Story of the Warsaw Ghetto. Bloom, Lloyd, illus. LC 89-7029. 48p. (gr. 3 up). 1990. SBE 13.95 (*0-689-31456-6*, Atheneum Child Bk) Macmillan Child Grp.

Tresselt, Alvin. Autumn Harvest. Duvoisin, Roger, illus. LC 51-8824. 32p. (ps-2). 1990. pap. 3.95 (*0-688-09925-4*, Mulberry) Morrow.

—Gift of the Tree. LC 90-2084. (ps-3). 1992. 14.00 (*0-688-10684-6*); PLB 13.93 (*0-688-10685-4*) Lothrop.

—Hide & Seek Fog. Duvoisin, Roger, illus. LC 65-14087. 32p. (ps-3). 1988. pap. 3.95 (*0-688-07813-3*, Mulberry) Morrow.

—The Mitten. Mills, Yaroslava, illus. LC 64-14436. 30p. (ps-3). 1989. pap. 4.95 (*0-688-09238-1*, Mulberry) Morrow.

—The Rabbit Story. Ewing, Carolyn, illus. LC 88-32594. 32p. (ps-2). 1989. 12.95 (*0-688-08650-0*); PLB 12.88 (*0-688-08651-9*) Lothrop.

—Rain Drop Splash. Weisgard, Leonard, illus. LC 46-11878. 28p. (ps-3). 1990. pap. 3.95 (*0-688-09352-3*, Mulberry) Morrow.

—Sun Up. (ps-3). 1991. 14.95 (*0-688-08656-X*) Lothrop.

—Sun Up. (ps-3). 1991. PLB 14.88 (*0-688-08657-8*) Lothrop.

—Wake Up, City! Ewing, Carolyn, illus. LC 88-32594. 32p. (ps-2). 1989. lib. bdg. 14.88 (*0-688-08653-5*) Lothrop.

—Wake up, Farm! Ewing, Carolyn, illus. LC 90-33646. 32p. (ps up). 1991. 14.95 (*0-688-08654-3*); PLB 14.88 (*0-688-08655-1*) Lothrop.

—White Snow Bright Snow. Duvoisin, Roger, illus. LC 88-10018. (ps-3). 1988. pap. 3.95 (*0-688-08294-7*, Mulberry) Morrow.

—White Snow, Bright Snow. Duvoisin, Roger, illus. (ps-3). 1989. 13.95 (*0-688-41161-4*); PLB 13.88 (*0-688-51161-9*) Lothrop.

Tresselt, Alvin R. Autumn Harvest. Duvoisin, Roger, illus. LC 51-8824. 32p. (gr. k-3). 1951. PLB 15.88 (*0-688-51155-4*) Lothrop.

—Hide & Seek Fog. Duvoisin, Roger, illus. LC 65-14087. 32p. (gr. k-2). PLB 14.88 (*0-688-51169-4*) Lothrop.

—Mitten. Mills, Yaroslava, illus. LC 64-14436. 30p. (gr. k-3). 1964. PLB 12.88 (*0-688-51053-1*) Lothrop.

Tretler, Marcia. Alan & Naomi: A Study Guide. (gr. 4-6). 1989. tchr's. ed. & wkbk. 14.95 (*0-88122-055-8*) LRN Links.

—Anne Frank: The Diary of a Young Girl: A Study Guide. (gr. 6-10). 1987. tchr's. ed. & wkbk. 14.95 (*0-88122-104-X*) LRN Links.

—Call It Courage: A Study Guide. (gr. 4-7). 1987. tchr's ed. & wkbk. 14.95 (*0-88122-080-9*) Lrn Links.

—The Cay: A Study Guide. (gr. 4-7). 1986. tchr's. ed. & wkbk. 14.95 (*0-88122-081-7*) LRN Links.

—From the Mixed-up Files of Mrs. Basil E. Frankweiler: A Study Guide. (gr. 4-7). 1987. tchr's. ed. & wkbk. 14.95 (*0-88122-084-1*) LRN Links.

—Hatchet: A Study Guide. Friedland, Joyce & Kessler, Rikki, eds. (gr. 9-12). 1990. pap. text ed. 14.95 (*0-88122-413-8*) Lrn Links.

—The Lottery Rose: A Study Guide. 22p. (gr. 9-12). 1990. pap. text ed. 14.95 (*0-88122-395-6*) Lrn Links.

—Luke Was There: A Study Guide. Friedland, Joyce & Kessler, Rikki, eds. 19p. (gr. 9-12). 1990. pap. text ed. 14.95 (*0-88122-400-6*) Lrn Links.

—The Outsiders - Study Guide. Friedland, Joyce & Kessler, Rikki, eds. (gr. 6-9). Date not set. pap. text ed. 14.95 (0-88122-030-2) Lrn Links.

—Sounder - Study Guide. Friedland, Joyce & Kessler, Rikki, eds. (gr. 6-9). Date not set. pap. text ed. 14.95 (0-88122-130-9) Lrn Links.

—The Summer of My German Soldier - Study Guide. Friedland, Joyce & Kessler, Rikki, eds. (gr. 6-9). Date not set. pap. text ed. 14.95 (0-88122-131-7) Lrn Links.

Tretler, Marcia, et al. Dear Mr. Henshaw: A Study Guide. (gr. 4-6). 1986. tchr's. ed. & wkbk. 14.95 (0-88122-074-4) LRN Links.

Trevant, Pierre, tr. see Cosby, Bill, et al.

Trevelyan, George M. English Revolution, Sixteen Eighty-Eight to Sixteen Eighty-Nine. (gr. 9 up). 1938. pap. 6.95 (0-19-500263-6) OUP.

Trevino, Elizabeth B. de see De Trevino, Elizabeth B.

Trevino, Elizabeth B. De see De Trevino, Elizabeth B.

Trevino, Elizabeth Borton De see De Trevino, Elizabeth Borton.

Trevor, William. Juliet's Story. LC 93-21790. 1994. pap. 14.00 (0-671-87442-X) S&S Trade.

Trezise, Percy. Children of the Great Lake. (ps-3). 1993. 10.00 (0-207-17677-9, Pub. by Angus & Robertson AT) HarpC.

—Lasca & Her Pups. (ps-3). 1992. pap. 6.95 (0-207-17003-7, Pub. by Angus & Robertson AT) HarpC.

Triado, Juan-Ramon. The Key to Baroque Art. (Illus.). 80p. (gr. 8 up). 1990. PLB 21.50 (0-8225-2056-7) Lerner Pubns.

—The Key to Painting. (Illus.). 80p. (gr. 8 up). 1990. PLB 21.50 (0-8225-2050-8) Lerner Pubns.

Tricker, Andy. Accidents Will Happen. 196p. (gr. 7-9). 1989. pap. 9.95 (0-233-98095-4, Pub. by A Deutsch England) Trafalgar.

Trifiletti, Don. Spirit Playmates: A Boy's Adventure with Music & Lyrics. 64p. (Orig.). (gr. 3-6). 1990. pap. 8.95 (1-56917-015-4) Am Literary Pr.

Triggs, Barbara. Wombats. LC 90-34042. (Illus.). 40p. (gr. 3-7). 1991. 14.45 (0-395-55993-6) HM.

Triggs, Tony P. Viking Warriors. LC 90-858. (Illus.). 24p. (gr. 2-5). 1991. PLB 10.90 (0-531-18356-4, Pub. by Bookwright Pr) Watts.

Triggs, Tracy. Discovering Virginia's Endangered Species: An Activity Book. (Illus.). 32p. (gr. 4 up). 1993. write for info. (0-9625801-5-5) VA Mus Natl Hist.

Trim, John. Ganz Spontan! (GER.). 352p. 1988. pap. text ed. 11.50 (0-8219-0346-2, 45295); tchr's. guide 5.95 (0-8219-0347-0, TG-45823) EMC.

Trimble, Marshall. Arizona: A Panoramic History of a Frontier State. LC 76-45265. 1977. pap. 14.95 (0-385-12806-1) Doubleday.

—It Always Rains after a Dry Spell. Graham, Jack, illus. 288p. (Orig.). (gr. 6 up). 1992. pap. 12.95 (0-918080-67-3) Treasure Chest.

Trimble, Stephen. The Village of Blue Stone. Dewey, Jennifer O. & Reade, Deborah, illus. LC 88-34194. 64p. (gr. 3-7). 1990. RSBE 14.95 (0-02-789501-7, Macmillan Child Bk) Macmillan Child Grp.

Trimby, Elisa see Moore, Clement C.

Trinca, Rod, jt. auth. see Argent, Kerry.

Trinkle, Timothy, et al. Practice, Practice, Practice, Plus, Bk. II: Proportions, Percents, Integers, Rationals, Equations, Area, Volume, Problem Solving, Combinations. 2nd ed. 224p. 1990. pap. 10.75 (0-685-35051-7); answer book 2.50 (0-685-35052-5) ST Two.

Tripp, C. J. Just Mole. Hudd, Stacy, illus. LC 87-71721. 137p. (Orig.). (gr. 4-6). 1989. pap. 7.00 (0-916383-39-3) Aegina Pr.

Tripp, Nathaniel. Thunderstorm! Wijngaard, Juan, illus. LC 93-4612. Date not set. write for info. (0-8037-1365-7); PLB write for info. (0-8037-1366-5) Dial Bks Young.

Tripp, Valerie. Baby Koala Finds a Home. Kalthoff, Sandra C., illus. LC 87-6325. 24p. (ps-2). 1987. pap. 3.95 (0-516-41577-8) Childrens.

—Baby Koala Finds a Home Big Book. (Illus.). 24p. (ps-2). 1990. PLB 30.60 (0-516-49515-1) Childrens.

—Changes for Felicity: A Winter Story. (Illus.). (gr. 2-5). 1992. PLB 12.95 (1-56247-038-8); pap. 5.95 (1-56247-037-X) Pleasant Co.

—Changes for Molly: A Winter Story. Backes, Nick, illus. 67p. (Orig.). (gr. 2-5). 1988. 12.95 (0-937295-96-5); pap. 5.95 (0-937295-49-3) Pleasant Co.

—Changes for Samantha: A Winter Story. Thieme, Jeanne, ed. Grace, Robert & Niles, Nancy, illus. 72p. (Orig.). (gr. 2-5). 1988. 12.95 (0-937295-46-9); PLB 12.95 (0-937295-95-7); pap. 5.95 (0-937295-47-7) Pleasant Co.

—Felicity, 6 bks. (Illus.). (gr. 2-5). 1991. Boxed Set. PLB 74.95 (1-56247-045-0); Boxed Set. pap. 34.95 (1-56247-044-2) Pleasant Co.

—Felicity Learns a Lesson. Andreasen, Dan, et al, illus. 80p. (Orig.). (gr. 2-5). 1991. 12.95 (1-56247-006-X); PLB 12.95 (1-56247-008-6); pap. 5.95 (1-56247-007-8) Pleasant Co.

—Felicity Saves the Day: A Summer Story. (Illus.). (gr. 2-5). 1992. PLB 12.95 (1-56247-035-3); pap. 5.95 (1-56247-034-5) Pleasant Co.

—Felicity's Surprise. Andreasen, Dan, et al, illus. 80p. (Orig.). (gr. 2-5). 1991. 12.95 (1-56247-009-4); PLB 12.95 (1-56247-011-6); pap. 5.95 (1-56247-010-8) Pleasant Co.

—Happy Birthday Felicity! A Springtime Story. (Illus.). 69p. (gr. 2-5). 1992. PLB 12.95 (1-56247-032-9); pap. 5.95 (1-56247-031-0) Pleasant Co.

—Happy Birthday Molly! A Springtime Story. Thieme, Jeanne, ed. Gaadt, David, illus. 72p. (gr. 2-5). 1987. 12.95 (0-937295-36-1); PLB 12.95 (0-937295-90-6); pap. 5.95 (0-937295-37-X) Pleasant Co.

—Happy Birthday Samantha! A Springtime Story. Thieme, Jeanne, ed. Grace, Robert & Niles, Nancy, illus. 72p. (gr. 2-5). 1987. 12.95 (0-937295-34-5); PLB 12.95 (0-937295-89-2); pap. 5.95 (0-937295-35-3) Pleasant Co.

—Happy, Happy Mother's Day! Martin, Sandra K., illus. LC 89-35757. 24p. (ps-2). 1989. pap. 3.95 (0-516-41521-2) Childrens.

—Meet Felicity. Andreasen, Dan, et al, illus. 80p. (Orig.). (gr. 2-5). 1991. 12.95 (1-56247-003-5); PLB 12.95 (1-56247-005-1); pap. 5.95 (1-56247-004-3) Pleasant Co.

—Meet Molly: An American Girl. Thieme, Jeanne, ed. Payne, C. F., illus. 72p. (gr. 2-5). 1986. 12.95 (0-937295-06-X); PLB 12.95 (0-937295-81-7); pap. 5.95 (0-937295-07-8) Pleasant Co.

—Molly, 6 bks. (Illus.). 432p. (gr. 2-5). 1991. Boxed Set. 74.95 (1-56247-014-0); Boxed Set. lib. bdg. 74.95 (1-56247-051-5); Boxed Set. pap. 34.95 (0-937295-78-7) Pleasant Co.

—Molly Learns a Lesson: A School Story. Thieme, Jeanne, ed. Payne, C. F., illus. 72p. (gr. 2-5). 1986. 12. 95 (0-937295-15-9); PLB 12.95 (0-937295-84-1); pap. 5.95 (0-937295-16-7) Pleasant Co.

—Molly Saves the Day: A Summer Story. Thieme, Jeanne, ed. Backes, Nick, illus. 72p. (gr. 2-5). 1988. 12.95 (0-937295-42-6); PLB 12.95 (0-937295-93-0); pap. 5.95 (0-937295-43-4) Pleasant Co.

—Molly's Surprise: A Christmas Story. Thieme, Jeanne, ed. Payne, C. F., illus. 72p. (gr. 2-5). 1986. 12.95 (0-937295-24-8); PLB 12.95 (0-937295-87-6); pap. 5.95 (0-937295-25-6) Pleasant Co.

—No Place Like Home. Callen, Liz, illus. 24p. (Orig.). (gr. 1-3). 1991. pap. text ed. 29.95 (1-56334-046-1); pap. text ed. 4.15 small bk. (1-56334-052-6) Hampton-Brown.

—The Penguins Paint. LC 87-14081. (Illus.). 24p. (ps-2). 1987. pap. 3.95 (0-516-41567-0) Childrens.

—Pequeno Coala Busca Casa (Baby Koala Finds a Home) Kalthoff, Sandra C., illus. LC 87-6325. (SPA & ENG.). 24p. (ps-2). 1989. PLB 12.33 (0-516-31577-3); pap. 3.95 (0-516-51577-2); pap. 30.60 big bk. (0-516-59515-6) Childrens.

—El Perro Cantor (The Singing Dog) Martin, Sandra K., illus. LC 86-14797. (SPA). 24p. (ps-2). 1990. PLB 12. 33 (0-516-31578-1); pap. 3.95 (0-516-51578-0) Childrens.

—Los Pinguinos Se Ponen a Pintar (The Penguins Paint) Martin, Sandra K., illus. LC 87-14081. (SPA). 24p. (ps-2). 1990. PLB 12.33 (0-516-31567-6); pap. 3.95 (0-516-51567-5) Childrens.

—Samantha Saves the Day: A Summer Story. Thieme, Jeanne, ed. Grace, Robert & Niles, Nancy, illus. 72p. (gr. 2-5). 1988. 12.95 (0-937295-40-X); PLB 12.95 (0-937295-92-2); pap. 5.95 (0-937295-41-8) Pleasant Co.

—Sillyhen's Big Surprise. Martin, Sandra K., illus. LC 89-35758. 24p. (ps-2). 1989. pap. 3.95 (0-516-41522-0) Childrens.

—La Sorpresa de Gallinita (Sillyhen's Big Surprise) Martin, Sandra K., illus. LC 89-35758. (SPA). 24p. (ps-2). 1990. pap. 3.95 (0-516-51522-9) Childrens.

—Squirrel's Thanksgiving Surprise. Martin, Sandra K., illus. LC 87-35518. 24p. (gr. k-2). 1988. PLB 12.33 (0-516-01568-0); pap. 3.95 (0-516-41568-9) Childrens.

Tripp, Valerie & Thieme, Jeanne. The American Girls Theater: Plays about Kirsten, Samantha, & Molly for You & Your Friends to Perform, 5 bks. Backes, Nick, et al, illus. 336p. (Orig.). (gr. 2-5). 1989. Set. pap. 14. 95 (0-937295-58-2) Pleasant Co.

Tripp, Wallace. Granfa' Grig Had a Pig & Other Rhymes Without Reason from Mother Goose. Tripp, Wallace, illus. 96p. (gr. 4-12). 1976. 19.95 (0-316-85282-1); pap. 10.95 (0-316-85284-8) Little.

—A Great Big Ugly Man Came up & Tied His Horse to Me: A Book of Nonsense Verse. (Illus.). 48p. (gr. k-12). 1974. lib. bdg. 14.95 (0-316-85280-5); pap. 6.95 (0-316-85281-3) Little.

Trisler, Alana & Cardiel, Patrice H. Words I Use When I Write. Trisler, Alana & Cardiel, Patrice H., illus. 36p. (Orig.). (gr. k-3). 1989. pap. text ed. 2.50 (0-935493-33-6) Programs Educ.

—Words I Use When I Write Poster Book: Alphabet, Theme & People Support Materials. (Illus.). 1992. wkbk. 8.95 (0-935493-39-5) Modern Learn Pr.

Trist, Alan. The Water of Life: A Tale of the Grateful Dead. Carpenter, Jim, illus. 52p. (gr. 2-12). 1990. PLB 12.95 (0-938493-12-4) Hulogosi Inc.

Tritten, Charles. Heidi Grows Up. 1988. pap. 4.95 (0-440-40107-0, Pub. by Yearling Classics) Dell.

Trivas, Irene. Annie... Anya: A Month in Moscow. LC 91-46433. (Illus.). 32p. (gr. k-2). 1992. 14.95 (0-531-05452-7); PLB 14.99 (0-531-08602-X) Orchard Bks Watts.

—Emma's Christmas: An Old Song Re-sung & Pictured. LC 88-1640. (Illus.). 32p. (ps-2). 1988. 14.95 (0-531-05780-1); PLB 14.99 (0-531-08380-2) Orchard Bks Watts.

—Emma's Christmas: An Old Song Re-sung & Pictured. LC 88-1640. (Illus.). 32p. (ps-2). 1992. pap. 5.95 (0-531-07022-0) Orchard Bks Watts.

Trivizas, Eugene. The Three Little Wolves & the Big Bad Pig. Oxenbury, Helen, illus. LC 92-24829. 32p. (gr. k-5). 1993. SBE 15.95 (0-689-50569-8, M K McElderry) Macmillan Child Grp.

Trodglen, James E., Jr. Super Origami: Book One. (Illus.). 44p. 1991. pap. 9.95 (1-879610-01-9) Origami Intl.

Troia, Lily. China Shelf Luxury. (Illus.). 32p. (gr. 2-4). 1990. PLB 29.28 clipper (0-8172-2787-3); PLB 17.96 (0-8172-2782-2) Raintree Steck-V.

—China Shelf Luxury. (ps-3). 1993. pap. 3.95 (0-8114-5212-3) Raintree Steck-V.

Troll. Black Beauty Activity Book. 64p. (ps-3). 1991. pap. 1.95 (0-8167-2290-0) Troll Assocs.

—Brain Teasers & Puzzles for Kids. 32p. (ps-3). 1991. pap. 1.95 (0-8167-2247-1) Troll Assocs.

—Kites That Really Fly. 14p. (gr. 5-9). 1991. pap. 5.95 (0-8167-2357-5) Troll Assocs.

—Legend of Sleepy Hollow Activity Book. 64p. (gr. 3-6). 1991. pap. 1.95 (0-8167-2284-6) Troll Assocs.

—Photo Fun Book Baby Animals. 12p. (ps-3). 1991. pap. 5.95 (0-8167-2085-1) Troll Assocs.

—Wizard of Oz Activity Book. 64p. (ps-3). 1991. pap. 1.95 (0-8167-2283-8) Troll Assocs.

Troll Books Staff. Goldilocks & the Three Bears, 4 vols. (ps). 1993. Boxed set. 9.95 (0-8167-2938-7) Troll Assocs.

—Last Action Hero Activity Book. (ps-3). 1993. pap. 2.50 (0-8167-3146-2) Troll Assocs.

—Wizard of Oz, 4 vols. (ps). 1993. Boxed set. 9.95 (0-8167-2996-4) Troll Assocs.

Troll, Morgan. The Ball, the Book, & the Drum. (Illus.). 32p. (gr. 2-4). 1990. PLB 29.28 clipper (0-8172-2786-5); PLB 17.96 (0-8172-2781-4) Raintree Steck-V.

Troll Press Staff. Home Alone Two: Lost in New York. (gr. 4-7). 1992. pap. 2.50 (0-8167-2847-X) Troll Assocs.

Troll Staff. Christmas Around the World. 12p. (ps-3). 1991. pap. 2.95 (0-8167-2189-0) Troll Assocs.

—Christmas Countdown. 10p. (ps). 1991. pap. 3.95 (0-8167-2183-1) Troll Assocs.

—Train Book. (ps). 1991. 4.95 (0-8167-2244-7) Troll Assocs.

Troop, Beth, ed. A Simply Monstrous Time: And Other Halloween Stories from Highlights. (Illus.). 32p. (Orig.). (gr. 2-7). 1993. pap. 4.95 (1-56397-085-6) Boyds Mills Pr.

Tropea, Judith. A Day in the Life of a Museum Curator. Halpern, John, photos by. LC 90-11060. (Illus.). 32p. (gr. 4-8). 1991. lib. bdg. 11.79 (0-8167-2212-9); pap. text ed. 2.95 (0-8167-2213-7) Troll Assocs.

Tropea, Judith, jt. auth. see Michels, Penny.

Tropea, Maria. Look & Look Again, Lost in the Haunted Mansion. Tallarico, Anthony, illus. 24p. (Orig.). (gr. 4-7). 1990. pap. 1.95 (1-878890-03-4) Palisades Prodns.

—Look & Look Again: Lost in the Haunted Mansion. Tallarico, A., illus. 24p. 1991. 2.98 (1-56156-044-8); pap. 1.95 (1-56156-050-2) Kidsbks.

—Look & Look Again: Missing Snowman. Tallarico, A., illus. 24p. 1991. 2.98 (1-56156-047-2); pap. 1.95 (1-56156-053-7) Kidsbks.

—Look & Look Again: Silly Schoolhouse. Tallarico, A., illus. 24p. 1991. pap. 1.95 (1-56156-051-0) Kidsbks.

—Look & Look Again: Silly Schoolhouse. Tallarico, A., illus. 24p. 1991. 2.98 (1-56156-045-6) Kidsbks.

—Look & Look Again: Where's Benjy Bunny? Tallarico, A., illus. 24p. 1991. 2.98 (1-56156-046-4); pap. 1.95 (1-56156-052-9) Kidsbks.

Tropea, S. BMX, A Photo-Fact Book. (Illus.). 24p. (Orig.). 1987. pap. 1.95 (0-942025-16-4) Kidsbks.

—Snakes, A Photo-Fact Book. (Illus.). 24p. (Orig.). 1988. pap. 1.95 (0-942025-15-6) Kidsbks.

Trosclair. A Cajun Night Before Christmas. Jacobs, Howard, ed. Rice, James, illus. LC 74-151725. 48p. (gr. 6-12). 1973. 12.95 (0-88289-002-6) Pelican.

—Cajun Night Before Christmas: Full-Color Edition. Jacobs, Howard, ed. Rice, James, illus. LC 92-8375. 48p. (gr. k-3). 1992. 14.95 (0-88289-940-6); ltd. boxed signed ed. 25.00 (0-88289-947-3); audio 9.95 (0-88289-914-7) Pelican.

Trost, Ed, ed. see Anderson, Stephen E.

Troth, Susan, jt. auth. see Ratliff, Gerald L.

Trotman, Felicity, as told by. The Sorcerer's Apprentice. (Illus.). 32p. (gr. k-5). 1985. PLB 17.96 (0-8172-2505-6) Raintree Steck-V.

Trotman, Felicity & Greenway, Shirley, eds. Davy Crockett. (Illus.). 32p. (gr. 2-5). 1985. PLB 17.96 (0-8172-2504-8) Raintree Steck-V.

Trott, Betty. Breathe on Me Butterflies. McGrew, Michelle, illus. LC 93-60232. 44p. (gr. k-3). 1994. pap. 8.95 (1-55523-603-0) Winston-Derek.

Trotter, Candace L., ed. see O'Connor, Patricia.

Trottier, Maxine, jt. auth. see McDowell, Margaret.

Troudet, Farideh. Trudy's Short Stories. 1993. pap. 8.95 (0-533-10451-3) Vantage.

Troughton, Joanna. Make-Believe Tales: A Folk Tale from Burma. Troughton, Joanna, illus. LC 90-48962. 32p. (gr. k-3). 1991. PLB 14.95 (0-87226-451-3, Bedrick Blackie) P Bedrick Bks.

—Mouse-Deer's Market: A Folk Tale from Borneo. Troughton, Joanna, illus. LC 84-11049. 32p. (gr. k-3). 1984. PLB 14.95 (0-911745-63-7, Bedrick Blackie) P Bedrick Bks.

—The Wizard Punchkin: A Folk Tale from India. Troughton, Joanna, illus. LC 87-11517. 32p. (gr. k-3). 1988. PLB 14.95 (*0-87226-162-X*, Bedrick Blackie) P Bedrick Bks.

Troughton, Joanna, retold by. & illus. How Night Came: A Folk Tale from the Amazon. LC 86-10917. 32p. (gr. k-3). 1986. PLB 14.95 (*0-87226-093-3*, Bedrick Blackie) P Bedrick Bks.

—How Rabbit Stole the Fire: A North American Indian Folk Tale. LC 85-15629. 32p. (gr. k-3). 1986. PLB 14.95 (*0-87226-040-2*, Bedrick Blackie) P Bedrick Bks.

—How the Birds Changed Their Feathers: A South American Folk Tale. LC 86-1251. 32p. (gr. k-3). 1986. PLB 14.95 (*0-87226-080-1*, Bedrick Blackie) P Bedrick Bks.

—How the Seasons Came: A North American Indian Folk Tale. LC 91-40499. 32p. (gr. k-3). 1992. PLB 14.95 (*0-87226-464-5*, Bedrick Blackie) P Bedrick Bks.

—The Magic Mill: A Finnish Folk Tale from the Kalevala. LC 88-24170. 32p. 1989. PLB 14.95 (*0-87226-405-X*, Bedrick Blackie) P Bedrick Bks.

—The Quail's Egg: A Folk Tale from Sri Lanka. LC 87-33376. 32p. (gr. k-3). 1988. PLB 14.95 (*0-87226-185-9*, Bedrick Blackie) P Bedrick Bks.

Troughton, Joanna, retold by. Tortoise's Dream: An African Folk Tale. Troughton, Joannna, illus. LC 85-15065. 28p. (ps-2). 1986. PLB 14.95 (*0-87226-039-9*, Bedrick Blackie) P Bedrick Bks.

Troughton, Joanna, retold by. & illus. Whale's Canoe: A Folk Tale from Australia. LC 92-43616. 32p. (gr. k-3). 1993. 14.95 (*0-87226-509-9*) P Bedrick Bks.

—What Made Tiddalik Laugh: An Australian Aborigine Folk Tale. LC 86-1234. 32p. (gr. k-3). 1986. PLB 14.95 (*0-87226-081-X*, Bedrick Blackie) P Bedrick Bks.

—Who Will Be the Sun? A North American Indian Folk Tale. LC 85-15074. 32p. (gr. k-3). 1986. PLB 14.95 (*0-87226-038-0*, Bedrick Blackie) P Bedrick Bks.

Trouillot, Michel-Rolph see Endore, Guy.

Trout. Joshua Mouse Lends a Hand. 1992. write for info. (*0-7814-0010-4*, Chariot Bks) Cook.

—Sheldon Squirrel Learns to Share. 1992. write for info. (*0-7814-0011-2*, Chariot Bks) Cook.

Trout, M. D., ed. see Allen, Joseph.

Trowell, Judith M., ed. Projects to Enrich School Mathematics: Level I. LC 89-14017. (Illus.). 168p. (gr. 4-6). 1990. pap. 14.50 (*0-87353-280-5*) NCTM.

Troy, John. Ben at Large. 1990. pap. 12.50 (*1-55971-048-9*) NorthWord.

Troyer, Terry L. Amish Life Style Illustrated. Smith, Tilman R., intro. by. LC 82-90105. (Illus.). 96p. (gr. 6-12). 1982. 19.95 (*0-943314-00-3*) TLT.

Trucano, Lucille, jt. auth. see Ames, Evelyn E.

True, Adiaha. Fire Deep in the Bones: Adventures in Time-Space & Spirit, Vols. 1 & 2. Akesson, Samuel K. & Ndachi, Teresa, eds. LC 82-73386. (Illus.). (gr. 7 up). 1983. pap. 5.00x ea. Vol. 1 (*0-918088-21-6*) Vol. 2. AFUA Ent.

True, Susan. Nursery Rhyme Crafts. 64p. (gr. k-2). 1985. 6.95 (*0-912107-33-2*) Monday Morning Bks.

Truelson, Thomas. Travels with Tiny Teddy: Cape Cod: The Great Escape. Burke, Kerry, illus. 40p. (Orig.). (gr. 1-3). 1988. pap. 3.95 (*0-685-19995-9*) Lighthse Bks MA.

Truit, Gloria A. Events of the Bible. (ps-3). 1992. pap. 1.89 (*0-570-06185-7*, 59-1312) Concordia.

Truitt, Gloria. Peter Set Free. Needham, James, illus. 24p. (gr. k-4). 1991. pap. 1.89 (*0-570-09027-X*) Concordia.

—The Raising of Jairus' Daughter. (Illus.). 24p. (gr. k-4). 1990. pap. 1.89 (*0-570-09023-7*, 59-1446) Concordia.

Truitt, Gloria A. Noah & God's Promise. 24p. (Orig.). (gr. k-4). 1985. pap. 1.89 (*0-570-06193-8*, 59-1294) Concordia.

—People of the Bible & Their Prayers. (Illus.). 24p. (ps-4). 1987. pap. 1.89 (*0-570-09005-9*, 59-1433) Concordia.

—People of the New Testament: Arch Book Supplement. LC 59-1311. 1983. pap. 1.89 (*0-570-06173-3*) Concordia.

—People of the Old Testament. LC 59-1310. (gr. k-4). 1983. pap. 1.89 (*0-570-06172-5*) Concordia.

—The Ten Commandments: Learning about God's Law. LC 56-1398. (gr. 1 up). 1983. pap. 3.99 (*0-570-08527-6*) Concordia.

Truman, Timothy. Wilderness: The True Story of Simon Girty. 1992. pap. 19.95 (*1-56060-167-1*) Eclipse Bks.

Truman, Timothy, jt. auth. see Siembieda, Kevin.

Trumbauer, Lisa. Runaway Valentines. Cote, Pamela, illus. LC 93-14181. (gr. k-2). 1993. pap. 2.95t (*0-8167-3264-7*) Troll Assocs.

Trumble, Mike. Rupert & the Black Imp. (Illus.). 32p. (gr. k-3). 1992. (BBC-Parkwest); pap. 3.95 (*0-563-20741-8*, BBC-Parkwest) Parkwest Pubns.

—Rupert & the Dragon Sweets. (Illus.). 32p. (gr. k-3). 1992. (BBC-Parkwest); pap. 3.95 (*0-563-20745-0*, BBC-Parkwest) Parkwest Pubns.

—Rupert & the Hazelnut. (Illus.). 32p. (gr. k-3). 1992. (BBC-Parkwest); pap. 3.95 (*0-563-20743-4*, BBC-Parkwest) Parkwest Pubns.

—Rupert & the Secret Boat. (Illus.). 32p. (gr. k-3). 1992. (BBC-Parkwest); pap. 3.95 (*0-563-20736-1*, BBC-Parkwest) Parkwest Pubns.

Trundle. People of the World. (gr. 4-9). 1978. (Usborne-Hayes); PLB 13.96 (*0-88110-116-8*); pap. 6.95 (*0-86020-189-9*) EDC.

Trussell, Margaret E. Sierra Summers: Fireside Tales to Share with Young & Old. Van Kleeck, Cynthia, illus. Trussell, Margaret E., et al, photos by. Bechtol, Bruce, intro. by. LC 89-51208. (Illus.). 200p. (Orig.). (gr. 8-9). 1989. pap. 10.95 (*0-9624235-1-3*) Talking Mntn.

Trussell-Cullen. I've Been Eating Blackberries. 1993. pap. 28.67 (*0-590-50151-8*) Scholastic Inc.

Trussell-Cullen, Alan. The Real Cinderella Rap. Webb, Philip, illus. LC 93-24528. 1994. 4.25 (*0-383-03771-9*) SRA Schl Grp.

Trutzschler, Wolf Von see Von Trutzschler, Wolf.

Truus. What Kouka Knows. LC 92-54428. (Illus.). 32p. (ps-3). 1993. 13.00 (*0-688-12381-3*) Lothrop.

Tryon, Leslie. Albert's Alphabet. Tryon, Leslie, illus. LC 90-38883. 40p. (ps-1). 1991. SBE 13.95 (*0-689-31642-9*, Atheneum Child Bk) Macmillan Child Grp.

—Albert's Field Trip. Tryon, Leslie, illus. LC 92-43686. 32p. (gr. k-3). 1993. SBE 14.95 (*0-689-31821-9*, Atheneum Child Bk) Macmillan Child Grp.

—Albert's Play. Tryon, Leslie, illus. LC 91-23145. 32p. (gr. k-3). 1992. SBE 13.95 (*0-689-31525-2*, Atheneum Child Bk) Macmillan Child Grp.

—One Gaping Wide-Mouthed Hopping Frog. Tryon, Leslie, illus. LC 92-11368. 32p. (ps-1). 1993. SBE 14.95 (*0-689-31785-9*, Atheneum Child Bk) Macmillan Child Grp.

Tryon, Leslie, jt. auth. see Evans, Joy.

Tryon, Leslie, jt. auth. see Moore, Jo E.

Tryon, Thomas. The Adventures of Opal & Cupid. (Illus.). 224p. 1992. 14.00 (*0-670-82239-6*) Viking Child Bks.

Trzeciak, Cathi. Worship: Our Gift to God. (Illus.). 24p. (gr. k-4). 1986. pap. 3.95 saddlestitched (*0-570-08531-X*, 56-1558) Concordia.

Tscharner, Renata von see Von Tscharner, Renata & Fleming, Ronald L.

Tsouras, Peter B., compiled by. Warriors' Words: A Quotation Book from Sesostris III to Schwarzkopf, 1871 BC to AD 1991. 528p. (gr. 10-12). 1992. 29.95 (*1-85409-088-7*, Pub. by Arms & Armour) Sterling.

Tsow, Ming. Chinese Spring Festival. (Illus.). 25p. (gr. 2-4). 1991. 12.95 (*0-237-60137-0*, Pub. by Evans Bros Ltd) Trafalgar.

—A Day with Ling. (Illus.). 25p. (gr. 2-4). 1991. 12.95 (*0-237-60117-6*, Pub. by Evans Bros Ltd) Trafalgar.

Tsuchiya, Yukio. Faithful Elephants. Dykes, Tomoko T., tr. from JPN. Lewin, Ted, illus. 32p. (ps up). 1988. 13.45 (*0-395-46555-9*) HM.

Tsumura, Ted K. & Jones, Lorraine H. Health & Safety for You. 6th ed. O'Neill, Martha, ed. 288p. (gr. 7-12). 1984. 30.32 (*0-07-065378-X*) McGraw.

Tsumura, Ted K., jt. auth. see Jones, Lorraine H.

Tsurmi, Masao, jt. auth. see Barnes, Jill.

Tsutakawa, Mayumi, jt. ed. see Geok-Lin Lim, Shirley.

Tsutsui, Yoriko. Anna in Charge. Hayashi, Akiko, illus. 32p. (ps-1). 1989. pap. 11.95 (*0-670-81672-8*) Viking Child Bks.

—Anna in Charge. Hayashi, Akiki, illus. 32p. (ps-3). 1991. pap. 3.95 (*0-14-050733-7*, Puffin) Puffin Bks.

—Anna's Secret Friend. Hayashi, Akiko, illus. 32p. (ps-1). 1989. pap. 3.99 (*0-14-050731-0*, Puffin) Puffin Bks.

—Anna's Special Present. Hayashi, Akiko, illus. 32p. (ps-3). 1988. pap. 11.95 (*0-670-81671-X*) Viking Child Bks.

—Anna's Special Present. Hayashi, Akiko, illus. 32p. (ps-3). 1990. pap. 3.95 (*0-14-054219-1*, Puffin) Puffin Bks.

Tubb, Jonathan. Bible Lands. Hills, Alan, photos by. LC 91-2388. (Illus.). 64p. (gr. 5 up). 1991. 15.00 (*0-679-81457-4*); lib. bdg. 15.99 (*0-679-91457-9*) Knopf Bks Yng Read.

Tubbs, Beth. Count to the Stars. Schmacker, Pam, illus. 28p. (ps). 1993. wiro-spiral bdg. 9.95 (*0-9632993-4-4*) Storytime Pub.

—Z Is for Zebra. Schmacker, Pam, illus. 32p. (ps). 1992. 9.95 (*0-9632993-3-6*) Storytime Pub.

Tubbs, Orrin, jt. auth. see Wilkinson, Jack.

Tubby, I. M. I'm a Little Airplane. Kraus, Robert, ed. (Illus.). 10p. (ps). 1982. pap. 3.95 vinyl (*0-671-45565-6*, Little Simon) S&S Trade.

Tubby, I. M., pseud. I'm a Little Fish. (Illus.). 10p. (ps up). 1982. pap. 2.95 vinyl (*0-671-44435-2*, Little Simon) S&S Trade.

—I'm a Little Tugboat. (Illus.). 10p. (ps up). 1982. pap. 3.95 vinyl (*0-671-44434-4*, Little Simon) S&S Trade.

Tuchman, Anita. The Black Pearl: A Study Guide. (gr. 7-12). 1984. tchr's. ed. & wkbk. 14.95 (*0-88122-106-6*) LRN Links.

Tuchman, Gail. Christmas KidDoodles, Bk. 3. Nethery, Susan, illus. 64p. (Orig.). (ps-2). 1991. pap. 0.99 activity pad (*1-56293-155-5*) McClanahan Bk.

—Halloween KidDoodles, No. 1. Solovic, Linda, illus. 64p. (ps-2). 1992. pap. 0.99 (*1-56293-259-4*) McClanahan Bk.

—Halloween KidDoodles, No. 2. Radtke, Becky, illus. 64p. (ps-2). 1992. pap. 0.99 (*1-56293-260-8*) McClanahan Bk.

Tucker, Dale, ed. Holiday Trimmings. (Orig.). 1992. pap. text 7.95 (*0-685-68820-8*) CPP Belwin.

Tucker, Dale, ed. see Scott, Michael.

Tucker, Dorothy, jt. auth. see Delton, Judy.

Tucker, Dorothy, ed. see Sabato, Olive.

Tucker, Iva J. Paul: The Missionary. Hester, Ron, illus. (gr. 1-6). 1976. 5.95 (*0-8054-4228-6*, 4242-28) Broadman.

Tucker, James C. & Wentworth, Anna. Goatie. (Illus.). 24p. (Orig.). (gr. 2-8). 1982. pap. 2.95 (*0-910341-00-1*) Blackwater Pub Co.

Tucker, Jeff & Tucker, Ramona. Life Oughta Come with Directions! Realistic Devotions for Teens. 112p. (Orig.). (gr. 9-12). 1990. pap. 5.99 (*0-87788-496-X*) Shaw Pubs.

—No Artificial Flavors: One Hundred Per Cent Friendship. LC 88-34710. 110p. (gr. 7 up). 1989. pap. 5.99 (*0-87788-582-6*) Shaw Pubs.

Tucker, Kathleen, ed. see Aseltine, Lorraine.

Tucker, Kathleen, ed. see Bahr, Mary.

Tucker, Kathleen, ed. see Bernstein, Joanne & Cohen, Paul.

Tucker, Kathleen, ed. see Borja, Corinne & Borja, Robert.

Tucker, Kathleen, ed. see Brooks, Ben.

Tucker, Kathleen, ed. see Bunting, Eve.

Tucker, Kathleen, ed. see Chevalier, Christa.

Tucker, Kathleen, ed. see Cross, Verda.

Tucker, Kathleen, ed. see Delton, Judy & Tucker, Dorothy.

Tucker, Kathleen, ed. see Ford, Barbara.

Tucker, Kathleen, ed. see Girard, Linda W.

Tucker, Kathleen, ed. see Hamm, Diane J.

Tucker, Kathleen, ed. see Kline, Suzy.

Tucker, Kathleen, ed. see Lasker, Joe.

Tucker, Kathleen, ed. see Lawlor, Laurie.

Tucker, Kathleen, ed. see Levine, Abby.

Tucker, Kathleen, ed. see Lindberg, Becky T.

Tucker, Kathleen, ed. see Litchfield, Ada B.

Tucker, Kathleen, ed. see Nixon, Joan L.

Tucker, Kathleen, ed. see Powers, Mary E.

Tucker, Kathleen, ed. see Rabe, Berniece.

Tucker, Kathleen, ed. see Sharmat, Marjorie.

Tucker, Kathleen, ed. see Simon, Norma.

Tucker, Kathleen, jt. ed. see Slavin, Bill.

Tucker, Kathleen, ed. see Stanek, Muriel.

Tucker, Kathleen, ed. see Sussman, Susan.

Tucker, Kathleen, ed. see Sussman, Susan & James, Robert.

Tucker, Kathleen, ed. see Tompert, Ann.

Tucker, Kathleen, ed. see Vigna, Judith.

Tucker, Kathleen, ed. see Wexler, Jerome.

Tucker, Kathleen, ed. see Whitelaw, Nancy.

Tucker, Kathy, ed. see Bernstein, Joanne E. & Cohen, Paul.

Tucker, Kathy, ed. see Blain, Diane.

Tucker, Kathy, ed. see Collins, Pat L.

Tucker, Kathy, ed. see Gay, Marie-Louise.

Tucker, Kathy, ed. see Girard, Linda.

Tucker, Kathy, ed. see Henriod, Lorraine.

Tucker, Kathy, ed. see Hooker, Ruth.

Tucker, Kathy, ed. see Johnson, Ryerson.

Tucker, Kathy, ed. see Lawlor, Laurie.

Tucker, Kathy, ed. see Levine, Abby.

Tucker, Kathy, ed. see Lindberg, Becky T.

Tucker, Kathy, ed. see Nerlove, Miriam.

Tucker, Kathy, ed. see Nims, Bonnie L.

Tucker, Kathy, ed. see Pirner, Connie.

Tucker, Kathy, ed. see Schlein, Miriam.

Tucker, Kathy, ed. see Schmidt, Diane.

Tucker, Kathy, ed. see Wallner, Alexandra.

Tucker, Kathy, ed. see Wexler, Jerome.

Tucker, Kathy, ed. see Wild, Margaret.

Tucker, Kerry, jt. auth. see Morgan, Hal.

Tucker, Kerry & Morgan, Hal, eds. The Kids' Bathtub Rhyme Book. Marsh, Susan, illus. 12p. (Orig.). (ps-1). 1988. pap. 4.95 (*0-942820-25-8*) Steam Pr MA.

—The Kids' Bathtub Songbook. Marsh, Susan, illus. 10p. (Orig.). (ps-3). 1985. pap. 4.95 (*0-942820-14-2*) Steam Pr MA.

Tucker, Martha, jt. auth. see Woodard, Judy.

Tucker, Nicholas. Adolescence. LC 90-21868. (Illus.). 64p. (gr. 5-9). 1991. PLB 19.92 (*0-8114-7805-X*) Raintree Steck-V.

—Childhood. LC 90-21867. (Illus.). 64p. (gr. 5-9). 1991. PLB 19.92 (*0-8114-7804-1*) Raintree Steck-V.

Tucker, Nicholas & McGough, Roger, eds. The Oxford One Two Three Book of Number Rhymes. (Illus.). 32p. 1992. bds. 13.95 (*0-19-910256-2*) OUP.

Tucker, Paul. Troubleshooting the Electrical System. Garman, Dave, ed. (gr. 10 up). Date not set. wkbk. 7.00 (*0-8064-0007-2*, A36) Bergwall.

Tucker, Ramona, jt. auth. see Tucker, Jeff.

Tucker, Shelley. Writing Poetry. 160p. (Orig.). (gr. 6-10). 1992. pap. 7.95 (*0-673-36039-3*) GdYrBks.

Tucker, Sian. At Home. 14p. (ps). 1991. 2.95 (*0-671-73399-0*, Little Simon) S&S Trade.

—Colors. (Illus.). 24p. (ps-k). 1992. pap. 2.95 (*0-671-76907-3*, Little Simon) S&S Trade.

—Going Out. 14p. (ps). 1991. pap. 2.95 (*0-671-73397-4*, S&S BFYR) S&S Trade.

—The Little Boat. (Illus.). 10p. (ps-k). 1993. pap. 2.95 (*0-671-79736-0*, Little Simon) S&S Trade.

—The Little Car. (Illus.). 10p. (ps-k). 1993. pap. 2.95 (*0-671-79737-9*, Little Simon) S&S Trade.

—The Little Plane. (Illus.). 10p. (ps-k). 1993. pap. 2.95 (*0-671-79735-2*, Little Simon) S&S Trade.

—The Little Train. (Illus.). 10p. (ps-k). 1993. pap. 2.95 (*0-671-79738-7*, Little Simon) S&S Trade.

—My Clothes. (ps). 1991. 2.95 (*0-671-73396-6*, Little Simon) S&S Trade.

—My Toys. 14p. (ps). 1991. 2.95 (*0-671-73398-2*) S&S Trade.

—Noises. (Illus.). 24p. (ps-k). 1992. pap. 2.95 (*0-671-76906-5*, Little Simon) S&S Trade.

—Numbers. (Illus.). 24p. (ps-k). 1992. pap. 2.95 (*0-671-76908-1*, Little Simon) S&S Trade.
—Nursery Board: Homes. (ps). 1994. pap. 2.95 (*0-671-88261-9*, Little Simon) S&S Trade.
—Nursery Board: Let's Go. (ps). 1994. pap. 2.95 (*0-671-88263-5*, Little Simon) S&S Trade.
—Nursery Board: Shopping. (ps-2). 1994. pap. 2.95 (*0-671-88262-7*, Little Simon) S&S Trade.
—Sizes. (Illus.). 24p. (ps-k). 1992. pap. 2.95 (*0-671-76909-X*, Little Simon) S&S Trade.
Tudor, Josh. Drawn from New England: A Portrait in Words & Pictures. LC 79-14230. (Illus.). 1979. 19.95 (*0-399-20835-6*, Philomel) Putnam Pub Group.
Tudor, T. Corgiville Fair. 1971. 14.95 (*0-690-21791-9*, Crowell Jr Bks) HarpC Child Bks.
Tudor, Tasha. A Is for Annabelle. Tudor, Tasha, illus. LC 60-15911. 64p. (ps-1). 1988. pap. 5.95 (*0-02-688534-4*, Aladdin) Macmillan Child Grp.
—Becky's Christmas. Tudor, Tasha, illus. LC 91-61679. 46p. (gr. 3 up). with autograph 25.00 (*0-9621753-5-8*) Jenny Wren Pr.
—A Book of Christmas. (Illus.). (ps up). 1987. 13.95 (*0-399-21475-5*, Philomel Bks) Putnam Pub Group.
—Corgiville Fair. Tudor, Tasha, illus. LC 72-154042. 56p. (ps-3). 1991. pap. 5.95 (*0-06-443236-X*, Trophy) HarpC Child Bks.
—Dolls' Christmas. Tudor, Tasha, illus. LC 59-12744. (gr. k-3). 1979. 6.95 (*0-8098-1026-3*); pap. 4.95 (*0-8098-2912-6*) McKay.
—First Delights: A Book About the Five Senses. Tudor, Tasha, illus. 32p. (ps-1). 1988. 8.95 (*0-448-09327-8*, G&D) Putnam Pub Group.
—First Graces. Tudor, Tasha, illus. LC 59-12017. (gr. k-3). 1978. pap. 6.95 (*0-8098-1953-8*) McKay.
—First Prayers. Tudor, Tasha, illus. LC 59-9631. (gr. k-3). 1978. protestant ed. 6.95 (*0-8098-1952-X*) McKay.
—Give Us This Day, the Lord's Prayer. (Illus.). (ps up). 1989. 9.95 (*0-399-21442-9*, Philomel Bks) Putnam Pub Group.
—Give Us This Day: The Lord's Prayer. 32p. (ps-3). 1992. mini ed. 4.95 (*0-399-21891-2*, Philomel Bks) Putnam Pub Group.
—The Jenny Wren Book of Valentines. Tudor, Tasha, illus. Wren, Jenny, intro. by. LC 88-51832. (Illus.). 16p. (Orig.). (gr. k up). 1989. pap. 6.95 (*0-9621753-1-5*) Jenny Wren Pr.
—The Lord Is My Shepherd: The Twenty-Third Psalm. 32p. (ps-3). 1992. pap. 4.95 (*0-399-21892-0*, Philomel Bks) Putnam Pub Group.
—Mother Goose. Tudor, Tasha, illus. LC 58-58523. (gr. k-3). 1980. 9.95 (*0-8098-1901-5*) McKay.
—Mother Goose. LC 88-30674. (Illus.). 96p. (ps-2). 1989. 8.95 (*0-394-84407-6*) Random Bks Yng Read.
—Mouse Mills Catalogue for Spring. Tudor, Tasha, illus. Mouse, Timothy D., tr. LC 89-50061. (Illus.). 40p. (gr. k up). 1989. pap. text ed. 6.95 (*0-9621753-2-3*) Jenny Wren Pr.
—One Is One. Tudor, Tasha, illus. LC 56-11381. (ps-1). 1988. pap. 4.95 (*0-02-688535-2*, Aladdin) Macmillan Child Grp.
—Pumpkin Moonshine. Tudor, Tasha, illus. LC 89-3543. 40p. (ps-2). 1989. pap. 5.95 (*0-394-84588-9*) Random Bks Yng Read.
—Rosemary for Remembrance. Rudor, Tasha, illus. 32p. (gr. 3-6). 1990. gift ed. 15.95 (*0-399-21816-5*, Philomel Bks) Putnam Pub Group.
—Seasons of Delight: A Year on an Old-Fashioned Farm. Tudor, Tasha, illus. 12p. (gr. 1 up). 1986. 14.95 (*0-399-21308-2*, Philomel) Putnam Pub Group.
—The Springs of Joy. Tudor, Tasha, illus. LC 79-66708. 64p. (ps up). 1988. SBE 12.95 (*0-02-689092-5*) Macmillan Child Grp.
—Take Joy: The Tasha Tudor Christmas Book. Tudor, Tasha, illus. LC 66-10645. (gr. k up). 1980. 18.95 (*0-399-20766-X*, Philomel) Putnam Pub Group.
—Tale for Easter. Tudor, Tasha, illus. LC 62-8626. (gr. k-3). 1985. 6.95 (*0-8098-1008-5*); pap. 4.95 (*0-8098-1807-8*) McKay.
—A Tale for Easter. LC 88-30675. (Illus.). 36p. (ps-2). 1989. Repr. of 1941 ed. 5.95 (*0-394-84404-1*) Random Bks Yng Read.
—A Tasha Tudor's Sampler: A Tale for Easter, Pumpkin Moonshine, The Dolls' Christmas. Tudor, Tasha, illus. (gr. k-3). 1977. 9.95 (*0-679-20412-1*) McKay.
—Tasha Tudor's Treasure, 3 vols. 144p. (gr. k-4). 1981. 13.95 (*0-679-20983-2*) McKay.
—A Time to Keep: The Tasha Tudor Book of Holidays. 2nd ed. LC 77-9067. (Illus.). (gr. k-3). 1988. SBE 13.95 (*0-02-789502-5*, Macmillan Child Bk) Macmillan Child Grp.
Tudor, Tasha, ed. & illus. All for Love. LC 83-21959. 96p. (gr. 6-8). 1984. 16.95 (*0-399-21012-1*, Philomel) Putnam Pub Group.
Tudor, Tasha, tr. First Graces. LC 88-30673. (Illus.). 48p. (ps-2). 1989. Repr. of 1955 ed. 6.95 (*0-394-84409-2*) Random Bks Yng Read.
Tudor, Tasha, illus. And It Was So: Words from the Scripture. 2nd, rev. ed. LC 87-16130. 48p. (ps up) 1988. 12.00 (*0-664-32724-9*, Westminster) Westminster John Knox.
—First Poems of Childhood. 32p. (ps-1). 1990. 9.95 (*0-448-09326-X*, G&D) Putnam Pub Group.
—The Lord Is My Shepherd: The Twenty-Third Psalm. LC 79-27134. 32p. (gr. 2 up). 1989. 9.95 (*0-399-20756-2*, Philomel) Putnam Pub Group.
Tuel, Patricia, jt. auth. see Smart, Margaret.

Tuer, Judy. Rocks. Vane, Mitch, illus. LC 92-30670. 1993. 2.50 (*0-383-03649-6*) SRA Schl Grp.
—Ten Crazy Caterpillars. Forss, Ian, illus. LC 92-30672. 1993. 2.50 (*0-383-03658-5*) SRA Schl Grp.
Tufts, Lorraine S. Secrets in the Grand Canyon, Zion & Bryce Canyon National Parks. Holmes, Tracey I., ed. 96p. (gr. 5 up). 1992. 29.95 (*0-9620255-4-2*); pap. 19.95 (*0-9620255-3-4*) Natl Photo Collections.
—Secrets in Yellowstone & Grand Teton National Parks. 2nd ed. Koteff, Ellen & Holmes, Tracey, eds. 88p. (gr. 4 up). 1990. 29.95 (*0-9620255-2-6*); pap. 19.95 (*0-9620255-1-8*) Natl Photo Collections.
Tufts, Mary L. The Wee Kitten Who Sucked Her Thumb. McQueen, Lucinda, illus. 32p. (ps-2). 1986. pap. 1.95 (*0-448-19076-1*, G&D) Putnam Pub Group.
Tuggle, Catherine & Weir, Gary. The Department of Energy. (Illus.). 112p. (gr. 5 up). 1990. 14.95 (*0-87754-839-0*) Chelsea Hse.
Tulchinsky, Dan. Human Reproductive Technologies. Head, J. J., ed. (Illus.). 16p. (Orig.). (gr. 10 up). 1992. pap. text ed. 2.75 (*0-89278-177-7*, 45-9777) Carolina Biological.
Tulku, Chagdud. The Kind King & the Magnanimous Mice: A Tibetan Folktale. 1993. pap. 9.95 (*1-881847-03-9*) Chagdud Gonpa-Padma.
Tulling, Virginia. Threatened Cultures. (Illus.). 48p. (gr. 5 up). 1990. lib. bdg. 18.60 (*0-86592-096-6*); lib. bdg. 13.95s.p. (*0-685-36381-3*) Rourke Corp.
Tulloch, Richard. Danny in the Toybox. Greder, Armin, illus. LC 90-24637. 32p. (ps-3). 1991. 13.95 (*0-688-10501-7*, Tambourine Bks) PLB 13.88 (*0-688-10502-5*, Tambourine Bks) Morrow.
—Rain for Christmas. Harris, Wayne, illus. 32p. 1990. 10.95 (*0-521-37085-X*) Cambridge U Pr.
—Stories from Our House. Vivas, Julie, illus. 32p. (ps-3). 1987. 11.95 (*0-521-33485-3*) Cambridge U Pr.
—Stories from Our Street. Vivas, Julie, illus. 32p. 1990. 11.95 (*0-521-36603-8*) Cambridge U Pr.
—The Strongest Man in Gundiwallanup. O'Loughlin, Sue, illus. 32p. 1990. 10.95 (*0-521-36651-8*) Cambridge U Pr.
Tully, Brock. Coming Together: A Ten Thousand Mile Bicycle Journey. 100p. (gr. 6 up). 1991. pap. 5.95 (*0-9693583-4-2*, Green Tiger) S&S Trade.
—Reflections for Living Life Fully. Thompson, Heidi, illus. 100p. (gr. 7 up). 1991. pap. 5.95 (*0-9693583-2-6*, Green Tiger) S&S Trade.
—Reflections for Sharing Dreams. Thompson, Heidi, illus. 100p. (gr. 6 up). 1991. pap. 5.95 (*0-9693583-5-0*, Green Tiger) S&S Trade.
—Reflections for Someone Special. Thompson, Heidi, illus. 100p. (gr. 6 up). 1991. 5.95 (*0-9693583-0-X*, Green Tiger) S&S Trade.
—Reflections for Touching Hearts. Thompson, Heidi, illus. 100p. (gr. 6 up). 1991. pap. 5.95 (*0-9693583-3-4*, Green Tiger) S&S Trade.
Tuma-Church, Deb. The Storytime Handbook. Tuma-Church, Deb, illus. 73p. (ps-5). 1988. wkbk. spiral bdg. 7.95 (*0-939644-37-1*) Media Pub.
Tunbo, Frances G. Stay Put, Robbie McAmis. Shaw, Charles, illus. LC 87-18123. 160p. (gr. 4 up). 1988. PLB 15.95 (*0-87565-025-2*) Tex Christian.
Tune, Suelyn C. How Maui Slowed the Sun. Burningham, Robin Y., illus. LC 88-4548. 32p. (gr. k up). 1988. 8.95 (*0-8248-1083-X*) UH Pr.
—Maui & the Secret of Fire. Burningham, Robin Y., illus. LC 90-27175. 32p. (ps-4). 1991. 9.95 (*0-8248-1391-X*, Kolowalu Bk) UH Pr.
Tune, Suelyn C., jt. auth. see Abernethy, Jane F.
Tung, Dana Y., jt. auth. see Wu, Dana Y.
Tunis, Edwin. Colonial Craftsmen: The Beginnings of American Industry. Tunis, Edwin, illus. LC 75-29612. 160p. (gr. 7 up). 1976. 25.00 (*0-690-01062-1*, Crowell Jr Bks) HarpC Child Bks.
—Colonial Living. Tunis, Edwin, illus. LC 75-29611. 160p. (gr. 7 up). 1976. 25.00 (*0-690-01063-X*, Crowell Jr Bks) HarpC Child Bks.
—Frontier Living. Tunis, Edwin, illus. LC 75-29639. 168p. (gr. 7 up). 1976. 26.00 (*0-690-01064-8*, Crowell Jr Bks) HarpC Child Bks.
—Indians. rev. ed. Tunis, Edwin, illus. LC 78-60175. 160p. (gr. 5 up). 1979. Repr. of 1959 ed. PLB 24.89 (*0-690-01283-7*, Crowell Jr Bks) HarpC Child Bks.
—Oars, Sails & Steam: A Picture Book of Ships. Tunis, Edwin, illus. LC 76-25453. 64p. (gr. 6 up). 1977. 25.00i (*0-690-01284-5*, Crowell Jr Bks) HarpC Child Bks.
—Weapons. LC 76-29699. (Illus.). 160p. (gr. 6 up). 1977. 25.00 (*0-690-01285-3*, Crowell Jr Bks) HarpC Child Bks.
Tunis, John R. All-American. 261p. (gr. 3-7). 1989. pap. 3.95 (*0-15-202292-9*, Odyssey) HarBrace.
—Champion's Choice. 206p. (gr. 3-7). 1990. pap. 3.95 (*0-15-216074-4*, Odyssey) HarBrace.
—City for Lincoln. 392p. (gr. 3-7). 1989. pap. 3.95 (*0-15-218580-1*, Odyssey) HarBrace.
—Duke Decides. 260p. (gr. 3-7). 1990. pap. 3.95 (*0-15-224308-9*, Odyssey) HarBrace.
—Highpockets. (gr. 4-7). 1990. pap. 4.95 (*0-688-09288-8*, Pub. by Beech Tree Bks) Morrow.
—Iron Duke. 262p. (gr. 3-7). 1990. pap. 3.95 (*0-15-238987-3*, Odyssey) HarBrace.
—Keystone Kids. Brooks, Bruce & Bacom, Paulintro. by. 239p. (gr. 3-7). 1990. pap. 3.95 (*0-15-242388-5*, Odyssey) HarBrace.
—The Kid from Tomkinsville. (gr. 3-7). 1988. 16.75 (*0-8446-6353-0*) Peter Smith.

—The Kid from Tomkinsville. Bacon, Paul, illus. Brooks, Bruce, intro. by. (Illus.). 278p. (gr. 3-7). 1989. pap. 3.95 (*0-15-242567-5*, Odyssey) HarBrace.
—Rookie of the Year. Brooks, Bruce & Bacom, Paulintro. by. 220p. (gr. 3-7). 1990. pap. 3.95 (*0-15-268880-3*, Odyssey) HarBrace.
—Schoolboy Johnson. LC 58-5728. 192p. (gr. 5 up). 1991. pap. 4.95 (*0-688-10150-X*, Pub. by Beech Tree Bks) Morrow.
—Schoolboy Johnson. LC 58-5728. 192p. (gr. 5 up). 1991. Repr. of 1958 ed. 11.95 (*0-688-10149-6*) Morrow Jr Bks.
—World Series. (gr. 3-7). 1988. 15.75 (*0-8446-6354-9*) Peter Smith.
—World Series. Bacon, Paul, illus. Brooks, Bruce, intro. by. (Illus.). 248p. (gr. 3-7). 1989. pap. 3.95 (*0-15-299646-X*, Odyssey) HarBrace.
—Yea! Wildcats. 319p. (gr. 3-7). 1989. pap. 3.95 (*0-15-299718-0*, Odyssey) HarBrace.
—Young Razzle. LC 49-9796. 192p. (gr. 5 up). 1991. pap. 4.95 (*0-688-10153-4*, Pub. by Beech Tree Bks) Morrow.
—Young Razzle. LC 49-9796. 192p. (gr. 5 up). 1991. Repr. of 1949 ed. 11.95 (*0-688-10152-6*) Morrow Jr Bks.
Tunmore, Gary, ed. see Bonagurio, Susan.
Tunmore, Gary, ed. see Cammarata, Joe.
Tunmore, Gary, ed. see Stauffer, P. Wayne.
Tunnell, Michael O. Beauty & the Beastly Children. Cymerman, John E., illus. LC 92-36757. 32p. (gr. k up). 1993. 15.00 (*0-688-12181-0*, Tambourine Bks); PLB 14.93 (*0-688-12182-9*, Tambourine Bks) Morrow.
—Chinook! Root, Barry, illus. LC 92-12711. 32p. (gr. k up). 1993. 14.00 (*0-688-10869-5*, Tambourine Bks); PLB 13.93 (*0-688-10870-9*, Tambourine Bks) Morrow.
—The Joke's on George. Osborn, Kathy, illus. LC 92-33312. 32p. (gr. k up). 1993. 14.00 (*0-688-11758-9*, Tambourine Bks); PLB 13.93 (*0-688-11759-7*, Tambourine Bks) Morrow.
Tunney, Christopher. Aircraft. LC 79-64384. (Illus.). 36p. (gr. 3-6). 1980. PLB 13.50 (*0-8225-1176-2*) Lerner Pubns.
—Midnight Animals. Atkinson, Mike & Francis, John, illus. LC 87-4792. 24p. (gr. 2-5). 1987. pap. 2.95 (*0-394-89213-5*, Random Juv) Random Bks Yng Read.
Turbak, Gary. America's Mountains. Ormsby, Lawrence, illus. 32p. (gr. 1 up). 1994. 14.95 (*0-87358-573-9*) Northland AZ.
—America's Oceans. Ormsby, Lawrence, illus. 32p. (gr. 1 up). 1994. 14.95 (*0-87358-574-7*) Northland AZ.
Turbek, Joan. The Little River & the Big, Big Bridge. LC 93-25968. 48p. 1993. 7.50 (*0-925168-18-1*) North Country.
Turck, Mary. Acid Rain. LC 90-35495. (Illus.). 48p. (gr. 5-6). 1990. RSBE 12.95 (*0-89686-547-9*, Crestwood Hse) Macmillan Child Grp.
—AIDS. LC 88-20259. (Illus.). 48p. (gr. 5-6). 1988. RSBE 12.95 (*0-89686-412-X*, Crestwood Hse) Macmillan Child Grp.
—Alcohol & Tobacco. LC 88-20253. (Illus.). 48p. (gr. 5-6). 1988. RSBE 12.95 (*0-89686-411-1*, Crestwood Hse) Macmillan Child Grp.
—Jewish Holidays. LC 89-25398. (Illus.). 48p. (gr. 3 up). 1990. RSBE 12.95 (*0-89686-502-9*, Crestwood Hse) Macmillan Child Grp.
Turck, Mary C. Crack & Cocaine. LC 89-25409. (Illus.). 48p. (gr. 4 up). 1990. RSBE 12.95 (*0-89686-491-X*, Crestwood Hse) Macmillan Child Grp.
Turcotte, Mary C. The Wind at My Back: The Life of St. Patrick. Bliss, Bob, illus. LC 88-13763. 115p. (gr. 3 up). 1991. 4.95 (*0-8198-8236-4*) St Paul Bks.
Turenne des Pres, Francois & California Afro-American Museum Foundation, Los Angeles Staff. Children of Yayoute: Folk Tales of Haiti. 96p. 1994. 19.95 (*0-87663-791-8*) Universe.
Turgenev, Ivan S. Fathers & Sons. Garnett, Constance, tr. Canon, R. R., intro. by. (gr. 11 up). 1967. pap. 1.95 (*0-8049-0129-5*, CL-129) Airmont.
—Fathers & Sons. Guerney, Bernard G., tr. 1950. pap. text ed. 6.49 (*0-07-553634-X*, T38) McGraw.
—A Month in the Country. (gr. 7-12). 1987. pap. 6.95 (*0-435-20966-3*, 20966) Heinemann.
Turin, Adela & Bosnia, Nella. Arthur & Clementine. (Illus.). 32p. (gr. 3-6). 1980. 6.95 (*0-904613-19-4*) Writers & Readers.
—The Real Story of the Bonobos Who Wore Spectacles. (Illus.). 32p. (gr. 3-6). 1980. 6.95 (*0-904613-18-6*) Writers & Readers.
Turin, Adela & Saccaro, Margherita. The Breadtime Story. (Illus.). 32p. (gr. 3-6). 1980. 6.95 (*0-904613-61-5*) Writers & Readers.
Turin, Adela & Selig, Syvie. Of Cannons & Caterpillars. (Illus.). 32p. (gr. 3-6). 1980. 4.95 (*0-904613-62-3*) Writers & Readers.
Turk, Ruth. Noises in the Night. Tolenen, Susan, illus. LC 93-1167. 1993. write for info. (*0-8368-0673-5*) Time-Life.
—They Reached for the Stars. Tripp, Ned, illus. (gr. 5-9). 1990. pap. 11.95 (*0-933025-20-3*) Blue Bird Pub.
Turkle, Brinton. Deep in the Forest. LC 76-21691. (Illus.). 32p. (ps-1). 1976. 12.95 (*0-525-28617-9*, DCB); pap. 3.95 (*0-525-44322-3*, DCB) Dutton Child Bks.
—Do Not Open. Turkle, Brinton, illus. LC 80-10289. 32p. (ps-2). 1981. pap. 13.95 (*0-525-28785-X*, 01258-370, DCB) Dutton Child Bks.

—Do Not Open. Turkle, Brinton, illus. LC 80-10289. 32p. (ps-2). 1985. pap. 3.95 (0-525-44224-3, DCB) Dutton Child Bks.

—Do Not Open. Turkle, Brinton, illus. (ps-3). 1993. pap. 4.99 (0-14-054747-9) Puffin Bks.

—Obadiah the Bold. Turkle, Brinton, illus. LC 65-13350. (gr. k-3). 1977. pap. 3.95 (0-14-050233-5, Puffin) Puffin Bks.

—Rachel & Obadiah. Turkle, Brinton, illus. LC 77-15661. (gr. k-3). 1978. 15.00 (0-525-38020-5, DCB) Dutton Child Bks.

—Rachel & Obadiah. Turkle, Brinton, illus. (gr. 1-3). 1987. pap. 4.95 (0-525-44303-7, DCB) Dutton Child Bks.

—Thy Friend, Obadiah. (Illus.). 40p. (gr. k-3). 1982. pap. 4.99 (0-14-050393-5, Puffin) Puffin Bks.

Turkle, Brinton, illus. If You Lived in Colonial Times. 1992. pap. 4.95 (0-590-45160-X) Scholastic Inc.

Turkovich, Marilyn, jt. auth. see Lane, Sarah.

Turkovich, Marilyn, et al. Omiyage. rev. ed. LC 90-42183. (Illus.). 220p. (gr. 6-12). 1990. looseleaf, incl. audio cass. 44.95 (0-930141-37-7) World Eagle.

—Nepal: From Kathmandu to Mt. Everest. 180p. (gr. 6-12). 1983. pap. 10.95 (0-685-55243-8, 5116) World Eagle.

Turnbull. Queen Cat. (gr. 4-7). 1992. pap. 2.99 (0-440-40511-4, YB) Dell.

Turnbull, Ann. Maroo of the Winter Caves. LC 84-4327. 144p. (gr. 4-7). 1984. 13.95 (0-89919-304-8, Clarion Bks) HM.

—Maroo of the Winter Caves. (gr. 4-7). 1990. pap. 4.80 (0-395-54795-4, Clarion Bks) HM.

—Rob Goes A-Hunting. Teasdale, Denise, illus. LC 90-30626. 32p. (ps-1). 1990. 13.95 (0-531-05877-8); PLB 13.99 (0-531-08477-9) Orchard Bks Watts.

—The Sand Horse. Foreman, Michael, illus. LC 89-9. 32p. (gr. k-3). 1989. SBE 13.95 (0-689-31581-3, Atheneum Child Bk) Macmillan Child Grp.

—Speedwell. LC 91-58757. (gr. 5-9). 1992. 14.95 (1-56402-112-2) Candlewick Pr.

—Speedwell. LC 91-58757. (gr. 4-7). 1994. pap. 3.99 (1-56402-281-1) Candlewick Pr.

—The Tapestry Cats. Morley, Carol, illus. 1992. 14.95 (0-316-85626-6) Little.

Turnbull, Harvey. The Guitar from the Renaissance to the Present Day. (Illus.). 168p. 1992. pap. 15.95 (0-933224-57-5) Bold Strummer Ltd.

Turner. Dust for Dinner. Date not set. 14.00 (0-06-023376-1, Festival); PLB 13.89 (0-06-023377-X, Festival) HarpC Child Bks.

—In the Heart. Date not set. 15.00 (0-06-023730-9, Festival); pap. 14.89 (0-06-023731-7, Festival) HarpC Child Bks.

—Jewish Festivals, Reading Level 4. (Illus.). 48p. (gr. 3-8). 1987. Set. PLB 15.74 (0-86592-977-7); 11.95s.p. (0-685-58771-1) Rourke Corp.

Turner, Ann. Apple Valley Year. Resnick, Sandi W., illus. LC 90-37733. 32p. (ps-3). 1993. RSBE 14.95 (0-02-789281-6, Macmillan Child Bk) Macmillan Child Grp.

—The Christmas House. Calder, Nancy E., illus. LC 93-12740. (gr. 3 up). Date not set. 15.00 (0-06-023429-6); PLB 14.89 (0-06-023432-6) HarpC Child Bks.

—Dakota Dugout. Himler, Ronald, illus. LC 85-3084. 32p. (gr. k-3). 1985. RSBE 13.95 (0-02-789700-1, Macmillan Child Bk) Macmillan Child Grp.

—Dakota Dugout. Himler, Ronald, illus. 32p. (ps-3). 1989. pap. 3.95 (0-689-71296-0, Aladdin) Macmillan Child Grp.

—Grass Songs: Poems. Moser, Barry, illus. LC 92-11684. (gr. 4 up). 1993. write for info. (0-15-136788-4) HarBrace.

—Grasshopper Summer. LC 88-13847. 144p. (gr. 3-7). 1989. SBE 13.95 (0-02-789511-4, Macmillan Child Bk) Macmillan Child Grp.

—Grasshopper Summer. 166p. (gr. 5-9). 1990. pap. 2.95 (0-8167-2262-5) Troll Assocs.

—Hedgehog for Breakfast. McCue, Lisa, illus. LC 88-8228. 32p. (ps-2). 1989. RSBE 13.95 (0-02-789241-7, Macmillan Child Bk) Macmillan Child Grp.

—Heron Street. Desimini, Lisa, illus. LC 87-24948. 32p. (gr. 1-4). 1989. 15.00i (0-06-026184-6); PLB 14.89 (0-06-026185-4) HarpC Child Bks.

—Katie's Trunk. Himler, Ronald, illus. LC 91-20409. 32p. (gr. k-3). 1992. RSBE 13.95 (0-02-789512-2, Macmillan Child Bk) Macmillan Child Grp.

—A Moon for Seasons. Norieka, Robert, illus. LC 92-36857. 40p. (gr. 1-5). 1994. RSBE 14.95 (0-02-789513-0, Macmillan Child Bk) Macmillan Child Grp.

—Nettie's Trip South. Himler, Ronald, illus. LC 86-18135. 32p. (gr. 1-5). 1987. SBE 13.95 (0-02-789240-9, Macmillan Child Bk) Macmillan Child Grp.

—Rainflowers. Blake, Robert J., illus. LC 90-39629. 32p. (gr. k-3). 1992. 14.00 (0-06-026041-6); PLB 13.89 (0-06-026042-4) HarpC Child Bks.

—Rosemary's Witch. LC 90-39779. 176p. (gr. 6 up). 1991. 14.00 (0-06-026128-7); PLB 13.89 (0-06-026128-5) HarpC Child Bks.

—Rosemary's Witch. LC 90-39779. 176p. (gr. 4-7). 1994. pap. 4.95 (0-06-440494-3, Trophy) HarpC Child Bks.

—Stars for Sarah. Teichman, Mary, illus. LC 89-26908. 32p. (ps-3). 1991. 13.95 (0-06-026186-2); PLB 13.89 (0-06-026187-0) HarpC Child Bks.

—Stars for Sarah. Teichman, Mary, illus. LC 89-36908. 32p. (ps-3). 1993. pap. 4.95 (0-06-443344-7, Trophy) HarpC Child Bks.

—Street Talk. (gr. 4-7). 1992. pap. 3.80 (0-395-61625-5) HM.

—Through Moon & Stars & Night Skies. Hale, James G., illus. LC 87-35044. 32p. (ps-3). 1990. 13.00 (0-06-026189-7); PLB 12.89 (0-06-026190-0) HarpC Child Bks.

—Through Moon & Stars & Night Skies. Hale, James G., illus. LC 87-35044. 32p. (ps-3). 1992. pap. 4.95 (0-06-443308-0, Trophy) HarpC Child Bks.

Turner, Barbie C. Hark the Herald Angels Sing. (ps-6). 1993. pap. 17.00 (0-671-87146-3, S&S BFYR) S&S Trade.

Turner, Bonnie. Haunted Igloo. 160p. (gr. 3-7). 1991. 13.45 (0-395-57037-9, Sandpiper) HM.

Turner, Charles. The Turtle & the Moon. Mathis, Melissa B., illus. LC 90-43841. 32p. (ps-2). 1991. 14.00 (0-525-44659-1, DCB) Dutton Child Bks.

Turner, Cynthia, jt. auth. see Sanders, Corine.

Turner, Dee. People. LC 92-53102. (Illus.). 48p. (Orig.). (gr. 3-8). 1992. pap. 5.95 (1-85697-810-9) Kingfisher Bks.

Turner, Derek. The Black Death. Reeves, Marjorie, ed. (Illus.). 96p. (gr. 7-12). 1978. pap. text ed. 10.02 (0-582-31097-0, 78068) Longman.

Turner, Dorothy. Bread. Yates, John, illus. 32p. (gr. 1-4). 1989. PLB 14.95 (0-87614-359-1) Carolrhoda Bks.

—Eggs. Yates, John, illus. 32p. (gr. 1-4). 1989. PLB 14.95 (0-87614-360-5) Carolrhoda Bks.

—Man-Made Wonders of the World. LC 86-1340. (Illus.). 32p. (gr. 2 up). 1986. RSBE 10.95 (0-87518-334-4, Dillon) Macmillan Child Grp.

—Milk. Yates, John, illus. 32p. (gr. 1-4). 1989. PLB 14.95 (0-87614-361-3) Carolrhoda Bks.

—Potatoes. Yates, John, illus. 32p. (gr. 1-4). 1989. PLB 14.95 (0-87614-362-1) Carolrhoda Bks.

Turner Educational Services, Inc. Staff & Clark, James I. Hawaii. 48p. (gr. 3 up). 1986. PLB 18.64 (0-8174-4516-1) Raintree Steck-V.

—Illinois. 48p. (gr. 3 up). 1986. PLB 18.64 (0-8174-4524-2) Raintree Steck-V.

Turner Educational Services, Inc. Staff, et al. Kentucky. 48p. (gr. 3 up). 1986. PLB 18.64 (0-8174-4532-3) Raintree Steck-V.

Turner Educational Services, Inc. Staff & Clark, James I. North Carolina. 48p. (gr. 3 up). 1986. PLB 18.64 (0-86514-454-0) Raintree Steck-V.

Turner Educational Services Inc. Staff & Clark, James I. Oklahoma. 48p. (gr. 3 up). 1986. text ed. 18.64 (0-86514-456-7) Raintree Steck-V.

Turner Educational Services, Inc. Staff & Clark, James I. South Carolina. 48p. (gr. 3 up). 1986. PLB 18.64 (0-86514-475-3) Raintree Steck-V.

Turner Educational Services, Inc. Staff, et al. South Dakota. 48p. (gr. 3 up). 1986. PLB 18.64 (0-86514-458-3) Raintree Steck-V.

Turner Educational Services, Inc. Staff & Clark, James I. Vermont. 48p. (gr. 3 up). 1986. PLB 18.64 (0-86514-459-1) Raintree Steck-V.

—Washington. 48p. (gr. 3 up). 1986. PLB 18.64 (0-86514-470-2) Raintree Steck-V.

Turner, Edwin A. The Adventures by the River Iki: Oscar Crow & Leapy Frog. (Illus.). 128p. 1992. 12.95 (0-8059-3299-2) Dorrance.

Turner, F. Bernadette. Faith of Little Creatures. (gr. 1-3). pap. 2.50 (0-8315-0138-3) Speller.

Turner, Geneva C., jt. auth. see Roy, Jessie H.

Turner, Glennette. Lewis Howard Latimer. (Illus.). 144p. (gr. 5-9). 1990. PLB 13.98 (0-382-09524-3); pap. 7.95 (0-382-24162-2) Silver Burdett Pr.

Turner, Glennette T. Running for Our Lives. Byrd, Samuel, illus. LC 93-28430. 208p. (gr. 8-12). 1994. 15.95 (0-8234-1121-4) Holiday.

—Take a Walk in Their Shoes. Fax, Elton C., illus. LC 89-9700. 176p. (gr. 4-8). 1989. 15.00 (0-525-65006-7, Cobblehill Bks) Dutton Child Bks.

—Take a Walk in Their Shoes: Biographies of Fourteen Outstanding African Americans - with Skits about Each to Act Out. Fax, Elton C., illus. LC 92-19524. 176p. (gr. 3-7). 1992. pap. 5.99 (0-14-036250-9) Puffin Bks.

Turner, Gwenda. Once Upon a Time. (ps). 1990. 9.95 (0-670-82551-4) Viking Child Bks.

—Opposites. Turner, Gwenda, illus. 24p. (ps-k). 1993. 9.99 (0-670-84813-1) Viking Child Bks.

—Shapes. (ps). 1991. 9.95 (0-670-83744-X) Viking Child Bks.

Turner, Herschel. The Black West Print Set. (gr. 4-6). 1992. 75.00 (1-882205-25-1) All Media Prods.

Turner, Herschell. The Black West Coloring Book. 32p. (gr. 4-6). 1992. pap. 3.95 (1-882205-01-4) All Media Prods.

Turner, Herschell & Blanchard, G. L. The Buffalo Soldiers Coloring Book. 32p. (gr. 4-6). 1992. pap. 3.95 (1-882205-02-2) All Media Prods.

Turner, Louise. It's a Great Day: The Story of Rusty, the Gunston Hall Fox. Sonnett, Barbie, illus. 45p. (Orig.). 1983. pap. 6.95 (1-884085-04-0) Bd Regents.

—Yesterday to Color at Gunston Hall. Alig, Mary J., illus. 15p. (Orig.). 1990. pap. 3.95 (1-884085-05-9) Bd Regents.

Turner, Margret & Scott, Alyson. Come on Everybody! Let's Go to the Fair. 32p. (ps-k). 1991. pap. write for info. (0-9630453-0-X) Lifeworks.

Turner, Morrie. All God's Chillun Got Soul. 64p. (gr. 6). 1980. pap. 7.00 (0-8170-0892-6) Judson.

Turner, Peggy & Brewer, Linda S. ABC Career Book for Girls: Introducing the Career Pals. Hollis, Myrlys, ed. Turner, Peggy, illus. Lincoln, Rebecca, intro. by. (Illus.). 32p. (gr. 1-4). 1992. pap. 6.95 (0-9622514-2-9) Columbia Sacramento.

Turner, Philip. The Bible Story. Wildsmith, Brian, illus. 142p. 1987. 19.95 (0-19-273104-1) OUP.

—Bible Story. Wildsmith, Brian, illus. 142p. (gr. k up). 1989. pap. 9.95 (0-19-273160-2) OUP.

Turner Program Services, Inc. Staff & Clark, James I. Arizona. LC 85-9978. 48p. (gr. 3 up). 1985. PLB 18.64 (0-8174-4257-X) Raintree Steck-V.

—Connecticut. 48p. (gr. 3 up). 1985. PLB 18.64 (0-8174-4265-0); pap. text ed. 9.27 (0-86514-501-6) Raintree Steck-V.

—Florida. 48p. (gr. 3 up). 1985. pap. text ed. 18.64 (0-8174-4273-1) Raintree Steck-V.

—Idaho. LC 85-12151. 48p. (gr. 3 up). 1985. PLB 18.64 (0-8174-4291-X) Raintree Steck-V.

—Indiana. LC 85-9977. 48p. (gr. 3 up). 1985. PLB 18.64 (0-8174-4303-7) Raintree Steck-V.

—Iowa. 48p. (gr. 3 up). 1985. PLB 18.64 (0-8174-4311-8) Raintree Steck-V.

—Louisiana. LC 85-9976. 48p. (gr. 3 up). 1985. PLB 18.64 (0-86514-432-X) Raintree Steck-V.

—Maine. LC 85-9975. 48p. (gr. 3 up). 1985. PLB 18.64 (0-86514-433-8) Raintree Steck-V.

—Maryland. 48p. (gr. 3 up). 1985. PLB 18.64 (0-86514-434-6) Raintree Steck-V.

—Massachusetts. LC 85-11915. 48p. (gr. 3 up). 1985. PLB 18.64 (0-86514-435-4) Raintree Steck-V.

—Missouri. LC 85-9979. 48p. (gr. 3 up). 1985. PLB 18.64 (0-86514-436-2) Raintree Steck-V.

Turner Program Services, Inc. Staff. Nevada. 48p. (gr. 3 up). 1985. PLB 18.64 (0-86514-437-0); pap. text ed. 9.27 (0-86514-512-1) Raintree Steck-V.

Turner Program Services, Inc. Staff & Clark, James I. New Jersey. LC 85-9981. 48p. (gr. 3 up). 1985. PLB 18.64 (0-86514-438-9) Raintree Steck-V.

—New Mexico. LC 85-10832. 48p. (gr. 3 up). 1985. PLB 18.64 (0-86514-439-7) Raintree Steck-V.

—North Dakota. LC 85-9974. 48p. (gr. 3 up). 1985. PLB 18.64 (0-86514-440-0) Raintree Steck-V.

—Oregon. LC 85-9973. 48p. (gr. 3 up). 1985. PLB 18.64 (0-86514-441-9) Raintree Steck-V.

—Pennsylvania. LC 85-9972. 48p. (gr. 3 up). 1985. PLB 18.64 (0-86514-442-7) Raintree Steck-V.

—Puerto Rico. 48p. (gr. 3 up). 1985. PLB 18.64 (0-86514-443-5) Raintree Steck-V.

—Tennessee. 48p. (gr. 3 up). 1985. PLB 18.64 (0-86514-444-3) Raintree Steck-V.

—Texas. LC 85-9980. 48p. (gr. 3 up). 1985. PLB 18.64 (0-86514-445-1) Raintree Steck-V.

—Utah. 48p. (gr. 3 up). 1985. PLB 18.64 (0-86514-446-X) Raintree Steck-V.

—Virginia. 48p. (gr. 3 up). 1985. PLB 18.64 (0-86514-447-8) Raintree Steck-V.

—Wisconsin. 48p. (gr. 3 up). 1985. PLB 18.64 (0-86514-448-6) Raintree Steck-V.

Turner Program Services, Inc. Staff, et al. Washington D. C. 48p. (gr. 4 up). 1986. PLB 18.64 (0-86514-472-9) Raintree Steck-V.

Turner Programs Services, Inc. Staff & Clark, James I. Georgia. 48p. (gr. 3 up). 1985. pap. text ed. 18.64 (0-8174-4281-2) Raintree Steck-V.

Turner Programs Services, Inc. Staff, et al. Rhode Island. 48p. (gr. 3 up). 1986. PLB 18.64 (0-86514-457-5) Raintree Steck-V.

Turner, R. Dale. Baseball Yearbook. (Illus.). 35p. (gr. 2-12). 1991. spiral bdg. 9.95 (0-9628939-0-0) SeaWard Graph.

Turner, Robyn M. Faith Ringgold. LC 92-42652. 1993. 15.95 (0-316-85652-5) Little.

—Frida Kahlo: Portraits of Women Artists for Children. (gr. 4-7). 1993. 15.95 (0-316-85651-7) Little.

—Georgia O'Keeffe. (ps-3). 1991. 15.95 (0-316-85649-5) Little.

—Georgia O'Keeffe: Portraits of Women Artist for Children. (gr. 4-7). 1993. pap. 6.95 (0-316-85654-1) Little.

—Mary Cassatt: Portraits of Women Artists for Children. (gr. 4-7). 1992. 15.95 (0-316-85650-9) Little.

—Rosa Bonheur. (ps-3). 1991. 15.95 (0-316-85648-7) Little.

—Rosa Bonheur: Portraits of Women for Children. (gr. 4-7). 1993. pap. 6.95 (0-316-85653-3) Little.

Turner, Teresa R. ABCs from the Book of Life. 32p. (gr. k-2). 1991. pap. 3.95 (0-9633509-3-5) T R Turner.

Turner, Thomas N. Hillbilly Night Afore Christmas. Rice, James, illus. LC 83-4120. 32p. (gr. 1-6). 1983. 12.95 (0-88289-367-X) Pelican.

Turner, Vernon K., ed. see Bolte, Carl E., Jr.

Turney, Ida V. Paul Bunyan, the Work Giant. (Illus.). (gr. 3 up). 1969. 7.95 (0-8323-0163-9) Binford Mort.

Turnwall, Ruth. G-O-S-P-E-L. Chappell, David, illus. 9p. (gr. k-6). 1982. visualized song 2.99 (3-90117-024-3) CEF Press.

—One Way. (Illus.). (gr. k-6). 1963. illustrated song 4.99 (3-90117-003-0) CEF Press.

—Wonderful Counselor. (gr. k-6). 1973. visualized song 4.25 (3-90117-022-7) CEF Press.

Turpin, Lorna. The Sultan's Snakes. (gr. 4 up). 1991. 7.95 (0-85953-511-8); pap. 3.95 (0-85953-512-6) Childs Play.

Turrentine, Jan. Acteens from A to Z. 24p. (Orig.). (gr. 7-12). 1988. pap. text ed. 1.50 (0-936625-47-3) Womans Mission Union.

—Always a Friend: The Story of Mildred McWhorter. 192p. (Orig.). (gr. 7-12). 1988. pap. 4.95 (0-936625-35-X, New Hope AL) Womans Mission Union.

Turrentine, Jan, ed. see Solomon, Marti.

Turvey, Peter. Inventions: Inventors & Ingenious Ideas. Kline, Marjory, ed. (Illus.). 48p. (gr. 4-9). 1992. 13.95 (0-531-15243-X) Watts.

Tusa, Tricia. Camilla's New Hairdo. (Illus.). 32p. (ps-3). 1991. 14.95 (0-374-31021-1) FS&G.

—Chicken. Tusa, Tricia, illus. LC 85-10591. 32p. (gr. k-3). 1986. RSBE 13.95 (0-02-789320-0, Macmillan Child Bk) Macmillan Child Grp.

—The Family Reunion. 32p. 1993. 15.00 (0-374-32268-6) FS&G.

—Maebelle's Suitcase. Tusa, Tricia, illus. LC 86-12434. 32p. (gr. k-3). 1987. SBE 13.95 (0-02-789250-6, Macmillan Child Bk) Macmillan Child Grp.

—Maebelle's Suitcase. Tusa, Tricia, illus. LC 90-40678. 32p. (gr. k-3). 1991. pap. 4.95 (0-689-71444-0, Aladdin) Macmillan Child Grp.

—Miranda. LC 85-10591. (Illus.). 32p. (ps up). 1985. RSBE 13.95 (0-02-789520-3, Macmillan Child Bk) Macmillan Child Grp.

—Miranda. LC 85-26769. (Illus.). 32p. (gr. k up). 1986. pap. 3.95 (0-689-71064-X, Aladdin) Macmillan Child Grp.

—Stay Away from the Junkyard! Tusa, Tricia, illus. LC 87-15274. 32p. (gr. k-3). 1988. RSBE 14.95 (0-02-789541-6, Macmillan Child Bk) Macmillan Child Grp.

—Stay Away from the Junkyard! Tusa, Tricia, illus. LC 91-38498. 32p. (gr. k-3). 1992. pap. 4.95 (0-689-71626-5, Aladdin) Macmillan Child Grp.

Tusan, Stan. Who Will Be My Pet? McKie, Roy, illus. 40p. (ps-1). 1992. write for info. (0-307-11582-8, 11582) Western Pub.

—Who Will Be My Pet? McKie, Roy, illus. 32p. (ps-1). 1993. pap. 3.25 (0-307-15972-8, 15972, Golden Pr) Western Pub.

Tusiani, Joseph. Dante's Inferno. Pfeiffer, Werner, illus. (gr. 5 up). 1965. 9.95 (0-8392-3046-X) Astor-Honor.

—Dante's Paradiso. Dore, Gustav, illus. (gr. 7 up). 1969. 9.95 (0-685-00563-1) Astor-Honor.

—Dante's Purgatorio. (Illus.). (gr. 5 up). 1968. 9.95 (0-8392-3053-2) Astor-Honor.

Tusquets, Eugenia, tr. see Wright, Bob.

Tutor, Pilar. Mayan Civilization. LC 92-37022. (Illus.). 36p. (gr. up). 1993. PLB 19.93 (0-516-08381-3); pap. 6.95 (0-516-48381-1) Childrens.

Tuttle, Dave. Forever Natural: How to Excel in Sports Drug-Free. (Illus.). 190p. (Orig.). (gr. 9 up). 1990. pap. text ed. 15.95 (0-9625740-0-7) Iron Bks.

Tuttle, Lisa, jt. auth. see Harrison, Mark.

Tuttle, Merlin D. America's Neighborhood Bats: Understanding & Learning to Live in Harmony with Them. (Illus.). 104p. (gr. 10-12). 1988. 19.95 (0-292-70403-8); pap. 9.95 (0-292-70406-2) U of Tex Pr.

Tuulikki, jt. auth. see Roes, Carol.

Tuyle, R. Helen Van see Van Tuyle, R. Helen.

Twain, Mark. The Adventures of Huckleberry Finn. LC 85-9576. (gr. 5 up). 1962. pap. 2.75 (0-8049-0004-3, CL-4) Airmont.

—Adventures of Huckleberry Finn. McKay, Donald & Polseno, Jo, illus. LC 85-9576. 448p. (gr. 4-6). 1981. 14.95 (0-448-06000-0, G&D); (G&D) Putnam Pub Group.

—Adventures of Huckleberry Finn. Smith, H. N., ed. LC 85-9576. (gr. 9 up). 1972. pap. 7.96 (0-395-05114-2, RivEd) HM.

—Adventures of Huckleberry Finn. LC 85-9576. 288p. (RL 7). 1959. pap. 1.75 (0-451-51912-4, Sig Classics) NAL-Dutton.

—Adventures of Huckleberry Finn. LC 85-9576. (gr. 3-7). 1983. pap. 2.99 (0-14-035007-1, Puffin Bks) Puffin Bks.

—Adventures of Huckleberry Finn. LC 85-9576. 187p. (gr. 4-6). 1983. Repr. PLB 15.95x (0-89966-468-7) Buccaneer Bks.

—The Adventures of Huckleberry Finn. LC 85-9576. 384p. (gr. 4-6). 1986. pap. 3.95 (0-14-039046-4) Viking Child Bks.

—Adventures of Huckleberry Finn. Gise, Joanne, adapted by. Burns, Ray, illus. LC 89-20353. 48p. (gr. 3-6). 1990. lib. bdg. 12.89 (0-8167-1857-1); pap. text ed. 3.95 (0-8167-1858-X) Troll Assocs.

—The Adventures of Huckleberry Finn. 288p. (gr. 9-12). 1959. pap. 2.50 (0-451-52373-3, Sig Classics) NAL-Dutton.

—Adventures of Huckleberry Finn. facsimile ed. (Illus.). 366p. 1990. Repr. of 1885 ed. miniature 60.00 (1-878582-01-1) Childs Min Bk Co.

—Adventures of Huckleberry Finn. (Illus.). (gr. 4-7). 1991. pap. 5.95 (0-582-03585-6) Longman.

—The Adventures of Huckleberry Finn. Fiore, Peter, illus. LC 92-10194. 1992. 12.99 (0-517-08128-8, Child Classics) Outlet Bk Co.

—Adventures of Huckleberry Finn. Kellogg, Steven, illus. Glassman, Peter, afterword by. LC 92-27398. (Illus.). 1993. write for info. (0-688-10656-0) Morrow Jr Bks.

—Adventures of Huckleberry Finn. Date not set. pap. 2.95 (0-590-43389-X) Scholastic Inc.

—The Adventures of Tom Sawyer. LC 63-19420. (gr. 5 up). 1964. pap. 2.95 (0-8049-0006-X, CL-6) Airmont.

—Adventures of Tom Sawyer. McKay, Donald & Polseno, Jo, illus. LC 62-19420. (gr. 4-6). 1981. 13.95 (0-448-06002-7, G&D); (G&D) Putnam Pub Group.

—Adventures of Tom Sawyer. LC 62-19420. 224p. (RL 7). 1959. pap. 2.25 (0-451-52355-5, Sig Classics) NAL-Dutton.

—The Adventures of Tom Sawyer. Dickey, James, intro. by. Incl. The Adventures of Huckleberry Finn. LC 62-19420. 512p. (RL 7). 1979. pap. 3.95 (0-451-51966-3, CL1613, Sig Classics) NAL-Dutton.

—The Adventures of Tom Sawyer. LC 62-19420. 224p. (gr. 3-7). 1983. pap. 2.99 (0-14-035003-9, Puffin) Puffin Bks.

—Adventures of Tom Sawyer. LC 62-19420. 167p. (gr. 4-6). 1983. Repr. PLB 15.95x (0-89966-467-9) Buccaneer Bks.

—The Adventures of Tom Sawyer. Moser, Barry, illus. Glassman, Peter, afterword by. LC 89-60838. (Illus.). 272p. (ps up). 1989. 21.95 (0-688-07510-X) Morrow Jr Bks.

Twain, Mark, pseud. Adventures of Tom Sawyer. Gise, Joanne, adapted by. James, Raymond, illus. LC 89-20559. 48p. (gr. 3-6). 1990. lib. bdg. 12.89 (0-8167-1859-8); pap. text ed. 3.95 (0-8167-1860-1) Troll Assocs.

Twain, Mark. Adventures of Tom Sawyer. 1989. 12.99 (0-517-68813-1) Outlet Bk Co.

—The Adventures of Tom Sawyer. facsimile ed. (Illus.). 267p. 1990. Repr. of 1876 ed. miniature 60.00 (1-878582-00-3) Childs Min Bk Co.

—The Adventures of Tom Sawyer. Aagaard, Gary, illus. 304p. (gr. 5 up). 1992. 24.95 (1-879329-08-5) Time Warner Libraries.

—Adventures of Tom Sawyer. 1991. pap. text ed. 5.95 (0-582-03588-0) Longman.

—Adventures of Tom Sawyer. 320p. 1992. 9.49 (0-8167-2546-2); pap. 2.95 (0-8167-2547-0) Troll Assocs.

—Adventures of Tom Sawyer. 1993. pap. 2.95 (0-590-43352-0) Scholastic Inc.

—Adventures of Tom Sawyer & Adventures of Huckleberry Finn. Dickey, James, intro. by. 1979. pap. 4.95 (0-451-52272-9) NAL-Dutton.

—Arabian Nights. Goodenow, Earle, illus. (gr. 4-9). 1981. (G&D); deluxe ed. 13.95 (0-448-06006-X) Putnam Pub Group.

Twain, Mark, pseud. Aventures de Tom Sawyer. Lapointe, Claude, illus. (FRE.). 296p. (gr. 5-10). 1987. pap. 10.95 (2-07-033449-X) Schoenhof.

Twain, Mark. The Celebrated Jumping Frog of Calaveras County. (CHI.). 32p. (gr. 6). 1990. PLB 13.95s.p. (0-88682-296-3) Creative Ed.

—Connecticut Yankee in King Arthur's Court. LC 83-9162. (gr. 5 up). 1964. pap. 3.25 (0-8049-0029-9, CL-29) Airmont.

—A Connecticut Yankee in King Arthur's Court. new & abr. ed. Fago, John N., ed. Redondo, Francisco, illus. LC 83-9162. (gr. 4-12). 1977. pap. text ed. 2.95 (0-88301-263-4) Pendulum Pr.

—A Connecticut Yankee in King Arthur's Court. Hyman, Trina S., illus. LC 87-62879. 384p. (gr. 5 up). 1988. 19.95 (0-688-06344-2); signed ltd. ed. 100.00 (0-688-08258-0, Morrow Jr Bks) Morrow Jr Bks.

—Family Mark Twain. 1462p. 1989. 29.95 (0-88029-264-4) Dorset Pr.

—Huckleberry Finn. Stewart, Diana, adapted by. Neidigh, Sherry, illus. LC 79-24312. 48p. (gr. 4 up). 1983. PLB 18.64 (0-8172-1651-0) Raintree Steck-V.

Twain, Mark, pseud. Huckleberry Finn. Vogel, Nathaele, illus. (FRE.). 380p. (gr. 5-10). 1990. pap. 9.95 (2-07-033230-6) Schoenhof.

—Huckleberry Finn. (gr. 4-7). 1993. pap. 4.95 (0-8114-6826-7) Raintree Steck-V.

Twain, Mark. Huckleberry Finn & Tom Sawyer among the Indians: And Other Unfinished Stories. 1989. pap. 10.00 (0-520-05110-6) U CA Pr.

—Innocents Abroad. Gemme, F. R., intro. by. (gr. 9 up). 1967. pap. 2.95 (0-8049-0151-1, CL-151) Airmont.

—The Jumping Frog. (Illus.). 78p. (gr. 1 up). 1986. 25.00 (0-932458-31-9); pap. 6.95 (0-932458-30-0) Star Rover.

—Life on the Mississippi. Willoughby, J., intro. by. (gr. 9 up). 1965. pap. 1.95 (0-8049-0055-8, CL-55) Airmont.

—The Man That Corrupted Hadleyburg: A Classic Story of Honesty. (Illus.). 72p. (gr. 6 up). 1986. PLB 13.95s.p. (0-88682-006-5) Creative Ed.

—Mark Twain: Short Stories & Tall Tales. 304p. (gr. 4 up). 1993. 5.98 (1-56138-323-6) Courage Bks.

—Mysterious Stranger & Other Stories. (RL 7). 1962. pap. 2.95 (0-451-52069-6, CE1651, Sig Classics) NAL-Dutton.

—The One Hundred-Thousand Pound Bank-Note. (gr. 5 up). 1992. PLB 13.95 (0-88682-508-3) Creative Ed.

—Prince & the Pauper. (gr. 5 up). 1964. pap. 2.50 (0-8049-0032-9, 32) Airmont.

—Prince & the Pauper. 223p. (RL 6). 1964. pap. 2.50 (0-451-52193-5, Sig Classics) NAL-Dutton.

—The Prince & the Pauper. 256p. (gr. 3-7). 1983. pap. 2.95 (0-14-035017-9, Puffin) Puffin Bks.

—The Prince & the Pauper. (gr. k-6). 1985. pap. 4.95 (0-440-47186-9, Pub. by Yearling Classics) Dell.

—The Prince & the Pauper. James, Raymond, ed. Couri, Kathryn A., illus. LC 89-33892. 48p. (gr. 3-6). 1990. lib. bdg. 12.89 (0-8167-1873-3); pap. text ed. 3.95 (0-8167-1874-1) Troll Assocs.

—The Prince & the Pauper. (Illus.). 304p. 1991. 9.99 (0-517-66845-9) Outlet Bk Co.

—The Prince & the Pauper. 256p. 1992. pap. 2.50 (0-8125-0477-1) Tor Bks.

—Pudd'nhead Wilson. Gemme, F. R., intro. by. (Illus.). (gr. 8 up). 1966. pap. 2.50 (0-8049-0124-4, CL-124) Airmont.

—Reader's Digest Best Loved Books for Young Readers: The Adventures of Huckleberry Finn. Ogburn, Jackie, ed. Falter, John, illus. 192p. (gr. 4-12). 1989. 3.99 (0-945260-30-X) Choice Pub NY.

—Reader's Digest Best Loved Books for Young Readers: The Adventures of Tom Sawyer. Ogburn, Jackie, ed. Falter, John, illus. 136p. (gr. 4-12). 1989. 3.99 (0-945260-19-9) Choice Pub NY.

—Roughing It. Girling, Z. N., intro. by. (Illus.). (gr. 8 up). 1967. pap. 2.95 (0-8049-0134-1, CL-134) Airmont.

—Roughing It. Kriegel, L., frwd. by. (RL 10). 1962. pap. 4.95 (0-451-52407-1, CE1829, Sig Classics) NAL-Dutton.

—Selected Shorter Writings of Mark Twain. Blair, Walter, ed. LC 62-51467. (gr. 9 up). 1974. pap. 9.16 (0-395-05155-X, RivEd) HM.

—Short Stories of Mark Twain. Franklin, B., intro. by. (gr. 8 up). 1968. pap. 3.95 (0-8049-0171-6, CL-171) Airmont.

—The Signet Classic Book of Mark Twain's Short Stories. 688p. (gr. 5 up). 1989. pap. 4.50 (0-451-52220-6, Sig Classics) NAL-Dutton.

—A Story Without an End. LC 85-30885. 32p. (gr. 4 up). 1986. PLB 13.95s.p. (0-88682-064-2) Creative Ed.

—Tom Sawyer. Edwards, June, adapted by. Naprstek, Joel, illus. LC 80-22095. 48p. (gr. 4 up). 1983. PLB 18.64 (0-8172-1665-0) Raintree Steck-V.

—Tom Sawyer. (Illus.). (gr. 3-5). 3.50 (0-7214-0977-6) Ladybird Bks.

Twain, Mark, pseud. Tom Sawyer. (Illus.). 1992. write for info. (0-89434-127-8) Ferguson.

—Tom Sawyer. (gr. 4-7). 1993. pap. 4.95 (0-8114-6843-7) Raintree Steck-V.

Twain, Mark. Tom Sawyer Abroad. Rowland, B., intro. by. Bd. with Tom Sawyer Detective. (gr. 5up). 1966. pap. 1.50 (0-8049-0126-0, CL-126) Airmont.

—Tom Sawyer, Abroad & Tom Sawyer, Detective. Busch, Frederick, afterword by. 224p. (ps-8). 1985. pap. 1.95 (0-451-51961-2, Sig Classics) NAL-Dutton.

Tweddle, Dominic. Growing up in Viking Times. McBride, Angus, illus. LC 91-41396. 32p. (gr. 3-5). 1993. PLB 11.89 (0-8167-2725-2); pap. text ed. 3.95 (0-8167-2726-0) Troll Assocs. Postponed.

Twedt, Curt, ed. see Prairie-Plains Resource Institute Staff & Whitney, William S.

Twentieth Century Fox Film Corporation Staff. Home Alone Two: Lost in New York. 16p. (ps-2). 1993. write for info. (1-883366-14-3) YES Ent.

Tweton, D. Jerome & Jelliff, Theodore B. North Dakota: The Heritage of a People. LC 76-27123. (Illus.). (gr. 7 up). 1976. 12.85 (0-911042-19-9) N Dak Inst.

Twin, Michael, jt. auth. see Adams, Pam.

Twining, Edith. Sandman. (ps-4). 1991. pap. 12.95 (0-385-41258-4) Doubleday.

Twinn, M. Paul Hunt's Night Diary. LC 92-10850. 1992. 11.95 (0-85953-925-3, Pub. by Childs Play UK) Childs Play.

—Who Cares about Animal Rights? Lavie, Arlette, illus. LC 92-10852. 1992. 7.95 (0-85953-358-1, Pub. by Childs Play UK) Childs Play.

Twinn, Michael & Adams, Pam. Lady Who Loved Animals. LC 90-46603. (Illus.). 32p. (ps-2). 1981. 7.95 (0-85953-121-X, Pub. by Child's Play England) Childs Play.

Twist, Clint. Christopher Columbus: The Discovery of the Americas. LC 93-19017. 1994. write for info. (0-8114-7253-1) Raintree Steck-V.

—Darwin: On the Trail of Evolution. LC 93-31789. 1994. write for info. (0-8114-7256-6) Raintree Steck-V.

—Deserts. LC 91-22471. (Illus.). 48p. (gr. 4-6). 1991. RSBE 13.95 (0-87518-490-1, Dillon) Macmillan Child Grp.

—Future Sources. LC 92-33918. (Illus.). 32p. (gr. k-4). 1993. PLB 11.90 (0-531-17395-X, Gloucester Pr) Watts.

—Hurricanes & Storms. LC 91-37269. (Illus.). 48p. (gr. 4-6). 1992. RSBE 13.95 (0-02-789685-4, New Discovery) Macmillan Child Grp.

—Ice Caps to Glaciers: Projects with Geography. LC 92-33917. 1993. 12.40 (0-531-17396-8, Gloucester Pr) Watts.

—Jungles & Forests: Projects with Geography. LC 92-33916. 1993. 12.40 (0-531-17397-6, Gloucester Pr) Watts.

—Magellan & Da Gama. LC 93-19303. 1994. write for info. (0-8114-7254-X) Raintree Steck-V.

—Marco Polo: Overland to Medieval China. LC 93-30744. 1994. write for info. (0-8114-7251-5) Raintree Steck-V.

—Nineteen Eighties. LC 92-40348. (Illus.). 47p. (gr. 6-7). 1993. PLB 22.80 (0-8114-3081-2) Raintree Steck-V.

—Nineteen Seventies. LC 92-39952. (Illus.). 47p. (gr. 6-7). 1993. PLB 22.80 (0-8114-3080-4) Raintree Steck-V.

—Rain to Dams: Projects with Water. 1990. PLB 12.40 (0-531-17199-X, Gloucester Pr) Watts.

—Reproduction to Birth: Projects with Biology. (Illus.). 32p. (gr. 5-8). 1991. PLB 12.40 (0-531-17294-5, Gloucester Pr) Watts.

—Seas & Oceans. LC 91-18086. (Illus.). 48p. (gr. 4-6). 1991. RSBE 13.95 (0-87518-491-X, Dillon) Macmillan Child Grp.

—Wind & Water Power. LC 92-33921. (Illus.). 32p. (gr. k-4). 1993. PLB 11.90 (*0-531-17377-1*, Gloucester Pr) Watts.
Two Can Publishing Ltd. Staff. Eagles. (Illus.). 32p. (gr. 2-7). 1991. pap. 3.50 (*0-87534-222-1*) Highlights.
—Elephants. (Illus.). 32p. (gr. 2-7). 1991. 3.50 (*0-87534-217-5*) Highlights.
—Pandas. (Illus.). 32p. (gr. 2-7). 1991. pap. 3.50 (*0-87534-225-6*) Highlights.
—Seals. (Illus.). 32p. (gr. 2-7). 1991. pap. 3.50 (*0-87534-218-3*) Highlights.
—Tigers. (Illus.). 32p. (gr. 2-7). 1991. pap. 3.50 (*0-87534-212-4*) Highlights.
—Whales. (Illus.). 32p. (gr. 2-7). 1991. pap. 3.50 (*0-87534-215-9*) Highlights.
Twohill, Maggie. Big Mouth. (gr. k-6). 1989. pap. 2.95 (*0-440-40223-9*, YB) Dell.
—Jeeter, Mason & the Magic Headset. (gr. 3-6). 1986. pap. 2.75 (*0-440-44220-6*, YB) Dell.
—Superbowl Upset. LC 90-47412. 160p. (gr. 3-6). 1991. SBE 13.95 (*0-02-789691-9*, Bradbury Pr) Macmillan Child Grp.
—Valentine Frankenstein. LC 90-24459. 144p. (gr. 3-6). 1991. SBE 13.95 (*0-02-789692-7*, Bradbury Pr) Macmillan Child Grp.
—Who Has the Lucky Duck in Class 4-B. (gr. k-6). 1986. pap. 2.50 (*0-440-49533-4*, YB) Dell.
—Who Has the Lucky-Duck in Class 4B? LC 83-15719. 112p. (gr. 3-5). 1984. SBE 12.95 (*0-02-789690-0*, Bradbury Pr) Macmillan Child Grp.
Twohy, Patrick J. Finding a Way Home. Raymond, Charlene T., illus. LC 83-90797. 296p. 1990. pap. text ed. 12.00 (*0-9623418-0-0*) P J Twohy.
Tworkov, Jack. The Camel Who Took a Walk. (Illus.). 32p. (gr. k-3). 1974. 13.95 (*0-525-27393-X*, DCB); (DCB) Dutton Child Bks.
—The Camel Who Took a Walk. Duvoisin, Roger, illus. 32p. (ps-3). 1989. pap. 3.95 (*0-525-44476-9*, DCB) Dutton Child Bks.
Tykal, Jack B. Etienne Provost: Man of the Mountains. Smith, Monte, ed. Smith, Ralph L., illus. Gowans, Fred, intro. by. (Illus.). 256p. (gr. 9 up). 1989. 15.95 (*0-943604-24-9*); pap. 9.95 perfect bdg. (*0-943604-23-0*) Eagles View.
Tykr, J. Treasure Trails. (ps-3). 1993. pap. 3.95 (*0-7460-1321-3*, Usborne) EDC.
Tyler. Brain Puzzles. (gr. 2-5). 1980. (Usborne-Hayes); PLB 12.96 (*0-88110-051-X*); pap. 4.50 (*0-86020-437-5*) EDC.
—Number Puzzles. (gr. 2-5). 1980. PLB 12.96 (*0-88110-050-1*, Usborne-Hayes); pap. 4.50 (*0-86020-435-9*) EDC.
—Picture Puzzles. (gr. 2-5). 1980. (Usborne-Hayes); PLB 12.96 (*0-88110-049-8*); pap. 4.50 (*0-86020-433-2*) EDC.
—The Seas. (gr. 3-6). 1976. pap. 6.95 (*0-86020-064-7*, Usborne-Hayes) EDC.
—World Geography. (Illus.). 160p. (gr. 3-6). 1986. 18.95 (*0-86020-193-7*) EDC.
Tyler, jt. auth. see Watts.
Tyler, Anne. Tumble Tower. Modarressi, Mitra, illus. LC 92-44524. 32p. (ps-2). 1993. 14.95 (*0-531-05497-7*); PLB 14.99 (*0-531-08647-X*) Orchard Bks Watts.
Tyler, Deborah. The Greeks & Troy. LC 93-18693. (Illus.). 32p. (gr. 6-8). 1993. RSBE 13.95 (*0-87518-537-1*, Dillon) Macmillan Child Grp.
—Japan. LC 93-3268. (Illus.). 32p. (gr. 4 up). 1993. RSBE 13.95 (*0-89686-773-0*, Crestwood Hse) Macmillan Child Grp.
Tyler, Diane M. & Tyler, James C. Start Exploring Oceans: A Fact-Filled Coloring Book. (Illus.). 128p. (Orig.). (gr. 3 up). 1990. pap. 8.95 (*0-89471-759-6*) Running Pr.
Tyler, Dick, jt. auth. see Columbu, Franco.
Tyler, J. Animal Words. 1989. 3.50 (*0-7460-0252-1*, Usborne) EDC.
—Brainbenders. (Illus.). 96p. 1993. pap. 10.95 (*0-7460-1629-8*, Usborne) EDC.
—Machines. (Illus.). 24p. (ps-2). 1991. pap. 3.50 (*0-7460-0606-3*, Usborne) EDC.
—On the Farm. (Illus.). 24p. (ps-2). 1991. pap. 3.50 (*0-7460-0595-4*, Usborne) EDC.
—Picture Atlas. (Illus.). 32p. (gr. 3-7). 1976. pap. 6.95 (*0-7460-0113-4*, Usborne) EDC.
Tyler, J. & Bryant-Mole, K. Starting to Add. (Illus.). 24p. (ps up). 1989. pap. 3.50 (*0-7460-0455-9*, Usborne) EDC.
—Starting to Subtract. (Illus.). 24p. (ps up). 1989. pap. 3.50 (*0-7460-0456-7*, Usborne) EDC.
Tyler, J. & Cartwright, S. Duck & His Friends. Cartwright, Stephen, illus. 16p. (ps). 1988. 3.50 (*0-7460-0184-3*); PLB 7.96 (*0-88110-326-8*) EDC.
—Duck in Trouble. Cartwright, Stephen, illus. 16p. (ps). 1988. 3.50 (*0-7460-0185-1*); PLB 7.96 (*0-88110-327-6*) EDC.
—Duck on Holiday. Cartwright, Stephen, illus. 16p. (ps). 1988. 3.50 (*0-7460-0183-5*); PLB 7.96 (*0-88110-328-4*) EDC.
—Stephen Cartwright's ABC. (Illus.). 32p. (ps). 1990. 8.95 (*0-7460-0434-6*, Usborne); lib. bdg. 13.96 (*0-88110-446-9*, Usborne) EDC.
Tyler, J. & Gee, R. Punctuation Puzzles. (Illus.). 32p. (gr. 2-6). 1993. pap. 4.95 (*0-7460-1054-0*) EDC.
—Spelling Puzzles. (Illus.). 32p. (gr. 2-5). 1992. pap. 4.95 (*0-7460-1053-2*) EDC.

Tyler, J. & Hawarth, L. Adventure Programs. Longworth, Mark, illus. 48p. (gr. 6 up). 1983. lib. bdg. 10.96 (*0-88110-143-5*); pap. 3.95 (*0-86020-741-2*) EDC.
Tyler, J. & Round, G. Counting up to Ten. (Illus.). 24p. (ps up). 1987. pap. 3.50 (*0-7460-0217-3*) EDC.
—Opposites. (Illus.). 24p. (ps up). 1987. pap. 3.50 (*0-7460-0219-X*) EDC.
—Ready for Reading. (Illus.). 24p. (ps up). 1989. pap. 3.50 (*0-7460-0267-X*, Usborne) EDC.
—Ready for Writing. (Illus.). 24p. (ps up). 1989. pap. 3.50 (*0-7460-0218-1*, Usborne) EDC.
—Sizes. (Illus.). 24p. (ps up). 1989. pap. 3.50 (*0-7460-0269-6*, Usborne) EDC.
—Starting to Count. (Illus.). 24p. (ps up). 1987. pap. 3.50 (*0-7460-0216-5*) EDC.
—Starting to Measure. (Illus.). 24p. (ps up). 1991. pap. 3.50 (*0-7460-0624-1*, Usborne) EDC.
Tyler, J. & Stitt, S. Bedtime Words. (Illus.). 16p. (ps up). 1988. 3.50 (*0-7460-0222-X*) EDC.
—Mealtime Words. (Illus.). 16p. (ps up). 1988. 3.50 (*0-7460-0221-1*) EDC.
—Outdoor Words. (Illus.). 16p. (ps). 1989. 3.50 (*0-7460-0435-4*, Usborne); (Usborne) EDC.
—Shopping Words. (Illus.). 16p. (ps). 1989. 3.50 (*0-7460-0436-2*, Usborne); lib. bdg. 6.96 (*0-88110-394-2*, Usborne) EDC.
—Toy Words. (Illus.). 16p. (ps up). 1988. 3.50 (*0-7460-0220-3*) EDC.
Tyler, J. & Waters, G. Mystery Stories. (Illus.). 144p. (gr. 3-8). 1987. pap. 9.95 (*0-7460-0014-6*, Usborne) EDC.
Tyler, J., jt. auth. see Bryant-Mole, K.
Tyler, J., jt. auth. see Gibson, R.
Tyler, J., et al. Our World. (Illus.). 96p. (gr. 3-7). 1993. pap. text ed. 12.95 (*0-86020-571-1*, Usborne) EDC.
Tyler, James C., jt. auth. see Tyler, Diane M.
Tyler, Jan. Holly Lolly. Mattingly, Jennie, ed. LC 87-50981. (Illus.). 44p. (gr. k-3). 1987. 7.95 (*1-55523-084-9*) Winston-Derek.
Tyler, Jane B., jt. auth. see Orr, C. Rob.
Tyler, Jenny. Creepy Computer Games. Round, Grahm, illus. 16p. (gr. 6 up). 1984. pap. 2.95 (*0-86020-780-3*) EDC.
Tyler, Jenny & Round, Graham. Escape from Blood Castle. (Illus.). 48p. (gr. 4-9). 1986. PLB 11.96 (*0-88110-388-8*); pap. 4.95 (*0-86020-950-4*) EDC.
Tyler, Jenny, jt. auth. see Blundell, Kim.
Tyler, Jenny, jt. auth. see Gemmell, Kathy.
Tyler, Laura & Renna, Giani. Anne Frank. (Illus.). 104p. (gr. 5-8). 1990. lib. bdg. 16.98 (*0-382-09975-3*); pap. 8.95 (*0-382-24002-2*) Silver Burdett Pr.
Tyler, Linda W. After Christmas Tree. (ps-3). 1990. 12.95 (*0-670-83045-3*) Viking Child Bks.
—The After-Christmas Tree. Davis, Susan, illus. LC 92-8616. (gr. 4 up). 1992. 3.99 (*0-14-054191-8*) Puffin Bks.
—My Brother Oscar Thinks He Knows It All. Davis, Susan, illus. 32p. (ps-3). 1991. pap. 3.95 (*0-14-050947-X*, Puffin) Puffin Bks.
—The Sick-in-Bed Birthday. Davis, Susan, illus. 32p. (ps-3). 1990. pap. 3.95 (*0-14-050783-3*, Puffin) Puffin Bks.
—Waiting for Mom. Davis, Susan, illus. 32p. (ps-2). 1989. pap. 3.95 (*0-14-050652-7*, Puffin) Puffin Bks.
Tyler, Robert. Spectre. 100p. (Orig.). 1987. pap. 4.95 (*0-943449-03-0*) Excel Pub.
Tyler, Sydney B. Just Think Program Series, 7 bks. Incl. Bk. 1. Teaching Early Primary Thinking. 82p. (ps-2). 1982. pap. 15.00 report cover (*0-912781-02-5*); Bk. 2. Developing Primary Thinking Skills. 176p. (gr. 1-2). 1982. pap. 25.00 report cover (*0-912781-03-3*); Bk. 3. Developing Primary or Early Intermediate Thinking Skills. 206p. (gr. 2-3). 1982. pap. 25.00 report cover (*0-912781-04-1*); Bk. 4. Developing Intermediate Thinking Skills. 172p. (Orig.). (gr. 3-4). pap. 25.00 report covert (*0-912781-05-X*); Bk. 5. Developing Intermediate or Early Upper Elementary Thinking Skills. 216p. (Orig.). (gr. 4-5). 1982. pap. 25.00 report cover (*0-912781-06-8*); Bk. 6. Developing Upper Elementay Thinking Skills, Pt. I. 178p. (Orig.). (gr. 5-8). 1983. pap. 25.00 report covert (*0-912781-07-6*); Bk. 7. Developing Upper Elementary Thinking Skills, Pt. II. 178p. (Orig.). (gr. 6-8). 1983. pap. 25.00 report cover (*0-912781-08-4*). pap. 5.95. Set. report cover 165.00 (*0-912781-00-9*) Thomas Geale.
—Stretch Think Program 1. 144p. (gr. k-2). 1984. pap. 35.00 (*0-912781-12-2*) Thomas Geale.
—Young Think Program Two. 90p. (Orig.). (gr. k-1). 1988. pap. text ed. 25.00 report cover (*0-912781-13-0*) Thomas Geale.
Tynan, D. M. Leonardo Da Vinci. (gr. 3-4). 1977. pap. 16.95 (*0-521-21209-X*) Cambridge U Pr.
Tyndale. Story of Creation. 1992. pap. 12.99 (*0-8423-5923-0*) Tyndale.
Tynes, Rick & Whittemore, Diane. Monster Dots: Connect the Dots & Color. (Illus.). 80p. (gr. 1-6). 1993. pap. 4.95 (*0-8069-8642-5*) Sterling.
Typpo, Marion H., jt. auth. see Hastings, Jill M.
Tyrrell, Esther Q. Hummingbirds: Jewels in the Sky. Tyrrell, Robert A., photos by. LC 91-40857. (Illus.). 36p. (gr. 1-5). 1992. 14.00 (*0-517-58390-9*); PLB 14.99 (*0-517-58391-7*) Crown Bks Yng Read.
Tyson, Cicely, narrated by see McKissack, Patricia C.
Tyson, Peter. Acid Rain. (Illus.). 128p. (gr. 5 up). 1992. lib. bdg. 19.95 (*0-7910-1577-7*) Chelsea Hse.
Tytla, Milan. Come to Your Senses. McLeod, Chum, illus. 96p. 1993. pap. 9.95 (*1-55037-292-0*, Pub. by Annick CN) Firefly Bks Ltd.

Tytla, Milan & Crystal, Nancy. You Won't Believe Your Eyes. Eldridge, Susan, illus. 88p. (gr. 2-8). 1992. pap. 9.95 (*1-55037-218-1*, Pub. by Annick CN) Firefly Bks Ltd.
Tzannes, Robin. Professor Puffendorf's Secret Potions. Paul, Korky, illus. 40p. (ps-5). 1992. 16.95 (*1-56288-267-8*) Checkerboard.
Tze-Si Huang, tr. see Demi.

U

U. S. A. Gymnastics Staff. I Can Do Gymnastics: Essential Skills for Intermediate Gymnasts. LC 92-43281. (Illus.). 144p. (Orig.). 1993. pap. 14.95 (*0-940279-54-1*) Masters Pr IN.
Uba, Gregory. Is a Mountain Just a Rock. Mitchell, Joanie, illus. LC 83-61882. 260p. (gr. 6-9). 1984. pap. 3.95 (*0-942610-03-2*) Mina Pr.
Uchello, Carlo. Virginians All. Barr, Marilyn, illus. LC 92-13634. 144p. (gr. 7-9). 1992. 11.95 (*0-88289-853-1*) Pelican.
Uchica, Yoshiko. The Invisible Thread. (gr. 8). 1992. write for info. (*0-663-56257-0*) Silver Burdett Pr.
Uchida, Yoshiko. The Best Bad Thing. LC 83-2833. 132p. (gr. 4-7). 1983. SBE 13.95 (*0-689-50290-7*, M K McElderry) Macmillan Child Grp.
—The Best Bad Thing. LC 85-26790. 136p. (gr. 4-7). 1986. pap. 4.95 (*0-689-71069-0*, Aladdin) Macmillan Child Grp.
—The Best Bad Thing. 2nd ed. 128p. (gr. 4-7). 1993. pap. 4.95 (*0-689-71745-8*, Aladdin) Macmillan Child Grp.
—The Bracelet. Yardley, Joanna, illus. LC 92-26196. 32p. (ps-3). 1993. 14.95 (*0-399-22503-X*, Philomel Bks) Putnam Pub Group.
—The Dancing Kettle. LC 86-70457. 184p. (gr. 5 up). 1986. pap. 7.95 (*0-88739-014-5*) Creative Arts Bk.
—The Happiest Ending. LC 85-6245. 120p. (gr. 3-7). 1985. SBE 13.95 (*0-689-50326-1*, M K McElderry) Macmillan Child Grp.
—Invisible Thread. 1991. 12.95 (*0-671-74164-0*, J Messner) S&S Trade.
—A Jar of Dreams. LC 81-3480. 144p. (gr. 5-7). 1981. SBE 13.95 (*0-689-50210-9*, M K McElderry) Macmillan Child Grp.
—A Jar of Dreams. 2nd ed. LC 92-18803. 144p. (gr. 4-7). 1993. pap. 3.95 (*0-689-71672-9*, Aladdin) Macmillan Child Grp.
—Journey Home. Robinson, Charles, illus. LC 78-8792. 144p. (gr. 5-7). 1978. SBE 13.95 (*0-689-50126-9*, M K McElderry) Macmillan Child Grp.
—Journey Home. 2nd ed. Robinson, Charles, illus. LC 91-40149. 144p. (gr. 3-7). 1992. pap. 3.95 (*0-689-71641-9*, Aladdin) Macmillan Child Grp.
—Journey to Topaz. rev. ed. Carrick, Donald, illus. LC 84-70422. 160p. (gr. 4-12). 1985. pap. 7.95 (*0-916870-85-5*) Creative Arts Bk.
—The Magic Listening Cap. Uchida, Yoshiko, illus. 160p. (Orig.). 1987. pap. 7.95 (*0-88739-016-1*) Creative Arts Bk.
—The Magic Purse. Narahashi, Keiko, illus. LC 92-30132. 32p. (gr. 1-4). 1993. SBE 15.95 (*0-689-50559-0*, M K McElderry) Macmillan Child Grp.
—The Rooster Who Understood Japanese. 8.95 (*0-684-14672-X*) JACP Inc.
—Samurai of Gold Hill. rev. ed. Forberg, Ati, illus. LC 84-20424. 128p. (gr. 4-12). 1985. pap. 5.95 (*0-916870-86-3*) Creative Arts Bk.
—The Terrible Leak. (gr. 4-12). Date not set. 13.95 (*0-88682-357-9*, 97223-098) Creative Ed.
Uchida, Yoshiko, retold by. The Wise Old Woman. Springett, Martin, illus. LC 92-46048. (gr. 4 up). 1994. write for info. (*0-689-50582-5*) Macmillan.
Uchitel, Sandra & Michaels, Serge. Endangered Animals of the Rain Forests. (Illus.). 32p. (gr. 3 up). 1992. 9.95 (*0-8431-2994-8*) Price Stern.
Udall, Stewart L. & Haury, Emil W. In Coronado's Footsteps. Priehs, T. J. & Jorgen, Randolph, eds. LC 91-62012. 36p. (Orig.). 1991. pap. 6.95 (*0-911408-99-1*) SW Pks Mnmts.
Ude, Wayne. Maybe I Will Do Something: Seven Coyote Tales. Rorer, Abigail, illus. LC 92-29392. 1993. 14.95 (*0-395-65233-2*) HM.
Uderzo, M., jt. auth. see De Goscinny, Rene.
Uderzo, M., jt. auth. see Goscinny, R.
Uderzo, M., jt. auth. see Goscinny, Rene.
Uderzo, M., jt. auth. see Goscinny, Rene de.
Uderzo, M., jt. auth. see Goscinny, Rene De.
Udry, Janice M. Glenda. Simont, Marc, illus. LC 69-14443. 64p. (gr. 1-5). 1991. pap. 3.95 (*0-06-440410-2*, Trophy) HarpC Child Bks.
—Let's Be Enemies. Sendak, Maurice, illus. LC 61-5777. 32p. (ps-1). 1961. 13.00 (*0-06-026130-7*); PLB 12.89 (*0-06-026131-5*) HarpC Child Bks.
—Let's Be Enemies. Sendak, Maurice, illus. LC 61-5777. 32p. (ps-2). 1988. pap. 4.50 (*0-06-443188-6*, Trophy) HarpC Child Bks.
—Moon Jumpers. Sendak, Maurice, illus. 32p. (gr. k-2). 1959. 15.00 (*0-06-026145-5*) HarpC Child Bks.
—Thump & Plunk. Schweninger, Ann, illus. LC 80-8443. 32p. (ps-3). 1981. 14.00 (*0-06-026149-8*); PLB 13.89 (*0-06-026150-1*) HarpC Child Bks.
—Tree Is Nice. Simont, Marc, illus. LC 56-5153. 32p. (ps-1). 1957. 14.00 (*0-06-026155-2*); PLB 13.89 (*0-06-026156-0*) HarpC Child Bks.

—A Tree Is Nice. Simont, Marc, illus. LC 56-5153. 32p. (ps-3). 1987. pap. 4.95 (*0-06-443147-9*, Trophy) HarpC Child Bks.

—What Mary Jo Shared. Mill, Eleanor, illus. LC 66-16082. 40p. (gr. k-2). 1966. PLB 13.95 (*0-8075-8842-3*) A Whitman.

Udry, Janice May. Is Susan Here? Gundersheimer, Karen, illus. LC 90-32044. 24p. (gr. k-3). 1993. 14.00 (*0-06-026142-0*); PLB 13.89 (*0-06-026143-9*) HarpC Child Bks.

—What Mary Jo Shared. Sayles, Elizabeth, illus. 32p. (ps-3). 1991. pap. 3.95 (*0-590-43757-7*) Scholastic Inc.

Uggla, Goran, illus. The Car Book. LC 93-4422. 1993. spiral bdg. 17.95 (*0-8118-0514-X*) Chronicle Bks.

Uhde, Anna & Atyeo, Marilyn. Birthdays: A Celebration. LC 83-83303. (Illus.). 160p. (Orig.). (ps-8). 1984. pap. 14.95 (*0-89334-075-8*) Humanics Ltd.

Uhing, Mary J. Windows of a Heart. Lauer, Alphonse, ed. Reyes, Augustine, illus. 72p. 1993. pap. 5.00 (*1-56788-013-4*, 20-002) BMH Pubns.

Uhland, Vicki. Miami Dolphins. (gr. 4-8). 1991. PLB 14.95s.p. (*0-88682-373-0*) Creative Ed.

Uhrich, Ethel. Manners in God's House. Hayes, Theresa, ed. Posey, Pam, illus. 16p. (gr. 3-6). 1992. wkbk. 7.99 (*0-87403-929-0*, 14-03501) Standard Pub.

Ujaama, E. James. Young People's Guide to Starting a Business Without Selling Drugs. 61p. (Orig.). 1991. pap. 12.95 (*0-91303-25-8*) Writers Pub Serv.

Ulitsch, Laura. Lil Guard Angel. Crowder, Debbie, illus. LC 91-67738. 64p. 1993. pap. 8.00 (*1-56002-137-3*, Univ Edtns) Aegina Pr.

Ullman, E., jt. auth. see Ullman, H. J.

Ullman, H. J. & Ullman, E. Spaniels. (Illus.). (gr. k-12). 1982. pap. 5.50 (*0-8120-2424-9*) Barron.

Ullman, James R. Banner in the Sky. LC 54-7296. 256p. (gr. 7 up). 1988. pap. 3.95 (*0-06-447048-2*, Trophy) HarpC Child Bks.

Ullom, A. Thomas. Come Aboard Boats: Ship-Shape 3-D Activities. Art In-Forms Staff, ed. Ullom, A. Thomas, illus. 20p. (Orig.). 1983. pap. 8.95 wkbk. (*0-911835-00-8*) Art In-Forms.

Ullrich, Annie. Fairy Tea. Rawley-Whitaker, Jena, illus. 52p. (ps up). 1992. 16.95g (*1-879244-35-7*) Windom Bks.

Ullrich, Marion C. The News Media As a Necessary Supplement to the Text in Education: Student Edition. 3rd, rev. ed. (Illus.). 6p. (Orig.). (gr. 7-12). 1981. write for info. M C Ullrich Pub.

—The Newspaper As a Necessary Supplement to the Text in Education: Teacher Edition. 3rd, rev. ed. (Illus.). 35p. (Orig.). (gr. 7-12). 1981. Repr. of 1979 ed. write for info. (*9617091-1-1*) M C Ullrich Pub.

Ullstein, Susan, adapted by see Gray, Charlotte.

Ulm, Chris, ed. see Cunningham, Lowell.

Ulm, Chris, ed. see Dunn, Ben.

Ulm, Chris, ed. see Gibson, Robert W.

Ulm, Chris, ed. see Mann, Roland.

Ulmer, Adam's Story. LC 59-1292. 24p. (Orig.). (gr. k-4). 1985. pap. 1.89 (*0-570-06191-1*) Concordia.

Ulmer, Louise. Good Friday. (Illus.). 24p. (Orig.). 1992. pap. 1.89 (*0-570-09028-8*) Concordia.

—Jesus' Twelve Disciples: Arch Bks. (gr. k-4). 1982. pap. 1.89 (*0-570-06160-1*, 59-1307) Concordia.

—The Man Who Learned to Give. (gr. k-2). 1977. pap. 1.89 (*0-570-06109-1*, 59-1227) Concordia.

—Samuel, the Judge. (Illus.). 24p. (gr. k-4). 1986. pap. 1.89 saddlestitched (*0-570-06200-4*, 59-1423) Concordia.

—The Son Who Said He Wouldn't. (gr. k-4). 1981. pap. 1.89 (*0-570-06145-8*, 59-1262) Concordia.

Ulrich, Cindy & Guild, Pat. No Sweat! How to Use Your Learning Style to Be a Better Student. Craig, Dorothy, ed. Hall, Mary A., illus. 52p. (gr. 8-12). 1986. wkbk. 5.95 (*0-317-92552-0*) Teaching Advisory.

Ulrich, George. The Spook Matinee: And Other Scary Poems for Kids. LC 91-28270. (Illus.). 32p. (gr. k-3). 1992. 13.00 (*0-385-30552-4*) Delacorte.

Umansky, Kaye. Broomnapped. large type ed. (gr. 1-8). 1991. 13.95 (*0-7451-1704-X*, Galaxy Child Lrg Print) Chivers N Amer.

—Phantasmagoria. Smedley, Chris, illus. 64p. (gr. 2-6). 14.95 (*0-7136-3072-8*, Pub. by A&C Black UK) Talman.

—Pongwiffy: A Witch of Dirty Habits. large type ed. 208p. 1992. 13.95 (*0-7451-1470-9*, Galaxy Child Lrg Print) Chivers N Amer.

Umansky, Kaye & Chamberlain, Margaret. Pass the Jam, Jim! (Illus.). 32p. (ps-1). 1993. 17.95 (*0-370-31662-2*, Pub. by Bodley Head UK) Trafalgar.

Umnik, Sharon D., ed. One Hundred Seventy-Five Easy-to-Do Easter Crafts: Easy-to-Do Projects with Easy-to-Do Things. Cary, C., photos by. (Illus.). 64p. (gr. k-5). 1994. pap. 6.95 (*1-56397-316-2*) Boyds Mills Pr.

Uncle Eric, pseud. Whatever Happened to Penny Candy? A Fast, Clear, & Fun Explanation of the Economics You Need for Success in Your Career, Business, & Investments. 3rd, rev. & enl. ed. Bixler, Nancy, illus. LC 92-36378. (gr. 5 up). 1993. 8.95 (*0-942617-15-0*) Blstckng Pr.

Uncle Hyggly, pseud. Tad Gonopolis & His Adventures in the Slumberyard, No. 3. Uncle Hyggly, illus. 48p. (gr. 3-6). 1987. pap. 8.95 (*0-935583-03-3*) Wounded Coot.

Underhill, Liz. Miss McTaffety's Cats. (Illus.). 32p. (ps-1). 1994. 19.95 (*0-224-03040-X*, Pub. by Jonathan Cape UK) Trafalgar.

—One, Two, Tie Up My Shoe: A New Look at an Old Nursery Rhyme. Underhill, Liz, illus. LC 89-28587. 32p. 1990. PLB 12.95 (*1-55670-142-X*) Stewart Tabori & Chang.

Underhill, Zoe D., ed. The Dwarf's Tailor, & Other Fairy Tales. LC 78-74521. (gr. 4-5). 1979. Repr. of 1896 ed. 21.75x (*0-8486-0224-2*) Roth Pub Inc.

Underwood, Jonathan, ed. see Russell, Bob.

Underwood, Lynn. Religions of the World. LC 90-20343. (Illus.). 64p. (gr. 4-6). 1991. PLB 19.93 (*0-8368-0022-2*) Gareth Stevens Inc.

Underwood, Oscar, tr. see Brady, Janeen.

Underwood, Shirley. The American Indian Coloring Book. Simmons, Shirley, illus. 20p. (gr. k-2). 1969. 3.50 (*0-935741-02-X*) Cherokee Pubns.

Underwood, Tom. Cherokee Legends & the Trail of Tears. Crowe, Amanda, illus. 32p. (gr. 4-12). 1956. 3.50 (*0-935741-00-3*) Cherokee Pubns.

Underwood, Tom B. The Magic Lake: A Mystical Healing Lake of the Cherokee. Simmons, Shirley, illus. 20p. (gr. 1-3). 1982. 3.50 (*0-935741-08-9*) Cherokee Pubns.

UNESCO Staff. Seven Hundred Science Experiments for Everyone. rev. ed. LC 64-10638. (Illus.). 252p. (gr. 5-9). 1964. new. pap. 15.00 (*0-385-05275-8*) Doubleday.

UNESCO Staff, et al. Rescue Mission - Planet Earth: A Global Handbook for the 21st Century. LC 93-20889. 1994. PLB 14.95 (*1-85697-982-2*); pap. 9.95 (*1-85697-944-X*) Kingfisher Bks.

Unfred, David W. Dinosaurs & the Bible. LC 90-80887. (Illus.). 47p. (gr. 3-8). 1990. 12.99 (*0-910311-70-6*) Huntington Hse.

Ungaro, Dan, jt. auth. see Borba, Michele.

Unger, Harlow G. But What If I Don't Want to Go to College? A Guide to Successful Careers Through Alternative Education. 176p. 1992. lib. bdg. 19.95x (*0-8160-2534-7*) Facts on File.

Ungerer, Tomi. Adelaide. (ps). 1991. pap. 3.99 (*0-440-40571-8*, YB) Dell.

—The Beast of Monsieur Racine. Ungerer, Tomi, illus. LC 74-149216. 32p. (ps-3). 1971. 15.95 (*0-374-30640-0*) FS&G.

—The Beast of Monsieur Racine. (Illus.). 32p. (ps up) 1986. pap. 5.95 (*0-374-40570-0*) FS&G.

—Christmas Eve at the Mellops. Ungerer, Tomi, illus. 32p. (gr. k-3). 1992. pap. 3.99 (*0-440-40728-1*, YB) Dell.

—Crictor. Ungerer, Tomi, illus. LC 58-5288. 32p. (ps-3). 1958. 13.00 (*0-06-026180-3*); PLB 12.89 (*0-06-026181-1*) HarpC Child Bks.

—Crictor. LC 58-5288. (Illus.). 32p. (ps-3). 1983. pap. 4.95 (*0-06-443044-8*, Trophy) HarpC Child Bks.

—Emile. Ungerer, Tomi, illus. 32p. (ps-2). 1992. pap. 3.99 (*0-440-40593-9*, YB) Dell.

—I Am Papa Snap & These Are My Favorite No Such Stories. Ungerer, Tomi, illus. (gr. k-3). 1992. 15.00 (*0-385-30653-9*) Delacorte.

—Mellops Go Diving for Treasure. (ps-3). 1993. pap. 3.99 (*0-440-40522-X*) Dell.

—The Mellops Go Spelunking. Ungerer, Tomi, illus. 32p. (gr. k-3). 1992. pap. 3.99 (*0-440-40727-3*, YB) Dell.

—Mellops Strike Oil. (ps-3). 1993. pap. 3.99 (*0-440-40523-8*) Dell.

—Moon Man. (ps-3). 1991. 16.00 (*0-385-30429-3*) Delacorte.

—No Kiss for Mother. (gr. 4-7). 1991. 13.00 (*0-385-30384-X*); PLB 13.99 (*0-385-30385-8*) Delacorte.

—No Kiss for Mother. 1993. pap. 4.99 (*0-440-40886-5*) Dell.

—Orlando. (ps-3). 1993. pap. 3.99 (*0-440-40594-7*) Dell.

—Rufus. (ps). 1991. pap. 3.99 (*0-440-40570-X*, YB) Dell.

—The Three Robbers. Ungerer, Tomi, illus. LC 87-11549. 32p. (ps-3). 1987. Repr. of 1962 ed. SBE 14.95 (*0-689-31391-8*, Atheneum Child Bk) Macmillan Child Grp.

—The Three Robbers. 2nd ed. Ungerer, Tomi, illus. LC 91-246. 40p. (gr. k-3). 1991. pap. 4.95 (*0-689-71511-0*, Aladdin) Macmillan Child Grp.

—Los Tres Bandidos - The Three Robbers. Azaola, Miguel, tr. Ungerer, Tomi, illus. (SPA.). 36p. (gr. 2-4). 1990. pap. write for info. (*84-204-5084-7*) Santillana.

—Zerlada's Ogre. (ps). 1991. 15.00 (*0-385-30386-6*) Delacorte.

UNICEF Staff. Children's Chorus. 32p. (ps up). 1989. 12.95 (*0-525-44545-5*, DCB) Dutton Child Bks.

Unicorn Game Pubs. Staff. Monsters, Magic & Sorcery. Garcia, Vince, ed. (Illus.). 80p. (Orig.). 1991. pap. text ed. 15.00 (*0-9628003-1-7*) Unicorn Game Pubns.

United Educators Staff. My Book House, 12 vols. rev. ed. LC 74-155096. (Illus.). (ps-8). 1993. 299.50 (*0-87566-012-6*); parent guide bks. avail. (*0-87566-006-1*) United Ed.

U. S. Department of Labor, Employment & Training Administration Staff. The Complete Guide for Occupational Exploration: An Easy-to-Use Guide to Exploring over 12,000 Job Titles Based on Interests, Experience, Skills, & Other Factors. Farr, J. Michael, ed. LC 92-39246. 936p. 1993. 44.95 (*1-56370-100-6*, CGOEH); pap. 34.95 (*1-56370-052-2*, CGOE) JIST Works.

U. S. Department of Labor Staff. Exploring Careers. rev. ed. JIST Staff, ed. LC 89-19881. (Illus.). 462p. (gr. 6-12). 1989. pap. 19.95 (*0-942784-27-8*, EXP) JIST Works.

United States Gymnastics Federation Staff. I Can Do Gymnastics: Essential Skills for Beginning Gymnasts. Wilson, Lynn, et al, illus. Feeney, Rik, intro. by. LC 92-2441. 144p. (Orig.). (gr. 1-5). 1993. pap. 14.95 (*0-940279-51-7*) Masters Pr IN.

—Make the Team: Gymnastics for Girls. (Illus.). (gr. 3-7). 1991. (Spts Illus Kids); pap. 5.95 (*0-316-88793-5*, Spts Illus Kids) Little.

U. S.-Japan Cross Culture Center, tr. see Los Angeles Children's Museum Staff.

United States Tennis Association Staff & Brewer, Lewis. Professional Tennis Drills. (gr. 7 up). 1985. pap. 13.00 (*0-684-18298-X*, Scribner) Macmillan.

University of Mexico City Staff, tr. El Alfabeto: Mentes Activas. Siede, George & Preis, Donna, photos by. Schwager, Istar, contrib. by. (SPA., Illus.). 24p. (ps-8). 1992. PLB 11.95 (*1-56674-036-3*) Forest Hse.

—Colores: Mentes Activas. Siede, George & Preis, Donna, photos by. Schwager, Istar, contrib. by. (SPA., Illus.). 24p. (ps-8). 1992. PLB 11.95 (*1-56674-037-1*) Forest Hse.

—Formas: Mentes Activas. Siede, George & Preis, Donna, photos by. Schwager, Istar, contrib. by. (SPA., Illus.). 24p. (ps-8). 1992. PLB 11.95 (*1-56674-041-X*) Forest Hse.

—Mi Dia: Mentes Activas. Siede, George & Preis, Donna, photos by. Schwager, Istar, contrib. by. (SPA., Illus.). 24p. (ps-8). 1992. PLB 11.95 (*1-56674-038-X*) Forest Hse.

—Numeros: Mentes Activas. Siede, George & Preis, Donna, photos by. Schwager, Istar, contrib. by. (SPA., Illus.). 24p. (ps-8). 1992. PLB 11.95 (*1-56674-039-8*) Forest Hse.

—Opuestos: Mentes Activas. Siede, George & Preis, Donna, photos by. Schwager, Istar, contrib. by. (SPA., Illus.). 24p. (ps-8). 1992. PLB 11.95 (*1-56674-040-1*) Forest Hse.

University of Mexico City Staff, tr. see Arem, Joel E.

University of Mexico City Staff, tr. see Dunn, Gary.

University of Mexico City Staff, tr. see Eugene, Toni.

University of Mexico City Staff, tr. see Jablonsky, Alice.

University of Mexico City Staff, tr. see Weidensaul, Scott.

Unkelbach, Kurt. Both Ends of the Leash: Selecting & Training Your Dog. Petie, Haris, illus. (gr. 3-7). 1968. P-H.

Unruh, John. Bright Eyes: The Life of a Baby Jack Rabbit. LC 80-18667. (Illus.). 112p. (Orig.). (gr. 4 up). 1980. pap. 4.95 (*0-914598-02-3*) Padre Prods.

Unruh, Sophia. Lenka of Emma Creek. Shelly, Maynard, ed. Unruh, Arch, illus. LC 89-81282. 32p. (Orig.). (ps-7). 1989. pap. 9.95 (*0-87303-136-9*) Faith & Life.

Unstead, R J. Nineteen Forties. 1990. PLB 13.40 (*0-531-14035-0*) Watts.

Unstead, R. J. Travel by Road Through the Ages. (Illus.). (gr. 7-10). 1983. 14.95 (*0-7136-1812-4*) Dufour.

Unstead, R. J., ed. see Hoare, Robert.

Untermeyer, Louis, ed. Rainbow in the Sky: Golden Anniversary Edition. Birch, Reginald, illus. LC 84-19306. 498p. (gr. 3-7). 1985. 19.95 (*0-15-265479-8*, HB Juv Bks) HarBrace.

Unus, Iqbal J. Up in the Sky. (Illus.). 24p. (Orig.). (gr. 3-6). 1983. pap. 1.50 (*0-89259-054-8*) Am Trust Pubns.

Unwin, Charlotte. Let's Pretend. Dann, Penny & Kindberg, Sally, illus. LC 87-19963. 24p. (ps-3). 1989. 4.95 (*0-8037-0507-7*) Dial Bks Young.

Unwin, M. Science Activities, Vol. II. (Illus.). 24p. (gr. 1-4). 1993. 12.95 (*0-7460-0978-X*) EDC.

—Science with Plants. (Illus.). 24p. (gr. 1-4). 1993. PLB 12.96 (*0-88110-620-8*); pap. 4.50 (*0-7460-0976-3*) EDC.

—Why Do Tigers Have Stripes? (Illus.). 24p. (gr. 1 up). 1993. PLB 11.96 (*0-88110-625-9*); pap. 3.95 (*0-7460-1300-0*) EDC.

Unwin, Pippa. Great Zoo Hunt! (ps-3). 1990. 13.99 (*0-385-41107-3*) Doubleday.

Updike, David. An Autumn Tale. Parker, Robert A., illus. 40p. (gr. 2 up). 1988. 14.95 (*0-945912-02-1*) Pippin Pr.

—Seven Times Eight. Lorenz, Lee, illus. 40p. (gr. 2-5). 1990. PLB 14.95 (*0-945912-10-2*) Pippin Pr.

—The Sounds of Summer. Parker, Robert A., illus. 40p. (gr. 2-5). 1993. 14.95 (*0-945912-20-X*) Pippin Pr.

—A Spring Story. Parker, Robert A., illus. 40p. (gr. 2 up). 1989. PLB 14.95 (*0-945912-06-4*) Pippin Pr.

Updike, John. A Child's Calendar. Burkert, Nancy E., illus. LC 61-21555. 32p. (gr. k-3). 1965. 11.95 (*0-394-81059-7*); PLB 12.99 (*0-394-91059-1*) Knopf Bks Yng Read.

—A Helpful Alphabet of Friendly Objects. Updike, David, photos by. LC 93-29922. (Illus.). Date not set. write for info. (*0-679-84324-8*); PLB write for info. (*0-679-94324-2*) Knopf.

Upgren, H. Ted, Jr. Across the Wheatgrass: A Collection of Hearthside Stories about Uncommon People, Wildlife, Days Afield, & Things, Times & Places of Some Centennial Years. Calkins, Burdette & Bruner, Mike, illus. LC 88-50045. 211p. (Orig.). (gr. 8-12). 1988. 18.95 (*0-9620122-0-3*); pap. 12.95 (*0-9620122-1-1*) Windfeather Pr.

Upham, Elizabeth. Grandmother's Locket. Hall, Maureen K., illus. 38p. (ps-1). 1985. 12.95 (*0-940696-10-X*) Monroe County Lib.

Upton, Arthur C. Ionizing Radiation & Health. Head, J. J., ed. Botzis, Ka, illus. LC 84-71145. 16p. (Orig.). (gr. 10 up). 1986. pap. text ed. 2.75 (*0-89278-199-8*, 45-9699) Carolina Biological.

Upton, H. Cattle Ranchers. (Illus.). 32p. (gr. 3-8). 1990. lib. bdg. 18.00 (0-86625-372-6) Rourke Corp.
—Indian Chiefs. (Illus.). 32p. (gr. 3-8). 1990. lib. bdg. 18.00 (0-86625-400-5); 13.50s.p. (0-685-58654-5) Rourke Corp.
—Trailblazers. (Illus.). 32p. (gr. 3-8). 1990. lib. bdg. 18.00 (0-86625-369-6); lib. bdg. 13.50s.p. (0-685-58653-7) Rourke Corp.
Upton, Pat. Who Does This Job? Novak, Matt, illus. LC 90-85722. 32p. (ps-1). 1991. 7.95 (1-878093-20-7) Boyds Mills Pr.
—Who Lives in the Woods? Upton, Pat & Schmidt, Karen L., illus. LC 90-85721. 32p. (ps-1). 1991. 7.95 (1-878093-19-3) Boyds Mills Pr.
Upton, Richard. The Indian As a Soldier at Fort Custer, Montana 1890-1895: Lieutenant Samuel C. Robertson's First Cavalry Crow Indian Contingent. Remington, Frederic & Goff, O. S., illus. LC 83-80826. 147p. (gr. 7-12). 1983. 27.50 (0-912783-00-1) Upton Sons.
Upton, Richard & Fair, Sharon. The Search for the Smell of Christmas. Buerkle, Bonnie K., illus. 32p. 1992. 14.95x (0-9633348-0-8) Aromatique.
Urban, Hal. Twenty Things I Want My Kids to Know. LC 92-15389. 1992. pap. 9.99 (0-8407-9153-4) Nelson.
Urban, Joan. Richard Wright. King, Coretta Scott, intro. by. (Illus.). (gr. 5 up). 1989. 17.95 (1-55546-618-4) Chelsea Hse.
Urbanski, Michael, jt. auth. see Garigan, Elizabeth.
Urbide, Fernanado & Engler, Dan. Columbus: Adventures to the Edge of the World. CCC of America Staff, illus. 35p. (Orig.). (ps-7). 1991. incl. video 21.95 (1-56814-005-3); pap. text ed. 4.95 book (0-685-62402-1) CCC of America.
Urbide, Fernando & Engler, Dan. Ben-Hur, A Race to Glory. CCC of America Staff, illus. 35p. (Orig.). (ps-8). 1992. incl. video 21.95 (1-56814-006-1); pap. text ed. 4.95 book (0-685-62399-8) CCC of America.
—Bernadette: The Princess of Lourdes. CCC of America Staff, illus. 35p. (Orig.). (ps-6). 1990. incl. video 21.95 (1-56814-004-5); pap. text ed. 4.95 book (0-685-62403-X) CCC of America.
Ure, Jean. If It Weren't For Sebastian. LC 84-15568. 192p. (gr. 7 up). 1985. 14.95 (0-385-29380-1) Delacorte.
—If It Weren't for Sebastian. (gr. k-12). 1987. pap. 2.95 (0-440-93996-8, LFL) Dell.
—One Green Leaf. (gr. 7 up). 1989. 14.95 (0-385-29751-3) Delacorte.
—The Other Side of the Fence. LC 87-27184. 176p. (gr. 7 up). 1988. 14.95 (0-385-29627-4) Delacorte.
—Plague. LC 93-18198. 224p. (gr. 7 up). 1993. pap. 3.99 (0-14-036283-5, Puffin) Puffin Bks.
—Plague. 218p. (gr. 5 up). 1991. 16.95 (0-15-262429-5, HB Juv Bks) HarBrace.
—See You Thursday. LC 83-5217. 224p. (gr. 7 up). 1983. pap. 12.95 (0-385-29303-8) Delacorte.
—What If They Saw Me Now? LC 83-14981. 160p. (gr. 7 up). 1984. 13.95 (0-385-29317-8) Delacorte.
—Wizard in the Woods. Anstey, David & Anstey, David, illus. LC 91-58770. 176p. (gr. 3-6). 1992. 14.95 (1-56402-110-6) Candlewick Pr.
—The Wizard in Wonderland. Anstey, David, illus. LC 92-53020. 176p. (gr. 3-6). 1993. 14.95 (1-56402-138-6) Candlewick Pr.
—You Win Some, You Lose Some. LC 85-16134. 182p. (gr. 7 up). 1986. pap. 14.95 (0-385-29434-4) Delacorte.
—You Win Some, You Lose Some. (gr. k-12). 1988. pap. 2.95 (0-440-99845-X, LFL) Dell.
Ureta, Floreal & Malve, Eduardo. Vive Lo Que Crees! - Live What You Believe! (SPA.). 96p. 1990. pap. 3.50 (0-311-12349-X) Casa Bautista.
Uri, Galila B. The Milah Chair. 250p. (gr. 7). 1992. write for info. (1-56062-143-5); pap. write for info. (1-56062-144-3) CIS Comm.
Uribe, Fernando & Engler, Dan. The Odyssey: A Journey Back Home. CCC of America Staff, illus. 36p. (Orig.). 1992. pap. text ed. write for info. (1-56814-007-X) CCC of America.
Urizar, Hugo, tr. see Sroka, Stephen R.
Urquhart, Jennifer C. Animals That Travel. Crump, Donald J., ed. LC 82-47856. 32p. (ps-3). 1982. PLB 13.95 (0-87044-463-8); lib. bdg. 16.95 (0-685-55634-4) Natl Geog.
—Lions & Tigers & Leopards: The Big Cats. (Illus.). (gr. k-4). 1990. Set. 13.95 (0-87044-820-X); Set. PLB 16.95 (0-87044-825-0) Natl Geog.
Urquhart, Jennifer C. see National Geographic Society Staff.
Urquhart, John, jt. auth. see Grauer, Rita.
Urquhart, John, et al. Fool of the World. (Orig.). (gr. k-3). 1987. pap. 4.50 playscript (0-87602-270-0) Anchorage.
—Nightingale (A Participation Play) (Orig.). (gr. k up). 1983. pap. 4.00 (0-87602-245-X) Anchorage.
Urshan, Benjamin D. & Smelser, Georgia. Survivor: The Life Story of Benjamin D. Urshan. Urshan, Nathaniel, intro. by. LC 90-33396. (Illus.). 208p. (Orig.). 1990. pap. 7.99 (0-932581-65-X) Word Aflame.
Urton, Andrea. Fifty Nifty Origami Crafts. Staunton, James, illus. 80p. (Orig.). (gr. 3-7). 1993. pap. 3.95 (1-56565-011-5) Lowell Hse.
—Fifty Nifty Ways to Earn Money. Manwaring, Kerry, illus. 80p. Date not set. pap. 4.95 (0-685-66755-3) Lowell Hse.
—Fifty Nifty Ways to Earn Money. (gr. 4-7). 1993. pap. 4.95 (1-56565-043-3) Lowell Hse.
—Great Predators of the Land. 1994. 13.95 (0-312-85480-3) Forge NYC.
—Great Predators of the Sea. 1994. 13.95 (0-312-85481-1) Forge NYC.
Uruno, M., jt. auth. see Rost, M.
Usher, Alice. The Sunny Hours. Kniffke, Sophie, illus. 40p. (Orig.). (ps-2). 1991. pap. 3.95 (0-671-75281-2, Green Tiger) S&S Trade.
Usher, Kerry. Heroes, Gods & Emperors from Roman Mythology. Sibbick, John, illus. 132p. (gr. 6 up). 1992. 22.50 (0-87226-909-4) P Bedrick Bks.
Usher, Michael A. & Bormuth, Robert. Experiencing Life Through Mathematics, Vol. 1. rev. ed. (Illus.). 128p. (Orig.). (gr. 8-12). 1978. pap. text ed. 4.92 (0-913688-18-5); tchrs. ed. 8.00x (0-913688-19-3) Pawnee Pub.
Ushinsky, Konstantin. How a Shirt Grew in the Field. Rudolph, Marguerita, adapted by. Weihs, Erika, illus. 32p. (ps-3). 1992. 13.45 (0-395-59761-7, Clarion Bks) HM.
Uspenski, Eduard. The Little Warranty People. Ignatowicz, Nina, tr. from RUS. LC 93-25259. 1994. 13.00 (0-679-82063-9) Knopf Bks Yng Read.
—Uncle Fedya, His Dog, & His Cat. Shpitalnik, Vladimir, illus. Heim, Michael, tr. from RUS. LC 92-44491. (Illus.). 144p. (gr. 1-5). 1993. 14.00 (0-679-82064-7) Knopf Bks Yng Read.
Ustinov. Fairytales. 1987. 12.95 (0-385-24096-1) Doubleday.
Utley, Derek. Espana Viva. (SPA.). 224p. 1988. pap. text ed. 11.50 (0-8219-0335-7, 70291); tchr's. guide 5.95 (0-8219-0336-5, TG-70826); text-wkbk. 18.95 (0-8219-0337-3, TXTWK-70662) EMC.
Utley, Robert. Fort Larned National Historic Site. Foreman, Ronald J. & Priehs, T. J., eds. 16p. (Orig.). 1992. pap. 2.95 (1-877856-15-0) SW Pks Mnmts.
—Fort Scott National Historic Site. Priehs, T. J. & Jorgen, Randolph, eds. LC 91-60460. (Orig.). 1991. pap. 2.95 (0-911408-97-5) SW Pks Mnmts.
Utter, Betty, jt. auth. see Pugh, Ann.

Utter, Jack. American Indians: Answers to Today's Questions. LC 92-62877. (Illus.). xx, 331p. Date not set. 21.95 (0-9628075-3-2); pap. 14.95 (0-9628075-2-4) Natl Woodlands Pub. BOOKLIST writes: "...a must for general libraries" & "...will be extremely valuable to high school libraries." INDIAN COUNTRY TODAY writes: "Jack Utter has painstakingly researched many of the issues most important to Indian people. ..This book...will be a resource asset to classrooms, newsrooms, & many research organizations...The book is a treasure." THE BAKERSFIELD CALIFORNIAN writes; "...comprehensive on contemporary issues." Amply illustrated, containing many tables, maps & photos. Comprehensive index, bibliography with 422 references, nine appendixes. Part I consists of a brief overview of the "Discovery" issue. Part II includes 115 questions & answers grouped under the following main sections: The Indian People; Indian Tribes; Treaties & Agreements; Myth, Misinformation, & Stereotype; Culture & Religion; Warfare; Land, Resources & Economics; Legal Status & Tribal Self-Government; The Bureau of Indian Affairs; Health; Education; Other Agencies & National Organizations; Alaska; The Future. Part III includes A Summary History of United States Indian Policy. The book is filled with information about Indian people, their concerns, & the main issues they face in American society. May be ordered directly from the publisher or from Publishers Distribution Service, phone (800) 345-0096. National Woodlands Publishing Company, 8846 Green Briar Road, Lake Ann, MI 49650. Phone: (616) 275-6735. *Publisher Provided Annotation.*

—Wounded Knee & the Ghost Dance Tragedy. LC 91-61211. (Illus.). iv, 29p. (Orig.). (gr. 10-12). 1991. pap. 3.95 (0-9628075-1-6) Natl Woodlands Pub. This Memorial Edition commemorates the 100th anniversary of the infamous massacre at Wounded Knee, South Dakota, on December 29, 1890. The author has condensed into very readable form the history leading up to & including that fateful event. Essentially, the confrontation marked the end of the major "battles" between U.S. government forces & the Indian nations. Wounded Knee became a milestone in U.S.-Indian history. Indian involvement in the ghost dance religion provided the U.S. military an excuse for killing Chief Sitting Bull & then subduing the Indians at Wounded Knee. All who have an interest in American Indian history will find this account compelling. The booklet is illustrated with two maps & six historical photographs courtesy of the Smithsonian Institution. Orders may be placed directly with National Woodlands Publishing Company, 8846 Green Briar Road, Lake Ann, MI 49650; Phone (616) 275-6735. *Publisher Provided Annotation.*

Uttley, Alison. Lavender Shoes: Eight Tales of Enchantment. Ede, Janina, illus. 84p. (gr. k-2). 1991. pap. 3.95 (0-571-15344-5) Faber & Faber.
—Stories for Christmas. Lines, Kathleen, ed. Rowes, Gavin, illus. 128p. (gr. 3-7). 1991. pap. 4.95 (0-571-16321-1) Faber & Faber.
—Ten Candelight Tales. Hawkins, Irene, illus. 112p. (gr. k-2). 1991. pap. 3.95 (0-571-14289-3) Faber & Faber.
—The Weather Cock & Other Tales. Innes, Nancy, illus. 111p. (gr. k-3). 1991. pap. 2.95 (0-571-14174-9) Faber & Faber.
Utton, Peter. The Witch's Hand. (ps up). 1989. 13.95 (0-374-38463-0) FS&G.
Utz. A Delightful Day with Bella Ballet. LC 75-190267. (Illus.). 32p. (gr. 2-3). 1972. PLB 9.95 (0-87783-056-8); pap. 3.94 deluxe ed. (0-87783-089-4) Oddo.
—The Houndstooth Check. LC 79-190268. (Illus.). 32p. (gr. 2-3). 1972. PLB 9.95 (0-87783-057-6); pap. 3.94 deluxe ed. (0-87783-095-9) Oddo.
—The King, the Queen, & the Lima Bean. LC 73-93020. (Illus.). 32p. (gr. k-3). 1974. PLB 9.95 (0-87783-121-1); pap. 3.94 deluxe ed. (0-87783-122-X) Oddo.
—The Simple Pink Bubble That Ended the Trouble with Jonathan Hubble. LC 78-190273. (Illus.). 32p. (gr. 2-3). 1972. PLB 9.95 (0-87783-062-2); pap. 3.94 deluxe ed. (0-87783-108-4) Oddo.
Uva, Kenneth, jt. auth. see Abramowitz, Jack.
Uva, Kenneth, jt. auth. see Abromowitz, Jack.

V

Va, Leong. A Letter to the King. Anderson, James, tr. from CHI. Va, Leong, illus. LC 91-9469. 32p. (gr. k-3). 1991. 14.95 (0-06-020079-0); PLB 14.89 (0-06-020070-7) HarpC Child Bks.
Vagin, Vladimir & Asch, Frank. Here Comes the Cat! Vagin, Vladimir & Asch, Frank, illus. LC 88-3083. (gr. k-3). 1989. pap. 11.95 (0-590-41859-9) Scholastic Inc.
Vagin, Vladimir, jt. auth. see Asch, Frank.
Vagin, Vladimir see Asch, Frank.
Vagin, Vladimir, jt. auth. see Asch, Frank.
Vagts, Detlev, jt. auth. see Beard, Charles A.
Vahila, Michael. Teaching Guitar to Children: A Complete Guide for Ages 5 to 12. LC 88-63797. (Illus.). 100p. (Orig.). (gr. k-7). 1988. pap. 9.95 (0-942253-01-9); book & cassette pkg. 18.95 (0-942253-02-7) PAZ Pub.
Vahnina, Galya. Den Meda: Annie's Day. Maidenberg, E., illus. (RUS.). 114p. (Orig.). 1987. pap. 14.95 (0-934393-16-8) Rector Pr.
Vail. A Kid's Best Friend. 1993. pap. 2.95 (0-590-42787-3) Scholastic Inc.
—Number Six All the Way Home. 1993. pap. 2.75 (0-590-43430-6) Scholastic Inc.
Vail, John. Fidel Castro. (Illus.). 112p. (gr. 5 up). 1986. lib. bdg. 17.95 (0-87754-566-9) Chelsea Hse.
—Nelson & Winnie Mandela. Schlesinger, Arthur M. (Illus.). 112p. (gr. 5 up). 1989. lib. bdg. 17.95 (1-55546-841-1) Chelsea Hse.

—Thomas Paine. Schlesinger, Arthur M., Jr., intro. by. (Illus.). 112p. (gr. 5 up). 1990. 17.95 (*1-55546-819-5*) Chelsea Hse.

—World War Two: The War in Europe. LC 91-23062. (Illus.). 112p. (gr. 5-8). 1991. PLB 17.95 (*1-56006-407-2*) Lucent Bks.

Vail, Linda. My Wicked Valentine. (Orig.). 1989. pap. 3.95 (*0-440-20233-7*) Dell.

Vail, Rachel. Do-Over. LC 92-6717. 160p. (gr. 6-12). 1992. 14.95 (*0-531-05460-8*); PLB 14.99 (*0-531-08610-0*) Orchard Bks Watts.

—Do-Over. large type ed. 178p. 1993. Repr. lib. bdg. 15. 95 (*1-56054-622-0*) Thorndike Pr.

—Ever After. LC 93-29802. 176p. (gr. 6-9). 1993. 14.95 (*0-531-06838-2*); lib. bdg. 14.99 RLB (*0-531-08688-7*) Orchard Bks Watts.

—Wonder. LC 91-10576. 128p. (gr. 6 up). 1991. 13.95 (*0-531-05964-2*); RLB 13.99 (*0-531-08564-3*) Orchard Bks Watts.

—Wonder. 128p. (gr. 5 up). 1993. pap. 3.99 (*0-14-036167-7*, Puffin) Puffin Bks.

Vail, Virginia. Good Sports. Bode, Daniel, illus. LC 89-31345. 128p. (gr. 4-6). 1990. lib. bdg. 9.89 (*0-8167-1629-3*); pap. text ed. 2.95 (*0-8167-1630-7*) Troll Assocs.

—Happy Trails. Bode, Daniel, illus. LC 89-30584. 128p. (gr. 4-6). 1990. PLB 9.89 (*0-8167-1627-7*); pap. text ed. 2.95 (*0-8167-1628-5*) Troll Assocs.

—Horse Play. Bode, Daniel, illus. LC 89-31347. 128p. (gr. 4-6). 1990. lib. bdg. 9.89 (*0-8167-1659-5*); pap. text ed. 2.95 (*0-8167-1660-9*) Troll Assocs.

—Horseback Summer. Bode, Daniel, illus. LC 89-30583. 128p. (gr. 4-6). 1990. lib. bdg. 9.89 (*0-8167-1625-0*); pap. text ed. 2.95 (*0-8167-1626-9*) Troll Assocs.

—Oh Deer! 128p. (gr. 3-7). 1990. pap. 2.75 (*0-590-42802-0*) Scholastic Inc.

—One Dog Too Many. (gr. 4-7). 1990. pap. 2.75 (*0-590-42800-4*) Scholastic Inc.

—Palomino. (gr. 4-7). 1992. pap. 3.50 (*0-06-106716-4*, Harp PBks) HarpC.

—Petnapped! (gr. 4-7). 1990. pap. 2.75 (*0-590-42799-7*) Scholastic Inc.

—Riding Home. Bode, Daniel, illus. LC 89-34548. 128p. (gr. 4-6). 1990. PLB 9.89 (*0-8167-1661-7*); pap. text ed. 2.95 (*0-8167-1662-5*) Troll Assocs.

—Surprise! Surprise! Bode, Daniel, illus. LC 89-31346. 128p. (gr. 4-6). 1990. lib. bdg. 9.89 (*0-8167-1657-9*); pap. text ed. 2.95 (*0-8167-1658-7*) Troll Assocs.

Vainio, Pirkko. The Snow Goose. James, J. Alison, tr. from GER. Vainio, Pirkko, illus. LC 92-31330. 32p. (gr. k-3). 1993. 14.95 (*1-55858-194-4*); lib. bdg. 14.88 (*1-55858-195-2*) North-South Bks NYC.

Valat, P. M. & Perols, S., illus. Couleur. (FRE.). (ps-1). 1989. 17.95 (*2-07-035706-6*) Schoenhof.

Valat, Pierre-Marie. Animal Faces: Fifteen Punch-Out Masks. (Illus.). 32p. (ps up). 1988. pap. 17.99 (*0-525-44440-8*, DCB) Dutton Child Bks.

—Dinosaur Faces. (Illus.). 16p. (ps up). 1990. 14.95 (*0-525-44631-1*, DCB) Dutton Child Bks.

—Fun Faces. (Illus.). 32p. (ps up). 1989. 15.95 (*0-525-44544-7*, DCB) Dutton Child Bks.

Valat, Pierre-Marie, illus. Pomme. (FRE.). (ps-1). 1989. 14.95 (*2-07-035702-3*) Schoenhof.

Valdez, Barbara. I Like Who I Am & It Shows. (ps-1). 1993. pap. 9.95 (*0-86653-952-2*) Fearon Teach Aids.

—I Relate Well to Others & It Shows. (gr. 5-7). 1993. pap. 9.95 (*0-86653-950-6*) Fearon Teach Aids.

—I Take Responsibility for Me & It Shows. (gr. 2-4). 1993. pap. 9.95 (*0-86653-951-4*) Fearon Teach Aids.

Valdivia, Rochelle, illus. Time for Rhyme: Stories, Poems, Games, Art Projects, Fun Sheets. 64p. (ps-k). 1988. pap. text ed. 8.95 (*0-943129-02-8*) Chatterbox Pr.

Valens, Amy. Danilo the Fruit Man. Valens, Amy, illus. LC 91-46893. 32p. (ps-3). 1993. 12.99 (*0-8037-1151-4*); PLB 12.89 (*0-8037-1152-2*) Dial Bks Young.

—Jesse's Day Care. Brown, Richard, illus. 32p. (ps-2). 1990. 13.45 (*0-395-53357-0*) HM.

Valenti-Hilliard, Beverly, jt. auth. see Hilliard, Dick.

Valentine. Educational Play: Math. (gr. 4-6). 1992. 8.00 (*0-89824-140-5*) Trillium Pr.

Valentine, Deborah. Educational Play: Language Arts. (gr. 4-6). 1986. 7.99 (*0-89824-170-7*) Trillium Pr.

Valentine, E. J. H. Norman Schwarzkopf. (gr. 4-7). 1991. pap. 3.50 (*0-553-15967-4*) Bantam.

—Pink Parrots, No. 5: Change-Up. Ellis, Lucy, created by. (gr. 3-7). 1991. pap. 3.95 (*0-316-74113-2*, Spts Illus Kids) Little.

Valentine, Johnny. The Daddy Machine. Schmidt, Lynette, illus. 48p. (Orig.). (gr. k-4). 1992. pap. 6.95 (*1-55583-107-9*, Alyson Wonderland) Alyson Pubns.

—The Day They Put a Tax on Rainbows. Schmidt, Lynette, illus. 32p. (gr. k-5). 1992. 12.95 (*1-55583-201-6*, Alyson Wonderland) Alyson Pubns.

—The Duke Who Outlawed Jelly Beans & Other Stories. Schmidt, Lynette, illus. 32p. (gr. k-5). 1991. 12.95 (*1-55583-199-0*) Alyson Pubns.

—The Duke Who Outlawed Jelly Beans & Other Stories. Schmidt, Lynette, illus. 32p. (gr. k-4). 1993. pap. 8.95 (*1-55583-219-9*) Alyson Pubns.

—One Dad, Two Dads, Brown Dad, Blue Dads. Sarecky, Melody, illus. 32p. (gr. 2-6). 1994. 10.95 (*1-55583-253-9*, Alyson Wonderland) Alyson Pubns.

—Two Moms, the Zark, & Me. Lopez, Angelo, illus. 48p. (gr. k-3). 1993. 12.95 (*1-55583-236-9*) Alyson Pubns.

Valentine, Tom, jt. auth. see Smith, Stan.

Valette. Spanish for Mastery One, 5 vols. large type ed. 1220p. (gr. 7-2). 1985. Repr. of 1984 ed. 17 pt. 242.50 (*0-317-01936-8, J-23380-00*); wkbk. 2 vols. 408p. 16 pt. 113.00 (*0-317-01937-6, J- 23390-00*) Am Printing Hse.

—Spanish for Mastery Two. large type ed. (gr. 7-12). Repr. of 1984 ed. 6 vols. 1300 p. 16-17 pt. 253.00 (*0-317-01938-4, J-23400-00*); wkbk. 3 vols. 518p. 16 pt. 142.00 (*0-317-01939-2, J-23410-00*) Am Printing Hse.

Valiappa, Al. Story of Our Rivers: Book II. Chakravarty, Pranab, illus. (gr. 1-9). 1979. pap. 2.50 (*0-89744-184-2*) Auromere.

Valier, Kathy. The Kaua'i Guide to Hiking Trails Less Traveled with Camping Information. (Illus.). 64p. (Orig.). 1989. pap. 2.50 (*0-942255-06-2, G5*) Magic Fishes Pr.

Valk, Gabriel, ed. see Mokrinskaia, Nina.

Valladares, Margaret M. Animal Heaven. Dalins, Astrid, illus. 24p. (Orig.). (gr. k-4). 1991. incl. coloring bk. & VHS 9.95 (*1-879588-01-3*) M Valladares.

Valle, Teresa La see Ralph, Margaret.

Vallejo, Mariano, et al. Great Indians of California. Knill, Harry, ed. (Illus.). 48p. (gr. 6). 1981. pap. 3.95 (*0-88388-087-3*) Bellerophon Bks.

Vallet, Cedric. Almost Finished. Vallet, Cedric, illus. 18p. (gr. k-3). 1992. pap. 11.95 (*1-895583-28-4*) MAYA Pubs.

—Mother, Where Is New York? Vallet, Cedric, illus. 11p. (gr. k-3). 1992. pap. 13.95 (*1-895583-27-6*) MAYA Pubs.

—Now Is the Time. Vallet, Cedric, illus. 16p. (gr. k-3). 1992. pap. 14.95 (*1-895583-25-X*) MAYA Pubs.

—A Trip to Paris. Vallet, Cedric, illus. 17p. (gr. k-3). 1992. pap. 15.95 (*1-895583-26-8*) MAYA Pubs.

—Where Is Here? Vallet, Cedric, illus. 19p. (gr. k-3). 1992. pap. 12.95 (*1-895583-29-2*) MAYA Pubs.

Vallet, Muriel. Camping Is Exciting. Vallet, Muriel, illus. 19p. (gr. k-3). 1992. pap. 13.95 (*1-895583-48-9*) MAYA Pubs.

—Chantal Takes Her First Steps. Vallet, Muriel, illus. 11p. (gr. k-3). 1992. pap. 6.95 (*1-895583-50-0*) MAYA Pubs.

—Dad, Can We Go Camping Tonight? Vallet, Muriel, illus. 16p. (gr. 1-6). 1992. pap. 13.95 (*1-56606-003-6*) Bradley Mann.

—How Many Times? Vallet, Muriel, illus. 13p. (gr. k-3). 1992. pap. 6.95 (*1-895583-47-0*) MAYA Pubs.

—Let's Take Turns. Vallet, Muriel, illus. 15p. (gr. k-3). 1993. pap. 10.95 (*1-895583-58-6*) MAYA Pubs.

—My Turn. Vallet, Muriel, illus. 17p. (gr. k-3). 1992. pap. 12.95 (*1-895583-46-2*) MAYA Pubs.

—Pinky Saves the Forest. Vallet, Muriel, illus. 12p. (gr. 1-3). 1992. pap. 6.95 (*1-895583-01-2*) MAYA Pubs.

—Take the Plane. Vallet, Muriel, illus. 10p. (gr. k-3). 1993. pap. 10.95 (*1-895583-59-4*) MAYA Pubs.

—Where on Earth Is Jean? Vallet, Muriel, illus. 17p. (gr. k-3). 1992. pap. 8.95 (*1-895583-49-7*) MAYA Pubs.

Vallet, Roxanne. The Balloon Book. Vallet, Roxanne, illus. 15p. (gr. 1-4). 1992. pap. 11.95 (*1-56606-008-7*) Bradley Mann.

—Children Can Be Scarry. Vallet, Roxanne, illus. 14p. (gr. k-3). 1993. pap. 12.95 (*1-56606-018-4*) Bradley Mann.

—Geography Is Fun. Vallet, Roxanne, illus. 13p. (gr. k-3). 1992. pap. 10.95 (*1-895583-37-3*) MAYA Pubs.

—Horses. Vallet, Roxanne, illus. 19p. (gr. k-3). 1992. pap. 10.95 (*1-895583-40-3*) MAYA Pubs.

—How Tall Is Too Tall? Vallet, Roxanne, illus. 12p. (gr. 1-3). 1992. pap. 10.95 (*1-56606-007-9*) Bradley Mann.

—Minochet. Vallet, Roxanne, illus. 19p. (gr. k-3). 1992. pap. 10.95 (*1-895583-36-5*) MAYA Pubs.

—Ralph Gets a Prize. Vallet, Roxanne, illus. 12p. (gr. k-3). 1993. pap. text ed. 12.95 (*1-56606-017-6*) Bradley Mann.

—Thinking. Vallet, Roxanne, illus. 14p. 1992. pap. 10.95 (*1-895583-39-X*) MAYA Pubs.

—Vacation to Marsailles. Vallet, Roxanne, illus. 15p. (gr. k-3). 1992. pap. 13.95 (*1-895583-38-1*) MAYA Pubs.

Vallo, Lawrence. Tales of a Pueblo Boy. LC 86-5876. (Illus.). 48p. (Orig.). 1987. pap. 5.95 (*0-86534-089-7*) Sunstone Pr.

Valloglise, P. Luc. The Search for the Rabbit. 138p. (gr. 7 up). 1988. pap. 10.00 (*0-934852-55-3*) Lorien Hse.

Valmiki. Ramayana: The Story of Rama. Bapu, illus., pseud. LC 74-77601. 72p. (gr. 5-12). 1975. 8.50 (*0-88253-292-8*); pap. 3.50 (*0-88253-291-X*) Ind-US Inc.

Van, Leeuwan J. Oliver Pig at School. LC 89-25607. (ps-3). 1990. 11.00 (*0-8037-0812-2*); PLB 10.89 (*0-8037-0813-0*) Dial Bks Young.

Vanage, jt. auth. see Amery.

Vanags. Empires & Barbarians. (Illus.). (gr. 4-9). 1979. (Usborne-Hayes); PLB 13.96 (*0-88110-109-5*); pap. 6.95 (*0-86020-142-2*) EDC.

Van Ahnan, Katherine & Young Bear, Joan A. Charlie Young Bear. Gilliland, Hap, ed. Hardgrove, Tanya, illus. 32p. (Orig.). (gr. 3-6). 1990. pap. 4.95 (*0-89992-128-0*) Coun India Ed.

Van Allen, Diane. Always Alvin. Reilly, Veronica, illus. (Orig.). (ps). 1984. pap. 3.95 (*0-939332-11-6*) J Pohl Assocs.

Van Allsburg, Chris. Ben's Dream. (Illus.). 32p. (gr. 2 up). 1982. 14.45 (*0-395-32084-4*) HM.

—The Garden of Abdul Gasazi. (Illus.). 32p. (gr. 1-12). 1979. 16.45 (*0-395-27804-X*) HM.

—Jumanji. Van Allsburg, Chris, illus. 32p. (gr. 3 up). 1981. 15. 95 (*0-395-30448-2*) HM.

—Just a Dream. (Illus.). 32p. (ps up). 1990. 17.45 (*0-395-53308-2*) HM.

—The Mysteries of Harris Burdick. LC 84-9006. (Illus.). 32p. (gr. 5 up). 1984. 16.95 (*0-395-35393-9*) HM.

—Polar Express. Van Allsburg, Chris, illus. LC 85-10907. 32p. (gr. 2 up). 1985. 17.45 (*0-395-38949-6*) HM.

—The Stranger. Van Allsburg, Chris, illus. LC 86-15235. 32p. (gr. 2-4). 1986. 16.45 (*0-395-42331-7*) HM.

—The Sweetest Fig. Van Allsburg, Chris, illus. LC 93-12692. (gr. 4 up). 1993. 17.95 (*0-395-67346-1*) HM.

—Two Bad Ants. Van Allsburg, Chris, illus. 32p. (ps up). 1988. 17.45 (*0-395-48668-8*) HM.

—The Widow's Broom. LC 92-7110. (Illus.). 32p. (gr. k-4). 1992. 17.95 (*0-395-64051-2*) HM.

—The Wreck of the Zephyr. Van Allsburg, Chris, illus. LC 82-23371. 32p. (ps up). 1983. 16.45 (*0-395-33075-0*) HM.

—The Wretched Stone. Van Allsburg, Chris, illus. 32p. 1991. 17.45 (*0-395-55307-4*, Sandpiper) HM.

—The Z Was Zapped: A Play in Twenty-Six Acts. Van Allsburg, Chris, illus. 56p. (ps up). 1987. 16.45 (*0-395-44612-0*, Clarion Bks) HM.

Van Antwerp, T. Cooper. Hereafter Rising. Graves, Helen, ed. LC 88-50121. 190p. (gr. 3-10). 1988. 8.95 (*1-55523-139-X*) Winston-Derek.

Van Beek, Tom. Degas, the Ballet, & Me. Peters, Thea, illus. 48p. (gr. 2-7). 1993. 12.95 (*1-56288-424-7*) Checkerboard.

Van Blaricom, Colleen, ed. Christmas Crafts: Merry Things to Make. Louise, Anita, illus. 32p. (Orig.). (ps-5). 1993. pap. 3.95 (*1-56397-083-X*) Boyds Mills Pr.

—Crafts from Recyclables: Great Ideas from Throwaways. LeHew, Ron, illus. LC 91-72872. 48p. (gr. 1-5). 1992. pap. 4.95 (*1-56397-015-5*) Boyds Mills Pr.

—Easter Crafts. Riggio, Anita, illus. LC 91-72873. 32p. (ps-3). 1992. pap. 3.95 (*1-56397-014-7*) Boyds Mills Pr.

—Halloween Craft Book: Spooky & Fun Things to Make. Palan, R. Michael, illus. 32p. (gr. 2-5). 1992. Set of 3 bks. pap. 11.85 (*1-56397-165-8*); pap. 3.95 (*1-56397-119-4*) Boyds Mills Pr.

Vance, Eleanor G. Tall Book of Fairy Tales. reissued ed. Sharp, William, illus. 128p. (ps-3). 1947. 9.95 (*0-06-025545-5*) HarpC Child Bks.

Vance, Eleanor G., ed. see Sewell, Anna.

Vance, Jim, ed. see Burns, Charles.

Vance, Joel M. Grandma & the Buck Deer. Colrus, Bill, illus. 173p. 1988. pap. text ed. 11.95 (*0-87691-322-2*) Cedar Glade Pr.

Vancil, Mark. NBA Slam Dunk All-Stars. (ps-3). 1993. pap. 2.25 (*0-307-12768-0*, Golden Pr) Western Pub.

VanCleave, Janice. A-Plus Projects in Biology: Winning Science Fair Ideas. 240p. 1993. 22.95 (*0-471-58629-3*); pap. 12.95 (*0-471-58628-5*) Wiley.
In this innovative new series, Janice VanCleave shows junior high & high school students how to devise & produce challenging science experiments without using complicated & expensive equipment. Each book features 30 fascinating experiment ideas --everything from studying weather by creating clouds in a soda bottle to exploring physiology by measuring the respiration of common house plants. Detailed background information & definitions are provided for each investigation. Once the experiment is completed, students are encouraged to probe deeper. They ask questions, create additional experiments, & develop their own theories & conclusions. Janice shows how to use these independent discoveries to produce science projects that get top grades, earn extra credit, & reveal how science really works. In BIOLOGY, potential science projects probe topics such as botany, zoology, physiology, cell division, photosynthesis & ecology.
Publisher Provided Annotation.

—A-Plus Projects in Chemistry: Winning Science Fair Ideas. 240p. (gr. 7 up). 1993. 22.95 (*0-471-58631-5*); pap. 12.95 (*0-471-58630-7*) Wiley.
In this innovative new series, Janice VanCleave shows junior high & high school students how to devise &

produce challenging science experiments without using complicated & expensive equipment. Each book features 30 fascinating experiment ideas --everything from studying weather by creating clouds in a soda bottle to exploring physiology by measuring the respiration of common house plants. Detailed background information & definitions are provided for each investigation. Once the experiment is completed, students are encouraged to probe deeper. They ask questions, create additional experiments, & develop their own theories & conclusions. Janice shows how to use these independent discoveries to produce science projects that get top grades, earn extra credit, & reveal how science really works. In CHEMISTRY, students develop projects involving weather, acids/bases, polymers, crystals, biochemistry, denaturing proteins, chromatography, & many more. Also available in the series is JANICE VANCLEAVE'S A-PLUS PROJECTS IN BIOLOGY. *Publisher Provided Annotation.*

—Janice VanCleave's Animals. 96p. (gr. 3 up). 1992. pap. text ed. 9.95 (0-471-55052-3) Wiley.
Every year, children, parents & teachers nationwide face the prospect of creating innovative & exciting science fair projects. Now they get a hand from none other than popular children's science book author, Janice VanCleave. In ANIMALS, one of six activity books in the SPECTACULAR SCIENCE PROJECTS series, junior scientists explore how elephants use their ears to cool their bodies, how chameleons change color, & much more. In this new series, Janice adds even more mind-boggling ideas for science exploration. Each book features 20 simple experiments on most kids' favorite topics plus lots of ideas for exploring each topic further. Janice then offers hints on transforming these explorations into the best science fair projects ever. Like all Janice VanCleave books, these include lively, detailed illustrations, are written in a simple, easy-to-understand style, & make use of everyday materials from around the house. The other books in the SPECTACULAR SCIENCE PROJECTS series include: EARTHQUAKES, GRAVITY, MACHINES, MAGNETS, & MOLECULES. "VanCleave's new SPECTACULAR SCIENCE PROJECTS series will be popular with students at science fair time." --Booklist. *Publisher Provided Annotation.*

—Janice Vancleave's Astronomy for Every Kid: 101 Easy Experiments That Really Work. 1991. pap. text ed. 10.95 (0-471-53573-7) Wiley.
—Janice Vancleave's Astronomy for Every Kid: 101 Easy Experiments That Really Work. 1991. text ed. 24.95 (0-471-54285-7); pap. 19.89 (0-685-47739-8) Wiley.
—Janice Vancleave's Astronomy for Every Kid. (Illus.). 240p. 1991. pap. 10.95 (0-685-41431-0) Wiley.
—Janice Vancleave's Earth Science for Every Kid: One Hundred One Easy Experiments That Really Work. (Illus.). 224p. (gr. 3-8). 1991. text ed. 24.95 (0-471-54389-6) Wiley.

—Janice VanCleave's Earthquakes. 88p. (Orig.). 1993. pap. 9.95 (0-471-57107-5) Wiley.
Every year, children, parents & teachers nationwide face the prospect of creating innovative & exciting science fair projects. Now they get a hand from none other than popular children's science book author, Janice VanCleave. In EARTHQUAKES, one of six activity books in the SPECTACULAR SCIENCE PROJECTS series, junior scientists explore how different conditions cause earthquakes, how a seismograph measures & much more. In this new series, Janice adds even more mind-boggling ideas for science exploration. Each book features 20 simple experiments on most kids' favorite topics plus lots of ideas for exploring each topic further. Janice then offers hints on transforming these explorations into the best science fair projects ever. Like all Janice VanCleave books, these include lively, detailed illustrations, are written in a simple, easy-to-understand style, & make use of everyday materials from around the house. The other books in the SPECTACULAR SCIENCE PROJECTS series include, ANIMALS, GRAVITY, MACHINES, MAGNETS, & MOLECULES. "VanCleave's new SPECTACULAR SCIENCE PROJECTS series will be popular with students at science fair time" --Booklist. *Publisher Provided Annotation.*

—Janice VanCleave's Geography for Every Kid. 240p. (gr. 3 up). 1993. text ed. 22.95 (0-471-59841-0); pap. text ed. 10.95 (0-471-59842-9) Wiley.
Janice VanCleave, the popular author who has made science & math fun for millions of children, now brings the kids fascinating world geography. Following the format of the wildly successful Science for Every Kid series, she captures the imagination of children & helps them learn basic geography terms & concepts as they participate in intriguing activities & explorations. The activities, presented in an easy step-by-step format, include making maps with clay, drawing a map of your neighborhood using simple symbols & symbol key, & using a string to measure the depth of a simulated ocean floor. GEOGRAPHY FOR EVERY KID is the perfect companion to any atlas & will become a welcome addition to your VanCleave library. Other topics covered in the SCIENCE FOR EVERY KID series include Astronomy, Biology, Chemistry, Earth Science, Math, & Physics. "An entertaining, educational, & nonthreatening aid to understanding earth science."--School Library Journal (for Earth Science for Every Kid). "A good selection for libraries looking for material on supplemental or remedial mathematics & a real boost to a weak section in most collections."--School Library Journal (Math for Every Kid). *Publisher Provided Annotation.*

—Janice VanCleave's Machines. 87p. (Orig.). (gr. 4 up). 1993. pap. write for info. (0-471-57108-3) Wiley.
—Janice VanCleave's Magnets. 87p. (Orig.). 1993. pap. 9.95 (0-471-57106-7) Wiley.

—Janice Vancleave's Math for Every Kid: Easy Activities That Make Learning Math Fun. 224p. 1991. text ed. 24.95 (0-471-54693-3); pap. text ed. 10.95 (0-471-54265-2) Wiley.

—Janice VanCleave's Microscopes & Magnifying Lenses: Mind-Boggling Chemistry & Biology Experiments You Can Turn Into Science Fair Projects. 112p. (gr. 3 up). 1993. pap. text ed. 9.95 (0-471-58956-X) Wiley.
This newest edition of the SPECTACULAR SCIENCE PROJECTS series takes children into a new world invisible to the naked eye. A child's first glance through a microscope opens up an entire new world. Janice VanCleave explains magnification & shows kids how they can use a microscope or magnifying lens to explore what lies beneath the surface of things around the house. With these imaginative investigations children embark into the hidden worlds of biology & chemistry in plants, minerals, protozoa & more. As with each book in the SPECTACULAR SCIENCE PROJECTS series the experiments include step-by-step instructions, background information, & suggestions for probing deeper into the topic & developing a winning science fair project. All that is required is a microscope or magnifying lens along with a spirit of scientific adventure. Other books in the series include ANIMALS, EARTHQUAKES, GRAVITY, MACHINES, MAGNETS, & MOLECULES. "VanCleave's new Spectacular Science Projects series will be popular with students at science fair time."--Booklist. *Publisher Provided Annotation.*

—Janice VanCleave's Two Hundred Gooey, Slippery, Slimy, Weird, & Fun Experiments. (Illus.). 128p. (gr. 3-7). 1992. pap. 12.95 (0-471-57921-1) Wiley.
Best-selling author Janice VanCleave's captivating collection of 200 zany, easy-to-do experiments offers great fun that's educational! Spanning five different science subjects, the book is bursting with the most popular & exciting activities for kids & includes experiments in biology, chemistry, physics, earth science, & astronomy. And, kids can safely perform these experiments at home or in the classroom with no elaborate or expensive equipment. An attractive, large format enhances the detailed instructions, clear scientific explanations, & drawings that both illustrate & entertain. *Publisher Provided Annotation.*

—Physics for Every Kid: One Hundred One Easy Experiments in Motion, Heat, Light, Machines & Sound. 1991. pap. text ed. 10.95 (0-471-52505-7) Wiley.
—Two Hundred Awesome, Magical, Bizarre, & Incredible Experiments. LC 93-29807. 1994. pap. write for info. (0-471-31011-5) Wiley.
Vancleave, Janice P. Biology for Every Kid: One Hundred & One Easy Experiments That Really Work. 1990. pap. text ed. 10.95 (0-471-50381-9) Wiley.
—Janice Vancleave's Earth Science for Every Kid: One Hundred & One Experiments That Really Work. (gr. 3-7). 1991. pap. text ed. 10.95 (0-471-53010-7) Wiley.
Van Curen, Barbara. When the Zebras Came for Lunch. Manierre, Betsy, illus. 64p. (ps-2). 1989. pap. text ed. 5.95 (0-922510-01-6) Lucky Bks.
Van Dam, Eva. The Magic Life of Milarepa: Tibet's Great Yogi. LC 90-43321. (Illus.). 80p. (Orig.). (gr. 6 up). 1991. pap. 16.00 (0-87773-473-9) Shambhala Pubns.

Van Deman, Barry A. & McDonald, Ed. Nuts & Bolts: A Matter of Fact Guide to Science Fair Projects. LC 79-93155. (Illus.). 64p. (Orig.). (gr. 7-12). 1980. pap. 7.95 tchr's. resource (0-936046-01-5) Science Man Pr.

Vanden Broeck, Fabricio, illus. Ah Bak's Strange New Crop. Goldman, Judy, adapted by. LC 92-11322. (Illus.). 1994. text ed. 14.95 (0-02-775657-2) Macmillan.

Vandenburg, Mary L. Coping with Being Shy. Rosen, Ruth, ed. (gr. 7-12). 1992. 13.95 (0-8239-1425-9) Rosen Group.

Van Denend, G. Mark in the Closet. Vreeman, J., ed. (Illus.). 16p. (Orig.). 1985. pap. 3.95 (0-918789-01-X) FreeMan Prods.

Van Denend, G. & Vreeman, J. Christopher & the Sycamore Tree. (Illus.). 16p. (Orig.). 1985. pap. 3.95 (0-918789-00-1) FreeMan Prods.

Van der Beek, Deborah. Melinda & the Class Photograph. 28p. (gr. k-4). 1991. PLB 18.95 (0-87614-694-9) Carolrhoda Bks.

Vander Els, Betty. The Bombers Moon. LC 85-47591. 129p. (gr. 4 up). 1985. 14.00 (0-374-30864-0) FS&G.
—The Bombers' Moon. 168p. (gr. 5 up). 1992. pap. 4.50 (0-374-40877-7, Sunburst) FS&G.
—Leaving Point. LC 87-23710. 176p. (gr. 7-12). 1987. 15.00 (0-374-34376-4) FS&G.

Vander Els, Betty see Vander Els, Betty.

VanderGriend, Donna. Faith Talk. 132p. (Orig.). (gr. 10-12). 1989. pap. text ed. 24.95 leader's guide (0-930265-56-4) CRC Pubns.

Van der Laan, Carrie. Active Listening Program (ALP) Baker, Robert T., illus. 113p. (Orig.). (gr. 5-12). 1986. Incl. manual, 36 3x5 cards, 50 4x6 cards, carrying tote. 39.00 (0-930599-02-0) Thinking Pubns.

Van der Linde, Laurel. The Devil in Salem Village: The Story of the Salem Witchcraft Trials. LC 91-24403. (Illus.). 64p. (gr. 4-6). 1992. PLB 14.40 (1-56294-144-5) Millbrook Pr.
—The Pony Express. LC 92-31756. (Illus.). 72p. (gr. 6 up). 1993. RSBE 14.95 (0-02-759056-9, New Discovery) Macmillan Child Grp.
—The White Stallions: The Story of the Dancing Horses of Lipizza. LC 93-18919. (Illus.). 72p. (gr. 6 up). 1994. RSBE 14.95 (0-02-759055-0, New Discovery Bks) Macmillan Child Grp.

Van der Linde, Polly & Van der Linde, Tasha. Around the World in Eighty Dishes. Lemke, Horst, illus. LC 71-160447. 88p. (gr. k-7). 10.95 (0-87592-007-1) Scroll Pr.

Van der Linde, Tasha, jt. auth. see Van der Linde, Polly.

Van der Meer, Altie, jt. auth. see Van der Meer, Ron.

Van Der Meer, Atie, jt. auth. see Van Der Meer, Ron.

Van der Meer, Atie, jt. auth. see Van der Meer, Ron.

Van der Meer, Mara. Family Bear Pop-up Book. Rohner, Thomas, illus. 10p. (gr. k-3). 1994. bds. 9.95 (0-689-71766-0, Aladdin) Macmillan Child Grp.

Van Der Meer, Ron. Amazing Animal Senses. (gr. 9-12). 1990. 10.95 (0-316-89624-1, Joy St Bks) Little.
—The Birthday Cake: A Lift-the-Flap Pop-up Book. Van der Meer, Ron, illus. LC 91-62464. 14p. (ps-1). 1993. 8.99 (0-679-82849-4) Random Bks Yng Read.
—The Fantastic Fairy Tale Pop-up Book. Thatcher, Fran & Williamson, Tracey, illus. LC 92-80742. 10p. (ps-3). 1993. 16.00 (0-679-83869-4) Random Bks Yng Read.
—What Is the Time. (ps-1). 1990. pap. 4.95 (0-8167-2176-9) Troll Assocs.
—The World's First Ever Pop-Up Games Book. Van der Meer, Ron, illus. 8p. (gr. k-3). 1982. 9.95 (0-440-06943-2) Delacorte.

Van der Meer, Ron & Ivory, Lesley A. Little Angels. Ivory, Lesley A., illus. LC 92-70261. 12p. 1992. Mini pop-up bk. in gift box. 10.00 (0-679-83472-9) Knopf Bks Yng Read.

Van der Meer, Ron & Van der Meer, Altie. Funny Shoes. Van der Meer, Ron & Van der Meer, Altie, illus. 14p. (ps-k). 1994. bds. 9.95 (0-689-71823-3, Aladdin) Macmillan Child Grp.

Van der Meer, Ron & Van der Meer, Atie. Funny Hats: A Lift-the-Flap Book. Van der Meer, Ron & Van der Meer, Atie, illus. LC 91-62463. 16p. (ps). 1992. 7.99 (0-679-82850-8) Random Bks Yng Read.
—Jumping Animals. (gr. 4 up). 1989. 4.95 (0-85953-261-5) Childs Play.
—Jumping Children. (gr. 4 up). 1989. 4.95 (0-85953-262-3) Childs Play.
—Jumping Clowns. (gr. 4 up). 1989. 4.95 (0-85953-263-1) Childs Play.
—Jumping Monsters. (gr. 4 up). 1989. 4.95 (0-85953-264-X) Childs Play.
—Your Amazing Senses: Thirty-Six Games, Puzzles & Tricks to Show How Your Senses Work. Van Der Meer, Ron & Van Der Meer, Atie, illus. 12p. (gr. 4-7). 1987. pap. 9.95 (0-689-71184-0, Aladdin) Macmillan Child Grp.

Van Der Meer, Ron, jt. auth. see Cole, Babette.

Vandermeulen, Carl. Photography for Student Publications. LC 79-89332. (gr. 7 up). 1979. pap. 12.95 (0-931940-01-X) Middleburg Pr.

Van der Plas, Rob. Roadside Bicycle Repairs: The Simple Guide to Fixing Your Bike. 2nd ed. Van der Plas, Rob, illus. LC 89-81203. 128p. 1990. pap. 4.95 (0-933201-27-3) Bicycle Books.

Van Der Plas, Robert. Mountain Bike Handbook. LC 91-13643. (Illus.). 128p. (gr. 10-12). 1992. pap. 10.95 (0-8069-8425-2) Sterling.

Van Der Rol, Ruud, jt. auth. see Verhoeven, Rian.

Vandersteen, Willy. The Circus Baron. Lahey, Nicholas J., tr. from FLE. LC 75-8497. (Illus.). 56p. (Orig.). (gr. 3 up). 1976. pap. 2.50 (0-915560-21-6, 21) Hiddigeigei.
—A Fool's Gold. Lahey, Nicholas J., tr. from FLE. LC 76-49377. (Illus., Orig.). (gr. 3-8). 1977. pap. 2.50 (0-915560-08-9, 08) Hiddigeigei.
—The Iron Flowerpotters. Lahey, Nicholas J., tr. from FLE. LC 76-49376. (Illus., Orig.). (gr. 3-8). 1977. pap. 2.50 (0-915560-11-9, 11) Hiddigeigei.
—An Island Called Hoboken. Lahey, Nicholas, tr. from FLE. LC 75-8496. (Illus.). 56p. (Orig.). (gr. 3 up). 1976. pap. 2.50 (0-915560-01-1, 1) Hiddigeigei.
—The King Drinks. Lahey, Nicholas J., tr. from FLE. LC 77-78696. (Illus., Orig.). (gr. 3-8). 1977. pap. 2.50 (0-915560-04-6) Hiddigeigei.
—The Merry Musketeers. Lahey, Nicholas J., tr. from FLE. LC 75-8495. (Illus., Orig.). (gr. 3 up). 1976. pap. 2.50 (0-915560-18-6, 18) Hiddigeigei.
—The Tender-Hearted Matador: Duck, Lambik, or Your Goose Is Cooked! Lahey, Nicholas J., tr. LC 75-8494. (Illus.). 56p. (Orig.). (gr. 3 up). 1976. pap. 2.50 (0-915560-10-0, 10) Hiddigeigei.
—The Zincshrinker. Lahey, Nicholas J., tr. from FLE. LC 76-49379. (Illus., Orig.). (gr. 3-8). 1977. pap. 2.50 (0-915560-03-8, 03) Hiddigeigei.

Vanderveld, Marjorie, jt. auth. see Levin, Beatrice.

Vandervelde, Marjorie. Across the Tundra. (gr. 4-12). 1972. 1.55 (0-89992-053-5) Coun India Ed.
—Could It Be Old Hiari. (gr. 5-9). 1975. 4.95 (0-89992-040-3) Coun India Ed.
—Sam & the Golden People. (gr. 4-9). 1972. 1.50 (0-89992-027-6) Coun India Ed.

Vander Vennen, Mark. Take Six: Behind the Scenes with the Parables. 64p. (Orig.). (gr. 9-12). 1992. pap. text ed. 3.25 (0-685-60748-8, 1210-3051); leader's guide 7.25 (1-56212-011-5, 1210-3043) CRC Pubns.

Vanderwater, Jeanette, ed. see Durbin, Carolyn.

VanderZee, Leonard. Can I Call after Midnight. 76p. (Orig.). (gr. 10-12). 1989. pap. text ed. 17.95 leader's guide (0-930265-70-X) CRC Pubns.

Vandevenne, Jean. Some Summer! (Illus.). 178p. (Orig.). (gr. 4-6). 1987. pap. 4.95 (0-89084-380-5) Bob Jones Univ Pr.

Van De Wetering, Janwillem. Hugh Pine. (Illus.). 96p. (gr. 3 up). 1980. 14.45 (0-395-29459-2) HM.
—Hugh Pine. ALC Staff, ed. Munsinger, Lynn, illus. LC 80-13652. 88p. (gr. 2-8). 1992. pap. 3.95 (0-688-11799-6, Pub. by Beech Tree Bks) Morrow.
—Hugh Pine & Something Else. Munsinger, Lynn, illus. 96p. (gr. 3 up). 1989. 13.45 (0-395-49216-5) HM.
—Hugh Pine & Something Else. ALC Staff, ed. Munsinger, Lynn, illus. LC 88-35801. 80p. (gr. 2-8). 1992. pap. 3.95 (0-688-11800-3, Pub. by Beech Tree Bks) Morrow.
—Hugh Pine & the Good Place. Munsinger, Lynn, illus. LC 86-3108. 80p. (gr. 3 up). 1986. 13.95 (0-395-40147-X) HM.
—Hugh Pine & the Good Place. ALC Staff, ed. Munsinger, Lynn, illus. LC 86-3108. 72p. 1992. pap. 3.95 (0-688-11801-1, Pub. by Beech Tree Bks) Morrow.

Van DeWeyer, Robert & Spenceley, Annabel. The Shepherd's Son. LC 92-40284. 24p. (gr. k-3). 1993. 10.00 (0-8170-1188-9) Judson.

Vandine, JoAnn. Lunch for Three. Tulloch, Coral, illus. LC 92-31954. 1993. 4.25 (0-383-03582-1) SRA Schl Grp.

Van Dine, S. S. The Green Murder Case. (gr. 5-6). Repr. lib. bdg. 24.95x (0-89190-514-6, Pub. by River City Pr) Amereon Ltd.

Van Dolson, Bobbie J., ed. see Jones, Lucile.

Van Doren, Liz, ed. see Anglund, Joan W.

Van Doren, Liz, ed. see Kaye, Marilyn.

Van Doren, Liz, ed. see Woolf, Virginia.

Van Duyn Southworth, John see Southworth, John V.

Van Dyke, Henry. Other Wise Man. Barrett, Robert, illus. 32p. (gr. k-3). 1989. 12.95 (0-8249-8396-3) Ideals.
—The Other Wise Man. Kennedy, Pamela, adapted by. Barrett, Robert, illus. 32p. (ps-3). 1992. pap. 4.95 (0-8249-8564-8, Ideals Child) Hambleton-Hill.

Van Dyke, Henry, jt. ed. see Wells, Ruth.

Vanek, Mona L. Behind These Mountains, 3 vols. (Illus.). 310p. 1986. Set. pap. 16.95 (0-940151-00-6) Statesman Exam.

Vanemst, Charlotte. Little Rabbit's Big Day, Vol. 1. (ps-3). 1990. 12.95 (0-316-89623-3, Joy Bks) Little.

Van Fleet, Matthew. One Yellow Lion: Fold-Out Fun with Numbers, Colors, Animals. LC 91-11972. (Illus.). 24p. (ps up). 1992. 7.95 (0-8037-1099-2) Dial Bks Young.

Van Fleet, Matthew, illus. Match It: A Fold-the-Flap Book. 10p. (ps-3). 1993. 11.95 (0-8037-1379-7) Dial Bks Young.

Van Gelder, Richard G., jt. auth. see Bancroft, Henrietta.

Van Gorden, Charles L. Olive, Char, Lizzie & Izzie: A Sea Otter Story. Moler, Kathy, illus. 44p. (gr. 1-4). 1991. pap. 4.95 saddle-stitched (1-56167-050-2) Am Literary Pr.

Van Gulik. Monkey & the Tiger. 1980. pap. 2.95 (0-684-16737-9, Scribner) Macmillan.

Van Hansel, E. Children's Treasury of Tales. Date not set. 10.95 (0-89906-416-7); pap. 7.95 (0-89906-417-5) Mesorah Pubns.

Van Hook, Beverly. Supergranny, No. 1: The Mystery of the Shrunken Heads. Wayson, Catherine, illus. 96p. (gr. 3-7). 1985. lib. bdg. 7.95 (0-916761-11-8); pap. 2.95 (0-916761-10-X) Holderby & Bierce.
—Supergranny, No. 2: The Case of the Riverboat Riverbelle. Wayson, Catherine, illus. 112p. (gr. 3-7). 1986. lib. bdg. 7.95 (0-916761-09-6); pap. 2.95 (0-916761-08-8) Holderby & Bierce.
—Supergranny, No. 3: The Ghost of Heidelberg Castle. Wayson, Catherine, illus. 112p. (gr. 3-7). 1987. lib. bdg. 7.95 (0-916761-07-X); pap. 2.95 (0-916761-06-1) Holderby & Bierce.
—Supergranny, No. 5: Character Who Came to Life. Nelken, Andrea, ed. Wayson, Catherine, illus. 112p. (Orig.). (gr. 3-6). 1989. lib. bdg. 7.95 (0-916761-13-4); pap. 2.95 (0-916761-12-6) Holderby & Bierce.
—Supergranny: Secret of Devil Mountain. Nelken, Andrea, ed. Wayson, Catherine, illus. 112p. (Orig.). (gr. 3-6). 1988. lib. bdg. 7.95 (0-916761-05-3); pap. 2.95 (0-916761-04-5) Holderby & Bierce.
—Supergranny 1: The Mystery of the Shrunken Heads. (Illus.). 96p. (gr. 3-7). 1985. PLB 9.95 (0-916761-17-7); pap. 3.25 (0-916761-16-9) Holderby & Bierce.
—Supergranny 2: The Case of the Riverboat Riverbelle. (Illus.). 112p. (gr. 3-7). 1986. PLB 9.95 (0-916761-23-1); pap. 3.25 (0-916761-22-3) Holderby & Bierce.
—Supergranny 3: The Ghost of Heidelberg Castle. (Illus.). 112p. (gr. 3-7). 1987. PLB 9.95 (0-916761-21-5); pap. 3.25 (0-916761-20-7) Holderby & Bierce.
—Supergranny 5: The Character Who Came to Life. (Illus.). 112p. (gr. 3-7). 1989. PLB 9.95 (0-916761-19-3); pap. 3.25 (0-916761-18-5) Holderby & Bierce.
—Supergranny 6: The Great College Caper, 6 bks. Nelken, Andrea, ed. Wayson, Catherine, illus. 112p. (gr. 3-7). 1991. Set. 53.00 (0-916761-15-0); 8.95 ea.; Set. app. 17.70 (0-916761-14-2); pap. 3.25 ea. Holderby & Bierce.

Van Horn, Brian & Van Horn, Chris. A Boy Full of Joy. Scott, Rita & Van Horn, Brian, illus. (ps-5). 1989. write for info. (1-877765-01-5) Lambgel Family.
—Lain Cain & Label Abel. Scott, Rita & Van Horn, Brian, illus. (gr. k-5). 1989. write for info. (1-877765-02-3) Lambgel Family.
—Leve Eve Believes Werpent the Serpent in the Garden of Eden. Scott, Rita & Van Horn, Brian, illus. (gr. k-5). 1989. write for info. (1-877765-03-1) Lambgel Family.
—Loah Noah & the Ark. Scott, Rita & Van Horn, Brian, illus. (gr. k-5). 1989. write for info. (1-877765-04-X) Lambgel Family.
—Lordy Lamb & the Twelve Lisciples. Mowdy, Sharon, ed. Scott, Rita & Van Horn, Brian, illus. 40p. (gr. k-5). 1989. 8.95 (1-877765-00-7) Lambgel Family.
—No Time in a Jam. Scott, Rita & Van Horn, Brian, illus. (gr. 2-8). 1989. write for info. (1-877765-05-8) Lambgel Family.

Van Horn, Chris, jt. auth. see Van Horn, Brian.

Van Horne, Carmon. The Three Big Pigs. Van Horne, Carmon, illus. LC 92-91035. 48p. (Orig.). (ps-3). 1993. incl. computer coloring disk 23.95 (1-882643-02-X); pap. 18.95 incl. computer coloring disk (1-882643-03-8); 12.95 (1-882643-00-3); pap. 7.95 (1-882643-01-1) V H Visionarts.
—The Three Big Pigs. Van Horne, Carmon, illus. LC 92-91035. 32p. (ps-3). 1993. PLB 13.95 (1-882643-04-6) V H Visionarts.

Van House, Charles L., Sr. & Swoszowski, Sarah M. Teen Self-Esteem: A Common Sense Path to Happiness & Success. 216p. (Orig.). (gr. 7-12). 1993. pap. 9.95 (0-9635745-7-4) Life Lines Pr.

Vanier, Jean. I Meet Jesus: He Tells Me "I Love You" LC 81-82109. 208p. (gr. k-5). 1984. pap. 5.50 (0-8091-2725-3) Paulist Pr.

Van Jacobs, Gregory. The Polka Dot Queen. 1992. 7.95 (0-533-09669-3) Vantage.

Van Kampen, Vlasta. Orchestranimals. 1990. pap. 12.95 (0-590-43149-8) Scholastic Inc.

VanKempen, Corrigan. Emily Umily. (Illus.). 24p. (ps-8). 1984. 12.95 (0-920236-96-0, Pub. by Annick CN); pap. 4.95 (0-920236-99-5, Pub. by Annick CN) Firefly Bks Ltd.

Van Kirk, Barbara D. The Person Who Had Feelings. Dunlap, Sam, illus. 44p. (Orig.). 1975. pap. 6.95 (0-9631751-0-6) New Begin OR.

Van Kirk, Eileen. Promise to Keep. 160p. (gr. 7 up). 1990. 14.95 (0-525-67319-9, Lodestar Bks) Dutton Child Bks.

Van Kleef Douthit, Gretchen. Inside Out: My Book about Who I Am & How I Feel. 96p. (gr. 3-10). 1991. perfect bdg. 8.00 (0-89486-757-1, T5151) Hazelden.

Van Laan, Nancy. The Legend of El Dorado. Vidal, Beatriz, illus. LC 89-7998. 40p. (ps-4). 1991. 16.00 (0-679-80136-7); lib. bdg. 15.99 (0-679-90136-1) Knopf Bks Yng Read.
—A Mouse in My House. Priceman, Marjorie, illus. LC 89-15591. 32p. (ps-3). 1990. 9.95 (0-679-80043-3); PLB 10.99 (0-679-90043-8) Knopf Bks Yng Read.
—People, People, Everywhere! Westcott, Nadine B., illus. LC 90-5303. 40p. (ps-2). 1992. 13.00 (0-679-81063-3); PLB 13.99 (0-679-91063-8) Knopf Bks Yng Read.
—Possum Come A-Knocking. Booth, George, illus. LC 88-12751. 32p. (ps-3). 1990. PLB 14.99 (0-394-92206-9) Knopf Bks Yng Read.

—Rainbow Crow. Vidal, Beatriz, illus. LC 88-12967. 40p. (ps-3). 1989. PLB 13.99 (0-394-99577-5) Knopf Bks Yng Read.
—This Is the Hat: A Story in Rhyme. (ps). 1992. 14.95 (0-316-89727-2, Joy St Bks) Little.
—The Tiny, Tiny Boy & the Big, Big Cow. Priceman, Marjorie, illus. LC 91-33738. 40p. (ps-2). 1993. 8.99 (0-679-82078-7); PLB 9.99 (0-679-92078-1) Knopf Bks Yng Read.
Van Lampen. Orchestranimals. 1993. pap. 28.67 (0-590-73163-7) Scholastic Inc.
Van Lawick-Goodall, Hugo, jt. auth. see Goodall, Jane.
Van Leeuwen, Jean. Amanda Pig & Her Big Brother Oliver. Schweninger, Ann, illus. LC 82-70188. 56p. (ps-3). 1982. pap. 4.95 (0-8037-0016-4) Dial Bks Young.
—Amanda Pig & Her Brother Oliver. (ps-3). 1992. pap. 4.99 (0-14-036176-6) Viking Child Bks.
—Amanda Pig on her Own. LC 90-3504. (Illus.). (ps-3). 1991. 9.95 (0-8037-0893-9); PLB 9.89 (0-8037-0894-7) Dial Bks Young.
—Benjy in Business. Apple, Margot, illus. LC 82-22158. 112p. (gr. 2-6). 1983. Dial Bks Young.
—Benjy the Football Hero. Owens, Gail, illus. LC 84-21459. 192p. (gr. 2-6). 1985. PLB 11.89 (0-8037-0190-X) Dial Bks Young.
—Bound for Oregon. LC 93-26709. 1994. write for info. (0-8037-1526-9); PLB write for info. (0-8037-1527-7) Dial Bks Young.
—Dear Mom, You're Ruining My Life. LC 88-3705. (Illus.). 160p. (gr. 4-7). 1989. 13.95 (0-8037-0572-7); PLB 13.89 (0-8037-0573-5) Dial Bks Young.
—Dear Mom You're Ruining My Life. (gr. 4 up). 1990. pap. 3.99 (0-14-034386-5, Puffin) Puffin Bks.
—Emma Bean. Wijngaard, Juan, illus. LC 92-29035. 40p. (ps-3). 1993. 13.99 (0-8037-1392-4); PLB 13.89 (0-8037-1393-2) Dial Bks Young.
—Going West. LC 90-20694. (Illus.). 48p. (ps-4). 1992. 15.00 (0-8037-1027-5); PLB 14.89 (0-8037-1028-3) Dial Bks Young.
—The Great Christmas Kidnapping Caper. Kellogg, Steven, illus. LC 75-9201. 144p. (gr. 2-6). 1975. 12.95 (0-685-01454-1) Dial Bks Young.
—The Great Christmas Kidnapping Caper. Kellogg, Steven, illus. 172p. (gr. 3 up). 1990. pap. 3.99 (0-14-034287-7, Puffin) Puffin Bks.
—The Great Rescue Operation. Apple, Margot, illus. LC 81-65851. 176p. (gr. 2-6). 1982. 10.95 (0-685-01455-X); PLB 10.89 (0-685-01456-8) Dial Bks Young.
—The Great Rescue Operation. Apple, Margot, illus. 144p. (gr. 3 up). 1990. pap. 3.95 (0-14-034288-5, Puffin) Puffin Bks.
—The Great Summer Camp Catastrophe. DeGroat, Diane, illus. LC 91-18487. 192p. (gr. 2-6). 1992. 13.00 (0-8037-1106-9); PLB 12.89 (0-8037-1107-7) Dial Bks Young.
—I Was a Ninety-Eight Pound Duckling. 96p. (gr. 5 up). 1976. pap. 1.50 (0-440-94190-3, LFL) Dell.
—More Tales of Oliver Pig. Lobel, Arnold, illus. LC 80-23289. (ps-3). 1981. PLB 9.89 (0-8037-8714-6); pap. 4.95 (0-8037-8713-8) Dial Bks Young.
—More Tales of Oliver Pig. Lobel, Arnold, illus. (gr. k-3). 1993. pap. 3.25 (0-14-036554-0, Puffin) Puffin Bks.
—Oliver, Amanda & Grandmother Pig. Schweninger, Ann, illus. LC 86-243326. 56p. (ps-3). 1987. 9.95 (0-8037-0361-9); PLB 9.89 (0-8037-0362-7) Dial Bks Young.
—Oliver, Amanda, & Grandmother Pig. 1990. pap. 4.95 (0-8037-0745-2, Dial Easy to Read) Puffin Bks.
—Oliver & Amanda's Christmas. Schweninger, Ann, illus. 9.95 (0-685-29542-7) Dial Bks Young.
—Oliver & Amanda's Christmas. 1989. 9.95 (0-8037-0636-7); PLB 9.89 (0-8037-0647-2) Dial Bks Young.
—Oliver & Amanda's Christmas. Schweninger, Ann, illus. 56p. (ps-3). 1992. pap. 3.99 (0-14-054566-2, Dial Easy to Read) Puffin Bks.
—Oliver & Amanda's Halloween. Schweninger, Ann, illus. LC 91-30941. 48p. (ps-3). 1992. 11.00 (0-8037-1237-5); PLB 10.89 (0-8037-1238-3) Dial Bks Young.
—Tales of Amanda Pig. Schweninger, Ann, illus. LC 82-23545. 56p. (ps-3). 1983. pap. 4.95 (0-8037-844J-0) Dial Bks Young.
—Tales of Amanda Pig. Schweninger, Ann, illus. LC 93-25615. (gr. k-3). 1994. pap. 3.25 (0-14-036840-X, Puffin) Puffin Bks.
—Tales of Amanda Pig: (Cuentos de la Cerdita Amanda) (SPA.). 6.95 (84-204-4013-2) Santillana.
—Tales of Oliver Pig. Lobel, Arnold, illus. LC 79-4276. 64p. (ps-3). 1979. PLB 9.89 (0-8037-8736-7); pap. 4.95 (0-8037-8737-5) Dial Bks Young.
—Tales of Oliver Pig. Lobel, Arnold, illus. (gr. k-3). 1993. pap. 3.25 (0-14-036549-4, Puffin) Puffin Bks.
Van Lindt, Carson. One Championship Season: The Story of the 1944 St. Louis Browns. (Illus.). 220p. 1994. pap. 10.95 (0-9632595-6-3) Marabou Pub.
Van Loan, Derek, jt. auth. see Keith, Ian.
Van Loon, Borin. DNA - the Marvellous Molecule. 32p. 1991. pap. 7.95 (0-906212-75-8, Pub. by Tarquin UK) Parkwest Pubns.
Van Loon, Joan & Van Loon, John. Jelly, Chips & Caramel Whips. (gr. 1-3). 1988. 13.95 (0-09-148830-3, Pub. by Hutchinson UK) Trafalgar.
Van Loon, John, jt. auth. see Van Loon, Joan.
Van Loon, Paul. Agarrar la Luna. Akkerman, Dinie, illus. LC 92-43067. 1993. 5.95 (0-8120-1676-9) Barron.

Van Loon, Paul, jt. auth. see Akkerman, Dinie.
Van Loy, Merrie, jt. auth. see Thompson, Denisse.
Van Matre, Nancy A., jt. auth. see Poppe, Carol A.
Vann, Donna R. Roberto & the Fountain of Lights. (Illus.). 32p. (gr. 4 up). 1988. 8.99 (0-7459-1277-X) Lion USA.
—Stefan's Secret Fear. Haysom, John, illus. 32p. (gr. 4-8). 1990. 11.95 (0-7459-1307-5) Lion USA.
Van Ness Seymour, Tryntje. The Gift of Changing Woman. LC 92-31833. (Illus.). 40p. (gr. 5-9). 1993. PLB 16.95 (0-8050-2577-4, Bks Young Read) H Holt & Co.
Van Nispen, Doug, jt. auth. see Haubrich-Casperson, Jane.
Van Nutt, Robert, adapted by. & illu see Irving, Washington.
Van Orden, M. D. U. S. Navy Ships & Coast Guard Cutters: A Naval Institute Book for Young Readers. Burke, Arleigh, frwd. by. LC 89-13539. (Illus.). 96p. (gr. 5-11). 1990. PLB 17.95 (0-87021-212-5) Naval Inst Pr.
Van Pallandt, Nicolas. The Butterfly Night of Old Brown Bear. (ps-3). 1992. bds. 15.00 jacketed (0-374-31009-2) FS&G.
Van Pelt, Nancy L. The Compleat Tween. Coffen, Richard W., ed. 96p. (Orig.). (gr. 5 up). 1986. pap. 7.50 (0-8280-0288-6) Review & Herald.
Van Raven, Pieter. The Great Man's Secret. LC 88-29204. 176p. (gr. 7 up). 1989. SBE 13.95 (0-684-19041-9, Scribners Young Read) Macmillan Child Grp.
—The Great Man's Secret. (Illus.). 176p. (gr. 5-9). 1991. pap. 3.95 (0-14-034390-3, Puffin) Puffin Bks.
—Pickle & Price. LC 89-10846. 224p. (gr. 7 up). 1990. SBE 14.95 (0-684-19162-8, Scribners Young Read) Macmillan Child Grp.
—A Time of Troubles. LC 90-31409. 192p. (gr. 7 up). 1990. SBE 13.95 (0-684-19212-8, Scribners Young Read) Macmillan Child Grp.
Van Rensselaer, Alexander. Your Book of Magic. (gr. 9 up). 1968. 7.95 (0-571-06939-8) Transatl Arts.
Van Rhijn, Patricia. El Nino Maicero: The Corn Boy. Suarez, Maribel, illus. (SPA.). 35p. (gr. k-4). 1990. 7.95 (968-494-042-4) Donars.
Van Riper, Guernsey, Jr. Babe Ruth: One of Baseball's Greatest. Fleishman, Seymour, illus. LC 86-10957. 192p. (gr. 2-6). 1986. pap. 3.95 (0-02-042130-3, Aladdin) Macmillan Child Grp.
—Jim Thorpe: Olympic Champion. Morrow, Gray, illus. LC 86-3478. 192p. (gr. 2-6). 1986. pap. 3.95 (0-02-042140-0, Aladdin) Macmillan Child Grp.
—Lou Gehrig: One of Baseball's Greatest. Robinson, Jerry, illus. LC 86-10951. 192p. (gr. 2-6). 1986. pap. 3.95 (0-02-041930-9, Aladdin) Macmillan Child Grp.
Van Ronzelen, George & Oberste, Kenneth, illus. TiL: A Book of Puzzles. LC 88-70805. 264p. (Orig.). (gr. 6 up). 1988. pap. 13.00 (0-934426-18-X) NAPSAC Reprods.
Van Rose, Susanna. Earth. LC 93-33102. 1994. write for info. (1-56458-476-3) Dorling Kindersley.
—Volcano & Earthquake. Stevenson, James, photos by. LC 92-4710. (Illus.). 64p. (gr. 5 up). 1992. 15.00 (0-679-81685-2); PLB 16.99 (0-679-91685-7) Knopf Bks Yng Read.
VanRynbach, Iris. Cecily's Christmas. LC 87-34083. (Illus.). 32p. (ps-1). 1988. 11.95 (0-688-07832-X); lib. bdg. 11.88 (0-688-07833-8) Greenwillow.
Van Rynbach, Iris. Everything from a Nail to a Coffin. LC 90-23035. (Illus.). 48p. (gr. 2-4). 1991. 15.95 (0-531-05941-3); RLB 15.99 (0-531-08541-4) Orchard Bks Watts.
VanRynbach, Iris. The Soup Stone. LC 86-31830. (Illus.). 32p. (ps-3). 1988. 11.95 (0-688-07254-2); lib. bdg. 11.88 (0-688-07255-0) Greenwillow.
Van Santvoord, George, ed. see Harris, Joel C.
Van Seters, Virginia A. Twenty-Six More Object Talks: For Children's Worship. Wimmer, Jan, illus. 48p. (gr. k-2). 1990. pap. 3.99 (0-87403-653-4, 14-02864) Standard Pub.
—Twenty-Six Object Talks for Children's Worship. Briggs, Richard, illus. 48p. 1988. pap. 3.99 (0-87403-497-3, 2877) Standard Pub.
—Twenty-Two Object Talks for Children's Worship. Briggs, Richard, illus. 48p. (ps-6). 1986. pap. 3.99 (0-87403-505-2, 2866) Standard Pub.
Van Shelton, Ricky. Quacker Meets Mrs. Moo: In Tales from a Duck Named Quacker. Williams, Shan, illus. 32p. (Orig.). Date not set. pap. write for info. (0-9634257-1-4) RVS Bks.
—Tales from a Duck Named Quacker: The Story Begins. 24p. 1992. pap. 7.00 (0-9634257-0-6) RVS Bks.
Van Sickle, Carol S. With Love, the Fairies. LC 89-51346. 44p. (gr. k-4). 1990. 5.95 (1-55523-240-X) Winston-Derek.
Van Steenwyk, Elizabeth. The California Gold Rush: West with the Forty-Niners. (Illus.). 64p. (gr. 5-8). 1991. PLB 12.90 (0-531-20032-9) Watts.
—Ida B. Wells-Barnett: Woman of Courage. Rich, Mary P., ed. LC 88-31376. (Illus.). 112p. (gr. 7-12). 1992. PLB 14.40 (0-531-13014-2) Watts.
—Levi Strauss: The Blue Jeans Man. (gr. 6-9). 1988. 13.95 (0-8027-6795-8); PLB 14.85 (0-8027-6796-6) Walker & Co.
—Three Dog Winter. (gr. 4-9). 1987. 13.95 (0-8027-6718-4) Walker & Co.

Van Stegeren, Theo. The Land & People of the Netherlands. LC 90-47650. (Illus.). 256p. (gr. 6 up). 1992. 17.95 (0-06-022537-8); PLB 17.89 (0-06-022538-6) HarpC Child Bks.
Van Straalen, Alice. The Book of Holidays Around the World. LC 86-11674. (Illus.). 192p. (ps up). 1986. 16.95 (0-525-44270-7, DCB) Dutton Child Bks.
Van Susteren, Margery. Prince. Rutherford, Donna, illus. 48p. 1991. pap. 7.95 (0-922510-05-9) Lucky Bks.
Van Treese, James B., ed. see Burbank, Linda.
Van Treese, James B., ed. see Goodin, Evelyn.
Van Treese, James B., ed. see Kohler, Jan.
Van Treese, James B., ed. see Merfield, LeAnn.
Van Treese, James B., ed. see Olson, Michelle.
Van Tuyle, R. Helen. Timely Tips & Treats for the Tenderfoot Homemaker. Engle, Arch, illus. 108p. (Orig.). 1987. wkbk. 9.95 (0-9617816-0-2) R H Van Tuyle.
Van Vleck, Jane, ed. see Olson, Jim.
Van Vorst, M. L. A Norse Lullaby. Tomes, Margot, illus. LC 87-31058. 32p. (ps-1). 1988. 12.95 (0-688-05812-4); PLB 12.88 (0-688-05813-2) Lothrop.
Van Walsum-Quispel, J. see Walsum-Quispel, J. van.
Van Wie, Eileen. Teenage Stress: How to Cope in a Complex World. LC 87-7742. (Illus.). 224p. (gr. 6 up). 1988. lib. bdg. 12.98 (0-671-63824-6, J Messner); lib. bdg. 6.95 (0-671-65980-4) S&S Trade.
Van Woerkom, Dorothy. Tall Corn: A Tall Tale. McKissack, Patricia & McKissack, Fredrick, eds. Boddy, Jo, illus. LC 87-61641. 32p. (Orig.). (gr. 1-3). 1987. text ed. 8.95 (0-88335-730-5); pap. text ed. 4.95 (0-88335-750-X) Milliken Pub Co.
Van Woerkom, Dorothy O. Old Devil Is Waiting: Three Folktales. Brett, Jan, illus. LC 85-919. 64p. (ps-3). 1985. (HB Juv Bks) HarBrace.
Van Zandt, Eleanor. Architecture. LC 89-21973. (Illus.). 48p. (gr. 6-11). 1990. PLB 19.92 (0-8114-2362-X) Raintree Steck-V.
—Dance. LC 89-21723. (Illus.). 48p. (gr. 6-11). 1990. PLB 19.92 (0-8114-2357-3) Raintree Steck-V.
Van Zwanenberg, Fiona. Caring for the Aged. LC 89-31783. (Illus.). 64p. (gr. 7-10). 1989. PLB 12.40 (0-531-17190-6, Pub. by Bookwright Pr) Watts.
Vard, Colin. Princess Finola: The Battle for Moytura. Kew, Tony, illus. 67p. (Orig.). (gr. 3-6). 1993. pap. 11.95 (1-897973-00-4, Pub. by Celtpress ER) Irish Bks Media.
Vardeman, Robert E. Road to the Stars. LC 87-45307. 224p. (gr. 7 up). 1988. HarpC Child Bks.
Vardy, Steven B. Attila. (Illus.). 112p. (gr. 5 up). 1991. 17.95 (1-55546-803-9) Chelsea Hse.
—The Hungarian Americans. Moynihan, Daniel P., intro. by. (Illus.). 112p. (gr. 5 up). 1990. lib. bdg. 17.95 (0-87754-884-6) Chelsea Hse.
Vare, Ethlie A. Adventurous Spirit: A Story about Ellen Richards. (ps-3). 1992. 14.95 (0-87614-733-3) Carolrhoda Bks.
Vare, Ethlie A. & Ptacek, Greg. Women Inventors & Their Discoveries. LC 92-38268. (Illus.). 160p. (gr. 5-12). 1993. PLB 14.95 (1-881508-06-4) Oliver Pr MN.
Varekamp, Marjolein. Little Sam Takes a Bath. LC 90-50866. (Illus.). 24p. (ps-1). 1991. 13.95 (0-531-05944-8) Orchard Bks Watts.
Varenhorst, Barbara B. Real Friends: Becoming the Friend You'd Like to Have. LC 82-48412. (Illus.). 160p. (Orig.). 1983. pap. 11.00 (0-06-250890-3, CN4048) Harper SF.
Vargo, Vanessa. Jaguar Talk. LC 92-4073. 1992. 3.95 (0-85953-396-4) Childs Play.
—Tiger Talk. (ps-3). pap. 5.95 (0-85953-397-2) Childs Play.
—Zebra Talk. LC 92-11028. 1991. pap. 3.95 (0-85953-395-6, Pub. by Childs Play UK) Childs Play.
Vargus, Jane A. Ashmouse & the Wrong Side of the Bed. Vargus, Jane A., illus. LC 92-61365. 44p. 1993. pap. 5.95 (1-55523-557-3) Winston-Derek.
Varley, C. Geography Encyclopedia. (Illus.). 128p. (gr. 3-6). 1993. PLB 16.96 (0-88110-600-3); pap. 12.95 (0-7460-0955-0) EDC.
Varley, C., jt. auth. see Watts, L.
Varley, M. C. White Rabbits Can't Jump. (gr. 4-7). 1993. pap. 3.95 (1-56282-516-X) Disney Pr.
—Wonderland Howl-oween. (gr. 4-7). 1993. pap. 3.95 (1-56282-515-1) Disney Pr.
Varley, Susan. Badger's Parting Gifts. Varley, Susan, illus. LC 83-17500. 32p. (gr. k-3). 1984. 13.95 (0-688-02699-0); lib. bdg. 13.88 (0-688-02703-2) Lothrop.
—Badger's Parting Gifts. LC 83-17500. (Illus.). 32p. (ps up). 1992. pap. 4.95 (0-688-11518-7, Mulberry) Morrow.
Varnai, Gyorgy. The Mouse & the Lion. Mark, Steve, illus. LC 92-43693. (gr. 3 up). Date not set. write for info. (1-56766-091-6) Childs World. Postponed.
Varney, Sharon. Cranberry Ridge Tales. 72p. (Orig.). (gr. 7 up). 1986. 7.95 (0-685-17323-2) S Varney.
Varona, Frank de see Codye, Corinn.
Varona, Frank de see De Varona, Frank.
Varona, Frank de see Gleiter, Jan.
Varvasovszky, Laszlo. Henry in Shadowland. Varvasovszky, Laszlo, illus. 32p. (gr. 2-7). 1989. 17.95 (0-87923-785-6) Godine.
Vary, Andree. Contes et Legendes de France: Intermediate. (FRE.). 128p. 1993. pap. 8.95 (0-685-66257-8, F1210-5, Natl Textbk) NTC Pub Grp.
Vasey, Andrew, jt. auth. see Walker, Sloan.
Vash, Peter, jt. auth. see Zak, Victoria.

Vasiliu, Mircea. A Day at the Beach. LC 76-24169. (ps-2). 1978. 2.25 (*0-394-83475-5*) Random Bks Yng Read.

Vasquez, Ely P., et al. The Story of Ana: La Historia de Ana. Guzman, Elia, illus. (SPA & ENG., Illus.). 28p. (Orig.). (gr. 3-6). 1985. PLB 8.95 (*0-932727-15-8*); pap. 3.95 (*0-932727-01-8*) Hope Pub Hse.

Vasquez, Juan J., ed. see Henrietta.

Vasquez, Juan J., ed. see Platt, Richard.

Vaszily, Diane A. & Perdue, Peggy K. Bones, Bodies, & Bellies. (Illus.). 128p. (Orig.). (gr. 3-6). 1993. pap. 9.95 (*0-673-36034-2*) GdYrBks.

Vaughan, Genevieve & Jackson. Sketching Drawing for Children. 1990. pap. 7.95 (*0-399-51619-0*) Putnam Pub Group.

Vaughan, Jenny. Man & Machines. 36p. (gr. 2-6). 1990. 3.99 (*0-517-69729-7*) Outlet Bk Co.

—The World of Science. (Illus.). 36p. (gr. 2-6). 1990. 3.99 (*0-517-69907-9*) Outlet Bk Co.

Vaughan, Marcia. How to Cook a Gooseberry Fool: Unusual Recipes from Around the World. Wolfe, Robert & Wolfe, Diane, photos by. LC 93-9117. 1993. 14.95 (*0-8225-0928-8*) Lerner Pubns.

—The Stick-Around Cloud. Smith, Craig, illus. LC 93-28962. 1994. 4.25 (*0-383-03777-8*) SRA Schl Grp.

Vaughan, Marcia & Mullins, Patricia. The Sea-Breeze Hotel. LC 91-22303. (Illus.). 32p. (ps-2). 1992. 14.00 (*0-06-020488-5*); PLB 13.89 (*0-06-020504-0*) HarpC Child Bks.

Vaughan, Marcia K. Wombat Stew. Lofts, Pamela, illus. LC 85-63492. 32p. (ps-3). 1985. 8.95 (*0-382-09211-2*); s.p. 6.71 (*0-382-24356-0*) Silver Burdett Pr.

Vaughn, Evelyn. Norwood & Eloise Waterhouse: Starters of Churches. LC 85-6718. (gr. k-3). 1985. 5.95 (*0-8054-4294-4*, 4242-94) Broadman.

Vaughn, Jenny. Russia. LC 89-26121. (Illus.). 32p. (gr. 2-5). 1990. PLB 15.96 (*0-8114-2549-5*); pap. 3.95 (*0-8114-7180-2*) Raintree Steck-V.

Vaughn, JIm. Jumbo Math Yearbook: Grade 3. 96p. (gr. 3). 1978. 18.00 (*0-8209-0032-X*, JMY 3) ESP.

—Jumbo Vocabulary Development Yearbook: Grade 7. 96p. (gr. 7-9). 1981. 18.00 (*0-8209-0056-7*, JVDY J) ESP.

Vaughn, Salle W. A Little One's Draw a Story Drawing Book. Vaughn, Jimmy, illus. 120p. (ps-5). 1990. wkbk, incl. protective envelope & rainbow drawing pencil 35. 00 (*0-9625832-0-0*) Crystal TX.

Vaughn-H, Shirley. Noby the Noble Nightwatchman with Three Strands of Hair. 1993. 7.95 (*0-533-10530-7*) Vantage.

Vaus, Steve. Anything under the Sun Activities Book. (Illus.). 25p. (ps-3). 1984. pap. text ed. 4.50 (*0-8497-5903-X*, WE6); pap. text ed. 4.50 record & songbook (*0-8497-5901-3*, RWE6) Kjos.

Vautier, Ghislaine. The Shining Stars. McLeish, Kenneth, adapted by. (Illus.). 1989. pap. 9.95 (*0-521-37914-8*) Cambridge U Pr.

—The Way of the Stars. McLeish, Kenneth, adapted by. (Illus.). 1989. pap. 8.95 (*0-521-37913-X*) Cambridge U Pr.

Vavrus, Toni, jt. auth. see Berk, Meridith.

Vazquez, Ana & Casas, Rosa. Cuba. LC 87-10235. (Illus.). 128p. (gr. 5-9). 1987. PLB 26.60 (*0-516-02758-1*) Childrens.

Vazquez, Ana M. Panama. LC 91-12667. 128p. (gr. 5-9). 1991. PLB 26.60 (*0-516-02604-6*) Childrens.

Veach, William N. The Gold Frog (Riddle) LC 92-80165. 128p. 1992. pap. 11.00 (*0-9632410-1-X*) Sundog Mining.

Veal, Janice, jt. auth. see Ashbach, Dawn.

Veaux, Alexis De see De Veaux, Alexis.

Veaux, Alexis de see De Veaux, Alexis.

Veaux, Alexis De see De Veaux, Alexis.

Veazey, Steve & Porter, John D., Jr. Flags in the History of Texas. McPeek, Ellen, illus. 40p. (gr. 4 up). 1991. pap. 6.95 (*0-937460-73-7*) Hendrick-Long.

Vecchione, Glen. World's Best Outdoor Games. LC 92-19101. (Illus.). 128p. (gr. 6 up). 1992. 12.95 (*0-8069-8436-8*) Sterling.

—World's Best Outdoor Games. (Illus.). 128p. (gr. 3-10). 1993. pap. 9.95 (*0-8069-8437-6*) Sterling.

—World's Best Street & Yard Games. Vecchione, Glen, illus. LC 88-38273. 128p. (gr. 2-8). 1990. pap. 4.95 (*0-8069-5762-X*) Sterling.

Vecere, Joel. Story about Courage. (gr. 4-7). 1993. pap. 3.95 (*0-8114-4307-8*) Raintree Steck-V.

Veer Reddy, G. P., jt. auth. see Pardee, Arthur B.

Veglahn, Nancy. Women Scientists. (Illus.). 128p. (gr. 6-10). 1992. lib. bdg. 16.95x (*0-8160-2482-0*) Facts on File.

Vehiller, Nina. The Haitian Americans. Moynihan, Daniel R., intro. by. (Illus.). 112p. (gr. 5 up). 1991. lib. bdg. 17.95 (*0-87754-882-X*) Chelsea Hse.

Veitch, Carol J. & Crawford, Jane. More Literature Puzzles for Elementary & Middle Schools. Mannerberg, Patricia A., illus. LC 86-7161. xiii, 90p. (gr. 1-7). 1986. pap. text ed. 15.50 (*0-87287-518-0*) Libs Unl.

Veith, Jan T. Boundless Imagination. 112p. (gr. 3-6). 1987. 9.95 (*0-912107-55-3*) Monday Morning Bks.

—Natural Wonders. 64p. (gr. 3-6). 1987. 9.95 (*0-912107-56-1*) Monday Morning Bks.

Velasquez, Eric, jt. auth. see Sobol, Donald J.

Velde, V. Dragon's Bait. 1992. write for info. (*0-15-200726-1*, J Yolen Bks) HarBrace.

Velde, Vande. User Unfriendly. (gr. 4-7). 1991. 16.95 (*0-15-200960-4*, HB Juv Bks) HarBrace.

Velez, Cesar P. Great Dinosaurs. 1989. 9.95 (*0-8167-1293-X*) Troll Assocs.

Velez, Jennicel. Poemas. Mendoza, Ester F., pref. by. LC 83-3526. (SPA). xvii, 51p. (gr. 3-7). 1983. pap. 2.50 (*0-8477-0063-1*) U of PR Pr.

Velez, Jose S. Cuando en Casa No Nos Comprenden - When We Are Not Understood at Home. (SPA). 112p. (Orig.). (gr. 9 up). 1991. pap. 4.90 (*0-311-46263-4*) Casa Bautista.

Velinsky, L., tr. see Nemcova, B.

Vellacott, Philip, tr. see Aeschylus.

Vellozi, Joseph A. Plane & Coordinate Geometry Study Aid. 1974. pap. 2.50 (*0-87738-040-6*) Youth Ed.

Velthuijs, Max. A Birthday Cake for Little Bear. Lanning, Rosemary, tr. Velthuijs, Max, illus. LC 87-73270. 32p. (gr. k-3). 1988. 9.95 (*1-55858-046-8*) North-South Bks NYC.

—Crocodile's Masterpiece. (Illus.). 32p. (ps-1). 1992. bds. 14.00 (*0-374-31658-9*) FS&G.

—Elephant & Crocodile. LC 90-55039. 32p. (gr. 4-8). 1990. 14.00 (*0-374-37675-1*) FS&G.

—Frog & the Birdsong. (ps-3). 1991. bds. 13.95 jacketed (*0-374-32467-0*) FS&G.

—Frog & the Stranger. Velthuijs, Max, illus. LC 93-26401. 32p. 1994. 14.00 (*0-688-13267-7*, Tambourine Bks) PLB 13.93 (*0-688-13268-5*, Tambourine Bks) Morrow.

—Frog in Love. Bell, Anthea, tr. (ps up). 1991. pap. 4.95 (*0-374-42470-5*) FS&G.

—Frog in Winter. Velthuijs, Max, illus. LC 92-20545. 32p. (ps up). 1993. 14.00 (*0-688-12306-6*, Tambourine Bks); PLB 13.93 (*0-688-12307-4*, Tambourine Bks) Morrow.

Velthuis, Max. Frog in Love. Bell, Anthea, tr. (ps up) 1989. 13.00 (*0-374-32465-4*) FS&G.

Velvin, Elaine. Discover Nature: A Child's Guide. rev. ed. (Illus.). 68p. (gr. 2-7). 1987. pap. 5.95 (*0-937460-18-4*) Hendrick-Long.

Venable, Bill, et al, eds. see Kansas City Barbeque Inner Circle Staff.

Venable, Fay. North to Rio Grande: Lorenzo de Zavala, First Vice President of the Republic of Texas. (Illus.). 56p. (gr. 5-7). 1985. 9.95 (*0-685-59075-5*) Eakin-Sunbelt.

Venable, James W., jt. auth. see Jorgensen, Karen L.

Vendrell, C. S., jt. auth. see Parramon, J. M.

Vendrell, Carme S., jt. auth. see Stuart, Alexander.

Venezia, Mike. Botticelli. Venezia, Mike, illus. LC 90-21645. 32p. (ps-4). 1991. PLB 15.00 (*0-516-02291-1*); pap. 4.95 (*0-516-42291-X*) Childrens.

—Da Vinci. Venezia, Mike, illus. LC 88-37715. 32p. (ps-4). 1989. PLB 15.00 (*0-516-02275-X*); pap. 4.95 (*0-516-42275-8*) Childrens.

—Edward Hopper. Venezia, Mike, illus. LC 90-2166. 32p. (ps-4). 1990. PLB 15.00 (*0-516-02277-6*); pap. 4.95 (*0-516-42277-4*) Childrens.

—Francisco Goya. Venezia, Mike, illus. LC 90-20887. 32p. (ps-4). 1991. PLB 15.00 (*0-516-02292-X*); pap. 4.95 (*0-516-42292-8*) Childrens.

—Georgia O'Keeffe. Venezia, Mike, illus. 32p. (ps-4). 1993. PLB 16.60 (*0-516-02297-0*) Childrens.

—How to Be an Older Brother or Sister. Venezia, Mike, illus. LC 85-27977. 32p. (ps-3). 1986. PLB 13.93 (*0-516-03494-4*); pap. 3.95 (*0-516-43494-2*) Childrens.

—Jackson Pollock. Moss, Meg, contrib. by. LC 93-36699. (Illus.). 1994. write for info. (*0-516-02298-9*) Childrens.

—Mary Cassatt. Venezia, Mike, illus. LC 90-2165. 32p. (ps-4). 1990. PLB 15.00 (*0-516-02278-4*); pap. 4.95 (*0-516-42278-2*) Childrens.

—Michelangelo. Venezia, Mike, illus. LC 91-555. 32p. (ps-4). 1991. PLB 15.00 (*0-516-02293-8*); pap. 4.95 (*0-516-42293-6*) Childrens.

—Monet. Venezia, Mike, illus. LC 89-25452. 32p. (ps-4). 1990. PLB 15.00 (*0-516-02276-8*); pap. 4.95 (*0-516-42276-6*) Childrens.

—Paul Gauguin. Venezia, Mike, illus. LC 91-35054. 32p. (ps-4). PLB 15.00, Apr. 1992 (*0-516-02295-4*); pap. 4. 95, Jul. 1992 (*0-516-42295-2*) Childrens.

—Paul Klee. Venezia, Mike, illus. LC 91-12554. 32p. (gr. 4). 1992. PLB 15.00 (*0-516-02294-6*); pap. 4.95 (*0-516-42294-4*) Childrens.

—Picasso. Venezia, Mike, illus. LC 87-33023. 32p. (ps-4). 1988. PLB 15.00 (*0-516-02271-7*); pap. 4.95 (*0-516-42271-5*) Childrens.

—Pieter Bruegel. Venezia, Mike, illus. LC 92-4810. 32p. (ps-4). 1992. PLB 15.00 (*0-516-02279-2*) Childrens.

—Pieter Bruegel. Venezia, Mike, illus. LC 92-4810. 32p. (ps-4). 1993. pap. 4.95 (*0-516-42279-0*) Childrens.

—Rembrandt. Venezia, Mike, illus. LC 87-33014. 32p. (ps-4). 1988. PLB 15.00 (*0-516-02272-5*); pap. 4.95 (*0-516-42272-3*) Childrens.

—Salvador Dali. Venezia, Mike, illus. LC 92-35053. 32p. (ps-4). 1993. PLB 15.00 (*0-516-02296-2*); pap. 4.95 (*0-516-42296-0*) Childrens.

—Van Gogh. Venezia, Mike, illus. LC 88-11842. 32p. (ps-4). 1988. PLB 15.00 (*0-516-02274-1*); pap. 4.95 (*0-516-42274-X*) Childrens.

Venino, Suzanne. Amazing Animal Groups. Crump, Donald J., ed. LC 81-47743. 32p. (ps-3). 1981. Set. lib. bdg. 16.95 (*0-87044-402-6*); Set. 13.95 (*0-87044-407-7*) Natl Geog.

—Animals Helping People. Crump, Donald J., ed. LC 83-13184. 32p. (ps-3). 1983. lib. bdg. 16.95 (*0-87044-493-X*) Natl Geog.

—Earth's Children. Maestas, Ken, illus. 64p. (Orig.). (gr. 4-6). 1991. pap. 5.95 (*1-877731-50-1*) Earthbooks Inc.

—What Happens in the Autumn? Crump, Donald J., ed. LC 82-47858. (ps-3). 1982. Set. 13.95 (*0-87044-452-2*); lib. bdg. 16.95 (*0-87044-465-4*) Natl Geog.

Venino, Suzanne see National Geographic Society Staff.

Vennema, Peter, jt. auth. see Stanley, Diane.

Vennen, Mark Vander see Vander Vennen, Mark.

Ven Shen Kai. An Exposition on the Buddhist Sutras, No. 2. LC 91-61744. (CHI). 400p. 1991. lib. bdg. (*1-56369-002-0*) Jen Chen Buddhism.

—The Unusual, No. II. LC 91-61740. (CHI., Illus.). 250p. 1991. (*1-56369-001-2*) Jen Chen Buddhism.

Venti, Pamela R. Why Should I? Asks Jeremy. Spiers, John, illus. 32p. (gr. 1-3). 1990. PLB 19.95 (*0-89565-700-7*); PLB 13.95s.p. (*0-685-56166-6*) Childs World.

Ventura, Anthony. Soccer, Play Like a Pro. LC 89-27292. (Illus.). 64p. (gr. 4-8). 1990. PLB 9.79 (*0-8167-1933-0*); pap. text ed. 2.95 (*0-8167-1934-9*) Troll Assocs.

Ventura, Cynthia L., jt. auth. see Carlson, Lori M.

Ventura, Cynthia L., jt. ed. see Carlson, Lori M.

Ventura, Marisa, jt. auth. see Ventura, Piero.

Ventura, Piero. Fourteen Ninety-Two: The Year of the New World. 96p. 1992. 19.95 (*0-399-22332-0*, Putnam) Putnam Pub Group.

—Great Composers. Ventura, Piero, illus. 128p. 1989. 24. 95 (*0-399-21746-0*, Putnam) Putnam Pub Group.

—Great Painters. Ventura, Piero, illus. LC 84-3423. 160p. (gr. 5 up). 1984. 24.95 (*0-399-21115-2*, Putnam) Putnam Pub Group.

—Houses: Structures, Methods, & Ways of Living. Casalini, Max, et al. LC 93-108. 1993. 16.95 (*0-395-66792-5*) HM.

—Michelangelo's World. Ventura, Piero, illus. 48p. (gr. 9-12). 1989. 13.95 (*0-399-21593-X*, Putnam) Putnam Pub Group.

Ventura, Piero & Ventura, Marisa. The Painter's Trick. Ventura, Piero & Ventura, Marisa, illus. LC 76-54411. (gr. k-2). 1977. lib. bdg. 6.99 (*0-394-93320-6*) Random Bks Yng Read.

Ventura, Pietro. Clothing: Garments, Styles, & Uses. Casalini, Max, et al. LC 93-107. 1993. 16.95 (*0-395-66791-7*) HM.

Venturi-Pickett, Stacy. Christmas Activity Book. Venturi-Pickett, Stacy, illus. 24p. (ps-3). 1993. pap. 4.95 (*0-8249-8621-0*, Ideals Child) Hambleton-Hill.

Venturi-Pickett, Stacy, illus. The Halloween Activity Book. 24p. (ps-3). 1992. pap. 4.95 (*0-8249-8573-7*, Ideals Child) Hambleton-Hill.

Vera, Rene, Jr. The Ninth Street Bridge. 1992. 7.95 (*0-533-09612-X*) Vantage.

Veray, Amaury. Villancico Yaucano. Camilli, Ivan, illus. 1992. 12.95 (*0-8477-2506-5*) U of PR Pr.

Verba, Joan M. North Dakota. Lerner Geography Department Staff, ed. (Illus.). 72p. (gr. 3-6). 1992. PLB 17.50 (*0-8225-2746-4*) Lerner Pubns.

—Voyager: Exploring the Outer Planets. 64p. (gr. 5 up). 1991. PLB 19.95 (*0-8225-1597-0*) Lerner Pubns.

Verbeeck, Carol, jt. auth. see Lowery, Lawrence.

Vercillo, Tony. One Hundred One Career Tips: Propel Yourself to the Top! Martin, Marilyn, ed. LC 91-76038. (Illus.). 135p. (Orig.). (gr. 9-11). 1992. pap. 12. 95 (*1-880530-01-5*) Del Sales.

Verdat, Jean-Pierre. The Sky: Stars & Night. Bogard, Vicki, tr. from FRE. Broutin, Christian, illus. LC 90-50776. 38p. (gr. k-5). 1991. 4.95 (*0-944589-32-4*, 324) Young Discovery Lib.

Verde, Thomas. Fiction Writers, 1900-1950. (Illus.). 128p. (gr. 7 up). 1993. PLB 16.95x (*0-8160-2573-8*) Facts on File.

Verdet, Jean-Pierre. The Earth & Sky. (Illus.). 1992. bds. 10.95 (*0-590-45268-1*, 040, Cartwheel) Scholastic Inc.

—Livre du Ciel. (FRE). 89p. (gr. 4-9). 1990. 13.95 (*2-07-039512-X*) Schoenhof.

VerDorn, Bethea. Day Breaks. Graham, Thomas, illus. 32p. (ps-3). 1992. 14.95 (*1-55970-187-0*) Arcade Pub Inc.

Ver Dorn, Bethea. Moon Glows. Graham, Thomas, illus. 32p. (ps-1). 1990. text ed. 14.95 (*1-55970-073-4*) Arcade Pub Inc.

Verdy, Violette. Of Swans, Sugarplums & Satin Slippers. Brown, Marcia, illus. 80p. 1991. 15.95 (*0-590-43484-5*, Scholastic Hardcover) Scholastic Inc.

Vere, Charles De see De Vere, Charles.

Vered, Ben. Why Is Hanukkah. (Illus.). (ps-5). 1961. pap. 2.50 (*0-914080-59-8*) Shulsinger Sales.

Vere-Hodge, Gwenda. Teddy Bear Island. 43p. (gr. 7-10). 1986. 23.00x (*0-7223-2006-X*, Pub. by A H Stockwell England) St Mut.

—Witches Are a Nuisance. 58p. 1987. 20.00x (*0-7223-2164-3*, Pub. by A H Stockwell) St Mut.

Verges, Gloria & Verges, Oriol. The Contemporary Age (Nineteenth & Twentieth Century) Rius, Maria & Peris, Carme, illus. (ENG & SPA). 32p. (gr. 2-4). 1988. 6.95 (*0-8120-3394-9*); La Edad Contemporanea. pap. 6.95 (*0-8120-3395-7*) Barron.

—The Greek & Roman Eras. Rius, Maria & Peris, Carme, illus. (ENG & SPA). 32p. (gr. 2-4). 1988. pap. 6.95 (*0-8120-3388-4*); La Edad Antigua. pap. 6.95 (*0-8120-3389-2*) Barron.

—The Middle Ages. Rius, Maria & Peris, Carme, illus. 32p. (gr. 2-4). 1988. pap. 6.95 (*0-8120-3386-8*); La Edad Media. pap. 6.95 (*0-8120-3387-6*) Barron.

—Modern Times (Seventeenth & Eighteenth Century) Rius, Maria & Peris, Carme, illus. 32p. (gr. 2-4). 1988. pap. 4.50 (*0-8120-3392-2*); La Edad Moderna. pap. 6.95 (*0-8120-3393-0*) Barron.

—Prehistory to Egypt. Rius, Maria, illus. (SPA & ENG.). 32p. (gr. 2-4). 1988. pap. 4.95 (*0-8120-3390-6*); La Prehistoria y el Antiguo Egipto. pap. 6.95 (*0-8120-3391-4*) Barron.
—The Renaissance. Rius, Maria & Peris, Carme, illus. 32p. (gr. 2-4). 1988. pap. 6.95 (*0-8120-3396-5*); El Renacimiento. pap. 6.95 (*0-8120-3397-3*) Barron.
Verges, Oriol, jt. auth. see Verges, Gloria.

Verheyden-Hilliard, Mary E. American Women in Science & Engineering, 15 bks. Biro, Scarlet & Rom, Holly M., illus. (gr. 1-4). 1988. Set. 75.00 (*0-932469-19-1*) Equity Inst. This illustrated, 15-book series presents contemporary African-American, American Indian, Asian-American, Hispanic, & Caucasian women who, in girlhood, overcame barriers of gender, race, language, & poverty to become scientists. Five of the books are about girls with physical disabilities who also went on to become scientists. "Inspiring group of biographies of women in science...Children in the lower grades will enjoy these biographies, & those in the upper grades with reading problems can use them for...biographical information."-- SCHOOL LIBRARY JOURNAL. "...useful to teachers who want to help girls become more positive towards mathematics & science... recommended."-- CURRICULUM REVIEW. "...smoothly written texts..."-- BOOKLIST. "...help children...see the connection...between determination to persevere in the face of disabilities & later 'payoff'...in a variety of very exciting careers."-- NEWSLETTER, Association of Black Women in Higher Education. "...warm, lively & true stories of young girls who went on to become successful scientists..."-- GIFTED CHILDREN MONTHLY. "...these books are so attractively produced that I can't imagine elementary classroom teaching without them."-- PERSPECTIVES, National Women Studies Association. Also available are tie-in Teaching Guide $10.00 (ISBN 0-932469-19-3), & video: "You Can Be a Scientist Too!" $46.00 (ISBN 0-932469-11-6). "Shows how exciting & fascinating science can be."-- BOOKLIST.
Publisher Provided Annotation.

—Engineer from the Comanche Nation, Nancy Wallace. Menzel, Marian, illus. LC 84-25935. 32p. (Orig.). (gr. 1-4). 1985. pap. 5.00 (*0-932469-10-8*) Equity Inst.
—Mathematician & Administrator, Shirley Mathis McBay. Biro, Scarlet, illus. LC 84-25983. 32p. (Orig.). (gr. 1-4). 1985. pap. 5.00 (*0-932469-04-3*) Equity Inst.
—Mathematician & Computer Scientist, Caryn Navy. Rom, Holly M., illus. LC 87-82595. 32p. (Orig.). (gr. 1-4). 1988. pap. 5.00 (*0-932469-12-4*) Equity Inst.
—Scientist & Activist, Phyllis Stearner. Rom, Holly M., illus. LC 87-82597. 32p. (Orig.). (gr. 1-4). 1988. pap. 5.00 (*0-932469-15-9*) Equity Inst.
—Scientist & Administrator, Antoinette Rodez Schiesler. Menzel, Marian, illus. LC 84-25978. 32p. (Orig.). (gr. 1-4). 1985. pap. 5.00 (*0-932469-08-6*) Equity Inst.
—Scientist & Astronaut, Sally Ride. Menzel, Marian, illus. LC 84-25940. 32p. (Orig.). (gr. 1-4). 1985. pap. 5.00 (*0-932469-07-8*) Equity Inst.
—Scientist & Governor, Dixy Lee Ray. Menzel, Marian, illus. LC 84-25986. 32p. (Orig.). (gr. 1-4). 1985. pap. 5.00 (*0-932469-06-X*) Equity Inst.
—Scientist & Physician, Judith Pachciarz. Stanier, Linda, illus. LC 87-82599. 32p. (Orig.). (gr. 1-4). 1988. pap. 5.00 (*0-932469-13-2*) Equity Inst.
—Scientist & Planner, Ru Chih Cheo Huang. Biro, Scarlet, illus. LC 84-25982. 32p. (Orig.). (gr. 1-4). 1985. pap. 5.00 (*0-932469-03-5*) Equity Inst.
—Scientist & Puzzle Solver, Constance Tom Noguchi. Menzel, Mary, illus. LC 84-25924. 32p. (Orig.). (gr. 1-4). 1985. pap. 5.00 (*0-932469-05-1*) Equity Inst.
—Scientist & Strategist, June Rooks. Rom, Holly M., illus. LC 87-82596. 32p. (Orig.). (gr. 1-4). 1988. pap. 5.00 (*0-932469-14-0*) Equity Inst.

—Scientist & Teacher, Anne Barrett Swanson. Rom, Holly M., illus. LC 87-82598. 32p. (Orig.). (gr. 1-4). 1988. pap. 5.00 (*0-932469-16-7*) Equity Inst.
—Scientist from Puerto Rico, Maria Cordero Hardy. Biro, Scarlet, illus. LC 84-25979. 32p. (Orig.). (gr. 1-4). 1985. pap. 5.00 (*0-932469-02-7*) Equity Inst.
—Scientist from the Santa Clara Pueblo, Agnes Naranjo Stroud-Lee. Menzel, Marian, illus. LC 84-25959. 32p. (Orig.). (gr. 1-4). 1985. pap. 5.00 (*0-932469-09-4*) Equity Inst.
—Scientist with Determination, Elma Gonzalez. Menzel, Marian, illus. LC 84-25981. 32p. (Orig.). (gr. 1-4). 1985. pap. 5.00 (*0-932469-01-9*) Equity Inst.
Verhoeven, Rian & Van Der Rol, Ruud. Anne Frank: Beyond the Diary. (Illus.). 112p. (gr. 5 up). 1993. 17.00 (*0-670-84932-4*) Viking Child Bks.
Verkouteren, J. Adrian. A Study of Numbers. 355p. (gr. 5-8). 1981. pap. text ed. 12.95 (*0-685-32862-7*) Longman.
Verlag, Mangold, tr. see Bohlke, Dorothee.
Verlag, Mangold, tr. see Mann, Marek.
Verlag, Mangold, tr. see Wolf, Andrea.
Vermeylen, Terry J. I Am Juma, Manatee. 88p. (gr. 4 up). 1987. pap. 6.95 (*0-8059-3055-8*) Dorrance.
Verne, Jules. The Adventures of the Rat Family. Copeland, Evelyn, tr. Taves, Brian, afterword by. LC 92-36983. 1993. 14.95 (*0-19-508114-5*) OUP.
—Around the World in Eighty Days. (gr. 8 up). 1964. pap. 2.25 (*0-8049-0024-8*, CL-24) Airmont.
—Around the World in Eighty Days. (gr. 5 up). 1964. pap. 2.95 (*0-440-90285-1*, LFL) Dell.
—Around the World in Eighty Days. new & abr. ed. Calhoun, D'Ann, ed. Redondo, Francisco, illus. (gr. 4-12). 1977. pap. text ed. 2.95 (*0-88301-261-8*) Pendulum Pr.
—Around the World in Eighty Days. Moser, Barry, illus. LC 87-62829. 256p. (gr. 5 up). 1988. 19.95 (*0-688-07508-8*); signed ltd. ed. 175.00 (*0-688-08257-2*, Morrow Jr Bks) Morrow Jr Bks.
—Around the World in Eighty Days. 1990. pap. 3.25 (*0-590-43053-X*) Scholastic Inc.
—Around the World in Eighty Days. 224p. (gr. 9-12). 1990. pap. 2.50 (*0-8125-0430-5*) Tor Bks.
—Around the World in Eighty Days. 1990. pap. 2.25 (*0-14-035114-0*, Puffin) Puffin Bks.
—De la Terre a la Lune. (gr. 7-12). 1970. pap. 5.95 (*0-88436-041-2*, 40275) EMC.
—De la Terre a la Lune. (FRE.). 246p. (gr. 5-10). 1977. pap. 8.95 (*2-07-033012-5*) Schoenhof.
—From the Earth to the Moon. Lowndes, R. A., intro. by. (gr. 8 up). 1967. pap. 1.75 (*0-8049-0142-2*, CL-142) Airmont.
—Journey to the Center of the Earth. Lowndes, R. A., intro. by. (gr. 6 up). 1965. pap. 3.50 (*0-8049-0060-4*, CL-60) Airmont.
—Journey to the Center of the Earth. 253p. (gr. 5 up). 1986. pap. 2.99 (*0-14-035049-7*, Puffin) Puffin Bks.
—A Journey to the Center of the Earth. James, Raymond, adapted by. Geehan, Wayne, illus. LC 89-20560. 48p. (gr. 3-6). 1990. lib. bdg. 12.89 (*0-8167-1867-9*); pap. text ed. 3.95 (*0-8167-1868-7*) Troll Assocs.
—A Journey to the Center of the Earth. 272p. (Orig.). 1992. pap. 2.50 (*0-8125-0471-2*) Tor Bks.
—Journey to the Centre of the Earth. (gr. 9 up). 1965. pap. 4.95 (*0-14-002265-1*, Penguin Bks) Viking Penguin.
—Master of the World. Lowndes, R. A., intro. by. (gr. 7 up). 1965. pap. 1.25 (*0-8049-0073-6*, CL-73) Airmont.
—Michael Strogoff. (gr. 8 up). 1964. pap. 1.50 (*0-8049-0048-5*, CL-48) Airmont.
—Mysterious Island. (gr. 8 up). 1965. pap. 1.95 (*0-8049-0077-9*, CL-77) Airmont.
—The Mysterious Island. reissued ed. Wyeth, N. C., illus. LC 88-3167. 512p. 1988. SBE 25.95 (*0-684-18957-7*, Scribners Young Read); deluxe ed. 100.00 limited ed. (*0-684-18991-7*, Scribner) Macmillan Child Grp.
—Reader's Digest Best Loved Books for Young Readers: Twenty Thousand Leagues under the Sea. Ogburn, Jackie, ed. Hildibrand, illus. 176p. (gr. 4-12). 1989. 3.99 (*0-945260-29-6*) Choice Pub NY.
—Round the Moon. (gr. 7 up). 1968. pap. 1.50 (*0-8049-0182-1*, CL-182) Airmont.
—Tour du Monde en Quatre-Vingts Jours. De Neuville, C. & Benett, L., illus. (FRE.). 333p. (gr. 5-10). 1988. pap. 10.95 (*2-07-033521-6*) Schoenhof.
—Twenty Thousand League under the Sea. 285p. 1992. pap. 3.25 (*0-590-45179-0*) Scholastic Inc.
—Twenty Thousand Leagues under the Sea. (gr. 8 up). 1964. pap. 3.25 (*0-8049-0012-4*, CL-12) Airmont.
—Twenty Thousand Leagues under the Sea. new ed. Binder, Otto, ed. Gamboa, Romy & Patricio, Ernie, illus. LC 73-75466. 64p. (Orig.). (gr. 5-10). 1973. pap. 2.95 (*0-88301-104-2*); student activity bk. 1.25 (*0-88301-180-8*) Pendulum Pr.
—Twenty Thousand Leagues under the Sea. Butz, Steve, illus. Nordlicht, Lillian, adapted by. LC 79-23887. 48p. (gr. 4 up). 1983. PLB 18.64 (*0-8172-1652-9*) Raintree Steck-V.
—Twenty Thousand Leagues under the Sea. James, Raymond, ed. Geehan, Wayne, illus. LC 89-34248. 48p. (gr. 3-6). 1990. PLB 12.89 (*0-8167-1879-2*); pap. text ed. 3.95 (*0-8167-1880-6*) Troll Assocs.
—Twenty Thousand Leagues under the Sea. new ed. rev. ed. Grund, Diane F., ed. (Illus.). 128p. 1990. pap. 2.95 (*0-942025-85-7*) Kidsbks.
—Twenty Thousand Leagues under the Sea. (gr. 4-7). 1993. pap. 4.95 (*0-8114-6846-1*) Raintree Steck-V.

Vernerey, Denise, jt. auth. see Descamps-Lequime, Sophie.
Vernier, David L., ed. Chaos in the Laboratory & Thirteen Other Science Projects Using the Apple II. LC 91-90900. (Illus.). 288p. (Orig.). (gr. 9 up). 1991. pap. 25.95 (*0-918731-46-1*) Vernier Soft.
Vernier, Louise. Your First Rabbit. (Illus.). 36p. (Orig.). 1991. pap. 1.95 (*0-86622-071-2*, YF-114) TFH Pubns.
Vernon, Judy L. All Ears: A Christmas Story. 25p. (Orig.). (gr. 2-8). 1989. pap. 4.95 (*0-9617776-4-8*) J Vernon.
Vernon, Louise A. Beggars Bible: An Illustrated Historical Fiction of John Wycliffe for the 9-14 Age-Group. LC 77-131534. (Illus.). 128p. (gr. 4-9). 1971. 5.95 (*0-8361-1732-8*) Herald Pr.
—Bible Smuggler. LC 67-15994. (Illus.). 138p. (gr. 4-9). 1967. pap. 5.95 (*0-8361-1557-0*) Herald Pr.
—Ink on His Fingers: The Life of Johannes Gutenberg. 127p. (gr. 4-8). 1993. pap. 6.95 (*1-882514-09-2*) Greenleaf TN.
—Night Preacher. LC 73-94378. (Illus.). 134p. (gr. 3-8). 1969. pap. 5.95 (*0-8361-1774-3*) Herald Pr.
—Secret Church. LC 67-15988. (Illus.). 128p. (gr. 3-8). 1967. pap. 5.95 (*0-8361-1783-2*) Herald Pr.
—Thunderstorm in Church: The Life of Martin Luther. 134p. (gr. 4-8). 1993. pap. 6.95 (*1-882514-08-4*) Greenleaf TN.
Vernon, Tannis. Adriana & the Magic Clockwork Train. LC 89-49368. (Illus.). 32p. 1990. PLB 13.99 (*0-517-57824-7*) Crown Bks Yng Read.
Verploegh, Harry, compiled by. The Next Chapter after the Last. Bester, Roger, photos by. LC 87-70164. 111p. (Orig.). 1988. pap. 7.99 (*0-87509-391-4*, PSPUM 35) Chr Pubns.
Verrier, Suzy. Titus Tidewater. Verrier, Suzy, illus. LC 70-112636. 48p. (gr. 2-4). 1990. Repr. of 1970 ed. 12.95 (*0-89272-289-4*) Down East.
Versailles, Elizabeth S. Hathaways Twelve Hundred to Nineteen-Eighty. 621p. 1980. lib. bdg. write for info. Versailles.
Verschuren, Ineke, compiled by. The Christmas Story Book. 430p. (gr. 4-8). Repr. of 1986 ed. 29.50 (*0-86315-077-2*, Pub. by Floris Bks UK) Gryphon Hse.
Versfield, Ruth. Why Are People Hungry? Franklin Watts Ltd., ed. LC 87-82886. (Illus.). 32p. (gr. k-3). 1988. 11.40 (*0-531-17082-9*, Gloucester Pr) Watts.
Verstraete, Elaine, illus. Games to Play. 32p. (ps-3). 1990. 4.95 (*1-56288-051-9*) Checkerboard.
Vert, John Le see LeVert, John.
Vertreace, Martha. Kelly in the Mirror. Speidel, Sandra, illus. LC 92-22655. 1993. 13.95 (*0-8075-4152-4*) A Whitman.
Vervoort & Mason. Calculator Math, 3 vols. (gr. 7-12). 1980. pap. 10.95 ea. Beginning Grades 5-7 (*0-8224-1200-4*) Intermediate Grades 6-8 (*0-8224-1201-2*) Advanced Grades 8-10 (*0-8224-1202-0*) Fearon Teach Aids.
Very, Lydia. Goody Two Shoes: Treasures from the Library of Congress. (Illus.). 16p. 1992. Repr. of 1865 ed. saddle wired 3.95 (*1-55709-169-2*) Applewood.
Very, Lydia L. Little Red Riding Hood: Treasures from the Library of Congress. (Illus.). 20p. 1992. Repr. of 1863 ed. saddle wired 3.95 (*1-55709-167-6*) Applewood.
Verzuh, Julie W. From the Heart of Lizzie. (gr. 7 up). 1983. pap. 7.50 (*0-87839-039-1*) North Star.
Vesco, Anne-Marie. Charlotte & Leo. (Illus.). 32p. (gr. 3-5). 1991. 18.50 (*0-89565-818-6*); 12.95s.p. (*0-685-55082-6*) Childs World.
Vesey, A. Merry Christmas, Thomas! (ps-3). 1988. pap. 3.95 (*0-14-050803-1*, Puffin) Puffin Bks.
—The Princess & the Frog. Vesey, A., illus. 32p. (ps-3). 1985. 14.95 (*0-316-90036-2*, 900362, Joy St Bks) Little.
Vesey, Amanda. Duncan & the Bird. LC 92-37335. 1993. 18.95 (*0-87614-785-6*) Carolrhoda Bks.
—Duncan's Tree House. LC 92-37334. 1993. 18.95 (*0-87614-784-8*) Carolrhoda Bks.
—Hector's New Sneakers. Vesey, Amanda, illus. 32p. (ps-3). 1993. 13.50 (*0-670-84882-4*) Viking Child Bks.
Vesey, Susan. Easter Activity Book. (Illus.). 32p. (gr. 1-5). 1993. pap. 5.99 (*0-7459-2371-2*) Lion USA.
Vesey, Susan & Doney, Meryl. The Christmas Activity Book (Mini) (Illus.). 48p. (gr. 1-6). 1990. pap. 0.99 (*0-7459-1507-8*) Lion USA.
Veslocki, Matthew, jt. auth. see Vuillequez, Richard J.
Vesper, Joan. Joey Becomes a Boomer. De Faye, Monique, illus. LC 85-70354. 63p. (Orig.). (ps-5). 1985. pap. 5.95 (*0-9615007-0-0*) Green Bough Pr.
Vessel, M. F. & Wong, H. H. Science Bulletin Boards. (gr. 1-8). 1962. pap. 6.95 (*0-8224-6290-7*) Fearon Teach Aids.
Vestal, J., ed. see Stacy, Tom.
Vestal, Jeanne, ed. see Meltzer, Milton.
Vestavia Elementary School Fourth Grade Class & Cockrell, Marcille. The Adventures of a Bubble-Bellied Bloopy Droopy Detective. (Illus.). 32p. (gr. k-5). 1989. pap. 3.95 (*0-943487-22-6*) Sevgo Pr.
Vesty, John. Adirontreks: Places & People in the Adirondacks. LC 90-82523. (Illus.). 268p. (Orig.). (gr. 8). 1991. pap. 19.95 (*0-9626876-0-X*) J Vesty Co.
Vetterlein, Millicent. The Blessing of Animals. 24p. (gr. k-2). 1992. pap. 7.95 (*0-9635447-0-5*) St George ME.
Vettori, Alessandro, tr. see Potter, Beatrix.

VGM Career Horizons Editors. Resumes for Communications Careers. LC 90-50723. 160p. (Orig.). (gr. 9 up). 1991. pap. 9.95 (0-8442-8546-3, VGM Career Bks) NTC Pub Grp.

Viamonte, Manuel. On Little Things, Challenges & Needs. Dorta, Teresa, illus. 80p. (Orig.). 1991. pap. 3.95 (1-56259-015-4) Editorial Amer.

Vianna, Fernando de Mello see Webster's New World Dictionaries Staff.

Vick, Helen H. Walker of Time. LC 92-46740. 216p. (Orig.). (gr. 6-12). 1993. 15.95 (0-943173-84-1); pap. 9.95 (0-943173-80-9) Harbinger AZ.

Vickery, Eugene L. Enchanted Hike: Children's Adventure Story in Verse. Meet Magical Rabbit in California. St. George, Adrianne B., illus. 20p. (Orig.). (gr. 1-8). 1987. pap. 3.95 (0-937775-04-5) Stonehaven Pubs.

—The Enchanted Mountain: Romantic & Science Fiction Story in Verse. St. George, Adrianne B., illus. (Orig.). (gr. 1-8). 1987. pap. 3.95 (0-937775-05-3) Stonehaven Pubs.

—Frontier Adventures: Stories in Verse of Young People in Kentucky & the South West. Vickery, Millie M., ed. Tolpo, Lily, illus. 40p. (Orig.). (gr. 1-8). 1987. pap. 4.95 perfect bdg. (0-937775-06-1) Stonehaven Pubs.

—New Friends in a New World: Thanksgiving Story of Children with New Friends. Tolpo, Lily, illus. 20p. (Orig.). (gr. k-8). 1986. pap. 1.95 (0-937775-03-7) Stonehaven Pubs.

—The Ramiluk Stories: Adventures of an Eskimo Family in the Prehistoric Arctic. Tolpo, Lily, illus. 124p. (Orig.). (gr. 5 up). 1989. 16.00 (0-937775-11-8); pap. 10.95 (0-937775-10-X) Stonehaven Pubs.

Vickery, Millie M., ed. see Vickery, Eugene L.

Victor, R. F. John Maynard Keynes: Father of Modern Economics. Rahmas, D. Steve, ed. 32p. (Orig.). (gr. 7-12). 1972. lib. bdg. 4.95 incl. catalog cards (0-87157-517-5) SamHar Pr.

Victor Raintree Publishers Inc. Staff. The Poles. LC 87-28697. (Illus.). 64p. (Orig.). (gr. 5-9). 1988. PLB 19.92 (0-8172-3078-5) Raintree Steck-V.

Videon, Lynn, et al. Take Me Along. 1987. pap. 9.95 (0-8224-6719-4) Fearon Teach Aids.

Viemeister, Peter. Microcars. LC 82-90754. (Illus.). 136p. (Orig.). (gr. 5 up). 1982. pap. 10.95 (0-9608598-0-2) Hamiltons.

Viera, Linda. The Ever-Living Tree: The Life & Times of a Coast Redwood. Canyon, Christopher, illus. LC 93-31688. 1994. write for info. (0-8027-8277-9); PLB write for info. (0-8027-8278-7) Walker & Co.

Viglucci, Pat C. Cassandra Robbins, Esq. 176p. (Orig.). (gr. 8-12). 1987. pap. 4.95 (0-938961-01-2, Stamp Out Sheep Pr) Sq One Pubs.

Vigna, Judith. Black Like Kyra, White Like Me. Tucker, Kathleen, ed. Vigna, Judith, illus. LC 92-1203. 32p. (gr. 2-6). 1992. 13.95g (0-8075-0778-4) A Whitman.

—Boot Weather. Fay, Ann, ed. Vigna, Judith, illus. LC 88-20563. 32p. (ps-2). 1989. 13.95 (0-8075-0837-3) A Whitman.

—Eric's Mom Has Cancer. LC 93-6533. (Illus.). 1993. write for info. (0-8075-2133-7) A Whitman.

—Grandma Without Me. Tucker, Kathleen, ed. Vigna, Judith, illus. LC 83-26031. 32p. (ps-3). 1984. PLB 13.95 (0-8075-3030-1) A Whitman.

—I Wish Daddy Didn't Drink So Much. Fay, Ann, ed. LC 88-108. (Illus.). 32p. (ps-3). 1988. PLB 13.95 (0-8075-3523-0); pap. 5.95 (0-8075-3526-5) A Whitman.

—Mommy & Me by Ourselves Again. Fay, Ann, ed. Vigna, Judith, illus. LC 87-2059. 32p. (ps-3). 1987. PLB 13.95 (0-8075-5232-1) A Whitman.

—My Big Sister Takes Drugs. Mathews, Judith, ed. Vigna, Judith, illus. LC 89-70736. 32p. (gr. k-3). 1990. PLB 13.95 (0-8075-5317-4) A Whitman.

—Nobody Wants a Nuclear War. Tucker, Kathleen, ed. Vigna, Judith, illus. LC 86-1654. 40p. (gr. 1-4). 1986. 13.95 (0-8075-5739-0) A Whitman.

—Saying Goodbye to Daddy. Levine, Abby, ed. Vigna, Judith, illus. LC 90-12757. 32p. (gr. k-2). 1991. 13.95 (0-8075-7253-5) A Whitman.

—She's Not My Real Mother. Fay, Ann, ed. Vigna, Judith, illus. LC 80-19073. 32p. (gr. 1-3). 1980. PLB 13.95 (0-8075-7340-X) A Whitman.

—When Eric's Mom Fought Cancer. (ps-3). 1993. 13.95 (0-8075-8883-0) A Whitman.

—Zio Pasquale's Zoo. LC 93-19360. 1993. write for info. (0-8075-9488-1) A Whitman.

Vigor, John. Danger, Dolphins, & Ginger Beer. LC 92-26182. (Illus.). 192p. (gr. 3-7). 1993. SBE 14.95 (0-689-31817-0, Atheneum Child Bk) Macmillan Child Grp.

Vila, Carmen. Tracy Knows Picasso: Children's Art History Read-Along Book. (Illus.). 24p. (gr. 1-3). Date not set. write for info. incl. tape (0-9635047-0-3) VILA Grp.

Vilain, Frederic, tr. see De Vries, C. M.

Vilain, Frederic, tr. see Wever, Hinke B.

Villa, Mickie, ed. The Comics That Ate My Brain. Wooley, John, intro. by. (Illus.). 114p. 1991. pap. 9.95 (0-944355-77-0) Malibu Graphics.

Villa, Mickie, ed. see Matsumoto, Leiji.

Villanella, Rosemary. Charlie & the Chocolate Factory: A Study Guide. (gr. 4-6). 1989. tchr's ed. & wkbk. 14.95 (0-18122-047-7) LRN Links.

—The Yearling - Study Guide. Friedland, Joyce & Kessler, Rikki, eds. (gr. 7-11). Date not set. pap. text ed. 14.95 (0-88122-061-2) Lrn Links.

Villanueva, Marciano, tr. see Pouts-Lajus, Serge.

Villanueva, Marie. Nene & the Horrible Math Monster. Unson, Ria, illus. LC 92-35425. 36p. (gr. 2-4). 1993. 12.95 (1-879965-02-X) Polychrome Pub.

Villarreal, Sylvia, jt. auth. see Quackenbush, Marcia.

Villasenor, David. Tapestries in Sand: The Spirit of Indian Sandpainting. rev. ed. (Illus.). 112p. (gr. 4 up). 1966. 16.95 (0-911010-23-8); pap. 8.95 (0-911010-22-X) Naturegraph.

Villasenor, Emma Z., tr. see Horton, Edna C. & Hadley, Roberta.

Villee, Claude A., Jr. Human Hormones. Head, J. J., ed. Johnson, Patricia & Steffen, Ann T., illus. LC 86-72197. 16p. (Orig.). (gr. 10 up). 1987. pap. text ed. 2.75 (0-89278-371-0, 45-9771) Carolina Biological.

Villeneuve, Jocelyne. The Legend of Greenmantle. Robert, Luc, illus. 80p. (ps-8). 1988. 9.95 (0-920806-95-3, Pub. by Penumbra Pr CN) U of Toronto Pr.

—Nanna Bijou: The Legend of the Sleeping Giant. Robert, Luc, illus. 46p. (ps-8). 1984. 6.95 (0-920806-26-0, Pub. by Penumbra Pr CN) U of Toronto Pr.

Villios, Lynne W. Cooking the Greek Way. Wolfe, Robert L., et al, illus. 52p. (gr. 5 up). 1984. PLB 14.95 (0-8225-0910-5) Lerner Pubns.

Vilsoni, Patricia H. South Pacific Islanders. (Illus.). 48p. (gr. 4-8). 1987. PLB 16.67 (0-86625-259-2); 12.50 (0-685-67606-4) Rourke Corp.

Vincent, jt. auth. see Hester.

Vincent, Gabrielle. Ernest & Celestine. LC 81-6392. (Illus.). (ps-3). 1986. 3.95 (0-688-06525-2, Mulberry) Morrow.

—Ernest & Celestine at the Circus. LC 88-23220. (Illus.). 32p. (ps up). 1989. 11.95 (0-688-08684-5); PLB 11.88 (0-688-08685-3) Greenwillow.

—Ernest & Celestine's Patchwork Quilt. Vincent, Gabrielle, illus. LC 84-25891. 16p. (ps-1). 1985. 5.25 (0-688-04557-X) Greenwillow.

—Ernest & Celestine's Picnic. Vincent, Gabrielle, illus. LC 82-2909. 24p. (gr. k-3). 1982. 15.95 (0-688-01250-7); PLB 15.88 (0-688-01252-3) Greenwillow.

—Ernest & Celestine's Picnic. LC 82-2909. (Illus.). 24p. (ps-3). 1988. pap. 3.95 (0-688-07809-5, Mulberry) Morrow.

—Feel Better, Ernest! LC 87-21074. (Illus.). 32p. (ps-3). 1988. Repr. of 1988 ed. 11.95 (0-688-07725-0); lib. bdg. 13.88 (0-688-07726-9) Greenwillow.

—Merry Christmas, Ernest & Celestine. Vincent, Gabrielle, illus. LC 83-14155. 32p. (gr. k-3). 1984. PLB 11.88 (0-688-02605-2); 12.00 (0-688-02606-0) Greenwillow.

—Merry Christmas, Ernest & Celestine. LC 83-14155. (ps-3). 1987. pap. 3.95 (0-688-07330-1, Mulberry) Morrow.

—Smile, Ernest & Celestine. LC 82-1075. (Illus.). 24p. (ps-3). 1982. 10.75 (0-688-01247-7); PLB 11.88 (0-688-01249-3) Greenwillow.

—Where Are You, Ernest & Celestine? Vincent, Gabrielle, illus. LC 85-17595. 28p. (gr. k-3). 1986. 11.75 (0-688-06234-2); PLB 14.93 (0-688-06235-0) Greenwillow.

Vincent, John. The Eiffel Target. (Illus.). 128p. (gr. 3-7). 1992. pap. 2.99 (0-14-036012-3) Puffin Bks.

—High Stakes. (Illus.). 128p. (gr. 3-7). 1992. pap. 2.99 (0-14-036048-4, Puffin) Puffin Bks.

—Live & Let's Dance. (Illus.). 128p. (gr. 3-7). 1992. pap. 2.99 (0-14-036013-1) Puffin Bks.

—Sandblast! (Illus.). 128p. (gr. 3-7). 1992. pap. 2.99 (0-14-036014-X) Puffin Bks.

—The Sword of Death. (Illus.). 128p. (gr. 3-7). 1992. pap. 2.99 (0-14-036049-2, Puffin) Puffin Bks.

—A View to a Thrill. (Illus.). 128p. (gr. 3-7). 1992. pap. 2.99 (0-14-036011-5) Puffin Bks.

Vincent, Richard J. Any Kid Can Cook: A Kid Friendly Cookbook. Tanaka, Rita K. & Brandes, Mary J., eds. Teague, Mark W., illus. LC 93-94116. 160p. (Orig.). (gr. 2-8). Date not set. pap. write for info. (0-9638354-0-8) Vision Pr CA.

Vinck, Christopher de see De Vinck, Christopher.

Vineberg, Ethel. Grandmother Came from Dworitz: A Jewish Love Story. Briansky, Rita, illus. 44p. (gr. 4 up). 1987. Repr. of 1978 ed. text ed. 3.95 (0-88776-195-X) Tundra Bks.

Viney, Peter, et al. Main Street Student Book. LC 92-22748. 1992. 7.95 (0-19-434485-1) OUP.

Vinge, Joan D. Psion. LC 82-70323. 256p. (gr. 7 up). 1982. pap. 12.95 (0-385-28780-1) Delacorte.

—Psion. 352p. (gr. k-12). 1985. pap. 2.95 (0-440-97192-6, LFL) Dell.

—Tarzan, King of the Apes. LC 83-42826. (Illus.). 128p. (gr. 5-9). 1983. lib. bdg. 4.99 (0-394-96212-5) Random Bks Yng Read.

Vining, Elizabeth J. Penn. Whitney, George G., illus. LC 86-63992. 298p. (gr. 8-12). 1986. pap. 9.00 (0-941308-06-5) Phila Yrly Mtg RSOF.

Vinje, Marie. Hanna's Butterfly. Hoffman, Joan, ed. (Illus.). 32p. (gr. k-2). 1992. pap. 3.95 (0-88743-428-2, 06080) Sch Zone Pub Co.

—Hanna's Butterfly. Hoffman, Joan, ed. 16p. (gr. k-2). 1992. pap. 2.25 (0-88743-267-0, 06034) Sch Zone Pub Co.

—I Don't Like Peas. Hoffman, Joan, ed. (Illus.). 32p. (gr. k-2). 1992. pap. 3.95 (0-88743-430-4, 06082) Sch Zone Pub Co.

—I Don't Like Peas. Hoffman, Joan, ed. (Illus.). 16p. (gr. k-2). 1992. pap. 2.25 (0-88743-269-7, 06036) Sch Zone Pub Co.

—The New Bike. Hoffman, Joan, ed. (Illus.). 32p. (gr. k-2). 1992. pap. 3.95 (0-88743-426-6, 06078) Sch Zone Pub Co.

—The New Bike. Hoffman, Joan, ed. (Illus.). 16p. (gr. k-2). 1992. pap. 2.25 (0-88743-265-4, 06032) Sch Zone Pub Co.

Vinson, Brown. Crazy Horse: Hoka Hey! LC 90-42985. (Illus.). 176p. (gr. 6-10). 1991. PLB 13.95 (1-55905-077-2) Marshall Cavendish.

Vinton, Iris. Look Out for Pirates. LC 61-7790. (Illus.). 72p. (gr. 1-2). 1961. lib. bdg. 8.99 (0-394-90022-7) Beginner.

Viola, Amy, tr. see Annable, Toni & Kaspar, Maria H.

Viola, Herman & Viola, Susan. Giuseppe Garibaldi. (Illus.). 112p. (gr. 5 up). 1988. 17.95 (0-87754-526-X) Chelsea Hse.

Viola, Herman, intro. by see Doss, Michael P.

Viola, Herman, intro. by see Iverson, Peter.

Viola, Herman, intro. by see Lowe, Felix C.

Viola, Herman, intro. by see Morrow, Mary F.

Viola, Herman, intro. by see Rivinus, Edward F.

Viola, Herman J. After Columbus: The Horse's Return to America. Thomas, Peter, narrated by. Howland, Deborah, illus. 32p. (gr. 2-5). 1992. 11.95 (0-924483-61-X); incl. audiocass. tape 16.95 (0-924483-60-1); incl. audiocass. tape & 13" stuffed mustang toy 39.95 (0-924483-58-X); incl. audiocass. tape & 9" stuffed mustang toy 25.95 (0-924483-59-8); audiocassette (0-924483-74-1) Soundprints.

—Andrew Jackson. Schlesinger, Arthur M., Jr., intro. by. (Illus.). 112p. (gr. 5 up). 1986. lib. bdg. 17.95 (0-87754-587-1) Chelsea Hse.

—Osceola. Miyake, Yoshi, illus. LC 92-5683. 32p. (gr. 4-5). 1992. PLB 17.96 (0-8114-6575-6); pap. 4.95 (0-8114-4098-2) Raintree Steck-V.

—Sitting Bull. (Illus.). 32p. (gr. 3-6). 1990. PLB 17.96 (0-8172-3401-2); pap. 4.95 (0-8114-4088-5) Raintree Steck-V.

Viola, Susan, jt. auth. see Viola, Herman.

Viola, Tom. Willy Brandt. Schlesinger, Arthur M., Jr., intro. by. (Illus.). 112p. (gr. 5 up). 1988. lib. bdg. 17.95 (0-87754-512-X) Chelsea Hse.

Viola, Vic. The Heart of Matter: A Nuclear Chemistry Module. Gardner, Marjorie, intro. by. (Illus.). 106p. (Orig.). (gr. 9-12). 1991. pap. text ed. 8.20 (1-879827-03-4) Vistas.

Viorst, Judith. Alexander & the Terrible, Horrible, No Good, Very Bad Day. Cruz, Ray, illus. LC 72-75289. 32p. (gr. k-4). 1972. RSBE 12.95 (0-689-30072-7, Atheneum Child Bk) Macmillan Child Grp.

—Alexander & the Terrible, Horrible, No Good, Very Bad Day. Cruz, Ray, illus. LC 87-31808. 32p. (gr. k-4). 1987. pap. 3.95 (0-689-71173-5, Aladdin) Macmillan Child Grp.

—Alexander, Que Era Rico el Domingo Pasado. Ada, Alma F., tr. Cruz, Ray, illus. (SPA.). 32p. (gr. k-4). 1989. 3.95 (0-689-71351-7, Aladdin) Macmillan Child Grp.

—Alexander, Que Era Rico el Domingo Pasado. Ada, Alma F., tr. Cruz, Ray, illus. (SPA.). 32p. (gr. k-4). 1989. SBE 12.95 (0-689-31590-2, Atheneum Child Bk) Macmillan Child Grp.

—Alexander Who Used to Be Rich Last Sunday. LC 77-1579. (Illus.). 32p. (ps-4). 1987. pap. 3.95 (0-689-71199-9, Aladdin) Macmillan Child Grp.

—Alexander, Who Used to Be Rich Last Sunday, Vol. 1. LC 77-1579. (Illus.). 32p. (ps-4). 1978. RSBE 13.95 (0-689-30602-4, Atheneum Child Bk) Macmillan Child Grp.

—Alexander y el Dia Terrible, Horrible, Espantoso, Horroso. Ada, Alma F., tr. Cruz, Ray, illus. (SPA.). 32p. (gr. k-4). 1989. pap. 3.95 (0-689-71350-9, Aladdin) Macmillan Child Grp.

—Alexander y el Dia Terrible, Horrible, Espantoso, Horroso. Ada, Alma F., tr. Cruz, Ray, illus. LC 89-33916. (SPA.). 32p. (gr. k-4). 1989. SBE 13.95 (0-689-31591-0, Atheneum Child Bk) Macmillan Child Grp.

—The Alphabet from Z to A: With Much Confusion on the Way. Hull, Richard, illus. LC 91-39338. 32p. (gr. 2-5). 1994. SBE 14.95 (0-689-31768-9, Atheneum Child Bk) Macmillan Child Grp.

—Earrings! Malone, Nola L., illus. LC 89-17846. 32p. (gr. 1-4). 1990. SBE 13.95 (0-689-31615-1, Atheneum Child Bk) Macmillan Child Grp.

—Earrings! Malone, Nola L., illus. LC 92-42984. 32p. (gr. 1-5). 1993. pap. 4.95 (0-689-71669-9, Aladdin) Macmillan Child Grp.

—The Good-Bye Book. Chorao, Kay, illus. LC 87-1778. 32p. (ps-1). 1988. SBE 13.95 (0-689-31308-X, Atheneum Child Bk) Macmillan Child Grp.

—The Good-Bye Book. Chorao, Kay, illus. LC 91-19916. 32p. (ps-1). 1992. pap. 4.95 (0-689-71581-1, Aladdin) Macmillan Child Grp.

—If I Were in Charge of the World & Other Worries. LC 81-2342. (Illus.). 64p. (gr. 2 up). 1984. pap. 3.95 (0-689-70770-3, Aladdin) Macmillan Child Grp.

—If I Were in Charge of the World & Other Worries: Poems for Children & Their Parents. Cherry, Lynn, illus. LC 81-2342. 64p. (gr. 3 up). 1981. SBE 14.95 (0-689-30863-9, Atheneum Child Bk) Macmillan Child Grp.

—I'll Fix Anthony. Lobel, Arnold, illus. LC 78-77942. (ps-3). 1969. 14.00i (0-06-026306-7); PLB 13.89 (0-06-026307-5) HarpC Child Bks.

—I'll Fix Anthony. Lobel, Arnold, illus. LC 87-18725. 32p. (gr. k-4). 1988. pap. 3.95 (0-689-71202-2, Aladdin) Macmillan Child Grp.

—My Mama Says There Aren't Any Zombies, Ghosts, Vampires, Creatures, Demons, Monsters, Fiends, Goblins, or Things. Chorao, Kay, illus. LC 73-76331. 48p. (gr. k-4). 1973. SBE 13.95 (0-689-30102-2, Atheneum Child Bk) Macmillan Child Grp.

—My Mama Says There Aren't Any Zombies, Ghosts, Vampires, Creatures, Demons, Monsters, Fiends, Goblins, or Things. Chorao, Kay, illus. LC 87-18733. 48p. (gr. k-4). 1987. pap. 3.95 (0-689-71204-9, Aladdin) Macmillan Child Grp.

—Rosie & Michael. Tomei, Lorna, illus. LC 74-75571. 40p. (gr. 1-4). 1974. SBE 13.95 (0-689-30439-0, Atheneum Child Bk) Macmillan Child Grp.

—Rosie & Michael. 2nd ed. Tomei, Lorna, illus. LC 86-13969. 40p. (gr. 1-4). 1988. pap. 3.95 (0-689-71272-3, Aladdin) Macmillan Child Grp.

—Sunday Morning. 2nd ed. Knight, Hilary, illus. LC 92-16928. 40p. (ps-3). 1992. RSBE 13.95 (0-689-31794-8, Atheneum Child Bk) Macmillan Child Grp.

—Sunday Morning. 2nd ed. Knight, Hilary, illus. LC 92-29561. 32p. (gr. k-3). 1993. pap. 3.95 (0-689-71702-4, Aladdin) Macmillan Child Grp.

—The Tenth Good Thing about Barney. Blegvad, Eric, illus. LC 71-154764. 32p. (gr. k-4). 1971. SBE 12.95 (0-689-20688-7, Atheneum Child Bk) Macmillan Child Grp.

—The Tenth Good Thing about Barney. Blegvad, Erik, illus. LC 86-25948. 32p. (gr. k-4). 1987. pap. 3.95 (0-689-71203-0, Aladdin) Macmillan Child Grp.

Vipont, Elfrida. The Elephant & the Bad Baby. Briggs, Raymond, illus. 32p. (ps-3). 1986. (Coward); pap. 6.95 (0-698-20625-8) Putnam Pub Group.

Virgil. Virgil's Aeneid. Dryden, John, tr. Andrews, C. A., intro. by. (gr. 11 up). 1968. pap. 1.95 (0-8049-0177-5, CL-177) Airmont.

Viscott, David, jt. auth. see Kalb, Jonah.

Vishwashrayananda, Swami. Ramakrishna for Children. Chakravarty, Purhachandra, illus. Bagchi, Santosh, tr. from BEN. (Illus.). 40p. (gr. 3-6). 1975. pap. 1.95 (0-87481-164-3) Vedanta Pr.

Vissell, Rami. Rami's Book: The Inner Life of a Child. Vissell, Rami, illus. Vissell, Barry, intro. by. LC 88-91345. (Illus.). 56p. 1990. 13.95 (0-9612720-4-X, 104) Ramira Pub.

Visual Education Corporation Staff. Macmillan Encyclopedia of Health, 8 vols. (gr. 7-12). 1993. Set. text ed. 335.00 (0-02-897439-5) Macmillan.

—Macmillan Encyclopedia of Health, 8 vols. (gr. 7-12). 1993. PLB 37.50 ea.; Vol. 1. text ed. 40.00 (0-02-897431-X); Vol. 2. text ed. 40.00 (0-02-897432-8); Vol. 3. text ed. 40.00 (0-02-897433-6); Vol. 4. text ed. 40.00 (0-02-897434-4); Vol. 5. text ed. 40.00 (0-02-897435-2); Vol. 6. text ed. 40.00 (0-02-897436-0); Vol. 7. text ed. 40.00 (0-02-897437-9); Vol. 8. text ed. 40.00 (0-02-897438-7) Macmillan.

Vita-finzi, Claudio. Planet Earth. 10p. 1989. pap. 13.95 casebound, pop-up (0-671-67573-7, S&S BFYR) S&S Trade.

—The Power Pop-up Book: Our Planet's Energy Resources: Production, Consumption, Conservation, & Innovation. Jacobs, Phil, illus. Wilgress, Paul, contrib. by. (Illus.). 10p. (gr. 3 up). 1991. pap. 13.95 casebound pop-up (0-671-73535-7, S&S BFYR) S&S Trade.

Vitale, Barbara M. Unicorns Are Real: A Right-Brained Approach to Learning. LC 82-83064. (Illus.). 144p. (Orig.). (gr. k-8). 1982. pap. 12.95 (0-915190-35-4, JP9035-4) Jalmar Pr.

Vitale, Miralla. Enciclopedia de la Nina. 3rd ed. (SPA.). 64p. 1979. 29.95 (0-8288-4738-X, S50471) Fr & Eur.

Vitalo, Valerie. Sweet Dreams, Sarah. DeVito, Pam, illus. LC 88-51277. 54p. (ps-4). 1989. 6.95 (0-932433-56-1) Windswept Hse.

Vitebsky, Piers. Saami of Lapland. LC 93-32424. (Illus.). 48p. (gr. 6-10). 1994. 16.95 (1-56847-159-9) Thomson Lrning.

Vitkus, Jessica. Beauty & Fitness with "Saved by the Bell" LC 91-42583. (Illus.). 64p. (Orig.). (gr. 5 up). 1992. pap. 6.95 (0-02-045425-2, Collier Young Ad) Macmillan Child Grp.

Vittitow, Mary L. & Liu, Sarah. Fun Things for Kids at Christmastime. Vittitow, Mary L., illus. 64p. (gr. 1-4). 1991. pap. 7.99 wkbk. (0-87403-843-X, 28-03063) Standard Hse.

Vittitow, Mary L., jt. auth. see Liu, Sarah.

Vivas, Julie. The Nativity. Vivas, Julia, illus. 34p. (ps up) 1988. 13.95 (0-15-200535-8, Gulliver Bks) HarBrace.

Vivelo, Jackie. Beagle in Trouble: Super Sleuth II. 112p. (gr. 4-7). 1992. pap. 2.95 (0-8167-1548-3) Troll Assocs.

—Mr. Scatter's Magic Spell. Chamberlain, Margaret, illus. LC 93-642. 32p. (gr. 2-5). 1993. 10.95 (1-56458-201-9) Dorling Kindersley.

—Reading to Matthew. Saflund, Birgitta, illus. LC 93-84912. 40p. (gr. 3-8). 1993. 15.95 (1-879373-60-2) R Rinehart.

—Super Sleuth. 96p. (gr. 4-7). 1992. pap. 2.95 (0-8167-1547-5) Troll Assocs.

—Super Sleuth & the Bare Bones: Super Sleuth III. 112p. (gr. 4-7). 1988. 12.95 (0-399-21536-0, Putnam) Putnam Pub Group.

Vivian, Charles. Science Experiments & Amusements for Children. Watts, S. A., photos by. LC 67-28142. (ps-6). 1967. pap. 2.95 (0-486-21856-2) Dover.

Vivian, E. Charles. Adventures of Robin Hood. Vivian, E. Charles, illus. (gr. 5 up). 1965. pap. 1.75 (0-8049-0067-1, CL-67) Airmont.

Viviano, Christy L. Haunted Louisiana: True Tales of Ghosts & Other Unearthly Creatures. 164p. (gr. 5-12). 1992. pap. 10.95 (1-881490-01-7); audiocassette 16.95 (1-881490-02-5) Tree House Pr.

Vlakos, Jon, illus. Ladle Rat Rotten Hut. 6th ed. 12p. 1988. pap. 2.00 (0-934714-05-3) Swamp Pr.

Vleck, Van Jane see Olson, Jim.

Vnenchak, Dennis. Lech Walesa & Poland. LC 92-40266. Date not set. write for info. (0-531-11128-8) Watts. Postponed.

Voake, Charlotte. Mrs. Goose's Baby. Voake, Charlotte, illus. 24p. (ps-1). 1989. 12.95 (0-316-90511-9, Joy St Bks) Little.

—Mrs. Goose's Baby. (ps) 1992. pap. 3.99 (0-440-40615-3) Dell.

Voake, Charlotte, retold by. & illus. The Three Little Pigs & Other Favorite Nursery Stories. LC 91-58759. 96p. (ps up). 1992. 18.95 (1-56402-118-1) Candlewick Pr.

Voake, Charlotte, illus. Over the Moon: A Book of Nursery Rhymes. LC 91-71826. 128p. (ps up) 1992. 19.95 (1-56402-038-X) Candlewick Pr.

Voce, Louise. Over in the Meadow: A Counting Rhyme. LC 93-21294. 1994. write for info. (1-56402-428-8) Candlewick Pr.

Vodopich, Darrell S., jt. auth. see Moore, Randy.

Vodraska, Cynthia L. & Vodraska, Kenneth F. Study Skills: Out-Line Format Reference Manual. 175p. (gr. 7-12). 1992. 3-ring binder 36.00 (0-9632356-0-5) OLF Pub Co.

Vodraska, Kenneth F., jt. auth. see Vodraska, Cynthia L.

Voelker, Joyce. Dear Terry. (Illus.). 97p. (Orig.). (gr. 3-6). 1990. pap. 4.95 (0-89084-526-3) Bob Jones Univ Pr.

Voeller, Edward. The Red-Crowned Crane. LC 89-11718. (Illus.). 60p. (gr. 3 up). 1990. RSBE 13.95 (0-87518-417-0, Dillon) Macmillan Child Grp.

Voelzke, Daryl E. Pierre Penguin: Finds a New Home. 24p. (ps-5). 1991. 11.95 (0-9630803-0-X) D E Voelzke.

Vogel, Carole G. Great Yellowstone Fire, Vol. 1. 1990. 15.95 (0-316-90522-4) Little.

Vogel, Carole G. & Goldner, Kathryn A. The Great Yellowstone Fire. (Illus.). (gr. 2-5). 1990. 14.95 (0-685-58504-2) Sierra.

—The Great Yellowstone Fire. (Illus.). 32p. (gr. 2-5). 1993. pap. 6.95 (0-316-90249-7) Sierra.

Vogel, Erwin. How to Start Minding Your Own (Mailorder, That Is) Business. (Illus.). 54p. (Microfiche avail., ISBN 0-912392-06-1). (gr. 9 up). 1969. pap. 8.95 (0-912392-02-9, MO1); pap. 6.75 incl. How to Write Collection Letters That Click & Collect (0-912392-07-X) E Wynn Vogel.

Vogel, Ilse-Margaret. Bad Times, Good Friends. 1992. write for info. (0-15-205528-2, HB Juv Bks) HarBrace.

Vogel, Richard, jt. auth. see Winans, Charles F.

Vogiel, Eva. One Tiny Spark. Hinlicky, Gregg, contrib. by. 176p. (gr. 8-12). 1989. 11.95 (0-935063-83-8); pap. 8.95 (0-935063-84-6) CIS Comm.

—A Problem Called Chavie. (Illus.). 152p. (gr. 4-7). 1985. 10.95 (0-87306-386-4); pap. 8.95 (0-87306-389-9) Feldheim.

Vogt, Carla, ed. see Nye, Julie.

Vogt, Esther. The Shiny Dragon. Converse, James, illus. LC 83-12981. 104p. (Orig.). (gr. 5-8). 1983. pap. 3.95 (0-8361-3348-X) Herald Pr.

Vogt, Esther L. God's Mountain Man: The Story of Jedediah Strong Smith. LC 90-25278. (Illus.). 160p. (gr. 6-8). 1991. pap. 5.95 (0-88243-563-9, 02-0563) Gospel Pub.

—A Race for Land. 112p. (Orig.). (gr. 4-7). 1992. pap. 4.95 (0-8361-3575-X) Herald Pr.

Vogt, Gregory. Apollo & the Moon Landing. (Illus.). 112p. (gr. 4-6). 1991. PLB 15.90 (1-878841-31-9) Millbrook Pr.

—The Hubble Space Telescope. LC 91-25771. (Illus.). 112p. (gr. 4-6). 1992. PLB 15.90 (1-56294-145-3) Millbrook Pr.

—Magellan & the Radar Mapping of Venus. LC 91-23494. (Illus.). 112p. (gr. 4-6). 1992. PLB 15.90 (1-56294-146-1) Millbrook Pr.

—Planets. 1995. write for info. (0-8050-3248-7); pap. write for info. (0-8050-3249-5) H Holt & Co.

—Predicting Earthquakes. LC 89-8996. (Illus.). 144p. (gr. 7-12). 1989. PLB 13.90 (0-531-10788-4) Watts.

—Predicting Volcanic Eruptions. (Illus.). 144p. (gr. 7-12). 1989. PLB 13.90 (0-531-10786-8) Watts.

—The Space Shuttle. (Illus.). 112p. (gr. 4-6). 1991. PLB 15.90 (1-56294-049-X) Millbrook Pr.

—Viking & the Mars Landing. (Illus.). 112p. (gr. 4-6). 1991. PLB 15.90 (1-878841-32-7) Millbrook Pr.

—Volcanoes. LC 92-23292. 1993. 12.90 (0-531-20151-1) Watts.

—Volcanoes. (Illus.). 64p. (gr. 5-8). 1993. pap. 5.95 (0-531-15667-2) Watts.

—Voyager. (Illus.). 112p. (gr. 4-6). 1991. PLB 15.90 (1-56294-050-3) Millbrook Pr.

Vogt, Gregory L. Jupiter. LC 92-30187. (Illus.). 32p. (gr. 2-4). 1993. PLB 12.40 (1-56294-329-4) Millbrook Pr.

—Mars. LC 91-11219. (Illus.). 32p. (gr. 2-4). 1994. PLB 12.40 (1-56294-392-8) Millbrook Pr.

—Mercury. LC 93-11218. (Illus.). 32p. (gr. 2-4). 1994. PLB 12.40 (1-56294-390-1) Millbrook Pr.

—Neptune. LC 92-30183. (Illus.). 32p. (gr. 2-4). 1993. PLB 12.40 (1-56294-331-6) Millbrook Pr.

—Pluto. LC 93-11224. (Illus.). 32p. (gr. 2-4). 1994. PLB 12.40 (1-56294-393-6) Millbrook Pr.

—Saturn. LC 92-30188. (Illus.). 48p. (gr. 2-4). 1993. PLB 12.40 (1-56294-332-4) Millbrook Pr.

—Uranus. LC 92-30184. (Illus.). 32p. (gr. 2-4). 1993. PLB 12.40 (1-56294-330-8) Millbrook Pr.

—Venus. LC 93-11217. (Illus.). 32p. (gr. 2-4). 1994. PLB 12.40 (1-56294-391-X) Millbrook Pr.

Vogt, Janice von see Cooper, Myrtle E.

Vogt, Lloyd. A Young Person's Guide to New Orleans Houses. LC 91-15213. (Illus.). 40p. 1991. pap. 5.95 (0-88289-829-9) Pelican.

Voight, Cynthia. A Solitary Blue. (gr. 7 up). 1993. pap. 3.95 (0-590-47157-0) Scholastic Inc.

—The Wings of a Falcon. (gr. 5 up). 1993. 14.95 (0-590-46712-3) Scholastic Inc.

Voigt, Cynthia. Building Blocks. LC 83-15853. 132p. (gr. 3-7). 1984. SBE 13.95 (0-689-31035-8, Atheneum Child Bk) Macmillan Child Grp.

—The Callender Papers. LC 82-13797. 224p. (gr. 4-8). 1983. SBE 14.95 (0-689-30971-6, Atheneum Child Bk) Macmillan Child Grp.

—The Callender Papers. (gr. 6 up). 1985. pap. 3.95 (0-449-70184-0, Juniper) Fawcett.

—Come a Stranger. LC 86-3610. 208p. (gr. 6 up). 1986. SBE 14.95 (0-689-31289-X, Atheneum Child Bk) Macmillan Child Grp.

—Come a Stranger. 240p. (gr. 6 up). 1991. pap. 3.95 (0-449-70246-4, Juniper) Fawcett.

—David & Jonathan. 208p. 1992. 14.95 (0-590-45165-0, Scholastic Hardcover) Scholastic Inc.

—Dicey's Song. LC 82-3882. 204p. (gr. 6 up). 1982. SBE 14.95 (0-689-30944-9, Atheneum Child Bk) Macmillan Child Grp.

—Dicey's Song. large type ed. 334p. 1990. Repr. lib. bdg. 15.95 (1-55736-166-5, Crnrstn Bks) BDD LT Grp.

—Homecoming. LC 80-36723. 320p. (gr. 5 up). 1981. SBE 15.95 (0-689-30833-7, Atheneum Child Bk) Macmillan Child Grp.

—Izzy, Willy-Nilly. LC 85-22933. 276p. (gr. 7 up). 1986. SBE 15.95 (0-689-31202-4, Atheneum Child Bk) Macmillan Child Grp.

—Izzy, Willy-Nilly. 1987. pap. 3.99 (0-449-70214-6, Juniper) Fawcett.

—Jackaroo. LC 85-7954. 320p. (gr. 8 up). 1985. SBE 15.95 (0-689-31123-0, Atheneum Child Bk) Macmillan Child Grp.

—Jackaroo. 304p. 1986. pap. 3.99 (0-449-70187-5, Juniper) Fawcett.

—On Fortune's Wheel. LC 89-39010. 288p. (gr. 6 up). 1990. SBE 15.95 (0-689-31636-4, Atheneum Child Bk) Macmillan Child Grp.

—On Fortune's Wheel. 304p. 1991. pap. 3.95 (0-449-70391-6, Juniper) Fawcett.

—Orfe. LC 91-46058. 128p. (gr. 9 up). 1992. SBE 12.95 (0-689-31771-9, Atheneum Child Bk) Macmillan Child Grp.

—The Runner. LC 84-21663. 192p. (gr. 8 up). 1985. SBE 14.95 (0-689-31069-2, Atheneum Child Bk) Macmillan Child Grp.

—The Runner. 224p. (gr. 5 up). 1987. pap. 3.95 (0-449-70294-4, Juniper) Fawcett.

—Seventeen Against the Dealer. LC 88-27488. 192p. (gr. 7 up). 1989. SBE 14.95 (0-689-31497-3, Atheneum Child Bk) Macmillan Child Grp.

—A Solitary Blue. LC 83-6007. 204p. (gr. 7 up). 1983. SBE 14.95 (0-689-31008-0, Atheneum Child Bk) Macmillan Child Grp.

—Sons from Afar. LC 87-1857. 224p. (gr. 7 up). 1987. SBE 14.95 (0-689-31349-7, Atheneum Child Bk) Macmillan Child Grp.

—Stories about Rosie. Kendrick, Dennis, illus. LC 86-3640. 48p. (gr. 1-4). 1986. SBE 13.95 (0-689-31296-2, Atheneum Child Bk) Macmillan Child Grp.

—Tell Me if the Lovers Are Losers. LC 81-8079. 252p. (gr. 7 up). 1982. SBE 15.95 (0-689-30911-2, Atheneum Child Bk) Macmillan Child Grp.

—Tree by Leaf. LC 87-17512. 208p. (gr. 4-8). 1988. SBE 14.95 (0-689-31403-5, Atheneum Child Bk) Macmillan Child Grp.

—The Vandemark Mummy. LC 91-7311. 244p. (gr. 5-9). 1991. SBE 14.95 (0-689-31476-0, Atheneum Child Bk) Macmillan Child Grp.

—The Vandemark Mummy. 1992. pap. 3.99 (0-449-70417-3, Juniper) Fawcett.

Volkmer, Jane A. Song of Chirimia - La Musica de la Chirimia: A Guatemalan Folktale - Folklore Guatemalteco. Volkmer, Jame A., illus. (SPA & ENG). 40p. (ps-4). 1990. PLB 18.95 (0-87614-423-7) Carolrhoda Bks.

—Song of the Chirimai: A Guatemalan Folktale; la Musica De la Chirimia; Folkloe Guatemalteco. (ps-3). 1992. pap. 6.95 (0-87614-592-6) Carolrhoda Bks.

Volkov, Alexander. Tales of Magic Land, No. 1. viii, 344p. 1991. pap. 11.95 (0-685-49966-9) Red Branch Pr.

The Wizard of Emerald City & Urfin Jus & His Wooden Soldiers. Blystone, Peter L., tr. from RUS. LC 90-62416. (gr. 4 up). 1991. pap. 11.95 (1-878941-16-X) Red Branch Pr. L. Frank Baum's The Wizard of Oz has been an American classic for over 90 years. But, during half that period, it's also been a Russian classic! Alexander Volkov published his

Russian rendition of it in 1939 &
revised it in 1959, retelling the tale &
giving it a uniquely Russian flavor.
Soviet children loved it so much that
Volkov eventually wrote five wonderful
"Magic Land" sequels for them. What
are these novels like? How does our
familiar tale look through Russian
eyes? This volume, with new
translations of the first two novels,
provides an answer. Volkov's WIZARD
differs considerably from Baum's: most
characters have new names, & the
young heroine, along with her other
problems, contends with an Ogre &
survives a deluge! The second novel
tells of her return to Magic Land to
defeat a wicked sorcerer who has
constructed an army of wooden soldiers
& seized power there. Anyone liking
the American WIZARD will enjoy
Volkov & want to read all six
delightful tales. Don't miss out! Order
your copy today! Address all orders to
Red Branch Press, P.O. Box 120221
Eltingville, Sta., Staten Island, NY
10312-0006 (phone & FAX 718-667-
3651).
Publisher Provided Annotation.

Volkov, Alexander M. The Seven
Underground Kings; & The Fiery God
of the Marrans. Blystone, Peter L., tr.
from RUS. & afterword by. LC 90-
83409. 384p. (Orig.). (gr. 4 up). 1993.
pap. 13.95 (*1-878941-18-6*) Red Branch
Pr.
This volume continues the publication
of the Soviet writer Alexander Volkov's
Oz-inspired "Magic Land" cycle of
children's novels. The two offered here
comprise the third & fourth in the
series of six, & are appearing in
English for the first time. THE
SEVEN UNDERGROUND KINGS is
about the inhabitants of an immense
cavern beneath Magic Land; they are
governed by seven kings who rule them
in turn, a month at a time, & those not
actually ruling are generally put to
sleep between reigns (along with their
hungry retinues) by means of some
magical water, to conserve the cavern's
resources. Chaos results when the
spring producing the water goes dry...
In the second story, Urfin Jus, villain
of TALES OF THE MAGIC LAND 1,
makes a second bid for power, this
time using an ordinary cigarette-lighter
to pass himself off as a god to the
Marran people, who are so primitive
that they do not even have fire, & he
molds their menfolk into a mighty
army & attacks the Emerald City...
Both stories are very popular in the
former Soviet Union, & deserve the
same popularity here! Order from Red
Branch Press, P.O. Box 120221,
Eltingville, Sta., Staten Island, NY
10312-0006. (Phone/FAX 718-667-
3651).
Publisher Provided Annotation.

Vollaro, Joseph. Skeletons in the Closet: A Collection of
Short Stories. Paretta, Joseph, ed. Van Brunt, Jon,
illus. 208p. (Orig.). (gr. 9-12). 1993. pap. 13.95
(*0-9633309-3-4*) Rightway Educ.
Vollbracht, James. The Way of the Circle. Foleen, Chris,
illus. 48p. (gr. 4-8). 1993. pap. 6.95 (*0-915166-76-3*)
Impact Pubs Cal.
Vollmer, Dennis. Joshua Disobeys. Vollmer, Dennis, illus.
LC 88-9464. 26p. (gr. k-3). 1988. PLB 14.95
(*0-933849-12-5*) Landmark Edns.

Volpe, Joseph & Volpe, Tracey. The Moon & the
Mistypips. (Illus.). 32p. (ps-4). 1991. pap. write for
info. (*0-9631215-1-0*); write for info. tchr's. ed.
(*0-9631215-2-9*) Hopewell Stories.
Volpe, Nancee. Good Apple & Seasonal Arts & Crafts.
144p. (gr. 3-7). 1982. 12.95 (*0-86653-087-8*, GA 438)
Good Apple.
Volpe, Tracey, jt. auth. see Volpe, Joseph.
Volz, Jim & Case, Evelyn C., eds. A Midsummer Night's
Dream: Simply Shakespeare. Barclay, Meg H., illus.
98p. (gr. 3-6). 1989. 14.95 (*0-929077-05-9*, Hopscotch
Bks); PLB 14.95 (*0-317-93769-3*) Watermark Inc.
Von Bulow, Hans, ed. see Cramer, J. B.
Von der Heide, John. Klemens von Metternich.
Schlesinger, Arthur M., Jr., intro. by. (Illus.). 112p.
(gr. 5 up). 1988. lib. bdg. 17.95 (*0-87754-541-3*)
Chelsea Hse.
Vondra, Lisa, jt. auth. see Vondra, Mary.
Vondra, Mary & Vondra, Lisa. This Time It's Me: For
Teens Who Have Just Found out They're Pregnant.
Borum, Shari, illus. 24p. (Orig.). 1985. pap. 2.65
(*1-56123-042-1*) Centering Corp.
Von Harrison, Grant. Is Kissing Sinful? 16p. 1985. pap.
text ed. (*0-929985-27-3*) Sonos.
Vonier, Sprague. Edward R. Murrow. LC 89-4344.
(Illus.). 64p. (gr. 5-6). 1989. PLB 18.60
(*0-8368-0100-8*) Gareth Stevens Inc.
Vonk, Idalee. Storytelling with the Flannel Board, Bk. 3.
LC 21-650. 313p. (ps). 1983. 15.95 (*0-513-01762-3*)
Denison.
Vonk, Idalee W. Fifty-Two Elementary Patterns. Karch,
Pat, illus. 48p. (Orig.). (gr. 1-6). 1979. pap. 6.99
(*0-87239-340-2*, 3366) Standard Pub.
Von Konigslow, A. Wayne. That's My Baby. (Illus.). 24p.
(ps-8). 1986. 12.95 (*0-920303-56-0*, Pub. by Annick
CN); pap. 4.95 (*0-920303-57-9*, Pub. by Annick CN)
Firefly Bks Ltd.
—Toilet Tales. (Illus.). 24p. (ps-8). 1985. PLB 14.95
(*0-920303-14-5*, Pub. by Annick CN); pap. 4.95
(*0-920303-13-7*, Pub. by Annick CN) Firefly Bks Ltd.
Von Konigslow, Andrea & Granfield, Linda. The Make-
Your-Own Button Book. LC 93-15230. (Illus.). 40p.
(gr. k-5). 1994. pap. 12.95 (*1-56282-486-4*) Hyprn
Ppbks.
Von Konigslow, Andrea W. Toilet Tales. Von Konigslow,
Andrea W., illus. 24p. (ps-2). 1989. pap. 0.99
(*0-920303-81-1*, Pub. by Annick CN) Firefly Bks Ltd.
Von Moshzisker, Felix. Playoff Champion. (gr. 4-7).
1993. pap. 3.25 (*0-553-56000-X*) Bantam.
Von Munchhausen, Angelita. The Real Munchhausen:
Baron of Bodenwerder. Carter, Harry, illus. 224p. (gr.
6 up). 1960. 10.00 (*0-8159-6701-2*) Devin.
Von Neumann-Cosel-Nebe, Isabelle. The Young Rider's
Book of Horses & Horsemanship. Von Newmann-
Cosel, Felicitas, ed. & tr. from GER. (Illus.). 208p. (gr.
4 up). 1992. 24.95 (*0-939481-24-3*) Half Halt Pr.
**Von Newmann-Cosel, Felicitas, ed. & tr. see Von
Neumann-Cosel-Nebe, Isabelle.**
Von Olfers, Sibylle. The Story of the Root Children. Von
Olfers, Sibylle, illus. (GER.). 32p. (ps-3). 1992. Repr.
of 1906 ed. 12.95 (*0-86315-106-X*, Pub. by Floris Bks
UK) Gryphon Hse.
Von Rosenberg, Marjorie. Cowboy Bob's Critters Visit
Texas Heroes. Von Rosenberg, Marjorie, illus. LC 93-
2908. 80p. (gr. 2-5). 1993. 12.95 (*0-89015-905-X*)
Eakin-Sunbelt.
—Elisabet Ney: Sculptor of American Heroes. Von
Roesnberg, Marjorie, illus. 64p. (gr. 4-7). 1990. 10.95
(*0-89015-747-2*) Eakin-Sunbelt.
—Max & Martha: Children from Germany in the Texas
Hill Country. (Illus.). 48p. (gr. 4-7). 1986. 8.95
(*0-89015-539-9*, Pub. by Panda Bks) Eakin-Sunbelt.
Vonsild, Fred. Tales from the "Ile" of Mulberry. 1989.
7.95 (*0-533-08213-7*) Vantage.
Von Tempski, Armine. Bright Spurs. Brown, Paul, illus.
LC 92-24540. x, 284p. 1992. pap. 14.95
(*0-918024-95-1*) Ox Bow.
—Judy of the Islands: A Story of the South Seas. Burger,
Carl, illus. LC 92-24539. viii, 280p. 1992. pap. 14.95
(*0-918024-97-8*) Ox Bow.
—Pam's Paradise Ranch: A Story of Hawaii. Brown, Paul,
illus. LC 92-24538. viii, 334p. 1992. pap. 14.95
(*0-918024-96-X*) Ox Bow.
Von Trutzschler, Wolf. Amanda. Von Trutzschler, Wolf,
illus. LC 89-82473. 48p. (ps-2). 1990. Repr. of 1941
ed. 14.95 (*0-944439-19-5*) Clark City Pr.
Von Tscharner, Renata & Fleming, Ronald L. New
Providence: A Changing Cityscape. Orloff, Denis,
illus. 26p. (ps up). 1987. 10.95 (*0-15-200540-4*,
Gulliver Bks) HarBrace.
—New Providence: A Changing Cityscape. Orloff, Denis,
illus. 32p. (gr. k-4). 1992. pap. 9.95 (*0-89133-191-3*)
Preservation Pr.
Vonvillain, Nancy. Black Hawk, Sac Rebel. LC 93-19330.
1993. write for info. (*0-7910-1711-7*); pap. write for
info. (*0-7910-1997-7*) Chelsea Hse.
Von Vogt, Janice, ed. see Cooper, Myrtle E.
Voran, Marilyn, jt. auth. see Mumaw, Catherine.
Vorhees, Duance & Mueller, Mark. The Faithful
Daughter Shim Ch'ong: The Little Frog Who Never
Listened. Kang, Mi-Sun & Kim, Yon-Kyong, illus.
46p. (gr. 2-5). 1990. PLB 9.95x (*0-930878-92-2*)
Hollym Intl.
—The Greedy Princess: The Rabbit & the Tiger. Pak, Mi-
Son & Kim, Yon-Kyong, illus. 46p. (gr. 2-5). 1990.
PLB 9.95x (*0-930878-90-6*) Hollym Intl.
—The Lazy Man. Kang, Mi-Suk, illus. 46p. (gr. 2-5).
1991. PLB 9.95x (*0-930878-73-6*) Hollym Intl.

—The Ogres' Magic Clubs. Kim, Yon-Kyong, illus. 46p.
(gr. 2-5). 1991. PLB 9.95x (*0-930878-88-4*) Hollym
Intl.
—The Seven Brothers & the Big Dipper. Pak, Mi-Son,
illus. 46p. (gr. 2-5). 1991. PLB 9.95x (*0-930878-74-4*)
Hollym Intl.
—The Snail Lady: The Magic Vase. Kang, Mi-Sun, illus.
46p. (gr. 2-5). 1990. PLB 9.95x (*0-930878-89-2*)
Hollym Intl.
—The Son of the Cinnamon Tree: The Donkey's Egg.
Kim, Yon-Kyong & Kang, Mi-Sun, illus. 46p. (gr. 2-5).
1990. PLB 9.95x (*0-930878-93-0*) Hollym Intl.
Vorhees, Duance & Mueller, Mark, eds. Mr. Moon &
Miss Sun. Kim, Yon-Kyong, illus. 45p. (gr. 2-5). 1990.
PLB 9.95x (*0-930878-72-8*) Hollym Intl.
—The Woodcutter & the Heavenly Maiden. Kim, Yon-
Kyong, illus. 45p. (gr. 2-5). 1990. PLB 9.95x
(*0-930878-71-X*) Hollym Intl.
Vornholt, John. How to Sneak into the Girls' Locker
Room. 96p. (Orig.). 1993. pap. 3.50 (*0-380-76859-3*,
Camelot) Avon.
—Mummies. 96p. 1991. pap. 3.50 (*0-380-76317-6*,
Camelot) Avon.
Vorspan, Albert & Saperstein, David. Tough Choices:
Jewish Perspectives on Social Justice. LC 92-31747.
1992. pap. 11.00 (*0-8074-0482-9*, 167275) UAHC.
Vorst, M. L. van see Van Vorst, M. L.
Vos, Catherine F. The Child's Story Bible. (Illus.). 432p.
(gr. 3 up). 1983. Repr. of 1934 ed. PLB 19.99
(*0-8028-5011-1*) Eerdmans.
Vos, Eric. Professor Filarsky's Miraculous Invention.
1980. 4.50 (*0-685-45738-9*) Anchorage.
Vos, Erik. The Dancing Donkey: Musical. 1965. 4.50
(*0-87602-117-8*) Anchorage.
Vos, Ida. Anna Is Still Here. Edelstein, Terese & Smidt,
Inez, trs. from DUT. LC 92-1618. 144p. (gr. 3-7).
1993. 13.45 (*0-395-65368-1*) HM.
—Hide & Seek. Edelstein, Terese & Smidt, Inez, trs. LC
90-4980. 144p. (gr. 3-7). 1991. 13.45 (*0-395-56470-0*)
HM.
Vosper, Alice. Rags to Riches. 222p. (gr. 7 up). 1983.
pap. 2.25 (*0-380-83873-7*, Flare) Avon.
Voss-Bark, Doris L. Philip the Fox & Other Stories.
Brown, Denise, illus. LC 66-10511. (gr. 3-6). 1967. 13.
95 (*0-8023-1105-9*) Dufour.
Vos-Wezeman, Phyllis. Benjamin Brody's Backyard Bag.
(Illus.). 32p. (Orig.). 1991. pap. 11.95 (*0-87178-091-7*)
Brethren.
Vos Wezeman, Phyllis & Fournier, Jude D. Counting the
Days: Twenty-Five Ways. 51p. (Orig.). 1989. pap.
9.95 (*0-940754-77-0*) Ed Ministries.
Vos Wezeman, Phyllis & Wiessner, Colleen A. A Day
with David. 30p. (Orig.). (gr. 1-6). 1988. pap. 5.95
(*0-940754-57-6*) Ed Ministries.
—Gleanings from Ruth. 25p. (Orig.). (gr. 1-6). 1988. pap.
5.95 (*0-940754-61-4*) Ed Ministries.
—Joseph's Jigsaw. 50p. (Orig.). (gr. 1-6). 1988. pap. 5.95
(*0-940754-59-2*) Ed Ministries.
—Lydia: Filling the Fibers with Faith. 24p. (Orig.). (gr.
1-6). 1989. pap. 5.95 (*0-940754-71-1*) Ed Ministries.
—Mary's Memories. 38p. (Orig.). (gr. 1-6). 1989. pap.
5.95 (*0-940754-72-X*) Ed Ministries.
—The Mosaic of Mary & Martha. 29p. (Orig.). (gr. 1-6).
1989. pap. 5.95 (*0-940754-73-8*) Ed Ministries.
—Noah's Noises. 33p. (Orig.). (gr. 1-6). 1988. pap. 5.95
(*0-940754-58-4*) Ed Ministries.
—On the Move with Moses. 33p. (Orig.). (gr. 1-6). 1988.
pap. 5.95 (*0-940754-60-6*) Ed Ministries.
—Saul to Paul: Enlightened to Serve. 32p. (Orig.). (gr.
1-6). 1989. pap. 5.95 (*0-940754-74-6*) Ed Ministries.
Vos Wezeman, Phyllis, jt. auth. see Wiessner, Colleen A.
Vouillemin, Jacques. Zebra, Reading Level 3-4. (Illus.). 28p. (gr.
2-5). 1983. PLB 16.67 (*0-86592-858-4*); PLB 12.50s.p.
(*0-685-58829-7*) Rourke Corp.
Vowles, A. Amazing Experiments. (Illus.). 32p. (gr. 2-6).
1985. pap. 5.95 (*0-88625-073-0*) Durkin Hayes Pub.
Vowles, Andrew. My Travel Book. Williams, Harland &
O'Halloran, Tim, illus. 32p. (gr. 1-5). 1985. pap. 2.95
(*0-88625-063-3*) Durkin Hayes Pub.
—Robotics. Bastien, Charles, illus. 32p. (gr. 5-9). 1985.
pap. 5.95 (*0-88625-113-3*) Durkin Hayes Pub.
Vowles, Andrew & Illingworth, Lynn. My Birthday Book.
Williams, Harland, illus. 32p. (gr. 1-5). 1985. pap. 2.95
(*0-88625-061-7*) Durkin Hayes Pub.
Vozar, David. Yo, Hungry Wolf! A Nursery Rap. Lewin,
Betsy, illus. LC 91-46264. (gr. 1-4). 1993. 15.00
(*0-385-30452-8*) Doubleday.
Vrana, Ronald, ed. The Nature of the Private Enterprise
Market System. rev. ed. (Illus.). 70p. (gr. 9-12). 1992.
Repr. of 1988 ed. tchr's. ed. 8.00 (*0-943447-12-7*) Free
Ent Partner.
—Productivity: The Worker & His Tools. rev. ed. (Illus.).
70p. (gr. 9-12). Repr. of 1988 ed. tchr's. ed. 8.00
(*0-943447-13-5*) Free Ent Partner.
Vrbova, Zuza. Budgerigars. McAulay, Robert, illus. 48p.
(gr. 2 up). 1990. PLB 9.95 (*0-86622-556-0*, J-006)
TFH Pubns.
—Guinea Pigs. McAulay, Robert, illus. 48p. 1990. PLB
9.95 (*0-86622-555-2*, J-005) TFH Pubns.
—Hamsters. (Illus.). 48p. (gr. 2 up). 1990. PLB 9.95
(*0-86622-554-4*, J-004) TFH Pubns.
—Junior Pet Care Koi for Ponds. McAulay, Robert, illus.
48p. (gr. 1-6). 1990. PLB 9.95 (*0-685-45484-3*, J-008)
TFH Pubns.
—Kittens. McAulay, Robert, illus. 48p. (gr. 2 up). 1990.
PLB 9.95 (*0-86622-553-6*, J-003) TFH Pubns.

—Mountains. Camm, Martin, et al, illus. LC 89-20299. 32p. (gr. 4-6). 1990. PLB 11.59 (0-8167-1973-X); pap. text ed. 3.95 (0-8167-1974-8) Troll Assocs.
—Puppies. McAulay, Robert, illus. 48p. (gr. 2 up). 1990. PLB 9.95 (0-86622-552-8, J-002) TFH Pubns.
—Rabbits. McAulay, Robert, illus. 48p. 1990. PLB 9.95 (0-86622-550-1, J-001) TFH Pubns.
—Snakes. McAulay, Robert, illus. 48p. 1990. PLB 9.95 (0-86622-557-9, J-007) TFH Pubns.
—Turtles. McAulay, Robert, illus. 48p. 1990. PLB 9.95 (0-86622-559-5, J-009) TFH Pubns.
—Volcanoes & Earthquakes. Roffe, Michael, et al, illus. LC 89-20334. 32p. (gr. 4-6). 1990. PLB 11.59 (0-8167-1977-2); pap. text ed. 3.95 (0-8167-1978-0) Troll Assocs.
Vredevelt, Pamela & Rodriguez, Kathryn. Surviving the Secret. 192p. (gr. 9-12). 1987. pap. 9.00 (0-8007-5333-X) Revell.
Vreeman, J. The Three Bears - Little Red Riding Hood. (Illus.). 16p. (Orig.). 1985. pap. 3.95 (0-918789-03-6) FreeMan Prods.
—We Wish You a Merry Christmas. (Illus.). 16p. (Orig.). 1985. pap. 3.95 (0-918789-02-8) FreeMan Prods.
Vreeman, J., jt. auth. see Van Denend, G.
Vreeman, J., ed. see Medema, K.
Vreeman, J., ed. see Van Denend, G.
Vriends, Matthew M., jt. auth. see Naether, Carl.
Vriends, Matthew M., ed. see Piers, Helen.
Vries, C. M. de see De Vries, C. M.
Vries, David De see De Vries, David.
Vries, Maggie de see Little, Jean & De Vries, Maggie.
Vries, Maggie De see Little, Jean & De Vries, Maggie.
Vrooman, Christine W. Willowby's World of Fluffits. Sidaras, Nanci, illus. 56p. (Orig.). (gr. 2-6). 1984. pap. 8.95 with stickers incl. (0-910349-02-9) Cloud Ten.
—Willowby's World of Unicorns. Kane, Sandy & Ogden, Peggy, eds. Sidaras, Nanci, illus. 56p. (gr. 2-6). 1982. pap. 8.95 with stickers incl. (0-685-06580-4) Cloud Ten.
Vu, Christine, tr. see Hutchinson, Hanna.
Vuillequez, Richard J. & Veslocki, Matthew. Technology & the Computer. Gregorio, Frank, ed. Edmonds, Keith, illus. 150p. (gr. 10 up). 1990. pap. text ed. 25.00x (0-9627537-0-X) TMC CT.
Vukelich see Sohn, David A.
Vulliamy, Clara. Bangd & Shout. LC 93-28123. 1994. write for info. reinforced bdg. (1-56402-409-1) Candlewick Pr.
—Blue Hat, Red Coat. LC 93-22737. (Illus.). Date not set. write for info. (1-56402-353-2) Candlewick Pr.
—Boo, Baby, Boo! LC 93-22736. Date not set. write for info. (1-56402-388-5) Candlewick Pr.
—Ellen & Penguin. Vulliamy, Clara, illus. LC 92-54590. 32p. (ps up). 1993. 13.95 (1-56402-193-9) Candlewick Pr.
—Yum Yum. LC 93-28124. (gr. 4 up). Date not set. write for info. (1-56402-408-3) Candlewick Pr.
Vuong, Lynette D. The Brocaded Slipper & Other Vietnamese Tales. Vo, Dinh M., illus. LC 84-40746. 96p. (gr. 3-7). 1992. PLB 13.89 (0-397-32508-8, Lipp Jr Bks) HarpC Child Bks.
—The Brocaded Slipper & Other Vietnamese Tales. Vo-Dinh Mai, illus. LC 81-19139. 128p. (gr. 2-5). 1992. pap. 3.95 (0-06-440440-4, Trophy) HarpC Child Bks.
—The Golden Carp, & Other Romantic Tales of Viet-Nam. Saito, Manabu, illus. LC 92-38208. (gr. k-5). 1993. write for info. (0-688-12514-X) Lothrop.
—Sky Legends of Vietnam. Vo-Dinh Mai, illus. LC 92-38345. 96p. (gr. 4 up). 1993. 14.00 (0-06-023000-2); PLB 13.89 (0-06-023001-0) HarpC Child Bks.
Vyner, Sue. Arctic Spring. Vyner, Tim, illus. LC 92-32280. (ps-3). 1993. 13.99 (0-670-84934-0) Viking Child Bks.
—The Stolen Egg. Vyner, Tim, illus. 32p. (ps-3). 1992. 14.00 (0-670-84460-8) Viking Child Bks.

W

Waas, Uli. Where's Molly? Waas, Uli, illus. Lanning, Rosemary, tr. from GER. (Illus.). 32p. (gr. k-3). 1993. 12.95 (1-55858-229-0); lib. bdg. 12.88 (1-55858-230-4) North-South Bks NYC.
Wabbes, Marie. Happy Birthday, Little Rabbit. Wabbes, Marie, illus. 24p. (ps-k). 1987. pap. 4.95 (0-87113-129-3, Joy St Bks) Little.
—How I Was Born. LC 91-8336. (Illus.). 32p. (gr. 1 up). 1991. 13.95 (0-688-10734-6, Tambourine Bks); PLB 13.88 (0-688-10735-4, Tambourine Bks) Morrow.
—It's Snowing, Little Rabbit. Wabbes, Marie, illus. 24p. (ps-k). 1987. pap. 4.95 (0-87113-128-5, Joy St Bks) Little.
Waber, Bernard. Anteater Named Arthur. Waber, Bernard, illus. LC 67-20374. 48p. (gr. k-3). 1977. 13.95 (0-395-20336-8); pap. 5.70 (0-395-25936-3) HM.
—Bernard. Waber, Bernard, illus. 48p. (gr. k-3). 1986. 13.45 (0-395-31865-3); pap. 5.70 (0-395-42648-0) HM.
—But Names Will Never Hurt Me. Waber, Bernard, illus. LC 75-40473. 32p. (gr. k-3). 1976. 14.45 (0-395-24383-1) HM.
—Funny, Funny Lyle. Waber, Bernard, illus. LC 86-27772. 40p. (gr. k-3). 1987. 13.45 (0-395-43619-2) HM.
—Funny, Funny Lyle. Waber, Bernard, illus. 40p. (gr. k-3). 1991. pap. 4.80 (0-395-60287-4, Sandpiper) HM.

—House on East Eighty-Eighth Street. (Illus.). 48p. (gr. k-3). 1973. 14.95 (0-395-18157-7) HM.
—The House on East Eighty-Eighth Street. Waber, Bernard, illus. LC 62-8144. 48p. (gr. k-4). 1975. pap. 4.80 (0-395-19970-0, Sandpiper) HM.
—The House on East Eighty-Eighth Street. Waber, Bernard, illus. (ps up). 1993. pap. 7.95 incl. cass. (0-395-48878-8) HM.
—I Was All Thumbs. Waber, Bernard, illus. LC 75-11689. 48p. (gr. k-3). 1975. pap. 4.80 (0-395-53969-2) HM.
—Ira Sleeps Over. Waber, Bernard, illus. LC 72-75605. 48p. (gr. k-3). 1973. 13.45 (0-395-13893-0) HM.
—Ira Sleeps Over. Waber, Bernard, illus. 48p. (gr. k-3). 1975. pap. 4.80 (0-395-20503-4, Sandpiper) HM.
—Ira Sleeps over. (gr. k-5). 1984. incl. cassette 19.95 (0-941078-36-1); pap. 12.95 incl. cassette (0-941078-34-5); incl. 4 bks., cassette, & guide 27.95 (0-941078-35-3); filmstrip 22.95 (0-941078-43-4) Live Oak Media.
—Ira Sleeps Over. (gr. 3 up). 1993. pap. 7.95 incl. cass. (0-395-45949-4) HM.
—Lovable Lyle. LC 69-14728. (Illus.). (gr. k-3). 1977. 14.95 (0-395-19858-5); pap. 5.95 (0-395-25378-0) HM.
—Lyle & the Birthday Party. (Illus.). (gr. k-3). 1966. 13.45 (0-395-15080-9) HM.
—Lyle & the Birthday Party. (Illus.). 48p. (gr. k-3). 1973. pap. 5.70 (0-395-17451-1, 4-97508, Sandpiper) HM.
—Lyle Finds His Mother. LC 74-5336. (Illus.). 48p. (gr. k-3). 1974. 13.95 (0-395-19489-X) HM.
—Lyle Finds His Mother. Waber, Bernard, illus. (gr. k-3). 1978. pap. 5.95 (0-395-27398-6) HM.
—Lyle, Lyle, Crocodile. (Illus.). (gr. k-3). 1965. 13.45 (0-395-16995-X) HM.
—Lyle, Lyle Crocodile. LC 65-19305. (ps-3). 1987. pap. 4.80 (0-395-13720-9) HM.
—Nobody Is Perfick. Waber, Bernard, illus. 128p. (gr. k-3). 1991. pap. write for info. (0-395-60288-2, Sandpiper) HM.
—Nobody Is Perfick. (ps-3). 1991. pap. 4.80 (0-395-31669-3) HM.
—Rich Cat, Poor Cat. (ps-3). 1990. pap. 3.95 (0-590-43091-2) Scholastic Inc.
—The Snake: A Very Long Love Story. Waber, Bernard, illus. (ps-1). 1978. PLB 7.95 (0-685-02310-9) HM.
—You Look Ridiculous Said the Rhinoceros to the Hippopotamus. (Illus.). (gr. k-3). 1973. reinforced bdg. 16.95 (0-395-07156-9) HM.
—You Look Ridiculous Said the Rhinoceros to the Hippopotamus. (Illus.). (gr. k-3). 1979. pap. 4.80 (0-395-28007-9) HM.
—You're a Little Kid with a Big Heart. (Illus.). (gr. k-3). 1980. 14.95 (0-395-29163-1) HM.
Wachter, Oralee. No More Secrets for Me. Aaron, Jane, illus. (gr. 1-4). 1984. pap. 4.95 (0-316-91491-6) Little.
Waddell, Martin. Can't You Sleep, Little Bear? Firth, Barbara, illus. LC 91-71858. 32p. (ps up). 1992. 14.95 (1-56402-007-X) Candlewick Pr.
—Can't You Sleep Little Bear? Firth, Barbara, illus. LC 91-71858. 32p. (ps up). 1993. 4.95 (1-56402-254-4) Candlewick Pr.
—Can't You Sleep, Little Bear? LC 91-71858. (ps-3). 1994. pap. 4.99 (1-56402-262-5) Candlewick Pr.
—Daisy's Christmas. 1993. pap. 3.99 (0-440-40876-8) Dell.
—Farmer Duck. Oxenbury, Helen & Oxenbury, Helen, illus. LC 91-71855. 40p. (ps up). 1992. 15.95 (1-56402-009-6) Candlewick Pr.
—Grandma's Bill. Johnson, Jane, illus. LC 90-43014. 32p. (ps-2). 1991. 12.95 (0-531-05923-5); PLB 12.99 (0-531-08523-6) Orchard Bks Watts.
—The Happy Hedgehog Band. Barton, Jill & Barton, Jill, illus. LC 91-71852. 32p. (ps). 1992. 14.95 (1-56402-011-8) Candlewick Pr.
—Happy Hedgehog Band. LC 91-71852. (ps-3). 1994. pap. 4.99 (1-56402-272-2) Candlewick Pr.
—Harriet & the Crocodiles. Burgess, Mark, illus. (gr. 3-7). 1984. 11.95 (0-316-91622-6, Joy St Bks) Little.
—Harriet & the Haunted School. Burgess, Mark, illus. (gr. 2-6). 1986. pap. 2.50 (0-671-62215-3, Minstrel Bks) PB.
—Harriet & the Robot. Burgess, Mark, illus. LC 86-17435. (gr. 3-7). 1987. 12.95 (0-316-91624-2, Joy St Bks) Little.
—Let's Go Home, Little Bear. Firth, Barbara, illus. LC 92-53003. 32p. (ps-3). 1993. 14.95 (1-56402-131-9) Candlewick Pr.
—Little Dracula at the Seashore. Wright, Joseph, illus. LC 91-71835. 32p. (ps up). 1992. pap. 3.95 (1-56402-026-6) Candlewick Pr.
—Little Dracula Goes to School. Wright, Joseph, illus. LC 91-71834. 32p. (ps up). 1992. pap. 3.95 (1-56402-027-4) Candlewick Pr.
—Little Dracula's Christmas. Wright, Joseph, illus. 32p. (gr. k up). 1986. pap. 3.95 (0-14-050658-6) Viking Child Bks.
—Little Dracula's First Bite. Wright, Joseph, illus. 32p. (gr. k up). 1986. pap. 3.95 (0-14-050657-8) Viking Child Bks.
—Little Mo. 1st U.S. ed. Barton, Jill, illus. LC 92-54410. 32p. (ps up). 1993. 14.95 (1-56402-211-0) Candlewick Pr.
—Little Obie & the Flood. Lennox, Elsie & Lennox, Elsie, illus. LC 91-58741. 80p. (gr. 3-6). 1992. 13.95 (1-56402-106-8) Candlewick Pr.
—Owl Babies. Benson, Patrick & Benson, Patrick, illus. LC 91-58750. 32p. (ps up). 1992. 14.95 (1-56402-101-7) Candlewick Pr.

—The Park in the Dark. Briley, D., ed. Firth, Barbara, illus. LC 88-9169. 32p. (ps-1). 1989. 11.95 (0-688-08516-4); PLB 11.88 (0-688-08517-2) Lothrop.
—The Pig in the Pond. Barton, Jill, illus. LC 91-58751. 32p. (ps up). 1992. 14.95 (1-56402-050-9) Candlewick Pr.
—Sailor Bear. Austin, Virginia & Miller, Virginia, illus. LC 91-71822. 32p. (ps). 1992. 14.95 (1-56402-040-1) Candlewick Pr.
—Sailor Bear. Austin, Virginia, illus. LC 91-71822. 32p. (ps up). 1993. 4.95 (1-56402-256-0) Candlewick Pr.
—Sam Vole & His Brothers. Firth, Barbara & Firth, Barbara, illus. LC 91-58755. 32p. (ps up). 1992. 14.95 (1-56402-082-7) Candlewick Pr.
—The Toymaker. Milne, Terry A. & Milne, Terry A., illus. LC 91-58762. 32p. (ps up). 1992. 13.95 (1-56402-103-3) Candlewick Pr.
—We Love Them. Firth, Barbara, illus. LC 89-8226. 32p. (ps-2). 1990. 12.95 (0-688-09331-0); lib. bdg. 12.88 (0-688-09332-9) Lothrop.
Waddell, Martin & Miller, Virginia. Squeak-a-Lot. LC 90-3568. (Illus.). 32p. (ps up). 1991. 13.95 (0-688-10244-1); PLB 13.88 (0-688-10245-X) Greenwillow.
Waddington-Feather, John. Quill's Adventures in Grozzieland, Bk. 3. Edmond, Doreen, illus. 132p. (gr. 3 up). 1991. pap. 5.95 (1-56261-017-1) John Muir.
—Quill's Adventures in the Great Beyond, Bk. 1. Edmond, Doreen, illus. 96p. (gr. 3 up). 1991. pap. 5.95 (1-56261-015-5) John Muir.
—Quill's Adventures in Wasteland, Bk. 2. Edmond, Doreen, illus. 132p. (gr. 3 up). 1991. pap. 5.95 (1-56261-016-3) John Muir.
Waddy, Lawrence, ed. First Bible Stories. Mitchell, Mark, illus. LC 93-34710. 1994. pap. 4.95 (0-8091-6613-5) Paulist Pr.
Wade, Alan. I'm Flying! Mathers, Petra, illus. LC 88-31360. 40p. (gr. k-4). 1990. 13.95 (0-394-84510-2) Knopf Bks Yng Read.
Wade, Barrie. Barley, Barley. (Illus.). 64p. 1991. jacketed 14.95 (0-19-276091-2) OUP.
—Little Monster. Kew, Katinka, illus. LC 89-37277. 32p. (ps-2). 1990. 13.95 (0-688-09596-8); lib. bdg. 13.88 (0-688-09597-6) Lothrop.
Wade, Evelyn A. God Is Here, I'm Not Afraid. Rogers, Kathy, illus. LC 88-83019. 32p. (Orig.). 1988. pap. 5.99 (0-8066-2382-9, 10-2646, Augsburg) Augsburg Fortress.
Wade, Gini, retold by. & illus. The Wonderful Bag: An Arabian Tale from the "Thousand & One Nights" LC 92-43615. 32p. (gr. k-3). 1993. 14.95 (0-87226-508-0) P Bedrick Bks.
Wade, L. Alamo: Battle of Honor & Freedom. 1991. 11.95s.p. (0-86592-470-8) Rourke Enter.
—Badlands: Beauty Carved from Nature. 1991. 11.95s.p. (0-86592-471-6) Rourke Enter.
—California: The Rush for Gold. 1991. 11.95s.p. (0-86592-467-8) Rourke Enter.
—Doors to America's Past Series, 8 bks. 1991. Set. 95.60s.p. (0-86592-464-3) Rourke Enter.
—Hannibal: Mark Twain's Boyhood Home. 1991. 11.95s.p. (0-86592-466-X) Rourke Enter.
—Plymouth: Pilgrims' Story of Survival. 1991. 11.95s.p. (0-86592-469-4) Rourke Enter.
—St. Augustine: America's Oldest City. 1991. 11.95s.p. (0-86592-468-6) Rourke Enter.
Wade, Larry. Whales in the Classroom, Vol. I: Oceanography. Bolles, Stephen, illus. 130p. (gr. 4-8). 1992. pap. text ed. 14.95 (0-9629395-0-1) Singing Rock.
—Whales in the Classroom, Vol. 1: Oceanography. 2nd ed. Bolles, Stephen, illus. 133p. (gr. 4-8). 1993. pap. 14.95 (0-9629395-1-X) Singing Rock.
Wade, Linda R. Andersonville: A Civil War Tragedy. LC 90-46576. 48p. (gr. 4-7). 1991. 11.95s.p. (0-86592-472-4) Rourke Enter.
—James Carter. LC 89-33754. 100p. (gr. 3 up). 1989. PLB 17.27 (0-516-01372-6) Childrens.
—Montgomery: Launching the Civil Rights Movement. LC 90-8974. 48p. (gr. 4-7). 1991. 11.95s.p. (0-86592-465-1) Rourke Enter.
—Warren G. Harding. LC 88-38057. (Illus.). 100p. (gr. 3 up). 1989. PLB 17.27 (0-516-01368-8) Childrens.
Wade, Mary D. Amelia Earhart: Flying for Adventure. LC 91-37645. (Illus.). 48p. (gr. 2-4). 1992. PLB 12.40 (1-56294-059-7) Millbrook Pr.
—Amelia Earhart: Flying for Adventure. (gr. 4-7). 1992. pap. 4.95 (0-395-64539-5) HM.
—Austin: The Son Becomes Father. Finney, Pat, illus. 64p. (gr. 3-5). 1993. 10.95 (1-882539-08-7); pap. 4.95 (1-882539-09-5); tchr's. guide 5.00 (1-882539-10-9) Colophon Hse.
—Cabeza De Vaca: Conquistador Who Cared. (Illus.). 64p. (gr. 3-5). 1994. 10.95 (1-882539-14-1); pap. 4.95 (1-882539-15-X); tchr's. guide 5.00 (1-882539-16-8) Colophon Hse.
—David Crockett: Sure He Was Right. Finney, Pat, illus. 64p. (gr. 2-3). 1992. 11.95 (0-89015-854-1) Eakin-Sunbelt.
—Easter Fires. Rucker, Patty L., illus. 48p. (gr. k-4). 1985. 10.95 (0-89015-469-4, Pub. by Panda Bks) Eakin-Sunbelt.
—Esteban: Walking Across America. Clark, Russell, illus. 48p. (gr. 1-3). 1994. 10.95 (1-882539-11-7); pap. 4.95 (1-882539-12-5); tchr's. guide 5.00 (1-882539-13-3) Colophon Hse.

—I Am Houston. (Illus.). 64p. (gr. 3-5). 1993. 10.95 (1-882539-05-2); pap. 4.95 (1-882539-06-0); tchr's. guide 5.00 (1-882539-07-9) Colophon Hse.
—Milk, Meat Biscuits & The Terraqueous Machine: The Story of Gail Borden. Roberts, Melissa, ed. (Illus.). 64p. (gr. 4-7). 1987. 9.95 (0-89015-605-0) Eakin-Sunbelt.

Wade, Theodore E., Jr. Fun on the Road: Travel Activities. Baptist, Michael, et al, illus. 40p. (Orig.). (gr. k-6). 1990. pap. 2.95 (0-930192-23-0) Gazelle Pubns.

Wade, Theodore E., Jr., ed. With Joy, Poems for Children. rev. ed. LC 88-72233. (Illus.). 48p. (gr. k-7). 1988. pap. 2.95 (0-930192-20-6) Gazelle Pubns.

Wade, Tom, jt. auth. see Bruggen, Bill.

Wadley, Verleen W. Four Winds of the Past. Webb, Glyn, ed. (Illus.). 215p. 1993. PLB 16.00x (0-9604726-6-5) Enterprise Pr.

Wadsworth, Ginger. John Muir: Wilderness Protector. (Illus.). 144p. (gr. 4-7). 1992. 21.50 (0-8225-4912-3) Lerner Pubns.
—Julia Morgan: Architect of Dreams. (Illus.). 128p. (gr. 5 up). 1990. PLB 21.50 (0-8225-4903-4) Lerner Pubns.
—Rachel Carson: Voice for the Earth. (Illus.). 128p. (gr. 5 up). 1991. PLB 21.50 (0-8225-4907-7) Lerner Pubns.
—Scenes along the Santa Fe Trail. Watling, James, illus. LC 93-6491. 1993. write for info. (0-8075-7258-6) A Whitman.
—Susan Butcher, Sled Dog Racer. LC 93-36093. 1994. 13.50 (0-8225-2878-9) Lerner Pubns.

Wadsworth, Ginger, retold by. Along the Santa Fe Trail: Marion Russell's Own Story. Watling, James, illus. (gr. 2-6). 1993. 16.95 (0-8075-0295-2) A Whitman.

Wadsworth, Olive A. Over in the Meadow. Keats, Ezra J., illus. (gr. k-3). 1985. 3.95 (0-590-44848-X) Scholastic Inc.
—Over in the Meadow. Rae, Mary M., illus. (gr. 1-5). 1986. pap. 3.99 (0-14-050606-3, Puffin) Puffin Bks.

Wadsworth, Olivia A. & Rae, Mary M. Over in the Meadow: A Counting-Out Rhyme. LC 84-19653. 32p. 1985. pap. 10.95 (0-670-53276-2) Viking Child Bks.

Waechter, F. K. & Campbell, Ken. Clown Plays. Stewart, Eve, illus. Eyre, Richard, intro. by. (Illus.). 129p. 1992. pap. 11.95 (0-413-66550-X, A0661) Heinemann.

Waechter, Friederich K. The Farmers in the Well. Dobak, Annelies, tr. LC 85-1240. (Illus.). (gr. k-3). 1985. 9.95 (0-915361-16-7) Modan-Adama Bks.

Wagenknecht, Edward, ed. see Irving, Washington.

Wagenman, Mark A. Aloha Bear ABC: Coloring & Activity Book. Wagenman, Mark A., illus. 24p. (ps-k). 1989. pap. 2.95 (0-89610-146-0) Island Heritage.
—Aloha Bear & Maui the Whale (the Adventures of) Wagenman, Mark A., illus. 28p. (ps-2). 1989. 7.95 (0-89610-148-7) Island Heritage.
—Aloha Bear: Color & Activity Book. Wagenman, Mark A., illus. 24p. (ps-k). 1988. pap. 2.95 (0-89610-023-5) Island Heritage.
—Atlantis the Submarine: Coloring & Activity Book. Wagenman, Mark A., illus. 24p. (ps-k). 1990. pap. 2.95 (0-89610-168-1) Island Heritage.
—Maui the Whale: Coloring & Activity Book. (Illus.). 24p. (ps-k). 1989. pap. 2.95 (0-89610-147-9) Island Heritage.

Waggoner, Carmen. Basic Structures - French, Bk. 1: A Textbook for the Learnables. (FRE., Illus.). 127p. (gr. 7 up). 1991. incl. 4 cass. 42.00 (0-939990-73-3) Intl Linguistics.
—Descriptions de Dessins: Picture Descriptions in French. Parr, Frederique & Winitz, Harris, eds. Baker, Syd, illus. (FRE.). 65p. (Orig.). (gr. 7 up). 1989. pap. text ed. 32.00 incl. 2 cassettes (0-939990-77-6) Intl Linguistics.
—Text for the Learnables, Bk. 1. (FRE.). 36p. (gr. 3 up). 1991. pap. text ed. 6.50 (0-939990-79-2) Intl Linguistics.

Waggoner, E. J. Christ & His Righteousness. 96p. (gr. 9 up). 1988. pap. 5.95 (0-945460-01-5) Upward Way.

Waggoner, Jeffrey. The Assassination of President Kennedy: Opposing Viewpoints. LC 89-37442. (Illus.). 112p. (gr. 5-8). 1989. PLB 14.95 (0-89908-068-5) Greenhaven.

Waggoner, Karen. Dad Gummit & Ma Foot. Riggio, Anita, illus. LC 89-70983. 32p. (ps-3). 1990. 14.95 (0-531-05891-3); PLB 14.99 (0-531-08491-4) Orchard Bks Watts.
—Lemonade Babysitter. (ps-3). 1992. 14.95 (0-316-91711-7, Joy St Bks) Little.

Waggoner, Sara M. Cheekie. 96p. (ps-3). 1988. 12.95 (0-8059-3114-7) Dorrance.

Wagman, Ellen, jt. auth. see Abbey, Nancy.

Wagner, Archibald C. Some Brief Cases of Inspector Alec Stuart of Scotland Yard. Wagner, Jane T., illus. 69p. (Orig.). 1992. pap. 12.95 (1-880664-01-1) E M Pr.

Wagner, Donald R. No Tears for My Mary. Horwitz, Janet, ed. LC 87-90522. 40p. (gr. 7 up). 1989. 8.95 (0-910583-02-1); pap. 4.95 (0-318-32717-1) Shamrock Pr.
—Once upon a Time Never Comes Again. Horwitz, Janet, ed. LC 86-62155. (Illus.). 60p. (Orig.). (gr. 7 up). 1989. 10.95 (0-910583-01-3); pap. 7.95 (0-910583-04-8) Shamrock Pr.

Wagner, E. Vernel. Dinosaurs & Prehistoric Animals Coloring Book. Wagner, E. Vernel, illus. 64p. (gr. 3-5). 1988. pap. 3.00 (0-941875-05-9) Wolverine Gallery.

Wagner, Ernst F. Foundation to Flute Playing: An Elementary Method. rev. ed. 120p. (Orig.). 1918. pap. 14.95 (0-8258-0054-4, 0223) Fischer Inc NY.

Wagner, Gerda. Konstantine. Barankova, Vlasta, illus. 28p. (ps-1). 1991. smythe sewn reinforced bdg. 9.95 (1-56182-023-7) Atomium Bks.

Wagner, Jane. J. T. Parks, Gordon, photos by. (Illus.). 128p. (gr. 3-8). 1972. pap. 3.50 (0-440-44275-3, YB) Dell.

Wagner, Jenny. John Brown, Rose, & the Midnight Cat. Brooks, Ron, illus. (gr. 5-8). 1980. pap. 3.99 (0-14-050306-4, Puffin) Puffin Bks.

Wagner, John & Grant, Alan. Batman - Judge Dredd: Judgement on Gotham. O'Neil, Dennis, ed. Bisley, Simon, illus. 64p. (Orig.). 1991. pap. 5.95 (1-56389-022-4) DC Comics.

Wagner, Karen. Animal Talk. (ps-1). 1990. pap. write for info. (0-307-11644-1, GOLDEN) Western Pub.
—Chocolate Chip Cookies. Preiss, Leah P., illus. 32p. (ps-2). 1990. 14.95 (0-8050-1268-0, Bks Young Read) H Holt & Co.
—Silly Fred. Chartier, Normand, illus. LC 88-22620. 32p. (gr. k-3). 1989. RSBE 13.95 (0-02-792280-4, Macmillan Child Bk) Macmillan Child Grp.

Wagner, Matt, et al. Grendel, No. 4. Wagner, Matt & Rankin, Rich, illus. 48p. (gr. 9-12). 1986. 29.95 (0-936211-02-4); pap. 5.95 (0-938695-01-0) Graphitti Designs.

Wagner, Paul. Thirteen, Vol. 1: Short Stories. 228p. (Orig.). (gr. 9-12). 1991. pap. text ed. 3.95 (0-9628653-0-3) USA Entrps.

Wagner, R. M., ed. see Lynn, Ruth.

Wagner, Roger. Assembly Lines the Book. rev., 2nd ed. (Illus.). 273p. (Orig.). pap. 19.95 (0-927796-99-6); Apple format disk 15.95 (0-927796-24-4) R Wagner Pub.

Wagner, Shelly. The Andrew Poems. LC 93-17769. (gr. 6 up). 1994. 16.50 (0-89672-319-4); pap. cancelled (0-89672-320-8) Tex Tech Univ Pr.

Wagner, Shirley A. Equality Now: Safeguarding Women's Rights. LC 92-9746. 1992. PLB 22.60 (0-86593-177-1); 16.95 s.p. (0-685-59280-4) Rourke Corp.

Wagner, Shirley L., ed. see Muchene, Barbara S. & Muchene, Munene.

Wagner, Viqi & Swisher, Karin L., eds. The Family in America: Opposing Viewpoints. LC 92-8150. (Illus.). 240p. (gr. 10 up). 1992. PLB 17.95 (0-89908-194-0); pap. text ed. 9.95 (0-89908-169-X) Greenhaven.

Wagoner, Jay J. Arizona! LC 79-15183. (Illus.). 270p. (gr. 4). 1983. text ed. 16.00 (0-87905-105-1, Peregrine Smith) Gibbs Smith Pub.
—Arizona's Heritage. LC 77-10778. (Illus.). 496p. (gr. 8-12). 1983. text ed. 21.00x (0-87905-028-4, Peregrine Smith) Gibbs Smith Pub.
—Oklahoma! Boutas, Nora, illus. LC 89-90110. 229p. 1989. lib. bdg. 20.00 (0-9622361-0-1) Thunderbird Bks.

Wagoner, Jean B. Abigail Adams: Girl of Colonial Days. LC 92-345. (Illus.). 192p. (gr. 7 up). 1992. pap. 3.95 (0-689-71657-5, Aladdin) Macmillan Child Grp.
—Martha Washington: America's First First Lady. Goldstein, Leslie, illus. LC 86-10737. 192p. (gr. 2-6). 1986. pap. 3.95 (0-02-042160-5, Aladdin) Macmillan Child Grp.

Wagonseller, Bill, et al. Coping in a Single-Parent Home. Rosen, Ruth, ed. (gr. 7-12). 1992. PLB 13.95 (0-8239-1491-7) Rosen Group.

Wahl, Jahn. Mooga Mega Mekki. Krahn, Fernando, illus. LC 73-16818. 48p. (gr. 2-4). 1974. 7.95 (0-87955-111-9) O'Hara.

Wahl, Jan. Doctor Rabbit's Foundling. 1990. pap. 3.95 (0-671-69008-6, Little Simon) S&S Trade.
—Doctor Rabbit's Lost Scout. 1990. pap. 3.95 (0-671-69007-8, Little Simon) S&S Trade.
—Dracula's Cat. LC 77-27051. (Illus.). (ps-3). 1981. 6.95 (0-685-03842-4); pap. 2.50 (0-685-03843-2) P-H.
—Dracula's Cat & Frankenstein's Dog. Chorao, Kay, illus. (ps-2). 1990. pap. 13.95 (0-671-70820-1) S&S Trade.
—The Furious Flycycle. 1994. pap. 3.99 (0-8125-2404-7) Tor Bks.
—A Gift for Miss Milo. Grove, Jeff, illus. 96p. 1990. 13. 95 (0-89815-339-5) Ten Speed Pr.
—How the Children Stopped the Wars. O'Keefe, Maureen, illus. LC 93-2479. 96p. 1993. Repr. of 1969 ed. 15.95 (1-883672-00-7) Tricycle Pr.
—Humphrey's Bear. Joyce, William, illus. LC 85-5541. 32p. (ps-2). 1987. 13.95 (0-8050-0332-0, Bks Young Read) H Holt & Co.
—Humphrey's Bear. Joyce, William, illus. LC 85-5541. 32p. (ps-2). 1989. pap. 5.95 (0-8050-1169-2, Bks Young Read) H Holt & Co.
—Little Eight John. Clay, Wil, illus. 32p. (gr. k-3). 1992. 14.00 (0-525-67367-9, Lodestar Bks) Dutton Child Bks.
—Little Gray One. Lessac, Frane, illus. LC 92-33776. 32p. (ps-up). 1993. 15.00 (0-688-12037-7, Tambourine Bks); PLB 14.93 (0-688-12038-5, Tambourine Bks) Morrow.
—Mrs. Owl & Mr. Pig. Christelow, Eileen, illus. 32p. (gr. k-3). 1991. 13.95 (0-525-67311-3, Lodestar Bks) Dutton Child Bks.
—My Cat Ginger. Naava, illus. LC 91-31883. 32p. (ps-2). 1992. 14.00 (0-688-10722-2, Tambourine Bks); PLB 13.93 (0-688-10723-0, Tambourine Bks) Morrow.
—Pleasant Fieldmouse. Sendak, Maurice, illus. LC 64-14684. 80p. (gr. k-3). 1964. PLB 14.89 (0-06-026331-8) HarpC Child Bks.
—Pleasant Fieldmouse. Sendak, Maurice, illus. LC 64-14684. 72p. (gr. k-3). 1992. pap. 7.95 (0-06-443226-2, Trophy) HarpC Child Bks.

—The Six Voyages of Pleasant Field Mouse. (Orig.). 1994. pap. 3.99 (0-8125-2403-9) Tor Bks.
—The Sleepytime Book. Johnson, Arden, illus. LC 91-10176. 32p. (ps-3). 1992. 15.00 (0-688-10275-1, Tambourine Bks); PLB 14.93 (0-688-10276-X, Tambourine Bks) Morrow.
—S.O.S. Bobomobile. 1994. pap. 3.99 (0-8125-2405-5) Tor Bks.
—Suzy & the Mouse King. Macaro, Catherine A., illus. 78p. 1992. lib. bdg. 12.95 (0-940696-34-7) Monroe County Lib.
—Sylvester Bear Overslept. Lorenz, Lee, illus. LC 79-4095. 48p. (ps-3). 1979. 5.95 (0-8193-1003-4); PLB 5.95 (0-8193-1004-2) Parents.
—Sylvester Bear Overslept. Lorenz, Lee, illus. LC 93-13039. write for info. (0-8368-0977-7) Gareth Stevens Inc.
—Tailypo! Clay, Wil, illus. LC 90-39491. 32p. (ps-2). 1991. 14.95 (0-8050-0687-7, Bks Young Read) H Holt & Co.
—Tim Kitten & the Red Cupboard. 1990. pap. 2.25 (0-671-70296-3, S&S BFYR) S&S Trade.
—The Toy Circus. Bowers, Tim, illus. LC 85-30186. 32p. (ps-3). 1986. 13.95 (0-15-200609-5, Gulliver Bks) HarBrace.

Wahl, John & Wahl, Stacey. I Can Count the Petals of a Flower. 2nd, rev. ed. LC 85-13670. (Illus.). 36p. (ps-1). 1985. 10.00 (0-87353-224-4) NCTM.

Wahl, Mark H. A Mathematical Mystery Tour: Higher Thinking Math Tasks. (Illus.). 256p. (gr. 5 up). 1988. pap. text ed. 24.95 (0-913705-26-8); Set of 5, mystery tour guide. 6.95 (0-913705-27-6) Zephyr Pr AZ.

Wahl, Mats. Grandfathers Laika. Nygren, Tord, illus. 32p. (gr. k-4). 1990. PLB 18.95 (0-87614-434-2) Carolrhoda Bks.

Wahl, Stacey, jt. auth. see Wahl, John.

Waidner, Mary, jt. auth. see Sheehan, Kathryn.

Waigandt, Alex, jt. auth. see Miller, Deborah A.

Wain, John. The Free Zone Starts Here. LC 83-14373. 196p. (gr. 7 up). 1984. 13.95 (0-385-29315-1) Delacorte.

Wainwright, James. Poetivities - Intermediate. 64p. (gr. 4-6). 1989. 7.95 (0-86653-488-1, GA1090) Good Apple.
—Poetivities - Primary. 64p. (gr. 1-3). 1989. 7.95 (0-86653-484-9, GA1089) Good Apple.

Wainwright, Richard M. Garden of Dreams. Dvorsack, Carolyn S., illus. LC 93-17974. 1994. write for info. (0-9619566-6-6) Family Life.
—The Gift from Obadiah's Ghost. Crompton, Jack, illus. 40p. 1990. 12.95 (0-9619566-2-3) Family Life.
—Montanas Escalar. Crompton, Jack, illus. (SPA.). 64p. 1991. 15.00 (0-9619566-5-8) Family Life.
—Mountains to Climb. Crompton, Jack, illus. 64p. 1990. 13.95 (0-9619566-3-1) Family Life.
—Poofin: The Cloud That Cried on Christmas. Crompton, Jack, illus. 40p. 1989. Repr. 12.95g (0-9619566-1-5) Family Life.
—A Tiny Miracle. Crompton, Jack, illus. 40p. 1986. Repr. 12.95g (0-9619566-0-7) Family Life.

Waite, Michael. Casey, the Greedy Young Cowboy. LC 37-35512. (Illus.). 32p. (ps-2). 1988. 8.99 (1-55513-615-X, Chariot Bks) Cook.
—Gilly Greenweed's Gift for Granny. (ps-3). 1992. pap. 8.99 (0-7814-0035-X) Cook.
—Sammy's Gadget Galaxy. (ps-3). 1992. pap. 8.99 (0-7814-0036-8) Cook.
—Sir Maggie, the Mighty. LC 87-35527. (Illus.). 32p. (ps-2). 1988. 8.99 (1-55513-616-8, Chariot Bks) Cook.
—Sylvester the Jester. (ps-3). 1992. pap. 8.99 (0-7814-0033-3) Cook.

Waite, Michael P. Boggin, Blizzy, & Sleeter the Cheater. LC 87-35510. (Illus.). 32p. (ps-2). 1988. 8.99 (1-55513-618-4, Chariot Bks) Cook.
—Buzzle Billy. LC 87-5282. (ps-2). 1987. 8.99 (1-55513-218-9, Chariot Bks) Cook.
—Eddy & His Amazing Pet. LC 88-16961. (Illus.). 112p. (gr. 3-7). 1988. pap. 4.49 (1-55513-641-9, Chariot Bks) Cook.
—Emma Wimble, Accidental Astronaut. LC 88-10946. 112p. (gr. 3-7). 1988. pap. 4.49 (1-55513-639-7, Chariot Bks) Cook.
—Handy-Dandy Helpful Hal. LC 87-5275. (ps-2). 1987. text ed. 8.99 (1-55513-221-9, Chariot Bks) Cook.
—Hoomania. LC 87-21279. (gr. 3-7). 1987. pap. 4.49 (1-55513-637-0, Chariot Bks) Cook.
—Max & the Big Fat Lie. LC 87-35511. (Illus.). 32p. (ps-2). 1988. 8.99 (1-55513-617-6, Chariot Bks) Cook.
—Miggy & Tiggy. 32p. (ps-2). 1987. 8.99 (1-55513-220-0, Chariot Bks) Cook.
—Suzy Swoof. LC 87-5269. (ps-2). 1987. 8.99 (1-55513-219-7, Chariot Bks) Cook.

Waite, Mitchell. The Lost Dutchman & Superstition Mountain Who's Who. Waite, Mitchell, illus. LC 93-83367. 150p. (Orig.). 1993. pap. text ed. 9.95 (1-881260-07-0) Southwest Pubns.

Wakcher, Bridget. Child Abuse: Is It Happening to You? Show, Michael, illus. 32p. (Orig.). (gr. 1 up). 1984. pap. 3.50 (0-930363-00-0) Teknek.

Wake, Susan. Advertising. Stefoff, Rebecca, ed. LC 90-3895. (Illus.). 32p. (gr. 4-8). 1991. PLB 17.26 (0-944483-95-X) Garrett Ed Corp.
—Butter. Yeats, John, illus. 32p. (gr. 1-4). 1990. PLB 14. 95 (0-87614-427-X) Carolrhoda Bks.
—Citrus Fruits. (Illus.). 32p. (gr. 1-4). 1990. PLB 14.95 (0-87614-389-3) Carolrhoda Bks.
—Vegetables. (Illus.). 32p. (gr. 1-4). 1990. PLB 14.95 (0-87614-390-7) Carolrhoda Bks.

Wakefield, David. How to Make Animated Toys. LC 86-42771. 310p. (gr. 10-12). 1987. pap. 14.95 (*0-943822-94-7*) Sterling.
—Making Dinosaur Toys in Wood. LC 90-9466. (Illus.). 260p. (Orig.). (gr. 10-12). 1990. pap. 12.95 (*0-8069-6956-3*) Sterling.
Wakefield, Pat & Carrara, Larry. A Moose for Jessica. Carrara, Larry, photos by. LC 87-13663. (Illus.). 32p. (gr. k up) 1987. 14.95 (*0-525-44342-8*, DCB) Dutton Child Bks.
Wakefield, Pat A. & Carrara, Larry. A Moose for Jessica. Carrara, Larry, photos by. (Illus.). 64p. (ps up). 1992. pap. 5.99 (*0-14-036134-0*, Puffin Unicorn) Puffin Bks.

Wakeland, Marcia A. The Big Fish: An Alaskan Fairy Tale. Sagan, Alexander, illus. 32p. (ps-4). 1993. 14.95 (*0-9635083-1-8*) Misty Mtn.
THE BIG FISH recounts the story of Lena, an Alaskan native girl, who has a dream of catching the great King Salmon. She thinks that she will become someone special if she catches the big fish. After repeated attempts, she is about to give up on her dream when suddenly the King Salmon grabs her line & pulls her into the magic river. There he shows her the fish of his kingdom doing wonderful things because they believe they can. Lena finally understands that she is already special & that she can do anything if she believes in herself. Brilliant, splashy illustrations cover each of the 32 pages of this delightful book, that not only strives to affirm children just as they are, but to intrigue the reader with the beauty & grandeur of America's last frontier. Order from Misty Mountain Publishing, P.O. Box 773042, Eagle River, AK 99577 or phone/FAX orders at (907) 696-8166. *Publisher Provided Annotation.*

—Big Fish: An Alaskan Fairy Tale. (Illus.). 32p. (ps-4). Date not set. pap. write for info. (*0-9635083-2-6*) Misty Mtn.
Wakeman, Cheryl A. Johnnie Ollie Carri III & His Friend. Womack, Fred, illus. 32p. (ps-3). 1985. 5.95 (*0-9614819-0-0*) R E Moen.
Wakeman, Diana, illus. Disney's Aladdin. LC 91-58974. 12p. (ps-3). 1993. 11.95 (*1-56282-242-X*) Disney Pr.
Wakin, Edward. Photos That Made U. S. History, Vol. II. (Illus.). (gr. 4-7). 1993. 13.95 (*0-8027-8270-1*); PLB 14.85 (*0-8027-8272-8*) Walker & Co.
Walbreck, Dirk. Benny's Hat. Poppel, Hans, illus. 28p. (ps-1). 1991. smythe sewn reinforced bdg. 9.95 (*1-56182-028-8*) Atomium Bks.
Walbruck, Harry A. Deutschland: Ein Neuer Anfang: Intermediate to Early Advanced. (GER.). 184p. pap. 9.95 (*0-685-62825-6*, F2052-3, Natl Textbk) NTC Pub Grp.
Walch, Timothy. John Paul Second. (Illus.). (gr. 5 up). 1990. 17.95 (*1-55546-839-X*) Chelsea Hse.
Wald, Ann. Choice Adventure: Counterfeit Collection. LC 92-36279. 1993. 4.99 (*0-8423-5049-7*) Tyndale.
Wald, Mike. What You Can Do for the Environment. (Illus.). 112p. (gr. 5 up). 1993. PLB 19.95 (*0-7910-1587-4*); pap. write for info. (*0-7910-1612-9*) Chelsea Hse.
Waldee, Lynne M. Cooking the French Way. LC 82-258. (Illus.). 48p. (gr. 5 up). 1982. PLB 14.95 (*0-8225-0904-0*) Lerner Pubns.
Walden, Daniel. Nutcracker. 1993. 9.98 (*1-56138-334-1*) Courage Bks.
Walden, Howard T., II. Big Stony. Weiler, Milton, illus. 401p. (gr. 10 up). 1993. Repr. of 1972 ed. 40.00 (*1-56416-045-9*) Derrydale Pr.
—Upstream & Down. Weiler, Milton, illus. 367p. (gr. 10 up). 1993. Repr. of 1972 ed. 40.00 (*1-56416-044-0*) Derrydale Pr.
Waldherr, Kris. Persephone & the Pomegranate: A Myth from Greece. Waldherr, Kris, illus. LC 92-21349. 32p. (ps-3). 1993. 14.99 (*0-8037-1191-3*); PLB 14.89 (*0-8037-1192-1*) Dial Bks Young.
Waldman, Bryna, illus. The First Christmas. 48p. 1992. 9.95 (*0-88101-229-7*) Unicorn Pub.
—The First Christmas. 48p. 1992. 12.95 (*0-88101-239-4*) Unicorn Pub.
Waldman, Carl. Encyclopedia of Native American Tribes. Braun, Molly, illus. 308p. 1987. 45.00x (*0-8160-1421-3*) Facts on File.
Waldman, David K. Crystal Moonlight. 48p. (gr. k-2). 1990. pap. 7.95 (*0-945522-01-0*) Rebecca Hse.

—How Teddy Bears Find Their Homes: The Story of Benjamin Tristan Bear.

Danner, Maggie, illus. LC 92-53786. 32p. (gr. k-2). 1993. casebound 12.95 (*0-945522-02-9*) Rebecca Hse.
Each Teddy Bear goes off to find a home with human children. This November 25th, Benjamin Tristan Bear sets off on his journey of the heart to find his new home. A classic story told by a grandmother to her granddaughter. Benjamin Bear is traced through the travels of several generations. A story for all ages. *Publisher Provided Annotation.*

Waldman, Sarah. Light: The First Seven Days. LC 92-8767. (ps-3). 1993. 14.95 (*0-15-220870-4*) HarBrace.
Waldo, Pattii. Problem Solver. (Orig.). (gr. 5-12). 1986. 35.00x (*0-930599-05-5*) Thinking Pubns.
Waldo, Pattii, jt. auth. see Mayo, Patty.
Waldron, Ann. Claude Monet. (Illus.). 92p. 1991. 19.95 (*0-8109-3620-8*) Abrams.
—Francisco Goya. (Illus.). 92p. 1992. 19.95 (*0-8109-3368-3*) Abrams.
Waldron, Linda & Montana, LeRoy. The Children's Handbook of Real Magic. 32p. (gr. 3-4). 1993. pap. 10.00 (*1-883783-00-3*) Crystal Oracle.
Waldrop, Ruth. Abigail Adams. LC 88-6137. (Illus.). 109p. (gr. 3 up). 1988. PLB 10.95 (*0-9616894-2-0*); pap. 6.95 (*0-9616894-1-2*) Rusk Inc.
—Bunny Rabbits in Mother Gooseland. Hendrix, Hurston H., illus. LC 86-61389. (Orig.). (ps-3). 1987. pap. 4.95 (*0-317-59032-4*); cassette 4.95 (*0-317-59033-2*) RuSk Inc.
—Dolly Madison. LC 89-61360. (Illus.). 112p. (gr. 3 up). 1989. PLB 10.95 (*0-318-50084-1*); pap. 6.95 (*0-9616894-3-9*) Rusk Inc.
—Martha Washington. Hendrix, Hurston H., illus. LC 87-61391. 112p. (gr. 3-6). 1987. PLB 10.95 (*0-317-59028-6*); pap. 6.95 (*0-317-59029-4*) RuSk Inc.
—Santa Grows up in Mother Goose Land. Hendrix, Hurston H., illus. 34p. (ps-3). 1986. pap. 4.95 (*0-9616894-0-4*); cassette incl. RuSk Inc.
Waldstreicher, David. Emma Goldman. Horner, Matina S., intro. by. (Illus.). 112p. (gr. 5 up). 1990. 17.95 (*1-55546-655-9*) Chelsea Hse.
Waldvogel, Merikay & Brackman, Barbara. Patchwork Souvenirs of the Nineteen Thirty-Three Chicago World's Fair: The Sears National Quilt Contest & Chicago's Century of Progress Exposition. LC 93-22421. (Illus.). 176p. (gr. 9 up). 1993. 26.95 (*1-55853-256-0*); pap. 19.95 (*1-55853-257-9*) Rutledge Hill Pr.
Walens, Stanley. The Kwakiutl. (Illus.). (gr. 5 up). 1992. 17.95 (*1-55546-711-3*) Chelsea Hse.
Walgamott, Charles S. Six Decades Back. Arrington, Leonard J., intro. by. LC 90-33649. (Illus.). 368p. 1990. pap. 15.95 (*0-89301-137-1*) U of Idaho Pr.
Walk Thru the Bible Staff. More Youthwalk: Faith, Dating, Friendship, & Other Topics for Teen Survival. 272p. 1992. pap. 9.99 (*0-310-54591-9*, Pub. by Daybreak) Zondervan.
—Youthwalk Again. 272p. 1993. pap. 9.99 (*0-310-54601-X*, Pub. by Daybreak Bks) Zondervan.
Walker. Alphabox. 1993. 28.95 (*0-8050-1581-7*) H Holt & Co.
Walker, A. & Deeter, C. Finding the Green Stone. 32p. (ps up) 1991. 16.95 (*0-15-227538-X*, HB Juv Bks) HarBrace.
Walker, Alice. Langston Hughes, American Poet. LC 73-9565. (Illus.). 40p. (gr. 2-5). 1974. PLB 14.89 (*0-690-00219-X*, Crowell Jr Bks) HarpC Child Bks.
—Langston Hughes, American Poet. rev. ed. Deeter, Catherine, illus. LC 92-28540. 48p. (gr. 3-6). Date not set. 15.00 (*0-06-021518-6*); PLB 14.89 (*0-06-021519-4*) HarpC Child Bks.
—To Hell with Dying. LC 86-27122. 1993. pap. 5.95 (*0-15-289074-2*) HarBrace.
Walker, Allen. Last Day Delusions: Insights for an Age of Confusion. 96p. (gr. 10). 1991. pap. 6.95 (*0-945460-11-2*) Upward Way.
Walker, Arthur L., et al, eds. How to Use Adding & Calculating Machines. 4th ed. (gr. 9-12). 1978. text ed. 16.96 (*0-07-067825-1*) McGraw.
Walker, Barbara. The Little House Cookbook: Frontier Foods from Laura Ingalls Wilder's Classic Stories. Williams, Garth, illus. LC 76-58733. 256p. (gr. 4 up). 1979. 15.00 (*0-06-026418-7*); PLB 14.89 (*0-06-026419-5*) HarpC Child Bks.
Walker, Barbara, ed. The Little House Diary. LC 84-48754. (Illus.). 160p. (ps up). 1985. pap. 9.95 (*0-06-446006-1*) HarpC Child Bks.
Walker, Barbara, ed. see Gravatt, Glenn.
Walker, Barbara K. Laughing Together: Giggles & Grins from Around the Globe. rev. ed. Taback, Simms, illus. LC 91-43784. 128p. (Orig.). (gr. k up). 1992. pap. 12.95 (*1-55793-37-7*) Free Spirit Pub.
—A Treasury of Turkish Folktales for Children. LC 88-6859. xii, 155p. (gr. 3 up). 1988. lib. bdg. 18.50 (*0-208-02206-6*, Linnet) Shoe String.
—Watermelons, Walnuts & the Wisdom of Allah: And Other Tales of the Hoca. Berson, Harold, illus. 72p. 1991. Repr. of 1967 ed. 17.50 (*0-89672-254-6*) Tex Tech Univ Pr.

Walker, Barbara K., retold by. The Dancing Palm Tree: & Other Nigerian Folktales. Siegl, Helen, illus. LC 89-27748. 112p. (gr. 3 up). 1990. Repr. of 1968 ed. 19.95 (*0-89672-216-3*) Tex Tech Univ Pr.
Walker, Barbara M. Little House Cookbook. LC 76-58733. (Illus.). 256p. (gr. 4 up). 1989. pap. 6.95 (*0-06-446090-8*, Trophy) HarpC Child Bks.
Walker, Cas. The Caribbean. (Illus.). 32p. (gr. 4-6). 1991. 17.95 (*0-237-60189-3*, Pub. by Evans Bros Ltd) Trafalgar.
Walker, Cheryl. Waterskiing & Kneeboarding. (Illus.). 48p. (gr. 3-6). 1992. PLB 12.95 (*1-56065-056-7*) Capstone Pr.
Walker, Chris. Dinosaurs: A New Discovery. (gr. 4-7). 1989. pap. 5.95 (*0-88625-235-0*) Durkin Hayes Pub.
Walker, Dava J. Animal Behavior. Nolte, Larry, illus. 48p. (gr. 3-6). Date not set. PLB 12.95 (*1-56065-116-4*) Capstone Pr. Postponed.
—Mathematics. Nolte, Larry, illus. 48p. (gr. 3-6). Date not set. PLB 12.95 (*1-56065-113-X*) Capstone Pr. Postponed.
Walker, David. Rick Tees Off. Wright, Malcolm, ed. Van Zandt, William, illus. Nicklaus, Jack, frwd. by. (Illus.). 112p. (Orig.). (gr. 4-9). 1985. pap. text ed. 3.95 (*0-9614856-0-4*) Pro Golfers.
Walker, Dick. Baseball: Play Like a Pro. LC 89-27392. (Illus.). 64p. (gr. 4-8). 1990. PLB 9.79 (*0-8167-1927-6*); pap. 2.95 (*0-8167-1928-4*) Troll Assocs.
—Softball: A Step-By-Step Guide. LC 89-27290. (Illus.). 64p. (gr. 4-8). 1990. PLB 9.79 (*0-8167-1937-3*); pap. 2.95 (*0-8167-1938-1*) Troll Assocs.
Walker, Doris, ed. see Osterman, Joe.
Walker, Erika D., ed. see Smyth, Virginia S.
Walker, Granville, Jr., ed. see Brown, Lynn.
Walker, Henry. Illustrated Baseball Dictionary for Young People. Kessler, Leonard, illus. (gr. 4 up). 1978. pap. 2.50 (*0-13-450924-2*, Pub. by Treehouse) P-H.
Walker, Jane. The Atmosphere in Danger. LC 93-29977. (Illus.). 32p. (gr. 5-7). 1993. PLB 12.40 (*0-531-17425-5*, Gloucester Pr) Watts.
—Avalanches & Landslides. LC 92-9085. (Illus.). 32p. (gr. 5-8). 1992. PLB 12.40 (*0-531-17363-1*, Gloucester Pr) Watts.
—Earthquakes. (Illus.). 32p. (gr. 5-9). 1992. PLB 12.40 (*0-531-17360-7*, Gloucester Pr) Watts.
—Famine, Drought, & Plague. LC 92-9086. 32p. (gr. 5-8). 1992. PLB 12.40 (*0-531-17341-0*, Gloucester Pr) Watts.
—Oil Spills. LC 92-37095. (Illus.). 32p. (gr. 5-8). 1993. PLB 12.40 (*0-531-17406-9*, Gloucester Pr) Watts.
—The Ozone Hole. LC 92-37096. (gr. 4-7). 1993. 17.71 (*0-531-17405-0*, Gloucester Pr) Watts.
—Tidal Waves & Flooding. LC 91-31099. (Illus.). 32p. (gr. 5-9). 1992. PLB 12.40 (*0-531-17361-5*, Gloucester Pr) Watts.
—Vanishing Habitats & Species. (Illus.). 32p. (gr. 5-7). 1993. PLB 12.40 (*0-531-17426-3*, Gloucester Pr) Watts.
Walker, Jane R. Exclusively for the Jetsitter. 36p. 1993. pap. 6.95 (*0-9639144-0-5*) Realistic Extremes.
Walker, Jim. Last of the Red Cars. (Illus.). 48p. (gr. 11). 1991. pap. 15.95 (*1-56342-001-5*) Interurban.
Walker, John C. In Other Words. Steiner, Connie, illus. 32p. 1993. lib. bdg. 14.95 (*1-55037-309-9*, Pub. by Annick CN); pap. 4.95 (*1-55037-310-2*, Pub. by Annick CN) Firefly Bks Ltd.
Walker, John R. Metal Projects, Bk. 3. LC 77-21602. (Illus.). 96p. (gr. 9 up). 1977. pap. 9.60 (*0-87006-238-7*); pap. 7.20 (*0-685-01929-2*) Goodheart.
Walker, Karen, illus. How to Draw Funny Faces. 32p. 1991. 3.98 (*1-56156-020-0*); pap. 2.95 (*1-56156-065-0*) Kidsbks.
—Make-a-Face: Monster Faces. 24p. (Orig.). 1990. pap. 1.95 (*0-942025-98-9*) Kidsbks.
Walker, Kate. Dragon of Mith. (Illus.). 128p. (Orig.). (gr. 1-5). 1993. pap. 7.95 (*0-94-928064-3*, Pub. by Allen & Unwin Aust Pty AT) IPG Chicago.
—Peter. LC 92-18948. 176p. (gr. 7 up). 1993. 13.95 (*0-395-64722-3*) HM.
Walker, Katherine S., jt. auth. see Butler, Joan.
Walker, Lester. Housebuilding for Children. Hogrogian, Nonny, intro. by. LC 76-47220. (Illus.). 176p. (gr. 2 up). 1977. 16.95 (*0-87951-059-5*) Overlook Pr.
—Housebuilding for Children. Hogrogian, Nonny, intro. by. (Illus.). 176p. (gr. 2 up). 1990. pap. 12.95 (*0-87951-332-2*) Overlook Pr.
Walker, Lois. Get Growing! Exciting Plant Projects for Kids. 96p. 1991. pap. text ed. 9.95 (*0-471-54488-4*) Wiley.
Walker, Lois, jt. auth. see Otis, Sharon.
Walker, Lou A. Hand, Heart, & Mind: The Story of the Education of America's Deaf People. LC 92-45631. 1994. 14.95t (*0-8037-1225-1*) Dial Bks Young.
—Roy Lichtenstein: The Artist at Work. Abramson, Michael, photos by. LC 93-2631. (Illus.). 48p. (gr. 3-7). 1994. 15.99 (*0-525-67435-7*, Lodestar Bks) Dutton Child Bks.
Walker, Lou Ann. Amy, the Story of a Deaf Child. Abramson, Michael, illus. LC 84-21152. 64p. (gr. 4-6). 1985. 14.95 (*0-525-67145-5*, Lodestar Bks) Dutton Child Bks.
Walker, Lydia. Challenge & Change: The Story of Civil Rights Activist, C. T. Vivian. Lewis, John. LC 93-60228. (Illus.). 61p. (Orig.). (gr. 6-8). 1993. pap. 8.95 (*1-877852-14-7*) Dreamkeeper Pr.

Walker, M. A-W Kids, Level 4. (Illus.). 1990. activity bk., 48p. 8.95 (*0-201-52135-0*); tchr's. ed., 128p. avail. (*0-201-52134-2*); cassette 17.25 (*0-201-52136-9*) Addison-Wesley.

—A-W Kids, Level 5. (Illus.). 1990. pap. text ed. 8.25 student ed., 80p. (*0-685-47383-X*); tchr's. ed., 128p. avail.; activity bk., 48p. 2.95 (*0-201-52139-3*); cassette pkg. 17.25 (*0-201-52140-7*) Addison-Wesley.

Walker, Margaret. October Journey. LC 73-82444. 38p. (gr. 12). 1973. pap. 7.00 (*0-910296-96-0*) Broadside Pr.

—Prophets for a New Day. LC 78-130304. 32p. (gr. 12). 1970. pap. 7.00 (*0-910296-21-9*) Broadside Pr.

Walker, Margaret, jt. auth. see Warner, John.

Walker, Mary A. The Scathatch & Maeve's Daughter. LC 90-141. 128p. (gr. 6-9). 1990. SBE 13.95 (*0-689-31638-0*, Atheneum Child Bk) Macmillan Child Grp.

Walker, Mary L., ed. A World of Children's Songs. Ortiz, Gloria, illus. LC 93-709103. 192p. (gr. 1-6). 1993. pap. 19.95 (*0-377-00260-7*) Friendship Pr.

Walker, Mort. Beetle Bailey: Three's a Crowd. 288p. (Orig.). 1986. pap. 2.95 (*0-8125-6111-2*) Tor Bks.

Walker, Mort & Browne, Dik. Hi & Lois: "Is Dinner Ready?" 288p. (Orig.). 1984. pap. 2.50 (*0-8125-6915-6*) Tor Bks.

—Hi & Lois: Trixie a la Mode. 128p. 1986. pap. 1.95 (*0-8125-6904-0*) Tor Bks.

Walker, P. Bigfoot & other Legendary Creatures. Noonan, W., illus. 1992. 15.95 (*0-15-207147-4*, HB Juv Bks) HarBrace.

Walker, Paul R. Big Men, Big Country: A Collection of American Tall Tales. LC 91-45128. (gr. 4-7). 1993. 16.95 (*0-15-207136-9*) HarBrace.

—Great Figures of the Wild West. (Illus.). 128p. (gr. 7-12). 1992. lib. bdg. 16.95x (*0-8160-2576-2*) Facts on File.

—Head for the Hills! The Amazing True Story of the Johnstown Flood. 96p. (Orig.). (gr. 2-5). 1993. PLB 9.99 (*0-679-94761-2*); pap. 2.99 (*0-679-84761-8*) Random Bks Yng Read.

—Method. 200p. (gr. 7 up). 1990. 14.95 (*0-15-200528-5*) HarBrace.

—Pride of Puerto Rico: The Life of Roberto Clemente. 132p. (gr. 3-7). 1988. 11.95 (*0-15-200562-5*, Gulliver Bks) HarBrace.

—Pride of Puerto Rico: The Life of Roberto Clemente. 157p. (gr. 3-7). 1990. pap. 4.95 (*0-15-263420-7*, Odyssey) HarBrace.

—The Sluggers Club: A Sports Mystery. LC 92-28201. 1993. 13.95 (*0-15-276163-2*) HarBrace.

—Spiritual Leaders. LC 93-31684. 1994. write for info. (*0-8160-2875-3*) Facts on File.

Walker, Richard. Japan. LC 92-10766. 96p. 1992. lib. bdg. 19.92 (*0-8114-2457-X*) Raintree Steck-V.

—Plants. LC 93-19075. 1993. 12.95 (*0-16458-383-X*) Dorling Kindersley.

Walker, Sally M. Born Near the Earth's Surface: Sedimentary Rocks. LC 90-42436. (Illus.). 64p. (gr. 6 up). 1991. lib. bdg. 15.95 (*0-89490-293-8*) Enslow Pubs.

—Glaciers: Ice on the Move. (Illus.). 48p. (gr. 3-6). 1990. PLB 19.95 (*0-87614-373-7*) Carolrhoda Bks.

—Volcanoes: Earth's Inner Fire. LC 93-23172. 1994. write for info. (*0-87614-812-7*) Carolrhoda Bks.

—Water Up, Water Down: The Hydrolic Cycle. 48p. (gr. 3-6). 1992. PLB 19.95 (*0-87614-695-7*) Carolrhoda Bks.

Walker, Sloan & Vasey, Andrew. The Only Other Crazy Car Book. LC 83-6546. (Illus.). 48p. (gr. 4 up). 1984. 10.95 (*0-8027-6504-1*); PLB 11.85 (*0-8027-6517-3*) Walker & Co.

—Supertrucks. LC 85-5379. (Illus.). 48p. (gr. 1-4). 1985. 12.95 (*0-8027-6586-6*); PLB 12.85 (*0-8027-6606-4*) Walker & Co.

Walker, Tim & Thompson, Marcia. Current Issues, 1993 Edition: Critical Issues Facing the Nation & the World. rev. ed. Sass, Charles, ed. (Illus.). 384p. (Orig.). (gr. 9-12). 1992. pap. text ed. 12.95 (*0-685-57438-5*, 1142-93); tchr's. ed., suppl. 14.95 (*0-685-57439-3*) Close Up.

Walker, Tom. Death of the Bronx Cop. LC 86-83147. 316p. (Orig.). 1987. pap. 4.95 (*0-9618132-0-2*) Inter Skills Pr.

Walker, Warren S., ed. Twentieth Century Short Story Explication New Series, 1989-1990, Vol. 1. LC 92-22790. vi, 366p. 1993. lib. bdg. 49.50 (*0-208-02340-2*) Shoe String.

Walker-Blondell, Becky. In My Mother's Arms. LC 93-60918. 186p. (gr. 6-12). 1994. 9.95 (*1-55523-647-2*) Winston-Derek.

Walkington, Ethlyn. Betsy Ross, Little Rebel. LC 89-25774. 140p. (Orig.). (gr. 4-6). 1990. pap. 8.95 (*0-944350-13-5*) Friends United.

Walkup, Jane, jt. auth. see Holley, Cynthia.

Wall, Dorothy. Blinky Bill's ABC. (ps-3). 1993. 7.00 (*0-207-17713-9*, Pub. by Angus & Robertson AT) HarpC.

—Complete Adventures of Blinky Bill. (gr. 4-7). 1993. pap. 7.00 (*0-207-16732-X*, Pub. by Angus & Robertson AT) HarpC.

—Tiny Story of Blinky Bill. (ps-3). 1993. 4.50 (*0-207-17468-7*, Pub. by Angus & Robertson AT) HarpC.

Wall, Lina Mao see Mao Wall, Lina & Spagnoli, Cathy.

Wallace. Rock & Roll Mystery, No. 69. 1987. pap. 2.25 (*0-553-26653-5*) Bantam.

Wallace, Annette H. Learning Centers Through the Year. Levin, Ina M., ed. Apodaca, Blanca, et al, illus. 384p. (gr. k-2). 1993. wkbk. 24.95 (*1-55734-059-5*) Tchr Create Mat.

Wallace, Art. Toby & the Phantoms of the Fourth Grade. LC 93-760. (Illus.). (gr. 4-7). 1993. Repr. of 1971 ed. 11.95 (*0-89015-917-3*) Eakin-Sunbelt.

Wallace, Barbara B. Peppermints in the Parlor. 2nd ed. LC 92-33031. 208p. (gr. 3-7). 1993. pap. 3.95 (*0-689-71680-X*, Aladdin) Macmillan Child Grp.

—The Twin in the Tavern. LC 92-36429. 192p. (gr. 3-7). 1993. SBE 14.95 (*0-689-31846-4*, Atheneum Child Bk) Macmillan Child Grp.

Wallace, Bill. Beauty. LC 88-6422. 192p. (gr. 3-7). 1988. 14.95 (*0-8234-0715-2*) Holiday.

—Beauty. (gr. 5). 1990. pap. write for info. (*0-663-56246-5*) Silver Burdett Pr.

—The Biggest Klutz in Fifth Grade. LC 92-52710. 144p. (gr. 3-7). 1992. 14.95 (*0-8234-0984-8*) Holiday.

—The Biggest Klutz in Fifth Grade. MacDonald, Pat, ed. 160p. 1994. pap. 2.99 (*0-671-86970-1*, Minstrel Bks) PB.

—Buffalo Gal. LC 91-28243. 192p. (gr. 5 up). 1992. 14.95 (*0-8234-0943-0*) Holiday.

—The Christmas Spurs. LC 90-55111. 128p. (gr. 3-7). 1990. 13.95 (*0-8234-0831-0*) Holiday.

—The Christmas Spurs. MacDonald, Patricia, ed. De Rosa, Dee, illus. 128p. (gr. 3-7). 1991. pap. 2.99 (*0-671-74505-0*, Minstrel Bks) PB.

—Danger in Quicksand Swamp. LC 89-83485. 196p. (gr. 3-7). 1989. 14.95 (*0-8234-0786-1*) Holiday.

—A Dog Called Kitty. LC 80-16293. 160p. (gr. 3-7). 1980. 14.95 (*0-8234-0376-9*) Holiday.

—Dog Called Kitty. (gr. 4-7). 1991. pap. 2.95 (*0-671-74389-9*, Archway) PB.

—Dog Called Kitty. (gr. 4-7). 1992. pap. 3.50 (*0-671-77081-0*, Minstrel Bks) PB.

—Ferret in the Bedroom, Lizards in the Fridge. LC 85-21996. 144p. (gr. 3-7). 1986. 14.95 (*0-8234-0600-8*) Holiday.

—Never Say Quit. LC 92-54420. 160p. (gr. 3-7). 1993. 14.95 (*0-8234-1013-7*) Holiday.

—Red Dog. LC 86-46202. 192p. (gr. 3-7). 1987. 14.95 (*0-8234-0650-4*) Holiday.

—Red Dog. 176p. (Orig.). (gr. 5-7). 1989. pap. 2.99 (*0-671-70141-X*, Archway) PB.

—Shadow on the Snow. LC 84-48743. 160p. (gr. 4-7). 1985. 14.95 (*0-8234-0557-5*) Holiday.

—Snot Stew. McCue, Lisa, illus. LC 88-31976. 96p. (gr. 3-7). 1989. 13.95 (*0-8234-0745-4*) Holiday.

—Snot Stew. McCue, Lisa, illus. 96p. 1990. pap. 2.99 (*0-671-69335-2*, Minstrel Bks) PB.

—Totally Disgusting! Morrill, Leslie, illus. LC 90-47561. 112p. (gr. 3-7). 1991. 13.95 (*0-8234-0873-6*) Holiday.

—Totally Disgusting. MacDonald, Pat, ed. 128p. 1992. pap. 2.99 (*0-671-75416-5*, Minstrel Bks) PB.

—Trapped in Death Cave. LC 83-48962. 176p. (gr. 4-7). 1984. 14.95 (*0-8234-0516-8*) Holiday.

Wallace, Brooks B. Argyle. Sandford, John, illus. LC 91-76021. 32p. (ps-3). 1992. 13.95 (*1-56397-043-0*) Boyds Mills Pr.

Wallace, Carol M. Should You Shut Your Eyes When You Kiss? Or, How to Survive "The Best Years of Your Life" Weston, Martha, illus. LC 83-5458. 112p. (gr. 7 up). 1983. 13.45i (*0-316-91998-5*) Little.

Wallace, Daisy, ed. Fairy Poems. Hyman, Trina S., illus. LC 79-18763. 32p. (ps-3). 1980. reinforced bdg. 13.95 (*0-8234-0371-8*) Holiday.

—Ghost Poems. LC 78-11028. (Illus.). 32p. (ps-3). 1979. reinforced bdg. 13.95 (*0-8234-0344-0*); pap. 4.95 (*0-8234-0849-3*) Holiday.

—Monster Poems. Chorao, Kay, illus. LC 75-17680. 32p. (ps-3). 1976. reinforced bdg. 13.95 (*0-8234-0268-1*); pap. 4.95 (*0-8234-0848-5*) Holiday.

—Witch Poems. Hyman, Trina S., illus. LC 76-9035. 32p. (ps-3). 1976. reinforced bdg. 13.95 (*0-8234-0281-9*); pap. 4.95 (*0-8234-0850-7*) Holiday.

Wallace, David. Money Basics: An Introduction for Young People. D'Amato, Janet, illus. 48p. 1984. 9.95 (*0-13-600479-2*) P-H.

Wallace, Don. Water Sports Basics. Petronella, Michael, illus. LC 84-22294. 48p. (gr. 3-7). 1985. 9.95 (*0-13-945957-X*) P-H.

Wallace, Dorathye, ed. see Morgan, Judith.

Wallace, Dorothy, ed. see Morgan, Judith.

Wallace, Ian. Chin Chiang & the Dragon's Dance. LC 83-13442. (Illus.). 32p. (gr. k-4). 1984. SBE 13.95 (*0-689-50299-0*, M K McElderry) Macmillan Child Grp.

—Morgan the Magnificent. Wallace, Ian, illus. LC 87-15482. 32p. (gr. k-4). 1988. SBE 13.95 (*0-689-50441-1*, M K McElderry) Macmillan Child Grp.

Wallace, Ian, et al. Bird Life. Quinn, David, et al, illus. 32p. (gr. 4-7). 1985. lib. bdg. 13.96 (*0-88110-172-9*); pap. 5.95 (*0-86020-841-9*) EDC.

Wallace, Jane. Poles & Gridwork, No. 26: Threshold Picture Guide. Vincer, Carole, illus. 24p. (Orig.). 1993. pap. 12.00 (*1-872082-44-0*, Pub. by Kenilworth Pr UK) Half Halt Pr.

—Solving Flatwork Problems, No. 25: Threshold Picture Guide. Vincer, Carole, illus. 24p. (Orig.). 1993. pap. 12.00 (*1-872082-43-2*, Pub. by Kenilworth Pr UK) Half Halt Pr.

Wallace, Jeffery S. Discovering the Four Seasons. Bittner, Bob, ed. LC 92-43796. (Illus.). 128p. (gr. 3-6). 1993. pap. 7.99 (*0-7459-2617-7*) Lion USA.

Wallace, Jim. Search for the Mountain Gorillas. 128p. (gr. 6 up). 1985. pap. 2.25 (*0-553-26062-6*) Bantam.

Wallace, Karen. My Hen is Dancing: Read & Wonder Bks. Jeram, Anita, illus. LC 93-930. (ps-3). 1994. 14.95 (*1-56402-303-6*) Candlewick Pr.

—Red Fox. Melnyczuk, Peter, illus. LC 93-32381. 1994. write for info. (*1-56402-422-9*) Candlewick Pr.

—Think of a Beaver. Manning, Mick, illus. LC 92-53132. 32p. (gr. k-4). 1993. 14.95 (*1-56402-179-3*) Candlewick Pr.

—Think of an Eel. Bostock, Mike, illus. LC 92-53131. 32p. (gr. k-4). 1993. 14.95 (*1-56402-180-7*) Candlewick Pr.

—Why Count Sheep? A Bedtime Book. Aggs, Patrice, illus. LC 92-56140. 32p. (ps-1). 1993. 13.95 (*1-56282-528-3*); PLB 13.89 (*1-56282-529-1*) Hyprn Child.

Wallace, Latressia & Wilson, Annette. Black Wallstreet Children's Storybook: A Black City Made of Gold! Wilson, Jay J. & Wallace, Ron, eds. Wilson, Mike, illus. 32p. (Orig.). (ps-5). 1993. pap. text ed. 8.95 (*1-884265-02-2*) Black Wallst.

Wallace, Lew. Ben Hur. Bennet, C. L., intro. by. (gr. 9 up). 1965. pap. 2.95 (*0-8049-0074-4*, CL-74) Airmont.

—Ben Hur. Larson, Dan, ed. Bohl, Al, illus. 224p. (Orig.). (gr. 6 up). 1990. pap. text ed. 2.50 (*1-55748-114-8*) Barbour & Co.

Wallace, Lewis. Ben Hur. 450p. 1981. Repr. lib. bdg. 27.95x (*0-89966-289-7*) Buccaneer Bks.

Wallace, M. Imelda, Sr. Outlaws of Ravenhurst. new ed. Schuster, L. A., illus. (gr. 6-10). 1950. 12.95 (*0-910334-25-0*); pap. 5.95 (*0-910334-26-9*) Cath Authors.

Wallace, Mary. How to Make Great Stuff for Your Room. Wallace, Mary, illus. 88p. 1992. pap. 8.95 (*0-920775-85-3*, Pub. by Greey de Pencier CN) Firefly Bks Ltd.

Wallace, Mary H. Profiles of Pentecostal Missionaries. Agnew, Tim, contrib. by. LC 86-15919. (Illus.). 352p. (Orig.). 1986. pap. 7.99 (*0-932581-00-5*) Word Aflame.

Wallace, Pamela. Partners in Crime. 1990. pap. 4.50 (*0-553-28472-X*) Bantam.

Wallace, Roger, jt. auth. see Burke, Amy M.

Wallace, Ron, ed. see Wallace, Latressia & Wilson, Annette.

Wallace, Zara & Cook, Elizabeth, eds. Gesar! The Wondrous Adventures of King Gesar of Tibet. Witwer, Julia, illus. LC 91-35260. 190p. (Orig.). (gr. 10-12). 1991. pap. 11.95 (*0-89800-223-0*) Dharma Pub.

Wallace-Brodeur, Ruth. The Godmother Tree. LC 91-17951. 128p. (gr. 3-7). 1992. 13.00 (*0-06-022457-6*); PLB 12.89 (*0-06-022458-4*) HarpC Child Bks.

—Home by Five. Graham, Mark, illus. LC 90-39854. 32p. (gr. k-4). 1992. SBE 13.95 (*0-689-50509-4*, M K McElderry) Macmillan Child Grp.

Wallach, Paul I., jt. auth. see Hepler, Donald E.

Wallach, Susan. Great Parties, How to Plan Them. Magnuson, Diana, illus. LC 90-46879. 128p. (gr. 5-9). 1991. PLB 10.89 (*0-8167-2291-9*); pap. text ed. 2.95 (*0-8167-2292-7*) Troll Assocs.

—Operation Isolation. (gr. 4-7). 1993. pap. 3.50 (*0-553-48068-5*) Bantam.

Wallenhorst, Ralph. Ralfs Stories - Princes, Monsters & Magic. Bennett, Gail, et al, illus. LC 89-38025. 128p. (Orig.). (gr. 3-6). 1989. 12.00x (*0-9622905-0-5*); pap. 6.00x (*0-9622905-1-3*) Dragon Tale.

Waller, Barrett. New Feet for Old. Stevenson, Harvey, illus. LC 90-21339. 32p. (gr. k-3). 1992. RSBE 13.95 (*0-02-792371-1*, Four Winds) Macmillan Child Grp.

Waller, Leslie. The Mob: The Story of Organized Crime in America. LC 73-6242. 160p. (gr. 7 up). 1973. pap. 5.95 (*0-440-05720-5*) Delacorte.

Waller, Lynn. How Do We Know the Bible Is True? Reasons a Kid Can Believe It. 64p. (gr. 3-7). 1991. pap. 4.99 (*0-310-53821-1*, Youth Bks) Zondervan.

Waller, Rayfield. Abstract Blues. LC 88-70737. (gr. 12 up). 1988. pap. 5.00 (*0-940713-01-2*) Broadside Pr.

Waller, Victoria, jt. auth. see Kramer, Estelle.

Waller, Victoria E., jt. auth. see Kramer, Estelle R.

Waller, Wanda W. Unicorns & Dreams. Lopez, Ron, ed. Perrin, Sandra, illus. 39p. (Orig.). (gr. k-6). 1985. pap. 4.95 (*0-930825-00-4*) Lola Library.

Walley, Dean & Ingle, Annie. A Visit to the Haunted House. Noel, Arlene, illus. 14p. (ps-3). 1992. 7.99 (*0-679-82450-2*) Random Bks Yng Read.

Walley, Deborah. Grandfather's Good Medicine. Thorne, Kate & Callou, Nadia, eds. Thompson, Tommy, illus. 72p. (Orig.). (gr. k up). 1993. pap. 9.95 (*0-9628329-6-0*) Thorne Enterprises. GRANDFATHER'S GOOD MEDICINE is a children's book for all ages; that is, a children's book that can be appreciated by adults as well as children. Its message is universal, its stories timeless & timely. It is a profound & poignant trilogy of stories containing an important message concerning man's relationship to his environment as seen through the Native

American eye & expressed through the imagination of three non-native children. In each of the three parts, GRANDFATHER tells a story to a young person in modern times that parallels his or her current situation, taking us back to a time when white man was only a rumor & the people still roamed freely over the land. The highly entertaining & thought provoking stories are based on Native American folklore & the MEDICINE WHEEL WAY. Exquisitely illustrated by renowned Navajo artist Tommy Thompson. This is a book to delight all ages. To order contact: THORNE ENTERPRISES, 149 Gambol Lane, Sedona, AZ 86336. (602) 282-7508. *Publisher Provided Annotation.*

Walley, Susan. Best of Friends. Lyall, Elizabeth, ed. Halverson, Tom, illus. 156p. (Orig.). (gr. 4-8). 1989. pap. 4.95 (0-89084-486-0) Bob Jones Univ Pr.
Wallin, Marie L. Tangles. 122p. (gr. 6-9). 1980. pap. 1.50 (0-440-99055-6, LFL) Dell.

Wallington, Dwight F. In the Child's Best Interest. 1993. 18.95 (1-881636-01-1) Forever Truth.
In a comprehensive defense of the abused child Dwight Wallington explores the shambles of divorce, habitual drunkeness & other family problems. He knows these problems inside & out from having been an abused child. He has constructive suggestions for helping children recover. One innovative idea is to provide a complaint &/or bright-idea-clipboard accessible to all family members. Another is to gradually enlist the child's help in routine chores & to establish duties, privileges & schedules to give children pride of accomplishment & security in the knowledge of what is expected. If you need in-depth practical solutions you will benefit from the mature wisdom of IN THE CHILD'S BEST INTEREST. Another special book by D. Wallington - a novel titled: The Maple Still Stands. Beyond the broken heart CAUSED BY ABUSE, there can be LOVE, YOU WILL WANT TO PLACE AN ORDER NOW FOR THIS THRILLING ROMANCE NOVEL, THOUGH LORAINE FALLS IN LOVE WITH MARK, AT TIMES HE RESPONDS, HE IS NEVER FREE OF THE STRINGS THAT HAD BECOME CORDS AROUND HIS HEART, OLD FRIENDS STANDING BENEATH THE TREE, A GATHERING OF CHILDREN WHO HAVE BEEN HELPED, LORAINE & A SPECIAL PERSON...WHO FINALLY IS ABLE TO READ THE TRUTH, where THE MAPLE STILL STANDS. *Publisher Provided Annotation.*

Wallington, Neil. Firefighters. Stefoff, Rebecca, ed. LC 91-41210. (Illus.). 32p. (gr. 5-9). 1992. PLB 17.26 (1-56074-044-2) Garrett Ed Corp.
Wallis, Diz. A Jar Full of Mice. Wallis, Diz, illus. LC 90-85919. 24p. 1991. 5.95 (1-878093-42-8) Boyds Mills Pr.
—Pip's Adventure. Wallis, Diz, illus. LC 90-85917. 24p. (ps up). 1991. 5.95 (1-878093-43-6) Boyds Mills Pr.
—Something Nasty in the Cabbages. Wallis, Diz, illus. LC 90-84007. 32p. 1991. 15.95 (1-878093-10-X); poster avail. (1-56397-000-7, Caroline Hse) Boyds Mills Pr.

Wallis, James & Siembieda, Kevin. Mutants in Avalon. Marciniszyn, Alex & Bartold, Thomas, eds. Fales, Kevin & MacDougall, Larry, illus. 80p. (Orig.). (gr. 8 up). 1991. pap. 9.95 (0-916211-47-9, 513) Palladium Bks.
Wallis, James & Sienbieda, Kevin. Mutants in Orbit. Marciniszyn, Alex, et al, eds. Gustovich, Mike & Ewell, Newton, illus. 112p. (Orig.). (gr. 8 up). 1992. pap. 11.95 (0-916211-48-7, 514) Palladium Bks.
Wallis, Lisa. Island Child. Haeffele, Deborah, illus. 32p. (gr. k-3). 1992. 14.00 (0-525-67324-5, Lodestar Bks) Dutton Child Bks.
Wallis, Reginald. The New Venture. (gr. 3-7). 1935. pap. 0.85 (0-87213-914-X) Loizeaux.
Wallner. Progressive Careers. 1991. 12.95s.p. (0-86593-123-2); 17.27 (0-685-59205-7) Rourke Corp.
Wallner, Alexander. Since Nineteen Twenty. LC 90-3646. (Illus.). 32p. (ps-3). 1992. pap. 15.00 (0-385-41216-9) Doubleday.
Wallner, Alexandra. Betsy Ross. Wallner, Alexandra, illus. LC 93-3559. 32p. (gr. 4-8). 1994. 15.95 (0-8234-1071-4) Holiday.
—Ghoulish Giggles & Monster Riddles. Tucker, Kathy, ed. Wallner, Alexandra, illus. LC 82-10969. 32p. (gr. 1-5). 1983. PLB 8.95 (0-8075-2863-3) A Whitman.
—Glitter Glow-Deck the Halls. Wallner, Alexandra, illus. 1989. 4.95 (1-55782-317-0, Pub. by Warner Juvenile Bks) Little.
—Glitter Glow-Jingle Bells. 1989. 4.95 (1-55782-315-4, Pub. by Warner Juvenile Bks) Little.
—Glitter Glow-Silent Night. 1989. 4.95 (1-55782-316-2, Pub. by Warner Juvenile Bks) Little.
—Glitter Glow-Twelve Days of Christmas. 1989. 4.95 (1-55782-318-9, Pub. by Warner Juvenile Bks) Little.
Wallner, John. City Mouse - Country Mouse & Two More Tales from Aesop. Wallner, John, illus. 32p. (Orig.). (gr. k-3). 1987. pap. 2.50 (0-590-41155-1) Scholastic Inc.
—Rumpelstiltskin. Wallner, John, illus. LC 83-19100. 32p. 1984. 10.95 (0-13-783747-X) P-H.
—Sleeping Beauty. (ps-3). 1987. pap. 7.95 (0-670-81708-2) Viking Child Bks.
Wallner, John, illus. Good King Wenceslas. 32p. 1990. 14.95 (0-399-21620-0, Philomel Bks) Putnam Pub Group.
Wallner, Rosemary. Barbara Bush. LC 91-73028. 32p. 1991. 12.94 (1-56239-079-1) Abdo & Dghtrs.
—Beverly Hills 90210. LC 92-16789. 1992. 12.94 (1-56239-139-9) Abdo & Dghtrs.
—Blossom. LC 92-14779. 1992. 12.94 (1-56239-141-0) Abdo & Dghtrs.
—Family Matters. LC 92-16788. 1992. 12.94 (1-56239-142-9) Abdo & Dghtrs.
—Fresh Prince of Bel Air. LC 92-16790. 1992. 12.94 (1-56239-140-2) Abdo & Dghtrs.
—Garth Brooks. LC 93-4175. 1993. 12.94 (1-56239-229-8) Abdo & Dghtrs.
—Julia Roberts. LC 91-73038. 1991. 12.94 (1-56239-055-4) Abdo & Dghtrs.
—Luke Perry. LC 92-16036. 1992. 12.94 (1-56239-146-1) Abdo & Dghtrs.
—M. C. Hammer. LC 91-73039. 202p. 1991. 12.94 (1-56239-054-6) Abdo & Dghtrs.
—Macaulay Culkin. LC 93-19061. (Illus.). 1993. 12.94 (1-56239-227-1) Abdo & Dghtrs.
—Michael Jackson. LC 91-73036. 202p. 1991. 12.94 (1-56239-057-0) Abdo & Dghtrs.
—Wynonna Judd. LC 91-73037. 202p. 1991. 12.94 (1-56239-056-2) Abdo & Dghtrs.
Wallner, Rosemary, jt. auth. see Espeland, Pamela.
Wallner, Rosemary, ed. see Bach, Julie.
Wallner, Rosemary, ed. see Dahlstrom, Lorraine M.
Wallner, Rosemary, ed. see Deegan, Paul J.
Wallner, Rosemary, ed. see Italia, Bob.
Wallner, Rosemary, ed. see Italia, Robert.
Wallner, Rosemary, ed. see Kallen, Stuart A.
Wallner, Rosemary, ed. see Karnes, Frances A. & Bean, Suzanne M.
Wallner, Rosemary, ed. see Nielsen, Shelly.
Wallner, Rosemary, ed. see Roberts, Gail C. & Guttormson, Lorraine.
Wallner, Rosemary, ed. see Wheeler, Jill.
Wallner, Rosie, ed. see Italia, Bob.
Wallner, S. J. Friendly Little Hobo. LC 68-56814. (Illus.). 48p. (gr. 2-4). 1968. PLB 10.95 (0-87783-013-4); pap. 3.94 deluxe ed. (0-87783-092-4) Oddo.
—Hans & the Golden Stirrup. LC 68-56815. (Illus.). 48p. (gr. 2-3). PLB 10.95 (0-87783-016-9); pap. 3.94 deluxe ed. (0-87783-093-2) Oddo.
Wallower, Lucille. All about Pennsylvania. Wholey, Ellen J., ed. Wallower, Lucille, illus. (gr. 3-4). 1984. pap. 4.55 (0-931992-05-2) Penns Valley.
—Indians of Pennsylvania Workshop. LC 76-12651. (gr. 3-4). 1985. pap. 4.90 (0-931992-53-2) Penns Valley.
—My Book about Abraham Lincoln. Gump, Patricia L., ed. (gr. 2-4). 1967. pap. 1.95 (0-931992-10-9) Penns Valley.
—The Pennsylvania Dutch. Gump, Patricia L., ed. (gr. 3-4). 1971. pap. 3.75 (0-931992-31-1) Penns Valley.
—Pennsylvania: The Keystone State. (gr. 4). 1987. 11.95 (0-931992-55-9) Penns Valley.
—Your Pennsylvania. Brebner, Daphne B. & Stevens, S. K., eds. (gr. 4-6). 1959. 6.35 (0-931992-07-9) Penns Valley.
—Your State: Pennsylvania. Gump, Patricia L., ed. (gr. 3-4). 1984. pap. 4.90 (0-931992-09-5) Penns Valley.

Wallower, Lucille & Wholey, Ellen J. They Came to Pennsylvania Workshop. LC 76-14140. (gr. 4-5). 1984. pap. 4.65 (0-931992-02-8) Penns Valley.
Wallower, Lucille & Wier, Bernice. The New Pennsylvania Primer. (gr. 3-4). 1984. 9.45 (0-931992-04-4) Penns Valley.
Walls, Jerry G. Your First Lizard. 34p. (Orig.). (gr. 1-6). 1991. pap. 1.95 (0-86622-068-2, YF-111) TFH Pubns.
Walls, Thomas K. The Japanese Texans. LC 87-50131. (Illus.). 256p. (gr. 8 up). 1987. 14.95 (0-86701-021-5); pap. 8.95 (0-86701-022-3) U of Tex Inst Tex Culture.
Walmer, M. Battleships. (Illus.). 48p. (gr. 3-8). 1989. lib. bdg. 18.60 (0-86625-083-2) Rourke Corp.
—Destroyers. (Illus.). 48p. (gr. 3-8). 1989. lib. bdg. 18.60 (0-86625-081-6) Rourke Corp.
—Frigates. (Illus.). 48p. (gr. 3-8). 1989. lib. bdg. 18.60 (0-86625-082-4); 13.95s.p. (0-685-58643-X) Rourke Corp.
Walmer, Max & Rawlinson, Jon. Sea Power Library, 6 bks, Reading Level 5. (Illus.). 288p. (gr. 3-8). 1989. Set. PLB 111.60 (0-86625-087-5); 18.60 (0-685-58760-6); 13.95 (0-685-58761-4) Rourke Corp.
Walne, Sarah W. Memphis Mazes. 32p. (gr. 1-6). 1992. text ed. 12.95 (1-881207-00-5); pap. text ed. 8.95 (1-881207-01-3); tchr's. manual 9.95 (1-881207-02-1); tape 7.95 (1-881207-03-X) City Mazes.
Walner, Rosemary, ed. see Italia, Bob.
Walner, Rosemary, ed. see Kallen, Stuart.
Walnum, Clayton. DataMania: A Child's Computer Organizer. (Illus., Orig.). (gr. k up). 1992. pap. 19.95 (0-672-30207-1) Alpha Bks IN.
Walpole, Brenda. One Hundred Seventy-Five Science Experiments to Amuse & Amaze Your Friends. Kuo Kang Chen & Bull, Peter, illus. LC 88-4526. 176p. (Orig.). (gr. 4-7). 1988. pap. 12.00 (0-394-89991-1) Random Bks Yng Read.
—Water. Stefoff, Rebecca, ed. Barber, Ed, photos by. LC 90-40381. (Illus.). 32p. (gr. 3-5). 1990. PLB 15.93 (0-944483-72-0) Garrett Ed Corp.
Walrond, H., jt. auth. see Longman, C. J.
Walser, David, tr. see Grimm, Jacob, et al.
Walsh, Abigail. Exploring the Numbers One to Ten. Dowling, Marilyn, illus. 24p. (ps-2). Date not set. PLB 11.95 (1-56065-108-3) Capstone Pr. Postponed.
—Exploring the Seasons. Dowling, Marilyn, illus. 24p. (ps-2). Date not set. PLB 11.95 (1-56065-109-1) Capstone Pr. Postponed.
Walsh, Abigail M. Momma Cat. Dowling, Marilyn, illus. LC 90-823. 112p. (gr. 2 up). 1990. 6.95 (0-934745-16-1) Acadia Pub Co.
Walsh, Adrian, jt. auth. see Harris, Paul.
Walsh, Amanda. The Buried Moon. Walsh, Amanda, illus. 32p. 1991. 14.45 (0-395-59349-2, Sandpiper) HM.
Walsh, Caroline. The Little Book of Prayers. Moore, Inga, illus. LC 92-30860. 1993. 7.95 (1-85697-888-5) Kingfisher Bks.
Walsh, Caroline, selected by. The Little Book of Poems. Marklew, Gilly, illus. LC 92-29126. 1993. 7.95 (1-85697-887-7) Kingfisher Bks.
Walsh, Chad. Knock & Enter. 208p. (gr. 6-9). 1953. pap. 4.95 (0-8192-1076-5) Morehouse Pub.
Walsh, Ellen S. Brunus & the New Bear. LC 92-29060. 1993. pap. 4.95 (0-15-212675-9) HarBrace.
—Hop Jump. LC 92-21037. 1993. 13.95 (0-15-292871-5) HarBrace.
—Mouse Count. D'Andrade, Diane, ed. Walsh, Ellen S., illus. 32p. (ps-1). 1991. 11.95 (0-15-256023-8) HarBrace.
—Mouse Paint. Walsh, Ellen S., illus. 32p. (ps-1). 1989. 11.95 (0-15-256025-4) HarBrace.
—Mouse Paint. (ps-1). 1991. pap. 19.95 (0-15-256026-2, HB Juv Bks) HarBrace.
—Pip's Magic. 1994. 13.95t (0-15-292850-2) HarBrace.
—You Silly Goose. 1992. 13.95 (0-15-299865-9, HB Juv Bks) HarBrace.
Walsh, Jeff. An Open Road & a Full Tank of Gas, Pt. 1. Bonner, Darlene, ed. (Illus.). 108p. (Orig.). 1993. pap. 8.95 (0-9636883-0-8) Walsh Assocs.
Walsh, Jill P. A Chance Child. 144p. (gr. 7 up). 1980. pap. 1.95 (0-380-48561-3, 48561-3, Flare) Avon.
—The Emperor's Winding Sheet. 288p. (gr. 7 up). 1992. pap. 4.95 (0-374-42121-8, Sunburst) FS&G.
—Matthew & the Sea Singer. (ps-3). 1993. 13.00 (0-374-34869-3) FS&G.
—When Grandma Came. Williams, Sophy, illus. 32p. (ps-3). 1992. 13.00 (0-670-83581-1) Viking Child Bks.
Walsh, Jill Paton see Paton Walsh, Jill.
Walsh, John see Hubbard, Kate & Berlin, Evelyn.
Walsh, John see Meyer, Linda D.
Walsh, Joy & Fuda, Siri, eds. Life Junkies: On Our Own. (Illus.). 200p. (gr. 9-12). 1990. pap. 8.00 (0-938838-51-2) Textile Bridge.
Walsh, Joy, ed. see Perry, Marion.
Walsh, Kevin, tr. see Biffi, Inos.
Walsh, Moira, jt. auth. see Cuyler, Juliana.
Walsh, Rita A. The Worst Show-and-Tell Ever. Tusan, Stan L., illus. LC 93-24844. 32p. (gr. 2-4). 1993. PLB 9.89 (0-8167-3176-4); pap. text ed. 2.95 (0-8167-3177-2) Troll Assocs.
Walsh, Vincent M. Prepare My People. 100p. (Orig.). 1986. pap. text ed. 5.00 (0-943374-13-8) Key of David.
Walsh, Vivian & Seibold, J. Otto. Mr. Lunch Takes a Plane Ride. Seibold, J. Otto, illus. 40p. (ps-3). 1993. RB 13.99 (0-670-84775-5) Viking Child Bks.
Walsh, White see Hubbard, Kate & Berlin, Evelyn.

Walshaw, Rachela & Walshaw, Sam. From Out of the Firestorm: A Memoir of the Holocaust. 260p. (gr. 5-8). 1990. pap. 10.95 (*1-56171-021-0*) Shapolsky Pubs.

Walshaw, Sam, jt. auth. see Walshaw, Rachela.

Walston, Mark. The Department of the Treasury. (Illus.). 128p. (gr. 5 up). 1989. 14.95 (*0-87754-848-X*) Chelsea Hse.

—The Education of an Egg. Walston, Dennis, illus. 48p. (Orig.). (gr. 7 up). 1982. pap. 6.95 (*0-9605776-2-9*) Sparhawk.

Walsum-Quispel, J. van. Tina's Island Home. Leeflang-Oudenarden, C., illus. LC 71-99920. 36p. (gr. k-5). 7.95 (*0-87592-053-5*) Scroll Pr.

Walt Disney Company Staff. Disney's Adventureland. (Illus.). (ps-1). 1989. Contains "Robin Hood & the Daring Mouse," "The Sword in the Stone: the Wizards' Duel," & "The Aristocats" write for info. (*0-307-15752-0*, Golden Pr) Western Pub.

—Disney's Christmas Stories. (Illus.). (ps-1). 1989. Contains "Donald Duck's Christmas Tree," "Santa's Toy Shop," & "Mickey's Christmas Carol" write for info. (*0-307-15750-4*, Golden Pr) Western Pub.

—Disney's Ducktales: Down the Drain. (Illus.). 24p. (ps-3). 1990. pap. write for info. (*0-307-11726-X*, Pub. by Golden Bks) Western Pub.

—Disney's Fantasyland. (Illus.). (ps-1). 1989. Contains "Mickey & the Beanstalk", "The Three Little Pigs," & "Mother Goose" write for info. (*0-307-15753-9*, Golden Pr) Western Pub.

—Disney's Mickey Mouse Stories. (Illus.). (ps-1). 1989. Repr. of 1971 ed. Contains "Mickey Mouse Heads for the Sky," "Mickey Mouse & Goofy: the Big Bear Scare," & "Mickey Mouse: Those Were the Days" write for info. (*0-307-15751-2*, Golden Pr) Western Pub.

—The New Walt Disney Treasury. (Illus.). (gr. 1-7). 1989. Repr. of 1971 ed. 8.95 (*0-685-50468-9*, Golden Pr) Western Pub.

—Reindeer Round-Up: A Merry Christmas at the North Pole. Walt Disney Company Staff, illus. 26p. (ps up). 1988. 19.95 (*1-55578-313-9*) Worlds Wonder.

—Walt Disney's Peter Pan. (Illus.). 24p. (ps-2). 1989. write for info. (*0-307-12081-3*, Pub. by Golden Bks) Western Pub.

Walt Disney Music Co. Staff, illus. Disney Afternoon Songbook. 80p. (Orig.). 1991. pap. 12.95 (*0-7935-0346-9*, 00490518) H Leonard Pub.

Walt Disney Productions. Rescuers Down Under. 1990. 6.98 (*0-8317-7389-8*) Viking Child Bks.

Walt Disney Staff. Aladdin. (ps-3). 1992. 6.98 (*0-453-03058-0*) Mouse Works.

—Aladdin Bath Book. (ps-3). 1992. 5.98 (*0-453-03060-2*) Mouse Works.

—Aladdin Little Library. (ps-3). 1992. 5.98 (*0-453-03059-9*) Mouse Works.

—Aladdin Puzzle Play Book. (ps-3). 1993. pap. 5.98 (*0-453-03062-9*) Mouse Works.

—Alice in Wonderland. 1988. 6.98 (*0-8317-0287-7*) Viking Child Bks.

—Bambi. (ps-3). 1992. 6.98 (*0-453-03019-X*) Viking-Penguin.

—Beauty & the Beast Bath Book. (ps-3). 1992. 5.98 (*0-453-03055-6*) Viking Child Bks.

—Beauty & the Beast Puzzle Play Book. (ps-3). 1993. pap. 5.98 (*0-453-03095-5*) Mouse Works.

—La Bella y la Bestia (Beauty & the Beast) (SPA.). (ps-3). 1992. 6.98 (*0-453-03016-5*) Viking-Penguin.

—Black Cauldron. (ps-3). 1993. 6.98 (*0-453-03154-4*) Viking Child Bks.

—Cars! Cars! Cars! Featuring "The Love Bug" & Other Fun on Wheels. LC 77-74465. (Illus.). (gr. 2-6). 1977. lib. bdg. 4.99 (*0-394-93598-5*) Random Bks Yng Read.

—Cinderella. 1987. 6.98 (*0-8317-1309-7*) Viking Child Bks.

—The Circus Book Featuring "Toby Tyler" LC 77-74462. (Illus.). (gr. 2-6). 1978. lib. bdg. 4.99 (*0-394-93597-7*) Random Bks Yng Read.

—Disney Babies Bath Books: I Can Spell. 1989. 5.98 (*0-8317-2480-3*) Viking Child Bks.

—Disney Babies Bath Books: I Love Opposites. 1989. 5.98 (*0-8317-2481-1*) Viking Child Bks.

—Disney's Princess Treasury Collection: Snow White & the Seven Dwarfs, Cinderella, Sleeping Beauty. (ps-3). 1993. 6.98 (*0-453-03100-5*) NAL-Dutton.

—Donald & His Friends. 1988. 6.98 (*0-8317-2392-0*) Viking Child Bks.

—Dumbo. 1987. 6.98 (*0-8317-2463-3*) Viking Child Bks.

—Follow that Squeak with Mickey Mouse. (ps-3). 1993. 6.98 (*0-453-03092-0*) Mouse Works.

—Fox & the Hound. 1988. 6.98 (*0-8317-3472-8*) Viking Child Bks.

—Great Mouse Detective. 1988. 6.98 (*0-8317-3993-2*) Viking Child Bks.

—Jungle Book. 1987. 6.98 (*0-8317-5291-2*) Viking Child Bks.

—Lady & the Tramp. 1987. 6.98 (*0-8317-5411-7*) Viking Child Bks.

—Little Mermaid. 1989. 6.98 (*0-8317-5605-5*) Viking Child Bks.

—Little Mermaid Disney Little Libraries. (ps-3). 1992. 5.98 (*0-453-03076-9*) Viking Child Bks.

—Meet the Seven Dwarfs: Interlocking Board Books. (ps). 1993. 5.98 (*0-453-03106-4*) NAL-Dutton.

—Mickey's Christmas Carol. 1988. 6.98 (*0-8317-5929-1*) Viking Child Bks.

—La Noche de las Narices Frias (One Hundred One Dalmatians) (SPA.). (ps-3). 1992. 6.98 (*0-453-03018-1*) Viking-Penguin.

—One Hundred One Dalmatians. (gr. 3 up). 1987. 6.98 (*0-453-03005-X*) Viking Penguin.

—Perils of Mickey: The Mail Pilot. (ps-3). 1993. pap. 2.25 (*0-307-12794-X*, Pub. by Golden Bks) Western Pub.

—Perils of Mickey: The Seven Ghosts. (ps-3). 1993. pap. 2.25 (*0-307-12793-1*, Pub. by Golden Bks) Western Pub.

—Peter Pan. 1987. 6.98 (*0-8317-6799-5*) Viking Child Bks.

—Peter Pan. (ps-3). 1992. 6.98 (*0-453-03053-X*) Viking Child Bks.

—Pinocchio. 1987. 6.98 (*0-8317-6889-4*) Viking Child Bks.

—Pinocchio. (ps-3). 1992. 6.98 (*0-453-03026-2*) Viking-Penguin.

—Pinocchio Bath Book. (ps). 1992. 5.98 (*0-453-03028-9*) Viking-Penguin.

—Pinocchio Little Library. (ps-3). 1992. 5.98 (*0-453-03027-0*) Viking-Penguin.

—Pop-Up Aladdin. (ps-3). 1993. pap. 5.98 (*0-453-03098-X*) Mouse Works.

—The Rescuers. (gr. 5-8). 1989. 6.98 (*0-8317-7388-X*) Viking Child Bks.

—Robin Hood. 1989. 6.98 (*0-8317-7408-8*) Viking Child Bks.

—Rub-a-Dub-Dub Seven Dwarfs & a Tub Bath Book. (ps). 1993. 5.98 (*0-453-03099-8*) NAL-Dutton.

—La Sirenita (The Little Mermaid) (SPA.). (ps-3). 1992. 6.98 (*0-453-03017-3*) Viking-Penguin.

—Sleeping Beauty. 1987. 6.98 (*0-8317-7863-6*) Viking Child Bks.

—Snow White & the Seven Dwarfs. 1987. 6.98 (*0-8317-7885-7*) Viking Child Bks.

—Snow White & the Seven Dwarfs Little Library. (ps). 1993. 5.98 (*0-453-03105-6*) NAL-Dutton.

—Snow White Meets the Dwarves Pop-up Book. (ps). 1993. 6.98 (*0-453-03097-1*) NAL-Dutton.

—Snuggle Up with Winnie the Pooh. (ps). 1993. 6.98 (*0-453-03104-8*) Mouse Works.

—Sorcerer's Apprentice. (ps-3). 1992. 5.98 (*0-453-03025-4*) Viking-Penguin.

—Sword in the Stone. 1988. 6.98 (*0-8317-8015-0*) Viking Child Bks.

—The Underwater Adventure Book Featuring "20,000 Leagues Under the Sea" LC 77-90198. (gr. 3-7). 1978. lib. bdg. 4.99 (*0-394-93602-7*) Random Bks Yng Read.

—Winnie the Pooh. 1992. 6.98 (*0-453-03014-9*) Mouse Works.

Walt Disney's Feature Animation Dept. Staff. Disney's Aladdin: An Animated Flip Book. 96p. 1992. bds. 3.95 (*1-56282-889-4*) Disney Pr.

—Disney's Beauty & the Beast: An Animated Flip Book. 96p. 1992. pap. 3.95 (*1-56282-888-6*) Disney Pr.

Walt Disney's Feature Animation Dept. Animators Staff. Walt Disney's Mickey Mouse in "The Little Whirlwind" An Animated Flip Book. 96p. 1993. pap. 3.95 (*1-56282-837-1*) Hyperion.

—Walt Disney's Snow White: An Animated Flip Book. (Illus.). 96p. 1993. pap. 3.95 (*1-56282-838-X*) Hyperion.

Walter, Dean S. Pages of My Mind. Teasley, Jamie. ed. 45p. 1990. pap. 4.95 (*1-55523-280-9*) Winston-Derek.

Walter, Elma, jt. auth. see Walter, Willard.

Walter, Eugene. Mobile Mardi Gras Annual 1948, Vol. 1, No. 2. Plummer, Cameron. ed. Walter, Eugene, illus. 32p. (gr. 7 up). 1948. pap. 10.00 (*0-940882-05-1*) HB Pubns.

Walter, F. Virginia. Fun with Paper Bags & Cardboard Tubes. Long, Teddy C., illus. LC 92-14944. 80p. (gr. 5 up). 1992. 17.95 (*1-895569-908-7*) Sterling.

—Great Newspaper Crafts. LC 90-20731. (Illus.). 80p. (gr. 3 up). 1991. pap. 17.95 (*0-920534-75-9*, Pub. by Hyperion Pr Ltd CN) Sterling.

—Great Newspaper Crafts. LC 90-20731. 80p. (gr. 4 up). 1993. pap. 9.95 (*0-920534-79-1*, Pub. by Tamos Bks CN) Sterling.

Walter, F. Virginia & Long, Teddy C. Super Toys & Games from Paper. LC 93-3161. (Illus.). 104p. (gr. 10-12). 1993. 17.95 (*1-895569-06-0*, Pub. by Tamos Bks CN) Sterling.

Walter, Marion. Look at Annette. Haber-Schaim, Navah, illus. LC 77-186592. 32p. (ps-3). 1977. 5.95 (*0-87131-071-6*) M Evans.

—Make a Bigger Puddle, Make a Smaller Worm. Walter, Marion, illus. LC 70-186593. 32p. (ps-3). 1970. 5.95 (*0-87131-073-2*) M Evans.

—The Mirror Puzzle Book. (Illus.). 32p. (gr. 2 up). 1985. pap. 6.95 (*0-906212-39-1*, Pub. by Tarquin UK) Parkwest Pubns.

Walter, Martin. S & S Young Readers Book of Animals. (gr. 4-7). 1991. pap. 7.95 (*0-671-73129-7*, S&S BFYR) S&S Trade.

Walter, Mary W., illus. Story Books for We Can Read. Incl. Eel, Ail, Ole (*0-917186-03-6*); Happenings (*0-917186-04-4*); We Learn at Play (*0-917186-05-2*); Things for All Seasons (*0-917186-06-0*); Tales & Tails (*0-917186-07-9*); Just Like Me (*0-917186-08-7*); All Around Me (*0-917186-09-5*); Bridging the Summer (*0-917186-10-9*). 5.40 ea McQueen.

Walter, Mildred P. Brother to the Wind. Dillon, Diane & Dillon, Leo, illus. LC 83-26800. 32p. (ps-2). 1985. PLB 14.88 (*0-688-03812-3*) Lothrop.

—Girl on the Outside. (gr. 4-7). 1993. pap. 3.25 (*0-590-46091-9*) Scholastic Inc.

—Have a Happy... Byard, Carole, illus. LC 88-8962. 144p. (gr. 3-6). 1989. 10.95 (*0-688-06923-1*) Lothrop.

—Have a Happy... 96p. 1990. pap. 2.99 (*0-380-71314-4*, Camelot) Avon.

—Justin & the Best Biscuits in the World. Stock, Catherine, illus. LC 86-7148. 128p. (gr. 3-7). 1986. 12.95 (*0-688-06645-3*) Lothrop.

—Mariah Keeps Cool. LC 89-23981. 144p. (gr. 3-7). 1990. SBE 13.95 (*0-02-792295-2*, Bradbury Pr) Macmillan Child Grp.

—Mariah Loves Rock. 128p. (gr. 3-9). 1989. pap. 2.95 (*0-8167-1838-5*) Troll Assocs.

—Mississippi Challenge. LC 92-6718. (Illus.). 224p. (gr. 6 up). 1992. SBE 18.95 (*0-02-792301-0*, Bradbury Pr) Macmillan Child Grp.

—My Mama Needs Me. Cummings, Pat, illus. LC 82-12654. 32p. (ps-1). 1983. 14.95 (*0-688-01670-7*); PLB 14.88 (*0-688-01671-5*) Lothrop.

—Tiger Ride. LC 92-40281. (Illus.). 32p. (ps-2). 1994. RSBE 14.95 (*0-02-792303-7*, Bradbury Pr) Macmillan Child Grp.

—Trouble's Child. LC 84-16387. 128p. (gr. 4 up). 1985. 11.95 (*0-688-04214-7*) Lothrop.

—Two & Too Much. LC 88-14888. (Illus.). 32p. (ps-2). 1990. RSBE 13.95 (*0-02-792290-1*, Bradbury Pr) Macmillan Child Grp.

—Ty's One-Man Band. Tomes, Margot, illus. 48p. (gr. k-3). 1984. pap. 3.95 (*0-590-40178-5*) Scholastic Inc.

—Ty's One-Man Band. Tomes, Margot, illus. LC 80-11224. 32p. (gr. k-3). 1987. Repr. of 1980 ed. RSBE 14.95 (*0-02-792300-2*, Pub. by Four Winds Pr) Macmillan Child Grp.

Walter, Nancy L. Inside of Me Series. Walter, Nancy L., photos by. (Illus.). 48p. (gr. k-2). 1993. pap. 18.95 (*0-9635127-9-X*) Naturally by Nan.

—Inside of Me There's a Storm a Brewing. 48p. (ps-2). 1994. pap. 10.95 (*0-9635127-7-3*) Naturally By Nan.

Walter, Willard & Walter, Elma. Heritage Hobbycraft. LC 77-19087. (Illus.). (gr. 5-12). 1978. 7.95 (*0-8313-0105-8*) Lantern.

Walters, Anna L., retold by. The Two-Legged Creature: An Otoe Story. Bowles, Carol, illus. LC 92-56510. 32p. 1993. 14.95 (*0-87358-553-4*) Northland AZ.

Walters, David. Being a Christian. Odell, Dave, illus. 40p. (Orig.). (gr. 2-10). Date not set. write for info. wkbk. (*0-9629559-2-2*) Good News Min.

—Fact or Fantasy. 48p. 1991. wkbk. 4.95 (*0-9629559-0-6*) Good News Min.

—Fruit of the Spirit. Henigman, Daniel, illus. 44p. (Orig.). Date not set. pap. 5.95 wkbk. (*0-9629559-3-0*) Good News Min.

Walters, Gregory J. Equal Access: Safeguarding Disability Rights. LC 92-11523. 1992. PLB 22.60 (*0-86593-174-7*); 16.95s.p. (*0-685-59328-2*) Rourke Corp.

Walters, Jean. Freedom or Fear. 32p. (Orig.). 1984. pap. 3.50 (*0-941992-21-7*) Los Arboles Pub.

Walters, Jennie. Gardening with Peter Rabbit. Potter, Beatrix, illus. 48p. (gr. k-4). 1992. 9.00 (*0-7232-3998-3*) Warne.

—Gardening with Peter Rabbit: A Gardening Kit. Potter, Beatrix, illus. 48p. (gr. k-4). 1992. pap. 14.50 (*0-7232-4024-8*) Warne.

Walters, Jerry. Walt Disney's Dumbo: On Land, on Sea, in the Air. (Illus.). (ps-3). 1973. 6.95 (*0-394-82518-7*); lib. bdg. 4.99 (*0-394-92518-1*) Random Bks Yng Read.

Walters, Julie & Kelly, Kathryn. God Loves Me: Three Psalms for Little Children. Kelly, Kathryn, illus. 96p. (gr. k-2). 1977. pap. 2.95 (*0-87793-138-0*) Ave Maria.

Walters, Martin, contrib. by. Earth Sciences. Trotman, Felicity. LC 92-15822. (Illus.). 160p. (gr. 4-10). 1992. pap. 19.00 (*0-13-681735-1*) P-H Gen Ref & Trav.

Walters, Michael E. Teaching Shakespeare to Gifted Students: An Examination of the Sensibility of Genius. (gr. 6-12). 1990. 12.00 (*0-910609-22-5*) Gifted Educ Pr.

Walters, Sarah. How Newspapers Are Made. (Illus.). 32p. 1989. 12.95x (*0-8160-2042-6*) Facts on File.

Walters-Lucy, Jean. Look Ma, I'm Flying. Tabesh, Delight, ed. & illus. LC 92-13953. 48p. (Orig.). (ps-5). 1992. pap. 6.95 perfect bdg. (*0-941992-28-4*) Los Arboles Pub.

Walther, Tom. Make Mine Music. Walther, Tom, illus. 128p. (Orig.). (gr. 3 up). 1981. pap. 9.95 (*0-316-92112-2*) Little.

Waltner, Elma. Carving Animal Caricatures. (Illus.). 104p. (Repr. of 1951 ed). (gr. 7-12). 1972. pap. 4.95 (*0-486-22813-4*) Dover.

Waltner, Elma, jt. auth. see Waltner, Willard.

Waltner, Willard & Waltner, Elma. Hobbycraft for Juniors. (Illus.). (gr. 2-10). 1975. 7.95 (*0-8313-0096-5*) Lantern.

—New Look at Old Crafts. LC 70-143700. (Illus.). 142p. (gr. 9 up). 1971. 7.19 (*0-8313-0098-1*) Lantern.

Walton, Ann & Walton, Rick. Alphabatty: Riddles from A to Z. Burke, Susan S., illus. (gr. 1-4). 1991. PLB 11.95 (*0-685-49141-2*) Lerner Pubns.

Walton, Ann, jt. auth. see Walton, Rick.

Walton, Darwin. What Color Are You? Franklin, Hal A., photos by. (Illus.). 64p. (gr. 5 up). 1973. 10.95 (*0-87485-045-2*) Johnson Chi.

Walton, Jim & Walton, Kim. Elijah & the Contest. (Illus.). (ps). 1987. pap. 3.49 (*1-55513-042-9*, Chariot Bks) Cook.

Walton, John. Tiny Tots Bible Story Book. (ps). 1993. 14.99 (*0-7814-0834-2*) Cook.

Walton, John & Walton, Kim. Abraham & His Big Family. LC 86-70678. (Illus.). (ps) 1986. pap. 3.49 (*1-55513-031-3*, Chariot Bks) Cook.
—Daniel & the Lions. (Illus.). (ps) 1987. pap. 3.49 (*1-55513-045-3*, Chariot Bks) Cook.
—David Fights Goliath. (ps) 1988. pap. 3.49 (*1-55513-239-1*, Chariot Bks) Cook.
—God & the World He Made. LC 86-70677. (Illus.). (ps) 1986. pap. 3.49 (*1-55513-030-5*, Chariot Bks) Cook.
—Jeroboam & the Golden Calves. LC 87-70613. (ps). 1988. pap. 3.49 (*1-55513-240-5*, Chariot Bks) Cook.
—Jesus, God's Son, Is Born. LC 87-70612. (ps) 1987. pap. 3.49 (*1-55513-230-8*, Chariot Bks) Cook.
—Jonah & the Big Fish. LC 86-70679. (Illus.). (ps) 1986. pap. 3.49 (*1-55513-035-6*, Chariot Bks) Cook.
—Paul & the Bright Light. LC 87-70611. (ps) 1987. pap. 3.49 (*1-55513-236-7*, Chariot Bks) Cook.
—Tiny Tots Bible Story Book. Craig, Alice, illus. (ps). 1993. 14.99 (*0-685-63498-1*, Chariot Bks) Cook.
Walton, Kim, jt. auth. see Walton, Jim.
Walton, Kim, jt. auth. see Walton, John.
Walton, Marilyn J. Chameleon's Rainbow. Salzman, Yuri, illus. LC 84-17760. 32p. (gr. 3-6). 1985. PLB 14.65 (*0-940742-45-4*); incl cassette 27.99 (*0-8172-2285-5*) Raintree Steck-V.
—Chameleons' Rainbow. (ps-3). 1993. pap. 4.95 (*0-8114-8402-5*) Raintree Steck-V.
Walton, O. F. Rosalie's Shepherd. (gr. 3-6). 1976. pap. 2.50 (*0-915374-16-1*) Rapids Christian.
Walton, Richard K. & Morrison, Gordon. A Field Guide to Endangered Wildlife Coloring Book. Walton, Richard K. & Morrison, Gordon, illus. 64p. 1991. pap. 4.80 (*0-395-57324-6*) HM.
Walton, Rick. Alphabatty: Riddles from A to Z. (ps-3). 1991. pap. 3.95 (*0-8225-9593-1*) Lerner Pubns.
—Hoop-la: Riddles about Basketball. (gr. 4-7). 1993. pap. 3.95 (*0-8225-9639-3*) Lerner Pubns.
—How Many, How Many, How Many. Jabar, Cynthia, illus. LC 92-54408. 32p. (ps up) 1993. 14.95 (*1-56402-062-2*) Candlewick Pr.
—Off Base: Riddles about Baseball. (gr. 4-7). 1993. pap. 3.95 (*0-8225-9638-5*) Lerner Pubns.
—Take a Hike: Riddles about Football. (gr. 4-7). 1993. pap. 3.95 (*0-8225-9640-7*) Lerner Pubns.
—Will You Still Love Me? Teare, Brad, illus. LC 92-341. 32p. (ps). 1992. 11.95 (*0-87579-582-X*) Deseret Bk.
Walton, Rick & Walton, Ann. Can You Match This? Jokes about Unlikely Pairs. Hanson, Joan, illus. 32p. (gr. 1-4). 1989. 11.95 (*0-8225-0973-3*) Lerner Pubns.
—Can You Match This? Jokes about Unlikely Pairs. Hanson, Joan, illus. 36p. pap. 2.95 (*0-8225-9565-6*) Lerner Pubns.
—Clowning Around! Jokes about the Circus. Hanson, Joan, illus. 32p. (gr. 1-4). 1989. 11.95 (*0-8225-0975-X*) Lerner Pubns.
—Dumb Clucks. 12p. 1992. text ed. 0.92 (*1-56956-110-9*) W A T Braille.
—Dumb Clucks! Jokes about Chickens. Hanson, Joan, illus. 32p. (gr. 1-4). 1987. PLB 11.95 (*0-8225-0991-1*) Lerner Pubns.
—Fossil Follies! Jokes about Dinosaurs. Hanson, Joan, illus. 32p. (gr. 1-4). 1989. 11.95 (*0-8225-0974-1*, First Ave Edns); pap. 2.95 (*0-8225-9560-5*, First Ave Edns) Lerner Pubns.
—Ho Ho Ho! Riddles about Santa Claus. (Illus.). 32p. (gr. 1-4). 1991. PLB 11.95 (*0-8225-2337-X*); pap. 3.95 (*0-8225-9595-8*) Lerner Pubns.
—Hoop-La: Riddles about Basketball. Burke, Susan S., illus. LC 92-25771. 1993. 11.95 (*0-8225-2339-6*) Lerner Pubns.
—I Toad You So: Riddles about Frogs & Toads. Burke, Susan S., illus. 32p. (gr. 1-4). 1991. PLB 11.95 (*0-8225-2331-0*); pap. 3.95 (*0-8225-9590-7*) Lerner Pubns.
—Kiss a Frog! Jokes about Fairy Tales, Knights, & Dragons. Hanson, Joan, illus. 32p. (gr. 1-4). 1989. 11.95 (*0-8225-0970-9*) Lerner Pubns.
—Kiss a Frog! Jokes about Fairy Tales, Knights, & Dragons. Hanson, Joan, illus. 40p. (gr. 1-4). pap. 2.95g (*0-8225-9566-4*) Lerner Pubns.
—Off Base: Riddles about Baseball. Burke, Susan S., illus. LC 92-19857. 1993. 11.95 (*0-8225-2338-8*) Lerner Pubns.
—On with the Show: Show Me Riddles. Burke, Susan S., illus. 32p. (gr. 1-4). 1989. PLB 11.95 (*0-8225-2327-2*) Lerner Pubns.
—Something's Fishy! Jokes about Sea Creatures. (Illus.). 32p. (gr. 1-4). 1987. PLB 11.95 (*0-8225-0993-8*, First Ave Edns); pap. 2.95 (*0-8225-9519-2*, First Ave Edns) Lerner Pubns.
—Take a Hike: Riddles about Football. Burke, Susan S., illus. LC 92-27011. 1993. 11.95 (*0-8225-2340-X*) Lerner Pubns.
—Weather or Not: Riddles for Rain & Shine. Burke, Susan S., illus. 32p. (gr. 1-4). 1989. PLB 8.95 (*0-8225-2329-9*) Lerner Pubns.
—What a Ham! Jokes about Pigs. Hanson, Joan, illus. 32p. (gr. 1-4). 1989. 11.95 (*0-8225-0972-5*) Lerner Pubns.
—What a Ham! Jokes about Pigs. Hanson, Joan, illus. 40p. (gr. 1-4). pap. 2.95 (*0-8225-9567-2*) Lerner Pubns.
—What's Your Name, Again? More Jokes about Names. Hanson, Joan, illus. 32p. (gr. 1-4). 1988. PLB 11.95 (*0-8225-0997-0*, First Ave Edns); pap. 2.95 (*0-8225-9553-2*, First Ave Edns) Lerner Pubns.
Walton, Rick, jt. auth. see Walton, Ann.

Walton, Robert. The Dragon & The Lemon Tree. Allen, Ginny, illus. LC 89-92122. 86p. (gr. 3-7). 1989. write for info. (*0-9623802-0-2*) Pisces Pr CA.
Walton, Robert M. Joel in Tananar. (Illus.). (gr. 4-9). 1982. 8.95 (*0-914598-05-8*) Pr MacDonald & Reinecke.
Walton, Sally & Walton, Stewart. Christmas Stencils. (Illus.). (ps-3). 1993. pap. 6.95 (*0-688-12942-0*, Tupelo Bks) Morrow.
—Stencil It! Over One Hundred Step-by-Step Projects. LC 92-36177. (Illus.). 80p. (gr. 4-10). 1993. 14.95 (*0-8069-0346-5*) Sterling.
Walton, Sally, jt. auth. see Walton, Stewart.
Walton, Sherry. Books Are for Eating. LC 89-11749. (Illus.). 24p. (ps-1). 1990. 11.95 (*0-525-44554-4*, DCB) Dutton Child Bks.
Walton, Simon. Flute, Recorder & Other Woodwind Instruments. (Illus.). 32p. (gr. 4-7). 1993. PLB 12.40 (*0-531-17421-2*, Gloucester Pr) Watts.
Walton, Stewart & Walton, Sally. Wild Animal Paperchains. (Illus.). 32p. (gr. 2 up) 1993. pap. 6.95 (*0-688-12608-1*, Pub. by Beech Tree Bks) Morrow.
Walton, Stewart, jt. auth. see Walton, Sally.
Waltz, Marjorie. The Dragon, the Winds & the Witches. Waltz, Catherine, illus. LC 86-72867. 64p. (Orig.). (gr. k-2). 1987. pap. 5.00 (*0-916383-14-8*) Aegina Pr.
Walworth, Nancy Z. Augustus Caesar. Schlesinger, Arthur M., Jr. (Illus.). 112p. (gr. 5 up). 1989. 17.95 (*1-55546-804-7*) Chelsea Hse.
—Constantine. (Illus.). 112p. (gr. 5 up). 1990. 17.95 (*1-55546-805-5*) Chelsea Hse.
Walz, Michael K. & Killen, M. Barbara. The Law & Economics: Your Rights As a Consumer. (Illus.). 88p. (gr. 5 up). 1990. PLB 21.50 (*0-8225-1779-5*) Lerner Pubns.
Walz, Richard, illus. The Pudgy Book of Mother Goose. 16p. (gr. k). 1984. 2.95 (*0-448-10212-9*, G&D) Putnam Pub Group.
Wamberg, Annie, jt. auth. see Wamberg, Steve.
Wamberg, Steve & Wamberg, Annie. Building Better Friendships. (Illus.). 48p. (gr. 6-8). 1992. pap. 7.99 (*1-55945-138-6*) Group Pub.
—Can Christians Have Fun? (Illus.). 48p. (gr. 6-8). 1992. pap. 7.99 (*1-55945-134-3*) Group Pub.
—Christmas: A Fresh Look. (Illus.). 48p. (gr. 6-8). 1991. pap. 7.99 (*1-55945-124-6*) Group Pub.
Wampamba, Mazzi. The Kingdom of the South: The Long Journey. Nobles, Henry, Jr., illus. (gr. 1-4). 1992. pap. 3.95 (*1-56411-045-1*) Untd Brothers.
Wanasundera, Nanda P. Sri Lanka. LC 91-18399. (Illus.). 128p. (gr. 5-9). 1991. PLB 21.95 (*1-85435-398-5*) Marshall Cavendish.
Wanbli Numpa Afraid of Hawk, jt. auth. see Wood, Ted.
Wandelmaier, Roy. Clouds. Jones, John, illus. LC 84-8643. 32p. (gr. k-2). 1985. PLB 11.59 (*0-8167-0338-8*); pap. text ed. 2.95 (*0-8167-0441-4*) Troll Assocs.
—The Great Rock 'n' Roll Mystery. Burns, Raymond, illus. LC 84-8753. 48p. (gr. 2-4). 1985. PLB 10.89 (*0-8167-0416-3*); pap. text ed. 3.50 (*0-8167-0417-1*) Troll Assocs.
—Mystery at Loch Ness. Mulkey, Kim, illus. LC 85-2532. 112p. (gr. 3-6). 1985. lib. bdg. 9.49 (*0-8167-0529-1*) Troll Assocs.
—Secret of the Old Museum. Smolinski, Dick, illus. LC 85-2533. 112p. (gr. 3-6). 1985. lib. bdg. 9.49 (*0-8167-0531-3*); pap. text ed. 2.95 (*0-8167-0532-1*) Troll Assocs.
—Shipwrecked on Mystery Island. Pinkney, Brian J. LC 85-2531. (Illus.). 112p. (gr. 3-6). 1985. lib. bdg. 9.49 (*0-8167-0533-X*); pap. text ed. 2.95 (*0-8167-0534-8*) Troll Assocs.
—Stars. Trivas, Irene, illus. LC 84-8642. 32p. (gr. k-2). 1985. PLB 11.59 (*0-8167-0339-6*); pap. text ed. 2.95 (*0-8167-0442-2*) Troll Assocs.
Wang, Mary L. The Ant & the Dove. Walters, Mary C., illus. LC 89-34414. 32p. (ps-2). 1989. PLB 11.93 (*0-516-02367-5*); pap. 3.95 (*0-516-42367-3*) Childrens.
—The Frog Prince. Connelly, Gwen, illus. LC 86-11796. 32p. (ps-2). 1986. PLB 11.93 (*0-516-03983-0*); pap. 3.95 (*0-516-43983-9*) Childrens.
—The Good Witch. Rosales, Melodye, illus. LC 89-34415. 32p. (ps-2). 1989. PLB 11.93 (*0-516-02368-3*); pap. 3.95 (*0-516-42368-1*) Childrens.
—El Leon y el Raton: The Lion & the Mouse. Dunnington, Tom, illus. LC 85-31441. (SPA.). 32p. (ps-2). 1988. PLB 11.93 (*0-516-33981-8*); pap. 3.95 (*0-516-53981-7*) Childrens.
—The Lion & the Mouse. Dunnington, Tom, illus. LC 85-31441. 32p. (ps-2). 1986. PLB 11.93 (*0-516-03981-4*); pap. 3.95 (*0-516-43981-2*) Childrens.
—El Principe Rana (The Frog Prince) Connelly, Gwen, illus. LC 86-11796. (SPA.). 32p. (ps-2). 1989. PLB 11.93 (*0-516-33983-4*); pap. 3.95 (*0-516-53983-3*) Childrens.
Wang, May S., tr. see La Fonatine, Jean de.
Wang, Rosalind. The Magical Starfruit Tree. Livingston, Julie, ed. Shao Wei Liu, illus. (gr. k-2). Date not set. 13.95 (*0-941831-89-2*) Beyond Words Pub.
—The Magical Starfruit Tree. Shao Wei Liu, illus. LC 93-3656. 1993. 13.95 (*0-09-843189-7*) Beyond Words Pub.
Wang, Rosalind C., retold by. The Fourth Question: A Chinese Folktale. Ju-Hong Chen, illus. LC 90-43536. 32p. (ps-3). 1991. reinforced 14.95 (*0-8234-0855-8*) Holiday.

Wang, Wally & Millard, Scott. Simple Computer Maintenance & Repair. Collier, Cynthia & Lingham, Gretchen, eds. Mozzini, Lisa, illus. 60p. (Orig.). (gr. 9 up). 1990. pap. 2.95 (*0-945776-10-1*) Comptr Pub Enterprises.
Wangerin, W., Jr. & Jennings, A. God, I've Gotta Talk to You. (Illus.). 32p. (gr. k-4). 1974. pap. 1.89 (*0-570-06086-9*, 59-1301) Concordia.
Wangerin, Walter. Branta & the Golden Stone. Healey, Deborah, illus. LC 92-34891. 1993. pap. 16.00 (*0-671-79693-3*, S&S BFYR) S&S Trade.
—Elisabeth & the Water-Troll. Healy, Deborah, illus. LC 90-4359. 64p. (gr. 3-7). 1991. HarpC Child Bks.
Wangerin, Walter, Jr. The Bible for Children. (Illus.). 416p. (ps up). 1987. pap. 14.95 (*1-56288-187-6*) Checkerboard.
—A Penny Is Everything. (Illus.). 32p. (gr. 1-4). 1974. pap. 1.89 (*0-570-06084-2*, 59-1204) Concordia.
Wangu, Madhu B. Buddhism. (Illus.). 128p. (gr. 7-12). 1992. bds. 17.95x (*0-8160-2442-1*) Facts on File.
Wangui wa Goro, tr. see Ngugi wa Thiong'o.
Warbelow, Willy L. Empire on Ice. Clark, Marvin, ed. (Illus.). 256p. (Orig.). (gr. 9 up). 1990. pap. 19.95 (*0-937708-21-6*) Great Northwest.
Warburg, Sandol S. Free. Oliver, Jenni, illus. LC 75-40013. 48p. (gr. 1 up). 1976. PLB 5.95 (*0-395-24210-X*) HM.
—Growing Time. Weisgard, Leonard, illus. LC 69-14729. (gr. k-3). 1975. 13.95 (*0-395-16966-6*) HM.
—Growing Time. Weisgard, Leonard, illus. 48p. (gr. k-3). 1975. pap. 1.50 (*0-395-19971-9*, Sandpiper) HM.
—Growing Time. Weisgard, Leonard, illus. (ps-3). 1989. pap. 4.80 (*0-395-51009-0*, Sandpiper) HM.
—I Like You. Chwast, Jacqueline, illus. LC 65-11020. 48p. (gr. 1-3). 1965. 5.70 (*0-395-07176-3*) HM.
Warburton, Lois. The Beginning of Writing. LC 90-6010. (Illus.). 112p. (gr. 5-8). 1990. PLB 14.95 (*1-56006-113-8*) Lucent Bks.
—The Chicago Fire. LC 89-33554. (Illus.). 64p. (gr. 5-8). 1989. PLB 11.95 (*1-56006-002-6*) Lucent Bks.
—Chief Joseph. LC 92-28010. (Illus.). 112p. (gr. 5-8). 1992. PLB 14.95 (*1-56006-003-4*) Lucent Bks.
—Human Origins: Tracing Humanity's Evolution. LC 92-24990. (Illus.). 96p. (gr. 5-8). 1992. PLB 15.95 (*1-56006-221-5*) Lucent Bks.
—Prisons. (Illus.). 112p. (gr. 5-8). 1993. PLB 14.95 (*1-56006-138-3*) Lucent Bks.
—Railroads: Bridging the Continents. LC 91-23857. (Illus.). 96p. (gr. 5-8). 1991. PLB 15.95 (*1-56006-216-9*) Lucent Bks.
—Rainforests. LC 90-46278. (Illus.). 96p. (gr. 5-8). 1991. PLB 14.95 (*1-56006-150-2*) Lucent Bks.
Warburton, Nick. Mr. Tite's Belongings. Warburton, Nick, illus. 32p. (ps-3). 1992. 13.95 (*0-670-84155-2*) Viking Child Bks.
Warburton, Thomas, tr. see Jansson, Tove.
Ward. I Am Eyes Ni Macho. 1993. pap. 28.67 (*0-590-71935-1*) Scholastic Inc.
Ward, Alan. Experimenting with Batteries, Bulbs, & Wires. Flax, Zena, illus. 48p. (gr. 2-7). 1991. lib. bdg. 12.95 (*0-7910-1516-5*) Chelsea Hse.
—Experimenting with Energy. Flax, Zena, illus. 48p. (gr. 2-7). 1991. lib. bdg. 12.95 (*0-7910-1510-6*) Chelsea Hse.
—Experimenting with Light & Illusions. Flax, Zena, illus. 48p. (gr. 2-7). 1991. lib. bdg. 12.95 (*0-7910-1514-9*) Chelsea Hse.
—Experimenting with Magnetism. Flax, Zena, illus. 48p. (gr. 2-7). 1991. lib. bdg. 12.95 (*0-7910-1509-2*) Chelsea Hse.
—Experimenting with Nature Study. Flax, Zena, illus. 48p. (gr. 2-7). 1991. lib. bdg. 12.95 (*0-7910-1515-7*) Chelsea Hse.
—Experimenting with Science about Yourself. Flax, Zena, illus. 48p. (gr. 2-7). 1991. lib. bdg. 12.95 (*0-7910-1512-2*) Chelsea Hse.
—Experimenting with Sound. (Illus.). 48p. (gr. 2-7). 1991. lib. bdg. 12.95 (*0-7910-1511-4*) Chelsea Hse.
—Experimenting with Surface Tension & Bubbles. Flax, Zena, illus. 48p. (gr. 2-7). 1991. lib. bdg. 12.95 (*0-7910-1513-0*) Chelsea Hse.
—Flight & Floating. King, Colin, illus. 64p. (gr. 3-6). 1983. pap. 4.95 (*0-86020-529-0*); lib. bdg. 11.96 (*0-88110-162-1*) EDc.
—Forces & Energy. LC 92-6260. (Illus.). 30p. (gr. k-4). 1992. PLB 11.40 (*0-531-14132-2*) Watts.
—Light & Color. LC 92-5140. (Illus.). 30p. (gr. k-4). 1992. PLB 11.40 (*0-531-14231-0*) Watts.
—Magnets & Electricity. (Illus.). 30p. (gr. k-4). 1992. PLB 11.40 (*0-531-14141-1*, Gloucester Pr) Watts.
—Plants & Animals. LC 92-14715. 1994. 11.40 (*0-531-14242-6*) Watts.
—Sky & Weather. LC 92-369. 1993. 11.40 (*0-531-14176-4*) Watts.
—Sound & Music. LC 92-370. 1993. 11.40 (*0-531-14237-X*) Watts.
—Water & Floating. LC 92-6260. (Illus.). 30p. (gr. k-4). 1992. PLB 11.40 (*0-531-14230-2*) Watts.
Ward, Ann. Peter Rabbit & Friends: Study Guide for Children for the Works of Beatrix Potter. 95p. Date not set. pap. text ed. 10.00 (*0-923463-96-8*) Noble Pub Assocs.
Ward, Annette, jt. auth. see Yorgason, Margaret.
Ward, Bernie, compiled by see Nash, Bruce & Zullo, Allan.
Ward, Betty, jt. auth. see Ward, Fred.

Ward, Brian. Bones & Joints: And Their Care. (Illus.). 32p. (gr. 5-8). 1991. PLB 12.40 (0-531-14175-6) Watts.
—Breathing: And Your Health. LC 90-31226. (Illus.). 32p. (gr. 5-8). 1991. PLB 12.40 (0-531-14094-6) Watts.
—Diet: And Health. LC 90-31200. (Illus.). 32p. 1991. PLB 12.40 (0-531-14095-4) Watts.
—Eyes: And Their Care. (Illus.). 32p. (gr. 5-8). 1990. PLB 12.40 (0-531-14071-7) Watts.
—Flying Models. LC 92-9908. 1993. 12.40 (0-531-14241-8) Watts.
—Skin. (Illus.). 32p. (gr. 5-8). 1990. PLB 12.40 (0-531-14072-5) Watts.
—Teeth: And Their Care. (Illus.). 32p. (gr. 5-8). 1991. PLB 12.40 (0-531-14174-8) Watts.
Ward, Carl. Hockey. (Illus.). 80p. (gr. 10-12). 1991. pap. 6.95 (0-7063-6770-7, Pub. by Ward Lock UK) Sterling.
Ward, Cindy. Cookie's Week. De Paola, Tomie, illus. 32p. (ps-1). 1988. 11.95 (0-399-21498-4, Putnam) Putnam Pub Group.
—Cookie's Week. De Paola, Tomie, illus. 32p. (ps) 1992. pap. 4.95 (0-399-22406-8, Putnam) Putnam Pub Group.
Ward, Dick, ed. see Branch, James H., III.
Ward, Elaine. Getting to Know You. 20p. (Orig.). (gr. 7-12). 1987. pap. 5.75 (0-940754-49-5) Ed Ministries.
—Roots & Wings. (Orig.). (gr. 1-6). 1983. pap. 3.95 (0-377-00130-9) Friendship Pr.
—Using God's World in Christian Education. 12p. (Orig.). (gr. 1-8). 1987. pap. 5.75 (0-940754-40-1) Ed Ministries.
Ward, Elaine M. Being Human: Learning Through Feelings. 57p. (Orig.). (gr. 1-6). 1988. pap. 9.95 (0-940754-63-0) Ed Ministries.
—Being with God: Advent Devotions. Lenzen, Diane, illus. 36p. (Orig.). (gr. 1-6). 1988. pap. 4.50 (0-940754-66-5) Ed Ministries.
—Gifts of the Spirit. 59p. (Orig.). (gr. 9-12). 1988. pap. 9.95 (0-940754-64-9) Ed Ministries.
—Growing with the Bible. 64p. (Orig.). (gr. 1-6). 1986. pap. 7.95 (0-940754-36-3) Ed Ministries.
—In the Summertime: What's There to Do? 1990. pap. 5.95 (0-940754-98-3) Ed Ministries.
—Movers of Mountains. 88p. (Orig.). (gr. 7-12). 1984. pap. 12.95 (0-940754-24-X, 8196) Ed Ministries.
—Old Testament Stories: For Church & Home. 70p. (Orig.). (gr. 1-8). 1984. pap. 7.95 (0-940754-19-3) Ed Ministries.
Ward, Elizabeth, ed. What Makes Popcorn Pop? First Questions & Answers about Food. (Illus.). (ps). 1994. write for info. (0-7835-0862-X); PLB write for info. (0-7835-0863-8) Time-Life.
Ward, Elizabeth, ed. see Time Life Inc. Editors.
Ward, Elizabeth, et al, eds. see Time Life Inc Staff.
Ward, Fred & Ward, Betty. About Sexual Abuse: A Program for Teens & Young Adults. Olszewski, Lema J. & Wolff, Kathy, eds. 85p. (Orig.). (gr. 9 up). 1990. pap. text ed. 9.95 (1-55896-175-5) Unitarian Univ.
Ward, Glenyse. Wandering Girl. LC 90-48825. 160p. (gr. 6 up). 1991. 14.95 (0-8050-1634-1, Bks Young Read) H Holt & Co.
Ward, Helen. The Golden Pear. Ward, Helen, illus. LC 91-9102. 40p. (ps-3). 1991. 14.95 (0-8249-8471-4, Ideals Child) Hambleton-Hill.
—The Golden Pear. Ward, Helen, illus. 40p. (ps-3). 1993. pap. 4.95 (0-8249-8639-3, Ideals Child) Hambleton-Hill.
—The Moonrat & the White Turtle. 40p. (ps-4). 1992. pap. 4.95 (0-8249-8580-X, Ideals Child) Hambleton-Hill.
Ward, Hiley H. Feeling Good about Myself. Novello, Joseph, intro. by. LC 82-25613. 166p. (gr. 6 up). 1983. 12.00 (0-664-32704-4, Westminster) Westminster John Knox.
Ward, James M. & Hong, Jane C. Pool of Radiance. LC 88-51726. 352p. (Orig.). 1989. pap. 3.95 (0-88038-735-1) TSR Inc.
Ward, Jane S. Tajar Tales. Drucklieb, Herman L. & Kerry, Jill, illus. LC 93-71385. 48p. (ps-4). 1993. Repr. of 1924 ed. Colorized pictures, music & song added. lib. bdg. 14.95 (1-883338-01-8); Book & cassette set. lib. bdg. 19.95 (1-883338-00-X) Classic Wrks.
Ward, John W. Andrew Jackson: Symbol for an Age. (gr. 9 up). 1955. pap. 9.95 (0-19-500699-2) OUP.
Ward, Kathy, jt. auth. see Avis, Jen.
Ward, Kay, jt. auth. see Simons, John.
Ward, Kay, ed. see Simons, John & Ward, Kay.
Ward, Ken. Mrs. Kitchen's Cats. (Illus.). 48p. 1990. 8.95 (1-55037-107-X, Pub. by Annick CN) Firefly Bks Ltd.
—Twelve Kids One Cow: Ken Ward's World. Ward, Ken, illus. 36p. 1989. pap. 4.95 (1-55037-076-6, Pub. by Annick CN) Firefly Bks Ltd.
Ward, Leila. I Am Eyes Ni Macho. Hogrogian, Nonny, illus. 32p. (gr. k-3). 1987. pap. 3.95 (0-590-40990-5, Blue Ribbon Bks) Scholastic Inc.
Ward Lock, Ltd. Staff. One Thousand Knock Knock Jokes for Kids. (gr. k up). 1986. pap. 4.99 (0-345-33481-7) Ballantine.
Ward, Lorrainie. A Walk in the Wild. 32p. 1993. PLB 15.00 (0-88106-480-7); pap. 7.95 (0-88106-478-5) Charlesbridge Pub.
Ward, Lynd. Biggest Bear. (Illus.). 88p. (gr. k-3). 1952. 14.45 (0-395-14806-5) HM.
—The Biggest Bear. Ward, Lynd, illus. LC 52-8730. 80p. (gr. k-3). 1973. pap. 5.70 (0-395-15024-8, Sandpiper) HM.

—Silver Pony. (ps-3). 1992. pap. 6.95 (0-395-64377-5) HM.
—The Silver Pony: A Story in Pictures. Ward, Lynd, illus. LC 72-5402. 192p. (gr. k-3). 1973. 17.95 (0-395-14753-0) HM.
Ward, Lynd, jt. auth. see Swift, Hildegarde H.
Ward, Nick. A Bag of Tricks. (Illus.). 16p. 1987. pap. 2.95 (0-19-272143-7) OUP.
—The Surprise Present. (Illus.). 16p. 1987. pap. 2.95 (0-19-272142-9) OUP.
Ward, Peter. The Adventures of Charles Darwin: A Story of the Beagle Voyage. LC 81-21751. (Illus.). 96p. (gr. 4-7). 1986. 12.95 (0-521-24510-9); pap. 5.95 (0-521-31074-1) Cambridge U Pr.
Ward, Peter D., jt. auth. see Fekete, Irene.
Ward, Richard J., jt. auth. see Pincus, Debbie.
Ward, Ruth M. Self Esteem: A Gift from God. (gr. 9 up). 1984. pap. 7.99 (0-8010-9664-2) Baker Bk.
Ward, Sally G. Punky Goes Fishing. LC 90-35538. (Illus.). 32p. (ps-1). 1991. 11.95 (0-525-44681-8, DCB) Dutton Child Bks.
Ward, Sally G. & Ward, Sally G. The Yawn Goes On. (Illus.). 16p. (ps). 1994. 4.99 (0-525-45076-9, DCB) Dutton Child Bks.
Wardlaw, Lee. Corey's Fire. 160p. (gr. 5). 1990. pap. 2.95 (0-380-75791-5, Flare) Avon.
—Don't Look Back. 160p. (Orig.). (gr. 5). 1993. pap. 3.50 (0-380-76419-9) Avon.
—The Eye & I. Stouffer, Deborah, illus. LC 88-15664. 75p. (Orig.). (gr. 3-6). 1988. pap. 3.50 (0-931093-10-4) Red Hen Pr.
—Me Plus Math Equals Headache. Hoy, Joanne H., illus. LC 86-20305. (Orig.). (gr. 1-3). 1986. pap. 3.50 (0-931093-07-4) Red Hen Pr.
—Operation Rhinoceros. Stouffer, Deborah, illus. LC 92-15933. 120p. (Orig.). (gr. 3-6). 1992. pap. 3.50 (0-931093-14-7) Red Hen Pr.
—Seventh Grade Weirdo. 176p. (gr. 3-7). 1992. 13.95 (0-590-44805-6, Scholastic Hardcover) Scholastic Inc.
—The Tales of Grandpa Cat. LC 92-39797. 32p. 1994. 13.99 (0-8037-1511-0); PLB 13.89 (0-8037-1512-9) Dial Bks Young.
Ware, Cindy. Summer Options for Teenagers. 576p. (Orig.). (gr. 8-12). 1990. pap. 16.95 (0-13-296443-0, Arco Test) P-H Gen Ref & Trav.
Ware, Derek. Stunt Performers. Stefoff, Rebecca, ed. LC 91-41209. (Illus.). 32p. (gr. 5-9). 1992. PLB 17.26 (1-56074-045-0) Garrett Ed Corp.
Ware, Martin E. Carly's & Amy's, Friends & Fables. (Illus.). 40p. (gr. 3-8). 1991. 7.50 (0-8059-3194-5) Dorrance.
Wareham, Alan. A Challenging Book of Logic Puzzles. (Illus.). 144p. (gr. 6-12). 1991. pap. 4.95 (0-7063-6946-7, Pub. by Ward Lock UK) Sterling.
Wareing, Eleanor J. The Cat Who Was Named Twice. Lynn, Susan K., illus. 141p. (Orig.). (gr. 3-6). 1990. pap. 6.95 (0-9629175-0-8) E J Wareing.
Warfield, B. B. Faith & Life. 458p. (gr. 7 up). 1991. 23.95 (0-85151-585-1) Banner of Truth.
Warhola, James, illus. The Pumpkinville Mystery. LC 87-2533. 32p. (gr. 1-4). 1987. PLB 10.95 (0-671-66905-2); pap. 5.95 (0-671-66906-0) S&S Trade.
—Rodgers & Hammerstein's "The Surrey with the Fringe on Top" Hammerstein, Oscar, II, contrib. by. LC 92-2462. (Illus.). 1993. pap. 14.00 (0-671-79456-6, S&S BFYR) S&S Trade.
Waring, Diana. History Alive Through Music America: The Heart of a New Land. (Illus.). 78p. (Orig.). (gr. 3-8). 1991. pap. 17.95 incl. cassette (1-879459-01-9); pap. 9.95 (1-879459-00-0); cassette 9.95 (1-879459-02-7) Hear & Learn Pubns.
—History Alive Through Music Westward Ho! The Heart of the Old West. (Illus.). 66p. (Orig.). (gr. 6-10). 1991. pap. 17.95 incl. cassette (1-879459-03-5); pap. 9.95 (1-879459-04-3); cassette 9.95 (1-879459-05-1) Hear & Learn Pubns.
Waring, Shirley B. What Happened to Benjamin: A True Story. Bergstrom, Lucy, illus. LC 92-83949. 44p. (Orig.). (gr. k-2). 1993. pap. 10.00 (0-9622808-2-8) S&T Waring.
Wark, Mary A. We Tell It to Our Children: The Story of Passover: A Haggadah for Seders with Young Children. 2nd ed. Oskow, Craig, illus. Lerner, Leigh D., frwd. by. LC 88-92282. (Illus.). 126p. (Orig.). (ps-6). 1988. pap. 5.95 wire bdg. (0-9619880-8-8) Mensch Makers Pr.

Wark, MaryAnn B. We Tell It to Our Children: The Story of Passover: A Haggadah for Seders with Young Children. Oskow, Craig, illus. Lerner, Leigh D., frwd. by. LC 87-63604. (Illus.). 150p. (Orig.). (ps-6). 1988. Leader's Edition with Puppets. pap. 11.95 wire-o bdg. (0-9619880-9-6) Mensch Makers Pr.
Children's active participatory Haggadah makes the Passover story into an engaging drama of the Exodus story. A complete guide, including multi-national recipes, for putting on the traditional Seder meal for

Passover. Text is a musical puppet show with Judaically-meaningful lyrics set to simple American folk tunes. Everyone participates in singing throughout the service. This Leader's edition has 9 cut out puppets who are the "guests" from the past, who in a "you-are-there" style tell the story of the Exodus. Parts for non-readers & early readers. Guest edition - no puppets with full text also available. Endorsed by rabbis, religious educators (Jewish & Christian), children's book store owners, preschool teachers, parents & grandparents nationwide. For home or model seders. Authentically Jewish; easy for non-Jews. Developmentally appropriate for children. Downright fun for adults. Other unique features include the Passover food symbols, like matzah, explained at the appropriate time in the story; special sections to personalize & teach about world Jewry. Difficult concepts like slavery are taught through action, songs, & pictures. Lyrics respond to children's thinking while tackling complicated issues surrounding freedom. Plentiful, detailed drawings emphasize immediacy of ideas & illustrate every idea & ceremonial symbol.
Publisher Provided Annotation.

Warlow, Aidan, ed. Start with Rhymes, Nos. 7-12: Little Miss Muffett; Baa Baa Black Sheep; 1, 2 Buckle My Shoe; Rain; In a Dark Dark Wood & Round the Moon, 6 bks. Smith, Lesley, et al, illus. 48p. (Orig.). (gr. k-1). 1988. Set. pap. text ed. 29.60 (1-55624-518-1) Wright Group.
Warmbold, Jean, jt. auth. see Steinbaum, Michael.
Warm Night Rain, jt. auth. see Chief Little Summer.
Warner, Gertrude C. Benny Uncovers a Mystery. (gr. 2-7). 1991. 10.95 (0-8075-0644-3); pap. 3.50 (0-8075-0645-1) A Whitman.
—Bicycle Mystery. Cunningham, David, illus. LC 79-126428. 128p. (gr. 2-7). 1971. PLB 10.95 (0-8075-0708-3); pap. 3.50 (0-8075-0709-1) A Whitman.
—Blue Bay Mystery. LC 61-15230. (Illus.). (gr. 2-7). 1961. PLB 10.95 (0-8075-0793-8); pap. 3.50 (0-8075-0794-6) A Whitman.
—Boxcar Children. LC 42-1418. (gr. 2-7). 1942. PLB 10.95 (0-8075-0851-9); pap. 3.50 (0-8075-0852-7); Set of 4, Nos. 1-4. pap. 14.00 boxed (0-8075-0854-3); Set of 4, Nos. 5-8. pap. 14.00 boxed (0-8075-0857-8) A Whitman.
—The Boxcar Children. (Illus.). 158p. 1992. Repr. PLB 14.95x (0-89966-902-6) Buccaneer Bks.
—Bus Station Mystery. Cunningham, David, illus. LC 74-8293. 128p. (gr. 2-7). 1974. PLB 10.95 (0-8075-0975-2); pap. 3.50 (0-8075-0976-0) A Whitman.
—Caboose Mystery. LC 66-10791. (Illus.). 128p. (gr. 2-7). 1966. PLB 10.95 (0-8075-1008-4); pap. 3.50 (0-8075-1009-2) A Whitman.
—The Castle Mystery. (gr. 4-7). 1993. 10.95 (0-8075-1078-5); pap. 3.50 (0-8075-1079-3) A Whitman.
—Houseboat Mystery. Cunningham, David, illus. LC 67-26521. 128p. (gr. 2-7). 1966. PLB 10.95 (0-8075-3412-9); pap. 3.50 (0-8075-3413-7) A Whitman.
—Lighthouse Mystery. Cunningham, David, illus. LC 63-20354. 128p. (gr. 2-7). 1963. PLB 10.95 (0-8075-4545-7); pap. 3.50 (0-8075-4546-5) A Whitman.
—Mike's Mystery. LC 60-8428. (Illus.). 128p. (gr. 2-7). 1960. PLB 10.95 (0-8075-5140-6); pap. 3.50 (0-8075-5141-4) A Whitman.
—Mountain Top Mystery. Cunningham, David, illus. LC 64-7722. 128p. (gr. 2-7). 1964. PLB 10.95 (0-8075-5292-5); pap. 3.50 (0-8075-5293-3) A Whitman.
—Mystery at the Dog Show. (Illus.). 128p. (gr. 2-7). 1993. PLB 10.95 (0-8075-5395-6); pap. 3.50 (0-8075-5394-8) A Whitman.
—Mystery Behind the Wall. Cunningham, David, illus. LC 72-13356. 128p. (gr. 2-7). 1973. PLB 10.95 (0-8075-5364-6); pap. 3.50 (0-8075-5367-0) A Whitman.
—The Mystery Horse. (Illus.). 128p. (gr. 2-7). 1993. PLB 10.95 (0-8075-5338-7); pap. 3.50 (0-8075-5339-5) A Whitman.

—Mystery in the Sand. Cunningham, David, illus. LC 70-165823. 128p. (gr. 2-7). 1971. PLB 10.95 (0-8075-5373-5); pap. 3.50 (0-8075-5372-7) A Whitman.
—The Mystery of the Lost Village. (gr. 4-7). 1993. 10.95 (0-8075-5400-6); pap. 3.50 (0-8075-5401-4) A Whitman.
—The Mystery of the Purple Pool. (gr. 4-7). 1994. pap. 3.50 (0-8075-5408-1) A Whitman.
—The Mystery of the Purple Pool. 1993. 10.95 (0-8075-5407-3) A Whitman.
—The Mystery on the Ice. (gr. 4-7). 1993. 10.95 (0-8075-5414-6); pap. 3.50 (0-8075-5413-8) A Whitman.
—Mystery Ranch. Gringhuis, Dirk, illus. LC 58-9953. 128p. (gr. 2-7). 1958. PLB 10.95 (0-8075-5390-5); pap. 3.50 (0-8075-5391-3) A Whitman.
—Schoolhouse Mystery. Cunningham, David, illus. LC 65-23889. 128p. (gr. 2-7). 1965. PLB 10.95 (0-8075-7262-4); pap. 3.50 (0-8075-7263-2) A Whitman.
—Snowbound Mystery. Cunningham, David, illus. LC 68-9124. (gr. 2-7). 1968. PLB 10.95 (0-8075-7517-8); pap. 3.50 (0-8075-7516-X) A Whitman.
—Surprise Island. Gehr, Mary, illus. LC 49-49618. (gr. 2-7). 1949. PLB 10.95 (0-8075-7673-5); pap. 3.50 (0-8075-7674-3) A Whitman.
—Tree House Mystery. Cunningham, David, illus. LC 77-91744. 128p. (gr. 2-7). 1969. PLB 10.95 (0-8075-8086-4); pap. 3.50 (0-8075-8087-2) A Whitman.
—Woodshed Mystery. LC 62-19726. (Illus.). 128p. (gr. 2-7). 1962. PLB 10.95 (0-8075-9206-4); pap. 3.50 (0-8075-9207-2) A Whitman.
—Yellow House Mystery. LC 53-13243. (Illus.). 128p. (gr. 2-7). 1953. PLB 10.95 (0-8075-9365-6); pap. 3.50 (0-8075-9366-4) A Whitman.
Warner, Gertrude C., created by. The Amusement Park Mystery. (Illus.). (gr. 2-7). 1992. 10.95 (0-8075-0320-7); pap. 3.50g (0-8075-0319-3) A Whitman.
—The Animal Shelter Mystery. (Illus.). (gr. 2-7). 1991. 10.95 (0-8075-0368-1); pap. 3.50g (0-8075-0367-3) A Whitman.
—The Camp-Out Mystery. (Illus.). 192p. (gr. 2-7). 1992. PLB 10.95 (0-8075-1053-X); pap. 3.50 (0-8075-1052-1) A Whitman.
—The Deserted Library Mystery. (Illus.). (gr. 2-7). 1991. 10.95g (0-8075-1561-2); pap. 3.50g (0-8075-1560-4) A Whitman.
—The Disappearing Friend Mystery. 192p. (gr. 2-7). 1992. 10.95g (0-8075-1627-9); pap. 3.50 (0-8075-1628-7) A Whitman.
—The Haunted Cabin Mystery. (Illus.). (gr. 2-7). 1991. 10.95g (0-8075-3179-0); pap. 3.50g (0-8075-3178-2) A Whitman.
—The Mystery Cruise. (Illus.). 192p. (gr. 2-7). 1992. PLB 10.95 (0-8075-5362-X); pap. 3.50 (0-8075-5368-9) A Whitman.
—The Mystery Girl. (Illus.). 192p. (gr. 2-7). 1992. PLB 10.95 (0-8075-5370-0); pap. 3.50 (0-8075-5371-9) A Whitman.
—The Mystery in the Snow. (Illus.). 192p. (gr. 2-7). 1992. 10.95g (0-8075-5392-1); pap. 3.50 (0-8075-5393-X) A Whitman.
—The Mystery of the Hidden Painting. (Illus.). (gr. 2-7). 1992. 10.95 (0-8075-5383-2); pap. 3.50g (0-8075-5379-4) A Whitman.
—The Mystery of the Mixed-Up Zoo. (Illus.). 192p. (gr. 2-7). 1992. PLB 10.95 (0-8075-5386-7); pap. 3.50 (0-8075-5385-9) A Whitman.
—The Mystery of the Singing Ghost. (Illus.). 192p. (gr. 2-7). 1992. 10.95g (0-8075-5397-2); pap. 3.50 (0-8075-5398-0) A Whitman.
—The Old Motel Mystery. (Illus.). (gr. 2-7). 1991. 10.95 (0-8075-5967-9); pap. 3.50g (0-8075-5966-0) A Whitman.
—The Pizza Mystery. Tang, Charles, illus. LC 92-32263. 128p. (gr. 2-7). 1993. PLB 10.95 (0-8075-6534-2); pap. 3.50 (0-8075-6535-0) A Whitman.
Warner, J. F. Rhode Island: Hello U. S. A. (gr. 4-7). 1993. 17.50 (0-8225-2731-6) Lerner Pubns.
—The U. S. Marine Corps. (Illus.). 80p. (gr. 5 up). 1991. PLB 22.95 (0-8225-1432-X) Lerner Pubns.
Warner, Jack. Map Attack: Understanding Globes & Maps. (Illus.). 176p. (gr. 5-8). 1991. pap. 5.25 (0-13-962903-3, 640122) P-H.
—Massachusetts. LC 93-37203. 1994. PLB write for info. (0-8225-2737-5) Lerner Pubns.
Warner, Jack & Warner, Margaret. Aliens & UFO's. 158p. (gr. 6-8). 1994. pap. 8.75 (0-89061-747-3) Jamestown Pubs.
Warner, Jerry S. Charlie McTwiddle & the Wobbly-Wheeled Sputter Putter Popper. Telfer, Judy, ed. Conlin, Jim, illus. LC 90-70308. 128p. (gr. 3-7). 1990. PLB 12.95 (0-9626293-0-8) Windsor Medallion.
Warner, John & Walker, Margaret. Apparitions. (Illus.). 160p. (gr. 6 up). 1987. pap. text ed. 7.75 (0-89061-465-2) Jamestown Pubs.
Warner, John F. Colonial American Home Life. (Illus.). 112p. (gr. 5-8). 1993. PLB 12.90 (0-531-12541-6) Watts.
Warner, Keith Q., tr. see Zobel, Joseph.
Warner, Laverne & Craycraft, Ken. Themetivities. (Illus.). 144p. (ps-2). 1992. wkbk. 11.95 (0-86653-680-9, 1414) Good Apple.

Warner, Laverne & Craycraft, Kenneth. Fun with Familiar Tunes. Filkins, Vanessa, illus. 128p. (ps-3). 1987. pap. 10.95 (0-86653-414-8, GA1014) Good Apple.
Warner, Lucille S. From Slave to Abolitionist: The Life of William Wells Brown. Feelings, Tom, illus. LC 76-2288. 144p. (gr. 6 up). 1993. 13.99 (0-8037-2743-7) Dial Bks Young.
Warner, Margaret, jt. auth. see Warner, Jack.
Warner, Margaret B., jt. auth. see Hayward, Ruth A.
Warner, Norma, jt. auth. see Goldstein, Nettie.
Warner, Rachel. Our Class. (Illus.). 25p. (gr. 2-4). 1991. 12.95 (0-237-60139-7, Pub. by Evans Bros Ltd) Trafalgar.
—Our Steel Band. (Illus.). 25p. (gr. 2-4). 1991. 12.95 (0-237-60143-5, Pub. by Evans Bros Ltd) Trafalgar.
Warner, Rachel, jt. auth. see Hasan, Khurshid.
Warner, Rita. Wonderful World of Horses Color & Story Album. (Illus.). 32p. (Orig.). (gr. 3 up). 1976. pap. 4.50 (0-8431-1709-5) Price Stern.
Warner, Rita, illus. North American Indians Color & Story Album. 32p. (Orig.). 1978. pap. 4.50 (0-8431-1727-3) Price Stern.
Warnke, Marie, jt. auth. see Gould, Toni S.
Warnock, Kitty. Mary Wollstonecraft. (Illus.). 64p. (gr. 6-10). 1991. 13.95 (0-237-60036-6, Pub. by Evans Bros Ltd) Trafalgar.
Warr, Michael. Painting Detail in Watercolour. (Illus.). 128p. (gr. 10-12). 1993. 24.95 (0-7153-9405-3, Pub. by David & Charles Pub UK) Sterling.
Warren, Andrea. Searching for Love. 240p. (Orig.). (gr. 7-12). 1987. pap. 2.95 (0-553-26292-0) Bantam.
Warren, Betsy. Explorers in Early Texas. Long, Joann M., ed. (Illus.). 128p. (gr. 4 up). 1992. 14.95 (0-937460-74-5) Hendrick-Long.
—Indians Who Lived in Texas. Warren, Betsy, illus. LC 71-76607. 48p. (gr. 2 up). 1981. Repr. of 1970 ed. lib. bdg. 10.95 (0-937460-02-8) Hendrick-Long.
—Let's Look Inside a Tepee. Warren, Betsy, illus. 28p. (Orig.). (gr. 3 up). 1989. pap. 3.50 (0-9618660-2-0) Ranch Gate Bks.
—Let's Remember Texas, the Twenty-Eighth State. (Illus.). 36p. (gr. 3-7). 1984. pap. 5.95 (0-937460-13-3) Hendrick-Long.
—Let's Remember When Texas Belonged to Spain. Warren, Betsy, illus. 32p. (gr. 3-7). 1982. pap. 5.95 (0-937460-04-4) Hendrick-Long.
—Let's Remember When Texas Was a Republic. Warren, Betsy, illus. 32p. (gr. 3-7). 1983. pap. 5.95 (0-937460-09-5) Hendrick-Long.
—Let's Remember...Indians of Texas. Warren, Betsy, illus. 32p. (gr. 3-7). 1981. pap. 5.95 (0-937460-03-6) Hendrick-Long.
—Let's Remember...When Texas Belonged to Mexico. (Illus.). 32p. (gr. 3-7). 1982. pap. 5.95 (0-937460-07-9) Hendrick Long.
—The Story of Texas: A History Picture Book. Warren, Betsy, illus. 46p. (gr. 3 up). 1988. pap. 3.50 (0-9618660-1-2) Ranch Gate Bks.
—Texas in Historic Sites & Symbols. Warren, Betsy, illus. 28p. (gr. k-3). 1982. pap. 5.50 (0-937460-05-2) Hendrick-Long.
—Twenty Texans, Historic Lives for Young Readers. LC 85-13926. (Illus.). 114p. (gr. 3-7). 1985. lib. bdg. 11.95 (0-937460-17-6) Hendrick-Long.
—Wilderness Walkers: Naturalists in Early Texas. La Freniere, Annette, ed. Warren, Betsy, illus. LC 55-7501. 112p. (gr. 4-8). 1987. PLB 12.95 (0-937460-26-5) Hendrick-Long.
Warren, Betsy & Ingerson, Martha. The Thirteen Colonies: A History Picture Book. (Illus.). 32p. (Orig.). (gr. 3 up). 1992. pap. 3.50 (0-9618660-3-9) Ranch Gate Bks.
Warren, Betsy, jt. auth. see Grisham, Noel.
Warren, Elizabeth. I Can Read About Baby Animals. LC 74-24879. (Illus.). (gr. 1-2). 1975. pap. 1.95 (0-89375-060-3) Troll Assocs.
—I Can Read About Bats. LC 74-24928. (Illus.). (gr. 2-4). 1975. pap. 1.95 (0-89375-064-6) Troll Assocs.
—I Can Read About Indians. LC 74-24880. (Illus.). (gr. 2-4). 1975. pap. 1.95 (0-89375-061-1) Troll Assocs.
—I Can Read About Trees & Plants. LC 74-24991. (Illus.). (gr. 2-4). 1975. pap. 1.95 (0-89375-069-7) Troll Assocs.
Warren, Hank, ed. see Corbett, Julia.
Warren, James A. Portrait of a Tragedy: America & the Vietnam War. Summers, Harry G., Jr., frwd. by. LC 88-39560. (Illus.). 208p. (gr. 5 up). 17.95 (0-688-07454-5) Lothrop. Postponed.
Warren, Jean. Alphabet & Number Rhymes. Bittinger, Gayle, ed. Walker-Carleson, Cora, illus. 160p. (Orig.). (ps-1). 1989. pap. text ed. 14.95 (0-911019-27-8) Warren Pub Hse.
—Animal Patterns. Bittinger, Gayle, ed. Mohrmann, Gary, illus. 240p. (Orig.). (ps-1). 1990. pap. text ed. 16.95 (0-911019-31-6) Warren Pub Hse.
—Animal Rhymes: Reproducible Pre-Reading Books for Young Children. Bittinger, Gayle, ed. Buskirk, Judith P., illus. 160p. (Orig.). (ps-1). 1990. pap. text ed. 14.95 (0-911019-34-0) Warren Pub Hse.
—Color, Shape & Season Rhymes: Reproducible Pre-Reading Books for Young Children. Bittinger, Gayle, ed. Walker-Carleson, Cora, illus. 160p. (Orig.). (ps-1). 1989. pap. text ed. 14.95 (0-911019-28-6) Warren Pub Hse.
—Crafts. 80p. (gr. k-2). 1983. 7.95 (0-912107-04-9) Monday Morning Bks.

—Ellie the Evergreen. Cubley, Kathleen, ed. Connelly, Gwen & Tourillotte, Barb, illus. LC 92-62825. 32p. (Orig.). (ps-2). 1993. 12.95 (0-911019-66-9); pap. text ed. 5.95 (0-911019-67-7) Warren Pub Hse.
—Everyday Patterns: Multi-Sized Patterns for Making Cut-Outs, Puppets, & Learning Games. Bittinger, Gayle, ed. Mohrmann, Gary, illus. 240p. (Orig.). (ps-1). 1990. pap. text ed. 16.95 (0-911019-35-9) Warren Pub Hse.
—The Gingerbread Kid. Cubley, Kathleen, ed. Shimono, Judy, illus. 8p. (Orig.). (ps-2). pap. 2.95 (0-911019-83-9) Warren Pub Hse.
—Goldilocks & the Three Bears. Cubley, Kathleen, ed. Shimono, Judy, illus. 8p. (Orig.). (ps-2). 1994. pap. 2.95 (0-911019-85-5) Warren Pub Hse.
—Henny Penny. Cubley, Kathleen, ed. Shimono, Judy, illus. 8p. (Orig.). (ps-2). 1994. pap. 2.95 (0-911019-84-7) Warren Pub Hse.
—Huff & Puff Around the World: A Totline Teaching Tale. Cubley, Kathleen, ed. Piper, Molly & Ekberg, Marion, illus. LC 93-5490. 32p. (Orig.). (ps-2). 1994. 12.95 (0-911019-81-2); pap. 5.95 (0-911019-80-4) Warren Pub Hse.
—Huff & Puff Go to School. Piper, Molly & Ekberg, Marion, illus. 1993. 12.95; pap. 5.95 (0-911019-94-4) Warren Pub Hse.
—Huff & Puff on Halloween. Cubley, Kathleen, ed. Isaacs, Jean & Tourtillotte, Barb, illus. LC 92-62824. 32p. (Orig.). (ps-2). 1993. 12.95 (0-911019-68-5); pap. text ed. 5.95 (0-911019-69-3) Warren Pub Hse.
—Huff & Puff on Thanksgiving: A Totline Teaching Tale. Cubley, Kathleen, ed. Piper, Molly & Ekberg, Marion, illus. LC 93-13545. 32p. (Orig.). (ps-2). 1993. 12.95 (0-911019-71-5); pap. 5.95 (0-911019-70-7) Warren Pub Hse.
—Huff & Puff's April Showers: A Totline Teaching Tale. Cubley, Kathleen, ed. Piper, Molly & Ekberg, Marion, illus. LC 93-5489. 32p. (Orig.). (ps-2). 1994. 12.95 (0-911019-79-0); pap. 5.95 (0-911019-78-2) Warren Pub Hse.
—Language Games. 80p. (gr. k-2). 1983. 7.95 (0-912107-05-7) Monday Morning Bks.
—Learning Games. 80p. (gr. k-2). 1983. 7.95 (0-912107-06-5) Monday Morning Bks.
—Little Red Riding Hood. Cubley, Kathleen, ed. Shimono, Judy, illus. 8p. (Orig.). (ps-2). 1994. pap. 2.95 (0-911019-88-X) Warren Pub Hse.
—Mini-Mini Musicals: Simple Musicals for Young Children Sung to Familiar Tunes. McKinnon, Elizabeth S., ed. Ekberg, Marion, illus. LC 86-51508. 80p. (Orig.). (ps-1). 1987. pap. 7.95 (0-911019-14-6) Warren Pub Hse.
—Movement Time. 80p. (gr. k-2). 1984. 7.95 (0-912107-17-0) Monday Morning Bks.
—Nature Patterns: Multi-Sized Patterns for Making Cut-Outs, Puppets & Learning Games. Bittinger, Gayle, ed. Mohrmann, Gary, illus. 240p. (Orig.). (ps-1). 1990. pap. text ed. 16.95 (0-911019-36-7) Warren Pub Hse.
—Nursery Rhyme Theme-a-Saurus: The Great Big Book of Nursery Rhyme Teaching Themes. Cubley, Kathleen, ed. (Illus.). 160p. (Orig.). (ps-1). 1993. pap. text ed. 14.95 (0-911019-55-3) Warren Pub Hse.
—Object Rhymes: Reproducible Pre-Reading Books for Young Children. Bittinger, Gayle, ed. Tourtillotte, Barb, illus. 160p. (Orig.). (ps-1). 1990. pap. text ed. 14.95 (0-911019-33-2) Warren Pub Hse.
—One - Two - Three Books. Bittinger, Gayle, ed. Walker, Cora, illus. LC 89-50120. 80p. (Orig.). (ps-1). 1989. pap. text ed. 7.95 (0-911019-23-5) Warren Pub Hse.
—One-Two-Three Art: Open-Ended Art Activities for Young Children. Ekberg, Marion H., illus. LC 85-50434. 160p. (Orig.). (ps-1). 1985. pap. 14.95 (0-911019-06-5) Warren Pub Hse.
—One-Two-Three Games: No-Lose Group Games for Young Children. McKinnon, Elizabeth, ed. Ekberg, Marion, illus. LC 85-50435. 80p. (Orig.). (ps-1). 1986. pap. 7.95 (0-911019-09-X) Warren Pub Hse.
—One-Two-Three Math. Ekberg, Marion, illus. LC 92-80528. 160p. 1992. 14.95 (0-911019-52-9, WPH 0409) Warren Pub Hse.
—One-Two-Three Murals: Simple Murals to Make Using Children's Open-Ended Art. Bittinger, Gayle, ed. Walker, Cora, illus. LC 89-50121. 80p. (Orig.). (ps-1). 1989. pap. 7.95 (0-911019-22-7) Warren Pub Hse.
—One-Two-Three Puppets: Simple Puppets to Make for Working with Young Children. Bittinger, Gayle, ed. Walker, Cora, illus. LC 89-50122. 80p. (Orig.). (ps-1). 1989. pap. 7.95 (0-911019-21-9) Warren Pub Hse.
—One-Two-Three Rhymes, Stories & Songs. Ekberg, Marion, illus. LC 91-67075. 80p. 1992. 8.95 (0-911019-50-2, WPH 0408) Warren Pub Hse.
—Storytime Theme-a-Saurus: The Great Big Book of Storytime Teaching Themes. Cubley, Kathleen, ed. (Illus.). 160p. (Orig.). (ps-1). 1993. pap. text ed. 14.95 (0-911019-56-1) Warren Pub Hse.
—Super Snacks. Mulvey, Glen, illus. 48p. 1992. 6.95 (0-911019-49-9, WPH 1601) Warren Pub Hse.
—Teeny-Tiny Folktales: Simple Folktales for Young Children Plus Flannelboard Patterns. McKinnon, Elizabeth S., compiled by. LC 86-51510. (Illus.). 80p. (Orig.). (ps-1). 1987. pap. 7.95 (0-911019-12-X) Warren Pub Hse.
—Theme-A-Saurus II: The Great Big Book of More Teaching Units. Bittinger, Gayle, ed. Walker-Carleson, Cora, illus. LC 89-51179. 280p. (Orig.). (ps-1). 1990. pap. text ed. 19.95 (0-911019-26-X) Warren Pub Hse.

—Theme-A-Saurus: The Great Big Book of Mini Teaching Topics. Bittinger, Gayle, ed. Walker, Cora L., illus. LC 88-51450. 280p. (Orig.). (ps-1). 1989. pap. text ed. 19.95 (0-911019-20-0) Warren Pub Hse.
—The Three Billy Goats. Cubley, Kathleen, ed. Shimono, Judy, illus. 8p. (Orig.). (ps-2). 1994. pap. 2.95 (0-911019-87-1) Warren Pub Hse.
—The Three Little Pigs. Cubley, Kathleen, ed. Shimono, Judy, illus. 8p. (Orig.). (ps-2). 1994. pap. 2.95 (0-911019-89-8) Warren Pub Hse.
—The Wishing Fish: A Totline Teaching Tale. Cubley, Kathleen, ed. Tourtillotte, Barbara, illus. LC 93-12523. 32p. (Orig.). (ps-2). 1994. 12.95 (0-911019-73-1); pap. 5.95 (0-911019-74-X) Warren Pub Hse.
Warren, Jean & McKinnon, Elizabeth S. Small World Celebrations: Multi-Cultural Holidays to Celebrate with Young Children. Bittinger, Gayle, ed. Ekberg, Marion H., illus. LC 88-50594. 160p. (Orig.). (ps-1). 1988. pap. 14.95 (0-911019-19-7) Warren Pub Hse.
Warren, Jean & Shroyer, Susan. Piggyback Songs to Sign. Kimmel, Joan, illus. LC 85-50433. 96p. 1992. 8.95 (0-911019-53-7, WPH 0209) Warren Pub Hse.
Warren, Jean, compiled by. More Piggyback Songs: New Songs Sung to the Tunes of Childhood Favorites. Ekberg, Marion H., illus. LC 84-90020. 96p. (Orig.). (ps-1). 1984. pap. 8.95 (0-911019-02-2) Warren Pub Hse.
—Piggyback Songs: New Song Sung to the Tunes of Childhood Favorites. Ekberg, Marion H., illus. LC 83-90111. 64p. (Orig.). (ps-1). 1983. pap. 7.95 (0-911019-01-4) Warren Pub Hse.
Warren, Jean & Bittinger, Gayle, eds. Holiday Patterns: Multi-Sized Patterns for Making Cut-Outs, Puppets & Learning Games. Mohrmann, Gary, illus. 240p. (Orig.). (ps-1). 1991. pap. text ed. 16.95 (0-911019-45-6) Warren Pub Hse.
—Piggyback Songs for School. Ekberg, Marion, illus. LC 85-50433. 96p. (Orig.). (ps-1). 1991. pap. text ed. 8.95 (0-911019-44-8) Warren Pub Hse.
Warren, Jean & McKinnon, Elizabeth, eds. Piggyback Songs in Praise of God. Ekberg, Marion H., illus. 80p. (Orig.). (ps-1). 1986. pap. 7.95 (0-911019-10-3) Warren Pub Hse.
—Piggyback Songs in Praise of Jesus: New Songs Sung to the Tunes of Childhood Favorites. Ekberg, Marion H., illus. 96p. (Orig.). (ps-1). 1986. pap. 8.95 (0-911019-11-1) Warren Pub Hse.
Warren, Jean, ed. see Bittinger, Gayle.
Warren, Jean, ed. see McKinnon, Elizabeth.
Warren, Jean, jt. ed. see McKinnon, Elizabeth S.
Warren, Jean, et al, eds. Alphabet Theme-a-Saurus: The Great Big Book of Letter Recognition. Mohrmann, Gary, illus. LC 90-71272. 280p. (ps-1). 1991. pap. text ed. 19.95 (0-911019-38-3) Warren Pub Hse.
Warren, Mary P. Lord, I'm Back Again: Story Devotions for Girls. LC 81-65651. 112p. (Orig.). 1981. pap. 5.99 (0-8066-1887-6, 10-4098, Augsburg) Augsburg Fortress.
Warren, Peggy. Where Love Goes. (Illus.). 36p. (gr. k-3). 1992. 5.95 (0-9628710-3-6) Art After Five.
—Where Love Is. (Illus.). (gr. k-3). 1992. 5.95 (0-9628710-2-8) Art After Five.
—Where Love Starts. LC 91-77291. (Illus.). 36p. (gr. k-3). 1992. 5.95 (0-9628710-4-4) Art After Five.
Warren, Robert. Facts of Wife (the)-for Teenage Girls from 13 to 53. Dean, Abner, illus. Berle, Milton, frwd. by. (Illus.). 1968. 3.95 (0-913830-01-1) Rodney.

Warren, Sandra & Pfleger, Deborah B. Arlie the Alligator. Thomas, Deborah, illus. LC 91-73758. 48p. (ps-3). Date not set. PLB 13.95 casebound (1-880175-13-4); bk. & cass. 19.90 (1-880175-11-8); audiocassette 5.95 (1-880175-12-6) Arlie Enter.
Arlie is a very curious alligator who longs to make friends with the strange creatures at the beach. Find out who the strange creatures are & what happens when he attempts to talk to them. The 10-minute audio cassette is fully produced with actors & actresses in mini-musical style. Four catchy tunes have children singing along the first time they listen. In beautiful color, this casebound, open-ended story book also includes a page about real alligators & sheet music. A creative use of fonts signals the change from song lyrics to dialogue. Non-readers enjoy the audio tape & pictures, while young readers & middle readers love to follow along, singing & reading, word-for-word, as the delightful story unfolds. Creative thinking is enhanced as children are encouraged to help Arlie find a way to communicate with the creatures. Unique in children's
literature, ARLIE THE ALLIGATOR makes a great addition to the children's books-on-tape section of the library, elementary music libraries, elementary classrooms, in homes or for that long trip in the car. Activity guide also available, making that important classroom connection.
Publisher Provided Annotation.

Warren, Sandra, ed. Being Gifted: Because You're Special from the Rest. 68p. (Orig.). (ps-6). 1987. pap. 9.99 (0-89824-173-1) Trillium Pr.
Warren, Scott S. Cities in the Sand: The Ancient Civilizations of the Southwest. Warren, Scott S., illus. 64p. (gr. 4-8). 1991. 10.95 (0-8118-0012-1) Chronicle Bks.
Warren, Shaun de see De Warren, Shaun.
Warren, Shirley, ed. see Sheetz, Russ.
Warren, Vic & Reasoner, Charles. Alpha Books. Woodman, Nancy, illus. (ps-1). 1991. miniature board books in a tray 14.95 (1-878624-66-0) McClanahan Bk.
—Alpha-Books & Count with Us. Woodman, Nancy, illus. (ps-1). 1991. miniature board books in a tray 19.95 (1-878624-83-0) McClanahan Bk.
—Count with Us. Woodman, Nancy, illus. (ps-1). 1991. miniature board books in a tray 9.95 (1-878624-67-9) McClanahan Bk.
Warren, William E. Footsteps in the Fog. Frascino, Edward, illus. 112p. (gr. 3-7). 1985. 11.95 (0-13-324807-0) P-H.
—The Graveyard: And Other Not-So-Scary Stories. Frascino, Ward, illus. 128p. 1984. 11.95 (0-13-363623-2) P-H.
—The Headless Ghost: True Tales of the Unexplained. Waldman, Neil, illus. LC 85-28214. 144p. (gr. 6 up). 1986. pap. 12.95 jacketed (0-671-67710-1, Little Simon) S&S Trade.
—The Screaming Skull: True Tales of the Unexplained. Waldman, Neil, illus. LC 87-6909. 144p. (gr. 5 up). 1987. pap. 11.95 jacketed (0-671-66809-9, S&S BFYR) S&S Trade.
Warren, William E. & Frascino, Edward. The Thing in the Swamp & More Not-So-Scary. LC 84-6769. (Illus.). 96p. (gr. 3-7). 1984. 10.95 (0-13-917196-7) P-H.
Warrener. Bunnykins in the Kitchen. 1987. 4.95 (0-670-80569-6) Viking Child Bks.
Warriner, J., et al. English Grammar & Composition: Heritage Edition. large type ed. Incl. First Course, 3 vols. 532p. (gr. 7-12). Set. 128.00 (0-317-02210-5, J-05500-00). (gr. 7-12). 1978. Repr. of 1977 ed. Am Printing Hse.
Warrior, MaRaDa H. Fly with the Heart. Free, Maya S., illus. (Orig.). (gr. 4 up). 1990. pap. text ed. write for info. (0-9622031-1-4) Woman Warrior Heart.
Warshawsky, Gale. Creative Puppetry for Jewish Kids. LC 85-70544. 192p. (Orig.). (gr. 4-7). 1985. pap. text ed. 13.50 (0-86705-017-9) A R E Pub.
Wartik, Nancy. French Canadians. (Illus.). 112p. (gr. 5 up). 1989. 17.95 (0-87754-879-X) Chelsea Hse.
—Memory & Learning. (Illus.). (gr. 6-12). 1992. 18.95 (0-7910-0022-2) Chelsea Hse.
Wartski, Maureen. Belonging. (Orig.). (gr. 7 up). 1993. pap. 3.99 (0-449-70419-X, Juniper) Fawcett.
—Dark Silence. (Orig.). (gr. 9-12). 1994. pap. 3.99 (0-449-70418-1, Juniper) Fawcett.
—My Name Is Nobody. (gr. 8-11). 1988. 16.95 (0-685-19001-3) Walker Pubns.
Wartski, Maureen C. My Brother Is Special. 144p. (gr. 7 up). 1981. pap. 3.50 (0-451-15856-3, Sig) NAL-Dutton.
Warwick, Catherine A. Love Is Like. Iscaro, Nancy L., ed. West Side High School Students, illus. 33p. (Orig.). (gr. 10-12). 1989. pap. text ed. write for info. West Side Pubns.
Warwick, James D. I Told the Spotted Fish. LC 90-84709. 48p. (Orig.). (gr. 9-12). 1993. pap. 7.95x (0-943864-62-3) Davenport.
Warwick Press, ed. see Wright, Jill & Wright, David.
Wasburn, Hope, jt. auth. see Hurwitz, Hilda A.
Wasburn, Mara H., ed. see Hurwitz, Hilda A. & Wasburn, Hope.
Washburn, JoAnn. Maude the Mare. LC 87-51039. (Illus.). 44p. (gr. k-3). 1988. 6.95 (1-55523-123-3) Winston-Derek.
Washburne, Carolyn K. A Multicultural Portrait of Colonial Life. LC 93-10320. (gr. 7 up). 1993. 18.95 (1-85435-657-7) Marshall Cavendish.
Washington, Anthony. Young Run Away. Adoma, Afua, illus. (Orig.). (gr. 3-6). 1984. pap. 2.98 (0-9613078-2-X) Detroit Black.
Washington, Booker T. Up from Slavery. Andrews, C. A., intro. by. (gr. 5 up). 1967. pap. 2.50 (0-8049-0157-0, CL-157) Airmont.
Washington, Dolores E. Begin Basic Budget Saving Shopping Spending, Vol. I. 13p. (gr. 11 up). 1989. wkbk. 2.50x (0-685-26101-8) Dew Educational.
Washington, Irving see York, Carol B.
Washington, Marian, ed. see Woodard, Lynette & Cook, Kevin.
Washington, Rosemary G. Gymnastics Is for Me. Oddie, Alan, photos by. LC 79-4496. (Illus.). 48p. (gr. 2-5). 1979. PLB 13.50 (0-8225-1078-2) Lerner Pubns.

—Karting: Racing's Fast Little Cars. LC 80-12385. (Illus.). 48p. (gr. 4-9). 1980. PLB 14.95 (0-8225-0435-9) Lerner Pubns.
Washington, Vivian E. I Am Somebody, I Am Me: A Black Child's Credo. Stockett, Thomas & Washington, Luther, illus. 35p. (gr. 2-6). 1986. pap. 8.50 (0-935132-07-4) C H Fairfax.
Washton, Arnold M. & Boundy, Donna. Cocaine & Crack: What You Need to Know. LC 88-16814. (Illus.). 96p. (gr. 6 up). 1989. lib. bdg. 16.95 (0-89490-162-1) Enslow Pubs.
Waskey, Leah. Monster Gallery Color & Story Album. Savee, Mark, illus. 32p. 1973. pap. 4.50 (0-8431-1728-1) Price Stern.
Waskow, Arthur, et al. Before There Was a Before. LC 84-11177. (Illus.). 88p. (gr. 1-6). 1984. 8.95 (0-915361-08-6) Modan-Adama Bks.
Wasser, Edward, jt. auth. see Greenbaum, David.
Wasserman, Dan, ed. see Cox, Mike, et al.
Wasserman, Dan, ed. see Cox, Mike & Cox, Kris.
Wasserman, Dan, ed. see Reese, Bob.
Wasserman, Dan, ed. see Schoder, Judy.
Wasserman, Dan, ed. see Shebar, Sharon.
Wasserman, Dan, ed. see Willoughby, Alana.
Wasserman, Dan, ed. see Winder, Jack.
Wasserman, Debra & Stahler, Charles, eds. I Love Animals & Broccoli. Ransom, Ruth, intro. by. 48p. (Orig.). 1985. pap. 5.00 (0-931411-01-7) Vegetarian Resc.
Wassermann, Jack, jt. auth. see Wassermann, Selma.
Wassermann, Selma & Wassermann, Jack. The Book of Comparing. Smith, Dennis, illus. 32p. (gr. k-3). 1990. lib. bdg. 12.85 (0-8027-6944-6); pap. 4.95 (0-8027-9451-3) Walker & Co.
—The Book of Deciding. Smith, Dennis, illus. LC 89-78073. (gr. k-3). 1990. lib. bdg. 12.85 (0-8027-6952-7); pap. 4.95 (0-8027-9456-4) Walker & Co.
—The Book of Hypotheses. Smith, Dennis, illus. LC 89-78082. 32p. (gr. k-3). 1990. PLB 12.85 (0-8027-6946-2); pap. 4.95 (0-8027-9452-1) Walker & Co.
—The Book of Imagining. Smith, Dennis, illus. LC 89-77869. 32p. (gr. k-3). 1990. PLB 12.85 (0-8027-6948-9); pap. 4.95 (0-8027-9454-8) Walker & Co.
—The Book of Judging. Smith, Dennis, illus. 32p. (gr. k-3). 1990. lib. bdg. 12.85 (0-8027-6950-0); pap. 4.95 (0-8027-9455-6) Walker & Co.
—The Book of Solving Problems. Smith, Dennis, illus. 32p. (gr. k-3). 1990. lib. bdg. 12.85 (0-8027-6954-3); pap. 4.95 (0-8027-9457-2) Walker & Co.
Wasserstein, Wendy see Lamb, Wendy.
Wasson, Valentina P. The Chosen Baby. 3rd ed. LC 76-41391. (gr. k-3). 1977. 15.00 (0-397-31738-7, Lipp Jr Bks) HarpC Child Bks.
Watanabe, Hitomi. Children of the World: Nepal. LC 86-42806. (Illus.). 64p. (gr. 5-6). 1987. PLB 19.93 (1-55532-166-6) Gareth Stevens Inc.
Watanabe, Shigeo. How Do I Put It on? Ohtomo, Yasuo, illus. LC 79-12714. (gr. 2-4). 1984. (Philomel); pap. 5.95 (0-399-21040-7, Philomel) Putnam Pub Group.
—I Can Take a Walk! Ohtomo, Yasuo, illus. 32p. 1991. (Philomel Bks); pap. 4.95 (0-399-21847-5, Philomel Bks) Putnam Pub Group.
—Let's Go Swimming. Ohtomo, Yasuo, illus. 32p. (ps-2). 1990. 10.95 (0-399-21896-3, Philomel Bks) Putnam Pub Group.
—What a Good Lunch! (Illus.). 32p. (ps-2). 1991. (Philomel Bks); pap. 5.95 (0-399-21845-9, Philomel Bks) Putnam Pub Group.
—Where's My Daddy? (Illus.). 32p. 1991. (Philomel Bks); pap. 5.95 (0-399-21851-3, Philomel Bks) Putnam Pub Group.
—Where's My Daddy? (ps-3). 1996. pap. 5.95 (0-399-22427-0, Philomel Bks) Putnam Pub Group.
Watanabe, Yuichi. Wally the Whale Who Loved Balloons. Ooka, D. T., tr. from JPN. Watanabe, Yuichi, illus. 32p. (ps-4). 1982. 11.95 (0-89346-150-4) Heian Intl.
Waterlow, Julia. The Amazon. Waterlow, Julia, photos by. LC 92-25446. (Illus.). 48p. (gr. 5-8). 1993. PLB 22.80 (0-8114-3101-0) Raintree Steck-V.
—Brazil. LC 91-48018. (Illus.). 48p. (gr. 5-8). 1992. PLB 13.90 (0-531-18439-0, Pub. by Bookwright Pr) Watts.
—China. (Illus.). 48p. (gr. 5-8). 1990. PLB 13.90 (0-531-18333-5, Pub. by Bookwright Pr) Watts.
—China. LC 90-25276. (Illus.). 32p. (gr. k-4). 1991. 12.40 (0-531-18393-9, Pub. by Bookwright Pr) Watts.
—China. LC 93-20428. 1994. write for info. (0-531-14271-X) Watts.
—The Explorer Through History. LC 93-5656. (Illus.). 48p. (gr. 5-8). 1994. 15.95 (1-56847-101-7) Thomson Lrning.
—Flood. LC 92-43946. (Illus.). 32p. (gr. 4-8). 1993. PLB 14.95t (1-56847-003-7) Thomson Lrning.
—Greece. LC 91-20086. (Illus.). 32p. (gr. k-4). 1992. PLB 12.40 (0-531-18447-1, Pub. by Bookwright Pr) Watts.
—Journeys. LC 93-6819. (Illus.). 32p. (gr. 4-6). 1993. 14.95 (1-56847-051-7) Thomson Lrning.
—The Nile. Waterlow, Julia, photos by. LC 92-39951. (Illus.). 48p. (gr. 5-6). 1993. PLB 22.80 (0-8114-3100-2) Raintree Steck-V.
Watermill. Midnight Fright: A Collection of Ghost Stories. (gr. 4-7). 1986. pap. 2.50 (0-89375-405-6) Troll Assocs.
Watermill Books Staff. Drawing Whales & Dolphins. (ps-3). 1989. pap. 1.95 (0-8167-1670-6) Troll Assocs.

Watermill Press Staff. Columbus Model Book. (gr. 4-7). 1992. pap. 9.95 (*0-8167-2748-1*) Troll Assocs.
—Drawing Funny Faces. (gr. 4-7). 1989. pap. 1.95 (*0-8167-1668-4*) Troll Assocs.
—Drawing Monsters. (gr. 4-7). 1989. pap. 1.95 (*0-8167-1666-8*) Troll Assocs.
—Drawing Things with Wings. (gr. 4-7). 1989. pap. 1.95 (*0-8167-1669-2*) Troll Assocs.
—Kid's Book of Magic Tricks. 80p. (gr. 4-7). 1992. pap. 4.95 (*0-8167-2739-2*, Pub. by Watermill Pr) Troll Assocs.
—Make It & Fly It. (gr. 4-7). 1992. pap. 5.95 (*0-8167-2848-8*, Pub. by Watermill Pr) Troll Assocs.
—Make It with Balloons. (gr. 4-7). 1992. pap. 5.95 (*0-8167-2849-6*, Pub. by Watermill Pr) Troll Assocs.
—Webster's Dictionary. (gr. 4-7). 1992. pap. 4.95 (*0-8167-2917-4*) Troll Assocs.
—Webster's English-French - Francais-Anglais Dictionary. 224p. (gr. 4-7). 1992. pap. 2.95 (*0-8167-2919-0*, Pub. by Watermill Pr) Troll Assocs.
—Webster's English-Spanish - Espanol-Ingles Dictionary. 224p. (gr. 4-7). 1992. pap. 2.95 (*0-8167-2918-2*, Pub. by Watermill Pr) Troll Assocs.
Wateron, Betty. Plain Noodles. Fitzgerald, Joanne, illus. 32p. 1993. pap. 4.95 (*0-88899-132-0*, Pub. by Groundwood-Douglas & McIntyre CN) Firefly Bks Ltd.
Waters. Computer Fun. Round, illus. 48p. (gr. 5-8). 1984. PLB 10.96 (*0-88110-212-1*); pap. 3.95 (*0-86020-803-6*) EDC.
—Sarah Morton's Day: A Day in the Life of a Pilgrim Girl. 1993. pap. 4.95 (*0-590-47400-6*) Scholastic Inc.
Waters, Alice. Fanny at Chez Panisse: A Child's Restaurant Adventure with Forty-Two Recipes. LC 92-52586. (Illus.). 1992. 23.00 (*0-06-016896-X*, HarpC) HarpC.
Waters, Elizabeth & Harris, Anne. Painting. (Illus.). 48p. (gr. 3-6). 1993. 14.95 (*1-56458-348-1*) Dorling Kindersley.
Waters, Fiona, ed. The Doubleday Book of Bedtime Stories. Dann, Penny, illus. LC 91-44298. 80p. (ps-3). 1992. 16.00 (*0-385-30790-X*) Doubleday.
—Whiskers & Paws. Julian-Ottie, Vanessa, illus. LC 89-77349. 32p. 1990. 9.95 (*0-940793-51-2*, Pub. by Crocodile Bks) Interlink Pub.
Waters, G. Agent Arthur on the Stormy Seas. (Illus.). 48p. 1990. PLB 11.96 (*0-88110-407-8*); pap. 4.95 (*0-7460-0143-6*) EDC.
—Deckchair Detectives. (Illus.). 48p. (gr. 4 up). 1993. PLB 11.96 (*0-88110-524-4*, Usborne); pap. 4.95 (*0-7460-0716-7*, Usborne) EDC.
—Ghost Train to Nowhere. (Illus.). 48p. (gr. 4 up). pap. 4.50 (*0-7460-0677-2*, Usborne) EDC.
—Ghost Train to Nowhere. (Illus.). 48p. (gr. 5 up). PLB 10.96 (*0-88110-519-8*, Usborne); pap. 4.50 (*0-685-48770-9*, Usborne) EDC.
—Haunted Tower. (gr. 4-7). 1989. pap. 4.95 (*0-7460-0332-3*, Usborne) EDC.
—Missing Clue. (Illus.). 48p. (gr. 4 up). PLB 10.96 (*0-88110-523-6*, Usborne); pap. 4.50 (*0-7460-0598-9*, Usborne) EDC.
—Time Train to Ancient Rome. (Illus.). 48p. (gr. 3-5). 1988. PLB 11.96 (*0-88110-302-0*); pap. 4.95 (*0-7460-0153-3*) EDC.
Waters, G., jt. auth. see Oliver, M.
Waters, G., jt. auth. see Tyler, J.
Waters, G., et al. Puzzle Adventures. (Illus.). 144p. (gr. 3-5). 1988. pap. 9.95 (*0-7460-0155-X*) EDC.
—Spinechillers. (Illus.). 144p. (gr. 4 up). pap. 9.95 (*0-7460-0718-3*, Usborne) EDC.
Waters, Gaby & Round, Graham. The Curse of the Lost Idol. (Illus.). 48p. (gr. 4-9). 1987. PLB 11.96 (*0-88110-387-X*); pap. 4.95 (*0-7460-0012-X*) EDC.
—Murder on the Midnight Plane. (Illus.). 48p. (gr. 4-9). 1987. PLB 11.96 (*0-88110-389-6*); pap. 4.95 (*0-86020-952-0*) EDC.
Waters, John. Flood! LC 90-45371. (Illus.). 48p. (gr. 5-6). 1991. RSBE 12.95 (*0-89686-596-7*, Crestwood Hse) Macmillan Child Grp.
Waters, John F. Deep-Sea Vents: Living Worlds Without Sun. LC 92-41111. (Illus.). 48p. (gr. 5 up). 1994. 14.99 (*0-525-65145-4*, Cobblehill Bks) Dutton Child Bks.
—Watching Whales. LC 90-28719. (Illus.). 48p. (gr. 4 up). 1991. 14.95 (*0-525-65072-5*, Cobblehill Bks) Dutton Child Bks.
Waters, Kate. Lion Dancer: Ernie Wan's Chinese New Year. (ps-3). 1991. pap. 3.95 (*0-590-43047-5*) Scholastic Inc.
—Samuel Eaton's Day: A Day in the Life of a Pilgrim Boy. Kendall, Russ, photos by. LC 92-32325. (gr. 4 up). 1993. 14.95 (*0-590-46311-X*) Scholastic Inc.
—Sarah Morton's Day: A Day in the Life of a Pilgrim Girl. Kendall, Russ, photos by. LC 88-35581. (Illus.). 32p. (gr. k-4). 1989. pap. 14.95 (*0-590-42634-6*) Scholastic Inc.
—Sarah Morton's Day: A Day in the Life of a Pilgrim Girl. Kendall, Russ, photos by. (Illus.). 32p. 1991. pap. 4.95 (*0-590-44871-4*, Blue Ribbon Bks) Scholastic Inc.
—The Story of the White House. 1991. 12.95 (*0-590-43335-0*, Scholastic Hardcover) Scholastic Inc.
—The Story of the White House. 1992. 4.95 (*0-590-43334-2*, Blue Ribbon Bks) Scholastic Inc.
Waters, Kate & Slovenz-Low, Madeline. Lion Dancer: Ernie Wan's Chinese New Year. Cooper, Martha, photos by. (Illus.). 32p. (ps-2). 1990. 13.95 (*0-590-43046-7*) Scholastic Inc.
Waters, Linda F. Slices of Chocolate Lives. 176p. (Orig.). 1993. pap. 4.95 (*0-9630887-0-X*) Ethnic Bks.

Waters, Mary. The Little Red Blanket. LC 93-61157. (Illus.). 40p. (ps-3). 1993. PLB 6.95 (*0-9638123-0-0*) WAI Pubng. Mikey receives a little red blanket on his sixth birthday which he takes everywhere. One day Mikey left the car door unlocked & the blanket was stolen. Harry the homeless man took the blanket to keep him warm in bad weather. The blanket is returned but Mikey, being concerned about the conditions of the homeless man, decides to give him the blanket as a gift. The story ends with a message that "it is better to give than to receive." To order contact: WAI Publishing Company, 1559 Rockville Pike, Rockville, MD 20852, 11/1993. $6.95. Sales Tax (5%). Special discount of 10% off the total price for bulk purchases of 10 or more books. Shipping & Handling (1-2 - $2.83; 3-4 - $3.74; 5-6 - $4.31; 7-8 - $4.77; 9-10 -5. 57, etc.).
Publisher Provided Annotation.

Waters, Sarah A. Animal Homes: Secrets of Nature. LC 93-77341. (ps-3). 1993. 9.95 (*0-89577-512-3*, Readers Digest Kids) RD Assn.
—Growing Up: Secrets of Nature. (ps-3). 1992. 9.95 (*0-89577-461-5*, Readers Digest Kids) RD Assn.
—Hidden Animals: Secrets of Nature. (ps-3). 1992. 9.95 (*0-89577-462-3*, Readers Digest Kids) RD Assn.
Waters, Tony. Sailor's Bride. (ps-3). 1991. pap. 13.95 (*0-385-41440-4*) Doubleday.
Waters, Virginia. Color Us Rational. Lee, Penny, illus. LC 78-71011. (ps-3). 1979. pap. 3.00 (*0-917476-15-8*) Inst Rational-Emotive.
—Rational Stories for Children. Rosenfeld, Eileen, illus. (ps-6). 1980. pap. 8.95 (*0-917476-18-2*) Inst Rational-Emotive.
Waterski Magazine Staff. Boating Watersports: The Ultimate Get Started Guide to Towing Fun. Robertson, Jo, ed. LC 89-52016. (Illus.). 100p. 1990. pap. 15.95 (*0-944406-07-6*) World Pub FL.
Waterson, Betty. Starring Quincy Rumpel. 115p. (gr. 3-5). 1991. pap. 5.95 (*0-88899-048-0*, Pub. by Groundwood-Douglas & McIntyre CN) Firefly Bks Ltd.
Waterston, Ellen. Barney's Joy. Pearce, Molly, illus. 32p. 1991. Repr. of 1990 ed. text ed. 14.95 (*0-9628129-2-7*) Sagebrush Bks.
Waterton, Betty. Baby Boat. Fitzgerald, Joanne, illus. LC 89-11173. 32p. (ps-1). 1990. PLB 11.99 (*0-679-90368-2*) Random Bks Yng Read.
—Morris Rumpel & the Wings of Icarus. 108p. (gr. 3-5). 1991. pap. 5.95 (*0-88899-099-5*, Pub. by Groundwood-Douglas & McIntyre CN) Firefly Bks Ltd.
—Pettranella. Blades, Ann, illus. 32p. 1991. pap. 4.95 (*0-88899-108-8*, Pub. by Groundwood-Douglas & McIntyre CN) Firefly Bks Ltd.
—Quincy Rumpel. 96p. (gr. 3-5). 1991. pap. 5.95 (*0-88899-036-7*, Pub. by Groundwood-Douglas & McIntyre CN) Firefly Bks Ltd.
—Quincy Rumpel, P. I. 116p. (gr. 3-5). 1991. pap. 5.95 (*0-88899-081-2*, Pub. by Groundwood-Douglas & McIntyre CN) Firefly Bks Ltd.
—A Salmon for Simon. Blades, Ann, illus. 32p. (ps-2). 1991. pap. 4.95 (*0-88899-107-X*, Pub. by Groundwood-Douglas & McIntyre CN) Firefly Bks Ltd.
Waterton, Kulyn. Orff, Twenty-Seven Dragons & a Snarkel. (Illus.). 24p. (ps-8). 1984. 12.95 (*0-920303-02-1*, Pub. by Annick CN); pap. 4.95 (*0-920303-03-X*, Pub. by Annick CN) Firefly Bks Ltd.
Watherwax, Richard, jt. auth. see Bissell, LeClair.
Watkins, Dawn. Zoli's Legacy, Pt. 1: Inheritance. (Illus.). 190p. (Orig.). (gr. 7-12). 1991. pap. 4.95 (*0-89084-596-4*) Bob Jones Univ Pr.
—Zoli's Legacy, Pt. 2: Bequest. 142p. (Orig.). (gr. 7-12). 1991. pap. 4.95 (*0-89084-597-2*) Bob Jones Univ Pr.
Watkins, Dawn L. The Cranky Blue Crab: A Tale in Verse. Smith, Anne, ed. Davis, Tim, illus. 32p. (Orig.). (gr. k-1). 1990. pap. write for info. (*0-89084-506-9*) Bob Jones Univ Pr.
—Jenny Wren. (Illus.). 138p. (gr. 4-5). 1986. pap. 4.95 (*0-89084-324-4*) Bob Jones Univ Pr.
—A King for Brass Cobweb. Smith, Anne, ed. Hannon, Holly, illus. (gr. k-1). 1990. pap. write for info. (*0-89084-505-0*) Bob Jones Univ Pr.
—The Medallion. (Illus.). 223p. (Orig.). (gr. 4). 1985. pap. 6.94 (*0-89084-282-5*) Bob Jones Univ Pr.
—Pocket Change: Five Small Fables. Habegger, Christa & Sidwell, Mark, eds. Davis, Tim, illus. 34p. (Orig.). (gr. 2-6). 1992. pap. 4.95 (*0-89084-645-6*) Bob Jones Univ Pr.

—Pulling Together. Cooper, Carolyn, ed. Pflug, Kathy, illus. 135p. (Orig.). (gr. 2-4). 1992. pap. 4.95 (*0-89084-609-X*) Bob Jones Univ Pr.
—The Spelling Window. Roberts, John, illus. LC 92-47049. 1993. write for info. (*0-89084-677-4*) Bob Jones Univ Pr.
—Very Like a Star. Thompson, Dana, illus. 30p. (Orig.). (ps). 1990. pap. 4.95 (*0-89084-533-6*) Bob Jones Univ Pr.
—Wait & See. Altizer, Suzanne R., photos by. (Illus.). 46p. (Orig.). (ps-1). 1991. pap. 4.95 (*0-89084-576-X*) Bob Jones Univ Pr.
Watkins, James N. Sex Is Not a Four-Letter Word. 1991. pap. 7.95 (*0-8423-7001-3*) Tyndale.
Watkins, Morris. Global Christianity. 64p. (Orig.). (gr. 7 up). 1987. pap. 6.95 (*0-939925-08-7*) R C Law & Co.
—Missions Resource Handbook. 128p. (Orig.). (gr. 7 up). 1987. pap. 9.95 (*0-939925-05-2*) R C Law & Co.
—Seven Worlds to Win. 240p. (Orig.). (gr. 7 up). 1987. pap. 19.95 (*0-939925-00-1*) R C Law & Co.
Watkins, Tracy D. Patrick the Pelaganty. Herbrechtsmeier, Keith, ed. Jones, Jerry D., illus. LC 93-83730. 40p. (ps-3). 1993. 8.99 (*1-883261-00-7*) Pelaganty.
Watkins, Will. Sid Seal, Houseman. Goffe, Toni, illus. LC 88-60095. 96p. (gr. 2-5). 1989. 14.95 (*0-531-05784-4*); PLB 14.99 (*0-531-08384-5*) Orchard Bks Watts.
Watkins, Willie L. Danny Pine & Patty Plum Tree. LC 88-51763. (Illus.). 40p. (Orig.). (gr. k-7). 1989. pap. 8.95 (*0-87516-595-8*) DeVorss.
Watkins, Yoko K. My Brother, My Sister, & I. 224p. (gr. 6 up). 1994. SBE 14.95 (*0-02-792526-9*, Bradbury Pr) Macmillan Child Grp.
—So Far from the Bamboo Grove. Fritz, Jean, intro. by. LC 85-15939. 192p. (gr. 6 up). 1986. 12.95 (*0-688-06110-9*) Lothrop.
—So Far from the Bamboo Grove. (gr. 5-9). pap. 3.95 (*0-317-62272-2*, Puffin) Puffin Bks.
—So Far from the Bamboo Grove. (Illus.). 192p. (gr. 6 up). 1994. pap. 3.95 (*0-688-13115-8*, Pub. by Beech Tree Bks) Morrow.
—Tales from the Bamboo Grove. Tseng, Jean & Mousien Tseng, illus. LC 91-38218. 64p. (gr. 4-11). 1992. SBE 14.95 (*0-02-792525-0*, Bradbury Pr) Macmillan Child Grp.
Watling, E. F., tr. see Sophocles.
Watrous, Merrill, jt. auth. see Tekerian, Irisa.
Watry, Charles A. & Hall, Duane L. Aerial Gunners: The Unknown Aces of World War II. LC 85-91368. (Illus.). 256p. (Orig.). 1986. pap. 12.95 (*0-914379-01-1*) Cal Aero Pr.
Watson. Aesop's Fables. (gr. k-4). 1982. (Usborne-Hayes); PLB 11.96 (*0-88110-093-5*); pap. 4.50 (*0-86020-667-X*) EDC.
—Animal Legends. (gr. k-4). 1982. (Usborne-Hayes); PLB 11.96 (*0-88110-094-3*); pap. 4.50 (*0-86020-672-6*) EDC.
—Grandpa's Slippers. 1993. pap. 28.67 (*0-590-75483-1*) Scholastic Inc.
—The House. (gr. k-2). 1980. (Usborne-Hayes); PLB 11.96 (*0-88110-068-4*); pap. 2.95 (*0-86020-388-3*) EDC.
—The Shop. (Illus.). (gr. k-2). 1980. (Usborne-Hayes); PLB 11.96 (*0-88110-069-2*); pap. 2.95 (*0-86020-390-5*) EDC.
—Simple Sums. Higham, illus. 28p. (ps-2). 1985. 2.95 (*0-86020-779-X*) EDC.
—The Town. (gr. k-2). 1980. (Usborne-Hayes); PLB 11.96 (*0-88110-070-6*); pap. 2.95 (*0-86020-392-1*) EDC.
Watson & Folliet. Round the World - English. (gr. 1-9). 1980. 11.95 (*0-86020-485-5*) English; French ed (*0-86020-488-X*) Spanish ed (*0-86020-484-7*) EDC.
Watson, Amy, jt. auth. see Abby Aldrich Rockefeller Folk Art Center Staff.
Watson, B. S. Arnold Schwarzenegger: Unauthorized Biography. (Illus.). 64p. (Orig.). 1991. pap. 2.95 (*1-56156-063-4*) Kidsbks.
—Hot Rappers. (Illus.). 64p. (Orig.). 1991. pap. 2.50 (*1-56156-049-9*) Kidsbks.
Watson, C. Shapes. Higham, David, illus. 24p. (gr. k-2). 1983. 2.95 (*0-86020-759-5*) EDC.
—Sizes. Higham, David, illus. 24p. (gr. k-2). 1983. 2.95 (*0-86020-760-9*) EDC.
Watson, Carol. Magical Animals. Price, Nick, illus. (gr. k-4). 1982. (Usborne-Hayes); PLB 11.96 (*0-88110-095-1*); pap. 4.50 (*0-86020-670-X*) EDC.
—My First Encyclopedia. LC 92-53477. (Illus.). 80p. (gr. k-3). 1993. 16.95 (*1-56458-214-0*) Dorling Kindersley.
—My Little Christmas Box, 4 bks. (Illus.). 32p. (ps-3). 1990. Set. casebound 10.95 (*0-7459-1837-9*) Lion USA.
—Prayers for a Fragile World. (ps-3). 1991. 12.95 (*0-7459-2212-0*) Lion USA.
Watson, Carol & De Saulles, Janet. Five Hundred French Words & Phrases for Children. McNicholas, Shelagh, illus. 32p. (gr. 1-2). 1994. 8.95 (*0-7818-0267-9*) Hippocrene Bks.
—Five Hundred Spanish Words & Phrases for Children. McNicholas, Shelagh, illus. (SPA & ENG). 32p. (gr. 1-2). 1994. 8.95 (*0-7818-0262-8*) Hippocrene Bks.
Watson, Carol, compiled by. Three Hundred Sixty-Five Children's Prayers. (Illus.). 160p. 1989. text ed. 12.95 (*0-7459-1454-3*); white ed. 24.95 (*0-7459-1721-6*) Lion USA.
Watson, Claire. Big Creatures from the Past: A Pop-up Book. Cremins, Robert, illus. 14p. (gr. k-4). 1990. 14.95 (*0-399-22159-X*, Putnam) Putnam Pub Group.

Watson, Clyde. Applebet: An ABC. Watson, Wendy, illus. 32p. (ps up). 1987. pap. 3.95 (*0-374-40427-5*) FS&G.
—Binary Numbers. Watson, Wendy, illus. LC 75-29161. 40p. (gr. 1-4). 1977. PLB 12.89 (*0-690-00993-3*, Crowell Jr Bks) Child Bks.
—Catch Me & Kiss Me & Say It Again. Watson, Wendy, illus. LC 78-17644. 64p. (gr. 1-12). 1983. (Philomel); pap. 7.95 (*0-399-20954-9*) Putnam Pub Group.
—Father Fox's Feast of Songs. Watson, Wendy, illus. 32p. 1992. PLB 14.95 (*1-878093-84-3*) Boyds Mills Pr.
—Father Fox's Pennyrhymes. Watson, Wendy, illus. LC 71-146291. 56p. (ps-3). 1987. pap. 5.95 (*0-06-443137-1*, Trophy) HarpC Child Bks.
—How Brown Mouse Kept Christmas. Watson, Wendy, illus. LC 80-18532. 32p. (ps-3). 1980. 10.00 (*0-374-33494-3*) FS&G.
—How Brown Mouse Kept Christmas. (ps-3). 1992. pap. 3.95 (*0-374-43315-1*) FS&G.
—Mister Toad. Watson, N. Cameron, illus. LC 91-24208. 32p. (gr. k-3). 1992. RSBE 13.95 (*0-02-792527-7*, Macmillan Child Bk) Macmillan Child Grp.
—Tom Fox & the Apple Pie. Watson, Wendy, illus. LC 74-171010. (ps-3). 1972. (Crowell Jr Bks) HarpC Child Bks.
—The Valentine Foxes. Watson, Wendy, illus. LC 88-22392. 32p. (ps-3). 1989. 13.95 (*0-531-05800-X*); PLB 13.99 (*0-531-08400-0*) Orchard Bks Watts.
—Valentine Foxes. Watson, Wendy, illus. LC 88-22392. 32p. (ps-3). 1992. pap. 5.95 (*0-531-07033-6*) Orchard Bks Watts.
Watson, D. Jeanene. Teresa of Calcutta. LC 84-60313. (gr. 3-6). 1984. pap. 6.95 (*0-88062-012-9*) Mott Media.
Watson, Elaine. Busy Feet. Loman, Roberta K., illus. 28p. (ps). 1992. 2.50 (*0-87403-952-5*, 24-03592) Standard Pub.
Watson, Elizabeth E. Tell Me about Jesus. (gr. 1 up). 1980. pap. 4.99 (*0-570-03484-1*, 56-1705) Concordia.
Watson, Harvey. Bob War & Poke. 144p. (gr. 5-9). 1991. 13.45 (*0-395-57038-7*, Sandpiper) HM.
Watson, James. Make Your Move. 160p. (gr. 6-10). 1991. 17.95 (*0-575-04397-0*, Pub. by Gollancz UK) Trafalgar.
—No Surrender. 160p. (gr. 7-10). 1993. 19.95 (*0-575-04893-X*, Pub. by Gollancz UK) Trafalgar.
—Where Nobody Sees. 160p. (gr. 6-9). 1990. 17.95 (*0-575-03977-9*, Pub. by Gollancz England) Trafalgar.
Watson, James A., jt. auth. see Rowzee, Janet Z.
Watson, Jane W., et al. My Friend the Doctor: A Read-Together Book for Parents & Children. rev. & updated ed. Smith, Catherine B., illus. 32p. (ps up). 1987. pap. 3.50 (*0-517-56485-8*) Crown Bks Yng Read.
—Sometimes a Family Has to Split Up. (Illus.). 32p. (ps-1). 1988. pap. 4.99 (*0-517-56811-X*) Crown Bks Yng Read.
Watson, John. We're the Noisy Dinosaurs. Watson, John, illus. LC 91-58764. 32p. (ps up). 1992. 14.95 (*1-56402-089-4*) Candlewick Pr.
Watson, Mary G. Beds & Bedding. Vincer, Carole, illus. 24p. (Orig.). (gr. 3 up). 1988. pap. 10.00 (*0-901366-27-7*, Pub. by Threshold Bks) Half Halt Pr.
—Feeds & Feeding. Vincer, Carole, illus. 24p. (Orig.). (gr. 3 up). 1988. pap. 10.00 (*0-901366-37-4*, Pub. by Threshold Bks) Half Halt Pr.
—Fields & Fencing. Vincer, Carole, illus. 24p. (Orig.). (gr. 3 up). 1988. pap. 10.00 (*0-901366-66-8*, Pub. by Threshold Bks) Half Halt Pr.
—Making Your Own Jumps. Vincer, Carole, illus. 24p. (Orig.). (gr. 3 up). 1988. pap. 10.00 (*0-901366-76-5*, Pub. by Threshold Bks) Half Halt Pr.
Watson, N. Cameron. The Little Pigs' First Cookbook. Watson, N. Cameron, illus. 48p. (gr. 1-3). 1987. 12.95 (*0-316-92467-9*) Little.
—Little Pigs Puppet Book. (gr. 4-8). 1990. 14.95 (*0-316-92468-7*) Little.
Watson, Nancy, et al. Our Violent Earth. LC 80-8797. (Illus.). 104p. (gr. 3-8). 1982. 8.95 (*0-87044-383-6*); lib. bdg. 12.50 (*0-87044-388-7*) Natl Geog.
Watson, Patricia. American Folklore Literature Guide. 96p. (gr. 7-12). 1992. pap. text ed. 10.95 (*0-944459-56-0*) ECS Lrn Systs.
—Inkblots: A Creative Writing Syllabus. 96p. (gr. 6-12). 1992. pap. text ed. 13.95 (*0-944459-60-9*) ECS Lrn Systs.
—To Kill a Mockingbird Literature Guide. 96p. (gr. 7-12). 1992. pap. text ed. 10.95 (*0-944459-53-6*) ECS Lrn Systs.
Watson, Percy. Building the Medieval Cathedrals. LC 74-19525. (Illus.). 48p. (gr. 7 up). 1976. pap. 7.50 limp bdg. (*0-521-08711-2*) Cambridge U Pr.
Watson, Pete. The Market Lady & the Mango Tree. Watson, Mary, illus. LC 93-7725. 32p. 1994. 14.00 (*0-688-12970-6*, Tambourine Bks); PLB 13.93 (*0-688-12971-4*, Tambourine Bks) Morrow.
Watson, Philip. Light Fantastic. Scruton, Clive & Fenton, Ronald, illus. LC 82-80989. 48p. (gr. 3-6). 1983. PLB 11.88 (*0-688-00969-7*) Lothrop.
—Light Fantastic. (Illus.). 48p. (gr. 3-6). 1983. pap. 7.95 (*0-688-00975-1*, Pub. by Beech Tree Bks) Morrow.
—Liquid Magic. Wood, Elizabeth & Fenton, Ronald, illus. LC 82-80988. 48p. (gr. 3-6). 1983. PLB 11.88 (*0-688-00967-0*) Lothrop.
—Liquid Magic. (Illus.). 48p. (gr. 3-6). 1983. pap. 7.95 (*0-688-00974-3*, Pub. by Beech Tree Bks) Morrow.
—Super Motion. Scruton, Clive & Falconer, Elizabeth, illus. LC 82-80990. 48p. (gr. 3-6). 1983. PLB 11.88 (*0-688-00971-9*) Lothrop.
—Super Motion. LC 82-80990. (Illus.). 48p. (gr. 3-6). 1983. pap. 7.95 (*0-688-00976-X*, Pub. by Beech Tree Bks) Morrow.
Watson, Richard J. Tom Thumb. (Illus.). 20p. (ps-3). 1989. 12.95 (*0-15-289280-X*) HarBrace.
—Tom Thumb. LC 87-12045. (ps-3). 1993. pap. 5.95 (*0-15-289281-8*, HB Juv Bks) HarBrace.
Watson, Wayne. Watercolour Ponies. (gr. 4 up). 1992. 12.99 (*0-8499-0976-7*) Word Inc.
Watson, Wendy. Boo! It's Halloween. Watson, Wendy, illus. 32p. (ps-3). 1992. 14.45 (*0-395-53628-6*, Clarion Bks) HM.
—Fox Went Out on a Chilly Night. LC 92-44157. (Illus.). (gr. k-4). 1993. write for info. (*0-688-10765-6*); PLB write for info. (*0-688-10766-4*) Lothrop.
—Happy Easter Day! Watson, Wendy, illus. 32p. (ps-1). 1993. 14.45 (*0-395-53629-4*, Clarion Bks) HM.
—Hurray for the Fourth of July. Watson, Wendy, illus. 32p. (ps-1). 1992. 14.45 (*0-395-53627-8*, Clarion Bks) HM.
—Tales for a Winter's Eve. LC 87-13467. (Illus.). 32p. (ps up). 1988. 13.00 (*0-374-37373-6*) FS&G.
—Tales for a Winter's Eve. (Illus.). 32p. (ps up). 1991. pap. 4.95 (*0-374-47419-2*) FS&G.
—Thanksgiving at Our House. Watson, Wendy, illus. 32p. (ps-1). 1991. 14.45 (*0-395-53626-X*, Clarion Bks) HM.
—A Valentine for You. Briley, Dorothy, ed. Watson, Wendy, illus. 32p. (ps-1). 1991. 14.45 (*0-395-53625-1*, Clarion Bks) HM.
—A Valentine for You. Watson, Wendy, illus. 32p. (gr. k-3). 1993. pap. 5.95 (*0-395-66411-X*, Clarion Bks) HM.
—Wendy Watson's Frog Went A-Courting. Watson, Wendy, illus. LC 89-63022. 32p. (ps-2). 1990. 13.95 (*0-688-06539-2*); lib. bdg. 13.88 (*0-688-06540-6*) Lothrop.
—Wendy Watson's Mother Goose. Watson, Wendy, illus. LC 88-37913. (ps-2). 1989. 19.95 (*0-688-05708-X*) Lothrop.
Watson-Russell & Harvey. So, You've Been Busted! A Guide to Court Procedures for Adolescents Charged under the Young Offenders Act. 48p. 1989. pap. 7.95 (*0-409-80985-3*) Butterworth Legal Pubs.
Watson-Russell, jt. auth. see Harvey.
Watt, Alec. Illustrated Dictionary of Geology in English with English-Arabic & Arabic English Glossaries. (gr. 8-12). 1982. 15.00x (*0-86685-353-7*) Intl Bk Ctr.
Watt, F. Planet Earth. (Illus.). 48p. (gr. 4-11). 1991. PLB 13.96 (*0-88110-510-4*, Usborne); pap. 7.95 (*0-7460-0637-3*, Usborne) EDC.
—Weather & Climate. (Illus.). 48p. (gr. 4-11). 1992. PLB 13.96 (*0-88110-511-2*, Usborne); pap. 7.95 (*0-7460-0683-7*, Usborne) EDC.
Wattenberg, Jane. Mrs. Mustard's Baby Faces. (Illus.). 6p. (ps). 1989. 4.95 (*0-87701-659-3*) Chronicle Bks.
—Mrs. Mustard's Beastly Babies. (Illus.). 7p. (ps). 1990. board book 4.95 (*0-87701-683-6*) Chronicle Bks.
—Mrs. Mustard's Name Games. LC 92-16128. (Illus.). 48p. 1993. 7.95 (*0-8118-0259-0*) Chronicle Bks.
Watterson, Bill. The Essential Calvin & Hobbes: A Calvin & Hobbes Treasury. Watterson, Bill, illus. Schulz, Charles. 256p. 1988. 19.95 (*0-8362-1809-4*); pap. 12.95 (*0-8362-1805-1*) Andrews & McMeel.
Watts & Tyler. Earth, The. (gr. 3-6). 1976. pap. 6.95 (*0-86020-062-0*, Usborne-Hayes) EDC.
Watts & Wunderli. Marty's World. pap. 5.95 (*0-88494-610-X*) Bookcraft Inc.
Watts, jt. auth. see Wunderli.
Watts, Alycyn. Moonlight Melody. 1993. pap. 2.99 (*0-553-29985-9*) Bantam.
Watts, Barrie. Ants. Watts, Barrie, photos by. (Illus.). 32p. (gr. k-4). 1991. PLB 11.40 (*0-531-14042-3*); pap. 4.95 (*0-531-15615-X*) Watts.
—Apple Tree. (Illus.). 24p. (gr. k-4). 1991. 3.95 (*0-382-09440-9*); PLB 9.98 (*0-382-09436-0*); pap. 3.95 (*0-382-24339-0*) Silver Burdett Pr.
—Beetles. (Illus.). 32p. (gr. k-4). 1989. PLB 11.40 (*0-531-10718-3*) Watts.
—Beetles. 32p. (gr. k-4). 1991. pap. 4.95 (*0-531-15619-2*) Watts.
—Birds' Nest. (Illus.). 25p. (gr. k-4). 1991. 6.95 (*0-382-09443-3*); PLB 9.98 (*0-382-09439-5*); pap. 3.95 (*0-382-24015-4*) Silver Burdett Pr.
—Butterflies & Moths. LC 90-46301. (Illus.). 32p. (gr. k-4). 1991. PLB 11.40 (*0-531-14160-8*); pap. 4.95 (*0-531-15617-6*) Watts.
—Butterfly & Caterpillar. LC 86-10050. (Illus.). 25p. (gr. k-4). 1991. 6.95 (*0-382-09291-0*) PLB 9.98 (*0-382-09282-1*); 3.95 (*0-382-09958-3*) Silver Burdett Pr.
—Caterpillars. 32p. (gr. k-4). 1991. pap. 4.95 (*0-531-15620-6*) Watts.
—Dandelion. (Illus.). 25p. (gr. k-4). 1991. 6.95 (*0-382-09442-5*); PLB 9.98 (*0-382-09438-7*); pap. 3.95 (*0-382-24016-2*) Silver Burdett Pr.
—Dragonfly. LC 88-18412. (Illus.). 25p. (gr. k-4). 1991. 6.95 (*0-382-09800-5*); PLB 9.98 (*0-382-09799-8*); pap. 3.95 (*0-382-24342-0*) Silver Burdett Pr.
—Earthworms. 32p. (gr. k-4). 1991. pap. 4.95 (*0-531-15621-4*) Watts.
—Grasshoppers & Crickets. LC 90-45996. (Illus.). 32p. (gr. k-4). 1991. PLB 11.40 (*0-531-14161-6*); pap. 4.95 (*0-531-15618-4*) Watts.
—Hamster. LC 86-10018. (Illus.). 25p. (gr. k-4). 1991. 6.95 (*0-382-09290-2*); pap. 3.95 (*0-382-09957-5*); PLB 9.98 (*0-382-09281-3*) Silver Burdett Pr.
—Honeybee. (Illus.). 25p. (gr. k-4). 1990. 6.95 (*0-382-24013-8*); PLB 9.98 (*0-382-24011-1*) Silver Burdett Pr.
—Ladybug. (Illus.). 25p. (gr. k-4). 1991. PLB 9.98 (*0-382-09437-9*); pap. 3.95 (*0-382-09960-5*) Silver Burdett Pr.
—Ladybugs. Watts, Barrie, photos by. (Illus.). 32p. (gr. k-4). 1991. PLB 11.40 (*0-531-14043-1*); pap. 4.95 (*0-531-15616-8*) Watts.
—Moth. (Illus.). 25p. (gr. k-4). 1991. 6.95 (*0-382-24220-3*); PLB 9.98 (*0-382-24218-1*); pap. 3.95 (*0-382-24241-6*) Silver Burdett Pr.
—Mushroom. LC 86-6659. (Illus.). 25p. (gr. k-4). 1986. 6.95 (*0-382-09301-1*); PLB 9.98 (*0-382-09287-2*); pap. 3.95 (*0-382-24017-0*) Silver Burdett Pr.
—Potato. LC 87-16702. (Illus.). 25p. (gr. k-4). 1988. 6.95 (*0-382-09528-6*); PLB 9.98 (*0-382-09527-8*); pap. 3.95 (*0-382-24018-9*) Silver Burdett Pr.
—Slugs & Snails. 32p. (gr. k-4). 1991. pap. 4.95 (*0-531-15623-0*) Watts.
—Spiders. 32p. (gr. k-4). 1991. pap. 4.95 (*0-531-15624-9*) Watts.
—Stick Insects. Kline, Marjory, ed. Watts, Barrie, photos by. (Illus.). 32p. (gr. k-4). 1992. PLB 11.40 (*0-531-14220-5*) Watts.
—Tomato. (Illus.). 25p. (ps-4). 1990. 6.95 (*0-382-24010-3*); 3.95s.p. (*0-685-58836-X*); PLB 9.98 (*0-382-24008-1*); PLB 7.49s.p. (*0-685-47004-0*); pap. 3.95 (*0-382-24344-7*) Silver Burdett Pr.
—Twenty-Four Hours in a Desert. (Illus.). 48p. (gr. 5-8). 1991. PLB 12.90 (*0-531-14187-X*) Watts.
—Twenty-Four Hours in a Forest. (Illus.). 48p. (gr. 5-8). 1990. PLB 12.90 (*0-531-14036-9*) Watts.
—Twenty-Four Hours in a Game Reserve. Kline, Marjory, ed. Watts, Barrie, photos by. (Illus.). 48p. (gr. 5-7). 1992. PLB 12.90 (*0-531-14173-X*) Watts.
—Twenty-Four Hours on a Seashore. (Illus.). 48p. (gr. 5-8). 1990. PLB 12.90 (*0-531-14037-7*) Watts.
—Wood Lice & Millipedes. Kline, Marjory, ed. Watts, Barrie, photos by. (Illus.). 32p. (gr. k-4). 1992. PLB 11.40 (*0-531-14162-4*) Watts.
Watts, Barrie, jt. auth. see Back, Christine.
Watts, Barrie, photos by. see Mouse. (Illus.). 24p. (gr. k-3). 1992. 6.95 (*0-525-67357-1*, Lodestar Bks) Dutton Child Bks.
—Rabbit. (Illus.). 24p. (gr. k-3). 1992. 6.95 (*0-525-67356-3*, Lodestar Bks) Dutton Child Bks.
—See How They Grow: Duck. (Illus.). 24p. (gr. k-3). 1991. 6.95 (*0-525-67346-6*, Lodestar Bks) Dutton Child Bks.
Watts, Barry. Amazing Magic Book. (gr. 4-7). 1992. pap. 3.95 (*0-207-15478-3*, Pub. by Angus & Robertson AT) HarpC.
—Amazing Magic Book. (gr. 4-7). 1992. pap. 3.95 (*0-207-17722-8*, Pub. by Angus & Robertson AT) HarpC.
—More Amazing Magic: Fantastic Tricks to Amuse, Confuse, & Mystify. (gr. 4-7). 1993. pap. 3.95 (*0-207-18172-1*, Pub. by Angus & Robertson AT) HarpC.
Watts, Bernadette. Goldilocks & the Three Bears. Watts, Bernadette, illus. LC 85-7192. (gr. k-3). 1985. 13.95 (*1-55858-039-5*); pap. 3.95 (*1-55858-040-9*) North-South Bks NYC.
—Tattercoats. Watts, Bernadette, illus. LC 87-30198. 32p. (gr. k-3). 1989. 13.95 (*1-55858-002-6*) North-South Bks NYC.
Watts, Carl. Steven Otto Nevets. LC 93-60236. (Illus.). 44p. (gr. k-3). 1993. 7.95 (*1-55523-602-2*) Winston-Derek.
Watts, Claire, jt. auth. see Nicholson, Robert.
Watts, Clare, et al. Do-It-Yourself. Tofts, Hannah & Barnes, Jon, illus. LC 93-21218. 48p. (gr. 3-7). 1994. 16.95 (*1-56847-147-5*) Thomson Lrning.
Watts, David, jt. auth. see Gulley, Greg.
Watts, Dorothy E. Stepping Stones. Woolsey, Raymond H., ed. 384p. (gr. 1 up). 1987. text ed. 9.95 (*0-8280-0384-X*) Review & Herald.
Watts, Gayle. Quotes for Kids & Teens: Motivational & Inspirational. 192p. 1992. pap. text ed. 13.95 (*0-945772-03-3*) Clarkston Pub.
Watts, Irene N. Great Theme Parties for Children. LC 90-47067. (Illus.). 128p. (gr. 1-10). 1991. 14.95 (*0-8069-7410-9*) Sterling.
Watts, Irene N., compiled by. Great Theme Parties for Children. 128p. (gr. k up). 1992. pap. 4.95 (*0-8069-7411-7*) Sterling.
Watts, James. The Irish Americans. Moynihan, Daniel P., intro. by. 112p. (Orig.). (gr. 5 up). 1988. 17.95 (*0-87754-855-2*); pap. 9.95 (*0-7910-0267-5*) Chelsea Hse.
Watts, L. & Inglis, L. Computers. (Illus.). 32p. (gr. 3-9). 1993. PLB 13.96 (*0-88110-595-3*); pap. 6.95 (*0-7460-1055-9*) EDC.
Watts, L. & Varley, C. Advanced Chess. (Illus.). 32p. (gr. 5 up). 1991. lib. bdg. 12.96 (*0-88110-503-1*, Usborne); pap. 6.95 (*0-7460-0617-9*, Usborne) EDC.
—Better Chess. (Illus.). 64p. (gr. 5 up). 1993. pap. 9.95 (*0-7460-1437-6*) EDC.
Watts, L., jt. auth. see Stockley, C.
Watts, Margaret. Trouble with Hairgrow. Smith, Craig, illus. LC 93-26298. 1994. 4.25 (*0-383-03782-4*) SRA Schl Grp.
Watts, Ramona, jt. auth. see Dickinson, Lavona.

Waugh, Charles & Greenberg, Martin, eds. The Newbery Award Reader. Hamilton, Virginia, intro. by. 252p. (gr. 7 up). 1984. 14.95 (0-15-257034-9, HB Juv Bks) HarBrace.
Waugh, Charles G., jt. ed. see Greenberg, Martin H.
Waugh, Michelle. Winning In Speech: A Workbook for Fluency. (Illus.). 98p. (gr. k-5). 1991. 16.95 (0-937857-29-7, 1594) Speech Bin.
Waugh, Sylvia. The Mennyms. LC 93-15901. 216p. (gr. 6 up). 1994. 14.00 (0-688-13070-4) Greenwillow.
Waura, Grace. The First Families of West Virginia. Waura, Grace M., illus. LC 90-70666. 70p. (Orig.). (gr. 3-6). 1991. pap. 6.00 (1-56002-007-5) Aegina Pr.
Waverly, Barney. How Big? How Fast? How Hungry? A Book about Cats. Henry, Steve, illus. 24p. (ps-2). 1990. PLB 14.60 (0-8172-3582-5); PLB 10.95 pkg. of 3 (0-685-58552-2) Raintree Steck-V.
Wax, Nina. Occupational Health. Garell, Dale C. & Snyder, Solomon H., eds. LC 93-3903. (Illus.). (gr. 6-12). 1994. PLB 19.95 (0-7910-0089-3, Am Art Analog); pap. write for info. (0-7910-0527-5) Chelsea Hse.
Wax, Wendy. Say No & Know Why: Kids Learn About Drugs. 64p. (gr. 2-5). 1992. 12.95 (0-8027-8140-3); PLB 13.85 (0-8027-8141-1) Walker & Co.
Wax, Wendy, compiled by. A Treasury of Christmas Poems, Carols, & Games to Share. Spier, John, illus. (ps-1). 1992. 10.00 (0-440-40731-1) Dell.
Waxter, Julia B. Science Cookbook. LC 79-57431. (gr. 4-8). 1981. pap. 9.95 (0-8224-6292-3) Fearon Teach Aids.
Way, Nancy. Our Town Redmond. Johnston, Helen, intro. by. (Illus.). (gr. 9-12). 1989. write for info. Marymoor Mus.
Way, P., jt. auth. see Cook, J.
Way, Voldi, jt. auth. see Douglas, Vincent.
Waybill, Marjorie. Chinese Eyes. Cutrell, Pauline, illus. LC 74-5751. 32p. (gr. k-2). 1974. 14.95 (0-8361-1738-7) Herald Pr.
—God Builds His Church: Activity Book. Converse, James, illus. 72p. (Orig.). (gr. 4-5). 1988. pap. 3.00 (0-8361-3457-5) Herald Pr.
—God's Family Activity Book. 64p. (Orig.). (ps-1). 1983. pap. 3.00 (0-8361-3336-6) Herald Pr.
—God's Justice: Activity Book. 88p. (Orig.). (ps-1). 1985. pap. 3.00 (0-8361-3397-8) Herald Pr.
Wayland, April H. It's Not My Turn to Look for Grandma. Booth, George, illus. LC 93-7018. 1994. 13.00 (0-679-84491-0); lib. bdg. 13.99 (0-679-94491-5) Knopf.
—Night Horse. 1991. 12.95 (0-590-42629-X, Scholastic Hardcover) Scholastic Inc.
—To Rabbittown. Spowart, Robin, illus. (gr. 2-5). 1989. pap. 12.95 (0-590-40852-6) Scholastic Inc.
—To Rabbittown. Spowart, Robin, illus. 32p. 1992. pap. 3.95 (0-590-44777-7, Blue Ribbon Bks) Scholastic Inc.
Wayman & Plum. Secrets & Surprises. 96p. (gr. k-8). 1977. 9.95 (0-916456-13-7, GA70) Good Apple.
Wayman, Joe. Colors of My Rainbow. (Illus.). 36p. (gr. k-8). 1988. pap. 7.95 (0-945799-03-9) Audio cassette 9.95. Pieces of Lrning.
—Don't Burn down the Birthday Cake. Wayman, Joe, illus. 90p. (gr. k up). 1989. 13.95 (0-945799-00-4) Audio cassette 12.95. Pieces of Lrning.
—I Like Me. (Illus.). 36p. (gr. k-8). 1988. pap. 7.95 (0-945799-02-0) Audio cassette 9.95. Pieces of Lrning.
—Let's Talk about It! Wayman, Joe, illus. 96p. (gr. 1-8). 1986. wkbk. 9.95 (0-86653-372-9, GA 799) Good Apple.
—The Other Side of Reading. 144p. (gr. k-8). 1980. 11.95 (0-916456-64-1, GA 183) Good Apple.
Wayman, Joseph. If You Promise Not to Tell. Wayman, Joseph, illus. 92p. (gr. k up). 1991. 13.95 (0-945799-04-7); Discussion Guide 5.95 (0-945799-05-5) Pieces of Lrning.
Wayne. Max, the Dog Who Refused to Die. (ps-7). 1987. pap. 2.25 (0-553-25160-0) Bantam.
Wayne, Kyra P. Li'l Ol' Charlie. Little, Nan K., illus. LC 39-438. 88p. (Orig.). 1989. pap. 8.95 (0-931866-41-3) Alpine Pubns.
Wayne, Matt. The Crystal Trap. Ashby, Ruth, ed. 128p. (Orig.). 1992. pap. 3.50 (0-671-74207-8, Archway) PB.
Weakland, Rembert G. Letters to Teens: Hopeful Words from an Archbishop. 48p. (Orig.). (gr. 8-12). 1988. pap. 1.75 (0-89243-290-X) Liguori Pubns.
Weaks, Charles. Leon's Big Day. rev. ed. 1993. 6.95 (0-8062-4747-9) Carlton.
Weatherford, Doris. American Women & World War Two. (Illus.). 384p. 1990. 29.95x (0-8160-2038-8) Facts on File.
Weatherhill, Craig. The Lyonesse Stone: A Novel of West Cornwall. (Illus.). 176p. 1992. pap. 9.95 (0-907018-85-8, Pub. by Tabb Hse Pubs UK) Seven Hills Bk Dists.
Weathers, Joseph, jt. auth. see Dennie, Joseph.
Weatherwax, Wilma M. The Blue-Eyed Chippewa: A Tragic Indian Story. 2nd ed. Perkins, Stan, contrib. by. (Illus.). 150p. 1987. 10.00 (0-9614640-6-2); pap. 7.50 (0-9614640-7-0) Broadblade Pr.
Weaver. Farm Team. Date not set. 14.00 (0-06-023588-8, Festival); PLB 13.89 (0-06-023589-6, Festival) HarpC Child Bks.
Weaver, jt. auth. see Hudson.
Weaver, Anna. Eyes for Benny. (gr. 6 up). 1984. 7.45 (0-318-01331-2) Rod & Staff.
Weaver, Charles. Hidden Logic Puzzles. 128p. (gr. 10-12). 1992. 12.95 (0-8069-8334-5) Sterling.
—Hidden Logic Puzzles. Hoffman, Sanford, illus. 128p. (gr. 5 up). 1993. pap. 4.95 (0-8069-8335-3) Sterling.
Weaver, Dorothy H. Arizona A to Z. Wacker, Kay, illus. 32p. (Orig.). (gr. k up). 1994. pap. 7.95 (0-87358-564-X) Northland AZ.
Weaver, Harriett E. Frosty: A Raccoon to Remember. Dewey, Jennifer O., illus. (gr. 5-7). 1986. pap. 2.50 (0-671-64088-7, Archway) PB.
Weaver, Jill. Meet the Alphabuddies. Maxwell, Cassandre, illus. LC 89-14599. 30p. (ps-4). 1990. 10.95 (0-8192-1518-X) Morehouse Pub.
Weaver, Lydia. Child Star: When Talkies Came to Hollywood. Laporte, Michele, illus. 64p. (gr. 2-6). 1992. PLB 12.00 (0-670-84039-4) Viking Child Bks.
—Close to Home: A Story of the Polio Epidemic. Arrington, Aileen, illus. LC 92-25937. 64p. (gr. 2-6). 1993. PLB 12.99 (0-670-84511-6) Viking Child Bks.
Weaver, Rebecca & Dale, Rodney. Machines in the Home. LC 92-21662. (Illus.). 64p. 1993. PLB 16.00 (0-19-520965-6) OUP.
Weaver, Rebecca, jt. auth. see Dale, Rodney.
Weaver, Will. Striking Out. LC 93-565. 80p. (gr. 5 up). 1993. 15.00 (0-06-023346-X); PLB 14.89 (0-06-023347-8) HarpC Child Bks.
Weaver, William, tr. see Eco, Umberto.
Weaver-Gelzer, Charlotte. In the Time of Trouble. LC 92-11146. 224p. (gr. 7 up). 1993. 15.99 (0-525-44973-6, DCB) Dutton Child Bks.
Webb & Amery. Ulysses. (Illus.). (gr. 3-6). 1981. (Usborne-Hayes); PLB 11.96 (0-88110-058-7); pap. 4.50 (0-86020-567-3) EDC.
Webb, Barbara O. The Lord's Prayer: The Prayer Jesus Taught. (Illus.). 24p. (Orig.). (gr. k-4). 1986. saddle stitch 3.99 (0-570-08529-2, 56-1156) Concordia.
—Now What, Lord? Bible Devotions for Girls. LC 85-22884. 112p. (Orig.). (gr. 3-7). 1985. pap. 5.99 (0-8066-2182-6, 10-4680, Augsburg) Augsburg Fortress.
Webb, C. Anne, et al, eds. Your Reading: A Booklist for Junior High & Middle School Students. 9th ed. LC 93-8652. 225p. (Orig.). (gr. 6-9). 1993. pap. write for info. (0-8141-5942-7) NCTE.
Webb, Charles. The Graduate. (RL 10). 1971. pap. 1.50 (0-451-08633-3, W8633, Sig) NAL-Dutton.
Webb, Dave. Adventures with the Santa Fe Trail: An Activity Book for Kids & Teachers. rev. ed. Buntin, Phillip R., illus. 76p. (gr. 4 up). 1993. pap. 7.95 (1-882404-05-X) KS Herit Ctr.
Webb, Equilla A. An Amateur's Guide to Basketball Recruiting. 60p. (Orig.). (gr. 9-12). 1989. pap. text ed. 9.95 (0-9624771-0-9) Equilla Enterprises.
Webb, Equilla B. An Amateur's Guide to Football & Recruiting. 192p. (Orig.). (gr. 9-12). 1990. pap. text ed. 45.00 (0-9624771-1-7) Equilla Enterprises.
Webb, Glyn, ed. see Wadley, Verleen W.
Webb, Jane C. & Duckett, Barbara. RULES Phonological Evaluation. Seeland, Rene K., illus. 140p. (ps-3). 1990. text ed. 49.95 (0-937857-12-2, 1577) Speech Bin.
Webb, Joan C. Devotions for Little Boys & Girls: New Testament. McCallum, Joanne V., illus. 112p. (ps-k). 1992. pap. 5.99 (0-87403-682-8, 12-02822) Standard Pub.
—Devotions for Little Boys & Girls: Old Testament. McCallum, Joanne V., illus. 112p. (Orig.). (ps-k). 1992. pap. 5.99 (0-87403-681-X, 12-02821) Standard Pub.
Webb, Marcus. Telephones, Words over Wires. LC 92-11400. (Illus.). 96p. (gr. 5-8). 1992. 15.95 (1-56006-219-3) Lucent Bks.
Webb, Margot. Coping with Compulsive Behavior. LC 93-29403. 1993. 13.95 (0-8239-1604-9) Rosen Group.
—Coping with Overprotective Parents. Rosen, Ruth, ed. (gr. 7-12). 1990. PLB 13.95 (0-8239-1088-1) Rosen Group.
—Coping with Parents Who Are Activists. Rosen, Ruth, ed. (gr. 7-12). 1992. 13.95 (0-8239-1416-X) Rosen Group.
—Coping with Street Gangs. rev. ed. Rosen, Roger, ed. 64p. (gr. 7-12). 1992. PLB 13.95 (0-8239-1600-6) Rosen Group.
—The Value of Loyalty. Rosen, Ruth, ed. (gr. 7-12). 1991. PLB 15.95 (0-8239-1243-4) Rosen Group.
Webb, Phila H. & Corby, Jane. Little Book of Hand Shadows. LC 90-52549. (Illus.). 80p. (gr. 1 up) 1990. 4.95 (0-89471-852-5) Running Pr.
Webb, Phila H. & Corby, Jose. Shadowgraphs: Anyone Can Make. LC 90-50896. (Illus.). 32p. (gr. 1-4). 1991. Repr. of 1927 ed. 8.95 (1-56138-014-8) Running Pr.
Webb, Sandra, ed. see Gunsher, Cheryl.
Webber, Andrew L., jt. auth. see Rice, Tim.
Webber, Helen. Good Night, Night. Webber, Helen, illus. (gr. k-6). 1968. 8.95 (0-8392-3054-0) Astor-Honor.
—How Long Is Long Ago & Other Poems. Webber, Helen, illus. (gr. k-6). 1968. 8.95 (0-8392-3068-0) Astor-Honor.
—My Kite Is the Magic Me. Webber, Helen, illus. (gr. k-6). 1968. 8.95 (0-8392-3055-9) Astor-Honor.
—Sea Is My Blanket. (Illus.). (gr. k-6). 1968. 8.95 (0-8392-3057-5) Astor-Honor.
—Summer Sun. Webber, Helen, illus. (gr. k-6). 1968. 8.95 (0-8392-3056-7) Astor-Honor.
—Webber Quartet, 4 Vols. (gr. k-6). Set. deluxe slipcase 35.00 (0-8392-3070-2) Astor-Honor.
Webber, Irma E. It Looks Like This. Webber, Irma E., illus. LC 76-43571. (ps up). 1976. text ed. 7.00x (0-918970-21-0) Intl Gen Semantics.

Weber. Action Family Handbook: Twil Aug. (gr. 3). 1985. 2.80 (0-02-658350-X) Macmillan.
—More Weird Moments in Sports. 1993. pap. 2.50 (0-590-43522-1) Scholastic Inc.
Weber, Ane & Krueger, Ron. A Tailor-Made Friendship. French, Marty & Iwai, Noel, illus. 26p. (ps up). 1988. incl. cassette 7.95 (1-55578-913-7) Worlds Wonder.
Weber, Ane, et al. The Bear That Was Chicken. French, Marty, et al, illus. 26p. (ps up). 1986. Book & Cassette. 7.95 (1-55578-101-2) Worlds Wonder.
—The Girl Who Wanted to Be Beautiful. French, Marty & Christman, Michael, illus. 26p. (ps up). 1986. Book & Cassette. 7.95 (1-55578-109-8) Worlds Wonder.
—The Girl Who Wanted to Be Beautiful. French, Marty & Christman, Michael, illus. 26p. (ps up). 1988. incl. cassette 7.95 (1-55578-915-3) Worlds Wonder.
—The Girl With the Pop-Up Garden. French, Marty, et al, illus. 26p. (ps up). 1986. Book & Cassette. 7.95 (1-55578-102-0) Worlds Wonder.
—Is It Soup Yet? French, Marty & Iwai, Noel, illus. 26p. (ps up). 1986. 7.95 (1-55578-105-5); cass. incl. Worlds Wonder.
—Is It Soup Yet? French, Marty & Iwai, Noel, illus. 26p. (ps up). 1988. incl. cassette 7.95 (1-55578-914-5) Worlds Wonder.
—A Tailor-Made Friendship. French, Marty & Iwia, Noel, illus. 26p. (ps up). 1986. Book & Cassette. 7.95 (1-55578-107-1) Worlds Wonder.
Weber, Bernard. Ira Says Goodbye. Weber, Bernard, illus. 40p. (ps-3). 1988. 13.45 (0-395-48315-8) HM.
—Ira Says Goodbye. (ps-3). 1991. pap. 4.80 (0-395-58413-2) HM.
Weber, Bruce. Babe Ruth: Classic Sports Shots. 1993. pap. 1.25 (0-590-47018-3) Scholastic Inc.
—Baseball Trivia and Fun Book. (gr. 4-7). 1993. pap. 2.50 (0-590-47174-0) Scholastic Inc.
—Bruce Weber's Inside Baseball 1992. (gr. 4-7). 1992. pap. 2.25 (0-590-45627-X, Apple Paperbacks) Scholastic Inc.
—Bruce Weber's Inside Pro Football, 1991. (gr. 4-7). 1991. pap. 2.50 (0-590-44707-6) Scholastic Inc.
—Bruce Weber's Inside Pro Football 1992. 1992. 2.50 (0-590-45626-1, 065) Scholastic Inc.
—The Indianapolis Five Hundred. 32p. (gr. 4). 1990. PLB 14.95s.p. (0-88682-321-8) Creative Ed.
—Jackie Robinson: Classic Sports Shots. 1993. pap. 1.25 (0-590-47021-3) Scholastic Inc.
—Lou Gehrig: Classic Sports Shots. 1993. pap. 1.25 (0-590-47023-X) Scholastic Inc.
—Mickey Mantle: Classic Sports Shots. 1993. pap. 1.25 (0-590-47024-8) Scholastic Inc.
—Pro Football Megastars, 1993. (gr. 4-7). 1993. pap. 3.95 (0-590-47433-2) Scholastic Inc.
—Sparky Anderson. LC 88-14985. (Illus.). 48p. (gr. 5-6). 1988. RSBE 11.95 (0-89686-379-4, Crestwood Hse) Macmillan Child Grp.
—Ted Williams: Classic Sports Shots. 1993. pap. 1.25 (0-590-47022-1) Scholastic Inc.
—Willie Mays: Classical Sports Shots. 1993. pap. 1.25 (0-590-47020-5) Scholastic Inc.
Weber, Chris, ed. Treasures, No. 2: Stories & Art by Students in Oregon. Kimmel, Eric, intro. by. 256p. (Orig.). (gr. k-12). 1988. pap. 11.95 (0-9616058-1-2) OR Students Writing.
Weber, Jil. A Happy Birthday Surprise! 1992. pap. 2.50 (1-878689-12-6) Frajil Farms.
Weber, Jill. Cat Flip Book. 1991. pap. 2.50 (1-878689-09-6) Frajil Farms.
—Santa Flip Book. 1991. pap. 2.50 (1-878689-03-7) Frajil Farms.
Weber, Judith E. The Family Heritage Cookbook. Bryant, Michael, illus. 64p. (gr. 1-3). 1994. PLB 11.95 (1-881889-53-X) Silver Moon.
—Forbidden Friendship. Golub, Nan, illus. 80p. (gr. 4-6). 1993. PLB 12.95 (1-881889-42-4) Silver Moon.
Weber, Kathryn. Midnite & Mark. Hamilton, Sandi, illus. LC 83-8622. 64p. (Orig.). (gr. 4-6). 1983. pap. 3.95 (0-88100-021-3) Ranch House Pr.
—Molly Moonshine & Timothy. Downey, Jane, illus. 44p. (gr. 2-4). 1990. pap. 2.95 (1-878438-01-8) Ranch House Pr.
Weber, Michael. Our National Parks. (Illus.). 48p. (gr. 2-4). 1994. 12.90 (1-56294-438-X) Millbrook Pr.
Weber, Peter J. Zodiac Degrees. (Illus.). 128p. (Orig.). 1989. 14.95 (0-940649-06-3); pap. 9.95 (0-940649-05-5) Parnell Pub.
Weber, Rhiannon. Signposts from Proverbs: An Introduction to Proverbs. Evans, Lawrence L., illus. 128p. (Orig.). 1988. spiral bdg. 9.95 (0-85151-517-7) Banner of Truth.
Weber, Sally & Glasscock, Paula. Castles, Pirates, Knights & Other Learning Delights. 104p. (gr. 5-8). 1980. 10.95 (0-916456-92-7, GA 158) Good Apple.
Weber, Susan B., ed. see Carbone, Elisa L.
Weber, Valerie, jt. auth. see Cummins, Ronnie.
Weber, Valerie, adapted by. The Wonder of Whales. Nicklin, Flip, photos by. LC 92-16946. (Illus.). 1992. PLB 18.60 (0-8368-0857-6) Gareth Stevens Inc.
Weber, Valerie & Rateliff, John D., eds. Egypt. Komatsu, Yoshio, photos by. LC 87-42579. (Illus.). 64p. (gr. 5-6). 1991. PLB 19.93 (1-55532-209-3) Gareth Stevens Inc.
Weber, Valerie, jt. ed. see Ackley, Meredith.
Weber, Valerie, jt. ed. see Pelnar, Tom.
Webster, Dan, jt. auth. see McAllister, Dawson.
Webster, David. And God Created... (Illus.). 52p. (gr. k-6). 1992. 3.95 (0-9633597-0-3) Doodle-bug.

—Exploring Nature Around the Year Series, 4 bks. (Illus.). 96p. (gr. 2-4). 1989. Set. PLB 43.92 (0-671-94109-7, J Messner); Set. pap. 19.80 (0-671-94110-0) S&S Trade.

—Fall. Steltenpohl, Jane, ed. Steadman, Barbara, illus. 48p. (gr. 2-4). 1989. (J Messner); lib. bdg. 5.95 (0-671-65985-5, J Messner) S&S Trade.

—Spring. Steadman, Barbara, illus. 48p. (gr. 2-4). 1990. lib. bdg. 10.98 (0-671-65858-1, J Messner); lib. bdg. 5.95 (0-671-65983-9) S&S Trade.

—Summer. Steadman, Barbara, illus. 48p. (gr. 2-4). 1990. lib. bdg. 10.98 (0-671-65859-X, J Messner); pap. 5.95 (0-671-65984-7) S&S Trade.

—Winter. Steltenpohl, Jane, ed. Steadman, Barbara, illus. 48p. (gr. 2-4). 1989. lib. bdg. 10.98 (0-671-65861-1, J Messner); lib. bdg. 5.95 (0-671-65986-3) S&S Trade.

Webster, David, jt. auth. see Gardner, Robert.

Webster, George P. & Nast, Thomas. Santa Claus & His Works. (Illus.). 12p. (gr. 1-8). 1972. pap. 3.25 (0-914510-03-7) Evergreen.

Webster, Harriet. Going Places: The Young Traveler's Guide & Activity Book. Owens, Gail, illus. LC 90-41234. 112p. (gr. 3-7). 1991. pap. 4.95 (0-689-71288-X, Aladdin) Macmillan Child Grp.

—Going Places: The Young Traveler's Guide & Activity Book. Owens, Gail, illus. LC 89-24201. 112p. (gr. 4-7). 1991. SBE 13.95 (0-684-19078-8, Scribners Young Read) Macmillan Child Grp.

—Winter Book. Trivas, Irene, illus. LC 88-4371. 128p. (gr. 3-7). 1988. SBE 13.95 (0-684-18891-0, Scribners Young Read) Macmillan Child Grp.

Webster, Jean. Daddy-Long-Legs. (Orig.). (gr. k-6). 1987. pap. 4.95 (0-440-41673-6, Pub. by Yearling Classics) Dell.

—Daddy-Long-Legs. Hearn, Michael P., afterword by. 1988. pap. 2.50 (0-451-52187-0, Sig Classics) NAL-Dutton.

—Daddy-Long-Legs. 256p. (gr. 5 up). 1989. pap. 3.95 (0-14-035111-6, Puffin) Puffin Bks.

—Daddy-Long-Legs. 176p. (gr. 5-8). 1988. pap. 3.25 (0-590-44094-2) Scholastic Inc.

—Daddy-Long-Legs. LC 92-55075. 1993. 12.95 (0-679-42312-5, Everymans Lib) Knopf.

—Dear Enemy. (gr. 4-7). 1991. pap. 3.50 (0-440-40440-1) Dell.

Webster, John see Bald, Robert C.

Webster, Vera. Experimentos Atmosfericos (Weather Experiments) Kratky, Lada, tr. LC 85-31425. (SPA., Illus.). 48p. (gr. k-4). 1986. PLB 15.27 (0-516-31662-1); pap. 4.95 (0-516-51662-0) Childrens.

—Experimentos Cientificos (Science Experiments) Kratky, Lada, tr. LC 85-31403. (SPA., Illus.). 48p. (gr. k-4). 1986. PLB 15.27 (0-516-31646-X); pap. 4.95 (0-516-51646-9) Childrens.

—Plant Experiments. LC 82-9448. (Illus.). 48p. (gr. k-4). 1982. PLB 15.27 (0-516-01638-5); pap. 4.95 (0-516-41638-3) Childrens.

—Science Experiments. LC 82-4429. 48p. (gr. k-4). 1982. PLB 15.27 (0-516-01646-6); pap. 4.95 (0-516-41646-4) Childrens.

—Weather Experiments. LC 81-17062. (Illus.). 48p. (gr. k-4). 1982. PLB 15.27 (0-516-01662-8); pap. 4.95 (0-516-41662-6) Childrens.

Webster-Doyle, Terrence. The Eye of the Hurricane: Tales of the Empty-Handed Masters. Cameron, Rod, illus. 128p. (gr. 4-8). 1992. PLB 17.95 (0-942941-25-X); pap. 12.95 (0-942941-24-1) Atrium Soc Pubns.

—Facing the Double Edged Sword: The Art of Karate for Young People. Cameron, Rod, illus. LC 73-83919. 90p. (Orig.). (gr. 5-9). 1988. 17.95 (0-942941-17-9); pap. 12.95 (0-942941-16-0) Atrium Soc Pubns.

—Fighting the Invisible Enemy: Understanding the Effects of Conditioning. (Illus.). 164p. (gr. 5-12). 1990. 17.95 (0-942941-19-5); pap. 12.95 (0-942941-18-7) Atrium Soc Pubns.

—Flight of the Golden Eagle: Tales of the Empty-Handed Masters. (Illus.). 112p. (gr. 5-12). 1992. 17.95 (0-942941-29-2); pap. 12.95 (0-942941-28-4) Atrium Soc Pubns.

—Maze of the Fire Dragon: Tales of the Empty-Handed Masters. (Illus.). 112p. (gr. 5-12). 1992. 17.95 (0-942941-27-6); pap. 12.95 (0-942941-26-8) Atrium Soc Pubns.

—Operation Warhawks: How Young People Become Warriors. (Illus.). 135p. (gr. 5-12). 1993. 17.95 (0-942941-31-4); pap. 12.95 (0-942941-30-6) Atrium Soc Pubns.

—Peace, the Enemy of Freedom: The Myth of Non-Violence. (Illus.). 157p. (gr. 5-12). 1991. pap. 9.95 (0-942941-12-8) Atrium Soc Pubns.

—Tug of War: Peace Through Understanding Conflict. (Illus.). 106p. (gr. 5-12). 1990. 17.95 (0-942941-21-7); pap. 12.95 (0-942941-20-9) Atrium Soc Pubns.

—Why Is Everybody Always Picking on Me? A Guide to Handling Bullies. (Illus.). (gr. 5-12). 1991. 17.95 (0-942941-23-3); pap. 12.95 (0-942941-22-5) Atrium Soc Pubns.

—Wrath of the Ancient Warriors: Breaking the Chains of the Past. (Illus.). 128p. (gr. 5-12). 1993. 17.95 (0-942941-33-0); pap. 12.95 (0-942941-32-2) Atrium Soc Pubns.

Webster's New World Dictionaries Staff. Webster's New World Children's Dictionary. Neufeldt, Victoria & De Mello Vianna, Fernando, eds. (Illus.). 912p. 1992. 15.95 (0-13-945726-7, Webster New Wrld) P-H Gen Ref & Trav.

Webster-Seek, Vesta. Old Ruff & Life on the Farm. LC 92-12956. (gr. k-3). 1993. write for info. (0-7814-0966-7, Chariot Bks) Cook.

Wechter, Nell W. Taffy of Torpedo Junction. Sparks, Mary W., illus. LC 57-9312. 134p. (gr. 5-9). 1990. pap. 7.95 (0-89587-076-2) Blair.

Weck, Thomas. Back-Back & the Lima Bear. Graves, Helen, ed. Taylor, Neil, illus. LC 85-51963. 64p. (gr. 1-6). 1986. 6.95 (0-938232-97-5) Winston-Derek.

Wedell, Robert F. Rolf & the Rainbow Christmas. M. J. Art Concepts Staff, illus. LC 89-91971. 133p. (Orig.). 1989. pap. 5.00 (0-9625221-1-2) Milrob Pr.

—Rolf the Green Ghost. Warners, Sheila B., illus. 69p. (Orig.). (ps-8). 1988. pap. 4.95 (0-685-30435-3) Milrob Pr.

—Save the Haunted House. Swidor, M. J., illus. 124p. (Orig.). 1991. pap. 6.95 (0-9625221-2-0) Milrob Pr.

Wedeven, Carol S. The Christmas Crib That Zack Built. Fisher, Nell F., illus. LC 89-263. 1989. casebound 9.95 (0-687-07816-4) Abingdon.

Wee, Jerrie. Taiwan. (Illus.). 96p. (gr. 5 up). 1988. 14.95 (1-55546-180-8) Chelsea Hse.

Wee, Jessie. Singapore. (Illus.). 96p. (gr. 5 up). 1988. 14.95 (0-222-00988-8) Chelsea Hse.

Weechees. Sun Boy & His Hunter's Bow. 32p. (gr. 4-8). 1988. pap. 4.95 (0-89992-115-9) Coun India Ed.

—Sun Boy & the Angry Panther. 32p. (gr. 4-8). 1988. pap. 4.95 (0-89992-114-0) Coun India Ed.

—Sun Boy & the Monster of To-Oh-Pah. 32p. (gr. 4-8). 1988. pap. 4.95 (0-89992-113-2) Coun India Ed.

—Sun Boy: Cou-Yan-Nai: Comanche Indian Story for Children. 32p. (gr. 4-9). 1983. pap. 1.95 (0-686-44422-1) Coun India Ed.

Weedn, Flavia. Flavia & the Dream Maker. Weedn, Flavia, illus. 56p. 1988. 14.95 (0-929632-00-1) deluxe limited 24.95 (0-929632-02-8) Applause Inc.

—Flavia & the Velveteen Rabbit. (Illus.). 52p. 1990. 16.00 (0-929632-10-9) Applause Inc.

Weedn, Flavia & Weedn, Lisa. Flavia & the Christmas Legacy. (Illus.). 52p. 1990. 16.00 (0-929632-11-7) Applause Inc.

Weedn, Lisa, jt. auth. see Weedn, Flavia.

Weeks, Jessica V. Television. LC 93-446. (Illus.). 59p. (gr. 5-6). 1994. RSBE 14.95 (0-89686-783-8, Crestwood Hse) Macmillan Child Grp.

Weeks, John. Pyramids. (Illus.). 48p. (gr. 7 up). 1971. pap. 7.50 (0-521-07240-9) Cambridge U Pr.

Weeks, Sarah. Hurricane City. Warhola, James, illus. LC 92-23389. 32p. (ps-1). 1993. 15.00 (0-06-021572-0); PLB 14.89 (0-06-021573-9) HarpC Child Grp.

Weeks, Wilfred H. The White Stone. Schlatter, Becky, illus. LC 85-51932. 37p. (Orig.). (gr. 4-9). 1990. pap. write for info. (0-9615677-0-8) Three Riv Ctr.

Weems, David B. Son of an Earl...Sold for a Slave. Magellan, Mauro, illus. LC 92-27917. 112p. (gr. 5 up). 1992. 11.95 (0-88289-921-X) Pelican.

Weems, John E. The Story of Texas. 2nd ed. (Illus., Orig.). (gr. 2-6). 1992. pap. 8.95 (0-940672-35-9) Shearer Pub.

Weerusinghe, Christabel. Happy New Year in Sri Lanka. Deepa, illus. 52p. (Orig.). (gr. 2 up). 1986. pap. 6.50 (0-941402-05-3) Devon Pub.

Wees, Dick, illus. & intro. by see Wees, Marty.

Wees, Marty. Fanny the Fanciful Frog - Coloring Book. Joyce, Susan, ed. Wees, Dick, illus. & intro. by. 30p. (gr. k-2). 1989. pap. write for info. Richmar Prodns.

Weese, Gene de see De Weese, Gene.

Weese, Gene De see De Weese, Gene.

Wegman, William. Cinderella. Wegman, William, illus. LC 92-72028. 40p. 1993. 16.95 (1-56282-348-5); PLB 16.89 (1-56282-349-3) Hyprn Child.

—Little Red Riding Hood. Wegman, William, illus. LC 92-54874. 40p. 1993. 16.95 (1-56282-416-3); PLB 16.89 (1-56282-417-1) Hyprn Child.

Wegrzecki, Lester L. Christmas Decoration: Eggshell-Wydmuski. Wegrzecki, Lester L., illus. Chrypinski, Anna, intro. by. (Illus.). 88p. (gr. 4 up). 1987. 9.50x (0-317-90582-1) L L Wegrzecki.

—Christmas Decoration: Eggshell-Wydmuszki. Chrypinski, Anna, intro. by. (Illus., Orig.). (gr. 4 up). 1987. pap. write for info. (0-9620774-0-2) L L Wegrzecki.

Wehrheim, Carol. The Great Parade: Learning about Women, Justice & the Church. (Orig.). 1992. pap. 7.95 incl. children's activity pages & tchr's. guide (0-377-00244-5) Friendship Pr.

Wehrli, K. Division. Reusable ed. (gr. 4). 1976. 6.00 (0-89039-180-7, Ann Arbor Div) Acad Therapy.

Wehrli, K., jt. ed. see Steele, B.

Wehrli, Kitty. Cues & Comprehension: Level 1. Reusable ed. (gr. 2). 1976. wkbk. 9.00 (0-87879-743-2, Ann Arbor Div) Acad Therapy.

—Cues & Comprehension: Level 2. Reusable ed. (gr. 2). 1976. wkbk. 9.00 (0-87879-744-0, Ann Arbor Div) Acad Therapy.

—Cues & Comprehension: Level 3. Reusable ed. (gr. 2). 1976. wkbk. 9.00 (0-87879-745-9, Ann Arbor Div) Acad Therapy.

—Cues & Comprehension: Level 4. Reusable ed. (gr. 2). 1976. wkbk. 9.00 (0-87879-746-7, Ann Arbor Div) Acad Therapy.

—Cues & Signals in Math, Book One: Number Tracking. Reusable Edition. 48p. (gr. 1 up). 1971. 9.00 (0-87879-757-2, Ann Arbor Div) Acad Therapy.

—Multiple Tracking: Math 2: A Self-Instruction Workbook for Visual Accuracy, Reusable Edition. Reusable ed. 88p. (gr. 1). 1971. 9.00 (0-87879-758-0, Ann Arbor Div) Acad Therapy.

—Numbers & Numerals. Reusable ed. (ps-2). 1976. 1.00 (0-89039-199-8, Ann Arbor Div); wkbk. 7.00 (0-89039-102-5) Acad Therapy.

—Subtraction 20-10, Levels 1 & 2. Reusable ed. (gr. 2-3). 1976. Level 1. wkbk 8.50 ea. (0-89039-178-5, Ann Arbor Div) Level 2 (0-89039-220-X) Acad Therapy.

—Thought Tracking Level 1: Simple Phrases. Reusable ed. (gr. 2). 1976. wkbk. 9.00 (0-87879-739-4, Ann Arbor Div) Acad Therapy.

—Thought Tracking Level 2: Sequential Phrases. Reusable ed. (gr. 2). wkbk. 6.50 (0-87879-740-8, Ann Arbor Div) Acad Therapy.

—Thought Tracking Level 3: Simple Sentences. Reusable ed. (gr. 2). 1976. wkbk. 6.50 (0-87879-741-6, Ann Arbor Div) Acad Therapy.

—Thought Tracking Level 4: Questions & Answers. Reusable ed. (gr. 2). 1976. wkbk. 6.50 (0-87879-742-4, Ann Arbor Div) Acad Therapy.

Weidensaul, Scott. Descubre Aves. University of Mexico City Staff, tr. from SPA. O'Neill, Pablo M. & Robare, Lorie, illus. 48p. (gr. 3-8). 1993. PLB 16.95 (1-56674-047-9, HTS Bks) Forest Hse.

—A Kid's First Book of Birdwatching. (Illus.). 64p. (ps up). 1990. incl. cassette 18.95 (0-89471-826-6) Running Pr.

Weider, Joe. Joe Weider's Bodybuilding System. rev. ed. (Illus.). 108p. (gr. 9). 1988. pap. 19.95 (0-945797-00-1) Weider Health.

Weidhorn, Manfred. Jackie Robinson. LC 92-15248. (Illus.). 160p. (gr. 5-9). 1993. SBE 14.95 (0-689-31644-5, Atheneum Child Bk) Macmillan Child Grp.

—Napoleon. LC 86-3352. (Illus.). 224p. (gr. 7 up). 1986. SBE 16.95 (0-689-31163-X, Atheneum Child Bk) Macmillan Child Grp.

—Robert E. Lee. LC 87-14500. (Illus.). 160p. (gr. 5 up). 1988. SBE 14.95 (0-689-31340-3, Atheneum Child Bk) Macmillan Child Grp.

Weidt, Maryann. Wild Bill Hickok. Casino, Steve, illus. LC 92-9732. 1992. write for info. (0-688-10089-9); lib. bdg. write for info. (0-688-10090-2) Lothrop.

Weidt, Maryann N. Mr. Blue Jeans: A Story about Levi Strauss. (gr. 4-7). 1992. pap. 5.95 (0-87614-588-8) Carolrhoda Bks.

—Presenting Judy Blume. 168p. (gr. 9-12). 1989. text ed. 19.95x (0-8057-8208-7, Twayne) Macmillan.

—Stateswoman to the World: A Story about Eleanor Roosevelt. Anderson, Lydia M., illus. LC 90-23216. 64p. (gr. 3-6). 1991. PLB 9.95 (0-87614-663-9) Carolrhoda Bks.

—Stateswoman to the World: A Story about Eleanor Roosevelt. (gr. 4-7). 1992. pap. 5.95 (0-87614-562-4) Carolrhoda Bks.

Weidt, Maryann N. & Anderson, Lydia M. Mr. Blue Jeans: A Story about Levi Strauss. (Illus.). 64p. (gr. 3-6). 1990. PLB 14.95 (0-87614-421-0) Carolrhoda Bks.

Weigand, Betty, ed. see De Bie, Catherine F.

Weigle, Marta. Follow My Fancy: The Book of Jacks & Jack Games. (Illus.). 94p. pap. 2.95 (0-486-22081-8) Dover.

Wei Jiang & Cheng An Jiang. La Heroina Hua Mulan-the Legend of Mu Lan: Una Leyenda De la Antigua China-a Heroine of Ancient China. (SPA & ENG., Illus.). 32p. (gr. 1 up). 1992. pap. 6.95 (1-878217-15-1) Victory Press.

—Hua Mu Lan De Gushi-the Legend of Mu Lan: Zhong Guo Gudai Nu Yingxiong-a Heroine of Ancient China. (CHI & ENG., Illus.). 32p. (gr. 1 up). 1992. pap. 6.95 (1-878217-14-3) Victory Press.

Weik, Mary H. The Jazz Man. 2nd ed. Grifalconi, Ann, illus. LC 93-9965. 48p. (gr. 3-7). 1993. pap. 3.95 (0-689-71767-9, Aladdin) Macmillan Child Grp.

Weikel, Ann T. The Very Best Me: Growing up Drug Free. John, Joseph, Jr., illus. Christian, Cora L., contrib. by. (Illus.). 60p. (Orig.). (gr. k-3). 1991. pap. 3.95 (0-935357-11-4) CRIC Prod.

Weil, Ann. Betsy Ross: Designer of Our Flag. Fiorentino, Al, illus. LC 86-10775. 192p. (gr. 2 up). 1986. pap. 3.95 (0-02-042120-6, Aladdin) Macmillan Child Grp.

—Eleanor Roosevelt. LC 89-37781. (Illus.). 192p. (gr. 2-6). 1989. pap. 3.95 (0-689-71348-7, Aladdin) Macmillan Child Grp.

—Red Sails to Capri. 160p. (gr. 5-9). 1988. pap. 3.95 (0-14-032858-0, Puffin) Puffin Bks.

—Red Sails to Capri. (gr. 5-9). 16.50 (0-8446-6413-8) Peter Smith.

Weil, Jennifer C. The Secret of Yellow. Farrington, Liz, created by. (Illus.). 40p. (gr. k-4). 1994. 14.95 (1-56844-006-5) Enchante Pub.

—William's Gift. Farrington, Liz, created by. (Illus.). 40p. (gr. k-4). 1994. 14.95 (1-56844-007-3) Enchante Pub.

Weil, Jennifer C., jt. auth. see Farrington, Liz.

Weil, Judith. School for One. (gr. 4 up). 1992. 11.95 (0-87306-620-0); pap. 9.95 (0-87306-621-9) Feldheim.

Weil, Lisl. Let's Go to the Circus. Weil, Lisl, illus. LC 87-25201. 32p. (ps-3). 1988. reinforced bdg. 13.95 (0-8234-0693-8) Holiday.

—Let's Go to the Library. Weil, Lisl, illus. LC 90-55105. 32p. (ps-3). 1990. reinforced 13.95 (0-8234-0829-9) Holiday.

—Let's Go to the Museum. Weil, Lisl, illus. LC 89-2078. 32p. (ps-3). 1989. reinforced 13.95 (0-8234-0784-5) Holiday.

—The Magic of Music. Weil, Lisl, illus. LC 88-21362. 32p. (ps-3). 1989. reinforced bdg. 13.95 (0-8234-0735-7) Holiday.

—Santa Claus Around the World. Weil, Lisl, illus. LC 87-45334. 32p. (ps-3). 1987. reinforced 13.95 (0-8234-0665-2) Holiday.
—Wolferl: The First Six Years in the Life of Wolfgang Amadeus Mozart. Weil, Lisl, illus. LC 90-47684. 33p. (ps-3). 1991. reinforced 14.95 (0-8234-0876-0) Holiday.
Weil, Zaro. Mud, Moon & Me. Burroughes, Jo, illus. 80p. (gr. 2-5). 1992. 13.45 (0-395-58038-2) HM.
Weiland, Jeanne, jt. auth. see Pravda, Myra.
Weilbacher, Mike. The Magnetism Exploration Kit: Discover One of Nature's Most Astonishing Forces. (Illus.). 64p. (gr. 3 up). 1993. incl. kit 16.95 (1-56138-240-X) Running Pr.
Weiler, Susan K. Mini-Myths & Maxi-Words. 1986. pap. text ed. 9.99 (0-88334-191-3, 76156) Longman.
Weilerstein, Sadie R. Best of K'tonton. Hirsh, Marilyn, illus. LC 80-20177. 96p. (gr. 1 up). 1980. pap. 9.95 (0-8276-0187-5) JPS Phila.
—Jewish Heroes, 2 bks. Cassel, Lili, illus. 208p. (gr. 2-3). pap. 4.25x ea. Bk. 1 (0-8381-0180-1) Bk. 2 (0-8381-0177-1) United Syn Bk.
—K'tonton in Israel, 3 bks. Safian, Elizabeth & Chernak, Judy, illus. (ps-6). 1988. Set of 3 bks. in zip loc bag. pap. 6.95 (0-944633-32-3); Set of 3 bks. & cassettes. pap. 29.95 (0-685-43967-4); pap. 2.95 ea. Bk. 1: A Visit with K'tonton & K'tonton on Kibbutz, 40p. Bk. 2: K'tonton in Jerusalem-I: Adventure on Yom Ha'atzma'ut, Israel's Independence Day, 32p. Bk. 3: K'tonton in Jerusalem-II: Adventure in the Old City, 36p. pap. 10.95 ea. bk. & cassette; cassette 8.95 ea. J Chernak.
—K'tonton in the Circus: A Hanukkah Adventure. Hirsh, Marilyn, illus. LC 81-11765. 96p. (gr. 2 up). pap. 8.95 (0-8276-0303-7) JPS Phila.
—K'tonton's Sukkot Adventure. Boddy, Joe, illus. LC 93-2990. 34p. (ps-3). 1993. 12.95 (0-8276-0502-1) JPS Phila.
—Ten & a Kid. Domanska, Janina, illus. LC 61-12600. 186p. (gr. 3 up). 1973. Repr. of 1961 ed. 8.95 (0-8276-0009-7) JPS Phila.
—What the Moon Brought. (Illus.). 159p. (gr. 1-3). 1942. pap. 7.95 (0-8276-0265-0) JPS Phila.
Weills, Christopher, ed. The Goodfellow Catalog of Wonderful Things for Kids of All Ages. LC 83-45398. (Illus.). 192p. (gr. 5 up). 1984. pap. 14.95 (0-317-61462-2) Goodfellow.
Weimann & Friedman. A-Choo. (Illus.). 30p. (gr. k-1). 1990. pap. 5.95 (0-89796-200-1) New Dimens Educ.
—A Buttonmat for Beautiful Buttons. (Illus.). 30p. (gr. k-1). 1990. pap. 5.95 (0-89796-201-X) New Dimens Educ.
—The Cotton Candy Caper. (Illus.). 30p. (gr. k-1). 1990. pap. 5.95 (0-89796-202-8) New Dimens Educ.
—A Dozen Delicious Doughnuts. (Illus.). 30p. (gr. k-1). 1990. pap. 5.95 (0-89796-203-6) New Dimens Educ.
—Fantastic Funny Feet. (Illus.). 30p. (gr. k-1). 1990. pap. 5.95 (0-89796-205-2) New Dimens Educ.
—Gooey Gum Is Not for Chewing. (Illus.). 30p. (gr. k-1). 1990. pap. 5.95 (0-89796-206-0) New Dimens Educ.
—Hat Helpers Hullabaloo. (Illus.). 30p. (gr. k-1). 1990. pap. 5.95 (0-89796-207-9) New Dimens Educ.
—The Incredible Inventor. (Illus.). 30p. (gr. k-1). 1990. pap. 5.95 (0-89796-208-7) New Dimens Educ.
—The Inimitable Mr. X. (Illus.). 30p. (gr. k-1). 1990. pap. 5.95 (0-89796-223-0) New Dimens Educ.
—Jingling, Jangling Joggers. (Illus.). 30p. (gr. k-1). 1990. pap. 5.95 (0-89796-209-5) New Dimens Educ.
—The Longest Kick. (Illus.). 30p. (gr. k-1). 1990. pap. 5.95 (0-89796-210-9) New Dimens Educ.
—Lovely Lemon Lollies. (Illus.). 30p. (gr. k-1). 1990. pap. 5.95 (0-89796-211-7) New Dimens Educ.
—Meet Me at the Market. (Illus.). 30p. (gr. k-1). 1990. pap. 5.95 (0-89796-212-5) New Dimens Educ.
—A Most Unusual Umbrella. (Illus.). 30p. (gr. k-1). 1990. pap. 5.95 (0-89796-220-6) New Dimens Educ.
—The Noisy Nose Nanny. (Illus.). 30p. (gr. k-1). 1990. pap. 5.95 (0-89796-213-3) New Dimens Educ.
—The Optimistic Optimist. (Illus.). 30p. (gr. k-1). 1990. pap. 5.95 (0-89796-214-1) New Dimens Educ.
—Popping Pointy Patches. (Illus.). 30p. (gr. k-1). 1990. pap. 5.95 (0-89796-215-X) New Dimens Educ.
—The Rubberbit Roundup. (Illus.). 30p. (gr. k-1). 1990. pap. 5.95 (0-89796-217-6) New Dimens Educ.
—Super Sock Sensation. (Illus.). 30p. (gr. k-1). 1990. pap. 5.95 (0-89796-218-4) New Dimens Educ.
—The Tale of Tall Toothbrush. (Illus.). 30p. (gr. k-1). 1990. pap. 5.95 (0-89796-219-2) New Dimens Educ.
—To Be or Not to Be...Quiet. (Illus.). 30p. (gr. k-1). 1990. pap. 5.95 (0-89796-216-8) New Dimens Educ.
—Vanishing Vests. (Illus.). 30p. (gr. k-1). 1990. pap. 5.95 (0-89796-221-4) New Dimens Educ.
—Wonderful Winks & Weather Wishes. (Illus.). 30p. (gr. k-1). 1990. pap. 5.95 (0-89796-222-2) New Dimens Educ.
—The Yawn Maker. (Illus.). 30p. (gr. k-1). 1990. pap. 5.95 (0-89796-224-9) New Dimens Educ.
—Zipping Zippers Save the Zoo. (Illus.). 30p. (gr. k-1). 1990. pap. 5.95 (0-89796-225-7) New Dimens Educ.
Weimann & Friedman, Rita. The Exercise Expert. (Illus.). 30p. (gr. k-1). 1990. pap. 5.95 (0-89796-204-4) New Dimens Educ.
Weimann, Elaine & Friedman, Rita. The Cotton Candy Caper. (Illus.). 30p. (ps-1). 1985. PLB 10.50 (0-89796-988-X) New Dimens Educ.
—A Dozen Delicious Doughnuts. (Illus.). 30p. (ps-1). 1988. PLB 10.50 (0-89796-803-4) New Dimens Educ.

—Gooey Gum Is Not for Chewing. (Illus.). 30p. (ps-1). 1985. PLB 10.50 (0-89796-989-8) New Dimens Educ.
—The Incredible Inventor. (Illus.). 30p. (ps-1). 1985. PLB 10.50 (0-89796-985-5) New Dimens Educ.
—The Inimitable Mr. X. (Illus.). 30p. (ps-1). 1986. PLB 10.50 (0-89796-992-8) New Dimens Educ.
—Jingling, Jangling Joggers. (Illus.). 30p. (ps-1). 1986. PLB 10.50 (0-89796-994-4) New Dimens Educ.
—The Longest Kick. (Illus.). 30p. (ps-1). 1986. PLB 10.50 (0-89796-990-1) New Dimens Educ.
—Lovely Lemon Lollies. (Illus.). 30p. (ps-1). 1978. PLB 10.50 (0-89796-802-6) New Dimens Educ.
—Meet Me at the Market. (Illus.). 30p. (ps-1). 1978. PLB 10.50 (0-89796-801-8) New Dimens Educ.
—A Most Unusual Umbrella. (Illus.). 30p. (ps-1). 1986. PLB 10.50 (0-89796-999-5) New Dimens Educ.
—The Noisy Nose Nanny. (Illus.). 30p. (ps-1). 1985. PLB 10.50 (0-89796-986-3) New Dimens Educ.
—The Optimistic Optimist. (Illus.). 30p. (ps-1). 1986. PLB 10.50 (0-89796-996-0) New Dimens Educ.
—Popping Pointy Patches. (Illus.). 30p. (ps-1). 1985. PLB 10.50 (0-89796-984-7) New Dimens Educ.
—The Rubberbit Roundup. (Illus.). 30p. (ps-1). 1986. PLB 10.50 (0-89796-998-7) New Dimens Educ.
—The Super Sock Sensation. (Illus.). 30p. (ps-1). 1985. PLB 10.50 (0-89796-987-1) New Dimens Educ.
—To Be or Not to Be...Quiet. (Illus.). 30p. (ps-1). 1986. PLB 10.50 (0-89796-997-9) New Dimens Educ.
—Vanishing Vests. (Illus.). 30p. (ps-1). 1978. PLB 10.50 (0-89796-804-2) New Dimens Educ.
—Wonderful Winks & Weather Wishes. (Illus.). 30p. (ps-1). 1986. PLB 10.50 (0-89796-995-2) New Dimens Educ.
—The Yawn Maker. (Illus.). 30p. (ps-1). 1986. PLB 10.50 (0-89796-993-6) New Dimens Educ.
—Zipping Zippers Save the Zoo. (Illus.). 30p. (ps-1). 1986. PLB 10.50 (0-89796-991-X) New Dimens Educ.
Weimann, Elayne & Friedman, Rita. The A-Choo Confusion. Callen, Elizabeth, illus. 30p. (ps-1). 1988. PLB 10.50 (0-89796-000-9) New Dimens Educ.
—The Best Quiet Meter. Callen, Elizabeth, illus. 30p. (ps-1). 1989. PLB 10.50 (0-89796-016-5) New Dimens Educ.
—Buttonyms for Safety. Callen, Elizabeth, illus. 30p. (ps-1). 1989. PLB 10.50 (0-89796-001-7) New Dimens Educ.
—The Cotton Candy Creature. Callen, Elizabeth, illus. 30p. (ps-1). 1989. PLB 10.50 (0-89796-002-5) New Dimens Educ.
—The Dictionary Doughnut Shop. Callen, Elizabeth, illus. 30p. (ps-1). 1989. PLB 10.50 (0-89796-003-3) New Dimens Educ.
—Exercise Excitement. Callen, Elizabeth, illus. 30p. (ps-1). 1988. PLB 10.50 (0-89796-004-1) New Dimens Educ.
—Fantastic Friendship. Callen, Elizabeth, illus. 30p. (ps-1). 1988. PLB 10.50 (0-89796-005-X) New Dimens Educ.
—Gooey Gumball Game. Callen, Elizabeth, illus. 30p. (ps-1). 1989. PLB 10.50 (0-89796-006-8) New Dimens Educ.
—The Hat House Hotel. Callen, Elizabeth, illus. 30p. (ps-1). 1988. PLB 10.50 (0-89796-007-6) New Dimens Educ.
—Inchy the Incredible Invention. Callen, Elizabeth, illus. 30p. (ps-1). 1988. PLB 10.50 (0-89796-008-4) New Dimens Educ.
—The Kazoo Kicker. Callen, Elizabeth, illus. 30p. (ps-1). 1989. PLB 10.50 (0-89796-010-6) New Dimens Educ.
—Lemonberry Lollipops. Callen, Elizabeth, illus. 30p. (ps-1). 1989. PLB 10.50 (0-89796-011-4) New Dimens Educ.
—Mr. J's Junkyard. Callen, Elizabeth, illus. 30p. (ps-1). 1989. PLB 10.50 (0-89796-009-2) New Dimens Educ.
—Mr. X's Mix-ups. Callen, Elizabeth, illus. 30p. (ps-1). 1989. PLB 10.50 (0-89796-023-8) New Dimens Educ.
—Munching Magic. Callen, Elizabeth, illus. 30p. (ps-1). 1988. PLB 10.50 (0-89796-012-2) New Dimens Educ.
—Ostrich Express. Callen, Elizabeth, illus. 30p. (ps-1). 1988. PLB 10.50 (0-89796-014-9) New Dimens Educ.
—Parking Pandemonium. Callen, Elizabeth, illus. 30p. (ps-1). 1989. PLB 10.50 (0-89796-015-7) New Dimens Educ.
—The Rubber Band Runner Champion. Callen, Elizabeth, illus. 30p. (ps-1). 1989. PLB 10.50 (0-89796-017-3) New Dimens Educ.
—Say No & Fly Away! Callen, Elizabeth, illus. 30p. (ps-1). 1988. PLB 10.50 (0-89796-013-0) New Dimens Educ.
—Super Socks for Courage. Callen, Elizabeth, illus. 30p. (ps-1). 1989. PLB 10.50 (0-89796-018-1) New Dimens Educ.
—Tall Toothbrush Retires. Callen, Elizabeth, illus. 30p. (ps-1). 1989. PLB 10.50 (0-89796-019-X) New Dimens Educ.
—Valuable Volunteers. Callen, Elizabeth, illus. 30p. (ps-1). 1989. PLB 10.50 (0-89796-021-1) New Dimens Educ.
—The Worry Machine. Callen, Elizabeth, illus. 30p. (ps-1). 1989. PLB 10.50 (0-89796-022-X) New Dimens Educ.
—Yawn-Maker Wanted. Callen, Elizabeth, illus. 30p. (ps-1). 1989. PLB 10.50 (0-89796-024-6) New Dimens Educ.
—You Forget Too. Callen, Elizabeth, illus. 30p. (ps-1). 1989. PLB 10.50 (0-89796-020-3) New Dimens Educ.
—Zip Codes. Callen, Elizabeth, illus. 30p. (ps-1). 1989. PLB 10.50 (0-89796-025-4) New Dimens Educ.

Weimer, Tonja E. Fingerplays & Action Chants: Animals, Vol. 1. Kozlina, Yvonne, illus. 42p. (Orig.). (gr. k-1). 1986. pap. text ed. 8.95 (0-936823-00-3); cassette 8.95 (0-936823-01-1) Pearce Evetts.
—Fingerplays & Action Chants: Family & Friends, Vol. 2. Kozlina, Yvonne, illus. 44p. (Orig.). (ps-1). 1986. pap. text ed. 8.95 (0-936823-02-X); cassette 8.95 (0-936823-03-8) Pearce Evetts.
—Space Songs for Children: Fun Songs & Activities about Outer Space. Kozlina, Yvonne, illus. 100p. (Orig.). (ps-3). 1993. 13.98 (0-936823-11-9); cassette 9.95 (0-936823-12-7) Pearce Evetts.
Wein, Elizabeth. The Winter Prince. LC 91-39129. 224p. (gr. 7 up). 1993. SBE 15.95 (0-689-31747-6, Atheneum Child Bk) Macmillan Child Grp.
Weinandy, Tom. What Must I Do? 32p. (Orig.). (gr. 8 up). 1988. pap. text ed. 9.95 10-pk. (0-932085-07-5) Word Among Us.
Weinbach, Shaindel. Shimmee & the Taste-Me Tree. Backman, Aidel, illus. (ps-2). 2.95 (0-87306-991-9) Feldheim.
—The Three Merchants: And Other Stories. Dershowitz, Y., illus. 160p. (gr. 6-12). 1983. 13.95 (0-89906-768-9); pap. 10.95 (0-89906-769-7) Mesorah Pubns.
Weinbach, Shaindel, tr. from HEB. Tales of Tzaddikim: Bamidbar. Bardugo, Miriam, illus. 320p. (gr. 7-12). 1988. 14.95 (0-89906-831-6); pap. 10.95 (0-89906-832-4) Mesorah Pubns.
—Tales of Tzaddikim: Vayikra. Bardugo, Miriam, illus. 320p. (gr. 7-12). 1988. 14.95 (0-89906-829-4); pap. 10.95 (0-89906-830-8) Mesorah Pubns.
Weinbach, Shaindel, tr. see Matov, G.
Weinbach, Shaindel, tr. see Piontac, Nechemiah.
Weinbach, Shaindel, tr. see Sofer, G.
Weinbaum, Helen, tr. see Ellenberger, W., et al.
Weinberg, Alyce T. Spirits of Frederick. LC 79-54039. (Illus.). 73p. (Orig.). 1979. pap. 3.95x (0-9604552-0-5) A T Weinberg.
Weinberg, Ben. Out to the Edge. Holmes, B., ed. 200p. (gr. 6-10). 1993. pap. 9.95 (0-932433-47-2) Windswept Hse.
Weinberg, Larry. The Curse. (gr. 7 up). 1984. pap. 2.50 (0-553-26549-0) Bantam.
—The Empire Strikes Back. LC 84-18030. (Illus.). 72p. (gr. 2-5). 1985. lib. bdg. 8.99 (0-394-96868-9) Random Bks Yng Read.
—Shivers & Shakes. Tavonatti, Mia, illus. LC 93-24445. 1993. pap. 2.95 (0-8167-3281-7) Troll Assocs.
—Universal Monsters: Dracula. (ps-3). 1993. pap. 3.50 (0-307-11475-9, Golden Pr) Western Pub.
—Universal Monsters: The Phantom of the Opera. (gr. 4-7). 1993. pap. 3.25 (0-307-22334-5, Golden Pr) Western Pub.
Weinberg, Larry, adapted by. The Legend of the Lone Ranger Storybook. (Illus.). (gr. 4-7). 1981. lib. bdg. 6.99 (0-394-94683-9) Random Bks Yng Read.
Weinberg, Larry, adapted by see Shelley, Mary Wollstonecraft.
Weinberg, Lawrence. Benjamin Franklin. Bloch, Alex, illus. 48p. (gr. 2-4). 1988. pap. 2.50 (0-681-40347-0) Longmeadow Pr.
—George Washington. Bloch, Alex, illus. 48p. (gr. 2-4). 1988. pap. 2.50 (0-681-40346-2) Longmeadow Pr.
—Jackie Robinson. Ford, George, illus. 48p. (gr. 2-4). 1988. pap. 2.50 (0-681-40690-9) Longmeadow Pr.
—Paul Revere. De John, Marie, illus. 48p. (gr. 2-4). 1988. pap. 2.50 (0-681-40688-7) Longmeadow Pr.
Weinberg, Michael. Thomas Edison. Ford, George, illus. 48p. (gr. 2-4). 1988. pap. 2.50 (0-681-40687-9) Longmeadow Pr.
Weinberg, Michael A. The Horrible Terrible Dragon: A Folktale. Weinberg, Kay, illus. 10p. (gr. 1-3). 1949. pap. 1.00 (0-9601014-3-8) Weinberg.
Weinberg, Robert see Effendi, Shoghi.
Weinberg, Shifra. Regards from Camp 2: Deepwater Dilemma. LC 93-72270. (Illus.). (gr. 5-8). 1993. write for info. (1-56062-200-8) CIS Comm.
Weinberg, Shnayer. Targilon for Haschalas Chumash: A Chumash Workbook for Beginners. (Illus.). 130p. (Orig.). pap. text ed. 5.50 (1-878895-00-1, A135) Torah Umesorah.
Weinberg, Susan, jt. auth. see Lumpkin, Susan.
Weinberger, Jane. Cory the Cormorant. LC 91-68128. (Illus.). 40p. (ps-4). 1992. pap. 9.95 (0-932433-92-8) Windswept Hse.
—Fanny & Sarah. 2nd ed. MacDonald, Karen, illus. LC 84-51987. 40p. (gr. k-4). 1986. pap. 3.95 (0-932433-02-2) Windswept Hse.
—Kiltie, the Laird of Kiltarnen. 2nd ed. Cap, photos by. (Illus.). 44p. (ps-5). 1987. 5.95 (0-932433-09-X) Windswept Hse.
—Lemon Drop. Berber, Richard, illus. LC 85-62023. 64p. (gr. 1-6). 1985. Repr. of 1953 ed. PLB 5.95 (0-932433-10-3) Windswept Hse.
—The Little Ones. LC 86-50874. (FRE & ENG., Illus.). 54p. (Orig.). (ps-4). 1987. pap. 5.95 (0-932433-29-4) Windswept Hse.
—Stormy. Kardas, Alek, illus. LC 85-62021. 54p. (gr. 1-6). 1985. 5.95 (0-932433-13-8) Windswept Hse.
—Tabitha Jones. 2nd ed. Jones, Renata S., illus. 40p. (Orig.). (ps-4). 1985. pap. 3.95 (0-932433-07-3) Windswept Hse.
—That's What Counts. Margit Studio, illus. LC 87-50549. 40p. (gr. k-4). 1988. pap. 5.95 (0-932433-33-2) Windswept Hse.

—Vim, a Very Important Mouse. 8th ed. Allen, Rosemary, illus. LC 84-50872. 40p. (ps-4.) 1989. 4.95 (0-932433-01-4) Windswept Hse.
—Wee Peter Puffin. LC 84-51988. (Illus.). 40p. (ps-8). 1984. 9.95 (0-932433-03-0) Windswept Hse.
Weinberger, Jane, ed. see Artes, Dorothy B.
Weinberger, Jane, ed. see Bacon, Joy.
Weinberger, Jane, ed. see Bullock, Gloria S. & Crocitto, Jane B.
Weinberger, Jane, ed. see Chesely, Mary.
Weinberger, Jane, ed. see DeVito, Pam.
Weinberger, Jane, ed. see Farrar, Susan C.
Weinberger, Jane, ed. see Fine, John C.
Weinberger, Jane, ed. see Fredeking, Jean T.
Weinberger, Jane, ed. see Friendly, Alfred.
Weinberger, Jane, ed. see Fuller, Ted.
Weinberger, Jane, ed. see Gould, Alberta.
Weinberger, Jane, ed. see Guglielmino, Terese.
Weinberger, Jane, ed. see Higa, Mandy.
Weinberger, Jane, ed. see Hornidge, Marilis.
Weinberger, Jane, ed. see Innis, Pauline.
Weinberger, Jane, ed. see Kittredge, Sonya.
Weinberger, Jane, ed. see Lupsewicz, Veronica-Ann.
Weinberger, Jane, ed. see McMahon, James P.
Weinberger, Jane, ed. see Marshall-Noke, Dorothy.
Weinberger, Jane, ed. see Morelli, Susan.
Weinberger, Jane, ed. see Pollard, Jean A.
Weinberger, Jane, ed. see Sargent, Ruth.
Weinberger, Jane, ed. see Scarpino, Jane.
Weinberger, Jane, ed. see Simcox, Helen E.
Weinberger, Jane, ed. see Stewart, Celeste.
Weinberger, Jane, ed. see Stone, Audrey.
Weinberger, Jane, ed. see White, Sylvia.
Weinboreir, Messody. Birds. Nodel, Norman, illus. Satat, Noah, photos by. (Illus.). 32p. (gr. 3-8). 1990. 10.95 (0-922613-33-8); pap. 8.95 (0-922613-34-6) Hachai Pubns.
Weinburg, Karen. Window of Time. Ratcliffe, Annelle W., illus. LC 90-20856. (gr. 2-4). 1991. pap. 9.95 (0-942597-18-4) White Mane Pub.
Weinburg, Larry. Guess a Rhyme: Poems to Complete! Riddles to Solve! reissued ed. McKie, Roy, illus. LC 81-15689. 32p. (ps-1). 1993. 2.25 (0-394-85062-9) Random Bks Yng Read.
Weiner, Beth L., illus. The Pudgy Book of Here We Go. 16p. (gr. k). 1984. pap. 2.95 (0-448-10208-0, G&D) Putnam Pub Group.
Weiner, Eric. The Civil War. LC 92-9461. (Illus.). 64p. (gr. 2-6). 1993. 7.98 (0-8317-2312-2) Smithmark.
—Ghostwriter: A Match of Wills. (ps-3). 1992. pap. 2.99 (0-553-29934-4) Bantam.
—The Kids Complete Baseball Catalogue. (Illus.). 256p. (gr. 5 up). 1990. lib. bdg. 14.98 (0-671-70196-7, J Messner); pap. 12.95 (0-671-70197-5) S&S Trade.
—Steer Clear of Haunted Hill. (gr. 1-3). 1993. pap. 2.99 (0-553-48087-1) Bantam.
—Story of Frederick Douglass: Voice of Freedom. (ps-3). 1992. pap. 3.25 (0-440-40560-2) Dell.
—Story of Henry Hudson. (gr. 4-7). 1991. pap. 2.99 (0-440-40513-0, YB) Dell.
Weiner, Eric & Storey, T. R. Full House: Behind the Scenes. LC 92-34522. (Illus.). 64p. (gr. 2-6). 1993. tchr's ed. 2.95 (0-8167-3037-7) Troll Assocs.
Weinerman, Eli, tr. The Black Swans (a Russian Folktale) Parker, Robert A., illus. Weinerman, Eli, retold by. (Illus.). 32p. (gr. k-3). 1994. 14.95 (0-945912-19-6) Pippin Pr.
Weingardt, Richard. Sound the Charge. Mayabb, Darrell, illus. LC 78-59321. 184p. (gr. 6-12). 9.95 (0-932446-00-0); pap. 4.95 (0-932446-01-9) Jacqueline Enter.
Weingarten, Elaine. The Dog Who Didn't Know about Snow. Sweeney, Phyllis, illus. 58p. (ps-3). 1988. text ed. 13.50 (0-89777-703-4, 97005) Soc Issues.
—Kenny the Caterpillar. Sweeney, Phyllis, illus. 30p. (ps-3). 1988. text ed. 13.50 (0-89777-702-6, 97003) Soc Issues.
—Old Doctor Monkey. Sweeney, Phyllis, illus. 44p. (ps-3). 1988. text ed. 13.50 (0-89777-704-2, 97004) Soc Issues.
—One Duck. Sweeney, Phyllis, illus. 56p. (ps-3). 1988. text ed. 13.50 (0-89777-700-X, 97001) Soc Issues.
—The Robin Who Was Afraid to Fly. Sweeney, Phyllis, illus. 50p. (ps-3). 1988. text ed. 13.50 (0-89777-701-8, 97002) Soc Issues.
Weininger, Rachel. Nightshade. Sawyer, Barbara, illus. LC 88-63135. 64p. (Orig.). (gr. 4-6). 1989. pap. 5.95 (0-931093-11-2) Red Hen Pr.
Weinman, Rosalind, jt. auth. see Sharmat, Marjorie W.
Weinman, Susan. Word Processing: Course Code S04-2. Schroeder, Bonnie, ed. Black, Jeanne, illus. 75p. (gr. 7). 1989. pap. text ed. 8.00 (0-917531-53-1) CES Compu-Tech.
Weinman, Susan, jt. auth. see Anderson, Jill.
Weinrich, Mark. Meet the Missionary. (Illus.). 24p. (Orig.). (gr. k-3). 1993. pap. 4.99 (0-87509-517-8) Chr Pubns.
—The Missing Missionary. (Illus.). 24p. (Orig.). (gr. k-3). 1993. pap. 4.99 (0-87509-518-6) Chr Pubns.
Weinstein, Nina. No More Secrets. LC 90-20603. 160p. (Orig.). 1991. pap. 8.95 (0-685-47511-5) Seal Pr Feminist.
Weinstein-Farson, Laurie. The Wampanoag. Porter, Frank, intro. by. (Illus.). 96p. (gr. 5 up). 1988. lib. bdg. 17.95x (1-55546-733-4); pap. 9.95 (0-7910-0368-X) Chelsea Hse.
Weinstock, Shaindel, tr. see Weinstock, Y.

Weinstock, Y. Tales from the Gemara, Vol. II: Shabbos. Weinstock, Shaindel, tr. from HEB. (Illus.). 160p. (gr. 5-12). 1989. 12.95 (0-89906-814-6); pap. 9.95 (0-89906-815-4) Mesorah Pubns.
Weir, Audrey B. Am I Still a Big Sister? Thomer, Susannah H., illus. LC 92-35395. 1992. 4.95 (0-9633243-0-6) Fall Leaf Pr.
Weir, Bob & Weir, Wendy. Baru Bay. LC 93-23325. (Illus.). 1994. incl. cassette 19.95 (1-56282-622-0); PLB 14.95 (1-56282-623-9) Hyprn Child.
—Panther Dream: A Story of the African Rainforest. Weir, Wendy, illus. LC 91-71385. 40p. (gr. k-5). 1991. PLB 14.89 (1-56282-075-3); PLB 19.95 incl. cassette (1-56282-076-1) Hyprn Child.
—Panther Dream: A Story of the African Rainforest. Weir, Wendy, illus. LC 91-71385. 40p. (gr. k-5). 1993. pap. 4.95 (1-56282-525-9); incl. cassette 8.95 (1-56282-591-7); Incl. tchr's. guide, 12 bks. & 1 cassette. classroom pkg. 32.95 (1-56282-548-8) Hyprn Ppbks.
Weir, Christy. The Very Best Book. Woodard, Virginia, ed. Brooks, Nan, illus. LC 92-32744. 35p. (ps-2). 1993. 12.99 (0-8307-1595-9, 5112262) Regal.
Weir, Gary, jt. auth. see Tuggle, Catherine.
Weir, Wendy, jt. auth. see Weir, Bob.
Weisberg, Barbara. The Big Golden Book of Knights & Castles. D'Achille, Gino, illus. 64p. (gr. 2-7). 1992. write for info. (0-307-17874-9, 17874, Golden Pr) Western Pub.
—Coronado's Golden Quest. Eagle, Mike, illus. LC 92-18078. 79p. (gr. 2-5). 1992. PLB 21.34 (0-8114-7232-9); pap. write for info. (0-8114-8072-0) Raintree Steck-V.
—Susan B. Anthony. Horner, Matina, intro. by. (Illus.). 112p. (gr. 5 up). 1988. lib. bdg. 17.95x (1-55546-639-7); pap. 9.95 (0-7910-0408-2) Chelsea Hse.
Weisberg, Eric J., jt. auth. see Shafner, R. L.
Weisberg, Lynette, jt. auth. see Deschaine, Scott.
Weisberg, Maggie, jt. auth. see Fuller, Melvin L.
Weisberg, Valerie H. English Verbs: Every Irregular Conjugation. Herrick, George H., intro. by. Bartz, Susie, illus. (SPA & ENG.). 168p. 1991. pap. 9.95x (0-941281-76-0); English verb wkbk. 3.95 (0-941281-52-3); with Spanish 15.50 (0-9610912-6-6) V H Pub.
—Students' Discourse: Comprehensive Examples & Explanations of All Expository Modes & Argument, Precis, Narrative, Examination Writing & MLA Reccomendations for Research Paper Documentation Writing Exposition. 2nd ed. 126p. 1990. pap. 9.95 (0-685-49571-X) V H Pub.
—Three Jolly Stories Include: Three Jollys, Jollys Visit L. A., Jolly Gets Mugged: An ESL Adult-Child Reader. Kolino, Olga, illus. 76p. (Orig.). (gr. 4 up). 1985. pap. text ed. 6.95x (0-9610912-4-X) V H Pub.
Weisbrot, Robert. Father Divine. (Illus.). 120p. (gr. 5 up). 1992. lib. bdg. 17.95 (0-7910-1122-4) Chelsea Hse.
Weiser, Jacob. The Lost Dutchman. (Illus.). 140p. (gr. 3-6). 1989. pap. 9.95 (0-944770-02-9) Discovery GA.
Weiser, M., jt. ed. see Speiser, E.
Weisfish, Chaya. Yedidut. (HEB.). 214p. (gr. 9-12). 1991. write for info. wkbk. (0-9630241-0-8) C Weisfish.
Weisgard, Leonard. The Plymouth Thanksgiving. (gr. k-3). 1990. hap. 10.00 (0-385-26754-1) Doubleday.
Weishampel, David B. Plant-Eating Dinosaurs. Rosoff, Iris, ed. (Illus.). 64p. (gr. 4-8). 1992. PLB 14.90 (0-531-11021-4) Watts.
Weishei, Eldon. Psalms for Teens. 128p. (Orig.). 1993. pap. 6.99 (0-570-04599-1) Concordia.
Weisheit, E. Sixty-One Worship Talks for Children. rev. ed. LC 68-20728. (gr. 3-6). 1975. pap. 7.99 (0-570-03714-X, 12-2616) Concordia.
Weisheit, Eldon. The Gospel for Kids: Series C. (gr. 3-6). 1979. 7.99 (0-570-03279-2, 15-2723) Concordia.
—The Gospel for Little Kids. 1980. pap. 5.99 (0-570-03811-1, 12-2920) Concordia.
Weisinger, Steve. The Little Book of Hugs. Davies, Sumiko, illus. LC 90-60083. 28p. (ps). 1991. bds. 2.95 (0-679-80755-1) Random Bks Yng Read.
—The Little Book of Kisses. Davies, Sumiko, illus. LC 90-60082. 28p. (ps). 1991. bds. 2.95 (0-679-80754-3) Random Bks Yng Read.
Weisman, Jill. Barbie & Her Friends. (gr. 4-7). 1991. pap. 2.95 (0-8431-2894-1) Price Stern.
—Barbie Travels Around the World. (gr. 4-7). 1991. pap. 2.95 (0-8431-2893-3) Price Stern.
Weisman, Joan. The Storyteller. Bradley, David, illus. LC 93-20460. 32p. 1993. 15.95 (0-8478-1742-3) Rizzoli Intl.
Weisman, Joanne B. Lowell Mill Girls: Life in the Factory. 48p. (gr. 5-12). 1991. pap. 4.95 (1-878668-06-4) Disc Enter Ltd.
Weisman, JoAnne B. & Deitch, Kenneth M. Christopher Columbus & the Great Voyage of Discovery: With a Message from President George Bush. Eldridge, Marion, illus. Bush, George, contrib. by. LC 90-81362. 40p. (gr. k-6). 1990. PLB 14.95 (1-878668-00-5); pap. 7.95g (1-878668-01-3) Disc Enter Ltd.
Weisman, JoAnne B., jt. auth. see Deitch, Kenneth M.
Weiss, et al. Holt Basic Reading Series. large type ed. (ps-8). 1985. Repr. of 1983 ed. write for info. Am Printing Hse.
Weiss, Andrea. Hanukkah Fun: Crafts & Games. Rhinelander, Mary F., illus. 32p. (gr. k-5). 1992. Set of 3 bks. pap. 14.85 (1-56397-170-4); pap. 4.95 (1-56397-059-7) Boyds Mills Pr.

Weiss, Ann E. Bioethics: Dilemmas in Modern Medicine. LC 85-11608. 128p. (gr. 6 up). 1985. lib. bdg. 17.95 (0-89490-113-3) Enslow Pubs.
—God & Government: The Separation of Church & State. 160p. (gr. 5-9). 1982. 9.95 (0-395-32085-2) HM.
—God & Government: The Separation of Church & State. 1990. pap. 4.80 (0-395-54977-9) HM.
—Good Neighbors? (gr. 5-8). 1985. 12.95 (0-317-38803-7) HM.
—Lies, Deception, & Truth. 160p. (gr. 6 up). 1993. pap. 4.80 (0-395-65750-4) HM.
—Lotteries: Who Wins, Who Loses? LC 90-26525. 112p. (gr. 6 up). 1991. lib. bdg. 17.95 (0-89490-242-3) Enslow Pubs.
—Money Games: The Business of Sports. LC 92-25002. 240p. (gr. 5-9). 1993. 14.45 (0-395-57444-7) HM.
—The Nuclear Arms Race-Can We Survive It? 160p. (gr. 5-9). 1983. 10.95 (0-395-34928-1) HM.
—Prisons: A System in Trouble. LC 88-431. 160p. (gr. 6 up). 1988. lib. bdg. 18.95 (0-89490-165-6) Enslow Pubs.
—Seers & Scientists: Can the Future Be Predicted? (Illus.). 80p. (gr. 7 up). 1986. 13.95 (0-15-272850-3, HB Juv Bks) HarBrace.
—The Supreme Court. LC 86-8929. 96p. (gr. 6 up). 1987. lib. bdg. 16.95 (0-89490-131-1) Enslow Pubs.
—Welfare: Helping Hand or Trap? LC 89-16843. 128p. (gr. 6 up). 1990. lib. bdg. 17.95 (0-89490-169-9) Enslow Pubs.
—Who's to Know? Information, the Media & Public Awareness. 192p. (gr. 5-9). 1990. 14.45 (0-395-49702-7) HM.
Weiss, Anne E. Lies, Deception, & Truth. 160p. (gr. 5-9). 1988. 13.45 (0-395-40486-X) HM.
Weiss, Christof. Snowboarding Know-How. LC 93-4748. 128p. (gr. 10-12). 1993. pap. 10.95 (0-8069-0502-6) Sterling.
Weiss, Clarence B. Grandpa Beaver: His Amazing Tales. Easson, Roger, ed. McKnight, Fred, illus. LC 87-20457. 98p. (Orig.). (gr. 5-12). 1987. pap. 6.95 (0-942179-01-3) Shelby Hse.
Weiss, E. & Friedman, M. The Poof Point. (gr. 3-7). 1992. 14.00 (0-679-83257-2); PLB 14.99 (0-679-93257-7) Knopf Bks Yng Read.
Weiss, Ellen. Baby Gonzo in Backwardsland. DiCicco, Sue, illus. 26p. (gr up). 1987. 12.95 (1-55578-603-0) Worlds Wonder.
—Muppet Babies: A to Z. (ps). 1993. 3.95 (0-307-12538-6, Golden Pr) Western Pub.
—Muppet Kids in I Want to Go Home. Brannon, Tom, illus. 32p. (ps-3). 1992. 1.95 (0-307-12650-1, 12650, Golden Pr) Western Pub.
—Muppet Kids in Piggy Takes a Dare. Brannon, Tom, illus. (ps-3). 1991. pap. 1.95 (0-307-12658-7, Golden Pr) Western Pub.
—Muppet Kids in Too Many Promises. Brannon, Tom, illus. 32p. (ps-3). 1991. 1.95 (0-307-12654-4, Golden Pr) Western Pub.
—Off to the Woods! (ps-3). 1993. pap. 1.95 (0-307-10553-9, Golden Pr) Western Pub.
—Oh Beans! Starring Bean Sprout. Hall, Susan, illus. LC 88-19980. 32p. (gr. k-3). 1989. lib. bdg. 8.79 (0-8167-1406-1); pap. text ed. 1.95 (0-8167-1407-X) Troll Assocs.
—Oh Beans! Starring Boston Bean. Hall, Susan, illus. LC 88-19981. 32p. (gr. k-3). 1989. lib. bdg. 8.79 (0-8167-1414-2); pap. text ed. 1.95 (0-8167-1415-0) Troll Assocs.
—Oh Beans! Starring Green Bean. Hall, Susan, illus. LC 88-19979. 32p. (gr. k-3). 1989. lib. bdg. 8.79 (0-8167-1398-7); pap. text ed. 1.95 (0-8167-1399-5) Troll Assocs.
—Oh Beans! Starring Half-Baked Bean. Hall, Susan, illus. LC 88-4901. 32p. (gr. k-3). 1989. PLB 8.79 (0-8167-1402-9); pap. text ed. 1.95 (0-8167-1403-7) Troll Assocs.
—Oh Beans! Starring Jelly Bean. Hall, Susan, illus. LC 88-4904. 32p. (gr. k-3). 1989. PLB 8.79 (0-8167-1404-5); pap. text ed. 1.95 (0-8167-1405-3) Troll Assocs.
—Oh Beans! Starring Lima Bean. Hall, Susan, illus. LC 88-19969. 32p. (gr. k-3). 1989. lib. bdg. 8.79 (0-8167-1394-4); pap. text ed. 1.95 (0-8167-1395-2) Troll Assocs.
—Oh Beans! Starring Mean Bean. Hall, Susan, illus. LC 88-19982. 32p. (gr. k-3). 1989. lib. bdg. 8.79 (0-8167-1400-2); pap. text ed. 1.95 (0-8167-1401-0) Troll Assocs.
—Oh Beans! Starring Snap Bean. Hall, Susan, illus. LC 88-4900. 32p. (gr. k-3). 1989. PLB 8.79 (0-8167-1410-X) Troll Assocs.
—Oh Beans! Starring String Bean. Hall, Susan, illus. LC 88-4907. 32p. (gr. k-3). 1989. PLB 8.79 (0-8167-1396-0); pap. text ed. 1.95 (0-8167-1397-9) Troll Assocs.
—Oh Beans! Starring Superbean. Hall, Susan, illus. LC 88-19979. 32p. (gr. k-3). 1989. lib. bdg. 8.79 (0-8167-1416-9); pap. text ed. 1.95 (0-8167-1417-7) Troll Assocs.
—Oh Beans! Starring Vanilla Bean. Hall, Susan, illus. LC 88-4903. 32p. (gr. k-3). 1989. PLB 8.79 (0-8167-1412-6); pap. text ed. 1.95 (0-8167-1413-4) Troll Assocs.
—Oh Beans! Starring Wax Bean. Hall, Susan, illus. LC 88-4902. 32p. (gr. k-3). 1989. PLB 8.79 (0-8167-1408-8); pap. text ed. 1.95 (0-8167-1409-6) Troll Assocs.

—Telephone Time: A First Book of Telephone Do's & Don'ts. Knight, Hilary, illus. LC 86-42560. 32p. (gr. k-3). 1986. lib. bdg. 5.99 (*0-394-98252-5*); pap. 1.95 (*0-394-88252-0*) Random Bks Yng Read.
—A Visit to the Sesame Street Zoo. Leigh, Tom, illus. LC 88-3201. 32p. (Orig.). (ps-1). 1988. lib. bdg. 5.99 (*0-394-90447-8*); pap. 2.25 (*0-394-80447-3*, Random Juv) Random Bks Yng Read.

Weiss, Ellen & Friedman, Mel. The Adventures of Ratman. Zimmer, Dirk, illus. LC 89-10869. 64p. (Orig.). (gr. 2-4). 1990. pap. 2.50 (*0-679-80531-1*) Random Bks Yng Read.
—The Poof Point. LC 91-34765. 168p. (gr. 3-7). 1993. pap. 3.99 (*0-679-82272-0*) Random Bks Yng Read.
—The Tiny Parents. LC 88-23103. 96p. (gr. 3-7). 1989. pap. 2.95 (*0-394-82418-0*) Knopf Bks Yng Read.

Weiss, Ellen, jt. auth. see Gikow, Louise.
Weiss, Ellen, jt. auth. see Perry, Philip.

Weiss, George D. Eight Days of Hanukah. 17p. 1991. incl. cassette 8.95 (*1-879756-00-5*) Holiday Time.

Weiss, George D. & Thiele, Bob. What a Wonderful World. Graef, Renee, illus. 24p. 1993. 12.95 (*0-7935-1840-7*, 00183009) H Leonard Pub Corp.

Weiss, Harvey. Machines & How They Work. LC 82-45925. (Illus.). 96p. (gr. 5-8). 1983. PLB 12.89 (*0-690-04300-7*, Crowell Jr Bks) HarpC Child Bks.
—Maps: Getting from Here to There. Weiss, Harvey, illus. 64p. (gr. 2-5). 1991. 14.45 (*0-395-56264-3*, Sandpiper) HM.
—Shelters: From Tepee to Igloo. Weiss, Harvey, illus. LC 87-47698. 80p. (gr. 5-8). 1988. (Crowell Jr Bks); PLB 12.89 (*0-690-04555-7*, Crowell Jr Bks) HarpC Child Bks.
—Submarines & Other Underwater Craft. Weiss, Harvey, illus. LC 89-37614. 64p. (gr. 5-8). 1990. (Crowell Jr Bks); PLB 12.89 (*0-690-04761-4*, Crowell Jr Bks) HarpC Child Bks.

Weiss, Jaqueline S. Young Brer Rabbit & Other Trickster Tales from the Americas. Arrowood, Clinton, illus. Pellowski, Anne, intro. by. (Illus.). 80p. (gr. 3-7). 1985. 14.95 (*0-88045-037-1*) Stemmer Hse.

Weiss, Karl, ed. The Prison Experience: An Anthology. LC 75-32920. 352p. (gr. 6 up). 1976. pap. 9.95 (*0-440-06017-6*) Delacorte.

Weiss, Leatie. My Teacher Sleeps in School. Weiss, Ellen, illus. LC 85-40449. 32p. (ps-3). 1985. pap. 4.50 (*0-14-050559-8*, Puffin) Puffin Bks.

Weiss, Malcolm E. One Sea, One Law? LC 81-47535. (Illus.). 120p. (gr. 5 up). 1982. 10.95 (*0-15-258690-3*, HB Juv Bks) HarBrace.
—Sky Watchers of Ages Past. McFadden, Eliza, illus. (gr. 5-9). 1982. 14.45 (*0-395-29525-4*) HM.

Weiss, Monica. The Biggest Pest, Comparisons. Berlin, Rosemary, illus. LC 91-16059. 24p. (gr. k-2). 1992. PLB 10.59 (*0-8167-2488-1*); pap. text ed. 2.95 (*0-8167-2489-X*) Troll Assocs.
—Birthday Cake Candles, Counting. Berlin, Rosemary, illus. LC 91-16033. 24p. (gr. k-2). 1992. PLB 10.59 (*0-8167-2496-2*); pap. text ed. 2.95 (*0-8167-2497-0*) Troll Assocs.
—Guess What! Drawing Conclusions. Berlin, Rosemary, illus. LC 91-17170. 24p. (gr. k-2). 1992. PLB 10.59 (*0-8167-2498-9*); pap. text ed. 2.95 (*0-8167-2499-7*) Troll Assocs.
—How Many? How Much? Measuring. Berlin, Rosemary, illus. LC 91-3992. 24p. (gr. k-2). 1992. PLB 10.59 (*0-8167-2500-4*); pap. text ed. 2.95 (*0-8167-2501-2*) Troll Assocs.
—Mmmm---Cookies! Simple Subtraction. Berlin, Rosemary, illus. LC 91-18648. 24p. (gr. k-2). 1992. PLB 10.59 (*0-8167-2486-5*); pap. text ed. 2.95 (*0-8167-2487-3*) Troll Assocs.
—Pop! ABC Letter & Sounds: Learning the Alphabet. Berlin, Rosemary, illus. LC 91-18704. 24p. (gr. k-2). 1992. PLB 10.59 (*0-8167-2492-X*); pap. text ed. 2.95 (*0-8167-2493-8*) Troll Assocs.
—Scoop! Fishbowl Fun, Simple Addition. Berlin, Rosemary, illus. LC 91-18657. 24p. (gr. k-2). 1992. PLB 10.59 (*0-8167-2484-9*); pap. text ed. 2.95 (*0-8167-2485-7*) Troll Assocs.
—Shopping Spree: Identifying Shapes. Berlin, Rosemary, illus. LC 91-3986. 24p. (gr. k-2). 1992. PLB 10.59 (*0-8167-2490-3*); pap. text ed. 2.95 (*0-8167-2491-1*) Troll Assocs.
—Snap! Charlie Gets the Whole Picture: Getting the Main Idea. Berlin, Rosemary, illus. LC 91-16499. (gr. k-2). 1992. PLB 10.59 (*0-8167-2494-6*); pap. 2.95 (*0-8167-2495-4*) Troll Assocs.

Weiss, Nicki. Barney Is Big. LC 87-8546. (Illus.). 24p. (ps-1). 1988. 11.95 (*0-688-07586-X*); lib. bdg. 11.88 (*0-688-07587-8*) Greenwillow.
—Dog Boy Cap Skate. LC 88-16390. (Illus.). 32p. (ps up). 1989. 11.95 (*0-688-08275-0*); PLB 11.88 (*0-688-08276-9*) Greenwillow.
—An Egg Is an Egg. (Illus.). 32p. (ps-1). 1990. 14.95 (*0-399-22182-4*, Putnam) Putnam Pub Group.
—A Family Story. Weiss, Nicki, illus. LC 85-27231. 24p. (ps-3). 1987. 11.75 (*0-688-06504-X*); PLB 11.88 (*0-688-06505-8*) Greenwillow.
—The First Night of Hanukkah. (Illus.). 48p. (gr. 1-3). 1992. PLB 3.50 (*0-448-40389-7*, G&D); (G&D) Putnam Pub Group.
—Hank & Dogie. (ps-3). 1991. pap. 2.75 (*0-553-15954-2*) Bantam.
—If You're Happy & You Know It. LC 86-753170. (Illus.). 40p. (gr. k-3). 1987. 14.95 (*0-688-06444-2*) Greenwillow.

—Maude & Sally. Weiss, Nicki, illus. LC 82-12003. 32p. (gr. k-3). 1983. 13.95 (*0-688-01859-9*); PLB 13.88 (*0-688-01861-0*) Greenwillow.
—On a Hot, Hot Day. Weiss, Nicki, illus. 32p. (ps-1). 1992. PLB 13.95 (*0-399-22119-0*, Putnam) Putnam Pub Group.
—Princess Pearl. Weiss, Nicki, illus. LC 85-17699. 24p. (gr. k-3). 1986. 11.75 (*0-688-05894-9*); PLB 11.88 (*0-688-05895-7*) Greenwillow.
—Stone Men. LC 92-3959. (Illus.). 32p. (ps up). 1993. 14.00 (*0-688-11015-0*); PLB 13.93 (*0-688-11016-9*) Greenwillow.
—Sun Sand Sea Sail. LC 88-16391. (Illus.). 32p. (ps up). 1989. 11.95 (*0-688-08270-X*); PLB 11.88 (*0-688-08271-8*) Greenwillow.
—Surprise Box. (Illus.). 32p. 1991. 13.95 (*0-399-22210-3*, Putnam) Putnam Pub Group.
—Where Does the Brown Bear Go? LC 87-36980. (Illus.). 24p. (ps up). 1989. 13.95 (*0-688-07862-1*); PLB 13.88 (*0-688-07863-X*) Greenwillow.
—Where Does the Brown Bear Go? (ps). 1990. pap. 3.95 (*0-14-054181-0*, Puffin) Puffin Bks.

Weiss, Trudy, jt. auth. see Karnofsky, Florence.
Weissberg, Ed. Arthur Ashe. King, Coretta Scott, intro. by. (Illus.). 112p. (gr. 5 up). 1991. lib. bdg. 17.95 (*0-7910-1115-1*) Chelsea Hse.
Weissberg, Ted. Arthur Ashe: Black Americans of Achievement. (gr. 4-7). 1992. pap. 7.95 (*0-7910-1141-0*) Chelsea Hse.
Weissenberg, Fran. The Streets Are Paved with Gold. LC 89-24413. (Illus.). 160p. (Orig.). (gr. 5 up). 1990. pap. 6.95 (*0-943173-51-5*) Harbinger AZ.
Weissenhorn, Mathilde, tr. see De Maupassant, Guy.
Weisser, M. My Synagogue. Rosenblum, R., illus. 25p. (gr. k-5). 1984. pap. text ed. 4.25 (*0-87441-386-9*) Behrman.
Weissman, Anne. The Castle of Chuchurumbel: El Castillo de Churchurumbel. Bailyn, Susan, illus. (ENG & SPA.). 19p. (gr. k-2). 1987. 8.95 (*968-6217-00-2*) Hispanic Bk Dist.
Weissman, Bari. Dial Playshapes: Circle. LC 91-73549. (Illus.). 10p. (ps). 1992. 3.95 (*0-8037-1144-1*) Dial Bks Young.
—Dial Playshapes: Square. LC 91-73550. (Illus.). 10p. (ps). 1992. 3.95 (*0-8037-1146-8*) Dial Bks Young.
—Dial Playshapes: Triangle. LC 91-73551. (Illus.). 10p. (Orig.). (ps). 1992. 3.95 (*0-8037-1147-6*) Dial Bks Young.
Weissman, Jackie. Higglety Pigglety Pop: Two Hundred Thirty-Three Playful Rhymes & Chants for Your Baby. (ps). 1991. pap. 9.95 (*0-939514-29-X*) Miss Jackie.
—My Toes are Starting to Wiggle. (ps-5). 1991. pap. 12.95 (*0-939514-12-5*) Miss Jackie.
—Sniggles, Squirrels & Chicken Pox: Forty Original Songs with Activities for Early Childhood. 64p. (ps-5). 1984. pap. 9.95 (*0-939514-06-0*); Vol. I. album 9.95 (*0-685-09111-2*); cassette 9.95 (*0-685-09112-0*); Vol. II. album 9.95 (*0-685-09113-9*); cassette 9.95 (*0-685-09114-7*) Miss Jackie.
Weissman, Julie, et al. Kids in Motion Creative Movement & Song Book. Schiff, Ronny S., ed. Miller, Wynn, illus. (ps-4). 1987. pap. text ed. 14.95 (*0-88284-356-7*, 2337) Alfred Pub.
Weissman, Paul & Harris, Alan. The Great Voyager Adventure. (Illus.). 64p. (gr. 5-9). 1990. 14.95 (*0-671-72539-4*, J Messner); lib. bdg. 16.98 (*0-671-72538-6*) S&S Trade.
Weissner, Colleen, jt. auth. see Wezeman, Phyllis.
Weist, Katherine, ed. Belle Highwalking: The Narrative of a Cheyenne Woman. (gr. 5 up). 1979. pap. 2.95 (*0-89992-075-6*) Coun India Ed.
Weist, Tom, jt. auth. see Henry Tall Bull.
Weist, Tom, jt. auth. see Tall Bull, Henry.
Weit, Kathryn, jt. auth. see Stewart, Judi.
Weitsman, Madeline. The Peace Corps. Schlesinger, Arthur M., Jr., intro. by. (Illus.). 128p. (gr. 5 up). 1989. 14.95 (*0-87754-832-3*) Chelsea Hse.
Weitz, Martin D. Poisoning the Land. LC 92-9090. (Illus.). 1992. PLB 12.40 (*0-531-17328-3*, Gloucester Pr) Watts.
Weitzman, David. Human Culture. LC 93-16791. (Illus.). 288p. (gr. 4-6). 1994. SBE 22.95 (*0-684-19438-4*, Scribners Young Read) Macmillan Child Grp.
—The Mountain Man & the President. Weiss, Charles, illus. LC 92-23040. 40p. (gr. 2-5). 1992. PLB 21.34 (*0-8114-7224-8*) Raintree Steck-V.
—My Backyard History Book. Robertson, James, illus. 128p. (gr. 4 up). 1975. 15.95 (*0-316-92901-8*); pap. 9.95 (*0-316-92902-6*) Little.
—Superpower: The Making of a Steam Locomotive. LC 86-46255. (Illus.). 1987. 24.95 (*0-87923-671-X*) Godine.

Wekesser, Carol, ed. Africa: Opposing Viewpoints. LC 91-42292. (Illus.). 264p. (gr. 10 up). 1992. PLB 17.95 (*0-89908-186-X*); pap. text ed. 9.95 (*0-89908-161-4*) Greenhaven.
—American Foreign Policy: Opposing Viewpoints. (Illus.). 264p. (gr. 10 up). 1993. PLB 17.95 (*0-89908-199-1*); pap. text ed. 9.95 (*0-89908-174-6*) Greenhaven.
—America's Children: Opposing Viewpoints. LC 90-24085. (Illus.). 240p. (gr. 10 up). 1991. PLB 17.95 (*0-89908-486-9*); pap. 9.95 (*0-89908-461-3*) Greenhaven.

—America's Defense: Opposing Viewpoints. LC 91-20163. (Illus.). 240p. (gr. 10 up). 1991. lib. bdg. 17.95 (*0-89908-184-3*); pap. 9.95 (*0-89908-159-2*) Greenhaven.
—The Death Penalty. LC 91-9931. (Illus.). 264p. (gr. 10 up). 1991. lib. bdg. 17.95 (*0-89908-180-0*); pap. text ed. 9.95 (*0-89908-155-X*) Greenhaven.
—Politics in America: Opposing Viewpoints. LC 91-42803. (Illus.). 264p. (gr. 10 up). 1992. PLB 17.95 (*0-89908-189-4*); pap. text ed. 9.95 (*0-89908-164-9*) Greenhaven.
Wekesser, Carol & Biskup, Michael D., eds. Europe. LC 92-23066. 200p. (gr. 10 up). 1992. PLB 16.95 (*1-56510-024-7*); pap. text ed. 9.95 (*1-56510-023-9*) Greenhaven.
Wekesser, Carol & Polesetsky, Matt, eds. Women in the Military. LC 91-25056. 200p. (gr. 10 up). 1991. PLB 16.95 (*0-89908-579-2*); pap. text ed. 9.95 (*0-89908-585-7*) Greenhaven.
Wekesser, Carol & Swisher, Karin, eds. Social Justice: Opposing Viewpoints. LC 90-42855. (Illus.). 240p. (gr. 10 up). 1990. PLB 17.95 (*0-89908-482-6*); pap. text ed. 9.95 (*0-89908-457-5*) Greenhaven.
Wekesser, Carol, jt. ed. see Biskup, Michael.
Wekesser, Carol, et al, eds. Central America: Opposing Viewpoints. LC 90-13922. (Illus.). 240p. (gr. 10 up). 1990. PLB 17.95 (*0-89908-484-2*); pap. text ed. 9.95 (*0-89908-459-1*) Greenhaven.
—Sexual Harassment. LC 92-23593. 200p. (gr. 10 up). 1992. PLB 16.95 (*1-56510-021-2*); pap. text ed. 9.95 (*1-56510-020-4*) Greenhaven.
Weksesser, Carol & Cozic, Charles P., eds. Gun Control. LC 92-91875. 200p. (gr. 10 up). 1992. PLB 16.95 (*1-56510-015-8*); pap. text ed. 9.95 (*1-56510-014-X*) Greenhaven.
Welber, Robert. Winter Picnic. Ray, Deborah, illus. LC 77-77418. (gr. 7 up). 1970. lib. bdg. 5.99 (*0-394-90444-3*) Pantheon.
—The Winter Picnic. Ray, Deborah, illus. (ps-3). 1973. pap. 0.95 (*0-394-82621-3*) Pantheon.
Welch, Catherine A. Clouds of Terror. Johnson, Laurie K., illus. LC 93-18416. (gr. 4 up). 1993. 10.95 (*0-87614-771-6*) Carolrhoda Bks.
—Danger at the Breaker. Shine, Andrea, illus. 48p. (gr. k-4). 1991. PLB 14.95 (*0-87614-693-0*) Carolrhoda Bks.
—Danger at the Breaker. (ps-3). 1992. pap. 5.95 (*0-87614-564-0*) Carolrhoda Bks.
Welch, Fay. The Magic Swap Shop. rev. ed. (gr. 3-12). 1985. pap. 6.00 play script (*0-88734-509-3*) Players Pr.
Welch, John. Charlie Brown's Piano Album. Schulz, Charles, illus. 38p. (Orig.). (gr. 1-6). 1989. pap. 5.50 (*1-56516-054-1*) Houston IN.
—Snoopy's Easy Piano Album. Schulz, Charles, illus. 38p. (Orig.). (gr. 1-6). 1989. pap. 5.50 (*1-56516-052-5*) Houston IN.
—Snoopy's Favorite Piano Solos. Schulz, Charles, illus. 38p. (Orig.). (gr. 1-6). 1989. pap. 5.50 (*1-56516-053-3*) Houston IN.
Welch, John, ed. Schroeder's Favorite Classics, Vol. 1. Schulz, Charles, illus. 38p. (Orig.). (gr. 1-6). 1989. pap. 5.50 (*1-56516-047-9*) Houston IN.
—Schroeder's Favorite Classics, Vol. 2. Schulz, Charles, illus. 38p. (Orig.). (gr. 1-6). 1989. pap. 5.50 (*1-56516-048-7*) Houston IN.
—Schroeder's Favorite Classics, Vol. 1: Clavinova Software. Schulz, Charles, illus. 38p. (Orig.). (gr. 1-6). 1992. pap. 34.95 (*1-56516-021-5*) Houston IN.
—Schroeder's First Recital. Schulz, Charles, illus. 38p. (Orig.). (gr. 1-6). 1989. pap. 5.50 (*1-56516-050-9*) Houston IN.
—Schroeder's First Recital Encores. Schulz, Charles, illus. 38p. (Orig.). (gr. 1-6). 1989. pap. 5.50 (*1-56516-051-7*) Houston IN.
Welch, Joyce. The Illustrated I Hate School Workbook. Gustafson, Dru, illus. 88p. (Orig.). (gr. 7-9). 1979. pap. 6.95 (*0-935996-00-1*) Wibat Pubns.
Welch, Karen, ed. see Tolliver, Ruby C.
Welch, Karen E., ed. see Matthews, Billie L. & Hurlburt, Virginia E.
Welch, R. C. Twisted Tales: The Dripping Head & Other Gruesome Stories. Fike, Scott, illus. 128p. (Orig.). (gr. 3-7). 1992. pap. 4.95 (*1-56288-314-3*) Checkerboard.
—Twisted Tales: The Slithering Corpse & Other Sinister Stories. Fike, Scott, illus. 128p. (Orig.). (gr. 3-7). 1992. pap. 4.95 (*1-56288-315-1*) Checkerboard.
—The Very Scary Dictionary: Who's Who in Fright. Warburton, Bartt, illus. 64p. 1993. pap. 4.95 (*1-56565-072-7*) Lowell Hse.
Welch, Robert. Scary Stories for Sleep-Overs. (Illus.). 128p. (Orig.). (gr. 3-6). 1991. pap. 4.99 (*0-8431-2914-X*) Price Stern.
Welch, Rose, jt. auth. see Cummins, Ronnie.
Welch, Sheila K. Don't Call Me Marda. Welch, Sheila K., illus. 138p. (gr. 4 up). 1990. 16.95 (*0-9611872-3-9*); pap. 12.95 (*0-9611872-4-7*) Our Child Pr.
Welcher, Rosalind. My Brother Says There's a Monster Living in Our Toilet. Welcher, Rosalind, illus. 96p. (Orig.). 1987. pap. 6.95 (*0-939775-01-8*) West Hill Pr.
Welchman-Tischler, Rosamond. How to Use Children's Literature to Teach Mathematics. LC 92-30867. (Illus.). 75p. (Orig.). (gr. k-6). 1992. pap. 8.50 (*0-87353-349-6*) NCTM.
—The Mathematical Toolbox. (Illus.). 90p. (gr. 1-8). 1992. pap. 9.50 (*0-938587-27-7*) Cuisenaire.

Welchons & Krickenberger. Tables of Square Roots, Logarithms, Etc. Taken from "Algebra: Bk. II," pp. 501-509. large type ed. 12p. (gr. 10 up). 1952. Repr. of 1949 ed. 3.31 (*0-317-01947-3*, 4-25070-00) Am Printing Hse.

Weldon, Louise B., jt. auth. see Mather, Anne D.

Welker, Dorothy W., jt. auth. see Harrison, William F.

Well, Rosemary. Max's Bedtime. Wells, Rosemary, illus. LC 84-14968. 12p. (ps-k). 1985. bds. 3.95 (*0-8037-0160-8*) Dial Bks Young.

Weller, Frances W. The Closet Gorilla. Smith, Cat B., illus. LC 90-40350. 32p. (gr. k-3). 1991. RSBE 13.95 (*0-02-792531-5*, Macmillan Child Bk) Macmillan Child Grp.

—Matthew Wheelock's Wall. Lewin, Ted, illus. LC 91-9608. 40p. (gr. k-3). 1992. RSBE 14.95 (*0-02-792612-5*, Macmillan Child Bk) Macmillan Child Grp.

—Riptide. Blake, Robert J., illus. 32p. (ps-3). 1990. 14.95 (*0-399-21675-8*, Philomel Bks) Putnam Pub Group.

Weller, Robert F. Sunken Treasure on Florida Reefs. 2nd, rev. ed. Richards, Ernie S., ed. (Illus.). 135p. 1987. pap. 12.95 (*0-9628359-1-9*) R Weller.

Welles, Laura & Welles, Ted. Will & Grandmother Change the Seashore. McCloskey, Maris, ed. Welles, Laura, illus. LC 92-62260. 40p. (Orig.). (gr. k-7). 1992. pap. 7.95 (*0-915189-07-0*) Oceanus.

—Will & Grandmother Change the Seashore. McCloskey, Maris, ed. Welles, Laura, illus. LC 92-62260. 40p. (Orig.). (gr. k-7). 1993. text ed. 24.00 (*0-915189-08-9*) Oceanus.

Welles, Samuel P., jt. auth. see Long, Robert A.

Welles, Ted. Van Buren, Wizard of O.K. & 8th U. S. A. President. Johnson, Mercy, ed. LC 87-60750. (Illus.). 96p. (Orig.). (gr. 6 up). 1987. July 30, 1987. lib. bdg. 12.00 (*0-915189-04-6*); June 30, 1987. pap. 5.95 (*0-915189-05-4*) Oceanus.

Welles, Ted, jt. auth. see Welles, Laura.

Wellington, Jerry. The Super Science Book of Space. Lloyd, Frances, illus. LC 93-24405. 32p. (gr. 4-8). 1993. 14.95 (*1-56847-129-7*) Thomson Lrning.

Wellington, Monica. All My Little Ducklings. Wellington, Monica, illus. LC 88-22841. 32p. (ps-k). 1989. 11.95 (*0-525-44459-9*, DCB) Dutton Child Bks.

—Mr. Cookie Baker. LC 91-43307. (Illus.). 32p. (ps-1). 1992. 12.50 (*0-525-44965-5*, DCB) Dutton Child Bks.

—Seasons of Swans. LC 89-28893. (Illus.). 32p. (ps-2). 1990. 12.95 (*0-525-44621-4*, DCB) Dutton Child Bks.

—The Sheep Follow. Wellington, Monica, illus. LC 91-3420. 32p. (ps-k). 1992. 13.00 (*0-525-44837-3*, DCB) Dutton Child Bks.

Wellnitz, William R. Be a Kid Physicist. LC 92-40506. 1993. 17.95 (*0-8306-4091-6*); pap. 9.95 (*0-8306-4092-4*) TAB Bks.

—Homemade Slime & Rubber Bones! Awesome Science Experiments. LC 92-41238. (gr. 3 up). 1993. 17.95 (*0-8306-4093-2*); pap. 9.95 (*0-8306-4094-0*) TAB Bks.

—Science Magic for Kids: Simple & Safe Experiments. (Illus.). 128p. 1990. 17.95 (*0-8306-8423-9*, 3423); pap. 9.95 (*0-8306-3423-1*) TAB Bks.

Wells. Noisy Nora. 1993. pap. 28.67 (*0-590-71436-8*) Scholastic Inc.

Wells, jt. auth. see Atwell.

Wells, Candace & Carroll, Jeri. Legendary Heroes. Foster, Tom, illus. 64p. (gr. k-4). 1987. pap. 7.95 (*0-86653-380-X*, GA1007) Good Apple.

Wells, Candace, jt. auth. see Carroll, Jeri.

Wells, Candace B. & Carroll, Jeri A. Learning about Spring & Summer Holidays. 112p. (ps-2). 1988. wkbk. 9.95 (*0-86653-442-3*, GA1047) Good Apple.

Wells, Candace B., jt. auth. see Carroll, Jeri A.

Wells, Candace, jt. auth. see Carroll, Jeri.

Wells, Carolyn. A Christmas Alphabet. (Illus.). 32p. 1989. 15.95 (*0-399-21683-9*, Putnam) Putnam Pub Group.

—Marjorie's Vacation. 232p. 1981. Repr. PLB 16.95x (*0-89966-337-0*) Buccaneer Bks.

—Marjorie's Vacation. 315p. 1980. Repr. PLB 12.95x (*0-89967-012-1*) Harmony Raine.

Wells, Christie. Babysitter Blues. LC 88-16948. 128p. (gr. 5-8). 1989. lib. bdg. 9.89 (*0-8167-1506-8*); pap. text ed. 2.95 (*0-8167-1507-6*) Troll Assocs.

—A Class Act. LC 88-16940. 128p. (gr. 5-8). 1989. lib. bdg. 9.89 (*0-8167-1500-9*); pap. text ed. 2.95 (*0-8167-1501-7*) Troll Assocs.

—Love Letters. LC 88-16938. 128p. (gr. 5-8). 1989. lib. bdg. 9.89 (*0-8167-1504-1*); pap. text ed. 2.95 (*0-8167-1505-X*) Troll Assocs.

—No More Promises. LC 88-16939. 128p. (gr. 5-8). 1989. lib. bdg. 9.89 (*0-8167-1502-5*); pap. text ed. 2.95 (*0-8167-1503-3*) Troll Assocs.

—Rival Roommates. LC 88-16954. 128p. (gr. 5-8). 1989. lib. bdg. 9.89 (*0-8167-1496-7*); pap. text ed. 2.95 (*0-8167-1497-5*) Troll Assocs.

—Secret Crush. LC 88-16941. 128p. (gr. 5-8). 1989. lib. bdg. 9.89 (*0-8167-1498-3*); pap. text ed. 2.95 (*0-8167-1499-1*) Troll Assocs.

Wells, Claudia E. Whiskers, the Bank Mouse. Shardin, Arthur, illus. LC 77-10823. (gr. 1-4). 1981. 4.50 (*0-930506-00-6*); pap. write for info. (*0-930506-01-4*) Popcorn Pubs.

Wells, Colin. Stick Like Glue. Parker, Liz, ed. Taylor, Marjorie, illus. 45p. (Orig.). (gr. 6-12). 1992. pap. text ed. 2.95 (*1-56254-058-0*) Saddleback Pubns.

Wells, D., jt. auth. see Tatchell, J.

Wells, David. Can You Solve These?, No. 2: Mathematical Problems to Test Your Thinking Powers. (Illus.). 80p. (Orig.). (gr. 5 up). 1985. pap. 6.95 (*0-906212-34-0*, Pub. by Tarquin UK) Parkwest Pubns.

Wells, Dawn, et al. Mary Ann's Gilligan's Island Cookbook. (Illus.). 256p. (gr. 10 up). 1993. comb. bdg. 12.95 (*1-55853-245-5*) Rutledge Hill Pr.

Wells, Dean F. Belle-Duck at the Peabody. Boyles, Renee, illus. 48p. (ps-8). 1984. 9.95 (*0-916242-24-2*) Yoknapatawpha.

Wells, Donna K. Pond Life: The Fishing Trip. Ching, illus. LC 90-1644. 32p. (ps-2). 1990. PLB 19.95 (*0-89565-581-0*); PLB 13.95s.p. (*0-685-56195-X*) Childs World.

—What Animals Give Us: So Many Things. Axeman, Lois, illus. LC 89-23991. 32p. (ps-2). 1990. PLB 21.35 (*0-89565-557-8*); PLB 14.95s.p. (*0-685-56178-X*) Childs World.

—Your Body: Treasures Inside. Endres, Helen, illus. LC 90-30632. 32p. (ps-2). 1990. PLB 19.95 (*0-89565-576-4*); PLB 13.95s.p. (*0-685-56192-5*) Childs World.

Wells, H. G. First Men in the Moon. Lowndes, R. A., intro. by. (gr. 7 up). 1965. pap. 1.25 (*0-8049-0078-7*, CL-78) Airmont.

—Food of the Gods. (gr. 7 up). 1965. pap. 0.95 (*0-8049-0059-0*, CL-59) Airmont.

—Guerre des Mondes. Bozellac, Anne, illus. (FRE.). 288p. (gr. 5-10). 1990. pap. 9.95 (*2-07-033567-4*) Schoenhof.

—In the Days of the Comet. Lowndes, R. A., intro. by. (gr. 7 up). pap. 1.25 (*0-8049-0111-2*, CL-111) Airmont.

—Invisible Man. (gr. 8 up). 1964. pap. 1.75 (*0-8049-0040-X*, CL-40) Airmont.

—Invisible Man. (gr. 4-7). 1990. pap. 2.95 (*0-590-44016-0*) Scholastic Inc.

—The Invisible Man. 192p. 1992. pap. 2.50 (*0-8125-0467-4*) Tor Bks.

—Invisible Man. (gr. 4-7). 1993. pap. 2.95 (*0-89375-415-3*) Troll Assocs.

—Island of Dr. Moreau. Lowndes, R. A., intro. by. (gr. 7 up). 1966. pap. 1.75 (*0-8049-0110-4*, CL-110) Airmont.

—Seven Science Fiction Novels. 1015p. (gr. 9 up). 24.95 (*0-486-20264-X*) Dover.

—The Strange Orchid. rev. ed. (gr. 9-12). 1989. Repr. of 1898 ed. multi-media kit 35.00 (*0-685-31127-9*) Balance Pub.

—This Misery of Boots. 48p. (ps-12). 1987. pap. text ed. 2.50 (*0-930997-01-8*, W-01) East Bay Bks.

—Time Machine. (gr. 7 up). 1964. pap. 2.50 (*0-8049-0044-2*, CL-44) Airmont.

—The Time Machine. Binder, Otto, ed. Nino, Alex, illus. LC 73-75467. 64p. (Orig.). (gr. 5-10). 1973. pap. 2.95 (*0-88301-102-6*) Pendulum Pr.

—The Time Machine. Powell, Ivan, illus. Wright, Betty R., adapted by. LC 81-4097. (Illus.). 48p. (gr. 4 up). 1983. PLB 18.64 (*0-8172-1675-8*) Raintree Steck-V.

—The Time Machine. abridged ed. Martin, Les, adapted by. Edens, John, illus. LC 89-39506. 96p. (Orig.). (gr. 2-6). 1990. lib. bdg. 5.99 (*0-679-90371-2*); pap. 2.95 (*0-679-80371-8*) Random Bks Yng Read.

—The Time Machine. James, Raymond, ed. Deal, Jim, illus. LC 92-5804. 48p. (gr. 3-6). 1992. PLB 12.89 (*0-8167-2872-0*); pap. text ed. 3.95 (*0-8167-2873-9*) Troll Assocs.

—War of the Worlds. (gr. 8 up). 1964. 2.50 (*0-8049-0045-0*, CL-45) Airmont.

—The War of the Worlds. (gr. 3 up). 1960. lib. bdg. 5.39 (*0-394-90471-0*) Random Bks Yng Read.

—The War of the Worlds. Evans, Mary A., adapted by. LC 90-52926. (Illus.). 96p. (Orig.). (gr. 2-7). 1991. lib. bdg. 5.99 (*0-679-91047-6*); pap. 2.95 (*0-679-81047-1*) Random Bks Yng Read.

—The War of the Worlds. 226p. 1993. pap. 2.50 (*0-8125-0515-8*) Tor Bks.

—War of the Worlds. (gr. 4-7). 1993. pap. 2.95 (*0-89375-347-5*) Troll Assocs.

Wells, Joel. The Manger Mouse. Anderson, Annette B., illus. (gr. k-5). 1990. 15.95 (*0-88347-255-4*) Thomas More.

Wells, John G., jt. auth. see Brusic, Sharon A.

Wells, Marian. Colorado Gold. LC 87-35333. 302p. (Orig.). (gr. 9-12). 1988. pap. 8.99 (*0-87123-966-3*) Bethany Hse.

—Out of the Crucible. LC 88-21121. 256p. (Orig.). 1988. pap. 8.99 (*1-55661-037-8*) Bethany Hse.

Wells, R. Basil. Harry-the-Mouse, Vol. 1: "Lonesome Harry" 1991. 6.95 (*0-533-08899-2*) Vantage.

Wells, Reuben F. On Land & Sea with Caesar. LC 61-28142. (Illus.). (gr. 7-11). 1926. 18.00 (*0-8196-0107-1*) Biblo.

—With Caesar's Legions. LC 60-16709. (Illus.). (gr. 7-11). 1951. 18.00 (*0-8196-0110-1*) Biblo.

Wells, Robert E. Is a Blue Whale the Biggest Thing There Is? LC 93-2703. (Illus.). (gr. 1-6). 1993. 13.95 (*0-8075-3655-5*); pap. 6.95 (*0-8075-3656-3*) A Whitman.

Wells, Rosemary. Benjamin & Tulip. Wells, Rosemary, illus. LC 73-6018. 32p. (ps-2). 1977. 12.00 (*0-8037-1808-X*); PLB 9.89 (*0-8037-2057-2*); pap. 4.50 (*0-8037-0545-X*) Dial Bks Young.

—Chut, Chut, Charlotte! (FRE.). 1990. pap. 7.95 (*2-07-039001-2*) Schoenhof.

—Don't Spill It Again, James. LC 77-71513. (Illus.). 48p. (ps-3). 1990. 8.95 (*0-8037-2118-8*); pap. 3.95 (*0-8037-0831-9*) Dial Bks Young.

—First Tomato. Wells, Rosemary, illus. LC 91-41599. 32p. (ps-3). 1992. PLB 12.89 (*0-8037-1175-1*) Dial Bks Young.

—Forest of Dreams. LC 88-3826. (Illus.). 24p. (ps-3). 1992. pap. 4.99 (*0-8037-1140-9*, Dial Pied Piper) Puffin Bks.

—Fritz & the Mess Fairy. LC 90-26671. (Illus.). 32p. (ps-2). 1991. 14.00 (*0-8037-0981-1*); PLB 13.89 (*0-8037-0983-8*) Dial Bks Young.

—Good Night, Fred. Wells, Rosemary, illus. LC 81-65849. 32p. (ps-3). 1981. Dial Bks Young.

—Hazel's Amazing Mother. Wells, Rosemary, illus. LC 85-1447. 32p. (ps-2). 1985. 13.95 (*0-8037-0209-4*); PLB 13.89 (*0-8037-0210-8*) Dial Bks Young.

—Hazel's Amazing Mother. Wells, Rosemary, illus. LC 85-1447. (ps-2). 1989. 3.95 (*0-8037-0703-7*) Dial Bks Young.

—Hazel's Amazing Mother. LC 85-1447. (Illus.). 32p. (ps-2). 1992. pap. 17.99 giant size (*0-14-054538-7*, Puffin Pied Piper) Puffin Bks.

—Hooray for Max. Wells, Rosemary, illus. (ps). 1986. Max doll 8.95 (*0-8037-0203-5*) Dial Bks Young.

—The Island Light. Wells, Rosemary, illus. LC 91-41598. 32p. (ps-3). 1992. PLB 12.89 (*0-8037-1178-6*) Dial Bks Young.

—A Lion for Lewis. Wells, Rosemary, illus. 32p. (ps-2). 1984. pap. 3.95 (*0-8037-0096-2*, Dial Pied Piper) Puffin Bks.

—Little Lame Prince. LC 89-23482. 32p. (ps-3). 1990. 12.95 (*0-8037-0788-6*); PLB 12.89 (*0-8037-0789-4*) Dial Bks Young.

—Man in the Woods. 1985. pap. 2.95 (*0-590-43732-1*) Scholastic Inc.

—The Man in the Woods. 232p. (gr. 7 up). 1991. pap. 2.95 (*0-590-43826-3*) Scholastic Inc.

—Max & Ruby's First Greek Myth. Wells, Rosemary, illus. LC 92-30332. 32p. (ps-3). 1993. 11.99 (*0-8037-1524-2*); PLB 11.89 (*0-8037-1525-0*) Dial Bks Young.

—Max's Bath. Wells, Rosemary, illus. LC 84-14969. 12p. (ps-k). 1985. bds. 3.95 (*0-8037-0162-4*) Dial Bks Young.

—Max's Birthday. Wells, Rosemary, illus. LC 84-14970. 12p. (ps-k). 1985. bds. 4.50 (*0-8037-0163-2*) Dial Bks Young.

—Max's Breakfast. Wells, Rosemary, illus. LC 84-14968. 12p. (ps-k). 1985. bds. 3.95 (*0-8037-0161-6*) Dial Bks Young.

—Max's Chocolate Chicken. Wells, Rosemary, illus. LC 88-14954. 32p. (ps-2). 1989. 9.95 (*0-8037-0585-9*); PLB 9.89 (*0-8037-0586-7*) Dial Bks Young.

—Max's Christmas. Wells, Rosemary, illus. LC 85-27547. 32p. (ps-2). 1986. 9.95 (*0-8037-0289-2*); PLB 9.89 (*0-8037-0290-6*) Dial Bks Young.

—Max's Dragon Shirt. Wells, Rosemary, illus. LC 90-43755. 32p. (ps-2). 1991. 12.00 (*0-8037-0944-7*); lib. bdg. 10.89 (*0-8037-0945-5*) Dial Bks Young.

—Max's First Word. Wells, Rosemary, illus. LC 79-59745. (ps-k). 1979. bds. 4.50 (*0-8037-6066-3*) Dial Bks Young.

—Max's New Suit. Wells, Rosemary, illus. LC 79-50747. (ps-k). 1979. bds. 3.95 (*0-8037-6065-5*) Dial Bks Young.

—Max's Ride. Wells, Rosemary, illus. LC 79-50746. (ps-k). 1979. bds. 3.95 (*0-8037-6069-8*) Dial Bks Young.

—Max's Toys: A Counting Book. Wells, Rosemary, illus. LC 79-50748. (ps-k). 1979. bds. 4.50 (*0-8037-6068-X*) Dial Bks Young.

—Morris's Disappearing Bag. giant ed. LC 75-9202. (ps-3). 1990. 17.99 (*0-8037-0839-4*) Dial Bks Young.

—Morris's Disappearing Bag. Wells, Rosemary, illus. 1975. 9.95 (*0-8037-5441-8*) Dial Bks Young.

—Moss Pillows. Wells, Rosemary, illus. LC 91-41600. 32p. (ps-3). 1992. PLB 12.89 (*0-8037-1177-8*) Dial Bks Young.

—Night Sounds. McPhail, David, illus. LC 93-31815. 1994. write for info. (*0-8037-1301-0*); PLB write for info. (*0-8037-1302-9*) Dial Bks Young.

—Noisy Nora. Wells, Rosemary, illus. LC 72-6068. 40p. (ps-2). 1973. 10.95 (*0-8037-6638-6*); PLB 10.89 (*0-8037-6639-4*) Dial Bks Young.

—Noisy Nora. Wells, Rosemary, illus. 40p. (ps-2). 1980. pap. 3.99 (*0-8037-6193-7*) Dial Bks Young.

—Peabody. LC 83-7207. (Illus.). 32p. (ps-2). 1983. 13.95 (*0-8037-0004-0*) Dial Bks Young.

—Shy Charles. Wells, Rosemary, illus. LC 87-27247. 32p. (ps-3). 1988. 11.95 (*0-8037-0563-8*); PLB 11.89 (*0-8037-0564-6*) Dial Bks Young.

—Shy Charles. LC 87-27247. (Illus.). 32p. (ps-3). 1992. pap. 3.99 (*0-14-054537-9*, Puffin Pied Piper) Puffin Bks.

—Shy Charles. (Illus.). 32p. (ps-3). 1992. pap. 17.99 giant bk. (*0-14-054570-0*, Puffin Pied Piper) Puffin Bks.

—Stanley & Rhoda. Wells, Rosemary, illus. LC 78-51874. 40p. (ps-2). 1981. pap. 4.95 (*0-8037-7995-X*, 0383-120) Dial Bks Young.

—Stanley & Rhoda. LC 78-51874. (Illus.). (ps-2). 1985. 13.95 (*0-8037-8248-9*) Dial Bks Young.

—Through the Hidden Door. LC 86-24273. 256p. (gr. 5 up). 1987. 14.95 (*0-8037-0276-0*) Dial Bks Young.

—Timothy Goes to School. Wells, Rosemary, illus. LC 80-20785. 32p. (ps-2). 1981. 13.95 (*0-8037-8948-3*); PLB 11.89 (*0-8037-8949-1*) Dial Bks Young.

—Unfortunately Harriet. Wells, Rosemary, illus. LC 76-181786. 32p. (ps-3). 1972. Dial Bks Young.
—Voyage to the Bunny Planet: First Tomato, Moss Pillows, the Island Light, 3 bks. Wells, Rosemary, illus. 32p. (ps-3). 1992. Boxed Set, 32p. ea. 13.00 (0-8037-1174-3) Dial Bks Young.
—Waiting for the Evening Star. Jeffers, Susan, illus. LC 92-30492. 40p. (gr. k-3). 1993. 15.00 (0-8037-1398-3); PLB 14.89 (0-8037-1399-1) Dial Bks Young.
—When No One Was Looking. 224p. (gr. 9up). 1991. pap. 2.95 (0-590-43514-0, Point) Scholastic Inc.
Wells, Rosemary & Jeffers, Susan. Forest of Dreams. LC 88-3826. (Illus.). 24p. (ps-3). 1988. 13.95 (0-8037-0569-7); PLB 13.89 (0-8037-0570-0) Dial Bks Young.
Wells, Ruth. A to Zen - A Book of Japanese Culture. Yoshi, illus. LC 91-14183. 28p. (gr. k up). 1992. pap. 15.95 (0-88708-175-4) Picture Bk Studio.
Wells, Ruth, retold by. The Poor God: A Japanese Folktale. Yoshi, illus. LC 93-18236. 1993. 15.95 (0-88708-330-7) Picture Bk Studio.
Wells, Ruth & Van Dyke, Henry, eds. The Other Wise Man. Moser, Barry, illus. LC 93-16259. (ps-8). 1993. 16.95 (0-88708-329-3) Picture Bk Studio.
Wells, Sue. Make Your Own Coral Reef: Includes Giant Three-Dimensional Press-Out Model. Tomblin, Gill, illus. Johnston, Damian, designed by. (Illus.). 18p. (gr. 3-7). 1994. 13.99 (0-525-67461-6, Lodestar Bks) Dutton Child Bks.
Wells, Sue & Hanna, Nick. The Greenpeace Book of Coral Reefs. LC 92-41504. (Illus.). 160p. (gr. 10-12). 1992. 35.00 (0-8069-8795-2); prepub. 29.95 (0-685-60094-7) Sterling.
Wells, Susan. Explore the World of Mighty Oceans. Quigley, Sebastian, illus. 48p. (gr. 3-7). 1992. write for info. (0-307-15609-5, 15609, Golden Pr) Western Pub.
—The Illustrated World of Oceans. LC 90-27361. (Illus.). 64p. (gr. 3-7). 1993. pap. 7.95 (0-671-77027-6, S&S BFYR) S&S Trade.
—The Illustrated World of Space. LC 90-20263. (Illus.). 64p. (gr. 3-7). 1993. pap. 7.95 (0-671-77033-0, S&S BFYR) S&S Trade.
Wells, Tom. Faith the Gift of God. 156p. (gr. 5 up). 1983. pap. 6.95 (0-85151-361-1) Banner of Truth.
Welser, Matthew W. God Promised Us a Savior. (Illus.). 24p. (ps-4). 1989. pap. 1.89 (0-570-09019-9, 59-1442) Concordia.
Welsh-Smith, Susan. Andy: An Alaskan Tale. Munoz, Rie, illus. 24p. 1988. 13.95 (0-521-35535-4) Cambridge U Pr.
Welty, Eudora. The Shoe Bird. Krush, Beth, illus. 88p. (gr. 4-6). 1993. 14.95 (0-87805-668-8) U Pr of Miss.
—A Worn Path. 1991. PLB 13.95s.p. (0-88682-471-0) Creative Ed.
Welty, Harry R. Visit to the Attic. Lee, Marlene K., illus. LC 92-90838. 250p. (Orig.). (gr. 6-8). 1992. pap. 6.95 (0-9632953-0-6) Welty Pr.
Wendell, Belew M. Ken Prickett: Man of Joy. LC 85-6208. (gr. 4-6). 1985. 5.99 (0-8054-4296-0, 4242-96) Broadman.
Wender, Leon. Little Brown Roadrunner: Who Did It Herself. O'Connor, Claiborne, illus. 24p. (Orig.). (gr. 1-3). 1992. pap. text ed. 4.00 (0-938513-14-1) Amador Pubs.
Wendland, Ernst H. God's Mission in the New Testament. Fischer, William E., ed. 40p. (Orig.). 1986. pap. 2.50 (0-938272-55-1) WELS Board.
Wendt, Allan, ed. see Johnson, Samuel & Boswell, James.
Wendt, Michael, ed. see Dickens, Charles.
Wenger, Rachelle & Wenger, Renee. Word of God, Priceless Treasure. Wenger, Ray M., ed. Wenger, Rachelle & Wenger, Renee, illus. 64p. (gr. 3-6). 1993. pap. 5.99 (0-9634616-1-3) Plumb Line Pr.
Wenger, Ray M., ed. see Wenger, Rachelle & Wenger, Renee.
Wenger, Renee, jt. auth. see Wenger, Rachelle.
Wenger, Win. A Method for Personal Growth & Development. (Illus.). 135p. (Orig.). (gr. 7-12). 1986. pap. 24.00 (0-931865-09-3) Psychegenics.
Wengrov, Charles. The Story of Hanukkah. (Illus.). (gr. k-7). 1965. pap. 2.50 (0-914080-52-0) Shulsinger Sales.
—The Story of Passover. (Illus.). (gr. k-7). 1965. pap. 2.50 (0-914080-54-7) Shulsinger Sales.
—The Story of Purim. (Illus.). (gr. k-7). 1965. pap. 2.50 (0-914080-53-9) Shulsinger Sales.
—The Story of Shavuot. (Illus.). (gr. k-7). 1965. pap. 2.50 (0-914080-55-5) Shulsinger Sales.
—Tales of King Saul. (Illus.). (gr. 5-10). 1969. 3.00 (0-914080-21-0) Shulsinger Sales.
—Tales of the Prophet Samuel. (Illus.). (gr. 5-10). 1969. 4.00 (0-914080-22-9) Shulsinger Sales.
Wengrow, Arnold, contrib. by. Pinocchio (Musical) (Orig.). 1991. Playscript. pap. 4.50 (0-87602-298-0) Anchorage.
Wenig, Laurin J. The Prophets: Showing Us the Way to Justice & Peace. (Illus.). 80p. (Orig.). (gr. 9-12). 1990. pap. text ed. 4.90 (0-937997-16-1); tchr's ed. 8.90 (0-937997-17-X) Hi-Time Pub.
Wenk, Laurie P. Francine Pascal's Sweet Valley High Slam Book. (gr. 7 up). 1988. pap. 3.95 (0-318-36514-6) Bantam.
Wenk, Richard. Batman & the Doomsday Prophecy. Delbo, Jose, illus. (gr. 3-6). 1989. pap. 2.99 (0-671-68312-8, Archway) PB.

Wenk, Richard, adapted by. Tales from the Crypt, Vol. 3: Introduced by the Vault-Keeper. Davis, Jack, illus. LC 90-23916. 96p. (gr. 4-7). 1991. pap. 2.99 (0-679-81801-4) Random Bks Yng Read.
Wenkart, Henny. Why Would Matthew Do Crack? (gr. 3-7). 1990. write for info. (0-911612-00-9) Wenkart.
Wensell, Ulises, illus. They Followed a Bright Star. LC 93-6065. 1994. write for info. (0-399-22706-7, Putnam) Putnam Pub Group.
Wentcrek, Ginger. Dandy Dictionary Skills. (gr. 2-4). 1986. pap. 5.95 (0-8224-1830-4) Fearon Teach Aids.
—Marvelous Maps & Graphs. (gr. 1-3). pap. 5.95 (0-8224-6332-6) Fearon Teach Aids.
Wentworth, Anna, jt. auth. see Tucker, James C.
Wenzel, Dorothy. Ann Bancroft: On Top of the World. LC 89-11980. (Illus.). 64p. (gr. 3 up). 1990. RSBE 13.95 (0-87518-418-9, Dillon) Macmillan Child Grp.
Wepman, Dennis. Adolf Hitler. (Illus.). 112p. (gr. 5 up). 1985. lib. bdg. 17.95 (0-87754-578-2); pap. 9.95 (0-7910-0575-5) Chelsea Hse.
—Alexander the Great. Schlesinger, Arthur M., Jr., intro. by. (Illus.). 112p. (gr. 5 up). 1986. lib. bdg. 17.95 (0-87754-594-4) Chelsea Hse.
—Benito Juarez. Schlesinger, Arthur M., Jr., intro. by. (Illus.). 112p. (gr. 5 up). 1987. lib. bdg. 17.95 (0-87754-537-5) Chelsea Hse.
—Desmond Tutu. LC 89-31010. (Illus.). 157p. (gr. 7 up). 1989. PLB 14.40 (0-531-10780-9) Watts.
—Helen Keller. Horner, Matina, intro. by. (Illus.). 112p. (Orig.). (gr. 5 up). 1987. 17.95 (1-55546-662-1); pap. 9.95 (0-7910-0417-1) Chelsea Hse.
—Hernando Cortes. Schlesinger, Arthur M., Jr., intro. by. (Illus.). 112p. (gr. 5 up). 1986. lib. bdg. 17.95 (0-87754-593-6) Chelsea Hse.
—Jomo Kenyatta. (Illus.). 112p. (gr. 5 up). 1985. lib. bdg. 17.95 (0-87754-575-8) Chelsea Hse.
—Simon Bolivar. (Illus.). 112p. (gr. 5 up). 1985. lib. bdg. 17.95 (0-87754-569-3) Chelsea Hse.
—Tamerlane. Schlesinger, Arthur M., Jr., intro. by. (Illus.). 112p. (gr. 5 up). 1987. lib. bdg. 17.95 (0-87754-442-5) Chelsea Hse.
Werenko, Lisa V. It Zwibble & the Greatest Clean-up Ever. 1991. pap. 2.50 (0-590-44840-4) Scholastic Inc.
—It Zwibble & the Hunt for the Rain Forest Treasure. 1992. pap. 2.50 (0-590-44841-2) Scholastic Inc.
Werges, Rosanne, jt. auth. see DeCloux, Tina.
Werges, Rosanne, ed. see DeCloux, Tina.
Werges, Rosanne, ed. see Mah, Ronald.
Wergin, Joseph P. Cribbage for Kids. Gansen, Ed, illus. Corvi, Becky S., intro. by. LC 90-82436. (Illus.). 116p. (Orig.). (gr. 4-6). 1990. pap. 12.50 (0-9627003-0-4); Deluxe gift set. 25.00 (0-685-58857-2) Intl Gamester.
Wergin, Joseph P. & Smith, Beatrice S. Poker for Kids. Grube, Karl W., intro. by. 1993. pap. 12.50 (0-685-63089-7); tchr's. ed. 20.00 (0-685-63090-0) Intl Gamester.
—Poker for Kids & Everyone Else. Grube, Karl W., intro. by. 124p. 1992. pap. 10.00 (0-685-60627-9); tchr's. ed. 20.00 (0-685-60628-7) Intl Gamester.
Werley, Judith G., ed. The Artist.., & the Legend: A Visit to China Is Remembered & the Legends Unfold... Domjan, Evelyn A., compiled by. Domjan, Joseph, illus. LC 74-81927. (gr. 7 up). 1974. 25.00 (0-933652-09-7) Domjan Studio.
Werlin, Mark, jt. auth. see Werlin, Marvin.
Werlin, Marvin & Werlin, Mark. The Savior. 480p. (gr. 9 up). 1979. pap. 2.75 (0-440-17748-0, LFL) Dell.
Werlin, Nancy. Are You Alone on Purpose? 1994. write for info. (0-395-67350-X) HM.
Wermert, Rosie & McClurg, Marie. Teddy Toast & Twelve Other Yummy Easy Recipes You Can Make Yourself: With a Little Help from a Grownup & a Very Special Cookie Cutter! Weissman, Bari, illus. 24p. (ps-2). 1992. bds. 7.99 plastic comb bdg. (0-679-80745-4) Random Bks Yng Read.
Werner, Meike, tr. see Potter, Beatrix.
Werner, Vivian. Dolls. 144p. 1991. pap. 2.95 (0-380-76044-4, Camelot) Avon.
Werner, Vivian, retold by. Petrouchka. Collier, John, illus. 32p. (gr. 5 up). 1992. 16.00 (0-670-83607-9) Viking Child Bks.
Wernham, Sara, jt. auth. see Lloyd, Sue.
Wersba, Barbara. The Best Place to Live Is the Ceiling. LC 90-30550. 192p. (gr. 7 up). 1990. PLB 13.89 (0-06-026409-8) HarpC Child Bks.
—The Carnival in My Mind. LC 81-48640. 224p. (gr. 7 up). 1982. PLB 12.89 (0-06-026410-1) HarpC Child Bks.
—Crazy Vanilla. LC 85-45956. 192p. (gr. 7 up). 1986. PLB 11.89 (0-06-026369-5) HarpC Child Bks.
—The Farewell Kid. LC 89-36401. 160p. (gr. 7 up). 1990. 12.95 (0-06-026378-4); PLB 12.89 (0-06-026379-2) HarpC Child Bks.
—Just Be Gorgeous. LC 87-45858. 160p. (gr. 7 up). 1988. PLB 11.89 (0-06-026360-1) HarpC Child Bks.
—Just Be Gorgeous. 1991. pap. 3.25 (0-440-20810-6) Dell.
—Let Me Fall Before I Fly. Hoys, James, illus. LC 86-2686. 48p. (gr. 6 up). 1986. PLB 13.95s.p. (0-88682-057-X) Creative Ed.
—Love Is the Crooked Thing. LC 87-171. 160p. (gr. 7 up). 1987. HarpC Child Bks.
—Love Is the Crooked Thing. 1990. 3.50 (0-440-20542-5, LFL) Dell.
—Wonderful Me. 1991. pap. 3.50 (0-440-20883-1) Dell.
—You'll Never Guess the End. LC 91-24771. 144p. (gr. 7 up). 1992. 14.00 (0-06-020448-6); PLB 13.89 (0-06-020449-4) HarpC Child Bks.

Wert, Debra. Mac's Choice Workbook. Anfenson-Vance, Deborah, et al, eds. Wilson, Miriam J., intro. by. (Illus.). 36p. (gr. 2-6). 1989. pap. 5.00 (0-944576-03-6) Rocky River Pubs.
Wert, Debra L. Mac's Choice: A Story about Choice & Drug Use. Anfenson-Vance, Deborah, et al, eds. Wilson, Miriam J., intro. by. (Illus.). 40p. (gr. 1 up). 1989. pap. 7.95 (0-944576-02-8) Rocky River Pubs.
Wertheim, J. & Oxlade, C. Dictionary of Chemistry. (Illus.). 128p. (gr. 6 up). 1987. PLB 15.96 (0-88110-230-X); pap. 9.95 (0-86020-821-4) EDC.
—Dictionary of Science: Physics, Chemistry & Biology Facts. (Illus.). 128p. (gr. 6 up). 1988. pap. 23.95 (0-86020-989-X) EDC.
Wertz, Marianna, ed. see Robinson, Amelia B.
Werz, Ed, jt. auth. see Gross, Cheryl.
Wesche, Alice. Wild Brothers of the Indians: As Pictured by the Ancient Americans. LC 77-79064. (Illus.). (gr. 3-8). 1977. pap. 4.95 (0-918080-21-5) Treasure Chest.
Wesche, Alice M. Runs Far, Son of the Chichimecs. (gr. 3-7). 1982. pap. 7.95 (0-89013-133-3) Museum NM Pr.
Wesley, Charles H. Neglected History. 1990. 5.95 (0-87498-012-7) Assoc Pubs DC.
—Richard Allen: An Apostle of Freedom. 1990. 12.95 (0-87498-078-X); pap. 9.95 (0-87498-079-8) Assoc Pubs DC.
Wesley, Mary. Haphazard House. LC 92-24590. 150p. (gr. 7 up). 1993. 14.95 (0-87951-470-1) Overlook Pr.
—The Sixth Seal. 194p. (gr. 7 up). 1993. 14.95 (0-87951-506-6) Overlook Pr.
—Speaking Terms. 128p. (gr. 7 up). 1994. 14.95 (0-87951-524-4) Overlook Pr.
Wesley, Valerie W., jt. auth. see Hudson, Wade.
Wessels, Florence, jt. auth. see Olivier, Pierre.
West, Alan. Jose Marti, Man of Poetry, Soldier of Freedom. LC 93-6258. 1994. PLB write for info. (1-56294-408-8) Millbrook Pr.
—Roberto Clemente: Baseball Legend. LC 92-33505. (Illus.). 32p. (gr. 2-4). 1993. PLB 12.40 (1-56294-367-7) Millbrook Pr.
West, Bobbie, tr. see Cutburth, Ronald W.
West, Cindy. Duck Tales Scrooge Mcduck. 1990. write for info. (0-307-11597-6, Golden Pr) Western Pub.
—Minnie 'n' Me: the Surprise Friend. (ps-3). 1990. write for info. (0-307-11588-7) Western Pub.
—The Superkids & the Singing Dog. Mathieu, Joe, illus. LC 81-50042. 48p. (gr. 1-4). 1982. lib. bdg. 4.99 (0-394-94924-2) Random Bks Yng Read.
—That Tickles! The Disney Book of Senses. Moore, Larry, illus. LC 92-53444. 32p. (ps-k). 1993. 9.95 (1-56282-383-3) Disney Pr.
—Three Bears. (ps-3). 1993. pap. 1.50 (0-307-11544-5, Golden Pr) Western Pub.
West, Colin. The Beginner's Book of Bad Behaviour. West, Colin, illus. 96p. (gr. 4-7). 1988. 13.95 (0-09-172120-2, Pub. by Hutchinson UK) Trafalgar.
—The Best of West. (Illus.). 192p. (gr. 5-8). 1992. 22.95 (0-09-173587-4, Pub. by Hutchinson UK) Trafalgar.
—Between the Sun, the Moon & Me. Banyard, Julie, illus. 32p. (ps-2). 1992. 15.95 (0-09-173644-7, Pub. by Hutchinson UK) Trafalgar.
—Go Tell It to the Toucan. West, Colin, illus. (ps-3). 1990. PLB 8.95 (0-553-05889-4, Little Rooster) Bantam.
—Have You Seen the Crocodile? West, Colin, illus. LC 85-45748. 24p. (ps-2). 1986. pap. 4.95 (0-06-443101-0, Trophy) HarpC Child Bks.
—The King's Toothache. Dalton, Anne, illus. LC 87-3713. 32p. (ps-2). 1988. (Lipp Jr Bks) HarpC Child Bks.
—One Little Elephant. LC 93-36273. 1994. write for info. (1-56402-375-3) Candlewick Pr.
—Pardon? Said the Giraffe. West, Colin, illus. LC 85-45747. 24p. (ps-2). 1986. pap. 4.95 (0-06-443102-9, Trophy) HarpC Child Bks.
—Shape Up, Monty! West, Colin, illus. LC 91-20316. 64p. (gr. 2-5). 1991. 10.95 (0-525-44777-6, DCB) Dutton Child Bks.
West, Cyndy. I Am Mickey Mouse. DiCicco, Sue, illus. (ps-k). 1991. 3.50 (0-307-12166-6, Golden Pr) Western Pub.
West, Dan. The Day the TV Blew Up. Levine, Abby, ed. LC 87-25348. (Illus.). 32p. (gr. 2-5). 1988. PLB 11.95 (0-8075-1491-8) A Whitman.
West, David. Why Is the Sky Blue? And Answers to Questions You Always Wanted to Ask. (Illus.). 64p. 1992. 14.95 (0-8120-6284-1); pap. 8.95 (0-8120-4884-9) Barron.
West, Delno C. & West, Jean M. Christopher Columbus: The Great Adventure & How We Know about It. LC 90-936. (Illus.). 144p. (gr. 5-9). 1991. SBE 15.95 (0-689-31433-7, Atheneum Child Bk) Macmillan Child Grp.
West, Irene C. Most Loved Christmas Stories. 96p. (gr. k-10). 1992. pap. 7.95 (0-9632452-7-9) Design Pub UT.
West, Jean M., jt. auth. see West, Delno C.
West, Jim, jt. auth. see Izen, Marshal.
West, Joanne, ed. & illus. see Sundeen, Poppy.
West, Keith. Little Pig's Special Day. (Illus.). (ps-3). 1991. 13.95 (0-399-22209-X, Putnam) Putnam Pub Group.
West, Mark I., ed. Before Oz: Juvenile Fantasy Stories from Nineteenth-Century America. LC 89-35643. (Illus.). 229p. 1989. lib. bdg. 29.50 (0-208-02234-1, Archon Bks) Shoe String.

—A Wondrous Menagerie: Animal Fantasy Stories from American Children's Literature. 172p. 1993. lib. bdg. 25.00 (0-208-02383-6, Pub. by Archon Bks) Shoe String.

West, Nick. The Mystery of the Coughing Dragon. LC 80-18982. 176p. (gr. 4-7). 1984. pap. 2.95 (0-394-86414-X) Random Bks Yng Read.

West, Pamela. Yours Truly, Jack the Ripper. 1989. pap. 3.50 (0-440-20259-0) Dell.

West, Patricia M. Hispanic Folk Songs of the Southwest: For Bilingual Programs (Part II) 33p. (gr. k-12). 1982. 5.00 (0-685-42610-6) U of Denver Teach.

West, Patricia M. & Otero, George G. Hispanic Folk Songs of the Southwest: An Introduction (Part I) updated ed. 33p. (Orig.). (gr. k-12). 1982. pap. 5.00 (0-943804-11-6) U of Denver Teach.

West, Robert, jt. auth. see Myers, Bill.

West, Robert E., jt. auth. see Myers, Bill.

West, Robin. Dinosaur Discoveries: How to Create Your Own Prehistoric World. Wolfe, Bob & Wolfe, Diane, illus. 72p. (gr. 1-5). 1989. PLB 19.95 (0-87614-351-6) Carolrhoda Bks.

—Far Out: How to Create Your Own Star World. Wolfe, Bob, photos by. (Illus.). 72p. (gr. k-4). 1987. lib. bdg. 19.95 (0-87614-279-X); pap. 5.95 (0-87614-463-6) Carolrhoda Bks.

—My Very Own Christmas: A Book of Cooking & Crafts. LC 92-8653. (Illus.). 1992. 19.95 (0-87614-722-8) Carolrhoda Bks.

—My Very Own Halloween. (ps-3). 1992. 19.95 (0-87614-725-2) Carolrhoda Bks.

—My Very Own Thanksgiving: A Book of Cooking & Crafts. Burke, Susan S., illus. Wolfe, Robert L. & Wolfe, Diane, photos by. LC 92-33234. (Illus.). (ps-3). 1993. 19.95 (0-87614-723-6) Carolrhoda Bks.

—My Very Own Valentine's Day: A Book of Cooking & Crafts. Wolfe, Robert L. & Wolfe, Diane, photos by. Burke, Susan S., illus. LC 92-22254. 1993. 19.95 (0-87614-724-4) Carolrhoda Bks.

West, Rose. Go & Have a Good Time. (gr. 2-8). 1990. pap. 10.95 (0-8224-3500-4) Fearon Teach Aids.

West, Timothy, read by see Potter, Beatrix.

West, Tracey. Fire in the Valley. Golub, Nan, illus. 80p. (gr. 4-6). 1993. PLB 12.95 (1-881889-32-7) Silver Moon.

—Mr. Peale's Bones. 80p. (gr. 4-6). 1994. PLB 12.95 (1-881889-50-5) Silver Moon.

—Voyage of the Half Moon. LC 93-16462. 64p. (Orig.). (gr. 4-6). 1993. PLB 12.95 (1-881889-18-1) Silver Moon.

West, Tracy. The Butterflies of Freedom. (gr. 6 up). 1988. pap. 2.25 (0-317-69512-6) S&S Trade.

West Virginia Writers, Inc., Staff & McClure, Patricia. Beyond the Magpie: A Selection of Winning Entries from Four Years - 1987, 1988, 1989, 1990 - of the West Virginia Writers, Inc. Annual Awards Competition. Carper, Helen, ed. Wahl, Diana, illus. Love, Patrick, contrib. by. 147p. (Orig.). 1991. pap. 9.40 (0-941092-23-2) Mtn St Pr.

Westall, Robert. Blitzcat. (gr. 7 up). 1989. pap. 12.95 (0-590-42770-9) Scholastic Inc.

—Blitzcat. 240p. (gr. 7 up). 1990. pap. 3.25 (0-590-42771-7) Scholastic Inc.

—The Call & Other Stories. 128p. (gr. 7 up). 1993. 13.00 (0-670-82484-4) Viking Child Bks.

—Demons & Shadows: The Ghostly Best Stories. (gr. 4-7). 1993. 15.00 (0-374-31768-2) FS&G.

—Echoes of War. 96p. (gr. 7 up). 1991. 13.95 (0-374-31964-2) FS&G.

—Ghost Abbey. LC 88-23945. (gr. 7 up). 1989. pap. 12. 95 (0-590-41692-8) Scholastic Inc.

—Ghost Abbey. 1990. pap. 2.95 (0-590-41693-6) Scholastic Inc.

—If Cats Could Fly. large type ed. Ross, Tony, illus. 1992. 13.95 (0-7451-1639-6, Galaxy Child Lrg Print) Chivers N Amer.

—In Camera: And Other Stories. LC 92-13815. 176p. (gr. 7 up). 1993. 13.95 (0-590-45920-1) Scholastic Inc.

—The Kingdom by the Sea. 176p. (gr. 5 up). 1991. 15.00 (0-374-34205-9) FS&G.

—Kingdom by the Sea. (ps-3). 1993. pap. 3.95 (0-374-44060-3) FS&G.

—The Machine Gunners. LC 76-13630. 186p. (gr. 5-9). 1976. PLB 13.88 (0-688-84055-8) Greenwillow.

—The Machine Gunners. LC 76-13630. 192p. (gr. 5 up). 1990. pap. 3.50 (0-679-80130-8) Random Bks Yng Read.

—The Promise. 208p. (gr. 5 up). 1991. 13.95 (0-590-43760-7, Scholastic Hardcover) Scholastic Inc.

—The Promise. (gr. 7 up). 1993. pap. 3.25 (0-590-43761-5) Scholastic Inc.

—Stones of Muncaster Cathedral. (gr. 4-7). 1993. 11.00 (0-374-37263-2) FS&G.

—The Stones of Muncaster Cathedral. large type ed. LC 93-10871. 1993. 14.95 (1-56054-766-9) Thorndike Pr.

—Stormsearch. (gr. 4-7). 1992. 14.00 (0-374-37272-1) FS&G.

—Urn Burial. LC 87-23816. 160p. (gr. 7 up). 1988. 11.95 (0-688-07595-9) Greenwillow.

—Yaxley's Cat. 208p. 1992. 13.95 (0-590-45175-8, Scholastic Hardcover) Scholastic Inc.

Westall, Robert, selected by. Ghost Stories. Eckett, Sean, illus. LC 92-26451. 256p. (gr. 4-9). 1993. 6.95 (1-85697-884-2) Kingfisher Bks.

Westberg, Barbara. Holiday Programs: Recitations, Exercises, Readings, Skits, Dramas, Musicals for All Ages, Vol. 2. Agnew, Tim, illus. LC 87-29786. 218p. (Orig.). 1993. pap. 6.99 (1-56722-012-6) Word Aflame.

—Rhymes, Riddles & Reasons, Vol. I: Genesis, A Devotional Book for Children. Agnew, Tim, illus. LC 90-38218. 224p. (Orig.). (gr. 3-7). 1991. pap. 7.99 (0-932581-75-7) Word Aflame.

—Rhymes, Riddles & Reasons, Vol. 2: Exodus Through Judges. Agnew, Tim, illus. LC 90-38218. 224p. (Orig.). (gr. 3-7). 1992. pap. 7.99 (0-932581-76-5) Word Aflame.

Westberg, Barbara, jt. auth. see Smelser, Georgia.

Westberg Peters, Lisa. Condor. LC 89-28270. (Illus.). 48p. (gr. 5 up). 1990. RSBE 12.95 (0-89686-515-0, Crestwood Hse) Macmillan Child Grp.

Westbrook, Charles L. The Talisman of the United States: The Mysterious Street Lines of Washington, D. C. (Illus.). 123p. (Orig.). (gr. 12). 1990. pap. 10.95x (0-9626554-0-6) Westcom NC.

Westbrook, Henry S. Burned at the Stake. Obaba, Al I., ed. 124p. (Orig.). 1991. pap. text ed. 9.95 (0-916157-88-1) African Islam Miss Pubns.

Westcott, A. & Symons, C. Whispering River. LC 78-108727. (Illus.). 48p. (gr. 3-5). 1970. PLB 10.95 (0-87783-049-5); pap. 3.94 deluxe ed (0-87783-116-5) Oddo.

Westcott, Alvin. Billy Lump's Adventure. LC 68-56817. (Illus.). 32p. (gr. 2-4). 1968. PLB 9.95 (0-87783-002-9) Oddo.

—Rockets & Crackers. LC 75-108729. (Illus.). 80p. (gr. 4 up). 1970. PLB 10.95 (0-87783-033-9); pap. 3.94 deluxe ed. (0-87783-105-X) Oddo.

—Word Bending with Aunt Sarah. LC 68-56821. (Illus.). 48p. (gr. 2-3). 1968. PLB 9.95 (0-87783-052-5); pap. 3.94 deluxe ed (0-87783-118-1) Oddo.

Westcott, Alvin & Schluep, J. Fun with Timothy Triangle. LC 66-11445. (Illus.). 64p. (gr. 4). 1970. pap. 3.94 deluxe ed. (0-87783-014-2); answer key 0. 39x (0-87783-164-5) Oddo.

Westcott, Alvin, jt. auth. see Symons.

Westcott, C. T. Silver Wings & Leather Jackets. (Orig.). 1989. pap. 3.50 (0-440-20239-6) Dell.

Westcott, Nadine B. Getting Up. Westcott, Nadine B., illus. LC 86-28721. (ps). 1987. pap. 4.95 (0-316-93131-4, Joy St Bks) Little.

—The Giant Vegetable Garden. (Illus.). 32p. (ps-3). 1981. 14.95i (0-316-93129-2, Pub. by Atlantic Monthly Pr); pap. 4.95 (0-316-93130-6) Little.

—Going to Bed. Westcott, Nadine B., illus. LC 86-28757. (ps). 1987. pap. 4.95 (0-316-93132-2, Joy St Bks) Little.

—House That Jack Built: Pop-up, Pull-tab, Playtime Book. (ps-3). 1991. 14.95 (0-316-93138-1) Little.

—I Know an Old Lady Who Swallowed a Fly. Westcott, Nadine B., illus. 32p. (gr. k-3). 1980. lib. bdg. 14.95 (0-316-93128-4, Joy St Bks); pap. 5.95 (0-316-93127-6) Little.

—The Lady with the Alligator Purse. (ps-3). 1990. pap. 4.95 (0-316-93136-5) Little.

—Peanut Butter & Jelly: A Play Rhyme. (Illus.). 24p. (ps-k). 1992. pap. 3.99 (0-14-054852-1) Puffin Bks.

—There's a Hole in the Bucket. Westcott, Nadine B., illus. LC 89-34538. 32p. (ps-2). 1990. 14.00 (0-06-026042-5); PLB 13.89 (0-06-026423-3) HarpC Child Bks.

—There's a Hole in the Bucket. Westcott, Nadine B., illus. LC 89-34538. 32p. (ps-2). 1993. pap. 4.95 (0-06-443195-9, Trophy) HarpC Child Bks.

Westcott, Nadine B., adapted by. & illus. The Lady with the Alligator Purse. Westcott, Nadine B., illus. LC 87-21368. (ps-3). 1988. 13.95 (0-316-93135-7, Joy St Bks) Little.

Westcott, Nadine B., ed. & illus. Never Take a Pig to Lunch: And Other Poems about the Fun of Eating. LC 93-11801. 64p. 1994. 16.95 (0-531-06834-X); lib. bdg. 16.99 RLB (0-531-08684-4) Orchard Bks Watts.

Westcott, Nadine B., adapted by. & illus. Skip to My Lou. 32p. (ps-3). 1989. 12.95 (0-316-93137-3, Joy St Bks) Little.

—Skip to My Lou. 32p. (ps-3). 1992. pap. 4.95 (0-316-93140-3, Joy St Bks) Little.

Westcott, Nadine B., illus. Peanut Butter & Jelly: A Play Rhyme. LC 86-32889. 32p. (ps-k). 1987. 13.00 (0-525-44317-7, DCB) Dutton Child Bks.

—Peanut Butter & Jelly: A Play Rhyme. LC 86-32889. 24p. (ps-k). 1992. pap. 3.99 (0-525-44885-3, DCB) Dutton Child Bks.

—Peanut Butter & Jelly: A Play Rhyme. giant ed. 24p. (ps-k). 1993. pap. 17.99 (0-14-054850-5) Puffin Bks.

—Peanut Butter & Jelly: A Play Rhyme. (ps-3). 1994. pap. 6.99 incl. cassette (0-14-095142-3, Puffin) Puffin Bks.

—Peanut Butter & Jelly Read-Aloud Set. (ps-k). 1993. Set incls. 1 Giant copy, 6 paperbacks, giant-sized bookmark & tchr's. guide in a free- standing easel. pap. 41.93 (0-14-778975-3) Puffin Bks.

—Raffi's Christmas Treasury: 14 Illustrated Songs & Musical Arrangements. (ps up). 1988. PLB 17.95 (0-517-56806-3) Crown Bks Yng Read.

Westdyk, Roxanne H., jt. auth. see Derrig, Leslie A.

Westell, Kerry. Amanda's Book. Ohi, Ruth, illus. 24p. (ps-1). 1991. PLB 15.95 (1-55037-185-1, Pub. by Annick CN); pap. 5.95 (1-55037-182-7, Pub. by Annick CN) Firefly Bks Ltd.

—Dinosaur Dreams. Ritchie, Scot, illus. 24p. (Orig.). (ps-2). 1989. pap. 0.99 (1-55037-049-9, Pub. by Annick CN) Firefly Bks Ltd.

Westerfeld, Scott. The Berlin Airlift. (Illus.). 64p. (gr. 5 up). 1989. PLB 16.98 (0-382-09833-1); pap. 8.95 (0-382-09852-8) Silver Burdett Pr.

—Watergate. (Illus.). 64p. (gr. 5 up). 1991. PLB 16.98 (0-382-24126-6); pap. 8.95 (0-382-24120-7) Silver Burdett Pr.

Western, Joan & Wilson, Ron. The Human Body. Atkinson, Mike, illus. LC 90-38929. 96p. (gr. 3-6). 1991. PLB 14.89 (0-8167-2234-X); pap. text ed. 6.95 (0-8167-2235-8) Troll Assocs.

Western Publishing Company, Inc. Staff. Poky Little Puppy's Friends. (Illus.). (ps). 1990. pap. write for info. (0-307-06039-X, Golden Pr) Western Pub.

Westfall, Tanja & Miles, Patrick. Decisions, 5 Vols. Karch, Cheri, ed. Tully, Carol & Rizzuto, Joe, illus. 160p. (gr. 4-7). 1989. Set. text ed. 38.95 (1-877618-00-4) APIX Intl.

—Decisions: Building Bricks - Crystal, Vol 3. Karch, Cherl, ed. Tully, Carol & Rizzuto, Joe, illus. 32p. (gr. 4-7). 1989. text ed. 7.79 (1-877618-03-9) APIX Intl.

—Decisions: Struggle in the Willow Tree, Vol. 1. Karch, Cheri, ed. Tully, Carol & Rizzuto, Joe, illus. 32p. (gr. 4-7). 1989. text ed. 7.79 (1-877618-01-2) APIX Intl.

—Decisions: The Edge - LSD, Vol. 5. Karch, Cheri, ed. Tully, Carol & Rizzuto, Joe, illus. 32p. (gr. 4-7). 1989. text ed. 7.79 ea. (1-877618-05-5) APIX Intl.

—Decisions: The Pit, Vol. 2. Karch, Cheri, ed. Tully, Carol & Rizzuto, Joe, illus. 32p. (gr. 4-7). 1989. text ed. 7.79 (1-877618-02-0) APIX Intl.

—Decisions: The Survivor, Vol. 4. Karch, Cheri, ed. Tully, Carol & Rizzuto, Joe, illus. 32p. (gr. 4-7). 1989. text ed. 7.84 (1-877618-04-7) APIX Intl.

Westheimer, Mary, ed. see Boatness, Marie E.

Westheimer, Ruth. Dr. Ruth Talks to Kids: Where You Came from, How Your Body Changes, & What Sex Is All About. DeGroat, Diane, illus. LC 92-11397. 96p. (gr. 4-9). 1993. SBE 13.95 (0-02-792532-3, Macmillan Child Bk) Macmillan Child Grp.

Westlake, Diane. The Will & the Grace. Galas, Julie, illus. 80p. (Orig.). (gr. 7 up). 1984. pap. 9.00 (0-9614438-0-4) Fen Winnie.

Westley, Christine, ed. see Swann, Jivan.

Westman, Barbara. Dancing Dogs: Charlotte & Emilio at the Circus. Westman, Barbara, illus. LC 90-23070. 32p. (ps-3). 1991. PLB 14.89 (0-06-022460-6) HarpC Child Bks.

Westman, Paul. Neil Armstrong: Space Pioneer. LC 80-10832. (Illus.). 64p. (gr. 4 up). 1980. PLB 13.50 (0-8225-0479-0) Lerner Pubns.

Westman, Randall P. Trust, AIDS & Your Dentist: Key Questions to Ask Your Dentist about Infection Control, HIV & Sterilization. (Illus.). 114p. (Orig.). 1993. pap. text ed. 11.95 (0-9637088-0-5) Sweettooth.

Westmoreland, Ronald P. The Wild Horses of Hidden Valley. Roberts, Melissa, ed. (Illus.). 96p. (gr. 4-7). 1990. 8.95 (0-89015-717-0) Eakin-Sunbelt.

Westmoreland, W. C. A Soldier Reports. 608p. (gr. 9 up). 1980. pap. 2.95 (0-440-10025-9) Dell.

West-Naus, Roberta. Art Aardvark. (Illus.). 72p. (gr. 1-6). 1981. 7.95 (0-88160-041-5, LW 226) Learning Wks.

Weston, A. A Step-by-Step Book about Lovebirds. (Illus.). 64p. (gr. 9-12). 1988. 3.95 (0-86622-456-4, SK-016) TFH Pubns.

Weston, Anthony. The Chinese Revolution. Yapp, Malcolm, et al, eds. (Illus.). 32p. (gr. 6-11). 1980. pap. text ed. 3.45 (0-89908-114-2) Greenhaven.

Weston, John & Spooner, Alan, eds. The Oxford Children's Dictionary. 3rd ed. Le Fever, Bill, et al, illus. LC 93-17585. 1993. 7.99 (0-19-861297-4) OUP.

Weston, Mark. The Land & People of Pakistan. LC 91-2847. (Illus.). 224p. (gr. 6 up). 1992. 18.00 (0-06-022789-3); PLB 17.89 (0-06-022790-7) HarpC Child Bks.

Weston, Martha. Bea's Four Bears. Weston, Martha, illus. 32p. (ps-k). 1992. 9.70 (0-395-57791-8, Clarion Bks) HM.

Weston, Marti & Decell, Florri. Washington! Adventure for Kids. 2nd ed. LC 90-70168. 64p. (gr. 1-9). 1990. pap. 6.95 (0-918339-13-8) Vandamere.

Weston, Reiko. Cooking the Japanese Way. LC 81-12656. (Illus.). 48p. (gr. 5 up). 1983. PLB 14.95 (0-8225-0905-9) Lerner Pubns.

Westphal, Arnold C. Paper & Scissors Truth Talks, No. 5. 1971. perfect bdg. 4.95 (0-915398-04-4) Visual Evangels.

Westphal, Patricia R. The Legend of Ice Breaker. LC 89-40245. 32p. (gr. 1-2). 1991. PLB 18.60 (0-8368-0119-9) Gareth Stevens Inc.

Westray, Kathleen. A Color Sampler. LC 93-19967. 1993. 14.95 (0-395-65940-X) Ticknor & Fields.

Westridge Young Writers Workshop. Kids Explore America's Hispanic Heritage. (Illus.). 112p. (Orig.). (gr. 3 up). 1992. pap. 7.95 (1-56261-034-1) John Muir.

Westridge Young Writers Workshop Staff. Kids Explore America's African-American Heritage. (Illus.). 112p. (Orig.). (gr. 3 up). Date not set. pap. 8.95 (1-56261-090-2) John Muir.

—Kids Explore America's Japanese Heritage. 112p. Date not set. pap. 8.95 (1-56261-155-0) John Muir.

—Kids Explore the Gifts of Children with Special Needs. 112p. (gr. 4-7). 1994. pap. 8.95 (1-56261-156-9) John Muir.

Westwood, Chris. Brother of Mine. LC 92-32020. (gr. 5 up). 1993. write for info. (0-395-66137-4, Clarion Bks) HM.

—Calling All Monsters. LC 91-19601. 224p. (gr. 7 up). 1993. 15.00 (0-06-022461-4); PLB 14.89 (0-06-022462-2) HarpC Child Bks.
—He Came from the Shadows. LC 90-38005. 224p. (gr. 7 up). 1991. 14.95 (0-06-021658-1); PLB 14.89 (0-06-021659-X) HarpC Child Bks.
—Shock Waves. 192p. (gr. 9 up). 1992. 13.45 (0-395-63111-4, Clarion Bks) HM.
Westwood, Dick. Champin' at the Bit: An Autobiography. (Illus.). 161p. (Orig.). (gr. 6-12). 1986. pap. 10.00x (0-9617118-1-7) Westwood Ent.
Westwood, Jennifer. Stories of Charlemagne. LC 74-12435. (gr. 6 up). 1976. 21.95 (0-87599-213-7) S G Phillips.
Westwood, Phoebe L. & Rohrbacher, Richard W. Yesteryear's Child: Golden Days & Summer Nights. LC 93-77688. 176p. (gr. 10). 1993. pap. 11.95 (0-9623048-7-5) Heritage West.
Wetering, Janwillem van de see Van De Wetering, Janwillem.
Wetering, Janwillem Van de see Van De Wetering, Janwillem.
Wetering, Janwillem van de see Van de Wetering, Janwillem.
Wetering, Janwillem Van De see Van de Wetering, Janwillem.
Wettasinghe, Sybil. The Umbrella Thief. (Illus.). 32p. (ps-3). 1987. 11.95 (0-916291-12-X) Kane-Miller Bk.
Wetterau, Bruce. Word Games. 352p. (gr. 9-12). 1990. 16.95 (0-13-947334-3, Webster New Wrld); pap. 9.95 (0-685-31180-5) P-H Gen Ref & Trav.
Wetterer, Margaret. Kate Shelley & the Midnight Express. Ritz, Karen, illus. 48p. (gr. k-4). 1990. PLB 14.95 (0-87614-425-3) Carolrhoda Bks.
Wetterer, Margaret K. The Boy Who Knew the Language of the Birds. Wright, Beth, illus. 48p. (gr. k-4). 1991. PLB 17.50 (0-87614-652-3) Carolrhoda Bks.
Wetzel, Charles. James Monroe. (Illus.). (gr. 5 up). 1989. 17.95 (1-55546-817-9) Chelsea Hse.
Wetzel, JoAnne, jt. auth. see Huberman, Caryn.
Wetzel, JoAnne S. The Christmas Box. Root, Barry, illus. LC 91-38911. 32p. (ps-3). 1992. 13.00 (0-679-81789-1); PLB 13.99 (0-679-91789-6) Knopf Bks Yng Read.
Wetzel, Rick. What Do You Eat? Wetzel, Rick, illus. LC 92-61623. 6p. (ps-1). 1993. 3.99 (0-679-83844-9) Random Bks Yng Read.
—What Do You Say? Wetzel, Rick, illus. LC 91-61624. 6p. (ps-1). 1993. 3.99 (0-679-83845-7) Random Bks Yng Read.
Wetzel, Rick & Swanson, Maggie. Big Bird's Bedtime Story. Wetzel, Rick & Swanson, Maggie, illus. LC 87-4764. 32p. (ps-1). 1987. lib. bdg. 5.99 (0-394-99126-5); 2.25 (0-394-89126-0) Random Bks Yng Read.
—Un Cuento Para la Hora De Dormir De Big Bird. Guibert, Rita, tr. from ENG. Wetzel, Rick & Swanson, Maggie, illus. LC 92-3815. (SPA.). 32p. (ps-3). 1992. pap. 2.25 (0-679-83500-8) Random Bks Yng Read.
Wever, Hinke B. Little Lights in the Darkness: Stories & Activities for Advent & Christmas. Vilain, Frederic, tr. from GER. Muller, Anna-Hermine, illus. LC 90-42800. 99p. (Orig.). 1990. pap. 9.95 (0-8198-4444-6) St Paul Bks.
Wexler, Jerome. Flowers, Fruits & Seeds. (gr. k-3). 1991. pap. 3.95 (0-671-73986-7, Little Simon) S&S Trade.
—Flowers Fruits Seeds. LC 86-30616. (Illus.). 32p. (ps-3). 1990. pap. 12.95 (0-671-66372-0, Little Simon) S&S Trade.
—Jack-in-the-Pulpit. Wexler, Jerome, illus. 40p. (gr. 2-6). 1993. 14.99 (0-525-45073-4, DCB) Dutton Child Bks.
—Pet Gerbils. Tucker, Kathy, ed. LC 89-5636. (Illus.). 48p. (gr. 3-6). 1990. PLB 14.95 (0-8075-6523-7) A Whitman.
—Pet Hamsters. Tucker, Kathleen, ed. Wexler, Jerome, photos by. (Illus.). 48p. (gr. 2-6). 1992. PLB 14.95 (0-8075-6525-3) A Whitman.
—Pet Mice. Tucker, Kathleen, ed. LC 88-2. (Illus.). 48p. (gr. 2-8). 1989. PLB 14.95 (0-8075-6524-5) A Whitman.
—Queen Anne's Lace. LC 93-29621. 1994. write for info. (0-8075-6710-8) A Whitman.
—Wonderful Pussy Willows. Wexler, Jerome, photos by. LC 91-32262. (Illus.). 32p. (ps-3). 1992. 14.50 (0-525-44867-5, DCB) Dutton Child Bks.
Wexler, Terry, ed. see Heath, Dixie.
Wexner, V. I., ed. see Higgins, Susan O.
Wexo, John B. Apes. 24p. (gr. 4). 1989. PLB 14.95s.p. (0-88682-265-3) Creative Ed.
—Baby Animals. 24p. (gr. 4). 1989. PLB 14.95.s.p. (0-88682-270-X) Creative Ed.
—Big Cats. 24p. 1989. PLB 14.95s.p. (0-88682-264-5) Creative Ed.
—Dinosaurs. 24p. (gr. 3 up). 1991. PLB 14.95 (0-88682-393-5) Creative Ed.
—Endangered Animals. 24p. (gr. 4). 1989. PLB 14.95s.p. (0-88682-269-6) Creative Ed.
—Flyers. 24p. (gr. 3 up). 1991. PLB 14.95 (0-88682-394-3) Creative Ed.
—Life Begins. 24p. (gr. 3 up). 1991. PLB 14.95s.p. (0-88682-387-0) Creative Ed.
—Mammals, Pt. I. 24p. (gr. 3 up). 1991. PLB 14.95s.p. (0-88682-395-1) Creative Ed.
—Mammals, Pt. II. 24p. (gr. 3 up). 1991. PLB 14.95s.p. (0-88682-396-X) Creative Ed.

—Out of the Water. 24p. (gr. 3 up). 1991. PLB 14.95s.p. (0-88682-391-9) Creative Ed.
—Owls. 24p. (gr. 4). 1989. PLB 14.95s.p. (0-88682-268-8) Creative Ed.
—Penguins. 24p. (gr. 4). 1989. PLB 14.95s.p. (0-88682-263-7) Creative Ed.
—Plants & Animals. 24p. (gr. 3 up). 1991. PLB 14.95s.p. (0-88682-389-7) Creative Ed.
—Reptiles. 24p. (gr. 3 up). 1991. PLB 14.95 (0-88682-392-7) Creative Ed.
—Seals, Sea Lions, Walruses. 24p. (gr. 4). 1989. PLB 14.95s.p. (0-88682-271-8) Creative Ed.
—Swimmers. 24p. (gr. 3 up). 1991. PLB 14.95 (0-88682-390-0) Creative Ed.
—Tigers. 24p. (gr. 4). 1989. PLB 14.95s.p. (0-88682-266-1) Creative Ed.
—Whales. 24p. (gr. 4). 1989. PLB 14.95s.p. (0-88682-272-6) Creative Ed.
—Wolves. 24p. (gr. 4). 1989. PLB 14.95s.p. (0-88682-267-X) Creative Ed.
Wexo, John G. Life Expands. 24p. (gr. 3 up). 1991. PLB 14.95s.p. (0-88682-388-9) Creative Ed.
Weyland, Jack. Brenda at the Prom. LC 88-14880. viii, 171p. (gr. 7-12). 1988. 9.95 (0-87579-150-6) Deseret Bk.
—Charly. LC 80-11216. 98p. (gr. 9-12). 1992. pap. 4.95 (0-87579-619-2) Deseret Bk.
—If Talent Were Pizza. 118p. (gr. 8-12). 1993. pap. 6.95 (0-87579-696-6) Deseret Bk.
—Jack Weyland. 672p. (gr. 9-12). 1992. Boxed set incls. Stephanie, Sara, Whenever I Hear Your Name, Sam, & Charly. pap. 16.00 (0-87579-596-X) Deseret Bk.
—Kimberly. LC 92-730. 151p. (gr. 9-12). 1992. 11.95 (0-87579-599-4) Deseret Bk.
—Megapowers: Can Science Fact Defeat Science Fiction. Steacy, Ken, illus. LC 92-5441. 1992. pap. 8.61 (0-201-58115-9) Addison-Wesley.
—A New Dawn. LC 83-24049. 181p. (gr. 8 up). 1988. pap. 4.95 (0-87579-163-8) Deseret Bk.
—Nicole. (gr. 8-12). 1993. write for info. Deseret Bk.
—Nicole. LC 93-27308. 1993. 11.95 (0-87579-787-3) Deseret Bk.
—Sam. LC 81-682. 168p. (gr. 9-12). 1992. pap. 4.95 (0-87579-122-0) Deseret Bk.
—Sara, Whenever I Hear Your Name. LC 86-29071. 152p. 1987. 9.95 (0-87579-070-4) Deseret Bk.
—Sara, Whenever I Hear Your Name. LC 86-29071. 168p. (gr. 9-12). 1992. pap. 4.95 (0-87579-621-4) Deseret Bk.
—A Small Light in the Darkness. LC 87-22281. 202p. (gr. 8-12). 1987. 10.95 (0-87579-105-0) Deseret Bk.
—Stephanie. LC 88-37541. 212p. (gr. 7 up). 1989. 9.95 (0-87579-203-0) Deseret Bk.
—Stephanie. LC 88-17541. 224p. (gr. 9-12). 1992. pap. 4.95 one of boxed set (0-87579-622-2) Deseret Bk.
Weyn, Suzanne. Adventures with Barbie: Ballet Debut. (gr. 4-7). 1992. pap. 2.99 (0-8431-3410-0) Price Stern.
—Adventures with Barbie: Holiday Magic. (gr. 4-7). 1992. pap. 2.99 (0-8431-3412-7) Price Stern.
—Adventures with Barbie: Rollerblade Crusade. (gr. 4-7). 1992. pap. 2.99 (0-8431-3413-5) Price Stern.
—Adventures with Barbie: The Phantom of Shrieking Pond. (gr. 4-7). 1992. pap. 2.99 (0-8431-3411-9) Price Stern.
—All Alone in the Eighth Grade. LC 91-10162. 128p. (gr. 6-9). 1992. lib. bdg. 9.89 (0-8167-2394-X); pap. text ed. 2.95 (0-8167-2395-8) Troll Assocs.
—Animal Escapades. (Illus.). 64p. (gr. 1-4). 1993. pap. 2.99 (0-8431-3618-9) Price Stern.
—Baby-Sitter Go Home. 96p. 1992. pap. 2.75 (0-590-43561-2) Scholastic Inc.
—Boy Trouble. LC 90-11142. 128p. (gr. 4-8). 1991. lib. bdg. 9.89 (0-8167-2011-8); pap. text ed. 2.95 (0-8167-2012-6) Troll Assocs.
—A Chance for Chris. LC 90-11026. (Illus.). 128p. (gr. 4-8). 1991. lib. bdg. 9.89 (0-8167-2009-6); pap. text ed. 2.95 (0-8167-2010-X) Troll Assocs.
—Checking In. LC 89-49703. 128p. (gr. 4-8). 1991. lib. bdg. 9.89 (0-8167-2003-7); pap. text ed. 2.95 (0-8167-2004-5) Troll Assocs.
—Collette's Magic Star. 96p. 1991. pap. 2.75 (0-590-43562-0) Scholastic Inc.
—Diana's Step-by-Step Family Scrapbook. (gr. 4-7). 1993. pap. 4.95 (0-590-47199-6) Scholastic Inc.
—Emma's Turn. Iskowitz, Joel, illus. LC 89-31348. 96p. (gr. 3-5). 1990. lib. bdg. 9.89 (0-8167-1623-4); pap. text ed. 2.95 (0-8167-1624-2) Troll Assocs.
—Green-Eyed Pearl. (Illus.). 1992. pap. 2.95 (1-56282-250-0) Disney Pr.
—Hilary & the Rich Girl. 80p. (gr. 2-5). 1991. 2.75 (0-590-43560-4) Scholastic Inc.
—Liza's Lucky Break. LC 89-77117. 128p. (gr. 4-8). 1991. lib. bdg. 9.89 (0-8167-2007-X); pap. text ed. 2.95 (0-8167-2008-8) Troll Assocs.
—Make Room for Patti. (gr. 4-7). 1991. pap. 2.75 (0-590-43559-0) Scholastic Inc.
—The Makeover Club. 128p. (gr. 7 up). 1986. pap. 2.50 (0-380-75007-4, Flare) Avon.
—The Makeover Summer. 128p. (gr. 7 up). 1988. pap. 2.95 (0-380-75521-1, Flare) Avon.
—Mermaid Island. (Illus.). 64p. (Orig.). 1993. pap. 2.99 (0-8431-3619-7) Price Stern.
—Nefazia Visits the Palace. LC 92-53937. (Illus.). 1992. pap. 2.95 (1-56282-247-0) Disney Pr.
—Nicole's Chance. LC 93-14022. (Illus.). 128p. (gr. 4-8). 1993. PLB 9.89 (0-8167-3235-3); pap. 2.95 (0-8167-3236-1) Troll Assocs.

—Patty's Big Problem. 96p. (gr. 2-5). 1992. pap. 2.75 (0-590-43564-7, Little Apple) Scholastic Inc.
—Pointing Toward Trouble. Iskowitz, Joel, illus. LC 89-34549. 96p. (gr. 3-5). 1990. PLB 9.89 (0-8167-1653-6); pap. text ed. 2.95 (0-8167-1654-4) Troll Assocs.
—Stage Fright. Iskowitz, Joel, illus. LC 89-31349. 96p. (gr. 3-5). 1990. lib. bdg. 9.89 (0-8167-1651-X); pap. text ed. 2.95 (0-8167-1652-8) Troll Assocs.
—Star Magic. LC 90-11151. 128p. (gr. 4-8). 1991. lib. bdg. 9.89 (0-8167-2013-4); pap. text ed. 2.95 (0-8167-2014-2) Troll Assocs.
—Starswept Adventure. (Illus.). 64p. (gr. 1-4). 1993. pap. 2.99 (0-8431-3616-2) Price Stern.
—Stepping Out. Iskowitz, Joel, illus. LC 89-30586. 96p. (gr. 3-5). 1990. PLB 9.89 (0-8167-1619-6); pap. text ed. 2.95 (0-8167-1620-X) Troll Assocs.
—Three for the Show. Iskowitz, Joel, illus. LC 89-34547. 96p. (gr. 3-5). 1990. PLB 9.89 (0-8167-1655-2); pap. text ed. 2.95 (0-8167-1656-0) Troll Assocs.
—Tracey's Tough Choice. LC 93-25185. (Illus.). 128p. (gr. 4-8). 1993. PLB 9.89 (0-8167-3237-X); pap. 2.95 (0-8167-3238-8) Troll Assocs.
—True Blue. LC 90-10830. 128p. (gr. 4-8). 1991. PLB 9.89 (0-8167-2005-3); pap. text ed. 2.95 (0-8167-2006-1) Troll Assocs.
—A Twist of Fate. Iskowitz, Joel, illus. LC 89-30585. 96p. (gr. 3-5). 1990. PLB 9.89 (0-8167-1621-8); pap. text ed. 2.95 (0-8167-1622-6) Troll Assocs.
—Wild Horse Run. (Illus.). 64p. (Orig.). (gr. 1-4). 1993. pap. 2.99 (0-8431-3617-0) Price Stern.
Wezeman, Phyllis & Weissner, Colleen. Seaside with the Savior. (Illus.). 144p. (gr. 1-6). 1989. 24.95 (1-55513-186-7, 68718) Cook.
Wezeman, Phyllis Vos & Wiessner, Colleen A. Fabric of Faith. Chase, Judith, illus. (Illus.). (gr. 4-8). 1990. pap. 7.50 (1-877871-04-4) Ed Ministries.
Wezeman, Phyllis Vos see Vos Wezeman, Phyllis & Fournier, Jude D.
Wezeman, Phyllis Vos see Vos Wezeman, Phyllis & Wiessner, Colleen A.
Wezeman, Phyllis Vos see Wezeman, Phyllis Vos & Wiessner, Colleen A.
Wezeman, Phyllis Vos see Wiessner, Colleen A. & Vos Wezeman, Phyllis.
Whale Museum Staff. Gentle Giants of the Sea. 2nd ed. 214p. (gr. k-6). pap. 15.95 (0-933331-25-8) Whale Museum.
Whalen, Terry. When I Grow up, I Can Go Anywhere for Jesus. (ps-3). 1992. pap. 7.99 (1-55513-488-2) Cook.
Whales, Bostune. Cherish Life. 25p. 1991. write for info. (0-9629599-1-X) Rainbow IA.
Whaley, Bo. Why the South Lost the War: And Other Things I Don't Understand. (Illus.). 160p. (Orig.). (gr. 10 up). 1992. pap. 5.95 (1-55853-161-0) Rutledge Hill Pr.
Whaley, Charles E. & Whaley, Helen F. Future Images: Future Studies for Grades 4-12. (gr. 4-12). 1985. 12.99 (0-89824-149-9) Trillium Pr.
Whaley, Helen F., jt. auth. see Whaley, Charles E.
Whaley, Jeanette, jt. auth. see Roberts, Paulette.
Whaley, Richie. Samuel: Prophet & Judge. Shelton, Dean, illus. (gr. 1-6). 1979. 5.95 (0-8054-4242-1, 4242-42) Broadman.
Whalin, Terry. Never Too Busy. Faltico, Mary L., illus. 28p. (ps-k). 1993. 4.99 (0-7847-0038-9, 24-03828) Standard Pub.
Whalley, Margaret. Experiment with Magnets & Electricity. LC 92-41109. 1993. 17.50 (0-8225-2457-0) Lerner Pubns.
Whalley, Mary & Whalley, Paul. Butterfly in the Garden. LC 86-5705. (Illus.). 32p. (gr. 4-6). 1986. PLB 15.93 (1-55532-068-6) Gareth Stevens Inc.
Whalley, Paul. Butterfly & Moth. Keates, Colin, et al, photos by. LC 88-1574. (Illus.). 64p. (gr. 5 up). 1988. 15.00 (0-394-89618-1); lib. bdg. 15.99 (0-394-99618-6) Knopf Bks Yng Read.
Whalley, Paul, jt. auth. see Whalley, Mary.
Wharton, Thomas. Hildegard Sings. (Illus.). 32p. (gr. k-3). 1991. 10.95 (0-374-33242-8) FS&G.
—Hildegard Sings. (ps-3). 1993. pap. 4.95 (0-374-43070-5, Sunburst) FS&G.
Whately, Bruce. Looking for Crabs. (ps-3). 1993. 12.00 (0-207-17596-9, Pub. by Angus & Robertson AT) HarpC.
Whatley, Michael E. Aloysius (Al-o-wish-us) the Long Haired Guinea Pig. Brown, Sheila, illus. LC 90-63585. 26p. (gr. 5). 1990. pap. 3.50 (0-9618300-1-8) Nauset Marsh.
Whatling, R. C. The Cat Story. 16p. (gr. 7-10). 1986. 35.00x (0-7223-2012-4, Pub. by A H Stockwell England) St Mut.
Whaton, M., jt. auth. see Davies, H.
Whayne, Susanne S. Night Creatures. Schindler, Steven, illus. LC 91-24654. 48p. (gr. 2-7). 1993. pap. 15.00 JRT (0-671-73395-8, S&S BFYR) S&S Trade.
—Watch the House. Morrill, Leslie, illus. LC 91-28071. 80p. (gr. k-3). 1992. pap. 12.00 jacketed (0-671-75886-1, S&S BFYR) S&S Trade.
—Watch the House. Morrill, Leslie, illus. LC 91-28071. 80p. (gr. k-3). 1993. 80p. pap. 2.95 (0-671-86700-8, Half Moon Bks) S&S Trade.
—The World of Insects. Dudley, Ebet, illus. 48p. (gr. 3-7). 1990. pap. 9.95 (0-671-69018-3, S&S BFYR) S&S Trade.

Wheat, Pam & Whorton, Brenda, eds. Clues from the Past: A Resource Book on Archeology. Thompson, Eileen, illus. LC 90-4991. 200p. (gr. 3 up). 1990. pap. 17.95 (0-937460-65-6) Hendrick-Long.

Wheatley, Jennie N. Pass It On! A Treasury of Virgin Island Tales. 100p. (gr. 9-10). 1991. pap. 7.00 (0-9630527-0-5) WSTD Pub.

Wheatley, Nadia. My Place. Rawlins, Donna, illus. LC 92-9006. 24p. (gr. 3 up). 1992. 14.95 (0-916291-42-1) Kane-Miller Bk.

Wheatly, Mark. Build the Alamo. Eakin, Ed, ed. (Illus.). 32p. (gr. 4-5). 1989. 10.95 (0-89015-721-9) Eakin-Sunbelt.

Whedbee, Charles H. Legends of the Outer Banks & Tar Heel Tidewater. LC 66-23049. (Illus.). 165p. (gr. 5 up). 1979. 9.95 (0-910244-41-3) Blair.

Wheeler. Fishes. (gr. 2-5). 1982. (Usborne-Hayes); PLB 11.96 (0-88110-075-7); pap. 3.95 (0-86020-626-2) EDC.

Wheeler, Benson. I, Becky Barrymore. Barrymore, Lionel, illus. (gr. 3 up). 8.95 (0-8315-0036-0) Speller.

Wheeler, Bernelda. The Bannock. Bekkering, Herman, illus. LC 92-34255. 1993. 4.25 (0-383-03617-8) SRA Schl Grp.

Wheeler, Cindy. Marmalade's Nap. LC 81-20868. (Illus.). 24p. (ps-1). 1983. PLB 9.99 (0-394-95022-4) Knopf Bks Yng Read.
—Rose. Wheeler, Cindy, illus. LC 83-19985. 32p. (ps-1). 1985. lib. bdg. 10.99 (0-394-96233-8) Knopf Bks Yng Read.

Wheeler, Gerald, ed. see Hardinge, Miriam.

Wheeler, Gerald, ed. see Minchin-Comm, Dorothy.

Wheeler, Gerald, ed. see Parker, Lois.

Wheeler, Gerald, ed. see Pyke, Helen.

Wheeler, Gerald, ed. see Ritchie, Jo-An.

Wheeler, Gerald, ed. see Robinson, Glen.

Wheeler, Gerald, ed. see Smith, David B.

Wheeler, Gerald, ed. see Wiggins, VeraLee.

Wheeler, Gerald, ed. see Wilson, Miriam J.

Wheeler, Jill. A. A. Milne: Creater of Winnie the Pooh. Wallner, Rosemary, ed. LC 92-16570. (gr. 4). 1992. PLB 13.99 (1-56239-114-3) Abdo & Dghtrs.
—Branch Out: A Book about Land. Kallen, Stuart, ed. LC 93-15450. 1993. 14.96 (1-56239-194-1) Abdo & Dghtrs.
—Corazon Aquino. LC 91-73025. 202p. 1991. 12.94 (1-56239-082-1) Abdo & Dghtrs.
—Dr. Seuss. Wallner, Rosemary, ed. LC 92-16569. (gr. 4). 1992. PLB 13.99 (1-56239-112-7) Abdo & Dghtrs.
—Earth Kids. LC 93-15330. (gr. 3 up). 1993. 14.96 (1-56239-199-2) Abdo & Dghtrs.
—Every Drop Counts: A Book about Water. LC 93-15463. 1993. 12.94 (1-56239-195-X) Abdo & Dghtrs.
—For the Birds: A Book about Air. LC 93-7751. 1993. 14.96 (1-56239-196-8) Abdo & Dghtrs.
—Laura Ingalls Wilder. Wallner, Rosemary, ed. LC 92-16568. (gr. 4). 1992. PLB 13.99 (1-56239-115-1) Abdo & Dghtrs.
—Michael Landon. Wallner, Rosemary, ed. LC 92-16571. (gr. 4). 1992. PLB 13.99 (1-56239-113-5) Abdo & Dghtrs.
—Mother Teresa. LC 92-16675. 1992. 12.94 (1-56239-119-4) Abdo & Dghtrs.
—Raisa Gorbachev. LC 92-16678. 1992. 12.94 (1-56239-118-6) Abdo & Dghtrs.
—The Story of Crazy Horse. Deegan, Paul, ed. Dodson, Liz, illus. LC 89-84913. 32p. (gr. 4). 1989. PLB 11.96 (0-939179-66-0) Abdo & Dghtrs.
—The Story of Geronimo. Deegan, Paul, ed. Dodson, Liz, illus. LC 89-84911. 32p. (gr. 4). 1989. PLB 11.96 (0-939179-68-7) Abdo & Dghtrs.
—The Story of Hiawatha. Deegan, Paul, ed. Dodson, Liz, illus. LC 89-84908. 32p. (gr. 4). 1989. PLB 11.96 (0-939179-71-7) Abdo & Dghtrs.
—The Story of Pontiac. Deegan, Paul, ed. Dodson, Liz, illus. LC 89-84910. 32p. (gr. 4). 1989. PLB 11.96 (0-939179-69-5) Abdo & Dghtrs.
—The Story of Sequoyah. Deegan, Paul, ed. Dodson, Liz, illus. LC 89-84909. 32p. (gr. 4). 1989. PLB 11.96 (0-939179-70-9) Abdo & Dghtrs.
—The Story of Sitting Bull. Deegan, Paul, ed. Dodson, Liz, illus. LC 89-94912. 32p. (gr. 4). 1989. PLB 11.96 (0-939179-67-9) Abdo & Dghtrs.

Wheeler, Jill, ed. see Hughes, Richard.

Wheeler, Jill C. Beastly Neighbors. Berg, Julie, ed. LC 93-19058. 32p. 1993. 14.96 (1-56239-197-6) Abdo & Dghtrs.
—Coretta Scott King. LC 92-16677. 1992. 12.94 (1-56239-116-X) Abdo & Dghtrs.
—Earth Day Every Day. LC 91-73070. 1991. 12.94 (1-56239-031-7) Abdo & Dghtrs.
—Earth Moves: Get There with Energy to Spare. LC 91-73066. 202p. 1991. 12.94 (1-56239-035-X) Abdo & Dghtrs.
—The Food We Eat. Kallen, Stuart A., ed. LC 91-73068. 202p. 1991. 17.95 (1-56239-033-3) Abdo & Dghtrs.
—Healthy Earth, Healthy Bodies. Kallen, Stuart A., ed. LC 91-73069. 202p. 1991. 12.94 (1-56239-032-5) Abdo & Dghtrs.
—Nancy R. Reagan. LC 91-73027. 202p. 1991. 12.94 (1-56239-080-5) Abdo & Dghtrs.
—The People We Live With. Kallen, Stuart A., ed. LC 91-73067. 1991. 12.94 (1-56239-034-1) Abdo & Dghtrs.
—Princess Caroline. LC 92-16676. 1992. 12.94 (1-56239-117-8) Abdo & Dghtrs.

—The Throw-Away Generation. Kallen, Stuart A., ed. LC 91-73071. 202p. 1991. 12.94 (1-56239-030-9) Abdo & Dghtrs.

Wheeler, Joan & Carter, Sharon. Brain Benders. 48p. (gr. 4-6). 1982. 5.95 (0-88160-048-2, LW 234) Learning Wks.

Wheeler, Jody, illus. The First Noel. LC 92-14438. 32p. 1992. 13.95 (0-8249-8565-6, Ideals Child) Hambleton-Hill.

Wheeler, Kim. Loves of the Cat: An Illustrated Anthology of Old & Modern Cat Poems. Wheeler, Kim, ed. LC 85-63189. (Illus.). 101p. (Orig.). (gr. 5 up). 1985. pap. 5.75 (0-9615937-0-9) Star City Pubns.

Wheeler, Leslie & Peacock, Judith. Events That Changed American History. Gerstle, Gary, contrib. by. LC 93-19007. (Illus.). 48p. (gr. 5-7). 1993. PLB 22.80 (0-8114-4927-0) Raintree Steck-V.

Wheeler, Leslie A. Jane Addams. Gallin, Richard, ed. (Illus.). 144p. (gr. 5-9). 1990. PLB 13.98 (0-382-09962-1); pap. 7.95 (0-382-09968-0) Silver Burdett Pr.
—Rachel Carson. (Illus.). 144p. (gr. 5-9). 1991. PLB 13.98 (0-382-24167-3); pap. 7.95 (0-382-24174-6) Silver Burdett Pr.

Wheeler, Lonnie. Story of Micky Mantle. 1990. (S&S BFYR); pap. 3.95 (0-671-69094-9, S&S BFYR) S&S Trade.

Wheeler, M. J. First Came the Indians. Houston, James, illus. LC 82-13916. 32p. (gr. 1-5). 1983. SBE 12.95 (0-689-50258-3, M K McElderry) Macmillan Child Grp.

Wheeler, Penny, ed. see Baumgardner, Mary A.

Wheeler, Penny E., ed. Morning Riser. 384p. (gr. 3-6). 1988. 9.50 (0-8280-0457-9) Review & Herald.

Wheeler, Penny E., ed. see Maniscalco, Joe.

Wheeler, Penny E., ed. see Reece, Colleen L.

Wheeler, Penny E., ed. see Rizzo, Kay D.

Wheeler, Post. Vasilissa the Beautiful. (gr. 4-12). Date not set. 13.95 (0-88682-354-4, 97226-098) Creative Ed.

Wheeler, Sharon. Opposites. Richesson, Robin, illus. (ps). 1984. wkbk 1.95 (0-916119-05-X) Creat Teach Pr.
—Sequencing. Richesson, Robin, illus. (ps). 1984. wkbk 1.95 (0-916119-10-6) Creat Teach Pr.
—Shapes. Richesson, Robin, illus. (ps). 1984. wkbk 1.95 (0-916119-00-9) Creat Teach Pr.

Wheeler, Sharon, ed. Alphabet. Koeller, Neena C., illus. (ps). 1984. wkbk 1.95 (0-916119-02-5) Creat Teach Pr.
—Classification. Richesson, Robin, illus. (ps). 1984. wkbk 1.95 (0-916119-06-8) Creat Teach Pr.
—Colors. Koeller, Neena C., illus. (ps). 1984. wkbk 1.95 (0-916119-01-7) Creat Teach Pr.
—Life Skills. Koeller, Neena C., illus. (ps). 1984. wkbk 1.95 (0-916119-11-4) Creat Teach Pr.
—Number Skills. Richesson, Robin, illus. (ps). 1984. wkbk 1.95 (0-916119-04-1) Creat Teach Pr.
—Same-Different. Koeller, Nina C., illus. (ps). 1984. wkbk 1.95 (0-916119-07-6) Creat Teach Pr.
—Visual Skills. Richesson, Robin, illus. (ps). 1984. wkbk 1.95 (0-916119-08-4) Creat Teach Pr.

Wheeler, Sharon, ed. see Forman-Hitt, Kathy & Young, Janet.

Wheeler, Sharon, ed. see Forman-Hitt, Kathy & YOung, Janet.

Wheeler, Sharon, ed. see Forman-Hitt, Kathy & Young, Janet.

Wheeler, Sharon, ed. see Garafalo, Lorraine.

Wheeler, Thomas G. All Men Tall. LC 70-77313. (gr. 8 up). 1969. 21.95 (0-87599-157-2) S G Phillips.
—Fanfare for the Stalwart. LC 67-22813. (gr. 8 up). 1967. 21.95 (0-87599-139-4) S G Phillips.
—Loose Chippings. LC 69-11990. (Illus.). (gr. 10 up). 1969. 21.95 (0-87599-152-1) S G Phillips.
—Lost Threshold. LC 68-16349. (Illus.). (gr. 7 up). 1968. 21.95 (0-87599-140-8) S G Phillips.

Wheelis, Mark, jt. auth. see Gonick, Larry.

Wheelus, Doris. Baton Twirling: A Complete Illustrated Guide. Bolle, Frank, illus. 144p. (gr. 5 up). 1975. PLB 11.95 (0-87460-310-2); pap. 7.95 (0-87460-311-0) Lion Bks.

Whelan, Gloria. Bringing the Farmhouse Home. LC 91-1641. (ps-3). 1992. pap. 15.00 (0-671-74984-6, S&S BFYR) S&S Trade.
—Goodbye, Vietnam. LC 91-3660. 112p. (gr. 3-7). 1992. 13.00 (0-679-82263-1); PLB 13.99 (0-679-92263-6) Knopf Bks Yng Read.
—Goodbye, Vietnam. LC 91-3660. 144p. (gr. 3-7). 1993. pap. 3.99 (0-679-82376-X) Random Bks Yng Read.
—Hannah. Bowman, Lealie, illus. LC 90-39554. 64p. (gr. 2-4). 1991. 10.95 (0-679-81397-7) Knopf Bks Yng Read.
—Hannah. Bowman, Leslie, illus. LC 92-24243. 64p. (gr. 2-4). 1993. RLB 11.99 (0-679-91397-1); pap. 2.50 (0-679-82698-X) Random Bks Yng Read.
—Next Spring an Oriole. Johnson, Pamela, illus. LC 87-4910. 64p. (gr. 2-4). 1987. lib. bdg. 6.99 (0-394-99125-7); pap. 1.95 (0-394-89125-2) Random Bks Yng Read.
—Night of the Full Moon. Bowman, Leslie, illus. LC 93-6706. 64p. (gr. 2-4). 1993. 13.00 (0-679-84464-3); PLB 13.99 (0-679-94464-8) Knopf Bks Yng Read.
—Silver. Marchesi, Stephen, illus. LC 87-26612. 64p. (Orig.). (gr. 2-4). 1988. lib. bdg. 5.99 (0-394-99611-9); 2.50 (0-394-89611-4) Random Bks Yng Read.
—Time to Keep Silent. (gr. 4-7). 1993. pap. 7.99 (0-8028-0118-8) Eerdmans.

—A Week of Raccoons. Munsinger, Lynn, illus. LC 87-16800. 40p. (ps-1). 1988. PLB 12.99 (0-394-98396-3) Knopf Bks Yng Read.

Whelchel, Sandy. Coloring Book of Pikes Peak Country: Follow the Pikes Peak Trail & See the Wonders of the Area. Brandt, Bill, illus. 38p. (Orig.). (gr. k-4). 1989. pap. 3.50 (1-878406-01-9) Parker Dstb.
—A Day in Blue: Follow Freddy Falcon on a Child's Tour of the U. S. Air Force Academy. Brandt, Bill, illus. 28p. (gr. k-4). 1986. pap. 2.95 (1-878406-00-0) Parker Dstb.
—Mile High Denver: Coloring Book. Brandt, Bill, illus. 30p. (Orig.). (gr. k-4). 1987. pap. 3.50 (0-685-29912-0) Parker Dstb.

Where's Waldo, Inc. Staff. Where's Waldo? Waldo in Dinoland. 16p. (ps-2). 1993. write for info. (1-883366-13-5) YES Ent.

Whicher, Stephen, ed. see Emerson, Ralph Waldo.

Whieldon, Tony. Fishing. Ashby, David, illus. LC 93-22781. 1994. 13.00 (0-679-83442-7); lib. bdg. 13.99 (0-679-93442-1) Random.

Whipple, A. B. Restless Oceans. (Illus.). 176p. (gr. 7 up). 1983. 18.60 (0-8094-4340-6); lib. bdg. 24.60 (0-8094-4341-4) Time-Life.

Whipple, Laura, compiled by. Celebrating America: A Collection of Poems & Images of the American Spirit. LC 92-26197. (Illus.). 1993. write for info. (0-399-22036-4, Philomel Bks) Putnam Pub Group.

Whishaw, Iona. Henry & the Cow Problem. McLeod, Chum, illus. (ps-1). 1992. 0.99 (1-55037-254-8, Pub. by Annick Pr) Firefly Bks Ltd.

Whitaker, Alexander. Dream Sister. 160p. (gr. k-6). 1989. pap. 2.95 (0-440-40156-9, YB) Dell.

Whitaker, Janet. Visiting Junjun & Meimei in China. (Illus.). 32p. (gr. 3-7). 1988. 10.95 (0-521-34575-8) Cambridge U Pr.

Whitcher, Susan. Moonfall. (ps-3). 1993. 14.00 (0-374-35056-6) FS&G.
—Real Mummies Don't Bleed: Friendly Tales for October Nights. (gr. 4-7). 1993. 15.00 (0-374-36213-0) FS&G.

Whitcomb, Norma A. Those Mysterious Dinosaurs: A Biblical Approach for Children, Their Parents & Their Teachers. 2nd ed. Job, Heather H., illus. Wyrtzen, Jack, frwd. by. (Illus.). 125p. (gr. 4 up). 1993. Spiral bdg. pap. 7.20x (0-685-67781-8); pap. text ed. 11.99 (0-9635049-0-8) Whitcomb Minist. Dino Mania has hit again! Children need to know that there is an alternative to the evolutionary, millions-of-years theory with which they are being bombarded. The pictures are designed to capture children's eyes & minds while the understandable text is substantiated with, "Thus said the Lord." Adults will be impacted & fascinated, as well, as they interpret captivating Biblical & scientific truths to curious young ones. Where did the dinosaurs come from? When were they here? Why aren't they around anymore? These are only a few of the baffling questions the book answers from God's Word. "Well researched & of scholarly excellence. A must for every school library, classroom, home." --Dr. Henry Morris, Pres., Institute for Creation Research. "An intriguing glimpse of those fascinating creatures from the creation-science point of view. ..well written."--Ellen Linduall, author. Also available in the set: A Christian video for children: DINOSAURS. To order contact: Whitcomb Ministries, Inc., BO, P.O. Box 277, Winona Lake, IN 46590-0277. *Publisher Provided Annotation.*

Whitcraft, John E., jt. auth. see Rosenberg, R. Robert.

White. Deinosuchus. (Illus.). 24p. 1984. PLB 14.00 (0-86592-524-0) Rourke Enter.
—Pachycephalosaurus. (Illus.). 24p. 1984. PLB 14.00 (0-86592-526-7) Rourke Enter.
—Parasaurolophus. (Illus.). 24p. 1984. PLB 14.00 (0-86592-529-1) Rourke Enter.

White & Swann. Dinosaur Library, 6 bks, Set V. (Illus.). 144p. 1984. Set. PLB write for info. (0-86592-523-2) Rourke Enter.
—Dinosaur Library, 6 bks, Set IV. (Illus.). 144p. 1989. Set. PLB write for info. (0-86592-516-X) Rourke Enter.

White, Alana. Come Next Spring. LC 89-37156. 170p. (gr. 6 up). 1990. 13.95 (0-395-52593-4, Clarion Bks) HM.

White, Carl P. Citizen Soldier: Opportunities in the Reserves. Rosen, Ruth, ed. (gr. 7-12). 1990. PLB 14.95 (0-8239-1023-7) Rosen Group.

White, Carolyn. The Children Who Lived in a Tree. Kromer, Christiane, illus. LC 92-46428. 1994. pap. 14.00 (0-671-79818-9, S&S BFYR) S&S Trade.

White, Celeste. The Legend of the Flying Hotdog. (Illus.). 32p. 1991. 11.95 (0-88138-131-4, Green Tiger) S&S Trade.

White, Cristine A. Matthew's Allowance. LC 89-51091. 44p. (gr. k-3). 1989. 5.95 (1-55523-249-3) Winston-Derek.

White, Curlie. Children's First Action Words. rev. ed. (gr. k-2). 1992. 7.95 (0-8062-4125-X) Carlton.

White, D. Anatosaurus. (Illus.). 24p. (gr. 3 up). 1989. PLB 14.60 (0-86592-520-8) Rourke Corp.
—Helicopters. (Illus.). 48p. (gr. 3-8). 1989. PLB 18.60 (0-86592-451-1); 13.95s.p. (0-685-58295-7) Rourke Corp.
—Rutiodon. (Illus.). 24p. (gr. 3 up). 1989. PLB 14.60 (0-86592-522-4); 10.95s.p. (0-685-58284-1) Rourke Corp.
—Scolosaurus. (Illus.). 24p. (gr. 3 up). 1989. PLB 14.60 (0-86592-519-4); 10.95 (0-685-58286-8) Rourke Corp.
—Spinosaurus. (Illus.). 24p. (gr. 3 up). 1989. PLB 14.60 (0-86592-517-8); PLB 10.95s.p. (0-685-58287-6) Rourke Corp.
—Submarines. (Illus.). 48p. (gr. 3-8). 1989. PLB 18.60 (0-86592-452-X) Rourke Corp.

White, Dana. High-Rise Workers. LC 88-11991. (Illus.). 48p. (gr. 5-6). 1988. RSBE 11.95 (0-89686-402-2, Crestwood Hse) Macmillan Child Grp.

White Deer of Autumn Staff. Native American Book of Knowledge. Roehm, Michelle, ed. (Illus.). 96p. (gr. 5-7). 1992. pap. 4.95 (0-941831-42-6) Beyond Words Pub.
—The Native American Book of Life. Roehm, Michelle, ed. (Illus.). 96p. (gr. 5-7). 1992. pap. 4.95 (0-941831-43-4) Beyond Words Pub.

White, Don. Poop Decks & Periwinkles: Emily & Jason Explore San Diego. LC 91-66464. 112p. (gr. 3-6). 1991. pap. 12.95 (0-942259-06-8) Westerfield Enter.

White, E. B. Charlotte's Web. Williams, Garth, illus. LC 52-9760. (gr. 3-6). 1952. 13.00 (0-06-026385-7); PLB 12.89 (0-06-026386-5) HarpC Child Bks.
—Charlotte's Web. LC 52-9760. (Illus.). 1974. pap. 3.95 (0-06-440055-7, Trophy) HarpC Child Bks.
—Charlotte's Web. (Illus.). 192p. (ps-8). 1990. Repr. lib. bdg. 21.95x (0-89966-696-5) Buccaneer Bks.
—E. B. White Boxed Set. Incl. Charlotte's Web; The Trumpet of the Swan; Stuart Little. (Illus.). (gr. 3 up). 1972. 39.00 (0-06-026399-7) HarpC Child Bks.
—E. B. White Boxed Set. Incl. Charlotte's Web; The Trumpet of the Swan; Stuart Little. (Illus.). (gr. 3 up). 1974. pap. 11.85 (0-06-440061-1, Trophy) HarpC Child Bks.
—Stuart Little. Williams, Garth, illus. LC 45-9585. 132p. (gr. 3-6). 1945. 13.00 (0-06-026395-4); PLB 12.89 (0-06-026396-2) HarpC Child Bks.
—Stuart Little. LC 45-9585. (Illus.). 132p. (gr. 3-7). 1974. pap. 3.95 (0-06-440056-5, Trophy) HarpC Child Bks.
—Tela Charlottae. Fox, Bernice, tr. Williams, Garth, illus. LC 90-55691. (LAT.). 256p. (gr. 2 up). 1991. 18.95 (0-06-026401-2) HarpC Child Bks.
—Trumpet of the Swan. Frascino, Edward, illus. LC 72-112484. (gr. 3-6). 1970. 13.00 (0-06-026397-0); PLB 12.89 (0-06-026398-9) HarpC Child Bks.
—The Trumpet of the Swan. Frascino, Edward, illus. LC 72-112484. 222p. (gr. 3 up). 1973. pap. 3.95 (0-06-440048-4, Trophy) HarpC Child Bks.

White, E. G. Christ Our Savior. (Illus.). 160p. (gr. 5 up). 1989. pap. 8.95 (0-945460-05-8) Upward Way.
—Christ Our Savior. (SPA., Illus.). 176p. (gr. 5 up). 1990. pap. 8.95 (0-945460-10-4) Upward Way.

White, Edwin C., et al. Acting & Stage Movement. Zapel, Michelle, illus. Wolfit, Donald, intro. by. LC 85-60573. (Illus.). 193p. (gr. 11-12). 1985. pap. text ed. 9.95 (0-916260-30-5, B187) Meriwether Pub.

White, Ellen E. Bo Jackson: Playing the Games. (Illus.). 96p. (Orig.). (gr. 3-7). 1990. pap. 2.95 (0-590-44075-6) Scholastic Inc.
—Friends for Life. 176p. (gr. 7 up). 1983. pap. 2.95 (0-380-82578-3, Flare) Avon.
—Life Without Friends. 256p. (gr. 7 up). 1988. pap. 3.25 (0-590-44628-2) Scholastic Inc.
—Long Live the Queen. (gr. 7 up). 1989. pap. 13.95 (0-590-40850-X) Scholastic Inc.
—Long Live the Queen. 1990. pap. 2.95 (0-590-40851-8) Scholastic Inc.
—Shaquille O'Neal. (gr. 8-12). 1994. pap. 2.95 (0-590-47785-4, Apple Paperbacks) Scholastic Inc.
—White House Autumn. (Orig.). (gr. 7 up). 1985. pap. 2.95 (0-380-89780-6, Flare) Avon.

White, Florence. Father Junipero Serra & the American. (Orig.). (gr. k-6). 1987. pap. 3.25 (0-440-42495-X, YB) Dell.

White, Frank, jt. auth. see Asimov, Isaac.

White, Frank, jt. auth. see Terrell, Sandy.

White, Glenn E. Folk Tales of Connecticut, Vol. I. Zangari, Rose M., illus. 61p. (Orig.). (gr. k-12). 1977. pap. 6.50 (0-9611926-0-7) GEF White.
—Folk Tales of Connecticut, Vol. II. Zangari, Rose M., illus. 62p. (gr. k-12). 1981. pap. 6.50 (0-9611926-1-5) GEF White.

White, Gregory. Emergency Childbirth: A Manual for the Non-Medically Trained. 2nd ed. Carson, Gordon, et al, eds. (Illus.). 64p. (gr. 12). 1993. Repr. of 1958 ed. spiral wire bdg. 15.95 (0-934426-57-0) NAPSAC Reprods.

White, J. Edson. Best Stories from the Best Book: And Thou Shalt Teach Them Diligently Unto Thy Children. (Illus.). 160p. (gr. 5 up). 1990. pap. 8.95 (0-945460-06-6) Upward Way.
—The Story of Joseph: From Shepherd Boy to a Ruler of Egypt. (Illus.). (gr. 3 up). 1990. pap. 4.95 (0-945460-07-4) Upward Way.

White, James E. The Triumphs of Trisha & Tripod: Tripod Finds a Home. Senf, Richard L., illus. 22p. 1991. pap. 7.95 (0-9629102-0-1) Pyramid TX.

White, Jesse. A Rime of Verdancy: Poems of Nature. Farr, Gina, illus. (Orig.). (gr. 12). Date not set. pap. 7.95 (0-9637176-9-3) Jesse White.

White, Joe. Looking for Love in All the Wrong Places. rev. & updated ed. 1991. pap. 3.95 (0-8423-3829-2) Tyndale.
—Over the Edge & Back. 192p. (gr. 8-12). 1992. pap. 7.99 (0-945564-58-9, Gold & Honey) Questar Pubs.
—Who Are My Real Friends; Peer Pressure: A Teen Survival Guide. 1992. pap. 7.99 (0-945564-40-6, Gold & Honey) Questar Pubs.

White, John. Gaal the Conqueror. Stockman, Jack, illus. LC 89-19821. 320p. (Orig.). (gr. 7-9). 1989. pap. 10.99 (0-87784-591-3, 591) InterVarsity.
—The Iron Sceptre. LC 80-36727. (Illus.). 408p. (Orig.). (gr. 4-7). 1981. pap. 10.99 (0-87784-589-1, 589) InterVarsity.
—The Sword Bearer. LC 86-2860. (Illus.). 295p. (Orig.). (gr. 4 up). 1986. pap. 10.99 (0-87784-590-5, 590) InterVarsity.
—The Tower of Geburah. LC 78-2078. (Illus.). 404p. (gr. 4 up). 1978. pap. 10.99 (0-87784-560-3, 560) InterVarsity.

White, John S., ed. see Plutarch.

White, Joseph A. The Three Little Mousies. LC 93-70959. 20p. (gr. k-3). 1993. pap. 3.95 (0-9636278-0-5) White DEI.

White, Judith. Summer Talk: Phrase-a-Day French for Families. Macbain, Carol, illus. (gr. ps-6). 1986. wkbk. 6.25 (0-937531-01-4) Fgn Lang Young Child.

White, Kathleen. Jim Elliott. 128p. (gr. 8 up). 1990. Repr. 4.99 (1-55661-125-0) Bethany Hse.

White, Kathy. Proverbs for Children. Haynes, Betty B., ed. Haynes, Rebecca, illus. 64p. (ps-3). 1985. pap. 6.95 (0-9616130-0-9) Naftaolh Pubns.

White, Larry & Broekel, Ray. Razzle Dazzle! Magic Tricks for You. Fay, Ann, ed. Seltzer, Meyer, illus. LC 87-6114. 48p. (gr. 3-8). 1987. PLB 11.95 (0-8075-6857-0) A Whitman.

White, Laurence, jt. auth. see Broekel, Ray.

White, Laurence B. Science Games & Puzzles. Brown, Marc T., illus. LC 84-40786. 1979. pap. 4.95 (0-201-08606-9, Lipp Jr Bks) HarpC Child Bks.
—Science Toys & Tricks. Brown, Marc T., illus. LC 84-40787. 1980. pap. 4.95 (0-201-08659-X, Lipp Jr Bks) HarpC Child Bks.

White, Laurence B., Jr. Science Games & Puzzles. Brown, Marc T., illus. LC 85-43035. 96p. (gr. 1-4). 1985. pap. 6.95 (0-06-446013-4, Trophy) HarpC Child Bks.
—Science Toys & Tricks. Brown, Marc T., illus. LC 85-43036. 96p. (gr. 1-4). 1985. pap. 6.95 (0-06-446014-2, Trophy) HarpC Child Bks.

White, Laurence B., Jr. & Broekel, Ray. Math-a-Magic: Number Tricks for Magicians. Mathews, Judith, ed. Seltzer, Meyer, illus. LC 89-35395. 48p. (gr. 3-6). 1990. 11.95 (0-8075-4994-0) A Whitman.
—Shazam! Simple Science Magic. Mathews, Judith, ed. Seltzer, Meyer, illus. LC 90-42441. 48p. (gr. 3-7). 1991. 11.95 (0-8075-7332-9) A Whitman.

White, Laurence B., Jr., jt. auth. see Broekel, Ray.

White, Laurie A. & Spencer, Steven L. Take Care with Yourself: A Young Person's Guide to Understanding, Preventing & Healing from the Hurts of Child Abuse. Cohen, Alice E., illus. 36p. (Orig.). (gr. k-7). 1983. English edition. pap. 5.95 (0-9612024-0-8); pap. Spanish edition avail. White & Spencer.

White, Lawrence B. & Broekel, Ray. Optical Illusions. Green, Anne C., illus. LC 86-10986. (gr. 4-9). 1986. PLB 10.90 (0-531-10220-3) Watts.

White, Logan, jt. auth. see McGuire, Barry.

White, Lori G., ed. see Miss Lori.

White, Marjorie L. Downtown Discovery Tour. rev. ed. (Illus.). 44p. (Orig.). (gr. 3-9). 1984. pap. 5.00 (0-317-42237-5) Birmingham Hist Soc.

White, Marjorie L. & Shannon, Katherine. Five Points Heritage Hike Guide. (Illus.). 32p. (Orig.). (gr. 3-9). 1983. pap. 2.00 (0-685-11943-2) Birmingham Hist Soc.

White, Nancy B. Meet John F. Kennedy. (Illus.). (gr. 2-5). 1965. 7.99 (0-394-80059-1) Random Bks Yng Read.
—Meet John F. Kennedy. LC 93-20057. 80p. (gr. 2-6). 1993. pap. 2.99 (0-679-83601-2) Random Bks Yng Read.

White, Paulette C. Love Poem to a Black Junkie. 37p. (gr. 7-12). 1975. pap. 4.00x (0-916418-04-9) Lotus.
—The Watermelon Dress: Portrait of a Woman. LC 83-82773. (Illus.). 61p. (gr. 7-12). 1984. pap. 6.00 (0-916418-53-7) Lotus.

White, Peter. Disabled People. LC 88-83085. (Illus.). 64p. (gr. 7-9). 1990. 12.40 (0-531-17146-9) Watts.

White, Rolf. The Last Word on Making Money. 288p. (Orig.). 1988. text ed. 17.95 (0-8184-0475-2); pap. 9.95 (0-8184-0480-9) Carol Pub Group.

White, Ruth. Sweet Creek Holler. 168p. (gr. 7 up). 1988. 16.00 (0-374-37360-4) FS&G.
—Sweet Creek Holler. (gr. 4-7). 1992. pap. 4.50 (0-374-47375-7) FS&G.
—Weeping Willow. 256p. (gr. 7 up). 1992. 16.00 (0-374-38255-7) FS&G.

White, Ryan & Cunningham, Ann M. Ryan White: My Own Story. (Illus.). 144p. (gr. 5 up). 1991. 16.95 (0-8037-0977-3) Dial Bks Young.

White, Sandra & Filisky, Michael. Sterling: The Rescue of a Baby Harbor Seal. (Illus.). 32p. (gr. 2-4). 1988. PLB 14.95 (0-517-57112-9) Crown Bks Yng Read.

White, Sarah g. Like Father, Like Son: Baseball's Major League Families. (gr. 4-7). 1993. pap. 2.95 (0-590-46027-7) Scholastic Inc.

White, Stephen. Baby Bop Discovers Shapes. Hartley, Linda, ed. Daste, Larry, illus. 20p. (ps-k). 1993. 4.95 (0-7829-0372-X) Barney Pub.
—Barney & Baby Bop: A Tent Too Full. Hartley, Linda, ed. Alger, Bill, illus. 24p. (ps-k). 1993. pap. 2.25 (0-7829-0378-9) Barney Pub.
—Barney's Favorite Mother Goose Rhymes, Vol. 1. Hartley, Linda, ed. Eubank, Mary G., illus. 32p. (ps-k). 1993. 7.95 (0-7829-0336-3) Barney Pub.
—Barney's Favorite Mother Goose Rhymes, Vol. 2. 1994. 7.95 (1-57064-012-2) Barney Pub.
—Barney's Favorite Mother Goose Rhymes, Vol. 2. Hartley, Linda, ed. Eubank, Mary G., illus. 32p. (ps-k). 1993. 7.95 (0-7829-0380-0) Barney Pub.

White, Stephen, ed. see Shrode, Mary.

White, Susan. Bad Baby-Sitter's Handbook. (gr. 4-7). 1992. pap. 2.99 (0-440-40633-1, YB) Dell.

White, Sylvia. Home Is Best. Weinberger, Jane & Black, Albert, eds. DeVito, Pamela, illus. LC 88-50315. 44p. (gr. 1-4). 1988. pap. 3.95 (0-932433-48-0) Windswept Hse.

White, T. H. The Book of Merlyn: The Unpublished Conclusion to "The Once & Future King." (Illus.). 159p. (gr. 10). 1988. pap. 10.95 (0-292-70769-X) U of Tex Pr.

White, Terence. What Happened to Sherlock Holmes? as Set to Rest In... The Legend of Wilson-The Amazing Athlete. Blackburn, Francis, et al, eds. Meade, Javier & Jamieson, Lindsey, illus. Barton, Hill, intro. by. LC 83-51870. 102p. 1984. 9.95 (0-9612698-0-4) Seagull Pub Co.

White, Terence H. The Sword in the Stone. Nolan, Dennis, illus. LC 92-24808. 256p. 1993. 18.95 (0-399-22502-1, Philomel Bks) Putnam Pub Group.

White, Theodore H. The Sword in the Stone. 288p. (gr. 7 up). 1978. pap. 3.99 (0-440-98445-9, LE) Dell.

White, Timothy. Nearest Faraway Place. 1994. 22.50 (0-8050-2266-X) H Holt & Co.

White, Valerie. **Choosing Your Children's Books: Beginning Readers 5 to 8 Years Old.** White, Trevor, illus. 32p. (Orig.). (gr. k-3). 1993. pap. 4.95 (1-882726-00-6) Bayley & Musgrave. CHOOSING YOUR CHILDREN'S BOOKS is a series of INEXPENSIVE, EASY-TO-USE guides to the best in children's literature, intended for teachers, parents, grandparents & children. BEGINNING READERS is the first in the series, & selects over 100 of the best books ever, for 5 to 8 year-olds. Selections are arranged in themes, such as EASY READERS, EVERYDAY LIFE & HUMOROUS, each lightly illustrated. Chosen from the classics, award winners & modern stories for today, each book is identified by title, author, publisher & ISBN number for loan request or purchase. Major awards such as Newbery & Caldecott are identified, & a brief outline of the story is given to help the reader choose. A full author & title index is provided. "A fabulous, concise guide...I am most impressed with the scope - from brand new titles to children's classics. Many multi-cultural authors & stories are included."--KATHLEEN SHELNUTT, Elementary School Media Specialist. "This book makes shopping for books a joy - many great classics, & so easy to find! A great resource."--ANNETTE SAVAGE, Owner of the National Award-winning store THE TOY SCHOOL, Atlanta,

GA. Bayley & Musgrave, 4949 Trailridge Pass, Atlanta, GA 30338. (404) 668-9738 or Baker & Taylor. *Publisher Provided Annotation.*

—Choosing Your Children's Books: Eight to Twelve Years Old. (Illus.). 80p. (Orig.). (gr. 3-7). 1994. 13.95 (*1-882726-14-6*); pap. 5.95 (*1-882726-12-X*) Bayley & Musgrave.

White, William, Jr. All about the Frog. LC 91-40812. (Illus.). 72p. (gr. 7-12). 1992. 14.95 (*0-8069-8274-8*) Sterling.
—All about the Turtle. LC 91-41301. (Illus.). 72p. (gr. 7-12). 1992. 14.95 (*0-8069-8276-4*) Sterling.

White Deer of Autumn. Ceremony-In the Circle of Life. San Souci, Daniel, illus. LC 83-7353. 32p. (gr. 3-6). 1983. PLB 14.65 (*0-940742-24-1*) Raintree Steck-V.
—Ceremony in the Circle of Life. San Souci, Daniel, illus. 32p. (gr. 2-6). 1991. pap. 6.95 (*0-941831-68-X*) Beyond Words Pub.
—The Great Change. (Illus.). 36p. (gr. k-5). 1992. 13.95 (*0-941831-79-5*) Beyond Words Pub.
—The Native American Book of Change. Begay, Shonto W., illus. LC 92-17001. 1992. write for info. (*0-941831-73-6*) Beyond Words Pub.
—The Native American Book of Wisdom. Begay, Shonto W., illus. LC 92-17002. 1992. 4.95 (*0-941831-74-4*) Beyond Words Pub.

Whitefeather, Willy. Willy Whitefeather's Outdoor Survival Handbook for Kids. Whitefeather, Willy, illus. LC 89-26929. 104p. (Orig.). (gr. 3 up). 1990. pap. 9.95 (*0-943173-47-7*) Harbinger AZ.
—Willy Whitefeather's River Book for Kids. Whitefeather, Willy, illus. 88p. (Orig.). (gr. 1-8). 1994. pap. write for info. (*0-943173-94-9*) Harbinger AZ.

Whitehead, Albert C. The Standard Bearer: A Story of Army Life in the Time of Caesar. (Illus.). (gr. 7-11). 1943. 20.00 (*0-8196-0116-0*) Biblo.

Whitehead, Arthur K. Odyssey of a Philippine Scout. (Illus.). 315p. (Orig.). 1989. pap. text ed. 11.95 (*0-9624089-0-5*) Whitehead Pub.

Whitehead, Nathalie W. Dear Mrs. Witch. 1992. 7.95 (*0-533-10268-5*) Vantage.

Whitehead, Pat. The Nutcracker. Rich, Beverly, illus. LC 87-10916. 32p. (gr. k-4). 1988. PLB 9.79 (*0-8167-1063-5*); pap. text ed. 1.95 (*0-8167-1064-3*) Troll Assocs.

Whitehead, Patricia. Arnold Plays Baseball. Karas, Brian, illus. LC 84-8827. 32p. (gr. k-2). 1985. PLB 11.59 (*0-8167-0367-1*); pap. text ed. 2.95 (*0-8167-0368-X*) Troll Assocs.
—Best Halloween Book. Britt, Stephanie, illus. LC 84-8828. 32p. (gr. k-2). 1985. PLB 11.59 (*0-8167-0373-6*); pap. text ed. 2.95 (*0-8167-0374-4*) Troll Assocs.
—Best Thanksgiving Book. Hall, Susan T., illus. LC 84-8831. 32p. (gr. k-2). 1985. PLB 11.59 (*0-8167-0371-X*); pap. text ed. 2.95 (*0-8167-0372-8*) Troll Assocs.
—Best Valentine Book. Harvy, Paul, illus. LC 84-8829. 32p. (gr. k-2). 1985. PLB 11.59 (*0-8167-0369-8*); pap. text ed. 2.95 (*0-8167-0370-1*) Troll Assocs.
—Christmas Alphabet Book. Borgo, Deborah C., illus. LC 84-8830. 32p. (gr. k-2). 1985. PLB 11.59 (*0-8167-0365-5*); pap. text ed. 2.95 (*0-8167-0366-3*) Troll Assocs.
—Dinosaur Alphabet Book. Snyder, Joel, illus. LC 84-8839. 32p. (gr. k-2). 1985. PLB 11.59 (*0-8167-0363-9*); pap. text ed. 2.95 (*0-8167-0364-7*) Troll Assocs.
—Here Comes Hungry Albert. Karas, G. Brian, illus. LC 84-8835. 32p. (gr. k-2). 1985. PLB 11.59 (*0-8167-0379-5*); pap. text ed. 2.95 (*0-8167-0380-9*) Troll Assocs.
—Let's Go to the Farm. Gold, Ethel, illus. LC 84-8834. 32p. (gr. k-2). 1985. lib. bdg. 11.59 (*0-8167-0377-9*); pap. 2.95 (*0-8167-0378-7*) Troll Assocs.
—Let's Go to the Zoo. Boyd, Patti, illus. LC 84-8832. 32p. (gr. k-2). 1985. PLB 11.59 (*0-8167-0375-2*); pap. text ed. 2.95 (*0-8167-0376-0*) Troll Assocs.
—Monkeys. Dodson, Bert, illus. LC 81-11439. 32p. (gr. k-2). 1982. PLB 11.59 (*0-89375-670-9*); pap. text ed. 2.95 (*0-89375-671-7*) Troll Assocs.
—What a Funny Bunny. Page, Don, illus. LC 84-8833. 32p. (gr. k-2). 1985. PLB 11.59 (*0-8167-0361-2*); pap. text ed. 2.95 (*0-8167-0362-0*) Troll Assocs.

Whitehead, Robert J. The Early School Years Read Aloud Program (Fall) LC 74-14891. 104p. (gr. k-2). 1975. 12.95 (*0-88280-028-0*); pap. 12.95 (*0-88280-029-9*) ETC Pubns.

Whitelaw, Nancy. A Beautiful Pearl. Tucker, Kathleen, ed. Friedman, Judith, illus. LC 90-28761. 32p. (gr. 2-5). 1991. 13.95 (*0-8075-0599-4*) A Whitman.
—Charles de Gaulle: I Am France. LC 91-13095. (Illus.). 112p. (gr. 4-6). 1991. RSBE 13.95 (*0-87518-486-3*, Dillon) Macmillan Child Grp.
—Josef Stalin: From Peasant to Premier. LC 92-5747. (Illus.). 160p. (gr. 5 up). 1992. RSBE 13.95 (*0-87518-557-6*, Dillon) Macmillan Child Grp.
—Margaret Sanger: Every Child a Wanted Child. LC 93-13635. (Illus.). 128p. (gr. 5). 1994. RSBE 13.95 (*0-87518-581-9*, Dillon) Macmillan Child Grp.
—Theodore Roosevelt Takes Charge. Levine, Abby, ed. LC 90-29181. 192p. (gr. 4-8). 1992. 11.95 (*0-8075-7849-5*) A Whitman.

Whiteley, Opal. Opal: The Journal of an Understanding Heart. Boulton, Jane, adapted by. LC 84-2418. (Illus.). 190p. (gr. 4 up). 1984. Repr. of 1976 ed. 14.95 (*0-935382-52-6*) Tioga Pub Co.

Whiteside, Kay H., jt. auth. see Healton, Sarah H.

Whiteside, Kay H., jt. ed. see Healton, Sarah H.

Whiteside, Rita G., jt. auth. see Whiteside, Sandra.

Whiteside, Sandra & Whiteside, Rita G. Primary Writing Fun. Whiteside, Saundra & Whiteside, Rita, illus. 80p. (gr. 1-3). 1983. wkbk. 8.95 (*0-86653-101-7*, GA 461) Good Apple.

Whitfield, Joanne, ed. see Whitfield, Vallie J.

Whitfield, Karen & Tackett, Eric. I Didn't Know Cops Did Things Like That. Hunsinger, Ruth A., ed. Whitfield, Karen, illus. 20p. (gr. k up). 1988. PLB 2.95 (*0-943155-03-7*) Laser Tech.

Whitfield, Philip. Macmillan Children's Guide to Dinosaurs & Other Prehistoric Animals. LC 91-45562. (Illus.). 96p. (gr. 2 up). 1992. SBE 16.95 (*0-02-762362-9*, Macmillan Child Bk) Macmillan Child Grp.
—Why Did the Dinosaurs Disappear? Questions about Life in the Past. 1991. 16.95 (*0-670-84055-6*) Viking Child Bks.

Whitfield, Philip & Pope, Joyce. Why Do the Seasons Change? Questions on Nature's Rhythms & Cycles Answered by the Natural History Museum. LC 87-40133. 96p. (ps up). 1987. pap. 16.95 (*0-670-81860-7*) Viking Child Bks.

Whitfield, Phillip. Why Do Volcanoes Erupt? Questions about Our Unique Planet. 1990. 16.95 (*0-670-83385-1*) Viking Child Bks.

Whitfield, Vallie J. Heritage History. 2nd ed. Whitfield, Joanne, ed. LC 87-50112. (Illus.). 265p. (gr. 10 up). 1988. 25.00 (*0-930920-19-8*) Whitfield Bks.

Whitin, David J. & Wilde, Sandra. Read Any Good Math Lately? Children's Books for Mathematical Learning, K-6. Goodman, Kenneth S., frwd. by. (Illus.). 206p. (gr. k-6). 1992. pap. text ed. 18.50 (*0-435-08334-1*, 08334) Heinemann.

Whiting, Charles. The Home Front: Germany. LC 81-21406. (Illus.). 208p. (gr. 7 up). 1982. lib. bdg. 25.93 (*0-8094-3420-2*, 0-8094-257-6); pap. 19.93 (*0-8094-2508-4*) Time-Life.

Whiting, Frank. Huckleberry Finn. 1948. 4.50 (*0-87602-138-0*) Anchorage.

Whiting, Helen A. Negro Art, Music, & Rhyme. Jones, Lois M., illus. (gr. 2). 1990. 4.25 (*0-87498-005-4*) Assoc Pubs DC.
—Negro Folk Tales. Jones, Lois M., illus. (gr. 1). 1990. 4.25 (*0-87498-006-2*) Assoc Pubs DC.

Whiting, Roger. Crime & Punishment: A Study Across Time. LC 87-50949. 220p. (Orig.). (gr. 9-12). 1987. pap. text ed. 16.95 (*0-685-19579-1*, Pub. by S Thornes) Dufour.
—Religions for Today. 3rd, rev. & updated ed. (Illus.). 270p. 1991. pap. 21.00x (*0-7487-0586-4*, Pub. by S Thornes UK) Dufour.

Whitlatch, Issac. Me & My Veggies. Whitlatch, Issac, illus. LC 87-2920. 24p. (gr. 1-7). 1987. PLB 14.95 (*0-933849-16-8*) Landmark Edns.

Whitley, Marvin, ed. see Capes, Richard.

Whitley, Shirley H. Sometimes Life Ain't Sweet: Stories of Rural Black Youth. 72p. (Orig.). (gr. 4-9). 1993. pap. 7.95 (*0-9637271-0-9*) I B Bold Pubns.

Whitlock, Susan L. Donovan Scares the Monsters. Abolafia, Yossi, illus. LC 86-4783. 24p. (gr. k-3). 1987. 11.75 (*0-688-06438-8*); PLB 11.88 (*0-688-06439-6*) Greenwillow.

Whitman, Bernard. New York State Map Skills Resource Guide. Whitman, Shirley, illus. 85p. (Orig.). (gr. 4-7). 1984. tchr's. ed. 18.00 (*0-918433-00-2*) In Educ.

Whitman, Bernard, ed. see Job, Kenneth.

Whitman, Edmund S. Little Pax. Ely, Gladys, illus. LC 74-182528. 120p. (gr. 5-9). 1972. 3.75 (*0-8356-0428-4*, Quest) Theos Pub Hse.

Whitman, Ken & Wilkey, Chris. Mutazoids. Sumner, Robert, ed. Radford, Stephan, illus. 98p. (Orig.). (gr. 10-12). 1989. pap. text ed. 12.95 (*0-685-29088-3*) Whit Prodns.

Whitman, Patricia, ed. see Armstrong, Virgil.

Whitman, Sylvia. Hernando de Soto & the Explorers of the American South. Goetzmann, William H., ed. Collins, Michael, intro. by. (Illus.). 112p. (gr. 5 up). 1991. lib. bdg. 18.95 (*0-7910-1301-4*) Chelsea Hse.
—V Is for Victory: The American Homefront During World War II. (Illus.). 80p. (gr. 5-12). 1992. PLB 17.50 (*0-8225-1727-2*) Lerner Pubns.

Whitman, Walt. Complete Poetry & Selected Prose. Miller, J. E., Jr., ed. LC 59-2805. (gr. 9 up). 1972. pap. 9.16 (*0-395-05132-0*, RivEd) HM.
—I Hear America Singing. Sabuda, Robert, illus. 32p. (ps-3). 1991. 14.95 (*0-399-21808-4*, Philomel) Putnam Pub Group.
—Leaves of Grass. Gemme, F. R., intro. by. (gr. 11 up). 1965. pap. 1.95 (*0-8049-0091-4*, CL-91) Airmont.

Whitmer, Lisa H. & Hutchcraft, Ronald P. Letters from the College Front: Girls' Edition. 96p. (gr. 9-12). 1993. 7.99 (*0-8010-9722-3*) Baker Bk.

Whitmore, Arvella. Bread Winner. (gr. 4-7). 1990. 13.45 (*0-395-53705-3*) HM.

Whitney, Alex. Sports & Games the Indians Gave Us. Ostberg, Marie & Ostberg, Nils, illus. (gr. 7 up). 1977. 7.95 (*0-679-20391-5*) McKay.

Whitney, Dorothy A. Creatures of an Exceptional Kind. LC 88-34736. (Illus.). 32p. (ps up). 1989. 12.95 (*0-89334-127-4*) Humanics Ltd.

Whitney, Jan, ed. see Prairie-Plains Resource Institute Staff & Whitney, William S.

Whitney, Julie & Sheffield, Linda J. Adventures in Science & Math: Integrated Activities for Young Children. 96p. (gr. k-3). 1991. pap. text ed. 8.95 (*0-938587-18-8*) Cuisenaire.

Whitney, Marceil. Teenie Tennis: A Love Game. 72p. (Orig.). (ps up). 1991. pap. write for info. (*0-9629089-0-8*) ATS Pub.

Whitney, Phyllis. Mystery of the Hidden Hand. 1991. pap. 3.99 (*0-449-70365-7*) Fawcett.

Whitney, Phyllis A. Mystery on the Isle of Skye. 192p. 1991. pap. 3.95 (*0-449-70364-9*, Juniper) Fawcett.
—Secret of the Samurai Sword. 1992. pap. 3.99 (*0-449-70367-3*, Juniper) Fawcett.

Whitney, Sharon. Totty - Young Eleanor Roosevelt. (Orig.). 1992. pap. 5.50 playscript (*0-87602-306-5*) Anchorage.

Whitney, Thomas P., tr. see Marshak, Samuel.

Whitney, William S., jt. auth. see Prairie-Plains Resource Institute Staff.

Whittaker, Bibby. Bears & Pandas. (Illus.). 32p. (gr. 4-6). 1991. 13.95 (*0-237-60171-0*, Pub. by Evans Bros Ltd) Trafalgar.

Whittaker, Dorothy. Angels of the Swamp. 160p. (gr. 6-9). 1992. 17.95 (*0-8027-8129-2*) Walker & Co.

Whittell, Giles. The Story of the Three Whales. Benson, Patrick, illus. LC 88-35630. 29p. (gr. 2-4). 1988. PLB 15.93 (*0-8368-0092-3*) Gareth Stevens Inc.

Whittemore, Diane, jt. auth. see Tynes, Rick.

Whittier, John Greenleaf. Barbara Frietchie. Parker, Nancy W., illus. LC 90-41755. 32p. (gr. 1 up). 1992. 14.00 (*0-688-09829-0*); PLB 13.93 (*0-688-09830-4*) Greenwillow.

Whittington, Mary K. The Patchwork Lady. Yolen, Jane, ed. Dyer, Jane, illus. 32p. (ps-3). 1991. 13.95 (*0-15-259580-5*) HarBrace.
—Troll Games. Day, Betsy, illus. LC 90-83. 32p. (gr. k-3). 1991. SBE 13.95 (*0-689-31630-5*, Atheneum Child Bk) Macmillan Child Grp.
—Winter's Child. Brown, Sue E., illus. LC 91-25011. 32p. (ps-3). 1992. SBE 14.95 (*0-689-31685-2*, Atheneum Child Bk) Macmillan Child Grp.

Whittle, Emily. The Fisherman's Tale. Burdick, Jeri, illus. LC 91-17386. 32p. 1991. 10.95 (*0-671-74760-6*, Green Tiger) S&S Trade.
—Sailor Cats. Burdick, Jeri, illus. LC 92-23418. 1993. 14.00 (*0-671-79933-9*, Green Tiger) S&S Trade.

Whittlesey, Lee H. Yellowstone Place Names. Haynes, F. Jay, illus. Manns, Timothy R., intro. by. LC 88-21610. (Illus.). xiii, 179p. (Orig.). (gr. 8 up). 1988. pap. 11.95 (*0-917298-15-2*); unabr. microfiche 8.95 (*0-685-45314-6*) MT Hist Soc.

Whittley, Marjorie T. The Dragon Will Survive. LC 89-17585. 1991. 13.95 (*0-87949-315-1*) Ashley Bks.

Wholey, Ellen J., jt. auth. see Wallower, Lucille.

Wholey, Ellen J., ed. see Wallower, Lucille.

Whordley, Derek, jt. auth. see Caballero, Jane A.

Whorton, Brenda, jt. auth. see Wheat, Pam.

Whybrow, Ian. Quacky Quack-Quack! Ayto, Russell, illus. LC 91-8388. 32p. (gr. k up). 1991. SBE 13.95 (*0-02-792741-5*, Four Winds) Macmillan Child Grp.

Whyte, Mal. North American Wildlife Color & Story Album. Whyte, Mal, illus. 32p. 1972. pap. 4.50 (*0-8431-1735-4*) Price Stern.

Whyte, Malcolm. Butterflies. (Illus.). 32p. (Orig.). (gr. 1-4). 1989. pap. 2.95 (*0-8431-1962-4*) Price Stern.
—Dinosaur Action Set. (Illus.). 24p. (gr. 2 up). 1987. pap. 5.95 (*0-8431-1758-3*) Troubador Pr.
—Dolphins & Whales Model Set. Smith, Daniel, illus. 24p. (gr. 1 up). 1992. 5.95 (*0-8431-2993-X*) Price Stern.
—Farm Animals. (Illus.). 32p. (Orig.). (gr. 1-4). 1989. pap. 2.95 (*0-8431-1960-8*) Price Stern.
—Great Whales. (Illus.). (gr. 2 up). pap. 3.99 (*0-8431-1953-5*) Price Stern.
—North American Birdlife Color & Story Album. (gr. 2 up). pap. 4.50 (*0-8431-1730-3*) Price Stern.
—Sea Creatures. (Illus.). 32p. (Orig.). (gr. 1-4). pap. 3.50 (*0-8431-1959-4*) Price Stern.
—The Second Dinosaur Action Set. Smith, Dan, illus. 24p. (gr. 7-11). 1988. 5.95 (*0-8431-1951-9*) Price Stern.
—Undersea Dinosaur Action Set. Smith, Dan, illus. 24p. (gr. 1 up). 1988. 5.95 (*0-8431-1954-3*) Price Stern.
—Zoo Animals. (Illus.). 32p. (Orig.). (gr. 1-4). pap. 3.95 (*0-8431-1961-6*) Price Stern.

Whyte, Malcolm, jt. auth. see Smith, Dan.

Whyte, Margaret. TestMaster SAT Review. Horner, Jill, ed. 110p. (gr. 10-12). 1992. tchr's. ed. 49.00 (*1-883859-05-0*); wkbk. 12.00 (*1-883859-04-2*) Resource Netwrk.

Whyte, Margaret & Horner, Jill. TestMaster ACT Review. 175p. (gr. 10-12). 1993. pap. 12.00 (*1-883859-01-8*); tchr's. ed. 49.00 (*1-883859-02-6*) Resource Netwrk.

Wiands, Catherine. Positive Strokes for Little Folks, Vols. 1-7. 2nd ed. Ziebarth, Pat, ed. 32p. (Orig.). (gr. 1-6). 1983. pap. 2.50 (*0-943262-00-3*); Set of 7. pap. write for info. Transitions.

Wibbelsman, Charles, jt. auth. see McCoy, Kathy.

Wibberley, Leonard. John Treegate's Musket. LC 59-10188. 224p. (gr. 5 up). 1986. pap. 3.95 (*0-374-43788-2*, Sunburst) FS&G.
—Mouse That Roared. (gr. 6-12). 1971. pap. 3.50 (*0-553-24969-X*) Bantam.

Wicentowski, Deborah. The New York Express. Scheinberg, Shepsil, illus. 127p. (gr. 3-5). 1988. 8.95 (0-935063-46-3); pap. 6.95 (0-935063-47-1) CIS Comm.

Wichman, Juliet R. Moki Learns to Fish. 1981. pap. 4.75 (0-686-86236-8) Kauai Museum.

Wichterman, Catherine, adapted by. Lost Horizon. Nicholas, Charles, illus. 32p. (Orig.). (gr. 3-5). 1979. pap. text ed. 2.25 (0-88301-309-6) Pendulum Pr.

Wick, Karen, jt. auth. see Mehrens, Gloria.

Wick, Ruth N. Diminutive Dinney. 1993. 8.95 (0-8062-4423-2) Carlton.

Wick, Walter, jt. auth. see Marzollo, Jean.

Wicke, Ed. The Muselings. LC 91-13346. 160p. (gr. 3-7). 1991. pap. 5.99 (0-8308-1351-9, 1351) InterVarsity.
—The Screeps. LC 92-12259. (Illus.). 180p. 1992. pap. 5.99 (0-8308-1352-7, 1352) InterVarsity.

Wickenden, Martha. A Day in the Life of a Newspaper Reporter. Plunkett, Michael & French, Larry, photos by. LC 90-37547. (Illus.). 32p. (gr. 4-8). 1991. lib. bdg. 11.79 (0-8167-2214-5); pap. text ed. 2.95 (0-8167-2215-3) Troll Assocs.

Wickens, Elaine. Anna Day & the O-Ring. (Illus.). 24p. (gr. 4-7). 1994. saddlestitched 6.95 (1-55583-252-0, Alyson Wonderland) Alyson Pubns.

Wicker, Ireene. How the Ocelots Got Their Spots. Perrot, Catherine, illus. 32p. (gr. 2-4). 1976. 6.95 (0-8184-0231-8) Carol Pub Group.

Wickham, Geoffrey. Rapid Perspective. (gr. 10 up). 9.95 (0-85458-050-6); pap. 7.95 (0-85458-051-4) Transatl Arts.

Wicks, Kathy. Texas Folklife Festival: A Children's Guide. (Illus.). 30p. 2.25 (0-86701-035-5) U of Tex Inst Tex Culture.

Wicks, Keith. Science Can Be Fun. Kostal, Pavel, illus. 32p. (gr. 4-7). 1988. PLB 14.95 (0-8225-0896-6, First Ave Edns); pap. 4.95 (0-8225-9559-1, First Ave Edns) Lerner Pubns.
—Working with Computers. (Illus.). 64p. (gr. 4-7). 15.95x (0-8160-1071-4) Facts on File.

Wickstrom, Lois. Ladybugs for Loretta. Mion, Francie & Johnson, Priscilla M., illus. (gr. k-6). 1978. pap. 2.00 (0-916176-04-5) Sproing.
—Oliver. Johnson, Priscilla M., illus. (gr. k-6). 1978. pap. 2.00 (0-916176-03-7) Sproing.
—Oliver: A Story about Adoption. (Illus.). 32p. 1991. 14. 95 (0-9611872-5-5) Our Child Pr.

Wickstrom, Sylvie K., illus. Wheels on the Bus. 32p. (ps-2). 1988. PLB 11.00 (0-517-56784-9) Crown Bks Yng Read.

Wickstrom, Thor. The Big Night Out. Wickstrom, Thor, illus. LC 91-46563. 32p. (ps-3). 1993. 13.99 (0-8037-1170-0); PLB 13.89 (0-8037-1171-9) Dial Bks Young.

Wickum, Mabel. The Egg. LC 88-51385. (Illus.). 44p. (gr. k-2). 1989. pap. 4.95 (1-55523-199-3) Winston-Derek.

Widdows, Richard. Mexico. (Illus.). 48p. (gr. 4-8). 1987. PLB 14.98 (0-382-09506-5) Silver Burdett Pr.

Widerberg, Siv. The Big Sister. Sjogren, Birgitta, tr. from SWE. Torudd, Cecilia, illus. 1989. 9.95 (91-29-59186-4, Pub. by R&S Bks) FS&G.
—The Boy & the Dog. Fisher, Richard E., tr. Ahlbom, Jens, illus. 28p. (ps-up). 1991. bds. 5.95 (91-29-59926-1, Pub. by R & S Bks) FS&G.

Widman, Christine. Housekeeper of the Wind. Desimini, Lisa, illus. LC 88-10979. 32p. (ps-3). 1990. PLB 15.89 (0-06-026468-3) HarpC Child Bks.
—The Hummingbird Garden. Ransome, James, illus. LC 91-27338. 32p. (ps-3). 1993. RSBE 14.95 (0-02-792761-X, Macmillan Child Bk) Macmillan Child Grp.
—The Lemon Drop Jar. Kieffer, Christa, illus. LC 91-11209. 32p. (gr. k-3). 1992. RSBE 14.95 (0-02-792759-8, Macmillan Child Bk) Macmillan Child Grp.
—The Star Grazers. Spowart, Robin, illus. LC 87-29377. 32p. (ps-3). 1989. HarpC Child Bks.
—The Willow Umbrella. Stock, Catherine, illus. LC 91-10989. 32p. (gr. k-3). 1993. RSBE 14.95 (0-02-792760-1, Macmillan Child Bk) Macmillan Child Grp.

Wiebe, Ann. Soap Films & Bubbles. (gr. 4-9). 1990. pap. text ed. 14.95 (1-881431-25-8) AIMS Educ Fnd.

Wiebe, Arthur. Domino Math, 2 bks. Creative Teaching Assocs. Staff, illus. 60p. Bks. A & B. write for info. set (1-878669-18-4, 4145); wkbk. 6.95 ea. Bk. A, Grades 1-4, 1973 (1-878669-19-2, 4145) Bk. B, Grades 2-6, 1974 (4146) Crea Tea Assocs.
—Picture Patterns, Set 1 & 2. Creative Teaching Assoc. Staff, illus. 24p. (gr. k-4). 1985. wkbk. 8.95 ea. (1-878669-32-X, CTA-4752, CTA-4755) Crea Tea Assocs.
—Picture Patterns Duplicating, Bk. 1. 24p. (gr. k-4). 1982. wkbk. 4.95 (1-878669-33-8, CTA-4752) Crea Tea Assocs.
—Picture Patterns Duplicating, Bk. 2. 24p. (gr. k-4). 1985. wkbk. 4.95 (1-878669-34-6, CTA-4755) Crea Tea Assocs.
—Rotation with Patterns Blocks. 24p. (gr. 3-9). 1985. wkbk. 4.95 (1-878669-31-1, CTA-4767) Crea Tea Assocs.
—Symmetry with Pattern Blocks. 24p. (gr. 3-9). 1985. wkbk. 4.95 (1-878669-30-3, CTA-4766) Crea Tea Assocs.

Wieck, Stephen, ed. see Rein-Hagen, Mark, et al.

Wiederhold, Margaret S., jt. auth. see Harst, Linda N.

Wiegand, Betty, ed. see Storr, Sherman.

Wiemann, Mary, jt. auth. see Sylvester, Diane.

Wiencek, Henry. The World of Lego Toys. (Illus.). 176p. 1987. pap. 19.95 (0-8109-2362-9) Abrams.

Wier, Bernice, jt. auth. see Wallower, Lucille.

Wier, Ester. Loner. (gr. 4-7). 1992. pap. 2.75 (0-590-44352-6) Scholastic Inc.

Wiersbe, Warren. Be Challenged! rev. ed. LC 82-12404. (gr. 7). 1982. pap. 4.50 (0-8024-1080-4) Moody.

Wiersma, Debbie B., ed. see Beers, V. Gilbert.

Wiese, George. Footsteps of the Great Sage. LC 93-77219. (gr. 1-3). 1993. spiral bdg. 8.95 (1-883251-02-8) Hgh Desert Pr.

Wiese, Kurt. Happy Easter. (Illus.). 32p. (ps-1). 1989. pap. 3.99 (0-670-88249-7, Puffin) Puffin Bks.

Wiese, Kurt, jt. auth. see Flack, Marjorie.

Wiesma, Debbie. Precious Moments: Forever Friends. (Illus.). 48p. (ps-2). 1992. write for info. (0-307-15605-2, 15605) Western Pub.

Wiesmuller, Dieter. Maury & the Nightpirates. 40p. (ps-8). 1990. 15.95 (0-87951-392-6) Overlook Pr.
—Pernix: The Adventures of a Small Dinosaur. Weismuller, Dieter, illus. LC 92-39419. 44p. (gr. 3-6). 1993. 14.99 (0-525-65127-6, Cobblehill Bks) Dutton Child Bks.

Wiesner, David. Free Fall. LC 87-22834. (Illus.). (gr. 1-5). 1988. 13.95 (0-688-05583-4); lib. bdg. 13.88 (0-688-05584-2) Lothrop.
—Free Fall. LC 87-22834. (Illus.). 32p. (ps-3). 1991. pap. 4.95 (0-688-10990-X, Mulberry) Morrow.
—Hurricane. Wiesner, David, illus. (k-3). 1990. 14.95 (0-395-54382-7, Clarion Bks) HM.
—Hurricane. (ps-3). 1992. pap. 5.70 (0-395-62974-8, Clarion Bks) HM.
—June 29, 1999. Wiesner, David, illus. 32p. (ps-3). 1992. 15.95 (0-395-59762-5, Clarion Bks) HM.
—Tuesday. Briley, Dorothy, ed. Wiesner, David, illus. 32p. (gr. k up). 1991. 15.45 (0-395-55113-7, Clarion Bks) HM.

Wiessner, Colleen A. & Vos Wezeman, Phyllis. Flavors of Faith. 70p. (gr. 1-6). 1991. pap. 7.50 (1-877871-27-3, 5873) Ed Ministries.

Wiessner, Colleen A., jt. auth. see Vos Wezeman, Phyllis.

Wiessner, Colleen A., jt. auth. see Wezeman, Phyllis Vos.

Wiethorn, Randall J. Rock Finds a Friend. Wiethorn, Randall J., illus. 32p. 1991. pap. 5.95 (0-88138-110-1, Green Tiger) S&S Trade.

Wiewandt, Thomas. The Hidden Life of the Desert. LC 89-22263. (Illus.). 40p. 1990. 15.00 (0-517-57355-5); PLB 13.99 (0-517-57356-3) Crown Bks Yng Read.

Wiggan, Kate D. Rebecca of Sunnybrook Farm. 320p. 1992. 9.49 (0-8167-2556-X); pap. 2.95 (0-8167-2557-8) Troll Assocs.

Wiggen, Kate D. Rebecca of Sunnybrook Farm. Bixler, Phyllis, afterword by. 1991. pap. 2.95 (0-451-52483-7, Sig Classics) NAL-Dutton.

Wiggers, Raymond. The Amateur Geologist: Explorations & Investigations. (Illus.). 144p. (gr. 6-9). 1993. PLB 12.90 (0-531-11112-1) Watts.
—Picture Guide to Tree Leaves. LC 90-47859. (Illus.). 64p. (gr. 3-5). 1991. PLB 12.90 (0-531-20025-6) Watts.
—Picture Guide to Tree Leaves. (Illus.). 64p. (gr. 5-8). 1992. pap. 5.95 (0-531-15646-X) Watts.

Wiggin, Kate D. The Birds' Christmas Carol. (Illus.). (gr. 4-6). 13.45 (0-395-07205-0) HM.
—The Birds' Christmas Carol. (Orig.). (gr. k-6). 1988. pap. 3.50 (0-440-40121-6, Pub. by Yearling Classics) Dell.
—The Birds' Christmas Carol. (Illus.). 66p. 1987. Repr. lib. bdg. 19.95x (0-89966-580-2) Buccaneer Bks.
—The Birds' Christmas Carol. (Illus.). 69p. 1990. Repr. of 1886 ed. 15.95 (0-9616844-6-1) Greenhouse Pub.
—Mother Carey's Chickens. Coven, Peggy, illus. Adams, Carole G., intro. by. Stephens, Alice B., illus. 368p. (gr. 4-8). 1991. pap. 14.00 (0-912498-10-2) F A C E.
—Rebecca of Sunnybrook Farm. (gr. 5 up). 1967. pap. 1.50 (0-8049-0144-9, CL-144) Airmont.
—Rebecca of Sunnybrook Farm. 239p. 1981. Repr. PLB 21.95x (0-89966-354-0) Buccaneer Bks.
—Rebecca of Sunnybrook Farm. 259p. 1981. Repr. PLB 21.95 (0-89967-028-8) Harmony Raine.
—Rebecca of Sunnybrook Farm. 288p. (gr. 4-6). 1988. pap. 3.25 (0-590-41343-0) Scholastic Inc.
—Rebecca of Sunnybrook Farm. (gr. k-6). 1986. pap. 4.95 (0-440-47533-3, Pub. by Yearling Classics) Dell.
—Rebecca of Sunnybrook Farm. 279p. (gr. 5 up). 1986. pap. 2.95 (0-14-035046-2, Puffin) Puffin Bks.
—Rebecca of Sunnybrook Farm. 92p. 38743. 1993. 12. 99 (0-517-09275-1, Child Classics) Outlet Bk Co.
—Rebecca of Sunnybrook Farm. 288p. (gr. 5-8). 1993. pap. 2.99 (0-87406-655-7) Willowisp Pr.

Wiggin, Kate D. & Smith, Nora A., eds. The Arabian Nights: Their Best-Known Tales. Parrish, Maxfield, illus. LC 92-38552. 368p. 1993. ltd. ed. 75.00 (0-684-19588-7, Scribners Young Read); text ed. 25.00 (0-684-19589-5, Scribners Young Read) Macmillan Child Grp.

Wiggin, Kate D., et al, eds. Pinafore Palace: A Book of Rhymes for the Nursery. LC 72-8290. (ps-1). Repr. of 1907 ed. 21.00 (0-8369-6399-7) Ayer.

Wiggins, VeraLee. Barbie. Wheeler, Gerald, ed. 128p. (Orig.). (gr. 7-12). 1990. pap. 4.95 (0-8280-0581-8) Review & Herald.
—Julius, the Perfectly Pesky Pet Parrot. LC 93-14254. 1994. write for info. (0-8163-1173-0) Pacific Pr Pub Assn.

—Shelby's Best Friend. LC 93-27279. 1994. write for info. (0-8163-1189-7) Pacific Pr Pub Assn.
—Shelby's Big Prayer. LC 93-11939. 1994. write for info. (0-8163-1188-9) Pacific Pr Pub Assn.
—Shelby's Big Scare. LC 93-31363. 1994. write for info. (0-8163-1190-0) Pacific Pr Pub Assn.

Wiggs, Susan. The Canary Who Sailed with Columbus. Roberts, Melissa, ed. Anderson, Sharon, illus. 48p. (ps-2). 1989. 12.95 (0-89015-719-7, Pub. by Panda Bks) Eakin-Sunbelt.

Wigner, Annabel. Elizabeth & Akbar: Portraits of Power. 52p. (gr. 11 up). 1987. pap. 7.95 (0-85950-541-3, Pub. by S Thornes UK) Dufour.

Wiingaard, Juan. Cat. LC 90-80860. (Illus.). 12p. (ps). 1991. bds. 3.95 (0-517-58202-3) Crown Bks Yng Read.

Wijnberg, Ellen. Alcohol. LC 93-25156. (Illus.). (gr. 6-9). 1993. PLB 21.34 (0-8114-3528-8) Raintree Steck-V.
—Parental Unemployment. LC 93-25154. (Illus.). 80p. (gr. 6-9). 1993. PLB 21.34 (0-8114-3525-3) Raintree Steck-V.

Wijngaard, Juan. Bear. Wijngaard, Juan, illus. LC 90-81897. 12p. (ps). 1991. bds. 3.95 (0-517-58201-5) Crown Bks Yng Read.
—Dog. Wijngaard, Juan, illus. LC 90-81895. 12p. (ps). 1991. bds. 3.95 (0-517-58203-1) Crown Bks Yng Read.
—Duck. Wijngaard, Juan, illus. LC 90-81896. 12p. (ps) 1991. bds. 3.95 (0-517-58204-X) Crown Bks Yng Read.

Wijngaard, Juan, illus. The Nativity. LC 90-5309. 29p. (gr. k up). 1990. write for info. (0-7445-1260-3) Lothrop.
—The Nativity: King James Bible Text. 32p. 1990. 13.95 (0-688-09870-3); PLB 13.88 (0-688-09871-1) Lothrop.

Wijs, Ivo De see De Wijs, Ivo.

Wik, Lars, photos by. Baby's First Words. LC 84-60700. (Illus.). 28p. (ps). 1985. 2.95 (0-394-86945-1) Random Bks Yng Read.

Wikler, Madeine, jt. auth. see Groner, Judyth.

Wikler, Madeline & Groner, Judye. I Have Four Questions. Radin, Chari M., illus. LC 88-83570. 12p. (ps). 1989. bds. 4.95 (0-930494-90-3) Kar Ben.
—Miracle Meals: Eight Nights of Chanukah Food & Fun. Radin, Chari, illus. LC 87-17325. 48p. (gr. k up). 1987. spiral bd. 6.95 (0-930494-71-7) Kar Ben.

Wikler, Madeline, jt. auth. see Groner, Judye.

Wikler, Madeline, jt. auth. see Groner, Judyth.

Wikler, Madeline, jt. auth. see Saypol, Judyth R.

Wilbourn, Debrah. Eddie Murphy. King, Coretta Scott, intro. by. (Illus.). 112p. (gr. 5 up). 1993. PLB 17.95 (0-7910-1879-2); pap. write for info. (0-7910-1908-X) Chelsea Hse.

Wilbur, C. Keith. Indian Handcrafts: How to Craft Dozens of Practical Objects Using Traditional Indian Techniques. LC 90-3522. (Illus.). 144p. (gr. 7 up). 1990. pap. 13.95 (0-87106-496-0) Globe Pequot.

Wilbur, Frances. Horse Called Holiday. (gr. 4-7). 1992. pap. 2.95 (0-590-44548-0) Scholastic Inc.

Wilbur, Richard. Loudmouse. D'Andrade, Diane, ed. Almquist, Don, illus. 32p. (gr. 1-5). 1991. 12.95 (0-15-249494-4) HarBrace.
—Opposites. D'Andrade, Diane, ed. (Illus.). 39p. (ps up) 1991. 11.95 (0-15-258720-9) HarBrace.
—Opposites. Drescher, Henrik, illus. LC 92-39472. 1994. write for info. (0-15-230563-7) HarBrace.

Wilbur, Richard, ed. see Shakespeare, William.

Wilburn, Kathy, illus. My Favorite Christmas Carols. LC 90-22390. 24p. (ps up) 1991. 2.95 (0-694-00366-2) HarpC Child Bks.
—The Pudgy Book of Babies. 16p. (gr. k). 1984. pap. 2.95 (0-448-10207-2, G&D) Putnam Pub Group.
—Pudgy Pals. 16p. (ps). 1983. pap. 2.95 (0-448-10203-X, G&D) Putnam Pub Group.
—The Pudgy Rock-a-Bye Book. 16p. (ps). 1983. pap. 2.95 (0-448-10206-4, G&D) Putnam Pub Group.

Wilcox, Cathy. Enzo the Wonderfish. LC 93-11021. 1994. 13.95 (0-395-68382-3) Ticknor & Fields.
—In the Old Gum Tree: Nursery Rhymes & Verse for Little Kids. Wilcox, Cathy, illus. 48p. (Orig.). (ps-3). 1993. pap. 6.95 (0-04-442216-4, Pub. by Allen & Unwin Aust Pty AT) IPG Chicago.

Wilcox, Charlotte. Mummies & Their Mysteries. LC 92-32160. 1993. 22.95 (0-87614-767-8) Carolrhoda Bks.
—A Skyscraper Story. Boucher, Jerry, photos by. (Illus.). 48p. (gr. p-4). 1990. PLB 19.95 (0-87614-392-3) Carolrhoda Bks.
—Trash! Bushey, Jerry, illus. 40p. (gr. k-4). 1988. PLB 19.95 (0-87614-311-7) Carolrhoda Bks.
—Trash! Bushey, Jerry, illus. 40p. (gr. k-4). 1989. pap. 5.95 (0-87614-511-X, First Ave Edns) Lerner Pubns.

Wilcox, Daniel, jt. auth. see Stiles, Norman.

Wilcox, Diane L., tr. see Azaad, Meyer.

Wilcox, Frank H. DNA: The Thread of Life. (Illus.). 80p. (gr. 5 up). 1988. PLB 17.50 (0-8225-1584-9) Lerner Pubns.

Wilcox, Kathleen, jt. auth. see Levine, Saul V.

Wilcox, Tamara. Mysterious Detectives: Psychics. LC 77-14315. (Illus.). 48p. (gr. 4 up). 1983. PLB 16.64 (0-8172-1061-X) Raintree Steck-V.

Wild, Anne. The Egyptians Pop-Up. (Illus.). 32p. (gr. 5-9). 1986. pap. 7.95 (0-906212-44-8, Pub. by Tarquin UK) Parkwest Pubns.
—Pop-up London. (Illus.). 32p. (gr. 3 up). 1985. pap. 7.95 (0-906212-30-8, Pub. by Tarquin UK) Parkwest Pubns.

Wild, Anne, jt. auth. see Jenkins, Gerald.

Wild, Jocelyn. Florence & Eric Take the Cake. LC 87-639. (Illus.). 32p. (ps-2). 1987. 11.95 (0-8037-0305-8) Dial Bks Young.
—Florence & Eric Take the Cake. (ps-3). 1990. pap. 3.95 (0-8037-0676-6, Dial Pied Piper) Puffin Bks.
Wild, Margaret. All the Better to See You With. Tucker, Kathy, ed. Reynolds, Pat, illus. LC 92-39127. 32p. (gr. 1-3). 1993. PLB 13.95 (0-8075-0284-7) A Whitman.
—Beast. LC 93-34596. 1994. 13.95 (0-590-47158-9) Scholastic Inc.
—But Granny Did! Forss, Ian, illus. LC 92-31906. 1993. 3.75 (0-383-03559-7) SRA Schl Grp.
—Going Home. Harris, Wayne, illus. LC 93-22975. 32p. (ps-3). 1994. 14.95 (0-590-47958-X) Scholastic Inc.
—Let the Celebrations Begin! Vivas, Julie, illus. LC 90-21606. 32p. (ps-1). 1991. 14.95 (0-531-05937-5); RLB 14.99 (0-531-08537-6) Orchard Bks Watts.
—Mr. Nick's Knitting. Huxley, Dee H., illus. 28p. (ps-3). 1989. 12.95 (0-15-200518-8, Gulliver Bks) HarBrace.
—My Dearest Dinosaur. Rawlins, Donna, illus. LC 91-46166. 32p. (ps-2). 1992. 14.95 (0-531-05453-5); PLB 14.99 (0-531-08603-8) Orchard Bks Watts.
—Our Granny. Vivas, Julie, illus. LC 93-11950. 1994. 14.95 (0-395-67023-3) Ticknor & Fields.
—The Queen's Holiday. O'Loughlin, Sue, illus. LC 91-14024. 32p. (ps-1). 1992. 13.95 (0-531-05973-1); PLB 13.99 (0-531-08573-2) Orchard Bks Watts.
—The Slumber Party. Cox, David, illus. LC 92-39783. 1993. 13.45 (0-395-66598-1) Ticknor & Fields.
—Space Travelers. Rogers, Gregory, illus. LC 91-30252. 40p. (gr. 1-4). 1993. 14.95 (0-590-45598-2) Scholastic Inc.
—Thank You, Santa. (Illus.). 1992. 12.95 (0-590-45805-1, Scholastic Hardcover) Scholastic Inc.
—Toby. Young, Noela, illus. LC 93-14394. Date not set. write for info. (0-395-67024-1) Ticknor & Fields.
—The Very Best of Friends. Vivas, Julie, illus. 30p. (ps-3). 1990. 13.95 (0-15-200625-7, Gulliver Bks) HarBrace.
Wild, Terri C., jt. auth. see Rothlein, Liz.
Wilde, Gary. Dealing with Death. (Illus.). 48p. (gr. 6-8). 1991. pap. 7.99 (1-55945-112-2) Group Pub.
—Handling Conflict. (Illus.). 48p. (gr. 6-8). 1991. pap. 7.99 (1-55945-125-4) Group Pub.
—Heaven & Hell. (Illus.). 48p. (gr. 6-8). 1992. pap. 7.99 (1-55945-131-9) Group Pub.
—Suicide: The Silent Epidemic. (Illus.). 48p. (gr. 6-8). 1992. pap. 7.99 (1-55945-145-9) Group Pub.
Wilde, Irma, illus. Baby's Farm Animals. 20p. (ps-1). 1986. bds. 4.95 (0-448-03094-2, G&D) Putnam Pub Group.
Wilde, Nicholas. Death Knell. (Illus.). 160p. (gr. 7 up). 1991. 14.95 (0-8050-1851-4, Bks Young Read) H Holt & Co.
—Down Came a Blackbird. LC 92-20209. 208p. (gr. 5 up). 1992. 15.95 (0-8050-2001-2, Bks Young Read) H Holt & Co.
—Into the Dark. 1990. 13.95 (0-590-43424-1) Scholastic Inc.
—Into the Dark. 1992. pap. 2.95 (0-590-43423-3, Apple Paperbacks) Scholastic Inc.
—Sir Bertie & the Wyvern: A Tale of Heraldry. LC 84-7779. (Illus.). 64p. (gr. 2-6). 1984. PLB 13.50 (0-87614-273-0) Carolrhoda Bks.
Wilde, Oscar. The Canterville Ghost. Zwerger, Lisbeth, illus. LC 86-8179. (gr. 4 up). 1991. pap. 15.95 (0-88708-027-8) Picture Bk Studio.
—The Canterville Ghost & Other Stories. (Illus.). 1991. pap. text ed. 4.87 (0-582-03589-9, 79118) Longman.
—Complete Fairy Tales of Oscar Wilde. Zipes, Jack, afterword by. 224p. 1990. pap. 3.95 (0-451-52435-7, Sig Classics) NAL-Dutton.
—The Devoted Friend. LC 86-2609. 32p. (gr. 4 up). 1986. PLB 13.95s.p. (0-88682-067-7) Creative Ed.
—The Devoted Friend. Batmanglij, N. Khalili, tr. from ENG. Fanta, illus. LC 87-31689. 28p. (gr. 4 up). 1988. 15.00 (0-934211-16-7); Bilingual Eng.-Persian. 15.00 (0-934211-10-8) Mage Pubs Inc.
—Five Major Plays. Incl. Lady Windermere's Fan; Importance of Being Earnest; Salome; Woman of No Importance; Ideal Husband. (gr. 10 up). 1970. pap. 2.75 (0-8049-0208-9, CL-208) Airmont.
—The Happy Prince. 32p. (gr. 6 up). 1983. PLB 13.95s.p. (0-87191-924-9) Creative Ed.
—The Happy Prince. Young, Ed, illus. LC 88-29694. (gr. 1-3). 1992. pap. 14.95 jacketed (0-671-67754-3, S&S BFYR); pap. 5.95 (0-671-77819-6, S&S BFYR) S&S Trade.
—Happy Prince & Other Stories. 1983. pap. 2.99 (0-14-035050-0, Puffin) Puffin Bks.
—The Happy Prince & Other Stories. Robinson, Charles, illus. Glassman, Peter, afterword by. LC 90-48353. (Illus.). 144p. 1991. Repr. of 1913 ed. 16.95 (0-688-10390-1) Morrow Jr Bks.
—The Nightingale & the Rose. Wright, Freire & Foreman, Michael, illus. (gr. 4 up). 1981. 14.95 (0-19-520231-7) OUP.
—Picture of Dorian Gray. (gr. 9 up). 1964. pap. 2.50 (0-8049-0039-6, CL-39) Airmont.
—The Picture of Dorian Gray. large type ed. (gr. 10 up). Repr. Set. write for info. NAVH.
—The Selfish Giant. Zwerger, Lisbeth, illus. LC 83-24930. 28p. (gr. 1 up). 1991. pap. 15.95 (0-907234-30-5) Picture Bk Studio.
—The Selfish Giant. LC 86-2593. 32p. (gr. 4 up). 1986. PLB 13.95s.p. (0-88682-068-5) Creative Ed.
—The Selfish Giant. Mansell, Dom, illus. LC 86-9356. 32p. (gr. 1-4). 1986. 10.95 (0-13-803586-5) P-H.

—The Selfish Giant. Mansell, Dom, illus. 1986. pap. 10.95 (0-671-66847-1) S&S Trade.
—The Selfish Giant. Zwerger, Lisbeth, illus. 1991. pap. 4.95 (0-590-44460-3) Scholastic Inc.
—The Selfish Giant. Gallagher, Saelig, illus. LC 93-10393. 1994. write for info. (0-399-22448-3) Putnam Pub Group.
—Stories for Children. Lynch, P. J., illus. LC 90-38854. 96p. (gr. 3 up). 1991. 14.95 (0-02-792765-2, Macmillan Child Bk) Macmillan Child Grp.
Wilde, Oscar & Riswold, G. Happy Prince. (gr. 1-4). 1971. pap. 1.95 (0-13-384057-3) P-H.
Wilde, Sandra, jt. auth. see Whitin, David J.
Wilde, Susie. Extraordinary Chester. Torrence, Susan, illus. LC 88-11441. 32p. (Orig.). (ps-2). 1988. 14.95 (0-931093-09-0); pap. 6.95 (0-931093-08-2) Red Hen Pr.
Wilder. My First Little House Cookbook. Date not set. 12.00 (0-06-024296-5, Festival); PLB 11.89 (0-06-024297-3, Festival) HarpC Child Bks.
Wilder, H., et al. This Is America's Story, 6 vols. 5th, large type ed. 1700p. (gr. 7-8). 1983. Set. 418.50 (0-317-01948-1, J-25540-00) Am Printing Hse.
Wilder, Laura I. By the Shores of Silver Lake. rev. ed. Williams, Garth, illus. LC 52-7529. 292p. (gr. 3-7). 1961. 15.00 (0-06-026416-0); PLB 14.89 (0-06-026417-9) HarpC Child Bks.
—By the Shores of Silver Lake. large type ed. 1990. Repr. lib. bdg. 15.95 (1-55736-176-2, Crnrstn Bks) BDD LT Grp.
—Dance at Grandpas. Graef, Renee, illus. LC 93-24535. 1994. 15.00 (0-06-023878-X, Festival); PLB 14.89 (0-06-023879-8, Festival) HarpC Child Bks.
—Farmer Boy. rev. ed. Williams, Garth, illus. LC 52-7527. (gr. 3-7). 1961. 15.00 (0-06-026425-X); PLB 14.89 (0-06-026421-7) HarpC Child Bks.
—First Four Years. Williams, Garth, illus. Macbride, R. L., intro. by. LC 76-135774. (Illus.). (gr. 3-7). 1971. 15.00 (0-06-026426-8); PLB 14.89 (0-06-026427-6) HarpC Child Bks.
—Going to Town. Graef, Renee, illus. LC 92-46722. (gr. k-3). 1994. 15.00 (0-06-023012-6); PLB 14.89 (0-06-023013-4) HarpC Child Bks.
—Little House Books, 9 vols. Williams, Garth, illus. Incl. Little House in the Big Woods. LC 52-7525. 1971. pap. 3.95 (0-06-440001-8); Little House on the Prairie. LC 52-7526. 1971. pap. 3.95 (0-06-440002-6); Farmer Boy. LC 52-7527. 1971. pap. 3.95 (0-06-440003-4); On the Banks of Plum Creek. LC 52-7528. 1971. pap. 3.95 (0-06-440004-2); By the Shores of Silver Lake. LC 52-7529. 1971. pap. 3.95 (0-06-440005-0); The Long Winter. LC 52-7530. 1971. pap. 3.95 (0-06-440006-9); Little Town on the Prairie. LC 52-7531. 1971. pap. 3.95 (0-06-440007-7); These Happy Golden Years. LC 52-7532. 1971. pap. 3.95 (0-06-440008-5); The First Four Years. LC 76-135774. 1972. pap. 3.95 (0-06-440031-X). (gr. 3-7). 1973. Boxed set. pap. 35.55 (0-06-440040-9, Trophy) HarpC Child Bks.
—Little House, Boxed set of 5 bks. Williams, Garth, illus. (gr. 3-7). 1993. pap. 19.75 (0-06-440476-5, Trophy) HarpC Child Bks.
—Little House Christmas Trees: Christmas Stories from the Little House Books. Williams, Garth, illus. LC 93-24537. 1994. 14.00 (0-06-024269-8, Festival); PLB 13.89 (0-06-024270-1, Festival) HarpC Child Bks.
—Little House in the Big Woods. rev. ed. Williams, Garth, illus. LC 52-7525. (gr. 3-7). 1961. 15.00 (0-06-026430-6); PLB 14.89 (0-06-026431-4) HarpC Child Bks.
—Little House on the Prairie. rev. ed. Williams, Garth, illus. LC 52-7526. 336p. (gr. 3-7). 1961. 15.00 (0-06-026445-4); PLB 14.89 (0-06-026446-2) HarpC Child Bks.
—Little House on the Prairie. (gr. 4-6). 1975. pap. 5.00 (0-06-080357-6, P357, PL) HarpC.
—The Little House on the Prairie. 250p. (gr. 4 up). 1991. Repr. lib. bdg. 19.95x (0-89966-868-2) Buccaneer Bks.
—Little Town on the Prairie. rev. ed. Williams, Garth, illus. LC 52-7531. 308p. (gr. 3-7). 1961. 15.00 (0-06-026450-0); PLB 14.89 (0-06-026451-9) HarpC Child Bks.
—The Long Winter. rev. ed. Williams, Garth, illus. LC 52-7530. 334p. (gr. 3-7). 1961. 15.00 (0-06-026460-8); PLB 14.89 (0-06-026461-6) HarpC Child Bks.
—On the Banks of Plum Creek. rev. ed. Williams, Garth, illus. LC 52-7528. 340p. (gr. 3-7). 1961. 15.00 (0-06-026470-5); PLB 14.89 (0-06-026471-3) HarpC Child Bks.
—On the Way Home. Lane, Rose W., ed. LC 62-17966. (Illus.). 112p. (gr. 7 up). 1962. 14.00 (0-06-026489-6); PLB 13.89 (0-06-026490-X) HarpC Child Bks.
—On the Way Home. Lane, Rose W., ed. LC 62-17966. (Illus.). 112p. (gr. 7 up). 1976. pap. 3.95 (0-06-440040-8, Trophy) HarpC Child Bks.
—These Happy Golden Years. rev. ed. Williams, Garth, illus. LC 52-7532. 289p. (gr. 5-9). 1961. 15.00 (0-06-026480-2); PLB 14.89 (0-06-026481-0) HarpC Child Bks.
—West from Home: Letters of Laura Ingalls Wilder, San Francisco 1915. MacBride, Roger L., ed. LC 73-14342. 176p. (gr. 7 up). 1974. 15.00 (0-06-024110-1); PLB 14.89 (0-06-024111-X) HarpC Child Bks.
—West from Home: Letters of Laura Ingalls Wilder, San Francisco 1915. MacBride, Roger L., ed. LC 73-14342. (Illus.). 176p. (gr. 7 up). 1976. pap. 3.95 (0-06-440081-6, Trophy) HarpC Child Bks.

—Winter Days in the Big Woods. Graef, Renee, illus. LC 92-45883. (gr. 1-8). 1994. 15.00 (0-06-023014-2); PLB 14.89 (0-06-023022-3) HarpC Child Bks.
Wilder, Lon, jt. auth. see Trautman, Neal E.
Wilderness Society Staff. Color the Ancient Forest. (Illus.). 48p. (Orig.). (ps-3). 1991. saddle-stitched 4.95 (1-879326-07-8) Living Planet Pr.
Wilding-White. UFO's. 32p. (gr. k-6). 1977. pap. 5.95 (0-86020-150-3) EDC.
Wildlife Education, Ltd. Staff. Alligators & Crocodiles. Hoopes, Barbara, illus. 20p. (Orig.). (gr. 5 up). 1984. pap. 2.75 (0-937934-25-9) Wildlife Educ.
—Animal Champions Two. (Illus.). 20p. (Orig.). 1990. pap. 2.75 (0-937934-64-X) Wildlife Educ.
—Animal Wonders. Stuart, Walter, illus. 20p. 1992. 13.95 (0-937934-74-7) Wildlife Educ.
—Apes. Hynes, Robert, et al, illus. 20p. (Orig.). (gr. 5 up). 1981. pap. 2.75 (0-937934-03-8) Wildlife Educ.
—Baby Animals. (Illus.). 20p. (Orig.). (gr. 5 up). 1981. pap. 2.75 (0-937934-06-2) Wildlife Educ.
—Baby Animals, Vol. 2. Francis, John & Stuart, Walter, illus. 20p. 1992. 13.95 (0-937934-75-5); pap. 2.75 (0-937934-58-5) Wildlife Educ.
—Bats. (Illus.). 20p. 1989. 2.75 (0-937934-59-3) Wildlife Educ.
—Big Cats. Meltzer, Dave, et al, illus. 20p. (Orig.). (gr. 5 up). 1981. pap. 2.75 (0-937934-04-6) Wildlife Educ.
—Birds of Prey. Goldman, Kenneth, et al, illus. 20p. (Orig.). (gr. 5 up). 1980. pap. 2.75 (0-937934-01-1) Wildlife Educ.
—Butterflies. Meltzer, Davis & Ripper, Chuck, illus. 20p. 1992. 13.95 (0-937934-76-3); pap. 2.75 (0-937934-65-8) Wildlife Educ.
—Camels. Orr, Richard, illus. 20p. (gr. 5 up). 1984. pap. 2.75 (0-937934-24-0) Wildlife Educ.
—Cheetahs. Stuart, Walter, et al, illus. 24p. 1992. 13.95 (0-937934-77-1); pap. 2.75 (0-937934-67-4) Wildlife Educ.
—Chimpanzees. (Illus.). 20p. 1990. 2.75 (0-937934-61-5) Wildlife Educ.
—Dinosaurs. Hallett, Mark, illus. 20p. (Orig.). (gr. k-12). 1985. pap. 2.75 (0-937934-34-8) Wildlife Educ.
—Dolphins - Porpoises. (Illus.). 20p. 1990. 2.75 (0-937934-62-3) Wildlife Educ.
—Eagles. 1983 ed. Boyer, Trevor, illus. 20p. (gr. 5 up). pap. 2.75 (0-937934-14-3) Wildlife Educ.
—Elephants. Hoopes, Barbara, et al, illus. 20p. (Orig.). (gr. 5 up). 1980. pap. 2.75 (0-937934-00-3) Wildlife Educ.
—Giraffes. Francis, John, et al, illus. 20p. (Orig.). (gr. 5 up). 1982. pap. 2.75 (0-937934-09-7) Wildlife Educ.
—Gorillas. Orr, Richard, et al, illus. 20p. (Orig.). (gr. 1-8). 1984. pap. 2.75 (0-937934-28-3) WildLife Educ.
—Gorillas. Orr, Richard & Stuart, Walter, illus. 24p. 1992. 13.95 (0-937934-78-X) Wildlife Educ.
—Hippos. Francis, John, illus. 24p. 1992. 13.95 (0-937934-79-8); pap. 2.75 (0-937934-54-2) Wildlife Educ.
—Kangaroos. Millsap, Darrel, illus. 24p. 1992. 13.95 (0-937934-80-1); pap. 2.25 (0-937934-63-1) Wildlife Educ.
—Koalas. Havlicek, Karel & Stuart, Walter, illus. 20p. (gr. 5 up). 1983. pap. 2.75 (0-937934-13-5) Wildlife Educ.
—Lions. Orr, Richard, illus. 24p. 1992. 13.95 (0-937934-81-X); pap. 2.75 (0-937934-42-9) Wildlife Educ.
—Little Cats. Orr, Richard & Stuart, Walter, illus. 200p. (gr. 5 up). 1983. pap. 2.75 (0-937934-16-X) Wildlife Educ.
—Little Cats. Orr, Richard & Stuart, Walter, illus. 24p. 1992. 13.95 (0-937934-82-8) Wildlife Educ.
—Night Animals. Stuart, Walter, illus. 20p. (Orig.). (gr. 5 up). 1984. pap. 2.75 (0-937934-26-7) Wildlife Educ.
—Old World Monkeys. Orr, Richard, illus. 24p. 1992. 13.95 (0-937934-92-5); pap. 2.75 (0-937934-69-0) Wildlife Educ.
—Orangutans. Meltzer, Dave, illus. 20p. (Orig.). (gr. 5 up). 1980. pap. 2.75 (0-937934-02-X) Wildlife Educ.
—Orangutans. (Illus.). 24p. (gr. 5 up). 1992. 13.95 (0-937934-83-6) Wildlife Educ.
—Ostriches. (Illus.). 1990. 2.75 (0-937934-60-7) Wildlife Educ.
—Owls. Boyer, Trevor, et al, illus. 20p. (Orig.). (gr. 5 up). 1985. pap. 2.75 (0-937934-32-1) Wildlife Educ.
—Parrots. Boyer, Trevor, illus. 20p. (gr. 5 up). 1984. pap. text ed. 2.75 (0-937934-27-5) Wildlife Educ.
—Parrots. Boyer, Trevor, illus. 24p. 1992. 13.95 (0-937934-84-4) Wildlife Educ.
—Penguins. Stuart, Walter & Boyer, Trevor, illus. 20p. (gr. 5 up). 1983. pap. 2.75 (0-937934-17-8) Wildlife Educ.
—Polar Bears. Espinoza, Rauol, et al, illus. 20p. (Orig.). (gr. k-12). 1985. pap. 2.75 (0-937934-36-4) Wildlife Educ.
—Polar Bears. Woods, Michael & Stuart, Walter, illus. 24p. 1992. 13.95 (0-937934-85-2) Wildlife Educ.
—Rattlesnakes. Hayward, Tim & Stuart, Walter, illus. 24p. 1992. 13.95 (0-937934-86-0); pap. 2.75 (0-937934-56-9) Wildlife Educ.
—Rhinos. Woods, Michael, et al, illus. 20p. (Orig.). (gr. 1-8). 1985. pap. 2.75 (0-937934-29-1) Wildlife Educ.
—Saving Our Animal Friends. (Illus.). 1990. 2.75 (0-937934-68-2) Wildlife Educ.
—Sea Birds. Hayward, Tim, illus. 24p. 1992. 13.95 (0-937934-90-9); pap. 2.75 (0-937934-66-6) Wildlife Educ.

—Sea Otters. Hayward, Tim & Stuart, Walten, illus. 1992. 13.95 (*0-937934-87-9*); pap. 2.75 (*0-937934-70-4*) Wildlife Educ.
—Seals & Sea Lions. Stuart, Walter, illus. 20p. (Orig.). (gr. 5 up). 1985. pap. 2.75 (*0-937934-33-X*) Wildlife Educ.
—Sharks. Hoopes, Barbara, illus. 20p. (gr. 5 up). 1983. pap. 2.75 (*0-937934-15-1*) Wildlife Educ.
—Snakes. Hoopes, Barbara & Oden, Dick, illus. 20p. (Orig.). (gr. 5 up). 1981. pap. 2.75 (*0-937934-05-4*) Wildlife Educ.
—Spiders. Stuart, Walter, et al, illus. 20p. (Orig.). (gr. 5 up). 1985. pap. 2.75 (*0-937934-39-9*) Wildlife Educ.
—Spiders. Stuart, Walter, illus. 24p. 1992. 13.95 (*0-937934-88-7*) Wildlife Educ.
—Tigers. Orr, Richard, et al, illus. 20p. (Orig.). (gr. k-12). 1985. pap. 2.75 (*0-937934-35-6*) Wildlife Educ.
—Turtles. Stuart, Walter & Hallett, Mark, illus. 20p. (Orig.). (gr. 5 up). 1985. pap. 2.75 (*0-937934-41-0*) Wildlife Educ.
—Turtles. Bliss, Rebecca & Stuart, Walter, illus. 24p. (gr. 5 up). 1992. 13.95 (*0-937934-89-5*) Wildlife Educ.
—Wild Horses. Hoopes, Barbara, illus. 20p. (Orig.). (gr. 5 up). 1982. pap. 2.75 (*0-937934-08-9*) Wildlife Educ.
—Zebras. Orr, Richard, illus. 24p. 1992. 13.95 (*0-937934-91-7*); pap. 2.75 (*0-937934-57-7*) Wildlife Educ.
Wildlife Education, Ltd. Staff, ed. Animal Champions, Vol. 1. (Illus.). 20p. 1992. 13.95 (*0-937934-73-9*) Wildlife Educ.
Wildsmith, Brian. All Fall Down. (Illus.). 16p. 1987. pap. 2.95 (*0-19-272135-6*) OUP.
—Animal Games. Wildsmith, Brian, illus. (ps-3). 1980. 9.95 (*0-19-279731-X*) OUP.
—Animal Games. (Illus.). 24p. (ps up). 1991. pap. 5.95 (*0-19-272177-1*, 12406) OUP.
—Animal Homes. Wildsmith, Brian, illus. (ps-3). 1980. 9.95 (*0-19-279732-8*) OUP.
—Animal Homes. (Illus.). 32p. (ps up). 1991. pap. 5.95 (*0-19-272176-3*, 12407) OUP.
—Animal Shapes. Wildsmith, Brian, illus. (ps-3). 1981. 9.95 (*0-19-279733-6*) OUP.
—Animal Shapes. (Illus.). 24p. (ps up). 1991. pap. 4.95 (*0-19-272174-7*, 12405) OUP.
—Animal Tricks. Wildsmith, Brian, illus. (ps-3). 1981. 9.95 (*0-19-279743-3*) OUP.
—Animal Tricks. (Illus.). 32p. (ps up). 1991. pap. 5.95 (*0-19-272173-9*, 12408) OUP.
—The Apple Bird. (Illus.). 16p. 1987. pap. 2.95 (*0-19-272136-4*) OUP.
—Bear's Adventure. Wildsmith, Brian, illus. LC 81-18814. 32p. (ps-2). 1982. 9.95 (*0-394-85295-8*); pap. 16.99 (*0-394-95295-2*) Pantheon.
—Birds by Brian Wildsmith. (Illus.). (gr. k-4). 1967. pap. 7.50 (*0-19-272117-8*) OUP.
—Cat on the Mat. (Illus.). 16p. 1987. pap. 2.95 (*0-19-272123-2*) OUP.
—A Christmas Story. Wildsmith, Brian, illus. LC 89-7959. 32p. (ps-3). 1989. 15.95 (*0-679-80074-3*) Knopf Bks Yng Read.
—A Christmas Story. Wildsmith, Brian, illus. LC 89-7959. (ps-3). 1993. 6.99 (*0-679-84726-X*) Knopf Bks Yng Read.
—The Circus. (Illus.). (ps-3). 1970. pap. 7.50x (*0-19-272102-X*) OUP.
—An Easter Story. Wildsmith, Brian, illus. LC 93-25097. 40p. (ps-3). 1994. 15.00 (*0-679-84727-8*) Knopf Bks Yng Read.
—Fishes. (Illus.). 32p. 1987. 16.00 (*0-19-279639-9*); pap. 7.50 (*0-19-272151-8*) OUP.
—Giddy Up. 16p. (ps-k). 1987. pap. 2.95 (*0-19-272183-6*) OUP.
—Goat's Trail. Wildsmith, Brian, illus. LC 86-2731. 40p. (gr. k-3). 1986. 10.95 (*0-394-88276-8*); lib. bdg. 12.99 (*0-394-98276-2*) Knopf Bks Yng Read.
—The Hunter & His Dog. Wildsmith, Brian, illus. 32p. (ps-2). 1979. 16.00 (*0-19-279725-5*); pap. 7.50 (*0-19-272147-X*) OUP.
—If I Were You. 16p. (ps-k). 1987. pap. 2.95 (*0-19-272182-8*) OUP.
—The Island. (Illus.). 16p. 1987. pap. 2.95 (*0-19-272137-2*) OUP.
—The Lazy Bear. (Illus.). 32p. (ps-1). 1987. 16.00 (*0-19-279693-3*); pap. 7.50 (*0-19-272158-5*) OUP.
—The Little Wood Duck. (Illus.). 32p. 1987. 16.00 (*0-19-279686-0*); pap. 7.50 (*0-19-272101-1*) OUP.
—The Miller, the Boy & the Donkey. Wildsmith, Brian, illus. 32p. (ps-1). 1987. 16.00 (*0-19-279652-6*); pap. 7.50 (*0-19-272114-3*) OUP.
—Mother Goose: Nursery Rhymes. (Illus.). 80p. (ps up) 1987. 16.00 (*0-19-279611-9*); pap. 8.95 (*0-19-272180-1*) OUP.
—My Dream. (Illus.). 16p. 1987. pap. 2.95 (*0-19-272161-5*) OUP.
—The Nest. (Illus.). 16p. 1987. pap. 2.95 (*0-19-272134-8*) OUP.
—One, Two, Three. (Illus.). 32p. 1987. bds. 12.95 laminated (*0-19-279613-5*) OUP.
—The Owl & the Woodpecker. (Illus.). 32p. 1987. 16.00 (*0-19-279676-3*) OUP.
—The Owl & the Woodpecker. (Illus.). 32p. 1992. pap. 7.50 (*0-19-272255-7*) OUP.
—Pelican. Wildsmith, Brian, illus. LC 82-12431. 64p. (ps-2). 1983. lib. bdg. 10.99 (*0-394-95668-0*) Pantheon.
—Professor Noah's Spaceship. Wildsmith, Brian, illus. 32p. (ps-3). 1980. 16.00 (*0-19-279741-7*); pap. 7.50 (*0-19-272149-6*) OUP.

—Python's Party. (Illus.). 32p. (ps up) 1991. pap. 7.50 (*0-19-272229-8*, 12355) OUP.
—Seasons. Wildsmith, Brian, illus. (ps-3). 1980. 9.95 (*0-19-279730-1*) OUP.
—Seasons. (Illus.). 32p. (ps up) 1991. pap. 5.95 (*0-19-272175-5*, 12409) OUP.
—Squirrels. (Illus.). 32p. 1987. pap. 7.50 (*0-19-272105-4*) OUP.
—Squirrels. (Illus.). 32p. 1992. bds. 16.00 (*0-19-279699-2*) OUP.
—Toot, Toot. (Illus.). 16p. 1987. pap. 2.95 (*0-19-272146-1*) OUP.
—The Trunk. (Illus.). 16p. 1987. pap. 2.95 (*0-19-272124-0*) OUP.
—What a Tale. (Illus.). 16p. 1987. pap. 2.95 (*0-19-272160-7*) OUP.
—What the Moon Saw. Wildsmith, Brian, illus. 32p. (ps-3). 1978. 16.00 (*0-19-279724-7*); pap. 7.50 (*0-19-272157-7*) OUP.
—Whose Shoes? (Illus.). 16p. 1987. pap. 2.95 (*0-19-272145-3*) OUP.
—Wild Animals. (Illus.). (ps) 1976. pap. 7.50 (*0-19-272103-8*) OUP.
Wildsmith, Brian & LaFontaine, Jean de. The Rich Man & the Shoe-Maker. (Illus.). (ps-3). 1965. pap. 7.50 (*0-19-272104-6*) OUP.
Wildsmith, Brian & Wildsmith, Rebecca. Jack & the Meanstalk. LC 93-30374. 1994. 10.99 (*0-679-85810-5*); pap. 16.99 (*0-679-95810-X*) Knopf Bks Yng Read.
—Look Closer. LC 92-17241. 1993. 6.95 (*0-15-200477-7*, Gulliver Bks); pap. write for info. (*0-15-200478-5*, Gulliver Bks) HarBrace.
—What Did I Find? LC 92-17666. 1993. 6.95 (*0-15-200688-5*); pap. write for info. (*0-15-200689-3*) HarBrace.
—Whose Hat Was That? LC 92-17237. 1993. 6.95 (*0-15-200691-5*); pap. write for info. (*0-15-200690-7*) HarBrace.
Wildsmith, Brian, jt. auth. see Wildsmith, Rebecca.
Wildsmith, Rebecca & Wildsmith, Brian. Wake up, Wake up. LC 92-18704. 1993. 6.95 (*0-15-200685-0*); pap. write for info. (*0-15-200686-9*) HarBrace.
Wildsmith, Rebecca, jt. auth. see Wildsmith, Brian.
Wiles, Mary J. The Alligator with a Toothache. (ps-3). 1978. pap. 1.75 (*0-8198-0355-3*) St Paul Bks.
Wiley, Chris. The Little Commission Handbook. 27p. 1991. pap. 1.95 (*0-8341-1421-6*) Beacon Hill.
Wiley, Jack. The Complete Book of Unicycling. LC 84-50464. (Illus.). 187p. (gr. 7 up). 1984. pap. 27.95 (*0-913999-05-9*) Solipaz Pub Co.
—Unicycles & Artistic Bicycles Illustrated. LC 86-61015. (Illus.). 168p. (gr. 7 up). 1986. pap. 26.95 (*0-913999-15-6*) Solipaz Pub Co.
Wiley, Larry. Introductory Geometrics. 278p. (Orig.). (gr. 10-12). 1986. pap. text ed. 15.00 (*0-89824-065-4*); tchr's. ed. 7.50 (*0-89824-066-2*) Trillium Pr.
Wilhelm, Carolyn. Early Childhood Bulletin Boards. 96p. (ps-1). 1987. 10.95 (*0-86653-393-1*, SS1825, Shining Star Pubns) Good Apple.
Wilhelm, Doug. The Mystery of the Forgotten Planet. (gr. 4-7). 1993. pap. 3.25 (*0-553-29303-6*) Bantam.
—Scene of the Crime. (gr. 4-7). 1993. pap. 3.25 (*0-553-56004-2*) Bantam.
—The Secret of Mystery Hill, No. 141. 1993. pap. 3.25 (*0-553-56001-8*) Bantam.
Wilhelm, Glenda, jt. auth. see Wilhelm, Tim.
Wilhelm, Hans. The Bremen Town Musicians. 32p. 1992. 13.95 (*0-590-44795-5*, Scholastic Hardcover) Scholastic Inc.
—Bunny Trouble. (Illus.). 40p. (Orig.). (ps-3). 1991. 3.95 (*0-590-45042-5*); pap. 6.95 (*0-590-63198-5*); Book & cassette. 6.95 (*0-590-63153-5*) Scholastic Inc.
—A Cool Kid - Like Me! LC 89-49370. (Illus.). 32p. (ps-2). 1990. 14.00 (*0-517-57821-2*); PLB 13.99 (*0-517-57822-0*) Crown Bks Yng Read.
—Don't Give Up, Josephine! Wilhelm, Hans, illus. LC 84-24849. 40p. (ps-3). 1985. lib. bdg. 7.99 (*0-394-97244-9*) Random Bks Yng Read.
—I'll Always Love You. Wilhelm, Hans, illus. LC 84-20060. 32p. (ps up). 1988. 15.00 (*0-517-55648-0*); pap. 3.99 (*0-517-57265-6*) Crown Bks Yng Read.
—More Bunny Trouble. (ps-3). 1990. pap. 3.95 (*0-590-41590-5*) Scholastic Inc.
—Pirates Ahoy! Wilhelm, Hans, illus. LC 87-30197. 40p. (ps-3). 1987. 5.95 (*0-8193-1162-6*) Parents.
—Pirates Ahoy. Wilhelm, Hans, illus. 48p. (ps-2). 1990. pap. 2.95 (*0-448-04340-8*, G&D) Putnam Pub Group.
—Schnitzel's First Christmas. (Illus.). 1989. pap. 13.95 jacketed (*0-671-67977-5*, S&S BFYR) S&S Trade.
—Schnitzel's First Christmas. LC 89-5858. (Illus.). 40p. (ps-1). 1991. pap. 5.00 (*0-671-74494-1*, S&S BFYR) S&S Trade.
—Tyrone the Double Dirty Rotten Cheater. Wilhelm, Hans, illus. 32p. (gr. 1-3). 1991. 12.95 (*0-590-44079-9*, Scholastic Hardcover) Scholastic Inc.
—Tyrone the Double Dirty Rotten Cheater. (Illus.). 1992. pap. 3.95 (*0-590-44080-2*) Scholastic Inc.
—Tyrone the Horrible. (ps). 1992. pap. 3.95 (*0-590-41472-0*) Scholastic Inc.
—Waldo, Tell Me about Christ. Wilhelm, Hans, illus. 40p. (gr. 3 up). 1988. 4.95 (*0-8378-1812-5*) Gibson.
—Waldo, Tell Me about Christmas. (Illus.). 40p. (gr. 3 up). 1989. 4.95 (*0-8378-1846-X*) Gibson.
—Waldo, Tell Me about God. Wilhelm, Hans, illus. 40p. (gr. 3 up). 1988. 4.95 (*0-8378-1809-5*) Gibson.

—Waldo, Tell Me about Guardian Angels. Wilhelm, Hans, illus. 40p. (gr. 3 up) 1988. 4.95 (*0-8378-1811-7*) Gibson.
—Waldo, Tell Me about Me. Wilhelm, Hans, illus. 40p. (gr. 3 up). 1988. 4.95 (*0-8378-1810-9*) Gibson.
—What Does God Do? 29p. 1987. write for info. (*0-8499-0712-8*) Word Inc.
Wilhelm, Tim & Wilhelm, Glenda. Bicycling Basics. Seiden, Art, illus. 48p. (gr. 3-7). 1985. pap. 4.95 (*0-13-077942-3*) P-H.
Wilker, Debbie A. Deadly Drugs: An Informative Coloring Book. Wilker, Debbie A., illus. (Orig.). (ps-3). 1990. pap. 5.95 (*1-878282-10-7*) St Johann Pr.
Wilker, Josh. The Lenape Indians. (Illus.). 80p. (gr. 2-5). 1993. PLB 13.95 (*0-7910-1665-X*, Am Art Analog); pap. 6.95 (*0-7910-2029-0*, Am Art Analog) Chelsea Hse.
Wilkerson, Tichi, jt. auth. see Borie, Marcia.
Wilkes. Catching Crooks. (gr. 2-5). 1979. (Usborne-Hayes); pap. 4.50 (*0-86020-229-1*) EDC.
—Colors Book. (gr. k-2). 1979. (Usborne-Hayes); PLB 11.96 (*0-88110-067-6*); pap. 2.95 (*0-86020-362-X*) EDC.
—Deserts. (gr. 4-6). 1980. (Usborne-Hayes); PLB 11.96 (*0-88110-080-3*); pap. 3.95 (*0-86020-470-7*) EDC.
—Gulliver's Travels. (gr. 3-6). 1982. PLB 11.96 (*0-88110-064-1*); pap. 4.50 (*0-86020-612-2*) EDC.
—Jungles. (gr. 4-6). 1980. (Usborne-Hayes); PLB 11.96 (*0-88110-078-1*); pap. 3.95 (*0-86020-466-9*) EDC.
—King Arthur. (Illus.). (gr. 3-6). 1981. (Usborne-Hayes); PLB 11.96 (*0-88110-061-7*); pap. 4.50 (*0-86020-551-7*) EDC.
—Mountains. 24p. (gr. 4-6). 1980. (Usborne-Hayes); PLB 11.96 (*0-88110-079-X*); pap. 3.95 (*0-7460-0755-8*) EDC.
—Simple Science. (Illus.). 38p. (gr. 2-5). 1983. 10.95 (*0-86020-761-7*) EDC.
—Treasure Island. (Illus.). (gr. 3-6). 1982. (Usborne-Hayes); PLB 11.96 (*0-88110-063-3*) EDC.
—Wild Places. (gr. 4-6). 1980. 11.95 (*0-86020-472-3*, Usborne-Hayes) EDC.
Wilkes & Zeff. First Book of Numbers. (gr. k-3). 1982. (Usborne-Hayes); pap. 8.95 (*0-7460-0214-9*) EDC.
Wilkes, A. Fakes & Forgeries. (Illus.). 64p. (gr. 3-7). 1979. (Usborne); pap. 4.50 (*0-86020-231-3*) EDC.
—First Cookbook. (Illus.). 24p. (gr. 1-4). 1993. pap. 10.95 (*0-7460-0233-5*, Usborne) EDC.
—Growing Things. (Illus.). 14p. (gr. 2-6). 1986. pap. 4.50 (*0-7460-0122-3*) EDC.
—Hot Things. (Illus.). 24p. (gr. 1-4). 1993. pap. 4.50 (*0-7460-0229-7*, Usborne) EDC.
—Party Things. (Illus.). 24p. (gr. 1-4). 1993. pap. 4.50 (*0-7460-0231-9*, Usborne) EDC.
—Sweet Things. (Illus.). 24p. (gr. 1-4). 1993. pap. 4.50 (*0-7460-0227-0*, Usborne) EDC.
Wilkes, A. & Garbera, C. Knitting. (Illus.). 48p. (gr. 6 up). 1986. PLB 14.96 (*0-88110-320-9*); pap. 6.95 (*0-86020-983-0*) EDC.
Wilkes, A. & Rosen, C. Making Presents. (Illus.). 14p. (gr. 2-6). 1986. pap. 4.50 (*0-7460-0123-1*) EDC.
—Simple Things to Make & Do. (Illus.). 72p. (gr. 2-6). 1986. pap. 8.95 (*0-7460-0549-0*, Usborne) EDC.
Wilkes, Angela. Colorful Animals. Lilly, Kenneth, illus. LC 92-52799. 24p. (ps-1). 1992. 3.95 (*1-56458-103-9*) Dorling Kindersley.
—Feathery Animals. Lilly, Kenneth, illus. LC 92-52800. 24p. (ps-1). 1992. 3.95 (*1-56458-104-7*) Dorling Kindersley.
—French for Beginners. (Illus.). 48p. (gr. 4 up). 1988. 7.95 (*0-8442-1413-2*, Passport Bks) NTC Pub Grp.
—Furry Animals. Lilly, Kenneth, illus. LC 92-52801. 24p. (ps-1). 1992. 3.95 (*1-56458-105-5*) Dorling Kindersley.
—German for Beginners. (Illus.). 48p. (gr. 4 up). 1988. 7.95 (*0-8442-2165-1*, Passport Bks) NTC Pub Grp.
—Italian for Beginners. 48p. (ps-1). 1988. 7.95 (*0-8442-8059-3*, Passport Bks) NTC Pub Grp.
—The Junior Visual Dictionary. LC 93-28753. 1994. write for info. (*1-56458-465-8*) Dorling Kindersley.
—Mon Premier Livre de Mots - My First French Word Book: A Bilingual Word Book. Heminway, Annie, tr. LC 92-54499. (ENG & FRE., Illus.). 48p. (gr. k-4). 1993. 12.95 (*1-56458-254-X*) Dorling Kindersley.
—My First Activity Book. LC 89-2640. (Illus.). 48p. (gr. 1-5). 1990. 13.00 (*0-394-86583-9*); PLB 13.99 (*0-394-96583-3*) Knopf Bks Yng Read.
—My First Cookbook. Johnson, David, photos by. LC 88-13798. (Illus.). 48p. (gr. 3-7). 1989. 13.00 (*0-394-80427-9*) Knopf Bks Yng Read.
—My First Garden Book. King, Dave, photos by. LC 90-40332. (Illus.). 48p. (gr. 2-5). 1992. 13.00 (*0-679-81412-4*); PLB 13.99 (*0-679-91412-9*) Knopf Bks Yng Read.
—My First Green Book. LC 91-4371. (Illus.). 48p. (gr. 2-5). 1991. 12.00 (*0-679-81780-8*); lib. bdg. 13.99 (*0-679-91780-2*) Knopf Bks Yng Read.
—My First Nature Book. LC 89-8019. (Illus.). 48p. (gr. 1-5). 1990. 13.00 (*0-394-86610-X*); PLB 13.99 (*0-394-96610-4*) Knopf Bks Yng Read.
—My First Party Book. LC 90-40331. (Illus.). 48p. (gr. 1-5). 1991. 13.00 (*0-679-80909-0*); PLB 12.99 (*0-679-90909-5*) Knopf Bks Yng Read.
—My First Science Book. (Illus.). 48p. (gr. 1-5). 1990. 13.00 (*0-679-80583-4*); PLB 13.99 (*0-679-90583-9*) Knopf Bks Yng Read.
—My First Spanish Word Book. LC 92-54500. (SPA & ENG., Illus.). 48p. (gr. k-4). 1993. 12.95 (*1-56458-255-8*) Dorling Kindersley.

—My First Word Book. LC 91-60897. (Illus.). 64p. (ps-3). 1991. 12.95 (*1-879431-21-1*); PLB 13.99 (*1-879431-36-X*) Dorling Kindersley.
—Prickly Animals. Lilly, Kenneth, illus. LC 92-52802. 24p. (ps-1). 1992. 3.95 (*1-56458-106-3*) Dorling Kindersley.
—Scaly Animals. Lilly, Kenneth, illus. LC 92-52803. 24p. (ps-1). 1992. 3.95 (*1-56458-107-1*) Dorling Kindersley.
—See How I Grow. LC 93-27039. 1994. write for info. (*1-56458-464-X*) Dorling Kindersley.
—Spanish for Beginners. 48p. (ps-1). 1988. 7.95 (*0-8442-7628-6*, Passport Bks) NTC Pub Grp.
—Spotty Animals. Lilly, Kenneth, illus. LC 92-52804. 24p. (ps-1). 1992. 3.95 (*1-56458-108-X*) Dorling Kindersley.
—Stripey Animals. Lilly, Kenneth, illus. LC 92-52805. 24p. (ps-1). 1992. 3.95 (*1-56458-109-8*) Dorling Kindersley.
—Wrinkly Animals. Lilly, Kenneth, illus. LC 92-52806. 24p. (ps-1). 1992. 3.95 (*1-56458-110-1*) Dorling Kindersley.
Wilkes, Angela & Borgia, Rubi. Mi Primer Libro de Palabras de Espanol. LC 92-56498. (SPA., Illus.). 64p. (ps-3). 1993. 12.95 (*1-56458-262-0*) Dorling Kindersley.
Wilkes, Angela & Heminway, Annie. Mon Premier Livre des Mots en Francais. LC 92-56499. (FRE., Illus.). 64p. (ps-3). 1993. 12.95 (*1-56458-261-2*) Dorling Kindersley.
Wilkes, Angela, compiled by. Animal Nursery Rhymes. LC 92-52818. (Illus.). 32p. (ps-k). 1992. 13.95 (*1-56458-122-5*) Dorling Kindersley.
Wilkes, Angela, ed. English Picture Dictionary. (Illus.). 96p. (gr. 1 up). 1988. 9.95 (*0-8442-5447-9*, Passport Bks) NTC Pub Grp.
—French Picture Dictionary. (Illus.). 96p. (gr. 1 up). 1988. 9.95 (*0-8442-1405-1*, Passport Bks) NTC Pub Grp.
—German Picture Dictionary. (Illus.). 96p. (gr. 1 up). 1988. 9.95 (*0-8442-2159-7*, Passport Bks) NTC Pub Grp.
—Spanish Picture Dictionary. (Illus.). 96p. (gr. 1 up). 1988. 9.95 (*0-8442-7630-8*, Passport Bks) NTC Pub Grp.
Wilkes, Donald L. & Hamilton-Wilkes, Viola. Teen Guide Job Search: Ten Easy Steps to Your Future. Carter, Carl, illus. 112p. (gr. 10-12). 1991. pap. 10.95 (*0-9628787-1-5*) Jem Job Educ.
Wilkes, J. The London Police in the Nineteenth Century. LC 76-57247. (Illus.). 48p. (gr. 7 up). 1977. pap. 7.50 (*0-521-21406-8*) Cambridge U Pr.
—Roman Army. (Illus.). 48p. (gr. 7 up). 1973. pap. 7.50 (*0-521-07243-3*) Cambridge U Pr.
Wilkes, Larry. The King's Egg Dance. Wilkes, Larry, illus. 32p. (gr. k-4). 1990. PLB 18.95 (*0-87614-446-6*) Carolrhoda Bks.
Wilkes, Marilyn. C.L.U.T.Z. Ross, Larry, illus. LC 81-68786. 128p. (gr. 3-7). 1982. 9.95 (*0-8037-1157-3*, 0966-290) Dial Bks Young.
Wilkes, Marilyn Z. C.L.U.T.Z. (gr. 2-3). 1983. pap. 2.50 (*0-553-15515-6*) Bantam.
Wilkes, Paul. My Book of Bedtime Prayers. Shields, Sandra S., illus. LC 92-70386. 32p. (ps-k). 1992. PLB 12.99 (*0-8066-2592-9*, 9-2592, Augsburg) Augsburg Fortress.
Wilkeshuis, Cornelis. The Best Gift of All. Van Bilsen, Rita, illus. LC 89-38122. 28p. (gr. k-2). 1989. 8.95 (*0-8198-1126-2*) St Paul Bks.
Wilkey, Chris, jt. auth. see Whitman, Ken.
Wilkie, E. Cleve. Just Lookin' Around. Smith, R. F., illus. Rogers, Dennis, intro. by. (Illus.). 224p. (Orig.). 1987. pap. 10.00 (*0-9617969-0-1*) E C Wilkie.
Wilkie, Katharine E. Daniel Boone: Taming the Wilds. Johnson, E. Harper, illus. 72p. (gr. 2-6). 1991. Repr. of 1960 ed. PLB 12.95 (*0-7910-1407-X*) Chelsea Hse.
—Helen Keller: From Tragedy to Triumph. Doremus, Robert, illus. LC 86-10719. 192p. (gr. 2-6). 1986. pap. 3.95 (*0-02-041980-5*, Aladdin) Macmillan Child Grp.
—Mary Todd Lincoln, Girl of the Bluegrass. Goldstein, Leslie, illus. LC 92-9782. 192p. (gr. 3-7). 1992. pap. 3.95 (*0-689-71655-9*, Aladdin) Macmillan Child Grp.
Wilkie, Katherine. Ferdinand Magellan: Noble Captain. Coyle, P., illus. (gr. 4-6). 1963. pap. 2.44 (*0-395-01751-3*, Piper) HM.
Wilkin, Eloise, illus. Baby's First Christmas. LC 80-80710. 14p. (ps). 1980. 3.95 (*0-394-84575-7*) Random Bks Yng Read.
—My Goodnight Book. 14p. (ps-k). 1981. write for info. (*0-307-12258-1*, Golden Bks.) Western Pub.
—Nursery Rhymes. LC 78-64606. (ps). 1979. bds. 3.95 (*0-394-84129-8*) Random Bks Yng Read.
—Rock-a-Bye Baby. LC 84-60029. (ps up). 1984. 5.95 (*0-394-86798-X*) Random Bks Yng Read.
—Three Best-Loved Tales: Play with Me; So Big; The Boy with a Drum. 80p. (ps-2). 1992. write for info. (*0-307-15632-X*, 15632, Golden Pr) Western Pub.
Wilkin, Fred. Machines. LC 85-30936. (Illus.). 48p. (gr. k-4). 1986. PLB 15.27 (*0-516-01283-5*) Childrens.
—Matter. LC 85-30882. (Illus.). 48p. (gr. k-4). 1986. PLB 15.27 (*0-516-01284-3*) Childrens.
—Microscopes & Telescopes. LC 83-7592. (Illus.). 48p. (gr. k-4). 1983. PLB 15.27 (*0-516-01696-2*); pap. 4.95 (*0-516-41696-0*) Childrens.
Wilkins, Frances. Family Life from Nineteen Thirty to the Nineteen Eighties. (Illus.). 72p. (gr. 7-12). 1986. 19.95 (*0-7134-4818-0*, Pub. by Batsford UK) Trafalgar.
—Gambia. (Illus.). 96p. (gr. 5 up). 1988. 14.95 (*0-222-01129-7*) Chelsea Hse.

—Morocco. (Illus.). 96p. (gr. 5 up). 1988. 14.95 (*1-55546-186-7*) Chelsea Hse.
Wilkins, Lorela N., jt. auth. see Stancil, Rosemary D.
Wilkins, Marne. The Long Ago Lake. Weston, Martha, illus. 160p. (gr. 4 up). 1990. pap. 7.95 (*0-87701-632-1*) Chronicle Bks.
Wilkins, Mary-Jane. Air, Light & Water. Forsey, Chris, illus. 40p. (gr. 4-5). 1991. PLB 12.40 (*0-531-19104-4*) Watts.
—Air, Light & Water. Bull, Peter, illus. LC 90-42620. 40p. (Orig.). (gr. 2-5). 1991. pap. 3.95 (*0-679-80859-0*) Random Bks Yng Read.
—Everyday Things & How They Work. Bull, Peter, illus. 40p. (gr. 4-5). 1991. PLB 12.40 (*0-531-19109-5*, Warwick) Watts.
Wilkins, Natalie, ed. see Smith, Josephine A.
Wilkins, Sarah. Sarah Wilkins, in Search of a Song, Vol. 7. Fisher, Barbara, ed. 22p. (Orig.). (gr. 5-8). 1984. pap. 2.00 (*0-934830-35-5*) Ten Penny.
Wilkins, Sarah & Mennella, Roxanna. Dolls. Fisher, Barbara, ed. Wilkins, Sarah & Mennella, Roxanna, illus. 27p. (Orig.). (gr. 4-6). 1984. pap. 2.00 (*0-934830-34-7*) Ten Penny.
Wilkins, Verna. Dave & the Tooth Fairy. (ps-3). 1993. pap. 3.95 (*0-85953-133-3*) Childs Play.
Wilkins, Verna & Mills, Elaine. Kay's Birthday Numbers Book. LC 93-6648. 1993. 6.95 (*1-870516-00-1*) Childs Play.
Wilkins, Verna & McLean, Gill, eds. Abena & the Rock: A Story from Ghana. Wilkinson, Barry, illus. Ramamurthy, Sita, contrib. by. LC 93-12122. (Illus.). 1993. 7.95 (*1-870516-08-7*) Childs Play.
—Five Things to Find: A Story from Tunisia. Wilkinson, Barry, illus. LC 93-12121. 1993. 7.95 (*1-870516-07-9*) Childs Play.
—Just a Pile of Rice: A Story from China. Wilkinson, Barry, illus. LC 93-6645. 1993. 7.95 (*1-870516-06-0*) Childs Play.
—The Snowball Rent: A Story from Scotland. Wilkinson, Barry, illus. LC 93-16156. 1993. 7.95 (*1-870516-09-5*) Childs Play.
Wilkins, Verna A. Ben Makes a Cake. Clipson, Helen, illus. LC 93-9290. 1993. 6.95 (*1-870516-02-8*) Childs Play.
—Finished Being Four. Pound, Claire, illus. LC 93-12120. 1993. 7.95 (*1-870516-10-9*) Childs Play.
—Mike & Lottie. Baker, Alan, illus. LC 93-6643. 1993. 9.95 (*1-870516-03-6*) Childs Play.
Wilkins, Verna A. & Mills, Elaine. Mum Can Fix It. LC 93-2804. 1993. 6.95 (*1-870516-01-X*) Childs Play.
Wilkinson, Barbara. Apples for the Missionaries. Dillard, Karen, illus. 32p. (Orig.). (gr. 1-3). 1989. pap. text ed. 2.95 (*0-936625-67-8*) Womans Mission Union.
Wilkinson, Beth. Coping When a Grandparent Has Alzheimer's Disease. Rosen, Ruth, ed. (gr. 7-12). 1992. PLB 13.95 (*0-8239-1415-1*) Rosen Group.
—Coping with Jealousy. Rosen, Ruth, ed. (gr. 7-12). 1992. 13.95 (*0-8239-1516-6*) Rosen Group.
Wilkinson, Brenda. Definitely Cool. LC 92-12112. 176p. (gr. 3-7). 1993. 13.95 (*0-590-46186-9*) Scholastic Inc.
—Jesse Jackson: Still Fighting for the Dream. Gallin, Richard, ed. Young, Andrew, intro. by. (Illus.). 128p. (gr. 5 up). 1990. lib. bdg. 16.98 (*0-382-09926-5*); pap. 7.95 (*0-382-24064-2*) Silver Burdett Pr.
—Ludell. LC 75-9390. 176p. (gr. 7 up). 1975. PLB 14.89 (*0-06-026492-6*) HarpC Child Bks.
—Ludell. LC 75-9390. 176p. (gr. 5 up). 1992. pap. 3.95 (*0-06-440419-6*, Trophy) HarpC Child Bks.
—Ludell & Willie. 144p. (gr. 6 up). 1985. pap. 2.25 (*0-553-24995-9*) Bantam.
—Ludell & Willie. LC 76-18402. (gr. 7 up). 1977. PLB 13.89 (*0-06-026488-8*) HarpC Child Bks.
Wilkinson, Elizabeth. Making Cents: Every Kid's Guide to Money, Vol. 1. 1989. 14.95 (*0-316-94101-8*); pap. 8.95 (*0-316-94102-6*) Little.
Wilkinson, Jack & Tubbs, Orrin. Spike Mosquito & the Flying Ants. Haigis, Debbie, ed. Tubbs, Orrin, illus. (Orig.). (gr. 1-6). 1991. pap. write for info. (*0-9629543-0-6*) Maine Heritage.
Wilkinson, Jean B., ed. see Reese, Lyn.
Wilkinson, Phil. Amazing Buildings. Donati, Paolo, illus. LC 92-54314. 48p. (gr. 3 up). 1993. 16.95 (*1-56458-234-5*) Dorling Kindersley.
Wilkinson, Philip & Dineen, Jacqueline. People Who Changed the World. Ingpen, Robert, illus. LC 93-31357. 1994. write for info. (*0-7910-2764-3*); pap. write for info. (*0-7910-2789-9*) Chelsea Hse.
Wilkinson, Philip & Pollard, Michael. Generals Who Changed the World. Ingpen, Robert, illus. LC 93-31358. 1994. write for info. (*0-7910-2761-9*); pap. write for info. (*0-7910-2786-4*) Chelsea Hse.
Wilkinson, Sally. Cats Are People Too: By PattySue, Herself. 47p. (Orig.). (gr. 5 up). 1989. pap. 6.95 (*0-9623354-5-2*) OP Inc.
Wilkon, Jozef & Moers, Hermann. Lullaby for a Newborn King. Wilkon, Jozef, illus. Lanning, Rosemary, tr. from GER. LC 91-11684. (Illus.). 32p. (gr. k-3). 1991. 14.95 (*1-55858-123-5*) North-South Bks NYC.
Wilkon, Jozef, jt. auth. see Wilkon, Piotr.
Wilkon, Piotr. The Brave Little Kittens. Wilkon, Jozef, illus. Graves, Helen, tr. from GER. LC 90-44095. (Illus.). 32p. (ps-k). 1991. 14.95 (*1-55858-103-0*) North-South Bks NYC.
—Katzenausflug. Wilkon, Jozef, illus. (GER.). 32p. (gr. k-3). 1992. 14.95 (*3-314-00536-9*) North-South Bks NYC.

—Noah's Ark. Wilkon, Jozef, illus. LC 92-2687. 32p. (gr. k-3). 1992. 14.95 (*1-55858-158-8*); PLB 14.88 (*1-55858-159-6*) North-South Bks NYC.
—Trois Chatons Intrepides. Wilkon, Jozef, illus. (FRE.). 32p. (gr. k-3). 1992. 14.95 (*3-314-20735-2*) North-South Bks NYC.
Wilkon, Piotr & Wilkon, Jozef. Escape from the Zoo! Lanning, Rosemary, tr. from GER. LC 92-31034. (Illus.). 32p. (gr. k-3). 1993. 14.95 (*1-55858-201-0*); PLB 14.88 (*1-55858-202-9*) North-South Bks NYC.
Wilks, Mike. The Ultimate Noah's Ark: Perfect Puzzle for All Ages. Wilks, Mike, illus. LC 93-4021. 80p. (gr. 7 up). 1993. 24.95 (*0-8050-2802-1*) H Holt & Co.
Wilks, Rick J. & Millyard, Anne W. Getting Along. LC 80-65478. (gr. 4-8). 1978. pap. 9.95 (*0-8224-3377-X*) Fearon Teach Aids.
Wilks, Shelley. What's It Like to Be a Grocer. Ramsey, Marcy D., illus. LC 89-34394. 32p. (gr. k-3). 1990. lib. bdg. 10.89 (*0-8167-1805-9*); pap. text ed. 2.95 (*0-8167-1806-7*) Troll Assocs.
Will & Nicolas. Finders Keepers. Nicolas, illus. LC 51-12326. 32p. (gr. k-4). 1951. 14.95 (*0-15-227529-0*, HB Juv Bks) HarBrace.
—Finders Keepers. Mordvinoff, Nicolas, illus. LC 51-12326. 32p. (gr. k-4). 1989. pap. 3.95 (*0-15-630950-5*, Voyager Bks) HarBrace.
Willan, Anne. Chicken Classics. LC 91-58569. (Illus.). 128p. 1992. 19.95 (*1-56458-030-X*) Dorling Kindersley.
Willard, Barbara. The Eldest Son. (gr. k-12). 1989. pap. 3.25 (*0-440-20412-7*, LFL) Dell.
—A Flight of Swans. (gr. k up). 1989. pap. 3.25 (*0-440-20458-5*, LFL) Dell.
—Harrow & Harvest. 1989. pap. 3.25 (*0-440-20480-1*, LFL) Dell.
—The Iron Lily. (gr. k-12). 1989. pap. 3.25 (*0-440-20434-8*, LFL) Dell.
—The Sprig of Broom. (Orig.). (gr. k-12). 1989. pap. 3.25 (*0-440-20347-3*, LFL) Dell.
Willard, Carolyn, jt. auth. see Barber, Jacqueline.
Willard, John. Ember & His Friends in the Forest. Elliot, Stephen C., illus. 25p. (Orig.). (gr. 2-6). 1991. pap. 3.95 (*0-9612398-4-0*) J A Willard.
Willard, N. Beauty & the Beast. Moser, B., illus. 1992. 19.95 (*0-15-206052-9*, HB Juv Bks) HarBrace.
Willard, N. & Dillon, L. D. Pish Posh, Said Hieronymous Bosch. 32p. (ps up). 1991. 18.95 (*0-15-262210-1*, HB Juv Bks) HarBrace.
Willard, Nancy. The Ballad of Biddy Early. Moser, Barry, illus. LC 88-29187. 48p. (gr. 5 up). 1989. lib. bdg. 14.99 (*0-394-98414-5*) Knopf Bks Yng Read.
—East of the Sun & West of the Moon: A Play. Moser, Barry, illus. 64p. (gr. 3 up). 1989. 14.95 (*0-15-224750-5*) HarBrace.
—Firebrat. Willard, Nancy, illus. 1992. pap. 3.50 (*0-553-15985-2*) Bantam.
—High Rise Glorious Skittle Skat Roarious Sky Pie Angel Food Cake. Watson, Richard J., illus. 54p. (gr. 3 up). 1990. 15.95 (*0-15-234332-6*) HarBrace.
—The Highest Hit. McCully, Emily, illus. LC 77-88970. (gr. 4-7). 1978. 6.95 (*0-15-234278-8*, HB Juv Bks) HarBrace.
—Highest Hit. LC 77-88970. (gr. 4-7). 1993. pap. 4.95 (*0-15-234279-6*) HarBrace.
—The Marzipan Moon. Sewall, Marcia, illus. LC 80-24221. 48p. (gr. 2-5). 1981. 9.95 (*0-15-252962-4*, HB Juv Bks) HarBrace.
—The Marzipan Moon. Sewall, Marcia, illus. LC 80-24221. 46p. (gr. 2-5). 1981. pap. 3.95 (*0-15-252963-2*, Voyager Bks) HarBrace.
—The Mountains of Quilt. De Paola, Tomie, illus. LC 86-19577. 32p. (ps-3). 1987. 12.95 (*0-15-256010-6*, HB Juv Bks) HarBrace.
—Night Story. Plume, Ilse, illus. LC 85-17677. 32p. (ps-3). 1986. 13.95 (*0-15-257348-8*, HB Juv Bks) HarBrace.
—The Nightgown of the Sullen Moon. McPhail, David, illus. LC 83-8472. (ps-3). 1983. 14.95 (*0-15-257429-8*, HB Juv Bks) HarBrace.
—The Nightgown of the Sullen Moon. McPhail, David, illus. LC 83-8472. 32p. (Orig.). (ps-3). 1987. pap. 4.95 (*0-15-257430-1*, Voyager Bks) HarBrace.
—Papa's Panda. Hoban, Lillian, illus. LC 78-31787. (ps-2). 1979. 5.95 (*0-15-259462-0*, HB Juv Bks) HarBrace.
—Sailing to Cythera. McPhail, David, illus. LC 74-5602. 72p. (gr. 5 up). 1985. pap. 5.95 (*0-15-269961-9*, Voyager Bks) HarBrace.
—Simple Pictures Are Best. De Paola, Tomie, illus. LC 78-6424. 32p. (ps-3). 1978. pap. 3.95 (*0-15-682625-9*, Voyager Bks) HarBrace.
—The Sorcerer's Apprentice. Dillon, Leo, et al, illus. LC 93-19912. 32p. (ps-6). 1993. 15.95 (*0-590-47329-8*) Scholastic Inc.
—Starlit Somersault Downhill. (ps-3). 1993. 15.95 (*0-316-94113-1*) Little.
—Telling Time: Angels, Ancestors, & Stories. LC 93-16390. (gr. 4-7). 1993. pap. 10.95 (*0-15-693130-3*, HB Juv Bks) HarBrace.
—Uncle Terrible: More Adventures of Anatole. McPhail, David, illus. LC 82-47940. 120p. (gr. 5 up). 1985. pap. 5.95 (*0-15-292794-8*, HB Juv Bks) HarBrace.
—A Visit to William Blake's Inn. Provensen, Nancy & Provensen, Martin, illus. LC 80-27403. 44p. (ps-3). 1982. pap. 5.95 (*0-15-293823-0*, Voyager Bks) HarBrace.

—A Visit to William Blake's Inn: Poems for Innocent & Experienced Travelers. Provensen, Alice & Provensen, Martin, illus. LC 80-27403. 44p. (ps-3). 1981. 14.95 (0-15-293822-2, HB Juv Bks) HarBrace.

—The Well-Mannered Balloon. D'Andrade, Diane, ed. Shekerjian, Hiag & Shekerjian, Regina, illus. 32p. (Orig.). (ps-3). 1991. pap. 3.95 (0-15-294986-0, HB Juv Bks) HarBrace.

Willard, Nancy, et al. The Voyage of the Ludgate Hill: A Journey with Robert Louis Stevenson. Provensen, Martin & Provensen, Alice, illus. LC 86-19502. 32p. (gr. k-3). 1987. 14.95 (0-15-294464-8) HarBrace.

Willcocks, David, jt. auth. see Jacques, Reginald.

Willcox, Ken, jt. auth. see Littmann, Mark.

Willcox Smith, Jessie. A Child's Book of Stories. (gr. k-6). 1986. 8.98 (0-685-16856-5, 618869) Outlet Bk Co.

Willcutt, Robert, jt. auth. see Davidson, Patricia.

Willcutt, Robert E., jt. auth. see Davidson, Patricia S.

Wille, Christopher M. Opportunities in Forestry Careers. (Illus.). 160p. 1991. 13.95 (0-8442-8571-4, VGM Career Bks); pap. 10.95 (0-8442-8572-2, VGM Career Bks) NTC Pub Grp.

Willey. Thanksgiving Uncles. Date not set. 15.00 (0-06-026469-1, Festival); PLB 14.89 (0-06-026474-8, Festival) HarpC Child Bks.

Willey, Bob. From All Sides: Memories of World War II. (Illus.). 160p. (gr. 7-12). 1990. pap. text ed. 10.00 (0-86299-678-3) A Sutton Pub.

Willey, Henry N., Jr. I'm Not Too Little. (Illus.). 8p. (gr. k-6). 1984. visualized song 3.50 (3-90117-028-6) CEF Press.

Willey, Margaret. The Bigger Book of Lydia. LC 82-48842. 224p. (gr. 7 up). 1988. 3.25 (0-06-447049-0, Trophy) HarpC Child Bks.

—If Not for You. LC 88-3343. 160p. (gr. 7 up). 1988. PLB 11.89 (0-06-026499-3) HarpC Child Bks.

—If Not for You. LC 88-3343. 160p. (gr. 7 up). 1990. pap. 3.25 (0-06-447015-6, Trophy) HarpC Child Bks.

—Saving Lenny. (gr. 7 up). 1990. 13.95 (0-553-05850-9, Starfire) Bantam.

—Saving Lenny. 160p. 1991. pap. 2.99 (0-553-29204-8, Starfire) Bantam.

Will-Harris, Toni. Hang Gliding. (Illus.). 48p. (gr. 3-6). 1992. PLB 12.95 (1-56065-058-3) Capstone Pr.

Willhoite, Michael. Daddy's Roommate. Willhoite, Michael, illus. 32p. (ps). 1990. 14.95 (1-55583-178-8) Alyson Pubns.

—Daddy's Roommate. Willhoite, Michael, illus. 32p. (ps-2). 1991. pap. 8.95 (1-55583-118-4) Alyson Pubns.

—The Entertainer. (Illus.). 32p. (ps-1). 1992. pamphlet 3.95 (1-55583-202-4, Alyson Wonderland) Alyson Pubns.

—Families: A Coloring Book. Willhoite, Michael, illus. 32p. (Orig.). 1991. pap. 2.95 saddle-stitched (1-55583-192-3) Alyson Pubns.

—Uncle What-Is-It Is Coming to Visit!!! (Illus.). 32p. (ps-5). 1993. 12.95 (1-55583-205-9) Alyson Pubns.

Willi, Denise. Martina Navratilova: Tennis Star. (Illus.). 64p. (gr. 3-7). 1994. PLB 14.95 (1-56711-014-2) Blackbirch.

William, Kate. Steven's Bride. large type ed. Pascal, Francine, created by. LC 93-1350. 1993. write for info. (1-56054-756-1) Thorndike Pr.

William, Mayne. Come, Come to My Corner. Lilly, Kenneth, illus. 32p. (ps-3). 1987. 9.95 (0-13-152497-6) P-H.

Williams, A. Susan. Canada. LC 91-9534. (Illus.). 32p. (gr. k-4). 1991. 12.40 (0-531-18390-4, Pub. by Bookwright Pr) Watts.

—The Greeks. LC 92-43639. 32p. (gr. 4-6). 1993. 14.95 (1-56847-059-2) Thomson Lrning.

Williams, Abbie, illus. Little Talks with God. Dumelle, Grace & Stong, Susantext by. LC 93-2782. (Illus.). 1993. write for info. (0-937739-17-0) Roman IL.

Williams, Alex, jt. auth. see Buckley, Richard.

Williams, Amy. The Coasting Kids' Adventures. 1992. 6.95 (0-533-09631-6) Vantage.

Williams, Ann. The Crusaders. 2nd ed. Reeves, Marjorie, ed. (Illus.). 95p. (gr. 7-12). 1975. pap. text ed. 8.60 (0-582-31096-2, 78069) Longman.

Williams, Arlene. Fairy Tales for the New Age. 160p. (gr. 4 up). 1992. pap. 12.95 (0-9605444-1-0, Waking Light Pr) Wee Smile.

Williams, Barbara. Albert's Toothache. Chorao, Kay, illus. LC 74-4040. 32p. (ps-1). 1974. (Dutton); pap. 3.95 (0-525-45037-8) NAL-Dutton.

—Albert's Toothache. Chorao, Kay, illus. LC 74-4040. 32p. (ps-1). 1988. pap. 3.95 (0-525-44363-0, 0383-120, DCB) Dutton Child Bks.

—Author & Squinty Gritt. LC 90-37021. 80p. (gr. 2-5). 1990. 12.95 (0-525-44655-9, DCB) Dutton Child Bks.

—Breakthrough: Women in Archaeology. LC 80-7687. (Illus.). 174p. 1981. 9.95 (0-8027-6406-1) Walker & Co.

—Chester Chipmunk's Thanksgiving. Chorao, Kay, illus. LC 77-20812. 32p. (gr. k-3). 1988. (DCB); (DCB) Dutton Child Bks.

—The Crazy Gang Next Door. LC 90-1350. 160p. (gr. 3-7). 1992. pap. 3.95 (0-06-440391-2, Trophy) HarpC Child Bks.

—Donna Jean's Disaster. Levine, Abby, ed. Apple, Margot, illus. LC 86-15817. 32p. (gr. 1-5). 1986. PLB 11.95 (0-8075-1682-1) A Whitman.

—If He's My Brother. De Paola, Tomie, illus. (ps-2). 1980. pap. 2.50 (0-13-450627-8, Pub. by Treehouse) P-H.

—Kevin's Grandma. LC 74-23713. (Illus.). 32p. (ps-1). 1991. pap. 3.95 (0-525-44785-7, Puffin) Puffin Bks.

—Mitzi & Frederick the Great. (gr. k-6). 1987. pap. 2.50 (0-440-45867-6, YB) Dell.

—Mitzi & the Terrible Tyrannosaurus Rex. McCully, Emily A., illus. 112p. (gr. 3-7). 1983. pap. 1.95 (0-440-45673-8, YB) Dell.

Williams, Betty. Portrait of a Decade: The 1920s. (Illus.). 72p. (gr. 7-10). 1989. 19.95 (0-7134-5816-X, Pub. by Batsford UK) Trafalgar.

Williams, Bill. The New Webster's Comprehensive Dictionary of the English Language. 2nd, rev. ed. Cayne, Bernard S. & Lechner, Doris E., eds. (Illus.). 1930p. (gr. 3 up). 1992. deluxe ed. 99.99 (0-9623476-0-4); lib. bdg. 99.99 (0-685-28124-8) Amer Intl Pr.

Williams, Bill, illus. Winnie-the-Pooh All Year Long. 14p. (ps). 1981. write for info. (0-307-12260-3, Golden Bks) Western Pub.

Williams, Bradley B. Out of the Miry Clay. (Orig.). 1989. pap. 5.95 (0-9620486-0-7) B B Williams.

Williams, Brenda & Williams, Brian. People & Places. Forsey, Chris, illus. 40p. (gr. 4-5). 1991. PLB 12.40 (0-531-19111-7) Watts.

—The Random House Book of One Thousand-One Wonders of Science. Kerrod, Robin, et al, illus. LC 89-3954. 160p. 1990. PLB 11.99 (0-679-90080-2); pap. 13.00 (0-679-80080-8) Random Bks Yng Read.

Williams, Brenda, jt. auth. see Williams, Brian.

Williams, Brian. Countries of the World: A Visual Factfinder. LC 92-40367. (Illus.). 96p. (gr. 5 up). 1993. 15.95 (1-85697-844-3); pap. 9.95 (1-85697-816-8) Kingfisher Bks.

—Farming. Green, Gwen, illus. LC 92-29905. 48p. (gr. 5-8). 1993. PLB 21.34 (0-8114-4786-3) Raintree Steck-V.

—Fishing. Robinson, Bernard, illus. LC 92-21389. 48p. (gr. 5-8). 1992. PLB 21.34 (0-8114-4788-X) Raintree Steck-V.

—George Washington. (Illus.). 32p. (gr. 3-8). 1988. PLB 10.95 (0-86307-924-5) Marshall Cavendish.

—Joan of Arc. (Illus.). 32p. (gr. 3-8). 1989. PLB 10.95 (1-85435-202-4) Marshall Cavendish.

—Karl Benz. (Illus.). 48p. (gr. 5-8). 1991. RLB 12.40 (0-531-18404-8, Pub. by Bookwright Pr) Watts.

—The Kingfisher Reference Atlas: An A-Z Guide to Countries of the World. Porter, Malcolm, illus. LC 92-54829. 216p. 1993. 19.95 (1-85697-838-9) Kingfisher Bks.

—Literature. LC 90-36113. (Illus.). 48p. (gr. 6-11). 1990. PLB 19.92 (0-8114-2365-4) Raintree Steck-V.

—The Living World. LC 92-41309. (Illus.). 96p. (Orig.). (gr. 5 up). 1993. 15.95 (1-85697-846-X); pap. 9.95 (1-85697-817-6) Kingfisher Bks.

—Mining. Morris, Tony, illus. LC 92-29906. 48p. (gr. 5-8). 1993. PLB 21.34 (0-8114-4789-8) Raintree Steck-V.

—On the Move. LC 92-21678. (Illus.). 128p. (ps-3). 1993. 10.00 (0-679-83694-2); PLB 11.99 (0-679-93694-7) Random Bks Yng Read.

—Pioneers of Flight. LC 90-9470. (Illus.). 48p. (gr. 4-8). 1990. PLB 19.92 (0-8114-2755-2) Raintree Steck-V.

—Science & Technology. LC 92-46589. (Illus.). 96p. (gr. 5 up). 1993. 15.95 (1-85697-850-8); pap. 9.95 (1-85697-849-4) Kingfisher Bks.

—The Sea. LC 91-10570. (Illus.). 48p. (gr. 5-8). 1991. PLB 13.90 (0-531-19146-X, Warwick) Watts.

—The Sea. LC 92-53090. (Illus.). 48p. (Orig.). (gr. 3-8). 1992. pap. 5.95 (1-85697-815-X) Kingfisher Bks.

—Trading. Robinson, Bernard, illus. LC 92-27031. 48p. (gr. 5-8). 1993. PLB 21.34 (0-8114-4787-1) Raintree Steck-V.

—Twenty Names in Space Exploration. LC 89-23901. (Illus.). 48p. (gr. 3-8). 1990. PLB 12.95 (1-85435-256-3) Marshall Cavendish.

—Under the Sea. Allen, Graham, et al, illus. LC 88-17654. 24p. (Orig.). (gr. 2-5). 1989. PLB 5.99 (0-394-99990-8); pap. 2.95 (0-394-89990-3) Random Bks Yng Read.

—Voyages of Discovery. LC 89-26337. (Illus.). 48p. (gr. 4-8). 1990. PLB 19.92 (0-8114-2756-0) Raintree Steck-V.

—War & Weapons. Berry, John, et al, illus. LC 86-26262. 24p. (gr. 2-5). 1987. lib. bdg. 5.99 (0-394-98971-6) Random Bks Yng Read.

—Winston Churchill. (Illus.). 32p. (gr. 3-8). 1988. PLB 10.95 (0-86307-925-3) Marshall Cavendish.

Williams, Brian & Williams, Brenda. First Encyclopedia of Science. LC 92-44792. (Illus.). 192p. (gr. 2-6). 1993. 19.00 (0-679-83698-5); PLB 21.99 (0-679-93698-X) Random Bks Yng Read.

—The Random House Library of Knowledge First Encyclopedia. LC 91-32817. (Illus.). 192p. (gr. 2-6). 1992. 18.00 (0-679-83059-6) Random Bks Yng Read.

Williams, Brian, jt. auth. see Williams, Brenda.

Williams, C. Fred. Adventure Tales of Arkansas: A Cartoon History of a Spirited People. Lisenby, Foy & Poole, Jerry D., illus. Clinton, Bill & Jonsson, Phillip R.intro. by. x, 38p. (Orig.). (gr. 5-7). 1986. pap. 5.95 (0-9616677-0-2); tchr's. ed. 3.50 (0-9616677-1-0) Signal Media.

Williams, Carol L. Kelly & Me. LC 92-20492. 1993. 13.95 (0-385-30897-3) Delacorte.

Williams, Cecil & Mirikitani, Janice, eds. I Have Something to Say about This Big Trouble: Children of the Tenderloin Speak Out. (Illus.). 128p. (Orig.). (gr. 3-7). 1989. pap. 9.95 (0-9622574-1-9) Glide Word.

Williams, Cecil J. see Clark, Barbara R.

Williams, Claudette, jt. auth. see Evans, David.

Williams, Connie. Right-Hand Man. Davis, Timothy N., illus. LC 92-19158. 108p. 1992. pap. 4.95 (0-89084-638-3) Bob Jones Univ Pr.

Williams, David. Grandma Essie's Covered Wagon. Sadowski, Wiktor, illus. 48p. (ps-3). 1993. 16.00 (0-679-80253-3); PLB 16.99 (0-679-90253-8) Knopf Bks Yng Read.

—Walking to the Creek. Allen, Tom, illus. LC 88-6763. 40p. (ps-3). 1990. PLB 13.99 (0-394-90598-9) Knopf Bks Yng Read.

Williams, Deniece. Lullabies to Dreamland. (ps-3). 1993. 12.99 (1-56507-149-2) Harvest Hse.

Williams, Dianna. The Pilgrims Thanksgiving: A Keepsake Book. Ross, Connie, illus. 32p. (gr. 2-6). 1992. pap. 2.75 (1-878893-27-0) Telcraft Bks.

—The Pilgrims Thanksgiving: With Thanksgiving Journal & Activities. Ross, Connie, illus. 32p. (gr. 2-6). 1991. pap. text ed. 1.95 (1-878893-16-5, Telecraft) Telcraft Bks.

Williams, Don & Bailey, Cathy, illus. Disney's Beauty & the Beast: Belle Explores the Castle. LC 92-52971. 18p. (ps-1). 1992. 9.95 (1-56282-271-3) Disney Pr.

Williams, Donna R., jt. auth. see Johnson, Patricia P.

Williams, Earl P., Jr. What You Should Know about the American Flag. rev. ed. Prosser, Les, illus. Sheads, Scott S., frwd. by. (Illus.). 68p. (gr. 4-6). 1989. pap. text ed. 4.95 (0-939631-10-5) Thomas Publications.

Williams, Effie M. A Hive of Busy Bees. (gr. 5 up). 1976. Repr. of 1939 ed. 3.40 (0-686-15479-7) Rod & Staff.

Williams, G. Walton & Kollock, John. The Best Friend. 1991. 10.95 (0-87844-098-4); pap. 6.95 (0-87844-103-4) Sandlapper Pub Co.

Williams, Garth. Chicken Book. (ps). 1992. pap. 3.99 (0-440-40600-5) Dell.

—Rabbits' Wedding. Williams, Garth, illus. LC 58-5285. 30p. (gr. k-3). 1958. 15.00 (0-06-026495-0) HarpC Child Bks.

Williams, Garth, illus. Three Best-Loved Tales: The Kitten Who Thought He Was a Mouse; My First Counting Book; Home for a Bunny. 80p. (ps-2). 1992. write for info. (0-307-15635-4, 15635, Golden Pr) Western Pub.

Williams, Geoff. Aliens Next Door: Book & Cassette in 3-D Sound. (Illus.). 32p. (gr. 2-5). 1989. bk. & cass. 6.95 (0-8431-2746-5); pap. 2.95 (0-8431-2376-1) Price Stern.

—Hello, Mars! (Illus.). 64p. (gr. 2-7). 1989. 10.95 (0-8431-2733-3); incl. cassette 13.95 (0-8431-2745-7) Price Stern.

Williams, Geoffrey & Regan, Dennis. Adventures in the Solar System. Svenson, Borje, illus. 64p. 1986. bk. only 9.95x (0-8431-1552-1); incl. cass. 13.95x (0-8431-1553-X) Price stern.

Williams, Geoffrey T. Adventures Beyond the Solar System Plentron & Me. Morgan, Pierr, illus. 64p. (gr. 2-7). 1988. 9.95 (0-8431-2298-6) Price Stern.

—Antarctica: The Last Frontier. (Illus.). 32p. (gr. 1-6). 1992. 14.95 (0-8431-2995-6) Price Stern.

—Dinosaur World. (Illus.). 32p. (Orig.). (gr. 2-5). 1985. pap. 2.95 (0-8431-1439-8); pap. 6.95 incl. cass. (0-8431-1424-X) Price Stern.

—Explorers in Dinosaur World. Cremins, Robert, illus. 32p. (gr. 1-6). 1988. pap. 2.95 (0-8431-2264-1); pap. 6.95 incl. cass. (0-8431-2265-X) Price Stern.

—Giants of the Insects World. (gr. 4-7). 1991. pap. 9.95 (0-8431-2832-1) Price Stern.

—I'm a Jet Pilot. Galloway, Nixon, illus. 32p. (gr. 1-4). 1992. 9.95 (0-8431-2928-X) Price Stern.

—Lost in Dinosaur World. Svensson, Borje, illus. 32p. (gr. 6-11). 1987. incl. audiocassette 6.95 (0-8431-1885-7) Price Stern.

—Saber Tooth: A Dinosaur World Adventure. Cremins, Robert, illus. 32p. (gr. 1-5). 1988. pap. 2.95 (0-8431-2308-7); pap. 6.95 incl. cass. (0-8431-2319-2) Price Stern.

Williams, George A. & Barnes, Richard. Physical Science. Siegelman, Irwin, ed. (gr. 9-12). 1978. text ed. 32.24 (0-07-070415-5) McGraw.

Williams, George F. Bullet & Shell: The Civil War As the Soldier Saw It. (Illus.). 480p. 1992. 9.98 (0-681-41497-9) Longmeadow Pr.

Williams, George, III. Hot Springs of the Eastern Sierra. 2nd, rev. ed. Dalton, Bill, ed. LC 87-16230. (Illus.). 80p. (gr. 8-12). 1993. text ed. 14.95 (0-935174-35-4); pap. 9.95 (0-935174-34-6) Tree by River.

Williams, George J., III. Mark Twain: His Adventures at Aurora & Mono Lake. LC 86-16021. (Illus.). 100p. (gr. 5 up). 1986. lib. bdg. 12.95 (0-935174-18-4); pap. 6.95 (0-935174-17-6) Tree by River.

—Mark Twain: His Life in Virginia City, Nevada. Dalton, Bill, ed. LC 85-16483. (Illus.). 200p. (gr. 5 up). 1986. 24.95 (0-935174-16-8); pap. 10.95 (0-935174-15-X) Tree by River.

—Mark Twain: Jackass Hill & the Jumping Frog. Dalton, Bill, ed. (Illus.). 112p. (gr. 5 up). 1989. text ed. 12.95 (0-935174-20-6); pap. 6.95 (0-935174-19-2) Tree by River.

Williams, Ginny. A Matter of Trust. 1994. pap. 3.99 (1-56507-207-3) Harvest Hse.

Williams, Guy. Billy Budd. LC 91-50833. 60p. (Orig.). 1992. pap. 5.00 play script (0-88734-415-1) Players Pr.

—The Burning Fiery Furnace: Shadrach, Meshach, & Abednego. LC 91-52608. (Orig.). 1991. pap. 5.00 play script (0-88734-413-5) Players Pr.

—David & Goliath. LC 90-53572. (Orig.). (gr. 3 up). 1991. pap. 5.00 play script (0-88734-411-9) Players Pr.

Williams, Guy R. Making Mobiles. (Illus.). (gr. 7 up). 1969. 11.95 (0-87523-167-5) Emerson.

Williams, H. Crazy Creatures. (Illus.). 32p. (gr. 1-4). 1989. pap. 2.95 (0-88625-222-9) Durkin Hayes Pub.

—Harland Draws Animals. (Illus.). 32p. (gr. 1-6). 1989. pap. 2.95 (0-88625-226-1) Durkin Hayes Pub.

—Harland Draws Cartoons. (Illus.). 32p. (gr. 1-6). 1989. pap. 2.95 (0-88625-224-5) Durkin Hayes Pub.

—Harland Draws Wacky & Wierd. (Illus.). 32p. (gr. 1-6). 1989. pap. 2.95 (0-88625-232-6) Durkin Hayes Pub.

—Harland Draws 3-D. (Illus.). 32p. (gr. 1-6). 1989. pap. 2.95 (0-88625-229-6) Durkin Hayes Pub.

—Lickety Split, Adventure Through Time. (Illus.). 32p. (gr. 1-4). 1988. pap. 2.95 (0-88625-173-7) Durkin Hayes Pub.

—Lickety Split, Lost Your Marbles. (Illus.). 32p. (gr. 1-4). 1988. pap. 2.95 (0-88625-178-8) Durkin Hayes Pub.

—Lickety Split, Meets Fire Puffin. (Illus.). 32p. (gr. 1-4). 1988. pap. 2.95 (0-88625-175-3) Durkin Hayes Pub.

—Lickety Split, Who Are You? (Illus.). 32p. (gr. 1-4). 1988. pap. 2.95 (0-88625-181-8) Durkin Hayes Pub.

Williams, Harry. Twins of Ceylon. Paton, Jane, illus. LC 65-12044. (gr. 6-9). 1965. 12.95 (0-8023-1108-3) Dufour.

Williams, Helen. Stories in Art. LC 91-32185. (Illus.). 48p. (gr. 2-6). 1992. PLB 13.90 (1-56294-174-7) Millbrook Pr.

—Stories in Art. (gr. 4-7). 1992. pap. 6.70 (0-395-64558-1) HM.

Williams, J., jt. auth. see Mors, A.

Williams, Jane A., ed. see Maybury, Richard J.

Williams, Jane S. Super Duck: A True Story. Pruett, Robert H., ed. Williams, Jane S., illus. 61p. (Orig.). (ps-4). 1990. pap. 9.95 (0-9627635-0-0) Brandylane.

Williams, Jay. Everyone Knows What a Dragon Looks Like. Mayer, Mercer, illus. LC 84-29589. 32p. (gr. k-3). 1984. RSBE 14.95 (0-02-793090-4, Four Winds) Macmillan Child Grp.

—Everyone Knows What a Dragon Looks Like. 32p. (gr. k-3). 1984. pap. 5.95 (0-02-045600-X, Aladdin) Macmillan Child Grp.

Williams, Jay & Abrashkin, Raymond. Danny Dunn & the Voice from Space. Summers, Leo, illus. LC 67-22974. (gr. 4-6). 1982. pap. 1.95 (0-671-42684-2, Archway) PB.

Williams, Jay & Williams, Victoria. The Water of Life. McQueen, Lucinda, illus. 40p. (gr. k-12). 1980. 15.00 (0-89486-721-0, T5129) Hazelden.

Williams, Jean. Let Me Out! Introducing Poetry to Elementary Students. (gr. 1-6). 1993. 5.95 (0-929917-08-1) Magnolia PA.

—Matthew Henson, Polar Explorer. LC 93-6101. 1994. write for info. (0-531-20006-X) Watts.

Williams, Jeanne. New Medicine. rev. ed. Taylor, Michael, illus. 168p. 1993. write for info. (0-937460-90-7); pap. write for info. (0-937460-93-1) Hendrick-Long.

—Tame the Wild Stallion. Conoly, Walle, illus. LC 84-16257. 182p. (gr. 4 up). 1985. 14.95 (0-87565-002-3); pap. 8.95 (0-87565-009-0) Tex Christian.

—Trails of Tears: American Indians Driven from Their Lands. rev. ed. Taylor, Michael, illus. LC 91-28849. 192p. (gr. 7 up). 1992. Repr. of 1972 ed. 15.95 (0-937460-76-1) Hendrick-Long.

Williams, Jeff T. Macao. (Illus.). 88p. (gr. 5 up). 1988. lib. bdg. 14.95 (1-55546-786-5) Chelsea Hse.

Williams, Jennifer. Stringbean's Trip to Shining Sea. 1990. pap. 4.95 (0-590-44851-X) Scholastic Inc.

Williams, Jenny. Everyday ABC. LC 91-9161. (Illus.). 32p. (ps-1). 1992. 10.95 (0-8037-1079-8) Dial Bks Young.

—Playtime 123. LC 91-4683. (Illus.). 32p. (ps-1). 1992. 10.95 (0-8037-1077-1) Dial Bks Young.

Williams, Jill. An Adventure in Mouseland. Christie, Robert D., illus. LC 92-61769. 61p. (gr. k-6). 1992. pap. 3.95 (0-931563-10-0) Wishing Rm.

Williams, Joanna, illus. Picture Word Book Four. 28p. (ps). 1991. 3.50 (0-7214-1437-0, 916-4) Ladybird Bks.

—Picture Word Book One. 28p. (ps). 1991. 3.50 (0-7214-1434-6, 916-1) Ladybird Bks.

Williams, John. The Life Cycle of a Frog. Caulkins, Janet, ed. LC 87-71472. (Illus.). 32p. (gr. k-6). 1988. PLB 11.90 (0-531-18161-8, Pub. by Bookwright Pr) Watts.

—Simple Science Projects with Air. LC 91-50543. (Illus.). 32p. (gr. 2-4). 1992. PLB 17.27 (0-8368-0765-0) Gareth Stevens Inc.

—Simple Science Projects with Color & Light. LC 91-50544. (Illus.). 32p. (gr. 2-4). 1992. PLB 17.27 (0-8368-0766-9) Gareth Stevens Inc.

—Simple Science Projects with Electricity. LC 91-50545. (Illus.). 32p. (gr. 2-4). 1992. PLB 17.27 (0-8368-0767-7) Gareth Stevens Inc.

—Simple Science Projects with Flight. LC 91-50546. (Illus.). 32p. (gr. 2-4). 1992. PLB 17.27 (0-8368-0768-5) Gareth Stevens Inc.

—Simple Science Projects with Machines. LC 91-50547. (Illus.). 32p. (gr. 2-4). 1992. PLB 17.27 (0-8368-0769-3) Gareth Stevens Inc.

—Simple Science Projects with Time. LC 91-50548. (Illus.). 32p. (gr. 2-4). 1992. PLB 17.27 (0-8368-0770-7) Gareth Stevens Inc.

—Simple Science Projects with Water. LC 91-50549. (Illus.). 32p. (gr. 2-4). 1992. PLB 17.27 (0-8368-0771-5) Gareth Stevens Inc.

—Simple Science Projects with Wheels. LC 91-50550. (Illus.). 32p. (gr. 2-4). 1992. PLB 17.27 (0-8368-0772-3) Gareth Stevens Inc.

Williams, Julie S. And the Birds Appeared. Burningham, Robin Y., illus. 32p. (ps-3). 1988. 8.95 (0-8248-1194-1, Kolowalu Bk) UH Pr.

—Maui Goes Fishing. Burningham, Robin Y., illus. LC 90-27176. 32p. (ps-4). 1991. 9.95 (0-8248-1390-1, Kolowalu Bk) UH Pr.

Williams, Karen L. Applebaum's Garage. LC 92-31336. 1993. 13.95 (0-395-65227-8, Clarion Bks) HM.

—Baseball & Butterflies. 80p. 1990. 12.95 (0-688-09489-9) Lothrop.

—First Grade King. Shiffman, Lena, illus. 112p. (gr. k-3). 1992. 13.95 (0-395-58583-X, Clarion Bks) HM.

—Galimoto. Stock, Catherine, illus. LC 89-2258. 32p. (gr. k-3). 1990. 13.95 (0-688-08789-2); lib. bdg. 13.88 (0-688-08790-6) Lothrop.

—Galimoto. Stock, Catherine, illus. LC 89-2258. 32p. (ps-3). 1991. pap. 4.95 (0-688-10991-8, Mulberry) Morrow.

—Galimoto. Stock, Catherine, illus. (gr. k-4). 1993. 13.95 (0-685-64814-1); audio cass. 11.00 (1-882869-77-X) Read Advent.

—Tap-Tap. Stock, Catherine, illus. LC 93-13006. 1994. write for info. (0-395-65617-6, Clarion Bks) HM.

—When Africa Was Home. Cooper, Floyd, illus. LC 90-7684. 32p. (ps-1). 1991. 14.95 (0-531-05925-1); PLB 14.99 (0-531-08525-2) Orchard Bks Watts.

—When Africa Was Home. Cooper, Floyd, illus. LC 90-7684. 32p. (ps-2). 1994. pap. 5.95 (0-531-07043-3) Orchard Bks Watts.

Williams, Karen S. Best Friends Are for Keeps. LC 92-10988. 1992. write for info. (0-8280-0660-1) Review & Herald.

Williams, Larry, jt. auth. see Humbert, Jack.

Williams, Lawrence. Deserts. LC 89-17340. (Illus.). 48p. (gr. 4-8). 1990. PLB 12.95 (1-85435-169-9) Marshall Cavendish.

—Famine & Hunger. LC 92-16903. (Illus.). 48p. (gr. 6 up). 1992. RSBE 13.95 (0-02-793025-4, New Discovery) Macmillan Child Grp.

—Jungles. LC 89-17322. (Illus.). 48p. (gr. 4-8). 1990. PLB 12.95 (1-85435-171-0) Marshall Cavendish.

—Mountains. LC 89-25349. (Illus.). 48p. (gr. 4-8). 1990. PLB 12.95 (1-85435-173-7) Marshall Cavendish.

—Oceans. LC 89-17341. (Illus.). 48p. (gr. 4-8). 1990. PLB 12.95 (1-85435-172-9) Marshall Cavendish.

—Polar Lands. LC 89-25350. (Illus.). 48p. (gr. 4-8). 1990. PLB 12.95 (1-85435-170-2) Marshall Cavendish.

—Space. LC 89-17338. (Illus.). 48p. (gr. 4-8). 1990. PLB 12.95 (1-85435-174-5) Marshall Cavendish.

Williams, Leslie. A Bear in the Air. Vendrell, Carme S., illus. LC 80-10290. 28p. (gr. k up). 1980. 7.95 (0-916144-54-2) Stemmer Hse.

Williams, Letty. Little Red Hen: La Pequena Gallina Roja. Williams, Herb, illus. LC 78-75684. (ENG & SPA.). (ps-3). 1969. (Pub. by Treehouse); pap. 3.95 (0-13-537894-X) P-H.

Williams, Linda. Big Golden Book of Riddles, Jokes, Giggles, & Rhymes. (gr. 4-7). 1993. 10.95 (0-307-17877-3, Golden Pr) Western Pub.

—The Little Old Lady Who Was Not Afraid of Anything. Lloyd, Megan, illus. LC 85-48250. 32p. (ps-2). 1986. 14.00 (0-690-04584-0, Crowell Jr Bks); PLB 13.89 (0-690-04586-7) HarpC Child Bks.

—The Little Old Lady Who Was Not Afraid of Anything. Lloyd, Megan, illus. LC 85-48250. 32p. (ps-2). 1988. pap. 4.95 (0-06-443183-5, Trophy) HarpC Child Bks.

Williams, Lorraine D., ed. Buck Rogers: The First 60 Years in the 25th Century. LC 88-50400. (Illus.). 368p. 1988. 24.95 (0-88038-604-5) TSR Inc.

Williams, Lucy. The American West. (Illus.). 24p. (gr. k-4). 1991. 10.90 (0-531-18387-4, Pub. by Bookwright Pr) Watts.

Williams, Lynn. NTC's Basic Japanese, Level 1: Beginning. (JPN.). 363p. 1993. text ed. 19.95 (0-685-62845-0, F8430-0, Natl Textbk); tchr's. manual, 288p. 14.95 (0-685-62846-9, F8432-7, Natl Textbk); wkbk., 208p. 5.95 (0-685-62847-7, F8433-5, Natl Textbk); 3 audiocassettes 69.95 (0-685-66260-8, F8378-X, Natl Textbk) NTC Pub Grp.

—NTC's Basic Japanese, Level 2: Intermediate. (JPN.). 336p. 1993. text ed. 21.95 (0-685-62849-3, F8440-8, Natl Textbk); tchr's. manual, 288p. 14.95 (0-685-62850-7, F8441-6, Natl Textbk); wkbk., 160p. 6.95 (0-685-62851-5, F8442-4, Natl Textbk); 3 audiocassettes 69.95 (0-685-62852-3, F8382-X, Natl Textbk) NTC Pub Grp.

Williams, Marcia. The First Christmas. Williams, Marcia, illus. LC 88-1961. 32p. (Orig.). (ps-1). 1988. 4.95 (0-394-80434-1) Random Bks Yng Read.

—Greek Myths for Young Children. Williams, Marcia, illus. LC 91-58733. 40p. (ps up). 1992. 17.95 (1-56402-115-7) Candlewick Pr.

—Joseph & His Magnificent Coat of Many Colors. Williams, Marcia, illus. LC 91-71843. 32p. (ps up). 1992. 13.95 (1-56402-019-3) Candlewick Pr.

—Joseph & His Magnificent Coat of Many Colors. LC 91-71843. (ps-3). 1994. pap. 3.99 (1-56402-265-X) Candlewick Pr.

—Sinbad the Sailor. LC 93-3531. (Illus.). 1994. write for info. (1-56402-310-9) Candlewick Pr.

Williams, Marcia, adapted by. & illus. Don Quixote. LC 92-52995. 32p. (gr. 3-6). 1993. 13.95 (1-56402-174-2) Candlewick Pr.

Williams, Margery. Margery Williams "The Velveteen Rabbit" Eastman, David, ed. Schindler, S. D., illus. LC 87-11269. 32p. (gr. k-4). 1988. PLB 9.79 (0-8167-1061-9); pap. text ed. 1.95 (0-8167-1062-7) Troll Assocs.

—Miniature Velveteen Rabbit Gift Set. Green, Michael, illus. 88p. (ps-8). 1991. net, incl. plush bunny 2.79 (0-89471-978-5) Running Pr.

—The Velveteen Rabbit. (Illus.). 40p. (gr. 1-9). 1994. pap. 2.95 (0-380-58156-6, Flare) Avon.

—Velveteen Rabbit. Nicholson, William, illus. 47p. (gr. 3-5). 1991. PLB (0-385-07748-3); pap. 9.95 (0-385-07725-4); pap. 15.95 slipcased (0-385-00913-5) Doubleday.

—Velveteen Rabbit. Klimo, Kate, ed. Ho, Tien, illus. 48p. 1983. pap. 8.95 (0-671-44498-0) S&S Trade.

—The Velveteen Rabbit. Nicholson, William, illus. 40p. (gr. k up). 1994. pap. 2.99 (0-380-00255-8, Camelot) Avon.

—The Velveteen Rabbit. LC 81-1454. (Illus.). (ps up). deluxe ed. 7.95 (0-89471-153-9); pap. 3.95 (0-89471-128-8) Running Pr.

—The Velveteen Rabbit. Jorgensen, David, illus. 48p. (ps up). 1985. with cassette 15.95 (0-394-87712-8); 11.95 (0-394-87711-X) Knopf Bks Yng Read.

—The Velveteen Rabbit. Graham, Florence, illus. 32p. (ps-2). 1987. pap. 2.25 (0-448-19083-4, Platt & Munk); (Platt & Munk) Putnam Pub Group.

—The Velveteen Rabbit. 48p. 1988. pap. 3.95 (0-8125-3627-4) Tor Bks.

—The Velveteen Rabbit. Green, Michael, illus. LC 89-42996. 88p. (gr. 1-8). 1989. 4.95 (0-89471-755-5) Running Pr.

—Velveteen Rabbit. 1988. 5.99 (0-517-61813-3) Outlet Bk Co.

—The Velveteen Rabbit. Jorgensen, David, illus. LC 85-4257. 48p. (ps-2). 1990. pap. 3.95 (0-679-80333-5) Knopf Bks Yng Read.

—Velveteen Rabbit. Miles, Elizabeth, illus. (ps-3). 1990. pap. 2.50 (0-590-42805-5) Scholastic Inc.

—Velveteen Rabbit. (ps-3). 1988. 2.95 (0-8249-8175-8, Ideals Child) Hambleton-Hill.

—Velveteen Rabbit. (ps-3). 1989. incl. wooden puzzle 7.95 (0-8249-7311-9) Ideals.

—The Velveteen Rabbit. Officer, Robyn, illus. 40p. 1991. 6.95 (0-8362-4910-0) Andrews & McMeel.

—The Velveteen Rabbit. Chandler, Jean, illus. 1991. Incl. book, cass. & toy rabbit. 14.99 (0-517-66810-6) Outlet Bk Co.

—The Velveteen Rabbit. 40p. 1992. 4.95 (0-8362-3022-1) Andrews & McMeel.

—The Velveteen Rabbit. 1991. PLB 13.95s.p. (0-88682-474-5) Creative Ed.

—The Velveteen Rabbit. Nicholson, William, illus. 48p. (gr. k-4). 1992. 4.99 (0-440-40722-2, YB) Dell.

—Velveteen Rabbit. LC 82-42887. (ps-3). 1994. pap. 4.95 (0-671-88248-1, Halfmoon) S&S Trade.

—The Velveteen Rabbit: A Board Book. Jorgensen, David, illus. LC 89-63161. 10p. (ps). 1990. bds. 3.95 (0-679-80644-X) Random Bks Yng Read.

—The Velveteen Rabbit: Or How Toys Become Real. Green, Michael, illus. LC 84-71843. 48p. (Orig.). (gr. k-12). 1984. 9.98 (0-89471-266-7); Book & plush toy gift set. 22.98 (0-89471-885-1) Courage Bks.

—The Velveteen Rabbit: Or, How Toys Become Real. Hague, Michael, illus. LC 82-15606. 48p. (gr. k up). 1983. 11.95 (0-8050-0209-X, Bks Young Read) H Holt & Co.

—The Velveteen Rabbit: Or How Toys Become Real. Plume, Ilse, illus. LC 86-33544. 32p. (ps-3). 1987. 10.95 (0-15-293500-2) HarBrace.

Williams, Mari. Revolt in the Valley. 1992. pap. 23.00x (0-86383-778-6, Pub. by Gomer Pr UK) St Mut.

Williams, Mary A. Parkside Pranks & Sunset Stunts: Growing Up with San Francisco. Sichen, Kali, ed. (Illus.). 83p. (gr. 4-9). 1986. pap. 7.95 (0-916299-02-3) North Scale Co.

Williams, Maxville B. First for Freedom. rev. ed. Grace, Eugene U., intro. by. (Illus.). 312p. (gr. 8-12). pap. 8.00 (0-685-68019-3) Scribere.

Williams, Michael. Crocodile Burning. 192p. (gr. 7 up). 1992. 15.00 (0-525-67401-2, Lodestar Bks) Dutton Child Bks.

—The Genuine Half-Moon Kid. 192p. (gr. 7 up). 1994. 15.99 (0-525-67470-5, Lodestar Bks) Dutton Child Bks.

—Into the Valley. LC 92-25116. 176p. (gr. 5-9). 1993. 14.95 (0-399-22516-1, Philomel Bks) Putnam Pub Group.

Williams, Michael J. Cousins in Wonderland. 1993. 7.95 (0-533-10273-1) Vantage.

Williams, Monique M. Peanut Tells His Story. Caroland, Mary, ed. LC 90-71225. (Illus.). 44p. (gr. k-3). 1991. pap. 4.95 (1-55523-382-1) Winston-Derek.

Williams, Oscar, ed. The Mentor Book of Major British Poets. 576p. (gr. 9-12). 1985. pap. 5.99 (0-451-62637-0, Ment) NAL-Dutton.

Williams, Owen. How Roads Are Made. (Illus.). 32p. 1989. 12.95x (0-8160-2041-8) Facts on File.

Williams, Philip C., jt. auth. see Garrett, Sandra G.

Williams, Phyllis S., jt. auth. see Kenda, Margaret.

Williams, R. A. The Amaerkan Diksunaere: Silis Silis. 160p. (Orig.). 1990. 19.95 (0-9623915-2-2); pap. 9.95 (0-9623915-3-0) Jackson Pub.

Williams, Randall. The Rosen Photo Guide to a Career in Magic. (Illus.). (gr. 7-12). 1988. lib. bdg. 12.95 (0-8239-0817-8) Rosen Group.

Williams, Rex. Joseph. (Illus.). 224p. (gr. 3 up). 1990. pap. 2.50 (1-55748-116-4) Barbour & Co.

Williams, Richard N. Handbook of Substance Abuse. 2nd ed. LC 91-60152. (Illus.). 120p. (gr. 6-12). 1991. text ed. 39.50 (*1-879278-00-6*) Pharmaco-Video Pubns.

Williams, Robert L. Cowboy's Caravan. (Illus.). 150p. 1990. 16.95 (*0-9627534-0-8*) Skyspec Pub.

Williams, Rose. What Am I? (ps). 1993. 7.99 (*1-56476-148-7*, Victor Books) SP Pubns.

—What Is It? (ps). 1993. 7.99 (*1-56476-149-5*, Victor Books) SP Pubns.

Williams, Ruth L. The Silver Tree. LC 91-16399. 224p. (gr. 3-7). 1992. 14.00 (*0-06-020296-3*); PLB 13.89 (*0-06-020297-1*) HarpC Child Bks.

Williams, S. Working Cotton. Byard, C., ed. 1992. 14.95 (*0-15-299624-9*, HB Juv Bks) HarBrace.

Williams, S. P. Ginger Goes on a Diet. Garafano, Marie, illus. LC 92-28950. 1993. 13.95 (*0-395-66077-7*) HM.

Williams, Sam. Rock-a-bye Baby Books & Cradle Set. (Illus.). 10p. (ps). 1992. 19.95 (*0-525-44925-6*, DCB) Dutton Child Bks.

Williams, Sarah. Pudding & Pie: Favorite Nursery Rhymes. Beck, Ian, illus. 48p. 1989. 14.95 (*0-19-279868-5*) OUP.

Williams, Sarah, ed. Ride a Cock-Horse. Beck, Ian, illus. 48p. (ps). 1988. 12.95 (*0-19-279831-6*); Cassette. 6.95 (*0-19-279867-7*) OUP.

—Round & Round the Garden. Beck, Ian, illus. 48p. (ps). 14.95 (*0-19-279766-2*); pap. 5.95 (*0-19-272132-1*); cassette 7.95 (*0-19-279852-9*) OUP.

Williams, Sarah & Beck, Ian, eds. Pudding & Pie: Favorite Nursery Rhymes. 48p. (ps up). 1991. cassette 7.95 (*0-19-279876-6*, 12354) OUP.

Williams, Selver B. Life's Battles. Lundberg, Louise, ed. Knotts, Richard, illus. 220p. (gr. 8 up). 1991. pap. 10.95 (*0-9626633-0-1*) Taliaferro IN.

Williams, Sheila. Loch Moose Monster: More Stories from Isaac Asimov's Science Fiction Magazine. LC 91-36291. 1993. 16.00 (*0-385-30600-8*) Doubleday.

Williams, Sheila & Ardai, Charles, eds. Why I Left Harry's All-Night Hamburgers: And Other Short Stories from Isaac Asimov's Science Fiction Magazine. 288p. (gr. 7 up). 1992. pap. 3.99 (*0-440-21394-0*, LFL) Dell.

Williams, Sheila & Manson, Cynthia, eds. Tales from Isaac Asimov's Science Fiction Magazine: Short Stories for Young Adults. Asimov, Isaac, intro. by. (gr. 7 up). 1986. 15.95 (*0-15-284209-8*) HarBrace.

Williams, Sheron. And in the Beginning... Roth, Robert, illus. LC 90-43094. 40p. (gr. 1-5). 1992. SBE 13.95 (*0-689-31650-X*, Atheneum Child Bk) Macmillan Child Grp.

Williams, Sophy. Nana's Garden. Williams, Sophy, illus. 32p. (ps-1). 1994. 14.99 (*0-670-85287-2*) Viking Child Bks.

Williams, Sue. I Went Walking. Vivas, Julie, illus. 30p. (ps-2). 1990. 13.95 (*0-15-200471-8*, Gulliver Bks) HarBrace.

—I Went Walking. Vivas, Julie, illus. 32p. (ps-2). 1991. pap. 19.95 (*0-15-238010-8*) HarBrace.

—I Went Walking. LC 89-7847. (ps-3). 1992. pap. 5.95 (*0-15-238011-6*, HB Juv Bks) HarBrace.

Williams, Sue, compiled by. Strawberry Fair. Rothero, Chris, illus. 96p. (gr. 1-6). 14.95 (*0-7136-2676-3*, Pub. by A&C Black UK) Talman.

Williams, Sunnie. The Nomie Book: Growing up from Shy. Crisamore, Naomi, illus. 104p. (Orig.). (gr. 3-6). 1981. pap. 2.75 (*0-9605444-0-2*) Wee Smile.

Williams, Suzanne. Mommy Doesn't Know My Name. Shachat, Andrew, illus. 48p. (ps). 1990. 13.45 (*0-395-54228-6*) HM.

Williams, Sylvia. Leontyne Price: Opera Superstar. rev. ed. LC 84-7617. (Illus.). 32p. (gr. 2-5). 1990. PLB 14.60 (*0-516-03531-2*); pap. 3.95 (*0-516-43531-0*) Childrens.

Williams, T. Harry. Lincoln & His Generals. (gr. 9 up). 1967. pap. text ed. 6.95 (*0-07-553705-2*) McGraw.

Williams, Tad & Hoffman, Nina K. Child of an Ancient City. LC 92-16802. (Illus.). 144p. (gr. 7 up). 1992. SBE 14.95 (*0-689-31577-5*, Atheneum Child Bk) Macmillan Child Grp.

Williams, Terry T. & Major, Ted. The Secret Language of Snow. Dewey, Jennifer, illus. LC 83-19410. 144p. (gr. 3-7). 1984. 10.95 (*0-394-86574-X*, Pant Bks Young) Pantheon.

Williams, Thelma. Our Family Table: Recipes & Food Memories from African-American Life Models. Cellino, Maria E. & Rolfes, Ellen, eds. Jackson, Al, illus. Cosby, Camille O., intro. by. (Illus.). 96p. (gr. 7 up). 1993. 14.95 (*1-879958-14-7*); PLB 14.95 (*1-879958-16-3*) Tradery Hse.

Williams, Tony L. West Virginia: Our State. Buckalew, Marshall, ed. Harvey, Eve S. & Harvey, Cliff, illus. 288p. (gr. 4). 1990. 20.00 (*0-914498-09-6*); punched for 3-ring binder tchr's. manual 25.00 (*0-685-25544-1*) WV Hist Ed Found.

Williams, Travis. Changes. Thatch, Nancy R., ed. Williams, Travis, illus. Melton, David, intro. by. LC 93-13420. (Illus.). 29p. (gr. 6-9). 1993. PLB 14.95 (*0-933849-44-3*) Landmark Edns.

Williams, Ursula M. Bogwoppit. large type ed. 288p. (ps-5). 1990. lib. bdg. 16.95x (*0-7451-1155-6*, Lythway Large Print) Hall.

—The Good Little Christmas Tree. Tyler, Gillian, illus. LC 90-4498. 48p. 1991. 14.95 (*0-679-81060-9*) Knopf Bks Yng Read.

—Spid. large type ed. 192p. (gr. 3-7). 1991. 13.95 (*0-7451-1321-4*, Galaxy Child Lrg Print) Chivers N Amer.

Williams, Vera. A Chair for My Mother. Marcuse, Aida, tr. from ENG. Williams, Vera, illus. (SPA.). 32p. (ps up). 1994. pap. 4.95 (*0-688-13200-6*, Mulberry) Morrow.

Williams, Vera B. A Chair for My Mother. Williams, Vera B., illus. LC 81-7010. 32p. (gr. k-3). 1982. 16.00 (*0-688-00914-X*); PLB 15.93 (*0-688-00915-8*) Greenwillow.

—A Chair for My Mother. LC 81-7010. (ps-3). 1988. pap. 7.95 incl. cassette (*0-688-08400-1*, Mulberry) Morrow.

—A Chair for My Mother. enl. ed. Williams, Vera B., illus. 32p. (ps). 1993. pap. 18.95 (*0-688-12612-X*, Mulberry) Morrow.

—Cherries & Cherry Pits. Williams, Vera B., illus. LC 85-17156. 40p. (ps up). 1986. 13.95 (*0-688-05145-6*); PLB 13.88 (*0-688-05146-4*) Greenwillow.

—Cherries & Cherry Pits. (Illus.). (ps-3). 1991. Repr. 3.95 (*0-688-10478-9*, Mulberry) Morrow.

—More More More, Said the Baby. LC 89-2023. (Illus.). 32p. (ps up). 1990. 12.95 (*0-688-09173-3*); PLB 12.88 (*0-688-09174-1*) Greenwillow.

—Music, Music for Everyone. Williams, Vera B., illus. LC 83-14196. 32p. (gr. k-3). 1984. 14.95 (*0-688-02603-6*); PLB 14.93 (*0-688-02604-4*) Greenwillow.

—Music, Music for Everyone. LC 83-14196. (Illus.). 32p. (ps-3). 1988. pap. 3.95 (*0-688-07811-7*, Mulberry) Morrow.

—Scooter. LC 90-38489. (Illus.). 160p. (gr. 4-7). 1993. 15.00 (*0-688-09376-0*); PLB 14.93 (*0-688-09377-9*) Greenwillow.

—Something Special for Me. Williams, Vera B., illus. LC 82-11884. 32p. (gr. k-3). 1983. 16.00 (*0-688-01806-8*); PLB 15.93 (*0-688-01807-6*) Greenwillow.

—Something Special for Me. LC 82-11884. (Illus.). (ps-3). 1986. 4.95 (*0-688-06526-0*, Mulberry) Morrow.

—Stringbean's Trip to The Shining Sea. Williams, Jennifer & Williams, Vera B., illus. LC 86-29502. 48p. (gr. k-3). 1988. 13.95 (*0-688-07161-9*); lib. bdg. 13.88 (*0-688-07162-7*) Greenwillow.

—Three Days on a River in a Red Canoe. LC 80-23893. (Illus.). 32p. (gr. k-3). 1981. 14.95 (*0-688-80307-5*); PLB 14.88 (*0-688-84307-7*) Greenwillow.

—Three Days on a River in a Red Canoe. LC 80-23893. (Illus.). 32p. (ps-3). 1986. pap. 3.95 (*0-688-04072-1*, Mulberry) Morrow.

Williams, Victoria, jt. auth. see Williams, Jay.

Williams-Ellis, Anabel. Tales from the Enchanted World. Kemp, Moira, illus. (gr. 3-7). 1988. 17.95 (*0-316-94133-6*) Little.

Williams-Garcia, Rita. Blue Tights. LC 87-17156. 160p. (gr. 7 up). 1988. 12.95 (*0-525-67234-6*, Lodestar Bks) Dutton Child Bks.

—Fast Talk on a Slow Track. 176p. (gr. 7 up). 1991. 15.00 (*0-525-67334-2*, Lodestar Bks) Dutton Child Bks.

—Fast Talk on a Slow Track. 1992. pap. 3.50 (*0-553-29594-2*) Bantam.

Williamson, Duncan. Don't Look Back Jack! Scottish Traveller Tales. 162p. (gr. 5 up). 1994. 13.95 (*0-86241-309-5*, Pub. by Cnngt UK) Trafalgar.

Williamson, Henry. Tarka the Otter: The Joyful Water-Life & Death in the Two Rivers. Finch, Robert, intro. by. LC 90-55169. (Illus.). 276p. 1990. pap. 9.95 (*0-8070-8507-3*) Beacon Pr.

Williamson, J. N. The Black School. (Orig.). 1989. pap. 3.50 (*0-440-20265-5*) Dell.

Williamson, Karina, ed. see Smart, Christopher.

Williamson, Kevin, illus. Heaven How to Get There. 6p. (gr. k-6). 1964. pap. text ed. 2.65 (*1-55976-125-3*) CEF Press.

Williamson, Louis. The Year Christmas Was Almost Spoiled. Galinat, William, illus. (gr. k-3). 1990. pap. 5.95 (*0-533-08481-4*) Vantage.

Williamson, Mel & Ford, George. Walk on. (Illus.). 32p. (gr. 3 up). 1972. 11.95 (*0-89388-042-6*) Okpaku Communications.

Williamson, Ray A. & Monroe, Jean G. First Houses: Native American Homes & Sacred Structures. Carlson, Susan, illus. LC 92-34900. 1993. 14.95 (*0-395-51081-3*) HM.

Williamson, Ray A., jt. auth. see Guard, Jean.

Williamson, Sarah & Williamson, Zachary. Kids Cook! Fabulous Food for the Whole Family. Williamson, Susan, ed. Trezzo, Loretta, illus. LC 91-38513. 160p. (Orig.). (gr. 2-12). 1992. pap. 12.95 (*0-913589-61-6*) Williamson Pub Co.

Williamson, Susan, ed. see Carlson, Laurie.

Williamson, Susan, ed. see Gordon, Patricia & Snow, Reed C.

Williamson, Susan, ed. see Milord, Susan.

Williamson, Susan, ed. see Williamson, Sarah & Williamson, Zachary.

Williamson, Tracey. Magic Shadow Show: Four Stories - Four Plays, 2 bks. (Illus.). 24p. (gr. k-4). 1991. 17.95 (*0-525-44765-2*, DCB) Dutton Child Bks.

Williamson, Walter. Early Stages: The Professional Theater & the Young Actor. LC 85-26467. (Illus.). 128p. (gr. 6 up). 1986. 12.95 (*0-8027-6624-2*); lib. bdg. 12.85 (*0-8027-6630-7*) Walker & Co.

Williamson, Zachary, jt. auth. see Williamson, Sarah.

Willingham, David. One Large Order of Faith to Go. Stoub, Paul, illus. Smit, Harvey A., intro. by. (Illus.). 99p. (Orig.). (gr. 6-8). 1991. pap. text ed. 6.25 (*1-56212-012-3*, 1701-0480) CRC Pubns.

Willis, Abigail. Halloween Fun: Great Things to Make & Do. Spenceley, Annabel, illus. LC 93-21712. 32p. (gr. 2-6). 1993. pap. 4.95 (*1-85697-864-8*) Kingfisher Bks.

Willis, Charles. Battle of Little Big Horn. (Illus.). 64p. 1990. PLB 16.98 (*0-382-09952-4*); pap. 8.95 (*0-382-09948-6*) Silver Burdett Pr.

Willis, Delta. The Leakey Family: Leaders in the Search for Human Origins. LC 92-12522. (Illus.). 128p. 1992. PLB 16.95 (*0-8160-2605-X*) Facts on File.

Willis, Doris. God's Wonderful World. (ps). 1990. 3.95 (*0-687-03121-4*) Abingdon.

—I Like to Come to My Church. (ps). 1990. 3.95 (*0-687-03122-2*) Abingdon.

—Jesus Grew. (ps). 1990. 3.95 (*0-687-03124-9*) Abingdon.

—Jesus, My Friend & Teacher. (ps). 1990. 3.95 (*0-687-03123-0*) Abingdon.

—Teacher's Guide to Pearl Makers. Lansdale, Paul, illus. 64p. (Orig.). 1989. pap. 5.95 (*0-377-00194-5*) Friendship Pr.

—Tell Me a Bible Story. LC 90-22423. 1991. pap. 3.95 (*0-687-03126-5*) Abingdon.

Willis, Irene, jt. auth. see Richards, Arlene K.

Willis, Jeanne. Earth Hounds, As Explained by Professor Xargle. LC 89-23696. (Illus.). 32p. (ps-2). 1990. 12.95 (*0-525-44600-1*, DCB) Dutton Child Bks.

—Earth Mobiles, As Explained by Professor Xargle. Ross, Tony, illus. LC 91-23500. 32p. (ps-2). 1992. 14.00 (*0-525-44892-6*, DCB) Dutton Child Bks.

—Earth Tigerlets, As Explained by Professor Xargle. Ross, Tony, illus. LC 90-19346. 32p. (ps-2). 1991. 13.95 (*0-525-44732-6*, DCB) Dutton Child Bks.

—Earth Weather As Explained by Professor Xargle. Ross, Tony, illus. LC 92-14067. (ps-2). 1993. Repr. of 1991 ed. 14.00 (*0-525-45025-4*, DCB) Dutton Child Bks.

—Earthlets, As Explained by Professor Xargle. Ross, Tony, illus. LC 88-23692. 32p. (ps-2). 1989. 14.00 (*0-525-44465-3*, DCB) Dutton Child Bks.

—The Monster Bed. Varley, Jeanne, illus. LC 86-10366. 32p. (ps-2). 1987. 12.95 (*0-688-06804-9*); PLB 12.88 (*0-688-06805-7*) Lothrop.

—Relativity, As Explained by Professor Xargle. Ross, Tony, illus. LC 93-32606. (gr. 5 up). 1994. write for info. (*0-525-45245-1*, DCB) Dutton Child Bks.

Willis, Kathy see Jones, Michael P.

Willis, Leydel J. Yesterday, Today, & Tomorrow, Bk. 2: Today. new ed. (gr. 8-12). 1977. 4.95 (*0-8187-0030-0*) Harlo Pr.

Willis, Lynn, ed. see Herber, Keith & Morrison, Mark.

Willis, Lynn, ed. see Isynwill, L. N. & Keith, Herbert.

Willis, Lynn, ed. see Love, Penelope & Morrison, Mark.

Willis, Lynn, ed. see Stafford, Greg.

Willis, Meredith S. The Legends of Marco. Lilly, Charles, illus. LC 93-14491. 1994. write for info. (*0-06-023558-6*); PLB write for info. (*0-06-023559-4*) HarpC Child Bks.

Willis, Patricia C. A Place to Claim As Home. Giblin, James, ed. 176p. (gr. 4-7). 1991. 13.45 (*0-395-55395-4*, Clarion Bks) HM.

Willis, Ted. The Bells of Autumn. 256p. 1991. 18.95 (*0-312-06303-2*) St Martin.

—A Problem for Mother Christmas. Bennett, Jill, illus. 160p. (gr. 3-5). 1991. 17.95 (*0-575-03884-5*, Pub. by Gollancz England) Trafalgar.

Willis, Terri. Land Use & Abuse. LC 92-8842. (Illus.). 128p. (gr. 4-8). 1992. PLB 26.60 (*0-516-05507-0*) Childrens.

Willis, Terri, jt. auth. see Black, Wallace B.

Willis, Val. The Mystery in the Bottle. Shelley, John, illus. 32p. (gr. k-3). 1991. bds. 14.95 (*0-374-35194-5*) FS&G.

—El Secreto en la Caja de Fostoros: The Secret in the Matchbox. (ps-3). 1993. 16.00 (*0-374-36701-9*, Mirasol) FS&G.

—Surprise in the Wardrobe. (gr. 4-8). 1990. 15.00 (*0-374-37309-4*) FS&G.

Willis, William M. The Children's Question Book: A Parent Teacher Guide. LC 81-83727. 115p. (Orig.). (gr. 1 up). 1981. pap. text ed. 7.95 (*0-9607028-1-4*) Ocean East.

Willner, Carl. Goblin-Gate & Eagle's Eyrie. (Illus.). 32p. (gr. 10-12). 1985. pap. 7.00 (*0-915795-40-X*, 8070) Iron Crown Ent Inc.

—Havens of Gondor, Land of Belfalas. Fenlon, Peter, ed. McBride, Angus, illus. 64p. (Orig.). (gr. 10-12). 1987. pap. 12.00 (*0-915795-25-6*, 3300) Iron Crown Ent Inc.

—Tower of Cirith Ungol & Shelob's Lair. (Illus.). 32p. (gr. 10-12). 1984. pap. 7.00 (*0-915795-21-3*, 8030) Iron Crown Ent Inc.

Willner-Pardo, Gina. Natalie Spitzer's Turtles. Levine, Abby, ed. Delaney, Molly, illus. LC 92-3342. 32p. (gr. k-3). 1992. 13.95g (*0-8075-5515-0*) A Whitman.

—What I'll Remember When I Am a Grownup. Krudop, Walter L., illus. LC 92-42148. 1994. write for info. (*0-395-63310-9*, Clarion Bks) HM.

Willoughby, Alana. My Dolly. Wasserman, Dan, ed. Reese, Bob, illus. (gr. k-1). 1979. 7.95 (*0-89868-075-1*); pap. 2.95 (*0-89868-086-7*) ARO Pub.

Willoughby, Bebe, jt. ed. see Etkin, Linda.

Willoughby, Elaine M. Boris & the Monsters. Munsinger, Lynn, illus. LC 80-25837. 32p. (gr. k-3). 1986. 13.45 (*0-395-29067-8*); pap. 4.80 (*0-395-42649-9*) HM.

Willow, Diane. At Home in the Rainforest. (Illus.). 32p. (ps-3). 1992. 14.95 (*0-88106-485-8*); PLB 15.00 (*0-88106-688-5*); pap. 6.95 (*0-88106-484-X*) Charlesbridge Pub.

—Dentro de la Selva Tropical (At Home in the Rain Forest) (Illus.). 32p. (ps-3). 1993. pap. 6.95 (*0-88106-421-1*) Charlesbridge Pub.

Willoya, William & Brown, Vinson. Warriors of the Rainbow: Strange & Prophetic Dreams of the Indian Peoples. (Illus.). 94p. (gr. 4 up). 1962. 15.95 (0-911010-25-4); pap. 7.95 (0-911010-24-6) Naturegraph.

Willrich, Lola. Penguins - a Thematic Unit. Fullam, Sue & Vasconcelles, Keith, illus. 80p. (gr. 1-3). 1991. wkbk. 7.95 (1-55734-277-6) Tchr Create Mat.

Wills, Charles. Pearl Harbor. (Illus.). 64p. (gr. 5 up). 1991. PLB 13.98 (0-382-24125-8); pap. 8.95 (0-382-24119-3) Silver Burdett Pr.

—The Tet Offensive. (Illus.). 64p. (gr. 5 up). 1989. PLB 16.98 (0-382-09849-8); pap. 8.95 (0-382-09855-2) Silver Burdett Pr.

Wills, John. Mountain: Four Seasons. 152p. (gr. 9 up). 1991. pap. text ed. 11.95 (1-880354-00-4) Qual-Tech.

Willson, Robina B. Mozart's Story. Lewis, Anthony, illus. 48p. (gr. 3 up). 1991. 14.95 (0-7136-3311-5, Pub. by A&C Black UK) Talman.

Wilmer, Diane. Gallop off & Go! rev. ed. Petrone, Valeria, illus. 32p. (gr. k-2). 1989. Repr. of 1989 ed. lib. bdg. 10.50 (1-878363-01-8) Forest Hse.

—Nuts about Nuts. rev. ed. Dowling, Paul, illus. 32p. (gr. k-2). 1990. Repr. of 1989 ed. PLB 10.50 (1-878363-09-3) Forest Hse.

—The Playground. rev. ed. Chamberlain, Margaret, illus. 32p. (gr. k-2). 1990. Repr. of 1986 ed. PLB 10.50 (1-878363-10-7) Forest Hse.

—Zap Zero - The Delivery Man. rev. ed. Dowling, Paul, illus. 32p. (gr. k-2). 1990. Repr. of 1989 ed. PLB 10.50 (1-878363-11-5) Forest Hse.

Wilmer, Diane & Currey, Anna. Mr. Pepino's Cabbage. rev. ed. Currey, Anna, illus. 32p. (gr. k-2). 1989. Repr. of 1989 ed. lib. bdg. 10.50 (1-878363-02-6) Forest Hse.

Wilmot, Zoe. Hook a Book: Bat. LC 93-77342. (ps-3). 1993. 3.99 (0-89577-509-3, Readers Digest Kids) RD Assn.

—Hook a Book: Lemur. LC 93-77343. (ps-3). 1993. 3.99 (0-89577-508-5, Readers Digest Kids) RD Assn.

—Hook a Book: Monkey. LC 93-77345. (ps-3). 1993. 3.99 (0-89577-510-7, Readers Digest Kids) RD Assn.

—Hook a Book: Opossum. LC 93-77344. (ps-3). 1993. 3.99 (0-89577-511-5, Readers Digest Kids) RD Assn.

Wilner, Barry. Soccer. Seiden, Art, illus. Photo Shoppe Staff, photos by. Charlton, Bobby, intro. by. LC 93-1525. 1993. write for info. (0-8114-5777-X) Raintree Steck-V.

Wilner, Isabel. B Is for Bethlehem: A Christmas Alphabet. Kleven, Elisa, illus. LC 89-49481. 32p. (ps up). 1990. 13.95 (0-525-44622-2, DCB) Dutton Child Bks.

—A Garden Alphabet. Wolff, Ashley, illus. LC 90-19619. 32p. (ps-2). 1991. 12.95 (0-525-44731-8, DCB) Dutton Child Bks.

—The Poetry Troupe: Poems to Read Aloud. LC 77-9439. (Illus.). 224p. (gr. 3-7). 1977. SBE 14.95 (0-684-15198-7, Scribners Young Read) Macmillan Child Grp.

Wilsdon, Christin. Blast with the Past: Puzzling History Mysteries. (gr. 4-7). 1994. pap. 1.25 (0-553-37285-8) Bantam.

Wilsdorf, Anne. Philomene. LC 90-24295. 1992. 14.00 (0-688-10369-3); PLB 13.93 (0-688-10370-7) Greenwillow.

—Princess: Based on Hans Christian Andersen's "The Princess & the Pea" LC 92-20636. (Illus.). 32p. (gr. up). 1993. 14.00 (0-688-11541-1); PLB 13.93 (0-688-11542-X) Greenwillow.

Wilson. Allosaurus. (Illus.). 24p. 1984. PLB 14.00 (0-86592-206-3) Rourke Enter.

—Chinese Americans. 1991. 13.95s.p. (0-86593-135-6) Rourke Corp.

—Diplodocus. (Illus.). 24p. 1984. PLB 14.00 (0-86592-202-0) Rourke Enter.

—Hypsilophodon. (Illus.). 24p. 1984. PLB 14.00 (0-86592-205-5) Rourke Enter.

—Mother Grumpy's Dog. 01#1991 ed. 12.95 (0-8050-1432-2) H Holt & Co.

—Pteranodon. (Illus.). 24p. 1984. PLB 14.00 (0-86592-201-2) Rourke Enter.

—Woolly Mammoth. (Illus.). 24p. 1984. PLB 14.00 (0-86592-203-9) Rourke Enter.

Wilson, jt. auth. see Oliver.

Wilson, ed. Ichthyosaurus. (Illus.). 24p. 1984. PLB 14.00 (0-86592-204-7) Rourke Enter.

Wilson, A. N. Hazel the Guinea Pig. Heale, Jonathan & Heale, Jonathan, illus. LC 91-71850. 96p. (gr. k-3). 1992. 13.95 (1-56402-013-4) Candlewick Pr.

—Tabitha. Fox-Davies, Sarah, illus. LC 88-19820. 48p. (gr. 3 up). 1989. 14.95 (0-531-05813-1); PLB 14.99 (0-531-08413-2) Orchard Bks Watts.

Wilson, Alice, et al. Flashback! (Orig.). (gr. k up). 1980. pap. 4.50 (0-87602-259-X) Anchorage.

Wilson, Annette, jt. auth. see Wallace, Latressia.

Wilson, April, illus. Look Again! The Second Ultimate Spot-the-Difference Book. Wood, A. J., notes by. LC 91-31214. (Illus.). 40p. (gr. 1 up). 1992. 13.00 (0-8037-0958-7) Dial Bks Young.

Wilson, Barbara. Icebergs & Glaciers. Leon, Vicki, ed. (Illus.). 40p. (Orig.). (gr. 5 up). 1990. pap. 7.95 (0-918303-23-0) Blake Pub.

Wilson, Barbara A. Study & Writing Skills Manual. 34p. 1992. tchr's ed. 8.00 (1-56778-042-3) Wilson Lang Trning.

Wilson, Barbara K. Acacia Terrace. 1990. 13.95 (0-590-42885-3) Scholastic Inc.

—Path Through the Woods. Stewart, Charles, illus. (gr. 7 up). 1958. 21.95 (0-685-40040-9) S G Phillips.

—Scottish Folk-Tales & Legends. Kiddell-Monroe, Joan, illus. 224p. (ps-7). 1990. pap. 10.95 (0-19-274141-1) OUP.

—Wishbones: A Folk Tale from China. So, Meilo, illus. LC 92-26993. 32p. (ps-2). 1993. SBE 14.95 (0-02-793125-0, Bradbury Pr) Macmillan Child Grp.

Wilson, Ben. UFOs. Gibbons, Tony & Kingstone, Martin, illus. LC 87-31480. 48p. (gr. 3-8). 1989. PLB 12.40 (0-531-18219-3, Pub. by Bookwright Pr) Watts.

Wilson, Bennett. The Magic Feather: An Adventure in Navajo Land. Wilson, Bennett, illus. 42p. (Orig.). (gr. 1-6). 1989. pap. 5.00 (0-918080-48-7) Treasure Chest.

Wilson, Beth P. Jenny. Johnson, Delores, illus. LC 89-8135. 32p. (gr. k-3). 1990. RSBE 13.95 (0-02-793120-X, Macmillan Child Bk) Macmillan Child Grp.

Wilson, Budge. The Leaving. 208p. (gr. 6 up). 1992. 14.95 (0-399-21878-5, Philomel Bks) Putnam Pub Group.

—The Leaving. 208p. (gr. 7 up). 1993. pap. 3.50 (0-590-46933-9, Point) Scholastic Inc.

—Thirteen Never Changes. 160p. 1991. pap. 2.95 (0-590-43488-8, Apple Paperbacks) Scholastic Inc.

Wilson, Christina. Ghostwriter: Trivia, Facts, & Fun. (gr. 1-3). 1993. pap. 1.25 (0-553-37157-6) Bantam.

Wilson, Claire. Quanah Parker. (Illus.). 112p. (gr. 5 up). 1992. lib. bdg. 17.95 (0-7910-1702-8) Chelsea Hse.

Wilson, Claire & Bolton, Jonathan. Joseph Brant. (Illus.). 112p. (gr. 5 up). 1992. lib. bdg. 17.95 (0-7910-1709-5) Chelsea Hse.

Wilson, Claire M., jt. auth. see Bolton, Jonathan W.

Wilson, Dana, ed. see Spainhower, Steven D.

Wilson, David A. Star Track. (Illus.). 152p. (Orig.). 1994. pap. 12.00 (0-934852-38-3) Lorien Hse.

Wilson, David C. Blackberry Organ. LC 91-67985. 48p. (gr. 7-4). 1992. pap. write for info. (0-9632765-6-5) Spirit Light.

Wilson, David M. The Vikings. (Illus.). (gr. 2-6). pap. 3.95 (0-7141-0549-X, Pub. by Brit Mus UK) Parkwest Pubns.

Wilson, Dorminster, jt. auth. see Rohmer, Harriet.

Wilson, Ellen. Annie Oakley. (Illus.). 192p. (gr. 2-6). 1989. pap. 3.95 (0-689-71346-0, Aladdin) Macmillan Child Grp.

Wilson, Etta. Daniel & the Lions. (Illus.). 1992. bds. 3.49 (0-8007-7123-0) Revell.

—Jesus & the Donkey. (Illus.). 1992. bds. 3.49 (0-8007-7125-7) Revell.

—Music in the Night. Koontz, Robin M., illus. LC 92-11575. (ps-2). 1993. 12.99 (0-525-65113-6, Cobblehill Bks) Dutton Child Bks.

—The Value of Excellence. (gr. 7-12). 1991. PLB 15.95 (0-8239-1289-2) Rosen Group.

Wilson, Etta & Jones, Sally L. Bible Atlas: A First Reference Book. Schindler, Stephen, illus. 24p. (gr. 3-5). 1993. text ed. 9.99 (0-7847-0080-X, 24-03620) Standard Pub.

—Bible Dictionary: A First Reference Book. Schindler, Stephen, illus. 24p. (gr. 3-5). 1993. text ed. 9.99 (0-7847-0079-6, 24-03619) Standard Pub.

Wilson, Etta, ed. My Play a Tune Book: Christmas Songs. Harrison, Susan, illus. 26p. (gr. k up). 1987. 15.95 (0-938971-05-0) JTG Nashville.

—My Play a Tune Book: Twelve Favorite Bible Songs. Mahan, Benton, illus. 26p. (ps up). 1988. 12.95 (0-687-27554-7) JTG Nashville.

Wilson, Forrest. What It Feels Like to Be a Building. rev. ed. Wilson, Forrest, illus. LC 88-22382. 80p. (gr. 2 up). 1988. pap. 10.95 (0-89133-147-6) Preservation Pr.

Wilson, Francis. The Weather Pop-Up Book. Jacobs, Philip, illus. Wilgrass, Paul, contrib. by. (Illus.). (gr. 5 up). 1987. pap. 15.00 (0-671-63699-5, S&S BFYR) S&S Trade.

Wilson, Frank. Twissington Ant's Great Discovery. 16p. (gr. 7-10). 1986. 15.00X (0-7223-2042-6, Pub. by A H Stockwell England) St Mut.

Wilson, Gahan, jt. auth. see Mendoza, George.

Wilson, Gina & Catley, Alison. I Hope You Know... (Illus.). 32p. (ps-2). 1992. 15.95 (0-09-174061-4, Pub. by Hutchinson UK) Trafalgar.

Wilson, Ginger. Questions! Questions! Questions!!! Sytsma, Cheryle, ed. LC 90-63620. (Illus.). 30p. (Orig.). (gr. k-5). 1991. pap. write for info. (1-879068-04-4) Ray-Ma Natsal.

Wilson, Jack. Glacier Wings & Tales. 2nd ed. Clark, Marvin, ed. Benson, Carl, intro. by. (Illus.). 220p. (gr. 9 up). 1990. pap. 19.95 (0-937708-18-6) Great Northwest.

Wilson, Jacqueline. The Suitcase Kid. large type ed. (gr. 1-8). 1991. 13.95 (0-7451-1703-1, Galaxy Child Lrg Print) Chivers N Amer.

Wilson, James. Native Americans. LC 93-36059. (Illus.). 48p. (gr. 6-10). 1994. 16.95 (1-56847-150-5) Thomson Lrning.

Wilson, Jay. Pope John Paul the Second: Religious Leader. (Illus.). 80p. (gr. 3-5). 1993. PLB 13.95 (0-7910-1758-3, Am Art Analog) Chelsea Hse.

Wilson, Jay J., ed. see Wallace, Latressia & Wilson, Annette.

Wilson, Jean. Crusader for Christ (Billy Graham) (gr. 6-9). 1979. illus. pap. 3.95 (0-87508-602-0) Chr Lit.

Wilson, Jean A. Caz & His Cat: Now We Like the Night. Wilson, Richard C., illus. 32p. 1994. 14.95 (0-685-68122-X) Wahr.

What does a 4-year old think about in bed after the lights are out? Watch this observant 4-year old with his cat (apparent at first only by a tail sticking out from under the bed) use a bed & a window to come up with the solution to his fears of the night. In her third book of verses for young children, Jean A. Wilson introduces Caz & his cat & takes the reader into the mind of a young child who uses what he calls his "thinking time" after he's in bed to solve being afraid in the dark. His progress is echoed by the gradual emergence of the cat until both cat & child are fully apparent to the reader, led by Ms. Wilson's sensitive verses. Both Jean Wilson, who writes the verses, & her husband Richard Wilson, who illustrated the book, know their 4-year olds, & deal with Caz's fears with knowledge, warmth & humor, allowing him to come up with his own answer to his problem. He does, with brilliance-- no pun intended. Watch Caz deal with what's in the room, what's "out there," until he's comfortable with his own solution. And so is the cat. From George Wahr Publishing Company, 304-1/2 S. State, Ann Arbor, MI 48104, (313) 668-6097/(800) 805-2497. *Publisher Provided Annotation.*

—Come Follow Me. Massmann, Jane H., illus. 26p. (ps-3). 1989. 12.95 (0-911586-01-6) Wahr.

Jean Wilson's second book of verses for children 3-7, follows the children through the seasons for discovery, learning & questioning. The children go to a supermarket; slide down a hill; ride a bike; go to a band concert; feel a live rabbit; & a horse; see their shadows; wonder about frost; leaves & snowmen, play jacks; go to a birthday party; wonder about raindrops & go to bed (but, according to the last verse, not without washing their feet). Reality based, vivid illustrations, accurate animal drawings & musical instruments. Again Wilson, adds another dimension to her whimsical verses through thoughtful questions posed by the child narrator. *Publisher Provided Annotation.*

Wilson, Jodi L. When I Grow Up. Anderson, Kari A., illus. 32p. (Orig.). (gr. 1-3). Date not set. pap. 4.95x (0-9628335-0-9) Wilander Pub.

Wilson, Joe, tr. see Crowder, Jack L. & Hill, Faith.

Wilson, John. Lucky & the Pot of Gold. (Illus.). (gr. 1-3). 1990. PLB 4.95 (0-9627193-2-3, 428-983) Wilson Investment.

Wilson, John H., ed. Six Restoration Plays. Incl. Country Wife. Wycherley, William; Man of Mode. Etherege, George; All for Love. Dryden, John; Venice Preserved. Otway, Thomas; Way of the World. Congreve, William; Beaux Stratagem. Farquhar, George. LC 59-1770. (gr. 9up). 1959. pap. 9.16 (0-395-05136-3, RivEd) HM.

Wilson, Johnniece M. Oh, Brother. 128p. (gr. 3-7). 1989. pap. 2.95 (0-590-41001-6, Apple Paperbacks) Scholastic Inc.

—Poor Girl, Rich Girl. 176p. 1992. 13.95 (0-590-44732-7, Scholastic Hardcover) Scholastic Inc.

—Robin on His Own. 160p. 1992. pap. 2.95 (0-590-41809-2, Apple Paperbacks) Scholastic Inc.

Wilson, Jonnie. AIDS. LC 89-12619. (Illus.). 96p. (gr. 5 up). 1989. PLB 14.95 (1-56006-105-7) Lucent Bks.

Wilson, Judy, jt. auth. see Koehler, Michael.

Wilson, Karen. Agha: The Terrible Demon. 2nd ed. Greene, Joshua, ed. Prubhupada, A. C., tr. from SAN. Dubois, Marie T., illus. 32p. (gr. 1-4). 1989. pap. 6.95 (0-89647-023-7) Bala Bks.

Wilson, Karle B. The Reindeer's Shoe & Other Stories. Montgomery, Charlotte B., illus. & intro. by. LC 88-2292. 112p. (ps-12). 1988. casebound 17.95 (0-936650-07-9) E C Temple.

Wilson, Kate. Earthquake! San Francisco, Nineteen Hundred Six. Courtney, Richard, illus. LC 92-18081. 62p. (gr. 2-5). 1992. PLB 21.34 (*0-8114-7216-7*) Raintree Steck-V.

Wilson, Kay. Arab Horses. (gr. 2-9). 1986. 7.95x (*0-86685-481-9*) Intl Bk Ctr.

Wilson, Kay W. Classics Then & Now: Around the World in Eighty Days, the Prince & the Pauper, the Legend of Sleepy Hollow. Kratoville, B. L., ed. (Illus.). 112p. (gr. 3 up). 1991. pap. text ed. 12.00 (*0-87879-919-2*, 919-2); wkbk. 10.00 (*0-87879-920-6*) High Noon Bks.

Wilson, Keith. Photography. LC 93-11574. (gr. 5 up). 1994. 13.00 (*0-679-83443-5*) Knopf Bks Yng Read.

Wilson, Lynn. Baby Whale. (Illus.). 32p. (ps-2). 1991. (G&D); pap. 1.95 (*0-448-40072-3*, G&D) Putnam Pub Group.

—Sharks! Courtney Studios, Inc. Staff, illus. 32p. (ps-3). 1992. (Platt & Munk Pubs); pap. 2.25 (*0-448-40300-5*, Platt & Munk Pubs) Putnam Pub Group.

—What's Out There? A Book about Space. Billin-Frye, Paige, illus. LC 92-24469. 32p. (ps-3). 1993. lib. bdg. 7.99 (*0-448-40518-0*, G&D); pap. 2.25 (*0-448-40517-2*, G&D) Putnam Pub Group.

Wilson, M. Two-by-Two: A Number Workbook for First & Second Grades Taken from Braille Edition Written Especially for the Blind. large type ed. 108p. (gr. 1-2). 1957. Repr. of 1956 ed. 27.00 (*0-317-01951-1*, J-26400-00) Am Printing Hse.

Wilson, M. L. Chester Himes. King, Coretta Scott, intro. by. LC 87-30961. (Illus.). 112p. (Orig.). (gr. 5 up). 1988. 17.95 (*1-55546-591-9*); pap. 9.95 (*0-7910-0212-8*) Chelsea Hse.

Wilson, Marie M. Nellie's Girl Two. (Illus.). 156p. (ps up). 1988. PLB 11.00 (*0-9615259-1-6*) Wilson Oregon.

Wilson, Marion M., ed. see Ferguson-Florissant Early Education Teachers Staff.

Wilson, Mark. Mark Wilson's Complete Course in Magic. LC 87-73058. (Illus.). 472p. 1988. Repr. of 1975 ed. 18.98 (*0-89471-623-9*) Courage Bks.

Wilson, Miriam J. Stress Stoppers for Children & Adolescents. 2nd ed. Wheeler, Gerald, ed. (Illus.). 111p. (gr. 9 up). 1988. pap. 6.95 (*0-944576-01-X*) Rocky River Pubs.

Wilson, Miriam W., ed. see Baumgardner, Mary A.

Wilson, Nancy H. Bringing Nettie Back. LC 92-7640. 160p. (gr. 3-7). 1992. SBE 13.95 (*0-02-793075-0*, Macmillan Child Bk) Macmillan Child Grp.

—The Reason for Janey. LC 93-22930. 176p. (gr. 3-7). 1994. SBE 14.95 (*0-02-793127-7*, Macmillan Child Bk) Macmillan Child Grp.

Wilson, Neil. Choice Adventures, No. 1: The Mysterious Old Church. (gr. 4-7). 1991. pap. 4.99 (*0-8423-5025-X*) Tyndale.

Wilson, Neil S. Choice Adventures, No. 9: The Tall Ship Shakedown. LC 92-30500. 1993. 4.99 (*0-8423-5046-2*) Tyndale.

Wilson, Patrick, ed. see DeCesare, Ruth.

Wilson, Raymond, jt. auth. see Isern, Thomas D.

Wilson, Reginald. Our Rights: Civil Liberties in the U. S. rev. ed. 160p. (gr. 7 up). 1993. PLB 15.85 (*0-8027-8127-6*); pap. 9.95 (*0-8027-7371-0*) Walker & Co.

—Think about Our Rights: Civil Liberties & the United States. LC 87-22989. 123p. 1988. 14.85 (*0-8027-6751-6*); pap. 5.95 (*0-8027-6752-4*) Walker & Co.

Wilson, Richard & Bridner, E. L., Jr. Maryland: Its Past & Present. 4th ed. 234p. (gr. 4). 1992. casebound 17. 75 (*0-917882-34-2*) MD Hist Pr.

Wilson, Robert, jt. auth. see Hafer, Jan.

Wilson, Robert A. Schrodinger's Cat Trilogy. 1988. pap. 13.95 (*0-440-50070-2*, Dell Trade Pbks) Dell.

Wilson, Ron, jt. auth. see Western, Joan.

Wilson, Sarah. Beware the Dragons! Wilson, Sarah, illus. LC 85-42164. 32p. (ps-3). 1988. pap. 4.95 (*0-06-443186-X*, Trophy) HarpC Child Bks.

—Christmas Cowboy. (ps-6). 1993. pap. 14.00 (*0-671-74780-0*, S&S BFYR) S&S Trade.

—The Day That Henry Cleaned His Room. (ps-3). 1990. pap. 13.95 (*0-671-69202-X*, S&S BFYR) S&S Trade.

—Garage Song. LC 91-393. (ps-3). 1994. pap. 4.95 (*0-671-88631-2*, Half Moon Bks) S&S Trade.

—June Is a Tune That Jumps on a Stair. LC 91-4053. (Illus.). 32p. 1992. pap. 14.00 jacketed (*0-671-73919-0*, S&S BFYR) S&S Trade.

—Muskrat, Muskrat, Eat Your Peas! Wilson, Sarah, illus. LC 88-29742. (ps). 1992. pap. 13.95 jacketed (*0-671-67515-X*, S&S BFYR) S&S Trade; pap. 3.95 (*0-671-77822-6*, S&S BFYR) S&S Trade.

—Three in a Balloon. 1990. pap. 12.95 (*0-590-42631-1*) Scholastic Inc.

—Uncle Albert's Flying Birthday. LC 90-36158. (gr. k-3). 1991. pap. 13.95 (*0-671-72793-1*) S&S Trade.

—Uncle Albert's Flying Birthday. LC 90-36158. (Illus.). 40p. (ps-3). 1993. pap. 7.95 (*0-671-79847-2*, S&S BYR) S&S Trade.

Wilson, Terry C. The Same: II Timothy 2: 2. 250p. (Orig.). (gr. 12). 1989. pap. 30.00 (*0-685-28038-1*) T C Wilson.

Wilson, Terry P. The Osage. Porter, Frank, intro. by. (Illus.). 111p. (gr. 5 up). 1988. lib. bdg. 17.95x (*1-55546-722-9*) Chelsea Hse.

Wilson, Tona, jt. auth. see Brusca, Maria C.

Wilson, Towana E. Sam, a Cocker: Sam & His Country Home. Wilson, Towana E., illus. LC 90-87585. (Orig.). (gr. 7 up). 1990. pap. 5.00 (*0-9623607-1-6*) BRAT Pubns.

—Sam, a Cocker: Sam & the Periwinkles. Wilson, Towana E., illus. LC 90-83106. (Orig.). (gr. 7 up). 1990. pap. 5.00 (*0-9623607-2-4*) BRAT Pubns.

—Sam a Cocker: Same Goes Home. Wilson, Towana E., illus. LC 89-92115. 24p. (Orig.). (gr. 5 up). 1989. pap. 5.00 (*0-9623607-0-8*) BRAT Pubns.

Wilson, Trevor. Let's Go Fishing. Miesen, Christine, illus. LC 93-26220. 1994. 4.25 (*0-383-03758-1*) SRA Schl Grp.

Wilson, Valerie & Hull, Shirley, eds. Preschoolers Sing & Say. (ps). 1976. wire spiral bdg. 3.50 (*0-87227-045-9*) Reg Baptist.

Wilson, Vesta. Little Mary Misfit. 1992. 6.95 (*0-533-09611-1*) Vantage.

Wilson, Yvonne M. Kitten Without A Name. (Illus.). 23p. (gr. 1-2). 1982. pap. 1.00 (*0-686-97302-X*) Bible Memory.

Wilson Story, Bettie. Gospel Trailblazer: The Exciting Story of Francis Asbury. 128p. (gr. 4-6). 1984. pap. 3.95 (*0-687-15652-1*) Abingdon.

Wiltshire, Teri. The Tale of Bella Brontosaurus. Archer, Rebecca, illus. LC 92-46250. (ps). 1993. 8.95 (*1-85697-857-5*) Kingfisher Bks.

—The Tale of Gus the Grumbly Grizzly. Archer, Rebecca, illus. LC 92-46248. (ps). 1993. 8.95 (*1-85697-856-7*) Kingfisher Bks.

—The Tale of Pepper the Pony. Archer, Rebecca, illus. LC 92-46249. (ps). 1993. 8.95 (*1-85697-858-3*) Kingfisher Bks.

Wiltshire, Terri. The Tale of Tiki Tiger. Archer, Rebecca, illus. LC 92-40364. 24p. (ps-k). 1993. 7.95 (*1-85697-859-1*) Kingfisher Bks.

Wimberly, Christine A. Exploring Prehistoric Alabama Through Archaeology. Anderson, John & Meredith, Marianne, illus. LC 80-70833. 96p. (Orig.). (gr. 5-12). 1981. pap. 8.95 (*0-9605938-3-7*); pap. text ed. 6.18 (*0-9605938-1-0*); tchr's ed. 9.49 (*0-9605938-2-9*) Explorer Bks.

—Poisonous Snakes of Alabama. DeJarnette, Tom, illus. 46p. (Orig.). (gr. 4-12). 1970. pap. 3.35 (*0-9605938-0-2*) Explorer Bks.

Wimberly, Potice, ed. see Avery, Louisia.

Wimer, David. Desmond Tutu: Religious Leader Devoted to Freedom. Lantier, Patricia, adapted by. LC 90-10044. (Illus.). 64p. (gr. 3-4). 1991. PLB 18.60 (*0-8368-0459-7*) Gareth Stevens Inc.

Winans, Charles F. & Vogel, Richard. Multiple Choice Questions in Preparation for the AP English Literature & Composition Examination. 3rd ed. 115p. (gr. 11-12). 1990. wkbk. 15.95 (*1-878621-14-9*); tchr's. manual, 73p. avail. (*1-878621-15-7*) D & S Mktg Syst.

—Multiple Choice Questions in Preparation for the AP English Language & Composition Examination. 2nd ed. 85p. (gr. 11-12). 1990. wkbk. 15.95 (*1-878621-16-5*); tchr's. manual, 71p. avail. (*1-878621-17-3*) D & S Mktg Syst.

Winborn, Marsha, illus. Inside Sesame Street. 22p. (ps) 1986. write for info. (*0-307-12142-9*, Pub. by Golden Bks.) Western Pub.

Winborn, Martha, jt. auth. see Baker, Barbara.

Winch, Bradley, ed. see Shles, Larry.

Winch, Bradley L., ed. see Shles, Larry.

Winch, Gordon. Enoch the Emu. Sherwood, Rhoda, ed. Gristwood, Doreen, illus. LC 88-42924. 32p. (gr. 2-3). 1988. PLB 18.60 (*1-55532-908-X*) Gareth Stevens Inc.

—Partly True Tales, 2 vols. Oliver, Tony & Gristwood, Doreen, illus. 64p. (gr. 2-3). 1988. Set. PLB 37.20 (*1-55532-938-1*) Gareth Stevens Inc.

—Samantha Seagull's Sandals. Sherwood, Rhoda, ed. Olliver, Tony, illus. LC 88-42923. 32p. (gr. 2-3). 1988. PLB 13.95 (*1-55532-909-8*) Gareth Stevens Inc.

Winch, Madeleine. Come by Chance. Winch, Madeleine, illus. LC 89-22157. 32p. (ps-2). 1990. PLB 11.99 (*0-517-57667-8*) Crown Bks Yng Read.

Winckler, Suzanne & Rodgers, Mary M. Our Endangered Planet: Antarctica. 64p. (gr. 4-6). 1991. PLB 21.50 (*0-8225-2506-2*) Lerner Pubns.

—Our Engandered Planet: Soil. LC 92-39902. 1993. PLB 21.50 (*0-8225-2508-9*) Lerner Pubns.

Wind, Betty, jt. auth. see Forell, Betty.

Windeatt, Mary F. Blessed Kateri Tekakwitha. Harmon, Gedge, illus. 32p. (gr. 1-5). 1989. Repr. of 1954 ed. wkbk. 3.00 (*0-89555-378-3*) TAN Bks Pubs.

—The Brown Scapular. Harmon, Gedge, illus. 32p. (gr. 1-5). 1989. Repr. of 1954 ed. wkbk. 3.00 (*0-89555-380-5*) TAN Bks Pubs.

—Catholic Story Coloring Books. Harmon, Gedge, illus. 32p. (gr. 1-5). 1989. Repr. of 1954 ed. Set of 24. 48.00 (*0-89555-381-3*) TAN Bks Pubs.

—The Children of Fatima & Our Lady's Message to the World. Harmon, Gedge, illus. LC 90-71828. 161p. (gr. 5-9). 1991. pap. 6.00 (*0-89555-419-4*) TAN Bks Pubs.

—The Cure of Ars: The Story of Saint John Vianney, Patron Saint of Parish Priests. Harmon, Gedge, illus. LC 90-71827. 211p. (gr. 5-9). 1991. pap. 9.00 (*0-89555-418-6*) TAN Bks Pubs.

—The Little Flower: The Story of Saint Therese of the Child Jesus. Harmon, Gedge, illus. LC 90-71829. 167p. (gr. 5-9). 1991. pap. 7.00 (*0-89555-413-5*) TAN Bks Pubs.

—The Miraculous Medal: The Story of Our Lady's Appearances to Saint Catherine of Laboure. Harmon, Gedge, illus. LC 90-71823. 107p. (gr. 5-9). 1991. pap. 5.00 (*0-89555-417-8*) TAN Bks Pubs.

—Our Lady of Banneux. Harmon, Gedge, illus. 32p. (gr. 1-5). 1989. Repr. of 1954 ed. wkbk. 3.00 (*0-89555-364-3*) TAN Bks Pubs.

—Our Lady of Beauraing. Harmon, Gedge, illus. 32p. (gr. 1-5). 1989. Repr. of 1954 ed. wkbk. 3.00 (*0-89555-363-5*) TAN Bks Pubs.

—Our Lady of Fatima. Harmon, Gedge, illus. 32p. (gr. 1-5). 1989. Repr. of 1954 ed. wkbk. 3.00 (*0-89555-357-0*) TAN Bks Pubs.

—Our Lady of Guadalupe. Harmon, Gedge, illus. 32p. (gr. 1-5). 1989. Repr. of 1954 ed. wkbk. 3.00 (*0-89555-359-7*) TAN Bks Pubs.

—Our Lady of Knock. Harmon, Gedge, illus. 32p. (gr. 1-5). 1989. Repr. of 1954 ed. wkbk. 3.00 (*0-89555-362-7*) TAN Bks Pubs.

—Our Lady of la Salette. Harmon, Gedge, illus. 32p. (gr. 1-5). 1989. Repr. of 1954 ed. wkbk. 3.00 (*0-89555-361-9*) TAN Bks Pubs.

—Our Lady of Lourdes. Harmon, Gedge, illus. 32p. (gr. 1-5). 1989. Repr. of 1954 ed. wkbk. 3.00 (*0-89555-358-9*) TAN Bks Pubs.

—Our Lady of Pellevoisin. Harmon, Gedge, illus. 32p. (gr. 1-5). 1989. Repr. of 1954 ed. wkbk. 3.00 (*0-89555-366-X*) TAN Bks Pubs.

—Our Lady of Pontmain. Harmon, Gedge, illus. 32p. (gr. 1-5). 1989. Repr. of 1954 ed. wkbk. 3.00 (*0-89555-365-1*) TAN Bks Pubs.

—Our Lady of the Miraculous Medal. Harmon, Gedge, illus. 32p. (gr. 1-5). 1989. Repr. of 1954 ed. wkbk. 3.00 (*0-89555-360-0*) TAN Bks Pubs.

—Patron Saint of First Communicants: The Story of Blessed Imelda Lambertini. Harmon, Gedge, illus. LC 90-71824. 85p. (gr. 5-9). 1991. pap. 4.00 (*0-89555-416-X*) TAN Bks Pubs.

—The Rosary. Harmon, Gedge, illus. 32p. (gr. 1-5). 1989. Repr. of 1954 ed. wkbk. 3.00 (*0-89555-379-1*) TAN Bks Pubs.

—St. Anthony of Padua. Harmon, Gedge, illus. 32p. (gr. 1-5). 1989. Repr. of 1954 ed. wkbk. 3.00 (*0-89555-369-4*) TAN Bks Pubs.

—St. Christopher. Harmon, Gedge, illus. 32p. (gr. 1-5). 1989. Repr. of 1954 ed. wkbk. 3.00 (*0-89555-376-7*) TAN Bks Pubs.

—St. Dominic Savio. Harmon, Gedge, illus. 32p. (gr. 1-5). 1989. Repr. of 1954 ed. wkbk. 3.00 (*0-89555-370-8*) TAN Bks Pubs.

—St. Frances Cabrini. Harmon, Gedge, illus. 32p. (gr. 1-5). 1989. Repr. of 1954 ed. wkbk. 3.00 (*0-89555-375-9*) TAN Bks Pubs.

—St. Francis of Assisi. Harmon, Gedge, illus. 32p. (gr. 1-5). 1989. Repr. of 1954 ed. wkbk. 3.00 (*0-89555-368-6*) TAN Bks Pubs.

—St. Joan of Arc. Harmon, Gedge, illus. 32p. (gr. 1-5). 1989. Repr. of 1954 ed. wkbk. 3.00 (*0-89555-367-8*) TAN Bks Pubs.

—St. Louis de Montfort: The Story of Our Lady's Slave. Grout, Paul A., illus. LC 90-71826. 211p. (gr. 5-9). 1991. pap. 9.00 (*0-89555-414-3*) TAN Bks Pubs.

—St. Maria Goretti. Harmon, Gedge, illus. 32p. (gr. 1-5). 1989. Repr. of 1954 ed. wkbk. 3.00 (*0-89555-374-0*) TAN Bks Pubs.

—St. Meinrad. Harmon, Gedge, illus. 32p. (gr. 1-5). 1989. Repr. of 1954 ed. wkbk. 3.00 (*0-89555-377-5*) TAN Bks Pubs.

—St. Philomena. Harmon, Gedge, illus. 32p. (gr. 1-5). 1989. Repr. of 1954 ed. wkbk. 3.00 (*0-89555-373-2*) TAN Bks Pubs.

—St. Pius X. Harmon, Gedge, illus. 32p. (gr. 1-5). 1989. Repr. of 1954 ed. wkbk. 3.00 (*0-89555-371-6*) TAN Bks Pubs.

—St. Teresa of Avila. Harmon, Gedge, illus. 32p. (gr. 1-5). 1989. Repr. of 1954 ed. wkbk. 3.00 (*0-89555-372-4*) TAN Bks Pubs.

Winder, Blanche, ed. Stories of King Arthur. Gotlieb, Jules, illus. (gr. 4 up). 1968. pap. 1.95 (*0-8049-0167-8*, CL-167) Airmont.

Winder, Blanche, ed. see Aesop.

Winder, Jack. Who's New at the Zoo? Wasserman, Dan, ed. Reese, Bob, illus. (gr. k-1). 1979. 7.95 (*0-89868-074-3*); pap. 2.95 (*0-89868-085-9*) ARO Pub.

Winder, Linda. Jesus. (ps). 1993. 8.93 (*0-7814-0120-8*) Cook.

—Jonah. (ps). 1993. 5.99 (*0-7814-0119-4*) Cook.

—Moses. (ps). 1993. 5.99 (*0-7814-0123-2*) Cook.

—My First Bible Dictionary: A Sticker-Fun Book. (Illus.). 48p. 1991. pap. 5.99 (*0-8010-9712-6*) Baker Bk.

—My First Question & Answer Book: A Sticker-Fun Book. (Illus.). 48p. 1991. pap. 5.99 (*0-8010-9713-4*) Baker Bk.

—Noah. 1993. 5.99 (*0-7814-0122-4*) Cook.

Windham, Joan. Sixty Saints for Boys. 416p. (gr. 1-6). 1988. pap. 13.95 (*0-87061-149-6*) Chr Classics.

—Sixty Saints for Girls. 384p. (gr. 1-6). 1988. pap. 13.95 (*0-87061-150-X*) Chr Classics.

Windham, Kathryn T. Jeffrey Introduces Thirteen More Southern Ghosts. Foster, Sharon, illus. LC 70-170663. 120p. (gr. 6 up). 1987. pap. 9.50t (*0-8173-0381-2*) U of Ala Pr.

—Jeffrey's Latest Thirteen: More Alabama Ghosts. Gilbert, John, illus. LC 82-50029. 152p. 1987. pap. 9. 50t (*0-8173-0380-4*) U of Ala Pr.

—Thirteen Georgia Ghosts & Jeffrey. Lanier, Frances, illus. LC 73-87004. 160p. (gr. 6 up). 1987. pap. 9.50t (*0-8173-0377-4*) U of Ala Pr.

—Thirteen Mississippi Ghosts & Jeffrey. Russell, H. R., illus. LC 74-15509. 152p. (gr. 6 up). 1987. pap. 9.50t (*0-8173-0379-0*) U of Ala Pr.

—Thirteen Tennessee Ghosts & Jeffrey. Brogdon, Lecia, illus. LC 73-87004. 160p. (gr. 6 up). 1987. pap. 9.50t (*0-8173-0378-2*) U of Ala Pr.

Windham, Kathryn T. & Figh, Margaret G. Thirteen Alabama Ghosts & Jeffrey. Atkins, Delores E., illus. LC 71-94443. 128p. (gr. 6 up). 1987. pap. 9.50t (0-8173-0376-6) U of Ala Pr.

Windle, Jeanette & Clements, Jan. Yandicu: From Witch Doctor to Evangelist. Espe, Marvin, illus. 44p. (gr. 2-7). 1992. pressboard cover, plastic bdg. 9.95 (0-9617490-2-4) Gospel Missionary.

Windridge, C. A Student's First Thesaurus. LC 92-45115. 144p. 1993. pap. 3.95 (0-681-45226-9) Longmeadow Pr.

Windrow, Martin & Hook, Richard. The Footsoldier. (Illus.). 80p. (ps-5). 1988. bds. 17.95 (0-19-273147-5) OUP.

—The Horse Soldier. (Illus.). 80p. (ps-5). 1988. bds. 17.95 (0-19-273157-2) OUP.

Windsor, Laura. Beating the Term Paper Deadline: A Student Guide to Getting Help at the Library - in Record Time. 24p. (Orig.). (ps-12). 1990. 4.95 (0-918734-34-7) Reymont.

Windsor, Patricia. The Christmas Killer. 192p. 1991. 13. 95 (0-590-43311-3, Scholastic Hardcover) Scholastic Inc.

—The Christmas Killer. 1992. pap. 3.25 (0-590-43310-5) Scholastic Inc.

—The Hero. LC 87-25658. 192p. (gr. 7 up). 1988. pap. 14.95 (0-385-29624-X) Delacorte.

—The Hero. (gr. k-12). 1990. pap. 3.25 (0-440-20638-3, LFL) Dell.

—How a Weirdo & a Ghost Can Change Your Entire Life. (gr. k-6). 1988. pap. 2.75 (0-440-40094-5) Dell.

—The Sandman's Eyes. LC 84-19888. 280p. (gr. 7 up). 1985. 15.95 (0-385-29381-X) Delacorte.

—The Sandman's Eyes. (gr. k-12). 1992. pap. 3.50 (0-440-97585-9, LFL) Dell.

—The Summer Before. 176p. (gr. 7 up). 1974. pap. 1.95 (0-440-98382-7, LFL) Dell.

—Two Weirdos & a Ghost. (gr. 4-7). 1991. pap. 3.25 (0-440-40515-7, YB) Dell.

—Very Weird & Moogly Christmas. (gr. 4-7). 1991. pap. 3.25 (0-440-40528-9, YB) Dell.

Wine, Jeanine. Mrs. Tibbles & the Special Someone. LC 87-14966. 32p. (ps-3). 1987. 12.95 (0-934672-54-7) Good Bks PA.

—Silly Tillie. LC 87-38311. 32p. (gr. k-3). 1990. 12.95 (0-934672-62-8) Good Bks PA.

Winefordner, Daivd. Activities for Individualized Career Exploration & Planning. rev. ed. 48p. (gr. 9-12). 1993. wkbk. pkg. of 10 24.95 (1-56191-196-8) Meridian Educ.

Winer, Yvonne. Pocketful of Puppets: Three Plump Fish & Other Short Stories. Keller, Merily H., ed. Renfro, Nancy, illus. 48p. (Orig.). (ps-4). 1982. pap. 9.95 (0-931044-08-1) Renfro Studios.

—Ssh, Don't Wake the Baby! Power, Margaret, illus. LC 92-34160. 1993. 3.75 (0-383-03655-0) SRA Schl Grp.

Wines, James, illus. Edward Lear's Nonsense. LC 93-20461. 1994. write for info. (0-8478-1682-6) Rizzoli Intl.

Winfield, Arthur. Rover Boys at College. 191p. 1981. Repr. PLB 12.95x (0-89966-330-3) Buccaneer Bks.

—The Rover Boys at College. 312p. 1980. Repr. PLB 12. 95x (0-89967-008-3) Harmony Raine.

—The Rover Boys at School. 302p. 1980. Repr. PLB 12. 95x (0-89967-009-1) Harmony Raine.

Winfield, Julia. Only Make-Believe. 176p. (Orig.). (gr. 7-12). 1987. pap. 2.50 (0-553-26418-4) Bantam.

—Private Eyes. 160p. (Orig.). (gr. 7-12). 1989. pap. 2.75 (0-553-25814-1) Bantam.

Winfrey, Buford A., illus. An Easter Parade of Verse. 24p. (Orig.). (ps-3). 1991. pap. 3.95 (0-8249-8504-4, Ideals Child) Hambleton-Hill.

Wing, Natasha. Hippity Hop, Frog on Top. McGraw, DeLoss, illus. LC 93-11473. 1994. write for info. (0-671-87045-9, S&S BFYR) S&S Trade.

Wing, Ralph. Just Do It! Time Management. Pangaea Press Staff, ed. 144p. (Orig.). (gr. 10 up). 1990. pap. text ed. 6.95 (0-9625534-0-9, P100) Pangaea Pr.

—The Whole World Done Gone Crazy! Pangaea Pr. Staff, ed. 214p. (gr. 10 up). 1990. pap. text ed. 7.95 (0-9625534-1-7, P101) Pangaea Pr.

Wingate, P. Essential Physics. (Illus.). 64p. 1992. lib. bdg. 12.96 (0-88110-507-4, Usborne); pap. 5.95 (0-7460-0703-5) EDC.

Wingate, Rosalee M. I'll Make It Happen Without Drugs. Sapenter, Marcellus, illus. 44p. (Orig.). (gr. 4-8). 1990. pap. 6.00 (0-9625391-0-4) R M Wingate.

Wingerd, William N. Understanding & Enjoying Adolescence. 1988. pap. text ed. 13.05 (0-8013-0215-3, 75873) Longman.

Wingfield, Angela, jt. auth. see Wingfield, Jack.

Wingfield, Jack & Wingfield, Angela. Growing up Now. (Illus.). 48p. (gr. 4-8). 1992. 14.95 (0-7459-1537-X) Lion USA.

Winhdam, Sophie. Read Me a Story: A Child's Book of Favorite Tales. (Illus.). 96p. 1991. 16.95 (0-590-44950-8, Scholastic Hardcover) Scholastic Inc.

Winik, J. T. Fun with Numbers. Winik, J. T., illus. 32p. (ps-k). 1985. pap. 2.95 (0-88625-104-4) Durkin Hayes Pub.

—Mysteries. Rowden, Rick, illus. 48p. (gr. 5-9). 1985. pap. 5.95 (0-88625-094-3) Durkin Hayes Pub.

Winik, J. T. & Pashuk, Lauren. Fun from A-Z. Winik, J. T. & Pashuk, Lauren, illus. 32p. (ps-k). 1985. pap. 2.95 (0-88625-105-2) Durkin Hayes Pub.

Winitz, Harris. Basic Structures - American English, Bk. 1: A Textbook for the Learnables. Baker, Syd, illus. 100p. (gr. 7 up). 1990. pap. text ed. 42.00 incl. 4 cass. tapes (0-939990-60-1) Intl Linguistics.

—Basic Structures - Spanish, Bk. 1: A Textbook for the Learnables. Sagarna, Blanca, tr. Baker, Syd, illus. 106p. (gr. 7 up). 1990. pap. text ed. 42.00 incl. 4 cass. tapes (0-939990-61-X) Intl Linguistics.

—Bildbeschreibungen: Picture Descriptions in German. Baker, Syd, illus. Rohrer, Josef, tr. (Illus.). (gr. 7 up). 1988. Incl. 2 cassettes. pap. 32.00 (0-939990-59-8) Intl Linguistics.

—Business, Bk. 2. Baker, Syd, illus. 50p. (Orig.). (gr. 7 up). 1986. pap. text ed. 22.00 incl. cass. (0-939990-46-6) Intl Linguistics.

—Hauser und Gebaude: Houses & Buildings in German. Rohrer, Josef, ed. Baker, Syd, illus. (GER.). 50p. (Orig.). (gr. 7 up). 1989. pap. text ed. 22.00 incl. cass. (0-939990-76-8) Intl Linguistics.

—School: All about Language Ser. Baker, Syd, illus. 50p. (Orig.). (gr. 7 up). 1987. pap. text ed. 31.00 incl. 2 cass. (0-939990-49-0) Intl Linguistics.

—The Telephone. Baker, Syd, illus. 50p. (Orig.). (gr. 7 up). 1987. pap. text ed. 22.00 incl. cass. (0-939990-50-4) Intl Linguistics.

—Text for the Learnables, American English, Bk. 1. 36p. (gr. 3 up). 1990. pap. text ed. 6.50 (0-939990-69-5) Intl Linguistics.

—Text for the Learnables, Spanish, Bk. 1. Sagarna, Blanca, tr. (SPA.). 36p. (gr. 3 up). 1990. pap. text ed. 6.50 (0-939990-68-7) Intl Linguistics.

—Weather. Baker, Syd, illus. 50p. (gr. 7 up). 1986. pap. text ed. 19.00 incl. cass. (0-939990-47-4) Intl Linguistics.

Winitz, Harris, ed. see Waggoner, Carmen.

Winkleman, Gretchen, ed. see Hoover, Evalyn, et al.

Winkler, Chris, ed. see Bhanji, Lindley.

Winkler, Christ, ed. see Polkinhorn, Harry.

Winkler, Ellen, ed. see Dixon, Franklin W.

Winkler, Ellen, ed. see Keene, Carolyn.

Winkler, Gershon. The Hostage Torah. Jones, Yochanan, illus. (gr. 7 up). 1981. pap. 5.95 (0-910818-34-7) Judaica Pr.

—The Secret of Sambatyon. Goldman, Bonnie, ed. Bloom, Lloyd, illus. 132p. (gr. 4 up). 1987. 6.95 (0-910818-68-1); pap. 5.95 (0-910818-69-X) Judaica Pr.

Winkler, Jude. Mass for Children. (ps-3). 14.95 (0-89942-215-2) Catholic Bk Pub.

—The Story of Noah & the Flood. 1989. 1.95 (0-685-28788-2) Catholic Bk Pub.

—The Story of the Birth of Jesus. 1989. 1.95 (0-685-28787-4) Catholic Bk Pub.

Winn, Chris. Archie's Acrobats. (Illus.). 32p. (gr. k-3). 1990. pap. 6.95 (0-575-04481-0, Pub. by Gollancz England) Trafalgar.

Winn, Marie & Miller, Allan. The Fireside Book of Children's Songs. Alcorn, John, illus. LC 65-17108. (gr. 3 up). 1966. 12.95 (0-671-25820-6) S&S Trade.

Winn, Marie, ed. The Fireside Book of Fun & Game Songs. Darrow, Whitney, Jr., illus. Miller, Allan, contrib. by. (Illus.). 224p. (gr. 1 up). 1974. 14.95 (0-671-65213-3) S&S Trade.

Winner, Cherie. Salamanders. LC 92-10430. 1993. 19.95 (0-87614-757-0) Carolrhoda Bks.

—Salamanders. (gr. 4-7). 1993. pap. 6.95 (0-87614-614-0) Carolrhoda Bks.

Winner, David. Desmond Tutu. LC 88-4883. (Illus.). 68p. (Orig.). 1990. pap. 7.95 (0-8192-1542-2) Morehouse Pub.

—Desmond Tutu: The Courageous & Eloquent Archbishop Struggling Against Apartheid in South Africa. Sherwood, Rhoda, ed. LC 88-4883. (Illus.). 68p. (gr. 5-6). 1989. PLB 18.60 (1-55532-822-9) Gareth Stevens Inc.

—Eleanor Roosevelt: Defender of Human Rights & Democracy. LC 91-291. (Illus.). 68p. (gr. 5-6). 1992. PLB 18.60 (0-8368-0218-7) Gareth Stevens Inc.

—Peter Beneson: Taking a Stand Against Injustice-Amnesty International. LC 90-47877. (Illus.). 68p. (gr. 5-6). 1992. PLB 18.60 (0-8368-0400-7) Gareth Stevens Inc.

Winner, David, jt. auth. see Nicholson, Michael.

Winnig, Das Romerzimmer. (gr. 7-12). pap. 4.95 (0-88436-041-5, 45261) EMC.

Winograd, Deborah. My Color Is Panda. Winograd, Deborah, illus. LC 92-17423. 32p. (ps-5). 1993. JRT 13.00 (0-671-79152-4, Green Tiger) S&S Trade.

Winslow, Mimi. Railroad Workers & Loggers. 1994. PLB write for info. (0-8050-2997-4) H Holt & Co.

Winslow, Phillips. The Alfalfabet. 26p. (gr. k). 1992. pap. text ed. 23.00 big bk. (1-56843-015-9); pap. text ed. 4.50 (1-56843-065-5) BGR Pub.

—A Number of Things You Can Count On. 16p. (ps-k). 1992. pap. text ed. 23.00 big bk. (1-56843-007-8); pap. text ed. 4.50 (1-56843-057-4) BGR Pub.

Winstanley, Rita. The Oxford Merry Christmas Book. 128p. (gr. 3-7). 1987. 14.95 (0-19-278120-0) OUP.

Winston, Barbara F. The Hardest Thing about Going to School. Wilson, James P., illus. (Orig.). (gr. k-5). 1987. pap. text ed. 33.00 big bk. (0-9622810-0-X) B Winston.

Winston, Clara, tr. see Schweitzer, Albert.

Winston, Lynn. Recreation & Sports: An Activity Guide. Garee, Betty, ed. LC 85-72420. 72p. (Orig.). (gr. 9-12). 1985. pap. 4.95 (0-915708-18-3, #1770) Cheever Pub.

Winston, Peggy D. Wild Cats. Crump, Donald J., ed. LC 81-47742. 32p. (ps-3). 1981. lib. bdg. 16.95 (0-87044-401-8) Natl Geog.

Winston, Peggy D. see National Geographic Society Staff.

Winston Press Editorial Staff, ed. Joy Five. rev. ed. (Illus.). (gr. 1-5). 1984. tchr's. manual 8.95 (0-03-041871-2) Harper SF.

Winston, Richard, tr. see Schweitzer, Albert.

Winstone, Harold. Gospel for Young Christians. Lescanff, Jacques, illus. 192p. (gr. 3-6). 1985. 3.95 (0-225-27392-6) Harper SF.

Winston-Hiller, Randy. Some Secrets Are For Sharing. Cleaveland, C. A. & McCreary, Jane, illus. 33p. (Orig.). (gr. 4 up). 1986. pap. 5.95 (0-910223-08-4) MAC Pub.
Timmy is all of nine years old--he plays ball--he loves to hear stories about the sea--Timmy is an abused child. SOME SECRETS ARE FOR SHARING is his story, told from the youngster's viewpoint. This book tells of the PROBLEM, REACTIONS, INTERVENTION, PROCESS & RECOVERY of both the child & the family. SOME SECRETS ARE FOR SHARING is a book for children to read or to read to children. The primary purposes are to help the abused child understand that there IS someone to listen & help & to give the involved adult reader insight & perspective about the abuse problem. Every year, over a million children are abused in one way or another. Most of these children are alone with their feelings. Even if they receive professional help, there is a strong likelihood that their experiences will not be shared with their peers. In SOME SECRETS ARE FOR SHARING, the reader is not only faced with the experience of a boy named Timmy who has been abused, but reads about the feelings, behaviors & struggles Timmy has to deal with as an abused child. By Randy Winston-Hiller. MAC Publishing, 5005 East 39th Avenue, Denver, CO 80207-1106. 303-331-0148. $5.95 plus $1.05 shipping.
Publisher Provided Annotation.

Winter, Donna, illus. Patterns for the Flannel Board. 32p. (ps-2). Date not set. 11.95 (1-56065-167-9) Capstone Pr. Postponed.

Winter, Frank H. Comet Watch: The Return of Halley's Comet. (Illus.). 64p. (gr. 4-10). 1986. PLB 13.50 (0-8225-1579-2) Lerner Pubns.

—The Filipinos in America. (Illus.). 80p. (gr. 5 up). 1988. 15.95 (0-8225-0237-2); pap. 5.95 (0-8225-1035-9) Lerner Pubns.

Winter, Ginny L. Ballet Book. Winter, Ginny L., illus. (gr. 1-5). 1962. 8.95 (0-8392-3001-X) Astor-Honor.

—Riding Book. Winter, Ginny L., illus. (gr. k-3). 1963. 8.95 (0-8392-3031-1) Astor-Honor.

—Skating Book. Winter, Ginny L., illus. (gr. k-3). 1963. 8.95 (0-8392-3035-4) Astor-Honor.

—Swimming Book. Winter, Ginny L., illus. (gr. k-3). 1964. 8.95 (0-8392-3037-0) Astor-Honor.

—What's in My Tree. Winter, Ginny L., illus. (gr. k-1). 1962. 8.95 (0-8392-3044-3) Astor-Honor.

Winter, Jane K. Chile. LC 90-22472. (Illus.). 128p. (gr. 5-9). 1991. PLB 21.95 (1-85435-383-7) Marshall Cavendish.

—Venezuela. LC 90-22470. (Illus.). 128p. (gr. 5-9). 1991. PLB 21.95 (1-85435-386-1) Marshall Cavendish.

—Women in Society: Brazil. Siow, Eric, illus. LC 92-34403. 1993. Set. write for info. (1-85435-554-6); 22. 95 (1-85435-558-9) Marshall Cavendish.

Winter, Jeanette. Klara's New World. Winter, Jeanette, illus. LC 91-30212. 48p. (gr. 2-7). 1992. 15.00 (0-679-80626-1); PLB 15.99 (0-679-90626-6) Knopf Bks Yng Read.

Winter, Jonah. Diego. Prince, Amy, tr. Winter, Jeanette, illus. LC 90-25923. (ENG & SPA.). 40p. (gr. k-4). 1991. 14.00 (0-679-81987-8); PLB 14.99 (0-679-91987-2) Knopf Bks Yng Read.

Winter, Magda & Peery, Meira. Heritage Language Program 1-3, 3 wkbks. pap. text ed. 4.25 ea. Behrman.

Winter, Milo. Aesop for Children. 1984. 12.95 (0-528-82134-2) Rand McNally.

Winter, Paula. The Bear & the Fly. Winter, Paula, illus. LC 76-2479. (ps-1). 1987. PLB 12.95 (*0-517-52605-0*) Crown Bks Yng Read.

Winter, Susan. I Can. Winter, Susan, illus. LC 92-54384. 24p. (ps-1). 1993. 9.95 (*1-56458-197-7*) Dorling Kindersley.

—Me, Too. Winter, Susan, illus. LC 92-54383. 24p. (ps-1). 1993. 9.95 (*1-56458-198-5*) Dorling Kindersley.

—My Shadow. LC 93-11437. (gr. 4 up). 1994. write for info. (*0-385-31066-8*) Doubleday.

Winterfeld, Henry. Castaways in Lilliput. Lattimore, Deborah N. & Hutchinson, William M., illus. 220p. (gr. 3-7). 1990. pap. 4.95 (*0-15-214822-1*, Odyssey) HarBrace.

—Detectives in Togas. 249p. (gr. 3-7). 1990. pap. 3.95 (*0-15-223415-2*, Odyssey) HarBrace.

—Mystery of the Roman Ransom. 217p. (gr. 3-7). 1990. pap. 3.95 (*0-15-256614-7*, Odyssey) HarBrace.

—Trouble at Timpetill. Lattimore, Deborah N. & Hutchinson, William M., illus. 199p. (gr. 3-7). 1990. pap. 4.95 (*0-15-290786-6*, Odyssey) HarBrace.

Winters, Jonathan, jt. ed. see Gleeson, Brian.

Winters, Kay. The Teacher's CopeBook: End the Year Better Than You Started. LC 80-81682. (gr. k-6). 1980. pap. 10.95 (*0-8224-6767-4*) Fearon Teach Aids.

Winther, Barbara. Plays from African Tales. (Orig.). 1992. pap. 13.95 (*0-8238-0296-5*) Plays.

Winthrop, Elizabeth. Asleep in a Heap. Morgan, Mary, illus. LC 92-11310. 32p. (ps-3). 1993. reinforced bdg. 15.95 (*0-8234-0992-9*) Holiday.

—The Battle for the Castle. LC 92-54490. 160p. (gr. 3-7). 1993. 14.95 (*0-8234-1010-2*) Holiday.

—Bear & Mrs. Duck. Brewster, Patience, illus. LC 87-25129. 32p. (ps-3). 1988. reinforced bdg. 14.95 (*0-8234-0687-3*); pap. 5.95 (*0-8234-0843-4*) Holiday.

—Bear's Christmas Surprise. Brewster, Patience, illus. LC 90-26414. 32p. (ps-3). 1991. reinforced 14.95 (*0-8234-0888-4*) Holiday.

—Being Brave Is Best. Cooke, Tom, illus. 40p. (ps-3). 1984. 5.95 (*0-910313-19-9*) Parker Bros.

—Belinda's Hurricane. Watson, Wendy, illus. LC 84-8028. 64p. (gr. 1-4). 1984. 10.95 (*0-525-44106-9*, DCB) Dutton Child Bks.

—Belinda's Hurricane. Watson, Wendy, illus. 64p. (gr. 2-6). 1989. pap. 3.95 (*0-14-032985-4*, Puffin) Puffin Bks.

—The Best Friends Club. Weston, Martha, illus. LC 88-13406. 32p. (ps-3). 1989. 12.95 (*0-688-07582-7*); PLB 12.88 (*0-688-07583-5*) Lothrop.

—The Castle in the Attic. Hyman, Trina S., illus. LC 85-5607. 192p. (gr. 4-7). 1985. 14.95 (*0-8234-0579-6*) Holiday.

—The Castle in the Attic. 192p. 1986. pap. 2.95 (*0-553-15483-8*) Bantam.

—Castle in the Attic. 1986. pap. 3.99 (*0-553-15601-2*) Bantam.

—A Child Is Born: The Christmas Story. Mikolaycak, Charles, photos by. LC 82-11728. (Illus.). 32p. (ps-3). 1983. reinforced bdg. 15.95 (*0-8234-0472-2*) Holiday.

—Grover Sleeps Over. Swanson, Maggie, illus. LC 83-83279. 32p. (ps). 1984. write for info. (*0-307-12010-4*, 12010, Golden Bks) Western Pub.

—I'm the Boss! Morgan, Mary, illus. LC 93-9029. 32p. (gr. 3-8). 1994. 15.95 (*0-8234-1113-3*) Holiday.

—Katharine's Doll. LC 83-1408. (Illus.). 32p. (gr. k-3). 1991. pap. 3.95 (*0-525-44738-5*, Puffin) Puffin Bks.

—Lizzie & Harold. Weston, Martha, illus. LC 83-14858. 32p. (gr. k-3). 1985. 12.95 (*0-688-02711-3*); PLB 12.88 (*0-688-02712-1*) Lothrop.

—Luke's Bully. Porter, Pat G., illus. 64p. (gr. 2-5). 1990. pap. 11.95 (*0-670-83103-4*) Viking Child Bks.

—Luke's Bully. Porter, Pat G., illus. 64p. (gr. 2-5). 1992. pap. 3.99 (*0-14-034329-6*, Puffin) Puffin Bks.

—Maggie & the Monster. De Paola, Tomie, illus. LC 86-19593. 32p. (ps-3). 1987. reinforced bdg. 15.95 (*0-8234-0639-3*); pap. 5.95 (*0-8234-0698-9*) Holiday.

—Marathon Miranda. (gr. 4 up). 1990. pap. 3.95 (*0-14-034391-1*, Puffin) Puffin Bks.

—Miranda in the Middle. (gr. 4 up). 1990. pap. 3.95 (*0-14-034392-X*, Puffin) Puffin Bks.

—Shoes. Joyce, William, illus. LC 85-45841. 32p. (ps-2). 1986. 14.00 (*0-06-026591-4*); PLB 13.89 (*0-06-026592-2*) HarpC Child Bks.

—Shoes. Joyce, William, illus. LC 85-45841. 32p. (ps-3). 1988. pap. 4.95 (*0-06-443171-1*, Trophy) HarpC Child Bks.

—Shoes. Joyce, William, illus. (ps-1). 1988. bk. & cassette 19.95 (*0-87499-113-7*); bk. & cassette 12.95 (*0-87499-112-9*); 4 cassettes & guide 27.95 (*0-87499-114-5*) Live Oak Media.

—Shoes Big Book. Joyce, William, illus. LC 85-45841. 24p. (ps-3). 1993. pap. 19.95 (*0-06-443320-X*, Trophy) HarpC Child Bks.

—Sledding. Wilson, Sarah, illus. LC 89-1761. 32p. (ps-2). 1989. PLB 13.89 (*0-06-026566-3*) HarpC Child Bks.

—Sloppy Kisses. Burgess, Anne, illus. (ps-3). 1983. pap. 3.95 (*0-14-050433-8*, Puffin) Puffin Bks.

—Sloppy Kisses. Burgess, Anne, illus. LC 90-105. 32p. (gr. k-3). 1990. pap. 4.95 (*0-689-71410-6*, Aladdin) Macmillan Child Grp.

—Story of the Nativity. 1986. pap. 2.50 (*0-671-63019-9*, Little Simon) S&S Trade.

—Strawberry Shortcake & the Big Balloon Race. Sustendal, Pat, illus. 40p. (ps-3). 1983. cancelled 5.95 (*0-910313-08-3*) Parker Bros.

—Tough Eddie. Hoban, Lillian, illus. LC 84-13664. 32p. (ps-2). 1989. pap. 3.95 (*0-525-44496-3*, DCB) Dutton Child Bks.

—Vasilissa the Beautiful. Koshkin, Alexander, illus. LC 89-26903. 40p. (gr. 1-5). 1994. pap. 5.95 (*0-06-443345-5*, Trophy) HarpC Child Bks.

—A Very Noisy Girl. LC 90-39175. (Illus.). 32p. (ps-3). 1991. reinforced 14.95 (*0-8234-0858-2*) Holiday.

Winthrop, Elizabeth, adapted by. He Is Risen: The Easter Story. Mikolaycak, Charles, illus. LC 84-15869. 32p. (gr. 4-6). 1985. reinforced bdg. 15.95 (*0-8234-0547-8*) Holiday.

—Vasilissa the Beautiful: A Russian Folktale. Koshkin, Alexander, illus. LC 89-26903. 40p. (gr. 1-5). 1991. 16.00 (*0-06-021662-X*); PLB 15.89 (*0-06-021663-8*) HarpC Child Bks.

Wintle, Sarah H., ed. see Kipling, Rudyard.

Winton, Tim. Lockie Leonard, Human Torpedo. (gr. 5 up). 1992. 13.95 (*0-316-94753-9*) Little.

Wippersberg, W. J. Bad Times for Ghosts. Bhend-Zaugg, Kathi, illus. LC 86-45058. 166p. (gr. 3-7). 1986. 13.95 (*0-15-200413-0*, Gulliver Bks); pap. 6.95 (*0-15-200414-9*) HarBrace.

Wirszup, Izaak & Streit, Robert. Developments in School Mathematics Education Around the World. 725p. (gr. k-12). 1987. pap. 22.00 (*0-87353-249-X*) NCTM.

Wirth, Victoria. Whisper from the Woods. (gr. 4-7). 1991. 17.00 (*0-671-74790-8*, S&S BFYR) S&S Trade.

Wirths. Your Power with Words. 1993. write for info. (*0-8050-3150-2*) H Holt & Co.

Wirths, Bowman-Kruhm Staff & Stren, Patti. Your Circle of Friends. (Illus.). 64p. (gr. 5-8). 1993. PLB 14.95 (*0-685-66709-X*) TFC Bks NY.

—Your Power with Words. (Illus.). 64p. (gr. 5-8). 1993. PLB 14.95 (*0-8050-2075-6*) TFC Bks NY.

Wirths, Claudine & Bowman-Kruhm, Mary. Your Circle of Friends. 64p. (gr. 5-8). 1993. PLB 14.95 (*0-8050-2073-X*) TFC Bks NY.

Wirths, Claudine G. & Bowman-Kruhm, Mary. How to Get up When Schoolwork Gets You Down. LC 93-3050. 1993. write for info. (*0-7814-0118-6*, Chariot Bks) Cook.

—I Hate School! How to Hang In & When to Drop Out. Stren, Patti, illus. LC 85-48248. 128p. (gr. 7 up). 1986. pap. 7.95 (*0-06-446054-1*, Trophy) HarpC Child Bks.

—I Hate School! How to Hang In & When to Drop Out. Stren, Patti, illus. LC 85-48248. 128p. (gr. 7 up). 1986. 12.95 (*0-690-04556-5*, Crowell Jr Bks); (Crowell Jr Bks) HarpC Child Bks.

—Where's My Other Sock? How to Get Organized & Drive Your Parents & Teachers Crazy. Coxe, Molly, illus. LC 88-39338. 128p. (gr. 5 up). 1989. (Crowell Jr Bks); PLB 13.89 (*0-690-04667-7*, Crowell Jr Bks) HarpC Child Bks.

—Your New School. Stren, Patti, illus. LC 93-8513. (gr. 5-8). 1993. 14.95 (*0-8050-2074-8*) TFC Bks NY.

Wirtzfeld, Beverly. Bear's Designs Unlimited, Vol. I. 60p. (gr. 4-10). Date not set. activity-coloring bk. 4.95 (*0-9638473-0-9*) Bears Designs.

Wisconsin Potato Growers Auxiliary Staff, ed. Team up to Unmask Potato Secrets. 14p. 1992. pap. 50.00 (*0-9635149-0-3*) WI Potato Grow.

Wise, Arthur & Wise, Sarah. Six Christian One-Act Plays for Young Adults. 52p. (gr. 7-12). pap. 5.00 (*0-88680-178-8*) I E Clark.

Wise, Beth A. Beginning to Read. Nayer, Judith E., ed. Banek, Yvette, illus. 32p. (gr. k-1). 1991. wkbk. 1.95 (*1-878624-62-8*) McClanahan Bk.

—Christmas KidDoodles, Bk. 2. Hoffman, Judy, illus. 64p. (Orig.). (ps-2). 1991. pap. 0.99 activity pad (*1-56293-154-7*) McClanahan Bk.

—Christmas KidDoodles, Bk. 4. Boyd, Patti, illus. 64p. (Orig.). (ps-2). 1991. pap. 0.99 activity pad (*1-56293-156-3*) McClanahan Bk.

—Colors, Shapes, & Sizes. Morgado, Richard, illus. 32p. (ps). 1992. wkbk. 1.95 (*1-56293-168-7*) McClanahan Bk.

—Follow Directions. Jordan, Polly, illus. 32p. (ps). 1992. wkbk. 1.95 (*1-56293-169-5*) McClanahan Bk.

—Get Ready to Read. Dorr, Mary A., illus. 32p. (ps). 1992. wkbk. 1.95 (*1-56293-173-3*) McClanahan Bk.

—KidDoodles, Bk. 2. Moffatt, Judy, illus. 64p. (Orig.). (ps-2). 1991. pap. 0.99 activity pad (*1-878624-51-2*) McClanahan Bk.

—KidDoodles, Bk. 4. Nethery, Susan, illus. 64p. (Orig.). (ps-2). 1991. pap. 0.99 activity pad (*1-878624-53-9*) McClanahan Bk.

—Letters & Sounds. Nayer, Judith E., ed. Regan, Dana & DeMarco, Susanne, illus. 32p. (gr. k-1). 1991. wkbk. 1.95 (*1-878624-60-1*) McClanahan Bk.

—My ABC's: Lowercase. Dorr, Mary A., illus. 32p. (ps). 1992. wkbk. 1.95 (*1-56293-167-9*) McClanahan Bk.

—My ABC's Uppercase. Nayer, Judith E., ed. Mahan, Ben, illus. 32p. (ps). 1991. wkbk. 1.95 (*1-56293-165-2*) McClanahan Bk.

—My First Math Book. Morgado, Richard, illus. 32p. (ps). 1992. wkbk. 1.95 (*1-56293-172-5*) McClanahan Bk.

—My First Words. McDonough, Chris, illus. 32p. (ps). 1992. wkbk. 1.95 (*1-56293-176-8*) McClanahan Bk.

—Sizes. Loh, Carolyn, illus. 16p. (ps). 1992. wkbk. 2.25 (*1-56293-187-3*) McClanahan Bk.

—Thinking. Loh, Carolyn, illus. 16p. (ps). 1992. wkbk. 2.25 (*1-56293-190-3*) McClanahan Bk.

Wise, Beth A. & Block, Arlene. Phonics Vowels. Nayer, Judith E., ed. Sims, Deborah & Lustig, Loretta, illus. 32p. (gr. k-1). 1991. wkbk. 1.95 (*1-878624-65-2*) McClanahan Bk.

Wise, Beth A. & Levin, Amy. I Can Read. Naver, Judith E., ed. Krupinski, Loretta, illus. 32p. (gr. k-1). 1991. wkbk. 1.95 (*1-878624-63-6*) McClanahan Bk.

Wise, Beth A. & Sokoloff, Myka-Lynne. Key Words to Reading. Nayer, Judith E., ed. Beckes, Shirley, illus. 32p. (gr. k-1). 1991. wkbk. 1.95 (*1-878624-61-X*) McClanahan Bk.

Wise, C. Dexter, III. Be a Man: Reflections on the Meaning of Manhood in Our Day (An Outline) 30p. (Orig.). (gr. 6 up). 1988. pap. text ed. 5.00 (*0-685-22586-0*) Wise Works Inc.

—I Ain't Into That: (The Book) 48p. (Orig.). (gr. 6-12). 1987. pap. text ed. 5.00 (*0-685-22587-9*); 6.00 (*0-685-22588-7*) Wise Works Inc.

Wise, Francis H. Ann. Wise, Joyce M., ed. & illus. 21p. (ps-1). 1983. pap. 1.50 (*0-915766-60-4*) Wise Pub.

—The Beach. Wise, Joyce M., ed. & illus. 21p. (ps-1). 1983. pap. 1.50 (*0-915766-63-9*) Wise Pub.

—Black Crow. Wise, Joyce M., ed. & illus. 21p. (gr. k-1). 1983. pap. 1.50 (*0-915766-62-0*) Wise Pub.

—Ed, 20 bks. 3rd ed. Wise, Joyce M., ed. (Illus.). 21p. (ps-1). 1983. pap. 1.50 (*0-915766-59-0*) Wise Pub.

—Youth & Drugs. Wise, Joyce M., illus. (gr. 10 up). Date not set. 4.95 (*0-686-86911-7*) Wise Pub.

Wise, Francis H. & Wise, Joyce M. Ann's Pans & Cans. Wise, Joyce, illus. 20p. (ps-1). 1974. pap. text ed. 1.50 (*0-915766-28-0*) Wise Pub.

—Bernie, the Saint. new ed. (Illus.). 21p. (Orig.). (gr. 1). 1980. pap. 1.50 (*0-915766-41-8*) Wise Pub.

—Dr. Wise Arithmetic Series, Vol. I. (Illus.). 105p. (ps-1). 1980. pap. text ed. 7.50 (*0-915766-55-8*) Wise Pub.

—Dr. Wise Arithmetic Series, Vol. II. (Illus.). 105p. (gr. k-1). 1980. pap. text ed. 7.50 (*0-915766-56-6*) Wise Pub.

—Dr. Wise Learn to Read Series, Vols. 1-4. Wise, Joyce M., illus. Incl. Vol. 1. Readers 1-5 Phonetic Reader Ser (*0-915766-42-6*); Vol. 2. Readers 6-10 in Phonetic Reader Ser (*0-915766-43-4*); Vol. 3. Readers 11-15 in Phonetic Reader Ser. 104p (*0-915766-64-7*); Readers 16-20 in Phonetic Learn to Read Ser. 105p. (Illus.). 105p. (ps-1). 1979. pap. 7.50 ea. Wise Pub.

—Ed's Red Bed. Wise, Joyce M., illus. 20p. (ps). 1974. pap. 1.50 (*0-915766-27-2*) Wise Pub.

—Fun in the Sun. Wise, Joyce M., illus. 21p. (ps-1). 1975. pap. 1.50 (*0-915766-30-2*) Wise Pub.

—Jack, the Rabbit. (Illus.). 21p. (gr. 1). 1976. pap. 1.50 (*0-685-42418-9*) Wise Pub.

—Jay's Fat Cat. Wise, Joyce M., illus. 20p. (ps-1). 1974. pap. text ed. 1.50 (*0-915766-29-9*) Wise Pub.

—Kites. (Illus.). (gr. 1). 1977. pap. 1.50 (*0-915766-38-8*) Wise Pub.

—Park the Car. Wise, Joyce M., illus. (ps-1). 1975. pap. text ed. 1.50 (*0-915766-32-9*) Wise Pub.

—Play Ball. Wise, Joyce M., illus. (ps-1). 1975. pap. text ed. 1.50 (*0-915766-31-0*) Wise Pub.

—Red Sail. (Illus.). (ps-1). 1978. pap. 1.50 (*0-915766-40-X*) Wise Pub.

—Sit By Me. Wise, Joyce M., illus. (ps-1). 1975. pap. text ed. 1.50 (*0-915766-33-7*) Wise Pub.

—Snowman. Wise, Joyce M., illus. (gr. 1). 1976. pap. 1.50 (*0-915766-37-X*) Wise Pub.

—Storybooks. (Illus.). 105p. (gr. k-1). 1979. pap. 7.50 (*0-685-05433-0*) Wise Pub.

Wise, Ira J. Bet Man. Raqchwerger, Lisa, et al, illus. 96p. (gr. 1-2). 1991. 4.95 (*0-933873-55-7*) Torah Aura.

Wise, Ira J. & Grishaver, Joel L. I Can Learn Torah, Vol. 2: Stories of the First Jewish Family. Blaicher, David, illus. 48p. (Orig.). (ps-2). 1992. pap. text ed. 2.45 (*0-933873-68-9*) Torah Aura.

Wise, Joyce M., jt. auth. see Wise, Francis H.

Wise, Joyce M., ed. see Wise, Francis H.

Wise, Joyce M., ed. & illus. see Wise, Francis H.

Wise, Lu C. Oklahoma's First Ladies. LC 83-82947. (Illus.). 88p. (gr. 5-12). 1984. 14.95 (*0-934188-10-6*) Evans Pubns.

Wise, Sarah, jt. auth. see Wise, Arthur.

Wise, William. Ten Sly Piranhas: A Counting Story in Reverse (A Tale of Wickedness - & Worse!) Chess, Victoria, illus. LC 91-33704. 32p. (ps-3). 1993. 13.50 (*0-8037-1200-6*); PLB 13.89 (*0-8037-1201-4*) Dial Bks Young.

Wise Brown, Margaret. Seashore Noisy Book. Weisgard, Leonard, illus. LC 92-31433. 48p. (ps-1). 1993. pap. 4.95 (*0-06-443329-3*, Trophy) HarpC Child Bks.

Wiseman, Ann. Making Musical Things: Improvised Instruments. Wiseman, Ann, illus. LC 79-4474. 64p. (gr. 3 up). 1979. SBE 14.95 (*0-684-16114-1*, Scribners Young Read) Macmillan Child Grp.

—Making Things: The Hand Book of Creative Discovery. Wiseman, Ann, illus. 192p. (gr. 4 up). 1973. pap. 14.95 (*0-316-94849-7*) Little.

Wiseman, Ann S. Nightmare Help: A Guide for Adults & Children. Wiseman, Ann S., et al, illus. 137p. (Orig.). (gr. 1-12). 1986. pap. text ed. 9.00 (*0-937369-00-4*) Ansayre Pr.

Wiseman, Anne, jt. auth. see McLean, Mollie.

Wiseman, B. Morris Goes to School. LC 75-77944. (Illus.). 64p. (gr. k-3). 1983. pap. 3.50 (*0-06-444045-1*, Trophy) HarpC Child Bks.

Wiseman, Bernard. Barber Bear. Wiseman, Bernard, illus. LC 86-27594. 48p. (gr. 1-3). 1987. pap. 11.95 (*0-316-94859-4*) Little.

—The Big Yellow School Bus. LC 91-58787. (Illus.). 48p. (gr. k-3). 1992. 9.95 (*1-56282-048-6*); PLB 9.89 (*1-56282-226-8*) Disney Pr.

—Cats! Cats! Cats! Wiseman, Bernard, illus. LC 83-27288. 48p. (ps-3). 1984. 5.95 (*0-8193-1127-8*) Parents.

—Cats! Cats! Cats! LC 93-15455. (Illus.). 1993. PLB 13.27 (0-8368-0965-3) Gareth Stevens Inc.
—Christmas with Morris & Boris. Wiseman, Bernard, illus. LC 83-11962. 44p. (gr. 1-3). 1983. 12.95 (0-316-94855-1) Little.
—Halloween with Morris & Boris. (gr. k-3). 1986. pap. 2.50 (0-590-41498-4) Scholastic Inc.
—Little New Kangaroo. Burns, Theresa, illus. LC 92-21955. 1993. 14.95 (0-395-65362-2, Clarion Bks) HM.
—Morris & Boris at the Circus. Wiseman, Bernard, illus. LC 87-45682. 64p. (gr. k-3). 1988. 14.00 (0-06-026477-2); PLB 13.89 (0-06-026478-0) HarpC Child Bks.
—Morris & Boris at the Circus. Wiseman, Bernard, illus. LC 87-45682. 64p. (gr. k-3). 1990. pap. 3.50 (0-06-444143-1, Trophy) HarpC Child Bks.
—Morris Goes to School. Wiseman, Bernard, illus. LC 75-77944. 64p. (gr. k-3). 1970. PLB 13.89 (0-06-026548-5) HarpC Child Bks.
—Morris the Moose. rev. ed. Wiseman, Bernard, illus. LC 87-33485. 32p. (ps-2). 1989. PLB 13.89 (0-06-026476-4) HarpC Child Bks.
—Morris the Moose. rev. ed. Wiseman, Bernard, illus. LC 87-33485. 32p. (ps-2). 1991. pap. 3.50 (0-06-444146-6, Trophy) HarpC Child Bks.
Wiseman, David. Jeremy Visick. (gr. 5 up). 1981. 13.95 (0-395-30449-0) HM.
—Jeremy Visick. (gr. 4-7). 1990. pap. 5.95 (0-395-56153-1) HM.
Wiseman, Loren K. American Combat Vehicle Handbook. Farley, A. C., illus. 104p. (Orig.). (gr. 9-12). 1990. pap. 12.00 (1-55878-061-0) Game Designers.
—Bangkok. 104p. (Orig.). 1991. pap. 12.00 (1-55878-074-2) Game Designers.
—Gazetteer. 64p. (Orig.). 1991. pap. 14.00 (1-55878-078-5) Game Designers.
—Heavy Weapons Handbook. Atlas, Nick, ed. 104p. (Orig.). 1992. pap. 12.00 (1-55878-100-5) Game Designers.
—Infantry Weapons of the World. Venters, Steve, illus. 104p. (Orig.). (gr. 9-12). 1991. pap. 12.00 (1-55878-068-8) Game Designers.
—Merc: Two Thousand. Larkin, Bob, illus. 120p. (Orig.). (gr. 9-12). 1990. pap. 16.00 (1-55878-072-6) Game Designers.
—More Tales from the Ether. Aulisio, Janet, illus. 64p. (Orig.). 1989. pap. 8.00 (1-55878-028-9) Game Designers.
—NATO Combat Vehicle Handbook. 104p. (Orig.). 1991. pap. 12.00 (1-55878-077-7) Game Designers.
—Nautical - Aviation Handbook. 104p. (Orig.). 1991. pap. 12.00 (1-55878-088-2) Game Designers.
—Soviet Combat Vehicle Handbook. Venters, Steve, illus. 104p. (Orig.). (gr. 9-12). 1990. pap. 12.00 (1-55878-067-X) Game Designers.
—Twilight Nightmares. 104p. (Orig.). 1991. pap. 12.00 (1-55878-095-5) Game Designers.
Wiseman, Loren K., ed. see Sheeley, Craig.
Wishik, Cindy. Kids Dish It up...Sugar-Free. LC 82-82188. (Illus.). 160p. (gr. k-3). 1982. pap. 9.95 (0-918146-22-4) Peninsula WA.
Wishinsky, Frieda. Oonga Boonga, Vol. 1. (ps-3). 1990. 13.95 (0-316-94872-1, Joy St Bks) Little.
Wishny, Judith, jt. auth. see Kaufman, Tanya.
Wisniewski, David. Rain Player. Wisniewski, David, illus. 32p. (gr. k-4). 1991. 15.45 (0-395-55112-9, Clarion Bks) HM.
Wiskur, Darrell. Mary's Merry Chase. Silver Dollar City, Inc. Staff, ed. Wiskur, Darrell, illus. (ps-1). 1977. 1.99g (0-686-19126-9) Silver Dollar.
—Silver Dollar City's ABC Words & Rhymes. Silver Dollar City, Inc. Staff, ed. Wiskur, Darrell, illus. (ps-1). 1977. 1.99g (0-686-19127-7) Silver Dollar.
Wisler, G. Clifton. Jericho's Journey. LC 92-36701. 144p. (gr. 5-9). 1993. 13.99 (0-525-67428-4, Lodestar Bks) Dutton Child Bks.
—Piper's Ferry. 144p. (gr. 5-9). 1990. 14.95 (0-525-67303-2, Lodestar Bks) Dutton Child Bks.
—Red Cap. 160p. (gr. 5-9). 1991. 15.00 (0-525-67337-7, Lodestar Bks) Dutton Child Bks.
—This New Land. LC 87-17749. (gr. 5 up). 1987. 13.95 (0-8027-6726-5); PLB 14.85 (0-8027-6727-3) Walker & Co.
Wismer, Donald. Starluck. LC 81-43375. 186p. 1982. 15.00 (0-89366-255-0) Ultramarine Pub.
Wisniewski, David. Elfwyn's Saga. 32p. 1990. 13.95 (0-688-09589-5); PLB 13.88 (0-688-09590-9) Lothrop.
—Sundiata: Lion King of Mali. Wisniewski, David, illus. 32p. (gr. k-4). 1992. 15.95 (0-395-61302-7, Clarion Bks) HM.
—The Warrior & the Wise Man. Wisniewski, David, illus. LC 88-21678. 32p. (gr. k-3). 1989. 13.95 (0-688-07889-3); PLB 13.88 (0-688-07890-7) Lothrop.
—The Wave of the Sea-Wolf. LC 93-18265. 1994. write for info. (0-395-66478-0, Clarion Bks) HM.
Wister, Owen. Virginian. (gr. 8 up). 1964. pap. 2.95 (0-8049-0046-9, CL-46) Airmont.
Wiswell, Phil. Kids' Games: Traditional Indoor & Outdoor Activities for Children of All Ages. LC 86-23955. (Illus.). 176p. (ps up). 1987. pap. 12.95 (0-385-23405-8) Doubleday.
Witcomb, Gerald, illus. The Moon. 32p. (gr. 3-5). 1985. 7.95x (0-86685-448-7) Intl Bk Ctr.
Witcombmsia, Gerald, illus. Paper. 32p. (gr. 3-5). 1985. 7.95x (0-86685-450-9) Intl Bk Ctr.

Witcover, Paul. Zora Neale Hurston. King, Coretta Scott, intro. by. (Illus.). 112p. (gr. 5 up). 1991. PLB 17.95 (0-7910-1129-1) Chelsea Hse.
—Zora Neale Hurston: Black Americans of Achievement. (gr. 4-7). 1992. pap. 7.95 (0-7910-1154-2) Chelsea Hse.
Witherow, Diane L. Gettysburg Children's Activity Book. (Illus.). 40p. (gr. 1-6). 1990. pap. 3.00 (0-939631-20-2) Thomas Publications.
Withers, Carl. Eenie-Meenie-Minie-Mo & Other Counting-Out Rhymes. Ripley, Elizabeth, illus. 44p. (ps up). 1970. pap. 2.50 (0-486-22414-7) Dover.
—A Rocket in My Pocket: The Rhymes & Chants of Young Americans. Suba, Sussanne, illus. LC 48-4881. 224p. (gr. 2-4). 1988. 14.95 (0-8050-0821-7, Bks Young Read); pap. 8.95 (0-8050-0804-7) H Holt & Co.
Withers, Tom. Basketball. LC 93-23275. 1993. write for info. (0-8114-5779-6) Raintree Steck-V.
Withington, W. A., ed. Southeast Asia. rev. ed. LC 87-83271. (Illus.). 160p. (gr. 6 up). 1988. text ed. 16.95 (0-685-01647-1); text ed. 16.95 (0-934291-32-2); tchr's. guide 9.95 (0-934291-33-0); mastery test packet 5.95 (0-934291-39-X) Gateway Pr MI.
Withrow, Marion O., ed. see Parkison, Ralph F.
Witkoski, Michael. Italian Americans. LC 91-15428. (Illus.). 104p. (gr. 5-9). 1991. 13.95s.p. (0-86593-137-2); PLB 18.60 (0-685-59185-9) Rourke Corp.
Witmer, Edith. Ray's Adventures with New Neighbors. (gr. 3 up). 1981. 6.85 (0-686-30774-7) Rod & Staff.
Witt, Dick, illus. Let's Look at Animals. Becker & Mayer. (Illus.). 12p. 1993. 5.95 (0-590-45700-4) Scholastic Inc.
—Let's Look at My World. Becker & Mayer. (Illus.). 12p. 1993. 5.95 (0-590-45699-7) Scholastic Inc.
Witt, Hannelore, tr. see Cutburth, Ronald W.
Witt, Matt. In Our Blood: Four Coal Mining Families. Dotter, Earl, photos by. LC 78-71518. (Illus., Orig.). (gr. 10-12). 1979. pap. text ed. 6.95 (0-9602226-1-8) Highlander.
Witt, Sandi. Across Five Aprils: A Study Guide. (gr. 9-12). 1990. pap. text ed. 14.95 (0-88122-394-8) Lrn Links.
Witt, Sandi & Petrovich, Janice. Daphne's Book: A Study Guide. Friedland, Joyce & Kessler, Rikki, eds. 20p. (gr. 9-12). 1990. pap. text ed. 14.95 (0-88122-397-2) Lrn Links.
Witt, Sorena De see Peaslee, Ann & De Witt, Sorena.
Wittanen, Etolin. Auke Lake Tales. Alenov, Nick & Alenov, Lydia, illus. 53p. (Orig.). (gr. 3-6). 1986. pap. 5.00 (0-911523-05-7) Synaxis Pr.
Witte, Eve & Witte, Pat. Touch Me Book. Rockwell, Harlow, illus. (ps). 1961. write for info (0-307-12146-1, Golden Bks) Western Pub.
Witte, Pat, jt. auth. see Witte, Eve.
Wittels, Harriet & Greisman, Joan. The Clear & Simple Thesaurus Dictionary. (Illus.). (gr. 3 up). 1976. pap. 8.95 (0-448-12198-0, G&D) Putnam Pub Group.
—A First Thesaurus. Block, Alex, illus. 144p. (gr. 2-4). 1985. pap. write for info. (0-307-15835-7, Pub. by Golden Bks) Western Pub.
—Things I Hate! LC 73-11053. (Illus.). 32p. (ps-3). 1973. 16.95 (0-87705-096-1) Human Sci Pr.
Wittenborn, Janet. God Makes Me His Child in Baptism. LC 85-7689. 24p. (gr. 2-5). 1985. pap. 2.99 (0-570-04126-0, 56-1537) Concordia.
Wittenborn, Sally, jt. auth. see Barth, Nancy.
Witter, Evelyn. Abigail Adams: First Lady of Faith & Courage. Hanzel, Linda & Hanzel, Linda, illus. LC 76-2416. (gr. 3-6). 1976. pap. 6.95 (0-915134-94-2) Mott Media.
—Mahalia Jackson: Born to Sing Gospel Music. (Illus.). (gr. 3-6). 1985. pap. 6.95 (0-88062-045-5) Mott Media.
—What's the Matter with Miss Taylor. McKissack, Patricia & McKissack, Fredrick, eds. Mitter, Kathy, illus. LC 87-61643. 32p. (Orig.). (gr. 1-3). 1987. text ed. 8.95 (0-88335-728-3); pap. text ed. 4.95 (0-88335-748-8) Milliken Pub Co.
Witter, Evelyn, jt. auth. see Collins, David R.
Witter, Evelyn, ed. More Stories Worth Reading. Penovich, Geraldine & Penovich, Beatrice A., eds. (Illus.). 1989. write for info. Printemps Bks.
Witters, Judith. When the Earth Was Bare. Cammarata, Kathleen, illus. LC 93-26930. 1994. 4.25 (0-383-03785-9) SRA Schl Grp.
Wittich, John. Discovering London Street Names. 96p. (Orig.). (gr. 6 up). 1977. pap. 3.00 (0-913714-09-7) Legacy Bks.
Wittles, Harriet & Greisman, Joan. How to Spell It: A Dictionary of Commonly Misspelled Words. Wittles, Harriet & Greisman, Joan, illus. 336p. (gr. 1 up). 1982. pap. 10.95 (0-448-14756-4, G&D) Putnam Pub Group.
Wittlinger, Ellen. Lombardo's Law. LC 92-28916. 1993. 13.95 (0-395-65969-8) HM.
Wittman, Sally. A Special Trade. Gundersheimer, Karen, illus. LC 77-25673. 32p. (ps-2). 1985. pap. 5.95 (0-06-443071-5, Trophy) HarpC Child Bks.
—Stepbrother Sabotage. McCully, Emily A., illus. LC 89-26804. 80p. (gr. 2-5). 1990. 13.00 (0-06-026561-2); PLB 12.89 (0-06-026562-0) HarpC Child Bks.
—Stepbrother Sabotage. McCully, Emily A., illus. LC 89-26804. 80p. (gr. 2-5). 1991. pap. 3.95 (0-06-440408-0, Trophy) HarpC Child Bks.

Wittmann, Patricia. Go Ask Giorgio! Hillenbrand, Will, illus. LC 91-2808. 32p. (gr. k-4). 1992. RSBE 14.95 (0-02-793221-4, Macmillan Child Bk) Macmillan Child Grp.
—Scrabble Creek. Poydar, Nancy, illus. LC 92-10810. 32p. (gr. k-3). 1993. RSBE 14.95 (0-02-793225-7, Macmillan Child Bk) Macmillan Child Grp.
Wittner, Seth H. Sounds Around Us. Nusbaum, Linda, illus. 32p. (Orig.). (ps). 1988. Incl. audio-cassette. pap. 9.95 (0-9619269-8-8) Sound World Record.
Wittstock, Laura W. Ininatig's Gift of Sugar: Traditional Native Sugarmaking. Kakkak, Dale, photos by. Dorris, Michael, frwd. by. LC 92-37980. (Illus.). 1993. 19.95 (0-8225-2653-0) Lerner Pubns.
—Ininatig's Gift of Sugar: Traditional Native Sugarmaking. (gr. 4-7). 1993. pap. 6.95 (0-8225-9642-3) Lerner Pubns.
Wittwer, Sylvan H. The Greenhouse Effect. Head, J. J., ed. Steffen, Ann T., illus. LC 84-45833. 16p. (Orig.). (gr. 10 up). 1988. pap. text ed. 2.75 (0-89278-363-X, 45-9763) Carolina Biological.
Witty, Bruce. A Different Tune. Hoffman, Joan, ed. Laurent, Richard, illus. 32p. (gr. k-2). 1987. wkbk. 1.99 (0-88743-103-8, 02603) Sch Zone Pub Co.
Witty, Bruce & Gregorich, Barbara. Noise in the Night: Reading Workbook. Hoffman, Joan, ed. Nerlove, Miriam & Pape, Richard, illus. 32p. (Orig.). (gr. k-2). 1988. 1.99 (0-88743-106-2) Sch Zone Pub Co.
—The Raccoon on the Moon: Reading Workbook. Hoffman, Joan, ed. Sandford, John & Pape, Richard, illus. 32p. (Orig.). (gr. k-2). 1988. 1.99 (0-88743-108-9) Sch Zone Pub Co.
Witty, Ken. A Day in the Life of an Illustrator. Sanacore, Stephen, photos by. LC 80-54100. (Illus.). 32p. (gr. 4-8). 1981. PLB 11.79 (0-89375-448-X); pap. 2.95 (0-89375-449-8); cassette avail. Troll Assocs.
Witty, Ken, jt. auth. see Witty, Margot.
Witty, Margot. A Day in the Life of an Emergency Room Nurse. Lewis, Sarah, photos by. LC 78-68842. (Illus.). 32p. (gr. 4-8). 1980. PLB 11.79 (0-89375-226-6); pap. 2.95 (0-89375-230-4); cassettes avail. Troll Assocs.
Witty, Margot & Witty, Ken. A Day in the Life of a Meteorologist. Sanacore, Stephen, photos by. LC 80-54098. (Illus.). 32p. (gr. 4-8). 1981. PLB 11.79 (0-89375-450-1); pap. 2.95 (0-89375-451-X); cassettes avail. Troll Assocs.
Woe, Jonathan. The Longneck Bird of Longboat Key: One of the Privileged Class. Woe, Jonathan, illus. 32p. 1992. 14.95 (0-9627946-6-X) Hawk FL.
—The Wing'ed Whale from Woefully. Constantine, R., ed. Woe, Jonathan, illus. 32p. 1992. 14.95 (0-9627946-3-5) Hawk FL.
Woelflein, Luise. Forest Animals. Gibson, Barbara, illus. 24p. 1993. 7.95 (0-590-46005-6) Scholastic Inc.
—Ultimate Bug Book: A Unique Introduction to the Fascinating World of Insects. (ps-3). 1993. 19.95 (0-307-17600-2, Artsts Writrs) Western Pub.
Woell, J. Fred. Gloucester: College Life Between Classes. Woell, J. Fred, illus. 144p. (Orig.). pap. 15.00x (0-9626935-2-9) Turtle Gal Edit.
Woerkom, Dorothy O. Van see Van Woerkom, Dorothy O.
Woerkom, Dorothy Van see Van Woerkom, Dorothy.
Wofford, Roberta A. Sidney & Sally: The Danger of Strangers. Wofford, Roberta A., illus. 38p. (gr. k-4). 1987. pap. text ed. 1.85 (0-9616198-0-5) Pt Orchard Spec.
Woggon, Guillermo. Alla en el Pesebre. Cranberry, Nola, tr. from ENG. (SPA., Illus.). 16p. (ps-2). 1987. pap. 1.40 (0-311-38562-1) Casa Bautista.
—Animales Que Dios Creo. Cranberry, Nola, tr. from ENG. (SPA., Illus.). 16p. (gr. 1-3). 1987. pap. 1.99 (0-311-38560-5) Casa Bautista.
—Cultivemos una Huerta. Granberry, Nola, tr. (SPA., Illus.). 16p. (gr. 1-3). 1987. pap. 1.40 (0-311-38564-8) Casa Bautista.
—Versiculos "Llave" Granberry, Nola, tr. (SPA., Illus.). 16p. (gr. 1-3). 1987. pap. 1.40 (0-311-38565-6) Casa Bautista.
Wohl, Lauren L. Matzoh Mouse. Keavney, Pamela, illus. LC 90-31976. 32p. (gr. k-3). 1991. 14.00 (0-06-026580-9) HarpC Child Bks.
—Matzoh Mouse. Keavney, Pamela, illus. LC 90-31976. 32p. (gr. k-3). 1993. pap. 4.95 (0-06-443323-4, Trophy) HarpC Child Bks.
Wohlberg, Myrna F., et al. Elementary Algebra Study Aid. 1980. pap. 2.50 (0-87738-037-6) Youth Ed.
Wohlfahrt, Franz. Easiest Elementary Method for Violin: Op. 38. 56p. 1894. pap. 7.50 (0-8258-0053-6, L1061) Fischer Inc NY.
Wojcicki, Marba, ed. see Cosby, Bill, et al.
Wojciechowska, Maia. Dreams of Golf. (Illus.). 52p. 1993. 14.50 (1-883740-01-0) Pebble Bch CA.
—Shadow of a Bull. LC 64-12563. (Illus.). 176p. (gr. 5 up). 1964. SBE 13.95 (0-689-30042-5, Atheneum Child Bk) Macmillan Child Grp.
—Shadow of a Bull. LC 91-27716. 160p. (gr. 3-7). 1992. pap. 3.95 (0-689-71567-6, Aladdin) Macmillan Child Grp.
—Shadow of a Bull. 180p. (gr. 5-8). 1984. 14.40 (0-685-63788-3, BR8256) W A T Braille.
—Shadow of a Bull. 180p. 1991. text ed. 14.40 (1-56956-316-0) W A T Braille.
Wojciechowska, Maja. Tuned Out. 128p. (gr. 7 up). 1969. pap. 1.50 (0-440-99139-0, LFL) Dell.

Wojciechowski, Susan. The Best Halloween of All. Meddaugh, Susan, illus. LC 91-9369. 32p. (ps-2). 1992. 10.00 (*0-517-57765-8*); PLB 10.99 (*0-517-57835-2*) Crown Bks Yng Read.
—Patty Dillman of Hot Dog Fame. LC 88-22565. 192p. (gr. 5 up). 1989. 13.95 (*0-531-05810-7*); PLB 13.99 (*0-531-08410-8*) Orchard Bks Watts.
—Promises to Keep. LC 90-23437. 160p. (gr. 4-8). 1991. 14.00 (*0-517-58186-8*); lib. bdg. 14.99 (*0-517-58187-6*) Crown Bks Yng Read.
Wojcieshowska, Maia. Dreams of Cycling. Karsky, A. K., illus. 52p. 1994. 14.50 (*1-883740-13-4*) Pebble Bch CA.
—Dreams of Fashion. Karsky, A. K., illus. 52p. 1994. 14. 50 (*1-883740-05-3*) Pebble Bch CA.
—Dreams of Ice Dancing. Karsky, A. K., illus. 52p. 1994. 14.50 (*1-883740-08-8*) Pebble Bch CA.
—Dreams of Soccer. Karsky, A. K., illus. 52p. 1994. 14. 50 (*1-883740-06-1*) Pebble Bch CA.
—Dreams of Super Bowl. Karsky, A. K., illus. 52p. 1993. 14.50 (*1-883740-03-7*) Pebble Bch CA.
—Dreams of the Deep. Karsky, A. K., illus. 52p. 1994. 14.50 (*1-883740-12-6*) Pebble Bch CA.
—Dreams of the Hoop. Karsky, A. K., illus. 52p. 1994. 14.50 (*1-883740-10-X*) Pebble Bch CA.
—Dreams of the Indy Five Hundred. Karsky, A. K., illus. 52p. 1994. 14.50 (*1-883740-11-8*) Pebble Bch CA.
—Dreams of the Kentucky Derby. Karsky, A. K., illus. 52p. 1994. 14.50 (*1-883740-07-X*) Pebble Bch CA.
—Dreams of the World Series. Karsky, A. K., illus. 52p. 1994. 14.50 (*1-883740-09-6*) Pebble Bch CA.
—Dreams of Wimbledon. Karsky, A. K., illus. 52p. 1993. 14.50 (*1-883740-02-9*) Pebble Bch CA.
—Dreams of Winter Gold. Karsky, A. K., illus. 52p. 1993. 14.50 (*1-883740-04-5*) Pebble Bch CA.
Wojcio, Michael D. & Gustason, Gerilee. Music in Motion: Twenty Two Songs in Signing Exact English, for Children. Norris, Carolyn, illus. 112p. (Orig.). 1982. 12.95 (*0-916708-07-1*) Modern Signs.
Wolak, Camilla H. Squire Gullible & the Dragon. rev. ed. LC 89-43530. (gr. 3-12). 1985. pap. 6.00 play script (*0-88734-508-5*) Players Pr.
Wolbers, Marian T. Burundi. (Illus.). 120p. (gr. 6 up). 1989. lib. bdg. 14.95 (*1-55546-785-7*) Chelsea Hse.
Wolcott, Patty. Double-Decker Double-Decker Double-Decker Bus. Barner, Bob, illus. LC 91-14210. 32p. (ps-2). 1991. 3.50 (*0-679-81930-4*); PLB 6.99 (*0-679-91930-9*) Random Bks Yng Read.
—Eeeeek! Delaney, Ned, illus. LC 91-12741. 32p. (ps-2). 1991. 3.50 (*0-679-81929-0*); PLB 6.99 (*0-679-91929-5*) Random Bks Yng Read.
—The Marvelous Mud Washing Machine. Brown, Richard, illus. LC 91-8196. 32p. (ps-2). 1991. 3.50 (*0-679-81926-6*); PLB 6.99 (*0-679-91926-0*) Random Bks Yng Read.
—Pickle Pickle Pickle Juice. Drawson, Blair, illus. LC 91-12774. 32p. (ps-2). 1991. 3.50 (*0-679-81928-2*); PLB 6.99 (*0-679-91928-7*) Random Bks Yng Read.
—Tunafish Sandwiches. Zander, Hans, illus. LC 91-13496. 32p. (ps-2). 1991. 3.50 (*0-679-81927-4*); PLB 6.99 (*0-679-91927-9*) Random Bks Yng Read.
—Where Did That Naughty Little Hamster Go? Hoffman, Rosekrans, illus. LC 91-12133. 32p. (ps-2). 1991. 3.50 (*0-679-81924-X*); PLB 6.99 (*0-679-91924-4*) Random Bks Yng Read.
Wolde, Gunilla. Betsy's First Day at Nursery School. LC 76-9322. (Illus.). (ps-k). 1982. 1.95 (*0-394-85381-4*) Random Bks Yng Read.
—Betsy's Fixing Day. Wolde, Gunilla, illus. LC 78-50056. 24p. (ps). 1990. 4.95 (*0-394-83781-9*) Random Bks Yng Read.
—This Is Betsy. Wolde, Gunilla, illus. LC 75-7566. 24p. (ps). 1990. 4.95 (*0-394-83161-6*) Random Bks Yng Read.
Wolf, A. El Cuento Verdadero de los Tres Cerditos. (ps-3). 1991. 14.95 (*0-670-84162-5*) Viking Child Bks.
—The True Story of the Three Little Pigs Gift Set. Scieszka, Jon & Scieszka, Jon, eds. Smith, Lane, illus. 32p. (ps-3). 1992. incl. cass. 24.95 (*0-670-89779-5*) Viking Child Bks.
Wolf, Aline D. A Book about Anna: For Children & Their Parents. Rajpar, Shamin & Wolf, Gerald, illus. LC 80-84874. 56p. (Orig.). (ps-k). 1981. 9.95x (*0-685-03953-6*); pap. 5.95x (*0-9601016-4-0*) Parent-Child Pr.
Wolf, Andrea. Valentino. Bradford, Elizabeth, ed. Verlag, Mangold, tr. from GER. Wolf, Alexander, illus. LC 91-21301. 32p. (gr. k-3). 1991. PLB 14.60 (*1-56074-030-2*) Garrett Ed Corp.
Wolf, Bernard. Beneath the Stone: A Mexican Zapotec Tale. Wolf, Bernard, photos by. LC 92-27103. (Illus.). 48p. (gr. k-6). 1994. 15.95 (*0-531-06835-8*); lib. bdg. 15.99 RLB (*0-531-08685-2*) Orchard Bks Watts.
Wolf, Bob. Bible Animal Stories, Bk. 1. Lautermilch, John, illus. 86p. (gr. 2-7). 1983. pap. 2.00 (*0-89323-044-8*) Bible Memory.
—Just Like Jesus. (Illus.). 24p. (Orig.). (gr. 1-4). 1982. pap. 0.50 (*0-89323-034-0*) Bible Memory.
—Uncle Bob's Bible Stories. Lautermilch, John, illus. 108p. (Orig.). (gr. 4-8). 1982. pap. 1.50 (*0-89323-028-6*) Bible Memory.
Wolf, Cathrine, jt. auth. see McMane, Fred.
Wolf, D. M. A Bird's Eye View of the Statue of Liberty: As Seen by Lorenzo the Parrot. McDaniel, Jerry, illus. 32p. (gr. 3-4). 1988. pap. 4.95 (*0-9617057-2-8*) Storyviews Pub.

—We the People: Bits, Bytes & Highlights of the U. S. Constitution & Bill of Rights from Honey Bees Tye & Sy. McDaniel, Jerry, illus. 32p. (Orig.). (gr. 3-5). 1987. pap. 4.95 (*0-9617057-1-X*) Storyviews Pub.
Wolf, Gerald P. Child-Size Masterpieces - Transportation in America. (Orig.). (ps-6). 1992. pap. 17.95 (*0-939195-05-4*) Parent-Child Pr.
Wolf, Jake. And Then What? LC 90-24644. (Illus.). 32p. (ps up). 1993. 14.00 (*0-688-10285-9*); PLB 13.93 (*0-688-10286-7*) Greenwillow.
Wolf, Janet. The Rosy Fat Magenta Radish. (ps-1). 1990. 14.95 (*0-316-95045-9*, Joy St Bks) Little.
Wolf, Jeannie, ed. see Rolliet, D. G.
Wolf, Jill. Bears in Toyland. 1988. pap. 2.50 (*0-89954-785-0*) Antioch Pub Co.
—Edward the Easter Bear. (ps up) 1990. pap. 2.50 (*0-89954-140-2*) Antioch Pub Co.
—The Story of Christmas. Rudegeair, Jean, illus. 24p. (gr. 3-7). 1986. pap. 2.50 (*0-89954-459-2*) Antioch Pub Co.
—Story of Easter. (ps up) 1990. pap. 2.50 (*0-89954-392-8*) Antioch Pub Co.
—Teddy Bear's Are Special Friends: Little Treasure Book. Wilson-Heaney, Kathyrn, illus. 24p. (gr. 3-7). 1985. pap. 2.50 (*0-89954-466-5*) Antioch Pub Co.
—Teddy Bear's Easter Picnic. Nelson, Linda K., illus. 24p. (gr. 3-7). 1985. pap. 2.50 (*0-89954-424-X*) Antioch Pub Co.
—Troll's Christmas. Till, Tom, illus. 24p. (gr. 3-7). 1981. pap. 2.50 (*0-89954-460-6*) Antioch Pub Co.
Wolf, Jill & Moore, Clement C. Teddy Bears Night Before Christmas. Rudegeair, Jean, illus. 24p. (gr. 3-6). 1985. pap. 2.50 (*0-89954-330-8*) Antioch Pub Co.
Wolf, Joyce. Between the Cracks. 176p. (gr. 5 up). 1992. 14.95 (*0-8037-1270-7*) Dial Bks Young.
Wolf, Sallie. Peter's Trucks. Levine, Abby, ed. Smith, Cat B., illus. LC 91-19251. 24p. (ps-1). 1992. PLB 13.95 (*0-8075-6519-9*) A Whitman.
Wolf, Stephen. A Day in the Life of a Stunt Person. Edwards, Al, photos by. LC 90-11101. (Illus.). 32p. (gr. 4-8). 1991. lib. bdg. 11.79 (*0-8167-2222-6*); pap. text ed. 7.95 (*0-8167-2223-4*) Troll Assocs.
Wolf, Susan, jt. auth. see Isenberg, Barbara.
Wolf, Tony. The First Christmas Book. (ps-2). 1992. 20. 00 (*1-56021-198-9*) W J Fantasy.
Wolf, William J. Benedict Arnold, a Novel. LC 89-63836. (Illus.). 413p. (gr. 10-12). 1990. 30.00 (*0-913993-13-1*) Paideia MA.
Wolf, Winfried. The Easter Bunny. Mathieu, Agnes, illus. LC 85-10115. 32p. (ps-3). 1987. 8.95 (*0-8037-0239-6*) Dial Bks Young.
Wolf, Winifried. The Easter Bunny. Mathieu, Agnes, illus. LC 85-10115. 24p. (ps-3). 1991. pap. 3.99 (*0-8037-0912-9*, Dial Pied Piper) Puffin Bks.
Wolfberg, Carrie. The Happy Dreidles: Hanukkah Adventure. Birenbaum, Barbara, illus. LC 86-12210. 28p. (ps-2). 1991. 8.50 (*0-935343-01-6*); pap. 3.50 (*0-935343-00-8*) Peartree.
Wolfe, Anne H. Wings of Love. (gr. 4-7). 1993. pap. 2.99 (*0-553-29978-6*) Bantam.
Wolfe, Bob & Wolfe, Diane, photos by. Holiday Cooking Around the World. Swofford, Jeannette, illus. 52p. (gr. 5 up). 1988. 15.95 (*0-8225-0922-9*) Lerner Pubns.
Wolfe, Charles. Mahalia Jackson. Horner, Matina S., intro. by. 112p. (gr. 5 up). 1990. 17.95 (*1-55546-661-3*) Chelsea Hse.
—Mahalia Jackson: American Women of Achievement. (gr. 4-7). 1992. pap. 7.95 (*0-7910-0440-6*) Chelsea Hse.
Wolfe, Cheri. Lt. Charles Wilkes & the Great U.S. Exploring Expedition. Goetzmann, William H., ed. Collins, Michael, intro. by. (Illus.). 112p. (gr. 6-12). 1991. PLB 18.95 (*0-7910-1320-0*) Chelsea Hse.
Wolfe, Constance. Search: A Research Guide for Science Fairs & Independent Study. 94p. (Orig.). (gr. 4-8). 1988. pap. text ed. 12.95 (*0-913705-30-6*) Zephyr Pr AZ.
Wolfe, Diane, jt. auth. see Wolfe, Robert L.
Wolfe, Elle. Lonely Heart. 1990. pap. 1.79 (*0-8125-1004-6*) Tor Bks.
—Palm Beach Prep, No. 3: The Girls Against the Boys. (gr. 4-7). 1990. pap. 2.95 (*0-8125-1063-1*) Tor Bks.
—Palm Beach Prep, No. 4: Screen Test. (gr. 4-7). 1990. pap. 2.95 (*0-8125-1062-3*) Tor Bks.
—Palm Beach Prep, No. 5: Troublemaker. (gr. 4-7). 1990. pap. 2.95 (*0-8125-1065-8*) Tor Bks.
—Palm Beach Prep, No. 6: Upstaged, No. 6. (gr. 4-7). 1990. pap. 2.95 (*0-8125-1077-1*) Tor Bks.
—Real Scoop. (gr. 4-7). 1990. pap. 2.95 (*0-8125-1005-4*) Tor Bks.
Wolfe, Gerard R. Spanish Study Aid. 1978. pap. 2.75 (*0-87738-033-3*) Youth Ed.
Wolfe, L. E. The Case of the Screaming Skates & Other Mysteries: Jack B. Quick, Sports Detective. (gr. 3-7). 1991. pap. 3.95 (*0-316-95095-5*, Spts Illus Kids) Little.
—The Case of the Sneaker Snatcher. 118p. (gr. 3-6). 1991. PLB 17.50 (*0-8225-3111-9*) Lerner Pubns.
—Case of the Sneaker Snatcher & Other Mysteries. (gr. 4-7). 1991. pap. 3.50 (*0-316-95097-1*, Spts Illus Kids) Little.
Wolfe, L E. Case of the Tour de Tricks & Other Mysteries. (gr. 4-7). 1991. pap. 3.50 (*0-316-95096-3*, Spts Illus Kids) Little.
Wolfe, L. E. The Case of the Tour de Tricks & Other Mysteries. 122p. (gr. 3-6). 1991. PLB 17.50 (*0-8225-3110-0*) Lerner Pubns.
Wolfe, Liz, tr. see Evans, Jo & Moore, Jo E.
Wolfe, Liz, tr. see Evans, Joy & Moore, Jo E.

Wolfe, Liz, tr. see Moore, Jo E. & Evans, Joy.
Wolfe, Rinna E. Charles Richard Drew, M. D. (Illus.). 64p. (gr. 3-6). 1991. PLB 12.90 (*0-531-20021-3*) Watts.
—Mary McLeod Bethune. Rich, Mary P., ed. LC 91-31660. (Illus.). 64p. (gr. 3-5). 1992. PLB 12.90 (*0-531-20103-1*) Watts.
Wolfe, Robert L. Vegetarian Cooking Around the World. (gr. 4-7). 1993. pap. 5.95 (*0-8225-9632-6*) Lerner Pubns.
Wolfe, Robert L. & Wolfe, Diane. Holiday Cooking Around the World. Swofford, Jeannette, illus. 52p. (gr. 5 up). pap. 5.95 (*0-8225-9573-7*) Lerner Pubns.
Wolfe, Robert L. & Wolfe, Diane, photos by. Desserts Around the World. (Illus.). 56p. (gr. 5 up). 1991. PLB 14.95 (*0-8225-0926-1*) Lerner Pubns.
—Vegetarian Cooking Around the World. (Illus.). 52p. (gr. 5-12). 1992. PLB 14.95 (*0-8225-0927-X*) Lerner Pubns.
Wolfe, Thomas, et al. A Southern Appalachian Reader. McNeil, Nellie, et al, eds. LC 87-19589. (Illus.). 500p. (gr. 10-12). 1988. pap. text ed. 14.95 (*0-913239-50-X*) Appalach Consortium.
Wolfe, William D. & Anderson, Sheryl J. A Message in a Minute: Lighthearted Minidramas for Churches. LC 92-5618. 104p. (Orig.). 1992. pap. 11.00 (*0-8170-1181-1*) Judson.
Wolfer, J. The Dog Who Cried Wolf: Based on Old Fairy Tale. Abell, ed. & illus. 50p. (Orig.). (gr. 1-3). 1993. 25.00 (*1-56611-058-0*); pap. text ed. 15.00 (*1-56611-061-0*) Jones.
Wolferman, Kristie, jt. auth. see Beachy, Mary D.
Wolfersperger, Shirley K. & Carlston, Eloise. Experimenting with Art: Twenty-Five Easy-to-Teach Lessons in Design & Color. (Illus.). 96p. (Orig.). (gr. 3-6). 1991. pap. 12.95 (*0-673-46411-3*) GdYrBks.
Wolff, Angelika. Mom, I Broke My Arm. Glueckselig, Leo, illus. LC 69-18646. (gr. k-3). 1969. PLB 11.95 (*0-87460-121-5*) Lion Bks.
—Mom, I Need Glasses. Hill, Dorothy, illus. Saltzman, S. L., intro. by. LC 74-112648. (Illus.). (gr. k-3). 1971. PLB 12.95 (*0-87460-139-8*) Lion Bks.
Wolff, Ashley. The Bells of London. (gr. k-3). 1984. 12. 95 (*0-396-08485-0*) Putnam Pub Group.
—Come with Me. LC 89-34482. (Illus.). 32p. (ps-2). 1990. 12.95 (*0-525-44555-2*, DCB) Dutton Child Bks.
—Only the Cat Saw. (Illus.). (ps-3). 1988. pap. 3.95 (*0-14-050853-8*, Puffin) Puffin Bks.
—Only the Cat Saw. (gr. k-3). 1985. 13.95 (*0-399-21698-7*, Putnam) Putnam Pub Group.
—Stella & Roy. Wolff, Ashley, illus. LC 92-27005. 32p. (ps-k). 1993. 12.99 (*0-525-45081-5*, DCB) Dutton Child Bks.
—A Year of Beasts. Wolff, Ashley, illus. LC 85-27419. 32p. (ps-1). 1986. 11.95 (*0-525-44240-5*, DCB) Dutton Child Bks.
—Year of Beasts. LC 85-27419. (Illus.). 32p. (ps-1). 1989. pap. 3.95 (*0-525-44541-2*, DCB) Dutton Child Bks.
—A Year of Birds. (ps-3). 1988. pap. 3.95 (*0-14-050854-6*, Puffin) Puffin Bks.
Wolff, B. The Little Pischna: Forty-Eight Preparatory Exercises for Piano. (ENG & GER.). 1907. pap. 4.00 (*0-8258-0122-2*, L 475) Fischer Inc NY.
Wolff, Barbara M. Mi Abuelito y Yo. Wolff, Barbara M., illus. (SPA.). 16p. (ps-1). 1992. PLB 13.95 (*1-879567-12-1*, Valeria Bks) Wonder Well.
—My Family & Me. Wolff, Barbara M., illus. 16p. (ps-1). 1993. PLB 13.95 (*0-685-59697-4*, Valeria Bks) Wonder Well.
—Pappa & Me. Wolff, Barbara M., illus. 16p. (ps-1). 1991. PLB 13.95 (*1-879567-11-3*, Valeria Bks) Wonder Well.
Wolff, Craig T. Wayne Gretzky: Profil d'un Joueur de Hockey. Curtis, Bruce, photos by. (FRE., Illus.). 64p. (ps-5). 1984. pap. 2.25 (*0-380-85753-7*, Camelot) Avon.
Wolff, Ferida. The Emperor's Garden. Osborn, Kathy, illus. LC 93-14751. 1994. write for info. (*0-688-11651-5*, Tambourine Bks); PLB write for info. (*0-688-11652-3*) Morrow.
—Pink Slippers, Bat Mitzvah Blues. (gr. 3-7). 1989. 13.95 (*0-8276-0332-0*) JPS Phila.
—Seven Loaves of Bread. Keller, Katie, illus. LC 92-34313. 32p. (ps up). 1993. 14.00 (*0-688-11101-7*, Tambourine Bks); PLB 13.93 (*0-688-11112-2*, Tambourine Bks) Morrow.
—Woodcutter's Coat. Wisdorf, Anne, illus. (ps-3). 1992. 15.95 (*0-316-95048-3*, Joy St Bks) Little.
Wolff, Ferida & Kozielski, Dolores. The Halloween Grab Bag: A Book of Tricks & Treats. Neuhouse, David, illus. 96p. (gr. 2-5). 1993. pap. 5.95 (*0-06-446148-3*, Trophy) HarpC Child Bks.
—On Halloween Night. Avendano, Dolores, illus. LC 93-26859. 1994. write for info. (*0-688-12972-2*, Tambourine Bks); PLB write for info. (*0-688-12973-0*, Tambourine Bks) Morrow.
Wolff, George. I Can Read About Cats & Kittens. LC 72-96959. (Illus.). (gr. 2-4). 1973. pap. 1.95 (*0-89375-056-5*) Troll Assocs.
Wolff, James H. Work Exploration Checklist. (gr. 7 up). 1989. 3.95 (*0-912486-60-0*) Finney Co.
Wolff, Kathy, ed. see Ward, Fred & Ward, Betty.
Wolff, Marion F. The Shrinking Circle: Memories of Nazi Berlin, 1933-39. 128p. (gr. 7-9). 1989. pap. 7.95 (*0-8074-0419-5*, 147501) UAHC.

Wolff, Mark R. The Illustrated Math Book on Animalcules. Wolff, Mark R., illus. 83p. (Orig.). (gr. 6-12). 1994. pap. text ed. 7.00 (0-9637132-0-5) M R Wolff.

Wolff, Patricia R. & Root, Kimberly B. The Toll-Bridge Troll. LC 93-32298. (gr. 3 up). 1995. write for info. (0-15-277665-6) Harbrace.

Wolff, Rick. Brooks Robinson. Murray, Jim, intro. by. (Illus.). 64p. (gr. 3 up). 1991. lib. bdg. 14.95 (0-7910-1186-0) Chelsea Hse.

—Mickey Mantle. Murray, Jim, illus. 64p. (gr. 3 up). 1991. lib. bdg. 14.95 (0-7910-1181-X) Chelsea Hse.

—Ted Williams. (Illus.). 64p. (gr. 3 up). 1994. PLB 14.95 (0-7910-1194-1, Am Art Analog) Chelsea Hse.

Wolff, Robert. Animals of Europe. Dallet, Robert, illus. LC 77-78379. 160p. (gr. 3-9). 1969. PLB 29.95 (0-87460-092-8) Lion Bks.

Wolff, Robert S. The Caves of Mars. LC 87-34252. 168p. (gr. 7 up). 1988. PLB 15.00 (0-208-02190-6, Linnet) Shoe String.

Wolff, Tobias. The Barracks Thief: And Selected Stories. 1989. pap. 7.95 (0-553-34675-X) Bantam.

Wolff, Virginia E. Make Lemonade. 160p. (gr. 5-9). 1993. PLB 15.95 (0-8050-2228-7, Bks Young Read) H Holt & Co.

—Make Lemonade. LC 93-21003. (gr. 9-12). 1993. 15.95 (0-7862-0056-1) Thorndike Pr.

—The Mozart Season. LC 90-23635. 208p. (gr. 6 up). 1991. 15.95 (0-8050-1571-X, Bks Young Read) H Holt & Co.

—The Mozart Season. 256p. (gr. 5 up). 1993. pap. 3.25 (0-590-45445-5, Point) Scholastic Inc.

—Probably Still Nick Swansen. 144p. (gr. 6 up). 1988. 13.95 (0-8050-0701-6, Bks Young Read) H Holt & Co.

Wolfman, Ira. Do People Grow on Family Trees? Genealogy for Kids & Other Beginners. LC 88-51586. (Illus.). 192p. (Orig.). (gr. 3-7). 1991. pap. 9.95 (0-89480-348-4, 1348) Workman Pub.

—My World & Globe. LC 91-50382. (Illus.). 64p. (Orig.). 1991. pap. 12.95 (0-89480-993-8, 1993) Workman Pub.

Wolfman, Marv. Deathstroke the Terminator: Full Cycle. Peterson, Jonathan, ed. (Illus.). 160p. (gr. 3 up). 1992. pap. 12.95 (0-930289-82-X) DC Comics.

Wolfman, Melvin S. So, You Want to Be a Veterinarian. Steinkraus, Edith, illus. 38p. (Orig.). (gr. 3-12). 1993. pap. 15.00 (0-9629806-3-3) Benjamin OH.
Wouldn't children love to read about a mule with a library card or a giraffe who wears a turtleneck sweater? They can with SO, YOU WANT TO BE A VETERINARIAN, written by Melvin S. Wolfman. The imagination is the limit in this interactive children's book. Thought provoking anecdotes allow children to provide their own solutions to unusual problems these many animals face; children actually share the writing credit with Mr. Wolfman. A bear wants to own a car repair shop so Mr. Wolfman gives the bear a screwdriver & then asks the reader "what would you do?" It is a wonderful tool for encouraging creativity. Illustrations are included & additional space is provided for the reader to draw his or her own pictures. SO, YOU WANT TO BE A VETERINARIAN is an outstanding introduction to the world of interactive media.
Publisher Provided Annotation.

Wolf-Morgenlander, Karl. The Orchestral Mage. (Orig.). Date not set. 9.95 (1-56883-012-2) Colonial Pr AL.

Wolfson, Alice, jt. auth. see Meyer, Ursula.

Wolfson, David, jt. auth. see Kimelman, Paul M.

Wolfson, Evelyn. American Indian Tools & Ornaments. 1981. 8.95 (0-679-20509-8) McKay.

—From Abenaki to Zuni: A Dictionary of Native American Tribes. Bock, William S., photos by. (gr. 5 up). 1988. 17.95 (0-8027-6789-3); PLB 18.85 (0-8027-6790-7) Walker & Co.

—Growing up Indian. Bock, William S., illus. LC 86-9053. 96p. (gr. 10 up). 1986. 10.95 (0-8027-6643-9); PLB 11.85 (0-8027-6644-7) Walker & Co.

—The Iroquois: People of the Northeast. LC 92-4642. (Illus.). 48p. (gr. 4-6). 1992. PLB 14.90 (1-56294-076-7) Millbrook Pr.

—The Teton Sioux: People of the Plains. LC 92-4633. (Illus.). 48p. (gr. 4-6). 1992. PLB 14.90 (1-56294-077-5) Millbrook Pr.

Wolfson, Mack, jt. auth. see Fass, Bernie.

Wolfstein, Luise. Desert Animals. Gibson, Barbara, illus. 24p. 1993. 7.95 (0-590-46006-4) Scholastic Inc.

Wolhart, Dayna. Anorexia & Bulimia. LC 88-21553. (Illus.). 48p. (gr. 5-6). 1988. RSBE 12.95 (0-89686-416-2, Crestwood Hse) Macmillan Child Grp.

—Emergency Vehicles. 48p. (gr. 3-4). 1991. PLB 11.95 (1-56065-079-6) Capstone Pr.

Wolitzer, Hilma. Introducing Shirley Braverman. (gr. 8 up). 1987. 3.50 (0-374-43597-9, Sunburst) FS&G.

—Silver. large type ed. 384p. 1989. lib. bdg. 20.95 (0-8161-4743-4, Large Print Bks); pap. 13.95 (0-8161-4933-X, Large Print Bks) Hall.

—Toby Lived Here. (gr. 5-11). 1986. pap. 3.45 (0-374-47924-0, Sunburst) FS&G.

Wolitzer, Hilmer. Wish You Were Here. 180p. (gr. 5 up). 1986. pap. 3.45 (0-374-48412-0, Sunburst) FS&G.

Wolitzer, Meg. Caribou. 176p. (gr. 7-12). 1986. pap. 2.50 (0-553-25560-6) Bantam.

—The Dream Book. 160p. (gr. 3-7). 1987. pap. 2.50 (0-380-70356-4, Camelot) Avon.

—Operation: Save the Teacher. 128p. (Orig.). (gr. 4-8). 1993. pap. 3.50 (0-380-76461-X, Camelot) Avon.

—Operation: Save the Teacher: Saturday Night Toast. 128p. (Orig.). 1993. pap. 3.50 (0-380-76462-8, Camelot) Avon.

—Operation: Save the Teacher: Tuesday Night Pie. 128p. (Orig.). 1993. pap. 3.50 (0-380-76460-1, Camelot) Avon.

Wolkoff, Judie. Happily Ever after...Almost. 224p. (gr. 5-9). 1984. pap. 2.95 (0-440-43366-5, YB) Dell.

—In a Pig's Eye. (gr. k-6). 1989. pap. 2.95 (0-440-40140-2, YB) Dell.

Wolkoff, Judie, jt. auth. see Beasley, Barbara.

Wolkomir, Joyce & Wolkomir, Richard. Junkyard Bandicoots & Other Tales of the World's Endangered Species. LC 92-11114. 128p. (gr. 4-7). 1992. pap. text ed. 9.95 (0-471-57261-6) Wiley.

Wolkomir, Richard, jt. auth. see Wolkomir, Joyce.

Wolkstein, Diane. The Banza. Brown, Marc, illus. LC 81-65845. 32p. (ps-3). 1981. Dial Bks Young.

—The Banza. Brown, Mark, illus. LC 81-65845. 32p. (gr. k-2). 1984. pap. 4.95 (0-8037-0058-X) Dial Bks Young.

—Little Mouse's Painting. Begin, Maryjane, illus. LC 91-16017. 32p. (ps up). 1992. 15.00 (0-688-07609-2); PLB 14.93 (0-688-07610-6) Morrow Jr Bks.

—The Magic Wings: A Tale from China. Parker, Robert A., illus. LC 83-1611. 32p. (gr. 2-4). 1983. (DCB); pap. 4.95 (0-525-44275-8, DCB) Dutton Child Bks.

—Oom Razoom or Go I Know Not Where, Bring Back I Know Not What. McDermott, Dennis, illus. LC 91-6308. 32p. (gr. k up). 1991. 14.95 (0-688-09416-3); PLB 14.88 (0-688-09417-1) Morrow Jr Bks.

—Step by Step. Smith, Joseph A., illus. LC 93-14667. 1994. write for info. (0-688-10315-4); PLB write for info. (0-688-10316-2) Morrow Jr Bks.

—White Wave: A Chinese Tale. Young, Ed, illus. LC 78-4781. (gr. 2 up). 1979. (Crowell Jr Bks) HarpC Child Bks.

Wolkstein, Diane, ed. The Magic Orange Tree: And Other Haitian Folktales. Henriquez, Elsa, illus. LC 79-22787. (gr. 10 up). 1987. pap. 16.00 (0-8052-0650-7) Schocken.

Wollard, Kathy. How Come? Solomon, Pedra, illus. 256p. (Orig.). (gr. 3-7). 1993. pap. 10.95 (1-56305-324-1, 3324) Workman Pub.

Wolman, Bernice, compiled by. Taking Turns: Poetry to Share. Stock, Catherine, illus. LC 90-46533. 32p. (gr. 1-4). 1992. SBE 13.95 (0-689-31677-1, Atheneum Child Bk) Macmillan Child Grp.

Wolman, Paul. The U. S. Mint. Schlesinger, Arthur M., Jr., intro. by. (Illus.). 96p. (gr. 5 up). 1987. lib. bdg. 14.95 (0-87754-829-3) Chelsea Hse.

Wolo & Wolo. Sir Archibald. LC 91-73411. (Illus.). 56p. (ps-1). 1991. Repr. of 1944 ed. 14.95 (0-944439-22-5) Clark City Pr.

Wolpert, Tom. Whale Magic for Kids. Nicklin, Flip, illus. LC 90-50718. 48p. (gr. 3-4). 1991. PLB 18.60 (0-8368-0660-3) Gareth Stevens Inc.

—Whitetail Magic for Kids. Cox, Daniel S., illus. LC 90-50719. 48p. (gr. 2-3). 1991. PLB 18.60 (0-8368-0661-1) Gareth Stevens Inc.

—Wolf Magic for Kids. Rogers, Lynn, illus. LC 90-50720. 48p. (gr. 2-3). 1991. PLB 18.60 (0-8368-0662-X) Gareth Stevens Inc.

Wolpert, Tom, jt. auth. see Klein, Tom.

Wolter, Annette. African Gray Parrots. (Illus.). 64p. (gr. 4 up). 1987. pap. 5.50 (0-8120-3773-1) Barron.

Wolterman, Jan, ed. see Isphording, Julie.

Wolters, Richard A. Home Dog. Hill, Gene, frwd. by. (Illus.). 160p. (gr. 7 up). 1984. 16.95 (0-525-24232-5, Dutton) NAL-Dutton.

Wolverton, Linda. Running Before the Wind. (gr. 6 up). 1987. 13.95 (0-395-42116-0) HM.

Womack, Randy L. South America Country Studies. (Illus.). 96p. (gr. 4 up). 1990. wkbk. 10.95 (1-56500-023-4) Gldn Educ.

Womack, Randy L. & Lew, Christina. Read 'n Draw: Following Directions, Bk. 1. (Illus.). 64p. (gr. 3-5). wkbk. 6.95 (0-685-57592-6) Gldn Educ.

—Read 'n Draw: Following Directions, Bk. 2. (Illus.). 48p. (gr. 4-6). 1992. wkbk. 6.95 (1-56500-032-3) Gldn Educ.

Wonder Kids Publication Staff, tr. see Wonder Kids Publications Group Staff (USA) & Hwa-I Publishing Co., Staff.

Wonder Kids Publications Group Staff (USA) & Hwa-I Publishing Co., Staff. Animal Tales: Chinese Children's Stories, Vols. 11-15. Ching, Emily, et al, eds. Wonder Kids Publication Staff, tr. from CHI. Hwa-I Publishing Co., Staff, illus. LC 90-60793. 28p. (gr. 3-6). 1991. Repr. of 1988 ed. Five vol. set, 28p. ea. bk. 39.75 (0-685-58702-9) Wonder Kids.

Wonder Kids Publications Group Staff. The Blind Man & the Cripple - Orchard Village: Folklore: English - Spanish Version. Ching, Emily, et al, eds. Wonder Kids Publications Staff, tr. from CHI. Hwa-I Publishing Co., Staff, illus. LC 90-60793. 28p. (gr. 3-6). 1992. Repr. of 1988 ed. 12.95 (1-56162-126-9) Wonder Kids.

—The Blind Man & the Cripple - Orchard Village: Folklore: English - Cambodian Version. Ching, Emily, et al, eds. Wonder Kids Publications Staff, tr. from CHI. Hwa-I Publishing Co., Staff, illus. 28p. (gr. 3-6). 1992. Repr. of 1988 ed. 12.95 (1-56162-128-5) Wonder Kids.

—The Blind Man & the Cripple - Orchard Village: Folklore: English - Vietnamese Version. Ching, Emily, et al, eds. Wonder Kids Publications Staff, tr. from CHI. Hwa-I Publishing Co., Staff, illus. 28p. (gr. 3-6). 1992. Repr. of 1988 ed. 12.95 (1-56162-127-7) Wonder Kids.

—Brother Cat & Brother Rat - The Rooster's Antlers: Twelve Beasts & the Years: English - Spanish Version. Ching, Emily, et al, eds. Wonder Kids Publications Staff, tr. from CHI. Hwa-I Publishing Co., Staff, illus. 28p. (gr. 3-6). 1992. Repr. of 1988 ed. 12.95 (1-56162-121-8) Wonder Kids.

—Brother Cat & Brother Rat - The Rooster's Antlers: Twelve Beasts & the Years: English - Cambodian Version. Ching, Emily, et al, eds. Wonder Kids Publications Staff, tr. from CHI. Hwa-I Publishing Co., Staff, illus. 28p. (gr. 3-6). 1992. Repr. of 1988 ed. 12.95 (1-56162-123-4) Wonder Kids.

—Brother Cat & Brother Rat - The Rooster's Antlers: Twelve Beasts & the Years: English - Vietnamese Version. Ching, Emily, et al, eds. Wonder Kids Publications Staff, tr. from CHI. Hwa-I Publishing Co., Staff, illus. 28p. (gr. 3-6). 1992. Repr. of 1988 ed. 12.95 (1-56162-122-6) Wonder Kids.

—Celebrating New Year - Miss Yuan-Shiau: Festivals: English - Cambodian Version. Ching, Emily, et al, eds. Wonder Kids Publications Staff, tr. from CHI. Hwa-I Publishing Co., Staff, illus. 28p. (gr. 3-6). 1992. Repr. of 1988 ed. 12.95 (1-56162-133-1) Wonder Kids.

—Celebrating New Year - Miss Yuan-Shiau: Festivals: English - Spanish Version. Ching, Emily, et al, eds. Wonder Kids Publications Staff, tr. from CHI. Hwa-I Publishing Co., Staff, illus. 28p. (gr. 3-6). 1992. Repr. of 1988 ed. 12.95 (1-56162-131-5) Wonder Kids.

—Celebrating New Year - Miss Yuan-Shiau: Festivals: English - Vietnamese Version. Ching, Emily, et al, eds. Wonder Kids Publications Staff, tr. from CHI. Hwa-I Publishing Co., Staff, illus. 28p. (gr. 3-6). 1992. Repr. of 1988 ed. 12.95 (1-56162-132-3) Wonder Kids.

Wonder Kids Publications Group Staff (USA) & Hwa-I Publishing Co., Staff. Chinese Sites: Chinese Children's Stories, Vols. 86-90. Ching, Emily, et al, eds. Wonder Kids Publications Staff, tr. from CHI. Hwa-I Publishing Co., Staff, illus. LC 90-60809. (gr. 3-6). 1991. Repr. of 1988 ed. Five vol. set, 28p. ea. bk. 39.75 (0-685-58717-7) Wonder Kids.

—Fables: Chinese Children's Stories, Vols. 16-20. Ching, Emily & Ching, Ko-Shee, eds. Wonder Kids Publications Staff, tr. from CHI. Hwa-I Publishing Co., Staff, illus. LC 90-60794. (gr. 3-6). 1991. Repr. of 1988 ed. Five vol. set, 28p. ea. bk. 39.75 (0-685-58703-7) Wonder Kids.

—Fairy Tales: Chinese Children's Stories, Vols. 46-50. Ching, Emily, et al, eds. Wonder Kids Publications Staff, tr. from CHI. Hwa-I Publishing Co., Staff, illus. LC 90-60801. (gr. 3-6). 1991. Repr. of 1988 ed. Five vol. set, 28p. ea. bk. 39.75 (0-685-58709-6) Wonder Kids.

—Festivals: Chinese Children's Stories, Vols. 26-30. Ching, Emily, et al, eds. Wonder Kids Publications Staff, tr. from CHI. Hwa-I Publishing Co., Staff, illus. LC 90-60797. (gr. 3-6). 1991. Repr. of 1988 ed. Five vol. set, 28p. ea. bk. 39.75 (0-685-58705-3) Wonder Kids.

—Filial Piety: Chinese Children's Stories, Vols. 51-55. Ching, Emily, et al, eds. Wonder Kids Publications Staff, tr. from CHI. Hwa-I Publishing Co., Staff, illus. LC 90-60802. (gr. 3-6). 1991. Repr. of 1988 ed. Five vol. set, 28p. ea. bk. 39.75 (0-685-58710-X) Wonder Kids.

—Folklore: Chinese Children's Stories, Vols. 1-5. Ching, Emily, et al, eds. Wonder Kids Publications Staff, tr. from CHI. Hwa-I Publishing Co., Staff, illus. LC 90-60791. 28p. (gr. 3-6). 1991. Repr. of 1988 ed. Five vol. set, 28p. ea. bk. 39.75 (0-685-58701-0); Set (100 vols.) 795.00 (1-56162-120-X) Wonder Kids.

—Heroes: Chinese Children's Stories, Vols. 76-80. Ching, Emily, et al, eds. Wonder Kids Publications Staff, tr. from CHI. Hwa-I Publishing Co., Staff, illus. LC 90-60807. (gr. 3-6). 1991. Repr. of 1988 ed. Five vol. set, 28p. ea. bk. 39.75 (0-685-58715-0) Wonder Kids.

—Historical Accounts: Chinese Children's Stories, Vols. 81-85. Ching, Emily, et al, eds. Wonder Kids Publications Staff, tr. from CHI. Hwa-I Publishing Co., Staff, illus. LC 90-60808. (gr. 3-6). 1991. Repr. of 1988 ed. Five vol. set, 28p. ea. bk. 39.75 (0-685-58716-9) Wonder Kids.

—Idioms: Chinese Children's Stories, Vols. 21-25. Ching, Emily, et al, eds. Wonder Kids Publications Staff, tr. from CHI. Hwa-I Publishing Co., Staff, illus. LC 90-60796. (gr. 3-6). 1991. Repr. of 1988 ed. Five vol. set, 28p. ea. bk. 39.75 (0-685-58704-5) Wonder Kids.

—Inventions: Chinese Children's Stories, Vols. 36-40. Ching, Emily, et al, eds. Wonder Kids Publications Staff, tr. from CHI. Hwa-I Publishing Co., Staff, illus. LC 90-60799. (gr. 3-6). 1991. Repr. of 1988 ed. Five vol. set, 28p. ea. bk. 39.75 (0-685-58707-X) Wonder Kids.

—Literature: Chinese Children's Stories, Vols. 66-70. Ching, Emily, et al, eds. Wonder Kids Publications Staff, tr. from CHI. Hwa-I Publishing Co., Staff, illus. LC 90-60805. (gr. 3-6). 1991. Repr. of 1988 ed. Five vol. set, 28p. ea. bk. 39.75 (0-685-58713-4) Wonder Kids.

—Mythology: Chinese Children's Stories, Vols. 61-65. Ching, Emily, et al, eds. Wonder Kids Publications Staff, tr. from CHI. Hwa-I Publishing Co., Staff, illus. LC 90-60804. (gr. 3-6). 1991. Repr. of 1988 ed. Five vol. set, 28p. ea. bk. 39.75 (0-685-58712-6) Wonder Kids.

—Popular Narratives: Chinese Children's Stories, Vols. 71-75. Ching, Emily, et al, eds. Wonder Kids Publications Staff, tr. from CHI. Hwa-I Publishing Co., Staff, illus. LC 90-60806. (gr. 3-6). 1991. Repr. of 1988 ed. Five vol. set, 28p. ea. bk. 39.75 (0-685-58714-2) Wonder Kids.

—Taiwanese Folklore: Chinese Children's Stories, Vols. 96-100. Ching, Emily, et al, eds. Wonder Kids Publication Staff, tr. from CHI. Hwa-I Publishing Co., Staff, illus. LC 90-60811. (gr. 3-6). 1991. Repr. of 1988 ed. Five vol. set, 28p. ea. bk. 39.75 (0-685-58719-3) Wonder Kids.

—Taiwanese Sites: Chinese Children's Stories, Vols. 91-95. Ching, Emily, et al, eds. Wonder Kids Publications Staff, tr. from CHI. Hwa-I Publishing Co., Staff, illus. LC 90-60810. (gr. 3-6). 1991. Repr. of 1988 ed. Five vol. set, 28p. ea. bk. 39.75 (0-685-58718-5) Wonder Kids.

—Tales about Food: Chinese Children's Stories, Vols. 31-35. Ching, Emily, et al, eds. Wonder Kids Publications Staff, tr. from CHI. Hwa-I Publishing Co., Staff, illus. LC 90-60798. (gr. 3-6). 1991. Repr. of 1988 ed. Five vol. set, 28p. ea. bk. 39.75 (0-685-58706-1) Wonder Kids.

Wonder Kids Publications Group Staff & Hwa-I Publishing Co., Staff. Tales about Plants: Chinese Children's Stories, 5 vols, Vols. 6-10. Ching, Emily, et al, eds. Haw-I Publishing Co., Staff, illus. LC 90-60792. 140p. (gr. 3-6). 1991. Repr. of 1988 ed. Set. 39.75 (0-685-59008-9) Wonder Kids.

Wonder Kids Publications Group Staff (USA) & Hwa-I Publishing Co., Staff. Twelve Beasts & the Years: Chinese Children's Stories, Vols. 41-45. Ching, Emily, et al, eds. Wonder Kids Publications Staff, tr. from CHI. Hwa-I Publishing Co., Staff, illus. LC 90-60800. (gr. 3-6). 1991. Repr. of 1988 ed. Five vol. set, 28p. ea. bk. 39.75 (0-685-58708-8) Wonder Kids.

—Wonder Kids: Chinese Children's Stories, Vols. 56-60. Ching, Emily, et al, eds. Wonder Kids Publications Staff, tr. from CHI. Hwa-I Publishing Co., Staff, illus. LC 90-60803. (gr. 3-6). 1991. Repr. of 1988 ed. Five vol. set, 28p. ea. bk. 39.75 (0-685-58711-8) Wonder Kids.

Wonder Kids Publications Staff, tr. see Hwa-I Publishing Co., Staff.

Wonder Kids Publications Staff, tr. see Wonder Kids Publications Group Staff.

Wonder Kids Publications Staff, tr. see Wonder Kids Publications Group Staff (USA) & Hwa-I Publishing Co., Staff.

Wonders, Allison & Edelheit, Jami. The Global Kidz Handbook, No. 2: Over 100 Self-Esteem & Environmental Hands-on Activities. 118p. (gr. 4 up). 1992. pap. write for info. (1-881497-01-1) Global Pr Wks.

—The Global Kidz Handbook: The Internal Self-Esteem & Environmental Program. 138p. (gr. 4 up). 1991. pap. text ed. write for info. (1-881497-00-3) Global Pr Wks.

Wong, H. H., jt. auth. see Vessel, M. F.

Wong, Helen & Rayson, Ann. Hawaii's Royal History. rev. ed. LC 87-70156. 240p. (gr. 6-8). 1987. 25.95 (0-935848-48-7); pap. 16.95 (1-880188-23-6) Bess Pr.

Wong, Herbert H. The Backyard Detective: A Guide for Beginning Naturalists. Greer, Deborah, illus. LC 92-63342. 64p. (Orig.). (gr. k-5). 1993. pap. 7.95 (1-882489-00-4) NatureVision.

THE BACKYARD DETECTIVE provides children with a headstart in science while they have fun exploring their own environment. This book & nature kit invite children to study nature by direct observation in easily accessible environments. With this fully-illustrated guide as an outdoor companion, they use simple science tools & basic comparison charts to investigate nature's clues & uncover their own areas of interest. Young Backyard Detectives will have the opportunity to examine, identify, measure, grow, feed, & collect organisms. They will learn how to keep their own nature journal. This book encourages children to enjoy & respect their natural environment. Dr. Herbert H. Wong, the author, is a zoologist & science educator whose children's science books have become standard favorites among children & their teachers. The ecological concepts he uses to form the framework for THE BACKYARD DETECTIVE are diversity, interrelationships, adaptations & change. THE BACKYARD DETECTIVE is available in book form only, & also with the complete exploration kit (carrying case, magnifier, observation jar, pencil & measuring tape). AVAILABLE THROUGH BOOKPEOPLE & QUALITY BOOKS. *Publisher Provided Annotation.*

Wong, Michael A. A Day in the Life of a Disc Jockey. Jann, Gayle, illus. LC 87-10943. 32p. (gr. 4-8). 1988. PLB 11.79 (0-8167-1125-9); pap. text ed. 2.95 (0-8167-1126-7) Troll Assocs.

Wong, Ovid. Experiments with Animal Behavior. LC 87-33779. (Illus.). 48p. (gr. k-4). 1988. PLB 15.27 (0-516-01214-2); pap. 4.95 (0-516-41214-0) Childrens.

—Giant Pandas. LC 87-10717. (Illus.). 48p. (gr. k-4). 1987. PLB 15.27 (0-516-01241-X); pap. 4.95 (0-516-41241-8) Childrens.

—Hands-On Ecology. LC 91-12751. (Illus.). 128p. (gr. 5 up). 1991. PLB 17.27 (0-516-00539-1) Childrens.

—Your Body & How It Works. Donahoe, Lindaanne, illus. LC 86-9686. 128p. (gr. 5 up). 1986. PLB 17.27 (0-516-00534-0) Childrens.

Wong, Ovid K. Experimenting with Electricity & Magnetism. LC 92-37672. (gr. 7-12). 1993. 13.40 (0-531-12547-5) Watts.

—Experimenting with Electricity & Magnetism. (Illus.). 128p. (gr. 7-12). 1993. pap. 6.95 (0-531-15681-8) Watts.

—Is Science Magic? LC 88-36961. (Illus.). 128p. (gr. 5 up). 1989. PLB 17.27 (0-516-00570-7) Childrens.

Wong, T. W., jt. auth. see Murray, D. M.

Wonsham, Genevieve. Cotton Carta: To Our City Cousins, Big Town, U. S. A. LC 77-83628. (Illus.). (ps-2). 1978. PLB 5.95 (0-89508-023-0) Rainbow Bks.

Woo, Diane. The Curious Carnival Caper. Yamamoto, Neal, illus. 64p. (Orig.). (gr. 2-6). 1992. pap. 3.95 (1-56288-217-1) Checkerboard.

—The Mystery of Cavanaugh's Mansion. Yamamoto, Neal, illus. 64p. (Orig.). (gr. 2-6). 1992. pap. 3.95 (1-56288-219-8) Checkerboard.

—The Riddle of Rattlesnake Gulch. Yamamoto, Neal, illus. 64p. (Orig.). (gr. 2-6). 1992. pap. 3.95 (1-56288-216-3) Checkerboard.

—The Secret of the S. S. Crimson. Yamamoto, Neal, illus. 64p. (Orig.). (gr. 2-6). 1992. pap. 3.95 (1-56288-218-X) Checkerboard.

Woo, Dianne. The Computer Munched My Homework. 128p. (Orig.). 1992. pap. 3.99 (0-8125-2050-5) Tor Bks.

—Werewolves, Ghost & Vampire Jokes You Can Sink Your Teeth Into. 128p. (Orig.). 1993. pap. 3.99 (0-8125-2049-1) Tor Bks.

Wood. Soviet Army. (Illus.). 48p. (gr. 3-8). 1987. PLB 18.60 (0-86625-334-3); PLB 13.95s.p. (0-685-58298-1) Rourke Corp.

Wood, A. Silly Sally. 1992. 13.95 (0-15-274428-2, HB Juv Bks) HarBrace.

Wood, A. & Wood, D. King Bidgood's in the Bathtub. Shaylen, J. & Shaylen, C., eds. 1991. incl. cassette 19.95 (0-15-242731-7, HB Juv Bks) HarBrace.

Wood, A. J. Amazing Animals. Ward, Helen, illus. LC 90-85906. 24p. (ps-1). 1991. 8.95 (1-878093-46-0) Boyds Mills Pr.

—Beautiful Birds. Ward, Helen, illus. LC 90-85907. 24p. (ps-1). 1991. 8.95 (1-878093-47-9) Boyds Mills Pr.

—Egg! A Dozen Eggs, What Will They Be? Unfold Each Page & You Will See! Stillwell, Stella, illus. LC 92-17930. 1993. 12.95 (0-316-81616-7) Little.

—Errata. LC 91-4394. (ps-3). 1991. 15.00 (0-671-77569-3, Green Tiger) S&S Trade.

—Look! The Ultimate Spot the Difference Book. (gr. 1 up). 1990. 13.00 (0-8037-0925-0) Dial Bks Young.

—Look! The Ultimate Spot-the-Difference Book. Wilson, April, illus. 40p. (gr. 1 up). 1993. pap. 4.99 (0-14-054879-3, Puffin Pied Piper) Puffin Bks.

—Sunny Stories: The Sheep that Liked to Sing. 1989. 1.98 (0-671-09892-6) S&S Trade.

—The Tale of the Napkin Rabbit. Downer, Maggie, illus. LC 93-9864. (gr. 3 up). 1993. 14.95 (0-307-17603-7, Artsts Writrs) Western Pub.

—The Treasure Hunt. Downer, Maggie, illus. LC 92-5515. 32p. (gr. k up). 1992. 13.95 (1-56566-018-8) Thomasson-Grant.

Wood, Angela, jt. auth. see Keene, Michael.

Wood, Audrey. Balloonia. Wood, Audrey, illus. LC 90-46602. 32p. (ps-2). 1981. 7.95 (0-85953-122-8, Pub. by Child's Play England); pap. 3.95 (0-85953-320-4, Pub. by Child's Play England) Childs Play.

—Elbert's Bad Word. Wood, Audrey & Wood, Don, illus. LC 86-7557. 32p. (ps-3). 1988. 13.95 (0-15-225320-3, HB Juv Bks) HarBrace.

—Heckedy Peg. Wood, Don, illus. LC 86-33639. 32p. (ps-3). 1987. 14.95 (0-15-233678-8, HB Juv Bks) HarBrace.

—Heckedy Peg. (ps-3). 1992. pap. write for info. (0-15-233679-6, HB Juv Bks) HarBrace.

—The Horrible Holidays. Hoffman, Rosekrans, illus. LC 87-30617. 48p. (ps-3). 1988. 9.95 (0-8037-0544-1); PLB 9.89 (0-8037-0546-8) Dial Bks Young.

—Horrible Holidays. LC 87-30617. 48p. (ps-3). 1990. pap. 3.95 (0-8037-0833-5) Dial Bks Young.

—Into the Napping House. Wood, Don, illus. Shaylen, Carl, contrib. by. (Illus.). (ps-2). 1990. Incl. cassette. 19.95 (0-15-256709-7) HarBrace.

—King Bidgood's in the Bathtub. Wood, Don, illus. LC 85-5472. 32p. (ps-3). 1985. 14.95 (0-15-242730-9, HB Juv Bks) HarBrace.

—King Bidgood's in the Bathtub. LC 85-5472. (ps-3). 1993. pap. 19.95 (0-15-242732-5) HarBrace.

—Little Penguin's Tale. 32p. (ps-1). 1989. 13.95 (0-15-246475-1) HarBrace.

—Little Penguin's Tale. (gr. k up). 1993. Repr. 5.95 (0-15-247476-5, Voyager Bks) HarBrace.

—Magic Shoelaces. Wood, Audrey, illus. LC 90-49097. 32p. (ps-2). 1989. 7.95 (0-85953-109-0); pap. 3.95 (0-85953-321-2) Childs Play.

—Moonflute. Wood, Don, illus. LC 86-4666. 25p. (ps-3). 1986. 14.95 (0-15-255337-1) HarBrace.

—The Napping House. Wood, Don, illus. LC 83-13035. 32p. (ps-3). 1984. 13.95 (0-15-256708-9, HB Juv Bks) HarBrace.

—The Napping House. Wood, Don, illus. 32p. (ps-3). 1991. pap. 19.95 (0-15-256711-9) HarBrace.

—Oh My Baby Bear! 32p. (ps-1). 1990. 12.95 (0-15-257698-3) HarBrace.

—Orlando's Littlewhile Friends. Wood, Audrey, illus. LC 90-45723. (ps-2). 1989. 11.95 (0-85953-111-2); pap. 5.95 (0-85953-106-6) Childs Play.

—Presto Change-o. LC 90-46912. 1989. 7.95 (0-85953-181-3); pap. 3.95 (0-85953-322-0) Childs Play.

—Princess & the Dragon. Wood, Audrey, illus. LC 90-49098. 32p. (ps-2). 1989. 7.95 (0-85953-150-3); pap. 3.95 (0-85953-013-2) Childs Play.

—Princess & the Dragon. (ps-3). 1989. pap. 2.50 (0-85953-305-0) Childs Play.

—The Rainbow Bridge. Florczak, Robert, illus. LC 92-17661. 1993. write for info. (0-15-265475-5) HarBrace.

—Rude Giants. LC 91-13015. (Illus.). 32p. (ps-3). 1993. 13.95 (0-15-269412-9, HB Juv Bks) HarBrace.

—Scaredy Cats. Wood, Audrey, illus. LC 90-46913. 32p. (ps-2). 1989. 7.95 (0-85953-110-4); pap. 3.95 (0-85953-323-9) Childs Play.

—Three Sisters. Hoffman, Rosekrans, illus. LC 85-29392. 48p. (ps-3). 1986. 9.95 (0-8037-0279-5); PLB 9.89 (0-8037-0280-9) Dial Bks Young.

—Three Sisters. Hoffman, Rosekrans, illus. LC 85-29392. 48p. (ps-3). 1989. 4.95 (0-8037-0597-2) Dial Bks Young.

—Tooth Fairy. LC 90-46911. 1989. 7.95 (0-85953-237-2); pap. 3.95 (0-85953-238-0) Childs Play.

—Tugford Wanted to Be Bad. Wood, Don, illus. LC 83-318. 32p. (ps-3). 1983. pap. 4.95 (0-15-291084-0, Voyager Bks) HarBrace.

—Twenty-Four Robbers. Wood, Audrey, illus. LC 90-46182. 32p. (ps-2). 1989. 7.95 (0-85953-100-7); pap. 3.95 (0-85953-324-7) Childs Play.

—Weird Parents. Fogelman, Phyllis J., ed. Wood, Audrey, illus. LC 88-25742. 32p. (ps-3). 1990. 12.99 (0-8037-0648-0); PLB 11.89 (0-8037-0649-9) Dial Bks Young.

Wood, Audrey & Wood, Audrey. Tugford Wanted to Be Bad. LC 83-318. (Illus.). 32p. (ps-3). 1983. 9.95 (0-15-291083-2, HB Juv Bks) HarBrace.

Wood, Audrey, retold by. When the Root Children Wake Up. Weatherby, Mark A., illus. LC 93-32737. 1995. Repr. of 1906 ed. 14.95 (0-590-42517-X) Scholastic Inc.

Wood, Barbara S. Messages Without Words. rev. ed. LC 87-23315. (Illus.). 48p. (gr. 2-6). 1987. PLB 18.64 (0-8172-3258-3) Raintree Steck-V.

Wood, Bill. Marty the Marathon Bear. Kaluza, Mary K. & Carreiro, Bob, illus. Kauffman, Helen, photos by. 136p. (Orig.). (gr. 3-7). 1988. pap. text ed. 6.95 (0-317-93376-0) Rallysport Video Prodns.

Wood, D. No Clothes. (Illus.). 40p. (ps-8). 1990. pap. 5.95 (1-55037-089-8, Pub. by Annick CN) Firefly Bks Ltd.

Wood, D., jt. auth. see Wood, A.

Wood, Don. Little Mouse, the Red Ripe Strawberry & the Big Hungry Bear. LC 90-46414. (ps-3). 1990. 11.95 (0-685-56131-3); pap. 5.95 (0-85953-012-4) Childs Play.

—Piggies. (ps-1). 1991. ltd. ed. 100.00 (*0-15-256344-X*) HarBrace.
—Piggies. 28p. (ps-1). 1991. 13.95 (*0-15-256341-5*) HarBrace.
—Quick As a Cricket. (ps-3). 1990. 11.95 (*0-85953-151-1*); pap. 5.95 (*0-85953-306-9*) Childs Play.
Wood, Dora. Five Hundred More Wild & Wacky Knock-Knock Jokes for Kids. (gr. 4-7). 1993. pap. 3.99 (*0-345-38161-0*) Ballantine.
Wood, Douglas. Old Turtle. Cheng-Khee Chee, illus. LC 91-73527. 48p. (ps-2). 1991. 17.95 (*0-938586-48-3*) Pfeifer-Hamilton.
Wood, Elizabeth. Fifty Nifty Magic Tricks. Yamamoto, Neal, illus. 64p. (ps-3). 1992. pap. 2.95 (*0-929923-93-6*) Lowell Hse.
Wood, Elizabeth L. Many Horses. Pollock, Dean, illus. (gr. 5-11). 1953. 7.95 (*0-8323-0175-2*) Binford Mort.
Wood, Ethel. Multiple Choice Questions in Preparation for the AP United States Government & Politics Examination. 75p. (gr. 11-12). 1991. wkbk. 15.95 (*1-878621-04-1*); tchr's. manual, 38p. avail. (*1-878621-05-X*) D & S Mktg Syst.
Wood, Heather. One Hundred One Marvelous Money-Making Ideas for Kids. 128p. (Orig.). 1993. pap. 3.50 (*0-8125-2060-2*) Tor Bks.
Wood, J. Moo Moo, Brown Cow. Bonner, R., illus. 1992. 12.95 (*0-15-200533-1*, HB Juv Bks) HarBrace.
Wood, Jakki. Animal Parade. Wood, Jakki, illus. LC 92-22826. 32p. (ps-k). 1993. SBE 14.95 (*0-02-793394-6*, Bradbury Pr) Macmillan Child Grp.
—Dads Are Such Fun. Bonner, Rog, illus. LC 91-21517. 32p. (ps). 1992. pap. 12.00 jacketed (*0-671-75342-8*, S&S BFYR) S&S Trade.
—Fiddle-I-Fee. Wood, Jakki, illus. LC 93-72322. 32p. (ps-1). 1994. SBE 14.95 (*0-02-793396-2*, Bradbury Pr) Macmillan Child Grp.
—One Bear with Bees in His Hair. Wood, Jakki, illus. LC 90-43211. 32p. (ps-1). 1991. 13.95 (*0-525-44695-8*, DCB) Dutton Child Bks.
—One Tortoise, Ten Wallabies. LC 93-23534. (gr. 2 up). 1994. write for info. (Bradbury Pr) Macmillan Child Grp.
Wood, Jenny. The Animal Kingdom. Bale, Andrew, illus. LC 91-14567. 32p. (ps-3). 1992. 14.95 (*0-02-793395-4*, Macmillan Child Bk) Macmillan Child Grp.
—Caves. (gr. 4 up). 1990. pap. 4.95 (*0-14-034464-0*, Puffin) Puffin Bks.
—Caves: An Underground Wonderland. LC 90-55463. (Illus.). 32p. (gr. 3-4). 1991. PLB 17.27 (*0-8368-0469-4*) Gareth Stevens Inc.
—Coral Reefs. (Illus.). 32p. (gr. 3-4). 1991. PLB 17.27 (*0-8368-0630-1*) Gareth Stevens Inc.
—Deserts. LC 91-15814. (Illus.). 32p. (gr. 3-4). 1991. PLB 17.27 (*0-8368-0631-X*) Gareth Stevens Inc.
—First Songs & Action Rhymes. McEwan, Chris, illus. LC 90-44773. 64p. (ps-k). 1991. POB 6.95 (*0-689-71472-6*, Aladdin) Macmillan Child Grp.
—Icebergs. (gr. 4 up). 1990. pap. 4.95 (*0-14-034467-5*, Puffin) Puffin Bks.
—Icebergs: Titans of the Oceans. LC 90-55462. (Illus.). 32p. (gr. 3-4). 1991. PLB 17.27 (*0-8368-0470-8*) Gareth Stevens Inc.
—Jungle Animals. (Illus.). 32p. (gr. k-4). 1990. PLB 11.40 (*0-531-19100-1*) Watts.
—My First Book of Animals. (ps). 1992. 9.95 (*0-316-95199-4*) Little.
—Rain Forests: Lush Tropical Paradise. (Illus.). 32p. (gr. 3-4). 1991. PLB 17.27 (*0-8368-0632-8*) Gareth Stevens Inc.
—Storm. LC 93-43947. (Illus.). 32p. (gr. 4-8). 1993. 14.95 (*1-56847-002-9*) Thomson Lrning.
—Storms. (gr. 4 up). 1990. pap. 4.95 (*0-14-034466-7*, Puffin) Puffin Bks.
—Storms: Nature's Fury. LC 90-55461. (Illus.). 32p. (gr. 3-4). 1991. PLB 17.27 (*0-8368-0471-6*) Gareth Stevens Inc.
—Under the Sea. Livingstone, Malcolm, illus. LC 91-7484. 32p. (gr. k-3). 1991. pap. 5.95 (*0-689-71488-2*, Aladdin) Macmillan Child Grp.
—Volcanoes. (gr. 4 up). 1990. pap. 4.95 (*0-14-034465-9*, Puffin) Puffin Bks.
—Volcanoes: Fire from Below. LC 90-55460. (Illus.). 32p. (gr. 3-4). 1991. PLB 17.27 (*0-8368-0472-4*) Gareth Stevens Inc.
—Waterfalls: Nature's Thundering Splendor. (Illus.). 32p. (gr. 3-4). 1991. PLB 17.27 (*0-8368-0633-6*) Gareth Stevens Inc.
—Wonderworks of Nature, 8 vols. (Illus.). 32p. (gr. 3-4). 1991. Set. PLB 138.16 (*0-8368-0757-X*) Gareth Stevens Inc.
Wood, Jenny & Munro, David. The Children's Atlas of People & Places. LC 92-28857. (Illus.). 96p. (gr. 2-6). 1993. PLB 18.90 (*1-56294-257-3*); pap. 10.95 (*1-56294-712-5*) Millbrook Pr.
Wood, Jessie, tr. see Pushkin, Aleksandr.
Wood, JoAnne, jt. auth. see Ottum, Bob.
Wood, John. Charlie & the Stinking Ragbags. (Illus., Orig.). (gr. 4-6). 1991. pap. 8.95 (*0-86327-298-3*, Pub. by Wolfhound Pr EIRE) Dufour.
—Trouble at Mrs. Portwine's. Nesbitt, Jan, illus. 96p. (gr. 5-9). 1990. 14.95x (*0-86327-147-2*, Pub. by Wolfhound Pr EIRE); pap. 8.95 (*0-86327-148-0*, Pub. by Wolfhound Pr EIRE) Dufour.
Wood, John, tr. see Moliere.

Wood, John N. Nature Hide & Seek: Jungles. Schulman, Janet, ed. Dean, Kevin, illus. LC 86-21450. 24p. (ps-4). 1987. 11.95 (*0-394-87802-7*) Knopf Bks Yng Read.
—Nature Hide & Seek: Oceans. Harrison, Mark, illus. LC 85-73. 24p. (gr. 1-4). 1985. 13.00 (*0-394-87583-4*) Knopf Bks Yng Read.
—Nature Hide & Seek: Rivers & Lake. Wood, John N. & Dean, Kevin, illus. LC 93-22501. (gr. 1-4). 1993. 13.00 (*0-679-83690-X*) Knopf Bks Yng Read.
—Woods & Forests. Silver, Maggie, illus. LC 93-22506. 22p. (gr. k-4). 1993. 13.00 (*0-679-83691-8*) Knopf Bks Yng Read.
Wood, Judy, et al. Sunakorn Drug Prevention Teaching Curriculum. 184p. (gr. k-5). 1989. 22.95 (*0-938021-42-7*) Turner Pub KY.
Wood, June R. The Man Who Loved Clowns. 192p. (gr. 5-9). 1992. 14.95 (*0-399-21888-2*, Putnam) Putnam Pub Group.
Wood, Karen, ed. Exploring Literature in the Classroom: Content & Methods. Strickland, Dorothy, frwd. by. 296p. (gr. k-8). 1991. pap. 14.95 (*0-926842-11-0*) CG Pubs Inc.
Wood, Kay. Sesame Street Little Library. Incl. Big Bird's Shape Book. LC 75-3943; Ernie & Bert's Counting Book. LC 75-3944; Grover's Favorite Color. LC 75-3945; The Monster's Alphabet. LC 75-3946. (ps-1). 1977. Set. 8.00 (*0-394-83262-0*) Random Bks Yng Read.
Wood, Keturah. A Medley of Youthful Verses. LC 93-90018. 68p. 1993. 11.00x (*0-8233-0484-1*) Golden Quill.
Wood, Leigh H. The Navajo Indians. (Illus.). 80p. (gr. 2-5). 1991. lib. bdg. 12.95 (*0-7910-1651-X*) Chelsea Hse.
—Navajos. (gr. 4-7). 1993. pap. 6.95 (*0-7910-2026-6*) Chelsea Hse.
Wood, Leslie. Bump, Bump, Bump. (Illus.). 16p. 1987. pap. 2.95 (*0-19-272162-3*) OUP.
—Dig Dig. (Illus.). 16p. (ps up) 1988. pap. 2.95 (*0-19-272185-2*) OUP.
—A Dog Called Mischief. (Illus.). 16p. 1987. pap. 2.95 (*0-19-272155-0*) OUP.
—The Frog & the Fly. (Illus.). 16p. 1987. pap. 2.95 (*0-19-272154-2*) OUP.
—My House. (Illus.). 16p. (ps up) 1988. pap. 2.95 (*0-19-272186-0*) OUP.
—Sam's Big Day. 16p. (ps-k). 1987. 2.95 (*0-19-272165-8*) OUP.
—Tom & His Tractor. (Illus.). 16p. 1987. pap. 2.95 (*0-19-272163-1*) OUP.
Wood, Marcia. Always, Julia. LC 91-40460. 128p. (gr. 5-9). 1993. SBE 13.95 (*0-689-31728-X*, Atheneum Child Bk) Macmillan Child Grp.
—The Search for Jim McGwynn. LC 88-36583. 160p. (gr. 5-9). 1989. SBE 13.95 (*0-689-31479-5*, Atheneum Child Bk) Macmillan Child Grp.
Wood, Marian. Ancient America. 1990. 17.95 (*0-8160-2210-0*) Facts on File.
Wood, Marina. Crayon Creations. Wood, Marina, illus. 40p. (Orig.). (gr. 4-8). 1984. pap. 6.00 (*0-932946-12-7*) Burdett CA.
Wood, Marion. Growing up in Aztec Times. Hook, Richard, illus. LC 91-39444. 32p. (gr. 3-5). 1993. PLB 11.89 (*0-8167-2723-6*); pap. text ed. 3.95 (*0-8167-2724-4*) Troll Assocs. Postponed.
—Spirits, Heroes & Hunters from North American Indian Mythology. Sibbick, John, illus. LC 91-38954. 132p. (gr. 6 up). 1992. 22.50 (*0-87226-903-5*) P Bedrick Bks.
Wood, Nancy. Many Winters. Howell, Frank, illus. LC 74-3554. 80p. (gr. 6 up). 1974. pap. 14.95 (*0-385-02226-3*) Doubleday.
—Many Winters. Howell, Frank, illus. LC 74-3554. 80p. (gr. 7 up). 1974. pap. 10.00 (*0-385-30865-5*) Doubleday.
—Spirit Walker: Poems. Howell, Frank, illus. LC 92-29376. 1993. pap. 19.95 (*0-385-30927-9*) Doubleday.
Wood, Nicholas. Touch...What Do You Feel? Willey, Lynne, illus. LC 90-10925. 32p. (gr. k-3). 1991. PLB 11.59 (*0-8167-2126-2*); pap. text ed. 3.95 (*0-8167-2127-0*) Troll Assocs.
Wood, Nicholas & Rye, Jennifer. Listen...What Do You Hear? Douglas, Julie, illus. LC 90-40136. 32p. (gr. k-3). 1991. lib. bdg. 11.59 (*0-8167-2120-3*); pap. text ed. 3.95 (*0-8167-2121-1*) Troll Assocs.
Wood, Paul, ed. see Katherine, Sharon.
Wood, Phyllis A. The Revolving Door Stops Here. Garrick, Jacqueline, illus. LC 89-23891. 192p. (gr. 6 up). 1990. 14.95 (*0-525-65022-9*, Cobblehill Bks) Dutton Child Bks.
—Song of the Shaggy Canary. LC 73-14785. 156p. (gr. 6 up). 1974. 9.00 (*0-664-32543-2*, Westminster) Westminster John Knox.
Wood, Randy. God, I Need to Talk! Nelson, Becky, ed. 26p. (gr. 7-12). 1993. pap. text ed. 4.95 (*1-56309-066-X*) Womans Mission Union.
Wood, Richard. The Builder Through History. Smith, Tony, illus. LC 93-24398. 48p. (gr. 5-8). 1994. 15.95 (*1-56847-102-5*) Thomson Lrning.
Wood, Robert M. Rand McNally Picture Atlas of Prehistoric Life. Hayward, Tim, illus. LC 92-5761. 1992. write for info. (*0-528-83525-4*) Rand McNally.
Wood, Robert W. Forty-Nine Easy Experiments with Acoustics. (Illus.). 224p. 1990. 16.95 (*0-8306-7392-X*, 3392); pap. 9.95 (*0-8306-3392-8*) TAB Bks.
—How to Tell the Birds from the Flowers. (Illus.). 64p. (gr. 4 up). 1959. pap. 1.95 (*0-486-20523-1*) Dover.

—Physics for Kids: Forty-Nine Easy Experiments with Electricity & Magnetism. (Illus.). 192p. 1990. 16.95 (*0-685-32939-9*, 3412); pap. 9.95 (*0-8306-3412-6*) TAB Bks.
—Physics For Kids: 49 Easy Experiments with Optics. (Illus.). 176p. 1990. 16.95 (*0-8306-8402-6*, 3402); pap. 9.95 (*0-8306-3402-9*) TAB Bks.
—Science for Kids: Thirty-nine Easy Engineering Experiments. (gr. 3-8). 1991. 16.95 (*0-8306-1946-1*); pap. 9.95 (*0-8306-1943-7*) TAB Bks.
—Thirty-Nine Easy Animal Biology Experiments. (Illus.). 160p. (gr. 3-8). 1991. 9.70 (*0-8306-6594-3*, 3594); pap. 9.95 (*0-8306-3594-7*) TAB Bks.
—Thirty-Nine Easy Astronomy Experiments. (Illus.). 160p. 1991. 16.95 (*0-8306-7597-3*, 3597); pap. 9.95 (*0-8306-3597-1*) TAB Bks.
—Thirty-Nine Easy Chemistry Experiments. (Illus.). 160p. 1991. 16.95 (*0-8306-7596-5*, 3596); pap. 9.95 (*0-8306-3596-3*) TAB Bks.
—Thirty-Nine Easy Geography Activities. 1991. 16.95 (*0-8306-2493-7*); pap. 9.95 (*0-8306-2492-9*) TAB Bks.
—Thirty-Nine Easy Geology Experiments. (Illus.). 160p. (gr. 3-8). 1991. 16.95 (*0-8306-6598-6*, 3598); pap. 9.95 (*0-8306-3598-X*) TAB Bks.
—Thirty-Nine Easy Meteorology Experiments. (Illus.). 160p. (gr. 3-8). 1991. 16.95 (*0-8306-6595-1*, 3595); pap. 9.95 (*0-8306-3595-5*) TAB Bks.
—Thirty-Nine Easy Plant Biology Experiments. 160p. 1991. 16.95 (*0-8306-1941-0*, 5003); pap. 9.95 (*0-8306-1935-6*) TAB Bks.
Wood, Sharon. The Portland Bridge Book. Alley, Joy D., illus. (Orig.). (ps-7). 1989. pap. 12.95 (*0-87595-211-9*) Oregon Hist.
Wood, Sydney. The British Welfare State 1900-1950. LC 81-3840. (Illus.). 48p. (gr. 7 up). 1982. pap. 5.95 (*0-521-22843-3*) Cambridge U Pr.
—Trains & Railroads. LC 91-58201. (Illus.). 64p. (gr. 3 up). 1992. 11.95 (*1-56458-001-6*); PLB 12.99 (*1-56458-002-4*) Dorling Kindersley.
Wood, Ted & Wanbli Numpa Afraid of Hawk. A Boy Becomes a Man at Wounded Knee. 42p. 1992. 15.95 (*0-8027-8174-8*); lib. bdg. 16.85 (*0-8027-8175-6*) Walker & Co.
Wood, Tim. Air Travel. LC 92-43977. (Illus.). 32p. (gr. 5-9). 1993. 14.95 (*1-56847-036-3*) Thomson Lrning.
—The Aztecs. (Illus.). 48p. (gr. 3-7). 1992. 15.00 (*0-670-84492-6*) Viking Child Bks.
—Gymnastics. Fairclough, Chris, photos by. LC 89-50205. (Illus.). 32p. (gr. k-3). 1989. PLB 11.90 (*0-531-10826-0*) Watts.
—Ice Skating. Fairclough, Chris, photos by. (Illus.). 32p. (gr. k-4). 1990. PLB 11.40 (*0-531-14051-2*) Watts.
—Motor Racing. Fairclough, Chris, photos by. LC 89-50201. (Illus.). 32p. (gr. k-3). 1989. PLB 11.40 (*0-531-10828-7*) Watts.
—Mountain Biking. Fairclough, Chris, photos by. (Illus.). 32p. (gr. k-4). 1989. PLB 11.40 (*0-531-10829-5*) Watts.
—Natural Disasters. LC 93-8525. 48p. (gr. 4-6). 1993. 15.95 (*1-56847-085-1*) Thomson Lrning.
—Our Planet Earth. Graham, Alastair, illus. LC 91-26681. 32p. (ps-2). 1992. pap. 5.95 (*0-689-71589-7*, Aladdin) Macmillan Child Grp.
—Out in Space. Wells, Tony, illus. LC 91-7483. 32p. (gr. k-3). 1991. pap. 5.95 (*0-689-71491-2*, Aladdin) Macmillan Child Grp.
—Racing Drivers. Stefoff, Rebecca, ed. LC 91-39098. (Illus.). 32p. (gr. 5-9). 1992. PLB 17.26 (*1-56074-042-6*) Garrett Ed Corp.
—The Renaissance. (Illus.). 48p. (gr. 3-7). 1993. 14.99 (*0-670-85149-3*) Viking Child Bks.
—Road Travel. LC 92-43978. (Illus.). 32p. (gr. 5-9). 1993. 14.95 (*1-56847-037-1*) Thomson Lrning.
Wood, Vivian B. You're a Very Special Person. Wood, David & Wood, Vivian B., illus. 38p. (Orig.). (gr. 1). 1988. pap. 5.95 (*0-9621567-0-1*) V B Wood.
Woodard, James & Purdy, Linda. One to Ten Count Again. (Illus.). (ps-k). 1972. PLB 6.89x (*0-914844-07-5*) J Alden.
Woodard, Judy & Tucker, Martha. The Legend of the SunaKorn. LC 89-50138. 40p. 1989. 12.95 (*0-938021-41-9*) Turner Pub Ky.
Woodard, Lynette & Cook, Kevin. Shoot for the Stars Basketball Handbook, Vol. 1. Bunch, Lewis & Washington, Marian, eds. Hankins, Rod & Ray, Dan, illus. 60p. (gr. 9-12). 1989. text ed. write for info. Worldwide Sports.
Woodard, Virginia, ed. see Weir, Christy.
Woodbridge, F. J. The Son of Apollo: Themes of Plato. 272p. (gr. 7 up). 1972. Repr. of 1929 ed. 24.00 (*0-8196-0278-7*) Biblo.
Woodburn, John H. Chemistry. (Illus.). 160p. (gr. 6 up). 1991. 13.95 (*0-8442-6137-8*, Passport Bks); pap. 10.95 (*0-8442-6138-6*, Passport Bks) NTC Pub Grp.
Woodburn, Marion L., tr. see Beskow, Elsa.
Woodcock, John. Trouble in Space. 64p. (Orig.). (gr. 6 up). 1984. pap. 2.25 (*0-553-15501-6*) Bantam.
Woodford, Protase E., et al. Espanol: A Sentirlo. 4th ed. Hearue, Jack, illus. (gr. 10 up). 1977. text ed. 31.40 (*0-07-071656-0*, W) McGraw.
Woodford, Susan. The Parthenon. (Illus.). 48p. (gr. 7 up). 1981. pap. 7.50 (*0-521-22629-5*) Cambridge U Pr.
Woodhull, Angela V. Easy Words: An Easy Way to Learn New Words. Eddy, Hal, et al, illus. 150p. (gr. 8 up). 1988. pap. 5.95 (*0-685-44299-3*) Woodhull Pubns.
Woodley, Richard. The Bad News Bears Go to Japan. 160p. (gr. 5 up). 1978. pap. 1.50 (*0-440-90427-7*) Dell.

Woodman, Allen & Kirby, David. The Bear Who Came To Stay. Stevenson, Harvey, illus. LC 92-7799. 32p. (ps-3). 1994. RSBE 14.95 (0-02-793397-0, Bradbury Pr) Macmillan Child Grp.
—The Cows Are Going to Paris. Demarest, Chris L., illus. LC 90-85733. 32p. (ps-3). 1991. 13.95 (1-878093-11-8) Boyds Mills Pr.
Woodman, Nancy, illus. Consonants. 6p. (gr. k-1). 1992. bds. 3.95 (1-56293-184-9) McClanahan Bk.
Woodrell, Daniel. Give Us a Kiss. (gr. 5 up). 1994. 22.95 (0-8050-2298-8) H Holt & Co.
Woodring, Carl R., ed. Prose of the Romantic Period. LC 61-16304. (gr. 9 up). 1961. pap. 9.16 (0-395-05154-1, RivEd) HM.
Woodrow, James I. The Christian College Advantage: A Student-Parent Guide to Colleges Affiliated with the Churches of Christ. 102p. (gr. 10-12). 1992. 11.95 (0-9631429-0-9) Inst Advan PHE.
Woodruff, Elvira. Awfully Short for the Fourth Grade. Hillenbrand, Will, illus. LC 89-2082. 112p. (gr. 3-6). 1989. 13.95 (0-8234-0785-3) Holiday.
—Awfully Short for the Fourth Grade. 1990. pap. 2.95 (0-440-40366-9, Pub. by Yearling Classics) Dell.
—Back in Action. Hillenbrand, Will, illus. LC 91-2093. 160p. (gr. 3-7). 1991. 13.95 (0-8234-0897-3) Holiday.
—Back in Action. (gr. 4-7). 1993. 3.50 (0-440-40808-3) Dell.
—Dear Levi: Letters from the Overland Trail. Peck, Beth, illus. LC 93-5315. 1994. 13.00 (0-679-84641-7); PLB 13.99 (0-679-94641-1) Knopf.
—Dear Napoleon, I Know You're Dead, But. Woodruff, Noah, contrib. by. LC 92-1128. 128p. (gr. 3-7). 1992. 13.95 (0-8234-0962-7) Holiday.
—The Disappearing Bike Shop. LC 91-29863. 176p. (gr. 3-7). 1992. 13.95 (0-8234-0933-3) Holiday.
—George Washington's Socks. (gr. 4-7). 1993. pap. 2.95 (0-590-44036-5) Scholastic Inc.
—Ghosts Don't Get Goosebumps. (gr. 4-7). 1993. 13.95 (0-8234-1035-8) Holiday.
—The Magnificent Mummy Maker. LC 93-7870. 160p. (gr. 4-7). 1994. 13.95 (0-590-45742-X) Scholastic Inc.
—The Secret Funeral of Slim Jim the Snake. LC 92-54419. 144p. (gr. 3-7). 1993. 13.95 (0-8234-1014-5) Holiday.
—Show-&-Tell. Brunkus, Denise, illus. LC 90-23588. 32p. (ps-3). 1991. reinforced 14.95 (0-8234-0883-3) Holiday.
—The Summer I Shrank My Grandmother. Coville, Katherine, illus. LC 90-55099. 160p. (gr. 3-7). 1990. 13.95 (0-8234-0832-9) Holiday.
—The Summer I Shrank My Grandmother. (gr. 4-7). 1992. 3.25 (0-440-40640-4, YB) Dell.
—Tubtime. Stevenson, Sucie, illus. LC 89-36609. 32p. (ps-3). 1990. reinforced bdg. 14.95 (0-8234-0777-2) Holiday.
—The Wing Shop. Gammell, Stephen, illus. LC 90-55094. 32p. (ps-3). 1991. reinforced 14.95 (0-8234-0825-6) Holiday.
Woodruff, Marian. Kiss Me, Creep. 192p. (gr. 7-12). 1984. pap. 2.25 (0-553-24150-8) Bantam.
Woods, et al. Lasers: Activities for the Classroom. (Illus.). 85p. (Orig.). 1990. pap. text ed. 13.81 (0-87192-216-9) Delmar.
Woods, Andrew. Young Abraham Lincoln, Log-Cabin President. Schories, Pat, illus. LC 91-26570. 32p. (gr. k-2). 1992. text ed. 11.59 (0-8167-2532-2); pap. text ed. 2.95 (0-8167-2533-0) Troll Assocs.
—Young George Washington: America's First President. Himmelman, John, illus. LC 91-26405. 32p. (gr. k-2). 1992. PLB 11.59 (0-8167-2540-3); pap. text ed. 2.95 (0-8167-2541-1) Troll Assocs.
—Young Orville & Wilbur Wright: First to Fly. Stuart, Dennis, illus. LC 91-26479. 32p. (gr. k-2). 1992. text ed. 11.59 (0-8167-2542-X); pap. text ed. 2.95 (0-8167-2543-8) Troll Assocs.
Woods, Becky. A Rocky Mountain Rabbit. LC 90-70093. (Illus.). 86p. (gr. 4-8). 1991. 12.95 (0-932433-65-0) Windswept Hse.
Woods, Bruce, jt. auth. see Schoonmaker, David.
Woods, Daniel W. Poverty in the U. S. Problems & Policies. LC 87-25246. 1992. PLB 14.85 (0-8027-6764-8); pap. 5.95 (0-8027-6765-6) Walker & Co.
Woods, Elsa & Lancaster, Beverly. Reading for Survival in Today's Society, Bk. 1. 2nd ed. (Illus.). 224p. (gr. 7-9). 1994. pap. 14.95 (0-673-36077-6) GdYrBks.
—Reading for Survival in Today's Society, Bk. 2. 2nd ed. (Illus.). 224p. (gr. 8 up). 1994. pap. 14.95 (0-673-36078-4) GdYrBks.
Woods, Geraldine. Jim Henson: From Puppets to Muppets. LC 86-11624. (Illus.). 64p. (gr. 3 up). 1987. RSBE 13.95 (0-87518-348-4, Dillon) Macmillan Child Grp.
—Oprah Winfrey. LC 91-7818. (Illus.). 80p. (gr. 3 up). 1991. RSBE 13.95 (0-87518-463-4, Dillon) Macmillan Child Grp.
—Science in Ancient Egypt. Rasof, Henry, ed. LC 87-23746. (Illus.). 96p. (gr. 5-8). 1988. PLB 10.90 (0-531-10486-9) Watts.
—Spain: A Shining New Democracy. (Illus.). (gr. 4 up). 1987. RSBE 14.95 (0-87518-363-8, Dillon) Macmillan Child Grp.
Woods, Geraldine, jt. auth. see Woods, Harold.
Woods, Harold & Woods, Geraldine. Bill Cosby: Making America Laugh & Learn. LC 82-23497. (Illus.). 48p. (gr. 3 up). 1989. RSBE 13.95 (0-87518-240-2, Dillon) Macmillan Child Grp.

—The Book of the Unknown. Mathieu, Joe, illus. LC 82-3683. 72p. (gr. 4-7). 1982. lib. bdg. 5.99 (0-394-95233-2) Random Bks Yng Read.
—Sandra Day O'Connor: Equal Justice: A Biography of Sandra Day O'Connor. LC 84-23042. (Illus.). 128p. (gr. 6 up). 1987. RSBE 13.95 (0-87518-292-5, Dillon) Macmillan Child Grp.
—Tarzan of the Apes. Gaydos, Tim, illus. LC 81-19873. 96p. (gr. 2-7). 1982. lib. bdg. 5.99 (0-394-95089-5); pap. 2.95 (0-394-85089-0, Random Juv) Random Bks Yng Read.
Woods, Judy F., jt. auth. see Greene, Jane F.
Woods, Julie N., ed. see Toomey, Marilyn M.
Woods, Karl M. The Sports Success Book: The Athlete's Guide to Sports Achievement. LC 84-19832. (Illus.). 256p. (Orig.). 1985. 17.95 (0-933857-00-4); pap. 12.95 (0-933857-01-2) Copperfield Pr.
Woods, Katherine, tr. see De Saint-Exupery, Antoine.
Woods, Katherine, tr. see Saint-Exupery, Antoine de.
Woods, P. Soccer Skills. (Illus.). 48p. (gr. 6-10). 1987. pap. 5.95 (0-7460-0167-3) EDC.
Woods, P., jt. ed. see Everett, F.
Woods, Paul. Advice to Young Christians: Exploring Paul's Letters. (Illus.). 48p. (gr. 6-8). 1992. pap. 7.99 (1-55945-146-7) Group Pub.
—Applying the Bible to Life. (Illus.). 48p. (gr. 6-8). 1991. pap. 7.99 (1-55945-116-5) Group Pub.
—Bible Heroes: Joseph, Esther, Mary & Peter. (Illus.). 48p. (gr. 6-8). 1992. pap. 7.99 (1-55945-137-8) Group Pub.
—Miracles! (Illus.). 48p. (gr. 6-8). 1991. pap. 7.99 (1-55945-117-3) Group Pub.
—The Ten Commandments. (Illus.). 48p. (gr. 6-8). 1992. pap. 7.99 (1-55945-127-0) Group Pub.
—What's a Christian? 48p. (Orig.). (gr. 6-8). 1990. pap. 7.99 (1-55945-105-X) Group Pub.
Woods, Samuel G., jt. auth. see Summer, Lila.
Woods, Samuel, Jr., jt. auth. see Diskavich, Laura.
Woods, Shirley E. Pip: The Adventures of a Deer Mouse. Wood, Bruce J., illus. 80p. (Orig.). (gr. k-3). 1992. pap. 6.95 (0-921054-98-X, Pub. by Nimbus Publishing Ltd CN) Chelsea Green Pub.
Woods, Tom & Schutz, Mary E. The Kelley Farm Activity Book. 32p. (ps up). 1985. pap. 3.50 (0-87351-183-2) Minn Hist.
Woodside, jt. auth. see Tison.
Woodside, John, jt. auth. see Boden, Arthur.
Woodson, Carter G. African Heroes & Heroines. (Illus.). 1990. 12.95 (0-87498-077-1); pap. 9.95 (0-87498-076-3) Assoc Pubs DC.
—The History of the Negro Church. (Illus.). 1990. 17.95 (0-87498-000-3) Assoc Pubs DC.
—Mis-Education of the Negro. 1990. pap. 12.95 (0-87498-001-1) Assoc Pubs DC.
—The Negro in Our History. rev. ed. Wesley, Charles H., contrib. by. 1990. 19.95 (0-87498-080-1); pap. 15.95 (0-87498-081-X) Assoc Pubs DC.
Woodson, Frank. Mean Waters. Parker, Liz, ed. Taylor, Marjorie, illus. 45p. (Orig.). (gr. 6-12). 1992. pap. text ed. 2.95 (1-56254-059-9) Saddleback Pubns.
Woodson, Jacqueline. Between Madison & Palmetto. LC 92-18743. (gr. 1-6). 1993. 13.95 (0-385-30906-6) Delacorte.
—Dear One. 1993. pap. 3.50 (0-440-21420-3) Dell.
—From the Notebooks of Melanin Sun. (gr. 4 up). 1995. 13.95 (0-590-45880-9) Scholastic Inc.
—I Hadn't Meant to Tell You This. LC 93-8733. 1994. 14.95 (0-385-32031-0) Delacorte.
—Last Summer with Maizon. 1990. 13.95 (0-385-30045-X) Doubleday.
—Last Summer with Maizon. 1992. pap. 3.50 (0-440-40555-6) Dell.
—Maizon at Blue Hill. LC 91-44295. 144p. (gr. 5-9). 1992. 14.00 (0-385-30796-9) Delacorte.
—Maizon at Blue Hill. (gr. 4-7). 1994. pap. 3.50 (0-440-40899-7) Dell.
—Martin Luther King, Jr. Brook, Bonnie, ed. Cooper, Floyd, illus. 32p. (gr. k-2). 1990. 6.95 (0-671-69112-0); PLB 10.98 (0-671-69106-6) Silver Pr.
Woodson, Jacqueline, et al. Let's Celebrate Series, 6 vols. Cooper, Floyd, et al, illus. 192p. (gr. k-2). 1990. Set. 41.70 (0-671-31231-6); Set. 26.78s.p. (0-685-54162-2); Set. PLB 65.88 (0-671-31230-8); Set. PLB 49.41s.p. (0-685-46998-0) Silver Pr.
Woodson, Meg. Turn It into Glory. Holmes, Marjorie, intro. by. 224p. (gr. 9 up). 1991. 13.99 (1-55661-178-1) Bethany Hse.
Woodward, Carol. Very Special Baby. (gr. 3-7). 1960. pap. 3.99 (0-8006-0420-2, 1-420, Fortress) Augsburg Fortress.
Woodward, Dan. Mo Artists Guide: Compendium of Missouri Artists. Ramsey-Woodward, Maureen, ed. 100p. (gr. 12). 1993. 12.95x (1-882935-01-2) Rolla Fine Arts.
—Out from the Trees: Poems of the 60s. 60p. (gr. 12). 1992. 12.95 (1-882935-00-4) Rolla Fine Arts.
Woodward, Deborah, jt. ed. see Egloff, Keith.
Woodward, K. Science in the Kitchen. (Illus.). 24p. (gr. 1-4). 1992. PLB 12.96 (0-88110-284-9); pap. 4.50 (0-7460-0974-7) EDC.
Woodward, Patricia. Journal Jumpstarts: Quick Topics & Tips for Journal Writing. 30p. (Orig.). (gr. 7-12). 1991. pap. text ed. 5.95 (1-877673-15-3) Cottonwood Pr.
Woodworth, Viki. Can You Grow a Popsicle? Woodworth, Viki, illus. (gr. 1-8). 1992. PLB 18.50 (0-89565-820-8); Resale. 12.95 (0-685-60958-8) Childs World.

—Fish Jokes. Woodworth, Viki, illus. LC 92-34646. Date not set. write for info. (1-56766-065-7) Childs World. Postponed.
—Food Riddles. Woodworth, Viki, illus. LC 92-38579. Date not set. write for info. (1-56766-064-9) Childs World. Postponed.
—Have You Heard a Kangaroo Buzz? Woodworth, Viki, illus. (gr. 1-8). 1992. PLB 12.95 (0-89565-822-4); Resale. 18.50 (0-685-60956-1) Childs World.
—Have You Seen a Green Gorilla? Woodworth, Viki, illus. (gr. 1-8). 1992. PLB 12.95 (0-89565-825-9); Resale. 18.50 (0-685-60953-7) Childs World.
—Have You Seen an Elephant's Nest? Woodworth, Viki, illus. (gr. 1-8). 1992. PLB 12.95 (0-89565-824-0); Resale. 18.50 (0-685-60954-5) Childs World.
—Jokes to Tell Your Dad. LC 93-15443. 1993. write for info. (1-56766-098-3) Childs World.
—Jokes to Tell Your Friends. LC 93-7834. 1993. write for info. (1-56766-099-1) Childs World.
—Jokes to Tell Your Mom. LC 93-15444. 1993. write for info. (1-56766-097-5) Childs World.
—Jungle Safari Jokes. Woodworth, Viki, illus. LC 92-38581. Date not set. write for info. (1-56766-062-2) Childs World. Postponed.
—Knock Knock Jokes. (Illus.). 32p. 1991. 19.95 (0-89565-729-5); 13.95s.p. (0-685-55124-5) Childs World.
—Mix & Match Jokes. Woodworth, Viki, illus. LC 92-38580. Date not set. write for info. (1-56766-063-0) Childs World. Postponed.
—School Jokes. (Illus.). 32p. 1991. 19.95 (0-89565-726-0); 13.95s.p. (0-685-55125-3) Childs World.
—Space Jokes. (Illus.). 32p. 1991. 19.95 (0-89565-730-9); 13.95s.p. (0-685-55126-1) Childs World.
—Sports Jokes. (Illus.). 32p. 1991. 19.95 (0-89565-727-9); 13.95s.p. (0-685-55127-X) Childs World.
—Teacher Jokes. (Illus.). 32p. 1991. 19.95 (0-89565-725-2); 13.95s.p. (0-685-55128-8) Childs World.
—Would You Spread a Turtle on Toast? Woodworth, Viki, illus. (gr. 1-8). 1992. PLB 12.95 (0-89565-823-2); Resale. 18.50 (0-685-60957-X) Childs World.
—Would You Wear a Snake? Woodworth, Viki, illus. (gr. 1-8). 1992. PLB 12.95 (0-89565-821-6); Resale. 18.50 (0-685-60955-3) Childs World.
Woody, Marilyn. First Christmas High Chair Devotions. (ps). 1993. pap. 6.99 (0-7814-0064-3) Cook.
—God Made My World. John, Joyce, illus. 14p. (ps). 1988. bds. 6.99 (1-55513-320-7, Chariot Bks) Cook.
Woody, Marilyn J. A Child's Book of Angels: Stories from the Bible about God's Special Messengers. LC 92-12862. 1992. write for info. (1-55513-756-3, Chariot Bks) Cook.
—God Cares for Me. John, Joyce, illus. 14p. (ps). 1988. bds. 6.99 (1-55513-319-3, Chariot Bks) Cook.
—High Chair Devotions: God Gave Me a Gift. John, Joyce, illus. 14p. (ps). 1989. bds. 6.99 spiral bdg. (1-55513-729-6, 37325, Chariot Bks) Cook.
—High Chair Devotions: God Is My Friend. John, Joyce, illus. 14p. (ps). 1989. bds. 6.99 spiral bdg. (1-55513-728-8, 37283, Chariot Bks) Cook.
Woody, Sandra. Run So Fast. Sytsma, Cheryle, ed. LC 90-63615. (Illus.). 25p. (Orig.). (gr. k-5). 1991. pap. write for info. (1-879068-05-2) Ray-Ma Natsal.
Woodyard, Chris. Haunted Ohio: Ghostly Tales from the Buckeye State. LC 91-75343. 224p. (Orig.). (gr. 6 up). 1991. pap. 9.95 (0-9628472-0-8) Kestrel Pubns.
Woofenden, Louise. Rainbow Colors in the Word: An Activity Book with Puzzles & Pictures to Color. Hill, Betty, ed. Woofenden, Louise, illus. 32p. (Orig.). 1992. pap. text ed. 2.50 (0-917426-08-8) Am New Church Sunday.
Woog, Dan, ed. see Russman, Penny & Wright, Sheila.
Wool, J., et al. Useful Arithmetic, 2 vols. rev., large type ed. (gr. 7-12). 1983. Repr. of 1981 ed. Vol. 1. 26.54 (0-317-01955-4, 4-26660-00); Vol. 2. 32.76 (0-317-01956-2, 4-26670- 00) Am Printing Hse.
Wool, John D. Buying Power, Bk. III. 64p. (gr. 3 up). 1987. pap. text ed. 3.75 (0-88323-241-3, 173); tchr's. key 1.50 (0-318-33410-0, 224) Pendergrass Pub.
—Counting My Money, Bk. I. 80p. (gr. 1 up). 1987. pap. text ed. 3.75 (0-88323-229-4, 171); tchr's. key 1.50 (0-318-33409-7, 224) Pendergrass Pub.
—Earning, Spending & Saving, Bk. IV. 64p. (gr. 3 up). 1987. pap. text ed. 3.75 (0-88323-228-6, 174); tchr's. key 1.50 (0-318-33411-9, 224) Pendergrass Pub.
Wool, John D. & Bohn, Raymond J. Learning about Writing: (Cursive) 56p. (gr. 1 up). 1988. pap. text ed. 3.75 (0-88323-234-0, 150) Pendergrass Pub.
Wooldridge, Rhoda. Hanah's Mill. LC 83-26515. (Illus.). (gr. 4-6). 1984. pap. 8.00 (0-8309-0386-0) Ind Pr MO.
—Johnny Tread Water. 1983. pap. 8.00 (0-8309-0354-2) Ind Pr MO.
Wooley, Catherine. Ginnie & Geneva. (gr. 5-7). 1988. pap. 3.95 (0-317-69651-3, Puffin) Puffin Bks.
Woolf, Betty E. Call Me Aunt. LC 88-51029. 167p. 1989. pap. 6.95 (1-55523-175-6) Winston-Derek.
Woolf, Felicity. Picture This: A First Introduction to Paintings. (gr. 3 up). 1990. 14.95 (0-385-41135-9) Doubleday.
—Picture This Century: An Introduction to Twentieth-Century Art. LC 92-9128. 1993. pap. 16.00 (0-385-30852-3) Doubleday.
Woolf, Virginia. Nurse Lugton's Curtain. Van Doren, Liz, ed. Vivas, Julie, illus. 32p. (gr. 2 up). 1991. 14.95 (0-15-200545-5, Gulliver Bks) HarBrace.

—The Widow & the Parrot. Bell, Julian, illus. Bell, Quentin, afterword by. (Illus.). 26p. (ps up). 1988. 12.95 (0-15-296783-4) HarBrace.
Woolfitt, Gabrielle. Blue. (ps-3). 1992. 15.95 (0-87614-704-X) Carolrhoda Bks.
—Green. (ps-3). 1992. 15.95 (0-87614-705-8) Carolrhoda Bks.
—Red. (ps-3). 1992. 15.95 (0-87614-706-6) Carolrhoda Bks.
—Yellow. (ps-3). 1992. 15.95 (0-87614-707-4) Carolrhoda Bks.
Woolfolk, Doug, ed. see Coltharp, Barbara.
Woolgar, Jack. Missing Gold Mystery. (gr. 7 up). 1977. PLB 7.19 (0-8313-0111-2) Lantern.
—Mystery in the Desert. (gr. 6-8). 1967. 7.19 (0-8313-0107-4); PLB 7.19 (0-685-13778-3) Lantern.
Woolger, David, ed. The Magic Tree: Poems of Fantasy & Mystery. (Illus.). 160p. 1987. pap. 8.95 (0-19-276046-7) OUP.
—Who Do You Think You Are? (Illus.). 128p. (gr. 6 up). 1990. jacketed 16.95 (0-19-276074-2) OUP.
Woolley, Alan. Rocks & Minerals. (Illus.). 64p. (gr. 7 up). 1992. pap. 4.50 (0-86020-112-0) EDC.
Woolley, Diane, jt. auth. see Brady, Janeen.
Woolley, Merle E. Say No to Drugs Color & Learn Book. Frising, Nic, illus. 20p. (gr. k-6). 1988. wkbk. 1.50 (0-9623773-0-9) Mapakam Inc.
—Say No to Drugs Color & Learn Book. Guitterez, Ruben, tr. Frising, Nic, illus. (SPA). 20p. (gr. k-6). 1990. 1.50 (0-9623773-1-7) Mapakam Inc.
Woolsey, Raymond H., ed. see Holmes, Jean E.
Woolsey, Raymond H., ed. see Ricchiuti, Paul B.
Woolsey, Raymond H., ed. see Schurch, Maylan.
Woolsey, Raymond H., ed. see Thomas, Heather S.
Woolsey, Raymond H., ed. see Watts, Dorothy E.
Wooten, Vernon. The Colonial Williamsburg Coloring Book. 36p. (Orig.). (gr. 1). 1979. pap. 3.95 (0-87935-052-0) Williamsburg.
Worcester, Donald. Lone Hunter & the Cheyennes. Pauley, Paige, illus. LC 85-4746. 78p. (gr. 4 up). 1985. Repr. of 1957 ed. 10.95 (0-87565-018-X) Tex Christian.
—Lone Hunter's Gray Pony. Pauley, Paige, illus. LC 84-16157. 70p. (gr. 4 up). 1985. 10.95 (0-87565-001-5) Tex Christian.
Worcester, Donald E. John Paul Jones. (gr. 4-6). 1961. 4.36 (0-395-01755-6, Piper) HM.
—Lone Hunter's Gray Pony & Lone Hunter & the Cheyennes & War Pony. 1992. Boxed set. 29.95 (0-87565-109-7) Tex Christian.
—War Pony. Pauley, Paige, illus. LC 83-40486. 96p. (gr. 4 up). 1984. Repr. of 1961 ed. 10.95 (0-912646-85-3) Tex Christian.
Word, Christine. Ghosts Along the Bayou: Tales of Haunted Places in Southwestern Louisiana. Fuchs, Jeff, illus. 160p. (gr. 6-12). 1988. 12.95 (0-937614-09-2) Acadiana Pr.
Wordmill Staff, tr. see Gilmore, Jackie.
Worland, Denyse. Playtime. Kelly, Geoff, illus. LC 92-31077. 1993. 4.25 (0-383-03590-2) SRA Schl Grp.
World Almanac Staff, ed. see McLoone-Basta, Margo & Siegel, Alice.
World Association of Girl Guides & Girl Scouts Staff. Trefoil 'Round the World. rev. ed. (Illus.). 304p. (gr. 4-12). 1992. 8.00 (0-900827-50-5, 23-965) Girl Scouts USA.
World Book Editors. Childcraft's Whole Wide World. (Illus.). 288p. 1992. lib. bdg. write for info. (0-7166-3244-6) World Bk.
—How We Get Things - The Childcraft Annual, 1990: A Supplement to Childcraft - The How & Why Library. LC 65-25105. (Illus.). 256p. (gr. k-4). 1990. PLB write for info. (0-7166-0690-9) World Bk.
—Pets & Other Animals: Childcraft Annual, 1992. LC 65-25105. (Illus.). 256p. (gr. 1-7). 1992. lib. bdg. write for info. (0-7166-0692-5) World Bk.
—Science Year - 1991: The World Book Annual Science Supplement. LC 65-21776. (Illus.). 400p. (gr. 7-12). 1990. PLB write for info. (0-7166-0591-0) World Bk.
—The World Book Learning Library, 7 vols. new ed. LC 89-51413. (Illus.). 896p. (gr. 6-9). 1990. Set. write for info. (0-7166-3222-5) World Bk.
—The World Book of Word Power, 2 vols. LC 90-72119. (Illus.). 726p. 1991. Set. write for info. (0-7166-3238-1) Vol. 1: Language. Vol. 2: Writing & Speaking. World Bk.
—The World Book Year Book - 1991. LC 62-4818. (Illus.). 576p. (gr. 6-12). 1991. write for info. (0-7166-0491-4) World Bk.
—World Book's Science Desk Reference. LC 91-65996. (Illus.). 415p. (gr. 4-6). 1991. lib. bdg. write for info. (0-7166-3242-X) World Bk.
—World Book's Young Scientist. LC 91-65812. (Illus.). (gr. 3-6). 1991. PLB write for info. (0-7166-2791-4) World Bk.
World Book, Inc. Staff, ed. Dinosaurs! LC 65-25105. (Illus.). 304p. (gr. 3-7). 1987. PLB write for info. (0-7166-0687-9) World BK.
—Play It Safe! With the Alphabet Pals: Hide- & -Seek Safety. (Illus.). 20p. (ps). 1989. lib. bdg. write for info. (0-7166-1901-6) World Bk.
—Put Your Best Foot Forward with the Alphabet Pals: Right Time for Rosie. LC 89-50457. (Illus.). 20p. (ps). 1989. lib. bdg. write for info. (0-7166-1902-4) World Bk.

World Book Staff, ed. Childcraft - The How & Why Library (1993 Edition, 15 vols. rev. ed. LC 92-64103. (Illus.). (ps-6). 1992. Set. PLB write for info. (0-7166-0193-1) World Bk.
—Childcraft Dictionary (1993) rev. ed. LC 92-64303. (Illus.). 900p. (gr. 3-6). 1993. PLB write for info. (0-7166-1493-6) World Bk.
—Childcraft Supplement, 5 vols. LC 91-65174. (Illus.). (gr. 2-6). 1991. Set. write for info. (0-7166-0666-6) Prehistoric Animals, 304p. About Dogs, 304p. The Magic of Words, 304p. The Indian Book, 304p. The Puzzle Book, 304p. World Bk.
—Childcraft Supplement: Prehistoric Animals, About Dogs, The Magic of Words, The Indian Book, The Puzzle Book, 5 vols. (Illus.). 1520p. (gr. 2-6). 1989. PLB write for info. (0-7166-0669-0) World Bk SW.
—Christmas in Russia. LC 92-64394. (Illus.). 80p. (gr. 6 up). 1992. write for info. (0-7166-0892-8) World Bk.
—Christmas in the Holy Land. LC 87-50393. (Illus.). 80p. (gr. 6 up). 1992. write for info. (0-7166-2009-X) World Bk.
—I Was Wondering, 1991 Annual: Supplement to "Childcraft - The How & Why Library" LC 65-25105. (Illus.). 256p. (gr. k-4). 1991. lib. bdg. write for info. (0-7166-0691-7) World Bk.
—Look at You, Zak! Feeling Good about Me with the Alphabet Pals. LC 90-70419. (Illus.). 22p. (ps). 1990. bds. write for info. (0-7166-1904-0) World Bk.
—Science Year - 1993: The World Book Annual Science Supplement. LC 65-21776. (Illus.). 400p. (gr. 6 up). 1992. PLB write for info. (0-7166-0593-7) World Bk.
—Science Year, 1992: The World Book Annual Science Supplement. LC 65-21776. (Illus.). 400p. (gr. 7-12). 1991. lib. bdg. write for info. (0-7166-0592-9) World Bk.
—Today Nineteen Ninety-Three: A Personal Record & Reference Book. LC 76-27228. (Illus.). 192p. (gr. 9 up). 1992. PLB write for info. (0-7166-0793-X) World Bk.
—Why Do We Have To? Learning Why We Have to with the Alphabet Pals. LC 90-71689. (Illus.). 24p. (ps). 1991. bds. write for info. (0-7166-1905-9) World Bk.
—The World Book Atlas. LC 92-80532. (Illus.). 432p. (gr. 7 up). 1992. PLB write for info. (0-7166-2695-0) World Bk.
—The World Book Encyclopedia (1993) rev. ed. LC 92-61262. (Illus.). 14000p. (gr. 4 up). 1993. PLB write for info. (0-7166-0093-5) World Bk.
—The World Book Health & Medical Annual - 1993. LC 87-648075. (Illus.). 400p. (gr. 6 up). 1992. PLB write for info. (0-7166-1193-7) World Bk.
—The World Book Health & Medical Annual, 1990. LC 87-648075. (Illus.). 400p. (gr. 6-12). 1989. lib. bdg. write for info. (0-7166-1190-2) World Bk SW.
—The World Book of Math Power, 2 vols. rev. ed. LC 90-70044. (Illus.). 800p. (gr. 6 up). 1992. write for info. (0-7166-1392-1) World Bk.
—The World Book Student Dictionary (1993) rev. ed. LC 92-64304. (Illus.). 900p. (gr. 3-6). 1993. write for info. (0-7166-1593-2) World Bk.
—The World Book Student Information Finder, 2 vols. LC 90-71009. (Illus.). 590p. (gr. 7-12). 1993. Set. PLB write for info. (0-7166-3247-0) Vol. 1: Language Arts & Social Studies. Vol. 2: Math & Science. World Bk.
—The World Book Year Book - 1993. LC 62-4818. (Illus.). 576p. (gr. 6-12). 1993. PLB write for info. (0-7166-0493-0) World Bk.
—The World Book Year Book, 1992. LC 62-4818. (Illus.). 576p. (gr. 6-12). 1992. write for info. (0-7166-0492-2) World Bk.
Worley, Daryl. Billy & the Attic Adventure. Daab, John, illus. 1989. 9.95 (0-924067-00-4) Tyke Corp.
—Billy & the Big Truck. Daab, John, illus. 32p. (ps). 1989. 9.95 (0-924067-06-3) Tyke Corp.
—Billy & the Bright Red Ball. Daab, John, illus. 32p. (ps). 1989. 9.95 (0-924067-05-5) Tyke Corp.
—Billy & the Chocolate Chip Cookies. Daab, John, illus. 32p. (ps). 1989. 9.95 (0-924067-02-0) Tyke Corp.
—Billy & the Christmas Present. Daab, John, illus. 32p. (gr. 2-4). 1989. 9.95 (0-924067-01-2) Tyke Corp.
—Billy & the Department Store. Daab, John, illus. 32p. (ps). 1989. 9.95 (0-924067-04-7) Tyke Corp.
—Billy & the Scary Things. Daab, John, illus. (ps). 1989. 9.95 (0-924067-03-9) Tyke Corp.
Wormell, Christopher. Alphabet of Animals. LC 90-2774. 64p. 1990. 17.95 (0-8037-0876-9) Dial Bks Young.
—A Number of Animals. (Illus.). 32p. (gr. 4-7). 1993. 19.95 (1-56846-083-X) Creat Editions.
Wormell, Christopher & Green, Kate. A Number of Animals. LC 93-17134. (Illus.). (ps-3). 1993. PLB 19.95s.p. (0-88682-625-X) Creative Ed.
Wormell, Mary. Hilda Hens' Search. (gr. 2 up). 1994. write for info. (0-15-200069-0) HarBrace.
Wormser, Richard. Allan Pinkerton: America's First Private Eye. (Illus.). 119p. (gr. 5 up). 1990. 17.95 (0-8027-6964-0); lib. bdg. 18.85 (0-8027-6965-9) Walker & Co.
—Growing up in the Great Depression. LC 93-20686. (Illus.). 96p. (gr. 5-9). 1994. SBE 15.95 (0-689-31711-5, Atheneum Child Bk) Macmillan Child Grp.
—The Iron Horse: How Railroads Changed America. LC 93-1128. (gr. 4-7). 1993. 16.95 (0-8027-8221-3); PLB 17.85 (0-8027-8222-1) Walker & Co.

—Lifer's Program: Learn the Truth at the Expense of Our Sorrow. 168p. (gr. 7 up). 1991. lib. bdg. 14.98 (0-671-72548-3, J Messner); pap. 8.95 (0-671-72549-1) S&S Trade.
Wormser, Richard L. Three Faces of Vietnam. LC 93-11099. (Illus.). 160p. (gr. 7-12). 1993. PLB 13.90 (0-531-11142-3) Watts.
Wornall, Ruthie. Three Ingredient Cookbook. Classic American Fundraisers Staff, illus. 64p. (gr. 9-12). 1988. pap. 5.95 (0-685-29002-6) R Wornall.
Worrall, Joyce. God Is So Great. Nielsen, Deborah B., illus. 19p. (gr. k-6). 1985. pap. text ed. 4.25 (1-55976-132-6) CEF Press.
Worsham, Genevieve. Cotton Carta. LC 77-83627. (Illus.). 32p. (gr. 2-4). 1978. PLB 9.95 (0-87783-144-0); pap. 3.94 deluxe ed. (0-87783-149-1) Oddo.
Worsley, Elizabeth. Baby Bunny's Day. (ps). 1992. bds. 1.95 (0-681-41486-3) Longmeadow Pr.
—Baby Bunny's Garden. (ps). 1992. bds. 1.95 (0-681-41488-X) Longmeadow Pr.
—Baby Bunny's Party. (ps). 1992. bds. 1.95 (0-681-41487-1) Longmeadow Pr.
—Baby Bunny's Picnic. (ps). 1992. bds. 1.95 (0-681-41489-8) Longmeadow Pr.
Worth, Bonnie. Bye-Bye, Blankie. Cooke, Tom, illus. 18p. (ps). 1992. bds. 3.50 (0-307-12329-4, 12329, Golden Pr) Western Pub.
—Full House Same to You Duck. (gr. 4-7). 1990. pap. 2.95 (0-440-40468-1) Dell.
—Hey Dude: Showdown at the Bar None. LC 90-86412. (Illus.). 96p. (Orig.). (gr. 2-6). 1992. pap. 2.95 (0-448-40203-3, G&D) Putnam Pub Group.
—I Can Dress Myself. Cooke, Tom, illus. 18p. (ps). 1993. bds. 3.50 (0-307-12204-2, 12204, Golden Pr) Western Pub.
—I Can Share. Cooke, Tom, illus. 18p. (ps). 1993. bds. 3.50 (0-307-12205-0, 12205, Golden Pr) Western Pub.
—The Lean, Green Urkel Machine. (gr. 4-7). 1992. pap. 3.25 (0-440-40739-7, YB) Dell.
—Peter Cottontail's Surprise. Hildebrandt, Greg, illus. LC 84-28031. 48p. (ps-2). 1985. 4.95 (0-88101-015-4) Unicorn Pub.
—Pretty Park. (ps-3). 1993. pap. 1.95 (0-307-10555-5, Golden Pr) Western Pub.
—Way to Go, Chipmunk Cheeks. (gr. 4-7). 1991. pap. 3.25 (0-440-40596-3, YB) Dell.
Worth, Richard. Edith Wharton. LC 93-23207. 1994. write for info. (0-671-86615-X, J Messner); pap. write for info. (0-671-86616-8, J Messner) S&S Trade.
—Robert Mugabe - Zimbawe. (Illus.). 128p. 1990. lib. bdg. 13.98 (0-671-68987-8, J Messner); pap. 7.95 (0-671-70684-5) S&S Trade.
—Single-Parent Families. LC 92-14230. (Illus.). 128p. (gr. 9-12). 1992. PLB 13.40 (0-531-11131-8) Watts.
Worth, Richard & Moskin, Marietta D. In Focus Biographies Series, 4 bks. (Illus.). 512p. (gr. 9 up). 1990. Set. PLB 55.92 (0-671-31236-7, J Messner); Set. PLB 41.94s.p. (0-685-47046-6); Set. pap. 31.80 (0-671-31237-5); Set. pap. 23.85s.p. (0-685-47047-4) S&S Trade.
Worth, Valerie. All the Small Poems. Babbitt, Natalie, illus. 192p. (gr. 3 up). 1987. pap. 3.95 (0-374-40344-9, Sunburst) FS&G.
—At Christmastime. Frasconi, Antonio, illus. LC 92-52693. 32p. (gr. k up). 1992. 15.00 (0-06-205019-2); PLB 14.89 (0-06-205020-6) HarpC Child Bks.
—Fox Hill. LC 85-81026. 148p. (gr. 7 up). 1986. 14.00 (0-374-32783-1) FS&G.
—Gypsy Gold. LC 83-20607. 176p. (gr. 12 up). 1986. pap. 3.45 (0-374-42820-4) FS&G.
—Small Poems Again. Babbitt, Natalie, illus. LC 85-47513. 48p. (gr. 3 up). 1986. 11.00 (0-374-37074-5) FS&G.
—Still More Small Poems. Babbitt, Natalie, illus. LC 78-11739. 48p. (gr. 3 up). 1978. 11.00 (0-374-37258-6) FS&G.
Worthington, Denise. En Nuestra Casa Habia un Raton. (Illus.). 8p. (gr. 1). 1993. 3.50 (1-880612-16-X) Seedling Pubns.
—Our House Had a Mouse. (Illus.). 8p. (gr. 1). 1993. pap. 3.50 (1-880612-29-1) Seedling Pubns.
Worthington, George. In Search of World Records. LC 80-82032. (gr. 10-12). 1980. 18.95 (0-938282-01-8) Hang Gliding.
Worthington, Joan & Worthington, Phoebe. Teddy Bear Farmer. (ps-1). pap. 2.95 (0-317-62188-2, Puffin) Puffin Bks.
Worthington, Phoebe, jt. auth. see Worthington, Joan.
Worthy, Judith. Eyes. 1989. pap. 9.95 (0-385-24965-9) Doubleday.
Worthylake, Mary M. The Pomo. LC 93-36666. 1994. write for info. (0-516-01057-3) Childrens.
Wortman, Alexandra & Hable, Mary P. BASIC Computer Literacy for Beginners. (Illus.). 57p. (Orig.). (gr. 2-4). 1984. pap. text ed. 5.95 (0-931983-03-7, BCLTXT-2) Basic Comp Lit.
Wortman, Mary, ed. see Dikis, Eloise.
Wosmek, Frances. ABC of Ecology. 2nd ed. LC 82-70224. (ENG, SPA & FRE., Illus.). 60p. (ps-3). 1990. 3.50 (0-943864-00-3) Davenport.
—A Brown Bird Singing. Lewin, Ted, illus. LC 85-24002. 160p. (gr. 5-10). 1985. 11.95 (0-688-06251-2) Lothrop.
—A Brown Bird Singing. Lewin, Ted, illus. LC 92-43784. 128p. (gr. 5 up). 1993. pap. 4.95 (0-688-04596-0, Pub. by Beech Tree Bks) Morrow.

—Neighbors. Wosmek, Frances, illus. LC 93-5079. 32p. (ps). 1993. 14.95 (*1-883280-01-X*); pap. 6.95 (*1-883280-02-8*) Font & Ctr Pr.
Wotzkow, Helm. Art of Hand-Lettering: Its Mastery & Practice. (Illus.). 320p. (gr. 9-12). pap. 6.95 (*0-486-21797-3*) Dover.
Wouters, Anne. This Book Is for Us. Wouters, Anne, illus. LC 91-23742. 32p. (ps-1). 1992. 8.95 (*0-525-44882-9*, DCB) Dutton Child Bks.
—This Book Is Too Small. Wouters, Anne, illus. LC 91-23743. 32p. (ps-1). 1992. 8.95 (*0-525-44881-0*, DCB) Dutton Child Bks.
Woychuk, Denis. The Other Side of the Wall. Howard, Kim, illus. LC 90-49415. 32p. (ps up). 1991. 13.95 (*0-688-09894-0*); PLB 13.88 (*0-688-09895-9*) Lothrop.
—Pirates. LC 91-3387. (ps-3). 1991. 14.00 (*0-688-10336-7*); PLB 13.93 (*0-688-10337-5*) Lothrop.
Woychuk, N. A. I Am: Memory Book for Pre-Schoolers. Jones, Mary E., illus. 33p. (Orig.). (ps). 1988. pap. 7.95 (*1-880960-10-9*) Script Memory FI.
Wrangham, Elizabeth. The Communications Revolution. Yapp, Malcolm, et al, eds. (Illus.). 32p. (gr. 10). 1980. pap. text ed. 3.45 (*0-89908-109-6*) Greenhaven.
Wrangham, Elizabeth, et al. The Family. Yapp, Malcolm, et al, eds. (Illus.). 32p. (gr. 6-11). 1980. pap. text ed. 3.45 (*0-89908-123-1*) Greenhaven.
Wray, Amanda. Wind Surfing. 48p. (gr. 3-4). 1991. PLB 11.95 (*1-56065-055-9*) Capstone Pr.
Wray, Kit, retold by. & illus. Hidden Picture Fairy Tales: Rapunzel. LC 90-85901. 32p. (gr. k-5). 1991. 7.95 (*1-878093-25-8*) Boyds Mills Pr.
—Hidden Picture Fairy Tales: Snow White. LC 90-85902. 32p. (gr. k-5). 1991. 7.95 (*1-878093-26-6*) Boyds Mills Pr.
Wray, Kit, as told by. & illus. King Arthur: A Hidden Picture Story. LC 91-76019. 32p. (ps-5). 1992. 7.95 (*1-56397-018-X*) Boyds Mills Pr.
Wray, Kit, retold by. & illus. Robin Hood: A Hidden Picture Story. LC 91-72976. 32p. (ps-3). 1992. 7.95 (*1-56397-020-1*) Boyds Mills Pr.
Wray, Rhonda, ed. see Lazicki, Ted.
Wray, Rhonda, ed. see Miller, Marianne M.
Wray, Rhonda, ed. see Olson, Judith.
Wrede, Patricia C. Calling on Dragons. LC 92-35469. 1993. write for info. (*0-15-200950-7*, J Yolen Bks) HarBrace.
—Dealing with Dragons. 212p. (gr. 7 up). 1990. 15.95 (*0-15-222900-0*, J Yolen Bks) HarBrace.
—Dealing with Dragons. 1992. pap. 3.25 (*0-590-45722-5*, Point) Scholastic Inc.
—Searching for Dragons. 242p. (gr. 7 up). 1991. 16.95 (*0-15-200898-5*, HB Juv Bks) HarBrace.
—Searching for Dragons. 1992. 3.25 (*0-590-45721-7*, 071, Point) Scholastic Inc.
—Talking to Dragons. LC 92-40719. 1993. 16.95 (*0-15-284247-0*, J Yolen Bks) HarBrace.
Wren. Flowers of Hawaii Coloring Book. Wren, illus. 32p. (ps-2). 1992. pap. 3.95 (*1-880188-42-2*) Bess Pr.
Wren & Maile. At the Beach. Wren, illus. (ENG & HAW.). 10p. (ps). 1992. bds. 3.95 (*1-880188-04-X*) Bess Pr.
—Local Colors. Wren, illus. (ENG & HAW.). 10p. (ps). 1992. bds. 3.95 (*1-880188-02-3*) Bess Pr.
—Na Holoholona Maoli: Native Animals. Wren, illus. (ENG & HAW.). 10p. (ps). 1992. bds. 3.95 (*1-880188-27-9*) Bess Pr.
—Na Mea Kanu: Plants. Wren, illus. (ENG & HAW.). 10p. (ps). 1992. bds. 3.95 (*1-880188-28-7*) Bess Pr.
—Na 'Olelo Hawaii: Words. Wren, illus. (ENG & HAW.). 10p. (ps). 1992. bds. 3.95 (*1-880188-29-5*) Bess Pr.
—One-Two-Three Counting Locally. Wren, illus. (ENG & HAW.). 10p. (ps). 1992. bds. 3.95 (*1-880188-01-5*) Bess Pr.
—Pi'a'pa: Alphabet. Wren, illus. (ENG & HAW.). 10p. (ps). 1992. bds. 3.95 (*1-880188-30-9*) Bess Pr.
—Say It in Hawaiian: My Body. Wren, illus. (ENG & HAW.). 10p. (ps). 1992. bds. 3.95 (*1-880188-03-1*) Bess Pr.
Wren, Percival C. Reader's Digest Best Loved Books for Young Readers: Beau Geste. Ogburn, Jackie, ed. Galli, Stan, illus. 160p. (gr. 4-12). 1989. 3.99 (*0-945260-33-4*) Choice Pub NY.

Wrenn, Romel. Super ABC's of the Human Body. Tripp, Charles, illus. 56p. (gr. k-4). 1993. Wkbk. write for info. (*0-9637869-0-3*) Chldrns Med. SUPER ABC'S OF THE HUMAN BODY is a MULTISENSORY tool. Its educational features include: Alphabet Chart, Printing Workbook, Human Anatomy, Alphabet Rhyme, Coloring Book. A is for ANKLE. I am Talus by name. I connect the leg & foot: that is my game. B is for BACK & Spine is my label. I can carry the load, because I am strong & able. Each alphabet has a super hero pointing to the appropriate part of the body. The opposing page has an anatomically correct illustration of the body part.

These are line drawings which may be colored by the students. Space is provided for printing of upper/lower case alphabets. Children ages 2-10 years are the target audience. The author, Dr. Romel C. Wrenn, M.D., has made this first of a planned series of books to be used for health education in primary school. SUPER ABC'S retails for $4.95. It may be obtained for $3.50 at quantities above 100. For more information, telephone Dr. Romel C. Wrenn at 318-445-9931/ 318-443-5524 or Ms. Theresa Rose at 318-445-3658. Mail inquiries to Children's Medical World, P.O. Drawer 8238, Alexandria, LA 71306. *Publisher Provided Annotation.*

Wright. A Ghost in the Window. 1993. pap. 2.75 (*0-590-43442-X*) Scholastic Inc.
—The Secret Window. 1993. pap. 2.95 (*0-590-42749-0*) Scholastic Inc.
Wright, Alexandra. At Home in the Tide Pool. (Illus.). 32p. (ps-4). 1993. 14.95 (*0-88106-483-1*); PLB 15.00 (*0-88106-481-5*) Charlesbridge Pub.
—Les Echaremo de Menos? Especies en Peligro de Extincion (Will We Miss Them? Endangered Species) (Illus.). 32p. (ps-3). 1993. pap. 6.95 (*0-88106-420-3*) Charlesbridge Pub.
—Will We Miss Them? (Illus.). 32p. (ps-8). 1991. 14.95 (*0-88106-489-0*); pap. 6.95 (*0-88106-488-2*) Charlesbridge Pub.
Wright, Annette T., jt. auth. see Stoops, Erik D.
Wright, Betty, ed. see Farquhar, Kristin.
Wright, Betty R. The Cat Next Door. Owens, Gail, illus. LC 90-29080. 32p. (ps-3). 1991. reinforced 14.95 (*0-8234-0896-5*) Holiday.
—Christina's Ghost. LC 85-42880. 128p. (gr. 3-7). 1985. 14.95 (*0-8234-0581-8*) Holiday.
—Christina's Ghost. 112p. (gr. 3-7). 1987. pap. 2.75 (*0-590-42709-1*) Scholastic Inc.
—The Day Our TV Broke Down. Bejna, Barbara & Jensen, Shirlee, illus. Holbrook, Thomas, intro. by. LC 80-14434. 32p. (gr. k-6). 1980. PLB 17.96 (*0-8172-1365-1*) Raintree Steck-V.
—The Dollhouse Murders. LC 83-6147. 160p. (gr. 3-7). 1983. 14.95 (*0-8234-0497-8*) Holiday.
—Dollhouse Murders. 160p. (gr. 3-7). 1985. pap. 2.75 (*0-590-43461-6*) Scholastic Inc.
—Un Fantasma en la Casa. (gr. 4-7). 1993. pap. 2.95 (*0-590-46860-X*) Scholastic Inc.
—The Ghost Comes Calling. LC 93-13969. 128p. (gr. 2-6). 1994. 13.95 (*0-590-47353-0*) Scholastic Inc.
—The Ghost in the House. 160p. 1991. 13.95 (*0-590-43606-6*, Scholastic Hardcover) Scholastic Inc.
—A Ghost in the House. 176p. (gr. 3-7). 1993. pap. 2.95 (*0-590-43603-1*, Apple Paperbacks) Scholastic Inc.
—A Ghost in the Window. LC 87-45331. 160p. (gr. 3-7). 1987. 14.95 (*0-8234-0661-X*) Holiday.
—The Ghost of Ernie P. LC 90-55108. 128p. (gr. 3-7). 1990. 14.95 (*0-8234-0835-3*) Holiday.
—The Ghost of Ernie P. 1992. pap. 2.95 (*0-590-45073-5*, Apple Paperbacks) Scholastic Inc.
—The Ghost of Popcorn Hill. Ritz, Karen, illus. LC 92-16391. 96p. (gr. 3-7). 1993. 13.95 (*0-8234-1009-9*) Holiday.
—Ghost Witch. (gr. 4-7). 1993. 13.95 (*0-8234-1036-6*) Holiday.
—Ghosts Beneath Our Feet. LC 84-47835. 144p. (gr. 3-7). 1984. 14.95 (*0-8234-0538-9*) Holiday.
—Ghosts Beneath Our Feet. 144p. (gr. 3-7). 1986. pap. 2.75 (*0-590-43444-6*) Scholastic Inc.
—The Ghosts of Mercy Manor. LC 92-21557. 1993. 13. 95 (*0-590-43601-5*) Scholastic Inc.
—I Like Being Alone. Toht, Don, illus. Okun, Barbara F., intro. by. LC 80-25513. (Illus.). 32p. (gr. k-6). 1981. PLB 17.96 (*0-8172-1367-8*) Raintree Steck-V.
—I Like Being Alone. (ps-3). 1993. pap. 3.95 (*0-8114-5208-5*) Raintree Steck-V.
—The Midnight Mystery. 144p. (gr. 4-7). 1991. pap. 3.25 (*0-590-43758-5*, Apple Paperbacks) Scholastic Inc.
—My New Mom & Me. Day, Betsy, illus. Silverman, Manuel S. LC 80-25529. (Illus.). (gr. k-6). 1981. PLB 16.67 (*0-8172-1368-6*) Raintree Pubs Ltd.
—My New Mom & Me. (ps-3). 1993. pap. 3.95 (*0-8114-7154-3*) Raintree Steck-V.
—My Sister Is Different. Cogancherry, Helen, illus. Nietupski, John, intro. by. LC 80-25508. (Illus.). 32p. (gr. k-6). 1981. PLB 16.67 (*0-8172-1369-4*) Raintree Pubs Ltd.
—My Sister Is Different. (ps-3). 1993. pap. 3.95 (*0-8114-7158-6*) Raintree Steck-V.
—The Pike River Phantom. LC 88-45276. 160p. (gr. 3-7). 1988. 14.95 (*0-8234-0721-7*) Holiday.
—The Pike River Phantom. 160p. (gr. 3-7). 1990. pap. 3.25 (*0-590-42808-X*) Scholastic Inc.
—Rosie & the Dance of the Dinosaurs. LC 89-2083. 112p. (gr. 3-7). 1989. 14.95 (*0-8234-0782-9*) Holiday.
—The Scariest Night. LC 91-55030. 166p. (gr. 3-7). 1991. 14.95 (*0-8234-0904-X*) Holiday.

—Scariest Night. (gr. 4-7). 1993. pap. 2.95 (*0-590-45918-X*) Scholastic Inc.
—The Secret Window. LC 82-80816. 160p. (gr. 3-7). 1982. 14.95 (*0-8234-0464-1*) Holiday.
—The Summer of Mrs. MacGregor. LC 86-45388. 160p. (gr. 3-7). 1986. 14.95 (*0-8234-0628-8*) Holiday.
—Why Do I Daydream? Glessner, Marc, illus. Silverman, Manuel S., intro. by. LC 80-25561. (Illus.). 32p. (gr. k-6). 1981. PLB 13.45 (*0-8172-1371-6*) Raintree Pubs Ltd.
Wright, Betty R., adapted by see Bronte, Emily.
Wright, Betty R., adapted by see Crane, Stephen.
Wright, Betty R., adapted by see Wells, H. G.
Wright, Blanche F., illus. The Real Mother Goose, 4 bks. 96p. (ps-2). Set Incl. cassettes. pap. 16.98 (*1-55886-018-5*) Smarty Pants.
—The Real Mother Goose, Vol. I. 24p. (ps-2). Incl. cassettes. pap. 5.98 (*1-55886-012-6*) Smarty Pants.
—The Real Mother Goose, Vol. II. 24p. (ps-2). Incl. cassettes. pap. 5.98 (*1-55886-013-4*) Smarty Pants.
—The Real Mother Goose, Vol. III. 24p. (ps-2). Incl. cassettes. pap. 5.98 (*1-55886-014-2*) Smarty Pants.
—The Real Mother Goose, Vol. IV. 24p. (ps-2). Incl. cassettes. pap. 5.98 (*1-55886-015-0*) Smarty Pants.
—Real Mother Goose. 128p. (ps-1). 1991. Repr. 12.95 (*1-56288-041-1*) Checkerboard.
Wright, Bob. Falling Star Mystery. bilingual ed. Bourne, Phyllis & Tusquets, Eugenia, trs. (SPA & ENG., Illus.). 96p. (gr. 1-5). 1989. pap. text ed. 4.95 (*0-87879-663-0*) High Noon Bks.
—Gold Coin Robbery. bilingual ed. Bourne, Phyllis & Tusquets, Eugenia, trs. (SPA & ENG., Illus.). 96p. (gr. 1-5). 1989. pap. text ed. 4.95 (*0-87879-667-3*) High Noon Bks.
—Mummy's Crown. bilingual ed. Bourne, Phyllis & Tusquets, Eugenia, trs. (SPA & ENG., Illus.). 96p. (gr. 1-5). 1989. pap. text ed. 4.95 (*0-87879-660-6*) High Noon Bks.
—On the Air, 5 plays in ea. set, 3 sets. (Illus.). (gr. 1-5). 1988. 6.50 ea. Missing Diamonds, 16p (*0-87879-578-2*) Zebra Mystery, 16p (*0-87879-579-0*) Mad Scientist, 16p (*0-87879-580-4*) High Noon Bks.
—Red Hair Robbery. bilingual ed. Bourne, Phyllis & Tusquets, Eugenia, trs. (SPA & ENG., Illus.). 96p. (gr. 1-5). 1989. pap. text ed. 4.95 (*0-87879-661-4*) High Noon Bks.
—Secret Staircase. bilingual ed. Bourne, Phyllis & Tusquets, Eugenia, trs. (SPA & ENG., Illus.). 96p. (gr. 1-5). 1989. pap. text ed. 4.95 (*0-87879-659-2*) High Noon Bks.
—Siamese Turtle Mystery. bilingual ed. Bourne, Phyllis & Tusquets, Eugenia, trs. (SPA & ENG., Illus.). 96p. (gr. 1-5). 1989. pap. text ed. 4.95 (*0-87879-658-4*) High Noon Bks.
—Silver Buckle Mystery. bilingual ed. Bourne, Phyllis & Tusquets, Eugenia, trs. (SPA & ENG., Illus.). 96p. (gr. 1-5). 1989. pap. text ed. 4.95 (*0-87879-664-9*) High Noon Bks.
—Thief in the Green Van. bilingual ed. Bourne, Phyllis & Tusquets, Eugenia, trs. (ENG & SPA., Illus.). 96p. (gr. 1-5). 1989. pap. text ed. 4.95 (*0-87879-666-5*) High Noon Bks.
—Tom & Ricky Mystery Series, 9 sets, 5 different novels per set. (Illus.). (gr. 1-5). 1983. Set. pap. 15.00 ea., 48p. ea. Set 1 (*0-87879-326-7*) Set 2 (*0-87879-336-4*) Set 3 (*0-87879-357-7*) Set 4 (*0-87879-363-1*) Set 5 (*0-87879-390-9*) Set 6 (*0-87879-396-8*) Set 7 (*0-87879-419-0*) Set 8 (*0-87879-425-5*) High Noon Bks.
—Tree House Mystery. bilingual ed. Bourne, Phyllis & Tusquets, Eugenia, trs. (ENG & SPA., Illus.). 96p. (gr. 1-5). 1989. pap. text ed. 4.95 (*0-87879-665-7*) High Noon Bks.
—Video Game Spy. bilingual ed. Bourne, Phyllis & Tusquets, Eugenia, trs. (ENG & SPA., Illus.). 96p. (gr. 1-5). 1989. pap. text ed. 4.95 (*0-87879-662-2*) High Noon Bks.
Wright, Bobby J., ed. see Quesenbury, Pat.
Wright, Carol L. Pegora the Witch: Musical. (gr. 1-7). 1966. 4.50 (*0-87602-171-2*) Anchorage.
Wright, Christine. Just Like Emma: How She Has Fun in God's World. LC 92-70792. 32p. (ps-3). 1992. 7.99 (*0-8066-2617-8*, 9-2617) Augsburg Fortress.
—My Sister Katie: How She Sees God's World. Hull, Biz, illus. LC 90-81702. 32p. (ps). 1990. text ed. 7.99 (*0-8066-2497-3*, 9-2497) Augsburg Fortress.
Wright, Cornelia H., jt. auth. see Patterson, Lillie.
Wright, Cynthia W. Hello, I Am a Manatee. (Illus.). 14p. (ps). 1986. 3.95 (*0-937961-01-9*) Primate Pub.
Wright, David & Wright, Jill. Facts on File Children's Atlas. updated ed. (Illus.). 96p. (gr. 6-10). 1991. 14.95 (*0-8160-2703-X*) Facts on File.
—The Facts on File Children's Atlas. LC 92-39432. 1993. write for info. (*0-8160-2925-3*) Facts on File.
—France. (Illus.). 32p. (gr. 4-6). 1991. 17.95 (*0-237-60184-2*, Pub. by Evans Bros Ltd) Trafalgar.
—Italy. (Illus.). 32p. (gr. 4-6). 1991. 17.95 (*0-237-60186-9*, Pub. by Evans Bros Ltd) Trafalgar.
—Spain. (Illus.). 32p. (gr. 4-6). 1991. 17.95 (*0-237-60183-4*, Pub. by Evans Bros Ltd) Trafalgar.
Wright, David, jt. auth. see Wright, Jill.
Wright, David, adapted by. & photos by Canada Is My Home. LC 92-17726. (Illus.). 1992. PLB 18.60 (*0-8368-0846-0*) Gareth Stevens Inc.
Wright, David, tr. Beowulf. (Orig.). (gr. 9 up). 1957. pap. 5.95 (*0-14-044070-4*) Viking Child Bks.
Wright, David K. Brunei. LC 91-22511. 128p. (gr. 5-9). 1991. PLB 26.60 (*0-516-02602-X*) Childrens.

—Burma. LC 90-21265. (Illus.). 128p. (gr. 5-9). 1991. PLB 26.60 (0-516-02725-5) Childrens.
—Canada. Wright, David K., photos by. LC 89-43197. (Illus.). (gr. 5-6). 1991. PLB 19.93 (0-8368-0256-X) Gareth Stevens Inc.
—Censorship. LC 92-19664. 1993. 17.50 (0-8225-2604-2) Lerner Pubns.
—Hong Kong. LC 90-9669. (Illus.). 64p. (gr. 5-6). 1991. PLB 19.93 (0-8368-0382-5) Gareth Stevens Inc.
—Malaysia. LC 87-33784. (Illus.). 128p. (gr. 5-9). 1988. PLB 26.60 (0-516-02702-6) Childrens.
—Singapore. LC 89-43196. (Illus.). 64p. (gr. 5-6). 1991. PLB 19.93 (0-8368-0255-1) Gareth Stevens Inc.
—The Story of the Vietnam Veterans Memorial. LC 89-713. (Illus.). 32p. (gr. 3-6). 1989. PLB 13.27 (0-516-04745-0); pap. 3.95 (0-516-44745-9) Childrens.
—Vietnam. LC 88-30486. (Illus.). 128p. (gr. 5-9). 1989. PLB 26.60 (0-516-02712-3) Childrens.
—War in Vietnam, Bks. I-IV. (Illus.). 144p. (gr. 4 up). 1989. PLB 85.27 (0-516-02285-7) Book I, Eve of Battle. Book II, A Wider War. Book III, Vietnamization. Book IV, The Fall of Vietnam. Childrens.
Wright, Friere & Foreman, Michael. Seven in One Blow. Wright, Friere & Foreman, Michael, illus. 32p. (ps-3). 1981. lib. bdg. 4.99 (0-394-93805-4) Random Bks Yng Read.
Wright, Gary. Track & Field: A Step-By-Step Guide. LC 89-27344. (Illus.). 64p. (gr. 4-8). 1990. PLB 9.79 (0-8167-1947-0); pap. text ed. 2.95 (0-8167-1948-9) Troll Assocs.
Wright, Gordon. In Quest of Healing. LC 83-82030. 176p. (Orig.). (gr. 12). 1984. pap. 4.95 (0-88243-614-7, 02-0614) Gospel Pub.
Wright, Harold B. Shepherd of the Hills. rev. ed. Phillips, Michael R., ed. LC 88-10311. 256p. 1988. pap. 7.99 (0-87123-916-7) Bethany Hse.
Wright, Janet. More Mandala Coloring Pad. 48p. (gr. 7 up). 1985. pap. 5.95 (0-385-19886-8, Dolp) Doubleday.
Wright, Jill. The Old Woman & the Jar of Ums. Rounds, Glen, illus. 32p. (ps-3). 1990. 14.95 (0-399-21736-3, Putnam) Putnam Pub Group.
Wright, Jill & Wright, David. Illustrated World Atlas. Warwick Press, ed. Streek, Tony, illus. 64p. (gr. 4-9). 1988. PLB 14.90 (0-531-19033-1, Warwick) Watts.
—The Simon & Schuster Young Readers' Atlas. Barish, Wendy, ed. Saunders, Mike & Wright, David, illus. 192p. 1984. pap. 7.95 (0-671-50657-9) S&S Trade.
Wright, Jill, jt. auth. see Wright, David.
Wright, Joan R., jt. auth. see Parker, Nancy W.
Wright, Lyndie. Puppets. Fairclough, Chris, photos by. (Illus.). 48p. (gr. 3-6). 1989. PLB 12.40 (0-531-10635-7) Watts.
—Toy Theaters. (Illus.). 48p. (gr. 5-8). 1991. PLB 12.40 (0-531-14196-9) Watts.
Wright, Lynn F. Just One Blade. Waters, Tony, illus. 32p. (gr. 1-4). 1993. 11.95 (1-881519-00-7) WorryWart.
—The Prison Bird. Donaho, K. Blythe, illus. LC 91-75180. 24p. (gr. 1-4). 1991. 11.95 (0-685-54896-1) WorryWart.
Wright, Malcolm, ed. see Walker, David.
Wright, Meg, illus. Three Stories from India. (gr. 1-8). 1984. pap. text ed. 9.50 (0-8658-166-2) BCM Pubn.
Wright, Nicola. Getting to Know France. Wooley, Kim, illus. 32p. (gr. 3-7). 1993. pap. 12.95 incl. 60 min. cassette (0-8120-8125-0) Barron.
—Getting to Know: France & French. Wooley, Kim, illus. 32p. (gr. 3-7). 1993. 12.95 (0-8120-6336-8); pap. 5.95 (0-8120-1532-0) Barron.
—Getting to Know: Germany & German. Wooley, Kim, illus. 32p. (gr. 3-7). 1993. 12.95 (0-8120-6337-6); pap. 5.95 (0-8120-1533-9) Barron.
—Getting to Know: Italy & Italian. Wooley, Kim, illus. 32p. (gr. 3-7). 1993. 12.95 (0-8120-6338-4); pap. 5.95 (0-8120-1534-7) Barron.
—Getting to Know: Spain & Spanish. Wooley, Kim, illus. 32p. (gr. 3-7). 1993. 12.95 (0-8120-6339-2); pap. 5.95 (0-8120-1535-5) Barron.
Wright, Nicola, jt. auth. see Butterfield, Moira.
Wright, Nicola, jt. auth. see Potter, Tony.
Wright, Patricia. Compute a Design - Fractions. Jacobs, Russell, ed. 50p. (Orig.). (gr. 5-9). 1987. pap. text ed. 11.95 (0-918272-14-9) Jacobs.
—Compute a Design - Percent. Jacobs, Russell, ed. 50p. (Orig.). (gr. 5-9). 1987. pap. text ed. 11.95 (0-918272-15-7) Jacobs.
—Compute a Design: Decimals. Jacobs, Russell, ed. 50p. (Orig.). (gr. 5-9). 1985. pap. text ed. 11.95 (0-918272-13-0) Jacobs.
—Compute a Design: Whole Numbers. Jacobs, Russell, ed. 50p. (gr. 5-9). 1985. pap. text ed. 11.95 (0-918272-12-2) Jacobs.
Wright, Rachel. Castles. (Illus.). 32p. (gr. 5-8). 1992. PLB 11.90 (0-531-14138-1) Watts.
—Egyptians. LC 92-7840. (Illus.). 32p. (gr. 5-8). 1993. PLB 11.90 (0-531-14209-4) Watts.
—Eyes, Ears & Noses. (ps-3). 1990. PLB 10.40 (0-531-14001-6) Watts.
—Greeks. LC 92-14718. 1993. 11.90 (0-531-14246-9) Watts.
—Knights. Kline, Marjory, ed. (Illus.). 32p. (gr. k-4). 1992. PLB 11.90 (0-531-14163-2) Watts.
—Pirates. (Illus.). 32p. (gr. k-4). 1991. PLB 11.90 (0-531-14156-X) Watts.
—Vikings. LC 92-4618. (Illus.). 32p. (gr. 5-8). 1993. PLB 11.90 (0-531-14210-8) Watts.

—Why Do I Eat? Trotter, Stuart, illus. LC 91-26683. 32p. (ps-2). 1992. pap. 5.95 (0-689-71588-9, Aladdin) Macmillan Child Grp.
Wright, Rachel, jt. auth. see Borlenghi, Patricia.
Wright, Rachel, jt. auth. see Chambers, Catherine.
Wright, Rachel, jt. auth. see Ganeri, Anita.
Wright, Rachel, jt. auth. see Lambert, David.
Wright, Richard. Rite of Passage. Rampersad, Arnold, afterword by. LC 93-2473. 128p. (gr. 7 up). 1994. 15.95 (0-06-023419-9); PLB 15.89 (0-06-023420-2) HarpC Child Bks.
Wright, Robert, jt. auth. see Collette, Paul.
Wright, Robin. Dinosaurs & Other Prehistoric Animals. Wazejewski, Don, et al, illus. LC 90-38028. 96p. (gr. 3-6). 1991. lib. bdg. 14.89 (0-8167-2232-3); pap. text ed. 6.95 (0-8167-2233-1) Troll Assocs.
Wright, Sandra, ed. The Teddy Bear Book. 34p. 1985. pap. 5.95 (0-89821-066-6) Reiman Pubns.
Wright, Sarah B. Islands of the Northeastern United States & Eastern Canada. (Illus.). 224p. (Orig.). 1990. pap. text ed. 9.95 (0-934601-99-2) Peachtree Pubs.
Wright, Sheila, jt. auth. see Russman, Penny.
Wright, Susan K. The Secret of the Old Graveyard. 184p. (Orig.). (gr. 4-8). 1993. pap. 5.95 (0-8361-3627-6) Herald Pr.
Wright, Tom. Bringing the Church to the World. 192p. (Orig.). 1993. pap. 8.99 (1-55661-318-0) Bethany Hse.
Wrighton, Charlene A., jt. auth. see Bradshaw, Georgene.
Wrighton, Charlene A., jt. auth. see Bradshaw, Georgene E.
Wrightson, Patricia. Balyet. LC 88-8298. 144p. (gr. 7 up). 1989. SBE 13.95 (0-689-50468-3, M K McElderry) Macmillan Child Grp.
—Balyet. 1990. pap. 3.95 (0-14-034339-3, Puffin) Puffin Bks.
—Moon-Dark. Young, Noela, illus. LC 87-3903. 176p. (gr. 4-7). 1988. SBE 14.95 (0-689-50451-9, M K McElderry) Macmillan Child Grp.
—The Nargun & the Stars. (gr. 7 up). 1988. pap. 3.95 (0-14-030780-X, Puffin) Puffin Bks.
—Night Outside. Peck, Beth, illus. LC 85-7529. 64p. (gr. 4-7). 1985. SBE 13.95 (0-689-50363-6, M K McElderry) Macmillan Child Grp.
—The Sugar-Gum Tree. Cox, David, illus. 64p. (gr. 2-6). 1992. 11.95 (0-670-83910-8) Viking Child Bks.
Wrigley, Heide S. May I Help You? (Illus.). 160p. (gr. 9-12). 1987. pap. text ed. 11.95 (0-201-09943-8); tchr's. guide 10.95 (0-201-09898-9) Addison-Wesley.
Wrinkle, Johanna. Canterbury Tales Literature Guide. 80p. (gr. 9-12). 1992. pap. text ed. 10.95 (0-944459-54-4) ECS Lrn Systs.
—ECS Literature Guide for "A Tale of Two Cities" 96p. (gr. 7-12). 1993. pap. text ed. 10.95 (0-944459-65-X) ECS Lrn Systs.
—Return of the Native Literature Guide. 96p. (gr. 7-12). 1992. pap. text ed. 10.95 (0-944459-57-9) ECS Lrn Systs.
—Wuthering Heights Literature Guide. 96p. (gr. 7-12). 1992. pap. text ed. 10.95 (0-944459-55-2) ECS Lrn Systs.
Writer, C. C., tr. see Amir, Tami.
Writer, C. C., tr. see Assaf, Yael.
Writer, C. C., tr. see Bar, Amos.
Writer, C. C., tr. see Baram, Bella.
Writer, C. C., tr. see Blatchford, Claire.
Writer, C. C., tr. see Burla, Oded.
Writer, C. C., tr. see Eitan, Ora.
Writer, C. C., tr. see Fleisher, Gila M.
Writer, C. C., tr. see Gelbart, Ofra.
Writer, C. C., tr. see Gelbert, Ofra.
Writer, C. C., tr. see Griffin, Gail M.
Writer, C. C., tr. see Harel, Nira.
Writer, C. C., tr. see Ofek, Uriel.
Writer, C. C., tr. see Sherrow, Victoria.
Writer, C. C., tr. see Shinhav, Chaya.
Writers' League of Washington Staff. A Diamond Anthology of Prose & Poetry: Seventy-Fifth Year. Ricketts, Marijane, et al, eds. Archambauer, Alan H., illus. Leighton, Frances S., intros. by. (Illus.). 112p. (gr. 8-12). 1992. pap. write for info. (0-9618223-2-5) M G Ricketts.
Wrixon, Fred B. Codes & Ciphers: An A to Z of Covert Communication, from the Clay Tablet to the Microdot. (Illus.). 288p. 1992. pap. 18.00 (0-13-277047-4) P-H Gen Ref & Trav.
Wroble, Lisa. Astronomy. Nolte, Larry, illus. 48p. (gr. 3-6). Date not set. PLB 12.95 (1-56065-110-5) Capstone Pr. Postponed.
—Natural Science. Nolte, Larry, illus. 48p. (gr. 3-6). Date not set. PLB 12.95 (1-56065-112-1) Capstone Pr. Postponed.
—Space Science. Nolte, Larry, illus. 48p. (gr. 3-6). Date not set. PLB 12.95 (1-56065-114-8) Capstone Pr. Postponed.
Wu, Dana Y. & Tung, Jeffrey D. The Chinese-American Experience. LC 92-15649. (Illus.). 64p. (gr. 4-6). 1993. PLB 14.90 (1-56294-271-9) Millbrook Pr.
Wu, Norbert. Beneath the Waves: Exploring the World of the Kelp Forest. Wu, Norbert, illus. (gr. 3-7). 1992. 12.95 (0-87701-835-9) Chronicle Bks.
—Fish Faces. LC 92-27343. (Illus.). 32p. (ps-2). 1993. PLB 15.95 (0-8050-1668-6, Bks Young Read) H Holt & Co.
—Life in the Oceans. (gr. 4-7). 1991. 17.95 (0-316-95638-4) Little.

Wu, William F. Hong on the Range. Hale, Phil & Anderson, Darrel, illus. LC 88-29329. 224p. (gr. 7 up). 1989. 17.95 (0-8027-6862-8) Walker & Co.
—Time Tours No. 1: Robin Hood Ambush. 1990. pap. 3.50 (0-06-106003-8, Harp PBks) HarpC.
Wubben, Pamela G. Living Genealogy for Children. 65p. (ps-7). 1981. pap. 9.95 (0-935442-03-0) One Percent.
Wujcik, Erick. Mutants of the Yucatan. Marciniszyn, Alex, ed. Fales, Kevin & Dombrowski, James, illus. 48p. (Orig.). (gr. 8 up). 1990. pap. 7.95 (0-916211-44-4, 511) Palladium Bks.
—Ninjas & Superspies. rev. ed. (Illus.). 176p. (gr. 8 up). 1987. pap. 15.95 (0-916211-31-2, 525) Palladium Bks.
—The Teenage Mutant Ninja Turtles Adventures. Marciniszyn, Alex, ed. Laird, Peter & Eastman, Kevin, illus. 48p. (Orig.). (gr. 8 up). 1986. pap. 7.95 (0-916211-16-9, 504) Palladium Bks.
—Teenage Mutant Ninja Turtles & Other Strangeness. Marciniszyn, Alex & Cartier, Randi, eds. Eastman, Kevin & Laird, Peter, illus. 112p. (Orig.). (gr. 8 up). 1985. pap. 11.95 (0-916211-14-2, 502) Palladium Bks.
—Teenage Mutant Ninja Turtles Guide to the Universe. Marciniszyn, Alex & Siembieda, Florence, eds. Eastman, Kevin, et al, illus. 48p. (Orig.). (gr. 8 up). 1987. pap. 7.95 (0-916211-25-8, 506) Palladium Bks.
Wujcik, Erick & Balent, Matthew. After the Bomb. Marciniszyn, Alex & Siembieda, Kevin, eds. Laird, Peter, illus. 48p. (Orig.). (gr. 8 up). 1986. pap. 7.95 (0-916211-15-0, 503) Palladium Bks.
Wujcik, Erick & Siembieda, Kevin. TMNT RPG Accessory Pack: Adventures in the Yucatan. Marciniszyn, Alex, ed. Dombrowski, James, illus. 24p. (Orig.). (gr. 8 up). 1990. pap. 11.95 (0-916211-45-2, 512) Palladium Bks.
Wulffson, Don L. Amazing True Stories. Jones, John R., illus. LC 90-28105. 128p. (gr. 4-9). 1991. 13.95 (0-525-65070-9, Cobblehill Bks) Dutton Child Bks.
—Extraordinary Stories: Behind the Inventions of Ordinary Things. Doty, Roy, illus. (gr. 3-7). 1991. pap. 3.50 (0-380-71294-6, Camelot) Avon.
—The Invention of Ordinary Things. Doty, Roy, illus. LC 80-17498. 96p. (gr. 3 up). 1981. PLB 12.88 (0-688-51978-4) Lothrop.
—More Incredible True Adventures. LC 89-1531. (Illus.). 112p. (gr. 4 up). 1989. 12.95 (0-525-65000-8, Cobblehill Bks) Dutton Child Bks.
Wunder, John R. The Kiowa. (Illus.). 112p. (gr. 5 up). 1989. 17.95 (1-55546-710-5) Chelsea Hse.
Wunderli & Watts. Adventure in the Wilderness. pap. 5.95 (0-88494-648-7) Bookcraft Inc.
Wunderli, jt. auth. see Watts.
Wunderli, Stephen. The Blue Between the Clouds. LC 91-28010. 80p. (gr. 5 up). 1992. 13.95 (0-8050-1772-0, Bks Young Read) H Holt & Co.
Wunnenberg, Helen. Three Questions. (Illus.). 12p. (gr. k-6). 1983. visualized song 3.99 (3-90117-027-8) CEF Press.
Wunsch, Marjory. Cabbie Abbie. LC 93-32617. 1995. write for info. (0-688-11626-4); PLB write for info. (0-688-11627-2) Lothrop.
—Spaceship Number Four: A Thanksgiving Story. Pearson, Susan, ed. LC 91-27552. (Illus.). 32p. (ps up). 1992. 13.00 (0-688-10472-X); PLB 12.93 (0-688-10473-8) Lothrop.
Wuorio, Eva-Lis. Detour to Danger: A Novel. LC 81-65501. 192p. (gr. 7 up). 1981. 12.95 (0-385-28206-0) Delacorte.
Wurfel, Nicole, jt. auth. see Barnett, Ada.
Wurmfeld, Hope H. Baby Blues. LC 92-5828. 80p. (gr. 7 up). 1992. 14.00 (0-670-84151-X) Viking Child Bks.
—Trucker. Wurmfeld, Hope H., illus. LC 89-13296. 64p. (gr. 3 up). 1990. RSBE 14.95 (0-02-793581-7, Macmillan Child Bk) Macmillan Child Grp.
Wurth, Shirley, ed. Books for You: A Booklist for Senior High Students. 11th ed. 257p. (Orig.). (gr. 9-12). 1992. pap. 16.95 (0-8141-0365-0) NCTE.
Wyatt, Elaine & Hinden, Stan. The Money Book & Bank. LC 91-13237. (Illus.). 64p. (gr. 2 up). 1991. pap. 11.95 (0-688-10365-0, Tambourine Bks) Morrow.
Wyatt, Margaret. My Friend Jesus. Wyatt, Tracey, illus. LC 86-90051. 20p. (Orig.). (ps-12). 1986. pap. 2.25 (0-9616117-0-7) M Wyatt.
Wyatt, Molly. Kim's Winter. (gr. 7 up). 1982. pap. 1.75 (0-317-00342-9, Sig Vista) NAL-Dutton.
Wyatt, Pam. I Can Go! Buell-Bakke, Karen, illus. (ps-1). 1988. lib. bdg. 9.95 (0-945286-00-7) Red Bus Pub.
Wycherley, William see Wilson, John H.
Wycoff, Cynthia. Language Treasure Chest: Extra Worksheets. (Illus.). 133p. (gr. k-6). 1987. wkbk. 29.95 (0-939161-02-8) Treas Chest Ent.
Wyeth, Sharon D. Amy's Song. (gr. k-6). 1990. pap. 2.95 (0-440-40260-3, YB) Dell.
—Annie K's Theater Book: The Mighty Dolphin. (gr. 4-7). 1991. pap. 2.75 (0-553-15853-8) Bantam.
—Annie K's Theater: The Dinosaur Tooth. (gr. 3-6). 1990. pap. 2.75 (0-553-15815-5) Bantam.
—Boy Crazy. (gr. 4-7). 1991. pap. 3.25 (0-440-40426-6, YB) Dell.
—Boy Project. (gr. 4-7). 1991. pap. 2.95 (0-440-40493-2) Dell.
—Boys Wanted. (gr. k-6). 1989. pap. 2.95 (0-440-40224-7, YB) Dell.
—The Chicken Pox Party. 1990. pap. 2.75 (0-553-15839-2) Bantam.
—The Ghost Show. 1990. pap. 2.75 (0-553-15829-5) Bantam.
—Handle with Care. (gr. k-6). 1990. 2.95 (0-440-40267-0, YB) Dell.

—Heartbreak Guy. (gr. 4-7). 1991. pap. 2.95 (*0-440-40412-6*) Dell.
—Lisa, We Miss You. 1990. pap. 2.95 (*0-440-40393-6*) Dell.
—Lisa's Secret. (Orig.). 1990. pap. 2.95 (*0-440-40346-4*, YB) Dell.
—No Creeps Need Apply. (gr. k-6). 1989. pap. 2.95 (*0-440-40241-7*, YB) Dell.
—P. S. Forget It. (gr. k-6). 1989. pap. 2.95 (*0-440-40230-1*, YB) Dell.
—Palmer at Your Service. (gr. 4 up). 1990. pap. 2.95 (*0-440-40343-X*, YB) Dell.
—Pen Pals: Stolen Pen Pals, No. 9. (gr. 4-7). 1990. pap. 2.95 (*0-440-40342-1*) Dell.
—Rocky Romance, No. 137. 192p. (Orig.). (gr. 7-12). 1988. pap. 2.50 (*0-553-26948-8*, Sweet Dreams) Bantam.
—Sam the Sham. (gr. k-6). 1989. pap. 2.95 (*0-440-40250-6*, YB) Dell.
—Sealed with a Kiss. (gr. k-6). 1990. pap. 2.95 (*0-440-40272-7*, YB) Dell.
—Summer Sizzle. (gr. 4-7). 1991. pap. 3.50 (*0-440-40470-3*) Dell.
—Super Pen Pals, No. 1. (Orig.). (gr. 4-7). 1990. pap. 3.50 (*0-440-40395-2*, Pub. by Yearling Classics) Dell.
—Too Cute for Words. (Orig.). (gr. k-6). 1989. pap. 2.95 (*0-440-40225-5*, YB) Dell.
—The Unknown Pen Pal. (Orig.). 1990. pap. 2.95 (*0-440-40345-6*) Dell.
—The World of Daughter McGuire. LC 93-15489. 1994. 14.95 (*0-385-31174-5*) Delacorte.

Wygant, Foster. School Art in American Culture, 1820-1970. (Illus.). 240p. (Orig.). 1993. pap. 21.95 (*0-9610376-1-X*) Interwood Pr. "An enormous achievement..a treasure!"--Dr. Diana Korzenik. THE ONLY BOOK PROVIDING THIS CONTENT. Six chapters: the 19th century; 1900-1915; 1915-30; 1930-45; 1945-60; 1960's. In each chapter: the conditions for art education in public schools (the influences in society & culture--events, attitudes, intellectual currents, literature, music, theatre, dance, visual arts, & education) & the response in art education (status, organizations, publications, purposes, issues, research, curriculum in drawing & painting, printmaking, sculpture, photography, design--graphic, industrial, home & community--ceramics, fibers, jewelry, other media, appreciation). The author, an emeritus professor, is an internationally respected historian of art education whose ART IN AMERICAN SCHOOLS IN THE NINETEENTH CENTURY (1983) has been widely praised & used as a text. This book, designed primarily for students & professionals, gives priority to detailed information rather than theoretical or critical interpretation. More than 100 illustrations: documents, extracts, & student artworks in 8" X 10" format. Interwood Press, 3562 Interwood Avenue, Cincinnati, OH 45220. Contact: Foster Wygant (513) 751-5239.
Publisher Provided Annotation.

Wykoff, Gerald L. Master Keys for Making Profits in Lapidary: A Complete Guide of Practical Tips & Methods That Can Help Hobbyists & Professionals Realize a Splendid, Dependable Income from Gemcutting. LC 93-28639. (Illus.). 204p. (Orig.). (gr. 12). 1994. pap. 19.95x (*0-9607892-8-6*) Adamas Pubs.
Wyland. The Art of Wyland. (Illus.). 32p. 1992. pap. text ed. 7.95 (*0-9631793-2-2*) Wyland Studios.
Wyler, Rose. Math Fun with Money Puzzlers. LC 92-351. (gr. 4-7). 1992. lib. bdg. 10.98 (*0-671-74313-9*, J Messner); lib. bdg. 5.95 (*0-671-74314-7*, J Messner) S&S Trade.
—Math Fun with Tricky Lines & Shapes. LC 92-351. (gr. 4-7). 1992. lib. bdg. 10.98 (*0-671-74315-5*, J Messner); pap. 5.95 (*0-671-74316-3*, J Messner) S&S Trade.
—Outdoor Science Series, 6 Bks. (Illus.). 64p. (gr. k-2). 1989. Set. lib. bdg. write for info. (*0-671-94099-6*, J Messner); Set. lib. bdg. write for info. (*0-671-94100-3*) S&S Trade.

—Puddles & Ponds. Petruccio, Steven, illus. 32p. (gr. k-2). 1990. lib. bdg. 11.98 (*0-671-66348-8*, J Messner) S&S Trade.
—Raindrops & Rainbows. Steltenpohl, Jane, ed. Petruccio, Steven, illus. 32p. (gr. k-2). 1989. (J Messner); lib. bdg. 4.95 (*0-671-66350-X*) S&S Trade.
—Science Fun Series, 6 vols. Stewart, Pat, illus. 288p. (gr. 2-4). 1987. Set. PLB 68.28 (*0-671-93016-8*, J Messner); Set. PLB 51.24s.p. (*0-685-47066-0*); Set. pap. 29.70 (*0-671-93018-4*); Set. pap. 22.26s.p. (*0-685-47067-9*) S&S Trade.
—Science Fun with a Homemade Chemistry Set. Stewart, Pat, illus. LC 86-21868. 48p. (gr. 2-4). 1987. lib. bdg. 11.38 (*0-671-55575-8*, J Messner); lib. bdg. 4.95 (*0-671-55570-7*); PLB 8.54s.p. (*0-685-47072-5*); pap. 3.71s.p. (*0-685-47073-1*) S&S Trade.
—Science Fun with Drums, Bells, & Whistles. Stewart, Pat, illus. LC 87-7838. 48p. (gr. 2-4). 1987. lib. bdg. 11.38 (*0-671-63783-5*, J Messner); lib. bdg. 4.95 (*0-671-64760-1*); PLB 8.54s.p. (*0-685-47070-9*); pap. 3.71s.p. (*0-685-47071-7*) S&S Trade.
—Science Fun With Mud & Dirt. Stewart, Pat, illus. 48p. (gr. 3). 1987. pap. 4.95 (*0-317-56794-2*) S&S Trade.
—Science Fun with Mud & Dirt. Stewart, Pat, illus. LC 86-8388. 48p. (gr. 2-4). 1986. lib. bdg. 11.38 (*0-671-55569-3*, J Messner); lib. bdg. 4.95 (*0-671-62904-2*); PLB 8.54s.p. (*0-685-47076-8*); pap. 3.71s.p. (*0-685-47077-6*) S&S Trade.
—Science Fun with Peanuts & Popcorn. Stewart, Pat, illus. 48p. (gr. 2-4). 1986. lib. bdg. 11.38 (*0-671-55572-3*, J Messner); lib. bdg. 4.95 (*0-671-62452-0*); PLB 8.54s.p. (*0-685-54164-9*); pap. 3.71s.p. (*0-685-54165-7*) S&S Trade.
—Science Fun with Toy Boats & Planes. Stewart, Pat, illus. 48p. (gr. 3). 1987. pap. 4.95 (*0-317-56816-7*) S&S Trade.
—Science Fun with Toy Boats & Planes. Stewart, Pat, illus. LC 85-8842. 48p. (gr. 2-4). 1986. lib. bdg. 11.38 (*0-671-55573-1*, J Messner); lib. bdg. 4.95 (*0-671-62453-9*); PLB 8.54s.p. (*0-685-47074-1*); pap. 3.71s.p. (*0-685-47075-X*) S&S Trade.
—Science Fun with Toy Cars & Trucks. Stewart, Pat, illus. LC 87-20326. 48p. (gr. 2-4). 1988. lib. bdg. 11.38 (*0-671-63784-3*, J Messner); lib. bdg. 4.95 (*0-671-65854-9*); PLB 8.54s.p. (*0-685-47068-7*); pap. 3.71s.p. (*0-685-47069-5*) S&S Trade.
—Seashore Surprises. (Illus.). 32p. (gr. k-3). 1991. lib. bdg. 11.98 (*0-671-69165-1*, J Messner); pap. 4.95 (*0-671-69167-8*) S&S Trade.
—The Starry Sky. Steltenpohl, Jane, ed. Petruccio, Steven, illus. 32p. (gr. k-2). 1989. lib. bdg. 11.98 (*0-671-66345-3*, J Messner); lib. bdg. 4.95 (*0-671-66349-6*) S&S Trade.
—Wonderful Woods. Petruccio, Steven, illus. 32p. (gr. k-3). 1990. (J Messner); lib. bdg. 4.95 (*0-671-69166-X*) S&S Trade.
Wyler, Rose & Ames, Gerald. Magic Secrets. rev. ed. Dorros, Arthur, illus. LC 89-35841. 64p. (gr. k-3). 1990. 14.00 (*0-06-026646-5*); PLB 13.89 (*0-06-026647-3*) HarpC Child Bks.
—Magic Secrets. rev. ed. Dorros, Arthur, illus. LC 89-35841. 64p. (gr. k-3). 1991. pap. 3.50 (*0-06-444153-9*, Trophy) HarpC Child Bks.
—Spooky Tricks. LC 68-16822. (Illus.). 64p. (gr. ps-3). 1968. PLB 11.89 (*0-06-026634-1*) HarpC Child Bks.
—Spooky Tricks. Schindler, Steven, illus. LC 92-47501. (ps-6). 1994. 14.00 (*0-06-023025-8*) HarpC Child Bks.
Wyler, Rose & Elting, Mary. Math Fun: Test Your Luck. LC 91-3919. (Illus.). 64p. (gr. 4-7). 1992. lib. bdg. 10.98 (*0-671-74311-2*, J Messner); pap. 5.95 (*0-671-74312-0*, J Messner) S&S Trade.
—Math Fun: With Pocket Calculator. LC 91-16265. (Illus.). 64p. (gr. 4-7). 1992. lib. bdg. 10.98 (*0-671-74308-2*, J Messner); lib. bdg. 5.95 (*0-671-74309-0*, J Messner) S&S Trade.
Wyler, Rose, jt. auth. see Ames, Gerald.
Wyles, Ames. Spooky Tricks. Date not set. PLB 13.89 (*0-06-023026-6*, Festival, Festival) HarpC Child Bks.
Wylie, D., jt. auth. see Wylie, J.
Wylie, David, jt. auth. see Wylie, Joanne.
Wylie, J. & Wylie, D. A Big Fish Story Big Book. (Illus.). 32p. (ps-2). 1987. PLB 30.60 (*0-516-49502-X*) Childrens.
Wylie, Joanne. Un Cuento Curioso de Colores. Kratky, Lada, tr. from ENG. Wylie, David, illus. LC 83-7448. (SPA.). 32p. (ps-2). 1984. PLB 15.00 (*0-516-32983-9*); pap. 3.95 (*0-516-52983-8*) Childrens.
—Un Cuento de Peces y Sus Formas (A Fishy Shape Story) Kratky, Lada, tr. Wylie, David, illus. LC 85-23264. (SPA.). 32p. (ps-2). 1986. PLB 15.00 (*0-516-32985-5*); pap. 3.95 (*0-516-52985-4*) Childrens.
—Un Cuento de un Pez Grande (A Big Fish Story) Kratky, Lada, tr. from ENG. Wylie, David, illus. LC 83-7449. (SPA.). 32p. (ps-2). 1984. PLB 15.00 (*0-516-32982-0*); pap. 3.95 (*0-516-52982-X*) Childrens.
—Sabes Donde Esta Tu Monstruo Esta Noche? Kratky, Lada, tr. Wylie, David, illus. LC 85-31423. (SPA.). 32p. (ps-2). 1986. PLB 15.00 (*0-516-34491-9*); pap. 3.95 (*0-516-54491-8*) Childrens.
Wylie, Joanne & Wylie, David. A Big Fish Story. LC 83-7449. (Illus.). 32p. (ps-2). 1983. pap. 3.95 (*0-516-42982-5*) Childrens.
—Cuantos Monstruos?: Un Cuento de Numeros (How Many Monsters? Learning about Counting) LC 85-15136. (SPA., Illus.). 32p. (ps-2). 1988. PLB 15.00 (*0-516-34494-3*); pap. 3.95 (*0-516-54494-2*) Childrens.

—Un Cuento de Peces, Mas o Menos (A More or Less Fish Story) LC 83-25223. (SPA., Illus.). 32p. (ps-2). 1987. PLB 15.00 (*0-516-32984-7*); pap. 3.95 (*0-516-52984-6*) Childrens.
—Un Cuento Gracioso de Peces (A Funny Fish Story) LC 83-24058. (ENG & SPA., Illus.). 32p. (ps-2). 1989. PLB 15.00 (*0-516-32986-3*); pap. 3.95 (*0-516-52986-2*) Childrens.
—A Fishy Alphabet Story. LC 83-7510. (Illus.). 32p. (ps-2). 1983. pap. 3.95 (*0-516-42981-7*) Childrens.
—A Fishy Color Story. LC 83-7448. (Illus.). 32p. (ps-2). 1983. pap. 3.95 (*0-516-42983-3*) Childrens.
—A Fishy Color Story Big Book. (Illus.). 32p. (ps-2). 1989. PLB 30.60 (*0-516-49511-9*) Childrens.
—A Fishy Shape Story. Wylie, David, illus. LC 83-25222. 32p. (ps-2). 1984. pap. 3.95 (*0-516-42985-X*) Childrens.
—A Funny Fish Story. Wylie, David, illus. LC 83-24058. 32p. (ps-2). 1984. pap. 3.95 (*0-516-42986-8*) Childrens.
—The Gumdrop Monster: Learning about Colors. LC 84-12133. (Illus.). 32p. (ps-2). 1984. pap. 3.95 (*0-516-44492-1*) Childrens.
—Has Abrazado Hoy a Tu Monstruo? Un Cuento de los Modales: Have You Hugged Your Monster Today? Learning about Manners. LC 86-21624. (Illus.). 32p. (ps-2). 1986. PLB 15.00 (*0-516-34493-5*); pap. 3.95 (*0-516-54493-4*) Childrens.
—Little Monster: Learning about Size. LC 85-14988. (Illus.). 32p. (ps-2). 1985. pap. 3.95 (*0-516-44495-6*) Childrens.
—A More or Less Fish Story. Wylie, David, illus. LC 83-25223. 32p. (ps-2). 1984. pap. 3.95 (*0-516-42984-1*) Childrens.
—El Pequeno Monstruo. LC 85-14988. (SPA., Illus.). 32p. (ps-2). 1988. PLB 15.00 (*0-516-34495-1*); pap. 3.95 (*0-516-54495-0*) Childrens.
—So You Think You Saw a Monster? Learning about Make-Believe. LC 85-16594. (Illus.). 32p. (ps-2). 1985. pap. 3.95 (*0-516-44496-4*) Childrens.
—Y Tu Crees Que Viste un Monstruo? Un Cuento de Fantasia: So You Think You Saw a Monster? A Make Believe Story. LC 86-21604. (Illus.). 32p. (ps-2). 1986. pap. 3.95 (*0-516-54496-9*) Childrens.
Wyllie, Stephen. Dinner with Fox. LC 89-25899. (Illus.). 24p. (ps-3). 1990. 12.95 (*0-8037-0796-7*) Dial Bks Young.
—Ghost Train: A Spooky Hologram Book. Lee, Brian, illus. LC 91-15719. 24p. (gr. k). 1992. 18.00 (*0-8037-1163-8*) Dial Bks Young.
—The Red Dragon: A 3-D Picture Book. Allen, Jonathan, illus. LC 92-26670. 20p. (ps-2). 1993. 13.99 (*0-8037-1452-1*) Dial Bks Young.
—The Wizards' Revenge. Heller, Julek, illus. LC 93-14494. Date not set. write for info. (*0-8037-1690-7*) Dial Bks Young.
Wyman, Andrea. Red Sky at Morning. LC 91-55029. 240p. (gr. 3-7). 1991. 13.95 (*0-8234-0903-1*) Holiday.
Wyman, Carolyn. Ella Fitzgerald: Jazz Singer Supreme. (Illus.). 144p. (gr. 9-12). 1993. PLB 14.40 (*0-531-13031-2*) Watts.
—Ella Fitzgerald: Jazz Singer Supreme. (Illus.). 144p. (gr. 7-12). 1993. pap. 6.95 (*0-531-15679-6*) Watts.
Wyndham, Robert. Chinese Mother Goose Rhymes. Young, Ed, illus. 48p. (ps-k). 1989. (Sandcastle Bks); pap. 5.95 (*0-399-21718-5*) Putnam Pub Group.
Wynn, Mychal. Don't Quit: Inspirational Poetry. Luckie, Anita, ed. (gr. 9 up). 1990. pap. 9.95 (*1-880463-28-8*) Rising Sun.
Wynne, Carrie E. That Looks Like a Nice House. LC 87-82078. (Illus.). 42p. (Orig.). (gr. 8). 1987. pap. 5.95 (*0-9613205-3-2*) Launch Pr.
Wynne, Diana, jt. auth. see Carlson, Anna L.
Wynne, Patricia, jt. auth. see Silver, Donald.
Wynne, Patricia, illus. The Animal ABC. LC 77-74470. 14p. (ps-k). 1977. bds. 3.95 (*0-394-83589-1*) Random Bks Yng Read.
Wynnejones, Pat. Village Tales, 4 bks. (Illus.). (ps-6). 1991. Set, 24p. ea. 14.95 (*0-7459-1830-1*) Lion USA.
Wynne-Jones, Tim. Builder of the Moon. Wallace, Ian, illus. LC 88-12703. (ps-3). 1989. SBE 14.95 (*0-689-50472-1*, M K McElderry) Macmillan Child Grp.
—Zoom at Sea. Beddows, Eric, illus. LC 92-14738. 32p. (ps-2). 1993. 15.00 (*0-06-021448-1*); PLB 14.89 (*0-06-021449-X*) HarpC Child Bks.
—Zoom Away. Beddows, Eric, illus. LC 92-41171. 32p. (ps-2). 1993. 15.00 (*0-06-022962-4*); PLB 14.89 (*0-06-022963-2*) HarpC.
Wynot, Jillian. The Mother's Day Sandwich. Chambliss, Maxie, illus. LC 89-35649. 32p. (ps-2). 1990. 14.95 (*0-531-05857-3*); PLB 14.99 (*0-531-08457-4*) Orchard Bks Watts.
Wyss, J. D. The Swiss Family Robinson. (gr. 4-6). 1986. pap. 2.95 (*0-14-035044-6*, Puffin) Puffin Bks.
Wyss, Johann. Swiss Family Robinson. (gr. 5 up). 1964. pap. 1.95 (*0-8049-0013-2*, CL-13) Airmont.
—Swiss Family Robinson. Ward, Lynd & Gregori, Lee, illus. (gr. 4-6). 1949. 14.95 (*0-448-06022-1*, G&D) Putnam Pub Group.
—The Swiss Family Robinson. James, Raymond, ed. Beier, Ellen, illus. LC 89-33888. 48p. (gr. 3-6). 1990. lib. bdg. 12.89 (*0-8167-1875-X*); pap. text ed. 3.95 (*0-8167-1876-8*) Troll Assocs.
—Swiss Family Robinson. 1993. 12.99 (*0-517-06022-1*) Outlet Bk Co.
Wyss, Johann D. The Swiss Family Robinson. 1990. pap. 2.95 (*0-451-52481-0*, Sig Classics) NAL-Dutton.

—Swiss Family Robinson. (gr. 4-7). 1991. pap. 3.25 *(0-590-44014-4)* Scholastic Inc.

—Swiss Family Robinson. (gr. 4-7). 1991. pap. 3.50 *(0-440-40430-4,* Pub. by Yearling Classics) Dell.

Wyss, Thelma H. Here at the Scenic-Vu Motel. LC 87-45308. 160p. (gr. 7 up). 1989. pap. 3.95 *(0-06-447001-6,* Trophy) HarpC Child Bks.

—A Stranger Here. LC 92-15307. 144p. (gr. 7 up). 1993. 14.00 *(0-06-021438-4);* PLB 13.89 *(0-06-021439-2)* HarpC Child Bks.

X

Xiong, Blia & Spagnoli, Cathy, eds. Nine-in-One Grr! Grr! LC 89-9891. (Illus.). 32p. (ps-5). 1989. 13.95 *(0-89239-048-4)* Childrens Book Pr.

Xiquan Publishing House Staff, ed. see Smarandache, Florentin.

Xydes, Georgia. Alexander Mackenzie & the Explorers of Canada. (Illus.). 112p. (gr. 5 up). 1992. lib. bdg. 18.95 *(0-7910-1314-6)* Chelsea Hse.

Y

Yaccarino, Dan. Big Brother Mike. Yaccarino, Dan, illus. LC 92-72017. 32p. (ps-2). 1993. 13.95 *(1-56282-329-9);* PLB 13.89 *(1-56282-330-2)* Hyprn Child.

—The House of Fun! 8p. (Orig.). (gr. 4-7). 1993. pap. 12. 95 *(1-55550-885-5)* Universe.

Yaconelli, Mike, jt. auth. see Rice, Wayne.

Yaconelli, Mike & Lynn, David, eds. Tension Getters. 128p. (Orig.). (gr. 8-12). 1985. pap. 9.99 *(0-310-45241-4,* 11371P) Zondervan.

Yaconelli, Mike, jt. ed. see Rice, Wayne.

Yacowitz, Caryn. The Jade Stone: A Chinese Folktale. Chen, Ju-Hong, illus. LC 91-17934. 32p. (ps-3). 1992. reinforced bdg. 14.95 *(0-8234-0919-8)* Holiday.

Yaffe, Rochel. Rambam: The Story of Rabbi Moshe Ben Maimon. Nodel, Norman, illus. 220p. (gr. 8 up). 1992. 10.95 *(0-922613-14-1);* pap. 8.95 *(0-922613-15-X)* Hachai Pubns.

Yagawa, Sumiko. The Crane Wife. Paterson, Katherine, tr. from JPN. Akaba, Suekichi, illus. LC 80-29278. 32p. (ps-3). 1981. pap. 4.95 *(0-685-03413-5,* Mulberry Bks) Morrow Jr Bks.

—Crane Wife. Paterson, Katherine, tr. from JPN. LC 80-29278. (Illus.). (ps-3). 1987. 4.95 *(0-688-07048-5,* Mulberry) Morrow.

—The Crane Wife. (ps-3). 1992. 17.50 *(0-8446-6589-4)* Peter Smith.

Yagelski, Robert. The Day the Lifting Bridge Stuck. Harris, Jennifer, illus. LC 90-33984. 32p. (ps-2). 1992. RSBE 14.95 *(0-02-793595-7,* Bradbury Pr) Macmillan Child Grp.

Yagyu, Genichiro. The Holes in Your Nose. Stinchecum, Amanda M., tr. from JPN. (Illus.). 32p. (ps). 1994. 11. 95 *(0-916291-50-2,* Cranky Nell Pr) Kane-Miller Bk.

Yahara, Mikio. Temple at Sengakigi. LC 93-77220. (gr. 1-3). 1993. spiral bdg. 8.95 *(1-883251-01-X)* Hgh Desert Pr.

Yajima, Minoru. The Firefly. Pohl, Kathy, ed. LC 85-28193. (Illus.). 32p. (gr. 3-7). 1986. pap. text ed. 17.96 *(0-8172-2535-8)* Raintree Steck-V.

Yakoyama, Masami. Children of the World: Spain. LC 86-42808. (Illus.). 64p. (gr. 5-6). 1987. PLB 19.93 *(1-55532-163-1)* Gareth Stevens Inc.

Yamaguchi, Marianne. The Sea of Gold & Other Tales from Japan. LC 87-72797. (Illus.). 144p. (gr. 7-12). 1988. pap. 7.95 *(0-88739-056-0)* Creative Arts Bk.

Yamamoto, Neil. Super Silly School Jokes & Riddles. (gr. 4-7). 1991. pap. 1.95 *(0-8125-9375-8)* Tor Bks.

Yamashita, Keiko. Paws, Wings, & Hooves: Mammals on the Move. Sekido, Isamu, photos by. LC 92-18506. (Illus.). 1993. 17.50 *(0-8225-2901-7)* Lerner Pubns.

Yamashita, Susan. The Menehune & the Nene. O'Connor, Barbara, illus. LC 84-3290. (gr. 3-6). 1984. 7.95 *(0-916630-42-0)* Pr Pacifica.

Yamate, Sandra S. Ashok by Any Other Name. (Illus.). 36p. (gr. k-4). 1992. 12.95 *(1-879965-01-1)* Polychrome Pub.

Yanagi, Akinobu. Children of the World: New Zealand. LC 86-42801. (Illus.). 64p. (gr. 5-6). 1987. PLB 19.93 *(1-55532-162-3)* Gareth Stevens Inc.

Yancey, Diane. Desperadoes & Dynamite: Train Robbery in the United States. LC 91-12149. (Illus.). 64p. (gr. 5-8). 1991. PLB 12.90 *(0-531-20038-8)* Watts.

—The Hunt for Hidden Killers: Ten Cases of Medical Mystery. LC 93-16638. (Illus.). 128p. (gr. 7 up). 1994. PLB 15.90 *(1-56294-389-8)* Millbrook Pr.

Yanda, Bill. Rads, Ergs, & Cheeseburgers: The Kid's Guide to Energy & the Environment. (Illus.). 108p. (Orig.). (gr. 3 up). 1991. pap. 12.95 *(0-945465-75-0)* John Muir.

Yanes, Audrey. Shaking Loose: Poetry. 2nd ed. 24p. 1991. pap. 6.95 *(0-938911-06-6)* Indiv Educ Syst.

Yanez, Juan, tr. see Bryan, Betsy & Cohen, Judith.

Yanez, Juan, tr. see Cohen, Judith L.

Yanez, Juan, tr. see Cohen, Judith L. & Siegel, Margot.

Yanez, Juan, tr. see Cohen, Judith L. & Thompson, Valerie.

Yanez, Juan, tr. see Gabriel, Diane & Cohen, Judith.

Yang, Jwing-Ming. YMAA Children's Book Series: Volume One, Stories One & Two. 32p. (Orig.). (gr. 4 up). 1989. pap. 3.95 *(0-940871-09-2)* Yangs Martial Arts.

Yannis, Alex. Soccer Basics. Gow, Bill, illus. Chinaglia, George, intro. by. (Illus.). 48p. (gr. 3-7). 1982. 9.95 *(0-13-815290-X)* P-H.

Yapp, Malcolm. The Ancient Near East. Killingray, Margaret, et al, eds. (Illus.). 32p. (gr. 6-11). 1980. pap. text ed. 3.45 *(0-89908-000-6)* Greenhaven.

—British Raj & Indian Nationalism. Killingray, Margaret & O'Connor, Edmund, eds. (Illus.). 32p. (gr. 6-11). 1980. pap. text ed. 3.45 *(0-89908-203-3)* Greenhaven.

—Chingis Khan & the Mongol Empire. Killingray, Margaret & O'Connor, Edmund, eds. (Illus.). 32p. (gr. 6-11). 1980. pap. text ed. 3.45 *(0-89908-005-7)* Greenhaven.

—Gandhi. Killingray, Margaret & O'Connor, Edmund, eds. (Illus.). 32p. (gr. 6-11). 1980. lib. bdg. 6.95 *(0-89908-128-2);* pap. text ed. 3.45 *(0-89908-103-7)* Greenhaven.

—The Growth of the State. Killingray, Margaret & O'Connor, Edmund, eds. (Illus.). 32p. (gr. 6-11). 1980. pap. text ed. 3.45 *(0-89908-204-1)* Greenhaven.

—Ibn Sina & the Muslim World. Killingray, Margaret & O'Connor, Edmund, eds. (Illus.). 32p. (gr. 6-11). 1980. pap. text ed. 3.45 *(0-89908-012-X)* Greenhaven.

—Nationalism. Killingray, Margaret & O'Connor, Edmund, eds. (Illus.). 32p. (gr. 6-11). 1980. pap. text ed. 3.45 *(0-89908-202-5)* Greenhaven.

Yapp, Malcolm, ed. see Addison, John, et al.

Yapp, Malcolm, ed. see Duckworth, John, et al.

Yapp, Malcolm, ed. see Harrison, John, et al.

Yapp, Malcolm, ed. see Heater, Derek & Owen, Gwyneth.

Yapp, Malcolm, ed. see Killingray, David.

Yapp, Malcolm, ed. see Killingray, Margaret.

Yapp, Malcolm, ed. see O'Connor, Edmund.

Yapp, Malcolm, ed. see Painter, Desmond.

Yapp, Malcolm, ed. see Painter, Desmond & Shepard, John.

Yapp, Malcolm, ed. see Pearson, Eileen.

Yapp, Malcolm, ed. see Tames, Richard.

Yapp, Malcolm, jt. auth. see Killingray, David.

Yapp, Malcolm, jt. auth. see Read, James.

Yapp, Malcolm, et al, eds. see Addison, John, et al.

Yapp, Malcolm, et al, eds. see Amey, Peter.

Yapp, Malcolm, et al, eds. see Amey, Peter, et al.

Yapp, Malcolm, et al, eds. see Amey, Peter.

Yapp, Malcolm, et al, eds. see Byres, Terence.

Yapp, Malcolm, et al, eds. see Clifford, Alan.

Yapp, Malcolm, et al, eds. see Cripwell, Kenneth.

Yapp, Malcolm, et al, eds. see Garrett, Sean.

Yapp, Malcolm, et al, eds. see Guyatt, John.

Yapp, Malcolm, et al, eds. see Kanitkar, Helen & Kanitkar, Hemant.

Yapp, Malcolm, et al, eds. see Killingray, David.

Yapp, Malcolm, et al, eds. see Killingray, David, et al.

Yapp, Malcolm, et al, eds. see Killingray, David.

Yapp, Malcolm, et al, eds. see Killingray, Margaret.

Yapp, Malcolm, et al, eds. see Knox, Diana.

Yapp, Malcolm, et al, eds. see Nicholson, Alasdair.

Yapp, Malcolm, et al, eds. see O'Connor, Edmund.

Yapp, Malcolm, et al, eds. see Painter, Desmond.

Yapp, Malcolm, et al, eds. see Tames, Richard.

Yapp, Malcolm, et al, eds. see Townson, Duncan.

Yapp, Malcolm, et al, eds. see Weston, Anthony.

Yapp, Malcolm, et al, eds. see Wrangham, Elizabeth.

Yapp, Malcolm, et al, eds. see Wrangham, Elizabeth, et al.

Yapp, Martin, ed. see Booth, Martin, et al.

Yarber, William L. STD & HIV: A Guide for Today's Young Adults. (Illus.). 106p. (Orig.). 1992. pap. text ed. 6.95 *(0-88314-533-2)* AAHPERD.

Yarber, Yvonne & Choy, Carol E. The Athabaskans: People of the Boreal Forest. Dickey, Terry P. & Smetzer, Mary B., eds. 39p. (Orig.). (gr. 7-12). 1983. tchr's. guide 4.00 *(0-931163-10-2);* pap. 9.95 *(0-931163-09-9)* U Alaska Museum.

Yarber, Yvonne Y., jt. auth. see Madison, Curt.

Yarbrough, Camille. Cornrows. Byard, Carole, illus. LC 78-24010. 48p. (Orig.). (gr. 2-6). 1981. (Coward); pap. 6.95 *(0-698-20529-4,* Coward) Putnam Pub Group.

—Cornrows. Byard, Carole, illus. (gr. 2-6). 1992. pap. 6.95 *(0-698-20709-2,* Sandcastle Bks) Putnam Pub Group.

—The Shimmershine Queens. 128p. (gr. 5-8). 1989. 14.95 *(0-399-21465-8,* Putnam) Putnam Pub Group.

Yarbrough, Jane, jt. auth. see Lewis, Judy.

Yardley, Joanna. The Red Ball. Yolen, Jane, ed. Yardley, Joanna, illus. 32p. (ps-3). 1991. 14.95 *(0-15-200894-2,* J Yolen Bks) HarBrace.

Yardley, Thompson. Buy Now, Pay Later! Smart Shopping Counts. LC 91-22497. (Illus.). 40p. (gr. 2-6). 1992. PLB 12.90 *(1-56294-149-6)* Millbrook Pr.

—Down the Drain: Explore Your Plumbing. LC 91-29900. (Illus.). 40p. (gr. 2-6). 1991. PLB 12.90 *(1-878841-28-9)* Millbrook Pr.

—Make a Splash! Care about the Ocean. LC 91-22963. (Illus.). 40p. (gr. 2-6). 1992. PLB 12.90 *(1-56294-147-X)* Millbrook Pr.

Yarmolinsky, Avraham, ed. see Babel, Issac.

Yashima, Mitsu & Yashima, Taro. Momo's Kitten. Yashima, Taro, illus. (gr. k-2). 1977. pap. 4.99 *(0-14-050200-9,* Puffin) Puffin Bks.

Yashima, Taro. Crow Boy. (Illus.). (gr. k-3). 1976. pap. 3.99 *(0-14-050172-X,* Puffin) Puffin Bks.

—Crow Boy. Yashima, T., illus. (gr. k-3). 1955. pap. 14. 99 *(0-670-24931-9)* Viking Child Bks.

—One-Inch Fellow. LC 93-10824. (ps-6). 1995. write for info. *(0-15-276897-1,* Browndeer Pr) HarBrace.

—Umbrella. Yashima, Taro, illus. (ps-1). 1977. pap. 3.99 *(0-14-050240-8,* Puffin) Puffin Bks.

—Umbrella. Yashima, T., illus. (ps-1). 1958. pap. 15.99 *(0-670-73858-1)* Viking Child Bks.

Yashima, Taro, jt. auth. see Yashima, Mitsu.

Yates, Alma J. Ghosts in the Baker Mine. LC 91-45230. 197p. (Orig.). (gr. 3-7). 1992. pap. 4.95 *(0-87579-581-1)* Deseret Bk.

—No More Strangers, Please! (gr. 7-12). 1994. write for info. *(0-87579-828-4)* Deseret Bk.

Yates, Brock, jt. auth. see Garlits, Don.

Yates, Diana. Chief Joseph: Thunder Rolling Down from the Mountains. (Illus.). 141p. (gr. 4 up). 1992. pap. 10. 95 *(0-9623380-8-7)* Ward Hill Pr.

—Chief Joseph: Thunder Rolling Down from the Mountains. (Illus.). 141p. (gr. 4 up). 1992. PLB 14.95 *(0-9623380-9-5)* Ward Hill Pr.

Yates, Elizabeth. Amos Fortune, Free Man. Unwin, Nora S., illus. (gr. 7 up). 1967. 15.00 *(0-525-25570-2,* DCB) Dutton Child Bks.

—Amos Fortune, Free Man. Unwin, Nora S., illus. 192p. (gr. 3-7). 1989. pap. 3.99 *(0-14-034158-7,* Puffin) Puffin Bks.

—Carolina's Courage. 131p. (Orig.). (gr. 2-4). 1989. pap. 4.95 *(0-89084-482-8)* Bob Jones Univ Pr.

—Hue & Cry. 182p. (gr. 7-12). 1991. pap. 4.95 *(0-89084-536-0)* Bob Jones Univ Pr.

—Journeyman. rev. ed. (Illus.). 161p. (gr. 9 up). 1990. pap. 4.95 *(0-89084-535-2)* Bob Jones Univ Pr.

—The Lighted Heart. Unwin, Nora S., illus. (gr. 7 up). 1974. pap. 8.95 *(0-87233-027-3)* Bauhan.

—Mountain Born. Unwin, Nora S., illus. LC 92-40545. 128p. (gr. 3-7). 1993. pap. 6.95 *(0-8027-7402-4)* Walker & Co.

—Sound Friendships: The Story of Willa & Her Hearing Dog. Leaman, Christine, ed. Roberts, John, illus. O'Brien, Sheila, frwd. by. (Illus.). 113p. (Orig.). (gr. 7-12). 1992. pap. 4.95 *(0-89084-650-2)* Bob Jones Univ Pr.

Yates, Janelle. Woody Guthrie. (Illus.). 128p. (gr. 4 up). 1993. pap. 10.95 *(0-9623380-5-2)* Ward Hill Pr.

—Woody Guthrie. (Illus.). 128p. (gr. 4 up). 1993. PLB 14.95 *(0-9623380-0-1)* Ward Hill Pr.

—Zora Neale Hurston: A Storyteller's Life. Adams, David, illus. 104p. (gr. 4 up). 1991. pap. 9.95 *(0-9623380-7-9)* Ward Hill Pr.

—Zora Neale Hurston: A Storyteller's Life. enl. ed. Adams, David, illus. 98p. (gr. 4-10). 1993. PLB 14.95 *(0-9623380-3-6);* pap. 9.95 *(0-9623380-1-X)* Ward Hill Pr.

Yates, Madeleine. It's School Picture Day. (ps-3). 1993. pap. 2.99 *(0-440-40781-8)* Dell.

Yates, Richard. Our Evergreen State Government: State & Local Government in Washington. Smith-Danell, Paula, illus. 190p. 1989. 13.95 *(0-911927-10-7)* Info Oregon.

Yawger, Kathleen S. Bible Story Crafts. 96p. (ps-5). 1991. 10.95 *(0-86653-637-X,* SS1895, Shining Star Pubns) Good Apple.

Yazaki, Setsuo. Little Bunny's Christmas Present. Ooka, D. T., tr. from JPN. Kuroi, Ken, illus. 32p. (ps-8). 1983. 11.95 *(0-89346-225-X)* Heian Intl.

Yazzie, Earl. More Monster Stories from the Navajo Country, Vol. 3. (Illus.). 43p. (Orig.). (gr. k-5). 1989. pap. 6.95 *(0-940113-12-0)* Sierra Oaks Pub. Postponed.

Yeager, David C. Instant Novels. 48p. (gr. 4-6). 1986. 5.95 *(0-88160-143-8,* LW261) Learning Wks.

Yeager, Doug, jt. auth. see Yeager, Nancy.

Yeager, Nancy & Yeager, Doug. A Tiny Little Story. 32p. (ps-k). 1993. pap. write for info. *(1-879911-01-9)* Rams Horn Bks.

—Where's Billy? 32p. (ps-k). 1991. pap. 4.95 *(1-879911-00-0)* Rams Horn Bks.

Yeatman, Linda. Buttons. Casson, Hugh, illus. 64p. (gr. 2-5). 1988. pap. 2.95 *(0-8120-3956-4)* Barron.

Yeatman, Linda, ed. A Child's Book of Prayers. Williamson, Tracey, illus. LC 91-37706. 93p. 1992. 19. 95 *(1-55670-251-5)* Stewart Tabori & Chang.

Yeats, William Butler. Fairy Tales of Ireland. Philip, Neil, selected by. Lynch, P. J., illus. Philip, Neil & Philip, Neilintro. by. (Illus.). 1990. 16.95 *(0-385-30249-5)* Delacorte.

Yedwab, Paul M. The Alef-Bet of Blessing. (Illus.). 80p. (Orig.). (gr. k-3). 1989. pap. text ed. 6.00x *(0-8074-0436-5,* 101094) 5.00 *(0-8074-0461-6,* 208029) UAHC.

Yee, Chiang. Men of the Burma Road. (Illus.). (gr. 4-6). 8.50 *(0-685-20604-1)* Transatl Arts.

Yee, Patrick. Baby Bear. (Illus.). 12p. (ps). 1994. bds. 3.99 *(0-670-85288-0)* Viking Child Bks.

—Baby Lion. (Illus.). 12p. (ps). 1994. bds. 3.99 *(0-670-85289-9)* Viking Child Bks.

—Baby Monkey. (Illus.). 12p. (ps). 1994. bds. 3.99 *(0-670-85290-2)* Viking Child Bks.

—Baby Penguin. (Illus.). 12p. (ps). 1994. bds. 3.99 *(0-670-85291-0)* Viking Child Bks.

—Little Buddy Goes Shopping. LC 92-16432. (ps). 1993. 10.95 *(0-670-84804-2)* Viking Child Bks.

—Winter Rabbit. (Illus.). 32p. (ps-1). 1994. 13.99 *(0-670-85383-6)* Viking Child Bks.

Yee, Paul. Roses Sing on New Snow: A Delicious Tale. Chan, Harvey, illus. LC 91-755. 32p. (ps-3). 1992. RSBE 13.95 (*0-02-793622-8*, Macmillan Child Bk) Macmillan Child Grp.
—Tales from Gold Mountain: Stories of the Chinese in the New World. Ng, Simon, illus. LC 89-12643. 64p. (ps up). 1990. RSBE 15.95 (*0-02-793621-X*, Macmillan Child Bk) Macmillan Child Grp.
Yee, Wong H. Big Black Bear. Yee, Wong H., illus. LC 92-40862. 1993. 14.95 (*0-395-66359-8*) HM.
—Eek! There's a Mouse in the House. LC 91-41823. (Illus.). 32p. (ps). 1992. 13.45 (*0-395-62303-0*) HM.
Yektai, Niki. Bears in Pairs. De Groat, Diane, illus. LC 86-18828. 32p. (ps-k). 1987. RSBE 14.95 (*0-02-793691-0*, Bradbury Pr) Macmillan Child Grp.
—Bears in Pairs. DeGroat, Diane, illus. LC 91-229. 32p. (ps-k). 1991. pap. 3.95 (*0-689-71500-5*, Aladdin) Macmillan Child Grp.
—Crazy Clothes. Stevenson, Sucie, illus. LC 93-19738. 32p. (gr. k-2). 1994. pap. 4.95 (*0-689-71781-4*, Aladdin) Macmillan Child Grp.
—Hi Bears, Bye Bears. DeGroat, Diane, illus. LC 89-37554. 32p. (ps-1). 1990. 12.95 (*0-531-05858-1*); PLB 12.99 (*0-531-08458-2*) Orchard Bks Watts.
—The Secret Room. LC 92-6720. 192p. (gr. 4-7). 1992. 14.95 (*0-531-05456-X*); PLB 14.99 (*0-531-08606-2*) Orchard Bks Watts.
—What's Missing. Ryan, Susannah, illus. LC 87-784. 32p. (ps-1). 1989. (Clarion Bks); pap. 4.95 (*0-317-04349-8*, Clarion Bks) HM.
—What's Silly? Ryan, Suzannah, illus. LC 88-22883. 32p. (gr. 2-4). 1989. 13.95 (*0-89919-746-9*, Clarion Bks) HM.
Yemm, Marta. Years to Grow. LC 81-68369. (Illus.). 600p. (Orig.). (ps-k). 1981. pap. 31.95 (*0-513-01724-0*) Denison.
Yen, Clara. Why Rat Comes First: The Story of the Chinese Zodiac. LC 90-26536. (Illus.). 32p. (gr. 3-4). 1991. PLB 21.34 (*0-89239-072-7*) Childrens Book Pr.
Yenawine, Philip. Colors. (Illus.). (gr. 2-5). 1991. 14.00 (*0-385-30254-1*); PLB 14.99 (*0-385-30314-9*) Delacorte.
—Lines. (Illus.). (gr. 2-5). 1991. 14.00 (*0-385-30253-3*); PLB 14.99 (*0-385-30313-0*) Delacorte.
—People. LC 92-11203. 1993. pap. 14.95 (*0-385-30901-5*) Dell.
—Places. LC 92-11202. 1993. 14.95 (*0-385-30900-7*) Dell.
—Shapes. (Illus.). (gr. 2-5). 1991. 14.00 (*0-385-30255-X*); PLB 14.99 (*0-385-30315-7*) Delacorte.
—Stories. (Illus.). (gr. 2-5). 1991. 14.00 (*0-385-30256-8*); PLB 14.99 (*0-385-30316-5*) Delacorte.
Yenne, Bill, retold by. Joseph & the Coat of Many Colors. LC 93-37474. (Illus.). 1994. write for info. (*0-7852-8330-7*); pap. write for info. (*0-7852-8326-9*) Nelson.
—Joshua & the Battle of Jericho. LC 93-35873. (gr. 3 up). 1994. write for info. (*0-7852-8331-5*); pap. write for info. (*0-7852-8327-7*) Nelson.
—The Story of Easter. LC 93-37475. (Illus.). 1994. write for info. (*0-7852-8332-3*); pap. write for info. (*0-7852-8328-5*) Nelson.
—The Story of Moses. LC 93-37476. 1994. write for info. (*0-7852-8329-3*); pap. write for info. (*0-7852-8325-0*) Nelson.
Yeo. The Girl in the Window. 1993. pap. 2.75 (*0-590-43153-6*) Scholastic Inc.
—The Stranger at Winifield House. 1993. pap. 2.75 (*0-590-43912-X*) Scholastic Inc.
Yeoman, John. Old Mother Hubbard's Dog Dresses Up. Blake, Quentin, illus. LC 89-27026. 24p. (ps-3). 1990. 6.70 (*0-395-53358-9*) HM.
—Old Mother Hubbard's Dog Learns to Play. Blake, Quentin, illus. LC 89-39863. 24p. (ps-3). 1990. 6.95 (*0-395-53360-0*) HM.
—Old Mother Hubbard's Dog Needs a Doctor. Blake, Quentin, illus. LC 89-24448. 24p. (ps-3). 1990. 6.70 (*0-395-53359-7*) HM.
—Old Mother Hubbard's Dog Takes up Sport. Blake, Quentin, illus. LC 89-39942. 24p. (ps-3). 1990. 6.70 (*0-395-53361-9*) HM.
—The Singing Tortoise: And Other Animal Folktales. Blake, Quentin, illus. LC 93-31208. 96p. (gr. 1 up). 1994. 18.00 (*0-688-13366-5*, Tambourine Bks) Morrow.
Yeomans, Thomas. For Every Child a Star: A Christmas Story. De Paola, Tomie, illus. LC 84-499. 32p. (ps-3). 1986. reinforced bdg. 14.95 (*0-8234-0526-5*) Holiday.
Yep, Laurence. American Dragons: Twenty-Five Asian American Voices. LC 92-28489. 256p. (gr. 7 up). 1993. 15.00 (*0-06-021494-5*); PLB 14.89 (*0-06-021495-3*) HarpC Child Bks.
—Butterfly Boy. (ps-3). 1993. 15.00 (*0-374-31003-3*) FS&G.
—Child of the Owl. 224p. (gr. 7 up). 1978. pap. 3.25 (*0-440-91230-X*, LFL) Dell.
—Child of the Owl. LC 76-24314. 224p. (gr. 7 up). 1977. PLB 12.89 (*0-06-026743-7*) HarpC Child Bks.
—Child of the Owl. LC 76-24314. 224p. (gr. 7 up). 1990. pap. 3.95 (*0-06-440336-X*, Trophy) HarpC Child Bks.
—The Curse of the Squirrel. Zimmer, Dirk, illus. LC 87-4612. 64p. (gr. 2-4). 1987. lib. bdg. 6.99 (*0-394-98200-2*); pap. 1.95 (*0-394-88200-8*, Random Juv) Random Bks Yng Read.
—Dragon Cauldron. LC 90-39584. (Illus.). 320p. (gr. 7 up). 1991. PLB 16.89 (*0-06-026754-2*) HarpC Child Bks.

—Dragon Cauldron. LC 90-39584. 320p. (gr. 7 up). 1994. pap. 4.95 (*0-06-440398-X*, Trophy) HarpC Child Bks.
—Dragon of the Lost Sea. LC 81-48644. 224p. (gr. 6 up). 1988. pap. 3.95 (*0-06-440227-4*, Trophy) HarpC Child Bks.
—Dragon Steel. LC 84-48338. 288p. (gr. 7 up). 1985. PLB 12.89 (*0-06-026751-8*) HarpC Child Bks.
—Dragon Steel. LC 84-48338. 288p. (gr. 7 up). 1993. pap. 4.95 (*0-06-440486-2*, Trophy) HarpC Child Bks.
—Dragon War. LC 91-28921. 320p. (gr. 7 up). 1992. 15.00 (*0-06-020302-1*); PLB 14.89 (*0-06-020303-X*) HarpC Child Bks.
—Dragon's Gate. LC 92-43649. 288p. (gr. 7 up). 1993. 15.00 (*0-06-022971-3*); PLB 14.89 (*0-06-022972-1*) HarpC Child Bks.
—Dragonwings. LC 74-2625. 256p. (gr. 7 up). 1975. PLB 14.89 (*0-06-026738-0*) HarpC Child Bks.
—Dragonwings. LC 74-2625. 256p. (gr. 6 up). 1977. pap. 3.95 (*0-06-440085-9*, Trophy) HarpC Child Bks.

—Dragonwings. large type ed. 282p. 1990. Repr. of 1975 ed. lib. bdg. 15.95 (*1-55736-168-1*, Crnrstn Bks) BDD LT Grp.
A Newbery Honor Book, 1976. "Moon Shadow's father works in the family laundry, but he is also a maker of fantastic kites & his dream is to build & fly an airplane. The pursuit of this dream unifies the story, which is enriched by Chinese folklore, details of family relationships, & problems of discrimination...An unusual historical novel, unique in its perspective of the Chinese in America & its portrayal of early 20th-century San Francisco."-- School Library Journal. WHILE YOU MIGHT INITIALLY ORDER THESE BEAUTIFUL HARDCOVER LARGE PRINT EDITIONS FOR VISUALLY IMPAIRED, LEARNING DISABLED, OR ESL CHILDREN, YOU'RE LIKELY TO FIND THAT ALL OF YOUR YOUNG READERS WILL BE DRAWN TO THEM. THESE POPULAR UNABRIDGED VERSIONS FEATURE ORIGINAL ILLUSTRATIONS & COVER ART, TOO. To order by phone or for answers to your questions, call toll-free 1-800-879-4459. MAIL YOUR ORDER TO: BANTAM DOUBLEDAY DELACORTE LIBRARY SERVICE, P.O. BOX 5001, WARMINISTER, PA 18974-0585 OR FAX IT TO US: 1-215-674-8402.
Publisher Provided Annotation.

—The Lost Garden. (Illus.). 128p. (gr. 5-7). 1991. 14.98 (*0-685-58838-6*, J Messner); 9.71s.p. (*0-685-47021-0*, J Messner); pap. 12.95 (*0-685-58839-4*, J Messner); pap. 11.24s.p. (*0-685-47022-9*, J Messner) S&S Trade.
—Lost Garden. 1991. 12.95 (*0-671-74160-8*, J Messner); lib. bdg. 14.98 (*0-671-74159-4*) S&S Trade.
—The Lost Garden. (gr. 8). 1990. write for info. (*0-663-56256-2*) Silver Burdett Pr.
—The Man Who Tricked a Ghost. Seltzer, Isadore, illus. LC 93-22202. 32p. (gr. k-4). 1993. PLB 15.95 (*0-8167-3030-X*); pap. text ed. write for info. (*0-8167-3031-8*) BrdgeWater.
—The Rainbow People. Wiesner, David, illus. LC 88-21203. 208p. (gr. 3-7). 1989. 16.00 (*0-06-026760-7*); PLB 15.89 (*0-06-026761-5*) HarpC Child Bks.
—The Rainbow People. Wiesner, David, illus. LC 89-21203. 208p. (gr. 3-7). 1992. pap. 3.95 (*0-06-440441-2*, Trophy) HarpC Child Bks.
—The Serpent's Children. LC 82-48855. 288p. (gr. 7 up). 1984. PLB 13.89 (*0-06-026812-3*) HarpC Child Bks.
—The Star Fisher. LC 90-23785. 150p. (gr. 3 up). 1991. 12.95 (*0-688-09365-5*) Morrow Jr Bks.
—The Star Fisher. 160p. (gr. 5 up). 1992. pap. 3.99 (*0-14-036003-4*, Puffin) Puffin Bks.
—Sweetwater. Noonan, Julia, illus. LC 72-9867. 224p. (gr. 5 up). 1983. pap. 3.50 (*0-06-440135-9*, Trophy) HarpC Child Bks.
—Tongues of Jade. Wiesner, David, illus. LC 91-2119. 208p. (gr. 3-7). 1991. 14.95 (*0-06-022470-3*); PLB 14.89 (*0-06-022471-1*) HarpC Child Bks.
Yep, Laurence, retold by. The Shell Woman & the King: A Chinese Folktale. Ming-Yi, Yang, illus. LC 92-9583. 32p. (gr. k-3). 1993. 13.99 (*0-8037-1394-0*); PLB 13.89 (*0-8037-1395-9*) Dial Bks Young.

Yep, Laurence, et al. The Boy Who Swallowed Snakes. Tseng, Jean & Tseng, Mou-Sien, illus. LC 93-21822. 32p. (gr. 5 up). 1994. 14.95 (*0-590-46168-0*) Scholastic Inc.
Yep, Lawrence. The Mark Twain Murders. LC 81-69510. 160p. (gr. 7 up). 1982. SBE 13.95 (*0-02-793670-8*, Four Winds) Macmillan Child Grp.
Yepsen, Roger. City Trains: Moving Through America's Cities by Rail. Yepsen, Roger, illus. LC 92-2395. 96p. (gr. 3-7). 1993. SBE 14.95 (*0-02-793675-9*, Macmillan Child Bk) Macmillan Child Grp.
—Humanpower: Cars, Planes, & Boats with Muscles for Motors. Yepsen, Roger, illus. LC 91-17575. 96p. (gr. 3-7). 1992. SBE 14.95 (*0-02-793615-5*, Macmillan Child Bk) Macmillan Child Grp.
—Smarten Up. (gr. 4-7). 1990. 13.95 (*0-316-96864-1*) Little.
YES Entertainment Corp. Staff. Dino Den. 2p. (ps-2). 1993. write for info. (*1-883366-03-8*) Yes Ent.
—My Doll House. 2p. (ps-2). 1993. write for info. (*1-883366-04-6*) Yes Ent.
—Police & Fire Station. 2p. (ps-2). 1993. write for info. (*1-883366-05-4*) Yes Ent.
YES! Entertainment Corporation Staff, ed. see Teitelbaum, Michael.
YES! Entertainment Corporation Staff. Cinderella: The Fairy Tale. 2p. (ps-2). 1993. write for info. (*1-883366-11-9*) YES Ent.
YES! Entertainment Corporation Staff, et al. Comes to Life Story Player & Berenstain Bears: Mysterious Numbers Book Set. 16p. (ps-2). 1993. write for info. (*1-883366-07-0*) YES Ent.
—Comes to Life Story Player (Phase I) & Berenstain Bears: Mysterious Numbers & Berenstain Bears Eager Beavers Books. 16p. (ps-2). 1993. write for info. (*1-883366-29-1*) YES Ent.
Yette, Frederick W., jt. auth. see Yette, Samuel F.
Yette, Samuel F. & Yette, Frederick W. Washington & Two Marches: 1963 & 1983. (Illus.). 1984. 25.00 (*0-911253-02-5*); pap. 16.95 (*0-911253-03-3*); deluxe ed. 50.00 deluxe ltd. ed (*0-317-11590-1*) Cottage Bks.
Yin-lien C. Chin & Center, Y. The Stone Lion & Other Chinese Detective Stories: The Wisdom of Lord Bau. Lu Wang, illus. LC 91-46520. 192p. (gr. 8-12). 1992. 24.95 (*0-87332-634-2*); pap. 13.95 (*0-87332-635-0*) M E Sharpe.
YMCA of the U. S. A. Staff. The Minnow Swim Book. 24p. 1990. pap. 2.00 (*0-87322-288-1*, LYMC5089) Human Kinetics.
—The Polliwog Swim Book. 24p. 1990. pap. 2.00 (*0-87322-274-1*, LYMC5087) Human Kinetics.
—Y Basketball Shooters Manual. Levin, Robert, ed. 44p. (gr. 7-9). 1985. pap. 5.00x (*0-931250-85-4*, LYMC4667, Pub. by YMCA USA) Human Kinetics.
Yoaker, Harry. The View. LC 91-13353. (Illus.). 32p. (ps-3). 1992. 14.00 (*0-8037-1105-0*) Dial Bks Young.
Yockey, R. Paul. Where's Joe? (Illus.). 144p. (Orig.). 1991. pap. 3.50 (*0-671-73942-5*, Archway) PB.
Yocom, Charles & Dasmann, Raymond. Pacific Coastal Wildlife Region. rev. ed. (Illus.). 120p. (gr. 4 up). 1965. 15.95 (*0-911010-05-X*); pap. 7.95 (*0-911010-04-1*) Naturegraph.
Yoder, Carolyn P., ed. see Baker, Charles F., III.
Yoder, Tamra, ed. see Richardson, Arleta.
Yoder, Walter D. Big American Pueblo Indian Activity Book. Smith, James C., Jr., ed. (Illus.). 48p. (Orig.). (gr. 3-9). 1993. pap. 7.95 (*0-86534-219-9*) Sunstone Pr.
—Big Camino Real Activity Book. (Illus.). 48p. (Orig.). (gr. 3-9). 1993. pap. 7.95 (*0-86534-218-0*) Sunstone Pr.
—Big Santa Fe Trail Activity Book. Smith, James C., Jr., ed. (Illus.). 48p. (Orig.). (gr. 3-9). 1993. pap. 7.95 (*0-86534-217-2*) Sunstone Pr.
Yogaville Children. Hatha Yoga for Kids - By Kids. Satchidananda, Sri S., intro. by. (Illus.). 112p. (Orig.). (gr. 1-8). 1990. spiral bdg. 13.95g (*0-932040-36-5*) Integral Yoga Pubns.
Yogeshananda, Swami. Way of the Hindu. (gr. 3-7). 1980. pap. 9.95 (*0-7175-0626-6*) Dufour.
Yogesvara dosa-Jyotirmayi. Gopal the Invincible. Bhaktivedanta Swami Prabhupado, A. C., tr. Sunita-devi dosa, illus. 15p. (gr. 3 up). 1983. 7.95 (*0-89647-017-2*) Bala Bks.
Yolen, J. & Nolan, D. Wings. 32p. (ps up). 1991. 15.95 (*0-15-297850-X*, HB Juv Bks) HarBrace.
Yolen, Jane. All in the Woodland Early: An ABC Book. Zalben, Jane B., illus. LC 91-70415. 32p. (ps-3). 1991. Repr. 14.95 (*1-878093-62-2*) Boyds Mills Pr.
—All Those Secrets of the World. (ps-3). 1991. 14.95 (*0-316-96891-9*) Little.
—All Those Secrets of the World. (ps-3). 1993. pap. 4.95 (*0-316-96895-1*) Little.
—Animal Fare: Zoological Nonsense Poems. Street, Janet, illus. LC 92-44931. (gr. 4 up). 1994. write for info (*0-15-203550-8*) Harbrace.
—Baby Bear's Bedtime Book. LC 89-2161. 29p. (ps-3). 1990. 13.95 (*0-15-205120-1*) HarBrace.
—Best Witches. Primavera, Elise, illus. 48p. (gr. k-4). 1989. 14.95 (*0-399-21539-5*, Putnam) Putnam Pub Group.
—Bird Watch. Lewin, Ted, illus. 48p. 1990. 15.95 (*0-399-21612-X*, Philomel Bks) Putnam Pub Group.
—Children of the Wolf. 144p. (gr. 7 up). 1993. pap. 3.99 (*0-14-036477-3*, Puffin) Puffin Bks.
—Commander Toad & the Big Black Hole. Degen, Bruce, illus. LC 82-23524. (gr. 1-4). 1983. (Coward); pap. 6.95 (*0-698-20594-4*) Putnam Pub Group.

—Commander Toad & the Dis-Asteroid. Degen, Bruce, illus. LC 84-1897. 64p. (gr. 4). 1985. (Coward); pap. 6.95 (0-698-20620-7, Coward) Putnam Pub Group.
—Commander Toad & the Intergalactic Spy. Degen, Bruce, illus. 64p. (ps-4). 1986. (Coward); pap. 6.95 (0-698-20623-1, Coward) Putnam Pub Group.
—Commander Toad & the Planet of the Grapes. Degen, Bruce, illus. 64p. (gr. 1-4). 1982. (Coward); pap. 6.95 (0-698-20540-5) Putnam Pub Group.
—Commander Toad & the Space Pirates. Degen, Bruce, illus. 64p. (gr. 1-4). 1987. (Coward); pap. 6.95 (0-698-20633-9, Coward) Putnam Pub Group.
—Commander Toad in Space. Degen, Bruce, illus. 64p. (gr. 3-5). 1980. (Coward); pap. 6.95 (0-698-20522-7) Putnam Pub Group.
—The Devil's Arithmetic. 160p. 1988. 13.00 (0-670-81027-4) Viking Child Bks.
—Devil's Arithmetic. 1990. pap. 3.99 (0-14-034535-3, Puffin) Puffin Bks.
—Dinosaur Dances. Degen, Bruce, illus. 40p. 1990. 14.95 (0-399-21629-4, Putnam) Putnam Pub Group.
—Dove Isabeau. Nolan, Dennis, illus. 32p. (gr. 3-7). 1989. 13.95 (0-15-224131-0) HarBrace.
—Dragon's Blood. LC 81-69668. 256p. (gr. 7 up). 1982. 14.95 (0-385-28226-5) Delacorte.
—Dragon's Blood. (gr. 7 up). 1984. pap. 3.50 (0-440-91802-2, LFL) Dell.
—The Dragon's Boy. LC 89-24642. 128p. (gr. 3-7). 1990. 14.00 (0-06-026789-5); PLB 13.89 (0-06-026790-9) HarpC Child Bks.
—Dream Weaver. Hague, Michael, illus. 80p. (gr. 10 up). 1989. 15.95 (0-399-22152-2, Philomel Bks) Putnam Pub Group.
—Eeny, Meeny, Miney Mole. Brown, K., illus. 1992. 13.95 (0-15-225350-5, HB Juv Bks) HarBrace.
—Elfabet: An ABC of Elves. Mills, Lauren, illus. (ps-3). 1990. 14.95 (0-316-96900-1) Little.
—The Emperor & the Kite. Young, Ed, illus. 32p. (ps-2). 1988. 15.95 (0-399-21499-2, Philomel Bks) Putnam Pub Group.
—Emperor & the Kite. Young, Ed, illus. 32p. (ps up). 1992. pap. 5.95 (0-399-22512-9, Philomel Bks) Putnam Pub Group.
—Encounter. Shannon, D., illus. 1992. 14.95 (0-15-225962-7, HB Juv Bks) HarBrace.
—The Faery Flag: Stories & Poems of Fantasy & the Supernatural. LC 88-34866. 128p. (gr. 5 up). 1989. 15.95 (0-531-05838-7); PLB 15.99 (0-531-08438-8) Orchard Bks Watts.
—Fever Dream. Pinkney, Jerry, illus. LC 93-10070. (gr. 4 up). Date not set. 14.00 (0-06-021482-1); PLB 13.89 (0-06-021483-X) Harpc Child Bks.
—The Gift of Sarah Barker. 160p. (gr. 5 up). 1992. pap. 3.99 (0-14-036027-1) Puffin Bks.
—The Girl in the Golden Bower. Dyer, Jane, illus. LC 92-37284. (gr. 5 up). 1994. 15.95 (0-316-96894-3) Little.
—The Girl Who Cried Flowers & Other Tales. Palladini, David, illus. LC 73-8903. 64p. (gr. 3-6). 1974. 12.95 (0-690-00216-5, Crowell Jr Bks); (Crowell Jr Bks) HarpC Child Bks.
—The Girl Who Loved the Wind. Young, Ed, illus. LC 71-171012. 32p. (ps-3). 1982. (Crowell Jr Bks); PLB 14.89 (0-690-33101-0, Crowell Jr Bks) HarpC Child Bks.
—The Girl Who Loved the Wind. reissue ed. Young, Ed, illus. LC 71-171012. 32p. (ps-3). 1987. pap. 5.95 (0-06-443088-X, Trophy) HarpC Child Bks.
—Good Griselle. Christiana, David, illus. LC 93-11691. 1994. 14.95 (0-15-231701-5) HarBrace.
—Greyling. (Illus.). 40p. (ps-3). 1991. 14.95 (0-399-22262-6, Philomel Bks) Putnam Pub Group.
—Heart's Blood. LC 83-14978. 224p. (gr. 7 up). 1984. 14.95 (0-385-29316-X) Delacorte.
—Heart's Blood. (Orig.). (gr. 6 up). 1986. pap. 3.50 (0-440-93385-4, LFL) Dell.
—Here There Be Dragons. Wilgus, David, illus. LC 92-23194. 1993. 16.95 (0-15-209888-7) HarBrace.
—Honkers. Baker, Leslie, illus. LC 92-24302. 1993. 14.95 (0-316-96893-5) Little.
—How Beastly! A Menagerie of Nonsense Poems. Marshall, James, illus. 48p. (gr. 2-6). 1994. 14.95 (1-56397-086-4) Boyds Mills Pr.
—An Invitation to the Butterfly Ball: A Counting Rhyme. Zalben, Jane B., illus. LC 91-70416. 32p. (ps-3). 1991. 14.95 (1-878093-61-4) Boyds Mills Pr.
—A Letter from Phoenix Farm. Stemple, Jason, illus. 32p. (gr. 2-5). 1992. 12.95 (1-878450-36-0) R Owen Pubs.
—Letting Swift River Go. (ps-3). 1992. 15.95 (0-316-96899-4) Little.
—The Lullaby Songbook. Mikolaycak, Charles, illus. LC 85-752885. 32p. (ps up). 1986. 13.95 (0-15-249903-2, HB Juv Bks) HarBrace.
—Mouse's Birthday. Degen, Bruce, illus. LC 92-15291. 32p. 1993. 14.95 (0-399-22189-1, Putnam) Putnam Pub Group.
—Owl Moon. Schoenherr, John, illus. (ps-1). 1987. 14.95 (0-399-21457-7, Philomel Bks) Putnam Pub Group.
—Picnic with Piggins. Dyer, Jane, illus. 32p. (ps-3). 1988. 14.95 (0-15-261534-2) HarBrace.
—Picnic with Piggins. LC 87-13564. (ps-3). 1993. pap. 4.95 (0-15-261535-0) HarBrace.
—Piggins. Dyer, Jane, illus. LC 86-22915. 32p. (ps-3). 1987. 14.95 (0-15-261685-3) HarBrace.
—Piggins. (ps-3). 1992. pap. 4.95 (0-15-261686-1) HarBrace.

—Piggins & the Royal Wedding. Dyer, Jane, illus. 32p. (ps-3). 1989. 13.95 (0-15-261687-X) HarBrace.
—Raining Cats & Dogs. LC 91-24295. (ps-3). 1993. 14.95 (0-15-265488-7, HB Juv Bks) HarBrace.
—Ring of Earth: A Child's Book of Seasons. Wallner, John, illus. LC 86-4800. 32p. (ps up). 1986. 14.95 (0-15-267140-4, HB Juv Bks) HarBrace.
—Sacred Places. Shannon, David, illus. LC 92-30323. 1994. write for info. (0-15-269953-8) HarBrace.
—The Seeing Stick. Charlip, Remy & Maraslis, Demetra, illus. LC 75-6946. 32p. (gr. k up). 1975. PLB 14.89 (0-690-00596-2, Crowell Jr Bks) HarpC Child Bks.
—A Sending of Dragons. McKeveny, Tom, illus. LC 87-6689. 240p. (gr. 7 up). 1987. pap. 14.95 (0-385-29587-1) Delacorte.
—A Sending of Dragons. (Orig.). (gr. k up). 1989. pap. 3.50 (0-440-20309-0, LFL) Dell.
—Sky Dogs. Moser, Barry, illus. LC 89-26960. 32p. (ps-3). 1990. 15.95 (0-15-275480-6); limited ed., numbered & s 100.00 (0-15-275481-4) HarBrace.
—Sleeping Ugly. (gr. 1-4). 1981. (Coward); pap. 6.95 (0-698-20617-7) Putnam Pub Group.
—Tam Lin. Mikolaycak, Charles, illus. LC 88-2280. 24p. (gr. 1-7). 1990. 14.95 (0-15-284261-6) HarBrace.
—Three Bears Holiday Book. Dyer, Jane, illus. LC 93-17252. 1994. write for info. (0-15-200932-9, J Yolen Bks) HarBrace.
—The Three Bears Rhyme Book. Dyer, Jane, illus. LC 86-19514. 32p. (ps-3). 1987. 14.95 (0-15-286386-9, HB Juv Bks) HarBrace.
—Touch Magic. 96p. (ps-8). 1992. pap. 10.95 (0-399-21897-1, Philomel Bks) Putnam Pub Group.
—Two Thousand Forty-One: Twelve Stories about the Future by Top Science Fiction Writers. 1994. pap. 3.99 (0-440-21898-5) Dell.
—Weather Report. 64p. 1993. 16.95 (1-56397-101-1) Boyds Mills Pr.
—Welcome to the Greenhouse. Regan, Laura, illus. 32p. (ps-3). 1993. PLB 14.95 (0-399-22335-5, Putnam) Putnam Pub Group.
—What Rhymes with Moon? Councell, Ruth T., illus. LC 92-7439. 40p. (ps). 1993. 15.95 (0-399-22501-3, Philomel Bks) Putnam Pub Group.
—Wizard's Hall. Ingber, Bonnie V., ed. 133p. (gr. 3-7). 1991. 13.95 (0-15-298132-2) HarBrace.
—Wizard's Hall. (gr. 4-7). 1993. pap. 2.95 (0-590-45811-6) Scholastic Inc.
Yolen, Jane & Councell, Ruth T. Old Dame Counterpane. LC 93-11528. 1994. write for info. (0-399-22686-9) Putnam Pub Group.
Yolen, Jane & Greenberg, Martin H. Vampires. LC 90-27888. 240p. (gr. 5 up). 1993. pap. 3.95 (0-06-440485-4, Trophy) HarpC Child Bks.
Yolen, Jane, ed. Camelot. LC 92-39322. 1994. write for info. (0-399-22540-4, Philomel Bks) Putnam Pub Group.
—Hark! A Christmas Sampler. De Paola, Tomie, illus. LC 90-42865. 128p. 1991. 19.95 (0-399-21853-X, Putnam) Putnam Pub Group.
—Jane Yolen's Mother Goose Songbook. Hoffman, Rosekrans, illus. Stemple, Adam, contrib. by. (Illus.). 96p. (ps-7). 1992. PLB 16.95 (1-878093-52-5) Boyds Mills Pr.
—Jane Yolen's Songs of Summer. Moore, Cyd, illus. Stemple, Adam, designed by. LC 92-85034. (Illus.). 32p. 1993. 12.95 (1-56397-110-0, Wordsong) Boyds Mills Pr.
Yolen, Jane, compiled by. The Lap-Time Song & Play Book. Tomes, Margot, illus. Stemple, Adam, contrib. by. (Illus.). 28p. (ps up). 1989. 15.95 (0-15-243588-3) HarBrace.
Yolen, Jane, retold by. Little Mouse & Elephant: A Tale from Turkey. Segal, John, illus. LC 92-21748. 1994. 10.00 (0-06-021502-X, HarpT); PLB 9.89 (0-06-021503-8, HarpT) HarpC.
—The Musicians of Bremen. Segal, John, illus. LC 92-18695. 32p. (ps-2). 1995. 10.00 (0-06-021498-8); PLB 9.89 (0-06-021499-6) HarpC Child Bks.
Yolen, Jane, ed. Sleep Rhymes Around the World. (Illus.). 40p. 1994. 16.95 (1-56397-243-3, Wordsong) Boyds Mills Pr.
—Street Rhymes Around the World. LC 91-66058. (Illus.). 40p. (ps-3). 1992. 16.95 (1-878093-53-3, Wordsong) Boyds Mills Pr.
Yolen, Jane & Greenberg, Martin H., eds. Things That Go Bump in the Night: A Collection of Original Stories. LC 88-39338. 288p. (gr. 5 up). 1989. 15.00 (0-06-026802-6); PLB 14.89 (0-06-026803-4) HarpC Child Bks.
—Vampires. LC 90-27888. 240p. (gr. 5 up). 1991. 15.00 (0-06-026800-X); PLB 14.89 (0-06-026801-8) HarpC Child Bks.
—Werewolves: A Collection of Original Stories. LC 87-45863. 288p. (gr. 5-9). 1988. 13.95 (0-06-026798-4); PLB 13.89 (0-06-026799-2) HarpC Child Bks.
Yolen, Jane, ed. see Coville, Bruce.
Yolen, Jane, ed. see Kirwan-Vogel, Anna.
Yolen, Jane, ed. see Oppenheim, Shulamith L.
Yolen, Jane, ed. see Whittington, Mary K.
Yolen, Jane, ed. see Yardley, Joanna.
Yolla Bolly Press Staff. Big Bugs. Yolla Bolly Press Staff, illus. LC 93-27516. 1994. write for info. (0-15-200693-1, Gulliver Bks) HarBrace.
—Nightprowlers. Yolla Bolly Press Staff, illus. LC 93-27547. 1994. write for info. (0-15-200694-X, Gulliver Bks) HarBrace.
Yonay, Rina, jt. auth. see Yonay, Shahar.

Yonay, Shahar & Yonay, Rina. Systematic Hebrew, Pt. C. Einat, Tzvi, illus. (gr. 7). 1986. 13.45 (0-9616783-0-5) S Yonay.
—Systematic Hebrew, Pt. D. (gr. 8-9). 1987. 14.95 (0-9616783-1-3) S Yonay.
—Systematic Hebrew, Pt. B. (gr. 6). 1988. 11.95 (0-9616783-3-X) S Yonay.
—Systematic Hebrew, Pt. A. (gr. 5). 1988. 11.95 (0-9616783-2-1) S Yonay.
—The Test. (gr. 7-12). 1988. 14.95 (0-9616783-4-8) S Yonay.
Yoo, Grace S. Two Korean Brothers: The Story of Hungbu & Nolbu. LC 73-18023. (gr. k-3). 1970. 6.95 (0-912580-01-1) Far Eastern Res.
Yopp, Hallie K., jt. auth. see Frazee, Charles.
Yopp, Hallie Kay, jt. auth. see Frazee, Charles.
Yorgason, Blaine & Yorgason, Brenton. The Problem with Immorality. 43p. 1990. pap. text ed. 3.50 (0-929985-15-X) Sonos.
Yorgason, Blaine M. & Yorgason, Brenton. Pardners: Three Stories on Friendship. Durfee, John C. & Durfee, Gaylie, illus. 64p. (Orig.). (gr. 9 up). 1988. pap. 3.95 (0-929985-05-2) Sonos.
Yorgason, Brenton, jt. auth. see Yorgason, Blaine.
Yorgason, Brenton, jt. auth. see Yorgason, Blaine M.
Yorgason, Margaret & Ward, Annette. All about Easter. 1993. pap. 3.95 (0-88494-874-9) Bookcraft Inc.
Yorimitsu, jt. auth. see Higa, Tomiko.
Yorinks, Arthur. Bravo, Minski. Egielski, Richard, illus. (ps up). 1988. 15.00 (0-374-30951-5) FS&G.
—Christmas in July. Egielski, Richard, illus. LC 91-55244. 32p. (ps-3). 1991. 14.95 (0-06-020256-4); PLB 14.89 (0-06-020257-2) HarpC Child Bks.
—Company's Coming. Small, David, illus. LC 87-13579. (ps-3). 1988. 12.95 (0-517-56751-2) Crown Bks Yng Read.
—Company's Coming. Small, David, illus. LC 87-13579. 32p. (ps-2). 1992. pap. 4.99 (0-517-58858-7) Crown Bks Yng Read.
—Hey, Al. Egielski, Richard, illus. LC 86-80955. 32p. (gr. k up). 1986. 15.00 (0-374-33060-3) FS&G.
—Hey, Al. Egielski, Richard, illus. 32p. (ps up). 1989. pap. 4.95 (0-374-42985-5, Sunburst) FS&G.
—It Happened in Pinsk. Egielski, Richard, illus. LC 83-1727. 32p. (ps up). 1983. 14.00 (0-374-33651-2) FS&G.
—It Happened in Pinsk. (Illus.). (ps up). 1987. pap. 3.95 (0-374-43649-5, Sunburst) FS&G.
—Louis the Fish. Egielski, Richard, illus. LC 80-16855. 32p. (ps up). 1980. 13.95 (0-374-34658-5) FS&G.
—Louis the Fish. Egielshi, Richard, illus. 32p. (ps up). 1986. pap. 4.95 (0-374-44598-2, Sunburst) FS&G.
—Oh, Brother. Egielski, Richard, illus. (ps up). 1989. 15.95 (0-374-35599-1) FS&G.
—Oh, Brother. Egielski, Richard, illus. 40p. (ps up). 1991. pap. 5.95 (0-374-45598-8, Sunburst) FS&G.
—Sid & Sol. (gr. 4-8). 1991. pap. 3.95 (0-374-46634-3, Sunburst) FS&G.
—Ugh. Egielski, Richard, illus. 32p. (ps-3). 1990. 13.95 (0-374-38028-7) FS&G.
—Ugh. (ps-3). 1993. pap. 4.95 (0-374-48050-8) FS&G.
York. Please Write... I Need Your Help! 1993. pap. 2.95 (0-590-46842-1) Scholastic Inc.
—The Secret House. 1992. pap. 2.75 (0-590-45051-4) Scholastic Inc.
York, Carol B. Casey Jones. new ed. LC 79-66313. (Illus.). 48p. (gr. 3-6). 1980. PLB 9.89 (0-89375-298-3); pap. 2.95 (0-89375-297-5) Troll Assocs.
—Christmas Dolls. (gr. 4-7). 1993. pap. 2.75 (0-590-42435-1) Scholastic Inc.
—Febold Feboldson, the Fix It Farmer. LC 79-66321. (Illus.). 48p. (gr. 3-6). 1980. lib. bdg. 9.89 (0-89375-312-2); pap. 2.95 (0-89375-311-4) Troll Assocs.
—The Good Day Mice. De Larrea, Victoria, illus. 112p. (gr. 3-7). 1989. 2.75 (0-553-15373-0, Skylark) Bantam.
—Johnny Appleseed. LC 79-66312. (Illus.). 48p. (gr. 3-6). 1980. lib. bdg. 9.89 (0-89375-296-7); pap. 2.95 (0-89375-295-9) Troll Assocs.
—Key to the Playhouse. Speirs, John, illus. LC 93-1800. 128p. (gr. 2-5). 1994. 13.95 (0-590-46258-X) Scholastic Inc.
—Mike Fink. LC 79-66315. (Illus.). 48p. (gr. 3-6). 1980. lib. bdg. 9.89 (0-89375-302-5); pap. 2.95 (0-89375-301-7) Troll Assocs.
—Miss Know It All... 96p. (Orig.). (gr. 4 up). 1985. pap. 2.50 (0-553-15408-7, Skylark) Bantam.
—Miss Know-It-All & the Magic House. Stock, Catherine, illus. (gr. 3-7). 1989. pap. 2.75 (0-318-41641-7, Skylark) Bantam.
—Miss Know-It-All & the Three Ring Circus. (Illus.). 96p. (Orig.). 1988. pap. 2.75 (0-553-15590-3, Skylark) Bantam.
—Miss Know It All Returns. 96p. 1985. pap. 2.25 (0-553-15351-X, Skylark) Bantam.
—Old Stormalong: The Seafaring Sailor. LC 79-66322. (Illus.). 48p. (gr. 3-6). 1980. lib. bdg. 9.89 (0-89375-314-9); pap. 2.95 (0-89375-313-0) Troll Assocs.
—On That Dark Night. 100p. (gr. 5-8). 1985. pap. 2.25 (0-553-25207-0) Bantam.
—Once upon a Dark November. LC 89-2021. 112p. (gr. 4-9). 1989. 13.95 (0-8234-0780-2) Holiday.
—Pudmuddles. Thiesing, Lisa, illus. LC 91-23596. 48p. (gr. 2-5). 1993. 13.00 (0-06-020436-2); PLB 12.89 (0-06-020437-0) HarpC Child Bks.

—Rabbit Magic. 128p. (gr. 2-5). 1991. pap. 2.50 (0-590-43894-8) Scholastic Inc.
—Sam Patch, the Big Time Jumper. new ed. LC 79-66318. (Illus.). 48p. (gr. 3-6). 1980. lib. bdg. 9.89 (0-89375-306-8); pap. 2.95 (0-89375-305-X); cassette avail. Troll Assocs.
York, Carol B., ed. Ichabod Crane & the Headless Horseman. Irving, Washington. LC 79-66323. (Illus.). 48p. (gr. 3-6). 1980. lib. bdg. 9.89 (0-89375-316-5); pap. 2.95 (0-89375-315-7) Troll Assocs.
—Rip Van Winkle. new ed. Washington, Irving. LC 79-66314. (Illus.). 48p. (gr. 3-6). 1980. lib. bdg. 9.89 (0-89375-300-9); pap. 2.95 (0-89375-299-1) Troll Assocs.
York, Jami. How Valentine's Day Began, 5 vols, Vol. I. 35p. (gr. 1-6). 1991. Repr. of 1979 ed. 12.95 (1-880108-04-6) Apple Valley.
York, Sherri, ed. see Kallstrom, Theresa.
York, Sherri, ed. see Zito, Penny.
York, Sheryl, ed. see Thatcher, Barbara B.
York, Susan. Kidding Around Santa Fe: A Young Person's Guide to the City. Blakemore, Sally, illus. 64p. (Orig.). (gr. 3 up). 1991. pap. 9.95 (0-945465-99-8) John Muir.
York, Susan P., ed. see Postell, Alice E.
Yorke, Malcolm. Miss Butterpat Goes Wild. Chamberlain, Margaret, illus. LC 93-20204. 32p. (gr. 1-5). 1993. 10.95 (1-56458-200-0) Dorling Kindersley.
—Ritchie F. Dweebly Thunders On. Chamberlain, Margaret, illus. LC 93-5003. 1994. write for info. (1-56458-199-3) Dorling Kindersley.
Yorke, Stephen. What's for Breakfast? Barrett, Trevor, illus. 8p. 1992. 3.95 (0-681-41548-7) Longmeadow Pr.
—What's for Dinner? Barrett, Trevor, illus. 8p. 1992. 3.95 (0-681-41550-9) Longmeadow Pr.
—What's for Lunch? Barrett, Trevor, illus. 8p. 1992. 3.95 (0-681-41549-5) Longmeadow Pr.
Yoshi. The Butterfly Hunt. Yoshi, illus. LC 90-7361. 32p. (gr. k up). 1991. pap. 14.95 (0-88708-137-1) Picture Bk Studio.
—The Butterfly Hunt. Yoshi, illus. LC 92-6631. 28p. (gr. k). 1993. Repr. Mini-bk. 4.95 (0-88708-270-X) Picture Bk Studio.
—One, Two, Three. Yoshi, illus. LC 90-23918. 28p. (gr. k up). 1991. pap. 15.95 (0-88708-159-2) Picture Bk Studio.
—Who's Hiding Here? LC 86-25455. (Illus.). 36p. (gr. up). 1991. pap. 15.95 (0-88708-041-3) Picture Bk Studio.
—Who's Hiding Here? Yoshi, illus. LC 92-6631. 32p. (ps up). 1992. pap. 4.95 minibk. (0-88708-277-7) Picture Bk Studio.
Yoshida, Toshi. Elephant Crossing. Yoshida, Toshi, illus. 40p. (gr. k-4). 1989. 14.95 (0-399-21745-2, Philomel Bks) Putnam Pub Group.
—Rhinoceros Mother. (Illus.). 40p. (gr. k-4). 1991. 14.95 (0-399-22270-7, Philomel Bks) Putnam Pub Group.
—Young Lions. Yoshida, Toshi, illus. 40p. (gr. 1-5). 1989. 14.95 (0-399-21546-8, Philomel Bks) Putnam Pub Group.
—Young Lions. Yoshida, Toshi, illus. 32p. (ps-3). 1992. pap. 5.95 (0-399-21886-6, Sandcastle Bks) Putnam Pub Group.
Yoslow, Mark. Drugs in the Body: Effects of Abuse. Cohn, Tom, ed. LC 91-39030. (Illus.). 144p. (gr. 9-12). 1992. PLB 14.40 (0-531-12507-6) Watts.
Yost, Carolyn K. Mother Rabbit Knew. Gardner, Katherine L., tr. (Illus.). 32p. (gr. k-2). 1989. pasted 2.50 (0-87403-595-3, 3855) Standard Pub.
—The Robins Knew. Gardner, Katherine W., illus. 32p. (gr. k-2). 1991. pasted 2.50 (0-87403-817-0, 24-03917) Standard Pub.
Yost, Graham. The CIA. (Illus.). 176p. 1989. 16.95x (0-8160-1941-X) Facts on File.
—The KGB. (Illus.). 160p. (gr. 8-12). 1989. 16.95x (0-8160-1940-1) Facts on File.
—Spies in the Sky. (Illus.). 144p. (gr. 8-12). 1989. lib. bdg. 16.95x (0-8160-1942-8) Facts on File.
Youdovin, Susan S. Why Does It Always Rain on Sukkot? Levine, Abby, ed. Nerlove, Miriam, illus. LC 90-11923. 32p. (ps-3). 1990. PLB 13.95 (0-8075-9079-7) A Whitman.
Young. Everyone Loves the Moon. Young, James, illus. 32p. (ps-3). 1992. 14.95 (0-316-97130-8) Little.
Young, Alida E. Dead Wrong. 128p. (gr. 5-8). 1992. pap. 2.99 (0-87406-602-6) Willowisp Pr.
—Is My Sister Dying? 144p. (Orig.). (gr. 5-8). 1991. pap. 2.99 (0-87406-541-0) Willowisp Pr.
Young, Barbara. Jesus Is My Very Best Friend. (ps-k). 1984. 5.99 (0-570-04097-3, 56-1465) Concordia.
Young, C. Castles, Pyramids & Palaces. (Illus.). 48p. (ps-8). 1990. lib. bdg. 13.96 (0-88110-411-6, Usborne); pap. 7.95 (0-7460-0463-X, Usborne) EDC.
—Diggers. (Illus.). 12p. (ps). 1993. bds. 4.50 (0-7460-1096-6) EDC.
—Diggers & Cranes. (Illus.). 32p. (ps-2). 1991. PLB 13.96 (0-88110-552-X, Usborne); pap. 5.95 (0-7460-0625-X, Usborne) EDC.
—Railways & Trains. (Illus.). 48p. (gr. 2 up). 1992. lib. bdg. 13.96 (0-88110-441-8, Usborne); pap. 7.95 (0-7460-0467-2, Usborne) EDC.
—Tractors. (Illus.). 32p. (ps-2). 1992. PLB 13.96 (0-88110-553-8, Usborne); pap. 5.95 (0-7460-0671-3, Usborne) EDC.
—Tractors. (Illus.). 12p. (ps). 1993. bds. 4.50 (0-7460-1097-4) EDC.
—Trucks. (Illus.). 32p. (ps-2). PLB 13.96 (0-88110-556-2, Usborne); pap. 5.95 (0-7460-0722-1, Usborne) EDC.

Young, Caroline & Castor, Harriet. Machines That Work. (Illus.). 96p. (gr. k-5). 1993. pap. 12.95 (0-7460-0990-9, Usborne) EDC.
Young, Christine, jt. auth. see Parolini, Stephen.
Young, David C. A Father's Love. Whitaker, Angela, illus. 24p. 1993. 14.00 (0-9638833-0-5) Yng & Yng Prods.
Young, Diana. Ferngully: The Last Rainforest Digest. 112p. 1992. pap. 2.95 (0-590-45433-1) Scholastic Inc.
Young, Douglas. A Primer of Christianity & Ethics. Hunting, Constance, ed. 200p. (Orig.). (gr. 9-12). 1985. pap. 12.95 (0-913006-34-3) Puckerbrush.
Young, Ed. Little Plum. LC 93-11526. 1994. write for info. (0-399-22683-4) Putnam Pub Group.
—The Other Bone. Young, Ed, illus. LC 83-47706. 32p. (ps-3). 1984. PLB 14.89 (0-06-026871-9) HarpC Child Bks.
—Red Thread. (Illus.). 32p. (ps-3). 1993. PLB 14.95 (0-399-21969-2, Philomel Bks) Putnam Pub Group.
—Seven Blind Mice. Young, Ed, illus. 40p. (ps-6). 1992. PLB 16.95 (0-399-22261-8, Philomel Bks) Putnam Pub Group.
—Up a Tree: A Wordless Picture Book. Young, Ed, illus. LC 82-47733. 32p. (ps-3). 1983. PLB 14.89 (0-06-026814-X) HarpC Child Bks.
Young, Ed, adapted by. Moon Mother: A Native American Creation Tale. LC 92-14981. (Illus.). 40p. (ps-3). 1993. 15.00 (0-06-021301-9); PLB 14.89 (0-06-021302-7) HarpC Child Bks.
Young, Ed, tr. from CHI. & illus. Lon Po Po: A Red Riding Hood Story from China. 32p. (gr. k-4). 1989. 14.95 (0-399-21619-7, Philomel Bks) Putnam Pub Group.
Young, Elaine, ed. see Hill, Fred D.
Young, Elaine, et al, eds. see Hill, Charlotte M.
Young, Elaine A., ed. see Hill, Fred & Hill, Charlotte M.
Young, Eleanor R. Basic Skills in Getting Around, No. 812542. (gr. 7-12). 1991. wkbk. 9.95 (0-86703-192-1) Opportunities Learn.
Young, Frederica. Super-Duper Jokes. (gr. 4-7). 1993. 13.00 (0-374-37301-9); pap. 4.95 (0-374-43753-6) FS&G.
Young, Frederica & Kohl, Marguerite. Jokes for Children. Patterson, Bob, illus. 128p. (gr. 2 up). 1983. pap. 4.95 (0-374-43832-3, Sunburst) FS&G.
—More Jokes for Children. Patterson, Bob, illus. (gr. 2-5). 1984. pap. 4.95 (0-374-45360-8, Sunburst) FS&G.
Young, Ginevra M. I Got My Report Card Today. LC 89-51084. (Illus.). 44p. (gr. k-3). 1990. pap. 5.95 (1-55523-254-X) Winston-Derek.
Young, Howard S. A Rational Counseling Primer. (Illus.). (gr. 6-12). 1974. pap. 2.50 (0-917476-01-8) Inst Rational-Emotive.
Young, James. Penelope & the Pirates. Young, James, illus. 32p. (ps-2). 1990. text ed. 12.95 (1-55970-074-2) Arcade Pub Inc.
Young, Janet, jt. auth. see Forman-Hitt, Kathy.
YOung, Janet, jt. auth. see Forman-Hitt, Kathy.
Young, Janet, jt. auth. see Forman-Hitt, Kathy.
Young, Jean. Versions of the Truth. LC 91-67099. 45p. (gr. 7 up). 1992. pap. 5.95 (1-55523-484-4) Winston-Derek.
Young, John. Heroes of Faith: Stories of Saints for Young & Old. 1989. pap. 6.95 (0-937032-61-1) Light&Life Pub Co MN.
Young, John K. Cells: Amazing Forms & Functions. LC 90-34262. (Illus.). 128p. (gr. 9-12). 1990. PLB 13.40 (0-531-10880-5) Watts.
—Hormones: Molecular Messengers. LC 92-40503. Date not set. write for info (0-531-12545-9) Watts. Postponed.
Young, Judy D., jt. auth. see Young, Richard.
Young, Judy D. & Young, Richard, eds. Stories from the Days of Columbus: A Multicultural Collection for Young Readers. 160p. 1992. 17.95 (0-87483-199-7); pap. 8.95 (0-87483-198-9) August Hse.
Young, Karen E. A Day at the Beach. 16p. (ps-1). 1991. pap. text ed. 21.00 big bk. (1-56843-034-5); pap. text ed. 4.25 (1-56843-082-5) BGR Pub.
—The Days of Josie. 19p. (gr. k). 1992. pap. text ed. 23.00 big bk. (1-56843-013-2); pap. text ed. 4.50 (1-56843-063-9) BGR Pub.
—The Great Space Race. 7p. (ps-1). 1991. pap. text ed. 21.00 big bk. (1-56843-033-7); pap. text ed. 4.25 (1-56843-081-7) BGR Pub.
—Hello, Mr. Bennett. 23p. (gr. 1). 1992. pap. text ed. 23.00 big bk. (1-56843-017-5); pap. text ed. 4.50 (1-56843-067-1) BGR Pub.
—Kind Mr. Spider. 15p. (gr. k-2). 1991. pap. text ed. 23.00 big bk. (1-56843-039-6); pap. text ed. 4.50 (1-56843-086-8) BGR Pub.
—Somewhere in Africa. 14p. (ps-1). 1991. pap. text ed. 21.00 big bk. (1-56843-030-2); pap. text ed. 4.25 (1-56843-078-7) BGR Pub.
—The Stuff of Dreams. 15p. (gr. k-2). 1991. pap. text ed. 23.00 big bk. (1-56843-043-4); pap. text ed. 4.50 (1-56843-090-6) BGR Pub.
Young, Lesley. Queen Victoria. (Illus.). 64p. (gr. 5-9). 1991. 11.95 (0-237-60001-3, Pub. by Evans Bros Ltd) Trafalgar.
Young, Marjabelle Y. & Buchwald, Ann. White Gloves & Party Manners. LC 65-25830. (gr. 7 up). 1988. 12.95 (0-88331-054-6) Luce.
Young, Mary M., illus. Bear with Me: Story & Coloring Book Adjusting to Life with a New Baby. 16p. (ps-3). 1989. pap. 7.95 (0-943114-20-9, CB100) Childbirth Graphics.

Young, Miriam. Miss Suzy's Easter Surprise. Lobel, Arnold, illus. LC 80-16966. 48p. (ps-3). 1984. Repr. of 1972 ed. RSBE 13.95 (0-02-793680-5, Four Winds) Macmillan Child Grp.
—Miss Suzy's Easter Surprise. LC 89-37842. (Illus.). 48p. (ps-3). 1990. pap. 4.95 (0-689-71374-6, Aladdin) Macmillan Child Grp.
Young, Patrick. Drugs & Pregnancy. (Illus.). 32p. (gr. 5 up). 1991. pap. 4.49 (0-7910-0001-X) Chelsea Hse.
Young, Philip G. The World That Was. Brumagin, Wayne, ed. Campbell, Susan, illus. 121p. (Orig.). (gr. 4 up). 1993. pap. 8.95 (1-880451-03-4) Rainbows End.
Young, Ralph C. The Better Grades Handbook. (Illus.). 92p. (Orig.). (gr. 6-11). 1991. pap. text ed. 8.95 (0-9631476-0-9) RCY Design.
Young, Richard & Young, Judy D. African-American Folktales. 1993. 18.95 (0-87483-308-6); pap. 9.95 (0-87483-309-4) August Hse.
—Favorite Scary Stories of American Children. Hall, Wendell E., illus. 112p. (Orig.). (ps-5). 1990. pap. 8.95 (0-87483-119-9). August Hse.
—Favorite Scary Stories of American Children. Hall, Wendell E., illus. 1991. 19.95 (0-87483-120-2) August Hse.
Young, Richard, ed. see Clemence, John.
Young, Richard, ed. see Govier, Heather.
Young, Richard, ed. see McClymont, Diane.
Young, Richard, ed. see Marshall, David.
Young, Richard, jt. ed. see Young, Judy D.
Young, Richard G., ed. see Akiko Sueyoshi.
Young, Richard G., ed. see Brown, Fern G.
Young, Richard G., ed. see Canadeo, Anne.
Young, Richard G., ed. see Carwardine, Mark.
Young, Richard G., ed. see Collins, David R.
Young, Richard G., ed. see Ellis, Rafaela.
Young, Richard G., ed. see Falkof, Lucille.
Young, Richard G., ed. see Fusako Ishinabe.
Young, Richard G., ed. see Gomi, Taro.
Young, Richard G., ed. see Green, Mary A.
Young, Richard G., ed. see Greenblatt, Miriam.
Young, Richard G., ed. see Horneck, Heribert.
Young, Richard G., ed. see Jones, Joan.
Young, Richard G., ed. see Koopman, Anne.
Young, Richard G., ed. see Law, Kevin J.
Young, Richard G., ed. see McInnes, Celia.
Young, Richard G., ed. see Mussari, Mark.
Young, Richard G., ed. see Nash, Paul.
Young, Richard G., ed. see Polikof, Barbara G.
Young, Richard G., ed. see Richman, Daniel A.
Young, Richard G., ed. see Robbins, Neal E.
Young, Richard G., ed. see Spiesman, Harriet.
Young, Richard G., ed. see Stefoff, Rebecca.
Young, Richard G., ed. see Stevens, Rita.
Young, Richard G., ed. see Tippins, Sherill.
Young, Richard G., ed. see Zickgraf, Ralph.
Young, Richard T. How Reading Came Back to Nowhere. (Illus.). 44p. (Orig.). (gr. 2 up). 1988. pap. 3.00 (0-88680-294-6); piano-vocal score 10.00 (0-88680-368-3); royalty on application 35.00 (0-685-58407-0) I E Clark.
Young, Richard Y., ed. see Asuka, Ken.
Young, Robert. The Chewing Gum Book. LC 88-31015. (Illus.). 72p. (gr. 3 up). 1989. RSBE 12.95 (0-87518-401-4, Dillon) Macmillan Child Grp.
—Christopher Columbus. Brook, Bonnie, ed. Stewart, Arvis, illus. 32p. (gr. k-2). 1990. 6.95 (0-671-69110-4); PLB 10.98 (0-671-69104-X) Silver Pr.
—Hiroshima: Fifty Years of Debate. LC 93-31261. 1994. write for info. (0-87518-610-6, Dillon) Macmillan Child Grp.
—Sneakers: The Shoes We Choose. LC 90-26473. (Illus.). 64p. (gr. 3 up). 1991. RSBE 14.95 (0-87518-460-X, Dillon) Macmillan Child Grp.
Young, Robert S. Action Figures. LC 92-7697. (Illus.). 64p. (gr. 5 up). 1992. RSBE 13.95 (0-87518-516-9, Dillon) Macmillan Child Grp.
—Dolls. LC 92-3498. (Illus.). 72p. (gr. 5 up). 1992. RSBE 13.95 (0-87518-517-7, Dillon) Macmillan Child Grp.
—Miniature Vehicles. LC 92-33010. (Illus.). 72p. (gr. 5 up). 1993. RSBE 13.95 (0-87518-518-5, Dillon) Macmillan Child Grp.
—Sports Cards. LC 92-33761. (Illus.). 72p. (gr. 5 up). 1993. RSBE 13.95 (0-87518-519-3, Dillon) Macmillan Child Grp.
—Teddy Bears. LC 92-4347. (Illus.). 64p. (gr. 5 up). 1992. RSBE 13.95 (0-87518-520-7, Dillon) Macmillan Child Grp.
Young, Robert W., tr. see Clark, Ann N.
Young, Robin. The Stock Market. (Illus.). 80p. (gr. 5 up). 1991. PLB 21.50 (0-8225-1780-9) Lerner Pubns.
Young, Roger & Caggiano, Rosemary. The Safari. 48p. (gr. k-8). 1979. pap. 14.95 (0-86704-006-8) Clarus Music.
Young, Ronder Y. Learning by Heart. LC 92-46887. 1993. 13.95 (0-395-65369-X) HM.
Young, Ruth. Daisy's Taxi. Sewall, Marcia, illus. LC 90-7735. 32p. (ps-1). 1991. 13.95 (0-531-05921-9); PLB 13.99 (0-531-08521-X) Orchard Bks Watts.
—Golden Bear. Isadora, Rachel, illus. 32p. (ps-1). 1992. PLB 14.00 (0-670-82577-8) Viking Child Bks.
—Golden Bear. Isadora, Rachel, illus. 32p. (ps-1). 1994. pap. 4.99 (0-14-050959-3) Puffin Bks.
—My Potty Chair. LC 87-6281. (ps-k). 1987. pap. 4.95 (0-670-81307-9) Viking Child Bks.
—The New Baby. LC 87-6280. (ps-k). 1987. pap. 4.95 (0-670-81304-4) Viking Child Bks.

—A Trip to Mars. Cocca-Leffler, Maryann, illus. LC 89-70936. 32p. (ps-1). 1990. 14.95 (*0-531-05892-1*); PLB 14.99 (*0-531-08492-2*) Orchard Bks Watts.

Young, Ruth & Rose, Mitchell, illus. Spider Magic. LC 89-61632. 12p. (ps-1). 1990. bds. 5.95 incl. finger puppet (*1-877779-03-2*) Schneider Educational.

—Turtle Magic. LC 89-61634. 12p. (ps-1). 1990. bds. 5.95 incl. finger puppet (*1-877779-01-6*) Schneider Educational.

Young, Selina. Ned. LC 92-33518. 26p. 1993. 14.95 (*1-56566-033-1*) Thomasson-Grant.

—Whistling in the Woods. Young, Selina, illus. LC 93-23765. 32p. 1994. 14.00 (*0-688-13073-9*, Tambourine Bks) Morrow.

Young, Sheila. Betty Bonnet Paper Dolls in Full Color. 1982. pap. 3.95 (*0-486-24415-6*) Dover.

—Lettie Lane Paper Doll. 1981. pap. 3.95 (*0-486-24089-4*) Dover.

Young, Sue K. The Scholastic Rhyming Dictionary. (Illus.). 224p. (gr. 3 up). 1994. 14.95 (*0-590-49460-0*, Scholastic Ref) Scholastic Inc.

Young, Tommy S. Tommy Scott Young Spins Magical Tales, 2 vols. Irvin, Nathanial, Jr., ed. Incl. Vol. I. Barney McCabe. LC 85-61698. 44p. 7.95 (*0-685-10585-7*); Vol. II. Tiny Hooty & the Percher. LC 85-61699. 36p. PLB 10.00 (*0-685-10586-5*). LC 85-6198. (gr. 1-8). 1985. PLB 13.95 Barney McCabe, vol. I, 44pgs. (*0-934721-01-7*); PLB 13.95 Tiny Hooty & the Percher, Vol. II, 36 pgs. (*0-934721-02-5*); PLB 29.95 Cassette & Book Package (*0-934721-07-6*); Cassette Tape Vol. I, 17 min. 30 sec. 11.95, Vol. II 18 min. 22 sec. (*0-934721-00-9*) Raspberry Rec.

Young, Virgil M. Story of Idaho: Centennial Edition. LC 89-36899. (Illus.). 304p. (ps-4). 1990. 22.95 (*0-89301-131-2*); tchr's. guide 35.95x (*0-89301-159-2*) U of Idaho Pr.

Young, William E. Moses: God's Helper. Meyers, William, illus. (gr. 1-6). 1976. 5.95 (*0-8054-4225-1*, 4242-25) Broadman.

—Ringle & Dingle: Santa's Christmas Elves. Hillenbach, Patricia, illus. 32p. (Orig.). 1991. pap. 5.95 (*0-9628122-1-8*) Pautuxet Pubns.

Young, Woody. Clockwise, Vol. One: Quotes on Life. White, Craig, illus. 50p. (Orig.). 1984. pap. text ed. 4.95 (*0-939513-01-3*) Joy Pub SJC.

—Clockwise, Vol. Two: Learn to Tell Time. White, Craig, illus. 48p. (Orig.). 1985. pap. text ed. 4.95 (*0-939513-02-1*) Joy Pub SJC.

—Moneywise. White, Craig, illus. 48p. (Orig.). (gr. 1-5). 1986. pap. text ed. 4.95 (*0-939513-30-7*) Joy Pub SJC.

—Smile Wise. White, Craig, illus. 48p. (Orig.). 1986. pap. text ed. 4.95 (*0-939513-21-8*) Joy Pub SJC.

—Song Wise, Three: Battle Hymn of the Republic. White, Craig, illus. 24p. (Orig.). 1986. pap. text ed. 2.95 (*0-939513-13-7*) Joy Pub SJC.

—Song Wise, Vol. Four: America. White, Craig, illus. 24p. (Orig.). 1986. pap. text ed. 2.95 (*0-939513-14-5*) Joy Pub SJC.

—Song Wise, Vol. One: The Star Spangled Banner. White, Craig, illus. 24p. (Orig.). 1986. pap. text ed. 2.95 (*0-939513-11-0*) Joy Pub SJC.

—Song Wise, Vol. Two: America the Beautiful. White, Craig, illus. 24p. (Orig.). 1986. pap. text ed. 2.95 (*0-939513-12-9*) Joy Pub SJC.

Young, Woody, jt. auth. see Stuart, Sally E.

Young, Woody C., jt. auth. see Stuart, Sally E.

Young Bear, Joan A., jt. auth. see Van Ahnan, Katherine.

Youngblood, Pete. Modeling Cajon. LC 85-19828. (Illus.). 72p. (gr. 11). 1990. pap. 13.95 (*0-87046-073-0*, Pub. by Trans-Anglo) Interurban.

Younger, Barbara & Flinn, Lisa. Making Scripture Stick. 108p. 1992. pap. 10.99 (*1-55945-093-2*) Group Pub.

Younger, Carol. Overcoming Insecurities. (Illus.). 48p. (gr. 9-12). 1991. pap. 7.99 (*1-55945-221-8*) Group Pub.

Younger, Jesse. The Fire Engine Book. Battaglia, Aurelius, illus. 24p. (ps-k). 1987. pap. write for info (*0-307-10082-0*, Pub. by Golden Bks) Western Pub.

Youngman, Bernard R. Patriarchs, Judges, & Kings. (gr. 8-12). 1979. pap. 9.95 (*0-7175-0414-X*) Dufour.

—Spreading the Gospel. (gr. 8-12). 1979. pap. 9.95 (*0-7175-0420-4*) Dufour.

Youngs, Bettie B. Friendship Is Forever, Isn't It? 141p. (Orig.). (gr. 4 up). 1990. pap. 8.95x (*0-940221-05-5*) Lrng Tools-Bilicki Pubns.

—Friendship Is Forever, Isn't It? 141p. (gr. 4-12). 1990. 8.95 (*0-915190-94-X*, JP 9094-X) Jalmar Pr.

—Goal Setting Skills for Young Adults. 64p. (gr. 5 up). 1990. 10.00 (*0-915190-91-5*, JP 9091-5) Jalmar Pr.

—Goal Setting Skills for Young People. 64p. (gr. 5-12). 1989. pap. 10.00 (*0-940221-04-7*); tchr's. ed. 10.00 (*0-685-27131-5*); wkbk. 10.00 (*0-685-27132-3*); lab manual 10.00 (*0-685-27133-1*) Lrng Tools-Bilicki Pubns.

—Problem Solving Skills for Children. 69p. (gr. k-6). 1989. pap. text ed. 9.95 (*0-940221-01-2*); tchr's. ed. 10.00 (*0-685-25381-3*); wkbk. 10.00 (*0-685-25382-1*); lab manual 10.00 (*0-685-25383-X*) Lrng Tools-Bilicki Pubns.

—Problem Solving Skills for Children. 69p. (ps-4). 1989. 10.00 (*0-915190-93-1*, JP 9093-1) Jalmar Pr.

—A Stress Management Guide for Young People. 6th ed. Nelson, Trish, illus. 88p. (gr. 6-12). 1986. pap. text ed. 9.95x (*0-940221-00-4*) Lrng Tools-Bilicki Pubns.

—A Stress Management Guide for Young People. 96p. (gr. 5 up). 1986. 9.95 (*0-915190-92-3*, JP 9092-3) Jalmar Pr.

—You & Self-Esteem: It's the Key to Happiness & Success. 160p. (gr. 5-12). 1992. pap. 16.95 (*0-915190-83-4*, JP-9083-4) Jalmar Pr.

Youngs, Bettie B. & Tracy, Brian S. Achievement, Happiness, Popularity & Success: A Self-Esteem Book for Young People. Baldwin, Cathy, ed. LC 88-90808. 169p. (Orig.). (gr. 5-12). 1989. pap. 12.95 (*0-929354-00-1*) Phoenix Educ Found.

—Achievement, Popularity, & Success: Getting What You Want from Life. 276p. (Orig.). (gr. 6-12). 1988. pap. 12.95 (*0-317-89982-1*) Phoenix Educ Found.

Younkin, Paula. Indians of the Arctic & Subarctic. (Illus.). 96p. (gr. 5-8). 1991. lib. bdg. 18.95x (*0-8160-2391-3*) Facts on File.

—The Spirit of St. Louis. LC 93-3292. (Illus.). 48p. (gr. 5-6). 1994. RSBE 13.95 (*0-89686-832-X*, Crestwood Hse) Macmillan Child Grp.

Yount, Christine. Responding to Injustice. (Illus.). 48p. (gr. 9-12). 1991. pap. 7.99 (*1-55945-214-5*) Group Pub.

—Telling Your Friends about Christ. (Illus.). 48p. (gr. 6-8). 1991. pap. 7.99 (*1-55945-114-9*) Group Pub.

Yount, Lisa. Black Scientists. (Illus.). (gr. 5-12). 1991. lib. bdg. 16.95x (*0-8160-2549-5*) Facts on File.

—Cancer. LC 91-23547. (Illus.). (gr. 5-8). 1991. PLB 14.95 (*1-56006-125-1*) Lucent Bks.

Yourcenar, Marguerite. Comment Wang-Fo Fut Sauve. Lemoine, Georges, illus. (FRE.). 48p. (gr. 3-7). 1990. pap. 7.95 (*2-07-031178-3*) Schoenhof.

Youyouseyah, jt. auth. see Mana, Tawa.

Ypsilantis, George, jt. auth. see McClard, Megan.

Yronwode, Catherine, ed. see Busiek, Kurt.

Yu, Ling. Cooking the Chinese Way. LC 82-263. (Illus.). 48p. (gr. 4-7). 1982. PLB 14.95 (*0-8225-0902-4*) Lerner Pubns.

—Cooking the Chinese Way. (gr. 4-7). 1993. pap. 5.95 (*0-8225-9631-8*) Lerner Pubns.

—A Family in Taiwan. (Illus.). 32p. (gr. 2-5). 1990. PLB 13.50 (*0-8225-1685-3*) Lerner Pubns.

Yuan Hsi Kuo & Louise Hsi Kuo. Chinese Folk Tales. LC 75-9082. (gr. 7 up). 1976. pap. 5.95 (*0-89087-074-8*) Celestial Arts.

Yue, Charlotte. The Pueblo. (gr. 4-7). 1990. pap. 6.95 (*0-395-54961-2*) HM.

—The Tipi: A Center of Native American Life. Yue, David, illus. LC 83-19529. 96p. (gr. 4-7). 1984. PLB 11.99 (*0-394-96177-3*) Knopf Bks Yng Read.

Yue, Charlotte & Yue, David. Christopher Columbus: How He Did It. Yue, David, illus. 144p. (gr. 3-6). 1992. 19.95 (*0-395-52100-9*) HM.

—The Igloo. LC 88-6154. (Illus.). 128p. (gr. 3-7). 1988. 13.45 (*0-395-44613-9*) HM.

—The Igloo. 128p. (gr. 3-7). 1992. pap. 4.80 (*0-395-62986-1*, Sandpiper) HM.

Yue, Charlotte, jt. auth. see Yue, David.

Yue, David & Yue, Charlotte. The Pueblo. (Illus.). (gr. 8-11). 1986. 13.45 (*0-395-38350-1*) HM.

Yue, David, jt. auth. see Yue, Charlotte.

Yulin, Betty. Una Guia Unica Para la Salud, Juventud y Longevidad. Elkan, Betty, intro. by. Yulin, Betty, tr. (SPA., Illus.). (gr. 5 up). 1993. pap. 5.00 (*0-9600148-9-6*) Juvenescent.

Yulin, Betty, tr. see Yulin, Betty.

Yun-Kan, Shio, jt. auth. see Merton, D.

Yurko, John. Video Basics. D'Amato, Janet, illus. LC 82-21543. 64p. (gr. 4-7). 1983. 9.95 (*0-13-941781-8*) P-H.

Yushij, Nima. When the Elephants Came. Evans, Mariam & Batmanglij, M., eds. Evans, Mariam, tr. from PER. Fanta, Illus. LC 87-31690. 32p. (gr. 4 up). 1988. 18.50 (*0-934211-15-9*); English-Persian Version. 18.50 (*0-934211-09-4*) Mage Pubs Inc.

Yusufali, Jabeen. Pakistan: An Islamic Treasure. (Illus.). 128p. (gr. 5 up). 1990. RSBE 14.95 (*0-87518-433-2*, Dillon) Macmillan Child Grp.

Yvart, Jacques. The Rising of the Wind: Adventures along the Beaufort Scale. Lazorthes, Jean, tr. from FRE. Forgeot, Claire, illus. LC 83-83203. 48p. (Fire.). (gr. 7 up). 1991. 12.95 (*0-88138-031-8*, Green Tiger) S&S Trade.

YWCA World Fellowship Committee - Tokyo. Japanese Etiquette: An Introduction. LC 59-9828. (Illus.). 171p. (gr. 7 up). 1959. pap. 9.95 (*0-8048-0290-4*) C E Tuttle.

Ywing-Ming Yang. The Mask of the King. Dougall, Alan, ed. Xieu-Lin, Li, illus. 52p. (gr. 4 up). 1990. 4.95 (*0-940871-11-4*) Yangs Martial Arts.

Yzermans, Vincent A. Jesus & Caesar Augustus: A Legend. Yell, Vonett & Bergmann, Melvin, illus. LC 89-50566. 180p. (Orig.). (gr. 7-12). 1989. pap. 7.95 (*0-89622-396-5*) Twenty-Third.

Z

Zabar, Abbie. Alphabet Soup. Zabar, Abbie, illus. 32p. 1990. 14.95 (*1-55670-154-3*) Stewart Tabori & Chang.

—A Perfectly Irregular Christmas Tree. Zabar, Abbie, illus. 40p. 1991. 14.00 (*0-517-58608-8*, C Potter Bks) Crown Pub Group.

Zabel, Morton D., ed. see Dickens, Charles.

Zable, Rona S. An Almost Perfect Summer. (gr. 7 up). 1989. pap. 2.95 (*0-553-27967-X*, Starfire) Bantam.

—Landing on Marvin Gardens. (gr. 7 up). 1989. 13.95 (*0-553-05839-8*, Starfire) Bantam.

—Landing on Marvin Gardens. 1991. pap. 3.50 (*0-553-29288-9*) Bantam.

—Love at the Laundromat. 160p. (gr. 7 up). 1992. pap. 3.50 (*0-553-27225-X*, Starfire) Bantam.

Zach, Cheryl. Benny & the Crazy Contest. LC 90-43903. (Illus.). 80p. (gr. 2-6). 1991. SBE 11.95 (*0-02-793705-4*, Bradbury Pr) Macmillan Child Grp.

—Benny & the No-Good Teacher. Wilson, Janet, illus. LC 91-30588. 80p. (gr. 2-6). 1992. SBE 12.95 (*0-02-793706-2*, Bradbury Pr) Macmillan Child Grp.

—Looking Out for Lacy. 1992. pap. 3.50 (*0-06-106772-5*, Harp PBks) HarpC.

—Los Angeles. (Illus.). 60p. (gr. 3 up). 1990. RSBE 13.95 (*0-87518-415-4*, Dillon) Macmillan Child Grp.

Zacharias, Thomas. Where Is the Green Parrot? 1990. 12.95 (*0-385-30091-3*) Doubleday.

Zachman, Linda, et al. ACHIEV-Red (Activities for Children Involving Everyday Vocabulary) Package. (ps-5). 1989. complete pkg. 192.70 (*1-55999-001-5*) LinguiSystems.

—ACHIEV-Red Books (Activities for Children Involving Everyday Vocabulary) (ps-5). 1985. spiral manuals 49.95 (*1-55999-005-8*) LinguiSystems.

Zack, Carol, jt. auth. see Gregorich, Barbara.

Zackon, Fred & McAulyfe, William E. Heroin: The Street Narcotic. (Illus.). 32p. (gr. 5 up). 1991. pap. 4.49 (*1-55546-999-X*) Chelsea Hse.

Zadra, Dan. Dare to Be Different. (Illus.). 32p. (gr. 6 up). 1986. PLB 12.95s.p. (*0-88682-016-2*) Creative Ed.

—Explorers of America: Champlain. rev. ed. (gr. 2-4). 1988. PLB 14.95s.p. (*0-88682-181-9*) Creative Ed.

—Explorers of America: Columbus. rev. ed. (gr. 2-4). 1988. PLB 14.95s.p. (*0-88682-184-3*) Creative Ed.

—Explorers of America: Coronado. rev. ed. (gr. 2-4). 1988. PLB 14.95s.p. (*0-88682-182-7*) Creative Ed.

—Explorers of America: DeSoto. rev. ed. (gr. 2-4). 1988. PLB 14.95s.p. (*0-88682-185-1*) Creative Ed.

—Explorers of America: Leif Erickson. (gr. 2-4). 1988. PLB 14.95s.p. (*0-88682-180-0*) Creative Ed.

—Explorers of America: Lewis & Clark. rev. ed. (gr. 2-4). 1988. PLB 14.95s.p. (*0-88682-183-5*) Creative Ed.

—Frontiersmen in America: Buffalo Bill. rev. ed. (gr. 2-4). 1988. PLB 11.50s.p. (*0-88682-194-0*); 14.95 (*0-318-32954-9*) Creative Ed.

—Frontiersmen in America: Daniel Boone. rev. ed. (gr. 2-4). 1988. PLB 11.50s.p. (*0-88682-191-6*); 14.45 (*0-318-32950-6*) Creative Ed.

—Frontiersmen in America: Davy Crocket. rev. ed. (gr. 2-4). 1988. PLB 11.50s.p. (*0-88682-195-9*); 14.95 (*0-318-32952-2*) Creative Ed.

—Frontiersmen in America: Francis Marion. rev. ed. (gr. 2-4). 1988. PLB 11.15s.p. (*0-88682-196-7*); 14.95 (*0-318-32955-7*) Creative Ed.

—Frontiersmen in America: Jim Bridgers. (gr. 2-4). 1988. PLB 11.50s.p. (*0-88682-179-7*); 14.95 (*0-318-32953-0*) Creative Ed.

—Frontiersmen in America: Kit Carson. rev. ed. (gr. 2-4). 1988. PLB 11.50s.p. (*0-88682-189-4*); 14.95 (*0-318-32951-4*) Creative Ed.

—How to Beat the Jitters. (Illus.). 32p. (gr. 6 up). 1986. PLB 12.95s.p. (*0-88682-018-9*) Creative Ed.

—Indians of America: Crazy Horse. rev. ed. (gr. 2-4). 1987. PLB 14.95s.p. (*0-88682-163-0*) Creative Ed.

—Indians of America: Geronimo. rev. ed. (gr. 2-4). 1987. PLB 14.95s.p. (*0-88682-159-2*) Creative Ed.

—Indians of America: Osceola. rev. ed. (gr. 2-4). 1987. PLB 14.95s.p. (*0-88682-162-2*) Creative Ed.

—Indians of America: Pontiac. rev. ed. (gr. 2-4). 1987. PLB 14.95s.p. (*0-88682-160-6*) Creative Ed.

—Indians of America: Squanto. rev. ed. (gr. 2-4). 1987. PLB 14.95s.p. (*0-88682-161-4*) Creative Ed.

—Just Keep on Keepin' On. (Illus.). 32p. (gr. 6 up). 1986. PLB 12.95s.p. (*0-88682-020-0*) Creative Ed.

—Mistakes Are Great! (Illus.). 32p. (gr. 6 up). 1986. PLB 12.95s.p. (*0-88682-019-7*) Creative Ed.

—More Good Time for You. (Illus.). 32p. (gr. 6 up). 1986. PLB 12.95s.p. (*0-88682-022-7*) Creative Ed.

—The Secrets to Goal-Setting. (Illus.). 32p. (gr. 6 up). 1986. PLB 12.95s.p. (*0-88682-017-0*) Creative Ed.

—Statesmen in America: John Paul Jones. rev. ed. (gr. 2-4). 1988. PLB 14.95s.p. (*0-88682-193-2*) Creative Ed.

—Statesmen in America: Lafayette. (gr. 2-4). 1988. PLB 14.95s.p. (*0-88682-190-8*) Creative Ed.

—Statesmen in America: Robert E. Lee. rev. ed. (gr. 2-4). 1988. PLB 14.95s.p. (*0-88682-192-4*) Creative Ed.

—Statesmen in America: Sam Houston. rev. ed. (gr. 2-4). 1988. PLB 14.95s.p. (*0-88682-187-8*) Creative Ed.

—Statesmen in America: Ulysses S. Grant. rev. ed. (gr. 2-4). 1988. PLB 14.95s.p. (*0-88682-188-6*) Creative Ed.

—Talk Like an Eagle. (Illus.). 32p. (gr. 6 up). 1986. PLB 12.95s.p. (*0-88682-021-9*) Creative Ed.

—There Will Never Be Another You. (Illus.). 32p. (gr. 6 up). 1986. PLB 12.95s.p. (*0-88682-015-4*) Creative Ed.

—Washington Bullets. 32p. (gr. 5 up). 1993. PLB 14.95 (*0-88682-523-7*) Creative Ed.

Zadra, Dan, jt. auth. see Grant, Matthew G.

Zadra, Dan, jt. auth. see Klingel, Cynthia.

Zagwyn, Deborah T. Pumpkin Blanket. (ps-5). 1991. 14.95 (*0-89087-637-1*) Celestial Arts.

Zahava, Irene, ed. Through Other Eyes: Animal Stories by Women. 200p. (Orig.). 1988. pap. 8.95 (*0-89594-314-X*) Crossing Pr.

Zahn, Ellsworth E. Dudley. Zahn, Ellsworth E., illus. 40p. (Orig.). Date not set. pap. text ed. 14.95 (*0-9637308-0-0*) L E Zahn.

Zahradka, Miroslav. The Un-Terrible Tiger. Zahradka, Miroslav, illus. LC 78-155815. 32p. (ps-3). 7.95 (*0-87592-056-X*) Scroll Pr.

Zak, Monica. Save My Rainforest. Runnerstrom, Bengt-Arne, illus. LC 91-40179. 29p. 1992. 14.95 (*0-912078-94-4*) Volcano Pr.

Zak, Victoria & Vash, Peter. The Dieter's Dictionary & Problem Solver: An A to Z Guide to Nutrition, Health, & Fitness. (Illus.). 352p. 1992. 19.95 (*1-55853-172-6*) Rutledge Hill Pr.

Zakalik, Leslie S. The Comprehension Carnival. 76p. (gr. 2-4). 1977. 7.95 (*0-88160-005-9*, LW 106) Learning Wks.

—Study Skills Sorcery. 48p. (gr. 4-6). 1978. 5.95 (*0-88160-028-8*, LW 213) Learning Wks.

—Super Science Fiction. 48p. (gr. 4-6). 1977. 5.95 (*0-88160-026-1*, LW 211) Learning Wks.

Zakhoder, Boris. Rosachok: A Russian Story. Mills, Yaroslava, illus. LC 72-10148. (gr. k-3). 1970. PLB 12.88 (*0-688-51113-9*) Lothrop.

Zakhoder's, Boris. The Good Stepmother. Rudolph, Marguerite, retold by. May, Darcy, illus. LC 90-10063. 40p. (ps-2). 1992. pap. 14.00 jacketed (*0-671-68270-9*, S&S BFYR) S&S Trade.

Zakim, Shelley P. Communication Workshop: Reproducible Manual & Role-Playing Cards for Social Communication. (gr. 4-12). 1986. spiral reproducible wkbk. 49.95 (*1-55999-031-7*) LinguiSystems.

Zakon, Miriam S. The Cohens of Tzefat. Dershowitz, Y., illus. 128p. (gr. 6-12). 1985. 12.95 (*0-89906-783-2*); pap. 9.95 (*0-89906-784-0*) Mesorah Pubns.

—The Egyptian Star. Gaelen, Nina, illus. 114p. (gr. 3-9). 1983. o. p. 6.95 (*0-910818-47-9*); pap. 5.95 (*0-910818-48-7*) Judaica Pr.

—Jerusalem Diaries & Other Stories. Dershowitz, Yosef, illus. 128p. (gr. 4-12). 1993. 12.95 (*0-89906-837-5*); pap. 9.95 (*0-89906-838-3*) Mesorah Pubns.

Zakutinsky, Adina. Ha Shem's World of Color. Geld, Goldie, illus. 12p. (ps). 1987. PLB 4.95x (*0-911643-10-9*); board book 4.95 (*0-685-55893-2*) Aura Bklyn.

Zakutinsky, Adina, jt. auth. see Sebarg, R.

Zakutinsky, Ruth. The House That Shlomo Built. Reason, Sharon, ed. Hakakian, Albert, illus. 24p. (ps-1). 1989. 9.95 (*0-911643-11-7*) Aura Bklyn.

—King David & the Frog. Kellman, A., ed. Backman, Aidel, illus. 32p. (gr. k-5). 1986. text ed. 9.95x (*0-911643-05-2*); pap. 5.95x (*0-911643-07-9*) Aura Bklyn.

—The Wonder Worm. Backman, Aidel, illus. 24p. (gr. k-3). 1992. PLB 6.95x (*0-911643-17-6*) Aura Bklyn.

Zakutinsky, Ruth, ed. see Goetz, Bracha.

Zakutinsky, Ruth, ed. see Rubinstein, Reva.

Zalben. Fortune Teller in 5B. 1991. 14.95 (*0-8050-1924-3*) H Holt & Co.

—Happy Passover Rosie. (gr. 4 up). 1991. 13.95 (*0-8050-1442-X*) H Holt & Co.

Zalben, Jane & Breskin. Papa's Latkes. 1994. write for info. (*0-8050-3099-9*) H Holt & Co.

Zalben, Jane B. Beni's First Chanukah. Zalben, Jane B., illus. LC 86-33634. 32p. (gr. k-3). 1988. 12.95 (*0-8050-0479-3*, Bks Young Read) H Holt & Co.

—Beni's Little Library, 4 bks. (Illus.). 32p. (gr. k-3). 1991. Boxed set, 32p. ea. pap. 19.95 (*0-8050-1879-4*, Bks Young Read) H Holt & Co.

—Buster Gets Braces. Zalben, Jane B., illus. LC 91-13967. 32p. (ps-2). 1992. 15.95 (*0-8050-1682-1*, Bks Young Read) H Holt & Co.

—Earth to Andrew O. Blechman. Zalben, Jane B., illus. (gr. 3-7). 1989. 14.00 (*0-374-31916-2*) FS&G.

—Fortune Teller in Five B. (gr. 4-7). 1993. pap. 2.95 (*0-590-46041-2*) Scholastic Inc.

—The Fortuneteller in 5B. (Illus.). 144p. (gr. 4-7). 1991. 14.95 (*0-8050-1537-X*, Bks Young Read) H Holt & Co.

—Goldie's Purim. LC 90-43153. (Illus.). 32p. (ps-2). 1991. 13.95 (*0-8050-1227-3*, Bks Young Read) H Holt & Co.

—Happy New Year, Beni. Zalben, Jane B., photos by. LC 92-25013. (Illus.). 32p. (gr. k-3). 1993. PLB 13.95 (*0-8050-1961-8*, Bks Young Read) H Holt & Co.

—Happy Passover, Rosie. Zalben, Jane B., illus. LC 89-19979. 32p. (ps-2). 1990. 13.95 (*0-8050-1221-4*, Bks Young Read) H Holt & Co.

—Here's Looking at You, Kid. (gr. k-12). 1987. pap. 2.50 (*0-440-49373-3*, LFL) Dell.

—Leo & Blossom's Sukkah. Zalben, Jane B., illus. LC 89-24596. 32p. (ps-2). 1990. 13.95 (*0-8050-1226-5*, Bks Young Read) H Holt & Co.

—Water from the Moon. LC 86-46439. 160p. (gr. 8 up). 1987. 15.00 (*0-374-38238-7*) FS&G.

Zaldivar, Raquel P. Roberto Goes Fishing - Roberto Va de Pesca. Bubiera, Sandra S., illus. 32p. (gr. 1-3). 1992. 12.95 (*1-880507-00-5*) Lectorum Pubns.

Zall, Paul M. Becoming American: Young People in the American Revolution. LC 92-40199. (Illus.). 208p. (gr. 6-12). 1993. PLB 22.50 (*0-208-02355-0*, Pub. by Linnet) Shoe String.

Zallinger, Peter. Dinosaurs. Zallinger, Peter, illus. LC 76-24178. (ps-1). 1977. pap. 2.25 (*0-394-83485-2*) Random Bks Yng Read.

—Dinosaurs & Other Archosaurs. Risom, Ole & Luke, Melinda, eds. Zallinger, Peter, illus. LC 85-42930. 96p. (gr. 5 up). 1986. lib. bdg. 9.99 (*0-394-94421-6*) Random Bks Yng Read.

—Prehistoric Animals. Zallinger, Peter, illus. 32p. (ps-3). 1981. 2.25 (*0-394-83737-1*) Random Bks Yng Read.

Zambreno, M. A Plague of Sorcerers. 257p. (gr. 4-9). 1991. 16.95 (*0-15-262430-9*, HB Juv Bks) HarBrace.

Zamojska-Hutchins, Danuta. Cooking the Polish Way. Wolfe, Robert, et al, illus. LC 84-11226. 52p. (gr. 5 up). 1984. PLB 14.95 (*0-8225-0909-1*) Lerner Pubns.

Zamora-Pearson, Marissa, tr. see Edge, Nellie.

Zamora-Pearson, Marissa, tr. see Ledbetter, H. & Lomax, John A.

Zamost, Barbara. Handstands in the Sand. Nalerio, Claudio, illus. 48p. (ps-6). 1992. 12.95 (*1-881970-00-0*) Saras Prints.

Zandt, Eleanor van see Van Zandt, Eleanor.

Zane, Alex. Osceola: Seminole Rebel. Baird, W. David, ed. LC 93-21750. (Illus.). (gr. 5 up). 1994. PLB 18.95 (*0-7910-1716-8*, Am Art Analog); pap. write for info. (*0-7910-1993-4*, Am Art Analog) Chelsea hse.

Zane, John, jt. auth. see Zane, Polly.

Zane, Polly & Zane, John. American Women: Four Centuries of Progress. 2nd, rev. ed. Zane, John, illus. (gr. 7 up). 1989. write for info. (*0-935070-03-6*) Proof Pr.

—The Native Americans. LC 76-5579. (gr. 1-12). 1982. tchrs' ed 32.00 (*0-935070-01-X*) Proof Pr.

Zanger, Walter. Jerusalem. (Illus.). 64p. (gr. 3-7). PLB 14.95 (*1-56711-022-3*) Blackbirch.

Zanini, G. The Dinosaur Book. (Illus.). 72p. (gr. k-6). 1985. 5.98 (*0-517-42525-4*) Outlet Bk Co.

Zanzig, Thomas. Learning to Meditate. Stamschror, Robert P., ed. (Illus.). 70p. (gr. 9-12). 1990. text ed. 2.50 stitched (*0-88489-226-3*); tchr's ed. 4.50 (*0-88489-227-1*) St Marys.

Zapata, Crystal. Cat That Barked. rev. ed. LC 88-36660. (gr. 2-6). 1989. 4.00 (*0-915541-71-8*) Star Bks Inc.

—The Galactic Rocking Chair. (Orig.). (gr. 4-9). 1990. pap. 4.00 (*0-915541-69-6*) Star Bks Inc.

Zapater, Beatriz M. Fiesta! Ortega, Jose, illus. 32p. (gr. 2-5). 1993. pap. 4.95 (*0-671-79842-1*, S&S BYR) S&S Trade.

Zapel, Arthur, ed. see Happy Jack Feder.

Zapel, Arthur, ed. see Kehret, Peg.

Zapel, Arthur L., ed. see Enscoe, Lawrence & Enscoe, Andrea.

Zapel, Arthur L., ed. see Kehret, Peg.

Zapel, Arthur L., ed. see Lazicki, Ted.

Zapel, Arthur L., ed. see Majeski, Bill.

Zapel, Arthur L., ed. see Novelly, Maria C.

Zapel, Theodore O., ed. see Krell-Oishi, Mary.

Zappler, George & Zappler, Lisbeth. Amphibians As Pets. LC 72-92252. 160p. (gr. 3-9). 1973. pap. 5.95 (*0-385-08581-8*) Doubleday.

Zappler, Lisbeth, jt. auth. see Zappler, George.

Zappler, Liz. A Day in the Life of the Monarch Butterfly. Eakin, Ed, ed. Morris, Aaron, illus. 48p. (gr. 2-6). 1989. 8.85 (*0-89015-616-6*) Eakin-Sunbelt.

Zar, Rose. In the Mouth of the Wolf. 224p. (gr. 6 up). 1983. pap. 8.95 (*0-8276-0382-7*) JPS Phila.

Zarambouka, Sofia. Irene. Zarambouka, Sofia & Loftin, Tee, trs. (Illus.). 42p. (gr. k-3). 1979. 8.95 (*0-934812-00-4*) Tee Loftin.

Zarchy, Harry. Let's Go Camping: A Guide to Outdoor Living. Zarchy, Harry, illus. (gr. 2 up). 1964. lib. bdg. 5.69 (*0-394-91328-0*) Knopf Bks Yng Read.

Zareef, Linda. Africa: A Glance at an Amazing Continent. (Illus.). (ps-6). 1989. write for info. (*0-9625787-0-3*) An Awareness.

Zarrin, Alireza. Az Qudesi Ta Sarzamin-e Khar: Two Long Poems. LC 88-82739. (PER.). 96p. (Orig.). (gr. 8 up). 1988. pap. 5.95 (*0-317-93236-5*) Alien Bks.

Zarzynski, Joseph W. Champ - Beyond the Legend. updated ed. Dinsale, Tim, intro. by. LC 88-60702. (Illus.). 240p. (gr. 7-12). 1988. pap. 12.95 (*0-937559-01-6*) M-Z Info.

Zaslavsky, Claudia. Count on Your Fingers African Style. Pinkney, Jerry, illus. LC 77-26586. 32p. (gr. k-3). 1980. (Crowell Jr Bks); (Crowell Jr Bks) HarpC Child Bks.

—Zero! Is It Something? Is It Nothing? Bassett, Jeni, illus. LC 88-38940. 32p. (gr. k-4). 1989. PLB 12.90 (*0-531-10693-4*) Watts.

Zaslow, David. A Rose by Any Other Name. (Illus.). 96p. (Orig.). 1980. pap. 4.95 (*0-89411-002-0*) Kids Matter.

—Somedays It Feels Like It Wants to Rain. Fink, Grace, illus. LC 76-46244. (gr. 2-6). 1976. pap. 3.95 (*0-89411-001-2*) Kids Matter.

Zaslow, David B. & Inada, Lawson F. Hey Diddle Rock. Bullock, Kathleen, illus. 32p. (Orig.). (ps-8). 1986. pap. 7.95 (*0-89411-006-3*) Kids Matter.

—Hickory Dickory Rock. Bullock, Kathleen, illus. 32p. (Orig.). (ps-8). 1986. pap. 7.95 (*0-89411-004-7*) Kids Matter.

—Humpty Dumpty Rock. Bullock, Kathleen, illus. 32p. (Orig.). (ps-8). 1986. pap. 7.95 (*0-89411-007-1*) Kids Matter.

—Rock-a-Doodle-Doo. Bullock, Kathleen, illus. 32p. (Orig.). (ps-8). 1986. pap. 7.95 (*0-89411-005-5*) Kids Matter.

Zavinski, Monique, tr. see D'Andrea, Deborah B.

Zavinski, Monique, tr. see D'Andrea, Joseph C.

Zavos, Judy. Murgatroyd's Garden. Zak, Drahos, illus. 32p. (gr. k-3). 1988. 9.95 (*0-312-01629-8*) St Martin.

Zavrel, Stepan. Vodnik. Zavrel, Stepan, illus. LC 72-121796. 32p. (ps-3). 8.95 (*0-87592-058-6*) Scroll Pr.

Zawadsky, Pat. The Secret in the Toy Room. 28p. (Orig.). (gr. 2-7). 1984. pap. 3.00 (*0-88680-225-3*); piano/vocal score 7.50 (*0-88680-226-1*); royalty on application 25.00 (*0-685-57940-9*) I E Clark.

Zawolkow, Esther, jt. auth. see Gustason, Gerilee.

Zebra, A. A Rumble in the Jungle. LC 89-82286. (Illus.). 96p. (Orig.). (gr. 2-6). 1990. pap. 7.95 (*0-86327-240-1*, Pub. by Wolfhound Pr EIRE) Dufour.

Zebrowski, George. The Stars Will Speak. LC 85-42638. 224p. (gr. 7 up). 1987. pap. 2.95 (*0-06-447050-4*, Trophy) HarpC Child Bks.

Zebrowski, Stephanie R., ed. see Stotz, Carl E.

Zech, Cindy O. SOS: Save Our Spines: A Backschool for Kids. rev. ed. Attebury, Kevan J., illus. 95p. (gr. 3-6). Date not set. wkbk. 10.95 (*0-9638765-1-1*); tchr's. ed. 18.95 (*0-9638765-0-3*) Prevent Educ.

Zechlin, Katharina. Creative Enameling & Jewelry-Making. Kuttner, Paul, tr. LC 65-20877. (gr. 10 up). 1965. 6.95 (*0-8069-5062-5*); PLB 6.69 (*0-8069-5063-3*) Sterling.

Zeck, Gerry. I Love to Dance! LC 82-4232. (Illus.). 64p. (gr. 2-5). 1982. lib. bdg. 13.50 (*0-87614-198-X*) Carolrhoda Bks.

Zeder, Susan. Ozma of Oz: A Tale of Time. (Orig.). (gr. 4 up). 1981. playscript 5.00 (*0-87602-233-6*) Anchorage.

Zeder, Suzan. Doors. (Orig.). (gr. 4 up). 1985. 4.50 (*0-87602-261-1*) Anchorage.

—Mother Hicks. 68p. (Orig.). (gr. k-3). 1986. pap. 5.50 playscript (*0-87602-263-8*) Anchorage.

—The Play Called Noah's Flood. (Orig.). (gr. 4 up). 1985. pap. 5.00 (*0-87602-247-6*) Anchorage.

—Step on a Crack. (gr. 1-9). 1976. 4.50 (*0-87602-207-7*) Anchorage.

—Wiley & the Hairy-Man. (gr. k up). 1978. 4.50 (*0-87602-219-0*) Anchorage.

Zeder, Suzan L. The Death & Life of Sherlock Holmes. (Orig.). 1991. Playscript. pap. 5.50 (*0-87602-296-4*) Anchorage.

—An Evening at Versailles. Moliere, J. B., contrib. by. 1989. Playscript. 5.00 (*0-87602-284-0*) Anchorage.

—In a Room Somewhere: (Musical) 60p. 1988. Playscript. 5.00 (*0-87602-282-4*) Anchorage.

Zeese, Dina. Sing a Song of Concepts. LC 87-83701. 112p. (Orig.). (ps-2). 1988. pap. 16.95 (*0-936485-01-9*) Lkng Glass Pubns.

Zeff. Animal Picture-English. (Illus.). (gr. 1-9). 1980. (Usborne-Hayes); French ed. 11.95 (*0-86020-556-8*); pap. 8.95 (*0-7460-0395-1*) EDC.

Zeff, jt. auth. see Wilkes.

Zeff, C. see Cartwright, Stephen.

Zeff, Robin L. Environmental Action Groups. (Illus.). 112p. (gr. 5 up). 1993. PLB 19.95 (*0-7910-1593-9*) Chelsea Hse.

Zeiderman, Howard. Worksheets for Touchstones, Vol. II, Pt. 1. 60p. (Orig.). (gr. 9-12). 1992. pap. 1.95 wkbk. (*1-878461-12-5*) CZM Pr.

Zeiderman, Howard, jt. auth. see Comber, Geoffrey.

Zeier, Joan T. The Elderberry Thicket. 90-90. 160p. (gr. 4-7). 1990. SBE 13.95 (*0-689-31612-7*, Atheneum Child Bk) Macmillan Child Grp.

—Stick Boy. LC 92-23326. 144p. (gr. 2-6). 1993. SBE 13.95 (*0-689-31835-9*, Atheneum Child Bk) Macmillan Child Grp.

Zeinert, Karen. The Warsaw Ghetto Uprising. LC 92-14758. (Illus.). 96p. (gr. 7 up). 1993. PLB 14.90 (*1-56294-282-4*) Millbrook Pr.

Zeinert, Karen, ed. see Sherburne, Andrew.

Zeitlin, Steve, jt. auth. see Jaffe, Nina.

Zelazny, Roger. The Courts of Chaos. 144p. (gr. 9 up). 1979. pap. 4.50 (*0-380-47175-2*) Avon.

—Creatures of Light & Darkness. 192p. (gr. 7 up). 1970. pap. 3.50 (*0-380-01122-0*) Avon.

—A Dark Traveling. LC 86-32437. (Illus.). 152p. (gr. 6 up). 1987. 14.95 (*0-8027-6686-2*) Walker & Co.

—The Hand of Oberon. 192p. (gr. 7 up). 1977. pap. 4.99 (*0-380-01664-8*) Avon.

—Nine Princes in Amber. 176p. (gr. 9 up). 1977. pap. 4.50 (*0-380-01430-0*) Avon.

—Sign of the Unicorn. 192p. (gr. 9 up). 1976. pap. 4.99 (*0-380-00831-9*) Avon.

Zelde, Janet S., jt. auth. see Liebowitz, Jay.

Zeldin, Florence. A Mouse in Our Jewish House. Rauchwerger, Lisa, illus. LC 89-40362. 32p. (ps). 1990. 11.95 (*0-933873-43-3*) Torah Aura.

Zeldis, Malcah, illus. Honest Abe. Kunhardt, Edith, photos by. LC 91-47191. (Illus.). 32p. (gr. k up). 1993. 15.00 (*0-688-11189-0*); PLB 14.93 (*0-688-11190-4*) Greenwillow.

Zeldis, Yona. Coping with Beauty, Fitness & Fashion. Rosen, Ruth, ed. Daven, Douglas, illus. LC 86-24850. 128p. (gr. 7 up). 1987. PLB 13.95 (*0-8239-0731-7*) Rosen Group.

—Coping with Social Situations: A Handbook of Correct Behavior. rev. ed. (gr. 7-12). 1987. PLB 13.95 (*0-8239-0767-8*) Rosen Group.

Zeleznak, Shirley. Camping. LC 80-425. (Illus.). 32p. (gr. 4 up). 1980. RSBE 9.95 (*0-89686-071-X*, Crestwood Hse) Macmillan Child Grp.

Zelinsky, Paul O. The Lion & the Stoat. Zelinsky, Paul O., illus. LC 83-16326. 40p. (gr. 1-3). 1984. PLB 10.88 (*0-688-02563-3*) Greenwillow.

—The Wheels on the Bus: With Pictures that Move. 16p. (ps). 1990. 14.95 (*0-525-44644-3*, DCB) Dutton Child Bks.

Zelinsky, Paul O., retold by. & illus. Enano Saltarin. (SPA.). 40p. (gr. k-6). 1992. 15.00 (*0-525-44903-5*, DCB) Dutton Child Bks.

Zelinsky, Paul O., adapted by. & illus. The Maid & the Mouse & the Odd-Shaped House. 32p. (ps-2). 1993. pap. 4.99 (*0-14-054946-3*, Puffin Unicorn) Puffin Bks.

—The Maid & the Mouse & the Odd-Shaped House. 32p. (ps-2). 1993. 14.99 (0-525-45095-5, DCB) Dutton Child Bks.
Zelinsky, Paul O., retold by. & illu see Grimm, Jacob & Grimm, Wilhelm K.
Zelinsky, Paul O., ed. see Grimm, Wilhelm K.
Zeller, Beatriz, tr. see Carrier, Roch.
Zeller, Paula K. Alerta a la Marihuana: Focus on Marijuana. Neuhaus, David, illus. (SPA.). 56p. (gr. 3-7). 1991. PLB 21.27 (0-516-37354-4) Childrens.
—Focus on Marijuana. (Illus.). 56p. (gr. 2-4). 1990. PLB 14.95 (0-941477-97-5) TFC Bks NY.
Zeller, Walter. Bildbeschreibungen: Picture Descriptions in German, 2 bks. Baker, Syd, illus. Winitz, Harris, intro. by. 130p. (gr. 7 up). 1988. Bk. I incl. 2 cassettes. 32.00 (0-939990-57-1); Bk. II incl. 2 cassettes. 32.00 (0-939990-58-X) Intl Linguistics.
Zellmer, Mary. R-Ticulation. (Illus.). (ps-4). 1986. incl. 40 3x5 cards 12.00 (0-930599-23-3) Thinking Pubns.
—S-Ticulation. (Illus.). (ps-4). 1987. incl. 40 3x5 cards 12.00 (0-930599-24-1) Thinking Pubns.
Zelonky, Joy. I Can't Always Hear You. Bejna, Barbara & Jensen, Shirlee, illus. Geist, Chris, intro. by. LC 79-23891. 32p. (gr. k-6). 1980. PLB 17.96 (0-8172-1355-4) Raintree Steck-V.
—I Can't Always Hear You. (ps-3). 1993. pap. 3.95 (0-8114-5205-0) Raintree Steck-V.
—My Best Friend Moved Away. Adams, Angela, illus. Silverman, Manuel, intro. by. LC 79-24111. (Illus.). (gr. k-6). 1980. PLB 17.96 (0-8172-1353-8) Raintree Steck-V.
—My Best Friend Moved Away. (ps-3). 1993. pap. 3.95 (0-8114-7157-8) Raintree Steck-V.
Zeltmann, Walter F. Human Rights. LC 90-71594. iii, 72p. (Orig.). 1990. 24.90 (0-9622705-2-0); pap. 9.90 (0-9622705-3-9) Yellow Hook Pr.
—The Roots of Prejudice. LC 93-93974. (Illus.). 93p. 1993. 24.90 (0-9622705-4-7) Yellow Hook Pr.
Zelver, Patricia. Don Octavio & the New Creature. Daste, Larry, illus. LC 93-29565. 1994. write for info. (0-688-13159-X, Tambourine Bks); PLB write for info. (0-688-13160-3, Tambourine Bks) Morrow.
—The Wedding of Don Octavio. Daste, Larry, illus. LC 92-12587. 32p. (gr. k up). 1993. 14.00 (0-688-11334-6, Tambourine Bks); PLB 13.93 (0-688-11335-4, Tambourine Bks) Morrow.
—The Wonderful Towers of Watts. Lessac, Frane, illus. LC 93-20344. 32p. 1994. 15.00 (0-688-12649-9, Tambourine Bks); PLB 14.93 (0-688-12650-2, Tambourine Bks) Morrow.
Zemach. Mother Goose Picture Book. (Illus.). Date not set. 15.00 (0-06-205046-X); PLB 14.89 (0-06-205047-8) HarpC Child Bks.
Zemach, Harve. Duffy & the Devil. Zemach, Margot, illus. LC 72-81491. 40p. (ps up). 1973. 17.00 (0-374-31887-5); pap. 4.95, 1986 (0-374-41897-7, Sunburst) FS&G.
—The Judge: An Untrue Tale. Zemach, Margot, illus. LC 79-87209. 48p. (ps-3). 1969. 17.00 (0-374-33960-0) FS&G.
—The Judge: An Untrue Tale. Zemach, Margot, illus. 48p. (ps up). 1988. pap. 5.95 (0-374-43962-1, Sunburst) FS&G.
—Mommy, Buy Me a China Doll. Zemach, Margot, illus. 32p. (ps up). 1989. pap. 4.95 (0-374-45286-5, Sunburst) FS&G.
—A Penny a Look. Zemach, Margot, illus. 48p. (ps up). 1989. pap. 4.95 (0-374-45758-1, Sunburst) FS&G.
—A Penny a Look: An Old Story. Zemach, Margot, illus. LC 71-161373. 48p. (ps-3). 1971. 16.00 (0-374-35793-5) FS&G.
Zemach, Harve & Zemach, Kaethe. The Princess & Froggie. Zemach, Margot, illus. (ps-3). 1992. pap. 4.95 (0-374-46011-6, Sunburst) FS&G.
Zemach, Kaethe, jt. auth. see Zemach, Harve.
Zemach, Margot. La Gallinita Roja: Un Cuento Viejo (the Little Red Hen: an Old Story) (ps-3). 1992. 14.00 (0-374-34285-7) FS&G.
—It Could Always Be Worse. (ps up). 1990. pap. 4.95 (0-374-43636-3, Sunburst) FS&G.
—Jake & Honeybunch Go to Heaven. LC 82-71752. (Illus.). 40p. (gr. 3 up). 1982. 16.00 (0-374-33652-0) FS&G.
—Jake & Honeybunch Go to Heaven. Zemach, Margot, illus. 40p. (ps up). 1987. pap. 4.95 (0-374-43714-9, Sunburst) FS&G.
—The Little Red Hen. (ps-3). 1987. pap. 3.95 (0-14-050567-9, Puffin) Puffin Bks.
—The Little Red Hen: An Old Story. Zemach, Margot, illus. LC 83-14159. 32p. (ps-3). 1983. 14.00 (0-374-34621-6) FS&G.
—Little Red Hen: An Old Story. (ps-3). 1993. pap. 4.95 (0-374-44511-7, Sunburst) FS&G.
—Siempre Puede Ser Peor: It Could Always Be Worse. Marcuse, Aida, tr. (SPA., Illus.). 32p. (ps-3). 1992. 17.00 (0-374-36907-0, Mirasol) FS&G.
—The Three Little Pigs. (Illus.). 32p. (ps up). 1991. pap. 3.95 (0-374-47717-5, Sunburst) FS&G.
—The Three Wishes: An Old Story. Zemach, Margot, illus. LC 86-80956. 32p. (ps up). 1986. 16.00 (0-374-37529-1) FS&G.
—Los Tres Deseos; un Viejo Cuento: The Three Wishes; an Old Story. (ps-3). 1993. pap. 16.00 (0-374-34662-3) FS&G.
Zemach-Bersin, Kaethe. The Funny Dream. LC 87-18769. (Illus.). 32p. (ps-3). 1988. 11.95 (0-688-07500-2); lib. bdg. 11.88 (0-688-07501-0) Greenwillow.

Zeman, Ludmila. Gilgamesh the King, Bk. 1. Zeman, Ludmila, illus. LC 91-67565. 24p. (gr. 3 up). 1992. 19.95 (0-88776-283-2) Tundra Bks.
—The Revenge of Ishtar, Bk. II: Gilgamesh the King. Zeman, Ludmila, illus. LC 93-60332. 24p. (gr. 3 up). Date not set. 19.95 (0-88776-315-4) Tundra Bks.
—Le Roi Gilgamesh. Boileau, Michele, tr. from ENG. Zeman, Ludmila, illus. LC 91-67565. (FRE.). 24p. (gr. 3 up). 1993. 19.95 (0-88776-288-3) Tundra Bks.
Zemke, Deborah. Shadow of Matilda Hunt. Zemke, Deborah, illus. LC 90-46140. 32p. (gr. k-3). 1991. 14.45 (0-395-55334-2) HM.
Zemoch, Margot. Three Wishes: An Old Story. (ps-3). 1993. pap. 4.95 (0-374-47728-0) FS&G.
Zenfell, Martha E. U. S. A. LC 88-18561. (Illus.). 48p. (gr. 4-8). 1988. PLB 14.98 (0-382-09515-4) Silver Burdett Pr.
Zenk, Heather. The Siberian Husky. LC 90-34315. (Illus.). 48p. (gr. 5-6). 1990. RSBE 12.95 (0-89686-535-5, Crestwood Hse) Macmillan Child Grp.
Zennert, Richard. Hank Aaron. King, Coretta Scott, intro. by. (Illus.). 112p. (gr. 5 up). 1993. PLB 17.95 (0-7910-1859-8); pap. write for info. (0-7910-1888-1) Chelsea Hse.
Zeplin, Zeno. Clowns to the Rescue. Brown, Bernice, illus. 48p. (gr. k-3). 1993. 9.95 (1-877740-12-8); pap. 5.50 (1-877740-13-6) Nel-Mar Pub.
—The Cross-Eyed Ghost. Jones, Judy, illus. 154p. (gr. 3-6). 1991. PLB 14.95 casebound (1-877740-05-5); pap. text ed. 7.95 (1-877740-06-3) Nel-Mar Pub.
—Discovery on Dusty Creek. Jones, Judy, illus. 112p. (gr. 3-6). 1994. 14.95 (1-877740-23-3); pap. 7.95 (1-877740-24-1) Nel-Mar Pub.
—Great Texas Christmas Legends. 2nd ed. Jones, Judy, illus. 156p. (gr. 4 up). 1987. 15.95 (0-9615760-2-2); pap. 7.95 (0-9615760-3-0) Nel-Mar Pub.
—The Haunted Classroom. Jones, Judy, illus. 136p. (gr. 4-7). 1989. text ed. 14.95 (0-9615760-8-1); pap. text ed. 7.95 (0-9615760-9-X) Nel-Mar Pub.
—Popcorn Is Missing: A Katy & Beth Mystery. Jones, Judy, illus. 48p. (gr. 2-4). 1990. lib. bdg. 7.95 casebound (1-877740-01-2); pap. text ed. 5.50 (1-877740-02-0) Nel-Mar Pub.
—Secret Magic. Jones, Judy, illus. 56p. (gr. 3-6). 1990. lib. bdg. 9.95 casebound (1-877740-03-9); pap. text ed. 5.50g (1-877740-04-7) Nel-Mar Pub.
Zeplin, Zeno & Jones, Judy. Apple Jack & the Big Storm: A Brave Horse to the Rescue. Ebersapacher, Margy, ed. Jones, Judy, illus. 48p. (gr. k-3). 1991. lib. bdg. 9.95 (1-877740-10-1); pap. text ed. 5.50 (1-877740-11-X) Nel-Mar Pub.
Zerbey, Richard J. Jam Plastic: Now You Can Play Lead Guitar with a Live Band. LC 85-754277. (Illus.). 24p. (Orig.). (gr. 7 up). 1986. lib. bdg. 21.95 incl. cassette (0-935565-07-8, JPHV-I); pap. 15.95 incl. cassette (0-935565-04-3); replacement (tape only) 7.99 (0-935565-10-8) Sound Ent.
—Jam Plastic: Now You Can Play Lead Guitar with a Live Band. LC 85-754101. (Illus.). 24p. (Orig.). (gr. 7 up). 1986. lib. bdg. 21.95 incl. cassette (0-935565-08-6); pap. 15.95 (0-935565-05-1); cassette incl.; replacement tape only 7.99 (0-935565-11-6) Sound Ent.
—Jam Plastic: Now You Can Play Lead Guitar with a Live Band. LC 85-754282. (Illus.). 24p. (Orig.). (gr. 7 up). 1986. lib. bdg. 21.95 incl. cassette (0-935565-06-X); pap. 15.95 (0-935565-03-5); cassette incl.; replacement tape only 7.99 (0-935565-09-4) Sound Ent.
Zeringue, Dona. I Am I. Thornton, Don, intro. by. Zeringue, Dona, illus. 32p. (Orig.). (gr. 6-12). Date not set. pap. 7.50 (1-882913-02-7) Thornton LA.
Zerman, Melvyn B. Beyond a Reasonable Doubt: Inside the American Jury System. Caldwell, John, illus. LC 80-2451. 224p. (gr. 7 up). 1981. PLB 12.89 (0-690-04095-4, Crowell Jr Bks) HarpC Child Bks.
—Taking on the Press: Constitutional Rights in Conflict. Rather, Dan, frwd. by. LC 85-47896. (Illus.). 192p. (gr. 7 up). 1986. (Crowell Jr Bks); (Crowell Jr Bks) HarpC Child Bks.
Zerner, Amy, illus. Zen ABC. LC 92-22940. 1993. 14.95 (0-8048-1806-1) C E Tuttle.
Zerner, Jesse, illus. Astro-Dots: Find the Constellations. 64p. (Orig.). (ps-7). 1985. pap. 3.95 (0-913319-01-5) Sunstone Pubns.
Zettner, Pat. The Shadow Warrior. LC 89-440. 224p. (gr. 7 up). 1990. SBE 14.95 (0-689-31486-8, Atheneum Child Bk) Macmillan Child Grp.
Zevin, Jack, ed. The Kingfisher Illustrated History of the World: 40,000 BC to Present Day. Magnusson, Magnus & Martell, Hazelfrwd. by. LC 92-29123. 808p. (gr. 3 up). 1993. 35.00 (1-85697-862-1) Kingfisher Bks.
Zharkova, Olga, illus. We Three Kings. LC 92-38571. 1993. 14.95 (0-590-46433-7) Scholastic Inc.
Zibart, Rosemary. Kidding Around San Francisco: A Young Person's Guide to the City. St. Marie, Janice, illus. 64p. (Orig.). (gr. 3 up). 1989. pap. 9.95 (0-945465-23-8) John Muir.
Zickgraf, Ralph. Laos. (Illus.). 112p. (gr. 5 up). 1991. 14.95 (0-7910-0159-8) Chelsea Hse.
—Norway. (Illus.). 128p. (gr. 5 up). 1990. 14.95 (0-7910-1100-3) Chelsea Hse.
—Sweden. (Illus.). 96p. (gr. 5 up). 1988. lib. bdg. 14.95 (1-55546-797-0) Chelsea Hse.

—William H. Gates: From Whiz Kid to Software King. Young, Richard G., ed. LC 91-32056. (Illus.). 64p. (gr. 4-8). 1992. PLB 17.26 (1-56074-016-7) Garrett Ed Corp.
Zidrou. Ms. Blanche, the Spotless Cow. Merveille, David, illus. LC 92-28673. 32p. (ps-k). 1993. PLB 14.95 (0-8050-2550-2, Bks Young Read) H Holt & Co.
Ziebarth, Pat, ed. see Schade, Charlene.
Ziebarth, Pat, ed. see Wiands, Catherine.
Ziebel, Peter. Look Closer. (ps-3). 1993. pap. 5.95 (0-395-66509-4, Clarion Bks) HM.
Ziefert, Harriet. Andy Toots His Horn. Hoffmann, Sanford, illus. (Orig.). (ps-3). 1988. pap. 3.50 (0-14-050813-9, Puffin) Puffin Bks.
—Animal Count. Baum, Susan, illus. 20p. (ps-1). 1989. pap. 4.95 (0-14-054174-8, Puffin) Puffin Bks.
—Animals for Baby. Baum, Susan, illus. 8p. (ps). 1993. 4.95 (0-694-00508-8, Festival) HarpC Child Bks.
—Animals of the Bible. Galli, Letizia, illus. LC 93-38568. 1995. write for info. (0-385-32084-1) Doubleday.
—Baby Ben's Bow-Wow Book. Gorbaty, Norman, illus. LC 83-63539. (ps). 1984. bds. 2.95 (0-394-86821-8) Random Bks Yng Read.
—Baby Ben's Go-Go Book. (Illus.). (ps). 1984. 2.95 (0-394-86820-X) Random Bks Yng Read.
—Baby Ben's Noisy Book. Gorbaty, Norman, illus. LC 83-63541. (ps). 1984. bds. 2.95 (0-394-86822-6) Random Bks Yng Read.
—Bear's Colors. Baum, Susan, illus. 12p. (ps). 1993. 4.50 (0-694-00454-5, Festival) HarpC Child Bks.
—Bear's Numbers. Baum, Susan, illus. 12p. (ps). 1993. 4.50 (0-694-00455-3, Festival) HarpC Child Bks.
—Bear's Shapes. Baum, Susan, illus. 12p. (ps). 1993. 4.50 (0-694-00456-1, Festival) HarpC Child Bks.
—Bear's Weather. Baum, Susan, illus. 12p. (ps). 1993. 4.50 (0-694-00457-X, Festival) HarpC Child Bks.
—The Big, Red Blanket. Jacobson, David, illus. 24p. (ps-3). 1992. 3.95 (0-694-00393-X) HarpC Child Bks.
—Big to Little, Little to Big. Baum, Susan, illus. 12p. (ps). 1992. 3.95 (0-694-00376-X) HarpC Child Bks.
—Bigger Than a Baby. Rader, Laura, illus. LC 90-20287. 32p. (ps-3). 1991. 13.95 (0-06-026902-2); PLB 13.89 (0-06-026903-0) HarpC Child Bks.
—Bob & Shirley: A Tale of Two Lobsters. Smith, Mavis, illus. LC 90-43150. 32p. (gr. k-3). 1991. PLB 11.89 (0-06-026908-1); pap. 3.95 (0-06-107427-6) HarpC Child Bks.
—Breakfast Time! Ernst, Lisa C., illus. (ps). 1988. pap. 3.95 (0-670-81579-9) Viking Child Bks.
—Bye, Bye, Daddy! Ernst, Lisa C., illus. (ps). 1988. pap. 3.95 (0-670-81581-0) Viking Child Bks.
—Can You Play. Smith, Mavis, illus. LC 88-24025. 24p. (Orig.). (ps-2). 1989. pap. 2.25 (0-394-82001-0) Random Bks Yng Read.
—A Car Trip for Mole & Mouse. Prebenna, David, illus. 32p. (ps-3). 1991. 8.95 (0-670-83858-6) Viking Child Bks.
—Cat Games. Schumacher, Claire, illus. LC 87-25805. 32p. (Orig.). (ps-3). 1988. pap. 3.50 (0-14-050809-0, Puffin) Puffin Bks.
—City Shapes. Baum, Susan, illus. 16p. (ps-1). 1991. pap. 4.95 (0-06-107417-9) HarpC Child Bks.
—A Clean House for Mole & Mouse. Prebenna, David, illus. (Orig.). (ps-3). 1988. pap. 3.50 (0-14-050810-4, Puffin) Puffin Bks.
—A Clean House for Mole & Mouse. Prebenna, David, illus. LC 87-25420. 32p. (ps-3). 1988. pap. 8.95 (0-670-82032-6) Viking Child Bks.
—Clothes on, Clothes off. Baum, Susan, illus. 12p. (ps). 1992. 3.95 (0-694-00375-1) HarpC Child Bks.
—Clown Games. Stevens, Larry, illus. 32p. (ps-3). 1993. 9.00 (0-670-84652-X) Viking Child Bks.
—Clown Games. Stevens, Larry, illus. 32p. (ps-3). 1993. pap. 3.50 (0-14-054581-6) Puffin Bks.
—Come out, Jessie! Smith, Mavis, illus. LC 90-41880. 32p. (ps-1). 1991. pap. 4.95 (0-06-107414-4) HarpC Child Bks.
—Come Visit My House! Three Books Inside: My Mommy; My Daddy; My Puppy, 3 bks. Smith, Mavis, illus. (ps-1). 1992. Set. bds. 12.00 (0-670-84485-3) Viking Child Bks.
—Count with Little Bunny. Ernst, Lisa C., illus. (ps-1). 1988. pap. 5.95 (0-670-82308-2) Viking Child Bks.
—Daddy, Can You Play with Me? Boon, Emilie, illus. (ps-k). 1988. pap. 5.95 (0-14-050895-3, Puffin) Puffin Bks.
—Dark Night, Sleepy Night. Baruffi, Andrea, illus. LC 87-25759. 32p. (ps-3). 1988. pap. 3.50 (0-14-050812-0, Puffin) Puffin Bks.
—Dark Night, Sleepy Night. Baruffi, Andrea, illus. (ps-2). 1993. pap. 3.25 (0-14-036538-9, Puffin) Puffin Bks.
—Dinner's Ready, Jessie! Smith, Mavis, illus. LC 90-55149. 32p. (ps-1). 1991. pap. 4.95 (0-06-107402-0) HarpC Child Bks.
—Dr. Cat. Mandel, Suzy, illus. LC 88-62152. 32p. (ps-3). 1989. pap. 3.50 (0-14-050985-2, Puffin) Puffin Bks.
—Don't Cry, Baby Sam. Brown, Richard, illus. 20p. (gr. 2-6). 1988. pap. 4.95 (0-14-050858-9, Puffin) Puffin Bks.
—A Dozen Dogs: A Read-&-Count Story. Nicklaus, Carol, illus. LC 84-17797. 32p. (ps-1). 1985. lib. bdg. 6.99 (0-394-96935-9); 3.50 (0-394-86935-4) Random Bks Yng Read.
—Dress Little Bunny. Ernst, Lisa C., illus. 12p. (ps-1). 1986. bds. 6.99 (0-670-80358-8) Viking Child Bks.
—Farm Friends. Baum, Susan, illus. 8p. (ps). 1993. 4.95 (0-694-00506-1, Festival) HarpC Child Bks.

—Feed Little Bunny. Ernst, Lisa C., illus. (ps-1). 1988. pap. 5.95 (0-670-82309-0) Viking Child Bks.
—Finding Robin Redbreast. 1988. pap. 4.95 (0-14-050839-2, Puffin) Puffin Bks.
—Follow Me! (Illus.). 32p. (ps-2). 1990. pap. 8.95 (0-670-83197-2) Viking Child Bks.
—Follow Me! (Illus.). 32p. (ps-3). 1990. pap. 3.50 (0-14-054220-5, Puffin) Puffin Bks.
—Getting Ready for New Baby. Rader, Laura, illus. LC 90-32197. 36p. (ps-3). 1990. PLB 13.89 (0-06-026897-2) HarpC Child Bks.
—Going on a Lion Hunt. Smith, Mavis, illus. 20p. (ps). 1989. pap. 5.95 (0-14-054083-0, Puffin) Puffin Bks.
—Good Luck - Bad Luck. (Illus.). 32p. (ps-3). 1992. pap. 3.50 (0-14-054461-5) Puffin Bks.
—Good Luck, Bad Luck. James, Lillie, illus. 32p. (ps-3). 1992. 8.95 (0-670-84275-3) Viking Child Bks.
—Good Morning Sun. 1988. pap. 3.95 (0-670-81578-0) Viking Child Bks.
—Goody New Shoes. Rader, Laura, illus. 32p. (ps-3). 1991. 8.95 (0-670-83859-4) Viking Child Bks.
—Halloween Parade. James, Lillie, illus. 32p. (ps-3). 1992. 9.00 (0-670-84568-X) Viking Child Bks.
—Halloween Parade. James, Lillie, illus. 32p. (ps-3). 1992. pap. 3.50 (0-14-054555-7) Puffin Bks.
—Harry Gets Ready for School. Smith, Mavis, illus. 32p. (ps-3). 1991. 8.95 (0-670-83861-6) Viking Child Bks.
—Harry Gets Ready for School. Smith, Mavis, illus. (ps-2). 1993. pap. 3.25 (0-14-036539-7, Puffin) Puffin Bks.
—Harry Goes to Day Camp. (Illus.). 32p. (ps-2). 1990. pap. 8.95 (0-670-83201-4) Viking Child Bks.
—Harry Goes to Day Camp. Smith, Mavis, illus. 32p. (ps-3). 1990. pap. 3.50 (0-14-054223-X, Puffin) Puffin Bks.
—Harry Goes to Fun Land. LC 88-82400. (Illus.). 32p. (ps-3). 1989. pap. 8.95 (0-670-82664-2) Viking Child Bks.
—Harry Goes to Fun Land. Smith, Mavis, illus. LC 88-62146. 32p. (ps-3). 1989. pap. 3.50 (0-14-050980-1, Puffin) Puffin Bks.
—Harry Takes a Bath. Smith, Mavis, illus. (ps-3). 1987. pap. 8.95 (0-670-81721-X, Puffin); pap. 3.50 (0-14-050746-9, Puffin) Puffin Bks.
—Harry Takes a Bath. Smith, Mavis, illus. LC 93-2718. (ps-2). 1993. pap. 3.25 (0-14-036537-0, Puffin) Puffin Bks.
—Harry's Bath. 1990. 9.95 (0-553-05863-0, Little Rooster) Bantam.
—Hello Reading. (ps-3). 1990. pap. 42.00 (0-14-778673-8) Puffin Bks.
—Henry's Wrong Turn, Vol. 1. 1989. 13.95 (0-316-98778-6) Little.
—Here Comes a Bus. 20p. (gr. 2-6). 1988. pap. 4.95 (0-14-050857-0, Puffin) Puffin Bks.
—Here Comes a Truck. Brown, Richard, illus. 20p. (ps-1). 1992. pap. 5.99 (0-14-054520-4) Puffin Bks.
—How Big Is Big? Baruffi, Andrea, illus. LC 88-612151. 32p. (ps-3). 1989. pap. 3.50 (0-14-050983-6, Puffin) Puffin Bks.
—I Hate Boots! Rader, Laura, illus. 24p. (ps-3). 1991. pap. 3.95 (0-06-107423-3) HarpC Child Bks.
—I Love Summer &... Baum, Susan, illus. 16p. (ps-3). 1992. incl. postcards 5.95 (0-694-00405-7) HarpC Child Bks.
—I Want to Sleep in Your Bed! Smith, Mavis, illus. LC 90-4456. 36p. (ps-1). 1990. HarpC Child Bks.
—In a Scary Old House. Smith, Mavis, illus. 20p. (ps). 1989. pap. 5.95 (0-14-054082-2, Puffin) Puffin Bks.
—Jason's Bus Ride. Taback, Simms, illus. (ps-3). 1987. pap. 8.95 (0-670-81718-X, Puffin); pap. 3.50 (0-14-050743-4, Puffin) Puffin Bks.
—Jason's Bus Ride. Taback, Simms, illus. LC 86-46224. 32p. (gr. 4-8). 1987. pap. 2.95 (0-317-63655-3, Puffin) Puffin Bks.
—Jason's Bus Ride. Taback, Simms, illus. (ps-2). 1993. pap. 3.25 (0-14-036536-2, Puffin) Puffin Bks.
—Later, Rover. (Illus.). 32p. (ps-3). 1992. pap. 3.50 (0-14-054387-2) Puffin Bks.
—Let's Get a Pet. Smith, Mavis, illus. 40p. (ps-5). 1993. PLB 13.50 (0-670-84550-7) Viking Child Bks.
—Let's Get Dressed. Ernst, Lisa C., illus. (ps-3). 1988. pap. 3.95 (0-670-81580-2) Viking Child Bks.
—Let's Trade. Morgan, Mary, illus. LC 88-62150. 32p. (ps-3). 1989. pap. 3.50 (0-14-050982-8, Puffin) Puffin Bks.
—Little Bunny's Melon Patch. Ernst, Lisa C., illus. 20p. (ps-3). 1990. pap. 4.95 (0-14-054262-0, Puffin) Puffin Bks.
—Little Bunny's Noisy Friends. Ernst, Lisa C., illus. 20p. (ps-3). 1990. pap. 4.95 (0-14-054263-9, Puffin) Puffin Bks.
—Measure Me. Baum, Susan, illus. 12p. (ps-3). 1991. 12.95 (0-694-00322-0) HarpC Child Bks.
—Mike & Tony: Best Friends. Siracusa, Catherine, illus. (ps-3). 1987. pap. 3.50 (0-14-050744-2, Puffin) Puffin Bks.
—Mike & Tony: Best Friends. Siracusa, Catherine, illus. LC 93-25617. (ps-2). 1994. pap. 3.25 (0-14-036853-1, Puffin) Puffin Bks.
—Mommy, Where Are You? Boon, Emilie, illus. (ps-k). 1988. pap. 5.95 (0-14-050894-5, Puffin) Puffin Bks.
—Move Over! Baum, Susan, illus. 24p. (ps-3). 1991. pap. 3.95 (0-06-107421-7) HarpC Child Bks.
—Music Lessons. Rader, Laura, illus. 24p. (ps-3). 1992. 3.95 (0-694-00390-1) HarpC Child Bks.
—My Apple Tree. Rader, Laura, illus. 24p. (ps-3). 1991. pap. 3.95 (0-06-107420-9) HarpC Child Bks.

—My Birthday Story Album. Smith, Mavis, illus. 10p. (ps-2). 1993. 6.95 (0-694-00445-6, Festival) HarpC Child Bks.
—My Camera. Rader, Laura, illus. 14p. (ps). 1993. 4.50 (0-694-00417-0, Festival) HarpC Child Bks.
—My Cassette Player. Rader, Laura, illus. 14p. (ps). 1993. 4.50 (0-694-00418-9, Festival) HarpC Child Bks.
—My Christmas Story Album. Smith, Mavis, illus. 10p. (ps up). 1992. 6.95 (0-694-00430-8, Festival) HarpC Child Bks.
—My Getting-Ready-for-Bed Book. Smith, Mavis, illus. LC 89-62012. 12p. (ps-1). 1990. 13.95 (0-694-00299-2) HarpC Child Bks.
—My Telephone. Rader, Laura, illus. 14p. (ps). 1993. 4.50 (0-694-00419-7, Festival) HarpC Child Bks.
—My Television. Rader, Laura, illus. 14p. (ps). 1993. 4.50 (0-694-00420-0, Festival) HarpC Child Bks.
—My Tooth is Loose. (Illus.). 32p. (ps-3). 1992. pap. 3.50 (0-14-054394-5) Puffin Bks.
—My Valentines. Baum, Susan, illus. 8p. (ps-2). 1993. incl. postcards 6.95 (0-694-00447-2, Festival) HarpC Child Bks.
—A New Coat for Anna. Lobel, Anita, illus. LC 86-2722. 40p. (ps-3). 1986. PLB 11.99 (0-394-97426-3) Knopf Bks Yng Read.
—A New Coat for Anna. Lobel, Anita, illus. LC 86-2722. 40p. (ps-3). 1988. pap. 4.95 (0-394-89861-3) Knopf Bks Yng Read.
—A New House for Mole & Mouse. Prebenna, David, illus. LC 86-46222. 32p. (ps-3). 1987. pap. 3.50 (0-14-050745-0, Puffin) Puffin Bks.
—New House for Mouse & Mole. Prebenna, David, illus. (ps-3). 1987. pap. 8.95 (0-670-81720-1) Viking Child Bks.
—Nicky Upstairs & Down. Brown, Richard, illus. (ps-3). 1987. (Puffin); pap. 3.50 (0-14-050742-6, Puffin) Puffin Bks.
—Nicky's Christmas Surprise. Brown, Richard, illus. LC 85-5681. 20p. (ps). 1985. pap. 5.99 (0-14-050555-5, Puffin) Puffin Bks.
—Nicky's Noisy Night. Brown, Richard, illus. 20p. (Orig.). (ps). 1986. pap. 4.95 (0-14-050583-0, Puffin) Puffin Bks.
—Nicky's Picnic. Brown, Richard, illus. 20p. (Orig.). (ps-k). 1986. pap. 4.95 (0-14-050584-9, Puffin) Puffin Bks.
—Nicky's Valentine. Brown, Richard, illus. (ps-1). 1987. pap. 4.95 (0-14-050706-X, Puffin) Puffin Bks.
—No More TV, Sleepy Dog. Gorbaty, Norman, illus. LC 88-26316. 24p. (Orig.). (ps-2). 1989. 2.25 (0-394-81996-9) Random Bks Yng Read.
—Noisy Barn! Taback, Simms, illus. 16p. (ps-1). 1991. pap. 4.95 (0-06-107405-5) HarpC Child Bks.
—Oh No, Nicky! Brown, Richard, illus. 20p. (ps-1). 1992. pap. 5.99 (0-14-054521-2) Puffin Bks.
—On Our Way to the Forest! Taback, Simms, illus. 16p. (ps-1). 1993. pap. 4.95 (0-694-00458-8, Festival) HarpC Child Bks.
—On Our Way to the Water! Taback, Simms, illus. 16p. (ps-1). 1993. pap. 4.95 (0-694-00459-6, Festival) HarpC Child Bks.
—Parade. 1990. 9.95 (0-553-05862-2, Little Rooster) Bantam.
—Penny Goes to the Movies. Rader, Laura, illus. 32p. (ps-3). 1990. pap. 3.50 (0-14-054225-6, Puffin) Puffin Bks.
—Pet Day (Mr. Rose's Class) Brown, Richard, illus. 64p. 1988. pap. 2.50 (0-553-15620-9, Skylark) Bantam.
—Piggety Pig Books, 6 of ea. title. Prebenna, David, illus. 96p. (ps-k). 1988. 2.95 (0-316-98758-1) Little.
—Play with Little Bunny. Ernst, Lisa C., illus. 12p. (ps-1). 1986. bds. 6.99 (0-670-80359-6) Viking Child Bks.
—Playtime for Baby. Baum, Susan, illus. 8p. (ps). 1993. 4.95 (0-694-00505-3, Festival) HarpC Child Bks.
—Please Let It Snow. Brown, Rick, illus. LC 88-62145. 32p. (ps-3). 1989. pap. 3.50 (0-14-050981-X, Puffin) Puffin Bks.
—The Prince Has a Boo-Boo. Alley, R. W., illus. LC 88-26322. 24p. (Orig.). (ps-2). 1989. PLB 2.25 (0-394-81999-3) Random Bks Yng Read.
—The Prince's Tooth Is Loose. Alley, R. W., illus. LC 89-36433. 24p. (Orig.). (ps-2). 1990. 2.25 (0-394-84840-3) Random Bks Yng Read.
—The Princess Needs a Bath. Gradisher, Martha, illus. 24p. (ps-3). 1992. 3.95 (0-694-00391-3) HarpC Child Bks.
—Sam & Lucy. Schumacher, Claire, illus. LC 90-46963. 36p. (ps-1). 1992. PLB 14.89 (0-06-026974-X) HarpC Child Bks.
—Say Good Night! Brown, Richard, illus. 32p. 1987. (Puffin); pap. 3.50 (0-14-050747-7, Puffin) Puffin Bks.
—Scooter's Christmas. Brown, Rick, illus. 16p. (ps-k). 1993. 10.95 (0-694-00484-7, Festival) HarpC Child Bks.
—Sleepy Dog: A Step One Book. Gorbaty, Norman, illus. LC 84-4775. (ps-2). 1984. PLB 7.99 (0-394-96877-8); pap. 3.50 (0-394-86877-3) Random Bks Yng Read.
—The Small Potatoes & the Birthday Party. 64p. (gr. k-6). 1985. pap. 7.95 (0-440-48035-3, YB) Dell.
—The Small Potatoes Club & the Small Potatoes & the Magic Show. Brown, Richard, illus. 64p. (Orig.). (gr. k-6). 1984. pap. 2.99 (0-440-48034-5, YB) Dell.
—So Hungry! Nicklaus, Carol, illus. LC 87-4763. 32p. (ps-1). 1987. lib. bdg. 7.99 (0-394-99127-3); 3.50 (0-394-89127-9) Random Bks Yng Read.

—So Sick. Nicklaus, Carol, illus. LC 85-1957. 32p. (ps-1). 1985. pap. 2.95 (0-394-87580-X) Random Bks Yng Read.
—Sometimes I Share. Nicklaus, Carol, illus. 24p. (ps-3). 1991. pap. 3.95 (0-06-107425-X) HarpC Child Bks.
—Stitches. Aitken, Amy, illus. 32p. (ps-3). 1990. pap. 3.50 (0-14-054224-8, Puffin) Puffin Bks.
—Stitches. Aitken, Amy, illus. LC 93-6553. (ps-2). 1993. pap. 3.25 (0-14-036553-2, Puffin) Puffin Bks.
—Surprise! Morgan, Mary, illus. LC 87-26217. 32p. (ps-3). 1988. pap. 8.95 (0-670-82036-9) Viking Child Bks.
—Take My Picture. Aitken, Amy, illus. 24p. (ps-3). 1991. pap. 3.95 (0-06-107424-1) HarpC Child Bks.
—Thank You, Nicky! (gr. 4 up). 1988. pap. 5.99 (0-14-050838-4, Puffin) Puffin Bks.
—Things That Go. Baum, Susan, illus. 8p. (ps). 1993. 4.95 (0-694-00507-X, Festival) HarpC Child Bks.
—Three Wishes. Jacobson, David, illus. 32p. (ps-3). 1993. 9.00 (0-670-84569-8) Viking Child Bks.
—Three Wishes. Jacobson, David, illus. 32p. (ps-3). 1993. pap. 3.50 (0-14-054556-5) Puffin Bks.
—Tim & Jim Take Off. Mandel, Suzy, illus. 32p. (ps-3). 1990. pap. 3.50 (0-14-054222-1, Puffin) Puffin Bks.
—Today Is Monday. (Illus.). 12p. (ps-3). 1992. 9.95 (0-694-00407-3) HarpC Child Bks.
—Trip Day (Mr. Rose's Class) Brown, Richard, illus. 64p. 1988. pap. 2.50 (0-553-15618-7, Skylark) Bantam.
—Under the Water. Mandel, Suzy, illus. 32p. (ps-3). 1990. pap. 3.50 (0-14-054221-3, Puffin) Puffin Bks.
—Under the Water. Mandel, Suzy, illus. (gr. k-3). 1993. pap. 3.25 (0-14-036535-4, Puffin) Puffin Bks.
—A Valentine for Ms. Vanilla. (Illus.). 32p. (ps-3). 1992. pap. 3.50 (0-14-054460-7) Puffin Bks.
—What Do I Hear? 1988. pap. 3.95 (0-553-05452-X) Bantam.
—What Do I See? 1988. 3.95 (0-553-05456-2) Bantam.
—What Do I Smell? 1988. pap. 3.95 (0-553-05457-0) Bantam.
—What Do I Taste? 1988. 3.95 (0-553-05453-8) Bantam.
—What Do I Taste: The Five Senses. Smith, Mavis, illus. (ps-1). 1988. pap. 3.95 (0-317-69282-8) Bantam.
—What Do I Touch? 1988. 3.95 (0-553-05454-6) Bantam.
—What Is Father's Day? Schumacher, Claire, illus. 16p. (ps-k). 1992. 5.95 (0-694-00383-2) HarpC Child Bks.
—What Is Halloween? Schumacher, Claire, illus. 16p. (ps). 1992. 5.95 (0-694-00381-6, Festival) HarpC Child Bks.
—What Is Mother's Day? Schumacher, Claire, illus. 16p. (ps-k). 1992. 5.95 (0-694-00382-4) HarpC Child Bks.
—What Is Passover? James, Lillie, illus. 16p. (ps). 1994. 5.95 (0-694-00482-0, Festival) HarpC Child Bks.
—What Is Thanksgiving? Schumacher, Claire, illus. 16p. (ps). 1992. 5.95 (0-694-00408-1, Festival) HarpC Child Bks.
—What Is Valentine's Day? Schumacher, Claire, illus. 16p. (ps-k). 1993. 5.95 (0-694-00413-8, Festival) HarpC Child Bks.
—What's a Birthday? Schumacher, Claire, illus. 16p. (ps-k). 1993. 5.95 (0-694-00380-8, Festival) HarpC Child Bks.
—What's a Vacation: A Lift-the Flap Bk. Schumacher, Claire, illus. 16p. (ps-k). 1993. 5.95 (0-694-00449-9, Festival) HarpC Child Bks.
—What's a Wedding? A Lift-the-Flap Bk. Schumacher, Claire, illus. 16p. (ps-k). 1993. 5.95 (0-694-00450-2, Festival) HarpC Child Bks.
—The Wheels on the Bus. Baruffi, Andrea, illus. LC 89-38100. 24p. (Orig.). (ps-2). 1990. pap. 2.25 (0-394-84870-5) Random Bks Yng Read.
—When Daddy Had the Chicken Pox. Kalish, Lionel, illus. LC 90-43559. 32p. (ps-3). 1991. PLB 13.89 (0-06-026907-3) HarpC Child Bks.
—When the TV Broke. Smith, Mavis, illus. LC 92-47097. (ps-2). 1993. pap. 3.25 (0-14-036540-0, Puffin) Puffin Bks.
—When Will Santa Come? Schumacher, Claire, illus. 16p. (ps-3). 1991. pap. 5.95 (0-06-107440-3) HarpC Child Bks.
—Where Is My Baby? 16p. (ps-2). 1994. 10.95 (0-694-00479-0, Festival) HarpC Child Bks.
—Where's Bobo? Rader, Laura, illus. LC 92-24495. 24p. (ps up). 1993. 10.95 (0-688-12327-9, Tambourine Bks) Morrow.
—Where's Daddy's Car? Baruffi, Andrea, illus. 16p. (ps). 1992. 5.95 (0-694-00378-6) HarpC Child Bks.
—Where's Mommy's Truck? Baruffi, Andrea, illus. 16p. (ps). 1992. 5.95 (0-694-00377-8) HarpC Child Bks.
—Where's My Easter Egg? Brown, Richard, illus. LC 84-62004. (gr. 2-6). 1985. pap. 5.99 (0-14-050537-7, Puffin) Puffin Bks.
—Where's the Halloween Treat? Brown, Richard, illus. LC 85-3632. 20p. (ps). 1985. pap. 5.99 (0-14-050556-3, Puffin) Puffin Bks.
—Who Can Boo the Loudest? Schumacher, Claire, illus. LC 90-4454. 36p. (ps-1). 1990. 13.95 (0-06-026898-0) HarpC Child Bks.
—Who Spilled the Milk? Gradisher, Martha, illus. 24p. (ps-3). 1992. 3.95 (0-694-00390-5) HarpC Child Bks.
—Worm Day (Mr. Rose's Class) Brown, Richard, illus. 64p. 1988. pap. 2.50 (0-553-15619-5, Skylark) Bantam.
—Zoo Parade! Taback, Simms, illus. 16p. (ps-1). 1991. pap. 4.95 (0-06-107404-7) HarpC Child Bks.
Ziefert, Harriet & Brown, Richard. Nicky Upstairs & Down. (ps-2). 1994. pap. 3.25 (0-14-036852-3) Puffin Bks.

Ziefert, Harriet & Gradisher, Martha. A Valentine for Ms. Vanilla. (Illus.). (gr. k-3). 1994. pap. 3.25 (0-14-036871-X) Puffin Bks.

Ziefert, Harriet & Nicklaus, Carol. Later, Rover. Jacobson, David, illus. 32p. (ps-3). 1992. 8.95 (0-670-83863-2) Viking Child Bks.

Ziefert, Harriet & Smith, Mavis. Harry Goes to Fun Land. (Illus.). (ps-2). 1994. pap. 3.25 (0-14-036885-X) Puffin Bks.

Ziegler, J. F. The Duck & the Fox: A Metaphysical Fairy Tale. Butler, Sandra L., ed. Gillard, Dianne & Kirkpatrick, Cindy F., illus. LC 88-32071. 75p. (ps-9). 1988. pap. 9.00 (0-9621235-0-1) Hallelujah Pr.

Ziegler, Jack. Mr. Knocky. Ziegler, Jack, illus. LC 91-34145. 32p. (ps-3). 1993. RSBE 14.95 (0-02-793725-9, Macmillan Child Bk) Macmillan Child Grp.

Ziegler, Judy. Judy Ziegler's Zany Fairytales: Hense, Toostel & Elepunzel. 1992. 1.99 (0-517-06686-6) Outlet Bk Co.

—Rhinorella & Rumplecatskin. 1992. pap. 1.99 (0-517-06685-8) Outlet Bk Co.

—Why Do Elephants Wear Purple Suspenders? 32p. (ps-3). 1992. pap. 3.95 (0-929923-96-0) Lowell Hse.

Ziegler, Sandra. Fairness. Endres, Helen, illus. LC 88-18976. 32p. (gr. k-3). 1989. PLB 21.35 (0-89565-390-7); PLB 14.95s.p. (0-685-55990-4) Childs World.

—Friends: A Handbook about Getting Along Together. Fleishman, Seymour, illus. LC 81-17025. 112p. (gr. 2-6). 1980. PLB 21.35 (0-89565-207-2); PLB 14.95s.p. (0-685-55480-5) Childs World.

—Manners. Hutton, Kathryn, illus. LC 88-15013. 32p. (gr. k-3). 1989. PLB 21.35 (0-89565-377-X); PLB 14.95s.p. (0-685-55992-0) Childs World.

—Our St. Patrick's Day Book. Connelly, Gwen, illus. LC 86-31726. 32p. (ps-3). 1987. PLB 19.95 (0-89565-344-3); PLB 13.95s.p. (0-685-55851-7) Childs World.

—Understanding. Williams, Jenny, illus. LC 88-23745. 32p. (gr. k-3). 1989. PLB 21.35 (0-89565-452-0); PLB 14.95s.p. (0-685-55991-2) Childs World.

—A Visit to the Airport. LC 87-35470. 32p. (ps-3). 1988. PLB 15.00 (0-516-01488-9); pap. 3.95 (0-516-41488-7) Childrens.

—A Visit to the Bakery. Pilot Productions Staff, photos by. LC 86-32647. (Illus.). 32p. (ps-3). 1987. PLB 15.00 (0-516-01495-1) Childrens.

—A Visit to the Dairy Farm. LC 87-19692. (Illus.). 32p. (ps-3). 1987. PLB 15.00 (0-516-01496-X); pap. 3.95 (0-516-41496-8) Childrens.

—A Visit to the Natural History Museum. LC 88-23268. 32p. (ps-3). 1988. PLB 15.00 (0-516-01489-7); pap. 3.95 (0-516-41489-5) Childrens.

—A Visit to the Post Office. Holmes, Dave, photos by. LC 89-35061. 32p. (ps-3). 1989. PLB 15.00 (0-516-01487-0); pap. 3.95 (0-516-41487-9) Childrens.

Ziegler, Sandra, jt. auth. see McDonnell, Janet.

Ziegler, Sandra K. Jokes & More Jokes. Magnuson, Diana, illus. LC 82-19742. 48p. (gr. 1-5). 1983. PLB 13.27 (0-516-01871-X) Childrens.

—Knock-Knocks, Limericks, & Other Silly Sayings. Magnuson, Diana, illus. LC 82-19764. 48p. (gr. 1-5). 1983. pap. 3.95 (0-516-41872-6) Childrens.

Ziemann, Debbie, jt. auth. see Todd, Cynthia.

Zierau, Lillee D. Amelia Earhart: Leading Lady of the Air Age. Rahmas, D. Steve, ed. LC 73-190237. 32p. (gr. 7-12). 1972. lib. bdg. 4.95 incl. catalog cards (0-87157-519-1) SamHar Pr.

Ziesk, Edra. Margaret Mead. Horner, Matina S., intro. by. (Illus.). 112p. (gr. 5 up). 1990. lib. bdg. 17.95 (1-55546-667-2) Chelsea Hse.

Ziglar, Zig. Confessions of a Happy Christian. Criswell, W. A., frwd. by. LC 78-6729. (gr. 6 up). 1982. 14.95 (0-88289-196-0); pap. 9.95 (0-88289-460-0) Pelican.

Zike, Dinah. The Earth Science Book: Activities for Kids. LC 92-46458. 119p. (gr. 3-7). 1993. pap. 12.95 (0-471-57166-0) Wiley.

Zilonka, Paul. God's Living Word. 1990. pap. 4.50 (0-89942-146-6) Catholic Bk Pub.

Zim, Herbert S. Dinosaurs. Irving, James G., illus. LC 54-5080. 64p. (gr. 3-7). 1954. PLB 11.88 (0-688-31239-X) Morrow Jr Bks.

—Snakes. Irving, James G., illus. LC 49-10266. 64p. (gr. 3-7). 1949. PLB 12.88 (0-688-31549-6) Morrow Jr Bks.

—Your Stomach & Digestive Tract. Martin, Rene, illus. LC 72-6734. 64p. (gr. 3-7). 1973. PLB 12.88 (0-688-31838-X, Morrow Jr Bks) Morrow Jr Bks.

Zim, Herbert S. & Baker, Robert H. Stars. rev. ed. Irving, James G., illus. (gr. 6 up). 1985. pap. write for info. (0-307-24493-8, Golden Pr) Western Pub.

Zim, Herbert S. & Gabrielson, Ira N. Birds. Irving, James G., illus. (gr. 7 up). 1956. PLB write for info. (0-307-24053-3); pap. write for info. (Golden Pr) Western Pub.

Zim, Herbert S. & Ingle, Lester. Seashores. Barlowe, Dorothea & Barlowe, Sy, illus. (gr. 5 up). 1955. pap. write for info. (0-307-24496-2, Golden Pr) Western Pub.

Zim, Herbert S. & Martin, Alexander C. Trees. Barlowe, Dorothea & Barlowe, Sy, illus. (gr. 6 up). 1952. pap. write for info. (0-307-24056-8, Golden Pr) Western Pub.

Zim, Herbert S. & Shaffer, Paul R. Rocks & Minerals. Perlman, Raymond, illus. (gr. 6 up). 1957. pap. write for info. (0-307-24499-7, Golden Pr) Western Pub.

Zim, Herbert S., jt. auth. see Cottam, Clarence.

Zim, Herbert S., jt. auth. see Mitchell, Robert.

Zim, Herbert S., ed. see Abbott, R. Tucker.

Zim, Herbert S., ed. see Brockman, C. Frank.

Zim, Herbert S., ed. see Levi, Herbert W. & Levi, Lorna R.

Zim, Herbert S., ed. see Reid, George K.

Zimelman, Nathan. The Great Adventure of Wo Ti. Downing, Julie, illus. LC 90-38150. 32p. (gr. k-3). 1992. RSBE 14.95 (0-02-793731-3, Macmillan Child Bk) Macmillan Child Grp.

—How the Second Grade Got 8,205.50 to Visit the Statue of Liberty. Mathews, Judith, ed. Slavin, Bill, illus. LC 92-996. 32p. (gr. k-3). 1992. 13.95g (0-8075-3431-5) A Whitman.

—Please Excuse Jaspar. (ps-3). 1993. pap. 2.99 (0-440-40783-4) Dell.

—Shaughnessy. Davenport, May, ed. Bd. with Humanization of Freddie Mouse. Blake, Richard. LC 81-71551. 64p. (Orig.). (gr. 3-5). 1984. pap. 3.50x (0-943864-38-0) Davenport.

—Treed by a Pride of Irate Lions. Goffe, Toni, illus. LC 89-30344. (gr. k-3). 1990. 14.95 (0-316-98802-2) Little.

Zimet, Susan & Goodman, Victor. The Great Cover-Up: A Condom Compendium. Silbur, Stephanie, illus. LC 88-92769. 136p. (Orig.). (gr. 10 up). 1989. pap. text ed. 7.95 (0-9621700-0-3) Civan Inc.

Zimmann, William C., Sr. The Legend of the Christmas Donkey. (gr. k-4). 1984. 1.95 (0-89536-989-3, 7540) CSS OH.

Zimmer-Loew, Helene & Moss, Anne. Der Spiegel: Aktuelle Themen in der Bundesrepublik Deutschland: Advanced. (GER.). pap. text ed. 16.95 (0-685-62826-4, F2280-1, Natl Textbk); tchr's. manual 3.95 (0-685-62827-2, F2282-8, Natl Textbk); 3 audiocassettes 34.95 (0-685-62828-0, F2283-X, Natl Textbk) NTC Pub Grp.

Zimmerman. Applesauce Cottage Cheese. Date not set. 15.00 (0-06-024277-9, Festival); PLB 14.89 (0-06-024278-7, Festival) HarpC Child Bks.

—Dictionary of Classical Mythology. (gr. 9 up). 1983. pap. 5.99 (0-553-25776-5) Bantam.

—Henny Penny. 1993. pap. 28.67 (0-590-71755-3) Scholastic Inc.

—Pollita Chiquita. (SPA.). 1993. pap. 28.67 (0-590-73225-0) Scholastic Inc.

Zimmerman, Andrea & Clemesha, David. The Cow Buzzed. Meisel, Paul, illus. LC 91-31905. 32p. (ps-1). 1993. 15.00 (0-06-020808-2); PLB 14.89 (0-06-020809-0) HarpC Child Bks.

Zimmerman, Andrea G. Riddle Zoo. 64p. (gr. 3-7). 1981. (Dutton) NAL-Dutton.

Zimmerman, Chanda K. Detroit. LC 88-35914. (Illus.). 60p. (gr. 3 up) 1989. RSBE 13.95 (0-87518-409-X, Dillon) Macmillan Child Grp.

Zimmerman, Dick, jt. auth. see Lewis, Shari.

Zimmerman, H. Werner. Alphonse Knows...A Circle Is Not a Valentine. (Illus.). 24p. (ps-2). 1991. bds. 9.95 laminated (0-19-540744-X) OUP.

—Henny Penny. 1989. pap. 9.95 (0-590-42390-8) Scholastic Inc.

—Pollita Chiquita: (Henny Penny) Freeman, Ann, tr. (SPA.). 32p. (gr. k-3). 1991. pap. 3.95 (0-590-44192-2) Scholastic Inc.

Zimmerman, Julie & Torumasu, Kimiaki. Wishing on Daruma. LC 91-76745. (Illus.). 112p. (Orig.). (gr. 5 up). 1992. pap. 9.95 (1-879418-05-3) Biddle Pub.

Zimmerman, Linda. Chicken Soup: Thirty-Eight Easy Recipes from Classic to New. Sturman, Sally, illus. LC 93-19280. (gr. 6 up). 1994. 12.00 (0-517-58622-3) Crown Bks Yng Read.

Zimmerman, Marjorie. The Mystery of the Old Castle. LC 88-6936. (gr. 3-7). 1988. pap. 4.49 (1-55513-584-6, Chariot Bks) Cook.

Zimmerman, Maureen, ed. see Miyazaki, Hayao.

Zimmerman, R. D. Bomb. 4p. 1987. incl. puzzle 17.95 (0-922242-01-1) Lombard Mktg.

Zimmerman, Thomas F., et al, eds. And He Gave Pastors. LC 78-50485. 500p. (gr. 12). 1979. 13.95 (0-88243-460-8, 02-0460) Gospel Pub.

Zimmermann, Robert. Sri Lanka. LC 91-35252. 128p. (gr. 5-9). 1992. PLB 26.60 (0-516-02606-2) Childrens.

Zindel, Bonnie. Hollywood Dream Machine. 192p. (gr. 7-12). 1985. pap. 2.50 (0-553-25240-2, Starfire) Bantam.

Zindel, Bonnie, jt. auth. see Zindel, Paul.

Zindel, Paul. The Amazing & Death-Defying Diary of Eugene Dingman. LC 82-47712. 224p. (gr. 7 up). 1987. 14.00 (0-06-026862-X); PLB 13.89 (0-06-026863-8) HarpC Child Bks.

—The Amazing & Death-Defying Diary of Eugene Dingman. (gr. 7 up). 1989. pap. 3.50 (0-553-27768-5, Starfire) Bantam.

—Attack of the Killer, No. 1. 1993. pap. 3.50 (0-553-48084-7) Bantam.

—A Begonia for Miss Applebaum. LC 88-11010. 192p. (gr. 7 up). 1989. 14.00i (0-06-026877-8); PLB 13.89 (0-06-026878-6) HarpC Child Bks.

—A Begonia for Miss Applebaum. (gr. 7 up). 1990. pap. 3.99 (0-553-28765-6, Starfire) Bantam.

—David & Della. LC 93-12719. (Illus.). 176p. (gr. 7 up). 1993. 14.00 (0-06-023353-2); PLB 13.89 (0-06-023354-0) HarpC Child Bks.

—Effect of Gamma Rays on Man-in-the-Moon Marigolds. Kingman, Dong, illus. (gr. 9 up). 1984. pap. 3.95 (0-553-28028-7) Bantam.

—Effect of Gamma Rays on Man-in-the-Moon Marigolds. Kingman, Dong, illus. LC 79-135772. 128p. (gr. 7 up). 1971. 18.00 (0-06-026829-8) HarpC Child Bks.

—The Fifth-Grade Safari. (gr. 4-7). 1993. pap. 3.50 (0-553-48085-5) Bantam.

—Fright Party. Mangiat, Jeff, illus. (gr. 4-7). 1993. pap. 3.50 (0-553-48082-0) Bantam.

—Harry & Hortense at Hormone High. LC 82-47697. 160p. (gr. 7 up). 1984. 14.00 (0-06-026864-6); PLB 13.89 (0-06-026869-7) HarpC Child Bks.

—Harry & Hortense at Hormone High. 160p. (gr. 7-12). 1985. pap. 2.95 (0-553-25175-9, Starfire) Bantam.

—I Never Loved Your Mind. 144p. (gr. 9 up). 1984. pap. 2.95 (0-553-27323-X) Bantam.

—I Never Loved Your Mind. LC 73-105476. 192p. (gr. 7 up). 1970. PLB 13.89 (0-06-026822-0) HarpC Child Bks.

—My Darling, My Hamburger. LC 70-85025. 176p. (gr. 7 up). 1969. PLB 13.89 (0-06-026824-7) HarpC Child Bks.

—One Hundred Percent Laugh Riot. (gr. 4-7). 1994. pap. 3.50 (0-553-48083-9) Bantam.

—Pardon Me, You're Stepping on My Eyeball. LC 75-25410. 272p. (gr. 7 up). 1976. PLB 19.89 (0-06-026838-7) HarpC Child Bks.

—The Pigman. LC 68-10784. 192p. (gr. 7 up). 1968. 14.00 (0-06-026827-1); PLB 13.89 (0-06-026828-X) HarpC Child Bks.

—The Pigman & Me. LC 91-35790. (Illus.). 178p. (gr. 7 up). 1992. 14.00 (0-06-020857-0); PLB 13.89 (0-06-020858-9) HarpC Child Bks.

—The Pigman's Legacy. 128p. (gr. 12 up). 1984. pap. 3.99 (0-553-26599-7) Bantam.

—The Pigman's Legacy. LC 79-2684. 192p. (gr. 7 up). 1980. PLB 13.89 (0-06-026854-9) HarpC Child Bks.

—The Undertaker's Gone Bananas. LC 78-54606. 256p. (gr. 7 up). 1978. PLB 16.89 (0-06-026846-8) HarpC Child Bks.

Zindel, Paul & Zindel, Bonnie. A Star for the Latecomer. 160p. (gr. 6 up). 1985. pap. 2.50 (0-553-25578-9) Bantam.

Zindel, Paul, jt. auth. see Dragonwagon, Crescent.

Ziner, Feenie. Squanto. LC 88-13982. x, 158p. (gr. 7 up). 1988. 17.50 (0-208-02218-X, Linnet); pap. 12.50 (0-208-02274-0, Linnet) Shoe string.

Ziner, Feenie & Thompson, Elizabeth. Time. LC 81-18080. (Illus.). 48p. (gr. k-4). 1982. PLB 15.27 (0-516-01651-2) Childrens.

Zingg, Eduard. African Elephants. Italia, Bob, ed. LC 93-3699. 40p. (gr. 5 up). 1993. 14.96 (1-56239-216-6) Abdo & Dghtrs.

—Animals of the Delta. Italia, Bob, ed. LC 93-3700. 40p. (gr. 5 up). 1993. 14.96 (1-56239-217-4) Abdo & Dghtrs.

—Giraffes of Botswana. LC 93-10265. 1993. 14.96 (1-56239-215-8) Abdo & Dghtrs.

—Rhino. Italia, Bob, ed. LC 93-7602. 1993. 14.96 (1-56239-219-0) Abdo & Dghtrs.

—Trumpa, the Cheetah. Italia, Bob, ed. LC 93-10263. (gr. 4 up). 1993. 14.96 (1-56239-214-X) Abdo & Dghtrs.

Zink, Richard M. Airline Industry Jobs: The New Job Manual. 4th ed. (Illus.). 50p. (gr. 9 up). 1992. pap. 14.95x (0-939469-27-8) Zinks Career Guide.

—Australia - New Zealand - South Sea Islands: The New Employment Manual. 3rd, rev. ed. (Illus.). 50p. (gr. 9 up). 1991. pap. 14.95x (0-939469-18-9) Zinks Career Guide.

—California Jobs - The New Employment Manual. 2nd ed. (Illus.). 50p. (Orig.). (gr. 9 up). 1993. pap. text ed. 14.95x (0-939469-30-8) Zinks Career Guide.

—Computer Jobs Worldwide: The Employment Manual. (Illus.). 50p. (Orig.). (gr. 9 up). 1993. pap. text ed. 14.95x (0-939469-32-4) Zinks Career Guide.

—Diplomas or Degrees: Fast, Legal, Inexpensive. 4th, rev. ed. (Illus.). 50p. (gr. 9 up). 1991. pap. 14.95x (0-939469-15-4) Zinks Career Guide.

—Foreign Travel: The Foreign Travelers Guide Book. 3rd ed. (Illus.). 50p. (gr. 9 up). 1992. pap. 14.95x (0-939469-26-X) Zinks Career Guide.

—Government Jobs: The New Employment Manual. 2nd, rev. ed. (Illus.). 50p. (gr. 9 up). 1991. pap. 14.95x (0-939469-17-0) Zinks Career Guide.

—Jobs - Jobs - Jobs: How to Earn Thirty Thousand Dollars Plus Yearly Without a College Degree. (Illus.). 50p. (Orig.). (gr. 9 up). 1992. pap. 14.95x (0-939469-25-1) Zinks Career Guide.

—Jobs: How to Get the Job You Want. 4th, rev. ed. (Illus.). 50p. (gr. 9 up). 1991. pap. 14.95x (0-939469-22-7) Zinks Career Guide.

—Nevada Jobs - The New Employment Manual. (Illus.). 50p. (Orig.). (gr. 9 up). 1993. pap. 14.95x (0-939469-31-6) Zinks Career Guide.

—Resumes for Overseas & Stateside Jobs. (Illus.). 50p. (gr. 9 up). 1993. pap. 14.95x (0-939469-29-4) Zinks Career Guide.

—Travel Industry & Resort Jobs: The New Employment Manual. 3rd ed. (Illus.). 50p. (gr. 9 up). 1992. pap. 14.95x (0-939469-28-6) Zinks Career Guide.

Zink, Richard M., ed. Overseas Exotic Employment - Unskilled, Skilled, Professionals: One Hundred Dollars to One Thousand Dollars Daily - Unskilled, Skilled, Professional. 7th, rev. ed. (Illus.). 64p. (gr. 9 up). 1993. pap. 14.95x (0-939469-33-2) Zinks Career Guide.

Zinkgraf, June & Bauman, Toni. Fall Fantasies. 240p. (gr. k-6). 1980. 15.95 (0-916456-61-7, GA 167) Good Apple.

Zinkgraf, June, jt. auth. see Bauman, Toni.

Zinsser, Hans. Rats, Lice & History. (gr. 9 up). 1984. (Pub. by Atlantic Monthly Pr); pap. 10.95 (0-316-98896-0) Little.

Zinsser, Nate. Dear Dr. Psych. (gr. 3-7). 1991. pap. 5.95 (*0-316-98898-7*, Spts Illus Kids) Little.

Zion, Gene. All Falling Down. Graham, Margaret B., illus. LC 51-12571. 32p. (ps-1). 1951. PLB 13.89 (*0-06-026831-X*) HarpC Child Bks.
—Harry & the Lady Next Door. Graham, Margaret B., illus. LC 60-9452. 64p. (gr. k-3). 1978. pap. 3.50 (*0-06-444008-7*, Trophy) HarpC Child Bks.
—Harry & the Lady Next Door. LC 60-9452. (Illus.). 64p. (gr. k-3). 1960. PLB 13.89 (*0-06-026852-2*) HarpC Child Bks.
—Harry by the Sea. Graham, Margaret B., illus. LC 65-21302. 32p. (gr. k-3). 1965. 14.00 (*0-06-026855-7*); PLB 13.89 (*0-06-026856-5*) HarpC Child Bks.
—Harry by the Sea. Graham, Margaret B., illus. LC 65-21302. 32p. (ps-3). 1976. pap. 4.95 (*0-06-443010-3*, JP 10, Trophy) HarpC Child Bks.
—Harry the Dirty Dog. Graham, Margaret B., illus. LC 56-8137. 32p. (gr. k-3). 1956. 15.00 (*0-06-026865-4*); PLB 14.89 (*0-06-026866-2*) HarpC Child Bks.
—Harry the Dirty Dog. Graham, Margaret B., illus. LC 56-8137. 32p. (ps-3). 1976. pap. 4.95 (*0-06-443009-X*, Trophy) HarpC Child Bks.
—No Roses for Harry. Graham, Margaret B., illus. LC 58-7752. (gr. k-3). 1958. 14.00 (*0-06-026890-5*); PLB 13.89 (*0-06-026891-3*) HarpC Child Bks.
—No Roses for Harry! Graham, Margaret B., illus. LC 58-7752. 32p. (ps-3). 1976. pap. 4.95 (*0-06-443011-1*, Trophy) HarpC Child Bks.

Ziong, Blia, as told by. Nine-in-One, Grr! Grr! Spagnoli, Cathy, adapted by. (Illus.). 32p. (ps-5). 1993. pap. 5.95 (*0-89239-110-3*) Childrens Book Pr.

Zipes, Jack, ed. & tr. from GER. Fairy Tales & Fables from Weimar Days. LC 89-40357. (Illus.). 221p. 1989. 30.00x (*0-87451-501-7*) U Pr of New Eng.

Zipko, Stephen J. Toxic Threat: How Hazardous Substances Poison Our Lives. LC 85-21563. (Illus.). 192p. (gr. 7 up). 1986. lib. bdg. 11.98 (*0-671-50963-2*, J Messner) S&S Trade.
—Toxic Threat: How Hazardous Substances Poison Our Lives. rev. ed. Steltenpohl, Jane, ed. 208p. (gr. 7 up). 1990. lib. bdg. 14.98 (*0-671-69330-1*, J Messner); lib. bdg. 5.95 (*0-671-69331-X*) S&S Trade.

Zirpoli, Jane. Roots in the Outfield. LC 87-33900. (gr. 3-7). 1988. 13.45 (*0-395-45184-1*) HM.

Zistel, Era. A Cat Called Christopher. (Illus.). 88p. (Orig.). (gr. 4 up). 1991. pap. 9.95 (*0-9617426-7-4*) J N Townsend.
—Orphan. Coombs, Christine, illus. 64p. (Orig.). (gr. 4 up). 1990. pap. 11.95 (*0-9617426-5-8*) J N Townsend.
—Wintertime Cat. rev. ed. Zistel, Era, illus. 64p. 1988. pap. 5.95 (*0-9617426-4-X*) J N Townsend.

Ziter, Cary B. When Turtles Come to Town. Bigger, Chuck, photos by. (Illus.). 64p. (gr. 3-5). 1989. PLB 12.90 (*0-531-10691-8*) Watts.

Zito, Penny. Through My Eyes - A Teenage Look at Life. York, Sherri, ed. LC 87-50257. (Illus.). 152p. (gr. 7 up). 1987. 7.95 (*1-55523-075-X*) Winston-Derek.

Zlatich, Marko. New England Soldiers. (gr. 1-9). 1992. pap. 3.95 (*0-88388-034-2*) Bellerophon Bks.
—Paper Soldiers of American Revolution. (gr. 1-9). 1992. pap. 3.95 (*0-88388-028-8*) Bellerophon Bks.

Zlotowitz, Bernard M. & Maiben, Dina. Abraham's Great Discovery. Sweeny, Raquel, illus. 32p. 1991. 12.95t (*0-911389-04-0*) NightinGale Res.

Zlotowitz, Bernard M., ed. see Segal, Abraham.

Zlotowitz, M. My Blessings for Food: Birchas Hamozon. Horen, Michael, illus. 32p. (gr. 1-6). 7.95 (*0-89906-799-9*) Mesorah Pubns.

Zlotowitz, Meir, jt. auth. see Scherman, Nosson.

Zobel, Joseph. Black Shack Alley. Warner, Keith Q., tr. from FRE. LC 78-13852. (Illus., Orig.). (gr. 9 up). 1991. pap. 10.50 (*0-914478-68-0*) Three Continents.

Zodrow, Brenda. Arkansas Coloring Book. (Illus.). 54p. (gr. k-4). 1990. 4.50 (*1-55728-179-3*) U of Ark Pr.

Zoehfeld. What's Alive. Date not set. 15.00 (*0-06-023443-1*, Festival); PLB 14.89 (*0-06-023444-X*, Festival) HarpC Child Bks.

Zoehfeld, Kathleen W. Dolphin's First Day. Petruccio, Steven, illus. LC 93-27270. 1994. 14.95 (*1-56899-024-3*); pap. 4.95 (*1-56899-025-1*) Soundprints.
—Seal Pup Grows Up: The Story of the Harbor Seal. Bonforte, Lisa, illus. LC 93-27269. 1994. 14.95 (*1-56899-026-X*); pap. 4.95 (*1-56899-027-8*) Soundprints.
—A Shell is Someone's Home. David, Helen K., illus. LC 93-12428. (gr. k-3). 1994. 14.00 (*0-06-022998-5*); PLB 13.89 (*0-06-022999-3*) HarpC Child Bks.

Zoglin, Suzanne, ed. see Delp, Debra.

Zohny, Sophia. History of the Prophets: A Workbook. 40p. (Orig.). (gr. 1-12). 1991. 5.00 (*0-89259-111-0*) Am Trust Pubns.

Zokeisha. Farm House. Klimo, Kate, ed. (Illus.). 16p. 1983. pap. 3.50 (*0-671-46130-3*, Little Simon) S&S Trade.
—Firehouse. Klimo, Kate, ed. Zokeisha, illus. 16p. (ps-k). 1983. pap. 3.50 (*0-671-46128-1*, Little Simon) S&S Trade.
—A Little Book of Baby Animals. Klimo, Kate, ed. Zokeisha, illus. 16p. 1982. pap. 2.95 (*0-671-44840-4*, Little Simon) S&S Trade.
—A Little Book of Colors. Klimo, Kate, ed. Zokeisha, illus. 16p. 1982. pap. 2.95 (*0-671-45570-2*, Little Simon) S&S Trade.
—Mother Goose House. Klimo, Kate, ed. Zokeisha, illus. 16p. (ps-k). 1983. pap. 3.50 (*0-671-46127-3*, Little Simon) S&S Trade.
—Mouse House. Klimo, Kate, ed. Zokeisha, illus. 16p. 1983. pap. 2.95 (*0-671-46129-X*, Little Simon) S&S Trade.
—Things I Like to Eat. Zokeisha, illus. 16p. (ps-k). 1981. pap. 2.95 (*0-671-44449-2*, Little Simon) S&S Trade.
—Things I Like to Look At. Zokeisha, illus. 16p. (ps-k). 1981. pap. 3.95 (*0-671-44451-4*, Little Simon) S&S Trade.
—Things I Like to Play With. Zokeisha, illus. 16p. (ps-k). 1981. pap. 2.95 (*0-671-44450-6*, Little Simon) S&S Trade.
—Things I Like to Wear. Zokeisha, illus. 16p. (ps-k). 1981. pap. 2.95 board (*0-671-44452-2*, Little Simon) S&S Trade.
—Zoo Animals. Zokeisha, illus. 16p. (ps). 1982. pap. 3.50 board (*0-671-44895-1*, Little Simon) S&S Trade.

Zola, Meguido. By Hook or by Crook: My Autograph Book. Pelham, Richard, illus. 48p. (gr. 1 up). 1987. 9.95 (*0-88776-201-8*) Tundra Bks.

Zollars, Jean A. Sillas Especiales. Montano, Macrina C., ed. Millar, Alejandra, tr. Knezevich, Joyce, illus. (SPA.). 95p. (Orig.). 1993. pap. 20.00 (*1-882632-02-8*); pap. 10.00 Third World Countries Nonprofits (*1-882632-04-2*) PAX Pr.
—Special Seating. Knezevich, Joyce, illus. 95p. (Orig.). 1993. pap. 20.00 (*1-882632-01-X*); pap. 10.00 Third World Countries Nonprofits (*1-882632-05-2*) PAX Pr.

Zollinger, Camma L. Sacrament. pap. 5.95 (*0-88494-261-9*) Bookcraft Inc.

Zolna, Ed. Fran an' Maabl: Rel. (Illus.). 64p. (Orig.). (gr. 9-12). 1988. pap. 2.50 (*0-945975-00-7*) E Zolna Inc.
—Fran an' Maabl, Vol. 1, No. 3: The Mantle of Command. (Illus.). 32p. (Orig.). (gr. 9-12). 1991. pap. 2.50 (*0-945975-01-5*) E Zolna Inc.

Zolotow, Charlotte. The Beautiful Christmas Tree. Robbins, Ruth, illus. 32p. (gr. k-3). 1983. 13.95 (*0-395-27676-4*); pap. 4.95 (*0-395-34925-7*) HM.
—Big Sister & Little Sister. Alexander, Martha, illus. 24p. (gr. k-3). 1966. 14.00 (*0-06-026925-1*) HarpC Child Bks.
—Big Sister & Little Sister. Alexander, Martha, illus. LC 66-8268. 32p. (gr. k-3). 1990. pap. 4.50 (*0-06-443217-3*, Trophy) HarpC Child Bks.
—The Bunny Who Found Easter. Peterson, Betty F., illus. 32p. (gr. k-3). 1983. 14.45 (*0-395-27677-2*); pap. 5.70 (*0-395-34068-3*) HM.
—But Not Billy. Chorao, Kay, illus. LC 82-47703. 32p. (ps-k). 1983. 12.95 (*0-06-026963-4*) HarpC Child Bks.
—Do You Know What I'll Do? Williams, Garth, illus. LC 58-7755. 32p. (ps-1). 1958. PLB 13.89 (*0-06-026940-5*) HarpC Child Bks.
—Everything Glistens & Everything Sings. Tomes, Margot, illus. LC 86-31917. 96p. (ps-3). 1987. 11.95 (*0-15-226488-4*, HB Juv Bks) HarBrace.
—A Father Like That. Shecter, Ben, illus. LC 70-135778. (ps-3). 1971. PLB 12.89 (*0-06-026950-2*) HarpC Child Bks.
—The Hating Book. Shecter, Ben, illus. LC 69-14444. 32p. (ps-3). 1969. 14.00 (*0-06-026923-5*); PLB 13.89 (*0-06-026924-3*) HarpC Child Bks.
—The Hating Book. Shecter, Ben, illus. LC 69-14444. 32p. (gr. k-3). 1989. pap. 3.95 (*0-06-443197-5*, Trophy) HarpC Child Bks.
—Hold My Hand. Reissue. ed. Di Grazia, Thomas, illus. LC 72-76506. 32p. (gr. k-3). 1972. PLB 12.89 (*0-06-026952-9*) HarpC Child Bks.
—I Know a Lady. Stevenson, James, illus. LC 83-25361. 24p. (gr. k-3). 1984. 14.95 (*0-688-03837-9*); PLB 14.88 (*0-688-03838-7*) Greenwillow.
—I Know a Lady. Stevenson, James, illus. LC 83-25361. 24p. (ps up). 1992. pap. 4.95 (*0-688-11519-5*, Mulberry) Morrow.
—I Like to Be Little. Blegvad, Erik, illus. LC 83-45056. 32p. (gr. k-4). 1987. (Crowell Jr Bks); PLB 12.89 (*0-690-04674-X*, Crowell Jr Bks) HarpC Child Bks.
—I Like to Be Little. Blegvad, Eric, illus. LC 83-45056. 32p. (gr. k-4). 1990. pap. 4.95 (*0-06-443248-3*, Trophy) HarpC Child Bks.
—If It Weren't for You. Reissue. ed. Shecter, Ben, illus. LC 66-15682. 32p. (gr. k-3). 1966. HarpC Child Bks.
—If You Listen. Reissue. ed. Simont, Marc, illus. LC 79-2688. 32p. (gr. k-3). 1980. PLB 13.89 (*0-06-027050-0*) HarpC Child Bks.
—It's Not Fair. Reissue. ed. Du Bois, William P., illus. LC 76-3387. 32p. (gr. k-3). 1976. 13.00 (*0-06-026934-0*); PLB 12.89 (*0-06-026935-9*) HarpC Child Bks.
—Janey. Himler, Ronald, illus. LC 72-9861. 24p. (ps-3). 1973. PLB 12.89 (*0-06-026928-6*) HarpC Child Bks.
—May I Visit? Reissue. ed. Blegvad, Erik, illus. LC 75-25405. 32p. (gr. k-3). 1976. PLB 12.89 (*0-06-026933-2*) HarpC Child Bks.
—Mister Rabbit & the Lovely Present. Sendak, Maurice, illus. LC 62-7590. 32p. (ps-3). 1962. 14.00 (*0-06-026945-6*); PLB 13.89 (*0-06-026946-4*) HarpC Child Bks.
—Mr. Rabbit & the Lovely Present. Sendak, Maurice, illus. LC 62-7590. 32p. (ps-3). 1977. pap. 4.50 (*0-06-443020-0*, Trophy) HarpC Child Bks.
—Mr. Rabbit & the Lovely Present. Sendak, Maurice, illus. (gr. k-3). 1987. incl. cassette 19.95 (*0-87499-047-5*); pap. 12.95 incl. cassette (*0-87499-046-7*); 4 paperbacks, cassette & guide 27.95 (*0-87499-048-3*) Live Oak Media.
—The Moon Was the Best. Hoban, Tana, photos by. LC 91-47748. (Illus.). 32p. (ps up). 1993. 15.00 (*0-688-09940-8*); PLB 14.93 (*0-688-09941-6*) Greenwillow.
—My Friend John. Shecter, Ben, illus. LC 68-10209. (gr. k-3). 1968. (C Zolotow Bks); PLB 13.89 (*0-06-026948-0*, C Zolotow Bks) HarpC Child Bks.
—My Grandson Lew. LC 73-14335. (Illus.). 32p. (gr. k-3). 1974. PLB 13.89 (*0-06-026962-6*) HarpC Child Bks.
—My Grandson Lew. Pene du Boid, William, illus. LC 73-1433. 32p. (ps-3). 1985. pap. 3.95 (*0-06-443066-9*, Trophy) HarpC Child Bks.
—Over & Over. Williams, Garth, illus. LC 56-8149. (gr. k-2). 1957. HarpC Child Bks.
—Over & Over. Reissue. ed. Williams, Garth, illus. LC 56-8149. 32p. (ps-3). 1987. PLB 14.89 (*0-06-026956-1*) HarpC Child Bks.
—Park Book. Rey, H. A., illus. LC 44-9471. 32p. (ps-1). 1986. PLB 13.89 (*0-06-026973-1*) HarpC Child Bks.
—Peter & the Pigeons. Gourgault, Martine, illus. LC 92-29405. 24p. (ps up). 1993. 14.00 (*0-688-12185-3*); PLB 13.93 (*0-688-12186-1*) Greenwillow.
—The Poodle Who Barked at the Wind. Otani, June, illus. LC 86-42992. 32p. (ps-3). 1987. HarpC Child Bks.
—The Quarreling Book. Lobel, Arnold, illus. LC 63-14445. 32p. (gr. k-3). 1963. 13.00 (*0-06-026975-8*); PLB 12.89 (*0-06-026976-6*) HarpC Child Bks.
—The Quarreling Book. Lobel, Arnold, illus. LC 63-14445. 32p. (gr. k-3). 1982. pap. 3.95 (*0-06-443034-0*, Trophy) HarpC Child Bks.
—The Quiet Mother & the Noisy Little Boy. Simont, Marc, illus. LC 88-936. 32p. (ps-3). 1989. 13.00 (*0-06-026978-2*); PLB 12.89 (*0-06-026979-0*) HarpC Child Bks.
—A Rose, a Bridge, & a Wild Black Horse. Spowart, Robin, illus. LC 86-25840. 32p. (ps-1). 1987. PLB 12.89 (*0-06-026939-1*, C Zolotow Bks) HarpC Child Bks.
—Say It! Stevenson, James, illus. LC 79-25115. 24p. (gr. k-3). 1980. PLB 14.88 (*0-688-84276-3*) Greenwillow.
—Say It! ALC Staff, ed. Stevenson, James, illus. LC 79-25115. 24p. (ps up). 1992. pap. 4.95 (*0-688-11711-2*, Mulberry) Morrow.
—The Seashore Book. Minor, Wendell, illus. LC 91-22783. 32p. (gr. k-3). 1992. 15.00 (*0-06-020213-0*); PLB 14.89 (*0-06-020214-9*) HarpC Child Bks.
—The Sky Was Blue. Williams, Garth, illus. LC 62-13328. (gr. k-3). 1963. PLB 14.89 (*0-06-027001-2*) HarpC Child Bks.
—Sleepy Book. Plume, Ilse, illus. LC 87-45861. 32p. (ps-1). 1988. PLB 12.89 (*0-06-026968-5*) HarpC Child Bks.
—Sleepy Book. Plume, Ilse, illus. LC 87-45861. 32p. (ps-1). 1990. pap. 5.95 (*0-06-443239-4*, Trophy) HarpC Child Bks.
—Snippets: A Gathering of Poems, Pictures, & Possibilities... Sweet, Melissa, illus. LC 91-37751. 48p. (ps-3). 1993. 16.00 (*0-06-020818-X*); PLB 15.89 (*0-06-020819-8*) HarpC Child Bks.
—Some Things Go Together. Gundersheimer, Karen, illus. LC 82-48694. 24p. (ps-2). 1987. pap. 4.95 (*0-06-443133-9*, Trophy) HarpC Child Bks.
—Someday. Lobel, Arnold, illus. LC 64-16654. 32p. (gr. k-3). 1965. PLB 12.89 (*0-06-027016-0*) HarpC Child Bks.
—Someday. LC 64-16654. (Illus.). 32p. (gr. k-3). 1989. pap. 4.95 (*0-06-443207-6*, Trophy) HarpC Child Bks.
—Someone New. Blegvad, Erik, illus. LC 77-11838. (ps-3). 1978. PLB 14.89 (*0-06-027018-7*) HarpC Child Bks.
—Something Is Going to Happen. Stock, Catherine, illus. LC 87-26661. 32p. (ps-3). 1988. PLB 13.89 (*0-06-027029-2*) HarpC Child Bks.
—Something Is Going to Happen. Stock, Catherine, illus. LC 87-26661. 32p. (ps-3). 1991. pap. 4.95 (*0-06-443274-2*, Trophy) HarpC Child Bks.
—Storm Book. Graham, Margaret B., illus. LC 52-7880. (gr. k-3). 1952. PLB 13.89 (*0-06-027026-8*) HarpC Child Bks.
—The Storm Book. Graham, Margaret B., illus. LC 52-7880. 32p. (ps-3). 1989. pap. 4.95 (*0-06-443194-0*, Trophy) HarpC Child Bks.
—The Summer Night. Shecter, Ben, illus. LC 88-44522. 32p. (ps-3). 1991. PLB 13.89 (*0-06-026917-0*) HarpC Child Bks.
—This Quiet Lady. Lobel, Anita, illus. LC 90-38485. 24p. (ps up). 1992. 14.00 (*0-688-09305-1*); PLB 13.93 (*0-688-09306-X*) Greenwillow.
—A Tiger Called Thomas. rev. ed. Stock, Catherine, illus. LC 86-20878. 40p. (ps-3). 1988. 12.95 (*0-688-06696-8*); PLB 12.88 (*0-688-06697-6*) Lothrop.
—Timothy Too! (ps-3). 1986. 13.45 (*0-395-39378-7*) HM.
—When I Have a Little Boy. Knight, Hilary, illus. LC 67-14072. 32p. (ps-3). 1988. pap. 3.95 (*0-06-443176-2*, Trophy) HarpC Child Bks.
—When I Have a Little Girl. Knight, Hilary, illus. LC 65-24656. 32p. (gr. k-3). 1965. 13.00 (*0-06-027045-4*) HarpC Child Bks.
—When I Have a Little Girl. Knight, Hilary, illus. LC 65-24656. 32p. (ps-3). 1988. pap. 3.95 (*0-06-443175-4*, Trophy) HarpC Child Bks.
—William's Doll. Pene Du Bois, William, illus. LC 70-183173. 32p. (ps-3). 1972. 14.00 (*0-06-027047-0*); PLB 13.89 (*0-06-027048-9*) HarpC Child Bks.
—William's Doll. Pene du Boid, William, illus. LC 70-183173. 32p. (ps-3). 1985. pap. 4.95 (*0-06-443067-7*, Trophy) HarpC Child Bks.

Zolotow, Charlotte & Stevenson, James. I Know a Lady. (Illus.). 32p. (ps-3). 1986. pap. 3.99 (*0-14-050550-4*, Puffin) Puffin Bks.

Zolotow, Charlotte, ed. Early Sorrow: Ten Stories of Youth. LC 79-2669. 224p. (gr. 7 up). 1986. PLB 14.89 (*0-06-026937-5*) HarpC Child Bks.
—An Overpraised Season. LC 73-5499. 204p. (gr. 7 up). 1973. PLB 12.89 (*0-06-026954-5*) HarpC Child Bks.
Zomberg, Paul G. Computers. LC 84-9792. (Illus.). 48p. (gr. 4-12). 1984. PLB 15.99 (*0-8172-1409-7*) Raintree Steck-V.
Zonderman, John & Shader, Laurel. Mononucleosis & Other Infectious Diseases. (Illus.). 112p. (gr. 6-12). 1989. 18.95 (*0-7910-0069-9*) Chelsea Hse.
Zone, Ray, jt. auth. see Aragones, Sergio.
Zook, Mary R. Little Missionaries. 184p. (ps-5). 1979. 6.95 (*0-686-30764-X*) Rod & Staff.
Zorc, R. David, jt. auth. see Sunio, Delicia.
Zorn, Steven. Classic American Folk Tales. LC 91-58125. (Illus.). 56p. 1992. 9.98 (*1-56138-062-8*) Courage Bks.
Zorn, Steven, jt. auth. see Martin, Mary.
Zorn, Steven, as told by. Mostly Ghostly: Eight Spooky Tales to Chill Your Bones. Brodley, John, illus. LC 91-71087. 56p. (gr. 2 up). 1991. 9.98 (*1-56138-033-4*) Courage Bks.
Zorn, Steven, retold by. Start Exploring Bulfinch's Mythology: Classic Tales of Heroes, Gods, & Magic. (Illus.). 128p. (Orig.). (gr. 2 up). 1989. pap. 8.95 (*0-89471-710-3*) Running Pr.
Zornes, Rocky see Stuart, Jesse.
Zortman, Bruce. TechOne: A Comprehensive Guide for Teaching the Skills of Technical Theater. LC 91-72924. 300p. (gr. 7-12). 1993. tchr's. ed. 29.95 (*0-9602498-7-7*) Firestein Bks.
Zovi, Lonnie D. Cantos, Rimos y Rimas. (SPA.). 67p. (Orig.). (gr. 5 up). 1990. pap. 22.95 (*0-935301-60-7*) Vibrante Pr.
Zuanich, Margaret A., jt. auth. see Lipscomb, Susan D.
Zuber, Sharon, jt. auth. see Friedman, Herbert.
Zubizarreta, Rosa, tr. see Ada, Alma F.
Zubizarreta, Rosalma, tr. see De Sauza, James.
Zubizarreta, Rosalma, tr. see Rohmer, Harriet.
Zubizarreta, Rosalma, tr. see Rohmer, Harriet & Gomez, Cruz.
Zubrowski, Bernie. Blinkers & Buzzers: Building & Experimenting with Electricity & Magnetism. Doty, Roy, illus. LC 90-44519. 112p. (gr. 3 up). 1991. pap. 6.95 (*0-688-09965-3*, Pub. by Beech Tree Bks) Morrow.
—Blinkers & Buzzers: Building & Experimenting with Electricity & Magnetism. Doty, Roy, illus. LC 90-44519. 112p. (gr. 3 up). 1991. PLB 12.88 (*0-688-09966-1*) Morrow Jr Bks.
—A Children's Museum Activity Book: Bubbles. Drescher, Joan, illus. LC 78-27497. (gr. 5-7). 1979. pap. 7.95 (*0-316-98881-2*) Little.

—Inks, Food Colors, & Papers. Vantage Art Staff, illus. 80p. (gr. 5-8). 1993. pap. text ed. 10.95 (*0-685-68097-5*) Cuisenaire.
—Making Waves: Finding Out about Rhythmic Motion. Doty, Roy, illus. LC 93-35455. 1994. lib. bdg. write for info. (*0-688-11787-2*) Morrow.
—Making Waves: Finding Out about Rhythmic Motion. Doty, Roy, illus. LC 93-35455. 1994. pap. write for info. (*0-688-11788-0*, Pub. by Beech Tree Bks) Morrow.
—Messing Around with Baking Chemistry: A Children's Museum Activity Book. Hanson, Signe, illus. 64p. (gr. 3-7). 1981. pap. 7.95 (*0-316-98879-0*) Little.
—Messing Around with Drinking Straw Construction: A Children's Museum Activity Book. Fleischer, Stephanie, illus. 64p. (gr. 3-7). 1981. 8.95 (*0-316-98875-8*); pap. 7.95 (*0-685-57751-1*) Little.
—Messing Around with Water Pumps & Siphons: A Children's Museum Activity Book. Lindblom, Steve, illus. 64p. (gr. 3-7). 1981. pap. 7.95 (*0-316-98877-4*) Little.
—Mirrors. Doty, Roy, illus. LC 91-29142. 112p. (gr. 3 up). 1992. pap. 6.95 (*0-688-10591-2*, Pub. by Beech Tree Bks) Morrow.
—Mirrors: Finding Out about the Properties of Light. Doty, Roy, illus. LC 91-29142. 96p. (gr. 3 up). 1992. PLB 13.93 (*0-688-10592-0*) Morrow Jr Bks.
—Mobiles. LC 92-28408. 1993. pap. 6.95 (*0-688-10589-0*, Pub. by Beech Tree Bks) Morrow.
—Mobiles: Building & Experimenting with Balancing Toys. Doty, Roy, illus. LC 92-28408. 104p. (gr. 3 up). 1993. Repr. PLB 13.93 (*0-688-10590-4*) Morrow Jr Bks.
—Structures. 64p. (gr. 5-8). 1993. pap. text ed. 9.95 (*0-938587-35-8*) Cuisenaire.

Zucker, David. Uncle Carmello. Miller, Lyle, illus. LC 91-15258. 32p. (ps-4). 1993. RSBE 14.95 (*0-02-793760-7*, Macmillan Child Bk) Macmillan Child Grp.
Zucker, William V., tr. see Seidelin, Anna S.
Zuckerman, Seth. Saving Our Ancient Forests. (Illus.). 128p. (Orig.). 1991. pap. 5.95 (*0-9626072-9-0*) Living Planet Pr.
Zuckerman, Susan, jt. auth. see Drutman, Ava.
Zuesse, Eric, tr. see Shakespeare, William.
Zullo, Allan, jt. auth. see Nash, Bruce.
Zuniega, Thelma M. The Haunted Cave. (Illus.). (ps-3). 1972. 3.00 (*0-686-09535-9*, Pub. by New Day Pub PI) Cellar.
Zurawiecka, Aska, tr. see Lehman, Patricia J. & Padzik, Alicja.
Zurlo, Tony. Japan: Superpower of the Pacific. rev. ed. LC 91-15412. (Illus.). 128p. (gr. 4-6). 1991. RSBE 14.95 (*0-87518-480-4*, Dillon) Macmillan Child Grp.

Zusman, Evelyn. The Passover Parrot. Kahn, Katherine J., illus. LC 83-22182. 40p. (ps-3). 1984. pap. 4.95 (*0-930494-30-X*) Kar Ben.
Zusman, Evelyn, jt. auth. see Chanover, Hyman.
Zutter, Hank De see De Zutter, Hank.
Zwahlen, Diana. Pee-U I Think There Is a Skunk in Our School. LC 93-60230. (Illus.). 44p. (ps-3). 1994. 7.95 (*1-55523-607-3*) Winston-Derek.
Zwanenberg, Fiona Van see Van Zwanenberg, Fiona.
Zwebner, Janet. The Animated Haggadah Activity Book. 48p. (ps-8). 1990. pap. 5.95 (*0-944007-46-5*) Shapolsky Pubs.
—Animated Menorah. (Illus.). 48p. (gr. 1-4). 1989. 9.95 (*0-685-28790-4*) Shapolsky Pubs.
—Animated Menorah Chanukah Activity. (gr. 4-7). 1991. pap. 5.95 (*0-944007-61-9*) Shapolsky Pubs.
—The Follow That Sleigh Christmas Activity Book. 48p. (gr. 1-5). 1990. wkbk. 5.95 (*0-944007-62-7*) Shapolsky Pubs.
—UH! OH! Jewish Holidays. (gr. 3-7). 1993. 12.95 (*0-943706-14-9*) Yllw Brick Rd.

Zweifel, Frances. The Make-Something Club: Fun with Crafts, Food & Gifts. Schweninger, Ann, illus. LC 93-2393. (ps-3). 1994. 13.99 (*0-670-82361-9*) Viking Child Bks.
—The Make-Something Club: Fun with Crafts, Food & Gifts. Schweninger, Ann, illus. 32p. (ps-3). 1994. pap. 4.99 (*0-14-050741-8*) Puffin Bks.

Zweig. Novellen. (gr. 7-12). pap. 5.95 (*0-88436-042-3*, 45273) EMC.
Zwerger, Lisbeth, selected by see Andersen, Hans Christian.
Zwerger, Lisbeth, illus. Aesop's Fables. (ps up). 1991. pap. 15.95 (*0-88708-108-5*); pap. 4.95 (*0-88708-179-7*) Picture Bk Studio.
Zwerin, Raymond, jt. auth. see Friedman, Audrey M.
Zwerin, Raymond A. & Marcus, Audrey F. But This Night Is Different. (Illus.). 48p. (gr. k-3). 1981. pap. 10.95 (*0-8074-0032-7*, 102561) UAHC.
Zwerin, Raymond A., jt. auth. see Marcus, Audrey F.
Zwerm, Raymond A. & Marcus, Audrey F. Purim Album. (Illus.). 32p. (gr. k-3). 1981. 10.95 (*0-8074-0154-4*, 101250) UAHC.
Zwicker, Linda. The Hope Chest of Arabella. (gr. 4-7). 1993. pap. 3.99 (*0-553-48036-7*) Bantam.
Zwocker, Ray. Who's Hot: Wesley Snipes. (gr. 4-7). 1993. pap. 1.49 (*0-440-21589-7*, YB) Dell.
Zyskind, Sara. The Struggle. 288p. (gr. 6 up). 1989. 22.95 (*0-8225-0772-2*) Lerner Pubns.
ZZ Top Staff. ZZ Top Greatest Hits. Cuellar, Carol & Stang, Aaron, eds. 220p. (Orig.). 1992. pap. text ed. 24.95 (*0-89898-638-9*) CPP Belwin.

ILLUSTRATOR INDEX

A

Aaestas, Ken. The National Wildlife Federation's Book of Dinosaurs & Other Pre-Historic Animals. Earthbooks, Inc. Staff. 64p. (Orig.). (gr. 4). 1991. pap. 5.95 (*1-877731-16-1*) Earthbooks Inc.

Aagaard, Gary. The Adventures of Tom Sawyer. Twain, Mark. 304p. (gr. 5 up). 1992. 24.95 (*1-879329-08-5*) Time Warner Libraries.

Aaron, Jane. No More Secrets for Me. Wachter, Oralee. (gr. 1-4). 1984. pap. 4.95 (*0-316-91491-6*) Little.

Aaron, Malcolm. My First Trip to Africa. Browder, Atlantis T. & Browder, Anthony T. Browder, Anne, ed. LC 91-70328. 38p. (Orig.). 1991. 16.95 (*0-924944-02-1*); pap. 8.95 (*0-924944-01-3*) Inst Karmic.

Aaseng, Nathan, photos by. Basketball's High Flyers. Aaseng, Nathan. LC 79-17137. 80p. (gr. 4 up). 1980. PLB 11.95 (*0-8225-1058-8*) Lerner Pubns.

—Football's Fierce Defenses. Aaseng, Nathan. LC 79-16315. 72p. (gr. 4 up). 1980. PLB 11.95 (*0-8225-1057-X*) Lerner Pubns.

Abantu Industries. The Color Your Way into Black History Book. Sealy, Adrienne V. 78p. (gr. 2-5). 1980. wkbk. 4.00 (*0-9602670-6-9*) Assn Family Living.

Abbatiello, Antonella. Star, Little Star. George, Lonnie. 24p. (ps). 1992. spiral bdg. 9.95 (*0-448-40487-7*, G&D) Putnam Pub Group.

Abbot, Elenore. Old-Fashioned Girl. Alcott, Louisa May. (gr. 7 up). 1969. 19.95 (*0-316-03096-1*) Little.

Abbott, Donald. How the Wizard Came to Oz. Abbott, Donald. (gr. 3 up). 1991. 19.95 (*0-929605-15-2*); pap. 9.95 (*0-685-59165-4*) Books Wonder.

Abel, J. Angle Iron: Basketball. Grubbs, J. 20p. (Orig.). 1992. pap. 18.00 (*1-56611-008-4*) Jones.

—Etruscans: Valentine's Day. rev. ed. Tab, Joan & Jon. 20p. (gr. 5-8). 1992. pap. 15.00 (*1-56611-007-6*) Jones.

—The House That Played Ball. rev. ed. Tab, Joan & Jon. 50p. (gr. k-2). 1992. pap. 18.00 (*1-56611-006-8*) Jones.

—Muscle Building. Grubbs, J. 36p. 1992. pap. 18.00 (*1-56611-010-6*) Jones.

—PH - Little Leaguer: Little League Peewee Baseball. Grubbs, Joan & Grubbs, Tori. 17p. (Orig.). (gr. 1-3). 1992. pap. 15.00 (*1-56611-009-2*) Jones.

Abel, Ray. Cousins & Circuses. Sypher, Lucy J. 250p. (gr. 3-7). 1991. pap. 3.95 (*0-14-034551-5*, Puffin) Puffin Bks.

—The Edge of Nowhere. Sypher, Lucy J. 211p. (gr. 3-7). 1991. pap. 3.95 (*0-14-034550-7*, Puffin) Puffin Bks.

—The Spell of the Northern Lights. Sypher, Lucy J. 256p. (gr. 3-7). 1991. pap. 4.95 (*0-14-034552-3*, Puffin) Puffin Bks.

—The Turnabout Year. Sypher, Lucy J. 224p. (gr. 3-7). 1991. pap. 4.95 (*0-14-034553-1*, Puffin) Puffin Bks.

Abel, Simone. The Backwards Watch. Houghton, Eric. LC 91-16951. 32p. (ps-2). 1991. 13.95 (*0-531-05968-5*); PLB 13.99 (*0-531-08568-6*) Orchard Bks Watts.

—Somebody & the Three Blairs. Tolhurst, Marilyn. LC 90-7747. 32p. (ps-1). 1991. 14.95 (*0-531-05878-6*); PLB 14.99 (*0-531-08478-7*) Orchard Bks Watts.

Abell. The Cat Who Returned Nine Times. Grubbs, Joan P. Abell, ed. 50p. (Orig.). (gr. 1-4). 1993. 25.00 (*1-56611-060-2*); pap. 15.00 (*0-685-68773-2*) Jones.

—Dog. Joan & Gene. Abell, ed. 50p. Date not set. 25.00 (*1-56611-048-3*); pap. 15.00 (*1-56611-049-1*) Jones.

—The Dog Who Cried Wolf: Based on Old Fairy Tale. Wolfer, J. Abell, ed. 50p. (Orig.). (gr. 1-3). 1993. 25.00 (*1-56611-058-0*); pap. text ed. 15.00 (*1-56611-061-0*) Jones.

—The Invisible Man & The Butler. Rebellion, Boxer. Abell, ed. (gr. 8 up). 1992. 24.00 (*1-56611-013-0*) Jones.

—The Rain Duck: A First Poem for Preschoolers & Kindergarten. Joan, et al. Abell, ed. 50p. (ps). Date not set. 25.00 (*1-56611-050-5*); pap. 15.00 (*1-56611-051-3*) Jones.

—Socks Changes His Mind: (The White House Cat, Bk. II. Abell-Grubbs, J. Abell, ed. (gr. 1 up). 1993. 23.00 (*1-56611-043-2*); pap. 15.00 (*1-56611-044-0*) Jones.

—The Survival Kit. rev. ed. Grubbs, J. Abell, ed. (gr. 7-8). Date not set. lib. bdg. 25.00 (*1-56611-011-4*); pap. 10.00 (*0-685-66203-9*) Jones.

—The Time Machine & The Chef. Baker. Abell, ed. (Orig.). (gr. 8 up). 1992. 24.00 (*1-56611-014-9*); pap. 7.00 (*0-685-66202-0*) Jones.

Abell, et al. C Little Leaguer: (A Little League Baseball Story) Grubbs, Joan, et al. Abell, ed. 50p. (gr. 1-4). 1993. 18.00 (*0-685-66007-9*); pap. 10.00 (*0-685-66008-7*) Jones.

Abell, J. Tori Had the Chicken-Pox: Halloween. Grubbs, T. Abell, J., ed. 36p. (Orig.). (gr. k-3). 1991. pap. 10.00 software looseleaf (*1-56611-002-5*) Jones.

Abell, J. & Abell, J. Where Do the Birds Go When It Storms. Grubbs, J., ed. (gr. 1-3). 1992. lib. bdg. 20.00 (*1-56611-012-2*); pap. 10.00 (*0-685-66201-2*) Jones.

Abell, J., jt. illus. see Grubbs, Tab.

Abell, Joan. Books for Young Ladies. rev. ed. Abell, Joan. Date not set. 22.00 (*1-56611-028-9*); PLB 22.00 (*0-685-65771-X*); pap. 10.00 (*0-685-65772-8*) Jones.

Abell, Joan P. You Will Be King: Gallantry, Bk. 2: Age Three. rev. ed. Abell, Joan P. 50p. (gr. 5-8). 1993. 22.00 (*1-56611-025-4*); PLB 22.00 (*0-685-65767-1*); pap. 10.00 (*0-685-65768-X*) Jones.

Abisch, Roz & Kaplan, Boche. Understanding Book. Pavao, John. Perle, Ruth L., ed. (gr. 1). 1977. pap. text ed. 1.75 (*0-89796-863-8*) New Dimens Educ.

Ablin, Barry. The Squiggly Wiggly Head Family. Osborne, Dwight. 16p. 1992. pap. 5.95 (*0-9632817-0-4*) Osborne Bks.

Abolafia, Yossi. Am I Beautiful? Minarik, Else H. LC 91-32562. 24p. (ps-4). 1992. 14.00 (*0-688-09911-4*); PLB 13.93 (*0-688-09912-2*) Greenwillow.

—The Birthday Thing. Kiser, SuAnn & Kiser, Kevin. LC 87-38085. 24p. (gr. k up). 1989. 11.95 (*0-688-07772-2*); PLB 11.88 (*0-688-07773-0*) Greenwillow.

—Busybody Brandy. Haas, Jessie. LC 93-29569. 1994. write for info. (*0-688-12792-4*); lib. bdg. write for info. (*0-688-12793-2*) Greenwillow.

—Donovan Scares the Monsters. Whitlock, Susan L. LC 86-4783. 24p. (gr. k-3). 1987. 11.75 (*0-688-06438-8*); PLB 11.88 (*0-688-06439-6*) Greenwillow.

—Harry Gets an Uncle. Porte, Barbara A. LC 90-39562. 48p. (gr. k up). 1991. 13.95 (*0-688-09389-2*); PLB 13.88 (*0-688-09390-6*) Greenwillow.

—Harry in Trouble. Porte, Barbara A. LC 87-21253. 48p. (gr. 1 up). 1989. 15.00 (*0-688-07633-5*); PLB 14.93 (*0-688-07722-6*) Greenwillow.

—Harry's Birthday. Porte, Barbara A. LC 93-18189. 48p. (gr. k up). 1994. write for info. (*0-688-12142-X*); PLB write for info. (*0-688-12143-8*) Greenwillow.

—Harry's Dog. Porte, Barbara A. LC 83-14129. 48p. (gr. 1-3). 1983. 13.95 (*0-688-02555-2*); PLB 13.88 (*0-688-02556-0*) Greenwillow.

—Harry's Mom. Porte, Barbara A. LC 84-25955. 48p. (gr. 1-4). 1985. 10.25 (*0-688-04817-X*); lib. bdg. 10.88 (*0-688-04818-8*) Greenwillow.

—It's Valentine's Day. Prelutsky, Jack. LC 83-1449. 48p. (gr. 1-3). 1983. 14.95 (*0-688-02311-8*); PLB 14.88 (*0-688-02312-6*) Greenwillow.

—It's Valentine's Day. Prelutsky, Jack. 48p. (gr. k-3). 1985. pap. 2.50 (*0-590-40979-4*) Scholastic Inc.

—It's Valentine's Day. Prelutsky, Jack. 48p. (gr. k-3). 1988. pap. 5.95 bk & cassette (*0-590-63172-1*) Scholastic Inc.

—Leo & Emily's Zoo. Brandenberg, Franz. LC 87-17907. 32p. (ps-1). 1988. 11.95 (*0-688-07457-X*); lib. bdg. 11.88 (*0-688-07458-8*) Greenwillow.

—My Parents Think I'm Sleeping. Prelutsky, Jack. LC 84-13640. 48p. (gr. 2-4). 1985. 13.95 (*0-688-04018-7*); lib. bdg. 13.88 (*0-688-04019-5*) Greenwillow.

—Stop, Thief! Kalan, Robert. LC 92-30081. 24p. (ps up). 1993. 14.00 (*0-688-11876-3*); PLB 13.93 (*0-688-11877-1*) Greenwillow.

—Taxicab Tales. Porte, Barbara A. LC 90-24609. 56p. 1992. 13.00 (*0-688-09908-4*) Greenwillow.

—Ten Old Pails. Heller, Nicholas. LC 92-31511. 24p. (ps up). 1994. write for info. (*0-688-12419-4*); PLB write for info. (*0-688-12420-8*) Greenwillow.

—A Turkey Drive & Other Tales. Porte, Barbara A. LC 91-48032. 64p. (gr. k up). 1993. 14.00 (*0-688-11336-2*) Greenwillow.

—What I Did Last Summer. Prelutsky, Jack. LC 83-11561. 48p. (gr. 1-3). 1984. 13.95 (*0-688-01754-1*) Greenwillow.

Abrahamson, Evie. The Hebrew Scriptures: The Biblical Story of God's Promise to Israel & to Us. Newland, Mary R. Nagel, Stephan, ed. 261p. (Orig.). (gr. 10-11). 1990. pap. text ed. 12.00 (*0-88489-231-X*); tchr's. ed. 18.95 (*0-88489-232-8*) St Marys.

Abrahamson, Evy, jt. illus. see McCormick, Keith.

Abramson, Michael. Amy, the Story of a Deaf Child. Walker, Lou Ann. LC 84-21152. 64p. (gr. 4-6). 1985. 14.95 (*0-525-67145-5*, Lodestar Bks) Dutton Child Bks.

Abramson, Michael, photos by. Roy Lichtenstein: The Artist at Work. Walker, Lou A. LC 93-2631. 48p. (gr. 3-7). 1994. 15.99 (*0-525-67435-7*, Lodestar Bks) Dutton Child Bks.

Abrera, Jess. Handyong. Abrera, Dette L. (Orig.). (gr. 7-9). 1985. pap. 5.75 (*971-10-0200-0*, Pub. by New Day Pub PI) Cellar.

Accardo, Anthony. Where Did You Get Those Eyes: A Guide to Discovering Your Family History. Cooper, Kay. (gr. 5 up). 1988. 13.95 (*0-8027-6802-4*); PLB 14.85 (*0-8027-6803-2*) Walker & Co.

—Who Put the Cannon in the Courthouse Square: A Guide to Uncovering the Past. Cooper, Kay. LC 84-17251. (gr. 4 up). 1984. PLB 12.85 (*0-8027-6561-0*) Walker & Co.

Accorsi, William. Friendship's First Thanksgiving. Accorsi, William. LC 91-45132. 32p. (ps-3). 1992. reinforced bdg. 14.95 (*0-8234-0963-5*) Holiday.

—My Name Is Pocahontas. Accorsi, William. LC 91-24218. 32p. (ps-3). 1992. reinforced bdg. 14.95 (*0-8234-0932-5*) Holiday.

Acheson, Robert B. A Candle Opera. Sparks, Richard W. 54p. (gr. 1-10). 1983. pap. 5.95 (*0-9614185-0-8*) S J F Co.

Acosta, Andres. Microbes & Bacteria. Sabin, Francene. LC 84-2749. 32p. (gr. 3-6). 1985. PLB 9.49 (*0-8167-0232-2*); pap. text ed. 2.95 (*0-8167-0233-0*) Troll Assocs.

—Prehistoric Animals. Bains, Rae. LC 84-2735. 32p. (gr. 3-6). 1985. PLB 9.49 (0-8167-0296-9); pap. text ed. 2.95 (0-8167-0297-7) Troll Assocs.
—Stars. Sabin, Louis. LC 84-2605. 32p. (gr. 3-6). 1985. PLB 9.49 (0-8167-0152-0); pap. text ed. 2.95 (0-8167-0153-9) Troll Assocs.
Acquistapace, David & Gary, N. C. When I Celebrate His Birthday. Gunn, Robin J. (ps). 1988. bds. 4.99 (1-55513-567-6, Chariot Bks) Cook.
—When I Go to the Park. Gunn, Robin J. (ps). 1988. bds. 4.99 (1-55513-589-7, Chariot Bks) Cook.
—When I Have a Babysitter. Gunn, Robin J. (ps). 1988. bds. 4.99 (1-55513-573-0, Chariot Bks) Cook.
—When I Help My Mommy. Gunn, Robin J. (ps). 1988. 4.99 (1-55513-566-8, Chariot Bks) Cook.
Adair, Dick. The Story of Aloha Bear. Adair, Dick. 24p. (ps-k). 1986. 7.95 (0-89610-049-9) Island Heritage.

Adair, Laura. The Rainbow Fairies. Boston, Gypsy D. 1991. 12.95 (0-9631503-0-8); pap. 4.95 (0-9631503-1-6) Gypsy Damaris. Pre-school & primary-grade children will delight in the folklore of this wonderfully written & beautifully illustrated book...& its size is perfect for small hands. "Who washes the flower's face?" "Who teaches baby owls to fly?" "Who colors the rainbow?" Why, the fairies -- of course!! Order directly from Gypsy Damaris Books, P.O. Box 8417, Shreveport, LA 71148-8417. *Publisher Provided Annotation.*

Adams, Adrienne. The Christmas Party. Adams, Adrienne. LC 78-16230. 32p. (ps-3). 1978. SBE 13.95 (0-684-15930-9, Scribners Young Read) Macmillan Child Grp.
—The Christmas Party. 2nd ed. Adams, Adrienne. LC 91-42159. 32p. (ps-3). 1992. pap. 3.95 (0-689-71630-3, Aladdin) Macmillan Child Grp.
—The Easter Bunny That Overslept. Friedrich, Priscilla & Friedrich, Otto. LC 82-13013. 1987. pap. 4.95 (0-688-07038-8, Mulberry) Morrow.
—The Easter Bunny That Overslept. Friedrich, Priscilla & Friedrich, Otto. 40p. (ps up). 1993. Repr. text ed. 4.95 (0-688-12667-7, Tupelo Bks) Morrow.
—The Easter Egg Artists. Adams, Adrienne. LC 75-39301. 32p. (ps-3). 1976. RSBE 13.95 (0-684-14652-5, Scribners Young Read) Macmillan Child Grp.
—The Easter Egg Artists. Adams, Adrienne. LC 90-1097. 32p. (ps-3). 1991. pap. 4.95 (0-689-71481-5, Aladdin) Macmillan Child Grp.
—The Great Valentine's Day Balloon Race. Adams, Adrienne. LC 80-19527. 32p. (ps-3). 1980. RSBE 14.95 (0-684-16640-2, Scribners Young Read) Macmillan Child Grp.
—The Great Valentine's Day Balloon Race. Adams, Adrienne. LC 86-3382. 32p. (ps-3). 1986. pap. 4.95 (0-689-71085-2, Aladdin) Macmillan Child Grp.
—A Halloween Happening. Adams, Adrienne. LC 81-8969. 32p. (ps-3). 1981. SBE 13.95 (0-684-17166-X, Scribners Young Read) Macmillan Child Grp.
—A Halloween Happening. Adams, Adrienne. LC 91-6907. 32p. (ps-3). 1991. pap. 3.95 (0-689-71502-1, Aladdin) Macmillan Child Grp.
—The Shoemaker & the Elves. Grimm, Jacob & Grimm, Wilhelm K. LC 60-12607. 32p. (ps-3). 1972. RSBE 13.95 (0-684-12982-5, Scribners Young Read) Macmillan Child Grp.
—Woggle of Witches. Adams, Adrienne. LC 70-161536. 32p. (ps-3). 1971. RSBE 13.95 (0-684-12506-4, Scribners Young Read) Macmillan Child Grp.
—A Woggle of Witches. Adams, Adrienne. LC 87-18703. 32p. (ps-1). 1985. pap. 4.95 (0-689-71050-X, Aladdin) Macmillan Child Grp.
Adams, Andrea. Why the Possum's Tail Is Bare: And Other North American Indian Nature Tales. Connolly, James E., ed. LC 84-26871. 64p. (gr. 4-8). 1992. 15.95 (0-88045-069-X); pap. 7.95 (0-88045-107-6) Stemmer Hse.
Adams, Angela. My Best Friend Moved Away. Zelonky, Joy. Silverman, Manuel, intro. by. LC 79-24111. (gr. k-6). 1980. PLB 17.96 (0-8172-1353-8) Raintree Steck-V.
Adams, Ben. How to Go from Geek to Chic (In Less Than 6 Weeks) Harmon, James, Jr. (Orig.). 1987. pap. 4.95 (0-942379-09-8) Wild Bore Bks.
Adams, Brian. MMXXVI - The Vision. Pannell, Gerard. LC 93-84363. 12p. (Orig.). 1993. pap. 9.50 (1-883588-00-6) PAAS Pr.
Adams, David. Zora Neale Hurston: A Storyteller's Life. Yates, Janelle. 104p. (gr. 4 up). 1991. pap. 9.95 (0-9623380-7-9) Ward Hill Pr.
—Zora Neale Hurston: A Storyteller's Life. enl. ed. Yates, Janelle. 98p. (gr. 4-10). 1993. PLB 14.95 (0-9623380-3-6); pap. 9.95 (0-9623380-1-X) Ward Hill Pr.

Adams, Jeanette. Sometimes I Think I Hear My Name. Avi. LC 81-38421. 160p. (gr. 7 up). 1982. 9.95 (0-394-85048-3); lib. bdg. 9.99 (0-394-95048-8) Pantheon.
Adams, Kathy R. Bouncy Bunny's Birthday: A Family Story about Bravery. Brown, Cathy J. & Paterson, Debi. LC 86-61065. 32p. (Orig.). (gr. 1-3). 1985. pap. 8.75 (0-9614796-0-4) C J Brown.
—Bouncy Bunny's Birthday: A Family Story about Bravery. Brown, Cathy J. & Paterson, Debi. 32p. (Orig.). (gr. 1-3). 1985. pap. 8.75 (0-318-19386-8) Offset Hse.
Adams, Lynn. Don Cooper's Musical Games. Cooper, Don, contrib. by. 32p. (Orig.). (ps-3). 1991. pap. 6.95 incl. 30-min. cassette (0-679-81935-5) Random Bks Yng Read.
—Kitty's First Airplane Trip. Falken, Linda C. 32p. (ps-2). 1993. pap. 2.50 (0-590-45788-8) Scholastic Inc.
Adams, Marylou. Brighten up at Breakfast: Helpful Tips for Heavenly Bodies. Adams, Marylou. LC 81-51601. 120p. (gr. 2-7). 1981. plastic comb 7.95 (0-9606248-0-5) Starbright.
Adams, Michael. Andersen's Classic Fairy Tales. 48p. (gr. k-5). 1993. 5.95 (0-88101-276-9) Unicorn Pub.
—Andersen's Fables & Fairy Tales. 48p. (gr. k-5). 1993. 5.95 (0-685-63134-6) Unicorn Pub.
—The Emperor's New Clothes. Ingram, John, ed. Adams, Michael. 48p. (gr. 1-4). 1990. 5.95 (0-88101-106-1) Unicorn Pub.
Adams, Norman. The Moon of the Fox Pups. new ed. George, Jean C. LC 90-22386. 48p. (gr. 3-7). 1992. 15.00 (0-06-022859-8); PLB 14.89 (0-06-022860-1) HarpC Child Bks.
Adams, P. The Child's Play Museum. LC 90-46592. (ps-2). 1976. 9.95 (0-85953-094-9, Pub. by Childs's Play England) Childs Play.
Adams, Pam. Alf 'N Bet. LC 92-14641. 1992. 5.95 (0-85953-167-8) Childs Play.
—Day Dreams. LC 90-45583. 32p. (Orig.). (ps-2). 1978. 11.95 (0-85953-105-8, Pub. by Child's Play England); pap. 5.95 (0-85953-082-5) Childs Play.
—The Gingerbread Man. LC 90-45757. 24p. (ps-2). 1981. 9.95 (0-85953-107-4, Pub. by Child's Play England) Childs Play.
—How Many? 16p. (Orig.). (ps-2). 1975. pap. 3.95 (0-85953-045-0, Pub. by Child's Play England) Childs Play.
—If I Weren't Me. LC 90-46184. 24p. (ps-2). 1981. 9.95 (0-85953-108-2, Pub. by Child's Play England) Childs Play.
—Letters & Words. 16p. (Orig.). (ps-2). 1975. pap. 3.95 (0-85953-046-9, Pub. by Child's Play England) Childs Play.
—Magic. LC 90-46518. 32p. (Orig.). (ps-2). 1978. 11.95 (0-85953-104-X, Pub. by Child's Play England); pap. 5.95 (0-85953-081-7) Childs Play.
—Mrs. Honey's Dream. Adams, Pam. LC 92-40124. 1993. 7.95 (0-85953-331-X); pap. 3.95 (0-85953-332-8) Childs Play.
—Mrs. Honey's Holiday. Adams, Pam. LC 92-41886. 1993. 7.95 (0-85953-755-2); pap. 3.95 (0-85953-756-0) Childs Play.
—Oh, Soldier! Soldier! LC 90-48946. 16p. (ps-2). 1978. 11.95 (0-85953-093-0, Pub. by Child's Play England) Childs Play.
—Old MacDonald Had a Farm. LC 90-46923. (Orig.). (ps-2). 1975. pap. 5.95 (0-85953-053-1, Pub. by Child's Play England) Childs Play.
—Same & Different. 16p. (Orig.). (ps-2). 1975. pap. 3.95 (0-85953-043-4, Pub. by Child's Play England) Childs Play.
—There Was an Old Lady Who Swallowed a Fly. LC 90-46921. 16p. (ps-2). 1989. pap. 5.99 (0-85953-018-3, Pub. by Child's Play UK) Childs Play.
—There Were Ten in the Bed. LC 90-45580. 24p. (ps-2). 1979. 9.95 (0-85953-095-7, Pub. by Childs's Play England) Childs Play.
—This Is the House That Jack Built. LC 90-46922. 16p. (Orig.). (ps-2). 1977. pap. 5.95 (0-85953-075-2, Pub. by Child's Play England) Childs Play.
—This Old Man. LC 90-34327. 16p. (Orig.). (ps-2). 1974. (Pub. by Child's Play England); pap. 5.95 (0-85953-026-4, Pub. by Child's Play England) Childs Play.
—What Is It? (Orig.). (ps-2). 1975. pap. 3.95 (0-85953-044-2, Pub. by Child's Play England) Childs Play.
Adams, Pam & Jones, Ceri. A Book of Ghosts. LC 90-45584. 32p. (Orig.). (ps-2). 1974. (Pub. by Child's Play England); pap. 5.95 (0-85953-028-0) Childs Play.
Adams, Susi. Naughty Ducklings. Cowley, Stewart. LC 92-60791. 22p. (ps). 1992. 6.99 (0-89577-444-5) RD Assn.
Adamson, Charlotte. Tinker's Journey Home. Lehner, Devony. Maloney, P. Dennis, ed. 34p. (ps-6). 12.95 (0-940305-00-3) P D Maloney.
Adinolfi, JoAnn. The Egyptian Polar Bear. Adinolfi, JoAnn. 1994. write for info. (0-395-68074-3) HM.
Adjoian, Eva M. The Miracle Santa's Beard. Mercurio, Helen C. Mercurio, Mary M., ed. 29p. 1985. 12.00 (0-9616079-0-4) Tiffany Pub.
Adkins, Bill, jt. photog. see Brown, Pamela.
Adkins, Jan. Moving Heavy Things. Adkins, Jan. 48p. (gr. 4-6). 1991. pap. 4.80 (0-395-60284-X, Sandpiper) HM.
—Solstice: A Mystery of the Season. Adkins, Jan. 128p. 1990. 12.95 (0-8027-6970-5); lib. bdg. 13.85 reinforced (0-8027-6971-3) Walker & Co.

—String: Tying It up, Tying It Down. Adkins, Jan. LC 91-25786. 48p. (gr. 5 up). 1992. SBE 13.95 (0-684-18875-9, Scribners Young Read) Macmillan Child Grp.
Adkins, Lynda. Big & Easy Art for Patriotic Holidays. Sullivan, Dianna J. 48p. (ps-2). 1987. wkbk. 5.95 (1-55734-085-4) Tchr Create Mat.
—Big & Easy Community Helpers. Sullivan, Dianna J. 48p. (ps-2). 1988. wkbk. 5.95 (1-55734-106-0) Tchr Create Mat.
—Big & Easy Dinosaurs. Sullivan, Dianna J. 48p. (ps-2). 1988. wkbk. 5.95 (1-55734-103-6) Tchr Create Mat.
—Big & Easy Health. Sullivan, Dianna J. 48p. (ps-2). 1988. wkbk. 5.95 (1-55734-104-4) Tchr Create Mat.
—Big & Easy Science. Sullivan, Dianna J. 48p. (ps-2). 1988. wkbk. 5.95 (1-55734-105-2) Tchr Create Mat.
—Gifts for Holidays & Everyday. Sullivan, Dianna J. 96p. (gr. k-4). 1987. wkbk. 9.95 (1-55734-091-9) Tchr Create Mat.
—Milk Carton Art Projects. Sullivan, Dianna J. 32p. (gr. 1-4). 1988. wkbk. 4.95 (1-55734-099-4) Tchr Create Mat.
—Paper Bag Art Projects. Sullivan, Dianna J. 32p. (gr. 1-4). 1988. wkbk. 4.95 (1-55734-100-1) Tchr Create Mat.
—Paper Plate Art Projects. Sullivan, Dianna J. 32p. (gr. 1-4). 1988. wkbk. 4.95 (1-55734-101-X) Tchr Create Mat.
Adoma, Afua. Neighbors & Family Coloring Book. Moore, Peggy A. 20p. (Orig.). (gr. k up). 1989. pap. 2.50 (0-9613078-4-6) Detroit Black.
—Young Run Away. Washington, Anthony. (Orig.). (gr. 3-6). 1984. pap. 2.98 (0-9613078-2-X) Detroit Black.
Adome, Afua. The Case of the Missing Bike & Other Things. 2nd, rev. ed. Moore, Peggy S. 40p. (Orig.). (gr. 4-6). 1992. pap. 5.95 (0-9613078-1-1) Detroit Black.
Agard-Smith, Nadema. The Chichi Hoohoo Bogeyman. Sneve, Virginia D. LC 93-15909. 64p. (ps-6). 1993. pap. 6.95 (0-8032-9219-8, Bison Books) U of Nebr Pr.
Agee, Jon. Flapstick! Agee, Jon. 24p. 1993. 10.99 (0-525-45124-2, DCB) Dutton Child Bks.
—Sitting in My Box. Lillegard, Dee. LC 89-31609. 32p. (ps-2). 1989. 12.95 (0-525-44528-5, DCB) Dutton Child Bks.
—Sitting in My Box. Lillegard, Dee. 32p. (ps-2). 1992. pap. 3.99 (0-14-054819-X, Puffin Unicorn) Puffin Bks.
—Sitting in My Box. Lillegard, Dee. 32p. (ps-2). 1993. pap. 17.99 (0-14-054886-6, Puffin Unicorn) Puffin Bks.
Agell, Charlotte. I Wear Long Green Hair in the Summer. Agell, Charlotte. LC 93-33612. 32p. (ps up). 1994. 6.95 (0-88448-121-2) Tilbury Hse.
—Mud Makes Me Dance in the Spring. Agell, Charlotte. LC 93-33610. 32p. (ps up). 1994. 6.95 (0-88448-112-3) Tilbury Hse.
—The Sailor's Book. Agell, Charlotte. 32p. (gr. 3-6). 1991. PLB 14.95 (0-920668-90-9); pap. 4.95 (0-920668-91-7) Firefly Bks Ltd.
Ageorges, Veronique. The Ancient Egyptians: Life in the Nile Valley. Koenig, Viviane. LaRose, Mary K., tr. from FRE. LC 91-25772. 64p. (gr. 4-6). 1992. PLB 14.90 (1-56294-161-5) Millbrook Pr.
—The Arabs: In the Golden Age. Moktefi, Mokhtar. LaRose, Mary K., tr. LC 92-4989. 64p. (gr. 4-6). 1992. PLB 14.90 (1-56294-201-8) Millbrook Pr.
—Asian Civilizations. Coblence, Jean-Michel. Lamb, Jane C., tr. from FRE. 77p. (gr. 7 up). 1988. 17.98 (0-382-09483-2); 13.49s.p. (0-685-18822-1) Silver Burdett Pr.
Aggs, Patrice. Florizella & the Wolves. Gregory, Philippa. LC 92-52998. 80p. (gr. 3-6). 1993. 13.95 (1-56402-126-2) Candlewick Pr.
—The Sleepy Book: A Lullaby. Hindley, Judy. LC 91-15787. 32p. (ps-1). 1992. 12.95 (0-531-05971-5); lib. bdg. 12.99 (0-531-08571-6) Orchard Bks Watts.
—Soft & Noisy. Hindley, Judy. LC 91-39110. 32p. (ps). 1992. 13.95 (1-56282-224-1); PLB 13.89 (1-56282-225-X) Hyprn Child.
—Why Count Sheep? A Bedtime Book. Wallace, Karen. LC 92-56140. 32p. (ps-1). 1993. 13.95 (1-56282-528-3); PLB 13.89 (1-56282-529-1) Hyprn Child.
—Why the Sea Is Salt. French, Vivian, retold by. LC 92-53138. 32p. (ps-3). 1993. 14.95 (1-56402-183-1) Candlewick Pr.
Agnew, Robin. Rebecca of Grand Hotel. Agnew, Robin. 72p. 1990. text ed. 15.95 (0-9627301-0-6) Grand Hotel.
Agnew, Tim. Behold the Nazarite Woman. Haney, Joy. LC 90-30639. 96p. (Orig.). 1990. pap. 5.99 (0-932581-63-3) Word Aflame.
—Challenges of the Heart. Miller, Cynthia P. LC 90-21432. 144p. (Orig.). 1991. pap. 6.99 (0-932581-79-X) Word Aflame.
—Heart-Shaped Pieces. Martin, LaJoyce. LC 90-22517. 160p. (Orig.). (gr. 9 up). 1991. pap. 6.99 (0-932581-78-1) Word Aflame.
—Holiday Programs: Recitations, Exercises, Readings, Skits, Dramas, Musicals for All Ages, Vol. 2. Westberg, Barbara. LC 87-29786. 218p. (Orig.). 1993. pap. 6.99 (1-56722-012-6) Word Aflame.
—In Search of Yesterday. Morehouse, Joyce M. LC 87-14741. 136p. (Orig.). (gr. 9 up). 1987. pap. 4.99 (0-932581-17-X) Word Aflame.

—The Marriage-Go-Round: Practical Guidelines for a Successful Marriage. Segraves, Judy. LC 90-30558. 138p. (Orig.). 1990. pap. 5.99 (0-932581-64-1) Word Aflame.

—May I Wash Your Feet. Haney, Joy. LC 91-21855. 100p. (Orig.). 1991. pap. 5.99 (0-932581-87-0) Word Aflame.

—Modesty. Pamer, Nan M. LC 90-30491. 50p. (Orig.). 1990. pap. 2.99 (0-932581-62-5) Word Aflame.

—Rhymes, Riddles & Reasons, Vol. I: Genesis, A Devotional Book for Children. Westberg, Barbara. LC 90-38218. 224p. (Orig.). (gr. 3-7). 1991. pap. 7.99 (0-932581-75-7) Word Aflame.

—Rhymes, Riddles & Reasons, Vol. 2: Exodus Through Judges. Westberg, Barbara. LC 90-38218. 224p. (Orig.). (gr. 3-7). 1992. pap. 7.99 (0-932581-76-5) Word Aflame.

Agnew, Tim & Kirchoff, Art. Love's Golden Wings. Martin, LaJoyce. LC 87-17346. 256p. (Orig.). (gr. 7 up). 1987. pap. 6.99 (0-932581-19-6) Word Aflame.

Agre, Patricia. My Brother Steven Is Retarded. Sobol, Harriet L. LC 76-46996. 32p. (gr. 3-6). 1977. RSBE 13.95 (0-02-785990-8, Macmillan Child Bk) Macmillan Child Grp.

Agre, Patricia A., photos by. A Dentist's Tools. DeSantis, Kenny. LC 87-36505. 48p. (gr. k-3). 1988. 10.99 (0-396-09043-5, Putnam); (Putnam) Putnam Pub Group.

Aguiar, Elithe & Sakamoto, Dean. Legends of Hawaii As Told By Lani Goose. Aguiar, Elithe. 20p. (gr. k up). 1986. pap. 8.95 incl. audio cassette (0-944264-00-X) Lani Goose Pubns.

Agustini, Michelle. The Adventures of Panchito & Miguel: Panchito's Guide to Computers. Rosales, Michael & Sider, Eva. 24p. (Orig.). (gr. 1-4). 1988. pap. text ed. 4.95 (0-929297-00-8, 301-158 (005996642)) R & S Books.

Aher, Jackie. My Feelings, My Self: Lynda Madaras' Growing-Up Guide for Girls. Madaras, Lynda & Madaras, Area. LC 86-23719. 160p. (gr. 3-10). 1993. cancelled (0-937858-87-0); pap. 9.95 (1-55704-157-1) Newmarket.

Ahgupuk, George. I Am Eskimo: Aknik My Name. Green, Paul & Abbott, Abbe. LC 59-15891. 1959. pap. 12.95 (0-88240-001-0) Alaska Northwest.

Ahlberg, Allan, jt. illus. see Ahlberg, Janet.

Ahlberg, Janet. The Bear Nobody Wanted. Ahlberg, Allan. 144p. (gr. 3-7). 1993. 15.00 (0-670-83982-5) Viking Child Bks.

—Burglar Bill. Ahlberg, Allan. 1992. pap. 3.99 (0-14-050301-3) Viking Child Bks.

—The Cinderella Show. Ahlberg, Allan. (ps-3). 1987. pap. 4.95 (0-670-81037-1) Viking Child Bks.

—Funnybones. Ahlberg, Allan. LC 79-24872. 32p. (gr. k-3). 1981. 12.88 (0-688-80238-9); PLB 11.88 (0-688-84238-0) Greenwillow.

—Funnybones. Ahlberg, Allan. 32p. (gr. k up). 1993. minibook 4.95 (0-688-12671-5, Tupelo Bks) Morrow.

—It Was a Dark & Stormy Night. Ahlberg, Allan. 32p. (ps-3). 1994. 13.99 (0-670-85159-0) Viking Child Bks.

—Starting School. Ahlberg, Allan. LC 88-50053. (ps-1). 1988. pap. 11.95 (0-670-82175-6) Viking Child Bks.

Ahlberg, Janet & Ahlberg, Allan. The Baby's Catalogue. Ahlberg, Janet & Ahlberg, Allan. 32p. (gr. k up). 1986. pap. 5.95 (0-316-02038-9) Little.

—Each Peach Pear Plum. Ahlberg, Janet & Ahlberg, Allan. 32p. (gr. 1). 1986. pap. 3.99 (0-14-050639-X, Puffin) Puffin Bks.

—The Jolly Postman. Ahlberg, Janet & Ahlberg, Allan. 32p. (gr. k-3). 1986. 16.95 (0-316-02036-2) Little.

Ahlbom, Jens. The Boy & the Dog. Widerberg, Siv. Fisher, Richard E., tr. 28p. (ps up). 1991. bds. 13.95 (91-29-59926-1, Pub. by R & S Bks) FS&G.

Ahlin, Per. The Night the Moon Came By. Alfredson, Hans. Nunnally, Tiina, tr. from SWE. LC 93-663. 1993. Repr. 13.00 (91-29-62246-8, Pub. by R & S Bks) FS&G.

Aho, Jennifer J. Learning About Sex: A Guide for Children & Their Parents. Aho, Jennifer J. & Petras, John W. LC 78-53949. 80p. (gr. 4-6). 1978. pap. 7.95 (0-8050-1078-5, Bks Young Read) H Holt & Co.

Aiello, Laurel. Birthday Buddies. Damon, Laura. LC 87-10866. 32p. (gr. k-2). 1988. PLB 11.59 (0-8167-1091-0); pap. text ed. 2.95 (0-8167-1092-9) Troll Assocs.

Ain, Diantha. What Do You Know about Succotash? Poems & Drawings. Ain, Diantha. 75p. (Orig.). (gr. 1-6). 1991. pap. 7.95 (0-925360-01-5) Geste Pub.

Aitken, Amy. My Tooth Is Loose. Silverman, Martin. 32p. (ps-3). 1992. 8.95 (0-670-83862-4) Viking Child Bks.

—The One in the Middle Is the Green Kangaroo. Blume, Judy. 48p. (gr. k-2). 1982. pap. 3.99 (0-440-46731-4, YB) Dell.

—Stitches. Ziefert, Harriet. 32p. (ps-3). 1990. pap. 3.50 (0-14-054224-8, Puffin) Puffin Bks.

—Stitches. Ziefert, Harriet. 32p. (ps-2). 1993. pap. 3.25 (0-14-036553-2, Puffin) Puffin Bks.

—Take My Picture. Ziefert, Harriet. 24p. (ps-3). 1991. pap. 9.95 (0-06-107424-1) HarpC Child Bks.

Aitken, J. Susan. My Daddy Is a Stranger. Cochran, Vicki. 24p. (Orig.). (gr. k up). 1992. pap. 3.75 (1-56123-049-9) Centering Corp.

Ajhar, Brian. Scarlett Angelina Wolverton-Manning. Ogburn, Jacqueline K. LC 92-41930. 1994. write for info. (0-8037-1376-2); PLB write for info. (0-8037-1377-0) Dial Bks Young.

Akaba, Suekichi. The Crane Wife. Yagawa, Sumiko. Paterson, Katherine, tr. from JPN. LC 80-29278. 32p. (ps-3). 1981. pap. 4.95 (0-685-03413-5, Mulberry Bks) Morrow Jr Bks.

—Tongue-Cut Sparrow. Ishii, Momoko. Paterson, Katherine, tr. LC 86-29314. 40p. (ps-3). 1987. 13.95 (0-525-67199-4, Lodestar Bks) Dutton Child Bks.

Akgulian, Nishan. The Hole by the Apple Tree. Polette, Nancy. LC 90-24646. 32p. 1992. 14.00 (0-688-10557-2); PLB 13.93 (0-688-10558-0) Greenwillow.

Akiko Hayashi. Jessica's Friend. Akiko Sueyoshi. Young, Richard G., ed. Kaisei-sha, tr. LC 89-12050. 32p. (gr. 1-3). 1989. PLB 14.60 (0-944483-47-X) Garrett Ed Corp.

Akinlana, Marcus. Morning of the Bright Bird. Mondo. 48p. 1993. pap. 8.95 (0-88378-136-0) Third World.

Akins, Kelly. My Dinosaur Library, 14 bks. (ps-2). 1992. bds. 17.95 (1-56293-201-2, Set, mini-board bks. in a tray) McClanahan Bk.

Akins, Linda. Ancient Egypt. Conway, Lorraine. 64p. (gr. 4-8). 1987. pap. 7.95 (0-86653-399-0, GA 1021) Good Apple.

—Chemistry Concepts. Conway, Lorraine. 64p. (gr. 5 up). 1983. wkbk. 7.95 (0-86653-100-9, GA 460) Good Apple.

—Earth Science: Tables & Tabulations. Conway, Lorraine. 64p. (gr. 5 up). 1984. wkbk. 7.95 (0-86653-154-8, GA 553) Good Apple.

—Energy. Conway, Lorraine. 64p. (gr. 5 up). 1985. wkbk. 7.95 (0-86653-267-6, GA 639) Good Apple.

—The Middle Ages. Conway, Lorraine. 64p. (gr. 4-8). 1987. pap. 7.95 (0-86653-400-8, GA 1022) Good Apple.

—Plants & Animals in Nature. Conway, Lorraine. 64p. (gr. 5 up). 1986. wkbk. 7.95 (0-86653-356-7, GA 797) Good Apple.

Akinsheye, Addae. African American Inventor Math Pack Workbook. Akinsheye, Dexter. Akinsheye, Dayo, ed. 20p. (Orig.). (gr. 2-5). 1992. pap. text ed. 2.50 (1-877835-53-6) TD Pub.

Akiwsheye, Dexter. I Want to Be... Akinsheye, Dexter & Akinsheye, Dayo. 56p. (gr. k-4). 1992. pap. 12.00 (1-877835-47-1); pap. text ed. 5.00 (1-877835-48-X) TD Pub.

Akkerman, Dinie. Agarrar la Luna. Van Loon, Paul. LC 92-43067. 1993. 5.95 (0-8120-1676-9) Barron.

Akmon, Roni. Come to My Tea Party: A Cookbook for Children. Akmon, Nancy C. 84p. (gr. 3-6). 1993. 10. 95 (0-926684-09-4) Eclectic Oregon.

Al-Amin, Abd A. Invincible Abdullah, Vol. 1: The Deadly Mountain Revenge. Hutchinson, Haji U. Siddiqui, Zeba, ed. 222p. (Orig.). (gr. 6-12). 1992. pap. 6.00 (0-89259-121-8) Am Trust Pubns.

Albers, Dave. Spider & the Sky God: An Akan Legend. Chocolate, Deborah M. LC 92-13277. 32p. (gr. 2-5). 1992. PLB 11.89 (0-8167-2811-9); pap. text ed. 3.95 (0-8167-2812-7) Troll Assocs.

—Talk, Talk: An Ashanti Legend. Chocolate, Deborah M. LC 92-13278. 32p. (gr. 2-5). 1992. PLB 11.89 (0-8167-2817-8); pap. text ed. 3.95 (0-8167-2818-6) Troll Assocs.

Albert, Gretchen D. Scribble Art: Kindergarten & Preschool. Albert, Gretchen D. 85p. (ps-3). 1980. pap. text ed. 5.80 (0-686-28105-5) GDA Pubns.

Albert, Julie D. Chansons de Chez-Nous. Douillard, Jeanne, ed. Snow, Suzanne. Blais, Lise M. (FRE.). 61p. (gr. k-6). 1978. pap. text ed. 1.00 (0-911409-01-7) Natl Mat Dev.

Albertson, Rebecca & Wilhelm, Pamela. The Complete Book of Macra-Tack. 4th, rev. ed. Albertson, Rebecca. 50p. (gr. 3-12). 1983. spiral 9.95 (0-9611536-0-1) Macra-Tack Inc.

Alborough, Jez. Beaky. Alborough, Jez. 32p. (ps-3). 1990. 13.45 (0-395-53348-1) HM.

—Can You Hear Me, Grandad? Thomson, Pat. 32p. (gr. k-2). 1988. pap. 8.95 (0-385-29559-5) Delacorte.

—Clothesline. Alborough, Jez. LC 92-54962. 32p. (ps). 1993. pap. 6.99 (1-56402-243-9) Candlewick Pr.

—Cuddly Dudley. Alborough, Jez. LC 92-52994. 32p. (ps). 1993. 14.95 (1-56402-095-9) Candlewick Pr.

—Martin's Mice. King-Smith, Dick. LC 88-20359. 128p. (gr. 3 up). 1988. 13.00 (0-517-57113-7) Crown Bks Yng Read.

—Where's My Teddy? Alborough, Jez. LC 91-58765. 32p. (ps up). 1992. 14.95 (1-56402-048-7) Candlewick Pr.

Albright, Nancy T. I Know an Old Lady Who Swallowed a Fly. (Orig.). (ps-6). 1985. pap. 3.50 (0-913545-10-4) Moonlight FL.

Albury, Mary. Color Me Special. Shepherd, Sue, et al. (ps-3). 1982. pap. text ed. 4.00 (0-937423-02-5) U M H & C.

—Stevie Has His Heart Examined. Sauer, Sue, et al. Goldstein, Nancy, ed. (ps-7). 1983. pap. text ed. 4.25 (0-937423-00-9) U M H & C.

—Stevie Has His Heart Repaired. Sauer, Sue, et al. Goldstein, Nancy, ed. (ps-7). 1979. pap. text ed. 4.25 (0-937423-01-7) U M H & C.

Alchemy II, Inc. Color Crazy. McKay, Sindy. 26p. (ps up). 1987. 12.95 (1-55578-609-X) Worlds Wonder.

—Muppet Babies on Twinkledink. Becker, Lois & Stratton, Mark. 26p. (ps up). 1987. 12.95 (1-55578-606-5) Worlds Wonder.

—Nanny Piggy. Baron, Michelle. 26p. (ps up). 1987. 12. 95 (1-55578-602-2) Worlds Wonder.

—Radio Station K-E-R-M. McKay, Sindy & Swerdlove, Larry. 26p. (ps up). 1987. 12.95 (1-55578-607-3) Worlds Wonder.

—Something's Fishy. McKay, Sindy. 26p. (ps up). 1986. 12.95 (1-55578-610-3) Worlds Wonder.

Alchemy II, Inc. Staff. Cinderella. Perrault, Charles. 26p. (ps). 1988. incl. cassette 9.95 (1-55578-911-0) Worlds Wonder.

—The Emperor's New Clothes. Andersen, Hans Christian. 26p. (ps). 1988. incl. cassette 9.95 (1-55578-901-3) Worlds Wonder.

—The Frog Prince. Grimm, Jacob & Grimm, Wilhelm K. 26p. (ps). 1988. incl. cassette 9.95 (1-55578-900-5) Worlds Wonder.

—Goldilocks & the Three Bears. 26p. 1988. incl. cassette 9.95 (1-55578-906-4) Worlds Wonder.

—Hey Diddle Diddle. Baron, Michelle. 26p. (ps). 1988. incl. cassette 9.95 (1-55578-919-6) Worlds Wonder.

—Hickory Dickory Dock. Baron, Michelle. 26p. (ps). 1988. incl. cassette 9.95 (1-55578-923-4) Worlds Wonder.

—Jack & the Beanstalk. 26p. (ps). 1988. incl. cassette 9.95 (1-55578-907-2) Worlds Wonder.

—Little Bo Peep. Baron, Michelle. 26p. (ps). 1988. incl. cassette 9.95 (1-55578-921-8) Worlds Wonder.

—Little Boy Blue. Baron, Michelle. 26p. (ps). 1988. incl. cassette 9.95 (1-55578-918-8) Worlds Wonder.

—Little Miss Muffet. Becker, Lois & Stratton, Mark. 26p. (ps). 1988. incl. cassette 9.95 (1-55578-922-6) Worlds Wonder.

—The Little Red Hen. 26p. (ps). 1988. incl. cassette 9.95 (1-55578-905-6) Worlds Wonder.

—Little Red Riding Hood. Grimm, Jacob & Grimm, Wilhelm K. 26p. (ps). 1988. incl. cassette 9.95 (1-55578-903-X) Worlds Wonder.

—Mistress Mary. Becker, Lois & Stratton, Mark. 26p. (ps). 1988. incl. cassette 9.95 (1-55578-920-X) Worlds Wonder.

—Peter & the Wolf. Prokofieff, Sergei. 26p. (ps). 1988. incl. cassette 9.95 (0-317-89541-9) Worlds Wonder.

—The Princess & the Pea. Andersen, Hans Christian. 26p. (ps). 1988. incl. cassette 9.95 (1-55578-909-9) Worlds Wonder.

—Rumpelstiltskin. Grimm, Jacob & Grimm, Wilhelm K. 26p. 1988. incl. cassette 9.95 (1-55578-910-2) Worlds Wonder.

—The Sleeping Beauty. Grimm, Jacob & Grimm, Wilhelm K. 26p. (ps). 1988. incl. cassette 9.95 (1-55578-908-0) Worlds Wonder.

—The Tortoise & the Hare. Aesop. 26p. 1988. incl. cassette 9.95 (1-55578-902-1) Worlds Wonder.

Alcola, Alfredo P. A Tale of Two Cities: Student Activity Book. Sohl, Marcia & Dackerman, Gerald. (gr. 4-10). 1976. pap. 1.25 (0-88301-196-4) Pendulum Pr.

Alcorn, John. The Fireside Book of Children's Songs. Winn, Marie & Miller, Allan. LC 65-17108. (gr. 3 up). 1966. 12.95 (0-671-25820-6) S&S Trade.

Alcorn, Stephen. Lincoln, in His Own Words. Melzer, Milton, ed. LC 92-17431. 1993. 22.95 (0-15-245437-3) HarBrace.

—Rembrandt's Beret. Alcorn, Johnny. LC 90-42330. 32p. (gr. 1 up). 1991. 13.95 (0-688-10206-9, Tambourine Bks); PLB 13.88 (0-688-10207-7, Tambourine Bks) Morrow.

Alda, Arlene, photos by. Arlene Alda's ABC. Alda, Arlene. 32p. (ps-2). 1993. Repr. of 1981 ed. 12.95 (0-89087-348-8) Tricycle Pr.

—Sheep, Sheep, Sheep: Help Me Fall Asleep. Alda, Arlene. LC 91-43006. 32p. (ps-2). 1992. pap. 13.50 (0-385-30791-8) Doubleday.

Alder, Andy. The Last Medal of Honor: A True Story of Unbelievable Valor. Billac, Pete. Davis, Sharon, et al, eds. LC 90-70069. 224p. (Orig.). (gr. 9 up). 1990. pap. 11.95 (0-685-32912-7) Swan Pub.

Alder, George. Help! Croser, Nigel. LC 89-35648. 28p. (gr. 1-2). 1989. PLB 15.93 (0-8368-0223-3) Gareth Stevens Inc.

Aldous, Kate. Meet Posy Bates. large type ed. Cresswell, Helen. 120p. 1991. 13.95 (0-7451-1404-0, Galaxy Child Lrg Print) Chivers N Amer.

—Meet Posy Bates. Cresswell, Helen. LC 91-24481. 96p. (gr. 1-4). 1992. SBE 12.95 (0-02-725375-9, Macmillan Child Bk) Macmillan Child Grp.

—Posy Bates, Again! Cresswell, Helen. LC 93-5789. 112p. (gr. k-4). 1994. SBE 13.95 (0-02-725372-4, Macmillan Child Bk) Macmillan Child Grp.

—The Real Tilly Beany. large type ed. Dalton, Annie. 1993. 15.95 (0-7451-1807-0, Galaxy Child Lrg Print) Chivers N Amer.

Aldrich, Cynthia. All I See Is Part of Me. Charaleone. 56p. (gr. 2-8). 1989. 14.95 (0-935699-03-1) Illum Arts.

—Fun Is a Feeling. Curtis, Chara M. 32p. (ps-2). 1992. 14.95 (0-935699-04-X) Illum Arts.

Aldrich, Kent A. Fine Print: A Story about Johann Gutenberg. Burch, Joann J. 64p. (gr. 3-6). 1991. lib. bdg. 14.95 (0-87614-682-5) Carolrhoda Bks.

Aldridge, George. Gold Star First Readers, 14 vols. Dodd, Lynley & Croser, Nigel. 360p. (gr. 1-2). 1989. Set. PLB 223.02 (0-8368-0775-8) Gareth Stevens Inc.

Aldworth, Susan. Claude Humphrey Dwickens: The Old Man with the Mustache. Herz, Roger J. 32p. (Orig.). (ps-6). 1988. pap. text ed. 3.95 (0-9619560-0-3) TGNW Pr.

—The Old Man of the Mountain. Herz, Roger J. 1989. pap. text ed. 3.95 (0-9619560-1-1) TGNW Pr.

Alegret, Nancy L. Desert Buddies. Philabaum, Dabney M. 40p. (gr. k-4). 1994. pap. 8.95 (0-9639215-0-9) Earth Buddies.

Alenov, Lydia, jt. illus. see Alenov, Nick.
Alenov, Nick & Alenov, Lydia. Auke Lake Tales. Wittanen, Etolin. 53p. (Orig.). (gr. 3-6). 1986. pap. 5.00 *(0-911523-05-7)* Synaxis Pr.
Alexander, Andrea. Why Do Mice Celebrate Christmas? And Other Fun Questions of the Season. Alexander, Andrea. 64p. (Orig.). (ps-5). 1991. pap. 13.95 *(0-9628006-0-0)* Zenon Pub.
Alexander, Barbara, et al. Alphabet Avalanche. Gregorich, Barbara. Hoffman, Joan, ed. 32p. (Orig.). (ps-1). wkbk. 1.99 *(0-88743-128-3)* Sch Zone Pub Co.
—Chicken Scratch. Gregorich, Barbara. Hoffman, Joan, ed. 32p. (Orig.). (ps-1). wkbk. 1.99 *(0-88743-127-5)* Sch Zone Pub Co.
—Counting Caterpillars. Gregorich, Barbara. Hoffman, Joan, ed. 32p. (Orig.). (ps-1). 1986. wkbk. 1.99 *(0-88743-126-7)* Sch Zone Pub Co.
—Reading Railroad. Gregorich, Barbara. Hofman, Joan, ed. 32p. (ps-1). 1986. wkbk. 1.99 *(0-88743-130-5,* 02506) Sch Zone Pub Co.
—Word Wagon. Gregorich, Barbara. Hoffman, Joan, ed. 32p. (Orig.). (ps-1). wkbk. 1.99 *(0-88743-129-1)* Sch Zone Pub Co.
Alexander, Eleanor. Dusty Was My Friend. Clardy, Andrea F. 32p. (gr. 5 up). 1984. 16.95 *(0-89885-141-6)* Human Sci Pr.
Alexander, Ellen. Fireflies in the Night. rev. ed. Hawes, Judith. LC 90-1587. 32p. (ps-1). 1991. PLB 13.89 *(0-06-022485-1)* HarpC Child Bks.
—Fireflies in the Night. rev. ed. Hawes, Judith. LC 90-4255. 32p. (ps-1). 1991. pap. 4.50 *(0-06-445101-1,* Trophy) HarpC Child Bks.
—Llama & the Great Flood: A Folktale from Peru. Alexander, Ellen. LC 88-1194. 40p. (gr. k-4). 1989. (Crowell Jr Bks); PLB 13.89 *(0-690-04729-0)* HarpC Child Bks.
Alexander, Gregory. The Jungle Book. Kipling, Rudyard. 120p. (gr. 1 up). 1991. 17.95 *(1-55970-127-7)* Arcade Pub Inc.
Alexander, Martha. A You're Adorable. Lippman, Sidney, et al. LC 93-931. 1994. write for info. *(1-56402-237-4)* Candlewick Pr.
—And My Mean Old Mother Will Be Sorry, Blackboard Bear. Alexander, Martha. LC 72-707. (gr. k-2). 1977. pap. 3.50 *(0-8037-0126-8)* Dial Bks Young.
—Big Sister & Little Sister. Zolotow, Charlotte. 24p. (gr. k-3). 1966. 14.00 *(0-06-026925-1)* HarpC Child Bks.
—Big Sister & Little Sister. Zolotow, Charlotte. LC 66-8268. 32p. (gr. k-3). 1990. pap. 4.50 *(0-06-443217-3,* Trophy) HarpC Child Bks.
—Blackboard Bear. Alexander, Martha. (Orig.). (ps-2). 1988. pap. 3.50 *(0-8037-0629-4)* Dial Bks Young.
—Emily & the Klunky Baby & the Next-Door Dog. Lexau, Joan M. LC 77-181789. 40p. (ps-3). 1972. 5.95 *(0-8037-2309-1)* Dial Bks Young.
—Even That Moose Won't Listen to Me. Alexander, Martha. 32p. (ps-k). 1988. PLB 11.89 *(0-8037-0188-8)* Dial Bks Young.
—Even That Moose Won't Listen to Me. Alexander, Martha. LC 85-4338. 32p. (ps-2). 1991. pap. 3.95 *(0-8037-0984-6,* Dial Pied Piper) Puffin Bks.
—Good Night, Lily. Alexander, Martha. LC 92-53005. 14p. (ps). 1993. 4.95 *(1-56402-164-5)* Candlewick Pr.
—How My Library Grew, By Dinah. Alexander, Martha. 32p. (gr. k-5). 1983. 18.00 *(0-8242-0679-7)* Wilson.
—I'll Protect You from the Jungle Beasts. Alexander, Martha. LC 73-6015. 32p. (ps-3). 1983. PLB 8.89 *(0-8037-4309-2)* Dial Bks Young.
—Lily & Willy. Alexander, Martha. LC 92-53004. 14p. (ps). 1993. 4.95 *(1-56402-163-7)* Candlewick Pr.
—Maggie's Moon. Alexander, Martha. LC 82-1575. 32p. (ps-2). 1982. Dial Bks Young.
—Maybe a Monster. Alexander, Martha. LC 68-28732. 32p. (ps-2). 1985. PLB 8.89 *(0-8037-5513-9)* Dial Bks Young.
—Move over, Twerp. Alexander, Martha. 32p. (ps-2). 1989. pap. 3.95 *(0-8037-5814-6)* Dial Bks Young.
—Nobody Asked Me If I Wanted a Baby Sister. Alexander, Martha. LC 78-153731. (ps-2). 1971. 10.95 *(0-8037-6401-4)*; PLB 10.89 *(0-8037-6402-2)* Dial Bks Young.
—Nobody Asked Me If I Wanted a Baby Sister. Alexander, Martha. (gr. k-2). 1977. pap. 3.95 *(0-8037-6410-3)* Dial Bks Young.
—Out, Out, Out. Alexander, Martha. LC 68-15251. (gr. k-3). 1968. PLB 6.95 *(0-685-01457-6)* Dial Bks Young.
—Sabrina. Alexander, Martha. LC 72-134855. 32p. (ps-2). 1991. pap. 2.95 *(0-8037-0842-4,* Dial Pied Piper) Puffin Bks.
—Sabrina. Alexander, Martha. 1991. 8.95 *(0-8037-7547-4)* Dial Bks Young.
—We Never Get to Do Anything. Alexander, Martha. (ps-3). 1985. Dial Bks Young.
—We're in Big Trouble, Blackboard Bear. Alexander, Martha. LC 79-20631. (ps-2). 1980. Dial Bks Young.
—When the New Baby Comes, I'm Moving Out. Alexander, Martha. LC 79-4275. (ps-2). 1979. PLB 9.89 *(0-8037-9558-0)* Dial Bks Young.
—Where's Willy? Alexander, Martha. LC 92-53006. 14p. (ps). 1993. 4.95 *(1-56402-161-0)* Candlewick Pr.
—Willy's Boot. Alexander, Martha. LC 92-53007. 14p. (ps). 1993. 4.95 *(1-56402-162-9)* Candlewick Pr.
Alger, Bill. Barney & Baby Bop: A Tent Too Full. White, Stephen. Hartley, Linda, ed. 24p. (ps-k). 1993. pap. 2.25 *(0-7829-0378-9)* Barney Pub.

Ali, Abdullah. ABC Rhymes for Young Muslims. Kishta, Leila. Quinlan, Hamid, ed. LC 83-70183. 32p. (gr. 1-6). 1983. pap. 3.00 *(0-89259-044-0)* Am Trust Pubns.
Alig, Mary J. Yesterday to Color at Gunston Hall. Turner, Louise. 15p. (Orig.). 1990. pap. 3.95 *(1-884085-05-9)* Bd Regents.
Aliki. Aliki's Dinosaur Dig: A Book & Card Game. Aliki. 32p. (gr. k-6). 1992. pap. 9.95 incl. cards *(0-694-00286-0)* HarpC Child Bks.
—At Mary Bloom's. Aliki. LC 75-45482. 32p. (gr. k-3). 1983. 11.25 *(0-688-02480-7)*; PLB 14.93 *(0-688-02481-5)* Greenwillow.
—Aunt Nina & Her Nephews & Nieces. Brandenberg, Franz. LC 82-12004. 32p. (gr. k-3). 1983. PLB 14.93 *(0-688-01870-X)*; 15.00 *(0-688-01869-6)* Greenwillow.
—Aunt Nina, Good Night. Brandenberg, Franz. LC 88-18777. 32p. (ps up). 1989. 12.95 *(0-688-07463-4)*; PLB 12.88 *(0-688-07464-2)* Greenwillow.
—Aunt Nina's Visit. Brandenberg, Franz. LC 83-16531. 32p. (gr. k-3). 1984. 15.00 *(0-688-01764-9)*; PLB 14. 93 *(0-688-01766-5)* Greenwillow.
—Christmas Tree Memories. Aliki. LC 90-45575. 32p. (ps-3). 1991. 15.00 *(0-06-020007-3)*; PLB 14.89 *(0-06-020008-1)* HarpC Child Bks.
—Corn Is Maize: The Gift of the Indians. Aliki. LC 75-6928. 40p. (gr. k-3). 1976. PLB 14.89 *(0-690-00975-5,* Crowell Jr Bks) HarpC Child Bks.
—Corn Is Maize: The Gift of the Indians. Aliki. LC 75-6928. 40p. (gr. k-3). 1986. pap. 4.50 *(0-06-445026-0,* Trophy) HarpC Child Bks.
—Digging up Dinosaurs. rev. ed. Aliki. LC 87-29949. 32p. (ps-3). 1988. 15.00i *(0-690-04714-2,* Crowell Jr Bks); PLB 14.89 *(0-690-04716-9)* HarpC Child Bks.
—Digging up Dinosaurs. rev. ed. Aliki. LC 85-42979. 32p. (gr. k-3). 1988. pap. 4.95 *(0-06-445078-3,* Trophy) HarpC Child Bks.
—Dinosaur Bones. Aliki. LC 85-48246. 32p. (ps-3). 1988. 15.00 *(0-690-04549-2,* Crowell Jr Bks); PLB 14.89 *(0-690-04550-6)* HarpC Child Bks.
—Dinosaur Bones. Aliki. 32p. (gr. k-4). 1990. pap. 4.50 *(0-06-445077-5,* Trophy) HarpC Child Bks.
—Dinosaurs Are Different. Aliki. LC 84-45332. 32p. (ps-3). 1985. 14.00 *(0-690-04456-9,* Crowell Jr Bks); PLB 13.89 *(0-690-04458-5)* HarpC Child Bks.
—Dinosaurs Are Different. Aliki. LC 84-45332. 32p. (ps-3). 1988. incl. cassette 7.95 *(0-694-00236-4,* Trophy); pap. 4.50 *(0-06-445056-2,* Trophy) HarpC Child Bks.
—Evolution. Cole, Joanna. LC 87-638. 32p. (gr. k-3). 1987. (Crowell Jr Bks); PLB 13.89 *(0-690-04598-0,* Crowell Jr Bks) HarpC Child Bks.
—Evolution. Cole, Joanna. LC 87-638. 32p. (ps-3). 1989. pap. 4.50 *(0-06-445086-4,* Trophy) HarpC Child Bks.
—Feelings. Aliki. LC 84-4098. 32p. (gr. k-3). 1984. 15.00 *(0-688-03831-X)*; PLB 14.93 *(0-688-03832-8)* Greenwillow.
—Fossils Tell of Long Ago. Aliki. LC 78-170999. 40p. (gr. k-3). 1972. PLB 12.89 *(0-690-31379-9,* Crowell Jr Bks) HarpC Child Bks.
—Fossils Tell of Long Ago. rev. ed. Aliki. LC 89-17247. 32p. (gr. k-4). 1990. 14.00 *(0-690-04844-0,* Crowell Jr Bks); PLB 13.89 *(0-690-04829-7,* Crowell Jr Bks) HarpC Child Bks.
—Fossils Tell of Long Ago. rev. ed. Aliki. LC 89-15468. 32p. (gr. k-4). 1990. pap. 4.95 *(0-06-445093-7,* JS093, Trophy) HarpC Child Bks.
—Go Tell Aunt Rhody. reissued ed. Aliki. LC 74-681. 32p. (ps-3). 1986. RSBE 14.95 *(0-02-700410-4,* Macmillan Child Bk) Macmillan Child Grp.
—How a Book Is Made. Aliki. LC 85-48156. 32p. (gr. 2 up). 1986. 14.00 *(0-690-04496-8,* Crowell Jr Bks); PLB 13.89 *(0-690-04498-4,* Crowell Jr Bks) HarpC Child Bks.
—How a Book Is Made. Aliki. LC 85-48156. 32p. (gr. k-4). 1988. pap. 5.95 *(0-06-446085-1,* Trophy) HarpC Child Bks.
—I Wish I Was Sick, Too! Brandenberg, Franz. LC 75-46610. 32p. (gr. k-3). 1976. PLB 15.88 *(0-688-84047-7)* Greenwillow.
—I Wish I Was Sick, Too! Brandenberg, Franz. LC 75-46610. 32p. (ps-3). 1990. pap. 3.95 *(0-688-09354-X,* Mulberry) Morrow.
—I'm Growing! Aliki. LC 91-14087. 32p. (ps-1). 1992. 14.00 *(0-06-020244-0)*; PLB 13.89 *(0-06-020245-9)* HarpC Child Bks.
—I'm Growing! Aliki. LC 91-14087. 32p. (ps-1). 1993. pap. 4.95 *(0-06-445116-X,* Trophy) HarpC Child Bks.
—It's Not My Fault. Brandenberg, Franz. LC 79-24157. 64p. (gr. 1-3). 1980. 14.00 *(0-688-80235-4)* Greenwillow.
—Jack & Jake. Aliki. LC 85-9911. 32p. (ps-1). 1986. 11. 75 *(0-688-06099-4)*; PLB 11.88 *(0-688-06100-1)* Greenwillow.
—Keep Your Mouth Closed, Dear. Aliki. LC 66-19310. (gr. k-3). 1966. PLB 13.89 *(0-8037-4418-8)* Dial Bks Young.
—The King's Day: Louis XIV of France. Aliki. LC 88-38179. 32p. (gr. 2-6). 1991. pap. 4.95 *(0-06-443268-8,* Trophy) HarpC Child Bks.
—Leo & Emily. Brandenberg, Franz. LC 80-19657. 56p. (gr. 1-3). 1981. 15.00 *(0-688-80292-3)* Greenwillow.
—Leo & Emily & the Dragon. Brandenberg, Franz. LC 83-14091. 56p. (gr. 1-3). 1984. 12.95 *(0-688-02531-5)*; PLB 12.88 *(0-688-02532-3)* Greenwillow.
—Leo & Emily's Big Ideas. Brandenberg, Franz. LC 81-6424. 56p. (gr. 1-3). 1982. 13.88 *(0-688-00754-6)*; PLB 13.95 *(0-688-00755-4)* Greenwillow.

—Listening Walk. Showers, Paul. LC 61-10495. 40p. (gr. k-3). 1961. PLB 13.89 *(0-690-49663-X,* Crowell Jr Bks) HarpC Child Bks.
—The Listening Walk. rev. ed. Showers, Paul. LC 90-30526. 32p. (ps-2). 1991. 14.00 *(0-06-021637-9)*; PLB 13.89 *(0-06-021638-7)* HarpC Child Bks.
—The Listening Walk. Showers, Paul. LC 90-30526. 32p. (ps-2). 1993. pap. 4.95 *(0-06-443322-6,* Trophy) HarpC Child Bks.
—The Many Lives of Benjamin Franklin. Aliki. 32p. (ps-3). 1988. pap. 12.95 *(0-671-66119-1,* S&S BFYR); pap. 5.95 *(0-671-66491-3,* S&S BFYR) S&S Trade.
—Mummies Made in Egypt. Aliki. LC 78-22139. 32p. (gr. 2-6). 1979. 14.00 *(0-690-03858-5,* Crowell Jr Bks); PLB 13.89 *(0-690-03859-3,* Crowell Jr Bks) HarpC Child Bks.
—Mummies Made in Egypt. Aliki. LC 85-42746. 32p. (gr. 2-6). 1985. pap. 5.95 *(0-06-446011-8,* Trophy) HarpC Child Bks.
—My Feet. Aliki. LC 89-49357. 32p. (ps-1). 1990. 14.00 *(0-690-04813-0,* Crowell Jr Bks); PLB 13.89 *(0-690-04815-7,* Crowell Jr Bks) HarpC Child Bks.
—My Feet. Aliki. LC 89-49357. 32p. (ps-1). 1992. pap. 4.50 *(0-06-445106-2,* Trophy) HarpC Child Bks.
—My Five Senses. rev. ed. Aliki. LC 88-35350. 32p. (ps-1). 1991. 19.95 *(0-06-020050-2)* HarpC Child Bks.
—My Five Senses. rev. ed. Aliki. LC 88-853500. 228p. (ps-3). 1989. 14.00 *(0-690-04792-4,* Crowell Jr Bks); PLB 13.89 *(0-685-58944-7)* HarpC Child Bks.
—My Hands. rev. ed. Aliki. LC 89-49158. 32p. (ps-1). 1990. 14.00 *(0-690-04878-5,* Crowell Jr Bks); PLB 13. 89 *(0-690-04880-7,* Crowell Jr Bks) HarpC Child Bks.
—My Hands. rev. ed. Aliki. LC 89-71728. 32p. (ps-1). 1992. pap. 4.50 *(0-06-445096-1,* Trophy) HarpC Child Bks.
—My Visit to the Aquarium. Aliki. LC 92-18678. 40p. (ps-3). 1993. 15.00 *(0-06-021458-9)*; PLB 14.89 *(0-06-021459-7)* HarpC Child Bks.
—My Visit to the Dinosaurs. rev. ed. Aliki. LC 85-47538. 32p. (ps-3). 1985. 14.00 *(0-690-04422-4,* Crowell Jr Bks); PLB 13.89 *(0-690-04423-2)* HarpC Child Bks.
—My Visit to the Dinosaurs. 2nd ed. Aliki. LC 85-42748. 32p. (ps-3). 1987. incl. cassette 7.95 *(0-694-00201-1,* Trophy); pap. 4.95 *(0-06-445020-1,* Trophy) HarpC Child Bks.
—My Visit to the Dinosaurs Big Book. Aliki. LC 85-47538. 32p. (ps-3). 1994. pap. 19.95 *(0-06-443350-1,* Trophy) HarpC Child Bks.
—Nice New Neighbors. Brandenberg, Franz. LC 77-1651. 56p. (gr. 1-4). 1977. PLB 13.88 *(0-688-84105-8)* Greenwillow.
—Nice New Neighbors. Brandenberg, Franz. 32p. (ps-2). 1990. pap. 2.75 *(0-590-44117-5)* Scholastic Inc.
—Nice New Neighbors. Brandenberg, Franz. LC 77-1651. 56p. (ps-3). 1991. pap. 4.95 *(0-688-10997-7,* Mulberry) Morrow.
—Overnight at Mary Bloom's. Aliki. LC 86-7719. 32p. (ps-3). 1987. 11.75 *(0-688-06764-6)*; lib. bdg. 11.88 *(0-688-06765-4)* Greenwillow.
—Story of Johnny Appleseed. Aliki. (ps-2). 1987. 11.95 *(0-13-850800-3)* P-H.
—The Story of William Penn. Aliki. LC 93-26289. (Orig.). Date not set. pap. 12.00 *(0-671-88558-8,* S&S BFYR) S&S Trade.
—This Is the House Where Jack Lives. Heilbroner, Joan. LC 62-7311. 64p. (gr. k-3). 1962. PLB 13.89 *(0-06-022286-7)* HarpC Child Bks.
—Use Your Head, Dear. Aliki. LC 82-11911. 48p. (gr. k-3). 1983. 13.95 *(0-688-01811-4)*; PLB 13.88 *(0-688-01812-2)* Greenwillow.
—We Are Best Friends. Aliki. LC 81-6549. 32p. (gr. k-3). 1982. 16.00 *(0-688-00822-4)*; PLB 15.93 *(0-688-00823-2)* Greenwillow.
—A Weed Is a Flower: The Life of George Washington Carver. Aliki. 32p. (ps-3). 1988. pap. 14.00 *(0-671-66118-3,* S&S BFYR); pap. 5.95 *(0-671-66490-5,* S&S BFYR) S&S Trade.
—Wild & Woolly Mammoths. Aliki. LC 76-18082. 40p. (gr. k-3). 1977. PLB 13.89 *(0-690-01276-4,* Crowell Jr Bks) HarpC Child Bks.
All, Wendy, jt. illus. see Paris, Pat.
Allan, Nicholas. Jesus' Christmas Party. Allan, Nicholas. LC 91-17092. 32p. 1992. 9.99 *(0-679-82688-2)* Random Bks Yng Read.
Allard, Harry & Marshall, James. The Stupids Take Off. Allard, Harry & Marshall, James. 32p. (gr. k-3). 1989. 13.45 *(0-395-50068-0)* HM.
Allard, Mike. The Ghost of Tomahawk Creek. Andrews, Jean F. LC 93-86006. (Orig.). (gr. 2-6). 1993. pap. text ed. 5.95 *(1-883120-01-2)* Northern St U.
Allen, Elizabeth M. Quien Es Quien? (Who Is Who?) McKissack, Patricia C. LC 83-7361. (SPA.). 32p. (ps-2). 1989. pap. 2.95 *(0-516-52042-3)* Childrens.
Allen, Gary. One Day in the Tropical Rain Forest. George, Jean C. LC 89-36583. 64p. (gr. 4-7). 1990. 14.00 *(0-690-04767-3,* Crowell Jr Bks); PLB 13.89 *(0-690-04769-X,* Crowell Jr Bks) HarpC Child Bks.
—One Day in the Woods. George, Jean C. LC 87-21712. 48p. (gr. 4-7). 1988. 14.00 *(0-690-04724-X,* Crowell Jr Bks); PLB 13.89 *(0-690-04724-X,* Crowell Jr Bks) HarpC Child Bks.
Allen, Ginny. The Dragon & The Lemon Tree. Walton, Robert. LC 89-92122. 86p. (gr. 3-7). 1989. write for info. *(0-9623802-0-2)* Pisces Pr CA.
Allen, Graham, jt. illus. see More, David.
Allen, Graham, et al. Under the Sea. Williams, Brian. LC 88-17654. 24p. (Orig.). (gr. 2-5). 1989. PLB 5.99 *(0-394-99990-8)*; pap. 2.95 *(0-394-89990-3)* Random Bks Yng Read.

Allen, Jonathan. Big Owl, Little Towel. Allen, Jonathan. LC 91-39349. 12p. (ps). 1992. 3.95 (*0-688-11783-X*, Tambourine Bks) Morrow.

—Boysie's First Birthday. Osband, Gillian. 32p. (gr. k-2). 1990. PLB 14.95 (*0-87614-404-0*) Carolrhoda Bks.

—Boysie's Kitten. Osband, Gillian. 32p. (ps-2). 1990. PLB 14.95 (*0-87614-403-2*) Carolrhoda Bks.

—Burton & Stanley. O'Rourke, Frank. (gr. 4-7). 1993. 15.95 (*0-87923-824-0*) Godine.

—The Great White Man-Eating Shark: A Cautionary Tale. Mahy, Margaret. (ps-3). 1990. 13.00 (*0-8037-0749-5*) Dial Bks Young.

—Mucky Moose. Allen, Jonathan. LC 90-6363. 32p. (ps-3). 1991. SBE 12.95 (*0-02-700251-9*, Macmillan Child Bk) Macmillan Child Grp.

—My Dog. Allen, Jonathan. LC 88-30857. 32p. (gr. 1-2). 1989. PLB 18.60 (*0-8368-0095-8*) Gareth Stevens Inc.

—One with a Bun. Allen, Jonathan. LC 91-44055. 12p. (ps). 1992. 3.95 (*0-688-11781-3*, Tambourine Bks) Morrow.

—Purple Sock, Pink Sock. Allen, Jonathan. LC 91-43379. 12p. (ps). 1992. 3.95 (*0-688-11782-1*, Tambourine Bks) Morrow.

—The Red Dragon: A 3-D Picture Book. Wyllie, Stephen. LC 92-26670. 20p. (ps-2). 1993. 13.99 (*0-8037-1452-1*) Dial Bks Young.

—The Three-Legged Cat. Mahy, Margaret. 32p. (ps-3). 1993. 13.99 (*0-670-85015-2*) Viking Child Bks.

—Up the Steps, Down the Slide. Allen, Jonathan. LC 91-44534. 12p. (ps). 1992. 3.95 (*0-688-11784-8*, Tambourine Bks) Morrow.

—Who's at the Door? Allen, Jonathan. LC 92-19618. 32p. (ps up). 1993. 11.95 (*0-688-12257-4*, Tambourine Bks) Morrow.

Allen, Laura H., jt. illus. see Allen, Thomas B.

Allen, Linda. The Mouse Bride: A Finnish Tale. Allen, Linda, retold by. 32p. (ps-3). 1992. PLB 14.95 (*0-399-22136-0*, Philomel Bks) Putnam Pub Group.

Allen, Mayme. One Hundred One Word Puzzlers. Allen, Mayme, et al. LC 92-26302. 128p. (gr. 6 up). 1992. pap. 4.95 (*0-8069-8722-7*) Sterling.

Allen, Pamela. Belinda. Allen, Pamela. 32p. (ps-3). 1993. 13.00 (*0-670-84372-5*) Viking Child Bks.

Allen, Rita. The Adventures of Monkey King. Gao, R. L., tr. from CHI. 132p. (Orig.). (gr. 2-5). 1989. pap. 6.95 (*0-9620765-1-1*) Victory Press.

Allen, Rosemary. Vim, a Very Important Mouse. 8th ed. Weinberger, Jane. LC 84-50872. 40p. (ps-4). 1989. 4.95 (*0-932433-01-4*) Windswept Hse.

Allen, Rowena. Amazing Monsters: Verses to Thrill & Chill. Fisher, Robert, ed. 96p. (gr. k-5). 1982. pap. 5.95 (*0-571-13925-6*) Faber & Faber.

Allen, Thomas. Littlejim. Houston, Gloria. 176p. 1990. 14.95 (*0-399-22220-0*, Philomel Bks) Putnam Pub Group.

Allen, Thomas B. Blackberries in the Dark. Jukes, Mavis. LC 85-4259. 48p. (gr. 2-6). 1993. 14.00 (*0-394-87599-0*) Knopf Bks Yng Read.

—The Chalk Box Kid. Bulla, Clyde R. LC 87-4683. 64p. (gr. 2-4). 1987. lib. bdg. 6.99 (*0-394-99102-8*); pap. 1.50 (*0-394-89102-3*) Random Bks Yng Read.

—Climbing Kansas Mountains. Shannon, George. 32p. (ps-2). 1993. RSBE 15.95 (*0-02-782181-1*, Bradbury Pr) Macmillan Child Grp.

—The Day Before Now. Brown, Margaret Wise. Blos, Joan W., ed. LC 93-12814. 1994. pap. 15.00 (*0-671-79628-3*, S&S BFYR) S&S Trade.

—Laura Ingalls Wilder. Blair, Gwenda. 64p. (gr. 1-4). 1981. (Putnam); pap. 6.95 (*0-399-20953-0*) Putnam Pub Group.

—Littlejim. Houston, Gloria. 176p. (gr. 5 up). 1993. pap. 4.95 (*0-688-12112-8*, Pub. by Beech Tree Bks) Morrow.

—The Most Beautiful Place in the World. Cameron, Ann. LC 88-4228. 64p. (ps-3). 1988. 11.95 (*0-394-89463-4*); lib. bdg. 12.99 (*0-394-99463-9*) Knopf Bks Yng Read.

—Never Fear, Flip the Dip Is Here. Hanft, Philip. LC 90-3385. 32p. (ps-3). 1991. 12.95 (*0-8037-0897-1*); PLB 12.89 (*0-8037-0899-8*) Dial Bks Young.

—On Grandaddy's Farm. Allen, Thomas B. LC 88-23374. 48p. (ps-3). 1989. 13.95 (*0-394-89613-0*); lib. bdg. 14.99 (*0-394-99613-5*) Knopf Bks Yng Read.

—Over Back. Major, Beverly. LC 91-19696. 32p. (gr. k-4). 1993. 15.00 (*0-06-020286-6*); PLB 14.89 (*0-06-020287-4*) HarpC Child Bks.

—The Random House Book of Sports Stories. Schulman, L. M., ed. LC 89-12834. 256p. (gr. 5 up). 1990. lib. bdg. 16.99 (*0-394-92874-1*); pap. 16.00 (*0-394-82874-7*) Random Bks Yng Read.

—The Secret Garden. Burnett, Frances H. Howe, James, adapted by. LC 86-17788. 72p. (gr. k-5). 1993. 13.95 (*0-394-86467-0*) Random Bks Yng Read.

—The Secret Garden. Burnett, Frances H. Howe, James, adapted by. LC 93-18509. 128p. (Orig.). (gr. 2-6). 1993. pap. 2.99 (*0-679-84751-0*) Random Bks Yng Read.

—Time to Go. Fiday, Beverly & Fiday, David. 30p. (ps-3). 1990. 14.95 (*0-15-200608-7*) HarBrace.

—Up the Tracks to Grandma's. Hendershot, Judy. LC 91-2749. 40p. (ps-2). 1993. 15.00 (*0-679-81964-9*); PLB 15.99 (*0-679-91964-3*) Knopf Bks Yng Read.

Allen, Thomas B. & Allen, Laura H. Where Does the Night Hide? Carlstrom, Nancy W. LC 89-32910. 32p. (ps-1). 1990. RSBE 13.95 (*0-02-717390-9*, Macmillan Child Bk) Macmillan Child Grp.

Allen, Tom. Walking to the Creek. Williams, David. LC 88-6763. 40p. (ps-3). 1990. PLB 13.99 (*0-394-90598-9*) Knopf Bks Yng Read.

Allender, David. Shake My Sillies Out. Simpson, Bert & Simpson, Bonnie. 32p. (ps-2). 1988. PLB 11.00 (*0-517-56646-X*) Crown Bks Yng Read.

—Shake My Sillies Out. Raffi. LC 87-750478. 32p. (ps-2). 1988. pap. 3.99 (*0-517-56647-8*) Crown Bks Yng Read.

Allert, Kathy. The Golden Nursery Song Book: Favorite Songs & Singing Games for Children. 48p. (ps-k). 1993. 7.95 (*0-307-15863-2*, 15863, Golden Pr) Western Pub.

—The Happy Little Engine. Nayer, Judy. 24p. (Orig.). (gr. k-1). 1990. pap. 0.99 (*1-878624-43-1*) McClanahan Bk.

—My First Answer Book. Packard, Mary. (ps-5). 1984. pap. 7.95 (*0-671-49312-4*, Little Simon) S&S Trade.

Alles, Hemesh. Behold! Spot the Difference Bible Stories. Madgwick, Wendy. LC 93-5506. 48p. (gr. k-3). 1994. 12.00 (*0-679-85333-2*) Knopf Bks Yng Read.

Alley, Joy D. The Portland Bridge Book. Wood, Sharon. (Orig.). (ps-7). 1989. pap. 12.95 (*0-87595-211-9*) Oregon Hist.

Alley, R. W. Amazing Space Facts. Moche, Dinah. Alley, R. W., photos by. LC 87-82370. 24p. (ps-3). 1992. pap. write for info. (*0-307-11815-0*, 11815-02, Golden Pr) Western Pub.

—Buck-Buck the Chicken. Ehrlich, Amy. LC 86-31639. 48p. (gr. 1-3). 1987. lib. bdg. 7.99 (*0-394-98804-3*); pap. 2.95 (*0-394-88804-9*) Random Bks Yng Read.

—Busy Farm Trucks. 12p. (ps up). 1986. 6.95 (*0-448-09883-0*, G&D) Putnam Pub Group.

—Family Reunion. Singer, Marilyn. LC 92-40336. 32p. (gr. 4 up). 1994. RSBE 14.95 (*0-02-782883-2*, Macmillan Child Bk) Macmillan Child Grp.

—The Giant Baby & Other Giant Tales. Leonard, Marcia. LC 93-6225. 1994. pap. 2.95 (*0-590-46892-8*) Scholastic Inc.

—How Many Trucks Can a Tow Truck Tow. Pomerantz, Charlotte. LC 89-3657. 24p. (ps-k). 1987. PLB 5.99 (*0-394-98775-6*); pap. 6.00 (*0-394-88775-1*) Random Bks Yng Read.

—Ice Cream Soup. Kent, Jack. Herman, Gail, retold by. LC 89-43680. 24p. (Orig.). (ps-2). 1990. pap. 2.25 (*0-679-80790-X*) Random Bks Yng Read.

—The Little Red Car. Ross, K. K. LC 88-63930. 28p. (ps). 1990. 2.95 (*0-394-85376-8*) Random Bks Yng Read.

—The Little Witch Sisters. Calmenson, Stephanie. LC 89-3320. 48p. (ps-3). 1989. 5.95 (*0-8193-1191-X*) Parents.

—The Little Witch Sisters. Calmenson, Stephanie. LC 93-15454. 1993. write for info. (*0-8368-0970-X*) Gareth Stevens Inc.

—Mrs. Toggle & the Dinosaur. Pulver, Robin. LC 90-35771. 32p. (ps-2). 1991. RSBE 12.95 (*0-02-775452-9*, Four Winds) Macmillan Child Grp.

—Mrs. Toggle's Beautiful Blue Shoe. Pulver, Robin. LC 92-40824. 32p. (ps-2). 1994. RSBE 14.95 (*0-02-775456-1*, Four Winds) Macmillan Child Grp.

—My Christmas Safari. Manushkin, Fran. LC 92-28643. 32p. (ps-1). 1993. 13.99 (*0-8037-1294-4*); PLB 13.89 (*0-8037-1295-2*) Dial Bks Young.

—Old MacDonald Had a Farm. 18p. (ps). 1991. 3.95 (*0-448-40106-1*, G&D) Putnam Pub Group.

—The Prince Has a Boo-Boo. Ziefert, Harriet. LC 88-26322. 24p. (Orig.). (ps-2). 1989. PLB 2.25 (*0-394-81999-3*) Random Bks Yng Read.

—The Prince's Tooth Is Loose. Ziefert, Harriet. LC 89-36433. 24p. (Orig.). (ps-2). 1990. pap. 2.25 (*0-394-84840-3*) Random Bks Yng Read.

—Recycled Songs. Cooper, Don. 32p. (ps-3). 1992. incl. cassette 7.99 (*0-679-82643-2*) Random Bks Yng Read.

—School Isn't Fair! Baehr, Patricia. LC 88-21461. 32p. (ps-k). 1989. RSBE 13.95 (*0-02-708130-3*, Four Winds) Macmillan Child Grp.

—School Isn't Fair. Baehr, Patricia. LC 91-38485. 32p. (ps-k). 1992. pap. 4.95 (*0-689-71544-7*, Aladdin) Macmillan Child Grp.

—Serena Katz. Pomerantz, Charlotte. LC 90-48672. 32p. (gr. k-3). 1992. RSBE 13.95 (*0-02-774901-0*, Macmillan Child Bk) Macmillan Child Grp.

—The Teeny Tiny Woman. O'Connor, Jane, retold by. LC 86-485. 32p. (ps-1). 1986. lib. bdg. 7.99 (*0-394-98320-3*); pap. 3.50 (*0-394-88320-9*, Random Juv) Random Bks Yng Read.

—Washington Irving's Tales of the Supernatural. Irving, Washington. Wagenknecht, Edward, ed. LC 80-29313. 288p. (gr. 6 up). 1982. 17.95 (*0-916144-64-X*) Stemmer Hse.

—Who Put the Pepper in the Pot? Cole, Joanna. LC 88-36625. 48p. (ps-3). 1989. 5.95 (*0-8193-1189-8*) Parents.

—Who Put the Pepper in the Pot? Cole, Joanna. 48p. (ps-2). 1991. pap. 2.95 (*0-448-41077-X*, G&D) Putnam Pub Group.

Alley, R. W., photos by. The Silliest Joke Book Ever. Hartman, Victoria. LC 92-22161. 1993. write for info. (*0-688-10109-7*); pap. write for info. (*0-688-10110-0*) Lothrop.

Alley, Robert. The Ghost in Dobbs Diner. Alley, Robert. LC 81-9684. 48p. (ps-3). 1982. PLB 13.95 (*0-8193-1055-7*); lib. bdg. 5.95 (*0-8193-1056-5*) Parents.

—Listening with Zachary. Slater, Teddy. 24p. (ps-1). 1991. 5.95 (*0-671-72986-1*); PLB 9.98 (*0-671-72985-3*) Silver Pr.

—Looking for Lewis. Slater, Teddy. 24p. (ps-1). 1991. 5.95 (*0-671-72988-8*); PLB 9.98 (*0-671-72987-X*) Silver Pr.

—Sheepish Riddles. Hall, Katy & Eisenberg, Lisa. LC 93-32212. 1995. write for info. (*0-8037-1535-8*); lib. bdg. write for info. (*0-8037-1536-6*) Dial Bks Young.

Alley, Robert & Hearn, Diane D. What Rhymes? Series. Slater, Teddy. (ps-1). 1991. Set, 24p. ea. 23.80 (*0-671-31245-6*); Set, 24p. ea. lib. bdg. 39.92 (*0-671-31244-8*) Silver Pr.

Alley, Robert W. Mrs. Toggle's Zipper. Pulver, Robin. LC 92-39355. 32p. (ps-2). 1993. pap. 3.95 (*0-689-71689-3*, Aladdin) Macmillan Child Grp.

—Who Put the Pepper in the Pot? Cole, Joanna. 42p. (ps-3). 1992. PLB 13.26 (*0-8368-0883-5*); PLB 13.26 s.p. (*0-685-61515-4*) Gareth Stevens Inc.

Allison, Diane. The Case of the Elevator Duck. Berends, Polly B. LC 88-23971. 64p. (gr. 2-4). 1989. PLB 6.99 (*0-394-92646-5*); pap. 2.50 (*0-394-82646-9*) Random Bks Yng Read.

Allison, Diane W. Julian, Secret Agent. Cameron, Ann. LC 88-4428. 64p. (Orig.). (gr. 2-4). 1988. lib. bdg. 6.99 (*0-394-91949-1*); pap. 2.50 (*0-394-81949-7*) Random Bks Yng Read.

—This Is the Key to the Kingdom. Allison, Diane W. 32p. (ps-3). 1992. 15.95 (*0-316-03432-0*) Little.

—Wishing at Dawn in Summer. Carlstrom, Nancy W. (ps-2). 1993. 14.95 (*0-316-12854-6*) Little.

Allison, Linda. Gee Wiz! How to Mix Art & Science or the Art of Thinking Scientifically. Allison, Linda & Katz, David. LC 83-9834. 128p. (gr. 4 up). 1983. 14.95 (*0-316-03444-4*); pap. 8.95 (*0-316-03445-2*) Little.

—The Reasons for Seasons: The Great Cosmic Megagalactic Trip Without Moving from Your Chair. Allison, Linda. 128p. (gr. 4 up). 1975. 14.95 (*0-316-03439-8*); pap. 9.95 (*0-316-03440-1*) Little.

—The Sierra Club Summer Book. Allison, Linda. 160p. (gr. 3-7). 1989. pap. 7.95 (*0-316-03433-9*) Sierra.

—The Wild Inside: Sierra Club's Guide to Great Outdoors. Allison, Linda. 144p. (gr. 3-7). 1988. pap. 7.95 (*0-316-03434-7*) Little.

Allison, Linda & Wells, William S. The Get-Well-Quick Kit. Allison, Linda & Ferguson, Tom. LC 92-42626. 1993. 14.38 (*0-201-63213-6*) Addison-Wesley.

—Living in Space. Kay, Jerry. 22p. (Orig.). (gr. 3-7). 1988. 9.95 (*0-929201-06-X*) Kay Productions.

Allnock, Sandy. Montana Wildlife: A Children's Field Guide to the State's Most Remarkable Animals. Shirley, Gayle C. 48p. (Orig.). 1993. pap. 6.95 (*1-56044-154-2*) Falcon Pr MT.

Allum, Lois Saarinen. Respite. Allum, Faith T. 48p. (Orig.). (gr. 6 up). 1985. pap. 3.00 (*0-9613349-2-4*) F T Allum.

Allwood, Suzanne E. The Adventures of Sugar-Gum. Allwood, Suzanne E. 1990. 6.95 (*0-533-08801-1*) Vantage.

Almada, Laura. The Six Wrinkled Woos. Czarnecki, Lois R. 32p. (gr. k-3). 1992. 17.95 (*0-9627275-0-4*) Ohana Pr.

Almaraz, Humberto. Santa Will Love My Tree (Play Format) Almaraz, Humberto. Almaraz, Humberto, intro. by. 12p. (Orig.). (ps-3). 1982. pap. 5.00 incl. 45 rpm record (*0-9616528-1-0*) Alpha-Beto Music.

—Santa Will Love My Tree (Story Format) Almaraz, Humberto. Almaraz, Humberto, intro. by. 12p. (Orig.). (ps-2). 1982. pap. 5.00 incl. 45 rpm record (*0-9616528-0-2*) Alpha-Beto Music.

Almeleh, Fiona. Plants & Flowers of the Desert. 32p. (gr. 3-5). 1985. 7.95x (*0-86685-446-0*) Intl Bk Ctr.

Almquist, Don. Loudmouse. Wilbur, Richard. D'Andrade, Diane, ed. 32p. (gr. 1-5). 1991. 12.95 (*0-15-249494-4*) HarBrace.

Aloise, Frank. George & Martha Washington at Home in New York. Siegel, Beatrice. LC 88-24534. 80p. (gr. 4-7). 1989. SBE 12.95 (*0-02-782721-6*, Four Winds) Macmillan Child Grp.

Aloof, Andrew. Animal Babies. Pope, Joyce. LC 91-45381. 32p. (gr. 3-6). 1993. PLB 11.59 (*0-8167-2773-2*); pap. text ed. 3.95 (*0-8167-2774-0*) Troll Assocs. Postponed.

—The Expeditions of Amundsen. Humble, Richard. Kline, Marjory, ed. 32p. (gr. 5-7). 1992. PLB 12.40 (*0-531-14200-0*) Watts.

Alpert, Lou. Dancing with the Shadows in My Room. Alpert, Lou. 32p. (ps-8). 1991. 12.95 (*1-879085-06-2*) Whsprng Coyote Pr.

—Emma & the Magic Dance. Alpert, Lou. 32p. (ps-8). 1991. smythe sewn reinforced bdg. 12.95 (*1-879085-01-1*) Whsprng Coyote Pr.

—Emma Giggled. Alpert, Lou. 32p. (ps-8). 1991. smythe sewn reinforced bdg. 12.95 (*1-879085-02-X*) Whsprng Coyote Pr.

—Emma Lights up the Sky. Alpert, Lou. 32p. (ps-8). 1991. smythe sewn reinforced bdg. 12.95 (*1-879085-03-8*) Whsprng Coyote Pr.

—Emma Swings. Alpert, Lou. 32p. (ps-8). 1991. smythe sewn reinforced bdg. 12.95 (*1-879085-04-6*) Whsprng Coyote Pr.

—Emma's Turn to Dance. Alpert, Lou. 32p. (ps-8). 1991. smythe sewn reinforced bdg. 12.95 (*1-879085-00-3*) Whsprng Coyote Pr.

—The Man in the Moon & His Flying Balloon. Alpert, Lou. 32p. (ps-8). 1991. smythe sewn reinforced bdg. 12.95 (*1-879085-05-4*) Whsprng Coyote Pr.

—Max & the Great Blueness. Alpert, Lou. LC 92-23313. 32p. (ps-12). 1993. smythe sewn reinforced 13.95 (*1-879085-38-0*) Whsprng Coyote Pr.

—You & Your Dad. Alpert, Lou. LC 91-44412. 32p. (ps-12). 1992. smythe sewn reinforced 12.95 (*1-879085-36-4*) Whsprng Coyote Pr.

Alred, Jean L. Making Your Own Nature Museum. MacFarlane, Ruth. LC 89-31826. 128p. (gr. 5 up). 1989. PLB 12.90 (*0-531-10809-0*) Watts.

Alston, Virgil. Little Dark Cloud. Fitzgerald, Bridget. Harman, Sandra L., intro. by. LC 78-189877. 44p. (gr. 1-2). 1973. 2.50 (*0-87884-012-5*) Unicorn Ent.

Altizer, Suzanne R., photos by. Wait & See. Watkins, Dawn L. 46p. (Orig.). (ps-1). 1991. pap. 4.95 (*0-89084-576-X*) Bob Jones Univ Pr.

Altman, Adelaide. Professor Pishposh & the Robots. Altman, Adelaide. 48p. (ps-2). 1988. 12.95 (*0-933905-05-X*); pap. 9.95 (*0-933905-16-5*) Claycomb Pr.

Altman, Robin W. Celeste. Shigezawa, Ruth. 28p. (gr. 2 up). 1993. 16.95 (*0-9637101-0-9*); pap. 7.95 (*0-9637101-1-7*) Cndlelght Pr. "Who will be our next leader?" Everyone asks that question around the assembly. The cloud clusters meet during their hundred-year reunion & eagerly await the news. When retiring leader, Great Great Grandfather Thundercloud, announces the name of their new leader, the assembly is in disbelief. The leader has always been a thundercloud of great rain-giving gifts. No one expects the chosen leader to be a female cloud named Celeste. So begins Celeste's initiation journey across the earth to learn about the creatures below. In the course of her odyssey, her already surprising life takes an even more astonishing turn. Against the advice of the Great Thundercloud, Celeste attempts to help a farming family who struggles to nurture the land they cultivate. Celeste rebels against ancient tradition & in an unusual way expresses her creative skills. She thus learns to give her special gifts in this modern fable about caring for nature, discovering a life's purpose, & listening to the true voice within. Order from Candlelight Press, P.O. Box 50187, Irvine, CA 92619-0187. *Publisher Provided Annotation.*

Altop, Tammy. Saving Our Planet. Brumley, Karen. 40p. (gr. 6). 1991. wkbk. 3.95 (*1-561894-06-0*) Amer Educ Pub.

—Saving Our Planet. Brumley, Karen. 40p. (gr. 5). 1991. wkbk. 3.95 (*1-561894-05-2*) Amer Educ Pub.

—Saving Our Planet. Brumley, Karen. 40p. (gr. 4). 1991. wkbk. 3.95 (*1-561894-04-4*) Amer Educ Pub.

Altshuler, Shanne. The Wood-Ash Stars. Poland, Marguerite. 64p. 1990. pap. 5.95 (*0-86486-089-7*, Pub. by D Philip South Africa) Interlink Pub.

Alvarado, Carol. Jimmy's Last Wish: A Story about Forever. Haines, Rashelle. 32p. 1992. 22.95 (*0-944963-23-4*); PLB 20.95 (*0-944963-32-5*); audio tape 9.95 (*0-944963-20-X*) Glastonbury Pr.

Alvarez, Juan. Chocolate, Chipmunks, & Canoes: An American Indian Words Coloring Book. Alvarez, Juan. LC 90-60331. 32p. (gr. 1-3). 1991. pap. 3.95 (*1-878610-03-1*) Red Crane Bks.

—Jose Rabbit's Southwest Adventures: An ABC Coloring Book with Spanish Words. Alvarez, Juan. 32p. (Orig.). (gr. 1-3). 1990. pap. 3.95 (*1-878610-00-7*) Red Crane Bks.

Ambler, Barbara H. Turtles, Toads, & Frogs. Fichter, George S. 36p. (gr. k-3). 1993. 4.95 (*0-307-11433-3*, 11433, Golden Pr) Western Pub.

Ambriz, Don & Reed, Libby. An Illustrated History of Kern County. Brock, John M. 83p. (gr. 3-8). 1976. pap. 5.00 (*0-943500-05-2*) Kern Historical.

Ambrus, Victor G. El Cid. McCaughrean, Geraldine. 128p. (gr. 5 up). 1989. 19.95 (*0-19-276077-7*) OUP.

Ambrus, Victor. Black Beauty. Sewell, Anna. LC 93-18939. 208p. (gr. 4-8). 1993. PLB 14.95 (*0-8050-2772-6*, Bks Young Read) H Holt & Co.

—The Bushbabies. Stevenson, William. (gr. 5-9). 1984. 16.00 (*0-8446-6167-8*) Peter Smith.

—Favorite Fairy Tales Told in France. Haviland, Virginia, compiled by. LC 93-29665. 1994. write for info. (*0-688-12596-4*, Pub. by Beech Tree Bks) Morrow.

—Gulliver's Travels. Swift, Jonathan. Riordan, James, ed. 96p. 1992. 18.00 (*0-19-279897-9*) OUP.

—Horse Stories. Pullein-Thompson, Christine, compiled by. Fyfe, Charlotte, contrib. by. LC 93-29422. 1994. pap. 6.95 (*1-85697-966-0*) Kingfisher Bks.

—An Illustrated Treasury of Myths & Legends. Riordan, James & Lewis, Brenda R. 152p. (gr. 7 up). 1991. 12. 95 (*0-87226-349-5*) P Bedrick Bks.

—Never Laugh at Bears: A Folk Tale from Transylvania. Ambrus, Victor, retold by. LC 91-40372. 32p. (gr. k-3). 1992. PLB 14.95 (*0-87226-465-3*, Bedrick Blackie) P Bedrick Bks.

—The Rabbi's Wisdom: A Jewish Folk Tale from Eastern Europe. Gordon, Erica, retold by. LC 90-44375. 32p. (gr. k-3). 1991. PLB 14.95 (*0-87226-446-7*, Bedrick Blackie) P Bedrick Bks.

—The Shoemaker's Boy. Aiken, Joan. LC 93-6613. (ps-6). 1994. pap. 13.00 (*0-671-86647-8*, S&S BFYR) S&S Trade.

—A Treasury of Stories from Around the World. Jennings, Linda, compiled by. LC 92-43153. 160p. (gr. k-4). 1993. write for info. (*1-85697-932-6*) Kingfisher Bks.

Ambrus, Victor G. The Canterbury Tales. McCaughrean, Geraldine, retold by. LC 85-60147. 128p. (gr. 4 up). 1985. 14.95 (*1-56288-259-7*) Checkerboard.

—Count, Dracula! Ambrus, Victor G. LC 91-40269. 24p. (ps-1). 1992. 3.99 (*0-517-58969-9*) Crown Bks Yng Read.

—Favorite Stories of the Ballet. Riordan, James. Nureyev, Rudolf, frwd. by. LC 84-42778. 128p. (gr. 4 up). 1991. 14.95 (*1-56288-252-X*) Checkerboard.

—Favorite Tales from Shakespeare. Miles, Bernard. 128p. (gr. 4-7). 1993. Repr. of 1976 ed. 14.95 (*1-56288-257-0*) Checkerboard.

—How the Reindeer Saved Santa. Haywood, Carolyn. LC 85-28456. 32p. (ps-3). 1986. 12.95 (*0-688-05903-1*); lib. bdg. 12.88 (*0-688-05904-X*) Morrow Jr Bks.

—How the Reindeer Saved Santa. Haywood, Carolyn. LC 85-28456. 64p. (ps-3). 1991. pap. 4.95 (*0-688-11073-8*, Mulberry) Morrow.

—The Odyssey. McCaughrean, Geraldine. 100p. (gr. 4 up). 1993. 14.95 (*1-56288-433-6*) Checkerboard.

—Peter & the Wolf. Riordan, James, retold by. 24p. (ps-6). 1987. 15.00 (*0-19-279824-3*) OUP.

—Peter & the Wolf. Riordan, James, retold by. 24p. (gr. k up). 1989. pap. 5.95 (*0-19-272201-8*) OUP.

—Pinocchio. Riordan, James. 96p. (gr. 3 up). 1988. 18.95 (*0-19-279855-3*) OUP.

—Robin Hood: His Life & Legend. Miles, Bernard. LC 79-64615. 128p. (gr. 4 up). 1991. 12.95 (*1-56288-412-3*) Checkerboard.

—Santa Claus Forever! Haywood, Carolyn. LC 83-1017. 32p. (gr. k-3). 1983. 11.95 (*0-688-10998-5*); lib. bdg. 11.88 (*0-688-02345-2*) Morrow Jr Bks.

—Tales from the Arabian Nights. Riordan, James. LC 84-62456. 128p. (gr. 4 up). 1985. 14.95 (*1-56288-258-9*) Checkerboard.

—Tales of Ancient Persia. Picard, Barbara. 176p. 1993. pap. 10.95 (*0-19-274154-3*) OUP.

—Tales of King Arthur. Riordan, James. LC 81-86152. 128p. (gr. 4-7). 1982. 14.95 (*1-56288-251-1*) Checkerboard.

—Well-Loved Tales from Shakespeare. Miles, Bernard. LC 85-63829. 128p. (gr. 2 up). 1986. 12.95 (*0-528-82758-8*) Checkerboard.

—What Time Is It, Dracula? Ambrus, Victor G. LC 91-41260. 24p. (ps-1). 1992. 3.99 (*0-517-58970-2*) Crown Bks Yng Read.

Ambrus, Victor G. & Ambrus, Victor G. A Valentine Fantasy. Haywood, Carolyn. LC 75-23083. 32p. (gr. k-3). 1976. PLB 14.88 (*0-688-32055-4*) Morrow Jr Bks.

Amendola, Dominique. Krishna, Master of All Mystics. Greene, Joshua, retold by. 16p. (gr. 1-4). 1981. pap. 4.00 (*0-89647-035-0*) Bala Bks.

America, Alexis. Team Earth: Show You Care. Pysz, Stephen. Patton, Sarah, ed. 32p. (gr. 2-5). 1992. pap. text ed. 4.95 wkbk. (*0-9630186-1-2*) Team Earth.

America, Alexis & Marcil, Beth. Team Earth: Advanced ABC Environmental Coloring Book. Pysz, Stephen. 56p. (gr. k-1). 1991. pap. text ed. 4.95 (*0-9630186-7-1*) Team Earth.

Ames, Lee J. Amazing Mouths & Menus. Blocksma, Mary. 64p. (gr. 2-6). 1986. 12.95 (*0-13-023854-6*) P-H.

—The Battle of the Dinosaurs. Knight, David C. 96p. (gr. 3-7). 1982. (Pub. by Treehouse); pap. 5.95 (*0-13-069518-1*) P-H.

Ammon, Richard. Trains at Work. Ammon, Richard. Peterson, Darrell, photos by. LC 92-33913. 32p. (gr. 1-5). 1993. SBE 14.95 (*0-689-31740-9*, Atheneum Child Bk) Macmillan Child Grp.

Amongo, Jo. Wuthering Heights. new & abr. ed. Bronte, Emily. Farr, Naunerle, ed. (gr. 4-12). 1977. pap. text ed. 2.95 (*0-88301-272-3*) Pendulum Pr.

Amos Bad Heart Bull, jt. illus. see Kills Two.

Amoss, Berthe. Cinderella. Amoss, Berthe. 10p. (ps-7). 1989. pap. 2.95 (*0-922589-04-6*) More Than Card.

—Hansel & Gretel. Amoss, Berthe. 10p. (ps-7). 1989. pap. 2.95 (*0-922589-05-4*) More Than Card.

—Jack & the Beanstalk. Amoss, Berthe. 10p. (ps-7). 1989. pap. 2.95 (*0-922589-00-3*) More Than Card.

—The Loup Garou. Amoss, Berthe. LC 79-20536. 48p. (ps-4). 1979. 9.95 (*0-88289-189-8*) Pelican.

—Mother Goose Rhymes. Amoss, Berthe. 10p. (ps-7). 1989. pap. 2.95 (*0-922589-02-X*) More Than Card.

—The Night Before Christmas. Moore, Clement C. 10p. (ps-7). 1989. pap. 3.95 (*0-922589-06-2*) More Than Card.

—Old Hannibal & the Hurricane. Amoss, Berthe. LC 91-71387. 32p. (ps-2). 1991. 14.95 (*1-56282-097-4*); PLB 14.89 (*1-56282-098-2*) Hyprn Child.

—Rumpelstiltskin. Amoss, Berthe. 10p. (ps-7). 1989. pap. 2.95 (*0-922589-03-8*) More Than Card.

—Snow White & the Seven Dwarfs. Amoss, Berthe. 10p. (ps-7). 1989. pap. 2.95 (*0-922589-01-1*) More Than Card.

Amsel, Sheri. Deserts. Amsel, Sheri. LC 92-8789. 32p. 1992. lib. bdg. 17.28 (*0-8114-6300-1*) Raintree Steck-V.

—Grasslands. Amsel, Sheri. LC 92-8788. 32p. 1992. lib. bdg. 17.28 (*0-8114-6302-8*) Raintree Steck-V.

—A Wetland Walk. Amsel, Sheri. 32p. (gr. k-3). 1993. PLB 14.90 (*1-56294-213-1*) Millbrook Pr.

Amsteen, Katy. I Can't Believe It's History! Guthrie, Donna. 32p. (gr. 4-7). 1993. pap. 3.99 (*0-8431-3621-9*) Price Stern.

Amstutz, Skeleton Crew. Ahlberg, Allan. ALC Staff, ed. LC 91-39161. 32p. (gr. k up). 1992. pap. 3.95 (*0-688-11660-4*, Mulberry) Morrow.

Amstutz, Andre. The Black Cat. Ahlberg, Allan. LC 90-2886. 32p. (ps up) 1990. 12.95 (*0-688-09903-3*); PLB 12.88 (*0-688-09904-1*) Greenwillow.

—The Black Cat. Ahlberg, Allan. LC 92-45621. 32p. (gr. k up). 1993. pap. text ed. 4.95 (*0-688-12679-0*, Mulberry) Morrow.

—The Ghost Train. Ahlberg, Allan. LC 91-39838. 32p. (ps-6). 1992. 14.00 (*0-688-11435-0*) Greenwillow.

—Ghost Train. Ahlberg, Allan. ALC Staff, ed. LC 91-39838. 32p. (gr. k up). 1992. pap. 3.95 (*0-688-11659-0*, Mulberry) Morrow.

—The Pet Shop. Ahlberg, Allan. LC 90-2881. 32p. (ps up). 1990. 12.95 (*0-688-09905-X*); PLB 12.88 (*0-688-09906-8*) Greenwillow.

—The Pet Shop. Ahlberg, Allan. LC 92-45657. 32p. (gr. k up). 1993. pap. 4.95 (*0-688-12680-4*, Mulberry) Morrow.

—Skeleton Crew. Ahlberg, Allan. LC 91-39161. 32p. (ps-6). 1992. 14.00 (*0-688-11436-9*) Greenwillow.

—Ten in a Bed. Ahlberg, Allan. 112p. 1989. pap. 12.95 (*0-670-82042-3*) Viking Child Bks.

—Ten in a Bed. Ahlberg, Allan. 112p. (gr. 2-6). 1991. pap. 3.99 (*0-14-032531-X*, Puffin) Puffin Bks.

—Who's a Bright Girl? Impey, Rose. 42p. (gr. 2-4). 1989. 3.95 (*0-8120-6144-6*) Barron.

Amstutz, Beverly. Sharing Is Fun. Amstutz, Beverly. 24p. (gr. k-7). 1979. pap. 2.50x (*0-937836-00-1*) Precious Res.

—Sprouts: A Diary for the Foster Child. Amstutz, Beverly. 38p. (Orig.). (gr. k-7). 1982. pap. 2.50x (*0-937836-07-9*) Precious Res.

Amundsen, Richard. Solemn Silence: The Complete Guide to Hood Canal, by Land, & Sea. Schweizer, William H. 304p. (Orig.). 1992. pap. write for info. (*0-925244-02-3*) EOS Pub.

Anand, B. M. Story of Mohammad the Prophet. Alladin, Bilzik. (gr. 3-10). 1979. 7.25 (*0-89744-139-7*) Auromere.

Anastasia, Karyn & Black, Jean. Skill Builders: Course Code 392-2. Anderson, Jill & Weinman, Susan. Schroeder, Bonnie & Doheny, Catherine, eds. 90p. (gr. 4). 1989. pap. text ed. 5.95 (*0-917531-88-4*) CES Compu-Tech.

Anastasia, Karyn & Knapp, William. Adventures in SeeLogo: Course Code 192-2. Kennedy, Sandra & MacDonald, James. Schroeder, Bonnie, ed. 91p. (Orig.). (gr. 4). 1989. wkbk. 6.95 (*0-917531-44-2*) CES Compu-Tech.

Anchor-Hoch, Timothy. Hunger, 1993: Third Annual Report on the State of World Hunger - Uprooted People. Cohen, Marc J., ed. 175p. (Orig.). (gr. 12 up). 1992. pap. text ed. 12.95 (*0-9628058-6-6*) Bread for the World.

Ancona, George. Artists of Handcrafted Furniture at Work. Rosenberg, Maxine B. LC 87-29342. 64p. (gr. 3 up). 1988. 14.95 (*0-688-06875-8*) Lothrop.

—Bananas: From Manolo to Margie. Ancona, George. 48p. (gr. 3-6). 1982. 15.95 (*0-89919-100-2*, Clarion Bks) HM.

—Being a Twin, Having a Twin. Rosenberg, Maxine B. LC 84-17159. 48p. (gr. 1-4). 1985. 11.95 (*0-688-04328-3*); lib. bdg. 11.88 (*0-688-04329-1*) Lothrop.

—Bodies. Brenner, Barbara. 1973. 13.95 (*0-525-26770-0*, DCB) Dutton Child Bks.

—Christmas on the Prairie. Anderson, Joan. LC 85-4095. 48p. (gr. 2-6). 1985. 14.95 (*0-89919-307-2*, Clarion Bks) HM.

—City! New York. Climo, Shirley. LC 89-13482. 64p. (gr. 3-7). 1990. RSBE 16.95 (*0-02-719020-X*, Macmillan Child Bk) Macmillan Child Grp.

—City! Washington, D. C. Climo, Shirley. LC 90-1785. 64p. (gr. 3-7). 1991. SBE 16.95 (*0-02-719036-6*, Macmillan Child Bk) Macmillan Child Grp.

—Dolphins at Grassy Key. Seligson, Marcia. LC 88-27143. 48p. (gr. 1 up). 1989. RSBE 15.95 (*0-02-781800-4*, Macmillan Child Bk) Macmillan Child Grp.

—Faces. Brenner, Barbara. LC 70-102737. 48p. (ps-2). 1970. 14.95 (*0-525-29518-6*, DCB) Dutton Child Bks.

—Handtalk: An ABC of Finger Spelling & Sign Language. Charlip, Remy & Miller, Mary B. LC 85-3667. 48p. (ps up). 1984. Repr. of 1974 ed. SBE 15.95 (*0-02-718130-8*, Four Winds) Macmillan Child Grp.

—Handtalk: An ABC of Finger Spelling & Sign Language. Charlip, Remy & Miller, Mary B. LC 86-20585. 48p. (ps-12). 1987. pap. 4.95 (*0-689-71108-5*, Aladdin) Macmillan Child Grp.

—Handtalk Birthday: A Number & Story Book in Sign Language. Charlip, Remy & Miller, Mary B. LC 86-22755. 48p. (ps up). 1987. SBE 15.95 (0-02-718080-8, Four Winds) Macmillan Child Grp.

—Handtalk Birthday: A Number & Story Book in Sign Language. Miller, Mary B. & Charlip, Remy. LC 91-1967. 48p. (ps-3). 1991. pap. 4.95 (0-689-71531-5, Aladdin) Macmillan Child Grp.

—Handtalk Zoo. Ancona, George & Miller, Mary B. LC 88-36861. 32p. (ps up). 1989. RSBE 14.95 (0-02-700801-0, Four Winds) Macmillan Child Grp.

—Joshua's Westward Journal. Anderson, Joan. LC 87-5509. 48p. (gr. 2-5). 1987. 13.00 (0-688-06680-1); lib. bdg. 12.88 (0-688-06681-X, Morrow Junior Books) Morrow Jr Bks.

—Living in Two Worlds. Rosenberg, Maxine B. Spivey, Philip, afterword by. LC 85-23990. 48p. (ps-3). 1986. 11.95 (0-688-06278-4); PLB 11.88 (0-688-06279-2) Lothrop.

—Making a New Home in America. Rosenberg, Maxine B. LC 85-11642. 48p. (gr. 1-4). 1986. 11.95 (0-688-05824-8); PLB 11.88 (0-688-05825-6) Lothrop.

—Man & Mustang. Ancona, George. LC 91-29513. 48p. (gr. 3-7). 1992. RSBE 15.95 (0-02-700802-9, Macmillan Child Bk) Macmillan Child Grp.

—Mom Can't See Me. Alexander, Sally. LC 89-13241. 48p. (gr. 1-5). 1990. RSBE 14.95 (0-02-700401-5, Macmillan Child Bk) Macmillan Child Grp.

—Mom's Best Friend. Alexander, Sally H. LC 91-43809. 48p. (gr. 1-5). 1992. RSBE 14.95 (0-02-700393-0, Macmillan Child Bk) Macmillan Child Grp.

—Richie's Rocket. Anderson, Joan. LC 92-38417. 32p. (gr. k up). 1993. 15.00 (0-688-11304-4); PLB 14.93 (0-688-11305-2) Morrow Jr Bks.

Ancona, George, photos by. Being Adopted. Rosenberg, Maxine B. LC 83-17522. 48p. (gr. 1-4). 1984. 13.95 (0-688-02672-9); lib. bdg. 13.88 (0-688-02673-7) Lothrop.

—Brothers & Sisters. Rosenberg, Maxine B. 32p. (gr. k-3). 1991. 14.45 (0-395-51121-6, Clarion Bks) HM.

—Earth Keepers. Anderson, Joan, text by. LC 92-38627. 1993. 17.95 (0-15-242199-8) HarBrace.

—Finding a Way: Living with Exceptional Brothers & Sisters. Rosenberg, Maxine B. LC 88-6776. 48p. (gr. 1-4). 1988. 12.95 (0-688-06873-1); PLB 12.88 (0-688-06874-X) Lothrop.

—The First Thanksgiving Feast. Anderson, Joan. LC 84-5803. 48p. (gr. 2-6). 1984. 14.95 (0-89919-287-4, Clarion Bks) HM.

—The First Thanksgiving Feast. Anderson, Joan. LC 84-58040. (gr. 3-6). 1989. pap. 5.70 (0-395-51886-5, Clarion Bks) HM.

—From Map to Museum: Uncovering Mysteries of the Past. Anderson, Joan. LC 87-31307. 64p. (gr. 3-7). 1988. 12.95 (0-688-06914-2); PLB 12.88 (0-688-06915-0, Morrow Jr Bks) Morrow Jr Bks.

—The Glorious Fourth at Prairietown. Anderson, Joan. LC 85-28417. 48p. (gr. 2-6). 1986. 11.95 (0-688-06246-6); lib. bdg. 11.88 (0-688-06247-4, Morrow Jr Bks) Morrow Jr Bks.

—Harry's Helicopter. Anderson, Joan. LC 89-28601. 32p. (gr. k up). 1990. 13.95 (0-688-09186-5); PLB 13.88 (0-688-09187-3, Morrow Jr Bks) Morrow Jr Bks.

—My Friend Leslie: The Story of a Handicapped Child. Rosenberg, Maxine B. LC 82-12734. (gr. 1-3). 1983. 13.95 (0-688-01690-1); PLB 13.88 (0-688-01691-X) Lothrop.

—My New Baby-Sitter. Loomis, Christine. LC 90-38527. 48p. (ps up). 1991. 13.95 (0-688-09625-5); PLB 13.88 (0-688-09626-3) Morrow Jr Bks.

—Over Here It's Different: Carolina's Story. Dawson, Mildred L. LC 92-44515. 48p. (gr. 3-7). 1993. RSBE 13.95 (0-02-726328-2, Macmillan Child Bk) Macmillan Child Grp.

—Powwow. LC 92-15912. 1993. write for info. (0-15-263268-9) HarBrace.

—Spanish Pioneers of the Southwest. Anderson, Joan. LC 88-16121. 64p. (gr. 3-6). 1989. 14.95 (0-525-67264-8, Lodestar Bks) Dutton Child Bks.

—Turtle Watch. Ancona, George. LC 87-9316. 48p. (gr. 1-5). 1987. RSBE 14.95 (0-02-700910-6, Macmillan Child Bk) Macmillan Child Grp.

—Twins on Toes: A Ballet Debut. Anderson, Joan. LC 92-35104. 32p. (gr. 3-7). 1993. 14.99 (0-525-67415-2, Lodestar Bks) Dutton Child Bks.

Anderasen, Norma, jt. illus. see Butcher, Sam.

Anderian, Kaffi & Johannsen, Rob. Acts of Courage. Donev, Mary K. & Donev, Stef. 48p. (gr. 5-9). 1985. pap. 5.95 (0-88625-091-9) Durkin Hayes Pub.

Andersen, Yvonne. Make Your Own Animated Movies & Videotapes, Vol. 1. Andersen, Yvonne. (gr. 7 up). 1991. 19.95 (0-316-03941-I) Little.

Anderson, Annette B. The Manger Mouse. Wells, Joel. (gr. k-5). 1990. 15.95 (0-88347-255-4) Thomas More.

Anderson, C. W. Blaze & the Lost Quarry: Story & Pictures. Anderson, C. W. LC 93-10721. 48p. (gr. k-3). 1994. pap. 3.95 (0-689-71775-X, Aladdin) Macmillan Child Grp.

—Blaze & the Mountain Lion: Billy & Blaze to the Rescue. Anderson, C. W. LC 92-27148. 48p. (gr. k-3). 1993. pap. 3.95 (0-689-71711-3, Aladdin) Macmillan Child Grp.

—Blaze & Thunderbolt: Billy & Blaze Head West. Anderson, C. W. LC 92-27153. 48p. (gr. k-3). 1993. pap. 3.95 PB (0-689-71712-1, Aladdin) Macmillan Child Grp.

—Blaze Shows the Way: Story & Pictures. Anderson, C. W. LC 93-1454. 48p. (gr. k-3). 1994. pap. 3.95 (0-689-71776-8, Aladdin) Macmillan Child Grp.

Anderson, Carol A. Books, Puppets & the Mentally Retarded Student. Champlin, John & Champlin, Connie. 162p. (Orig.). 1981. pap. 15.95 (0-938594-00-1) Spec Lit Pr.

Anderson, Cindy & Flippin, Terry. Revelation & Apocalyptic Symbols: Bible Stories of the Planets & Stars. Bilderback, Allen H. 180p. (gr. 8 up). 1992. 24.95 (0-9630710-1-7); pap. 19.95 (0-9630710-0-9) ABCO Pub.

Anderson, Darrel, jt. illus. see Hale, Phil.

Anderson, Debby. Friends. Anderson, Debby. 32p. (ps). 1986. plastic comb bdg. 3.95 (0-89191-932-5, 59329, Chariot Bks) Cook.

—God Is with Me. Anderson, Debby. 32p. (gr. k-2). 1991. pasted 2.50 (0-87403-821-9, 24-03921) Standard Pub.

—God Loves Even Me. Anderson, Debby. 32p. (gr. k-2). 1991. pasted 2.50 (0-87403-820-0, 24-03920) Standard Pub.

Anderson, Doug. The World's Best Party Games. Barry, Sheila A. LC 86-30038. 128p. (gr. 6-10). 1987. pap. 4.95 (0-8069-6484-7) Sterling.

Anderson, Fred. Soul of Christmas. King, Helen. 32p. (gr. k-4). 1972. 4.50 (0-87485-057-6) Johnson Chi.

Anderson, Gary. Friendship in the Forest. Hogg, Gary. (gr. k-6). 1991. 11.95 (0-89868-204-5); pap. 4.95 (0-89868-205-3) ARO Pub.

—The Half-Hearted Hare. Hogg, Gary. (gr. k-6). 1991. 11.95 (0-89868-206-1); pap. 4.95 (0-89868-207-X) ARO Pub.

—Happy Hawk Series, 6 bks. Hogg, Gary. (gr. k-6). 1991. Set. 71.70 (0-89868-243-6); Set. pap. 29.70 (0-89868-242-8) ARO Pub.

—I Heard of a Nerd Bird. Hogg, Gary. (gr. k-6). 1991. 11.95 (0-89868-200-2); pap. 4.95 (0-89868-201-0) ARO Pub.

—The Lion Who Couldn't Roar. Hogg, Gary. (gr. k-6). 1991. 11.95 (0-89868-210-X); pap. 4.95 (0-89868-211-8) ARO Pub.

—Lizzie Learns About Lying. Hogg, Gary. (gr. k-6). 1991. 11.95 (0-89868-202-9); pap. 4.95 (0-89868-203-7) ARO Pub.

—Sir William the Worm. Hogg, Gary. (gr. k-6). 1991. 11.95 (0-89868-208-8); pap. 4.95 (0-89868-209-6) ARO Pub.

Anderson, John & Meredith, Marianne. Exploring Prehistoric Alabama Through Archaeology. Wimberly, Christine A. LC 80-70833. 96p. (Orig.). (gr. 5-12). 1981. pap. 8.95 (0-9605938-3-7); pap. text ed. 6.18 (0-9605938-1-0); tchr's ed. 9.49 (0-9605938-2-9) Explorer Bks.

Anderson, Judith. Let's Get Cooking. Pemberton, Judy. 103p. (Orig.). (gr. 3-12). 1984. text ed. 7.95 (0-317-02695-X) King Fisher Pr.

Anderson, Kari A. When I Grow Up. Wilson, Jodi L. 32p. (Orig.). (gr. 1-3). Date not set. pap. 4.95x (0-9628335-0-9) Wilander Pub.

Anderson, Keith O. Whole Grain: Collected Poems 1958-1989. Emanuel, James A. LC 90-61082. 400p. (gr. 9-12). 1991. 25.00 (0-916418-79-0) Lotus.

Anderson, L., jt. illus. see Swanberg, Nancy.

Anderson, Lena. Anna's Garden Songs. Steele, Mary Q. LC 88-5660. 32p. (gr. k up). 1989. 11.95 (0-688-08217-3); PLB 11.88 (0-688-08218-1) Greenwillow.

—Anna's Summer Songs. Steele, Mary Q. LC 86-27109. (SWE.). 32p. (gr. k-3). 1988. 11.95 (0-688-07180-5); lib. bdg. 11.88 (0-688-07181-3) Greenwillow.

—Bunny Bath. Anderson, Lena. LC 89-63049. (ps-k). 1991. bds. 3.95 (91-29-59652-1) R & S Books.

—Bunny Party. (ps). 1989. bds. 3.95 (91-29-59134-1, Pub. by R & S Bks) FS&G.

—Bunny Story. (ps). 1989. bds. 3.95 (91-29-59132-5, Pub. by R & S Bks) FS&G.

—Bunny Surprise. Anderson, Lena. LC 89-63050. (ps-k). 1991. bds. 3.95 (91-29-59654-8) R & S Books.

—Elliot's Extraordinary Cookbook. Bjork, Christina. Sandin, Joan, tr. 60p. 1991. 11.95 (91-29-59658-0, Pub. by R & S Bks) FS&G.

—Linnea in Monet's Garden. Bjork, Christina. Sandin, Joan, tr. from SWE. 56p. (gr. 3-6). 1987. 11.95 (91-29-58314-4, Pub. by R & S Bks) FS&G.

—Linnea's Almanac. Bjork, Christina. Sandin, Joan, tr. (gr. k-3). 1989. 11.95 (91-29-59176-7, Pub. by R & S Bks) FS&G.

—Linnea's Windowsill Garden. Bjork, Christina. 60p. 1988. 11.95 (91-29-59064-7, Pub. by R & S Bks) FS&G.

—Nicky the Nature Detective. Svedberg, Ulf. Selberg, Ingrid, tr. 52p. (gr. 5 up) 1988. 12.95 (91-29-58786-7, R & S Bks) FS&G.

Anderson, Lin. And This I Know. 2nd ed. Cambridge, Barbara S. Blackburn, Jim, contrib. by. 24p. 1987. pap. write for info. (0-9621018-1-8) CBridge Pubns.

—And This I Know: Affirmations for Children. rev. ed. Cambridge, Barbara S. 28p. 1987. pap. 6.95 (0-317-91380-8) CBridge Pubns.

Anderson, Linda. On Top of Old Smoky: A Collection of Songs & Stories from Appalachia. Kidd, Ronald. LC 92-14437. 40p. 1992. 13.95 (0-8249-8569-9, Ideals Child); PLB 14.00 (0-8249-8586-9); incl. 60-min. cassette 17.95 (0-8249-7513-8) Hambleton-Hill.

Anderson, Lydia M. Stateswoman to the World: A Story about Eleanor Roosevelt. Weidt, Maryann N. LC 90-23216. 64p. (gr. 3-6). 1991. PLB 9.95 (0-87614-663-9) Carolrhoda Bks.

Anderson, Nancy. Experiments with Plants. Byles, Monica. LC 92-43117. 1993. 17.50 (0-8225-2456-2) Lerner Pubns.

Anderson, Peggy P. Azulin Visita a Mexico (Blue Bug Visits Mexico) Poulet, Virginia. LC 89-25420. (SPA.). 32p. (ps-3). 1990. PLB 15.00 (0-516-33429-8); pap. 3.95 (0-516-53429-7) Childrens.

—Blue Bug Goes to Paris. Poulet, Virginia. LC 85-31390. 32p. (ps-3). 1986. pap. 3.95 (0-516-43480-2) Childrens.

—Blue Bug Goes to School. Poulet, Virginia. LC 84-23161. 32p. (ps-3). 1985. PLB 15.00 (0-516-03416-2); pap. 3.95 (0-516-43416-0) Childrens.

—Blue Bug Goes to the Library. Poulet, Virginia. LC 79-15219. 32p. (ps-3). 1979. PLB 15.00 (0-516-03430-8) Childrens.

—Blue Bug Visits Mexico. Poulet, Virginia. LC 89-25420. 32p. (ps-3). 1990. PLB 15.00 (0-516-03429-4); pap. 3.95 (0-516-43429-2) Childrens.

—Blue Bug's Book of Colors. Poulet, Virginia. LC 80-23229. 32p. (ps-3). 1981. PLB 15.00 (0-516-03442-1); pap. 3.95 (0-516-43442-X) Childrens.

—Danger on the Homestead. rev. ed. Heck, Bessie H. LC 93-71892. 160p. (gr. 3-6). 1993. Repr. of 1991 ed. 14.95 (0-9637259-0-4) Dinosaur Pr. What Others Say About DANGERS ON THE HOMESTEAD: "Todd, 9, accompanies his father on the expedition to find & legally register a new home. While the father goes to file on the claim, Todd stays on it overnight & is compelled to defend it against Blackjack Bice, an outlaw who tries to steal it while Todd's father is gone. This is an excellent story about the 1889 run into the Unassigned Lands of what is today central Oklahoma. The author's rich research of this aspect of the run lends a delightful authenticity to this historical novel for boys & girls."--Harold Keith, Two-Time Winner of the Newbery Award. "I love Peggy Anderson's lively drawings. I expect to see more good things from this talented young illustrator."--Gail Haley, Winner of the Caldecott & Kate Greenaway Medals. "It has a strong story line, well-developed characters, it is well researched, accurate in frontier detail; a real good book."--Ken Jackson, Editor, World of Books, Sunday Tulsa World. "It is very exciting...I'm promoting it for a class "reader" in the whole language program."--Sybil Connolly, Library Media Specialist, Windsor Hills Elementary, Oklahoma City, OK. "My fourth grade class learned more about that run from DANGER ON THE HOMESTEAD than from their text books.--Barbara Marks, Barnes Elementary, Owasso, OK. Send orders to: Dinosaur Press, P.O. Box 50414, Tulsa, OK 74150-0414. *Publisher Provided Annotation.*

—The Ugly Little Duck. McKissack, Patricia & McKissack, Fredrick. LC 85-31428. 32p. (ps-2). 1986. PLB 11.93 (0-516-03982-2); pap. 3.95 (0-516-43982-0) Childrens.

Anderson, Richard. Mystery of the Maya. large type ed. Montgomery, Raymond A. 134p. (gr. 3-7). 1987. Repr. of 1977 ed. 8.95 (0-942545-00-1); PLB 9.95 (0-942545-06-0, Dist. by Grolier) Grey Castle.

Anderson, Scoular. Rex, the Most Special Car in the World. Osborne, Victor. 24p. (ps-3). 1989. PLB 17.50 (0-87614-357-5) Carolrhoda Bks.

Anderson, Sharon. The Canary Who Sailed with Columbus. Wiggs, Susan. Roberts, Melissa, ed. 48p. (ps-2). 1989. 12.95 (0-89015-719-7, Pub. by Panda Bks) Eakin-Sunbelt.

Anderson, Stephen E. Wee-Sitt Babysitting Guide. Anderson, Stephen E. Trost, Ed, ed. (Orig.). (gr. 6-9). 1989. pap. 4.95 (0-685-29145-6) Chimurenga.

Anderson, Terri. Zwort's Nature Report Think 'n' Do Book: Forest, Ocean, Safari. Agy, Christine. 100p. (ps-4). 1991. spiral bdg., wkbk. 3.95 (*1-55999-159-3*) LinguiSystems.
Anderson, Terry, et al. The Hosanna Bible. Abraham, Angela & Abraham, Ken. LC 93-593. 448p. (ps-3). 1993. 15.99 (*0-8499-1036-6*) Word Inc.
Anderson, Walter. The Magic Carpet & Other Tales. Douglas, Ellen. LC 87-10434. (ps up). 1987. 35.00 (*0-87805-327-1*) U Pr of Miss.
—Walter Anderson for Children: An Activity Book from the Mississippi State Historical Museum. Black, Patti & Morrison, Ann, eds. 64p. (Orig.). (ps-8). 1984. pap. 12.95 (*0-685-09182-1*) Mississippi Archives.
Anderson, Wayne. Dragons: Truth, Myth, & Legend. Passes, David. LC 92-44745. (gr. 7 up). 1993. 14.95 (*0-307-17500-6*, Artsts & Writers Guild) Western Pub.
Anderson-Miller, Julia. Mr. Raccoon & His Friends. McCarthy, Eugene J. 112p. 1992. 16.00 (*0-89733-377-2*); pap. 6.95 (*0-89733-374-8*) Academy Chi Pubs.
Andersson, Benny. The Soft Secret Word. Aylott, Jane. 32p. 1992. 12.00 (*0-9631440-0-6*) Winged Peoples.
Andre, John. Traitor: The Case of Benedict Arnold. Fritz, Jean. (gr. 3-7). 1981. 15.95 (*0-399-20834-8*, Putnam) Putnam Pub Group.
Andreasen, Dan. The Bite of the Gold Bug: A Story of the Alaskan Gold Rush. DeClements, Barthe. 64p. (gr. 2-6). 1992. 13.00 (*0-670-84495-0*) Viking Child Bks.
—The Boonsville Bombers. Herzig, Alison C. 96p. (gr. 3-7). 1993. pap. 3.99 (*0-14-034578-7*, Puffin) Puffin Bks.
—By the Dawn's Early Light: The Story of the Star Spangled Banner. Kroll, Steven. LC 92-27101. 40p. (ps-5). 1994. 14.95 (*0-590-45054-9*) Scholastic Inc.
—Joshua T. Bates Takes Charge. Shreve, Susan. LC 92-19708. 112p. (gr. 3-5). 1993. 15.00 (*0-394-84362-2*) Knopf Bks Yng Read.
—Love, David. Case, Dianne. 144p. (gr. 3-7). 1991. 14.95 (*0-525-67350-4*, Lodestar Bks) Dutton Child Bks.
—The President Is Dead: A Story of the Kennedy Assassination. Gross, Virginia. 64p. (gr. 2-6). 1993. reinforced bdg. 12.99 (*0-670-85156-6*) Viking Child Bks.
Andreasen, Dan, et al. Felicity Learns a Lesson. Tripp, Valerie. 80p. (Orig.). (gr. 2-5). 1991. 12.95 (*1-56247-006-X*); PLB 12.95 (*1-56247-008-6*); pap. 5.95 (*1-56247-007-8*) Pleasant Co.
—Felicity's Surprise. Tripp, Valerie. 80p. (Orig.). (gr. 2-5). 1991. 12.95 (*1-56247-009-4*); PLB 12.95 (*1-56247-011-6*); pap. 5.95 (*1-56247-010-8*) Pleasant Co.
—Meet Felicity. Tripp, Valerie. 80p. (Orig.). (gr. 2-5). 1991. 12.95 (*1-56247-003-5*); PLB 12.95 (*1-56247-005-1*); pap. 5.95 (*1-56247-004-3*) Pleasant Co.
Andreasen, Norma. Moses, Vol. I. Overholtzer, Ruth. 50p. (gr. k-6). 1957. pap. text ed. 9.45 (*1-55976-007-9*) CEF Press.
—Moses, Vol. II. Overholtzer, Ruth. 50p. (gr. k-6). 1967. pap. text ed. 9.45 (*1-55976-008-7*) CEF Press.
Andreko, John A. Rainshine & Sundrops: Language Fun for Young Children. Lee, Billie W. Lee, Billie W., intro. by. 40p. (Orig.). 1987. 6.95 (*0-9619675-0-1*) P&M Bear Pubns.
Andrew, Robert. Castles. Osband, Gillian. LC 91-60082. 16p. 1991. 15.95 (*0-531-05949-9*) Orchard Bks Watts.
—Machines: A Book of Moving Pop-Ups. Reeve, Tim. LC 92-5752. 22p. (gr. 1 up). 1993. 15.95 (*0-399-21974-9*, Philomel Bks) Putnam Pub Group.
Andrews, Benny. The Last Radio Baby: A Memoir. Andrews, Raymond. LC 90-41751. 224p. 1990. 15.95 (*1-56145-004-9*) Peachtree Pubs.
Andrews, Douglas. Pomo Indians of California & Their Neighbors. Brown, Vinson. Elsasser, Albert B., ed. LC 78-13946. 64p. (Orig.). (gr. 4 up). 1969. 15.95 (*0-911010-31-9*); pap. 7.95 (*0-911010-30-0*) Naturegraph.
Andrews, Duane. The Sun Dance & Other Poems. Kulkarni, Shyamkant. LC 91-90016. iv, 32p. (Orig.). (gr. 5 up). 1991. pap. 5.50 (*0-9627083-1-3*) S Kulkarni.
Andrews, Jane, jt. illus. see Newton, Martin.
Anelay, Henry. The Mother's Picture Alphabet. Stockham, Peter, ed. 64p. (ps-3). 1975. pap. 4.50 (*0-486-23089-9*) Dover.
Anema, George. Just Beyond Reach. Nims, Bonnie L. 48p. 1992. 13.95 (*0-590-44077-2*, Scholastic Hardcover) Scholastic Inc.

Anestey, Caroline. Blancanieves y los Siete Enanitos (Snow White & the Seven Dwarfs) Hayes, Sarah. Puncel, Maria, tr. from ENG. (SPA.). 32p. (gr. 2-4). 1990. Incl. cass. 11.95 (*84-372-8053-2*) Santillana.
Beautifully illustrated version of the traditional story in Spanish. A cassette with original music & dramatic narrations presented by Alma Flor Ada & Suni Paz accompanies the storybook. Two other stories are also included in the collection: UNA MUJERCITA CON SURTE (Lucky

Woman) & TRES CHIVOS TESTARUDOS (Three Billy Goats Gruff). To order: Santillana, 901 West Walnut, Compton, CA 90220. Telephone 1-310-763-0455.
Publisher Provided Annotation.

Angelini, George. Martina Navratilova: Tennis Power. Knudson, R. R. LC 85-40832. 64p. (gr. 2-6). 1986. pap. 10.95 (*0-670-80665-X*) Viking Child Bks.
Angelo, Valenti. Roller Skates. Sawyer, Ruth. 192p. (gr. 4-7). 1969. pap. 1.50 (*0-440-47499-X*, YB) Dell.
—Roller Skates. Sawyer, Ruth. 184p. (gr. 5-9). 1986. pap. 3.99 (*0-14-030358-8*, Puffin) Puffin Bks.
Anglund, Joan W. All about My Family. Anglund, Joan W. 48p. (ps up). 1987. pap. 6.95 (*0-590-40828-3*) Scholastic Inc.
—Baby's First Book. Anglund, Joan W. 12p. (ps). 1985. 3.99 (*0-394-87470-6*) Random Bks Yng Read.
—Christmas Is a Time of Giving. Anglund, Joan W. LC 61-10106. 28p. (ps up). 1961. 9.95 (*0-15-217863-5*, HB Juv Bks) HarBrace.
—A Friend Is Someone Who Likes You: Silver Anniversary Edition. Anglund, Joan W. LC 58-8624. 32p. (ps up). 1983. 8.95 (*0-15-229678-6*, HB Juv Bks) HarBrace.
—How Many Days Has Baby To Play? Anglund, Joan W. LC 87-19665. 21p. (ps-k). 1988. 7.95 (*0-15-200460-2*, Gulliver Bks) HarBrace.
—In a Pumpkin Shell. Anglund, Joan W. LC 60-10243. 32p. (ps-2). 1977. pap. 3.95 (*0-15-644425-9*, Voyager Bks) HarBrace.
—In a Pumpkin Shell: A Mother Goose ABC. Anglund, Joan W. LC 60-10243. (ps-2). 1960. 10.95 (*0-15-238269-0*, HB Juv Bks) HarBrace.
—The Joan Walsh Anglund Coloring Book. Anglund, Joan W. 64p. (ps-3). 1984. pap. 2.95 saddle-stitched (*0-394-86875-7*) Random Bks Yng Read.
—The Joan Walsh Anglund I Love You Book & Doll Set. Anglund, Joan W. LC 88-60060. 24p. (ps-1). 1988. book & doll pkg. 5.95 (*0-394-89338-7*) Random Bks Yng Read.
—Morning Is a Little Child. Anglund, Joan W. LC 69-11592. (gr. 4-6). 1969. 7.95 (*0-15-255652-4*, HB Juv Bks) HarBrace.
—A Mother Goose Book. Anglund, Joan W. Van Doren, Liz, ed. 32p. (ps up). 1991. 7.95 (*0-15-200529-3*, Gulliver Bks) HarBrace.
—Nibble Nibble Mousekin: A Tale of Hansel & Gretel. Anglund, Joan W. LC 62-14422. 32p. (gr. k-3). 1962. 10.95 (*0-15-257400-X*, HB Juv Bks) HarBrace.
—Nibble Nibble Mousekin: A Tale of Hansel & Gretel. Anglund, Joan W. LC 62-14422. 32p. (gr. k-3). 1977. pap. 4.95 (*0-15-665588-8*, Voyager Bks) HarBrace.
—Spring Is a New Beginning. Anglund, Joan W. LC 63-7892. 32p. (ps up). 1991. 8.95 (*0-15-278161-7*, HB Juv Bks) HarBrace.
Anholt, Catherine. Here Come the Babies. Anholt, Catherine. LC 92-54584. 32p. (gr. 3 up). 1993. 13.95 (*1-56402-209-9*) Candlewick Pr.
—Tom's Rainbow Walk, Vol. 1. Anholt, Catherine. 32p. (ps-3). 1990. 12.95 (*0-316-04261-7*, Joy St Bks) Little.
—When I Was a Baby. Anholt, Catherine. 32p. (ps-3). 1989. 11.95 (*0-316-04262-5*, Joy St Bks) Little.
Anholt, Catherine & Anholt, Laurence. Kids. Anholt, Catherine & Anholt, Laurence. LC 91-58739. 32p. (ps up). 1992. 13.95 (*1-56402-097-5*) Candlewick Pr.
—Toddlers. Anholt, Catherine & Anholt, Laurence. LC 92-54588. 24p. (ps). 1993. 5.95 (*1-56402-242-0*) Candlewick Pr.
—Twins, Two by Two. Anholt, Catherine & Anholt, Laurence. LC 91-71820. 32p. (ps). 1992. 13.95 (*1-56402-041-X*) Candlewick Pr.
Anholt, Catherine, jt. illus. see Anholt, Laurence.
Anholt, Laurence. The Forgotten Forest. Anholt, Laurence. 32p. (ps-3). 1992. 14.95 (*0-87156-569-2*) Sierra.
Anholt, Laurence & Anholt, Catherine. Bear & Baby. Anholt, Catherine & Anholt, Laurence. LC 92-54581. 24p. (ps). 1993. 5.95 (*1-56402-235-8*) Candlewick Pr.
Anholt, Laurence, jt. illus. see Anholt, Catherine.
Animation Cottage Staff. The Jungle Book: Based on the Mowgli Tales from "The Jungle Book" by Rudyard Kipling. Kipling, Rudyard. Oliver, Tony, ed. LC 90-64201. 36p. (Orig.). (gr. 3-4). 1990. pap. 2.95 (*1-879551-50-0*) Saban Pub.
Annen, Charles. Chantefables. Desnos, Robert. Annen, Sharon, tr. from FRE. LC 84-61257. 60p. (gr. 1-6). 1988. 17.95 (*0-9613938-0-7*) Penstemon Pr.
Annis, Scott E. Color in Nebraska Coloring Album. Isham, Joy & Annis, Scott E. 32p. (gr. 1-5). 1985. pap. 3.95 (*0-9615584-1-5*) Little Gnome.
Anno, Mitsumasa. Anno's Aesop: A Book of Fables by Aesop & Mr. Fox. Anno, Mitsumasa, retold by. LC 88-60087. 64p. (ps-2). 1989. 18.95 (*0-531-05774-7*); PLB 18.99 (*0-531-08374-8*) Orchard Bks Watts.
—Anno's Alphabet: An Adventure in Imagination. Anno, Mitsumasa. LC 73-21652. 64p. (gr. k up). 1975. 16.00 (*0-690-00540-7*, Crowell Jr Bks); PLB 15.89 (*0-690-00541-5*) HarpC Child Bks.
—Anno's Alphabet: An Adventure in Imagination. Anno, Mitsumasa. LC 73-21652. 64p. (ps up). 1988. pap. 7.95 (*0-06-443190-8*, Trophy) HarpC Child Bks.

—Anno's Counting Book. Anno, Mitsumasa. LC 76-28977. 32p. (ps-3). 1977. 16.00 (*0-690-01287-X*, Crowell Jr Bks); PLB 15.89 (*0-690-01288-8*) HarpC Child Bks.
—Anno's Faces. Anno, Mitsumasa. 32p. (ps). 1989. 11.95 (*0-399-21711-8*, Philomel Bks) Putnam Pub Group.
—Anno's Math Games II. Anno, Mitsumasa. 104p. (gr. 1-4). 1989. 19.95 (*0-399-21615-4*, Philomel Bks) Putnam Pub Group.
—Anno's Medieval World. Anno, Mitsumasa. LC 79-28367. 56p. (gr. 3 up). 1990. 16.95 (*0-399-20742-2*, Philomel Bks) Putnam Pub Group.
—Anno's Mysterious Multiplying Jar. Anno, Mitsumasa. LC 82-22413. 48p. (gr. 3 up). 1983. 16.95 (*0-399-20951-4*, Philomel Bks) Putnam Pub Group.
—Anno's Twice Told Tales: The Fisherman & His Wife & The Four Clever Brothers. Grimm, Jacob & Grimm, Wilhelm K. Anno, Mitsumasa, retold by. LC 92-25307. 64p. (ps up). 1993. PLB 17.95 (*0-399-22005-4*, Philomel Bks) Putnam Pub Group.
Ansari, Said S. Modern Hypnosis: Theory & Practice. Ansari, Masud. 232p. (gr. 5). 1982. pap. 6.95 (*0-685-05553-1*) MAS-Pr.
Anstey, Carolina. The Glass Bird. Richemont, Enid. LC 92-54585. 112p. (gr. 3-6). 1993. 14.95 (*1-56402-195-5*) Candlewick Pr.
Anstey, Caroline. Moles Can Dance. Edwards, Richard. LC 93-2462. 1994. write for info. (*1-56402-361-3*) Candlewick Pr.
Anstey, David. Balancing. Jennings, Terry. LC 88-83615. 28p. (gr. k-4). 1989. PLB 10.90 (*0-531-17175-2*, Gloucester Pr) Watts.
—The Big Book of Animal Masks. Holroyd, Angela. 32p. (gr. k-4). 1990. pap. 8.95 heavy card (*0-671-72580-7*, Little Simon) S&S Trade.
—The Big Book of Monster Masks. Holroyd, Angela. 32p. (gr. k-4). 1990. pap. 8.95 heavy card (*0-671-72579-3*, Little Simon) S&S Trade.
—Bouncing & Rolling. Jennings, Terry. Franklin Watts Ltd., ed. LC 87-82971. 24p. (gr. k-3). 1988. PLB 10.90 (*0-531-17085-3*, Gloucester Pr) Watts.
—Colors. Jennings, Terry. LC 88-93098. 24p. (ps-2). 1989. PLB 10.90 (*0-531-17129-9*, Gloucester Pr) Watts.
—Hot & Cold. Jennings, Terry. LC 88-83099. 24p. (ps-2). 1989. PLB 10.90 (*0-531-17127-2*, Gloucester Pr) Watts.
—Seeds. Jennings, Terry. Franklin Watts Ltd., ed. 24p. (gr. k-3). 1988. PLB 10.90 (*0-531-17087-X*, Gloucester Pr) Watts.
—Slugs & Snails. Jennings, Terry. LC 88-83101. 24p. (ps-2). 1989. PLB 10.90 (*0-531-17128-0*, Gloucester Pr) Watts.
—Spiders. Jennings, Terry. LC 88-83614. 24p. (gr. 1-3). 1989. PLB 10.40 (*0-531-17176-0*) Denison.
—Trees. Jennings, Terry. Kline, M., ed. 24p. (gr. 1-3). 1991. PLB 10.90 (*0-531-17276-7*, Gloucester Pr) Watts.
—The Wizard in Wonderland. Ure, Jean. LC 92-53020. 176p. (gr. 3-6). 1993. 14.95 (*1-56402-138-6*) Candlewick Pr.
Anstey, David & Anstey, David. Wizard in the Woods. Ure, Jean. LC 91-58770. 176p. (gr. 3-6). 1992. 14.95 (*1-56402-110-6*) Candlewick Pr.
Anthony, Stephen R. & Suvari, Mari-Ann. Best-Selling Chapters: Advanced Level. Harris, Raymond. 496p. (gr. 9 up). 1978. text ed. 17.00 (*0-89061-706-6*, 621H); pap. text ed. 13.25 (*0-89061-702-3*, 621) Jamestown Pubs.
Antolik, Jerry. Little Spotted Moo. Sims, Larry K. 24p. (Orig.). 1991. pap. text ed. 3.95 (*1-880706-00-8*) Goldrock Bks.
Anton, Karen. Two Are Twins. Albertsen, June. LC 86-70195. 31p. (ps-3). 1987. pap. 5.95 (*0-9615839-0-8*) Double Talk.
Antonie, Joy. Julie Rescues Big Mack. Hall, Roger. LC 93-26217. 1994. 4.25 (*0-383-03755-7*) SRA Schl Grp.
Antonucci, Emil. My Letter from Grandma. Cullen, Ruth V. LC 92-34381. 32p. 1993. pap. 4.95 (*0-8091-6610-0*) Paulist Pr.
—The Tree That Survived the Winter. Fahy, Mary. 64p. (gr. 8-12). 1989. pap. 8.95 (*0-8091-0432-6*) Paulist Pr.
Apodaca, Blanca. American History Simulations. Fischer, Max W. 96p. (gr. 5-8). 1993. wkbk. 9.95 (*1-55734-480-9*) Tchr Create Mat.
Apodaca, Blanca & Vasconcelles, Keith. Making Big & Little Books. Sterling, Mary E. 80p. (Orig.). (gr. k-3). 1991. wkbk. 7.95 (*1-55734-133-8*) Tchr Create Mat.
Apodaca, Blanca, et al. Connecting Math & Literature. Carratello, John & Carratello, Patty. Vasconcelles, Keith, intro. by. 144p. (gr. k-3). 1991. wkbk. 12.95 (*1-55734-342-X*) Tchr Create Mat.
—Connecting Science & Literature. Cerbus, Deborah P. & Rice, Cheryl F. 144p. (gr. k-3). 1991. wkbk. 12.95 (*1-55734-341-1*) Tchr Create Mat.
—Learning Centers Through the Year. Wallace, Annette H. Levin, Ina M., ed. 384p. (gr. k-2). 1993. wkbk. 24.95 (*1-55734-059-5*) Tchr Create Mat.
—Native Americans - A Thematic Unit. Severson, Leigh. 80p. (Orig.). (gr. k-3). 1991. wkbk. 7.95 (*1-55734-276-8*) Tchr Create Mat.
Apodaca, Blanqui. April Monthly Activities. Hale, Janet. 80p. (gr. 1-5). 1990. wkbk. 7.95 (*1-55734-158-3*) Tchr Create Mat.
—Newspaper Reporters. Brown, Marzella. Coan, Sharon, ed. 48p. (gr. 3-6). 1990. wkbk. 5.95 (*1-55734-137-0*) Tchr Create Mat.

—Seasons - a Thematic Unit. Graube, Ireta S. 80p. (ps-1). 1990. wkbk. 7.95 (*1-55734-251-2*) Tchr Create Mat.
Apodaca, Blanqui & Spence, Paula. February Monthly Activities. Hale, Janet. 80p. (gr. 1-5). 1989. wkbk. 7.95 (*1-55734-156-7*) Tchr Create Mat.
—January Monthly Activities. Hale, Janet. 80p. (gr. 1-5). 1989. wkbk. 7.95 (*1-55734-155-9*) Tchr Create Mat.
—June Monthly Activities. Hale, Janet. 80p. (gr. 1-5). 1990. wkbk. 7.95 (*1-55734-164-8*) Tchr Create Mat.
Apodaca, Blanqui & Vasconcelles, Keith. Literature & Critical Thinking. Carratello, Patty. 96p. (gr. 5-8). 1990. wkbk. 9.95 (*1-55734-316-0*) Tchr Create Mat.
Apodaca, Blanqui & Wright, Theresa. Literature & Critical Thinking. Carratello, Patty & Carratello, John. 96p. (gr. 3-5). 1989. wkbk. 9.95 (*1-55734-312-8*) Tchr Create Mat.
—Masterpiece of the Month. Thomas, Jennifer. 96p. (gr. k-5). 1990. wkbk. 9.95 (*1-55734-018-8*) Tchr Create Mat.
Apodaca, Blanqui, et al. August Monthly Activities. Hale, Janet. 80p. (gr. 1-5). 1990. wkbk. 7.95 (*1-55734-166-4*) Tchr Create Mat.
—July Monthly Activities. Hale, Janet. 80p. (gr. 1-5). 1990. wkbk. 7.95 (*1-55734-165-6*) Tchr Create Mat.
—Literature & Critical Thinking. Carratello, John & Carratello, Patty. 96p. (gr. 5-8). 1990. wkbk. 9.95 (*1-55734-314-4*) Tchr Create Mat.
—March Monthly Activities. Hale, Janet. 80p. (gr. 1-5). 1990. wkbk. 7.95 (*1-55734-157-5*) Tchr Create Mat.
—May Monthly Activities. Hale, Janet. 80p. (gr. 1-5). 1990. wkbk. 7.95 (*1-55734-159-1*) Tchr Create Mat.
—Literature & Critical Thinking. Carratello, John & Carratello, Patty. 96p. (gr. 3-5). 1990. wkbk. 9.95 (*1-55734-315-2*) Tchr Create Mat.
Apodaca-LaBounty, Blanca & Wright, Theresa M. Whole Language Units for the Alphabet. Stone, Sylvia & Bye, Holly. 144p. (ps-1). 1993. wkbk. 12.95 (*1-55734-202-4*) Tchr Create Mat.
Appelbaum, Neil. Is There a Hole in Your Head? Appelbaum, Neil. (gr. k-3). 1963. 8.95 (*0-8392-3012-5*) Astor-Honor.
Appell-Mertiny, Helene. Animals That Wear Disguises. Duprez, Martine. LC 93-20967. 1994. 14.95 (*0-88106-673-7*) Charlesbridge Pub.
Apple, M. Star Baby. Lawson, A. 1992. 15.95 (*0-15-200905-1*, HB Juv Bks) HarBrace.
Apple, Margot. Angel's Mother's Baby. Delton, Judy. 144p. (gr. 2-5). 1989. 13.45 (*0-395-50926-2*) HM.
—Angel's Mother's Boyfriend. Delton, Judy. LC 82-27054. 176p. (gr. 2-5). 1986. 12.95 (*0-395-39968-8*) HM.
—Benjy in Business. Van Leeuwen, Jean. LC 82-22158. 112p. (gr. 2-6). 1983. Dial Bks Young.
—Blanket. Apple, Margot. 32p. (ps-3). 1990. 13.45 (*0-395-51522-X*) HM.
—The Boy Who Ate Dog Biscuits. Sachs, Betsy. LC 89-3905. 64p. (gr. 2-4). 1989. PLB 7.99 (*0-394-94778-9*); pap. 2.50 (*0-394-84778-4*) Random Bks Yng Read.
—Bunny's Night Out. Schotter, Roni. 32p. (ps-3). 1989. 13.95 (*0-316-77465-0*, Joy St Bks) Little.
—The Chocolate Touch. Catling, Patrick S. LC 78-31100. 96p. (gr. 4-6). 1979. Repr. of 1952 ed. PLB 11.88 (*0-688-32187-9*) Morrow Jr Bks.
—Donna Jean's Disaster. Williams, Barbara. Levine, Abby, ed. LC 86-15817. 32p. (gr. 1-5). 1986. PLB 11.95 (*0-8075-1682-1*) A Whitman.
—Don't Forget Michael. Thompson, Jean. LC 79-16637. 64p. (gr. k-3). 1979. 11.95 (*0-688-22196-3*); (Morrow Jr Bks) Morrow Jr Bks.
—The Great Rescue Operation. Van Leeuwen, Jean. LC 81-65851. 176p. (gr. 2-6). 1982. 10.95 (*0-685-01455-X*); PLB 10.89 (*0-685-01456-8*) Dial Bks Young.
—The Great Rescue Operation. Van Leeuwen, Jean. 144p. (gr. 3 up). 1990. pap. 3.95 (*0-14-034288-5*, Puffin) Puffin Bks.
—Have I Got Dogs! Cole, William. 32p. (ps-3). 1993. reinforced bdg. 13.99 (*0-670-83070-4*) Viking Child Bks.
—Just Like My Dad. Gardella, Tricia. LC 90-4403. 32p. (ps-3). 1993. 15.00 (*0-06-021937-8*); PLB 14.89 (*0-06-021938-6*) HarpC Child Bks.
—Mystery of the Witch's Shoes. new ed. Supraner, Robyn. LC 78-60125. 48p. (gr. 2-4). 1979. PLB 10.89 (*0-89375-090-5*); pap. 3.50 (*0-89375-078-6*) Troll Assocs.
—Sheep in a Jeep. Shaw, Nancy. LC 86-3101. 32p. (ps-k). 1986. 13.95 (*0-395-41105-X*) HM.
—Sheep in a Jeep. Shaw, Nancy. 32p. (ps-k). 1991. pap. 3.80 (*0-395-47030-7*, Sandpiper); pap. 7.70 incl. cassette (*0-395-60167-3*, Sandpiper) HM.
—Sheep in a Shop. Shaw, Nancy. LC 90-4139. 32p. (ps-k). 1991. 13.45 (*0-395-53681-2*) HM.
—Sheep on a Ship. Shaw, Nancy. (ps). 1989. 13.45 (*0-395-48160-0*) HM.
—Sheep Out to Eat. Shaw, Nancy. LC 91-38425. 32p. (ps-1). 1992. 13.45 (*0-395-61128-8*) HM.
—Sheep Take a Hike. Shaw, Nancy. LC 93-30725. 1994. write for info. (*0-395-68394-7*) HM.
—Susie Goes Shopping. Greydanus, Rose. 32p. (gr. k-2). 1980. PLB 7.89 (*0-89375-389-0*); pap. 1.95 (*0-89375-289-4*) Troll Assocs.
—Sybil Rides for Independence. Brown, Drollene. Levine, Abby, ed. LC 84-17219. 48p. (gr. 2-5). 1985. 11.95 (*0-8075-7684-0*) A Whitman.

—Tale of Peter Rabbit. new ed. Potter, Beatrix. LC 78-18071. 32p. (gr. k-3). 1979. PLB 9.79 (*0-89375-124-3*); pap. 1.95 (*0-89375-102-2*) Troll Assocs.
—The Trouble with Santa. Sachs, Betsy. LC 89-24257. 64p. (Orig.). (gr. 2-4). 1990. pap. 2.50 (*0-679-80410-2*) Random Bks Yng Read.
—You Push, I Ride. Levine, Abby. Tucker, Kathleen, ed. LC 87-36852. 32p. (ps-k). 1989. PLB 13.95 (*0-8075-9444-X*) A Whitman.
Apple, Margot. The Chocolate Touch. Catling, Patrick S. 96p. 1981. pap. 2.75 (*0-553-15479-6*) Bantam.
Appleby, Barrie. Ghosts, Monsters & Legends. Bradley, Susannah, ed. 48p. (gr. 3-6). 1992. pap. 2.95 (*1-56680-005-6*) Mad Hatter Pub.
Appleby, Ellen. All about Me. Muntean, Michaela. 48p. (ps-3). 1984. 5.95 (*0-8193-1123-5*) Parents.
—Beginning to Add. Jonson, Liz & Silliman, Emery. Nayer, Judith E., ed. 32p. (gr. k-1). 1991. wkbk. 1.95 (*1-878624-55-5*) McClanahan Bk.
—I'd Like to Be. Kroll, Steven. LC 86-25215. 48p. (ps-3). 1987. 5.95 (*0-8193-1141-3*) Parents.
—A Merry Scary Halloween. 16p. (ps-k). 1990. pap. 3.95 casebound (*0-671-70721-3*, Little Simon) S&S Trade.
—One Little Monkey. Calmenson, Stephanie. LC 82-7958. 48p. (ps-3). 1982. pap. 5.95 (*0-8193-1091-3*); PLB 5.95 (*0-8193-1092-1*) Parents.
—Peek-A-Boo. 16p. (ps-k). 1990. pap. 3.95 casebound (*0-671-70722-1*, Little Simon) S&S Trade.
—Pets I Wouldn't Pick. Schmeltz, Susan A. LC 81-11071. 48p. (ps-3). 1982. 5.95 (*0-8193-1073-5*); PLB 5.95 (*0-8193-1074-3*) Parents.
—Where Will the Animals Stay? Calmenson, Stephanie. LC 83-13479. 48p. (ps-3). 1984. 5.95 (*0-8193-1119-7*) Parents.
Appleton, Doug. Barbie & the Beat Play Set. 24p. 1991. 6.95 (*0-8431-2920-4*) Price Stern.
Aragon, Hilda. Blue & Red. Ortiz, Simon. 14p. (Orig.). (ps-7). 1981. pap. 3.75 (*0-915347-08-3*) Pueblo Acoma Pr.
—Mother Deer & Her Spotted Fawns. Chavez, Juana. 14p. (Orig.). (ps-7). 1981. pap. 3.75 (*0-915347-10-5*) Pueblo Acoma Pr.
—My Birthday on Christmas Day. Gracia, Debbie. 30p. (Orig.). (ps-7). 1980. pap. 3.75 (*0-915347-05-9*) Pueblo Acoma Pr.
—My First Nursery Rhyme Book. 28p. (Orig.). (ps-7). 1981. pap. 3.75 (*0-915347-07-5*) Pueblo Acoma Pr.
—A Pueblo Village. 8p. (Orig.). (ps-7). 1982. pap. 4.00 (*0-915347-17-2*) Pueblo Acoma Pr.
Aragon, Loretta. Cosmic Reader of the Southwest for Young People. Salaz, Ruben D. (gr. 4 up). 1976. pap. 6.95 (*0-932492-00-2*) Cosmic Hse NM.
Aragon, Sherry. A Girlfriend at Acoma, Siyu, & an Invitation to Supper. Garcia, Lola. 14p. (Orig.). (ps-7). 1981. pap. 3.75 (*0-915347-09-1*) Pueblo Acoma Pr.
—My Grandfather & the Boys. Ortiz, Mamie. 14p. (Orig.). (ps-7). 1982. pap. 3.75 (*0-915347-03-2*) Pueblo Acoma Pr.
Aragones, Sergio. Aragones 3-D. Aragones, Sergio & Zone, Ray. 64p. (Orig.). (gr. 9-12). 1989. pap. 4.95 (*0-317-93126-1*) Three-D Zone.
Aragones, Sergio, et al. Visions of Arzach. L'Officier, Randy & L'Officier, Jean-Marc, eds. Ellison, Harlan, frwd. by. 64p. (gr. 6 up). 1993. Repr. of 1992 ed. 14.95 (*0-87816-233-X*) Kitchen Sink.
Arai, Tomie. Sachiko Means Happiness. Sakai, Kimiko. LC 90-2248. 32p. (gr. k-5). 1990. 13.95 (*0-89239-065-4*) Childrens Book Pr.
Arakaki, Daryl. Let's Call Him Lau-Wili-Wili-Humu-Humu-Nukuauku-Nukunukai-Apuaa-Oioi. Myers, Tim. LC 93-72767. 24p. (ps-3). 1993. 12.95 (*1-880188-67-8*); pap. 5.95 (*0-685-68878-X*) Bess Pr.
Araten, Harry. Classic Bible Stories for Jewish Children. Kolatch, Alfred J. LC 93-10165. 72p. (gr. 3 up). 1993. 14.95 (*0-8246-0362-1*) Jonathan David.
—Two by Two: Favorite Bible Stories. Araten, Harry. LC 90-46841. 32p. (gr. k-3). 1991. pap. 7.95 (*0-929371-54-2*) Kar Ben.
Arbuckle, Jane & Krupinsky, Lisa. Look Out for Loons. Krupinsky, Jacquelyn S. Krupinsky, Lisa A., ed. 28p. (Orig.). (gr. k-3). 1983. pap. 5.95 (*0-912123-01-X*) Woodbury Pr.
Arbuckle, Kathy. The Bedtime Bible Story Book. Hurlbut, Jesse L. Sortor, Toni, ed. 1989. text ed. 17.95 (*1-55748-096-6*); pap. text ed. 9.95 (*1-55748-095-8*); leather bdg. 24.95 (*1-55748-113-X*) Barbour & Co.
Arbuckle, Scott. Miracles & Wonders. Seims, Tom. 32p. (Orig.). 1993. 7.99 (*1-56476-046-4*, Victor Books) SP Pubns.
—People & Places. Seims, Tom. 32p. (Orig.). 1993. 7.99 (*1-56476-047-2*, Victor Books) SP Pubns.
Arcade, Greg. The Backcountry. Scott, Bob. 24p. (gr. 4-12). 1989. cardstock cover 5.00 (*0-9621201-0-3*) B Scott Bks.
Arcaris, Mary. A Tale of a Teddy Bear. LeRoque, Ellen E. 28p. (Orig.). (ps-2). 1985. pap. 3.95 (*0-932967-03-5*) Pacific Shoreline.
Archambauer, Alan H. A Diamond Anthology of Prose & Poetry: Seventy-Fifth Year. Writers' League of Washington Staff. Ricketts, Marijane, et al, eds. Leighton, Frances S., intros. by. 112p. (gr. 8-12). 1992. pap. write for info. (*0-9618223-2-5*) M G Ricketts.
Archambault, Alan. Civil War Heroes. Canon, Jill & Archambault, Alan. 48p. (Orig.). (gr. 7). 1988. pap. 3.95 (*0-88388-130-6*) Bellerophon Bks.

—Civil War Heroines. Canon, Jill. (Orig.). (gr. 7 up). 1989. pap. 3.95 (*0-88388-147-0*) Bellerophon Bks.
—The Story of Early California to 1849, Vol. 1. Knill, Harry. 48p. (Orig.). (gr. 4 up). 1988. pap. 3.95 (*0-88388-129-2*) Bellerophon Bks.
Archambault, Matthew. The Mystery of Sadler Marsh. Pritts, Kim D. 112p. (Orig.). (gr. 3-7). 1993. pap. 4.95 (*0-8361-3618-7*) Herald Pr.
Archer, Pat. Discover Nature at the Seashore: Things to Know & Things to Do. Lawlor, Elizabeth P. LC 91-17260. 224p. 1992. pap. 12.95 (*0-8117-3079-4*) Stackpole.
—Discover Nature Close to Home: Things to Know & Things to Do. Pawlor, Elizabeth P. 224p. (Orig.). (gr. 8 up). 1993. pap. 14.95 (*0-8117-3077-8*) Stackpole.
Archer, Rebecca. Beginner's Guide to French. Bradley, Susannah, ed. 48p. (gr. 3-6). 1992. pap. 2.95 (*1-56680-004-8*) Mad Hatter Pub.
—Farmyard: Stories for under Fives. Stimson, Joan. 44p. (ps-k). 1992. 3.50 (*0-7214-1506-7*) Ladybird Bks.
—How to Draw Cartoons. Bradley, Susannah. 48p. (gr. 3-6). 1992. pap. 2.95 (*1-56680-003-X*) Mad Hatter Pub.
—The Tale of Bella Brontosaurus. Wiltshire, Teri. LC 92-46250. (ps). 1993. 8.95 (*1-85697-857-5*) Kingfisher Bks.
—The Tale of Gus the Grumbly Grizzly. Wiltshire, Teri. LC 92-46248. (ps). 1993. 8.95 (*1-85697-856-7*) Kingfisher Bks.
—The Tale of Pepper the Pony. Wiltshire, Teri. LC 92-46249. (ps). 1993. 8.95 (*1-85697-858-3*) Kingfisher Bks.
—The Tale of Tiki Tiger. Wiltshire, Terri. LC 92-40364. 24p. (ps-k). 1993. 7.95 (*1-85697-859-1*) Kingfisher Bks.
Archipowa, Anastassija. The Goose Maiden. Grimm, Jacob & Grimm, Wilhelm K. 24p. 1990. 5.99 (*0-517-05388-8*) Outlet Bk Co.
—Rapunzel, & The Seven Ravens. Grimm, Jacob & Grimm, Wilhelm K. 24p. 1990. 3.99 (*0-517-05386-1*) Outlet Bk Co.
—Sleeping Beauty, & The Frog Prince. Grimm, Jacob & Grimm, Wilhelm K. 24p. 1990. 5.99 (*0-517-05385-3*) Outlet Bk Co.
Archives of the Kauai Museum Staff & Bernice P. Bishop Museum Staff. The Kaua'i Guide on Ni'ihau: UniNi'ihau: M-m-m, What a Sweet Potato. Oyama, Kaikilani E. (Orig.). 1988. pap. 2.50 (*0-942255-04-6*, G3) Magic Fishes Pr.
Archo, Mayra. Two Way Bilingual Songs for Elementary School. Ronnholm, Ursula O. 41p. (gr. k-12). 1987. pap. text ed. 8.00 (*0-941911-06-3*); cassettes incl. Two Way Bilingual.
Arciero, Susan. Nat, Nat, the Nantucket Cat. Barnes, Peter W. 30p. 1993. 15.95 (*0-9637688-0-8*) Vacation Spot.
Ardizzone, Edward. A Child's Christmas in Wales. Thomas, Dylan. LC 80-66216. 48p. 1980. 14.95 (*0-87923-339-7*); pap. 9.95 (*0-87923-529-2*) Godine.
—Exploits of Don Quixote. Reeves, James, retold by. LC 85-11170. (gr. 5 up). 1985. 12.95 (*0-87226-025-9*, Bedrick Blackie); (Bedrick Blackie) P Bedrick Bks.
—A Likely Place. Fox, Paula. LC 87-5542. 64p. (gr. 2-6). 1987. Repr. SBE 13.95 (*0-02-735761-9*, Macmillan Child Bk) Macmillan Child Grp.
—Pinky Pye. Estes, Eleanor. LC 58-5708. (gr. 3-7). 1958. 10.95 (*0-15-262076-1*, HB Juv Bks) HarBrace.
—Pinky Pye. Estes, Eleanor. LC 75-31581. 192p. (gr. 3-7). 1976. pap. 1.75 (*0-15-671840-5*, Voyager Bks) HarBrace.
—Stories from the Bible: From the Garden of Eden to the Promised Land. De La Mare, Walter. 418p. (gr. 3 up). 1985. pap. 8.95 (*0-571-11086-X*) Faber & Faber.
—Tim & Ginger. Ardizzone, Edward. 48p. (ps-3). 1987. pap. 6.95 (*0-19-272113-5*) OUP.
—Tim's Friend Towser. Ardizzone, Edward. 48p. (ps-3). 1987. pap. 6.95 (*0-19-272112-7*) OUP.
Ardizzone, Edward, jt. illus. see Hewitt, Kathryn.
Arehart, Betsy H. Alaska Wildlife: A Coloring Book. Roebuck, Susan H. Holen, Anne M., ed. Heshiki, Kazumi, tr. from ENG. (JPN.). 48p. (Orig.). (gr. 3-8). 1990. pap. 5.95 (*0-922127-01-8*) Paisley Pub.

Arehart, Betsy L. Arctic Animal Babies. Holen-Roebuck, Susan D. 40p. (Orig.). (ps-3). 1993. pap. 4.95 (*0-922127-04-2*) Paisley Pub.
This high-quality, educational coloring book features 40 simple, beautiful, accurate pictures of baby animals of the Arctic in their natural habitat. Illustrated by Alaskan artist Betsy L. Arehart. The cover printed on coated cover stock, is colorful & brilliant, the inside pages are high quality 70# recycled vellum. Children age 3 & up will love using paints, crayons, or markers to color pictures of playful polar bear cubs leaving their den for the first time in spring, a caribou calf kicking up his heels while his mother grazes in the background, a walrus pup

& his watchful mother "hauled out" on an ice floe, a beluga whale calf swimming beneath the sea ice with a pod of other belugas, a family of river otters sliding down a snowy river bank. A line or two of descriptive text accompanies each drawing. Each drawing includes a border & the name of the animal in inch-high "open" lettering, that can be colored in. Paisley Publishing also Publishes ALASKAN WILDLIFE (ISBN 0-922127-00-X) an educational coloring book for children age 8 & up featuring 20 of Alaska's animals with a full page of text accompanying each picture. To order: Paisley Publishing, P.O. Box 201853, Anchorage, AK 99520; or call (907) 272-6604.
Publisher Provided Annotation.

Arehart, Betsy L. & Holen, Susan D. Alaska's Wild Activity Book. Holen, Susan D. 48p. (gr. 3-8). 1994. pap. 4.95 (0-922127-03-4) Paisley Pub.
Arem, Joel, jt. photog. see Boltin, Lee.
Arenson, Roberta. The World Is Round. Stein, Gertrude. LC 93-562. 160p. Repr. of 1939 ed. 6.00 (1-56957-905-9) Shambhala Pubns.
Argent, Kerry. Derek the Knitting Dinosaur. Blackwood, Mary. 32p. (ps-3). 1990. PLB 18.95 (0-87614-400-8) Carolrhoda Bks.
—One Woolly Wombat. Argent, Kerry & Trinca, Rod. 32p. (ps-1). 1987. pap. 6.95 (0-916291-10-3) Kane-Miller Bk.
—Sebastian Lives in a Hat. Catterwell, Thelma. 32p. (ps-1). 1990. 13.95 (0-916291-30-8) Kane-Miller Bk.
Argent, Philip. Sing Nowell! 64p. (gr. 1-6). 1991. pap. 14.95 (0-7136-5695-6, Pub. by A&C Black UK) Talman.
Ariel, Liat B. Tali's Slippers, Tova's Shoes. Ganz, Yaffa. 32p. (gr. k-6). 1989. 6.95 (0-89906-502-3) Mesorah Pubns.
—The Wonderful World We Live In. Ganz, Yaffa. 48p. (gr. k-6). 1989. 10.95 (0-89906-964-9); pap. 6.95 (0-89906-965-7) Mesorah Pubns.
Aries, Ruby. Dream & Play with Us: Come Share Tim's & Lisa's Adventures & Learn How to Play Their Games. Aries, Ruby. Loft, Randi, ed. 115p. (Orig.). (gr. k-4). 1990. pap. 14.95 (0-9626570-5-0) Perk-Lo Pk Prodns.
Arisman, Marshall. Fitcher's Bird. Grimm, Jacob & Grimm, Wilhelm K. 32p. (gr. 9 up). 1983. PLB 13.95s.p. (0-87191-942-7) Creative Ed.

Arkenberg, Rebecca N. The Magic Box. Bulla, Dale. 24p. (gr. 2-6). 1993. 12.95 (1-884197-00-0) N Horizon Educ.
As a poor couple work in their garden, they discover a box that reproduces anything that is placed into it. The choices they make are reminiscent of a modern day rags to riches story. The mixture of old to new, past & present, rich & poor, provide a playful adaptation of an ancient tale. When youngsters read or listen to this story, they may be encouraged to talk about the mistakes made & issues raised as they think about the consequences of their choices. Children may be asked, "What would you do if you found such a box?" Storyteller Dale Bulla shares this comical retelling of an old folktale which is the most often requested story in his repertoire.
Publisher Provided Annotation.

Arkinstall, Eva. Silky, the Woods Cat. Moss, Helen. 80p. (gr. 2-4). 1993. 10.95 (0-89015-867-3) Eakin-Sunbelt.
Arkle, Dave, jt. illus. see Taylor, Karen.
Arlitt, Nancy. Waldo, the Goat Dog. Ebeling, Jean. Roberts, Melissa, ed. 48p. (gr. 4-7). 1987. 8.95 (0-89015-588-7, Pub. by Panda Bks) Eakin-Sunbelt.
Arlt, Bob. Learn about Growing Friendships with Little Bud. rev. ed. Holstead, Christy & Linder, Pamela. (ps-3). 1992. activity bk. 3.98 (1-881037-00-2) McGreen Wisdom.
Armer, Laura A. Waterless Mountain. Armer, Laura A. (gr. 5-8). 1931. 11.95 (0-679-20233-1) Random Bks Yng Read.
Armitage, David. The Cuckoo Bird. Corbalis, Judy. LC 90-22576. 32p. (gr. 1-4). 1991. PLB 14.89 (0-06-021698-0) HarpC Child Bks.

Arms, William. Storytelling with the Flannel Board, 3 Bks, Bk. 2. Anderson, Paul S. LC 21-650. 260p. (ps). 1970. 15.95 (0-513-00137-9) Denison.
Armstrong, Bev. Classifying Cat. Isaak, Betty. 24p. (ps). 1982. wkbk. 2.95 (0-88160-087-3, LW 123) Learning Wks.
—Dinosaur Detective. Armstrong, Bev. 32p. (gr. k-3). 1979. 3.95 (0-88160-075-X, LW 808) Learning Wks.
—Handwriting Hamburger. Schwartz, Linda. 32p. (gr. 3-6). 1979. wkbk. 3.95 (0-88160-073-3, LW 806) Learning Wks.
—Handwriting Hot Dog. Schwartz, Linda. 32p. (gr. k-3). 1979. wkbk. 3.95 (0-88160-078-4, LW 811) Learning Wks.
—Have Fun Following Directions. Armstrong, Bev. 32p. (gr. 1-3). 1979. wkbk. 3.95 (0-88160-077-6, LW 810) Learning Wks.
—Perception Panda. Isaak, Betty. 24p. (ps). 1982. wkbk. 2.95 (0-88160-088-1, LW 122) Learning Wks.
—Sequencing Seal. Isaak, Betty. 24p. (ps). 1982. wkbk. 2.95 (0-88160-090-3, LW 124) Learning Wks.
—Who's Following Directions? Armstrong, Bev. 32p. (gr. 4-7). 1979. wkbk. 3.95 (0-88160-072-5, LW 805) Learning Wks.
Armstrong, Beverly. Como Darle una Mano a los Perros y los Gatos: (How to Be a Helping Hand for Dogs & Cats) Montgomery, Charlotte B. (SPA & ENG.). 32p. (Orig.). (gr. k). Date not set. wkbk. 3.00 (0-941246-07-8) NAHEE.
—Earth Book for Kids: Activities to Help Heal the Environment. Schwartz, Linda. LC 90-91737. 184p. (Orig.). (gr. 3-6). 1990. pap. 9.95x (0-88160-195-0, LW 289) Learning Wks.
—My Earth Book: Puzzles, Projects, Facts & Fun. Schwartz, Linda. LC 92-60123. 64p. (gr. 1-4). 1991. pap. 7.95 (0-88160-201-9, LW153) Learning Wks.
—What Would You Do? A Kid's Guide to Tricky & Sticky Situations. Schwartz, Linda. LC 90-63597. 184p. (gr. 3-7). 1991. pap. 9.95 (0-88160-196-9, LW294) Learning Wks.
Armstrong, Bruce. A Dragon Drinks Just One Drop. Armstrong, Vicki. 32p. (gr. 1-6). 1990. wkbk. 5.99 (0-933367-01-5) See the Sounds.
—Pigs Pet People. Armstrong, Vicki. (ps-4). 1985. wkbk. 5.99 (0-933367-00-7) See the Sounds.

Armstrong, Camilla B. Robert Nathaniel's Tree. Schlitt, RaRa S. 36p. (gr. k up). 1993. 14.95 (0-9630017-3-6) Light-Bearer.
"This 36-page children's book was created by a young mother to help her oldest child better understand the death of his infant brother. As intended, ROBERT NATHANIEL'S TREE offers a source of inspiration for families facing loss; but this gentle, simple book is equally a celebration of life. The book addresses sensitive subject matter & will help countless families better deal with the tragedy of a child's death. Upon the loss of a child, comfort is most commonly & understandably directed toward the parents; but brothers & sisters face a loss, as well. ROBERT NATHANIEL'S TREE will help bring some peace & comfort into the lives of grieving families."--Midwest Book Review, August 1993. Already in many school libraries, ROBERT NATHANIEL'S TREE meets a vital need. Beautiful picture-book format suitable for all ages.
Publisher Provided Annotation.

Armstrong, Julie, et al. Fire Safety with Teddy Ruxpin. Baron, Phil. 22p. (ps). 1988. write for info. incl. pre-programmed audiotape (0-934323-75-5) Alchemy Comms.
—Safe at Home with Teddy Ruxpin. Baron, Michelle. 34p. (ps). 1988. write for info. incl. audio tape (0-934323-70-4) Alchemy Comms.
—Water Safety with Teddy Ruxpin. Baron, Michelle. 34p. (ps). 1988. incl. audio tape 9.95 (0-934323-74-7) Alchemy Comms.
Armstrong, M. J. Little Princess' Symphony Adventures. Sharp, Vera. 76p. (ps-6). 1985. incl. 2 cassettes 49.00 (0-9616987-0-5) V Sharp.
Armstrong, Nicholas. Ant. Chinery, Michael. Watts, Barrie, photos by. LC 90-10947. 32p. (gr. 4-6). 1991. PLB 11.59 (0-8167-2098-3); pap. text ed. 3.95 (0-8167-2099-1) Troll Assocs.
Armstrong, Robert. A Frog's Tale. Book, Linda. 32p. (Orig.). (gr. k-6). 1990. PLB 5.00 (0-9626294-0-5) Words & Muse Prodns.

Armstrong, Tom. Lets Make Piano Music with Marvin, Bk. 2. Patrick, Ann. 48p. (gr. k-7). 1986. pap. text ed. 6.95 (0-931759-13-7) Centerstream Pub.
Armstrong, Tom & Davis, Florence. Jonah & the Worm. Briscoe, Jill. 143p. (gr. 6). 1989. pap. write for info. Jilcoe.
Arnal, Encarna. Tierra del Sur. Larcada, Luis I. (SPA.). 48p. 1993. lib. bdg. 7.00 (0-937509-09-4) Edit Arcos.
Arndt, Ursula. Fireworks, Picnics, & Flags: The Story of the Fourth of July Symbols. Giblin, James C. LC 82-9612. 96p. (gr. 3-6). 1983. 14.95 (0-89919-146-0, Clarion Bks); pap. 4.95 (0-89919-174-6, Clarion Bks) HM.
—Hearts, Cupids, & Red Roses: The Story of the Valentine Symbols. Barth, Edna. LC 73-7128. 64p. (gr. 3-6). 1982. pap. 5.95 (0-89919-036-7, Clarion Bks) HM.
—Holly, Reindeer, & Colored Lights: The Story of the Christmas Symbols. Barth, Edna. LC 71-157731. 96p. (gr. 3-6). 1981. pap. 5.95 (0-89919-037-5, Clarion Bks) HM.
—Holly, Reindeer, & Colored Lights: The Story of the Christmas Symbols. Barth, Edna. LC 71-157731. 96p. (gr. 3-6). 1979. 15.45 (0-395-28842-8, Calrion Bks) HM.
—Lilies, Rabbits, & Painted Eggs: The Story of the Easter Symbols. Barth, Edna. LC 74-79033. (gr. 3-6). 1979. (Clarion Bks); pap. 5.95 (0-395-30550-0, Clarion Bks) HM.
—Shamrocks, Harps, & Shillelaghs: The Story of the St. Patrick's Day Symbols. Barth, Edna. LC 77-369. 96p. (gr. 3-6). 1982. 15.45 (0-395-28845-2, Clarion Bks) HM; pap. 5.95 (0-89919-038-3, Clarion) HM.
—Turkeys, Pilgrims, & Indian Corn: The Story of the Thanksgiving Symbols. Barth, Edna. LC 75-4703. 96p. (gr. 3-6). 1981. pap. 4.95 (0-89919-039-1, Clarion Bks) HM.
—Turkeys, Pilgrims, & Indian Corn: The Story of the Thanksgiving Symbols. Barth, Edna. LC 75-4703. 96p. (gr. 3-6). 1979. 13.95 (0-395-28846-0, Clarion Bks) HM.
—Witches, Pumpkins & Grinning Ghosts: The Story of the Halloween Symbols. Barth, Edna. LC 72-75705. 96p. (gr. 3-6). 1981. 4.95 (0-89919-040-5, Clarion Bks); pap. 4.95 (0-317-03145-7, Clarion Bks) HM.
—Witches, Pumpkins & Grinning Ghosts: The Story of the Halloween Symbols. Barth, Edna. LC 72-75705. 96p. (gr. 3-6). 1979. 13.45 (0-395-28847-9, Clarion Bks) HM.
Arno, Enrico. Brendan the Navigator. Fritz, Jean. LC 78-13247. (gr. 2-5). 1979. 14.95 (0-698-20473-5, Coward) Putnam Pub Group.
Arnoff, Julie, jt. illus. see Jackson, Jett.
Arnold, Arthur. A Walk on the Great Barrier Reef. Arnold, Caroline. 48p. (gr. 2-5). 1988. pap. 6.95 (0-87614-501-2, First Ave Edns) Lerner Pubns.
Arnold, Elaine. Little Fox & the Golden Hawk. Berry, Gail. Kremer, John, intro. by. 32p. (gr. 1-9). 1991. 9.50 (0-912411-36-8) Open Horizons.
—Snake In, Snake Out. Banchek, Linda. 32p. (ps-1). 1992. pap. 2.99 (0-440-40738-9, YB) Dell.
—Wee Green Witch. Leister, Mary. LC 78-12380. 44p. (ps up). 1978. 9.95 (0-916144-30-5) Stemmer Hse.
Arnold, Jeanne. Carlos & the Squash Plant: Carlos y la Planta Calabaza. Stevens, Jan R. LC 92-82137. (SPA & ENG.). 32p. (gr. k). 1993. 14.95 (0-87358-559-3) Northland AZ.
—When You Were Just a Little Girl. Hennessy, B. G. 32p. (ps-3). 1994. pap. 4.99 (0-14-054172-1) Puffin Bks.
Arnold, Katya. Baba Yaga: A Russian Folktale. Arnold, Katya, retold by. LC 92-38199. 32p. (gr. k-3). 1993. 14.95 (1-55858-208-8); PLB 14.88 (1-55858-209-6) North-South Bks NYC.
Arnold, Nick, jt. photog. see Keates, Colin.
Arnold, Rist. If I Were a Cat I Would Sit in a Tree. Cutler, Ebbitt. 28p. (gr. k-4). 1985. text ed. 7.95 (0-88776-177-1, Dist. by U of Toronto Pr) Tundra Bks.
Arnold, Tedd. Actions. 16p. (ps). 1992. pap. 3.95 (0-671-77824-2, Little Simon) S&S Trade.
—Colors. 16p. (ps). 1992. pap. 3.95 (0-671-77825-0, Little Simon) S&S Trade.
—Green Wilma. Arnold, Tedd. LC 91-31501. 32p. (ps-3). 1993. 13.99 (0-8037-1313-4); PLB 13.89 (0-8037-1314-2) Dial Bks Young.
—My First Baking Book. Coyle, Rena. LC 87-40646. 144p. (gr. 1-5). 1988. pap. 9.95 (0-89480-579-7, 1579) Workman Pub.
—My Working Mom. Glassman, Peter. LC 93-22036. 1994. write for info. (0-688-12259-0); PLB write for info. (0-688-12260-4) Morrow Jr Bks.
—No Jumping on the Bed! Arnold, Tedd. LC 86-13501. 32p. (ps-2). 1987. 14.00 (0-8037-0038-5); PLB 13.89 (0-8037-0039-3) Dial Bks Young.
—Ollie Forgot. Arnold, Tedd. 32p. (ps-3). 1991. pap. 3.95 (0-8037-0985-4, Dial Pied Piper) Puffin Bks.
—Opposites. 16p. (ps). 1992. pap. 3.95 (0-671-77823-4, Little Simon) S&S Trade.
—The Signmaker's Assistant. Arnold, Tedd. LC 90-19537. 32p. (ps-3). 1992. 14.00 (0-8037-1010-0); PLB 13.89 (0-8037-1011-9) Dial Bks Young.
—Sounds. 16p. (ps). 1992. pap. 3.95 (0-671-77826-9, Little Simon) S&S Trade.
Arnold, Tim. Least of All. Purdy, Carol. LC 86-12613. 32p. (gr. 1-4). 1987. SBE 12.95 (0-689-50404-7, M K McElderry) Macmillan Child Grp.

—Least of All. Purdy, Carol. LC 92-19964. 32p. (gr. k-3). 1993. pap. 3.95 (0-689-71681-8, Aladdin) Macmillan Child Grp.
—Natural History from A to Z: A Terrestrial Sampler. Arnold, Tim. LC 88-26879. 64p. (gr. 5-9). 1991. SBE 15.95 (0-689-50467-5, M K McElderry) Macmillan Child Grp.
—The Three Billy Goats Gruff. Arnold, Tim, retold by. LC 92-23992. 32p. (ps-3). 1993. SBE 14.95 (0-689-50575-2, M K McElderry) Macmillan Child Grp.
—Worlds I Know & Other Poems. Livingston, Myra C. LC 85-7344. 64p. (gr. 4-7). 1985. SBE 13.95 (0-689-50332-6, M K McElderry) Macmillan Child Grp.

Arnosky, Jim. Crinkleroot's Book of Animal Tracking. Arnosky, Jim. LC 88-15353. 48p. (gr. k-5). 1989. RSBE 13.95 (0-02-705851-4, Bradbury Pr) Macmillan Child Grp.
—Crinkleroot's Guide to Knowing the Birds. Arnosky, Jim. LC 91-38234. 32p. (gr. k-5). 1992. RSBE 14.95 (0-02-705857-3, Bradbury Pr) Macmillan Child Grp.
—Crinkleroot's Guide to Knowing the Trees. Arnosky, Jim. LC 91-18651. 40p. (gr-5). 1992. RSBE 13.95 (0-02-705855-7, Bradbury Pr) Macmillan Child Grp.
—Crinkleroot's Guide to Walking in Wild Places. Arnosky, Jim. LC 89-38427. 32p. (gr. k-5). 1990. RSBE 13.95 (0-02-705842-5, Bradbury Pr) Macmillan Child Grp.
—Crinkleroot's Guide to Walking in Wild Places. Arnosky, Jim. LC 92-45775. 32p. (gr. k-5). 1993. pap. 4.95 (0-689-71753-9, Aladdin) Macmillan Child Grp.
—Crinkleroot's Twenty-Five Birds Every Child Should Know. Arnosky, Jim. LC 92-36059. 32p. (gr. k-3). 1993. RSBE 12.95 (0-02-705859-X, Bradbury Pr) Macmillan Child Grp.
—Crinkleroot's Twenty-Five Fish Every Child Should Know. Arnosky, Jim. LC 92-39381. 32p. (gr. k-3). 1993. RSBE 12.95 (0-02-705844-1, Bradbury Pr) Macmillan Child Grp.
—Crinkleroot's Twenty-Five Mammals Every Child Should Know. Arnosky, Jim. LC 93-7585. 32p. (ps-3). 1994. RSBE 12.95 (0-02-705845-X, Bradbury Pr) Macmillan Child Grp.
—Crinkleroot's Twenty-Five More Mammals Every Child Should Know. Arnosky, Jim. LC 93-7584. 32p. (ps-3). 1994. RSBE 12.95 (0-02-705846-8, Bradbury Pr) Macmillan Child Grp.
—Drawing from Nature. Arnosky, Jim. LC 82-15327. 64p. (Orig.). 1987. 13.95 (0-688-01295-7) Lothrop.
—Drawing Life in Motion. Arnosky, Jim. LC 83-25129. 48p. (Orig.). 1987. 12.95 (0-688-03803-4) Lothrop.
—The Empty Lot. Fife, Dale H. 32p. (gr. k-4). 1991. 14.95 (0-316-28167-0) Sierra.
—Every Autumn Comes the Bear. Arnosky, Jim. LC 92-30515. 32p. (ps-1). 1993. 14.95 (0-399-22508-0, Putnam) Putnam Pub Group.
—Flies in the Water, Fish in the Air: A Personal Introduction to Fly Fishing. Arnosky, Jim. Randolph, John, frwd. by. 96p. (gr. 6-12). 1992. pap. 10.00 (0-88150-246-4) Countryman.
—I Was Born in a Tree & Raised by Bees. Arnosky, Jim. LC 88-6121. 48p. (gr. k-5). 1988. Repr. of 1977 ed. RSBE 13.95 (0-02-705841-7, Bradbury Pr) Macmillan Child Grp.
—A Kettle of Hawks. Arnosky, Jim. LC 89-12459. 32p. (gr. k-4). 1990. 13.95 (0-688-09279-9); lib. bdg. 13.88 (0-688-09280-2) Lothrop.
—Long Spikes. Arnosky, Jim. 96p. (gr. 3-7). 1992. 12.70 (0-395-58830-8, Clarion Bks) HM.
—Raccoons & Ripe Corn. Arnosky, Jim. LC 87-4243. 32p. (ps-3). 1987. 13.95 (0-688-05455-2); PLB 13.88 (0-688-05456-0) Lothrop.
—Sketching Outdoors in Spring. Arnosky, Jim. LC 86-21308. 48p. (gr. 4 up). 1987. 12.95 (0-688-06284-9) Lothrop.

Arnow, Jan, photos by. Louisville Slugger: The Making of a Baseball Bat. Arnow, Jan. LC 84-7049. 48p. (gr. 3-7). 1984. 11.95 (0-394-86297-X, Pant Bks Young); lib. bdg. 14.00 (0-394-96297-4) Pantheon.

Arnsteen, Katy. Grandpa Doesn't Know It's Me: A Family Adjusts to Alzheimer's Disease. Guthrie, Donna W. Aronson, Miriam, intro. by. 1986. 14.95 (0-89885-302-8); pap. 9.95 (0-89885-308-7) Human Sci Pr.

Arnsteen, Katy K. Mommy Loves Jesus. Snider, Catherine. LC 93-13354. 24p. (Orig.). (ps-6). 1993. pap. 3.95 (0-8198-4731-3) St Paul Bks.
—Mrs. Gigglebelly Is Coming to Tea. Guthrie, Donna. 32p. (ps-2). 1993. pap. 2.50 (0-671-79605-4, Little Simon) S&S Trade.
—Not for Babies. Guthrie, Donna. 24p. (ps-1). 1993. pap. 2.50 (0-685-63280-6, Little Simon) S&S Trade.
—What Babies Can Do. Morton, Jane. 12p. (ps). 1993. bds. 2.99 (1-56476-081-2, Victor Books) SP Pubns.
—What Ones Can Do. Morton, Jane. 12p. (ps). 1993. bds. 2.99 (1-56476-082-0, Victor Books) SP Pubns.
—What Threes Can Do. Morton, Jane. 12p. (ps). 1993. bds. 2.99 (1-56476-084-7, Victor Books) SP Pubns.
—What Twos Can Do. Morton, Jane. 12p. (ps). 1993. bds. 2.99 (1-56476-083-9, Victor Books) SP Pubns.
—The Witch Has an Itch. Guthrie, Donna. 24p. (ps-1). 1990. pap. 2.50 (0-671-70346-3, Little Simon) S&S Trade.
—The Young Author's Do-It-Yourself Book: How to Write, Illustrate, & Produce Your Own Book. Guthrie, Donna, et al. LC 93-9736. 64p. (gr. 2-4). 1994. PLB 14.90 (1-56294-350-2) Millbrook Pr.

Armstrong, Beverly. Animal Places & Faces: A Drawing Book for Kids Who Care. Holden, Lorraine & Malcarne, Vanessa. 30p. 1983. 3.50 (0-317-60991-2) NAHEE.

Aronson, Lou. Stalwart Men of Early Texas. McCall, Edith. LC 78-101296. 128p. (gr. 3-10). 1980. PLB 15.00 (0-516-03371-9) Childrens.
—The Story of the Lewis & Clark Expedition. Stein, R. Conrad. LC 78-4648. 32p. (gr. 3-6). 1978. pap. 3.95 (0-516-44620-7) Childrens.

Arostu, Salma. Fatima's Surprise. Kezzeiz, Ediba. 21p. (Orig.). (ps-1). 1991. pap. 3.50 (0-89259-114-5) Am Trust Pubns.

Arpino, Alaria. Domino: Traditional Children's Songs, Proverbs & Culture from the American Virgin Islands. Ellis, Karen S., intro. by. 96p. (Orig.). (gr. 1-6). 1990. Set. pap. 21.50 (0-9625560-7-6); pap. text ed. 14.50 (0-9625560-3-3); incl. audio tape 10.00 (0-9625560-0-9) Guavaberry Bks.

Arquette, Mary F. Children of the Morning Light: Wampanoag Tales As Told by Manitonquat. Medicine Story. LC 92-32328. 80p. (gr. 1). 1994. SBE 18.95 (0-02-765905-4, Macmillan Child Bk) Macmillan Child Grp.

Arrants, Cheryl & Arrants, Dennis. Thimbelina & the Notion Parade. Arrants, Cheryl & Arrants, Dennis. 32p. (Orig.). (gr. k-4). 1983. pap. text ed. 2.50 (0-943704-03-0) Arrants & Assoc.

Arrants, Dennis, jt. illus. see Arrants, Cheryl.

Arrendondo, Francisco. Fascinating World of Birds. Julivert, Maria A. LC 92-5684. (gr. 4-7). 1992. pap. 7.95 (0-8120-1378-6) Barron.

Arridondo, F. El Fascinante Mundo: Las Serpientes, The Fascinating World of Snakes. Julivert, Maria A. Marcel Socias Studio Staff, ed. (gr. 3-7). Date not set. pap. 7.95 (0-8120-1799-4) Barron.
—El Fascinante Mundo, The Fascinating World: Las Ranas y Los Sapos, Of Frogs & Toads. Julivert, Maria A. Marcel Socias Studio Staff, ed. 32p. (gr. 3-7). Date not set. pap. 7.95 (0-8120-1795-1) Barron.

Arrigo, Joseph. The Louisiana Plantation Coloring Book. Dartez, Cecilia C. 32p. (Orig.). (ps-4). 1985. pap. 2.95 (0-88289-473-0) Pelican.

Arrington, Aileen. Close to Home: A Story of the Polio Epidemic. Weaver, Lydia. LC 92-25937. 64p. (gr. 2-6). 1993. PLB 12.99 (0-670-84511-6) Viking Child Bks.

Arrowood, Clinton. Alligators & Music. Elliott, Donald. LC 84-13862. (gr. 8). 1984. (Pub. by Gambit); pap. 8.95 (0-87645-118-0, Pub. by Gambit) Harvard Common Pr.
—Frogs & Ballet. Elliott, Donald. LC 78-19566. (gr. 1 up). 1979. smythe sewn 12.95 (0-87645-099-0, Pub. by Gambit); pap. 8.95 (0-87645-119-9) Harvard Common Pr.
—Young Brer Rabbit & Other Trickster Tales from the Americas. Weiss, Jaqueline S. Pellowski, Anne, intro. by. 80p. (gr. 3-7). 1985. 14.95 (0-88045-037-1) Stemmer Hse.

Arroyo, John. The Cure: A World in Distress. Fifth Period LEAP & Honors English Classes. Hames, Karen & Martin, Peggy, eds. 142p. (Orig.). (gr. 6-8). 1990. pap. 3.00 (0-9623607-9-1) BRAT Pubns.

Art, Eve. Lebanon: Bridge between East & West. Abood, Doris M. Thomas, Danny, intro. by. LC 73-84565. 40p. (gr. 5-10). 1973. 3.50 (0-913228-07-9) Dillon-Liederbach.

Artell, Mike. T'was the Night Before Christmas. LC 93-37281. 1994. write for info. (0-689-71801-2, Aladdin) Macmillan Child Grp.
—Who Said Moo? Artell, Mike. 12p. (ps-k). 1994. pap. 7.95 (0-689-71811-X, Aladdin) Macmillan Child Grp.

Arthur, James & Morrow, Gray. Robert E. Lee: Young Confederate. Monsell, Helen A. LC 86-10736. 192p. (gr. 2-6). 1986. pap. 3.95 (0-02-042020-X, Aladdin) Macmillan Child Grp.

Arthur, John. Cheeky Rubs. Stiles, Barbara J. LC 89-164732. 20p. (ps-5). 1989. text ed. 12.95 (0-9622057-1-0); pap. text ed. 7.95 (0-9622057-0-2) Manzanita Canyon.

Arthur, Lorraine. Anytime Parties for Children. Reid, Mary. 80p. (gr. 1-5). 1987. wkbk. 5.99 (0-87403-290-3, 2802) Standard Pub.

Artzybasheff, Boris. Gay-Neck: The Story of a Pigeon. Mukerji, Dhan G. LC 68-13419. 192p. (gr. 4 up). 1968. 15.00 (0-525-30400-2, DCB) Dutton Child Bks.

Aruego, Jose. Leo the Late Bloomer. Reissue. ed. Kraus, Robert. LC 70-159154. 32p. (gr. k-3). 1971. 15.00 (0-87807-042-7, Crowell Jr Bks); PLB 14.89 (0-87807-043-5) HarpC Child Bks.
—Leo the Late Bloomer. Krauss, Robert. LC 80-12511. (ps). 1987. pap. 5.95 (0-671-66271-6, S&S BFYR) S&S Trade.
—Leo the Late Bloomer. Kraus, Robert. LC 70-159154. 32p. (gr. k-3). 1994. pap. 4.95 (0-06-443348-X, Trophy) HarpC Child Bks.
—Look What I Can Do! Aruego, Jose. LC 87-21743. 32p. (ps-1). 1988. pap. 3.95 (0-689-71205-7, Aladdin) Macmillan Child Grp.
—Whose Mouse Are You? Kraus, Robert. LC 70-89931. 32p. (ps-k). 1986. pap. 4.95 (0-689-71142-5, Aladdin) Macmillan Child Grp.
—Whose Mouse Are You? Kraus, Robert. LC 70-89931. 32p. (ps-k). 1970. RSBE 13.95 (0-02-751190-1, Macmillan Child Bk) Macmillan Child Grp.

Aruego, Jose & Dewey, Ariane. Alligator Arrived with Apples: A Potluck Alphabet Feast. Dragonwagon, Crescent. LC 86-37. 40p. (gr. k-3). 1987. RSBE 15.95 (0-02-733090-7, Macmillan Child Bk) Macmillan Child Grp.
—Alligator Arrived with Apples: A Potluck Alphabet Feast. Dragonwagon, Crescent. LC 91-38490. 40p. (gr. k-3). 1992. pap. 4.95 (0-689-71613-3, Aladdin) Macmillan Child Grp.
—Alligators & Others All Year Long! A Book of Months. Dragonwagon, Crescent. LC 91-2831. 32p. (ps-3). 1993. RSBE 14.95 (0-02-733091-5, Macmillan Child Bk) Macmillan Child Grp.
—Another Mouse to Feed. Kraus, Robert. LC 78-21259. 32p. (gr. 4 up). 1987. P-H.
—Another Mouse to Feed. Kraus, Robert. 32p. (ps-1). 1988. pap. 6.95 bk. & cassette (0-671-67146-4, S&S BFYR) S&S Trade.
—Another Mouse to Feed. Kraus, Robert. LC 78-21259. (ps). 1987. pap. 13.95 jacketed (0-671-66522-7, S&S BFYR); pap. 5.95 (0-671-66688-6, S&S BFYR) S&S Trade.
—Boris Bad Enough. Kraus, Robert. 32p. (ps-3). 1988. pap. 12.95 jacketed (0-671-66894-3, S&S BFYR); pap. 5.95 (0-671-66895-1, S&S BFYR) S&S Trade.
—The Chick & the Duckling. Ginsburg, Mirra. Suteyev, V., tr. from RUS. LC 74-188773. 32p. (ps-1). 1972. RSBE 14.95 (0-02-735940-9, Macmillan Child Bk) Macmillan Child Grp.
—The Chick & the Duckling. Ginsburg, Mirra. 32p. (ps-1). 1988. pap. 4.95 (0-689-71226-X, Aladdin) Macmillan Child Grp.
—Dance Away! Shannon, George. LC 81-6391. 32p. (gr. k-3). 1982. 13.95 (0-688-00838-0); PLB 13.88 (0-688-00839-9) Greenwillow.
—Dance Away. Shannon, George. LC 81-6391. 32p. (ps-3). 1991. pap. 3.95 (0-688-10483-5, Mulberry) Morrow.
—Five Little Ducks. Raffi. LC 88-3752. 32p. (ps-2). 1992. pap. 3.99 (0-517-58360-7) Crown Bks Yng Read.
—Gregory, the Terrible Eater. Sharmat, Mitchell. LC 79-19172. 32p. (gr. k-3). 1980. RSBE 14.95 (0-02-782250-8, Four Winds) Macmillan Child Grp.
—Gregory, the Terrible Eater. Sharmat, Mitchell. 32p. (gr. k-3). 1984. pap. 3.95 (0-590-43350-4) Scholastic Inc.
—Herman the Helper. Kraus, Robert. LC 73-9319. (ps). 1987. pap. 12.95 jacketed (0-671-66887-0, S&S BFYR); pap. 5.95 (0-671-66270-8, S&S BFYR) S&S Trade.
—Lizard's Song. Shannon, George. LC 80-21432. 32p. (gr. k-3). 1981. 14.95 (0-688-80310-5); PLB 14.88 (0-688-84310-7) Greenwillow.
—Lizard's Song. Marcuse, Aida, tr. from ENG. (SPA.). 32p. (ps up). 1994. pap. 3.95 (0-688-13201-4, Mulberry) Morrow.
—Merry-Go-Round: Four Stories. Ginsburg, Mirra. LC 90-30439. 48p. 1992. 15.00 (0-688-09256-X); PLB 14.93 (0-688-09257-8) Greenwillow.
—Mert the Blurt. Kraus, Robert. LC 80-1458. 32p. (gr. 4 up). 1987. 10.95 (0-13-577164-1) P-H.
—Mert the Blurt. Krauss, Robert. LC 80-14508. (ps). 1987. pap. 10.95 jacketed (0-671-66537-5, S&S BFYR); (S&S BFYR) S&S Trade.
—Milton the Early Riser. Krauss, Robert. LC 81-9460. (ps). 1987. pap. 13.95 jacketed (0-671-66272-4, S&S BFYR); pap. 5.95 (0-671-66911-7, S&S BFYR) S&S Trade.
—Mitchell Is Moving. Sharmat, Marjorie W. LC 85-47782. 48p. (gr. 1-4). 1985. pap. 3.95 (0-02-045260-8, Aladdin) Macmillan Child Grp.
—Mitchell Is Moving. Sharmat, Marjorie W. LC 78-6816. 48p. (gr. 1-4). 1978. RSBE 11.95 (0-02-782410-1, Macmillan Child Bk) Macmillan Child Grp.
—Mushroom in the Rain. Ginsburg, Mirra. LC 72-92438. 32p. (ps-1). 1987. RSBE 13.95 (0-02-736241-8, Macmillan Child Bk) Macmillan Child Grp.
—Musical Max. Kraus, Robert. LC 89-77079. 40p. 1990. pap. 13.95 jacketed (0-671-68681-X, Little Simon) S&S Trade.
—Noel the Coward. Kraus, Robert. 32p. (ps-3). 1988. pap. 12.95 jacketed (0-671-66845-5, S&S BFYR); pap. 5.95 (0-671-66846-3, S&S BFYR) S&S Trade.
—One Duck, Another Duck. Pomerantz, Charlotte. LC 83-20767. 24p. (ps-1). 1984. 10.25 (0-688-03744-5); PLB 13.93 (0-688-03745-3) Greenwillow.
—Owliver. Kraus, Robert. LC 80-13664. (ps). 1987. pap. 13.95 jacketed (0-671-66523-5, S&S BFYR) S&S Trade.
—Pork & Beans: Play Date. Stine, Jovial Bob. (ps-2). 1989. pap. 12.95 (0-590-41579-4) Scholastic Inc.
—The Surprise. Shannon, George. LC 83-1434. 32p. (gr. k-3). 1983. 13.95 (0-688-02313-4) Greenwillow.
—Two Greedy Bears: Adapted from a Hungarian Folk Tale. Ginsburg, Mirra. LC 76-8819. 32p. (ps-2). 1976. RSBE 13.95 (0-02-736450-X, Macmillan Child Bk) Macmillan Child Grp.
—Where Are You Going, Little Mouse? Kraus, Robert. LC 84-25868. 32p. (ps-1). 1986. 15.00 (0-688-04294-5); PLB 14.93 (0-688-04295-3) Greenwillow.
—Where Does the Sun Go at Night? Ginsburg, Mirra. LC 79-16151. 32p. (gr. k-3). 1980. 10.95 (0-688-80245-1); PLB 10.88 (0-688-84245-3) Greenwillow.

—Where Does the Sun Go at Night? Ginsburg, Mirra. LC 79-16151. 32p. (ps-3). 1987. pap. 4.95 (0-688-07041-8, Mulberry) Morrow.

Arvego, Jose & Dewey, Ariane. Lizard's Song. Shannon, George. LC 80-21432. 32p. (ps up). 1992. pap. 3.95 (0-688-11516-0, Mulberry) Morrow.

—Three Friends. Kraus, Robert. (gr. k-3). 1975. (Dutton); pap. 2.95 (0-525-62346-9) NAL-Dutton.

Aryai, Sia, photos by. Baby Bright Board Books: ABC's. Aryai, Sia. 1993. 5.95 (1-56565-049-2) Lowell Hse.

—Baby Bright Board Books: Colors. Aryai, Sia. 1993. 5.95 (1-56565-050-6) Lowell Hse.

—Baby Bright Board Books: Shapes. Aryai, Sia. 1993. 5.95 (1-56565-051-4) Lowell Hse.

Asala, Jason. The Green Knight: A Tale of Ancient Britain - Arthurian Romance about Sir Gawain & the Green Knight. Asala, Joanne. 64p. (gr. 3). 1992. pap. 6.95 (1-880954-00-1) Kalevala Bks.

Asare, Meshack. Bury My Bones But Keep My Words: African Tales for Retelling. Fairman, Tony. 192p. 1993. 15.95 (0-8050-2333-X, Bks Young Read) H Holt & Co.

Asch, Connie. Brenda the Cow & the Little White Hen. Swan, Walter. Swan, Deloris, ed. 16p. (Orig.). (gr. 2-3). 1989. pap. 1.50 (0-927176-02-5) Swan Enterp.

—The Little Green Tractor. Swan, Walter. Swan, Deloris, ed. 16p. (Orig.). (gr. 2-4). 1989. pap. 1.50 (0-927176-04-1) Swan Enterp.

—Stick 'em up! I've Got You Covered! Swan, Walter. Swan, Deloris, ed. 16p. (Orig.). (ps-8). 1989. pap. 1.50 (0-927176-03-3) Swan Enterp.

—Teeny Weeny. Swan, Walter. Swan, Deloris, ed. 16p. (Orig.). (ps). 1989. pap. 1.50 (0-927176-01-7) Swan Enterp.

Asch, Connie, et al. Adventure Stories. Swan, Walter. Swan, Deloris, ed. 252p. (gr. k-5). 1991. 19.95 (0-927176-08-4) Swan Enterp.

Asch, Frank. Bear Shadow. Asch, Frank. LC 82-18250. 32p. (ps-2). 1988. pap. 14.00 jacketed (0-671-66279-1, S&S BFYR); pap. 4.95 (0-671-66866-8, S&S BFYR) S&S Trade.

—Bear's Bargain. Asch, Frank. LC 85-6355. (ps-2). 1989. pap. 12.95 jacketed (0-671-66690-8, S&S BFYR); pap. 4.95 (0-671-67838-8, S&S BFYR) S&S Trade.

—Bread & Honey. Asch, Frank. LC 81-16893. 48p. (ps-3). 1982. 5.95 (0-8193-1077-8); PLB 5.95 (0-8193-1078-6) Parents.

—The Flower Faerie. Asch, Frank & Vagin, Vladimir. Vagin, Vladimir. LC 91-33763. 32p. (gr. 1-4). 1993. 14.95 (0-590-45493-5) Scholastic Inc.

—Goodbye House. Asch, Frank. LC 85-19263. (ps-2). 1989. pap. 12.95 jacketed (0-671-67054-9, Little Simon); pap. 4.95 (0-671-67927-9, Little Simon) S&S Trade.

—Goodnight, Horsey. Asch, Frank. LC 81-7332. 32p. (ps up). 1989. pap. 12.95 jacketed (0-671-66277-5, Little Simon); pap. 4.95 (0-671-66278-3, Little Simon) S&S Trade.

—Happy Birthday Moon. Asch, Frank. 32p. (ps-1). 1988. Bk. & cassette. pap. 7.95 (0-671-67145-6, Little Simon) S&S Trade.

—The Last Puppy. Asch, Frank. LC 80-215. 32p. (ps up). 1989. pap. 14.00 (0-671-66276-7, S&S BFYR); pap. 4.95 (0-671-66687-8, S&S BFYR) S&S Trade.

—Mooncake. Asch, Frank. 32p. 1986. pap. 4.95 (0-671-66451-4) S&S Trade.

—Moondance. Asch, Frank. LC 92-12358. 32p. (gr. k-3). 1993. 12.95 (0-590-45487-0) Scholastic Inc.

—Oats & Wild Apples. Asch, Frank. LC 87-17742. 32p. (ps-3). 1988. reinforced bdg. 14.95 (0-8234-0677-6) Holiday.

—Pearl's Pirates. Asch, Frank. LC 86-19621. 160p. (gr. k-3). 1987. pap. 13.95 (0-385-29546-4) Delacorte.

—Pearl's Promise. Asch, Frank. LC 83-17153. 160p. (gr. 4-6). 1984. PLB 12.95 (0-385-29321-6); pap. 12.95 (0-385-29325-9) Delacorte.

—Popcorn. Asch, Frank. LC 79-216. 48p. (ps-3). 1979. 5.95 (0-8193-1001-8); lib. bdg. 5.95 (0-8193-1002-6) Parents.

—Popcorn. Asch, Frank. 48p. (gr. 3-7). 1990. pap. 2.95 (0-448-04333-5, G&D) Putnam Pub Group.

—Sand Cake. Asch, Frank. LC 78-11183. 48p. (ps-3). 1979. 5.95 (0-8193-0985-0); lib. bdg. 5.95 (0-8193-0986-9) Parents.

—Sand Cake. Asch, Frank. 48p. (ps-2). 1990. pap. 2.95 (0-448-04341-6, G&D) Putnam Pub Group.

—Skyfire. Asch, Frank. LC 88-3193. 32p. (ps-2). 1988. (Little Simon); pap. 4.95 (0-671-66861-7, Little Simon) S&S Trade.

Asch, Frank & Vladimir, Vagin. Here Comes the Cat! Asch, Frank & Vagin, Vladimir. 1991. pap. 3.95 (0-590-41854-8) Scholastic Inc.

Asch, Frank, jt. illus. see Vagin, Vladimir.

Aschenbrenner, Gerald. Jack, the Seal, & the Sea. Aschenbrenner, Gerald. Fink, Joanne, adapted by. 30p. (gr. 2-5). 1988. PLB 14.98 (0-382-09985-0); PLB 11.24s.p. (0-685-46995-6); pap. 6.95 (0-382-09986-9); pap. 5.21s.p. (0-685-46996-4) Silver Burdett Pr.

Ascherman, Herbert, Jr., photos by. Over the Falls: A Child's Guide to Chagrin Falls. Cockley, David H. 24p. (Orig.). (gr. 1-6). 1981. pap. 2.25 (0-940900-00-9) Aschley Pr.

Aschwanden, Peter, jt. illus. see Gadbois, Nick.

Asensio, Agusti. Don Gil y el Paraguas Magico: Sir Gil & the Magic Umbrella. Company, Merce. Serra, Aurora M., tr. from GER. (SPA.). 26p. (gr. 1-4). 1990. 13.95 (968-6465-03-0) Hispanic Bk Dist.

—Sleeping Beauty: A Classic Tale. Perrault, Charles. Jose, Eduard, adapted by. Moncure, Jane B., tr. from SPA. LC 88-35212. 32p. (gr. 1-4). 1988. PLB 19.95 (0-89565-478-4); PLB 13.95s.p. (0-685-56040-6) Childs World.

Asensio, Augusti. Cinderella: A Classic Tale. Grimm, Jacob & Grimm, Wilhelm K. Jose, Eduard, adapted by. Moncure, Jane B., tr. from SPA. LC 88-35317. 32p. (gr. 1-4). 1988. PLB 19.95 (0-89565-483-0); PLB 13.95s.p. (0-685-56029-5) Childs World.

—Hansel & Gretel: A Classic Tale. Grimm, Jacob & Grimm, Wilhelm K. Jose, Eduard, adapted by. Riehecky, Janet, tr. LC 88-35212. 32p. (gr. 1-4). 1988. PLB 19.95 (0-89565-480-6); PLB 13.95s.p. (0-685-56039-2) Childs World.

—The Old Sandman: A Classic Tale. Jose, Eduard, adapted by. Riehecky, Janet, tr. LC 88-36793. 32p. (gr. 1-4). 1988. PLB 19.95 (0-89565-461-X); PLB 13.95s.p. (0-685-56042-2) Childs World.

—Pinocchio: A Classic Tale. Collodi, Carlo. Jose, Eduard, adapted by. Moncure, Jane B., tr. from SPA. LC 88-35308. 32p. 1988. PLB 19.95 (0-89565-458-X); PLB 13.95s.p. (0-685-56023-6) Childs World.

—Puss in Boots: A Classic Tale. Perrault, Charles. Jose, Eduard, adapted by. Suire, Diane D., tr. LC 88-35316. 32p. (gr. 1-4). 1988. PLB 19.95 (0-89565-482-2); PLB 13.95s.p. (0-685-56028-7) Childs World.

—Rumpelstiltskin: A Classic Tale. Grimm, Jacob & Grimm, Wilhelm K. Moncure, Jane B., tr. from SPA. LC 88-35315. 32p. (gr. 1-4). 1988. PLB 19.95 (0-89565-463-6); PLB 13.95s.p. (0-685-56025-2) Childs World.

—Snow White & the Seven Dwarfs: A Classic Tale. Jose, Eduard, adapted by. McDonnell, Janet, tr. LC 88-35210. 32p. (gr. 1-4). 1988. PLB 19.95 (0-89565-479-2); PLB 13.95s.p. (0-685-56035-X) Childs World.

—The Steadfast Tin Soldier: A Classic Tale. Andersen, Hans Christian. Jose, Eduard, adapted by. Moncure, Jane B., tr. LC 88-35207. 32p. (gr. 1-4). 1988. PLB 19.95 (0-89565-468-7); PLB 13.95s.p. (0-685-56024-4) Childs World.

—The Three Little Pigs: A Classic Tale. Jose, Eduard, adapted by. McDonnell, Janet, tr. LC 88-35314. 32p. (gr. 1-4). 1988. PLB 19.95 (0-89565-459-8); PLB 13.95s.p. (0-685-58429-1) Childs World.

—The Ugly Duckling: A Classic Tale. Andersen, Hans Christian. Jose, Eduard, adapted by. McDonnell, Janet, tr. LC 88-36795. 32p. (gr. 1-4). 1988. PLB 19.95 (0-89565-474-1); PLB 13.95s.p. (0-685-56044-9) Childs World.

—The Vain Little Mouse: A Classic Tale. Jose, Eduard, adapted by. Riehecky, Janet, tr. LC 88-35214. 32p. (gr. 1-4). 1988. PLB 19.95 (0-89565-464-4); PLB 13.95s.p. (0-685-56021-X) Childs World.

Ashabranner, Jennifer. A Memorial for Mr. Lincoln. Ashabranner, Brent. 128p. (gr. 5-9). 1992. 15.95 (0-399-22273-1, Putnam) Putnam Pub Group.

Ashabranner, Jennifer, photos by. Always to Remember: The Story of the Vietnam Veterans Memorial. Ashabranner, Brent. 40p. (gr. 6 up). 1988. pap. 14.95 (0-399-22031-3, Putnam) Putnam Pub Group.

—Crazy about German Shepherds. Ashabranner, Brent. LC 90-1303. 96p. (gr. 5 up). 1990. 14.95 (0-525-65032-6, Cobblehill Bks) Dutton Child Bks.

—Still a Nation of Immigrants. Ashabranner, Brent. LC 92-44335. 144p. (gr. 5 up). 1993. 15.99 (0-525-65130-6, Cobblehill Bks) Dutton Child Bks.

Ashby, David. Fishing. Whieldon, Tony. LC 93-22781. 1994. 13.00 (0-679-83442-7); lib. bdg. 13.99 (0-679-93442-1) Random.

Ashforth, Camilla. Calamity. Ashforth, Camilla. LC 92-54956. 32p. (ps up). 1993. 15.95 (1-56402-252-8) Candlewick Pr.

—Horatio's Bed. Ashforth, Camilla. LC 91-58737. 32p. (ps up). 1992. 15.95 (1-56402-057-6) Candlewick Pr.

—Monkey Tricks. Ashforth, Camilla. LC 92-53013. 32p. (ps-3). 1993. 15.95 (1-56402-170-X) Candlewick Pr.

Ashley, Bryan. Lion & the Ostrich Chicks & Other African Folk Tales. Bryan, Ashley. LC 86-3349. 96p. (gr. 2-6). 1986. SBE 13.95 (0-689-31311-X, Atheneum Child Bk) Macmillan Child Grp.

Ashley, Yvonne. Try Again, Sally Jane. Diestel-Feddersen, Mary. LC 86-42810. 30p. (gr. 2-3). 1987. PLB 18.60 (1-55532-150-X) Gareth Stevens Inc.

Ashman, Iain. Chemistry. Chisholm, J. & Lynnington, M. 48p. (gr. 6 up). 1983. lib. bdg. 13.96 (0-88110-151-6); pap. 6.95 (0-86020-709-9) EDC.

—Human Body. Graham, Meredith & Lissauer, T. 32p. (gr. 6 up). 1983. lib. bdg. 13.96 (0-88110-150-8); pap. 6.95 (0-86020-747-1) EDC.

—Information Revolution. Myring, L. & Graham, I. 48p. (gr. 6 up). 1983. lib. bdg. 13.96 (0-88110-153-2); pap. 6.95 (0-86020-726-9) EDC.

Ashman, Iain, jt. illus. see McCaig, Rob.

Ashmead, Hal. The Phantom Coach. Edwards, Amelia B. Richardson, I. M., adapted by. LC 81-19862. 32p. (gr. 5-10). 1982. PLB 10.79 (0-89375-634-2); pap. text ed. 2.95 (0-89375-635-0) Troll Assocs.

—The Signalman. Dickens, Charles. Richardson, I. M., adapted by. LC 81-19819. 32p. (gr. 5-10). 1982. PLB 10.79 (0-89375-630-X); pap. text ed. 2.95 (0-89375-631-8) Troll Assocs.

Ashton, Frederick, jt. illus. see Clarke, Mary.

Ashwill, Betty. The Runaways. Ashwill, Beverley. LC 87-72441. 48p. (gr. 4-8). 1988. 12.95 (0-941381-02-1); pap. 5.95 (0-941381-01-3) BJO Enterprises.

Ashwill, Betty J. The Blue-Eyed Ninja Warrior. Ashwill, Beverley. LC 90-83313. 43p. (gr. 3-9). 1990. pap. 5.98 (0-941381-05-6) BJO Enterprises.

—Charley the Fearless Zoo Keeper. Ashwill, Beverly. LC 90-83311. 20p. (ps-3). 1990. pap. 3.98 (0-941381-07-2) BJO Enterprises.

—Heather & the New Baby. Ashwill, Beverley B. LC 88-63168. 23p. (Orig.). (ps-5). 1988. pap. 3.98 (0-941381-03-X) BJO Enterprises.

—The Invisible Dawn. Ashwill, Beverly. LC 90-83310. 24p. (ps-5). 1990. pap. 3.98 (0-685-37787-3) BJO Enterprises.

—Jeffrey, the Littlest Pig. Ashwill, Beverly. LC 90-83312. 24p. (ps-3). 1990. pap. 3.98 (0-941381-06-4) BJO Enterprises.

—Marlina & McGee. Ashwill, Beverley. LC 86-73031. 32p. (ps-3). 1987. pap. 5.95 (0-941381-00-5) BJO Enterprises.

—Too Little, Too Big, Just Right. Ashwill, Beverley. LC 90-83314. 18p. (ps-3). 1990. pap. 3.98 (0-941381-04-8) BJO Enterprises.

Aska, Warabe. Who Hides in the Park. Aska, Warabe. (ENG, FRE, JPN & CHI.). 36p. (gr. k up). 1990. pap. 7.95 (0-88776-244-1) Tundra Bks.

Askew, Rebecca T. The Wedding of G. Washington Bear. Pittman, Rachel N. 42p. (Orig.). (ps-5). 1986. pap. 6.95 (0-9615382-1-X) Pittman Pub.

Asklin, William O. Commander the Gander. McKelvey, David. LC 84-72455. 48p. (gr. 4-6). 1984. lib. bdg. 10.95 (0-931722-31-4); pap. 3.95 (0-931722-30-6) Corona Pub.

Asmann, Lynn. Baby Basics. Asmann, Lynn & Sprague, Jane. (gr. 5 up). 1980. pap. 4.95 (0-938416-00-6) BCS Educ Aids.

Assel, Steven. World War II Resistance Stories. Prager, Arthur & Prager, Emily. 96p. (gr. 7 up). 1980. pap. 2.25 (0-440-99800-X, LFL) Dell.

Astley-Maberly, C. T. The Hunter Is Death. Bulpin, Tom V. 348p. (gr. 10 up). 1987. Repr. of 1962 ed. 30.00 (0-940143-08-9) Safari Pr.

Astrom, Lena. Easy Art. Smith, Mary & Robison, Phyllis. 48p. (gr. k-3). 1982. wkbk. 5.95 (1-55734-004-8) Tchr Create Mat.

Astrop, John. John Astrop's Ghastly Games. Astrop, John. 24p. (ps-3). 1983. pop-up bk. 5.95 (0-385-29307-0) Delacorte.

Asuka, Ken. Smile for Toto. Barnes, Jill & Asuka, Ken. Rubin, Caroline, ed. Japan Foreign Rights Centre Staff, tr. from JPN. LC 90-37747. 32p. (gr. k-4). 1990. PLB 14.60 (0-944483-87-9) Garrett Ed Corp.

—Toto in Trouble. Barnes, Jill & Asuka, Ken. Rubin, Caroline, ed. Japan Foreign Rights Centre Staff, tr. from JPN. LC 90-37749. 32p. (gr. k-4). 1990. PLB 14.60 (0-944483-86-0) Garrett Ed Corp.

—Toto Visits Mystic Mountain. Asuka, Ken. Young, Richard Y., ed. Kaisei-sha, tr. LC 89-11754. 32p. (gr. 1-3). 1989. PLB 14.60 (0-944483-46-1) Garrett Ed Corp.

Atcheson, Marguerite. Copito: The Christmas Chihuahua. Nelson-Erichsen, Jean. Davenport, May, intro. by. LC 82-72080. 80p. (gr. k-5). 1982. pap. 3.50x (0-943864-07-0) Davenport.

Atherton, Lisa. Wally the Wordworm. Fadiman, Clifton. LC 83-9181. (gr. 3 up). 1984. 12.95 (0-88045-038-X); cassette & bk. 21.90 (0-88045-101-7); cassette only 8.95 (0-88045-098-3) Stemmer Hse.

Atkins, Delores E. Thirteen Alabama Ghosts & Jeffrey. Windham, Kathryn T. & Figh, Margaret G. LC 71-94443. 128p. (gr. 6 up). 1987. pap. 9.50t (0-8173-0376-6) U of Ala Pr.

Atkins, Linda. Body Systems. Conway, Lorraine. 64p. (gr. 5 up). 1984. wkbk. 7.95 (0-86653-153-X, GA 552) Good Apple.

Atkinson, Allen. Babes in Toyland. Howe, James. 79p. (gr. 3-7). 1988. pap. 9.95 (0-15-200410-6) HarBrace.

—The Cat & the Fiddle & Other Favorites. 64p. (Orig.). (gr. k). 1985. pap. 2.50 (0-553-15321-8) Bantam.

—Cecily Parsley's Nursery Rhymes. Potter, Beatrix. 1983. pap. 2.25 (0-553-15229-7) Bantam.

—Humpty Dumpty & Other Favorites. 64p. (Orig.). (gr. k). 1985. pap. 2.50 (0-553-15340-4) Bantam.

—Jack & Jill & Other Favorites. 64p. (Orig.). 1986. pap. 2.50 (0-553-15354-4) Bantam.

—Little Bo-Peep & Other Favorites. 64p. (Orig.). 1986. pap. 2.50 (0-553-15353-6) Bantam.

—Little Boy Blue & Other Favorites. 64p. (Orig.). (gr. k). 1985. pap. 2.50 (0-553-15320-X) Bantam.

—Mary Had a Little Lamb & Other Favorites. (Orig.). (gr. k). 1985. pap. 2.50 (0-553-15319-6) Bantam.

—Mystery of the Windy Meadow. Michaels, Ski. LC 85-14019. 48p. (Orig.). (gr. 1-3). 1986. PLB 10.59 (0-8167-0630-1); pap. text ed. 3.50 (0-8167-0631-X) Troll Assocs.

—Peter & the Wolf. Eastman, David. LC 87-11275. 32p. (gr. k-3). 1988. PLB 9.79 (0-8167-1057-0); pap. text ed. 1.95 (0-8167-1058-9) Troll Assocs.

—Simple Simon & Other Favorites (Mother Goose) 64p. (Orig.). 1986. pap. 2.50 (0-553-15322-6) Bantam.

—The Tailor of Gloucester. Potter, Beatrix. 1984. pap. 2.25 (0-553-15220-3) Bantam.

—The Tale of Benjamin Bunny. Potter, Beatrix. 64p. 1984. pap. 2.25 (0-553-15203-3) Bantam.

—The Tale of Mr. Jeremy Fisher. Potter, Beatrix. 1983. pap. 2.25 (0-553-15221-1) Bantam.

—The Tale of Mrs. Tiggy-Winkle. Potter, Beatrix. 1984. pap. 2.25 (0-553-15204-1) Bantam.

—The Tale of Peter Rabbit. Potter, Beatrix. 64p. (Orig.). 1984. pap. 2.50 (0-553-15470-2) Bantam.

—The Tale of Squirrel Nutkin. Potter, Beatrix. 64p. 1984. pap. 2.25 (0-553-15205-X) Bantam.

—The Tale of Tom Kitten. Potter, Beatrix. 1983. pap. 2.25 (0-553-15224-6) Bantam.

Atkinson, Mary. A Bird's-Eye View of California. Hoyt, George & Hoyt, Doris. 48p. (Orig.). (gr. k-4). 1989. pap. 4.95 (0-9622364-4-6) Adona Pub.

Atkinson, Mike. The Age of Dinosaurs. Langley, Glynis. 64p. (gr. k-5). 1992. pap. 6.95 (0-8249-8537-0, Ideals Child) Hambleton-Hill.

—The Age of Steam. Rutland, Jonathan. LC 87-4788. 24p. (gr. 2-5). 1987. pap. 2.95 (0-394-89216-X, Random Juv) Random Bks Yng Read.

—Built to Speed. Rutland, Jonathan. LC 87-4790. 24p. (gr. 2-5). 1987. lib. bdg. 5.99 (0-394-99215-6); (Random Juv) Random Bks Yng Read.

—The Human Body. Western, Joan & Wilson, Ron. LC 90-38929. 96p. (gr. 3-6). 1991. PLB 14.89 (0-8167-2234-X); pap. text ed. 6.95 (0-8167-2235-8) Troll Assocs.

Atkinson, Mike & Francis, John. Midnight Animals. Tunney, Christopher. LC 87-4792. 24p. (gr. 2-5). 1987. pap. 2.95 (0-394-89213-5, Random Juv) Random Bks Yng Read.

Attalides, Stephanos. Journey into Space: Adventure Box IV. Attalides, Stephanos. 12p. (ps up). 1988. 4.95 (0-694-00266-6) HarpC Child Bks.

Attebury, Kevan J. SOS: Save Our Spines: A Backschool for Kids. rev. ed. Zech, Cindy O. 95p. (gr. 3-6). Date not set. wkbk. 10.95 (0-9638765-1-1); tchr's. ed. 18.95 (0-9638765-0-3) Prevent Educ.

Attinello, Lauren. Kermit's Mixed-up Message. Barkan, Joanne. 32p. (Orig.). (gr. 1-4). 1987. pap. 2.75 (0-590-44011-X) Scholastic Inc.

—Muppet Babies & the Magic Garden. Gikow, Louise. 26p. (ps up). 1987. 12.95 (1-55578-608-1) Worlds Wonder.

Atwell, Debby. The Day Hans Got His Way. Atwell, David L. LC 91-43945. 32p. (ps-3). 1992. 14.45 (0-395-58772-7) HM.

Aubrey, Meg K. Andrew's Own Place. Riecken, Nancy. LC 92-22953. 1993. 14.95 (0-395-64723-1) HM.

—Grandmother's Chair. Scott, Ann H. 32p. (ps-1). 1990. 13.45 (0-395-52001-0, Clarion Bks) HM.

Auch, Mary J. Bird Dogs Can't Fly. Auch, Mary J. LC 93-2746. (ps-3). 1993. reinforced bdg. 15.95 (0-8234-1050-1) Holiday.

—The Easter Egg Farm. Auch, Mary J. LC 91-15681. 32p. (ps-3). 1992. reinforced bdg. 15.95 (0-8234-0917-1) Holiday.

Auclair, Joan. Big Talk. rev. ed. Schlein, Miriam. LC 89-35343. 32p. (ps-1). 1990. RSBE 13.95 (0-02-781231-6, Bradbury Pr) Macmillan Child Grp.

—The Dancer. Burstein, Fred. LC 91-41429. 40p. (ps-3). 1993. RSBE 14.95 (0-02-715625-7, Bradbury Pr) Macmillan Child Grp.

Audette, Anna H. Click, Rumble, Roar: Poems about Machines. Hopkins, Lee B., ed. LC 86-47746. 48p. (gr. 2-6). 1987. (Crowell Jr Bks); PLB 13.89 (0-690-04589-1, Crowell Jr Bks) HarpC Child Bks.

Augenstine, Erin. Little Match Girl. Andersen, Hans Christian. 32p. (ps-3). 1992. 6.95 (0-8362-4931-3) Andrews & McMeel.

Augestine, Erin. Snow White. Grimm, Jacob & Grimm, Wilhelm K. Greenway, Jennifer, retold by. 1991. 6.95 (0-8362-4906-2) Andrews & McMeel.

August, Louise. In the Month of Kislev: A Story for Hanukkah. Jaffe, Nina. 32p. (ps-3). 1992. 15.00 (0-670-82863-7) Viking Child Bks.

—Sunday Potatoes, Monday Potatoes. Shiefman, Vicky. LC 92-46112. (gr. 3 up). 1994. pap. 14.00 (0-671-86596-X, S&S BFYR) S&S Trade.

Augustine, Victoria C. Conny the Clown. Augustine, Nicholas & Augustine, Victoria C. 32p. (Orig.). 1991. pap. write for info. (1-879783-00-2) Staccato Prodns.

—Little Lady Star. Augustine, Nicholas & Augustine, Victoria C. 32p. 1991. pap. write for info. (1-879783-01-0) Staccato Prodns.

Aulisio, Janet. Beastman of Mars. Smith, Lester W. 64p. (Orig.). 1989. pap. 8.00 (1-55878-022-X) Game Designers.

—The Body Bank. Brinkley, Chad & Barrett, Kevin. 32p. (Orig.). (gr. 12). 1990. pap. 10.00 (1-55806-128-2, 5104) Iron Crown Ent Inc.

—Cloud Captains of Mars. Chadwick, Frank. 64p. (Orig.). 1989. pap. 8.00 (1-55878-043-2) Game Designers.

—Cyber Rogues. Bouton, Steve. Barrett, Kevin, ed. 32p. (Orig.). (gr. 12). 1990. pap. 10.00 (1-55806-125-8, 5103) Iron Crown Ent Inc.

—Deathwatch Program. Smith, Lester W. 64p. (Orig.). 1990. pap. 8.00 (1-55878-051-3) Game Designers.

—More Tales from the Ether. Wiseman, Loren K. 64p. (Orig.). 1989. pap. 8.00 (1-55878-028-9) Game Designers.

—Rotten to the Core. Martin, Julia. 64p. (Orig.). 1990. pap. 8.00 (1-55878-059-9) Game Designers.

Aulisio, Janet, jt. illus. see Gibbons, Lee.

Aulisio, Janet, et al. Death Game 2090. Armintrout, W. G. Barrett, Kevin, ed. 48p. (Orig.). (gr. 12). 1990. pap. 9.00 (1-55806-132-0, 5106) Iron Crown Ent Inc.

Aunt Eeebs. The Dinosaur Debut. rev. ed. Aunt Eeebs. 24p. (ps-2). 1991. pap. write for info. (1-878908-00-6) Rivercrest Indus.

—The Happy Campers. Aunt Eeebs. 24p. (Orig.). (ps-2). 1991. pap. write for info. (1-878908-02-2) Rivercrest Indus.

Aushenker, Michael. Get That Goat! Aushenker, Michael. Thatch, Nancy R., ed. Melton, David, intro. by. LC 90-5930. 26p. (gr. k-4). 1990. PLB 14.95 (0-933849-28-1) Landmark Edns.

Austen, Alice. Alice's World: The Life & Photography of an American Original: Alice Austen, 1866-1952. Novotny, Ann. LC 76-18489. (gr. 7-9). 1976. 22.50 (0-85699-128-7) Chatham Pr.

Austin, Alicia. Solomon Leviathan's Nine Hundred Thirty-First Trip Around the World. Le Guin, Ursula K. 40p. (gr. 7 up). 1983. 70.00 (0-941826-03-1) Cheap St.

Austin, Caroline. The Great Wall of China. Thompson, Brenda & Overbeck, Cynthia. LC 76-22443. 24p. (gr. k-3). 1977. PLB 7.95 (0-8225-1357-9) Lerner Pubns.

Austin, Erwin H. Spooks of the Valley: Ghost Stories for Boys & Girls. Jones, Louis C. 111p. pap. 11.95 (0-910746-10-9, SOT01) Hope Farm.

Austin, Kent, photos by. Acrobatics. Pulley, Maxine. (gr. 3-7). 1981. 8.95 (0-13-003079-1) P-H.

Austin, Virginia. Sailor Bear. Waddell, Martin. LC 91-71822. 32p. (ps up) 1993. 4.95 (1-56402-256-0) Candlewick Pr.

Austin, Virginia & Miller, Virginia. Sailor Bear. Waddell, Martin. LC 91-71822. 32p. (ps). 1992. 14.95 (1-56402-040-1) Candlewick Pr.

Auth, Tony. Kids' Talk. Harris, Linda K. LC 93-16169. 96p. 1993. pap. 6.95 (0-8362-8019-9) Andrews & McMeel.

—The Tree of Here. Potok, Chaim. LC 92-28412. (gr. k-4). 1993. 13.00 (0-679-84010-9); PLB 13.99 (0-679-94010-3) Knopf Bks Yng Read.

Avendano, Dolores. On Halloween Night. Wolff, Ferida & Kozielski, Dolores. LC 93-26859. 1994. write for info. (0-688-12972-2, Tambourine Bks); PLB write for info. (0-688-12973-0, Tambourine Bks) Morrow.

Averill, Esther. Fire Cat. Averill, Esther. LC 60-10234. 64p. (gr. k-3). 1960. PLB 13.89 (0-06-020196-7) HarpC Child Bks.

—Jenny's Birthday Book. Averill, Esther. LC 54-6589. 32p. (gr. k-3). 1954. PLB 14.89 (0-06-020251-3) HarpC Child Bks.

—The School for Cats & Jenny's Moonlight Adventure. Averill, Esther. (gr. k-3). 1990. pap. 2.95 (0-553-15362-5) Bantam.

Avery, Bob. The House That Jack Built. Rawles, Jess, ed. 32p. 1994. 3.95 (1-879384-24-8) Cypress Hse.

Avery, Milton. Paul. Kuskin, Karla. 48p. (gr. k-3). 1994. 16.95 (0-06-023568-3); PLB 16.89 (0-06-023573-X) HarpC Child Bks.

Avishai, Susan. Bat Time. Horowitz, Ruth. LC 90-35772. 32p. (ps-2). 1991. RSBE 13.95 (0-02-744541-0, Four Winds) Macmillan Child Grp.

—My Brother's Bar Mitzvah. Gallant, Janet. LC 90-4879. 32p. (ps-3). 1990. 12.95 (0-929371-20-8); pap. 4.95 (0-929371-21-6) Kar Ben.

—Sophie & the Sidewalk Man. Tolan, Stephanie S. LC 91-17317. 80p. (gr. 2-4). 1992. SBE 12.95 (0-02-789365-0, Four Winds) Macmillan Child Grp.

—A Visit to the Big House. Butterworth, Oliver. LC 92-9787. 48p. (gr. 2-5). 1993. 13.95 (0-395-52805-4) HM.

Axelsen, Jenny, jt. illus. see Axelsen, Stephen.

Axelsen, Stephen. The Old Car. Marshall, Val & Tester, Bronwyn. LC 92-27264. 1993. 3.75 (0-383-03644-5) SRA Schl Grp.

—Troublesome Snout. Hessell, Jenny. LC 92-34274. 1993. 14.00 (0-383-03662-3) SRA Schl Grp.

Axelsen, Stephen & Axelsen, Jenny. Little Sisters. Axelsen, Stephen & Axelsen, Jenny. LC 92-34261. 1993. 4.25 (0-383-03637-2) SRA Schl Grp.

Axeman, Linda. In the Detective's Lab. Baker, Eugene. LC 80-17787. 32p. (gr. 2-5). 1980. PLB 18.50 (0-89565-154-8); PLB 12.95s.p. (0-685-55489-9) Childs World.

Axeman, Lois. Are You Listening? Gambill, Henrietta. LC 85-10349. 32p. (gr. k-2). 1985. PLB 21.35 (0-89565-332-X); PLB 14.95s.p. (0-685-55764-2) Childs World.

—At the Scene of the Crime. Baker, Eugene. LC 80-14091. 32p. (gr. 2-5). 1980. PLB 18.50 (0-89565-151-3); PLB 12.95s.p. (0-685-55474-0) Childs World.

—The Five Senses: Treasures Outside. Moncure, Jane B. LC 90-30635. 32p. (ps-2). 1990. PLB 19.95 (0-89565-575-6); PLB 13.95s.p. (0-685-56191-7) Childs World.

—Fue Carmelita (Katie Did It) McDaniel, Becky B. LC 83-7260. (SPA.). 32p. (ps-2). 1988. PLB 11.93 (0-516-32043-2); pap. 2.95 (0-516-52043-1) Childrens.

—Happy Healthkins. Moncure, Jane B. LC 82-14794. (ps-2). 1982. PLB 19.95 (0-89565-243-9); PLB 13.95s.p. (0-685-55640-9) Childs World.

—Healthkins Help. Moncure, Jane B. LC 82-14713. 32p. (ps-2). 1982. PLB 19.95 (0-89565-242-0); PLB 13.95s.p. (0-685-55642-5) Childs World.

—Holidays. LC 84-9429. (gr. k-3). 1984. PLB 21.35 (0-89565-266-8); PLB 14.95s.p. (0-685-55700-6) Childs World.

—Igual Que Yo (Just Like Me) Neasi, Barbara J. LC 83-23154. (SPA.). 32p. (ps-2). 1988. PLB 11.93 (0-516-32047-5); PLB 30.60 big bk (0-516-59506-7); pap. 2.95 (0-516-52047-4) Childrens.

—Just Like Me. Neasi, Barbara. LC 83-23154. 32p. (ps-2). 1984. lib. bdg. 11.93 (0-516-02047-1); pap. 2.95 (0-516-42047-X) Childrens.

—Katie Can. McDaniel, Becky B. LC 87-5190. 32p. (ps-2). 1987. PLB 11.93 (0-516-02082-X); pap. 2.95 (0-516-42082-8) Childrens.

—Katie Couldn't. McDaniel, Becky B. LC 85-11666. 30p. (gr. 1-2). 1985. PLB 11.93 (0-516-02069-2); pap. 2.95 (0-516-42069-0) Childrens.

—Let's Take a Walk in the City. O'Connor, Karen & Crowdy, Deborah. LC 86-20746. 32p. (ps-2). 1986. PLB 21.35 (0-89565-355-9); PLB 14.95s.p. (0-685-55819-3) Childs World.

—Let's Take a Walk in the Park. Crowdy, Deborah. LC 86-17598. 32p. (ps-2). 1986. PLB 21.35 (0-89565-357-5); PLB 14.95s.p. (0-685-55820-7) Childs World.

—Let's Take a Walk in the Zoo. Moncure, Jane B. LC 86-20744. 32p. (ps-2). 1986. PLB 21.35 (0-89565-356-7); PLB 14.95s.p. (0-685-55821-5) Childs World.

—Let's Take a Walk on the Beach. O'Connor, Karen. LC 86-9551. 32p. (ps-2). 1986. PLB 21.35 (0-89565-354-0); PLB 14.95s.p. (0-685-55822-3) Childs World.

—The Look Book. Moncure, Jane B. LC 82-4517. 32p. (ps-3). 1982. pap. 3.95 (0-516-43251-6) Childrens.

—Master of Disguise. Baker, Eugene. LC 80-11297. 32p. (gr. 2-5). 1980. PLB 18.50 (0-89565-149-1); PLB 12.95s.p. (0-685-55504-6) Childs World.

—Mine, Yours, Ours. Albert, Burton, Jr. LC 77-9408. (ps-1). 1977. PLB 10.95 (0-8075-5148-1) A Whitman.

—Please? Thanks! I'm Sorry. Moncure, Jane B. LC 85-11664. 32p. (gr. k-2). 1985. PLB 21.35 (0-89565-331-1); PLB 14.95s.p. (0-685-55774-X) Childs World.

—Shadowing the Suspect. Baker, Eugene. LC 80-13982. 32p. (gr. 2-5). 1980. PLB 18.50 (0-89565-152-1); PLB 12.95s.p. (0-685-55542-9) Childs World.

—Sounds All Around. Moncure, Jane B. LC 82-4516. 32p. (ps-3). 1982. pap. 3.95 (0-516-43252-4) Childrens.

—Spotting the Fakes-Forgeries & Counterfeits. Baker, Eugene. LC 80-15998. 32p. (gr. 2-5). 1980. PLB 18.50 (0-89565-153-X); PLB 12.95s.p. (0-685-55551-8) Childs World.

—A Tasting Party. Moncure, Jane B. LC 82-4411. 32p. (ps-3). 1982. pap. 3.95 (0-516-43253-2) Childrens.

—The Touch Book. Moncure, Jane B. LC 82-4154. (ps-3). 1982. pap. 3.95 (0-516-43254-0) Childrens.

—What? Reece, Colleen L. LC 83-7308. 32p. (gr. k-2). 1983. pap. 3.95 (0-516-46591-0) Childrens.

—What Animals Give Us: So Many Things. Wells, Donna K. LC 89-23991. 32p. (ps-2). 1990. PLB 21.35 (0-89565-557-8); PLB 14.95s.p. (0-685-56178-X) Childs World.

—What Was It Before It Was Ice Cream? Reece, Colleen L. LC 85-13262. 32p. (gr. k-2). 1985. PLB 21.35 (0-89565-325-7); PLB 14.95s.p. (0-685-55776-6) Childs World.

—What Your Nose Knows! Moncure, Jane B. LC 82-9464. 32p. (ps-3). 1982. pap. 3.95 (0-516-43255-9) Childrens.

—When. Alden, Laura. LC 83-7305. 32p. (gr. k-2). 1983. pap. 3.95 (0-516-46592-9) Childrens.

—Where? Moncure, Jane B. LC 83-7307. 32p. (gr. k-2). 1983. pap. 3.95 (0-516-46593-7) Childrens.

—Why? Clark, Roberta. LC 83-7306. 32p. (gr. k-2). 1983. pap. 3.95 (0-516-46594-5) Childrens.

—Word Bird's Easter Words. Moncure, Jane B. 32p. (gr. k-2). 1987. PLB 21.35 (0-89565-363-X); PLB 14.95s.p. (0-685-55880-0) Childs World.

Axeman, Lois, jt. illus. see Rubin, Caroline.

Axing, Xi. Chinese Myths. Jin, Yu, et al. 96p. (gr. 2). 1987. pap. 6.95 (0-8351-1795-2) China Bks.

Axworthy, Anni. Along Came Toto. Axworthy, Anni. LC 92-52992. 32p. (ps-3). 1993. 12.95 (1-56402-172-6) Candlewick Pr.

—Anni's India Diary. Axworthy, Anni. LC 92-17524. 32p. (ps-12). 1992. smyth sewn reinforced 14.95 (1-879085-59-3) Whsprng Coyote Pr.

—Count Me In. Hunt, Brian, introduced by. 64p. (ps-3). 12.95 (0-7136-2622-4, Pub. by A&C Black UK) Talman.

Ayer, M. Anna & the King of Siam. Landon, Margaret. 1944. 16.95 (0-381-98135-5, A05201); 16.45 (0-685-02093-2) HarpC Child Bks.

Ayers, Alan. Maxi, the Star. Barracca, Sal & Barracca, Debra. LC 91-44962. 32p. (ps-3). 1993. 13.99 (0-8037-1348-7); PLB 13.89 (0-8037-1349-5) Dial Bks Young.

Ayers, Donna. Jennifer's Rabbit. Paxton, Tom. LC 87-14113. 32p. (ps-1). 1988. 12.95 (0-688-07431-6); lib. bdg. 12.88 (0-688-07432-4, Morrow Jr Bks) Morrow Jr Bks.

—The Sign Painter's Secret: The Story of a Revolutionary Girl. Hoobler, Dorothy & Hoobler, Thomas. 64p. (gr. 4-6). 1991. 11.95 (0-382-24150-9); PLB 13.98 (0-382-24143-6); pap. 7.95 (0-382-24345-5) Silver Burdett Pr.

Ayers, Michael B. Count with Me 1, 2, 3. D'Andrea, Deborah B. Guenther, Luisa, tr. (SPA.). 12p. (ps). 4.99 (1-878338-35-8) Picture Me Bks.

—Count With Me 1, 2, 3. D'Andrea, Deborah B. Zavinski, Monique, tr. (FRE.). 12p. (ps). 4.99 (0-685-63815-4) Picture Me Bks.

—Count with Me 1,2,3. D'Andrea, Deborah. 12p. (ps-k). 1991. 4.99 (1-878338-07-2) Picture Me Bks.

—If I Played Baseball: Or Football, or Soccer, or... D'Andrea, Joseph. 12p. (ps-k). 1991. 4.99 (1-878338-05-6) Picture Me Bks.

—If I Played Baseball, Or Football, Or Soccer, Or... D'Andrea, Joseph C. Guenther, Luisa, tr. (SPA.). 12p. (ps). 4.99 (1-878338-40-4) Picture Me Bks.

—If I Played Baseball, Or Football, Or Soccer, Or... D'Andrea, Joseph C. Zavinski, Monique, tr. (FRE.). 12p. (ps). 4.99 (1-878338-34-X) Picture Me Bks.
—If I Were a Bunny, Or a Panda, Or a Monkey, Or... D'Andrea, Deborah B. 12p. (ps-1). 1989. bds. 4.99 (1-878338-00-5) Picture Me Bks.
—If I Were a Bunny, Or a Panda, Or a Monkey, Or... D'Andrea, Deborah B. Zavinski, Monique, tr. (FRE.). 12p. (ps). 4.99 (1-878338-30-7) Picture Me Bks.
—If I Were a Bunny, Or a Panda, Or a Monkey, Or... D'Andrea, Deborah B. Guenther, Luisa, tr. (SPA.). 12p. (ps). 4.99 (1-878338-36-6) Picture Me Bks.
—If I Were a Chicago Bear. D'Andrea, Joseph C. 28p. (ps-5). pap. 5.95 (1-878338-08-0) Picture Me Bks.
—If I Were a Dallas Cowboy. D'Andrea, Joseph C. 28p. (ps-5). pap. 5.95 (1-878338-11-0) Picture Me Bks.
—If I Were a Fairy, Or a Ballerina, Or a Witch, Or... D'Andrea, Deborah B. 12p. (ps-1). 1989. bds. 4.99 (1-878338-01-3) Picture Me Bks.
—If I Were a Fairy, Or a Ballerina, Or a Witch, Or... D'Andrea, Deborah B. Guenther, Luisa, tr. (SPA.). 12p. (ps). 4.99 (1-878338-38-2) Picture Me Bks.
—If I Were a Fairy, Or a Ballerina, Or a Witch, Or... D'Andrea, Deborah B. Zavinski, Monique, tr. (FRE.). 12p. (ps). 4.99 (1-878338-32-3) Picture Me Bks.
—If I Were a Firefighter: Or a Doctor, Or an Astronaut, or... D'Andrea, Deborah. 12p. (ps-k). 1991. 4.99 (1-878338-04-8) Picture Me Bks.
—If I Were a Firefighter, Or a Doctor, Or an Astronaut, Or... D'Andrea, Deborah B. Guenther, Luisa, tr. (SPA.). 12p. (ps). 4.99 (1-878338-39-0) Picture Me Bks.
—If I Were a Firefighter, Or a Doctor, Or an Astronaut, Or... D'Andrea, Deborah B. Zavinski, Monique, tr. (FRE.). 12p. (ps). 4.99 (1-878338-33-1) Picture Me Bks.
—If I Were a Green Bay Packer. D'Andrea, Joseph C. 28p. (ps-5). pap. 5.95 (1-878338-29-3) Picture Me Bks.
—If I Were a Los Angeles Raider. D'Andrea, Joseph C. 28p. (ps-5). pap. 5.95 (1-878338-10-2) Picture Me Bks.
—If I Were a Miami Dolphin. D'Andrea, Joseph C. 28p. (ps-5). pap. 5.95 (1-878338-24-2) Picture Me Bks.
—If I Were a Minnesota Viking. D'Andrea, Joseph C. 28p. (ps-5). pap. 5.95 (1-878338-27-7) Picture Me Bks.
—If I Were a New Orleans Saint. D'Andrea, Joseph C. 28p. (ps-5). pap. 5.95 (1-878338-13-7) Picture Me Bks.
—If I Were a New York Giant. D'Andrea, Joseph C. 28p. (ps-5). pap. 5.95 (1-878338-12-9) Picture Me Bks.
—If I Were a Philadelphia Eagle. D'Andrea, Joseph C. 28p. (ps-5). pap. 5.95 (1-878338-26-9) Picture Me Bks.
—If I Were a Pirate, Or a Cowboy, Or a Knight, Or... D'Andrea, Deborah B. 12p. (ps-1). 1989. bds. 4.99 (1-878338-02-1) Picture Me Bks.
—If I Were a Pirate, Or a Cowboy, Or a Knight, Or... D'Andrea, Deborah B. Guenther, Luisa, tr. (SPA.). 12p. (ps). 4.99 (1-878338-37-4) Picture Me Bks.
—If I Were a Pirate, Or a Cowboy, Or a Knight, Or... D'Andrea, Deborah B. Zavinski, Monique, tr. (FRE.). 12p. (ps). 4.99 (1-878338-31-5) Picture Me Bks.
—If I Were a Pittsburgh Steeler. D'Andrea, Joseph C. 28p. (ps-5). pap. 5.95 (1-878338-28-5) Picture Me Bks.
—If I Were a San Francisco 49er. D'Andrea, Joseph C. 28p. (ps-5). pap. 5.95 (1-878338-23-4) Picture Me Bks.
—If I Were a Washington Redskin. D'Andrea, Joseph C. 28p. (ps-5). pap. 5.95 (1-878338-22-6) Picture Me Bks.
—Learn Letters with Me ABC. D'Andrea, Deborah. 12p. (ps-k). 1991. 4.99 (1-878338-06-4) Picture Me Bks.
Ayliffe, Alex. Bus Stop Bop. Kingsland, Robin. 32p. (ps-3). 1991. 14.95 (0-670-83919-1) Viking Child Bks.
—Funny Walks. Hindley, Judy. LC 93-28446. 32p. (ps-2). 1993. PLB 13.95 (0-8167-3313-9); pap. 3.95t (0-8167-3314-7) Troll Assocs.
—I Hate You, Marmalade. Kulling, Monica. 32p. (ps-3). 1992. 14.00 (0-670-84480-2) Viking Child Bks.
—Number Nine Duckling. Akass, Susan. 32p. (ps-1). 1993. 13.95 (1-56397-224-7) Boyds Mills Pr.
Ayrai, Sia, photos by. Baby Bright Board Books: 123's. Ayrai, Sia. 1993. 5.95 (1-56565-048-4) Lowell Hse.
Ayres, Carter M., photos by. Illusions Illustrated: A Professional Magic Show for Young Performers. Baker, James W. Swofford, Jeanette. LC 83-19549. 120p. (gr. 6 up). 1984. PLB 22.95 (0-8225-0768-4, First Ave Edns); pap. 6.95 (0-8225-9512-5, First Ave Edns) Lerner Pubns.
Ayto, Russell. Quacky Quack-Quack! Whybrow, Ian. LC 91-8388. 32p. (gr. k up). 1991. SBE 13.95 (0-02-792741-5, Four Winds) Macmillan Child Grp.
Azarian. Sea Gifts. Shannon, George. LC 88-45429. (gr. 2-4). 1989. 11.95 (0-87923-770-8) Godine.
Azarian, Mary. Gridley Firing. Hayford, James. LC 87-61473. 160p. (Orig.). (gr. 4 up). 1987. pap. 9.95 (0-933050-49-6) New Eng Pr VT.
—The Man Who Lived Alone. Hall, Donald. LC 84-47655. 36p. (gr. 2 up). 1984. 12.50 (0-87923-538-1) Godine.

B

Baba, Noboru. Eleven Cats & a Pig. Baba, Noboru. LC 88-9596. 48p. (gr. k-4). 1988. lib. bdg. 18.95 (0-87614-338-9) Carolrhoda Bks.
—Eleven Cats & Albatrosses. Baba, Noboru. LC 88-9598. 48p. (gr. k-4). 1988. lib. bdg. 18.95 (0-87614-335-4) Carolrhoda Bks.
—Eleven Cats in a Bag. Baba, Noboru. LC 88-9597. 48p. (gr. k-4). 1988. lib. bdg. 18.95 (0-87614-336-2) Carolrhoda Bks.
Babbitt, Natalie. All the Small Poems. Worth, Valerie. 192p. (gr. 3 up). 1987. pap. 3.95 (0-374-40344-9, Sunburst) FS&G.
—Bub or The Very Best Thing. Babbitt, Natalie. LC 93-78758. 32p. (gr. k up). 1994. 15.00 (0-06-205044-3); PLB 14.89 (0-06-205045-1) HarpC Child Bks.
—The Devil's Storybook. Babbitt, Natalie. LC 74-5488. 102p. (gr. 3-7). 1984. pap. 3.95 (0-374-41708-3) FS&G.
—Kneeknock Rise. Babbitt, Natalie. LC 79-105622. 96p. (gr. 3 up). 1970. 15.00 (0-374-34257-1); pap. 3.95, 1984 (0-374-44260-6, Sunburst) FS&G.
—Nellie: A Cat on Her Own. Babbitt, Natalie. (ps up). 1989. 14.00 (0-374-35506-1) FS&G.
—The Search for Delicious. Babbitt, Natalie. LC 69-20374. 176p. (gr. 3 up). 1969. 15.00 (0-374-36534-2) FS&G.
—Small Poems Again. Worth, Valerie. LC 85-47513. 48p. (gr. 3 up). 1986. 11.00 (0-374-37074-5) FS&G.
—The Something. Babbitt, Natalie. LC 70-125143. 40p. (ps-3). 1987. 11.00 (0-374-37137-7) FS&G.
—Still More Small Poems. Worth, Valerie. LC 78-11739. 48p. (gr. 3 up). 1978. 11.00 (0-374-37258-6) FS&G.
Babcock, Patricia. Christmas Magic: A Modern Christmas Fable. Hamilton, Mary M. Miles, Leona & Kelly, Robert T., eds. 208p. 1989. lib. bdg. 15.95 (0-317-93677-8) Havet Pr.

Babson, Jane F. Babson's Bestiary. Babson, Jane F. LC 90-71155. 32p. (ps-4). 1991. casebound 10.95 (0-940787-02-4) Winstead Pr. Second in a learning to read series for children & adults. Illustrated with original art, writing designed to stimulate interest, curiosity & intellectual skills. Thought-provoking. Acid-free paper. Special discounts to libraries, literacy programs. "The art book offers a superior presentation... includes some fun animal rhymes within the alphabet form...intriguing, unusual art.--THE MIDWEST BOOK REVIEW. "Attractive alphabet primer with its well-executed illustrations, a fun & funny book about animals."-- THE BLOOMSBURY REVIEW. *Publisher Provided Annotation.*

—The Nest on the Porch. Babson, Jane F. LC 88-51084. 32p. (Orig.). (ps up) 1989. pap. 4.95 (0-940787-01-6) Winstead Pr.
Bacchini, Lisa. I'm in the Spotlight! A Journal of Discovery for Young Writers. Euretig, Mary. 160p. (Orig.). (gr. 1-5). 1993. pap. 11.95 (0-9628216-1-6) Dream Tree Pr.
—Rainbow Writing: A Journal with Activities for Budding Young Writers. Euretig, Mary & Kreisberg, Darlene. (Orig.). (gr. 1-3). 1990. pap. 11.95 (0-9628216-0-8) Dream Tree Pr.
Bach, Katharina. Meet Mrs. Wiggywaggle: Mrs. Wiggywaggle Goes to Town. Biser, Len. 32p. (ps-1). 1991. write for info. (1-880015-29-3) Petra Pub Co.
Bacha, Andy. Two Weeks with the Queen. Gleitzman, Morris. 144p. (gr. 3-7). 1993. pap. 3.95 (0-06-440482-X, Trophy) HarpC Child Bks.
Bachleda, F. Lynn. An Easter Celebration: Traditions & Customs from Around the World. Kennedy, Pamela. 32p. (gr. 1-5). 1991. 10.95 (0-8249-8506-0, Ideals Child) Hambleton-Hill.
Bachman, Barbara. Frisky Phonics Fun I. Bachman, Barbara. 152p. (gr. 1-3). 1984. wkbk. 11.95 (0-86653-195-5, GA 548) Good Apple.
—Frisky Phonics Fun II. Bachman, Barbara. 152p. (gr. 1-3). 1984. wkbk. 11.95 (0-86653-212-9, GA 549) Good Apple.
Bachmann, Mark, et al. Oregon River Watch: A Contemporary History of Oregon's Waterways, Vol. 1. Jones, Michael P., ed. 48p. (Orig.). 1985. text ed. 9.95 (0-89904-143-4); pap. text ed. 5.00 (0-89904-144-2); composition 8.00 (0-89904-145-0) Crumb Elbow Pub.
—Oregon River Watch: A Contemporary History of Oregon's Waterways, Vol. 2. Jones, Michael P., ed. 50p. (Orig.). 1985. text ed. 9.95 (0-89904-146-9); pap. text ed. 5.00 (0-89904-147-7); composition 8.00 (0-89904-148-5) Crumb Elbow Pub.

Backes, Nick. Changes for Molly: A Winter Story. Tripp, Valerie. 67p. (Orig.). (gr. 2-5). 1988. 12.95 (0-937295-96-5); pap. 5.95 (0-937295-49-3) Pleasant Co.
—Molly Saves the Day: A Summer Story. Tripp, Valerie. Thieme, Jeanne, ed. 72p. (gr. 2-5). 1988. 12.95 (0-937295-42-6); PLB 12.95 (0-937295-93-0); pap. 5.95 (0-937295-43-4) Pleasant Co.
—Our New Baby. Rowland, Pleasant T. Thieme, Jeanne, ed. (ps). 1990. White Version. 19.95 ea. (0-937295-64-7); African-American Version. 19.95 (0-937295-65-5) Pleasant Co.
—Our New Baby - Asian Version. Rowland, Pleasant T. 14p. (ps-k). 1991. 19.95 (1-56247-000-0) Pleasant Co.
Backes, Nick, et al. The American Girls Diary: A Journal for Writing Your Secrets - An American Girls' Tradition. Thieme, Jeanne. 96p. (Orig.). (gr. 2-5). 1989. pap. 9.95 (0-937295-56-6) Pleasant Co.
—The American Girls Theater: Plays about Kirsten, Samantha, & Molly for You & Your Friends to Perform, 5 bks. Tripp, Valerie & Thieme, Jeanne. 336p. (Orig.). (gr. 2-5). 1989. Set. pap. 14.95 (0-937295-58-2) Pleasant Co.
Backhaus, Kenn. Sing Raposo, Joe. 24p. 1993. 12.95 (0-7935-1800-1, 00183012) H Leonard Pub Corp.
Backman, Aidel. Guess Who's Coming for Shabbos? Siff, Shoshana M. 14p. (Orig.). (ps-2). 1987. 4.95 (0-685-67641-2); PLB 5.95 (0-685-55892-4) Aura Bklyn.
—King David & the Frog. Zakutinsky, Ruth. Kellman, A., ed. 32p. (gr. k-5). 1986. text ed. 9.95x (0-911643-05-2); pap. 5.95x (0-911643-07-9) Aura Bklyn.
—Passport to Russia. Gross, Sukey S. 158p. (gr. 5-8). 1989. 10.95 (0-935063-59-5); pap. 7.95 (0-935063-60-9) CIS Comm.
—The Secret Diary. Gross, Sukey S. (gr. 5-8). 1989. 10.95 (0-935063-67-6); pap. 7.95 (0-935063-68-4) CIS Comm.
—Shimmee & the Taste-Me Tree. Weinbach, Shaindel. (ps-2). 2.95 (0-87306-991-9) Feldheim.
—The Wonder Worm. Zakutinsky, Ruth. 24p. (gr. k-3). 1992. PLB 6.95x (0-911643-17-6) Aura Bklyn.
Bacon, Paul. The Kid from Tomkinsville. Tunis, John R. Brooks, Bruce, intro. by. 278p. (gr. 3-7). 1989. pap. 3.95 (0-15-242567-5, Odyssey) HarBrace.
—Sandburg Treasury: Prose & Poetry for Young People. Sandburg, Carl. LC 79-120818. 480p. (gr. 7 up). 1970. 24.95 (0-15-270180-X, HB Juv Bks) HarBrace.
—Susanna of the Alamo: A True Story. Jakes, John. LC 85-27143. 32p. (gr. 1-5). 1986. 13.95 (0-15-200592-7, Gulliver Bks) HarBrace.
—Teammates. Golenbock, Peter. (gr. 1-4). 1990. 15.95 (0-15-200603-6) HarBrace.
—World Series. Tunis, John R. Brooks, Bruce, intro. by. 248p. (gr. 3-7). 1989. pap. 3.95 (0-15-299646-X, Odyssey) HarBrace.
Badenhop, Mary. The Boy Who Remembered Everything. Abbott, Jennie. LC 87-14986. 96p. (gr. 5-8). 1988. PLB 9.89 (0-8167-1183-6); pap. text ed. 2.95 (0-8167-1184-4) Troll Assocs.
—Costume Party. Abbott, Jennie. LC 87-14987. 96p. (gr. 5-8). 1988. PLB 9.89 (0-8167-1189-5); pap. text ed. 2.95 (0-8167-1190-9) Troll Assocs.
—The Ghost of Hanover Hill. Abbott, Jennie. LC 87-14983. 96p. (gr. 5-8). 1988. PLB 9.89 (0-8167-1185-2); pap. text ed. 2.95 (0-8167-1186-0) Troll Assocs.
—The Most Beautiful Dog in the World. Abbott, Jennie. LC 87-14985. 96p. (gr. 5-8). 1988. PLB 9.89 (0-8167-1187-9); pap. text ed. 2.95 (0-8167-1188-7) Troll Assocs.
Baden-Powell, Robert. My Adventures As a Spy. Baden-Powell, Robert. 132p. (Orig.). Date not set. pap. 16.95 (0-9632054-8-X) Stevens Pub.
—Scouting for Boys: A Handbook for Instruction in Good Citizenship. Baden-Powell, Robert. 273p. (Orig.). 1992. pap. 17.95 (0-9632054-1-2) Stevens Pub.
Baer, Dale, jt. illus. see Baer, Jane.
Baer, Gene. Have You Seen My Finger? Baer, Gene. LC 91-61251. 16p. (ps-k). 1992. 5.99 (0-679-81382-9) Random Bks Yng Read.
Baer, Jane & Baer, Dale. The Littlest Mule. Barrett, John. Silver Dollar City, Inc. Staff, ed. (ps-5). 1977. 2.99g (0-686-19125-0) Silver Dollar.
Baer, Mary A. Brave Sir Laughalot. Matthews, Morgan. LC 85-14010. 48p. (Orig.). (gr. 1-3). 1986. PLB 10.59 (0-8167-0594-1); pap. text ed. 3.50 (0-8167-0595-X) Troll Assocs.
Baerg, Harry, jt. illus. see James, Elden.
Baeten, Lieve. The Thirteen Hours of Halloween. Regan, Dian C. LC 92-41207. 1993. write for info. (0-8075-7876-2) A Whitman.
Baginski, Frank. Illustrated Basketball Dictionary for Young People. Clark, Steve. (gr. 4 up). 1978. pap. 2.50 (0-13-450940-4, Pub. by Treehouse) P-H.
Bagley, Michael. Peter Parrot, Private Eye. Nickerson, Sara. Counts, Sandra J, frwd. by. LC 88-63800. 43p. (Orig.). (gr. 2-6). 1988. pap. 8.00 (0-935529-07-1) Comprehen Health Educ.
Bagley, Pat. If You Were a Boy in the Time of the Nephites. Bagley, Pat. 48p. (gr. 3-6). 1989. pap. 4.95 (0-87579-250-2) Deseret Bk.
—If You Were a Girl in the Time of the Nephites. Bagley, Pat. 48p. (gr. 3-6). 1989. pap. 4.95 (0-87579-249-9) Deseret Bk.

—Norman the Nephite & Rover-Hah Coloring Book. Bagley, Pat. 32p. (Orig.). (gr. 1-6). 1992. pap. 1.95 (0-87579-673-7) Deseret Bk.

—Where Have All the Nephites Gone? Bagley, Pat. (gr. 3-12). 1993. 12.95 (0-87579-757-1) Deseret Bk.

Bagley, Tom, photos by. The Romance of Country Inns: A Decorating Book for Your Home. Greco, Gail. 288p. (gr. 10 up). 1993. 29.95 (1-55853-175-0) Rutledge Hill Pr.

Bagley, Val & Barwald, Diana. Times Tables the Fun Way: A Picture Method of Learning the Multiplication Facts. Rodriguez, David & Rodriguez, Judy. 86p. (gr. 2-8). 1992. 19.95 (1-883841-25-9) Key Pubs UT. Times tables come alive with this revolutionary method of learning the multiplication facts. The facts are presented as part of a complete mini-story of colorful cartoon characters. Children easily visualize the animated scene, & then remember the characters which trigger the answer to the fact. Proven by numerous studies, visualization & association enhance retention of facts in long term memory. To teach six times six, the story tells of twin sixes who travel across the desert to visit cousins. The twin sixes get low on water becoming thirsty sixes, a word play on 36. The picture shows perspiring, hot & drooping sixes crossing the Sahara. A reminder under the illustration reads: When 6 is with 6, they are very thirsty sixes (36). The book covers the multiplication facts through the nines. Numerical tricks & association are used to teach the ones, twos, fives, & nines while the remaining facts have their own picture & story. Studies have shown a 33% increase in retention with the picture-story method versus conventional methods. Children are eager to learn the stories & parents & teachers enjoy the refreshing approach of the picture method. Also available are the TIMES TABLES THE FUN WAY Flash Cards, Student Workbook, & Teacher's Manual. *Publisher Provided Annotation.*

—Times Tables the Fun Way Book for Kids: A Picture Method of Learning the Multiplication Facts. 2nd, rev. ed. Rodriguez, David & Rodriguez, Judy. 86p. (gr. 2-8). 1993. 19.95 (1-883841-26-7); 54p. 7.95 (1-883841-27-5); tchr's. manual, 56p. 39.00 (1-883841-28-3); flash cards 4.95 (1-883841-29-1) Key Pubs UT.

Bagley, Val C. What Do I Do Now, Mom? Growing-up Guidance for Young Teen-age Girls. Crowther, Jean D. LC 80-82257. 86p. (gr. 9-12). 1980. 8.95 (0-88290-134-6) Horizon Utah.

Bahlinger, Nanette M. The Jekyll Island Historic District Coloring Book. Bahlinger, Nanette M. 32p. (Orig.). (gr. 5). 1993. wkbk. 4.00 (0-9638256-1-5) N M Bahlinger.

Bahti, Tom. When Clay Sings. Baylor, Byrd. LC 70-180743. 32p. (ps-3). 1987. Repr. of 1977 ed. SBE 13.95 (0-684-18829-5, Scribners Young Read) Macmillan Child Grp.

—When Clay Sings. Baylor, Byrd. LC 86-20587. 32p. (gr. 1-4). 1987. pap. 3.95 (0-689-71106-9, Aladdin) Macmillan Child Grp.

Bailey, Cathy, jt. illus. see Williams, Don.

Bailey, Karen. Irish Family Names. Grehan, Ida. 96p. (Orig.). 1985. map. 7.95 (0-86281-133-3, Pub. by Appletree Pr ER) Irish Bks Media.

Bailey-Jones, Suzanne & Jones, Michael R. The Baby Leopard: An African Folktale. Goss, Linda & Goss, Clay. 32p. (ps-3). 1989. audiocassette 7.95 (0-318-41503-8) Bantam.

Bailyn, Susan. The Castle of Chuchurumbel: El Castillo de Churchurumbel. Weissman, Anne. (ENG & SPA.). 19p. (gr. k-2). 1987. 8.95 (968-6217-00-2) Hispanic Bk Dist.

Bain, Gordon. Air: All about Cyclones, Rainbows, Clouds, Ozone & More. Allen, David 32p. 1993. pap. 5.95 (1-895688-08-6, Pub. by Greey dePencier CN) Firefly Bks Ltd.

Bair, Michael, jt. illus. see Birch, J. J.

Baird, Anne. The Christmas Lamb. Baird, Anne. LC 88-5137. 32p. (ps-2). 1989. 12.95 (0-688-07774-9); PLB 12.88 (0-688-07775-7, Morrow Jr Bks) Morrow Jr Bks.

Baird, Robin L. Red Is Best. Stinson, Kathy. 32p. (gr. k-3). 1982. PLB 14.95 (0-920236-24-3, Pub. by Annick CN); pap. 4.95 (0-920236-26-X, Pub. by Annick CN) Firefly Bks Ltd.

Baird Lewis, Robin. Big Or Little. Stinson, Kathy. 32p. (gr. k-2). 1983. PLB 14.95 (0-920236-30-8, Pub. by Annick CN); pap. 4.95 (0-920236-32-4, Pub. by Annick CN) Firefly Bks Ltd.

Bak, Linda. The Greedy Pup. Fanning, Margaret & Bak, Linda. 18p. (Orig.). 1992. Set of 2 scripts. pap. text ed. 6.00 (1-882063-25-2) Cottage Pr MA.

Bakacs, George. Respiratory System: How Living Creatures Breathe. Silverstein, Alvin & Silverstein, Virginia B. (gr. 3-7). 1969. 10.95 (0-13-774547-8) P-H.

Baker, Alan. Benjamin's Portrait. Baker, Alan. LC 86-10396. 32p. (ps-2). 1987. PLB 11.88 (0-688-06878-2) Lothrop.

—Frogs & Toads. Petty, Kate. 32p. (gr. k-3). 1990. pap. 3.95 (0-531-15154-9) Watts.

—Mike & Lottie. Wilkins, Verna A. LC 93-6643. 1993. 9.95 (1-870516-03-6) Childs Play.

—Mr. Toad to the Rescue. Petty, Kate. 24p. (ps-2). 1992. 8.95 (0-8120-6273-6) Barron.

—Stop, Look & Listen, Mr. Toad. Petty, Kate. 24p. (ps-2). 1991. 8.95 (0-8120-6230-2) Barron.

—Two Tiny Mice. Baker, Alan. LC 90-13939. 32p. (ps-1). 1991. 12.95 (0-8037-0973-0) Dial Bks Young.

—What on Earth? Poems with a Conservation Theme. Nicholls, Judith, ed. 132p. (gr. 2 up). 1989. pap. 8.95 (0-571-15262-7) Faber & Faber.

—Where's Mouse? Baker, Alan. LC 92-53117. 16p. (ps-k). 1992. 12.95 (1-85697-821-4) Kingfisher Bks.

Baker, Anthony. Storytime with the Millers. Martin, Mildred A. 96p. (Orig.). (ps-3). 1992. pap. 4.50 (0-9627643-1-0) Green Psturs Pr.

Baker, Carl, photos by. Please Don't Say Hello: Living with Childhood Autism. Gold, Phyllis. LC 74-13185. 48p. (gr. 1-5). 1975. 14.95 (0-87705-211-5); pap. 9.95 (0-89885-199-8) Human Sci Pr.

Baker, Darrell. Baby Donald's Busy Play Group. LC 87-81947. 14p. (ps-1). 1988. write for info. (0-307-12316-2) Western Pub.

—Disney Babies Nursery Rhymes. LC 87-83006. 12p. (ps). 1988. write for info. (0-307-06082-9) Western Pub.

—Disney Babies on the Go. LC 87-83008. 12p. (ps). 1988. write for info. (0-307-06099-3) Western Pub.

—Disney Babies Rock-a-Bye. LC 87-83007. 12p. (ps). 1988. write for info. (0-307-06084-5) Western Pub.

—Disney Babies: What Does Baby Mickey Find? North, Carol. (ps-k). 1991. bds. 1.80 (0-307-06113-2, Golden Pr) Western Pub.

—Disney Babies What's up High? LC 87-83009. 12p. (ps). 1988. write for info. (0-307-06100-0) Western Pub.

—Disney's Aladdin. Kreider, Karen. 24p. (ps-3). 1992. write for info. (0-307-12348-0, 12348, Golden Pr) Western Pub.

—Disney's Beauty & the Beast Word Book. Bazaldua, Barbara. 14p. (ps-k). 1992. write for info. (0-307-12391-X, 12391) Western Pub.

—Disney's Winnie the Pooh Helping Hands: Oh, Bother! Somebody's Grumpy! Birney, Betty. 24p. (ps-3). 1992. write for info. (0-307-12667-6, 12667) Western Pub.

—The Great Big Walt Disney Word Book. Silverman, Maida. 48p. (ps-2). 1992. write for info. (0-307-15604-4, 15604, Golden Pr) Western Pub.

—Piglet Bakes Half a Haycorn Pie. Birney, Betty. 24p. (ps-2). 1992. write for info. (0-307-12338-3, 12338) Western Pub.

—The Tortoise & the Hare. Lang, Jenny, adapted by. 24p. (ps-k). 1993. 9.00 (0-307-74814-6, 64814, Golden Pr) Western Pub.

—Walt Disney's Goofy Joke Book. Bazaldua, Barbara. 24p. (ps-3). 1993. pap. 1.95 (0-307-12683-8, 12683, Golden Pr) Western Pub.

—Walt Disney's Winnie the Pooh: Pooh Can... Can You? North, Carol. 12p. (ps). 1993. bds. 1.95 (0-307-06081-0, 6081, Golden Pr) Western Pub.

Baker, Gary G. There Once Was a Cook. Spence, Lora T., et al. (gr. k up). 1985. pap. 12.95 (0-9614501-0-X) Wesley Inst.

Baker, Howard & Netherton, John, photos by. Big South Fork Country. Baker, Howard, text by. 120p. (gr. 9 up). 1993. 29.95 (1-55853-258-7) Rutledge Hill Pr.

Baker, Jeannie. Home in the Sky. Baker, Jeannie. LC 83-25379. 32p. (gr. k-3). 1984. 13.00 (0-688-03841-7); PLB 11.96 (0-688-03842-5) Greenwillow.

—Home in the Sky. Baker, Jeannie. 32p. (ps-3). 1993. pap. 4.95 (0-590-44704-1) Scholastic Inc.

Baker, Joe. I Am Wings. Fletcher, Ralph. 48p. (gr. 5-9). 1994. SBE 12.95 (0-02-735395-8, Bradbury Pr) Macmillan Child Grp.

Baker, Karen. The Beaver Boys. Pryor, Bonnie. LC 90-38515. 40p. (ps-up). 1992. 15.00 (0-688-08702-7); lib. bdg. 14.93 (0-688-08703-5) Morrow Jr Bks.

Baker, Karen L. Leaving Home with a Pickle Jar. Dugan, Barbara. LC 91-48256. 32p. (gr. k up). 1993. 14.00 (0-688-10836-9); PLB 13.93 (0-688-10837-7) Greenwillow.

—Mama Bought Me a Floppy Teddy Bear. Lillie, Patricia. LC 93-26516. 1994. write for info. (0-688-12570-0); lib. bdg. write for info. (0-688-12571-9) Greenwillow.

Baker, Keith. The Dove's Letter. Baker, Keith. LC 87-8530. 32p. (ps-3). 1988. 14.95 (0-15-224133-7, HB Juv Bks) HarBrace.

—Who Is the Beast? Baker, Keith. 28p. (ps-3). 1991. pap. 19.95 (0-15-296059-7) HarBrace.

—Who Is the Beast? Baker, Keith. LC 89-29365. 28p. (ps-2). 1990. 12.95 (0-15-296057-0) HarBrace.

Baker, Leslie. The Antique Store Cat. Baker, Leslie. 32p. (ps-3). 1992. 14.95 (0-316-07837-9) Little.

—Honkers. Yolen, Jane. LC 92-24302. 1993. 14.95 (0-316-96893-5) Little.

—September Song. Hippely, Hilary H. LC 93-32625. (gr. 5 up). 1995. write for info. (0-399-22646-X, Putnam) Putnam Pub Group.

Baker, Lisa H. Animals in Action. Barrett, Katharine. Bergman, Lincoln & Fairwell, Kay, eds. Barrett, Reginald & Craig, Rose, photos by. 44p. (Orig.). (gr. 6-9). 1986. pap. 8.50 (0-912511-10-9) Lawrence Science.

—Buzzing a Hive. Echols, Jean C. Bergman, Lincoln & Fairwell, Kay, eds. Curtis, Elizabeth, et al, photos by. 97p. (Orig.). (gr. 1-3). 1987. pap. 12.00 (0-912511-12-5) Lawrence Science.

Baker, Lisa H. & Bevilacqua, Carol. Earth, Moon, & Stars. Sneider, Cary I. Bergman, Lincoln & Fairwell, Kay, eds. Sneider, Cary I., photos by. 50p. (Orig.). (gr. 5-9). 1986. pap. 10.00 (0-912511-18-4) Lawrence Science.

—Mapping Animal Movements. Barrett, Katharine. Bergman, Lincoln & Fairwell, Kay, eds. Barrett, Reginald, et al, photos by. 41p. (Orig.). (gr. 5-9). 1987. pap. 8.50 (0-912511-60-5) Lawrence Science.

Baker, Lisa H. & Byal, Chris. Hot Water & Warm Homes from Sunlight. Gould, Alan. Bergman, Lincoln & Fairwell, Kay, eds. Sneider, Cary I., photos by. 40p. (Orig.). (gr. 4-8). 1986. pap. 8.50 (0-912511-24-9) Lawrence Science.

Baker, Lisa H. & Craig, Rose. Chemical Reactions. Barber, Jacqueline. Bergman, Lincoln & Fairwell, Kay, eds. Barber, Jacqueline, et al, photos by. 24p. (Orig.). (gr. 7-10). 1986. pap. 7.50 (0-912511-13-3) Lawrence Science.

Baker, Lisa H. & Klofkorn, Lisa. Hide a Butterfly. Echols, Jean C. Bergman, Lincoln & Fairwell, Kay, eds. Callaway, Jane, et al, photos by. 28p. (Orig.). (gr. 1-3). 1986. pap. 7.50 (0-912511-23-0) Lawrence Science.

Baker, Lisa H. & Peterson, Adria. Oobleck: What Do Scientists Do? rev. ed. Sneider, Cary I. Bergman, Lincoln & Fairwell, Kay, eds. Sneider, Cary I., photos by. 28p. (gr. 4-8). 1988. pap. 8.50 (0-912511-64-8) Lawrence Science.

—Solids, Liquids, & Gases. Barber, Jacqueline. Bergman, Lincoln & Fairwell, Kay, eds. Barber, Jacqueline, et al, photos by. 56p. (Orig.). (gr. 3-6). 1986. pap. 10.00 (0-912511-69-9) Lawrence Science.

Baker, Lisa H., jt. illus. see Sneider, Cary I.

Baker, Lisa H., et al. Bubble-ology. Barber, Jacqueline. Bergman, Lincoln & Fairwell, Kay, eds. Barber, Jacqueline & Sneider, Cary I., photos by. 53p. (gr. 5-9). 1987. pap. 8.50 (0-912511-11-7) Lawrence Science.

Baker, Robert T. Active Listening Program (ALP) Van der Laan, Carrie. 113p. (Orig.). (gr. 5-12). 1986. Incl. manual, 36 3x5 cards, 50 4x6 cards, carrying tote. 39.00 (0-930599-02-0) Thinking Pubns.

—Transfer Activities: Thinking Skill Vocabulary Development. Mayo, Patty & Gajewski, Nancy. 202p. (gr. 5-12). 1987. pap. text ed. 31.00 (0-930599-13-6) Thinking Pubns.

Baker, Syd. Basic Structures - American English, Bk. 1: A Textbook for the Learnables. Winitz, Harris. 100p. (gr. 7 up). 1990. pap. text ed. 42.00 incl. 4 cass. tapes (0-939990-60-1) Intl Linguistics.

—Basic Structures - Spanish, Bk. 1: A Textbook for the Learnables. Winitz, Harris. Sagarna, Blanca, tr. 106p. (gr. 7 up). 1990. pap. text ed. 42.00 incl. 4 cass. tapes (0-939990-61-X) Intl Linguistics.

—Beforderung. Brinckmann, Caren, et al. Winitz, Harris, intro. by. (GER.). 40p. (gr. 7 up). 1990. Incls. cass. tape. pap. text ed. 22.00 (0-939990-71-7) Intl Linguistics.

—Beginning Spanish: A Teacher's Manual: Comprehension Based Activities for the Learnables, Book One. Bouwman, Constance, et al. 163p. (gr. 7 up). 1989. pap. text ed. 28.00 (0-939990-78-4) Intl Linguistics.

—Bildbeschreibungen: Picture Descriptions in German. Winitz, Harris. Rohrer, Josef, tr. (gr. 7 up). 1988. Incl. 2 cassettes. pap. 32.00 (0-939990-59-8) Intl Linguistics.

—Bildbeschreibungen: Picture Descriptions in German, 2 bks. Zeller, Walter. Winitz, Harris, intro. by. 130p. (gr. 7 up). 1988. Bk. I incl. 2 cassettes. 32.00 (0-939990-57-1); Bk. II incl. 2 cassettes. 32.00 (0-939990-58-X) Intl Linguistics.

—Business, Bk. 2. Winitz, Harris. 56p. (Orig.). (gr. 7 up). 1986. pap. text ed. 22.00 incl. cass. (0-939990-46-6) Intl Linguistics.

—Descriptions de Dessins: Picture Descriptions in French. Waggoner, Carmen. Parr, Frederique & Winitz, Harris, eds. (FRE.). 65p. (Orig.). (gr. 7 up). 1989. pap. text ed. 32.00 incl. 2 cassettes (0-939990-77-6) Intl Linguistics.

—Entertainment: Movies. Moore, Douglas. 50p. (Orig.). (gr. 7 up). 1986. incl. cass. 22.00 (0-939990-48-2) Intl Linguistics.

—Gehen. Hildebrand, Sigrid S. & Hildebrand, Eckart. Rohrer, Josef, ed. Winitz, Harris, intro. by. (GER.). 85p. (gr. 7 up). 1990. Incls. cass. tape. pap. 22.00 (0-939990-64-4) Intl Linguistics.

—Hauser und Gebaude: Houses & Buildings in German. Winitz, Harris. Rohrer, Josef, ed. (GER.). 50p. (Orig.). (gr. 7 up). 1989. pap. text ed. 22.00 incl. cass. (0-939990-76-8) Intl Linguistics.

—Medios de Transporte: Transportation - Spanish. Sagarna, Blanca. Winitz, Harris, intro. by. (SPA.). 50p. (gr. 7 up). 1989. pap. text ed. 22.00 incl. cass. (0-939990-75-X) Intl Linguistics.

—School: All about Language Ser. Winitz, Harris. 50p. (Orig.). (gr. 7 up). 1987. pap. text ed. 31.00 incl. 2 cass. (0-939990-49-0) Intl Linguistics.

—Stellen, Legen und Setzen. Hildebrand, Sigrid S. & Hildebrand, Eckart. Rohrer, Josef, ed. Winitz, Harris, intro. by. (GER.). 80p. (Orig.). (gr. 7 up). 1990. Incls. cass. tape. pap. text ed. 22.00 (0-939990-65-2) Intl Linguistics.

—Telefon. Beeck, Johannes, et al. Winitz, Harris, intro. by. (GER.). 50p. (gr. 7 up). 1990. Incls. cass. tape. pap. text ed. 22.00 (0-939990-70-9) Intl Linguistics.

—The Telephone. Winitz, Harris. 50p. (Orig.). (gr. 7 up). 1987. pap. text ed. 22.00 incl. cass. (0-939990-50-4) Intl Linguistics.

—Weather. Winitz, Harris. 50p. (gr. 7 up). 1986. pap. text ed. 19.00 incl. cass. (0-939990-47-4) Intl Linguistics.

Baker, Wendy. The Dressing-up Book. James, Diane. LC 93-36430. 48p. (gr. 4-8). 1994. 16.95 (1-56847-136-X) Thomson Lrning.

—Fashion. James, Diane. LC 93-21215. 48p. (gr. 3-7). 1994. 16.95 (1-56847-145-9) Thomson Lrning.

—Knitting. Diane, James. LC 93-21217. 48p. (gr. 3-7). 1994. 16.95 (1-56847-146-7) Thomson Lrning.

Bakke, Eric. Danger sur la Cote d'azur: Reader 4. Conroy, Joseph F. LC 81-7820. (FRE.). 40p. (Orig.). (gr. 7-12). 1982. pap. 2.95 (0-88436-857-2, 40262) EMC.

—Destination: France! Reader 1. Conroy, Joseph F. LC 81-7816. (FRE.). 40p. (Orig.). (gr. 7-12). 1982. pap. 2.95 (0-88436-854-8, 40259) EMC.

—Un Grabado de Goya: Reader 3. Jarvis-Sladky, Kay. LC 81-7783. (SPA.). 40p. (Orig.). (gr. 7-12). 1982. pap. 2.75 (0-88436-860-2, 70261) EMC.

—La Guitarra Misteriosa: Reader 1. Jarvis-Sladky, Kay. LC 81-7785. (SPA.). 40p. (Orig.). (gr. 7-12). 1982. pap. 2.95 (0-88436-858-0, 70259) EMC.

—El Penitente Elusivo: Reader 4. Jarvis-Sladky, Kay. LC 81-7842. (SPA., Orig.). (gr. 7-12). 1982. pap. 2.95 (0-88436-861-0, 70262) EMC.

—Secretos de Famalia: Reader 2. Jarvis-Sladky, Kay. LC 81-7780. (SPA.). 40p. (Orig.). (gr. 7-12). 1982. pap. 2.95 (0-88436-859-9, 70260) EMC.

—Sur la Route de la Contrebande. Conroy, Joseph F. LC 81-7817. (FRE.). 40p. (Orig.). (gr. 7-12). pap. 2.95 (0-88436-856-4, 40261) EMC.

Bala, Virginia. Los Tres Osos: (The Three Bears) McKissack, Patricia C. & McKissack, Fredrick. LC 85-12765. (SPA.). 32p. (ps-2). 1989. PLB 11.93 (0-516-32364-4); pap. 3.95 (0-516-52364-3) Childrens.

Balcomb, Philip E. The Clock Repair First Reader: Second Steps for the Beginner. Balcomb, Philip E. 160p. (Orig.). (gr. 9 up). 1989. pap. 14.95 (0-9620456-1-6) Tempus Pr.

Baldridge, Cyrus L. Jesus - the Carpenter's Son. rev. ed. Fahs, Sophia L. 160p. 1990. pap. 14.95 (1-55896-191-7) Unitarian Univ.

Baldwin, Bob, et al, photos by. The Wonder of Wolves. Lantier-Sampon, Patricia, adapted by. LC 92-16948. 1992. PLB 18.60 (0-8368-0859-2) Gareth Stevens Inc.

Baldwin-Ford, Pamela. Amazing World of Dinosaurs. Granger, Judith. LC 84-7476. 32p. (gr. 2-4). 1982. PLB 11.59 (0-89375-562-1); pap. text ed. 2.95 (0-89375-563-X) Troll Assocs.

—Tatterhood & Other Tales. Phelps, Ethel J., ed. Phelps, Ethel, intro. by. LC 78-9352. 192p. (Orig.). (gr. 1 up). 1978. o. p. 11.95 (0-912670-49-5); pap. 9.95 (0-912670-50-9) Feminist Pr.

—Wonders of the Desert. Sabin, Louis. LC 81-7397. 32p. (gr. 2-4). 1982. PLB 11.59 (0-89375-574-5); pap. text ed. 2.95 (0-89375-575-3) Troll Assocs.

Bale, Andrew. The Animal Kingdom. Wood, Jenny. LC 91-14567. 32p. (ps-3). 1992. 14.95 (0-02-793395-4, Macmillan Child Bk) Macmillan Child Grp.

—Bears. Gilks, Helen. LC 92-37693. (gr. 3 up). 1993. 15. 45 (0-395-66899-9) Ticknor & Fields.

Bales, Carol A., photos by. Tales of the Elders: A Memory Book of Men & Women Who Came to America as Immigrants, 1900-1930. Bales, Carol A. LC 92-46729. 160p. (gr. 5 up). 1993. Repr. of 1977 ed. 10.98 (0-382-24373-0); PLB 12.98 (0-382-24364-1) Silver Burdett Pr.

Bales, Marcia. The Best Manners Book Ever. Mehew, Randall & Mehew, Karen. 68p. 1990. pap. text ed. 5.95 (0-929985-55-9) Sonos.

—Gospel Basic Busy Book, Vol. II. Mehew, Randall & Mehew, Karen. 100p. 1990. pap. text ed. 6.95 (0-910613-08-7) Millenial Pr.

Balian, Lorna. Amelia's Nine Lives. Balian, Lorna. 32p. (ps-3). 1987. Repr. of 1986 ed. 7.50 (0-687-37096-5) Humbug Bks.

—Amelia's Nine Lives. Balian, Lorna. 32p. (ps-3). 1986. PLB 13.95 (0-687-01250-3) Humbug Bks.

—The Aminal. Balian, Lorna. 32p. (ps-3). 1987. Repr. of 1972 ed. 7.50 (0-687-37101-5) Humbug Bks.

—Bah! Humbug? Balian, Lorna. 32p. (ps-3). 1988. Repr. of 1978 ed. 7.50 (0-687-37107-4) Humbug Bks.

—A Garden for a Groundhog. Balian, Lorna. 32p. (gr. k up). 1985. PLB 13.95 (0-687-14009-9) Humbug Bks.

—Humbug Potion: An A-B-Cipher. Balian, Lorna. 32p. (ps-3). 1988. Repr. of 1985 ed. 7.50 (0-687-37102-3) Humbug Bks.

—Humbug Potion: An A-B-Cipher. Balian, Lorna. 32p. (ps-3). 1985. PLB 12.95 (0-687-18021-X) Humbug Bks.

—Humbug Rabbit. Balian, Lorna. 32p. (ps-3). 1987. Repr. of 1975 ed. 7.50 (0-687-37098-1) Humbug Bks.

—Humbug Witch. Balian, Lorna. 32p. (gr. k up). 1992. Repr. of 1987 ed. PLB 13.95 (1-881772-24-1) Humbug Bks.

—I Love You, Mary Jane. Balian, Lorna. 48p. (ps-3). 1988. Repr. of 1966 ed. 7.50 (0-687-37100-7) Humbug Bks.

—Leprechauns Never Lie. Balian, Lorna. 32p. (ps-3). 1988. Repr. of 1981 ed. 7.50 (0-687-37110-4) Humbug Bks.

—Mother's, Mother's Day. Balian, Lorna. 32p. (ps-3). 1987. Repr. of 1982 ed. 7.50 (0-687-37097-3) Humbug Bks.

—The Socksnatchers. Balian, Lorna. 32p. (ps-3). 1988. PLB 12.95 (0-687-39047-8) Humbug Bks.

—Sometimes It's Turkey, Sometimes It's Feathers. Balian, Lorna. 32p. (ps-3). 1987. Repr. of 1973 ed. 7.50 (0-687-37106-6) Humbug Bks.

—A Sweetheart for Valentine. Balian, Lorna. 32p. (ps-3). 1988. Repr. of 1980 ed. 7.50 (0-687-37109-0) Humbug Bks.

—Wilbur's Space Machine. Balian, Lorna. LC 90-55095. 32p. (ps-3). 1990. reinforced 14.95 (0-8234-0836-1) Holiday.

Balistreri, Francis. Casey Jones. Gleiter, Jan & Thompson, Kathleen. 32p. (gr. 2-5). 1987. PLB 17.96 (0-8172-2653-2); pap. 9.27 (0-685-67542-4) Raintree Steck-V.

—Paul Revere. Gleiter, Jan & Thompson, Kathleen. 32p. (gr. 2-5). 1986. PLB 17.96 (0-8172-2644-3) Raintree Steck-V.

Balkovek, James. Dell & His Dot. Cory, Beverly. 64p. (Orig.). (ps-4). 1993. pap. 9.95 (0-8449-4252-9); FRE Translation Tool, "Trans-it" 4.95 (0-8449-4281-2); CHI Translation Tool, "Trans-it" 4.95 (0-8449-4283-9); GER Translation Tool, "Trans-it" 4.95 (0-8449-4282-0); SPA Translation Tool, "Trans-it" 4.95 (0-8449-4280-4) Good Morn Tchr.

—The Gob-Gob-Goblin's Feast. Buchanan, D. H. 64p. (ps-4). 1993. pap. 9.95 (0-8449-4275-8); FRE Translation Tool, "Trans-it" 4.95 (0-8449-4289-8); CHI Translation Tool, "Trans-it" 4.95 (0-8449-4291-X); GER Translation Tool, "Trans-it" 4.95 (0-8449-4290-1); SPA Translation Tool, "Trans-it" 4.95 (0-8449-4288-X) Good Morn Tchr.

—Gork & the Mop Tops. Cory, Beverly. 64p. (Orig.). (ps-4). 1993. pap. 9.95 (0-8449-4251-0); FRE Translation Tool, "Trans-it" 4.95 (0-8449-4285-5); CHI Translation Tool, "Trans-it" 4.95 (0-8449-4287-1); GER Translation Tool, "Trans-it" 4.95 (0-8449-4286-3); SPA Translation Tool, "Trans-it" 4.95 (0-8449-4284-7) Good Morn Tchr.

—Simon & His Shrinking Socks. Steinbaum, Michael & Cohen, Diana. 64p. (ps-4). 1993. pap. 9.95 (0-8449-4253-7); FRE Translation Tool, "Trans-it" 4.95 (0-8449-4293-6); CHI Translation Tool, "Trans-it" 4.95 (0-8449-4295-2); GER Translation Tool, "Trans-it" 4.95 (0-8449-4294-4); SPA Translation Tool, "Trans-it" 4.95 (0-8449-4292-8) Good Morn Tchr.

—The Tumble-Down Tower. Steinbaum, Michael & Warmbold, Jean. (ps-4). 1993. pap. 9.95 (0-8449-4254-5); FRE Translation Tool, "Trans-it" 4.95 (0-8449-4297-9); CHI Translation Tool, "Trans-it" 4.95 (0-8449-4299-5); GER Translation Tool, "Trans-it" 4.95 (0-8449-4298-7); SPA Translation Tool, "Trans-it" 4.95 (0-8449-4296-0) Good Morn Tchr.

Balkovek, Jim. The Great Seed Mystery. Henry, Peggy. Copeland, Alan & Shapiro, Barry, photos by. LC 92-20193. 1993. 7.95 (1-880281-11-2) NK Lawn & Garden.

Ball, Dave. You Can Make It! You Can Do It! 101 E-Z Holiday Craft-Tivities for Children. Peaslee, Ann & Kille, Jullien. 120p. (Orig.). (gr. 3-6). 1991. pap. 9.95 (0-89346-337-X) Heian Intl.

Ball, Robert. The Gold-Laced Coat. rev. ed. Orton, Helen F. 226p. (gr. 4-8). 1988. pap. 5.95 (0-941967-07-7) Old Fort Niagara Assn.

—My Shooting Box. 2nd ed. Forester, Frank. 187p. (gr. 10 up). 1990. Repr. of 1941 ed. 35.00 (1-56416-014-9) Derrydale Pr.

—The Treasure in the Little Trunk. Orton, Helen F. 208p. (gr. 4). 1989. pap. text ed. 5.95 (0-685-29125-1) Niagara Cnty Hist Soc.

—Warwick Woodlands. 2nd ed. Forester, Frank. 200p. (gr. 10 up). 1990. Repr. of 1934 ed. 35.00 (1-56416-015-7) Derrydale Pr.

Balla, Laszlo. When Will Summer Come? Rollini, Art. LC 90-70904. 21p. (ps-6). 1991. pap. 5.95 (1-55523-354-6) Winston-Derek.

Ballagh, Robert. Spike & the Professor. Hickey, Tony. LC 89-51005. 160p. (Orig.). (gr. 4-7). 1989. pap. 5.95 (1-85371-039-3, Pub. by Poolbeg Press Ltd Eire) Dufour.

Ballard, Robin. The Scrap Doll. Rosenberg, Liz. LC 90-35668. 32p. (ps-3). 1991. PLB 13.89 (0-06-024865-3) HarpC Child Bks.

Ballestar, Vincenc & Martinez, Francesc. Wax Crayon. Rovira, Albert. 48p. 1991. pap. 7.95 (0-8120-4718-4) Barron.

Ballman, Jean. Visiting Olympia. Dumond, Val. 24p. (Orig.). (gr. 1-4). 1983. pap. 2.75 (0-933992-39-4) Coffee Break.

Ballonga, Jordi. Barmi: A Mediterranean City Through the Ages. Comes, Pilar & Hernandez, Xavier. 64p. (gr. 5 up). 1990. 14.45 (0-395-54227-8) HM.

Ballonga, Jordi & Escofet, Josep. San Rafael: A Central American City Through the Ages. Hernandez, Xavier. LC 91-39906. 64p. (gr. 4-7). 1992. 17.45 (0-395-60645-4) HM.

Ballouhey, Pierre. Goodbye U. S. A. - Ola Mexico! Bovaird, Anne. (gr. 3-7). 1994. 12.95 (0-8120-6374-0); pap. 5.95 (0-8120-1388-3) Barron.

Balterman, Lee. Girders & Cranes: A Skyscraper Is Built. Balterman, Lee. Levine, Abby, ed. LC 90-37028. 32p. (gr. k-4). 1991. PLB 14.95 (0-8075-2923-0) A Whitman.

Balthis, Frank, et al, photos by. Tidepools: The Bright World of the Rocky Shoreline. rev. ed. Barnhart, Diana & Leon, Vicki. LC 93-21338. 48p. (gr. 5 up). 1993. pap. 9.95 (0-918303-37-0) Blake Pub.

Banazi, Pauline. Busy Bee Pack. Bradley, Susannah. (gr. 3-6). 1992. pap. 7.95 (1-56680-503-1) Mad Hatter Pub.

—Cuddly Teddies' Activity Book. Bradley, Susannah. (gr. 3-6). 1992. pap. 5.95 (1-56680-507-4) Mad Hatter Pub.

—A "Spot-It" Guide to Nature. Border, Rosy. 48p. (gr. 3-6). 1992. pap. 2.95 (1-56680-012-9) Mad Hatter Pub.

Bancroft, Bronwyn. Kun-Man-Gur the Rainbow Serpent. Cowan, James. LC 93-32319. 1994. 16.00 (1-56957-906-7) Barefoot Bks.

Bancroft-Hunt, Norman. A Midsummer Night's Dream. Mulherin, Jennifer. LC 87-37229. 32p. (gr. 6-12). 1988. 10.96g (0-382-09690-8) Silver Burdett Pr.

Bandk, Yvette. Amazing Aunt Agatha. Samton, Sheila. 24p. (ps-2). 1990. PLB 14.60 (0-8172-3575-2); pap. 10.95 pkg. of 3 (0-8114-2932-6) Raintree Steck-V.

Banek, Yvette. Beginning to Read. Wise, Beth A. Nayer, Judith E., ed. 32p. (gr. k-1). 1991. wkbk. 1.95 (1-878624-62-8) McClanahan Bk.

—Let's Investigate Magical, Mysterious Meteorites. Carlisle, Madelyn. LC 92-12776. (gr. 4-7). 1992. pap. 4.95 (0-8120-4733-8) Barron.

Banek, Yvette & Cushman, Doug. The Elves & the Shoemaker. Leonard, Marcia. Brook, Bonnie, ed. 24p. (ps-1). 1990. 5.95 (0-671-69351-4); PLB 9.98 (0-671-69347-6) Silver Pr.

—Goldilocks & the Three Bears. Leonard, Marcia. Brook, Bonnie, ed. 24p. (ps-1). 1990. 5.95 (0-671-69350-6); PLB 9.98 (0-671-69346-8) Silver Pr.

—Rumplestilskin. Leonard, Marcia. Brook, Bonnie, ed. 24p. (ps-1). 1990. 5.95 (0-671-69352-2); PLB 9.98 (0-671-69348-4) Silver Pr.

—The Three Little Pigs. Leonard, Marcia. Brook, Bonnie, ed. 24p. (ps-1). 1990. 5.95 (0-671-69349-2); PLB 9.98 (0-671-69345-X) Silver Pr.

Banek, Yvette, jt. illus. see Cushman, Doug.

Banek, Yvette S. Let's Investigate Soft, Shimmering Sand. Carlisle, Madelyn W. 32p. (gr. 3-7). 1993. pap. 4.95 (0-8120-4972-1) Barron.

—Let's Investigate Weird & Wonderful Sea Creatures. Carlisle, Madelyn W. LC 92-45206. 32p. (gr. 3-7). 1993. pap. 4.95 (0-8120-4974-8) Barron.

Banerjee, Ramananda. Story of Vivekananda. Ray, Irene R. & Gupta, Mallika C. (gr. 4-7). 1971. pap. 1.95 (0-87481-125-2) Vedanta Pr.

Banfill, A. Scott. The Forest Child. McGee, Marni. LC 92-37148. 1994. 15.00 (0-671-86608-7, Green Tiger) S&S Trade.

Bang, Molly. David's Landing. Richardson, Judith B. LC 84-22084. 150p. (gr. 3-7). 1984. write for info. (0-9611374-1-X) Woods Hole Hist.

—Delphine. Bang, Molly. LC 87-34958. 32p. (gr. 2 up). 1988. 12.95 (0-688-05636-9); PLB 12.88 (0-688-05637-7, Morrow Jr Bks) Morrow Jr Bks.

—The Goblins Giggle & Other Stories. Bang, Molly, ed. (gr. 3-5). 1988. 17.25 (0-8446-6360-3) Peter Smith.

—The Paper Crane. Bang, Molly. LC 84-13546. 32p. (gr. k-3). 1985. 13.95 (0-688-04108-6); lib. bdg. 13.93 (0-688-04109-4) Greenwillow.

—Red Dragonfly on My Shoulder: Haiku. Cassedy, Sylvia & Suetake, Kunihiro. LC 91-18443. 32p. (gr. k-5). 1992. 15.00 (0-06-022624-2); PLB 14.89 (0-06-022625-0) HarpC Child Bks.

—Ten, Nine, Eight. Bang, Molly. LC 81-20106. 24p. (ps-1). 1983. 14.00 (0-688-00906-9); PLB 13.93 (0-688-00907-7) Greenwillow.

—Yellow Ball. Bang, Molly. LC 90-46077. 24p. (ps up). 1991. 55.99 (0-688-06314-4); PLB 12.88 (0-688-06315-2, Morrow Jr Bks) Morrow Jr Bks.

Bang, Molly, et al. From Sea to Shining Sea. Cohn, Amy, selected by. LC 92-30598. 1993. 29.95 (0-590-42868-3) Scholastic Inc.

Bang, Molly G. Wiley & the Hairy Man: Adapted from an American Folk Tale. Bang, Molly. LC 75-38581. 64p. (gr. 1-4). 1976. RSBE 11.95 (0-02-708370-5, Macmillan Child Bk) Macmillan Child Grp.

—Wiley & the Hairy Man: Adapted from an American Folk Tale. Bang, Molly G. LC 87-2540. 64p. (gr. 1-4). 1987. pap. 3.95 (0-689-71162-X, Aladdin) Macmillan Child Grp.

Banish, Roslyn. A Forever Family: A Book About Adoption. Banish, Roslyn. LC 90-28725. 48p. (gr. k-3). 1992. 14.00 (0-06-021673-5); PLB 13.89 (0-06-021674-3) HarpC Child Bks.
—A Forever Family: A Book About Adoption. Banish, Roslyn. LC 90-28726. 48p. (gr. k-3). 1992. pap. 5.95 (0-06-446116-5, Trophy) HarpC Child Bks.
Banse, Charles. Life of Christ, Vol. III. Hershey, Katherine. 51p. (gr. k-6). 1978. pap. text ed. 9.45 (1-55976-002-8) CEF Press.
—Life of Christ, Vol. IV. Hershey, Katherine. 49p. (gr. k-6). 1978. pap. text ed. 9.45 (1-55976-003-6) CEF Press.
Banse, Charles & Chappell, David. Life of Christ, Vol. I. Hershey, Katherine. 54p. (gr. k-6). 1987. pap. text ed. 9.45 (1-55976-000-1) CEF Press.
Bansemer, Roger. Rachael's Splendiflous Adventure. May, Daryl & Bansemer, Roger. Little, Carl, ed. LC 91-66032. 40p. (Orig.). (ps-4). 1992. PLB 10.95 (0-932433-83-9) Windswept Hse.
Banta, Susan. Animals. 10p. (ps-1). 1993. bds. 2.95 (1-56293-311-6) McClanahan Bk.
—Colors. 10p. (ps-1). 1993. bds. 2.95 (1-56293-309-4) McClanahan Bk.
—Observing. Rutman, Shereen G. 16p. (ps). 1992. wkbk. 2.25 (1-56293-189-X) McClanahan Bk.
—Opposites. 10p. (ps-1). 1993. bds. 2.95 (1-56293-312-4) McClanahan Bk.
—Shapes. 10p. (ps-1). 1993. bds. 2.95 (1-56293-310-8) McClanahan Bk.
—Sorting. Rutman, Shereen G. 16p. (ps). 1992. wkbk. 2.25 (1-56293-186-5) McClanahan Bk.
Bantock, Nick. Runners, Sliders, Bouncers, Climbers: A Pop-up Look at Animals in Motion. Bantock, Nick. 15p. (gr. 1-5). 1992. 14.95 (1-56282-219-5) Hyprn Child.
—Solomon Grundy: A Pop-up Rhyme. Bantock, Nick, retold by. 12p. 1992. 8.95 (0-670-84319-9) Viking Child Bks.
—There Was an Old Lady. Bantock, Nick, retold by. (gr. 4 up). 1990. pap. 8.95 (0-670-83194-8) Viking Child Bks.
—Wings: A Pop-up Book of Things That Fly. Bantock, Nick. LC 90-60979. 12p. (ps-5). 1991. 14.95 (0-679-81041-2) Random Bks Yng Read.
Banyard, Julie. Between the Sun, the Moon & Me. West, Colin. 32p. (ps-2). 1992. 15.95 (0-09-173644-7, Pub. by Hutchinson UK) Trafalgar.
Baptist, Michael, et al. Fun on the Road: Travel Activities. Wade, Theodore E., Jr. 40p. (Orig.). (gr. k-6). 1990. pap. 2.95 (0-930192-23-0) Gazelle Pubns.
Bapu, pseud. Ramayana: The Story of Rama. Valmiki. LC 74-77601. 72p. (gr. 5-12). 1975. 8.50 (0-88253-292-8); pap. 3.50 (0-88253-291-X) Ind-US Inc.
Barankova, Vlasta. Konstantine. Wagner, Gerda. 28p. (ps-1). 1991. smythe sewn reinforced bdg. 9.95 (1-56182-023-7) Atomium Bks.

Barath, Judith. El Agua y Tu. Kohen, Clarita. (SPA.). 16p. (gr. k-5). 1993. PLB 7.50x (1-56492-101-8) Laredo. A creative way of educating children about the importance of water conservation. An historical link with the past & present towards the future. Fully illustrated in color with simple, repetitive text. In Spanish. *Publisher Provided Annotation.*

Barb, Arlene. Jeremy's Jack-O-Lantern. Mueller, Amelia. 24p. (gr. k-3). 1992. pap. 5.95 (0-945530-06-4) Wordsworth KS.
Barbaresi, Nina. Specs: The True Story of Baseball Player George Toporcer. Motomora, Mitchell. 24p. (ps-2). 1990. 14.60 (0-8172-3585-X); PLB 10.95 pkg. of 3 (0-685-58557-3) Raintree Steck-V.
Barbaresi, Nina, jt. illus. see Bracken, Carolyn.
Barber, Ed, photos by. Bread. Baskerville, Judith. Stefoff, Rebecca, ed. LC 91-18189. 32p. (gr. 3-5). 1991. PLB 15.93 (1-56074-001-9) Garrett Ed Corp.
—Bricks. Cash, Terry. Stefoff, Rebecca, ed. LC 90-40249. 32p. (gr. 3-5). 1990. PLB 15.93 (0-944483-68-2) Garrett Ed Corp.
—Clay. Dixon, Annabelle. Stefoff, Rebecca, ed. LC 90-40369. 32p. (gr. 3-5). 1990. PLB 15.93 (0-944483-69-0) Garrett Ed Corp.
—Glass. Chandler, Jane. Stefoff, Rebecca, ed. LC 91-18191. 32p. (gr. 3-5). 1991. PLB 15.93 (1-56074-004-3) Garrett Ed Corp.
—New Bike. Petty, Kate. 32p. (gr. 2 up). 1992. bds. 12.95 (0-7136-3482-0, Pub. by A&C Black UK) Talman.
—New Car. Petty, Kate. 32p. (gr. 2 up). 1992. bds. 12.95 (0-7136-3484-7, Pub. by A&C Black UK) Talman.
—New Shampoo. Petty, Kate. 32p. (gr. 2 up). 1992. bds. 12.95 (0-7136-3481-2, Pub. by A&C Black UK) Talman.
—New Shoes. Petty, Kate. 32p. (gr. 2 up). 1992. bds. 12.95 (0-7136-3483-9, Pub. by A&C Black UK) Talman.
—Paper. Dixon, Annabelle. Stefoff, Rebecca, ed. LC 91-18188. 32p. (gr. 3-5). 1991. PLB 15.93 (1-56074-003-5) Garrett Ed Corp.
—Plastics. Cash, Terry. Stefoff, Rebecca, ed. LC 90-40368. 32p. (gr. 3-5). 1990. PLB 15.93 (0-944483-70-4) Garrett Ed Corp.
—Rocks. Jennings, Terry J. Stefoff, Rebecca, ed. LC 91-18190. 32p. (gr. 3-5). 1991. PLB 15.93 (1-56074-000-0) Garrett Ed Corp.
—Water. Walpole, Brenda. Stefoff, Rebecca, ed. LC 90-40381. 32p. (gr. 3-5). 1990. PLB 15.93 (0-944483-72-0) Garrett Ed Corp.
—Wood. Jennings, Terry J. Stefoff, Rebecca, ed. LC 91-18187. 32p. (gr. 3-5). 1991. PLB 15.93 (1-56074-002-7) Garrett Ed Corp.
—Wool. Dixon, Annabelle. Stefoff, Rebecca, ed. LC 90-40366. 32p. (gr. 3-5). 1990. PLB 15.93 (0-944483-73-9) Garrett Ed Corp.
Barber, Joel. Wild Fowl Decoys. 2nd ed. Barber, Joel. 151p. (gr. 10 up). 1989. Repr. of 1934 ed. 39.95 (1-56416-002-5) Derrydale Pr.
Barber, Liz A. Uncle Wiley Whiskers: Tells How the Catfish Got Its name. Bullock, Judy. 16p. (gr. k-6). 1992. pap. 4.95 (0-937552-49-6) Quail Ridge.
Barberis, Franco. Would You Like a Parrot? Barberis, France. LC 67-28671. 32p. (ps-k). 8.95 (0-87592-060-8) Scroll Pr.
Barbier, Suzette. One Red Rooster. Carroll, Kathleen S. 32p. (ps). 1992. 13.45 (0-395-60195-9) HM.
Barbour, Karen. Flamboyan. Adoff, Arnold. 32p. (ps-3). 1988. 14.95 (0-15-228404-4, HB Juv Bks) HarBrace.
—Street Music: City Poems. Adoff, Arnold. LC 92-28539. 1992. 15.00 (0-06-021522-4); PLB 14.89 (0-06-021523-2) HarpC Child Bks.
—When I Dance. Berry, James. Ingber, Bonnie V., ed. 120p. (gr. 7 up). 1991. 15.95 (0-15-295568-2) HarBrace.
Barcita, Pamela. Boots & the Spooky House. James, Sara. 24p. 1993. PLB 3.98 (1-56156-133-9) Kidsbks.
—Boots Goes to School. James, Sara. 24p. 1993. 3.98 (1-56156-132-0) Kidsbks.
—Boots Loses a Tooth. James, Sara. 7p. 1993. 4.98 (1-56156-126-6) Kidsbks.
—Boots Loses a Tooth. James, Sara. 14p. (ps-k). 1993. 4.98 (0-8317-0608-2) Smithmark.
—Boots Plays Hide & Seek. James, Sara. 7p. 1993. 4.98 (1-56156-127-4) Kidsbks.
—Boots Plays Hide & Seek. James, Sara. 14p. (ps-k). 1993. 4.98 (0-8317-0607-4) Smithmark.
—Boots Sleeps Over. James, Sara. 24p. 1993. 3.98 (1-56156-135-5) Kidsbks.
—Boots Sleeps Over. James, Sara. 24p. (ps-k). 1993. 3.98 (0-8317-0604-X) Smithmark.
—Boots Visits Grandma. James, Sara. 24p. 1993. PLB 3.98 (1-56156-134-7) Kidsbks.
—Boots Visits Grandma. James, Sara. 24p. (ps-k). 1993. 3.98 (0-8317-0603-1) Smithmark.
—What Does Boots Hear? James, Sara. 6p. 1993. 2.98 (1-56156-129-0) Kidsbks.
—What Does Boots Hear? James, Sara. 12p. (ps). 1993. 2.98 (0-8317-9606-5) Smithmark.
—What Does Boots See? James, Sara. 6p. 1993. 2.98 (1-56156-128-2) Kidsbks.
—What Does Boots See? James, Sara. 12p. (ps). 1993. 2.98 (0-8317-9605-7) Smithmark.
—What Does Boots Smell? James, Sara. 6p. 1993. PLB 2.98 (1-56156-130-4) Kidsbks.
—What Does Boots Smell? James, Sara. 12p. (ps). 1993. 2.98 (0-8317-9607-3) Smithmark.
—What Does Boots Touch? James, Sara. 6p. 1993. PLB 2.98 (1-56156-131-2) Kidsbks.
—What Does Boots Touch? James, Sara. 12p. (ps). 1993. 2.98 (0-8317-9608-1) Smithmark.
Barclay, Meg H. A Midsummer Night's Dream: Simply Shakespeare. Volz, Jim & Case, Evelyn C., eds. 98p. (gr. 3-6). 1989. 14.95 (0-929077-05-9, Hopscotch Bks); PLB 14.95 (0-317-93769-3) Watermark Inc.
Bardugo, Miriam. The Arizal: The Life & Times of Rabbi Yitzchak Luria. Piontac, Nechemiah. Weinbach, Shaindel, tr. from HEB. 288p. (gr. 5-12). 1988. 12.95 (0-89906-835-9); pap. 9.95 (0-89906-836-7) Mesorah Pubns.
—A Story a Day, Vol. I: Tishrei-Cheshvan. Sofer, G. Weinbach, Shaindel, tr. from HEB. 206p. (gr. 7-12). 1989. 12.95 (0-89906-950-9); pap. 9.95 (0-89906-951-7) Mesorah Pubns.
—A Story a Day, Vol. II: Kislev-Teves. Sofer, G. Weinbach, Shaindel, tr. from HEB. 232p. (gr. 7-12). 1988. 14.95 (0-89906-952-5); pap. 10.95 (0-89906-953-3) Mesorah Pubns.
—A Story a Day, Vol. III: Shevat-Adar. Sofer, G. Weinbach, Shaindel, tr. from HEB. 224p. (gr. 7-12). 1989. 14.95 (0-89906-954-1); pap. 10.95 (0-89906-955-X) Mesorah Pubns.
—A Story a Day, Vol. IV: Nissan-Iyar. Sofer, G. Weinbach, Shaindel, tr. from HEB. 210p. (gr. 7-12). 1989. 14.95 (0-89906-956-8); pap. 10.95 (0-89906-957-6) Mesorah Pubns.
—A Story a Day, Vol. V: Sivan-Tammuz. Sofer, G. Weinbach, Shaindel, tr. from HEB. 210p. (gr. 7-12). 1989. 14.95 (0-89906-958-4); pap. 10.95 (0-89906-959-2) Mesorah Pubns.
—A Story a Day, Vol. VI: Ev-Elul. Sofer, G. Weinbach, Shaindel, tr. from HEB. 210p. (gr. 7-12). 1989. 14.95 (0-89906-960-6); pap. 10.95 (0-89906-961-4) Mesorah Pubns.
—Tales of Tzaddikim: Bamidbar. Weinbach, Shaindel, tr. from HEB. 320p. (gr. 7-12). 1988. 14.95 (0-89906-831-6); pap. 10.95 (0-89906-832-4) Mesorah Pubns.
—Tales of Tzaddikim: Bereishis. Matov, G. Weinbach, Shaindel, tr. from HEB. 320p. (gr. 7-12). 1987. 14.95 (0-89906-825-1); pap. 10.95 (0-89906-826-X) Mesorah Pubns.
—Tales of Tzaddikim: Devarim. Matov, G. Weinbach, Shaindel, tr. 320p. (gr. 7-12). 1988. 14.95 (0-89906-833-2); pap. 10.95 (0-89906-834-0) Mesorah Pubns.
—Tales of Tzaddikim: Vayikra. Weinbach, Shaindel, tr. from HEB. 320p. (gr. 7-12). 1988. 14.95 (0-89906-829-4); pap. 10.95 (0-89906-830-8) Mesorah Pubns.
Bardugo, Miriam. Tales of Tzaddikim: Sh'emos. Matov, G. Weinbach, Shaindel, tr. from HEB. 320p. (gr. 7-12). 1988. 14.95 (0-89906-827-8); pap. 10.95 (0-89906-828-6) Mesorah Pubns.
Bare, Arnold E. The Play Party Book: Singing Games for Children. Durlacher, Ed, ed. 38p. (ps-5). 1945. 9.50 (0-8159-6505-2) Devin.
Bare, Colleen S., photos by. Busy, Busy Squirrels. Bare, Colleen S. LC 90-44219. 32p. (gr. 1-4). 1991. 12.95 (0-525-65063-6, Cobblehill Bks) Dutton Child Bks.
—Elephants on the Beach. Bare, Colleen S. LC 89-32267. 32p. (ps-3). 1990. 12.95 (0-525-65018-0, Cobblehill Bks) Dutton Child Bks.
—Never Grab a Deer by the Ear. Bare, Colleen S. LC 92-7702. 32p. (gr. 1-4). 1993. 13.00 (0-525-65112-8, Cobblehill Bks) Dutton Child Bks.
—This Is a House. Bare, Colleen S. 32p. (gr. 1-5). 1992. 14.00 (0-525-65090-3, Cobblehill Bks) Dutton Child Bks.
—Who Comes to the Water Hole? Bare, Colleen S. LC 91-7915. 32p. (ps-3). 1991. 13.95 (0-525-65073-3, Cobblehill Bks) Dutton Child Bks.
Barham, Scott. Lion in the Lake - Le Lion dans le Lac. Oberman, Sheldon. (ENG & FRE.). 56p. (gr. k-3). 1988. 14.95 (0-920541-36-4) Peguis Pubs Ltd.
—Of the Jigsaw. 248p. (Orig.). (gr. 5-8). 1986. pap. 12.95 (0-920541-07-0); tchr's. guide, 51p. 5.95 (0-920541-48-8) Peguis Pubs Ltd.
—Pieces. 120p. (Orig.). (gr. k-4). 1986. pap. 12.95 (0-920541-05-4); tchr's. guide, 24p. 5.95 (0-920541-46-1) Peguis Pubs Ltd.
—Puzzle. 178p. (Orig.). (gr. 9-12). 1986. pap. 12.95 (0-920541-09-7); tchr's. guide, 44p. 5.95 (0-920541-50-X) Peguis Pubs Ltd.
Barich, Mike, et al. Indian Bead-Weaving Patterns: Chain Weaving Designs & Bead Loom Weaving-An Illustrated "How-To" Guide. Goodhue, Horace R. LC 84-71456. 64p. (gr. 3 up). 1984. pap. 4.95 (0-9613503-0-X) Bead Craft.
Barker, Bill. Nevada: A History of Changes. Thompson, David. Dickerson, Donald, ed. Thompson, David, intro. by. LC 86-82332. 232p. (Orig.). 1986. pap. text ed. 17.50 (0-913205-09-5); special price 10.50 Grace Dangberg.
Barker, Chris. The Little Christmas Tree. Jeffs, Stephanie. 16p. (ps-8). 1991. 12.95 (0-7459-2118-3) Lion USA.
Barker, Cicely M. Flower Fairies of the Garden. Barker, Cicely M. (ps up). 1991. 5.95 (0-7232-3758-1) Warne.
—Flower Fairies of the Spring. Barker, Cicely M. (ps up). 1991. 5.95 (0-7232-3753-0) Warne.
—Flower Fairies of the Summer. Barker, Cicely M. (ps up). 1991. 5.95 (0-7232-3754-9) Warne.
—Flower Fairies of the Trees. Barker, Cicely M. (ps up). 1991. 5.95 (0-7232-3760-3) Warne.
—A Flower Fairies Postcard Book. 30p. (ps up). 1991. pap. 7.95 (0-7232-3710-7) Warne.
—Old Rhymes for All Times. 112p. (gr. 4-7). 1994. 12.99 (0-7232-3751-4) Warne.
Barker, Melissa & Logan, Ann. A Banana for Rosie. Haines, Joan. 16p. (Orig.). (ps-1). 1985. pap. 2.65 (0-936652-03-9, Pub. by Ed Concern Pubns) Two Ems.
—Meet Rosie Posie. Haines, Joan. 16p. (Orig.). (ps-1). 1985. pap. 2.65 (0-936652-00-4, Pub. by Ed Concern Pubns) Two Ems.
—Rosie Posie Has a Bath. Haines, Joan. 16p. (ps-1). 1985. pap. 2.65 (0-936652-02-0, Pub. by Ed Concern Pubns) Two Ems.
Barker, Scott J. Benny, the Lazy Beaver. Fisk, George W. LC 90-45200. 32p. 1991. 10.99 (0-9620507-1-7) Cosmic Concepts Pr.
Barklem, Jill. The Secret Staircase. Barklem, Jill. 32p. (ps-3). 1989. pap. 5.95 (0-399-21726-6, Sandcastle Bks) Putnam Pub Group.
—Spring Story. Barklem, Jill. LC 80-15300. 32p. (gr. 1 up). 1986. 10.95 (0-399-20746-5, Philomel) Putnam Pub Group.
—Summer Story. Barklem, Jill. LC 80-15423. 32p. (gr. 1 up). 1986. 10.95 (0-399-20747-3, Philomel) Putnam Pub Group.
—Winter Story. Barklem, Jill. LC 80-15422. 32p. (gr. 1 up). 1986. 10.95 (0-399-20748-1, Philomel) Putnam Pub Group.
Barkley, James. Sounder. Armstrong, William H. LC 70-85030. 128p. (gr. 6 up). 1972. pap. 3.95 (0-06-440020-4, Trophy) HarpC Child Bks.
—Sounder. large type ed. Armstrong, William H. 99p. (gr. 2-6). 1987. Repr. of 1969 ed. lib. bdg. 13.95 (1-55736-003-0, Crnrstn Bks) BDD LT Grp.
Barkman, Aidel. The Shushan Chronicle: The Story of Purim. Gottlieb, Yaffa L. 56p. (gr. 4-6). 1991. 11.95 (0-922613-39-7); pap. 9.95 (0-922613-40-0) Hachai Pubns.
Barks, Carl. Uncle Scrooge McDuck: His Life & Times. Summer, Edward, ed. Lucas, George, intro. by. LC 81-66953. 376p. (ps-3). 1987. pap. 34.95 (0-89087-510-3); text ed. 59.95 (0-89087-511-1) Celestial Arts.

—Walt Disney's Comics in Color, Vol. 4. rev. ed. 192p. 1990. pap. 19.95 (0-944599-42-7) Gladstone Pub.
—Walt Disney's Donald & Daisy Comic Album. Barks, Carl. Blum, Geoffrey, intro. by. 48p. (Orig.). (ps up). 1988. pap. 5.95 (0-944599-11-7) Gladstone Pub.
—Walt Disney's Donald Duck Adventures Album. Barks, Carl. Blum, Geoffrey, intro. by. 48p. (Orig.). (ps up). 1988. pap. 5.95 (0-944599-08-7) Gladstone Pub.
—Walt Disney's Donald Duck Adventures Album. Barks, Carl. Blum, Geoffrey, intro. by. 48p. (Orig.). (ps up). 1988. pap. 5.95 (0-944599-13-3) Gladstone Pub.
—Walt Disney's Donald Duck Adventures Album. Barks, Carl. Blum, Geoffrey, intro. by. 48p. (Orig.). (ps up). 1989. pap. 5.95 (0-944599-15-X) Gladstone Pub.
—Walt Disney's Donald Duck Adventures Comic Album. Barks, Carl. Blum, Geoffrey, intro. by. 48p. (Orig.). (ps up). 1988. pap. 5.95 (0-944599-04-4) Gladstone Pub.
—Walt Disney's Donald Duck Album. Barks, Carl. Blum, Geoffrey, intro. by. 48p. (Orig.). (ps up) 1988. pap. 5.95 (0-944599-06-0) Gladstone Pub.
—Walt Disney's Donald Duck Comic Album. Barks, Carl. Blum, Geoffrey, intro. by. 48p. (Orig.). (ps up) 1987. pap. 5.95 (0-944599-01-X) Gladstone Pub.
—Walt Disney's Uncle Scrooge Album. Barks, Carl. Blum, Geoffrey, intro. by. 48p. (Orig.). (ps up) 1988. pap. 5.95 (0-944599-14-1) Gladstone Pub.
—Walt Disney's Uncle Scrooge Comic Album. Barks, Carl. Blum, Geoffrey, intro. by. 48p. (Orig.). (ps up) 1987. pap. 5.95 (0-944599-02-8) Gladstone Pub.
—Walt Disney's Uncle Scrooge Comic Album. Barks, Carl. Blum, Geoffrey, intro. by. 48p. (Orig.). (ps up) 1988. pap. 5.95 (0-944599-05-2) Gladstone Pub.
—Walt Disney's Uncle Scrooge Comic Album. Barks, Carl. Blum, Geoffrey, intro. by. 48p. (Orig.). (ps up) 1987. pap. 5.95 (0-944599-00-1) Gladstone Pub.
—Walt Disney's Uncle Scrooge Comic Album. Barks, Carl. Blum, Geoffrey, intro. by. 48p. (Orig.). (ps up) 1988. pap. 5.95 (0-944599-10-9) Gladstone Pub.
—Walt Disney's Uncle Scrooge Comic Album. Barks, Carl. Blum, Geoff, intro. by. 48p. (Orig.). 1989. pap. 5.95 (0-944599-16-8) Gladstone Pub.
—Walt Disney's Uncle Scrooge Comic Album. Barks, Carl. Blum, Geoff, intro. by. 48p. (Orig.). 1989. pap. 5.95 (0-944599-19-2) Gladstone Pub.
Barks, Carl & Gollub, Mo. Walt Disney's Comics in Color, Vol. 1. rev. ed. 192p. 1990. pap. 19.95 (0-944599-39-7) Gladstone Pub.
Barks, Carl & Gottfredson, Floyd. Walt Disney's Comics in Color. rev. ed. 192p. (ps up). 1990. pap. 19.95 (0-944599-35-4) Gladstone Pub.
—Walt Disney's Comics in Color, Vol. 2. rev. ed. 192p. 1990. pap. 19.95 (0-944599-40-0) Gladstone Pub.
—Walt Disney's Comics in Color, Vol. 3. rev. ed. 192p. 1990. pap. 19.95 (0-944599-41-9) Gladstone Pub.
—Walt Disney's Comics in Color, Vol. 5. rev. ed. 200p. 1990. pap. 19.95 (0-944599-38-9) Gladstone Pub.
—Walt Disney's Comics in Color, Vol. 6. rev. ed. 184p. (ps up) 1990. pap. 19.95 (0-944599-37-0) Gladstone Pub.
Barks, Carl & Hannah, Jack. Walt Disney's Donald Duck Giant Comic Album. Barks, Carl & Hannah, Jack. Blum, Geoff, intro. by. 72p. (gr. k up) 1989. pap. 8.95 (0-944599-20-6) Gladstone Pub.
Barks, Carl & Rosa, Don. Walt Disney's Comics in Color, Vol. 7. rev. ed. 206p. (ps up) 1990. pap. 19.95 (0-944599-36-2) Gladstone Pub.
Barlowe, Dorothea & Barlowe, Sy. Dinosaurs. LC 77-70862. (ps-3). 1977. 8.99 (0-394-83538-7) Random Bks Yng Read.
—Seashores. Zim, Herbert S. & Ingle, Lester. (gr. 5 up). 1955. pap. write for info. (0-307-24496-2, Golden Pr) Western Pub.
—Trees. Zim, Herbert S. & Martin, Alexander C. (gr. 6 up). 1952. pap. write for info. (0-307-24056-8, Golden Pr) Western Pub.
Barlowe, Dorothy. Insects Do the Strangest Things. Hornblow, Leonora & Hornblow, Arthur. LC 88-30201. 64p. (gr. 2-4). 1990. lib. bdg. 6.99 (0-394-94306-6); pap. 3.95 (0-394-84306-1) Random Bks Yng Read.
Barlowe, Dot & Barlowe, Sy. Who Lives Here? Barlowe, Dot & Barlowe, Sy. LC 79-27494. 32p. (ps-3). 1980. pap. 2.25 (0-394-83740-1) Random Bks Yng Read.
Barlowe, Sy. Prehistoric Monsters Did the Strangest Things. abr. ed. Hornblow, Leonora & Hornblow, Arthur. LC 88-30212. 64p. (gr. 2-4). 1990. Repr. lib. bdg. 6.99 (0-394-94307-4); 4.99 (0-394-84307-X) Random Bks Yng Read.
Barlowe, Sy, jt. illus. see Barlowe, Dorothea.
Barlowe, Sy, jt. illus. see Barlowe, Dot.
Barnard, Anna. Look at Rainbow Colors. rev. ed. Kirkpatrick, Rena K. LC 84-26250. 32p. (gr. 2-4). 1985. PLB 17.28 (0-8172-2356-8); pap. 4.95 (0-8114-6902-6) Raintree Steck-V.
Barnard, Bryn. Night of the Milky Way Railway. Kenji, Miyazawa. Strong, Sarah M., tr. & intro. by. LC 91-6608. 192p. (gr. 7 up). 1991. 22.50 (0-87332-820-5) M E Sharpe.
Barner, Bob. Double-Decker Double-Decker Double-Decker Bus. Wolcott, Patty. LC 91-14210. 32p. (ps-2). 1991. 3.50 (0-679-81930-4); PLB 6.99 (0-679-91930-9) Random Bks Yng Read.
—Pick up Your Ears, Henry. Demuth, Patricia B. LC 91-27162. 32p. (ps-1). 1992. RSBE 13.95 (0-02-728465-4, Macmillan Child Bk) Macmillan Child Grp.
Barnes, Jon, jt. illus. see Tofts, Hannah.

Barnes-Murphy, Rowan. The Baron of Grogzwig. Dickens, Charles. Greenway, Shirley, ed. LC 93-18627. 1993. write for info. (1-879085-81-X) Whsprng Coyote Pr.
—The Emergency Handbook. McGee, Eddie. Arico, Diane, ed. 176p. (gr. 8-12). 1985. lib. bdg. 9.79 (0-671-60484-8); pap. 4.95 (0-671-60483-X) S&S Trade.
—Let's Sing about Silly People. Charney, Steve. LC 92-24713. 32p. (gr. k-2). 1992. PLB 11.89 (0-8167-2978-6); pap. text ed. 3.95 (0-8167-2979-4) Troll Assocs.
—My Tricks & Treats: Halloween Stories, Songs, Poems, Recipes, Crafts & Fun for Kids. Dewhirst, Carin & Dewhirst, Joan. 80p. (ps-3). 1993. 9.98 (0-8317-5172-X) Smithmark.
—Opposites. Barnes-Murphy, Rowan. 16p. (ps). 1993. bds. 3.95 (0-8249-8611-3, Ideals Child) Hambleton-Hill.
—Shapes. Barnes-Murphy, Rowan. 16p. (ps). 1993. bds. 3.95 (0-8249-8606-7, Ideals Child) Hambleton-Hill.
—Sherman the Sheep. Kiser, Kevin. LC 92-22745. 32p. (gr. k-3). 1994. RSBE 14.95 (0-02-750825-0, Macmillan Child Bk) Macmillan Child Grp.
Barnes-Murphy, Rowan S. The Legend of Sleepy Hollow. Jensen, Patricia A. LC 93-24803. (gr. k-3). 1993. PLB 9.89 (0-8167-3168-3); pap. text ed. 2.95 (0-8167-3169-1) Troll Assocs.
Barnet, Nancy. Dream Meadow. Griffith, Helen V. LC 93-18175. 24p. (ps up). 1994. write for info. (0-688-12293-0); PLB write for info. (0-688-12294-9) Greenwillow.
Barnett, Isa. Reader's Digest Best Loved Books for Young Readers: The Red Badge of Courage. Crane, Stephen. Ogburn, Jackie, ed. 120p. (gr. 4-12). 1989. 3.99 (0-945260-34-2) Choice Pub NY.
Barnett, Moneta. A Glorious Age in Africa: The Story of Three Great African Empires. Chu, Daniel & Skinner, Eliott. LC 90-80150. 124p. (gr. 6-12). 1990. 19.95 (0-86543-166-3); pap. 7.95 (0-86543-167-1) Africa World.
—Me & Neesie. Greenfield, Eloise. LC 74-23078. 40p. (gr. 1-4). 1975. PLB 13.89 (0-690-00715-9, Crowell Jr Bks) HarpC Child Bks.
—Me & Neesie. Greenfield, Eloise. LC 74-23078. 40p. (gr. k-3). 1984. pap. 4.95 (0-06-443057-X, Trophy) HarpC Child Bks.
—Sister. Greenfield, Eloise. LC 73-22182. 96p. (gr. 5-12). 1974. 15.00 (0-690-00497-4, Crowell Jr Bks) HarpC Child Bks.
—Sister. Greenfield, Eloise. LC 73-22182. 96p. (gr. 5-8). 1987. pap. 3.95 (0-06-440199-5, Trophy) HarpC Child Bks.
Barnhart, Philo. The Haunted Palace. Applegate, Katherine. LC 93-70936. 80p. (gr. 1-4). 1993. pap. 2.95 (1-56282-503-8) Disney Pr.
—King Triton, Beware! Applegate, Katherine. LC 93-71030. 80p. (gr. 1-4). 1993. pap. 2.95 (1-56282-502-X) Disney Pr.
Barnum, Jay H. Boats on the River. Flack, Marjorie. 32p. (ps-3). 1991. 14.95 (0-670-83918-3) Viking Child Bks.
Baron, Alan. What Is a Wall, After All? Allen, Judy. LC 92-54623. 32p. (ps up). 1993. PLB 14.95 (1-56402-218-8) Candlewick Pr.
Baron, Elaine, photos by. The Cat Lover's Diary. Tanaka, Shelley. Fanelli, Jenny, ed. Reynolds, Nancy L. & Macpherson, Elaine, illus. 176p. (gr. 5 up). 1984. pap. 8.95 (0-394-86613-4) Random Bks Yng Read.
Baron, Nancy. Getting Started in Calligraphy. Baron, Nancy. LC 78-66311. (gr. 7 up). 1979. spiral bdg. 9.95 (0-8069-8840-1) Sterling.
Barr, Charlotte & Cook, Tonya. To Be a Doctor: A Health Education Workbook. Skolnick, Georgette B. 215p. (Orig.). (gr. 6-9). 1982. student's wkbk. 8.00 (0-913855-00-6) GBS CA.
Barr, Ken. Frankenstein. Shelley, Mary Wollstonecraft. Weinberg, Larry, adapted by. LC 87-23543. 96p. (gr. 2-6). 1993. pap. 2.99 (0-394-84827-6) Random Bks Yng Read.
—Frankenstein. Shelley, Mary Wollstonecraft. Weinberg, Larry, adapted by. 96p. (gr. 3-7). 1992. pap. 6.99 incl. cass. (0-679-82443-X) Random Bks Yng Read.
Barr, Loel. Business Is Looking Up: Featuring Renaldo Rodriguez. Aiello, Barbara & Shulman, Jeffrey. 48p. (gr. 3-6). 1988. PLB 13.95 (0-941477-00-2) TFC Bks NY.
—Friends for Life: Featuring Amy Wilson. Aiello, Barbara & Shulman, Jeffrey. LC 88-29251. 48p. (gr. 3-6). 1988. PLB 13.95 (0-941477-03-7) TFC Bks NY.
—Hometown Hero: Featuring Scott Whittaker. Aiello, Barbara & Shulman, Jeffrey. 48p. (gr. 3-6). 1989. PLB 13.95 (0-941477-04-5) TFC Bks NY.
—How & Why? A Kid's Book about the Body. O'Neil, Catherine. 144p. (Orig.). (gr. 2 up). 1987. pap. 9.95 (0-89043-099-3) Consumer Reports.
—It's Your Turn at Bat: Featuring Mark Riley. Aiello, Barbara & Shulman, Jeffrey. 48p. (gr. 3-6). 1988. PLB 13.95 (0-8050-3070-0) TFC Bks NY.
—On with the Show! Featuring Brenda Dubrowski. Aiello, Barbara & Shulman, Jeffrey. 56p. (gr. 3-6). 1989. PLB 13.95 (0-941477-06-1) TFC Bks NY.
—Secrets Aren't (Always) for Keeps: Featuring Jennifer Hauser. Aiello, Barbara & Shulman, Jeffrey. 48p. (gr. 3-6). 1988. PLB 13.95 (0-8050-3069-7) TFC Bks NY.
—Trick or Treat or Trouble: Featuring Brian McDaniel. Aiello, Barbara & Shulman, Jeffrey. 56p. (gr. 3-6). 1989. PLB 13.95 (0-941477-07-X) TFC Bks NY.

Barr, Marilyn. Hillel Builds a House. Lepon, Shoshana. LC 92-39383. 1993. cancelled (0-929371-41-0); pap. 5.95 (0-929371-42-9) Kar Ben.
—Virginians All. Uchello, Carlo. LC 92-13634. 144p. (gr. 7-9). 1992. 11.95 (0-88289-853-1) Pelican.
Barr, Marilynn G. ABC: Board Games. Lieberman, Lillian. 64p. (ps-2). 1991. pap. 7.95 (1-878279-31-9) Monday Morning Bks.
—ABC: Box Games. Lieberman, Lillian. 64p. (ps-2). 1991. pap. 7.95 (1-878279-30-0) Monday Morning Bks.
—ABC: Folder Games. Lieberman, Lillian. 64p. (ps-2). 1991. pap. 7.95 (1-878279-29-7) Monday Morning Bks.
—How to Be President of the U. S. A. Suid, Murray. 80p. (Orig.). (gr. 3-8). 1992. pap. text ed. 9.95 (1-878279-47-5, MM1963) Monday Morning Bks.
—Playkits. Jones, Candy & McGee, Lea. 64p. (ps-2). 1991. pap. 7.95 (1-878279-26-2) Monday Morning Bks.
—Story Kits. Jones, Candy & McGee, Lea. 64p. (ps-2). 1991. pap. 7.95 (1-878279-28-9) Monday Morning Bks.
Barrenger, Nick. The Super Joke Book. Brandreth, Gyles. LC 83-397. 128p. (gr. 3 up). 1985. 12.95 (0-8069-4672-5); pap. 3.95 (0-8069-6200-3) Sterling.
Barrett, Angela. Beware, Beware. Hill, Susan. LC 92-54960. 32p. (ps up). 1993. 14.95 (1-56402-245-5) Candlewick Pr.
—Proud Knight, Fair Lady: The Twelve Lais of Marie de France. Lewis, Naomi, tr. 128p. (gr. 5 up). 1989. pap. 19.95 (0-670-82656-1) Viking Child Bks.
—The Random House Book of Ghost Stories. Hill, Susan, ed. LC 87-3818. 224p. (gr. 3-7). 1991. 18.95 (0-679-81234-2); lib. bdg. 19.99 (0-679-91234-7) Random Bks Yng Read.
—The Snow Queen. Andersen, Hans Christian. Lewis, Naomi, retold by. LC 92-54412. 48p. (ps up). 1993. 16.95 (1-56402-215-3) Candlewick Pr.
—The Witches & the Singing Mice: A Celtic Tale. Nimmo, Jenny, retold by. LC 92-37642. 32p. (gr. 1 up). 1993. 14.99 (0-8037-1509-9) Dial Bks Young.
—The Woman in the Moon & Other Tales of Forgotten Heroines. Riordan, James. LC 84-20050. 96p. (ps up). 1985. 13.00 (0-8037-0194-2) Dial Bks Young.
Barrett, Brett K. The Flight of Fancy. Barrett, Kirt K. LC 89-60346. 38p. (gr. 3-9). 1989. PLB 12.95 (0-9622496-0-2) Roanoke Park.
Barrett, Deborah. The Adventures of Puppycat. Kriegman, Mitchell. (ps-3). 1990. PLB 8.95 (0-553-05888-6, Little Rooster) Bantam.
Barrett, Jennifer. I Know I'm Myself Because... Greenberg, Polly. 32p. (ps-3). 1986. 16.95 (0-89885-045-2); pap. 9.95 (0-89885-200-5) Human Sci Pr.
—Imagine That!!! Exploring Make-Believe. Strauss, Joyce. LC 82-1089. 32p. (ps-3). 1983. 16.95 (0-89885-128-9); pap. 9.95 (0-89885-306-0) Human Sci Pr.
—Promise Not to Tell. Polese, Carolyn. LC 84-19767. 66p. (gr. 3 up). 1985. 16.95 (0-89885-239-0) Human Sci Pr.
—Promise Not to Tell. Polese, Carolyn. LC 92-24599. 64p. (gr. 4 up). 1993. pap. 3.95 (0-688-12026-1, Pub. by Beech Tree Bks) Morrow.
—Seven Treasure Hunts. Byars, Betsy. LC 90-32043. 80p. (gr. 2-6). 1991. 14.00 (0-06-020885-6); PLB 13.89 (0-06-020886-4) HarpC Child Bks.
—The Seven Treasure Hunts. Byars, Betsy. LC 90-32043. 80p. (gr. 2-6). 1992. pap. 3.95 (0-06-440435-8, Trophy) HarpC Child Bks.
Barrett, Jerry. Y Basketball Dribblers Manual: For 5th-6th Grade Players. Levin, Robert, ed. 58p. (gr. 5-6). 1984. pap. text ed. 5.00 (0-931250-84-6, LYMC4666, Pub. by YMCA USA) Human Kinetics.
Barrett, Jery. Y Basketball Passers Manual: For 3rd-4th Grade Players. Levin, Robert, ed. 36p. (gr. 3-4). 1984. pap. 5.00x (0-931250-83-8, LYMC4665, Pub. by YMCA USA) Human Kinetics.
Barrett, John E., photos by. Big Bird Is Yellow: A Sesame Street Book of Colors. LC 89-63996. 14p. (ps). 1990. bds. 3.95 (0-679-80752-7) Random Bks Yng Read.
—Big Bird's Farm. Sesame Street Staff. LC 81-50537. 14p. (ps). 1981. bds. 3.95 (0-394-84812-8) Random Bks Yng Read.
—Grover's New Kitten. Sesame Street Staff. LC 81-50538. 14p. (ps). 1981. bds. 3.95 (0-394-84872-1) Random Bks Yng Read.
—One Rubber Duckie. Sesame Street Staff. LC 81-86375. (ps). 1982. 3.95 (0-394-85309-1) Random Bks Yng Read.
Barrett, John E. & View-Master International, photos by. Big Bird's Mother Goose. LC 83-63404. 28p. (ps). 1984. bds. 2.95 (0-394-86745-9) Random Bks Yng Read.
Barrett, Lindsey. Macmillan Illustrated Almanac for Kids. Elwood, Ann, et al. LC 81-82099. 400p. (gr. 4 up). 1984. SBE 12.95 (0-02-535420-5, Macmillan Child Bk); pap. 7.95 (0-02-043040-X) Macmillan Child Grp.
—Macmillan Illustrated Almanac for Kids. Elwood, Ann, et al. LC 83-26296. 448p. (gr. 4 up). 1986. pap. 10.95 (0-02-043100-7, Aladdin) Macmillan Child Grp.
Barrett, Peter. Dinosaur Babies: A Step One Book. Penner, Lucille R. LC 90-36045. 32p. (Orig.). (ps-1). 1991. lib. bdg. 7.99 (0-679-91207-X); pap. 2.95 (0-679-81207-5) Random Bks Yng Read.

—Don't Wake the Animals. Ingle, Annie. LC 91-67720. 14p. (ps-k). 1992. bds. 3.99 (*0-679-83433-8*) Random Bks Yng Read.
—Glow-in-the-Dark Dinosaur Skeletons. Ingle, Annie. LC 92-18176. 16p. (ps-1). 1993. pap. 4.99 (*0-679-84366-3*) Random Bks Yng Read.
—Moses the Kitten. Herriot, James. LC 84-50930. 32p. (ps up). 1984. 13.00 (*0-312-54905-9*) St Martin.
—Moses the Kitten. Herriot, James. 1991. pap. 6.95 (*0-312-06419-5*) St Martin.
—Only One Woof. Herriot, James. 32p. (ps up). 1985. 13.00 (*0-312-58583-7*) St Martin.
—Only One Woof. Herriot, James. 32p. (gr. 1-8). 1993. pap. 6.95 (*0-312-09129-X*) St Martin.
—The World of Animals. Morris, Desmond. 128p. 1993. 22.50 (*0-670-85184-1*) Viking Child Bks.
Barrett, Randy. The Case of the Goofy Game Show. Hope, Laura L. Greenberg, Anne, ed. 96p. (Orig.). 1991. pap. 2.95 (*0-671-69296-8*, Minstrel Bks) PB.
—The Monster Mouse Mystery. Hope, Laura L. Greenberg, Ann, ed. 96p. (Orig.). 1991. pap. 2.95 (*0-671-69295-X*, Minstrel Bks) PB.
Barrett, Rob. Birds & Their Environments. Stewart, Frances T. & Stewart, Charles P. 22p. (ps up). 1988. sticker bk. 7.95 (*0-694-00257-7*) HarpC Child Bks.
Barrett, Robert. Other Wise Man. Van Dyke, Henry. 32p. (gr. k-3). 1989. 12.95 (*0-8249-8396-3*) Ideals.
—The Other Wise Man. Van Dyke, Henry. Kennedy, Pamela, adapted by. 32p. (ps-3). 1992. pap. 4.95 (*0-8249-8564-8*, Ideals Child) Hambleton-Hill.
Barrett, Ron. Animals Should Definitely Not Act Like People. Barrett, Judi. LC 80-13364. 32p. (ps-2). 1980. SBE 13.95 (*0-689-30768-3*, Atheneum Child Bk) Macmillan Child Grp.
—Animals Should Definitely Not Act Like People. Barrett, Judi. 32p. (ps-1). 1988. pap. 3.95 (*0-689-71287-1*, Aladdin) Macmillan Child Grp.
—Animals Should Definitely Not Wear Clothing. Barrett, Judi. LC 70-115078. 32p. (ps-2). 1970. SBE 13.95 (*0-689-20592-9*, Atheneum Child Bk) Macmillan Child Grp.
—Animals Should Definitely Not Wear Clothing. Barrett, Judi. 32p. (ps-1). 1988. pap. 3.95 (*0-689-70807-6*, Aladdin) Macmillan Child Grp.
—Animals Should Definitely Not Wear Clothing. Barrett, Judi. 32p. (gr. k-3). 1990. incl. cass. 19.95 (*0-87499-147-1*); pap. 12.95 incl. cass. (*0-87488-146-3*); Set; incl. 4 bks., cass., & guide. pap. 27.95 (*0-87499-148-X*) Live Oak Media.
—Benjamin's Three Hundred Sixty-Five Birthdays. reissue ed. Barrett, Judi. LC 92-2497. 40p. (ps-1). 1992. RSBE 13.95 (*0-689-31791-3*, Atheneum Child Bk) Macmillan Child Grp.
—Benjamin's 365 Birthdays. 2nd ed. Barrett, Judi. LC 92-2497. 40p. (ps-1). 1992. pap. 4.95 (*0-689-71635-4*, Aladdin) Macmillan Child Grp.
—Cloudy with a Chance of Meatballs. Barrett, Judi. LC 78-2945. 32p. (ps-3). 1978. RSBE 14.95 (*0-689-30647-4*, Atheneum Child Bk) Macmillan Child Grp.
—Cloudy with a Chance of Meatballs. Barrett, Judi. (gr. 2-5). 1985. pap. 12.95 incl. cassette (*0-941078-91-4*); PLB incl. cassette 19.95 (*0-941078-93-0*); incl. cassette, 4 paperbacks guide 27.95 (*0-941078-92-2*) Live Oak Media.
—Ghastlies, Goops & Pincushions: Nonsense Verse. Kennedy, X. J. LC 88-28663. 64p. (gr. 3 up). 1989. SBE 13.95 (*0-689-50477-2*, M K McElderry) Macmillan Child Grp.
—Wackysaurus: Dinosaur Jokes. Phillips, Louis. LC 93-15134. 64p. (gr. 2-5). 1993. pap. 3.99 (*0-14-034687-2*, Puffin) Puffin Bks.
Barrett, Trevor. What's for Breakfast? Yorke, Stephen. 8p. 1992. 3.95 (*0-681-41548-7*) Longmeadow Pr.
—What's for Dinner? Yorke, Stephen. 8p. 1992. 3.95 (*0-681-41550-9*) Longmeadow Pr.
—What's for Lunch? Yorke, Stephen. 8p. 1992. 3.95 (*0-681-41549-5*) Longmeadow Pr.
Barrett George, Lindsay. Box Turtle at Long Pond. George, William T. Grammer, Red, narrated by. 24p. (ps-3). 1989. incl. audiocassette 19.95 (*0-924483-21-0*) Soundprints.
Barrett-Plecas, Jennifer. What about My Goldfish? Greenwood, Pamela D. LC 92-11281. 1993. 14.95 (*0-395-64337-6*, Clarion Bks) HM.
Barrios, David. Ballpoint Bananas & Other Jokes for Kids. Keller, Charles. LC 72-7338. 96p. (gr. 3-7). 1976. pap. 5.95 (*0-671-66965-6*, S&S BFYR) S&S Trade.
Barron, Rex, photos by. The Day the Daisies Danced. Lillegard, Dee. LC 93-30583. 1995. write for info. (*0-399-22661-3*, Putnam) Putnam Pub Group.
Barrow, Ann. A Visit from Dr. Katz. Le Guin, Ursula K. LC 87-1783. 32p. (gr. k-3). 1988. SBE 12.95 (*0-689-31332-2*, Atheneum Child Bk) Macmillan Child Grp.

Barrows, Jack. Socks Says! Finch, Carolyn B. 40p. (Orig.). 1993. pap. 8.95 (*1-882956-00-1*) Bogart Comm. SOCKS SAYS!, another book by Carolyn Finch, professional speaker noted for UNIVERSAL HANDTALK & PORTRAITS OF SOUNDS, has written this poetic plea for a positive self-image. The story narrated by the President Clinton family cat is for ages one to one hundred & one. Cartoon illustrations & calligraphy give uniqueness to this delightful poetic plea for a positive self-image. Cartoon illustrations by artist Jack Barrows make the story come alive. Steve Allen, author, musician, & entertainer writes: "Thank you for permitting me to see a pre-publication copy of your charming book SOCKS SAYS! I plan to take it home this evening & share it with my grandchildren. I'm sure they'll enjoy it as much as I did." The book with black & white drawings is $8.95 or (pkg. B) with Crayola pencils in a zip lock bag for travel, $10.95. The book is available through not-for-profit groups & organizations who need to help themselves & wish to use the books as a fund raiser. This is especially good for schools, hospitals & health care organizations. It is also available in book stores & gift shops. ORDER FROM: Bogart Communications, Inc., 51 Cedar Drive, Danbury CT 06811. 203-792-4833, FAX: 203-794-0945. *Publisher Provided Annotation.*

Barry, Mark. Car Books & Puzzle. Barry, Mark. (ps). 1993. Gift box set of 4 bks., 12p. ea. bds. 14.95 (*1-56828-039-4*) Red Jacket Pr.
Barry, Pat. Blast off with Book Reports. Robertson, Debbie. 64p. (gr. 3-8). 1985. wkbk. 7.95 (*0-86653-327-3*, GA 682) Good Apple.
Barry, Richard E. Seward, Alaska: A History of the Gateway City, Vol. II: 1914-1923. Barry, Mary J. 225p. (gr. 8 up). 1993. pap. 25.00 (*0-9617009-2-0*) M J P Barry.
Barry, Robert. Mr. Willowby's Christmas Tree. Barry, Robert. 32p. (ps-2). 1992. pap. 3.99 (*0-440-40726-5*, YB) Dell.
Barrymore, Lionel. I, Becky Barrymore. Wheeler, Benson. (gr. 3 up). 8.95 (*0-8315-0036-0*) Speller.
Barss, William. Words from the Myths. Asimov, Isaac. 224p. (gr. 5-10). 1961. 14.95 (*0-395-06568-2*) HM.
Bartel, Marvin. My Own Picture Book about Getting Older. Bartel, Marvin. LC 89-80248. 43p. (ps-7). 1989. wkbk. 4.95 (*0-87303-135-0*) Faith & Life.
Bartelt, Robert. Once There Was a Knight & You Can Be One too! Hindley, Judy & Reyes, Gregg. LC 87-20485. 32p. (ps-2). 1988. lib. bdg. 5.99 (*0-394-99007-2*) Random Bks Yng Read.
Barter, Nan. Why Do You Call Me Chocolate Boy? Parker, Carol. LC 93-79098. 28p. (Orig.). (gr. 2-6). 1993. pap. 5.95 (*0-9637267-0-6*) Gull Crest.
Barth, Gillian. In & Out the Windows: Happy Poems for Children. Eastwick, Ivy O. Swinger, Marlys. LC 73-90841. 80p. (ps-3). 1969. 8.00 (*0-87486-007-5*) Plough.
Bartholomew. Every Kid's Guide to Being Special. Berry, Joy. 48p. (gr. 3-7). 1987. 5.95 (*0-516-21401-2*) Childrens.
—Every Kid's Guide to Handling Family Arguments. Berry, Joy. 48p. (gr. 3-7). 1987. 4.95 (*0-516-21402-0*) Childrens.
—Every Kid's Guide to Handling Feelings. Berry, Joy. 48p. (gr. 3-7). 1987. 4.95 (*0-516-21403-9*) Childrens.
—Every Kid's Guide to Handling Fights with Brothers & Sisters. Berry, Joy. 48p. (gr. 3-7). 1987. 5.95 (*0-516-21404-7*) Childrens.
—Every Kid's Guide to Making & Managing Money. Berry, Joy. 48p. (gr. 3-7). 1986. 4.95 (*0-516-21405-5*) Childrens.
—Every Kid's Guide to Making Friends. Berry, Joy. 48p. (gr. 3-7). 1987. 5.95 (*0-516-21406-3*) Childrens.
Bartholomew. About Change & Moving. Berry, Joy. 48p. (gr. 3 up). 1990. PLB 15.00 (*0-516-02951-7*) Childrens.
—About Death. Berry, Joy. 48p. (gr. 3 up). 1990. PLB 15.00 (*0-516-02952-5*) Childrens.
—About Divorce. Berry, Joy. 48p. (gr. 3 up). 1990. PLB 15.00 (*0-516-02953-3*) Childrens.
—About Physical Disabilities. Berry, Joy. 48p. (gr. 3 up). 1990. PLB 15.00 (*0-516-02954-1*) Childrens.
—About Step Families. Berry, Joy. 48p. (gr. 3 up). 1990. 15.00 (*0-516-02955-X*) Childrens.
—About Substance Abuse. Berry, Joy. 48p. (gr. 3 up). 1990. PLB 15.00 (*0-516-02956-8*) Childrens.
—Big Bug Book of Counting. McKissack, Patricia & McKissack, Fredrick. LC 87-61655. 24p. (Orig.). (gr. k-1). 1987. spiral bdg. 14.95 (*0-88335-762-3*); pap. text ed. 4.95 (*0-88335-772-0*) Milliken Pub Co.

—Big Bug Book of Exercise. Duyff, Roberta L. McKissack, Patricia & McKissack, Fredrick, eds. LC 87-61656. 24p. (Orig.). (gr. k-1). 1987. spiral bdg. 14.95 (*0-88335-761-5*); pap. text ed. 4.95 (*0-88335-771-2*) Milliken Pub Co.
—Big Bug Book of Opposites. McKissack, Patricia & Mckissack, Fredrick. LC 87-61654. 24p. (Orig.). (gr. k-1). 1987. spiral bdg. 14.95 (*0-88335-763-1*); pap. text ed. 4.95 (*0-88335-773-9*) Milliken Pub Co.
—Big Bug Book of Places to Go. McKissack, Patricia & McKissack, Fredrick. LC 87-61652. 24p. (Orig.). (gr. k-1). 1987. spiral bdg. 14.95 (*0-88335-765-8*); pap. text ed. 4.95 (*0-88335-775-5*) Milliken Pub Co.
—Big Bug Book of the Alphabet. McKissack, Patricia & McKissack, Fredrick. LC 87-61653. 24p. (Orig.). (gr. k-1). 1987. spiral bdg. 14.95 (*0-88335-764-X*); pap. text ed. 4.95 (*0-88335-774-7*) Milliken Pub Co.
—Big Bug Book of Things to Do. McKissack, Patricia & McKissack, Fredrick. LC 87-61651. 24p. (Orig.). (gr. k-1). 1987. spiral bdg. 14.95 (*0-88335-766-6*); pap. text ed. 4.95 (*0-88335-776-3*) Milliken Pub co.
—Crassy the Crude Beastie: A Beastie Book about Good Manners. Berry, Ron, et al. 48p. (ps-1). 1993. write for info. (*1-883761-03-4*) Fmly Life Prods.
—Every Kid's Guide to Coping with Childhood Traumas. Berry, Joy. 48p. (gr. 3-7). 1988. 5.95 (*0-516-21426-8*) Childrens.
—Every Kid's Guide to Decision Making & Problem Solving. Berry, Joy. 48p. (gr. 3-7). 1987. 4.95 (*0-516-21410-1*) Childrens.
—Every Kid's Guide to Laws That Relate to Parents & Children. Berry, Joy. 48p. (gr. 3-7). 1987. 4.95 (*0-516-21411-X*) Childrens.
—Every Kid's Guide to Laws That Relate to School & Work. Berry, Joy. 48p. (gr. 3-7). 1987. 4.95 (*0-516-21412-8*) Childrens.
—Every Kid's Guide to Watching TV Intelligently. Berry, Joy. 48p. (gr. 3-7). 1987. 4.95 (*0-516-21417-9*) Childrens.
—Fritter the Wasteful Beastie: A Beastie Book about Conserving Resources. Berry, Ron, et al. 48p. (ps-1). 1993. write for info. (*1-883761-02-6*) Fmly Life Prods.
—Glumby the Grumbler: A Beastie Book about Being Grateful. Berry, Ron, et al. 48p. (ps-1). 1993. write for info. (*1-883761-00-X*) Fmly Life Prods.
—Hogger the Hoarding Beastie: A Beastie Book about Sharing. Berry, Ron, et al. 48p. (ps-1). 1993. write for info. (*1-883761-01-8*) Fmly Life Prods.
—It's the Truth, Christopher. McKissack, Patricia C. LC 84-71376. 32p. (Orig.). (ps-1). 1984. pap. 5.99 (*0-8066-2111-7*, 10-3457, Augsburg) Augsburg Fortress.
—Lights Out, Christopher. McKissack, Patricia A. LC 84-71375. 32p. (Orig.). (ps-1). 1984. pap. 5.99 (*0-8066-2110-9*, 10-3870, Augsburg) Augsburg Fortress.
—Millicent Eats Her Supper. Noonan, Janet & Calvert, Jacquelyn. (ps-2). 1990. 3.79 (*1-55513-984-1*, Chariot Bks) Cook.
—Millicent Goes to the Shopping Mall. Noonan, Janet & Calvert, Jacquelyn. (ps-2). 1990. 3.79 (*1-55513-970-1*, Chariot Bks) Cook.
—Millicent Has a Party. Noonan, Janet & Calvert, Jacquelyn. (ps-2). 1990. 3.79 (*1-55513-983-3*, Chariot Bks) Cook.
—Millicent Plays at the Park. Noonan, Janet & Calvert, Jacquelyn. (ps-2). 1990. 3.79 (*1-55513-982-5*, Chariot Bks) Cook.
—Moogie the Messy Beastie: A Beastie Book about Being Neat. Berry, Ron, et al. 48p. (ps-1). 1993. write for info. (*1-883761-05-0*) Fmly Life Prods.
—Scrappy the Squabbler: A Beastie Book about Getting along with Others. Berry, Ron, et al. 48p. (ps-1). 1993. write for info. (*1-883761-04-2*) Fmly Life Prods.
—Speak Up, Christopher: Christopher Learns the Difference Between Right & Wrong. McKissack, Patricia. LC 87-73523. 32p. (ps-6). 1988. pap. 5.99 (*0-8066-2355-1*, 10-5966, Augsburg) Augsburg Fortress.
—A Troll in a Hole. McKissack, Patricia & McKissack, Fredrick. LC 88-60384. 32p. (Orig.). (gr. 1-3). 1988. text ed. 8.95 (*0-88335-782-8*); pap. text ed. 4.95 (*0-88335-794-1*) Milliken Pub Co.
Bartick, Robert. Popular Careers. Funes, Marilyn & Lazarus, Alan. Piltch, Benjamin, ed. 64p. (gr. 7 up). 1980. 3.95 (*0-934618-01-1*) Learning Well.
—School Events. Kaufman, Tanya & Wishny, Judith. Piltch, Benjamin, ed. 64p. (gr. 2-5). 1983. 4.00 (*0-934618-04-6*) Learning Well.
Bartle, Brian. Here Comes Bulldozer. Breverton, David. 12p. (ps-1). 1992. 4.95 (*0-448-40590-3*, G&D) Putnam Pub Group.
—Here Comes Dump Truck. Breverton, David. 12p. (ps-1). 1992. 4.95 (*0-448-40591-1*, G&D) Putnam Pub Group.
—Here Comes Fire Truck. Breverton, David. 12p. (ps-1). 1992. 4.95 (*0-448-40592-X*, G&D) Putnam Pub Group.
—Here Comes Tow Truck. Bartle, Brian. 12p. (ps-1). 1992. 4.95 (*0-448-40593-8*, G&D) Putnam Pub Group.
Barto, Bobbi. Happy Bear, Christmas Star. Gerver, Jane E. LC 90-60174. 32p. (ps-3). 1990. pap. 2.25 (*0-679-80858-2*) Random Bks Yng Read.
—Ten Little Care Bears Counting Book. Katz, Bobbi. LC 83-60084. 14p. (ps-k). 1983. 4.95 (*0-394-86088-8*) Random Bks Yng Read.

Barto, Renzo. Detective Tricks You Can Do. Conaway, Judith. LC 85-28881. 48p. (gr. 1-5). 1986. PLB 11.89 (*0-8167-0672-7*); pap. text ed. 3.50 (*0-8167-0673-5*) Troll Assocs.
—Dollhouse Fun! Furniture You Can Make. Conaway, Judith. LC 86-16133. 48p. (gr. 1-5). 1987. PLB 11.89 (*0-8167-0862-2*); pap. text ed. 3.50 (*0-8167-0863-0*) Troll Assocs.
—Easy-to-Make Christmas Crafts. Conaway, Judith. LC 85-16475. 48p. (gr. 1-5). 1986. PLB 11.89 (*0-8167-0674-3*); pap. text ed. 3.50 (*0-8167-0675-1*) Troll Assocs.
—Fun-to-Make Nature Crafts. Conaway, Judith. LC 80-23999. 48p. (gr. 1-5). 1981. PLB 11.89 (*0-89375-440-4*); pap. 3.50 (*0-89375-441-2*) Troll Assocs.
—Fun with Paper. Supraner, Robyn. LC 80-19859. 48p. (gr. 1-5). 1981. PLB 11.89 (*0-89375-430-7*); pap. 3.50 (*0-89375-431-5*) Troll Assocs.
—Great Gifts to Make. Conaway, Judith. LC 85-16498. 48p. (gr. 1-5). 1986. PLB 11.89 (*0-8167-0676-X*); pap. text ed. 3.50 (*0-8167-0677-8*) Troll Assocs.
—Great Masks to Make. Supraner, Robyn. LC 80-24077. 48p. (gr. 1-5). 1981. PLB 11.89 (*0-89375-436-6*); pap. 3.50 (*0-89375-437-4*) Troll Assocs.
—Happy Day! Things to Make & Do. Conaway, Judith. LC 86-7131. 48p. (gr. 1-5). 1987. PLB 11.89 (*0-8167-0842-8*); pap. text ed. 3.50 (*0-8167-0843-6*) Troll Assocs.
—Happy Halloween: Things to Make & Do. Supraner, Robyn. LC 80-23889. 48p. (gr. 1-5). 1981. lib. bdg. 11.89 (*0-89375-420-X*); pap. 3.50 (*0-89375-421-8*) Troll Assocs.
—Happy Haunting: Halloween Costumes You Can Make. Conaway, Judith. LC 85-28840. 48p. (gr. 1-5). 1986. PLB 11.89 (*0-8167-0666-2*); pap. text ed. 3.50 (*0-8167-0667-0*) Troll Assocs.
—Happy Thanksgiving: Things to Make & Do. Conaway, Judith. LC 85-16463. 48p. (gr. 1-5). 1986. PLB 11.89 (*0-8167-0668-9*); pap. text ed. 3.50 (*0-8167-0669-7*) Troll Assocs.
—I Wonder Why. Pansini, Anna, ed. LC 90-44455. 48p. (gr. k-2). 1991. PLB 10.89 (*0-8167-2304-4*); pap. text ed. 2.50 (*0-8167-2305-2*) Troll Assocs.
—Kids' Question & Answer Book. Pansini, Anna, ed. LC 90-43969. 48p. (gr. 2-4). 1991. PLB 10.89 (*0-8167-2306-0*); pap. text ed. 2.95 (*0-8167-2307-9*) Troll Assocs.
—Magic Tricks You Can Do! Supraner, Robyn. LC 80-19780. 48p. (gr. 1-5). 1981. PLB 11.89 (*0-89375-418-8*); pap. text ed. 3.50 (*0-89375-419-6*) Troll Assocs.
—Make Your Own Costumes & Disguises. Conaway, Judith. LC 86-11212. 48p. (gr. 1-5). 1987. PLB 11.89 (*0-8167-0840-1*); pap. text ed. 3.50 (*0-8167-0841-X*) Troll Assocs.
—Merry Christmas: Things to Make & Do. Supraner, Robyn. LC 80-23884. 48p. (gr. 1-5). 1981. PLB 11.89 (*0-89375-422-6*); pap. 3.50 (*0-89375-423-4*) Troll Assocs.
—Plenty of Puppets to Make. Supraner, Robyn & Supraner, Lauren. LC 80-23785. 48p. (gr. 1-5). 1981. PLB 11.89 (*0-89375-432-3*); pap. 3.50 (*0-89375-433-1*) Troll Assocs.
—Quick & Easy Cookbook. Supraner, Robyn. LC 80-24021. 48p. (gr. 1-5). 1981. PLB 11.89 (*0-89375-438-2*); pap. 3.50 (*0-89375-439-0*) Troll Assocs.
—Science Secrets. Supraner, Robyn. LC 80-23794. 48p. (gr. 1-5). 1981. PLB 11.89 (*0-89375-426-9*); pap. 3.50 (*0-89375-427-7*) Troll Assocs.
—Springtime Surprises: Things to Make & Do. Conaway, Judith. LC 85-16497. 48p. (gr. 1-5). 1986. PLB 11.89 (*0-8167-0670-0*); pap. text ed. 3.50 (*0-8167-0671-9*) Troll Assocs.
—Stop & Look! Illusions. Supraner, Robyn. LC 80-23799. 48p. (gr. 1-5). 1981. PLB 11.89 (*0-89375-434-X*); pap. 3.50 (*0-89375-435-8*) Troll Assocs.
—Things That Go! How to Make Toy Boats, Cars, & Planes. Conaway, Judith. LC 86-7130. 48p. (gr. 1-5). 1987. PLB 11.89 (*0-8167-0838-X*); pap. text ed. 3.50 (*0-8167-0839-8*) Troll Assocs.
—Valentine's Day: Things to Make & Do. Supraner, Robyn. LC 80-23780. 48p. (gr. 1-5). 1981. PLB 11.89 (*0-89375-424-2*); pap. 3.50 (*0-89375-425-0*) Troll Assocs.
Barton, Byron. Airport. Barton, Byron. LC 79-7816. 32p. (ps-k). 1982. 15.00 (*0-690-04168-3*, Crowell Jr Bks); PLB 14.89 (*0-690-04169-1*) HarpC Child Bks.
—Airport. Barton, Byron. LC 79-7816. 32p. (ps-1). 1987. pap. 4.95 (*0-06-443145-2*, Trophy) HarpC Child Bks.
—Al's Blind Date. Greene, Constance C. 128p. (gr. 5-9). 1991. pap. 3.95 (*0-14-034171-4*, Puffin) Puffin Bks.
—Arthur's New Power. Hoban, Russell. LC 77-11550. (gr. 1-5). 1978. PLB 12.89 (*0-690-01371-X*, Crowell Jr Bks) HarpC Child Bks.
—Ask Anybody. Greene, Constance C. 160p. (gr. 5-9). 1991. pap. 3.95 (*0-14-034787-9*, Puffin) Puffin Bks.
—Boats. Barton, Byron. LC 85-47900. 32p. (ps-k). 1986. 4.95 (*0-694-00059-4*, Crowell Jr Bks); PLB 12.89 (*0-690-04536-0*) HarpC Child Bks.
—Bones, Bones, Dinosaur Bones. Barton, Byron. LC 89-71306. 32p. (ps-1). 1990. 11.00 (*0-690-04825-4*, Crowell Jr Bks); PLB 12.89 (*0-690-04827-0*, Crowell Jr Bks) HarpC Child Bks.
—Dinosaurs, Dinosaurs. Barton, Byron. LC 88-22938. 40p. (ps-1). 1989. 10.95 (*0-694-00269-0*, Crowell Jr Bks); PLB 13.89 (*0-690-04768-1*) HarpC Child Bks.

—Dinosaurs, Dinosaurs. Barton, Byron. LC 88-22938. 40p. (ps-1). 1991. 19.95 (*0-06-020410-9*) HarpC Child Bks.
—Dinosaurs, Dinosaurs. Barton, Byron. LC 88-22938. 40p. (ps-1). 1993. pap. 4.95 (*0-06-443298-X*, Trophy) HarpC Child Bks.
—Gila Monsters Meet You at the Airport. Sharmat, Marjorie W. LC 80-12264. 32p. (gr. k-3). 1980. RSBE 14.95 (*0-02-782450-0*, Macmillan Child Bk) Macmillan Child Grp.
—A Girl Called Al. Greene, Constance C. (gr. 6-8). 1969. pap. 15.00 (*0-670-34153-3*) Viking Child Bks.
—A Girl Called Al. Greene, Constance C. 128p. (gr. 5-9). 1991. pap. 3.99 (*0-14-034786-0*, Puffin) Puffin Bks.
—Good Morning, Chick. Ginsburg, Mirra. LC 80-11352. 32p. (ps). 1980. PLB 12.88 (*0-688-84284-4*) Greenwillow.
—Good Morning Chick. Ginsburg, Mirra. 32p. (ps up). 1993. Repr. text ed. 4.95 (*0-688-12666-9*, Tupelo Bks) Morrow.
—I Want to Be an Astronaut. Barton, Byron. LC 87-24311. 32p. (ps-1). 1988. 7.95 (*0-694-00261-5*, Crowell Jr Bks); PLB 12.89 (*0-690-04744-4*) HarpC Child Bks.
—I Want to Be an Astronaut. Barton, Byron. LC 87-24311. 32p. (ps-1). 1992. pap. 4.95 (*0-06-443280-7*, Trophy) HarpC Child Bks.
—Jump, Frog, Jump! Kalin, Robert. 32p. (gr. k-3). Big Book. 19.95 (*0-590-71722-7*); pap. 2.95 (*0-590-71723-5*) Scholastic Inc.
—Little Red Hen. Barton, Byron. LC 91-4051. 32p. (ps-1). 1993. 12.95 (*0-06-021675-1*); PLB 12.89 (*0-06-021676-X*) HarpC Child Bks.
—Machines at Work. Barton, Byron. LC 86-24221. 32p. (ps-1). 1987. 14.00 (*0-694-00190-2*, Crowell Jr Bks); PLB 13.89 (*0-690-04573-5*) HarpC Child Bks.
—Roman Numerals. Adler, David A. LC 77-2270. 40p. (gr. 1-4). 1977. PLB 14.89 (*0-690-01302-7*, Crowell Jr Bks) HarpC Child Bks.
—The Snopp on the Sidewalk & Other Poems. Prelutsky, Jack. LC 76-46323. 32p. (gr. 3 up). 1977. PLB 15.93 (*0-688-84084-1*) Greenwillow.
—The Tamarindo Puppy. reissued ed. Pomerantz, Charlotte. LC 79-16584. 32p. (ps up). 1993. 14.00 (*0-688-11902-6*); PLB 13.93 (*0-688-11903-4*) Greenwillow.
—The Tamarindo Puppy & Other Poems. Pomerantz, Charlotte. 32p. (ps). 1993. pap. 4.95 (*0-688-11514-4*, Mulberry) Morrow.
—The Three Bears. Barton, Byron, retold by. LC 90-43151. 32p. (ps-1). 1991. 15.00 (*0-06-020423-0*); PLB 14.89 (*0-06-020424-9*) HarpC Child Bks.
—Trains. Barton, Byron. LC 85-47898. 32p. (ps-k). 1986. 4.95 (*0-694-00061-2*, Crowell Jr Bks); PLB 12.89 (*0-690-04534-4*) HarpC Child Bks.
—Truck Song. Siebert, Diane. LC 83-46173. 32p. (ps-3). 1984. (Crowell Jr Bks); PLB 14.89 (*0-690-04411-9*) HarpC Child Bks.
—Truck Song. Siebert, Diane. (gr. k-3). 1988. bk. & cassette 19.95 (*0-87499-093-9*); bk. & cassette 12.95 (*0-87499-092-0*); 4 cassettes & guide 27.95 (*0-87499-094-7*) Live Oak Media.
—Trucks. Barton, Byron. LC 85-47901. 32p. (ps-k). 1986. 4.95 (*0-694-00062-0*, Crowell Jr Bks); PLB 12.89 (*0-690-04530-1*) HarpC Child Bks.
—Where's the Bear? Pomerantz, Charlotte. LC 83-1697. 32p. (ps-1). 1984. 15.00 (*0-688-01752-5*); PLB 14.93 (*0-688-01753-3*) Greenwillow.
—Where's the Bear. Pomerantz, Charlotte. LC 83-1697. 32p. (ps-3). 1991. pap. 3.95 (*0-688-10999-3*, Mulberry) Morrow.
Barton, David. Changes in Youth Morality: What Caused Them, No. 1. rev. ed. Barton, Charles D. 40p. 1988. pap. 3.00 (*0-317-93057-5*) Wallbuilders.
—What Happened to SAT Scores, No. 1. rev. ed. Barton, Charles D. 52p. 1988. pap. 3.00 (*0-317-93056-7*) Wallbuilders.
Barton, Harriett. Books & Libraries. Knowlton, Jack. LC 89-70804. 48p. (gr. 2-5). 1993. pap. 5.95 (*0-06-446153-X*, Trophy) HarpC Child Bks.
Barton, Harriett. Books & Libraries. Knowlton, Jack. LC 89-70804. 48p. (gr. 2-5). 1991. PLB 14.89 (*0-06-021610-7*) HarpC Child Bks.
—Deserts of the World. Knowlton, Jack. LC 92-19169. 48p. (gr. 2-5). 1995. 15.00 (*0-06-021309-4*); PLB 14.89 (*0-06-021310-8*) HarpC Child Bks.
—Geography from A to Z: A Picture Glossary. Knowlton, Jack. LC 86-4594. 48p. (gr. 2-5). 1988. 14.00 (*0-690-04616-2*, Crowell Jr Bks); PLB 13.89 (*0-690-04618-9*) HarpC Child Bks.
—In the Witch's Kitchen: Poems for Halloween. Brewton, John E., et al. LC 79-7822. 96p. (gr. 2-5). 1980. PLB 13.89 (*0-690-04062-8*, Crowell Jr Bks) HarpC Child Bks.
—Learning to Sew. Hoffman, Christine. LC 92-9516. 32p. (gr. 2-5). 1994. 11.00 (*0-06-021146-6*); PLB 10.89 (*0-06-021147-4*) HarpC Child Bks. Postponed.
—Maps & Globes. Knowlton, Jack. LC 85-47537. 48p. (gr. 2-5). 1985. 15.00 (*0-690-04457-7*, Crowell Jr Bks); PLB 14.89 (*0-690-04459-3*) HarpC Child Bks.
—Maps & Globes. Knowlton, Jack. LC 85-47537. 48p. (gr. 2-5). 1986. pap. 4.95 (*0-06-446049-5*, Trophy) HarpC Child Bks.
—Rain & Hail. Branley, Franklyn M. LC 83-45058. 40p. (gr. k-3). 1983. PLB 13.89 (*0-690-04353-8*, Crowell Jr Bks) HarpC Child Bks.

Barton, Jill. Little Mo. 1st U.S. ed. Waddell, Martin. LC 92-54410. 32p. (ps up). 1993. 14.95 (*1-56402-211-0*) Candlewick Pr.
—The Pig in the Pond. Waddell, Martin. LC 91-58751. 32p. (ps up). 1992. 14.95 (*1-56402-050-9*) Candlewick Pr.
Barton, Jill & Barton, Jill. The Happy Hedgehog Band. Waddell, Martin. LC 91-71852. 32p. (ps). 1992. 14.95 (*1-56402-011-8*) Candlewick Pr.
Barton, Kent. What Happens to Me When I Fish the Sea & a Fish Catches Me. Thelma. LC 76-12929. 36p. (Orig.). (gr. 1-3). 1976. pap. 3.50 (*0-89317-009-7*) Windward Pub.
Barton, Patrice. My Body Is My House: A Coloring Book about Alcohol, Drugs & Health. Engelmann, Jeanne. 16p. (gr. k-5). 1990. pap. 1.50 (*0-89486-735-0*) Hazelden.
—Wonder What I Feel Today? A Coloring Book about Feelings. Engelmann, Jeanne. 16p. (gr. k-5). 1991. pap. 1.50 (*0-89486-744-X*) Hazelden.
Bartusch, Nancy. Alphabet in Signs: ABC's in Fingerspelling. Geiger, Michael. 60p. (Orig.). (ps-3). 1984. pap. 5.00 (*0-916708-13-6*) Modern Signs.
Bartz, Susie. English Verbs: Every Irregular Conjugation. Weisberg, Valerie H. Herrick, George H., intro. by. (SPA & ENG.). 168p. 1991. pap. 9.95x (*0-941281-76-0*); English verb wkbk. 3.95 (*0-941281-52-3*); with Spanish 15.50 (*0-9610912-6-6*) V H Pub.
Baruffa, Joan, et al. The Times of Our Constitution. 2nd ed. Haener, Donald R. & Fry, Janice. Ridge, Tom, intro. by. 24p. (gr. 2-6). 1987. pap. 3.00 (*0-942661-03-6*) Discovry Enterp.
Baruffa, Joanne & Tunis, Edwin. The Era & Our Constitution. rev. ed. Haener, Donald R. & Fry, Janice K. (gr. 6 up). 1988. pap. text ed. 5.00 (*0-942661-02-8*) Discovry Enterp.
Baruffi, Andrea. Dark Night, Sleepy Night. Ziefert, Harriet. LC 87-25759. 32p. (Orig.). (ps-3). 1988. pap. 3.50 (*0-14-050812-0*, Puffin) Puffin Bks.
—Dark Night, Sleepy Night. Ziefert, Harriet. (ps-2). 1993. pap. 3.25 (*0-14-036538-9*, Puffin) Puffin Bks.
—How Big Is Big? Ziefert, Harriet. LC 88-612151. 32p. (ps-3). 1989. pap. 3.50 (*0-14-050983-6*, Puffin) Puffin Bks.
—Return of the Shadows. Farber, Norma. LC 91-27517. 40p. (gr. k-3). 1992. 15.00 (*0-06-020518-0*); PLB 14.89 (*0-06-020519-9*) HarpC Child Bks.
—The Wheels on the Bus. Ziefert, Harriet. LC 89-38100. 24p. (Orig.). (ps-2). 1990. pap. 2.25 (*0-394-84870-5*) Random Bks Yng Read.
—Where's Daddy's Car? Ziefert, Harriet. 16p. (ps). 1992. 5.95 (*0-694-00378-6*) HarpC Child Bks.
—Where's Mommy's Truck? Ziefert, Harriet. 16p. (ps). 1992. 5.95 (*0-694-00377-8*) HarpC Child Bks.
—Yours 'Til the Ice Cracks: A Book of Valentines. Geringer, Laura. LC 91-22687. 32p. (gr. 1-7). 1992. 10.00 (*0-06-020399-4*) HarpC Child Bks.
Barwald, Diana, jt. illus. see Bagley, Val.
Barwick, Mary. The Alabama Angels. 3rd ed. Barwick, Mary. 28p. (gr. 1-6). 1989. pap. 8.95 (*0-9622815-1-4*) Black Belt Pr.
—The Alabama Angels in Anywhere, L. A. (Lower Alabama) Barwick, Mary. 32p. (gr. Orig.). 1991. pap. 8.95 (*0-9622815-6-5*) Black Belt Pr.
—Little Girls Have to Sleep. Muir, Jim. Moore, Robert, contrib. by. LC 92-37456. 1992. 19.50 (*1-881320-03-0*) Black Belt Pr.
Base, Graeme. Animalia. Base, Graeme. 32p. (ps up). 1987. 17.95 (*0-8109-1868-4*) Abrams.
—Jabberwocky: From Lewis Carroll's Through the Looking Glass. 32p. 1989. 16.95 (*0-8109-1150-7*) Abrams.
Bash, Barbara. Desert Giant: The World of the Saguaro Cactus. Bash, Barbara. 32p. (gr. 1-5). 1989. 15.95 (*0-316-08301-1*) Little.
—Tiger Lilies & Other Beastly Plants. Ring, Elizabeth. LC 84-7499. 32p. (gr. 3 up). 1985. 9.95 (*0-8027-6540-8*) Walker & Co.
—Urban Roosts: Where Birds Nest in the City. Bash, Barbara. (gr. 1-5). 1990. 15.95 (*0-316-08306-2*) Little.
—Urban Roosts: Where Birds Nest in the City. Bash, Barbara. 32p. (gr. 4-7). 1992. pap. 5.95 (*0-316-08312-7*) Little.
Baskerville, Leana. Spot, the Guinea Pig. Hughes, Barb. Bogan, Rachel, ed. 32p. (gr. k-3). 1992. pap. 7.95 (*1-878036-10-6*) Hughes Taylor. Postponed.
Baskin, Leonard. Alberic the Wise. Juster, Norton. LC 92-7807. 28p. (gr. 1 up). 1992. 16.95 (*0-88708-243-2*) Picture Bk Studio.
—The Book of Adam to Moses. Segal, Lore. LC 87-2581. 144p. (gr. k up). 1987. lib. bdg. 14.99 (*0-394-96757-7*) Knopf Bks Yng Read.
—Did You Say Ghosts? Michelson, Richard. LC 92-30134. 32p. (ps up). 1993. RSBE 14.95 (*0-02-766915-7*, Macmillan Child Bk) Macmillan Child Grp.
—Leonard Baskin's Miniature Natural History. Baskin, Leonard. 28p. (gr. k up). 1993. Repr. 14.95 (*0-88708-265-3*) Picture Bk Studio.
—On Passover. Fishman, Cathy. LC 91-43110. 32p. (gr. k up). 1994. RSBE 14.95 (*0-02-735320-6*, Macmillan Child Bk) Macmillan Child Grp.
Basquiat, Jean-Michel. Life Doesn't Frighten Me. Angelou, Maya. Boyers, Sara J., ed. LC 92-40409. (gr. 7 up). 1993. write for info. (Dist. by Workman Pub.) Stewart Tabori & Chang.

Bass, Jo Ann. What's a Girl to Do? Quesenbury, Pat. Wright, Bobby J., ed. Haynes, Glenda, intro. by. 133p. (Orig.). (gr. 7 up). 1981. pap. 3.50 (0-89114-108-1) Baptist Pub Hse.

Bass, Marilyn. The Alef-Bet Primer Reading Practice Book. Shumsky, Adaia & Shumsky, Abraham. 80p. (gr. k-3). 1984. pap. text ed. 5.00 (0-8074-0257-5, 405315) UAHC.

Bass, Marilyn & Goldman, Marvin. Alef-Bet: A Hebrew Primer. Shumsky, Abraham & Shumsky, Adaia. (gr. k-3). 1979. pap. text ed. 7.00 (0-8074-0026-2, 405309) UAHC.

Bass, Michael. The Boy Who Turned into a TV Set. Manes, Stephen. 32p. (Orig.). (gr. 2-5). 1983. pap. 2.50 (0-380-62000-6, Camelot) Avon.

Bass, Rachel. Bubble Gum. Noble, Kate. 32p. (ps-3). 1992. 14.95 (0-9631798-0-2) Silver Seahorse.

—Oh Look, It's a Nosserus. Noble, Kate. 32p. (ps-4). 1993. 14.95 (0-9631798-2-9) Silver Seahorse.
Robbi is a young rhino who lives in a game park in Africa. He can't wait to have a horn as beautiful as his Mama's; he gets teased for being clumsy, & he sets out to save his friends from terrible danger. Children who loved & laughed with Kimbi in BUBBLE GUM will be delighted to meet Robbi & his zebra & giraffe friends. Once again, Rachel Bass creates the beauty of Africa & the charm of its animals in her vivid paintings. BUBBLE GUM. Kate Noble (Africa Stories Ser.) (Illus. by Rachel Bass). 32p. 1992. 14.95 (0-9631798-0-2) Silver Seahorse Press. Kimbi is a young baboon who lives in a park in Africa. He wishes tourists didn't pay so much attention to lions. He loves sweets, & he stumbles into an amazing adventure. The illustrations for this delightful story capture the magic of the African landscape. There's also a learning plus: the details of animal behavior are correct, & the pictures show both black & white children & adults. A kindergarten teacher who previewed the boards writes "I can't wait to read it to children."
Publisher Provided Annotation.

Bassett, Jeni. The Biggest Pumpkin Ever. Kroll, Steven. LC 83-18492. 32p. (ps-3). 1984. reinforced bdg. 14.95 (0-8234-0505-2) Holiday.

—The Biggest Pumpkin Ever. Kroll, Steven. 32p. (gr. k-3). 1985. pap. 2.50 (0-590-41113-6) Scholastic Inc.

—The Biggest Pumpkin Ever. Kroll, Steven. 32p. (ps-1). 1993. pap. 2.50 (0-590-46463-9, Cartwheel) Scholastic Inc.

—Bunches & Bunches of Bunnies. Mathews, Louise. 32p. (gr. k-3). 1991. pap. 3.95 (0-590-44766-1) Scholastic Inc.

—The Bunny's Alphabet Eggs. Bassett, Lisa. LC 92-37987. (gr. 2 up). 1993. 3.99 (0-517-08153-9) Outlet Bk Co.

—But Not Like Mine. Facklam, Margery. LC 86-33588. 18p. (gr. 3-5). 1988. 6.95 (0-15-200585-4, Gulliver Bks) HarBrace.

—It's April Fools' Day! Kroll, Steven. LC 88-28434. 32p. (ps-3). 1990. reinforced bdg. 14.95 (0-8234-0747-0) Holiday.

—It's Groundhog Day! Kroll, Steven. LC 86-22924. 32p. (ps-3). 1987. reinforced bdg. 14.95 (0-8234-0643-1) Holiday.

—Koala Christmas. Bassett, Lisa. LC 90-47628. 32p. (ps-2). 1991. 12.95 (0-525-65065-2, Cobblehill Bks) Dutton Child Bks.

—Mister Momboo's Hat. Leemis, Ralph. LC 90-34397. 24p. (ps-k). 1991. 11.95 (0-525-65045-8, Cobblehill Bks) Dutton Child Bks.

—The Pigrates Clean Up. Kroll, Steven. LC 92-21823. 32p. (ps-k). 1993. PLB 14.95 (0-8050-2368-2, Bks Young Read) H Holt & Co.

—So Can I. Facklam, Margery. LC 86-33720. 28p. (ps-k). 1988. 6.95 (0-15-200419-X, Gulliver Bks) HarBrace.

—The Squirrels' Thanksgiving. Kroll, Steven. LC 89-77513. 32p. (ps-3). 1991. reinforced 14.95 (0-8234-0823-X) Holiday.

—Ten Little Bunnies. Bassett, Lisa. LC 92-37986. (gr. 2 up). 1993. 3.99 (0-517-08154-7) Outlet Bk Co.

—Zero! Is It Something? Is It Nothing? Zaslavsky, Claudia. LC 88-38940. 32p. (gr. k-4). 1989. PLB 12.90 (0-531-10693-4) Watts.

Bassett, Jeni, photos by. The Chicks' Trick. Bassett, Jeni, text by. LC 93-18471. 1994. write for info. (0-525-65152-7, Cobblehill Bks) Dutton Child Bks.

Bassett, Scott. Artemus & the Alphabet. Bassett, Scott & Bassett, Tammy. 32p. (ps-k). 1980. 6.95x (0-9605548-0-7); PLB 6.95x (0-9605548-1-5) Bassett & Brush.

Basso, Bill. Ghost Dog. Leroe, Ellen. LC 92-72020. 64p. (gr. 2-5). 1993. 12.95 (1-56282-268-3); PLB 12.89 (1-56282-269-1) Hyprn Child.

—Rhyme Time with the Rymons: My Think-Along Funbook. Simms, Susan R. Dallgas-Frey, Paul, contrib. by. 100p. (ps-4). 1991. wkbk. 3.95 (1-55999-158-5) LinguiSystems.

—Rhyme Time with the Rymons: My Think 'n' Do Book. Simms, Susan R. 100p. (ps-3). 1990. pap. 3.95 spiral bdg., wkbk. (1-55999-139-9) LinguiSystems.

Bastien, Charles. Robotics. Vowles, Andrew. 32p. (gr. 5-9). 1985. pap. 5.95 (0-88625-113-3) Durkin Hayes Pub.

Bastien, Charles & Livingston, Richard. Planets & Galaxies. Mackie, Dan. 32p. (gr. 5-9). 1985. pap. 5.95 (0-88625-102-8) Durkin Hayes Pub.

Bastien, Charles & Rowden, Rick. Electricity. Mackie, Dan. Goshorn, Bill, ed. 32p. (gr. 4). 1986. PLB 14.65 (0-88625-133-8); pap. 5.95 (0-685-30764-6) Durkin Hayes Pub.

Basu, R. K. Stories from the Arabian Nights. Thomas, Vernon. (gr. 8-12). 1979. 7.50 (0-89744-142-7) Auromere.

—The Story of Buddha. Landaw, Jonathan. (gr. 3-10). 1979. 7.95 (0-89744-140-0) Auromere.

—Tales from Indian Classics. Gupta, Rupa. 136p. (gr. 1-9). 1981. 7.50 (0-89744-233-4, Pub. by Hemkunt India) Auromere.

Batchelor, John. Airliners. Chant, Chris. LC 88-28762. 63p. (gr. 3 up). 1990. PLB 16.95 (1-85435-088-9) Marshall Cavendish.

—Sailing Ships. Chant, Chris. LC 88-28706. 63p. (gr. 3 up). 1990. PLB 16.95 (1-85435-091-9) Marshall Cavendish.

—Steam Locomotives. Chant, Chris. LC 88-28763. 63p. (gr. 3-9). 1989. PLB 16.95 (1-85435-087-0) Marshall Cavendish.

—Steamships. Chant, Chris. LC 88-28764. 63p. (gr. 3-9). 1989. PLB 16.95 (1-85435-086-2) Marshall Cavendish.

Batchelor, John & Lapper, Ivan. The Fighting Ship. Brett, Bernard. 96p. (gr. 7 up). 1988. 17.95 (0-19-273155-6) OUP.

Batdorf, Carol. Tinka: A Day in a Little Girl's Life. Batdorf, Carol. 32p. (Orig.). (gr. 1-6). 1990. pap. 5.95 (0-88839-249-4) Hancock House.

Bateman, Noel, jt. illus. see Loftus, Barbara.

Bates, Dawn, jt. illus. see Sanford, James, Jr.

Bates, Louise. My First ABC. Slier, Debby. 24p. (Orig.). (gr. k-1). 1990. pap. 0.99 (1-878624-36-9) McClanahan Bk.

—Rhymes to Count On. Nayer, Judy, ed. 24p. (ps-2). 1992. pap. 0.99 (1-56293-104-0) McClanahan Bk.

—Serafina's Birthday. Ada, Alma F. LC 91-15389. 32p. (ps-2). 1992. SBE 13.95 (0-689-31516-3, Atheneum Child Bk) Macmillan Child Grp.

—Teddy Bear Bedtime Stories. Hollander, Cass. 24p. (ps-2). 1992. pap. 0.99 (1-56293-115-6) McClanahan Bk.

—Teddy's Day in the Forest. Eldrid, Brenda. 24p. (ps-2). 1993. pap. text ed. 0.99 (1-56293-341-8) McClanahan Bk.

Bates, Matt. What Is Columbus Day? Parker, Margot. LC 85-12748. 48p. (ps-3). 1985. PLB 15.00 (0-516-03781-1) Childrens.

—What Is Martin Luther King, Jr. Day? Parker, Margot. LC 89-29254. 48p. (ps-3). 1990. 15.00 (0-516-03784-6); pap. 4.95 (0-516-43784-4) Childrens.

—What Is Thanksgiving Day? Parker, Margot. LC 88-11112. 48p. (ps-3). 1988. PLB 15.00 (0-516-03783-8); pap. 4.95 (0-516-43783-6) Childrens.

—What Is Veterans Day? Parker, Margot. LC 86-11732. 48p. (ps-3). 1986. PLB 15.00 (0-516-03782-X) Childrens.

Bates, Stephen. Chris Finds the Answer. Klaus, Sandra. 20p. (gr. k-6). 1988. pap. text ed. 4.25 (1-55976-127-X) CEF Press.

—God Speaks to Me. Lashbrook, Marilyn. 52p. (gr. k-6). 1985. pap. text ed. 8.99 (1-55976-030-3) CEF Press.

—Is Satan Real? Leslie, Elsie. (gr. k-6). 1987. pap. 4.25 (1-55976-153-9) CEF Press.

—Loving God's Way. Middleton, Barth & Middleton, Sally. 55p. (gr. k-6). 1988. pap. text ed. 7.50 (1-55976-033-8) CEF Press.

Bates, Stephen & Williamson, Kevin. The Message of a Star. Hershey, Katerine. 9p. (gr. k-6). 1982. pap. 4.25 (1-55976-133-4) CEF Press.

Bates, Steve. Digging for Buried Treasure. Lashbrook, Marilyn. 12p. (gr. k-6). 1984. pap. text ed. 4.25 (1-55976-141-5) CEF Press.

—Living God's Way. Middleton, Barth & Middleton, Sally. 64p. (gr. k-6). 1985. pap. text ed. 11.99 (1-55976-031-1) CEF Press.

—Pythons & Book Reports. Klaus, Sandra. 51p. (gr. k-6). 1987. pap. text ed. 6.99 (1-55976-147-4) CEF Press.

Bates, Steve, jt. illus. see Chappell, David.

Bates, Virginia. Betsy Bigmouth. Hoffecker, Felicity. LC 89-13254. 28p. (gr. 2-5). 1990. 7.95 (0-8192-1519-8) Morehouse Pub.

Bateson, Ian. People of the Ice: How the Inuit Lived. Siska, Heather S. 48p. (gr. 4-7). 1992. pap. 7.95 (0-88894-404-7, Pub. by Groundwood-Douglas & McIntyre CN) Firefly Bks Ltd.

—People of the Longhouse: How the Iroquoian Tribes Lived. Ridington, Jillian & Ridington, Robin. 48p. (gr. 3-7). 1992. pap. 7.95 (1-55054-221-4, Pub. by Groundwood-Douglas & McIntyre CN) Firefly Bks Ltd.

—People of the Trail: How the Northern Forest Indians Lived. Ridington, Robin & Ridington, Jillian. 40p. (gr. 3-7). 1992. pap. 7.95 (0-88894-412-8, Pub. by Groundwood-Douglas & McIntyre CN) Firefly Bks Ltd.

Batherman, Muriel. The Alphabet Tale. Garten, Jan. (ps up). 1994. write for info. (0-688-12702-9); PLB write for info. (0-688-12703-7) Greenwillow.

—Before Columbus. Batherman, Muriel. 32p. (gr. k-3). 1990. pap. 4.80 (0-395-54954-X) HM.

Batholomew. Give It with Love, Christopher: Christopher Learns about Gifts & Giving. McKissack, Patricia. LC 87-73524. 32p. (ps-3). 1988. pap. 5.99 (0-8066-2354-3, 10-2554, Augsburg) Augsburg Fortress.

Batki, Laszlo. King Arthur's Camelot: A Pop-up Castle & Four Storybooks. Rojany, Lisa, adapted by. (ps up). 1993. Set, 12p. ea. 18.99 (0-525-45026-2, DCB) Dutton Child Bks.

Battaglia, Aurelius. Animal Sounds. 22p. (ps). 1981. write for info. (0-307-12122-4, Golden Bks) Western Pub.

—The Fire Engine Book. Younger, Jesse. 24p. (ps-k). 1987. pap. write for info (0-307-10082-0, Pub. by Golden Bks) Western Pub.

—Seasons. LC 76-43128. 16p. (ps-1). 1978. 3.95 (0-448-46514-0, G&D) Putnam Pub Group.

—Three Little Pigs. LC 76-24170. 32p. (ps-2). 1982. lib. bdg. 5.99 (0-394-93459-8) Random Bks Yng Read.

Batten, John D. Celtic Fairy Tales. Jacobs, Joseph, ed. LC 67-24223. xvi, 267p. (ps-6). 1968. pap. 5.95 (0-486-21826-0) Dover.

—Celtic Fairy Tales. Jacobs, Joseph. 18.25 (0-8446-2302-4) Peter Smith.

—English Fairy Tales. Jacobs, Joseph, ed. LC 67-19703. xv, 261p. (gr. 3-6). 1898. pap. 5.95 (0-486-21818-X) Dover.

—Indian Fairy Tales. Jacobs, Joseph, ed. xvi, 255p. (ps-4). 1969. pap. 6.95 (0-486-21828-7) Dover.

—More Celtic Fairy Tales. Jacobs, Joseph, ed. LC 67-24224. x, 234p. (ps-6). 1968. pap. 5.95 (0-486-21827-9) Dover.

Batten, Linda. The Hero. Bridges, Christina. 29p. (gr. k-6). 1981. pap. text ed. 8.95 (0-917002-39-3) Joyce Media.

Battersby, Sarah. Archibald & the Crunch Machine. Nelson, Jenny. 40p. (gr. 2-4). 1990. pap. 5.95 (1-55037-114-2, Pub. by Annick CN) Firefly Bks Ltd.

Battles-Herron, Linda & Newman, Beth. Mastodon Hunters to Mound Builders: North American Archaeology. Nichols, Peter & Nichols, Belia. 112p. (gr. 4-7). 1992. 12.95 (0-89015-748-0) Eakin-Sunbelt.

Bauer, Eleanor L. Byron's Double Discovery. Braithwaite, Pamela A. 120p. (Orig.). (gr. 4-10). 1991. pap. 4.00 (1-880960-00-1) Script Memory FI.

Bauer, Erwin & Bauer, Peggy, photos by. Save Our Forests. Hirschi, Ron. LC 92-37385. 1992. write for info. (0-553-09521-8); pap. write for info. (0-553-37239-4) Bantam.

—Save Our Prairies & Grasslands. Hirschi, Ron. LC 93-4985. 1994. 17.95 (0-385-31149-4); pap. 9.95 (0-385-31199-0) Delacorte.

—Save Our Wetlands. Hirschi, Ron. LC 93-4984. 1994. 17.95 (0-385-31152-4); pap. 9.95 (0-385-31197-4) Delacorte.

Bauer, Erwin A. & Bauer, Peggy, photos by. Save Our Oceans & Coasts. Hirschi, Ron. LC 92-37384. (gr. 5 up). 1993. write for info. (0-553-09520-X) Bantam.

Bauer, John. Great Swedish Fairy Tales. Lundbergh, Holger, tr. from SWE. LC 73-132364. 224p. (gr. 4-6). 1973. (Sey Lawr). pap. 10.95 (0-440-03041-2) Delacorte.

Bauer, Louise, jt. illus. see Cheney, Paul.

Bauer, Peggy, jt. photog. see Bauer, Erwin.

Bauer, Peggy, jt. photog. see Bauer, Erwin A.

Baum, Ann. Mike's Lonely Summer. Nystrom, Carolyn. 48p. (gr. 1-6). 1986. 7.99 (0-7459-1016-5) Lion USA.

—Otter Rescue. Bailey, Jill. LC 91-19277. 48p. (gr. 3-7). 1992. PLB 18.60 (0-8114-2710-2); pap. 4.95 (0-8114-6548-9) Raintree Steck-V.

—Save the Macaw. Bailey, Jill. LC 91-19871. 48p. (gr. 3-7). 1992. PLB 18.60 (0-8114-2712-9); pap. 4.95 (0-8114-6549-7) Raintree Steck-V.

Baum, Susan. Animal Count. Ziefert, Harriet. 20p. (ps-1). 1989. pap. 4.95 (0-14-054174-8, Puffin) Puffin Bks.

—Animals for Baby. Ziefert, Harriet. 8p. (ps). 1993. 4.95 (0-694-00508-8, Festival) HarpC Child Bks.

—Beach. Baum, Susan. 16p. (ps-1). 1991. pap. 4.95 (0-06-107416-0) HarpC Child Bks.

—Bear's Colors. Ziefert, Harriet. 12p. (ps). 1993. 4.50 (0-694-00454-5, Festival) HarpC Child Bks.

—Bear's Numbers. Ziefert, Harriet. 12p. (ps). 1993. 4.50 (0-694-00455-3, Festival) HarpC Child Bks.

—Bear's Shapes. Ziefert, Harriet. 12p. (ps). 1993. 4.50 (0-694-00456-1, Festival) HarpC Child Bks.

—Bear's Weather. Ziefert, Harriet. 12p. (ps). 1993. 4.50 (0-694-00457-X, Festival) HarpC Child Bks.

—Big to Little, Little to Big. Ziefert, Harriet. 12p. (ps). 1992. 3.95 (0-694-00376-X) HarpC Child Bks.

—City Shapes. Ziefert, Harriet. 16p. (ps-1). 1991. pap. 4.95 (0-06-107417-9) HarpC Child Bks.
—Clothes on, Clothes off. Ziefert, Harriet. 12p. (ps). 1992. 3.95 (0-694-00375-1) HarpC Child Bks.
—Farm Friends. Ziefert, Harriet. 8p. (ps). 1993. 4.95 (0-694-00506-1, Festival) HarpC Child Bks.
—I Love Summer &... Ziefert, Harriet. 16p. (ps-3). 1992. incl. postcards 5.95 (0-694-00405-7) HarpC Child Bks.
—Measure Me. Ziefert, Harriet. 12p. (ps-3). 1991. 12.95 (0-694-00322-0) HarpC Child Bks.
—My Valentines. Ziefert, Harriet. 8p. (ps-2). 1993. incl. postcards 6.95 (0-694-00447-2, Festival) HarpC Child Bks.
—Playtime for Baby. Ziefert, Harriet. 8p. (ps). 1993. 4.95 (0-694-00505-3, Festival) HarpC Child Bks.
—Things That Go. Ziefert, Harriet. 8p. (ps). 1993. 4.95 (0-694-00507-X, Festival) HarpC Child Bks.
Baumann, Ann. Legs: The Story of a Giraffe. Barber, Phyllis. LC 90-47679. 80p. (gr. 4-7). 1991. SBE 13.95 (0-689-50526-4, M K McElderry) Macmillan Child Grp.
Baumgardner, Mary A. Alexandra, Keeper of Dreams. Baumgardner, Mary A. Wheeler, Penny & Wilson, Miriam W., eds. 37p. (gr. k-4). 1993. 12.95 (0-944576-08-7) Rocky River Pubs.
Baumgart, Klaus. Anna & the Little Green Dragon. Baumgart, Klaus. LC 91-26639. 32p. (ps-3). 1992. 12.95 (1-56282-166-0); PLB 12.89 (1-56282-167-9) Hyprn Child.
—The Little Green Dragon Steps Out. Baumgart, Klaus. LC 92-5120. 32p. (ps-3). 1992. Repr. of 1989 ed. PLB 12.89 (1-56282-255-1); text ed. 12.95 (1-56282-254-3) Hyprn Child.
—Where Are You, Little Green Dragon? Baumgart, Klaus. LC 92-72026. 32p. (ps-3). 1993. 12.95 (1-56282-344-2); PLB 12.89 (1-56282-345-0) Hyprn Child.
Baumli, Othmar, photos by. An Apple Tree Through the Year. Schnieper, Claudia. 48p. (gr. 2-5). 1987. PLB 19.95 (0-87614-248-X); pap. 6.95 (0-87614-483-0) Carolrhoda Bks.
Baviera, Rocco. A Boy Called Slow. Bruchac, Joseph. LC 93-21233. 1994. write for info. (0-399-22692-3, Philomel Bks) Putnam Pub Group.
Bavilacqua, Carol & Craig, Rose. Acid Rain. Hocking, Colin, et al. Bergman, Lincoln & Fairwell, Kay, eds. Hoyt, Richard & Bergman, Lincoln, photos by. 168p. (gr. 6-10). 1990. pap. 12.00 (0-912511-74-5) Lawrence Science.
Bawden, Nina. White Horse Gang. Bawden, Nina. 176p. (gr. 4-7). 1992. 13.95 (0-395-58709-3, Clarion Bks) HM.
Baxter, Leon. The Drawing Book. Baxter, Leon. 64p. (ps-4). 1990. 13.95 (0-8249-8475-7, Ideals Child) Hambleton-Hill.
—The Drawing Book. Baxter, Leon. 64p. (ps-4). 1993. pap. 5.95 (0-8249-8633-4, Ideals Child) Hambleton-Hill.
—Famous Ships. Baxter, Leon. 48p. (gr. 2-5). 1993. pap. 7.95 (0-685-65409-5, Ideals Child) Hambleton-Hill.
Baxter, Robert. The Adventures of Eros & Psyche. Richardson, I. M. LC 82-16057. 32p. (gr. 4-8). 1983. PLB 11.79 (0-89375-861-2); pap. text ed. 2.95 (0-89375-862-0) Troll Assocs.
—The Adventures of Hercules. Richardson, I. M. LC 82-16557. 32p. (gr. 4-8). 1983. PLB 11.79 (0-89375-865-5); pap. text ed. 2.95 (0-89375-866-3) Troll Assocs.
—American Revolution. Sabin, Francene. LC 84-2582. 32p. (gr. 3-6). 1985. PLB 9.49 (0-8167-0136-9); pap. text ed. 2.95 (0-8167-0137-7) Troll Assocs.
—Demeter & Persephone: The Seasons of Time. Richardson, I. M. LC 82-16023. 32p. (gr. 4-8). 1983. PLB 11.79 (0-89375-863-9); pap. text ed. 2.95 (0-89375-864-7) Troll Assocs.
—Frog Prince. Grimm, Jacob & Grimm, Wilhelm K. LC 78-18073. 32p. (gr. k-4). 1979. PLB 9.79 (0-89375-126-X); pap. 1.95 (0-89375-104-9) Troll Assocs.
—Indians of the Plains. Bains, Rae. LC 84-2645. 32p. (gr. 3-6). 1985. PLB 9.49 (0-8167-0188-1); pap. text ed. 2.95 (0-8167-0189-X) Troll Assocs.
—Jason & the Golden Fleece. Naden, C. J., adapted by. LC 80-50068. 32p. (gr. 4-8). 1980. PLB 11.79 (0-89375-360-2); pap. 2.95 (0-89375-364-5) Troll Assocs.
—Perseus & Medusa. Naden, C. J., adapted by. LC 80-50083. 32p. (gr. 4-8). 1980. PLB 11.79 (0-89375-362-9); pap. 2.95 (0-89375-366-1) Troll Assocs.
—Prometheus & the Story of Fire. Richardson, I. M. LC 82-15979. 32p. (gr. 4-8). 1983. PLB 11.79 (0-89375-859-0); pap. text ed. 2.95 (0-89375-860-4) Troll Assocs.
—Teddy Roosevelt, Rough Rider. Sabin, Lou. LC 85-1090. 48p. (gr. 4-6). 1986. lib. bdg. 10.79 (0-8167-0555-0); pap. text ed. 3.50 (0-8167-0556-9) Troll Assocs.
—Theseus & the Minotaur. Naden, C. J., adapted by. LC 80-50067. 32p. (gr. 4-8). 1980. PLB 11.79 (0-89375-363-7); pap. 2.95 (0-89375-367-X) Troll Assocs.
—Young Thomas Jefferson. Sabin, Francene. LC 85-1093. 48p. (gr. 4-6). 1985. lib. bdg. 10.79 (0-8167-0561-5); pap. text ed. 3.50 (0-8167-0562-3) Troll Assocs.

Baxter, Rosario. Jane Long - Frontier Woman. Crawford, Ann F. 64p. (gr. 4-7). 1990. lib. bdg. 12.95 (0-87443-090-9) Benson.
Bayard, E. Sans Famille, Tome 1. Malot, Hector. (FRE.). 351p. (gr. 5-10). 1990. pap. 10.95 (2-07-033612-3) Schoenhof.
—Sans Famille, Tome 2. Malot, Hector. (FRE.). 417p. (gr. 5-10). 1991. pap. 10.95 (2-07-033617-4) Schoenhof.
Bayard, Emile. Francois le Bossu. De Segur. (FRE.). 250p. (gr. 5-10). 1981. pap. 8.95 (2-07-033196-2) Schoenhof.
—General Dourakine. De Segur. (FRE.). 220p. (gr. 5-10). 1979. pap. 8.95 (2-07-033092-3) Schoenhof.
Bayer, Breindy. A Blick of Tzurik. Chana Faiga Brander. 126p. (Orig.). (gr. 4). 1990. pap. text ed. 9.50 (0-9629684-0-4) K K Aharon.
Bayes, Pilarin. Lord, I Am One of Your Little Ones. Puig, Enric. 93p. (gr. 3-6). 1987. 8.95 (0-8294-0545-3) Loyola.
Bayles, Arthur. Si Bantay, Si Puti, at Si Ngaw. Bayles, Miriam. (TAG., Orig.). (gr. k-2). 1988. pap. 3.75x (971-10-0359-7, Pub. by New Day Pub PI) Cellar.
Bayley, Nicola. Copycats. Bayley, Nicola. LC 91-58722. 96p. (ps up). 1992. 14.95 (1-56402-114-9) Candlewick Pr.
—Fun with Mrs. Thumb & Ginger Paw. Mark, Jan. LC 92-54955. 32p. (ps up). 1993. 9.95 (1-56402-247-1) Candlewick Pr.
—The Mousehole Cat. Barber, Antonia. LC 90-31533. 40p. (gr. k-3). 1990. SBE 14.95 (0-02-708331-4, Macmillan Child Bk) Macmillan Child Grp.
Bayly, Clifford. Troll Young People's Dictionary. Smith, David & Newton, Derek. Goldsmith, Evelyn, rev. by. LC 89-27331. 128p. (gr. 1-4). 1991. PLB 14.89 (0-8167-2255-2); pap. 9.95 (0-8167-2256-0) Troll Assocs.
Baynes, Pauline. Bilbo's Last Song. Tolkien, J. R. R. 32p. 1990. 14.45 (0-395-53810-6) HM.
—Bilbo's Last Song. Tolkien, J. R. R. LC 89-48659. 32p. 1992. pap. 6.99 (0-679-82710-2) Knopf Bks Yng Read.
—The Chronicles of Narnia. Lewis, C. S. (gr. 4 up). 1988. Boxed set. SBE 89.95 (0-02-758801-7, Macmillan Child Bk) Macmillan Child Grp.
—The Cobweb Curtain: A Christmas Story. Koralek, Jenny. LC 88-27035. 32p. (ps-2). 1989. 13.95 (0-8050-1051-3, Bks Young Read) H Holt & Co.
—Four Dolls. Godden, Rumer. LC 83-14157. 144p. (gr. 4-6). 1984. reinforced 13.00 (0-688-02801-2) Greenwillow.
—The Horse & His Boy. Lewis, C. S. LC 85-29978. 202p. (gr. 4 up). 1986. pap. 5.95 (0-02-044410-9, Collier Young Ad) Macmillan Child Grp.
—The Horse & His Boy. Lewis, C. S. LC 54-12817. 202p. (gr. 4 up). 1988. SBE 12.95 (0-02-757650-7, Macmillan Child Bk); pap. 3.95 (0-02-044200-9, Collier) Macmillan Child Grp.
—The Horse & His Boy. Lewis, C. S. LC 93-14300. (gr. 5 up). Date not set. 15.00 (0-06-023488-1); PLB 14.89 (0-06-023489-X) HarpC Child Bks.
—Land of Narnia: Brian Sibley Explores the World of C. S. Lewis. Sibley, Brian. LC 90-4192. 96p. (gr. 5 up). 1990. 19.95 (0-06-025625-7); PLB 19.89 (0-06-025626-5) HarpC Child Bks.
—The Last Battle. reissued ed. Lewis, C. S. LC 56-9362. 184p. (gr. 4 up). 1988. SBE 12.95 (0-02-757900-X, Macmillan Child Bk) Macmillan Child Grp.
—The Last Battle. Lewis, C. S. LC 93-14302. Date not set. 15.00 (0-06-023493-8) HarpC Child Bks.
—Let There Be Light. Baynes, Pauline. LC 90-44572. 32p. (gr. 1 up). 1991. SBE 13.95 (0-02-708542-2, Macmillan Child Bk) Macmillan Child Grp.
—The Lion, the Witch & the Wardrobe. Lewis, C. S. LC 50-10611. 160p. (gr. 4 up). 1988. 12.95 (0-02-758120-9, Macmillan Child Bk) Macmillan Child Grp.
—The Lion, the Witch, & the Wardrobe. Lewis, C. S. LC 93-8889. (gr. 5 up). 1994. 15.00 (0-06-023481-4) HarpC Child Bks.
—The Magician's Nephew. Lewis, C. S. LC 85-29973. 176p. (gr. 4 up). 1986. pap. 5.95 (0-02-044390-0, Collier Young Ad) Macmillan Child Grp.
—The Magician's Nephew. Lewis, C. S. LC 55-14869. 192p. (gr. 4 up). 1988. SBE 12.95 (0-02-758340-6, Macmillan Child Bk) Macmillan Child Grp.
—The Naming. Greaves, Margaret. 32p. (ps-3). 1993. 14.95 (0-15-200534-X) HarBrace.
—Prince Caspian. Lewis, C. S. LC 85-18999. 192p. (gr. 4 up). 1986. pap. 5.95 (0-02-044430-3, Collier Young Ad) Macmillan Child Grp.
—Prince Caspian. Lewis, C. S. LC 51-12799. 192p. (gr. 4 up). 1988. SBE 12.95 (0-02-758580-8, Macmillan Child Bk) Macmillan Child Grp.
—Prince Caspian. LC 93-11514. (gr. 5 up). 1994. 15.00 (0-06-023483-0); PLB 14.89 (0-06-023484-9) HarpC Child Bks.
—The Silver Chair. Lewis, C. S. LC 85-29984. 216p. (gr. 4 up). 1986. pap. 5.95 (0-02-044420-6, Collier Young Ad) Macmillan Child Grp.
—The Silver Chair. Lewis, C. S. LC 53-12553. 216p. (gr. 4 up). 1988. SBE 12.95 (0-02-758780-0, Macmillan Child Bk); pap. 3.50 (0-02-044250-5, Collier) Macmillan Child Grp.
—The Silver Chair. Lewis, C. S. LC 93-14299. (gr. 5 up). 1994. 15.00 (0-06-023495-4) HarpC Child Bks.

—Thanks Be to God: Prayers from Around the World. Baynes, Pauline, compiled by. LC 89-28622. 32p. (ps up). 1990. 12.95 (0-02-708541-4, Macmillan Child Bk) Macmillan Child Grp.
—The Voyage of the "Dawn Treader" Lewis, C. S. LC 85-29979. 218p. (gr. 4 up). 1986. pap. 5.95 (0-02-044440-0, Collier Young Ad) Macmillan Child Grp.
—Voyage of the "Dawn Treader" Lewis, C. S. LC 52-4219. 224p. (gr. 4 up). 1988. SBE 13.95 (0-02-758820-3, Macmillan Child Bk); pap. 3.50 (0-02-044260-2, Collier) Macmillan Child Grp.
—The Voyage of the Dawn Treader. Lewis, C. S. LC 93-11515. (gr. 4 up). 1994. 15.00 (0-06-023486-5); PLB 14.89 (0-06-023487-3) HarpC Child Bks.
Baynton, Martin. Mousewing. Mayne, William. 32p. (ps-3). 1988. 9.95 (0-13-604240-6) P-H.
Beach, Bettye. My Funny Cloud. Peebles, J. Winston. LC 81-50915. 36p. (ps-3). 1981. 4.95 (0-938232-00-2) Winston-Derek.
Beach-Balthis, Judy. Ano Nuevo: A Children's Guide. Beach-Balthis, Judy. Balthis, Frank S., ed. 24p. (Orig.). (gr. k-8). 1985. pap. 2.95 (0-918355-02-8) Firehole Pr.
—Point Reyes: A Children's Guide. Beach-Balthis, Judy. Balthis, Frank S., ed. 24p. (Orig.). (gr. k-8). 1983. pap. 2.95 (0-685-53258-5) Firehole Pr.
—Yellowstone: A Children's Guide. Beach-Balthis, Judy. Balthis, Frank, ed. 36p. (Orig.). (gr. k-8). 1981. pap. 2.95 (0-918355-01-X) Firehole Pr.
Bear, Alice. The Planet of the Dinosaurs. Carr, Barbara. LC 92-9287. 32p. (gr. k-3). 1992. 12.95 (0-89334-161-4, 161-4) Humanics Ltd.
Beard, Derrick. Max Science & the Glowing Firefly. Edwards, Roger. Sanchez, Brenda L., ed. 26p. (gr. k-5). 1991. pap. 3.95 (1-879350-01-7) Max Sci Pub.
—Max Science & the Thunderstorm. Sanchez, Brenda L. Sanchez, J. A., ed. 26p. (gr. k-5). 1991. pap. 3.95 (1-879350-02-5) Max Sci Pub.
Bearden, Romare. A Visit to the Country. Johnson, Herschel. LC 87-25083. 32p. (ps-3). 1989. PLB 13.89 (0-06-022854-7) HarpC Child Bks.
Bearman, Jane. David. Bearman, Jane. LC 65-21753. (gr. 3 up). 1975. 3.95 (0-8246-0085-1) Jonathan David.
—Jonathan. Bearman, Jane. LC 65-21754. (gr. 3 up). 1975. 3.95 (0-8246-0089-4) Jonathan David.
Bearson, Lee. Bible Stories for Little Children, Bk. 1. rev. ed. Hollender, Betty R. 80p. (Orig.). (gr. 1-3). 1985. pap. text ed. 6.00 (0-8074-0309-1, 103100) UAHC.
Beasley, Roberta. Baby's Cradle Songs. 12p. (ps). 1986. 3.99 (0-394-88242-3) Random Bks Yng Read.
Beath, Mary. Manatees & Dugongs: A Coloring Book in English & Spanish. Kuzmier, Kerrie & McCann, Jennifer. Inchaustegui, Sixto, tr. (ENG & SPA.). 28p. (Orig.). (gr. 3-6). 1991. pap. text ed. 4.00 (0-685-39509-X) Ctr Marine Cnsrv.
Beaton, Clare. Cards. Beaton, Clare. 24p. (gr. k-4). 1990. PLB 10.90 (0-531-19096-X); pap. 2.95 (0-531-15159-X) Watts.
—Christmas Activity Book. Bruzzone, Catherine. 24p. (gr. k-5). 1993. pap. 3.95 (0-8120-1745-5) Barron.
—Costumes. Beaton, Clare. LC 89-21520. 24p. (gr. k-4). 1990. PLB 10.90 (0-531-19094-3); pap. 2.95 (0-531-15160-3) Watts.
—Face Painting. Beaton, Clare. LC 90-11956. 24p. (gr. k-4). 1990. PLB 10.90 (0-531-19095-1); pap. 2.95 (0-531-15161-1) Watts.
—Hats. Beaton, Clare. 24p. (gr. k-4). 1990. PLB 10.90 (0-531-19097-8); pap. 2.95 (0-531-15162-X) Watts.
—Masks. Beaton, Clare. 24p. (gr. k-4). 1990. PLB 10.90 (0-531-19098-6); pap. 2.95 (0-531-15163-8) Watts.
—T-Shirt Painting. Beaton, Clare. 24p. (gr. k-4). 1990. PLB 10.90 (0-531-19099-4); pap. 2.95 (0-531-15164-6) Watts.
Beattie, Linda D. The Little Cloud That Couldn't: An Environmental Story for Children. Arnold, Jeanne G. LC 90-62422. 76p. (Orig.). (gr. 3-7). 1990. pap. 4.95 (0-9620887-1-4) Media Serv Unltd.
Beauvais, Denis, jt. illus. see Long, Kevin.
Bech, Bente. Hot on the Scent. Lind, Peter, contrib. by. LC 92-8782. 32p. (ps-3). 1993. PLB 17.27 (0-8368-0510-0); PLB 17.27 s.p. (0-685-61501-4) Gareth Stevens Inc.
Becher, Ivy. The Ballad of Padre Island, Vol. 1. Meltabarger, P. J. Samuelson, Arnold & Samuelson, Billie, eds. Miller, Jesse A., intro. by. 28p. (Orig.). (gr. 1-5). 1987. pap. text ed. 3.95 (0-923133-00-3) JM Pub.
—The Karankawa Indians, Pt. 2. Meltabarger, P. J. Samuelson, Arnold & Samuelson, Billie, eds. Miller, Jesse A., intro. by. 28p. (Orig.). (gr. 1-5). 1988. pap. text ed. 3.95 (0-923133-01-1) JM Pub.
—Livingston: The Pedigreed Pooch of Padre Island. Meltabarger, P. J. Samuelson, Arnold & Samuelson, Billie, eds. Lynn, E. Russell, intro. by. 150p. (gr. 7-10). 1988. 19.95 (0-923133-02-X) JM Pub.
Becicka, Lori. Chooch. Schultz, Betty K. LC 90-91639. 64p. (gr. k-3). 1990. 14.95 (0-929568-00-1) Raspberry IL.
Beck, Arthello, jt. illus. see Davis, Rhonda K.
Beck, Connie & O'Toole, Tim. Elizabeth's Castle Adventure: A Just Suppose(TM) Story. Rayburn, Cherie. Gress, Jonna, ed. 4p. (gr. 1-7). 1992. 18.80 (0-944943-07-1) Current Inc.
Beck, Ian. Pudding & Pie: Favorite Nursery Rhymes. Williams, Sarah. 48p. 1989. 14.95 (0-19-279868-5) OUP.

—Read Me a Fairy Tale: A Child's Book of Classic Fairy Tales. Impey, Rose, as told by. LC 92-41949. (gr. k up). 1993. 14.95 (0-590-49431-7) Scholastic Inc.
—Ride a Cock-Horse. Williams, Sarah, ed. 48p. (ps up). 1988. 12.95 (0-19-279831-6); Cassette. 6.95 (0-19-279867-7) OUP.
—Round & Round the Garden. Williams, Sarah, ed. 48p. (ps). 14.95 (0-19-279766-2); pap. 5.95 (0-19-272132-1); cassette 7.95 (0-19-279852-9) OUP.
Beck, Michael. Geography: United States: Geography - History - Maps - Flags (Through Research Activities) Beck, Michael & Scott, Judy. 240p. (Orig.). (gr. 4-6). 1990. pap. text ed. 20.00 (0-927867-00-1) Skippingstone Pr.
Becker, Richard, jt. illus. see McAllister, Mimi.
Becker, Wayne. A Funny Man. Jensen, Patricia. LC 92-36007. 1993. 3.95 (0-590-46190-7) Scholastic Inc.
Beckes, Shirley. Fire Engine to the Rescue. Dubowski, Cathy E. 24p. (Orig.). (gr. k-1). 1990. pap. 0.99 (1-878624-37-7) McClanahan Bk.
—Key Words to Reading. Wise, Beth A. & Sokoloff, Myka-Lynne. Nayer, Judith E., ed. 32p. (gr. k-1). 1991. wkbk. 1.95 (1-878624-61-X) McClanahan Bk.
—The Little School Bus That Talked. Eldrid, Brenda M. 24p. (ps-2). 1992. pap. 0.99 (1-56293-113-X) McClanahan Bk.
—My First Spring Day. Lambert, Matthew. 1994. write for info. (0-8114-4459-7) Raintree Steck-V.
Beckes, Shirley V. A Very Scraggly Christmas Tree. Pippen, Christie. (gr. 2-4). 1988. 17.96 (0-8172-2754-7) Raintree Steck-V.
Beckett, Bob. Take a Deep Breath: The Kids' Play-Away Stress Book. Shelton, Laura S. & Shapiro, Lawrence E. 100p. (Orig.). (gr. k-6). 1992. pap. 16.95 (1-882732-02-2) Ctr Applied Psy.
Beckett, Sheila. Three-Minute Bible Stories. Leale, Judy. 24p. (ps-k). 1993. 5.98 (0-8317-8298-6) Smithmark.
Beckett, Sheilah. The Christmas Story: Based on the Gospels According to St. Matthew & St. Luke. Hautzig, Deborah, ed. LC 83-60411. 24p. (ps-2). 1983. 2.95 (0-394-86124-8) Random Bks Yng Read.
—Three-Minute Bible Stories. Leale, Judy. 32p. 1992. 9.95 (1-56156-152-5) Kidsbks.
—Wynken, Blynken, & Nod. Field, Eugene. 18p. (ps). 1986. 3.95 (0-448-10225-0, G&D) Putnam Pub Group.
Beckman, Per. Lisa Can't Sleep. Beckman, Kaj. 28p. (ps). 1990. 7.95 (91-29-59768-4, Pub. by R & S Bks) FS&G.
Beddows, Eric. The Cave of Snores. Haseley, Dennis. LC 85-48845. 40p. (gr. k-4). 1987. HarpC Child Bks.
—Joyful Noise: Poems for Two Voices. Fleischman, Paul. LC 87-45280. 64p. (gr. 3-8). 1988. 14.00 (0-06-021852-5); PLB 13.89 (0-06-021853-3) HarpC Child Bks.
—Joyful Noise: Poems for Two Voices. Fleischman, Paul. LC 87-45280. 64p. (gr. 3 up). 1992. pap. 3.95 (0-06-446093-2, Trophy) HarpC Child Bks.
—Shadow Play. Fleischman, Paul. LC 89-26874. 48p. (gr. 2 up). 1990. PLB 14.89 (0-06-021865-7) HarpC Child Bks.
—The Rooster's Gift. Conrad, Pam. LC 93-14490. 1995. write for info. (0-06-023603-5); PLB write for info. (0-06-023604-3) HarpC Child Bks.
—Who Shrank My Grandmother's House? Poems of Discovery. Esbensen, Barbara J. LC 90-39631. 48p. (gr. 3-7). 1992. 15.00 (0-06-021827-4); PLB 14.89 (0-06-021828-2) HarpC Child Bks.
—Zoom at Sea. Wynne-Jones, Tim. LC 92-14738. 32p. (ps-2). 1993. 15.00 (0-06-021448-1); PLB 14.89 (0-06-021449-X) HarpC Child Bks.
—Zoom Away. Wynne-Jones, Tim. LC 92-41171. 32p. (ps-2). 1993. 15.00 (0-06-022962-4); PLB 14.89 (0-06-022963-2) HarpC.
Bedford, F. D. Peter Pan. Barrie, J. M. LC 92-53172. 224p. 1992. 12.95 (0-679-41792-3, Evrymans Lib Childs Class) Knopf.
Bedford, F. D., jt. illus. see White, Flora.
Beebe, Mark & Filkins, Vanessa. Creative Encounters with Creative People. Gudeman, Janice. 144p. (gr. 4 up). 1984. wkbk. 11.95 (0-86653-258-7, GA 623) Good Apple.
Beecham, Thomas. Davy Crockett: Hero of the Wild Frontier. Moseley, Elizabeth R. 80p. (gr. 2-6). 1991. Repr. of 1967 ed. lib. bdg. 12.95 (0-7910-1409-6) Chelsea Hse.
Beeching, Mark. Caterpillar. Aunt Peggy. 24p. 1992. pap. 6.95 (0-9636185-0-4); Coloring bk. 8.95 (0-9636185-3-9) Aunt Peggys Pub.

—Caterpillar. 2nd ed. Aunt Peggy. 24p. (ps-k). 1994. 13.95 (0-9636185-2-0) Aunt Peggys Pub.
A beautifully illustrated, twenty-four page picture book for children ages 2 to 6 yrs. In this book there are three words that explain the working of nature--COCOON--HIBERNATE--& METAMORPHOSIS. Available in: HARDCOVER--PAPERBACK-- COLORING BOOK or "FUN PACK", PAPERBACK/COLOR BOOK. Order from: Aunt Peggy's Publishing, P.O. Box 395, Lowell, IN 46356. 219-

---

696-8707.
Publisher Provided Annotation.

—Caterpillar: Fun Pack. Aunt Peggy. 24p. (ps-k). 1994. Set, Story bk. & color bk. 8.95 (0-9636185-4-7) Aunt Peggys Pub.
—How Did You Come to School Today. Aunt Peggy. LC 93-90173. 42p. 1993. pap. 6.95 (0-9636185-1-2) Aunt Peggys Pub.
Beelaerts, Marie, jt. illus. see Guell, Fernando.
Beerhorst, Adrian. Hudson Taylor. Kiefer, James. 53p. (gr. k-6). 1973. pap. text ed. 8.99 (1-55976-054-0) CEF Press.
—Life of Peter. Overholtzer, Ruth P. 21p. (gr. k-6). 1964. pap. text ed. 9.45 (1-55976-013-3) CEF Press.
Beeson, Bob. Ten Little Circus Mice. Beeson, Bob. 32p. (ps-1). 1993. 11.95 (0-8249-8616-4, Ideals Child) Hambleton-Hill.
Beeson, D. Biology. Chisholm, J. 48p. (gr. 3-6). 1984. PLB 13.96 (0-88110-166-4); pap. 6.95 (0-86020-707-2) EDC.
—Book of Science. Chisholm, J. 48p. (gr. 3-6). 1984. 14.95 (0-86020-721-8) EDC.
Begay, Shonto. The Mud Pony: A Traditional Skidi Pawnee Tale. Cohen, Caron Lee, adapted by. LC 87-23451. 32p. (gr. k-4). 1988. pap. 14.95 (0-590-41525-5) Scholastic Inc.
Begay, Shonto W. The Native American Book of Change. White Deer of Autumn. LC 92-17001. 1992. write for info. (0-941831-73-6) Beyond Words Pub.
—The Native American Book of Wisdom. White Deer of Autumn. LC 92-17002. 1992. 4.95 (0-941831-74-4) Beyond Words Pub.
Begin, Maryjane. Little Mouse's Painting. Wolkstein, Diane. LC 91-16017. 32p. (ps up). 1992. 15.00 (0-688-07609-2); PLB 14.93 (0-688-07610-6) Morrow Jr Bks.
—The Porcupine Mouse. Pryor, Bonnie. LC 87-12305. 32p. (ps-2). 1988. 13.95 (0-688-07153-8); PLB 13.88 (0-688-07154-6, Morrow Jr Bks) Morrow Jr Bks.
Begin-Callanan, Maryjane. Before I Go to Sleep. Hood, Thomas. 32p. (ps-3). 1990. 14.95 (0-399-21638-3, Putnam) Putnam Pub Group.
—Before I Go to Sleep. Hood, Thomas. 32p. (ps-1). 1992. pap. 4.95 (0-399-22440-8, Putnam) Putnam Pub Group.
Beguinot, Brigitte. The Mouse Party: An Open-the-Door Book. Beguinot, Brigitte. 12p. (ps-3). 1992. bds. 10.95 (1-878093-50-9) Boyds Mills Pr.
Behl, Deborah. Jesus Is Caring for You. Mayfield, Larry. 20p. (gr. k-6). 1982. visualized song 5.99 (3-90117-026-X) CEF Press.
Behm, Kim, et al. Teenage Pregnancy: A New Beginning. rev. ed. Barr, Linda & Monserrat, Catherine. Jones, Lyn, et al, photos by. 112p. (gr. 6-12). 1992. pap. 14.95 (0-945886-07-1) New Futures.
Behr, J. The Best Joke Book for Kids, No. 1. Eckstein, Joan & Gleit, Joyce. 48p. (gr. 7-12). 1977. pap. 2.99 (0-380-01734-2, Camelot) Avon.
Behr, Joyce. Biggest Riddle Book in the World. Rosenbloom, Joseph. LC 76-1165. (gr. 5 up). 1979. pap. 5.95 (0-8069-8884-3) Sterling.
—Doctor Knock-Knock's Official Knock-Knock Dictionary. Rosenbloom, Joseph. LC 76-19796. 128p. (gr. 3 up). 1980. 12.95 (0-8069-4536-2); pap. 3.95 (0-8069-8936-X) Sterling.
—Funny Insults & Snappy Put-Downs. Rosenbloom, Joseph. LC 82-50547. 128p. (gr. 4 up). 1982. pap. 3.95 (0-8069-7644-6) Sterling.
—Gigantic Joke Book. Rosenbloom, Joseph. LC 77-93310. 256p. (gr. 4-6). 1981. pap. 5.95 (0-8069-7514-8); 16.95 (0-8069-4590-7) Sterling.
—Sneaky Tricks to Fool Your Friends. Chuchill, E. Richard. LC 86-14448. 128p. (gr. 6-12). 1987. pap. 3.95 (0-8069-4808-6) Sterling.
—World's Best Funny Songs. Nelson, Esther. LC 87-753871. 128p. (gr. 1-8). 1989. pap. 4.95 (0-8069-6893-1) Sterling.
Behrens, Terry. Hanukkah. Behrens, June. LC 82-17890. 32p. (gr. k-4). 1983. PLB 15.00 (0-516-02386-1); pap. 3.95 (0-516-42386-X) Childrens.
—Passover. Behrens, June. LC 87-5161. 32p. (gr. k-4). 1987. pap. 3.95 (0-516-42389-4) Childrens.
Beier, Ellen. Centerfield Ballhawk. Christopher, Matt. 64p. (gr. 2-4). 1992. 11.95 (0-316-14079-1) Little.
—John Lennon, Young Rock Star. Santrey, Laurence. LC 89-33938. 48p. (gr. 4-6). 1990. lib. bdg. 10.79 (0-8167-1781-8); pap. text ed. 3.50 (0-8167-1782-6) Troll Assocs.
—Ludwig Van Beethoven: Young Composer. Sabin, Louis. LC 91-18616. 48p. (gr. 4-6). 1992. PLB 10.79 (0-8167-2511-X); pap. text ed. 3.50 (0-8167-2512-8) Troll Assocs.
—Mrs. Peachtree & the Eighth Avenue Cat. Silverman, Erica. LC 92-16973. 32p. (ps-3). 1994. RSBE 14.95 (0-02-782684-8, Macmillan Child Bk) Macmillan Child Bk.
—The Swiss Family Robinson. Wyss, Johann. James, Raymond, ed. LC 89-33888. 48p. (gr. 3-6). 1990. lib. bdg. 12.89 (0-8167-1875-X); pap. text ed. 3.95 (0-8167-1876-8) Troll Assocs.
—Young Albert Einstein. Santrey, Laurence. LC 89-33940. 48p. (gr. 4-6). 1990. PLB 10.79 (0-8167-1777-X); pap. text ed. 3.50 (0-8167-1778-8) Troll Assocs.

—Young Harriet Tubman: Freedom Fighter. Benjamin, Anne. LC 91-26404. 32p. (gr. k-2). 1992. PLB 11.59 (0-8167-2538-1); pap. text ed. 2.95 (0-8167-2539-X) Troll Assocs.
Beingessner, Laura. Boys Don't Knit. Schoop, Janice. 30p. (ps-3). 1988. pap. 4.95 (0-86543-077-2) Africa World.
Beinicke, Steve. Andrew & the Wild Bikes. Morgan, Allen. 32p. (ps-2). 1990. 12.95 (1-55037-083-9, Pub. by Annick CN); pap. 4.95 (1-55037-082-0, Pub. by Annick CN) Firefly Bks Ltd.
—The Dog Who Wouldn't Be Left Behind. Finnigan, Joan. 32p. (ps-2). 1991. 12.95 (0-88899-057-X, Pub. by Groundwood-Douglas & McIntyre CN) Firefly Bks Ltd.
—The Heat Is On: Facing Our Energy Problem. Tanaka, Shelly. 56p. (gr. 3-7). 1991. pap. 9.95 (0-920668-94-1) Firefly Bks Ltd.
—I Am Not Jenny. Kaner, Steve. 32p. (ps-2). 1991. 13.95 (0-88899-142-8, Pub. by Groundwood-Douglas & McIntyre CN) Firefly Bks Ltd.
—Trash Attack: Garbage, & What We Can Do about It. Savage, Candace. 56p. (gr. 3-7). 1991. pap. 9.95 (0-920668-73-9) Firefly Bks Ltd.
Beinieke, Steven. Ellie & the Ivy. Morgan, Allen. 32p. (gr. 2 up). 1990. bds. 12.95 laminated (0-19-540726-1) OUP.
Beirne, Barbara, photos by. A Pianist's Debut: Preparing for the Concert Stage. Beirne, Barbara. 56p. (gr. 2-5). 1990. PLB 21.50 (0-87614-432-6) Carolrhoda Bks.
Beisert, Heide H. My Magic Cloth: A Story for a Whole Week. Beisert, Heide H. Lewis, Naomi, tr. LC 86-60490. 32p. (gr. k-3). 1986. 14.95 (1-55858-069-7) North-South Bks NYC.
Beisner, Monica. Under the Sea. Thompson, Brenda & Overbeck, Cynthia. LC 76-22470. 24p. (gr. k-3). 1977. PLB 7.95 (0-8225-1363-3) Lerner Pubns.
Beisner, Monika. Secret Spells & Curious Charms. Beisner, Monika. LC 85-45323. 32p. (ps up). 1986. 15.00 (0-374-36692-6) FS&G.
Beittel, Kenneth R. Ralph & Deno in Vermont. Beittel, Kenneth R. & Beittel, Joan N. LC 90-86028. 32p. (Orig.). (gr. 5 up). 1990. pap. 6.00 (0-9628511-0-8) HVHA.
Bejna, Barbara & Jensen, Shirlee. The Day Our TV Broke Down. Wright, Betty R. Holbrook, Thomas, intro. by. LC 80-14434. 32p. (gr. k-6). 1980. PLB 17.96 (0-8172-1365-1) Raintree Steck-V.
—I Can't Always Hear You. Zelonky, Joy. Geist, Chris, intro. by. LC 79-23891. 32p. (gr. k-6). 1980. PLB 17.96 (0-8172-1355-4) Raintree Steck-V.
Bekkering, Herman. The Bannock. Wheeler, Bernelda. LC 92-34255. 1993. 4.25 (0-383-03617-8) SRA Schl Grp.
Belanger, Ray, et al. Black Image Makers. Gaines, Edith M., et al. Adrine-Robinson, Kenyette, ed. Gregory, Dick, frwd. by. (Orig.). (gr. 5-9). 1988. pap. 5.00 (0-913678-17-1) New Day Pr.
Belcastro, Jani. The Old House on the Hill. Belcastro, Jani. LC 92-59951. 44p. (gr. k-3). 1993. 6.95 (1-55523-575-1) Winston-Derek.
Belcher, Cynthia. Discover Dinosaurs: Activity Book. Esslinger, Jessica. 20p. (gr. 1-6). 1988. wkbk. 2.95 (0-911239-26-X) Carnegie Mus.
Belcher, Cynthia, jt. illus. see Girdler, Netta.
Belding, Pam. Certain Choices. Haensel, Phyllis C. Hoff, Marshall G. & Bock, Glenn H., eds. 32p. (Orig.). (gr. 7-9). 1984. pap. text ed. write for info. (0-940210-01-0) Minn Med Found.
Belding, Pam & Lasley, Susan K. Someone Special. Bock, Glenn N & Hoff, Marshall G., eds. 32p. (gr. k-6). 1981. write for info. (0-940210-00-2) Minn Med Found.
Belknap, Barbara. An Anasazi Welcome. Matthews, Kay. LC 92-796. 40p. (gr. 1-6). 1992. pap. 8.95 (1-878610-27-9) Red Crane Bks.
Bell, Anthea. Buster, the Sheikh of Hope Street. Reuter, Bjarne. LC 91-19397. 144p. (gr. 4 up). 1991. 13.95 (0-525-44772-5, DCB) Dutton Child Bks.
Bell, Bill. Dr. Drabble's Astounding Musical Mesmerizer. Brouwer, Sigmund & Davidson, Wayne. 24p. (ps-2). 1991. 5.99 (0-89693-904-9) SP Pubns.
—Dr. Drabble's Incredible Identical Robot Innovation. Brouwer, Sigmund & Davidson, Wayne. 24p. (ps-2). 1991. 5.99 (0-89693-902-2) SP Pubns.
—Dr. Drabble's Phenomenal Anti-Gravity Dust Machine. Brouwer, Sigmund & Davidson, Wayne. 24p. (ps-2). 1991. 5.99 (0-89693-901-4) SP Pubns.
—Let's Pretend: Poems Collected by Natalie Bober. 72p. (ps-3). 1990. pap. 4.95 (0-14-032132-2, Puffin) Puffin Bks.
Bell, Julian. The Widow & the Parrot. Woolf, Virginia. Bell, Quentin, afterword by. 26p. (ps up). 1988. 12.95 (0-15-296783-4) HarBrace.
Bell, Martha. A Box of Peppermints. Stopple, Libby. Dromgoole, Dick, ed. LC 75-20957. 96p. (gr. 2-10). 1975. 12.95 (0-913632-08-2); pap. 7.95 (0-913632-07-4) Am Univ Artforms.
Bell, Owain. Bertie the Bus Wheel Book. Awdry, W. 14p. (ps-k). 1993. 4.99 (0-679-84469-4) Random Bks Yng Read.
—Breakfast-Time for Thomas: Based on the Railway Series. Awdry, W. LC 89-62527. 32p. (Orig.). (ps-3). 1990. pap. 1.50 (0-679-80409-9) Random Bks Yng Read.

—Catch Me, Catch Me! A Thomas the Tank Engine Story. Awdry, W. LC 89-37547. 24p. (Orig.). (ps-2). 1990. pap. 2.25 (*0-679-80485-4*) Random Bks Yng Read.
—Choo-Choo, Peek-a-Boo. Awdry, W. LC 91-61250. 14p. (ps). 1992. 3.99 (*0-679-82262-3*) Random Bks Yng Read.
—Good Morning, James. Awdry, W. 12p. (ps). 1992. 3.99 (*0-679-82707-2*) Random Bks Yng Read.
—Happy Birthday, Thomas! A Step 1 Book - Preschool-Gr 1. Awdry, W. LC 89-49649. 32p. (Orig.). (ps-1). 1990. lib. bdg. 7.99 (*0-679-90809-9*); pap. 3.50 (*0-679-80809-4*) Random Bks Yng Read.
—Henry & the Elephant: Based on the Railway Series. Awdry, W. LC 89-62528. 32p. (Orig.). (ps-3). 1990. pap. 1.50 (*0-679-80408-0*) Random Bks Yng Read.
—James the Red Engine. Awdry, W. 7p. (ps-k). 1991. bds. 7.00 with plastic wheels (*0-679-81590-2*) Random Bks Yng Read.
—The Midnight Ride of Thomas the Tank Engine. LC 93-26587. 1994. 4.99 (*0-679-85643-9*) Random Bks Yng Read.
—Thomas & the Freight Train. Awdry, W. LC 90-62371. 22p. (ps). 1991. bds. 2.95 (*0-679-81599-6*) Random Bks Yng Read.
—Thomas & the Hide-&-Seek Animals: A Thomas the Tank Engine Flap Book. Awdry, W. LC 90-62114. 24p. (ps-1). 1991. 7.95 (*0-679-81316-0*) Random Bks Yng Read.
—Thomas the Tank Engine & the Great Race. Awdry, W. 7p. (ps-k). 1989. bds. 7.00 with plastic wheels (*0-679-80000-X*) Random Bks Yng Read.
—Thomas the Tank Engine & the School Trip. Awdry, W. LC 92-33711. 32p. (ps-1). 1993. PLB 7.99 (*0-679-94365-X*); pap. 3.50 (*0-679-84365-5*) Random Bks Yng Read.
—Thomas the Tank Engine Says Goodnight. 12p. (ps-k). 1990. sponge filled 3.99 (*0-679-80791-8*) Random Bks Yng Read.
—Thomas the Tank Engine Visits a Farm. Awdry, W. 10p. (ps). 1991. vinyl 3.95 (*0-679-81580-5*) Random Bks Yng Read.
—Thomas the Tank Engine's Noisy Trip. Awdry, W. LC 89-60089. 28p. 1989. bds. 2.95 (*0-679-80083-2*) Random Bks Yng Read.
—Thomas's Big Railway Pop-up Book. Awdry, W. 14p. (ps up). 1992. 13.00 (*0-679-83465-6*) Random Bks Yng Read.
—Thomas's Carousel Book. Awdry, W. 5p. (ps-3). 1993. 8.00 (*0-679-84819-3*) Random Bks Yng Read.
—Wave Hello to Thomas! A Thomas the Tank Engine Lift-&-Peek-a-Board Book. Awdry, W., contrib. by. LC 92-80747. 14p. (ps-k). 1993. bds. 3.99 (*0-679-83877-5*) Random Bks Yng Read.
Bell, Thomas P. The Fox Who Found Christmas. Pochocki, Ethel F. LC 90-82095. 56p. (Orig.). 1990. pap. 5.95 (*0-87793-431-2*) Ave Maria.
Bellew, Mike. Fun Projects for Kids: A Teacher's Guide to Classroom Art. Neal, Judith. LC 83-7657. 136p. (gr. k-6). 1983. PLB 21.27 (*0-516-00821-8*) Childrens.
Belli, Fred. Little Red Riding Hood "Puzzle 'n Book" Tailor, Z. 8p. (gr. k up). 1989. PLB write for info. ABC Child Bks.
Bellows, Cathy. Toad School. Bellows, Cathy. LC 89-212562. 32p. (ps-3). 1990. RSBE 13.95 (*0-02-708835-9*, Macmillan Child Bk) Macmillan Child Grp.
Bellville, Cheryl W. The Airplane Book. Bellville, Cheryl W. 48p. (gr. k-4). 1991. PLB 19.95 (*0-87614-686-8*) Carolrhoda Bks.
—Theater Magic: Behind the Scenes at a Children's Theater. Bellville, Cheryl W. LC 86-9757. 48p. (gr. k-4). 1986. PLB 19.95 (*0-87614-278-1*) Carolrhoda Bks.
Bellville, Cheryl W., photos by. Cranberries: Fruit of the Bogs. Burns, Diane. LC 93-29620. 1994. write for info. (*0-87614-822-4*) Carolrhoda Bks.
Bellwood, Shirley. Jenny & Grandpa: What Is It Like to Grow Old? Nystrum, Carolyn. 48p. (gr. 9-12). 1988. 7.99 (*0-7459-1396-2*) Lion USA.
Belsky, Vera. King Philip, the Indian Chief. Averill, Esther. LC 92-32156. v, 147p. (gr. 6-12). 1993. lib. bdg. 17.50 (*0-208-02357-7*, Pub. by Linnet); (Pub. by Linnet) Shoe String.
Beltier, Pam. My "A" Sound Box. Moncure, Jane. 32p. (gr. k-2). 1993. pap. text ed. 5.95 (*1-56189-384-6*) Amer Educ Pub.
—My "U" Sound Box. Moncure, Jane. 32p. (gr. k-2). 1993. pap. text ed. 5.95 (*1-56189-383-8*) Amer Educ Pub.
Bemelmans, Ludwig. Madeline. Bemelmans, Ludwig. LC 39-21791. (gr. k-3). 1977. pap. 4.50 incl. cassette (*0-14-050198-3*, Puffin) Puffin Bks.
—Madeline. Bemmelmans, Ludwig. LC 68-666. (gr. k-3). 1958. pap. 15.00 (*0-670-44580-0*) Viking Child Bks.
—Madeline & the Bad Hat. Bemelmans, Ludwig. LC 57-62. (gr. k-3). 1977. pap. 4.99 (*0-14-050206-8*, Puffin) Puffin Bks.
—Madeline & the Bad Hat. Bemmelmans, Ludwig. (gr. k-3). 1957. pap. 14.00 (*0-670-44614-9*) Viking Child Bks.
—Madeline & the Gypsies. Bemelmans, Ludwig. 56p. (ps-3). 1977. pap. 4.50 (*0-14-050261-0*) Puffin Bks.
—Madeline & the Gypsies. Bemelmans, Ludwig. (gr. k-3). 1959. pap. 14.99 (*0-670-44682-3*) Viking Child Bks.
—Madeline in London. Bemelmans, Ludwig. 56p. (ps-3). 1977. pap. 4.50 (*0-14-050199-1*, Puffin) Puffin Bks.

—Madeline in London. Bemmelmans, Ludwig. (gr. k-3). 1961. pap. 15.00 (*0-670-44648-3*) Viking Child Bks.
—Madeline's House: Includes: Madeline; Madeline's Rescue; Madeline & the Bad Hat. Bemelmans, Ludwig. (ps-3). 1989. pap. 12.50 (*0-14-095028-1*, Puffin) Puffin Bks.
—Madeline's Rescue. Bemelmans, Ludwig. 64p. (gr. k-3). 1977. pap. 4.50 (*0-14-050207-6*, Puffin) Puffin Bks.
—Madeline's Rescue. Bemelmans, Ludwig. LC 53-8709. 56p. (gr. k-3). 1953. pap. 14.00 (*0-670-44716-1*) Viking Child Bks.
—Rosebud. Bemelmans, Ludwig. LC 92-47046. 40p. (ps-2). 1993. 8.99 (*0-679-84913-0*); PLB 9.99 (*0-679-94913-5*) Knopf Bks Yng Read.
Ben-Ami, Doron. Magic Comes in Its Time. Rabe, Berniece. LC 92-19260. 1993. pap. 13.00 (*0-671-79454-X*, S&S BFYR) S&S Trade.
Benarde, Anita. Games from Many Lands. Benarde, Anita. Winskill, Mary, frwd. by. LC 71-86975. 64p. (gr. 3-7). 1971. PLB 13.95 (*0-87460-147-9*) Lion Bks.
Bendall-Brunello, John. Seven-&-One-Half Labors of Hercules. Bendall-Brunello, John. LC 91-36176. 64p. (gr. 2-5). 1991. 10.95 (*0-525-44780-6*, DCB) Dutton Child Bks.
Bender, Robert. A Moving Experience: Dance for Lovers of Children & the Child Within. Benzwie, Teresa. 216p. (ps-6). 1988. pap. text ed. 21.95 (*0-913705-25-X*) Zephyr Pr AZ.
—The Three Billy Goats Gruff. Bender, Robert. LC 92-41077. 32p. (ps-2). 1993. PLB 14.95 (*0-8050-2529-4*, Bks Young Read) H Holt & Co.
Bendix, Jane. Mi'Ca: Buffalo Hunter. Bendix, Jane. 189p. (Orig.). (gr. 5-10). 1992. 14.95 (*0-89992-431-X*); pap. 9.95 (*0-89992-131-0*) Coun India Ed.

Benedict, Jennifer S. The Little Green Hummingbird. Linn, James R. Huston, Dwayne L., ed. LC 92-75969. 44p. (gr. 3). 1993. pap. 7.98 (*1-882798-01-5*) Erth & Sky Pub.
For every child there are times when common day occurrences are magical. They are most magical when the child is first encountering logical thinking but still has a sense of wonderment. This is a story told by an adult but seen through the eyes of his own inner child. Aided by beautifully realistic illustrations from a gifted artist, the author gives a portrayal of two urban families. A family of four follows a hummingbird as she raises two offspring in view of their dining room window. Together with help from their neighbor, the family tries to share the perils of the smallest of all birds. Full of humor & human drama, there are traces of issues important to children who face the start of the next century. Community, schooling, wildlife conservation & instinctive parenting are lightly touched upon. Written so that it is easy reading for third graders & up, it is also a pleasant exercise for adults who will be reading it to younger children. The illustrations will hold the attention of even the most active youngster. The mood will make adults remember their own inner child. *Publisher Provided Annotation.*

Benett, L., jt. illus. see De Neuville, C.
Benigni, M. Luisa. Hosanna to You, Jesus! A Palm Sunday Experience. Mignolli, Marisa. 32p. (Orig.). (ps-3). 1993. pap. 3.95 (*0-8198-3368-1*) St Paul Bks.
Benjamin, Ann, jt. illus. see Maley, Matthew.
Benjamin, Carol L. Cartooning for Kids. Benjamin, Carol L. LC 81-43876. 80p. (gr. 3-7). 1982. PLB 12.89 (*0-690-04208-6*, Crowell Jr Bks) HarpC Child Bks.
—Writing for Kids. Benjamin, Carol L. LC 85-47542. 80p. (gr. 3-7). 1985. PLB 12.89 (*0-690-04490-9*, Crowell Jr Bks) HarpC Child Bks.
Benner, Cheryl. Applesauce. Kurtz, Shirley. LC 92-32017. 32p. (Orig.). (ps-5). 1992. pap. 6.95 (*1-56148-065-7*) Good Bks PA.
Benner, Cheryl A. Amos & Susie: An Amish Story. Good, Merle. 24p. (ps-3). 1993. 12.95 (*1-561480-88-6*); pap. 4.95 (*0-934672-46-6*) Good Bks PA.
—The Boy & the Quilt. Kurtz, Shirley. 32p. (ps-5). 1991. pap. 6.95 (*1-56148-009-6*) Good Bks PA.
Benner, Patti. Damos Gracias: Libro de la Eucaristia para Ninos. Hart, Corinne. Silva, P. Fidencio & Di Raimondo, P. Domenico, trs. from ENG. (SPA.). 32p. (ps-2). 1991. pap. 1.90 (*1-55944-006-6*) Franciscan Comns.

—Pedimos Perdon: Libro de Reconciliacion para Ninos. Shannon, Ellen & Hart, Corinne. Silva, P. Fidencio & Di Raimondo, P. Domenico, trs. from ENG. (SPA.). 32p. (ps-2). 1991. pap. 1.90 (*1-55944-007-4*) Franciscan Comns.
—We Ask Forgiveness: A Young Child's Book for Reconciliation. rev. ed. Hart, Corinne & Shannon, Ellen. 32p. (ps-2). 1991. pap. 1.90 (*1-55944-005-8*) Franciscan Comns.
—We Say Thanks: A Young Child's Book for Eucharist. rev. ed. Hart, Corinne. 32p. (ps-2). 1991. pap. 1.90 (*1-55944-004-X*) Franciscan Comns.
Bennet, Jill. The Faber Book of Christmas Stories. Corrin, Sara & Corrin, Stephen, eds. LC 84-13552. 150p. (gr. 3-7). 1984. pap. 9.95 (*0-571-13348-7*) Faber & Faber.
Bennett, Charlotte. Teach Me Japanese. Mahoney, Judy. Satoh, Naomi, tr. 20p. (ps-6). 1990. pap. 11.95 incl. audiocassette (*0-934633-17-7*); tchr's. ed. 5.95 (*0-934633-30-4*) Teach Me.
Bennett, Gail, et al. Ralf's Stories - Princes, Monsters & Magic. Wallenhorst, Ralph. LC 89-38025. 128p. (Orig.). (gr. 3-6). 1989. 12.00x (*0-9622905-0-5*); pap. 6.00x (*0-9622905-1-3*) Dragon Tale.

Bennett, Geraldine M. Opening the Door to Your Inner Self: My Lessons. Bennett, Geraldine M. 122p. (Orig.). (gr. 2 up). 1993. pap. 12.98 (*0-9630718-5-8*, 1-87122) New Dawn NY.
OPENING THE DOOR TO YOUR INNER SELF, MY LESSONS, emphasizes the positive, teaching love using Happy faces versus Ugly bugs. Carefully formatted steps teach both young & old how to be the best person they possibly can be by taking the reader on a journey of self-discovery which builds self-confidence & self-respect. Emphasis is placed on the free will to choose which path to take. Charts, fun filled exercises, & clear illustrated demonstrations make this choice very clear, & it is the hope of the author that the majority prefer to travel the path of the Happy faces or Love. The beginning to understanding one's own inner nature & how to apply it to daily living. Order from The New Dawn Publishing Company, RD 1, Box 133, Dexter, NY 13634. Phone: 315-639-6764. *Publisher Provided Annotation.*

Bennett, Jill. Chris & the Dragon. Sampson, Fay. 96p. (gr. 4-6). 1987. 14.95 (*0-575-03661-3*, Pub. by Gollancz England) Trafalgar.
—Danny: The Champion of the World. Dahl, Roald. 208p. (gr. 3 up). 1975. 16.00 (*0-394-83103-9*); PLB 15.99 (*0-394-93103-3*) Knopf Bks Yng Read.
—A Problem for Mother Christmas. Willis, Ted. 160p. (gr. 3-5). 1991. 17.95 (*0-575-03884-5*, Pub. by Gollancz England) Trafalgar.
Bennett, Pearl. My ABC Book. Bennett, Nancy & Bennett, Pearl. 54p. (ps-1). 1988. wkbk. 12.00 (*0-9622242-0-0*) Red Baron Pub Co.
Bennish, Gracia. Bats. Kendall, Cindy. Dudley, Dick, created by. LC 93-3114. (ps). 1994. 4.99 (*0-8037-1272-3*) Dial Bks Young.
—Butterflies. Kendall, Cindy. Dudley, Dick. LC 93-3117. (ps). 1994. pap. 3.95 (*0-8037-1275-8*) Dial Bks Young.
Benscoter, Robert. The Ultimate Baseball Players Yearbook. Newberger, Joe & Hendricks, Elrod. 96p. (gr. 3-9). 1991. wkbk. 12.95 (*0-9629307-0-9*) Batboy Pr.
Benson, John. Outflowing Love: Auntie-Bai, Effie Southworth's Life. Root, Loretta P. Benson, Mary C., ed. 124p. (Orig.). 1989. pap. 5.95 (*0-89367-142-8*) Light & Life.
Benson, Patrick. Charles Dicken's "A Christmas Carol" 1st U.S. ed. French, Vivian, abridged by. LC 93-54577. 48p. (gr. 4 up). 1993. 15.95 (*1-56402-204-8*) Candlewick Pr.
—Robin Hood. Haynes, Sarah, retold by. LC 89-33419. 80p. (gr. 4-6). 1989. 12.95 (*0-8050-1206-0*, Bks Young Read) H Holt & Co.
—The Story of the Three Whales. Whittell, Giles. LC 88-35630. 29p. (gr. 2-4). 1988. PLB 15.93 (*0-8368-0092-3*) Gareth Stevens Inc.
Benson, Patrick & Benson. Owl Babies. Waddell, Martin. LC 91-58750. 32p. (ps up). 1992. 14.95 (*1-56402-101-7*) Candlewick Pr.
Benson, Robert, photos by. I Will Sing Life: Voices from the Hole in the Wall Gang Camp. Berger, Larry B. & Lithwick, Dahlia, eds. Newman, Paul, intro. by. 288p. 1992. 22.95 (*0-316-09273-8*) Little.

Bent, Jennifer. The Calypso Alphabet. Agard, John. LC 89-945617. 32p. (ps-2). 1989. 13.95 (*0-8050-1177-3*, Bks Young Read) H Holt & Co.
—Tower to Heaven. Dee, Ruby. LC 90-34131. 32p. (ps-2). 1991. 14.95 (*0-8050-1460-8*, Bks Young Read) H Holt & Co.
Bentley, Nancy. I've Got Your Nose! Madden, John. 1991. 12.00 (*0-685-59973-6*) Dell.
Benton, Peter, et al. A Fourth Poetry Book. Foster, John, compiled by. 128p. 1987. 11.95 (*0-19-918152-7*); pap. 5.95 (*0-19-918151-9*) OUP.
Ben-Yosef, Yisrael. The Little Old Lady Who Couldn't Fall Asleep. Ganz, Yaffa. 32p. (gr. k-6). 1989. 6.95 (*0-89906-501-5*) Mesorah Pubns.
Benziger, John & Benziger, Mary. The Corpuscles: Adventurers in Inner Space. Benziger, John. LC 88-92390. 64p. (gr. k-6). 1989. 11.95 (*0-9620961-0-5*) Corpuscles Intergalactica.
—The Corpuscles Meet the Virus Invaders. Benziger, John. LC 90-80327. 30p. (gr. 3-6). 1990. 14.95 (*0-9620961-1-3*) Corpuscles Intergalactica.
Benziger, Mary, jt. illus. see Benziger, John.
Berber, Richard. Lemon Drop. Weinberger, Jane. LC 85-62023. 64p. (gr. 1-6). 1985. Repr. of 1953 ed. PLB 5.95 (*0-932433-10-3*) Windswept Hse.
Bercasio, E. Captains Courageous. new & abr. ed. Kipling, Rudyard. Fago, John N., ed. (gr. 4-12). 1977. pap. text ed. 2.95 (*0-88301-262-6*) Pendulum Pr.
Berelson, Howard. Viva Mexico! The Story of Benito Juarez & Cinco de Mayo. Palacios, Argentina. LC 92-18071. 32p. (gr. 2-5). 1992. PLB 21.34 (*0-8114-7214-0*) Raintree Steck-V.
Berenstain, Jan & Berenstain, Stan. The Berenstain Bears & the New Girl in Town. Berenstain, Stan & Berenstain, Jan. LC 92-32570. 112p. (Orig.). (gr. 2-6). 1993. PLB 7.99 (*0-679-93613-0*); pap. 2.99 (*0-679-83613-6*) Random Bks Yng Read.
Berenstain, Jan, jt. illus. see Berenstain, Stan.
Berenstain, Janice & Berenstain, Stan. The Berenstain Bears & the Messy Room. Berenstain, Stan & Berenstain, Janice. Lerner, Sharon, ed. 32p. (ps-2). 1983. lib. bdg. 5.99 (*0-394-95639-7*); pap. 2.25 (*0-394-85639-2*) Random Bks Yng Read.
—The Berenstain Bears Get in a Fight. Berenstain, Janice & Berenstain, Stan. LC 81-15866. 32p. (ps-1). 1982. lib. bdg. 5.99 (*0-394-95132-8*); pap. 2.25 (*0-394-85132-3*) Random Bks Yng Read.
—The Berenstain Bears Go to Camp. Berenstain, Janice & Berenstain, Stan. LC 81-15864. 32p. (ps-1). 1982. pap. 2.25 (*0-394-85131-5*) Random Bks Yng Read.
Berenstain, Janice, jt. illus. see Berenstain, Stan.
Berenstain, Michael. The Day of the Dinosaur. Berenstain, Stan & Berenstain, Janice. LC 87-9828. 32p. (gr. k-3). 1987. lib. bdg. 5.99 (*0-394-99130-3*); pap. 2.25 (*0-394-89130-9*) Random Bks Yng Read.
—Flying Dinosaurs - Pterodactyls. Berenstain, Michael. (ps-3). 1991. pap. 1.75 (*0-307-12620-X*, Golden Pr) Western Pub.
—Michael Berenstain's Butterfly Book. Berenstain, Michael. 24p. (ps-k). 1992. pap. write for info. laminated covers (*0-307-10023-5*, 10023, Golden Pr) Western Pub.
—Peat Moss & Ivy's Backyard Adventure. Berenstain, Michael. LC 85-43097. 32p. (ps-3). 1986. lib. bdg. 5.99 (*0-394-97604-5*); pap. 1.95 (*0-394-87604-0*) Random Bks Yng Read.
—Who Am I? A First Book of Famous People. Berenstain, Michael. 40p. (gr. 2-4). 1992. write for info. (*0-307-11551-8*, 11551, Golden Pr) Western Pub.
Berenstain, Stan. The Berenstain Bears' Almanac. Berenstain, Stan & Berenstain, Janice. LC 73-2298. 72p. (ps-4). 1984. pap. 6.99 (*0-394-86601-0*) Random Bks Yng Read.
Berenstain, Stan & Berenstain, Jan. The Berenstain Bears Accept No Substitutes. Berenstain, Stan & Berenstain, Jan. 112p. (Orig.). (gr. 2-6). 1993. PLB 7.99 (*0-679-94035-9*); pap. 2.99 (*0-679-84035-4*) Random Bks Yng Read.
—The Berenstain Bears & Mama's New Job. Berenstain, Stan & Berenstain, Janice. LC 84-4787. 32p. (ps-1). 1984. lib. bdg. 5.99 (*0-394-96881-6*); pap. 2.25 (*0-394-86881-1*) Random Bks Yng Read.
—The Berenstain Bears & the Bully. Berenstain, Stan & Berenstain, Jan. 32p. (ps-3). 1993. PLB 5.99 (*0-679-94805-8*); pap. 2.25 (*0-679-84805-3*) Random Bks Yng Read.
—The Berenstain Bears & the Drug Free Zone. Berenstain, Stan & Berenstain, Jan. LC 92-31604. 112p. (Orig.). (gr. 2-6). 1993. PLB 7.99 (*0-679-93612-2*); pap. 2.99 (*0-679-83612-8*) Random Bks Yng Read.
—The Berenstain Bears & the Female Fullback. Berenstain, Stan & Berenstain, Jan. 112p. (Orig.). (gr. 2-6). 1993. PLB 7.99 (*0-679-93611-4*); pap. 2.99 (*0-679-83611-X*) Random Bks Yng Read.
—The Berenstain Bears & the Nerdy Nephew. Berenstain, Stan & Berenstain, Jan. LC 92-32564. 112p. (Orig.). (gr. 2-6). 1993. PLB 7.99 (*0-679-93610-6*); pap. 2.99 (*0-679-83610-1*) Random Bks Yng Read.
—The Berenstain Bears & the Red-Handed Thief. Berenstain, Stan & Berenstain, Jan. 112p. (Orig.). (gr. 2-6). 1993. PLB 7.99 (*0-679-94033-2*); pap. 2.99 (*0-679-84033-8*) Random Bks Yng Read.
—The Berenstain Bears & the School Scandal Sheet. Berenstain, Stan & Berenstain, Jan. 112p. (Orig.). (gr. 2-6). 1994. PLB 7.99 (*0-679-95812-6*); pap. 2.99 (*0-679-85812-1*) Random Bks Yng Read.

—The Berenstain Bears & the Trouble with Grownups. Berenstain, Stan & Berenstain, Jan. LC 91-27430. 32p. (Orig.). (ps-1). 1992. PLB 5.99 (*0-679-93000-0*); pap. 2.25 (*0-679-83000-6*) Random Bks Yng Read.
—The Berenstain Bears & the Wheelchair Commando. Berenstain, Stan & Berenstain, Jan. 112p. (Orig.). (gr. 2-6). 1993. PLB 7.99 (*0-679-94034-0*); pap. 2.99 (*0-679-84034-6*) Random Bks Yng Read.
—The Berenstain Bears & Too Much Pressure. Berenstain, Stan & Berenstain, Jan. LC 92-6544. 32p. (Orig.). (ps-1). 1992. PLB 5.99 (*0-679-93671-8*); pap. 2.25 (*0-679-83671-3*) Random Bks Yng Read.
—The Berenstain Bears & Too Much TV. Berenstain, Stan & Berenstain, Janice. LC 83-22887. (gr. 3-6). 1984. lib. bdg. 5.99 (*0-394-96570-1*); pap. 2.25 (*0-394-86570-7*) Random Bks Yng Read.
—The Berenstain Bears Don't Pollute (Anymore) Berenstain, Stan & Berenstain, Jan. 32p. (ps-1). 1993. incl. cass. 5.95 (*0-679-83889-9*) Random Bks Yng Read.
—The Berenstain Bears Gotta Dance. Berenstain, Stan & Berenstain, Jan. LC 92-32565. 112p. (Orig.). (gr. 2-6). 1993. PLB 7.99 (*0-679-94032-4*); pap. 2.99 (*0-679-84032-X*) Random Bks Yng Read.
—Berenstain Bears Learn about Strangers. Berenstain, Stan & Berenstain, Janice. LC 84-43157. 32p. (ps-1). 1985. lib. bdg. 5.99 (*0-394-97334-8*); 2.25 (*0-394-87334-3*) Random Bks Yng Read.
—The Berenstain Bears Meet Santa Bear. Berenstain, Stan & Berenstain, Janice. LC 84-4829. 32p. (ps-1). 1984. lib. bdg. 5.99 (*0-394-96880-8*); pap. 2.25 (*0-394-86880-3*) Random Bks Yng Read.
—The Berenstain Bears' Nature Guide. Berenstain, Stan & Berenstain, Janice. LC 75-8070. 72p. (ps-4). 1984. pap. 7.95 (*0-394-86602-9*) Random Bks Yng Read.
—Los Osos Berenstain en la Oscuridad. Berenstain, Stan & Berenstain, Jan. Guibert, Rita, tr. from ENG. LC 91-51092. (SPA.). 32p. (ps-3). 1992. pap. 2.25 (*0-679-83471-0*) Random Bks Yng Read.
—Los Osos Berenstain y Demasiada Fiesta. Berenstain, Stan & Berenstain, Jan. Guibert, Rita, tr. LC 92-45874. (SPA.). 32p. (ps-3). 1993. pap. 2.25 (*0-679-84745-6*) Random Bks Yng Read.
—Los Osos Berenstain y Demasiada Television. Berenstain, Stan & Berenstain, Jan. Guibert, Rita, tr. LC 92-16251. (SPA.). 32p. (ps-3). 1993. pap. 2.25 (*0-679-84007-9*) Random Bks Yng Read.
—Los Osos Berenstain y el Cuarto Desordenado. Berenstain, Stan & Berenstain, Jan. Guibert, Rita, tr. from ENG. LC 50191. (SPA.). 32p. (ps-3). 1992. pap. 2.25 (*0-679-83470-2*) Random Bks Yng Read.
—Los Osos Berenstain y la Ninera. Berenstain, Stan & Berenstain, Jan. Guibert, Rita, tr. LC 92-46719. (SPA.). 32p. (ps-3). 1993. pap. 2.25 (*0-679-84746-4*) Random Bks Yng Read.
—Los Osos Berenstain y las Peleas Entre Amigos. Berenstain, Stan & Berenstain, Jan. Guibert, Rita, tr. LC 92-14807. (SPA.). 32p. (ps-3). 1993. pap. 2.25 (*0-679-84006-0*) Random Bks Yng Read.
Berenstain, Stan & Berenstain, Janice. After the Dinosaurs. Berenstain, Stan & Berenstain, Janice. LC 88-42588. 32p. (Orig.). (gr. k-3). 1988. lib. bdg. 5.99 (*0-394-90518-0*); (Random Juv) Random Bks Yng Read.
—The Bear Detectives. Berenstain, Stan & Berenstain, Janice. LC 75-1603. 48p. (gr. k-3). 1975. 6.95 (*0-394-83127-6*); lib. bdg. 7.99 (*0-394-93127-0*) Beginner.
—The Bear Detectives. Berenstain, Stan & Berenstain, Janice. 48p. (ps-1). 1988. pap. 5.95 bk. & cassette pkg. (*0-394-80499-6*) Random Bks Yng Read.
—Bear Scouts. Berenstain, Stan & Berenstain, Janice. LC 67-21919. 72p. (gr. k-3). 1967. 6.95 (*0-394-80046-X*) Beginner.
—The Bears' Christmas. Berenstain, Stan & Berenstain, Janice. 64p. (ps-1). 1988. pap. 6.95 bk. & cassette pkg. (*0-394-89835-4*) Random Bks Yng Read.
—Bears' Vacation. Berenstain, Stan & Berenstain, Janice. LC 68-28460. 72p. (gr. k-3). 1968. 6.95 (*0-394-80052-4*) Beginner.
—The Bears' Vacation. Berenstain, Stan & Berenstain, Janice. 64p. (ps-1). 1987. 6.95 (*0-394-88848-0*) Random Bks Yng Read.
—El Bebe de los Osos Berenstain: (The Berenstain Bears' New Baby) Berenstain, Stan & Berenstain, Janice. De Cuenca, Pilar & Alvarez, Ines, trs. from ENG. LC 81-12193. (SPA.). 32p. (Orig.). (ps-3). 1982. lib. bdg. 5.99 (*0-394-95144-1*); pap. 2.25 (*0-394-85144-7*) Random Bks Yng Read.
—The Berenstain Bears & the Bad Dream. Berenstain, Stan & Berenstain, Janice. LC 87-27295. 32p. (ps-1). 1988. lib. bdg. 5.99 (*0-394-97341-0*); pap. 2.25 (*0-394-87341-6*) Random Bks Yng Read.
—The Berenstain Bears & the Bad Habit. Berenstain, Stan & Berenstain, Janice. LC 86-3205. 32p. (ps-1). 1987. lib. bdg. 5.99 (*0-394-97340-2*); pap. 2.25 (*0-394-87340-8*) Random Bks Yng Read.
—The Berenstain Bears & the Big Election. Berenstain, Stan & Berenstain, Janice. LC 83-62399. 32p. (ps-3). 1984. pap. 1.50 (*0-394-86542-1*) Random Bks Yng Read.
—The Berenstain Bears & the Big Road Race. Berenstain, Stan & Berenstain, Janice. LC 87-4581. 32p. (gr. k-3). 1987. lib. bdg. 5.99 (*0-394-99134-6*); pap. 2.25 (*0-394-89134-1*) Random Bks Yng Read.
—The Berenstain Bears & the Dinosaurs. Berenstain, Stan & Berenstain, Janice. LC 84-60384. 32p. (ps-3). 1984. pap. 1.50 (*0-394-86883-8*) Random Bks Yng Read.

—The Berenstain Bears & the Double Dare. Berenstain, Stan & Berenstain, Janice. LC 87-27296. 32p. (ps-1). 1988. lib. bdg. 5.99 (*0-394-99748-4*); pap. 2.25 (*0-394-89748-X*) Random Bks Yng Read.
—The Berenstain Bears & the Ghost of the Forest. Berenstain, Stan & Berenstain, Janice. LC 88-42586. 32p. (Orig.). (gr. k-3). 1988. lib. bdg. 5.99 (*0-394-90565-2*); 2.25 (*0-394-80565-8*, Random Juv) Random Bks Yng Read.
—The Berenstain Bears & the Missing Dinosaur Bone. Berenstain, Stan & Berenstain, Janice. LC 79-3458. 48p. (ps-3). 1980. lib. bdg. 7.99 (*0-394-94447-X*) Beginner.
—The Berenstain Bears & the Missing Honey. Berenstain, Stan & Berenstain, Janice. LC 87-4549. 32p. (ps-3). 1987. lib. bdg. 5.99 (*0-394-99133-8*); pap. 2.25 (*0-394-89133-3*) Random Bks Yng Read.
—The Berenstain Bears & the Prize Pumpkin. Berenstain, Stan & Berenstain, Janice. LC 90-32865. 32p. (Orig.). (ps-1). 1990. lib. bdg. 5.99 (*0-679-90847-1*); pap. 2.25 (*0-679-80847-7*) Random Bks Yng Read.
—The Berenstain Bears & the Sitter. Berenstain, Stan & Berenstain, Janice. LC 81-50046. 32p. (ps-1). 1981. lib. bdg. 5.99 (*0-394-94837-8*); pap. 2.25 (*0-394-84837-3*) Random Bks Yng Read.
—The Berenstain Bears & the Sitter. Berenstain, Stan & Berenstain, Janice. 32p. (ps-1). 1987. 2.95 (*0-394-88890-1*) Random Bks Yng Read.
—The Berenstain Bears & the Slumber Party. Berenstain, Stan & Berenstain, Janice. LC 89-55223. 32p. (Orig.). 1990. PLB 5.99 (*0-679-90419-0*); pap. 2.25 (*0-679-80419-6*) Random Bks Yng Read.
—The Berenstain Bears & the Trouble with Friends. Berenstain, Stan & Berenstain, Janice. LC 85-30165. 32p. (ps-1). 1987. lib. bdg. 5.99 (*0-394-97339-9*); pap. 2.25 (*0-394-87339-4*) Random Bks Yng Read.
—The Berenstain Bears & the Truth. Berenstain, Stan & Berenstain, Janice. LC 83-3304. 32p. (ps-1). 1988. bk. & cassette pkg. 5.95 (*0-394-89771-4*) Random Bks Yng Read.
—The Berenstain Bears & the Week at Grandma's. Berenstain, Stan & Berenstain, Janice. LC 85-25743. (ps-1). 1986. lib. bdg. 5.99 (*0-394-97335-6*); pap. 2.25 (*0-394-87335-1*) Random Bks Yng Read.
—The Berenstain Bears & the Week at Grandma's. Berenstain, Stan & Berenstain, Janice. LC 85-25743. 32p. (ps-1). 1990. pap. 3.50 incl. puppet (*0-394-82714-7*) Random Bks Yng Read.
—The Berenstain Bears & Too Much Birthday. Berenstain, Stan & Berenstain, Janice. LC 85-14529. 32p. (ps-1). 1986. lib. bdg. 5.99 (*0-394-97332-1*); pap. 2.25 (*0-394-87332-7*) Random Bks Yng Read.
—The Berenstain Bears & Too Much Junk Food. Berenstain, Stan & Berenstain, Janice. Lerner, Sharon, ed. LC 84-40393. 32p. (ps-2). 1985. lib. bdg. 5.99 (*0-394-97217-1*); pap. 2.25 (*0-394-87217-7*) Random Bks Yng Read.
—The Berenstain Bears & Too Much TV. Berenstain, Stan & Berenstain, Janice. (ps-1). 1989. bk. & cassette 5.95 (*0-394-82894-1*) Random Bks Yng Read.
—The Berenstain Bears & Too Much Vacation. Berenstain, Stan & Berenstain, Janice. LC 88-32094. 32p. (ps-1). 1990. pap. 5.95 (*0-679-80311-4*); cass. incl. Random Bks Yng Read.
—The Berenstain Bears Are a Family. Berenstain, Stan & Berenstain, Janice. LC 90-63082. 24p. (Orig.). (ps). 1991. 2.95 (*0-679-80746-2*) Random Bks Yng Read.
—The Berenstain Bears at the Super-Duper Market. Berenstain, Stan & Berenstain, Janice. LC 90-63080. 24p. (Orig.). (ps). 1991. 2.95 (*0-679-80748-9*) Random Bks Yng Read.
—The Berenstain Bears' Bath Book. Berenstain, Stan & Berenstain, Janice. 10p. (ps). 1985. vinyl 3.95 (*0-394-87116-2*) Random Bks Yng Read.
—The Berenstain Bears Blaze a Trail. Berenstain, Stan & Berenstain, Janice. LC 87-4552. 32p. (ps-1). 1987. lib. bdg. 5.99 (*0-394-99132-X*); pap. 2.25 (*0-394-89132-5*) Random Bks Yng Read.
—The Berenstain Bears' Christmas Tree. reissue ed. Berenstain, Stan & Berenstain, Janice. 64p. (ps-2). 1991. incl. 20-min. cassette 8.95 (*0-679-81974-6*) Random Bks Yng Read.
—The Berenstain Bears Don't Pollute (Anymore) Berenstain, Stan & Berenstain, Janice. LC 91-9147. 32p. (Orig.). (ps-1). 1991. lib. bdg. 5.99 (*0-679-92351-9*); pap. 2.25 (*0-679-82351-4*) Random Bks Yng Read.
—Berenstain Bears Forget Their Manners. Berenstain, Stan & Berenstain, Janice. LC 84-43156. 32p. (gr. k-3). 1985. lib. bdg. 5.99 (*0-394-97333-X*); pap. 2.25 (*0-394-87333-5*) Random Bks Yng Read.
—The Berenstain Bears Forget Their Manners. Berenstain, Stan & Berenstain, Janice. 32p. (ps-1). 1986. pap. 5.95 with cassette (*0-394-88343-8*) Random Bks Yng Read.
—The Berenstain Bears' Four Seasons. Berenstain, Stan & Berenstain, Janice. LC 90-63079. 24p. (Orig.). (ps). 1991. 2.95 (*0-679-80749-7*) Random Bks Yng Read.
—The Berenstain Bears Get in a Fight. Berenstain, Stan & Berenstain, Janice. 32p. (ps-1). 1987. pap. 3.50 (*0-394-88893-6*) Random Bks Yng Read.
—The Berenstain Bears Get in a Fight. Berenstain, Stan & Berenstain, Janice. 32p. (ps-1). 1988. pap. 4.95 bk. & cassette pkg. (*0-394-89778-1*) Random Bks Yng Read.

—The Berenstain Bears Get Stage Fright. Berenstain, Stan & Berenstain, Janice. LC 85-25716. 32p. (gr. 3-6). 1986. lib. bdg. 5.99 (0-394-97337-2); pap. 2.25 (0-394-87337-8) Random Bks Yng Read.
—The Berenstain Bears Get the Gimmies. Berenstain, Stan & Berenstain, Janice. LC 88-42587. 32p. (Orig). (ps-1). 1988. lib. bdg. 5.99 (0-394-90566-0); pap. 2.25 (0-394-80566-6) Random Bks Yng Read.
—The Berenstain Bears Get the Gimmies. Berenstain, Stan & Berenstain, Janice. LC 88-42587. 32p. (ps-1). 1990. pap. 5.95 (0-679-80313-0); cass. incl. Random Bks Yng Read.
—The Berenstain Bears Go Out for the Team. reissued ed. Berenstain, Stan & Berenstain, Janice. LC 85-30164. 32p. (ps-1). 1991. pap. 5.95 incls. cassette (0-679-81495-7) Random Bks Yng Read.
—The Berenstain Bears Go to Camp. Berenstain, Stan & Berenstain, Janice. (ps-1). 1989. 5.95 (0-394-82896-8) Random Bks Yng Read.
—The Berenstain Bears Go to the Doctor. Berenstain, Stan & Berenstain, Janice. LC 81-50043. 32p. (ps-1). 1981. lib. bdg. 5.99 (0-394-94835-1); pap. 2.25 (0-394-84835-7) Random Bks Yng Read.
—The Berenstain Bears' Make & Do Book. Berenstain, Stan & Berenstain, Janice. 64p. (ps-3). 1984. pap. 3.95 (0-394-86895-1) Random Bks Yng Read.
—The Berenstain Bears Meet Santa Bear. Berenstain, Stan & Berenstain, Janice. LC 84-4829. 32p. (ps-1). 1989. pap. 5.95 incl. cassette (0-394-85228-1) Random Bks Yng Read.
—The Berenstain Bears' Moving Day. Berenstain, Stan & Berenstain, Janice. LC 81-50044. 32p. (ps-1). 1981. lib. bdg. 5.99 (0-394-94838-6); pap. 2.25 (0-394-84838-1) Random Bks Yng Read.
—The Berenstain Bears' New Baby. Berenstain, Stan & Berenstain, Janice. LC 74-2535. 32p. (Orig). (ps-1). 1974. pap. 2.25 (0-394-82908-5) Random Bks Yng Read.
—The Berenstain Bears' New Baby. Berenstain, Stan & Berenstain, Janice. 32p. (gr. 1-3). 1985. pap. 5.95 incl. cass. (0-394-87661-X) Random Bks Yng Read.
—The Berenstain Bears: No Girls Allowed. Berenstain, Stan & Berenstain, Janice. LC 85-18246. 32p. (ps-1). 1986. pap. 2.25 (0-394-87331-9) Random Bks Yng Read.
—The Berenstain Bears on the Job. Berenstain, Stan & Berenstain, Janice. LC 87-9739. 32p. (gr. k-3). 1987. lib. bdg. 5.99 (0-394-99131-1); pap. 2.25 (0-394-89131-7) Random Bks Yng Read.
—The Berenstain Bears on the Moon. Berenstain, Stan & Berenstain, Janice. LC 84-20428. 48p. (ps-3). 1985. 6.95 (0-394-87180-4); lib. bdg. 7.99 (0-394-97180-9) Random Bks Yng Read.
—The Berenstain Bears Ready, Set, Go! Berenstain, Stan & Berenstain, Janice. LC 88-42589. 32p. (Orig). (gr. k-3). 1988. lib. bdg. 5.99 (0-394-90564-4); 2.25 (0-394-80564-X) Random Bks Yng Read.
—The Berenstain Bears Say Good Night. Berenstain, Stan & Berenstain, Janice. LC 90-63081. 24p. (Orig). (ps). 1991. 2.95 (0-679-80747-0) Random Bks Yng Read.
—The Berenstain Bears' Science Fair. Berenstain, Stan & Berenstain, Janice. LC 76-8121. (gr. 1-4). 1977. PLB 11.99 (0-394-93294-3) Random Bks Yng Read.
—The Berenstain Bears' Science Fair. Berenstain, Stan & Berenstain, Janice. LC 76-8121. 72p. (ps-4). 1984. pap. 6.95 (0-394-86603-7) Random Bks Yng Read.
—The Berenstain Bears Shoot the Rapids. Berenstain, Stan & Berenstain, Janice. LC 83-62400. 32p. (ps-3). 1984. pap. 1.50 (0-394-86543-X) Random Bks Yng Read.
—The Berenstain Bears Trick or Treat. Berenstain, Stan & Berenstain, Janice. LC 89-30884. 32p. (Orig). (ps-1). 1989. PLB 5.99 (0-679-90091-8); pap. 2.25 (0-679-80091-3) Random Bks Yng Read.
—The Berenstain Bears Trick or Treat. reissue ed. Berenstain, Stan & Berenstain, Janice. 32p. (ps-1). 1991. incl. 20-min. cassette 6.00 (0-679-81497-3) Random Bks Yng Read.
—The Berenstain Bears' Trouble at School. Berenstain, Stan & Berenstain, Janice. LC 86-4999. 32p. (ps-1). 1987. lib. bdg. 5.99 (0-394-97336-4); pap. 2.25 (0-394-87336-X) Random Bks Yng Read.
—The Berenstain Bears' Trouble at School. Berenstain, Stan & Berenstain, Janice. LC 86-4999. 32p. (ps-1). 1990. pap. 3.50 incl. puppet (0-394-82715-5) Random Bks Yng Read.
—The Berenstain Bears' Trouble with Pets. Berenstain, Stan & Berenstain, Janice. LC 90-32956. 32p. (Orig). (ps-1). 1990. lib. bdg. 5.99 (0-679-90848-X); pap. 2.25 (0-679-80848-5) Random Bks Yng Read.
—The Berenstain Bears Visit the Dentist. Berenstain, Stan & Berenstain, Janice. LC 81-50045. 32p. (ps-1). 1981. lib. bdg. 5.99 (0-394-94836-X); pap. 2.25 (0-394-84836-5) Random Bks Yng Read.
—The Berenstain Kids: I Love Colors. LC 87-9722. (ps-3). 1987. PLB 5.99 (0-394-99129-X); pap. 2.25 (0-394-89129-5) Random Bks Yng Read.
—He Bear, She Bear. Berenstain, Stan & Berenstain, Janice. LC 74-5518. 48p. (ps-1). 1974. 6.95 (0-394-82997-2); lib. bdg. 7.99 (0-394-92997-7) Random Bks Yng Read.
—He Bear She Bear & Bears on Wheels. Berenstain, Stan & Berenstain, Janice. (ps-1). 1989. bk. & cassette 7.95 (0-394-82952-2) Random Bks Yng Read.
Berenstain, Stan & Berentstain, Jan. The Berenstain Bears on Wheels. Berenstain, Stan & Berenstain, Jan. 14p. (ps-k). 1992. bds. 3.99 (0-679-83245-9) Random Bks Yng Read.

Berenstain, Stan, jt. illus. see Berenstain, Jan.
Berenstain, Stan, jt. illus. see Berenstain, Janice.
Berentstain, Jan, jt. illus. see Berenstain, Stan.
Berenzy, Alix. Cannonball River Tales. Rounds, David. LC 92-11374. 136p. (gr. 4-7). 1992. 15.95 (0-87156-577-3) Sierra.
—A Frog Prince. Berenzy, Alix. 32p. (ps up). 1989. 14.95 (0-8050-0426-2, Bks Young Read) H Holt & Co.
—A Frog Prince. Berenzy, Alix, retold by. LC 88-29628. 32p. (ps up). 1991. pap. 4.95 (0-8050-1848-4, Owlet BYR) H Holt & Co.
—The Last Slice of Rainbow: And Other Stories. Aiken, Joan. LC 87-45271. 160p. (gr. 3-7). 1988. PLB 12.89 (0-06-020043-X) HarpC Child Bks.
—The Last Slice of Rainbow: And Other Stories. Aiken, Joan. LC 87-45271. 160p. (gr. 3-7). 1988. pap. 3.50 (0-06-440334-3, Trophy) HarpC Child Bks.
—Touch the Moon. Bauer, Marion Dane. LC 87-663. 96p. (gr. 4-7). 1987. 12.95 (0-89919-526-1, Clarion Bks) HM.
Berg, Bjorn. Mrs. Pepperpot Again. Proysen, Alf. (gr. 1-4). 1961. 12.95 (0-8392-3023-0) Astor-Honor.
—Mrs. Pepperpot & the Moose. Proysen, Alf. Fisher, Richard E., tr. 28p. (ps up). 1991. bds. 13.95 (91-29-59924-5, Pub. by R & S Bks) FS&G.
—Mrs. Pepperpot in the Magic Wood. Proysen, Alf. 128p. (gr. 1-4). 1988. pap. 3.95 (0-14-030538-6, Puffin) Puffin Bks.
Berg, Bjorn, photos by. Mrs. Pepperpot to the Rescue. Proysen, Alf. (gr. 1-4). 1988. pap. 3.50 (0-317-69648-3, Puffin) Puffin Bks.
Berg, Joan. Oh, Brother Juniper. Benedict, Rex. (gr. 5-6). 1963. lib. bdg. 4.99 (0-394-91457-0) Pantheon.
Berg, Julie. Beverly Cleary. Berg, Julie. LC 93-12958. (gr. 6 up). 1993. 13.99 (1-56239-222-0) Abdo & Dghtrs.
—Tomie de Paola. Berg, Julie. LC 93-12960. 1993. 13.95 (1-56239-223-9) Abdo & Dghtrs.
Berger, Barbara H. The Donkey's Dream. Berger, Barbara H. LC 84-18905. 32p. (ps-5). 1986. 14.95 (0-399-21233-7, Philomel) Putnam Pub Group.
—Grandfather Twilight. Berger, Barbara H. 32p. (ps-3). 1986. 14.95 (0-399-20996-4, Philomel) Putnam Pub Group.
—When the Sun Rose. Berger, Barbara H. LC 86-2484. 32p. (ps-2). 1986. 14.95 (0-399-21360-0, Philomel) Putnam Pub Group.
Berger, Dan, et al. Teenage Mutant Ninja Turtles, Vol. 1. Brown, Ryan, et al. 150p. 1990. pap. 9.95 (1-879450-00-3) Tundra MA.
Berger, Joshua. Estimate! Calculate! Evaluate! Calculator Activities for the Middle Grades. Bloom, Marjorie W. & Galton, Grace C. 88p. (gr. 5-8). 1990. pap. text ed. 9.50 (0-938587-12-9) Cuisenaire.
Berghauer, Meri H. Isadore the Dinosaur. LaFleur, Tom & Brennan, Gale. 16p. (Orig). (gr. k-6). 1981. pap. 1.25 (0-685-02456-3) Brennan Bks.
Bergin, James E. You...& Being a Teenager. rev. ed. Bergin, Feryl J. 112p. 1991. 6.95 (0-936955-00-7) Eminent Pubns.
Bergin, Mark. A Medieval Castle. Macdonald, Fiona. 48p. (gr. 5 up). 1993. pap. 8.95 sewn (0-87226-258-8) P Bedrick Bks.
—A Medieval Castle: Inside Story. MacDonald, Fiona. 48p. (gr. 5 up). 1990. 17.95 (0-87226-340-1) P Bedrick Bks.
—The Story of Flight. Pearl, Lizzy. LC 91-33412. 32p. (gr. 1-4). 1993. PLB 11.89 (0-8167-2709-0); pap. text ed. 3.95 (0-8167-2710-4) Troll Assocs. Postponed.
—A World War Two Submarine. Humble, Richard. 48p. (gr. 5 up). 1991. 17.95 (0-87226-351-7) P Bedrick Bks.
Bergin, Mark & James, John. An Egyptian Pyramid. Morley, Jacqueline. 48p. (gr. 5 up). 1993. pap. 8.95 (0-87226-255-3) P Bedrick Bks.
—An Egyptian Pyramid: Inside Story. Morley, Jacqueline. 48p. (gr. 5 up). 1991. 17.95 (0-87226-346-0) P Bedrick Bks.
Bergin, Mark, jt. illus. see Scrace, Carolyn.
Bergman, Thomas. Don't Turn Away, 8 vols. Bergman, Thomas. 56p. (gr. 4-5). 1989. Set. PLB 138.16 (0-8368-0759-6) Gareth Stevens Inc.
—Going Places: Children Living with Cerebral Palsy. Bergman, Thomas. LC 90-48266. 48p. (gr. 4-5). 1991. PLB 17.27 (0-8368-0199-7) Gareth Stevens Inc.
Bergman, Melvin, jt. illus. see Yell, Vonett.
Bergsma, Jody. Touching. Coalition for Child Advocacy Staff. 32p. (Orig). (ps). 1985. pap. 5.95 (0-934671-00-1) Whatcom Cty Opp.
Bergstrom, Gunilla. Who's Scaring Alfie Atkins? Bergstrom, Gunilla. Sandin, Joan, tr. from SWE. 32p. (ps up). 1987. 6.95 (91-29-58318-7, Pub. by R & S Bks) FS&G.
Bergstrom, Lucy. What Happened to Benjamin: A True Story. Waring, Shirley B. LC 92-83949. 44p. (Orig). (gr. k-2). 1993. pap. 10.00 (0-9622808-2-8) S&T Waring.
Bergum, Connie. A Is for Animals. Shirley, Gayle. 56p. (ps-3). 1991. pap. 8.95 (1-56044-025-2) Falcon Pr MT.
—C Is for Colorado. Shirley, Gayle. LC 89-83793. 40p. (Orig). (gr. k-3). 1989. 12.95 (0-937959-85-5) Falcon Pr MT.
—Seya's Song. Hirschi, Ron. 32p. (gr. 1 up). 1993. pap. 7.95 (0-912365-91-9) Sasquatch Bks.
Bergum, Constance. M Is for Montana. Shirley, Gayle. LC 87-73310. 32p. (Orig). 1988. pap. 7.95 (0-937959-32-4, ABC Press) Falcon Pr MT.

Bergum, Constance R. Seya's Song. Hirschi, Ron. LC 92-5029. 32p. (ps up). 1992. text ed. 14.95 (0-912365-62-5) Sasquatch Bks.
Berker, Melissa & Logan, Ann. Rosie Posie Makes Friends. Haines, Joan. 16p. (Orig). (ps-1). 1985. pap. 2.65 (0-936652-01-2, Pub. by Ed Concern Pubns) Two Ems.
Berkowitz, Henry. Amphibians & Reptiles. Berkowitz, Henry. 32p. (Orig). (gr. 1-9). 1985. pap. 2.50 (0-317-66182-5) Banyan Bks.
—The Dinosaurs: An Educational Coloring Book. Berkowitz, Henry. 32p. (Orig). (gr. 1-9). 1986. pap. 2.50 (0-938059-00-9) Henart Bks.
Berlin, Rosemary. The Biggest Pest, Comparisons. Weiss, Monica. LC 91-16059. 24p. (gr. k-2). 1992. PLB 10.59 (0-8167-2488-1); pap. text ed. 2.95 (0-8167-2489-X) Troll Assocs.
—Birthday Cake Candles, Counting. Weiss, Monica. LC 91-16033. 24p. (gr. k-2). 1992. PLB 10.59 (0-8167-2496-2); pap. text ed. 2.95 (0-8167-2497-0) Troll Assocs.
—Guess What! Drawing Conclusions. Weiss, Monica. LC 91-17170. 24p. (gr. k-2). 1992. PLB 10.59 (0-8167-2498-9); pap. text ed. 2.95 (0-8167-2499-7) Troll Assocs.
—How Many? How Much? Measuring. Weiss, Monica. LC 91-3992. 24p. (gr. k-2). 1992. PLB 10.59 (0-8167-2500-4); pap. text ed. 2.95 (0-8167-2501-2) Troll Assocs.
—Kid Wise Talks to Kids about Drugs. Di Silvestro, Frank. 22p. (gr. 1-8). 1990. pap. write for info. (0-934591-02-4) Songs & Stories.
—Mmmm---Cookies! Simple Subtraction. Weiss, Monica. LC 91-18648. 24p. (gr. k-2). 1992. PLB 10.59 (0-8167-2486-5); pap. text ed. 2.95 (0-8167-2487-3) Troll Assocs.
—Pop! ABC Letter & Sounds: Learning the Alphabet. Weiss, Monica. LC 91-18704. 24p. (gr. k-2). 1992. PLB 10.59 (0-8167-2492-X); pap. text ed. 2.95 (0-8167-2493-8) Troll Assocs.
—Scoop! Fishbowl Fun, Simple Addition. Weiss, Monica. LC 91-18657. 24p. (gr. k-2). 1992. PLB 10.59 (0-8167-2484-9); pap. text ed. 2.95 (0-8167-2485-7) Troll Assocs.
—Shopping Spree: Identifying Shapes. Weiss, Monica. LC 91-3986. 24p. (gr. k-2). 1992. PLB 10.59 (0-8167-2490-3); pap. text ed. 2.95 (0-8167-2491-1) Troll Assocs.
—Snap! Charlie Gets the Whole Picture: Getting the Main Idea. Weiss, Monica. LC 91-16499. (gr. k-2). 1992. PLB 10.59 (0-8167-2494-6); pap. 2.95 (0-8167-2495-4) Troll Assocs.
Bernal, Richard. Jack & the Beanstalk. Greenway, Jennifer, retold by. 1991. 6.95 (0-8362-4903-8) Andrews & McMeel.
—Peter & the Wolf. Easton, Samantha, retold by. 32p. (ps-3). 1992. 6.95 (0-8362-4921-6) Andrews & McMeel.
Bernardin, James. My Christmas Stocking: Stories, Songs, Poems, Recipes, Crafts & Fun for Kids. Elish, Dan. Palubniak, Nancy, photos by. 80p. (ps-3). 1993. 9.98 (0-8317-5173-8) Smithmark.
Bernbaum, Israel. I Am a Star: Child of the Holocaust. Auerbacher, Inge. LC 92-31444. 80p. (gr. 3-7). 1993. pap. 4.99 (0-14-036401-3) Puffin Bks.
Bernhard, Durga. Dragonfly. Bernhard, Emery. LC 92-39930. 32p. (ps-3). 1993. reinforced bdg. 15.95 (0-8234-1033-1) Holiday.
—Eagles: Lions of the Sky. Bernhard, Emery. LC 93-1833. 32p. (gr. 4-8). 1994. 15.95 (0-8234-1105-2) Holiday.
—How Snowshoe Hare Rescued the Sun: A Yuit Folktale. Bernhard, Emery, retold by. LC 92-47124. (ps-3). 1993. reinforced bdg. 15.95 (0-8234-1043-9) Holiday.
—Ladybug. Bernhard, Emery. LC 92-52714. 32p. (ps-3). 1992. reinforced bdg. 14.95 (0-8234-0986-4) Holiday.
—Spotted Eagle & Black Crow: A Lakota Legend. Bernhard, Emery, retold by. LC 92-23950. 32p. (ps-3). 1993. reinforced bdg. 15.95 (0-8234-1007-2) Holiday.
—The Tree That Rains: The Flood Myth of the Huichol Indians of Mexico. Berhard, Emery, retold by. LC 93-8294. (gr. 4-8). 1994. 15.95 (0-8234-1108-7) Holiday.
—What's Maggie up To? Bernhard, Durga. LC 91-42915. 32p. (ps-3). 1992. reinforced bdg. 14.95 (0-8234-0969-4) Holiday.
Bernice P. Bishop Museum Staff, jt. illus. see Archives of the Kauai Museum Staff.
Bernstein, Dianne. Choosing Your Pet. McPherson, Mark. LC 84-226. 48p. (gr. 3-7). 1985. PLB 9.89 (0-8167-0111-3) Troll Assocs.
Bernstein, Marianne. Caring for Your Cat. McPherson, Mark. LC 84-223. 48p. (gr. 3-7). 1985. PLB 9.89 (0-8167-0115-6); pap. text ed. 2.95 (0-8167-0116-4) Troll Assocs.
—Caring for Your Dog. McPherson, Mark. LC 84-222. 48p. (gr. 3-7). 1985. PLB 9.89 (0-8167-0113-X); pap. 2.95 (0-8167-0114-8) Troll Assocs.
—Caring for Your Fish. McPherson, Mark. LC 84-8563. 48p. (gr. 3-7). 1985. PLB 9.89 (0-8167-0109-1); pap. text ed. 2.95 (0-8167-0110-5) Troll Assocs.
Bernstein, Michael. Class Dismissed! High School Poems. Glenn, Mel. LC 81-38441. 112p. 1991. pap. 5.70 (0-395-58111-7, Clarion Bks) HM.
Bernstein, Michael, photos by. Special Parents, Special Children. Bernstein, Joanne E. & Fireside, Bryna. Mathews, Judith, ed. LC 90-42442. 64p. (gr. 3-7). 1991. 11.95 (0-8075-7559-3) A Whitman.

Bernstein, Michael J., photos by. Back to Class: Poems by Mel Glenn. Glenn, Mel. LC 88-2835. 112p. (gr. 7 up). 1988. 13.95 (0-89919-656-X, Clarion Bks) HM.
—Class Dismissed Two: More High School Poems. Glenn, Mel. LC 86-2671. 96p. (gr. 8 up). 1986. 13.95 (0-89919-443-5, Clarion Bks) HM.
Bernstein, Zena. Mrs. Frisby & the Rats of NIMH. O'Brien, Robert C. LC 74-134818. 240p. (gr. 3-7). 1971. SBE 14.95 (0-689-20651-8, Atheneum Child Bk) Macmillan Child Grp.
Berret, Lisa. Who Am I? Birney, Betty. 16p. (ps) 1992. pap. 5.95 pop-up bk. (0-671-76914-6, Little Simon) S&S Trade.
Berridge, Celia. Forget-Me-Not. Rogers, Paul T. 32p. (ps-k). 1986. pap. 3.50 (0-685-43615-2, Puffin) Puffin Bks.
—Puffin First Picture Dictionary. Thompson, Brian. 38p. (ps-3). 1989. pap. 3.95 (0-14-050777-9, Puffin) Puffin Bks.
Berry, Anno. Ntombi's Song. Seed, Jenny. LC 88-39522. 48p. (gr. k-3). 1989. lib. bdg. 14.95 (0-8070-8318-6, NL6) Beacon Pr.
Berry, Cathy. Up & down the Blood Sugar Trail. Payne, Mary. Smith, Lendon H., intro. by. (Orig.). (gr. k-4). 1987. pap. 1.98 (0-9619326-0-0) MstrWorks Pub.
Berry, Don. North American Indian Sign Language. Liptak, Karen. LC 90-12337. 64p. (gr. 5-8). 1990. PLB 12.90 (0-531-10869-4) Watts.
Berry, Gaynor. First Five Hundred Words. 28p. 1993. 3.50 (0-7214-1520-2) Ladybird Bks.
—First Picture Dictionary. 26p. 1993. 3.50 (0-7214-1519-9) Ladybird Bks.
—First Words for Me. 26p. 1993. 3.50 (0-7214-1522-9) Ladybird Bks.
Berry, John, et al. War & Weapons. Williams, Brian. LC 86-26262. 24p. (gr. 2-5). 1987. lib. bdg. 5.99 (0-394-98971-6) Random Bks Yng Read.
Berry, William D. Buffalo Land. Berry, William D. 48p. (gr. 5-8). 1985. pap. 9.95 (0-938271-01-6) Press N Amer.
Berselli, Remo. The Americas in the Colonial Era. Dambrosio, Monica & Barbieri, Roberto. Ianni, Mary D., tr. from ITA. LC 92-19154. 72p. (gr. 5-6). 1992. PLB 17.97 (0-8114-3326-9) Raintree Steck-V.
—The Birth of Modern Europe. Dambrosio, Monica & Barbieri, Roberto. Di Ianni, Mary, tr. LC 92-22076. (ITA & ENG). 72p. (gr. 5-6). 1992. PLB 17.97 (0-8114-3325-0) Raintree Steck-V.
Berson, Harold. Children's Book of Irish Folktales. Danaher, Kevin. 108p. 1987. pap. 11.95 (0-85342-718-6, Pub. by Mercier Press Ltd Eire) Dufour.
—My Trip to Alpha I. Slote, Alfred. LC 78-6463. 96p. (gr. 2-5). 1992. (Lipp Jr Bks); PLB 13.89 (0-397-32510-X, Lipp Jr Bks) HarpC Child Bks.
—My Trip to Alpha I. Slote, Alfred. LC 85-45394. 96p. (gr. 2-5). 1986. pap. 3.95 (0-06-440166-9, Trophy) HarpC Child Bks.
—Watermelons, Walnuts & the Wisdom of Allah: And Other Tales of the Hoca. Walker, Barbara K. 72p. 1991. Repr. of 1967 ed. 17.50 (0-89672-254-6) Tex Tech Univ Pr.
Berst, Barbara. We Are Farmers. Berst, Barbara. 24p. (Orig.). (ps-2). 1990. acid-free cotton paper 25.00, (0-9614126-3-1); pap. 9.95 (0-9614126-2-3) Natl Lilac Pub.
Berthiaume, Tom, photos by. On Monday When It Rained. Kachenmeister, Cherryl. 40p. (gr. k-3). 1989. 11.95 (0-395-51940-3) HM.
Berthon, Prue. Answering the Call. 40p. 1991. 17.95 (0-9629140-0-2) White Dove NM.
—Light Bears, Bk. 2: Planting the Seeds. Fritz & Angel. 38p. (Orig.). (ps-1). 1991. pap. 17.95 (0-9629140-1-0) Fritz & Angel.
Bertschmann, Harry. Crow. Sampson, Mary Y. & Bertschmann, Harry. Bertschmann, Mary, ed. 48p. 1989. pap. 8.00x (0-935505-05-9) Bank St Pr.
—The Golden Falcon. Sampson, Mary Y. Bertschmann, Mary, ed. 120p. (Orig.). 1993. pap. 25.00 fine print, letter press ed. (0-935505-08-3) Bank St Pr.
Beskow, Elsa. The Flowers' Festival. Beskow, Elsa. 32p. (gr. k-4). 1991. Repr. of 1914 ed. 14.95g (0-86315-120-5, Pub. by Floris Bks UK) Gryphon Hse.
—Ollie's Ski Trip. Beskow, Elsa. Ernest Benn Ltd. Staff, tr. from SWE. (ps-2). Repr. of 1960 ed. 14.95 (0-86315-091-8, Pub. by Floris Bks UK) Gryphon Hse.
—Pelle's New Suit. Beskow, Elsa. 16p. (ps-1). 1929. PLB 13.89 (0-06-020496-6) HarpC Child Bks.
—Pelle's New Suit. Beskow, Elsa. Woodburn, Marion L., tr. from SWE. 32p. (ps-2). Repr. of 1979 ed. 14.95 (0-86315-092-6, Pub. by Floris Bks UK) Gryphon Hse.
—The Tale of the Little, Little Old Woman. Beskow, Elsa. (ps) 1989. 10.95 (0-86315-079-9, 20246) Gryphon Hse.
Bessie, Dan. The Immune System: Your Magic Doctor. Garvy, Helen. LC 91-91575. 76p. (gr. 4 up). 1992. lib. bdg. 15.00 (0-918828-09-0); pap. 10.00 (0-918828-10-4) Shire Pr.
Best, Charles. Quest for King Arthur, No. 23. Garrick, Liz. 144p. (gr. ps-6). 1988. pap. 2.50 (0-553-27126-1) Bantam.
Bester, Roger, photos by. The Next Chapter after the Last. Verploegh, Harry, compiled by. LC 87-70164. 111p. (Orig.). 1988. pap. 7.99 (0-87509-391-4, PSPUM 35) Chr Pubns.

Betco, Boboy. Filipino Word Book. Ramos, Teresita V. & Clausen, Josie. (ENG & ILO & TAG.). 112p. (gr. k-6). 1993. pap. 11.95 (1-880188-44-9) Bess Pr.
Betera, Carol. Hugo & the Sunshine Girl. Dhuibhne, Eilis N. 129p. (Orig.). (gr. 5-9). 1991. pap. 7.95 (1-85371-160-8, Pub. by Poolbeg Pr ER) Dufour.
Bethards, David. Meditation for Little People. Langford, Anne. LC 75-46191. 40p. (gr. k-4). 1976. pap. 6.95 (0-87516-211-8) DeVorss.
Bethel, Steve. Camp-Out. Maynard, Joyce. LC 85-5504. 32p. (ps-3). 1985. 12.95 (0-15-214077-8, HB Juv Bks) HarBrace.
—New House. Maynard, Joyce. 32p. (gr. k-3). 1987. 12.95 (0-15-257042-X) HarBrace.
Betteridge, Deirdre. The Boy Who Wouldn't Speak. Berry, Steve. 32p. 1992. PLB 14.95 (1-55037-231-9, Pub. by Annick CN); pap. 4.95 (1-55037-230-0, Pub. by Annick CN) Firefly Bks Ltd.
Bettoli, Delana. Aesop's Fables. Poskanzer, Susan C., retold by. 64p. (gr. 2 up). 1992. 15.95 (0-671-74116-0); lib. bdg. 16.98 (0-671-74117-9) Silver Pr.
—Animal Footnotes: A Nature's Footprints Guide. Pearce, Q. L. 40p. (ps-3). 1990. PLB 12.98 (0-671-69116-3); pap. 8.95 (0-671-69117-1) Silver Pr.
—In the African Grasslands. Pearce, Q. L. & Pearce, W. L. Brook, Bonnie, ed. 24p. (ps-1). 1990. 5.95 (0-671-68831-6); PLB 9.98 (0-671-68827-8) Silver Pr.
—In the Barnyard. Pearce, Q. L. & Pearce, W. J. Brook, Bonnie, ed. 24p. (ps-1). 1990. 5.95 (0-671-68828-6); PLB 9.98 (0-671-68824-3) Silver Pr.
—In the Desert. Pearce, Q. L. & Pearce, W. L. Brook, Bonnie, ed. 24p. (ps-1). 1990. 5.95 (0-671-68829-4); PLB 9.98 (0-671-68825-1) Silver Pr.
—In the Forest. Pearce, Q. L. & Pearce, W. L. Brook, Bonnie, ed. 24p. (ps-1). 1990. 5.95 (0-671-68830-8); PLB 9.98 (0-671-68826-X) Silver Pr.
—Nature's Footprints Series, 4 vols. Pearce, Q. L. & Pearce, W. J. 96p. (ps-1). 1990. Set. 23.80 (0-671-94431-2); Set. 17.85s.p. (0-685-46999-9); Set. PLB 39.92 (0-671-94430-4); Set. PLB 29.94s.p. (0-685-47000-8) Silver Pr.
Betts, Ethel F., et al. The Complete Mother Goose. Shapiro, Ellen S. 288p. (ps-1). 1988. 12.99 (0-517-63383-3) Outlet Bk Co.
Beuth, Eugene. We Love Our New Home. Beuth, Eugene. LC 93-77946. 34p. (Orig.). (ps) 1993. pap. 12.95 (0-9636417-2-7) Make-Hawk Pub.
Beveren, Margaret V. My Tree. Marie, Evelyn. 24p. (gr. k-2). 1987. pap. 3.95 (0-9614746-5-3) Berry Bks.
Bevilacqua, Carol. Animal Defenses. Echols, Jean C. Bergman, Lincoln & Fairwell, Kay, eds. Barrett, Reginald & Craig, Rose, photos by. 27p. (Orig.). (ps-k). 1987. pap. 7.50 (0-912511-09-5) Lawrence Science.
—More Than Magnifiers. Sneider, Cary I. Bergman, Lincoln & Fairwell, Kay, eds. Hoyt, Richard, photos by. 47p. (Orig.). (gr. 6-9). 1988. pap. 8.50 (0-912511-62-1) Lawrence Science.
—Paper Towel Testing. Sneider, Cary I. & Barber, Jacqueline. Bergman, Lincoln & Fairwell, Kay, eds. Hoyt, Richard, photos by. 29p. (Orig.). (gr. 5-9). 1987. pap. 8.50 (0-912511-65-6) Lawrence Science.
—Vitamin C Testing. Barber, Jacqueline. Bergman, Lincoln & Fairwell, Kay, eds. Barber, Jacqueline & Hoyt, Richard, photos by. 48p. (Orig.). (gr. 4-8). 1988. pap. 8.50 (0-912511-70-2) Lawrence Science.
Bevilacqua, Carol & Klofkorn, Lisa. The Wizard's Lab. Sneider, Cary I. & Gould, Alan. Bergman, Lincoln & Fairwell, Kay, eds. Hoyt, Richard, photos by. 72p. 1989. pap. 20.00 (0-912511-71-0) Lawrence Science.
Bevilacqua, Carol, jt. illus. see Baker, Lisa H.
Beyer, Beverly. Volunteer Firefighter. Marion, Kenneth P. 32p. (ps-2). 1990. pap. 4.00 (0-945878-00-1) JK Pub.
Beyer, Paul. Little Elk's Miracle. Benander, Carl D. Teasley, Jamie, ed. LC 89-51758. 45p. (gr. k-3). 1991. 7.95 (0-685-31291-7) Winston-Derek.
Beylon, Cathy. Baby Lamb Chop Loves Animals. Lewis, Shari. 12p. (ps-k). 1991. bds. 3.95 (0-679-81723-9) Random Bks Yng Read.
—Baby Lamb Chop Loves Numbers. Lewis, Shari. 12p. (ps-k). 1991. bds. 3.95 (0-679-81724-7) Random Bks Yng Read.
—Baby Lamb Chop Loves Nursery School. Lewis, Shari. 12p. (ps-k). 1991. bds. 3.95 (0-679-81725-5) Random Bks Yng Read.
—Baby Lamb Chop Loves the Beach. Lewis, Shari. 12p. (ps-k). 1991. bds. 3.95 (0-679-81726-3) Random Bks Yng Read.
—Big Horn Trees: From an Original Article which Appeared in Ranger Rick Magazine, Copyright National Wildlife Federation. Boyle, Doe & Thomas, Peter, eds. 20p. (gr. k-3). 1993. 6.95 (0-924483-84-9); incl. audio tape 9.95 (0-924483-84-9); incl. audio tape & 13 inch plush toy 35.95 (0-924483-87-3); incl. 9 inch plush toy 21.95 (0-924483-88-1) Soundprints.
—Count by Twos. Nelson, JoAnne. 16p. (Orig.). (gr. k-2). 1990. pap. 3.95 (1-878624-10-5) McClanahan Bk.
—Earth Day Every Day: From an Original Article which Appeared in Ranger Rick Magazine, Copyright National Wildlife Federation. Boyle, Doe & Thomas, Peter, eds. 20p. (gr. k-3). 1993. 6.95 (0-924483-82-2); incl. audio tape 9.95 (0-924483-85-7); incl. audio tape & 13 inch plush toy 35.95 (0-924483-86-5); incl. 9 inch plush toy 21.95 (0-924483-88-1) Soundprints.

—Gift from the Trees from an Original Article Which Appeared in Ranger Rick Magazine, Copyright National Wildlife Federation. Boyle, Doe & Thomas, Peter, eds. 20p. (gr. k-3). 1993. 6.95 (1-56899-022-7); incl. audiocassette 9.95 (1-56899-021-9); incl. audiocassette, 13 in. plush toy 35.95 (1-56899-019-7); incl. 13 in. plush toy 21.95 (1-56899-020-0) Soundprints.
—Operation Beaver: From an Original Article Which Appeared in Ranger Rick Magazine, Copyright National Wildlife Federation. Boyle, Doe & Thomas, Peter, eds. Luther, Sallie, contrib. by. 20p. (gr. k-3). 1992. 6.95 (0-924483-57-1); incl. audiocass. tape & 13" toy 35.95 (0-924483-54-7); incl. 9" toy 21.95 (0-924483-55-5); incl. audiocass. tape 9.95 (0-924483-56-3); write for info. audiocass. tape (0-924483-81-4) Soundprints.
—Over in the Meadow. 28p. (ps). 1990. 2.95 (0-02-689484-X) Checkerboard.
—Wynken, Blynken, & Nod. 24p. (ps). 1992. bds. write for info. (0-307-06141-8, 6141, Golden Pr) Western Pub.
Bhanji, Lindley. Cocoon. Bhanji, Lindley. Winkler, Chris, ed. 28p. (Orig.). (gr. 10 up). 1988. pap. 2.00 saddle stapled (0-929611-00-4) Plutonium Pr.
Bhend, Kathi. Duck & the Owl. Johansen, Hanna. LC 91-33011. 64p. (gr. 2-5). 1992. 12.95 (0-525-44828-4, DCB) Dutton Child Bks.
—En Suenos Puedo Volar: In His Dreams He Could Fly. Hasler, Eveline. Krohn, Hildegard M., tr. from GER. (SPA.). 26p. (gr. ps-5). 1990. 13.95 (968-6465-05-7) Hispanic Bk Dist.
—Rabbit Spring. Michels, Tilde. LC 87-18107. 96p. (gr. 1-4). 1990. pap. 2.95 (0-679-80153-7) Knopf Bks Yng Read.
Bhend, Kathi, jt. illus. see James, J. Alison.
Bhend-Zaugg, Kathi. Bad Times for Ghosts. Wippersberg, W. J. LC 86-45058. 166p. (gr. 3-7). 1986. 13.95 (0-15-200413-0, Gulliver Bks); pap. 6.95 (0-15-200414-9) HarBrace.
Bhusan, Rboti. The Donkey on the Bridge. Jafa, Manorama. 24p. (Orig.). (gr. k-3). 1980. pap. 2.50 (0-89744-209-1, Pub. by Childrens Bk Trust IA) Auromere.
Bhusan, Reboti. Stories from Panchatantra: Book II. Shivkumar. (gr. 1-9). 1979. 4.50 (0-89744-163-X); pap. 3.00 (0-685-57662-0) Auromere.
Bhushan, Reboti. Aesop's Fables. Thomas, Vernon. 135p. (gr. 1-7). 1981. 7.50 (0-89744-231-8, Pub. by Hemkunt IA) Auromere.
—Stories from Panchatantra. Choudhary, Bani R. (gr. 3-10). 1979. 7.25 (0-89744-136-2) Auromere.
Bial, Raymond. Amish Home. Bial, Raymond. 40p. (gr. 4-7). 1993. 14.45 (0-395-59504-5) HM.
—County Fair. Bial, Raymond. 40p. (gr. 3-6). 1992. 14.45 (0-395-57644-X) HM.
Biamonte, Daniel. A Village Called Harmony - A Fable. 2nd ed. Kavanaugh, James. LC 90-62063. 70p. 1990. pap. 7.95 (1-878995-06-5) S J Nash Pub.
Biancalana, Tim. Party Shakers. Martin, Kathy. Martin, Kathy. LC 82-21729. 47p. (gr. k-8). 1982. pap. 3.95 (0-942752-00-7) C A M Co.
Bianchi, John. The Dingles. Levchuk, Helen. 24p. (ps-2). 1991. 4.95 (0-88899-044-8, Pub. by Groundwood-Douglas & McIntyre CN) Firefly Bks Ltd.
—Exploring the Night Sky: The Equinox Astronomy Guide for Beginners. Dickinson, Terence. 72p. (Orig.). (gr. 5 up). 1989. 17.95 (0-920656-64-1, Pub. by Camden Hse CN); pap. 9.95 (0-920656-66-8, Pub. by Camden Hse CN) Firefly Bks Ltd.
—Flight of the Space Quester. Bianchi, John. 24p. 1993. lib. bdg. 14.95 (0-921285-31-0, Pub. by Bungalo Bks CN); pap. 4.95 (0-921285-30-2, Pub. by Bungalo Bks CN) Firefly Bks Ltd.
—For the Birds. Atwood, Margaret. 56p. (gr. 8-12). 1991. pap. 9.95 (0-920668-32-1) Firefly Bks Ltd.
—Grandma Mooner Lost Her Voice. Bianchi, John & Edwards, Frank B. 24p. (ps-2). 1992. PLB 14.95 (0-921285-19-1, Pub. by Bungalo Bks CN); pap. 4.95 (0-921285-17-5, Pub. by Bungalo Bks CN) Firefly Bks Ltd.
—Penelope Penguin: The Incredibly Good Baby. Bianchi, John. 24p. (ps-3). 1992. PLB 14.95 (0-921285-13-2, Pub. by Bungalo Bks CN); pap. 4.95 (0-921285-11-6, Pub. by Bungalo Bks CN) Firefly Bks Ltd.
—The Short Tree & the Bird That Could Not Sing. Foon, Dennis. 32p. (ps-2). 1991. pap. 4.95 (0-88899-120-7, Pub. by Groundwood-Douglas & McIntyre CN) Firefly Bks Ltd.
—Snowed in at Pokeweed Public School. Bianchi, John. 24p. (gr. 6-9). 1991. 14.95 (0-921285-07-8, Pub. by Bungalo Bks CN); pap. 4.95 (0-921285-05-1, Pub. by Bungalo Bks CN) Firefly Bks Ltd.
Bible, William. Baton Twirling Is for Me. Hawkins, Jim W. LC 82-245. 48p. (gr. 2-5). 1982. PLB 13.50 (0-8225-1134-7) Lerner Pubns.
Biedrzycki, David. The Kids' Book of Fishing. Rosen, Michael J. LC 90-50949. 96p. (Orig.). (gr. 2-6). 1991. pap. 12.95 (0-89480-866-4, 1866) Workman Pub.
Biegel, Michael D. Ghost Hunters. Deem, James M. 128p. (Orig.). 1992. pap. 3.50 (0-380-76682-5, Camelot) Avon.
Biel, Bill. Elisha. Overholtzer, Ruth. 33p. (gr. k-6). 1967. pap. text ed. 9.45 (1-55976-010-9) CEF Press.
Biel, Bill, et al. The Christian Soldier. Hershey, Katherine. 10p. (gr. k-6). 1981. pap. text ed. 4.25 (1-55976-138-5) CEF Press.

Biene, Susanna & Moneli. Sing Through the Seasons: Ninety-Nine Songs for Children. Society of Brothers Staff, ed. LC 70-164916. 144p. (gr. k-6). 1972. 17.00 (0-87486-006-7); cassette 7.00 (0-87486-048-2) Plough.

Bierhorst, Jane B. In the Trail of the Wind: American Indian Poems & Ritual Orations. Bierhorst, John, ed. (gr. 8 up). 1987. pap. 4.95 (0-374-43576-6) FS&G.

Biesty, Stephan. Explore the World of Man-Made Wonders. Adams, Simon. (gr. 3-7). 1991. 7.95 (0-685-54426-5, Golden Pr) Western Pub.

Biesty, Stephen. Ancient Egypt. Hart, George. LC 88-30065. 64p. (gr. 3-7). 1989. 14.95 (0-15-200449-1) HarBrace.

—Incredible Cross Sections. Platt, Richard. LC 91-27439. 48p. 1992. 20.00 (0-679-81411-6) Knopf Bks Yng Read.

—The Middle Ages. Oakes, Catherine. 28p. (gr. 3-7). 1989. 14.95 (0-15-200451-3, Gulliver Bks) HarBrace.

Biesty, Steven. Man-of-War. Biesty, Stephen & Platt, Richard. LC 92-21227. 32p. (gr. 3 up). 1993. 16.95 (1-56458-321-X) Dorling Kindersley.

Bietsy, Stephen. Del Interior de las Cosas - Incredible Cross-Sections. Platt, Richard. Puncel, Maria & Vasquez, Juan J., eds. Bermejo, Ana & Aixela, Javier F., trs. (SPA.). 48p. (gr. 5-12). 1992. write for info. (84-372-4524-9) Santillana.

Bigelow, Holly. Greek Roots. Duncan, Leonard C. 82p. (Orig.). (gr. 6-12). 1982. pap. 10.00 (0-941414-01-9) LCD.

Bigger, Chuck, photos by. When Turtles Come to Town. Ziter, Cary B. 64p. (gr. 3-5). 1989. PLB 12.90 (0-531-10691-8) Watts.

Biggers, John. I, Momolu. Graham, Lorenz. LC 87-82944. 240p. (gr. 7-12). 1988. pap. 9.95 (0-9619521-0-5) Graham Bks.

Bileck, Marvin. Rain Makes Applesauce. Scheer, Julian. 36p. (ps-3). 1964. 15.95 (0-8234-0091-3) Holiday.

Bilezikian, Gary. While I Slept. Bilezikian, Gary. LC 90-52514. 32p. (ps-1). 1990. 12.95 (0-531-05875-1); PLB 12.99 (0-531-08475-2) Orchard Bks Watts.

Billin-Frye, Paige. Alice's Adventures in Wonderland. Carroll, Lewis. Hitchner, Earle, adapted by. LC 89-33889. 48p. (gr. 3-6). 1990. PLB 12.89 (0-8167-1861-X); pap. text ed. 3.95 (0-8167-1862-8) Troll Assocs.

—Dinosaur Bones! Thompson, C. E. 32p. (ps-3). 1992. 6.95 (0-448-41087-7, G&D) Putnam Pub Group.

—Ghastly Giggles & Ghoulish Guffaws. Teitelbaum, Michael. LC 91-60998. 96p. (Orig.). (gr. 1-6). 1992. pap. 2.99 (0-679-81787-5) Random Bks Yng Read.

—Inside Your Busy Body. Demuth, Patricia. LC 92-44173. 32p. (ps-3). 1993. pap. 2.25 (0-448-40189-4, G&D) Putnam Pub Group.

—The Neighbor Game: A Pop-up, Figure-It-Out Book. Shapiro, Arnold. LC 93-11199. Date not set. write for info. (0-8037-1239-1) Dial Bks Young.

—Skeletons! Skeletons! All about Bones. Hall, Katy. LC 90-82153. 32p. (ps-3). 1991. (G&D); pap. 2.25 (0-448-40108-8, G&D) Putnam Pub Group.

—The Sleepy Little Puppy. 12p. (ps). 1993. bds. 4.95 (0-448-40541-5, G&D) Putnam Pub Group.

—The Three Pups. Porter, Mark & Aymerich, Angela F. 16p. (Orig.). (gr. 1-3). 1991. pap. text ed. 29.95 big bk. (1-56334-049-6); pap. text ed. 4.15 small bk. (1-56334-055-0) Hampton-Brown.

—Los Tres Perritos. Aymerich, Angela F. (SPA.). 16p. (Orig.). (gr. 1-3). 1991. pap. text ed. 29.95 big bk. (1-56334-021-6); pap. text ed. 6.00 small bk. (1-56334-035-6) Hampton-Brown.

—What's Out There? A Book about Space. Wilson, Lynn. LC 92-24469. 32p. (ps-3). 1993. lib. bdg. 7.99 (0-448-40518-0, G&D); pap. 2.25 (0-448-40517-2, G&D) Putnam Pub Group.

—Why Did the Vampire Cross the Road? And Other Horrific Howlers. Teitelbaum, Michael. LC 91-61001. 96p. (Orig.). (gr. 1-6). 1992. pap. 2.99 (0-679-81788-3) Random Bks Yng Read.

Billinghurst, P. J. A Hundred Fables of La Fontaine. La Fontaine, Jean de. 208p. (gr. 2-6). 2.98 (0-517-40206-8) Outlet Bk Co.

Billington, James. Cowboys. Sandler, Martin W. LC 93-20386. 96p. (gr. 3 up). 1994. 19.95 (0-06-023318-4); PLB 20.89 (0-06-023319-2) HarpC Child Bks.

Billout, Guy. By Camel or by Car: A Look at Transportation. Billout, Guy. 32p. 1983. 8.95 (0-13-109603-6, Pub. by Treehouse); pap. 5.95 (0-13-109595-1) P-H.

—The Journey. Billout, Guy. LC 93-17094. 1993. PLB 16.95 (0-88682-626-8) Creative Ed.

—Squid & Spider: A Look at the Animal Kingdom. Billout, Guy. 32p. (Orig.). (gr. 6 up). 1982. 10.95 (0-13-839928-X) P-H.

Bimler, Rich. Sex & the New You. 64p. (gr. 6-9). 1988. pap. 7.99 (0-570-08484-9, 14-1624) Concordia.

Binachi, John. Snow: Learning for the Fun of It. Bianchi, John & Edwards, Frank B. 48p. (gr. 5 up). 1992. PLB 17.95 (0-921285-15-9, Pub. by Bungalo Bks CN); pap. 7.95 (0-921285-09-4, Pub. by Bungalo Bks CN) Firefly Bks Ltd.

By combining a wealth of factual information about snow with the cartoon illustrations of John Bianchi, this book serves up science in a painless way that both kids & adults will love. Bianchi & author Frank B. Edwards examine snow from dozens of perspectives, keeping their approach light & the facts interesting. Their explanation of snowflake formation is accompanied by a sidebar about the meteorological pioneer who devoted his lifetime to photographing snowflakes (yes, he died of pneumonia). The movement of glaciers is introduced with an illustration of an advancing icesheet creeping along the main street of a city, eroding office towers instead of mountains. After explaining how animals adapt to snow, the book offers a blueprint of the ultimate winter beast--the long-eared snow scooter. Advice on tracking species in the snow includes abominable snowmen as well as rabbits & birds. After thoroughly tracing how snow has affected the planet & how people have learned to cope with its inevitable presence (through such inventions as the snow shovel, skis & the igloo), the book presents a romp through the snow hall of fame, a useful collection of snow trivia that is guaranteed to delight readers.
Publisher Provided Annotation.

Binch, Caroline. Billy the Great. Guy, Rosa. LC 92-34704. 32p. (gr. k-3). 1992. 15.00 (0-385-30666-0) Delacorte.

—Hue Boy. Mitchell, Rita P. LC 92-18560. (ps-3). 1993. 13.99 (0-8037-1448-3) Dial Bks Young.

—Paris, Pee Wee & Big Dog. Guy, Rosa. LC 85-1654. 112p. (gr. 4-6). 1985. 13.95 (0-385-29407-7) Delacorte.

—Twisters. Cate, Dick. 160p. (gr. 5-8). 1989. 17.95 (0-575-04099-8, Pub. by Gollancz England) Trafalgar.

Bindel, Binah T. My Upsheren Book. Gottlieb, Yaffa L. 32p. (ps-1). 1991. 8.95 (0-922613-37-0); pap. 6.95 (0-922613-38-9) Hachai Pubns.

Binder, Pat. Bluebonnet at the State Fair. Casad, Mary B. 40p. (gr. 2-4). 1985. 11.95 (0-89015-530-5) Eakin-Sunbelt.

—Bluebonnet of the Hill Country. Casad, Mary B. (gr. k-4). 1983. 11.95 (0-89015-395-7, Pub. by Panda Bks) Eakin-Sunbelt.

Bindon, John. Air Scare. O'Neill, Mary. LC 89-49626. 32p. (gr. 3-6). 1991. lib. bdg. 12.89 (0-8167-2082-7); pap. text ed. 3.95 (0-8167-2083-5) Troll Assocs.

—Dinosaur Mysteries. O'Neill, Mary. LC 89-4789. 32p. (gr. 3-7). 1989. lib. bdg. 12.89 (0-8167-1635-8); pap. text ed. 3.95 (0-8167-1636-6) Troll Assocs.

—A Family of Dinosaurs. O'Neill, Mary. LC 89-4792. 32p. (gr. 3-7). 1989. lib. bdg. 12.89 (0-8167-1633-1); pap. text ed. 3.95 (0-8167-1634-X) Troll Assocs.

—Life after the Dinosaurs. O'Neill, Mary. LC 89-31164. 32p. (gr. 3-7). 1989. lib. bdg. 12.89 (0-8167-1639-0); pap. text ed. 3.95 (0-8167-1640-4) Troll Assocs.

—Nature in Danger. O'Neill, Mary. LC 90-37437. 32p. (gr. 3-6). 1991. lib. bdg. 12.89 (0-8167-2285-4); pap. text ed. 3.95 (0-8167-2286-2) Troll Assocs.

—Power Failure. O'Neill, Mary. LC 90-11148. 32p. (gr. 3-6). 1991. PLB 12.89 (0-8167-2288-9); pap. text ed. 3.95 (0-8167-2289-7) Troll Assocs.

—Water Squeeze. O'Neill, Mary. LC 89-77456. 32p. (gr. 3-6). 1989. PLB 12.89 (0-8167-2080-0); pap. text ed. 3.95 (0-8167-2081-9) Troll Assocs.

—Where Are All the Dinosaurs? O'Neill, Mary. LC 89-31165. 32p. (gr. 2-6). 1989. lib. bdg. 12.89 (0-8167-1637-4); pap. text ed. 3.95 (0-8167-1638-2) Troll Assocs.

Binford, Dale. Rabbits Can't Dance! Binford, Dale. LC 89-42640. 24p. (gr. 1-2). 1989. PLB 18.60 (0-8368-0106-7) Gareth Stevens Inc.

Bingham, Edith. If Tiny Little Dinosaurs Played House... Shaine, Frances. 30p. (Orig.). (ps-3). 1993. pap. 4.95 (1-884217-02-8) Wellford.

—My Doll Is Just Like Me. Shaine, Frances. 30p. (Orig.). (ps-2). 1993. pap. 4.95 (1-884217-03-6) Wellford.

—A Walk in the Alphabet Zoo. Shaine, Frances. 30p. (Orig.). (ps-2). 1993. pap. 4.95 (1-884217-00-1) Wellford.

—A Walk Through the Alphabet Garden. Shaine, Frances. 30p. (Orig.). (ps-3). 1993. pap. 4.95 (1-884217-01-X) Wellford.

Binns, Brenda S. Travel Tales: A Mobility Storybook. Halpern-Gold, Julia & Adler, Robin W. LC 88-62588. 107p. (Orig.). (ps-3). 1988. pap. text ed. 20.00 (0-922637-00-8) Most Mobil.

Binyamini-Ariel, Liat. B. Y. Times: Running Away. Prenzlau, Sheryl. Zakon, Miriam, contrib. by. 120p. (Orig.). (gr. 2-6). 1993. pap. 5.95 (1-56871-018-6) Targum Pr.

Bionoi, Janet. D Is for Dolphin. Berg, Cami. 64p. 1991. 18.95 (1-879244-01-2) Windom Bks.

Birch, J. J. & Bair, Michael. The Catwoman: Her Sister's Keeper. Newell, Mindy. O'Neil, Dennis, ed. 104p. (Orig.). 1991. pap. 9.95 (0-930289-97-8) DC Comics.

Birch, Linda. When the People Are Away. Jungman, Ann. 32p. (ps-3). 1993. 12.95 (1-56397-202-6) Boyds Mills Pr.

Birch, Reginald. Rainbow in the Sky: Golden Anniversary Edition. Untermeyer, Louis, ed. LC 84-19306. 498p. (gr. 3-7). 1985. 19.95 (0-15-265479-8, HB Juv Bks) HarBrace.

Bircham, Don. Texas Cool Cat Coloring Book. Sommers, Maxine S. 10p. (Orig.). (gr. k-1). 1991. pap. 1.95 size: 8 1/2" x 11" (0-943991-20-X) Pound Sterling Pub.

Birchoff, Ilse. Gigi: The Story of a Merry-Go-Round Horse. Foster, Elizabeth. 124p. (gr. 4-8). pap. 9.95 (0-913028-55-X) North Atlantic.

Birchum, Donald. A Children's Texas Cool Cat Cookbook. large type ed. Sommers, Maxine S. 10p. (Orig.). (gr. 1-9). 1991. pap. 3.25 (0-943991-22-6) Pound Sterling Pub.

—The Magical Powers of "Frank" the World Famous Texas Cool Cat! large type ed. Sommers, Maxine. 10p. (gr. k-2). 1991. pap. 1.95 (0-943991-23-4) Pound Sterling Pub.

Bird, E. J. The Blizzard of Eighteen Ninety-Six. Bird, E. J. 72p. (gr. 2-6). 1990. PLB 14.95 (0-87614-651-5) Carolrhoda Bks.

—How Do Bears Sleep? Bird, E. J. 32p. (ps-3). pap. 5.95 (0-87614-522-5) Carolrhoda Bks.

Bird, Malcolm. The Witch's Handbook. Bird, Malcolm. LC 88-911. 96p. (ps up). 1988. POB 7.95 (0-689-71237-5, Aladdin) Macmillan Child Grp.

Birdsall, Josh. Christmas Trees. Hoffman, Robert B., Jr. 62p. (Orig.). (gr. 3 up). 1991. pap. 9.95 (0-9633156-0-9) R B Hoffman.

A Christmas storybook & diary for all ages. If you like Christmas & Christmas trees -- you will enjoy these five stories that tell the spirit of giving, receiving, sharing, love & fellowship during the Christmas season. You will never look at a Christmas tree again without thinking about these stories. According to the Alaska News Agency, these stories out-sell other Christmas books in Alaska bookstores 6 to 1. LITTLE TREE: A little Christmas tree doesn't "think" it will be picked for Christmas because of its small size. THE MOST BEAUTIFUL CHRISTMAS TREE EVER: A little boy decides a tree you can see from his home will be his own special Christmas tree. THE PAINTED TREE: An old Indian "spirit" woman helps the members of a lost wagon train find their way to safe haven. THE TREASURE TREE: A young boy's father plants a tree & years later its treasure is discovered. THE LAST CHRISTMAS TREE: A broken down tree is left on a tree lot the night before Christmas with a "free" tag on it. To order: write or call -- Robert B. Hoffman, Jr., 7761 Ingram Street, Anchorage, AK 99502. (907) 243-0626.
Publisher Provided Annotation.

Birenbaum, Barbara. Candle Talk. Birenbaum, Barbara. LC 90-33299. 54p. (gr. 2-5). 1991. 10.95 (0-935343-10-5); pap. 5.95g (0-935343-15-6) Peartree.

—The Cupdeer. Birenbaum, Barbara. LC 92-33093. 1993. PLB write for info. (0-935343-04-0); pap. write for info. (0-935343-02-4) Peartree.

—The Gooblins Night. Birenbaum, Barbara. LC 85-62585. 44p. (gr. 2-5). 1985. 10.95 (0-935343-32-6); pap. 5.95 (0-935343-31-8) Peartree.

—The Happy Dreidels: Hanukkah Adventure. Wolfberg, Carrie. LC 86-12210. 28p. (ps-2). 1991. 8.50 (0-935343-01-6); pap. 3.50 (0-935343-00-8) Peartree.

—The Hidden Shadow. Birenbaum, Barbara. LC 86-12187. 54p. (gr. 1-4). 1986. 10.95 (0-935343-42-3); pap. 5.95 (0-935343-43-1) Peartree.

—Lady Liberty's Light. Birenbaum, Barbara. LC 85-32061. 50p. (gr. 3-5). 1986. 10.95 (0-935343-12-1); pap. 5.95 (0-935343-11-3) Peartree.

—The Lost Side of the Dreydl. Birenbaum, Barbara. 50p. (gr. 3-5). 1987. 10.95 (0-935343-17-2); pap. 5.95 (0-935343-16-4) Peartree.
Birenbaum, Barbara & Sapp, Patt. The Lighthouse Christmas. Birenbaum, Barbara. LC 90-7284. 48p. (Orig.). (gr. k-5). 1991. 10.95 (0-935343-26-1); pap. 5.95 (0-935343-25-3) Peartree.
Birkett, Rachel. Hans Andersen's Fairy Tales. Andersen, Hans Christian. Kingsland, L. W., tr. 268p. (ps-6). 1987. 18.95 (0-19-274532-8) OUP.
Birkinshaw, Linda. It Was a Dark & Stormy Night: A Pop-up Mystery Whodunit. Moseley, Keith. 14p. (gr. 1-4). 1991. 12.95 (0-8037-1021-6) Dial Bks Young.
Birling, Paul. Brooklyn Doesn't Rhyme. Blos, Joan W. 96p. (gr. 3-6). 1994. SBE 12.95 (0-684-19694-8, Scribners Young Read) Macmillan Child Grp.
Birmingham, Lloyd. Dinosaurs. Greenberg, Judith E. & Carey, Helen H. 32p. (gr. 2-4). 1990. PLB 17.96 (0-8172-3751-8) Raintree Steck-V.
—Heat. Santrey, Laurence. LC 84-2711. 32p. (gr. 3-6). 1985. PLB 9.49 (0-8167-0306-X); pap. text ed. 2.95 (0-8167-0307-8) Troll Assocs.
Birmingham, Lucy, et al, photos by. Nicaragua. Ackley, Meredith, et al, eds. LC 89-43174. (gr. 3-8). PLB 19.93 (0-8368-0221-7); PLB 19.93 s.p. (0-685-61532-4) Gareth Stevens Inc.
Biro, Scarlet. Mathematician & Administrator, Shirley Mathis McBay. Verheyden-Hilliard, Mary E. LC 84-25983. 32p. (Orig.). (gr. 1-4). 1985. pap. 5.00 (0-932469-04-3) Equity Inst.
—Scientist & Planner, Ru Chih Cheo Huang. Verheyden-Hilliard, Mary E. LC 84-25982. 32p. (Orig.). (gr. 1-4). 1985. pap. 5.00 (0-932469-03-5) Equity Inst.
—Scientist from Puerto Rico, Maria Cordero Hardy. Verheyden-Hilliard, Mary E. LC 84-25979. 32p. (Orig.). (gr. 1-4). 1985. pap. 5.00 (0-932469-02-7) Equity Inst.

Biro, Scarlet & Rom, Holly M. American Women in Science & Engineering, 15 bks. Verheyden-Hilliard, Mary E. (gr. 1-4). 1988. Set. 75.00 (0-932469-19-1) Equity Inst.

This illustrated, 15-book series presents contemporary African-American, American Indian, Asian-American, Hispanic, & Caucasian women who, in girlhood, overcame barriers of gender, race, language, & poverty to become scientists. Five of the books are about girls with physical disabilities who also went on to become scientists. "Inspiring group of biographies of women in science...Children in the lower grades will enjoy these biographies, & those in the upper grades with reading problems can use them for...biographical information."-- SCHOOL LIBRARY JOURNAL. "...useful to teachers who want to help girls become more positive towards mathematics & science... recommended."-- CURRICULUM REVIEW. "...smoothly written texts..."-- BOOKLIST. "...help children...see the connection...between determination to persevere in the face of disabilities & later 'payoff'...in a variety of very exciting careers."-- NEWSLETTER, Association of Black Women in Higher Education. "...warm, lively & true stories of young girls who went on to become successful scientists..."-- GIFTED CHILDREN MONTHLY. "...these books are so attractively produced that I can't imagine elementary classroom teaching without them."-- PERSPECTIVES, National Women Studies Association. Also available are tie-in Teaching Guide $10.00 (ISBN 0-932469-19-3), & video: "You Can Be a Scientist Too!" $46.00 (ISBN 0-932469-11-6). "Shows how exciting & fascinating science can be."-- BOOKLIST.
Publisher Provided Annotation.

Biro, Val. Hungarian Folk-Tales. Biro, Val, retold by. 192p. (gr. 4 up). 1992. pap. 10.95 (0-19-274148-9) OUP.

—Rub-a-Dub-Dub: Val Biro's Seventy-Seven Favorite Nursery Rhymes. Biro, Val. LC 90-14402. 62p. (ps). 1991. PLB 16.95 (0-87226-449-1, Bedrick Blackie) P Bedrick Bks.
—The Silly Silly Ghost. Todd, H. E. 32p. (gr. k-3). 1989. 13.95 (0-340-41155-4, Pub. by Hodder & Stoughton UK) Trafalgar.
—Tobias & the Dragon: A Hungarian Folk Tale. Biro, Val. LC 89-18492. 32p. (gr. k-3). 1990. PLB 12.95 (0-87226-427-0, Bedrick Blackie) P Bedrick Bks.
—What's up the Coconut Tree? Benjamin, A. 32p. (ps up). 1992. laminated boards 11.95 (0-19-279896-0) OUP.
—When I Was Your Age. Adams, Ken. 32p. (ps-2). 1991. incl. dust jacket 12.95 (0-8120-6249-3) Barron.
Birrer, Cynthia & Birrer, William. The Lady & the Unicorn. Birrer, Cynthia & Birrer, William. LC 86-20872. 32p. (ps-3). 1987. 12.95 (0-688-04037-3) Lothrop.
Birrer, William, jt. illus. see Birrer, Cynthia.
Birt, Jane L. The Chess Set & Other Stories. Baggiani, J. M. & Tewell, V. M. 21p. (gr. 2-3). 1966. pap. 3.50 (0-934329-07-9) Baggiani-Tewell.
—In the Country. Baggiani, J. M. & Tewell, V. M. 26p. (gr. 2-4). 1966. pap. 3.50 (0-934329-08-7) Baggiani-Tewell.
—Phonics; a Tool for Better Reading & Spelling, Bk. I. Baggiani, J. M. & Tewell, V. M. (gr. 1-2). 1982. pap. 9.50 student's copy (0-934329-00-1); tchr's. manual 10.75 (0-934329-01-X) Baggiani-Tewell.
—Read & Draw. Baggiani, J. M. & Tewell, V. M. 12p. (gr. 1-3). 1966. pap. 2.00 (0-934329-06-0) Baggiani-Tewell.
Bischoff, Ilse. Gigi: The Story of a Merry-Go-Round Horse. Foster, Elizabeth. Israel, Nancy M., intro. by. 118p. (gr. 2-6). 1990. Repr. of 1943 ed. 14.95 (0-9626165-0-8) Paper Memories.
Biser, Dee. The Birthday Present. Glyman, Caroline A. 32p. (gr. k-3). 1992. PLB 12.95 (1-878363-79-4) Forest Hse.
—Learning Your ABC's of Nutrition. Glyman, Caroline A. 32p. (gr. k-3). 1992. PLB 12.95 (1-878363-75-1) Forest Hse.
—What's above the Sky? A Book about the Planets. Glyman, Caroline A. 32p. (gr. k-3). 1992. PLB 12.95 (1-878363-76-X) Forest Hse.
Bishop, Bonnie. Miracle at Egg Rock: A Puffin's Story. Gove, Doris. LC 85-7050. 48p. (Orig.). (gr. 1-4). 1985. pap. 6.95 (0-89272-205-3) Down East.
Bishop, Michael. The Secret Garden. Burnett, Frances H. 200p. 1993. 25.00 (0-88363-202-0) H L Levin.
Bishop, Roma. Christmas Songs & Prayers for Children. 32p. (ps). 1993. 3.98 (0-8317-5168-1) Smithmark.
Biske, Joel & Nielson, Mike. London Sourcebook. Sargent, Carl. Ippolito, Donna & Mulvihill, Sharon T., eds. 152p. (gr. 7 up). 1991. pap. 15.00 (1-55560-131-6, 7203) FASA Corp.
Biske, Joel, jt. illus. see Nelson, Jim.
Bisley, Simon. Batman - Judge Dredd: Judgement on Gotham. Wagner, John & Grant, Alan. O'Neil, Dennis, ed. 64p. (Orig.). 1991. pap. 5.95 (1-56389-022-4) DC Comics.
Bissex, Thelma & Turner, Elizabeth. Horses & Ponies. Dell, Catherine. LC 88-17652. 24p. (Orig.). (gr. 2-5). 1989. PLB 5.99 (0-394-99987-8) Random Bks Yng Read.
Biswas, Dolly. Sherlock Holmes & the Jewel & Other Short Plays. Chokai, M. 169p. (gr. 6). 1983. pap. 3.95x (0-86131-330-5) Apt Bks.
Biswas, Pulak. Maya of Mohenjo-Daro. 3rd ed. Anand, Mulk R. 24p. (Orig.). (gr. k-3). 1980. pap. 2.50 (0-89744-214-8, Pub. by Childrens Bk Trust IA) Auromere.
—Stories from Panchatantra: Book I. Shivkumar. (gr. 1-9). 1979. 4.50 (0-89744-162-1); pap. 3.00 (0-685-57661-2) Auromere.
—Stories from Panchatantra: Book IV. Shivkumar. (gr. 1-9). 1979. 4.50 (0-89744-165-6); pap. 3.00 (0-685-57664-7) Auromere.
—Tales from Indian Classics, Bk. I. Savitri. (gr. 3-9). 1979. 4.50 (0-89744-167-2); pap. 3.00 (0-685-57665-5) Auromere.
—Tales from Indian Classics, Bk. II. Savitri. (gr. 3-9). 1979. 4.50 (0-89744-168-0); pap. 3.00 (0-685-57666-3) Auromere.
Bivens, Chris. The Perfect Tree. Bivens, Tom. 48p. (ps-2). 1991. 6.95 (0-88101-179-7) Unicorn Pub.
Bivens, Christopher. The Perfect Tree & Favorite Christmas Carols. Ingram, John W., & Bivens, Christopher. LC 90-34514. 48p. (ps-2). 1990. 4.95 (0-88101-104-5) Unicorn Pub.
Bixler, Nancy. Whatever Happened to Penny Candy? A Fast, Clear, & Fun Explanation of the Economics You Need for Success in Your Career, Business, & Investments. 3rd, rev. & enl. ed. Uncle Eric, pseud. LC 92-36378. (gr. 5 up). 1993. 8.95 (0-942617-15-0) Blstckng Pr.
Bizette, Genevieve. Nell's Aviary. (ps) 1993. Gift box set of 4 bks., 12p. ea. incl 4 hanging birds. bds. 14.95 (1-56828-018-2-3) New Dawn NY.
Bjorke, Drew. Arne & Loki. Bjorke, Drew. 12p. (ps). 1993. 4.95 (1-56828-033-5) Red Jacket Pr.
—Arne the Viking. Bjorke, Drew. (ps). 1993. Gift box set of 4 bks., 12p. ea. incl. viking ship. bds. 14.95 (1-56828-037-8) Red Jacket Pr.
—The Artic Trip. Bjorke, Drew. 12p. (ps). 1993. 4.95 (1-56828-035-1) Red Jacket Pr.

—The Magic Sail. Bjorke, Drew. 12p. (ps). 1993. 4.95 (1-56828-036-X) Red Jacket Pr.
—The Viking Counting Book. Bjorke, Drew. 12p. (ps). 1993. 4.95 (1-56828-034-3) Red Jacket Pr.
Bjorklund, L. Young Mark Twain & the Mississippi. Kane, Harnett T. LC 87-4531. 176p. (gr. 5-9). 1987. lib. bdg. 8.99 (0-394-90413-3); pap. 4.99 (0-394-89182-1) Random Bks Yng Read.
Bjorklund, Lorence. My Pardner. Evans, Max. LC 75-187421. 104p. (gr. 5-9). 1972. 3.95 (0-395-13725-X) HM.
Bjorkman, Dale. Harold's Dog Horace Is Scared of the Dark. Skoglund, Elizabeth. 48p. (gr. 2). 1992. pap. 2.99 (0-8423-1047-9) Tyndale.
Bjorkman, George. Seeds. Shannon, George. LC 92-40738. 1994. write for info. (0-395-66990-1) HM.
Bjorkman, Steve. Aliens for Breakfast. Etra, Jonathan & Spinner, Stephanie. LC 88-6653. 64p. (Orig.). (gr. 2-4). 1988. lib. bdg. 6.99 (0-394-92093-7); pap. 2.50 (0-394-82093-2) Random Bks Yng Read.
—Aliens for Lunch. Etra, Jon & Spinner, Stephanie. LC 90-39417. 64p. (Orig.). (gr. 2-4). 1991. PLB 6.99 (0-679-91056-5); pap. 2.50 (0-679-81056-0) Random Bks Yng Read.
—I Hate English! Levine, Ellen. (gr. k-2). 1989. pap. 13.95 (0-590-42305-3) Scholastic Inc.
—This Is the Way We Go to School. Baer, Edith. 32p. (ps-1). 1992. pap. 3.95 (0-590-43162-5, Blue Ribbon Bks) Scholastic Inc.
Bjorkman, Steven. In Fourteen Ninety-Two. Marzollo, Jean. 40p. 1991. 14.95 (0-590-44413-1, Scholastic Hardcover) Scholastic Inc.
Bjorksten, Gus, et al. Perils of the Young Kingdoms. Behrendt, Fred, et al. Brooks, Les, ed. 128p. (Orig.). (gr. 7 up). 1991. pap. text ed. 18.95 (0-933635-82-6, 2113) Chaosium.
—Tales of the Miskatonic Valley. Behrendt, Fred, et al. Brooks, Les, ed. 128p. (Orig.). (gr. 7 up). 1992. pap. text ed. 18.95 (0-933635-83-4, 2334) Chaosium.
Blachon, Roger. Livre de Tous les Francais. Tissot, Olivier. (FRE.). 92p. (gr. 4-9). 1989. 14.95 (2-07-039526-X) Schoenhof.
Black, Candice N. The Shelby Avenue Gang. Black, Auguste R. 66p. (Orig.). (gr. 2-5). 1990. pap. 3.95 (0-9628010-0-3) A R Black.
Black, Diane, jt. illus. see Gruettner, Diane.
Black, Don. Donkeys. Noonan, Diana. LC 93-28998. 1994. 4.25 (0-383-03741-7) SRA Schl Grp.
—Houses That Move. Noonan, Diane. LC 92-27085. 1993. 14.00 (0-383-03574-0) SRA Schl Grp.
—X-Rays. Morrison, Rob. LC 93-28983. 1994. 4.25 (0-383-03789-1) SRA Schl Grp.
Black, Jean, jt. illus. see Anastasia, Karyn.
Black, Jeanne. Word Processing: Course Code S04-2. Weinman, Susan. Schroeder, Bonnie, ed. 75p. (gr. 7). 1989. pap. text ed. 8.00 (0-917531-53-1) CES Compu-Tech.
Black, Robert. Wow! What a Wonderful World. Frasier, Elizabeth. 32p. (Orig.). (gr. k-4). 1990. pap. 4.50 (1-879253-00-3) Apex Creat.

Blackard, Sandy. Terrific Bee on Terrific Me. Conkle, Nancy E. 32p. (Orig.). (ps-1). 1993. pap. 9.50 (0-9639061-0-0) N Conkle.

A brightly colored picture book that uses repetitive language to describe the adventures of Terrific Bee. The flight line can be traced as the bee flys from one body part to another. Fun & understanding can be enhanced through the use of a bee hand puppet or bee stickers that the children enjoy placing on each body part as the story is read. The characters are from various ethnic backgrounds & some children have a handicap. All children are in play situations & aside from a fun way to learn body parts the book also gives adults an opportunity to satisfy a child's natural curiosity by talking about apparatus that some children need for more efficient function. As understanding develops differences become less significant.
Publisher Provided Annotation.

Blacke, Terry L. Pabulum Pig: The Yule Swine. Blacke, Terry L. & Hill, Donald. 30p. (gr. 4). 1992. pap. 7.98 (0-9630718-2-3) New Dawn NY.
Blacklock, Craig, photos by. Wild Boars. Nicholson, Darrell. 48p. (gr. 2-5). 1987. PLB 19.95 (0-87614-308-7) Carolrhoda Bks.
Blackshear, Ami. Diamonds & Toads: A Classic Fairy Tale. Schecter, Ellen. LC 93-14096. Date not set. write for info. (0-553-09046-1); pap. write for info. (0-553-37339-0) Bantam.

Blackstone, Ann. Extra Book, Level One. Thurston, Cheryl M. 46p. (Orig.). (gr. 5-12). 1988. pap. text ed. 12.95 (*1-877673-05-6*) Cottonwood Pr.
—Grandmother's Adobe Dollhouse. Smith, MaryLou M. 32p. (gr. k-6). 1988. PLB 12.95 (*0-937206-03-2*); pap. 6.95 (*0-937206-07-5*) New Mexico Mag.
—What's in a Name? rev. ed. Thurston, Cheryl M. 24p. (Orig.). (gr. 5-12). 1993. pap. text ed. 8.95 (*1-877673-04-8*) Cottonwood Pr.
—Writing Your Life: Autobiographical Writing Activities for Young People. Borg, Mary. 46p. (gr. 5-12). 1989. pap. text ed. 14.95 (*1-877673-09-9*) Cottonwood Pr.
Blades, Ann. A Candle for Christmas. Speare, Jean. LC 86-61560. 32p. (gr. k-4). 1987. SBE 13.95 (*0-689-50417-9*, M K McElderry) Macmillan Child Grp.
—A Dog Came, Too: A True Story. Manson, Ainslie. LC 91-44891. 32p. (gr. 1-5). 1993. SBE 13.95 (*0-689-50567-1*, M K McElderry) Macmillan Child Grp.
—Fall. Blades, Ann. (ps-k). 1990. bds. 4.95 (*0-688-09232-2*) Lothrop.
—Ida & the Wool Smugglers. Alderson, Sue A. LC 87-15487. 32p. (gr. k-4). 1988. SBE 13.95 (*0-689-50440-3*, M K McElderry) Macmillan Child Grp.
—Pettranella. Waterton, Betty. 32p. 1991. pap. 4.95 (*0-88899-108-8*, Pub. by Groundwood-Douglas & McIntyre CN) Firefly Bks Ltd.
—A Salmon for Simon. Waterton, Betty. 32p. (ps-2). 1991. pap. 4.95 (*0-88899-107-X*, Pub. by Groundwood-Douglas & McIntyre CN) Firefly Bks Ltd.
—The Singing Basket. Pearson, Kit, retold by. 32p. (ps-3). 1991. 13.95 (*0-88899-104-5*, Pub. by Groundwood-Douglas & McIntyre CN) Firefly Bks Ltd.
—Spring. Blades, Ann. LC 89-2424. 10p. (ps). 1990. board 4.95 (*0-688-09230-6*) Lothrop.
—Winter. Blades, Ann. (ps-k). 1990. bds. 4.95 (*0-688-09233-0*) Lothrop.
Blaebst, Werner. Maxi's Bed Magicians. Blaebst, Werner. 28p. (ps-k). 1991. smythe sewn reinforced bdg. 9.95 (*1-56182-020-2*) Atomium Bks.
Blaicher, David. I Can Learn Torah, Vol. 2: Stories of the First Jewish Family. Wise, Ira J. & Grishaver, Joel L. 48p. (Orig.). (ps-2). 1992. pap. text ed. 2.45 (*0-933873-68-9*) Torah Aura.
Blair, Culverson. Afro-Bets: Book of Colors. Brown, Margery W. LC 91-76333. 24p. (Orig.). (ps-1). 1991. pap. 3.95 (*0-940975-29-7*) Just Us Bks.
—Afro-Bets: Book of Shapes. Brown, Margery W. LC 91-76334. 24p. (Orig.). (ps-1). 1991. pap. 3.95 (*0-940975-28-9*) Just Us Bks.
—Afro-Bets Kids: I'm Gonna Be! Hudson, Wade. LC 92-72000. 32p. (Orig.). (ps up). 1992. pap. 6.95 (*0-940975-40-8*) Just Us Bks.
Blair, Janice, jt. illus. see Blattel, Carolyn.
Blair, Jay. We Didn't Mean to. Addy, Sharon. McDermot, Gerald, intro. by. LC 80-24976. 32p. (gr. k-6). 1981. PLB 16.67 (*0-8172-1370-8*) Raintree Pubs Ltd.
Blair, Mary. I Can Fly. reissued ed. Krauss, Ruth. 24p. (ps-k). 1992. write for info. (*0-307-00146-6*, 312-12, Golden Pr) Western Pub.
Blair, Susan M. Unexpected Company. Blair, Susan M. 56p. (ps-7). 1992. 19.95 (*0-9631956-0-3*) Pendant Pr.
Blaisdell, Elinore. Rhymes & Verses: Collected Poems for Young People. De la Mare, Walter. LC 88-45278. 370p. (gr. 2-4). 1988. 15.95 (*0-8050-0847-0*, Bks Young Read); pap. 7.95 (*0-8050-0848-9*) H Holt & Co.
Blake, Amy. Sound All Around. ps-4 ed. Susen, Phyllis B., ed. 40p. (Orig.). 1992. pap. 8.50 (*0-9635667-0-9*) Phila Orchestra.
Blake, Quentin. Alphabeasts. King-Smith, Dick. LC 91-38435. 64p. (gr. 1 up). 1992. SBE 14.95 (*0-02-750720-3*, Macmillan Child Bk) Macmillan Child Grp.
—The BFG. Dahl, Roald. LC 85-566. 221p. (gr. 1 up). 1982. 16.00 (*0-374-30469-6*) FS&G.
—The BFG. Dahl, Roald. 1989. pap. 4.50 (*0-14-034019-X*, Puffin) Puffin Bks.
—Custard & Company. Nash, Ogden. 128p. (gr. 2-6). 1985. pap. 6.95 (*0-316-59855-0*) Little.
—The Dahl Diary, 1992. Dahl, Roald. 208p. (ps up) 1991. pap. 8.95 (*0-14-034647-3*, Puffin) Puffin Bks.
—Dirty Beasts. Dahl, Roald. LC 85-594. 32p. (gr. 1 up). 1986. pap. 4.99 (*0-14-050435-4*, Puffin) Puffin Bks.
—Down at the Doctor's: The Sick Book. Rosen, Michael. 24p. (gr. k-4). 1988. 10.95 (*0-13-218942-9*, Little Simon) S&S Trade.
—The Enormous Crocodile. reissue ed. Dahl, Roald. LC 77-5081. 32p. (ps-3). 1978. 14.00 (*0-394-83594-8*); lib. bdg. 14.99 (*0-394-93594-2*) Knopf Bks Yng Read.
—The Enormous Crocodile. Dahl, Roald. 32p. (gr. 1-5). 1993. pap. 3.99 (*0-14-036556-7*, Puffin) Puffin Bks.
—Esio Trot. Dahl, Roald. 1990. 14.95 (*0-670-83451-3*) Viking Child Bks.
—Esio Trot. Dahl, Roald. LC 92-16931. 64p. (gr. 3-7). 1992. pap. 3.99 (*0-14-036099-9*) Puffin Bks.
—The Giraffe & the Pelly & Me. Dahl, Roald. LC 86-43079. 32p. (ps-3). 1987. pap. 4.99 (*0-14-050566-0*, Puffin) Puffin Bks.
—Great Day for Up! Dr. Seuss. LC 74-5517. 36p. (ps-1). 1974. 6.95 (*0-394-82913-1*); lib. bdg. 7.99 (*0-394-92913-6*) Random Bks Yng Read.

—The Great Piratical Rumbustification & The Librarian & The Robbers. Mahy, Margaret. LC 92-46599. 64p. (gr. 5 up). 1993. pap. 3.95 (*0-688-12469-0*, Pub. by Beech Tree Bks) Morrow.
—Great Piratical Rumbustification the Librarian & the Robbers. Mahy, Margaret. LC 85-45966. 64p. 1986. 11.95 (*0-87923-629-9*) Godine.
—Hard-Boiled Legs: The Breakfast Book. Rosen, Michael. LC k-4). 1986. 10.95 (*0-13-383746-7*) P-H.
—Here Comes McBroom. Fleischman, Sid. LC 91-32689. 80p. (gr. 1 up). 1992. 14.00 (*0-688-11160-2*) Greenwillow.
—Joseph & the Amazing Technicolor Dreamcoat. Rice, Tim & Webber, Andrew L. 32p. (gr. k-3). 1993. pap. 11.95 (*1-85793-119-X*, Pub. by Pavilion UK) Trafalgar.
—McBroom's Wonderful One-Acre Farm. Fleischman, Sid. LC 91-31906. 64p. (gr. 1 up). 1992. 14.00 (*0-688-11159-9*) Greenwillow.
—The Marzipan Pig. Hoban, Russell. LC 86-24253. 40p. (gr. 1-4). 1987. 13.00 (*0-374-34859-6*) FS&G.
—The Marzipan Pig. Hoban, Russell. 40p. (gr. 1 up). 1989. pap. 3.50 (*0-374-44750-0*) FS&G.
—Matilda. Dahl, Roald. 224p. (gr. 3-7). 1988. pap. 14.95 (*0-670-82439-9*) Viking Child Bks.
—Mind Your Own Business. Rosen, Michael. LC 74-9969. 96p. (gr. 3 up). 1974. 21.95 (*0-87599-209-9*) S G Phillips.
—Monsters. Hoban, Russell. 1990. 13.95 (*0-590-43422-5*) Scholastic Inc.
—Monsters. Hoban, Russell. 32p. (ps-2). 1993. pap. 4.95 (*0-590-43421-7*) Scholastic Inc.
—My Year. Dahl, Roald. 64p. (gr. 4-7). 1994. 14.99 (*0-670-85397-6*) Viking Child Bks.
—Nonstop Nonsense. Mahy, Margaret. LC 88-8401. 128p. (gr. 1-5). 1989. SBE 12.95 (*0-689-50483-7*, M K McElderry) Macmillan Child Grp.
—Of Quarks, Quasars, & Other Quirks: Quizzical Poems for the Supersonic Age. Brewton, Sara, et al, eds. LC 76-54747. 128p. (gr. 5 up). 1990. PLB 13.89 (*0-690-04885-8*, Crowell Jr Bks) HarpC Child Bks.
—Old Mother Hubbard's Dog Dresses Up. Yeoman, John. LC 89-27026. 24p. (ps-3). 1990. 6.70 (*0-395-53358-9*) HM.
—Old Mother Hubbard's Dog Learns to Play. Yeoman, John. LC 89-39863. 24p. (ps-3). 1990. 6.95 (*0-395-53360-0*) HM.
—Old Mother Hubbard's Dog Needs a Doctor. Yeoman, John. LC 89-24448. 24p. (ps-3). 1990. 6.70 (*0-395-53359-7*) HM.
—Old Mother Hubbard's Dog Takes up Sport. Yeoman, John. LC 89-39942. 24p. (ps-3). 1990. 6.70 (*0-395-53361-9*) HM.
—Potion Magique de Georges Bouillon. Dahl, Roald. (FRE.). 148p. (gr. 5-10). 1990. pap. 8.95 (*2-07-033463-5*) Schoenhof.
—The Rain Door. Hoban, Russell. LC 86-47719. 32p. (ps-3). 1987. (Crowell Jr Bks) HarpC Child Bks.
—Rhyme Stew. Dahl, Roald. 80p. (gr. 4 up). 1990. pap. 14.95 (*0-670-82916-1*) Viking Child Bks.
—Roald Dahl's Revolting Rhymes. Dahl, Roald. LC 82-15263. 48p. (gr. 3-6). 1983. 14.00 (*0-394-85422-5*); lib. bdg. 14.99 (*0-394-95422-X*) Knopf Bks Yng Read.
—Simpkin. Blake, Quentin. 32p. (ps-1). 1994. 14.99 (*0-670-85371-2*) Viking Child Bks.
—The Singing Tortoise: And Other Animal Folktales. Yeoman, John. LC 93-31208. 96p. (gr. 1 up). 1994. 18.00 (*0-688-13366-5*, Tambourine Bks) Morrow.
—The Twits. Dahl, Roald. 96p. (gr. 2-6). 1991. pap. 3.99 (*0-14-034640-6*, Puffin) Puffin Bks.
—Under the Bed. Rosen, Michael. 32p. 1986. 10.95 (*0-13-935412-3*) P-H.
—The Vicar of Nibbleswicke. Dahl, Roald. 24p. 1992. 12. 50 (*0-670-84384-9*) Viking Child Bks.
—Willie the Squowse. Allan, Ted. (gr. 2 up). 1991. Repr. of 1978 ed. 9.95 (*0-8038-9341-8*) Hastings.
—The Witches. Dahl, Roald. LC 85-519. 200p. (gr. 3-7). 1985. pap. 3.95 (*0-14-031730-9*) Viking Child Bks.
Blake, Quentin, photos by. The Witches. Dahl, Roald. LC 83-14195. 208p. (gr. 3-9). 1983. 16.00 (*0-374-38457-6*); ltd. ed. o.s.i. 35.00 (*0-374-38458-4*) FS&G.
Blake, Robert J. The Perfect Spot. Blake, Robert J. 32p. (ps-8). 1992. PLB 14.95 (*0-399-22132-8*, Philomel Bks) Putnam Pub Group.
—Rainflowers. Turner, Ann. LC 90-39629. 32p. (gr. k-3). 1992. 14.00 (*0-06-026041-6*); PLB 13.89 (*0-06-026042-4*) HarpC Child Bks.
—Riptide. Weller, Frances W. 32p. (ps-3). 1990. 14.95 (*0-399-21675-8*, Philomel Bks) Putnam Pub Group.
Blakemore, Sally. Kidding Around Boston: A Young Person's Guide. 2nd ed. Byers, Helen. 64p. (gr. 3 up). 1993. pap. 9.95 (*1-56261-092-9*) John Muir.
—Kidding Around Chicago: A Young Person's Guide. 2nd ed. Davis, Lauren. 64p. (gr. 3 up). 1993. pap. 9.95 (*1-56261-094-5*) John Muir.
—Kidding Around New York City: A Young Person's Guide. 2nd ed. Lovett, Sarah. 64p. (gr. 3 up). 1993. pap. 9.95 (*1-56261-095-3*) John Muir.
—Kidding Around Santa Fe: A Young Person's Guide to the City. York, Susan. 64p. (Orig.). (gr. 3 up). 1991. pap. 9.95 (*0-945465-99-8*) John Muir.
Blakemore, Sally & Sundstrom, Mary. Extremely Weird Primates. Lovett, Sarah. 48p. (Orig.). (gr. 3 up). 1991. pap. 9.95 (*1-56261-018-X*) John Muir.
—Extremely Weird Reptiles. Lovett, Sarah. 48p. (Orig.). (gr. 3 up). 1991. pap. 9.95 (*1-56261-036-8*) John Muir.
Blakemore, Sally, jt. illus. see Sundstrom, Mary.

Blanc, Henry. Playing Tennis with Bouncy & Fuzzy. Barbic, Ivo. 96p. 1987. pap. 9.95 (*0-88289-654-7*) Pelican.
Blaney, Christine. My Dog's Day: A Moving Picture Book. Blaney, Christine. 8p. (ps). 1993. 11.99 (*0-670-85202-3*) Viking Child Bks.
Blank, Diane. The Quest of the Junior Blue Knights. Jagen, Edward J. Jagen, E. J., intro. by. 32p. (gr. k-7). 1990. wkbk. 4.95 (*0-9625641-1-7*) White Feather & Co.
Blank, Diane, et al. A Good Knight Story: The Quest for the Missing Children. Jagen, Edward J. Gregory, G., et al, eds. McCarthy, Dennis, intro. by. 64p. (Orig.). (gr. k-7). 1990. pap. 14.95x (*0-9625641-0-9*); wkbk. 4.95 (*0-9625641-2-5*) White Feather & Co.
Blankenship, Judy. Teddy Beddy Bear's Bedtime Songs & Poems. LC 84-4837. 32p. (ps). 1984. pap. 2.25 saddle-stitched (*0-394-86826-9*) Random Bks Yng Read.
Blankley, Kathy. The King & the Tortoise. Mollel, Tololwa M. LC 92-12485. 32p. (gr. k-3). 1993. 14.45 (*0-395-64480-1*, Clarion Bks) HM.
Blanton, Betty. The Flying Mule Car. Piequet, Miriam. Anyone Can Read Staff, ed. 149p. (Orig.). (gr. 4-6). 1988. pap. 15.00 (*0-914275-11-9*) Anyone Can Read Bks.
Blass, Jacqueline. My Playhouse. Blass, Jacqueline. 8p. (ps-4). 1989. bds. 6.99 (*1-55037-033-2*, Pub. by Annick CN) Firefly Bks Ltd.
Blattel, Carolyn & Blair, Janice. Father Gander Nursery Rhymes. Father Gander, pseud. LC 85-72785. 47p. (ps up). 1985. 15.95 (*0-911655-12-3*, Dist. by Ingram Bookpeople) Advocacy Pr.
Blau, Judith. Bunny Mitten's Book. Blau, Judith. 7p. (ps). 1991. incl. puppet 5.95 (*0-679-81315-2*) Random Bks Yng Read.
—Ducky Mitten's Book. Blau, Judith. 7p. (ps). 1991. incl. puppet 5.95 (*0-679-81314-4*) Random Bks Yng Read.
—Kitten Mitten's Stocking. Blau, Judith. 7p. (ps). 1992. incl. puppet 5.99 (*0-679-83046-4*) Random Bks Yng Read.
—Puppy Mitten's Present. Blau, Judith. 7p. (ps). 1992. incl. puppet 5.99 (*0-679-83045-6*) Random Bks Yng Read.
—Stop & Go Potty. Blau, Judith. LC 92-61706. 6p. (ps). 1993. 6.99 (*0-679-84021-4*) Random Bks Yng Read.
Blaustein, Muriel. Play Ball, Zachary! Blaustein, Muriel. LC 87-45274. 32p. (ps-2). 1988. HarpC Child Bks.
Blazek, Scott R. Clovis Crawfish & Batiste Bete Puante. Fontenot, Mary A. LC 93-1249. 32p. (gr. k-3). 1993. 14.95 (*0-88289-952-X*) Pelican.
—Clovis Crawfish & Bertile's Bon Voyage. Fontenot, Mary A. LC 90-22160. 32p. (ps-3). 1991. 12.95 (*0-88289-825-6*) Pelican.
—Clovis Crawfish & Etienne Escargot. Fontenot, Mary A. LC 91-26896. 32p. (ps-3). 1992. 12.95 (*0-88289-826-4*) Pelican.
—Clovis Crawfish & Michelle Mantis. Fontenot, Mary A. LC 88-30305. 32p. (ps-3). 1989. 12.95 (*0-88289-730-6*) Pelican.
—Clovis Crawfish & Simeon Suce-Fleur. Fontenot, Mary A. LC 89-35370. 32p. (ps-3). 1990. 12.95 (*0-88289-751-9*) Pelican.
Bleck, Cathie. Aloha Means Come Back: The Story of a World War II Girl. Hoobler, Dorothy & Hoobler, Thomas. 64p. (gr. 4-6). 1992. 11.95 (*0-382-24156-8*); PLB 13.98 (*0-382-24148-7*); pap. 7.95 (*0-382-24349-8*) Silver Burdett Pr.
—KidSkills Interpersonal Skill Series, An Island Adventure: Self-Esteem: Being a Friend to Myself. Morse, J. Thomas, et al. Gouge, Betty, et al, eds. LC 85-45429. 47p. (gr. 2-3). 1985. PLB 9.95 (*0-934275-01-7*); bk. & cassette 13.95 (*0-934275-14-9*) Fam Skills.
—KidSkills Interpersonal Skill Series, A Lasting Friend: Friendship: Making Friends. Morse, J. Thomas, et al. Gouge, Betty, et al, eds. LC 85-45422. 45p. (gr. 2-3). 1985. PLB 9.95 (*0-934275-06-8*); bk. & cassette 13.95 (*0-934275-20-3*) Fam Skills.
—KidSkills Interpersonal Skill Series, Lair of the Jade Tiger: Friendship: Keeping Friends. Morse, J. Thomas, et al. Gouge, Betty, et al, eds. LC 85-81270. 48p. (gr. 2-3). 1986. PLB 9.95 (*0-934275-07-6*); bk. & cassette 13.95 (*0-934275-21-1*) Fam Skills.
—KidSkills Interpersonal Skill Series, The Feeling Fun House: Feelings: Dealing with Feelings. Morse, J. Thomas, et al. Gouge, Betty, et al, eds. LC 85-45423. 45p. (gr. 2-3). 1985. PLB 9.95 (*0-934275-03-3*); bk. & cassette 13.95 (*0-934275-17-3*) Fam Skills.
—KidSkills Interpersonal Skill Series, The Land of Listening: Listening: Getting & Giving Attention. Morse, J. Thomas, et al. Gouge, Betty, et al, eds. LC 85-45429. 45p. (gr. 2-3). 1985. PLB 9.95 (*0-934275-00-9*); bk. & cassette 13.95 (*0-934275-15-7*) Fam Skills.
Bleck, Cathie, jt. illus. see Bleck, Linda.
Bleck, Linda & Bleck, Cathie. KidSkills Interpersonal Skill Series, Choices! Choices! Choices! Responsibility: Making & Living with Choices. Gouge, Betty, et al. Morse, J. Thomas, ed. LC 86-45001. 45p. (ps). 1986. PLB 8.95 (*0-934275-09-2*); bk. & cassette 11.95 (*0-934275-23-8*) Fam Skills.
—KidSkills Interpersonal Skill Series, Let's Share: Friendship: Sharing. Gouge, Betty, et al. Morse, J. Thomas, et al, eds. LC 86-81270. 48p. (ps). 1986. PLB 8.95 (*0-934275-13-0*); bk. & cassette 11.95 (*0-934275-27-0*) Fam Skills.

—KidSkills Interpersonal Skill Series, My Feelings & Me: Feelings: Experiencing Feelings. Gouge, Betty, et al. Morse, J. Thomas, et al, eds. LC 85-81270. 44p. (ps) 1986. 8.95 (0-934275-10-6); bk. & cassette 11.95 (0-934275-24-6) Fam Skills.

—KidSkills Interpersonal Skill Series, The Rules at My House: Responsibility: Understanding & Accepting Limits. Gouge, Betty, et al. Morse, J. Thomas, et al, eds. 44p. (ps) 1986. PLB 8.95 (0-934275-11-4); bk. & cassette 11.95 (0-934275-25-4) Fam Skills.

—KidSkills Interpersonal Skill Series, Wonderful You: Self-Awareness: Accepting & Knowing Myself. Gouge, Betty, et al. Morse, J. Thomas, et al, eds. LC 85-81270. 42p. (ps). 1986. PLB 8.95 (0-934275-12-2); bk. & cassette 11.95 (0-934275-26-2) Fam Skills.

Blegvad, Erik. Little, Little Sister. Curry, Jane L. LC 88-13079. 32p. (ps-3). 1989. SBE 12.95 (0-689-50459-4, M K McElderry) Macmillan Child Grp.

Blegvad, Erik. The Fragile Flag. Langton, Jane. LC 83-49471. 224p. (gr. 3-7). 1984. PLB 14.89 (0-06-023699-X) HarpC Child Bks.

Blegvad, Erik. I Like to Be Little. Zolotow, Charlotte. LC 83-45056. 32p. (gr. k-4). 1990. pap. 4.95 (0-06-443248-3, Trophy) HarpC Child Bks.

—The Tenth Good Thing about Barney. Viorst, Judith. LC 71-154764. 32p. (gr. k-4). 1971. SBE 12.95 (0-689-20688-7, Atheneum Child Bk) Macmillan Child Grp.

Blegvad, Erik. Anna Banana & Me. Blegvad, Lenore. LC 84-547. 32p. (gr. k-3). 1985. SBE 13.95 (0-689-50274-5, M K McElderry) Macmillan Child Grp.

—Anna Banana & Me. Blegvad, Lenore. LC 86-22220. 32p. (ps-3). 1987. pap. 3.95 (0-689-71114-X, Aladdin) Macmillan Child Grp.

—Anna Banana & Me. Blegvad, Lenore. (gr. 1-3). 1988. bk. & cassette 19.95 (0-87499-104-8); bk. & cassette 12.95 (0-87499-103-X); 4 cassettes & guide 27.95 (0-87499-105-6) Live Oak Media.

—Bed-Knob & Broomstick. large type ed. Norton, Mary. 296p. (gr. 3-7). 1989. lib. bdg. 14.95 (0-8161-4786-8, Large Print Bks) Hall.

—Cat Walk. Stolz, Mary. LC 82-47576. 128p. (gr. 3-7). 1983. HarpC Child Bks.

—Cat Walk. Stolz, Mary. LC 82-47576. 128p. (gr. 3-7). 1985. pap. 3.95 (0-06-440155-3, Trophy) HarpC Child Bks.

—The Diamond in the Window. Langton, Jane. LC 62-7312. 256p. (gr. 5 up). 1973. pap. 3.95 (0-06-440042-5, Trophy) HarpC Child Bks.

—I Like to Be Little. Zolotow, Charlotte. LC 83-45056. 32p. (gr. k-4). 1987. (Crowell Jr Bks); PLB 12.89 (0-690-04674-X, Crowell Jr Bks) HarpC Child Bks.

—May I Visit? Reissue. ed. Zolotow, Charlotte. LC 75-25405. 32p. (gr. k-3). 1976. PLB 12.89 (0-06-026933-2) HarpC Child Bks.

—Someone New. Zolotow, Charlotte. LC 77-11838. (ps-3). 1978. PLB 14.89 (0-06-027018-7) HarpC Child Bks.

—The Tenth Good Thing about Barney. Viorst, Judith. LC 86-25948. 32p. (gr. k-4). 1987. pap. 3.95 (0-689-71203-0, Aladdin) Macmillan Child Grp.

—Twelve Tales. Andersen, Hans Christian. Blegvad, Erik, tr. LC 93-6927. 1994. write for info. (0-689-50584-1, M K McElderry) Macmillan Child Grp.

—Water Pennies & Other Poems. Bodecker, N. M. LC 90-6477. 64p. 1991. SBE 12.95 (0-689-50517-5, M K McElderry) Macmillan Child Grp.

—The Winter Bear. Craft, Ruth. LC 74-18178. 32p. (ps-3). 1975. SBE 13.95 (0-689-50017-3, M K McElderry) Macmillan Child Grp.

—The Winter Bear. Craft, Ruth. LC 89-31866. 32p. (ps-3). 1989. pap. 3.95 (0-689-71342-8, Aladdin) Macmillan Child Grp.

Blegvad, Lenore. Once upon a Time & Grandma. Blegvad, Lenore. LC 92-7407. 32p. (ps-3). 1993. SBE 14.95 (0-689-50548-5, M K McElderry) Macmillan Child Grp.

Bleicher, David. Building Jewish Life Prayers & Blessings. Berman, Melanie. 32p. (Orig.). (gr. k-2). 1991. pap. text ed. 1.85 (0-933873-66-2) Torah Aura.

—Tanta Teva & the Magic Booth. Grishaver, Joel L. LC 93-13193. 1993. 11.95 (1-881283-00-3) Alef Design.

Blevins, Wade. And Then the Feather Fell. Blevins, Wade. Sargent, Dave, intro. by. 48p. (gr. k-8). 1993. text ed. 11.95 (1-56763-060-X); pap. text ed. 5.95 (0-685-67465-7) Ozark Pub.

—Ganseti & the Legend of the Little People. Blevins, Wade. Sargent, Dave, intro. by. 48p. (Orig.). (gr. k-8). 1993. text ed. 11.95 (1-56763-065-0); pap. text ed. 5.95 (1-56763-066-9) Ozark Pub.

—Legend of Little Deer. Blevins, Wade. Sargent, Dave, intro. by. 48p. (Orig.). (gr. k-8). 1993. text ed. 11.95 (1-56763-073-1); pap. text ed. 5.95 (1-56763-074-X) Ozark Pub.

—Path of Destiny. Blevins, Wade. Sargent, Dave, intro. by. 48p. (Orig.). (gr. k-8). 1993. text ed. 11.95 (1-56763-071-5); pap. text ed. 5.95 (1-56763-072-3) Ozark Pub.

—The Wisdom Circle. Blevins, Wade. Sargent, Dave, intro. by. 48p. (Orig.). (gr. k-8). 1993. text ed. 11.95 (1-56763-075-8); pap. text ed. 5.95 (1-56763-076-6) Ozark Pub.

Bliss, Bob. Cry of the Eagle. Signer, Billie T. 190p. (Orig.). (gr. 5-8). 1990. pap. 4.95 (0-8198-1455-5) St Paul Bks.

—Shetland Summer. Signer, Billie T. LC 88-18480. 125p. (Orig.). (gr. 5-8). 1990. pap. 3.95 (0-8198-6884-1) St Paul Bks.

—The Wind at My Back: The Life of St. Patrick. Turcotte, Mary C. LC 88-13763. 115p. (gr. 3 up). 1991. 4.95 (0-8198-8236-4) St Paul Bks.

Bliss, Phil, jt. illus. see Ortiz, Juan.

Bliss, Rebecca & Stuart, Walter. Turtles. Wildlife Education, Ltd. Staff. 24p. (gr. 5 up). 1992. 13.95 (0-937934-89-5) Wildlife Educ.

Bloch, Alex. Benjamin Franklin. Weinberg, Lawrence. 48p. (gr. 2-4). 1988. pap. 2.50 (0-681-40347-0) Longmeadow Pr.

—George Washington. Weinberg, Lawrence. 48p. (gr. 2-4). 1988. pap. 2.50 (0-681-40346-2) Longmeadow Pr.

—Harriet Tubman. Polcovar, Jane. 48p. (gr. 2-4). 1988. pap. 2.50 (0-681-40357-8) Longmeadow Pr.

Bloch, Lucienne. Starfish. Hurd, Edith T. LC 62-7742. 40p. (gr. k-2). 1962. PLB 13.89 (0-690-77069-3, Crowell Jr Bks) HarpC Child Bks.

Bloch, Serge. Lily Is in Love. De Saint Mars, Dominique. LC 93-10988. 1993. write for info. (1-56766-101-7) Childs World.

—Max Doesn't Like School. De Saint Mars, Dominique. LC 93-23773. 1993. write for info. (1-56766-103-3) Childs World.

—Max Is Crazy about Video Games. De Saint Mars, Dominique. LC 93-10987. 1993. write for info. (1-56766-102-5) Childs World.

—Mystere. Murail, Marie-Aude. (FRE.). 64p. (gr. 1-5). 1987. pap. 8.95 (2-07-031217-8) Schoenhof.

—Zoe's Parents Are Getting Divorced. De Saint Mars, Dominique. LC 93-19767. 1993. write for info. (1-56766-104-1) Childs World.

Block, Alex. A First Thesaurus. Wittels, Harriet & Greisman, Joan. 144p. (gr. 2-4). 1985. pap. write for info. (0-307-15835-7, Pub. by Golden Bks) Western Pub.

—The Mix & Match Book of Dinosaurs. Sanders, George. 10p. (ps-6). 1992. pap. 7.95 (0-671-76911-1, Little Simon) S&S Trade.

Block, Lori. The Great Coaster Ride. Sanders, Lawrence. Sargent, Dave, intro. by. 135p. (Orig.). (gr. k-8). 1993. text ed. 11.95 (1-56763-099-5); pap. text ed. 5.95 (1-56763-100-2) Ozark Pub.

—Harpo's Horrible Secret. Kelley, Barbara. Sargent, Dave, intro. by. 120p. (Orig.). (gr. k-8). 1993. text ed. 16.95 (1-56763-058-8); pap. text ed. 8.95 (1-56763-059-6) Ozark Pub.

—Slow Joe. Kassel, April. Sargent, Dave, intro. by. 36p. (Orig.). (gr. k-8). 1993. text ed. 12.95 (1-56763-067-7); pap. text ed. 5.95 (1-56763-068-5) Ozark Pub.

Block, Ruth W. Benji Bear's Race. Shelton, Ingrid. 35p. (Orig.). (ps-2). 1992. pap. 2.50 (0-919797-74-1) Kindred Pr.

Blocker, Kearn. Multicultural Social Studies Unit: Who Am I? Clarke, Joy A. 150p. (gr. 3-8). 1991. 3-ring binder 79.95 (0-9626984-1-5); pap. 69.95 (0-685-62443-9) Clarke Enterprise.

Blonder, Ellen. Bunny's ABC Box. Silverman, Maida. 24p. (ps-1). 1986. pap. 3.95 (0-448-01464-5, G&D) Putnam Pub Group.

—My Very First Things. (ps) 1988. bds. 2.50 (0-448-09253-0, G&D) Putnam Pub Group.

Blonski, Maribeth. Story of the Christmas Bear. Foreman, Donna. 40p. (gr. k-3). 1992. 7.95 (1-880851-02-4) Greene Bark Pr.

Bloom, Lloyd. Arthur, for the Very First Time. MacLachlan, Patricia. LC 79-2007. 128p. (gr. 4-7). 1980. PLB 13.89 (0-06-024047-4) HarpC Child Bks.

—Arthur, for the Very First Time. MacLachlan, Patricia. LC 79-2007. 128p. (gr. 3-6). 1989. pap. 3.95 (0-06-440288-6, Trophy) HarpC Child Bks.

—But No Candy. Houston, Gloria. 30p. (ps-3). 1992. PLB 14.95 (0-399-22142-5, Philomel Bks) Putnam Pub Group.

—Ghost Catcher. Haseley, Dennis. LC 91-4426. 40p. (gr. 1-5). 1991. PLB 15.89 (0-06-022247-6) HarpC Child Bks.

—Goathered & the Shepherdess. Hort, Lenny. LC 93-18178. 1994. 14.99 (0-8037-1352-5); PLB 14.89 (0-8037-1353-3) Dial Bks Young.

—The Green Book. Paton Walsh, Jill. LC 81-12620. 80p. (gr. 5 up). 1982. 13.00 (0-374-32778-5) FS&G.

—Grey Cloud. Graeber, Charlotte T. LC 79-14673. 128p. (gr. 3-7). 1984. SBE 12.95 (0-02-736910-2, Four Winds) Macmillan Child Grp.

—Hear O Israel: A Story of the Warsaw Ghetto. Treseder, Terry W. LC 89-7029. 48p. (gr. 3 up). 1990. SBE 13.95 (0-689-31456-6, Atheneum Child Bk) Macmillan Child Grp.

—Like Jake & Me. Jukes, Mavis. LC 83-8380. 32p. (gr. k up). 1984. PLB 13.99 (0-394-95608-7) Knopf Bks Yng Read.

—Like Jake & Me. Jukes, Mavis. LC 83-8380. 32p. (gr. 1-5). 1987. pap. 6.00 (0-394-89263-1) Knopf Bks Yng Read.

—The Maid of the North: Feminist Folk Tales from Around the World. Phelps, Ethel J. LC 80-21500. 196p. (gr. 4-6). 1981. (Bks Young Read); pap. 9.95 (0-8050-0679-6) H Holt & Co.

—A Man Named Thoreau. Burleigh, Robert. LC 85-7947. 48p. (gr. 3 up). 1985. SBE 13.95 (0-689-31122-2, Atheneum Child Bk) Macmillan Child Grp.

—Poems for Jewish Holidays. Livingston, Myra C., selected by. LC 85-27179. 32p. (ps-4). 1986. reinforced bdg. 13.95 (0-8234-0606-7) Holiday.

—The Secret of Sambatyon. Winkler, Gershon. Goldman, Bonnie, ed. 132p. (gr. 4 up). 1987. 6.95 (0-910818-68-1); pap. 5.95 (0-910818-69-X) Judaica Pr.

—Yonder. Johnston, Tony. LC 86-11549. 32p. (ps-3). 1988. 12.95 (0-8037-0277-9); PLB 12.89 (0-8037-0278-7) Dial Bks Young.

—Yonder. Johnston, Tony. LC 86-11549. 32p. (ps-3). 1991. pap. 4.95 (0-8037-0987-0, Dial Pied Piper) Puffin Bks.

Bloom, Suzanne. A Family for Jamie: An Adoption Story. Bloom, Suzanne. LC 90-42589. 24p. (ps-1). 1991. 13.00 (0-517-57492-6, Clarkson Potter); PLB 13.99 (0-517-57493-4, C N Potter Bks) Crown Bks Yng Read.

—We Keep a Pig in the Parlor. Bloom, Suzanne. 32p. (ps-1). 1988. 13.95 (0-517-56829-2, Clarkson Potter) Crown Bks Yng Read.

Bloom, Tom. Vicki Cobb's Papermaking Book & Kit. Cobb, Vicki. 32p. (gr. 2-6). 1993. 16.95 (0-694-00467-7, Festival) HarpC Child Bks.

Bluestone, Sara. Crab-Bags & Other Bean-Beings. Park, Margaret. (gr. 5 up). 1979. pap. 2.95 (0-915556-05-7) Great Ocean.

Blumenfeld, Rochelle. The Little Leaf. Sharfstein, Chana. Rosenfeld, Dina, ed. 32p. (gr. k-4). 1989. 8.95 (0-922613-18-4); pap. 6.95 (0-922613-19-2) Hachai Pubns.

Blumenschein, E. L. Indian Boyhood. Eastman, Charles A. LC 68-58282. (gr. 3-7). 1971. pap. 4.95 (0-486-22037-0) Dover.

Blumenstein, Amy. Henry: The Heron. MacHaffie, Ingeborg. Mouck, Mike, frwd. by. 55p. (Orig.). (ps). 1988. lib. bdg. 7.95 (0-9609374-3-9) Skribent.

Blundell, Tony. Funny Stories. Rosen, Michael, compiled by. LC 92-26447. 256p. (gr. 4-9). 1993. 6.95 (1-85697-883-4) Kingfisher Bks.

Blythe, Gary. The Whales' Song. Sheldon, Dyan. LC 90-46722. 32p. (ps-3). 1991. 15.99 (0-8037-0972-2) Dial Bks Young.

—When the Earth Was Large. Sheldon, Dyan. LC 93-11711. 1994. write for info. (0-8037-1670-2) Dial Bks Young.

Boardman, Diane. Hands on Puget Sound: An Interactive Workbook for the Young & Curious. Kolb, James A. 80p. (Orig.). (gr. 3-7). 1994. pap. text ed. 5.95 (1-57061-000-2) Sasquatch Bks.

—Red Hot Peppers. Boardman, Bob. 64p. (Orig.). (gr. 3 up). 1993. pap. 12.95 incl. speed rope (0-912365-78-1) Sasquatch Bks.

—Red Hot Peppers: The Skookum Book of Jump Rope Games, Rhymes, & Fancy Footwork. Boardman, Bob. 64p. (Orig.). (gr. 3 up). 1993. pap. 8.95 (0-912365-74-9) Sasquatch Bks.

Bobak, Cathy. Bernie, the Beagle Who Liked German Cooking. Rossbach, Jean. LC 90-21782. 64p. (gr. 1-7). 1991. SBE 13.95 (0-02-777787-1, Bradbury Pr) Macmillan Child Grp.

—Burton & the Giggle Machine. Haas, Dorothy. LC 91-25411. 160p. (gr. 5-8). 1992. SBE 13.95 (0-02-738203-6, Bradbury Pr) Macmillan Child Grp.

—Burton's Zoom Zoom Va-Rooom Machine. Haas, Dorothy. LC 89-77426. 144p. (gr. 5-8). 1990. SBE 13.95 (0-02-738201-X, Bradbury Pr) Macmillan Child Grp.

—Tom Foolery. Parkinson, Curtis. LC 92-7852. 32p. (ps-2). 1993. RSBE 13.95 (0-02-770025-9, Bradbury Pr) Macmillan Child Grp.

—When Your Parents Get a Divorce. Banks, Ann. 64p. (gr. 3 up). 1990. pap. 7.95 (0-14-034340-7, Puffin) Puffin Bks.

Bobak, Molly. Toes in My Nose: And Other Poems. Fitch, Sheree. 48p. (gr. 1-5). 1993. pap. 6.95 (1-56397-127-5, Wordsong) Boyds Mills Pr.

Bobbish, John. Trail Fever: The Life of a Texas Cowboy. Lightfoot, D. J. LC 92-5458. 1992. write for info. (0-688-11537-3) Lothrop.

Bochak, Grayce. Paper Boats. Tagore, Rabindranath. LC 91-72987. 32p. (ps-3). 1992. 14.95 (1-878093-12-6) Boyds Mills Pr.

Bock, William S. Blackbeard the Pirate & Other Stories of the Pine Barrens. Homer, Larona. 96p. (gr. 3-5). 1987. pap. 8.95 (0-912608-04-8) Mid Atlantic.

—Fur Trappers & Traders: The Indians, the Pilgrims, & the Beaver. Siegel, Beatrice. LC 80-7671. 64p. (gr. 3-7). 1987. PLB 11.85 (0-8027-6397-9) Walker & Co.

—Growing up Indian. Wolfson, Evelyn. LC 86-9053. 96p. (gr. 10 up). 1986. 10.95 (0-8027-6643-9); PLB 11.85 (0-8027-6644-7) Walker & Co.

—Jamestown: The Beginning. Campbell, Elizabeth A. 96p. (gr. 4-6). 1974. lib. bdg. 15.95 (0-316-12599-7) Little.

—Only the Names Remain: The Cherokees & the Trail of Tears. Bealer, Alex. (gr. 4-6). 1972. lib. bdg. 15.95 (0-316-08520-0) Little.

—The Shore Ghosts & Other Stories of New Jersey. Homer, Larona. 154p. (gr. 4-8). 1986. 8.95 (0-912608-14-5) Mid Atlantic.

—The World of Young George Washington. Hilton, Suzanne. LC 86-13296. 112p. (gr. 5-9). 1987. 12.95 (0-8027-6657-9); PLB 12.85 (0-8027-6658-7) Walker & Co.

—The World of Young Tom Jefferson. Hilton, Suzanne. 96p. (gr. 3-6). 1986. 12.95 (0-8027-6621-8); lib. bdg. 12.85 (0-8027-6622-6) Walker & Co.

Bock, William S. & Jensen, Debbie. Malcolm Yucca Seed. rev. ed. Gessner, Lynne. 64p. (gr. 3-8). pap. 5.95 (0-918080-63-0) Treasure Chest.
Bock, William S., photos by. From Abenaki to Zuni: A Dictionary of Native American Tribes. Wolfson, Evelyn. (gr. 5 up). 1988. 17.95 (0-8027-6789-3); PLB 18.85 (0-8027-6790-7) Walker & Co.
Boddy, Jo. Tall Corn: A Tall Tale. Van Woerkom, Dorothy. McKissack, Patricia & McKissack, Fredrick, eds. LC 87-61641. 32p. (Orig.). (gr. 1-3). 1987. text ed. 8.95 (0-88335-730-5); pap. text ed. 4.95 (0-88335-750-X) Milliken Pub Co.
Boddy, Joe. Blue Ben. Greene, Carol. McKissack, Patricia & McKissack, Fredrick, eds. LC 87-61649. 32p. (Orig.). (gr. 1-3). 1987. text ed. 8.95 (0-88335-722-4); pap. text ed. 4.95 (0-88335-742-9) Milliken Pub Co.
—A Christmas Carol. Dickens, Charles. LC 91-9054. 48p. (ps-2). 1991. Animal version. 6.95 (0-88101-160-6) Unicorn Pub.
—A Christmas Carol. 48p. (ps-2). 1992. 5.95 (0-88101-263-7) Unicorn Pub.
—Countdown to Christmas. 48p. (ps). 1992. 6.95 (0-88101-230-0) Unicorn Pub.
—First Steamboat down the Mississippi. Fichter, George S. LC 88-30308. 112p. (gr. 4-6). 1989. 9.95 (0-88289-715-2) Pelican.
—The First Zoo. Gambill, Henrietta G. 32p. (gr. k-2). 1989. pasted 2.50 (0-87403-592-9, 3852) Standard Pub.
—Hallelujah the Clown: A Story of Blessing & Discovery. Long, Kathy. LC 92-70384. 32p. (ps-k). 1992. pap. 4.99 (0-8066-2560-0, 9-2560, Augsburg) Augsburg Fortress.
—K'tonton's Sukkot Adventure. Weilerstein, Sadie R. LC 93-2990. 34p. (ps-3). 1993. 12.95 (0-8276-0502-1) JPS Phila.
—Mixed-Up Sam. Moore, Elaine. McKissack, Patricia & McKissack, Fredrick, eds. LC 88-60390. 32p. (Orig.). (gr. 1-3). 1988. text ed. 8.95 (0-88335-786-0); pap. text ed. 4.95 (0-88335-798-4) Milliken Pub Co.
—The Mystery of the Fallen Tree. Christian, Mary B. (ps-8). 1991. 8.95 (0-88335-274-5, AH56); pap. 4.95 (0-88335-288-5, AS56) Milliken Pub Co.
—The Mystery of the Message from the Sky. Christian, Mary B. (ps-8). 1991. 8.95 (0-88335-298-2, AH57); pap. 4.95 (0-88335-289-3, AS57) Milliken Pub Co.
—The Mystery of the Message from the Sky. Christian, Mary B. 32p. 1991. pap. 4.95 (0-685-50187-6) Milliken Pub Co.
—The Mystery of the Midnight Raider. Christian, Mary B. (ps-8). 1991. 8.95 (0-88335-271-0, AH53); pap. 4.95 (0-88335-285-0, AS53) Milliken Pub Co.
—The Mystery of the Missing Red Wagon. Christian, Mary B. (ps-8). 1991. 8.95 (0-88335-286-9, AH54); pap. 4.95 (0-88335-272-9, AS54) Milliken Pub Co.
—The Mystery of the Missing Scarf. Christian, Mary B. Bolinske, Janet L., ed. LC 88-60630. 32p. (Orig.). (gr. 1-3). 1989. text ed. 8.95 (0-88335-596-5); pap. text ed. 4.95 (0-88335-549-3) Milliken Pub Co.
—The Mystery of the Polluted Stream. Christian, Mary B. (ps-8). 1991. 8.95 (0-88335-299-0, AH58); pap. 4.95 (0-88335-290-7, AS58) Milliken Pub Co.
—The Mystery of the Unsigned Valentine. Christian, Mary B. (ps-8). 1991. 8.95 (0-88335-273-7, AH55); pap. 4.95 (0-88335-287-7, AS55) Milliken Pub Co.
—The North Pole Mystery. Christian, Mary B. Bolinske, Janet L., ed. LC 88-60633. 32p. (Orig.). (gr. 1-3). 1989. text ed. 8.95 (0-88335-593-0); pap. text ed. 4.95 (0-88335-597-3) Milliken Pub Co.
—The Pet Day Mystery. Christian, Mary B. Bolinske, Janet L., ed. LC 88-60631. 32p. (Orig.). (gr. 1-3). 1989. text ed. 8.95 (0-88335-595-7); pap. text ed. 4.95 (0-88335-599-X) Milliken Pub Co.
—Robinson Rabbit, What Do You Hear? Laird, Rebecca. LC 89-82550. 32p. (ps-k). 1990. pap. 5.99 (0-8066-2463-9, 9-2463) Augsburg Fortress.
—The Sherlock Street Detectives Package. Christian, Mary B. Bolinske, Janet L., ed. (Orig.). (gr. 1-3). 1989. text ed. 32.00 (0-88335-591-4); pap. text ed. 18.00 (0-88335-592-2) Set of 4 books, 32 pp. each. Milliken Pub Co.
—Silent Night: A Mouse Tale. Hernandez, Betsy & Monk, Donny. 48p. (ps-5). 1992. write for info. (0-917143-17-5) Sparrow TN.
—Special Strengths. Radley, Gail. 64p. (gr. 2-6). 1984. pap. 6.50 (0-87743-702-5, Pub. by Bellwood Pr) Bahai.
—The UFO Mystery. Christian, Mary B. Bolinske, Janet L., ed. LC 88-60632. 32p. (Orig.). (gr. 1-3). 1989. text ed. 8.95 (0-88335-594-9); pap. text ed. 4.95 (0-88335-598-1) Milliken Pub Co.
Boddy, Joe & Boddy, Joe. Bremen Town Musicians. Evans, Eugene. LC 90-10974. 48p. (gr. 1-5). 1990. 5.95 (0-88101-102-9) Unicorn Pub.
Bode, Daniel. Good Sports. Vail, Virginia. LC 89-31345. 128p. (gr. 4-6). 1990. lib. bdg. 9.89 (0-8167-1629-3); pap. text ed. 2.95 (0-8167-1630-7) Troll Assocs.
—Happy Trails. Vail, Virginia. LC 89-30584. 128p. (gr. 4-6). 1990. PLB 9.89 (0-8167-1627-7); pap. text ed. 2.95 (0-8167-1628-5) Troll Assocs.
—Horse Play. Vail, Virginia. LC 89-31347. 128p. (gr. 4-6). 1990. lib. bdg. 9.89 (0-8167-1659-5); pap. text ed. 2.95 (0-8167-1660-9) Troll Assocs.
—Horseback Summer. Vail, Virginia. LC 89-30583. 128p. (gr. 4-6). 1990. lib. bdg. 9.89 (0-8167-1625-0); pap. text ed. 2.95 (0-8167-1626-9) Troll Assocs.

—Riding Home. Vail, Virginia. LC 89-34548. 128p. (gr. 4-6). 1990. PLB 9.89 (0-8167-1661-7); pap. text ed. 2.95 (0-8167-1662-5) Troll Assocs.
—Surprise! Surprise! Vail, Virginia. LC 89-31346. 128p. (gr. 4-6). 1990. lib. bdg. 9.89 (0-8167-1657-9); pap. text ed. 2.95 (0-8167-1658-7) Troll Assocs.
Bodecker, N. M. Half Magic. Eager, Edward. LC 54-5153. 217p. (gr. 3-7). 1954. 14.95 (0-15-233078-X, HB Juv Bks) HarBrace.
—Knight's Castle. Eager, Edward. (gr. 4-6). 16.75 (0-8446-6232-1) Peter Smith.
—Magic or Not? Eager, Edward. (gr. 4-6). 1984. 16.75 (0-8446-6154-6) Peter Smith.
—The Time Garden. Eager, Edward. (gr. 4-6). 17.50 (0-8446-6233-X) Peter Smith.
Bodecker, N. M., jt. illus. see Treherne, Katie T.
Boden, Art. Boden's Beasts. Boden, Arthur & Woodside, John. (gr. 1-5). 1964. 8.95 (0-8392-3045-1) Astor-Honor.
Bodmer, Karl. An Indian Winter. Freedman, Russell. LC 91-24205. 96p. (gr. 5 up). 1992. 21.95 (0-8234-0930-9) Holiday.
Bodmer, Karl, jt. illus. see Catlin, George.
Boe, David. Make Your Own Video. Schwartz, Perry. 64p. (gr. 5 up). 1991. PLB 19.95 (0-8225-2301-9) Lerner Pubns.
Boehm, Terrie W. Tap the Deck. Knight, Tanis & Lewin, Larry. Hrebic, Herbert J., ed. (Orig.). (gr. 5-6). 1985. text ed. 9.10 (0-933282-18-4); pap. text ed. 6.00 (0-933282-17-6) Stack the Deck.
Boeller, Cheryl. Do I Have a Daddy? A Story about a Single-Parent Child. 2nd ed. Lindsay, Jeanne W. LC 90-49676. 48p. (ps-1). 1991. 12.95 (0-930934-45-8); pap. 5.95 (0-930934-44-X) Morning Glory.
—Yo Tengo Papa? Do I Have a Daddy? Un Cuento Sobre Un Nino de Madre Soltera, A Story about a Single-Parent Child. Lindsay, Jeanne W. Palacios, Argentina, tr. (SPA.). 48p. (Orig.). (ps-3). Date not set. 12.95 (0-930934-83-0); pap. 5.95 (0-930934-82-2) Morning Glory.
Boerke, Carol. Toddlers Bedtime Storybook. Beers, V. Gilbert. 352p. (ps). 1993. 14.99 (1-56476-181-9, Victor Books) SP Pubns.
Boerke, Carole. Little Bear Finds a Friend. Meyer, Kathleen. 32p. (gr. k-2). 1991. pasted 2.50 (0-87403-815-4, 24-03915) Standard Pub.
—Little Bear's Big Adventure. Meyer, Kathleen A. 32p. (gr. k-2). 1990. pasted 2.50 (0-87403-706-9, 24-03906) Standard Pub.
Boethner, Sandra, jt. illus. see Sioles, Anna M.
Bogacki, Tomek. Crackling Brat. Matthews, Andrew. 32p. (gr. k-3). 1993. PLB 15.95 (0-8050-2608-8, Bks Young Read) H Holt & Co.
—The Giant from the Little Island. Kreye, Walter. LC 89-43726. 32p. (ps-3). 1990. 13.95 (1-55858-085-9) North-South Bks NYC.
Bogan, Paulette. One Hundred One Ways to Do Better in School. Colman, Penny. LC 93-30872. 1993. pap. write for info. (0-8167-3285-X) Troll Assocs.
Bogart, Ann, photos by. Thinking Green: My Home. 24p. (ps-k). 1993. 3.98 (0-8317-2530-3) Smithmark.
—Thinking Green: My Neighborhood. 24p. (ps-k). 1993. 3.98 (0-8317-2529-X) Smithmark.
Bogdanovic, Toma. The Snow Queen. Andersen, Hans Christian. Lewis, Naomi, adapted by. LC 68-17218. 32p. (ps-5). 9.95 (0-87592-048-9) Scroll Pr.
—The Ugly Duckling. Andersen, Hans Christian. LC 75-145207. 32p. (ps-3). 9.95 (0-87592-055-1) Scroll Pr.
Bogdanowicz, Basia. Asleep at Last. Lipniacka, Ewa. LC 92-33326. 1993. 6.95 (1-56656-118-3, Crocodile Bks) Interlink Pub.
—It's Mine! Lipniacka, Ewa. LC 92-33324. 1993. 6.95 (1-56656-119-1, Crocodile Bks) Interlink Pub.
—School Trip. Lipniacka, Ewa. LC 92-33325. 1993. 6.95 (1-56656-121-3, Crocodile Bks) Interlink Pub.
—To Bed...or Else! Lipniacka, Ewa. LC 91-22118. 32p. (ps-3). 1992. 13.95 (0-940793-85-7, Crocodile Bks) Interlink Pub.
—Tooth Fairy. Lipniacka, Ewa. LC 92-33328. 1993. 6.95 (1-56656-120-5, Crocodile Bks) Interlink Pub.
Bohl, Al. Ben Hur. Wallace, Lew. Larson, Dan, ed. 224p. (Orig.). (gr. 6 up). 1990. pap. text ed. 2.50 (1-55748-114-8) Barbour & Co.
—The Dark Secret of the Ouija. Modica, Terry A. 224p. (gr. 9-12). 1990. pap. text ed. 2.50 (1-55748-138-5) Barbour & Co.
—Jesus. Larsen, Dan. 224p. (gr. 4-8). 1989. pap. text ed. 2.50 (1-55748-100-8) Barbour & Co.
—The Pilgrim's Progress. Bunyan, John. Larsen, Dan, ed. 224p. (gr. 4-8). 1989. pap. text ed. 2.50 (1-55748-099-0) Barbour & Co.
—Zaanan: Fatal Limit. Bohl, Al. 224p. (gr. 4-8). 1989. pap. text ed. 2.50 (1-55748-101-6) Barbour & Co.
Bohlke, Dorothee. Cokolina & the Wild Island. Bohlke, Dorothee. Max, Jill & Bradford, Elizabeth, eds. Verlag, Mangold, tr. LC 91-24337. 24p. (gr. k-3). 1991. PLB 14.60 (1-56074-032-9) Garrett Ed Corp.
—Mr. Chang & the Yellow Robe. Bohlke, Dorothee. Bradford, Elizabeth, ed. Verlag, Mangold, tr. from GER. LC 91-21303. 32p. (gr. k-3). 1991. PLB 14.60 (1-56074-029-9) Garrett Ed Corp.
Bohonek, Jan & Bohonek, Stan B. How Peter Molar Looked for a Smile. Bohonek, Jan B. & Bohonek, Stan B. Johnsen, David C. LC 83-73507. 32p. (gr. 1-3). 1984. PLB 9.95 (0-914827-00-6) Adonis Studio.
Bohonek, Stan B., jt. illus. see Bohonek, Jan.

Boix, Manuel. The Magic Box, Level 3. Brenner, Barbara. 1990. PLB 9.99 (0-553-05896-7, Little Rooster); pap. 3.50 (0-553-34926-0, Little Rooster) Bantam.
—Socrates. Moessinger, Pierre. LC 92-44060. 1993. 14.95 (0-88682-606-3) Creative Ed.
Bolam, Emily. The Elephant's Child. Kipling, Rudyard. LC 91-19378. 24p. (gr. k up). 1992. 13.95 (0-525-44862-4, DCB) Dutton Child Bks.
—House That Jack Built. (gr. k up). 1993. 14.00 (0-525-44972-8, DCB) Dutton Child Bks.
Boldorini, Maria G. My First Bible. 12p. (ps-1). 1994. 6.99 (0-679-85621-8) Random Bks Yng Read.
Bolduc, Susan. A Gift to America. Gardner, Jane M. 32p. (gr. k-3). 1986. pap. 3.95 (0-9617183-0-7) Gardner Pub.
Boldway, John. Believing in Yourself: Songbook for Children. Stevens, Jill & Gaskill, Rebecca. Sacks, Jonathan. 70p. (Orig.). (ps up). 1987. pap. 10.95 spiral bound (1-877614-00-9) Two Wings.
—We Are Free! Songbook: Children's Songs of America. Stevens, Jill. Sacks, Jonathan, contrib. by. 72p. (Orig.). (ps-5). 1989. pap. 10.95 spiral bound (1-877614-04-1) Two Wings.
Boldway, John & Stevens, Jill. A Happy Life Songbook: Imagination Songs for Children. Stevens, Jill. Sacks, Jonathan, contrib. by. 63p. (Orig.). (ps-5). 1988. pap. 10.95 spiral bound (1-877614-02-5) Two Wings.
Boles, Terry. Can Elephants Drink Through Their Noses? The Strange Things People Say about Animals at the Zoo. Dennard, Deborah. LC 92-9956. 1992. 19.95 (0-87614-720-1) Carolrhoda Bks.
Bolle, Frank. The Case of the Silk King. large type ed. Gilligan, Shannon. 114p. (gr. 3-7). 1987. Repr. of 1986 ed. 8.95 (0-942545-14-1); PLB 9.95 (0-942545-19-2, Dist. by Grolier) Grey Castle.
—Great Horror Stories. Ross, Harriet, ed. 160p. (gr. 3-9). 1992. pap. 11.95 (0-87460-188-6) Lion Bks.
—Great Mystery Stories. Ross, Harriet, compiled by. 160p. (gr. 3-9). 1993. pap. 8.95 (0-87460-194-0) Lion Bks.
—Great Stories about Horses. Ross, Harriet, compiled by. LC 63-18759. 160p. (gr. 3-9). 1992. PLB 10.95 (0-87460-202-5) Lion Bks.
—Soccer: The Game & How to Play It. rev. ed. Rosenthal, Gary. LC 72-129116. 256p. (gr. 3-9). 1978. PLB 14.95 (0-87460-258-0) Lion Bks.
Bollen, Roger. Alistair & the Alien Invasion. Sadler, Marilyn. LC 92-22828. 1994. pap. 14.00 (0-671-75957-4, S&S BFYR) S&S Trade.
—Alistair's Elephant. Sadler, Marilyn. 44p. (Orig.). (gr. k-3). 1986. pap. 5.95 (0-13-022773-0) P-H.
—Alistair's Time Machine. Sadler, Marilyn. 40p. (ps up). 1992. pap. 13.95 jacketed (0-671-66679-7, S&S BFYR); pap. 5.95 (0-671-68493-0, S&S BFYR) S&S Trade.
—Bedtime for Bunnies. Sadler, Marilyn. 14p. (ps). 1994. bds. 3.99 (0-679-83868-6) Random Bks Yng Read.
—Elizabeth & Larry. Sadler, Marilyn. LC 89-11552. 1992. pap. 13.95 jacketed (0-671-69189-9, S&S BFYR); pap. 4.95 (0-671-77817-X, S&S BFYR) S&S Trade.
—It's Not Easy Being a Bunny. Sadler, Marilyn. LC 83-2680. 48p. (gr. k-3). 1983. 6.95 (0-394-86102-7); lib. bdg. 7.99 (0-394-96102-1) Beginner.
—Knock, Knock, It's P. J. Funnybunny! Sadler, Marilyn. 24p. (ps-1). 1992. 8.00 (0-679-81733-6) Random Bks Yng Read.
—Nanny Goat & the Lucky Kid. Sadler, Marilyn. (ps-k). 1991. pap. write for info. (0-307-11514-3, Golden Pr) Western Pub.
—P.J. The Spoiled Bunny. Sadler, Marilyn. LC 85-19650. 32p. (ps-k). 1986. lib. bdg. 5.99 (0-394-97245-7); pap. 2.25 (0-394-87245-2) Random Bks Yng Read.
Bolles, Stephen. Whales in the Classroom, Vol. I: Oceanography. Wade, Larry. 130p. (gr. 4-8). 1992. pap. text ed. 14.95 (0-9629395-0-1) Singing Rock.
—Whales in the Classroom, Vol. 1: Oceanography. 2nd ed. Wade, Larry. 133p. (gr. 4-8). 1993. pap. 14.95 (0-9629395-1-X) Singing Rock.
Bollinger, Kristine. Songs for a Merry Christmas. Roth, Kevin. 24p. (Orig.). (ps-1). 1992. pap. 9.95 incl. cass. (0-679-83253-X) Random Bks Yng Read.
Bolognese, Don. Big & Little. Smith, William J. LC 91-66057. 32p. (gr. 5 up). 1992. 15.95 (1-56397-023-6, Wordsong) Boyds Mills Pr.
—Buffalo Bill & the Pony Express. Coerr, Eleanor. LC 93-24261. 1995. write for info. (0-06-023372-9); PLB write for info. (0-06-023373-7) HarpC Child Bks.
—George the Drummer Boy. Benchley, Nathaniel. LC 76-18398. 64p. (gr. k-3). 1977. PLB 13.89 (0-06-020501-6) HarpC Child Bks.
—George the Drummer Boy. Benchley, Nathaniel. LC 76-18398. 64p. (gr. k-3). 1987. pap. 3.50 (0-06-444106-7, Trophy) HarpC Child Bks.
—Ghost of Windy Hill. Bulla, Clyde R. LC 68-11059. (gr. 3-7). 1968. PLB 13.89 (0-690-32764-1, Crowell Jr Bks) HarpC Child Bks.
—The Skeleton Inside You. Balestrino, Philip. LC 85-42982. 40p. (ps-3). 1986. pap. 4.95 (0-06-445039-2, Trophy) HarpC Child Bks.
—Wagon Wheels. newly illus. ed. Brenner, Barbara. LC 92-18780. 64p. (gr. k-3). 1978. 14.00 (0-06-020668-3); PLB 13.89 (0-06-020669-1) HarpC Child Bks.
—The Warrior Goddess: Athena. Gates, Doris. (gr. 3-7). 1982. pap. 4.99 (0-14-031530-6, Puffin) Puffin Bks.

Bolognese, Don & Raphael, Elaine. Letters to Horseface: Young Mozart's Travels in Italy. Monjo, F. N. 96p. (gr. 3 up). 1991. pap. 7.95 *(0-14-034801-8,* Puffin) Puffin Bks.
—The Way to Draw & Color Dinosaurs. Bolognese, Don & Raphael, Elaine. LC 90-8636. 48p. (Orig.). (gr. 1-7). 1991. lib. bdg. 10.99 *(0-679-90477-8);* pap. 6.00 *(0-679-80477-3)* Random Bks Yng Read.
—The Way to Draw & Color Monsters. Bolognese, Don & Raphael, Elaine. LC 90-8637. 48p. (Orig.). (gr. 1-7). 1991. lib. bdg. 10.99 *(0-679-90478-6);* pap. 5.99 *(0-679-80478-1)* Random Bks Yng Read.
Bolognese, Don, jt. illus. see Raphael, Elaine.
Bologneze, Don. Wagon Wheels. newly illustrated ed. Brenner, Barbara. LC 92-18780. 64p. (gr. k-3). 1984. pap. 3.50 *(0-06-444052-4,* Trophy) HarpC Child Bks.
Bolster, Rob. Going Lobstering. Pallotta, Jerry. 32p. (Orig.). (ps-4). 1990. 15.95 *(0-88106-475-0);* pap. 7.95 *(0-88106-474-2)* Charlesbridge Pub.
Bolt, John. Moods & Emotions. Odor, Ruth S. LC 81-17008. 112p. (gr. 2-6). 1980. PLB 21.35 *(0-89565-210-2);* PLB 14.95s.p. *(0-685-55505-4)* Childs World.
—You & Me. Moncure, Jane B. LC 81-17009. 112p. (gr. 2-6). 1980. PLB 21.35 *(0-89565-212-9);* PLB 14.95s.p. *(0-685-55563-1)* Childs World.
Boltin, Lee & Arem, Joel, photos by. Rocks & Minerals. Arem, Joel. LC 91-74106. 160p. (gr. 7-12). 1991. pap. 8.95 *(0-945005-06-7)* Geoscience Pr.
Bolurchian, Flora. A Persian Reader Bk. 1: Farsi Biyamuzim: Ketab-E Aval. 2nd, rev. ed. Ayman, Lily. LC 93-61060. (PER.). 104p. (Orig.). (gr. 1). 1994. pap. text ed. 9.95x *(0-936347-34-1)* Iran Bks.
Bomzer, Barry. Dirt Bike Racer. Christopher, Matt. LC 79-745. (gr. 4-6). 1986. 14.95 *(0-316-13977-7);* pap. 3.95 *(0-316-14053-8)* Little.
Bonaforte, Lisa. Whales. Berger, Gilda. LC 86-16500. 48p. (gr. k-3). 1987. 11.99 *(0-685-18308-4);* PLB 10. 95 *(0-685-18309-2)* Doubleday.
Bonagurio, Susan. Animal Count. Bonagurio, Susan. Tunmore, Gary, ed. 22p. (ps). 1991. 12.95 *(0-924649-09-7);* PLB 15.95 *(0-924649-08-9);* pap. text ed. 9.95 *(0-685-48844-6)* Scribblers Pub.
Bond, Barbara H. Young Martin's Promise. Myers, Walter D. LC 92-18070. 32p. (gr. 2-5). 1992. PLB 21. 34 *(0-8114-7210-8)* Raintree Steck-V.
Bond, Bruce. Autumn. Allington, Richard L. & Krull, Kathleen. LC 80-25190. 32p. (gr. k-3). 1985. PLB 15. 96 *(0-8172-1343-0);* pap. text ed. 3.95 *(0-8114-8242-1)* Raintree Steck-V.
—Woolly the Wolf. LaFleur, Tom & Brennan, Gale. 16p. (Orig.). (gr. k-6). 1981. pap. 1.25 *(0-685-02459-8)* Brennan Bks.
Bond, Denny. The School Picnic. Steffy, Jan. LC 87-14867. 32p. (ps-3). 1987. 12.95 *(0-934672-52-0)* Good Bks PA.
Bond, Felicia. The Big Green Pocketbook. Ransom, Candice. LC 92-29393. 32p. (ps-2). 1993. 14.00 *(0-06-020848-1);* PLB 13.89 *(0-06-020849-X)* HarpC Child Bks.
—Big Red Barn. rev. ed. Brown, Margaret W. LC 85-45814. 32p. (ps-1). 1989. 14.00 *(0-06-020748-5);* PLB 13.89 *(0-06-020749-3)* HarpC Child Bks.
—Big Red Barn. Brown, Margaret W. LC 85-45814. 32p. (ps-1). 1991. 19.95 *(0-06-020750-7)* HarpC Child Bks.
—Big Red Barn. Brown, Margaret W. 32p. (ps-1). 1993. pap. 5.95 *(0-06-443349-8,* Trophy) HarpC Child Bks.
—Four Valentines in a Rainstorm. Bond, Felicia. LC 82-45586. 32p. (gr. k-3). 1990. pap. 3.95 *(0-06-443216-5,* Trophy) HarpC Child Bks.
—The Halloween Performance. Bond, Felicia. LC 82-45920. 32p. (ps-3). 1987. pap. 4.95 *(0-06-443155-X,* Trophy) HarpC Child Bks.
—How to Think Like a Scientist: Answering Questions by the Scientific Method. Kramer, Stephen P. LC 85-43604. 48p. (gr. 3-7). 1987. 14.00 *(0-690-04563-8,* Crowell Jr Bks);* PLB 13.89 *(0-690-04565-4,* Crowell Jr Bks)* HarpC Child Bks.
—If You Give a Moose a Muffin. Numeroff, Laura J. LC 91-2207. 32p. (ps-2). 1991. 14.00 *(0-06-024405-4);* PLB 13.89 *(0-06-024406-2)* HarpC Child Bks.
—If You Give a Muffin Big Book. Numeroff, Laura J. LC 91-2207. 32p. (ps-2). 1994. pap. 19.95 *(0-06-443366-8,* Trophy) HarpC Child Bks.
—If You Give a Mouse a Cookie. Numeroff, Laura J. LC 84-48343. 32p. (ps-2). 1985. 13.00 *(0-06-024586-7);* PLB 12.89 *(0-06-024587-5)* HarpC Child Bks.
—If You Give a Mouse a Cookie Box & Doll. Numeroff, Laura J. LC 91-46093. 32p. (ps-2). 1992. 16.95 *(0-694-00416-2,* Festival) HarpC Child Bks.
—Poinsettia & Her Family. Bond, Felicia. LC 81-43035. 32p. (ps-3). 1981. PLB 13.89 *(0-690-04145-4,* Crowell Jr Bks)* HarpC Child Bks.
—Poinsettia & Her Family. Bond, Felicia. LC 81-43035. 32p. (ps-3). 1985. pap. 4.95i *(0-06-443076-6,* Trophy) HarpC Child Bks.
—Poinsettia & the Firefighters. Bond, Felicia. LC 83-46169. 32p. (ps-3). 1988. pap. 4.95 *(0-06-443160-6,* Trophy) HarpC Child Bks.
—The Right Number of Elephants. Sheppard, Jeff. LC 90-4148. 32p. (ps-3). 1990. 12.95 *(0-06-025615-X);* PLB 12.89 *(0-06-025616-8)* HarpC Child Bks.
—The Right Number of Elephants. Sheppard, Jeff. LC 90-4148. 32p. (ps-3). 1992. pap. 4.95 *(0-06-443299-8,* Trophy) HarpC Child Bks.
—The Right Number of Elephants Big Book. Sheppard, Jeff. 32p. (ps-3). 1993. pap. 19.95 *(0-06-443338-2,* Trophy) HarpC Child Bks.

—The Sky Is Full of Stars. Branley, Franklyn M. LC 81-43037. 40p. (gr. k-3). 1983. pap. 4.50 *(0-06-445002-3,* Trophy) HarpC Child Bks.
Bond, Higgins. Ancient Rome. Cohen, Daniel. LC 90-1410. 48p. (gr. 2-6). 1992. 13.00 *(0-385-26066-0)* Doubleday.
—When I Was Little. Igus, Toyomi. LC 92-72006. 32p. (Orig.). (gr. 1 up). 1992. 14.95 *(0-940975-32-7);* pap. 6.95 *(0-940975-33-5)* Just Us Bks.
Bond, Janice. Elizabeth Cady Stanton: A Biography for Young Children. Schlank, Carol H. & Metzger, Barbara. 32p. (ps-2). 1991. lib. bdg. 14.95 *(0-87659-177-2);* pap. 6.95 *(0-87659-176-4)* Gryphon Hse.
Bond, Lahki. Spinning Tales, Weaving Hope: Stories, Storytelling & Activities for Peace, Justice, & the Environment. Brody, Ed, et al, eds. 288p. (Orig.). 1992. lib. bdg. 49.95 *(0-86571-228-X);* pap. 22.95 *(0-86571-229-8)* New Soc Pubs.
Bond, Magi. Mystery at Indian Rocks. Moore, Ruth N. LC 80-25803. 192p. (gr. 5-10). 1981. pap. 4.95 *(0-8361-1944-4)* Herald Pr.
Bond, Reed. Betsy's Butter. Bond, Reed. 16p. (Orig.). (gr. 1-3). 1992. pap. 4.50 *(0-9631992-1-8)* Bonding Place.
Boney, Lesley. Cities. 48p. (gr. k-5). 1988. pap. 2.95 *(0-8431-2248-X)* Price Stern.
—Dinosaurs. 48p. (gr. k-5). 1988. pap. 2.95 *(0-8431-2245-5)* Price Stern.
—Space. 48p. (gr. k-5). 1988. pap. 2.95 *(0-8431-2247-1)* Price Stern.
—Wild Animals. 48p. (gr. k-5). 1988. pap. 2.95 *(0-8431-2246-3)* Price Stern.
Boney, Leslie. All about Dinosaurs. Pearce, Q. L. (gr. 2 up). 1989. pap. 7.95 *(0-671-64517-X,* Little Simon) S&S Trade.
Bonforte, Lisa. Animal Babies. Dickinson, Rebecca. LC 87-81765. 22p. (ps). 1988. write for info. *(0-307-12116-X,* Pub. by Golden Bks) Western Pub.
—Giants of the Land. Pearce, Q. L. 48p. (gr. 3-7). 1993. pap. 5.95 *(1-56565-041-7)* Lowell Hse.
—Reptiles & Amphibians. Smith, Howard E. LC 89-29384. 1991. write for info. *(0-385-41177-4);* PLB write for info. *(0-385-41178-2)* Doubleday.
—Seal Pup Grows Up: The Story of the Harbor Seal. Zoehfeld, Kathleen W. LC 93-27269. 1994. 14.95 *(1-56899-026-X);* pap. 4.95 *(1-56899-027-8)* Soundprints.
—Whales & Sharks. Miller, Suzanne S. Klimo, Kate, ed. 48p. 1982. pap. 9.95 *(0-671-45148-0,* S&S BFYR) S&S Trade.
Bonin, Diana R. Button Breaker. Cosgrove, Stephen. 32p. (gr. k-5). 1993. PLB 12.95 *(1-56674-043-6,* HTS Bks) Forest Hse.
—Snicker Doodle. Cosgrove, Stephen. 32p. (gr. k-5). 1993. PLB 12.95 *(1-56674-044-4,* HTS Bks) Forest Hse.
—Tinkling. Cosgrove, Stephen. 32p. (gr. k-5). 1993. PLB 12.95 *(1-56674-045-2,* HTS Bks) Forest Hse.
—Tizzy. Cosgrove, Stephen. 32p. (gr. k-5). 1993. PLB 12. 95 *(1-56674-046-0,* HTS Bks) Forest Hse.
Bonner, R. Moo Moo. Brown Cow. Wood, J. 1992. 12.95 *(0-15-200533-1,* HB Juv Bks) HarBrace.
Bonner, Rog. Dads Are Such Fun. Wood, Jakki. LC 91-21517. 32p. (ps). 1992. pap. 12.00 jacketed *(0-671-75342-8,* S&S BFYR) S&S Trade.
Bonners, Susan. Cold Stars & Fireflies: Poems for the Four Seasons. Esbensen, Barbara J. LC 83-45051. 80p. (gr. 3-7). 1984. PLB 14.89 *(0-690-04363-5,* Crowell Jr Bks) HarpC Child Bks.
—I Am Four. Fitzhugh, Louise. LC 82-70309. 48p. (ps-k). 1982. pap. 8.95 *(0-385-28444-6);* pap. 8.89 *(0-385-28445-4)* Delacorte.
—Inside Turtle's Shell & Other Poems of the Field. Ryder, Joanne. LC 84-833. 64p. (gr. 2-5). 1985. RSBE 12.95 *(0-02-778010-4,* Macmillan Child Bk) Macmillan Child Grp.
—A Penguin Year. Bonners, Susan. LC 79-53595. 48p. (ps-3). 1981. 11.95 *(0-685-01398-7);* PLB 12.95 *(0-385-28022-X)* Delacorte.
—Rain Shadow. Newton, James R. LC 82-45927. 32p. (gr. 2-6). 1983. (Crowell Jr Bks); (Crowell Jr Bks) HarpC Child Bks.
Bonnett, Niki. Gilly the Goose. Mister Tom. 32p. (gr. 2-4). 1978. write for info. Oddo.
—Gilly the Goose. Mister Tom. 32p. (Orig.). (gr. k-4). 1989. pap. 5.95 *(0-925237-02-7)* Ten Pubns.
Bonno, Chris, jt. illus. see Deschaine, Scott.
Bonsall, Crosby. The Case of the Cat's Meow. Bonsall, Crosby. LC 65-11451. 64p. (gr. k-3). 1978. pap. 3.50 *(0-06-444017-6,* Trophy) HarpC Child Bks.
—The Case of the Hungry Stranger. newly illustrated ed. Bonsall, Crosby. LC 91-14365. 64p. (gr. k-3). 1980. pap. 3.50 *(0-06-444026-5,* Trophy) HarpC Child Bks.
—The Day I Had to Play with My Sister. Bonsall, Crosby. LC 72-76507. 32p. (ps-2). 1988. pap. 3.50 *(0-06-444117-2,* Trophy) HarpC Child Bks.
—Go Away, Dog. Nodset, Joan L. LC 63-11162. 32p. (ps-3). 1963. PLB 9.89 *(0-06-024556-5)* HarpC Child Bks.
—Go Away, Dog! reissued ed. Nodset, Joan L. LC 63-11162. (ps-3). 1963. 10.00 *(0-06-024555-7)* HarpC Child Bks.
—Mine's the Best. Bonsall, Crosby N. LC 72-9863. 32p. (ps-2). 1973. PLB 13.89 *(0-06-020578-4)* HarpC Child Bks.
—Piggle. Bonsall, Crosby N. LC 73-5478. 64p. (gr. k-3). 1973. PLB 13.89 *(0-06-020580-6)* HarpC Child Bks.

—Who's a Pest? Bonsall, Crosby. LC 62-13310. 64p. (gr. k-3). 1986. pap. 3.50 *(0-06-444099-0,* Trophy) HarpC Child Bks.
—Who's Afraid of the Dark? Bonsall, Crosby. LC 79-2700. 32p. (ps-2). 1985. pap. 3.50 *(0-06-444071-0,* Trophy) HarpC Child Bks.
Bonsall, Crosby N. Case of the Cat's Meow. Bonsall, Crosby N. LC 65-11451. 64p. (gr. k-3). 1965. PLB 13. 89 *(0-06-020561-X)* HarpC Child Bks.
—Case of the Dumb Bells. Bonsall, Crosby N. LC 66-8267. 64p. (gr. k-3). 1966. PLB 13.89 *(0-06-020624-1)* HarpC Child Bks.
—Case of the Hungry Stranger. newly illus. ed. Bonsall, Crosby N. LC 91-13345. 64p. (gr. k-3). 1963. 13.00 *(0-06-020570-9);* PLB 12.89 *(0-06-020571-7)* HarpC Child Bks.
—The Day I Had to Play with My Sister. Bonsall, Crosby N. LC 72-76507. 32p. (ps-2). 1972. PLB 13.89 *(0-06-020576-8)* HarpC Child Bks.
—It's Mine: A Greedy Book. Bonsall, Crosby N. LC 64-11839. 32p. (gr. k-3). 1964. PLB 13.89 *(0-06-020585-7)* HarpC Child Bks.
—What Spot? Bonsall, Crosby N. LC 63-8005. 64p. (gr. k-3). 1963. PLB 13.89 *(0-06-020611-X)* HarpC Child Bks.
—Who's a Pest? Bonsall, Crosby N. LC 62-13310. 64p. (gr. k-3). 1962. PLB 13.89 *(0-06-020621-7)* HarpC Child Bks.
Bookless, Nan. It Happens to Boys Too... Satullo, Jane, et al. 36p. (Orig.). (ps-6). 1988. pap. 6.50 *(0-9618618-0-0)* RCC-Berkshires Pr.
Boon, Emilie. A Cake for Barney. Dunbar, Joyce. LC 87-15294. 32p. (ps-2). 1988. 12.95 *(0-531-05735-6);* PLB 12.99 *(0-531-08335-7)* Orchard Bks Watts.
—Daddy, Can You Play with Me? Ziefert, Harriet. (ps-k). 1988. pap. 5.95 *(0-14-050895-3,* Puffin) Puffin Bks.
—It's Spring, Peterkin. Boon, Emilie. LC 85-62015. 14p. (ps). 1986. bds. 3.95 *(0-394-87997-X)* Random Bks Yng Read.
—Mommy, Where Are You? Ziefert, Harriet. (ps-k). 1988. pap. 5.95 *(0-14-050894-5,* Puffin) Puffin Bks.
Boonthanakit, Ted & Chacon, Joe. Demons Rule. Brown, Charles. Bell, Rob, ed. 32p. (Orig.). (gr. 12). 1990. pap. 7.00 *(1-55806-110-X,* 412) Iron Crown Ent Inc.
Booten, Kevin. Great American English Handbook. rev. ed. National Curriculum Publishing Editors. Snodgrass, Mary E., ed. 256p. (gr. 7 up). 1991. Repr. of 1987 ed. lib. bdg. 10.80 *(0-8000-2426-5,* 122550) Perma-Bound.
Booth, George. It's Not My Turn to Look for Grandma. Wayland, April H. LC 93-7018. 1994. 13.00 *(0-679-84491-0);* lib. bdg. 13.99 *(0-679-94491-5)* Knopf.
—Possum Come A-Knocking. Van Laan, Nancy. LC 88-12751. 32p. (ps-3). 1990. PLB 14.99 *(0-394-92206-9)* Knopf Bks Yng Read.
—Wacky Wednesday. Le Sieg, Theodore. LC 74-5520. 48p. (gr. k-4). 1974. 6.95 *(0-394-82912-3);* lib. bdg. 7.99 *(0-394-92912-8)* Beginner.
Booth, Graham. Henry the Explorer. Taylor, Mark. 48p. (ps-3). 1988. pap. 5.95 *(0-316-83384-3)* Little.
—My Tang's Tungled & Other Ridiculous Situations. Brewton, Sara, et al, eds. LC 73-254. 128p. (gr. 5 up). 1989. PLB 13.89 *(0-690-04778-9,* Crowell Jr Bks) HarpC Child Bks.
Booth, Tim. Silas Rat & the Nuclear Tail. O'Donovan, Dermot. 125p. 1988. pap. 7.95 *(0-947962-22-0,* Pub. by Children's Pr) Irish Bks Media.
Bootman, Collin. Young Frederick Douglass: The Slave Who Learned to Read. Girard, Linda W. LC 93-28245. 1994. write for info. *(0-8075-9463-6)* A Whitman.
Boratynski, Katrina & Giles, William B. The Magic Gem: A Story Coloring Book. Dass, Baba H. LC 76-10032. 32p. (Orig.). (ps-2). 1976. pap. 2.50 *(0-918100-07-0)* Sri Rama.
Boren, James H. The Case of the Pelican's Feather: An Ocean City, Maryland Novel. Fleetwood, Wade B. LC 91-77403. 296p. 1992. pap. 5.95 *(0-9631466-0-2)* W B Fleetwood.
Borgo, Deborah. The Brave Little Mouse. Rosenbluth, Rosalyn. 24p. (ps-2). 1993. pap. text ed. 0.99 *(1-56293-346-9)* McClanahan Bk.
—The Fuzzy Duckling. Teitelbaum, Michael, retold by. (ps-2). 1991. 5.25 *(0-307-15700-8,* Golden Pr) Western Pub.
—Just Like Mommy, Just Like Daddy. Leeka, M. C. 24p. (ps-2). 1993. pap. text ed. 0.99 *(1-56293-345-0)* McClanahan Bk.
—Scaredy-Cat Kitten. Rosenbluth, Rosalyn. 24p. (ps-2). 1993. pap. text ed. 0.99 *(1-56293-352-3)* McClanahan Bk.
Borgo, Deborah C. Christmas Alphabet Book. Whitehead, Patricia. LC 84-8830. 32p. (gr. k-2). 1985. PLB 11.59 *(0-8167-0365-5);* pap. text ed. 2.95 *(0-8167-0366-3)* Troll Assocs.
—Thomas the Tank Engine - Shapes & Sizes. Awdry, W., contrib. by. 14p. (ps). 1993. bds. 2.29 *(0-679-81643-7)* Random Bks Yng Read.
—Thomas the Tank Engine Counts to Ten. Awdry, W., contrib. by. 14p. (ps). 1993. bds. 2.29 *(0-679-81644-5)* Random Bks Yng Read.
—Umbrella Parade. Feczko, Kathy. LC 84-8650. 32p. (gr. k-2). 1985. PLB 11.59 *(0-8167-0356-6);* pap. text ed. 2.95 *(0-8167-0436-8)* Troll Assocs.
Borguald, Pamela M. I Think Divorce Stinks. Lebowitz, Marcia L. 16p. (Orig.). (gr. 7-10). 1989. pap. 4.95 *(0-935769-05-6)* CDC Pr.

Borja, Corinne & Borja, Robert. Making Chinese Paper Cuts. Borja, Corinne & Borja, Robert. Tucker, Kathleen, ed. LC 79-18358. (gr. 3-8). 1980. PLB 13.95 (0-8075-4948-7) A Whitman.

Borja, Robert. Explorers in a New World. McCall, Edith. LC 60-6675. 128p. (gr. 3-10). 1980. PLB 15.00 (0-516-03318-2) Childrens.

—Steamboats to the West. McCall, Edith. LC 59-3665. 128p. (gr. 3-10). 1980. PLB 15.00 (0-516-03368-9) Childrens.

Borja, Robert, jt. illus. see Borja, Corinne.

Bork, Beatrice. Free the Horses: Storybook & Songbook. Popkin, Michael H. Greathead, Susan D. & Sardinas-Wyssling, Karen, eds. 80p. (gr. 1-3). 1991. pap. 6.95 (0-9618020-7-3) Active Parenting.

Born, Flint. An Alphabet in Five Acts. Andersen, Karen B. LC 92-26947. 32p. 1993. 13.99 (0-8037-1440-8); PLB 13.89 (0-8037-1441-6) Dial Bks Young.

Bornschlegel, Ruth. Little Brother. Brown, Regina. (gr. 3-7). 1962. 8.95 (0-8392-3019-2) Astor-Honor.

Bornstein, Ruth. Little Gorilla. Bornstein, Ruth. LC 75-25508. 32p. (ps-3). 1986. 15.45 (0-395-28773-1, Clarion Bks); pap. 4.95 (0-89919-421-4, Clarion Bks) HM.

—Mama One, Mama Two. MacLachlan, Patricia. LC 81-47795. 32p. (gr. 1-3). 1982. 13.00 (0-06-024081-4); PLB 13.89 (0-06-024082-2) HarpC Child Bks.

Borovsky, Paul. George. Borovsky, Paul. LC 89-2022. (ps up). 1990. 12.95 (0-688-09150-4); PLB 12.88 (0-688-09151-2) Greenwillow.

—Nico. Borovsky, Paul. LC 92-13924. 32p. (ps-2). 1993. 14.00 (0-517-58854-4); PLB 14.99 (0-517-58855-2) Crown Bks Yng Read.

—The Strange Blue Creature. Borovsky, Paul. LC 92-54864. 32p. (ps-2). 1993. 13.95 (1-56282-434-1); PLB 13.89 (1-56282-435-X) Hyprn Child.

Borowik, Kathleen. You're the Detective! Twenty-Four Solve-Them-Yourself Picture Mysteries. Treat, Lawrence. LC 82-49346. 80p. (Orig.). (gr. 3-6). 1983. pap. 7.95 (0-87923-478-4) Godine.

Borowitz, Franz. Joey & Sam: A Heartwarming Storybook about Autism, a Family, & a Brother's Love. Katz, Illana & Ritvo, Edward. LC 92-38812. 40p. (gr. k-6). 1993. smythe sewn 16.95 (1-882388-00-3) Real Life Strybks.

—Show Me Where It Hurts. Katz, Illana & Rosenthal, Alan D. 40p. (gr. k-6). 1993. smythe sewn 16.95 (1-882388-01-1) Real Life Strybks.

—Uncle Jimmy. Katz, Illana. Schwartz, Stanley, epilogue by. 40p. (gr. k-6). 1993. Smythe Sewn 16.95 (1-882388-03-8) Real Life Strybks.

Borum, Shari. The Class in Room Forty-Four: When a Classmate Dies. Blackburn, Lynn B. Johnson, Joy, ed. 24p. (Orig.). (gr. 1-6). 1990. pap. 3.50 (1-56123-025-1) Centering Corp.

—Hurting Yourself: For Teens Who Have Attempted Suicide. Johnson, Joy & Johnson, Marvin. 24p. (Orig.). (gr. 9-12). 1986. pap. 2.65 (1-56123-038-3) Centering Corp.

—I Know I Made It Happen: A Book about Children & Guilt. Blackburn, Lynn B. Johnson, Joy, ed. 24p. (Orig.). (ps-6). 1990. pap. 3.50 (1-56123-016-2) Centering Corp.

—Katie's Premature Brother. Hawkins-Walsh, Elizabeth. Johnson, Joy, ed. 24p. (Orig.). (ps). 1990. pap. 2.65 (1-56123-005-7) Centering Corp.

—New Baby: A Coloring Book for Big Sisters & Brothers. Johnson, Joy & Johnson, Marvin. 24p. (Orig.). (ps). 1981. pap. 1.00 (1-56123-018-9) Centering Corp.

—No New Baby. Gryte, Marilyn. 24p. 1988. pap. 3.25 (1-56123-041-3) Centering Corp.

—Tell Me, Papa: A Family Book for Children's Questions about Death & Funerals. Johnson, Joy & Johnson, Marvin. 24p. (gr. 2-7). 1978. pap. 3.25 (1-56123-011-1) Centering Corp.

—This Time It's Me: For Teens Who Have Just Found out They're Pregnant. Vondra, Mary & Vondra, Lisa. 24p. (Orig.). 1985. pap. 2.65 (1-56123-042-1) Centering Corp.

—Timothy Duck: The Story of the Death of a Friend. Blackburn, Lynn B. Johnson, Joy, ed. 24p. (Orig.). (gr. 1-6). 1989. pap. 3.25 (1-56123-013-8) Centering Corp.

—Tim's Dad: A Story about a Boy Whose Father Dies. Hitchcock, Ruth. 24p. (gr. 4-6). 1988. pap. 2.65 (1-56123-045-6) Centering Corp.

—Where's Jess? Goldstein, Ray & Goldstein, Jody. 24p. (Orig.). 1982. pap. 3.25 (1-56123-009-X) Centering Corp.

Bosco, James & Carter, Fred. The Misadventures of Wags & Freckles Kid-Pak: A Lesson in the Dangers of Alcohol. rev. ed. Bosco, James. Lupo, Ann, ed. 28p. (ps-3). 1991. pap. text ed. 3.95 (1-56230-136-5); pap. text ed. 4.95 incl. audiotape (1-56230-126-8) Syndistar.

Bose, R. K. Legends from Northern India. Hasija, Nipla, retold by. (gr. 5-10). 1981. 7.25 (0-89744-241-5, Pub. by Hemkunt India) Auromere.

—More Stories from the Arabian Nights. Thomas, Vernon. 135p. (gr. 1 up). 1981. 7.50 (0-89744-232-6, Pub. by Hemkunt India) Auromere.

Bosmans, Serge. The Bloody Lotus. Mitchetz, Marc. Hansom, Dick, tr. from FRE. 49p. (Orig.). (gr. 12 up). 1990. pap. 7.95 (0-87416-103-7, Comcat Comics) Catalan Comunications.

Bosni, Nella. Two Little Monkeys. Magni, Laura. 18p. (ps-k). 1992. Set of 3 books. bds. 11.85 (1-56397-159-3); bds. 3.95 (1-56397-154-2) Boyds Mills Pr.

Boss, Jackie. A Hear Do'n Sing Book: Little Bitty You Little Bitty Me. Chadwick, Kenneth E. (ps). 1979. 4.25 (0-9603698-0-5) Bet-Ken Prods.

Bosson, Jo-Ellen. Fenton's Leap. Gray, Libba M. LC 92-19648. 1994. pap. 14.00 (0-671-79196-6, S&S BFYR) S&S Trade.

—Jackrabbit & the Prairie Fire: Story of a Black-Tailed Jackrabbit. Saunders, Susan. Thomas, Peter, narrated by. LC 91-61144. 32p. (ps-3). 1991. 11.95 (0-924483-29-6); incl. audiocassette 16.95 (0-924483-30-X); incl. audiocassette & toy combination 39.95 (0-924483-31-8); incl. audiocassette & small toy combination 25.95 (0-924483-38-5); write for info audiocassette (0-924483-32-6) Soundprints.

—Platypus. Bosson, Jo-Ellen. 10p. (ps-1). 1992. bds. 2.95 (1-56293-218-7) McClanahan Bk.

—Robin. Bosson, Jo-Ellen. 10p. (ps-1). 1992. bds. 2.95 (1-56293-217-9) McClanahan Bk.

—Seasons of a Red Fox. Saunders, Susan. Thomas, Peter, narrated by. LC 91-61145. 32p. (ps-3). 1991. 11.95 (0-924483-25-3); incl. audiocassette 16.95 (0-924483-26-1); incl. audiocassette & toy combination 39.95 (0-924483-27-X); incl. audiocassette & small toy combination 25.95 (0-924483-40-7); write for info. audiocassette (0-924483-28-8) Soundprints.

—Swan. Bosson, Jo-Ellen. 10p. (ps-1). 1992. bds. 2.95 (1-56293-216-0) McClanahan Bk.

—Swan Flyway: The Tundra Swan. Limpert, Dana. Thomas, Peter, narrated by. (ps-3). 1993. 11.95 (0-924483-95-4); incl. audiocassette tape 16.95 (0-924483-96-2); incl. audiocassette tape & 8" toy 25.95 (0-924483-97-0); incl. audiocassette tape & 13" toy 39.95 (0-924483-98-9); audiocassette tape only avail. (0-924483-99-7) Soundprints.

—Turtle. Bosson, Jo-Ellen. 10p. (ps-1). 1992. bds. 2.95 (1-56293-219-5) McClanahan Bk.

—Wild & Free: The Story of a Black-Footed Ferret. Bosson, Jo-Ellen. Thomas, Peter, narrated by. 32p. (ps-3). 1992. 11.95 (0-924483-68-7); incl. audiocassette 16.95 (0-924483-67-9); incl. audiocassette tape & 16 inch stuffed animal toy 39.95 (0-924483-66-0); write for info. audiocass. tape (0-924483-75-X) Soundprints.

Bostic, Alex. The Lonely Ten: A Book of Counting for Preschool & Above. Shearer, Marilyn J. 16p. (Orig.). (ps-6). 1989. pap. 19.95 (0-685-30094-3) L Ashley & Joshua.

—The Lonely Ten: A Book of Simple Addition for Preschool & Above. Shearer, Marilyn J. 16p. (Orig.). (ps-6). 1989. 19.95 (0-685-30093-5) L Ashley & Joshua.

Bostic, Angela. Ranger. Nilsen, David. 64p. (Orig.). 1989. pap. 8.00 (1-55878-016-5) Game Designers.

Bostick, Matthew, jt. illus. see Soto, Zachary.

Bostick, Mike. Think of an Eel. Wallace, Karen. LC 92-53131. 32p. (gr. k-4). 1993. 14.95 (1-56402-180-7) Candlewick Pr.

Boston, Peter. The Chimneys of Green Knowe. large type ed. Boston, Lucy M. 272p. (gr. 3 up). 1990. 18.95 (0-7451-1175-0) G K Hall.

—The River at Greene Knowe. large type ed. Boston, Lucy M. 208p. 1992. 13.95 (0-7451-1467-9, Galaxy Child Lrg Print) Chivers N Amer.

—Sea Egg. Boston, Lucy M. LC 67-10200. (gr. 2-6). 1967. 8.95 (0-15-271050-7, HB Juv Bks) HarBrace.

—Stranger at Green Knowe. Boston, Lucy M. LC 61-10108. (gr. 5-9). 1961. 9.95 (0-15-281752-2, HB Juv Bks) HarBrace.

Boston, Peter, jt. illus. see Deeter, Catherine.

Boswell, Kathryn. The ABC's of Prayer...for Children. O'Connor, Francine M. 32p. (gr. 1-5). 1989. pap. 2.95 (0-89243-317-5) Liguori Pubns.

—ABCs of the Mass...for Children. O'Connor, Francine M. 32p. (Orig.). (ps-4). 1988. pap. text ed. 2.95 (0-89243-291-8) Liguori Pubns.

—ABCs of the Old Testament...for Children. O'Connor, Francine M. 32p. (gr. 1-5). 1989. pap. 2.95 (0-89243-310-8) Liguori Pubns.

Boswell, Kathryn. The ABC's Lessons of Love: Sermon on the Mount for Children. O'Connor, Francine M. 48p. (gr. 6-8). 1991. pap. text ed. 4.95 (0-89243-345-0) Liguori Pubns.

Botero, Kirk. Daddy, There's a Hippo in the Grapes. Dobkins, Lucy M. LC 92-20321. 64p. (gr. 3-7). 1992. 12.95 (0-88289-889-2) Pelican.

Bottner, Barbara. Messy. Bottner, Barbara. LC 78-50420. (gr. k-2). 1979. 6.95 (0-440-05492-3); pap. 6.46 (0-440-05493-1) Delacorte.

Botto, Lisa. A Picture Book of Farm Animals. Scott, Mary. LC 90-44888. 24p. (gr. 1-4). 1991. lib. bdg. 9.59 (0-8167-2150-5); pap. text ed. 2.50 (0-8167-2151-3) Troll Assocs.

Botto, Lisa C. How to Draw Wild Animals. Simpson, Anne. LC 91-26928. 32p. (gr. 2-6). 1991. text ed. 10.65 (0-8167-2481-4); pap. text ed. 1.95 (0-8167-2482-2) Troll Assocs.

Bottomley, Jane. Chanticleer. Berrill, Margaret. LC 86-6746. 32p. (gr. 2-5). 1992. PLB 17.96 (0-8172-2626-5) Raintree Steck-V.

Botwinick, Allan. The Man in the Blue Truck. Sheetz, Russ. Warren, Shirley, ed. 12p. (ps-k). 1990. pap. 3.95 (0-685-33385-X) Still Waters.

Botzis, Ka. AIDS & HIV Diseases. Fox, Cecil H. Head, J. J., ed. 16p. (Orig.). (gr. 10 up). 1991. pap. text ed. 2.75 (0-89278-120-3, 45-9620) Carolina Biological.

—Animal Movement. Alexander, R. McNeill. Head, J. J., ed. LC 84-45834. 16p. (Orig.). (gr. 10 up). 1985. pap. text ed. 2.75 (0-89278-364-8, 45-9764) Carolina Biological.

—Ionizing Radiation & Health. Upton, Arthur C. Head, J. J., ed. LC 84-71145. 16p. (Orig.). (gr. 10 up). 1986. pap. text ed. 2.75 (0-89278-199-8, 45-9699) Carolina Biological.

Boucher, Jerry, photos by. A Skyscraper Story. Wilcox, Charlotte. 48p. (ps-4). 1990. PLB 19.95 (0-87614-392-3) Carolrhoda Bks.

Boucher, Joelle. The Seventh Walnut. Petit, Genevieve. Aubertin, Marc, contrib. by. LC 92-10588. 1992. 13.95 (0-922984-10-7) Wellington IL.

—Undersea Giants. Geistdoefer, Patrick. LC 87-34531. 38p. (gr. k-5). 1988. 4.95 (0-944589-02-2, 022) Young Discovery Lib.

Boucher, Michel. Port Englouti. Cassabois, Jacques. (FRE.). 79p. (gr. 3-7). 1989. pap. 8.95 (2-07-031204-6) Schoenhof.

Boughton, Narda, jt. illus. see Colucci, Kristina.

Boulet, Susan B. Poor Gabriella: A Christmas Story. Forrester, Victoria. LC 86-3607. 32p. 1986. SBE 14.95 (0-689-31265-2, Atheneum Child Bk) Macmillan Child Grp.

Bouma, Paddy. One More Time. Baum, Louis. LC 85-31050. 32p. (ps-k). 1986. lib. bdg. 11.88 (0-688-06587-2, Morrow Jr Bks) Morrow Jr Bks.

—One More Time. Baum, Louis. ALC Staff, ed. LC 85-31050. 32p. (ps up). 1992. pap. 3.95 (0-688-11698-1, Mulberry) Morrow.

Bouman, Carol & Codor, Dick. RV & the Haunted Garage. Gilden, Mel. (gr. k-3). 1988. pap. 2.25 (0-671-63901-3) S&S Trade.

Bour, Daniele. Little Brown Bear Is Ill. Lebrun, Claude. 14p. (gr. k-3). 1982. 4.95 (0-8120-5499-7) Barron.

—Livre d'Hiver. Ottenheimer, Laurence. (FRE.). 93p. (gr. 4-9). 1983. 14.95 (2-07-039505-7) Schoenhof.

—Pierrot ou les Secrets de la Nuit. Tournier, Michel. (FRE.). 56p. (gr. 3-7). 1989. pap. 8.95 (2-07-031205-4) Schoenhof.

Bour, Laura. The Living Pond. Tordjman, Nathalie. Bogard, Vicki, tr. from FRE. LC 90-50780. 38p. (gr. k-5). 1991. 4.95 (0-944589-38-3, 383) Young Discovery Lib.

—The River. Jeunesse, Gallimard & Bour, Laura, eds. LC 92-41415. 1993. 11.95 (0-590-47128-7) Scholastic Inc.

—Whales. Bour, Laura. LC 92-41413. 24p. (ps-3). 1993. 11.95 (0-590-47130-9, Cartwheel) Scholastic Inc.

Bourke, Linda. Eye Spy: A Mysterious Alphabet. Bourke, Linda. 64p. (ps up) 1991. 15.95 (0-87701-805-7) Chronicle Bks.

—A Show of Hands: Say It in Sign Language. Sullivan, Mary B., et al. LC 84-48782. 96p. (gr. 2-6). 1985. pap. 4.95 (0-06-446007-X, Trophy) HarpC Child Bks.

Boutas, Nora. Oklahoma! Wagoner, Jay J. LC 89-90110. 229p. 1989. lib. bdg. 20.00 (0-9622361-0-1) Thunderbird Bks.

Bove, Eugene. Uncle Gene's Breadbook for Kids! Bove, Eugene. 64p. (gr. 5-12). 1986. pap. 11.95 (0-937395-00-5) Happibook Pr.

Bowdren, John. A December Gift from the Shoals. Jesep, Paul P. 16p. (Orig.). (gr. 4). 1993. pap. 5.95 (0-9634360-1-5) Seacoast Pubns New Eng.

—The Witch & the Sunflower Garden. Jesep, Paul P. LC 92-62305. 20p. (Orig.). (gr. 4-5). 1993. pap. 9.95 (0-9634360-3-1) Seacoast Pubns New Eng.

Bowen, Betsy. Antler, Bear, Canoe: A Northwoods Alphabet Year. Bowen, Betsy. 32p. (ps-3). 1991. 15.95 (0-316-10376-4, Joy St Bks) Little.

Bowen, Keith. Snowy. Doherty, Berlie. LC 91-47519. 32p. (ps-3). 1993. 14.00 (0-8037-1343-6) Dial Bks Young.

Bowen, Richard. The First Helping. Bowen, Richard. (gr. k-6). Date not set. pap. 9.95 (1-56883-009-2) Colonial Pr AL.

Bower, Adele. About Ballet Class. Sanchez, Sharon S., ed. 32p. (ps up). 1990. pap. 5.95 (0-9626651-0-X) Dance Data.

—About Ballet Performance. Sanchez, Sharon S. 32p. (ps up). 1990. pap. 5.95 (0-9626651-1-8) Dance Data.

Bower, J. R. Big Boss Charger. Kienlen, Helen & Sandercock, Lois. 16p. (gr. k-4). 1989. pap. text ed. 4.00 (0-9626864-1-7) Holistic Learning.

—Llamas. Kienlen, Helen & Sandercock, Lois. 16p. (Orig.). (gr. k-4). 1989. pap. text ed. 4.00 (0-9626864-0-9) Holistic Learning.

Bower, Tom. Albert Blows a Fuse. Bower, Tom. 32p. (gr. 5-8). 1991. 11.95 (0-7459-1906-5) Lion USA.

Bowers, Helen M. Jonathan Michael & Mother Nature's Fury. Harper-Deiters, Cyndi. Ruggles, Robert & Ruggles, Grace, eds. 36p. (Orig.). (gr. 2-4). 1993. pap. text ed. 4.95x (0-9632513-2-5) Cntry Home.

—Jonathan Michael & the Perilous Flight. Harper-Deiters, Cyndi. Ruggles, Robert & Ruggles, Grace, eds. 34p. (gr. 2-4). Date not set. pap. 4.95 (0-9632513-3-3) Cntry Home.

—Jonathan Michael & the Uninvited Guest. Harper-Deiters, Cyndi. Ruggles, Robert & Ruggles, Grace, eds. 34p. (Orig.). (gr. 2-4). 1992. pap. text ed. 4.95x (0-9632513-1-7) Cntry Home.

— The Jonathan Michael Series. Harper-Deiters, Cyndi. Ruggles, Robert & Ruggles, Grace, eds. (Orig.). (gr. 2-5). 1993. pap. text ed. write for info. (0-9632513-4-1) Cntry Home.

This series is designed to encourage 2-5 grade readers to problem-solve without the use of physical violence. The complete set will include ten books, with two books being released annually. The masterful illustrations by HELEN M. BOWERS depict the events of each story as they unfold. Meet JONATHAN MICHAEL & his barnyard friends in the introductory story, JONATHAN MICHAEL THE RESIDENT ROOSTER. Mrs. Skunk & her babies move in underneath the house porch in the second book, JONATHAN MICHAEL & THE UNINVITED GUEST. Can JONATHAN MICHAEL through advisory problem-solving methods convince her to move before they are discovered & destroyed? JONATHAN MICHAEL & MOTHER NATURE'S FURY, the third book, emphasizes completing a task regardless of the obstacles. Will JONATHAN MICHAEL'S rescue mission for a lost chick in the violent storm come in time? Find out the importance of team work in the FORTHCOMING fourth book, JONATHAN MICHAEL & THE PERILOUS FLIGHT. Will JONATHAN MICHAEL & his barnyard friends find a south-bound flock for Ercella, a young duck, to join before it is too late? Country Home Publishers, 930 N. Osborn, White Cloud, MI 49349. (616) 924-0817. *Publisher Provided Annotation.*

Bowers, Tim. Pajamas. Taylor, Livingston & Taylor, Maggie. 32p. (ps-3). 1988. 13.95 (*0-15-200564-1*, Gulliver Bks) HarBrace.
—The Toy Circus. Wahl, Jan. LC 85-30186. 32p. (ps-3). 1986. 13.95 (*0-15-200609-5*, Gulliver Bks) HarBrace.
Bowes, Clare. The Hippo Bus. Bowes, Clare. LC 92-34264. 1993. 14.00 (*0-383-03629-1*) SRA Schl Grp.
Bowler, Ray. The Beast & the Babysitter. Stevens, Kathleen. LC 88-42917. 32p. (gr. 2-3). 1989. PLB 18.60 (*1-55532-929-2*) Gareth Stevens Inc.
—The Beast in the Bathtub. Stevens, Kathleen. LC 86-45074. 32p. (ps-3). 1987. pap. 5.95 (*0-06-443121-5*, Trophy) HarpC Child Bks.
—The Beast in the Bathtub. Stevens, Kathleen. LC 85-12691. 32p. (gr. 2-3). 1985. PLB 18.60 (*0-918831-15-6*) Gareth Stevens Inc.
—Bully for the Beast! Stevens, Kathleen. LC 88-33090. 32p. (gr. 2-3). 1990. PLB 18.60 (*0-8368-0020-6*) Gareth Stevens Inc.
Bowles, Carol. The Two-Legged Creature: An Otoe Story. Walters, Anna L., retold by. LC 92-56510. 32p. 1993. 14.95 (*0-87358-553-4*) Northland AZ.
Bowling, Patricia H. Clean up Your Act, Dirty Dinjy Daryl. Bowling, David L. 32p. (Orig.). (gr. 1-4). 1993. 9.95 (*0-939700-06-9*); PLB 13.95 (*0-939700-05-0*); pap. 5.95 (*0-939700-04-2*) I D I C P.
—Dirty Dingy Daryl. Bowling, David L. & Bowling, Patricia H. Martz, John, ed. LC 81-83120. 24p. (ps-4). 1981. 6.00 (*0-939700-00-X*); pap. 3.00 (*0-939700-01-8*) I D I C P.
—Dirty Dingy Daryl for President. Bowling, David L. & Bowling, Patricia H. Martz, John, ed. LC 83-82273. 40p. (gr. 1-4). 1983. 6.00 (*0-939700-02-6*); pap. 3.00 (*0-939700-03-4*) I D I C P.
Bowman, Joyce & Guest, Mary J. The Aunt Rocker: Songs of Sottong, Vol. 8. Sottong, Mary L. LC 89-92205. 64p. (Orig.). (ps-3). 1989. pap. 5.98 (*0-9624136-1-5*) Songs Sottongs.
Bowman, Leslie. The Canada Geese Quilt. Kinsey-Warnock, Natalie. 60p. (gr. 5 up). 1992. pap. 3.50 (*0-440-40719-2*, YB) Dell.
—A Christmas Sonata. Paulsen, Gary. LC 90-46891. 80p. (gr. 3-7). 1992. 14.00 (*0-385-30441-2*) Delacorte.
—The Cuckoo Child. King-Smith, Dick. LC 92-72029. 128p. (gr. 3-6). 1993. 13.95 (*1-56282-350-7*); PLB 13.89 (*1-56282-351-5*) Hyprn Child.
—The Fourth-Grade Four. Levinson, Marilyn. LC 89-31109. 64p. (gr. 2-4). 1989. 12.95 (*0-8050-1082-3*, Bks Young Read) H Holt & Co.
—The Fourth-Grade Four. Levinson, Marilyn. LC 89-31109. 64p. (gr. 2-4). 1991. pap. 4.95 (*0-8050-1640-6*, Owlet BYR) H Holt & Co.
—Hannah. Whelan, Gloria. LC 90-39554. 64p. (gr. 2-4). 1991. 10.95 (*0-679-81397-7*) Knopf Bks Yng Read.

—Hannah. Whelan, Gloria. LC 92-24243. 64p. (gr. 2-4). 1993. RLB 11.99 (*0-679-91397-1*); pap. 2.50 (*0-679-82698-X*) Random Bks Yng Read.
—Hello, Crow. Marion, Jeff D. LC 91-18561. 32p. (ps-2). 1992. 13.95 (*0-531-05975-8*); PLB 13.99 (*0-531-08575-9*) Orchard Bks Watts.
—The Man on Stilts. Ransom, Candice. LC 92-39358. 1994. write for info. (*0-399-22537-4*, Philomel Bks) Putnam Pub Group.
—Night of the Full Moon. Whelan, Gloria. LC 93-6706. 64p. (gr. 2-4). 1993. 13.00 (*0-679-84464-3*); PLB 13.99 (*0-679-94464-8*) Knopf Bks Yng Read.
—The Pennywhistle Tree. Smith, Doris B. LC 90-23119. 144p. (gr. 5-9). 1991. 14.95 (*0-399-21840-8*, Putnam) Putnam Pub Group.
—Shadows. Haseley, Dennis. 80p. (gr. 2-6). 1991. 12.95 (*0-374-36761-2*) FS&G.
Bowman, Leslie W. The Canada Geese Quilt. Kinsey-Warnock, Natalie. LC 88-32661. 64p. (gr. 4 up). 1989. 13.00 (*0-525-65004-0*, Cobblehill Bks) Dutton Child Bks.
—The Fiddler of the Northern Lights. Kinsey-Warnock, Natalie. LC 92-36703. 1994. write for info. (*0-525-65143-8*, Cobblehill Bks) Dutton Child Bks.
—El Guero. De Trevino, Elizabeth B. 112p. (gr. 3 up). 1989. 14.00 (*0-374-31995-2*) FS&G.
—The Night the Bells Rang. Kinsey-Warnock, Natalie. LC 91-3053. 80p. (gr. 4 up). 1991. 12.95 (*0-525-65074-1*, Cobblehill Bks) Dutton Child Bks.
Bowman, Margret. Blue-Footed Booby: Bird of the Galapagos. Bowman, Margret & Millhouse, Nicholas. LC 85-27617. 32p. (gr. 1-7). 1986. 11.95 (*0-8027-6628-5*); lib. bdg. 11.85 (*0-8027-6629-3*) Walker & Co.
Bowman, Patricia. Magic Monsters Halloween. Tester, Sylvia R. LC 79-25183. (gr. k-3). 1980. PLB 21.35 (*0-89565-121-1*); PLB 13.95s.p. (*0-685-55496-1*) Childs World.
—Magic Monsters Learn about Weather. Tester, Sylvia R. LC 79-24826. (gr. k-3). 1980. PLB 21.35 (*0-89565-120-3*); PLB 14.95s.p. (*0-685-55501-1*) Childs World.
Bowman, Peter. Grandpa Baxter & the Photographs. Castle, Caroline. LC 92-44192. 32p. (ps-1). 1993. 14.95 (*0-531-05487-X*); PLB 14.99 (*0-531-08637-2*) Orchard Bks Watts.
Bowring, Isabel. Gruesome Land Creatures. Hoy, Ken. 5p. (ps-3). 1993. 12.95 (*0-8249-8617-2*, Ideals Child) Hambleton-Hill.
Bowring, Isabel, jt. illus. see Hargreaves, Anglea.
Bowring, Isabel, et al. Rivers. Stephen, Richard. LC 89-20303. 32p. (gr. 4-6). 1990. PLB 11.59 (*0-8167-1975-6*); pap. text ed. 3.95 (*0-8167-1976-4*) Troll Assocs.
Bowring, Joanne. Where the Sun Kisses the Sea. Gabel, Susan L. LC 89-16296. 32p. (ps-5). 1989. 12.95 (*0-944934-00-5*) Perspect Indiana.
Bowser, Carolyn E. Seasons in God's World. Beckmann, Beverly. 24p. (gr. 2-5). 1985. 6.99 (*0-570-04127-9*, 56-1538) Concordia.
Bowser, M. Tobias, Vol. I, Bk. I: Follow Me to Yesterday. Bowser, Milton. MacLean, Alistair, ed. 72p. 1993. PLB 20.00 (*0-685-65016-2*) (*0-940178-30-3*) Sitare.
Boyce, Kenneth. Davy's Dawg. Matthews, Billie L. & Hurlburt, Virginia E. Welch, Karen E., ed. LC 88-32832. 64p. (gr. 3-8). 1989. PLB 9.95 (*0-937460-58-3*) Hendrick-Long.
Boyd, L. M. Clancy's Treasure Book for Children. Boyd, L. M. 166p. (Orig.). (gr. k-5). 1981. pap. 7.95 (*0-941620-34-4*) Carson Ent.
Boyd, Lizi. Black Dog Red House. Boyd, Lizi. (ps-2). 1993. 12.95 (*0-316-10443-4*) Little.
—Sweet Dreams, Willy. Boyd, Lizi. 32p. (ps-1). 1992. PLB 12.50 (*0-670-84382-2*) Viking Child Bks.
—What Would You Do If You Lived at the Zoo? Carlstrom, Nancy W. LC 93-7036. 1993. 13.95 (*0-316-12867-8*) Little.
Boyd, Patti. All about Deserts. Sanders, John. LC 83-4857. 32p. (gr. 3-6). 1984. lib. bdg. 10.59 (*0-89375-965-1*); pap. text ed. 2.95 (*0-89375-966-X*) Troll Assocs.
—Amazing World of Plants. Marcus, Elizabeth. LC 83-4836. 32p. (gr. 3-6). 1984. lib. bdg. 10.59 (*0-89375-967-8*); pap. text ed. 2.95 (*0-89375-968-6*) Troll Assocs.
—Christmas KidDoodles, Bk. 4. Wise, Beth A. 64p. (Orig.). (ps-2). 1991. pap. 0.99 activity pad (*1-56293-156-3*) McClanahan Bk.
—Dino-Songs. Cooper, Don. 32p. (ps-3). 1988. bk. & cassette pkg. 6.95 (*0-394-89810-9*) Random Bks Yng Read.
—KidDoodles, Bk. 1. Herman, Emmi S. 64p. (ps-2). 1991. pap. 0.99 activity pad (*1-878624-50-4*) McClanahan Bk.
—Let's Go to the Zoo. Whitehead, Patricia. LC 84-8832. 32p. (gr. k-2). 1985. PLB 11.59 (*0-8167-0375-2*); pap. text ed. 2.95 (*0-8167-0376-0*) Troll Assocs.
—Oh So Noisy! 12p. (ps). 1993. bds. 4.95 (*0-448-40538-5*, G&D) Putnam Pub Group.
—Our Amazing Sun. Adams, Richard. LC 82-17419. 32p. (gr. 3-6). 1983. PLB 10.59 (*0-89375-890-6*); pap. text ed. 2.95 (*0-89375-891-4*) Troll Assocs.
—Our Wonderful Seasons. Marcus, Elizabeth. LC 82-17372. 32p. (gr. 3-6). 1983. PLB 10.59 (*0-89375-896-5*); pap. text ed. 2.95 (*0-89375-897-3*) Troll Assocs.

—You Look Funny! Kim, Joy. LC 86-30839. 32p. (gr. k-2). 1988. PLB 7.89 (*0-8167-0976-9*); pap. text ed. 1.95 (*0-8167-0977-7*) Troll Assocs.
Boyer, Ralph. A Tomato Can Chronicle. 2nd ed. Smith, Edmund W. 189p. (gr. 10 up). 1991. Repr. of 1937 ed. 35.00 (*1-56416-018-1*) Derrydale Pr.
—Tranquility. 2nd ed. Sheldon, Harold P. 216p. (gr. 10 up). 1991. Repr. of 1936 ed. 35.00 (*1-56416-021-1*) Derrydale Pr.
Boyer, Trevor. Eagles. 1983 ed. Wildlife Education, Ltd. Staff. 20p. (gr. 5 up). pap. 2.75 (*0-937934-14-3*) Wildlife Educ.
—Parrots. Wildlife Education, Ltd. Staff. 20p. (gr. 5 up). 1984. pap. text ed. 2.75 (*0-937934-27-5*) Wildlife Educ.
—Parrots. Wildlife Education, Ltd. Staff. 24p. 1992. 13.95 (*0-937934-84-4*) Wildlife Educ.
Boyer, Trevor, jt. illus. see Stuart, Walter.
Boyer, Trevor, et al. Owls. Wildlife Education, Ltd. Staff. 20p. (Orig.). (gr. 5 up). 1985. pap. 2.75 (*0-937934-32-1*) Wildlife Educ.
Boyle, Kenneth. Night Light: A Story for Children Afraid of the Dark. Dutro, Jack. LC 91-19612. 32p. (ps-4). 1991. 16.95 (*0-945354-37-1*); pap. 6.95 (*0-945354-38-X*) Imagination Pr.
—Night Light: A Story for Children Afraid of the Dark. Dutro, Jack. LC 92-56873. 1993. PLB 17.26 (*0-8368-0934-3*) Gareth Stevens Inc.
Boyles, Renee. Belle-Duck at the Peabody. Wells, Dean F. 48p. (ps-8). 1984. 9.95 (*0-916242-24-2*) Yoknapatawpha.
Boynton, David, photos by. The Kaua'i Guide to Freshwater Sport Fishing. Ikemoto, Glenn Y. 64p. (Orig.). 1989. pap. 2.50 (*0-942255-07-0*, G6) Magic Fishes Pr.
Boynton, Lee. The Day They Left the Bay. 2nd ed. Blackistone, Mick. (gr. 1-6). 1991. Repr. of 1988 ed. PLB 14.95 (*0-9627726-3-1*) Blue Crab MD.
Boynton, Sandra. A to Z. Boynton, Sandra. 14p. (ps). 1984. 3.95 (*0-671-49317-5*, Little Simon) S&S Trade.
—But Not the Hippopotamus. Boynton, Sandra. Klimo, Kate, ed. 14p. (ps-k). 1982. 3.95 (*0-671-44904-4*, Little Simon) S&S Trade.
—The Going to Bed Book. Boynton, Sandra. Klimo, Kate, ed. 14p. (ps-k). 1982. 3.95 (*0-671-44902-8*, Little Simon) S&S Trade.
—Good Night, Good Night. Boynton, Sandra. LC 85-2098. 40p. (ps-1). 1985. 6.95 (*0-394-87285-1*) Random Bks Yng Read.
—Moo Baa La La La. Boynton, Sandra. Klimo, Kate, ed. 14p. 1982. 3.95 (*0-671-44901-X*, Little Simon) S&S Trade.
—Opposites. Boynton, Sandra. Klimo, Kate, ed. (ps-k). 1982. 3.95 (*0-671-44903-6*, Little Simon) S&S Trade.
Boytin, Michael. Barefeet & Bellybuttons: Poems & Activities to Tickle a Child. Goodrich, Patricia. 46p. (gr. k-4). 1989. pap. 5.00 (*0-9625348-1-1*) P Goodrich.
Bozellac, Anne. Guerre des Mondes. Wells, H. G. (FRE.). 288p. (gr. 5-10). 1990. pap. 9.95 (*2-07-033567-4*) Schoenhof.
Bozzo, Frank. The Beasts of Never. McHargue, Georgess. LC 86-29374. 128p. (gr. 7 up). 1987. pap. 14.95 (*0-385-29573-1*) Delacorte.
Bracken, Carolyn. The Airplane Book. Kunhardt, Edith. 24p. (ps-k). 1987. pap. write for info. (*0-307-10083-9*, Pub. by Golden Bks) Western Pub.
—All Aboard! Stuart, Doris. LC 87-81766. 22p. (ps). 1988. write for info. (*0-307-12117-8*, Pub. by Golden Bks) Western Pub.
—The Busy School Bus. 12p. (ps up). 1986. 6.95 (*0-448-09880-6*, G&D) Putnam Pub Group.
—The Care Bears' Book of ABC's. Kahn, Peggy. LC 82-18538. 40p. (ps-2). 1983. lib. bdg. 4.99 (*0-394-95808-X*) Random Bks Yng Read.
—The Care Bears' Circus of Shapes. Kahn, Peggy. LC 83-51590. 14p. (ps-1). 1984. bds. 3.95 (*0-394-86726-2*) Random Bks Yng Read.
—The Care Bears' Garden. Maison, Della. LC 82-61566. 32p. (gr. 1-6). 1983. pap. 1.25 saddle-stitched (*0-394-85827-1*) Random Bks Yng Read.
—Fast Rolling Fire Trucks. (ps). 1984. 6.95 (*0-448-09876-8*, G&D) Putnam Pub Group.
—Santa's Pockets. (ps). 1983. pap. 3.95 (*0-671-47660-2*, Little Simon) S&S Trade.
—Teddy Bear's Pockets. 8p. (ps). 1983. pap. 3.95 washable (*0-671-46448-5*, Little Simon) S&S Trade.
—Wee Sing Pop-up Nursery Rhymes. Beall, Pamela C. & Nipp, Susan H. 7p. 1993. 13.95 (*0-8431-3599-9*) Price Stern.
Bracken, Carolyn & Barbaresi, Nina. Baby Seal. (ps). 1984. pap. 2.95 vinyl (*0-671-50031-7*, Little Simon) S&S Trade.
—Duckling. (ps). 1984. pap. 2.95 vinyl (*0-671-50030-9*, Little Simon) S&S Trade.
Bracy, Norma M. Light Bulbs. Bracy, Norma M. 22p. (gr. k up). 1984. pap. text ed. 2.00 (*0-915783-01-0*) Book Binder.
—Rule of Gold. Bracy, Norma M. 20p. (gr. k-12). 1983. pap. text ed. 2.00g (*0-915783-00-2*) Book Binder.
Bradbury, Frances. American Hooked Rug Patterns. Bradbury, Frances M. 48p. (Orig.). 1986. pap. 5.95 (*0-88045-084-3*) Stemmer Hse.
Bradley, David. The Storyteller. Weisman, Joan. LC 93-20460. 32p. 1993. 15.95 (*0-8478-1742-3*) Rizzoli Intl.
Bradley, John. Alice's Adventures in Wonderland. abr. ed. Carroll, Lewis. Blair, David, retold by. LC 91-58124. 56p. 1992. 9.98 (*1-56138-100-4*) Courage Bks.
Bradley, John, jt. illus. see Marshall, Ray.

Bradley, Maureen. Twin & Super-Twin. Cross, Gillian. LC 90-55098. 176p. (gr. 3-7). 1990. 13.95 (0-8234-0840-X) Holiday.

Bradstreet, Tim, jt. illus. see Laubenstein, Jeff.

Brady, Irene. America's Horses & Ponies. Brady, Irene. 202p. (gr. 4 up). 1976. pap. 15.45 (0-395-24050-6, Sandpiper) HM.

—Gorilla. McClung, Robert M. LC 84-718. 96p. (gr. 3-7). 1984. 11.00 (0-688-03875-1) Morrow Jr Bks.

—Lili: A Giant Panda of Sichuan. McClung, Robert M. LC 87-28271. 96p. (gr. 3-7). 1988. 12.95 (0-688-06942-8); PLB 12.88 (0-688-06943-6, Morrow Jr Bks) Morrow Jr Bks.

—Peeping in the Shell: A Whooping Crane Is Hatched. McNulty, Faith. LC 85-45837. 64p. (gr. 3-7). 1986. PLB 11.89 (0-06-024135-7) HarpC Child Bks.

—Whitetail. McClung, Robert M. LC 86-18183. 96p. (gr. 3-7). 1987. 12.95 (0-688-06126-5); lib. bdg. 12.88 (0-688-06127-3, Morrow Jr Bks) Morrow Jr Bks.

Brady, Jennifer. Jambi & the Lions. Brady, Jennifer. Thatch, Nancy R., ed. Melton, David, intro. by. LC 92-17593. 26p. (gr. 3-5). 1992. PLB 14.95 (0-933849-41-9) Landmark Edns.

Brady, Kathleen. Oh, A-Hunting We Will Go Big Book. (ps-2). 1988. pap. text ed. 14.00 (0-922053-14-6) N Edge Res.

Brady, Steve. Amazing Alphabet Animals. RuDenski, Kathy. LC 91-65792. 44p. (gr. k-3). 1992. 8.95 (1-55523-447-X) Winston-Derek.

Brady, Susan. Find My Blanket. Brady, Susan. LC 87-45310. 32p. (ps-1). 1988. (Lipp Jr Bks) HarpC Child Bks.

Bragg, Michael. Monday's Child. 32p. (ps-1). 1989. 15.95 (0-575-04097-1, Pub. by Gollancz England) Trafalgar.

Bragg, Ruth. Mrs. Muggle's Sparkle. Bragg, Ruth. LC 89-31371. 28p. (ps up). 1991. pap. 15.95 (0-88708-106-1) Picture Bk Studio.

Bragg, Ruth G. The Birthday Bears. Bragg, Ruth G. LC 90-7385. 28p. (gr. k up). 1991. pap. 14.95 (0-88708-139-8) Picture Bk Studio.

—Colors of the Day. Bragg, Ruth G. LC 92-7790. 40p. 1992. pap. 14.95 (0-88708-245-9) Picture Bk Studio.

Brahm, Sumishta. Would You Rather? Menzel, Barbara J. LC 81-6810. 32p. (ps-3). 1982. 16.95 (0-89885-076-2) Human Sci Pr.

Braille International, Inc. Staff. All Things Change: Maylene the Mermaid. Daniells, Trenna. Henry, James. (Orig.). (gr. 1). 1992. pap. 10.95 (1-56956-004-8) W A T Braille.

—All Things Change: Maylene the Mermaid. Daniells, Trenna. Henry, James. (Orig.). (gr. 2). 1992. pap. 10. 95 (1-56956-029-3) W A T Braille.

—Be True to Yourself: I Don't Want to Be a Lion Anymore. Daniells, Trenna. Henry, James. 11p. (Orig.). (gr. 1). 1992. pap. 10.95 (1-56956-001-3) W A T Braille.

—Be True to Yourself: I Don't Want to Be a Lion Anymore. Daniells, Trenna. Henry, James. (Orig.). (gr. 2). 1992. pap. 10.95 (1-56956-026-9) W A T Braille.

—Don't Blame Others: Timothy Chicken Learns to Lead. Daniells, Trenna. Henry, James. (Orig.). (gr. 1). 1992. pap. 10.95 (1-56956-007-2) W A T Braille.

—Don't Blame Others: Timothy Chicken Learns to Lead. Daniells, Trenna. Henry, James. (Orig.). (gr. 2). 1992. pap. 10.95 (1-56956-016-1) W A T Braille.

—It's Okay to Be Different: Oliver's Adventures on Monkey Island. Daniells, Trenna. Henry, James. (Orig.). (gr. 1). 1992. pap. 10.95 (1-56956-008-0) W A T Braille.

—It's Okay to Be Different: Oliver's Adventures on Monkey Island. Daniells, Trenna. Henry, James. (Orig.). (gr. 2). 1992. pap. 10.95 (1-56956-017-X) W A T Braille.

—No More Nightmares: Keeper of the Dreams. Daniells, Trenna. Henry, James. (Orig.). (gr. 2). 1992. pap. 10. 95 (1-56956-027-7) W A T Braille.

—Taking the Problems Out of Bedtime. Daniells, Trenna. Henry, James. (Orig.). (gr. 2). 1992. pap. 10.95 (1-56956-031-5) W A T Braille.

—Travis & the Dragon: Accepting Others As They Are. Daniells, Trenna. Henry, James. (Orig.). (gr. 1). 1992. pap. 10.95 (1-56956-005-6) W A T Braille.

—Travis & the Dragon: Accepting Others As They Are. Daniells, Trenna. Henry, James. (Orig.). (gr. 2). 1992. pap. 10.95 (1-56956-030-7) W A T Braille.

—When Jokes Aren't Fun: The Hyena Who Teased Too Much. Daniells, Trenna. Henry, James. 20p. (Orig.). (gr. 1). 1992. pap. 10.95 (1-56956-003-X) W A T Braille.

—When Jokes Aren't Fun: The Hyena Who Teased Too Much. Daniells, Trenna. Henry, James. (Orig.). (gr. 2). 1992. pap. 10.95 (1-56956-028-5) W A T Braille.

Braille International, Inc. Staff & Henry, James. No More Nightmares: Keeper of the Dreams. 17p. (Orig.). (gr. 1). 1992. pap. 10.95 (1-56956-002-1) W A T Braille.

Bramley, Peter. Florida's Vanishing Wildlife. 32p. (Orig.). (gr. k-4). 1992. pap. 2.95 (0-8200-1101-0) Great Outdoors.

Bramos, Ann S. My Favorite Bed Time Stories. Bramos, Helen. Bramos, Ann S., tr. LC 91-76687. 63p. (Orig.). 1992. pap. 7.00 (1-56002-152-7) Aegina Pr.

—My Red Storybook. Bramos, Helen. Bramos, Ann S., tr. from GRE & FRE. 77p. (Orig.). (ps-7). 1993. pap. 8.00 (0-9635333-1-2) A S Bramos.

Brand, Jennifer. Making Dreams Come True. Lindo, Howard. 1993. 7.95 (0-533-10406-8) Vantage.

Brande, Marlie. Danish Fairy Tales & Rhymes for Children & Adults: Folke Eventyr Og Remse. Seidelin, Anna S. Zucker, William V., tr. from DAN. 147p. (Orig.). 1992. pap. 15.00 (0-9634440-1-8) Lester St Pub.

Brandenberg, Aliki. Welcome Little Baby: Miniature Edition. Brandenberg, Aliki. 32p. (ps up). 1993. Repr. text ed. 4.95 (0-688-12665-0, Tupelo Bks) Morrow.

Brandenburg, Alexa. A Fun Weekend. Brandenburg, Franz. LC 89-77502. 24p. (ps up). 1991. 13.95 (0-688-09720-0); PLB 13.88 (0-688-09721-9) Greenwillow.

Brandes, Louis G. Can You Believe What You See? Illusions. Brandes, Louis G. Laycock, Mary, ed. 96p. (Orig.). (gr. 4-10). 1988. pap. 12.50 (0-918932-92-0) Activity Resources.

Brandi, Leonard, jt. illus. see Shortall, Leonard.

Brandi, Lillian & Shortall, Leonard. Encyclopedia Brown & the Case of the Midnight Visitor. Sobol, Donald J. LC 77-22159. 96p. (gr. 3-5). 1979. 12.50 (0-525-67221-4, Lodestar Bks) Dutton Child Bks.

Brandi, Lillian, jt. illus. see Shortall, Leonard.

Brandi, Shortall, jt. illus. see Shortall, Leonard.

Brandt, Bill. Coloring Book of Pikes Peak Country: Follow the Pikes Peak Trail & See the Wonders of the Area. Whelchel, Sandy. 38p. (Orig.). (gr. k-4). 1989. pap. 3.50 (1-878406-01-9) Parker Dstb.

—A Day in Blue: Follow Freddy Falcon on a Child's Tour of the U. S. Air Force Academy. Whelchel, Sandy. 28p. (gr. k-4). 1986. pap. 2.95 (1-878406-00-0) Parker Dstb.

—Mile High Denver: Coloring Book. Whelchel, Sandy. 30p. (Orig.). (gr. k-4). 1987. pap. 3.50 (0-685-29912-0) Parker Dstb.

Brandt, Bill, jt. illus. see Dirks, Nathan.

Brannon, Tom. Eureeka's Castle: Magellan Saves the Day. McGuire, Leslie. (ps-k). 1991. pap. 1.25 (0-307-11512-7, Golden Pr) Western Pub.

—I Want to Be President. Muntean, Michaela. 24p. (ps-k). 1993. pap. 1.95 (0-307-13118-1, 13118, Golden Pr) Western Pub.

—Jim Henson's Muppet Babies' Christmas Book. 48p. (ps-2). 1992. 6.95 (0-307-15955-8, 15955, Golden Pr) Western Pub.

—Muppet Babies & the Time Machine. Prady, Bill. 26p. (ps up). 1987. 12.95 (1-55578-605-7) Worlds Wonder.

—The Muppet Babies in Let's Imagine...Music Everywhere. Barken, Joanne, et al. 26p. (ps up) 1987. pap. 14.95 (1-55578-807-6) Worlds Wonder.

—Muppet Kids in I Want to Go Home. Weiss, Ellen. 32p. (ps-3). 1992. 1.95 (0-307-12650-1, 12650, Golden Pr) Western Pub.

—Muppet Kids in Piggy Takes a Dare. Weiss, Ellen. (ps-3). 1991. pap. 1.95 (0-307-12658-7, Golden Pr) Western Pub.

—Muppet Kids in Too Many Promises. Weiss, Ellen. 32p. (ps-3). 1991. 1.95 (0-307-12654-4, Golden Pr) Western Pub.

—Sesame Street: Little Elmo's Toy Box. (ps). 1990. pap. write for info. (0-307-06038-1, Golden Pr) Western Pub.

—Sesame Street: Little Ernie Loves Rubber Duckie. 12p. (ps). 1992. write for info. nontoxic, washable (0-307-06064-0, 6064, Golden Pr) Western Pub.

—Sesame Street: Little Grover Takes a Walk. (ps-k). 1991. pap. write for info. (0-307-06062-4, Golden Pr) Western Pub.

—Too Little! Alexander, Liza. 32p. (ps-k). 1992. write for info. (0-307-12009-0, 12009) Western Pub.

—What Does Baby Kermit Say? 12p. (ps). 1993. pap. 1.95 (0-307-06036-5, 6036, Golden Pr) Western Pub.

Brannon, Tom & Cooke, Tom. Open Sesame Multilevel Book. Baigelman, Simon, photos by. pap. 7.95 (0-19-434261-1) OUP.

Braren, Loretta. EcoArt! Earth-Friendly Art & Craft Experiences for 3- to 9-Year-Olds. Carlson, Laurie. LC 92-21347. 160p. (Orig.). (ps-5). 1993. pap. 12.95 (0-913589-68-3) Williamson Pub Co.

Braren, Loretta T. Kids & Weekends! Creative Ways to Make Special Days. Hart, Avery & Mantell, Paul. Weathers, Marcy, contrib. by. LC 91-25314. 176p. (Orig.). (gr. k-7). 1992. pap. 12.95 (0-913589-47-0) Williamson Pub Co.

—Kids Create! Art & Craft Experiences for 3- to 9-Year-Olds. Carlson, Laurie. Williamson, Susan, ed. LC 90-33677. 160p. (Orig.). (gr. k-3). 1990. pap. 12.95 (0-913589-51-9) Williamson Pub Co.

Bratun, Katy. Beauty & the Beast. Carr, Jan. 32p. (ps-3). 1993. pap. 2.50 (0-590-46451-5, Cartwheel) Scholastic Inc.

—The Bunnies' Ball. Ingle, Annie. 32p. (ps-1). 1993. pap. 2.50 (0-685-68188-2) Random Bks Yng Read.

—The Bunnies' Ball. Ingle, Annie. LC 93-8536. 1994. write for info.; PLB write for info. Random Bks Yng Read.

—The Little Pumpkin Book. Ross, Katharine. LC 91-67669. 22p. 1992. bds. 2.95 (0-679-83384-6) Random Bks Yng Read.

—Rabbits' Carnival. Ross, Katharine. LC 92-29930. 1994. write for info. (0-679-83503-2); lib. bdg. write for info. (0-679-93503-7) Random Bks Yng Read.

—Sshaboom! Mangas, Brian. LC 91-24764. 40p. (ps-1). 1993. pap. 14.00 JRT (0-671-75538-2, S&S BFYR) S&S Trade.

—Where Is Sammy's Smile: A Lift-the-Flap Book. Lewison, Wendy C. 24p. (ps-k). 1989. 10.95 (0-448-40150-9, G&D) Putnam Pub Group.

Braun, Molly. Encyclopedia of Native American Tribes. Waldman, Carl. 308p. 1987. 45.00x (0-8160-1421-3) Facts on File.

Braun, Wendy. Missing Angel Juan. Block, Francesca L. LC 92-38299. 144p. (gr. 7 up). 1993. 14.00 (0-06-023004-5); PLB 13.89 (0-06-023007-X) HarpC Child Bks.

Bray, Vivieene. Little Bear's Bedtime. 10p. (ps-2). 1993. bds. 16.95 (1-56293-317-5) McClanahan Bk.

—Little Bear's Breakfast. 10p. (ps-2). 1993. bds. 16.95 (1-56293-318-3) McClanahan Bk.

Brazell, Derek. Cleversticks. Ashley, Bernard. LC 91-34669. 32p. (ps-2). 1992. 10.00 (0-517-58878-1); PLB 10.99 (0-517-58879-X) Crown Bks Yng Read.

—My Brother Is a Visitor from Another Planet. Sheldon, Dyan. LC 92-53420. 96p. (gr. 3-6). 1993. 13.95 (1-56402-141-6) Candlewick Pr.

Breathed, Berkeley. A Wish for Wings That Work: An Opus Christmas Story. Breathed, Berkeley. 32p. 1991. 14.95 (0-316-10758-1) Little.

Bredius, Rein. Little Stories. Franco, Eloise. (gr. k-5). 1979. pap. 4.50 (0-87516-384-X) DeVorss.

Bree, Marlin. Kid's Vacation Diary: A Fun Diary & Vacation Book for Use While Traveling! Marlor Editors. 96p. (Orig.). (gr. 1-7). 1991. pap. 6.95 (0-943400-56-2) Marlor Pr.

Breeden, Teisha. Finding a Friend. Booth, Zilpha M. LC 86-50987. 54p. (gr. 1-5). 1987. pap. 3.95 (0-932433-22-7) Windswept Hse.

Breeze, Lynn. This Little Baby Goes Out. Morris, Ann, text by. LC 92-30880. (ps). 1993. 5.95 (0-316-10854-5) Little.

—This Little Baby's Bedtime. Morris, Ann, text by. LC 92-30879. (ps). 1993. 5.95 (0-316-58419-3) Little.

—This Little Baby's Morning. Morris, Ann, text by. LC 92-30881. (ps). 1993. 5.95 (0-316-58420-7) Little.

—This Little Baby's Playtime. Morris, Ann, text by. LC 92-30878. (ps). 1993. 5.95 (0-316-10855-3) Little.

Brendon, Stuart. Children's Giant World Atlas. Lye, Keith, contrib. by. 14p. (gr. k-4). 1987. 19.95 (0-681-40268-7) Longmeadow Pr.

Brenes, Irma M. River of Miracles. Schoepfer, G. R. Schoepfer, Virginia B., ed. (gr. 1-11). 1978. pap. text ed. 2.75x (0-931436-01-X, Children's Books) G R Schoepfer.

Brennan, Christine. Moses Goodleaf Learns to Walk: A Short Tale of Discovery. Bridge, Michael. 32p. 1992. PLB 22.95 (0-944963-18-8); pap. 16.95 (0-944963-19-6); audio tape 7.95 (0-944963-33-1) Glastonbury Pr.

Brennan, Nancy. The Squirrel & the Frog. McDowell, Mildred. Harman, Sandra L., intro. by. LC 76-133256. 44p. (gr. 1-2). 1971. 2.50 (0-87884-007-9) Unicorn Ent.

Brenner, Barbara. A Snake-Lover's Diary. Brenner, Barbara. LC 84-43136. 96p. (gr. 4-6). 1990. PLB 15.89 (0-06-020697-7) HarpC Child Bks.

Brenner, Fred. The Drinking Gourd. newly illustrated ed. Monjo, F. N. LC 92-10823. 64p. (gr. k-3). 1983. pap. 3.50 (0-06-444042-7, Trophy) HarpC Child Bks.

—One Day in the Desert. George, Jean C. LC 82-45924. 48p. (gr. 5-7). 1983. PLB 13.89 (0-690-04341-4, Crowell Jr Bks) HarpC Child Bks.

—The Tremendous Tree Book. Brenner, Barbara & Garelick, May. LC 91-73753. 40p. (ps-3). 1992. 14.95 (1-878093-56-8) Boyds Mills Pr.

Brenner, Fred, photos by. The Drinking Gourd. newly illus. ed. Monjo, F. N. LC 92-10823. 64p. (gr. k-3). 1970. 14.00 (0-06-024329-5); PLB 13.89 (0-06-024330-9) HarpC Child Bks.

Brent, Isabelle. An Alphabet of Animals. LC 92-54652. 1993. 12.95 (0-316-10852-9) Little.

—Just So Stories. Kipling, Rudyard. Philip, Neil, frwd. by. 160p. 1993. 19.99 (0-670-85196-5) Viking Child Bks.

Brent, Jenny. Come Home Soon, Baba. Hampton, Janie. 32p. (gr. 4 up). 1993. 12.95 (0-87226-511-0, Bedrick Blackie) P Bedrick Bks.

Bretlinger, Ted. Fuzzy Buzzard. Mister Tom. 32p. (gr. 2-4). 1978. write for info. Oddo.

Brett, Jan. Annie & the Wild Animals. Brett, Jan. LC 84-19818. 32p. (gr. k-3). 1985. 14.95 (0-395-37800-1); pap. 7.95 (0-395-53962-5) HM.

—Annie & the Wild Animals. Brett, Jan. (ps-3). 1989. pap. 4.80 (0-395-51006-6, Sandpiper) HM.

—Beauty & the Beast. Brett, Jan. LC 88-16965. 48p. (gr. 1-7). 1989. 14.95 (0-89919-497-4, Clarion Bks) HM.

—Christmas Trolls. Brett, Jan. LC 93-10106. 32p. (ps-3). 1993. PLB 15.95 (0-399-22507-2, Putnam) Putnam Pub Group.

—Fritz & the Beautiful Horses. Brett, Jan. 32p. (gr. k-3). 1987. 13.45 (0-395-30850-X); pap. 4.80 (0-395-45356-9) HM.

—The Great Rescue. Taylor, Mark. LC 83-25113. 40p. (gr. 1-5). 1984. 6.95 (0-910313-28-8); incl. cassette 7.95 (0-910313-61-X) Parker Bros.

—Happy Birthday, Dear Duck. Bunting, Eve. LC 87-15694. 32p. (ps-1). 1988. 13.95 (0-89919-541-5, Clarion Bks) HM.

—Happy Birthday, Dear Duck. Bunting, Eve. LC 87-15694. 32p. (ps). 1990. pap. 4.80 (0-395-52594-2, Clarion Bks) HM.

—The Mitten: A Ukrainian Folktale. Brett, Jan. 32p. (ps-3). 1990. 15.95 (0-399-21920-X, Putnam) Putnam Pub Group.

—The Mother's Day Mice. Bunting, Eve. LC 85-13991. (ps-3). 1986. 13.95 (0-89919-387-0, Clarion Bks) HM.

—The Mother's Day Mice. Bunting, Eve. (gr. 4 up). 1988. pap. 4.95 (*0-89919-702-7*, Clarion Bks) HM.
—Noelle of the Nutcracker. Jane, Pamela. 64p. (gr. 2-5). 1986. 13.95 (*0-395-39969-6*) HM.
—Old Devil Is Waiting: Three Folktales. Van Woerkom, Dorothy O. LC 85-919. 64p. (ps-3). 1985. (HB Juv Bks) HarBrace.
—St. Patrick's Day in the Morning. Bunting, Eve. LC 79-15934. 32p. (ps-3). 1983. 13.95 (*0-395-29098-8*, Clarion Bks); pap. 5.95 (*0-89919-162-2*, Clarion Bks) HM.
—Scary, Scary Halloween. Bunting, Eve. LC 86-2642. 32p. (ps-3). 1988. 12.95 (*0-89919-414-1*, Clarion Bks); pap. 5.95 (*0-89919-799-X*, Clarion Bks) HM.
—The Valentine Bears. Bunting, Eve. 32p. (gr. 3). 1985. 14.95 (*0-89919-138-X*, Clarion Bks); pap. 4.95 (*0-89919-313-7*, Clarion) HM.
—The Wild Christmas Reindeer. Brett, Jan. 32p. (ps-3). 1990. 14.95 (*0-399-22192-1*, Putnam) Putnam Pub Group.
Brett, Jan, photos by. The Enchanted Book: A Tale from Krakow. Porazinska, Janina. Smith, Bozena, tr. LC 86-22918. 32p. (gr. k-4). 1987. 13.95 (*0-15-225950-3*) HarBrace.
Breviek, Phil. Entice Their Imaginations. Short, David & Short, Pat. 64p. (gr. k-6). 1985. wkbk. 7.95 (*0-86653-324-9*, GA 658) Good Apple.
Brewis, Henry. Pigs in the Playground. Terry, John. 208p. 1986. pap. 7.95 (*0-85236-158-0*, Pub by Farming Pr UK); pap. text ed. 6.95 (*0-317-47058-2*, Pub. by Farming Pr UK) Diamond Farm Bk.
Brewster, Karen, et al. Discovering Torrance: A Guide & Coloring Book. Brewster, Dorothy P. Haggott, Mikko, tr. 52p. (Orig.). (gr. 3). 1987. pap. 4.50 (*0-9619944-0-1*); tchr's. manual 8.00 (*0-9619944-1-X*); write for info. Japanese suppl. (*0-9619944-2-8*) Rodor & Co.
Brewster, Patience. Bear & Mrs. Duck. Winthrop, Elizabeth. LC 87-25129. 32p. (ps-3). 1988. reinforced bdg. 14.95 (*0-8234-0687-3*); pap. 5.95 (*0-8234-0843-4*) Holiday.
—Bear's Christmas Surprise. Winthrop, Elizabeth. LC 90-26414. 32p. (ps-3). 1991. reinforced 14.95 (*0-8234-0888-4*) Holiday.
—Don't Touch My Room. Lakin, Patricia. 32p. (ps-3). 1988. 12.95 (*0-316-51230-3*); pap. 5.95 (*0-316-51228-1*) Little.
—The Fannie Farmer Junior Cook Book. rev. ed. Scobey, Joan. LC 92-42632. 1993. 19.95 (*0-316-77624-6*) Little.
—Good As New. Douglass, Barbara. LC 80-21406. 32p. (ps-1). 1982. 13.00 (*0-688-41983-6*); PLB 12.88 (*0-688-51983-0*) Lothrop.
—Good As New! Douglas, Barbara. LC 80-21406. (ps). 1989. pap. 3.95 (*0-688-08739-6*, Mulberry) Morrow.
—Princess Abigail & the Wonderful Hat. Kroll, Steven. LC 90-39213. 32p. (ps-3). 1991. reinforced 14.95 (*0-8234-0853-1*) Holiday.
—Queen of the May. Kroll, Steven. LC 92-16393. 32p. (ps-3). 1993. reinforced bdg. 15.95 (*0-8234-1004-8*) Holiday.
—There's More...Much More. Alexander, Sue. LC 86-33632. 32p. (ps-3). 1987. 12.95 (*0-15-200605-2*, Gulliver Bks) HarBrace.
Briansky, Rita. Grandmother Came from Dworitz: A Jewish Love Story. Vineberg, Ethel. 44p. (gr. 4 up). 1987. Repr. of 1978 ed. text ed. 3.95 (*0-88776-195-X*) Tundra Bks.
Brich, Reginald. Little Men. Alcott, Louisa May. (gr. 7 up). 1971. 17.95 (*0-316-03094-5*) Little.
Brickman, Robin. I Am an Artist. Collins, Pat L. LC 91-42071. 32p. (gr. k-3). 1992. 14.95 (*1-56294-702-8*); PLB 14.90 (*1-56294-082-1*) Millbrook Pr.
—Insects. Brandt, Keith. LC 84-2659. 32p. (gr. 3-6). 1985. PLB 9.49 (*0-8167-0184-9*); pap. text ed. 2.95 (*0-8167-0185-7*) Troll Assocs.
Bridgman, Allison. Thomasina & the Tommyknocker. Browne, Juanita K. LC 93-13732. viii, 85p. (Orig.). (gr. 4-7). 1993. pap. 8.75 (*0-9636621-0-4*) Browne Bks.
Bridgman, L. T. Finger Plays for Nursery & Kindergarten. Poulsson, Emilie. LC 74-165397. (ps-k). 1971. pap. 2.25 (*0-486-22588-7*) Dover.
Bridwell, Norman. Clifford & the Grouchy Neighbors. Bridwell, Norman. 32p. (gr. k-3). 1989. pap. 2.25 (*0-590-44261-9*); pap. 5.95 incl. cass. (*0-590-63437-2*) Scholastic Inc.
—Clifford Gets a Job. Bridwell, Norman. 32p. (gr. k-3). 1985. pap. 2.25 (*0-590-44296-1*) Scholastic Inc.
—Clifford Goes to Hollywood. Bridwell, Norman. 32p. (gr. k-3). 1990. pap. 2.25 (*0-590-44289-9*); pap. 5.95 incl. cass. (*0-590-63435-6*) Scholastic Inc.
—Clifford the Big Red Dog. Bridwell, Norman. (ps-3). 1988. 2.25 (*0-590-44297-X*); pap. 5.95 incl. cassette (*0-590-63212-4*) Scholastic Inc.
—Clifford the Big Red Dog. Bridwell, Norman. 32p. (ps-3). 1988. 10.95 (*0-590-40743-0*, Pub. by Scholastic Hardcover) Scholastic Inc.
—Clifford's Birthday Party. Bridwell, Norman. 32p. (Orig.). (gr. k-3). 1991. 8.95 (*0-590-44232-5*); pap. 5.95 incl. cassette (*0-590-63237-X*) Scholastic Inc.
—Clifford's Christmas. Bridwell, Norman. 32p. (Orig.). (gr. k-3). 1987. 2.25 (*0-590-44288-0*); incl. cassette 5.95 (*0-590-63210-8*) Scholastic Inc.
—Clifford's Family. Bridwell, Norman. 32p. (gr. k-3). 1984. pap. 2.25 (*0-590-44290-2*) Scholastic Inc.
—Clifford's Good Deeds. Bridwell, Norman. 32p. (gr. k-3). 1985. pap. 2.25 (*0-590-44292-9*) Scholastic Inc.

—Clifford's Halloween. Bridwell, Norman. 32p. (gr. k-3). 1989. pap. 2.25 (*0-590-44287-2*); pap. 5.95 (*0-590-63436-4*) Scholastic Inc.
—Clifford's Happy Days: A Pop-up Book. Bridwell, Norman. 16p. (Orig.). (gr. k-3). 1990. pap. 12.95 (*0-590-42926-4*) Scholastic Inc.
—Clifford's Kitten. Bridwell, Norman. 32p. (gr. k-3). 1984. pap. 2.25 (*0-590-44280-5*) Scholastic Inc.
—Clifford's Manners. Bridwell, Norman. 32p. (gr. k-3). 1987. pap. 2.25 (*0-590-44285-6*) Scholastic Inc.
—Clifford's Pals. Bridwell, Norman. 32p. (gr. k-3). 1985. pap. 2.25 (*0-590-44295-3*) Scholastic Inc.
—Clifford's Riddles. Bridwell, Norman. 32p. (gr. k-3). 1984. pap. 2.25 (*0-590-44282-1*) Scholastic Inc.
—Clifford's Sticker Book. Bridwell, Norman. 24p. (ps-3). 1984. pap. 5.95 (*0-590-33657-6*) Scholastic Inc.
—Clifford's Tricks. Bridwell, Norman. 32p. (gr. k-3). 1986. pap. 2.25 (*0-590-44291-0*) Scholastic Inc.
—Clifford's Word Book. Bridwell, Norman. 32p. (Orig.). (ps-1). 1990. pap. 2.25 (*0-590-43095-5*) Scholastic Inc.
—The Witch Next Door. Bridwell, Norman. 32p. (gr. k-3). 1986. pap. 2.50 (*0-590-40433-4*) Scholastic Inc.
—The Witch's Christmas. Bridwell, Norman. 32p. (gr. k-3). 1972. pap. 1.50 (*0-590-09216-2*) Scholastic Inc.
—The Witch's Christmas. Bridwell, Norman. 32p. (gr. k-3). 1986. pap. 1.95 (*0-590-40434-2*) Scholastic Inc.
—The Witch's Vacation. Bridwell, Norman. 32p. (Orig.). (gr. k-3). 1987. pap. 2.50 (*0-590-40558-6*) Scholastic Inc.
Brier, Peggy. Southern Fried Rat & Other Gruesome Tales. Cohen, Daniel. LC 82-25120. 128p. (gr. 7 up). 1982. 9.95 (*0-87131-400-2*) M Evans.
Briere, Euphemia. The Nativity of Our Lord: The Birth of the Messiah. Briere, Euphemia. (Orig.). (gr. 1-3). 1993. pap. 6.00 (*0-913026-38-7*) St Nectarios.
Brierley, Louise. The Fisherwoman. Carter, Anne. 32p. (gr. 1-4). 1991. 14.95 (*0-688-09872-X*); PLB 14.88 (*0-688-09873-8*) Lothrop.
—Lightning Inside You: And Other Native American Riddles. Bierhorst, John, ed. & tr. LC 91-21744. 112p. (gr. 2 up). 1992. 14.00 (*0-688-09582-8*) Morrow Jr Bks.
Briggs, Raymond. The Elephant & the Bad Baby. Vipont, Elfrida. 32p. (ps-3). 1986. (Coward); pap. 6.95 (*0-698-20625-8*) Putnam Pub Group.
—Jim & the Beanstalk. Briggs, Raymond. 40p. (ps-2). 1989. pap. 5.95 (*0-698-20641-X*, Sandcastle Bks) Putnam Pub Group.
—The Mother Goose Treasury. Briggs, Raymond. 1986. pap. 8.95 (*0-440-46408-0*, YB) Dell.
—The Snowman. Briggs, Raymond. LC 78-55904. 32p. (Orig.). (ps-2). 1986. pap. 4.95 book & doll pkg. (*0-394-88466-3*) Random Bks Yng Read.
—The Snowman. Briggs, Raymond. LC 78-55904. 32p. (ps-3). 1978. 13.95 (*0-394-83973-0*) Random Bks Yng Read.
—The Snowman Clock Book. Briggs, Raymond. LC 91-67874. 16p. (ps-3). 1992. pap. 7.99 (*0-679-83261-0*) Random Bks Yng Read.
—The Snowman Cuddle Cloth Book. Briggs, Raymond. 12p. (ps). 3.99 (*0-679-82696-3*) Random Bks Yng Read.
—The Snowman Storybook. Briggs, Raymond. LC 90-8029. 24p. (ps). 1990. 6.00 (*0-679-80840-X*) Random Bks Yng Read.
Briggs, Richard. Twenty-Six Object Talks for Children's Worship. Van Seters, Virginia A. 48p. 1988. pap. 3.99 (*0-87403-497-3*, 2877) Standard Pub.
—Twenty-Two Object Talks for Children's Worship. Van Seters, Virginia A. 48p. (gr. s-6). 1986. pap. 3.99 (*0-87403-055-2*, 2866) Standard Pub.
Bright, M. D., jt. illus. see Tanghal, Romeo.
Bright, Mark, jt. illus. see Johnston, Dirk.
Bright, Robert. Georgie. Bright, Robert. 44p. (gr. k-1). 1944. pap. 7.95 (*0-385-07307-0*) Doubleday.
—Georgie & the Robbers. Bright, Robert. LC 63-11384. 28p. (ps-1). 1963. pap. 5.95 (*0-385-04483-6*); pap. 2.50 (*0-385-13341-3*) Doubleday.
Brightling, Geoff. Cowboy. Murdoch, David H. LC 93-12768. 64p. (gr. 5 up). 1993. 15.00 (*0-679-84014-1*); PLB 15.99 (*0-679-94014-6*) Knopf Bks Yng Read.
Brigman, Chris. Bizarre & Beautiful Feelers. Santa Fe Writers Group. LC 93-2034. 48p. 1993. text ed. 14.95 (*1-56261-125-9*) John Muir.
—Bizarre & Beautiful Tongues. Santa Fe Writer's Group Staff. 48p. (gr. 4-7). 1993. text ed. 14.95 (*1-56261-123-2*) John Muir.
Brillhart, Julie. Anna's Goodbye Apron. Brillhart, Julie. Mathews, Judith, ed. LC 89-49362. 32p. (ps-1). 1990. PLB 13.95 (*0-8075-0375-4*) A Whitman.
—Story Hour - Starring Megan! Brillhart, Julie. Levine, Abby, ed. LC 91-19523. 32p. (ps-2). 1992. PLB 13.95 (*0-8075-7628-X*) A Whitman.
Brimner, Larry D., photos by. Snowboarding. Brimner, Larry D. LC 89-9088. 64p. (gr. 4-6). 1989. PLB 12.90 (*0-531-10748-5*) Watts.
Brimoh, Peregrino. Mr. B. Saro-Wiwa, Ken. 154p. (Orig.). (gr. 6 up). pap. text ed. 8.50x (*1-87071-601-9*) Three Continents.
Brinckloe, Julie. Fireflies! Brinckloe, Julie. LC 84-20158. 32p. (gr. k-3). 1985. RSBE 13.95 (*0-02-713310-9*, Macmillan Child Bk) Macmillan Child Grp.
—The Hunky-Dory Dairy. Lindbergh, Anne M. LC 85-16408. 147p. (gr. 4-6). 1986. 14.95 (*0-15-237449-3*, HB Juv Bks) HarBrace.

—Lotta on Troublemaker Street. Lindgren, Astrid. Bothmer, Gerry, tr. LC 90-25169. 64p. (gr. 1-4). 1991. pap. 2.95 (*0-689-71443-2*, Aladdin) Macmillan Child Grp.
—Playing Marbles. Brinckloe, Julie. LC 88-1608. 32p. (gr. k-3). 1988. 12.95 (*0-688-07143-0*); PLB 12.88 (*0-688-07144-9*, Morrow Jr Bks) Morrow Jr Bks.
Brindle, John. Melvin's Cold Feet. Crust, Linda. LC 90-47201. 32p. (gr. 2-3). 1991. PLB 18.60 (*0-8368-0356-6*) Gareth Stevens Inc.
Brindle, Susan A., jt. illus. see Hooker, Irene H.
Bringle, Beverly. Rising Fawn & the Fire Mystery. Awiakta, Marilou. Easson, Roger R., ed. LC 83-13824. 48p. (Orig.). (gr. 5 up). 1984. pap. 11.95 (*0-918518-29-6*) Iris Pr.
Brison-Stack, Guy. The Hebrew Primer. Strauss, Ruby, et al. 128p. (Orig.). (gr. 1-6). 1985. pap. 4.95 (*0-87441-392-3*); tchr's guide 12.50x (*0-87441-396-6*) Behrman.
British Museum. Money. Cribb, Joe. LC 89-15589. 64p. (gr. 5 up). 1990. 13.95 (*0-679-80438-2*); PLB 15.99 (*0-679-90438-7*) Knopf Bks Yng Read.
Britt, Gary. Birds. Kuchalla, Susan. LC 81-11412. 32p. (gr. k-2). 1982. lib. bdg. 11.59 (*0-89375-656-3*); pap. 2.95 (*0-89375-657-1*) Troll Assocs.
Britt, Stephanie. Best Halloween Book. Whitehead, Patricia. LC 84-8828. 32p. (gr. k-2). 1985. PLB 11.59 (*0-8167-0373-6*); pap. text ed. 2.95 (*0-8167-0374-4*) Troll Assocs.
—Fir Tree. Andersen, Hans Christian. 24p. (ps-3). 1989. pap. 2.95 (*0-8249-8389-0*, Ideals Child) Hambleton-Hill.
—Monster under My Bed. Gruber, Suzanne. LC 84-45687. 32p. (gr. k-2). 1985. PLB 10.89 (*0-8167-0456-2*); pap. text ed. 2.95 (*0-8167-0457-0*) Troll Assocs.
—Prayers at Eastertime. Kennedy, Pamela. 24p. (ps-k). 1990. pap. 3.95 (*0-8249-8422-6*, Ideals Child) Hambleton-Hill.
—Saturday with Little Rabbit. Murray, Marjorie D. LC 91-48362. 48p. (gr. k-3). 1993. RSBE 13.95 (*0-02-767753-2*, Macmillan Child Bk) Macmillan Child Grp.
—Story of Daniel & the Lions. Pingry, Patricia. 24p. (Orig.). (ps-3). 1988. pap. 3.95 (*0-8249-8179-0*, Ideals Child) Hambleton-Hill.
—The Story of Moses & the Ten Commandments. Pingry, Patricia. (ps-3). 1990. pap. 3.95 (*0-8249-8418-8*, Ideals Child) Hambleton-Hill.
—The Story of Passover for Children. Silberg, Francis B. 24p. (ps-2). 1989. pap. 3.95 (*0-8249-8309-2*, Ideals Child) Hambleton-Hill.
Britt, Stephanie M. The Day Bird Almost Flew the Coop at Peanut Butter Pond. Littke, Lael. 36p. (ps-1). 1991. pap. 4.95 incl. audiocassette (*1-55999-145-3*) LinguiSystems.
—The Day Porcupine Put on the Dog at Peanut Butter Pond. Littke, Lael. 36p. (ps-1). 1990. pap. 4.95 incl. audiocassette (*1-55999-123-2*) LinguiSystems.
—The Day Snake Saved Time at Peanut Butter Pond. Littke, Lael. 36p. (ps-1). 1990. pap. 4.95 incl. audiocassette (*1-55999-122-4*) LinguiSystems.
—The Day the Critter Sitters Hung It up at Peanut Butter Pond. Littke, Lael. 36p. (ps-1). 1991. pap. 4.95 incl. audiocassette (*1-55999-146-1*) LinguiSystems.
—The Day They Smelled a Skunk at Peanut Butter Pond. Littke, Lael. 36p. (ps-1). 1991. pap. 4.95 incl. audiocassette (*1-55999-144-5*) LinguiSystems.
—The Day Woodchuck Would Chuck Wood at Peanut Butter Pond. Littke, Lael. 36p. (ps-1). 1990. pap. 4.95 incl. audiocassette (*1-55999-124-0*) LinguiSystems.
—Don't Rock the Boat: The Story of the Miraculous Catch. Lashbrook, Marilyn. LC 88-63779. 32p. (ps). 1989. 5.95 (*0-86606-435-4*, 867) Roper Pr.
—Get Lost, Little Brother: The Story of Joseph. Lashbrook, Marilyn. LC 87-62503. 32p. (ps). 1988. 5.95 (*0-86606-432-X*, 863) Roper Pr.
—I Don't Want to: The Story of Jonah. Lashbrook, Marilyn. LC 87-60264. 32p. (ps). 1987. 5.95 (*0-86606-428-1*, 844) Roper Pr.
—I May be Little: The Story of David's Growth. Lashbrook, Marilyn. LC 87-60262. 32p. (ps). 1987. 5.95 (*0-86606-429-X*, 843) Roper Pr.
—My Little Prayers. Ward, Brenda C., compiled by. LC 93-578. (gr. 3 up). 1993. pap. 5.99 (*0-8499-1064-1*) Word Pub.
—No Tree for Christmas: The Story of Jesus' Birth. Lashbrook, Marilyn. LC 88-62025. 32p. (ps). 1989. 5.95 (*0-86606-434-6*, 866) Roper Pr.
—Now I See: The Story of the Man Born Blind. Lashbrook, Marilyn. LC 86-62520. 32p. (ps). 1989. 5.95 (*0-86606-437-0*, 869) Roper Pr.
—Prayers at Christmastime. Kennedy, Pamela. 24p. (ps-k). 1990. 3.95 (*0-8249-8480-3*, Ideals Child) Hambleton-Hill.
—Someone to Love: The Story of Creation. Lashbrook, Marilyn. LC 87-60261. 32p. (ps). 1987. 5.95 (*0-86606-426-5*, 841) Roper Pr.
—Two by Two: The Story of Noah's Faith. Lashbrook, Marilyn. LC 87-60263. 32p. (ps). 1987. 5.95 (*0-86606-427-3*, 842) Roper Pr.
—The Wall That Did Not Fall: The Story of Rahab's Faith. Lashbrook, Marilyn. LC 87-63420. 32p. (ps). 1988. 5.95 (*0-86606-433-8*, 864) Roper Pr.
—Who Needs a Boat? The Story of Moses. Lashbrook, Marilyn. LC 87-83295. 32p. (ps). 1988. 5.95 (*0-86606-431-1*, 862) Roper Pr.

Britton, Colleen. Palestine Thirty A. D. You Are There. Britton, Colleen. 73p. (Orig.). (ps-6). 1987. pap. 12.95 (*0-940754-38-X*) Ed Ministries.

Brix-Henker, Silke. The Giant Apple. Scheffler, Ursel. 32p. (gr. k-3). 1990. PLB 18.95 (*0-87614-413-X*) Carolrhoda Bks.

—Stop Your Crowing, Kasimir! Scheffler, Ursel. 32p. (gr. k-3). 1988. lib. bdg. 18.95 (*0-87614-323-0*) Carolrhoda Bks.

Broda, Ron. The Little Crooked Christmas Tree. Cutting, Michael. 24p. 1991. 13.95 (*0-590-45204-5*, Scholastic Hardcover) Scholastic Inc.

Broderick, Michael. Daniel & the Sand Angel: A Florida Christmas Story. Anderson, Debbie S. 32p. (Orig.). (ps-4). 1988. pap. 9.95 (*0-936417-11-0*) Axelrod Pub.

Brodie, Caroline. The Planets: Neighbors in Space. Bendick, Jeanne. 32p. (gr. k-2). 1991. PLB 12.40 (*1-878841-03-3*) Millbrook Pr.

—The Stars: Lights in the Night Sky. Bendick, Jeanne. 32p. (gr. k-2). 1991. PLB 12.40 (*1-878841-00-9*) Millbrook Pr.

—The Sun: Our Very Own Star. Bendick, Jeanne. 32p. (gr. k-2). 1991. PLB 12.40 (*1-878841-02-5*) Millbrook Pr.

—The Universe: Think Big! Bendick, Jeanne. 32p. (gr. k-2). 1991. PLB 12.40 (*1-878841-01-7*) Millbrook Pr.

Brodie, Cynthia. Mother Goose. Nayer, Judy, ed. 24p. (ps-2). 1992. pap. 0.99 (*1-56293-105-9*) McClanahan Bk.

Brodley, John. Mostly Ghostly: Eight Spooky Tales to Chill Your Bones. Zorn, Steven, as told by. LC 91-71087. 56p. (gr. 2 up). 1991. 9.98 (*1-56138-033-4*) Courage Bks.

Brodsky, Harry. The Big Parade. Mockrin, Ida. 16p. (ps-1). 1983. pap. 2.00 (*0-9612244-0-1*) Honeycomb Pr.

Brogdon, Lecia. Thirteen Tennessee Ghosts & Jeffrey. Windham, Kathryn T. LC 73-87004. 160p. (gr. 6 up). 1987. pap. 9.50t (*0-8173-0378-2*) U of Ala Pr.

Brogger, Lilian. Wildebeest. Berliner, Franz. Gyldendal, tr. LC 90-82449. 32p. (ps-2). 1991. 13.95 (*0-8249-8488-9*, Ideals Child) Hambleton-Hill.

Brook, Anne C. A Trip to a Pow Wow. Red Hawk, Richard. 45p. (Orig.). (gr. k-3). 1988. pap. 6.95 (*0-940113-14-7*) Sierra Oaks Pub.

Brooke, L. Leslie. Golden Goose Book. Brooke, L. Leslie. 96p. (ps-3). 1992. 16.45 (*0-395-61303-5*, Clarion Bks) HM.

—Ring O'Roses. Brooke, L. Leslie. 96p. (ps-3). 1992. 16.95 (*0-395-61304-3*, Clarion Bks) HM.

Brooke, Leonard L. Nonsense Poems of Edward Lear. Lear, Edward. 128p. 1991. 18.45 (*0-395-57001-8*, Clarion Bks) HM.

Brooks, Nan. Nicole Digs a Hole. Gregorich, Barbara. Hoffman, Joan, ed. 32p. (gr. k-2). 1987. wkbk. 1.99 (*0-88743-101-1*, 02601) Sch Zone Pub Co.

—The Very Best Book. Weir, Christy. Woodard, Virginia, ed. LC 92-32744. 35p. (ps-2). 1993. 12.99 (*0-8307-1595-9*, 5112262) Regal.

Brooks, Ron. Bianca & Roja. Brinsmead, Hesba. 112p. (Orig.). (gr. 2-6). 1993. pap. 7.95 (*1-86373-082-6*, Pub. by Allen & Unwin Aust Pty AT) IPG Chicago.

—John Brown, Rose, & the Midnight Cat. Wagner, Jenny. (gr. 5-8). 1980. pap. 3.99 (*0-14-050306-4*, Puffin) Puffin Bks.

—This Baby. McClelland, Julia. LC 92-43756. 1994. write for info. (*0-395-66613-9*) HM.

Broomfield, Robert. Saint Joan: The Girl in Armour. Smith, Dorothy. 1990. 2.95 (*0-8091-6594-5*) Paulist Pr.

—Thomas More: The King's Good Servant. Smith, Dorothy. 1990. 2.95 (*0-8091-6595-3*) Paulist Pr.

Brophy, Paul. No Monkey Too Big. Spacone, Carl. Hoffman, John, ed. 224p. (Orig.). (gr. 9 up). 1987. 8.95 (*0-944712-00-2*); pap. text ed. 8.95 (*0-318-23727-X*) Spacone Pub.

Brost, Victoria. The Tale of Humphrey the Humpback Whale. Heus, John & Robinson, Tom. 32p. (Orig.). (ps-3). 1985. pap. 6.95 (*0-9616109-0-5*) Brost Heus.

Brostrom, Eileen. Dot's Pot. Carratello, Patty. Spivak, Darlene, ed. 16p. (gr. k-2). 1988. wkbk. 1.95 (*1-55734-389-6*) Tchr Create Mat.

—My Truck & My Pup. Carratello, Patty. Spivak, Darlene, ed. 16p. (gr. k-2). 1988. wkbk. 1.95 (*1-55734-390-X*) Tchr Create Mat.

—This Is Fred. Carratello, Patty. Spivak, Darlene, ed. 16p. (gr. k-2). 1988. wkbk. 1.95 (*1-55734-391-8*) Tchr Create Mat.

Brother Theo. What Kwanzaa Means to Me. Oni, Sauda. 36p. (gr. k-3). Date not set. pap. 3.95 (*0-912444-38-X*) DARE Bks.

Brough, Hazel. The Charm of the Bear Claw Necklace. Searcy, Margaret Z. LC 89-78044. 80p. (gr. 3-7). 1990. 12.95 (*0-88289-821-3*); pap. 6.95 (*0-88289-777-2*) Pelican.

—Wolf Dog of the Woodland Indians. Searcy, Margaret Z. LC 90-26215. 112p. (Orig.). (ps-8). 1991. pap. 5.95 (*0-88289-778-0*) Pelican.

Broutin, Christian. Arbre. (FRE.). (ps-1). 1989. 14.95 (*2-07-035712-0*) Schoenhof.

—Boats. Jeunesse, Gallimard, created by. LC 92-41414. 1993. 11.95 (*0-590-47131-7*) Scholastic Inc.

—Living on a Tropical Island. Planche, Bernard. Matthews, Sarah, tr. from FRE. LC 87-34592. 38p. (gr. k-5). 1988. 4.95 (*0-944589-13-8*, 138) Young Discovery Lib.

—On the Banks of the Pharaoh's Nile. Courtalon, Corinne. LC 87-37195. 38p. (gr. k-5). 1988. 4.95 (*0-944589-07-3*, 073) Young Discovery Lib.

—The Sky: Stars & Night. Verdat, Jean-Pierre. Bogard, Vicki, tr. from FRE. LC 90-50776. 38p. (gr. k-5). 1991. 4.95 (*0-944589-32-4*, 324) Young Discovery Lib.

Brouwer, Jack, jt. illus. see Poindexter, Cathlene.

Brower, Bob. Latter-Day Saints Temple Coloring Book. 80p. (Orig.). (gr. 2-6). 1993. pap. 5.95 (*0-910523-22-3*) Grandin Bk Co.

—Presidents of the LDS Church Coloring Book. 50p. (Orig.). (gr. 2-6). 1993. pap. 5.95 (*0-910523-21-5*) Grandin Bk Co.

Brower, R. K. Joseph Smith's First Vision: A Book for Little Saints. Literski, Nicholas D. LC (ps). 1991. 4.95 (*0-9628778-0-8*) Eagle Gate UT.

Brown, Amy L. Do-It-Yourself Story Puzzle Book. Lasley, Mary. 2p. (ps). 1988. 9.95 (*0-9622406-0-5*) MOL Bks.

Brown, Anthony. Gorilla. Brown, Anthony. LC 85-13. 32p. (ps-2). 1989. pap. 6.00 (*0-394-82225-0*) Knopf Bks Yng Read.

Brown, Barbara. The First Christmas. Billington, Rachel. LC 87-20383. 32p. (gr. k-5). 1987. pap. 6.95 (*0-8192-1410-8*) Morehouse Pub.

Brown, Becky. Leave, Retard, Leave! Brown, Towana J. 127p. (Orig.). (gr. 8-12). 1988. pap. 3.50 (*0-9622060-0-8*) T J Brown.

—Raglagger. Brown, Towana J. LC 89-90647. 168p. (Orig.). (gr. 5-7). 1989. pap. 3.50 (*0-9622060-2-4*) T J Brown.

Brown, Becky E. Scottie. Brown, Towana J. LC 88-93029. 150p. (Orig.). (gr. 5-6). 1989. pap. 3.50 (*0-9622060-1-6*) T J Brown.

Brown, Bernice. Clowns to the Rescue. Zeplin, Zeno. 48p. (gr. k-3). 1993. 9.95 (*1-877740-12-8*); pap. 5.50 (*1-877740-13-6*) Nel-Mar Pub.

—The Magic Caterpillar. Brown, Bernice. Eberspacher, Jeff, ed. 48p. (gr. k-3). 1992. PLB 9.95 casebound (*1-877740-19-5*); pap. 5.50 (*1-877740-20-9*) Nel-Mar Pub.

Brown, Blanche M. What's Keeping You, Santa? A Christmas Musical Program Package. Pickett, Margaret E. 74p. (gr. k-12). 1983. Incl Production Guide with choir arranged songs, cass of songs, thirty slides from bk. 49.95 (*0-913939-01-3*) TP Assocs.

—What's Keeping You, Santa? A Christmas Story Book. Pickett, Margaret E. LC 83-50122. 64p. (gr. k-5). 1983. PLB 24.95 (*0-913939-00-5*); read a long Cassette 4.95 (*0-913939-03-X*) TP Assocs.

Brown, Bob, et al. Batman: Tales of the Demon. O'Neil, Dennis. Levitz, Paul, et al, eds. 208p. (Orig.). 1991. pap. 17.95 (*0-930289-94-3*) DC Comics.

Brown, Christine M. Peer Listing in the Middle School: Training Activities for Students. Hazouri, Sandra P. & Smith, Miriam F. LC 91-75586. 134p. (Orig.). (gr. 6-8). 1991. pap. text ed. 8.95x (*0-932796-34-6*) Ed Media Corp.

Brown, Craig. Big Thunder Magic. Strete, Craig K. LC 89-34613. 32p. (ps up). 1990. 12.95 (*0-688-08853-8*); PLB 12.88 (*0-688-08854-6*) Greenwillow.

Brown, Craig M. The Gossamer Tree: A Christmas Fable. Knapp, Toni, ed. LC 88-90759. 32p. (Orig.). (gr. 2 up). 1988. 14.95 (*1-882092-00-7*); pap. 8.95 (*1-882092-02-3*) Travis Ilse.

—Ornery Morning. Demuth, Patricia B. LC 90-40188. 24p. (ps-1). 1991. 13.95 (*0-525-44688-5*, DCB) Dutton Child Bks.

—The Six Bridges of Humphrey the Whale. Knapp, Toni, ed. LC 89-8417. 48p. (gr. 8 up). 1989. 15.95 (*1-882092-01-5*) Travis Ilse.

—Snips the Tinker. Roop, Peter & Roop, Connie. McKissack, Patricia & McKissack, Fredrick, eds. LC 88-60385. 32p. (gr. k-3). 1990. text ed. 8.95 (*0-88335-785-2*); pap. text ed. 4.95 (*0-88335-797-6*) Milliken Pub Co.

—The Talking Bird & the Story Pouch. Lawson, Amy. LC 86-45493. 96p. (gr. 5up). 1987. HarpC Child Bks.

Brown, Denise. Philip the Fox & Other Stories. Voss-Bark, Doris L. LC 66-10511. (gr. 3-6). 1967. 13.95 (*0-8023-1105-9*) Dufour.

Brown, Diane B. GAIA Celebration for Children: A Workshop & Activities Book. Hawthorne, Terri B. & Brown, Diane B. 32p. 1990. pap. 5.99 (*0-929404-02-5*) Tara Educ Servs.

—Winter Solstice Celebrations Through the Ages: A Coloring Book for All Ages. Hawthorne, Terri B. & Brown, Diane B. 32p. 1990. pap. 5.99 (*0-929404-01-7*) Tara Educ Servs.

Brown, Elizabeth. The Great Asparagus War. Ford, Beatrice. Duthie, Dorothy B., ed. 1991. pap. write for info. (*1-88017-250-X*) Storyteller.

Brown, Jane C. Defenders of the Universe. Kelleher, D. V. LC 92-1617. 128p. (gr. 3-5). 1993. 13.45 (*0-395-60515-6*) HM.

—The Smallest Cow in the World. new ed. Paterson, Katherine. LC 90-30521. 64p. (gr. k-3). 1991. 14.00 (*0-06-024690-1*); PLB 13.89 (*0-06-024691-X*) HarpC Child Bks.

—Smallest Cow in the World. new ed. Paterson, Katherine. LC 90-30521. 64p. (gr. k-3). 1993. pap. 3.50 (*0-06-444164-4*, Trophy) HarpC Child Bks.

Brown, Jean. Spin-a-Story, the Haunted Banana & Other Wacky Mysteries. Daniel, Jennifer. 24p. (Orig.). (gr. 4-7). 1990. pap. 2.95 (*1-878890-02-6*) Palisades Prodns.

—Spin-a-Story, Twenty Thousand French Fries under the Sea & Other Crazy Classics. Daniel, Jennifer. 24p. (gr. 4-7). 1990. pap. 2.95 (*1-878890-01-8*) Palisades Prodns.

Brown, Jim, jt. illus. see Runyon, Anne.

Brown, Judith. Melvil & Dewey in the Chips. Swallow, Pamela C. LC 86-61092. 48p. (Orig.). (gr. 1-3). 1986. o. p 9.95 (*0-936915-02-1*); pap. 4.95 (*0-936915-03-X*) Shoe Tree Pr.

—Melvil & Dewey in the Fast Lane. Swallow, Pamela C. LC 89-17926. 48p. (gr. k-3). 1989. pap. 4.95 (*1-55870-134-6*) Shoe Tree Pr.

Brown, Judith G. The Best Christmas Pageant Ever. Robinson, Barbara. LC 72-76501. 96p. (gr. 3 up). 1972. 14.00 (*0-06-025043-7*); PLB 13.89 (*0-06-025044-5*) HarpC Child Bks.

—The Best Christmas Pageant Ever. Robinson, Barbara. LC 72-76501. 96p. (gr. 3 up). 1988. pap. 28.00 (*0-06-440278-9*, Trophy); pap. 3.95 (*0-685-44099-0*) HarpC Child Bks.

—I Sing a Song of the Saints of God. Scott, Lesbia, text by. LC 91-10393. 32p. (ps-5). 1991. Repr. 10.95 (*0-8192-1561-9*) Morehouse Pub.

—Mandy. Edwards, Julie. LC 76-157901. 224p. (gr. 3-6). 1989. 3.95 (*0-06-440296-7*, Trophy) HarpC Child Bks.

—Mandy. reissued ed. Edwards, Julie. LC 76-157901. 192p. (gr. 4-7). 1990. PLB 13.89 (*0-06-021803-7*) HarpC Child Bks.

—Maudie in the Middle. Naylor, Phyllis R. & Reynolds, Lura S. LC 87-3470. 176p. (gr. 2-6). 1988. SBE 13.95 (*0-689-31395-0*, Atheneum Child Bk) Macmillan Child Grp.

—New Treasury of Children's Poetry. Cole, Joanna. LC 83-20821. 224p. (ps-8). 1984. pap. 18.50 (*0-385-18539-1*) Doubleday.

—An Orphan for Nebraska. Talbot, Charlene J. LC 78-12179. 216p. (gr. 4-6). 1979. SBE 14.95 (*0-689-30698-9*, Atheneum Childrens Bks) Macmillan Child Grp.

—Ring Around the Moon: Two Hundred Songs, Tongue Twisters, Riddles & Rhymes for Children. Fowke, Edith. 160p. (gr. k-5). 1987. pap. 12.95 (*1-55021-006-8*, Pub. by NC Press CN) U of Toronto Pr.

Brown, Judy. The Do-It-Yourself Genius Kit, 4 bks. Brandeth, Gyles. (ps-3). 1989. Gift Set. pap. 3.95 (*0-14-095331-0*, Puffin) Puffin Bks.

—The Emergency Excuses Kit, 4 bks. Brandeth, Gyles. (gr. 2-5). 1992. Boxed Set. pap. 4.50 (*0-14-034832-8*) Puffin Bks.

—The Emergency Joke Kit. Brandeth, Gyles. (Orig.). (ps-3). 1988. pap. 3.95 (*0-14-095322-1*, Puffin) Puffin Bks.

—The Emergency Joke Kite. Brandeth, Gyles. (ps-3). 1988. pap. 3.50 (*0-317-69598-3*, Puffin) Puffin Bks.

—An Oxford Book of Christmas Stories. Pepper, Dennis, ed. 224p. (gr. 3 up). 1988. 16.95 (*0-19-278119-7*); pap. 10.95 1988 (*0-19-278124-3*) OUP.

Brown, K. Eeny, Meeny, Miney Mole. Yolen, Jane. 1992. 13.95 (*0-15-225350-5*, HB Juv Bks) HarBrace.

Brown, Ken. The King of the Woods. Day, David. LC 93-9410. 32p. (ps-2). 1993. Repr. of 1993 ed. RSBE 13.95 (*0-02-726361-4*, Four Winds) Macmillan Child Grp.

Brown, Kenneth. Barn House Book: Rhymes, Riddles, & Jokes. Brown, Kenneth. Date not set. 12.95 (*1-56743-046-5*) Amistad Pr.

—Dollhouse Book: Color & Counting Concepts. 1994. 12.95 (*1-56743-044-9*) Amistad Pr.

Brown, Laurene K. The Bionic Bunny Show. Brown, Marc. 32p. (ps-3). 1985. 14.95 (*0-316-11120-1*, Joy St Bks); pap. 5.95 (*0-316-10992-4*, Joy St Bks) Little.

Brown, M. K. Let's Go Swimming with Mr. Sillypants. Brown, M. K. LC 85-29900. 32p. (ps-2). 1992. pap. 4.99 (*0-517-59030-1*) Crown Bks Yng Read.

Brown, Marc. Arthur Goes to Camp. Brown, Marc. LC 81-15588. 32p. (ps-3). 1984. 14.95 (*0-316-11218-6*, Joy St Bks); pap. 4.95 (*0-316-11058-2*, Joy St Bks) Little.

—Arthur's Birthday. Brown, Marc. 32p. (ps-3). 1989. 14.95 (*0-316-11073-6*, Joy St Bks) Little.

—Arthur's Christmas. Brown, Marc. LC 84-4373. (ps-3). 1985. 14.95 (*0-316-11180-5*, Joy St Bks); pap. 4.95 (*0-316-10993-2*) Little.

—Arthur's Eyes. Brown, Marc. LC 79-11734. (ps-3). 1979. lib. bdg. 14.95 (*0-316-11063-9*, Joy St Bks) Little.

—Arthur's Eyes. Brown, Marc. 32p. (ps-3). 1986. pap. 4.95 (*0-316-11069-8*, Joy St Bks) Little.

—Arthur's Halloween. Brown, Marc. LC 82-14286. 32p. (ps-3). 1983. 14.95 (*0-316-11116-3*, Joy St Bks); pap. 4.95 (*0-316-11059-0*, Joy St Bks) Little.

—Arthur's Nose. Brown, Marc. 32p. (ps-3). 1986. lib. bdg. 14.95 (*0-316-11193-7*, Joy St Bks); pap. 4.95 (*0-316-11070-1*, Joy St Bks) Little.

—Arthur's Teacher Trouble. Brown, Marc. 32p. (ps-3). 1989. 13.95 (*0-316-11244-5*, Joy St Bks); pap. 4.95 (*0-316-11186-4*, Joy St Bks) Little.

—Arthur's Thanksgiving. Brown, Marc. LC 83-798. 32p. (gr. 1-3). 1984. 14.95 (*0-316-11060-4*, Joy St Bks); pap. 4.95 (*0-316-11232-1*) Little.

—Arthur's Tooth. Brown, Marc. 32p. (ps-3). 1985. 14.95 (*0-316-11245-3*, Joy St Bks) Little.

—Arthur's Valentine. Brown, Marc. (ps-3). 1980. 14.95 (*0-316-11062-0*, Joy St Bks) Little.

—Arthur's Valentine. Brown, Marc. 32p. (ps-3). 1988. pap. 4.95 (*0-316-11187-2*, Joy St Bks) Little.

—The Banza. Wolkstein, Diane. LC 81-65845. 32p. (ps-3). 1981. Dial Bks Young.
—Can You Jump Like a Frog? 8p. (ps-k). 1989. 5.95 (0-525-44463-7, DCB) Dutton Child Bks.
—D. W. All Wet. Brown, Marc. (ps-3). 1988. 10.95 (0-316-11077-9, Joy St Bks) Little.
—D. W. Flips. Brown, Marc. (ps-2). 1987. 12.95 (0-316-11239-9, Joy St Bks) Little.
—Dinosaurs Divorce: A Guide for Changing Families. Brown, Laurene K. & Brown, Marc. 32p. (ps-3). 1988. 14.95 (0-316-11248-8); pap. 5.95 (0-316-10996-7) Little.
—Dinosaurs to the Rescue: A Guide to Protecting Our Planet. Brown, Laurie K. & Brown, Marc. (ps-3). 1992. 14.95 (0-316-11087-6, Joy St Bks) Little.
—Dinosaurs Travel: A Guide for Families on the Go. Brown, Laurene K. & Brown, Marc. 32p. (ps-3). 1988. 13.95 (0-316-11076-0) Little.
—The Family Read-Aloud Christmas Treasury. Low, Alice, compiled by. (ps up). 1989. 17.95 (0-316-53371-8, Joy St Bks) Little.
—The Family Read-Aloud Holiday Treasury. Low, Alice. 1991. 19.95 (0-316-53368-8) Little.
—Go West, Swamp Monsters. Christian, Mary B. LC 84-12686. 48p. (ps-3). 1985. 8.95 (0-8037-0091-1) Dial Bks Young.
—Hand Rhymes. Brown, Marc. 32p. (ps-1). 1993. pap. 4.99 (0-14-054939-0, Puffin Unicorn) Puffin Bks.
—Happy Birthday Little Witch. Hautzig, Deborah. 1985. pap. 2.95 (0-394-87365-3) Random Bks Yng Read.
—Little Witch's Big Night. Hautzig, Deborah. LC 84-3309. 48p. (ps-2). 1984. PLB 7.99 (0-394-96587-6); pap. 2.95 (0-394-86587-1) Random Bks Yng Read.
—Little Witch's Book of Magic Spells. Hautzig, Deborah. LC 87-63196. 24p. (ps-1). 1993. 2.99 (0-679-84769-3) Random Bks Yng Read.
—Oh, Kojo! How Could You? Aardema, Verna. LC 84-1710. 32p. (ps-3). 1984. 14.00 (0-8037-0006-7); PLB 12.89 (0-8037-0007-5) Dial Bks Young.
—Oh, Kojo! How Could You! Aardema, Verna. LC 84-1710. 32p. (ps-3). 1988. pap. 4.99 (0-8037-0449-6) Dial Bks Young.
—One, Two Buckle My Shoe. 8p. (ps-k). 1989. 5.95 (0-525-44462-9, DCB) Dutton Child Bks.
—Party Rhymes. Brown, Marc, compiled by. LC 88-17680. 48p. (ps-3). 1988. 13.95 (0-525-44402-5, DCB) Dutton Child Bks.
—Pickle Things. Brown, Marc. LC 80-10540. 48p. (ps-3). 1980. 5.95 (0-8193-1027-1) Parents.
—Play Rhymes. Brown, Marc, compiled by. LC 87-13537. 32p. (ps-1). 1987. 12.95 (0-525-44336-3, DCB) Dutton Child Bks.
—Play Rhymes. Brown, Marc, compiled by. 32p. (ps-1). 1993. pap. 4.99 (0-14-054936-6, Puffin Unicorn) Puffin Bks.
—Rabbit's New Rug. Delton, Judy. LC 79-16639. 40p. (ps-3). 1980. 5.95 (0-8193-1009-3); PLB 5.95 (0-8193-1010-7) Parents.
—Rabbit's New Rug. Delton, Judy. 48p. (ps-2). 1992. pap. 2.95 (0-448-40318-8, G&D) Putnam Pub Group.
—Rabbit's New Rug. Delton, Judy. LC 93-15453. 1993. write for info. (0-8368-0972-6) Gareth Stevens Inc.
—Read-Aloud Rhymes for the Very Young. Prelutsky, Jack, ed. Trelease, Jim, intro. by. LC 86-7147. 112p. (ps-3). 1988. bk. & cassette pkg. 19.95 (0-394-89833-8) Knopf Bks Yng Read.
—Read Aloud Rhymes for the Very Young. Prelutsky, Jack, ed. Trelease, Jim, intro. by. LC 86-7147. 112p. (ps-3). 1986. 17.00 (0-394-87218-5); PLB 16.99 (0-394-97218-X) Knopf Bks Yng Read.
—Rex & Lilly at Play. Brown, Laurie K. LC 93-25877. 1994. 12.95 (0-316-11386-7) Little.
—The Silly Tail Book. Brown, Marc. LC 83-2250. 48p. (ps-3). 1983. 5.95 (0-8193-1109-X); pap. 2.95 (0-8193-1158-8) Parents.
—Swamp Monsters. Christian, Mary B. LC 82-1574. 56p. (ps-3). 1983. pap. 4.95 (0-8037-7614-4) Dial Bks Young.
—Swamp Monsters. Christian, Mary B. LC 93-25616. (gr. 1-4). 1994. pap. 3.25 (0-14-036841-8, Puffin) Puffin Bks.
—Teddy Bear, Teddy Bear. 8p. (ps-k). 1989. 5.95 (0-525-44531-5, DCB) Dutton Child Bks.
—There's No Place Like Home. Brown, Marc. LC 84-4229. 48p. (ps-3). 1984. 5.95 (0-8193-1125-1) Parents.
—Toddler Time: A Book to Share with Your Toddler. Brown, Laurie K. 48p. 1990. 14.95 (0-316-11263-1, Joy St Bks) Little.
—The True Francine. Brown, Marc. 32p. (ps-3). 1981. 15.95 (0-316-11212-7, Joy St Bks) Little.
—The True Francine. Brown, Marc. (ps-3). 1987. pap. 5.95 (0-316-11243-7, Joy St Bks) Little.
—Two Little Monkeys. 8p. (ps-k). 1989. 5.95 (0-525-44533-1, DCB) Dutton Child Bks.
—What Do You Call a Dumb Bunny? & Other Rabbit Riddles, Games, Jokes & Cartoons. Brown, Marc. LC 82-21650. 32p. (ps-3). 1983. (Joy St Bks); pap. 4.95 (0-316-11119-8, Joy St Bks) Little.
—What's So Funny, Ketu? Aardema, Verna. LC 82-70195. 32p. (ps-3). 1989. pap. 4.95 (0-8037-0646-4) Dial Bks Young.
—Why the Tides Ebb & Flow. Bowden, Joan. 48p. (gr. k-3). 1990. pap. 5.95 (0-395-54952-3) HM.
—Witches Four. Brown, Marc. LC 79-5263. 48p. (ps-3). 1980. 5.95 (0-8193-1013-1); PLB 5.95 (0-8193-1014-X) Parents.
—Witches Four. Brown, Marc. 48p. (ps-2). 1991. pap. 2.95 (0-448-41079-6, G&D) Putnam Pub Group.

—A World Full of Monsters. McQueen, John T. LC 85-48257. 32p. (ps-3). 1986. (Crowell Jr Bks) HarpC Child Bks.
—Your First Garden Book. Brown, Marc. (gr. 1 up). 1981. 12.45i (0-316-11217-8, Pub. by Atlantic Pr); pap. 6.95 (0-316-11215-1) Little.
Brown, Marc & Krensky, Stephen. Dinosaurs, Beware! A Safety Guide. Brown, Marc & Krensky, Stephen. LC 82-15207. 32p. (ps-3). 1984. 14.95 (0-316-11228-3, Joy St Bks); pap. 6.95 (0-316-11219-4, Joy St Bks) Little.
Brown, Marc T. Science Games & Puzzles. White, Laurence B. LC 84-40786. 1979. pap. 4.95 (0-201-08606-9, Lipp Jr Bks) HarpC Child Bks.
—Science Games & Puzzles. White, Laurence B., Jr. LC 85-43035. 96p. (gr. 1-4). 1985. pap. 6.95 (0-06-446013-4, Trophy) HarpC Child Bks.
—Science Toys & Tricks. White, Laurence B. LC 84-40757. 1980. pap. 4.95 (0-201-08659-X, Lipp Jr Bks) HarpC Child Bks.
—Science Toys & Tricks. White, Laurence B., Jr. LC 85-43036. 96p. (gr. 1-4). 1985. pap. 6.95 (0-06-446014-2, Trophy) HarpC Child Bks.
Brown, Marcia. Cinderella. 2nd ed. Perrault, Charles. Brown, Marcia, tr. from FRE. LC 87-34920. 32p. (ps-3). 1988. pap. 4.50 (0-689-71261-8, Aladdin) Macmillan Child Grp.
—Dick Whittington & His Cat. Brown, Marcia. LC 50-9157. 32p. (gr. k-3). 1988. Repr. of 1950 ed. RSBE 14.95 (0-684-18998-4, Scribners Young Read) Macmillan Child Grp.
—Of Swans, Sugarplums & Satin Slippers. Verdy, Violette. 80p. 1991. 15.95 (0-590-43484-5, Scholastic Hardcover) Scholastic Inc.
—Once a Mouse. Brown, Marcia. LC 61-14769. 32p. (ps-3). 1972. SBE 13.95 (0-684-12662-1, Scribners Young Read) Macmillan Child Grp.
—Once a Mouse. Brown, Marcia. LC 89-32057. 32p. (gr. k-4). 1989. pap. 3.95 (0-689-71343-6, Aladdin) Macmillan Child Grp.
—Shadow. Cendrars, Blaise. Brown, Marcia, tr. from FRE. LC 81-9424. 40p. (gr. 2 up). 1982. SBE 16.95 (0-684-17226-7, Scribners Young Read) Macmillan Child Grp.
—Shadow. Brown, Marcia. LC 86-3432. 38p. (ps up). 1986. pap. 3.95 (0-689-71084-4, Aladdin) Macmillan Child Grp.
—Sopa de Piedras. Brown, Marcia. Mlawer, Teresa, tr. from ENG. (gr. 5-7). 1991. PLB 12.95 (0-9625162-1-X) Lectorum Pubns.
—Stone Soup. Brown, Marcia. LC 47-11630. 48p. (ps-4). 1979. RSBE 13.95 (0-684-92296-7, Scribners Young Read); (Scribner) Macmillan Child Grp.
—Stone Soup. reissued ed. Brown, Marcia. LC 86-10964. 48p. (ps-2). 1986. pap. 3.95 (0-689-71103-4, Aladdin) Macmillan Child Grp.
—Stone Soup. Brown, Marcia. (gr. 1-4). 1987. incl. cassette 19.95 (0-87499-053-X); pap. 12.95 incl. cassette (0-87499-052-1); 4 paperbacks, cassette & guide 27.95 (0-87499-054-8) Live Oak Media.
—The Three Billy Goats Gruff. Asbjornsen, P. C. & Moe, J. E. 28p. (ps-3). 1991. pap. 3.95 (0-15-690150-1) HarBrace.
Brown, Margaret W. Three Best-Loved Tales: Mister Dog; The Color Kittens; Seven Little Postmen. 80p. (ps-2). 1992. write for info. (0-307-15634-6, 15634, Golden Pr) Western Pub.
Brown, Margery. Dori the Mallard. Allred, Gordon. (gr. 5 up). 1968. 8.95 (0-8392-3052-4) Astor-Honor.
—Old Crackfoot. Allred, Gordon. (gr. 5 up). 1965. 8.95 (0-8392-3051-6) Astor-Honor.
Brown, Mark. The Banza. Wolkstein, Diane. LC 81-65845. 32p. (gr. k-2). 1984. pap. 4.95 (0-8037-0058-X) Dial Bks Young.
Brown, Mary B. Joshua & the Big Bad Blue Crabs. Childress, Mark. LC 93-30351. 1995. reinforced bdg. 15.95 (0-316-14118-6) Little.
—Playful Slider: The North American River Otter. Esbensen, Barbara J. LC 92-13783. 1993. 15.95 (0-316-24977-7) Little.
—Tiger with Wings: The Great Horned Owl. Esbensen, Barbara J. LC 90-23034. 32p. (gr. 2-4). 1991. 14.95 (0-531-05940-5); RLB 14.99 (0-531-08540-6) Orchard Bks Watts.
Brown, Matt & Sahloff, Carl, photos by. Friends Together: More Alike Than Different. Bunnett, Rochelle. 12p. (gr. k-4). 1993. tchr's. ed. 24.95 (1-56288-429-8) Checkerboard.
Brown, Mik. Off the Wall: A Very Silly Story Book. Rosen, Michael. LC 93-28643. 1994. pap. 2.95 (1-85697-949-0) Kingfisher Bks.
Brown, Pamela & Adkins, Bill, photos by. Anne Abrams: Engineering Drafter. Bryant, Jennifer. 40p. (gr. 2-4). 1991. PLB 15.95 (0-941477-51-7) TFC Bks NY.
—Carol Thomas-Weaver: Music Teacher. Bryant, Jennifer. 40p. (gr. 2-4). 1991. PLB 15.95 (0-941477-56-8) TFC Bks NY.
—Jane Sayler: Veterinarian. Bryant, Jennifer. 40p. (gr. 2-4). 1991. PLB 15.95 (0-941477-55-X) TFC Bks NY.
—Karen Strange: Children's Theater Producer. Shulman, Jeffrey. 40p. (gr. 2-4). 1991. PLB 15.95 (0-941477-57-6) TFC Bks NY.
—Sharon Oehler: Pediatrician. Bryant, Jennifer. 40p. (gr. 2-4). 1991. PLB 15.95 (0-941477-53-3) TFC Bks NY.
—Ubel Velez: Lawyer. Bryant, Jennifer. 40p. (gr. 2-4). 1991. PLB 15.95 (0-941477-52-5) TFC Bks NY.
—Zoe McCully: Park Ranger. Bryant, Jennifer. 40p. (gr. 2-4). 1991. PLB 15.95 (0-941477-54-1) TFC Bks NY.

Brown, Paul. Bright Spurs. Von Tempski, Armine. LC 92-24540. x, 284p. 1992. pap. 14.95 (0-918024-95-1) Ox Bow.
—Colonel Weatherford's Young Entry: Being an Account of the South Dorchester Ratters & Other Genteel Diversions Suitable for Children. Grand, Gordon. 214p. (gr. 10 up). 1991. Repr. of 1935 ed. 40.00 (1-56416-028-9) Derrydale Pr.
—Pam's Paradise Ranch: A Story of Hawaii. Von Tempski, Armine. LC 92-24538. viii, 334p. 1992. pap. 14.95 (0-918024-96-X) Ox Bow.
Brown, Regina. Play at Your House. Brown, Regina. (gr. 3-7). 1962. 8.95 (0-8392-3027-3) Astor-Honor.
Brown, Richard. Don't Cry, Baby Sam. Ziefert, Harriet. 20p. (gr. 2-6). 1988. pap. 4.95 (0-14-050858-9, Puffin) Puffin Bks.
—Fletcher & the Great Big Dog. Hilleary, Jane K. 32p. (gr. k-3). 1988. 13.45 (0-395-46761-6) HM.
—Fletcher & the Great Big Dog. Hilleary, Jane K. 32p. (gr. k-3). 1992. pap. 4.80 (0-395-62982-9, Sandpiper) HM.
—Gone Fishing. Long, Earlene R. LC 83-22558. 32p. (ps-3). 1987. 13.95 (0-395-55570-2, 5-90090); pap. 4.80 (0-395-44236-2) HM.
—Gulliver's Travels: A Kid's Guide to Southern California. 135p. (gr. 1 up). 1988. 6.95 (0-318-33430-5, Gulliver Bks) HarBrace.
—Here Comes a Truck. Ziefert, Harriet. 20p. (ps-1). 1992. pap. 5.99 (0-14-054520-4) Puffin Bks.
—Jesse's Day Care. Valens, Amy. 32p. (ps-2). 1990. 13.45 (0-395-53357-0) HM.
—The Kids' Complete Guide to Money. Kyte, Kathy S. LC 84-3962. 96p. (gr. 5 up). 1984. lib. bdg. 10.99 (0-394-96672-4) Knopf Bks Yng Read.
—A Kid's Guide to National Parks. 160p. (gr. 1 up). 1989. pap. 6.95 (0-318-37140-5, Gulliver Bks) HarBrace.
—A Kid's Guide to New York City. 138p. (gr. 1 up). 1988. pap. 6.95 (0-15-200458-0, Gulliver Bks) HarBrace.
—A Kid's Guide to Southern California. 135p. (gr. 1 up). 1988. pap. 6.95 (0-15-200457-2, Gulliver Bks) HarBrace.
—The Marvelous Mud Washing Machine. Wolcott, Patty. LC 91-8196. 32p. (ps-2). 1991. 3.50 (0-679-81926-6); PLB 6.99 (0-679-91926-0) Random Bks Yng Read.
—Muchas Palabras Sobre Animals. (SPA). 32p. (ps-1). 1989. pap. 3.95 (0-15-200531-5) HarBrace.
—Muchas Palabras Sobre Mi Casa. (SPA). 28p. (ps-1). 1989. pap. 3.95 (0-15-200532-3, Gulliver Bks) HarBrace.
—Nicky Upstairs & Down. Ziefert, Harriet. (ps-3). 1987. (Puffin); pap. 3.50 (0-14-050742-6, Puffin) Puffin Bks.
—Nicky's Christmas Surprise. Ziefert, Harriet. LC 85-5681. 20p. (ps). 1985. pap. 5.99 (0-14-050555-5, Puffin) Puffin Bks.
—Nicky's Noisy Night. Ziefert, Harriet. 20p. (Orig.). (ps). 1986. pap. 4.95 (0-14-050583-0, Puffin) Puffin Bks.
—Nicky's Picnic. Ziefert, Harriet. 20p. (Orig.). (ps-k). 1986. pap. 4.95 (0-14-050584-9, Puffin) Puffin Bks.
—Nicky's Valentine. Ziefert, Harriet. 20p. (ps-1). 1987. pap. 4.95 (0-14-050706-X, Puffin) Puffin Bks.
—Oh No, Nicky! Ziefert, Harriet. 20p. (ps-1). 1992. pap. 5.99 (0-14-054521-2) Puffin Bks.
—One Hundred Words about Animals. Brown, Richard. LC 86-22774. 27p. (ps-k). 1987. 5.95 (0-15-200550-1, Gulliver Bks) HarBrace.
—One Hundred Words about Animals. (ps-1). 1989. pap. 4.95 (0-15-200554-4, Voy B) HarBrace.
—One Hundred Words about Animals. Brown, Richard. (gr. k-2). 1990. incl. cass. 19.95 (0-87488-183-8); pap. 12.95 incl. cass. (0-87499-182-X); Set; incl. 4 bks., cass., & guide. pap. 27.95 (0-87499-184-6) Live Oak Media.
—One Hundred Words about My House. (ps-1). 1989. pap. 3.95 (0-15-200556-0, Voy B) HarBrace.
—One Hundred Words about Transportation. Brown, Richard. LC 86-22781. 27p. (ps-k). 1987. 5.95 (0-15-200551-X, Gulliver Bks) HarBrace.
—One Hundred Words about Transportation. (ps-1). 1989. pap. 3.95 (0-15-200555-2, Voy B) HarBrace.
—One Hundred Words about Working. (ps-1). 1989. pap. 3.95 (0-15-200557-9, Voy B) HarBrace.
—Pet Day (Mr. Rose's Class) Ziefert, Harriet. 64p. 1988. pap. 2.50 (0-553-15620-9, Skylark) Bantam.
—Say Good Night! Ziefert, Harriet. 32p. 1987. (Puffin); pap. 3.50 (0-14-050747-7, Puffin) Puffin Bks.
—Sesame Street, Cookie Monster's Book of Cookie Shapes. 24p. (ps). 1979. pap. write for info (0-307-10074-X, Pub. by Golden Bks) Western Pub.
—The Small Potatoes Club & the Small Potatoes & the Magic Show. Ziefert, Harriet. 64p. (Orig.). (gr. k-6). 1984. pap. 2.99 (0-440-48034-5, YB) Dell.
—Trip Day (Mr. Rose's Class) Ziefert, Harriet. 64p. 1988. pap. 2.50 (0-553-15618-7, Skylark) Bantam.
—Where's My Easter Egg? Ziefert, Harriet. LC 84-62004. (gr. 2-6). 1985. pap. 5.99 (0-14-050537-7, Puffin) Puffin Bks.
—Where's the Halloween Treat? Ziefert, Harriet. LC 85-3632. 20p. (ps). 1985. pap. 5.99 (0-14-050556-3, Puffin) Puffin Bks.
—Worm Day (Mr. Rose's Class) Ziefert, Harriet. 64p. 1988. pap. 2.50 (0-553-15619-5, Skylark) Bantam.
Brown, Richard, photos by. View from the Air: Charles Lindbergh's Earth & Sky. Lindbergh, Reeve. 32p. 1992. 15.00 (0-670-84660-0) Viking Child Bks.

Brown, Rick. Baseball, Football, Daddy & Me. Friend, David. 32p. (ps-3). 1990. 12.95 (*0-670-82420-8*) Viking Child Bks.
—Baseball, Football, Daddy & Me. Friend, David. 32p. (ps-3). 1992. pap. 3.99 (*0-14-050914-3*) Puffin Bks.
—The Day Porkchop Climbed the Christmas Tree. Pearson, Susan. (gr. k-3). 9.95 (*0-317-62031-2*) P-H.
—The Day Porkchop Climbed the Christmas Tree. Pearson, Susan. (ps up) 1989. pap. 9.95 (*0-671-66370-4*, S&S BFYR); (S&S BFYR) S&S Trade.
—Kate Heads West. Brisson, Pat. LC 89-27590. 40p. (gr. k-3). 1990. RSBE 13.95 (*0-02-714345-7*, Bradbury Pr) Macmillan Child Grp.
—Kate on the Coast. Brisson, Pat. LC 91-17046. 40p. (gr. 2-5). 1992. RSBE 13.95 (*0-02-714341-4*, Bradbury Pr) Macmillan Child Grp.
—Old MacDonald Had a Farm. (ps-k). 1993. 9.99 (*0-670-85157-4*) Viking Child Bks.
—Please Let It Snow. Ziefert, Harriet. LC 88-62145. 32p. (ps-3). 1989. pap. 3.50 (*0-14-050981-X*, Puffin) Puffin Bks.
—Porkchop's Halloween. Pearson, Susan. LC 88-4427. 32p. (gr. k-3). 1988. pap. 13.00 jacketed (*0-671-66732-7*, S&S BFYR) S&S Trade.
—Porkchop's Halloween. Pearson, Susan. 32p. (ps up) 1989. pap. 4.00 (*0-671-68872-3*, S&S BFYR) S&S Trade.
—The Princess & the Potty. Lewison, Wendy C. LC 93-7853. (gr. 2 up). 1994. pap. 14.00 (*0-671-87284-2*, S&S BFYR) S&S Trade.
—Rockaby Farm. Hamm, Diane J. LC 91-19127. 40p. (ps-1). 1992. pap. 14.00 jacketed (*0-671-74773-8*, S&S BFYR) S&S Trade.
—Scooter's Christmas. Ziefert, Harriet. 16p. (ps-k). 1993. 10.95 (*0-694-00484-7*, Festival) HarpC Child Bks.
—Uncle Chuck's Truck. Coulter, Hope N. LC 91-42638. 32p. (ps-1). 1993. RSBE 13.95 (*0-02-724825-9*, Bradbury Pr) Macmillan Child Grp.
—What Rhymes with Snake? A Word & Picture Flap Book. Brown, Rick. LC 92-37870. 24p. 1994. 11.95 (*0-688-12328-7*, Tambourine Bks) Morrow.
—Who Built the Ark? (ps-3). 1994. fold-outs 9.99 (*0-670-85160-4*) Viking Child Bks.
—Your Best Friend, Kate. Brisson, Pat. LC 88-6037. 40p. (gr. k-3). 1989. RSBE 13.95 (*0-02-714350-3*, Bradbury Pr) Macmillan Child Grp.
—Your Best Friend, Kate. Brisson, Pat. LC 91-15245. 40p. (gr. 1-7). 1992. pap. 4.50 (*0-689-71545-5*, Aladdin) Macmillan Child Grp.
Brown, Ron, jt. illus. see Shand, Jim.
Brown, Ruth. Blossom Comes Home. Herriot, James. 1988. 13.00 (*0-312-02169-0*) St Martin.
—Blossom Comes Home. Herriot, James. 32p. (gr. 1-8). 1993. pap. 6.95 (*0-312-09131-1*) St Martin.
—Bonny's Big Day. Herriot, James. 32p. (gr. k up). 1987. 13.00 (*0-312-01000-1*) St Martin.
—Bonny's Big Day. Herriot, James. 32p. 1991. pap. 6.95 (*0-312-06571-X*) St Martin.
—Christmas Day Kitten. Herriot, James. LC 86-13890. (ps up). 1986. 12.95 (*0-312-13407-X*) St Martin.
—A Dark Dark Tale. Brown, Ruth. LC 81-66798. 32p. (ps-3). 1981. 12.95 (*0-8037-1672-9*); PLB 12.89 (*0-8037-1673-7*) Dial Bks Young.
—A Dark Dark Tale. Brown, Ruth. LC 81-66798. 32p. (ps-3). 1984. pap. 3.95 (*0-8037-0093-8*) Dial Bks Young.
—The Grizzly Revenge. Brown, Ruth. 32p. (gr. 3-6). 1987. 15.95 (*0-86264-024-5*, Pub. by Anderson Pr UK) Trafalgar.
—If at First You Do Not See. Brown, Ruth. LC 82-15527. 48p. (ps-2). 1983. 14.95 (*0-8050-1053-X*, Bks Young Read) H Holt & Co.
—Ladybug, Ladybug. Brown, Ruth. LC 88-14852. 32p. (ps-1). 1988. 12.95 (*0-525-44423-8*, DCB) Dutton Child Bks.
—The Market Square Dog. Herriot, James. 32p. 1989. 13.00 (*0-312-03397-4*) St Martin.
—The Market Square Dog. Herriot, James. 32p. 1991. pap. 6.95 (*0-312-06567-1*) St Martin.
—One Stormy Night. Brown, Ruth. LC 92-27004. 32p. (ps-1). 1993. 13.99 (*0-525-45091-2*, DCB) Dutton Child Bks.
—Oscar, Cat-about-Town. Herriot, James. 32p. (gr. 1-3). 1993. pap. 6.95 (*0-312-09130-3*) St Martin.
—Our Cat Flossie. Brown, Ruth. LC 86-19895. 32p. (ps-1). 1986. 10.95 (*0-525-44256-1*, DCB) Dutton Child Bks.
—Our Cat Flossie. Brown, Ruth. LC 86-19895. 32p. (ps-1). 1990. pap. 3.95 (*0-525-44608-7*, DCB) Dutton Child Bks.
—Smudge, the Little Lost Lamb. Herriot, James. 32p. 1991. 12.95 (*0-312-06404-7*) St Martin.
—The World That Jack Built. Brown, Ruth. LC 90-25034. 32p. (ps-1). 1991. 13.95 (*0-525-44635-4*, DCB) Dutton Child Bks.
Brown, Sheila. Aloysius (Al-o-wish-us) the Long Haired Guinea Pig. Whatley, Michael E. LC 90-63585. 26p. (gr. 5). 1990. pap. 3.50 (*0-9618300-1-8*) Nauset Marsh.
Brown, Sue E. Winter's Child. Whittington, Mary K. LC 91-25011. 32p. (ps-3). 1992. SBE 14.95 (*0-689-31685-2*, Atheneum Child Bk) Macmillan Child Grp.
Brown, Trillie. Chinch Bugs, Chinky Pins, & Chinie-Berry Beads. Brown, Faye. 191p. (Orig.). 1990. pap. 9.95 (*0-943487-24-2*) Sevgo Pr.

Brown, Virginia. Vowel Fun. Jenkins, Betty. 96p. (gr. 1-3). 1983. wkbk. 9.95 (*0-86653-107-6*, GA 465) Good Apple.
Brown, Wynne. The Secret: A Child's Story of Sex Abuse, Ages 7-10. McCoy, Diana L. Sgroi, Suzanne, intro. by. 32p. (Orig.). (gr. 2-5). 1986. pap. text ed. 6.00 (*0-9619250-1-9*) Magic Lantrn.
—A Special Place: A Child's Story about Entering Counseling for Children Ages 4 Through 6. McCoy, Diana L. 24p. (Orig.). (ps-1). 1988. pap. 5.50 (*0-9619250-2-7*) Magic Lantrn.
—A Special Place: A Child's Story about Entering Counseling for Children Ages 7 Through 10. McCoy, Diana L. 32p. (gr. 2-5). 1988. pap. text ed. 5.50 (*0-9619250-3-5*) Magic Lantrn.
Browne, Anthony. Changes. Browne, Anthony. LC 90-4283. 32p. (ps-3). 1991. Repr. of 1990 ed. 14.95 (*0-679-81029-3*); PLB 15.99 (*0-679-91029-8*) Knopf Bks Yng Read.
—Gorilla. Browne, Anthony. LC 85-13. 32p. (ps-3). 1985. PLB 13.99 (*0-394-97525-1*) Knopf Bks Yng Read.
—Gorilla: Miniature Edition. Browne, Anthony. 32p. (ps-3). 1991. 4.95 (*0-679-81453-1*) Knopf Bks Yng Read.
—Knock, Knock! Who's There? Grindley, Sally. LC 86-112. 32p. (ps-2). 1986. PLB 7.95 (*0-394-88400-0*) Knopf Bks Yng Read.
—The Night Shimmy. Strauss, Gwen. LC 91-11294. 32p. (ps-2). 1992. 15.00 (*0-679-82384-0*); PLB 15.99 (*0-679-92384-5*) Knopf Bks Yng Read.
—Piggybook. Browne, Anthony. LC 86-3008. 32p. (ps-3). 1986. 14.95 (*0-394-88416-7*); lib. bdg. 14.99 (*0-394-98416-1*) Knopf Bks Yng Read.
—Trail of Stones. Strauss, Gwen. LC 89-38358. 40p. 1990. 6.95 (*0-679-80582-6*); PLB 9.99 (*0-679-90582-0*) Knopf Bks Yng Read.
—The Tunnel. Browne, Anthony. (gr. 4-8). 1990. 14.00 (*0-394-84582-X*); lib. bdg. 12.99 (*0-394-94582-4*) Random Bks Yng Read.
—Willy & Hugh. Browne, Anthony. LC 90-4938. 32p. (ps-3). 1991. 13.00 (*0-679-81446-9*); lib. bdg. 13.99 (*0-679-91446-3*) Knopf Bks Yng Read.
—Willy the Wimp. Browne, Anthony. LC 84-14320. 32p. (ps-3). 1985. PLB 13.99 (*0-394-97061-6*) Knopf Bks Yng Read.
—Willy the Wimp. Browne, Anthony. LC 84-14320. 32p. (ps-2). 1989. Repr. of 1985 ed. 5.99 (*0-394-82610-8*) Knopf Bks Yng Read.
—Zoo. Browne, Anthony. LC 92-11708. 32p. 1993. lib. bdg. 15.99 (*0-679-93946-6*) Knopf Bks Yng Read.
Browne, Eileen. Where's That Bus? Browne, Eileen. LC 90-20885. 32p. (ps-1). 1991. pap. 13.95 jacketed (*0-671-73810-0*, S&S BFYR) S&S Trade.
Browne, Gerard. The Aircraft Lift-the-Flap Book. 18p. (gr. 2-5). 1992. 13.00 (*0-525-67351-2*, Lodestar Bks) Dutton Child Bks.
Browne, Gerard & Browne, Gerard. The Car & Truck Lift-the-Flap Book. LC 88-29994. 18p. (gr. 2-5). 1989. 12.95 (*0-525-67273-7*, Lodestar Bks) Dutton Child Bks.
Browne, James. Chai. Mittelstaedt, Robert C. LC 93-80043. 32p. (ps-2). 1994. 15.00 (*0-9630976-3-6*) Morgin Pr.
Browne, Jane. My Wicked Stepmother. Leach, Norman. LC 92-19674. 32p. (ps-3). 1993. SBE 13.95 (*0-02-754700-0*, Macmillan Child Bk) Macmillan Child Grp.
Browne, Rob. Friendship. Miller, E. Lorraine. LC 77-79105. (ps up) 1977. 5.00 (*0-89566-000-8*) Miller Ent.
Browning, Colleen. Can't Sit Still. Lotz, Karen E. LC 92-28853. 48p. (ps-3). 1993. 13.99 (*0-525-45066-1*, DCB) Dutton Child Bks.
—Every Man Heart Lay Down. Graham, Lorenz. 48p. (gr. 3 up). 1993. 15.95 (*1-56397-184-4*) Boyds Mills Pr.
Brown-Wing, Katherine. Living Lights: Creatures That Glow in the Dark. Filisky, Michael. LC 90-27880. 24p. (gr. k-4). 1991. 15.00 (*0-517-58162-0*); lib. bdg. 15.99 (*0-517-58163-9*) Crown Bks Yng Read.
Bruandet, Jerome. Frogs in Three Dimensions. Bailey, Jill. 12p. (ps). 1992. 16.00 (*0-670-84336-9*) Viking Child Bks.
Brubaker, Lee W. But Everybody Does It: Peer Pressure. Christian, Mary B. LC 85-17112. 72p. (Orig.). (gr. 4-7). 1986. pap. 3.99 (*0-570-03636-4*, 39-1098) Concordia.
Bruce, Kathy. The Human Body: A Thematic Unit. Jefferies, David. 80p. (gr. 3-5). 1993. wkbk. 7.95 (*1-55734-235-0*) Tchr Create Mat.
Bruce, Linda. Al Phillip Bettle. Bruce, Linda. (gr. k-3). 1965. 8.95 (*0-8392-3050-8*) Astor-Honor.
Bruce, Michael. Please Understand Us! Is the World As I See It?; My Little World Book; Open Minded Kids!; Fence Me In...with Understanding, 33 vols. Mohr-Stephens, Judy. Riegert, Evelyn, ed. 500p. (gr. k-8). 1990. Set. 139.95 (*0-935323-00-7*) Barrington Hse.
Bruce, T. Taylor. Quest for the Crystal Castle. Millman, Dan. LC 92-70302. 32p. (ps-5). 1992. 13.95 (*0-915811-41-3*) H J Kramer Inc.
Bruck, Victoria. Chinese Portraits. Hoobler, Dorothy & Hoobler, Thomas. LC 92-13617. 96p. (gr. 7-8). 1992. PLB 22.80 (*0-8114-6375-3*) Raintree Steck-V.
Bruckner, Roger. A Question of Yams: A Missionary Story Based on True Events. Repp, Gloria. Daniels, Karen, ed. 67p. (Orig.). (gr. 2-4). 1992. pap. 4.95 (*0-89084-614-6*) Bob Jones Univ Pr.
Bruemmer, Fred. Seals. Grace, Eric S. (gr. 3-6). 1991. 15.95 (*0-316-32279-2*) Little.

Bruemmer, Fred, photos by. Land of Dark, Land of Light: The Arctic National Wildlife Refuge. Pandell, Karen. LC 92-40405. 32p. (ps-3). 1993. 14.99 (*0-525-45094-7*, DCB) Dutton Child Bks.
Bruere, Julian. Grandma's Hospital. McCartney, Jenny. LC 92-29958. 1993. 4.25 (*0-383-03570-8*) SRA Schl Grp.
—Have You Ever Found a Beetle? Ray, Stephen & Murdoch, Kathleen. LC 92-27265. 1993. 3.75 (*0-383-03627-5*) SRA Schl Grp.
—What Are You Called? Anderson, Honey & Reinholtd, Bill. LC 92-31953. 1993. 3.75 (*0-383-03604-6*) SRA Schl Grp.
Bruhn, Joan. Children's Chillers & Thrillers. Johnson, Liliane & Dufton, Jo S. 136p. (Orig.). Date not set. pap. 10.00 (*0-930069-04-8*) Jasmine Pr.
Bruijn, Ruud. Looking for Vincent. Dubelaar, Thea. 56p. (gr. 2-8). 1992. 9.95 (*1-56288-300-3*) Checkerboard.
Bruncus, Denise. The Pizza Monster. Sharmat, Marjorie W. & Sharmat, Mitchell. (ps up) 1989. 12.95 (*0-385-29722-X*) Delacorte.
Brunelle, Lynn. Incredible Edible Science: The Amazing Things That Happen When You Cook. Seelig, Tina L. LC 93-33480. 1994. write for info. (*0-7167-6501-2*, Sci Am Yng Rdrs); pap. write for info. (*0-7167-6507-1*) W H Freeman.
Bruner, Mike, jt. illus. see Calkins, Burdette.
Bruner, Stephen, photos by. Simple Machines. Horvatic, Anne. LC 88-29997. 32p. (gr. 1-4). 1989. 13.95 (*0-525-44492-0*, DCB) Dutton Child Bks.
Brunkus, Denise. The Case of the Wandering Weathervanes: A McGurk Mystery. Hildick, E. W. LC 87-13171. 160p. (gr. 3-7). 1988. SBE 13.95 (*0-02-743970-4*, Macmillan Child Bk) Macmillan Child Grp.
—Junie B. Jones & a Little Monkey Business. Park, Barbara. LC 92-56706. 80p. (Orig.). (gr. 1-4). 1993. PLB 9.99 (*0-679-93886-9*); pap. 2.99 (*0-679-83886-4*) Random Bks Yng Read.
—Junie B. Jones & Her Big Fat Mouth. Park, Barbara. LC 92-50957. 80p. (Orig.). (gr. 1-4). 1993. PLB 9.99 (*0-679-94407-9*); pap. 2.99 (*0-679-84407-4*) Random Bks Yng Read.
—Junie B. Jones & Some Sneaky Peeky Spying. Park, Barbara. LC 93-5557. 1994. write for info. (*0-679-85101-1*); PLB write for info. (*0-679-95101-6*) Random Bks Yng Read.
—Junie B. Jones & the Stupid Smelly Bus. Park, Barbara. LC 91-51104. 80p. (Orig.). (gr. 1-4). 1992. PLB 9.99 (*0-679-92642-9*); pap. 2.99 (*0-679-82642-4*) Random Bks Yng Read.
—Newsman Ned & the Broken Rules. Kroll, Steven. 32p. (Orig.). (ps-1). 1989. pap. 2.95 (*0-590-41368-6*) Scholastic Inc.
—The Princess of the Fillmore Street School. Sharmat, Marjorie W. & Sharmat, Mitchell. LC 89-1106. (gr. 2-4). 1989. 12.95 (*0-385-29811-0*) Delacorte.
—The Principal's New Clothes. Calmenson, Stephanie. (ps-3). 1989. pap. 12.95 (*0-590-41822-X*) Scholastic Inc.
—The Principal's New Clothes. Calmenson, Stephanie. 40p. (ps-2). 1991. pap. 3.95 (*0-590-44778-5*, Blue Ribbon Bks) Scholastic Inc.
—Show-&-Tell. Woodruff, Elvira. LC 90-23588. 32p. (ps-3). 1991. reinforced 14.95 (*0-8234-0883-3*) Holiday.
—Three Smart Pals. Rocklin, Joanne. 48p. (ps-4). 1994. pap. 3.50 (*0-590-47431-6*, Cartwheel) Scholastic Inc.
Brunn, Peter. Brain: What It Is, What It Does. Bruun, Ruth D. & Bruun, Bertel. LC 88-21182. 64p. 1989. 12.95 (*0-688-08453-2*); PLB 12.88 (*0-688-08454-0*) Greenwillow.
Bruno, Clara E. The Raindrop Children, Vol. 1. Charley, Aunt, pseud. 24p. (gr. 1-2). 1991. pap. 5.95 (*1-880945-00-2*) Animated Elements.
Bruns, Stan & Capron, Michael W. Stories Worth Reading. Ball, Douglas H., et al. 192p. (Orig.). (gr. 8-11). 1989. pap. text ed. write for info. (*0-9621844-0-3*) Printemps Bks.
Brunswick, G. The Haunted House Three-D Coloring Book. 32p. (Orig.). (gr. 4-7). 1988. pap. 3.95 (*0-942025-57-1*) Kidsbks.
—Wild Wheels Three-D Coloring Book. 32p. (Orig.). (gr. 4-7). 1988. pap. 3.95 (*0-942025-60-1*) Kidsbks.
Brunza-Horn, Nanette. The Asthma Attack by Bo B. Bear. Casterline, Charlotte L. (Orig.). (ps-6). 1988. pap. 5.95 (*0-9617218-2-0*) Info All Bk.
Brusca, Maria C. The Blacksmith & the Devils. Brusca, Maria C. & Wilson, Tona. LC 92-176. 40p. (gr. 1-4). 1992. 15.95 (*0-8050-1954-5*, Bks Young Read) H Holt & Co.
—The Cook & the King. Brusca, Maria C. & Wilson, Tona. LC 92-25812. 40p. (gr. 1-4). 1993. 14.95 (*0-8050-2355-0*, Bks Young Read) H Holt & Co.
—Mama Went Walking. Berry, Christine. LC 89-39789. 32p. (ps-2). 1990. 14.95 (*0-8050-1261-3*, Bks Young Read) H Holt & Co.
—On the Pampas. Brusca, Maria C. LC 90-40938. 40p. (ps-2). 1991. 14.95 (*0-8050-1548-5*, Bks Young Read) H Holt & Co.
—On the Pampas. Brusca, Maria C. LC 90-40938. 40p. (ps-2). 1993. pap. 5.95 (*0-8050-2919-2*, Bks Young Read) H Holt & Co.
—The Zebra-Riding Cowboy: A Folk Song of the Old West. Medearis, Angela S., compiled by. LC 91-27941. 32p. (ps-2). 1992. 14.95 (*0-8050-1712-7*, Bks Young Read) H Holt & Co.

Brusch, Beat. The Story of Paper. Limousin, Odile. Matthews, Sarah, tr. from FRE. LC 87-31752. 38p. (gr. k-5). 1988. 4.95 (*0-944589-16-2*, 162) Young Discovery Lib.

Bruvelaitis, Lisa. Nearly Noodles. Bruvelaitis, Lisa. 24p. (Orig.). (ps-2). 1990. pap. 0.99 (*1-55037-128-2*, Pub. by Annick CN) Firefly Bks Ltd.

Bryan, Ashley. All Night, All Day: A Child's First Book of African-American Spirituals. Bryan, Ashley. LC 90-753145. 48p. (ps-4). 1991. SBE 14.95 (*0-689-31662-3*, Atheneum Child Bk) Macmillan Child Grp.

—Beat the Story-Drum, Pum-Pum. Bryan, Ashley. LC 86-20598. 80p. (gr. 4-6). 1987. pap. 7.95 (*0-689-71107-7*, Aladdin) Macmillan Child Grp.

—Christmas Gif' An Anthology of Christmas Poems, Songs, & Stories, Written by & about Black People. Rollins, Charlemae, ed. Baker, Augusta, intro. by. LC 92-18976. 128p. 1993. lib. bdg. 13.93 (*0-688-11668-X*) Morrow.

—Christmas Gif' An Anthology of Christmas Poems, Songs, & Stories Written by & about African-Americans. Rollins, Charlemae H., ed. Baker, Augusta, intro. by. LC 92-18976. 128p. 1993. 15.00 (*0-688-11667-1*) Morrow Jr Bks.

—The Dancing Granny. Bryan, Ashley. LC 87-1140. 64p. (gr. k-4). 1987. pap. 6.95 (*0-689-71149-2*, Aladdin) Macmillan Child Grp.

—The Ox of the Wonderful Horns: And Other African Folktales. reissue ed. Bryan, Ashley, LC 75-154749. 48p. (ps-4). 1993. RSBE 14.95 (*0-689-31799-9*, Atheneum Child Bk) Macmillan Child Grp.

—The Story of Lightning & Thunder. Bryan, Ashley. LC 92-40509. 32p. (ps-3). 1993. SBE 14.95 (*0-689-31836-7*, Atheneum Child Bk) Macmillan Child Grp.

—Turtle Knows Your Name. Bryan, Ashley. LC 89-2. 32p. (ps-2). 1989. SBE 13.95 (*0-689-31578-3*, Atheneum Child Bk) Macmillan Child Grp.

—Turtle Knows Your Name. Bryan, Ashley, retold by. LC 92-33553. 32p. (ps-3). 1993. pap. 4.95 (*0-689-71728-8*, Aladdin) Macmillan Child Grp.

—What a Morning! The Christmas Story in Black Spirituals. Langstaff, John. LC 87-750130. 32p. 1987. SBE 14.95 (*0-689-50422-5*, M K McElderry) Macmillan Child Grp.

Bryan, Brigitte. The Beggar in the Blanket. Graham, Gail B. LC 77-85548. 96p. (gr. 1-5). 1988. PLB 12.89 (*0-8037-0663-4*) Dial Bks Young.

Bryan, Diana. The Fisherman & His Wife. Grimm, Jacob & Grimm, Wilhelm K. Metaxas, Eric, tr. from GER. LC 89-28445. 32p. (ps up). 1991. pap. 14.95 (*0-88708-122-3*, Rabbit Ears); includes cassette 19.95 (*0-88708-123-1*) Picture Bk Studio.

Bryan, Tony, jt. illus. see Sarson, Peter.

Bryant, Larkin. Chamber Music Primer: Four Piano Trio Pieces. Taylor, Ann. (Orig.). (gr. 1-6). 1983. pap. 6.75 (*0-943644-01-1*); cassette 5.98 (*0-685-06794-7*) Ivory Pal.

Bryant, Michael. Bein' with You This Way. Nikola-Lisa, W. LC 93-5164. 1994. 14.95 (*1-880000-05-9*) Lee & Low Bks.

—Family Celebrations. Patrick, Diane. LC 93-18456. 64p. (ps-4). 1993. PLB 11.95 (*1-881889-04-1*) Silver Moon.

—The Family Heritage Cookbook. Weber, Judith E. 64p. (gr. 1-3). 1994. PLB 11.95 (*1-881889-53-X*) Silver Moon.

Bryant, Micheal. Our People. Medearis, Angela S. LC 92-44499. 32p. (gr. k-3). 1994. SBE 14.95 (*0-689-31826-X*, Atheneum Child Bk) Macmillan Child Grp.

Bryant, Samuel. King's Fifth. O'Dell, Scott. (gr. 7-10). 1966. 14.45 (*0-395-06963-7*) HM.

Brychta, Alex. Oxford Activity Books for Children. Clark, Christopher. (gr. k-4). 1985. Bk. 4. pap. 3.95x (*0-19-421833-3*); Bk. 5. pap. 3.95x (*0-19-421834-1*); Bk. 6. pap. 3.95x (*0-19-421835-X*); Bk. 3. pap. 3.95x (*0-19-421832-5*); Bk. 1. pap. 3.95x (*0-19-421830-9*); Bk. 2. pap. 3.95x (*0-19-421831-7*) OUP.

Bryer, Debbie. Are We Almost There? The Kids' Book of Travel Fun. LaPlaca, Annette. 45p. (Orig.). (gr. 1-5). 1992. pap. 4.99 wkbk. (*0-87788-051-4*) Shaw Pubs.

—How Long 'til Christmas? The Kid's Book of Holiday Fun. LaPlaca, Annette. 48p. (Orig.). (gr. 3-6). 1993. pap. 4.99 saddle-stitch (*0-87788-369-6*) Shaw Pubs.

Bryson, Bernarda. Shepherd of the Sun. Appel, Benjamin. (gr. 5 up). 1961. 10.95 (*0-8392-3033-8*) Astor-Honor.

Buba, Joy. Lyrico. 2nd ed. Foster, Elizabeth V. 230p. (gr. 6-8). 1991. pap. 10.95 (*0-930407-21-0*) Parabola Bks.

Bubiera, Sandra S. Roberto Goes Fishing - Roberto Va de Pesca. Zaldivar, Raquel P. 32p. (gr. 1-3). 1992. 12. 95 (*1-880507-00-5*) Lectorum Pubns.

Buchanan, Yvonne. Follow the Drinking Gourd. Connelly, Bernardine. LC 93-19247. 1993. 14.95 (*0-88708-336-6*, Rabbit Ears); incl. cass. 19.95 (*0-88708-335-8*, Rabbit Ears) Picture Bk Studio.

—The Science of Music. Berger, Melvin. LC 87-24921. 160p. (gr. 5-9). 1989. (Crowell Jr Bks); PLB 13.89 (*0-690-04647-2*, Crowell Jr Bks) HarpC Child Bks.

—Uranus: The Seventh Planet. Branley, Franklyn M. LC 87-35046. 64p. (gr. 3-6). 1988. (Crowell Jr Bks); PLB 12.89 (*0-690-04687-1*, Crowell Jr Bks) HarpC Child Bks.

Buchmiller, Therese. A Special Gift to God. Iakovina, Theodore. 38p. (gr. k-4). 1986. PLB write for info. Amnos Pubns.

Bucholtz-Ross, Linda. Dr. Zed's Dazzling Book of Science Activities. Penrose, Gordon. 48p. 1993. pap. 7.95 (*0-919872-78-6*, Pub. by Greey dePencier CN) Firefly Bks Ltd.

Buck, Eunice & Clapp, E. J. Repairing Christian Lifestyles. 2nd ed. Clapp, Steve & Mauck, Sue I. 174p. (gr. 7-12). 1983. pap. 6.00 (*0-914527-26-6*); pap. 5.00 leader's guide (*0-914527-27-4*) C-Four Res.

Buckingham, Nash, photos by. Mark Right. 2nd ed. Buckingham, Nash. 250p. (gr. 10 up). 1989. Repr. 35. 00 (*1-56416-005-X*) Derrydale Pr.

Buckley, Cicely. Thoughts for the Free Life: Lao Tsu to the Present. 2nd ed. Taylor, Phoebe, ed. 110p. (Orig.). (gr. 8 up). 1989. pap. 10.00 (*0-9617481-5-X*) Oyster River Pr.

Buckley, F. Reid, Jr. A Day in the Life of an Actress. Smith, Betsy C. LC 84-8678. 32p. (gr. 4-8). 1985. PLB 11.79 (*0-8167-0105-9*); pap. text ed. 2.95 (*0-8167-0106-7*); cassettes avail. Troll Assocs.

Buckley, James. Swamps & Marshes. Arvetis, Chris & Palmer, Carole. LC 93-33675. (gr. 4 up). 1994. write for info. (*0-528-83676-5*) Rand McNally.

Bucknall, Caroline. One Bear All Alone. Bucknall, Caroline. LC 85-6968. 32p. (ps-2). 1989. pap. 4.95 (*0-8037-0645-6*) Dial Bks Young.

—One Bear in the Hospital. Bucknall, Caroline. LC 90-2994. 32p. (ps-2). 1991. 11.95 (*0-8037-0847-5*) Dial Bks Young.

—The Three Little Pigs. Bucknall, Caroline. LC 86-16716. 32p. (ps-2). 1987. 10.95 (*0-8037-0100-4*) Dial Bks Young.

Bucur, Mike. Get It Together: Group Projects for Creative Bulletin Boards. Molyneux, Lynn. 160p. (gr. k-4). 1983. perfect bdg. 9.95 (*0-685-29141-3*) Trellis Bks Inc.

—Your Own Thing: Individual Art Projects for Primary Grades. Molyneux, Lynn & Bucur, Mike. 160p. (gr. k-6). 1983. perfect bdg. 9.95 (*0-685-29140-5*) Trellis Bks Inc.

Buehner, Mark. The Adventures of Taxi Dog. Barracca, Sal & Barracca, Debra. Fogelman, Phyllis J., ed. LC 89-1056. 32p. (ps-3). 1990. 13.00 (*0-8037-0671-5*); PLB 12.89 (*0-8037-0672-3*) Dial Bks Young.

—A Job for Wittilda. Buehner, Caralyn. LC 91-15630. 32p. (ps-3). 1993. 13.99 (*0-8037-1149-2*); lib. bdg. 13. 89 (*0-8037-1150-6*) Dial Bks Young.

—Maxi, the Hero. Barracca, Debra & Barracca, Sal. (ps-3). 1991. 12.95 (*0-8037-0939-0*); PLB 12.89 (*0-8037-0940-4*) Dial Bks Young.

Buell, Carl. Humphrey the Wayward Whale. Callenbach, Ernest & Leefeldt, Christine. 24p. (Orig.). (gr. k-6). 1986. pap. 9.95 (*0-930588-23-1*) Heyday Bks.

Buell-Bakke, Karen. I Can Go! Wyatt, Pam. (ps-1). 1988. lib. bdg. 9.95 (*0-945286-00-7*) Red Bus Pub.

Buerkle, Bonnie K. The Search for the Smell of Christmas. Upton, Richard & Fair, Sharon. 32p. 1992. 14.95x (*0-9633348-0-8*) Aromatique.

Buffet, Guy. Spooky Stuffs: Hawaiian Ghost Stories. Knudsen, Eric A. Kaye, Sally, ed. LC 74-80510. 64p. 1987. pap. 7.95 (*0-89610-047-2*) Island Heritage.

Bugbee, Harold D. Maverick Town: The Story of Old Tascosa. McCarty, John L. Sonnichsen, C. L., frwd. by. LC 87-5946. 320p. (gr. 6-12). 1968. pap. 12.95 (*0-8061-2089-4*) U of Okla Pr.

Buguet, Anne. On Cat Mountain. Richard, Francoise. Levine, Arthur A., adapted by. LC 93-11408. 1994. write for info. (*0-399-22608-7*, Putnam) Putnam Pub Group.

Buhler, Cheryl. Explorers: A Thematic Unit. Sterling, Mary E. 80p. (Orig.). (gr. 5-8). 1992. pap. 7.95 wkbk. (*1-55734-288-1*) Tchr Create Mat.

—Tide Pools & Coral Reefs. King, Jeanne. Sima, Patricia M., ed. 80p. (gr. 1-3). 1993. wkbk. 7.95 (*1-55734-249-0*) Tchr Create Mat.

—World History Simulations. Fischer, Max W. 96p. (gr. 5-8). 1993. wkbk. 9.95 (*1-55734-481-7*) Tchr Create Mat.

Buhler, Cheryl, et al. Literature Activities for Reluctant Readers: Intermediate. Carratello, John & Carratello, Patty. 112p. (gr. 3-5). 1991. wkbk. 10.95 (*1-55734-354-3*) Tchr Create Mat.

—Thematic Bibliography. Buhler, Cheyl, et al. 176p. (gr. k-8). 1993. wkbk. 14.95 (*1-55734-373-X*) Tchr Create Mat.

—Elections. Rayburn, Richard. 96p. (Orig.). (gr. 4-8). 1992. wkbk. 9.95 (*1-55734-069-2*) Tchr Create Mat.

Bu Ho Choi. Taekwondo for Children: The Ultimate Reference Guide for Children Interested in the World's Most Popular Martial Art. Park, Y. H. & Leibowitz, Jeff. 128p. (Orig.). (gr. 4-8). 1993. PLB 9.95 (*0-9637151-0-0*) YH Pk Taekwondo. This book (endorsed by The World Taekwondo Federation) explains the philosophy & basic techniques of the ancient Korean martial art & modern day sport of taekwondo in simple terms. Taekwondo is recognized as an official Olympic sport & the Co-Author was Coach of the 1988 USA Olympic Team. The book stresses how taekwondo's philosophy of strength tempered by gentleness can help a youngster in all aspects of his or her life. It describes how children can improve academic performance, boost self-esteem & confidence & learn to respect themselves & others. It dispels many myths that had previously made parents apprehensive about taekwondo. Taekwondo teaches highly effective self-defense, mainly with its devastating kicks. But it also teaches an individual how to be his or her very best-- physically & mentally. Its emphasis is on what attitudinal changes a child can & should strive toward as he undertakes the study of taekwondo. Negative outlets from reality such as drugs, alcohol & abusive language & behavior have no place in the life of a taekwondo practitioner. This book illustrates why & suggests that taekwondo practice can profoundly improve the life of any child. *Publisher Provided Annotation.*

Bull, Charles L. Animal Fairy Tales. Baum, L. Frank. 48p. (ps-3). 1989. pap. 7.95 (*0-929605-04-7*) Books Wonder.

Bull, Kris F. The Pemaquid Loon from Temple. McIntire, Donald. 1988. pap. 5.99 (*0-317-92307-2*) Herit Print Co.

Bull, Peter. Air, Light & Water. Wilkins, Mary-Jane. LC 90-42620. 40p. (Orig.). (gr. 2-5). 1991. pap. 3.95 (*0-679-80859-0*) Random Bks Yng Read.

—The First Men on the Moon. Furniss, Tim. LC 88-24166. 32p. (gr. 4-6). 1989. PLB 11.90 (*0-531-18240-1*, Pub. by Bookwright Pr) Watts.

—Sun, Stars & Planets. Stacy, Tom. LC 90-42979. 40p. (Orig.). (gr. 2-5). 1991. pap. 3.95 (*0-679-80862-0*) Random Bks Yng Read.

—The Travels of Marco Polo. Rosen, Mike. LC 88-23375. 32p. (gr. 4-6). 1989. PLB 11.90 (*0-531-18241-X*, Pub. by Bookwright Pr) Watts.

—The Voyage of the Beagle. Hyndley, Kate. LC 88-28695. 32p. (gr. 5-9). 1989. PLB 11.90 (*0-531-18272-X*, Pub. by Bookwright Pr) Watts.

—Wings, Wheels & Sails. Stacy, Tom. LC 90-42977. 40p. (Orig.). (gr. 2-5). 1991. pap. 3.95 (*0-679-80863-9*) Random Bks Yng Read.

Bull, Peter & Chen, Kuo K. Weather. Parker, Steve. 40p. (gr. 5-8). 1990. PLB 12.90 (*0-531-19086-2*, Warwick) Watts.

Bull, Peter & Johnson, Paul. Natural World. Ganeri, Anita & Butterfield, Maira. LC 89-11349. 48p. (gr. 4-5). 1989. PLB 17.27 (*0-8368-0133-4*) Gareth Stevens Inc.

Bull, Peter & Moores, Ian. Everyday Things & How They Work. Parker, Steve. LC 91-213. 40p. (Orig.). (gr. 2-5). 1991. pap. 3.99 (*0-679-80866-3*) Random Bks Yng Read.

Bull, Peter, jt. illus. see Chen, Kuo K.

Bull, Peter, jt. illus. see Kuo Kang Chen.

Bull, Peter, jt. illus. see Smith, Guy.

Bull, Peter, et al. Green Thumbs Up! The Science of Growing Plants. Taylor, Barbara. LC 91-4290. 40p. (Orig.). (gr. 2-5). 1992. pap. 4.95 (*0-679-82042-6*) Random Bks Yng Read.

—More Power to You! The Science of Batteries & Magnets. Taylor, Barbara. LC 91-4293. 40p. (Orig.). (gr. 2-5). 1992. pap. 4.95 (*0-679-82040-X*) Random Bks Yng Read.

—Over the Rainbow! The Science of Color & Light. Taylor, Barbara. LC 91-4291. 40p. (Orig.). (gr. 2-5). 1992. pap. 4.95 (*0-679-82041-8*) Random Bks Yng Read.

—Up, Up & Away! The Science of Flight. Taylor, Barbara. LC 91-4292. 40p. (Orig.). (gr. 2-5). 1992. pap. 4.95 (*0-679-82039-6*) Random Bks Yng Read.

—Get It in Gear! The Science of Movement. Taylor, Barbara. LC 90-42617. 40p. (Orig.). (gr. 2-5). 1991. pap. 4.95 (*0-679-80812-4*) Random Bks Yng Read.

—Hear! Hear! The Science of Sound. Taylor, Barbara. LC 90-42617. 40p. (Orig.). (gr. 2-5). 1991. pap. 4.95 (*0-679-80813-2*) Random Bks Yng Read.

—Seeing Is NOT Believing! The Science of Shadow & Light. Taylor, Barbara. LC 90-42974. 40p. (Orig.). (gr. 2-5). 1991. pap. 4.95 (*0-679-80814-0*) Random Bks Yng Read.

—Sink or Swim! The Science of Water. Taylor, Barbara. LC 90-42618. 40p. (Orig.). (gr. 2-5). 1991. pap. 4.95 (*0-679-80815-9*) Random Bks Yng Read.

Buller, Jon. Hello! Hello! Schade, Susan. 32p. (ps). 1993. pap. 2.25 (*0-671-79608-9*, Little Simon) S&S Trade.

—Howie Merton & the Magic Dust. Reeves, Faye C. LC 90-38341. 64p. (Orig.). (gr. 2-4). 1991. lib. bdg. 6.99 (*0-679-91527-3*); pap. 2.50 (*0-679-81527-9*) Random Bks Yng Read.

—No Tooth, No Quarter! A Step 3 Book. Buller, Jon &
Schade, Susan. LC 89-30250. 48p. (Orig.). (gr. 2-3).
1989. lib. bdg. 7.99 (0-394-94956-0); pap. 3.50
(0-394-84956-6, Random Juv) Random Bks Yng Read.
—Railroad Toad. Schade, Susan & Buller, Jon. LC 92-
23303. 32p. (ps-1). 1993. PLB 7.99 (0-679-93934-2);
pap. 3.50 (0-679-83934-8) Random Bks Yng Read.
—Shari Lewis Presents One Hundred & One Things for
Kids to Do. Lewis, Shari. LC 86-43065. 96p. (gr. 1-5).
1987. lib. bdg. 9.99 (0-394-98966-X); pap. 7.95
(0-394-88966-5) Random Bks Yng Read.
—Shari Lewis Presents One Hundred-One Magic Tricks
for Kids to Do. Lewis, Shari & Zimmerman, Dick. LC
89-10360. 96p. (Orig.). 1990. PLB 9.99
(0-394-92059-7); pap. 6.95 (0-394-82059-2) Random
Bks Yng Read.
—Space Rock. Schade, Susan, ed. LC 87-12762. 48p.
(Orig.). (gr. 2-3). 1988. lib. bdg. 7.99 (0-394-99384-5);
pap. 2.95 (0-394-89384-0) Random Bks Yng Read.
—Toad on the Road. Buller, Jon & Schade, Susan. LC
91-4246. 32p. (Orig.). (ps-1). 1992. PLB 7.99
(0-679-92689-5); pap. 3.50 (0-679-82689-0) Random
Bks Yng Read.
—Twenty-Thousand Baseball Cards under the Sea: A
Step Three Book. Buller, Jon & Schade, Susan. LC 90-
40704. 48p. (Orig.). (gr. 2-3). 1991. lib. bdg. 7.99
(0-679-91569-9); pap. 3.50 (0-679-81569-4) Random
Bks Yng Read.
—Woodchuck Nation. Saltzman, Mark. LC 93-4641.
1994. 15.00 (0-679-85107-0) Knopf Bks Yng Read.
Buller, Jon & Schade, Susan. Yo! It's Captain Yo-Yo.
Buller, Jon & Schade, Susan. LC 92-44306. 48p. (gr.
2-3). 1993. PLB 3.50 (0-448-40192-4, G&D); (G&D)
Putnam Pub Group.
Bullock, Kathleen. Composition & Creative Writing for
the Middle Grades. Forte, Imogene & MacKenzie,
Joy. Lewis, Sherri Y., intro. by. 80p. (Orig.). (gr. 5-8).
1991. pap. text ed. 7.95 (0-86530-176-X, IP 192-1)
Incentive Pubns.
—Hey Diddle Rock. Zaslow, David B. & Inada, Lawson
F. 32p. (Orig.). (ps-8). 1986. pap. 7.95
(0-89411-006-3) Kids Matter.
—Hickory Dickory Rock. Zaslow, David B. & Inada,
Lawson F. 32p. (Orig.). (ps-8). 1986. pap. 7.95
(0-89411-004-7) Kids Matter.
—Humpty Dumpty Rock. Zaslow, David B. & Inada,
Lawson F. 32p. (Orig.). (ps-8). 1986. pap. 7.95
(0-89411-007-1) Kids Matter.
—It Chanced to Rain. Bullock, Kathleen. LC 87-32070.
(ps-1). 1992. pap. 13.95 jacketed (0-671-66005-5, S&S
BFYR); pap. 3.95 (0-671-77820-X, S&S BFYR) S&S
Trade.
—Rock-a-Doodle-Doo. Zaslow, David B. & Inada,
Lawson F. 32p. (Orig.). (ps-8). 1986. pap. 7.95
(0-89411-005-5) Kids Matter.
—Shakin' Loose with Mother Goose. Allen, Steve &
Meadows, Jayne. 128p. (ps-2). 1987. 4 bks. & 2 forty
minute tapes in gift box ed. 19.95 (0-89411-010-1)
Kids Matter.
Bullock, Robert. Wilderness Habitat: The Great Plains -
A Young Reader's Journal. Bullock, Robert. LC 86-
81461. 64p. (Orig.). (gr. k-8). 1987. pap. 5.95
(0-943972-10-8) Homestead WY.
—Wilderness Habitat: The Rocky Mountains: A Young
Reader's Journal. Bullock, Robert. LC 93-77117. 64p.
(Orig.). (gr. k-5). 1993. pap. 7.95 (0-943972-18-3)
Homestead WY.
Bumgarner-Kirby, Claudia. Gwendolyn's Gifts. Sheehan,
Patty. LC 91-12335. 32p. 1991. 14.95 (0-88289-845-0)
Pelican.
Bunson, Margaret. Kateri Tekakwitha. Bunson, Margaret
& Bunson, Matthew. LC 92-61548. 56p. (Orig.). 1993.
9.95 (0-87973-786-7, 786); pap. 6.95 (0-87973-560-0,
560) Our Sunday Visitor.
—St. Patrick. Bunson, Margaret & Bunson, Matthew. LC
92-61547. 56p. (Orig.). 1993. 9.95 (0-87973-785-9,
785); pap. 6.95 (0-87973-559-7, 559) Our Sunday
Visitor.
Buntin, Phillip R. Adventures with the Santa Fe Trail:
An Activity Book for Kids & Teachers. rev. ed. Webb,
Dave. 76p. (gr. 4 up). 1993. pap. 7.95
(1-882404-05-X) KS Herit Ctr.
Bunting, Eve. How Many Days to America: A
Thanksgiving Story. Bunting, Eve. 32p. (ps-3). 1990.
pap. 5.70 (0-395-54777-6, Clarion Bks) HM.
Burdick, Jeri. The Fisherman's Tale. Whittle, Emily. LC
91-17386. 32p. 1991. 10.95 (0-671-74760-6, Green
Tiger) S&S Trade.
—Sailor Cats. Whittle, Emily. LC 92-23418. 1993. 14.00
(0-671-79933-9, Green Tiger) S&S Trade.
Bureloff, Morris. Brain-Busting Decode Puzzles. Bureloff,
Morris. Laycock, Mary, ed. 64p. (gr. 7-10). 1985. pap.
7.95 (0-918932-86-6) Activity Resources.
Burford, Kay. Kimako's Story. Jordan, June. 42p. (gr.
k-3). 1991. pap. 3.80 (0-395-60338-2, Sandpiper) HM.
Burger, Carl. The Incredible Journey. Burnford, Sheila.
(gr. 4-8). 1990. 16.00 (0-553-05874-6, Skylark)
Bantam.
—Judy of the Islands: A Story of the South Seas. Von
Tempski, Armine. LC 92-24539. viii, 280p. 1992. pap.
14.95 (0-918024-97-8) Ox Bow.
Burger, Dan, jt. illus. see Lawson, Jim.
Burgeson, Marjorie. A Birthday for General Washington.
Johnston, Johanna. LC 75-38545. 32p. (gr. k-4). 1976.
PLB 15.93 (0-516-08881-5, Golden Gate) Childrens.
Burgess, Anne. Sloppy Kisses. Winthrop, Elizabeth.
(ps-3). 1983. pap. 3.95 (0-14-050433-8, Puffin) Puffin
Bks.

—Sloppy Kisses. Winthrop, Elizabeth. LC 90-105. 32p.
(gr. k-3). 1990. pap. 4.95 (0-689-71410-6, Aladdin)
Macmillan Child Grp.
Burgess, Gelett. Goops & How to Be Them: A Manual of
Manners for Polite Infants. Burgess, Gelett. LC 68-
55630. 96p. (ps-4). 1968. pap. 3.95 (0-486-22233-0)
Dover.
—More Goops & How Not to Be Them: A Manual of
Manners for Impolite Infants. Burgess, Gelett. LC 68-
55531. 96p. (ps-4). 1968. pap. 3.95 (0-486-22234-9)
Dover.
Burgess, Mark. Harriet & the Crocodiles. Waddell,
Martin. (gr. 3-7). 1984. 11.95 (0-316-91622-6, Joy St
Bks) Little.
—Harriet & the Haunted School. Waddell, Martin. (gr.
2-6). 1986. pap. 2.50 (0-671-62215-3, Minstrel Bks)
PB.
—Harriet & the Robot. Waddell, Martin. LC 86-17435.
(gr. 3-7). 1987. 12.95 (0-316-91624-2, Joy St Bks)
Little.
—Huff Puff & Ruffly. Edmiston, Jim. 96p. (gr. 2-4). 1993.
18.95 (0-460-88123-X, Pub. by J M Dent & Sons)
Trafalgar.
—Surprise, Surprise, Queen Loonia! Groves, Richard.
32p. (ps-1). 1992. pap. 5.95 (0-8120-4582-3) Barron.
Burgest, David R., II. Proverbs for the Young...& the
Not So Young. Burgest, David R. 75p. (Orig.). (gr. 7-
12). 1989. pap. write for info. Self-Taught Pubs.
Burgevin, Daniel. Iroquois Stories: Heroes & Heroines,
Monsters & Magic. Bruchac, Joseph. LC 85-5705.
198p. (gr. 3-7). 1985. pap. 8.95 (0-89594-234-8)
Crossing Pr.
Burgoyne, John. The Twits. Dahl, Roald & Tannen,
Mary. LC 80-18410. (ps-5). 1981. 12.00
(0-394-84599-4); lib. bdg. 12.99 (0-394-94599-9)
Knopf Bks Yng Read.
Burgoyne, Mari-Ann S. Best Short Stories: Advanced
Level. Harris, Raymond. 560p. (Orig.). (gr. 9 up).
1980. text ed. 17.00 (0-89061-705-8, 620H); pap. text
ed. 13.25 (0-89061-701-5, 620) Jamestown Pubs.
Burke, Ann & Burke, Ann. Cocoa Puppy. Burke,
Timothy. LC 89-50890. 32p. (Orig.). (ps-3). 1989.
5.00 (0-9623227-0-9) Thunder & Ink.
Burke, Dianne O. Creepy Cuisine. Monroe, Lucy. LC 92-
41654. 80p. (gr. 4-7). 1993. pap. 4.99 (0-679-84402-3)
Random Bks Yng Read.
—My First Science Dictionary. Rabkin, Sarah. 64p. (gr.
k-3). 1992. 10.95 (1-56288-215-5) Checkerboard.
Burke, Edgar. Blood Lines. 2nd ed. Buckingham, Nash.
Davis, Henry P., intro. by. 227p. (gr. 10 up). 1991.
Repr. of 1938 ed. 35.00 (1-56416-004-1) Derrydale Pr.
Burke, Kerry. Travels with Tiny Teddy: Cape Cod: The
Great Escape. Truelson, Thomas. 40p. (Orig.). (gr.
1-3). 1988. pap. 3.95 (0-685-19995-9) Lighthse Bks
MA.
Burke, Rod. Johannes Kepler: Giant of Faith & Science.
Tiner, John H. LC 77-558. (gr. 3-6). 1977. pap. 6.95
(0-915134-11-X) Mott Media.
Burke, Susan S. Alphabatty: Riddles from A to Z.
Walton, Ann & Walton, Rick. 32p. (gr. 1-4). 1991.
PLB 11.95 (0-685-49141-2) Lerner Pubns.
—Help Wanted: Riddles about Jobs. Adler, Larry. 32p.
(gr. 1-4). 1989. PLB 11.95 (0-8225-2325-6) Lerner
Pubns.
—Here's to Ewe: Riddles about Sheep. Burns, Diane L. &
Scholten, Dan. 32p. (gr. 1-4). 1989. PLB 11.95
(0-8225-2326-4) Lerner Pubns.
—Hoop-La: Riddles about Basketball. Walton, Rick &
Walton, Ann. LC 92-25771. 1993. 11.95
(0-8225-2339-6) Lerner Pubns.
—Hot Stuff: Riddles about Deserts. Swanson, June. LC
93-26294. 1994. 11.00 (0-8225-2343-4) Lerner Pubns.
—I Toad You So: Riddles about Frogs & Toads. Walton,
Rick & Walton, Ann. 32p. (gr. 1-4). 1991. PLB 11.95
(0-8225-2331-0); pap. 3.95 (0-8225-9590-7) Lerner
Pubns.
—My Very Own Thanksgiving: A Book of Cooking &
Crafts. West, Robin. Wolfe, Robert L. & Wolfe, Diane,
photos by. LC 92-33234. (ps-3). 1993. 19.95
(0-87614-723-6) Carolrhoda Bks.
—Off Base: Riddles about Baseball. Walton, Rick &
Walton, Ann. LC 92-19857. 1993. 11.95
(0-8225-2338-8) Lerner Pubns.
—On with the Show: Show Me Riddles. Walton, Rick &
Walton, Ann. 32p. (gr. 1-4). 1989. PLB 11.95
(0-8225-2327-2) Lerner Pubns.
—Out on a Limb: Riddles about Trees & Plants. Peterson,
Scott K. 32p. (gr. 1-4). 1989. PLB 11.95
(0-8225-2328-0) Lerner Pubns.
—Summit Up: Riddles about Mountains. Swanson, June.
LC 93-19157. 1994. PLB 11.95 (0-8225-2342-6)
Lerner Pubns.
—Take a Hike: Riddles about Football. Walton, Rick &
Walton, Ann. LC 92-27011. 1993. 11.95
(0-8225-2340-X) Lerner Pubns.
—That's for Shore: Riddles from the Beach. Swanson,
June. 32p. (gr. 1-4). 1991. PLB 11.95 (0-8225-2332-9)
Lerner Pubns.
—Weather or Not: Riddles for Rain & Shine. Walton,
Rick & Walton, Ann. 32p. (gr. 1-4). 1989. PLB 8.95
(0-8225-2329-9) Lerner Pubns.
—What's Gnu? Riddles from the Zoo. Mase, Thomas.
32p. (gr. 1-4). 1989. PLB 11.95 (0-8225-2330-2)
Lerner Pubns.
Burke, Susan S., photos by. Home on the Range: Ranch-
Style Riddles. Burnes, Diane & Burns, Andy. LC 93-
19158. (gr. 4 up). 1994. 11.95 (0-8225-2341-8) Lerner
Pubns.

Burkel, Dietrich. The Shark Watcher's Guide. Dingerkus,
Guido. 176p. (gr. 7 up). 1989. lib. bdg. 10.98
(0-671-50234-4, J Messner); lib. bdg. 5.95
(0-671-68815-4) S&S Trade.
Burkert, Nancy E. A Child's Calendar. Updike, John. LC
61-21555. 32p. (gr. k-3). 1965. 11.95 (0-394-81059-7);
PLB 12.99 (0-394-91059-1) Knopf Bks Yng Read.
—The Fir Tree. Andersen, Hans Christian. LC 73-
121800. 48p. (ps up). 1986. pap. 5.95 (0-06-443109-6,
Trophy) HarpC Child Bks.
—James & the Giant Peach. Dahl, Roald. (gr. 3 up).
1961. 15.00 (0-394-81282-4); PLB 15.99
(0-394-91282-9) Knopf Bks Yng Read.
—Nightingale. Andersen, Hans Christian. Le Gallienne,
Eva, tr. LC 64-18574. 48p. (gr. 3 up). 1965. PLB 14.
89 (0-06-023781-3) HarpC Child Bks.
—The Nightingale. Andersen, Hans Christian. Le
Gallienne, Eva, tr. from DAN. LC 64-18574. 48p. (gr.
2-6). 1985. pap. 7.95 (0-06-443070-7, Trophy) HarpC
Child Bks.
—Scroobious Pip. Lear, Edward & Nash, Ogden. LC 68-
10373. (gr. 3 up). 1968. HarpC Child Bks.
—Snow-White & the Seven Dwarfs. Grimm, Jacob &
Grimm, Wilhelm K. Jarrell, Randall, tr. from GER.
LC 28-1489. 32p. (ps up). 1972. 17.00
(0-374-37099-0) FS&G.
—Snow-White & the Seven Dwarfs. Grimm, Jacob &
Grimm, Wilhelm K. Jarrell, Randall, tr. from GER.
32p. (ps up). 1987. pap. 5.95 (0-374-46868-0,
Sunburst) FS&G.
—Valentine & Orson. Burkert, Nancy E. 56p. (gr. 5 up).
1989. 16.95 (0-374-38078-3) FS&G.
Burkhart, Joyce L. Scripture Concepts for Children
Activity-Story Book: Building Godly Character, Vol.
2. Burkhart, Joyce L. & Mercer, Deborah B. 43p.
(ps-2). 1992. pap. 7.95 (0-9633166-1-3) Penta Ent.
—Scripture Concepts for Children Activity-Story Book,
Vol. 1: Building Godly Self-Esteem. Burkhart, Joyce
L. & Mercer, Deborah B. 43p. (ps-2). 1991. pap. 7.95
(0-9633166-0-5) Penta Ent.
Burkholder, Edith. Missionary Stories & the Millers.
Martin, Mildred A. 208p. (gr. 3 up). 1993. pap. 6.00
(0-9627643-4-5) Green Psturs Pr.
—Wisdom & the Millers: Proverbs for Children. 2nd ed.
Martin, Mildred A. 159p. (gr. 2-8). 1993. 9.50
(0-685-68129-7); pap. 6.00 (0-9627643-5-3) Green
Psturs Pr.
Burleson, Joe. The Witch Returns. Naylor, Phyllis R. LC
91-32370. 192p. (gr. 3-6). 1992. 14.00
(0-385-30601-6) Delacorte.
—Witch Weed. Naylor, Phyllis R. 192p. (gr. 4-7). 1992.
pap. 3.50 (0-440-40708-7, YB) Dell.
Burn, Doris. Christina Katerina & the Box. Gauch,
Patricia L. 48p. 1980. pap. 6.95 (0-698-20524-3,
Coward) Putnam Pub Group.
Burn, Jeffery. The Days of the Week. Hughes, Paul.
Harris, Peter, ed. LC 89-11758. 62p. (gr. 4-7). 1989.
PLB 17.26 (0-944483-32-1) Garrett Ed Corp.
—The Months of the Year. Hughes, Paul. Harris, Peter,
ed. LC 89-11759. 62p. (gr. 4-7). 1989. PLB 17.26
(0-944483-33-X) Garrett Ed Corp.
Burness, Tad. Joshua. Burness, Tad. 90p. (Orig.). (gr. 3
up). 1987. pap. 4.95 (1-55523-082-2) Winston-Derek.
Burnett, Lindy. My Jesus Pocketbook of a Very Special
Birth Day. Stirrup Associates, Inc. Staff. Harvey,
Bonnie C. & Phillips, Cheryl M., eds. LC 84-50919.
32p. (ps). 1984. pap. 0.69 (0-937420-15-8) Stirrup
Assoc.
—My Jesus Pocketbook of the Beginning. Stirrup
Associates, Inc. Staff. Harvey, Bonnie C. & Phillips,
Cheryl M., eds. LC 84-50918. 32p. (Orig.). (ps-3).
1984. pap. 0.69 (0-937420-14-X) Stirrup Assoc.
Burningham, John. Aldo. Burningham, John. LC 91-
19589. 32p. (ps-2). 1992. 15.00 (0-517-58701-7); PLB
15.99 (0-517-58699-1) Crown Bks Yng Read.
—Avocado Baby. Burningham, John. LC 81-43844. 24p.
(ps-3). 1982. 16.00 (0-690-04243-4, Crowell Jr Bks);
PLB 15.89 (0-690-04244-2) HarpC Child Bks.
—Chitty-Chitty-Bang-Bang. Fleming, Ian. LC 64-21282.
112p. (gr. 3-7). 1989. pap. 2.95 (0-394-81948-9) Knopf
Bks Yng Read.
—Come Away from the Water, Shirley. Burningham,
John. LC 77-483. 32p. (gr. 1-2). 1977. (Crowell Jr
Bks); PLB 14.89 (0-690-01361-2) HarpC Child Bks.
—Granpa. Burningham, John. LC 84-17464. 32p. (ps-1).
1985. 14.00 (0-517-55643-X) Crown Bks Yng Read.
—Harvey Slumfenberger's Christmas Present.
Burningham, John. LC 92-54957. 32p. (ps up). 1993.
15.95 (1-56402-246-3) Candlewick Pr.
—Hey! Get off Our Train. Burningham, John. LC 89-
15802. 48p. (ps-4). 1990. 15.00 (0-517-57638-4); PLB
15.99 (0-517-57643-0) Crown Bks Yng Read.
—John Burningham's ABC. Burningham, John. LC 92-
42765. 64p. (ps-2). 1993. 13.00 (0-517-59503-6); PLB
13.99 (0-517-59504-4) Crown Bks Yng Read.
—Mr. Gumpy's Motor Car. Burningham, John. LC 75-
4582. 48p. (ps-3). 1976. PLB 14.89 (0-690-00799-X,
Crowell Jr Bks) HarpC Child Bks.
—Time to Get out of the Bath, Shirley. Burningham,
John. LC 76-58503. 32p. (gr. k-2). 1978. 13.95
(0-690-01378-7, Crowell Jr Bks); PLB 13.89
(0-690-01379-5) HarpC Child Bks.
—The Wind in the Willows. Grahame, Kenneth. 240p.
(gr. 1 up). 1983. 15.75 (0-670-77120-1) Viking Child
Bks.
—The Wind in the Willows. Grahame, Kenneth. 240p.
(gr. 4-6). 1984. pap. 2.95 (0-14-031544-6) Viking
Child Bks.

—Would You Rather... Burningham, John. LC 78-7088. 32p. (ps-3). 1978. 17.00 (0-690-03917-4, Crowell Jr Bks); PLB 16.89 (0-690-03918-2, Crowell Jr Bks) HarpC Child Bks.

Burningham, Robin. Ka Mea Ho'ala, the Awakener: The Story of Henry Obookiah. Kikukawa, Cecily H. LC 82-70246. 100p. (Orig.). (gr. 7-10). 1982. pap. 6.95 (0-935848-10-X) Bess Pr.

Burningham, Robin Y. And the Birds Appeared. Williams, Julie S. 32p. (ps-3). 1988. 8.95 (0-8248-1194-1, Kolowalu Bk) UH Pr.

—How Maui Slowed the Sun. Tune, Suelyn C. LC 88-4548. 32p. (gr. k up). 1988. 8.95 (0-8248-1083-X) UH Pr.

—Maui & the Secret of Fire. Tune, Suelyn C. LC 90-27175. 32p. (ps-4). 1991. 9.95 (0-8248-1391-X, Kolowalu Bk) UH Pr.

—Maui Goes Fishing. Williams, Julie S. LC 90-27176. 32p. (ps-4). 1991. 9.95 (0-8248-1390-1, Kolowalu Bk) UH Pr.

Burnnett, Carroll. Kikko's Tracks. Burnnett, Carroll. 28p. (Orig.). (ps up). 1988. pap. 6.95 (0-9619414-1-3) Foto Fantasi Pr.

Burns, Elizabeth. Hanky Panky: Traditional Handkerchief Toys. Burns, Elizabeth. 24p. (ps-6). 1989. pap. 4.50 (0-9624152-0-0) E Burns.

Burns, Howard M. The Boy Who Saved the Town. Seabrooke, Brenda. LC 89-52027. 30p. (gr. 2-5). 1990. 7.95 (0-87033-405-0) Tidewater.

Burns, Kathy. Gramma Curlychief's Pawnee Indian Stories. 3rd ed. Howell, War Cry. LC 82-71948. 88p. (Orig.). (gr. 5-12). 1991. pap. 4.95x (0-943864-22-4) Davenport.

Burns, Ray. Adventures of Huckleberry Finn. Twain, Mark. Gise, Joanne, adapted by. LC 89-20353. 48p. (gr. 3-6). 1990. lib. bdg. 12.89 (0-8167-1857-1); pap. text ed. 3.95 (0-8167-1858-X) Troll Assocs.

—All about Animal Migrations. Sanders, John. LC 83-6630. 32p. (gr. 3-6). 1984. PLB 10.59 (0-89375-977-5); pap. text ed. 2.95 (0-89375-978-3) Troll Assocs.

—All about Islands. Rydell, Wendy. LC 83-4833. 32p. (gr. 3-6). 1984. lib. bdg. 10.59 (0-89375-975-9); pap. text ed. 2.95 (0-89375-976-7) Troll Assocs.

—Backyard Tent. Daniel, Kira. LC 85-14068. 48p. (Orig.). (gr. 1-3). 1986. PLB 10.59 (0-8167-0626-3); pap. text ed. 3.50 (0-8167-0627-1) Troll Assocs.

—Discovering Fossils. Rydell, Wendy. LC 83-4832. 32p. (gr. 3-6). 1984. lib. bdg. 10.59 (0-89375-973-2); pap. text ed. 2.95 (0-89375-974-0) Troll Assocs.

—Ghost in the House. Bolton, Elizabeth. LC 84-20530. 48p. (gr. 2-4). 1985. PLB 10.89 (0-8167-0418-X); pap. 3.50 (0-8167-0419-8) Troll Assocs.

—The Upside-Down Boy. Palazzo-Craig, Janet. LC 85-14067. 48p. (Orig.). (gr. 1-3). 1986. PLB 10.59 (0-8167-0604-2); pap. text ed. 3.50 (0-8167-0605-0) Troll Assocs.

—Who's Who at the Zoo! Palazzo-Craig, Janet. LC 85-14123. 48p. (Orig.). (gr. 1-3). 1986. PLB 10.59 (0-8167-0658-1); pap. text ed. 3.50 (0-8167-0659-X) Troll Assocs.

—Young Mark Twain. Sabin, Louis. LC 89-33982. 48p. (gr. 4-6). 1990. PLB 10.79 (0-8167-1783-4); pap. text ed. 3.50 (0-8167-1784-2) Troll Assocs.

Burns, Raymond. Air. Brandt, Keith. LC 84-2608. 32p. (gr. 3-6). 1985. PLB 9.49 (0-8167-0130-X); pap. text ed. 2.95 (0-8167-0131-8) Troll Assocs.

—All about the Moon. Adler, David. LC 82-17422. 32p. (gr. 3-6). 1983. PLB 10.59 (0-89375-886-8); pap. text ed. 2.95 (0-89375-887-6) Troll Assocs.

—Energy & Fuels. Santrey, Laurence. LC 84-2704. 32p. (gr. 3-6). 1985. PLB 9.49 (0-8167-0290-X); pap. text ed. 2.95 (0-8167-0291-8) Troll Assocs.

—The Great Rock 'n' Roll Mystery. Wandelmaier, Roy. LC 84-8753. 48p. (gr. 2-4). 1985. PLB 10.89 (0-8167-0416-3); pap. text ed. 3.50 (0-8167-0417-1) Troll Assocs.

—Our Wonderful Solar System. Adams, Richard. LC 82-17413. 32p. (gr. 3-6). 1983. PLB 10.59 (0-89375-872-8); pap. text ed. 2.95 (0-89375-873-6) Troll Assocs.

—Seasons. Sabin, Francene. LC 84-2713. 32p. (gr. 3-6). 1985. PLB 9.49 (0-8167-0308-6); pap. text ed. 2.95 (0-8167-0309-4) Troll Assocs.

—What's It Like to Be a Doctor. Bauer, Judith. LC 89-34398. 32p. (gr. k-3). 1990. lib. bdg. 10.89 (0-8167-1801-6); pap. text ed. 2.95 (0-8167-1802-4) Troll Assocs.

—World of Weather. Adler, David. LC 82-17398. 32p. (gr. 3-6). 1983. PLB 10.59 (0-89375-870-1); pap. text ed. 2.95 (0-89375-871-X) Troll Assocs.

Burns, Robert. Caves. Rigby, Susan. LC 91-45082. 32p. (gr. 4-6). 1993. PLB 11.59 (0-8167-2749-X); pap. text ed. 3.95 (0-8167-2750-3) Troll Assocs. Postponed.

—Glaciers. Patchett, Lynne. LC 91-45080. 32p. 1993. PLB 11.59 (0-8167-2751-1); pap. text ed. 3.95 (0-8167-2752-X) Troll Assocs. Postponed.

—Journey Through India. Ganeri, Anita. LC 91-46176. 32p. (gr. 3-5). 1993. PLB 11.89 (0-8167-2761-9); pap. text ed. 3.95 (0-8167-2762-7) Troll Assocs. Postponed.

—Journey Through Italy. Clark, Colin. LC 91-46174. 32p. (gr. 3-5). 1993. PLB 11.89 (0-8167-2763-5); pap. text ed. 3.95 (0-8167-2764-3) Troll Assocs. Postponed.

—Oceans. Oldershaw, Callie. LC 91-45079. 32p. (gr. 4-6). 1993. PLB 11.59 (0-8167-2753-8); pap. text ed. 3.95 (0-8167-2754-6) Troll Assocs. Postponed.

—Swamps. Gore, Sheila. LC 91-45081. 32p. (gr. 4-6). 1993. PLB 11.59 (0-8167-2755-4); pap. text ed. 3.95 (0-8167-2756-2) Troll Assocs. Postponed.

Burns, Theresa. Little New Kangaroo. Wiseman, Bernard. LC 92-21955. 1993. 14.95 (0-395-65362-2, Clarion Bks) HM.

Burris, Priscilla. Here a Mom, There a Mom. Jenks, Graham. 1994. write for info. (0-7852-8215-7) Nelson.

Burroughes, Jo. Mud, Moon & Me. Weil, Zaro. 80p. (gr. 2-5). 1992. 13.45 (0-395-58038-2) HM.

Burroughes, Joanna. My Grandma Has Black Hair. Hoffman, Mary. LC 87-24654. 32p. (ps-3). 1988. 9.95 (0-8037-0510-7) Dial Bks Young.

Burroughs, John, photos by. The Little Character That's Me, Vol. I. Schwartz, Barbara. 65p. (Orig.). (ps-6). 1988. wkbk. 11.95 (0-685-22570-4); audio cassette 14.95 (0-685-22571-2) Little Prodns.

Burrowes, Adjoa J. Ballad of Harriet Tubman. Plumpp, Sterling. 1993. 18.95 (0-88378-062-3) Third World.

—Paul Robeson. Plumpp, Sterling. 1992. pap. 5.95 (0-88378-065-8) Third World.

Burrus, Sue. Fun Guide to Anchorage. Madison, Kathy. Lauzen, Elizabeth, ed. 32p. (Orig.). (gr. 1-6). 1987. pap. 3.50 incl. wkbk. (0-942553-00-4) Madison Aves.

Bursik, Rose. Amelia's Fantastic Flight. Bursik, Rose. LC 91-28809. 32p. (ps-2). 1992. 14.95 (0-8050-1872-7, Bks Young Read) H Holt & Co.

Burstein, Chaya. A Kid's Catalog of Israel. Burstein, Chaya M. 288p. (gr. 3 up). 1988. 14.95 (0-8276-0263-4) JPS Phila.

—My Very Own Haggadah. Rev. ed. Saypol, Judyth R. & Wikler, Madeline. LC 83-6. 32p. (ps-3). 1983. pap. text ed. 2.95 (0-930494-23-7) Kar Ben.

Burstein, Chaya M. A First Jewish Holiday Cookbook. Burstein, Chaya M. (gr. 3-8). 1979. (Bonim Bks); pap. 8.95 (0-88482-775-5, Bonim Bks) Hebrew Pub.

—The Jewish Kids Catalog. Burstein, Chaya M. 224p. (gr. 3-7). 1983. pap. 14.95 (0-8276-0215-4) JPS Phila.

—Jewish Kids Hebrew-English Wordbook. Burstein, Chaya M. 40p. (gr. 1 up). 1993. 16.95 (0-8276-0381-9) JPS Phila.

—The Mystery of the Coins. Burstein, Chaya M. 160p. (Orig.). (gr. 4-6). 1988. pap. text ed. 9.95 (0-8074-0350-4, 123000) UAHC.

—The UAHC Kids Catalog of Jewish Living. Burstein, Chaya M. LC 91-42815. 32p. (gr. 4-6). 1992. pap. 8.95 (0-8074-0464-0, 123934) UAHC.

Burtick, Lyn M. Lori Lamb. Oana, Katherine. Baird, Tate, ed. 16p. (Orig.). (ps-k). 1989. pap. 4.52 (0-914127-09-8) Univ Class.

Burton, Bruce. Wide Awake in Dreamland. Duel, John. LC 91-66837. 239p. (gr. 4-8). 1992. 15.95 (0-9630923-0-8) Stargaze Pub.

Burton, Jane. Baby Animals Growing Up, 12 vols. Burton, Jane. 384p. (gr. 2-3). 1989. Set. PLB 191.16 (0-8368-0201-2) Gareth Stevens Inc.

—The First Dinosaurs. Dixon, Dougal. LC 87-6460. 32p. (gr. 2-3). 1987. PLB 15.93 (1-55532-258-1) Gareth Stevens Inc.

—Hunting the Dinosaurs. Dixon, Dougal. LC 87-6461. 32p. (gr. 2-3). 1987. PLB 15.93 (1-55532-259-X) Gareth Stevens Inc.

—The Jurassic Dinosaurs. Dixon, Dougal. LC 87-6462. 32p. (gr. 2-3). 1987. PLB 15.93 (1-55532-260-3) Gareth Stevens Inc.

—The Last Dinosaurs. Dixon, Dougal. LC 87-6463. 32p. (gr. 2-3). 1987. PLB 15.93 (1-55532-261-1) Gareth Stevens Inc.

Burton, Jane & Taylor, Kim. Animal Activities, 4 vols. Burton, Jane. 128p. (gr. 2-3). 1989. Set. PLB 63.72 (0-8368-0184-9) Gareth Stevens Inc.

Burton, Jane, photos by. Caper the Kid. Burton, Jane. LC 89-11566. 32p. (gr. 2-3). 1989. PLB 15.93 (0-8368-0203-9) Gareth Stevens Inc.

—Chick. 24p. (gr. k-3). 1992. 6.95 (0-525-67355-5, Lodestar Bks) Dutton Child Bks.

—Dabble the Duckling. Burton, Jane. LC 89-11398. 32p. (gr. 2-3). 1989. PLB 15.93 (0-8368-0205-5) Gareth Stevens Inc.

—Ginger the Kitten. Burton, Jane. LC 87-16660. 24p. (ps-3). 1988. pap. 2.25 (0-394-89638-6) Random Bks Yng Read.

—See How They Grow: Kitten. 24p. (gr. k-3). 1991. 6.95 (0-525-67343-1, Lodestar Bks) Dutton Child Bks.

—See How They Grow: Puppy. 24p. (gr. k-3). 1991. 6.95 (0-525-67342-3, Lodestar Bks) Dutton Child Bks.

Burton, Jane & King, Dave, photos by. Mammal. Parker, Steve. LC 88-22656. 64p. (gr. 5 up). 1989. 15.00 (0-394-82258-7); lib. bdg. 15.99 (0-394-92258-1) Knopf Bks Yng Read.

Burton, Jane & Taylor, Kim, photos by. The Egg Book. Burton, Robert. LC 93-28365. 1994. 14.95 (1-56458-460-7) Dorling Kindersley.

—Keeping Clean. Burton, Jane. LC 89-11557. 32p. (gr. 2-3). 1989. PLB 15.93 (0-8368-0187-3) Gareth Stevens Inc.

—Keeping Cool. Burton, Jane. LC 89-11412. 32p. (gr. 2-3). 1989. PLB 15.93 (0-8368-0188-1) Gareth Stevens Inc.

—Keeping Safe. Burton, Jane. LC 89-11416. 32p. (gr. 2-3). 1989. PLB 15.93 (0-8368-0186-5) Gareth Stevens INc.

—Keeping Warm. Burton, Jane, ed. LC 89-11411. 32p. (gr. 2-3). 1989. PLB 15.93 (0-8368-0185-7) Gareth Stevens Inc.

Burton, Jane, jt. photog. see Taylor, Kim.

Burton, Jene. The New Dinosaur Library, 4 vols. Dixon, Douglas. 128p. (gr. 2-3). 1988. Set. PLB 63.73 (1-55532-262-X) Gareth Stevens Inc.

Burton, Marilee R. Tail Toes Eyes Ears Nose. Burton, Marilee R. LC 87-33276. 32p. (ps-1). 1988. PLB 11.89 (0-06-020874-0) HarpC Child Bks.

—Tail Toes Eyes Ears Nose. Burton, Marilee R. LC 87-33276. 32p. (ps-1). 1992. pap. 4.95 (0-06-443260-2, Trophy) HarpC Child Bks.

Burton, Terry. Weird & Wonderful Science Facts. Pyke, Magnus. LC 83-24288. 128p. (gr. 5 up). 1985. pap. 3.95 (0-8069-6254-2) Sterling.

Burton, Tim. The Nightmare Before Christmas. Burton, Tim. LC 92-54867. 40p. 1993. 15.95 (1-56282-411-2); PLB 15.89 (1-56282-412-0) Hyprn Child.

Burton, Virginia L. Choo Choo: The Story of a Little Engine Who Ran Away. Burton, Virginia L. LC 37-19461. 56p. (Orig.). (gr. k-8). 1988. pap. 4.80 (0-395-47942-8) HM.

—The Emperor's New Clothes. Andersen, Hans Christian. LC 83-19610. 48p. (gr. k-3). 1979. pap. 5.70 (0-395-28594-1) HM.

—Katy & the Big Snow. Burton, Virginia L. 40p. (gr. k-3). 1974. pap. 4.80 (0-395-18562-9, Sandpiper) HM.

Buschini, Henny & Buschini, Luciano. The Ship in the Field. Buschini, Henny & Buschini, Luciano. LC 77-174719. 32p. (gr. k-3). 1973. 6.95 (0-87592-045-4) Scroll Pr.

Buschini, Luciano, jt. illus. see Buschini, Henny.

Bush, Florence C. & Bush, Margaret C. If Life Gives You Scraps, Make a Quilt: Short Stories of the Smoky Mountains. Bush, Florence C. 180p. (Orig.). 1993. pap. 9.95 (0-9634680-0-6) Misty Cove Pr.

Bush, Margaret C., jt. illus. see Bush, Florence C.

Bush, Timothy. James in the House of Aunt Prudence. Bush, Timothy. LC 92-40127. 32p. (ps-2). 1993. 13.00 (0-517-58881-1); PLB 13.99 (0-517-58882-X) Crown Bks Yng Read.

Bush, William. Big Red & the Fence Post. Parkison, Ralph F. Withrow, Marion O., ed. 53p. (Orig.). (gr. 2-8). 1988. pap. write for info. Little Wood Bks.

—Days. Parkison, Ralph F. Withrow, Marion O., ed. 60p. (Orig.). (gr. 2-8). 1988. pap. write for info. Little Wood Bks.

—Eovl. Parkison, Ralph F. Withrow, Marion O., ed. 36p. (Orig.). (gr. 2-8). 1988. pap. write for info. Little Wood Bks.

—In the Middle of the Corn Patch. Parkison, Ralph F. Withrow, Marion O., ed. 55p. (Orig.). (gr. 2-8). 1988. pap. write for info. Little Wood Bks.

—The Little Flea. Parkison, Ralph F. Withrow, Marion O., ed. 21p. (Orig.). (gr. 2-8). 1988. pap. write for info. Little Wood Bks.

—The Little Girl & the Inchworm. Parkison, Ralph F. Withrow, Marion O., ed. 75p. (Orig.). (gr. 2-8). 1988. pap. write for info. Little Wood Bks.

—The Little Girl, the Lillipop, & the Green Bird, Bk. 1. Parkison, Ralph F. Withrow, Marion O., ed. 31p. (Orig.). (gr. 2-6). 1988. pap. 4.25 (0-929949-00-5) Little Wood Bks.

—The Old Goat. Parkison, Ralph F. Withrow, Marion O., ed. 112p. (Orig.). (gr. 2-8). 1988. pap. write for info. Little Wood Bks.

—The Pea in the Pod, Bk. 3. Parkison, Ralph F. Withrow, Marion O., ed. 10p. (Orig.). (gr. 2-6). 1988. pap. text ed. 3.00 (0-929949-02-1) Little Wood Bks.

—The Pencil. Parkison, Ralph F. Withrow, Marion O., ed. 47p. (Orig.). (gr. 2-8). 1988. pap. write for info. Little Wood Bks.

—Santa's Wheat Kernels. Parkison, Ralph F. Withrow, Marion O., ed. 60p. (Orig.). (gr. 2-8). 1988. pap. write for info. Little Wood Bks.

—Seeds & Seeds & Seeds. Parkison, Ralph F. Withrow, Marion O., ed. 65p. (Orig.). (gr. 2-8). 1988. pap. write for info. Little Wood Bks.

—The Soda Pop Can & the Road Sign, Bk. 4. Parkison, Ralph F. Withrow, Marion O., ed. 13p. (Orig.). (gr. 2-6). 1988. pap. text ed. 3.73 (0-929949-03-X) Little Wood Bks.

—The Spot on the Ground. Parkison, Ralph F. Withrow, Marion O., ed. 83p. (Orig.). (gr. 2-8). 1988. pap. write for info. Little Wood Bks.

—A This or a That. Parkison, Ralph F. Withrow, Marion O., ed. 53p. (Orig.). (gr. 2-8). 1988. pap. write for info. Little Wood Bks.

—The Twig & the Mouse, Bk. 2. Parkison, Ralph F. Withrow, Marion O., ed. 17p. (Orig.). (gr. 2-6). 1988. pap. 4.25 (0-929949-01-3) Little Wood Bks.

—Yodeling. Parkison, Ralph F. Withrow, Marion O., ed. 71p. (Orig.). (gr. 2-8). 1988. pap. write for info. Little Wood Bks.

Bushe, Claire & Ripley, Edward. Angels, Prophets, Rabbis & Kings: From the Stories of the Jewish People. Patterson, Jose. 132p. (gr. 6 up). 1991. 22.50 (0-87226-912-4) P Bedrick Bks.

Bushell, Isobel. Frere Jacques. Books, Emma K. 14p. (ps). 1994. 5.95 (0-694-00574-6, Festival) HarpC Child Bks.

—Rudolph the Red-Nosed Reindeer: Musical Board Book. Emma Kemp Books. 12p. (ps). 1993. 5.95 (0-694-00564-9) HarpC Child Bks.

—Santa Claus Is Coming to Town: Musical Board Book. 12p. (ps). 1993. 5.95 (0-694-00563-0) HarpC Child Bks.

—Twinkle, Twinkle, Little Star. Books, Emma K. 12p. (ps). 1994. 5.95 (0-694-00575-4, Festival) HarpC Child Bks.

Bushey, Jerry. Trash! Wilcox, Charlotte. 40p. (gr. k-4). 1988. PLB 19.95 (0-87614-311-7) Carolrhoda Bks.
—Trash! Wilcox, Charlotte. 40p. (gr. k-4). 1989. pap. 5.95 (0-87614-511-X, First Ave Edns) Lerner Pubns.
Bushey, Jerry, photos by. Farming the Land: Modern Farmers & Their Machines. Bushey, Jerry. 40p. (gr. k-4). 1987. PLB 13.50 (0-87614-314-1) Carolrhoda Bks.
Buskirk, Judith P. Animal Rhymes: Reproducible Pre-Reading Books for Young Children. Warren, Jean. Bittinger, Gayle, ed. 160p. (ps-1). 1990. pap. text ed. 14.95 (0-911019-34-0) Warren Pub Hse.
Buskohl, Esther E. Honey: Story of a Little Brown Mule. Buskohl, Esther E. LC 85-80216. 80p. (Orig.). (gr. 3-5). 1985. 9.95 (0-9614991-0-9); pap. 4.95 (0-9614991-1-7) EEBART.
Butcher, Jim. Jackie Robinson & the Story of All-Black Baseball. O'Connor, Jim. LC 88-18466. 48p. (Orig.). (gr. 2-4). 1989. PLB 7.99 (0-394-92456-8); pap. 3.50 (0-394-82456-3) Random Bks Yng Read.
Butcher, Sam. David, Vol. I. Hershey, Katherine. 52p. (gr. k-6). 1972. pap. text ed. 9.45 (1-55976-020-6) CEF Press.
—David, Vol. II. Hershey, Katherine. 55p. (gr. k-6). 1973. pap. text ed. 9.45 (1-55976-021-4) CEF Press.
—Elijah. Overholtzer, Ruth. 36p. (gr. k-6). 1967. pap. text ed. 9.45 (1-55976-009-5) CEF Press.
—First Christians. George, Alan. 56p. (gr. k-6). 1991. pap. text ed. 9.45 (1-55976-023-0) CEF Press.
—Gifts & Rewards. Johnson, Betty. 13p. (gr. k-6). 1981. pap. text ed. 9.45 (1-55976-137-7) CEF Press.
—Give What You Can. Hutchcroft, Vera. 20p. (gr. k-6). 1984. pap. text ed. 4.25 (1-55976-142-3) CEF Press.
—The One Who Was Different. Haskin, Dorothy. 16p. (gr. k-6). 1983. pap. text ed. 4.25 (1-55976-130-X) CEF Press.
—Parables of Christ. Kratavil, Helen S. 64p. (gr. k-6). 1974. pap. text ed. 11.50 (1-55976-015-X) CEF Press.
—Precious Moments Bedtime Stories. Butcher, Samuel J. LC 88-24047. 248p. 1989. 14.99 (0-8010-0959-6) Baker Bk.
—Rejoicing with Joy. Harner, Ruth. 21p. (gr. k-6). 1988. pap. text ed. 4.25 (1-55976-145-8) CEF Press.
—Run Ma Run. Dick, Lois H. 57p. (gr. k-6). 1978. pap. text ed. 8.99 (1-55976-055-9) CEF Press.
—Ruth. Alexander, Matilda. 48p. (gr. k-6). 1972. pap. text ed. 9.45 (1-55976-017-6) CEF Press.
—The Tabernacle. Smith, Jane D. 38p. (gr. k-6). 1972. pap. text ed. 9.45 (1-55976-022-2) CEF Press.
Butcher, Sam & Anderasen, Norma. Joshua. Overholtzer, Ruth. 62p. (gr. k-6). 1987. pap. text ed. 9.45 (1-55976-012-5) CEF Press.
Butcher, Sam & Geraldo, Esteban. Children of the Bible. Seger, Doris. 64p. (gr. k-6). 1967. pap. text ed. 8.99 (1-55976-028-1) CEF Press.
Butcher, Sam & Hilterbrand, Greg. My Wonderful Lord. George, Alan. 61p. (gr. k-6). 1987. pap. text ed. 8.99 (1-55976-029-X) CEF Press.
Butcher, Samuel J. Precious Moments Stories from the Bible. Haan, Sheri D. LC 78-97507. 288p. (gr. 1-6). 1987. 14.99 (0-8010-4311-5) Baker Bk.
—Precious Moments Children's Bible: Easy-to-Read, New Life Version. Ledyard, Gleason H., tr. LC 90-36671. 1424p. 1991. 24.99 (0-8010-5664-0) Baker Bk.
—Precious Moments Through-the-Day Stories. Beers, V. Gilbert. LC 90-1265. 256p. 1991. 14.99 (0-8010-0992-8) Baker Bk.
—Precious Moments Through-the-Year Stories. Beers, V. Gilbert, text by. LC 89-17848. 288p. (gr. 2-6). 1989. 14.99 (0-8010-0973-1) Baker Bk.
Butcher, Solomon. Prairie Visions: The Life & Times of Solomon Butcher. Conrad, Pam. LC 90-38658. 96p. (gr. 5 up). 1994. pap. 8.95 (0-06-446135-1, Trophy) HarpC Child Bks.
Butenhoff, Lisa K. Nina's Magic. Butenhoff, Lisa K. Thatch, Nancy R., ed. Melton, David, intro. by. LC 92-18293. 26p. (gr. 3-4). 1992. PLB 14.95 (0-933849-40-0) Landmark Edns.
Butenko, Bohdan. How Pleasant to Know Mr. Lear. Lear, Edward. 64p. (gr. k-4). Date not set. 14.95 (0-88045-126-2) Stemmer Hse. Postponed.
Butler, John. Animal Families of the Forest. Strong, Stacie & Butler, John. 6p. (gr. 1-6). 1993. 14.99 (0-8431-3391-0) Price Stern.
—Animal Families of the Wild: A Read-Aloud Collection of Animal Literature. Russell, William F., ed. LC 89-22226. 96p. (gr. 2 up). 1990. 12.95 (0-517-57358-X); PLB 13.99 (0-517-57359-8) Crown Bks Yng Read.
—Apes. Lemmon, Tess. LC 92-37692. (gr. 3 up). 1993. 15.45 (0-395-66901-4) Ticknor & Fields.
—Baby Animals: Five Stories of Endangered Species. Hall, Derek. LC 91-71861. 64p. (ps up). 1992. 14.95 (1-56402-004-5) Candlewick Pr.
—The Fish: The Story of the Stickleback. Lane, Margaret. 32p. (gr. k-4). 1994. pap. 4.99 (0-14-055276-6, Puffin Pied Piper) Puffin Bks.
—Giant Book of Animal Worlds. Ganeri, Anita. 14p. (gr. 2-5). 1992. 19.95 (0-525-67369-5, Lodestar Bks) Dutton Child Bks.
—Shadow the Deer. Radcliffe, Theresa. 32p. (ps-1). 1993. 13.99 (0-670-83852-7) Viking Child Bks.
Butler, John & McIntyre, Brian. Grassland Animals. Chinery, Michael. LC 91-53145. 40p. (Orig.). (gr. 2-5). 1992. PLB 8.99 (0-679-92045-5); pap. 4.99 (0-679-82045-0) Random Bks Yng Read.

—Questions & Answers about Polar Animals. Chinery, Michael. LC 93-29426. 1994. 5.95 (1-85697-964-4) Kingfisher Bks.
Butler, Nate & Evans, Beth. Tracing Our German Roots. Silver, Leda. 48p. (gr. 4-7). 1993. text ed. 12.95 (1-56261-150-X) John Muir.
—Tracing Our Irish Roots. Moscinski, Sharon. LC 93-2070. 48p. 1993. text ed. 12.95 (1-56261-148-8) John Muir.
—Tracing Our Italian Roots. Lee, Kathleen. 48p. (gr. 4-7). 1993. text ed. 12.95 (1-56261-149-6) John Muir.
—Tracing Our Jewish Roots. Sagan, Miriam. 48p. (gr. 4-7). 1993. text ed. 12.95 (1-56261-151-8) John Muir.
Butler, Paul. Practical English Structure, Vol. 1. Bordman, Marcia Beth, et al. LC 80-85299. 200p. (gr. 9-12). 1981. text ed. 15.95 (0-913580-66-X, Clerc Bks) Gallaudet Univ Pr.
—Practical English Structure, Vol. 2. Bordman, Marcia B., et al. LC 80-85299. 224p. (gr. 9-12). 1981. text ed. 15.95 (0-913580-67-8, Clerc Bks) Gallaudet Univ Pr.
—Practical English Structure, Vol. 3. Bordman, Marcia B., et al. LC 80-85299. 220p. (gr. 9-12). 1981. text ed. 15.95 (0-913580-68-6, Clerc Bks) Gallaudet Univ Pr.
—Practical English Structure, Vol. 4. Bordman, Marcia B., et al. LC 80-85299. 218p. (gr. 9-12). 1981. text ed. 15.95 (0-913580-69-4, Clerc Bks) Gallaudet Univ Pr.
—Practical English Structure, Vol. 5. Bordman, Marcia B., et al. LC 80-85299. 340p. (gr. 9-12). 1982. text ed. 15.95 (0-913580-70-8, Clerc Bks) Gallaudet Univ Pr.
Butler, Ralph. You've Got the Power: A Recovery Guide for Young People with Drug & Alcohol Problems. Read, Edward M. & Daley, Dennis C. Gondles, James A., Jr., frwd. by. 98p. (Orig.). 1993. pap. 10.00 (0-929310-87-X, 349) Am Correctional.
Butler, Stephen. Henny Penny. Butler, Stephen. LC 90-35115. 32p. (ps-1). 1991. 12.95 (0-688-09921-1, Tambourine Bks); PLB 12.88 (0-688-09922-X, Tambourine Bks) Morrow.
—Little Bird. Pirotta, Saviour. LC 91-25413. 32p. (ps-3). 1992. 14.00 (0-688-11289-7, Tambourine Bks); PLB 13.93 (0-688-11290-0, Tambourine Bks) Morrow.
—The Mouse & the Apple. Butler, Stephen. LC 93-15951. 32p. (ps up). 1994. 15.00 (0-688-12810-6, Tambourine Bks); PLB 14.93 (0-688-12811-4, Tambourine Bks) Morrow.
Butler, Steven, jt. illus. see Byrd, Mitch.
Butler, Synovia. Understanding Numbers. Singletary, Helen P., et al. 47p. (Orig.). (gr. p-6). 1991. pap. text ed. 20.00 (1-880850-04-4) Comp Trng Clinic.
Butrick, Lyn M. Chirpy Chipmunk. Oana, Katherine. Baird, Tate, ed. LC 88-51854. 16p. (Orig.). (ps) 1989. pap. 4.52 (0-914127-08-X) Univ Class.
—If This... & That.. Then What. Butrick, Lyn M. Cooper, William R., ed. LC 83-50783. 27p. (gr. 1-3). 1983. Set. pap. 15.80 (0-914127-13-6); Vol. 1. 3.93 (0-914127-04-7) Univ Class.
—Kippy Koala. Oana, Katherine. Cooper, William, ed. LC 85-51823. 16p. (Orig.). (ps up). 1985. pap. text ed. 3.72 (0-914127-21-7) Univ Class.
—Minnie Muskrat. Oana, Katherine. Baird, Tate, ed. LC 88-51856. 16p. (ps-k). 1989. pap. 4.52 (0-914127-10-1) Univ Class.
—The Young Christian Observes the Law. Shuster, Albert H., et al. Cooper, William H., ed. LC 83-80868. 106p. (gr. 4-8). 1983. pap. text ed. 5.27 (0-914127-02-0) Univ Class.
—The Young Citizen Observes the Law. Shuster, Albert H. & Miller, Russell H. Cooper, William H., ed. LC 83-80867. 93p. (gr. 4-8). 1983. pap. text ed. 5.27 (0-914127-03-9); tchr's. ed. 4.88 (0-685-07834-5) Univ Class.
—Zippy Zebra. Oana, Katherine. Baird, Tate, ed. LC 88-51853. 16p. (Orig.). (ps) 1989. pap. 4.52 (0-914127-11-X) Univ Class.
Butterworth, Nick. Busy People. Butterworth, Nick. LC 91-58719. 32p. (ps). 1992. 9.95 (1-56402-056-8) Candlewick Pr.
—Making Faces. Butterworth, Nick. LC 92-54578. 32p. (ps). 1993. 12.95 (1-56402-212-9) Candlewick Pr.
—My Dad Is Awesome. Butterworth, Nick. LC 91-71832. 32p. (ps up). 1992. pap. 4.99 (1-56402-033-9) Candlewick Pr.
—My Grandma Is Wonderful. Butterworth, Nick. LC 91-58747. 32p. (ps up). 1992. pap. 4.99 (1-56402-100-9) Candlewick Pr.
—My Grandpa Is Amazing. Butterworth, Nick. LC 91-58746. 32p. (ps up). 1992. pap. 4.99 (1-56402-099-1) Candlewick Pr.
Butterworth, Nick & Inkpen, Mick. The Good Stranger. Butterworth, Nick & Inkpen, Mick. 32p. (ps-3). 1992. 3.99 (0-551-02507-7) HarpC.
—The Little Gate. Butterworth, Nick & Inkpen, Mick. 32p. (ps-3). 1992. pap. 3.99 (0-551-02506-9) HarpC.
—The Rich Farmer. Butterworth, Nick & Inkpen, Mick. 32p. (ps-3). 1992. pap. 3.99 (0-551-02508-5) HarpC.
—The Ten Silver Coins. Butterworth, Nick & Inkpen, Mick. 32p. (ps-3). 1992. 3.99 (0-551-02505-0) HarpC.
—Who Made Me? Doney, Malcolm & Doney, Meryl. 38p. (ps-3). 1987. 9.99 (0-310-55660-0, 19064) Zondervan.
—Who Made Me? Doney, Malcolm, text by. LC 92-20748. 1992. write for info. (0-551-01476-8) Zondervan.
Button, Mary. Handicapped...How Does It Feel: Activity Packet. Fox, C. Lynn. Lovelady, Janet, ed. 48p. (gr. k-12). 1982. pap. 5.95 (0-935266-13-5, BW6613-5) B L Winch.

Butts, Donna R. UFO Contact, the Four. Butts, Donna R. & Corder, S. Scott. Stevens, Wendelle C., ed. Caulfield, William, intro. by. (gr. 9-12). 1989. PLB 17.95 (0-934269-18-1) UFO Photo.
Butz, Steve. Twenty Thousand Leagues under the Sea. Verne, Jules. Nordlicht, Lillian, adapted by. LC 79-23887. 48p. (gr. 4 up). 1983. PLB 18.64 (0-8172-1652-6) Raintree Steck-V.
Buxton, John. Secret Treasures. LC 93-9767. 1993. write for info. (0-87044-956-7) Natl Geog.
Buzzanco, Eileen M. Beezle's Bravery. Elliott, Joey. Chapin, Tom, narrated by. 32p. (gr. k-4). 1989. 11.95 (0-924483-17-2); incl. audiocassette 16.95 (0-924483-15-6); incl. audiocassette & toy combination 39.95 (0-924483-13-X); incl. audiocassette & small toy combination 25.95 (0-924483-35-0); write for info. audiocassette (0-924483-19-9) Soundprints.
—Delver's Danger. Thompson-Hoffman, Susan. Chapin, Tom, narrated by. LC 88-64152. 32p. (gr. k-4). 1989. 11.95 (0-924483-02-4); incl. audiocassette 16.95 (0-924483-05-9); incl. audiocassette & toy combination 39.95 (0-924483-08-3); audiocassette and small toy combination 25.95__incl. (0-924483-36-9); write for info. audiocassette (0-924483-11-3) Soundprints.
—Frolic's Dance. Harms, Valerie. Chapin, Tom, narrated by. LC 88-64155. 32p. (gr. k-4). 1989. 11.95 (0-924483-01-6); incl. audiocassette 16.95 (0-924483-04-0); incl. audiocassette & toy combination 39.95 (0-924483-07-5); incl. audiocassette & small toy combination 25.95 (0-924483-37-7); pap. 5.95 (0-924483-77-6); write for info. (0-924483-10-5) Soundprints.
—Scamp's New Home. Elliott, Joey. Chapin, Tom, narrated by. 32p. (gr. k-4). 1989. 11.95 (0-924483-16-4); incl. audiocassette 16.95 (0-924483-14-8); incl. audiocassette & toy combination 39.95 (0-924483-12-1); incl. audiocassette & small toy combination 25.95 (0-924483-39-3); write for info. audiocassette (0-924483-18-0) Soundprints.
—Tassel's Mission. Thompson-Hoffman, Susan. Chapin, Tom, narrated by. LC 88-64151. 32p. (gr. k-4). 1989. 11.95 (0-924483-00-8); incl. audiocassette 16.95 (0-924483-03-2); incl. audiocassette & toy combination 39.95 (0-924483-06-7); incl. audiocassette & small toy combination 25.95 (0-924483-41-5); write for info. audiocassette (0-924483-09-1) Soundprints.
Byal, Chris, jt. illus. see Baker, Lisa H.
Byard, Carole. Africa Dream. Greenfield, Eloise. LC 77-5080. 32p. (ps-3). 1989. PLB 13.89 (0-690-04776-2, Crowell Jr Bks) HarpC Child Bks.
—Africa Dream. Greenfield, Eloise. LC 77-5080. 32p. (ps-3). 1992. pap. 4.95 (0-06-443277-7, Trophy) HarpC Child Bks.
—The Black Snowman. Mendez, Phil. (gr. 2-5). 1989. 14.95 (0-590-40552-7) Scholastic Inc.
—The Black Snowman. Mendez, Phil. 48p. 1991. pap. 4.95 (0-590-44873-0, Blue Ribbon Bks) Scholastic Inc.
—Cornrows. Yarbrough, Camille. LC 78-24010. 48p. (Orig.). (gr. 2-6). 1981. (Coward); pap. 6.95 (0-698-20529-4, Coward) Putnam Pub Group.
—Cornrows. Yarbrough, Camille. (gr. 2-6). 1992. pap. 6.95 (0-698-20709-2, Sandcastle Bks) Putnam Pub Group.
—Grandmama's Joy. Greenfield, Eloise. LC 79-11403. 32p. (gr. 2-5). 1980. 13.95 (0-399-21064-4, Philomel) Putnam Pub Group.
—I Can Do It by Myself. Little, Lessie J. & Greenfield, Eloise. LC 77-11554. (gr. k-2). 1978. (Crowell Jr Bks); PLB 14.89 (0-690-03851-8) HarpC Child Bks.
Byars, Betsy. The Computer Nut. large type ed. Byars, Betsy. 200p. 1993. 13.95 (0-7451-1680-9, Galaxy Child Lrg Print) Chivers N Amer.
Byars, Guy. The Computer Nut. Byars, Betsy C. 144p. (gr. 3-7). 1986. pap. 3.99 (0-14-032086-5, Puffin) Puffin Bks.
Bye, C. J., et al. Work-Game Sheets for Magnet Magic Etc. Hoyt, Marie A. 28p. (Orig.). (gr. 2-8). 1984. pap. text ed. 2.50 (0-914911-03-1) Educ Serv Pr.
Byer, Carol. Henny Penny. LC 80-28146. 32p. (gr. k-3). 1981. PLB 9.79 (0-89375-490-0); pap. text ed. 1.95 (0-89375-491-9) Troll Assocs.
Byers, Helen. Count Your Way Through Germany. Haskins, Jim. 24p. (gr. 1-4). 1990. PLB 17.50 (0-87614-407-5) Carolrhoda Bks.
—Count Your Way Through Mexico. Haskins, Jim. 24p. (gr. 1-4). 1989. 17.50 (0-87614-349-4); pap. 5.95 (0-87614-517-9) Carolrhoda Bks.
Byers, Reggie. The Esteem Team in "The Best I Can Be" Byers, Reggie. 48p. (gr. k-4). 1993. 9.95 (1-882732-05-7) Ctr Applied Psy.
Byfield, Barbara N. The Cable Car & the Dragon. Caen, Herb. LC 85-32004. 40p. 1986. 9.95 (0-87701-390-X) Chronicle Bks.
Byrd, Bob, photos by. The Young Scientist's Guide to Successful Science Projects. Markle, Sandra. LC 89-45290. 128p. (gr. 3-7). lib. bdg. 12.88 (0-688-07217-8) Lothrop. Postponed.
—The Young Scientist's Guide to Successful Science Projects. Markle, Sandra. LC 89-45290. 128p. (gr. 3-7). 1990. pap. 6.95 (0-688-09137-7, Pub. by Beech Tree Bks) Morrow.
Byrd, Mitch & Butler, Steven. Cat & Mouse Collection. Mann, Roland. Ulm, Chris, ed. 139p. 1990. pap. 9.95 (0-944735-70-3) Malibu Graphics.

Byrd, N. Kalomo. A Brand New Flavor. Ebo, Runett N. 28p. (Orig.). (gr. 9-12). 1993. pap. 8.00 (1-883753-02-3) Jwand Ent.

Byrd, Robert. The Bear & the Bird King. Grimm, Jacob & Grimm, Wilhelm K. Byrd, Robert, retold by. LC 93-15741. 32p. (ps-3). 1994. 14.99 (0-525-45118-8, DCB) Dutton Child Bks.

—The Children's Aesop: Selected Fables. Calmenson, Stephanie, retold by. LC 91-73884. 64p. (ps-3). 1992. 11.95 (1-56397-041-4) Boyds Mills Pr.

—Dinosaurs & Dragons. Roth, Kevin, read by. 24p. (ps-1). 1991. pap. 9.95 incls. cassette (0-679-81744-1) Random Bks Yng Read.

—The Emperor's New Clothes. Andersen, Hans Christian. Levinson, Riki, retold by. LC 89-23820. 40p. (ps-2). 1991. 14.95 (0-525-44611-7, DCB) Dutton Child Bks.

Byrd, Samuel. Abraham Lincoln: A Man for All the People: A Ballad. Livingston, Myra C. LC 93-2731. 1993. 15.95 (0-8234-1049-8) Holiday.

—Dancing with the Indians. Medearis, Angela S. LC 90-28666. 32p. (ps-3). 1991. reinforced 14.95 (0-8234-0893-0) Holiday.

—Dancing with the Indians: A Reading Rainbow Review Book. Medearis, Angela S. (ps-3). 1993. pap. 5.95 (0-8234-1023-4) Holiday.

—Let Freedom Ring: A Ballad of Martin Luther King, Jr. Livingston, Myra C. LC 91-28245. 32p. (ps-3). 1992. reinforced bdg. 15.95 (0-8234-0957-0) Holiday.

—A Picture Book of Frederick Douglass. Adler, David A. LC 92-17378. 32p. (ps-3). 1993. reinforced bdg. 14.95 (0-8234-1002-1) Holiday.

—A Picture Book of Harriet Tubman. Adler, David A. LC 91-19628. 32p. (ps-3). 1992. reinforced bdg. 14.95 (0-8234-0926-0) Holiday.

—A Picture Book of Sitting Bull. Adler, David A. LC 92-47119. (ps-3). 1993. reinforced bdg. 15.95 (0-8234-1044-7) Holiday.

—Running for Our Lives. Turner, Glennette T. LC 93-28430. 208p. (gr. 8-12). 1994. 15.95 (0-8234-1121-4) Holiday.

Byrne, Connell. Millions of Miles to Mars. Kelch, Joseph W. LC 93-33798. (gr. 3 up). 1994. write for info. (0-671-88249-X, J Messner); pap. write for info. (0-671-88250-3, J Messner) S&S Trade.

Byrnes, Lynne. The Three Little Pigs. 24p. (ps-1). 1991. pap. 1.25 (0-7214-5305-8, S9016-6 SER.) Ladybird Bks.

—The Ugly Duckling. 24p. (ps-1). 1991. pap. 1.25 (0-7214-5304-X, S9016-5) Ladybird Bks.

Byron, Barton. The Paper Airplane Book. Simon, Seymour. (gr. 4-6). 1971. pap. 12.95 (0-670-53797-7) Viking Child Bks.

Byron, Kevin, photos by. The Insect Almanac: A Year-Round Activity Guide. Russo, Monica. LC 90-22438. 136p. (gr. 4-10). 1992. pap. 7.95 (0-8069-7455-9) Sterling.

—The Tree Almanac: A Year-Round Activity Guide. Russo, Monica. LC 92-41347. (gr. 3 up). 1993. 14.95 (0-8069-1252-9) Sterling.

Bywaters, Lynn. Cinderella. Easton, Samantha, retold by. 32p. (ps-3). 1992. 6.95 (0-8362-4905-4) Andrews & McMeel.

—Sleeping Beauty. Easton, Samantha, retold by. 32p. (ps-3). 1992. 6.95 (0-8362-4915-1) Andrews & McMeel.

C

Caban, Janice. Cinderella, Vol. 512. rev. ed. Lipton, Alfred. Caban, Janice, ed. 10p. (gr. k). 1989. pap. 2.00 (1-878501-01-1) Ntrl Science Indus.

—Goldilox & the Three Bears, Vol. 514. rev. ed. Lipton, Alfred. Caban, Janice, ed. 10p. (gr. k). 1989. pap. 2.00 (1-878501-02-X) Ntrl Science Indus.

—Jack & the Beanstalk, Vol. 510. rev. ed. Lipton, Alfred. Caban, Janice, ed. 10p. (gr. k). 1989. pap. 2.00 (1-878501-00-3) Ntrl Science Indus.

—Little Red Riding Hood, Vol. 520. rev. ed. Lipton, Alfred. Caban, Janice, ed. 10p. (gr. k). 1989. pap. 2.00 (1-878501-05-4) Ntrl Science Indus.

—Pinocchio, Vol. 516. rev. ed. Lipton, Alfred. Caban, Janice, ed. 10p. (gr. k). 1989. pap. 2.00 (1-878501-03-8) Ntrl Science Indus.

—Sleeping Beauty, Vol. 518. rev. ed. Lipton, Alfred. Caban, Janice, ed. 10p. (gr. k). 1989. pap. 2.00 (1-878501-04-6) Ntrl Science Indus.

Cabat, Erni. Erni Cabat's Magical ABC: Animals Around the Farm. Rule, Michael, notes by. LC 90-5242. 64p. (ps-2). 1992. 15.95 (0-943173-73-6) Harbinger AZ.

—Erni Cabat's Magical World of Monsters. Cohen, Daniel, text by. 32p. (gr. 4 up). 1992. 14.00 (0-525-65087-3, Cobblehill Bks) Dutton Child Bks.

Cable, Annette. End of Winter. Chmielarz, Sharon. LC 91-30304. 32p. (ps-3). 1992. 14.00 (0-517-58745-9); PLB 14.99 (0-517-58746-7) Crown Bks Yng Read.

Cabrera, Ralph. How to Get into & Graduate from College in Four Years with Good Grades, a Useful Major, a Little Debt, Great Friends, Happy Parents, Maximum Party Attendance, Minimal Weight Gain, Decent Habits, Fewer Hassles, a Career Goal, & a Super Attitude All While Remaining Extremely Cool. Spethman, Martin J. 192p. (Orig.). (gr. 11-12). 1993. pap. 10.95 (0-9633598-0-0) Westgate Pub & Ent.

Cabuco, et al. Quest of the Ancients. Garcia, Vince. 224p. (Orig.). (gr. 9-12). 1990. pap. 23.00 (0-9628003-0-9) Unicorn Game Pubns.

Caddell, Foster. Catcher with a Glass Arm. Christopher, Matt. (gr. 4-6). 1985. pap. 3.95 (0-316-13985-8) Little.

—Miracle at the Plate. Christopher, Matt. 144p. (gr. 3-6). 1989. pap. 3.95 (0-316-13926-2) Little.

—Touchdown for Tommy. Christopher, Matt. 145p. (gr. 4-6). 1985. pap. 3.95 (0-316-13982-3) Little.

—The Year Mom Won the Pennant. Christopher, Matt. 160p. (gr. 4 up). 1986. pap. 3.95 (0-316-13988-2) Little.

Cady, Harrison. The Adventures of Buster Bear. Burgess, Thornton W. Kliros, Thea, adapted by. LC 92-36949. 96p. 1993. pap. 1.00 (0-486-27564-7) Dover.

—The Adventures of Chatterer the Red Squirrel. unabr. ed. Burgess, Thornton W. Kliros, Thea, adapted by. LC 92-14627. 96p. 1992. pap. 1.00 (0-486-27399-7) Dover.

—The Adventures of Grandfather Frog. unabr. ed. Burgess, Thornton W. Kliros, Thea, adapted by. LC 92-13146. 96p. 1992. pap. text ed. 1.00 (0-486-27400-4) Dover.

—The Adventures of Jimmy Skunk. Burgess, Thornton W. 128p. (ps-3). 1987. pap. 2.95 (0-316-11662-9) Little.

—The Dear Old Briar-Patch. Burgess, Thornton W. 192p. (ps-3). 1983. pap. 8.95 (0-316-11654-8) Little.

—Mother West Wind's Children. Burgess, Thornton W. 156p. (ps-3). 1985. pap. 8.95 (0-316-11657-2) Little.

—Mother West Wind's Neighbors. Burgess, Thornton W. LC 68-21862. (gr. 1 up). 1985. pap. 8.95 (0-316-11656-4) Little.

—Old Mother West Wind. golden anniversary ed. Burgess, Thornton W. (gr. 1 up). 1985. 16.95 (0-316-11648-3); pap. 8.95 (0-316-11655-6) Little.

—Racketty-Packetty House: As Told by Queen Crosspatch. Burnett, Frances H. 72p. (gr. 3-6). 1992. 4.99 (0-517-07249-1, Pub. by Derrydale Bks) Outlet Bk Co.

—The Spring Cleaning: As Told by Queen Crosspatch. Burnett, Frances H. 56p. (gr. 3-6). 1992. 4.99 (0-517-07248-3, Pub. by Derrydale Bks) Outlet Bk Co.

—The Troubles of Queen Silver-Bell: As Told by Queen Crosspatch. Burnett, Frances H. 56p. (gr. 3-6). 1992. 4.99 (0-517-07247-5, Pub. by Derrydale Bks) Outlet Bk Co.

Cady, Harrison & Kliros, Thea. The Adventures of Danny Meadow Mouse. Burgess, Thornton W. LC 92-36950. 96p. 1993. pap. 1.00 (0-486-27565-5) Dover.

Cafferata, Sue. Sound-a-Likes One: One, Won. Fowler, Allan. 32p. (gr. k-2). 1993. PLB 10.95 (1-878363-97-2) Forest Hse.

—Sound-a-Likes Two: Two, To, Too. Fowler, Allan. 32p. (gr. 2-4). 1993. PLB 10.95 (1-878363-98-0) Forest Hse.

Caffin, Liz. Blossom. Butler, Dale. LC 92-34265. 1993. 14.00 (0-383-03620-8) SRA Schl Grp.

Cahoun, Cindy. The Woodland Gang & the Dinosaur Bones. Schultz, Irene. 128p. (gr. 3 up). 1988. pap. 4.95 (0-201-50056-6) Addison-Wesley.

—The Woodland Gang & the Secret Spy Code. Schultz, Irene. 128p. (Orig.). (gr. 3 up). 1988. pap. 4.95 (0-201-50052-3) Addison-Wesley.

Caigoy, Faustino. Ying-Ying: Pieces of a Childhood. Joe, Jeanne. 112p. (Orig.). (gr. 4 up). 1982. pap. 4.95 (0-934788-02-2) E-W Pub Co.

Cain, David. Copier Creations: Using Copy Machines to Make Decals, Silhouettes, Flip Books, Films, & Much More! Fleischman, Paul. LC 91-45413. 128p. (gr. 3 up). 1993. 14.00 (0-06-021052-4); PLB 13.89 (0-06-021053-2) HarpC Child Bks.

—Science Experiments You Can Eat. rev. ed. Cobb, Vicki. LC 93-13679. 1994. Repr. of 1972 ed. 15.00 (0-06-023534-9); PLB 14.89 (0-06-023551-9) HarpC Child Bks.

Caines, Kelly. The Girls of Summer. Cornwell, Anita. LC 88-64051. 100p. (Orig.). (gr. 6 up). 1989. pap. 12.95 (0-938678-11-6) New Seed.

Caito, Mike. So You Want to Serve. DeHart, Jack. 189p. (Orig.). 1990. pap. 6.95 (0-932581-77-3) Word Aflame.

Cajacob, Thomas, photos by. Close to the Wild: Siberian Tigers in a Zoo. Cajacob, Thomas & Burton, Teresa. 48p. (gr. 2-5). 1986. PLB 19.95 (0-87614-227-7); pap. 6.95 (0-87614-451-2) Carolrhoda Bks.

Calatanotto, Peter. Soda Jerk. Ryland, Cynthia. 48p. (gr. 7 up). 1993. pap. 3.95 (0-688-12654-5, Pub. by Beech Tree Bks) Morrow.

Calder, Nancy E. The Christmas House. Turner, Ann. LC 93-12740. (gr. 3 up). Date not set. 15.00 (0-06-023429-6); PLB 14.89 (0-06-023432-6) HarpC Child Bks.

Caldwell, Clyde, et al. Island at the Edge of the World. Siembieda, Kevin & Bartold, Thomas. Marciniszyn, Alex & Osten, James, eds. 144p. (Orig.). (gr. 8 up). 1993. pap. 15.95 (0-916211-61-4, 458) Palladium Bks.

Caldwell, Herschel V. Black & Beautiful: A Self-Discovery Coloring Book. McNair, Wallace Y. 26p. (Orig.). (gr. 2 up). 1992. pap. 10.00 (0-9627600-3-X) Wstrn Images.

Caldwell, John. Any Number Can Play. Sullivan, George. LC 89-35501. 128p. (gr. 3-7). 1990. (Crowell Jr Bks); (Crowell Jr Bks) HarpC Child Bks.

—Beyond a Reasonable Doubt: Inside the American Jury System. Zerman, Melvyn B. LC 80-2451. 224p. (gr. 7 up). 1981. PLB 12.89 (0-690-04095-4, Crowell Jr Bks) HarpC Child Bks.

Caliger, Roberta. Soccer Is Our Game. Gemme, Leila B. LC 79-13245. 32p. (gr. k-3). 1979. PLB 15.93 (0-516-03615-7); pap. 3.95 (0-516-43615-5) Childrens.

Calkins, Burdette & Bruner, Mike. Across the Wheatgrass: A Collection of Hearthside Stories about Uncommon People, Wildlife, Days Afield, & Things, Times & Places of Some Centennial Years. Upgren, H. Ted, Jr. LC 88-50045. 211p. (Orig.). (gr. 8-12). 1988. 18.95 (0-9620122-0-3); pap. 12.95 (0-9620122-1-1) Windfeather Pr.

Callahan, Kevin. The Funniest Moments in Sports. Masin, Herman L. LC 73-86219. 128p. (gr. 4 up). 1973. 5.95 (0-87131-133-X) M Evans.

Callen, Elizabeth. The A-Choo Confusion. Weimann, Elayne & Friedman, Rita. 30p. (ps-1). 1988. PLB 10.50 (0-89796-000-9) New Dimens Educ.

—The Best Quiet Meter. Weimann, Elayne & Friedman, Rita. 30p. (ps-1). 1989. PLB 10.50 (0-89796-016-5) New Dimens Educ.

—Buttonyms for Safety. Weimann, Elayne & Friedman, Rita. 30p. (ps-1). 1989. PLB 10.50 (0-89796-001-7) New Dimens Educ.

—The Cotton Candy Creature. Weimann, Elayne & Friedman, Rita. 30p. (ps-1). 1989. PLB 10.50 (0-89796-002-5) New Dimens Educ.

—The Dictionary Doughnut Shop. Weimann, Elayne & Friedman, Rita. 30p. (ps-1). 1989. PLB 10.50 (0-89796-003-3) New Dimens Educ.

—Exercise Excitement. Weimann, Elayne & Friedman, Rita. 30p. (ps-1). 1988. PLB 10.50 (0-89796-004-1) New Dimens Educ.

—Fantastic Friendship. Weimann, Elayne & Friedman, Rita. 30p. (ps-1). 1988. PLB 10.50 (0-89796-005-X) New Dimens Educ.

—Gooey Gumball Game. Weimann, Elayne & Friedman, Rita. 30p. (ps-1). 1989. PLB 10.50 (0-89796-006-8) New Dimens Educ.

—The Hat House Hotel. Weimann, Elayne & Friedman, Rita. 30p. (ps-1). 1988. PLB 10.50 (0-89796-007-6) New Dimens Educ.

—Inchy the Incredible Invention. Weimann, Elayne & Friedman, Rita. 30p. (ps-1). 1988. PLB 10.50 (0-89796-008-4) New Dimens Educ.

—The Kazoo Kicker. Weimann, Elayne & Friedman, Rita. 30p. (ps-1). 1989. PLB 10.50 (0-89796-010-6) New Dimens Educ.

—Lemonberry Lollipops. Weimann, Elayne & Friedman, Rita. 30p. (ps-1). 1989. PLB 10.50 (0-89796-011-4) New Dimens Educ.

—Mr. J's Junkyard. Weimann, Elayne & Friedman, Rita. 30p. (ps-1). 1989. PLB 10.50 (0-89796-009-2) New Dimens Educ.

—Mr. X's Mix-ups. Weimann, Elayne & Friedman, Rita. 30p. (ps-1). 1989. PLB 10.50 (0-89796-023-8) New Dimens Educ.

—Munching Magic. Weimann, Elayne & Friedman, Rita. 30p. (ps-1). 1988. PLB 10.50 (0-89796-012-2) New Dimens Educ.

—Ostrich Express. Weimann, Elayne & Friedman, Rita. 30p. (ps-1). 1988. PLB 10.50 (0-89796-014-9) New Dimens Educ.

—Parking Pandemonium. Weimann, Elayne & Friedman, Rita. 30p. (ps-1). 1989. PLB 10.50 (0-89796-015-7) New Dimens Educ.

—The Rubber Band Runner Champion. Weimann, Elayne & Friedman, Rita. 30p. (ps-1). 1989. PLB 10.50 (0-89796-017-3) New Dimens Educ.

—Say No & Fly Away! Weimann, Elayne & Friedman, Rita. 30p. (ps-1). 1988. PLB 10.50 (0-89796-013-0) New Dimens Educ.

—Super Socks for Courage. Weimann, Elayne & Friedman, Rita. 30p. (ps-1). 1989. PLB 10.50 (0-89796-018-1) New Dimens Educ.

—Tall Toothbrush Retires. Weimann, Elayne & Friedman, Rita. 30p. (ps-1). 1988. PLB 10.50 (0-89796-019-X) New Dimens Educ.

—Valuable Volunteers. Weimann, Elayne & Friedman, Rita. 30p. (ps-1). 1989. PLB 10.50 (0-89796-021-1) New Dimens Educ.

—The Worry Machine. Weimann, Elayne & Friedman, Rita. 30p. (ps-1). 1989. PLB 10.50 (0-89796-022-X) New Dimens Educ.

—Yawn-Maker Wanted. Weimann, Elayne & Friedman, Rita. 30p. (ps-1). 1989. PLB 10.50 (0-89796-024-6) New Dimens Educ.

—You Forget Too. Weimann, Elayne & Friedman, Rita. 30p. (ps-1). 1989. PLB 10.50 (0-89796-020-3) New Dimens Educ.

—Zip Codes. Weimann, Elayne & Friedman, Rita. 30p. (ps-1). 1989. PLB 10.50 (0-89796-025-4) New Dimens Educ.

Callen, Liz. Baseball Bloopers. Hall, Katy & Eisenberg, Lisa. LC 89-62210. 96p. (Orig.). (gr. 2-6). 1991. pap. 2.95 (0-679-80335-1) Random Bks Yng Read.

—No Place Like Home. Tripp, Valerie. 24p. (Orig.). (gr. 1-3). 1991. pap. text ed. 29.95 (1-56334-046-1); pap. text ed. 4.15 small bk. (1-56334-052-6) Hampton-Brown.

—Oddball Baseball. Hall, Katy & Eisenberg, Lisa. LC 89-62206. 96p. (Orig.). (gr. 2-6). 1991. pap. 2.95 (0-679-80336-X) Random Bks Yng Read.

—El Patio de Mi Casa: Cuento Basado en una Rima Tradicional. Ada, Alma F. (SPA.). 24p. (Orig.). (gr. 1-3). 1991. pap. text ed. 29.95 big bk. (1-56334-018-6); pap. text ed. 3.50 small bk. (1-56334-044-5) Hampton-Brown.

Calles, Rosa M. Dodo the Bird & Other Stories. De Aragon, Ray J. 105p. (Orig.). (gr. 1-12). pap. 5.95 (*0-932906-21-4*) Pan-AM Publishing Co.

Calsbeek, Craig. Seeing Stars: A Book & Poster about the Constellations. Seiger, Barbara. LC 92-43199. 24p. (gr. 2-6). 1993. pap. 7.95 (*0-448-40198-3*, G&D) Putnam Pub Group.

Calvin, James. Talk about a Family. reissued ed. Greenfield, Eloise. LC 77-16423. 64p. (gr. 2-5). 1991. PLB 12.89 (*0-397-32504-5*, Lipp Jr Bks) HarpC Child Bks.

Camburn, Herbert. Old House, New House. Gaughenbaugh, Michael & Camburn, Herbert. 56p. (gr. 4-6). 1993. 16.95 (*0-89133-236-7*) Preservation Pr.

Cameron, Don. Picture Stories from the Bible: The New Testament in Full-Color Comic-Strip Form. Gaines, M. C., ed. LC 80-51593. 144p. (gr. 3-10). 1980. Repr. of 1946 ed. 12.95 (*0-934386-02-1*) Scarf Pr.

—Picture Stories from the Bible: The Old Testament in Full-Color Comic-Strip Form. Gaines, M. C., ed. LC 79-66064. 222p. (gr. 3-10). 1979. Repr. of 1943 ed. 12.95 (*0-934386-01-3*) Scarf Pr.

Cameron, Rod. The Eye of the Hurricane: Tales of the Empty-Handed Masters. Webster-Doyle, Terrence. 128p. (gr. 4-8). 1992. PLB 17.95 (*0-942941-25-X*); pap. 12.95 (*0-942941-24-1*) Atrium Soc Pubns.

—Facing the Double Edged Sword: The Art of Karate for Young People. Webster-Doyle, Terrence. LC 73-83919. 90p. (Orig.). (gr. 5-9). 1988. 17.95 (*0-942941-17-9*); pap. 12.95 (*0-942941-16-0*) Atrium Soc Pubns.

Cameron, Scott. Beethoven Lives Upstairs. Nichol, Barbara. LC 93-5774. 1994. 15.95 (*0-531-06828-5*) Orchard Bks Watts.

Cameron, Tracey. Telling Fortunes: Love Magic, Dream Signs, & Other Ways to Learn the Future. Schwartz, Alvin. LC 85-45174. 128p. (gr. 4 up). 1987. 12.95 (*0-397-32132-5*, Lipp Jr Bks); PLB 12.89 (*0-397-32133-3*, Lipp Jr Bks) HarpC Child Bks.

—Telling Fortunes: Love Magic, Dream Signs, & Other Ways to Learn the Future. Schwartz, Alvin. LC 85-45174. 128p. (gr. 4 up). 1990. pap. 4.95 (*0-06-446094-0*, Trophy) HarpC Child Bks.

Camhi, Morrie, jt. illus. see Noren, Catherine.

Camilli, Ivan. Villancico Yaucano. Veray, Amaury. 1992. 12.95 (*0-8477-2506-5*) U of PR Pr.

Camm, Martin. Dolphin. Houghton, Sue. LC 91-44819. 32p. (gr. 4-6). 1993. lib. bdg. 11.59 (*0-8167-2767-8*); pap. text ed. 3.95 (*0-8167-2768-6*) Troll Assocs. Postponed.

—Journey Through Australia. Cooper, Rod. LC 91-46173. 32p. (gr. 3-5). 1993. PLB 11.89 (*0-8167-2757-0*); pap. text ed. 3.95 (*0-8167-2758-9*) Troll Assocs. Postponed.

—Monkeys & Apes. Carwardine, Mark. Young, Richard G., ed. LC 89-32808. 45p. (gr. 3-5). 1989. PLB 14.60 (*0-944483-28-3*) Garrett Ed Corp.

—Night Animals. Carwardine, Mark. Young, Richard G., ed. LC 89-7880. 45p. (gr. 3-5). 1989. PLB 14.60 (*0-944483-30-5*) Garrett Ed Corp.

—Water Animals. Carwardine, Mark. Young, Richard G., ed. LC 89-7879. 45p. (gr. 3-5). 1989. PLB 14.60 (*0-944483-31-3*) Garrett Ed Corp.

—Weather. Lambert, David. LC 89-20304. 32p. (gr. 4-6). 1990. PLB 11.59 (*0-8167-1979-9*); pap. text ed. 3.95 (*0-8167-1980-2*) Troll Assocs.

Camm, Martin, et al. Forests. Lambert, David. LC 89-20311. 32p. (gr. 4-6). 1990. PLB 11.59 (*0-8167-1971-3*); pap. text ed. 3.95 (*0-8167-1972-1*) Troll Assocs.

—Journey Through Canada. Tames, Richard. LC 90-10934. 32p. (gr. 3-5). 1991. lib. bdg. 11.89 (*0-8167-2110-6*); pap. text ed. 3.95 (*0-8167-2111-4*) Troll Assocs.

—Journey Through Mexico. Bulmer-Thomas, Barbara. LC 90-10950. 32p. (gr. 3-5). 1991. PLB 11.89 (*0-8167-2116-5*); pap. text ed. 3.95 (*0-8167-2117-3*) Troll Assocs.

—Mountains. Vrbova, Zuza. LC 89-20299. 32p. (gr. 4-6). 1990. PLB 11.59 (*0-8167-1973-X*); pap. text ed. 3.95 (*0-8167-1974-8*) Troll Assocs.

—Journey Through China. Steele, Philip. LC 90-10943. 32p. (gr. 3-5). 1991. PLB 11.89 (*0-8167-2112-2*); pap. text ed. 3.95 (*0-8167-2113-0*) Troll Assocs.

—Journey Through Japan. Tames, Richard. LC 90-10944. 32p. (gr. 3-5). 1991. PLB 11.89 (*0-8167-2114-9*); pap. text ed. 3.95 (*0-8167-2115-7*) Troll Assocs.

Cammack, Phyllis. From Here to There & Back Again. Hockett, Betty M. LC 84-81034. 80p. (Orig.). (gr. 3-8). 1984. pap. 3.50 (*0-943701-09-0*) George Fox Pr.

Cammarata, Kathleen. When the Earth Was Bare. Witters, Judith. LC 93-26930. 1994. 4.25 (*0-383-03785-9*) SRA Schl Grp.

Cammarata, Sharon. Student Survival Guide. Cammarata, Joe. Tunmore, Gary, ed. 108p. (gr. 6-12). 1991. wkbk. 9.95 (*0-924649-03-8*) Scribblers Pub.

Campana, Manny. I Am Curious about Me. Carr, Jan. 48p. (ps-2). 1990. pap. 1.95 (*0-590-44032-2*) Scholastic Inc.

Campbell, Aileen. The Wee Scot Book: Scottish Poems & Stories. Greenberg, Linda, ed. LC 93-28728. 1994. write for info. (*1-56554-018-2*) Pelican.

Campbell, Caroline. Escape from Zarcay. Cartwright, Pauline. LC 90-10075. 32p. (gr. 4-5). 1990. PLB 17.28 (*0-8114-2694-7*) Raintree Steck-V.

—Just Right for the Night. Ray, Stephen & Murdoch, Kathleen. LC 92-21398. (gr. 4 up). 1993. 4.25 (*0-383-03580-5*) SRA Schl Grp.

—Rosa's Diary. Benson, Rita. LC 93-28972. 1994. 4.25 (*0-383-03772-7*) SRA Schl Grp.

Campbell, Carolinee. Snake. Ray, Stephen & Murdoch, Kathleen. LC 92-21453. 1993. 4.25 (*0-383-03653-4*) SRA Schl Grp.

Campbell, Donna P. So Many Gifts. Pierce, Anne M. 30p. (ps up). 1989. 14.95 (*0-685-44721-9*); 7.50x (*0-685-27188-9*) Forword MN.

—So Many Gifts. Pierce, Anne M. 32p. (gr. k-6). 1989. Repr. of 1990 ed. 14.95g (*0-9623937-0-3*) Forword MN.

Campbell, Dwayne. The Rise & Fall of Ilsa: (The Female Lady Giant) High, Jackie L. Hillen, Rodolfo, ed. 26p. (ps-3). 1991. laminated 8.95x (*1-880605-00-7*) J Laverne Mus.

Campbell, E. Simms. Popo & Fifina. Bontemps, Arna & Hughes, Langston. Rampersad, Arnold & Rampersad, Arnold.intro. by. 120p. 1993. jacketed 14.95 (*0-19-508765-8*) OUP.

Campbell, Elisa L., jt. illus. see Sydlik, Danilea.

Campbell, Jay. Hump-Free Goes to Galapagos. Eisemann, Henry. 26p. (Orig.). (gr. k-6). 1990. pap. 7.95g (*0-938129-04-X*) Emprise Pubns.

—Hump-Free Heads for Hawaii. Eisemann, Henry. 24p. (Orig.). (gr. k-6). 1989. pap. 6.95 (*0-938129-02-3*) Emprise Pubns.

—Hump-Free Visits Vancouver Expo. Eisemann, Henry. (Orig.). (gr. k-6). 1986. pap. 6.95 (*0-938129-01-5*) Emprise Pubns.

Campbell, Jim. Baseball's Greatest Pitchers. Kramer, S. A. LC 91-27892. 48p. (Orig.). (gr. 2-4). 1992. PLB 7.99 (*0-679-92149-4*); pap. 3.50 (*0-679-82149-X*) Random Bks Yng Read.

—Comeback! Four True Stories. O'Connor, Jim. LC 91-25028. 48p. (Orig.). (gr. 2-4). 1992. PLB 7.99 (*0-679-92666-6*); pap. 3.50 (*0-679-82666-1*) Random Bks Yng Read.

Campbell, Loreen. ABC Come See Wyoming. Kidner, Maria C. 56p. (Orig.). (gr. k-3). 1990. pap. 4.95 (*0-9625920-0-5*) Rainbow Rhapsody.

Campbell, Lorene. ABC Come See Wyoming. Rev. ed. Kidner, Maria C. 56p. (gr. k-3). 1990. pap. 4.95 (*0-9625920-1-3*) Rainbow Rhapsody.

Campbell, Rod. Dear Zoo. Campbell, Rod. LC 82-83224. 22p. (ps-1). 1983. bds. 10.95 (*0-02-716440-3*, Four Winds) Macmillan Child Grp.

—Dear Zoo. Campbell, Rod. 24p. (ps-1). 1988. bds. 3.95 (*0-689-71230-8*, Aladdin) Macmillan Child Grp.

—My Presents. Campbell, Rod. 24p. (ps-1). 1989. Repr. of 1989 ed. POB 3.95 (*0-689-71286-3*, Aladdin) Macmillan Child Grp.

—Oh Dear! Campbell, Rod. LC 84-3993. 20p. (ps-1). 1986. bds. 8.95 (*0-02-716430-6*, Four Winds) Macmillan Child Grp.

—Oh Dear! Campbell, Rod. 20p. (ps-k). 1994. Repr. of 1986 ed. bds. 4.95 (*0-689-71774-1*, Aladdin) Macmillan Child Grp.

Campbell, Sid, jt. illus. see Evans, Ed.

Campbell, Susan. The World That Was. Young, Philip G. Brumagin, Wayne, ed. 121p. (Orig.). (gr. 4 up). 1993. pap. 8.95 (*1-880451-03-4*) Rainbows End.

Campbell, V. Floyd. The Roosevelt Bears: Their Travels & Adventures. Eaton, Seymour. 192p. (gr. 1 up). 1979. pap. 5.95 (*0-486-23819-9*) Dover.

Campbell, V. Floyd & Culver, R. K. The Roosevelt Bears Go to Washington. Eaton, Seymour. 192p. (gr. 6 up). 1981. pap. 4.50 (*0-486-24163-7*) Dover.

Canaday, Ralph. The Story of Sherman's March to the Sea. Kent, Zachary. LC 86-31054. 32p. (gr. 3-6). 1987. PLB 13.27 (*0-516-04728-0*); pap. 3.95 (*0-516-44728-9*) Childrens.

—The Story of Susan B. Anthony. Clinton, Susan. LC 86-9613. 32p. (gr. 3-6). 1986. PLB 13.27 (*0-516-04705-1*) Childrens.

—The Story of the Election of Abraham Lincoln. Kent, Zachary. LC 85-23277. 32p. (gr. 3-6). 1986. pap. 3.95 (*0-516-44669-X*) Childrens.

—The Story of the Salem Witch Trials. Kent, Zachary. LC 86-9632. 32p. (gr. 3-6). 1986. pap. 3.95 (*0-516-44704-1*) Childrens.

—The Story of the United Nations. Stein, R. Conrad. LC 85-31356. 32p. (gr. 3-6). 1986. pap. 3.95 (*0-516-44698-3*) Childrens.

Canley, Lorinda B. The Ugly Duckling. Cauley, Lorinda B. LC 79-12340. 40p. (gr. k-3). 1979. pap. 4.95 (*0-15-692528-1*, Voyager Bks) HarBrace.

Cann., Alison. Talking about Divorce & Separation: A Dialogue Between Parent & Child. Grollman, Earl A. LC 75-5289. (gr. k-4). pap. 9.00 (*0-8070-2375-2*, BP524) Beacon Pr.

Canning, Celia. The MacMagics: A Spell for My Sister. Dicks, Terrance. 96p. (gr. 3-6). 1992. pap. 3.50 (*0-8120-4881-4*) Barron.

—The MacMagics: My Brother the Vampire. Dicks, Terrance. 96p. (ps-3). 1992. pap. 3.50 (*0-8120-4883-0*) Barron.

—Meet the MacMagics. Dicks, Terrance. 96p. (gr. 3-6). 1992. pap. 3.50 (*0-8120-4882-2*) Barron.

Cannizzo, John. A Very Special Christmas Present. Sowerby, Lynda. 1991. 6.95 (*0-533-09198-5*) Vantage.

Cannon, Annie. Whistle Home. Honeycutt, Natalie. LC 92-47052. 32p. (ps-1). 1993. 14.95 (*0-531-05490-X*); PLB 14.99 (*0-531-08640-2*) Orchard Bks Watts.

—You Hold Me & I'll Hold You. Carson, Jo. LC 91-16370. 32p. (ps-2). 1992. 14.95 (*0-531-05895-6*); lib. bdg. 14.99 (*0-531-08495-7*) Orchard Bks Watts.

Cannon, Christy. Old Mother Bear's Book of Hug Rhymes. Landgren, Le. LC 88-38973. 40p. (ps-9). 1989. pap. 6.95 (*0-943367-02-6*) Princess Pub.

Canter, Barbara. The Last Teenage Suicide. Geller, Norman. (Orig.). (gr. 6-12). 1988. pap. 7.95 (*0-915753-13-8*) N Geller Pub.

Canterbury, Joyce C. Time We Talk: The Pre-Teen Years. Canterbury, Joyce C. LC 92-73621. 24p. (Orig.). (gr. 4-7). 1993. pap. 4.25 (*0-9634737-0-0*) Hoffman Spec.

Cantrell, Ray. Saucer Sam. Bowser, Milton & Haramilio, Alyce, eds. 72p. 1992. 10.00 (*0-940178-38-9*) Sitare.

Cantwell, Jim. I Say...You Say! Dowell, Ruth I. 104p. (ps-2). 1991. pap. 9.95 (*0-945842-12-0*) Pollyanna Prodns.

—Let's Talk! Dowell, Ruth I. 24p. (ps-6). 1986. pap. 6.00 (*0-945842-03-1*) Pollyanna Prodns.

—Mother Ruth's Rhymes. Dowell, Ruth I. 104p. (ps-6). 1991. pap. 9.95 (*0-945842-13-9*) Pollyanna Prodns.

Canyon, Christopher. The Ever-Living Tree: The Life & Times of a Coast Redwood. Viera, Linda. LC 93-31688. 1994. write for info. (*0-8027-8277-9*); PLB write for info. (*0-8027-8278-7*) Walker & Co.

Cap, photos by. Kiltie, the Laird of Kiltarnen. 2nd ed. Weinberger, Jane. 44p. (ps-5). 1987. 5.95 (*0-932433-09-X*) Windswept Hse.

Capdevila, Roser. Let's Count. Ballar, Elisabet, text by. LC 92-2813. 44p. (ps-3). 1992. 13.95 (*1-56566-011-0*) Thomasson-Grant.

Capek, Jindra. A Child Is Born. Capek, Jindra. (gr. 5 up). 1987. 12.95 (*1-55774-007-0*) Modan-Adama Bks.

Capello, Joe. Universal Speaking Pictures, No. 2. Gast, Natalie. (Orig.). 1984. wkbk., 36 p. 7.45 (*0-916177-01-7*); pap. 1.45 ans. key, 8 p. (*0-685-50631-2*) Am Eng Pubns.

Capezio, Betsy. To Grow by Storybook Phonics Readers. Friend, Janet. (gr. k-3). 1990. Set. pap. text ed. 44.95 (*0-910311-69-2*) Huntington Hse.

Caple, Kathy. The Biggest Nose. Caple, Kathy. LC 84-19745. 32p. (gr. k-3). 1985. 14.45 (*0-395-36894-4*); pap. 5.70 (*0-395-47943-6*) HM.

—The Coolest Place in Town. Caple, Kathy. 32p. (gr. k-3). 1990. 13.45 (*0-395-51523-8*) HM.

—Fox & Bear. Caple, Kathy. 40p. (gr. k-3). 1992. 13.45 (*0-395-55634-1*) HM.

—Harry's Smile. Caple, Kathy. LC 87-5094. 32p. (gr. k-3). 1987. 13.95 (*0-395-43417-3*) HM.

—The Purse. Caple, Kathy. LC 86-2889. 32p. (gr. k-3). 1986. 13.95 (*0-395-41852-6*) HM.

Capocy, Edward J. The Magic of Christmas. rev. ed. Capocy, Edward J. 48p. 1991. 14.00 (*1-880210-00-2*); PLB 18.00 (*1-880210-01-0*); pap. 4.50 (*1-880210-02-9*); coloring bk. 2.29 (*1-880210-03-7*) Am Classic Ent.

Caponigro, John P. Ghost in the House. Cohen, Daniel. LC 92-37858. (gr. 3-5). 1993. 13.99 (*0-525-65131-4*, Cobblehill Bks) Dutton Child Bks.

Capron, Michael W., jt. illus. see Bruns, Stan.

Cara, Costas & Cara, Stephen, photos by. The Nutcracker: A Story & A Ballet. Switzer, Ellen. LC 85-7463. 112p. (gr. 4-6). 1985. SBE 16.95 (*0-689-31061-7*, Atheneum Child Bk) Macmillan Child Grp.

Cara, Stephen, jt. photog. see Cara, Costas.

Carabis, Anne. The Magic Rocking Chair. Carabis, Anne. 28p. (Orig.). (ps-3). 1980. pap. 3.50 (*0-9605802-0-4*) Carabis.

Caravana, Anton. The Best of O. Henry. abr. ed. Porter, William S. Fago, John N., ed. (gr. 4-12). 1977. pap. 2.95 (*0-88301-268-5*) Pendulum Pr.

Caravana, Tony & Cruz, Nardo. Babe Ruth-Jackie Robinson. Farr, Naunerle C. (gr. 4-12). 1979. pap. text ed. 2.95 (*0-88301-359-2*); wkbk 1.25 (*0-88301-383-5*) Pendulum Pr.

—Vincent Lombardi-Pele. Fago, John N. (gr. 4-12). 1979. text ed. 7.50 (*0-88301-370-3*); pap. text ed. 2.95 (*0-88301-358-4*); wkbk. 1.25 (*0-88301-382-7*) Pendulum Pr.

Caraway, Caren. Sign Language Talk. Greene, Laura & Dicker, Eva B. Solomon, Maury, ed. 96p. (gr. 5 up). 1989. PLB 11.90 (*0-531-10597-0*) Watts.

—Sign-Me-Fine: Experiencing American Sign Language. Greene, Laura & Dicker, Eva B. LC 90-5148. 120p. (gr. 7-12). 1989. pap. 5.95 (*0-930323-76-9*, Pub. by K Green Pubns) Gallaudet Univ Pr.

Carbonnean, Lana. Jack Snake. Bush, Don. 48p. (gr. k up). 1985. 5.50x (*0-943978-01-7*) Rolling Hills Pr.

Cardiel, Patrice H., jt. illus. see Trisler, Alana.

Cardin, George. Floridians All. Fichter, George S. LC 91-9858. 96p. (ps-8). 1991. 15.95 (*0-88289-804-3*) Pelican.

Cardinal, Michael S. The Dynamo's Guide to the Lowlife. Cardinal, Michael S. Baruch, Andrea, ed. LC 89-90015. 64p. (Orig.). 1989. pap. 8.95 (*0-9623902-0-8*) Dreamworld.

Cardo, Ras. Ras Cardo, the Man, the Legend & Reggae Music: Where Reggae Legends Trod. Scott, Ricardo A. 150p. (Orig.). Date not set. write for info. (*1-883427-23-1*) Crnerstone GA.

Cardona, Jose. Disney's Beauty & the Beast. Balducci, Rita. 24p. (ps-k). 1992. write for info. (*0-307-10021-9*, 10021) Western Pub.

—Pop-Up Book of Actions. LC 92-70935. 12p. (ps-k). 1993. 7.95 (*1-56282-506-2*) Disney Pr.

—A Pop-up Book of Things That Go. LC 92-56160. 12p. (ps-k). 1993. 7.95 (*1-56282-509-7*) Disney Pr.

Cardoni, Paolo. Albert Einstein. Lepscky, Ibi. 24p. (gr. k-3). 1992. pap. 4.95 (*0-8120-1452-9*) Barron.

—Amadeus Mozart. Lepscky, Ibi. 24p. (gr. k-3). 1992. pap. 4.95 (0-8120-1493-6) Barron.
—Leonardo da Vinci. Lepscky, Ibi. 24p. (gr. k-3). 1992. pap. 4.95 (0-8120-1451-0) Barron.
—Marie Curie. Lepscky, Ibi. 24p. (gr. k-3). 1993. 9.95 (0-8120-6340-6); pap. 4.95 (0-8120-1558-4) Barron.
—Pablo Picasso. Lepscky, Ibi. 24p. (gr. k-3). pap. 4.95 (0-8120-1450-2) Barron.
—William Shakespeare. Lepscky, Ibi. 28p. (gr. k-3). 1989. 7.95 (0-8120-6106-3) Barron.
Carey, Joanna. Spooky: Stories of the Supernatural. Lonsdale, Pamela, ed. LC 84-26425. 144p. (gr. 5 up). 1985. 12.95 (0-13-835463-4) P-H.
Carey, Vicky. Mark T-W-A-I-N! A Story about Samuel Clemens. Collins, David R. LC 93-15164. 1993. write for info. (0-87614-801-1) Carolrhoda Bks.
Carle, Eric. All Around Us. Carle, Eric. LC 86-9354. (ps up). 1991. bds. 11.95 3 friezes, incl. carry case (0-88708-016-2) Picture Bk Studio.
—The Art of Eric Carle. Carle, Eric. LC 91-646. 124p. (gr. k up). 1993. pap. 29.95 (0-88708-176-2) Picture Bk Studio.
—Brown Bear, Brown Bear, What Do You See? Martin, Bill, Jr. LC 83-12779. 24p. (ps-k). 1983. 14.95 (0-8050-0201-4, Bks Young Read) H Holt & Co.
—Brown Bear, Brown Bear, What Do You See? 25th Anniversary Edition. Martin, Bill, Jr. LC 91-29115. 32p. (ps-k). 1992. 14.95 (0-8050-1744-5, Bks Young Read) H Holt & Co.
—Do You Want to Be My Friend? Carle, Eric. LC 70-140643. 32p. (ps-2). 1971. 15.00 (0-690-24276-X, Crowell Jr Bks); PLB 14.89 (0-690-01137-7, Crowell Jr Bks) HarpC Child Bks.
—Do You Want to Be My Friend? Carle, Eric. LC 70-140643. 32p. (ps-2). 1987. pap. 5.95 (0-06-443127-4, Trophy) HarpC Child Bks.
—Dragons Dragons & Other Creatures That Never Were. Carle, Eric. 72p. (ps up). 1991. 18.95 (0-399-22105-0, Philomel) Putnam Pub Group.
—The Eric Carle Slipcase Collection: The Very Hungry Caterpillar; the Very Bust Spider; the Very Quiet Cricket. Carle, Eric. 32p. (ps-3). Date not set. 52.85 (0-399-22623-0, Philomel) Putnam Pub Group. Postponed.
—Eric Carle's Treasury of Classic Stories for Children. Aesop, et al. Carle, Eric, retold by. LC 87-22072. 160p. (ps-4). 1988. 21.95 (0-531-05742-9) Orchard Bks Watts.
—The Follish Fortoise. Buckley, Richard. LC 93-20123. (gr. 1-8). 1993. map. 4.95 (0-88708-323-4) Picture Bk Studio.
—The Foolish Fortoise & the Greedy Python. Buckley, Richard. LC 86-25468. 48p. (ps). 1991. pap. 12.95 (0-88708-039-1) Picture Bk Studio.
—The Greedy Python. Buckley, Richard. LC 92-6633. 28p. (ps). 1993. Repr. Mini-bk. 4.95 (0-88708-268-8) Picture Bk Studio.
—The Grouchy Ladybug. Carle, Eric. LC 77-3170. 48p. (ps-1). 1977. 15.00i (0-690-01391-4, Crowell Jr Bks); PLB 14.89 (0-690-01392-2) HarpC Child Bks.
—Have You Seen My Cat? Carle, Eric. 1991. pap. 3.95 (0-590-44461-1, Blue Ribbon Bks) Scholastic Inc.
—The Hole in the Dike. Green, Norma, retold by. 32p. (ps-2). 1993. pap. 4.95 (0-590-46146-X) Scholastic Inc.
—The Hole in the Dyke. Green, Norma. LC 74-23562. 32p. (gr. k-3). 1975. (Crowell Jr Bks); PLB 15.89 (0-690-00676-4) HarpC Child Bks.
—A House for Hermit Crab. Carle, Eric. LC 90-25388. 32p. (gr. k up). 1991. pap. 4.95 (0-88708-168-1) Picture Bk Studio.
—The Lamb & the Butterfly. Sundgaard, Arnold. LC 88-60092. 32p. (ps-2). 1988. 14.95 (0-531-05779-8); PLB 14.99 (0-531-08379-9) Orchard Bks Watts.
—La Mariquita Malhumorada. Carle, Eric. LC 91-28582. 48p. (ps-3). 1992. 15.00 (0-06-020549-0); PLB 14.89 (0-06-020569-5) HarpC Child Bks.
—La Mariquita Malhumorada. Carle, Eric. LC 91-28582. 48p. (gr. k-3). 1992. pap. 5.95 (0-06-443301-3, Trophy) HarpC Child Bks.
—The Mixed-Up Chameleon. 2nd ed. Carle, Eric. LC 83-45950. 32p. (ps-3). 1984. 15.00 (0-690-04396-1, Crowell Jr Bks); PLB 14.89 (0-690-04397-X) HarpC Child Bks.
—Mixed-up Chameleon: Miniature Edition. Carle, Eric. LC 91-2497. 32p. (ps-3). 1991. 4.95 (0-06-020103-7) HarpC Child Bks.
—The Mixed-up Chameleon Sticker Book. Carle, Eric. LC 75-5505. 32p. (ps-2). 1993. 7.95 (0-694-00448-0, Festival) HarpC Child Bks.
—The Mountain That Loved a Bird. McLerran, Alice. LC 85-9391. 32p. (ps up). 1991. pap. 15.95 (0-88708-000-6) Picture Bk Studio.
—My Very First Book of Colors. reissued ed. Carle, Eric. LC 72-83776. 10p. (ps-1). 1985. 4.95 (0-694-00011-6, Crowell Jr Bks) HarpC Child Bks.
—My Very First Book of Food. Carle, Eric. LC 85-45259. 10p. (ps-k). 1986. 2.95 (0-694-00130-9, Crowell Jr Bks) HarpC Child Bks.
—My Very First Book of Heads & Tails. Carle, Eric. LC 85-45260. 10p. (ps-k). 1986. 2.95 (0-694-00128-7, Crowell Jr Bks) HarpC Child Bks.
—My Very First Book of Numbers. reissued ed. Carle, Eric. LC 72-83777. 10p. (ps-1). 1985. 4.95 (0-694-00012-4, Crowell Jr Bks) HarpC Child Bks.
—My Very First Book of Shapes. reissued ed. Carle, Eric. LC 72-83778. 10p. (ps-1). 1985. 4.95 (0-694-00013-2, Crowell Jr Bks) HarpC Child Bks.

—My Very First Book of Tools. Carle, Eric. LC 85-45258. 10p. (ps-k). 1986. 2.95 (0-694-00129-5, Crowell Jr Bks) HarpC Child Bks.
—My Very First Book of Touch. Carle, Eric. LC 84-47894. 10p. (ps-k). 1986. 2.95 (0-694-00095-7, Crowell Jr Bks) HarpC Child Bks.
—My Very First Book of Words. Carle, Eric. LC 72-83779. 10p. (ps-1). 1985. 4.95 (0-694-00014-0, Crowell Jr Bks) HarpC Child Bks.
—Pancakes, Pancakes! Carle, Eric. LC 88-32438. 36p. (gr. k up). 1991. pap. 15.95 (0-88708-120-7) Picture Bk Studio.
—Pancakes, Pancakes! Carle, Eric. LC 92-6633. 28p. 1992. pap. 4.95 minibk. (0-88708-275-0) Picture Bk Studio.
—Polar Bear, Polar Bear, What Do You Hear? Martin, Bill, Jr. 32p. (ps). 1991. 14.95 (0-8050-1759-3, Bks Young Read) H Holt & Co.
—Polar Bear, Polar Bear, What Do You Hear? Martin, Bill, Jr. 32p. (ps-2). 1993. PLB 16.95 incl. plush toy (0-8050-2815-3, Bks Young Read) H Holt & Co.
—Polar Bear, Polar Bear, What Do You Hear? Big Book. Martin, Bill, Jr. LC 91-13322. 32p. (ps-2). 1993. pap. 18.95 (0-8050-2346-1, Bks Young Read) H Holt & Co.
—Por Que Noe Eligio la Paloma: Why Noah Chose the Dove. Singer, Isaac Bashevis. Marcuse, Aida, tr. (SPA.). 32p. (ps up). 1992. 16.00 (0-374-36085-5, Mirasol) FS&G.
—Rooster's Off to See the World. Carle, Eric. LC 91-15246. 28p. (gr. k up). 1992. pap. 4.95 (0-88708-178-9) Picture Bk Studio.
—Secret Birthday Message. Carle, Eric. LC 75-168726. 26p. (ps-3). 1972. 15.00 (0-690-72347-4, Crowell Jr Bks); PLB 14.89 (0-690-72348-2) HarpC Child Bks.
—Secret Birthday Message. Carle, Eric. LC 85-45403. 26p. (ps-3). 1986. pap. 5.95 (0-06-443099-5, Trophy) HarpC Child Bks.
—The Secret Birthday Message: Miniature Edition. Carle, Eric. LC 91-8306. 26p. (ps-3). 1991. 4.95 (0-06-020102-9) HarpC Child Bks.
—The Tiny Seed. Carle, Eric. LC 86-2534. 32p. (gr. k up). 1991. pap. 15.95 (0-88708-015-4) Picture Bk Studio.
—The Tiny Seed. 2nd ed. Carle, Eric. LC 86-2534. 36p. (gr. k up). 1991. pap. 4.95 (0-88708-155-X) Picture Bk Studio.
—Today Is Monday. Carle, Eric. 32p. (ps-3). 1993. 14.95 (0-399-21966-8, Philomel Bks) Putnam Pub Group.
—The Very Busy Spider. Carle, Eric. 32p. (ps-2). 1989. 16.95 (0-399-21166-7, Philomel Bks); mini ed. 5.95 (0-399-21592-1) Putnam Pub Group.
—The Very Hungry Caterpillar. Carle, Eric. LC 70-82764. (ps-2). 1981. 15.95 (0-399-20853-4, Philomel) Putnam Pub Group.
—The Very Hungry Caterpillar. Carle, Eric. (ps up). 1986. miniature ed. 4.95 (0-399-21301-5, Putnam) Putnam Pub Group.
—The Very Hungry Caterpillar: Mini & Plush Package. Carle, Eric. 32p. (ps-3). 1991. 13.95 (0-399-22049-6, Philomel) Putnam Pub Group.
Carley, Nathan B. Louisianians All. Frois, Jeanne. LC 92-19208. 96p. 1991. 11.95 (0-88289-824-8) Pelican.
Carlisle, Kim. The Empty Place: A Child's Guide Through Grief. Temes, Roberta. LC 92-60613. 48p. (Orig.). (gr. k-5). 1992. pap. 6.95 (0-88282-118-0) New Horizon NJ.

Carlos, Christina. Earth Day Lessons from Planet Mars. Frank-Mosenson, Sandra. 72p. (Orig.). (gr. 4 up). 1991. Perfect bdg. 10.95 (0-9629607-3-X) Wisdom Pr IL.
1993 NATIONAL BOOK AWARD recipient for the "BEST CHILDREN'S BOOK OF THE YEAR" from the Writer's Foundation of America. Chosen to represent the United States at the International Children's Book Fair, it is currently a part of a thirty-month state-wide tour of all Illinois libraries. New age fairy tales told in poem with clear lyrical quality & sense of purpose. A review by HEARTLAND JOURNAL: "This is a book of poetic imagery, emotion & gentle wisdom, with a mission, stimulating children to a commitment to their Earth, helping them to realize the importance of all families of all species to live in a non-violent world." Accompanied by intriguing black & white illustrations, printed with soy-based ink on acid-free 100% recycled 80lb. text paper. "Small frogs golden/ living in harmony beneath the mimosa/ Lonely cheetah crying his mornful song/ as man grows closer." The

reviewer continues, "As a mother of four, I loved this book, including the glossary & environmental resource list. I encourage you to add this book to your children's collection, & by all means, share the message & the moments." To order, call WISDOM PRESS, (312) 477-3737 or BAKER & TAYLOR, (800) 775-1800. *Publisher Provided Annotation.*

Carlson, Bruce, jt. illus. see **Thomas, Tony.**
Carlson, Faith. A Cookie Christmas. Carlson, Faith. 28p. (Orig.). (ps-2). 1986. pap. 5.00 (0-932591-05-1) Baggeboda Pr.
Carlson, Jeanne, et al. A King, a Hunter & a Golden Goose. Tulku, Tarthang, intro. by. LC 86-24154. 32p. (gr. 1-4). 1987. PLB 14.95 (0-89800-155-2) Dharma Pub.
Carlson, John. Summer & Shiner. Carlson, Nolan. LC 92-71256. 158p. 1992. pap. text ed. 8.95 (0-9627947-4-0) Hearth KS.
Carlson, Kathleen. The Nautical Alphabet. Sargent, Ruth. 32p. (ps-1). 1984. saddle-stitched 3.95 (0-89272-190-1) Down East.
Carlson, Nancy. The Baby & the Bear. Pearson, Susan. (ps-k). 1987. pap. 3.95 (0-670-81299-4) Viking Child Bks.
—Bunnies & Their Hobbies. Carlson, Nancy. LC 83-23161. 32p. (ps-3). 1984. PLB 13.50 (0-87614-257-9) Carolrhoda Bks.
—Halloween. Kessel, Joyce K. 48p. (gr. k-4). 1987. pap. 3.95 (0-87614-475-X, First Ave Edns) Lerner Pubns.
—Harriet & the Garden. Carlson, Nancy. 32p. (ps-3). 1985. pap. 3.95 (0-14-050466-4, Puffin) Puffin Bks.
—Harriet & the Garden. Carlson, Nancy. (gr. k-3). 1985. bk. & cassette 19.95 (0-941078-66-3); pap. 12.95 bk. & cassette (0-317-14686-6); cassette, 4 paperbacks & guide 27.95 (0-317-14687-4) Live Oak Media.
—Harriet & the Roller Coaster. Carlson, Nancy. (gr. k-3). 1985. bk. & cassette 19.95 (0-941078-59-0); pap. 12.95 bk. & cassette (0-941078-54-X); cassette, 4 paperbacks & guide 27.95 (0-941078-55-8) Live Oak Media.
—Harriet & Walt. Carlson, Nancy. (gr. k-3). 1984. bk. & cassette 19.95 (0-941078-59-0); pap. 12.95 bk. & cassette (0-317-14688-2); cassette, 4 paperbacks & guide 27.95 (0-317-14689-0) Live Oak Media.
—Harriet's Halloween Candy. Carlson, Nancy. (gr. k-3). 1985. bk. & cassette 19.95 (0-941078-53-1); pap. 12.95 bk. & cassette (0-941078-51-5); cassette, 4 paperbacks & guide 27.95 (0-941078-52-3) Live Oak Media.
—Harriet's Recital. Carlson, Nancy. (gr. k-3). 1985. bk. & cassette 19.95 (0-941078-69-8); pap. 12.95 bk. & cassette (0-941078-67-1); cassette, 4 paperbacks & guide 27.95 (0-941078-68-X) Live Oak Media.
—Lenore's Big Break. Pearson, Susan. 32p. (gr. k up). 1992. PLB 14.00 (0-670-83474-2) Viking Child Bks.
—Lenore's Big Break. Pearson, Susan. 32p. (ps-3). 1994. pap. 4.99 (0-14-054294-9) Puffin Bks.
—Life Is Fun! Carlson, Nancy. 32p. (ps-3). 1993. reinforced bdg. 13.99 (0-670-84206-0) Viking Child Bks.
—Louanne Pig in Making the Team. Carlson, Nancy. (ps-3). 1986. pap. 3.99 (0-14-050601-2, Puffin) Puffin Bks.
—Louanne Pig in Making the Team. Carlson, Nancy. (gr. k-3). 1987. 19.95 (0-685-18332-7); pap. 12.95 (0-87499-038-6); 4 paperbacks, cassette & guide 27.95 (0-87499-036-X) Live Oak Media.
—Louanne Pig in the Mysterious Valentine. Carlson, Nancy. (gr. 1-3). 1988. bk. & cassette 19.95 (0-87499-087-4); bk. & cassette 12.95 (0-87499-086-6); 4 cassettes & guide 27.95 (0-87499-088-2) Live Oak Media.
—Louanne Pig in The Perfect Family. Carlson, Nancy. (gr. k-3). 1987. incl. cassette 19.95 (0-87499-037-8); pap. 12.95 incl. cassette (0-87499-035-1); 4 paperbacks, cassette & guide 27.95 (0-685-18333-5) Live Oak Media.
—Louanne Pig in the Talent Show. Carlson, Nancy. 32p. (ps-3). 1986. pap. 3.95 (0-14-050603-9, Puffin) Puffin Bks.
—Louanne Pig in The Talent Show. Carlson, Nancy. (gr. k-3). 1987. incl. cassette 19.95 (0-87499-065-3); pap. 12.95 incl. cassette (0-87499-064-5); 4 paperbacks, cassette & guide 27.95 (0-87499-066-1) Live Oak Media.
—Louanne Pig in the Witch Lady. Carlson, Nancy. 32p. (ps-3). 1986. pap. 3.95 (0-14-050602-0, Puffin) Puffin Bks.
—Louanne Pig in Witch Lady. Carlson, Nancy. (gr. k-3). 1987. incl. cassette 19.95 (0-87499-068-8); pap. 12.95 incl. cassette (0-87499-067-X); 4 paperbacks, guide & cassette 27.95 (0-87499-069-6) Live Oak Media.
—Loudmouth George & the Big Race. Carlson, Nancy. 32p. (ps-3). 1986. pap. 3.95 (0-14-050516-4, Puffin) Puffin Bks.
—Loudmouth George & The Big Race. Carlson, Nancy. (gr. k-3). 1986. incl. cassette 19.95 (0-317-59227-0); pap. 12.95 incl. cassette (0-87499-029-7); 4 paperbacks, cassette & guide 27.95 (0-87499-031-9) Live Oak Media.

—Loudmouth George & the Cornet. Carlson, Nancy. (gr. k-3). 1986. pap. 12.95 incl. cassette (0-87499-011-4); PLB incl. cassette 19.95 (0-87499-013-0); incl. cassette 4 paperbacks guide 27.95 (0-87499-012-2) Live Oak Media.
—Loudmouth George & the Fishing Trip. Carlson, Nancy. (gr. k-3). 1986. pap. 12.95 incl. cassette (0-87499-017-3); PLB incl. cassette 19.95 (0-87499-019-X); write for info. incl. cassette, 4 paperbacks guide (0-87499-018-1) Live Oak Media.
—Loudmouth George & the New Neighbors. Carlson, Nancy. (ps-3). 1986. pap. 3.99 (0-14-050515-6, Puffin) Puffin Bks.
—Loudmouth George & The New Neighbors. Carlson, Nancy. (gr. k-3). 1987. incl. cassette 19.95 (0-87499-034-3); pap. 12.95 incl. cassette (0-87499-032-7); 4 paperbacks, cassette & guide 27.95 (0-87499-033-5) Live Oak Media.
—Loudmouth George & the Sixth Grade Bully. Carlson, Nancy. (gr. k-3). 1986. pap. 12.95 incl. cassette (0-87499-014-9); incl. cassette 19.95 (0-87499-016-5); incl. cassette, 4 paperbacks guide 27.95 (0-317-40166-1) Live Oak Media.
—Making the Team. Carlson, Nancy. LC 85-3775. 32p. (ps-3). 1985. PLB 13.50 (0-87614-281-1) Carolrhoda Bks.
—The Masked Marvel. Ogburn, Jacqueline. LC 92-1669. 1994. write for info. (0-688-11049-5); PLB write for info. (0-688-11050-9) Lothrop.
—The Perfect Family. Carlson, Nancy. LC 85-4123. 32p. (ps-3). 1985. PLB 13.50 (0-87614-280-3) Carolrhoda Bks.
—The Talent Show. Carlson, Nancy. LC 85-4122. 32p. (ps-3). 1985. PLB 13.50 (0-87614-284-6) Carolrhoda Bks.
—Watch Out for These Weirdos. Kline, Rufus. 32p. (ps-3). 1990. pap. 12.95 (0-670-82376-7) Viking Child Bks.
—Watch Out for These Weirdos! Kline, Rufus. 32p. (ps-3). 1992. pap. 3.99 (0-14-050907-0, Puffin) Puffin Bks.
—What If It Never Stops Raining? Carlson, Nancy. 32p. (ps-3). 1992. 14.00 (0-670-81775-9) Viking Child Bks.
—Witch Lady. Carlson, Nancy. LC 85-3756. 32p. (ps-3). 1985. PLB 13.50 (0-87614-283-8) Carolrhoda Bks.
Carlson, Nancy L. Halloween. Kessel, Joyce K. LC 80-15890. 48p. (gr. k-4). 1980. PLB 14.95 (0-87614-132-7) Carolrhoda Bks.
Carlson, Susan. First Houses: Native American Homes & Sacred Structures. Williamson, Ray A. & Monroe, Jean G. LC 92-34900. 1993. 14.95 (0-395-51081-3) HM.
Carmen, Dave. God Answers Children's Prayers Too. Noble, Trudy V. LC 85-217377. 30p. (ps-4). 1990. write for info. (0-9620133-0-7) Joy Deliverance Bks.
Carmi, Eugenio. The Bomb & the General. Eco, Umberto. Weaver, William, tr. 40p. (ps up) 1989. 12. 95 (0-15-209700-7) HarBrace.
—The Three Astronauts. Eco, Umberto. (gr. 1 up) 1989. 12.95 (0-15-286383-4, HB Juv Bks) HarBrace.
Carmi, Giora. The Chanukkah Guest. Kimmel, Eric A. LC 89-20073. 32p. (ps-3). 1990. reinforced bdg. 14.95 (0-8234-0788-8); pap. 5.95 (0-8234-0978-3) Holiday.
—The Chanukkah Tree. Kimmel, Eric A. LC 88-4510. 32p. (ps-3). 1988. reinforced bdg. 14.95 (0-8234-0705-5) Holiday.
—Deena the Damselfly. Rosman, Steven S. LC 91-43472. (gr. k-3). 1992. 10.95 (0-8074-0477-2, 101069) UAHC.
—The Greatest of All: A Japanese Folktale. Kimmel, Eric A., retold by. LC 90-23658. 32p. (ps-3). 1991. reinforced 14.95 (0-8234-0885-X) Holiday.
—Happy Thanksgiving! Barkin, Carol & James, Elizabeth. LC 86-33734. 96p. (gr. 4-7). 1987. 12.95 (0-688-06800-6); PLB 12.88 (0-688-06801-4) Lothrop.
—Like a Maccabee. Marcus, Audrey F. & Zwerin, Raymond A. (gr. k-3). 1991. 11.95 (0-8074-0445-4, 102564) UAHC.
—The Little Menorah Who Forgot Chanukah. Sperling, Jerry. (Orig.). 1993. pap. 12.95 incl. cassette (0-8074-0508-6, 101971) UAHC.
—My First One Hundred Hebrew Words: A Young Person's Dictionary of Judaism. Bogot, Howard I. (gr. k-3). 1993. 11.95 (0-8074-0509-4, 101716) UAHC.
—The Old Woman & Her Pig. Kimmel, Eric A., adapted by. LC 91-44185. 32p. (ps-3). 1992. reinforced bdg. 14.95 (0-8234-0970-8) Holiday.
—A Torah Commentary for Our Times: Genesis, Vol. I. Fields, Harvey J., ed. LC 89-28478. (gr. 7 up). 1990. pap. text ed. 12.00 (0-8074-0308-3, 164000) UAHC.
—A Torah Commentary for Our Times, Vol. 2: Exodus & Leviticus. Fields, Harvey J. LC 89-28478. (gr. 7-9). 1991. pap. text ed. 12.00x (0-8074-0334-2, 164010) UAHC.
Carnabuci, Anthony. Sleep Tight. Hennessy, B. G. 32p. (ps-1). 1992. RB 14.00 (0-670-83567-6) Viking Child Bks.
Carney, Christina S. Story of Adoption: Why Do I Look Different? Lowe, Darla. LC 87-46273. (Orig.). (gr. 3-6). 1987. pap. 5.95 (0-9606090-2-4) EastWest Pr.
Carow, Leslie. Marjory Stoneman Douglas: Guardian of the Everglades. Sawyer, Kem A. 72p. (gr. 5-12). 1994. PLB 16.95 (1-878668-20-X); pap. 7.95 (1-878668-28-5) Disc Enter Ltd.
Carpenter, Jim. The Water of Life: A Tale of the Grateful Dead. Trist, Alan. 52p. (gr. 2-12). 1990. PLB 12.95 (0-938493-12-4) Hulogosi Inc.

Carpenter, Joe. The Pos Activity Book. Fettig, Art. LC 86-83237. 48p. (gr. k-7). 1984. pap. 5.95 (0-9601334-5-3) Growth Unltd.
—The Three Robots Discover Their Pos-Abilities: A Lesson in Goal Setting. Fettig, Art. LC 84-81461. (gr. k-7). 1984. pap. 3.95 (0-916927-00-8) Growth Unltd.
—The Three Robots Find a Grandpa. Fettig, Art. LC 84-80378. 96p. (Orig.). (gr. k-7). 1984. pap. 3.95 (0-9601334-8-8); cassette incl. Growth Unltd.
—The Three Robots Learn about Drugs. Fettig, Art. LC 86-83041. 96p. (gr. k-7). 1987. pap. 3.95 (0-916927-04-0) Growth Unltd.
Carpenter, Mimi G. Mermaid in a Tidal Pool. Carpenter, Mimi G. 32p. (Orig.). (ps-6). 1985. pap. 8.95 (0-9614628-0-9) Beachcomber Pr.
—What the Sea Left Behind. Carpenter, Mimi G. LC 81-66251. 32p. (gr. 1-4). 1981. pap. 7.95 (0-89272-123-5) Down East.
Carpenter, Nancy. At Taylor's Place. Denslow, Sharon P. LC 89-23898. 32p. (ps-2). 1990. RSBE 13.95 (0-02-728685-1, Bradbury Pr) Macmillan Child Grp.
—Bus Riders. Denslow, Sharon P. LC 92-14109. 32p. (ps-2). 1993. RSBE 14.95 (0-02-728682-7, Four Winds) Macmillan Child Grp.
—Lester's Dog. Hesse, Karen. LC 92-27674. 32p. (ps-2). 1993. 13.00 (0-517-58357-7); PLB 13.99 (0-517-58358-5) Crown Bks Yng Read.
—Masai & I. Kroll, Virginia. LC 91-24561. 32p. (gr. k-2). 1992. RSBE 13.95 (0-02-751165-0, Four Winds) Macmillan Child Grp.
—Our Mountain. Showell, Ellen H. LC 90-2392. 80p. (gr. 2-6). 1991. SBE 12.95 (0-02-782551-5, Bradbury Pr) Macmillan Child Grp.
—Riding with Aunt Lucy. Denslow, Sharon P. LC 90-37803. 32p. (ps-2). 1991. RSBE 13.95 (0-02-728686-X, Bradbury Pr) Macmillan Child Grp.
—Sitti's Secrets. Nye, Naomi S. LC 93-19742. 32p. (ps-3). 1994. RSBE 15.95 (0-02-768460-1, Four Winds) Macmillan Child Grp.
—Treasure in the Stream: The Story of a Gold Rush Girl. Hoobler, Dorothy & Hoobler, Thomas. 64p. (gr. 4-6). 1991. 11.95 (0-382-24151-7); PLB 13.98 (0-382-24144-4); pap. 7.95 (0-382-24346-3) Silver Burdett Pr.
—The Tree That Came to Stay. Quindlen, Anna. LC 91-31957. 32p. (ps-4). 1992. 13.00 (0-517-58145-0) Crown Bks Yng Read.
—The Velveteen Rabbit. abr. ed. Kass, Kimberly, retold by. LC 92-6036. 22p. (ps). 1993. 3.25 (0-679-83617-9) Random Bks Yng Read.
Carpenter, Stephen. New Adventures of Mother Goose: Gentle Rhymes for Happy Times. Lansky, Bruce. LC 93-11129. 32p. 1993. 15.00 (0-88166-201-1) Meadowbrook.
—The New Adventures of Mother Goose: Gentle Rhymes for Happy Times. Lansky, Bruce. LC 93-11129. 1993. 15.00 (0-671-87288-5) S&S Trade.
Carr, Ed. Lifting by Levers. Dunn, Andrew. LC 93-6828. 32p. (gr. 3-6). 1993. 13.95 (1-56847-016-9) Thomson Lrning.
—Simple Slopes. Dunn, Andrew. LC 93-6836. 32p. (gr. 3-6). 1993. 13.95 (1-56847-017-7) Thomson Lrning.
Carr, Linda. A Picture Book. Cannon, Frances A. Petz, Rita K., ed. (gr. 4-6). write for info. Rapcom Enter.
Carrara, Larry, photos by. A Moose for Jessica. Wakefield, Pat & Carrara, Larry. LC 87-13663. 32p. (gr. k up). 1987. 14.95 (0-525-44342-8, DCB) Dutton Child Bks.
—A Moose for Jessica. Wakefield, Pat A. & Carrara, Larry. 64p. (ps up). 1992. pap. 5.99 (0-14-036134-0, Puffin Unicorn) Puffin Bks.
Carratello, John, jt. illus. see Carratello, Patricia.
Carratello, Patricia. Food & Nutrition. Carratello, Patricia. 40p. (gr. 1-4). 1980. wkbk. 5.95 (1-55734-212-1) Tchr Create Mat.
—My Body. Carratello, Patricia. 38p. (gr. 1-4). 1980. wkbk. 5.95 (1-55734-211-3) Tchr Create Mat.
Carratello, Patricia & Carratello, John. Let's Investigate Space. Carratello, Patricia & Carratello, John. 48p. (gr. 1-4). 1984. wkbk. 5.95 (1-55734-216-4) Tchr Create Mat.
Carreiro, Bob, jt. illus. see Kaluza, Mary K.
Carrick, Donald. The Accident. Carrick, Carol. LC 76-3532. 32p. (ps-3). 1981. (Clarion Bks); pap. 5.95 (0-89919-041-3) HM.
—Ben & the Porcupine. Carrick, Carol. LC 80-214020. 32p. (ps-3). 1985. pap. 5.70 (0-89919-348-X, Clarion Bks) HM.
—Big Jeremy. Kroll, Steven. LC 88-35812. 32p. (ps-3). 1989. reinforced bdg. 14.95 (0-8234-0759-4) Holiday.
—Big Old Bones: A Dinosaur Tale. Carrick, Carol. 32p. (gr. k-2). 1989. 13.95 (0-89919-734-5, Clarion Bks) HM.
—The Crocodiles Still Wait. Carrick, Carol. LC 79-23519. 32p. (gr. 1-4). 1980. 14.45 (0-395-29102-X, Clarion Bks) HM.
—Doctor Change. Cole, Joanna. LC 86-881. 32p. (ps-3). 1986. 12.95 (0-688-06135-4); lib. bdg. 13.88 (0-688-06136-2, Morrow Jr Bks) Morrow Jr Bks.
—The Elephant. Carrick, Carol. write for info. (Clarion Bks) HM.
—The Elephant in the Dark. Carrick, Carol. LC 88-2591. 144p. (gr. 3-7). 1988. 13.95 (0-89919-757-4, Clarion Bks) HM.
—The Foundling. Carrick, Carol. LC 77-1587. 32p. (ps-4). 1979. 14.45 (0-395-28775-8, Clarion Bks) HM.
—The Foundling. Carrick, Carol. LC 77-1587. 32p. (ps-3). 1986. pap. 4.95 (0-89919-466-4, Clarion Bks) HM.

—Ghost's Hour, Spook's Hour. Bunting, Eve. LC 86-31674. 32p. (ps-1). 1987. 14.45 (0-89919-484-2, Clarion Bks) HM.
—Ghost's Hour, Spook's Hour. Bunting, Eve. LC 86-31674. 32p. (ps). 1989. pap. 4.95 (0-395-51583-1, Clarion Bks) HM.
—Ghost's Hour, Spook's Hour. Bunting, Eve. 1990. pap. 7.70 incl.cassette (0-395-56244-9, Clarion Bks) HM.
—Going the Moose Way Home. Latimer, Jim. LC 87-9762. 32p. (gr. 1-3). 1988. SBE 13.95 (0-684-18890-2, Scribners Young Read) Macmillan Child Grp.
—Harald & the Great Stag. Carrick, Donald. LC 87-17875. 32p. (gr. k-4). 1988. 14.95 (0-89919-514-8, Clarion Bks) HM.
—Harald & the Great Stag. Carrick, Donald. 32p. (ps-3). 1990. pap. 4.80 (0-395-52596-9, Clarion Bks) HM.
—Here I Am, an Only Child. Shyer, Marlene F. LC 87-1112. 32p. (ps-3). 1987. pap. 3.95 (0-689-71156-5, Aladdin) Macmillan Child Grp.
—In the Moonlight, Waiting. Carrick, Carol. 32p. (ps-1). 1990. 13.95 (0-89919-867-8) Clarion Pr.
—Journey to Topaz. rev. ed. Uchida, Yoshiko. LC 84-70422. 160p. (gr. 4-12). 1985. pap. 7.95 (0-916870-85-5) Creative Arts Bk.
—Left Behind. Carrick, Carol. LC 88-1040. 32p. (gr. k-3). 1988. 13.95 (0-89919-535-0, Clarion Bks) HM.
—Left Behind. Carrick, Carol. 32p. (ps-3). 1991. pap. 4.80 (0-395-54380-0, Clarion Bks) HM.
—Lost in the Storm. Carrick, Carol. LC 74-1051. 32p. (ps-3). 1979. 14.45 (0-395-28776-6, Clarion Bks) HM.
—Lost in the Storm. Carrick, Carol. (ps-3). 1987. pap. 5.95 (0-89919-493-1, Clarion Bks) HM.
—Milk. Carrick, Donald. LC 84-25879. 24p. (ps-1). 1985. lib. bdg. 13.88 (0-688-04823-4) Greenwillow.
—Moss Gown. Hooks, William H. (gr. k-4). 1987. 13.95 (0-89919-460-5, Clarion Bks) HM.
—Moss Gown. Hooks, William H. (ps-3). 1990. pap. 5.70 (0-395-54793-8, Clarion Bks) HM.
—Octopus. Carrick, Carol. 32p. (ps-3). 1991. pap. 5.70 (0-395-59759-5, Clarion Bks) HM.
—Old Mother Witch. Carrick, Carol. LC 75-4609. 32p. (ps-4). 1979. 14.45 (0-395-28778-2, Clarion Bks) HM.
—Old Mother Witch. Carrick, Carol. LC 75-4609. 32p. (ps). 1989. pap. 4.80 (0-395-51584-X, Clarion Bks) HM.
—Patrick's Dinosaurs. Carrick, Carol. LC 83-2049. 32p. (gr. k-3). 1983. 13.95 (0-89919-189-4, Clarion Bks) HM.
—Patrick's Dinosaurs. Carrick, Carol. LC 83-2049. (gr. k-3). 1985. pap. 7.95 (0-89919-402-8, Clarion Bks) HM.
—Paul's Christmas Birthday. Carrick, Carol. LC 77-28408. 32p. (gr. k-3). 1978. PLB 13.88 (0-688-84159-7) Greenwillow.
—Rosalie. Hewett, Joan. LC 86-7333. 32p. (ps-2). 1987. 13.95 (0-688-06228-8); PLB 13.88 (0-688-06229-6) Lothrop.
—Sand Tiger Shark. Carrick, Carol. 32p. (ps-3). 1991. pap. 5.70 (0-395-59701-3, Clarion Bks) HM.
—Secrets of a Small Brother. Margolis, Richard J. LC 84-3478. 40p. (gr. 1-4). 1984. RSBE 12.95 (0-02-762280-0, Macmillan Child Bk) Macmillan Child Grp.
—Sleep Out. Carrick, Carol. LC 72-88539. 32p. (gr. 1-3). 1979. (Clarion Bks); pap. 4.95 (0-89919-083-9, Clarion) HM.
—Some Friend. Carrick, Carol. LC 79-11490. 112p. (gr. 3-6). 1987. pap. 5.70 (0-89919-525-3, Clarion Bks) HM.
—Stay Away from Simon. Carrick, Carol. LC 84-14289. 64p. (gr. 2-5). 1985. 12.95 (0-89919-343-9, Clarion Bks) HM.
—Stay Away from Simon! Carrick, Carol. (gr. 3-6). 1989. pap. 5.70 (0-89919-849-X, Clarion Bks) HM.
—The Wednesday Surprise. Bunting, Eve. 32p. (ps-3). 1990. pap. 4.80 (0-395-54776-8, Clarion Bks) HM.
—What a Wimp! Carrick, Carol. LC 82-9597. (gr. 3-6). 1988. pap. 3.95 (0-89919-703-5, Clarion Bks) HM.
—What Happened to Patrick's Dinosaurs? Carrick, Carol. LC 85-13989. (gr. k-3). 1988. 14.95 (0-89919-406-0, Clarion Bks); pap. 5.95 (0-89919-797-3, Clarion Bks) HM.
—When Moose Was Young. Latimer, Jim. LC 89-10059. 32p. (gr. 1-3). 1990. SBE 13.95 (0-684-18932-1, Scribners Young Read) Macmillan Child Grp.
—Yellow Blue Jay. Hurwitz, Johanna. LC 85-25868. 128p. (gr. 2-5). 1986. 11.95 (0-688-06078-1) Morrow Jr Bks.
—Yellow Blue Jay. Hurwitz, Johanna. LC 92-24597. 128p. (gr. 3 up). 1993. pap. 3.95 (0-688-12278-7, Pub. by Beech Tree Bks) Morrow.
Carrick, Donald, photos by. The Elephant in the Dark. Carrick, Carol. write for info. (Clarion Bks) HM.
Carrick, Doral. What Happened to Patrick's Dinosaurs? Carrick, Carol. 1988. pap. 7.70 incl. cass. (0-89919-838-4, Clarion Bks) HM.
Carrier, Lark. A Perfect Spring. Carrier, Lark. LC 89-49262. 32p. (ps up). 1991. pap. 14.95 (0-88708-131-2) Picture Bk Studio.
—Scout & Cody. Carrier, Lark. LC 86-883. 28p. (ps up). 1991. pap. 14.95 (0-88708-013-8) Picture Bk Studio.
—Snowy Path: A Christmas Journey. Carrier, Lark. LC 89-8449. 28p. (ps up). 1991. pap. 15.95 (0-88708-121-5) Picture Bk Studio.
—There Was a Hill... Carrier, Lark. LC 84-25536. 40p. (ps up). 1991. pap. 15.95 (0-907234-70-4) Picture Bk Studio.

Carrillo, Fred. The Call of the Wild. new ed. London, Jack. Platt, Kin, ed. LC 73-75461. 64p. (Orig.). (gr. 5-10). 1973. pap. 2.95 (*0-88301-095-X*) Pendulum Pr.
—The Last of the Mohicans. new & abr. ed. Cooper, James Fenimore. Farr, Naunerle, ed. (gr. 4-12). 1977. pap. text ed. 2.95 (*0-88301-267-7*) Pendulum Pr.
—White Fang. new & abr. ed. London, Jack. Farr, Naunerle, ed. (gr. 4-12). 1977. pap. text ed. 2.95 (*0-88301-271-5*) Pendulum Pr.
Carrillo, Fred & Cruz, E. R. George Washington-Thomas Jefferson. Farr, Naunerle C. (gr. 4-12). 1979. pap. text ed. 2.95 (*0-88301-355-X*); wkbk. 1.25 (*0-88301-379-7*) Pendulum Pr.
Carrillo, Fred & Redondo, Nestor. Davy Crockett-Daniel Boone. Farr, Naunerle C. (gr. 4-12). 1979. pap. text ed. 2.95 (*0-88301-351-7*); wkbk. 1.25 (*0-88301-375-4*) Pendulum Pr.
Carrillo, Fred, jt. illus. see Redondo, Frank.
Carrillo, Graciela. The Legend of Food Mountain (La montana del alimento) Rohmer, Harriet, adapted by. LC 81-71634. 24p. (gr. k-8). 1982. 13.95 (*0-89239-022-0*) Childrens Book Pr.
Carroll, David, photos by. Make Your Own Chess Set. Carroll, David. (gr. 5 up). 1975. (Pub. by Treehouse); pap. 2.95 (*0-13-547786-7*) P-H.
Carroll, Gary. Our Communities & Others: Study Book. Davis, James. Hawke, Sharryl D. & Combs, Eunice A., eds. Calvin, Eunice, photos by. 57p. (gr. 3). 1983. pap. 4.50 (*0-943068-74-6*) Graphic Learning.
Carroll, Lewis. Alice's Adventures Underground. Carroll, Lewis. Gardner, Martin. 128p. (gr. 4-9). 1965. pap. 2.95 (*0-486-21482-6*) Dover.
Carroll, Marilee. Zoo Animals. Cortright, Sandy. 80p. (ps). 1990. pap. 6.95 (*0-8120-4436-3*) Barron.
Carroll, Pamela. Birds for Pets & Pleasure. Haley, Neale. LC 80-68740. 224p. (gr. 7 up). 1981. PLB 8.95 (*0-385-28053-X*); pap. 4.95 (*0-440-00475-6*) Delacorte.
—The Largest Dinosaurs. Simon, Seymour. LC 85-24088. 32p. (gr. k-3). 1986. RSBE 13.95 (*0-02-782910-3*, Macmillan Child Bk) Macmillan Child Grp.
—Little Giants. Simon, Seymour. LC 82-14139. 48p. (gr. k-5). 1983. PLB 14.88 (*0-688-01731-2*) Morrow Jr Bks.
Carroll, Pamela & Carroll, Walter. The Dolphins & Me. Reed, Don C. 144p. (gr. 5 up). 1989. 14.95 (*0-316-73659-7*) Little.
Carroll, Walter, jt. illus. see Carroll, Pamela.
Carruthers, Sandy. The Men in Black. Cunningham, Lowell. Ulm, Chris, ed. 76p. 1990. pap. 7.95 (*0-944735-60-6*) Malibu Graphics.
Carson, Carol D. The Rebus Treasury. Marzollo, Jean. LC 85-16133. 64p. (ps up). 1986. Dial Bks Young.
—The Rebus Treasury. Marzollo, Jean, compiled by. LC 85-16133. 64p. (ps up). 1989. pap. 5.95 (*0-8037-0644-8*) Dial Bks Young.
Carter, Abby. Baseball Ballerina. Cristaldi, Kathryn. LC 90-20234. 48p. (Orig.). (gr. 1-3). 1992. PLB 7.99 (*0-679-91734-9*); pap. 3.50 (*0-679-81734-4*) Random Bks Yng Read.
—Busy O'Brien & the Great Bubble Gum Blowout. Poploff, Michelle. 96p. (gr. 2-5). 1990. 12.95 (*0-8027-6983-7*); lib. bdg. 13.85 (*0-8027-6984-5*) Walker & Co.
—Busy O'Brien & the Great Bubblegum Blowout. Poploff, Michelle. MacDonald, Pat, ed. 96p. 1992. pap. 2.99 (*0-671-74082-2*, Minstrel Bks) PB.
—Great-Uncle Dracula. Harvey, Jayne. LC 91-31460. 80p. (Orig.). (gr. 2-4). 1992. PLB 6.99 (*0-679-92448-5*); pap. 2.50 (*0-679-82448-0*) Random Bks Yng Read.
—Great-Uncle Dracula & the Dirty Rat. Harvey, Jayne. LC 92-39018. 64p. (gr. 2-4). 1993. PLB 6.99 (*0-679-93457-X*); pap. 2.50 (*0-679-83457-5*) Random Bks Yng Read.
—I Thought I'd Take My Rat to School: Poems for September to June. Kennedy, Dorothy M., et al, eds. Soto, Gary & Kuskin, Karla. LC 92-12775. 1993. 15.95 (*0-316-48893-3*) Little.
—Never Babysit the Hippopotamuses! Johnson, Doug. LC 93-18341. 32p. (ps-2). 1993. PLB 14.95 (*0-8050-1873-5*, Bks Young Read) H Holt & Co.
—New Kid on Spurwick Ave. Crowley, Michael. 32p. (gr. k-3). 1992. 14.95 (*0-316-16230-2*) Little.
—Snakes Are Nothing to Sneeze At. Charbonnet, Gabrielle. 80p. (gr. 2-4). 1990. 13.95 (*0-8050-1373-3*, Bks Young Read) H Holt & Co.
—Snakes Are Nothing to Sneeze At. Charbonnet, Gabrielle. LC 89-26919. 80p. (gr. 2-4). 1991. pap. 4.95 (*0-8050-1842-5*, Bks Young Read) H Holt & Co.
—Tess & Tim. Gave, Marc. LC 88-12418. 48p. (ps-3). 1988. 5.95 (*0-8193-1185-5*) Parents.
—Travels with Tess & Tim. Gave, Marc. LC 89-16401. 48p. (ps-3). 1990. 5.95 (*0-8193-1192-8*) Parents.
—Twin Surprises. Pfeffer, Susan B. 64p. (gr. 2-4). 1991. 13.95 (*0-8050-1850-6*, Redfeather BYR) H Holt & Co.
—Twin Surprises. Pfeffer, Susan B. LC 91-13968. 64p. (gr. 2-4). 1993. pap. 4.95 (*0-8050-2626-6*, Redfeather BYR) H Holt & Co.
—Twin Troubles. Pfeffer, Susan B. LC 92-5773. 1992. write for info. (*0-8050-2146-9*, Redfeather BYR) H Holt & Co.
Carter, Carl. Teen Guide Job Search: Ten Easy Steps to Your Future. Wilkes, Donald L. & Hamilton-Wilkes, Viola. 112p. (gr. 10-12). 1991. pap. 10.95 (*0-9628787-1-5*) Jem Job Educ.

Carter, David. I'm a Little Mouse. Carter, Noelle. LC 90-80318. 12p. (ps-2). 1991. 10.95 (*0-8050-1420-9*, Bks Young Read) H Holt & Co.
—Merry Christmas, Little Mouse: A Lift-the-Flap, Scratch-the-Scent Book. Carter, Noelle & Carter, David. 12p. (ps). 1993. PLB 11.95 (*0-8050-2712-2*, Bks Young Read) H Holt & Co.
—Peek-a-Boo, Little Mouse. Carter, Noelle. LC 91-78193. 12p. (ps). 1992. 10.95 (*0-8050-2253-8*, Bks Young Read) H Holt & Co.
Carter, David A. How to Be an Ocean Scientist in Your Own Home. Simon, Seymour. LC 87-45988. 144p. (gr. 5-9). 1988. (Lipp Jr Bks); PLB 13.89 (*0-397-32292-5*, Lipp Jr Bks) HarpC Child Bks.
—Snack Attack: A Tasty Pop Up Book. Ruschak, Lynette. 12p. (ps-3). 1990. pap. 8.95 (*0-671-70448-6*, S&S BFYR) S&S Trade.
—What's at the Beach? A Lift-the-Flap, Pop-up Book. Seymour, Peter. LC 84-81819. 18p. (ps-2). 1993. PLB 11.95 (*0-8050-2869-2*, Bks Young Read) H Holt & Co.
—What's in My Pocket? A Pop-up & Peek-in Book. Carter, David A. 10p. (ps-k). 1989. 8.95 (*0-399-21685-5*, Putnam) Putnam Pub Group.
—What's in the Cave? A Lift-the-Flap, Pop-up Book. Seymour, Peter. LC 84-81820. 18p. (ps-2). 1993. PLB 11.95 (*0-8050-2868-4*, Bks Young Read) H Holt & Co.
—What's in the Deep Blue Sea? Seymour, Peter. LC 90-80884. 18p. (ps-2). 1990. 10.95 (*0-8050-1449-7*, Bks Young Read) H Holt & Co.
—What's in the Jungle. Seymour, Peter. LC 87-81818. 18p. (ps-2). 1988. 10.95 (*0-8050-0688-5*, Bks Young Read) H Holt & Co.
—What's in the Prehistoric Forest? Seymour, Peter. LC 90-80885. 18p. (ps-2). 1990. 10.95 (*0-8050-1450-0*, Bks Young Read) H Holt & Co.
Carter, Debby L. Help Save Us Stickerbooks of Wild Animals, Bks. 1 & 2. 16p. (ps-2). 1989. Bk. 1. 4.95 (*0-525-44460-2*, DCB); Bk. 2 pap. 4.95 (*0-525-44461-0*, DCB) Dutton Child Bks.
—Ida's Doll. Goodman, Louise. LC 87-25085. 32p. (ps-3). 1989. HarpC Child Bks.
Carter, Dorothy. The Day They Stole the Letter J. Mahiri, Jabari. (Orig.). (gr. 3-5). 1981. pap. 3.95 (*0-88378-084-4*) Third World.
Carter, Fred, jt. illus. see Bosco, James.
Carter, Gail G. Mac & Marie & the Train Toss Surprise. Howard, Elizabeth F. LC 92-17918. 32p. (ps-2). 1993. RSBE 14.95 (*0-02-744640-9*, Four Winds) Macmillan Child Grp.
Carter, Harry. The Real Munchhausen: Baron of Bodenwerder. Von Munchhausen, Angelita. 224p. (gr. 6 up). 1960. 10.00 (*0-8159-6701-2*) Devin.
Carter, Noelle. Where's My Squishy Ball? A Lift & Touch Book. Carter, Noelle. 14p. (ps). 1993. 6.95 (*0-590-47385-9*, Cartwheel) Scholastic Inc.
Carter, Penny. A New House for the Morrisons. Carter, Penny. LC 93-12463. 32p. (ps-1). 1993. 12.99 (*0-670-84567-1*) Viking Child Bks.
—Rub-a-Dub Suds. Peters, Sharon. LC 86-30856. 32p. (gr. k-2). 1988. PLB 7.89 (*0-8167-0984-X*); pap. text ed. 1.95 (*0-8167-0985-8*) Troll Assocs.
—Secret of the Old Barn. Robert, Adrian. LC 84-8743. 48p. (gr. 2-4). 1985. PLB 10.89 (*0-8167-0412-0*); pap. text ed. 3.50 (*0-8167-0413-9*) Troll Assocs.
Carter, Terry & George, Bob. Card Games for Children. Collis, Len. 96p. (ps up). 1989. pap. 5.95 (*0-8120-4290-5*) Barron.
—Magic Tricks for Children. Collis, Len. 96p. (gr. 3 up). 1989. pap. 4.95 (*0-8120-4289-1*) Barron.
Cartlidge, Michelle. Baby Mice at Home. Cartlidge, Michelle. 24p. (ps). 1992. bds. 2.95 (*0-525-44840-3*, DCB) Dutton Child Bks.
—Bear in the Forest. Cartlidge, Michelle. 12p. (ps). 1991. bds. 3.50 (*0-525-44674-5*, DCB) Dutton Child Bks.
—Bears on the Go. Cartlidge, Michelle. 24p. (ps). 1992. bds. 2.95 (*0-525-44841-1*, DCB) Dutton Child Bks.
—Bunny's Birthday. Cartlidge, Michelle. 24p. (ps). 1992. bds. 2.95 (*0-525-44843-8*, DCB) Dutton Child Bks.
—Doggy Days. Cartlidge, Michelle. 24p. (ps). 1992. bds. 2.95 (*0-525-44844-6*, DCB) Dutton Child Bks.
—Duck in the Pond. Cartlidge, Michelle. 12p. (ps). 1991. bds. 3.50 (*0-525-44675-3*, DCB) Dutton Child Bks.
—Elephant in the Jungle. Cartlidge, Michelle. 12p. (ps). 1991. bds. 3.50 (*0-525-44676-1*, DCB) Dutton Child Bks.
—Good Night, Teddy. Cartlidge, Michelle. LC 91-58732. 24p. (ps). 1992. 5.95 (*1-56402-076-2*) Candlewick Pr.
—Mouse in the House. Cartlidge, Michelle. 12p. (ps). 1991. bds. 3.50 (*0-525-44678-8*, DCB) Dutton Child Bks.
—Mouse Letters. Cartlidge, Michelle. 24p. (ps). 1993. 4.99 (*0-525-45089-0*, DCB) Dutton Child Bks.
—Mouse Time. Cartlidge, Michelle. 24p. (ps). 1991. 3.95 (*0-525-44766-0*, DCB) Dutton Child Bks.
—Teddy's Friends. Cartlidge, Michelle. LC 91-58758. 24p. (ps). 1992. 5.95 (*1-56402-077-0*) Candlewick Pr.
Cartwrigh, Stephen. First Thousand Words in Spanish. Amery, Heather. 50p. (ps-7). 1979. 11.95 (*0-86020-277-1*) EDC.
Cartwright. At the Seaside. Amery. 20p. (ps). 1985. 3.95 (*0-86020-855-9*, Pub. by Usborne) EDC.
Cartwright, Reg. Birds, Beasts, & Fishes: A Selection of Animal Poems. Carter, Ann, compiled by. & intros. by. LC 90-21493. 64p. (ps up). 1991. SBE 16.95 (*0-02-717776-9*, Macmillan Child Bk) Macmillan Child Grp.

—The Firebird. Hastings, Selina. LC 92-52997. 40p. (gr. 1-8). 1993. 15.95 (*1-56402-096-7*) Candlewick Pr.
—My Cat. Taylor, Judy. LC 88-22127. 32p. (ps-2). 1989. pap. 3.95 (*0-689-71209-X*, Aladdin) Macmillan Child Grp.
—My Dog. Taylor, Judy. LC 88-19441. 32p. (ps-2). 1989. pap. 3.95 (*0-689-71210-3*, Aladdin) Macmillan Child Grp.
—Peter & the Wolf. Hastings, Selina. LC 86-27004. 32p. (ps-2). 1990. 5.95 (*0-8050-1362-8*, Bks Young Read) H Holt & Co.
Cartwright, S. Apple Tree Farm: Press Out Model. Cartwright, S. & Ashman, I. 32p. 1991. pap. 8.95 (*0-7460-0664-0*, Usborne) EDC.
Cartwright, Shannon. Alaska Mother Goose. Gill, Shelley R. 36p. (Orig.). (gr. k-6). 1987. 13.95 (*0-934007-05-5*); pap. 8.95 (*0-934007-02-0*) Charlesbridge Pub.
—Alaska's Three Bears. Gill, Shelly. 32p. (ps-3). 1992. 13.95 (*0-934007-10-1*); pap. 7.95 (*0-934007-11-X*) Paws Four Pub.
—Kiana's Iditarod. Gill, Shelley R. 52p. (Orig.). (gr. 2-6). 1984. pap. 8.95 (*0-934007-00-4*) Paws Four Pub.
—The Loop Train. Kreeger, Charlene. 48p. 1991. pap. 11.95 (*0-933914-02-4*) Lone Raven.
—Mammoth Magic. Gill, Shelley R. 36p. (Orig.). (gr. k-6). 1986. pap. 7.95 (*0-934007-01-2*) Paws Four Pub.
Cartwright, Stephen. Bedtime Stories. Hawthorn, Philip. (ps-4). 1992. 10.95 (*0-7460-0538-5*, Usborne) EDC.
—Duck & His Friends. Tyler, J. & Cartwright, S. 16p. (ps). 1988. 3.50 (*0-7460-0184-3*); PLB 7.96 (*0-88110-326-8*) EDC.
—Duck in Trouble. Tyler, J. & Cartwright, S. 16p. (ps). 1988. 3.50 (*0-7460-0185-1*); PLB 7.96 (*0-88110-327-6*) EDC.
—Duck on Holiday. Tyler, J. & Cartwright, S. 16p. (ps). 1988. 3.50 (*0-7460-0183-5*); PLB 7.96 (*0-88110-328-4*) EDC.
—Find the Bird. Cartwright, Stephen & Zeff, C. 12p. (ps). 1984. bds. 3.50 (*0-86020-719-6*, Pub. by Usborne) EDC.
—Find the Duck. Cartwright, Stephen & Zeff, C. 12p. (ps). 1984. bds. 3.50 (*0-86020-714-5*, Pub. by Usborne) EDC.
—Find the Kitten. Cartwright, Stephen & Zeff, C. 12p. (ps). 1984. bds. 3.50 (*0-86020-718-8*, Pub. by Usborne) EDC.
—Find the Piglet. Cartwright, Stephen & Zeff, C. 12p. (ps). 1984. bds. 3.50 (*0-86020-716-1*, Pub. by Usborne) EDC.
—Find the Puppy. Cartwright, Stephen & Zeff, C. 12p. (ps). 1984. bds. 3.50 (*0-86020-717-X*, Pub. by Usborne) EDC.
—Find the Teddy. Cartwright, Stephen & Zeff, C. 12p. (ps). 1984. bds. 3.50 (*0-86020-715-3*, Pub. by Usborne) EDC.
—The First Hundred Words. Amery, Heather & Cartwright, Stephen. 32p. (ps up). 1988. PLB 11.96 (*0-88110-322-5*); pap. 7.95 (*0-7460-0186-X*) EDC.
—First Stories. Amery, H. 48p. 1988. 8.95 (*0-7460-0191-6*) EDC.
—First Thousand Words in French. Amery, Heather. 50p. (ps-7). 1980. 11.95 (*0-86020-267-4*) EDC.
—First Thousand Words in German. Amery, Heather. 50p. (ps-7). 1979. 11.95 (*0-86020-268-2*) EDC.
—First Thousand Words in Hebrew. Amery & Haron. 62p. (ps-6). 1985. PLB 11.95 (*0-86020-863-X*, Pub. by Usborne) EDC.
—Going to School. 16p. (ps up). 1986. pap. 3.95 (*0-7460-1269-1*) EDC.
—Goldilocks & the Three Bears. Amery, H. 16p. (ps-2). 1988. PLB 6.96 (*0-88110-318-7*) EDC.
—Little Red Riding Hood. Amery, H. 16p. (ps-2). 1987. 2.95 (*0-7460-0138-X*); PLB 6.96 (*0-88110-290-3*) EDC.
—Moving House. 16p. (ps up). 1986. PLB write for info.; pap. 3.95 (*0-685-58332-5*) EDC.
—The New Baby. 16p. (ps up). 1986. 3.95 (*0-86020-966-0*) EDC.
—On the Farm. Amery. 20p. (ps). 1984. 3.95 (*0-86020-853-2*, Pub. by Usborne) EDC.
—Stories for Young Children. Rawson, C. 32p. (gr. 1-4). 1990. 12.95 (*0-7460-0800-7*, Usborne) EDC.
—Things People Do. Civardi, Anne. 38p. (ps-4). 1986. 10.95 (*0-86020-864-8*, Pub. by Usborne); PLB 12.96 (*0-88110-236-9*) EDC.
—Three Little Pigs. Amery, H. 16p. (ps-2). 1987. 3.95 (*0-7460-0189-4*); PLB 6.96 (*0-88110-293-8*) EDC.
—Word Detective in French. Amery, Heather. 50p. (gr. 3-7). 1983. 8.95 (*0-7460-0399-4*) EDC.
—Word Detective in German. Amery, Heather. 50p. (gr. 3-7). 1983. 11.95 (*0-86020-664-5*) EDC.
—Word Finder in German. Civardi, Anne. 48p. (gr. k-3). 1984. 11.95 (*0-86020-771-4*) EDC.
Carver, Douglas, photos by. Michael Andretti at Indianapolis. Andretti, Michael, et al. LC 91-38815. 64p. (gr. 3-7). 1993. pap. 5.95 (*0-671-79674-7*, S&S BFYR) S&S Trade.
Carvin, Ruth. Color It Christmas: With Three Christmas Posters. Carvin, Ruth. 8p. (gr. 3 up). 1987. write for info. Carvin Pub.

Cary. The Corduroy Road. Clyne, Patricia E. (gr. 5-9). 1984. 15.25 (*0-8446-6163-5*) Peter Smith.
—Eli Whitney: Great Inventor. Latham, Jean L. 80p. (gr. 2-6). 1991. Repr. of 1963 ed. lib. bdg. 12.95 (*0-7910-1453-3*) Chelsea Hse.
—Martha Washington: First Lady of the Land. Anderson, LaVere. 80p. (gr. 2-6). 1991. Repr. of 1973 ed. lib. bdg. 12.95 (*0-7910-1452-5*) Chelsea Hse.
—Mary Todd Lincoln: President's Wife. Anderson, LaVere. 80p. (gr. 2-6). 1991. Repr. of 1975 ed. lib. bdg. 12.95 (*0-7910-1415-0*) Chelsea Hse.

Cary, Bob. CampSights. Cook, Sam. LC 91-62787. 192p. (gr. 10-12). 1991. 16.95 (*0-938586-49-1*) Pfeifer-Hamilton.

Cary, C., photos by. One Hundred Seventy-Five Easy-to-Do Easter Crafts: Easy-to-Do Projects with Easy-to-Do Things. Umnik, Sharon D., ed. 64p. (gr. k-5). 1994. pap. 6.95 (*1-56397-316-2*) Boyds Mills Pr.

Casad, Michael. Harmony. Cosgrove, Stephen. LC 89-83842. 72p. (gr. 7 up). 1991. 24.95 (*1-55868-008-X*) Gr Arts Ctr Pub.

Casale, Paul. My Stepfather Shrank! Dillon, Barbara. LC 91-23901. 128p. (gr. 3-6). 1994. pap. 3.95 (*0-06-440459-5*, Trophy) HarpC Child Bks.
—Return of the Home Run Kid. Christopher, Matt. 168p. (gr. 3-7). 1992. 14.95 (*0-316-14080-5*) Little.

Case, Bernard. Chemistry Experiments for Children. Mullin, Virginia L. LC 68-9306. (gr. 3-10). 1968. pap. 2.95 (*0-486-22031-1*) Dover.

Caseley, Judith. Apple Pie & Onions. Caseley, Judith. LC 86-9804. 32p. (gr. 1-4). 1987. 11.75 (*0-688-06762-X*); PLB 11.88 (*0-688-06763-8*) Greenwillow.
—Hurricane Harry. Caseley, Judith. LC 93-6991. 112p. (gr. 2 up). 1994. pap. 3.95 (*0-688-12549-2*, Pub. by Beech Tree Bks) Morrow.
—Starring Dorothy Kane. Caseley, Judith. LC 93-6992. 160p. (gr. 2 up). 1994. pap. 3.95 (*0-688-12548-4*, Pub. by Beech Tree Bks) Morrow.
—When Grandpa Came to Stay. Caseley, Judith. LC 85-12616. 32p. (gr. k-2). 1986. 11.75 (*0-688-06128-1*); PLB 11.88 (*0-688-06129-X*) Greenwillow.

Caselli, Giovanni. An Egyptian Craftsman. Caselli, Giovanni. LC 85-30685. 32p. (gr. 3-6). 1991. lib. bdg. 12.95 (*0-87226-100-X*) P Bedrick Bks.
—The Everyday Life of a Cathedral Builder. Caselli, Giovanni. LC 87-29787. 32p. (gr. 3-6). 1992. PLB 12.95 (*0-87226-115-8*) P Bedrick Bks.
—The Everyday Life of a Florentine Merchant. Caselli, Giovanni. LC 86-4365. 32p. (gr. 3-6). 1991. PLB 12.95 (*0-87226-107-7*) P Bedrick Bks.
—Gods & Heroes from Viking Mythology. Branston, Brian. LC 92-29705. 1993. write for info. (*0-87226-905-1*) P Bedrick Bks.
—A Greek Potter. Caselli, Giovanni. LC 85-30637. 32p. (gr. 3-6). 1991. lib. bdg. 12.95 (*0-87226-101-8*) P Bedrick Bks.
—An Ice Age Hunter. Caselli, Giovanni. LC 91-33261. 32p. (gr. 3-6). 1992. lib. bdg. 12.95 (*0-87226-103-4*) P Bedrick Bks.
—The Middle Ages. Caselli, Giovanni. 48p. (gr. 5 up). 1993. pap. 8.95 sewn (*0-685-66005-2*) P Bedrick Bks.
—The Renaissance & The New World. Caselli, Giovanni. LC 85-22900. 48p. (gr. 5 up). 1986. 16.95 (*0-87226-050-X*) P Bedrick Bks.
—A Viking Settler. Caselli, Giovanni. LC 86-3302. 32p. (gr. 3-6). 1991. lib. bdg. 12.95 (*0-87226-104-2*) P Bedrick Bks.

Casey, Marjorie. Billy. Miller, Shirley J. 60p. (Orig.). (gr. 2-6). 1993. pap. 6.95 (*1-878580-92-2*) Asylum Arts.
—My House, Your House. Miller, Shirley J. 60p. (Orig.). (gr. 2-6). 1993. pap. 6.95 (*1-878580-91-4*) Asylum Arts.
—School Days. Miller, Shirley J. 80p. (Orig.). (gr. 2-6). 1993. pap. 6.95 (*1-878580-90-6*) Asylum Arts.

Casey, Patricia. I Like Monkeys Because. Hansard, Peter. LC 92-54409. 32p. (ps up) 1993. 14.95 (*1-56402-196-3*) Candlewick Pr.

Casilla, Robert. Con Mi Hermano with My Brother. Roe, Eileen. LC 90-33983. 32p. (ps-3). 1991. RSBE 12.95 (*0-02-777373-6*, Bradbury Pr) Macmillan Child Grp.
—Jackie Robinson: He Was the First. Adler, David A. LC 88-32394. 48p. (gr. 2-5). 1990. pap. 4.95 (*0-8234-0799-3*) Holiday.
—Un Libro Ilustrado Sobre Martin Luther King, Hijo. Adler, David A. Mlawer, Teresa, tr. from ENG. (SPA.). 32p. (ps-3). 1992. reinforced bdg. 14.95 (*0-8234-0982-1*); pap. 5.95 (*0-8234-0991-0*) Holiday.
—The Little Painter of Sabana Grande. Markun, Patricia M. LC 91-35230. 32p. (ps-2). 1993. RSBE 14.95 (*0-02-762205-3*, Bradbury Pr) Macmillan Child Grp.
—Martin Luther King, Jr. Free at Last. Adler, David A. LC 86-4670. 48p. (gr. 2-5). 1986. reinforced bdg. 14.95 (*0-8234-0618-0*); pap. 4.95 (*0-8234-0619-9*) Holiday.
—A Picture Book of Eleanor Roosevelt. Adler, David A. LC 90-39212. 32p. (ps-3). 1991. reinforced 14.95 (*0-8234-0856-6*) Holiday.
—A Picture Book of Jackie Robinson. Adler, David A. LC 93-27224. 32p. (gr. 3 up). 1994. write for info. (*0-8234-1122-7*) Holiday.
—A Picture Book of Jesse Owens. Adler, David A. LC 91-44735. 32p. (ps-3). 1992. reinforced bdg. 14.95 (*0-8234-0966-X*) Holiday.
—A Picture Book of John F. Kennedy. Adler, David A. LC 90-23589. 32p. (ps-3). 1991. reinforced 14.95 (*0-8234-0884-1*); pap. 5.95 (*0-8234-0976-7*) Holiday.

—A Picture Book of Martin Luther King, Jr. Adler, David A. LC 89-81930. 32p. (ps-3). 1989. reinforced bdg. 14.95 (*0-8234-0770-5*); pap. 5.95 (*0-8234-0847-7*) Holiday.
—A Picture Book of Rosa Parks. Adler, David A. LC 92-41826. 32p. (ps-3). 1993. reinforced bdg. 15.95 (*0-8234-1041-2*) Holiday.
—A Picture Book of Simon Bolivar. Adler, David A. LC 91-19419. 32p. (ps-3). 1992. reinforced bdg. 14.95 (*0-8234-0927-9*) Holiday.
—Poems for Fathers. Livingston, Myra C., ed. LC 88-17010. 32p. (ps-3). 1989. reinforced bdg. 13.95 (*0-8234-0729-2*) Holiday.
—The Pool Party. Soto, Gary. LC 92-34407. 1993. 13.95 (*0-385-30890-6*) Delacorte.
—Rodeo Day. Toriseva, Jonelle. LC 92-39475. 32p. (ps-2). 1994. RSBE 14.95 (*0-02-789405-3*, Bradbury Pr) Macmillan Child Grp.
—The Train to Lulu's. Howard, Elizabeth F. LC 86-33429. 32p. (ps-2). 1988. RSBE 14.95 (*0-02-744620-4*, Bradbury Pr) Macmillan Child Grp.

Casino, Steve. Wild Bill Hickok. Weidt, Maryann. LC 92-9732. 1992. write for info. (*0-688-10089-9*); lib. bdg. write for info. (*0-688-10090-2*) Lothrop.

Cassatt, Mary. Lullabies & Good Night. 32p. 1989. 13.95 (*0-8249-8441-2*, Ideals Child); incl. 60-min. cassette 17.95 (*0-8249-7351-8*) Hambleton-Hill.

Casseau, Vera. Fairy Minstrel of Glenmalure & Other Stories for Children. Leamy, Edmund. LC 76-9901. (gr. 4-6). 1976. Repr. of 1913 ed. 15.00x (*0-8486-0210-2*) Roth Pub Inc.

Cassel, Lili. Jewish Heroes, 2 bks. Weilerstein, Sadie R. 208p. (gr. 4-5). 1976. pap. 4.25x ea. Bk. 1 (*0-8381-0180-1*) Bk. 2 (*0-8381-0177-1*) United Syn Bk.

Cassell, Robert. Ruth: Woman of Courage. Parris, Paula. (gr. 1-6). 1977. bds. 5.95 (*0-8054-4229-4*, 4242-29) Broadman.

Cassels, Jean. Armies of Ants. Retan, Walter. LC 93-29782. 48p. (ps-4). 1994. pap. 3.50 (*0-590-47616-5*, Cartwheel) Scholastic Inc.
—Dinosaurs & Their Relatives in Action. Gay, Tanner O. 16p. (ps-3). 1990. POB 7.95 (*0-689-71434-3*, Aladdin) Macmillan Child Grp.
—The Mystery of the Phantom Pony. Hall, Lynn. 64p. (Orig.). (gr. 2-4). 1993. POB 6.99 (*0-679-94335-8*); pap. 2.50 (*0-679-84335-3*) Random Bks Yng Read.
—The Random House Book of Horses & Horsemanship. Rodenas, Paula. Farley, Walter, frwd. by. LC 86-42934. 192p. (gr. 3-7). 1991. 17.95 (*0-394-88705-0*); PLB 18.99 (*0-394-98705-5*) Random Bks Yng Read.
—Sharks in Action. Gay, Tanner O. 16p. (ps-4). 1990. POB 7.95 (*0-689-71435-1*, Aladdin) Macmillan Child Grp.
—Snakes & Other Reptiles in Action. Gay, Tanner O. 16p. (gr. k-4). 1991. POB 7.95 (*0-689-71536-6*, Aladdin) Macmillan Child Grp.
—Whales & Dolphins in Action. Gay, Tanner O. 16p. (gr. k-4). 1991. POB 7.95 (*0-689-71535-8*, Aladdin) Macmillan Child Grp.

Cassidy, Christophe. The Black Rose. Keckeis, M. B. Steiner, Frank, et al, trs. (ENG, SPA, FRE & GER.). 256p. (gr. 3-9). 1991. 23.50 (*1-879870-54-1*) Pro Lingua Pr.
—The Black Rose. 2nd ed. Keckeis, M. B., et al. Steiner, Frank & Mercer, Denis, trs. (ENG, SPA, FRE & GER.). 256p. (gr. 6-10). 1993. Repr. of 1991 ed. 23.50 (*1-879870-55-X*) Pro Lingua Pr.
—The White Dove. Keckeis, M. B. & Beaubeau, Anne. Steiner, Frank, tr. (ENG, SPA, FRE & GER.). 256p. (gr. 6-10). 1993. 23.50 (*1-879870-56-8*) Pro Lingua Pr.

Cassidy, Dianne. The Thanksgiving Day Parade Mystery. Markham, Marion M. LC 86-4618. 48p. (gr. 2-5). 1986. 10.95 (*0-395-41855-0*) HM.
—The Thanksgiving Day Parade Mystery. Markham, Marion M. 64p. 1990. pap. 2.95 (*0-380-70967-8*, Camelot) Avon.

Casson, Hugh. Buttons. Yeatman, Linda. 64p. (gr. 2-5). 1988. pap. 2.95 (*0-8120-3956-4*) Barron.

Castelli, H. Les Malheurs de Sophie. Segur, C. (FRE.). 220p. (gr. 5-10). 1988. pap. 9.95 (*2-07-033496-1*) Schoenhof.

Castiano, Robert. Pueblo Indians of New Mexico: Activities & Adventures for Kids. Hallett, Bill & Hallett, Jane. (Orig.). (gr. 3-8). 1991. activity bk. 3.95 (*1-877827-08-8*) Look & See.

Castille, Robert. The Train to Lulu's. Howard, Elizabeth F. LC 93-255565. 32p. 1994. pap. 4.95 (*0-689-71797-0*, Aladdin) Macmillan Child Grp.

Castillo, Consuelo M. Atariba & Niguayona. Rohmer, Harriet & Guerrero Rea, Jesus. LC 76-17495. (ENG & SPA.). 24p. (gr. 2-6). 1988. 13.95 (*0-89239-026-3*) Childrens Book Pr.

Castillo, L. A Mexican Legend: Quetzalcoat! The Bird-Serpent. Parapan, S. M. 24p. (Orig.). (gr. k-3). 1989. pap. text ed. write for info.; write for info. tchr's. activity guide Parapan.

Castillo, Romulo & Paul, Frank A. Noah. new ed. Fant, Louie J., Jr. 14p. (gr. 3-4). 1973. pap. text ed. 5.00 (*0-917002-70-9*) Joyce Media.

Castillo, Steve. Maximum Happiness: Jack & Jill Discover True Love. Castillo, Steve. 58p. (Orig.). (gr. 9). 1989. 5.95 (*0-317-93187-3*) Paisley Bks.

Castle, Barry. Cry Wolf & Other Aesop Fables. Lewis, Naomi. 32p. (ps up). 1988. 18.00 (*0-19-520710-6*) OUP.

Castro, Antonio. Barry: The Bravest Saint Bernard. Hall, Lynn. LC 92-1228. 48p. (Orig.). (gr. 2-4). 1992. PLB 7.99 (*0-679-93054-X*); pap. 3.50 (*0-679-83054-5*) Random Bks Yng Read.
—Jane Goodall: Living with the Chimps. Fromer, Julie. 72p. (gr. 4-7). 1992. PLB 14.95 (*0-8050-2116-7*) TFC Bks NY.
—John Muir: At Home in the Wild. Talmadge, Katherine S. LC 92-36292. 80p. (gr. 4-7). 1993. PLB 14.95 (*0-8050-2123-X*) TFC Bks NY.
—The Life of Charles Drew. Talmadge, Katherine S. 80p. (gr. 4-7). 1991. PLB 13.95 (*0-941477-65-7*) TFC Bks NY.
—The Life of Dorothea Dix. Schleichert, Elizabeth. 80p. (gr. 4-7). 1991. PLB 13.95 (*0-941477-68-1*) TFC Bks NY.
—The Life of Elizabeth Blackwell. Schleichert, Elizabeth. 80p. (gr. 4-7). 1991. PLB 13.95 (*0-941477-66-5*) TFC Bks NY.
—The Life of Louis Pasteur. Newfield, Marcia. 84p. (gr. 4-7). 1991. PLB 13.95 (*0-941477-67-3*) TFC Bks NY.
—Margaret Murie: A Wilderness Life. Bryant, Jennifer. 80p. (gr. 4-7). 1993. PLB 14.95 (*0-8050-2220-1*) TFC Bks NY.
—Theodore Roosevelt: Conservation President. DeStefano, Susan. 80p. (gr. 4-7). 1993. PLB 14.95 (*0-8050-2122-1*) TFC Bks NY.

Castro, Carlos & Dunn, Ben. Ninja High School, Vol. 1: Graphic Album. 2nd ed. Dunn, Ben. 126p. (gr. 10). 1990. pap. 9.95 (*0-944735-13-4*) Malibu Graphics.

Caswell, Edmund. Peter Pan: A Changing Picture & Lift-the-Flap Book. abr. ed. Barrie, J. M. 32p. (ps-3). 1992. 15.95 (*0-670-83608-7*) Viking Child Bks.

Caswell, Helen. God Must Like to Laugh. Caswell, Helen. LC 87-1362. (ps-3). 1987. pap. 5.95 (*0-687-15188-0*) Abingdon.
—God's Love Is for Sharing. Caswell, Helen. LC 87-11580. (gr. k-3). 1987. pap. 5.95 (*0-687-15335-2*) Abingdon.
—Parable of the Bridesmaids. Caswell, Helen. 24p. (ps-3). 1992. 11.95 (*0-687-30022-3*) Abingdon.
—Parable of the Good Samaritan. Caswell, Helen. 24p. (ps-3). 1992. 11.95 (*0-687-30023-1*) Abingdon.
—Parable of the Leaven. Caswell, Helen. LC 92-15161. 24p. (ps-3). 1992. pap. 5.95 (*0-687-30024-X*) Abingdon.
—Parable of the Mustard Seed. Caswell, Helen. LC 92-15160. 24p. (ps-3). 1992. pap. 5.95 (*0-687-30025-8*) Abingdon.

Caswell, Helen R. God's World Makes Me Feel So Little. Caswell, Helen R. LC 84-14545. 32p. (gr. k-3). 1988. 5.95 (*0-687-15510-X*) Abingdon.

Caswell, Philip. Family Dinner. Cutler, Jane. 112p. (gr. 3 up). 1992. 13.95 (*0-374-32267-8*) FS&G.

Catalano, Dominic. The Bear Who Loved Puccini. Sundgaard, Arnold. 32p. (ps-3). 1992. PLB 14.95 (*0-399-22135-2*, Philomel Bks) Putnam Pub Group.
—Monsieur Cochon. Schotter, Roni. LC 92-26223. 1993. write for info. (*0-399-22023-2*, Philomel Bks) Putnam Pub Group.
—Rabbit Surprise. Houck, Eric L., Jr. LC 92-1318. 32p. (ps-2). 1993. 14.00 (*0-517-58777-7*); PLB 14.99 (*0-517-58778-5*) Crown Bks Yng Read.
—Rise & Shine. Carlstrom, Nancy W. LC 92-21696. 32p. (ps-2). 1993. 15.00 (*0-06-021451-1*); PLB 14.89 (*0-06-021452-X*) HarpC Child Bks.

Catalano, Sal. The Moon of the Deer. George, Jean C. LC 91-14607. 48p. (gr. 3-7). 1992. 15.00 (*0-06-020261-0*); PLB 14.89 (*0-06-020262-9*) HarpC Child Bks.
—The Moon of the Gray Wolves. new ed. George, Jean C. LC 90-38166. 48p. (gr. 3-7). 1991. 15.00 (*0-06-022442-8*); PLB 14.89 (*0-06-022443-6*) HarpC Child Bks.

Catalanotto, Peter. All I See. Rylant, Cynthia. LC 88-42547. 32p. (gr. k-2). 1988. 15.95 (*0-531-05777-1*); PLB 15.99 (*0-531-08377-2*) Orchard Bks Watts.
—All I See. Rylant, Cynthia. LC 88-42547. 32p. (gr. k-2). 1994. pap. 5.95 (*0-531-07048-4*) Orchard Bks Watts.
—An Angel for Solomon Singer. Rylant, Cynthia. LC 91-15957. 32p. 1992. 14.95 (*0-531-05978-2*); lib. bdg. 14.99 (*0-531-08578-3*) Orchard Bks Watts.
—The Catspring Somersault Flying One-Handed Flip-Flop. Kiser, SuAnn. LC 92-44519. 32p. (ps-2). 1993. 14.95 (*0-531-05493-4*); PLB 14.99 (*0-531-08643-7*) Orchard Bks Watts.
—Cecil's Story. Lyon, George-Ella. LC 90-7775. 32p. (gr. k-2). 1991. 14.95 (*0-531-05912-X*); PLB 14.99 (*0-531-08512-0*) Orchard Bks Watts.
—Dark Cloud Strong Breeze. Patron, Susan. LC 93-4873. (gr. 5 up). 1994. write for info. (*0-531-06815-3*); PLB write for info. (*0-531-08665-8*) Orchard Bks Watts.
—Dreamplace. Lyon, George-Ella. LC 92-25102. 32p. (ps-2). 1993. 15.95 (*0-531-05466-7*); PLB 15.99 (*0-531-08616-X*) Orchard Bks Watts.
—Dylan's Day Out. Catalanotto, Peter. LC 88-36440. 32p. (ps-1). 1993. pap. 5.95 (*0-531-07034-4*) Orchard Bks Watts.
—Mr. Mumble. Catalanotto, Peter. LC 89-48940. 32p. (ps-2). 1990. 14.95 (*0-531-05880-8*); PLB 14.99 (*0-531-08480-9*) Orchard Bks Watts.
—Soda Jerk. Rylant, Cynthia. LC 89-35654. 48p. (gr. 7 up). 1990. 14.95 (*0-531-05864-6*); PLB 14.99 (*0-531-08464-7*) Orchard Bks Watts.
—Who Came Down That Road? Lyon, George-Ella. LC 91-20742. 32p. (ps-2). 1992. 15.95 (*0-531-05987-1*); PLB 15.99 (*0-531-08587-2*) Orchard Bks Watts.

Catchpole, Diane. Amanda & the Star Child. Greaves, Margaret. 32p. (ps-1). 1993. pap. 8.95 (*0-460-88138-8*, Pub. by J M Dent & Sons) Trafalgar.

Cates, Emily. The Ghost in the Attic. Cates, Emily. (gr. 3-7). 1990. pap. 2.95 (*0-553-15826-0*, Skylark) Bantam.

Cates, Joe W. Buzbee. Cates, Joe W. 96p. (gr. 3-8). 1987. PLB write for info. (*0-942403-04-5*) J Barnaby Dist.
—Carl the Cactus. Cates, Joe W. 64p. (Orig.). (gr. k-6). 1986. PLB 9.95 (*0-942403-03-7*); pap. 7.00 (*0-942403-01-0*) J Barnaby Dist.
—The Crooked Tree. Cates, Joe W. 48p. (Orig.). (gr. k-6). 1986. PLB 9.95 (*0-942403-02-9*); pap. 6.00 (*0-942403-00-2*) J Barnaby Dist.

Cathcart, Yvonne. Katherine & the Garbage Dump. Morris, Martha. 24p. (gr. 1-4). 1992. 12.95 (*0-929005-39-2*, Pub. by Second Story Pr CN); pap. 5.95 (*0-929005-38-4*, Second Story Pr CN) InBook.

Cathleen, Mella. Book Report Poster Party. Thorne, Randy. Sussman, Ellen, intro. by. 12p. (Orig.). (gr. 3-6). 1989. text ed. 6.95 (*0-933606-73-7*) E Sussman Educ.

Catlett, Elizabeth. Lift Every Voice & Sing. Johnson, James Weldon. 36p. 1993. 14.95 (*0-8027-8250-7*); PLB 15.85 (*0-8027-8251-5*) Walker & Co.

Catlin, George. George Catlin: Painter of the Indian West. Sufrin, Mark. LC 90-19813. 160p. (gr. 5-9). 1991. SBE 14.95 (*0-689-31608-9*, Atheneum Child Bk) Macmillan Child Grp.

Catlin, George & Bodmer, Karl. Among the Plains Indians. Engel, Lorenz. LC 74-102895. 108p. (gr. 5 up). 1970. PLB 14.95 (*0-8225-0564-9*) Lerner Pubns.

Catrow, David. The Attic Mice. Pochocki, Ethel. LC 90-32064. 128p. (gr. 2-4). 1990. 13.95 (*0-8050-1298-2*, Bks Young Read) H Holt & Co.
—The Cataract of Lodore. Southey, Robert. LC 91-29748. 32p. (gr. 1-3). 1992. 15.95 (*0-8050-1945-6*, Bks Young Read) H Holt & Co.
—Good Cats, Bad Cats. Ghigna, Charles. LC 92-52984. 40p. 1992. 7.95 (*1-56282-292-6*); PLB 10.89 (*1-56282-293-4*) Hyprn Child.
—Good Dogs, Bad Dogs. Ghinga, Charles. LC 92-52985. 32p. 1992. 7.95 (*1-56282-290-X*); PLB 10.89 (*1-56282-291-8*) Hyprn Child.
—The Million Dollar Bear. Kotzwinkle, William. LC 93-6262. 1994. write for info. (*0-679-85295-6*); PLB write for info. (*0-679-95295-0*) Knopf Bks Yng Read.
—That's Good! That's Bad! Cuyler, Margery. LC 90-49353. 32p. (ps-2). 1991. 15.95 (*0-8050-1535-3*, Bks Young Read) H Holt & Co.
—That's Good! That's Bad! Cuyler, Margery. LC 90-49353. 32p. (ps-2). 1993. pap. 5.95 (*0-8050-2954-0*, Bks Young Read) H Holt & Co.

Catrow, David A. Backstage with Clawdio. Schwartz, Harriet B. LC 92-21683. 40p. (ps-4). 1993. 15.00 (*0-679-81763-8*); PLB 15.99 (*0-679-91763-2*) Knopf Bks Yng Read.

Catrow, David, III. The Story of the Trail of Tears. Stein, R. Conrad. LC 84-28507. 32p. (gr. 3-6). 1985. PLB 13.27 (*0-516-04683-7*); pap. 3.95 (*0-516-44683-5*) Childrens.

Catrow, David J., III. The Story of the Battle of Bull Run. Kent, Zachary. LC 86-9642. 32p. (gr. 3-6). 1986. PLB 13.27 (*0-516-04703-5*); pap. 3.95 (*0-516-44703-3*) Childrens.

Caudill-Paye, Judythe. This Book Is Just for You. Schmeltz, Susan A., ed. LC 81-11928. 100p. (gr. k-6). 1981. 11.95g (*0-9606586-0-2*) Quality MO.

Cauley, Lorinda B. The Beginning of the Armadillos. Kipling, Rudyard. LC 85-5444. 43p. (ps-3). 1985. 14.95 (*0-15-206380-3*, Pub. by HJ) HarBrace.
—Clap Your Hands. Cauley, Lorinda B. 32p. (ps-1). 1992. PLB 14.95 (*0-399-22118-2*, Putnam) Putnam Pub Group.
—The Elephant's Child. Kipling, Rudyard. LC 85-9098. 48p. (ps-3). 1988. pap. 4.95 (*0-15-225386-6*, HB Juv Bks) HarBrace.
—The Elephant's Child. Kipling, Rudyard. 44p. (ps-3). 1983. 14.95 (*0-15-225385-8*, Voyager Bks) HarBrace.
—Goldilocks & the Three Bears. Cauley, Lorinda B., retold by. 32p. (ps-2). 1981. 14.95 (*0-399-20794-5*, Putnam) Putnam Pub Group.
—Goldilocks & the Three Bears. Cauley, Lorinda B., retold by. (ps-3). 1992. pap. 5.95 (*0-399-22326-6*, Sandcastle Bks) Putnam Pub Group.
—The Goodnight Circle. Lesser, Carolyn. LC 84-4501. 30p. (ps-3). 1984. 14.95 (*0-15-232158-6*, HB Juv Bks) HarBrace.
—Old MacDonald Had a Farm. 32p. (ps-3). 1989. 14.95 (*0-399-21628-6*, Putnam) Putnam Pub Group.
—The Trouble with Tyrannosaurus Rex. Cauley, Lorinda B. 32p. (ps-3). 1988. 14.95 (*0-15-290880-3*) HarBrace.

Cauper, David. The Story of Christopher Columbus & Our October 12th Holiday for Kindergarten Children. Cauper, Eunice. 16p. (Orig.). (gr. k-3). 1985. pap. 3.95 (*0-9617551-0-5*) E Cauper.
—The Story of the Pilgrims & Their Indian Friends: A Thanksgiving Story for Children. 5th ed. Cauper, Eunice. 15p. (gr. k). 1990. pap. 4.95 (*0-9617551-1-3*) E Cauper.

Cavallotti, Carolina. Don't Steal My Blocks! The Children's Storybook of Operation Desert Storm. Jain, Ash. 12p. (Orig.). (ps-3). 1991. pap. 2.95 (*0-9629992-1-0*) Arlington Pr.

Cavin, Diantha S. Scripture by Picture: Make Memorizing the Bible Fun & Easy. Cavin, Diantha S. 78p. (Orig.). (ps-6). 1992. pap. 10.95 (*0-9628012-3-2*) Dexter KS.

Cawley, Jacqueline. After-School Crafts. Dondiego, Barbara L. 144p. 1992. 22.95 (*0-8306-3868-7*, 4138); pap. 12.95 (*0-8306-3869-5*, 4138) TAB Bks.

Cazet, Denys. Annie, Bea, & Chi Chi Dolores: A School Day Alphabet. Maurer, Donna. LC 92-25104. 32p. (ps-k). 1993. 14.95 (*0-531-05467-5*); PLB 14.99 (*0-531-08617-8*) Orchard Bks Watts.
—Born in the Gravy. Cazet, Denys. LC 92-44523. 32p. (ps-1). 1993. 14.95 (*0-531-05488-8*); PLB 14.99 (*0-531-08638-0*) Orchard Bks Watts.
—Christmas Moon. Cazet, Denys. LC 84-10969. 32p. (ps-2). 1984. RSBE 13.95 (*0-02-717810-2*, Bradbury Pr) Macmillan Child Grp.
—Christmas Moon. Cazet, Denys. LC 87-37434. 32p. (ps-2). 1988. pap. 4.95 (*0-689-71259-6*, Aladdin) Macmillan Child Grp.
—Daydreams. Cazet, Denys. LC 89-48939. 32p. (ps-2). 1990. 14.95 (*0-531-05881-6*); PLB 14.99 (*0-531-08481-7*) Orchard Bks Watts.
—December Twenty-Fourth. Cazet, Denys. LC 86-8247. 32p. (ps-2). 1986. RSBE 13.95 (*0-02-717950-8*, Bradbury Pr) Macmillan Child Grp.
—A Fish in His Pocket. Cazet, Denys. LC 87-5462. 32p. (ps-2). 1987. 13.95 (*0-531-05713-5*); PLB 13.99 (*0-531-08313-6*) Orchard Bks Watts.
—Frosted Glass. Cazet, Denys. LC 86-26822. 32p. (ps-2). 1987. RSBE 13.95 (*0-02-717960-5*, Bradbury Pr) Macmillan Child Grp.
—Good Morning, Maxine! Cazet, Denys. LC 88-2889. 32p. (ps-1). 1989. RSBE 13.95 (*0-02-717940-0*, Bradbury Pr) Macmillan Child Grp.
—The Great Squirrel Uprising. Elish, Dan. LC 91-27145. 128p. (gr. 4 up). 1992. 14.95 (*0-531-05995-2*); lib. bdg. 14.99 (*0-531-08595-3*) Orchard Bks Watts.
—Great-uncle Felix. Cazet, Denys. LC 87-24682. 32p. (ps-1). 1988. 12.95 (*0-531-05750-X*); PLB 12.99 (*0-531-08350-0*) Orchard Bks Watts.
—I'm Not Sleepy. Cazet, Denys. LC 91-15958. 32p. (ps-1). 1992. 14.95 (*0-531-05898-0*); lib. bdg. 14.99 (*0-531-08498-1*) Orchard Bks Watts.
—Never Spit on Your Shoes. Cazet, Denys. LC 89-35164. 32p. (ps-1). 1993. pap. 5.95 (*0-531-07039-5*) Orchard Bks Watts.
—Saturday. Cazet, Denys. LC 87-2388. 64p. (gr. 1-4). 1988. pap. 3.95 (*0-689-71065-8*, Aladdin) Macmillan Child Grp.

CCC of America Staff. Ben-Hur, A Race to Glory. Urbide, Fernando & Engler, Dan. 35p. (Orig.). (ps-8). 1992. incl. video 21.95 (*1-56814-006-1*); pap. text ed. 4.95 book (*0-685-62399-8*) CCC of America.
—Bernadette: The Princess of Lourdes. Urbide, Fernando & Engler, Dan. 35p. (Orig.). (ps-6). 1990. incl. video 21.95 (*1-56814-004-5*); pap. text ed. 4.95 book (*0-685-62403-X*) CCC of America.
—Columbus: Adventures to the Edge of the World. Urbide, Fernando & Engler, Dan. 35p. (Orig.). (ps-7). 1991. incl. video 21.95 (*1-56814-005-3*); pap. text ed. 4.95 book (*0-685-62402-1*) CCC of America.
—The Day the Sun Danced: The True Story of Fatima. Father Robert J. Fox. 60p. (Orig.). (gr. k-6). 1989. incl. video 21.95 (*1-56814-001-0*); book 4.95 (*0-685-62401-3*) CCC of America.
—Francis: The Knight of Assisi. Nichols, Terri V. 61p. (Orig.). (ps-6). 1990. incl. video 21.95 (*1-56814-002-9*); pap. text ed. 4.95 book (*0-685-62404-8*) CCC of America.
—If You Love Me...Show Me! Family of the America's Staff & Sincro Communications Staff. 41p. (Orig.). (gr. 5-7). 1992. incl. video 21.95 (*1-56814-400-8*); pap. text ed. 6.95 book (*0-685-62406-4*) CCC of America.
—Nicholas: The Boy Who Became Santa. CCC of America Staff. 35p. (Orig.). (ps-4). 1989. incl. video 21.95 (*1-56814-003-7*); pap. text ed. 2.95 book (*0-685-62400-5*) CCC of America.
—The Odyssey: A Journey Back Home. Uribe, Fernando & Engler, Dan. 36p. (Orig.). 1992. pap. text ed. write for info. (*1-56814-007-X*) CCC of America.

Celestri, John. The Christian Crusader: The Quest Begins. rev. ed. Celestri, John. 80p. 1992. pap. 3.99 (*0-9634183-1-9*) CC Comics.

Cellini, Joseph. Canal Boat to Freedom. 2nd ed. Fall, Thomas. (gr. 4-6). pap. write for info. (*0-9636532-0-2*) Neversink Valley.

Chabela, Elizabeth H. Peregrinations: Adventures with the Green Parrot. Klein, Gerda W. LC 86-80966. 48p. (gr. 3-4). 1986. 12.95 (*0-9616699-0-X*); pap. 5.95 (*0-9616699-1-8*) CHB Goodyear Comm.

Chabrian, Deborah. Naomi's Geese. Evans, Sanford. LC 92-44109. (gr. 5 up). 1993. pap. 15.00 (*0-671-75623-0*, S&S BFYR) S&S Trade.

Chacon, Joe, jt. illus. see Boonthanakit, Ted.

Chacon, Rick. Big & Easy Art. Chacon, Rick. 32p. (ps-1). 1986. wkbk. 4.95 (*1-55734-074-9*) Tchr Create Mat.
—Grocery Bag Art: Farm. Chacon, Rick. 48p. (ps-3). 1986. wkbk. 5.95 (*1-55734-071-4*) Tchr Create Mat.
—Grocery Bag Art: Holidays. Chacon, Rick. 48p. (ps-3). 1986. wkbk. 5.95 (*1-55734-073-0*) Tchr Create Mat.
—I Can Capitalize. Carratello, Patricia. 32p. (gr. 3-6). 1983. wkbk. 4.95 (*1-55734-331-4*) Tchr Create Mat.
—I Can Give a Speech. Carratello, Patricia. 32p. (gr. 3-6). 1981. 4.95 (*1-55734-327-6*) Tchr Create Mat.
—I Can Punctuate. Carratello, Patricia. 32p. (gr. 3-6). 1983. wkbk. 4.95 (*1-55734-332-2*) Tchr Create Mat.
—I Can Write a Book Report. Carratello, Patricia. 32p. (gr. 3-6). 1985. wkbk. 4.95 (*1-55734-336-5*) Tchr Create Mat.
—I Can Write a Letter. Carratello, Patricia. 32p. (gr. 3-6). 1983. wkbk. 4.95 (*1-55734-333-0*) Tchr Create Mat.

—I Can Write a Paragraph. Carratello, Patricia. 32p. (gr. 3-6). 1981. wkbk. 4.95 (*1-55734-330-6*) Tchr Create Mat.
—I Can Write a Poem. Carratello, Patricia. 32p. (gr. 3-6). 1981. wkbk. 4.95 (*1-55734-326-8*) Tchr Create Mat.
—I Can Write a Research Paper. Carratello, Patricia. 32p. (gr. 3-6). 1985. wkbk. 4.95 (*1-55734-334-9*) Tchr Create Mat.
—I Can Write a Short Story. Carratello, Patricia. 32p. (gr. 3-6). 1985. wkbk. 4.95 (*1-55734-335-7*) Tchr Create Mat.
—Let's Investigate the Senses. Carratello, Patricia & Carratello, John. 48p. (gr. 1-4). 1984. wkbk. 5.95 (*1-55734-213-X*) Tchr Create Mat.

Chadwick, Peter, photos by. Bird. Burnie, David. LC 87-26441. 64p. (gr. 5 up). 1988. 15.00 (*0-394-89619-X*); lib. bdg. 15.99 (*0-394-99619-4*) Knopf Bks Yng Read.
—Tree. Burnie, David. LC 88-1572. 64p. (gr. 5 up). 1988. 15.00 (*0-394-89617-3*); lib. bdg. 15.99 (*0-394-99617-8*) Knopf Bks Yng Read.

Chadwick, Valerie A. Book of Mormon Story & Coloring Book. (Orig.). (gr. 3-6). Date not set. pap. 4.95 (*0-87579-702-4*) Deseret Bk.

Chaffee, Dan. Look up Look Down Look All Around El Morro National Monument. Hallett, Bill & Hallett, Jane. 32p. (Orig.). (gr. 3-8). 1988. pap. 3.45 activity bk. (*0-943087-04-X*) Look & See.

Chaffin, Donald. Fantastic Mr. Fox. Dahl, Roald. LC 74-118704. 72p. (gr. 3-6). 1986. 14.95 (*0-394-80497-X*); lib. bdg. 14.99 (*0-394-90497-4*) Knopf Bks Yng Read.

Chaffin, Maureen A. Elmer Bair's Story: 1899-1987, Vol. 1. Bair, Elmer O. Mangan, Velda B., ed. LC 87-80294. 484p. (gr. 9 up). 1987. 20.00 (*0-9618269-0-8*) Elmer Bair.

Chagoya, Enrique. Mr. Sugar Came to Town (La visita del Senor Azucar) Rohmer, Harriet & Gomez, Cruz, eds. Zubizarreta, Rosalma, tr. (SPA & ENG.). 32p. (ps-5). 1989. 13.95 (*0-89239-045-X*) Childrens Book Pr.

Chai, Florence. With Sound & Color: An Intermediate Chinese-English Reader. Chang, Florence C. LC 80-68257. 71p. (Orig.). (gr. 7-9). 1980. pap. 6.00x (wkbk. incl.) (*0-936620-01-3*) Ginkgo Hut.

Chaiko, Ted. The Tall Book of Bible Stories. reissued ed. Gibson, Katherine. LC 57-10952. 128p. (ps-3). 1957. 9.95 (*0-06-021935-1*) HarpC Child Bks.

Chakravarty, Biswaranjan. The Story of Ramakrishna. Smaranananda, Swami. (Orig.). (gr. k-5). 1976. pap. 1.95 (*0-87481-168-6*) Vedanta Pr.
—Story of Sarada Devi. Smaranananda. 36p. (Orig.). (gr. k-4). 1987. pap. 1.95 (*0-87481-229-1*, Pub. by Advaita Ashram IA) Vedanta Pr.
—Tales from Ramakrishna. Ramakrishna, Swami. Ray, Irene R. & Gupta, Mallika C.retold by. 54p. (Orig.). (gr. 1-5). 1975. pap. 1.95 (*0-87481-152-X*) Vedanta Pr.

Chakravarty, Pranab. Story of Our Rivers: Book II. Valiappa, Al. (gr. 1-9). 1979. pap. 2.50 (*0-89744-184-2*) Auromere.

Chakravarty, Purhachandra. Ramakrishna for Children. Vishwashrayananda, Swami. Bagchi, Santosh, tr. from BEN. 40p. (gr. 3-6). 1975. pap. 1.95 (*0-87481-164-3*) Vedanta Pr.

Chalk, Gary. The Boy Who Cried Wolf! Schecter, Ellen, retold by. (gr. 4 up). 1994. 10.95 (*0-553-09043-7*) Bantam.
—Mossflower. Jacques, Brian. LC 88-17921. 432p. (gr. 5 up). 1988. 16.95 (*0-399-21549-2*, Philomel Bks) Putnam Pub Group.
—Salamandastron: A Tale from Red Wall. Jacques, Brian. 400p. (gr. 5 up). 1993. 17.95 (*0-399-21992-7*, Philomel Bks) Putnam Pub Group.
—Yankee Doodle. Chalk, Gary. LC 92-53482. 48p. (gr. k-3). 1993. 14.95 (*1-56458-202-7*) Dorling Kindersley.

Chalmers, Mary. A Christmas Story. Chalmers, Mary. LC 56-8143. 24p. (ps-1). 1962. Repr. of 1956 ed. PLB 12.89 (*0-06-021191-1*) HarpC Child Bks.
—Easter Parade. Chalmers, Mary. LC 87-45277. 32p. (ps-1). 1988. PLB 11.89 (*0-06-021233-0*) HarpC Child Bks.
—Easter Parade. Chalmers, Mary. LC 87-45277. 32p. (ps-1). 1990. pap. 4.95 (*0-06-443219-X*, Trophy) HarpC Child Bks.
—Marigold & Grandma on the Town. Calmenson, Stephanie. LC 89-31147. 64p. (gr. k-3). 1994. 14.00 (*0-06-020812-0*); PLB 13.89 (*0-06-020813-9*) HarpC Child Bks.
—Secret Language. Nordstrom, Ursula. LC 60-7701. 192p. (gr. 3-5). 1960. PLB 12.89 (*0-06-024576-X*) HarpC Child Bks.
—Take a Nap, Harry. Chalmers, Mary. LC 89-77655. 32p. (ps-1). 1991. PLB 13.89 (*0-06-021244-6*) HarpC Child Bks.
—Three to Get Ready. Boegehold, Betty. LC 62-8042. (gr. k-3). 1965. PLB 13.89 (*0-06-020551-2*) HarpC Child Bks.
—Throw a Kiss, Harry. Chalmers, Mary. LC 89-49064. 32p. (ps-2). 1990. 12.95 (*0-06-021246-2*) HarpC Child Bks.
—When Will It Snow? Hoff, Syd. LC 64-16657. 32p. (gr. k-3). 1971. HarpC Child Bks.

Chamberlain, Margaret. Angela's New Sister. Mutarasso, Janet. 24p. 1988. 11.95 (*0-521-35640-7*) Cam. ridge U Pr.
—Best Thing of All. Thomson, Pat. 32p. (gr. 1-4). 1990. 13.95 (*0-575-04578-7*, Pub. by Gollancz UK) Trafalgar.

—The Best Thing of All. Thomson, Pat. 32p. (ps-1). 1993. pap. 6.95 (0-575-05159-0, Pub. by Gollancz UK) Trafalgar.
—The Birthday Burglar & a Very Wicked Head Mistress. large type ed. Mahy, Margaret. 184p. 1991. 13.95 (0-7451-1407-5, Galaxy Child Lrg Print) Chivers N Amer.
—The Birthday Burglar: And A Very Wicked Headmistress. Mahy, Margaret. LC 92-43777. 144p. (gr. 5 up). 1993. pap. 4.95 (0-688-12470-4, Pub. by Beech Tree Bks) Morrow.
—A Busy Day for a Good Grandmother. Mahy, Margaret. LC 93-77331. 32p. (ps-3). 1993. SBE 14.95g (0-689-50595-7, M K McElderry) Macmillan Child Grp.
—The Little Christmas Fold-Out Book. 28p. (ps-4). 1991. accordian bk. 4.99 (0-7459-2121-3) Lion USA.
—Miss Butterpat Goes Wild. Yorke, Malcolm. LC 93-20204. 32p. (gr. 1-5). 1993. 10.95 (1-56458-200-0) Dorling Kindersley.
—Mr. Scatter's Magic Spell. Vivelo, Jackie. LC 93-642. 32p. (gr. 2-5). 1993. 10.95 (1-56458-201-9) Dorling Kindersley.
—A Piece of String Is a Wonderful Thing. Hindley, Judy. LC 92-53137. 32p. (gr. k-3). 1993. 14.95 (1-56402-147-5) Candlewick Pr.
—The Pirates' Mixed-up Voyage. Mahy, Margaret. LC 92-3931. 192p. (gr. 4-8). 1993. 13.99 (0-8037-1350-9) Dial Bks Young.
—The Playground. rev. ed. Wilmer, Diane. 32p. (gr. k-2). 1990. Repr. of 1986 ed. PLB 10.50 (1-878363-10-7) Forest Hse.
—Ritchie F. Dweebly Thunders On. Yorke, Malcolm. LC 93-5003. 1994. write for info. (1-56458-199-3) Dorling Kindersley.
—Tattercoats. Greaves, Margaret. 32p. (ps-2). 1990. 13.95 (0-517-58026-8) Crown Bks Yng Read.

Chamberlain, Sarah. Friendly Beasts: A Traditional Christmas Carol. LC 91-2115. 24p. (ps-2). 1991. 13.95 (0-525-44773-3, DCB) Dutton Child Bks.
—My Yellow Ball. Lillegard, Dee. LC 92-27003. (gr. k-3). 1993. 12.99 (0-525-45078-5, DCB) Dutton Child Bks.

Chambers, Alma, et al. Church Humor Digest. Graham, Billy, et al. Ingram, William R. & Goodman, Charles, eds. 106p. (Orig.). 1991. pap. 7.95 (0-916693-15-5) Castle Bks.

Chambers, Margaret. Why Can't You Grow Up? Matarasso, Janet. LC 85-25539. 24p. (ps-2). 1986. 11.95 (0-521-32125-5) Cambridge U Pr.

Chambless-Rigie, Jane. Uncle Wiggily to the Rescue. Garis, Howard R. 32p. (ps-2). 1987. pap. 1.95 (0-448-34305-3, G&D) Putnam Pub Group.

Chambliss, Maxie. Andrew's Amazing Monsters. Berlan, Kathryn H. LC 91-39131. 32p. (ps-2). 1993. SBE 13.95 (0-689-31739-5, Atheneum Child Bk) Macmillan Child Grp.
—Come & Play, Hippo. Thaler, Mike. LC 87-33489. 64p. (gr. k-3). 1991. 14.00 (0-06-026176-5); PLB 13.89 (0-06-026177-3) HarpC Child Bks.
—Come & Play, Hippo. Thaler, Mike. LC 87-33489. 64p. (ps-3). 1993. pap. 3.50 (0-06-444165-2, Trophy) HarpC Child Bks.
—Dad's Car Wash. Sutherland, Harry A. LC 87-15183. 32p. (ps-1). 1988. RSBE 13.95 (0-689-31335-7, Atheneum Child Bk) Macmillan Child Grp.
—Dad's Car Wash. Sutherland, Harry A. LC 93-28734. 32p. (gr. k-3). 1994. pap. 4.95 (0-689-71807-1, Aladdin) Macmillan Child Grp.
—Eggs over Easy. Kenah, Katharine. 96p. (gr. 2-5). 1993. 13.99 (0-525-45071-8, DCB) Dutton Child Bks.
—Fat Fanny, Beanpole Bertha, & the Boys. Porte, Barbara A. LC 90-7686. 112p. (gr. 3-5). 1991. 14.95 (0-531-05928-6); PLB 14.99 (0-531-08528-7) Orchard Bks Watts.
—Favorite Fairy Tales Told in England. Haviland, Virginia, compiled by. LC 93-29707. 1994. write for info. (0-688-12595-6, Pub. by Beech Tree Bks) Morrow.
—The Giggle Book. Calmenson, Stephanie. LC 87-9085. 48p. (ps-3). 1987. 5.95 (0-8193-1140-5) Parents.
—Go Away Monsters, Lickety Split! Cooney, Nancy E. 32p. (ps-1). 1990. 13.95 (0-399-21935-8, Putnam) Putnam Pub Group.
—I Can't Get My Turtle to Move. O'Donnell, Elizabeth L. LC 88-22046. 32p. (ps-1). 1989. 11.95 (0-688-07323-9); PLB 11.88 (0-688-07324-7, Morrow Jr Bks) Morrow Jr Bks.
—I Know an Old Lady. 1987. pap. 6.99 incl. audiocassette (0-553-45901-5) Bantam.
—The Little Bunny. Calmenson, Stephanie. (gr. 2-6). 1986. 4.95 (0-671-62079-7, Little Simon) S&S Trade.
—The Mother's Day Sandwich. Wynot, Jillian. LC 89-35649. 32p. (ps-2). 1990. 14.95 (0-531-05857-3); PLB 14.99 (0-531-08457-4) Orchard Bks Watts.
—One Up, One Down. Snyder, Carol. LC 93-36282. 1994. 15.95 (0-689-31828-6, Atheneum) Macmillan.
—Ten Furry Monsters. Calmenson, Stephanie. LC 84-4998. 48p. (ps-3). 1985. 4.95 (0-8193-1128-6) Parents.
—We're Going on a Trip. Loomie, Christine. LC 93-17592. 1994. write for info. (0-688-10173-9); PLB write for info. (0-688-10172-0) Morrow Jr Bks.
—When Aunt Lucy Rode A Mule & Other Stories. Porte, Barbara A. LC 93-4874. 1994. write for info. (0-531-06816-1); PLB write for info. (0-531-08666-6) Orchard Bks Watts.

—When Grandma Almost Fell off the Mountain & Other Stories. Porte, Barbara A. LC 91-41174. 32p. (ps-2). 1993. 14.95 (0-531-05965-0); PLB 14.99 (0-531-08565-1) Orchard Bks Watts.
—Where's Rufus? Calmenson, Stephanie. LC 88-4092. 48p. (ps-3). 1988. 5.95 (0-8193-1177-4) Parents.
—You Cheat! Gilson, Jamie. LC 91-13886. 64p. (gr. 1-4). 1992. SBE 13.95 (0-02-735993-X, Bradbury Pr) Macmillan Child Grp.

Chambliss, Maxie & Iosa, Ann W. Gregory & Mr. Grump. Leonard, Marcia. Brook, Bonnie, ed. 24p. (ps-1). 1990. 5.95 (0-671-70406-0); lib. bdg. 9.98 (0-671-70402-8) Silver Pr.
—Hannah the Hamster Hunter. Leonard, Marcia. Brook, Bonnie, ed. 24p. (ps-1). 1990. 5.95 (0-671-70404-4); lib. bdg. 9.98 (0-671-70399-4) Silver Pr.
—How Did That Happen? Series, 4 vols. Leonard, Marcia. 96p. (ps-1). 1990. Set. 23.80 (0-671-31235-9); Set. 14.85s.p. (0-685-37312-6); Set. PLB 39.92 (0-671-31234-0); Set. PLB 29.94s.p. (0-685-37313-4) Silver Pr.
—Jeffrey Lee, Future Fireman. Leonard, Marcia. Brook, Bonnie, ed. LC 90-31299. 24p. (ps-1). 1990. 5.95 (0-671-70407-9); lib. bdg. 9.98 (0-671-70403-6) Silver Pr.

Champlin, Dale. Down by the Bay Big Book. (ps-2). 1988. pap. text ed. 14.00 (0-922053-02-2) N Edge Res.
—The Wheels on the Bus Big Book. (ps-2). 1988. pap. text ed. 14.00 (0-922053-15-4) N Edge Res.

Chan, Anthony. Grandma's Band. Bowles, Brad. 48p. (gr. k-4). 1989. PLB 14.95 (0-88045-112-2) Stemmer Hse.

Chan, Barbara J. Kid Pix Around the World: A Computer & Activities Book. Chan, Barbara J. LC 92-46141. 1993. pap. 12.95 (0-201-62226-2) Addison-Wesley.

Chan, Bonnie. Very Shy. Hazen, Barbara S. LC 81-6809. 32p. (ps-3). 1983. 16.95 (0-89885-067-3) Human Sci Pr.

Chan, Harvey. Amazing Investigations: Twins. Ingram, Jay. (gr. 3 up). 1989. pap. 12.95 (0-671-66263-5) S&S Trade.
—Roses Sing on New Snow: A Delicious Tale. Yee, Paul. LC 91-755. 32p. (ps-3). 1992. RSBE 13.95 (0-02-793622-8, Macmillan Child Bk) Macmillan Child Grp.

Chan, Peter. The Adventure of the Wandering Wolves in Vulcan's Vent. Kelly, Karla, et al. Crosby, Harriet, ed. 40p. (Orig.). (gr. 1-6). 1993. pap. 6.95 (1-883871-01-8) Nature Co.

Chan, Shirley. Mr. Silver & Mrs. Gold. Fink, Dale B. LC 79-15924. 32p. (ps-3). 1980. 16.95 (0-87705-447-9) Human Sci Pr.

Chan, Wilson. Why Does That Man Have Such a Big Nose? Quinsey, Mary Beth. LC 85-63760. 32p. (Orig.). (ps-1). 1986. lib. bdg. 16.95 (0-943990-25-4); pap. 5.95 (0-943990-24-6) Parenting Pr.

Chance, Tony J. Tales from Perrault. Perrault, Charles. Lawrence, Ann, tr. 118p. (gr. 3-7). 1989. jacketed 18.95 (0-19-274533-6) OUP.

Chandler, Alton, jt. illus. see Still, Wayne A.

Chandler, Alton, et al. Black Women: A Salute to Black Inventors. rev. ed. Chandler, Ann. Ivery, Evelyn L., ed. Chandler, Alton, intro. by. 24p. (gr. 3-7). 1992. pap. text ed. 1.50 (1-877804-06-1) Chandler White.
—Communication: A Salute to Black Inventors. rev. ed. Howell, Ann C. Ivery, Evelyn L., ed. Chandler, Alton, intro. by. 24p. (gr. 3-7). 1992. pap. text ed. 1.50 (1-877804-05-3) Chandler White.
—Old West: A Salute to Black Inventors. rev. ed. Howell, Ann C. Ivery, Evelyn L., ed. Chandler, Alton, pref. by. 24p. (gr. 3-7). 1992. pap. text ed. 1.50 (1-877804-03-7); tchr's. guide 1.75 (1-877804-07-X) Chandler White.
—Safety: A Salute to Black Inventors. rev. ed. Howell, Ann C. Ivery, Evelyn L., ed. Chandler, Alton H., intro. by. 24p. (gr. 3-7). 1992. pap. text ed. 1.50 (1-877804-02-9) Chandler White.
—Transportation - Food - Safety - Old West - Working Easier - Communication - Black Women: A Salute to Black Inventors. rev. ed. Howell, Ann C. Ivery, Evelyn L., ed. 24p. (gr. 3-7). 1992. pap. text ed. 10.50 (1-877804-10-X) Chandler White.
—Working Easier: A Salute to Black Inventors. rev. ed. Howell, Ann C. Ivery, Evelyn L., ed. Chandler, Alton, intro. by. 24p. (gr. 3-7). 1992. pap. text ed. 1.50 (1-877804-04-5) Chandler White.

Chandler, Alton H., et al. Black Science Working Easier: Coloring - Learning Activities. Howell, Ann C. & Massey, Grace C. Ivery, Evelyn L., ed. Chandler, Alton, intro. by. (Orig.). (gr. 1-6). 1987. pap. text ed. 1.50 (0-685-26058-5) Chandler White.

Chandler, Jean. The Best Color of All. Dykstra, Mary A. 24p. (ps-k). 1993. 9.00 (0-307-74816-2, 64816, Golden Pr) Western Pub.
—My First Golden Dictionary. Thoburn, Tina, compiled by. LC 87-81750. 24p. 1988. write for info. (0-307-11992-0, Pub. by Golden Bks) Western Pub.
—The Poky Little Puppy. Lowrey, Janette S. Hansen, Rosanna, adapted by. 14p. (ps-k). 1992. bds. write for info. (0-307-12333-2, 12333, Golden Pr) Western Pub.
—The Velveteen Rabbit. Williams, Margery. 1991. Incl. book, cass. & toy rabbit. 14.99 (0-517-66810-6) Outlet Bk Co.

Chandler, Karen. Edgar Allan Poe's Tales of Terror. Poe, Edgar Allan. Martin, Les, adapted by. LC 90-52926. 96p. (Orig.). (gr. 2-7). 1991. lib. bdg. 5.99 (0-679-91046-8); pap. 2.95 (0-679-81046-3) Random Bks Yng Read.

Chandrasekhar, Aruna. Oliver & the Oil Spill. Chandrasekhar, Aruna. Thatch, Nancy R., ed. Melton, David, intro. by. LC 91-3340. 26p. (gr. k-4). 1991. PLB 14.95 (0-933849-33-8) Landmark Edns.

Chang, Heidi. Elaine & the Flying Frog. Chang, Heidi. LC 90-33721. 64p. (Orig.). (gr. 2-4). 1991. PLB 6.99 (0-679-90870-6); pap. 2.50 (0-679-80870-1) Random Bks Yng Read.
—Henry & the Boy Who Thought Numbers Were Fleas. Kaplan, Marjorie. LC 90-43852. 80p. (gr. 2-4). 1991. SBE 12.95 (0-02-749351-2, Four Winds) Macmillan Child Grp.

Chang, Phillip. The Beautiful Chick. Rausiri, Supa. Rodriguez, Gloria F., ed. Pinta, Thanom, tr. (gr. k-2). 1979. pap. 3.00x (0-686-26620-X, Pub. by New Day Pub PI) Cellar.
—The Poor Lizard. Kemvichanuvat, Cherdchai. Rodriguez, Gloria F., ed. Pinta, Thanom, tr. (gr. k-3). 1979. pap. 3.50 (0-686-26621-8, Pub. by New Day Pub PI) Cellar.

Chang, Shou-Jen. Believe It or Not: An Anthology of Ancient Tales Retold. Chang, Florence C. LC 80-68258. 80p. (gr. 10-12). 1980. pap. 6.25x (wkbk. incl.) (0-936620-02-1) Ginkgo Hut.

Chang, Tao-Yuan. Maomao & Mimi. Chang, Florence C. LC 81-80784. 80p. (Orig.). (gr. 5-6). 1981. pap. 4.15x incl. exercises (0-936620-05-6) Ginkgo Hut.
—Puppy's Tail. Chang, Florence C. LC 81-82176. 72p. (Orig.). (gr. 1-2). 1981. pap. 4.15x incl. exercises (0-936620-06-4) Ginkgo Hut.

Channell, Jim. Animals in the Cold. Carwardine, Mark. Young, Richard G., ed. LC 89-32827. 45p. (gr. 3-5). 1989. PLB 14.60 (0-944483-26-7) Garrett Ed Corp.

Channell, Jim & Maddison, Kevin. Dinosaur & Other Prehistoric Animal Factfinder. Benton, Michael. LC 92-53119. 256p. (Orig.). (gr. 4-8). 1992. pap. 12.95 (1-85697-802-8) Kingfisher Bks.

Channell, Jim, et al. The Dinosaur Encyclopedia. Benton, Michael J. Barish, Wendy, ed. 192p. (gr. 3-7). 1984. (S&S BFYR); pap. 7.95 (0-671-51046-0, S&S BFYR) S&S Trade.

Chanowitz, Elise. The World's Strangest "True" Ghost Stories. Macklin, John. LC 89-26125. 96p. 1990. 12.95 (0-8069-5784-0) Sterling.
—World's Strangest "True" Ghost Stories. Macklin, John. LC 89-26125. 96p. (gr. 4 up). 1991. pap. 3.95 (0-8069-5785-9) Sterling.

Chansler, Jim. Zacchaeus. Jenkins, Lee. Greeno, Ron, frwd. by. 32p. (Orig.). (ps-3). 1993. pap. 6.95 (1-883952-03-4) Hse of Steno.

Chapin, Patrick O. The Green Team: The Adventures of Mitch & Molly. O'Connor, Karen. LC 92-24643. 80p. (Orig.). (gr. 1-4). 1993. pap. 4.95 (0-570-04726-9) Concordia.
—The Water Detectives: The Adventures of Mitch & Molly. O'Connor, Karen. LC 92-24649. 80p. (Orig.). (gr. 1-4). 1993. pap. 4.95 (0-570-04727-7) Concordia.

Chapman, Bettina B. Characters in Mythology. Farrell, William R. 60p. (gr. k-10). 1992. spiral bdg. 9.25 (0-939507-38-2, B423) Amer Classical.

Chapman, Donna & Doege, Erwin. Ozark Tales & Superstitions. Steele, Phillip W. LC 82-22425. 96p. (gr. 6 up). 1983. pap. 5.95 (0-88289-404-8) Pelican.

Chapman, Gaynor. Wheels: First Readers. Harding, Jacqueline. 28p. (ps-k). 1992. 3.50 (0-7214-1483-4) Ladybird Bks.

Chapman, Shirley. Kathryn's Mouse. Anderson, Myra. 48p. (gr. k-6). 1991. 16.95 (0-9625620-4-1) DOT Garnet.

Chapman, Wendy. Lucinda the Late. Ross, Eileen. LC 92-14092. 32p. (ps-2). Date not set. 11.95 (1-56065-164-4) Capstone Pr. Postponed.

Chappell, David. Five Things God Cannot Do. 16p. (gr. k-6). 1989. pap. text ed. 4.25 (1-55976-129-6) CEF Press.
—G-O-S-P-E-L. Turnwall, Ruth. 9p. (gr. k-6). 1982. visualized song 2.99 (3-90117-024-3) CEF Press.

Chappell, David & Bates, Steve. Are You Afraid. Kraft, Victoreen. 20p. (gr. k-6). 1983. pap. text ed. 4.25 (1-55976-139-3) CEF Press.

Chappell, David, jt. illus. see Banse, Charles.

Chappell, Warren. The Dark Frigate. rev. ed. Hawes, Charles B. (gr. 7 up). 1971. 18.95 (0-316-35096-6, Joy St Bks) Little.
—Wolf Story. McCleery, William. LC 87-25977. 82p. (gr. 1-6). 1988. Repr. of 1947 ed. PLB 15.00 (0-208-02191-4, Linnet) Shoe String.

Chappick, Joseph. Junior High Champs. Perkins, Thornton. 49p. (Orig.). (gr. 6-9). 1989. pap. 3.00 (0-9623407-0-7) NVEM.

Charles, Donald. El Libro de Ejercicios de Gato Galano (Calico Cat's Exercise Book) Charles, Donald. Kratky, Lada, tr. from ENG. LC 82-9640. (SPA.). 32p. (ps-3). 1984. pap. 3.95 (0-516-53457-2) Childrens.

Charles, Donald. El Ano de Gato Galano (Calico Cat's Year) Charles, Donald. Kratky, Lada, tr. from GER. (SPA.). 32p. (ps-3). 1984. PLB 15.00 (0-516-33461-1); pap. 3.95 (0-516-53461-0) Childrens.
—Blue Bug's Safety Book. Poulet, Virginia. LC 72-8348. 32p. (gr. k-3). 1973. PLB 15.00 (0-516-03419-7) Childrens.

—Blue Bug's Vegetable Garden. Poulet, Virginia. LC 73-8896. 32p. (gr. k-3). 1973. PLB 15.00 (0-516-03421-9) Childrens.

—Calico Cat at the Zoo. Charles, Donald. LC 80-25380. 32p. (gr. 3). 1981. PLB 15.00 (0-516-03443-X) Childrens.

—Calico Cat Looks at Shapes. Charles, Donald. LC 75-12947. 32p. (ps-3). 1975. PLB 15.00 (0-516-03436-7) Childrens.

—Calico Cat's Sunny Smile. Charles, Donald. LC 90-37981. 32p. (ps-3). 1990. PLB 15.00 (0-516-03482-0) Childrens.

—Count on Calico Cat. Charles, Donald. LC 74-8007. 32p. (ps-3). 1974. PLB 15.00 (0-516-03435-9) Childrens.

—Cuenta con Gato Galano (Count on Calico Cat) Charles, Donald. Kratky, Lada, tr. from ENG. LC 74-8007. (SPA.). 32p. (ps-3). 1984. PLB 15.00 (0-516-33479-4); pap. 3.95 (0-516-53479-3) Childrens.

—Gordito, Gordon Gato Galano: (Fat, Fat Calico Cat) Charles, Donald. LC 77-7154. (SPA.). 32p. (ps-2). 1988. PLB 15.00 (0-516-33456-5); pap. 3.95 (0-516-53456-4) Childrens.

—Shaggy Dog's Birthday. Charles, Donald. LC 86-9566. 32p. (ps-3). 1986. PLB 15.00 (0-516-03576-2) Childrens.

—Shaggy Dog's Tall Tale. Charles, Donald. LC 79-26493. 32p. (ps-3). 1980. PLB 15.00 (0-516-03616-5) Childrens.

Charlet, James D. North Carolina: Our People, Places, & Past Student Workbook. Charlet, James D., et al. 300p. 1988. wkbk. 49.95 (0-935911-13-8) Cornucop Pub.

Charlip, Remy. David's Little Indian. Brown, Margaret W. 48p. (gr. 2-5). 1989. Repr. of 1954 ed. 10.95 (0-929077-02-4, Hopscotch Bks); PLB 10.95 (0-317-92547-4, Hopscotch Bks) Watermark Inc.

—The Dead Bird. Brown, Margaret W. LC 84-43124. 48p. (gr. k-3). 1989. Repr. of 1958 ed. PLB 11.89 (0-06-020758-2) HarpC Child Bks.

—Fortunately. Charlip, Remy. LC 80-36956. 48p. (ps-3) 1980. Repr. of 1964 ed. RSBE 14.95 (0-02-718100-6, Four Winds) Macmillan Child Grp.

—Fortunately. Charlip, Remy. LC 92-22794. 48p. (ps-3). 1993. pap. 4.95 (0-689-71660-5, Aladdin) Macmillan Child Grp.

—Four Fur Feet. Brown, Margaret W. 48p. (gr. 1-3). 1989. Repr. of 1961 ed. 13.95 (0-929077-03-2, Hopscotch Bks); PLB 12.95 (0-317-92548-2, Hopscotch Bks) Watermark Inc.

—The Tree Angel. Martin, Judith & Charlip, Remy. 40p. (gr. k-3). 1992. pap. 3.25 (0-440-40725-7, YB) Dell.

Charlip, Remy & Maraslis, Demetra. The Seeing Stick. Yolen, Jane. LC 75-6946. 32p. (gr. k up). 1975. PLB 14.89 (0-690-00596-2, Crowell Jr Bks) HarpC Child Bks.

Charlot, Jean. And Now Miguel. Krumgold, Joseph. LC 53-8415. 245p. (gr. 5 up). 1987. 15.00 (0-690-09118-4, Crowell Jr Bks) HarpC Child Bks.

—And Now Miguel. Krumgold, Joseph. LC 53-8415. 245p. (gr. 5 up). 1984. pap. 3.95 (0-06-440143-X, Trophy) HarpC Child Bks.

—The Boy Who Could Do Anything: And Other Mexican Folktales. Brenner, Anita. LC 92-3903. 128p. (gr. 3-7). 1992. Repr. of 1942 ed. lib. bdg. 17.50 (0-208-02353-4, Pub. by Linnet) Shoe String.

—A Child's Good Night Book. Brown, Margaret W. LC 84-43123. 32p. (ps-2). 1986. pap. 4.95 (0-06-443114-2, Trophy) HarpC Child Bks.

—A Child's Good Night Book. Brown, Margaret W. LC 91-45340. 32p. (ps-3). 1992. 10.00 (0-06-021028-1); PLB 9.89 (0-06-020752-3) HarpC Child Bks.

—The Corn Grows Ripe. Rhoads, Dorothy. LC 92-24888. (gr. 8-12). 1993. 4.99 (0-14-036313-0, Puffin) Puffin Bks.

—Secret of the Andes. Clark, Ann N. (gr. 3-7). 1976. pap. 4.99 (0-14-030926-8, Puffin) Puffin Bks.

—Secret of the Andes. Clark, Ann N. (gr. 4-8). 1952. pap. 14.99 (0-670-62975-8) Viking Child Bks.

—Sneakers: Seven Stories about a Cat. Brown, Margaret W. (ps-3). 1985. PLB 14.89 (0-06-020767-1) HarpC Child Bks.

Charlot, Jean, et al. Newbery Award Library II:...And Now Miguel - Bridge to Terabithia - Sarah, Plain & Tall - The Wheel on the School, 4 bks. Krumgold, Joseph, et al. (gr. 4-6). 1988. Set. pap. 11.95 (0-06-440277-0, Trophy) HarpC Child Bks.

Charlton, Michael. Mandy & the Hospital. Coles, Allison. 28p. (ps up) 1985. 3.95 (0-88110-269-5) EDC.

—Michael & the Sea. Coles, Allison. 28p. (ps up). 1985. 3.95 (0-88110-268-7) EDC.

—Michael in the Dark. Coles, Allison. 28p. (ps up). 1985. 3.95 (0-88110-267-9) EDC.

Charrier, Michel. Rois Mages. Tournier, Michel. (FRE.). 160p. (gr. 5-10). 1978. pap. 7.95 (2-07-033280-2) Schoenhof.

Chartier, Norm. Big Bird's Rhyming Book. Sesame Street Staff. LC 78-68790. (ps-3). 1979. 7.95 (0-394-84140-9) Random Bks Yng Read.

Chartier, Normand. All Stuck Up. Hayward, Linda. LC 89-34675. 32p. (Orig.). (ps-1). 1990. PLB 7.99 (0-679-90216-3); pap. 2.95 (0-679-80216-9) Random Bks Yng Read.

—Boris the Boring Boar. Jackson, Ellen. LC 91-48670. 32p. (gr. k-3). 1992. RSBE 14.95 (0-02-747662-6, Macmillan Child Bk) Macmillan Child Grp.

—Grover Goes to School. Elliott, Dan. LC 81-15398. 40p. (ps-3). 1992. pap. 2.99 (0-679-82397-2) Random Bks Yng Read.

—Grover Learns to Read. Elliott, Dan. LC 84-27692. 40p. (ps-3). 1985. 4.95 (0-394-87498-6) Random Bks Yng Read.

—Grover Learns to Read. Elliott, Dan. LC 84-27692. 40p. (ps-3). 1993. pap. 2.99 (0-679-83949-6) Random Bks Yng Read.

—Grover's Lucky Jacket. Hautzig, Deborah. LC 89-30102. 40p. (ps-3). 1989. PLB 6.99 (0-679-90077-2); pap. 4.95 (0-679-80077-8) Random Bks Yng Read.

—January Brings the Snow. Coleridge, Sara. (ps-3). 1990. (Little Simon); pap. 2.25 (0-671-72338-3) S&S Trade.

—Jingle Bells. 1986. pap. 2.25 (0-671-63022-9, Little Simon) S&S Trade.

—Keep Looking! Selsam, Millicent E. & Hunt, Joyce. LC 88-1416. 32p. (gr. k-3). 1989. RSBE 14.95 (0-02-781840-3, Macmillan Child Bk) Macmillan Child Grp.

—McCrephy's Field. Myers, Christopher A. & Myers, Lynne B. 32p. (gr. 2-5). 1991. 14.45 (0-395-53807-6, Sandpiper) HM.

—Open Sesame. Ross, Anna. LC 91-67671. 14p. (ps-k). 1992. bds. 3.99 (0-679-83063-4) Random Bks Yng Read.

—Oscar's Rotten Birthday. Elliott, Dan. LC 81-2398. 40p. (ps-3). 1992. pap. 2.99 (0-679-82400-6) Random Bks Yng Read.

—Pack 109. Thaler, Mike. LC 87-30493. 48p. (ps-2). 1988. 9.95 (0-525-44393-2, 0966-290, DCB) Dutton Child Bks.

—Pack 109. Thaler, Mike. (gr. k-3). 1993. pap. 3.25 (0-14-036548-6, Puffin) Puffin Bks.

—Silly Fred. Wagner, Karen. LC 88-22620. 32p. (gr. k-3). 1989. RSBE 13.95 (0-02-792280-4, Macmillan Child Bk) Macmillan Child Grp.

Chartier, Normand, et al. The Sesame Street Treasury: Featuring Jim Henson's Sesame Street Muppets. Alexander, Liza, et al. LC 93-8326. Date not set. write for info. (0-679-84655-7); PLB write for info. (0-679-94655-1) Random.

Chartler, Normand. Happy Mother's Day. Hautzig, Deborah. LC 88-14002. 32p. (Orig.). (ps-1). 1989. PLB 7.99 (0-394-92204-2); pap. 2.95 (0-394-82204-8) Random Bks Yng Read.

Chase, Andra. Bailey's Birthday. Happy, Elizabeth. LC 93-32519. 32p. (gr. 1-4). 1994. 16.95 (1-55942-059-6, 7658); video, tchr's. guide & storybook 79.95 (1-55942-062-6, 9377) Marshfilm.

—BJ Bernard Grows up. Duckworth, Marion. 28p. (ps-k). 1993. 4.99 (0-7847-0065-6, 24-03845) Standard Pub.

—Celebrate the Birth of Jesus. Hayes, Theresa. 16p. (gr. 3-6). 1992. wkbk. 7.99 (0-87403-930-4, 14-03502) Standard Pub.

—God Keeps His Promises. Odor, Ruth S. LC 91-67212. 32p. (gr. 5-7). 1992. saddle-stitch 5.99 (0-87403-931-2, 24-03561) Standard Pub.

—Jomo & Mata. Chase, Alyssa. LC 93-25206. 32p. (gr. 1-4). 1993. 16.95 (1-55942-051-0, 7656); video, tchr's. guide & storybook 79.95 (1-55942-054-5, 9375) Marshfilm.

—Where Are We Going Today? Tester, Sylvia. 12p. (ps). 1992. deluxe ed. 4.99 (0-87403-996-7, 24-03116) Standard Pub.

Chase, Jan B. The Golden Song. Chase, Jan B. 32p. (gr. k-3). 1993. 16.95 (1-880158-01-9) J N Townsend.

Chase, John. Louisiana Purchase: An American Story. Chase, John. 96p. 1991. 4.95 (0-911116-24-9); pap. 8.95 (0-911116-68-0) Pelican.

—The Pirate Lafitte & the Battle of New Orleans. Tallant, Robert. 192p. (gr. 5 up). 1992. pap. 7.95 (0-88289-931-7) Pelican.

Chase, Judith. Fabric of Faith. Wezeman, Phyllis Vos & Wiessner, Colleen A. 47p. (Orig.). (gr. 4-8). 1990. pap. 7.50 (1-877871-04-4) Ed Ministries.

Chase, Victoria. Princess Gorilla & a New Kind of Water. Aardema, Verna. LC 86-32888. 32p. (ps-3). 1988. 10.95 (0-8037-0412-7); PLB 10.89 (0-8037-0413-5) Dial Bks Young.

—Slugs. Greenberg, David. LC 82-10017. 32p. (gr. k-5). 1983. 13.95 (0-316-32658-5, Joy St Bks); pap. 4.95i (0-316-32659-3, Joy St Bks) Little.

Chast, Roz. Gabby the Shrew. Olsen, Alfa-Betty & Efron, Marshall. LC 92-31902. 1994. lib. bdg. write for info. (0-679-94467-2) Random.

—Now Everybody Really Hates Me. Martin, Jane R. & Marx, Patricia. LC 92-13075. 32p. (gr. k-3). 1993. 14.00 (0-06-021293-4); PLB 13.89 (0-06-021294-2) HarpC Child Bks.

Chastain, Madye L. The Cow-Tail Switch & Other West African Stories. Courlander, Harold & Herzog, George. LC 47-30108. 160p. (gr. 2-4). 1988. 12.95 (0-8050-0288-X, Bks Young Read) H Holt & Co.

Chatterjee, Sukumar. Tales from Indian Classics, Bk. III. Savitri. (gr. 3-9). 1979. 4.50 (0-89744-169-9); pap. 3.00 (0-685-57667-1) Auromere.

Chatterji, Sukumar. Books Forever. Das, Manoj. (gr. 2-8). 1979. pap. 2.50 (0-89744-175-3) Auromere.

Chatterton, Martin. Look at Me in a Funny Hat! Johnson, Richard. LC 93-32379. 1994. 4.99 (1-56402-414-8) Candlewick Pr.

—Look at Me in Funny Clothes! Johnson, Richard. LC 93-32380. 1994. 4.99 (1-56402-415-6) Candlewick Pr.

Chatton, Ray. God's Mother Is My Mother. Mulqueen, Jack & Chatton, Ray. 28p. (Orig.). (gr. 1-3). 1978. pap. 2.50 (0-913382-49-3, 103-13) Prow Bks-Franciscan.

—Soldier of God. Treece, Patricia. 32p. (gr. 1-8). 1982. pap. 1.00 (0-913382-22-1, 111-1) Prow Bks-Franciscan.

Chauhan, Man har. The Muppet Babies in Let's Imagine.. ..A Trip to the Stars. Barkan, Joanne, et al. 26p. (ps up). 1987. pap. 14.95 (1-55578-806-8) Worlds Wonder.

Chauhan, Manhar. Baby Piggy at the Bat. Gikow, Louise. LC 86-62182. 32p. (ps-3). 1987. 1.25 (0-394-88783-2) Random Bks Yng Read.

—Muppet Babies Take a Bath. 10p. (ps). 1992. vinyl 3.95 (0-394-86362-3) Random Bks Yng Read.

—Muppet Kids in I'm Mad at You! Gikow, Louise. 24p. (ps-3). 1992. 1.95 (0-307-12648-X, 12648) Western Pub.

Chavis, Ken. Monte Superstition Gold. Andrist, Earl W. 170p. (Orig.). 1990. pap. 7.95 (1-878431-02-1) Artist Profile Pub.

Chbosky, Stacy. Who Owns the Sun? Chbosky, Stacy. LC 88-12694. 26p. (gr. 3-12). 1988. PLB 14.95 (0-933849-14-1) Landmark Edns.

Cheairs, Nancy & Robinson, Susan. Chasing the Moon to China. McLean, Virginia O. Mitler, Ellen, et al, photos by. LC 87-60411. 40p. (gr. k-6). 1987. PLB 15.95 incl. record (0-9606046-1-8) Redbird.

Cheese, Bernard, jt. illus. see Harris, Frank.

Chellton, Anna. All about Science Fairs. Carratello, John & Carratello, Patty. 96p. (gr. 1-8). 1989. wkbk. 9.95 (1-55734-228-8) Tchr Create Mat.

—Problem Solving Science Investigations. Carratello, John & Carratello, Patty. 96p. (gr. 1-8). 1989. wkbk. 9.95 (1-55734-229-6) Tchr Create Mat.

—World Geography. Carratello, John & Carratello, Patty. 48p. (gr. 3-6). 1989. wkbk. 5.95 (1-55734-161-3) Tchr Create Mat.

—Writing a Country Report. Carratello, John & Carratello, Patty. 48p. (gr. 3-6). 1989. wkbk. 5.95 (1-55734-163-X) Tchr Create Mat.

—Writing a State Report. Carratello, John & Carratello, Patty. 48p. (gr. 3-6). 1989. wkbk. 5.95 (1-55734-162-1) Tchr Create Mat.

Chellton, Anna, et al. Literature & Critical Thinking. Carratello, John & Carratello, Patty. 96p. (gr. k-3). 1989. wkbk. 9.95 (1-55734-361-6) Tchr Create Mat.

—Literature & Critical Thinking. Carratello, John & Carratello, Patty. 96p. (gr. 3-5). 1989. wkbk. 9.95 (1-55734-362-4) Tchr Create Mat.

—United States Geography. Carratello, John & Carratello, Patty. 48p. (gr. 3-6). 1989. wkbk. 5.95 (1-55734-160-5) Tchr Create Mat.

Chen, Chih-hsien. Square Beak. Sun, Chyng F. LC 92-19093. 40p. (gr. k-3). 1993. 13.95 (0-395-64567-0) HM.

Chen, Ju-Hong. The Jade Stone: A Chinese Folktale. Yacowitz, Caryn. LC 91-17934. 32p. (ps-3). 1992. reinforced bdg. 14.95 (0-8234-0919-8) Holiday.

—The Tale of Aladdin & the Wonderful Lamp. Arabian Nights Staff. Kimmel, Eric A., retold by. LC 91-814. 32p. (ps-3). 1992. reinforced bdg. 14.95 (0-8234-0938-4) Holiday.

—Tiddalick the Frog. Nunes, Susan. LC 89-1. 32p. (gr. k-3). 1989. SBE 13.95 (0-689-31502-3, Atheneum Child Bk) Macmillan Child Grp.

Chen, Kuo K. & Bull, Peter. Sound. Cash, Terry. 40p. (gr. 5-6). 1989. PLB 12.90 (0-531-19064-1, Warwick) Watts.

Chen, Kuo K., jt. illus. see Bull, Peter.

Chen, Tony. Animals Showing Off. Crump, Donald J., ed. (ps-5). 1988. Set. 21.95 (0-87044-724-6) Natl Geog.

—A Child's First Bible. Stoddard, Sandol. 96p. (ps-3). 1991. 15.99 (0-8037-0941-2) Dial Bks Young.

—Doubleday Illustrated Children's Bible. Stoddard, Sandol. LC 82-45340. 384p. (gr. 4-6). 1983. pap. 25.00 (0-385-18521-9) Doubleday.

Cheney, Glenn L. Cookbook for Kids: The Kids Can Cook, Too, Cookbook. Ferguson, David L. Ferguson, Jane, ed. LC 90-86154. 56p. (Orig.). (gr. 3-6). 1991. cerlox bound 9.95 (0-9628148-0-6) Abigail Pubns.

Cheney, Paul & Bauer, Louise. The Mike Schmidt Hitting Study, Youth Version: Building a Foundation. Schmidt, Mike & Ellis, Rob. 80p. (Orig.). (gr. 4-10). 1993. pap. 8.95 (0-9634609-3-5) McGriff & Bell.

Cheney, Tracy. Totem Poles: An Ancient Art. Batdorf, Carol. 24p. (Orig.). (gr. 1-6). 1990. pap. 4.95 (0-88839-248-6) Hancock House.

Cheng, Yang Zhr. China's Long March: 6000 Miles of Danger. Fritz, Jean. LC 87-31171. 128p. (gr. 7 up). 1988. 15.95 (0-399-21512-3, Putnam) Putnam Pub Group.

Cheng-Khee Chee. Old Turtle. Wood, Douglas. LC 91-73527. 48p. (ps-2). 1991. 17.95 (0-938586-48-3) Pfeifer-Hamilton.

Cheny, Roland J., jt. illus. see Hedge-Cheney, Jacquelyn.

Cherbak, Yvonne. Monster Math Workbook. Cron, Mary. 48p. (Orig.). (gr. 1-3). 1993. pap. 2.95 (1-56565-030-1) Lowell Hse.

Cherin, Robin & Reyes, Roger I. My Aunt Otilia's Spirits: Los espiritus de mi Tia Otilia. Garcia, Richard. Guerrero Rea, Jesus, tr. LC 86-17129. (ENG & SPA.). 24p. (gr. 2-9). 1987. 13.95 (0-89239-029-8) Childrens Book Pr.

Chermayeff, Ivan. Three Languages. Grimm, Jacob & Grimm, Wilhelm K. 32p. (gr. 4 up). 1984. PLB 13.95s.p. (0-87191-940-0) Creative Ed.

Chernak, Judy, jt. illus. see Safian, Elizabeth.

Cherry, Eric. Alien Prey. Peel, John. 144p. (gr. 3-7). 1993. pap. 3.50 (0-448-40529-6, G&D) Putnam Pub Group.

—Blood Wolf. Peel, John. 144p. (gr. 3-7). 1993. pap. 2.95 (0-448-40527-X, G&D) Putnam Pub Group.
—Grave Doubts. Peel, John. 144p. (gr. 3-7). 1993. pap. 2.95 (0-448-40528-8, G&D) Putnam Pub Group.
—Night Wings. Peel, John. 144p. (gr. 3-7). 1993. pap. 2.95 (0-448-40526-1, G&D) Putnam Pub Group.
Cherry, Lynn. If I Were in Charge of the World & Other Worries: Poems for Children & Their Parents. Viorst, Judith. LC 81-2342. 64p. (gr. 3 up). 1981. SBE 14.95 (0-689-30863-9, Atheneum Child Bk) Macmillan Child Grp.
—The Snail's Spell. Ryder, Joan. (gr. 3-8). 1988. pap. 4.99 (0-14-050891-0, Puffin) Puffin Bks.
Cherry, Lynne. Chipmunk Song. Ryder, Joanne. LC 86-19786. 32p. (ps-3). 1987. 13.95 (0-525-67191-9, Lodestar Bks); pap. 4.95 (0-525-67312-1, Lodestar Bks) Dutton Child Bks.
—Emir's Education in the Proper Use of Magical Powers. Roberts, Jane. 138p. (gr. 3 up). 1984. pap. 8.95 (0-913299-08-1, Dist. by PGW) Stillpoint.
—The Snail's Spell. Ryder, Joanne. 32p. (ps-3). 1992. PLB 14.00 (0-670-84385-7) Viking Child Bks.
—Snow Leopard. LC 86-24033. 12p. (ps). 1987. (DCB); book & toy package 13.95 (0-685-14571-9, DCB) Dutton Child Bks.
—Where Butterflies Grow. Ryder, Joanne. LC 88-37989. 32p. (ps-3). 1989. 14.00 (0-525-67284-2, Lodestar Bks) Dutton Child Bks.
—Who's Sick Today? Cherry, Lynne. LC 87-22185. 24p. (ps-1). 1988. 11.95 (0-525-44380-0, 01160-350, DCB) Dutton Child Bks.
Cherry, Winky. My First Embroidery Book. Cherry, Winky. 40p. (ps-6). 1990. pap. 12.00 (0-317-93838-X) ITS Pub.
—My First Machine Sewing Book. Cherry, Winky. 40p. (Orig.). (gr. 2 up). 1989. pap. 12.00 (0-317-93839-8) ITS Pub.
—My First Sewing Book. Cherry, Winky. 40p. (Orig.). (ps-6). 1984. pap. 10.00 (0-317-93840-1) ITS Pub.
Chess, V. Slither McCreep & His Brother, Joe. Johnston, T. 1992. 13.95 (0-15-276100-4, HB Juv Bks) HarBrace.
Chess, Victoria. The Bigness Contest. Heide, Florence P. LC 92-12663. 1993. 14.95 (0-316-35444-9, Joy St Bks) Little.
—Ghosts! Ghostly Tales from Folklore. Schwartz, Alvin. LC 90-21746. 64p. (gr. k-3). 1991. 14.00 (0-06-021796-0); PLB 13.89 (0-06-021797-9) HarpC Child Bks.
—Ghosts! Ghostly Tales from Folklore. Schwartz, Alvin, retold by. LC 90-21746. 64p. (gr. k-3). 1993. pap. 3.50 (0-06-444170-9, Trophy) HarpC Child Bks.
—Good Night, Dinosaurs. Sierra, Judy. LC 93-8855. Date not set. write for info. (0-395-65016-X, Clarion Bks) HM.
—Grim & Ghastly Goings-On. Heide, Florence P. Pearson, Susan, ed. LC 89-8071. 24p. (gr. k up). 1992. 14.00 (0-688-08319-6); PLB 13.93 (0-688-08322-6) Lothrop.
—A Hippopotamusn't: And Other Animal Poems. Lewis, J. Patrick. 40p. (ps-3). 1994. pap. 4.99 (0-14-055273-1, Puffin Pied Piper) Puffin Bks.
—A Hippopotamusn't: And Other Animal Verses. Lewis, Patrick. Fogelman, Phyllis J., ed. LC 87-24579. 40p. (ps-3). 1990. 12.95 (0-8037-0518-2); PLB 12.89 (0-8037-0519-0) Dial Bks Young.
—Jim, Who Ran Away from His Nurse, & Was Eaten by a Lion. Belloc, Hilaire. (gr. 2 up). 1987. pap. 4.95 (0-316-13816-9) Little.
—Once Around the Block. Henkes, Kevin. LC 85-24901. 24p. (gr. k-3). 1987. 11.75 (0-688-04954-0); PLB 11.88 (0-688-04955-9) Greenwillow.
—Princess Gorilla & a New Kind of Water. Aardema, Verna. LC 86-32888. 32p. (ps-3). 1991. pap. 3.95 (0-8037-0914-5, Dial Pied Piper) Puffin Bks.
—The Queen of Eene. Prelutsky, Jack. LC 77-17311. 32p. (gr. k-3). 1978. PLB 14.88 (0-688-84144-9) Greenwillow.
—Rolling Harvey Down the Hill. Prelutsky, Jack. LC 79-18236. 32p. (gr. k-3). 1980. 14.95 (0-688-80258-3); PLB 12.88 (0-688-84258-5) Greenwillow.
—Rolling Harvey Down the Hill. Prelutsky, Jack. LC 92-24606. 40p. (gr. 2 up). 1993. pap. 4.95 (0-688-12270-1, Mulberry) Morrow.
—The Sheriff of Rottenshot. Prelutsky, Jack. LC 81-6420. 32p. (gr. k-3). 1982. 12.95 (0-688-00205-6); PLB 14.93 (0-688-00198-X) Greenwillow.
—Spider Kane & the Mystery at Jumbo Nightcrawler's. Osborne, Mary P. LC 91-10983. 128p. (gr. 1-5). 1993. 14.00 (0-679-80856-6) Knopf Bks Yng Read.
—Spider Kane & the Mystery under the May-Apple. Osborne, Mary P. LC 90-33524. 128p. (gr. 1-7). 1992. 13.00 (0-679-80855-8); PLB 13.99 (0-679-90855-2) Knopf Bks Yng Read.
—Spider Kane & the Mystery under the May-Apple. Osborne, Mary P. LC 90-33524. 128p. (gr. 1-7). 1993. pap. 3.50 (0-679-84174-1, Bullseye Bks) Knopf Bks Yng Read.
—Tales for the Perfect Child. Heide, Florence P. 80p. (gr. 3-6). 1985. 14.95 (0-688-03892-1); PLB 14.88 (0-688-03893-X) Lothrop.
—Ten Sly Piranhas: A Counting Story in Reverse (A Tale of Wickedness - & Worse!) Wise, William. LC 91-33704. 32p. (ps-3). 1993. 13.50 (0-8037-1200-6); PLB 13.89 (0-8037-1201-4) Dial Bks Young.
—Tommy at the Grocery Store. Grossman, Bill. LC 88-35756. 32p. (ps-2). 1989. 13.00 (0-06-022408-8); PLB 12.89 (0-06-022409-6) HarpC Child Bks.

—Tommy at the Grocery Store. Grossman, Bill. LC 88-35756. 32p. (ps-2). 1991. pap. 4.95 (0-06-443266-1, Trophy) HarpC Child Bks.
—Tommy at the Grocery Store Big Book. Grossman, Bill. LC 88-35756. 32p. (ps-1). 1992. 19.95 (0-694-00387-5) HarpC Child Bks.
—The Twisted Witch & Other Spooky Riddles. Adler, David A. LC 85-909. 64p. (gr. 1-4). 1985. reinforced bdg. 11.95 (0-8234-0571-0) Holiday.
—Tyrannosaurus Wrecks. Sterne, Noelle. LC 78-22499. 32p. (gr. 1-4). 1983. pap. 4.95 (0-06-443043-X, Trophy) HarpC Child Bks.
—Tyrannosaurus Wrecks: A Book of Dinosaur Riddles. Sterne, Noelle. LC 78-22499. 32p. (gr. 1-4). 1979. PLB 13.89 (0-690-03960-3, Crowell Jr Bks) HarpC Child Bks.
Chessare, Michele. The Daddies Boat. Monfried, Lucia. 32p. (ps-3). 1993. pap. 4.99 (0-14-054938-2, Puffin Unicorn) Puffin Bks.
—The Ghost from Beneath the Sea. Brittain, Bill. LC 92-1091. 148p. (gr. 4-7). 1992. 14.00 (0-06-020827-9); PLB 13.89 (0-06-020828-7) HarpC Child Bks.
—His Majesty, Queen Hatshepsut. Carter, Dorothy S. LC 85-45855. 256p. (gr. 5 up). 1987. (Lipp Jr Bks); PLB 13.89 (0-397-32179-1, Lipp Jr Bks) HarpC Child Bks.
—A Lion to Guard Us. Bulla, Clyde R. LC 80-2455. (gr. 2-5). 1981. (Crowell Jr Bks); PLB 13.89 (0-690-04097-0, Crowell Jr Bks) HarpC Child Bks.
—Rainy Day: Stories & Poems. Bauer, Caroline F., ed. LC 85-45170. 96p. (gr. 2-5). 1986. (Lipp Jr Bks); PLB 13.89 (0-397-32105-8, Lipp Jr Bks) HarpC Child Bks.
—Roomrimes. Cassedy, Sylvia. LC 86-4583. 80p. (gr. k-3). 1987. (Crowell Jr Bks); PLB 12.89 (0-690-04467-4, Crowell Jr Bks) HarpC Child Bks.
—Who Knew There'd Be Ghosts? Brittain, Bill. LC 84-48496. 128p. (gr. 4-7). 1985. PLB 13.89 (0-06-020700-0) HarpC Child Bks.
—Who Knew There'd Be Ghosts? Brittain, Bill. LC 84-48496. 128p. (gr. 4-7). 1988. pap. 3.95 (0-06-440224-X, Trophy) HarpC Child Bks.
—Zoomrimes: Poems About Things That Go. Cassedy, Sylvia. LC 90-1463. 64p. (gr. 3-7). 1993. 14.00 (0-06-022632-3); PLB 13.89 (0-06-022633-1) HarpC Child Bks.
Chestney, P. L. When the Animals Left. Chestney, P. L. 52p. (gr. 1-6). 1994. pap. 12.95 (1-883533-00-7) PL&R Chestney.
Chestnutt, David. Beauty & the Beast. LC 78-54959. 32p. (Orig.). (gr. k-4). 1991. pap. 2.25 (0-394-83954-4) Random Bks Yng Read.
Chesworth, Michael. Alvin's Famous No-Horse. Harding, William H. LC 92-13834. 64p. (gr. 2-4). 1992. alk. paper 14.95 (0-8050-2227-9, Redfeather BYR) H Holt & Co.
—The Curse of the Trouble Dolls. Regan, Dian C. LC 91-28572. 64p. (gr. 2-4). 1992. 14.95 (0-8050-1944-8, Bks Young Read) H Holt & Co.
—The Curse of the Trouble Dolls. Regan, Dian C. LC 91-28572. 64p. (gr. 2-4). 1993. pap. 4.95 (0-8050-2952-4, Bks Young Read) H Holt & Co.
—Gentle Willow: A Story for Children about Dying. Mills, Joyce C. LC 93-22770. 1993. 16.95 (0-945354-54-1); pap. 8.95 (0-945354-53-3) Magination Pr.
—Gran-Gran's Best Trick: A Story for Children Who Have Lost Someone They Love. Holden, L. Dwight. LC 89-8336. 48p. 1989. 16.95 (0-945354-19-3); pap. 6.95 (0-945354-16-9) Magination Pr.
—Little Tree: A Story for Children with Serious Medical Problems. Mills, Joyce C. LC 92-19654. 32p. 1992. 16.95 (0-945354-52-5); pap. 6.95 (0-945354-51-7) Magination Pr.
—The Riddle Streak. Pfeffer, Susan B. 64p. (gr. 2-4). 1993. PLB 14.95 (0-8050-2147-7, Bks Young Read) H Holt & Co.
—Trouble Will Find You. Lexau, Joan M. LC 93-6813. (ps-6). 1994. write for info. (0-395-64380-5) HM.
Chesworth, Michael D. The Monster in Room 202. Korman, Justine H. LC 93-2215. 32p. (gr. 2-4). 1993. pap. text ed. 2.95 (0-8167-3182-9); pap. 2.95 (0-8167-3183-7) Troll Assocs.
Chetwin, Grace. Jason's Seven Magical Night Rides. Chetwin, Grace. 128p. (gr. 2-5). 1994. SBE 14.95 (0-02-718221-5, Bradbury Pr) Macmillan Child Grp.
Chevalier, Christa. Spence & the Sleepytime Monster. Chevalier, Christa. Tucker, Kathleen, ed. LC 83-25988. 32p. (ps-1). 1984. PLB 11.95 (0-8075-7574-7) A Whitman.
—Spence Is Small. Chevalier, Christa. Levine, Abby, ed. LC 87-2054. (ps-1). 1987. PLB 11.95 (0-8075-7567-4) A Whitman.
—Spence Isn't Spence Anymore. Chevalier, Christa. Levine, Abby, ed. LC 84-29195. 32p. (ps-1). 1985. 11.95 (0-8075-7565-8) A Whitman.
Chevance, Audrey. Tutu. Chevance, Audrey. LC 91-3506. 32p. (ps-6). 1991. 13.95 (0-525-44769-5, DCB) Dutton Child Bks.
Chew, Ruth. No Such Thing As a Witch. Chew, Ruth. LC 79-18153. (gr. 2 up). 1980. 8.95 (0-8038-5073-5) Hastings.
—Shark Lady: True Adventures of Eugenie Clark. reissued ed. McGovern, Ann. LC 78-22126. 96p. (gr. 3-7). 1984. 12.95 (0-02-767060-0, Four Winds) Macmillan Child Grp.
Chewning, Paul. Where Does the Garbage Go? rev. ed. Showers, Paul. LC 91-46115. 32p. (gr. k-4). 1994. pap. 4.95 (0-06-445114-3, Trophy) HarpC Child Bks.

Chewning, Randy. Glow-in-the-Dark Constellations: A Field Guide for Young Stargazers. Thompson, C. E. 32p. (gr. 1-5). 1989. 11.95 (0-448-09070-8, G&D) Putnam Pub Group.
—Hammers, Nails, Planks & Paint. Jackson, Thomas C. 32p. (ps-3). 1994. pap. 2.50 (0-590-44642-8, Cartwheel) Scholastic Inc.
—Space Words: A Dictionary. Simon, Seymour. LC 90-37402. 48p. (gr. 2-5). 1991. 15.00 (0-02-722532-7); PLB 14.89 (0-06-022533-5) HarpC Child Bks.
—Where Does the Garbage Go? rev. ed. Showers, Paul. LC 91-46115. 32p. (gr. k-2). 1994. 15.00 (0-06-021054-0); PLB 14.89 (0-06-021057-5) HarpC Child Bks.
—You Can Name 100 Trucks! Becker, Jim. 14p. (ps). 1994. bds. 8.95 (0-590-46302-0, Cartwheel) Scholastic Inc.
Chhuy, Dorothy H. Dark Horse. Doty, Jean S. LC 82-21651. 122p. (gr. 4-6). 1983. 12.95 (0-688-01703-7) Morrow Jr Bks.
Chiasson, John, photos by. African Journey. Chiasson, John. LC 86-8233. 64p. (gr. 3-6). 1987. SBE 17.95 (0-02-718530-3, Bradbury Pr) Macmillan Child Grp.
Chichester-Clark, Emma. Time & the Clock Mice, Etcetera. Dickinson, Peter. LC 93-11434. 1994. write for info. (0-385-32038-8) Delacorte.
Chien-Erikson, Nancy. Paul & Mary & their Magic Crystals. Silbey, Uma. 48p. (Orig.). (ps-3). 1988. pap. 9.95 (0-938925-07-5) U-Music.
Child, Charles. A Book of Americans. Benet, Stephen Vincent & Benet, Rosemary. LC 33-27433. 128p. (gr. 4-6). 1944. 12.95 (0-8050-0284-7, Bks Young Read); pap. 5.95 (0-8050-0297-9) H Holt & Co.
Childers, Norman. Tears for Ashan. Marie, D. LC 88-63766. 32p. (ps-3). 1989. 11.95 (0-9621681-0-6) Creative Pr Works.
—Water Babies. Kingsley, Charles. Adam, G. Mercer, ed. (gr. k-4). Repr. of 1905 ed. 12.95 (0-940561-09-3) White Rose Pr.
Childers, Norman H. The Great Monkey Debate. Childers, Norman H. 44p. (gr. k-5). 1988. 14.95g (0-940561-12-3) White Rose Pr.
Childers, Peggy, jt. illus. see Crofts, Trudy.
Children at Sunrise Ranch. Songs for the Joy of Living. 50p. (gr. 1-10). 1985. ring-bound 11.95 (0-932869-01-7) Emissaries Divine.
Childress, Rhonda. The Fence Was Too High. Esh, Olivia. LC 93-34499. 1994. write for info. (0-8114-4460-0) Raintree Steck-V.
Ching. Animal Talk: Barks, Growls, Hisses, Howls. McDonnell, Janet. LC 89-23990. 32p. (ps-2). 1990. PLB 21.35 (0-89565-558-6); PLB 14.95s.p. (0-685-56179-8) Childs World.
—Cat Purrs. Halloran, Phyllis. McKissack, Patricia & McKissack, Fredrick, eds. LC 87-61648. 32p. (Orig.). (gr. 1-3). 1987. text ed. 8.95 (0-88335-723-2); pap. text ed. 4.95 (0-88335-743-7) Milliken Pub Co.
—God Made Something Wonderful. McKissack, Patricia & McKissack, Fredrick. LC 89-84938. 32p. (Orig.). (gr. 3-5). 1989. pap. 5.99 (0-8066-2434-5, 9-2434) Augsburg Fortress.
—Hypsilophodon. Riehecky, Janet. 32p. (gr. k-4). 1990. PLB 21.35 (0-89565-628-0); PLB 14.95s.p. (0-685-56213-1) Childs World.
—Ornithomimus. Alden, Laura. 32p. (gr. k-4). 1990. PLB 21.35 (0-89565-630-2); PLB 14.95s.p. (0-685-56215-8) Childs World.
—Pond Life: The Fishing Trip. Wells, Donna K. LC 90-1644. 32p. (ps-2). 1990. PLB 19.95 (0-89565-581-0); PLB 13.95s.p. (0-685-56195-X) Childs World.
Ching, Patrick. Exotic Animals in Hawaii. Ching, Patrick. 32p. (Orig.). (ps-6). 1988. pap. 3.95 (0-935848-56-8) Bess Pr.
—Helu Papa-Counting in Hawaiian: Pi'a Pa-Hawaiian Alphabet. Beamer, Nona. 40p. 1991. text ed. write for info. (0-9627294-0-X) Hawaiian Resources.
—Native Animals of Hawaii. Ching, Patrick. 32p. (Orig.). (ps-6). 1988. pap. 3.95 (0-935848-55-X) Bess Pr.
Chiostri, Carlo. Pinocchio. Collodi, Carlo. (FRE.). 235p. (gr. 5-10). 1985. pap. 9.95 (2-07-033283-7) Schoenhof.
Chodkowski, Dick. Snakes Alive! It's Reptile Clive! Chodkowski, Dick. McKissack, Patricia & McKissack, Fredrick, eds. LC 88-60391. 32p. (Orig.). (gr. 1-3). 1990. text ed. 8.95 (0-88335-787-9); pap. text ed. 4.95 (0-88335-799-2) Milliken Pub Co.
Choi, Dong Ho. Blindman's Daughter. Adams, Edward B., ed. 32p. (gr. 3). 1981. 8.95 (0-8048-1472-4, Pub. by Seoul Intl Tourist SK) C E Tuttle.
Choi, Dong-Ho. Herdboy & Weaver. Adams, Edward B. 32p. (gr. 3). 1981. 8.95 (0-8048-1470-8, Pub by Seoul Intl Publishing House) C E Tuttle.
Choi, Dong Ho. Korean Cinderella. Adams, Edward B., ed. 32p. (gr. 3). 1982. 8.95 (0-8048-1473-2, Pub. by Seoul Intl Tourist SK) C E Tuttle.
Choi, Dong-Ho. Woodcutter & Nymph. Adams, Edward B. 32p. (gr. 3). 1982. 8.95 (0-8048-1471-6, Pub by Seoul Intl Publishing House) C E Tuttle.
Chojnacki, Cathy. Yellow Submarine. Lennon, John & McCartney, Paul. 24p. 1993. 12.95 (0-7935-1859-8, 00183013) H Leonard Pub Corp.
Chong, Jonathon. Dry Bones & Other Fossils. Parker, Gary. LC 79-51174. (gr. 2-4). 1979. pap. 5.95 (0-89051-117-0) Master Bks.
Chorao, Kay. Albert's Toothache. Williams, Barbara. LC 74-4040. 32p. (ps-1). 1974. (Dutton); pap. 3.95 (0-525-45037-8) NAL-Dutton.

—Albert's Toothache. Williams, Barbara. LC 74-4040. 32p. (ps-1). 1988. pap. 3.95 (0-525-44363-0, 0383-120, DCB) Dutton Child Bks.
—The Baby's Bedtime Book. Chorao, Kay. LC 84-6067. 64p. (ps). 1989. 13.95 (0-525-44149-2, DCB); bk & cassette 18.95 (0-525-44506-4) Dutton Child Bks.
—Baby's Christmas Treasury. Chorao, Kay, compiled by. LC 90-45872. 48p. (ps). 1991. 10.00 (0-679-80198-7); lib. bdg. 10.99 (0-679-90198-1) Random Bks Yng Read.
—Baby's Good Morning Book. Collins, Judy, contrib. by. LC 86-6415. 64p. (ps). 1990. 13.95 (0-525-44257-X, DCB); incl. audio cass. 17.95 (0-525-44627-3, DCB) Dutton Child Bks.
—The Baby's Story Book. Chorao, Kay. LC 84-26005. 64p. (ps-1). 1989. 13.95 (0-525-44200-6, DCB); bk. & cassette 17.95 (0-525-44507-2) Dutton Child Bks.
—But Not Billy. Zolotow, Charlotte. LC 82-47703. 32p. (ps-k). 1983. 12.95 (0-06-026963-4) HarpC Child Bks.
—Cathedral Mouse. Chorao, Kay. LC 87-33398. 32p. (ps-2). 1988. 12.95 (0-525-44400-9, DCB) Dutton Child Bks.
—The Cherry Pie Baby. Chorao, Kay. LC 88-2630. 32p. (ps-3). 1989. 12.95 (0-525-44435-1, DCB) Dutton Child Bks.
—Chester Chipmunk's Thanksgiving. Williams, Barbara. LC 77-20812. 32p. (gr. k-3). 1988. (DCB); (DCB) Dutton Child Bks.
—The Child's Story Book. Chorao, Kay. LC 87-8899. 64p. (ps-3). 1987. 12.95 (0-525-44328-2, 01258-370, DCB) Dutton Child Bks.
—Clyde Monster. Crowe, Robert L. LC 76-10733. 32p. (ps-3). 1987. (DCB); pap. 3.95 (0-525-44289-8, DCB) Dutton Child Bks.
—Dracula's Cat & Frankenstein's Dog. Wahl, Jan. (ps-2). 1990. pap. 13.95 (0-671-70820-1) S&S Trade.
—The Good-Bye Book. Viorst, Judith. LC 87-1778. 32p. (ps-1). 1988. SBE 13.95 (0-689-31308-X, Atheneum Child Bk) Macmillan Child Grp.
—The Good-Bye Book. Viorst, Judith. LC 91-19916. 32p. (ps-1). 1992. pap. 4.95 (0-689-71581-1, Aladdin) Macmillan Child Grp.
—Ida & Betty & the Secret Eggs. Chorao, Kay. Giblin, James, ed. 32p. (ps-2). 1991. 13.45 (0-395-52591-8, Clarion Bks) HM.
—I'm Terrific. Sharmat, Marjorie W. LC 76-9094. 32p. (ps-3). 1977. reinforced bdg. 13.95 (0-8234-0282-7) Holiday.
—I'm Terrific. Sharmat, Marjorie W. LC 76-9094. 32p. (ps-3). 1992. pap. 4.95 (0-8234-0955-4) Holiday.
—Monster Poems. Wallace, Daisy, ed. LC 75-17680. 32p. (ps-3). 1976. reinforced bdg. 13.95 (0-8234-0268-1); pap. 4.95 (0-8234-0848-5) Holiday.
—Mother Goose Magic. LC 92-37160. 64p. (ps-k). 1994. 15.99 (0-525-45064-5, DCB) Dutton Child Bks.
—My Mama Says There Aren't Any Zombies, Ghosts, Vampires, Creatures, Demons, Monsters, Fiends, Goblins, or Things. Viorst, Judith. LC 73-76331. 48p. (gr. k-4). 1973. SBE 13.95 (0-689-30102-2, Atheneum Child Bk) Macmillan Child Grp.
—My Mama Says There Aren't Any Zombies, Ghosts, Vampires, Creatures, Demons, Monsters, Fiends, Goblins, or Things. Viorst, Judith. LC 87-18733. 48p. (gr. k-4). 1987. pap. 3.95 (0-689-71204-9, Aladdin) Macmillan Child Grp.
—The Nutcracker. Hoffmann, E. T. Schulman, Janet, adapted by. LC 79-11223. 64p. (gr. 3-7). 1988. pap. 2.95 (0-394-82018-5) Knopf Bks Yng Read.
—Rock, Rock, My Baby. Chorao, Kay. LC 92-61268. 22p. (ps). 1993. 3.25 (0-679-84333-7) Random Bks Yng Read.
—Tyler Toad & the Thunder. Crowe, Robert L. LC 80-347. 32p. (ps-1). 1980. 9.95 (0-525-41795-8, DCB) Dutton Child Bks.
—Tyler Toad & the Thunder. Crowe, Robert L. LC 80-347. 32p. (ps-1). 1986. pap. 4.95 (0-525-44243-X, DCB) Dutton Child Bks.
—Visiting Pamela. Klein, Norma. LC 78-72203. (ps-3). 1979. Dial Bks Young.
Choroa, Kay. The Boy with the Helium Head. Naylor, Phyllis R. (ps-3). 1992. 2.99 (0-440-40644-7, YB) Dell.
Chow, Adam. Amy & Gully in Rainbowland. Rowe, W. W. LC 92-9075. 84p. (Orig.). (gr. k-4). 1992. pap. 5.95 (1-55939-003-4) Snow Lion.
Christa. Raymond Floyd Goes to Africa: or There Are No Bears in Africa. Mrs. Moose. 32p. (gr. 1-4). 1993. 14.95 (0-86543-375-5); pap. 6.95 (0-86543-376-3) Africa World.
Christelow, Eileen. Annie's Four Grannies. Kroll, Steven. LC 85-27193. 32p. (ps-3). 1986. reinforced bdg. 12.95 (0-8234-0605-9) Holiday.
—Celeste & Crabapple Sam. Brutschy, Jennifer. LC 92-1587. (gr. k-3). 1994. 14.99 (0-525-67416-0, Lodestar Bks) Dutton Child Bks.
—The Completed Hickory Dickory Dock. Aylesworth, Jim. LC 89-38484. 32p. (ps-2). 1990. SBE 13.95 (0-689-31606-2, Atheneum Child Bk) Macmillan Child Grp.
—Dilly Dilly Piccalilli: Poems for the Very Young. Livingston, Myra C. (gr. 1 up). 1989. SBE 12.95 (0-689-50466-7, M K McElderry) Macmillan Child Grp.
—Don't Wake up Mama! Another Five Little Monkeys Story. Christelow, Eileen. 32p. (ps-3). 1992. 13.45 (0-395-60176-2, Clarion Bks) HM.

—A Fish Named Yum: Mr. Pin, Vol. IV. Monsell, Mary E. LC 93-25731. 64p. (ps-4). 1994. SBE 13.95 (0-689-31882-0, Atheneum Child Bk) Macmillan Child Grp.
—Five Little Monkeys Jumping on the Bed. Christelow, Eileen. (ps-3). 1993. pap. 5.70 (0-395-55701-1, Clarion Bks); pap. 7.95 incl. cassette (0-395-60115-0, Clarion Bks) HM.
—Five Little Monkeys Sitting in a Tree. Christelow, Eileen. Giblin, James, ed. 32p. (ps-1). 1991. 13.45 (0-395-54434-3, Clarion Bks) HM.
—Five Little Monkeys Sitting in a Tree. Christelow, Eileen. 32p. (gr. k-3). 1993. pap. 5.70 (0-395-66413-6, Clarion Bks) HM.
—Gertrude, the Bulldog Detective. Christelow, Eileen. 32p. (gr. k-3). 1992. 13.45 (0-395-58701-8, Clarion Bks) HM.
—Henry & the Dragon. Christelow, Eileen. LC 83-14405. 32p. (ps-2). 1984. 13.45 (0-89919-220-3, Clarion Bks) HM.
—Henry & the Red Stripes. Christelow, Eileen. 32p. (ps-3). 1982. 14.45 (0-89919-118-5, Clarion Bks) HM.
—Jerome & the Witchcraft Kids. Christelow, Eileen. LC 88-2597. 32p. (gr. k-3). 1988. 13.95 (0-89919-742-6, Clarion Bks) HM.
—Jerome & the Withcraft Kids. Christelow, Eileen. 32p. (ps-3). 1990. pap. 4.80 (0-395-54428-9, Clarion Bks) HM.
—Jerome the Babysitter. Christelow, Eileen. LC 84-12738. 32p. (ps-3). 1987. pap. 4.95 (0-89919-520-2, Clarion Bks) HM.
—Mr. Pin: The Chocolate Files. Monsell, Mary E. LC 89-78228. 64p. (gr. 2-5). 1990. SBE 12.95 (0-689-31639-9, Atheneum Child Bk) Macmillan Child Grp.
—Mrs. Owl & Mr. Pig. Wahl, Jan. 32p. (gr. k-3). 1991. 13.95 (0-525-67311-3, Lodestar Bks) Dutton Child Bks.
—The Mysterious Cases of Mr. Pin. Monsell, Mary E. LC 88-8102. 64p. (gr. 2-5). 1989. SBE 12.95 (0-689-31435-3, Atheneum Child Bk) Macmillan Child Grp.
—Olive & the Magic Hat. Christelow, Eileen. LC 87-672. 32p. (gr. k-3). 1987. 12.95 (0-89919-513-X, Clarion Bks) HM.
—Oliver Dibbs & the Dinosaur Cause. Steiner, Barbara. LC 86-9941. 128p. (gr. 3-7). 1986. SBE 13.95 (0-02-787880-5, Four Winds) Macmillan Child Grp.
—Oliver Dibbs to the Rescue! Steiner, Barbara. LC 85-42801. 96p. (gr. 3-5). 1985. SBE 12.95 (0-02-787890-2, Four Winds) Macmillan Child Grp.
—Oliver Dibbs to the Rescue! Steiner, Barbara. 128p. 1988. pap. 2.50 (0-380-70465-X, Camelot) Avon.
—The Spy Who Came North from the Pole: Mr. Pin, Vol. II. Monsell, Mary E. LC 92-24646. 64p. (gr. 1-4). 1993. SBE 12.95 (0-689-31754-9, Atheneum Child Bk) Macmillan Child Grp.
—Two Terrible Frights. Aylesworth, Jim. LC 86-25859. 32p. (ps-2). 1987. SBE 13.95 (0-689-31327-6, Atheneum Child Bk) Macmillan Child Grp.
—Zucchini. Dana, Barbara. LC 80-8448. 128p. (gr. 3-6). 1982. PLB 12.89 (0-06-021395-7) HarpC Child Bks.
—Zucchini. Dana, Barbara. 160p. (gr. 3-6). 1984. pap. 2.95 (0-553-15437-0, Skylark) Bantam.
Christen-Pallo, Susan & Hennessy, Jim. Where Does It Belong? Interactive Language Activities Featuring Vocabulary & Question Forms. Toomey, Marilyn M. (ps-8). 1989. cards & worksheets 16.95 (0-923573-13-5) Circuit Pubns.
Christensen, Carrie. Where the Wind Goes. Heyes, Eileen. 32p. (ps-2). Date not set. 11.95 (1-56065-148-2) Capstone Pr. Postponed.
Christensen, Don. Student Inventors Lesson Plan. Fuller, Melvin L. & Weisberg, Maggie. 75p. (Orig.). (gr. 4-12). 1989. pap. 14.95x (0-685-25993-5) M&M Assocs.
Christian, Marilynn V. Feathers. Marshall-Noke, Dorothy. Weinberger, Jane, ed. LC 88-51278. 64p. (gr. 1-4). 1990. pap. 7.95 (0-932433-52-9) Windswept Hse.
Christian, Raleta. Sonny. Signer, Billie T., pseud. Ervis, K. Leroy, intro. by. LC 90-82038. 134p. (gr. 5-8). 1990. lib. bdg. 17.95 (0-944419-28-3) Everett Cos Pub.
Christian, Releta. Alabama's Youngest Admirals. Estes, James L. Krauel, Mary E., ed. 132p. (Orig.). (gr. 4-12). 1991. pap. 8.95 (0-9628634-0-8) J L Estes.
Christiana, David. Fat Man in a Fur Coat: And Other Bear Stories. Schwartz, Alvin. LC 84-4161. 167p. (gr. 3 up). 1984. 14.00 (0-374-32291-0) FS&G.
—Fat Man in a Fur Coat: And Other Bear Stories. Schwartz, Alvin. (gr. 5 up). 1987. pap. 3.50 (0-374-42273-7) FS&G.
—Good Griselle. Yolen, Jane. LC 93-11691. 1994. 14.95 (0-15-231701-5) HarBrace.
—Run for Your Sweet Life. Benedict, Rex. LC 86-45507. 128p. (gr. 5 up). 1986. 14.00 (0-374-36359-5) FS&G.
—Tales of Trickery from the Land of Spoof. Schwartz, Alvin, ed. LC 85-16004. 87p. (gr. 4 up). 1985. 14.00 (0-374-37378-7) FS&G.
—Tales of Trickery from the Land of Spoof. Schwartz, Alvin. 88p. (gr. 3 up). 1988. pap. 3.50 (0-374-47426-5) FS&G.
Christiansen, Lee & Selwyn, Paul. Julia's World, Pt. 1: Better Times. Boluch, Kathleen A. 58p. 1990. 14.95 (0-9626365-0-9) Swarovski Amer Ltd.

Christiansen, Per. How the Leopard Got His Claws. Achebe, Chinua & Iroaganachi, John. LC 72-93382. 32p. (gr. 6 up). 1973. 11.95 (0-89388-056-6) Okpaku Communications.
Christie, Robert D. An Adventure in Mouseland. Williams, Jill. LC 92-61769. 61p. (gr. k-6). 1992. pap. 3.95 (0-931563-10-0) Wishing Rm.
—Shy Ann. Ball, Nancy. LC 88-51305. 55p. (Orig.). (gr. k-4). 1989. pap. 3.95 (0-931563-03-8) Wishing Rm.
Christman, Catherine. Dr. Christman's Learn to Read Book. Christman, Ernest. 256p. (Orig.). 1990. pap. 15.95 (0-933025-17-3) Blue Bird Pub.
Christman, Catherine A. Progressive Phonics, Level 1. Christman, Ernest H. LC 90-71304. 84p. 1990. pap. text ed. 15.95 perfect bdg. (0-912329-06-8) Tutorial Press.
Christman, Michael, jt. illus. see French, Marty.
Christopher, Debbonnaire. The Day the Ohio Canal Turned Eerie. Christopher, Debbonnaire. LC 93-6614. 1993. 3.00 (1-880443-10-4) Roscoe Village.
Christopherson, Jerry. Gospel Basic Busy Book, Vol. I. Mehew, Randall & Mehew, Karen. 100p. 1989. pap. text ed. 6.95 (0-910613-13-3) Millenial Pr.
Christy-Pallo, Susan. Verbs Past & Present. Toomey, Marilyn M. 77p. 1989. wkbk. & cards 17.95 (0-923573-09-7) Circuit Pubns.
Chu, Charles. Halcyon Time. Hennedy, Hugh. 160p. (Orig.). 1993. pap. 12.95 (1-552291-54-5) Oyster River Pr.
Chudnovsky, Elynne. Bare, Beautiful Feet & Other Missionary Stories. (gr. 1-5). 1992. 3.99 (0-87509-485-6) Chr Pubns.
—The Potato Story & Other Missionary Stories. (gr. 1-5). 1992. 3.99 (0-87509-484-8) Chr Pubns.
Chung, Simon T. The Gods Must Be Angry. Miller, Sheila & Murray, Ian. 34p. (gr. 1-4). 1990. 2.95 (9971-972-93-X) OMF Bks.
Church, Caroline. Little Ghost. Khdir, Kate & Nash, Sue. 32p. (ps-2). 1991. incl. dust jacket 12.95 (0-8120-6203-5); pap. 5.95 (0-8120-4779-6) Barron.
—Little Witch. Smith, Iris. LC 92-39671. 28p. (ps-2). 1993. 12.95 (0-8120-5791-0); pap. 5.95 (0-8120-1552-5) Barron.
—My First Family Tree Book. Bruzzone, Catherine. 24p. (gr. k-2). 1992. pap. 3.95 (0-8249-8546-X, Ideals Child) Hambleton-Hill.
Church, Caroline J. All about Me. Bruzzone, Catherine & Morton, Lone. 24p. (Orig.). (gr. k-3). 1993. pap. 3.95 (0-8249-8605-9, Ideals Child) Hambleton-Hill.
Chusid, Nancy. Favorite Folk Songs. Chusid, Nancy. 32p. (Orig.). (gr. 2-6). 1990. pap. 6.95 incl. cassette (1-878624-07-5) McClanahan Bk.
—Favorite Lullabies. Chusid, Nancy. 32p. (Orig.). (gr. 2-6). 1990. pap. 6.95 incl. cassette (1-878624-06-7) McClanahan Bk.
—Favorite Nursery Songs. Chusid, Nancy. 32p. (Orig.). (gr. 2-6). 1990. pap. 6.95 incl. cassette (1-878624-05-9) McClanahan Bk.
Chwast, Jacqueline. I Like You. Warburg, Sandol S. LC 65-11002. 48p. (gr. 1-3). 1965. 5.70 (0-395-07176-3) HM.
—The Perilous Pit. Protopopescu, Orel O. LC 92-290. 40p. (ps-1). 1993. JRT 14.00 (0-671-76910-3, Green Tiger) S&S Trade.
Chwast, Seymour. Bushy Bride: Norwegian Fairy Tale. LC 83-71174. 32p. (gr. 6 up). 1983. PLB 13.95 s.p. (0-87191-952-4) Creative Ed.
—Just Enough Is Plenty: A Hannukkah Tale. Goldin, Barbara D. (ps-3). 1988. pap. 12.95 (0-670-81852-6) Viking Child Bks.
Cieslawski, Steve. At the Crack of the Bat. Morrison, Lillian, ed. LC 91-28946. 64p. (gr. 2-5). 1992. 14.95 (1-56282-176-8); lib. bdg. 14.89 (1-56282-177-6) Hyprn Child.
Cilchrist, Jan S. Sweet Baby Coming. Greenfield, Eloise. 14p. (ps). 1994. 4.95 (0-694-00578-9, Festival) HarpC Child Bks.
Claflin, Dale. Boris Bear Remembers His Manners. Doray, Andrea. Gress, Jonna C., ed. LC 91-78098. 18p. (Orig.). (gr. k-3). 1992. pap. 11.60 (0-944943-06-3) Current Inc.
Clapp, E. J., jt. illus. see Buck, Eunice.
Claridy, Jimmy. The Good, the Bad & the Two Cookie Kid: The Two Cookie Kid. Kelley, Shirley. Herbst, Eric & Genee, Gloria, eds. Cash, Johnny, intro. by. 32p. (ps-4). 1993. 9.95 (1-882436-02-4) Better Pl Pub.
—The Rainy Day Blues. Kelley, Shirley. Herbst, Eric & Genee, Gloria, eds. Kay, B. B., intro. by. 32p. (ps-4). 1993. 9.95 (1-882436-01-6) Better Pl Pub.
Clark, Alan M. The Homecoming. Longyear, Barry B. 224p. 1989. 15.95 (0-8027-6863-6) Walker & Co.
—The Twilight Gate. Salsitz, Rhondi V. LC 92-22040. 192p. (gr. 7 up). 1993. 16.95 (0-8027-8213-2) Walker & Co.
Clark, Brenda. Big Sarah's Little Boots. Bourgeois, Paulette. LC 89-4224. (ps-k). 1989. pap. 11.95 (0-590-42622-2) Scholastic Inc.
—Big Sarah's Little Boots. Bourgeois, Paulette. 1992. pap. 3.95 (0-590-42623-0, Blue Ribbon Bks) Scholastic Inc.
—Franklin in the Dark. Bourgeois, Paulette. 32p. (ps-2). 1987. pap. 3.95 (0-590-44506-5) Scholastic Inc.
—Little Fingerling. Hughs, Monica, as told by. 32p. (gr. k-3). 1992. 13.95 (0-8249-8553-2, Ideals Child) Hambleton-Hill.
—Sadie & the Snowman. Morgan, Allan. 32p. (ps-2). 1987. pap. 2.50 (0-590-41826-2) Scholastic Inc.

Clark, Cindy & Kuska, George. Live Again Our Mission Past: California Missions Through Children's Eyes. Linse, Barbara B. & Kuska, George, eds. 200p. (gr. 7-12). 1984. pap. 13.95 (*0-9607458-1-5*) Arts Pubns.
Clark, Cindy, jt. illus. see Links, Marty.
Clark, David. Peculiar Zoo. Polisar, Barry L. 32p. (gr. k-6). 1993. 14.95 (*0-938663-14-3*) Rainbow Morn.
—The Snake Who Was Afraid of People. Polisar, Barry L. 32p. (gr. k-4). 1993. Repr. of 1988 ed. 14.95 (*0-938663-16-X*) Rainbow Morn.
—Snakes & the Boy Who Was Afraid of Them. Polisar, Barry L. 32p. (gr. 1-6). 1993. Repr. of 1988 ed. 14.95 (*0-938663-15-1*) Rainbow Morn.
—The Trouble with Ben. Polisar, Barry L. 32p. (gr. k-4). 1992. 14.95 (*0-938663-13-5*) Rainbow Morn.
Clark, Emma C. Beware of the Aunts! Thomson, Pat. LC 90-28928. 32p. (gr. k-3). 1992. SBE 14.95 (*0-689-50538-8*, M K McElderry) Macmillan Child Grp.
—Boo! Young Scary Stories. Cecil, Laura, compiled by. LC 90-2824. (ps up). 1990. 20.00 (*0-688-09842-8*) Greenwillow.
—Goodnight, Stella. McMullan, Kate. LC 93-876. Date not set. write for info. (*1-56402-065-7*) Candlewick Pr.
—I Never Saw a Purple Cow. 96p. (ps-3). 1991. 18.95 (*0-316-14500-9*) Little.
—Listen to This. Cecil, Laura. LC 87-8556. 96p. (ps-3). 1988. 15.00 (*0-688-07617-3*) Greenwillow.
—Stuff & Nonsense. Cecil, Laura. LC 89-1647. 96p. (ps up). 1989. 15.95 (*0-688-08898-8*) Greenwillow.
—A Thousand Years of Sea. Cecil, Laura, compiled by. LC 91-35687. 80p. (ps up). 1993. 18.00 (*0-688-11437-7*) Greenwillow.
—Wild Robert. large type ed. Jones, Diana W. 120p. 1992. 13.95 (*0-7451-1471-7*, Galaxy Child Lrg Print) Chivers N Amer.
Clark, Emma Chichester. The Minstrel & the Dragon Pup. Sutcliff, Rosemary. LC 92-53012. 48p. (ps-3). 1993. 16.95 (*1-56402-098-3*) Candlewick Pr.
Clark, Irene. Zoo-Phonics. Bradshaw, Georgene E. & Wrighton, Charlene A. 32p. (gr. k-4). 1986. pap. text ed. 10.00 (*0-9617342-0-5*); tchr's manual (incl. basic kit) 50.00 (*0-685-17464-6*) Zoo-Phonics.
—A Zoo-Phonics Reader: Level A. Bradshaw, Georgene E. & Wrighton, Charlene A. 32p. (ps-1). 1986. pap. text ed. 3.50 (*0-9617342-1-3*) Zoo-Phonics.
Clark, Linda F. Baby's Dinner. Lanton, Sandy. 32p. (ps-2). Date not set. 11.95 (*1-56065-145-8*) Capstone Pr. Postponed.
Clark, Mary. The Life & Adventures of Santa Claus. Baum, L. Frank. Gardner, Martin, intro. by. (gr. 3-8). 18.25 (*0-8446-5450-7*) Peter Smith.
Clark, Matthew. The Magic of Myrna C. Waxweather. Dutton, Sandra. LC 86-20579. 96p. (gr. 2-5). 1987. SBE 12.95 (*0-689-31273-3*, Atheneum Child Bk) Macmillan Child Grp.
Clark, Melissa & Johnson, Gloria. Children's Stories Two: Coloring Nature's Harmony. Johnson, Ralph E. Johnson, Paul T., ed. Johnson, Paul & Johnson, Paul. 100p. (Orig.). (gr. k-12). 1989. pap. write for info. (*0-9621929-0-2*) J-p Press.
Clark, Patricia. Seawolf: Building a Canoe. Batdorf, Carol. 24p. (Orig.). (gr. 1-6). 1990. pap. 4.95 (*0-88839-247-8*) Hancock House.
Clark, Penny. A Coloring Book of Bible Proverbs. 32p. (ps-5). 1988. 2.50 (*0-9618608-2-0*) Lynn's Bookshelf.
—A Coloring Book of Bible Verses from Proverbs. NIV ed. Decker, Barbara, ed. 32p. (Orig.). (ps-8). 1991. 2.50 (*0-9618608-6-3*) Lynn's Bookshelf.
—A Coloring Book of Bible Verses from the Epistles. Decker, Barbara, ed. 32p. (Orig.). 1989. coloring bk 2.50 (*0-9618608-4-7*) Lynn's Bookshelf.
—A Coloring Book of Bible Verses from the Epistles. Decker, Barbara, ed. 32p. (ps-5). 1992. 2.50 (*0-9618608-9-8*) Lynn's Bookshelf.
Clark, Roland. Gunner's Dawn. 2nd ed. Clark, Roland. 125p. (gr. 10 up). 1991. Repr. of 1937 ed. 40.00 (*1-56416-017-3*) Derrydale Pr.
Clark, Ron G. Animal Jokes. Chmielewski, Gary. LC 86-17684. (gr. 2-3). 1986. 13.27 (*0-86592-687-5*); 9.95s.p. (*0-685-58362-7*) Rourke Corp.
—Riddles. Chemielewski, Gary. LC 86-17720. (gr. 2-3). 1986. PLB 13.27 (*0-86592-686-7*); 9.95 (*0-685-58363-5*) Rourke Corp.
—Sports Jokes. Chmielewski, Gary. (gr. 2-3). 1986. 13.27 (*0-86592-683-2*); lib. bdg. 9.95 (*0-685-58364-3*) Rourke Corp.
—Teacher Jokes. Chmielewski, Gary. LC 86-17773. (gr. 2-3). 1986. 13.27 (*0-86592-688-3*); 9.95s.p. (*0-685-58365-1*) Rourke Corp.
—Tongue Twisters. Chmielewski, Gary. LC 86-17701. (gr. 2-3). 1986. 13.27 (*0-86592-685-9*); 9.95s.p. (*0-685-58366-X*) Rourke Corp.
Clark, Russell. Esteban: Walking Across America. Wade, Mary D. 48p. (gr. 1-3). 1994. 10.95 (*1-882539-11-7*); pap. 4.95 (*1-882539-12-5*); tchr's guide 5.00 (*1-882539-13-3*) Colophon Hse.
Clarke, Dorothy J. The ABC's of Family Court: A Children's Guide. Alberton, Kathleen. LC 88-120423. 54p. (gr. 1-12). 1987. pap. 1.50 (*0-9619599-0-8*) NYC Law Dept.
Clarke, Gus. Anthony & the Aardvark. Sloss, Lesley. LC 90-6528. 32p. (ps up). 1991. 13.95 (*0-688-10302-2*); PLB 13.88 (*0-688-10303-0*) Lothrop.
—E I E I O: The Story of Old MacDonald, Who Had a Farm. LC 92-53462. (gr. 3 up). 1993. write for info. (*0-688-12215-9*) Lothrop.

Clarke, Karen. The Very Special Visitors. Odor, Ruth S. 28p. (ps). 1992. 2.50 (*0-87403-955-X*, 24-03595) Standard Pub.
Clarke, Lea A. Think Pink. Cossi, Olga. LC 93-5556. 1994. write for info. (*0-88289-995-3*) Pelican.
Clarke, Mary & Ashton, Frederick. Antoinette Sibley. Ashton, Frederick, intro. by. 128p. (gr. 8-12). 1981. 29.95 (*0-903102-64-1*, Pub. by Dance Bks UK) Princeton Bk Co.
Clarke, Sue. Passover! A Three-Dimensional Celebration. Freedland, Sara. LC 93-34026. 8p. (ps-3). 1994. 15.99 (*0-670-85111-6*) Viking Child Bks.
Clarkson & Twede. Someone Special - You! Brady, Janeen. 26p. (gr. k-9). 1991. activity bk. 2.25 (*0-944803-76-8*); cassette & bklt. 9.95 (*0-944803-74-1*) Brite Intl.
Clarkson, Doris. I am a Try-Frog, Vol. 4. Seeley, Mae. 32p. (ps-2). 1990. 4.95 (*0-9624309-3-5*) MYLAC Pub Co.
—I am Unique, Vol. 3. Seeley, Mae. 32p. (ps-2). 1990. 4.95 (*0-9624309-2-7*) MYLAC Pub Co.
Classen, Martin. Tide Pools. Rood, Ronald. LC 92-2581. 48p. (gr. 2-5). 1993. 12.00 (*0-06-027074-8*); PLB 11.89 (*0-06-027075-6*) HarpC Child Bks.
—Tide Pools. Rood, Ronald. LC 92-2581. 48p. (gr. 2-5). 1993. pap. 7.95 (*0-06-446151-3*, Trophy) HarpC Child Bks.
Classic American Fundraisers Staff. Three Ingredient Cookbook. Wornall, Ruthie. 64p. (gr. 9-12). 1988. pap. 5.95 (*0-685-29002-6*) R Wornall.
Claverie, Jean. Billy the Brave. Chapouton, Anne-Marie. Bell, Anthea, tr. from FRE. LC 85-63307. 32p. (gr. k-2). 1986. 8.95 (*1-55858-070-0*) North-South Bks NYC.
—Die Drei Kleinen Schweinchen. Claverie, Jean. (GER.). 32p. (gr. k-3). 1992. 13.95 (*3-85825-330-8*) North-South Bks NYC.
—Little Lou. Claverie, Jean. LC 90-1531. 48p. 1990. 16.95 (*1-55670-162-4*) Stewart Tabori & Chang.
—Little Lou. Claverie, Jean. 48p. (gr. 3 up). 1990. PLB 17.95s.p. (*0-88682-329-3*) Creative Ed.
—Livre d'Ete. Ottenheimer, Laurence. (FRE.). 88p. (gr. 4-9). 1983. 13.95 (*2-07-039508-1*) Schoenhof.
—Peekaboo! Price, Mathew. 24p. (ps). 1993. 5.99 (*0-679-84031-1*) Knopf Bks Yng Read.
—The Three Little Pigs. Claverie, Jean. Crawford, Elizabeth, tr. from GER. LC 88-25327. 32p. (gr. k-3). 1989. 13.95 (*1-55858-004-2*) North-South Bks NYC.
—Les Trois Petits Cochons. Claverie, Jean. (FRE.). 32p. (gr. k-3). 1992. 13.95 (*3-314-20655-0*) North-South Bks NYC.
Clay, Cliff. Fireside Tales. Moore, Mary S. 21p. (Orig.). (gr. 5-12). 1990. pap. 7.95 (*0-913678-18-X*); paper & audiocassette 10.00 (*0-913678-19-8*) New Day Pr.
—Freedom Light: Underground Railroad Stories from Ripley, Ohio. Gaines, Edith M. (Orig.). (gr. 5-8). 1991. pap. 6.95 (*0-913678-20-1*) New Day Pr.
Clay, Jesse, jt. illus. see Pacheco, David.
Clay, Marilyn. Exploring Forces & Structures. Bardon, Keith. LC 91-38318. 48p. (gr. 4-8). 1992. PLB 19.92 (*0-8114-2602-5*) Raintree Steck-V.
—Exploring Variety of Life. Stephenson, Robert & Browne, Roger. LC 92-34357. 48p. (gr. 4-8). 1992. PLB 19.92 (*0-8114-2606-8*) Raintree Steck-V.
Clay, Wil. Little Eight John. Wahl, Jan. 32p. (gr. k-3). 1992. 14.00 (*0-525-67367-9*, Lodestar Bks) Dutton Child Bks.
—The Real McCoy: The Life of an African-American Inventor. Towle, Wendy. LC 91-38895. 32p. (gr. k-4). 1993. 14.95 (*0-590-43596-5*) Scholastic Inc.
—Tailypo! Wahl, Jan. LC 90-39491. 32p. (ps-2). 1991. 14.95 (*0-8050-0687-7*, Bks Young Read) H Holt & Co.
—Themba. Sacks, Margaret. LC 92-9754. 48p. (gr. 2-5). 1992. 12.00 (*0-525-67414-4*, Lodestar Bks) Dutton Child Bks.
—Two Hundred Thirteen Valentines. Cohen, Barbara. LC 91-7151. 64p. (gr. 2-4). 1991. 13.95 (*0-8050-1536-1*, Redfeather BYR) H Holt & Co.
—Two Hundred Thirteen Valentines. Cohen, Barbara. LC 91-7151. 64p. (gr. 2-4). 1993. pap. 4.95 (*0-8050-2627-4*, Redfeather BYR) H Holt & Co.
Clay, Wil, photos by. The House in the Sky. San Souci, Robert D. LC 92-39958. 1995. 13.99 (*0-8037-1284-7*); PLB 13.89 (*0-8037-1285-5*) Dial Bks Young.
Claycamp, Micah. My Mother Doesn't Like to Cook. Phillips, Wanda C. 28p. (Orig.). (ps-5). 1993. pap. 6.95 (*0-936981-20-2*) ISHA Enterprises.
Clayson, David N. Guess What Day It Is? Peaslee, Ann & De Witt, Sorena. 216p. (gr. 3-6). 1988. pap. 14.50 (*0-89346-305-1*) Heian Intl.
Clayton, Elaine. Pup in School. Clayton, Elaine. LC 92-18457. 24p. (ps-1). 1993. 12.00 (*0-517-59085-9*); PLB 12.99 (*0-517-59086-7*) Crown Bks Yng Read.
Clayton, Gordon, photos by. Calf. Ling, Mary. LC 92-53486. 24p. (ps-1). 1993. 7.95 (*1-56458-205-1*) Dorling Kindersley.
—Lamb. 24p. (gr. k-3). 1992. 6.95 (*0-525-67359-8*, Lodestar Bks) Dutton Child Bks.

Cleaveland, C. A. & McCreary, Jane. Some Secrets Are For Sharing. Winston-Hiller, Randy. 33p. (Orig.). (gr. 4 up). 1986. pap. 5.95 (*0-910223-08-4*) MAC Pub.

Timmy is all of nine years old--he plays ball--he loves to hear stories about the sea--Timmy is an abused child. SOME SECRETS ARE FOR SHARING is his story, told from the youngster's viewpoint. This book tells of the PROBLEM, REACTIONS, INTERVENTION, PROCESS & RECOVERY of both the child & the family. SOME SECRETS ARE FOR SHARING is a book for children to read or to read to children. The primary purposes are to help the abused child understand that there IS someone to listen & help & to give the involved adult reader insight & perspective about the abuse problem. Every year, over a million children are abused in one way or another. Most of these children are alone with their feelings. Even if they receive professional help, there is a strong likelihood that their experiences will not be shared with their peers. In SOME SECRETS ARE FOR SHARING, the reader is not only faced with the experience of a boy named Timmy who has been abused, but reads about the feelings, behaviors & struggles Timmy has to deal with as an abused child. By Randy Winston-Hiller. MAC Publishing, 5005 East 39th Avenue, Denver, CO 80207-1106. 303-331-0148. $5.95 plus $1.05 shipping.
Publisher Provided Annotation.

Cleaver, Elizabeth, photos by. The Loon's Necklace. Cleaver, Elizabeth. Toye, William, retold by. 24p. (ps up). 1990. pap. 7.50 (*0-19-540675-3*) OUP.
Cleaver, William. The Case of the Missing Mother. Howe, James. LC 82-13287. 32p. (gr. 1-6). 1983. pap. 1.95 (*0-394-85729-1*) Random Bks Yng Read.
Clement, Frederic. The Painter & the Wild Swans. Clement, Claude. LC 86-2154. 32p. (gr. k up). 1986. 13.95 (*0-8037-0268-X*) Dial Bks Young.
—The Voice of the Wood. Clement, Claude. 32p. (gr. k-8). 1993. pap. 5.99 (*0-14-054594-8*) Puffin Bks.
Clement, Frederic, photos by. The Voice of the Wood. Clement, Claude. LC 88-22892. 32p. (gr. k up). 1989. 14.95 (*0-8037-0635-9*) Dial Bks Young.
Clement, Gary. Eat Up! Savage, Candace. 56p. 1993. pap. 9.95 (*1-895565-13-8*) Firefly Bks Ltd.
—Get Growing: How the Earth Feeds Us. Savage, Candace. 56p. (gr. 3-7). 1991. pap. 9.95 (*0-920668-95-X*) Firefly Bks Ltd.
Clement, Rod. Snail Mail. Edwards, Hazel. 32p. (gr. k-3). 1991. pap. 7.95 (*0-7322-7206-8*, Pub. by Angus & Robertson AT) HarpC.
—When Hippo Was Hairy & Other Tales from Africa. Greaves, Nick. 144p. (gr. 3-12). 1988. 12.95 (*0-8120-4131-3*) Barron.
—When Hippo Was Hairy & Other Tales from Africa. Greaves, Nick. 144p. (gr. k up). 1991. pap. 8.95 (*0-8120-4548-3*) Barron.
—When Lion Could Fly: And Other Tales from Africa. Greaves, Nick. LC 93-21841. 144p. (gr. 3 up). 1993. 13.95 (*0-8120-6344-9*); pap. 8.95 (*0-8120-1625-4*) Barron.
Clements, Gillian. The Truth about Castles. Clements, Gillian. 40p. (gr. 2-6). 1990. PLB 18.95 (*0-87614-401-6*) Carolrhoda Bks.
Clements, Jehan. Alfred the Ant: The First Storytelling "Flip Over" Picture Book. Clements, Jehan. LC 89-61138. 48p. (gr. k-3). 1991. 20.00 (*0-9622500-0-7*) Strytllr Co.
Clementson, J. How the Animals Got Their Colors: Animal Myths from Around the World. Rosen, M. 1992. 14.95 (*0-15-236783-7*, HB Juv Bks) HarBrace.
Clementson, John. How Giraffe Got Such a Long Neck--& Why Rhino Is So Grumpy: A Tale from East Africa. Rosen, Michael, retold by. LC 92-46662. 32p. (ps-3). 1993. 13.99 (*0-8037-1621-4*) Dial Bks Young.
Clemmons, Bradley & Witwer, Julia. The Fish King's Power of Truth. Tulku, Tarthang, intro. by. LC 86-24159. 32p. (gr. k-4). 1987. PLB 14.95 (*0-89800-158-7*); pap. 7.95 (*0-89800-144-7*) Dharma Pub.
Cleveland, Fred. Apache Legends: Songs of the Wind Dancer. Cuevas, Lou. Brown, Keven, ed. 128p. (Orig.). 1991. 16.95 (*0-87961-218-5*); pap. text ed. 8.95 (*0-87961-219-3*) Naturegraph.
—The Navajo Brothers & the Stolen Herd. Grammer, Maurine. Rushing, Jack, frwd. by. LC 92-15018. 120p. (gr. 6-8). 1992. pap. 9.95 (*1-878610-23-6*) Red Crane Bks.

Cliff, Don. Two for America: The True Story of a Swiss Immigrant. Jacobson, Gloria. 36p. (gr. 4). 1989. pap. 8.50 (*0-9618399-1-0*) G Jacobson.

Clifford, Rowan. Head in the Sand. Cole, Michael. LC 90-30086. 24p. (ps-3). 1990. PLB 13.50 (*0-87614-435-0*) Carolrhoda Bks.

Clifford, Sandy. Good for Me! All about Food in 32 Bites. Burns, Marilyn. LC 78-6727. (gr. 5 up). 1978. pap. 9.95 (*0-316-11747-1*) Little.
—Only Human: Why We Are the Way We Are. Bell, Neill. LC 83-9826. 128p. (gr. 4 up). 1983. 14.95 (*0-316-08816-1*); pap. 9.95 (*0-316-08818-8*) Little.
—Pig Tales: The Adventures of Arnold the Chinese Potbelly Miniature Pig. Kujoko. 21p. (Orig.). (ps-8). 1988. pap. 4.95 (*0-9623210-0-1*) Kiyoko & Co.

Clift, Eva. Frankenstein. Shelley, Mary Wollstonecraft. Arneson, D. J., retold by. 128p. 1992. pap. 2.95 (*1-56156-142-8*) Kidsbks.
—Gulliver's Travels. Swift, Jonathan. Arneson, D. J., retold by. 128p. 1992. pap. 1.95 (*1-56156-143-6*) Kidsbks.
—Peter Pan. Barrie, J. M. Arneson, D. J., retold by. 128p. 1991. pap. 2.95 (*1-56156-029-4*) Kidsbks.
—Robin Hood. abr. ed. Pyle, Howard. Arneson, D. J., retold by. 128p. 1991. pap. 2.95 (*1-56156-028-6*) Kidsbks.

Clifton-Dey, Richard. Space: A Three-Dimensional Journey. Jones, Brian. 14p. (gr. k-4). 1991. 15.95 (*0-8037-0759-2*) Dial Bks Young.

Cline, Paul. Amy & Nathaniel. Poltarnees, Welleran. 32p. 1991. 11.95 (*0-88138-118-7*, Green Tiger) S&S Trade.
—The Angel Who Forgot. Bartone, Elisa. LC 91-34233. 48p. (Orig.). (ps up). 1992. 10.00 (*0-671-76037-8*, Green Tiger) S&S Trade.

Cline, Paul & Sieck, Judyth. Booboo's Dream. Cline, Paul. 32p. (ps-8). 1990. 12.95 (*0-9625261-1-8*) Medlicott Pr.

Clipson, Bill. The Colonial Wars: Clashes in the Wilderness. Carter, Alden R. 64p. (gr. 5-8). 1992. PLB 12.90 (*0-531-20079-5*) Watts.

Clipson, Helen. Ben Makes a Cake. Wilkins, Verna A. LC 93-9290. 1993. 6.95 (*1-870516-02-8*) Childs Play.

Clo, Kathy. La Historia De Jean Baptiste DuSable: El Padre De Chicago. Thompson-Peters, Flossie E. Nolasco-Carrandi, Guadalupe, tr. from ENG. (SPA.). 32p. (gr. 3-8). 1994. pap. 4.70 (*1-880784-09-2*) Atlas Pr.
—Jan, the Shoeman: The Story of Jan Matzeliger. Thompson-Peters, Flossie E. 32p. (Orig.). (gr. 3-9). 1985. pap. text ed. 4.70 (*1-880784-01-7*) Atlas Pr.
—The Story of Benjamin Banneker. Thompson-Peters, Flossie E. 32p. (Orig.). (gr. 1-6). 1986. pap. text ed. 4.70 (*1-880784-02-5*) Atlas Pr.
—The Story of Jean Baptiste DuSable: Father of Chicago. Thompson-Peters, Flossie E. 32p. (Orig.). (gr. 3-9). 1986. pap. text ed. 4.70 (*1-880784-03-3*) Atlas Pr.

Clonan, Barbara. The Night Before Christmas. Moore, Clement C. LC 89-6560. 28p. (gr. k-3). 1990. PLB 12.95 (*0-87226-416-5*, Bedrick Blackie) P Bedrick Bks.

Cloonan, Paula. The Twelve Days of Christmas. 24p. (gr. k-3). 1990. PLB 14.95 (*0-87226-438-6*, Bedrick Blackie) P Bedrick Bks.

Clore, Chuck. I'm Scared to Witness! Bonnici, Roberta L. 48p. (Orig.). (gr. 9-12). 1979. pap. 1.50 (*0-88243-931-6*, 02-0931); leader's guide 3.95 (*0-88243-330-X*, 02-0330) Gospel Pub.
—Your Right to Be Different. Bonnici, Roberta L. 48p. (gr. 9-12). 1982. pap. 1.50 (*0-88243-842-5*, 02-0842); leader's guide 3.95 (*0-88243-333-4*, 02-0333) Gospel Pub.

Clouse, Nancy. Sebgugugu the Glutton. Aardema, Verna. 40p. (gr. k-4). 1993. text ed. 14.99 (*0-8028-5073-1*) Eerdmans.

Clouse, Nancy L. Puzzle Maps U. S. A. Clouse, Nancy L. LC 89-24604. 32p. (ps-2). 1990. 15.95 (*0-8050-1143-9*, Bks Young Read) H Holt & Co.

Cloutier, James. This Day in Oregon. Cloutier, James. LC 80-83719. 128p. 1981. pap. 6.95 (*0-918966-06-X*) Image West.

Clover, Barbara. Santa & the Captain: A Mystic Christmas Tale. Tift, Tom. LC 89-81337. 24p. (Orig.). (gr. 2-4). 1989. pap. 6.95 (*0-9624607-0-2*) Hickory Ridge Pr.

Club de Madres Virgen del Carmen Staff. Por Fin Es Carnaval. Dorros, Arthur. Dorros, Sandra M., tr. LC 90-36222. (SPA.). 32p. (ps-3). 1991. 13.95 (*0-525-44690-7*, DCB) Dutton Child Bks.
—Tonight Is Carnaval. Dorros, Arthur. LC 90-32391. 32p. (gr. k-3). 1991. 13.95 (*0-525-44641-9*, DCB) Dutton Child Bks.

Cluet, Jaume. Come to the Park. Magni, Laura. 16p. (ps up). 1989. 8.95 (*0-8120-5994-8*) Barron.

Clutterbuck, Mary. Animals & Birds of the Desert. 32p. (gr. 3-5). 1985. 7.95x (*0-86685-445-2*) Intl Bk Ctr.

Co-Op Kids. Stories & Poems by the Co-Op Kids. Higgins, Susan O. & Co-Op Kids. 70p. (Orig.). (ps-3). 1987. pap. 4.00 (*0-939973-04-9*) Pumpkin Pr Pub Hse.

Coady, Christopher. Little Star. Conlon-McKenna, Marita. LC 92-22132. 1993. 13.95 (*0-316-15375-3*) Little.
—Red Riding Hood. Coady, Christopher, retold by. LC 91-25567. 32p. (ps-6). 1992. 15.00 (*0-525-44896-9*, DCB) Dutton Child Bks.

Coalson, Glo. On Mother's Lap. Scott, Ann H. 32p. (ps-k). 1992. 14.45 (*0-395-58920-7*, Clarion Bks); pap. 5.70 (*0-395-62976-4*, Clarion Bks) HM.

Coates, Ross. Creation of a California Tribe: Grandfather's Maidu Indian Tale. Trafzer, Clifford E. & Smith-Trafzer, Lee A. LC 88-61007. 45p. (Orig.). (gr. 3-6). 1988. pap. 6.95 (*0-940113-18-X*) Sierra Oaks Pub.
—When Hopi Children Were Bad: A Monster Story. Mana, Tawa & Youyouseyah. 41p. (Orig.). (gr. k-5). 1989. pap. 6.95 (*0-940113-20-1*) Sierra Oaks Pub.

Coats, Carolyn. Come Cook with Me! A Cookbook for Kids. Coats, Carolyn & Smith, Pamela. 133p. 1989. pap. 10.00 spiral bound (*1-878722-06-9*) C Coats Bestsellers.

Coats, Laura J. Alphabet Garden. Coats, Laura J. LC 92-6235. 32p. (ps-1). 1993. 13.95 (*0-02-719042-0*, Macmillan Child Bk) Macmillan Child Grp.
—Mr. Jordan in the Park. Coats, Laura J. LC 88-13295. 32p. (gr. k-3). 1989. RSBE 14.95 (*0-02-719053-6*, Macmillan Child Bk) Macmillan Child Grp.
—Ten Little Animals. Coats, Laura J. LC 89-36778. 32p. (ps-1). 1990. RSBE 12.95 (*0-02-719054-4*, Macmillan Child Bk) Macmillan Child Grp.

Cobb, Theo. Chemically Active! Experiments You Can Do at Home. Cobb, Vicki. LC 83-49490. 160p. (gr. 5-8). 1985. (Lipp Jr Bks); PLB 14.89 (*0-397-32080-9*, Lipp Jr Bks) HarpC Child Bks.
—Chemically Active: Experiments You Can Do at Home. reissue ed. Cobb, Vicki. LC 83-49490. 160p. (gr. 6-8). 1990. pap. 4.95 (*0-06-446101-7*, Trophy) HarpC Child Bks.
—Light Action! Amazing Experiments with Optics. Cobb, Vicki & Cobb, Joshua. LC 92-25528. 208p. (gr. 6 up). 1993. 15.00 (*0-06-021436-8*); PLB 14.89 (*0-06-021437-6*) HarpC Child Bks.
—The Secret Life of Cosmetics: A Science Experiment Book. Cobb, Vicki. LC 85-40097. 128p. (gr. 5-9). 1985. 14.00 (*0-397-32121-X*, Lipp Jr Bks); PLB 13.89 (*0-397-32122-8*, Lipp Jr Bks) HarpC Child Bks.
—Sneakers Meet Your Feet. Cobb, Vicki. 48p. (gr. 4-6). 1985. 11.95 (*0-316-14896-2*) Little.

Cober, Alan. The Dark Is Rising. Cooper, Susan. LC 72-85916. 232p. (gr. 5 up). 1973. SBE 14.95 (*0-689-30317-3*, M K McElderry) Macmillan Child Grp.

Cober, Alan E. Viollet. Cunningham, Julia. (gr. 4-7). 1966. PLB 6.99 (*0-394-91821-5*) Pantheon.

Cocca, Maryann. Beginning Math. Jonson, Liz & Silliman, Emery. Nayer, Judith E., ed. 32p. (gr. k-1). 1991. wkbk. 1.95 (*1-878624-59-8*) McClanahan Bk.
—Oh, So Silly! Schmeltz, Susan A. LC 83-23754. 48p. (ps-3). 1984. 5.95 (*0-8193-1122-7*) Parents.

Cocca-Leffler, Maryann. Alphabet Bandits: An ABC Book. Leonard, Marcia. LC 89-4933. 24p. (gr. k-2). 1990. PLB 9.59 (*0-8167-1718-4*); pap. text ed. 1.95 (*0-8167-1719-2*) Troll Assocs.
—Big Time Bears. Krensky, Stephen. LC 88-30793. (ps-k). 1989. 14.95 (*0-316-50375-4*) Little.
—Count the Days Till Christmas. Cocca-Leffler, Maryann. LC 92-82915. 16p. (ps-3). 1993. pap. 3.95 (*0-590-46929-0*, Cartwheel) Scholastic Inc.
—The Elves & the Shoemaker. 18p. (ps). 1993. bds. 3.95 (*0-448-40177-0*, G&D) Putnam Pub Group.
—Grandma & Me. Cocca-Leffler, Maryann. LC 90-61044. 28p. (ps). 1991. bds. 2.95 (*0-679-80758-6*) Random Bks Yng Read.
—Hey Diddle Diddle: My First Book of Nursery Rhymes. 18p. (ps). 1991. 3.95 (*0-448-40107-X*, G&D) Putnam Pub Group.
—The Kitten Twins: A Book about Opposites. Leonard, Marcia. LC 89-4945. 24p. (gr. k-2). 1990. PLB 9.59 (*0-8167-1724-9*); pap. text ed. 1.95 (*0-8167-1725-7*) Troll Assocs.
—My First Numbers. Nayer, Judy. 32p. (ps). 1991. wkbk. 1.95 (*1-56293-166-0*) McClanahan Bk.
—Something Fishy. Schindel, John. LC 91-19223. 32p. (ps-1). 1993. page. 13.00 JRT (*0-671-74777-0*, S&S BFYR) S&S Trade.
—Thanksgiving at the Tappletons' Spinelli, Eileen. LC 84-40793. 32p. (gr. k-3). 1984. 11.95 (*0-201-15892-2*, Lipp Jr Bks) HarpC Child Bks.
—Thanksgiving at the Tappletons' newly illustrated ed. Spinelli, Eileen. LC 91-33250. 32p. (gr. k-3). 1989. pap. 4.95 (*0-06-443204-1*, Trophy) HarpC Child Bks.
—Thanksgiving at the Tappletons' newly illus. ed. Spinelli, Eileen. LC 91-33250. 32p. (ps-3). 1992. 15.00 (*0-06-020871-6*); PLB 14.89 (*0-06-020872-4*) HarpC Child Bks.
—A Trip to Mars. Young, Ruth. LC 89-70936. 32p. (ps-1). 1990. 14.95 (*0-531-05892-1*); PLB 14.99 (*0-531-08492-2*) Orchard Bks Watts.

Cochran, Marie. The Sweetest Berry on the Bush. Kai, Nubia. LC 92-63010. 121p. (Orig.). 1993. pap. 8.00 (*0-88378-059-3*) Third World.

Cocklin-Ray, Christine. The Roller Coaster: A Story of Alcoholism & the Family. Fitzmahan, Don. Black, Claudia, intro. by. LC 88-63798. 36p. (Orig.). (gr. 6). 1986. pap. 8.00 (*0-935529-11-X*) Comprehen Health Educ.

CoConis, Constantine. The Golden God: Apollo. Gates, Doris. 110p. (gr. 3-7). 1983. pap. 4.99 (*0-14-031647-7*, Puffin) Puffin Bks.
—Two Queens of Heaven: Aphrodite & Demeter. Gates, Doris. 94p. (gr. 3-7). 1983. pap. 4.99 (*0-14-031646-9*, Puffin) Puffin Bks.

CoConis, Ted. The Summer of the Swans. Byars, Betsy C. 144p. 1981. pap. 3.99 (*0-14-031420-2*, Puffin) Puffin Bks.
—Summer of the Swans. Byars, Betsy C. (gr. 7 up). 1970. pap. 14.00 (*0-670-68190-3*) Viking Child Bks.

Codd, Michael. Children's Bible in Story. Couch, Frank. 320p. 1989. 12.95 (*0-8249-8355-6*, Ideals Child) Hambleton-Hill.

Codd, Mike. King Midas. Storr, Catherine. LC 84-18307. 32p. (gr. 2-5). 1985. PLB 17.96 (*0-8172-2112-3*) Raintree Steck-V.
—The Trojan Horse. Storr, Catherine. LC 84-18292. 32p. (gr. 2-5). 1985. PLB 17.96 (*0-8172-2114-X*) Raintree Steck-V.

Codor, Dick, jt. illus. see Bouman, Carol.

Codor, Dick, jt. illus. see Couman, Carol.

Cody, Brian. Feelings. Allington, Richard L. & Krull, Kathleen. LC 79-27549. 32p. (ps-2). 1985. pap. text ed. 3.95 (*0-8114-8236-7*) Raintree Steck-V.

Cody, Iron Eyes. Indian Talk: Hand Signals of the North American Indians. Cody, Iron Eyes. LC 73-16246. 112p. (gr. 1 up). 1970. 14.95 (*0-911010-83-1*); pap. 6.95 (*0-911010-82-3*) Naturegraph.

Cofer, Camilla. Caterfly. DePaul, Don. LC 76-39691. (gr. 7 up). 1977. pap. 4.25 (*0-8356-0490-X*, Quest) Theos Pub Hse.

Coffman, Gina. If You Print This, Please Don't Use My Name: Questions from Teens & Their Parents about Things That Matter. Keltner, Nancy, compiled by. & intro. by. LC 91-36306. 256p. (Orig.). (gr. 7-12). 1992. pap. 8.95 (*0-944176-03-8*) Terra Nova.

Cogancherry, Helen. Children Do, Grownups Don't. Simon, Norma. Tucker, Kathleen, ed. LC 87-2205. (ps-3). 1987. PLB 13.95 (*0-8075-1144-7*) A Whitman.
—Don't Call Me Fatso. Philips, Barbara. Okun, Barbara, intro. by. LC 85-24341. 32p. (gr. k-6). 1980. PLB 17.96 (*0-8172-1350-3*) Raintree Steck-V.
—Fourth of July Bear. Lasky, Kathryn. LC 90-37422. 40p. (gr. k up). 1991. 13.95 (*0-688-08287-4*); PLB 13.88 (*0-688-08288-2*, Morrow Jr Bks) Morrow Jr Bks.
—Here Comes the Mystery Man. Sanders, Scott R. LC 92-24572. 32p. (gr. k-5). 1993. RSBE 15.95 (*0-02-778145-3*, Bradbury Pr) Macmillan Child Grp.
—I Am Not a Crybaby! Simon, Norma. Tucker, Kathleen, ed. LC 88-21698. 40p. (gr. k-4). 1989. 13.95 (*0-8075-3447-1*) A Whitman.
—I Am Not a Crybaby. Simon, Norma. 32p. (ps-3). 1991. pap. 3.95 (*0-14-054216-7*, Puffin) Puffin Bks.
—Millie Cooper, Take a Chance. Herman, Charlotte. LC 88-11081. 112p. (gr. 3 up). 1989. 11.95 (*0-525-44442-4*, DCB) Dutton Child Bks.
—Millie Cooper, Take a Chance. Herman, Charlotte. 112p. (gr. 3 up). 1990. pap. 3.95 (*0-14-034119-6*, Puffin) Puffin Bks.
—Millie Cooper, 3B. Herman, Charlotte. 80p. (gr. 3-7). 1986. pap. 3.95 (*0-14-032072-5*, Puffin) Puffin Bks.
—Millie Cooper, 3B. Herman, Charlotte. LC 84-25951. 112p. (gr. 2-6). 1985. 11.95 (*0-525-44157-3*, DCB) Dutton Child Bks.
—My Sister Is Different. Wright, Betty R. Nietupski, John, intro. by. LC 80-25508. 32p. (gr. k-6). 1981. PLB 16.67 (*0-8172-1369-4*) Raintree Pubs Ltd.
—Pride & Prejudice. Austen, Jane. Stewart, Diana, adapted by. LC 81-5215. 48p. (gr. 4 up). 1983. PLB 18.64 (*0-8172-1673-1*) Raintree Steck-V.
—Real Tooth Fairy. Kaye, Marilyn. 32p. (ps-3). 1990. 12.95 (*0-15-265780-0*) HarBrace.
—Sarah, Also Known As Hannah. Ross, Lillian H. LC 93-29601. 1994. write for info. (*0-8075-7237-3*) A Whitman.
—Sometimes My Mom Drinks Too Much. Kenny, Kevin & Krull, Helen. Neidengard, Ted, intro. by. LC 80-14515. 32p. (gr. k-6). 1980. PLB 17.96 (*0-8172-1366-X*) Raintree Steck-V.
—Whispering in the Park. Burstein, Fred. LC 91-239. 32p. (ps-2). 1992. SBE 13.95 (*0-02-715621-4*, Bradbury Pr) Macmillan Child Grp.
—Who Is a Stranger & What Should I Do? Girard, Linda W. Levine, Abby, ed. LC 84-17313. 32p. (gr. 2-6). 1985. PLB 11.95 (*0-8075-9014-2*); pap. 4.95 (*0-8075-9016-9*) A Whitman.
—Words in Our Hands. Litchfield, Ada B. Tucker, Kathleen, ed. LC 79-28402. (gr. 2-4). 1980. PLB 13.95 (*0-8075-9212-9*) A Whitman.
—Wuthering Heights. Bronte, Emily. Wright, Betty R., adapted by. LC 81-15786. 48p. (gr. 4 up). 1982. PLB 18.64 (*0-8172-1682-0*) Raintree Steck-V.

Cogbill, Catherine, jt. illus. see Ottenstein, Claire.

Coghlan, Jeanne A. There's an Elephant in the Bathtub. Albee, Jo. 24p. (Orig.). (gr. k-1). 1990. pap. 0.99 (*1-878624-39-3*) McClanahan Bk.

Cohen, A. R. Chadwick & the Garplegrungen. Cummings, Priscilla. LC 87-71087. 32p. (gr. k-4). 1987. 8.95 (*0-87033-377-1*) Tidewater.
—The Chadwick Coloring Book. Cummings, Priscilla. 32p. (Orig.). (gr. k-4). 1988. pap. 3.95 (*0-87033-389-5*) Tidewater.
—Chadwick Forever. Cummings, Priscilla. 30p. (gr. 4-8). 1993. bds. 8.95 (*0-87033-450-6*) Tidewater.
—Chadwick the Crab. Cummings, Priscilla. LC 85-41005. 32p. (gr. k-4). 1986. 8.95 (*0-87033-347-X*) Tidewater.
—Chadwick's Wedding. Cummings, Priscilla. LC 88-51677. 30p. (gr. k-4). 1989. 8.95 (*0-87033-390-9*) Tidewater.
—Oswald & the Timberdoodles. Cummings, Priscilla. LC 90-70723. 30p. (gr. k-5). 1990. 8.95 (*0-87033-411-5*) Tidewater.
—Sid & Sal's Famous Channel Marker Diner. Cummings, Priscilla. LC 91-65255. 30p. (gr. k-5). 1992. 8.95 (*0-87033-423-9*) Tidewater.

Cohen, Alice E. Take Care with Yourself: A Young Person's Guide to Understanding, Preventing & Healing from the Hurts of Child Abuse. White, Laurie A. & Spencer, Steven L. 36p. (Orig.). (gr. k-7). 1983. English edition. pap. 5.95 (0-9612024-0-8); pap. Spanish edition avail. White & Spencer.

Cohen, Barbara. The Long Way Home. Cohen, Barbara. 1992. pap. 3.50 (0-553-15984-4) Bantam.

Cohen, Donald. Calculus by & for Young People: (Ages 7, Yes 7 & Up) Cohen, Donald. 177p. (Orig.). (gr. 2 up). 1988. pap. 12.00 spiral bdg. (0-9621674-0-1) D Cohen Mathman.

Cohen, Dorothy P. Danger-Watch Out! Sears, Jeanne. 12p. (ps-3). 1988. pap. 1.95 (0-9621086-0-X) J Sears.

Cohen, Helena. Baby Safari. Cohen, Seth. 28p. (ps). 1993. 3.25 (0-679-83608-X) Random Bks Yng Read.

Cohen, Marsha. Baby's Favorite Things. 12p. (ps). 1986. 3.95 (0-394-88243-1) Random Bks Yng Read.

Cohen, Sharon. Does Candy Grow on Trees? Rice, Karen. LC 83-40407. 32p. (gr. 2-5). 1984. 9.95 (0-8027-6555-6) Walker & Co.

Cohen, Sheldon. The Boxing Champion. Carrier, Roch. LC 90-70133. 24p. (gr. 3 up). 1991. 14.95 (0-88776-249-2) Tundra Bks.

—The Boxing Champion. Carrier, Roch. 24p. (gr. 3 up). 1993. pap. 6.95 (0-88776-308-1) Tundra Bks.

—Un Champion. Carrier, Roch. LC 90-70134. (FRE.). 24p. (gr. 3 up). 1991. 14.95 (0-88776-250-6) Tundra Bks.

—Le Chandail de Hockey. Carrier, Roch. (FRE.). 24p. (Orig.). (gr. 1 up). 1985. pap. 6.95 (0-88776-176-3, Dist. by U of Toronto Pr); 14.95 (0-88776-171-2) Tundra Bks.

—The Hockey Sweater. Carrier, Roch. Fischman, Sheila, tr. from FRE. 24p. (gr. 1 up). 1984. text ed. 14.95 (0-88776-169-0, Dist. by U of Toronto Pr); pap. 6.95 (0-88776-174-7) Tundra Bks.

—El Jonron Mas Largo. Carrier, Roch. Zeller, Beatriz, tr. (SPA.). 24p. (gr. 3 up). 1993. 14.95 (0-88776-304-9) Tundra Bks.

—The Longest Home Run. Carrier, Roch. Fischman, Sheila, tr. from FRE. LC 92-62364. 24p. (gr. 3 up). 1993. 14.95 (0-88776-300-6) Tundra Bks.

—Le Plus Long Circuit (The Longest Home Run) Carrier, Roch. LC 92-62362. (FRE.). 24p. (gr. 2 up). 1993. 14.95 (0-88776-301-4) Tundra Bks.

Cohen, Susan J. The Donkey's Story. Cohen, Barbara, adapted by. LC 85-27. 32p. (gr. k-5). 1988. 12.95 (0-688-04104-3); PLB 12.88 (0-688-04105-1) Lothrop.

Cohen, Toby M. Do You Know What I'm Going to Be? I'm Going to Be a Yeshiva Bochur. Finkelstein, Ruth. 16p. (Orig.). (ps-k). 1991. pap. 4.50 (0-9628157-0-5) R Finkelstein.

Cohen, Vivien. A Better Safe Than Sorry Book: A Family Guide for Sexual Assault Prevention. Gordon, Sol & Gordon, Judith. 44p. (gr. 2-7). 1992. pap. 8.95 (0-934978-13-1) Prometheus Bks.

—Changes in You for Boys: A Clearly Illustrated, Simply Worded Explanation of the Changes of Puberty for Boys. Siegel, Peggy C. LC 90-86238. 44p. (Orig.). (gr. 4-8). 1991. pap. 8.95 (0-9628687-1-X) Fam Life Ed.

—Changes in You for Girls: A Beautifully Illustrated, Simply Worded Explanation of the Changes of Puberty for Girls. Siegel, Peggy C. LC 90-86237. 52p. (Orig.). (gr. 4-8). 1991. pap. 8.95 (0-9628687-0-1) Fam Life Ed.

—Did the Sun Shine Before Your Were Born? Gordon, Sol & Gordon, Judith. 48p. (Orig.). (gr. k-5). 1992. pap. 8.95 (0-87975-723-X) Prometheus Bks.

—Facts about Sex: For Today's Youth. Gordon, Sol. 50p. (gr. 2-5). 1992. pap. 8.95 (0-934978-01-8) Prometheus Bks.

—Girls Are Girls & Boys Are Boys: So What's the Difference? Gordon, Sol. 48p. (Orig.). (gr. 3-7). 1991. pap. 9.95 (0-87975-686-1) Prometheus Bks.

—How Can You Tell If You're Really in Love? Everly, Kathleen & Gordon, Sol. 20p. (gr. 7-12). 1983. pap. 1.95 (0-934978-06-9) Ed-U Pr.

Cohn, Ronald H., photos by. Koko's Kitten. Patterson, Francine. 50p. (gr. k up). 1985. pap. 13.95 (0-590-40952-2) Scholastic Inc.

—Koko's Story. Patterson, Francine. 40p. 1988. pap. 5.95 (0-590-41364-3) Scholastic Inc.

Cokendolpher, Jean, jt. illus. see **Dean, David.**

Coker, Paul, Jr. Giggle Puss: Pet Jokes for Kids. Keller, Charles. LC 76-44837. (gr. 3-7). 1977. (Pub. by Treehouse); pap. 3.95 (0-13-356303-0) P-H.

—Minibikes! Jennings, Gordon. (gr. 5 up). 1974. P-H.

Colaquian, Val. Journey to the Center of the Earth: Student Activity Book. Sohl, Marcia & Dackerman, Gerald. (gr. 4-10). 1976. 1.25 (0-88301-191-3) Pendulum Pr.

Colbert, Margaret. Discovering Dinosaur Babies. Schlein, Miriam. LC 89-23496. 40p. (gr. 1-5). 1991. RSBE 14.95 (0-02-778091-0, Four Winds) Macmillan Child Grp.

Cole, Babette. Prince Cinders. Cole, Babette. 32p. (gr. 1-3). 1988. 14.95 (0-399-21502-6, Putnam) Putnam Pub Group.

—Prince Cinders. Cole, Babette. 32p. (ps-3). 1992. pap. 5.95 (0-399-21882-3, Sandcastle Bks) Putnam Pub Group.

—Princess Smartypants. Cole, Babette. LC 86-12381. (ps-3). 1987. 13.95 (0-399-21409-7, Putnam) Putnam Pub Group.

—Tarzanna. Cole, Babette. 32p. (ps-3). 1992. 14.95 (0-399-21837-8, Putnam) Putnam Pub Group.

—The Trouble with Mom. Cole, Babette. 32p. (gr. 5-8). 1984. 13.95 (0-698-20597-9, Putnam); pap. 5.95 (0-698-20681-9, Sandcastle Bks) Putnam Pub Group.

—Winni Allfours. Cole, Babette. LC 93-28447. (gr. k-4). 1993. PLB 13.95 (0-8167-3307-4); pap. 3.95t (0-8167-3308-2) Troll Assocs.

Cole, Bradley. Fingernail Souffle. DeWitt, Jim. 136p. (Orig.). (gr. 4-12). 1987. pap. 6.00 (0-915199-03-3) Pen Dec.

—Sharpshooting at Kinkajous. DeWitt, Jim. 136p. (gr. 4-12). 1987. pap. 6.00 (0-915199-06-8) Pen Dec.

Cole, Brock. Gaffer Samson's Luck. Paton Walsh, Jill. LC 84-10180. 112p. (gr. 5 up). 1984. 14.00 (0-374-32498-0) FS&G.

—Gaffer Samson's Luck. Paton Walsh, Jill. 128p. (gr. 3-7). 1990. pap. 3.50 (0-374-42513-2, Sunburst) FS&G.

—The Indian in the Cupboard. Banks, Lynne R. 192p. (gr. 4-7). 1982. pap. 3.99 (0-380-60012-9, Camelot) Avon.

—The Indian in the Cupboard. Banks, Lynne R. LC 80-2835. (gr. 4). 1985. 15.00 (0-385-17051-3) Doubleday.

Cole, Gwen. The Dangerous Life of the Sea Horse. Schlein, Miriam. LC 85-26857. 40p. (gr. 3-6). 1986. SBE 13.95 (0-689-31180-X, Atheneum Child Bk) Macmillan Child Grp.

Cole, Henry. Bats: Let's Read & Find Out About Science Ser. Earle, Ann. LC 93-11052. (gr. 4 up). 1994. 15.00 (0-06-023479-2); PLB 14.89 (0-06-023480-6) HarpC Child Bks.

Cole, Jeff. A Child's Guide to Historical Places. Cole, Deena. 64p. (ps-6). 1993. pap. 3.95 (1-878893-32-7); tchr's. guide 6.95 (1-878893-31-9) Telcraft Bks.

—A Child's Guide to Natural Wonders. Cole, Deena. 64p. (ps-6). 1993. pap. 3.95 (1-878893-34-3); tchr's. guide 6.95 (1-878893-33-5) Telcraft Bks.

Cole, Robin H. Pablo & the Miracle of Saint Anton. Cole, Robin H. LC 89-37973. 48p. 1990. pap. 3.95 (0-8091-6590-2) Paulist Pr.

Coleman, Bernice. The Ballad of the Men at Mier: The Black Bean Expedition. Seale, Jan E. 46p. (gr. 4-8). 1986. lib. bdg. 10.95 (0-936927-14-3); pap. 7.95 (0-936927-15-1) Knowing Pr.

Coleman, Debbie. Bugs - Bugs - Bugs, Vol. 10. Barone, Shirley A. 44p. (Orig.). (ps-2). 1989. pap. write for info. Toad Hse Bks.

—Easter Parade, Vol. 6. Barone, Shirley A. 44p. (Orig.). (ps-2). 1990. pap. write for info. Toad Hse Bks.

—Funny Dinosaurs, Vol. 4. Barone, Shirley A. 44p. (Orig.). (ps-2). 1989. pap. write for info. Toad Hse Bks.

—Halloween Fun for Everyone, Vol. 1. Barone, Shirley A. 44p. (Orig.). (ps-2). 1989. pap. 1.69 (0-685-30447-7) Toad Hse Bks.

—Happy Valentines, Vol. 5. Barone, Shirley A. 44p. (Orig.). (ps-2). 1990. pap. text ed. write for info. Toad Hse Bks.

—I Know My ABC's, Vol. 13. Barone, Shirley A. 44p. (Orig.). (ps-2). 1989. pap. write for info. Toad Hse Bks.

—I Know My Numbers, Vol. 14. Barone, Shirley A. 44p. (Orig.). (ps-2). 1989. pap. write for info. Toad Hse Bks.

—I Like Monsters, Vol. 9. Barone, Shirley A. 44p. (Orig.). (ps-2). 1989. pap. write for info. Toad Hse Bks.

—In My Toy Box, Vol. 8. Barone, Shirley A. 44p. (Orig.). (ps-2). 1989. pap. write for info. Toad Hse Bks.

—Kittens & Puppies, Vol. 11. Barone, Shirley A. 44p. (Orig.). (ps-2). 1989. pap. write for info. Toad Hse Bks.

—Let's Give Thanks, Vol. 2. Barone, Shirley A. 44p. (Orig.). (ps-2). 1989. pap. 1.75 (0-685-30448-5) Toad Hse Bks.

—Meet My Friends: Children of the World, Vol. 15. Barone, Shirley A. 44p. (Orig.). (ps-2). 1989. pap. write for info. Toad Hse Bks.

—My Teddy Bears, Vol. 12. Barone, Shirley A. 44p. (Orig.). (ps-2). 1989. pap. write for info. Toad Hse Bks.

—A Shoe for You, Vol. 7. Barone, Shirley A. 44p. (Orig.). (ps-2). 1989. pap. write for info. Toad Hse Bks.

—A Time for Joy (Christmas, Vol. 3. Barone, Shirley A. 44p. (Orig.). (ps-2). 1989. pap. write for info. Toad Hse Bks.

Coling, Jerome F. John Forbes & Company & the War of 1812 in the Spanish Borderlands. Coker, William S. 37p. (gr. 7 up). 1979. pap. 2.50 (0-933776-08-X) Perdido Bay.

Collard, Derek. At the Circus. Booth, Eugene. LC 77-7946. 24p. (gr. k-3). 1985. PLB 13.32 (0-8393-0112-X); pap. text ed. 9.27 (0-8393-0162-6) Raintree Steck-V.

—At the Fair. Booth, Eugene. LC 77-7961. 24p. (gr. k-3). 1985. PLB 13.32 (0-8393-0114-6); pap. text ed. 9.27 (0-8393-0163-4) Raintree Steck-V.

Collas, Daniel. My 911 Book for Help. Melle, Julie. LC 92-71606. 16p. (ps-6). 1992. pap. text ed. 9.99g (1-881402-00-2) CA Storybook.

Collete, Rondi. Socorro, Daughter of the Desert. Papagapitos, Karen. Kleinman, Estelle, ed. 64p. (gr. 1-4). 1993. 6.95 (0-9637328-0-3) Kapa Hse Pr.
SOCORRO, DAUGHTER OF THE

DESERT is the story of a young girl, who knows the answer to a mystery that nobody else seems to see. It is through the eyes of Socorro Hernandez that we find out who the mysterious phantom of the desert road is, & why he wants to warn people of any danger that might lie in their path. Socorro's family is going through a difficult period at the same time, & through this young girl's hard work & perseverance they manage to weather the father's bout with malaria. This book profiles the resourcefulness, courage & hope women historically have exhibited in trying times. Young readers should enjoy the several appearances of the mysterious phantom & still come away from the conclusion with a strong respect for women & their strength in an often unsettled world.
Publisher Provided Annotation.

Collette, Rondi. Caring for My Things. Moncure, Jane B. 32p. (ps-2). 1990. PLB 18.50 (0-89565-670-1); PLB 12.95s.p. (0-685-58739-8) Childs World.

—Space Travel: Blast-Off Day. McDonnell, Janet. LC 89-23999. 32p. (ps-2). 1990. PLB 19.95 (0-89565-556-X); PLB 13.95s.p. (0-685-56177-1) Childs World.

—What Plants Give Us: The Gift of Life. Riehecky, Janet. LC 90-30374. 32p. (ps-2). 1990. PLB 19.95 (0-89565-570-5); PLB 13.95s.p. (0-685-56186-0) Childs World.

Colley, Molly. Adventures of the Ballenger Bears. Ballenger, Sharon. 62p. (Orig.). (ps-6). 1992. Spiral bdg. pap. 11.95 (1-880734-00-1) SharLew Ent.
How many of us have treasured a Teddy Bear friend? Lots of people have them as children but more & more adults have become engrossed in the wonderful world of Teddy Bears & live "real life adventures" with them. This book is composed of 12 stories, each of which recounts a new adventure had by members of a very large collection of Teddy Bears. "...you will enjoy this book for the entertaining stories about Teddy Bears entering the world & looking for adventure. This is just the sort of whimsy loved by all our readers!" (The Teddy Tribune, May, 1993). These stories are illustrated by over 30 charming, gentle drawings that make these characters look so real you could just reach out & give them a hug. While stories aren't preachy, they do encourage the reader to share, to set goals & meet them, to care for family & friends, & to try new things as the Bears do. You will find yourself smiling when you read about the Bears calling on Grandma Bear to help finish up the apricot pie adventure, or trying to learn the polite way to eat cupcakes & drink tea at Bear School. This is definitely a "feel good" book, one which makes you feel you've spent an afternoon with good friends. Order from: SharLew Enterprises, P.O. Box 971, Ridgecrest, CA 93556. (619) 375-8540.
Publisher Provided Annotation.

Collier, Jaunell. I Love You. Collier, Jaunell & Hill, Marie. 27p. (Orig.). 1983. write for info. (0-918464-58-7) Irresistible.

Collier, John. In My Backyard. Collier, John. 32p. (ps-3). 1993. reinforced bdg. 14.99 (0-670-83609-5) Viking Child Bks.

—Petrouchka. Werner, Vivian, retold by. 32p. (gr. 5 up). 1992. 16.00 (0-670-83607-9) Viking Child Bks.

—The Sleeping Beauty in the Woods. Perrault, Charles. 32p. (gr. 6 up). 1984. PLB 13.95s.p. (0-87191-944-3) Creative Ed.

Collier, Michael, photos by. Black Canyon of the Gunnison National Monument. Houk, Rose. Priehs, T. J. & Jorgen, Randolph, eds. LC 91-60464. 16p. (Orig.). 1991. pap. 2.95 (0-911408-93-2) SW Pks Mnmts.

Collier, Roberta. One-Minute Jewish Stories. Lewis, Shari, adapted by. (ps-3). 1989. 10.00 (0-385-24447-9) Doubleday.

—Sing with Me Lullabies. (ps-1). 1987. Incl cassette. 5.95 (0-394-88811-1) Random Bks Yng Read.

Collier-Morales, Roberta. If I Ran the Family. Johnson, Lee & Johnson, Sue K. Espeland, Pamela, ed. LC 92-948. 32p. (ps-3). 1992. 13.95 (0-915793-41-5) Free Spirit Pub.

Collington, Peter. The Angel & the Soldier Boy. miniature ed. Collington, Peter. 32p. (ps-3). 1991. 4.95 (0-679-81441-8) Knopf Bks Yng Read.

—The Coming of the Surfman. Collington, Peter. LC 92-41844. 32p. (gr. 3 up). 1994. 16.00 (0-679-84721-9) Knopf Bks Yng Read.

—The Midnight Circus. Collington, Peter. 32p. (ps-2). 1993. 15.00 (0-679-83262-9); PLB 15.99 (0-679-93262-3) Knopf Bks Yng Read.

—On Christmas Eve. Collington, Peter. LC 90-4202. 32p. 1990. 14.95 (0-679-80830-2); PLB 15.99 (0-679-90830-7) Knopf Bks Yng Read.

Collins, Dane. Good Morning Mr. President: A Story about Carl Sandburg. Mitchell, Barbara. LC 88-7265. 56p. (gr. 3-6). 1988. PLB 14.95 (0-87614-329-X) Carolrhoda Bks.

Collins, Heather. Bare Naked Book. Stinson, Kathy. 32p. (gr. k-2). 1986. PLB 14.95 (0-920303-52-8, Pub. by Annick CN); pap. 4.95 (0-920303-53-6, Pub. by Annick CN) Firefly Bks Ltd.

—The Kids Cottage Book. Drake, Jane & Love, Ann. LC 93-2524. 1994. 13.95 (0-395-68711-X); pap. 10.95 (0-395-68709-8) Ticknor & Fields.

Collins, Judi. Squirrel's Adventure in Alphabet Town. Alden, Laura. LC 92-1314. 32p. (ps-2). 1992. PLB 14. 60 (0-516-05419-8) Childrens.

Collins, Patrick. The Tainos: The People Who Welcomed Columbus. Jacobs, Francine. 112p. (gr. 5-9). 1992. 15. 95 (0-399-22116-6, Putnam) Putnam Pub Group.

Collins, Tim. No Luck. Salem, Lynn & Stewart, Josie. 12p. (gr. 1). 1993. pap. 3.50 (1-880612-07-0) Seedling Pubns.

Collman, Martha R. Ballads & Other Island Things. Collman, Marthamarie C. 104p. (Orig.). (gr. 9 up). 1992. pap. 8.95 (0-9631903-0-X) M R Collman.

Colloms, Alisa. Know & Tell: A Workbook for Parents & Children on How to Prevent Child Abuse. 2nd ed. Lehman, Yvette K. Naeb, Yuli, tr. from CHI. 46p. (ps-4). 1993. write for info. (0-9638555-2-2) Y K Lehman.

—Saber y Decir: El Manual Para Padres e Hijos Sobre Como Prevenir el Abuso a los Ninos. 2nd ed. Lehman, Yvette K. Chavez, Vivian & Costas, Gloria, trs. from ENG. 46p. (ps-4). 1993. wkbk. 9.00 (0-9638555-1-4) Y K Lehman.

Collopy, George F. Happenings! Hilliard, Dick & Valenti-Hilliard, Beverly. LC 81-52715. 60p. (gr. 1 up). 1981. pap. text ed. 4.95 (0-89390-033-8) Resource Pubns.

—Surprises! Hilliard, Dick & Valenti-Hilliard, Beverly. LC 81-52714. 64p. (Orig.). (gr. 1 up). 1981. pap. text ed. 4.95 (0-89390-031-1) Resource Pubns.

—Wonders! Hilliard, Dick & Valenti-Hilliard, Beverly. LC 81-52713. 64p. (Orig.). (gr. 1 up). 1981. pap. text ed. 4.95 (0-89390-032-X) Resource Pubns.

Collot, Pierre. Wind of Chance. Guillot, Rene. Dale, Norman, tr. (gr. 6-9). 1958. 21.95 (0-87599-048-7) S G Phillips.

Colon, Odette E. The Song of the Whango-Whee. Smith, John F. Hannaford, Joey, contrib. by. 24p. (ps-5). 1993. 13.95 (1-884375-00-6) Chinky-Po Tree.

Colorado, Nani. Harry Dresses Himself. Gaban, Jesus. 16p. (ps-1). 1992. PLB 13.27 (0-8368-0715-4) Gareth Stevens Inc.

—Harry the Hippo, 4 vols. Gaban, Jesus. 16p. (ps-1). 1992. Set. PLB 53.08 (0-8368-0714-6) Gareth Stevens Inc.

—Harry's Mealtime Mess. Gaban, Jesus. 16p. (ps-1). 1992. PLB 13.27 (0-8368-0717-0) Gareth Stevens Inc.

—Harry's Sandbox Surprise. Gaban, Jesus. 16p. (ps-1). 1992. PLB 13.27 (0-8368-0716-2) Gareth Stevens Inc.

—Tub Time for Harry. Gaban, Jesus. 16p. (ps-1). 1992. PLB 13.27 (0-8368-0718-9) Gareth Stevens Inc.

Colquhoun, Diana. Animals. rev. ed. McCracken, Marlene J. & McCracken, Robert A. 83p. (gr. k-4). 1985. pap. 11.95 (0-920541-12-7) Peguis Pubs Ltd.

—Celebrations. rev. ed. McCracken, Marlene J. & McCracken, Robert A. 67p. (gr. k-4). 1986. pap. 11.95 (0-920541-72-0) Peguis Pubs Ltd.

—Fall. McCracken, Marlene J. & McCracken, Robert A. 88p. (gr. k-4). 1987. pap. 11.95 (0-920541-16-X) Peguis Pubs Ltd.

—Fantasy. 4th ed. McCracken, Marlene J. & McCracken, Robert A. 39p. (Orig.). (gr. k-4). 1992. pap. 11.95 (0-920541-02-X) Peguis Pubs Ltd.

—Halloween. rev. ed. McCracken, Marlene J. & McCracken, Robert A. 74p. (gr. k-4). 1984. pap. 11.95 (0-920541-76-2) Peguis Pubs Ltd.

—Myself. rev. ed. McCracken, Marlene J. & McCracken, Robert A. 84p. (gr. k-4). 1984. pap. 11.95 (0-920541-78-X) Peguis Pubs Ltd.

—The Sea & Other Water. rev. ed. McCracken, Marlene J. & McCracken, Robert A. 71p. (gr. k-4). 1985. pap. 11.95 (0-920541-80-1) Peguis Pubs Ltd.

—Spring. rev. ed. McCracken, Marlene J. & McCracken, Robert A. 83p. (gr. k-4). 1987. pap. 11.95 (0-920541-14-3) Peguis Pubs Ltd.

—Winter. rev. ed. McCracken, Marlene J. & McCracken, Robert A. 67p. (gr. k-4). 1987. pap. 11.95 (0-920541-10-0) Peguis Pubs Ltd.

Colquhoun, Jean. Angel Baskets: A Little Story about the Shakers. Ray, Mary L. LC 87-50789. 32p. (Orig.). 1987. pap. write for info. (0-9609384-3-5) M Wetherbee.

—Christmas in Water Village. Maxfield, Christine. 32p. (ps-5). 1989. 15.95 (0-9621029-0-3) Prima Design.

Colrus, Bill. Grandma & the Buck Deer. Vance, Joel M. 173p. 1988. pap. text ed. 11.95 (0-87691-322-2) Cedar Glade Pr.

—KidDoodles, Bk. 3. Herman, Emmi S. 64p. (Orig.). (ps-2). 1991. pap. 0.99 activity pad (1-878624-52-0) McClanahan Bk.

Coltharpe, Barbara A. Mr. Rumples Recycles. Coltharpe, Barbara A. Gullic, Bob, ed. 30p. (Orig.). (gr. 3-7). 1989. pap. 4.25x (0-9622752-0-4) Hyacinth Hse.

Colucci, Kristina & Boughton, Narda. The Pizza Boogie Songbook. Olshansky, Joanne. 33p. (Orig.). (gr. k-6). 1990. pap. 9.95 (0-9626239-0-3) JHO Music.

Colville, Jeane, et al. The Magic Handbook. Eldin, Peter. LC 85-171061. 192p. (gr. 4 up). 1985. lib. bdg. 9.79 (0-671-55040-3, J Messner); pap. 6.95 (0-685-42988-1) S&S Trade.

Combs, Jonathan. The Quitters. Starkman, Neal. LC 91-16797. 28p. (Orig.). (gr. 4). 1991. pap. 7.00 (0-935529-26-8) Comprehen Health Educ.

Compass Productions Staff. The Horrors of Howling Hall. Skwarek, Skip. LC 91-46526. 10p. (gr. k-4). 1992. 4.95 (0-8037-1185-9) Dial Bks Young.

—In the Deep Dark Dungeon. Skwarek, Skip. LC 91-45515. 10p. (gr. k-4). 1992. 4.95 (0-8037-1187-5) Dial Bks Young.

—The Mystery of Maggoty Mill. Skwarek, Skip. LC 91-47021. 10p. (gr. k-4). 1992. 4.95 (0-8037-1186-7) Dial Bks Young.

—The Weirdies of Wailing Wood. Skwarek, Skip. LC 91-46916. 10p. (gr. k-4). 1992. 4.95 (0-8037-1188-3) Dial Bks Young.

Compere, Janet. I'm Growing. Syme, Daniel & Bogot, Howard. 32p. (ps-1). 1982. pap. 4.00 (0-8074-0167-6, 101095) UAHC.

—Louis Braille: The Boy Who Invented Books for the Blind. Davidson, Margaret. 80p. 1991. pap. 2.75 (0-590-44350-X) Scholastic Inc.

Compton, Annette. God's Paintbrush. Sasso, Sandy E. LC 92-15493. 32p. (gr. k-4). 1992. 15.95 (1-879045-22-2) Jewish Lights.

Compton, Joanne, jt. illus. see Compton, Kenn.

Compton, Kenn. Ashpet: An Appalachian Tale. Compton, Joanne. LC 93-16034. 40p. (gr. 4-8). 1994. 15.95 (0-8234-1106-0) Holiday.

—Happy Christmas to All! Compton, Kenn. LC 90-29078. 32p. (ps-3). 1991. reinforced 14.95 (0-8234-0890-6) Holiday.

Compton, Kenn & Compton, Joanne. Little Rabbit's Easter Surprise. Compton, Kenn & Compton, Joanne. LC 91-17957. 32p. (ps-3). 1992. reinforced bdg. 14.95 (0-8234-0920-1) Holiday.

Comstock, David A. Feliciana's California Miracle. Comstock, Esther J. LC 85-9707. xiv, 178p. (Orig.). (gr. 6). 1985. 14.50 (0-933994-03-6); pap. 8.75 (0-933994-04-4) Comstock Bon.

Comstock, Floyd B. Vallejo & the Four Flags. Comstock, Esther J. LC 79-21636. xvi, 142p. (gr. 4). 1988. 12.50 (0-933994-01-X); pap. 8.75 (0-933994-07-9) Comstock Bon.

Comyns, Nantz. Blazing Bear. Deans, Sis B. LC 92-60478. 40p. (gr. 3-7). 1992. pap. 9.95 (0-932433-94-4) Windswept Hse.

Conahan, Carolyn. The Day Small Circle Changed His Shape. Bell, Jo G. 32p. (ps-2). Date not set. 11.95 (1-56065-160-1) Capstone Pr. Postponed.

—Hide & Seek with Colors. Bell, Jo G. 32p. (ps-2). Date not set. 11.95 (1-56065-158-X) Capstone Pr. Postponed.

—Sometimes I Wish I Were Big. Bell, Jo G. 32p. (ps-2). Date not set. 11.95 (1-56065-159-8) Capstone Pr. Postponed.

Conant, Roger, et al. Peterson First Guide to Reptiles & Amphibians. Conant, Roger, et al. 128p. (gr. 5 up). 1992. pap. 4.80 (0-395-62232-8) HM.

Conaway, James. Brachiosaurus. Riehecky, Janet. LC 89-22069. 32p. 1989. PLB 21.35 (0-89565-542-X); PLB 14.95s.p. (0-685-56084-8) Childs World.

—Troodon. Riehecky, Janet. 32p. (gr. k-4). 1990. PLB 21.35 (0-89565-636-1); PLB 14.95s.p. (0-685-58731-2) Childs World.

Conaway, Jim. Baryonyx. Riehecky, Janet. 32p. (gr. k-4). 1990. PLB 21.35 (0-89565-622-1); PLB 14.95s.p. (0-685-56207-7) Childs World.

—Diplodocus. Riehecky, Janet. 32p. (gr. k-4). 1990. PLB 21.35 (0-89565-627-2); PLB 14.95s.p. (0-685-56212-3) Childs World.

Concept of Design Staff. Learning How: BMX Riding. Boulais, Sue. James, Jody, ed. 48p. (gr. 4-7). 1992. lib. bdg. 14.95 (0-944280-36-6); pap. 5.95 (0-944280-41-2) Bancroft-Sage.

—Learning How: Football. Boulais, Sue. James, Jody, ed. 48p. (gr. 4-7). 1992. lib. bdg. 14.95 (0-944280-37-4); pap. 5.95 (0-944280-43-9) Bancroft-Sage.

—Learning How: Gymnastics. Leder, Jane M. James, Jody, ed. 48p. (gr. 4-7). 1992. lib. bdg. 14.95 (0-944280-35-8); pap. 5.95 (0-944280-40-4) Bancroft-Sage.

—Learning How: Karate. Leder, Jane M. James, Jody, ed. 48p. (gr. 4-7). 1992. lib. bdg. 14.95 (0-944280-34-X); pap. 5.95 (0-944280-39-0) Bancroft-Sage.

—Learning How: Skateboarding. Leder, Jane M. James, Jody, ed. 48p. (gr. 4-7). 1992. lib. bdg. 14.95 (0-944280-33-1); pap. 5.95 (0-944280-42-0) Bancroft-Sage.

—Learning How: Soccer. Leder, Jane M. James, Jody, ed. 48p. (gr. 4-7). 1992. lib. bdg. 14.95 (0-944280-32-3); pap. 5.95 (0-944280-38-2) Bancroft-Sage.

Cone, Patrick, photos by. Avalanche. Kramer, Stephen. 48p. (gr. 1-4). 1991. PLB 17.50 (0-87614-422-9) Carolrhoda Bks.

—Grand Canyon. Cone, Patrick. LC 93-31066. 1994. write for info. (0-87614-820-8) Carolrhoda Bks.

—Lightning. Kramer, Stephen. 48p. (gr. 1-4). 1991. PLB 17.50 (0-87614-659-0) Carolrhoda Bks.

Cone, William. The Night Before Christmas. Moore, Clement C. LC 92-22712. 40p. 1992. 14.95 (0-88708-261-0, Rabbit Ears); incl. cassette 19.95 (0-88708-260-2, Rabbit Ears) Picture Bk Studio.

Coner, Nancy. Cork & Wood Crafts. Newsome, Arden. LC 72-112370. 64p. (gr. k-3). 1971. PLB 12.95 (0-87460-229-7) Lion Bks.

Conforth, Kellie. A Picture Book of Arctic Animals. Conforth, Kellie. LC 90-44896. 24p. (gr. 1-4). 1991. lib. bdg. 9.59 (0-8167-2144-0); pap. text ed. 2.50 (0-8167-2145-9) Troll Assocs.

—A Picture Book of Australian Animals. Conforth, Kellie. LC 91-18706. 24p. (gr. 1-4). 1992. PLB 9.59 (0-8167-2470-9); pap. 2.50 (0-8167-2471-7) Troll Assocs.

Conkle, Nancy. California Authors. Tomb, Eric & Knill, Henry. 68p. (gr. 1-9). pap. 3.95 (0-88388-178-0) Bellerophon Bks.

—Early Composers. Tomb, Eric. 48p. (Orig.). (gr. 7). 1988. pap. 3.95 (0-88388-124-1) Bellerophon Bks.

—Great Composers, Bk. 1. Brownell, David. (gr. 7 up). 1978. pap. 3.95 (0-88388-058-X) Bellerophon Bks.

—Great Doctors. Nunis, Doyce B., Jr. 64p. (Orig.). (gr. 8). 1991. pap. 3.95 (0-88388-144-6) Bellerophon Bks.

—Great Lawyers. Brownell, David. 48p. (Orig.). (gr. 8). 1988. pap. 3.95 (0-88388-133-0) Bellerophon Bks.

—Horses & Riding. Anderson, John K. 48p. (gr. 7-9). 1979. pap. 3.95 (0-88388-066-0) Bellerophon Bks.

—New England Authors. Tomb, Eric. 64p. (gr. 8). 1991. pap. text ed. 3.95 (0-88388-149-7) Bellerophon Bks.

Conkle, Nancy & Neary, D. Great Dancers. Menning, Viiu. (Orig.). (gr. 8). 1978. pap. 3.95 (0-88388-065-2) Bellerophon Bks.

Conklin, Paul. An Ancient Heritage: The Arab-American Minority. Ashabranner, Brent. LC 90-30641. 160p. (gr. 3-7). 1991. PLB 14.89 (0-06-020049-9) HarpC Child Bks.

—City Kids in China. Thomson, Peggy. LC 90-1993. 128p. (gr. 3-7). 1991. 14.95 (0-06-021654-9) HarpC Child Bks.

—Dark Harvest: Migrant Farmworkers in America. Ashabranner, Brent. x, 150p. (gr. 7 up). 1993. Repr. of 1985 ed. PLB 16.50 (0-208-02391-7, Pub. by Linnet) Shoe String.

Conklin, Paul, photos by. A New Frontier: The Peace Corps in Eastern Europe. Ashabranner, Brent. LC 93-38535. (gr. 5 up). 1994. write for info (Cobblehill Bks) Dutton Child Bks.

Conklin, Paul, et al, photos by. Land of Yesterday, Land of Tomorrow: Discovering Chinese Central Asia. Ashabranner, Brent. text by. 96p. (gr. 5 up). 1992. 16. 00 (0-525-65086-5, Cobblehill Bks) Dutton Child Bks.

Conklin, Paul S., photos by. Keepers & Creatures at the National Zoo. Thomson, Peggy. LC 87-47697. 208p. (gr. 3-7). 1988. 13.95 (0-690-04710-X, Crowell Jr Bks); PLB 13.89 (0-690-04712-6, Crowell Jr Bks) HarpC Child Bks.

Conlin, Jim. Charlie McTwiddle & the Wobbly-Wheeled Sputter Putter Popper. Warner, Jerry S. Telfer, Judy, ed. LC 90-70308. 128p. (gr. 3-7). 1990. PLB 12.95 (0-9626293-0-8) Windsor Medallion.

Connelly, Gwen. Adventures. LC 83-25212. 32p. (gr. k-3). 1984. PLB 21.35 (0-89565-265-X); PLB 14.95s.p. (0-685-55698-0) Childs World.

—After You. Riehecky, Janet. 32p. (ps-2). 1989. PLB 18. 50 (0-89565-538-1); PLB 12.95s.p. (0-685-25650-2) Childs World.

—El Alfabeto: A Child's Introduction to the Letters & Sounds of Spanish. 32p. 1990. 7.95 (0-8442-7564-6, Natl Textbk) NTC Pub Grp.

—Caring for My Home. Moncure, Jane B. 32p. (ps-2). 1990. PLB 18.50 (0-89565-667-1); PLB 12.95s.p. (0-685-56168-2) Childs World.

—Excuse Me. Richecky, Janet. 32p. (ps-2). 1989. PLB 18.50 (0-89565-539-X); PLB 12.95s.p. (0-685-25652-9) Childs World.

—Feeling Afraid. Barsuhn, Rochelle N. LC 82-19946. (gr. 1-2). 1983. PLB 21.35 (0-89565-246-3); PLB 14.95s.p. (0-685-55658-1) Childs World.

—The Frog Prince. Wang, Mary L. LC 86-11796. 32p. (ps-2). 1986. PLB 11.93 (0-516-03983-0); pap. 3.95 (0-516-43983-9) Childrens.

—The King's New Clothes. McKissack, Patricia & McKissack, Fredrick. LC 86-33422. 32p. (ps-3). 1987. PLB 11.93 (0-516-02365-9); pap. 3.95 (0-516-42365-7) Childrens.

—The Luck of the Irish. Paulsen, Brendan P. (gr. 2-4). 1988. 17.96 *(0-8172-2752-0)* Raintree Steck-V.
—May I? Riehecky, Janet. LC 88-16838. 32p. (ps-2). 1989. PLB 18.50 *(0-89565-388-5)*; PLB 12.95s.p. *(0-685-55996-3)* Childs World.
—My First Thanksgiving Book. Moncure, Jane B. LC 84-9433. 32p. (ps-2). 1984. PLB 15.00 *(0-516-02903-7)*; pap. 3.95 *(0-516-42903-5)* Childrens.
—Our St. Patrick's Day Book. Ziegler, Sandra. LC 86-31726. 32p. (ps-3). 1987. PLB 19.95 *(0-89565-344-3)*; PLB 13.95s.p. *(0-685-55851-7)* Childs World.
—Please. Riehecky, Janet. LC 88-16841. 32p. 1989. PLB 18.50 *(0-89565-386-9)*; PLB 12.95s.p. *(0-685-55998-X)* Childs World.
—El Principe Rana (The Frog Prince) Wang, Mary L. LC 86-11796. (SPA.). 32p. (ps-2). 1989. PLB 11.93 *(0-516-33983-4)*; pap. 3.95 *(0-516-53983-3)* Childrens.
—Saying Thank You. Reece, Colleen L. LC 82-21992. 32p. (gr. 1-2). 1983. PLB 21.35 *(0-89565-249-8)*; PLB 14.95s.p. *(0-685-55662-X)* Childs World.
—Seasons. Suire, Diane D. LC 89-773. 32p. (gr. k-3). 1989. PLB 21.35 *(0-89565-503-9)*; PLB 14.95s.p. *(0-685-56083-X)* Childs World.
—The Story of Shadrach, Meshach & Abednego. Colburn, Rhonda. 24p. (ps-3). 1990. pap. 3.95 *(0-8249-8421-8, Ideals Child)* Hambleton-Hill.
—Thank-You. Riehecky, Janet. LC 88-16840. 32p. (ps-2). 1989. PLB 18.50 *(0-89565-387-7)*; PLB 12.95s.p. *(0-685-55997-1)* Childs World.
—Wind: What Can It Do? McDonnell, Janet. LC 89-24011. 32p. (ps-2). 1990. PLB 19.95 *(0-89565-555-1)*; PLB 13.95s.p. *(0-685-56176-3)* Childs World.
Connelly, Gwen & Tourillotte, Barb. Ellie the Evergreen. Warren, Jean. Cubley, Kathleen, ed. LC 92-62825. 32p. (Orig.). 1993. 12.95 *(0-911019-66-9)*; pap. text ed. 5.95 *(0-911019-67-7)* Warren Pub Hse.
Connelly, Gwen, jt. illus. see Stasiak, Krystyna.
Conner, Eulala. Amazing World of Ants. Sabin, Francene. LC 81-7492. 32p. (gr. 2-4). 1982. PLB 11.59 *(0-89375-558-3)*; pap. text ed. 2.95 *(0-89375-559-1)* Troll Assocs.
—Look - a Butterfly. Cutts, David. LC 81-11369. 32p. (gr. k-2). 1982. PLB 11.59 *(0-89375-662-8)*; pap. text ed. 2.95 *(0-89375-663-6)* Troll Assocs.
—Opposites. Allington, Richard L. LC 79-20525. 32p. (gr. k-3). 1985. pap. 3.95 *(0-8114-8237-5)* Raintree Steck-V.
Connolly, Jay. Dwight D. Eisenhower: Man of Many Hats; With a Message from John S. D. Eisenhower. Deitch, Kenneth M. & Weisman, JoAnne B. Eisenhower, John S., intro. by. LC 90-82588. 48p. (gr. 5-12). 1990. PLB 14.95 *(1-878668-02-1)* Disc Enter Ltd.
Connolly, Peter. The Greeks. Burrell, Roy. 112p. (gr. 7 up). 1997. 17.95 *(0-19-917161-0)* OUP.
—Oxford First Ancient History. Burrell, Roy. 320p. 1993. bds. 35.00 *(0-19-521058-1)* OUP.
—The Romans. Burrell, Roy. 112p. (gr. 5-9). 1991. bds. 17.95 *(0-19-917162-9, 5084)* OUP.
Connor, Bil. Splash & Trickle. Green, Ivah. (gr. 2-3). 1978. pap. 1.25 *(0-89508-062-1)* Rainbow Bks.
Connor, Eulala. Fright Night. Albright, Molly. LC 88-12388. 96p. (gr. 3-6). 1989. PLB 9.89 *(0-8167-1486-X)*; pap. text ed. 2.95 *(0-8167-1487-8)* Troll Assocs.
—Here Comes Jack Frost. Peters, Sharon. LC 81-4093. 32p. (gr. k-2). 1981. PLB 11.59 *(0-89375-513-3)*; pap. text ed. 2.95 *(0-89375-514-1)* Troll Assocs.
—The Mascot Mess. Albright, Molly. LC 88-15879. 96p. (gr. 3-6). 1989. PLB 9.89 *(0-8167-1484-3)*; pap. text ed. 2.95 *(0-8167-1485-1)* Troll Assocs.
—The Room of Doom. Albright, Molly. LC 88-15912. 96p. (gr. 3-6). 1989. PLB 9.89 *(0-8167-1482-7)*; pap. text ed. 2.95 *(0-8167-1483-5)* Troll Assocs.
—Video Stars. Albright, Molly. LC 88-15880. 96p. (gr. 3-6). 1989. PLB 9.89 *(0-8167-1480-0)*; pap. text ed. 2.95 *(0-8167-1481-9)* Troll Assocs.
Connor, Genevieve. God's Children Share Their Faith with You. Herbst, Helen. 48p. (gr. 1-4). 1988. coloring bk. 2.50 *(0-913382-55-8, 103-20)* Prow Bks-Franciscan.
Conoly, Walle. Duster. Roderus, Frank. LC 85-14759. 266p. (gr. 4 up). 1987. 14.95 *(0-87565-055-4)*; pap. 10.95 *(0-87565-095-3)* Tex Christian.
—Tame the Wild Stallion. Williams, Jeanne. LC 84-16257. 182p. (gr. 4 up). 1985. 14.95 *(0-87565-002-3)*; pap. 8.95 *(0-87565-009-0)* Tex Christian.
Conoly, Walli. Luke & the Van Zandt County War. Alter, Judith M. LC 84-101. 132p. (gr. 4 up). 1984. 10.95 *(0-912646-88-8)* Tex Christian.
Conover, Chris. The Little Humpbacked Horse. Hodges, Margaret. 32p. (ps up). 1987. pap. 3.95 *(0-374-44495-1)* FS&G.
—Moon Song. Meigs, Mildred P. LC 89-32942. 32p. (ps up). 1990. 14.95 *(0-688-08160-6)*; PLB 14.88 *(0-688-08707-8)*, Morrow Jr Bks) Morrow Jr Bks.
Conoway, Judith. Establishing Sequence. Tilkin, Sheldon L. 24p. (gr. 3-4). 1980. wkbk. 2.95 *(0-89403-570-3)* EDC.
—Finding the Main Idea. Tilkin, Sheldon L. 24p. (gr. 3-4). 1980. wkbk. 2.95 *(0-89403-569-X)* EDC.
—Following Directions. Tilkin, Sheldon L. 24p. (gr. 3-4). 1980. wkbk. 2.95 *(0-89403-571-1)* EDC.
—Recalling Details. Tilkin, Sheldon L. 24p. (gr. 4-5). 1980. wkbk. 2.95 *(0-89403-568-1)* EDC.
Conran, Sebastian. My First ABC Book. Conran, Sebastian. LC 87-14562. 64p. (ps-k). 1988. POB 6.95 *(0-689-71198-0, Aladdin)* Macmillan Child Grp.

—My First 1-2-3 Book. Conran, Sebastian. LC 88-6275. 64p. (ps-1). 1988. POB 7.95 *(0-689-71267-7, Aladdin)* Macmillan Child Grp.
Conteh-Morgan, Jane. Arnold Always Answers. Kotter, Deborah. LC 92-18578. 1993. 14.95 *(0-385-30905-8, Zephyr-BFYR)* Doubleday.
—Around the Church, Around the Year: Unitarian Universalism for Children. Evans-Tiller, Jan. Lewis, Kathryn, et al, eds. 144p. (Orig.). (gr. k-3). 1990. pap. text ed. 29.95 *(1-55896-174-7)* Unitarian Univ.
—Colors. 9p. (ps-1). 1993. bds. 4.95 *(0-448-40522-9, G&D)* Putnam Pub Group.
—Noah's Ark. 18p. (ps-1). 1994. bds. 3.95 *(0-448-40185-1, G&D)* Putnam Pub Group.
Converse, James. Amanda Fair. Hamilton, Dorothy. LC 80-25073. 136p. (gr. 5-10). 1981. pap. 3.95 *(0-8361-1943-6)* Herald Pr.
—Crisis at Pemberton Dike. Roberts, Rachel S. LC 83-18664. 152p. (gr. 7-10). 1984. pap. 4.95 *(0-8361-3350-1)* Herald Pr.
—Gina In-Between. Hamilton, Dorothy. LC 81-13387. 128p. (Orig.). (gr. 5 up). 1982. pap. 3.95 *(0-8361-1986-X)* Herald Pr.
—God Builds His Church. MacMaster, Eve B. LC 87-2875. 184p. (Orig.). (gr. 3 up). 1987. pap. 5.95 *(0-8361-3446-X)* Herald Pr.
—God Builds His Church: Activity Book. Waybill, Marjorie. 72p. (Orig.). (gr. 4-5). 1988. pap. 3.00 *(0-8361-3457-5)* Herald Pr.
—God Comforts His People. MacHaster, Eve B. LC 95-835. 176p. (Orig.). (gr. 3 up). 1985. pap. 5.95 *(0-8361-3393-5)* Herald Pr.
—God Comforts His People: Activity Book. Kauffman, Suzanne. 84p. (Orig.). (gr. k-6). 1986. pap. 3.00 *(0-8361-3411-7)* Herald Pr.
—God Rescues His People: Stories of God & His People: Exodus, Leviticus, Numbers & Deuteronomy. MacMaster, Eve. LC 82-2849. 176p. (Orig.). (ps-1). 1982. pap. 5.95 *(0-8361-1994-0)* Herald Pr.
—God Sends His Son. MacMaster, Eve B. LC 86-18342. 160p. (Orig.). (gr. 3-9). 1986. pap. 5.95 *(0-8361-3420-6)* Herald Pr.
—God's Chosen King. MacMaster, Eve. LC 83-12736. 190p. (Orig.). (gr. 5-6). 1983. pap. 5.95 *(0-8361-3344-7)* Herald Pr.
—God's Family. MacMaster, Eve. LC 81-6551. 168p. (gr. 3 up). 1981. pap. 5.95 *(0-8361-1964-9)* Herald Pr.
—God's Justice. MacMaster, Eve. LC 84-20514. 168p. (Orig.). (ps-1). 1984. pap. 5.95 *(0-8361-3381-1)* Herald Pr.
—God's Suffering Servant. MacMaster, Eve B. LC 86-19526. 120p. (Orig.). (gr. 3-9). 1987. pap. 5.95 *(0-8361-3422-2)* Herald Pr.
—God's Wisdom & Power. MacMaster, Eve. LC 84-8974. 168p. (Orig.). (gr. 3-8). 1984. pap. 5.95 *(0-8361-3362-5)* Herald Pr.
—In Search of Liberty, Vol. 1. Moore, Ruth N. LC 83-10827. 168p. (Orig.). (gr. 7-10). 1983. pap. 4.95 *(0-8361-3340-4)* Herald Pr.
—Last One Chosen. Hamilton, Dorothy. LC 82-3150. 112p. (Orig.). (gr. 5-10). 1982. pap. 3.95 *(0-8361-3306-4)* Herald Pr.
—My Friend, My Brother. Swartley, David W. LC 79-26273. 104p. (gr. 6 up). 1980. pap. 3.95 *(0-8361-1916-9)* Herald Pr.
—Mystery of the Lost Heirloom. Moore, Ruth N. LC 85-27334. 152p. (Orig.). (gr. 6-9). 1985. pap. 5.95 *(0-8361-3408-7)* Herald Pr.
—Mystery of the Missing Stallions. Moore, Ruth N. LC 84-19. 136p. (Orig.). (gr. 3-8). 1984. pap. 5.95 *(0-8361-3376-5)* Herald Pr.
—Mystery of the Secret Code. Moore, Ruth N. LC 85-5441. 128p. (Orig.). (gr. 7-9). 1985. pap. 5.95 *(0-8361-3394-3)* Herald Pr.
—Remember the Eagle Day. Martin, Guenn. LC 83-26376. 128p. (gr. 7-9). 1983. pap. 4.95 *(0-8361-3351-X)* Herald Pr.
—The Shiny Dragon. Vogt, Esther. LC 83-12981. 104p. (Orig.). (gr. 5-8). 1983. pap. 3.95 *(0-8361-3348-X)* Herald Pr.
—Winter Caboose. Hamilton, Dorothy. LC 83-10816. 104p. (Orig.). (gr. 4-8). 1983. pap. 3.95 *(0-8361-3341-2)* Herald Pr.
Converse, James, photos by. God Gives the Land. Macmaster, Eve. LC 83-182. 168p. (Orig.). (ps-1). 1983. pap. 5.95 *(0-8361-3332-3)* Herald Pr.
Converse, James L., photos by. Ken's Bright Room. Hamilton, Dorothy. LC 82-23351. 88p. (Orig.). (gr. 7-10). 1982. pap. 3.95 *(0-8361-3328-5)* Herald Pr.
Conway, Lisa. I Like Ketchup Sandwiches. Conway, Lisa. LC 90-64218. 24p. (Orig.). (ps-2). 1991. pap. 2.25 *(0-679-81719-0)* Random Bks Yng Read.
Conway, Robin & Nguyen, Peter. Our Power to Love. Nerbun, Ann. LC 91-73633. 100p. 1990. pap. 6.00 *(0-89870-382-4)* Ignatius Pr.
Cony, Frances. Chicken Pox. Roddie, Shen. LC 92-53851. 1993. 14.95 *(0-316-75347-5, Joy St Bks)* Little.
Cony, Sue. Colors. 8p. (ps-k). 1991. bds. 4.95 *(1-56293-148-2)* McClanahan Bk.
—Opposites. 8p. (ps-k). 1991. bds. 4.95 *(1-56293-150-4)* McClanahan Bk.
—Shapes. 8p. (ps-k). 1991. bds. 4.95 *(1-56293-149-0)* McClanahan Bk.
—Where Do We Live? 8p. (ps-k). 1991. bds. 4.95 *(1-56293-151-2)* McClanahan Bk.
Cook, Allen, jt. illus. see Hough, Bonnie J.
Cook, Beth A., jt. illus. see Means, Gary.

Cook, Chris. Advanced Multiplication & Division. Palmer, Martha. Hoffman, Joan, ed. 32p. (gr. 5-6). 1980. wkbk. 1.99 *(0-938256-36-X)* Sch Zone Pub Co.
—Alphabet. rev. ed. Hoffman, Joan. 32p. (ps-1). 1987. wkbk. 1.99 *(0-938256-03-3)* Sch Zone Pub Co.
—Beginning Addition & Subtraction. Palmer, Martha. Hoffman, Joan, ed. 32p. (gr. 1). 1980. wkbk. 1.99 *(0-938256-29-7)* Sch Zone Pub Co.
—Beginning Multiplication & Division. Palmer, Martha. Hoffman, Joan, ed. 32p. (gr. 3-4). 1980. wkbk. 1.99 *(0-938256-34-3)* Sch Zone Pub Co.
—Blends. Gregorich, Barbara. Hoffman, Joan, ed. 32p. (gr. 1-3). 1981. wkbk. 1.99 *(0-938256-39-4)* Sch Zone Pub Co.
—Consonants. Gregorich, Barbara. Hoffman, Joan, ed. 32p. (gr. 1-3). 1981. wkbk. 1.99 *(0-938256-37-8)* Sch Zone Pub Co.
—Cursive Writing. Hoffman, Joan. 32p. (gr. 3-4). 1981. wkbk. 1.99 *(0-938256-02-5)* Sch Zone Pub Co.
—Fractions. Palmer, Martha. Hoffman, Joan, ed. 32p. (gr. 5-6). 1981. wkbk. 1.99 *(0-938256-43-2)* Sch Zone Pub Co.
—Long Vowels. Gregorich, Barbara. Hoffman, Joan, ed. 32p. (gr. 1-3). 1981. wkbk. 1.99 *(0-938256-41-6)* Sch Zone Pub Co.
—Math: Grade 1. Bannister, Roberta. Hoffman, Joan, ed. 32p. (gr. 1). 1979. wkbk. 1.99 *(0-938256-28-9)* Sch Zone Pub Co.
—Math: Grade 2. Bannister, Roberta. Hoffman, Joan, ed. 32p. (gr. 2). 1979. wkbk. 1.99 *(0-938256-30-0)* Sch Zone Pub Co.
—Math: Grade 3. Bannister, Roberta. Hoffman, Joan, ed. 32p. (gr. 3). 1979. wkbk. 1.99 *(0-938256-31-9)* Sch Zone Pub Co.
—Math: Grade 4. Bannister, Roberta. Hoffman, Joan, ed. 32p. (gr. 4). 1979. wkbk. 1.99 *(0-938256-33-5)* Sch Zone Pub Co.
—Math: Grades 5-6. Bannister, Roberta. Hoffman, Joan, ed. 32p. (gr. 5-6). 1980. wkbk. 1.99 *(0-938256-35-1)* Sch Zone Pub Co.
—Numbers One to Twelve. rev. ed. Hoffman, Joan. 32p. (ps-1). 1987. wkbk. 1.99 *(0-938256-26-2)* Sch Zone Pub Co.
—Phonics Review. Henkel, Arlene. Hoffman, Joan, ed. 32p. (gr. 2-3). 1980. wkbk. 1.99 *(0-938256-08-4)* Sch Zone Pub Co.
—Reading Readiness, Bk. 1. Hoffman, Joan. 32p. (ps-1). 1980. wkbk. 1.99 *(0-938256-04-1)* Sch Zone Pub Co.
—Reading Readiness, Bk. 2. Hoffman, Joan. 32p. (ps-1). 1980. wkbk. 1.99 *(0-938256-05-X)* Sch Zone Pub Co.
—Reading Sentences, Grade 1. Schwaller, Catherine. Hoffman, Joan, ed. 32p. (gr. 1). 1979. wkbk. 1.99 *(0-938256-06-8)* Sch Zone Pub Co.
—Reading Sentences, Grade 2. Lane, Shirley. Hoffman, Joan, ed. 32p. (gr. 2). 1979. wkbk. 1.99 *(0-938256-09-2)* Sch Zone Pub Co.
—Reading Sentences, Grades 3-4. Syswerda, Jean. Hoffman, Joan, ed. 32p. (gr. 3-4). 1980. wkbk. 1.99 *(0-938256-11-4)* Sch Zone Pub Co.
—Reading Stories, Grade 1. Schwaller, Catherine. Hoffman, Joan, ed. 32p. (gr. 1). 1979. wkbk. 1.99 *(0-938256-07-6)* Sch Zone Pub Co.
—Reading Stories, Grade 2. Lane, Shirley. Hoffman, Joan, ed. 32p. (gr. 2). 1979. wkbk. 1.99 *(0-938256-10-6)* Sch Zone Pub Co.
—Rhyming Families. Gregorich, Barbara. Hoffman, Joan, ed. 32p. (gr. 1-3). 1981. wkbk. 1.99 *(0-938256-38-6)* Sch Zone Pub Co.
—Short Vowels. Gregorich, Barbara. Hoffman, Joan, ed. 32p. (gr. 1-3). 1981. wkbk. 1.99 *(0-938256-40-8)* Sch Zone Pub Co.
—Spelling Puzzles: Grade 1. Syswerda, Jean. Hoffman, Joan, ed. 32p. (gr. 1). 1980. wkbk. 1.99 *(0-938256-16-5)* Sch Zone Pub Co.
—Spelling Puzzles: Grade 2. Syswerda, Jean. Hoffman, Joan, ed. 32p. (gr. 2). 1979. wkbk. 1.99 *(0-938256-17-3)* Sch Zone Pub Co.
—Spelling Puzzles: Grade 3. Syswerda, Jean. Hoffman, Joan, ed. 32p. (gr. 3). 1979. wkbk. 1.99 *(0-938256-18-1)* Sch Zone Pub Co.
—Spelling Puzzles: Grade 4. Syswerda, Jean. Hoffman, Joan, ed. 32p. (gr. 4). 1979. wkbk. 1.99 *(0-938256-19-X)* Sch Zone Pub Co.
—Story Problems: Grades 1-2 Math. Gregorich, Barbara. Hoffman, Joan, ed. 32p. (gr. 1-2). 1982. wkbk. 1.99 *(0-938256-45-9)* Sch Zone Pub Co.
—Story Problems: Grades 3-4 Math. Gregorich, Barbara. Hoffman, Joan, ed. 32p. (gr. 3-4). 1982. wkbk. 1.99 *(0-938256-46-7)* Sch Zone Pub Co.
—Transition Math. Palmer, Martha. Hoffman, Joan, ed. 32p. (gr. k-1). 1979. wkbk. 1.99 *(0-938256-27-0)* Sch Zone Pub Co.
Cook, David. Land Animals. Cook, David. LC 84-12072. 32p. (gr. 3-7). 1985. bds. 5.95 *(0-517-55430-5)* Crown Bks Yng Read.
Cook, Debbie. Conversations with Children. Jones, James A., III. LC 85-40201. 96p. (gr. 4-8). 1985. 8.95 *(0-938232-72-X)* Winston-Derek.
Cook, Donald. Hanukkah Songs & Games. Cooper, Don. 32p. (ps-3). 1989. pap. 6.95 incl. cassette *(0-679-80041-7)* Random Bks Yng Read.
—The Headless Horseman. Standiford, Natalie, retold by. LC 90-53228. 48p. (Orig.). (ps-2). 1992. PLB 7.99 *(0-679-91241-X)*; pap. 3.50 *(0-679-81241-5)* Random Bks Yng Read.
—White Bird. Bulla, Clyde R. LC 89-70231. 64p. (Orig.). (gr. 2-4). 1990. lib. bdg. 6.99 *(0-679-90662-2)*; pap. 2.50 *(0-679-80662-8)* Random Bks Yng Read.

Cook, Germaine. Sammy the Elephant & Mr. Camel: A Story to Help Children Overcome Bedwetting While Discovering Self-Appreciation. Mills, Joyce C. & Crowley, Richard J. LC 88-13581. 48p. (gr. 1 up). 1988. PLB 16.95 (0-945354-09-6); pap. 6.95 (0-945354-08-8) Magination Pr.

Cook, Joel. Whistling the Morning in New Poems by Lillian Morrison: New Poems. Morrison, Lillian. 40p. 1992. PLB 16.95 (1-56397-035-X) Boyds Mills Pr.

Cook, Richard J. The Life to Come: Stories for Children about the Spiritual World. Keith, Gretchen L. 89p. (Orig.). (gr. 3-7). 1990. pap. 5.00 (0-945003-03-X) General Church.

Cook, Scott. A Christmas Carol. abr. ed. Dickens, Charles. LC 89-24076. 72p. (gr. 2 up). 1990. 14.95 (0-394-82239-0); PLB 15.99 (0-394-92239-5) Random Bks Yng Read.

—Mother Goose. Cook, Scott, selected by. LC 92-18296. 1993. write for info. (0-679-80949-X); PLB write for info. (0-679-90949-4) Knopf.

—Nettie Jo's Friends. McKissack, Patricia C. LC 87-14080. 40p. (gr. k-4). 1989. 15.00 (0-394-89158-9); lib. bdg. 15.99 (0-394-99158-3) Knopf Bks Yng Read.

Cook, Tim. How to Be Slimmer, Trimmer & Happier: An Action Plan for Young People with a Step-by-Step Guide to Losing Weight Through Positive Living. rev. ed. Berg, Francie M. LC 82-90690. 200p. (Orig.). (gr. 9 up). 1983. 11.95 (0-918532-10-8); pap. 6.95 (0-918532-11-6); Leader's Guide 64p. 4.95 (0-918532-12-4) Healthy Liv Inst.

Cook, Tom. Keep on Caring. Rosenblatt, Arthur. 40p. (ps-3). 1985. 5.95 (0-910313-84-9) Parker Bros.

—A Walk to Grow On. Plummer, Louise. 40p. (ps-3). 1985. 5.95 (0-910313-85-7) Parker Bros.

Cook, Tonya, jt. illus. see Barr, Charlotte.

Cook, Veronica L. Mike the Copycat: Adventures & Stories of Cat Tails. Cook, Veronica L. 50p. (Orig.). (ps up) 1989. pap. text ed. write for info. Ronnie Two Pub.

Cooke, Andy. One Cow Moo Moo. Bennett, David. LC 90-32065. 32p. (ps-2). 1990. 11.95 (0-8050-1416-0, Bks Young Read) H Holt & Co.

Cooke, Jeff. Kids Can Write Songs, Too! Cooke, Frank E. & Franck, Eddie. 120p. (gr. 6-12). 1993. pap. 10.95 (0-940076-02-0) Fiesta City.

Cooke, Ralph W. What Is a California Sea Otter? Graves, Jack A. (gr. 3 up). 1977. pap. 3.95 (0-910286-61-2) Boxwood.

Cooke, Tom. The Adventures of Ernie & Bert at the South Pole. Elliott, Dan. LC 84-60187. 32p. (ps-3). 1984. pap. 1.50 (0-394-86299-6) Random Bks Yng Read.

—The Baby Hugs Bear & Baby Tugs Bear Counting Book. Haas, Dorothy. 40p. (ps). 1984. 5.95 (0-910313-71-7) Parker Bros.

—The Baby Hugs Bear & Baby Tugs Bear Look & Find Book. Mason, Evelyn. 40p. (ps). 1984. 5.95 (0-910313-73-3) Parker Bros.

—Baby Rowlf & the Boomtown Bandits. Gikow, Louise. 26p. (ps up). 1987. 12.95 (1-55578-600-6) Worlds Wonder.

—Being Brave Is Best. Winthrop, Elizabeth. 40p. (ps-3). 1984. 5.95 (0-910313-19-9) Parker Bros.

—Ben's New Buddy. Johnson, Ward. 40p. (ps-3). 1984. 5.95 (0-910313-16-4) Parker Bros.

—Bert & Ernie on the Go. LC 80-54574. 16p. (ps-2). 1981. 8.99 (0-394-84869-1) Random Bks Yng Read.

—Bert's Little Garden: A Sesame Street Book. LC 90-61311. 22p. (ps). 1991. bds. 2.95 (0-679-81061-7) Random Bks Yng Read.

—Big Bird Goes to the Doctor. Sommers, Tish. LC 85-81562. 32p. (ps-k). 1986. write for info. (0-307-12019-8, Pub. by Golden Bks) Western Pub.

—Big Bird's Animal Game. 14p. (ps). 1993. bds. 3.95 (0-307-12395-2, 12395, Golden Pr) Western Pub.

—Big Bird's Big Bike. Ross, Anna. LC 92-60305. 22p. (ps). 1993. 3.25 (0-679-83271-8) Random Bks Yng Read.

—Big Bird's New Nest & Other Good-Night Stories. Korman, Justine. (ps-1). 1989. write for info. (0-307-12060-0, 12060) Western Pub.

—Bye-Bye, Blankie. Worth, Bonnie. 18p. (ps). 1992. bds. 3.50 (0-307-12329-4, 12329, Golden Pr) Western Pub.

—Bye-Bye, Pacifier. Gikow, Louise. 18p. (ps). 1992. bds. 3.50 (0-307-12330-8, 12330, Golden Pr) Western Pub.

—The Care Bears' Book of Favorite Bedtime Stories. Pepper, Bob. 48p. (ps-3). 1984. 5.95 (0-910313-20-2) Parker Bros.

—Caring Is What Counts. Johnson, Ward. 40p. (ps-3). 1983. 5.95 (0-685-06604-5, 7004) Parker Bros.

—The Count's Counting Book. Sesame Street Staff. LC 79-56535. 16p. (ps-3). 1980. pap. 8.99 (0-394-84436-X) Random Bks Yng Read.

—Elmo's Little Playhouse. Ross, Anna. LC 91-68111. 22p. (ps). 1993. 3.25 (0-679-83270-X) Random Bks Yng Read.

—Ernie Gets Lost. Campbell, Louisa. 32p. (gr. k-3). 1985. write for info. (0-307-12015-5, Pub. by Golden Bks) Western Pub.

—Ernie's Little Toolbox: A Sesame Street Book. Ingle, Annie. LC 90-61312. 22p. (ps). 1991. bds. 2.95 (0-679-80905-8) Random Bks Yng Read.

—Follow the Monsters. Lerner, Sharon. LC 84-18031. 32p. (ps-1). 1985. pap. 2.95 (0-394-87126-X) Random Bks Yng Read.

—Grover & the New Kid. Smith, Jennifer. LC 86-42965. 40p. (ps-3). 1987. 4.95 (0-394-88519-8) Random Bks Yng Read.

—Grover, Grover, Come on Over: A Step 1 Book - Preschool-Grade 1. Ross, Katharine. LC 90-33947. 32p. (Orig.). (ps-1). 1991. PLB 7.99 (0-679-91117-0); pap. 2.95 (0-679-81117-6) Random Bks Yng Read.

—Grover's Adventure under the Sea. LC 88-61629. 14p. (ps). 1989. bds. 3.99 (0-394-81951-9) Random Bks Yng Read.

—Grover's Super Surprise Book. Sesame Street Staff. LC 77-93776. (ps-3). 1978. 8.99 (0-394-83841-6) Random Bks Yng Read.

—Hide & Seek Camping Trip: A Sesame Street Book. LC 89-61021. 14p. (ps). 1990. bds. 3.99 (0-679-80138-3) Random Bks Yng Read.

—Hide-&-Seek with Big Bird: A Sesame Street Book. LC 89-64284. 14p. (ps). 1991. bds. 3.99 (0-679-80785-3) Random Bks Yng Read.

—The Hugs & Tugs Counting Book. Haas, Dorothy. (ps). 5.95 (0-317-13462-0) Parker Bros.

—I Can Dress Myself. Worth, Bonnie. 18p. (ps). 1993. bds. 3.50 (0-307-12204-2, 12204, Golden Pr) Western Pub.

—I Can Share. Worth, Bonnie. 18p. (ps). 1993. bds. 3.50 (0-307-12205-0, 12205, Golden Pr) Western Pub.

—I Spy. Hayward, Linda. 32p. (Orig.). (ps-1). 1993. PLB 7.99 (0-679-94979-8); pap. 3.50 (0-679-84979-3) Random Bks Yng Read.

—I Want to Be a Veterinarian. Muntean, Michaela. 24p. (ps-k). 1992. pap. write for info. (0-307-13116-5, 13116, Golden Pr) Western Pub.

—Just Like Ernie. Thompson, Emily. LC 87-81762. 32p. (ps-k). 1988. write for info. (0-307-12025-2, Pub. by Golden Bks) Western Pub.

—Muppet Kids in Frogs Only! Gikow, Louise. 32p. (ps-3). 1992. 1.95 (0-307-12651-X, 12651, Golden Pr) Western Pub.

—Muppet Kids in Mom's Having a Baby. Gikow, Louise. (ps-3). 1991. 1.95 (0-307-12661-7, Golden Pr) Western Pub.

—My First Muppet Dictionary. Gikow, Louise, et al. 112p. (ps-2). 1992. 9.95 (0-307-15610-9, 15610, Golden Pr) Western Pub.

—Nothing to Do. Alexander, Liza. LC 87-81761. 32p. (ps-k). 1988. write for info. (0-307-12024-4, Pub. by Golden Bks) Western Pub.

—Oh, I Am So Embarrassed! Dickson, Anna H. LC 87-81782. 32p. (ps-1). 1988. write for info. (0-307-12027-9) Western Pub.

—Open Sesame Picture Dictionary. Malecki, Ed, designed by. (ENG & JPN.). 1987. pap. 7.75 (0-19-434170-4) OUP.

—Open Sesame Picture Dictionary: Featuring Jim Henson's Sesame Street Muppets, Children's Television Workshop. Schimpff, Jill W. (gr. k-6). 1982. 12.75x (0-19-503201-2); pap. 7.75x (0-19-503035-4); activity book 4.95 (0-19-434253-0); Picture Dictionary, English-Chinese. 7.75 (0-19-583744-4) OUP.

—Scared of the Dark. Alexander, Liza. 32p. (ps-k). 1986. write for info. (0-307-12020-1, Pub by Golden Bks) Western Pub.

—Sesame Street: Come to the Playground. Clasing, Elisabeth. 12p. (ps). 1992. write for info. (0-307-12003-1, 12003, Golden Pr) Western Pub.

—Sesame Street Hide-&-Seek Safari. LC 87-61638. 14p. (ps). 1988. bds. 3.99 (0-394-89474-X) Random Bks Yng Read.

—Sesame Street Sign Language ABC with Linda Bove. Bove, Linda. Shevett, Anita & Shevett, Anita, photos by. LC 85-1845. 32p. (gr. 3-8). 1985. lib. bdg. 5.99 (0-394-97516-2); 2.25 (0-394-87516-8) Random Bks Yng Read.

—Sesame Street Sign Language Fun. Sesame Street Staff. Selkirk, Neil, photos by. LC 79-5570. 72p. (ps-3). 1980. 10.00 (0-394-84212-X) Random Bks Yng Read.

—Sweet Dreams for Sally. Hubert, Amelia. 40p. (ps-3). 1983. 5.95 (0-910313-01-6, 7002) Parker Bros.

—That Makes Me Angry. Best, Anthony. (ps-3). 1990. pap. write for info. (0-307-12026-0, Pub. by Golden Bks) Western Pub.

—Tiger's Bedtime. Calrenson, Stephanie. (ps-k). 1991. pap. write for info. (0-307-11510-0, Golden Pr) Western Pub.

—Twinkle, Twinkle, Little Bug: A Sesame Street Book. Ross, Katharine. LC 90-61760. 24p. (Orig.). (ps-2). 1991. pap. 2.25 (0-679-81372-1) Random Bks Yng Read.

—Voyage of the Micronauts: A Book about the Human Body. Time Life Inc. Editors. Fallow, Allan, ed. 64p. (ps-2). 1992. write for info. (0-8094-9295-4); PLB write for info. (0-8094-9296-2) Time-Life.

—What's in Oscar's Trash Can? And Other Good-Night Stories. Muntean, Michaela. (ps-1). 1991. 3.25 (0-307-12342-1, Golden Pr) Western Pub.

—When Is My Birthday? Sipherd, Ray. LC 88-80284. 32p. (ps-1). 1988. write for info. (0-307-12028-7) Western Pub.

—Who's Hiding? Children's Television Workshop Staff. LC 84-81602. 14p. (ps-k). 1986. write for info. (0-307-12157-7, Pub. by Golden Bks) Western Pub.

—Why Are You So Mean to Me? Hautzig, Deborah. LC 85-18434. 40p. (ps-3). 1992. pap. 2.99 (0-679-82402-2) Random Bks Yng Read.

—The Witch down the Street. Morgan, Stephanie. 40p. (ps-3). 1983. cancelled 5.95 (0-910313-02-4, 7003) Parker Bros.

Cooke, Tom, jt. illus. see Brannon, Tom.

Cooke, Tom, et al. The Sesame Street Bedtime Storybook. Geiss, Tony, et al. LC 77-93774. (ps-2). 1978. 10.00 (0-394-83843-2); lib. bdg. 7.99 (0-394-93843-7) Random Bks Yng Read.

Cooley, Gary. Rumpelstiltskin. Grimm, Jacob & Grimm, Wilhelm K. 32p. (ps-3). 1992. 6.95 (0-8362-4922-4) Andrews & McMeel.

Cooley, Nance. The Parable of Jesus & Santa. Grimes, Bobbie M. LC 84-90331. 40p. (ps-5). 1984. 14.95 (0-9613328-0-8) B & D Pub.

Coolidge, Archibald C., jt. illus. see Van Santvoord, George.

Coombs, Christine. Orphan. Zistel, Era. 64p. (Orig.). (gr. 4 up). 1990. pap. 11.95 (0-9617426-5-8) J N Townsend.

Coombs, Patricia. Dorrie & the Blue Witch. Coombs, Patricia. 48p. (gr. k-6). 1980. pap. 1.50 (0-440-42210-8, YB) Dell.

—Dorrie & the Dreamyard Monsters. Coombs, Patricia. 48p. (gr. k-6). 1982. pap. 2.25 (0-440-40896-2, YB) Dell.

—Dorrie & the Haunted Schoolhouse. Coombs, Patricia. 32p. (ps-3). 1992. 13.45 (0-395-60116-9, Clarion Bks) HM.

—Dorrie & the Screebit Ghost. Coombs, Patricia. LC 79-4443. (gr. 1-4). 1979. 9.95 (0-688-41883-X) Lothrop.

—Dorrie & the Witches' Camp. Coombs, Patricia. LC 82-9986. 48p. (gr. 1-5). 1983. PLB 12.88 (0-688-01508-5) Lothrop.

—Dorrie & the Wizard's Spell. Coombs, Patricia. LC 68-27601. 48p. (gr. 1-5). 1968. PLB 12.88 (0-688-51083-3) Lothrop.

—The Magician & McTree. Coombs, Patricia. LC 83-11984. (gr. 1-4). 1984. 11.95 (0-688-02109-3) Lothrop.

Coombs, Roy. Dogs. Boorer, Wendy. LC 88-17653. 24p. (Orig.). (gr. 2-5). 1989. lib. bdg. 5.99 (0-394-99988-6) Random Bks Yng Read.

Cooney, Barbara. American Folk Songs for Children. Seeger, Ruth C. 192p. (gr. k-12). 1980. pap. 12.00 (0-385-15788-6, Zephyr-BFYR) Doubleday.

—Animal Folk Songs for Children. Seeger, Ruth C. LC 92-767692. 90p. (gr. 1-6). 1992. PLB 22.50 (0-208-02364-X, Pub. by Linnet); pap. 13.95 (0-208-02365-8, Pub. by Linnet) Shoe String.

—Bambi. Salten, Felix. (ps up). 1988. pap. 3.50 (0-671-66607-X, Minstrel Bks) PB.

—The Best Christmas. Kingman, Lee. (gr. 2-5). 1984. 16.50 (0-8446-6160-0) Peter Smith.

—The Best Christmas. Kingman, Lee. LC 92-21152. 96p. (gr. 5 up). 1993. pap. 3.95 (0-688-11838-0, Pub. by Beech Tree Bks) Morrow.

—Chanticleer & the Fox. Chaucer, Geoffrey. LC 58-10449. 40p. (ps-3). 1982. 14.00 (0-690-18561-8, Crowell Jr Bks); PLB 13.89 (0-690-18562-6); pap. 3.95 (0-690-04318-X) HarpC Child Bks.

—Chanticleer & the Fox. Chaucer, Geoffrey. LC 58-10449. 32p. (gr. k-3). 1982. pap. 5.95 (0-06-443087-1, Trophy) HarpC Child Bks.

—Christmas in the Barn. Brown, Margaret W. LC 52-7858. 32p. (gr. k-3). 1961. PLB 13.89 (0-690-19272-X, Crowell Jr Bks) HarpC Child Bks.

—Christmas in the Barn. Brown, Margaret W. LC 85-42738. 32p. (ps-3). 1985. pap. 4.95 (0-06-443082-0, Trophy) HarpC Child Bks.

—Emily. Bedard, Michael. LC 91-41806. 40p. (gr. k-3). 1992. 16.00 (0-385-30697-0) Doubleday.

—Hattie & the Wild Waves. Cooney, Barbara. (ps-3). 1990. 14.95 (0-670-83056-9) Viking Child Bks.

—Hattie & the Wild Waves: A Story from Brooklyn. Cooney, Barbara. LC 92-40723. 40p. 1993. pap. 4.99 (0-14-054193-4, Puffin) Puffin Bks.

—The Little Fir Tree. Brown, Margaret W. LC 85-42743. 40p. (ps-3). 1985. 4.95 (0-06-443083-9, Trophy) HarpC Child Bks.

—The Little Fir Tree. Brown, Margaret W. LC 54-5534. 24p. (gr. k-3). 1979. PLB 13.89 (0-690-04016-4, Crowell Jr Bks) HarpC Child Bks.

—Louhi, Witch of North Farm. De Gerez, Toni. LC 84-21600. 32p. (ps-3). 1986. 13.95 (0-670-80556-4) Viking Child Bks.

—Louhi, Witch of North Farm: A Finnish Tale. Gerez, Toni de, retold by. (ps-3). 1988. pap. 4.99 (0-14-050529-6, Puffin) Puffin Bks.

—Miss Rumphius. Cooney, Barbara. LC 82-2837. 32p. (gr. k-3). 1982. pap. 14.95 (0-670-47958-6) Viking Child Bks.

—Miss Rumphius. Cooney, Barbara. (ps-3). 1994. pap. 6.99 incl. cassette (0-14-095026-5, Puffin) Puffin Bks.

—Ox-Cart Man. Hall, Donald. LC 79-14466. (gr. k-3). 1979. pap. 15.00 (0-670-53328-9) Viking Child Bks.

—Ox-Cart Man. Hall, Donald. 40p. (ps-3). 1983. pap. 4.99 (0-14-050441-9, Puffin) Puffin Bks.

—Peter & the Wolf Pop-up-Book. Prokofiev, Sergei. (gr. k-12). 1986. pap. 17.00 (0-670-80849-0) Viking Child Bks.

—Roxaboxen. McLerran, Alice. 32p. (ps-3). 1992. pap. 4.99 (0-14-054475-5, Puffin) Puffin Bks.

—Seven Little Rabbits. Becker, John. 32p. 1991. pap. 3.95 (0-590-44849-8, Blue Ribbon Bks) Scholastic Inc.

—Spirit Child: A Story of the Nativity. Bierhorst, John, tr. LC 84-720. 32p. (ps-2). 1990. pap. 4.95 (0-688-09926-2, Mulberry) Morrow.

—Squawk to the Moon, Little Goose. Preston, Edna M. LC 84-22296. 32p. (ps-1). 1985. pap. 3.95 (0-14-050546-6, Puffin) Puffin Bks.

—The Story of Holly & Ivy. Godden, Rumer. LC 84-25799. 32p. (ps-5). 1985. pap. 15.00 (0-670-80622-6) Viking Child Bks.

—The Story of Holly & Ivy. Godden, Rumer. (gr. k-5). 1987. pap. 4.99 (0-14-050723-X, Puffin) Puffin Bks.
—Tortillitas Para Mama: And Other Nursery Rhymes, Spanish & English. Griego, Margo C., et al. LC 81-4823. 32p. (ps-2). 1981. 14.95 (0-8050-0285-5, Bks Young Read) H Holt & Co.
—The Year of the Perfect Christmas Tree: An Appalachian Story. Houston, Gloria M. LC 87-245515. 32p. (ps-3). 1988. 14.95 (0-8037-0299-X); PLB 14.89 (0-8037-0300-7) Dial Bks Young.
Cooney, Cynthia D., jt. illus. see Schmitt, Judy.
Coontz, Otto. Hiccups, Hiccups. Bains, Rae. LC 81-4638. 32p. (gr. k-2). 1981. PLB 11.59 (0-89375-537-0); pap. text ed. 2.95 (0-89375-538-9) Troll Assocs.
Cooper, Andrea. Let's Talk about...S-E-X: A Read & Discuss Guide for People 9 to 12 & Their Parents. Gitchel, Sam & Foster, Lorri. 59p. (gr. 4-8). 1983. pap. 4.95 (0-9610122-0-X) Plan Par Ctrl CA.
Cooper, Floyd. Be Good to Eddie Lee. Fleming, Virginia. 32p. (ps-3). 1993. write for info. (Philomel Bks) Putnam Pub Group.
—Be Good to Eddie Lee. Fleming, Virginia. 32p. (ps-3). 1993. PLB 14.95 (0-399-21993-5, Philomel Bks) Putnam Pub Group.
—Brown Honey in Broomwheat Tea. Thomas, Joyce C. LC 91-46043. 32p. (gr. k up). 1993. 15.00 (0-06-021087-7); PLB 14.89 (0-06-021088-5) HarpC Child Bks.
—Chita's Christmas Tree. Howard, Elizabeth F. LC 88-26250. 32p. (ps-2). 1989. RSBE 14.95 (0-02-744621-2, Bradbury Pr) Macmillan Child Grp.
—Chita's Christmas Tree. Howard, Elizabeth F. LC 92-44482. 32p. (gr. k-2). 1993. pap. 4.95 (0-689-71739-3, Aladdin) Macmillan Child Grp.
—Coyote Walks on Two Legs. Hausman, Gerald, compiled by. LC 92-25115. 1993. write for info. (0-399-22018-6, Philomel Bks) Putnam Pub Group.
—From Miss Ida's Porch. Belton, Sandra. LC 92-31239. 40p. (gr. 2-5). 1993. RSBE 14.95 (0-02-708915-0, Four Winds) Macmillan Child Grp.
—The Girl Who Loved Caterpillars. Merrill, Jean. 32p. (ps up). 1992. PLB 14.95 (0-399-21871-8, Philomel Bks) Putnam Pub Group.
—Grandpa's Face. Greenfield, Eloise. LC 87-16729. 32p. (ps-2). 1988. 14.95 (0-399-21525-5, Philomel Bks) Putnam Pub Group.
—Grandpa's Face. Greenfield, Eloise. 32p. (ps-3). 1991. pap. 5.95 (0-399-22106-9, Sandcastle Bks) Putnam Pub Group.
—Grandpa's Face. Greenfield, Eloise. (SPA.). 32p. (ps up). 1993. pap. 5.95 (0-399-22511-0, Philomel Bks) Putnam Pub Group.
—Imani's Gift at Kwanzaa. Burden-Patmon, Denise. 32p. (gr. 2-5). 1993. pap. 4.95 (0-671-79841-3, S&S BYR) S&S Trade.
—King Sejong's Secret. Farley, Carol. LC 93-12967. 1995. write for info. (0-688-12776-2); lib. bdg. write for info. (0-688-12777-0) Lothrop.
—Langston Hughes. Cooper, Floyd. LC 93-36332. 1994. write for info. (0-399-22682-6, Philomel Bks) Putnam Pub Group.
—Laura Charlotte. Galbraith, Kathryn. 32p. (ps-3). 1990. 14.95 (0-399-21613-8, Philomel Bks) Putnam Pub Group.
—Laura Charlotte. Galbraith, Kathryn O. 32p. (ps up). 1993. pap. 5.95 (0-399-22514-5, Philomel Bks) Putnam Pub Group.
—Martin Luther King, Jr. Woodson, Jacqueline. Brook, Bonnie, ed. 32p. (gr. k-2). 1990. 6.95 (0-671-69112-0); PLB 10.98 (0-671-69106-6) Silver Pr.
—Meet Danitra Brown. Grimes, Nikki. LC 92-43707. (gr. 4 up). 1995. write for info. (0-688-12073-3) (0-688-12074-1) Lothrop.
—Papa Tells Chita a Story. Howard, Elizabeth F. LC 93-1252. 1994. write for info. (0-02-744623-9, Four Winds) Macmillan Child Grp.
—Pass It On: African-American Poetry for Children. Hudson, Wade, compiled by. LC 92-16034. 32p. (gr. k-4). 1993. 14.95 (0-590-45770-5) Scholastic Inc.
—Pulling the Lion's Tail. Kurtz, Jane. LC 93-22836. 1994. pap. 14.00 (0-671-88183-3, S&S BFYR) S&S Trade.
—When Africa Was Home. Williams, Karen L. LC 90-7684. 32p. (ps-1). 1991. 14.95 (0-531-05925-1); PLB 14.99 (0-531-08525-2) Orchard Bks Watts.
—When Africa Was Home. Williams, Karen L. LC 90-7684. 32p. (ps-2). 1994. pap. 5.95 (0-531-07043-3) Orchard Bks Watts.
Cooper, Floyd, et al. Let's Celebrate Series, 6 vols. Woodson, Jacqueline, et al. 192p. (gr. k-2). 1990. Set. 41.70 (0-671-31231-6); Set. 26.78s.p. (0-685-54162-2); Set. PLB 65.88 (0-671-31230-8); Set. PLB 49.41s.p. (0-685-46998-0) Silver Pr.
Cooper, Gail. Promises: A Teen's Guide to Pregnancy. Brinkley, Ginny & Sampson, Sherry. Mahan, Charles, pref. by. 48p. (gr. 7-12). 1993. pap. text ed. write for info. (0-9622585-4-7) Pink Inc.
Cooper, Gail S. Joven y Embarazada: Un Libro Para Usted. Brinkley, Ginny & Sampson, Sherry. Salmon, Otilia & Rodriquez, Judy, trs. from ENG. Mahan, Charles S., pref. by. (SPA.). 80p. (gr. 7-12). 1992. pap. text ed. 4.95 (0-9622585-3-9) Pink Inc.
—Usted y Su Nuevo Bebe: Un Libro Para Madres Jovenes. Brinkley, Ginny & Sampson, Sherry. Salmon, Otilia & Rodriquez, Judy, trs. from ENG. LC 92-80146. (SPA.). 80p. (gr. 7-12). 1992. pap. text ed. 4.95 (0-9622585-2-0) Pink Inc.

—You & Your New Baby: A Book for Young Mothers. Brinkley, Ginny & Sampson, Sherry. 70p. (Orig.). (gr. 7 up). 1991. pap. text ed. 3.95 (0-9622585-1-2) Pink Inc.
—Young & Pregnant: A Book for You. Brinkley, Ginny & Sampson, Sherry. Mahan, Charles, intro. by. 80p. (Orig.). (gr. 7-12). 1989. pap. text ed. 4.95x (0-317-93681-6) Pink Inc.
Cooper, Heather. Black Unicorn. Lee, Tanith. LC 91-15646. 144p. (gr. 7 up). 1991. SBE 14.95 (0-689-31575-9, Atheneum Child Bk) Macmillan Child Grp.
—Woosh! I Heard a Sound. Heam, Emily. 24p. (ps-1). 1987. pap. 0.99 (0-920303-21-8, Pub. by Annick CN) Firefly Bks Ltd.
Cooper, Helen. The Bear under the Stairs. Cooper, Helen. LC 92-23840. (ps-2). 1993. 12.99 (0-8037-1279-0) Dial Bks Young.
—Ella & the Rabbit. Cooper, Helen. LC 90-34499. 32p. (ps-3). 1990. 12.95 (0-940793-62-8, Crocodile Bks) Interlink Pub.
Cooper, Martha, photos by. Lion Dancer: Ernie Wan's Chinese New Year. Waters, Kate & Slovenz-Low, Madeline. 32p. (ps-2). 1990. 13.95 (0-590-43046-7) Scholastic Inc.
—My Two Worlds. Gordon, Ginger. LC 92-39271. (gr. 5 up). 1993. 14.45 (0-395-58704-2, Clarion Bks) HM.
Cooper, Ryan M. Good Questions. Kaminski, Gerald. 32p. (Orig.). (gr. k-3). 1980. pap. 5.95 (0-931896-00-2) Cove View.
Cooper-Brown, Jean. Chick-in-a-Box. Gaw, Robyn. LC 93-11735. 1994. 4.25 (0-383-03799-9) SRA Schl Grp.
Copelman, Evelyn. The First Woman Doctor. Baker, Rachel. 192p. (gr. 4-6). 1987. pap. 2.95 (0-590-44767-X) Scholastic Inc.
Copelman, Evelyn, et al. Wizard of Oz. Baum, L. Frank. (gr. 4-6). 1956. il. jr. lib. o.p. 5.95 (0-448-05826-X, G&D); deluxe ed. 12.95 (0-448-06026-4) Putnam Pub Group.
Coplans, Peta. Dottie. Coplans, Peta. LC 92-41955. 1994. write for info. (0-395-66788-7) HM.
—Spaghetti for Suzy. Coplans, Peta. LC 92-21611. 32p. (gr. k-3). 1993. 13.95 (0-395-65232-4) HM.
Copp, Brent. The Air Around Us: An Air Pollution Primer. Luoma, Jon R. Smith, Richard H., photos by. 20p. (Orig.). (gr. 5 up). 1989. pap. 9.95 (0-935577-10-6) Acid Rain Found.
Copping, Harold. Children's Stories from Dickens. Copping, Harold. LC 92-37666. 1993. 8.99 (0-517-08485-6, Pub. by Derrydale Bks) Outlet Bk Co.
Corbella, Luciano. Flight & Flying Machines. Parker, Steve. LC 92-54316. 64p. (gr. 3-7). 1993. 12.95 (1-56458-236-1) Dorling Kindersley.
—The Oceans Atlas. Ganeri, Anita. LC 93-28724. 1994. write for info. (1-56458-475-5) Dorling Kindersley.
Corbella, Luciano, jt. illus. see Gornari, Giuliano.
Corbett, Susanne. How Babies & Family Are Made-There Is More Than One Way! Schaffer, Patricia. LC 86-23087. 64p. (gr. k-4). 1988. pap. 6.95 (0-935097-17-3) Tabor Sarah Bks.
Corbett, Sylvia. Little Freddie at the Kentucky Derby. Cocquyt, Kathryn. LC 91-23540. 128p. (gr. 4-7). 1992. 13.95 (0-88289-856-6) Pelican.
—Little Freddie's Legacy. Cocquyt, Kathryn. LC 93-5558. 1994. write for info. (1-56554-000-X) Pelican.
Corcoran, Mark. The Beanstalk Incident. Paulson, Tim. 1992. pap. 8.95 (0-8065-1313-6, Citadel Pr) Carol Pub Group.
—Brave Little Tailor. Grimm, Jacob & Grimm, Wilhelm K. LC 78-18075. 32p. (gr. 1-4). 1979. PLB 9.79 (0-89375-137-5); pap. 1.95 (0-89375-115-4) Troll Assocs.
—The Bremen Town Musicians. Grimm, Jacob & Grimm, Wilhelm K. Easton, Samantha, retold by. 1991. 6.95 (0-8362-4925-9) Andrews & McMeel.
—Jack & the Beanstalk & the Beanstalk Incident. Paulson, Tim. (ps-2). 1992. 12.95 (0-685-38934-0, Birch Ln Pr) Carol Pub Group.
Corderoc'h, Jean-Pierre. Can We Help You, Saint Nicholas? Scheidl, Gerda M. Lanning, Rosemary, tr. from GER. LC 92-5231. 32p. (gr. k-3). 1992. 14.95 (1-55858-154-5); PLB 14.88 (1-55858-155-3) North-South Bks NYC.
—Coriander's Easter Adventure. Ostheeren, Ingrid. Lanning, Rosemary, tr. from GER. LC 91-26867. 32p. (gr. k-3). 1992. 14.95 (1-55858-136-7); lib. bdg. 14.88 (1-55858-150-2) North-South Bks NYC.
—Little Ben. Moers, Hermann. Lanning, Rosemary, tr. from GER. LC 90-47030. 32p. (gr. k-3). 1991. 14.95 (1-55858-105-7) North-South Bks NYC.
—The New Dog. Ostheeren, Ingrid. James, J. Alison, tr. from GER. 32p. (gr. k-3). 1993. 14.95 (1-55858-218-5); lib. bdg. 14.88 (1-55858-219-3) North-South Bks NYC.
Cordoba, Liglia. Small Folk Quilters. Rogler, Ingrid. Moss, Pamela. ed. 68p. (gr. 3-10). 1989. pap. text ed. 9.95 (0-9622565-0-1) Chitra Pubns.
Corey, Donna. Manatee: A First Book. rev. ed. Corey, Donna. Strykowski, Joe, photos by. LC 92-60557. 48p. (ps-6). 1993. pap. 5.00 (1-882533-15-1) Star Thrower.
—Where is Manatee: A First Book. rev. ed. Corey, Donna. Strykowski, Joe, photos by. LC 92-60557. 48p. (ps-6). 1992. pap. 4.95 (1-879488-00-0) Sundiver.
Corfield, Robin B. Zoe's Tower. Rogers, Paul & Rogera, Emma. LC 90-48291. 32p. (ps-1). 1991. pap. 13.95 jacketed (0-671-73811-9, S&S BFYR) S&S Trade.

Cori, Nathan. Friends Forever. Reinsma, Carol. 48p. (Orig.). (gr. 1-3). 1993. pap. 3.99 (0-7847-0096-6, 24-03946) Standard Pub.
—The Picnic Caper. Reinsma, Carol. LC 93-29567. 48p. (Orig.). (gr. k-3). 1994. pap. 3.99 (0-7847-0006-0, 24-03956) Standard Pub.
—A Place in the Palace. Reinsma, Carol. 48p. (Orig.). (gr. 1-3). 1993. pap. 3.99 (0-7847-0095-8, 24-03945) Standard Pub.
—The Shimmering Stone. Reinsma, Carol. 48p. (Orig.). (gr. k-3). 1994. pap. 3.99 (0-7847-0007-9, 24-03957) Standard Pub.
Corke, Philip. Rivers. 32p. (gr. 3-5). 1985. 7.95x (0-86685-452-5) Intl Bk Ctr.
Cormi, Giora. A Torah Commentary for Our Times, Vol. 3: Numbers & Deuteronomy. Fields, Harvey J. LC 89-28478. (Orig.). (gr. 7-9). 1993. pap. text ed. 12.00x (0-8074-0511-6, 164020) UAHC.
Cornell, Donald. Ice Told Tales. Cornell, Donald. Rosoff, Barbara, tr. (ENG & FRE.). 58p. (Orig.). (ps-2). 1991. pap. 4.00 (0-9620738-1-4) D Cornell.
Cornell, Laura. Annie Bananie. Komaiko, Leah. LC 86-45767. 32p. (ps-3). 1987. 15.00 (0-06-023259-5) HarpC Child Bks.
—Annie Bananie. Komaiko, Leah. LC 86-45767. 32p. (gr. k-3). 1989. pap. 4.95 (0-06-443198-3, Trophy) HarpC Child Bks.
—Earl's Too Cool for Me. Komaiko, Leah. LC 87-30803. 40p. (gr. k-3). 1988. 14.00 (0-06-023281-1) HarpC Child Bks.
—Earl's Too Cool for Me. Komaiko, Leah. LC 87-30803. 40p. (gr. k-3). 1990. pap. 5.95 (0-06-443245-9, Trophy) HarpC Child Bks.
—Leonora O'Grady. Komaiko, Leah. LC 91-23208. 32p. (gr. k-3). 1992. 15.00 (0-06-021766-9); PLB 14.89 (0-06-021767-7) HarpC Child Bks.
—Traveling Backwards. Forward, Toby. LC 93-32514. 1994. write for info. RTE (0-688-13076-3, Tambourine Bks) Morrow.
—When I Was Little: A Four-Year-Old's Memoir of Her Youth. Curtis, Jamie L. LC 91-46188. 32p. (gr. k-3). 1993. 14.00 (0-06-021078-8); PLB 13.89 (0-06-021079-6) HarpC Child Bks.
Corni, Francesco. Lebek: A City of Northern Europe Through the Ages. Hernandez, Xavier & Ballonga, Jordi. Leverich, Kathleen, tr. 64p. 1991. 16.45 (0-395-57442-0, Sandpiper) HM.
—Umm el Madayan: An Islamic City Through the Ages. Ayoub, Abderrahaman, et al. LC 93-757. (ENG.). (gr. 5 up). 1994. 16.95 (0-395-65967-1) HM.
Corns, Marvin A. The Sloppy Monster. Kracht, Susan. LC 92-60289. 44p. (ps-3). 1992. 5.95 (1-55523-527-1) Winston-Derek.
Cornwall, Peter. Ships. Humble, Richard. LC 93-19705. 32p. (gr. 4-6). 1993. PLB 19.97 (0-8114-6158-0) Raintree Steck-V.
Corpening, Gene S., jt. illus. see James, Linda.
Corrigan, Barbara. Tom Glazer's Christmas Songbook. Glazer, Tom. 1989. 16.00 (0-685-29548-6) Doubleday.
—Tom Glazer's Christmas Songbook. Glazer, Tom. 128p. (gr. 3 up). 1989. pap. 16.00 (0-385-24641-2, Zephyr-BFYR) Doubleday.
Corrigan, Wendy O. The Saratoga Yearling. Reed, Kevin J. Herold, Meri G., ed. 110p. (Orig.). (gr. 5-9). 1985. pap. 3.95 (0-9614546-0-1) Chowder Pr.
—A Season for Dreams. Reed, Kevin. LC 89-90670. 152p. (gr. 5-7). 1989. pap. 5.95 (0-9614546-3-6) Chowder Pr.
Corvey, Linda. Brain Gym Surfer. Hinsley, Sandra. 6.00 (0-685-64789-7, 5) Edu-Kinesthetics.
Corvi, Donna. The Moon. Greenberg, Judith E. & Carey, Helen H. 32p. (gr. 2-4). 1990. PLB 17.96 (0-8172-3752-6) Raintree Steck-V.
Corwin, Judith H. Birthday Fun. Corwin, Judith H. 64p. (gr. 3 up). 1986. lib. bdg. 10.98 (0-671-55519-7, J Messner); lib. bdg. 5.95 (0-671-60126-1); PLB 7.71s.p. (0-685-47048-2); pap. 3.71s.p. (0-685-47049-0) S&S Trade.
—Christmas Fun. Corwin, Judith H. 64p. (gr. 3 up). 1983. lib. bdg. 10.98 (0-671-45944-9, J Messner); lib. bdg. 5.95 (0-671-49583-6); PLB 7.71s.p. (0-685-47052-0); pap. 4.46s.p. (0-685-47053-9) S&S Trade.
—Colonial American Crafts: The Village. Corwin, Judith H. LC 89-8966. 48p. (gr. 4-7). 1989. PLB 12.40 (0-531-10715-9) Watts.
—Cookie Fun. Corwin, Judith H. 64p. (gr. 3 up). 1985. lib. bdg. 10.98 (0-671-50797-4, J Messner); lib. bdg. 5.95 (0-671-55019-5); PLB 7.71s.p. (0-685-47050-4); pap. 3.71s.p. (0-685-47051-2) S&S Trade.
—Easter Fun. Corwin, Judith H. 64p. (gr. 3 up). 1984. (J Messner); lib. bdg. 5.95 (0-671-53108-5); PLB 7.71s.p. (0-685-47054-7); pap. 4.46s.p. (0-685-47055-5) S&S Trade.
—Halloween Fun. Corwin, Judith H. LC 83-8289. 64p. (gr. 3 up). 1983. (J Messner); lib. bdg. 5.95 (0-671-49756-1); PLB 7.71s.p. (0-685-47056-3); pap. 4.46s.p. (0-685-47057-1) S&S Trade.
—Jewish Holiday Fun. Corwin, Judith H. LC 86-16201. 64p. (gr. 3 up). 1987. (J Messner); lib. bdg. 5.95 (0-671-60127-X); PLB 7.71s.p. (0-685-47058-X); pap. 4.46s.p. (0-685-47059-8) S&S Trade.
—Mapmaking. Mango, Karin N. LC 83-25084. 112p. (gr. 4 up). 1984. lib. bdg. 9.29 (0-671-45518-4, J Messner) S&S Trade.
—Messner Holiday Library, 9 bks. Corwin, Judith H. (gr. 3 up). 1990. Set, 64p. ea. lib. bdg. 92.61 (0-671-92641-1, J Messner); Set, 64p. ea. pap. 49.55 (0-671-92642-X) S&S Trade.

—Papercrafts. Corwin, Judith H. IRosoff, ed. LC 87-21611. 72p. (gr. 2-4). 1988. PLB 12.90 (0-531-10465-6) Watts.

—Patriotic Fun. Corwin, Judith H. LC 85-18730. 64p. (gr. 3 up). 1986. lib. bdg. 10.98 (0-671-50799-0, J Messner); PLB 7.71s.p. (0-685-47060-1); pap. 3.71s.p. (0-685-47061-X) S&S Trade.

—Thanksgiving Fun. Corwin, Judith H. 64p. (gr. 3 up). 1984. lib. bdg. 10.98 (0-671-49422-8, J Messner); lib. bdg. 5.95 (0-671-50849-0); PLB 7.71s.p. (0-685-47062-8); pap. 4.46s.p. (0-685-47063-6) S&S Trade.

—Valentine Fun. Corwin, Judith H. LC 82-6047. 64p. (gr. 3 up). 1983. (J Messner); lib. bdg. 5.95 (0-671-49755-3); PLB 7.71s.p. (0-685-47064-4); pap. 4.46s.p. (0-685-47065-2) S&S Trade.

Cory, Fanny Y. The Fairy Alphabet of F. Y. Cory. Cory, Fanny Y. 32p. 1991. 14.95 (1-56037-006-8) Am Wrld Geog.

Cosgrove, Colleen B. Cisco & the Twin Foals. Field, Arthur W. LC 83-61713. 160p. (gr. 8 up). 1983. 12.00 (0-935356-06-1) Mills Pub Co.

Cosgrove, Jim. Texans: The Story of Texan Cultures for Young People. Stanush, Barbara E. LC 88-50983. 122p. (gr. 4-7). 1988. 19.95 (0-86701-040-1) U of Tex Inst Tex Culture.

Cosgrove, John O. Carry on, Mr. Bowditch. Latham, Jean L. LC 55-5219. 256p. (gr. 6 up). 1973. pap. 5.70 (0-395-13713-6, Sandpiper) HM.

—Carry on, Mr. Bowditch. Latham, Jean L. (gr. 6 up). 1955. 14.95 (0-395-06881-9) HM.

Costa, Nicoletta. Look Inside Your Brain. Alexander, Heather. LC 90-85544. 16p. (ps-3). 1991. 11.95 (0-448-40186-X, G&D) Putnam Pub Group.

—My Poke & Look Busy Book Two. 32p. (ps-2). 1992. bds. 14.95 (0-448-40390-0, G&D) Putnam Pub Group.

Costabel, Eva D. The Early People of Florida. Costabel, Eva D. LC 92-16283. 40p. (gr. 2-6). 1993. SBE 13.95 (0-689-31500-7, Atheneum Child Bk) Macmillan Child Grp.

—Jews of New Amsterdam. Costabel, Eva D. LC 87-27873. 32p. (gr. 2-6). 1988. SBE 13.95 (0-689-31351-9, Atheneum Child Bk) Macmillan Child Grp.

Costanzo, Lana. Playbook for Kids About Sex. Blank, Joani. 56p. (gr. 2-6). 1980. pap. 5.00 (0-9602324-6-X, Yes Pr) Down There Pr.

Costello, Melina P. Tutti-Frutti Town: Blinky Blueberry Finds a Friend. Costello, Melina P. 32p. (Orig.). (gr. k-3). 1991. pap. 6.50 (1-878130-01-3) Bang A Drum.

Costeloe, Brenda. Busy Bees. Scarffe, Bronwen. LC 92-31958. 1993. 3.75 (0-383-03558-9) SRA Schl Grp.

—How to Make Cheese Muffins. Bissett, Isabel. LC 93-21247. 1994. 4.25 (0-383-03748-4) SRA Schl Grp.

—The Storm. Drew, David. LC 92-30671. 1993. write for info. (0-383-03656-9) SRA Schl Grp.

—Waves. Beveridge, Barbara. LC 92-31948. 1993. 3.75 (0-383-03603-8) SRA Schl Grp.

Costner, Howard. Juneteenth. rev. ed. Barrett, Anna P. Goodman, Frances B., ed. 64p. (gr. k-8). 1993. pap. 9.95 (0-89896-111-4) Larksdale.

—The Tenth Rifle. Marvin, Isabelle. 128p. (Orig.). (gr. 3-8). 1993. pap. 9.95 (0-89896-109-2) Larksdale.

Cote, Nancy. Palm Trees. Cote, Nancy. LC 92-18938. 40p. (ps-2). 1993. RSBE 14.95 (0-02-724760-0, Four Winds) Macmillan Child Grp.

—Ruby's Storm. Hest, Amy. LC 92-31242. 32p. (ps-2). 1994. RSBE 14.95 (0-02-743160-6, Four Winds) Macmillan Child Grp.

Cote, Nancy, jt. illus. see Harris, Denise.

Cote, Pamela. Runaway Valentines. Trumbauer, Lisa. LC 93-14181. (gr. k-2). 1993. pap. 2.95t (0-8167-3264-7) Troll Assocs.

—Somethins Is Coming. Chardiet, Bernice. 20p. (ps-1). 1994. pap. 4.99 (0-14-054996-X) Puffin Bks.

Cote, Phyllis N. Gigi in America: The Further Adventures of a Merry-Go-Round Horse. Foster, Elizabeth. 130p. (gr. 4-8). 1990. pap. 9.95 (0-913028-69-X) North Atlantic.

Cotler, Joanna. Sky Above Earth Below. Cotler, Joanna. LC 89-26743. 32p. (ps-k). 1990. 14.95 (0-06-021365-5) HarpC Child Bks.

Couch, Greg. The Man in the Moon in Love. Brumbeau, Jeff. LC 91-37804. 32p. 1992. 14.95 (1-55670-229-9) Stewart Tabori & Chang.

Couderc, Agnes. The Amazing Fate of Raoul Raccoon, Vol. 1. Couderc, Agnes. (ps-3). 1993. 12.95 (0-316-15829-1) Little.

Coulter, Gene. Tales, Trails & Tommyknockers: Stories from Colorado's Past. Friggens, Myriam. LC 79-84876. 144p. (gr. 6 up). 1979. pap. 7.95 (0-933472-01-3) Johnson Bks.

Couman, Carol & Codor, Dick. Pokey to the Rescue. Gilden, Mel. (gr. k-3). 1988. pap. 2.25 (0-671-63900-5) S&S Trade.

Councell, Ruth T. Country Bear's Surprise. Brimner, Larry D. LC 90-7717. 32p. (ps-2). 1991. 12.95 (0-531-05811-5); PLB 12.99 (0-531-08411-6) Orchard Bks Watts.

—Handel: And the Famous Sword Swallower of Halle. Stevens, Bryna. 32p. (ps-3). 1990. 14.95 (0-399-21548-4, Philomel Bks) Putnam Pub Group.

—What Rhymes with Moon? Yolen, Jane. LC 92-7439. 40p. (ps). 1993. 15.95 (0-399-22501-3, Philomel Bks) Putnam Pub Group.

County Studio Staff. The Doll's Tea Party. Leeka, M. C. 24p. (ps-2). 1993. pap. text ed. 0.99 (1-56293-343-4) McClanahan Bk.

—Pershey the Rabbit. Eldrid, Brenda. 24p. (ps-2). 1993. pap. text ed. 0.99 (1-56293-342-6) McClanahan Bk.

Coupland, Gill. The Harris Visits the Garden of Everything. De Warren, Shaun. 32p. (ps-3). 1985. cloth 12.95 (0-913299-21-9, Dist. by PGW) Stillpoint.

Couri, Kathryn A. The Prince & the Pauper. Twain, Mark. James, Raymond, ed. LC 89-33892. 48p. (gr. 3-6). 1990. lib. bdg. 12.89 (0-8167-1873-3); pap. text ed. 3.95 (0-8167-1874-1) Troll Assocs.

Couri, Kathy. The Best Thing about Easter. Tangvald, Christine H. 28p. (ps). 1993. PLB 4.99 (0-7847-0035-4, 24-03825) Standard Pub.

—Friends from Galilee: A Bible-Times Visit with Micah & Hannah. Stewart, Dana. 28p. (ps). 1994. 4.99 (0-7847-0003-6, 24-03869) Standard Pub.

Courtney. Dolphins. Bakoske, Sharon & Davidson, Margaret. 48p. (Orig.). (gr. 1-3). 1993. PLB 7.99 (0-679-94437-0); pap. 3.50 (0-679-84437-6) Random Bks Yng Read.

—Volcanoes & Earthquakes. Elting, Mary. LC 89-37107. 48p. (gr. 3-7). 1990. pap. 9.95 (0-671-67217-7, S&S BFYR) S&S Trade.

Courtney, Richard. All Aboard Trains. Harding, Mary. 32p. (Orig.). (ps-2). 1989. pap. 2.25 (0-448-19111-3, Platt & Munk Pubs) Putnam Pub Group.

—All Aboard Trucks. Conrad, Lynn. 32p. (Orig.). (ps-2). 1989. pap. 2.25 (0-448-19094-X, Platt & Munk Pubs) Putnam Pub Group.

—The Big Book of Real Trains. Retan, Walter. 48p. (gr. 1-4). 1987. 7.95 (0-448-19178-4, G&D) Putnam Pub Group.

—Dinosaurs: Giants of the Earth. Moseley, Keith, designed by. 12p. (ps-3). 1988. 6.95 (0-448-19302-7, G&D) Putnam Pub Group.

—Earthquake! San Francisco, Nineteen Hundred Six. Wilson, Kate. LC 92-18081. 62p. (gr. 2-5). 1992. PLB 21.34 (0-8114-7216-7) Raintree Steck-V.

Courtney Studios, Inc. Staff. Sharks! Wilson, Lynn. 32p. (ps-3). 1992. (Platt & Munk Pubs); pap. 2.25 (0-448-40300-5, Platt & Munk Pubs) Putnam Pub Group.

Cousins, Luch. Maisy Goes to Bed. Cousins, Lucy. (ps). 1990. 12.95 (0-316-15832-1) Little.

Cousins, Lucy. Country Animals. Cousins, Lucy. LC 90-35894. (ps). 1991. bds. 3.95 (0-688-10070-8, Tambourine Bks) Morrow.

—Farm Animals. Cousins, Lucy. LC 90-35893. (ps). 1991. bds. 3.95 (0-688-10071-6, Tambourine Bks) Morrow.

—Flower in the Garden. Cousins, Lucy. LC 91-71854. 8p. (ps). 1992. 4.95 (1-56402-029-0) Candlewick Pr.

—Garden Animals. Cousins, Lucy. LC 90-36259. (ps). 1991. bds. 3.95 (0-688-10072-4, Tambourine Bks) Morrow.

—Hen on the Farm. Cousins, Lucy. LC 91-71849. 8p. (ps). 1992. 4.95 (1-56402-032-0) Candlewick Pr.

—Kite in the Park. Cousins, Lucy. LC 91-71842. 8p. (ps). 1992. 4.95 (1-56402-031-2) Candlewick Pr.

—Maisy Goes to School. Cousins, Lucy. LC 91-58743. 16p. (ps). 1992. 12.95 (1-56402-085-1) Candlewick Pr.

—Maisy Goes to the Playground. Cousins, Lucy. LC 91-58742. 16p. (ps). 1992. 12.95 (1-56402-084-3) Candlewick Pr.

—Noah's Ark. Cousins, Lucy, retold by. LC 92-54589. 40p. (gr. 2 up). 1993. 14.95 (1-56402-213-7) Candlewick Pr.

—Pet Animals. Cousins, Lucy. LC 90-36260. (ps). 1991. bds. 3.95 (0-688-10073-2, Tambourine Bks) Morrow.

—Teddy in the House. Cousins, Lucy. LC 91-71821. 8p. (ps). 1992. 4.95 (1-56402-030-4) Candlewick Pr.

Coutney, Richard. How Tough Was a Tyrannosaurus? More Fascinating Facts about Dinosaurs. Sereno, Paul C. 32p. (ps-7). 1989. pap. 2.25 (0-448-19116-4, Platt & Munk Pubs) Putnam Pub Group.

Couture, Christin. The Lizard of Oz. Seltzer, Richard W., Jr. LC 74-20172. 128p. (Orig.). (gr. 7 up). 1974. pap. 4.50 (0-915232-01-4) B & R Samizdat.

Covell, Joan. Nursery Songs & Lap Games. Kennedy, Pamela, compiled by. 32p. 1990. 13.95 (0-8249-8486-2, Ideals Child); incl. 50-min. cassette 17.95 (0-8249-7399-2) Hambleton-Hill.

Coven, Peggy. Joel: A Boy of Galilee. Johnston, Annie F. Slater, Rosalie J., intro. by. LC 92-75820. 254p. (gr. 4-8). 1992. pap. 12.00 (0-912498-11-0) F A C E.

—Mother Carey's Chickens. Wiggin, Kate D. Adams, Carole G., intro. by. Stephens, Alice B. 368p. (gr. 4-8). 1991. pap. 14.00 (0-912498-10-2) F A C E.

Cover, Marilyn. Peggy's Problem. Gillespie, Bonita. 35p. (gr. 3-8). 1987. 6.95 (1-55523-058-X) Winston-Derek.

Coverly, Dave. Smart Learning: A Study Skills Guide for Teens. Christen, William & Murphy, Thomas. Strother, Deborah B. & Strother, William C., eds. LC 91-48274. 120p. (Orig.). (gr. 6 up). 1992. pap. 10.95 (0-9628556-5-0) Grayson Bernard Pubs.

Covert, Susan. Eagle Eyes: A Child's Guide to Paying Attention. 2nd ed. Gehret, Jeanne. 40p. (gr. 1-5). 1991. 13.95 (0-9625136-5-2); pap. 8.95 perfect bdg. (0-9625136-4-4) Verbal Images Pr.

Coville, Bruce. Space Brat Two: Blork's Evil Twin. Coville, Bruce. 80p. (Orig.). (gr. 2-4). 1993. 12.00 (0-671-87038-6, Minstrel Bks); pap. 3.50 (0-671-77713-0, Minstrel Bks) PB.

Coville, Bruce & Coville, Katherine. Sarah's Unicorn. Coville, Bruce & Coville, Katherine. LC 85-42749. 48p. (gr. 1-4). 1985. pap. 4.95 (0-06-443084-7, Trophy) HarpC Child Bks.

Coville, Katherine. Aliens Ate My Homework. Coville, Bruce. 160p. (gr. 3-6). 1993. 12.00 (0-671-87249-4, Minstrel Bks); pap. 3.50 (0-671-72712-5, Minstrel Bks) PB.

—The Foolish Giant. Coville, Bruce. LC 77-18522. 48p. (ps-2). 1990. pap. 3.95 (0-06-443229-7, Trophy) HarpC Child Bks.

—Goblins in the Castle. Coville, Bruce. MacDonald, Pat, ed. 176p. (Orig.). 1992. pap. 3.50 (0-671-72711-7, Minstrel Bks) PB.

—The Monster's Ring. Coville, Bruce. LC 82-3436. 96p. (gr. 8-11). 1982. lib. bdg. 9.99 (0-394-95320-7) Pantheon.

—Mostly Michael. Smith, Robert K. LC 86-19618. 192p. (gr. 4-6). 1987. pap. 13.95 (0-385-29545-6) Delacorte.

—The Scary Halloween Costume Book. Barkin, Carol & James, Elizabeth. LC 81-14249. (gr. 3-6). 1983. 12.95 (0-688-00956-5); PLB 12.88 (0-688-00957-3) Lothrop.

—Space Brat. Coville, Bruce. MacDonald, Pat, ed. 80p. (Orig.). 1992. pap. 3.50 (0-671-74567-0, Minstrel Bks) PB.

—Space Brat. Coville, Bruce. MacDonald, Pat, ed. 1993. 12.00 (0-671-87059-9, Minstrel Bks) PB.

—The Summer I Shrank My Grandmother. Woodruff, Elvira. LC 90-55099. 160p. (gr. 3-7). 1990. 13.95 (0-8234-0832-9) Holiday.

—Take Care of Things, Edward Said. Buckley, Helen. LC 88-1578. 32p. (ps up). 1991. 13.95 (0-688-07731-5); PLB 13.88 (0-688-07732-3) Lothrop.

Coville, Katherine, jt. illus. see Coville, Bruce.

Coville, Katherine D. Bible Stories from the New Testament. Hopkins, Margaret. 96p. (ps-3). 1989. 12.95 (0-448-19184-9, G&D) Putnam Pub Group.

Cowcher, Helen. Antarctica. Cowcher, Helen. Red Grammer Staff, narrated by. 32p. (ps-3). 1990. incl. audiocassette 19.95 (0-924483-24-5); incl. audio cass. tape & stuffed penguin toy 44.95 (0-924483-65-2) Soundprints.

—Tigress. Cowcher, Helen. Thomas, Peter, narrated by. 32p. (gr. k-4). incls. cassette 19.95 (0-924483-33-4, 3530) Soundprints.

Cowen-Fletcher, Jane. Mama Zooms. Cowen-Fletcher, Jane. LC 92-15553. 32p. (ps-1). 1993. 14.95 (0-590-45774-8) Scholastic Inc.

Cox, Anne. Phonics for the New Reader: Step-by-Step. Fields, Harriette. LC 90-70334. 128p. (Orig.). (ps-2). 1991. 17.95x (0-9625802-0-1); pap. 8.95 (0-9625802-1-X) Words Pub CO. "The author provides a ready-to-use blueprint for helping young children understand phonics & provides the necessary tools for that understanding," says former President of the National Association of State Boards of Education, Roseann Bentley. "This book provides clear, well-organized directions," & "I think this would be an excellent book for people striving to learn English as a second language." TABLE OF CONTENTS: Lesson 1- Letter Names, Shapes & Sounds; Lesson 2- Short Vowels; Lesson 3- Long Vowels; Lesson 4- Special Words & Letters; Lesson 5- Reading Consonant Combinations; Lesson 6- Reading Vowel Combinations; Lesson 7- Special Vowel Combinations; Lesson 8- Reading Vowel-Consonant Combinations. *Publisher Provided Annotation.*

Cox, Carolyn. My Own Book of Bible Stories. 2nd ed. Alexander, Pat, as told by. LC 92-36252. 128p. (gr. k-3). 1993. text ed. 14.95 (0-7459-2635-5) Lion USA.

Cox, Daniel J., photos by. Loon Lake. Hirschi, Ron. LC 90-34396. 32p. (ps-3). 1991. 13.95 (0-525-65046-6, Cobblehill Bks) Dutton Child Bks.

—The Wonder of Whitetails. Lantier-Sampon, Patricia, adapted by. LC 92-16947. 1992. PLB 18.60 (0-8368-0858-4) Gareth Stevens Inc.

Cox, Daniel S. Whitetail Magic for Kids. Wolpert, Tom. LC 90-50719. 48p. (gr. 2-3). 1991. PLB 18.60 (0-8368-0661-1) Gareth Stevens Inc.

Cox, David. The Slumber Party. Wild, Margaret. LC 92-39783. 1993. 13.45 (0-395-66598-1) Ticknor & Fields.

—The Sugar-Gum Tree. Wrightson, Patricia. 64p. (gr. 2-6). 1992. 11.95 (0-670-83910-8) Viking Child Bks.

Cox, Palmer. The Brownies' Merry Adventures. Cox, Palmer. LC 93-563. 224p. 1993. 6.00 (1-56957-901-6) Shambhala Pubns.

Coxe, Molly. The Big Dipper. rev. ed. Branley, Franklyn M. LC 90-33198. 32p. (ps-1). 1991. pap. 4.95 (0-06-445100-3, Trophy) HarpC Child Bks.

—The Big Dipper. rev. ed. Branley, Franklyn M. LC 90-31199. 32p. (ps-1). 1991. 13.95 (0-06-020511-3); PLB 13.89 (0-06-020512-1) HarpC Child Bks.

—Ducks, Ducks, Ducks. Otto, Carolyn B. LC 90-42089. 32p. (ps-1). 1991. PLB 14.89 (*0-06-024639-1*) HarpC Child Bks.

—Louella & the Yellow Balloon. Coxe, Molly. LC 87-30379. 32p. (ps-2). 1988. (Crowell Jr Bks) HarpC Child Bks.

—Where's My Other Sock? How to Get Organized & Drive Your Parents & Teachers Crazy. Wirths, Claudine G. & Bowman-Kruhm, Mary. LC 88-39338. 128p. (gr. 5 up). 1989. (Crowell Jr Bks); PLB 13.89 (*0-690-04667-7*, Crowell Jr Bks) HarpC Child Bks.

Coxon, Michele. The Cat Who Lost His Purr. Coxon, Michele. 32p. (gr. k-3). 1991. 12.95 (*0-87226-453-X*, Bedrick Blackie) P Bedrick Bks.

Coxon, Michelle. Who Will Play with Me? Coxon, Michelle. LC 91-40498. 32p. (gr. k-3). 1992. PLB 12.95 (*0-87226-469-6*, Bedrick Blackie) P Bedrick Bks.

Coy, Michael. Darkness Creeping: Tales to Trouble Your Sleep. Shusterman, Neal. LC 93-13792. 128p. 1993. pap. 4.95 (*1-56565-069-7*) Lowell Hse.

Coy, Venture. Do I Like Myself? Holt, Janice M. LC 82-82332. 119p. (gr. 3-9). 1983. pap. 39.95 (*0-9608812-1-2*) Greenlf Pubns.

Coyle, P. Ferdinand Magellan: Noble Captain. Wilkie, Katherine. (gr. 4-6). 1963. pap. 2.44 (*0-395-01751-3*, Piper) HM.

Coyne, John P. Suzie Q. Mouse Adventures. Sternburg, Sharon. 39p. (Orig.). (ps-1). 1993. pap. 5.99 (*0-9633513-1-1*) S M Resar Pub.

—Suzie Q. Mouse Adventures: Coloring Book. Sternburg, Sharon. 39p. (Orig.). (ps-1). Date not set. pap. 1.99x (*0-9633513-0-3*) S M Resar Pub.

Cozzolino, Sandra, jt. illus. see Majewski, Dawn.

Cozzolino, Sandra, jt. illus. see Steiner, Pat.

Cracchiolo, Rachelle & Smith, Mary D. Holiday Hats. Cracchiolo, Rachelle & Smith, Mary D. 16p. (gr. k-4). 1979. wkbk. 6.50 (*1-55734-002-1*) Tchr Create Mat.

Crachiolo, Rachelle & Smith, Mary D. Christmas Activities. Cracchiolo, Rachelle & Smith, Mary D. 32p. (gr. 1-3). 1985. wkbk. 4.95 (*1-55734-013-7*) Tchr Create Mat.

—Halloween Activities. Cracchiolo, Rachelle & Smith, Mary D. 32p. (gr. 1-3). 1980. wkbk. 4.95 (*1-55734-011-0*) Tchr Create Mat.

—Thanksgiving Activities. Cracchiolo, Rachelle & Smith, Mary D. 32p. (gr. 1-3). 1985. wkbk. 4.95 (*1-55734-012-9*) Tchr Create Mat.

Craft, Kinuko Y. Bailey's Window. Lindbergh, Anne M. LC 83-18360. 115p. (gr. 3-7). 1984. 14.95 (*0-15-205642-4*, HB Juv Bks) HarBrace.

—The Elephant. Hogan, Paula Z. LC 79-13307. (gr. 1-4). 1979. PLB 29.28 incl. cassette (*0-8172-1844-0*); PLB 17.96 (*0-8172-1505-0*); pap. 4.95 (*0-8114-8177-8*); pap. 9.95 incl. cassette (*0-8114-8185-9*) Raintree Steck-V.

—Tales of the Ugly Ogres. Denan, Corinne. LC 79-66333. 48p. (gr. 3-6). 1980. PLB 9.89 (*0-89375-332-7*); pap. text ed. 2.95 (*0-89375-331-9*) Troll Assocs.

—Treasure Island. Stevenson, Robert Louis. Edwards, Jane, adapted by. LC 79-24100. (gr. 4-12). 1983. PLB 18.64 (*0-8172-1655-3*) Raintree Steck-V.

—Twelve Dancing Princess. Mayer, Marianna. LC 83-1034. 40p. (ps up). 1989. 14.95 (*0-688-08051-0*); PLB 14.88 (*0-688-02026-7*, Morrow Jr Bks) Morrow Jr Bks.

—Wolf & the Seven Kids. new ed. Grimm, Jacob & Grimm, Wilhelm K. LC 78-18076. 32p. (gr. 1-4). 1979. PLB 9.79 (*0-89375-138-3*); pap. 1.95 (*0-89375-116-2*) Troll Assocs.

Craft, Mary. Sea Otters Cruz & Slick. Craft, Mary. 24p. (Orig.). 1991. pap. write for info. (*0-9624842-2-9*) M Craft.

—Tiger. Lorenzen, Anna L. 22p. (Orig.). (gr. 1-2). 1989. pap. text ed. 2.95 (*0-9626133-0-4*) ALL Ventura Pub.

Craft, Mary L. Little Orphan Otter. Craft, Mary L. 20p. (Orig.). (gr. k-12). 1989. pap. text ed. 5.25 (*0-9624842-0-2*) M Craft.

Craghead, Gary. Ready, Willing & Terrified: A Coward's Guide to Risk-Taking. Chaney, Casey. Moffett, Berdell & Rhiannon, Thea, eds. 144p. (Orig.). 1991. pap. 10.95 (*0-9626403-1-X*) Mocha Pub.

Craig, Alice. Tiny Tots Bible Story Book. Walton, John & Walton, Kim. (ps). 1993. 14.99 (*0-685-63498-1*, Chariot Bks) Cook.

Craig, Bobby. Amazing Facts about Your Body. Brandreth, Gyles. LC 80-1088. 32p. (gr. 5-8). 1981. pap. 2.95 (*0-385-17018-1*, Zephyr-BFYR) Doubleday.

Craig, Helen. Alexander & the Dragon. Holabird, Katharine. 24p. (ps-2). 1988. 13.00 (*0-517-56996-5*, Clarkson Potter) Crown Bks Yng Read.

—Alexander & the Magic Boat. Holabird, Katharine. 24p. (ps-2). 1990. 11.95 (*0-517-58142-6*); PLB 12.99 (*0-517-58149-3*) Crown Bks Yng Read.

—Angelina & Alice. Holabird, Katharine. (ps-2). 1988. 14.00 (*0-517-56074-7*, Clarkson Potter) Crown Bks Yng Read.

—Angelina at the Fair. Holabird, Katharine. LC 84-28931. 24p. (ps-2). 1988. 13.00 (*0-517-55744-4*, Clarkson Potter) Crown Bks Yng Read.

—Angelina Ballerina. Holabird, Katharine. LC 83-8233. (ps-2). 1988. 13.00 (*0-517-55083-0*, Clarkson Potter) Crown Bks Yng Read.

—Angelina Ballerina. miniature ed. Holabird, Katharine. 24p. (ps-2). 1990. 4.99 (*0-517-57668-6*, Clarkson Potter) Crown Bks Yng Read.

—Angelina Book & Doll Package. Holabird, Katharine. LC 83-8233. 32p. (ps-2). 1989. book & doll 20.00 (*0-517-57089-0*, Clarkson Potter) Crown Bks Yng Read.

—Angelina Dances. Holabird, Katharine. LC 92-80524. 6p. (ps-k). 1992. bds. 5.99 (*0-679-83484-2*) Random Bks Yng Read.

—Angelina Ice Skates. Holabird, Katharine. 32p. (ps-2). 1993. 15.00 (*0-517-59619-9*) Crown Bks Yng Read.

—Angelina on Stage. Holabird, Katharine. 24p. (ps-2). 1988. 14.00 (*0-517-56073-9*, Clarkson Potter) Crown Bks Yng Read.

—Angelina's Birthday Surprise. Holabird, Katharine. LC 89-3513. 32p. (ps-2). 1989. 14.00 (*0-517-57325-3*, Clarkson Potter) Crown Bks Yng Read.

—Angelina's Christmas. Holabird, Katharine. LC 85-12389. 32p. (gr. 1 up). 1986. 13.00 (*0-517-55823-8*, Clarkson Potter); pap. 4.95 (*0-685-22929-7*, C N Potter Bks) Crown Bks Yng Read.

—Christmas with Angelina. Holabird, Katharine. LC 92-80523. 6p. (ps-k). 1992. bds. 5.99 (*0-679-83485-0*) Random Bks Yng Read.

—I See the Moon, & the Moon Sees Me. Craig, Helen. LC 92-18996. 48p. (ps-2). 1993. 16.00 (*0-06-021453-8*); PLB 15.89 (*0-06-021454-6*) HarpC Child Bks.

—Jam. Mahy, Margaret. 32p. (ps-3). 1986. 12.95 (*0-316-54396-9*, 543969, Joy St Bks) Little.

—The Knight, the Princess & the Dragon. Craig, Helen. LC 84-19419. 32p. (ps-2). 1985. lib. bdg. 8.99 (*0-394-97212-0*) Knopf Bks Yng Read.

—Mary Mary. Hayes, Sarah. LC 90-5964. 32p. (gr. k-3). 1990. SBE 13.95 (*0-689-50514-0*, M K McElderry) Macmillan Child Grp.

—The One & Only Robin Hood. Gray, Nigel. LC 87-2680. 32p. (ps-3). 1987. 12.95 (*0-316-32578-3*, Joy St Bks) Little.

—This Is the Bear. Hayes, Sarah. LC 92-53421. 32p. (ps). 1993. 12.95 (*1-56402-189-0*) Candlewick Pr.

—This Is the Bear & the Picnic Lunch. Hayes, Sarah. 32p. (ps-1). 1989. 12.95 (*0-316-35248-9*, Joy St Bks) Little.

—This Is the Bear & the Scary Night. Hayes, Sarah. (ps-1). 1992. 13.95 (*0-316-35250-0*, Joy St Bks) Little.

—The Town Mouse & the Country Mouse. Craig, Helen, retold by. LC 91-58761. 32p. (ps up). 1992. 13.95 (*1-56402-102-5*) Candlewick Pr.

—The Wrestling Princess & Other Stories. large type ed. Corbalis, Judy. 208p. 1992. 13.95 (*0-7451-1551-9*, Galaxy Child Lrg Print) Chivers N Amer.

—The Yellow House. Morrison, Blake. 32p. (ps-3). 1987. 12.95 (*0-15-299820-9*, HB Juv Bks) HarBrace.

Craig, Helen & Craig, Helen. Crumbling Castle. Hayes, Sarah. LC 91-58723. 80p. (gr. 3-6). 1992. 13.95 (*1-56402-108-4*) Candlewick Pr.

Craig, Jennifer. The Adventures of Nicolet. Brandt, Betty. Brandt, Laura, ed. 160p. (Orig.). (gr. 8-12). 1991. 12.95 (*0-9622014-2-1*) Beaver Valley.

Craig, Michael. Kitten in the Country. Heupel, DuWayne. 32p. (gr. 1-2). 1993. text ed. 10.95 (*1-882841-05-0*) Educare CO.

Craig, Rose & Noll, Sally. Get It Together: Math Problems for Groups Grades 4-12. Erickson, Tim. 180p. (Orig.). (gr. 4-12). 1989. pap. 15.00 (*0-912511-53-2*) Lawrence Science.

Craig, Rose, jt. illus. see Baker, Lisa H.

Craig, Rose, jt. illus. see Bavilacqua, Carol.

Craig, Rose, jt. illus. see Klofkorn, Lisa.

Craighead, John, et al. Operation Grizzly Bear. Calabro, Marian. LC 88-37497. 112p. (gr. 5 up). 1989. SBE 12.95 (*0-02-716241-9*, Four Winds) Macmillan Child Grp.

Cram, L. D. Carcajou. Montgomery, Rutherford G. LC 36-6665. (gr. 6-8). 1936. 4.95 (*0-87004-105-3*) Caxton.

Crampton, Kayle. Walk in Peace: Legends & Stories of the Michigan Indians. 2nd ed. Otto, Simon. Bussey, M. T., ed. 50p. (gr. 3-4). 1992. pap. 9.95 (*0-9617707-5-9*) Grnd Rpds Intertribal.

Crane, Charles. Modeling: How to Make It in Modeling Without Having to Go to Modeling School. rev. ed. Stafford, Marilyn. Terschluse, Ann, ed. Lee, Sharon, intro. by. 150p. (gr. 7 up). 1990. Set. incl. video 55.90 (*0-685-36259-0*); video avail. MidCoast Comns.

Crane, Walter. Favorite Poems of Childhood. LC 92-42770. 1993. 14.00 (*0-671-86614-1*, Green Tiger) S&S Trade.

—Household Stories of the Brothers Grimm. Grimm, Jacob & Grimm, Wilhelm K. Crane, Lucy, tr. x, 269p. (gr. 3-9). 1886. pap. 4.95 (*0-486-21080-4*) Dover.

Cranford, Kay K., et al. Creative Conflict Solving for Kids: Grades 5-9. 2nd., rev. ed. Schmidt, Fran & Friedman, Alice. 80p. (gr. 4-9). 1985. Incl. poster. pap. text ed. 21.95 (*1-878227-00-9*) Peace Educ.
CREATIVE CONFLICT SOLVING FOR KIDS challenges your students to deal creatively & constructively with conflict. The activities can easily be incorporated into your social studies, science & language arts programs. The curriculum comes with 40 student pages & an extensive teacher's guide with many enjoyable extending activities. Your students will be actively involved in brainstorming, role playing, problem solving & decision making as they learn the skills of creative communication, active listening, fighting fair, critical thinking, & cooperation. Students will: develop positive interpersonal skills; respect human differences; understand the dynamics of conflict; practice conflict resolution strategies; learn ways to handle frustration & anger; explore conflict as a positive force of change. "My students just love CREATIVE CONFLICT SOLVING FOR KIDS. They enjoy all of the activities & I can honestly say that the program has made a significant difference in the way the children treat each other. Name calling & put downs are rarely heard & when they occur they are handled before they turn into a fight."-- Joanne Sweeney, Fifth Grade, New York, New York. Students are involved in problem solving, brainstorming, role playing, & responsible decision making. *Publisher Provided Annotation.*

Crask, Tammy & Setzer, Debra. Science Fair Spelled W-I-N. Tant, Carl. 112p. (Orig.). (gr. 7-12). 1992. pap. 14.95 (*1-880319-02-0*) Biotech.

—Seeds, etc... Tant, Carl. LC 91-76151. 160p. (gr. 6-9). 1992. pap. 13.95 (*1-880319-01-2*) Biotech.

Cravath, Lynne. Three Two One Day. Driscoll, Debbie. LC 92-23420. 1994. pap. 14.00 (*0-671-79330-6*, S&S BFYR) S&S Trade.

Crawford, Dale. The Secret Garden: A Young Reader's Edition of the Classic Story. Abr. ed. Burnett, Francis H. LC 90-80198. 56p. (gr. 1 up). 1990. 9.98 (*0-89471-860-6*) Courage Bks.

Crawford, David, photos by. Teen Dads: Rights, Responsibilities & Joys. Lindsay, Jeanne W. 192p. (Orig.). (gr. 7 up). 1993. 15.95 (*0-930934-77-6*); pap. 9.95 (*0-930934-78-4*); tchr's. guide 2.50 (*0-930934-80-6*); wkbk. 2.50 (*0-930934-79-2*) Morning Glory.

Crawford, Kimberly Ann. Farnagle's Fables for Children & Adults. Farnagle, A. E. & Smith, W. Hovey. 64p. (Orig.). (gr. 1-5). 1984. pap. 4.25 (*0-916565-04-1*) Whitehall Pr.

Crawford, Mel. How Do I Grow? rev. ed. Carola, Robert. 32p. (gr. 2-4). 1990. Repr. of 1988 ed. PLB 9.95 (*1-878363-14-X*) Forest Hse.

—How Do I Know? Carola, Robert. 32p. (gr. 2-4). 1990. Repr. of 1988 ed. PLB 9.95 (*1-878363-12-3*) Forest Hse.

Crawford, Mel & Hultgren, Ken. Walt Disney's Bambi Comic Album. Salten, Felix. Blum, Geoffrey, intro. by. 48p. (Orig.). (ps up). 1988. pap. 5.95 (*0-944599-09-5*) Gladstone Pub.

Creative Company Staff. Discover African Wildlife: Activity Book. Beattie, Laura C. 24p. (Orig.). (gr. 3-7). 1993. wkbk. 2.95 (*0-911239-38-3*) Carnegie Mus.

—Discover Rocks & Minerals: Activity Book. Beattie, Laura C. 24p. (gr. 3-8). 1991. wkbk. 2.95 (*0-911239-36-7*) Carnegie Mus.

Creative Studios 1, Inc. Staff. Bear, Your Manners Are Showing. Meyer, Kathleen A. 32p. (gr. k-2). 1987. 2.50 (*0-87403-271-7*, 3771) Standard Pub.

Creative Teaching Assoc. Staff. Picture Patterns, Set 1 & 2. Wiebe, Arthur. 24p. (gr. k-4). 1985. wkbk. 8.95 ea. (*1-878669-32-X*, CTA-4752, CTA-4755) Crea Tea Assocs.

Creative Teaching Assocs. Staff. Domino Math, 2 bks. Wiebe, Arthur. 60p. Bks. A & B. write for info. set (*1-878669-18-4*, 4145); wkbk. 6.95 ea. Bk. A, Grades 1-4, 1973 (*1-878669-19-2*, 4145) Bk. B, Grades 2-6, 1974 (4146) Crea Tea Assocs.

—States & Capitals, 2 bks. Silvani, Harold. (gr. 3-6). 1975. Bks. A & B. write for info. set (*1-878669-12-5*, 4348); wkbk. 6.95 ea. Bk. A, 28p (*1-878669-13-3*, 4348) Bk. B, 53p (4395) Crea Tea Assocs.

Credit, Alfred A. Ribbons & Tadpoles. Potulny, Janice C. 56p. (ps-4). 1990. 6.95 (*0-8059-3174-0*) Dorrance.

Cregan, Nannette. Star Seed. Fontenot, Mary A. LC 86-12171. 32p. (gr. k-4). 1986. Repr. 7.95 (*0-88289-628-8*) Pelican.

Crema, Laura. Look Inside the Ocean. Malfatti, Patrizia. 16p. (ps-3). 1993. bds. 11.95 (*0-448-40488-5*, G&D) Putnam Pub Group.

Cremins, Bob. The Amazing Rhino. Bowden, Joan. Moseley, Keith, contrib. by. LC 92-18891. (ps-3). 1993. 7.99 (*0-8037-1383-5*) Dial Bks Young.

—A World Without Elephants. Bowden, Joan. Moseley, Keith, contrib. by. LC 92-18889. (ps-3). 1993. 7.99 (*0-8037-1382-7*) Dial Bks Young.

—A World Without Tigers. Bowden, Joan. Moseley, Keith, contrib. by. LC 92-18890. (ps-3). 1993. 7.99 (*0-8037-1381-9*) Dial Bks Young.

Cremins, Robert. Animal Acrobats. Eugene, Toni. LC 93-9768. 1993. write for info. (*0-87044-955-9*) Natl Geog.

—Big Creatures from the Past: A Pop-up Book. Watson, Claire. 14p. (gr. k-4). 1990. 14.95 (*0-399-22159-X*, Putnam Pub Group.

—Explorers in Dinosaur World. Williams, Geoffrey T. 32p. (gr. 1-6). 1988. pap. 2.95 (*0-8431-2264-1*); pap. 6.95 incl. cass. (*0-8431-2265-X*) Price Stern.

—Pooh & Some Bees. Milne, A. A. 10p. (ps up). 1987. 7.95 (*0-525-44339-8*, 0674-210, DCB) Dutton Child Bks.

—Pooh Goes Visiting. Milne, A. A. 10p. (ps up). 1987. 7.95 (*0-525-44337-1*, 0674-210, DCB) Dutton Child Bks.

—Saber Tooth: A Dinosaur World Adventure. Williams, Geoffrey T. 32p. (gr. 1-5). 1988. pap. 2.95 (*0-8431-2308-7*); pap. 6.95 incl. cass. (*0-8431-2319-2*) Price Stern.

Crescenzo, Phil. Dating Etiquette for Christian Teens. Diorio, MaryAnn L. 48p. (Orig.). (gr. 6-12). 1984. pap. 3.95 (*0-930037-00-6*) Daystar Comm.

Crespi, Francesca. The Sleeping Beauty. Richardson, Jean. 32p. (ps-1). 1991. 14.95 (*1-55970-142-0*) Arcade Pub Inc.

Crespo, George. How the Sea Began. Crespo, George. 32p. (gr. k-3). 1993. 14.95 (*0-395-63033-9*, Clarion Bks) HM.

Crews, Donald. Bigmama's. Crews, Donald. LC 90-33142. 32p. (ps up). 1991. 15.00 (*0-688-09950-5*); PLB 13.88 (*0-688-09951-3*) Greenwillow.

—Bigmama's. Crews, Donald. (gr. k-4). 1993. text ed. 3.95 (*0-685-64817-6*); audio cass. 11.00 (*1-882869-75-3*) Read Advent.

—Blue Sea. Kalan, Robert. LC 78-18396. 24p. (gr. k-3). 1979. 14.95 (*0-688-80184-6*); PLB 14.88 (*0-688-84184-8*) Greenwillow.

—Blue Sea. Kalan, Robert. LC 78-18396. 24p. (ps up). 1992. pap. 3.95 (*0-688-11509-8*, Mulberry) Morrow.

—Carousel. Crews, Donald. LC 82-3062. 32p. (ps-1). 1982. PLB 13.88 (*0-688-00909-3*) Greenwillow.

—Each Orange Had Eight Slices: A Counting Book. Giganti, Paul, Jr. LC 90-24167. 24p. (ps up). 1992. 14.00 (*0-688-10428-2*); PLB 13.93 (*0-688-10429-0*) Greenwillow.

—Each Orange Has Eight Slices. Giganti, Paul, Jr. 32p. (ps up). 1994. pap. 18.95 (*0-688-13116-6*, Mulberry) Morrow.

—Eclipse: Darkness in Daytime. rev. ed. Branley, Franklyn M. LC 87-47692. 32p. (ps-3). 1988. (Crowell Jr Bks); PLB 14.89 (*0-690-04619-7*, Crowell Jr Bks) HarpC Child Bks.

—Eclipse: Darkness in Daytime. rev. ed. Branley, Franklyn M. LC 87-45276. 32p. (ps-3). 1988. pap. 4.50 (*0-06-445081-3*, Trophy) HarpC Child Bks.

—Flying. Crews, Donald. LC 85-27022. 32p. (ps-3). 1986. 14.95 (*0-688-04318-6*); PLB 14.88 (*0-688-04319-4*) Greenwillow.

—Harbor. Crews, Donald. LC 81-6607. 32p. (ps-1). 1982. 11.75 (*0-688-00861-5*); PLB 14.93 (*0-688-00862-3*) Greenwillow.

—Parade. Crews, Donald. LC 82-20927. 32p. (gr. k-3). 1983. 14.00 (*0-688-01995-1*); PLB 13.93 (*0-688-01996-X*) Greenwillow.

—Rain. Kalan, Robert. LC 77-25312. 24p. (gr. k-3). 1978. PLB 13.93 (*0-688-84139-2*) Greenwillow.

—School Bus. Crews, Donald. LC 83-18681. 32p. (gr. k-3). 1984. 15.00 (*0-688-02807-1*); PLB 14.93 (*0-688-02808-X*) Greenwillow.

—Ten Black Dots. rev. ed. Crews, Donald. LC 85-14871. 32p. (ps-3). 1986. 15.00 (*0-688-06067-6*); PLB 14.93 (*0-688-06068-4*) Greenwillow.

—Truck. enl. ed. Crews, Donald. 32p. (ps up). 1993. pap. 18.95 (*0-688-12611-1*, Mulberry) Morrow.

—We Read: A to Z. Crews, Donald. LC 83-25453. 64p. (ps-1). 1984. 15.95 (*0-688-03843-3*); PLB 15.88 (*0-688-03844-1*) Greenwillow.

—When This Box Is Full. Lillie, Patricia. LC 92-28743. 24p. 1993. 14.00 (*0-688-12016-4*); PLB 13.93 (*0-688-12017-2*) Greenwillow.

Crews, Terry. Psalm One Hundred Thirty-Nine: An Illustrated Bible Chapter for Young Children. Meyer, David & Meyer, Alice, eds. LC 91-90825. 48p. (Orig.). (ps-4). 1991. pap. 12.95 incl. cassette (*1-879099-03-9*) Thy Word.

Cribbs, Dianna G. A Kid's Guide to Fishing & Fun Things to Do! Cribbs, Dianna G. 113p. (gr. 1-5). 1990. pap. 6.95 (*0-943487-27-7*) Sevgo Pr.

Crillis, Carla. I Can Help. 14p. (ps). 1991. Repr. bds. 5.50 (*0-86315-123-X*) Gryphon Hse.

Crisamore, Naomi. The Nomie Book: Growing up from Shy. Williams, Sunnie. 104p. (Orig.). (gr. 3-6). 1981. pap. 2.75 (*0-9605444-0-2*) Wee Smile.

Criscuolo, Edna. Once upon a Rhyme. Swan, Frances M. 48p. 1984. pap. 2.00 (*0-9602126-2-0*) F M Swan.

Cristini, Ermanno & Puricelli, Luigi. In My Garden. Cristini, Ermanno & Puricelli, Luigi. LC 85-9402. 28p. (ps up). 1991. pap. 12.95 (*0-907234-05-4*) Picture Bk Studio.

—In the Pond. Cristini, Ermanno & Puricelli, Luigi. LC 84-972. 28p. (ps up). 1991. pap. 12.95 (*0-907234-43-7*) Picture Bk Studio.

—In the Woods. Cristini, Ermanno & Puricelli, Luigi. LC 83-8153. 28p. (ps up). 1991. pap. 12.95 (*0-907234-31-3*) Picture Bk Studio.

Crocker, Russell. Gloria Goes to Gay Pride. Newman, Leslea. 48p. (Orig.). (ps-2). 1991. pap. 7.95 (*1-55583-185-0*) Alyson Pubns.

Crofts, Trudy & Childers, Peggy. The Hunter & the Quail. 32p. (gr. 1-6). 1993. pap. 7.95 (*0-89800-250-8*) Dharma Pub.

Crofut, bob. Emmy. Green, Connie J. LC 92-1513. 160p. (gr. 5-9). 1992. SBE 13.95 (*0-689-50556-6*, M K McElderry) Macmillan Child Grp.

Croll, Carolyn. Big Balloon Race. newly illus. ed. Coerr, Eleanor. LC 91-13607. 64p. (gr. k-3). 1984. pap. 3.50 (*0-06-444053-2*, Trophy) HarpC Child Bks.

—The Big Balloon Race. newly illus. ed. Coerr, Eleanor. LC 91-13606. 64p. (gr. k-3). 1981. 13.00 (*0-06-021352-3*); PLB 12.89 (*0-06-021353-1*) HarpC Child Bks.

—Clara & the Bookwagon. Levinson, Nancy S. LC 86-45773. 64p. (gr. k-3). 1988. PLB 13.89 (*0-06-023838-0*) HarpC Child Bks.

—Clara & the Bookwagon. Levinson, Nancy S. LC 86-45773. 64p. (gr. k-3). 1991. pap. 3.50 (*0-06-444134-2*, Trophy) HarpC Child Bks.

—The Little Snowgirl. Croll, Carolyn, adapted by. 32p. (ps-k). 1989. 14.95 (*0-399-21691-X*, Putnam) Putnam Pub Group.

—Music. Santrey, Laurence. LC 84-2648. 32p. (gr. 3-6). 1985. PLB 9.49 (*0-8167-0218-7*); pap. text ed. 2.95 (*0-8167-0219-5*) Troll Assocs.

—Questions. Hopkins, Lee B., selected by. LC 90-21745. 64p. (gr. k-3). 1992. 13.00 (*0-06-022412-6*); PLB 12.89 (*0-06-022413-4*) HarpC Child Bks.

—Switch On, Switch Off. Berger, Melvin. LC 88-17638. 32p. (gr. k-3). 1989. (Crowell Jr Bks); PLB 13.89 (*0-690-04786-X*, Crowell Jr. Bks) HarpC Child Bks.

—Switch on, Switch Off. Berger, Melvin. LC 88-17638. 32p. (gr. k-3). 1990. pap. 4.50 (*0-06-445097-X*, Trophy) HarpC Child Bks.

—The Three Brothers: A German Folktale. Croll, Carolyn, adapted by. (ps-3). 1991. 14.95 (*0-399-22195-6*, Whitebird Bks) Putnam Pub Group.

—Too Many Babas. newly illus. ed. Croll, Carolyn. LC 92-18779. 64p. (gr. k-3). 1979. 14.00 (*0-06-021383-3*); PLB 13.89 (*0-06-021384-1*) HarpC Child Bks.

—Too Many Babas. newly illus. ed. Croll, Carolyn. LC 92-18779. 64p. (gr. k-4). 1994. pap. 3.50 (*0-06-444168-7*, Trophy) HarpC Child Bks.

—What Will the Weather Be? DeWitt, Lynda. LC 90-1446. 32p. (gr. k-4). 1991. 13.95 (*0-06-021596-8*); PLB 13.89 (*0-06-021597-6*) HarpC Child Bks.

—What Will the Weather Be? DeWitt, Lynda. LC 90-1446. 32p. (gr. k-4). 1993. pap. 4.50 (*0-06-445113-5*, Trophy) HarpC Child Bks.

Croll, Carolyn & Ray, Deborah K. Chang's Paper Pony. Coerr, Eleanor. LC 87-45679. 64p. (gr. k-3). 1993. pap. 3.50 (*0-06-444163-6*, Trophy) HarpC Child Bks.

Croly, Donald. Eye of the Changer. Ringstad, Muriel. LC 83-7121. 96p. (Orig.). (gr. 4 up). 1984. pap. 9.95 (*0-88240-251-X*) Alaska Northwest.

Crompton, Jack. The Gift from Obadiah's Ghost. Wainwright, Richard M. 40p. 1990. 12.95 (*0-9619566-2-3*) Family Life.

—Montanas Escalar. Wainwright, Richard M. (SPA.). 64p. 1991. 15.00 (*0-9619566-5-8*) Family Life.

—Mountains to Climb. Wainwright, Richard M. 64p. 1990. 13.95 (*0-9619566-3-1*) Family Life.

—Poofin: The Cloud That Cried on Christmas. Wainwright, Richard M. 40p. 1989. Repr. 12.95g (*0-9619566-1-5*) Family Life.

—A Tiny Miracle. Wainwright, Richard M. 40p. 1986. Repr. 12.95g (*0-9619566-0-7*) Family Life.

Crompton, T. The Good Samaritan: Retold by Catherine Storr. 32p. (gr. k-4). 1984. 14.65 (*0-8172-1988-9*, Raintree Childrens Books Belitha Press Ltd. - London) Raintree Steck-V.

Crosby, Alexander L., photos by. Crazy to Be Alive in Such a Strange World: Poems about People. Larrick, Nancy. LC 76-49667. 192p. (gr. 5 up). 1989. pap. 6.95 (*0-87131-566-1*) M Evans.

Cross, Genevieve. The Engine That Lost Its Whistle. 10th ed. Cross, Genevieve. 32p. (gr. 1-3). 1988. pap. 12.50 (*0-9621162-0-3*) Van Buren Cty Hist Soc.

Cross, Jeanne. Simple Printing Methods. Cross, Jeanne. LC 72-39812. 48p. (gr. 6 up). 1972. 21.95 (*0-87599-192-0*) S G Phillips.

Cross, Peter. The Adventures of Dudley Dormouse. Taylor, Judy. Cross, Peter, created by. LC 91-58717. 80p. (ps up). 1992. 9.95 (*1-56402-043-6*) Candlewick Pr.

—Trouble for Trumpets. Cross, Peter. LC 83-43115. (gr. 3 up). 1984. 9.95 (*0-394-86513-8*) Random Bks Yng Read.

Crossett, Warren. Down at the Billabong. Culton, Wilma. LC 92-31951. 1993. 3.75 (*0-383-03565-1*) SRA Schl Grp.

—Monsters! Just Imagine. Morrison, Rob & Morrison, James. LC 93-26927. 1994. 4.25 (*0-383-03763-8*) SRA Schl Grp.

—The Stream. Beveridge, Barbara. LC 92-33738. 1993. 3.75 (*0-383-03657-7*) SRA Schl Grp.

—Walter Hottle Bottle. Scarffe, Bronwen. LC 92-34271. 1993. 14.00 (*0-383-03664-X*) SRA Schl Grp.

Crossland, Caroline. Ten Tall Oak Trees. Edwards, Richard. LC 92-41771. 32p. (ps-k). 1993. 15.00 (*0-688-04620-7*, Tambourine Bks); PLB 14.93 (*0-688-04621-5*, Tambourine Bks) Morrow.

Crouch, Ellen, jt. illus. see Palm, Felix.

Crow, James L. & Finkel, Becky. Traces: The Story of Lexington's Past. Ryen, Dag. 177p. (gr. 4 up). 1987. text ed. 13.95 (*0-912839-08-2*) Lexington-Fayette.

Crowder, Beth. Among These Hills: A Child's History of Harrison County. Pool, James M. 240p. 1985. 12.95 (*0-9615566-0-9*) Clarksburg-Harrison Bicent.

Crowder, Debbie. Lil Guard Angel. Ulitsch, Laura. LC 91-67738. 64p. 1993. pap. 8.00 (*1-56002-137-3*, Univ Edtns) Aegina Pr.

Crowder, Jack L., photos by. Tonibah & the Rainbow. Crowder, Jack L. & Hill, Faith. Tohtsonie, Clara & Wilson, Joe, trs. (ENG & NAV.). 32p. (Orig.). (gr. 7 up). 1986. pap. 6.95 (*0-9616589-1-6*) Upper Strata.

Crowder, Susan. Daniel au Repaire des Lions. Crowder, Susan. (FRE.). 36p. (Orig.). 1993. pap. 4.00x (*0-912927-57-7*, D018) St John Kronstadt.

—Daniel in the Lions' Den. 36p. (Orig.). 1984. pap. 3.00 (*0-912927-08-9*, X008) St John Kronstadt.

—The Great Flood. Crowder, Susan. 28p. (Orig.). 1988. pap. 2.50 (*0-912927-27-5*, X027) St John Kronstadt.

—The Three Children in the Furnace. Crowder, Susan. 37p. (Orig.). 1984. pap. 2.50 (*0-912927-11-9*, X011) St John Kronstadt.

Crowe, Amanda. Cherokee Legends & the Trail of Tears. Underwood, Tom. 32p. (gr. 4-12). 1956. 3.50 (*0-935741-00-3*) Cherokee Pubns.

Crowe, Elizabeth. Jirohattan. Mori, Hana. Kurosaki, Tamiko & Crowe, Elizabeth, trs. from JPN. LC 93-72833. 80p. (gr. 4-8). 1993. pap. 5.95 (*1-880188-69-4*) Bess Pr.

Crowe, Patricia. Belonging. Scott, Virginia M. LC 85-31135. 176p. (gr. 7-12). 1987. pap. 9.95 (*0-930323-33-5*, Kendall Green Pubns) Gallaudet Univ Pr.

Crowell, James. The Fall of the House of Usher. Poe, Edgar Allan. Cutts, David E., adapted by. LC 81-15958. 32p. (gr. 5-10). 1982. PLB 10.79 (*0-89375-624-5*); pap. text ed. 2.95 (*0-89375-625-3*) Troll Assocs.

Crowell, Pers. Christmas Horse. Balch, Glenn. Woodward, Tim, intro. by. 1990. pap. 9.95 (*0-931659-10-8*) Limberlost Pr.

Crowther, Robert. All the Fun of the Fair. Crowther, Robert. LC 91-71863. 12p. (ps up). 1992. 15.95 (*1-56402-001-0*) Candlewick Pr.

—Animal Rap! Crowther, Robert. LC 92-54586. 10p. (ps). 1993. 9.95 (*1-56402-207-2*) Candlewick Pr.

—Animal Snap! Crowther, Robert. LC 92-54587. 10p. (ps). 1993. 9.95 (*1-56402-208-0*) Candlewick Pr.

—The Most Amazing Hide & Seek Counting Book. Crowther, Robert. 14p. (ps-3). 1981. pap. 13.95 (*0-670-48997-2*) Viking Child Bks.

—Most Amazing Hide & Seek Opposites Book. Crowther, Robert. LC 85-42757. 12p. (ps-3). 1985. pap. 12.95 pop-up (*0-670-80121-6*) Viking Child Bks.

—Who Lives in the Country? Crowther, Robert. LC 91-58766. 10p. (ps). 1992. 6.95 (*1-56402-090-8*) Candlewick Pr.

—Who Lives in the Garden? Crowther, Robert. LC 91-58767. 10p. (ps). 1992. 6.95 (*1-56402-091-6*) Candlewick Pr.

Crozat, Francois. Lazy Cat. Danner, Thomas. 28p. (ps-3). 1994. prepub. 12.95 (*1-56397-353-7*) Boyds Mills Pr.

Cruchow, Jane C. Color Me Happy: It's Rosh Hashannah & Yom Kippur. Geller, Norman. 36p. (gr. k-4). 1986. pap. 2.95 (*0-915753-10-3*) N Geller Pub.

Cruickshank, Kathy. The Baby Book. Cruickshank, Kathy. (ps-k). 1991. pap. 1.50 (*0-307-10029-4*, Golden Pr) Western Pub.

Crum, Anna M. The Adventures of Paz in the Land of Numbers. Bowden, Miriam. LC 89-71741. 32p. (ps-3). 1992. 12.95 (*0-89334-150-9*, 150-9) Humanics Ltd.

—On the River ABC. Stutson, Caroline. LC 92-61907. 32p. (gr. k-3). 1993. lib. bdg. 12.95 (*1-879373-46-7*) R Rinehart.

Crump, Fred. Afrotina & the Three Bears: (A Retold Story) Crump, Fred. LC 88-51222. 44p. (gr. k-2). 1991. pap. 6.95 (*1-55523-195-0*) Winston-Derek.

—Jamako & the Beanstalk. Crump, Fred, Jr. 44p. (gr. k-3). 1992. pap. 8.95 incl. cass. (*1-55523-481-X*) Winston-Derek.

—Little Red Riding Hood: (A Retold Story) Crump, Fred. LC 88-51219. 44p. (gr. k-2). 1989. pap. 6.95 (*1-55523-193-4*) Winston-Derek.

—Mother Goose: A Retold Story. Crump, Fred. LC 88-51224. 44p. (gr. k-2). 1989. pap. 6.95 (*1-55523-194-2*) Winston-Derek.

—Rumpelstiltskin. Crump, Fred, Jr. 44p. (gr. k-2). 1991. pap. 6.95 (*1-55523-409-7*) Winston-Derek.

—Thumblina: A Retold Story. Crump, Fred. LC 88-51223. 44p. (gr. k-2). 1989. pap. 6.95 (*1-55523-191-8*) Winston-Derek.

Crump, Fred, Jr. Beauty & the Beast. Crump, Fred, Jr. 44p. (gr. k-2). 1991. pap. 5.95 (*1-55523-379-1*) Winston-Derek.

—Cinderella: A Retold Story. Crump, Fred, Jr. LC 89-51789. 44p. (gr. k-2). 1990. pap. 6.95 (*1-55523-299-X*) Winston-Derek.

—Ebony Duckling. Crump, Fred, Jr. LC 91-75090. 44p. (gr. k-3). 1991. pap. 6.95 (*1-55523-457-7*) Winston-Derek.

—Hakim & Grenita: A Retold Story. Crump, Fred, Jr. LC 89-51790. 44p. (gr. k-2). 1991. pap. 6.95 (*1-55523-298-1*) Winston-Derek.

—Jamako & the Beanstalk: A Retold Story. Crump, Fred, Jr. LC 89-51792. 44p. (gr. k-2). 1990. pap. 6.95 (*1-55523-296-5*) Winston-Derek.

—MGambo & the Tiger. Crump, Fred, Jr. 44p. (gr. k-2). 1991. pap. 6.95 (*1-55523-410-0*) Winston-Derek.
—The Other Little Angel. Crump, Fred, Jr. LC 93-60369. 44p. (gr. k-3). 1993. pap. 6.95 (*1-55523-624-3*) Winston-Derek.
—Rapunzel. Crump, Fred, Jr. 272p. (gr. k-2). 1991. pap. 6.95 (*1-55523-408-9*) Winston-Derek.
—Rapunzel. Crump, Fred, Jr. LC 91-67499. 44p. (gr. k-3). 1992. pap. 8.95 incl. cass. (*1-55523-482-8*) Winston-Derek.
—Sleeping Beauty: A Retold Story. Crump, Fred, Jr. LC 89-51788. 44p. (gr. k-2). 1991. pap. 6.95 (*1-55523-300-7*) Winston-Derek.
Cruz, E. R. Benjamin Franklin-Martin Luther King Jr. Alico, Stella H. (gr. 4-12). 1979. pap. text ed. 2.95 (*0-88301-353-3*); wkbk 1.25 (*0-88301-377-0*) Pendulum Pr.
—The Great Adventures of Sherlock Holmes: Student Activity Book. Sohl, Marcia & Dackerman, Gerald. (gr. 4-10). 1976. wkbk 1.25 (*0-88301-187-5*) Pendulum Pr.
—Gulliver's Travels: Student Activity Book. Sohl, Marcia & Dackerman, Gerald. (gr. 4-10). 1976. wkbk 1.25 (*0-88301-188-3*) Pendulum Pr.
—Hound of the Baskervilles. new & abr. ed. Doyle, Arthur Conan. Fago, John N., ed. (gr. 4-12). 1977. pap. text ed. 2.95 (*0-88301-264-2*) Pendulum Pr.
—Mysterious Island: Student Activity Book. Sohl, Marcia & Dackerman, Gerald. (gr. 4-10). 1976. wkbk. 1.25 (*0-88301-193-X*) Pendulum Pr.
—The New World, 1500-1750. Farr, Naunerle. Calhoun, D'Ann & Bloch, Lawrence W., eds. (gr. 4-12). 1977. Pendulum Pr.
—The Red Badge of Courage. Crane, Stephen. Shapiro, Irwin, ed. LC 73-75464. 64p. (Orig.). (gr. 5-10). 1973. pap. 2.95 (*0-88301-101-8*) Pendulum Pr.
—The Red Badge of Courage: Student Activity Book. Sohl, Marcia & Dackerman, Gerald. 16p. (gr. 4-10). 1976. pap. 1.25 (*0-88301-184-0*) Pendulum Pr.
—Tom Sawyer. new ed. Clemens, Samuel. Shapiro, Irwin, ed. LC 73-75465. 64p. (Orig.). (gr. 5-10). 1973. pap. 2.95 (*0-88301-103-4*); student activity bk. 1.25 (*0-88301-179-4*) Pendulum Pr.
Cruz, E. R. & Guanlao, Ernie. Elvis Presley - The Beatles. Alico, Stella H. (gr. 4-12). 1979. pap. text ed. 2.95 (*0-88301-352-5*); wkbk 1.25 (*0-88301-376-2*) Pendulum Pr.
Cruz, E. R. & Henson, Tenny. Houdini - Walt Disney. Fago, John N. & Toan, Debbie. (gr. 4-12). 1979. pap. text ed. 2.95 (*0-88301-350-9*); wkbk 1.25 (*0-88301-374-6*) Pendulum Pr.
Cruz, E. R., jt. illus. see Carrillo, Fred.
Cruz, Ernesto. Two Years Before the Mast. new & abr. ed. Dana, Richard H. Fago, John N., ed. (gr. 4-12). 1977. pap. text ed. 2.95 (*0-88301-270-7*) Pendulum Pr.
Cruz, Harry H. Famous People - Women. Silvani, Harold. 52p. (gr. 4-8). 1975. wkbk. 6.95 (*1-878669-22-2*, 4345) Crea Tea Assocs.
Cruz, Manuel. A Chicano Christmas Story. Cruz, Manuel & Cruz, Ruth. LC 80-69444. (SPA.). 48p. (Orig.). (ps-5). 1981. pap. text ed. 3.95 (*0-86624-000-4*, RM7) Bilingual Ed Serv.
Cruz, Nardo. Frankenstein. Shelley, Mary Wollstonecraft. Binder, Otto, ed. LC 73-75462. 64p. (Orig.). (gr. 5-10). 1973. pap. 2.95 (*0-88301-097-6*); student activity bk. 1.25 (*0-88301-177-8*) Pendulum Pr.
Cruz, Nardo, jt. illus. see Caravana, Tony.
Cruz, Ray. Alexander & the Terrible, Horrible, No Good, Very Bad Day. Viorst, Judith. LC 72-75289. 32p. (gr. k-4). 1972. RSBE 12.95 (*0-689-30072-7*, Atheneum Child Bk) Macmillan Child Grp.
—Alexander & the Terrible, Horrible, No Good, Very Bad Day. Viorst, Judith. LC 87-1087. 32p. (gr. k-4). 1987. pap. 3.95 (*0-689-71173-5*, Aladdin) Macmillan Child Grp.
—Alexander, Que Era Rico el Domingo Pasado. Viorst, Judith. Ada, Alma F., tr. (gr. k-4). 1989. pap. 3.95 (*0-689-71351-7*, Aladdin) Macmillan Child Grp.
—Alexander, Que Era Rico el Domingo Pasado. Viorst, Judith. Ada, Alma F., tr. LC 89-6503. (SPA.). 32p. (gr. k-4). 1989. SBE 12.95 (*0-689-31590-2*, Atheneum Child Bk) Macmillan Child Grp.
—Alexander y el Dia Terrible, Horrible, Espantoso, Horroso. Viorst, Judith. Ada, Alma F., tr. (SPA.). 32p. (gr. k-4). 1989. pap. 3.95 (*0-689-71350-9*, Aladdin) Macmillan Child Grp.
—Alexander y el Dia Terrible, Horrible, Espantoso, Horroso. Viorst, Judith. Ada, Alma F., tr. LC 89-33916. (SPA.). 32p. (gr. k-4). 1989. SBE 13.95 (*0-689-31591-0*, Atheneum Child Bk) Macmillan Child Grp.
—Baseball Fever. Hurwitz, Johanna. LC 81-5633. 128p. (gr. 4-6). 1981. 12.95 (*0-688-00710-4*); PLB 12.88 (*0-688-00711-2*, Morrow Jr Bks) Morrow Jr Bks.
—Baseball Fever. Hurwitz, Johanna. LC 81-5633. 128p. (gr. 3 up). 1991. pap. 3.95 (*0-688-10495-9*, Pub. by Beech Tree Bks) Morrow.
—Felita. Mohr, Nicholasa. LC 79-50149. (gr. 3-6). 1979. Dial Bks Young.
—The Gorilla Did It. Hazen, Barbara S. LC 73-84828. 32p. (ps-1). 1974. RSBE 13.95 (*0-689-30138-3*, Atheneum Child Bk) Macmillan Child Grp.
—In Trouble Again, Zelda Hammersmith. Hall, Lynn. 138p. (gr. 3-5). 1987. 13.95 (*0-15-238780-3*) HarBrace.
—Storybook Cookbook. Mac Gregor, Carol. (gr. 3-7). pap. 1.95 (*0-13-850842-9*, Pub. by Treehouse) P-H.

—What Are We Going to Do about Andrew? Sharmat, Marjorie W. LC 88-3357. 32p. (gr. k-4). 1988. pap. 3.95 (*0-689-71264-2*, Aladdin) Macmillan Child Grp.
Cudworth, Chris. Running to the Top of the Mountain. Durkin, John F. & Newton, Joe. 350p. (Orig.). (gr. 9-12). 1988. pap. text ed. 24.95 (*0-9621313-0-X*) J & J Win Edge.
Cuebas, Alma. Just Pretend: A Freethought Book for Children. Barker, Dan. 72p. (Orig.). (ps-6). 1988. pap. 10.00 (*0-318-42495-9*) Freedom Rel Found.
Cufari, Richard. The Far Side of Evil. Engdahl, Sylvia. 288p. (gr. 7 up). 1989. pap. 3.95 (*0-02-043041-8*, Collier Young Ad) Macmillan Child Grp.
Cuffani, Richard. The Testing of Tertius. Newman, Robert. (gr. 5-9). 19.75 (*0-8446-6188-0*) Peter Smith.
Cuffari, Richard. The Cartoonist. Byars, Betsy C. LC 77-12782. 128p. (gr. 3-7). 1978. pap. 13.95 (*0-670-20556-7*) Viking Child Bks.
—The Cartoonist. Byars, Betsy C. (gr. 3-7). 1987. pap. 3.99 (*0-14-032309-0*, Puffin) Puffin Bks.
—Hunter's Stew & Hangtown Fry. Perl, Lila. LC 77-5366. 176p. (gr. 6 up). 1979. 13.95 (*0-395-28922-X*, Clarion Bks) HM.
—I'm Nobody, Who Are You: The Story of Emily Dickinson. Barth, Edna. LC 72-129211. 128p. (gr. 3-6). 1979. 15.45 (*0-395-28843-6*, Clarion Bks) HM.
—Mightiest of Mortals: Heracles. Gates, Doris. 96p. (gr. 3-7). 1984. pap. 4.95 (*0-14-031531-4*, Puffin) Puffin Bks.
—Nothing Is Impossible - The Story of Beatrix Potter. Aldis, Dorothy. (gr. k-6). 1988. 18.75 (*0-8446-6359-X*) Peter Smith.
—Old Ben. rev. ed. Stuart, Jesse. Gifford, James M. & Charles, Chuck D., eds. LC 91-35578. 64p. (gr. 3-6). 1992. 10.00 (*0-945084-22-6*); pap. 3.00 (*0-945084-23-4*) J Stuart Found.
—The Perilous Gard. Pope, Elizabeth M. LC 73-21648. 272p. (gr. 6 up). 1974. 16.95 (*0-395-18512-2*) HM.
—The Perilous Gard. Pope, Elizabeth M. LC 91-23898. (gr. 7 up). 1992. pap. 4.99 (*0-14-034912-X*) Puffin Bks.
—Slumps, Grunts, & Snickerdoodles: What Colonial America Ate & Why. Perl, Lila. LC 75-4894. 128p. (gr. 6 up). 1979. 14.95 (*0-395-28923-8*, Clarion Bks) HM.
—Teetoncey. Taylor, Theodore. (gr. 3-7). 1991. pap. 3.50 (*0-380-71024-2*, Camelot) Avon.
—Teetoncey & Ben O'Neal. Taylor, Theodore. 192p. (gr. 5-7). 1991. pap. 3.50 (*0-380-71025-0*, Camelot) Avon.
—Thank You, Jackie Robinson. Cohen, Barbara. LC 87-29341. (gr. 3-6). 1988. PLB 13.95 (*0-688-07909-1*) Lothrop.
—Toliver's Secret. Brady, Esther W. 176p. (gr. 3-7). 1988. pap. 4.99 (*0-517-56910-8*) Crown Bks Yng Read.
—The TV Kid. Byars, Betsy C. 128p. (gr. 4-6). 1976. pap. 12.95 (*0-670-73331-8*) Viking Child Bks.
—The TV Kid. Byars, Betsy C. (gr. 2-7). 1987. pap. 3.99 (*0-14-032308-2*, Puffin) Puffin Bks.
—What's Going to Happen to Me? When Parents Separate or Divorce. reissued ed. LeShan, Eda. LC 78-4340. 144p. (gr. 3-7). 1984. 13.95 (*0-02-759230-8*, Four Winds) Macmillan Child Grp.
—What's Going to Happen to Me? When Parents Separate or Divorce. rev. ed. LeShan, Eda. LC 86-10769. 144p. (gr. 3-7). 1986. pap. 3.95 (*0-689-71093-3*, Aladdin) Macmillan Child Grp.
—The Winged Colt of Casa Mia. Byars, Betsy. 132p. (gr. 3-7). 1981. pap. 2.95 (*0-380-00201-9*, Camelot) Avon.
Cugat, Xavier. Pepito: The Little Dancing Dog. Evans, Mark. LC 78-65354. (gr. k-4). 1979. 6.95 (*0-87592-063-2*) Scroll Pr.
Culic, Ned. Burger Time. Taylor, Carol. LC 93-9281. 1994. pap. write for info. (*0-383-03678-X*) SRA Schl Grp.
—Mr. McGillicuddy's Clocks. Best, Elizabeth. LC 93-26928. 1994. 4.25 (*0-383-03765-4*) SRA Schl Grp.
—Why Not? Matthews, Cecily. LC 93-9280. 1994. write for info. (*0-383-03727-1*) SRA Schl Grp.
Culio, Ned. Jock Jerome. Drew, David. LC 92-31133. 1993. 2.50 (*0-383-03636-4*) SRA Schl Grp.
—Looking for Felix. Hathorn, Libby. LC 92-34259. 1993. 4.25 (*0-383-03638-0*) SRA Schl Grp.
Cullen-Clark, Patricia. Penny in the Road. Precek, Katharine W. LC 88-13331. 32p. (gr. k-3). 1989. RSBE 14.95 (*0-02-774970-3*, Macmillan Child Bk) Macmillan Child Grp.
Cullinan, Dorothy K. & Podgorski, Mary E. Archeology Search Book. Snyder, Thomas F. O'Neill, Martha, ed. 32p. (gr. 4-12). 1982. pap. text ed. 8.08 (*0-07-059467-8*) McGraw.
—Community Search Apple Set. Snyder, Thomas F. & O'Neill, Martha. (gr. 4-12). 1982. Set. 219.76 (*0-07-079006-X*) McGraw.
—Community Searchbook. Snyder, Thomas F. & O'Neill, Martha. 32p. (gr. 4 up). 1982. pap. text ed. 8.08 reorders (*0-07-059463-5*) McGraw.
Cullo, Ned. Clothes. Calderwood, Simone. LC 92-27086. 1993. 2.50 (*0-383-03560-0*) SRA Schl Grp.
—My Dog Ben. Matthews, Cecily. LC 92-31946. 1993. 3.75 (*0-383-03585-6*) SRA Schl Grp.
—One Foggy Night. Parkes, Brenda. LC 92-32514. 1993. 4.25 (*0-383-03585-6*) SRA Schl Grp.
Culver, R. K., jt. illus. see Campbell, V. Floyd.
Cumings, Art. The Cat's Pajamas. Chittum, Ida. 48p. (ps-3). 1980. 3.95 (*0-8193-1029-8*) Parents.
—Ecosystems & Food Chains. Sabin, Francene. LC 84-2707. 32p. (gr. 3-6). 1985. PLB 9.49 (*0-8167-0282-9*); pap. text ed. 2.95 (*0-8167-0283-7*) Troll Assocs.

—Magic Growing Powder. Quin-Harkin, Janet. LC 80-18019. 48p. (ps-3). 1981. 5.95 (*0-8193-1037-9*); PLB 5.95 (*0-8193-1038-7*) Parents.
—Mountains. Brandt, Keith. LC 84-2577. 32p. (gr. 3-6). 1985. PLB 9.49 (*0-8167-0154-7*); pap. text ed. 2.95 (*0-8167-0155-5*) Troll Assocs.
—Ohm on the Range: Robot & Computer Jokes. Keller, Charles. 48p. (gr. 3-7). 1982. 8.95 (*0-13-633552-7*) P-H.
—One-Minute Bedtime Stories. Lewis, Shari & O'Kun, Lan. LC 79-8024. 48p. (ps-3). 1982. pap. 10.00 (*0-385-15292-2*) Doubleday.
—Septimus Bean & His Amazing Machine. Quin-Harkin, Janet. LC 79-163. 48p. (ps-3). 1980. 5.95 (*0-8193-0999-0*) Parents.
Cumings, Arthur. Please Try to Remember the First of Octember. Le Sieg, Theodore. LC 77-4504. 48p. (gr. 1-4). 1977. lib. bdg. 7.99 (*0-394-93563-2*) Beginner.
Cumming, David. The Rhine. Smalley, Mark. LC 92-24041. 48p. (gr. 5-6). 1993. PLB 22.80 (*0-8114-3102-9*) Raintree Steck-V.
Cummings, Ann L. Harrow Sparrow. Briscoe, Jill. 143p. (gr. 6). 1989. pap. write for info. Jilcoe.
Cummings, Art. Ohm on the Range. Keller, Charles. 48p. (gr. 3-7). 1985. pap. 4.95 (*0-13-633546-2*) P-H.
Cummings, B. Martin. The Rotten Chicken: A Modern Fable. rev., 2nd ed. Solomon, L. Ursa. Lewis, Benjamin G., frwd. by. 34p. 1989. Repr. of 1984 ed. wire 7.95 (*0-9615756-3-8*) Henchanted Bks.
Cummings, Pat. Carousel. Cummings, Pat. LC 93-8708. 40p. (ps-3). 1994. RSBE 14.95 (*0-02-725512-3*, Bradbury Pr) Macmillan Child Grp.
—Chilly Stomach. Caines, Jeannette. LC 85-45250. 32p. (ps-2). 1986. HarpC Child Bks.
—Clean Your Room, Harvey Moon! Cummings, Pat. LC 89-23863. 32p. (ps-2). 1991. RSBE 13.95 (*0-02-725511-5*, Bradbury Pr) Macmillan Child Grp.
—Clean Your Room, Harvey Moon! Cummings, Pat. LC 93-20571. 32p. (gr. k-3). 1994. pap. 4.95 (*0-689-71798-9*, Aladdin) Macmillan Child Grp.
—Go Fish. Stolz, Mary. LC 90-4860. 80p. (gr. 2-6). 1991. 13.00 (*0-06-025820-9*); PLB 12.89 (*0-06-025822-5*) HarpC Child Bks.
—Go Fish. Stolz, Mary. LC 90-4860. 80p. (gr. 2-6). 1993. pap. 3.95 (*0-06-440466-8*, Trophy) HarpC Child Bks.
—I Need a Lunch Box. Caines, Jeannette. LC 85-45829. 32p. (ps-1). 1993. 14.00i (*0-06-020984-4*); PLB 13.89 (*0-06-020985-2*) HarpC Child Bks.
—I Need a Lunch Box. Caines, Jeannette. LC 85-45829. 32p. (ps-1). 1993. pap. 4.95 (*0-06-443341-2*, Trophy) HarpC Child Bks.
—Just Us Women. Caines, Jeannette. LC 81-48655. (gr. k-3). 1982. PLB 14.89 (*0-06-020942-9*) HarpC Child Bks.
—Just Us Women. Caines, Jeannette. LC 81-48655. 32p. (gr. k-3). 1984. pap. 4.95 (*0-06-443056-1*, Trophy) HarpC Child Bks.
—My Mama Needs Me. Walter, Mildred P. LC 82-12654. 32p. (ps-1). 1983. 14.95 (*0-688-01670-7*); PLB 14.88 (*0-688-01671-5*) Lothrop.
—Petey Moroni's Camp Runamok Diary. Cummings, Pat. LC 91-45774. 32p. (gr. k-5). 1992. SBE 14.95 (*0-02-725513-1*, Bradbury Pr) Macmillan Child Grp.
—Storm in the Night. Stolz, Mary. LC 85-45838. 32p. (gr. k-3). 1988. 15.00 (*0-06-025912-4*); PLB 14.89 (*0-06-025913-2*) HarpC Child Bks.
—Storm in the Night. Stolz, Mary. LC 85-45838. 32p. (gr. k-3). 1990. pap. 4.95 (*0-06-443256-4*, Trophy) HarpC Child Bks.
—Willie's Not the Hugging Kind. Barrett, Joyce D. LC 89-1868. 32p. (gr. k-3). 1989. 14.00 (*0-06-020416-8*); PLB 13.89 (*0-06-020417-6*) HarpC Child Bks.
—Willie's Not the Hugging Kind. Barrett, Joyce D. LC 89-1868. 32p. (gr. k-3). 1991. pap. 4.95 (*0-06-443264-5*, Trophy) HarpC Child Bks.
Cummings, Richard. Make Your Own Model Forts & Castles. Cummings, Richard. (gr. 6 up). 1977. 8.95 (*0-679-20400-8*) McKay.
Cummins, James. What Would You Do? A Child's Book about Divorce. Cain, Barbara & Benedek, Elissa P. 50p. 1976. text ed. 9.00 (*0-88048-300-8*) Am Psychiatric.
Cummins, Jim. The Christmas Eve Mystery. Nixon, Joan L. Fay, Ann, ed. LC 81-345. 32p. (gr. 1-3). 1981. PLB 8.95 (*0-8075-1150-1*) A Whitman.
—The Happy Birthday Mystery. Nixon, Joan L. Ann, Fay, ed. LC 79-18362. 32p. (gr. 1-3). 1980. PLB 8.95 (*0-8075-3150-2*) A Whitman.
—The New Year's Mystery. Nixon, Joan L. Pacini, Kathy, ed. LC 79-172. 32p. (gr. 1-3). 1979. PLB 8.95 (*0-8075-5592-4*) A Whitman.
—The Thanksgiving Mystery. Nixon, Joan L. Fay, Ann, ed. LC 79-27346. 32p. (gr. 1-3). 1979. PLB 8.95 (*0-8075-7820-7*) A Whitman.
—The Valentine Mystery. Nixon, Joan L. Tucker, Kathleen, ed. LC 79-17055. 32p. (gr. 1-3). 1979. PLB 8.95 (*0-8075-8450-9*) A Whitman.

Cummins, Lisa. Trouble - of the Northwest Territory. Greegor, Katherine. LC 92-61031. 100p. (Orig.). (gr. 3-8). 1992. pap. 5.95 (*0-9633091-7-X*) Promise Land Pubs. An ornery pet raccoon named Trouble & twelve-year-old Jeremiah find plenty

of adventure in TROUBLE--OF THE NORTHWEST TERRITORY. The setting is in Ohio before it became a state, near the place where missionary David Zesiberger established a settlement of converted Indians & taught them how to live a Christian life. While Jeremiah struggles with acceptance of his parents' Christian values & the loss of his friends back East, Trouble's antics lead Jeremiah to a terrifying meeting with one of those Indians. It's all complicated by the fact that the new neighbor, sixteen-year-old Jedd, hates all Indians. There's plenty of excitement in the forests of Ohio & along her rivers as the boys learn about the spirit of forgiveness & other Christian principles. Even adults enjoy & learn from this book. Book review: There is a happy balance achieved by the author, making the spiritual elements of the story to be conspicuously evident without detracting from the exciting adventures that form the developing plot of the book. The book fulfills a real need for high-quality Christian reading for children & young people. We recommend it gladly.--THE SWORD OF THE LORD.
Publisher Provided Annotation.

Cunningham, David. Bicycle Mystery. Warner, Gertrude C. LC 79-126428. 128p. (gr. 2-7). 1971. PLB 10.95 (*0-8075-0708-3*); pap. 3.50 (*0-8075-0709-1*) A Whitman.
—Bus Station Mystery. Warner, Gertrude C. LC 74-8293. 128p. (gr. 2-7). 1974. PLB 10.95 (*0-8075-0975-2*); pap. 3.50 (*0-8075-0976-0*) A Whitman.
—Children's Atlas of Native Americans Rand McNally: Native Cultures of North & South America. Rand McNally Staff & Reddy, Francis. Adelman, Elizabeth, ed. 78p. (gr. 3-12). Date not set. 14.95 (*0-685-66563-1*); PLB write for info. (*1-878363-99-9*) Forest Hse.
—Houseboat Mystery. Warner, Gertrude C. LC 67-26521. 128p. (gr. 2-7). 1966. PLB 10.95 (*0-8075-3412-9*); pap. 3.50 (*0-8075-3413-7*) A Whitman.
—Lighthouse Mystery. Warner, Gertrude C. LC 63-20354. 128p. (gr. 2-7). 1963. PLB 10.95 (*0-8075-4545-7*); pap. 3.50 (*0-8075-4546-5*) A Whitman.
—The Memory Box. Bahr, Mary. Tucker, Kathleen, ed. LC 91-21628. 32p. (gr. 1-4). 1992. PLB 13.95 (*0-8075-5052-3*) A Whitman.
—Mountain Top Mystery. Warner, Gertrude C. LC 64-7722. 128p. (gr. 2-7). 1964. PLB 10.95 (*0-8075-5292-5*); pap. 3.50 (*0-8075-5293-3*) A Whitman.
—Mystery Behind the Wall. Warner, Gertrude C. LC 72-13356. 128p. (gr. 2-7). 1973. PLB 10.95 (*0-8075-5364-6*); pap. 3.50 (*0-8075-5367-0*) A Whitman.
—Mystery in the Sand. Warner, Gertrude C. LC 70-165823. 128p. (gr. 2-7). 1971. PLB 10.95 (*0-8075-5373-5*); pap. 3.50 (*0-8075-5372-7*) A Whitman.
—Schoolhouse Mystery. Warner, Gertrude C. LC 65-23889. 128p. (gr. 2-7). 1965. PLB 10.95 (*0-8075-7262-4*); pap. 3.50 (*0-8075-7263-2*) A Whitman.
—Snowbound Mystery. Warner, Gertrude C. LC 68-9124. 128p. (gr. 2-7). 1968. PLB 10.95 (*0-8075-7517-8*); pap. 3.50 (*0-8075-7516-X*) A Whitman.
—Tree House Mystery. Warner, Gertrude C. LC 77-91744. 128p. (gr. 2-7). 1969. PLB 10.95 (*0-8075-8086-4*); pap. 3.50 (*0-8075-8087-2*) A Whitman.
Cunningham, Imogen & Richardson, David. Two Dogs Plus. Campbell, John C. 95p. (Orig.). (gr. 8 up). 1984. pap. text ed. 9.95 (*0-9613596-0-9*); pap. 7.95 (*0-685-09160-0*) Deer Creek Pr.
Cunningham, Richard W. Anita of Rancho del Mar. O'Brien, Elaine F. LC 90-19711. 176p. (Orig.). (gr. 4-8). 1991. pap. 8.95 (*0-931832-79-9*) Fithian Pr.
Cupples, Pat. Earthwatch: Earthcycles & Ecosystems. Savan, Beth. 96p. 1992. pap. 8.61 (*0-201-58148-5*) Addison-Wesley.
—Take Action: An Environmental Book for Kids. Love, Ann & Drake, Jane. LC 92-30412. 96p. (gr. 3 up). 1993. Repr. PLB 13.93 (*0-688-12464-X*, Tambourine Bks) Morrow.
Curlee, Jane. My Number Book. Krampe, Leesa. 126p. (ps-1). 1986. pap. text ed. 3.95 (*0-932957-99-4*) Natl School.

Curlee, Lynn. Horses with Wings. Haseley, Dennis. LC 92-29869. 32p. (gr. k up). 1993. 16.00 (*0-06-022885-7*); PLB 15.89 (*0-06-022886-5*) HarpC Child Bks.
Curless, Allan, et al. Spaceways: An Anthology of Space Poetry. Foster, John, compiled by. 128p. 1987. bds. 14.00 (*0-19-276056-4*) OUP.
—A Third Poetry Book. Foster, John, compiled by. 128p. 1987. 11.95 (*0-19-918140-3*); pap. 5.95 (*0-19-918139-X*) OUP.
Curley, Ed. A Bible Way of the Cross for Children. Costello, Gwen. 32p. (Orig.). (gr. 4-6). 1988. pap. 1.95 (*0-89622-353-1*) Twenty-Third.
Currey, Anna. Mr. Pepino's Cabbage. rev. ed. Wilmer, Diane & Currey, Anna. 32p. (gr. k-2). 1989. Repr. of 1989 ed. lib. bdg. 10.50 (*1-878363-02-6*) Forest Hse.
Currie, Mary. The Singing Sack. East, Helen, compiled by. 80p. (gr. 2 up). 16.95 (*0-7136-3115-5*, Pub. by A&C Black UK) Talman.
Curt, Kaufman. Hotel Boy. Kaufman, Curt & Kaufman, Gita. LC 86-25925. 40p. (gr. k-3). 1987. SBE 12.95 (*0-689-31287-3*, Atheneum Child Bk) Macmillan Child Grp.
Curti, Anna M. Angel of God. Paltro, Piera. Daughters of St. Paul Staff, tr. from ITA. 14p. (Orig.). (ps-1). 1981. pap. 2.50 (*0-8198-0739-7*, CH0031P) St Paul Bks.
—Eternal Rest: A Prayer for People Who Have Died. Paltro, Piera. Daughters of St. Paul Staff, tr. from ITA. 15p. (Orig.). (gr. k-3). 1992. pap. 2.50 (*0-8198-2332-5*) St Paul Bks.
—Glory to the Father. Paltro, Piera. Daughters of St. Paul Staff, tr. from ITA. 24p. (Orig.). (ps up). 1987. pap. 2.50 (*0-8198-3043-7*, CH0227) St Paul Bks.
—Hail, Holy Queen. Paltro, Piera. Daughters of St. Paul Staff, tr. from ITA. 16p. (Orig.). (gr. k-3). 1992. pap. 2.50 (*0-8198-3365-7*) St Paul Bks.
—Hail Mary. Paltro, Piera. Daughters of St. Paul Staff, tr. from ITA. 24p. (gr. k-3). 1992. pap. 2.50 (*0-8198-3316-9*) St Paul Bks.
—I Believe: The Profession of Faith or Creed. Paltro, Piera. Daughters of St. Paul Staff, tr. from ITA. 29p. (Orig.). (gr. k-3). 1992. pap. 2.50 (*0-8198-3664-8*) St Paul Bks.
—My Mass. Paltro, Piera. Daughters of St. Paul Staff, tr. from ITA. 31p. (Orig.). (gr. k-3). 1992. pap. 2.50 (*0-8198-4765-8*) St Paul Bks.
—Our Father. Paltro, Piera. Daughters of St. Paul Staff, tr. from ITA. 24p. (Orig.). (ps-1). 1991. pap. 2.50 (*0-8198-5416-6*, CH0416P) St Paul Bks.
Curtis, Bruce, photos by. Wayne Gretzky: Profil d'un Joueur de Hockey. Wolff, Craig T. (FRE.). 64p. (ps-5). 1984. pap. 2.25 (*0-380-85753-7*, Camelot) Avon.
Curtis, Charmaine. Only Soldiers Go to War. Kennaley, Lucinda H. LC 91-65288. 42p. (ps-4). 1991. 14.95 (*0-9628067-1-4*) Thoth MO.
Curtis, Dorris. Skammy: Prince of Troy. Curtis, Dorris. 231p. (gr. 5-9). 1988. lib. bdg. 18.50 (*0-944436-04-8*) Univ Central AR Pr.
Curtis, Neil. The Lunch That Mom Made. Beames, Margaret. LC 92-21454. 1993. 4.25 (*0-383-03639-9*) SRA Schl Grp.
Curtis, Peggy H. Pee Wee Saves Christmas. Lyman, et al. 80p. 1983. 14.95 (*0-317-03904-0*) Imagination Dust.
Curtner, Rondi. Seventy-Two Ways to Have Fun with My Mind. Fearn, Leif & Golisz-Benson, Ursula. 80p. (Orig.). (gr. 4-6). 1976. 5.00 (*0-940444-03-8*) Kabyn.
Curtner, Rondi L. Forty-Two Ways to Have Fun with My Mind. Fearn, Leif & Goliaz-Benson, Ursula. 58p. (ps-6). 1976. 5.00 (*0-940444-00-3*) Kabyn.
Cushman, Doug. ABC Mystery. Cushman, Doug. LC 92-9621. 32p. (ps-2). 1993. 14.00 (*0-06-021226-8*); PLB 13.89 (*0-06-021227-6*) HarpC Child Bks.
—An Alligator Named...Alligator. Grambling, Lois. 32p. (ps-1). 1991. lib. bdg. 12.95 (*0-8120-6224-8*); pap. 5.95 (*0-8120-4756-7*) Barron.
—Aunt Eater Loves a Mystery. Cushman, Doug. LC 87-73. 64p. (gr. k-3). 1987. 13.00 (*0-06-021326-4*); PLB 13.89 (*0-06-021327-2*) HarpC Child Bks.
—Aunt Eater Loves a Mystery. Cushman, Doug. LC 87-73. 64p. (ps-3). 1989. pap. 3.50 (*0-06-444126-1*, Trophy) HarpC Child Bks.
—Aunt Eater's Mystery Vacation. Cushman, Doug. LC 91-25059. 64p. (gr. k-3). 1992. 13.00 (*0-06-020513-X*); PLB 13.89 (*0-06-020514-8*) HarpC Child Bks.
—Aunt Eater's Mystery Vacation. Cushman, Doug. LC 91-25059. 64p. (gr. k-3). 1993. pap. 3.50 (*0-06-444169-5*, Trophy) HarpC Child Bks.
—Aunt Morbelia & the Screaming Skulls. Carris, Joan. (gr. 3-7). 1990. 14.95 (*0-316-12945-3*) Little.
—Aunt Morbelia & the Screaming Skulls. Carris, Joan. MacDonald, Pat, ed. 144p. (gr. 3-6). 1992. pap. 2.99 (*0-671-74784-3*, Minstrel Bks) PB.
—Bedtime Story. Greydanus, Rose. LC 86-30858. 32p. (gr. k-2). 1988. PLB 7.89 (*0-8167-0996-3*); pap. text ed. 1.95 (*0-8167-0997-1*) Troll Assocs.
—Benny's Bad Day. Pellowski, Michael J. LC 85-14016. 48p. (Orig.). (gr. 1-3). 1986. PLB 10.59 (*0-8167-0620-4*); pap. text ed. 3.50 (*0-8167-0621-2*) Troll Assocs.
—Bicycle Bear. Muntean, Michaela. LC 83-3980. 48p. (ps-3). 1983. 5.95 (*0-8193-1103-0*); PLB 5.95 (*0-8193-1103-0*) Parents.
—Bicycle Bear. Muntean, Michaela. LC 93-15458. 1994. PLB 13.27 (*0-8368-0963-7*) Gareth Stevens Inc.
—Bicycle Bear Rides Again. Muntean, Michaela. LC 89-27823. 48p. (ps-3). 1989. 5.95 (*0-8193-1193-6*) Parents.

—Bicycle Bear Rides Again. Muntean, Michaela. LC 93-15470. 1993. write for info. (*0-8368-0964-5*) Gareth Stevens Inc.
—Camp Big Paw. Cushman, Doug. LC 89-26867. 64p. (gr. k-3). 1990. PLB 11.89 (*0-06-021368-X*) HarpC Child Bks.
—Chatty Chipmunk's Nutty Day. Gruber, Suzanne. LC 84-8665. 32p. (gr. k-2). 1985. PLB 11.59 (*0-8167-0360-4*); pap. text ed. 2.95 (*0-8167-0440-6*) Troll Assocs.
—The Fourth Little Pig. Celsi, Teresa. 24p. (ps-3). 1990. PLB 14.60 (*0-8172-3577-9*); pap. 10.95 pkg. of 3 (*0-685-67711-7*) Raintree Steck-V.
—Halloween Mice! Roberts, Bethany. LC 93-17192. 1994. write for info. (*0-395-67064-0*, Clarion Bks) HM.
—Itsy-Bitsy Giant. Martin, Melanie. LC 88-1234. 48p. (Orig.). (gr. 1-4). 1989. PLB 10.59 (*0-8167-1335-9*); pap. text ed. 3.50 (*0-8167-1336-7*) Troll Assocs.
—The Jolly Monsters. Gordon, Sharon. LC 87-10867. 32p. (gr. k-2). 1988. PLB 11.59 (*0-8167-1079-1*); pap. text ed. 2.95 (*0-8167-1080-5*) Troll Assocs.
—Mixed-up Magic. Pellowski, Michael J. LC 88-1312. 48p. (Orig.). (gr. 1-4). 1989. PLB 10.59 (*0-8167-1327-8*); pap. text ed. 3.50 (*0-8167-1328-6*) Troll Assocs.
—Porcupine's Pajama Party. Harshman, Terry W. LC 87-45681. 64p. (gr. k-3). 1988. PLB 13.89 (*0-06-022249-2*) HarpC Child Bks.
—Porcupine's Pajama Party. Harshman, Terry W. LC 87-45681. 64p. (gr. k-3). 1990. pap. 3.50 (*0-06-444140-7*, Trophy) HarpC Child Bks.
—The Pudgy Fingers Counting Book. 16p. (ps-3). 1983. pap. 2.95 (*0-448-10202-1*, G&D) Putnam Pub Group.
—Tillie & Mert. Luttrell, Ida. LC 85-42641. 64p. (gr. k-3). 1992. pap. 3.50 (*0-06-444159-8*, Trophy) HarpC Child Bks.
—Uncle Foster's Hat Tree. Cushman, Doug. LC 88-3573. 48p. (ps-3). 1988. 9.95 (*0-525-44410-6*, DCB) Dutton Child Bks.
Cushman, Doug & Banek, Yvette. What's Missing? Ser, 4 vols. Leonard, Marcia. 96p. (ps-1). 1990. Set. 23.80 (*0-671-94433-9*); Set. 14.85s.p. (*0-685-46991-3*); Set. PLB 39.92 (*0-671-94432-0*); Set. PLB 29.94s.p. (*0-685-46992-1*) Silver Pr.
Cushman, Doug, jt. illus. see Banek, Yvette.
Cushman, Douglas E. The Witch Who Couldn't Fly. Packard, Mary E. LC 93-2212. (gr. k-3). 1993. pap. 2.95 (*0-8167-3256-6*) Troll Assocs.
Custard Paste Art Staff. Revelations in a Schoolroom: And Other Recollections As Remembered in the Year 1984. Gilman, Alma B. & Gilman, Clarence R. Loweree, Paul & Gilman, C. R., illus. Kelley, Win, intro. by. 56p. (Orig.). 1984. pap. 3.75 (*0-9613914-0-5*) A B Gilman.
Cuthbert, Peter. Faces of the World. Hegler, Michele & Hegler, Jodi. 79p. (gr. 9-12). 1989. pap. 7.95 (*0-945362-02-1*) Best Sllrs TX.
—Willing to Grow. Higman, Anita. 45p. (gr. 9-12). 1988. pap. 4.95 (*0-945362-01-3*) Best Sllrs TX.
Cutrell, Pauline. Chinese Eyes. Waybill, Marjorie. LC 74-5751. 32p. (gr. k-2). 1974. 14.95 (*0-8361-1738-7*) Herald Pr.
Cutri, Anne, jt. illus. see Cutri, Anne C.
Cutri, Anne C. & Cutri, Anne. Henry, the Hesitant Heron. Krupinsky, Jacquelyn S. 32p. (Orig.). (gr. k-3). 1987. pap. 6.95 (*0-912123-02-8*) Woodbury Pr.
Cutter, Priscilla. The Surprise Box. Hathorn, Libby. LC 93-28957. 1994. 4.25 (*0-383-03778-6*) SRA Schl Grp.
Cymerman, John. How's the Weather? Berger, Melvin & Berger, Gilda. 48p. (gr. 1-5). 1993. PLB 12.00 (*0-8249-8599-0*, Ideals Child); pap. 13.95 (*0-8249-8641-5*) Hambleton-Hill.
—Round & Round the Money Goes. Berger, Melvin & Berger, Gilda. 48p. (gr. 1-5). 1993. PLB 12.00 (*0-8249-8640-7*, Ideals Child); pap. 3.95 (*0-8249-8598-2*) Hambleton-Hill.
Cymerman, John E. Beauty & the Beastly Children. Tunnell, Michael O. LC 92-36757. 32p. (gr. k up). 1993. 15.00 (*0-688-12181-0*, Tambourine Bks); PLB 14.93 (*0-688-12182-9*, Tambourine Bks) Morrow.
—The Man Who Was Too Lazy to Fix Things. Krasilovsky, Phyllis. LC 91-435. 32p. (ps-3). 1992. 15.00 (*0-688-10394-4*, Tambourine Bks); PLB 14.93 (*0-688-10395-2*, Tambourine Bks) Morrow.
—Stinky Stanley. Hodgman, Ann. MacDonald, Pat, ed. 128p. (Orig.). (gr. 3-6). 1993. pap. 2.99 (*0-671-78548-6*, Minstrel Bks) PB.
—Stinky Stanley Stinks Again. Hodgman, Ann. MacDonald, Pat, ed. 128p. (Orig.). 1993. pap. 2.99 (*0-671-78560-5*, Minstrel Bks) PB.
—The Woman Who Saved Things. Krasilovsky, Phyllis. LC 92-5126. 32p. (gr. k up). 1993. 14.00 (*0-688-11162-9*, Tambourine Bks); PLB 13.93 (*0-688-11163-7*, Tambourine Bks) Morrow.
Czap, Daniel, photos by. Eclairs & Brown Bears. Rosin, Arielle. Collomb, Etienne. LC 93-24971. Date not set. write for info. (*0-395-68380-7*) Ticknor & Fields.
—Pizzas & Punk Potatoes. Rosin, Arielle. Collomb, Etienne, contrib. by. LC 93-24970. Date not set. 13.95 (*0-395-68381-5*) Ticknor & Fields.
Czapla, Carole. The Christmas Polar Bear. Bishop, Adela. 32p. (gr. k-3). 1991. 12.95 (*0-9625620-2-5*) DOT Garnet.
—The Easter Wolf. Bishop, Adela. 28p. (ps-3). 1991. 12.95 (*0-9625620-1-7*) DOT Garnet.

Czernecki, Stefan. Nina's Treasures. Czernecki, Stefan & Rhodes, Timothy. 40p. (gr. k-4). 1994. pap. 4.95 (*1-56282-487-2*) Hyprn Ppbks.
—Pancho's Pinata. Czernecki, Stefan & Rhodes, Timothy. LC 92-7325. 40p. (gr. k-4). 1992. 14.95 (*1-56282-277-2*); PLB 14.89 (*1-56282-278-0*) Hyprn Child.
—The Singing Snake. Czernecki, Stefan & Rhodes, Timothy. LC 92-85515. 40p. (ps-2). 1993. 14.95 (*1-56282-399-X*); PLB 14.89 (*1-56282-400-7*) Hyprn Child.
—The Sleeping Bread. Czernecki, Stefan & Rhodes, Timothy. LC 91-75422. 40p. (gr. k-4). 1993. pap. 4.95 (*1-56282-519-4*) Hyprn Ppbks.
Czerniak, Jerry. Young Scientists Explore: The Weather. DeBruin, Jerry. 32p. (gr. 4 up). 1983. wkbk. 5.95 (*0-86653-129-7*, GA 456) Good Apple.
Czernick, Charlene. Young Scientists Explore: Inner & Outer Space. DeBruin, Jerry. 32p. (gr. 4 up). 1983. wkbk. 5.95 (*0-86653-152-1*, GA 457) Good Apple.

D

Daab, John. Billy & the Attic Adventure. Worley, Daryl. (ps). 1989. 9.95 (*0-924067-00-4*) Tyke Corp.
—Billy & the Big Truck. Worley, Daryl. 32p. (ps). 1989. 9.95 (*0-924067-06-3*) Tyke Corp.
—Billy & the Bright Red Ball. Worley, Daryl. 32p. (ps). 1989. 9.95 (*0-924067-05-5*) Tyke Corp.
—Billy & the Chocolate Chip Cookies. Worley, Daryl. 32p. (ps). 1989. 9.95 (*0-924067-02-0*) Tyke Corp.
—Billy & the Christmas Present. Worley, Daryl. 32p. (gr. 2-4). 1989. 9.95 (*0-924067-01-2*) Tyke Corp.
—Billy & the Department Store. Worley, Daryl. 32p. (ps). 1989. 9.95 (*0-924067-04-7*) Tyke Corp.
—Billy & the Scary Things. Worley, Daryl. (ps). 1989. 9.95 (*0-924067-03-9*) Tyke Corp.
Dabcovich, Lydia. Feathers. Gordon, Ruth. LC 92-26164. 32p. (gr. k-3). 1993. RSBE 14.95 (*0-02-736511-5*, Macmillan Child Bk) Macmillan Child Grp.
—Hurry Home, Grandma! Olson, Arielle N. LC 84-1529. 32p. (ps-1). 1984. 9.95 (*0-525-44113-1*, DCB) Dutton Child Bks.
—Mrs. Huggins & Her Hen Hannah. Dabcovich, Lydia. LC 85-4406. 24p. (ps-2). 1988. 12.95 (*0-525-44203-0*, DCB); pap. 3.95 (*0-525-44368-1*, DCB) Dutton Child Bks.
—The Night Ones. Grossman, Patricia. D'Andrade, Diane, ed. 32p. (ps-3). 1991. 13.95 (*0-15-257438-7*) HarBrace.
—Sleepy Bear. Dabcovich, Lydia. 32p. (ps-2). 1982. 12.95 (*0-525-39465-6*, DCB) Dutton Child Bks.
—Sleepy Bear. Dabcovich, Lydia. 32p. (ps-2). 1985. pap. 4.95 (*0-525-44196-4*, DCB) Dutton Child Bks.
—Up North in Winter. Hartley, Deborah. 32p. (ps-3). 1993. pap. 4.99 (*0-14-054943-9*, Puffin Unicorn) Puffin Bks.
—William & Grandpa. Schertle, Alice. Stevenson, D., ed. LC 88-666. 32p. (gr. k-3). 1988. 12.95 (*0-688-07580-0*); PLB 12.88 (*0-688-07581-9*) Lothrop.
Dabney, Joy. A Book about Me. 32p. (gr. k-3). 1987. wkbk. 2.50 (*0-939985-00-4*) Creative Dimensions.
D'Achille, Gino. The Big Golden Book of Knights & Castles. Weisberg, Barbara. 64p. (gr. 2-7). 1992. write for info. (*0-307-17874-9*, 17874, Golden Pr) Western Pub.
—Twenty-Thousand Leagues under the Sea. Conaway, Judith, adapted by. 96p. (gr. 2-5). 1983. 2.95 (*0-394-85333-4*); lib. bdg. 4.99 (*0-394-95333-9*) Random Bks Yng Read.
D'Adamo, Anthony. All about Trees. Dickinson, Jane. LC 82-17382. 32p. (gr. 3-6). 1983. PLB 10.59 (*0-89375-892-2*); pap. text ed. 2.95 (*0-89375-893-0*) Troll Assocs.
—Amazing World of Animals. Jefferies, Lawrence. LC 82-20061. 32p. (gr. 3-6). 1983. PLB 10.59 (*0-89375-898-1*); pap. text ed. 2.95 (*0-89375-899-X*) Troll Assocs.
Dadd, Elvira. A Child's First Book of Prayers. Newman, Marjorie. 24p. (ps-1). 1991. 10.00 (*0-8007-7129-X*) Revell.
Dagan, Bernard. Living in South America. Henry-Biabaud, Chantal. Bogard, Vicki, tr. from FRE. LC 90-50773. 38p. (gr. k-5). 1991. 4.95 (*0-944589-28-6*, 286) Young Discovery Lib.
Daggett, R. M. The Legends & Myths of Hawaii: The Fables & Folk-Lore of a Strange People. Kalakaua, David. Daggett, R. M., ed. LC 72-77519. 530p. (gr. 9 up). 1972. pap. 12.95 (*0-8048-1032-X*) C E Tuttle.
D'Agostino, Anthony. Kidding Around Spain: A Young Person's Guide. Biggs, Betsey. 108p. (Orig.). (gr. 3 up). 1991. pap. 12.95 (*0-945465-97-1*) John Muir.
Dahar, Andre. Louis Braille, l'Enfant de la Nuit. Davidson, Margaret. (FRE.). 103p. (gr. 3-7). 1990. pap. 10.95 (*2-07-031225-9*) Schoenhof.
Dahl, Sharon. King Leonard's Great Grape Harvest. Lane, Christopher. 32p. 1991. text ed. 7.99 (*0-89693-268-0*, Victor Books) SP Pubns.
—Mrs. Beaver & the Wolf at the Door. Lane, Christopher. 32p. 1991. text ed. 7.99 (*0-89693-269-9*, Victor Books) SP Pubns.
Daily, Don. The Wind in the Willows. Grahame, Kenneth. 56p. (gr. 2 up). 1993. 9.98 (*0-685-65070-7*) Courage Bks.

Daines, Cameron K. What Is a California Gray Whale? Graves, Jack A. 48p. (gr. 1-4). 1991. pap. 4.95 (*0-929526-13-9*) Double B Pubns.
Dalby, C. Reginald. Thomas the Tank Engine Starter Library, 4 bks. Awdry, W. (gr. 1-5). 1990. Repr. of 1945 ed. boxed set 19.95 (*0-679-80792-6*) Random Bks Yng Read.
Dale, Penny. All about Alice. Dale, Penny. LC 92-52991. 32p. (ps-3). 1993. 13.95 (*1-56402-171-8*) Candlewick Pr.
—Bet You Can't. Dale, Penny. LC 87-3780. 32p. (ps-1). 1988. (Lipp Jr Bks) HarpC Child Bks.
—Wake up, Mr. B.! Dale, Penny. LC 91-58763. 32p. (ps up). 1992. 14.95 (*1-56402-104-1*) Candlewick Pr.
Daley, Natalie, jt. illus. see Hafer, Dick.
Dalins, Astrid. Animal Heaven. Valladares, Margaret M. 24p. (Orig.). (gr. k-4). 1991. incl. coloring bk. & VHS 9.95 (*1-879580-01-3*) M Valladares.
Dallet, Robert. Animals of Europe. Wolff, Robert. LC 77-78379. 160p. (gr. 3-9). 1969. PLB 29.95 (*0-87460-092-8*) Lion Bks.
Dallgas-Frey, Paul. Rhyme Time with the Rymons: A Better Way Than Throw Away. Simms, Susan R. 36p. (ps-4). 1991. pap. 4.95 incl. audiocassette (*1-55999-151-8*) LinguiSystems.
—Rhyme Time with the Rymons: Birds, Frogs, & Puppydogs. Simms, Susan R. 36p. (ps-4). 1991. pap. 4.95 incl. audiocassette (*1-55999-150-X*) LinguiSystems.
—Rhyme Time with the Rymons: Kitchen Magician. Simms, Susan R. 36p. (ps-3). 1990. pap. 4.95 incl. audiocassette (*1-55999-136-4*) LinguiSystems.
—Rhyme Time with the Rymons: Remedy for Emily. Simms, Susan R. 36p. (ps-3). 1991. pap. 4.95 incl. audiocassette (*1-55999-149-6*) LinguiSystems.
—Rhyme Time with the Rymons: Squeeze for the Keys. Simms, Susan R. 36p. (ps-3). 1990. pap. 4.95 incl. audiocassette (*1-55999-138-0*) LinguiSystems.
—Rhyme Time with the Rymons: Wakin' to the Bacon. Simms, Susan R. 36p. (ps-3). 1990. pap. 4.95 incl. audiocassette (*1-55999-137-2*) LinguiSystems.
Dally, Tim. Supercat. Hubbell, Andra. LC 88-63735. 16p. (ps-3). 1989. PLB 16.95 (*0-9621759-1-9*); PLB 11.95 (*0-317-93727-8*) Rochester Pub Lib Dist.
Dalton, Anne. The King's Toothache. West, Colin. LC 87-3713. 32p. (ps-2). 1988. (Lipp Jr Bks) HarpC Child Bks.
—The Twelve Dancing Princesses. Grimm, Jacob & Grimm, Wilhelm K. Carter, Anne, retold by. LC 88-13794. 32p. (ps-4). 1989. (Lipp Jr Bks) HarpC Child Bks.
Daly, Jude. The Dove. Stewart, Dianne. LC 91-45798. 32p. (ps up). 1993. 14.00 (*0-688-11264-1*); PLB 13.93 (*0-688-11265-X*) Greenwillow.
Daly, Niki. All the Magic in the World. Hartmann, Wendy. LC 92-38289. 32p. (gr. k-3). 1993. 12.99 (*0-525-45092-0*, DCB) Dutton Child Bks.
—The Day of the Rainbow. Craft, Ruth. 32p. (ps-3). 1991. pap. 4.95 (*0-14-050935-6*, Puffin) Puffin Bks.
—I Want to See the Moon. Baum, Louis. LC 88-33061. 32p. (ps-3). 1989. cloth 11.95 (*0-87951-367-5*) Overlook Pr.
—Not So Fast, Songololo. Daly, Niki. LC 85-70134. 32p. (gr. k-3). 1986. SBE 13.95 (*0-689-50367-9*, M K McElderry) Macmillan Child Grp.
—One Round Moon & a Star for Me. Mennen, Ingrid. LC 93-9628. 32p. (ps-2). 1994. 14.95 (*0-531-06804-8*); PLB 14.99 (*0-531-08654-2*) Orchard Bks Watts.
—Papa Lucky's Shadow. Daly, Niki. LC 91-24283. 32p. (gr. k-3). 1992. SBE 14.95 (*0-689-50541-8*, M K McElderry) Macmillan Child Grp.
D'Amato, Alex, jt. illus. see D'Amato, Jane.
D'Amato, Alex, jt. illus. see D'Amato, Janet.
D'Amato, Jane & D'Amato, Alex. Cardboard Carpentry. D'Amato, Janet & D'Amato, Alex. Thompson, Morton, intro. by. (gr. 2-5). PLB 13.95 (*0-87460-085-5*) Lion Bks.
D'Amato, Janet. Aerobics Basics. Liptak, Karen. 48p. (gr. 3-7). 1983. 9.95 (*0-13-018218-4*) P-H.
—Ecology Basics. Stevens, Lawrence. 48p. (gr. 3-7). 1986. 10.95 (*0-13-223215-4*) P-H.
—Money Basics: An Introduction for Young People. Wallace, David. 48p. 1984. 9.95 (*0-13-600479-2*) P-H.
—Video Basics. Yurko, John. LC 82-21543. 64p. (gr. 4-7). 1983. 9.95 (*0-13-941781-8*) P-H.
D'Amato, Janet & D'Amato, Alex. Handicrafts for Holidays. D'Amato, Janet & D'Amato, Alex. (gr. 1-4). 1967. PLB 13.95 (*0-87460-086-3*) Lion Bks.
—Indian Crafts. D'Amato, Janet & D'Amato, Alex. (gr. 2-5). PLB 13.95 (*0-87460-088-X*) Lion Bks.
D'Amato, Janet P. How on Earth Do We Recycle Plastic? D'Amato, Janet P. & Carter, Laurel S. LC 91-22430. 64p. (gr. 4-6). 1992. PLB 12.90 (*1-56294-143-7*) Millbrook Pr.
D'Amboise, Carolyn G., photos by. I Feel Like Dancing: A Year with Jacques D'Amboise & the National Dance Institute. Barboza, Steven. LC 91-28439. 48p. (gr. 2-6). 1992. 13.00 (*0-517-58454-9*); PLB 13.99 (*0-517-58455-7*) Crown Bks Yng Read.
Damon, Valerie. Marty's Monster. Hird, Nancy E. 48p. (Orig.). (gr. 1-3). 1993. pap. 3.99 (*0-7847-0098-2*, 24-03948) Standard Pub.
Damon, Valerie H. Grindle Lamfoon & the Procurnious Fleekers. Damon, Valerie H. Damon, Dave, ed. LC 78-64526. (gr. 1-12). 1979. 12.95 (*0-932356-05-2*); fleeker ed. 14.95 (*0-932356-06-0*) Star Pubns MO.

Danciger, Leila N. ABC Bible & Holiday Stories. Aronoff, Daisy P. 58p. (ps-7). 1992. pap. 15.95 (*1-878612-28-X*) Sunflower Co.
Dandola, John. Rogers' Rangers. Dandola, John. 24p. (Orig.). (gr. k-6). 1992. pap. 3.95 (*1-878452-08-8*) Tory Corner Editions.
D'Andrea, Domenick. Black Beauty. reissued ed. Sewell, Anna. Norby, Lisa, adapted by. LC 89-62772. 96p. (Orig.). (gr. 2-6). 1993. lib. bdg. 5.99 (*0-679-90370-4*); pap. 2.99 (*0-679-80370-X*) Random Bks Yng Read.
—The Black Stallion: Golden Anniversary Edition. Farley, Walter. LC 90-53670. 224p. (gr. 4 up). 1991. Repr. of 1941 ed. gift ed. 15.00 (*0-679-81349-7*); lib. bdg. 15.99 gift ed. (*0-679-91349-1*) Random Bks Yng Read.
—Robin Hood. reissued ed. Ingle, Annie, adapted by. LC 90-23078. 96p. (Orig.). (gr. 2-6). 1993. pap. 2.99 (*0-679-81045-5*) Random Bks Yng Read.
Danforth, Liz & Martin, David. The Necromancer's Lieutenant. Ney, Jessica, ed. 32p. (Orig.). (gr. 12). 1990. pap. 7.00 (*1-55806-113-4*, 8113) Iron Crown Ent Inc.
Danforth, Liz, jt. illus. see Hook, Richard.
Danforth, Liz, jt. illus. see McBride, Angus.
Daniel, Alan. Bunnicula: A Rabbit Tale of Mystery. Howe, Deborah & Howe, James. LC 78-11472. 112p. (gr. 4-6). 1979. SBE 12.95 (*0-689-30700-4*, Atheneum Child Bk) Macmillan Child Grp.
—Bunnicula: A Rabbit-Tale of Mystery. Howe, Deborah & Howe, James. 100p. (gr. 3-7). 1980. pap. 3.99 (*0-380-51094-4*, Camelot) Avon.
—The Bunnicula Fun Book. Howe, James. LC 92-34561. 176p. 1993. pap. 9.95 (*0-688-11952-2*) Morrow Jr Bks.
—The Grand Escape. Naylor, Phyllis R. LC 91-40816. 160p. (gr. 3-7). 1993. SBE 13.95 (*0-689-31722-0*, Atheneum Child Bk) Macmillan Child Grp.
—I'll Never Love Anything Ever Again. Delton, Judy. Fay, Ann, ed. LC 84-17271. 32p. (gr. k-3). 1985. PLB 11.95 (*0-8075-3521-4*) A Whitman.

—**The Orchestra.** Rubin, Mark. 48p. (gr. k-3). 1992. pap. 7.95 (*0-920668-99-2*) Firefly Bks Ltd.
THE ORCHESTRA, a non-fiction book for children, introduces musical instruments, basic musical concepts & the symphonic orchestra. The very straightforward text is accompanied by playful but accurate drawings. A number of musical concepts are explored, among them harmony, tempo & dynamics. The role of the composer & conductor are explored & each musical instrument described. A subplot, apparent only through the illustrations, shows two children who wend their way through the orchestra's rehearsal, visiting the instrument families, & culminates in a full-dress concert. Comprehensive but simple in its approach, the book combines solid information with an enjoyable format. Mark Rubin has produced a number of films & television shows for young children. Victor Feldbrill, conductor of the Toronto Symphony program for young children, has reviewed the text for accuracy. Alan Daniel has illustrated a number of books, among them FLYING & SWIMMING CREATURES & THE BAIT CHOPPER. *Publisher Provided Annotation.*

—Rabbit Cadabra! Howe, James. LC 91-34656. 48p. (gr. k up). 1993. 15.00 (*0-688-10402-9*); PLB 14.93 (*0-688-10403-7*) Morrow Jr Bks.
Daniel, Frank. Chanukah. 20p. (ps). 1993. bds. 3.95 (*0-689-71733-4*, Aladdin) Macmillan Child Grp.
—Christmas. 20p. (ps). 1993. bds. 3.95 (*0-689-71734-2*, Aladdin) Macmillan Child Grp.
—Halloween. 20p. (ps). 1993. bds. 3.95 (*0-689-71736-9*, Aladdin) Macmillan Child Grp.
—One Hundred One Easy-to-Do Magic Tricks. unabr., unaltered ed. Tarr, Bill. LC 92-22895. 224p. 1992. pap. text ed. 7.95t (*0-486-27367-9*) Dover.
—Spooky Tunes. Cooper, Don. 32p. (Orig.). (ps-3). 1990. pap. 6.95 incl. cassette (*0-679-80303-3*) Random Bks Yng Read.
—Thanksgiving. 20p. (ps). 1993. bds. 3.95 (*0-689-71735-0*, Aladdin) Macmillan Child Grp.
Daniels, Alan. Return to Howliday Inn. Howe, James. LC 91-29505. 176p. (gr. 3-7). 1992. SBE 13.95 (*0-689-31661-5*, Atheneum Child Bk) Macmillan Child Grp.

Daniels, Neil. Ozzie: An Odyssey of Love. Hudson, Anne & Daniels, Neil. LC 83-81305. 72p. (Orig.). (gr. 1-6). 1983. pap. 3.95 (*0-940258-10-2*) Kripalu Pubns.

Dann, Geoff, photos by. Three Hundred First Words. Root, Betty. 156p. (ps). 9.95 (*0-8120-6356-2*) Barron.

—Three Hundred First Words - Palabras Primeras. Root, Betty. (ENG & SPA.). 156p. (ps). 9.95 (*0-8120-6358-9*) Barron.

—Three Hundred First Words - Premiers Mots. Root, Betty. (ENG & FRE.). 156p. (ps). 1993. 9.95 (*0-8120-6357-0*) Barron.

Dann, Penny. Beryl's Box. Taylor, Lisa. LC 92-44990. 32p. (ps-2). 1993. 12.95 (*0-8120-6355-4*); pap. 5.95 (*0-8120-1673-4*) Barron.

—Brutus the Wonder Poodle. Gondosch, Linda. LC 89-39377. 64p. (Orig.). (gr. 2-4). 1990. PLB 5.99 (*0-679-90573-1*); pap. 1.95 (*0-679-80573-7*) Random Bks Yng Read.

—Dirt, Wonderful Dirt! Murray, Peter. LC 92-42741. Date not set. write for info. (*1-56766-079-7*) Childs World. Postponed.

—The Doubleday Book of Bedtime Stories. Waters, Fiona, ed. LC 91-44298. 80p. (ps-3). 1992. 16.00 (*0-385-30790-X*) Doubleday.

—Funny Folk: Poems about People. Fisher, Robert, ed. 80p. (ps-3). 1992. pap. 5.95 (*0-571-16214-2*) Faber & Faber.

—How Green Are You? Bellamy, David. LC 90-19453. 32p. (gr. 1-4). 1991. 14.95 (*0-517-58429-8*, Clarkson Potter); PLB 15.99 (*0-517-58447-6*, C N Potter Bks) Crown Bks Yng Read.

—A Little Book of Courage. Flynn, Kristee, compiled by. LC 93-6640. 1993. write for info. (*1-56766-094-0*) Childs World.

—A Little Book of Friendship. Dann, Penny, compiled by. LC 93-12918. 1993. write for info. (*1-56766-095-9*) Childs World.

—Mountain Bike Madness. Sachs, Betsy. LC 93-29929. 1994. PLB 7.99 (*0-679-93395-6*); pap. 2.99 (*0-679-83395-1*) Random Bks Yng Read.

—The Perfect Pizza. Murray, Peter. LC 93-4032. (gr. 7-8). Date not set. write for info. (*1-56766-080-0*) Childs World. Postponed.

Dann, Penny & Kindberg, Sally. Let's Pretend. Unwin, Charlotte. LC 87-19963. 24p. (ps-3). 1989. 4.95 (*0-8037-0507-7*) Dial Bks Young.

Dannen, Donna, jt. photog. see Dannen, Kent.

Dannen, Kent & Dannen, Donna, photos by. Rocky Mountain Seasons: From Valley to Mountaintop. Burns, Diane. LC 92-22833. 32p. (gr. 1-5). 1993. RSBE 14.95 (*0-02-716142-0*, Macmillan Child Bk) Macmillan Child Grp.

Danner, Maggie. How Teddy Bears Find Their Homes: The Story of Benjamin Tristan Bear. Waldman, David K. LC 92-53786. 32p. (gr. k-2). 1993. casebound 12.95 (*0-945522-02-9*) Rebecca Hse.
Each Teddy Bear goes off to find a home with human children. This November 25th, Benjamin Tristan Bear sets off on his journey of the heart to find his new home. A classic story told by a grandmother to her granddaughter. Benjamin Bear is traced through the travels of several generations. A story for all ages. *Publisher Provided Annotation.*

Danner, Robert W. Calendar Capers: A Child's School Year in Celebration. LoPresti, Joan. LC 90-36812. 32p. (gr. k-3). 1990. PLB 18.60 (*0-8368-0428-7*) Gareth Stevens Inc.

Danziger, Jeff. Think about Space: Where Have We Been? Where Are We Going? Asimov, Isaac & White, Frank. LC 88-36731. 120p. (gr. 6 up). 1989. PLB 14.85 (*0-8027-6766-4*); pap. 5.95 (*0-8027-6767-2*) Walker & Co.

Darby's Designs. Holiday Cards. Cracchiolo, Rachelle. 32p. (gr. 1-6). 1982. wkbk. 4.95 (*1-55734-031-5*) Tchr Create Mat.

D'Arcy, Adele. Fishing for Angels: The Magic of Kites. Evans, David. 88p. (Orig.). (gr. 5 up). 1991. pap. 12.95 (*1-55037-162-2*, Pub. by Annick CN) Firefly Bks Ltd.

Darcy, Tom. A Tree for Me. LeValley, Norma. LC 87-70974. 50p. (ps-2). 1987. pap. 5.95 (*0-9618740-0-7*) Caring Tree.

Da Rif, Andrea. Where Did You Put Your Sleep? Newfield, Marcia. LC 83-2785. 32p. (gr. k-4). 1983. SBE 13.95 (*0-689-50286-9*, M K McElderry) Macmillan Child Grp.

Da Riff, Andrea. Puss in Boots. new ed. Perrault, Charles. LC 78-18061. 32p. (gr. k-3). 1979. PLB 9.79 (*0-89375-130-8*); pap. 1.95 (*0-89375-108-1*) Troll Assocs.

Darke, Alison C. The Ice Journey. Greaves, Margaret. 32p. (ps-1). 1994. 22.95 (*0-460-88133-7*, Pub. by J M Dent & Sons) Trafalgar.

—The Nightingale. Andersen, Hans Christian. 32p. (ps-3). 1989. 13.95 (*0-385-26081-4*, Zephyr-BFYR); (Zephyr-BFYR) Doubleday.

Darling, Louis. Beezus & Ramona. Cleary, Beverly. LC 55-7623. 192p. (gr. 3-7). 1955. 12.95 (*0-688-21076-7*); PLB 12.88 (*0-688-31076-1*, Morrow Jr Bks) Morrow Jr Bks.

—Ellen Tebbits. Cleary, Beverly. LC 51-11430. 160p. (gr. 3-7). 1951. 12.95 (*0-688-21264-6*); PLB 12.88 (*0-688-31264-0*, Morrow Jr Bks) Morrow Jr Bks.

—The Enormous Egg. Butterworth, Oliver. (gr. 4-6). 1956. 14.95 (*0-316-11904-0*, Pub. by Atlantic Monthly Pr) Little.

—Henry & Beezus. Cleary, Beverly. LC 52-5930. 192p. (gr. 3-7). 1952. 13.95 (*0-688-21383-9*); PLB 13.88 (*0-688-31383-3*, Morrow Jr Bks) Morrow Jr Bks.

—Henry & Ribsy. Cleary, Beverly. LC 54-6402. 192p. (gr. 3-7). 1954. 12.95 (*0-688-21382-0*); PLB 12.88 (*0-688-31382-5*, Morrow Jr Bks) Morrow Jr Bks.

—Henry & the Clubhouse. Cleary, Beverly. LC 62-7161. (gr. 3-7). 1962. 12.95 (*0-688-21381-2*); PLB 12.88 (*0-688-31381-7*, Morrow Jr Bks) Morrow Jr Bks.

—Henry & the Paper Route. Cleary, Beverly. LC 57-8562. (gr. 3-7). 1957. 15.95 (*0-688-21380-4*); PLB 15.80 (*0-688-31380-9*) Morrow Jr Bks.

—Henry Huggins. Cleary, Beverly. LC 50-8615. (gr. 3-7). 1950. 13.95 (*0-688-21385-5*); PLB 13.88 (*0-688-31385-X*, Morrow Jr Bks) Morrow Jr Bks.

—Mr. Bass's Planetoid. Cameron, Eleanor. (gr. 3-7). 1958. 14.95 (*0-316-12525-3*, Joy St Bks) Little.

—The Mouse & the Motorcycle. Cleary, Beverly. LC 65-20956. (gr. 2-6). 1965. 13.95 (*0-688-21698-6*); PLB 13.88 (*0-688-31698-0*) Morrow Jr Bks.

—Otis Spofford. Cleary, Beverly. LC 53-6660. 192p. (gr. 3-7). 1953. 12.95 (*0-688-21720-6*); PLB 12.88 (*0-688-31720-0*) Morrow Jr Bks.

—Ramona the Pest. Cleary, Beverly. LC 68-12981. (gr. 3-7). 1968. 13.95 (*0-688-21721-4*); PLB 13.88 (*0-688-31721-9*) Morrow Jr Bks.

—Ribsy. Cleary, Beverly. 192p. (gr. 3-7). 1982. pap. 3.50 (*0-440-47456-6*, YB) Dell.

—Ribsy. Cleary, Beverly. LC 64-13263. (gr. 3-7). 1964. 15.95 (*0-688-21662-5*); PLB 15.88 (*0-688-31662-X*) Morrow Jr Bks.

—Shag: Last of the Plains Buffalo. McClung, Robert M. LC 91-7508. 96p. (gr. 3-7). 1991. Repr. of 1960 ed. PLB 15.00 (*0-208-02313-5*, Linnet) Shoe String.

Darling, Tara, photos by. Kangaroos on Location. Darling, Kathy. LC 92-38418. 1993. write for info. (*0-688-09728-6*); lib. bdg. write for info. (*0-688-09729-4*) Lothrop.

—Tasmanian Devil: On Location. Darling, Kathy. Pearson, Susan, ed. LC 91-27561. 40p. (gr. 2 up). 1992. 15.00 (*0-688-09726-X*); PLB 14.93 (*0-688-09727-8*) Lothrop.

—Walrus: On Location. Darling, Kathy. LC 90-33376. 40p. (gr. 2 up). 1991. 14.95 (*0-688-09032-X*); PLB 14.88 (*0-688-09033-8*) Lothrop.

Darlington, Joan R. Is It Poison Ivy? Darlington, Joan R. 32p. (Orig.). (gr. 1-8). 1993. pap. 9.00g (*1-882291-53-0*) Oyster River Pr.

Darrell, Gail O. The Young Musician's Series. Epstein, Melvin H. LC 92-80357. (Orig.). (gr. 4-9). 1992. Five vol. set. pap. text ed. 65.00 (*1-881136-00-0*) Vol. 1: The Basics of Music (*1-881136-01-9*) Vol. 2: Melody. pap. text ed. 14.95 (*1-881136-02-7*); Vol. 3: Harmony. pap. text ed. 14.94 (*1-881136-03-5*); Vol. 4: Time & Rhythm. pap. text ed. 12.95 (*1-881136-04-3*); Vol. 5: Special Effects. pap. text ed. 12.95 (*1-881136-05-1*) Word Hse.

Darrow, Whitney, Jr. The Fireside Book of Fun & Game Songs. Winn, Marie, ed. Miller, Allan, contrib. by. 224p. (gr. 1 up). 1974. 14.95 (*0-671-65213-3*) S&S Trade.

Darwin, Beatrice. Daniel in the Lions' Den: Berg, Jean H. Jareaux, Robin, contrib. by. 32p. (Orig.). (gr. k-3). 1973. pap. 9.95 incl. audiocassette (*0-87510-178-X*) Christian Sci.

—God Keeps His Promise: A Bible Story Book for Young Children. Lehn, Cornelia. LC 76-90377. (gr. k-4). 1970. 12.95 (*0-87303-291-8*) Faith & Life.

—If You Lived with the Sioux Indians. 1992. pap. 4.95 (*0-590-45162-6*) Scholastic Inc.

—Socks. Cleary, Beverly. LC 72-10298. 160p. (gr. 3-7). 1973. 11.95 (*0-688-20067-2*); PLB 11.88 (*0-688-30067-7*, Morrow Jr Bks) Morrow Jr Bks.

Das, Arup. The Hidden Pool. Bond, Ruskin. 64p. (Orig.). (gr. k-3). 1980. pap. 2.75 (*0-89744-211-3*, Pub. by Childrens Bk Trust IA) Auromere.

Das, Prodeepta, photos by. Rice. Thomson, Ruth. Stefoff, Rebecca, ed. LC 90-40367. 32p. (gr. 3-5). 1990. PLB 15.93 (*0-944483-71-2*) Garrett Ed Corp.

Dasa, Puskar. A Gift of Love: The Story of Sudama Brahmin. Dasa, Yogesvara & Dasi, Jyotirmayi-Devi. LC 82-8874. 32p. (gr. 5-8). 1982. PLB 7.00 (*0-89647-015-6*) Bala Bks.

Dassow, Laura. Winter Watch. Ramsey, James. 154p. (Orig.). (gr. 10). 1989. pap. 9.95 (*0-88240-329-X*) Alaska Northwest.

Daste, Larry. Baby Bop Discovers Shapes. White, Stephen. Hartley, Linda, ed. 20p. (ps-k). 1993. 4.95 (*0-7829-0372-X*) Barney Pub.

—Don Octavio & the New Creature. Zelver, Patricia. LC 93-29565. 1994. write for info. (*0-688-13159-X*, Tambourine Bks); PLB write for info. (*0-688-13160-3*, Tambourine Bks) Morrow.

—A Griffin in the Garden. Marston, Elsa. LC 92-35399. 32p. (gr. k up). 1993. 15.00 (*0-688-10981-0*, Tambourine Bks); PLB 14.93 (*0-688-10982-9*, Tambourine Bks) Morrow.

—Teenage Mutant Ninja Turtles: The Final Lesson. Holm, Astrid. 32p. (Orig.). (ps-3). 1990. pap. 1.25 (*0-679-80669-5*) Random Bks Yng Read.

—The Wedding of Don Octavio. Zelver, Patricia. LC 92-12587. 32p. (gr. k up). 1993. 14.00 (*0-688-11334-6*, Tambourine Bks); PLB 13.93 (*0-688-11335-4*, Tambourine Bks) Morrow.

—Where Are My Shoes? Dudko, Mary A. & Larsen, Margie. Hartley, Linda, ed. 24p. (ps-k). 1993. pap. 2.25 (*0-7829-0375-4*) Barney Pub.

Datz, Margot. Amy the Dancing Bear. Simon, Carly. (ps-3). 1989. 12.95 (*0-385-26637-5*) Doubleday.

—Boy of the Bells. Simon, Carly. 1990. 14.95 (*0-385-41587-7*); PLB 15.99 (*0-385-41736-5*) Doubleday.

—The Nightime Chauffeur. Simon, Carly. LC 92-44934. 1993. pap. 16.00 (*0-385-47009-6*) Doubleday.

Daugherty, James. Abe Lincoln Grows Up. Sandburg, Carl. LC 74-17180. 222p. (gr. 7 up). 1985. 19.95 (*0-15-201037-8*, HB Juv Bks); pap. 5.95 (*0-15-602615-5*) HarBrace.

—Andy & the Lion. Daugherty, James. LC 38-27390. 80p. (gr. 1-4). 1938. pap. 13.95 (*0-670-12433-8*) Viking Child Bks.

—Early Moon. Sandburg, Carl. LC 77-16488. 136p. (gr. 5 up). 1978. pap. 1.95 (*0-15-627326-8*, Voyager Bks) HarBrace.

—Joe Magarac & His U. S. A. Citizen Papers. Shapiro, Irwin. LC 78-66070. 58p. (gr. 1-8). 1979. pap. 5.95 (*0-8229-5305-6*) U of Pittsburgh Pr.

Daughters of St. Paul Staff. The Holy Mass Coloring Book. rev. ed. Daughters of St. Paul Staff. 16p. (gr. 1-4). 1993. pap. 0.95 (*0-8198-3343-6*) St Paul Bks.

D'Aulaire, Edgar P., jt. illus. see D'Aulaire, Ingri.

D'Aulaire, Ingri & D'Aulaire, Edgar P. D'Aulaire's Book of Greek Myths. D'Aulaire, Ingri & D'Aulaire, Edgar P. LC 62-15877. 1980. 20.00 (*0-385-01583-6*, Zephyr-BFYR); PLB 19.99 (*0-385-07108-6*); (Zephyr-BFYR) Doubleday.

—George Washington. D'Aulaire, Ingri & D'Aulaire, Edgar P. LC 36-27417. 64p. (gr. 1-4). 1936. pap. 13.95 (*0-385-07306-2*) Doubleday.

Davalos, Felipe. The Hummingbird King: A Guatemalan Legend. Palacios, Argentina. LC 92-21437. 32p. (gr. 2-5). 1993. lib. bdg. 11.89 (*0-8167-3051-2*); pap. text ed. 3.95 (*0-8167-3052-0*) Troll Assocs.

—The Sea Serpent's Daughter: A Brazilian Legend. Lippert, Margaret H. LC 92-21438. 32p. (gr. 2-5). 1993. lib. bdg. 11.89 (*0-8167-3053-9*); pap. text ed. 3.95 (*0-8167-3054-7*) Troll Assocs.

Daven, Douglas. Coping with Beauty, Fitness & Fashion. Zeldis, Yona. Rosen, Ruth, ed. LC 86-24850. 128p. (gr. 7 up). 1987. PLB 13.95 (*0-8239-0731-7*) Rosen Group.

Davenport, May. Pigalee Pink & Other Stories. Dorio, Evelyn. Davenport, May, intro. by. LC 79-56540. 95p. (gr. 3-6). 1979. 4.50x (*0-9603118-5-8*); pap. text ed. 1.25 (*0-9603118-4-X*) Davenport.

—Pompey Poems... Celebrating a Cat. Langill, Ellen. LC 86-91603. 64p. (Orig.). (gr. 7-12). 1986. 10.25x (*0-943864-28-3*); pap. 3.50x (*0-943864-26-7*) Davenport.

David, Helen K. The Great Buffalo Race: How the Buffalo Got His Hump: a Seneca Tale. Esbensen, Barbara J., retold by. LC 92-23410. 1994. 14.95 (*0-316-24982-3*) Little.

—He Wakes Me. James, Betsy. LC 90-28920. 32p. (ps-1). 1991. 14.95 (*0-531-05954-5*); RLB 14.99 (*0-531-08554-6*) Orchard Bks Watts.

—A Shell Is Someone's Home. Zoehfeld, Kathleen W. LC 93-12428. 32p. (gr. k-3). 1994. 14.00 (*0-06-022998-5*); PLB 13.89 (*0-06-022999-3*) HarpC Child Bks.

David, Susan. Animal Babies One Two Three. Spencer, Eve. 24p. (ps-2). 1990. PLB 14.60 (*0-8172-3581-7*); pap. 10.95 pkg. of 3 (*0-8114-2930-X*) Raintree Steck-V.

David, Thomas. Birth of a Foal. Isenbart, Hans-Heinrich. LC 85-17406. 48p. (gr. 2-5). 1986. lib. bdg. 19.95 (*0-87614-239-0*) Carolrhoda Bks.

Davids, Paul, photos by. The Fountain of Youth. Davids, Paul. 56p. (Orig.). (gr. 5-9). Date not set. pap. text ed. 9.95 (*0-939031-01-9*) Pictorial Legends.

Davidson, Andrew. The Mink War. Kemp, Gene. 48p. (Orig.). (gr. 5 up). 1992. pap. 8.95 (*0-571-16312-2*) Faber & Faber.

Davidson, Dennis. Moonwalk: The First Trip to the Moon. Donnelly, Judy. LC 88-23668. 48p. (Orig.). (gr. 2-4). 1989. PLB 7.99 (*0-394-92457-6*); pap. 3.50 (*0-394-82457-1*) Random Bks Yng Read.

Davidson, Diane. Hamlet for Young People. Shakespeare, William. Davidson, Diane, ed. 64p. (gr. 5-8). 1993. pap. text ed. 4.95 (*0-934048-24-X*) Swan Books.

—Henry the Fifth for Young People. Shakespeare, William. Davidson, Diane, ed. LC 91-20093. 64p. (gr. 5-8). 1991. pap. text ed. 4.95 (*0-934048-23-1*) Swan Books.

Davidson, Gordon, jt. illus. see Howett, Andrew.

Davidson, Penny. Wild Jake Hiccup: The History of America's First Frontiersman. Davidson, Sol M. LC 91-19499. 160p. (Orig.). (gr. 2-9). 1992. 16.95 (*1-56412-003-1*); pap. 9.95

(*1-56412-004-X*); audio cassette 6.95 (*1-56412-001-5*) Hse Nine Muses. "The story of our tallest unknown folk hero, from his early days in colonial western "Pennsylvanny" to his epic battle with the young Paul Bunyan. Jacob grew up to play no small role in history: he is credited with single-handedly driving the French from Fort Duquense; suggesting a design for the U.S. flag based on George Washington's pajamas; making Mike Fink the victim of the first April Fool's joke; urging Audubon to add a few birds to his paintings; & inspiring John Chapman, later known as Johnny Peachfuzz - no, Johnny Peanutshell... Johnny Apricotpit something like that. The tale is told in "countrified" prose, illustrated with small, simple line drawings. Readers can absorb a fair dose of history while enjoying the droll adventures of this animal-loving, generally peacable giant."--KIRKUS REVIEWS, Aug. 1, 1992. "DELICIOUS!"--Mrs. M. Cunningham, 3rd grade teacher, Wash., D.C. "DELIGHTFUL!"--R. Messineo, Administrator, Passaic, N.J. Schools. "CHARMING!"--Mr. J. Wodden, Curriculum Dir., Des Moines, IA, Public Schools. "This book is funny & full of historical information. Overall, this book is very good & on a scale of one to ten, I would give it an eight & a half."--Megan Melamed, Age 12, The Gifted Child Today Magazine (GCT). Also ENJOYING AMERICAN HISTORY: Teacher's Guide to the Mining the Rich Vein of Ideas in Wild Jake Hiccup. Over 200 stimulating projects to make learning American History FUN! 80 pages. Illustrated. ISBN 1-56412-002-3. (softcover.) $5.95. For librarians, parents, grandparents to use with youngsters. Also THE BALLAD OF WILD JAKE HICCUP, audio cassette. Approx. 40 mins. Original words & music composed by John Deltenre & his Pioneer Band. $6. 95. ISBN 1-56412-001-5. Publisher Provided Annotation.

Davie, Helen. Sing with Me Christmas Carols. 24p. (ps up). 1987. pap. 5.95 incl. cassette (*0-394-89060-4*) Random Bks Yng Read.

Davie, Helen K. Ladder to the Sky: How the Gift of Healing Came to the Ojibway Nation. Esbensen, Barbara J. (ps-3). 1989. 15.95 (*0-316-24952-1*) Little.

—The Star Maiden: An Ojibway Tale. Esbensen, Barbara J. (ps-3). 1988. 14.95 (*0-316-24951-3*) Little.

—The Star Maiden: An Ojibway Tale. Esbensen, Barbara J. (ps-3). 1991. pap. 4.95 (*0-316-24955-6*) Little.

Davies, Joy D. Kelly Bear Behavior. Davies, Leah G. LC 88-82603. 28p. (Orig.). (ps-3). 1988. pap. 4.50 (*0-9621054-1-4*) Kelly Bear Pr.

—Kelly Bear Feelings. rev. ed. Davies, Leah G. LC 88-82577. 28p. (ps-3). 1988. pap. 4.50 (*0-9621054-0-6*) Kelly Bear Pr.

—Kelly Bear Health. Davies, Leah G. LC 89-85159. 28p. (Orig.). (ps-3). 1989. pap. 4.50 (*0-9621054-2-2*) Kelly Bear Pr.

Davies, Kate. Five Little Kittens: A Magic Window Board Book. Cowley, Stewart. 22p. (ps). 1992. 6.99 (*0-89577-454-2*) RD Assn.

—Patterns. Teeny Books Staff. 10p. (ps). 1993. 4.95 (*0-448-40534-2*, G&D) Putnam Pub Group.

—Pictures. Teeny Books Staff. 10p. (ps). 1993. 4.95 (*0-448-40535-0*, G&D) Putnam Pub Group.

Davies, Sumiko. The Little Book of Hugs. Weisinger, Steve. LC 90-60083. 28p. (ps). 1991. bds. 2.95 (*0-679-80755-1*) Random Bks Yng Read.

—The Little Book of Kisses. Weisinger, Steve. LC 90-60082. 28p. (ps). 1991. bds. 2.95 (*0-679-80754-3*) Random Bks Yng Read.

Da Vinci, Leonardo. Leonardo da Vinci. Raboff, Ernest. LC 87-45146. 32p. (gr. 1 up). 1987. pap. 7.95 (*0-06-446076-2*, Trophy) HarpC Child Bks.

Davis, Allen. Benito Juarez, Hero of Modern Mexico. Bains, Rae. LC 92-2291. 48p. (gr. 4-6). 1992. lib. bdg. 10.79 (*0-8167-2825-9*); pap. 3.50 (*0-8167-2826-7*) Troll Assocs.

—Chipmunk at Hollow Tree Lane. Sherrow, Victoria. LC 93-27267. 1994. 14.95 (*1-56899-028-6*); pap. 4.95 (*1-56899-029-4*) Soundprints.

—I Love to Laugh. Nordlicht, Lillian. Silverman, Manuel, intro. by. LC 80-14399. 32p. 1980. 17.96 (*0-8172-1364-3*) Raintree Steck-V.

—Save the Everglades! Stamper, Judith B. LC 92-18085. 56p. (gr. 2-5). 1992. PLB 21.34 (*0-8114-7219-1*) Raintree Steck-V.

—Skunk at Hemlock Circle. Sherrow, Victoria. LC 93-35511. 1994. 14.95 (*1-56899-031-6*); pap. 4.95 (*1-56899-032-4*) Soundprints.

Davis, Alton. Summer Coat, Winter Coat: The Story of a Snowshoe Hare. Boyle, Doe. Komisar, Alexi, narrated by. 32p. (gr. k-3). 1993. 11.95 (*1-56899-015-4*); incl. audiocassette, 8 in. brown plush toy 25.95 (*1-56899-018-9*); incl. audiocassette 16.95 (*1-56899-014-6*); incl. audiocassette, 11 in. white plush toy 39.95 (*1-56899-012-X*); incl. audiocassette, 11 in. brown plush toy 39.95 (*1-56899-017-0*); incl. audiocassette, 8 in. white plush toy 25.95 (*1-56899-013-8*) Soundprints.

Davis, Annelies. Fun with Nature. Hayes, Dympna & Lehman, Melanie. Kelly, Teri, ed. 32p. (gr. 2). 1987. PLB 14.97 (*0-88625-154-0*); pap. 2.95 (*0-685-30766-2*) Durkin Hayes Pub.

—Fun with Rhymes. Hayes, Dympna. 32p. (gr. 1). 1987. PLB 14.97 (*0-88625-165-6*); pap. 2.95 (*0-88625-144-3*) Durkin Hayes Pub.

—Fun with Sizes & Shapes. Buddle, Jacqueline. 32p. (gr. k). 1988. PLB 14.97 (*0-88625-162-1*); pap. 2.95 (*0-88625-143-5*) Durkin Hayes Pub.

—Fun with Words. Buddle, Jackie. 32p. (gr. 2). 1988. PLB 14.97 (*0-88625-164-8*); pap. 2.97 (*0-88625-161-3*) Durkin Hayes Pub.

Davis, Beverly. Brickhouse Dreams: Young Benjamin E. Mays. De Gree, Melvin. 140p. (Orig.). (gr. 3-10). 1992. pap. 11.95 (*0-9632895-0-0*) Trail of Success.

Davis, Carolyn. Color Fun. Brown, Charlene & Davis, Carolyn. 64p. (Orig.). (gr. k up). 1990. pap. 5.95 (*0-929261-27-5*, BA02) W Foster Pub.

—Colored Pencil Fun: How to Use Color Pencils. Brown, Charlene & Davis, Carolyn. 64p. (Orig.). (gr. k up). 1990. pap. 5.95 (*1-56010-058-3*, BA10) W Foster Pub.

—Craft Painting Fun: How to Paint on Objects. Brown, Charlene & Davis, Carolyn. Sprague, Sydney, ed. 64p. (Orig.). 1991. pap. 5.95 (*1-56010-071-0*, BA12) W Foster Pub.

—Drawing Fun. Brown, Charlene & Davis, Carolyn. 64p. (Orig.). (gr. k up). 1988. pap. 5.95 (*0-929261-26-7*, BA01) W Foster Pub.

—Felt Tip Fun: How to Use Felt Tip Pens. Brown, Charlene & Davis, Carolyn. 64p. (Orig.). (gr. k up). 1990. pap. 5.95 (*1-56010-057-5*, BA09) W Foster Pub.

—Paper Art Fun. Brown, Charlene & Davis, Carolyn. 64p. (gr. k up). 1988. pap. 5.95 (*0-929261-31-3*, BA06) W Foster Pub.

Davis, Deborah. The Secret of the Seal. Davis, Deborah. (gr. 2 up). 1988. 13.95 (*0-517-56725-3*) Crown Bks Yng Read.

Davis, Dennas. The Beginner's Bible: Timeless Children's Stories. Henley, Karyn. 528p. (ps-8). 1989. 16.99 (*0-945564-31-7*, Gold & Honey) Questar Pubs. STILL NUMBER ONE on the children's bestseller list in BOOKSTORE JOURNAL (ever since March 1990), this one has sold more than 1,000,000 copies! Ideal for ages two through eight, THE BEGINNER'S BIBLE includes ninety-five Bible stories told chronologically from Genesis to Revelation. Children will love the more than five hundred pages of Bible stories - with a full-sized, full-color picture on every page! There's also a thorough index to "Favorite Characters, Topics, & Stories," & each story is tagged with a reference line indicating the story's Scripture source. With its clear, young-hearted writing style & charming illustrations, this book is a proven winner! Order from Questar Publishers, P.O. Box 1720, Sisters, OR 97759, 503-549-1144. Publisher Provided Annotation.

—My First Hymnal: Seventy-Five Favorite Bible Songs & What They Mean. Henley, Karyn. 160p. 1994. incl. cass. 14.95 (*0-917143-35-3*) Sparrow TN.

Davis, Don. Exploring the Night Sky with Binoculars. Chandler, David. 48p. (Orig.). 1983. pap. 4.95 (*0-9613207-0-2*) D Chandler.

Davis, Florence, jt. illus. see Armstrong, Tom.

Davis, Florence S. Holt & the Cowboys. McCafferty, Jim. LC 93-16618. 40p. (gr. 4-8). 1993. 12.95 (*0-88289-985-6*) Pelican.

—Holt & the Teddy Bear. McCafferty, Jim. LC 90-44060. 40p. (gr. 4-8). 1991. 12.95 (*0-88289-823-X*) Pelican.

Davis, Jack. Tales from the Crypt, Vol. 1: Introduced by the Crypt-Keeper. Fremont, Eleanor, adapted by. LC 90-23916. 96p. (Orig.). (gr. 4-7). 1991. pap. 2.99 (*0-679-81799-9*) Random Bks Yng Read.

—Tales from the Crypt, Vol. 2: Introduced by the Old Witch. Fremont, Eleanor, adapted by. LC 90-23916. 96p. (Orig.). (gr. 4-7). 1991. pap. 2.99 (*0-679-81800-6*) Random Bks Yng Read.

—Tales from the Crypt, Vol. 3: Introduced by the Vault-Keeper. Wenk, Richard, adapted by. LC 90-23916. 96p. (gr. 4-7). 1991. pap. 2.99 (*0-679-81801-4*) Random Bks Yng Read.

Davis, James A. Times Table Secrets. Davis, James A. 12p. (gr. 3-5). 1994. incls. flash cards 10.00 (*0-9634088-1-X*) Simp Solns.

Davis, Jim. Garfield's Ghost Stories. Kraft, Jim & Fentz, Mike. 32p. 1992. 10.95 (*0-448-40577-6*, G&D) Putnam Pub Group.

Davis, Lambert. Baby Whales Drink Milk. Esbensen, Barbara J. LC 92-30375. 32p. (ps-1). 1994. 15.00 (*0-06-021551-8*); PLB 14.89 (*0-06-021552-6*) HarpC Child Bks.

—Baby Whales Drink Milk. Esbensen, Barbara J. LC 92-30375. 32p. (ps-2). 1994. pap. 4.95 (*0-06-445119-4*, Trophy) HarpC Child Bks.

—The Dark Way: Stories from the Spirit World. Hamilton, Virginia. 154p. (gr. 3 up). 1990. 19.95 (*0-15-222340-1*); Numbered, signed & Ltd. ed. 100.00 (*0-15-222341-X*) HarBrace.

—The Jolly Man. Buffett, Jimmy & Buffett, Savannah J. (ps-3). 1990. Incl. cassette. 19.95 (*0-15-240531-3*) HarBrace.

—The Jolly Mon. Buffett, Jimmy & Buffet, Savannah J., eds. 32p. (gr. 4-8). 1988. 14.95 (*0-15-240530-5*) HarBrace.

—The Terrible Hodag. Arnold, Caroline. 30p. (ps-3). 1989. 14.95 (*0-15-284750-2*) HarBrace.

—Trouble Dolls. Buffett, Jimmy & Buffett, Savannah J. Ingber, Bonnie V., intro. by. 32p. (gr. 1 up). 1991. 14. 95 (*0-15-290790-4*) HarBrace.

Davis, Lloyd S., photos by. Penguin: A Season in the Life of the Adelie Penguin. Davis, Lloyd S., text by. LC 93-36407. 1994. 17.95 (*0-15-200070-4*, HB Juv Bks) HarBrace.

Davis, maggie S. Roots of Peace, Seeds of Hope: A Journey for Peacemakers. Davis, Maggie S. 60p. (gr. 5-12). 1994. pap. 8.95 (*0-9638813-0-2*) Heartsong Bks.

Davis, Marc. Chanticleer & the Fox. Chaucer, Geoffrey. Roberts, Fulton, retold by. LC 91-71341. 32p. 1991. 13.95 (*1-56282-022-2*); PLB 13.89 (*1-56282-072-9*) Disney Pr.

Davis, Marguerite. Magical Melons. Brink, Carol R. LC 90-144. 208p. (gr. 3-7). 1990. pap. 3.95 (*0-689-71416-5*, Aladdin) Macmillan Child Grp.

—Under the Lilacs. Alcott, Louisa May. (gr. 7 up). 1977. 17.95 (*0-316-03099-6*) Little.

Davis, Mary I., jt. illus. see Jacobson, Mary M.

Davis, Nancy M. April & Easter. Davis, Nancy M., et al. 45p. (Orig.). (ps-2). 1986. pap. 5.95 (*0-937103-10-1*) DaNa Pubns.

—Colors. Davis, Nancy M., et al. (Orig.). (ps-2). 1986. pap. 4.95 (*0-937103-13-6*) DaNa Pubns.

—Fall & September. Davis, Nancy M., et al. 25p. (Orig.). (ps-2). 1986. pap. 4.95 (*0-937103-00-4*) DaNa Pubns.

—February & Valentines. Davis, Nancy M., et al. 29p. (Orig.). (ps-2). 1986. pap. 4.95 (*0-937103-07-1*) DaNa Pubns.

—Indians. Davis, Nancy M. & Moon, Teresa. 33p. (Orig.). (ps-5). 1986. pap. 4.95 (*0-937103-03-9*) DaNa Pubns.

—November & Thanksgiving. Davis, Nancy M., et al. 31p. (Orig.). (ps-2). 1986. pap. 4.95 (*0-937103-02-0*) DaNa Pubns.

—Numbers. Davis, Nancy M., et al. 26p. (Orig.). (ps-2). 1986. pap. 4.95 (*0-937103-14-4*) DaNa Pubns.

—October & Halloween. Davis, Nancy M, et al. 28p. (Orig.). (ps-4). 1986. pap. 4.95 (*0-937103-01-2*) DaNa Pubns.

—Patriotism. Davis, Nancy M., et al. 34p. (Orig.). (ps-5). 1986. pap. 4.95 (*0-937103-19-5*) DaNa Pubns.

—St. Patrick's. Davis, Nancy M., et al. 29p. (Orig.). (ps-4). 1986. pap. 4.95 (*0-937103-08-X*) DaNa Pubns.

—Spring & May. Davis, Nancy M., et al. 46p. (Orig.). (ps-4). 1986. pap. 5.95 (*0-937103-11-X*) DaNa Pubns.

—Winter. Davis, Nancy M., et al. 29p. (ps-2). 1986. pap. 4.95 (*0-937103-05-5*) DaNa Pubns.

Davis, Nelle. Munching: Poems about Eating. Hopkins, Lee B., ed. 48p. (gr. 3-6). 1985. 14.95 (*0-316-37269-2*) Little.

—The Mystery of Sleep. Silverstein, Alvin & Silverstein, Virginia. 48p. (gr. 2-5). 1987. 12.95 (*0-316-79117-2*) Little.

—Save the Earth: An Action Handbook for Kids. Miles, Betty. LC 90-46514. 128p. (Orig.). (gr. 5 up). 1991. 13.99 (*0-679-91731-4*); pap. 6.95 (*0-679-81731-X*) Knopf Bks Yng Read.

Davis, Rhonda K. & Beck, Arthello. Sons & Daughters of Autumn, Vol. I. Davis, Rhonda K. 32p. (Orig.). (ps-4). 1992. pap. 3.00 (*1-881967-14-X*) Express In Writing.

Davis, Richard. Lumpy Bumpy Pumpkin. rev. ed. Robbins, Sandra. 32p. (ps-4). Date not set. pap. 9.98 incl. cass. (*1-882601-18-1*) See-Mores Wrkshop.

Davis, Susan. The After-Christmas Tree. Tyler, Linda W. LC 92-8616. (gr. 4 up). 1992. 3.99 (*0-14-054191-8*) Puffin Bks.

—Birthday Moon. Duncan, Lois. 32p. (ps-3). 1989. 13.95 (*0-670-82238-8*) Viking Child Bks.

—The Dinosaur Who Lived in My Backyard. Hennessy, B. G. LC 87-19867. 32p. (ps-1). 1988. pap. 12.95 (*0-670-81685-X*) Viking Child Bks.

—The Dinosaur Who Lived in My Backyard. Hennessy, B. G. 32p. (ps-3). 1990. pap. 3.99 (*0-14-050736-1*, Puffin) Puffin Bks.

—My Brother Oscar Thinks He Knows It All. Tyler, Linda W. 32p. (ps-3). 1991. pap. 3.95 (*0-14-050947-X*, Puffin) Puffin Bks.

—The Sick-in-Bed Birthday. Tyler, Linda W. 32p. (ps-3). 1990. pap. 3.95 (*0-14-050783-3*, Puffin) Puffin Bks.

—Waiting for Mom. Tyler, Linda W. 32p. (ps-2). 1989. pap. 3.95 (*0-14-050652-7*, Puffin) Puffin Bks.

Davis, Tim. The Cranky Blue Crab: A Tale in Verse. Watkins, Dawn L. Smith, Anne, ed. 32p. (Orig.). (gr. k-1). 1990. pap. write for info. (*0-89084-506-9*) Bob Jones Univ Pr.

—Grandpa's Gizmos. Menken, John. Skaggs, Keith A., ed. 28p. (Orig.). (gr. 2-6). 1992. pap. 4.95 (*0-89084-663-4*) Bob Jones Univ Pr.

—Pocket Change: Five Small Fables. Watkins, Dawn L. Habegger, Christa & Sidwell, Mark, eds. 34p. (Orig.). (gr. 2-6). 1992. pap. 4.95 (*0-89084-645-6*) Bob Jones Univ Pr.

Davis, Timothy N. Right-Hand Man. Williams, Connie. LC 92-19158. 108p. 1992. pap. 4.95 (*0-89084-638-3*) Bob Jones Univ Pr.

Davisson, Vanessa. The Adventures of Inquisitive Englebert. Hutchison, Wick. 64p. (gr. k-3). 1991. pap. 7.95 (*0-929690-11-7*) Herit Pubs AZ.

DaVolls, Andy. Tano & Binti: Two Chimpanzees Return to the Wild. DaVolls, Linda. LC 93-25403. 1994. write for info. (*0-395-68701-2*, Clarion Bks) HM.

Davot, Francois. Descubrir la Tierra (Discover the Earth) Beautier, Francois. Calzada, Francisco-Javier, tr. (SPA). 96p. (gr. 4 up). 1992. PLB 15.90 (*1-56294-175-5*) Millbrook Pr.

—Robots y Ordenadores (Robots & Computers) Pouts-Lajus, Serge. Villanueva, Marciano, tr. (SPA). 96p. (gr. 4 up). 1992. PLB 15.90 (*1-56294-178-X*) Millbrook Pr.

Dawnay-Timms, Romayne. The Champions of Appleby Magna. Dawnay-Timms, Romayne. 160p. (gr. 3-7). 1994. SBE 14.95 (*0-02-789355-3*, Four Winds) Macmillan Child Grp.

Dawson, Dave. Money. Ockenga, Earl & Rucker, Walt. 16p. (gr. 1). 1990. pap. text ed. 1.25 (*1-56281-125-8*, M125) Extra Eds.

—Place Value to One Hundred. Ockenga, Earl & Rucker, Walt. 16p. (gr. 1). 1990. pap. text ed. 1.25 (*1-56281-115-0*, M115) Extra Eds.

—Subtracting from Eighteen or Less. Ockenga, Earl & Rucker, Walt. 16p. (gr. 1). 1990. pap. text ed. 1.25 (*1-56281-135-5*, M135) Extra Eds.

—Subtracting from Ten or Less. Ockenga, Earl & Rucker, Walt. 16p. (gr. 1). 1990. pap. text ed. 1.25 (*1-56281-110-X*, M110) Extra Eds.

—Sums Through Eighteen. Ockenga, Earl & Rucker, Walt. 16p. (gr. 1). 1990. pap. text ed. 1.25 (*1-56281-130-4*, M130) Extra Eds.

—Sums Through Ten. Ockenga, Earl & Rucker, Walt. 16p. (gr. 1). 1990. pap. text ed. 1.25 (*1-56281-105-3*, M105) Extra Eds.

—Telling Time. Ockenga, Earl & Rucker, Walt. 16p. (gr. 1). 1990. pap. text ed. 1.25 (*1-56281-120-7*, M120) Extra Eds.

Dawson, Diane. Mother, Mother, I Want Another. Polushkin, Maria. 32p. (ps-1). 1988. pap. 5.99 (*0-517-55947-1*) Crown Bks Yng Read.

Dawson, Nancy, jt. illus. see Osawa, Yasu.

Day, Alexandra. The Blue Faience Hippopotamus. Grant, Joan. LC 91-17133. 32p. (Orig.). (gr. 7-9). 1991. Repr. of 1942 ed. 11.95 (*0-671-74977-3*, Green Tiger) S&S Trade.

—Carl Goes Shopping. Day, Alexandra. (ps) 1992. 6.00x (*0-374-31101-3*) FS&G.

—Carl's Afternoon in the Park. Day, Alexandra. (ps). 1992. 6.00x (*0-374-31104-8*) FS&G.

—Carl's Christmas. Day, Alexandra. 32p. 1990. bds. 11. 95 (*0-374-31114-5*) FS&G.

—Carl's Christmas. Day, Alexandra. (ps). 1992. 6.00 (*0-374-31102-1*) FS&G.

—Frank & Ernest. Day, Alexandra. 40p. (gr. k-3). 1988. 13.95 (*0-590-41557-3*, Pub. by Scholastic Hardcover) Scholastic Inc.

—Frank & Ernest. Day, Alexandra. 1991. pap. 3.95 (*0-590-41556-5*, Blue Ribbon Bks) Scholastic Inc.

—Frank & Ernest Play Ball. Day, Alexandra. LC 89-10312. (gr. k-3). 1990. 12.95 (*0-590-42548-X*) Scholastic Inc.

—Good Dog, Carl. Day, Alexandra. 36p. (Orig.). (ps up) 1991. 11.95 (*0-88138-062-8*, Green Tiger) S&S Trade.

—Paddy's Pay Day. Day, Alexandra. 32p. (ps-3). 1989. 14.00 (*0-670-82598-0*, Puffin) Puffin Bks.

—Paddy's Pay-Day. Day, Alexandra. (ps-3). 1991. pap. 4. 00x (*0-14-050963-1*, Puffin) Puffin Bks.

—The Teddy Bears' Picnic. Kennedy, Jimmy. LC 91-24944. 40p. (ps-2). 1991. 13.00 (*0-671-75589-7*, Green Tiger); incl. cass. tape 19.95 (*0-671-74902-1*); incl. record 15.95 (*0-671-74903-X*) S&S Trade.

—Teddy Bears' Picnic Cookbook. Darling, Abigail. LC 92-28174. 1993. 4.99 (*0-14-054157-8*) Puffin Bks.

Day, Betsy. Hazel Saves the Day. Kiser, SuAnn. LC 92-34782. 1994. write for info. (*0-8037-1488-2*); PLB write for info. (*0-8037-1489-0*) Dial Bks Young.

—My New Mom & Me. Wright, Betty R. Silverman, Manuel S. LC 80-25529. (gr. k-6). 1981. PLB 16.67 (*0-8172-1368-6*) Raintree Pubs Ltd.

—Next Time I Will: An Old English Tale. Orgel, Doris, retold by. LC 92-10772. 1993. 9.99 (*0-553-09031-3*); pap. 3.50 (*0-553-37147-9*) Bantam.

—Stefan & Olga. Day, Betsy. LC 89-23647. 32p. (ps-3). 1991. 12.95 (*0-8037-0816-5*); PLB 12.89 (*0-8037-0817-3*) Dial Bks Young.

—Troll Games. Whittington, Mary K. LC 90-83. 32p. (gr. k-3). 1991. SBE 13.95 (*0-689-31630-5*, Atheneum Child Bk) Macmillan Child Grp.

Day, Brant. Humphrey & Ralph. Andres, Katherine. LC 93-11478. 1994. write for info. (*0-671-88129-9*, S&S BFYR) S&S Trade.

Day, Marie. Dragon in the Rocks: A Story Based on the Childhood of the Early Paleontologist, Mary Anning. Day, Marie. 32p. (ps up) 1992. 12.95 (*0-920775-76-4*, Pub. by Greey de Pencier CN) Firefly Bks Ltd.

Day, O. M. ABC's of Bugs & Beasts. Day, O. M. 31p. (Orig.). (gr. 3-12). 1991. pap. 11.95 (*0-9629795-1-1*) Klar-Iden Pub.

Day, Richard. The Conners of Conner Prairie. Hale, Janet. Baxter, Nancy N., ed. LC 89-80212. 120p. (gr. 4-6). 1989. 13.95 (*0-9617367-5-5*) Guild Pr IN.

—Hoosier Sports Heroes. Ogden, Dale. LC 90-84308. 192p. 1990. 19.95 (*1-878208-01-2*) Guild Pr In.

Day, Susan. Tad & Dad. Mooser, Stephen & Oliver, Lin. LC 87-40340. (ps-2). 1990. 4.95 (*1-55782-023-6*, Pub. by Warner Juvenile Bks) Little.

Deach, Carol. It's My Body. Freeman, Lory. 32p. (ps-3). 1983. lib. bdg. 15.95 (*0-943990-02-5*); pap. 4.95 (*0-943990-03-3*) Parenting Pr.

—Loving Touches. Freeman, Lory. LC 85-62434. 32p. (Orig.). (ps). 1985. PLB 15.95 (*0-943990-21-1*); pap. 4.95 (*0-943990-20-3*) Parenting Pr.

—Mi Cuerpo Es Mio. Freeman, Lory. Dunn, Lois, tr. from ENG. LC 85-62435. (SPA.). 32p. (Orig.). (ps). 1985. pap. 4.95 (*0-943990-19-X*) Parenting Pr.

—Something Happened & I'm Scared to Tell: A Book for Young Children Victims of Abuse. Kehoe, Patricia. LC 86-62032. 32p. (Orig.). (ps-1). 1987. PLB 15.95 (*0-943990-29-7*); pap. 4.95 (*0-943990-28-9*) Parenting Pr.

Deal, Jim. The Time Machine. Wells, H. G. James, Raymond, ed. LC 92-5804. 48p. (gr. 3-6). 1992. PLB 12.89 (*0-8167-2872-0*); pap. text ed. 3.95 (*0-8167-2873-9*) Troll Assocs.

—Whales & Other Creatures of the Sea. Milton, Joyce. LC 92-2409. 32p. (ps-4). 1993. PLB 7.99 (*0-679-93899-0*); pap. 2.25 (*0-679-83899-6*) Random Bks Yng Read.

Deal, L. Kate & Neill, Eileen M. The Boxcar Children Cookbook. Blain, Diane. Tucker, Kathy, ed. LC 91-15080. 96p. (gr. 2-8). 1991. 13.95g (*0-8075-0859-4*); pap. 9.95g (*0-8075-0856-X*) A Whitman.

Deal, Peggy B. Alan & the Baron. Hamilton, Ron. 50p. (Orig.). (gr. 3-7). 1983. pap. 2.95x (*0-913072-54-0*) Natl Assn Deaf.

Dean, Abner. Facts of Wife (the)-for Teenage Girls from 13 to 53. Warren, Robert. Berle, Milton, frwd. by. 1968. 3.95 (*0-913830-01-1*) Rodney.

Dean, Bessie. Aprendamos el Plan de Dios. Dean, Bessie. Balderas, Eduardo, tr. LC 80-82256. (SPA.). 64p. (gr. k-3). 1980. pap. text ed. 5.95 (*0-88200-135-4*) Horizon Utah.

—Lessons Jesus Taught. Dean, Bessie. 72p. (Orig.). (gr. k-5). 1980. pap. 5.95 (*0-88290-146-X*) Horizon Utah.

—Let's Go to Church. Dean, Bessie. LC 76-3995. 63p. (ps-3). 1993. pap. 3.98 (*0-88290-062-5*) Horizon Utah.

—Living the Articles of Faith. Dean, Bessie. 88p. (gr. k-4). 1988. pap. 6.95 (*0-88290-336-5*) Horizon Utah.

Dean, David & Cokendolpher, Jean. An Ancient Watering Hole: The Lubbock Lake Landmark Story. Johnson, Eileen, ed. LC 90-90258. 32p. (Orig.). (gr. 2-5). 1990. pap. 3.00 (*0-89672-218-X*) Tex Tech Univ Pr.

Dean, Kevin. Nature Hide & Seek: Jungles. Wood, John N. Schulman, Janet, ed. LC 86-21450. 24p. (ps-4). 1987. 11.95 (*0-394-87802-7*) Knopf Bks Yng Read.

Dean, Kevin, jt. illus. see Wood, John N.

Dean, Robyn. A Black Cat Named Smokey: On Vacation. Dean, Robyn. LC 92-93502. 64p. (Orig.). (gr. k-3). 1992. pap. 7.95 (*0-9633466-0-1*) Zyxalon Pr.

Dean, Theresa. Pocket Full of School Memories. Dean, Theresa & Lucadamo, Rhonda. 26p. (ps-8). 1992. 18. 95 (*1-881511-00-6*) Pockets Pr.

Dean, W. A. Twelve Years a Slave, Eighteen Forty-One to Eighteen Fifty-Three. Northup, Soloman. Eakin, Sue, retold by. LC 89-82295. 205p. (gr. 6-12). 1990. lib. bdg. 16.50 (*0-944419-27-5*); pap. text ed. 9.95x (*0-944419-17-8*) Everett Cos Pub.

Dean, Wayne. The Incredible, Spreadable, Magic, Drawing Book. Dean, Wayne. Harryman, Diana L. & Leatherbury, Leven C., eds. 56p. (gr. 3-9). 1983. pap. 9.95 (*0-9616161-0-1*) W Dean Editions.

Dean, William R. The Gift of Hope. Pennywell, Sylvia C. 21p. 1992. pap. 12.00 (*0-9637324-0-4*) Silver Grace Pubs.

—The Gift of Peace. Pennywell, Sylvia C. 21p. (Orig.). 1993. pap. 12.00 (*0-9637324-1-2*) Silver Grace Pubs.

De Anda, Ruben. A Crack in the Wall. Haggerty, Mary E. LC 92-59952. 32p. (gr. k-3). 1993. 14.95 (*1-880000-03-2*) Lee & Low Bks.

De Angeli, Marguerite. Book of Nursery & Mother Goose Rhymes. De Angeli, Marguerite. (gr. k-5). 1954. Doubleday.

—The Door in the Wall: Story of Medieval London. De Angeli, Marguerite. LC 64-7025. 111p. (gr. 3-6). 1989. pap. 14.95 (*0-385-07283-X*) Doubleday.

—The Lion in the Box. De Angeli, Marguerite. 80p. (gr. 2-5). 1992. pap. 3.50 (*0-440-40740-0*, YB) Dell.

—Marguerite De Angeli's Book of Nursery & Mother Goose Rhymes. De Angeli, Marguerite. LC 54-9838. (gr. k-5). 1979. pap. 18.95 (*0-685-01499-1*, Zephyr BFYR); pap. 7.95 (*0-385-15291-4*) Doubleday.

De Angulo, Jaime. Indian Tales. De Angulo, Jaime. 256p. (gr. 5 up). 1984. 10.95 (*0-374-52163-8*, Am Century) FS&G.

De Armond, Dale. Berry Woman's Children. De Armond, Dale. LC 84-29760. 40p. (gr. 1 up). 1985. 10.25 (*0-688-05814-0*); lib. bdg. 10.88 (*0-688-05815-9*) Greenwillow.

DeArmond, Dale. The Seal Oil Lamp. DeArmond, Dale. 48p. (gr. k-4). 1988. 14.95 (*0-316-17786-5*) Little.

Dearth, D. L., jt. illus. see Zimmerman, Paul.

Deas, Michael J. Deadly Game at Stony Creek. Cohen, Peter Z. LC 93-9364. 96p. (gr. 5 up). 1993. 3.99 (*0-14-036476-5*, Puffin) Puffin Bks.

De Batuc, Alfredo & Grim, Ellen. The Missions: California's Heritage, No. 18: Mission San Luis Rey de Francia, 21 Bks. Boule, Mary N. 24p. (Orig.). (gr. 4). 1988. pap. 3.50 (*1-877599-17-4*) Merryant Pubs.

De Batuc, Alfredo, jt. illus. see Grim, Ellen.

De Beer, Hans. Ahoy There, Little Polar Bear. De Beer, Hans. LC 88-42533. 32p. (gr. k-3). 1988. 13.95 (*1-55858-028-X*) North-South Bks NYC.

—Ahoy There, Little Polar Bear. De Beer, Hans. 32p. (gr. k-3). 1991. pap. 2.95 (*1-55858-109-X*) North-South Bks NYC.

—The Big Squirrel & the Little Rhinoceros. Damjan, Mischa. Hort, Lenny, tr. from GER. LC 91-17865. 32p. (gr. k-3). 1991. 14.95 (*1-55858-117-0*) North-South Bks NYC.

—Das Eichhorn und das Nashornchen. Damjan, Mischa. (GER). 32p. (gr. k-3). 1992. 14.95 (*3-314-00538-5*) North-South Bks NYC.

—La Foret Aux Milles Ombres. Damjan, Mischa. (FRE.). 32p. (gr. k-3). 1992. 14.95 (*3-314-20740-9*) North-South Bks NYC.

—Kleiner Eisbar, Komm Bald Wieder! De Beer, Hans. (GER). 32p. (gr. k-3). 1992. 13.95 (*3-85825-316-2*) North-South Bks NYC.

—Kleiner Eisbar, Nimm Mich Mit! De Beer, Hans. (GER). 320p. (gr. k-3). 1992. 22.50 (*3-314-00344-7*, Bradford Bks) North-South Bks NYC.

—Kleiner Eisbar, Wohin Fahrst Du? De Beer, Hans. (GER.). 32p. (gr. k-3). 1992. 13.95 (*3-85825-290-5*) North-South Bks NYC.

—Little Polar Bear. De Beer, Hans. LC 86-33208. 32p. (gr. k-3). 1989. 13.95 (*1-55858-024-7*); pap. 2.95 (*1-55858-030-1*) North-South Bks NYC.

—Little Polar Bear Address Book. De Beer, Hans. 128p. 1990. 7.95 (*1-55858-080-8*) North-South Bks NYC.

—Little Polar Bear & the Brave Little Hare. De Beer, Hans. James, J. Alison, tr. from GER. LC 92-9803. 32p. (gr. k-3). 1992. 12.95 (*1-55858-179-0*); PLB 12. 88 (*1-55858-180-4*) North-South Bks NYC.

—Little Polar Bear Birthday Book. De Beer, Hans. 120p. 1990. 7.95 (*1-55858-081-6*) North-South Bks NYC.

—Little Polar Bear Finds a Friend. De Beer, Hans. LC 89-43727. (ps-3). 1990. 13.95 (*1-55858-092-1*) North-South Bks NYC.

—Little Polar Bear Finds a Friend. De Beer, Hans. 32p. (gr. k-3). 1992. pap. 2.95 (*1-55858-144-8*) North-South Bks NYC.

—Olli, der Kleine Elefant. Bos, Burny. (GER). 32p. (gr. k-3). 1992. 13.95 (*3-85825-328-6*) North-South Bks NYC.

—Olli, le Petit Elephant. Bos, Burny. (FRE.). 32p. (gr. k-3). 1992. 13.95 (*3-85539-659-0*) North-South Bks NYC.

—Ollie the Elephant. Bos, Burny. LC 89-42608. 32p. (gr. k-3). 1989. 13.95 (*1-55858-012-3*) North-South Bks NYC.

—Ollie the Elephant. Bos, Burny. 32p. (gr. k-3). 1991. pap. 2.95 (*1-55858-110-3*) North-South Bks NYC.

—Plume en Bateau. De Beer, Hans. (FRE.). 32p. (gr. k-3). 1992. 13.95 (*3-85539-647-7*) North-South Bks NYC.

—Plume S'Echappe. De Beer, Hans. (FRE.). 32p. (gr. k-3). 1992. 13.95 (*3-314-20719-0*) North-South Bks NYC.

—Le Prince Ferdinand. Bos, Burny. (FRE.). 32p. (gr. k-3). 1992. 13.95 (*3-85539-703-1*) North-South Bks NYC.

—Prince Valentino. Bos, Burny. LC 89-43247. 32p. (gr. k-3). 1990. 13.95 (*1-55858-089-1*) North-South Bks NYC.

—Valentino Frosch und das Himbeerrote Cabrio. Bos, Burny. (GER). 32p. (gr. k-3). 1992. 13.95 (*3-85825-346-4*) North-South Bks NYC.

—Le Voyage de Plume. De Beer, Hans. (FRE.). 32p. (gr. k-3). 1992. 13.95 (*3-314-20619-4*) North-South Bks NYC.

De Bello, Rosario. Gina's Saturday Adventure. De Bello, Rosario. LC 93-5845. 32p. (ps-3). 1994. pap. 4.95 (*0-8091-6612-7*) Paulist Pr.

DeBiase, Judith. Daniel's Question: A Cesarean Birth Story. Allinson, Elaine S. 13p. (ps-5). 1981. staple bdg. 2.95 (*0-9606960-0-8*) Willow Tree NY.

DeBiasi, Antoinette. The Air I Breathe. Kalman, Bobbie & Schaub, Janine. 32p. (Orig.). (gr. k-8). 1993. PLB 15.95 (*0-86505-556-4*); pap. 7.95 (*0-86505-582-3*) Crabtree Pub Co.

—Eighteenth Century Clothing. Kalman, Bobbie. 32p. (Orig.). (gr. 3-6). 1993. PLB 15.95 (*0-86505-492-4*); pap. 7.95 (*0-86505-512-2*) Crabtree Pub Co.

—Nineteenth Century Clothing. Kalman, Bobbie. 32p. (Orig.). (gr. 3-6). 1993. PLB 15.95 (*0-86505-493-2*); pap. 7.95 (*0-86505-513-0*) Crabtree Pub Co.

De Brunhoff, Jean. Babar & Father Christmas. De Brunhoff, Jean. 40p. (gr. k-3). 1987. 16.95 (*0-394-89265-8*) Random Bks Yng Read.

—Babar & Father Christmas. De Brunhoff, Jean. LC 90-61863. 48p. 1991. 4.95 (*0-679-81483-3*) Random Bks Yng Read.

—The Story of Babar. De Brunhoff, Jean. 48p. (ps-1). 1984. Oversized Facsimile ed. 19.00 (*0-394-86823-4*) Random Bks Yng Read.

—The Story of Babar. De Brunhoff, Jean. LC 90-61704. 48p. 1991. miniature ed. 4.95 (*0-679-81049-8*) Random Bks Yng Read.

—The Travels of Babar. De Brunhoff, Jean. LC 85-2236. 48p. (ps up). 1985. 18.95 (*0-394-87453-6*) Random Bks Yng Read.

De Brunhoff, Jean & De Brunhoff, Laurent. Babar's Anniversary Album. reissued ed. De Brunhoff, Jean & De Brunhoff, Laurent. Sendak, Maurice, intro. by. LC 81-5182. 144p. (ps-3). 1993. 18.00 (*0-394-84813-6*); lib. bdg. 16.99 (*0-394-94813-0*) Random Bks Yng Read.

De Brunhoff, Laurent. Babar & the Ghost. De Brunhoff, Laurent. LC 80-5753. 32p. (gr. k-3). 1981. PLB 11.99 (*0-394-94660-X*) Random Bks Yng Read.

—Babar & the Ghost: An Easy-to-Read Version: A Step Two Book. De Brunhoff, Laurent. LC 85-11841. 48p. (gr. 1-3). 1986. pap. 2.95 (*0-394-87908-2*) Random Bks Yng Read.

—Babar Learns to Cook. De Brunhoff, Laurent. LC 78-11769. (ps-3). 1979. 2.25 (*0-394-84108-5*) Random Bks Yng Read.

—Babar Loses His Crown. De Brunhoff, Laurent. LC 67-21918. 72p. (gr. k-3). 1967. lib. bdg. 7.99 (*0-394-90045-6*) Beginner.

—Babar's Bath Book. De Brunhoff, Laurent. 10p. (ps). 1992. vinyl bdg. 3.99 (*0-679-83434-6*) Random Bks Yng Read.

—Babar's Battle. De Brunhoff, Laurent. LC 91-53169. 36p. (ps). 1992. 10.00 (*0-679-81068-4*); PLB 10.99 (*0-679-91068-9*) Random Bks Yng Read.

—Babar's Book of Color. De Brunhoff, Laurent. LC 84-42737. 36p. (ps-2). 1984. 12.00 (*0-394-86896-X*); lib. bdg. 10.99 (*0-394-96896-4*) Random Bks Yng Read.

—Babar's Busy Week. De Brunhoff, Laurent. LC 89-64400. 22p. (ps). 1990. bds. 2.95 (*0-679-80664-4*) Random Bks Yng Read.

—Babar's Busy Year: a Book about Seasons: Just Right for 2's & 3's. De Brunhoff, Laurent. LC 88-35726. 24p. (ps). 1989. 6.00 (*0-394-82882-8*) Random Bks Yng Read.

—Babar's Car. De Brunhoff, Laurent. 14p. (ps-k). 1992. bds. 3.99 (*0-679-83242-4*) Random Bks Yng Read.

—Babar's Counting Book. De Brunhoff, Laurent. LC 85-19652. 36p. (ps). 1986. 10.00 (*0-394-87517-6*); PLB 10.99 (*0-394-97517-0*) Random Bks Yng Read.

—Babar's Family Album: Five Favorite Stories. De Brunhoff, Laurent. LC 90-8748. 112p. (ps-3). 1991. 17.00 (*0-679-81167-2*); lib. bdg. 17.99 (*0-679-91167-7*) Random Bks Yng Read.

—Babar's Little Circus Star. De Brunhoff, Laurent. LC 87-14149. 32p. (Orig.). (ps-1). 1988. lib. bdg. 7.99 (*0-394-98959-7*); pap. 3.50 (*0-394-88959-2*) Random Bks Yng Read.

—Babar's Little Girl. De Brunhoff, Laurent. LC 68-42962. 36p. (ps-3). 1987. 11.00 (*0-394-88689-5*); lib. bdg. 9.99 (*0-394-98689-X*) Random Bks Yng Read.

—Babar's Little Library: Stories About Earth, About Fire, About Air, About Water, 4 bks. De Brunhoff, Laurent. (ps-2). 1992. Set of mini-bks. in slipcase incls. Air, Water, 48 pgs. ea. & Earth & Fire, 32 pgs. ea. 8.99 (*0-394-84365-7*) Random Bks Yng Read.

—Babar's Peekaboo Fair. De Brunhoff, Laurent. LC 92-64269. 14p. (ps). 1993. bds. 3.99 (*0-679-83935-6*) Random Bks Yng Read.

—Babar's Picnic. De Brunhoff, Laurent. LC 90-61349. 24p. (Orig.). (ps-2). 1991. pap. 2.25 (*0-679-81245-8*) Random Bks Yng Read.

—Hello, Babar! De Brunhoff, Laurent. 12p. (ps). 1991. foam filling 3.99 (*0-679-81073-0*) Random Bks Yng Read.

—Isabelle's New Friend: A Babar Book. De Brunhoff, Laurent. LC 89-3727. 32p. (ps-1). 1990. PLB 5.99 (*0-394-92880-6*); pap. 2.25 (*0-394-82880-1*) Random Bks Yng Read.

—Meet Babar & His Family. De Brunhoff, Laurent. 32p. (ps-1). 1985. pap. 5.95 incl. cassette (*0-394-87653-9*) Random Bks Yng Read.

—The One Pig with Horns. De Brunhoff, Laurent. Howard, Richard, tr. from FRE. LC 78-4917. (gr. k-3). 1979. Pantheon.

—The Pop-up Travels of Babar. De Brunhoff, Jean. LC 91-60192. 12p. (ps-1). 1991. 13.00 (*0-679-82151-1*) Random Bks Yng Read.

—The Rescue of Babar. De Brunhoff, Laurent. LC 92-50958. 36p. (ps-3). 1993. 20.00 (*0-679-83897-X*) Random Bks Yng Read.

De Brunhoff, Laurent, jt. illus. see De Brunhoff, Jean.

DeChristoper, Marlowe. Deer in the Hollow. Holmes, Efner T. 32p. (ps-3). 1993. 15.95 (*0-399-21735-5*, Philomel) Putnam Pub Group.

De Christopher, Marlowe. Greencoat & the Swanboy. De Christopher, Marlowe. 32p. (ps-3). 1991. 14.95 (*0-399-22165-4*, Philomel) Putnam Pub Group.

Decker, Tim. Billy Groat. Munger, Carol V. LC 87-71679. 23p. (Orig.). 1990. pap. 4.00 (*0-916383-45-8*) Aegina Pr.

—Boots: The Story of a Saint. Ball, Nancy. LC 88-72340. 44p. (Orig.). (gr. 2-5). 1989. pap. 5.00 (*0-916383-72-5*) Aegina Pr.

—Captain & Joey & the Tumbled down Cabin. Joachim, Mary J. LC 89-81198. 47p. (Orig.). 1990. pap. 4.95 (*0-916383-99-7*) Aegina Pr.

Deckert, Dianne T. My Book of Bible Rhymes. Knapp, John, II. (ps-1). 1987. 13.95 (*1-55513-161-1*, 51615, Chariot Bks) Cook.

Dedieu, Thierry. The Little Christmas Soldier. Dedieu, Thierry. LC 92-40172. 32p. (ps-2). 1993. PLB 15.95 (*0-8050-2612-6*, Bks Young Read) H Holt & Co.

Dee, Jeff. Quest for Clues, No. III. Addams, Shay, ed. 198p. 1990. pap. 24.99 (*0-685-41032-3*) Origin Syst.

Dee, Jeff, jt. illus. see Gustovich, Michael.

Deel, Guy. Reader's Digest Best Loved Books for Young Readers: Great Cases of Sherlock Holmes. Doyle, Arthur Conan. Ogburn, Jackie, ed. 184p. (gr. 4-12). 1989. 3.99 (*0-945260-22-9*) Choice Pub NY.

Deepa. Happy New Year in Sri Lanka. Weerusinghe, Christabel. 52p. (Orig.). (gr. 2 up). 1986. pap. 6.50 (*0-941402-05-3*) Devon Pub.

Deeter, Catherine. Langston Hughes, American Poet. rev. ed. Walker, Alice. LC 92-28540. 48p. (gr. 3-6). Date not set. 15.00 (*0-06-021518-6*); PLB 14.89 (*0-06-021519-4*) HarpC Child Bks.

Deeter, Catherine & Boston, Peter. The Children of Green Knowe. Boston, Lucy. 183p. (gr. 3-7). 1989. pap. 3.95 (*0-15-217151-7*, Odyssey) HarBrace.

—An Enemy at Green Knowe. Boston, Lucy. 176p. (gr. 4-7). 1989. pap. 3.95 (*0-15-225973-2*, Odyssey) HarBrace.

—A Stranger at Green Knowe. Boston, Lucy. 199p. (gr. 3-7). 1989. pap. 3.95 (*0-15-281755-7*, Odyssey) HarBrace.

—Treasure of Green Knowe. Boston, Lucy. 214p. (gr. 3-7). 1989. pap. 3.95 (*0-15-289982-0*, Odyssey) HarBrace.

Deeter, Theresa. A Little Peoples' Beginning on Michigan. Parker, Lois & McConnell, David. 32p. (Orig.). (gr. 1-2). 1981. pap. 5.50 (*0-910726-06-X*) Hillsdale Educ.

—A Puzzle Book for Young Michiganians. McConnell, David B. 24p. (Orig.). (gr. 3-6). 1982. pap. 5.50 (*0-910726-17-5*) Hillsdale Educ.

De Faye, Monique. Joey Becomes a Boomer. Vesper, Joan. LC 85-70354. 63p. (Orig.). (ps-5). 1985. pap. 5.95 (*0-9615007-0-0*) Green Bough Pr.

DeFazio, Deborah. Emma's Happy Birthday Piano. Bailey, Bobbi M. 36p. (gr. k-4). 1991. pap. 7.95 (*0-9625005-1-8*) Wee Pr.

Degano, Marino. Hobee Scrogneenee. Rocard, Ann. 28p. (ps-4). 1991. smythe sewn reinforced bdg. 9.95 (*1-56182-000-8*) Atomium Bks.

—Hobee Scrogneenee at Joey's School. Rocard, Ann. 28p. (ps-4). 1991. smythe sewn reinforced bdg. 9.95 (*1-56182-001-6*) Atomium Bks.

Degen, Bruce. A Beautiful Feast for a Big King Cat. Archambault, John & Martin, Bill, Jr. LC 92-32331. 32p. (ps-3). 1994. 15.00 (*0-06-022903-9*); PLB 14.89 (*0-06-022904-7*) HarpC Child Bks. Postponed.

—Better Not Get Wet, Jesse Bear. Carlstrom, Nancy W. LC 87-10810. 32p. (ps-1). 1988. RSBE 13.95 (*0-02-717280-5*, Macmillan Child Bk) Macmillan Child Grp.

—Commander Toad & the Big Black Hole. Yolen, Jane. LC 82-23524. (gr. 1-4). 1983. (Coward); pap. 6.95 (*0-698-20594-4*) Putnam Pub Group.

—Commander Toad & the Dis-Asteroid. Yolen, Jane. LC 84-1897. 64p. (gr. 4). 1985. (Coward); pap. 6.95 (*0-698-20620-7*, Coward) Putnam Pub Group.

—Commander Toad & the Intergalactic Spy. Yolen, Jane. 64p. (ps-4). 1986. (Coward); pap. 6.95 (*0-698-20623-1*, Coward) Putnam Pub Group.

—Commander Toad & the Planet of the Grapes. Yolen, Jane. 64p. (gr. 1-4). 1982. (Coward); pap. 6.95 (*0-698-20540-5*) Putnam Pub Group.

—Commander Toad & the Space Pirates. Yolen, Jane. 64p. (gr. 1-4). 1987. (Coward); pap. 6.95 (*0-698-20633-9*, Coward) Putnam Pub Group.

—Commander Toad in Space. Yolen, Jane. 64p. (gr. 3-5). 1980. (Coward); pap. 6.95 (*0-698-20522-7*) Putnam Pub Group.

—Dinosaur Dances. Yolen, Jane. 40p. 1990. 14.95 (*0-399-21629-4*, Putnam) Putnam Pub Group.

—Encyclopedia Brown's Record Book of Weird & Wonderful Facts. Sobol, Donald J. (gr. 3-7). 1981. pap. 1.75 (*0-440-42361-9*, YB) Dell.

—Encyclopedia Brown's Second Record Book of Weird & Wonderful Facts. Sobol, Donald J. LC 81-790. 160p. (gr. 4-6). 1981. 10.95 (*0-385-28243-5*); PLB 10.95 (*0-685-01395-2*) Delacorte.

—Goblin Walk. Johnston, Tony. LC 90-22985. 32p. (gr. 3-6). 1991. 14.95 (*0-399-22238-3*, Putnam) Putnam Pub Group.

—The Good-Luck Pencil. Stanley, Diane. LC 85-13122. 32p. (gr. k-2). 1986. RSBE 12.95 (*0-02-786800-1*, Four Winds) Macmillan Child Grp.

—Grandpa Bear. Pryor, Bonnie. LC 84-25545. 32p. (ps-1). 1985. 12.95 (*0-688-04551-0*) Morrow Jr Bks.

—Grandpa Bear's Christmas. Pryor, Bonnie. LC 85-29707. 32p. (ps-1). 1986. 12.95 (*0-688-06063-3*); lib. bdg. 12.88 (*0-688-06064-1*) Morrow Jr Bks.

—Happy Birthday, Jesse Bear! Carlstrom, Nancy W. LC 93-25180. 1994. write for info. (*0-02-717277-5*, Macmillan Child Bk) Macmillan Child Grp.

—How Do You Say It Today, Jesse Bear? Carlstrom, Nancy W. LC 91-21939. 32p. (ps-1). 1992. RSBE 13.95 (*0-02-717276-7*, Macmillan Child Bk) Macmillan Child Grp.

—If You Were a Writer. Nixon, Joan L. LC 88-402. 32p. (gr. k-3). 1988. RSBE 14.95 (*0-02-768210-2*, Four Winds) Macmillan Child Grp.

—In the Middle of the Puddle. Thaler, Mike. LC 85-45830. 32p. (ps-1). 1988. HarpC Child Bks.

—In the Middle of the Puddle. Thaler, Mike. LC 85-45830. 32p. (ps-1). 1992. pap. 4.95 (*0-06-443288-2*, Trophy) HarpC Child Bks.

—It's About Time, Jesse Bear: And Other Rhymes. Carlstrom, Nancy W. LC 88-8511. 32p. (ps-1). 1990. RSBE 13.95 (*0-02-717351-8*, Macmillan Child Bk) Macmillan Child Grp.

—Jamberry. Degen, Bruce. (gr. k-3). 1986. incl. cassette 19.95 (*0-87499-028-9*); pap. 12.95 incl. cassette (*0-87499-026-2*); 4 paperbacks, cassette & guide 27.95 (*0-87499-027-0*) Live Oak Media.

—Jamberry. Degen, Bruce. LC 82-47708. 32p. (ps-1). 1983. 14.00 (*0-06-021416-3*) HarpC Child Bks.

—Jamberry: Big Book. Degen, Bruce. LC 82-47708. 32p. (ps-3). 1992. pap. 19.95 (*0-06-443311-0*, Trophy) HarpC Child Bks.

—Jesse Bear, What Will You Wear? Carlstrom, Nancy W. LC 85-10610. 32p. (ps-k). 1986. RSBE 13.95 (*0-02-717350-X*, Macmillan Child Bk) Macmillan Child Grp.

—The Josefina Story Quilt. Coerr, Eleanor. LC 85-45260. 64p. (gr. k-3). 1986. 14.00 (*0-06-021348-5*); PLB 13.89 (*0-06-021349-3*) HarpC Child Bks.

—The Josefina Story Quilt. Coerr, Eleanor. LC 85-45260. 64p. (gr. k-3). 1989. pap. 3.50 (*0-06-444129-6*, Trophy) HarpC Child Bks.

—Lion & Lamb, Level 3. Hooks, William H. & Brenner, Barbara. (ps-3). 1989. pap. 3.50 (*0-553-34692-X*) Bantam.

—Lion & Lamb: Level 3. Hooks, William H. & Brenner, Barbara A. (ps-3). 1989. 9.99 (*0-553-05829-0*) Bantam.

—Little Chick's Friend Duckling. Kwitz, Mary D. LC 90-5027. 32p. (ps-2). 1992. 13.00 (*0-06-023638-8*); PLB 12.89 (*0-06-023639-6*) HarpC Child Bks.

—The Little Witch & the Riddle. Degen, Bruce. LC 78-19475. 64p. (gr. k-3). 1988. pap. 3.50 (*0-06-444125-3*, Trophy) HarpC Child Bks.

—The Magic School Bus at the Waterworks. Cole, Joanna. 40p. (gr. 1-4). 1988. pap. 3.95 (*0-590-40360-5*, Scholastic Hardcover) Scholastic Inc.

—The Magic School Bus: In the Time of the Dinosaurs. Cole, Joanna. LC 93-5753. 1994. 14.95 (*0-590-44688-6*) Scholastic Inc.

—The Magic School Bus Inside the Earth. Cole, Joanna. LC 87-4563. 48p. (gr. k-3). 1987. 14.95 (*0-590-40759-7*, Scholastic Hardcover) Scholastic Inc.

—The Magic School Bus Inside the Earth. Cole, Joanna. 1989. pap. 3.95 (*0-590-40760-0*, Scholastic Hardcover) Scholastic Inc.

—The Magic School Bus Inside the Human Body. Cole, Joanna. 1992. pap. 3.95 (*0-685-53602-5*) Scholastic Inc.

—The Magic School Bus Lost in the Solar System. Cole, Joanna. (ps-3). 1990. 14.95 (*0-590-41428-3*, Scholastic Hardcover) Scholastic Inc.

—The Magic School Bus Lost in the Solar System. Cole, Joanna. 40p. 1992. pap. 3.95 (*0-590-41429-1*, Scholastic Hardcover) Scholastic Inc.

—Mouse's Birthday. Yolen, Jane. LC 92-15291. 32p. 1993. 14.95 (*0-399-22189-1*, Putnam) Putnam Pub Group.

—Teddy Bear Towers. Degen, Bruce. LC 90-31937. 32p. (ps-1). 1991. 14.00 (*0-06-021420-1*); PLB 13.89 (*0-06-021430-9*) HarpC Child Bks.

—Upchuck Summer. Schwartz, Joel L. 144p. (gr. 3-7). 1983. pap. 3.50 (*0-440-49264-5*, YB) Dell.

—Upchuck Summer. Schwartz, Joel L. LC 81-65838. 144p. (gr. 4-6). 1982. 10.95 (*0-385-29099-3*); pap. 10.95 (*0-385-29100-0*) Delacorte.

—Upchuck Summer. Schwartz, Joel L. LC 81-69670. 144p. (gr. 4-8). 9.95 (*0-440-09264-7*); PLB 9.89 (*0-440-09269-8*) Delacorte.

—Will You Give Me a Dream? Nixon, Joan L. LC 91-19581. 40p. (ps-1). 1994. RSBE 14.95 (*0-02-768211-0*, Four Winds) Macmillan Child Grp.

Deger, Bruce. The Magic School Bus Inside the Human Body. Cole, Joanna. (ps-3). 1990. pap. 3.95 (*0-590-41427-5*, Scholastic Hardcover) Scholastic Inc.

De Gogorza, Maitland. Jane's Island. Allee, Marjorie H. 236p. (gr. 6 up). 1988. Repr. of 1931 ed. 13.95 (*0-96411374-2-8*) Woods Hole Hist.

DeGrazia, Ted. Tortillas. Gordon, Alvin J. 20p. (Orig.). (gr. 1-3). 1971. pap. 6.95 (*0-916955-06-0*) ARCUS Pub.

De Groat, Diane. Albert the Running Bear Gets the Jitters. Isenberg, Barbara & Wolf, Susan. 40p. (gr. k-4). 1987. 13.95 (*0-89919-517-2*, Clarion Bks); (Clarion Bks) HM.

—Albert the Running Bear's Exercise Book. Isenberg, Barbara & Jaffe, Marjorie. LC 84-7064. 64p. (Orig.). (ps-4). 1984. (Clarion Bks) HM.

—Aldo Peanut Butter. Hurwitz, Johanna. LC 90-35366. 128p. (gr. 2 up). 1990. 12.95g (*0-688-09751-0*) Morrow Jr Bks.

DeGroat, Diane. Aldo Peanut Butter. Hurwitz, Johanna. 112p. (gr. 3-7). 1992. pap. 3.99 (*0-14-036020-4*) Puffin Bks.

—All about Sam. Lowry, Lois. 144p. (gr. k-6). 1989. pap. 3.50 (*0-440-40221-2*, YB) Dell.

—Amanda & April. Pryor, Bonnie. LC 85-15308. 32p. (ps-1). 1986. 15.95 (*0-688-05869-8*); lib. bdg. 15.88 (*0-688-05870-1*) Morrow Jr Bks.

De Groat, Diane. Amy Dunn Quits School. Shreve, Susan. LC 92-41772. 96p. (gr. 3 up). 1993. 13.00 (*0-688-10320-0*, Tambourine Bks) Morrow.

—Anastasia Again! Lowry, Lois. 160p. (gr. 3-6). 1981. 14.45 (*0-395-31147-0*) HM.

—Anastasia at Your Service. Lowry, Lois. LC 82-9231. 160p. (gr. 3-6). 1982. 13.45 (*0-395-32865-9*) HM.

—Animal Fact - Animal Fable. reissued ed. Simon, Seymour. LC 78-14866. 48p. (gr. 1-5). 1992. PLB 12.99 (*0-517-58846-3*) Crown Bks Yng Read.

—Animal Fact: Animal Fable. Simon, Seymour. LC 78-14866. (gr. k-3). 1986. pap. 7.00 (*0-517-53794-X*) Crown Bks Yng Read.

—Attaboy, Sam! Lowry, Lois. 128p. (gr. 2-6). 1992. 13.45 (*0-395-61588-7*) HM.

DeGroat, Diane. The Bad Dreams of a Good Girl. Shreve, Susan R. LC 92-24593. 96p. (gr. 4 up). 1993. pap. 3.95 (*0-688-12113-6*, Pub. by Beech Tree Bks) Morrow.

De Groat, Diane. Bears in Pairs. Yektai, Niki. LC 86-18828. 32p. (ps-k). 1987. RSBE 14.95 (*0-02-793691-0*, Bradbury Pr) Macmillan Child Grp.

DeGroat, Diane. Bears in Pairs. Yektai, Niki. LC 91-229. 32p. (ps-k). 1991. pap. 3.95 (*0-689-71500-5*, Aladdin) Macmillan Child Grp.

De Groat, Diane. The Christmas Revolution. Cohen, Barbara. LC 86-21340. 96p. (gr. 3-6). 1987. 12.95 (*0-688-06806-5*) Lothrop.

Degroat, Diane. The Christmas Revolution. Cohen, Barbara. 176p. (gr. 4 up). 1988. pap. 2.95 (*0-553-15642-X*, Skylark) Bantam.

De Groat, Diane. DeDe Takes Charge! Hurwitz, Johanna. LC 84-9085. 128p. (gr. 3-7). 1984. 12.95 (*0-688-03853-0*) Morrow Jr Bks.

—DeDe Takes Charge! Hurwitz, Johanna. LC 84-9085. 144p. (gr. 4 up). 1992. pap. 3.95 (*0-688-11499-7*, Pub. by Beech Tree Bks) Morrow.

DeGroat, Diane. Dr. Ruth Talks to Kids: Where You Came from, How Your Body Changes, & What Sex Is All About. Westheimer, Ruth. LC 92-11397. 96p. (gr. 4-9). 1993. SBE 13.95 (*0-02-792532-3*, Macmillan Child Bk) Macmillan Child Grp.

—Don't Be Mad, Ivy. McDonnell, Christine. LC 81-65850. 80p. (gr. 1-5). 1981. Dial Bks Young.

De Groat, Diane. An Elephant Never Forgets Its Snorkel: How Animals Survive Without Tools & Gadgets. Evans, Lisa G. LC 91-31828. 40p. (gr. 1-5). 1992. 10.00 (*0-517-58401-8*); PLB 10.99 (*0-517-58404-2*) Crown Bks Yng Read.

—The Flunking of Joshua T. Bates. Shreve, Susan. LC 83-19636. 96p. (gr. 2-6). 1984. PLB 13.99 (*0-394-96380-6*) Knopf Bks Yng Read.

DeGroat, Diane. Fruit Flies. LeMieux, A. C. LC 93-29606. 1994. write for info. (*0-688-13299-5*, Tambourine Bks) Morrow.

De Groat, Diane. The Gray Whales Are Missing. Thrush, Robin A., ed. LC 87-17822. 113p. (gr. 3-7). 1987. 14.95 (*0-15-200455-6*, Gulliver Bks) HarBrace.

DeGroat, Diane. Great Advice from Lila Fenwick. McMillan, Kate. LC 87-24513. 160p. (gr. 3-7). 1988. PLB 11.89 (*0-8037-0532-8*) Dial Bks Young.

De Groat, Diane. The Great Eggspectations of Lila Fenwick. McMullan, Kate. 148p. (gr. 3-7). 1991. bds. 13.95 jacketed (*0-374-32774-2*) FS&G.

—The Great Ideas of Lila Fenwick. McMullan, Kate. (gr. 2-5). 1988. pap. 3.95 (*0-14-032499-2*, Puffin) Puffin Bks.

DeGroat, Diane. The Great Summer Camp Catastrophe. Van Leeuwen, Jean. LC 91-18487. 192p. (gr. 2-6). 1992. 13.00 (*0-8037-1106-9*); PLB 12.89 (*0-8037-1107-7*) Dial Bks Young.

—Hi Bears, Bye Bears. Yektai, Niki. LC 89-37554. 32p. (ps-1). 1990. 12.95 (*0-531-05858-1*); PLB 12.99 (*0-531-08458-2*) Orchard Bks Watts.

De Groat, Diane. Hurricane Elaine. Hurwitz, Johanna. LC 86-12409. 112p. (gr. 5-8). 1986. 12.95 (*0-688-06461-2*) Morrow Jr Bks.

—Itchy Richard. Gilson, Jamie. 64p. (gr. 1-5). 1991. 13.45 (*0-395-59282-8*, Clarion Bks) HM.

—Jace the Ace. Rocklin, Joanne. LC 90-34095. 112p. (gr. 2-6). 1990. SBE 12.95 (*0-02-777445-7*, Macmillan Child Bk) Macmillan Child Grp.

—Just for the Summer. McDonnell, Christine. LC 87-8201. (gr. 2-5). 1987. pap. 11.95 (*0-670-80059-7*) Viking Child Bks.

—Just for the Summer. McDonnell, Christine. 128p. (gr. 2-6). 1989. pap. 3.95 (*0-14-032147-0*, Puffin) Puffin Bks.

—Little Rabbit's Loose Tooth. Bate, Lucy. LC 75-6833. 32p. (gr. k-3). 1988. PLB 15.00 (*0-517-52240-3*); pap. 4.99 (*0-517-55122-5*) Crown Bks Yng Read.

—Lullabies for Little Dreamers. Roth, Kevin. 24p. (ps-1). 1992. incl. cassette 9.95 (*0-679-82382-4*) Random Bks Yng Read.

—Merry Christmas, Amanda & April. Pryor, Bonnie. LC 89-39723. 32p. (ps up). 1990. 13.95 (*0-688-07544-4*); PLB 13.88 (*0-688-07545-2*, Morrow Jr Bks) Morrow Jr Bks.

—Never Trust a Sister over Twelve. Roos, Stephen. LC 92-34406. 1993. 13.95 (*0-385-31048-X*) Delacorte.

DeGroat, Diane. The Orphan Game. Cohen, Barbara. LC 87-29340. (gr. 3-6). 1988. PLB 12.95 (*0-688-07615-7*) Lothrop.

De Groat, Diane. Our Teacher's Having a Baby. Bunting, Eve. 32p. (ps-3). 1992. 13.45 (*0-395-60470-2*, Clarion Bks) HM.

—Peter's Song. Saul, Carol P. LC 91-24674. 40p. (ps-1). 1992. pap. 14.00 jacketed (*0-671-73812-7*, S&S BFYR) S&S Trade.

—Stories from the Big Chair. Brodeur, Ruth W. LC 88-35230. 48p. (gr. 1-4). 1989. SBE 12.95 (*0-689-50481-0*, M K McElderry) Macmillan Child Grp.

—Sunshine Home. Bunting, Eve. LC 93-570. Date not set. write for info. (*0-395-63309-5*, Clarion Bks) HM.

—Toad Food & Measle Soup. McDonnell, Christine. 112p. 1984. pap. 3.99 (*0-14-031724-4*, Puffin) Puffin Bks.

—A Turkey for Thanksgiving. Bunting, Eve. 32p. (ps-1). 1991. 13.95 (*0-89919-793-0*, Clarion Bks) HM.

—Wait for Me. Shreve, Susan. LC 91-30233. 112p. (gr. 3 up). 1992. 13.00 (*0-688-11120-3*, Tambourine Bks) Morrow.

—When Mom & Dad Divorce. Nickman, Steven L. 80p. (gr. 3-6). 1986. lib. bdg. 10.98 (*0-671-60153-9*, J Messner); pap. 4.95 (*0-671-62878-X*) S&S Trade.

DeGroat, Diane. Where Is Everybody? Merriam, Eve. LC 88-19800. (ps-1). 1992. pap. 14.95 jacketed (*0-671-64964-7*, S&S BFYR); pap. 4.95 (*0-671-77821-8*, S&S BFYR) S&S Trade.

De Groat, Diane. The Wrong-Way Rabbit. Slater, Teddy. LC 92-14334. 32p. (ps-2). 1993. pap. 2.95 (*0-590-45359-9*) Scholastic Inc.

—You Don't Know Beans about Bats. Gilson, Jamie. LC 93-559. 1994. write for info. (*0-395-67063-2*, Clarion Bks) HM.

De Groat, Diane, photos by. Don't Be Mad, Ivy. McConnell, Christine. (gr. 2-5). 1988. pap. 3.95 (*0-14-032329-5*, Puffin) Puffin Bks.

De Hugo, Pierre. Animals in Jeopardy. Costa de Beauregard, Diane. Bogard, Vicki, tr. from FRE. LC 90-50779. 38p. (gr. k-5). 1991. 4.95 (*0-944589-37-5*, 375) Young Discovery Lib.

Deis, Ishaq, et al. Treasures of the Heart: Sufi Stories for Young Children. Muhaiyaddeen, M. R. Steele, Christine, ed. Balamore, Usha, tr. 110p. (ps). 1993. 10.00 (*0-914390-33-3*) Fellowship Pr PA.

Deiss, Veronique. Ogron. Serres, Alain. (FRE.). 104p. (gr. 3-7). 1991. pap. 10.95 (*2-07-031218-6*) Schoenhof.

Deitrick, David. Ironclads & Ether Flyers. Chadwick, Frank. 112p. (Orig.). 1990. pap. 12.00 (*0-943580-96-X*) Game Designers.

Deitrick, David R. Tales from the Ether. 64p. (Orig.). (gr. 9-12). 1989. pap. 8.00 (*1-55878-011-4*) Game Designers.

DeJarnette, Tom. Poisonous Snakes of Alabama. Wimberly, Christine A. 46p. (Orig.). (gr. 4-12). 1970. pap. 3.35 (*0-9605938-0-2*) Explorer Bks.

De John, Marie. Call of the Wild. London, Jack. Hitchner, Earle, ed. LC 89-33890. 48p. (gr. 3-6). 1990. PLB 12.89 (*0-8167-1863-6*); pap. text ed. 3.95 (*0-8167-1864-4*) Troll Assocs.

—Paul Revere. Weinberg, Lawrence. 48p. (gr. 2-4). 1988. pap. 2.95 (*0-681-40688-7*) Longmeadow Pr.

DeJohn, Marie. Roberto Clemente: Young Baseball Hero. Sabin, Louis. LC 91-17851. 48p. (gr. 4-6). 1992. PLB 10.79 (*0-8167-2509-8*); pap. text ed. 3.50 (*0-8167-2510-1*) Troll Assocs.

De John, Marie. Treasure Island. Stevenson, Robert Louis. Hitchner, Earle, ed. LC 89-20561. 48p. (gr. 3-6). 1990. lib. bdg. 12.89 (*0-8167-1877-6*); pap. text ed. 3.95 (*0-8167-1878-4*) Troll Assocs.

DeJohn, Marle. The Story of Daniel Boone. Retan, Walter. 112p. (Orig.). (gr. 2-5). 1992. pap. 3.25 (*0-440-40711-7*, YB) Dell.

De Jonge, Reint. Bible Stories to Live by, Old Testament. Beers, V. Gilbert & Beers, Ronald A. 96p. (gr. k-3). 1991. 12.99 (*0-8407-3506-5*) Nelson.

De Keefte, Kees. What Is a Family? Super, Gretchen. 56p. (gr. k-3). 1991. PLB 15.95 (*0-941477-63-0*) TFC Bks NY.

—What Kind of Family Do You Have? Super, Gretchen. 56p. (gr. k-3). 1991. PLB 15.95 (*0-941477-64-9*) TFC Bks NY.

De Kiefte, Kees. Family Traditions. Super, Gretchen. 48p. (gr. k-3). 1992. PLB 15.95 (*0-8050-2218-X*) TFC Bks NY.

—Sisters & Brothers. Super, Gretchen. 48p. (gr. k-3). 1992. PLB 15.95 (*0-8050-2219-8*) TFC Bks NY.

—Story of the Christmas Rose. Richardson, I. M. LC 87-13817. 32p. (gr. k-4). 1988. PLB 9.79 (*0-8167-1069-4*); pap. text ed. 6.99 (*0-8167-1070-8*) Troll Assocs.

—Yang the Youngest & his Terrible Ear. Namioka, Lensey. 112p. (gr. 3-7). 1992. 14.95 (*0-316-59701-5*, Joy St Bks) Little.

De Lacey, Honey. The Lost Ones. Greaves, Margaret. 96p. (gr. 4-6). 1993. 16.95 (*0-460-88053-5*, Pub. by J M Dent & Sons) Trafalgar.

—The Woman Who Went to Fairyland: A Welsh Folk Tale. Kerven, Rosalind, retold by. LC 91-40382. 32p. (gr. k-3). 1992. PLB 14.95 (*0-87226-466-1*, Bedrick Blackie) P Bedrick Bks.

DeLacre, Lulu. Aloysius Sebastian Mozart Mouse. Leigh, Oretta. 32p. (gr. k-2). 1984. 6.95 (*0-685-09671-8*, J Messner) S&S Trade.

—Arroz Con Leche. Delacre, Lulu. 1992. pap. 3.95 (*0-590-41886-6*, Blue Ribbon Bks); cassette 4.95 (*0-590-60035-4*, Blue Ribbon Bks) Scholastic Inc.

—The Bossy Gallito: A Traditional Cuban Folk Tale. Gonzalez, Lucia M., retold by. LC 93-15541. 32p. (ps-2). 1994. 14.95 (*0-590-46843-X*) Scholastic Inc.

—Peter Cottontail's Easter Book. Delacre, Lulu. 32p. (ps-1). 1991. 12.95 (*0-590-43338-5*, Scholastic Hardcover) Scholastic Inc.

—Sing with Me Mother Goose. (ps-1). 1987. incl. cassette 5.95 (*0-394-88812-X*) Random Bks Yng Read.

—Time for School, Nathan! Delacre, Lulu. 32p. (ps-2). 1991. pap. 2.50 (*0-590-45688-1*) Scholastic Inc.

Delamare, David. The Hawk's Tale. Balaban, John. LC 87-14938. 148p. (gr. 3-7). 1988. 14.95 (*0-15-200462-9*, Gulliver Bks) HarBrace.

—The Nutcracker. Hoffmann, E. T. LC 91-2167. 48p. (gr. 1-5). 1991. 9.95 (*0-88101-115-0*) Unicorn Pub.

—Nutcracker. 48p. (gr. 1-5). 1992. 12.95 (*0-88101-235-1*) Unicorn Pub.

—Nutcracker. 48p. (ps-3). 1992. 4.95 (*0-88101-244-0*) Unicorn Pub.

—Steadfast Tin Soldier. Ingram, John W., ed. Delamare, David. LC 90-10927. 48p. (gr. 1-5). 1990. 9.95 (*0-88101-077-4*) Unicorn Pub.

—Steadfast Tin Soldier. 48p. (ps-3). 1992. 4.95 (*0-88101-245-9*) Unicorn Pub.

—Steadfast Tin Soldier. 48p. (ps-3). 1990. 12.95 (*0-88101-237-8*) Unicorn Pub.

—Twelve Days of Christmas. 48p. 1992. 12.95 (*0-88101-238-6*) Unicorn Pub.

—Twelve Days of Christmas. 48p. 1992. 5.95 (*0-88101-264-5*) Unicorn Pub.

—Twelve Days of Christmas (Fairy Tale Classic) 48p. 1992. 9.95 (*0-88101-228-9*) Unicorn Pub.

Delaney, A. Sesame Street Big Bird & Little Bird's Book of Big & Little. Kingsley, Emily P. 24p. (ps-k). 1977. pap. write for info (*0-307-10073-1*, Pub. by Golden Bks) Western Pub.

Delaney, Antoinette. The Gunnywolf. Delaney, Antoinette. LC 87-29351. 32p. (ps-3). 1992. pap. 4.95 (*0-06-443304-8*, Trophy) HarpC Child Bks.

Delaney, Jacqueline K. Oliver & Ophelia: A Tale of Opossums. Demers, Paul. LC 85-6020. 20p. (Orig.). (gr. 1-6). 1986. pap. 2.95 (*0-916897-04-4*) Andrew Mtn Pr.

Delaney, Molly. Andrew Wants a Dog. Kroll, Steven. LC 91-25637. 64p. (gr. 2-6). 1992. 11.95 (*1-56282-118-0*); PLB 11.89 (*1-56282-119-9*) Hyprn Child.

—Birthday Blizzard. Pryor, Bonnie. LC 92-1713. 32p. (gr. k up). 1993. 15.00 (*0-688-09423-6*); PLB 14.93 (*0-688-09424-4*) Morrow Jr Bks.

—The Farmer in the Soup. Littledale, Freya. 32p. (Orig.). (gr. k-3). 1987. pap. 2.50 (*0-590-42535-8*) Scholastic Inc.

—Natalie Spitzer's Turtles. Willner-Pardo, Gina. Levine, Abby, ed. LC 92-3342. 32p. (gr. k-3). 1992. 13.95g (*0-8075-5515-0*) A Whitman.

Delaney, Ned. Aren't You Forgetting Something, Fiona? Cole, Joanna. LC 83-13457. 48p. (ps-3). 1984. 5.95 (*0-8193-1121-9*) Parents.

—The Cactus Flower Bakery. Allard, Harry. LC 90-36565. 32p. (ps-3). 1991. PLB 14.89 (*0-06-020047-2*) HarpC Child Bks.

—The Cactus Flower Bakery. Allard, Harry. LC 90-36565. 32p. (ps-3). 1993. pap. 4.95 (*0-06-443297-1*, Trophy) HarpC Child Bks.

—Eeeeeek! Wolcott, Patty. LC 91-12741. 32p. (ps-2). 1991. 3.50 (*0-679-81929-0*); PLB 6.99 (*0-679-91929-5*) Random Bks Yng Read.

—Old Enough for Magic. Pickett, Anola. LC 88-30320. 64p. (gr. k-3). 1989. PLB 13.89 (*0-06-024732-0*) HarpC Child Bks.

—Old Enough for Magic. Pickett, Anola. LC 88-30320. 64p. (gr. k-3). 1993. pap. 3.50 (*0-06-444161-X*, Trophy) HarpC Child Bks.

—Otto. Kroll, Steven. LC 82-19024. 48p. (ps-3). 1983. 5.95 (*0-8193-1105-7*); PLB 5.95 (*0-8193-1106-5*) Parents.

Delany, Dan & Walker, Jan. Alpine to Alkali. Freeman, Marie E. & Davis, Maria H. LC 83-80807. 150p. (Orig.). (gr. 7-12). 1983. pap. text ed. 7.95 (*0-913205-01-X*) Grace Dangberg.

Delany, Molly. Andrew Wants a Dog. Kroll, Steven. LC 91-25637. 64p. (gr. 2-4). 1993. pap. 2.95 (*1-56282-521-6*) Hyprn Ppbks.

DeLapp, Tom & Whittaker, Jessica L. Woven with Love. Marshall, Ann E. 36p. (Orig.). (gr. 2-5). 1988. pap. 4.50 (*0-934351-02-3*) Heard Mus.

De Larrea, Victoria. Candles, Cakes, & Donkey Tails: Birthday Symbols & Celebrations. Perl, Lila. LC 84-5803. 80p. (gr. 3-6). 1984. (Clarion Bks) HM.

—The Good Day Mice. York, Carol B. 112p. (gr. 3-7). 1989. pap. 2.75 (*0-553-15373-0*, Skylark) Bantam.

—Halloween Treats. Haywood, Carolyn. LC 81-3959. 176p. (gr. 4-6). 1981. lib. bdg. 12.88 (*0-688-00709-0*) Morrow Jr Bks.

—Lisa & Lottie. Kastner, Erich. Books, Cyrus, tr. 136p. (gr. 3-7). 1982. pap. 2.95 (*0-380-57117-X*, Camelot) Avon.

—Pinatas & Paper Flowers-Pinatas y Flores de Papel: Holidays of the Americas in English & Spanish. Perl, Lila & Ada, Alma F. LC 82-12211. 91p. (gr. 3-6). 1983. 12.95 (*0-89919-112-6*, Clarion Bks); pap. 5.95 (*0-89919-155-X*, Clarion Bks) HM.
Delbo, Jose. Batman & the Doomsday Prophecy. Wenk, Richard. (gr. 3-6). 1989. pap. 2.99 (*0-671-68312-8*, Archway) PB.
De Leon, Romeo. Abadeha: The Philippine Cinderella. De La Paz, Myrna J. 28p. (gr. k-7). 1991. 13.95 (*0-9629255-0-0*) Pazific Queen.
Delessert, Etienne. Albert Einstein. Einstein, Albert. Redpath, Ann, ed. 32p. (gr. 9 up). 1986. PLB 12.95s.p. (*0-88682-011-1*) Creative Ed.
—Albert Schweitzer. Schweitzer, Albert. Repath, Ann, ed. Winston, Richard & Winston, Clara, trs. 32p. (gr. 9 up). 1986. PLB 12.95s.p. (*0-88682-013-8*) Creative Ed.
—Ashes, Ashes. Delessert, Etienne. 32p. (gr. 1-12). Date not set. lib. bdg. 16.95 RLB smythe-sewn (*0-88682-628-4*, 97855-098) Creative Ed.
—At Home. Delessert, Etienne. LC 93-27456. 1993. write for info. (*0-88682-646-2*) Creative Ed.
—Beauty & the Beast. Madame de Villeneuve. 48p. (gr. 4 up). 1984. PLB 13.95s.p. (*0-87191-946-X*) Creative Ed.
—The Bee-Man of Orn. Stockton, Frank. LC 85-23272. 40p. (gr. 4 up). 1986. PLB 13.95s.p. (*0-88682-055-3*) Creative Ed.
—Bertrand Russell. Russell, Bertrand. Redpath, Ann, ed. 32p. (gr. 9 up). 1986. PLB 12.95s.p. (*0-88682-012-X*) Creative Ed.
—Best Friends. Delessert, Etienne. LC 93-27461. 1993. write for info. (*0-88682-639-X*) Creative Ed.
—The Black Cat. Poe, Edgar Allan. Redpath, Ann, ed. 32p. (gr. 9 up). 1985. PLB 13.95s.p. (*0-88682-001-4*) Creative Ed.
—A Christmas Memory. Capote, Truman. 40p. (gr. 4 up). 1984. PLB 13.95s.p. (*0-87191-956-7*) Creative Ed.
—Dance! Delessert, Etienne. 32p. (gr. 1-8). Date not set. RLB smythe-sewn 16.95 (*0-88682-627-6*, 97938-098) Creative Ed.
—The Earthworm. Benedict, Kitty. Soutter-Perrot, Andrienne, concept by. LC 92-15024. (gr. 5 up). 1992. PLB 10.95 (*0-88682-566-0*) Creative Ed.
—The Fifty-First Dragon. Broun, Heywood. Redpath, Ann, ed. 32p. (gr. 4 up). 1985. PLB 13.95s.p. (*0-88682-005-7*) Creative Ed.
—For the Birds. Delessert, Etienne. LC 93-27462. 1993. write for info. (*0-88682-638-1*) Creative Ed.
—I Hate to Read. Marshall, Rita. 1992. PLB 16.95 (*0-88682-531-8*) Creative Ed.
—It's Such a Beautiful Day. Asimov, Isaac. Redpath, Ann, ed. 64p. (gr. 4 up). 1985. PLB 13.95s.p. (*0-88682-008-1*) Creative Ed.
—Let's Play. Delessert, Etienne. LC 93-27459. 1993. write for info. (*0-88682-649-7*) Creative Ed.
—Magic Tricks. Delessert, Etienne. LC 93-31972. 1993. write for info. (*0-88682-642-X*) Creative Ed.
—Mahatma Gandhi. Gandhi, Mahatma. Redpath, Ann, ed. 32p. (gr. 4 up). 1985. PLB 12.95s.p. (*0-88682-010-3*) Creative Ed.
—Moonlight. Delessert, Etienne. LC 93-27458. 1993. write for info. (*0-88682-648-9*) Creative Ed.

—My First Nature Book Series, 12 bks. Benedict, Kitty. 32p. (Orig.). (gr. 1-4). 1993. Set. pap. 35.40 (*1-56189-149-5*) Amer Educ Pub.
What is soil made of? What happens when an earthworm is cut in half? What do toads eat? Children will find the answers to these questions & more in twelve Nature Books--& they'll have a lot of fun along the way! MY FIRST NATURE BOOKS are designed to arouse & encourage a child's curiosity about the world around us. Each book introduces a fascinating topic--from essentials of life such as air & earth, to the beneficial cow & the mighty oak tree. The text is engagingly simple & there's a charming illustration on each page. Children will quickly take to heart the most important fact of all: that learning about nature is a natural thing to do! Titles include: Air, ISBN 1-56189-167-3, $2.95; Earth, ISBN 1-56189-168-1, $2.95; Water, ISBN 1-56189-169-X, $2.95; The Oak, ISBN 1-56189-170-3, $2.95; The Gnat, ISBN 1-56189-171-1, $2.95; The Wolf, ISBN 1-56189-172-X, $2.95; Fire, ISBN 1-56189-173-8, $2.95; The Ant, ISBN 1-56189-174-6, $2.95; The Egg, ISBN 1-56189-175-4, $2.95; The Earthworm, ISBN 1-56189-176-2, $2.95; The Cow,

ISBN 1-56189-177-0, $2.95; The Toad, ISBN 1-56189-178-9, $2.95.
Publisher Provided Annotation.

—My Oedipus Complex. O'Connor, Frank. LC 85-32526. 40p. (gr. 4 up). 1986. PLB 13.95s.p. (*0-88682-062-6*) Creative Ed.
—Nonsense. Delessert, Etienne. LC 93-27464. 1993. write for info. (*0-88682-641-1*) Creative Ed.
—Nuts! Delessert, Etienne. LC 93-27454. 1993. write for info. (*0-88682-644-6*) Creative Ed.
—The Sire de Maletroit's Door. Stevenson, Robert Louis. Redpath, Ann, ed. 58p. (gr. 6 up). 1985. PLB 13.95s.p. (*0-87191-967-2*) Creative Ed.
—Snowflakes. Delessert, Etienne. LC 93-27457. 1993. write for info. (*0-88682-647-0*) Creative Ed.
—Surprises. Delessert, Etienne. LC 93-27453. 1993. write for info. (*0-88682-643-8*) Creative Ed.
—Two Friends. De Maupassant, Guy. Redpath, Ann, ed. 32p. (gr. 4 up). 1985. PLB 13.95s.p. (*0-88682-003-0*) Creative Ed.
—Weird? Delessert, Etienne. LC 93-27455. 1993. write for info. (*0-88682-645-4*) Creative Ed.
—What a Circus! Delessert, Etienne. LC 93-27463. 1993. write for info. (*0-88682-640-3*) Creative Ed.
Delf, Brian. Picture Atlas of the World. LC 92-37056. 1992. write for info. (*0-528-83564-5*) Rand McNally.
D'Elgin, Tershia. See You Later Alligator. Strauss, Barbara & Friedland, Helen. 28p. 1986. 6.95 (*0-8431-1554-8*) Price Stern.
Delia. The ABC's of Texas. Lewein, David A. Lewein, Mary J., ed. 64p. 1989. pap. 4.95 (*0-685-29420-X*) TX Pride Pubns.
De Lisle, Elizabeth, et al. Treasury of Christmas. Miles, John C., ed. LC 90-39372. 96p. (gr. 2-5). 1991. lib. bdg. 14.89 (*0-8167-2236-6*); pap. text ed. 6.95 (*0-8167-2237-4*) Troll Assocs.
Delmonte, Patti. An Apple a Day! Over Twenty Apple Projects for Kids. Gillis, Jennifer S. 64p. (Orig.). (gr. k-4). 1993. pap. 8.95 (*0-88266-849-8*, Garden Way Pub) Storey Comm Inc.
—Hearts & Crafts: Over Twenty Projects for Fun-Loving Kids. Gillis, Jennifer S. Steege, Gwen, ed. LC 93-4841. 64p. (gr. k-4). 1994. pap. 9.95 (*0-88266-844-7*) Storey Comm Inc.
—In a Pumpkin Shell: Over Twenty Pumpkin Projects for Kids. Gillis, Jennifer S. LC 91-50604. 64p. (gr. k-4). 1992. (Garden Way Pub); pap. 8.95 (*0-88266-771-8*, Garden Way Pub) Storey Comm Inc.
Delstanche, Albert. Flemish Legends. De Coster, Charles T. Taylor, Harold, tr. LC 78-74513. (gr. 7 up). 1979. Repr. of 1920 ed. 18.75x (*0-8486-0217-X*) Roth Pub Inc.
Delton, Alan T. The Artificial Grandma. Judy. 1990. pap. 2.95 (*0-440-40315-4*, YB) Dell.
—Huckleberry Hash. 1990. pap. 2.95 (*0-440-40325-1*, YB) Dell.
De Luna, Betty, jt. illus. see De Luna, Tony.
De Luna, Tony & De Luna, Betty. Starting School. Stanek, Muriel. Fay, Ann, ed. LC 81-297. 32p. (ps-1). 1981. PLB 10.95 (*0-8075-7617-4*) A Whitman.
DeMarco, Susanne. Snap the Clam. Rutman, Shereen. 16p. (ps). 1993. wkbk. 2.25 (*1-56293-326-4*) McClanahan Bk.
DeMarco, Susanne, jt. illus. see Regan, Dana.
Demarest, Chris. Bob & Jack: A Boy & His Yak. Moss, Jeff. LC 92-17458. 64p. (gr. 4 up). 1992. 15.00 (*0-553-08931-5*) Bantam.
—The Butterfly Jar. Moss, Jeffrey. (ps up) 1989. 15.00 (*0-553-05704-9*) Bantam.
—Hooray for Grandma Jo! McKean, Thomas. LC 93-16376. (ps-6). 1994. 14.00 (*0-517-57842-5*); PLB 14.99 (*0-517-57843-3*) Crown Bks Yng Read.
—Not Now! Said the Cow: Level 2. Oppenheim, Joanne. 1989. 9.99 (*0-553-05826-6*) Bantam.
—Tree House Fun. Greydanus, Rose. 32p. (gr. k-2). 1980. PLB 7.89 (*0-89375-391-2*); pap. 1.95 (*0-89375-291-6*) Troll Assocs.
—Uh-oh! Cawed the Crow. Oppenheim, Joanne. LC 92-1629. 1993. 9.99 (*0-553-09387-8*, Little Rooster); pap. 3.50 (*0-553-37186-X*, Little Rooster) Bantam.
Demarest, Chris, et al. The Scary Book. Cole, Joanna & Calmenson, Stephanie, eds. LC 90-26330. 128p. (gr. 2 up). 1991. 12.95 (*0-688-10654-4*) Morrow Jr Bks.
Demarest, Chris L. The Cows Are Going to Paris. Woodman, Allen & Kirby, David. LC 90-85733. 32p. (ps-3). 1991. 13.95 (*1-878093-11-8*) Boyds Mills Pr.
—How Do You Wrap a Horse? Klemin, Diana. 32p. (ps-3). 1993. 14.95 (*1-56397-187-9*) Boyds Mills Pr.
—Lindbergh. Demarest, Chris L. LC 92-41845. 40p. (ps-4). 1993. 15.99 (*0-517-58718-1*); PLB 15.99 (*0-517-58719-X*) Crown Bks Yng Read.
—Morton & Sidney. Demarest, Chris L. LC 92-44153. 32p. (gr. k-2). 1993. pap. 4.95 (*0-689-71740-7*, Aladdin) Macmillan Child Grp.
—My Little Red Car. Demarest, Chris L. 32p. (ps-1). 1992. PLB 14.95 (*1-878093-86-X*) Boyds Mills Pr.
—No Peas for Nellie. Demarest, Chris L. LC 90-39986. 32p. (gr. k-3). 1991. pap. 3.95 (*0-689-71474-2*, Aladdin) Macmillan Child Grp.
—Today I'm Going Fishing with My Dad. Sharp, N. L. 32p. (ps-3). 1993. 14.95 (*1-56397-107-0*) Boyds Mills Pr.
—Two Badd Babies. Gordon, Jeffie R. LC 91-72869. 32p. (ps-3). 1992. 13.95 (*1-878093-85-1*) Boyds Mills Pr.

—What's on the Menu? Goldstein, Bobbye S., compiled by. 32p. (ps-3). 1992. PLB 12.50 (*0-670-83031-3*) Viking Child Bks.
—When Cows Come Home. Harrison, David L. 32p. (ps-3). 1994. 14.95 (*1-56397-143-7*) Boyds Mills Pr.
De Matharel, Laure. Musical Chairs & Dancing Bears. Rocklin, Joanne. LC 92-41078. 32p. (ps-2). 1993. PLB 14.95 (*0-8050-2374-7*, Bks Young Read) H Holt & Co.
De Mejo, Oscar. La Bella Magellona: And the Little Cavalier. De Mejo, Oscar. 32p. (gr. k-4). 1992. PLB 14.95 (*0-399-22138-7*, Philomel Bks) Putnam Pub Group.
—Does God Have a Big Toe? Stories about Stories in the Bible. Gellman, Marc. LC 89-1893. 96p. (gr. 4 up). 1989. 16.00 (*0-06-022432-0*); PLB 15.89 (*0-06-022433-9*) HarpC Child Bks.
—Does God Have a Big Toe? Stories about Stories in the Bible. Gellman, Marc. LC 89-1893. 96p. (gr. 4 up). 1993. pap. 7.95 (*0-06-440453-6*, Trophy) HarpC Child Bks.
—Oscar de Mejo's ABC. De Mejo, Oscar. LC 91-28768. 32p. (ps up). 1992. 17.00 (*0-06-020516-4*); PLB 16.89 (*0-06-020517-2*) HarpC Child Bks.
Demeyer, Paul. Dial D for Disaster. Thomson, Pat. 32p. (gr. 1-4). 1990. 13.95 (*0-575-04572-8*, Pub. by Gollancz UK) Trafalgar.
—Goblin Party. Hill, Douglas. 44p. (gr. 3-5). 1990. 13.95 (*0-575-04338-5*, Pub. by Gollancz England) Trafalgar.
Demi. The Artist & the Architect. Demi. LC 90-40936. 32p. (ps-2). 1991. 15.95 (*0-8050-1580-9*, Bks Young Read); PLB 15.89 (*0-8050-1685-6*) H Holt & Co.
—Bamboo Hats & a Rice Cake: A Tale Adapted from Japanese Folklore. Tompert, Ann. LC 92-26849. 32p. (ps-3). 1993. 13.00 (*0-517-59272-X*); PLB 13.99 (*0-517-59273-8*) Crown Bks Yng Read.
—A Chinese Zoo: Fables & Proverbs. LC 86-33562. 32p. (ps-3). 1987. 14.95 (*0-15-217510-5*, HB Juv Bks) HarBrace.
—Chingis Khan. Demi. LC 90-28807. 64p. (gr. 3-5). 1991. 19.95 (*0-8050-1708-9*, Bks Young Read) H Holt & Co.
—Cuddly Chick. Demi. 12p. (ps). 1987. bds. 6.95 (*0-448-19154-7*, G&D) Putnam Pub Group.
—Demi's Count the Animals One-Two-Three. Demi. LC 85-81653. 48p. (ps-2). 1986. PLB 12.95 (*0-448-18980-1*, G&D) Putnam Pub Group.
—Demi's Dozen Farm Friends, 12 bks. Demi. (ps-2). 1992. Set. 9.95 (*0-8050-1956-1*, Bks Young Read) H Holt & Co.
—Demi's Dragons & Fantastic Creatures. Demi. 50p. (ps-2). 1993. PLB 19.95 (*0-8050-2564-2*, Bks Young Read) H Holt & Co.
—Demi's Find the Animal ABC. Demi. LC 85-70285. 48p. (ps up). 1985. 12.95 (*0-448-18970-4*, G&D) Putnam Pub Group.
—Demi's Opposites: An Animal Game Book. Demi. (ps-2). 1990. 10.95 (*0-448-18995-X*, G&D) Putnam Pub Group.
—Demi's Secret Garden. Demi, compiled by. LC 92-27204. 50p. (ps-2). 1993. PLB 19.95 (*0-8050-2553-7*, Bks Young Read) H Holt & Co.
—Downy Duckling. Demi. 12p. (ps). 1987. bds. 6.95 (*0-448-19153-9*, G&D) Putnam Pub Group.
—The Empty Pot. Demi. LC 89-39062. 32p. (ps-2). 1990. 15.95 (*0-8050-1217-6*, Bks Young Read) H Holt & Co.
—Find Demi's Dinosaurs: An Animal Game Book. Demi. 50p. (ps-3). 1989. 15.95 (*0-448-19020-6*, G&D) Putnam Pub Group.
—Find Demi's Sea Creatures. Demi. 1991. 14.95 (*0-399-22112-3*) Putnam Pub Group.
—Fleecy Lamb. Demi. 12p. (gr. 4 up). 1987. 6.95 (*0-448-19152-0*, G&D) Putnam Pub Group.
—In the Eyes of the Cat. Demi, selected by. Tze-Si Huang, tr. from JPN. LC 91-27709. 80p. (gr. 1-3). 1992. 15.95 (*0-8050-1955-3*, Bks Young Read) H Holt & Co.
—Liang & the Magic Paintbrush. Demi. LC 80-11351. 32p. (ps-2). 1988. pap. 5.95 (*0-8050-0801-2*, Bks Young Read) H Holt & Co.
—Light Another Candle: The Story & Meaning of Hanukkah. 1987 ed. Chaikin, Miriam. (gr. 7 up). 1981. pap. 6.95 (*0-89919-057-X*, Clarion Bks) HM.
—Little Baby Lamb. Demi. 12p. (ps). 1993. bds. 3.95 (*0-448-40580-6*, G&D) Putnam Pub Group.
—Little Bitty Bunny. Demi. LC 90-85828. 12p. (ps). 1992. 3.95 (*0-448-41089-3*, G&D) Putnam Pub Group.
—Little Chick Chick. Demi. LC 90-85829. 12p. (ps). 1992. 3.95 (*0-448-41090-7*, G&D) Putnam Pub Group.
—Little Lucky Ducky. Demi. 12p. (ps). 1993. bds. 3.95 (*0-448-40581-4*, G&D) Putnam Pub Group.
—The Magic Boat. Demi. LC 90-4425. 32p. (ps-2). 1990. 15.95 (*0-8050-1141-2*, Bks Young Read) H Holt & Co.
—The Magic Tapestry: A Chinese Folktale. Demi, retold by. LC 93-11426. 1994. write for info. (*0-8050-2810-2*) H Holt & Co.
—Make Noise, Make Merry: The Story & Meaning of Purim. Chaikin, Miriam. LC 82-12926. 96p. (gr. 3-6). 1986. pap. 4.95 (*0-89919-424-9*, Clarion Bks) HM.
—The Nightingale. Andersen, Hans Christian. 32p. (ps-3). 1988. pap. 3.95 (*0-15-257428-X*, Voyager Bks) HarBrace.
—So Soft Kitty. Demi. 12p. (ps). 1986. pap. 6.95 (*0-448-18986-0*, G&D) Putnam Pub Group.

—Watch Harry Grow! Demi. LC 84-60109. 26p. (ps-1). 1984. bds. 3.50 (0-394-86857-9) Random Bks Yng Read.

—Where Is Willie Worm? Demi. LC 80-53680. 24p. (ps-1). 1981. 3.95 (0-394-84759-8) Random Bks Yng Read.

Deming, Susan. The Desert: A Nature Panorama. Deming, Susan. 7p. (ps-3). 1991. bds. 5.95 (0-8118-0291-4) Chronicle Bks.

—The Ocean: A Nature Panorama. Deming, Susan. 7p. (ps-3). 1992. bds. 5.95 (0-8118-0158-6) Chronicle Bks.

—The River: A Nature Panorama. Deming, Susan. 7p. (ps-3). 1991. bds. 5.95 (0-87701-812-X) Chronicle Bks.

De Miskey, Julian. Chucaro: Wild Pony of the Pampa. Kalnay, Francis. 115p. 1993. pap. 6.95 (0-8027-7387-7) Walker & Co.

Dempster, Al & Justice, Bill. Walt Disney's Uncle Remus Stories. Harris, Joel C. Palmer, Marion, ed. (gr. 3-5). 1964. write for info. (0-307-15551-X, Golden Bks) Western Pub.

Denetsosie, Hoke. Little Herder in Autumn. Clark, Ann N. Harrington, John P., ed. Young, Robert W., tr. LC 88-70848. (ENG & NAV.). 96p. (gr. 1-5). 1988. pap. 9.95 (0-941270-46-7) Ancient City Pr.

—Lucy Learns to Weave: Gathering Plants. Hoffman, Virginia. LC 74-4894. 46p. (gr. 1-4). 1974. pap. 7.00 (0-89019-009-7) Rough Rock Pr.

De Neuville, C. & Benett, L. Tour du Monde en Quatre-Vingts Jours. Verne, Jules. (FRE.). 333p. (gr. 5-10). 1988. pap. 10.95 (2-07-033521-6) Schoenhof.

Dengler, Sandy. Smokey, a Simple Country Bear Who Made Good. Dengler, Sandy. 31p. (gr. 3-5). 1987. pap. text ed. 3.00 (0-914019-15-5) NW Interpretive.

Denman, Cherry. The Little Peacock's Gift: A Folk Tale from China. Denman, Cherry. LC 87-17504. 32p. (gr. k-3). 1988. PLB 14.95 (0-87226-175-1, Bedrick Blackie) P Bedrick Bks.

Denn, et al. Rack 'em Daddy! By the Pied Piper of Pool. Denn, Jon. LC 92-73955. 128p. (Orig.). (gr. 3). 1992. pap. 13.95 (0-9634187-5-0) Colburn Pr.

Dennen, Susan. Ticket to the Twenties: A Time Traveler's Guide. Blocksma, Mary. LC 92-24303. 1993. 19.95 (0-316-09974-0) Little.

Dennis, David M. Snakes: Their Place in the Sun. McClung, Robert. 64p. (gr. 2-4). 1991. 14.95 (0-8050-1718-6, Bks Young Read) H Holt & Co.

—Snakes: Their Place in the Sun. McClung, Robert M. LC 91-692. 64p. (gr. 2-4). 1993. pap. 4.95 (0-8050-2893-5, Bks Young Read) H Holt & Co.

Dennis, Lynne. The Alphabet Between. McGee, Marni. LC 91-25489. 32p. (ps-1). 1994. SBE 14.95 (0-689-31753-0, Atheneum Child Bk) Macmillan Child Grp.

—The Quiet Farmer. McGee, Marni. LC 90-37930. 32p. (ps-1). 1991. SBE 12.95 (0-689-31678-X, Atheneum Child Bk) Macmillan Child Grp.

Dennis, Wesley. Album of Horses. Henry, Marguerite. LC 92-33009. 112p. (gr. 2-5). 1993. pap. 9.95 (0-689-71709-1, Aladdin) Macmillan Child Grp.

—Brighty: Of the Grand Canyon. reissued ed. Henry, Marguerite. LC 53-7233. 224p. (gr. 3-7). 1991. SBE 13.95 (0-02-743664-0, Macmillan Child Bk) Macmillan Child Grp.

—Brighty: Of the Grand Canyon. Henry, Marguerite. LC 90-28636. 224p. (gr. 3-7). 1991. pap. 3.95 (0-689-71485-8, Aladdin) Macmillan Child Grp.

—Flip. Dennis, Wesley. (ps-1). 1977. pap. 3.95 (0-14-050203-3, Puffin) Puffin Bks.

—Flip & the Morning. Dennis, Wesley. LC 51-13521. (ps-1). 1977. pap. 3.95 (0-14-050204-1, Puffin) Puffin Bks.

—Justin Morgan Had a Horse. 2nd ed. Henry, Marguerite. LC 91-13973. 176p. (gr. 3-7). 1991. pap. 3.95 (0-689-71534-X, Aladdin) Macmillan Child Grp.

—Kentucky Derby Champion. rev. ed. Pace, Mildred M. Gifford, James M., et al, eds. 144p. (gr. 3 up). 1993. Repr. of 1955 ed. 12.00 (0-945084-36-6) J Stuart Found.

—King of the Wind: The Story of the Godolphin Arabian. 2nd ed. Henry, Marguerite. LC 48-8773. 176p. (gr. 3-7). 1990. SBE 13.95 (0-02-743629-2, Macmillan Child Bk) Macmillan Child Grp.

—King of the Wind: The Story of the Godolphin Arabian. Henry, Marguerite. 176p. (gr. 3-7). 1991. pap. 3.95 (0-689-71486-6, Aladdin) Macmillan Child Grp.

—Misty of Chincoteague. reissued ed. Henry, Marguerite. LC 47-11404. 176p. (gr. 3-7). 1990. SBE 13.95 (0-02-743622-5, Macmillan Child Bk); pap. 3.95 (0-02-688759-2) Macmillan Child Grp.

—Misty of Chincoteague. Henry, Marguerite. LC 90-27237. 176p. (gr. 3-7). 1991. pap. 3.95 (0-689-71492-0, Aladdin) Macmillan Child Grp.

—The Red Pony. reissue ed. Steinbeck, John. (gr. 7 up). 1986. pap. 15.95 (0-670-59184-X) Viking Child Bks.

—Stormy, Misty's Foal. Henry, Marguerite. LC 90-27306. 224p. (gr. 3-7). 1991. pap. 3.95 (0-689-71487-4, Aladdin) Macmillan Child Grp.

—The White Stallion of Lipizza. Henry, Marguerite. LC 93-86024. 112p. (gr. 3-7). 1994. Repr. of 1964 ed. SBE 15.95 (0-02-743628-4, Macmillan Child Bk) Macmillan Child Grp.

—White Stallion of Lipizza. Henry, Marguerite. 112p. 1994. pap. 9.95 (0-689-71824-1, Aladdin) Macmillan Child Grp.

Dennison, Graham, jt. illus. see Hall, Douglas.

Dennison, Graham, jt. illus. see Oak-Rhind, Mary.

Denslow, W. W. Denslow's Picture Book Treasury. 80p. (ps-2). 1990. 17.95 (1-55970-071-8) Arcade Pub Inc.

—The Wizard of Oz Waddle Book. Baum, L. Frank. LC 93-10069. 1993. 24.95 (1-55709-205-2); ltd. collector's ed. 85.00 (1-55709-203-6) Applewood.

—Wonderful Wizard of Oz. Baum, L. Frank. Gardner, Martin, intro. by. vii, 268p. (gr. k-6). 1960. pap. 7.95 (0-486-20691-2) Dover.

—Wonderful Wizard of Oz. Baum, L. Frank. (gr. 4 up). 19.25 (0-8446-1610-9) Peter Smith.

—The Wonderful Wizard of Oz. Baum, L. Frank. Glassman, Peter, afterword by. LC 86-62556. 316p. (ps up). 1987. 19.95 (0-688-06944-4) Morrow Jr Bks.

—The Wonderful Wizard of Oz. large type ed. Baum, L. Frank. 188p. (gr. 2-6). 1987. lib. bdg. 13.95 (1-55736-013-8, Crnrstn Bks) BDD LT Grp.

—The Wonderful Wizard of Oz. Baum, L. Frank. LC 92-53173. 192p. 1992. 12.95 (0-679-41794-X, Evrymans Lib Childs Class) Knopf.

Denton, Kady M. Before I Go to Sleep: A Collection of Bible Stories, Poems & Prayers for Children. Pilling, Ann. LC 89-7816. 96p. 1990. PLB 15.99 (0-517-58019-5) Crown Bks Yng Read.

—Granny Is a Darling. Denton, Kady M. LC 89-18397. 32p. (ps-2). 1990. pap. 4.95 (0-689-71207-3, Aladdin) Macmillan Child Grp.

—Janet's Horses. Denton, Kady M. 32p. (ps-2). 1991. 12.70 (0-395-51601-3, Clarion Bks) HM.

—The Kingfisher Children's Bible. Pilling, Ann, retold by. LC 92-42679. 1993. 18.95 (1-85697-840-0) Kingfisher Bks.

—Realms of Gold: Myths & Legends from Around the World. Pilling, Ann. LC 92-30858. 1993. 16.95 (1-85697-913-X) Kingfisher Bks.

—Til All the Stars Have Fallen: A Collection of Poems for Children. Booth, David, selected by. 96p. (ps-3). 1994. pap. 6.99 (0-14-034438-1) Puffin Bks.

—The Traveling Musicians of Bremen. Page, P. K., retold by. 32p. (ps-3). 1992. 13.95 (0-316-68836-3, Joy St Bks) Little.

Denton, Terry. Home Is the Sailor. Denton, Terry. 32p. (gr. k-3). 1989. 13.45 (0-395-51525-4) HM.

—The School for Laughter. Denton, Terry. 32p. (gr. k-3). 1990. 13.45 (0-395-53353-8) HM.

—The Story of Imelda, Who Was Small. Lurie, Morris. 32p. (gr. k-3). 1988. 13.45 (0-395-48663-7) HM.

Denver Museum of Art Staff. Bats: Swift Shadows of the Twilight. Cooper, Ann. 64p. (gr. 3-6). 1993. pap. text ed. 7.95x (1-879373-52-1) R Rinehart.

De Paola, Tomie. The Art Lesson. De Paola, Tomie. 32p. (ps-3). 1989. 13.95 (0-399-21688-X, Putnam) Putnam Pub Group.

—The Badger & the Magic Fan: A Japanese Folktale. Johnston, Tony. 32p. (ps-3). 1990. 13.95 (0-399-21945-5, Putnam) Putnam Pub Group.

—The Baseball Birthday Party. Prager, Annabelle. LC 93-25258. 1994. write for info. (0-679-84171-7); PLB write for info. (0-679-94171-1) Random Bks Yng Read.

—Beat the Drum: Independence Day Has Come. Hopkins, Lee B., selected by. LC 92-85033. 32p. (gr. 1-4). 1993. reinforced 9.95 (1-878093-60-6, Wordsong) Boyds Mills Pr.

—Big Anthony & the Magic Ring. De Paola, Tomie. LC 78-23631. 32p. (gr. k up). 1979. 14.95 (0-15-207124-5); pap. 4.95 (0-15-611907-2) HarBrace.

—Bill & Pete. De Paola, Tomie. LC 78-5330. (gr. k-2). 1978. 14.95 (0-399-20646-9, Putnam); pap. 5.95 (0-399-20650-7, Putnam) Putnam Pub Group.

—Bill & Pete Go Down the Nile. De Paola, Tomie. 32p. (ps-1). 1987. 14.95 (0-399-21395-3, Putnam) Putnam Pub Group.

—The Carsick Zebra & Other Animal Riddles. Adler, David A. LC 82-48750. 64p. (gr. 1-4). 1983. reinforced bdg. 12.95 (0-8234-0479-X) Holiday.

—The Carsick Zebra & Other Animal Riddles. Adler, David A. 64p. (Orig.). (gr. 1). 1985. pap. 2.25 (0-553-15487-7) Bantam.

—The Cloud Book. De Paola, Tomie. LC 74-34493. 32p. (ps-3). 1975. reinforced bdg. 14.95 (0-8234-0259-2); pap. 5.95 (0-8234-0531-1) Holiday.

—The Clown of God. De Paola, Tomie. LC 78-3845. (gr. k up). 1978. 13.95 (0-15-219175-5, HB Juv Bks) HarBrace.

—The Clown of God. De Paola, Tomie. LC 78-3845. 45p. (ps-3). 1978. pap. 5.95 (0-15-618192-4, Voyager Bks) HarBrace.

—Cookie's Week. Ward, Cindy. 32p. (ps-1). 1988. 11.95 (0-399-21498-4, Putnam) Putnam Pub Group.

—Cookie's Week. Ward, Cindy. 32p. (ps). 1992. pap. 4.95 (0-399-22406-8, Putnam) Putnam Pub Group.

—Danny & His Thumb. Ernst, Kathryn F. (ps-3). 1975. (Pub. by Treehouse); pap. 4.95 (0-13-196808-4) P-H.

—An Early American Christmas. De Paola, Tomie. LC 86-3102. 32p. (ps-3). 1987. reinforced bdg. 15.95 (0-8234-0617-2); pap. 5.95 (0-8234-0979-1) Holiday.

—For Every Child a Star: A Christmas Story. Yeomans, Thomas. LC 84-499. 32p. (ps-3). 1986. reinforced bdg. 14.95 (0-8234-0526-5) Holiday.

—Four Stories for Four Seasons. De Paola, Tomie. LC 76-8837. (ps-3). 1977. PLB 9.95 o. p. (0-13-330175-3, Pub. by Treehouse); pap. 3.95 (0-13-330100-1) P-H.

—Francis: The Poor Man of Assisi. De Paola, Tomie. LC 81-6984. 48p. (ps-3). 1982. reinforced bdg. 16.95 (0-8234-0435-8); pap. 6.95 (0-8234-0812-4) Holiday.

—The Friendly Beasts: An Old English Christmas Carol. De Paola, Tomie. 32p. (ps-2). 1981. (Putnam); pap. 7.95 (0-399-20777-5, Putnam) Putnam Pub Group.

—The Ghost with the Halloween Hiccups. Mooser, Stephen. 32p. (gr. k-3). 1978. pap. 2.95 (0-380-40287-4, Camelot) Avon.

—The Good Giants & The Bad Pukwudgies. Fritz, Jean. 40p. (gr. 3-7). 1982. 15.95 (0-399-21732-0, Sandcastle Bks); pap. 5.95 (0-399-21732-0, Sandcastle Bks) Putnam Pub Group.

—The Great Adventure of Christopher Columbus. Fritz, Jean. 1992. 15.95 (0-399-22113-1, Putnam) Putnam Pub Group.

—Haircuts for the Woolseys. De Paola, Tomie. 24p. (ps-1). 1989. 5.95 (0-399-21662-6, Putnam) Putnam Pub Group.

—Hark! A Christmas Sampler. Yolen, Jane, ed. LC 90-42865. 128p. 1991. 19.95 (0-399-21853-X, Putnam) Putnam Pub Group.

—Helga's Dowry. De Paola, Tomie. LC 76-54953. 32p. (gr. k-3). 1977. 15.95 (0-15-233701-6, HB Juv Bks) HarBrace.

—Helga's Dowry. De Paola, Tomie. LC 76-54953. 32p. (gr. k-3). 1977. pap. 4.95 (0-15-640010-3, Voyager Bks) HarBrace.

—Hey Diddle Diddle: And Other Mother Goose Rhymes. (gr. 1 up). 1988. pap. 5.95 (0-399-21589-1, Putnam) Putnam Pub Group.

—I Love You, Mouse. Graham, John. LC 76-8022. (ps-2). 1976. 12.95 (0-15-238005-1, HB Juv Bks) HarBrace.

—I Love You, Mouse. Graham, John. LC 78-6214. 32p. (ps-2). 1990. pap. 3.95 (0-15-644106-3, Voyager Bks) HarBrace.

—If He's My Brother. Williams, Barbara. (ps-2). 1980. pap. 2.50 (0-13-450627-8, Pub. by Treehouse) P-H.

—John Fisher's Magic Book. Fisher, John. (gr. 5-8). 1975. pap. 1.95 (0-13-510222-7, Pub. by Treehouse) P-H.

—The Lady of Guadalupe. De Paola, Tomie. LC 79-19610. 48p. (ps-4). 1980. reinforced bdg. 16.95 (0-8234-0373-4); pap. 6.95 (0-8234-0403-X) Holiday.

—The Legend of Old Befana. De Paola, Tomie. LC 80-12293. 32p. (gr. 1-5). 1980. 14.95 (0-15-243816-5, HB Juv Bks) HarBrace.

—The Legend of Old Befana. De Paola, Tomie. LC 80-12293. 32p. (gr. 1-5). 1980. pap. 3.95 (0-15-243817-3, Voyager Bks) HarBrace.

—The Legend of the Bluebonnet: An Old Tale of Texas. De Paola, Tomie, retold by. LC 82-12391. 32p. (ps-3). 1983. 14.95 (0-399-20937-9, Putnam); pap. 5.95 (0-399-20938-7, Putnam) Putnam Pub Group.

—The Legend of the Indian Paintbrush. De Paola, Tomie, ed. LC 87-20160. 40p. (ps-2). 1988. 14.95 (0-399-21534-4, Putnam) Putnam Pub Group.

DePaola, Tomie. La Leyenda Del Pincel Indio: The Legend of the Indian Paintbrush. De Paola, Tomie. 32p. (ps-2). 1993. pap. 5.95 (0-399-22604-4, Putnam) Putnam Pub Group.

—Little Grunt & the Big Egg. DePaola, Tomie. (ps-3). 1993. pap. 5.95 (0-8234-1027-7) Holiday.

De Paola, Tomie. Little Grunt & the Big Egg: A Prehistoric Fairy Tale. De Paola, Tomie. LC 88-17009. 32p. (ps-3). 1990. reinforced bdg. 14.95 (0-8234-0730-6) Holiday.

—Maggie & the Monster. Winthrop, Elizabeth. LC 86-19593. 32p. (ps-3). 1987. reinforced bdg. 15.95 (0-8234-0639-3); pap. 5.95 (0-8234-0698-9) Holiday.

—Marianna May & Nursey. De Paola, Tomie. LC 82-9364. 32p. (ps-3). 1983. reinforced bdg. 14.95 (0-8234-0473-0); pap. 5.95 (0-8234-0623-7) Holiday.

—Mary Had a Little Lamb. Hale, Sarah J. LC 83-22369. 32p. (ps-3). 1984. reinforced bdg 14.95 (0-8234-0509-5); pap. 5.95 (0-8234-0519-2) Holiday.

—Mary Had a Little Lamb. Hale, Sarah J. (ps-2). 1989. bk. & cassette 19.95 (0-87499-125-0); pap. 12.95 bk. & cassette (0-87499-124-2); pap. 27.95 4 cassettes & guide (0-87499-126-9) Live Oak Media.

—Merry Christmas, Strega Nona. De Paola, Tomie. LC 86-4639. 32p. (ps-3). 1986. 14.95 (0-15-253183-1, HB Juv Bks) HarBrace.

—Michael Bird-Boy. De Paola, Tomie. LC 74-23563. 32p. (gr. 4 up). 1987. 12.95 (0-317-63504-2) P-H.

—Miracle on Thirty-Fourth Street. Davies, Valentine. (gr. k up). 1984. 16.95 (0-15-254526-3, HB Juv Bks) HarBrace.

—The Miracles of Jesus. De Paola, Tomie. LC 86-18297. 32p. (gr. k-4). 1987. reinforced bdg. 15.95 (0-8234-0635-0) Holiday.

—The Mountains of Quilt. Willard, Nancy. LC 86-19577. 32p. (ps-3). 1987. 12.95 (0-15-256010-6, HB Juv Bks) HarBrace.

—My First Chanukah. De Paola, Tomie. 12p. (ps-k). 1989. 5.95 (0-399-21780-0, Putnam) Putnam Pub Group.

—The Mysterious Giant of Barletta. De Paola, Tomie. LC 83-18445. 32p. (ps-3). 1988. pap. 3.95 (0-15-256349-0, Voyager Bks) HarBrace.

—Nana Upstairs & Nana Downstairs. new ed. De Paola, Tomie. 32p. (ps-3). 1973. 13.95 (0-399-21417-8, Putnam) Putnam Pub Group.

—Nicholas Bentley Stoningpot III. reissue ed. McGovern, Ann. 32p. (ps-3). 1992. PLB 14.95 (1-56397-104-6) Boyds Mills Pr.

—The Night Before Christmas. Moore, Clement C. LC 80-11758. 32p. (ps up). 1980. reinforced bdg. 14.95 (0-8234-0414-5); pap. 5.95 (0-8234-0417-X) Holiday.

—The Night Before Christmas. Moore, Clement C. (gr. k-3). 1984. incl. cassette 19.95 (0-317-07112-2); pap. 12.95 incl. cassette (0-941078-37-X); incl. 4 bks., cassette, & guide 27.95 (0-685-08869-3) Live Oak Media.

—Noah & the Ark. De Paola, Tomie. 40p. (Orig.). (ps-4). 1985. pap. 5.95 (0-685-07222-3) Harper SF.
—Now One Foot, Now the Other. De Paola, Tomie. 48p. (gr. 3-7). 1981. 13.95 (0-399-20774-0, Putnam); pap. 5.95 (0-399-20775-9) Putnam Pub Group.
—Oh, Such Foolishness! Poems Selected by William Cole. Cole, William, selected by. LC 78-1622. 96p. (gr. 4-6). 1991. PLB 13.89 (0-397-32502-9, Lipp Jr Bks) HarpC Child Bks.
—Oliver Button Is a Sissy. De Paola, Tomie. LC 78-12624. 48p. (gr. k-3). 1979. 11.95 (0-15-257852-8, HB Juv Bks) HarBrace.
—Oliver Button Is a Sissy. De Paola, Tomie. LC 78-12624. 46p. (ps-3). 1979. pap. 4.95 (0-15-668140-4, Voyager Bks) HarBrace.
—Pages of Music. Johnston, Tony. 32p. (gr. k-3). 1988. PLB 13.95 (0-399-21436-4, Putnam) Putnam Pub Group.
—Pancakes for Breakfast. De Paola, Tomie. LC 77-15523. 32p. (ps-2). 1978. 14.95 (0-15-259455-8, HB Juv Bks) HarBrace.
—Pancakes for Breakfast. De Paola, Tomie. LC 77-15523. 32p. (ps-2). 1978. pap. 4.95 (0-15-670768-3, Voyager Bks) HarBrace.
—The Parables of Jesus. De Paola, Tomie. LC 86-18323. 32p. (gr. k-4). 1987. reinforced bdg. 15.95 (0-8234-0636-9) Holiday.
—Patrick: Patron Saint of Ireland. De Paola, Tomie. LC 91-19417. 32p. (ps-3). 1992. reinforced bdg. 15.95 (0-8234-0924-4) Holiday.
—Petook: An Easter Story. Houselander, Caryll. LC 87-21228. 32p. (ps-3). 1988. reinforced bdg. 15.95 (0-8234-0681-4) Holiday.
—The Prince of the Dolomites. De Paola, Tomie. LC 79-18524. 46p. (gr. 1-5). 1980. pap. 4.50 (0-15-674432-5, Voyager Bks) HarBrace.
—The Quilt Story. Johnston, Tony. LC 84-18212. 32p. (gr. k-2). 1992. 14.95 (0-399-21009-1, Putnam); pap. 5.95 (0-399-22403-3, Putnam) Putnam Pub Group.
—Santa's Crash-Bang Christmas. Kroll, Steven. LC 77-3025. 32p. (gr. k-3). 1977. reinforced bdg. 14.95 (0-8234-0302-5); pap. 5.95 (0-8234-0621-0) Holiday.
—Shh! We're Writing the Constitution. Fritz, Jean. 64p. (gr. 3-7). 1987. 14.95 (0-399-21403-8, Putnam); pap. 6.95 (0-399-21404-6, Putnam) Putnam Pub Group.
—Simple Pictures Are Best. Willard, Nancy. LC 78-6424. 32p. (ps-3). 1978. pap. 3.95 (0-15-682625-9, Voyager Bks) HarBrace.
—Sing, Pierrot, Sing: A Picture Book in Mime. De Paola, Tomie. LC 83-8403. 32p. (ps-3). 1983. 12.95 (0-15-274988-8, HB Juv Bks) HarBrace.
—Songs of Praise. Krull, Kathleen, selected by. 32p. (ps up). 1989. 15.95 (0-15-277108-5) HarBrace.
—The Spooky Halloween Party. Prager, Annabelle. LC 81-1945. 48p. (gr. 1-4). 1981. 6.95 (0-394-84370-3); lib. bdg. 7.99 (0-394-94370-8) Pantheon.
—The Spooky Halloween Party. reissue ed. Prager, Annabelle. 48p. (gr. k-4). 1992. pap. 6.99 incl. cass. (0-679-83056-1) Random Bks Yng Read.
—The Spooky Halloween Party: A Step 2 Book. Prager, Annabelle. LC 88-37571. 48p. (gr. 1-3). 1989. lib. bdg. 7.99 (0-394-94961-7); pap. 2.95 (0-394-84961-2) Random Bks Yng Read.
DePaola, Tomie. Strega Nona Meets Her Match. DePaola, Tomie. 32p. (ps-3). 1993. 14.95 (0-685-66597-6, Putnam) Putnam Pub Group.
De Paola, Tomie. Strega Nona's Magic Lessons. De Paola, Tomie. LC 80-28260. 32p. (gr. k up). 1982. 13.95 (0-15-281785-9, HB Juv Bks) HarBrace.
—Strega Nona's Magic Lessons. De Paola, Tomie. 32p. (gr. k up). 1984. pap. 4.95 (0-15-281786-7, Voyager Bks) HarBrace.
—The Surprise Party. Prager, Annabelle. LC 87-20649. 48p. (Orig.). (gr. 1-3). 1988. PLB 7.99 (0-394-99596-1); 3.50 (0-394-89596-7) Random Bks Yng Read.
—The Tale of Rabbit & Coyote. Johnston, Tony. LC 92-43652. 1994. write for info. (0-399-22258-8, Putnam) Putnam Pub Group.
—Tattie's River Journey. Murphy, Shirley R. LC 82-45508. 32p. (ps-3). 1983. 11.95 (0-8037-8767-7) Dial Bks Young.
—Teeny Tiny. Bennett, Jill. LC 85-12347. 32p. (ps-1). 1986. 10.95 (0-399-21293-0) Putnam Pub Group.
—Tomie de Paola's Favorite Nursery Tales. De Paola, Tomie, selected by. 128p. (gr. 1 up). 1986. 18.95 (0-399-21319-8, Putnam) Putnam Pub Group.
DePaola, Tomie. Tomie DePaola's Book of Christmas Carols. De Paola, Tomie. LC 86-755157. 82p. (gr. 1 up). 1987. 19.95 (0-399-21432-1, Putnam) Putnam Pub Group.
—Tomie dePaola's Mother Goose. LC 84-26314. 127p. (ps-2). 1985. 18.95 (0-399-21258-2, Putnam) Putnam Pub Group.
De Paola, Tomie. Tony's Bread. De Paola, Tomie. 32p. (ps-3). 1989. 14.95 (0-399-21693-6, Whitebird Bks) Putnam Pub Group.
—Too Many Hopkins. De Paola, Tomie. 24p. (ps-1). 1989. 5.95 (0-399-21661-8, Putnam) Putnam Pub Group.
—The Triumphs of Fuzzy Fogtop. Rose, Anne. LC 78-72204. (gr. k-3). 1979. Dial Bks Young.
—The Tyrannosaurus Game. Kroll, Steven. LC 75-37078. 40p. (ps-3). 1976. reinforced bdg. 14.95 (0-8234-0275-4); pap. 5.95 (0-8234-0620-2) Holiday.

—The Tyrannosaurus Game. Kroll, Steven. 1988. bk. & cassette 19.95 (0-87499-096-3); bk. & cassette 12.95 (0-87499-095-5); 4 cassettes & guide 27.95 (0-87499-097-1) Live Oak Media.
—The Vanishing Pumpkin. Johnston, Tony. 32p. (ps-2). 1990. (Putnam); pap. 5.95 (0-399-20992-1, Putnam) Putnam Pub Group.
—Who's a Friend of the Water-Spurting Whale? Baker, Sanna A. 32p. (ps-1). 1987. 9.99 (0-89191-587-7, Chariot Bks) Cook.
—The Wuggie Norple Story. Pinkwater, Daniel. LC 88-878. 40p. (gr. k-4). 1988. pap. 4.50 (0-689-71257-X, Aladdin) Macmillan Child Grp.
De Paolo, Tomie. Can't You Make Them Behave, King George? Fritz, Jean. 48p. (gr. 3-6). 1982. 13.95 (0-698-20315-1, Coward); pap. 6.95 (0-698-20542-1) Putnam Pub Group.
DePauw, Sandra A. The Don't-Give-up Kid & Learning Differences: Learning Differences. 2nd ed. Gehret, Jeanne. 40p. (gr. 1-5). 1992. 13.95 (0-9625136-3-6); pap. 8.95 (0-9625136-2-8) Verbal Images Pr.
De Puthod, Daisy. The Story of Things. Morgan, Kate. 32p. (gr. 3-7). 1991. 14.95 (0-8027-6918-7); lib. bdg. 15.85 (0-8027-6919-5) Walker & Co.
DeRan, David. Morning Milking. Morris, Linda L. LC 91-13103. 32p. (gr. k up). 1991. pap. 16.95 (0-88708-173-8) Picture Bk Studio.
Deraney, Michael J. Molly's Pilgrim. Cohen, Barbara. LC 83-797. 32p. (gr. 2-5). 1983. 12.95 (0-688-02103-4); PLB 12.88 (0-688-02104-2) Lothrop.
—Molly's Pilgrim. Cohen, Barbara. (gr. k-3). 1990. pap. 3.25 (0-553-15833-3) Bantam.
—Warm in Winter. Silverman, Erica. LC 88-22691. 32p. (gr. k-3). 1989. RSBE 13.95 (0-02-782661-9, Macmillan Child Bk) Macmillan Child Grp.
—Yussel's Prayer. Cohen, Barbara. LC 80-25377. 32p. (gr. k-4). 1981. PLB 12.88 (0-688-00461-X) Lothrop.
—Yussel's Prayer: A Yom Kippur Story. Cohen, Barbara, retold by. LC 92-44551. 32p. 1993. pap. 4.95 (0-688-04581-2, Mulberry) Morrow.
DeRoo, Sally. Exploring Our Environment: A Resource Guide-Manual: Animals. DeRoo, Sally. 207p. (gr. 3-6). 1979. tchr's. ed. 5.00 (0-87879-827-7, Ann Arbor Div) Acad Therapy.
—Exploring Our Environment: Animals Student Materials One. DeRoo, Sally. 22p. (gr. 3-6). 1979. wkbk. 1.00 (0-87879-828-5, Ann Arbor Div) Acad Therapy.
—Exploring Our Environment: Animals Student Materials Two. DeRoo, Sally. 32p. (gr. 3-6). 1979. wkbk. 1.00 (0-87879-829-3, Ann Arbor Div) Acad Therapy.
De Rosa, Dee. The Amazing Adventures of Albert & His Flying Machine. Sant, Thomas. 160p. (gr. 4-7). 1990. 13.95 (0-525-67302-4, Lodestar Bks) Dutton Child Bks.
DeRosa, Dee. And the Winner Is... Roos, Stephen. LC 88-27519. 128p. (gr. 3-7). 1989. SBE 13.95 (0-689-31300-4, Atheneum Child Bk) Macmillan Child Grp.
—Best Friends. Albright, Molly. LC 87-13874. 96p. (gr. 3-6). 1988. PLB 9.89 (0-8167-1151-8); pap. text ed. 2.95 (0-8167-1152-6) Troll Assocs.
—The Big Showoffs. Albright, Molly. LC 87-13872. 96p. (gr. 3-6). 1988. PLB 9.89 (0-8167-1155-0); pap. text ed. 2.95 (0-8167-1156-9) Troll Assocs.
—The Boy Who Could Make His Mother Stop Yelling. Sondheimer, Ilse. 32p. (ps-6). 1982. lib. bdg. 9.95 (0-943156-00-9); pap. 2.95 (0-943156-01-7) Rainbow Pr NY.
De Rosa, Dee. The Christmas Spurs. Wallace, Bill. MacDonald, Patricia, ed. 128p. (gr. 3-7). 1991. pap. 2.99 (0-671-74505-0, Minstrel Bks) PB.
DeRosa, Dee. The Dream Team. Albright, Molly. LC 87-13821. 96p. (gr. 3-6). 1988. PLB 9.89 (0-8167-1153-4); pap. text ed. 2.95 (0-8167-1154-2) Troll Assocs.
De Rosa, Dee. An Elf for Christmas. Hollands, Judith. MacDonald, Patricia, ed. 80p. (Orig.). (gr. 2-5). 1990. pap. 2.99 (0-671-70170-3, Minstrel Bks) PB.
DeRosa, Dee. The Fair-Weather Friends. Roos, Stephen. LC 86-17246. 128p. (gr. 3-6). 1987. SBE 13.95 (0-689-31297-0, Atheneum Child Bk) Macmillan Child Grp.
—Leap Frog Friday. Leroe, Ellen. LC 92-8284. 48p. (gr. 2-5). 1992. 12.00 (0-525-67370-9, Lodestar Bks) Dutton Child Bks.
—The Magic of Pomme. Sondheimer, Ilse. LC 86-62731. (gr. k-4). 1990. PLB 13.95 (0-943156-02-5); pap. 4.95 (0-943156-03-3) Rainbow Pr NY.
—Meet Miss Dracula. Albright, Molly. LC 87-13871. 96p. (gr. 3-6). 1988. PLB 9.89 (0-8167-1157-7); pap. text ed. 2.95 (0-8167-1158-5) Troll Assocs.
—My Favorite Ghost. Roos, Stephen. LC 87-15186. 128p. (gr. 3-7). 1988. SBE 13.95 (0-689-31301-2, Atheneum Child Bk) Macmillan Child Grp.
—Olympia Odette Presents: My Think-Along Funbook. Nowiszewski, Nancy. 100p. (gr. k-4). 1991. wkbk. 3.95 (1-55999-157-7) LinguiSystems.
—Olympia Odette Presents: My Think 'n' Do Adventure Book. Nowiszewski, Nancy. 100p. (ps-3). 1990. spiral bdg., wkbk. 3.95 (1-55999-132-1) LinguiSystems.
—The Secret of the Haunted Doghouse. Hollands, Judith. 80p. (Orig.). (gr. 2-5). 1990. pap. 2.99 (0-671-66812-9, Minstrel) PB.
—Sticks & Stones & Skeleton Bones. Gilson, Jamie. (gr. 3-6). 1991. 12.95 (0-688-10098-8) Lothrop.

Dershowitz, Y. The Cohens of Tzefat. Zakon, Miriam S. 128p. (gr. 6-12). 1985. 12.95 (0-89906-783-2); pap. 9.95 (0-89906-784-0) Mesorah Pubns.
—Jerusalem Gems: Great Tales about Everyday People In Old Jerusalem. Sonnenfeld, Shlomo Z. 160p. 1987. 12.95 (0-89906-839-1); pap. 9.95 (0-89906-840-5) Mesorah Pubns.
—The Story of Reb Yisrael Salanter: The Legendary Founder of the Mussar Movement. Finkelman, Shimon. 96p. (gr. 6-12). 1986. 11.95 (0-89906-797-2); pap. 8.95 (0-89906-798-0) Mesorah Pubns.
—The Story of Reb Yosef Chaim: The Life & Times of Rabbi Yosef Chaim Sonnefeld, the Guardian of Jerusalem. Finkelman, S. 160p. (gr. 6-12). 1984. 11.95 (0-89906-779-4); pap. 8.95 (0-89906-780-8) Mesorah Pubns.
—The Three Merchants: And Other Stories. Weinbach, Shaindel. 160p. (gr. 6-12). 1983. 13.95 (0-89906-768-9); pap. 10.95 (0-89906-769-7) Mesorah Pubns.
Dershowitz, Yosef. The Exiles of Crocodile Island. Meyer, Henye. 224p. (gr. 6-12). 1984. 12.95 (0-89906-772-7); pap. 9.95 (0-89906-773-5) Mesorah Pubns.
—Jerusalem Diaries & Other Stories. Zakon, Miriam S. 128p. (gr. 4-12). 1993. 12.95 (0-89906-837-5); pap. 9.95 (0-89906-838-3) Mesorah Pubns.
—The Story of Reb Elchonon: The Life of Rabbi Elchonon Wasserman. Finkelman, Shimon. 160p. (gr. 6-12). 1984. 11.95 (0-89906-770-0); pap. 8.95 (0-89906-771-9) Mesorah Pubns.
—The Story of Reb Nachum'ke: The Nineteenth Century Tzaddik - A Legend in His Time. Finkelman, Shimon. 144p. (gr. 6-12). 1985. 11.95 (0-89906-781-6); pap. 8.95 (0-89906-782-4) Mesorah Pubns.
—The Story of the Chofetz Chaim. Scherman, Nosson & Gevirtz, Eliezer. 160p. (gr. 6-12). 1987. 11.95 (0-89906-766-2); pap. 8.95 (0-89906-767-0) Mesorah Pubns.
—The Story of the Sha'agas Aryeh: The Man Behind the Legend. Finkelman, Shimon. 96p. (gr. 4-12). 1986. 11.95 (0-89906-793-X); pap. 8.95 (0-89906-794-8) Mesorah Pubns.
Dershowitz, Yosef & Horen, Michael. Reb Yitzchak's Jewel: Rashi's Father Gets a Reward. Scherman, Nosson. 32p. (gr. k-6). 1988. 6.95 (0-89906-525-2) Mesorah Pubns.
DeSaix, Debbi D. The Girl Who Danced with Dolphins. DeSaix, Frank. 32p. (gr. k-3). 1991. 14.95 (0-374-32626-6) FS&G.
DeSalvo, Antonio. Bioscience II: An Advanced Biology Course Manual. rev. ed. DeFina, Anthony V. 396p. (gr. 12). 1993. tchr's. ed. 27.50 (0-916209-10-5); wkbk. student's ed. 25.00 (0-916209-11-3) Owlet Pubns.
DeSalvo-Ryan, DyAnne. The Half-Birthday Party. Pomerantz, Charlotte. LC 84-4963. 48p. (gr. 1-4). 1984. 13.95 (0-89919-273-4, Clarion Bks) HM.
—Two Dog Biscuits. rev. ed. Cleary, Beverly. LC 85-18816. 32p. (ps-1). 1986. 11.95 (0-688-05847-7); lib. bdg. 11.88 (0-688-05848-5, Morrow Jr Bks) Morrow Jr Bks.
De Santo, Rita, et al. Young People's Nature Guide. Benton, Allen H. & Bunting, Richard L. 177p. (gr. 2-4). 1978. pap. text ed. 3.00 (0-942788-05-2) Marginal Med.
De Saulles, Tony. Body Talk. Nelson, Nigel. LC 93-27780. 32p. (gr. k-2). 1993. 12.95 (1-56847-099-1) Thomson Lrning.
—Signs & Symbols. Nelson, Nigel. LC 93-27779. 32p. (gr. k-2). 1993. 12.95 (1-56847-100-9) Thomson Lrning.
Desch, Christine. Jeremy's Muffler. Nielsen, Laura F. 1994. write for info. (0-02-768135-1, Bradbury Pr) Macmillan Child Grp.
Deschaine, Scott & Bonno, Chris. Head On. Deschaine, Scott & Bonno, Chris. 36p. 1990. pap. 2.00 (1-878181-02-5) Discovery Comics.
Deschaine, Scott & Weisberg, Lynette. A Bug's Gift. Deschaine, Scott & Weisberg, Lynette. 20p. 1991. pap. 1.95 (1-878181-01-7) Discovery Comics.
De Seve, Peter. Finn McCoul. Gleeson, Brian. 40p. (gr. k up). 1993. incl. cass. 19.95 (0-88708-272-6, Rabbit Ears); 14.95 (0-88708-271-8, Rabbit Ears) Picture Bk Studio.
Design in Demand Staff. Dad: Are People Using Alcohol & Drugs As an Alternative to Problem Solving? Tate, Albert J., III. 68p. (Orig.). (gr. 10). 1992. pap. 12.95 (0-9622996-9-3) Unique Memphis.
De Silva, Jessica. Learn to Be the Master Student: How to Develop Self-Confidence & Effective Study Skills. Rooney, Robert & Lipuma, Anthony. LC 92-80281. 248p. (Orig.). (gr. 9-12). 1992. pap. 14.95 (0-9632530-8-5) Maydale Pub.
Desimini, Lisa. Adelaide & the Night Train. Rosenberg, Liz. LC 88-39948. 32p. (ps-2). 1989. HarpC Child Bks.
—Fish & Flamingo. Carlstrom, Nancy W. (ps-3). 1993. 14.95 (0-316-12859-7) Little.
—The Great Peace March. Near, Holly. LC 92-25170. 32p. (gr. 2-5). 1993. PLB 15.95 (0-8050-1941-3, Bks Young Read) H Holt & Co.
—Heron Street. Turner, Ann. LC 87-24948. 32p. (gr. 1-4). 1989. 15.00i (0-06-026184-6); PLB 14.89 (0-06-026185-4) HarpC Child Bks.
—Housekeeper of the Wind. Widman, Christine. LC 88-10979. 32p. (ps-3). 1990. PLB 15.89 (0-06-026468-3) HarpC Child Bks.

—How the Stars Fell into the Sky. Oughton, Jerrie. 32p. (gr. k-3). 1992. 14.45 (0-395-58798-0) HM.

—I Am Running Away Today. Desimini, Lisa. LC 91-25341. 32p. (ps-3). 1992. 13.95 (1-56282-120-2); PLB 13.89 (1-56282-121-0) Hyprn Child.

—The Magic Weaver of Rugs. Oughten, Jerrie. LC 93-4850. 1994. write for info. (0-395-66140-4) HM.

—Moon Soup. Desimini, Lisa. LC 92-55041. 32p. (ps-3). 1993. 14.95 (1-56282-463-5); PLB 14.89 (1-56282-464-3) Hyprn Child.

—The Passerby. Atlan, Liliane. Owens, Rochelle, tr. 96p. (gr. 7 up). 1993. PLB 13.95 (0-8050-3054-9, Bks Young Read) H Holt & Co.

DesJarlait, Robert. Sparrow Hawk. Le Sueur, Meridel. LC 87-80573. 176p. (gr. 7 up). 1987. Repr. of 1950 ed. 13.95 (0-930100-22-0) Holy Cow.

Desputeaux, Helene. The Extraordinary Ordinary Everything Room. Tregebov, Rhea. (gr. k-2). 1991. pap. 5.95 (0-929005-24-4, Pub. by Second Story Pr CN) InBook.

—Melinda's No's Gold. Chislett, Gail. 32p. (ps-2). 1991. PLB 14.95 (1-55037-196-7, Pub. by Annick CN); pap. 4.95 (1-55037-198-3, Pub. by Annick CN) Firefly Bks Ltd.

—My Uncle Max. Casson, Lee. 24p. (Orig.). (ps-2). 1990. pap. 0.99 (1-55037-130-4, Pub. by Annick CN) Firefly Bks Ltd.

—Purple, Green & Yellow. Munsch, Robert. 32p. (ps-2). 1992. PLB 14.95 (1-55037-255-6, Pub. by Annick Pr); pap. 4.95 (1-55037-256-4, Pub. by Annick Pr) Firefly Bks Ltd.

—Sasha & the Wiggly Tooth. Tregeebov, Rhea. 24p. 1993. 12.95 (0-317-05541-0, Pub. by Second Story Pr CN); pap. 5.95 (0-929005-50-3, Second Story Pr CN) InBook.

—Violet, Vert et Jaune: Purple, Green & Yellow in French. Munsch, Robert. 32p. 1992. pap. 5.95 (1-55037-272-6, Pub. by Annick Pr) Firefly Bks Ltd.

Dessereau, April & Present, David. Alaska, Uncle Jim & Me. Arnold, Marti. Lesko, Marian, ed. 146p. (Orig.). (gr. 6 up). 1983. pap. 5.95 (0-912683-00-7) Fireweed.

Detmold, Maurice, et al. The Jungle Book. Kipling, Rudyard. 320p. 1989. 12.99 (0-517-67902-7) Outlet Bk Co.

De Toulouse-Lautrec, Henri. Henri de Toulouse-Lautrec. Raboff, Ernest. LC 87-17703. 32p. (gr. 1 up). 1988. pap. 7.95 (0-06-446070-3, Trophy) HarpC Child Bks.

Detterbeck, Nancy. Coming Home: Children's Stories for Adult Children of Alcoholics. Anderson, Peggy K. LC 87-73388. 136p. (Orig.). (gr. 5-10). 1988. pap. 7.95 (0-934125-06-6) Glen Abbey Bks.

De Tuerk, Lif. The Little White Ladybug. Jones, Renata. LC 90-70475. 54p. (ps-3). 1990. 8.95 (0-932433-67-7) Windswept Hse.

Detwiler, Susan. The First Teddy Bear. Kay, Helen. LC 85-25706. 40p. (gr. 1 up). 1985. 12.95 (0-88045-042-8) Stemmer Hse.

Deuchar, Ian. The Piper's Ring. Scott, Michael. 32p. (gr. 1-3). 1993. 17.95 (0-460-88130-2, Pub. by J M Dent & Sons) Trafalgar.

Deutsch, Nicholas. The Big Good Wolf. Loring, Honey & Harris, John. 28p. (ps-6). 1990. pap. text ed. 2.75 (0-9626566-0-7) Gone Dogs.

DeVaney, Janet S. ConverStations: The Go Anywhere Speech Book. Shaw DeVaney, Janet. 48p. (gr. 2-6). 1986. 16.95 (0-937857-00-9, 1551) Speech BIn.

—Speech Stations: The One-Stop Speech Book. DeVaney, Janet S. 205p. (ps-5). 1987. 24.95 (0-937857-03-3, 1552) Speech Bin.

DeVelasco, Joe. Acts 13-28: Missions Accomplished. Fromer, Margaret & Nystrom, Carolyn. 93p. (gr. 7-12). 1979. saddle-stitched tchr's. ed. 4.99 (0-87788-011-5); saddle- stitched student ed. 3.99 (0-87788-010-7) Shaw Pubs.

Deverell, Christine, jt. illus. see Deverell, Richard.

Deverell, Richard & Deverell, Christine. How They Lived in Bible Times. Jones, Graham. LC 91-30420. 48p. (gr. 1-8). 1992. 12.99 (0-8307-1574-6, 5112125) Regal.

De Vico, Elvira. The Night of the Shepherds: A Christmas Experience. Quaglini, Juliana. Flanagan, Anne J., tr. from ITA. LC 93-25027. 32p. (gr. 4 up). 1993. pap. 3.95 (0-8198-5128-0) St Paul Bks.

Devi-Doolin, Daya. Dormck. Devi-Doolin, Daya. LC 89-8613. 10p. (Orig.). (gr. 2-5). 1989. pap. 4.50 (1-877945-01-3) Padarin Pubns.

Devi-Doolin, Daya & Joiner, Eddie. Dabney, Dormck & Wiggle's Slakadunan Adventure. Devi-Doolin, Daya. 50p. (Orig.). (gr. 4-8). 1989. pap. text ed. 6.50 (1-877945-02-1) Padaran Pubns.

Devito, Anna. If You Sailed on the May Flower. McGovern, Ann. 80p. 1991. pap. 3.95 (0-590-45161-8) Scholastic Inc.

DeVito, Pam. Lydia & the Purple Paint. DeVito, Pam. Weinberger, Jane, ed. LC 89-50681. 52p. (ps-4). 1989. pap. 5.95 (0-932433-59-6) Windswept Hse.

—Oliver Bean. Bacon, Joy. Weinberger, Jane, ed. LC 90-70907. 68p. (ps-3). 1991. 12.95 (0-932433-71-5); pap. 9.95 (0-932433-73-1) Windswept Hse.

—The Other Side of the Desk. Bunt, Sandra K. LC 90-71374. 135p. (Orig.). (gr. 3-6). 1992. pap. 9.95 (0-932433-80-4) Windswept Hse.

—Shopping at the Ani-Mall. Bullock, Gloria S. & Crocitto, Jane B. Weinberger, Jane, ed. LC 90-70475. 44p. (ps-3). 1991. pap. 9.95 (0-932433-72-3) Windswept Hse.

—Sweet Dreams, Sarah. Vitalo, Valerie. LC 88-51277. 54p. (ps-4). 1989. 6.95 (0-932433-56-1) Windswept Hse.

Devito, Pam, jt. illus. see Gorski, Paul.

DeVito, Pamela. Barney the Bus. Fuller, Ted. Weinberger, Jane, ed. LC 88-51276. 48p. (ps-4). 1989. pap. 7.95 (0-932433-49-9) Windswept Hse.

—Christmas Tales. Hornidge, Marilis. Weinberger, Jane, ed. LC 88-51378. 72p. (gr. 1-6). 1988. pap. 7.95 (0-932433-50-2) Windswept Hse.

—Dinni, the Dinosaur. Stone, Audrey. Weinberger, Jane, ed. LC 87-51330. 64p. (Orig.). (gr. 2-6). 1988. pap. 4.95 (0-932433-41-3) Windswept Hse.

—Dragomir. Friendly, Alfred. Weinberger, Jane & Black, Albert, eds. LC 88-50316. 46p. (ps up) 1988. pap. 9.95 (0-932433-44-8) Windswept Hse.

—Home Is Best. White, Sylvia. Weinberger, Jane & Black, Albert, eds. LC 88-50315. 44p. (gr. 1-4). 1988. pap. 3.95 (0-932433-48-0) Windswept Hse.

—The Island Merry-Go-Round. Sargent, Ruth. Weinberger, Jane, ed. LC 88-52077. 46p. (Orig.). (gr. 1-4). 1988. pap. 5.95 (0-932433-46-4) Windswept Hse.

—Merry Berry. Stewart, Celeste. Weinberger, Jane & Black, Albert, eds. LC 88-51280. 88p. (gr. 4-8). 1990. pap. 5.00 (0-932433-53-7) Windswept Hse.

Devlin, Harry. Cranberry Birthday. Devlin, Wende & Devlin, Harry. LC 92-23541. 40p. (ps-3). 1993. pap. 4.95 (0-689-71697-4, Aladdin) Macmillan Child Grp.

—Cranberry Christmas. Devlin, Wende & Devlin, Harry. LC 80-16971. 40p. (ps-3). 1984. Repr. of 1976 ed. RSBE 13.95 (0-02-729900-7, Four Winds) Macmillan Child Grp.

—Cranberry Easter. Devlin, Wende & Devlin, Harry. LC 88-21370. 40p. (gr. k-3). 1990. RSBE 13.95 (0-02-729935-X, Four Wind) Macmillan Child Grp.

—Cranberry Summer. Devlin, Wende & Devlin, Harry. LC 90-24560. 40p. (gr. k-3). 1992. RSBE 13.95 (0-02-729181-2, Four Winds) Macmillan Child Grp.

—Cranberry Thanksgiving. Devlin, Wende & Devlin, Harry. LC 80-17070. 48p. (ps-3). 1984. Repr. of 1971 ed. RSBE 13.95 (0-02-729930-9, Four Winds) Macmillan Child Grp.

—Old Black Witch. 2nd ed. Devlin, Wende & Devlin, Harry. LC 92-19897. 32p. (gr. k-3). 1992. RSBE 13.95 (0-02-729185-5, Four Winds) Macmillan Child Grp.

Devlin, Harry, jt. illus. see Devlin, Wende.

Devlin, Wende & Devlin, Harry. Cranberry Birthday. Devlin, Wende & Devlin, Harry. LC 88-294. 40p. (gr. k-3). 1988. RSBE 13.95 (0-02-729210-X, Four Winds) Macmillan Child Grp.

—Cranberry Christmas. Devlin, Wende & Devlin, Harry. LC 91-1988. 40p. (gr. k-3). 1991. pap. 3.95 (0-689-71510-2, Aladdin) Macmillan Child Grp.

—Cranberry Halloween. Devlin, Wende & Devlin, Harry. LC 89-18666. 40p. (gr. k-3). 1990. pap. 3.95 (0-689-71428-9, Aladdin) Macmillan Child Grp.

—Cranberry Thanksgiving. Devlin, Wende & Devlin, Harry. LC 89-18642. 40p. (gr. k-3). 1990. pap. 3.95 (0-689-71429-7, Aladdin) Macmillan Child Grp.

—Cranberry Valentine. Devlin, Wende & Devlin, Harry. LC 85-24047. 32p. (gr. k-3). 1986. SBE 13.95 (0-02-729200-2, Four Winds) Macmillan Child Grp.

—Cranberry Valentine. Devlin, Wende & Devlin, Harry. LC 91-6915. 40p. (gr. k-3). 1992. pap. 3.95 (0-689-71509-9, Aladdin) Macmillan Child Grp.

—Old Black Witch. Devlin, Wende & Devlin, Harry. LC 91-42133. 32p. (gr. k-3). 1992. pap. 3.95 (0-689-71636-2, Aladdin) Macmillan Child Grp.

Dew, Heather, jt. illus. see Sibbeck, John.

Dewagian, Jeanette. Beginning Math at Home. Peterson, Elizabeth J. 75p. (ps-1). 4 sets 10.95, (0-938911-01-5) Indiv Educ Syst.

—Beginning Reading at Home. Peterson, Elizabeth J. 136p. (ps-1). 1992. Repr. of 1986 ed. write for info. (0-938911-00-7) Indiv Educ Syst.

Dewan, Ted. Inside Dinosaurs & Other Prehistoric Creatures. Parker, Steve. LC 93-10045. (gr. 1-8). 1994. 16.95 (0-385-31143-5); pap. 10.95 (0-385-31189-3) Delacorte.

Dewar, Bob. Ivan: Stories of Old Russia. Crouch, Marcus. 80p. (gr. 3-7). 1989. jacketed 18.95 (0-19-274135-7) OUP.

Dewey, Ariane. Gib Morgan, Oilman. Dewey, Ariane. LC 86-284. 48p. (gr. 1-3). 1987. 11.75 (0-688-06566-X); PLB 11.88 (0-688-06567-8) Greenwillow.

—The Narrow Escapes of Davy Crockett. Dewey, Ariane. LC 88-34902. (gr. 1 up). 1990. 13.95 (0-688-08914-3); PLB 13.88 (0-688-08915-1) Greenwillow.

—Pecos Bill. Dewey, Ariane. 56p. (gr. 1 up). 1994. pap. 4.95 (0-688-13108-5, Mulberry) Morrow.

—Sally Ann Thunder Ann Whirlwind Crockett. Cohen, Caron Lee. LC 84-7978. 40p. (gr. 1-3). 1985. 11.75 (0-688-04006-3); PLB 11.88 (0-688-04007-1) Greenwillow.

—Sally Ann Thunder Ann Whirlwind Crockett. Cohen, Caron L., retold by. LC 92-24585. 40p. 1993. pap. 4.95 (0-688-12331-7, Mulberry) Morrow.

—The Tea Squall. Dewey, Ariane. 40p. (gr. 1 up). 1994. pap. 4.95 (0-688-04582-0, Mulberry) Morrow.

Dewey, Ariane, jt. illus. see Aruego, Jose.

Dewey, Ariane, jt. illus. see Arvego, Jose.

Dewey, Ariane, jt. illus. see Dewey, Jose.

Dewey, Jennifer. New Questions & Answers about Dinosaurs. Simon, Seymour. LC 88-36226. 48p. (gr. k up). 1990. 13.95 (0-688-08195-9); PLB 13.88 (0-688-08196-7, Morrow Jr Bks) Morrow Jr Bks.

—New Questions & Answers about Dinosaurs. Simon, Seymour. LC 92-25546. 48p. (gr. 2 up). 1993. pap. 4.95 (0-688-12271-X, Mulberry) Morrow.

—The Secret Language of Snow. Williams, Terry T. & Major, Ted. LC 83-19410. 144p. (gr. 3-7). 1984. 10.95 (0-394-86574-X, Pant Bks Young) Pantheon.

—Song of the Sea Otter. Hurd, Edith T. LC 83-4675. 48p. (gr. 2-7). 1983. (Pant Bks Young); PLB 9.95 (0-394-86191-4) Pantheon.

—Song of the Sea Otter. Hurd, Edith T. 40p. (gr. 2-5). 1989. pap. 5.95 (0-316-38323-6) Sierra.

—Young Kangaroo. Brown, Margaret W. 48p. (ps-3). 1993. 13.95 (1-56282-409-0); PLB 13.89 (1-56282-410-4) Hyprn Child.

Dewey, Jennifer O. The Adelie Penguin. Dewey, Jennifer O. LC 88-13010. 48p. (gr. 3-6). 1989. 15.95 (0-316-18207-9) Little.

—All about Arrowheads & Spear Points. Smith, Howard E., Jr. LC 88-39089. 80p. (gr. 4-6). 1989. 14.95 (0-8050-0892-6, Bks Young Read) H Holt & Co.

—At the Edge of the Pond. Dewey, Jennifer O. 48p. (gr. 1-5). 1987. 14.95 (0-316-18208-7) Little.

—Creatures of Earth, Sea, & Sky. Heard, Georgia. LC 91-65978. 32p. (gr. 1-4). 1992. 15.95 (1-56397-013-9, Wordsong) Boyds Mills Pr.

—Frosty: A Raccoon to Remember. Weaver, Harriett E. (gr. 5-7). 1986. pap. 2.50 (0-671-64088-7, Archway) PB.

—The Wandering Albatross. Dewey, Jennifer O. LC 88-31419. 48p. (gr. 3-6). 1989. 15.95 (0-316-18209-5) Little.

Dewey, Jennifer O. & Reade, Deborah. The Village of Blue Stone. Trimble, Stephen. LC 88-34194. 64p. (gr. 3-7). 1990. RSBE 14.95 (0-02-789501-7, Macmillan Child Bk) Macmillan Child Grp.

Dewey, Jose & Dewey, Ariane. Where Are You Going, Little Mouse? Kraus, Robert. LC 84-25868. (ps up). 1989. 4.95 (0-688-08747-7, Mulberry) Morrow.

DeWind, June & Katsma, Candi. First Corinthians Thirteen: An Illustrated Bible Chapter for Young Children. Meyer, David & Meyer, Alice, eds. LC 90-71555. 48p. (Orig.). (ps-4). 1990. pap. 12.95 incl. cassette (1-879099-01-2) Thy Word.

DeWitt, Jim. The En-Dec System of Writing & Reading. DeWitt, Jim. 52p. (Orig.). (gr. 9-12). 1987. pap. 6.95 (0-915199-74-2) Pen-Dec.

DeWitt, Nancy. Heroes & Heroines in Tlingit-Haida Legend. Beck, Mary L. LC 89-14931. 126p. (Orig.). (gr. 8 up). 1989. pap. 12.95 (0-88240-334-6) Alaska Northwest.

DeWitt, Pat & DeWitt, Robin. The Pied Piper of Hamelin. Chmielarz, Sharon, adapted by. 40p. (gr. k-6). 1990. 14.95 (0-88045-115-7) Stemmer Hse.

DeWitt, Pat, jt. illus. see DeWitt, Robin.

DeWitt, Patricia, jt. illus. see DeWitt, Robin.

DeWitt, Robin & DeWitt, Pat. Under the Greenwood Tree. Shakespeare, William. Holdridge, Barbara, ed. Rowse, A. L., pref. by. 80p. (gr. 4 up). 1986. 21.95 (0-88045-028-2); pap. 14.95 (0-88045-029-0); cass. & bk. 23.90 (0-88045-103-3); cassette only 8.95 (0-88045-100-9) Stemmer Hse.

DeWitt, Robin & DeWitt, Patricia. The Peach Tree. Pike, Norman. 36p. (ps up). 1984. 10.95 (0-88045-014-2) Stemmer Hse.

DeWitt, Robin, jt. illus. see DeWitt, Pat.

Dexter, Alison. Grandma. Dexter, Alison. LC 92-6473. 32p. (ps-2). 1993. 15.00 (0-06-021143-1); PLB 14.89 (0-06-021144-X) HarpC Child Bks.

Deyhle, Karen, jt. illus. see Phipps, Weston.

DiaGrammatics Staff. I Am a Star. Harrill, Suzanne E. 50p. (Orig.). (gr. 1-6). 1992. pap. write for info. (0-9625996-3-8); business-size cards 8.95 (0-685-52563-5) Innerworks Pub.

Diamantes, Kitty. Favorite Tales from Grimm. 96p. (gr. 3 up). 1988. 9.95 (0-02-689060-7) Checkerboard.

Diamanti, Gina. Bradley's Christmas Adventure. Connolly, Brian A. 38p. (Orig.). (gr. 1-6). 1989. pap. 7.95 (0-9624282-0-5) Steele Hollow.

Diamond, Donna. The Arrow & the Lamp: The Story of Psyche. Hodges, Margaret. LC 86-2728. (gr. 4-8). 1989. 14.95 (0-316-36790-7) Little.

—Bridge to Terabithia. Paterson, Katherine. LC 77-2221. (gr. 5 up). 1977. 14.00 (0-690-01359-0, Crowell Jr Bks) HarpC Child Bks.

—Bridge to Terabithia. Paterson, Katherine. LC 77-2221. 144p. (gr. 5-9). 1987. pap. 3.95 (0-06-440184-7, Trophy) HarpC Child Bks.

—Bridge to Terabithia. Paterson, Katherine. LC 77-2221. 144p. (gr. 5 up). 1987. Repr. of 1977 ed. PLB 13.89 (0-690-04635-9, Crowell Jr Bks) HarpC Child Bks.

—Bridge to Terabithia. large type ed. Paterson, Katherine. 155p. (gr. 2-6). 1987. Repr. of 1977 ed. lib. bdg. 14.95 (1-55736-010-3, Crnrstn Bks) BDD LT Grp.

—Dorothea Lange: Life Through the Camera. Meltzer, Milton. Lange, Dorothea, photos by. 64p. (gr. 2-6). 1986. pap. 3.95 (0-14-032105-5, Puffin) Puffin Bks.

—A Gift for Mama. Hautzig, Esther. 64p. (gr. 3-7). 1987. pap. 3.95 (0-14-032384-8, Puffin) Puffin Bks.

—Helen Keller. Kudlinski, Kathleen V. 64p. (gr. 2-6). 1991. 3.95 (0-14-032902-1) Puffin Bks.

—Helen Keller: A Light for the Blind. Kudlinski, Kathleen V. 64p. (gr. 2-6). 1989. pap. 10.95 (0-670-82460-7) Viking Child Bks.

—Horses of Dreamland. Duncan, Lois. 32p. (ps-3). 1986. 12.95 (0-316-19554-5) Little.

—Mustard. Graeber, Charlotte. 64p. 1988. pap. 2.75 (0-553-15674-8, Skylark) Bantam.

—The Remembering Box. Clifford, Eth. 64p. (gr. 2-5). 1985. 13.45 (0-395-38476-1) HM.
—Riches. Hautzig, Esther. LC 89-26904. 32p. (gr. 3 up). 1992. 14.00 (0-06-022259-X); PLB 13.89 (0-06-022260-3) HarpC Child Bks.
—The Song of the Christmas Mouse. Murphy, Shirley R. LC 89-19744. 96p. (gr. 2-5). 1990. 13.00 (0-06-024357-0); PLB 12.89 (0-06-024358-9) HarpC Child Bks.
—Zeppelin. Haugen, Tormod. Jacobs, David R., tr. from NOR. LC 92-8319. 128p. (gr. 4-7). 1992. 15.00 (0-06-020881-3); PLB 14.89 (0-06-020882-1) HarpC Child Bks. Postponed.
Diamond, Lynnell & Mueller, Marge. Let's Discover the San Juan Islands. Diamond, Lynnell & Mueller, Marge. 48p. (Orig.). 1989. pap. 4.95 (0-89886-220-5) Mountaineers.
Dian, Russell. A Man Can Be... Kempler, Susan, et al. (ps-3). 1984. 16.95 (0-89885-046-0); pap. 9.95 (0-89885-208-0) Human Sci Pr.
Dias, Ron. Disney's Beauty & the Beast. Singer, A. L., adapted by. LC 91-71340. 96p. 1991. 14.95 (1-56282-049-4); PLB 14.89 (1-56282-050-8) Disney Pr.
—Disney's the Little Mermaid: Illustrated Classic. Singer, A. L., adapted by. LC 92-74259. 96p. 1993. 14.95 (1-56282-429-5); PLB 14.89 (1-56282-430-9) Disney Pr.
—Disney's the Little Mermaid: Junior Novelization. Singer, A. L., adapted by. LC 92-74260. 64p. (gr. 2-6). 1993. pap. 2.95 (1-56282-436-8) Disney Pr.
—Walt Disney's Dumbo. Slater, Teddy, adapted by. LC 88-80740. 24p. (ps-1). 1988. write for info. (0-307-11994-7) Western Pub.
Dias, Ron, jt. illus. see Langley, Bill.
Diaz, D. Neighborhood Odes. Soto, G. 1992. 15.95 (0-15-256879-4, HB Juv Bks) HarBrace.
Diaz, David. Smoky Night. Bunting, Eve. LC 93-14885. (gr. 4 up). 1994. write for info (0-15-269954-6) Harbrace.
Diaz, Jose. Drugs, Sex, & Integrity: What Does Judaism Say? Polish, Daniel F., et al. LC 90-28763. (gr. 7-9). 1991. pap. 10.00 (0-8074-0459-4, 168505) UAHC.

Diaz, Michael A. Courageous Pacers: The Complete Guide to Running, Walking & Fitness for Kids (Ages 8-108) Erson, Tim. 250p. (Orig.). (gr. 2 up). 1993. Incl. logbook & journal. 18.95 (0-9636547-0-5) PRO-ACTIV Pubns.

Courage, Confidence, Fitness & Friendship are the themes of this book which introduces children to life skills of fun & athletics through running & walking. Inspiring & humorous, it includes 20 delightfully illustrated chapters & teaches the Courageous Pacer philosophy of respect for oneself, respect for others, & respect for the community. It also emphasizes goal setting & working through the ups & downs of goal completion. Practical advice about getting started, training, how & where to enter events, nutrition, & injury care are neatly folded into true stories of sports heroes, courageous dreamers, communities, winners & more. Excellent source for youth & adults interested in combining sports, fitness & personal growth. It's the book parents have been waiting for that will inspire champions & everyday heroes alike. Author Tim Erson, M.S., P.T., is a graduate of Columbia University's Program in Physical Therapy & a returned Peace Corps Volunteer. He has been recognized for positive & motivational leadership in youth fitness programs since 1981. Timely & intergenerational. A book for families, individuals, or groups. To order, call: (512) 884-8351, or write: PRO-ACTIV Publications, P.O. Box 331186, Corpus Christi, TX 78463-1186.

Publisher Provided Annotation.

Di Benedetto, Angelo. How the Donkeys Came to Haiti & Other Folk Tales. Johnson, Gyneth. 124p. (gr. 4-9). 12.95 (0-8159-5706-8) Devin.

Dibner, Ellen J. & Gustafson, Ronald. Book Finders for Kids: The "Easy to Use" Subject Guide to Finding Non-fiction Books in a Library. Dibner, Ellen J. & Gustafson, Ronald. LC 88-61646. 16p. (Orig.). (gr. 2-8). 1988. pap. 2.95 (0-9620888-0-3) Point Publications.
DiCicco, Dan. The Mayday Rampage. Bess, Clayton. LC 92-74268. 208p. (gr. 9-12). 1993. 14.95 (1-882405-00-5); pap. 7.95 (1-882405-01-3); 3 audiocassettes, incl. AIDS curriculum unit w/ tchr's. guide 21.95 (1-882405-02-1) Lookout Pr.
DiCicco, Gil. The Villains Collection: Stories from the Films. Strasser, Todd. Rifkin, Mark, contrib. by. LC 93-70882. 80p. 1993. 14.95 (1-56282-500-3); PLB 14. 89 (1-56282-501-1) Disney Pr.
—Walt Disney's One Hundred One Dalmatians. Braybrooks, Ann, adapted by. LC 90-85425. 72p. (Orig.). (gr. 2-6). 1991. pap. 2.95 (1-56282-013-3) Disney Pr.
DiCicco, Sue. Baby Gonzo in Backwardsland. Weiss, Ellen. 26p. (ps up). 1987. 12.95 (1-55578-603-0) Worlds Wonder.
—Disney's Darkwing Duck in Clean Money. Bazaldua, Barbara. 24p. (ps-3). 1992. write for info. (0-307-12668-4, 12668) Western Pub.
—Disney's The Little Mermaid: Ariel's Secret. Patrick, Denise L. 14p. (ps-k). 1992. bds. write for info. (0-307-12393-6, 12393, Golden Pr) Western Pub.
—I Am Mickey Mouse. West, Cyndy. (ps-k). 1991. 3.50 (0-307-12166-6, Golden Pr) Western Pub.
—Oh, Bother! Someone's Baby-Sitting! Disney's Winnie the Pooh Helping Hands Book. Grimes, N. 24p. (ps-k). 1991. pap. write for info. (Golden Pr) Western Pub.
—Walt Disney's Alice in Wonderland: Book of Colors. Balducci, Rita. 12p. (ps). 1993. bds. 1.95 (0-307-06079-9, 6079, Golden Pr) Western Pub.
Dick, Jo A. & Ferreri, Donna. T. A. for Tots: (& Other Prinzes) rev. ed. Freed, Alvyn M. 144p. (ps-5). 1991. pap. 14.95 (0-915190-73-7, JP9073-7) Jalmar Pr.
Dick, Joann. A Warm Fuzzy Tale. Steiner, Claude. Freed, Alvyn M., intro. by. LC 77-77981. (Orig.). (gr. k up). 1977. 8.95 (0-915190-08-7, JP9008-7) Jalmar Pr.
Dickens, Earl. Real Fossils. Benanti, Carol. Frank, Michael, ed. 32p. (Orig.). (gr. 3-8). Date not set. pap. 6.95 (1-880592-06-1) Pace Prods.
Dickens, Frank. Albert Herbert Hawkins: The Naughtiest Boy in the World. Dickens, Frank. LC 72-149044. 32p. (ps-3). 7.95 (0-87592-000-4) Scroll Pr.
Dickens, Lucy. Dancing Class. Dickens, Lucy. 32p. (ps-3). 1992. 14.00 (0-670-84484-5) Viking Child Bks.
Dickenson, Ken. Disciple of a Master (How to Hit a Baseball to Your Potential) Ferroli, Stephen J. 200p. (Orig.). (gr. 7-12). 1986. pap. 9.95 (0-939905-00-0) Line Drive.
Dickins, Robert. The Sombrero. Brown, Hayden & Dickins, Roberts. LC 93-6633. 1994. write for info. (0-383-03714-X) SRA Schl Grp.
Dickinson, Charles. Eucharistic Manual for Children. Garrison, Eileen & Albanese, Gayle. LC 84-60217. 28p. (gr. 1-8). 1984. pap. 4.75 (0-8192-1343-8) Morehouse Pub.
Dickson, Mona. Tales of an Ashanti Father. Appiah, Peggy. LC 88-19059. 160p. (gr. 2-6). 1989. lib. bdg. 12.95 (0-8070-8312-7); pap. 6.95 (0-8070-8313-5, NL4) Beacon Pr.
Didier, J., jt. illus. see Dore, G.
Didier, Les. Carlos Finlay. Sumption, Christine & Thompson, Kathleen. De Varona, Frank, intro. by. (SPA & ENG.). 32p. (gr. 3-6). 1990. PLB 15.96 (0-8172-3378-4) Raintree Steck-V.
Dieneman, Debbie. Classic Poems for Children. Eisen, Armand, ed. LC 92-13078. 32p. 1992. 6.95 (0-8362-4909-7) Andrews & McMeel.
—The Easter Bunny. Egan, Louise B., retold by. LC 92-32435. 1993. 6.95 (0-8362-4935-6) Andrews & McMeel.
—Puss in Boots. Easton, Samantha, retold by. (ps-3). 1992. 6.95 (0-8362-4932-1) Andrews & McMeel.
—The Three Little Pigs. Greenway, Jennifer, retold by. 1991. 6.95 (0-8362-4904-6) Andrews & McMeel.
Difiori, Larry. The Bunny Hop. Slater, Teddy. 32p. 1992. pap. 2.95 (0-590-45354-8, Cartwheel) Scholastic Inc.
—Muffin Mouse's New House. DiFiori, Larry. (ps-k). 1991. pap. write for info. (0-307-10028-6, Golden Pr) Western Pub.
Di Fiori, Lawrence. A Toad for Tuesday. Erickson, Russell. LC 73-19900. 64p. (gr. k-4). 1974. PLB 12.88 (0-688-51569-X) Lothrop.
DiFiori, Lawrence. The Truck Book. DiFiori, Lawrence. LC 83-83106. (ps). 1984. write for info. (0-307-12299-9, Golden Bks) Western Pub.
Di Fiori, Lawrence. Warton & the Contest. Erickson, Russell E. LC 86-102. 96p. (gr. k-4). 1986. 11.95 (0-688-05818-3); PLB 11.88 (0-688-05819-1) Lothrop.
Di Fiori, Lawrence, photos by. A Toad for Tuesday. Erickson, Russell E. LC 92-24595. 64p. (gr. 3 up). 1993. pap. 3.95 (0-688-12276-0, Pub. by Beech Tree Bks) Morrow.
Digby, Desmond. Waltzing Matilda. Paterson, A. B. 32p. (gr. k-3). 1991. pap. 7.95 (0-207-17098-3, Pub. by Angus & Robertson AT) HarpC.
Di Grazia, Thomas. Hold My Hand. Reissue. ed. Zolotow, Charlotte. LC 72-76506. 32p. (gr. k-3). 1972. PLB 12.89 (0-06-026952-9) HarpC Child Bks.

DiGrazia, Thomas. Holiday Tales of Sholom Aleichem. Aleichem, Sholom. Shevrin, Aliza, tr. LC 79-753. 145p. (gr. 5 up). 1985. pap. 5.95 (0-689-71034-8, Aladdin) Macmillan Child Grp.
—Miss Maggie. Rylant, Cynthia. LC 82-18206. 32p. (gr. k-3). 1983. 12.95 (0-525-44048-8, DCB) Dutton Child Bks.
Digregorio, Elizabeth. Littlest Dinosaur Finds a Friend. James, Sara. 24p. (Orig.). 1992. pap. 2.50 (1-56156-110-X) Kidsbks.
Dijs, Carla. Are You My Daddy? Dijs, Carla. 12p. (ps). 1990. pap. 5.95 casebound, pop-up (0-671-70227-0, Little Simon) S&S Trade.
—Are You My Mommy? Dijs, Carla. 12p. (ps). 1990. pap. 5.95 casebound, pop-up (0-671-70226-2, Little Simon) S&S Trade.
—A Giraffe Needs to Laugh: Pop-up Book. Dijs, Carla. 10p. (gr. k-2). 1993. 7.99 (0-8431-3480-1) Price Stern.
—Who Sees You? At Night. 12p. (ps). 1993. 5.95 (0-448-40079-0, G&D) Putnam Pub Group.
—Who Sees You? Underground. 12p. (ps). 1993. 5.95 (0-448-40080-4, G&D) Putnam Pub Group.
DiLella, Barbara. The Anne of Green Gables Cookbook. Macdonald, Kate. 48p. 1987. 11.95 (0-19-540496-3) OUP.
Dillard, Karen. Apples for the Missionaries. Wilkinson, Barbara. 32p. (Orig.). (gr. 1-3). 1989. pap. text ed. 2.95 (0-936625-67-8) Womans Mission Union.
—Guess What I Made!?! Recipes for Children from Around the World. Sledge, Sharlande. 64p. (Orig.). (gr. 1-6). 1988. pap. 4.95 (0-936625-39-2, New Hope AL) Womans Mission Union.
Dilley, Romilda. Bible Double Trouble Puzzles. Beegle, Shirley. 64p. (gr. 5 up). 1992. wkbk. 6.99 (0-87403-671-2, 28-02791) Standard Pub.
Dillon, Diane & Dillon, Leo. Ashanti to Zulu: African Traditions. Musgrove, Margaret W. LC 76-6610. (gr. k-4). 1976. 17.00 (0-8037-0357-0); PLB 15.89 (0-8037-0358-9) Dial Bks Young.
—Brother to the Wind. Walter, Mildred P. LC 83-26800. 32p. (ps-2). 1985. PLB 14.88 (0-688-03812-3) Lothrop.
—Honey, I Love: And Other Love Poems. Greenfield, Eloise. LC 77-2845. 48p. (gr. 1-3). 1978. 13.00 (0-690-01334-5, Crowell Jr Bks); PLB 12.89 (0-690-03845-3) HarpC Child Bks.
—Honey, I Love & Other Love Poems. Greenfield, Eloise. LC 85-45398. 48p. (gr. 1-4). 1986. pap. 3.95 (0-06-443097-9, Trophy) HarpC Child Bks.
Dillon, Diane, jt. illus. see Dillon, Leo.
Dillon, Jana. Jeb Scarecrow's Pumpkin Patch. Dillon, Jana. LC 91-16423. 32p. (ps-3). 1992. 14.45 (0-395-57578-8) HM.
Dillon, Leo & Dillon, Diane. Ashanti to Zulu: African Traditions. Musgrove, Margaret W. LC 76-6610. 32p. (gr. k up). 1980. pap. 4.95 (0-8037-0308-2, Dial Pied Piper) Puffin Bks.
—The Color Wizard: Level 1. Brenner, Barbara A. (ps-3). 1989. 9.99 (0-553-05825-8) Bantam.
—The Color Wizard: Level 1. Brenner, Barbara. (ps-3). 1989. pap. 3.50 (0-553-34690-3) Bantam.
—Happy Birthday Grampie. Pearson, Susan. LC 86-31105. 32p. (ps-3). 1987. PLB 10.89 (0-8037-3458-1) Dial Bks Young.
—The Hundred-Penny Box. Mathis, Sharon B. 48p. (gr. k-3). 1975. pap. 15.00 (0-670-38787-8) Viking Child Bks.
—The Hundred-Penny Box. Mathis, Sharon B. 48p. (gr. 1-4). 1986. pap. 3.99 (0-14-032169-1, Puffin) Puffin Bks.
—Many Thousand Gone: African-Americans from Slavery to Freedom. Hamilton, Virginia. LC 89-19988. 160p. (gr. 4-9). 1992. 16.00 (0-394-82873-9); PLB 16.99 (0-394-92873-3) Knopf Bks Yng Read.
—Moses & Noah's Ark: Stories from the Bible. Bach, Alice & Exum, J. Cheryl. LC 89-1069. 181p. 1989. 14.95 (0-385-29778-5) Delacorte.
—Moses' Ark: Stories from the Bible. Bach, Alice & Exum, Cheryl. (gr. 4-8). 1989. 14.95 (0-685-30899-5) Delacorte.
—Northern Lullaby. Carlstrom, Nancy. 32p. (ps-3). 1992. PLB 15.95 (0-399-21806-8, Philomel Bks) Putnam Pub Group.
—The People Could Fly. Hamilton, Virginia. LC 84-25020. 192p. (gr-12). 1985. 18.00 (0-394-86925-7); lib. bdg. 18.99 (0-394-96925-1) Knopf Bks Yng Read.
—The People Could Fly: American Black Folktales. Hamilton, Virginia. LC 85-25020. 192p. 1993. pap. 10.00 (0-679-84336-1) Knopf Bks Yng Read.
—The People Could Fly: American Black Folktales. Hamilton, Virginia. Jones, James E., contrib. by. 192p. 1994. pap. 15.00 incl. cass. (0-679-85465-7) Knopf Bks Yng Read.
—The Race of the Golden Apples. Martin, Claire. LC 85-16290. 32p. (ps-3). 1991. 14.95 (0-8037-0248-5); PLB 14.89 (0-8037-0249-3) Dial Bks Young.
—Switch on the Night. Bradbury, Ray. LC 92-25321. 40p. (ps-2). 1993. 8.99 (0-394-80486-4); PLB 9.99 (0-394-90486-9) Knopf Bks Yng Read.
—The Tale of the Mandarin Ducks. Paterson, Katherine. (gr. k-3). 1990. 15.00 (0-525-67283-4, Lodestar Bks) Dutton Child Bks.
—Who's in Rabbit's House? Aardema, Verna, retold by. LC 77-71514. 32p. (gr. k-3). 1977. PLB 14.89 (0-8037-9551-3) Dial Bks Young.
—Who's in Rabbit's House? Aardema, Verna, retold by. LC 77-71514. 32p. (ps-3). 1979. pap. 4.95 (0-8037-9549-1) Dial Bks Young.

—Why Mosquitoes Buzz in People's Ears: A West African Tale. Aardema, Verna. LC 77-71514. (ps-3). 1978. pap. 4.95 (0-8037-6088-4, Dial Pied Piper) Puffin Bks.
—Why Mosquitoes Buzz in People's Ears: A West African Tale. Aardema, Verna. LC 74-2886. 32p. (ps-3). 1975. 15.00 (0-8037-6089-2); PLB 14.89 (0-8037-6087-6) Dial Bks Young.
—Why Mosquitoes Buzz in People's Ears: A West African Tale. giant ed. Aardema, Verna, retold by. 32p. (ps-3). 1993. pap. 17.99 (0-14-054589-1) Puffin Bks.
—Why Mosquitoes Buzz in People's Ears: A West African Tale. Aardema, Verna, retold by. 32p. (ps-3). Date not set. pap. 4.99 (0-14-054905-6) Puffin Bks.
—Why Mosquitoes Buzz in People's Ears Read-Aloud Set. Aardema, Verna, retold by. (ps-3). 1993. Set incls. 1 Giant copy, 6 paperbacks, giant-sized bookmark & tchr's. guide in a free- standing easel. pap. 47.93 (0-14-778979-6) Puffin Bks.
Dillon, Leo, jt. illus. see Dillon, Diane.
Dillon, Leo, et al. The Sorcerer's Apprentice. Willard, Nancy. LC 93-19912. 32p. (ps-6). 1993. 15.95 (0-590-47329-8) Scholastic Inc.
Dillon, Paul. Children of the Sea. Levine, Gloria. 48p. (Orig.). (gr. 4-8). 1991. pap. 5.95 (0-913839-98-1) Bk Lures.
—Earthwatch. Polette, Nancy. 48p. (gr. 3-6). 1993. pap. 5.95 (1-879287-26-9) Bk Lures.
—Enjoying Tall Tales. Polette, Nancy & Mealy, Virginia. 48p. (Orig.). (gr. 3-6). 1991. 5.95 (0-913839-90-6) Bk Lures.
—First Literature Experiences. Lance, Janice. 48p. (gr. k-3). 1991. pap. 5.95 (1-879287-01-3) Bk Lures.
—Literature Activities for Primary Social Studies. Jones, Charla. 128p. (Orig.). (gr. 1-4). 1993. pap. 12.95 (1-879287-24-2) Bk Lures.
—Literature-Based Spelling & Writing Activities for Primary Grades. Polette, Nancy. 48p. (Orig.). (gr. 1-4). 1993. pap. 5.95 (1-879287-23-4) Bk Lures.
—Multi-Cultural Literature: Books & Activities. Polette, Nancy. 48p. (Orig.). (gr. 3-6). 1993. pap. 5.95 (1-879287-22-6) Bk Lures.
—Read, Write, Now! Polette, Keith. 44p. (gr. 5-9). 1993. pap. text ed. 5.95 (1-879287-20-X) Bk Lures.
—Reading the World with Folktales. Polette, Nancy. 124p. (Orig.). (gr. 2-4). 1993. pap. 12.95 (1-879287-19-6) Bk Lures.
—Research Without Copying. 2nd, expanded ed. Polette, Nancy. 48p. (gr. 4-9). 1991. pap. 5.95 (0-913839-91-4) Bk Lures.
—Survival. Polette, Nancy. 48p. (Orig.). (gr. 4-8). 1991. pap. 5.95 (0-913839-93-0) Bk Lures.
—Trials. Albert, Kristine & Polette, Nancy. 48p. (Orig.). (gr. 4-8). 1991. pap. 5.95 (0-913839-89-X) Bk Lures.
—Unforgettable Characters. Polette, Nancy. 48p. (Orig.). (gr. 3-6). 1991. pap. 5.95 (0-913839-97-3) Bk Lures.
—Write Your Own Fairy Tale. enl. ed. Polette, Nancy. 48p. (Orig.). (gr. 3-7). 1993. pap. 5.95 (1-879287-25-0) Bk Lures.
—Young Heroines. Polette, Nancy. 48p. (Orig.). (gr. 4-8). 1991. pap. 5.95 (0-913839-96-5) Bk Lures.
Dillon, Sharon Saseen. Where Did My Feather Pillow Come From? Taylor, Audilee Boyd. LC 81-71027. 32p. (ps-3). 1982. 10.00 (0-942250-00-1) Castlemarsh.
Dillow, John. Baby's Day: Board Books. 10p. (ps) 1991. bds. 3.50 (0-7214-9136-7) Ladybird Bks.
—Baby's Toys: Little Ladybird Board Book. 8p. (ps) 1991. bds. 3.50 (0-7214-9137-5, S851-15) Ladybird Bks.
—Picture Atlas of the World. 45p. 1993. 11.95 (0-7214-5354-6) Ladybird Bks.
Dimalanta, Ariel. Liberation Nineteen Forty-Four: The Pictorial History of Guam. Farrell, Don A. Koontz, Phyllis, ed. (gr. 8-12). 1984. Repr. 15.95 (0-930839-00-5) Micronesian.
DiMino, Frank. Hot Rods. DiMino, Frank. 32p. (Orig.). (gr. k-2). 1993. pap. 3.99 (0-8431-3514-X) Troubador Pr.
Di Mino, Frank. Hot Trucks. Di Mino, Frank. (gr. k-2). 1993. pap. 4.50 (0-8431-3515-8) Price Stern.
Dimond, Jasper. Dinosaurs. Dimond, Jasper. 48p. (gr. 3-7). 1985. pap. 10.95 (0-13-214628-2) P-H.
Dinan, Carolyn. Alfred Mouse. Dinan, Carolyn. 80p. (ps) 1992. laminated bds. 15.95 (0-571-16500-1) Faber & Faber.
Dinardo, Jeffrey. Come Out, Mouse. Chardiet, Bernice. 20p. (ps-1). 1994. pap. 4.99 (0-14-054997-8) Puffin Bks.
—Timothy & the Night Noises. Dinardo, Jeffrey. LC 86-9383. 32p. (ps-2). 1986. 11.95 (0-13-922048-8) P-H.
Dines, Glen. Sir Cecil & the Bad Blue Beast. Dines, Glen. LC 70-125868. (gr. k-2). 1970. 20.95 (0-87599-175-0) S G Phillips.
Dinkelman, Craig. Face to Face. Starkman, Neal. (Orig.). (gr. 6-9). 1988. pap. 5.00 (0-935529-09-8) Comprehen Health Educ.
Dinkels, Rochel. Baila Wants a Bicycle Bell. Finkelstein, Ruth. 24p. (ps-4). 1992. 8.95 (0-9628157-1-3) Feldheim.
Di Palma, Gaetano. Animals in Winter. Bancroft, Henrietta & Van Gelder, Richard G. 40p. (gr. k-3). pap. 1.95 (0-590-01321-1) Scholastic Inc.
Dirgo, Ray. Show! Don't Tell! How to Personalize College Applications. Barth, Shannon. Berescik, Susan, ed. 175p. (Orig.). (gr. 11-12). 1993. plastic comb 19.95 (0-9638297-0-X) Intl Editing.

Dirks, Nathan & Brandt, Bill. God's Love for Happiness: A Return to Family Values. Rummel, Mary. LC 92-91032. 64p. (Orig.). (gr. k up) 1992. pap. 9.95 (0-9635091-0-1) Olive Brnch.
Dirks, Ray. Journey with Justice. Lehman, Paula D. Hull, Eddy & Shelly, Maynard, eds. LC 90-81509. 100p. (Orig.). 1990. pap. 7.95 (0-87303-139-3) Faith & Life.
Dirksen, Helen. More Than a Number Book. Hooge, Selma. 32p. (ps-k). 1990. pap. 7.95 (0-919797-95-4) Kindred Pr.
DiSalvo-Ryan, DyAnne. The Christmas Knight. Curry, Jane L. LC 92-2277. 32p. (gr. k-4). 1993. SBE 14.95 (0-689-50572-8, M K McElderry) Macmillan Child Grp.
—George Washington's Mother. Fritz, Jean. 48p. (gr. 2-4). 1992. 3.50 (0-448-40385-4, G&D); (G&D) Putnam Pub Group.
—The Go-Between. Hest, Amy. LC 90-24561. 32p. (gr. k-3). 1992. RSBE 14.95 (0-02-743632-2, Four Winds) Macmillan Child Grp.
—The Growing-Up Feet. Cleary, Beverly. LC 86-12585. 32p. (ps-1). 1987. 11.95 (0-688-06619-4); lib. bdg. 11.88 (0-688-06620-8) Morrow Jr Bks.
—The Growing up Feet. Cleary, Beverly. (gr. k-6). 1988. pap. 3.95 (0-440-40109-7, YB) Dell.
—Janet's Thingamajigs. Cleary, Beverly. (gr. k-6). 1988. pap. 4.95 (0-440-40108-9, YB) Dell.
—The Mommy Exchange. Hest, Amy. LC 87-7539. 32p. (ps-2). 1988. RSBE 13.95 (0-02-743650-0, Pub. by Four Winds Pr) Macmillan Child Grp.
—The Mommy Exchange. Hest, Amy. LC 90-40596. 32p. (ps-2). 1991. pap. 3.95 (0-689-71450-5, Aladdin) Macmillan Child Grp.
—Nina, Nina, Ballerina. O'Connor, Jane. LC 92-24465. 32p. (ps-1). 1993. lib. bdg. 7.99 (0-448-40512-1, G&D); pap. 3.50 (0-448-40511-3, G&D) Putnam Pub Group.
—Sam Ellis's Island. Siegel, Beatrice. LC 85-42799. 128p. (gr. 3-7). 1985. SBE 13.95 (0-02-782720-8, Four Winds) Macmillan Child Grp.
—Uncle Willie & the Soup Kitchen. DiSalvo-Ryan, Dyanne. LC 90-6375. 32p. (gr. 1 up). 1991. 13.95 (0-688-09165-2); PLB 13.88 (0-688-09166-0, Morrow Jr Bks) Morrow Jr Bks.
—Why Is Baby Crying? Johnson, Ryerson. Tucker, Kathy, ed. LC 89-5380. 32p. (ps-2). 1989. PLB 13.95 (0-8075-9084-3) A Whitman.
Disney Staff. My Trip to Walt Disney World Resort: A Photolog Book. Horowitz, Janet & Faggella, Kathy. 48p. 1991. 9.95 (1-55670-141-1) Stewart Tabori & Chang.
Disney Studios Staff. Donald's Wild Adventure. Hill, Stephanie. 24p. (Orig.). (ps-7). 1992. pap. 8.98 incl. cassette (0-943351-55-3, XD 1002) Astor Bks.
—Mickey's Marching Band. Hill, Stephanie. 24p. (Orig.). (ps-7). 1992. pap. 8.95 incl. cassette (0-943351-54-5, XD 1001) Astor Bks.
DiVito, Anna. The Biggest Mouth in Baseball. McMullan, Kate. LC 92-24467. 48p. (gr. 2-4). 1993. lib. bdg. 7.99 (0-448-40516-4, G&D); pap. 3.50 (0-448-40515-6, G&D) Putnam Pub Group.
—I Want Answers & a Parachute. Petersen, P. J. LC 92-38262. (gr. 6 up). 1993. pap. 13.00 (0-671-86577-3, S&S BFYR) S&S Trade.
Dixon, David. The Adventure of Fifi's Honey Bee Bears & the Big Bee Hive. Schroeder, Ruth. 32p. (gr. k-5). 1987. PLB 8.95 (0-935087-24-9) R & D Bks.
—The Honey Bee Bears in Bluer Than Blueberries. Schroeder, Ruth E. 22p. (gr. k-5). 1989. 8.95 (0-685-26760-1); PLB 8.95 (0-685-26761-X) R & D Bks.
—The Story of Smartworms: The Journey Begins. Dickson, Sandy L. Barrow, Madeline H., ed. 34p. (gr. k-5). 1989. write for info.; PLB write for info.; pap. write for info. Smartworm Corp.
Dixon, Jim. The Zoo Is Blue: And Should Be Read. Dixon, Jim. 36p. (gr. k-2). 1991. 12.95 (1-880453-01-0) J Hefty Pub.
Dixon, Tennessee. Berchick, My Mother's Horse. Blanc, Esther S. LC 87-37172. 36p. (gr. k-5). 1989. 14.95 (0-912078-81-2) Volcano Pr.
—The Heroine of the Titanic: A Tale Both True & Otherwise of the Life of Molly Brown. Blos, Joan W. LC 90-35369. 40p. (gr. 1 up). 1991. 14.95 (0-688-07546-0); PLB 14.88 (0-688-07547-9) Morrow Jr Bks.
—Jessica & the Wolf: A Story for Children Who Have Bad Dreams. Lobby, Theodore E. LC 89-29688. 32p. (gr. k-3). 1990. 16.95 (0-945354-22-3); pap. 6.95 (0-945354-21-5) Magination Pr.
—Jessica & the Wolf: A Story for Children Who Have Bad Dreams. Lobby, Ted. LC 92-56872. 1993. PLB 17.26 (0-8368-0933-5) Gareth Stevens Inc.
—The Princess & the Peacocks: Or, the Story of the Room. Merrill, Linda. LC 92-72019. 32p. (gr. k-4). 1993. 14.95 (1-56282-327-2); PLB 14.89 (1-56282-328-0) Hyprn Child.
Dixon, Tom. King of the Birds. O'Huigin, Sean. 36p. (ps-5). 1992. pap. 4.95 (0-88753-168-7, Pub. by Black Moss Pr CN) Firefly Bks Ltd.
Dobbs, Holly J. Tales of Wonder: Reading Level 2-3. Reiff, Tana, retold by. LC 93-16083. 1993. 4.00 (0-88336-459-X); read-along tape 10.00 (0-88336-524-3) New Readers.
Dobson, Clive. Fred's TV. Dobson, Clive. 32p. (ps-5). 1989. 12.95 (0-920668-60-7); pap. 4.95 (0-920668-59-3) Firefly Bks Ltd.

Dobson, Steven. Abraham Lincoln: President of a Divided Country. Greene, Carol. LC 89-33845. 48p. (gr. k-3). 1989. PLB 15.93 (0-516-04206-8); pap. 4.95 (0-516-44206-6) Childrens.
—Benjamin Franklin: A Man with Many Jobs. Greene, Carol. LC 88-15011. 48p. (gr. k-3). 1988. PLB 15.93 (0-516-04202-5); pap. 4.95 (0-516-44202-3) Childrens.
—Christopher Columbus: A Great Explorer. Greene, Carol. LC 88-37943. 48p. (gr. k-3). 1989. PLB 15.93 (0-516-04204-1); pap. 4.95 (0-516-44204-X) Childrens.
—Daniel Boone: Man of the Forests. Greene, Carol. LC 89-25346. 48p. (gr. k-3). 1990. PLB 15.93 (0-516-04210-6); pap. 4.95 (0-516-44210-4) Childrens.
—Elizabeth Blackwell: First Woman Doctor. Greene, Carol. LC 90-20001. 48p. (gr. k-3). 1991. PLB 15.93 (0-516-04217-3); pap. 4.95 (0-516-44217-1) Childrens.
—Elizabeth the First: Queen of England. Greene, Carol. LC 90-2204. 48p. (gr. k-3). 1990. PLB 15.93 (0-516-04214-9); pap. 4.95 (0-516-44214-7) Childrens.
—George Washington Carver: Scientist & Teacher. Greene, Carol. LC 92-7374. 48p. (gr. k-3). 1992. PLB 15.93 (0-516-04250-5) Childrens.
—George Washington Carver: Scientist & Teacher. Greene, Carol. LC 92-7374. 48p. (gr. k-3). 1993. pap. 4.95 (0-516-44250-3) Childrens.
—George Washington: First President of the United States. Greene, Carol. LC 90-22195. 48p. (gr. k-3). 1991. PLB 15.93 (0-516-04218-1); pap. 4.95 (0-516-44218-X) Childrens.
—Hans Christian Andersen: Prince of Storytellers. Greene, Carol. LC 90-19998. 48p. (gr. k-3). 1991. PLB 15.93 (0-516-04219-X); pap. 4.95 (0-516-44219-8) Childrens.
—Jackie Robinson: Baseball's First Black Major Leaguer. Greene, Carol. LC 89-28816. 48p. (gr. k-3). 1990. PLB 15.93 (0-516-04211-4); pap. 4.95 (0-516-44211-2) Childrens.
—Jacques Cousteau: Man of the Oceans. Greene, Carol. LC 90-2162. 48p. (gr. k-3). 1990. PLB 15.93 (0-516-04215-7); pap. 4.95 (0-516-44215-5) Childrens.
—Johann Sebastian Bach: Great Man of Music. Greene, Carol. LC 92-7373. 48p. (gr. k-3). 1992. PLB 15.93 (0-516-04251-3) Childrens.
—Johann Sebastian Bach: Great Man of Music. Greene, Carol. LC 92-7373. 48p. (gr. k-3). 1993. pap. 4.95 (0-516-44251-1) Childrens.
—John Muir: Man of the Wild Places. Greene, Carol. LC 90-19993. 48p. (gr. k-3). 1991. PLB 15.93 (0-516-04220-3); pap. 4.95 (0-516-44220-1) Childrens.
—Katherine Dunham: Black Dancer. Greene, Carol. LC 92-8769. 48p. (gr. k-3). 1992. PLB 15.93 (0-516-04252-1) Childrens.
—Katherine Dunham: Black Dancer. Greene, Carol. LC 92-8769. 48p. (gr. k-3). 1993. pap. 4.95 (0-516-44252-X) Childrens.
—Laura Ingalls Wilder: Author of the Little House Books. Greene, Carol. LC 89-25362. 48p. (gr. k-3). 1990. PLB 15.93 (0-516-04212-2); pap. 4.95 (0-516-44212-0) Childrens.
—Louis Pasteur: Enemy of Disease. Greene, Carol. LC 90-2197. 48p. (gr. k-3). 1990. PLB 15.93 (0-516-04216-5); pap. 4.95 (0-516-44216-3) Childrens.
—Ludwig Van Beethoven: Musical Pioneer. Greene, Carol. LC 89-15849. 48p. (gr. k-3). 1989. PLB 15.93 (0-516-04208-4); pap. 4.95 (0-516-44208-2) Childrens.
—Martin Luther King, Jr. A Man Who Changed Things. Greene, Carol. LC 88-37714. 48p. (gr. k-3). 1989. PLB 15.93 (0-516-04205-X); pap. 4.95 (0-516-44205-8) Childrens.
—Pocahontas: Daughter of a Chief. Greene, Carol. LC 88-11978. 48p. (gr. k-3). 1988. PLB 15.93 (0-516-04203-3); pap. 4.95 (0-516-44203-1) Childrens.
—Rachel Carson: Friend of Nature. Greene, Carol. LC 91-39446. 48p. (gr. k-3). 1992. PLB 15.93 (0-516-04229-7) Childrens.
—Rachel Carson: Friend of Nature. Greene, Carol. LC 91-39446. 48p. (gr. k-3). 1993. pap. 4.95 (0-516-44229-5) Childrens.
—Robert E. Lee: Leader in War & Peace. Greene, Carol. LC 89-33749. 48p. (gr. k-3). 1989. PLB 15.93 (0-516-04209-2); pap. 4.95 (0-516-44209-0) Childrens.
Dockery, Della. Cami & Other Familiar Friends. Dockery, Della. 20p. (ps). 1987. pap. 2.95 (0-943487-05-6) Sevgo Pr.
Dodd, John & Taylor, Leigh. Lessons in Love. RanDelle, B. J. & Marshbum, Sandra. LC 24-476. 64p. (gr. k-4). 1982. text ed. 5.95 (0-910445-00-1) Randelle Pubns.
Dodd, Lynley. The Apple Tree. Dodd, Lynley. LC 85-9774. 26p. (gr. 1-2). 1985. PLB 15.93 (0-918831-08-3) Gareth Stevens Inc.
—Dragon in a Wagon. Dodd, Lynley. Sherwood, Rhoda, ed. LC 88-42925. 32p. (gr. 1-2). 1988. PLB 15.93 (1-55532-911-X) Gareth Stevens Inc.
—Hairy Maclary from Donaldson's Dairy. Dodd, Lynley. LC 85-9773. 38p. (gr. 1-2). 1988. 15.93 (0-918831-05-9) Gareth Stevens Inc.
—Hairy Maclary-Scattercat. Dodd, Lynley. LC 86-42797. 32p. (gr. 1-2). 1988. PLB 15.93 (1-55532-123-2) Gareth Stevens Inc.
—Hairy Maclary's Bone. Dodd, Lynley. LC 85-9772. 32p. (gr. 1-2). 1985. PLB 15.93 (0-918831-06-7) Gareth Stevens Inc.
—Hairy Maclary's Caterwaul Caper. Dodd, Lynley. LC 88-42926. 32p. (ps-2). 1989. PLB 15.93 (1-55532-910-1) Gareth Stevens Inc.
—Hairy Maclary's Rumpus at the Vet. Dodd, Lynley. LC 89-43120. 28p. (gr. 1-2). 1989. PLB 15.93 (0-8368-0126-1) Gareth Stevens Inc.

—Slinky Malinki. Dodd, Lynley. LC 90-44686. 32p. (gr. 1-2). 1991. PLB 15.93 (0-8368-0197-0) Gareth Stevens Inc.
—Smallest Turtle. Dodd, Lynley. LC 85-9771. 29p. (gr. 1-2). 1985. PLB 15.93 (0-918831-07-5) Gareth Stevens Inc.
—Wake Up Bear. Dodd, Lynley. LC 86-42798. 32p. (gr. 1-2). 1988. PLB 15.93 (1-55532-124-0) Gareth Stevens Inc.
Dodd, Margaret. Charlsie's Chuckle. Berkus, Clara W. LC 91-46655. 32p. (gr. k-6). 1992. 14.95 (0-933149-50-6) Woodbine House.
Dodd, Maurice. Jim Button: And Luke the Engine Driver. Ende, Michael. Bell, Anthea, tr. 244p. (gr. 3 up). 1990. 13.95 (0-87951-391-8) Overlook Pr.
Dodds, Siobhan. Babies, Babies, Babies. Dahl, Tessa. 32p. (ps-2). 1991. 12.95 (0-670-83921-3) Viking Child Bks.
—Charles Tiger. Dodds, Siobhan. (ps-3). 1988. 9.95 (0-316-18817-4, Joy Street Bks) Little.
—Elizabeth Hen. Dodds, Siobhan. (ps-3). 1988. 9.95 (0-316-18818-2, Joy Street Bks) Little.
—Grandpa Bud. Dodds, Siobhan. LC 92-53135. 32p. (ps-3). 1993. 13.95 (1-56402-175-0) Candlewick Pr.
—Words & Pictures: Reading with Picture Clues. Dodds, Siobhan. LC 91-71817. 32p. (ps). 1992. 14.95 (1-56402-042-8) Candlewick Pr.
Dodge, Katherine. Tongue Dancing. Swann, Brian. 56p. (gr. 7-12). 1984. 12.95g (0-937672-12-2) Rowan Tree.
Dodge, Nancy C. Sharing with Thumpy: My Story of Love & Grief. Lamb, Jane M. 48p. (gr. k-12). 1985. pap. 8.95 workbook (0-918533-10-4) Prairie Lark.
Dodson, Bert. The Great Baseball Card Hunt. Greenberg, Daniel A. Lewis, Glenn. 112p. (gr. 2-6). 1992. pap. 12.00 (0-671-72927-6, S&S BFYR) S&S Trade.; pap. 2.95 (0-671-72931-4, S&S BFYR) S&S Trade.
—A Guide Dog Goes to School: The Story of a Dog Trained to Lead the Blind. Smith, Elizabeth S. LC 87-11056. 64p. (gr. 1-4). 1987. 12.95 (0-688-06844-8); lib. bdg. 12.88 (0-688-06846-4, Morrow Jr Bks) Morrow Jr Bks.
—Hannah's Fancy Notions: A Story of Industrial New England. Ross, Pat. LC 92-20286. 64p. (gr. 2-6). 1992. pap. 3.99 (0-14-032389-9) Puffin Bks.
—Hero over Here. Kudlinski, Kathleen V. 64p. (gr. 2-6). 1990. pap. 13.00 (0-670-83050-X) Viking Child Bks.
—Hero over Here: A Story of World War I. Kudlinski, Kathleen V. 64p. (gr. 2-6). 1992. pap. 3.99 (0-14-034286-9, Puffin) Puffin Bks.
—Jason & the Argonauts. Evslin, Bernard. LC 86-32114. 176p. (gr. 5 up). 1986. 13.00 (0-688-06245-8) Morrow Jr Bks.
—Lazy Jack. LC 78-18070. 32p. (gr. k-4). 1979. PLB 9.79 (0-89375-123-5); pap. 1.95 (0-89375-101-4) Troll Assocs.
—The Missing Championship Ring. Greenberg, Daniel A. Lewis, Glenn. 112p. (gr. 2-6). 1992. (Little Simon); pap. 2.95 (0-671-72933-0, Little Simon) S&S Trade.
—Monkeys. Whitehead, Patricia. LC 81-11439. 32p. (gr. k-2). 1982. PLB 11.59 (0-89375-670-9); pap. text ed. 2.95 (0-89375-671-7) Troll Assocs.
—Mystery at the Zoo. new ed. Supraner, Robyn. LC 78-60126. (gr. 2-4). 1979. PLB 10.89 (0-89375-091-3); pap. 3.50 (0-89375-079-4) Troll Assocs.
—Rapunzel. Grimm, Jacob & Grimm, Wilhelm K. LC 78-18066. 32p. (gr. k-3). 1979. PLB 9.79 (0-89375-135-9); pap. 1.95 (0-89375-113-8) Troll Assocs.
—The Stolen Signs. Otfinoski, Steven. Lewis, Glenn. 112p. (gr. 2-6). 1992. (S&S BFYR); pap. 2.95 (0-671-72930-6, S&S BFYR) S&S Trade.
—What Makes the Wind? Santrey, Laurence. LC 81-7486. 32p. (gr. 2-4). 1982. PLB 11.59 (0-89375-584-2); pap. text ed. 2.95 (0-89375-585-0); cassette avail. Troll Assocs.
—Who Stole Home Plate? Otfinoski, Steven. Lewis, Glenn. 112p. (gr. 2-6). 1992. (S&S BFYR); pap. 2.95 (0-671-72932-2, S&S BFYR) S&S Trade.
—Wonders of the Sea. Sabin, Louis. LC 81-3334. 32p. (gr. 2-4). 1982. PLB 11.59 (0-89375-578-8); pap. text ed. 2.95 (0-89375-579-6) Troll Assocs.
—Young Frederick Douglass: Fight for Freedom. Santrey, Laurence. LC 82-15993. 48p. (gr. 4-6). 1983. PLB 10.79 (0-89375-857-4); pap. text ed. 3.50 (0-89375-858-2) Troll Assocs.
Dodson, Deborah, jt. illus. see Schepp, Warren.
Dodson, Liz. The Story of Crazy Horse. Wheeler, Jill. Deegan, Paul, ed. LC 89-84913. 32p. (gr. 4). 1989. PLB 11.96 (0-939179-66-0) Abdo & Dghtrs.
—The Story of Geronimo. Wheeler, Jill. Deegan, Paul, ed. LC 89-84911. 32p. (gr. 4). 1989. PLB 11.96 (0-939179-68-7) Abdo & Dghtrs.
—The Story of Hiawatha. Wheeler, Jill. Deegan, Paul, ed. LC 89-84908. 32p. (gr. 4). 1989. PLB 11.96 (0-939179-71-7) Abdo & Dghtrs.
—The Story of Pontiac. Wheeler, Jill. Deegan, Paul, ed. LC 89-84910. 32p. (gr. 4). 1989. PLB 11.96 (0-939179-69-5) Abdo & Dghtrs.
—The Story of Sequoyah. Wheeler, Jill. Deegan, Paul, ed. LC 89-84909. 32p. (gr. 4). 1989. PLB 11.96 (0-939179-70-9) Abdo & Dghtrs.
—The Story of Sitting Bull. Wheeler, Jill. Deegan, Paul, ed. LC 89-94912. 32p. (gr. 4). 1989. PLB 11.96 (0-939179-67-9) Abdo & Dghtrs.
Dodson, Liz B. Count Your Way Through India. Haskins, Jim. (gr. 1-4). 1990. PLB 17.50 (0-87614-414-8) Carolrhoda Bks.

—Korean Holidays & Festivals. Koh, Frances M. 32p. (gr. 2-5). 1990. PLB 14.95 (0-9606090-5-9) EastWest Pr.
Doege, Erwin, jt. illus. see Chapman, Donna.
Dolan, Tom, jt. illus. see Kaicher, Sally.
Dolce, J. Ellen. Baby's Mother Goose. LC 87-81921. 12p. (ps). 1988. write for info. (0-307-06066-7, Pub. by Golden Bks) Western Pub.
—Christmas Carols. Schulte, Karl, compiled by. 1990. pap. write for info. (0-307-02979-4, Golden Pr) Western Pub.
Dole, Bob. Congressperson. Sabin, Louis, LC 84-2651. 32p. (gr. 3-6). 1985. PLB 9.49 (0-8167-0266-7); pap. text ed. 2.95 (0-8167-0267-5) Troll Assocs.
—Freedom Documents. Sabin, Francene. LC 84-8596. 32p. (gr. 3-6). 1985. PLB 9.49 (0-8167-0238-1); pap. text ed. 2.95 (0-8167-0239-X) Troll Assocs.
—The Lion & the Mouse. Aesop. LC 80-28154. 32p. (gr. k-3). 1981. PLB 9.79 (0-89375-466-8); pap. text ed. 1.95 (0-89375-467-6) Troll Assocs.
—President. Brandt, Keith. LC 84-2652. 32p. (gr. 3-6). 1985. PLB 9.49 (0-8167-0268-3); pap. text ed. 2.95 (0-8167-0269-1) Troll Assocs.
—Santa's New Sled. Peters, Sharon. LC 81-5028. 32p. (gr. k-2). 1981. PLB 11.59 (0-89375-523-0); pap. text ed. 2.95 (0-89375-524-9) Troll Assocs.
—State & Local Government. Santrey, Laurence. LC 84-8440. 32p. (gr. 3-6). 1985. PLB 9.49 (0-8167-0270-5); pap. text ed. 2.95 (0-8167-0271-3) Troll Assocs.
—Supreme Court. Bains, Rae. LC 84-2736. 32p. (gr. 3-6). 1985. PLB 9.49 (0-8167-0272-1); pap. text ed. 2.95 (0-8167-0273-X) Troll Assocs.
—Using the Library. Santrey, Laurence. LC 84-2590. 32p. (gr. 3-6). 1985. PLB 9.49 (0-8167-0122-9); pap. text ed. 2.95 (0-8167-0123-7) Troll Assocs.
Dollar, Diane. Candy the Zoo Truck. Harwell, Helen B. 32p. 1987. 3.95 (0-938991-37-X) Colonial Pr AL.
Dolobowsky, Mena. Cleaning Up: How Trash Becomes Treasure. Stwertka, Eve & Stwertka, Albert. LC 91-28777. 40p. (gr. 2-5). 1993. lib. bdg. 10.98 (0-671-69461-8, J Messner); pap. 5.95 (0-671-69467-7, J Messner) S&S Trade.
—Tuning in the Sounds of the Radio: The Sounds of the Radio. Stwertka, Eve & Stwertka, Albert. LC 91-16058. 40p. (gr. 2-5). 1993. lib. bdg. 10.98 (0-671-69460-X, J Messner); pap. 5.95 (0-671-69466-9, J Messner) S&S Trade.
—A Visit to New Orleans Coloring Book. Carvin, Ruth. 28p. (gr. k-4). 1986. 3.50 (0-9616390-0-8) Carvin Pub.
—A Visit to New Orleans: With Pictures to Color & Verses to Read. rev. ed. Carvin, Ruth. 32p. (gr. k-4). 1988. coloring bk. 3.50 (0-9616390-2-4) Carvin Pub.
—What's It Like to Be a Police Officer. Pellowski, Michael J. LC 89-34395. 32p. (gr. k-3). 1990. lib. bdg. 10.89 (0-8167-1811-3); pap. text ed. 2.95 (0-8167-1812-1) Troll Assocs.
Domanska, Janina. Busy Monday Morning. Domanska, Janina. LC 83-25362. 32p. (ps-1). 1985. 13.00 (0-688-03833-6); PLB 14.93 (0-688-03834-4) Greenwillow.
—The First Noel. LC 85-27084. 24p. (ps up). 1986. 11.75 (0-688-04324-0); PLB 11.88 (0-688-04325-9) Greenwillow.
—If All the Seas Were One Sea. reissued ed. LC 73-146621. 32p. (ps-2). 1987. SBE 14.95 (0-02-732540-7, Macmillan Child Bk) Macmillan Child Grp.
—Mischievous Meg. Lindgren, Astrid. Bothmer, Gerry, tr. LC 85-575. (ps-k). 1985. pap. 4.99 (0-14-031954-9, Puffin) Puffin Bks.
—Ten & a Kid. Weilerstein, Sadie R. LC 61-12600. 186p. (gr. 3 up). 1973. Repr. of 1961 ed. 8.95 (0-8276-0009-7) JPS Phila.
—The Trumpeter of Krakow. Kelly, Eric P. LC 66-16712. 224p. (gr. 7 up). 1966. 14.95 (0-02-750140-X, Collier Young Ad); (Aladdin) Macmillan Child Grp.
—The Trumpeter of Krakow. Kelly, Eric P. LC 91-26879. 224p. (gr. 3-7). 1992. pap. 3.95 (0-689-71571-4, Aladdin) Macmillan Child Grp.
—Under the Green Willow. Coatsworth, Elizabeth. LC 84-1471. 24p. (gr. k-3). 1984. 9.25 (0-688-03845-X); PLB 8.59 (0-688-03846-8) Greenwillow.
Dombrowski, James. TMNT RPG Accessory Pack: Adventures in the Yucatan. Wujcik, Erick & Siembieda, Kevin. Marciniszyn, Alex, ed. 24p. (Orig). (gr. 8 up). 1990. pap. 11.95 (0-916211-45-2, 512) Palladium Bks.
Dombrowski, James, jt. illus. see Fales, Kevin.
Dominguez, Angel. Classic Animal Stories. O'Mara, Lesley, ed. 160p. (gr. 1 up). 1991. 18.95 (1-55970-143-9) Arcade Pub Inc.
Dominiak, Dana M., et al. Mr. Everybody's Musical Apartment, Bk. 1. Feltenberger, Myles. LC 92-96919. 40p. 1993. pap. 9.95 (0-9634218-0-8) Myles Music.
Dominquez, Angel. Diary of a Victorian Mouse. Dominquez, Angel. 32p. (ps up) 1991. 14.95 (1-55970-121-8) Arcade Pub Inc.
Domjan, Joseph. The Artist.., & the Legend: A Visit to China Is Remembered & the Legends Unfold... Werley, Judith G., ed. Domjan, Evelyn A., compiled by. LC 74-81927. (gr. 7 up). 1974. 25.00 (0-933652-09-7) Domjan Studio.
Domm, Jeff. Gray Wolf Pup. Boyle, Doe. Thomas, Peter, narrated by. 32p. (gr. k-3). 1993. 11.95 (1-56899-010-3); incl. audiocassette 16.95 (1-56899-009-X); incl. audiocassette 14 in. plush toy 39.95 (1-56899-007-3); incl. audiocassette, 8 in. plush toy 25.95 (1-56899-008-1) Soundprints.

Donaho, K. Blythe. The Prison Bird. Wright, Lynn F. LC 91-75180. 24p. (gr. 1-4). 1991. 11.95 (0-685-54896-1) WorryWart.
Donahoe, Lindaanne. Your Body & How It Works. Wong, Ovid. LC 86-9686. 128p. (gr. 5 up). 1986. PLB 17.27 (0-516-00534-0) Childrens.
Donahue, Dorothy. Maybe Yes, Maybe No, Maybe Maybe. Patron, Susan. LC 92-34067. 96p. (gr. 3-5). 1993. 14.95 (0-531-05482-9); PLB 14.99 (0-531-08632-1) Orchard Bks Watts.
Donaldson, Judith E. Travel Games: Vol. 2, Five to Ten Years. Donaldson, Judith E. Brown, George H., ed. 36p. (gr. k-5). pap. text ed. 1.50 (0-939942-06-2) Larkspur.
Donatelli, Betty. A Good Book to Toot About. Donatelli, Betty. 11p. (Orig). (gr. 1-2). 1984. pap. 2.00 (0-912981-10-5) Hse BonGiovanni.
—Growing in Reading. Donatelli, Betty. 11p. (Orig). (gr. 1-2). 1984. pap. 2.00 (0-912981-07-5) Hse BonGiovanni.
—Merry Words for You. Donatelli, Betty. 11p. (Orig). (gr. 1-2). 1984. pap. 2.00 (0-912981-09-1) Hse BonGiovanni.
—Sounding Words with Roy & Joy. Donatelli, Betty. 11p. (Orig). (gr. k-2). 1984. pap. 1.00 (0-912981-06-7) Hse BonGiovanni.
—Sunny, Funny Stories. Donatelli, Betty. 11p. (Orig). (gr. 1-2). 1984. pap. 1.00 (0-912981-08-3) Hse BonGiovanni.
Donati, Paolo. Amazing Buildings. Wilkinson, Phil. LC 92-54314. 48p. (gr. 3 up). 1993. 16.95 (1-56458-234-5) Dorling Kindersley.
Doney, Todd. Kentucky Frontiersmen: The Adventures of Henry Ware, Hunter & Border Fighter. rev. ed. Altsheler; Joseph A. Kenton, Nathaniel, ed. LC 88-50581. 256p. (gr. 5-10). 1988. 16.95 (0-929146-01-8) Voyageur Pub.
Doney, Todd L. Sleeping Beauty: The Ballet Story. Horosko, Marian, retold by. LC 93-14399. 1994. text ed. 15.95 (0-689-31885-5, Atheneum) Macmillan.
—The Stone Lion. Schroeder, Alan. LC 93-38257. 32p. (gr. 1-3). 1994. SBE 14.95 (0-684-19578-X, Scribners Young Read) Macmillan Child Grp.
Dong-Ho, Choi. Two Brothers & Their Magic Gourds. Adams, Edward B., ed. 32p. (gr. 3). 1981. 8.95 (0-8048-1474-0, Pub. by Seoul Intl Tourist SK) C E Tuttle.
Doniger, Nancy. Talk about English: How Words Travel & Change. Klausner, Janet. LC 89-49116. 208p. (gr. 5 up). 1990. 14.95 (0-690-04831-9, Crowell Jr Bks); (Crowell Jr Bks) HarpC Child Bks.
Donnelly, Liza. Dinosaur Beach. Donnelly, Liza. 32p. (Orig). (ps-3). 1991. 2.50 (0-590-42176-X); pap. 2.50 (0-685-43744-2) Scholastic Inc.
Donnelly, Marlene H. How to Be a Nature Detective. Selsam, Millicent. LC 93-28523. 1995. write for info. (0-06-023447-4); PLB write for info. (0-06-023448-2) HarpC Child Bks.
—Wetlands. Rood, Ronald. LC 92-47140. (gr. 1-4). 1994. 14.00 (0-06-023010-X); PLB 13.89 (0-06-023011-8) HarpC Child Bks.
Donohoe, Bill & Townsend, Tony. Stars & Planets. Lambert, David. LC 93-28282. 1994. write for info. (0-8114-9246-X) Raintree Steck-V.
Donovan, Bob. Bird Meets Fish. Chipangu, Florita. 36p. 1993. pap. 2.50 (1-878181-07-6) Discovery Comics.
—Monster Love. Deschaine, Scott. 36p. 1993. pap. 2.50 (1-878181-05-X) Discovery Comics.
—Popcorn! Deschaine, Scott. 68p. 1993. pap. 4.95 (1-878181-06-8) Discovery Comics.
Donovan, Karen. The Golden Gate Bridge Troll. Fitzgerald, Jean. 48p. (Orig). (gr. k-2). 1978. pap. 6.95x (0-9618225-0-3) Bridge Troll Pr.
Donze, Lisa. Squanto & the First Thanksgiving. Kessel, Joyce K. LC 82-10313. 48p. (gr. k-4). 1983. PLB 14.95 (0-87614-199-8); pap. 5.95 (0-87614-452-0) Carolrhoda Bks.
Donze, Mary T. I Can Pray the Rosary! Donze, Mary T. 48p. (Orig). (gr. 2-4). 1991. pap. 2.95 (0-89243-335-3) Liguori Pubns.
Doody, Jim. Fibber E. Frog. Newman, Al. LC 93-77685. 32p. (ps-3). 1993. text ed. 13.95 (0-89334-213-0); pap. 4.95 (0-89334-217-3) Humanics Ltd.
—Fraid E. Cat. Newman, Al. LC 93-77687. 32p. (ps-3). 1993. 13.95 (0-89334-215-7); pap. 4.95 (0-89334-219-X) Humanics Ltd.
—Giggle E. Goose. Newman, Al. LC 93-77684. 32p. (ps-3). 1993. 13.95 (0-89334-212-2); pap. 4.95 (0-89334-216-5) Humanics Ltd.
—Grub E. Dog. Newman, Al. LC 93-77686. 32p. (ps-3). 1993. 13.95 (0-89334-214-9); pap. 4.95 (0-89334-218-1) Humanics Ltd.
Dool, Jan. The Witch of Pungo. Kyle, Louisa V. 87p. (gr. 3). 1973. 12.95 (0-927044-00-5) Four Oclock Farms.
Dooling, Michael. Astrid Lindgren. Hurwitz, Johanna. 64p. (gr. 2-6). 1991. 3.95 (0-14-032692-8) Puffin Bks.
—Astrid Lindgren: Storyteller to the World. Hurwitz, Johanna. 64p. (gr. 2-6). 1989. pap. 10.95 (0-670-82207-8) Viking Child Bks.
—The Hundred & One Dalmatians. Smith, Dodie. (gr. 4 up). 1989. pap. 3.95 (0-318-41739-1, Puffin) Puffin Bks.
—Lights on the River. Thomas, Jane R. LC 93-33636. Date not set. 14.95; PLB 14.89 Hyprn Child.
—A Long Way to Go. Oneal, Zibby. 64p. (gr. 2-6). 1990. pap. 11.95 (0-670-82532-8) Viking Child Bks.

—A Long Way to Go: A Story of Women's Right to Vote. Oneal, Zibby. 64p. (gr. 2-6). 1992. pap. 3.99 (*0-14-032950-1*, Puffin) Puffin Bks.
—Mary McLean & the St. Patrick's Day Parade. Kroll, Steven. 32p. (ps-3). 1991. 13.95 (*0-590-43701-1*, Scholastic Hardcover) Scholastic Inc.
—The One Hundred & One Dalmatians. Smith, Dodie. (gr. 5-9). 1989. pap. 3.99 (*0-14-034034-3*, Puffin) Puffin Bks.
—Thomas Jefferson: A Picture Book Biography. Giblin, James C. LC 93-23340. 1994. 14.95 (*0-590-44838-2*) Scholastic Inc.
—Uncle James. Harshman, Marc. 32p. (gr. 1-4). 1993. reinforced bdg. 13.99 (*0-525-65110-1*, Cobblehill Bks) Dutton Child Bks.
Dooling, Mike. Rip Van Winkle. Littledale, Freya. 40p. 1991. pap. 3.95 (*0-590-43113-7*) Scholastic Inc.
—Straw Sense. Rupert, Rona. LC 92-8775. 1993. pap. 14.00 (*0-671-77047-0*, S&S BFYR) S&S Trade.
Doolittle, Jerry. Pollyanna Herself. Dowell, Ruth I. 44p. (ps-6). 1988. pap. 6.00 (*0-945842-08-2*) Pollyanna Prodns.

Doolittle, Jerry, et al. Move Over, Mother Goose Series. Dowell, Ruth I. (Orig.). (ps-6). 1991. pap. write for info. (*0-945842-24-4*) Pollyanna Prodns.
Move Over Mother Goose!, ISBN 0-945842-00-7 $6.00; Jiggle on the Doorknob, ISBN 0-945842-01-5 $4.00; Watch Out, Pollyanna!, ISBN 0-945842-02-3 $4.00; Let's Talk!, ISBN 0-945842-03-1 $6.00; Think About It, ISBN 0-945842-04-X $3.00; Alphabet-ter Letter Rhymes, ISBN 0-945842-05-8 $6.00; Busy Being Me, ISBN 0-945842-07-4 $6.00; Pollyanna Herself, ISBN 0-945842-08-2 $6.00; I Say...You Say!, ISBN 0-945842-12-0 $9.95; Mother Ruth's Rhymes, ISBN 0-945842-13-9 $12.00; Alphabet-ter Letter Rhymes Activity Book, ISBN 0-945842-14-7 $6.00. Fingerplays, action verses & a wide subject range of rhymes to grow by. Indexed for concepts & the curriculum: story rhymes that "grab children & hold on!" *Publisher Provided Annotation.*

Dooney, Michael. Teenage Mutant Ninja Turtles. Eastman, Kevin & Laird, Peter. (gr. 2-6). 1989. bk. & cassette 5.95 (*0-394-84169-7*) Random Bks Yng Read.
Dora. Captain Orkle's Treasure. Micocci, Harriet. (gr. 3-7). 1961. 10.95 (*0-8392-3003-6*) Astor-Honor.
Dore, G. & Didier, J. Nouveaux Contes de Fees. De Segur. (FRE.). 216p. (gr. 5-10). 1980. pap. 8.95 (*2-07-033149-0*) Schoenhof.
Dore, Gustav. Dante's Paradiso. Tusiani, Joseph. (gr. 7 up). 1969. 9.95 (*0-685-00563-1*) Astor-Honor.
Dore, Gustave. Contes de Ma Mere l'Oye. Perrault, Charles. (FRE.). 223p. (gr. 5-10). 1988. pap. 8.95 (*2-07-033443-0*) Schoenhof.
—Perrault's Fairy Tales. Perrault, Charles. LC 72-79522. viii, 117p. (gr. 4-6). 1969. pap. 5.95 (*0-486-22311-6*) Dover.
Doremus, Robert. Albert Einstein: Young Thinker. Hammontree, Marie. LC 86-10730. 192p. (gr. 2-6). 1986. pap. 3.95 (*0-02-041860-4*, Aladdin) Macmillan Child Grp.
—Daniel Boone: Young Hunter & Tracker. Stevenson, Augusta. LC 86-10795. 192p. (gr. 2-6). 1986. pap. 3.95 (*0-02-041830-2*, Aladdin) Macmillan Child Grp.
—Harry S. Truman: Missouri Farm Boy. Hudson, Wilma J. LC 92-7513. 192p. (gr. 3-7). 1992. pap. 3.95 (*0-689-71658-3*, Aladdin) Macmillan Child Grp.
—Helen Keller: From Tragedy to Triumph. Wilkie, Katharine E. LC 86-10719. 192p. (gr. 2-6). 1986. pap. 3.95 (*0-02-041980-5*, Aladdin) Macmillan Child Grp.
—Knute Rockne: Young Athlete. Riper, Guernsey V., Jr. LC 86-10791. 192p. (gr. 2-6). 1986. pap. 3.95 (*0-02-042110-9*, Aladdin) Macmillan Child Grp.
—Sacagawea: American Pathfinder. Seymour, Flora W. LC 90-23267. 192p. (gr. 3-7). 1991. pap. 3.95 (*0-689-71482-3*, Aladdin) Macmillan Child Grp.
—Wilbur & Orville Wright: Young Fliers. Stevenson, Augusta. LC 86-10747. 192p. (gr. 2-6). 1986. pap. 3.95 (*0-02-042170-2*, Aladdin) Macmillan Child Grp.
Dorenkamp, Michelle. The Bread That Grew. Duyff, Roberta L. McKissack, Patricia & McKissack, Fredrick, eds. LC 87-61646. 32p. (Orig.). (gr. 1-3). 1987. text ed. 8.95 (*0-88335-725-9*); pap. text ed. 4.95 (*0-88335-745-3*) Milliken Pub Co.
—My First Diary. Simon, Mary M. 80p. (Orig.). (gr. 2-5). 1992. pap. 4.99 (*0-570-04721-8*) Concordia.

—Smiles for Smiles. Duyff, Roberta L. McKissack, Patricia & McKissack, Fredrick, eds. LC 88-60386. 32p. (Orig.). (gr. 1-3). 1988. text ed. 8.95 (*0-88335-780-1*); pap. text ed. 4.95 (*0-88335-792-5*) Milliken Pub Co.
Dornisch, Alcuin. Prey Animals. Aaseng, Nathan. 48p. (gr. k-3). 1987. PLB 10.95 (*0-8225-1121-5*) Lerner Pubns.
Dornisch, Alcuin C. Animal Specialists. Aaseng, Nathan. 48p. (gr. k-3). 1987. PLB 10.95 (*0-8225-1120-7*) Lerner Pubns.
—Horned Animals. Aaseng, Nathan. 48p. (gr. k-3). 1987. PLB 10.95 (*0-8225-1119-3*) Lerner Pubns.
—Meat-Eating Animals. Aaseng, Nathan. 48p. (gr. k-3). 1987. PLB 10.95 (*0-8225-1118-5*) Lerner Pubns.
Dorr, Mary A. A Child's Garden of Verses. Stevenson, Robert Louis. 24p. (ps-2). 1993. pap. text ed. 0.99 (*1-56293-351-5*) McClanahan Bk.
—Get Ready to Read. Wise, Beth A. 32p. (ps). 1992. wkbk. 1.95 (*1-56293-173-3*) McClanahan Bk.
—My ABC's: Lowercase. Wise, Beth A. 32p. (ps). 1992. wkbk. 1.95 (*1-56293-167-9*) McClanahan Bk.
Dorros, Arthur. Alligator Shoes. Dorros, Arthur. LC 82-2409. (ps-k). 1982. 3.95 (*0-525-44001-1*, Dutton) NAL-Dutton.
—Alligator Shoes. Dorros, Arthur. LC 82-2409. 24p. (ps-k). 1988. pap. 3.95 (*0-525-44428-9*) Dutton Child Bks.
—Ant Cities. Dorros, Arthur. LC 85-48244. 32p. (ps-3). 1987. (Crowell Jr Bks); PLB 14.89 (*0-690-04570-0*, Crowell Jr Bks) HarpC Child Bks.
—Ant Cities. Dorros, Arthur. LC 85-48244. 32p. (gr. k-3). 1988. pap. 4.95 (*0-06-445079-1*, Trophy) HarpC Child Bks.
—Feel the Wind. Dorros, Arthur. LC 88-18961. 32p. (ps-3). 1989. (Crowell Jr Bks); PLB 13.89 (*0-690-04741-X*, Crowell Jr Bks) HarpC Child Bks.
—Feel the Wind. Dorros, Arthur. LC 88-18961. 32p. (ps-3). 1990. pap. 4.50 (*0-06-445095-3*, Trophy) HarpC Child Bks.
—Follow the Water from Brook to Ocean. Dorros, Arthur. LC 90-1438. 32p. (gr. k-4). 1991. 15.00 (*0-06-021598-4*); PLB 14.89 (*0-06-021599-2*) HarpC Child Bks.
—Magic Secrets. rev. ed. Wyler, Rose & Ames, Gerald. LC 89-35841. 64p. (gr. k-3). 1990. 14.00 (*0-06-026646-5*); PLB 13.89 (*0-06-026647-3*) HarpC Child Bks.
—Magic Secrets. rev. ed. Wyler, Rose & Ames, Gerald. LC 89-35841. 64p. (gr. k-3). 1991. pap. 3.50 (*0-06-444153-9*, Trophy) HarpC Child Bks.
—What Makes Day & Night? rev. ed. Branley, Franklyn M. LC 85-40657. 32p. (gr. k-3). 1986. pap. 4.95 (*0-06-445050-3*, Trophy) HarpC Child Bks.
—What Makes Day & Night? rev. ed. Branley, Franklyn M. LC 85-47903. 32p. (ps-3). 1986. PLB 14.89 (*0-690-04524-7*, Crowell Jr Bks) HarpC Child Bks.
Dorsey, Kim. Rhymin' Simon's Small Talk: Self Discovery Stress Management. Dorsey, Marilyn M. 83p. (gr. 4 up). 1991. pap. 6.95 (*0-916369-18-8*) Magnolia Pr.
Dorta, Teresa. On Little Things, Challenges & Needs. Viamonte, Manuel. 80p. (Orig.). 1991. pap. 3.95 (*1-56259-015-4*) Editorial Amer.
Dotter, Earl, photos by. In Our Blood: Four Coal Mining Families. Witt, Matt. LC 78-71518. (Orig.). (gr. 10-12). 1979. pap. text ed. 6.95 (*0-9602226-1-8*) Highlander.
Doty, Eldon C. Zoo Clues: Making the Most of Your Visit to the Zoo. Gerstenfeld, Sheldon L. 128p. (gr. 2-5). 1991. 13.95 (*0-670-82362-7*) Viking Child Bks.
—Zoo Clues: Making the Most of Your Visit to the Zoo. Gerstenfeld, Sheldon. 120p. (gr. 2 up). 1993. pap. 4.99 (*0-14-032813-0*, Puffin) Puffin Bks.
Doty, Roy. Blinkers & Buzzers: Building & Experimenting with Electricity & Magnetism. Zubrowski, Bernie. LC 90-44519. 112p. (gr. 3 up). 1991. pap. 6.95 (*0-688-09965-3*, Pub. by Beech Tree Bks) Morrow.
—Blinkers & Buzzers: Building & Experimenting with Electricity & Magnetism. Zubrowski, Bernie. LC 90-44519. 112p. (gr. 3 up). 1991. PLB 12.88 (*0-688-09966-1*) Morrow Jr Bks.
—Extraordinary Stories: Behind the Inventions of Ordinary Things. Wulffson, Don L. (gr. 3-7). 1991. pap. 3.50 (*0-380-71294-6*, Camelot) Avon.
—The First Travel Guide to the Moon: What to Pack, How to Go, & What to See When You Get There. Blumberg, Rhoda. LC 84-28757. 96p. (gr. 3-7). 1984. Repr. of 1980 ed. 13.95 (*0-02-711680-8*, Four Winds) Macmillan Child Grp.
—Freebies for Sports Fans. Nash, Bruce & Zullo, Allan. 96p. (gr. 1 up). 1990. pap. 4.95 (*0-671-70339-0*, S&S BFYR) S&S Trade.
—Girls Can Be Anything. Klein, Norma. LC 72-85258. 32p. (ps-1). 1975. 11.95 (*0-525-30662-5*, DCB); pap. 3.95 (*0-525-45029-7*, DCB) Dutton Child Bks.
—How to Be School Smart: Secrets of Successful Schoolwork. James, Elizabeth & Barkin, Carol. LC 87-2899. 96p. (gr. 4-7). 1988. pap. 6.95 (*0-688-06798-0*, Pub. by Beech Tree Bks) Morrow.
—How to Write Your Best Book Report. James, Elizabeth & Barkin, Carol. LC 86-8597. 80p. (gr. 3-7). 1986. 11.88 (*0-688-05744-6*) Lothrop.
—How to Write Your Best Book Report. James, Elizabeth & Barkin, Carol. LC 86-8597. 80p. (gr. 3-7). 1986. pap. 6.00 (*0-688-05743-8*, Pub. by Beech Tree Bks) Morrow.

—The Invention of Ordinary Things. Wulffson, Don L. LC 80-17498. 96p. (gr. 3 up). 1981. PLB 12.88 (*0-688-51978-4*) Lothrop.
—Jobs for Kids. Barkin, Carol & James, Elizabeth. LC 89-45900. 128p. (gr. 5-9). 1989. lib. bdg. 11.88 (*0-688-09324-8*) Lothrop.
—Jobs for Kids. Barkin, Carol & James, Elizabeth. LC 89-45900. 128p. (gr. 5-9). 1991. pap. 6.95 (*0-688-09323-X*, Pub. by Beech Tree Bks) Morrow.
—Kid Camping from Aaaaiii! to Zip. McManus, Patrick F. LC 79-13152. (gr. 3-8). 1979. 12.95 (*0-688-41910-0*) Lothrop.
—Kid Camping from AAAAIII! to Zip. McManus, Patrick F. 144p. (gr. 6-7). 1991. pap. 3.50 (*0-380-71311-X*, Camelot) Avon.
—Making Waves: Finding Out about Rhythmic Motion. Zubrowski, Bernie. LC 93-35455. 1994. lib. bdg. write for info. (*0-688-11787-2*) Morrow.
—Making Waves: Finding Out about Rhythmic Motion. Zubrowski, Bernie. LC 93-35455. 1994. pap. write for info. (*0-688-11788-0*, Pub. by Beech Tree Bks) Morrow.
—Mirrors. Zubrowski, Bernie. LC 91-29142. 112p. (gr. 3 up). 1992. pap. 6.95 (*0-688-10591-2*, Pub. by Beech Tree Bks) Morrow.
—Mirrors: Finding Out about the Properties of Light. Zubrowski, Bernie. LC 91-29142. 96p. (gr. 3 up). 1992. PLB 13.93 (*0-688-10592-0*) Morrow Jr Bks.
—Mobiles: Building & Experimenting with Balancing Toys. Zubrowski, Bernie. LC 92-28408. 104p. (gr. 3 up). 1993. Repr. PLB 13.93 (*0-688-10590-4*) Morrow Jr Bks.
—Tales of a Fourth Grade Nothing. Blume, Judy. LC 70-179050. 128p. (gr. 2-5). 1972. 11.95 (*0-525-40720-0*, DCB) Dutton Child Bks.
—Tales of a Fourth Grade Nothing. large type ed. Blume, Judy. 174p. (gr. 2-6). 1987. Repr. of 1972 ed. lib. bdg. 14.95 (*1-55736-015-4*, Crnrstn Bks) BDD LT Grp.
—You Can Speak up in Class. Gilbert, Sara. 64p. (gr. 3 up). 1991. pap. 6.95 (*0-688-10304-9*, Pub. by Beech Tree Bks) Morrow.
—You Can Speak up in Class. Gilbert, Sara. LC 90-19268. 64p. (gr. 3 up). 1991. PLB 12.88 (*0-688-09867-3*) Morrow Jr Bks.
Doty, Roy, photos by. How to Be School Smart: Secrets of Successful Schoolwork. James, Elizabeth & Barkin, Carol. Greenlaw, M. Jean, intro. by. LC 87-2899. (gr. 4-7). 1988. lib. bdg. 12.88 (*0-688-06799-9*) Lothrop.
Doubet, Amy. Over the Top. Novak, Greg. 120p. (Orig.). (gr. 9-12). 1990. pap. 12.00 (*1-55878-012-2*) Game Designers.
Doubilet, David, photos by. Under the Sea from A to Z. Doubilet, Anne. LC 90-1355. 32p. (gr. k-6). 1991. 15.00 (*0-517-57836-0*); PLB 15.00 (*0-517-57837-9*) Crown Bks Yng Read.
Doubilet, David, et al. Shark. Chinery, Michael. LC 90-33361. 32p. (gr. 4-6). 1991. lib. bdg. 11.59 (*0-8167-2104-1*); pap. text ed. 3.95 (*0-8167-2105-X*) Troll Assocs.
Dougherty, Charles, et al. Faeries: A Complete Handbook of the Seelie. Link, Sarah, et al. 144p. (Orig.). (gr. 11 up). 1991. pap. text ed. 17.95 (*0-9627790-5-9*) White Wolf.
Dougherty, Edie. Developing Creative Thinking. Juntune, Joyce E. 30p. (gr. k-4). 1984. pap. 5.00 (*0-912773-09-X*) One Hund Twenty Creat.
—Developing Creative Thinking: Fun Book, No. 2. Juntune, Joyce E. 26p. (gr. k-4). 1984. pap. 5.00 (*0-912773-08-1*) One Hund Twenty Creat.
—Developing Creative Thinking: Fun Book, No. 3. Juntune, Joyce E. (ps-5). 1985. pap. 6.00 (*0-912773-10-3*) One Hund Twenty Creat.
Doughty, Virgina. Pen Pals, Vol. 1: The Beginning. Gunn, Jeffrey. (Orig.). (gr. 3). 1990. pap. write for info. (*1-879146-01-0*) Knowldg Pub.
—Pen Pals, Vol. 5: Facts about Dust. Gunn, Jeffrey. (Orig.). (gr. 3). 1990. pap. write for info. (*1-879146-05-3*) Knowldg Pub.
Douglas, Cal. Brave Little Blackfoot. Toussant, Eliza. 32p. (Orig.). (gr. 1 up). 1993. pap. text ed. write for info. (*0-9630583-3-9*) E Toussant.

—The Cootie Dragons. Toussant, Eliza. 120p. (gr. 4 up). 1993. pap. text ed. write for info. (*0-9630583-2-0*) E Toussant.
THE COOTIE DRAGONS was written to help children to better understand HIV & AIDS. The AIDS virus is a health problem that has been identified as "Public Enemy Number One." Children hear about AIDS, just as we all do. But the real question is, just how much do they understand? Before printing THE COOTIE DRAGONS, I gathered twenty students & asked them one by one to tell me what they knew about AIDS. Just as I expected they knew very little & were very confused about the subject. I gave each of the students a

rough draft of THE COOTIE DRAGONS to take home with them & read. Three days later I met with the same group of children & asked them again what they knew about AIDS. Their knowledge level had improved one hundred percent. Basic health education should be started as early as possible, in keeping with parental & community standards. It is very important that middle school students (those entering their teens) learn to protect themselves from the AIDS virus. Children must also be taught values & responsibility, as well as skills to help them resist peer pressure that might lead to risky behavior. These skills can be reinforced by religious & community groups. However, final responsibility rests with the parents. As a parent, I encourage you to read THE COOTIE DRAGONS, & discuss the book with your children. *Publisher Provided Annotation.*

Douglas, Julie. How Do Things Grow? Althea. LC 90-10923. 32p. (gr. k-3). 1991. PLB 11.59 (*0-8167-2118-1*); pap. text ed. 3.95 (*0-8167-2119-X*) Troll Assocs.
—Listen...What Do You Hear? Wood, Nicholas & Rye, Jennifer. LC 90-40136. 32p. (gr. k-3). 1991. lib. bdg. 11.59 (*0-8167-2120-3*); pap. text ed. 3.95 (*0-8167-2121-1*) Troll Assocs.
Douglas, Virginia. Birdwatch: A Young Person's Introduction to Birding. MacPherson, Mary. 144p. (Orig.). (gr. 6 up). 1989. pap. 9.95 (*0-920197-57-4*, Pub. by Summerhill CN) Sterling.
Douglas-Hamilton, Iain, photos by. The Elephant Family Book. Douglas-Hamilton, Oria. LC 89-77319. 56p. (ps up). 1991. pap. 15.95 (*0-88708-126-6*) Picture Bk Studio.
Douglas-Hamilton, Oria. African Elephants: Giants of the Land. Patent, Dorothy H. LC 91-55028. 40p. (gr. 3-7). 1991. reinforced 14.95 (*0-8234-0911-2*) Holiday.
Douglass, S. Multicultural Stories. Branch, James H., III. Ward, Dick, ed. LC 92-93449. 29p. 1992. 12.50 (*0-9635840-0-6*) Guttenburg Pub.
Dove, Sally. The Mischief Maker. Pitcher, Diana. 64p. 1990. pap. 5.95 (*0-86486-106-0*, Pub. by D Philip South Africa) Interlink Pub.

Dow, Bill, photos by. The Cats of Shambala. rev. ed. Hedren, Tippi & Taylor, Theodore. 300p. (gr. 6 up). 1992. pap. 14.95 (*0-9631549-0-7*) Tiger Isld Pr.
Here is the riveting, lavishly illustrated saga of how actress Tippi Hedren, in the process of making a feature film as a plea to save wildlife, came to share her home & hearth with its "stars" - some hundred lions, tigers, leopards, cheetahs, & cougars - on a 180 acre preserve in California. Over a hundred photos bring the big cats, & the humans who worked, lived, raised them from cubs & sometimes slept with them, vividly to life. "An exciting read..."--Library Journal. "An intriguing tale of obsession..."--Kirkus Review. "This is a rare & captivating book... fascinating, unusual & engrossing"--John Barkham Reviews. "Animal lovers will have difficulty putting Hedren's book down..."--Charleston Evening Post.
Publisher Provided Annotation.

Dow, Bonnie. God Loves Children. Hughes, Barbara & Dwiggins, Gwen. (ps-3). 1987. 0.99 (*0-8091-6562-7*) Paulist Pr.
—God Loves Colors. Hughes, Barbara & Dwiggins, Gwen. (ps-3). 1987. 0.99 (*0-8091-6566-X*) Paulist Pr.
—God Loves Fun. Hughes, Barbara & Dwiggins, Gwen. (ps-3). 1987. 0.99 (*0-8091-6564-3*) Paulist Pr.
—God Loves Love. Hughes, Barbara & Dwiggins, Gwen. (ps-3). 1987. 0.99 (*0-8091-6565-1*) Paulist Pr.
—God Loves Seasons. Hughes, Barbara & Dwiggins, Gwen. (ps-3). 1987. 0.99 (*0-8091-6563-5*) Paulist Pr.

Dow, Jill. Our Changing World: The Forest. Bellamy, David. 24p. (gr. 1-4). 1988. bds. 12.00 (*0-517-56800-4*, Clarkson Potter) Crown Bks Yng Read.
—Our Changing World: The River. Bellamy, David. 24p. (gr. 1-4). 1988. bds. 12.00 (*0-517-56801-2*, Clarkson Potter) Crown Bks Yng Read.
—Our Changing World: The Rock Pool. Bellamy, David. 32p. (gr. 1-5). 1988. 9.95 (*0-517-56977-9*, Clarkson Potter) Crown Bks Yng Read.
Dowd, Ken. Island Eyes: The Adventures of a Shell. Lee, A. Laney. LC 85-8972. 112p. (gr. 2-5). 1987. 12.95 (*0-688-06094-3*) Lothrop.
Dowd, Vic. Henry Clay: Leader in Congress. Stone-Peterson, Helen. 80p. (gr. 2-6). 1991. Repr. of 1964 ed. lib. bdg. 12.95 (*0-7910-1457-6*) Chelsea Hse.
Dowden, Anne O. The Clover & the Bee: A Book of Pollination. Dowden, Anne O. LC 87-30116. 96p. (gr. 5 up). 1990. 18.00 (*0-690-04677-4*, Crowell Jr Bks); PLB 17.89 (*0-690-04679-0*, Crowell Jr Bks) HarpC Child Bks.
—Consider the Lilies: Flowers of the Bible. Paterson, John & Paterson, Katherine. LC 85-43603. 48p. (gr. 7 up). 1986. 14.00 (*0-690-04461-5*, Crowell Jr Bks) HarpC Child Bks.
—The Lore & Legends of Flowers. Crowell, Robert L. LC 79-7829. 88p. (gr. 7 up). 1982. (Crowell Jr Bks); (Crowell Jr Bks) HarpC Child Bks.
—Plants of Christmas. Borland, Hal. LC 87-552. 32p. (gr. 3 up). 1987. Repr. of 1969 ed. 14.95 (*0-690-04649-9*, Crowell Jr Bks); (Crowell Jr Bks) HarpC Child Bks.
—Shakespeare's Flowers. Kerr, Jessica. LC 68-13585. 96p. (gr. 7 up). 1982. (Crowell Jr Bks); (Crowell Jr Bks) HarpC Child Bks.
—Shakespeare's Flowers. Kerr, Jessica. 86p. (gr. 7 up). 1992. PLB 16.89 (*0-06-022877-6*) HarpC Child Bks.
—State Flowers. Reissue. ed. Dowden, Anne O. LC 78-41927. 96p. (gr. 5 up). 1978. PLB 14.89 (*0-690-03884-4*, Crowell Jr Bks) HarpC Child Bks.
Dowden, D. D. Arizona Wildflowers. Magley, Beverly. 32p. (gr. 1-8). 1991. pap. 5.95 (*1-56044-096-1*) Falcon Pr MT.
—California Wildflowers. Magley, Beverly. LC 88-83883. 32p. (Orig.). (gr. 3-6). 1989. pap. 4.95 (*0-937959-58-8*) Falcon Pr MT.
—The Fire Mountains: The Story of the Cascade Volcanos. Magley, Beverly. LC 88-83884. 32p. (Orig.). (gr. 3-6). 1989. pap. 5.95 (*0-937959-57-X*) Falcon Pr MT.
—Minnesota Wildflowers: Childrens Field Guide. Magley, Beverly. 32p. (Orig.). (gr. 4-7). 1992. pap. 5.95 (*1-56044-117-8*) Falcon Pr MT.
—Montana Wildflowers. Magley, Beverly. 32p. (Orig.). (gr. 4-7). 1992. pap. 5.95 (*1-56044-118-6*) Falcon Pr MT.
—North Carolina Wildflowers: A Children's Field Guide to the State's Most Common Flowers. Magley, Beverly. 32p. (Orig.). 1993. pap. 5.95 (*1-56044-184-4*) Falcon Pr MT.
—Oregon Wildflowers: Childrens Field Guide. Magley, Beverly. 32p. (Orig.). (gr. 4-7). 1992. pap. 5.95 (*1-56044-035-X*) Falcon Pr MT.
—Texas Wildflowers: A Children's Field Guide to the State's Most Common Flowers. Magley, Beverly. 32p. (Orig.). 1993. pap. 5.95 (*1-56044-183-6*) Falcon Pr MT.
—The Tree Giants. Schnieder, Bill. LC 88-80225. 32p. 1988. pap. 4.95 (*0-937959-40-5*) Falcon Pr MT.
Dowell, Philip, photos by. Pond & River. Parker, Steve. LC 88-1575. 64p. (gr. 5 up). 1988. 15.00 (*0-394-89615-7*); lib. bdg. 15.99 (*0-394-99615-1*) Knopf Bks Yng Read.
—Skeleton. Parker, Steve. LC 87-26314. 64p. (gr. 5 up). 1988. 15.00 (*0-394-89620-3*); lib. bdg. 15.99 (*0-394-99620-8*) Knopf Bks Yng Read.
Dowley, May. Being Cool, Going to School. Smith, Josephine A. Wilkins, Natalie, ed. LC 92-74244. 64p. (Orig.). 1994. pap. text ed. 2.99 (*1-881958-02-7*) Hickle Pickle.

— Hickle the Pickle. rev. ed. Smith, Josephine A. LC 92-96864. 40p. 1992. pap. 2.99 (*1-881958-00-0*, TX2-116-470) Hickle Pickle.
HICKLE THE PICKLE; is a delightful children's book written in story & rhyme by Josephine A. Smith & illustrated by May Dowley. Follow the adventures of Hickle the Pickle, who as a special cucumber seed only used by pickle factories, gets mixed up with a bunch of wrong seeds & is planted in someone's backyard garden. As a cucumber who would not settle for being sliced as bread & butter pickles, or being put into potato salad, Hickle leaves his clinging vine in search of adventure. "HICKLE THE PICKLE has been on local & national news & is becoming quite an interesting dill!" HICKLE THE

PICKLE is the first in a series of eight Hickle books. ISBN 1-881958-00-0. OFF THE VINE DOIN' FINE; The second in a series also in story & rhyme, written by Josephine A. Smith & illustrated by May Dowley. On the way to the pickle factory Hickle saw some interesting things. Boys on the playground playing on swings. Children eating ice cream cones & having fun. Hickle decided at that point, "I WANT TO BE A LITTLE BOY!!!" He causes quite a mess when he escapes from the vat & hides, only to be found & taken home with one of the workers. Sarah tries to help Hickle adjust to the outside world, which is a full time job. ISBN: 1-881958-01-9.
Publisher Provided Annotation.

—Off the Vine, Doin' Fine. Smith, Josephine A. LC 92-96865. 48p. (Orig.). 1992. pap. 2.99 (*1-881958-01-9*, TXU328879*) Hickle Pickle.
Dowling, Marilyn. Exploring the Numbers One to Ten. Walsh, Abigail. 24p. (ps-2). Date not set. PLB 11.95 (*1-56065-108-3*) Capstone Pr. Postponed.
—Exploring the Seasons. Walsh, Abigail. 24p. (ps-2). Date not set. PLB 11.95 (*1-56065-109-1*) Capstone Pr. Postponed.
—Momma Cat. Walsh, Abigail M. LC 90-823. 112p. (gr. 2 up). 1990. 6.95 (*0-934745-16-1*) Acadia Pub Co.
Dowling, Paul. Are You Sleepy, Puff? Dowling, Paul. LC 92-72934. 32p. (ps-k). 1993. 9.95 (*1-56282-393-0*) Hyprn Child.
—Meg & Jack Are Moving. Dowling, Paul. 32p. (ps-3). 1990. 10.70 (*0-395-53514-X*) HM.
—Meg & Jack's New Friends. Dowling, Paul. 32p. (ps-3). 1990. 10.70 (*0-395-53513-1*) HM.
—Nuts about Nuts. rev. ed. Wilmer, Diane. 32p. (gr. k-2). 1990. Repr. of 1989 ed. PLB 10.50 (*1-878363-09-3*) Forest Hse.
—Poonam's Pets. Davies, Andrew & Davies, Diana. 32p. (ps-2). 1990. pap. 12.95 (*0-670-83321-5*) Viking Child Bks.
—Splodger. Dowling, Paul. 32p. (ps). 1991. 13.45 (*0-395-57443-9*, Sandpiper) HM.
—You Can Do It, Rabbit. Dowling, Paul. LC 91-48352. 32p. (ps-k). 1992. Repr. text ed. 9.95 (*1-56282-252-7*) Hyprn Child.
—You Need a Bath, Mustard. Dowling, Paul. LC 92-72933. 32p. (ps-k). 1993. 9.95 (*1-56282-392-2*) Hyprn Child.
—Zap Zero - The Delivery Man. rev. ed. Wilmer, Diane. 32p. (gr. k-2). 1990. Repr. of 1989 ed. PLB 10.50 (*1-878363-11-5*) Forest Hse.
Downer, Maggie. The Tale of the Napkin Rabbit. Wood, A. J. LC 93-9864. (gr. 3 up). 1993. 14.95 (*0-307-17603-7*, Artsts Writrs) Western Pub.
—The Treasure Hunt. Wood, A. J. LC 92-5515. 32p. (gr. k up). 1992. 13.95 (*1-56566-018-8*) Thomasson-Grant.
Downey, Jane. Molly Moonshine & Timothy. Weber, Kathryn. 44p. (gr. 2-4). 1990. pap. 2.95 (*1-878438-01-8*) Ranch House Pr.
Downey, William R. Poisonous Snakes. Simon, Seymour. LC 85-24202. 80p. (gr. 3-7). 1984. SBE 14.95 (*0-02-782850-6*, Four Winds) Macmillan Child Grp.
Downing, Johnette. A Squirrel Jumped Out of the Tree. Downing, Johnette. (ps). 1990. pap. 2.50 (*0-938991-57-4*) Colonial Pr AL.
Downing, Julie. Cabbage Rose. Helldorfer, M. C. LC 91-9833. 32p. (ps-3). 1993. RSBE 14.95 (*0-02-743513-X*, Bradbury Pr) Macmillan Child Grp.
—Daniel's Gift. Helldorfer, M. C. LC 87-5160. 32p. (ps-3). 1987. RSBE 13.95 (*0-02-743511-3*, Bradbury Pr) Macmillan Child Grp.
—Daniel's Gift. Helldorfer, M. C. LC 90-186. 32p. (gr. k-3). 1990. pap. 4.95 (*0-689-71440-8*, Aladdin) Macmillan Child Grp.
—The Great Adventure of Wo Ti. Zimelman, Nathan. LC 90-38150. 32p. (gr. k-3). 1992. RSBE 14.95 (*0-02-793731-3*, Macmillan Child Bk) Macmillan Child Grp.
—I Had a Cat. Reeves, Mona R. LC 87-37608. 32p. (ps-1). 1989. RSBE 13.95 (*0-02-775731-5*, Bradbury Pr) Macmillan Child Grp.
—Mr. Griggs' Work. Rylant, Cynthia. LC 88-1484. 32p. (ps-2). 1989. 14.95 (*0-531-05769-0*); PLB 14.99 (*0-531-08369-1*) Orchard Bks Watts.
—Mr. Griggs' Work. Rylant, Cynthia. LC 88-1484. 32p. (ps-2). 1993. pap. 5.95 (*0-531-07037-9*) Orchard Bks Watts.
—Mozart Tonight. Downing, Julie. LC 90-34479. 40p. 1991. RSBE 15.95 (*0-02-732881-3*, Bradbury Pr) Macmillan Child Grp.
—Mozart Tonight. Downing, Julie. LC 93-27445. 40p. 1994. pap. 5.95 (*0-685-68187-4*, Aladdin) Macmillan Child Grp.
—Prince Boghole. Haugaard, Erik C. LC 86-61. 32p. (gr. k-3). 1987. SBE 14.95 (*0-02-743440-0*, Macmillan Child Bk) Macmillan Child Grp.

—Pulling My Leg. Carson, Jo. LC 89-70978. 32p. (ps-2). 1990. 14.95 *(0-531-05817-4)*; PLB 14.99 *(0-531-08417-5)* Orchard Bks Watts.
—Pulling My Leg. Carson, Jo. LC 89-70978. 32p. (ps-2). 1994. pap. 5.95 *(0-531-07046-8)* Orchard Bks Watts.
—A Ride on the Red Mare's Back. Le Guin, Ursula K. LC 91-21677. 48p. (gr. 1-4). 1992. 15.95 *(0-531-05991-X)*; PLB 15.99 *(0-531-08591-0)* Orchard Bks Watts.
—Sonia Begonia. Rocklin, Joanne. LC 85-23120. 96p. (gr. 3-7). 1986. SBE 12.95 *(0-02-777310-8,* Macmillan Child Bk) Macmillan Child Grp.
—White Snow - Blue Feather. Downing, Julie. LC 89-815. 32p. (ps-1). 1989. RSBE 13.95 *(0-02-732530-X,* Bradbury Pr) Macmillan Child Grp.
Downing, Julie, photos by. Soon, Annala. Levinson, Riki. LC 92-44588. 32p. (ps-2). 1993. 14.95 *(0-531-05494-2)*; PLB 14.99 *(0-531-08644-5)* Orchard Bks Watts.
Downs, Peter, photos by. Amazing Bikes. Lord, Trevor. LC 92-911. 32p. (Orig.). (gr. 1-5). 1992. PLB 9.99 *(0-679-92772-7)*; pap. 7.99 *(0-679-82772-2)* Knopf Bks Yng Read.
Doyle, A. Bean Sprouts - a How to Story Rhyme & Activity Workbook. Story Time Stories That Rhyme Staff. 30p. (Orig.). (gr. 4-7). 1992. pap. text ed. 17.95 *(0-939476-82-7,* Pub. by Biblio Pr) Prosperity & Profits.
Doyle, A. C. Fish Convention Plus Twenty-Five Stories, Story Rhyme Coloring & Activity Book. rev. ed. Story Rhyme Staff. 12p. (Orig.). (gr. 4-8). 1993. notebk. 19.95 *(0-913597-48-1,* Pub. by Alpha Pyramis) Prosperity & Profits.
Doyle, Richard. The King of the Golden River or the Black Brother. Ruskin, John. LC 74-82199. viii, 56p. (gr. 1 up). 1974. pap. 2.95 *(0-486-20066-3)* Dover.
Drake, Charles, jt. illus. see Zerner, Amy.
Draper, Angie. Black Stallion's Ghost. Farley, Walter. (gr. 5-9). 1978. lib. bdg. 10.99 *(0-394-90618-7)*; pap. 3.95 *(0-394-83919-6)* Random Bks Yng Read.
Draper, Tani. Magic Penny Big Book. Reynolds, Malvina. (ps-2). 1988. pap. text ed. 14.00 *(0-922053-19-7)* N Edge Res.
—Peanut Butter & Jelly Big Book. (ps-2). 1988. pap. text ed. 14.00 *(0-922053-10-3)* N Edge Res.
Drath, Bill. If I Found a Wistful Unicorn: A Gift of Love. Ashford, Ann. 40p. 1992. 6.95 *(1-56145-047-2)* Peachtree Pubs.
—When Someone Dies. Greenlee, Sharon. 40p. (gr. 1-7). 1992. 12.95 *(1-56145-044-8)* Peachtree Pubs.
Drawson, Blair. Pickle Pickle Pickle Juice. Wolcott, Patty. LC 91-12774. 32p. (ps-2). 1991. 3.50 *(0-679-81928-2)*; PLB 6.99 *(0-679-91928-7)* Random Bks Yng Read.
Dreamer, Sue. Happy Silly Birthday to Me. McGovern, Ann. 32p. (gr. k-3). 1994. pap. 2.50 *(0-590-46365-9,* Cartwheel Bks) Scholastic Inc.
—A Teddy Bear Christmas. Dreamer, Sue. 10p. (ps-1). 1992. bds. 7.95 *(1-56397-121-6)* Boyds Mills Pr.
Dreany, E. J. George Washington: Young Leader. Stevenson, Augusta. LC 86-10914. 192p. (gr. 2-6). 1986. pap. 3.95 *(0-02-042150-8,* Aladdin) Macmillan Child Grp.
Dreany, F. Joseph. Buffalo Bill: Frontier Daredevil. Stevenson, Augusta. LC 90-23767. 192p. (gr. 3-7). 1991. pap. 3.95 *(0-689-71479-3,* Aladdin) Macmillan Child Grp.
Drescher, Henrik. Brer Rabbit & the Wonderful Tar Baby. Harris, Joel C. & Metaxas, Eric, eds. LC 90-7166. 32p. (gr. k up). 1991. pap. 14.95 *(0-88708-144-4,* Rabbit Ears); pap. 19.95 incl. cass. *(0-88708-145-2,* Rabbit Ears) Picture Bk Studio.
—Brer Rabbit & the Wonderful Tar Baby. Harris, Joel C. 64p. 1992. Repr. of 1990 ed. Mini-bk. incl. cass. 9.95 *(0-88708-250-5,* Rabbit Ears) Picture Bk Studio.
—The Fool & the Flying Ship. Metaxas, Eric. LC 91-40669. 40p. (gr. k up). 1992. pap. 14.95 *(0-88708-228-9,* Rabbit Ears); incl. cass. 19.95 *(0-88708-229-7,* Rabbit Ears) Picture Bk Studio.
—No Plain Pets! Barasch, Marc I. LC 90-22518. 40p. (ps-3). 1991. 14.95 *(0-06-022472-X)*; PLB 14.89 *(0-06-022473-8)* HarpC Child Bks.
—Opposites. Wilbur, Richard. LC 92-39472. 1994. write for info. *(0-15-230563-7)* HarBrace.
—Pat the Beastie: A Pull-&-Poke Book. Drescher, Henrik. 18p. (ps). 1993. 9.95 *(1-56282-407-4)* Hyprn Child.
—Poems of A. Nonny Mouse. Prelutsky, Jack, intro. by. LC 89-31672. 48p. (gr. 1-7). 1989. 12.95 *(0-394-88711-5)*; lib. bdg. 14.99 *(0-394-98711-X)* Knopf Bks Yng Read.
—Whose Furry Nose? Drescher, Henrik. LC 87-45151. 32p. (gr. k-3). 1987. (Lipp Jr Bks) HarpC Child Bks.
—Whose Scaly Tail? Drescher, Henrik. LC 87-45152. 32p. (gr. k-3). 1987. (Lipp Jr Bks) HarpC Child Bks.
Drescher, Joan. The Birth-Order Blues. Drescher, Joan. 32p. (ps-3). 1993. RB 13.99 *(0-670-83621-4)* Viking Child Bks.
—The Caption Workbook. Decker, Nan. 27p. (gr. 5-8). 1984. pap. text ed. 1.95 *(0-913072-61-3)* Natl Assn Deaf.
—A Children's Museum Activity Book: Bubbles. Zubrowski, Bernie. LC 78-27497. (gr. 5-7). 1979. pap. 7.95 *(0-316-98881-2)* Little.
—Eaton Stanley & the Mind Control Experiment. Adler, David A. LC 84-21135. 96p. (gr. 2-6). 1985. 11.95 *(0-525-44117-4,* DCB) Dutton Child Bks.
—I'm in Charge. Drescher, Joan. (gr. 1-3). 1981. 9.95 *(0-316-19330-5,* Pub. by Atlantic Pr) Little.
—Max & Rufus. Drescher, Joan. (gr. k-3). 1982. write for info. HM.
—My Mother's Getting Married. Drescher, Joan. LC 84-18642. 32p. (ps-3). 1986. PLB 10.89 *(0-8037-0176-4)* Dial Bks Young.
—My Mother's Getting Married. Drescher, Joan. LC 84-18642. 32p. (ps-3). 1989. pap. 4.95 *(0-8037-0642-1)* Dial Bks Young.
—Your Family, My Family. Drescher, Joan. 32p. (gr. 2-5). 1980. PLB 13.85 *(0-8027-6383-9)* Walker & Co.

Drew, James. Rackstraw: The Magical Thoughts & Adventures of A Brilliant Young Art Mouse. Drew, James. George, Mary G., ed. LC 93-71718. 168p. (gr. 2-9). 1994. 18.95 *(0-9625023-9-1)* Art Pr Intl.
In this world of Art Mice, magic & art shape the lives of Rackstraw & his family, leading to mysterious & exciting adventures that include a ghost, hornets, menacing hawks, & dancing spiders. Woven into the fabric of this multilayered, humorous fantasy are some of the world's greatest artists, real & imagined, from Bach to Picasso to the Art Mouse in Prague known simply as Bela - all supported by the values & traditions that are essential for the survival of our culture. RACKSTRAW celebrates children's dreams, their aspirations, & their imaginations & it reflects the best qualities in all of us. In the words of concert pianist Lorin Hollander, "RACKSTRAW is deeply sensitive & very moving; it captures the interest & heart of those who enter in on its journey." Noted educators Frances Clark & Louise Goss declare that "RACKSTRAW surely deserves to become a children's classic." Pulitzer Prize winner Donald Martino states, "RACKSTRAW should be required reading for all of us - young & old." Adults will enjoy reading this story to the young child; junior readers (ages 9-13) will read RACKSTRAW themselves, & will find encouragement for their own artistic adventures, for this is an Art Mouse's spiritual odyssey. Order from: Artistry Press International, P.O. Box 741111, Orange City, FL 32774-1111; 904-775-6407.
Publisher Provided Annotation.

Driggs, Helen. Start Exploring Folktales of Native Americans: A Story-Filled Coloring Book. Borgenicht, David. 128p. (Orig.). (gr. 3 up). 1993. pap. 8.95 *(1-56138-303-1)* Running Pr.
—Start Exploring Insects: A Fact-Filled Coloring Book. Glenn, George S., Jr. 128p. (Orig.). (gr. 3 up). 1991. pap. 8.95 *(1-56138-043-1)* Running Pr.
—Start Exploring Masterpieces of American Art: A Fact-Filled Coloring Book. Gartenhaus, Alan. 128p. (Orig.). 1992. pap. 8.95 *(1-56138-083-0)* Running Pr.
—Start Exploring Space: A Fact-Filled Coloring Book. Mammana, Dennis. 128p. (Orig.). (gr. 3 up). 1991. pap. 8.95 *(0-89471-864-9)* Running Pr.
Dr. Seuss. Bartholomew & the Oobleck. Dr. Seuss. (gr. k-3). 1949. 11.00 *(0-394-80075-3)*; lib. bdg. 11.99 *(0-394-90075-8)* Random Bks Yng Read.
—The Butter Battle Book. Dr. Seuss. LC 83-21286. 48p. (gr. 5 up). 1984. 12.00 *(0-394-86580-4)*; lib. bdg. 12.99 *(0-394-96580-9)* Random Bks Yng Read.
—Cat in the Hat. Dr. Seuss. LC 56-5470. 72p. (gr. 1-2). 1957. 6.95 *(0-394-80001-X)*; lib. bdg. 7.99 *(0-394-90001-4)* Random Bks Yng Read.
—The Cat in the Hat. Dr. Seuss. 64p. (ps-1). 1987. book & cassette 6.95 *(0-394-89218-6)* Random Bks Yng Read.
—The Cat in the Hat - el Gato Ensombrerado. Dr. Seuss. (ENG & SPA.). 72p. (gr. 3). 1993. incl. cass. 6.95 *(0-679-84329-9)* Random Bks Yng Read.
—Cat in the Hat Comes Back. Dr. Seuss. LC 58-9017. 72p. (gr. k-3). 1958. 6.95 *(0-394-80002-8)*; lib. bdg. 7.99 *(0-394-90002-2)* Random Bks Yng Read.
—The Cat in the Hat in English & Spanish. Dr. Seuss. Rivera, Carlos, tr. LC 67-5819. 72p. (gr. 1-2). 1967. 6.95 *(0-394-81626-9)* Beginner.
—Did I Ever Tell You How Lucky You Are? Dr. Seuss. (ps-4). 1973. 11.00 *(0-394-82719-8)*; PLB 11.99 *(0-394-92719-2)* Random Bks Yng Read.
—Did I Ever Tell You How Lucky You Are? Dr. Seuss. 64p. (Orig.). (ps up). 1993. incl. cass. 13.00 *(0-679-84993-9)* Random Bks Yng Read.
—Dr. Seuss Beginner Book Classics, 5 bks. Dr. Seuss. (ps-3). 1992. Boxed set incls. The Cat in the Hat, Dr. Seuss's ABC, Fox in Socks, Green Eggs & Ham & One Fish Two Fish Red Fish Blue Fish, 72 pgs. ea. 50.00 *(0-679-83846-5)* Random Bks Yng Read.
—Dr. Seuss from Then to Now. San Diego Museum of Art Staff, compiled by. LC 87-4838. 96p. (ps up). 1987. 12.95 *(0-394-89268-2)* Random Bks Yng Read.
—Dr. Seuss's ABC. Dr. Seuss. LC 63-9810. 72p. (gr. k-3). 1963. 6.95 *(0-394-80030-3)*; lib. bdg. 7.99 *(0-394-90030-8)* Random Bks Yng Read.
—Dr. Seuss's Sleep Book. Dr. Seuss. (gr. 3-7). 1962. 13.00 *(0-394-80091-5)*; lib. bdg. 13.99 *(0-394-90091-X)* Random Bks Yng Read.
—Foot Book. Dr. Seuss. LC 68-28462. (ps-1). 1968. 6.95 *(0-394-80937-8)*; lib. bdg. 7.99 *(0-394-90937-2)* Random Bks Yng Read.
—Fox in Socks. Dr. Seuss. LC 65-10484. 72p. (gr. k-3). 1965. 6.95 *(0-394-80038-9)*; lib. bdg. 7.99 *(0-394-90038-3)* Random Bks Yng Read.
—Green Eggs & Ham. Dr. Seuss. LC 60-13493. 72p. (gr. 1-2). 1960. 6.95 *(0-394-80016-8)*; lib. bdg. 7.99 *(0-394-90016-2)* Random Bks Yng Read.
—Green Eggs & Ham. Dr. Seuss. 64p. (ps-1). 1987. pap. 6.95 incl. cassette *(0-394-89220-8)* Random Bks Yng Read.
—Happy Birthday to You. Dr. Seuss. (gr. 1-5). 1959. 13.00 *(0-394-80076-1)*; PLB 13.99 *(0-394-90076-6)* Random Bks Yng Read.
—Hop on Pop. Dr. Seuss. LC 63-9810. 72p. (gr. 1-2). 1963. 6.95 *(0-394-80029-X)*; lib. bdg. 7.99 *(0-394-90029-4)* Random Bks Yng Read.
—Hop on Pop. Dr. Seuss. 64p. (ps-1). 1987. pap. 6.95 incl. cassette *(0-394-89222-4)* Random Bks Yng Read.
—Horton Hatches the Egg. Dr. Seuss. (gr. k-3). 1940. 11.95 *(0-394-80077-X)*; lib. bdg. 13.99 *(0-394-90077-4)* Random Bks Yng Read.
—Horton Hatches the Egg. reissued ed. Dr. Seuss. Crystal, Billy, read by. LC 40-27753. 64p. (ps up). 1991. pap. 10.95 incls. cassette *(0-394-82956-5)* Random Bks Yng Read.
—Horton Hears a Who. Dr. Seuss. (gr. k-3). 1954. 12.00 *(0-394-80078-8)*; PLB 12.99 *(0-394-90078-2)* Random Bks Yng Read.
—How the Grinch Stole Christmas. Dr. Seuss. (gr. k-3). 1957. 8.95 *(0-394-80079-6)*; PLB 9.99 *(0-394-90079-0)* Random Bks Yng Read.
—How the Grinch Stole Christmas! Dr. Seuss. Matthau, Walter, contrib. by. 64p. (ps-1). 1988. bk. & cassette pkg. 10.00 *(0-394-81339-1)* Random Bks Yng Read.
—Hunches in Bunches. Dr. Seuss. 48p. (gr. 1-5). 1982. lib. bdg. 10.99 *(0-394-95502-1)*; pap. 10.95 *(0-394-85502-7)* Random Bks Yng Read.
—I Can Draw It Myself: By Me, Myself with a Little Help from My Friend Dr. Seuss. Dr. Seuss. LC 75-117541. 48p. (ps-4). 1987. pap. 9.00 *(0-394-80097-4)* Beginner.
—I Can Lick Thirty Tigers Today & Other Stories. Dr. Seuss. (gr. k-3). 1969. 13.00 *(0-394-80094-X)* Random Bks Yng Read.
—I Can Read with My Eyes Shut! Dr. Seuss. LC 78-7193. (gr. 1-3). 1978. 6.95 *(0-394-83912-9)*; lib. bdg. 7.99 *(0-394-93912-3)* Random Bks Yng Read.
—I Can Read with My Eyes Shut! Dr. Seuss. 40p. (ps-1). 1987. Incl. cassette. pap. 6.95 *(0-394-88767-0)* Random Bks Yng Read.
—I Had Trouble in Getting to Solla Sollew. Dr. Seuss. LC 65-23994. 64p. (gr. 1-4). 1992. 13.00 *(0-394-80092-3)* Random Bks Yng Read.
—If I Ran the Circus. Dr. Seuss. (gr. k-3). 1956. 13.00 *(0-394-80080-X)*; lib. bdg. 10.99 *(0-394-90080-4)* Random Bks Yng Read.
—If I Ran the Zoo. Dr. Seuss. (gr. k-3). 1950. 13.00 *(0-394-80081-8)*; lib. bdg. 13.99 *(0-394-90081-2)* Random Bks Yng Read.
—King's Stilts. Dr. Seuss. (gr. k-3). 1939. 9.95 *(0-394-80082-6)*; lib. bdg. 9.99 *(0-394-90082-0)* Random Bks Yng Read.
—Lorax. Dr. Seuss. (gr. 2-3). 1971. 12.00 *(0-394-82337-0)*; lib. bdg. 12.99 *(0-394-92337-5)* Random Bks Yng Read.
—The Lorax. Dr. Seuss. Danson, Ted, narrated by. 64p. (ps up). 1992. incl. cassette 13.00 *(0-679-82273-9)* Random Bks Yng Read.
—McElligot's Pool. Dr. Seuss. (gr. k-3). 1947. 11.00 *(0-394-80083-4)*; lib. bdg. 11.99 *(0-394-90083-9)* Random Bks Yng Read.
—Marvin K. Mooney, Will You Please Go Now. Dr. Seuss. (ps-2). 1972. 6.95 *(0-394-82490-3)*; lib. bdg. 7.99 *(0-394-92490-8)* Random Bks Yng Read.
—Mister Brown Can Moo, Can You. Dr. Seuss. (ps-1). 1970. 6.95 *(0-394-80622-0)*; lib. bdg. 7.99 *(0-394-90622-5)* Random Bks Yng Read.
—Mr. Brown Can Moo! Can You? - The Foot Book, 2 bks. reissue ed. Dr. Seuss. (ps-1). 1991. Set, 32p. ea. incl. 2 20-min. cassette 8.95 *(0-679-82036-1)* Random Bks Yng Read.

—Oh, Say Can You Say? Dr. Seuss. LC 78-20716. (gr. 1-4). 1979. 6.95 (0-394-84255-3, BYR); lib. bdg. 7.99 (0-394-94255-8) Beginner.

—Oh Say Can You Say? Dr. Seuss. 40p. (ps-1). 1987. Incl. cassette. 6.95 (0-394-88769-7) Random Bks Yng Read.

—Oh, the Places You'll Go! Dr. Seuss. LC 89-36892. 48p. (gr. k up). 1993. 20.00 (0-679-84736-7) Random Bks Yng Read.

—Oh! The Thinks You Can Think! Dr. Seuss. LC 75-1602. 48p. (ps-1). 1975. 6.95 (0-394-83129-2); lib. bdg. 7.99 (0-394-93129-7) Beginner.

—On Beyond Zebra. Dr. Seuss. (ps-3). 1955. 12.00 (0-394-80084-2); lib. bdg. 12.99 (0-394-90084-7) Random Bks Yng Read.

—One Fish Two Fish Red Fish Blue Fish. Dr. Seuss. LC 60-7180. 72p. (gr. 1-2). 1960. 6.95 (0-394-80013-3); PLB 7.99 (0-394-90013-8) Random Bks Yng Read.

—One Fish Two Fish Red Fish Blue Fish. Dr. Seuss. 64p. (ps-1). 1987. pap. 6.95 incl. cassette (0-394-89224-0) Random Bks Yng Read.

—Scrambled Eggs Super! Dr. Seuss. (gr. k-3). 1953. lib. bdg. 13.99 (0-394-90085-5) Random Bks Yng Read.

—Scrambled Eggs Super! Dr. Seuss. LC 53-5013. 64p. (gr. 1-4). 1992. 13.00 (0-394-80085-0) Random Bks Yng Read.

—Six by Seuss: A Treasury of Dr. Seuss Classics. Dr. Seuss. LC 91-6311. 352p. 1991. 25.00 (0-679-82148-1) Random Bks Yng Read.

—Sneetches & Other Stories. Dr. Seuss. (gr. k-4). 1961. 9.95 (0-394-80089-3); lib. bdg. 13.99 (0-394-90089-8) Random Bks Yng Read.

—There's a Wocket in My Pocket! Dr. Seuss. LC 74-5516. 36p. (ps-1). 1974. 6.95 (0-394-82920-4); lib. bdg. 7.99 (0-394-92920-9) Random Bks Yng Read.

—There's a Wocket in My Pocket & Marvin K. Mooney Will You Please Go Now! Dr. Seuss. (ps-1). 1989. bk. & cassette 7.95 (0-394-82954-9) Random Bks Yng Read.

—Thidwick, the Big-Hearted Moose. Dr. Seuss. (gr. k-3). 1948. 11.00 (0-394-80086-9); lib. bdg. 11.99 (0-394-90086-3) Random Bks Yng Read.

—Thidwick the Big-Hearted Moose. Dr. Seuss. 48p. (ps-6). 1993. incl. cass. 12.00 (0-679-84338-8) Random Bks Yng Read.

—Yertle the Turtle & Other Stories. Dr. Seuss. (gr. k-3). 1958. 13.00 (0-394-80087-7); PLB 13.99 (0-394-90087-1) Random Bks Yng Read.

—Yertle the Turtle & Other Stories. reissue ed. Dr. Seuss. Lithgow, John, narrated by. 80p. (ps). 1992. pap. 14.00 incl. cass. (0-679-83229-7) Random Bks Yng Read.

Drucklieb, Herman L. & Kerry, Jill. Tajar Tales. Ward, Jane S. LC 93-71385. 48p. (ps-4). 1993. Repr. of 1924 ed. Colorized pictures, music & song added. lib. bdg. 14.95 (1-883338-01-8); Book & cassette set. lib. bdg. 19.95 (1-883338-00-X) Classic Wrks.

Drum & Spear Collective Staff. Children of Africa: A Coloring Book. Drum & Spear Collective Staff. LC 92-63013. 24p. (ps-3). 1993. pap. 5.95 (0-88378-076-3) Third World.

Drum, Stacy. Is That Our Car? Lanton, Sandy. 32p. (ps-2). Date not set. 11.95 (1-56065-143-1) Capstone Pr. Postponed.

—Moving Through Your ABC's. Marie, Jeanne. LC 92-9944. 32p. (ps-2). Date not set. 11.95 (1-56065-166-0) Capstone Pr. Postponed.

Drummond, Allan. The Willow Pattern Story. Drummond, Allan. LC 91-46239. 32p. (gr. k-3). 1992. 14.95 (1-55858-171-5); PLB 14.88 (1-55858-172-3) North-South Bks NYC.

Dryhurst, Dinal. Railway Children. Nesbit, Evelyn. 192p. 1992. 9.99 (0-517-07011-1, Pub. by Derrydale Bks) Outlet Bk Co.

D'Souza, Edgar. Madison Squid & the Ghost of Slapstick: Hilarious Children's Books for Grown-ups. Crumble, Mortimer. LC 93-79348. 144p. 1994. 19.95 (0-9636606-1-6) Crumble Bks.

Duarte, Pamela. Barbie Rockin' Rappin' Dancin' World Tour Pop-up Book. Strong, Stacie. 12p. (ps-2). 1992. write for info. (0-307-16560-4, 16560, Golden Pr) Western Pub.

—Barbie: Show Time! Jensen, Patricia. 24p. (ps-3). 1992. pap. write for info. (0-307-12691-9, 12691, Golden Pr) Western Pub.

—Dancing the Night Away. St. Pierre, Stephanie. 64p. (Orig.). (gr. 1-2). 1991. pap. 2.95 (0-8431-2906-9) Price Stern.

—The Mysterious Dude of Ghost Ranch. St. Pierre, Stephanie. 64p. (Orig.). (gr. 1-2). 1991. pap. 2.95 (0-8431-2905-0) Price Stern.

—Soda Shop Surprise. St. Pierre, Stephanie. 64p. (Orig.). (gr. 1-2). 1991. pap. 2.95 (0-8431-2919-0) Price Stern.

—Wildlife Rescue. St. Pierre, Stephanie. 64p. (Orig.). (gr. 1-2). 1991. pap. 2.95 (0-8431-2918-2) Price Stern.

Duarte, Steven. The Magic of Green. Griffith, Neysa. LC 93-34811. 1994. 4.95 (1-56844-028-6) Enchante Pub.

—The Magic of Orange. Griffith, Neysa. LC 93-35439. 1994. 4.95 (1-56844-026-X) Enchante Pub.

—The Magic of Red. Griffith, Neysa. LC 93-34813. 1994. 4.95 (1-56844-025-1) Enchante Pub.

—The Magic of Yellow. Griffith, Neysa. LC 93-34812. 1994. 4.95 (1-56844-027-8) Enchante Pub.

Dubanevich, Arlene. Do Bunnies Talk? Dodds, Dayle A. LC 91-13434. 32p. (ps-1). 1992. 15.00 (0-06-020248-3); PLB 14.89 (0-06-020249-1) HarpC Child Bks.

—Invisible Oink: Pig Jokes. Phillips, Louis. LC 92-24803. 64p. 1993. 11.99 (0-670-84387-3) Viking Child Bks.

—Pig William. Dubanevich, Arlene. LC 85-5776. 32p. (ps-2). 1985. RSBE 13.95 (0-02-733200-4, Bradbury Pr) Macmillan Child Grp.

—Pigs at Christmas. Dubanevich, Arlene. LC 86-6891. 32p. (ps-2). 1986. RSBE 13.95 (0-02-733160-1, Bradbury Pr) Macmillan Child Grp.

—Pigs at Christmas. Dubanevich, Arlene. LC 89-32229. 32p. (ps-3). 1989. pap. 3.95 (0-689-71344-4, Aladdin) Macmillan Child Grp.

—Pigs in Hiding. Dubanevich, Arlene. LC 83-1409. 32p. (ps-1). 1983. RSBE 13.95 (0-02-732140-1, Four Winds) Macmillan Child Grp.

—Pigs in Hiding. Dubanevich, Arlene. 32p. (gr. k-3). 1989. pap. 3.95 (0-590-44503-0) Scholastic Inc.

—Way Out! Jokes from Outer Space. Phillips, Louis. LC 89-14700. 58p. (gr. 4-8). 1989. pap. 10.95 (0-670-82755-X) Viking Child Bks.

Dubin, Jill. Cat & Kittens. Estep, Don. 28p. (ps). 1990. 2.95 (0-02-689487-4) Checkerboard.

—Lucy's Early Day. Estep, Don. 28p. (ps). 1990. 2.95 (0-02-689485-8) Checkerboard.

—Rebecca Goes Out. Richards, Selena. 18p. (ps). 1992. 3.50 (1-56288-269-4) Checkerboard.

—Rebecca Goes to the Country. Richards, Selena. 18p. (ps). 1992. 3.50 (1-56288-270-8) Checkerboard.

—Rebecca Goes to the Park. Richards, Selena. 18p. (ps). 1992. 3.50 (1-56288-271-6) Checkerboard.

—Rebecca's Rainy Day. Richards, Selena. 18p. (ps). 1992. 3.50 (1-56288-272-4) Checkerboard.

Dubina, Alan. Caterpillar Had a Dream: A Story about Dreams Coming True. Bartlett, Jaye. 38p. (Orig.). (ps up). 1990. PLB 11.95 incl. cassette (1-878064-00-2) New Age CT.

—Freddy the Elephant: The Story of a Sensitive Leader. Bartlett, Jaye. 45p. (Orig.). (ps up). 1991. pap. 11.95 incl. cassette (1-878064-01-0) New Age CT.

Dubnansky, Marsha L. The Story of Punxsutawney Phil, "The Fearless Forecaster" Moutran, Julia S. LC 86-82950. 64p. (ps-5). 1987. 14.95 (0-9617819-2-0); pap. 8.95 (0-9617819-0-4); audiocassette 10.95 (0-9617819-3-9) Lit Pubns.

Dubois, Marie T. Agha: The Terrible Demon. 2nd ed. Wilson, Karen. Greene, Joshua, ed. Prubhupada, A. C., tr. from SAN. 32p. (gr. 1-4). 1989. pap. 6.95 (0-89647-023-7) Bala Bks.

DuBois, William P. Bear in Mind: A Book of Bear Poems. Goldstein, Bobbye. 32p. (ps-3). 1989. 12.95 (0-670-81907-7) Viking Child Bks.

Du Bois, William P. It's Not Fair. Reissue. ed. Zolotow, Charlotte. LC 76-3387. 32p. (gr. k-3). 1976. 13.00 (0-06-026934-0); PLB 12.89 (0-06-026935-9) HarpC Child Bks.

—The Sick Day. MacLachlan, Patricia. LC 78-11686. (gr. k-3). 1979. 6.95 (0-394-83876-9) Pantheon.

—The Twenty-One Balloons. Du Bois, William P. 184p. (gr. 5-9). 1986. pap. 3.99 (0-14-032097-0, Puffin) Puffin Bks.

DuBosque, D. C. Learn to Draw Now! DuBosque, D. C. 64p. (Orig.). (gr. 3-9). 1991. pap. 7.95 (0-939217-16-3) Peel Prod.

—Naro, the Ancient Spider. Joyce, Susan. (gr. 4). 1990. 12.00 (0-939217-04-X) Peel Prod.

—Peel, el Elefant Extraordinario. Joyce, Susan. Sampson, Jennifer, tr. from ENG. (SPA). 48p. (ps-7). 1990. lib. bdg. 13.95x (0-939217-02-3); pap. 7.95 (0-939217-03-1) Peel Prod.

—Peel, the Extraordinary Elephant. Joyce, Susan. LC 86-61990. 48p. (ps up). 1988. pap. 7.95 sewn bdg. (0-939217-01-5) Peel Prod.

—Pilon, el Extraordinario Elefanton. Joyce, Susan. Marcuse, Aida, tr. from ENG. LC 92-35437. (SPA). 48p. (Orig.). (gr. 1-6). 1993. pap. 8.95 (0-939217-05-8) Peel Prod.

Dubowski, Mark. Cave Boy. Dubowski, Cathy E. LC 87-23427. 32p. (ps-1). 1988. lib. bdg. 7.99 (0-394-99571-6); pap. 2.95 (0-394-89571-1) Random Bks Yng Read.

—Pretty Good Magic. Dubowski, Cathy W. LC 87-4784. 48p. (gr. 1-3). 1987. lib. bdg. 7.99 (0-394-99068-4); 3.50 (0-394-89068-X) Random Bks Yng Read.

Duca, Bill. Do You See Me God? Murphy, Elspeth C. 32p. (ps). 1989. text ed. 7.95 (1-55513-457-2, Chariot Bks) Cook.

—Mrs. Rosey-Posey & the Chocolate Cherry Treat. Gunn, Robin J. 32p. (ps-2). 1991. pap. 4.49 (1-55513-370-3, 33704, Chariot Bks) Cook.

—Mrs. Rosey-Posey & the Treasure Hunt. Gunn, Robin J. 32p. (ps-2). 1991. pap. 4.49 (1-55513-372-X, 33720, Chariot Bks) Cook.

Ducey, Beth. My Peanut Butter Pond Think 'n' Do Book. Sargent, Lynne. 100p. (ps-1). 1990. wkbk. 3.95 (1-55999-125-9) LinguiSystems.

Ducey, Elizabeth P. My Peanut Butter Pond Think-Along Funbook. Keiser, Gayle, et al. Britt, Stephanie M., contrib. by. 100p. (ps-4). 1991. wkbk., spiral bdg. 3.95 (1-55999-156-9) LinguiSystems.

DuCharme, Tracy. Friends All Around. Nelson, JoAnne. LC 92-4657. 24p. (Orig.). (gr. k-2). 1993. pap. 5.95 (0-935529-17-9) Comprehen Health Educ.

Du Charme, Tracy. Where's Mittens? Nelson, JoAnne. LC 91-9373. 24p. (Orig.). (gr. k-2). 1993. pap. 5.95 (0-935529-14-4) Comprehen Health Educ.

Duckworth, Ruch. The Life of St. Nicholas: A Cloud of Witnesses, Vol. 3. Seco, Nina S. (Orig.). (gr. k-3). 1993. pap. 6.00 (0-913026-36-0) St Nectarios.

Duckworth, Ruth. A Cloud of Witnesses Series. Seco, Nina, et al. (Orig.). (ps-1). 1991. pap. write for info. (0-913026-27-1) St Nectarios.

—The Life of St. Nina. Seco, Nina. (Orig.). (ps-1). 1991. pap. 6.00 (0-913026-28-X) St Nectarios.

—Saints Adrian & Natalie. Seco, Nina & Pilutik, Anastasia D. (Orig.). (ps-1). 1991. pap. write for info. (0-913026-29-8) St Nectarios.

Dudley, Ebet. The World of Insects. Whayne, Susanne S. 48p. (gr. 3-7). 1990. pap. 9.95 (0-671-69018-3, S&S BFYR) S&S Trade.

Duell, Nancy. Different & Alike. McConnell, Nancy P. LC 87-73309. 40p. (gr. 1-6). 1982. pap. text ed. 6.85 (0-944943-00-4) Current Inc.

—Different & Alike. 3rd ed. McConnell, Nancy P. Cliff, Donna, ed. LC 93-70957. 40p. (gr. 1-6). 1993. pap. 6.85 (0-944943-32-2, CODE 22164-6) Current Inc.

—Ladybug's Color Book. Silverman, Maida. 24p. (ps-1). 1986. 3.95 (0-448-01461-0, G&D) Putnam Pub Group.

Duerrstein, Richard. Dentro Fuera: Un Libro Disney de Opuestos. Santacruz, Daniel, tr. (SPA.). 12p. 1993. 5.95 (1-56282-458-9) Disney Pr.

—In - Out: A Disney Book of Opposites. LC 91-58979. 12p. (ps). 1992. bds. 5.95 (1-56282-266-7) Disney Pr.

—Mickey Esta Feliz: Un Libro Disney de Emociones. Santacruz, Daniel, tr. (SPA). 12p. 1993. 5.95 (1-56282-459-7) Disney Pr.

—Mickey Is Happy: A Disney Book of Feelings. LC 92-52974. 12p. (ps). 1992. bds. 5.95 (1-56282-267-5) Disney Pr.

—Un Raton Mickey: Un Libro Disney de Numeros. Santacruz, Daniel, tr. (SPA). 12p. 1993. 5.95 (1-56282-460-0) Disney Pr.

Duerstein, Richard. One Mickey Mouse: A Disney Book of Numbers. LC 92-52973. 12p. (ps). 1992. 5.95 (1-56282-251-9) Disney Pr.

Duff, Leo. Life Story. Maddern, Eric. LC 87-73253. 32p. (gr. 1 up). 1988. 11.95 (0-8120-5941-7) Barron.

Duffield, Francesca. ABC Rhymes. LC 92-75611. 10p. (ps). 1993. bds. 5.95 (1-85697-941-5) Kingfisher Bks.

—A Bedtime Story. LC 92-75613. 10p. 1993. 5.95 (1-85697-915-6) Kingfisher Bks.

—Lullabies. LC 92-75609. (ps-k). 1993. 5.95 (1-85697-916-4) Kingfisher Bks.

—Nursery Rhymes. LC 92-75584. 10p. (ps-k). 1993. 5.95 (1-85697-917-2) Kingfisher Bks.

—One-Two-Three Rhymes. LC 92-75610. 10p. (ps). 1993. bds. 5.95 (1-85697-942-3) Kingfisher Bks.

—A Teddy Tale. LC 92-75612. 10p. (ps). 1993. 5.95 (1-85697-918-0) Kingfisher Bks.

Duffy, Daniel M. The Great Pony Hassle. Springer, Nancy. LC 92-34781. (gr. 3-7). 1993. 12.99 (0-8037-1306-1); PLB 13.89 (0-8037-1308-8) Dial Bks Young.

Dugan, Karen. Christmas Around the World. Lankford, Mary D. LC 93-38566. 1994. write for info. (0-688-12166-7, Tambourine Bks); PLB write for info. (0-688-12167-5, Tambourine Bks) Morrow.

—Fly Away Home. Dugan, Karen. 26p. (ps up). 1994. 11.95 (0-8431-3687-1) Price Stern.

Dugan, LeRoy. Falling Off Cloud Nine & Other High Places. Peterson, Lorraine. LC 81-38465. 159p. (Orig.). (gr. 8-12). 1981. pap. 7.99 (0-87123-167-0) Bethany Hse.

—Why Isn't God Giving Cash Prizes? Peterson, Lorraine. LC 82-17866. 160p. (gr. 8-12). 1982. pap. 6.99 (0-87123-626-5) Bethany Hse.

Dugan, Terry & Slonim, David. Hide em in Your Heart: Activity Book. Hernandez, Frank & Hernandez, Betsy. 40p. (Orig.). (ps-6). 1991. pap. 7.95 (0-917143-06-X) Sparrow TN.

Dugger, Kim. The Truth Shall Make You Free: An Inquiry into the Legend of God. Steiner, Robert A. Patterson, John W., intro. by. LC 80-80646. 47p. (Orig.). (gr. 6 up). 1980. pap. 4.95 (0-9604044-0-6) Wide-Awake Bks.

Dugin, Andrej & Dugina, Olga. The Fine Round Cake. Esterl, Arnica. Hejl, Pauline, tr. from GER. LC 91-6411. 24p. (ps-2). 1991. SBE 14.95 (0-02-733568-2, Four Winds) Macmillan Child Grp.

Dugina, Olga, jt. illus. see Dugin, Andrej.

Duitsman, Penny, jt. illus. see Splane, Lily.

Duke, Kate. Aunt Isabel Tells a Good One. Duke, Kate. LC 91-14598. 32p. (ps-2). 1992. 14.00 (0-525-44835-7, DCB) Dutton Child Bks.

—Bedtime. Duke, Kate. LC 84-73140. 12p. (ps). 1986. bds. 2.95 (0-525-44207-3, DCB) Dutton Child Bks.

—Clean-Up Day. Duke, Kate. LC 84-73139. 12p. (ps). 1986. bds. 2.95 (0-525-44208-1, DCB) Dutton Child Bks.

—Don't Tell the Whole World! Cole, Joanna. LC 89-29283. 32p. (gr. k-3). 1992. pap. 4.95 (0-06-443292-0, Trophy) HarpC Child Bks.

—The Guinea Pig ABC. Duke, Kate. LC 83-1410. 32p. (ps-1). 1983. 12.95 (0-525-44058-5, DCB) Dutton Child Bks.

—Guinea Pigs Far & Near. Duke, Kate. LC 84-1580. 24p. (ps-1). 1984. 9.95 (0-525-44112-3, DCB) Dutton Child Bks.

—Guinea Pigs Far & Near. Duke, Kate. LC 84-1580. 24p. (ps-1). 1989. pap. 3.95 (0-525-44480-7, DCB) Dutton Child Bks.

—If You Walk Down This Road. Duke, Kate. LC 92-27685. 32p. (ps-k). 1993. 13.99 (0-525-45072-6, DCB) Dutton Child Bks.

—It's Too Noisy. Cole, Joanna. LC 88-3865. 32p. (ps-3). 1989. (Crowell Jr Bks); PLB 12.89 (0-690-04737-1, Crowell Jr Bks) HarpC Child Bks.

—Let's Go Dinosaur Tracking! Schlein, Miriam. LC 90-39632. 48p. (gr. 2-5). 1991. PLB 14.89 (0-06-025139-5) HarpC Child Bks.

—The Playground. Duke, Kate. LC 84-73141. 12p. (ps). 1986. bds. 2.95 (0-525-44206-5, DCB) Dutton Child Bks.
—Tingalayo. (ps-2). 1988. 9.95 (0-517-56926-4) Crown Bks Yng Read.
—Tingalayo. Raffi. LC 88-3562. 32p. 1993. pap. 3.99 (0-517-88099-7) Crown Bks Yng Read.
—What Bounces? Duke, Kate. LC 84-73138. 12p. (ps) 1986. 2.95 (0-525-44209-X, DCB) Dutton Child Bks.
Duke, Pat, et al. Captain Harlock Returns. Gibson, Robert W. Ulm, Chris, ed. 86p. 1991. pap. 9.95 (0-944735-75-4) Malibu Graphics.
Dulac, Edmund. Dulac's the Snow Queen: And Other Stories. Andersen, Hans Christian. Haugaard, Erik C., tr. LC 76-7308. 144p. (ps up). 1976. 9.95 (0-385-11678-0) Doubleday.
—Fairy Tales of the World. Dulac, Edmund. Cott, Jonathan, ed. LC 93-24486. 200p. 1994. 15.00 (1-56957-914-8) Barefoot Bks.
Dulac, Glen J. & Dulac, John J. The Color Coded Alphabet, an Alphabet for Easy Reading: The Alphabet as It Has Never Been Seen Before. Dulac, Glen J. (ps-2). 1990. 49.50 (0-9628227-2-8) Desert Bks.
Dulac, John J., jt. illus. see Dulac, Glen J.
Dumas, Philippe. Odette: A Springtime in Paris. Fender, Kay. 32p. (ps-3). 1991. 10.95 (0-916291-33-2) Kane-Miller Bk.
—Voyage d'Alice ou Comment Sont Nes les Droits de l'Enfant. Heron, Jean O. (FRE.). 151p. (gr. 3-7). 1990. pap. 11.95 (0-685-60281-8) Schoenhof.
Dumas, Phillipe. The Queen Bee. Grimm, Jacob & Grimm, Wilhelm K. 32p. (gr. 4 up). 1984. PLB 13.95s.p. (0-87191-939-7) Creative Ed.
Dummer, H. Boylston. Adventures of the Animal Town Aviators, Bk. I. Dummer, H. Boylston. 118p. (ps-3). 1989. 17.95 (0-87510-198-4) Monitor Bks.
—Adventures of the Animal Town Aviators, Bk. II. Dummer, H. Boylston. 118p. (ps-3). 1989. 17.95 (0-87510-199-2) Monitor Bks.
Dunbar, James. I Want a Blue Banana. Dunbar, Joyce. 32p. (ps). 1991. 13.45 (0-395-57579-6, Sandpiper) HM.
—Why Is the Sky Up? Dunbar, Joyce. 32p. (ps). 1991. 13.45 (0-395-57580-X, Sandpiper) HM.
Duncan, Beverly. Red-Spotted Newt. Gove, Doris. LC 91-34497. 1993. write for info. (0-689-31697-6, Aladdin) Macmillan Child Grp.
—A Water Snake's Year. Gove, Doris. LC 90-673. 40p. (gr. 2-6). 1991. SBE 13.95 (0-689-31597-X, Atheneum Child Bk) Macmillan Child Grp.
Duncan, Bob. A Day in the Life of a Medical Detective. Carter, Adam. LC 84-8851. 32p. (gr. 4-8). 1985. PLB 11.79 (0-8167-0097-4); pap. text ed. 2.95 (0-8167-0098-2) Troll Assocs.
Duncan, Riana. A Nutcracker in a Tree: A Book of Riddles. Duncan, Riana. LC 80-67492. 32p. (gr. k-3). 1981. PLB 8.95 (0-385-28733-X); pap. 8.95 (0-385-28732-1) Delacorte.
—When Emily Woke up Angry. Duncan, Riana. 32p. (ps-1). 1989. incl. dust jacket 9.95 (0-8120-5985-9) Barron.
Duncan, Robert. Amber on the Mountain. Johnston, Tony. LC 93-16292. (ps-6). 1994. write for info. (0-8037-1219-7); pap. write for info. (0-8037-1220-0) Dial Bks Young.
Dunham, Meredith. Colors: How Do You Say It? Dunham, Meredith. LC 86-27739. 24p. (ps up) 1987. 9.25 (0-688-06948-7); PLB 9.88 (0-688-06949-5) Lothrop.
—In My Treehouse. Schertle, Alice. LC 82-10016. 32p. (gr. k-3). 1983. 11.95 (0-688-01638-3) Lothrop.
—Shapes: How Do You Say It? Dunham, Meredith. LC 86-27740. 24p. (ps up) 1987. PLB 9.88 (0-688-06953-3) Lothrop.
Dunlap, Hope. The Little Lame Prince. Dunlap, Hope. LC 92-37665. 1993. 8.99 (0-517-08484-8, Pub. by Derrydale Bks) Outlet Bk Co.
Dunlap, Loren. Edgar Allan. Neufeld, John. LC 68-31175. (gr. 5-8). 1968. 21.95 (0-87599-149-1) S G Phillips.
Dunlap, Sam. The Person Who Had Feelings. Van Kirk, Barbara D. 44p. (Orig.). 1975. pap. 6.95 (0-9631751-0-6) New Begin OR.
Dunmire, Marj. Mountain Wildlife. Dunmire, Marj. 48p. (Orig.). (gr. 2 up). 1986. pap. 3.95 (0-942559-03-7) Pegasus Graphics.
—Not Even Footprints. Dunmire, Marj. 72p. (Orig.). (gr. 2-7). 1987. pap. 4.95 (0-942559-04-5) Pegasus Graphics.
—Water Birds. Dunmire, Marj. 48p. (gr. 2-8). 1990. pap. 3.95 (0-942559-06-1) Pegasus Graphics.
—Wildlife of Cactus & Canyon Country. Dunmire, Marj. 48p. (gr. 2-6). 1988. pap. 3.95 (0-942559-05-3) Pegasus Graphics.
Dunn, Ben. Ninja High School, Vol. 2: Beware of Dog. Dunn, Ben. Ulm, Chris, ed. 121p. 1990. pap. 9.95 (0-944735-59-2) Malibu Graphics.
Dunn, Ben, jt. illus. see Castro, Carlos.
Dunn, Ben, jt. illus. see Phillips, Joe.
Dunn, Benn, et al. Mekton II. 2nd ed. Pondsmith, Michael. Bryant, Linda, et al, eds. 93p. (gr. 7-12). 1987. game bk. 12.00 (0-937279-04-8, MK 1002) R Talsorian.
Dunn, Joan W. Waiting for Baby Joe. Collins, Pat L. Tucker, Kathy, ed. LC 89-21457. 48p. (ps-2). 1990. PLB 11.95 (0-8075-8625-0) A Whitman.

Dunn, Joyce E. Riding on a School Bus. rev. ed. Dunn, Joyce E. Doyle, James M., intro. by. 56p. (gr. k-1). 1989. pap. 4.95 (0-9624280-0-0) SPI Pub.
Dunn, Patricia. Math Trivial Pursuit - Intermediate Level. Dunn, Patricia. 64p. (gr. 4-6). 1989. wkbk. 12. 95 (0-86653-468-7, GA1073) Good Apple.
—Math Trivial Pursuit - Junior High Level. Dunn, Patricia. 64p. (gr. 7-9). 1989. wkbk. 12.95 (0-86653-469-5, GA1074) Good Apple.
—Math Trivial Pursuit - Primary Level. Dunn, Patricia. 64p. (gr. 1-3). 1989. wkbk. 12.95 (0-86653-492-X, GA1072) Good Apple.
Dunn, Phoebe. The Little Goat. Dunn, Judy. LC 77-91658. (ps-1). 1979. lib. bdg. 5.99 (0-394-93872-0); pap. 2.25 (0-394-83872-6) Random Bks Yng Read.
—The Little Lamb. Dunn, Judy. LC 76-24167. (ps-2). 1978. lib. bdg. 5.99 (0-394-93455-5); pap. 2.25 (0-394-83455-0) Random Bks Yng Read.
—The Little Puppy. Dunn, Judy. LC 84-2031. 32p. (ps-3). 1984. lib. bdg. 5.99 (0-394-96595-7); saddle-stitched 2.25 (0-394-86595-2) Random Bks Yng Read.
—The Little Rabbit. Dunn, Judy. LC 79-5241. 32p. (ps-2). 1980. lib. bdg. 5.99 (0-394-94377-5); pap. 2.25 (0-394-84377-0) Random Bks Yng Read.
Dunn, Phoebe, photos by. Baby's Animal Friends. LC 87-61462. 28p. (ps). 1988. bds. 2.95 (0-394-89583-5) Random Bks Yng Read.
—I'm a Baby! LC 86-61904. 14p. 1987. 2.99 (0-394-88605-4) Random Bks Yng Read.
—The Little Duck. Dunn, Judy. LC 75-36467. 32p. (ps-1). 1976. 2.25 (0-394-83247-7) Random Bks Yng Read.
—The Little Kitten. Dunn, Judy. LC 82-16711. 32p. (ps-4). 1983. lib. bdg. 5.99 (0-394-95818-7); 2.25 (0-394-85818-2) Random Bks Yng Read.
—The Little Pig. Dunn, Judy. LC 86-42956. 32p. (ps-3). 1987. pap. 2.25 (0-394-88774-3) Random Bks Yng Read.
Dunn, Phoebe & Lee, Vincent B., photos by. How Many? A Matchem Counting Bk. LC 87-61521. 18p. (ps). 1988. bds. 4.95 (0-394-89388-3) Random Bks Yng Read.
Dunne, Jeanette. Badger, Beano & the Magic Mushroom. Scoltock, Jack. 125p. (Orig.). (gr. 2-6). 1990. pap. 8.95 (0-86327-263-0, Pub. by Poolbeg Pr ER) Dufour.
—Lightning over Giltspur. MacRaois, Cormac. 139p. (gr. 4-6). 1991. 14.95 (0-86327-308-4, Pub. by Wolfhound Pr EIRE) Dufour.
—Mission West: Journey of Mystery & Adventure to the Edge of the World. Langenus, Ron. (Orig.). 1990. pap. 8.95 (0-86327-239-8, Pub. by Wolfhound Pr EIRE) Dufour.
—Sea Wolves from the North. Mullen, Michael. 112p. (gr. 3-9). 1989. 10.95 (0-905473-94-9, Pub. by Wolfhound Pr EIRE); pap. 7.95 (0-86327-023-9, Pub. by Wolfhound Pr IE) Dufour.
Dunne, Jeanette. Lightning over Giltspur. MacRaois, Cormac. 144p. (gr. 4-8). 1993. pap. 9.95 (0-86327-332-7, Pub. by Wolfhound Pr EIRE) Dufour.
—Run to the Ark. McCaughren, Tom. 208p. (gr. 4-8). 1993. 13.95 (0-86327-304-1, Pub. by Wolfhound Pr EIRE); pap. 9.95 (0-86327-342-4, Pub. by Wolfhound Pr EIRE) Dufour.
Dunning, Mike, photos by. Amazing Birds of Prey. Parry-Jones, Jemima. LC 92-909. 32p. (Orig.). (gr. 1-5). 1992. PLB 9.99 (0-679-92771-9); pap. 7.99 (0-679-82771-4) Knopf Bks Yng Read.
—Amazing Flying Machines. Kerrod, Robin. LC 91-53137. 32p. (Orig.). (gr. 1-5). 1992. PLB 9.99 (0-679-92765-4); pap. 6.95 (0-679-82765-X) Knopf Bks Yng Read.
—Train. Coiley, John. LC 92-4711. 64p. (gr. 5 up). 1992. 15.00 (0-679-81684-4); PLB 16.99 (0-679-91684-9) Knopf Bks Yng Read.
Dunning, Mike & Moller, Ray, photos by. Amazing Boats. Lincoln, Margaret. LC 92-3045. 32p. (Orig.). (gr. 1-5). 1992. PLB 9.99 (0-679-92770-0); pap. 7.99 (0-679-82770-6) Knopf Bks Yng Read.
Dunnington, T. Goat's Adventure in Alphabet Town. McDonnell, Janet. LC 91-20548. 32p. (ps-2). 1992. PLB 14.60 (0-516-05407-4) Childrens.
Dunnington, Tom. Addition Annie. Gisler, David. LC 91-17654. 32p. (ps-2). 1991. PLB 11.93 (0-516-02007-2); pap. 2.95 (0-516-42007-0) Childrens.
—Animal Babies. Hamsa, Bobbie. LC 84-27459. 32p. (ps-2). 1985. lib. bdg. 11.93 (0-516-02066-8); pap. 2.95 (0-516-42066-6) Childrens.
—Animal Habitats: The Best Home of All. Pemberton, Nancy. LC 90-30633. 32p. (ps-2). 1990. PLB 21.35 (0-89565-578-0); PLB 14.95s.p. (0-685-56194-1) Childs World.
—Animals. LC 83-25213. 32p. (gr. k-3). 1984. PLB 21.35 (0-89565-264-1); PLB 14.95s.p. (0-685-55699-9) Childs World.
—Bobby's Zoo. Lunn, Carolyn. LC 88-36865. 32p. (ps-2). 1989. PLB 11.93 (0-516-02089-7); pap. 2.95 (0-516-42089-5) Childrens.
—A Buzz Is Part of a Bee. Lunn, Carolyn. LC 89-25434. 32p. (ps-2). 1990. PLB 11.93 (0-516-02062-5); pap. 2.95 (0-516-42062-3) Childrens.
—Cinderella. McKissack, Patricia & McKissack, Fredrick. LC 85-12764. (gr. 1-2). 1985. PLB 11.93 (0-516-02361-6); pap. 3.95 (0-516-42361-4) Childrens.
—Columbus & Frankie the Cat. Greene, Carol. LC 88-33067. 32p. (ps-2). 1989. pap. 3.95 (0-516-43462-4) Childrens.

—Constance Stumbles. McKissack, Patricia & McKissack, Fredrick. 32p. (ps-2). 1988. PLB 11.93 (0-516-02086-2); pap. 2.95 (0-516-42086-0) Childrens.
—Count the Possums. Punnett, Richard D. LC 81-21773. 32p. (ps-2). 1982. PLB 21.35 (0-89565-215-3); PLB 14.95s.p. (0-685-57678-7) Childs World.
—Los Gatos Me Gustan Mas (I Love Cats) Matthias, Catherine. LC 83-7215. (SPA.). 32p. (ps-2). 1988. pap. 2.95 (0-516-52041-5) Childrens.
—Good Health: A Visit from Droopy. McDonnell, Janet. LC 90-1871. 32p. (ps-2). 1990. PLB 19.95 (0-89565-582-9); PLB 13.95s.p. (0-685-56196-8) Childs World.
—The Great Bug Hunt. Dobkin, Bonnie. LC 93-10333. 32p. (ps-2). 1993. PLB 13.27 (0-516-02017-X) Childrens.
—Help Jumbo Escape. Punnett, Richard D. LC 81-21667. 32p. (ps-2). 1982. PLB 21.35 (0-89565-214-5); PLB 14.95s.p. (0-685-55535-6) Childs World.
—I Love Fishing. Dobkin, Bonnie. LC 92-38506. 32p. (ps-2). 1993. PLB 11.93 (0-516-02013-7); pap. 2.95 (0-516-42013-5) Childrens.
—If I Were an Ant. Moses, Amy. LC 92-12947. 32p. (ps-2). 1992. PLB 11.93 (0-516-02011-0) Childrens.
—If I Were an Ant. Moses, Amy. LC 92-12947. 32p. (ps-2). 1993. pap. 2.95 (0-516-42011-9) Childrens.
—King Midas & His Gold. McKissack, Patricia & McKissack, Fredrick. LC 86-11744. 32p. (ps-2). 1986. PLB 11.93 (0-516-03984-9); pap. 3.95 (0-516-43984-7) Childrens.
—El Leon y el Raton: The Lion & the Mouse. Wang, Mary L. LC 85-31441. (SPA.). 32p. (ps-2). 1988. PLB 11.93 (0-516-33981-8); pap. 3.95 (0-516-53981-7) Childrens.
—The Lion & the Mouse. Wang, Mary L. LC 85-31441. 32p. (ps-2). 1986. PLB 11.93 (0-516-03981-4); pap. 3.95 (0-516-43981-2) Childrens.
—Name Lizzy's Colors. Punnett, Richard D. LC 82-1172. 32p. (ps-2). 1982. PLB 21.35 (0-89565-216-1); PLB 14.95s.p. (0-685-55533-X) Childs World.
—Name Patty's Pets. Punnett, Richard D. LC 81-18056. 32p. (ps-2). 1982. PLB 21.35 (0-89565-213-7); PLB 14.95s.p. (0-685-55534-8) Childs World.
—Osos, osos, aqui y alli: (Bears, Bears, Everywhere) Milios, Rita. LC 87-33780. (ENG & SPA.). 32p. (ps-2). 1989. PLB 11.93 (0-516-32085-8); pap. 2.95 (0-516-52085-7) Childrens.
—The Perky Little Pumpkin. Friskey, Margaret. LC 90-38376. 32p. (ps-3). 1990. PLB 15.00 (0-516-03564-9); pap. 4.95 (0-516-43564-7) Childrens.
—A Pet for Pat. Snow, Pegeen. LC 83-23159. 32p. (ps-2). 1984. PLB 11.93 (0-516-02049-8); pap. 2.95 (0-516-42049-6) Childrens.
—The Pilgrims Are Marching. Greene, Carol. LC 88-20219. 32p. (ps-2). 1988. PLB 15.00 (0-516-08234-5); pap. 3.95 (0-516-48234-3) Childrens.
—Spiders & Webs. Lunn, Carolyn. LC 89-34665. 32p. (ps-2). 1989. PLB 11.93 (0-516-02093-5); pap. 2.95 (0-516-42093-3) Childrens.
—The Story of D-Day. Stein, R. Conrad. LC 77-5089. 32p. (gr. 3-6). 1977. pap. 3.95 (0-516-44609-6) Childrens.
—The Story of Mississippi Steamboats. Stein, R. Conrad. 32p. (gr. 3-6). 1987. pap. 3.95 (0-516-44726-2) Childrens.
—Story of Old Ironsides. Richards, Norman. LC 67-20099. 32p. (gr. 3-6). 1967. pap. 3.95 (0-516-44628-2) Childrens.
—Talk-along-Help Dress Priscilla. Punnett, Dick. LC 84-23030. 32p. (ps). 1985. PLB 21.35 (0-89565-217-X); PLB 14.95s.p. (0-685-55714-6) Childs World.
—Three Billy Goats Gruff. McKissack, Patricia & McKissack, Fredrick. LC 86-33450. 32p. (ps-2). 1987. PLB 11.93 (0-516-02366-7); pap. 3.95 (0-516-42366-5) Childrens.
—Los Tres Chivitos. McKissack, Patricia & McKissack, Fredrick. LC 86-33450. (SPA.). 32p. (ps-2). 1988. PLB 11.93 (0-516-32366-0); pap. 3.95 (0-516-52366-X) Childrens.
—Wait, Skates! Johnson, Mildred. LC 82-22228. 32p. (ps-2). 1983. PLB 11.93 (0-516-02039-0); pap. 2.95 (0-516-42039-9) Childrens.
—What Plants Need: The Rabbit Who Knew. Moncure, Jane B. LC 89-24001. 32p. (ps-2). 1990. PLB 19.95 (0-89565-559-4); PLB 13.95s.p. (0-685-56180-1) Childs World.
Dunrea, Olivier. Deep Down Underground. Dunrea, Olivier. LC 88-13534. 32p. (ps-2). 1989. RSBE 13.95 (0-02-732861-9, Macmillan Child Bk) Macmillan Child Grp.
—Deep down Underground. Dunrea, Olivier. LC 92-45273. 32p. (gr. k-3). 1993. pap. 4.95 (0-689-71756-3, Aladdin) Macmillan Child Grp.
—Eppie M. Says... Dunrea, Olivier. LC 89-8134. 32p. (ps-2). 1990. RSBE 13.95 (0-02-733205-5, Macmillan Child Bk) Macmillan Child Grp.
—Fergus & Bridey. Dunrea, Olivier. 32p. (ps-3). 1992. pap. 3.99 (0-440-40691-9, YB) Dell.
—Mogwogs on the March. Dunrea, Olivier. LC 85-5493. 32p. (ps-1). 1985. pap. 5.95 (0-8234-0845-0) Holiday.
—Skara Brae: The Story of a Prehistoric Village. Dunrea, Olivier. LC 85-42882. 40p. (gr. 3-7). 1986. reinforced bdg. 13.95 (0-8234-0583-4) Holiday.
Dunton, Mary J. Something New Begins: New & Selected Poems. Moore, Lilian. LC 82-1723. 128p. (gr. 3 up). 1982. SBE 12.95 (0-689-30818-3, Atheneum Child Bk) Macmillan Child Grp.

Duntze, Dorothee. The Emperor's New Clothes. Andersen, Hans Christian. LC 86-2509. 32p. (gr. k-3). 1986. 14.95 (*1-55858-036-0*) North-South Bks NYC.
—The Golden Goose. Grimm, Jacob & Grimm, Wilhelm K. Bell, Anthea, tr. LC 87-32108. 32p. (gr. k-3). 1988. 13.95 (*1-55858-047-6*) North-South Bks NYC.
—The Life of Jesus. LC 93-28776. 1993. write for info. (*0-8146-2303-4*) Liturgical Pr.
—The Princess & the Pea. Andersen, Hans Christian. LC 85-7199. 32p. (gr. k-2). 1985. 14.95 (*1-55858-034-4*) North-South Bks NYC.
—The Swineherd. Andersen, Hans Christian. Lewis, Naomi, tr. LC 86-62521. 32p. (gr. k-3). 1987. 14.95 (*1-55858-038-7*) North-South Bks NYC.
—The Twelve Days of Christmas. Duntze, Dorothee. LC 91-32359. 32p. (gr. k-3). 1992. 14.95 (*1-55858-151-0*); PLB 14.88 (*1-55858-152-9*) North-South Bks NYC.
Dupre, Rick. Agassu: Legend of the Leopard King. Dupre, Rick. 40p. (gr. 1-4). 1993. 18.95 (*0-87614-764-3*) Carolrhoda Bks.
DuQuette, Keith. Happy As a Tapir. Carbone, Terry. 32p. 1992. 13.00 (*0-670-84227-3*) Viking Child Bks.
—Hotel Animal. DuQuette, Keith. LC 93-14531. 32p. (ps-3). 1994. PLB 13.99 (*0-670-85056-X*) Viking Child Bks.
Duranceau, Suzanne. Hickory, Dickory, Dock. Muller, Robin. LC 92-37588. 32p. (ps-6). 1994. 15.95 (*0-590-47278-X*) Scholastic Inc.
—Millicent & the Wind. Munsch, Robert. 32p. (gr. k-3). 1984. PLB 14.95 (*0-920236-98-7*, Pub. by Annick CN); pap. 4.95 (*0-920236-93-6*, Pub. by Annick CN) Firefly Bks Ltd.
—Millicent & the Wind. Munsch, Robert. 24p. (Orig.). (ps-2). 1989. pap. 0.99 (*1-55037-010-3*, Pub. by Annick CN) Firefly Bks Ltd.

Durant, Charlotte T. Kristina & Diabetes: How Kristina Faced the Disease. Fennoy, Thelma R. 56p. (Orig.). (gr. 2 up). 1993. pap. text ed. 5.00 (*0-9637350-0-4*) T R Fennoy. This book is designed for young children, especially those who have diabetes. It depicts real-life episodes in the life of Kristina, a ten-year old diabetic, & gives fresh & personal view of how it feels to have this disease as a young person. This information is both vital & accurate. It explains what happens to the body when diabetes occurs & what role the child can play in coping with the disease. This is a book filled with hope, encouragement & courage. "This book should be very helpful to children who have been recently diagnosed with diabetes."--Carl R. Turner, M.D., F.A.A.P. "I enjoyed reading Mrs. Fennoy's KRISTINA & DIABETES, & I feel that this booklet helps to fill a void in instructive literature for those children affected with juvenile diabetes. I feel that the booklet will be of benefit to both the child & the child's parents."--Peter Pappas, Jr., M.D. KRISTINA & DIABETES-HOW KRISTINA FACED THE DISEASE, Cost $5.00 plus $3.00 shipping & handling. Order from: T.R. Fennoy, Publisher, Route 2, Box 173, Jefferson, TX 75657. *Publisher Provided Annotation.*

—Miss Mary McLeod Bethune: The Life of a Beautiful African American Woman. Durant, Charlotte T. Pye, Ethel, ed. 40p. (Orig.). (ps-1). 1992. pap. 4.00 (*0-913678-21-X*) New Day Pr.
Durdee, Becky. Children's Parties Made Easy. Fulk, Penny. 142p. (Orig.). pap. 6.00 (*0-941951-00-6*) JJJ Pubs.
Durenceau, Andre. Butterflies & Moths. Mitchell, Robert & Zim, Herbert S. (gr. 5 up). 1964. PLB write for info. (*0-307-24052-5*); pap. write for info. (Golden Pr) Western Pub.
Durer, Albrecht. Albrecht Durer. Raboff, Ernest. LC 87-17702. 32p. (gr. 1 up). 1988. pap. 5.95 (*0-06-446071-1*, Trophy) HarpC Child Bks.
Durfee, Gaylie, jt. illus. see Durfee, John C.
Durfee, John C. & Durfee, Gaylie. Pardners: Three Stories on Friendship. Yorgason, Blaine M. & Yorgason, Brenton. 64p. (Orig.). (gr. 9 up). 1988. pap. 3.95 (*0-929985-05-2*) Sonos.
Durham, Robert. Ghost in the Library. Pellowski, Michael J. LC 88-1236. 48p. (Orig.). (gr. 1-4). 1989. PLB 10.59 (*0-8167-1337-5*); pap. text ed. 3.50 (*0-8167-1338-3*) Troll Assocs.

Durham, Robert C. Children. Lucas, Daryl. 18p. (gr. 2). 1992. 7.99 (*0-8423-1013-4*) Tyndale.
—Heroes. Lucas, Daryl. 18p. (gr. 2). 1992. 8.99 (*0-8423-1009-6*) Tyndale.
—Heroines. Lucas, Daryl. 18p. (gr. 2). 1992. 8.99 (*0-8423-1012-6*) Tyndale.
—Prophets. Lucas, Daryl. (gr. 2). 1992. 8.99 (*0-8423-1011-8*) Tyndale.
Durham-Moulin, Francoise. Jill & the Jogero. Thompson, Richard. 24p. (ps-2). 1992. PLB 14.95 (*1-55037-245-9*, Pub. by Annick Pr); pap. 4.95 (*1-55037-246-7*, Pub. by Annick Pr) Firefly Bks Ltd.
Duris, Ellen. Hopes, Dreams & Wishes, 3 bks. Coleman, Nancy, et al. 24p. (Orig.). (ps-k). 1991. Set. pap. 8.95 (*0-8249-7419-0*, Ideals Child) Hambleton-Hill.
Durkee, Noura. Cheng Ho's Voyage. Clyde, Ahmad. LC 81-66951. 32p. (Orig.). (gr. 3-7). 1981. pap. 2.00 (*0-89259-021-1*) Am Trust Pubns.
Duroussy, Nathalie. The Crystal Ball. Scheidl, Gerda M. Lanning, Rosemary, tr. from GER. LC 92-44762. 32p. (gr. k-3). 1993. 14.95 (*1-55858-197-9*); PLB 14.88 (*1-55858-198-7*) North-South Bks NYC.
Durrand, Diana. A Peanut Butter Waltz. Stutchner, Joan B. 24p. (Orig.). (ps-2). 1990. pap. 0.99 (*1-55037-126-6*, Pub. by Annick CN) Firefly Bks Ltd.
Durrell, Dennis. Lady & the Tramp: Pop-up Book. LC 93-71380. 12p. (ps-3). 1994. 11.95 (*1-56282-612-3*) Disney Pr.
Durrell, Dennis, jt. illus. see Gonzalez, Ric.
Durrell, Julie. Easter Holiday Grab Bag. Stamper, Judith. LC 92-10132. 48p. (gr. 2-5). 1992. PLB 11.89 (*0-8167-2912-3*); pap. text ed. 3.95 (*0-8167-2913-1*) Troll Assocs.
—The Lettuce Leaf Birthday Letter. Taylor, Linda. LC 93-16906. 1994. 13.99 (*0-8037-1454-8*); PLB 13.89 (*0-8037-1455-6*) Dial Bks Young.
—Lizzie Logan Wears Purple Sunglasses. Spinelli, Eileen. LC 93-29104. 1994. write for info. (*0-671-74685-5*, S&S BFYR) S&S Trade.
—Merry Christmas from Eddie. Haywood, Carolyn. LC 86-2466. 112p. (gr. 1-4). 1986. 12.95 (*0-688-05828-0*) Morrow Jr Bks.
—Mouse Tails. Durrell, Julie. LC 84-12638. 32p. (ps-1). 1985. 6.95 (*0-517-55592-1*) Crown Bks Yng Read.
—My Gingerbread Fairy Tale House, 4 bks. Nash, Corey & Nash, Corey, eds. LC 87-40689. (ps). 1990. Set. bds. 6.95 (*1-55782-056-2*, Pub. by Warner Juvenile Bks) Little.
—Peek-a-Boo. Durrell, Julie. Bahr, Amy C. & Klimo, Kate, eds. 8p. (ps). 1982. pap. 3.95 (*0-671-45546-X*, Little Simon) S&S Trade.
—Professor Possum's Great Adventure. Pellowski, Michael J. LC 88-1281. 48p. (Orig.). (gr. 1-4). 1988. PLB 10.59 (*0-8167-1341-3*); pap. text ed. 3.50 (*0-8167-1342-1*) Troll Assocs.
—The Pudgy Book of Farm Animals. 16p. (gr. k). 1984. 2.95 (*0-448-10211-0*, G&D) Putnam Pub Group.
—The Pudgy Book of Toys. 16p. (ps-3). 1983. pap. 2.95 (*0-448-10201-3*, G&D) Putnam Pub Group.
—Summer Fun. Haywood, Carolyn. LC 85-25864. 128p. (gr. 1-4). 1986. 11.95 (*0-688-04958-3*) Morrow Jr Bks.
—The Tiny Christmas Elf. Peters, Sharon. LC 86-30849. 32p. (gr. k-2). 1988. PLB 7.89 (*0-8167-0988-2*); pap. text ed. 1.95 (*0-8167-0989-0*) Troll Assocs.
—Windy Day. Craig, Janet. LC 87-10909. 32p. (gr. k-2). 1988. PLB 7.89 (*0-8167-0982-3*); pap. text ed. 1.95 (*0-8167-0983-1*) Troll Assocs.
—Young Helen Keller: Woman of Courage. Benjamin, Anne. LC 91-26406. 32p. (gr. k-2). 1992. PLB 11.59 (*0-8167-2530-6*); pap. text ed. 2.95 (*0-8167-2531-4*) Troll Assocs.
Duskin, Leisia. Octavia & Other Poems. Madgett, Naomi L. LC 87-51637. 117p. (Orig.). (gr. 9-12). 1988. pap. 8.00 (*0-88378-121-2*) Third World.
Duvoisin, Roger. Autumn Harvest. Tresselt, Alvin R. LC 51-8824. 32p. (gr. k-3). 1951. PLB 15.88 (*0-688-51155-4*) Lothrop.
—Autumn Harvest. Tresselt, Alvin. LC 51-8824. 32p. (ps-2). 1990. pap. 3.95 (*0-688-09925-4*, Mulberry) Morrow.
—The Camel Who Took a Walk. Tworkov, Jack. 32p. (ps-3). 1989. pap. 3.95 (*0-525-44476-9*, DCB) Dutton Child Bks.
—Hide & Seek Fog. Tresselt, Alvin R. LC 65-14087. 32p. (gr. k-2). PLB 14.88 (*0-688-51169-4*) Lothrop.
—Hide & Seek Fog. Tresselt, Alvin. LC 65-14087. 32p. (ps-3). 1988. pap. 3.95 (*0-688-07813-3*, Mulberry) Morrow.
—Hungry Leprechaun. Calhoun, Mary. LC 62-7214. 32p. (gr. k-3). 1962. PLB 12.88 (*0-688-31713-8*) Morrow Jr Bks.
—Petunia. Duvoisin, Roger. (gr. k-3). 1962. lib. bdg. 9.99 (*0-394-90865-1*) Knopf Bks Yng Read.
—Petunia, Beware! Duvoisin, Roger. (gr. 1-3). 1964. lib. bdg. 12.99 (*0-394-90867-8*) Knopf Bks Yng Read.
—Petunia, Beware! Duvoisin, Roger. LC 72-580009. 32p. (ps-2). 1990. pap. 3.95 (*0-679-80334-3*) Knopf Bks Yng Read.
—Petunia the Silly Goose Stories: Five Read-Aloud Classics. Duvoisin, Roger. LC 86-2783. 160p. (ps-3). 1987. PLB 15.99 (*0-394-98292-4*) Knopf Bks Yng Read.
—Petunia's Christmas. Duvoisin, Roger. (gr. k-3). 1963. lib. bdg. 12.99 (*0-394-90868-6*) Knopf Bks Yng Read.
—Rain Puddle. Holl, Adelaide. LC 65-22026. 32p. (gr. k-3). 1965. PLB 14.88 (*0-688-51096-5*) Lothrop.

—White Snow Bright Snow. Tresselt, Alvin. LC 88-10018. (ps-3). 1988. pap. 3.95 (*0-688-08294-7*, Mulberry) Morrow.
—White Snow, Bright Snow. Tresselt, Alvin. (ps-3). 1989. 13.95 (*0-688-41161-4*); PLB 13.88 (*0-688-51161-9*) Lothrop.
—Wobble the Witch Cat. Calhoun, Mary. LC 58-5018. 32p. (gr. k-3). 1958. PLB 13.88 (*0-688-31621-2*) Morrow Jr Bks.
Dvorak, David, Jr. A Sea of Grass: The Tallgrass Prairie. Dvorak, David, Jr. LC 93-19507. 32p. (gr. 1-4). 1994. RSBE 14.95 (*0-02-733245-4*, Macmillan Child Bk) Macmillan Child Grp.
Dvorsack, Carolyn S. Garden of Dreams. Wainwright, Richard M. LC 93-17974. 1994. write for info. (*0-9619566-6-6*) Family Life.
Dwight, Laura. Hello School. Slier, Debby, ed. 28p. (ps). 1990. 2.95 (*0-02-689483-1*) Checkerboard.
—Me & My Dad. Slier, Debby, ed. 28p. (ps). 1990. 2.95 (*1-56288-380-1*) Checkerboard.
—Me & My Mom. Slier, Debby, ed. 28p. (ps). 1990. 2.95 (*1-56288-379-8*) Checkerboard.
—What Happens Next? Christian, Cheryl, ed. 12p. (ps). 1991. 4.95 (*1-56288-131-0*) Checkerboard.
—Where's the Baby? Christian, Cheryl, ed. 12p. (ps). 1992. 4.95 (*1-56288-128-0*) Checkerboard.
—Where's the Kitten? Christian, Cheryl, ed. 12p. (ps). 1992. 4.95 (*1-56288-130-2*) Checkerboard.
—Where's the Puppy? Christian, Cheryl, ed. 12p. (ps). 1992. 4.95 (*1-56288-129-9*) Checkerboard.
Dwight, Laura, photos by. All My Things. 28p. (ps). 1992. bds. 2.95 (*1-56288-185-X*) Checkerboard.
—Babies All Around. 28p. (ps). 1992. bds. 2.95 (*1-56288-184-1*) Checkerboard.
—Me & My Grandma. Slier, Debby, ed. 28p. (ps). 1992. bds. 2.95 (*1-56288-183-3*) Checkerboard.
—Me & My Grandpa. Slier, Debby, ed. 28p. (ps). 1992. bds. 2.95 (*1-56288-182-5*) Checkerboard.
Dyck, Lavonne. Christmas Goose. Harder, Geraldine & Harder, Milton. Shelly, Maynard, ed. LC 90-84535. 80p. (Orig.). (gr. k-6). 1990. pap. 5.95 (*0-87303-146-6*) Faith & Life.
Dyer, Jane. Babyland: A Book for Babies. Dyer, Jane, selected by. LC 93-4244. 1994. 17.95 (*0-316-19766-1*) Little.
—Cozy in the Woods. Ross, K. K. LC 88-63931. 28p. (ps). 1990. 2.95 (*0-394-85400-4*) Random Bks Yng Read.
—The Girl in the Golden Bower. Yolen, Jane. LC 92-37284. (gr. 5 up). 1994. 15.95 (*0-316-96894-3*) Little.
—Goldilocks & the Three Bears. 16p. (ps). 1984. 3.95 (*0-448-10213-7*, G&D) Putnam Pub Group.
—Little Red Riding Hood. Aesop. LC 85-70289. 18p. (ps). 1985. 3.95 (*0-448-10227-7*, G&D) Putnam Pub Group.
—Moo, Moo Peekaboo. Dyer, Jane. LC 85-61530. (ps). 1986. 3.99 (*0-394-87883-3*) Random Bks Yng Read.
—My Book of Christmas Carols. Rosenkrans, B., compiled by. 32p. (ps-2). 1986. pap. 1.95 (*0-448-19079-6*, G&D) Putnam Pub Group.
—The Patchwork Lady. Whittington, Mary K. Yolen, Jane, ed. 32p. (ps-3). 1991. 13.95 (*0-15-259580-5*) HarBrace.
—Penrod Again. Christian, Mary B. LC 86-21846. 56p. (gr. 1-4). 1987. RSBE 11.95 (*0-02-718550-8*, Macmillan Child Bk) Macmillan Child Grp.
—Penrod Again. Christian, Mary B. LC 90-29. 56p. (gr. 1-4). 1990. pap. 3.95 (*0-689-71432-7*, Aladdin) Macmillan Child Grp.
—Penrod's Pants. Christian, Mary B. LC 85-11545. 56p. (gr. 1-4). 1986. RSBE 11.95 (*0-02-718520-6*, Macmillan Child Bk) Macmillan Child Grp.
—Picnic with Piggins. Yolen, Jane. 32p. (ps-3). 1988. 14.95 (*0-15-261534-2*) HarBrace.
—Piggins. Yolen, Jane. LC 86-22915. 32p. (ps-3). 1987. 14.95 (*0-15-261685-3*) HarBrace.
—Piggins & the Royal Wedding. Yolen, Jane. 32p. (ps-3). 1989. 13.95 (*0-15-261687-X*) HarBrace.
—The Snow Speaks. Carlstrom, Nancy W. (ps-3). 1992. 14.95 (*0-316-12861-9*) Little.
—Talking Like the Rain: A First Book of Poems. Kennedy, X. J. & Kennedy, Dorothy M., eds. (ps up). 1992. 18.95 (*0-316-48889-5*) Little.
—Three Bears Holiday Book. Yolen, Jane. LC 93-17252. 1994. write for info. (*0-15-200932-9*, J Yolen Bks) HarBrace.
—The Three Bears Rhyme Book. Yolen, Jane. LC 86-19514. 32p. (ps-3). 1987. 14.95 (*0-15-286386-9*, HB Juv Bks) HarBrace.
—Time for Bed. Fox, Mem. LC 92-19771. 1993. 13.95 (*0-15-288183-2*) HarBrace.
Dyer, Jane & Krush, Beth. Gone-Away Lake. Enright, Elizabeth. 256p. (gr. 3-7). 1990. pap. 4.95 (*0-15-231649-3*, Odyssey) HarBrace.
—Return to Gone-Away. Enright, Elizabeth. 212p. (gr. 3-7). 1990. pap. 4.95 (*0-15-266377-0*, Odyssey) HarBrace.
Dzierzawska, Malgorzata. Little Mouse's Rescue: Little Animal Adventures Ser. Chottin, Ariane. Jensen, Patricia, adapted by. LC 93-2949. (ps-3). 1993. write for info. (*0-89577-505-0*) RD Assn.

E

Eachus, Jennifer. In the Middle of the Night. Henderson, Kathy. LC 91-29982. 32p. (ps-1). 1992. 13.95 (0-02-743545-8, Macmillan Child Bk) Macmillan Child Grp.

Eaddy, Susan. Young Children Rap to Learn about Famous African-Americans. Meissel, Chris. Keeling, Jan, ed. 80p. (Orig.). 1993. pap. text ed. 8.95 (0-86530-265-0) Incentive Pubns.

Eads, Nancy. The Story of Valley Forge. Stein, R. Conrad. LC 84-23203. 32p. (gr. 3-6). 1985. PLB 13.27 (0-516-04681-0) Childrens.

Eagle, Ellen. The Case of the Gobbling Squash. Levy, Elizabeth. (gr. 2-4). 1989. pap. 10.95 jacketed (0-671-63655-3, S&S BFYR); pap. 2.95 (0-671-68873-1, S&S BFYR) S&S Trade.
—The Case of the Mind-Reading Mommies. Levy, Elizabeth. 1990. pap. 2.95 (0-671-69435-9) S&S Trade.
—The Case of the Tattletale Heart. Levy, Elizabeth. 64p. (gr. 2-4). 1992. pap. 3.00 (0-671-74064-4, S&S BFYR) S&S Trade.
—The Ghost of Whispering Rock. Robinson, Nancy K. LC 92-52856. 64p. (gr. 2-6). 1992. 13.95 (0-8234-0944-9) Holiday.
—Gypsy's Cleaning Day. Eagle, Ellen. LC 89-34315. 32p. (ps-up). 1990. 13.95 (0-688-07391-3); PLB 13.88 (0-688-07392-1, Morrow Jr Bks) Morrow Jr Bks.
—The Jenny Summer. Greene, Carol. LC 87-45283. 80p. (gr. 1-4). 1988. PLB 12.89 (0-06-022209-3) HarpC Child Bks.
—Star Guide. Branley, Franklyn M. LC 82-45928. 64p. (gr. 3-6). 1987. (Crowell Jr Bks); PLB 12.89 (0-690-04351-1, Crowell Jr Bks) HarpC Child Bks.
—What Do We Do Now, George? McCann, Helen. LC 91-2329. 160p. (gr. 4-7). 1993. pap. 2.95 (0-671-86691-5, Half Moon Bks) S&S Trade.
—What's French for Help, George? McCann, Helen. LC 91-41563. 460p. (gr. 5-9). 1993. pap. 13.00 JR3 (0-671-74689-8, S&S BFYR) S&S Trade.
—Will Somebody Please Marry My Sister? Clifford, Eth. 128p. (gr. 3-6). 1992. 13.45 (0-395-58037-4) HM.

Eagle, Michael. Pompeii... Buried Alive! Kunhardt, Edith. LC 87-4512. 48p. (gr. 2-3). 1987. lib. bdg. 6.99 (0-394-98866-3); 3.50 (0-394-88866-9) Random Bks Yng Read.
—The Trojan Horse: How the Greeks Won the War. Little, Emily. LC 87-43118. 48p. (Orig.). (gr. 2-4). 1988. lib. bdg. 7.99 (0-394-99674-7); pap. 2.95 (0-394-89674-2) Random Bks Yng Read.

Eagle, Mike. Adios, Berry. Shinhav, Chaya. Writer, C. C. & Nielsen, Lisa C., trs. (SPA.). 24p. (Orig.). (ps). 1992. pap. text ed. 3.00x (1-56134-154-1) Dushkin Pub.
—An Afternoon at Emmi's. Griffin, Gail. 24p. (Orig.). (ps). 1992. pap. text ed. 3.00x (1-56134-163-0) Dushkin Pub.
—El Cielo Azul de Shawna. Blatchford, Claire. Writer, C. C. & Nielsen, Lisa C., trs. (SPA.). 24p. (Orig.). (ps). 1992. pap. text ed. 3.00x (1-56134-174-6) Dushkin Pub.
—Coronado's Golden Quest. Weisberg, Barbara. LC 92-18078. 79p. (gr. 2-5). 1992. PLB 21.34 (0-8114-7232-9); pap. write for info. (0-8114-8072-0) Raintree Steck-V.
—Dan Goes to First Grade. Fleisher, Gila M. Kriss, David, tr. from HEB. 24p. (Orig.). (ps). 1992. pap. text ed. 3.00x (1-56134-166-5) Dushkin Pub.
—Daniel Entra Al Primer Grado. Fleisher, Gila M. Writer, C. C. & Nielsen, Lisa C., trs. (SPA.). 24p. (Orig.). (ps). 1992. pap. text ed. 3.00x (1-56134-176-2) Dushkin Pub.
—David Bushnell & His Turtle: The Story of America's First Submarine. Swanson, June. LC 90-628. 40p. (gr. 2-5). 1991. SBE 13.95 (0-689-31628-3, Atheneum Child Bk) Macmillan Child Grp.
—Down the Path. Blatchford, Claire. 24p. (Orig.). (ps). 1992. pap. text ed. 3.00x (1-56134-142-8) Dushkin Pub.
—La Escuela de Maria. Harel, Nira. Writer, C. C. & Nielsen, Lisa C., trs. (SPA.). 24p. (Orig.). (ps). 1992. pap. text ed. 3.00x (1-56134-153-3) Dushkin Pub.
—A Flag for Our Country. Spencer, Eve. LC 92-14414. 32p. (gr. 2-5). 1992. PLB 21.34 (0-8114-7211-6) Raintree Steck-V.
—Goodbye, Berry. Shinhav, Chaya. Kriss, David, tr. from HEB. 24p. (Orig.). (ps). 1992. pap. text ed. 3.00x (1-56134-144-4) Dushkin Pub.
—Maria's School. Harel, Nira. Kriss, David, tr. from HEB. 24p. (Orig.). (ps). 1992. pap. text ed. 3.00x (1-56134-143-6) Dushkin Pub.
—The Pigs Got Out. Sherrow, Victoria. 24p. (Orig.). (ps). 1992. pap. text ed. 3.00x (0-685-60664-3) Dushkin Pub.
—Por el Camino. Blatchford, Claire. Writer, C. C. & Nielsen, Lisa C., trs. (SPA.). 24p. (Orig.). (ps). 1992. pap. text ed. 3.00x (1-56134-152-5) Dushkin Pub.
—Los Puerquitos Se Escaparon. Sherrow, Victoria. Writer, C. C. & Nielsen, Lisa C., trs. (SPA.). 24p. (Orig.). (ps). 1992. pap. text ed. 3.00x (1-56134-171-1) Dushkin Pub.
—Shawna's Bit of Blue Sky. Blatchford, Claire. 24p. (Orig.). (ps). 1992. pap. text ed. 3.00x (1-56134-164-9) Dushkin Pub.

—Sonidos Que Oigo. Gelbart, Ofra. Writer, C. C. & Nielsen, Lisa C., trs. (SPA.). 24p. (Orig.). (ps). 1992. pap. text ed. 3.00x (1-56134-148-7) Dushkin Pub.
—Una Sorpresa para Reggie. Blatchford, Claire. Writer, C. C. & Nielsen, Lisa C., trs. (SPA.). 24p. (Orig.). (ps). 1992. pap. text ed. 3.00x (1-56134-151-7) Dushkin Pub.
—Sounds I Hear. Gelbart, Ofra. Kriss, David, tr. from HEB. 24p. (Orig.). (ps). 1992. pap. text ed. 3.00x (1-56134-138-X) Dushkin Pub.
—A Surprise for Reggie. Blatchford, Claire. 24p. (Orig.). (ps). 1992. pap. text ed. 3.00x (1-56134-141-X) Dushkin Pub.
—Una Tarde en la Casa de Emmi. Griffin, Gail M. Writer, C. C. & Nielsen, Lisa C., trs. (SPA.). 24p. (Orig.). (ps). 1992. pap. text ed. 3.00x (1-56134-173-8) Dushkin Pub.
—Voyagers from Space: Meteors & Meteorites. Lauber, Patricia. LC 86-47745. 80p. (gr. 5 up). 1989. (Crowell Jr Bks); PLB 15.89 (0-690-04634-0, Crowell Jr Bks) HarpC Child Bks.
—Who Discovered America? Mysteries & Puzzles of the New World. new ed. Lauber, Patricia. LC 90-43604. 80p. (gr. 2-6). 1992. 16.00 (0-06-023728-7); PLB 15.89 (0-06-023729-5) HarpC Child Bks.

Eames, David. Nature Detective: How to Solve Outdoor Mysteries. Docekal, Eileen M. LC 89-31387. 128p. (gr. 3-10). 1991. pap. 7.95 (0-8069-6845-1) Sterling.

Earle, James H. Masterson & Roosevelt. DeMattos, Jack. DeArment, Robert K., photos by. LC 84-17591. 151p. (gr. 9 up). 1984. 18.95 (0-932702-31-7) Creative Texas.

Early, Margaret. William Tell. Early, Margaret, retold by. 32p. 1991. 17.95 (0-8109-3854-5) Abrams.

Easley, Jeff. Universal Monsters: Frankenstein. Henry, Robert. 48p. (gr. 2-4). 1992. pap. write for info. (0-307-11467-8, 11467, Golden Pr) Western Pub.

Easmon, Carol. Amoko & Efua Bear. Appiah, Sonia. LC 88-8343. 32p. (ps-1). 1989. SBE 13.95 (0-02-705591-4, Macmillan Child Bk) Macmillan Child Grp.

Easterling, Mae L. Leola et la pirogue. Theriot, David. (FRE.). 39p. (gr. 3). 1979. pap. text ed. 1.25 (0-911409-03-3) Natl Mat Dev.
—Les Trois Petits Amis et la Decouverte du Gumbo. Theriot, David. (FRE.). 41p. (gr. 3). 1979. pap. 1.25 (0-911409-04-1) Natl Mat Dev.

Eastman, Kevin & Laird, Peter. Teenage Mutant Ninja Turtles & Other Strangeness. Wujcik, Erick. Marciniszyn, Alex & Cartier, Randi, eds. 112p. (Orig.). (gr. 8 up). 1985. pap. 11.95 (0-916211-14-2, 502) Palladium Bks.
—Teenage Mutant Ninja Turtles in Intergalactic Wrestling & Other Adventures. Eastman, Kevin & Laird, Peter. 96p. (Orig.). (gr. 2-8). 1991. pap. 6.95 incls. cassette (0-679-81747-6) Random Bks Yng Read.

Eastman, Kevin, jt. illus. see Laird, Peter.

Eastman, Kevin, et al. Teenage Mutant Ninja Turtles Guide to the Universe. Wujcik, Erick. Marciniszyn, Alex & Siembieda, Florence, eds. 48p. (Orig.). (gr. 8 up). 1987. pap. 7.95 (0-916211-25-8, 506) Palladium Bks.

Eastman, P. D. Are You My Mother? - Eres Tu Mi Mama? Eastman, P. D. (ENG & SPA.). 64p. (ps-3). 1993. incl. cass. 6.95 (0-679-84430-9) Random Bks Yng Read.
—Flap Your Wings. Eastman, Philip D. 32p. (ps-1). 1985. pap. 4.95 incl. cassette (0-394-87655-5) Random Bks Yng Read.
—Perro Grande...Perro Pequeno: (Big Dog...Little Dog) Eastman, P. D. De Cuenca, Pilar & Alvarez, Ines, trs. LC 81-12070. (SPA.). 32p. (ps-3). 1982. lib. bdg. 5.99 (0-394-95142-5); pap. 2.25 (0-394-85142-0) Random Bks Yng Read.

Eastman, Philip D. The Alphabet Book. Eastman, Philip D. LC 73-16859. 32p. (ps-3). 1974. pap. 2.25 (0-394-82808-6) Random Bks Yng Read.
—Best Nest. Eastman, Philip D. LC 68-28459. 72p. (gr. k-3). 1968. 6.95 (0-394-80051-6); lib. bdg. 7.99 (0-394-90051-0) Beginner.

Eaton, John. Fairy Tales. Cummings, e. e. LC 65-18727. 39p. (gr. k up). 1975. pap. 3.95 (0-15-629895-3, Voyager Bks) HarBrace.

Eaton, Lewis. Journey to Freedom. Leeson, Muriel. 128p. (Orig.). (gr. 4-8). 1989. pap. 4.95 (0-8361-3498-2) Herald Pr.

Eaton, Tom. One Hundred & One Pet Jokes. Hirsch, Phil & Hirsch, Hope. 96p. (Orig.). (gr. 3-7). 1981. pap. 1.95 (0-590-30380-5, Schol Pap) Scholastic Inc.

Eberbach, Andrea. Sportsathon Puzzles, Jokes, Facts & Games. Braden, Vic & Phillips, Louis. (ps-k). 1986. pap. 4.95 (0-14-032028-8, Puffin) Puffin Bks.
—Willie the Slowpoke. Greydanus, Rose. 32p. (gr. k-2). 1980. PLB 7.89 (0-89375-394-7); pap. 1.95 (0-89375-294-0); cassette 8.95 (0-685-04954-X) Troll Assocs.

Eberly, Keith. Alone Together. Boulden, Jim. 32p. (Orig.). (gr. 1-7). 1991. pap. 4.95 (1-878076-09-4) Boulden Pub.
—Saying Goodbye. rev. ed. Boulden, Jim. 32p. (Orig.). (gr. 1-7). 1991. pap. 3.95 (1-878076-12-4) Boulden Pub.

Ebert, Len. My Read-&-Do Bible Storybook. O'Neal, Debbie T. LC 89-15184. 128p. (Orig.). (gr. 3-8). 1989. pap. 14.99 kivar (0-8066-2431-0, 9-2431) Augsburg Fortress.

Eccles, Anne. Colorado Activity & Coloring Book. Eccles, Anne. 32p. (ps-8). 1986. pap. 2.95 (0-9618555-0-9) Anne M Eccles.

Eccles, Anne M. United States Activity & Coloring Book. Eccles, Anne M. 36p. (ps-8). 1992. activity/coloring bk. 3.95 (0-9618555-2-5) Anne M Eccles.

Eckart, Chuck. How the Forest Grew. Jaspersohn, William. LC 79-16286. 56p. (gr. 1 up). 1989. Repr. of 1980 ed. 13.95 (0-688-80232-X) Greenwillow.
—How the Forest Grew. Jaspersohn, William. LC 79-16286. 56p. (gr. k up). 1992. pap. 4.95 (0-688-11508-X, Mulberry) Morrow.

Ecke, Wolfgang. The Face at the Window. Ecke, Wolfgang. LC 79-15628. (gr. 5-9). 1979. 9.95 (0-13-299115-2) P-H.

Ecker, Beverly. Big & Easy Art for Fall. Sullivan, Dianna J. 48p. (ps-2). 1987. wkbk. 5.95 (1-55734-082-X) Tchr Create Mat.
—Big & Easy Art for Spring & Summer. Sullivan, Dianna J. 64p. (ps-2). 1987. wkbk 6.95 (1-55734-084-6) Tchr Create Mat.
—Big & Easy Art for Winter. Sullivan, Dianna J. 48p. (ps-2). 1987. wkbk. 5.95 (1-55734-083-8) Tchr Create Mat.
—Decorations & Clip Art for Holidays & Everyday. Sullivan, Dianna J. 96p. (gr. k-4). 1987. wkbk. 9.95 (1-55734-092-7) Tchr Create Mat.
—Make Your Own Adventure Books. Sullivan, Dianna. 48p. (gr. 1-4). 1988. wkbk. 5.95 (1-55734-395-0) Tchr Create Mat.
—Make Your Own Fable & Fairy Tale Books. Sullivan, Dianna. 48p. (gr. 1-4). 1988. wkbk. 5.95 (1-55734-392-6) Tchr Create Mat.
—Make Your Own Happy Times Books. Sullivan, Dianna. 48p. (gr. 1-4). 1988. wkbk. 5.95 (1-55734-394-2) Tchr Create Mat.
—Make Your Own Holiday Books. Sullivan, Dianna. 48p. (gr. 1-4). 1988. wkbk. 5.95 (1-55734-393-4) Tchr Create Mat.

Eckett, Sean. Ghost Stories. Westall, Robert, selected by. LC 92-26451. 256p. (gr. 4-9). 1993. 6.95 (1-85697-884-2) Kingfisher Bks.

Eclov, Homer. Acid Rain Reader. Stubbs, Harriett S., et al. 20p. (Orig.). (gr. 4-8). 1989. pap. 5.95 (0-935577-12-2); pap. 2.50 (0-685-17881-1) Acid Rain Found.

Eddy, Hal, et al. Easy Words: An Easy Way to Learn New Words. Woodhull, Angela V. 150p. (gr. 8 up). 1988. pap. 5.95 (0-685-44299-3) Woodhull Pubns.

Ede, Janina. Lavender Shoes: Eight Tales of Enchantment. Uttley, Alison. 84p. (gr. k-2). 1991. pap. 3.95 (0-571-15344-5) Faber & Faber.

Edelman, Heinz. Prince Ring: Icelandic Fairy Tale. 32p. (gr. 6 up). 1983. PLB 13.95s.p. (0-87191-951-6) Creative Ed.

Edelson, Wendy. Derby Downs. Cosgrove, Stephen E. 32p. (ps-3). 1990. PLB 21.35 (0-89565-659-0); PLB 14.95s.p. (0-685-58733-9) Childs World.
—Easter Bunnies. Cosgrove, Stephen. 32p. (Orig.). (gr. k-4). 1992. pap. 4.95 (0-8249-8538-9, Ideals Child) Hambleton-Hill.
—Fiddler. Cosgrove, Stephen E. 32p. (ps-3). 1990. PLB 21.35 (0-89565-665-5); PLB 14.95s.p. (0-685-58735-5) Childs World.
—Gossamer. Cosgrove, Stephen E. 32p. (ps-3). 1990. PLB 21.35 (0-89565-662-0); PLB 14.95s.p. (0-685-56225-5) Childs World.
—Hannah & Hickory. Cosgrove, Stephen E. 32p. (ps-3). 1990. PLB 21.35 (0-89565-664-7); PLB 14.95s.p. (0-685-56229-8) Childs World.
—Heidi's Rose. Cosgrove, Stephen. LC 90-71079. 32p. (gr. 3-6). 1991. 14.95 (1-55868-033-0) Gr Arts Ctr Pub.
—Ira Wordworthy. Cosgrove, Stephen E. 32p. (ps-3). 1990. PLB 21.35 (0-89565-658-2); PLB 14.95s.p. (0-685-58732-0) Childs World.
—Persimmony. Cosgrove, Stephen E. 32p. (ps-3). 1990. PLB 21.35 (0-89565-661-2); PLB 14.95s.p. (0-685-58736-3) Childs World.
—Read on Rita. Cosgrove, Stephen E. 32p. 1993. PLB 12.95 (1-56674-042-8, HTS Bks) Forest Hse.
—Shadow Chaser. Cosgrove, Stephen E. 32p. (ps-3). 1990. PLB 21.35 (0-89565-663-9); PLB 14.95s.p. (0-685-58734-7) Childs World.
—T. J. Flopp. Cosgrove, Stephen E. 32p. (ps-3). 1990. PLB 14.95 (0-89565-660-4); PLB 14.95s.p. (0-685-56224-7) Childs World.

Edelson, Wendy, photos by. The Baker's Dozen: A St. Nicholas Tale. Shepard, Aaron. LC 92-38261. (gr. 1-8). 1994. write for info. (0-684-19577-1, Scribner) Macmillan.

Edens, Cooper. Caretakers of Wonder. Edens, Cooper. LC 91-24035. 40p. (gr. 3 up). 1991. 11.95 (0-671-75193-X, Green Tiger) S&S Trade.
—If You're Afraid of the Dark, Remember the Night Rainbow. Edens, Cooper. LC 91-15823. 1991. 11.95 (0-671-74952-8, Green Tiger) S&S Trade.
—The Starcleaner Reunion. Edens, Cooper. 1991. (Green Tiger); pap. 8.95 (0-671-74969-2) S&S Trade.

Edens, John. Glorious Days, Dreadful Days: The Battle of Bunker Hill. Kirby, Philippa. LC 92-18084. 88p. (gr. 2-5). 1992. PLB 21.34 (0-8114-7226-4) Raintree Steck-V.
—Meet Christopher Columbus. De Kay, James T. LC 88-19068. 72p. (gr. 2-4). 1989. PLB 6.99 (0-394-91963-7); pap. 2.99 (0-394-81963-2) Random Bks Yng Read.

—The Time Machine. abridged ed. Wells, H. G. Martin, Les, adapted by. LC 89-39506. 96p. (Orig.). (gr. 2-6). 1990. lib. bdg. 5.99 (0-679-90371-2); pap. 2.95 (0-679-80371-8) Random Bks Yng Read.

Edgell, Kyle. Danny. Hubbard, Inez. LC 84-62082. 48p. (Orig.). (gr. k-3). 1984. pap. 3.95 (0-931571-00-6) Lifetime Pr.

—Good Morning Dogs! Newton, Jane. 20p. (Orig.). (ps) 1991. pap. text ed. 4.95 (0-931571-08-1) Lifetime Pr.

Edgerton, Jean. The Year of Our Lord: A Primer. Edgerton, Jean & Rolff, Ray. 102p. (Orig.). 1989. pap. 15.95 wkbk. (0-9624794-0-3) Lilium Pr.

Ediger, Kristin. Nicholas. Schrag, J. O. 35p. (Orig.). (gr. k-3). 1991. pap. 7.95 (0-945530-05-6) Wordsworth KS.

Edington, Jo A. Hinds Feet on High Places. Hurnard, Hannah. Layton, Barry & Layton, Dian, eds. 112p. (gr. 2-5). 1993. PLB 19.95 (1-56043-111-3) Destiny Image.

—Tag-along Timothy Tours Alaska. Richardson, Jean. Eakin, Edwin M., ed. 48p. (gr. 2-3). 1989. 12.95 (0-89015-706-5, Pub. by Panda Bks) Eakin-Sunbelt.

Edler, Jules. Time in God's World. Beckmann, Beverly. 24p. (gr. 2-5). 1985. 6.99 (0-570-04128-7, 56-1539) Concordia.

Edler, Timothy J. The Adventures of Crawfish-Man. Edler, Timothy J. 40p. (gr. k-8). 1979. pap. 6.00x (0-931108-04-7) Little Cajun Bks.

Edmond, Doreen. Quill's Adventures in Grozzieland, Bk. 3. Waddington-Feather, John. 132p. (gr. 3 up). 1991. pap. 5.95 (1-56261-017-1) John Muir.

—Quill's Adventures in the Great Beyond, Bk. 1. Waddington-Feather, John. 96p. (gr. 3 up). 1991. pap. 5.95 (1-56261-015-5) John Muir.

—Quill's Adventures in Wasteland, Bk. 2. Waddington-Feather, John. 132p. (gr. 3 up). 1991. pap. 5.95 (1-56261-016-3) John Muir.

Edmonds, Keith. Technology & the Computer. Vuillequez, Richard J. & Veslocki, Matthew. Gregorio, Frank, ed. 150p. (gr. 10 up). 1990. pap. text ed. 25. 00x (0-9627537-0-X) TMC CT.

Edwards, Al, photos by. A Day in the Life of a Stunt Person. Wolf, Stephen. LC 90-11101. 32p. (gr. 4-8). 1991. lib. bdg. 11.79 (0-8167-2222-6); pap. text ed. 2.95 (0-8167-2223-4) Troll Assocs.

Edwards, Bruce. The Complete Juggler. 2nd, rev. ed. Finnigan, Dave. Strong, Todd, contrib. by. LC 91-61138. 576p. (gr. 9-12). 1991. lib. bdg. 19.95 (0-9615521-1-5); pap. 14.95 (0-9615521-0-7) Jugglebug.

—The Joy of Juggling. rev. ed. Finnigan, Dave. 100p. (gr. 4-9). 1993. pap. 6.00 (0-9615521-3-1, 09001) Jugglebug.

—Scarf Juggling. Finnigan, Dave. 24p. (Orig.). (gr. 2-7). 1991. pap. 7.95 (0-9615521-8-2, 04000) Jugglebug.

Edwards, Christy. Robert's Tall Friend: A Story of the Fire Island Lighthouse. Farrell, Vivian. LC 87-35246. 64p. (gr. 4-7). 1988. write for info. (0-9619832-0-5) Island-Metro Pubns.

Edwards, Diana. Being Me & Drug Free Kid-Pak. rev. ed. Lupo, Ann. Fox, Greg, ed. 16p. (gr. k-3). 1991. pap. text ed. 3.95 (1-56230-135-7); pap. text ed. 4.95 incl. audiotape (1-56230-125-X) Syndistar.

—Healthy Bodies Don't Need Drugs Kid-Pak. rev. ed. Lupo, Ann. Fox, Greg, ed. 20p. (gr. 3-5). 1991. pap. text ed. 3.95 (1-56230-138-1); pap. text ed. 4.95 incl. audiotape (1-56230-128-4) Syndistar.

—Red the Firedog's How to Plan for a Safe Escape Kid-Pak. rev. ed. Lupo, Ann. Fox, Greg, ed. 20p. (ps-3). 1991. pap. text ed. 3.95 (1-56230-137-3); pap. text ed. 4.95 incl. audiotape (1-56230-134-9) Syndistar.

Edwards, Don. Cartooning. Edwards, Don. Stieglitz, Cliff, ed. 64p. (Orig.). (gr. 7 up). 1993. pap. 12.95 (0-9637336-0-5) Airbrush Act.

Edwards, Gunvor. Little Women. Alcott, Louisa May. Gliberry, Lysbeth, retold by. 48p. (gr. 7-12). 1975. pap. text ed. 3.25x (0-19-421804-X) OUP.

—What Is a Kumquat? And Other Poems. Cowling, Sue. 64p. (Orig.). (gr. 2 up). 1991. pap. 6.95 (0-571-16065-4) Faber & Faber.

Edwards, Jason, jt. illus. see Smith, George W., Jr.

Edwards, Joan. There Are Those. Levy, Nathan & Levy, Janet. LC 82-81111. 32p. (ps up). 1990. 21.95 (0-9608240-0-6) NL Assoc Inc.

Edwards, Linda S. Call Me Friday the Thirteenth. Bates, Betty. 112p. (gr. 3-7). 1985. pap. 2.50 (0-440-40984-5, LFL) Dell.

—The Downtown Day. Edwards, Linda S. LC 82-4645. 48p. (gr. k-3). 1983. 9.95 (0-394-85407-1) Pantheon.

—Four-B Goes Wild. Gilson, Jamie. LC 83-948. 160p. (gr. 4-6). 1983. 12.95 (0-688-02236-7) Lothrop.

—Four-B Goes Wild. Gilson, Jamie. MacDonald, Pat, ed. (gr. 3-6). 1989. pap. 2.99 (0-671-68063-3, Minstrel Bks) PB.

—Gus Wanders Off. Schertle, Alice. LC 86-21311. 32p. (ps-2). 1988. 12.95 (0-688-04984-2); PLB 12.88 (0-688-04985-0) Lothrop.

—Thirteen Ways to Sink a Sub. Gilson, Jamie. (gr. 3-7). 1982. 12.95 (0-688-01304-X) Lothrop.

—The Turtle Street Trading Co. Klevin, Jill R. LC 82-70312. 144p. (gr. 4-6). 1982. 11.95 (0-385-29043-8); PLB 11.95 (0-685-05625-2) Delacorte.

—Turtles Together Forever! Klevin, Jill R. LC 82-70313. 160p. (gr. 4-6). 1982. 9.95 (0-385-29045-4); pap. 9.89 (0-385-29046-2) Delacorte.

Edwards, Michelle. Alef-Bet: A Hebrew Alphabet Book. Edwards, Michelle. Pearson, Susan, ed. LC 91-31011. 32p. (ps-3). 1992. 15.00 (0-688-09724-3); PLB 14.93 (0-688-09725-1) Lothrop.

—And Sunday Makes Seven. Baden, Robert. Mathews, Judith, ed. LC 89-37823. 40p. (ps-3). 1990. 13.95 (0-8075-0356-8) A Whitman.

—Chicken Man. Edwards, Michelle. 32p. (ps up). 1994. pap. 4.95 (0-688-13106-9, Mulberry) Morrow.

—Dora's Book. Edwards, Michelle. 32p. (gr. k-4). 1990. PLB 19.95 (0-87614-411-3) Carolrhoda Bks.

—Y Domingo, Siete. Baden, Robert. Mathews, Judith, ed. Ada, Alma F., tr. LC 89-37823. (SPA.). 40p. (ps-3). 1990. 13.95 (0-8075-9355-9) A Whitman.

Edwards, Ron. Cinderella & the Glass Slipper: A Retelling. Shearer, Marilyn J. LC 90-60394. 16p. (ps-6). 1990. 19.95 (0-685-33063-X); pap. 10.95 (1-878389-02-5) L Ashley & Joshua.

Effinger, Michael. Bunker & Me: Summer Adventures of Best Friends, Vol. I. Effinger, Marta. Lawrence & Penny, ed. Washington, Pat, intro. by. 30p. (gr. 3-5). 1990. 12.95x (0-929917-02-2) Magnolia PA.

Egenberger, Carl. Becky. Hirsch, Karen. LC 80-27619. 40p. (gr. 1-4). 1981. PLB 13.50 (0-87614-144-0) Carolrhoda Bks.

Eggenhofer, Nicholas. The Boy in the Alamo. Cousins, Margaret. LC 83-72585. 180p. (gr. 5-7). 1983. pap. 5.95 (0-931722-26-8) Corona Pub.

Eggenhoffer, Nicholas. The Trail to Santa Fe. rev. ed. Lavender, David. LC 58-9634. 112p. (gr. 4-8). 1988. pap. 8.95 (0-939729-15-6) Trails West Pub.

Eggert, John F. Fish Do the Strangest Things. Hornblow, Leonora & Hornblow, Arthur. LC 88-30202. 64p. (gr. 2-4). 1990. Repr. lib. bdg. 6.99 (0-394-94309-0); 4.99 (0-394-84309-6) Random Bks Yng Read.

Egielshi, Richard. Louis the Fish. Yorinks, Arthur. 32p. (ps up). 1986. pap. 4.95 (0-374-44598-2, Sunburst) FS&G.

Egielski, Richard. Amy's Eyes. Kennedy, Richard. LC 82-48841. 448p. (ps up). 1985. 15.00 (0-06-023219-6) HarpC Child Bks.

—Amy's Eyes. Kennedy, Richard. LC 82-48841. 448p. (gr. 5 up). 1988. pap. 10.95 (0-06-440220-7, Trophy) HarpC Child Bks.

—Bravo, Minski. Yorinks, Arthur. (ps up) 1988. 15.00 (0-374-30951-5) FS&G.

—Christmas in July. Yorinks, Arthur. LC 91-55244. 32p. (ps-3). 1991. 14.95 (0-06-020256-4); PLB 14.89 (0-06-020257-2) HarpC Child Bks.

—Hey, Al. Yorinks, Arthur. LC 86-80955. 32p. (gr. k up). 1986. 15.00 (0-374-33060-3) FS&G.

—Hey, Al. Yorinks, Arthur. (ps up). 1989. pap. 4.95 (0-374-42985-5, Sunburst) FS&G.

—It Happened in Pinsk. Yorinks, Arthur. LC 83-1727. 32p. (ps up). 1983. 14.00 (0-374-33651-2) FS&G.

—The Letter, the Witch, & the Ring. Bellairs, John. LC 75-28968. (gr. 4-7). 1976. Dial Bks Young.

—The Letter, the Witch, & the Ring. Bellairs, John. LC 92-31361. 208p. (gr. 3 up). 1993. pap. 3.50 (0-14-036338-6, Puffin) Puffin Bks.

—The Little Father. Burgess, Gelett. LC 84-46171. 32p. (ps up). 1985. 14.00 (0-374-34596-1) FS&G.

—The Lost Sailor. Conrad, Pam. LC 91-39640. 32p. (gr. k-4). 1992. 15.00 (0-06-021695-6); PLB 14.89 (0-06-021696-4) HarpC Child Bks.

—Louis the Fish. Yorinks, Arthur. LC 80-16855. 32p. (ps up). 1980. 13.95 (0-374-34658-5) FS&G.

—Oh, Brother. Yorinks, Arthur. (ps up) 1989. 15.95 (0-374-35599-1) FS&G.

—Oh, Brother. Yorinks, Arthur. 40p. (ps up) 1991. pap. 5.95 (0-374-45598-8, Sunburst) FS&G.

—A Telling of the Tales: Five Stories. Brooke, William J. LC 89-36588. 144p. (gr. 3-7). 1990. 13.00 (0-06-020688-8); PLB 12.89 (0-06-020689-6) HarpC Child Bks.

—A Telling of the Tales: Five Stories. Brooke, William J. LC 89-36588. 144p. (gr. 3-7). 1993. pap. 5.95 (0-06-440467-6, Trophy) HarpC Child Bks.

—The Tub Grandfather. Conrad, Pam. LC 92-31770. 32p. (gr. k-3). 1993. 15.00 (0-06-022895-4); PLB 14.89 (0-06-022896-2) HarpC Child Bks.

—The Tub People. Conrad, Pam. LC 88-32804. 32p. (ps-3). 1989. 15.00 (0-06-021340-X); PLB 14.89 (0-06-021341-8) HarpC Child Bks.

—The Tub People. Conrad, Pam. LC 88-32804. 32p. (gr. k-3). 1995. pap. 4.95 (0-06-443306-4, Trophy) HarpC Child Bks.

—Ugh. Yorinks, Arthur. 32p. (ps-3). 1990. 13.95 (0-374-38028-7) FS&G.

Ehlert, Lois. Chicka Chicka Boom Boom. Martin, Bill, Jr. & Archambault, John. (gr. 2-6). 1989. pap. 13.95 jacketed (0-671-67949-X, S&S BFYR) S&S Trade.

—Circus. Ehlert, Lois. LC 91-12067. 40p. (ps-1). 1992. 15.00 (0-06-020252-1); PLB 14.89 (0-06-020253-X) HarpC Child Bks.

—Color Farm. Ehlert, Lois. LC 89-13561. 40p. (ps-k). 1990. 12.95 (0-397-32440-5, Lipp Jr Bks); PLB 12.89 (0-397-32441-3, Lipp Jr Bks) HarpC Child Bks.

—Color Zoo. Ehlert, Lois. LC 87-17065. 32p. (ps-1). 1989. 14.00 (0-397-32259-3, Lipp Jr Bks); PLB 13.89 (0-397-32260-7) HarpC Child Bks.

—Fish Eyes: A Book You Can Count On. Ehlert, Lois. 32p. (ps-1). 1990. 14.95 (0-15-228050-2) HarBrace.

—Growing Vegetable Soup. Ehlert, Lois. 32p. (ps-3). 1991. pap. 19.95 (0-15-232581-6) HarBrace.

—Shapes. Allington, Richard L. LC 79-19852. 32p. (gr. k-3). 1985. pap. 3.95 (0-8114-8238-3) Raintree Steck-V.

—Sing a Song of Sound. Silvers, Vicki. LC 72-90695. 32p. (ps-2). 1973. 7.95 (0-87592-046-2) Scroll Pr.

—Thump, Thump, Rat-a-Tat-Tat. Baer, Gene. LC 88-28469. 32p. (ps-1). 1991. pap. 4.95 (0-06-443265-3, Trophy) HarpC Child Bks.

—Thump, Thump, Rat-a-Tat-Tat Big Book. Baer, Gene. LC 88-28469. 32p. (ps-1). 1992. 19.95 (0-694-00386-7) HarpC Child Bks.

Ehrlich, Gary. The Cosmological Milkshake: A Semi-Serious Look at the Size of Things. Ehrlich, Robert. LC 93-28135. 1994. 29.95 (0-8135-2045-2); pap. 14.95 (0-8135-2046-0) Rutgers U Pr.

Eichenauer, Gabriele G. The King's Forest. Golden, Silvia. 1988. 14.95 (0-86315-085-3, 20247) Gryphon Hse.

Eichenberg, Fritz. Ape in a Cape: An Alphabet of Odd Animals. Eichenberg, Fritz. LC 52-6908. 26p. (ps-3). 1952. 15.95 (0-15-203722-5, HB Juv Bks) HarBrace.

—Ape in a Cape: An Alphabet of Odd Animals. Eichenberg, Fritz. LC 52-6908. 32p. (ps-3). 1988. pap. 4.95 (0-15-607830-9, Voyager Bks) HarBrace.

—Dancing in the Moon: Counting Rhymes. Eichenberg, Fritz. LC 75-8514. 25p. (gr. k-1). 1975. pap. 3.95 (0-15-623811-X, Voyager Bks) HarBrace.

—Rainbows Are Made: Poems by Carl Sandburg. Hopkins, Lee B., ed. LC 82-47934. 82p. (gr. k up). 1982. 17.95 (0-15-265480-1, HB Juv Bks) HarBrace.

Eichorn, Chris & Nelson, Lois. Becoming Friends, What Friends Believe. Barratt, Dorothy, et al. 78p. (gr. 5-6). 1990. tchr's. ed. 7.50 (0-943701-16-3) George Fox Pr.

Eide, Joyce. How the Tooth Fairy Got Her Job. Henry, Gilson. LC 87-62126. 24p. (ps-5). 1987. pap. 3.95 (0-943925-03-7) Purple Turtle Bks.

Eide, Lucille. My UFO. Eide, Lucille. LC 81-90261. 84p. (Orig.). 1980. pap. 4.95 (0-9610668-1-4) L Eide.

Eidregevicius, Stasys. Little Pig. Ramachander, Akumal. 32p. 1992. 15.00 (0-670-84350-4) Viking Child Bks.

Eidrigevicius, Stasys. The Hungry One. Baumann, Kurt. Lewis, Naomi, tr. from GER. LC 92-31030. 32p. (gr. k-3). 1993. 14.95 (1-55858-121-9); PLB 14.88 (1-55858-196-0) North-South Bks NYC.

—Johnny Longnose. Kruss, James & Lewis, Naomi. LC 89-42612. 32p. (gr. k-3). 1990. 13.95 (1-55858-023-9) North-South Bks NYC.

Eidrigewcius, Stasys, jt. illus. see Hess, Dick.

Eimon, Mina H. Why Cats Chase Mice: A Story of the 12 Zodiac Signs. Eimon, Mina H. 32p. (gr. k-6). 1993. 11.95 (0-89346-533-X) Heian Intl.

Einat, Tzvi. Systematic Hebrew, Pt. C. Yonay, Shahar & Yonay, Rina. (gr. 7). 1986. 13.45 (0-9616783-0-5) S Yonay.

Einsiedel, Andreas, photos by. Shell. Arthur, Alex. LC 88-13449. 64p. (gr. 5 up). 1989. 15.00 (0-394-82256-0); lib. bdg. 15.99 (0-394-92256-5) Knopf Bks Yng Read.

Einsiedel, Andreas, jt. photog. see Keates, Colin.

Eisenberg, Linda, jt. illus. see Kaufman, Richard.

Eisenbery, Monroe. The Pit & the Pendulum. Poe, Edgar Allan. Cutts, David E., adapted by. LC 81-16432. 32p. (gr. 5-10). 1982. PLB 10.79 (0-89375-626-1); pap. text ed. 2.95 (0-89375-627-X); cassettes avail. Troll Assocs.

Eisenhardt, Ann. Ready Reading. Crow, Faye. 135p. (Orig.). (ps-2). 1987. pap. 10.95 (0-9617529-0-4) Ready Work.

Eitan, Ora. Night Is Calling. Leuck, Laura. LC 93-22837. 1994. pap. 14.00 (0-671-86940-X, S&S BFYR) S&S Trade.

—No Milk! Ericsson, Jennifer A. LC 92-21806. 32p. (ps up). 1993. 14.00 (0-688-11306-0, Tambourine Bks); PLB 13.93 (0-688-11307-9, Tambourine Bks) Morrow.

Eitan, Ora, photos by. Garden Song. Mallett, David. 1995. write for info. (0-06-024303-1, Festival); PLB write for info. (0-06-024304-X, Festival) HarpC Child Bks.

Eitzen, Allan. California Gold Rush: Search for Treasure. Chambers, Catherine E. LC 83-18280. 32p. (gr. 5-9). 1984. PLB 11.59 (0-8167-0051-6); pap. text ed. 2.95 (0-8167-0052-4) Troll Assocs.

—Log Cabin Home: Pioneers in the Wilderness. Chambers, Catherine E. LC 83-18277. 32p. (gr. 5-9). 1984. PLB 11.59 (0-8167-0041-9); pap. text ed. 2.95 (0-8167-0042-7) Troll Assocs.

Eitzen, Allan. Africa. Sabin, Francene. LC 84-10560. 32p. (gr. 3-6). 1985. PLB 9.49 (0-8167-0236-5); pap. text ed. 2.95 (0-8167-0237-3) Troll Assocs.

—Arctic & Antarctic Regions. Sabin, Francene. LC 84-2730. 32p. (gr. 3-6). 1985. PLB 9.49 (0-8167-0234-9); pap. text ed. 2.95 (0-8167-0235-7) Troll Assocs.

—Asia. Sabin, Louis. LC 84-10559. 32p. (gr. 3-6). 1985. PLB 9.49 (0-8167-0274-8); pap. text ed. 2.95 (0-8167-0275-6) Troll Assocs.

—Australia. Santrey, Laurence. LC 84-2636. 32p. (gr. 3-6). 1985. PLB 9.49 (0-8167-0124-5); pap. text ed. 2.95 (0-8167-0125-3) Troll Assocs.

—Canada. Sabin, Louis. LC 84-40437. 32p. (gr. 3-6). 1985. PLB 9.49 (0-8167-0302-7); pap. text ed. 2.95 (0-8167-0303-5) Troll Assocs.

—Cherry Tree. Bond, Ruskin. LC 90-85731. 32p. (ps-3). 1991. 14.95 (1-878093-21-5) Boyds Mills Pr.

—Europe. Bains, Rae. LC 84-8598. 32p. (gr. 3-6). 1985. PLB 9.49 (0-8167-0304-3); pap. text ed. 2.95 (0-8167-0305-1) Troll Assocs.

—Fisherman. Craig, Janet. LC 88-10045. 32p. (gr. 1-3). 1989. PLB 10.89 (0-8167-1438-X); pap. text ed. 2.95 (0-8167-1439-8) Troll Assocs.

—The Great Houdini, Daring Escape Artist. Sabin, Louis. LC 89-5170. 48p. (gr. 4-6). 1990. PLB 10.79 (0-8167-1769-9); pap. text ed. 3.50 (0-8167-1770-2) Troll Assocs.
—Marie Curie. Sabin, Louis. LC 84-2654. 32p. (gr. 3-6). 1985. PLB 9.49 (0-8167-0162-8); pap. text ed. 2.95 (0-8167-0163-6) Troll Assocs.
—Mexico & Central America. Brandt, Keith. LC 84-2668. 32p. (gr. 3-6). 1985. PLB 9.49 (0-8167-0264-0); pap. text ed. 2.95 (0-8167-0265-9) Troll Assocs.
—North America. Sabin, Louis. LC 84-8625. 32p. (gr. 3-6). 1985. PLB 9.49 (0-8167-0240-3); pap. text ed. 2.95 (0-8167-0241-1) Troll Assocs.
—Sanitation Worker. Poskanzer, Susan C. LC 88-10044. 32p. (gr. k-3). 1989. PLB 10.89 (0-8167-1436-3); pap. text ed. 2.95 (0-8167-1437-1) Troll Assocs.
—Sherlock Holmes: The Adventure of the Empty House. Eastman, David, adapted by. LC 81-11673. 32p. (gr. 5-9). 1982. PLB 10.79 (0-89375-616-4); pap. 2.95 (0-89375-617-2) Troll Assocs.
—Sherlock Holmes: The Final Problem. Eastman, David, adapted by. LC 81-11609. 32p. (gr. 5-9). 1982. PLB 10.79 (0-89375-612-1); pap. 2.95 (0-89375-613-X) Troll Assocs.
—Sherlock Holmes: The Red-Headed League. Eastman, David, adapted by. LC 81-11619. 32p. (gr. 5-9). 1982. PLB 10.79 (0-89375-614-8); pap. 2.95 (0-89375-615-6) Troll Assocs.
—South America. Sabin, Francene. LC 84-8586. 32p. (gr. 3-6). 1985. PLB 9.49 (0-8167-0292-6); pap. text ed. 2.95 (0-8167-0293-4) Troll Assocs.
—Thomas Jefferson. Santrey, Laurence. LC 84-2579. 32p. (gr. 3-6). 1985. PLB 9.49 (0-8167-0176-8); pap. text ed. 2.95 (0-8167-0177-6) Troll Assocs.
—What's It Like to Be an Astronaut. Poskanzer, Susan C. LC 89-34393. 32p. (gr. k-3). 1990. PLB 10.89 (0-8167-1793-1); pap. text ed. 2.95 (0-8167-1794-X) Troll Assocs.
—The White Feather. Eitzen, Ruth. LC 86-31786. 64p. (gr. 3-4). 1987. 12.95 (0-8361-3439-7) Herald Pr.
—Young Martin Luther King, Jr. I Have a Dream. Mattern, Joanne. LC 91-26478. 32p. (gr. k-2). 1992. text ed. 11.59 (0-8167-2544-6); pap. text ed. 2.95 (0-8167-2545-4) Troll Assocs.
Eitzen, Allen. The Christmas Surprise. Moore, Ruth N. 160p. (Orig.). (gr. 4-8). 1989. pap. 5.95 (0-8361-3499-0) Herald Pr.
Eitzen, David. Sherlock Holmes: The Adventure of the Speckled Band. Eastman, David, adapted by. LC 81-11694. 32p. (gr. 5-9). 1982. PLB 10.79 (0-89375-618-0); pap. 2.95 (0-89375-619-9); cassettes avail. Troll Assocs.
Ekberg, Marion. Great Big Holiday Celebrations: Activities for Celebrating Major Holidays with Young Children. McKinnon, Elizabeth. Bittinger, Gayle, ed. LC 91-65045. 224p. (Orig.). (ps-1). 1991. pap. text ed. 16.95 (0-911019-43-X) Warren Pub Hse.
—Mini-Mini Musicals: Simple Musicals for Young Children Sung to Familiar Tunes. Warren, Jean. McKinnon, Elizabeth S., ed. LC 86-51508. 80p. (Orig.). (ps-1). 1987. pap. 7.95 (0-911019-14-6) Warren Pub Hse.
—One-Two-Three Games: No-Lose Group Games for Young Children. Warren, Jean. McKinnon, Elizabeth, ed. LC 85-50435. 80p. (Orig.). (ps-1). 1986. pap. 7.95 (0-911019-09-X) Warren Pub Hse.
—One-Two-Three Math. Warren, Jean. LC 92-80528. 160p. 1992. 14.95 (0-911019-52-9, WPH 0409) Warren Pub Hse.
—One-Two-Three Rhymes, Stories & Songs. Warren, Jean. LC 91-67075. 80p. 1992. 8.95 (0-911019-50-2, WPH 0408) Warren Pub Hse.
—Piggyback Songs for School. Warren, Jean & Bittinger, Gayle, eds. LC 85-50433. 96p. (Orig.). (ps-1). 1991. pap. text ed. 8.95 (0-911019-44-8) Warren Pub Hse.
—Short-Short Stories: Simple Stories for Young Children Plus Seasonal Activities. McKinnon, Elizabeth S. & Warren, Jean, eds. LC 86-51509. 80p. (Orig.). (ps-1). 1987. pap. 7.95 (0-911019-13-8) Warren Pub Hse.
Ekberg, Marion, jt. illus. see Piper, Molly.
Ekberg, Marion H. Holiday Piggyback Songs. Bittinger, Gayle, ed. Warren, Jean, compiled by. LC 88-50593. 96p. (Orig.). (ps-1). 1988. pap. 8.95 (0-911019-18-9) Warren Pub Hse.
—More Piggyback Songs: New Songs Sung to the Tunes of Childhood Favorites. Warren, Jean, compiled by. LC 84-90020. 96p. (Orig.). (ps-1). 1984. pap. 8.95 (0-911019-02-2) Warren Pub Hse.
—One-Two-Three Art: Open-Ended Art Activities for Young Children. Warren, Jean. LC 85-50434. 160p. (Orig.). (ps-1). 1985. pap. 14.95 (0-911019-06-5) Warren Pub Hse.
—One-Two-Three Colors: Activities for Introducing Color to Young Children. McKinnon, Elizabeth S., ed. Warren, Jean, compiled by. LC 87-51241. 160p. (Orig.). (ps-1). 1988. pap. 14.95 (0-911019-17-0) Warren Pub Hse.
—Piggyback Songs for Infants & Toddlers. McKinnon, Elizabeth S. & Warren, Jean, eds. LC 85-50433. 80p. (Orig.). (ps-k). 1985. pap. 7.95 (0-911019-07-3) Warren Pub Hse.
—Piggyback Songs in Praise of God. Warren, Jean & McKinnon, Elizabeth, eds. 80p. (Orig.). (ps-1). 1986. pap. 7.95 (0-911019-10-3) Warren Pub Hse.
—Piggyback Songs in Praise of Jesus: New Songs Sung to the Tunes of Childhood Favorites. Warren, Jean & McKinnon, Elizabeth, eds. 96p. (Orig.). (ps-1). 1986. pap. 8.95 (0-911019-11-1) Warren Pub Hse.

—Piggyback Songs: New Song Sung to the Tunes of Childhood Favorites. Warren, Jean, compiled by. LC 83-90111. 64p. (Orig.). (ps-1). 1983. pap. 7.95 (0-911019-01-4) Warren Pub Hse.
—Small World Celebrations: Multi-Cultural Holidays to Celebrate with Young Children. Warren, Jean & McKinnon, Elizabeth S. Bittinger, Gayle, ed. LC 88-50594. 160p. (Orig.). (ps-1). 1988. pap. 14.95 (0-911019-19-7) Warren Pub Hse.
—Special Day Celebrations: Seasonal Mini Celebrations to Enjoy with Young Children. McKinnon, Elizabeth. Bittinger, Gayle, ed. LC 89-50765. 128p. (Orig.). (ps-1). 1989. pap. text ed. 14.95 (0-911019-24-3) Warren Pub Hse.
—Yankee Doodle Birthday Celebrations: All-American Birthdays to Celebrate with Young Children. McKinnon, Elizabeth. Bittinger, Gayle, ed. LC 90-70414. 128p. (Orig.). (ps-1). 1990. pap. text ed. 12.95 (0-911019-32-4) Warren Pub Hse.
Ekman, Marlene. The Reluctant Dragon. Grahame, Kenneth. Richardson, I. M., ed. LC 87-10906. 32p. (gr. k-4). 1988. lib. bdg. 9.79 (0-8167-1059-7); text ed. 1.95 (0-8167-1060-0) Troll Assocs.
Elam, Keith. The Sun Is On. rev. ed. Baron, Lindamichelle. Dee, Ruby, intro. by. 48p. (gr. 1-6). 1982. pap. 5.95 (0-940938-02-2) Harlin Jacque.
Elcanan. Sometimes Big, Sometimes Small. Eitan, Ora. Kriss, David, tr. from HEB. 24p. (Orig.). (ps). 1992. pap. text ed. 3.00x (1-56134-139-8) Dushkin Pub.
Elchanan. A Veces Grande, a Veces Pequeno. Eitan, Ora. Writer, C. C. & Nielsen, Lisa C., trs. (SPA.). 24p. (Orig.). (ps). 1992. pap. text ed. 3.00x (1-56134-149-5) Dushkin Pub.
—Beware! Ducks Crossing. Ofek, Uriel. Kriss, David, tr. from HEB. 24p. (Orig.). (ps). 1992. pap. text ed. 3.00x (1-56134-145-2) Dushkin Pub.
—The Brave Frog. Amir, Tami. Kriss, David, tr. from HEB. 24p. (Orig.). (ps). 1992. pap. text ed. 3.00x (1-56134-158-4) Dushkin Pub.
—The Cat Who Looked for a House. Baram, Bella. Kriss, David, tr. from HEB. 24p. (Orig.). (ps). 1992. pap. text ed. 3.00x (1-56134-140-1) Dushkin Pub.
—Cien Cuartos. Shinhav, Chaya. Writer, C. C. & Nielsen, Lisa C., trs. (SPA.). 24p. (Orig.). (ps). 1992. pap. text ed. 3.00x (1-56134-169-X) Dushkin Pub.
—Cuidado! Patos Cruzando. Ofek, Uriel. Writer, C. C. & Nielsen, Lisa C., trs. (SPA.). 24p. (Orig.). (ps). 1992. pap. text ed. 3.00x (1-56134-155-X) Dushkin Pub.
—Gary el Jardinero. Bar, Amos. Writer, C. C. & Nielsen, Lisa C., trs. (SPA.). 24p. (Orig.). (ps). 1992. pap. text ed. 3.00x (1-56134-172-X) Dushkin Pub.
—Gary the Gardener. Bar, Amos. Kriss, David, tr. from HEB. 24p. (Orig.). (ps). 1992. pap. text ed. 3.00x (1-56134-162-2) Dushkin Pub.
—La Gata Que Buscaba un Hogar. Baram, Bella. Writer, C. C. & Nielsen, Lisa C., trs. (SPA.). 24p. (Orig.). (ps). 1992. pap. text ed. 3.00x (1-56134-150-9) Dushkin Pub.
—A Hundred Rooms. Shinhav, Chaya. Kriss, David, tr. from HEB. 24p. (Orig.). (ps). 1992. pap. text ed. 3.00x (1-56134-159-2) Dushkin Pub.
—El Nombre Secreto. Burla, Oded. Writer, C. C. & Nielsen, Lisa C., trs. (SPA.). 24p. (Orig.). (ps). 1992. pap. text ed. 3.00x (1-56134-156-8) Dushkin Pub.
—Otra Cosa. Gelbert, Ofra. Writer, C. C. & Nielsen, Lisa C., trs. (SPA.). 24p. (Orig.). (ps). 1992. pap. text ed. 3.00x (1-56134-175-4) Dushkin Pub.
—Pete & the Vegetable Soup. Assaf, Yael. Kriss, David, tr. from HEB. 24p. (Orig.). (ps). 1992. pap. text ed. 3.00x (1-56134-160-6) Dushkin Pub.
—Pete y la Sopa de Verduras. Assaf, Yael. Writer, C. C. & Nielsen, Lisa C., trs. (SPA.). 24p. (Orig.). (ps). 1992. pap. text ed. 3.00x (1-56134-170-3) Dushkin Pub.
—La Rana Valiente. Amir, Tami. Writer, C. C. & Nielsen, Lisa C., trs. (SPA.). 24p. (Orig.). (ps). 1992. pap. text ed. 3.00x (1-56134-168-1) Dushkin Pub.
—The Secret Name. Burla, Oded. Kriss, David, tr. from HEB. 24p. (Orig.). (ps). 1992. pap. text ed. 3.00x (1-56134-146-0) Dushkin Pub.
—Something Else. Gelbert, Ofra. Kriss, David, tr. from HEB. 24p. (Orig.). (ps). 1992. pap. text ed. 3.00x (1-56134-165-7) Dushkin Pub.
Elchoness, Monte. Why Can't Anyone Hear Me? A Guide for Surviving Adolescence. 2nd, rev. ed. Elchoness, Monte. LC 86-737. 200p. (gr. 6-12). 1989. pap. 10.95 (0-936781-06-8, Dist. by Publishers Group West) Monroe Pr.
Elder, John. L Is for Liberty. Stewart, Bonnie. 32p. (gr. 1 up). 1993. 15.95g (1-879244-00-4) Windom Bks.
Eldridge, Alexandra. The Sleepy Baker: A Collection of Stories & Recipes for Children. Field Drake, Christin. LC 92-56509. 56p. (gr. k-5). 1993. 14.95 (0-87358-551-8) Northland AZ.
Eldridge, Marion. Christopher Columbus & the Great Voyage of Discovery: With a Message from President George Bush. Weisman, JoAnne B. & Deitch, Kenneth M. Bush, George, contrib. by. LC 90-81362. 40p. (gr. k-6). 1990. PLB 14.95 (1-878668-00-5); pap. 7.95g (1-878668-01-3) Disc Enter Ltd.
Eldridge, Susan. You Won't Believe Your Eyes. Tytla, Milan & Crystal, Nancy. 88p. (gr. 2-8). 1992. pap. 9.95 (1-55037-218-1, Pub. by Annick CN) Firefly Bks Ltd.
Elena, Horacio. El Superzorro - Fantastic Mr. Fox. Dahl, Roald. Buckley, Ramon, tr. (SPA.). 153p. (gr. 2-4). 1992. pap. write for info. (84-204-0013-0) Santillana.

Elfring, Harriet. Ilana & the Monsters. Cohen, Milton. 40p. (Orig.). Date not set. pap. 3.00 (0-9616076-0-2) Jomilt Pubns.
Elfstrand, Elizabeth. Mount St. Helens Is My Home. Garlie, Gina. 40p. (gr. k-3). 1993. pap. 5.95 (0-9637878-0-2, 574180) Lupine Pr.
Ellen, G. & Sasaki, Joy. Z's Gift. Starkman, Neal. LC 88-71483. 52p. (Orig.). (gr. 4-6). 1988. pap. 7.00 (0-935529-08-X) Comprehen Health Educ.
Elley, Charles, jt. illus. see Warp, Eric.
Ellinger, Debra. Mac Club! Schepp, Debra & Schepp, Brad. LC 93-8520. 1993. 19.60 (0-8306-4253-6) TAB Bks.
—Mac Party! Schepp, Debra & Schepp, Brad. LC 93-8519. 1993. 19.60 (0-8306-4250-1) TAB Bks.
Elliot, Glen, photos by. The Colors That I Am. Sheehan, Cilla. LC 80-25351. 32p. (ps-5). 1981. 16.95 (0-89885-047-9) Human Sci Pr.
Elliot, Stephen C. Ember & His Friends in the Forest. Willard, John. 25p. (Orig.). (gr. 2-6). 1991. pap. 3.95 (0-9612398-4-0) J A Willard.
Elliott, Tony. High Country Wildlife. Elliott, Tony. LC 86-2218. 64p. (Orig.). (gr. 1-6). 1988. pap. 2.50 (0-914565-20-6, 20-6) Capstan Pubns.
—Test of the Tenderfoot. Saban, Vera. LC 89-9729. 147p. (gr. 5-8). 1989. 6.95 (0-914565-35-4, Timbertrails) Capstan Pubns.
—Texas Outdoors: Read 'n Color Book. Elliott, Tony. (gr. 1-8). 1986. pap. 3.95 (0-914565-24-9, 24-9, Timbertrails) Capstan Pubns.
—This Is Wyoming: Read 'n Color Book. Elliott, Tony. LC 89-469. (gr. 3-6). 1989. pap. 3.95 (0-914565-39-7, 39-7, Timbertrails) Capstan Pubns.
Ellis, Andy. Edd the Astronaut. MacKay-Robinson, Christina. 32p. (gr. k-3). 1992. pap. 4.95 (0-563-36062-3, BBC-Parkwest) Parkwest Pubns.
—Piggo & the Nosebag. Ayres, Pam. 32p. (gr. k-3). 1991. 9.95 (0-563-20922-4, BBC-Parkwest) Parkwest Pubns.
—Piggo Has a Train Ride. Ayres, Pam. 32p. (gr. k-3). 1992. 9.95 (0-563-20921-6, BBC-Parkwest) Parkwest Pubns.
Ellis, Debbie. Lottie Moon Storybook. Jones, Carolyn E. 20p. (gr. k-4). 1984. pap. 2.50 (0-9616996-0-4) Honor Pub.
Ellis, Elizabeth. Life in the Pond. Curran, Eileen. LC 84-16285. 32p. (gr. k-2). 1985. lib. bdg. 11.59 (0-8167-0452-X); pap. text ed. 2.95 (0-8167-0453-8) Troll Assocs.
Ellis, Jan D. Mush! Across Alaska in the World's Longest Sled-Dog Race. Seibert, Patricia. LC 91-38883. 32p. (gr. 2-4). 1992. PLB 14.90 (1-56294-053-8) Millbrook Pr.
—The Winter Solstice. Jackson, Ellen. LC 92-45065. 32p. (gr. 2-4). 1994. PLB 14.90 (1-56294-400-2) Millbrook Pr.
Ellis, Kevin. Fighting Ships. Miller, Marc W. 96p. (Orig.). 1990. pap. 10.00 (1-55878-050-5) Game Designers.
Ellis, Kim. A Charlie Brown Christmas. Schulz, Charles M. Namm, Diane, adapted by. LC 87-83488. 40p. (gr. 1 up). 1988. write for info. (0-307-13723-6) Western Pub.
Ellis, Tim. Chicken Socks: And Other Contagious Poems. Bagert, Brod. 32p. (gr. 3-7). 1994. 15.95 (1-56397-292-1) Boyds Mills Pr.
Ellison, Chris. The Servant. Harwell, Ivy E. 180p. (Orig.). (gr. 9 up). 1993. pap. 7.98 (1-882671-09-0) Wrds of Life.
Ellison, Mick. Hank Greenberg: Hall-of-Fame Slugger. Berkow, Ira. LC 90-43005. 108p. (gr. 3-7). 1991. 12.95t (0-8276-0376-2) JPS Phila.
Elmore, Larry. Visions of Fantasy. Asimov, Isaac & Greenberg, Martin H., eds. 192p. (gr. 5 up). 1989. 14.95 (0-385-26359-7, Zephyr-BFYR) Doubleday.

Elovson, Andrea K. The Kindergarten Survival Handbook: The Before School Checklist & a Guide for Parents. rev. ed. Elovson, Allana. 96p. (Orig.). (gr. k). 1993. Spanish ed. pap. text ed. 12.95 perfect bdg. (1-879888-07-6); English ed. pap. text ed. 12.95 (1-879888-06-8) Parent Ed.
"SMALLER THAN A BOX OF RICE KRISPIES, THE KINDERGARTEN SURVIVAL HANDBOOK IS WORTH ITS WEIGHT IN GOLD!"-- The Harrisburg, PA Patriot News. Coming to school ready to learn is crucial to children's self-esteem, attitude toward school & subsequent school achievement & is the Number One goal of Education 2000, our national education strategy. Written in simple language accessible to parents of every socio-economic level & cultural backround, the charmingly illustrated KINDERGARTEN SURVIVAL HANDBOOK & its Spanish language version EL MANUAL DE COMO

SOBRE VIVIR EL JARDIN DE NINOS, present the whys, the whats & the hows of kindergarten readiness. First, THE BEFORE SCHOOL CHECKLIST identifies the skills & information that prepare children to THRIVE as well as survive in kindergarten. Then, A GUIDE FOR PARENTS & THE NEXT STEP offer simple, enjoyable, inexpensive ways to use everyday experiences to transform a child's world into an exciting learning environment & establish a beneficial relationship with school & teachers. An invaluable resource for all parents including teens & immigrant parents; teachers, pre-schools, schools, parent educators, & for community & training programs of all kinds. Strongly endorsed by educators, teachers, child-care professionals, parents & reviewers throughout the country: "THE KINDERGARTEN SURVIVAL HANDBOOK IS FABULOUS, & HAS BEEN NEEDED FOR A LONG, LONG TIME!" says Cherry Belanger, Kindergarten Teacher, L.A. Available from major wholesalers & Publishers' Services, P. O. Box 2510, Novato, CA 94948.
Publisher Provided Annotation.

Elston, Dino. The Magical Tree. Lavranos, Destini & Rithcie, Sheri. 2p. (ps-k). 1993. 14.95 (0-9638393-0-6) Bedtime Bks.

Elwell, Peter. Hans Brinker. Dodge, Mary M. Betts, Louise, adapted by. LC 87-15472. 48p. (gr. 3-6). 1988. PLB 12.89 (0-8167-1205-0); pap. text ed. 3.95 (0-8167-1206-9) Troll Assocs.
—Margaret Ziegler Is Horse Crazy. Dragonwagon, Crescent. LC 87-23975. 32p. (gr. 1-4). 1988. RSBE 12.95 (0-02-733230-6, Macmillan Child Bk) Macmillan Child Grp.
—The Muppet Guide to Magnificent Manners. Howe, James. LC 83-25063. 64p. (gr. 3-7). 1984. lib. bdg. 5.99 (0-394-96351-2); pap. 4.95 (0-394-86351-8) Random Bks Yng Read.
—Three Brave Women. Martin, C. L. G. LC 89-77770. 32p. (gr. k-3). 1991. RSBE 13.95 (0-02-762445-5, Macmillan Child Bk) Macmillan Child Grp.
—Time Out. Cresswell, Helen. LC 89-36798. 80p. (gr. 2-5). 1990. SBE 13.95 (0-02-725425-9, Macmillan Child Bk) Macmillan Child Grp.

Ely, Gladys. Little Pax. Whitman, Edmund S. LC 74-182528. 120p. (gr. 5-9). 1972. 3.75 (0-8356-0428-4, Quest) Theos Pub Hse.
—Popo: The Adventures of a Mexican Donkey. Streiber, William R. & Rizzoto, Flora M. LC 70-146604. (gr. 1-4). 1971. 3.75 (0-8356-0420-9, Quest) Theos Pub Hse.

Elzaurdia, Sharon. Sandbox Betty. Petrie, Catherine. LC 81-15547. 32p. (ps-2). 1982. PLB 11.93 (0-516-03578-9); pap. 2.95 (0-516-43578-7) Childrens.

Elzbieta. Dikou & the Baby Star. Elzbieta. LC 88-302. 32p. (ps-3). 1989. (Crowell Jr Bks) HarpC Child Bks.
—Dikou & the Mysterious Moon Sheep. Elzbieta. LC 87-13587. 32p. (ps-3). 1988. (Crowell Jr Bks) HarpC Child Bks.
—Mimi's Scary Theater: A Play in Nine Scenes for Seven Chartacters & an Egg. Elzbieta. LC 92-54868. 18p. (ps-3). 1993. 14.95 (1-56282-415-5) Hyprn Child.

Emberley, Barbara & Emberley, Ed E. The BASIC Book. Simon, Seymour. LC 85-42736. 32p. (gr. k-4). 1985. pap. 4.50 (0-06-445015-5, Trophy) HarpC Child Bks.
—Flash, Crash, Rumble & Roll. Branley, Franklyn M. LC 84-48532. 32p. (ps-3). 1987. (Trophy); pap. 4.50 (0-06-445012-0, Trophy) HarpC Child Bks.
—The Moon Seems to Change. rev. ed. Branley, Franklyn M. LC 86-47747. 32p. (ps-3). 1987. (Crowell Jr Bks); PLB 13.89 (0-690-04585-9) HarpC Child Bks.
—The Moon Seems to Change. rev. ed. Branley, Franklyn M. LC 86-27097. 32p. (ps-3). 1987. pap. 4.50 (0-06-445065-1, Trophy) HarpC Child Bks.
—Turtle Talk: A Beginner's Book of Logo. Simon, Seymour. LC 85-47890. 32p. (gr. 1-4). 1986. (Crowell Jr Bks); PLB 13.89 (0-690-04522-0, Crowell Jr Bks) HarpC Child Bks.
—Turtle Talk: A Beginner's Book of Logo. Simon, Seymour. LC 85-47890. 32p. (gr. 1-4). 1986. pap. 4.50 (0-06-445051-1, Trophy) HarpC Child Bks.

Emberley, Barbara, jt. illus. see Emberley, Ed E.
Emberley, Ed. One Wide River to Cross. Emberley, Barbara, adapted by. 32p. (ps-3). 1992. pap. 4.95 (0-316-23445-1) Little.
—The Story of Paul Bunyan. Emberley, Barbara. LC 93-11791. 1994. pap. 14.00 (0-671-88557-X, S&S BFYR) S&S Trade.

Emberley, Ed E. Drummer Hoff. Emberley, Barbara. LC 74-8201. 32p. (gr. k-4). 1985. pap. 12.95 jacketed (0-671-66682-7, S&S BFYR); pap. 5.95 (0-671-66745-9, S&S BFYR) S&S Trade.
—Ed Emberley's Big Green Drawing Book. Emberley, Ed E. LC 79-16247. (gr. k up). 1979. 15.95 (0-316-23595-4); pap. 8.95 (0-316-23596-2) Little.
—Ed Emberley's Big Purple Drawing Book. Emberley, Ed E. (gr. 1 up). 1981. 14.95 (0-316-23422-2); pap. 8.95 (0-316-23423-0) Little.
—Ed Emberley's Drawing Book: Make a World. Emberley, Ed E. LC 70-154962. (gr. 2 up). 1972. lib. bdg. 14.95 (0-316-23598-9) Little.
—Ed Emberley's Drawing Book of Faces. Emberley, Ed E. 32p. (gr. k-3). 1975. lib. bdg. 14.95 (0-316-23609-8) Little.
—Ed Emberley's Great Thumbprint Drawing Book. Emberley, Ed E. (gr. 1 up). 1977. lib. bdg. 14.95 (0-316-23613-6) Little.
—Ed Emberley's Picture Pie: A Book of Circle Art. Emberley, Ed E. 48p. 1984. 15.95 (0-316-23425-7); pap. 7.95 (0-316-23426-5) Little.
—First Words: Animals. (ps). 1987. pap. 3.50 (0-316-23428-1) Little.
—First Words: Cars, Boats, & Planes. (ps). 1987. pap. 3.50 (0-316-23430-3) Little.
—First Words: Home. (ps). 1987. pap. 3.50 (0-316-23433-8) Little.
—Straight Hair, Curly Hair. Goldin, Augusta. LC 66-12669. 40p. (gr. k-3). 1966. PLB 13.89 (0-690-77921-6, Crowell Jr Bks) HarpC Child Bks.
—The Wing on a Flea: A Book about Shapes. Emberley, Ed E. (ps-3). 1988. lib. bdg. 14.95 (0-316-23600-4) Little.

Emberley, Ed E. & Emberley, Barbara. Flash, Crash, Rumble, & Roll. rev. ed. Branley, Franklyn M. LC 84-45333. 32p. (ps-3). 1985. PLB 13.89 (0-690-04425-9, Crowell Jr Bks) HarpC Child Bks.

Emberley, Ed E. & Emberley, Rebecca. Ed Emberley's Big Red Drawing Book, Vol. 1. Emberley, Ed E. & Emberley, Rebecca. 96p. (gr. 1-5). 1987. 14.95 (0-316-23434-6); pap. 8.95 (0-316-23435-4) Little.

Emberley, Ed E., jt. illus. see Emberley, Barbara.
Emberley, Michael. Dinosaurs! A Drawing Book. Emberley, Michael. 48p. (gr. 3 up). 1985. pap. 5.95 (0-316-23631-4) Little.
—More Dinosaurs! And Other Prehistoric Beasts. Emberley, Michael. LC 83-9822. 64p. (gr. 3 up). 1983. 13.95 (0-316-23424-9) Little.
—More Dinosaurs! & Other Prehistoric Beasts. Emberley, Michael. 64p. (ps-3). 1992. pap. 5.95 (0-316-23441-9) Little.
—Rudolph's Second Christmas. May, Robert L. LC 92-18416. (ps-3). 1992. 9.95 (1-55709-192-7) Applewood.

Emberley, Rebecca. City Sounds. Emberley, Rebecca. 32p. (ps-1). 1989. 15.95 (0-316-23635-7) Little.
—Jungle Sounds. Emberley, Rebecca. 32p. (ps-1). 1989. 13.95 (0-316-23636-5) Little.
—My House, Mi Casa: A Book in Two Languages. Emberley, Rebecca. LC 89-12893. (ps-2). 1990. 15.95 (0-316-23637-3) Little.

Emberley, Rebecca, jt. illus. see Emberley, Ed E.
Emmerich, Donald. An Air Show Adventure. Crisfield, Deborah. LC 89-34372. 32p. (gr. 3-6). 1990. PLB 10.79 (0-8167-1735-4); pap. text ed. 2.95 (0-8167-1736-2) Troll Assocs.
—Let's Visit a Spaghetti Factory. Corey, Melinda. LC 89-5110. 32p. (gr. 2-4). 1990. PLB 10.79 (0-8167-1741-9); pap. text ed. 2.95 (0-8167-1742-7) Troll Assocs.

Emmet, Mary. Fifty-Two Ways to Have Fun with My Mind. Fearn, Leif & Golisz-Benson, Ursula. 62p. (gr. 1-3). 1975. 5.00 (0-940444-01-1) Kabyn.

Emu, Namae. Road Roller Saves the Day. Barnes, Jill & Kanabe, Junkichi. Rubin, Caroline, ed. Japan Foreign Rights Centre Staff, tr. from JPN. LC 90-3841. 40p. (gr. k-3). 1990. PLB 15.93 (0-944483-81-X) Garrett Ed Corp.

Enbody, Shari B. A Bunch of Balloons: A Book - Workbook for Grieving Children. Ferguson, Dorothy. (Orig.). (gr. 1-6). 1992. pap. 5.95 (1-56123-054-5) Centering Corp.

End, Simone & Woodcock, John. Plantas - Plants. Gomez-Navarro, Maria J., et al, eds. Del Carmen Blazquez, Maria, tr. (SPA.). 64p. (gr. 5-12). 1993. write for info. (84-372-4529-X) Santillana.

Endersby, Frank. The Boy & the Horse. Endersby, Frank. LC 90-46601. 16p. (ps-2). 1976. 11.95 (0-85953-098-1, Pub. by Child's Play England) Childs Play.
—Time for Bed. Kennedy, Fiona. 26p. (ps-k). 1992. pap. 5.95 (0-8120-4974-6) Barron.

Endes, Helen. Caring. rev. ed. Moncure, Jane B. LC 80-27506. (gr. k-3). 1981. PLB 21.35 (0-89565-201-3); PLB 14.95s.p. (0-685-55475-9) Childs World.
—Courage. rev. ed. Moncure, Jane B. LC 80-39515. 32p. (gr. k-3). 1981. PLB 21.35 (0-89565-202-1); PLB 14.95s.p. (0-685-55478-3) Childs World.

Endicott, James. Listen to the Rain. Martin, Bill, Jr. & Archambault, John. LC 88-6502. 32p. (ps-3). 1988. 14.95 (0-8050-0682-6, Bks Young Read) H Holt & Co.
—Trees. Behn, Harry. LC 91-25179. 32p. (ps-2). 1992. 14.95 (0-8050-1926-X, B Martin BYR) H Holt & Co.

Endo, Teruyo. The Adventures of the One Inch Boy. Okawa, Essei. Ooka, D. T., tr. from JPN. 32p. (gr. k-6). 1985. 11.95 (0-89346-258-6) Heian Intl.

Endres, Helen. Christmas in Other Lands. McDonnell, Janet. LC 93-7632. 1993. write for info. (0-516-00682-7) Childrens.
—Discovering Dinosaurs. Riehecky, Janet. 32p. (gr. k-4). 1990. PLB 21.35 (0-89565-620-5); PLB 14.95s.p. (0-685-56205-0) Childs World.
—Does Anyone Have a Spare Bear? Punnett, Dick. LC 84-23009. 32p. (gr. k-3). 1985. PLB 19.95 (0-89565-304-4); PLB 13.95s.p. (0-685-55732-4) Childs World.
—Fairness. Ziegler, Sandra. LC 88-18976. 32p. (gr. k-3). 1989. PLB 21.35 (0-89565-390-7); PLB 14.95s.p. (0-685-55990-4) Childs World.
—Growing up with God's Friends. Beers, V. Gilbert. LC 87-81046. 94p. (Orig.). (ps-7). 1987. 12.99 (0-89081-528-3) Harvest Hse.
—Growing up with Jesus. Beers, V. Gilbert. LC 87-81043. 94p. (Orig.). (ps-7). 1987. 12.99 (0-89081-525-9) Harvest Hse.
—The Healthkin Food Train. Moncure, Jane B. LC 82-14710. 32p. (ps-2). 1982. PLB 19.95 (0-89565-240-4); PLB 13.95s.p. (0-685-55643-3) Childs World.
—Healthkins Exercise! Moncure, Jane B. LC 82-14712. 32p. (ps-2). 1982. PLB 19.95 (0-89565-241-2); PLB 13.95s.p. (0-685-55641-7) Childs World.
—How Seeds Travel: Popguns & Parachutes. Moncure, Jane B. LC 89-71171. 32p. (ps-2). 1990. PLB 19.95 (0-89565-569-1); PLB 13.95s.p. (0-685-56185-2) Childs World.
—Jesus Grows Up. Hillert, Margaret. 24p. (gr. k-1). 1988. 4.99 (0-87403-459-0, 24-03698) Standard Pub.
—Magic Monsters Act the Alphabet. Moncure, Jane B. LC 79-23841. (ps-2). 1980. PLB 21.35 (0-89565-116-5); PLB 14.95s.p. (0-685-55493-7) Childs World.
—Magic Monsters Learn about Health. Moncure, Jane B. LC 79-24240. (ps-3). 1980. PLB 21.35 (0-89565-117-3); PLB 14.95s.p. (0-685-57681-7) Childs World.
—My First Martin Luther King Book. Lillegard, Dee. LC 86-31670. 32p. (ps-2). 1987. PLB 15.00 (0-516-02908-8); pap. 3.95 (0-516-42908-6) Childrens.
—Now I Am Five! Moncure, Jane B. LC 83-25264. 32p. (ps-2). 1984. pap. 3.95 (0-516-41879-3) Childrens.
—Obedience. rev. ed. Buerger, Jane. LC 80-39520. 32p. (gr. k-3). 1981. PLB 21.35 (0-89565-206-4); PLB 14.95s.p. (0-685-55536-4) Childs World.
—Our Birthday Book. Moncure, Jane B. LC 86-30976. 32p. (ps-3). 1987. PLB 19.95 (0-89565-349-4); PLB 13.95s.p. (0-685-55999-8) Childs World.
—Our Easter Book. Rev. ed. Moncure, Jane B. LC 86-29876. 32p. (ps-3). 1987. PLB 19.95 (0-89565-345-1); PLB 13.95s.p. (0-685-55850-9) Childs World.
—Our Martin Luther King Book. McKissack, Patricia. LC 86-6785. 32p. (ps-3). 1986. PLB 19.95 (0-89565-342-7); PLB 13.95s.p. (0-685-55831-2) Childs World.
—Polka-Dot Puppy. Moncure, Jane B. LC 87-15813. 32p. (ps-2). 1987. PLB 21.35 (0-89565-407-5); PLB 14.95s.p. (0-685-55926-2) Childs World.
—Prince Charles. Gilleo, Alma. LC 78-18938. (gr. k-4). 1978. PLB 19.95 (0-89565-029-0); PLB 13.95s.p. (0-685-55540-2) Childs World.
—Raccoon's Adventure in Alphabet Town. McDonnell, Janet. LC 92-1066. 32p. (ps-2). 1992. PLB 14.60 (0-516-05418-X) Childrens.
—Sharing Hanukkah. McDonnell, Janet. LC 93-13250. 1993. write for info. (0-516-00685-1) Childrens.
—Short A & Long A Play a Game. Moncure, Jane B. LC 79-10300. (gr. k-2). 1979. PLB 21.35 (0-89565-089-4); PLB 14.95s.p. (0-685-55544-5) Childs World.
—Short E & Long E Play a Game. Moncure, Jane B. LC 79-10305. (gr. k-2). 1979. PLB 21.35 (0-89565-090-8); PLB 14.95s.p. (0-685-55545-3) Childs World.
—Short I & Long I Play a Game. Moncure, Jane B. LC 79-10303. (gr. k-2). 1979. PLB 21.35 (0-89565-091-6); PLB 14.95s.p. (0-685-55546-1) Childs World.
—Short O & Long O Play a Game. Moncure, Jane B. LC 79-10304. (gr. k-2). 1979. PLB 21.35 (0-89565-092-4); PLB 14.95s.p. (0-685-55547-X) Childs World.
—Short U & Long U Play a Game. Moncure, Jane B. LC 79-10306. (gr. k-2). 1979. PLB 21.35 (0-89565-093-2); PLB 14.95s.p. (0-685-55548-8) Childs World.
—The Sun: Our Daytime Star. Moncure, Jane B. LC 89-24009. 32p. (ps-2). 1990. PLB 19.95 (0-89565-551-9); PLB 13.95s.p. (0-685-56172-0) Childs World.
—Surprise at Muddy Creek. Anderson, Leone C. 32p. (gr. 1-3). 1990. PLB 19.95 (0-89565-698-1); PLB 13.95s.p. (0-685-56164-X) Childs World.
—Terry's Turn-Around. Moncure, Jane B. LC 82-19898. 32p. (gr. 3-4). 1982. PLB 19.95 (0-89565-250-1); PLB 13.95 (0-685-57929-8) Childs World.
—What Was It Before It Was My Sweater? Schreckhise, Roseva. LC 85-11401. 32p. (ps-2). 1985. PLB 21.35 (0-89565-324-9); PLB 14.95s.p. (0-685-55778-2) Childs World.
—Your Body: Treasures Inside. Wells, Donna K. LC 90-30632. 32p. (ps-2). 1990. PLB 19.95 (0-89565-576-4); PLB 13.95s.p. (0-685-56192-5) Childs World.

Engel, Diana. Eleanor, Arthur, & Claire. Engel, Diana. LC 91-21781. 32p. (gr. k-3). 1992. RSBE 14.95 (0-02-733462-7, Macmillan Child Bk) Macmillan Child Grp.
—Fishing. Engel, Diana. LC 91-47705. 32p. (gr. k-3). 1993. RSBE 14.95 (0-02-733463-5, Macmillan Child Bk) Macmillan Child Grp.

—Gino Badino. Engel, Diana. LC 90-36456. 32p. (ps up). 1991. 13.95 (*0-688-09502-X*); PLB 13.88 (*0-688-09503-8*, Morrow Jr Bks) Morrow Jr Bks.
—Josephina Hates Her Name. Engel, Diana. LC 88-1500. 32p. (ps-2). 1989. 13.95 (*0-688-07795-1*); PLB 13.88 (*0-688-07796-X*, Morrow Jr Bks) Morrow Jr Bks.
—Josephina, the Great Collector. Engel, Diana. LC 87-20358. 32p. (ps-2). 1988. 12.95 (*0-688-07542-8*); PLB 12.88 (*0-688-07543-6*, Morrow Jr Bks) Morrow Jr Bks.
—The Little Lump of Clay. Engel, Diana. LC 88-22049. 32p. (ps up). 1989. 13.95 (*0-688-08969-0*); PLB 13.88 (*0-688-08407-9*, Morrow Jr Bks) Morrow Jr Bks.
—The Shelf-Paper Jungle. Engel, Diana. LC 93-21772. 32p. (gr. k-3). 1994. RSBE 14.95 (*0-02-733464-3*, Macmillan Child Bk) Macmillan Child Grp.
Engel, Michael. Bamboo & Friends. Atkinson, John. LC 88-50844. 104p. (gr. 1-12). 1988. 13.95 (*0-929155-05-X*) Windward Bks.
Engelland, Tim. Basketball Basics. Morris, Greggory. LC 75-34142. (gr. 2-6). 1979. 6.95 (*0-13-072256-1*, Pub. by Treehouse) P-H.
Englander, Alice. Not Just a Witch. large type ed. Ibbotson, Eve. 240p. 1992. 13.95 (*0-7451-1552-7*, Galaxy Child Lrg Print) Chivers N Amer.
—Stephen's Feast. Richardson, Jean. (ps-3). 1991. 15.95 (*0-316-74435-2*) Little.
Engle, Arch. Timely Tips & Treats for the Tenderfoot Homemaker. Van Tuyle, R. Helen. 108p. (Orig.). 1987. wkbk. 9.95 (*0-9617816-0-2*) R H Van Tuyle.
English, Betty L. Women at Their Work. English, Betty L. LC 76-42924. 48p. (gr. k-4). 1988. pap. 4.95 (*0-8037-0496-8*) Dial Bks Young.
English, Mark. Reader's Digest Best Loved Books for Young Readers: Little Women. Alcott, Louisa May. Ogburn, Jackie, ed. 176p. (gr. 4-12). 1989. 3.99 (*0-945260-25-3*) Choice Pub NY.
English, Sarah J. Habitats. Hickman, Pamela M. LC 93-12683. 1993. write for info. (*0-201-62651-9*); pap. 9.57 (*0-201-62618-7*) Addison-Wesley.
Enik, Ted. Encyclopedia Brown's Book of the Wacky Outdoors. Sobol, Donald J. LC 87-7851. 112p. (gr. 3-7). 1987. 12.95 (*0-688-06635-6*) Morrow Jr Bks.
—Encyclopedia Brown's Book of Wacky Animals. Sobol, Donald J. LC 84-22608. 128p. (gr. 3-7). 1985. 11.95 (*0-688-04152-3*) Morrow Jr Bks.
—Encyclopedia Brown's Book of Wacky Cars. Sobol, Donald J. LC 86-23556. 128p. (gr. 3-7). 1987. 11.95 (*0-688-06222-9*) Morrow Jr Bks.
—Encyclopedia Brown's Book of Wacky Cars. Sobol, Donald J. 128p. (gr. 3-7). 1987. pap. 2.75 (*0-553-15512-1*) Skylark) Bantam.
—Encyclopedia Brown's Book of Wacky Crimes. Sobol, Donald J. LC 82-9683. 128p. (gr. 3-5). 1982. 12.95 (*0-525-66786-5*, Lodestar Bks) Dutton Child Bks.
—Encyclopedia Brown's Book of Wacky Crimes. Sobol, Donald J. 1983. pap. 2.25 (*0-553-15358-7*) Bantam.
—Encyclopedia Brown's Book of Wacky Spies. Sobol, Donald J. LC 83-17179. 128p. (gr. 3-7). 1984. 13.95 (*0-688-02744-X*) Morrow Jr Bks.
—Encyclopedia Brown's Book of Wacky Spies. Sobol, Donald J. 112p. (gr. 4-6). 1984. pap. 2.25 (*0-553-15369-2*, Skylark) Bantam.
—Encyclopedia Brown's Book of Wacky Sports. Sobol, Donald J. LC 82-84250. 128p. (gr. 3-7). 1984. 11.95 (*0-688-03884-0*) Morrow Jr Bks.
—Encyclopedia Brown's Book of Wacky Sports. Sobol, Donald J. 128p. (Orig.). (gr. 3-7). 1984. pap. 2.50 (*0-553-15497-4*, Skylark) Bantam.
—The Glow-in-the-Dark Planetarium Book. Ingle, Annie. LC 92-29932. 16p. (Orig.). (ps-1). 1993. pap. 4.99 (*0-679-84367-1*) Random Hse Yng Read.
—Making up Your Mind about Drugs. Berger, Gilda. LC 88-3609. 80p. (gr. 4-6). 1988. (Lodestar Bks); pap. 4.95 (*0-525-67256-7*, Lodestar Bks) Dutton Child Bks.
—The Old Barn. Miller, Rose. LC 92-35283. 32p. (gr. 2-6). 1992. PLB 17.96 (*0-8114-3581-4*) Raintree Steck-V.
—Why Can't You Unscramble an Egg? Cobb, Vicki. LC 89-33465. 40p. (gr. 2-5). 1990. 12.95 (*0-525-67293-1*, Lodestar Bks) Dutton Child Bks.
—Why Doesn't the Earth Fall Up? And Other Not Such Dumb Questions about Motion. Cobb, Vicki. LC 88-11108. 40p. (gr. 2-5). 1989. 13.00 (*0-525-67253-2*, Lodestar Bks) Dutton Child Bks.
—Why Doesn't the Sun Burn Out? Cobb, Vicki. 40p. (gr. 2-5). 1990. 13.95 (*0-525-67301-6*, Lodestar Bks) Dutton Child Bks.
Enrees, Michael B. It's Your Constitution! rev. ed. Scesney, Gladys. 32p. (gr. 1-6). 1987. pap. 1.50 (*0-9618667-1-3*) Scesney Pubns.
Enright, Beverley R. Exits & Entrances. Madgett, Naomi L. LC 77-91712. 69p. (gr. 9-12). 1978. pap. 5.00 perfect bdg. (*0-916418-13-8*) Lotus.
Enright, Elizabeth. The Saturdays. Enright, Elizabeth. LC 41-30925. 196p. (gr. 4-6). 1988. 12.95 (*0-8050-0291-X*, Bks Young Read) H Holt & Co.
—Then There Were Five. Enright, Elizabeth. (gr. k-6). 1987. pap. 2.95 (*0-440-48806-0*, YB) Dell.
—Thimble Summer. Enright, Elizabeth. LC 38-27586. 124p. (gr. 6 up). 1938. 15.95 (*0-8050-0306-1*, Bks Young Read) H Holt & Co.
Enrique, Miguel M. My Book of Words, Songs & Sentences. Ronnholm, Ursula O. & Ronnholm, Paul F. 91p. (gr. k-3). 1986. pap. text ed. 7.00 (*0-941911-03-9*) Two Way Bilingual.

Enriquez, Edmund C. The Golden Gospel: A Pictorial History of the Restoration. Enriquez, Edmund C. 96p. (gr. 6-12). 1981. pap. 7.95 (*0-88290-198-2*) Horizon Utah.
Enriquez, Jesse B. The Magic Seed. Intia, Perla S. 20p. (Orig.). (gr. k-2). 1989. pap. 3.50x (*971-10-0327-9*, Pub. by New Day Pub PI) Cellar.
Ensing-Keelean, Jan. Now I Understand. LaMore, Gregory S. LC 85-20639. 56p. (gr. 3-6). 1986. 8.95 (*0-930323-13-0*, Kendall Green Pubns) Gallaudet Univ Pr.
Ensor, Robert. Nellie, the Light House Dog. Scarpino, Jane. Weinberger, Jane, ed. 40p. (ps-3). 1993. pap. 9.95 (*0-932433-23-5*) Windswept Hse.
Entwisle, Mark. The Walking Catfish. Day, David. LC 91-9144. 32p. (gr. k-3). 1992. 13.95 (*0-02-726360-6*, Macmillan Child Bk) Macmillan Child Grp.
Eppinga, Jane. Kids Can Cook with Billy the Kid. Eppinga, Jane. 67p. (gr. 4-6). 1979. pap. 4.95x (*0-9618890-0-4*) BK Pubns.
Epps, Melanie. Into the Jungle. Hindley, Judy. 1994. write for info. (*1-56402-423-7*) Candlewick Pr.
Epps, Sarah. The Staffordshire Bull Terrier in America. Eltinge, et al. Eltinge, Steve, ed. & intro. by. 140p. (gr. 4 up). 1986. pap. 24.95 (*0-9617204-0-9*) MIP Pub.
Epstein, Len. Frontier Farmer: Kansas Adventures. Chambers, Catherine E. LC 83-18279. 32p. (gr. 5-9). 1984. PLB 11.59 (*0-8167-0053-2*); pap. text ed. 2.95 (*0-8167-0054-0*) Troll Assocs.
—Mr. Lion Goes to Lunch. Frost, Erica. LC 85-14012. 48p. (Orig.). (gr. 1-3). 1986. PLB 10.59 (*0-8167-0638-7*); pap. text ed. 3.50 (*0-8167-0639-5*) Troll Assocs.
—Teddy on Time. Pellowski, Michael J. LC 85-14127. 48p. (Orig.). (gr. 1-3). 1986. PLB 10.59 (*0-8167-0582-8*); pap. text ed. 3.50 (*0-8167-0583-6*) Troll Assocs.
Epstein, Len, et al. My First Book of Space Coloring & Activity Book. Bell, Robert. 160p. (gr. 1 up). 1986. pap. 6.95 (*0-671-62407-5*, Little Simon) S&S Trade.
Epstein, Vivian S. History of Women for Children. Epstein, Vivian S. 32p. (ps-5). 1984. 12.95 (*0-9601002-4-5*); pap. 5.95 (*0-9601002-3-7*) V S Epstein.
—History of Women in Science for Young People. Epstein, Vivian S. 40p. (Orig.). (gr. 4-9). 1993. 14.95 (*0-9601002-8-8*); pap. 7.95 (*0-9601002-7-X*) V S Epstein.
Era, Diane. My A, B, C, D, E Thinking, Feeling & Doing Book. Goldman, Margaret F. Ellis, Albert, intro. by. LC 83-90397. 48p. (ps up). 11.95 (*0-914237-00-4*) L & M Bks.
Erb, Sherry. Buckethead Bunch: Bossy, Loser, Show-off & Angry. Epperley, Mike. LC 92-85592. 40p. (Orig.). (gr. k-6). 1992. pap. 5.98x (*1-882183-24-X*) Computer Pr.
—The Buckethead Families: Givers & Takers. rev. ed. Epperley, Mike. LC 92-85597. 32p. (gr. k-6). 1992. pap. 5.98 (*1-882183-23-1*) Computer Pr.
—The Three Bucketeers: Commander, Thinker, Player. Epperley, Mike. 40p. (Orig.). (gr. k-6). 1993. pap. 5.98 (*1-882183-22-3*) Computer Pr.
Erdoes, R. Come Over to My House. Le Sieg, Theodore. LC 66-10686. 72p. (gr. k-3). 1966. lib. bdg. 7.99 (*0-394-90044-8*) Beginner.
Erdtmann, Greta. The Path to Math. Erdtmann, Greta. Doman, Glenn, intro. by. 60p. (ps). 1981. 8.95 (*0-936676-11-6*) Better Baby.
Ericksen, Mary. A Monster is Bigger than Nine. Ericksen, Claire, ed. 48p. (Orig.). 1991. pap. 8.95 (*0-88138-099-7*, Green Tiger) S&S Trade.
Erickson, Cindy R. The Magic Treble Tree. Rhoton, Jessian L. 48p. 1989. PLB write for info. Happy Music Pub.
—The Magic Treble Tree. Rhoton, Jessian L. 48p. 1990. write for info. (*0-9624162-9-0*) Happy Music Pub.
Erikkson, Eva. The Wild Baby. Lindgren, Barbro. Prelutsky, Jack, tr. from SWE. LC 81-2151. (gr. k-3). 1981. PLB 15.88 (*0-688-00601-9*) Greenwillow.
Eriksson, Ake. Joel, Jesper, & Julia. Eriksson, Ake. LC 89-25116. 32p. (ps-4). 1990. PLB 18.95 (*0-87614-419-9*) Carolrhoda Bks.
Eriksson, Eva. The Horrible Spookhouse. Stridh, Kicki. LC 93-22076. 1993. write for info. (*0-87614-811-9*) Carolrhoda Bks.
—If You Didn't Have Me. Nilsson, Ulf. Blecher, Lone T. & Blecher, George, trs. LC 86-21327. 128p. (gr. 2-5). 1987. SBE 12.95 (*0-689-50406-3*, M K McElderry) Macmillan Child Grp.
—Is It Magic? Lagercrantz, Rose & Lagercrantz, Samuel. Norlen, Paul, tr. from SWE. LC 89-63054. (gr. k-3). 1990. 13.95 (*91-29-59182-1*, Pub. by R & S Bks) FS&G.
—Mimi & the Biscuit Factory. Sundvall, Viveca. Bibb, Eric, tr. 32p. (ps up). 1989. 12.95 (*91-29-59142-2*, Pub. by R & S Bks) FS&G.
—Mimi Gets a Grandpa. Sundvall, Viveca. Fisher, Richard E., tr. 32p. (ps up). 1991. bds. 13.95 (*91-29-59864-8*, Pub. by R&S Bks) FS&G.
—Sam's Bath. Lindgren, Barbro. LC 83-724. 32p. (ps-k). 1983. 6.95 (*0-688-02362-2*) Morrow Jr Bks.
—Sam's Car. Lindgren, Barbro. LC 82-3437. 32p. (gr. k-3). 1982. 6.95 (*0-688-01263-9*) Morrow Jr Bks.
—Sam's Cookie. Lindgren, Barbro. LC 82-3419. 32p. (gr. k-3). 1982. 6.95 (*0-688-01267-1*) Morrow Jr Bks.
—Sam's Potty. Lindgren, Barbro. LC 86-864. 32p. (ps-k). 1986. 6.95 (*0-688-06603-8*) Morrow Jr Bks.

—Sam's Teddy Bear. Lindgren, Barbro. LC 82-3418. 32p. (gr. k-3). 1982. 5.95 (*0-688-01270-1*) Morrow Jr Bks.
—Sam's Wagon. Lindgren, Barbro. LC 86-865. 32p. (ps-k). 1986. 6.95 (*0-688-05802-7*) Morrow Jr Bks.
—The Wild Baby Gets a Puppy: Swedish Edition. Lindgren, Barbro. Prelutsky, Jack, tr. LC 87-212. 32p. (ps-3). 1988. Repr. of 1985 ed. 11.95 (*0-688-06711-5*); lib. bdg. 11.88 (*0-688-06712-3*) Greenwillow.
Eriksson, Inga-Karin. The Other Alice: The Story of Alice Liddell & Alice in Wonderland. Bjork, Christina. Sandlin, Joan, tr. from SWE. LC 93-662. 1993. 18.00 (*91-29-62242-5*, Pub. by R & S Bks) FS&G.
Erkel, Michael. The Farmhouse Mouse. Erkel, Cynthia R. LC 92-27040. 1993. write for info. (*0-399-22444-0*, Putnam) Putnam Pub Group.
Erkmann, Chris. Why Frogs Go to School & Other Weird Facts You Never Learned. Keats, Robin. 96p. (Orig.). 1992. pap. 3.50 (*0-380-76718-X*, Camelot) Avon.
Ernst, Lisa C. Breakfast Time! Ziefert, Harriet. (ps). 1988. pap. 3.95 (*0-670-81579-9*) Viking Child Bks.
—Bye, Bye, Daddy! Ziefert, Harriet. (ps). 1988. pap. 3.95 (*0-670-81581-0*) Viking Child Bks.
—Count with Little Bunny. Ziefert, Harriet. (ps-1). 1988. pap. 5.95 (*0-670-82308-2*) Viking Child Bks.
—Dress Little Bunny. Ziefert, Harriet. 12p. (ps-1). 1986. bds. 6.99 (*0-670-80358-8*) Viking Child Bks.
—Feed Little Bunny. Ziefert, Harriet. (ps-1). 1988. pap. 5.95 (*0-670-82309-0*) Viking Child Bks.
—Ginger Jumps. Ernst, Lisa C. LC 89-38706. 32p. (ps-2). 1990. RSBE 14.95 (*0-02-733565-8*, Bradbury Pr) Macmillan Child Grp.
—Gumshoe Goose, Private Eye. Kwitz, Mary D. LC 86-29331. 48p. (ps-3). 1988. 9.95 (*0-8037-0423-2*); PLB 9.89 (*0-8037-0424-0*) Dial Bks Young.
—Let's Get Dressed. Ziefert, Harriet. (ps). 1988. pap. 3.95 (*0-670-81580-2*) Viking Child Bks.
—Little Bunny's Melon Patch. Ziefert, Harriet. 20p. (ps-3). 1990. pap. 4.95 (*0-14-054262-0*, Puffin) Puffin Bks.
—Little Bunny's Noisy Friends. Ziefert, Harriet. 20p. (ps-3). 1990. pap. 4.95 (*0-14-054263-9*, Puffin) Puffin Bks.
—Miss Penny & Mr. Grubbs. Ernst, Lisa C. LC 90-43175. 40p. (ps-2). 1991. RSBE 14.95 (*0-02-733563-1*, Bradbury Pr) Macmillan Child Grp.
—Play with Little Bunny. Ziefert, Harriet. 12p. (ps-1). 1986. bds. 6.99 (*0-670-80359-6*) Viking Child Bks.
—Squirrel Park. Ernst, Lisa C. LC 92-27920. 40p. (ps-2). 1993. RSBE 15.95 (*0-02-733562-3*, Bradbury Pr) Macmillan Child Grp.
—Walter's Tail. Ernst, Lisa C. LC 91-19948. 40p. (ps-2). 1992. RSBE 14.95 (*0-02-733564-X*, Bradbury Pr) Macmillan Child Grp.
—When Bluebell Sang. Ernst, Lisa C. LC 88-22262. 32p. (ps-1). 1989. RSBE 13.95 (*0-02-733561-5*, Bradbury Pr) Macmillan Child Grp.
—When Bluebell Sang. Ernst, Lisa C. LC 91-15552. 40p. (ps-1). 1992. pap. 4.95 (*0-689-71584-6*, Aladdin) Macmillan Child Grp.
Eros, Keith. The Slave Dancer. Fox, Paula. LC 73-80642. 192p. (gr. 5-8). 1982. SBE 14.95 (*0-02-735560-8*, Bradbury Pr) Macmillan Child Grp.
Erost. Be Patient, Little Chick. Clement, Claude. Jensen, Patricia, adapted by. LC 93-2951. 1993. write for info. (*0-89577-503-4*, Readers Digest Kids) RD Assn.
Errickson, Shirley V. Duck, Duck: The Different Duck. Petrie, Mildred M. LC 87-80921. 40p. 1987. 12.95 (*0-9618241-0-7*) Enfield Pubs.
Erspamer, Steve. Lectionary for Masses with Children: Sundays - Year A. Hoffman, Elizabeth, ed. American Bible Society Staff, tr. Gregory, Wilton, intro. by. (gr. 1-8). Date not set. text ed. 42.00 (*0-929650-71-9*); pap. text ed. 10.00 (*1-56854-000-0*) Liturgy Tr Pubns.
—Lectionary for Masses with Children: Sundays - Year B. Hoffman, Elizabeth, ed. American Bible Society Staff, tr. Gregory, Wilton, intro. by. 291p. (gr. 1-8). 1993. 42.00 (*0-929650-73-5*); pap. 10.00 (*1-56854-002-7*) Liturgy Tr Pubns.
—Lectionary for Masses with Children: Sundays - Year C. Hoffman, Elizabeth, ed. American Bible Society Staff, tr. Gregory, Wilton, intro. by. (gr. 1-8). 1994. 42.00 (*0-929650-74-3*); pap. 10.00 (*1-56854-003-5*) Liturgy Tr Pubns.
—Lectionary for Masses with Children: Weekdays. Hoffman, Elizabeth, ed. American Bible Society Staff, tr. Gregory, Wilton, intro. by. 503p. (gr. 1-8). 1993. 49.00 (*0-929650-72-7*); pap. 10.00 (*1-56854-001-9*) Liturgy Tr Pubns.
Ertmann, Caren L. & Read, Jacqueline P. The Legend of Natural Tunnel: La Leyenda del Tunel Natural. Fugate, Clara T. Calvera, Elizabeth C., ed. Socarras-Roufagalas, Gilda, tr. LC 85-30068. (SPA & ENG.). 80p. (Orig.). (gr. 6-12). 1986. pap. 5.95 (*0-936015-02-0*) Pocahontas Pr.
Erwin, Julie. The Birthday Gift That Beeped. Laster, Jim. Knight, George, ed. LC 83-176266. 56p. (gr. k-4). 1983. 10.95 (*0-9612780-0-5*) J Laster Pub Co.
Escofet, Josep, jt. illus. see Ballonga, Jordi.
Escriba, Vivi. Olmo y la Mariposa Azul. Ada, Alma F., ed. 24p. (gr. k-3). 1992. pap. 7.50x (*1-56492-095-X*) Laredo.

Escriva, Vivi. In the Cow's Backyard - La Hamaca De La Vaca. Ada, Alam F. (SPA & ENG.). 23p. (gr. k-2). 1991. English ed. 6.95 (*1-56014-275-8*);

Spanish ed. 6.95 (*1-56014-219-7*) Santillana.
Young readers will be enchanted with the menagerie of animal characters in this whimsical selection. A hospitable cow discovers an ant in her hammock, then a frog, then a chick. a hen, & a goose. But, sys the cow, "There's always room for one more friend." This selection makes an enjoyable counting book, while the rhyming text makes for easy reading. English & Spanish versions are available to entertain children in both languages. To order: Santillana, 901 West Walnut, Compton, CA 90220. Telephone 1-310-763-0455. *Publisher Provided Annotation.*

—**The Kite - El Papalote.** Ada, Alma F. (SPA & ENG.). 23p. (gr. k-2). 1992. English ed. 6.95 (*1-56014-228-6*); Spanish ed. 6.95 (*1-56014-227-8*) Santillana. **A resourceful mother helps her children make & fly a kite in this entertaining selection. A surprise ending adds to the reading experience. Predictable language patterns help young readers to decode the text easily. English & Spanish versions are available to delight children in both languages. To order: Santillana, 901 West Walnut, Compton, CA 90220. Telephone 1-310-763-0455.** *Publisher Provided Annotation.*

—**A Strange Visitor - Una Extrana Visita.** Ada, Alam F. (SPA & ENG.). 26p. (Orig.). (gr. k-2). 1989. English ed. 3.95 (*0-88272-802-4*); Spanish Ed. 3.95 (*0-88272-793-1*) Santillana. **A delightful collection of animals gather to play various musical instruments: cows with maracas, crickets with fiddles, & mice playing accordions. Days of the week & counting are also introduced in this entertaining book. The story is available in both English & Spanish with rhyming text in both languages. Ingeniously drawn illustrations by Vivi Escriva add to the fun. To order: Santillana, 901 West Walnut, Compton, CA 90220. Telephone 1-310-763-0455.** *Publisher Provided Annotation.*

—**Who's Hatching Here? - Quien Nacera Aqui?** Ada, Alma F. (SPA & ENG.). 24p. (gr. k-2). 1989. English ed. 3.95 (*0-88272-811-3*); Spanish ed. 3.95 (*0-88272-800-8*) Santillana. **Charming story by the incomparable Alma Flor Ada portraying the habitats & birth cycles of numerous animals & insects: chicks, mosquitoes, frogs, turtles, & butterflies are included. Water color illustrations by Vivi Escriva add to young readers' enjoyment. To order: Santillana, 901 West Walnut, Compton, CA 90220. Telephone 1-310-763-0455.** *Publisher Provided Annotation.*

Eskander, Stefanie C. Mac & Zach from Hackensack. Rogers, George L. 32p. (gr. k-6). 1992. PLB 12.95 (*0-938399-07-1*); pap. 4.95 (*0-938399-06-3*) Acorn Pub MN.

Espada, Frank, jt. illus. see Ordonez, Maria A.

Esparza, Thomas, Jr. Humpty Dumpty & Friends in the Southwest, Bk. I. Esparza, Esther L. & Esparza, Thomas, Jr. 28p. (Orig.). (ps-9). 1991. pap. text ed. 6.95 (*1-879817-05-5*); pap. text ed. 12.95 incl. cassette (*1-879817-15-2*); cassette 9.95 (*1-879817-10-1*) Star Light Pr.
—Humpty Dumpty & Friends in the Southwest, Bk. II. Esparza, Esther L. & Esparza, Thomas, Jr. 28p. (Orig.). (ps-9). 1991. pap. text ed. 6.95 (*1-879817-06-3*); pap. text ed. 12.95 incl. cassette (*1-879817-16-0*); cassette 9.95 (*1-879817-11-X*) Star Light Pr.
—Humpty Dumpty & Friends in the Southwest, Bk. III. Esparza, Esther L. & Esparza, Thomas, Jr. 28p. (Orig.). (ps-9). 1991. pap. text ed. 6.95 (*1-879817-07-1*); pap. text ed. 12.95 incl. cassette (*1-879817-17-9*); cassette 9.95 (*1-879817-12-8*) Star Light Pr.
—Humpty Dumpty & Friends in the Southwest, 3 vols, Bks. I, II & III. Esparza, Esther L. & Esparza, Thomas, Jr. (Orig.). (ps-9). 1991. Set. pap. text ed. 19.95 (*1-879817-08-X*); Set. pap. text ed. 35.95 incl. cassettes (*1-879817-14-4*); Set. cassettes 24.95 (*1-879817-13-6*) Star Light Pr.

Espe, Marvin. Discovering with God. Dick, Lois H. 22p. (gr. k-6). 1984. pap. text ed. 4.25 (*1-55976-143-1*) CEF Press.
—Mustapha's Secret: A Muslim Boy's Search to Know God. Klaus, Sandra. 42p. (gr. 2-7). 1988. pressboard cover, plastic bdg. 9.95 (*0-9617490-1-6*) Gospel Missionary.
—Ringu of India's Forest. Allison, Carol. 52p. (gr. k-6). 1987. pap. text ed. 8.99 (*1-55976-050-8*) CEF Press.
—Surrounded by Headhunters. Klaus, Sandra. 32p. (gr. 2-7). 1986. pressboard cover, plastic bdg. 9.95 (*0-9617490-0-8*) Gospel Missionary.
—Yandicu: From Witch Doctor to Evangelist. Windle, Jeanette & Clements, Jan. 44p. (gr. 2-7). 1992. pressboard cover, plastic bdg. 9.95 (*0-9617490-2-4*) Gospel Missionary.

Espinosa, Tony. The Big Bad Wolf in Texas. Huebel, Russ. 48p. (Orig.). 1983. pap. 6.25 (*0-9611604-2-X*) C Del Grullo.

Espinoza, Rauol, et al. Polar Bears. Wildlife Education, Ltd. Staff. 20p. (Orig.). (gr. k-12). 1985. pap. 2.75 (*0-937934-36-4*) Wildlife Educ.

Esquivel, Jim & Leaf, Richard. Badges of the United States Marshals. Sherrard, Raymond & Stumpf, George. LC 89-61859. (Orig.). 1991. 35.45 (*0-914503-02-2*); pap. 22.45 (*0-914503-03-0*) RHS Ent.

Essley, Roger. Appointment. Maugham, W. Somerset. Benjamin, Alan, adapted by. LC 92-391. (ps-3). 1993. 16.00 (*0-671-75887-X*, Green Tiger) S&S Trade.
—Wildflower Tea. Pochocki, Ethel. LC 92-29872. 1993. 14.00 (*0-671-78115-4*, Green Tiger) S&S Trade.

Estes, Eleanor. Ginger Pye. Estes, Eleanor. LC 51-10446. (gr. 3-7). 1950. 13.95 (*0-15-230930-6*, HB Juv Bks) HarBrace.
—The Moffat Museum. Estes, Eleanor. LC 83-8427. 262p. (gr. 3-7). 1983. 10.95 (*0-15-255086-0*, HB Juv Bks) HarBrace.

Estrada, Pau. The April Fool's Day Mystery. Markham, Marion M. LC 90-41318. 48p. (gr. 2-6). 1991. 13.45 (*0-395-56235-X*) HM.
—The Birthday Party Mystery. Markham, Marion M. (gr. 2 up). 1989. 13.45 (*0-395-49698-5*) HM.
—Button Soup. Orgel, Doris. LC 93-14087. 1994. write for info. (*0-553-09045-3*); pap. write for info. (*0-553-37341-2*) Bantam.
—Just Not the Same. Lacoe, Addie. LC 91-44041. 32p. (ps-3). 1992. 14.45 (*0-395-59347-6*) HM.
—Opal in the Closet. Knight, Joan. LC 91-659. 28p. (gr. k up). 1992. pap. 14.95 (*0-88708-174-6*) Picture Bk Studio.

Estrada, Zilia C. If I Were a Bird. Estrada, Zilia C. (Orig.). (gr. 1 up). 1988. pap. write for info. Blue Flame Pr.

Etow, Carole. What Goes Inside? 8p. (ps). 1992. 5.95 (*0-8431-2998-0*) Price Stern.
—Where Does It Come From? 8p. (ps). 1992. 5.95 (*0-8431-2999-9*) Price Stern.
—Who Makes This? Strong, Stacie. 8p. (ps). 1992. 5.95 (*0-8431-2997-2*) Price Stern.
—Whose Footprints Are These? 8p. (ps). 1992. 5.95 (*0-8431-3358-9*) Price Stern.

Etre, Lisa. One White Sail. Garne, S. T. LC 91-24662. 32p. 1992. 14.00 (*0-671-75579-X*, Green Tiger) S&S Trade.

Ets, Marie H. Gilberto & the Wind. Ets, Marie H. LC 63-8527. (gr. k-3). 1978. pap. 3.99 (*0-14-050276-9*, Puffin) Puffin Bks.
—Gilberto & the Wind. Ets, Marie H. (ps-1). 1963. pap. 14.00 (*0-670-34025-1*) Viking Child Bks.
—Just Me. Ets, Marie H. (ps-2). 1965. pap. 14.95 (*0-670-41109-4*) Viking Child Bks.
—Just Me. Ets, Marie H. (gr. k-3). 1985. bk. & cassette 19.95 (*0-941078-75-2*); pap. 12.95 bk. & cassette (*0-941078-73-6*); cassette, 4 paperbacks & guide 27.95 (*0-941078-74-4*) Live Oak Media.
—Nine Days to Christmas. Ets, Marie H. & Labastida, Aurora. (ps-2). 1959. pap. 13.95 (*0-670-51350-4*) Viking Child Bks.
—Play with Me. Ets, Marie H. (ps-1). 1955. pap. 13.95 (*0-670-55977-6*) Viking Child Bks.

Eubank, Mary G. Barney's Favorite Mother Goose Rhymes, Vol. 1. White, Stephen. Hartley, Linda, ed. 32p. (ps-k). 1993. 7.95 (*0-7829-0336-3*) Barney Pub.
—Barney's Favorite Mother Goose Rhymes, Vol. 2. White, Stephen. Hartley, Linda, ed. 32p. (ps-k). 1993. 7.95 (*0-7829-0380-0*) Barney Pub.
—Friends Are Helpers. Beers, V. Gilbert. 12p. (ps-2). 1991. bds. 3.99 (*0-8010-0997-9*) Baker Bk.
—Friends Give Good Gifts. Beers, V. Gilbert. 12p. (ps-2). 1991. bds. 3.99 (*0-8010-0998-7*) Baker Bk.
—Friends Play Together. Beers, V. Gilbert. 12p. (ps-2). 1991. bds. 3.99 (*0-8010-0999-5*) Baker Bk.
—Friends Share. Beers, V. Gilbert. 12p. (ps-2). 1991. bds. 3.99 (*0-8010-0996-0*) Baker Bk.
—Journey to Jesus: A Four-in-One Story. Hollingsworth, Mary. 32p. 1993. 13.99 (*0-8010-4371-9*) Baker Bk.
—Just Imagine, with Barney. Shrode, Mary. White, Stephen, ed. 32p. (ps-k). 1992. 7.95g (*0-7829-0137-9*) Lyons Group.
—Little Red Riding Hood. Balducci, Rita, retold by. (ps-k). 1991. pap. 1.25 (*0-307-11511-9*, Golden Pr) Western Pub.

Eugol, Trebor. Space Needle: Journey to Mars. 2nd ed. Idore. 37p. (Orig.). (ps-3). 1991. pap. 4.95 (*0-926060-08-2*) Anschell Pub Co.

Eula, Joe. Tiffany's Table Manners for Teenagers. Hoving, Walter. LC 88-23964. 96p. (gr. 5 up). 1989. Repr. of 1962 ed. 13.00 (*0-394-82877-1*) Random Bks Yng Read.

Eulalie. A Child's Garden of Verses. Stevenson, Robert Louis. LC 85-12766. 86p. (ps-3). 1957. 15.95 (*0-448-40510-5*, G&D); (G&D) Putnam Pub Group.

Eutemey, Loring. Magic Made Easy. new. ed. Kettelkamp, Larry. Klotzbeacher, Donovan, photos by. LC 80-22947. 96p. (gr. 3-7). 1981. 13.95 (*0-688-00458-X*); PLB 13.88 (*0-688-00377-X*, Morrow Jr Bks) Morrow Jr Bks.

Euvremer, Teryl. The Thieves of Peck's Pocket. Euvremer, Teryl. LC 89-23845. 32p. (ps-2). 1990. PLB 13.99 (*0-517-57538-8*) Crown Bks Yng Read.
—Triple Whammy. Euvremer, Teryl. LC 91-44240. 32p. (gr. k-4). 1993. 15.00 (*0-06-021060-5*); PLB 14.89 (*0-06-021061-3*) HarpC Child Bks.

Evangelist, Gary. Reading Skills Songbook, Vol. 1: Read, Rapp, & Rock to the Skills of Reading. Bryer, James. 48p. (Orig.). (gr. 2-6). 1989. pap. 14.95 incl. audiocassette (*0-9622499-0-4*) Soundbox Pubns.

Evans, Beth, jt. illus. see Butler, Nate.

Evans, Beth, jt. illus. see Sundstrom, Mary.

Evans, Christine, et al. The Handbook of Historically Black Colleges & Universities, Premier Edition 1992-94: Comprehensive Profiles & Photos of Black Colleges & Universities. Hodge-Wright, Toni, et al, eds. LC 92-71364. 248p. (gr. 10 up). 1992. 19.95 (*0-9632669-0-X*) Jireh & Assocs.

Evans, Dolly B., jt. illus. see Evans, Wendy M.

Evans, Ed & Campbell, Sid. Mastering Bruce Lee's Devastating 1 & 3 Inch Punch...with the BRUTUS Power Punch System. Campbell, Sid. Campbell, Sid, intro. by. 16p. 1986. pap. 1.00 (*0-318-20215-8*) Gong Prods.

Evans, Graci. David Has AIDS. Sanford, Doris. LC 89-3162. 29p. (gr. k-4). 1989. 6.99 (*0-88070-299-0*, Gold & Honey) Questar Pubs.
—Don't Look at Me: A Child's Book about Feeling Different. Sanford, Doris. LC 86-185484. 27p. (gr. k-6). 1986. 7.99 (*0-88070-150-1*, Gold & Honey) Questar Pubs.
—Don't Make Me Go Back, Mommy. Sanford, Doris. (gr. k-6). 1990. 7.99 (*0-88070-367-9*, Gold & Honey) Questar Pubs.
—Filling' Up. Littleton, Mark. 168p. 1993. 8.99 (*0-945564-72-4*, Gold & Honey Books) Questar Pubs.
—For Your Own Good. Sanford, Doris. 28p. (gr. k-6). 1993. 7.99 (*0-88070-604-X*, Gold & Honey) Questar Pubs.
—I Can't Talk about It: A Child's Book about Sexual Abuse. Sanford, Doris. LC 86-831. 32p. (gr. k-6). 1986. 7.99 (*0-88070-149-8*, Gold & Honey) Questar Pubs.
—It Must Hurt a Lot: A Child's Book about Death. Sanford, Doris. LC 86-25009. 32p. (gr. k-6). 1985. 7.99 (*0-88070-131-5*, Gold & Honey) Questar Pubs.
—It Won't Last Forever. Sanford, Doris. 28p. (gr. k-6). 1993. 7.99 (*0-88070-605-8*, Gold & Honey) Questar Pubs.
—Lisa's Parents Fight. Sanford, Doris. Davis, Deena, ed. LC 89-31409. 28p. (gr. k-4). 1989. 6.99 (*0-88070-301-6*, Gold & Honey) Questar Pubs.
—Maria's Grandma Gets Mixed Up. Sanford, Doris. LC 89-3161. 31p. (gr. k-4). 1989. 6.99 (*0-88070-298-2*, Gold & Honey) Questar Pubs.
—Please Come Home: A Child's Book about Divorce. Sanford, Doris. LC 86-106753. 32p. (ps-5). 1985. 7.99 (*0-88070-138-2*, Gold & Honey) Questar Pubs.

Evans, Graci Help! Fire! Escaping with My Life. Sanford, Doris. Heaney, Liz, ed. 1992. 9.99 (*0-88070-520-5*, Gold & Honey) Questar Pubs.
—My Friend, the Enemy: Surviving a Prison Camp. Sanford, Doris. 1992. 9.99 (*0-88070-518-3*, Gold & Honey) Questar Pubs.
—My Real Family. Sanford, Doris. 28p. (gr. k-6). 1993. 7.99 (*0-88070-466-7*, Gold & Honey) Questar Pubs.
—No Longer Afraid: Living with Cancer. Sanford, Doris. 1992. 9.99 (*0-88070-519-1*, Gold & Honey) Questar Pubs.
—Yes, I Can: Challenging Cerebral Palsy. Sanford, Doris. Heaney, Liz, ed. 32p. 1992. 9.99 (*0-88070-510-8*, Gold & Honey) Questar Pubs.

Evans, K. Chicken Little Count-To-Ten. Friskey, Margaret. 32p. (gr. k-3). 1946. PLB 15.00 (0-516-03431-6) Childrens.
—Pollito Pequenito Cuenta hasta Diez - Chicken Little Count-to-Ten. Friskey, Margaret. Kratky, Lada, tr. from ENG. (SPA.). 32p. (gr. k-3). 1984. PLB 15.00 (0-516-33431-X); pap. 3.95 (0-516-53431-9) Childrens.
Evans, Lawrence L. Signposts from Proverbs: An Introduction to Proverbs. Weber, Rhiannon. 128p. (Orig.). 1988. spiral bdg. 9.95 (0-85151-517-7) Banner of Truth.
Evans, Leslie. The Flower Alphabet Book. Pallotta, Jerry. 32p. (ps-3). 1989. 14.95 (0-88106-459-9); pap. 6.95 (0-88106-453-X) Charlesbridge Pub.
—From Top Hats to Baseball Caps, from Bustles to Blue Jeans: Why We Dress the Way We Do. Perl, Lila. LC 89-77717. 118p. (gr. 5-8). 1990. 14.45 (0-89919-872-4, Clarion Bks) HM.
Evans, Michael. Nativity Press-Out. Evans, Michael. 12p. (ps-5). 1993. pap. 7.95 (0-8249-8635-0, Ideals Child) Hambleton-Hill.
—Noah's Ark: With Press-Out Model Ark, Animals, People & More. Evans, Michael. 16p. (Orig.). (gr. k-4). 1993. pap. 7.95 (0-8249-8600-8, Ideals Child) Hambleton-Hill.
Evans, Nate. My Book of Funny Valentines. Lundell, Margo. 32p. (ps-3). 1993. pap. 2.50 (0-590-44187-6) Scholastic Inc.
Evans, Robert R. As Ancient Is This Hostelry: The Story of the Wayside Inn. Ridley, Alison & Garfield, Curtis F. 335p. (Orig.). (gr. 7 up). 1989. pap. 14.00 (0-9621976-0-2) Porcupine Enter.
Evans, Ted. Angles. Smoothey, Marion. LC 92-36222. 1993. 15.95 (1-85435-466-3) Marshall Cavendish.
—Area & Volume. Smoothey, Marion. LC 92-10579. 1992. 15.95 (1-85435-460-4) Marshall Cavendish.
—Circles. Smoothey, Marion. 64p. (gr. 4-8). 1992. text ed. 15.95 (1-85435-456-6) Marshall Cavendish.
—Communications. Kerrod, Robin. LC 93-1913. 1993. write for info. (1-85435-624-0) Marshall Cavendish.
—Force & Motion. Kerrod, Robin. LC 93-4550. 1993. Set. write for info.; pap. 15.95 (1-85435-622-4) Marshall Cavendish.
—Let's Investigate Series, 6 vols. Smoothey, Marion. 64p. (gr. 4-8). 1993. Set, Group 1. PLB 101.70 (1-85435-455-8); Set, Group 2. PLB write for info. (1-85435-463-9) Marshall Cavendish.
—Number Patterns. Smoothey, Marion. 64p. (gr. 4-8). 1992. text ed. 16.95 (1-85435-458-2) Marshall Cavendish.
—Numbers. Smoothey, Marion. 64p. (gr. 4-8). 1992. text ed. 16.95 (1-85435-457-4) Marshall Cavendish.
—Quadrilaterals. Smoothey, Marion. LC 92-10436. 1992. 15.95 (1-85435-459-0) Marshall-Cavendish.
—Shape Patterns. Smoothey, Marion. LC 92-36223. 1993. 15.95 (1-85435-465-5) Marshall Cavendish.
—Shapes. Smoothey, Marion. LC 92-36224. 1993. 15.95 (1-85435-464-7) Marshall Cavendish.
—The Solar System. Kerrod, Robin. LC 93-4339. 1993. Set. write for info. (1-85435-620-8); pap. 15.95 (1-85435-621-6) Marshall Cavendish.
—Solids. Smoothey, Marion. LC 92-36220. 1993. 15.95 (1-85435-469-8) Marshall Cavendish.
—Statistics. Smoothey, Marion. LC 92-35574. 1993. 15.95 (0-685-62557-5) Marshall Cavendish.
—Statistics. Smoothey, Marion. 64p. (gr. 4-8). 1993. text ed. 16.95 (1-85435-468-X) Marshall Cavendish.
—Time, Distance, & Speed. Smoothey, Marion. LC 92-36225. 1993. 15.95 (1-85435-467-1) Marshall Cavendish.
—Triangles. Smoothey, Marion. LC 92-12156. 1992. 15.95 ea. (1-85435-461-2) Marshall-Cavendish.
Evans, Timothy. Ernestine or the Pig in the Potting Shed. Innis, Pauline. Weinberger, Jane, ed. 128p. 1992. pap. 9.95 (0-932433-97-9) Windswept Hse.
Evans, Valeria. The Whale's Tale. Evans-Smith, Deborah. LC 85-51791. 25p. (gr. 2-6). 1986. 8.95 (0-917507-02-9) Sea Fog Pr.
Evans, Wendy M. & Evans, Dolly B. Sex Respect: The Option of True Sexual Freedom: A Public Health Manual for Teachers. Mast, Coleen K. 61p. (Orig.). (gr. 7-9). 1986. pap. 12.95 (0-945745-00-1) Respect Inc.
—Sex Respect: The Option of True Sexual Freedom: A Public Health Guide for Parents. Mast, Coleen K. 61p. (Orig.). (gr. 7-9). 1986. pap. text ed. 8.95 (0-945745-01-X) Respect Inc.
—Sex Respect: The Option of True Sexual Freedom: A Public Health Workbook for Students. Mast, Coleen K. 61p. (Orig.). (gr. 7-9). 1986. pap. text ed. 7.95 (0-945745-02-8) Respect Inc.
Evelyne Johnson Associates Staff. Teen Guide. 6th ed. Chamberlain, Valerie M. & Buddinger, Peyton B. O'Neill, Martha, ed. 528p. 1985. text ed. 30.00 (0-07-007842-4); pap. text ed. 11.68 (0-07-007831-9) McGraw.
Evelyn-Marie. Pick Your Own Strawberries. rev. ed. Evelyn-Marie. 32p. (gr. k-3). 1983. pap. 3.00 (0-9614746-3-7) Berry Bks.
Everett, Mimi. Beginners Guide to Magic. Border, Rosy. 48p. (gr. 3-6). 1992. pap. 2.95 (1-56680-008-0) Mad Hatter Pub.
—Cinderella. 24p. 1991. pap. 1.25 (0-7214-5300-7, S9016-1 SER.) Ladybird Bks.
—Snow White & the Seven Dwarfs. 24p. (ps-1). 1991. pap. 1.25 (0-7214-5306-6, S9016-7) Ladybird Bks.

Everitt, Betsy. The Happy Hippopotami. Martin, Bill, Jr. Johnston, Allyn, ed. 32p. (ps-3). 1991. 12.95 (0-15-233380-0) HarBrace.
Everitt-Stewart, Andy & Moseley, Dudley. Pop-Up Dinosaurs. Malam, John. LC 90-60818. 10p. (gr. 1 up). 1991. 7.95 (0-679-80871-X) Random Bks Yng Read.
Everitt-Stewart, Andy & Mutimer, Ray. Pop-Up Machines. Malam, John. LC 90-60819. 10p. (gr. 1 up). 1991. 7.95 (0-679-80872-8) Random Bks Yng Read.
Everix, Nancy. More Windows to the World. Everix, Nancy. 128p. (gr. 2-8). 1985. wkbk. 11.95 (0-86653-316-8, GA 640) Good Apple.
—Windows to the World. Everix, Nancy. 128p. (gr. 2-8). 1984. wkbk. 11.95 (0-86653-173-4, GA 527) Good Apple.
Evers, June V. The Dreidle Champ & Other Holiday Stories. Sidi, Smadar S. 120p. (gr. 3-9). 1987. 13.95 (0-915361-89-2) Modan-Adama Bks.
—The Original Book of Recipes for Horses. Evers, June V., ed. 1994. 19.95 (0-9638814-1-8) Horse Hollow.
Evers, Melissa. Daddy, Me & the Adventures of Growing Up. Lemberg, Ray & Lemberg, Alexis. 32p. (Orig.). (gr. k-4). 1988. pap. 6.45 (0-9619208-5-8) Small Hands Pr.
Ewart, Claire. The Dwarf, the Giant, & the Unicorn: A Tale of King Arthur. Giblin, James C., retold by. LC 92-34031. 1994. write for info. (0-395-60520-2, Clarion Bks) HM.
—The Legend of the Persian Carpet. DePaola, Tomie. 32p. (ps-3). 1993. 14.95 (0-399-22415-7, Putnam-Whitebird) Putnam Pub Group.
—Sister Yessa's Story. Greenfield, Karen R. LC 91-15634. 32p. (gr. k-4). 1992. 15.00 (0-06-020278-5); PLB 14.89 (0-06-020279-3) HarpC Child Bks.
—Time Train. Fleischman, Paul. LC 90-27357. 32p. (gr. k-4). 1991. 15.00 (0-06-021709-X); PLB 14.89 (0-06-021710-3) HarpC Chiid Bks.
—Time Train. Fleischman, Paul. LC 90-27357. 32p. (gr. k-4). 1994. 4.95 (0-06-443351-X, Trophy) HarpC Child Bks.
Ewell, Newton, jt. illus. see Gustovich, Mike.
Ewers, Joe. The Best Prize of All. Taylor, Mark. 40p. (ps-3). 1985. 5.95 (0-910313-86-5) Parker Bros.
—The Biggest Cookie in the World. Hayward, Linda. LC 88-36247. 24p. (Orig.). (ps-1). 1989. pap. 2.25 (0-394-84049-6) Random Bks Yng Read.
—The Care Bears Battle the Freeze Machine. Rosenblatt, Arthur S. 40p. (ps-3). 1984. 5.95 (0-910313-15-6) Parker Bros.
—The Case of the Funny Money Man. Alexander, William. LC 89-36358. 96p. (gr. 4-7). 1990. PLB 9.89 (0-8167-1692-7); pap. text ed. 2.95 (0-8167-1693-5) Troll Assocs.
—The Case of the Gumball Bandits. Alexander, William. LC 89-36558. 96p. (gr. 4-7). 1990. PLB 9.89 (0-8167-1696-X); pap. text ed. 2.95 (0-8167-1697-8) Troll Assocs.
—The Case of the Pizza Pie Spy. Alexander, William. LC 89-20156. 96p. (gr. 4-7). 1990. PLB 9.89 (0-8167-1698-6); pap. text ed. 2.95 (0-8167-1699-4) Troll Assocs.
—The Ghost of Shockly Manor. Alexander, William. LC 89-36544. 96p. (gr. 4-7). 1990. PLB 9.89 (0-8167-1694-3); pap. text ed. 2.95 (0-8167-1695-1) Troll Assocs.
—The Happy Birthday Hug. Anderson, Janet S. LC 85-9476. 32p. (ps-3). 1985. pap. 0.99 (0-87372-006-7); 3.50 (0-910313-90-3) Parker Bros.
—Hugs from the Heart. Creighton, Susan. 32p. (ps-3). 1985. pap. 0.99 (0-87372-005-9) Parker Bros.
—I Want to Be a Cowboy. Alexander, Liza. 24p. (ps-k). 1992. write for info. (0-307-13117-3) Western Pub.
—Little Yellow School Bus. 14p. (ps-k). 1992. bds. 3.99 (0-679-83243-2) Random Bks Yng Read.
—Popple Opposites. Kahn, Peggy. LC 85-63459. 28p. (ps). 1986. 2.95 (0-394-88266-0) Random Bks Yng Read.
—Runners to the Rescue. Rosenblatt, Arthur S. 40p. (ps-3). write for info (0-910313-76-8) Parker Bros.
—Sesame Street Busy Little Neighborhood, 4 bks. Ross, Anna. (ps). 1991. Set, 12p. ea. bds. 8.00 (0-679-80252-5) Random Bks Yng Read.
—The Wacky Rulebook. Havel, Jennifer. 40p. (ps-3). write for info (0-910313-77-6) Parker Bros.
—We're Counting on You, Grover! Muntean, Michaela. (ps-k). 1991. write for info. (0-307-12050-3, Golden Pr) Western Pub.
—Your Best Wishes Can Come True. Cowell, Phyllis F. 40p. (ps-3). 1984. 5.95 (0-910313-18-0) Parker Bros.
Ewers, Joe & Sustendal, Pat. Pitch in & Play Fair. Hartsell, Lynn. 40p. (ps-3). write for info (0-910313-75-X) Parker Bros.
Ewers, Joseph. Sesame Street: Going Places. Smith, Jessie. LC 87-81768. 24p. (ps-k). 1988. pap. write for info. (0-307-10057-X, Pub. by Golden Bks) Western Pub.
Ewing, Carolyn. Branigan's Cat & the Halloween Ghost. Kroll, Steven. LC 89-77509. 32p. (ps-3). 1990. reinforced 14.95 (0-8234-0822-1) Holiday.
—The Cold & Hot Winter. Hurwitz, Johanna. LC 88-5144. 144p. (gr. 3-7). 1988. 12.95 (0-688-07839-7) Morrow Jr Bks.
—Dog on Third Base. Hiser, Constance. LC 90-29062. 64p. (gr. 2-6). 1991. 13.95 (0-8234-0898-1) Holiday.

—The Happy Birthday Book: A Party-Time Book with Lights & Music. Seymour, Peter. 12p. (ps-1). 1992. POB 10.95 (0-689-71585-4, Aladdin) Macmillan Child Grp.
—I Love Christmas: A Wonderful Collection of Christmas Stories, Poems, Carols, & More. Retan, Walter, compiled by. 96p. (gr. k up). 1992. write for info. (0-307-15875-6, 15875, Golden Pr) Western Pub.
—Jingle Bells: A Holiday Book with Lights & Music. 10p. (ps-1). 1990. 10.95 (0-689-71431-9, Aladdin) Macmillan Child Grp.
—Moose & Friends. Latimer, Jim. LC 91-14047. 32p. (ps-3). 1993. SBE 14.95 (0-684-19335-3, Scribners Young Read) Macmillan Child Grp.
—No Bean Sprouts, Please! Hiser, Constance. LC 89-1817. 64p. (gr. 2-5). 1989. 13.95 (0-8234-0760-8) Holiday.
—The Nutcracker Ballet. Hautzig, Deborah, retold by. LC 92-3320. 48p. (Orig.). (gr. 1-3). 1992. PLB 7.99 (0-679-92385-3); pap. 3.50 (0-679-82385-9) Random Bks Yng Read.
—Phoebe's Parade. Mills, Claudia. LC 93-21861. 32p. (gr. k-3). 1994. RSBE 14.95 (0-02-767012-0, Macmillan Child Bk) Macmillan Child Grp.
—Wake Up, City! Tresselt, Alvin. LC 88-32594. 32p. (ps-2). 1989. lib. bdg. 14.88 (0-688-08653-5) Lothrop.
—Wake up, Farm! Tresselt, Alvin. LC 90-33646. 32p. (ps up). 1991. 14.95 (0-688-08654-3); PLB 14.88 (0-688-08655-1) Lothrop.
Ewing, Carolyn S. Dog on Third Base. Hiser, Constance. MacDonald, Pat, ed. 80p. (gr. 2-4). 1993. pap. 2.99 (0-671-78962-7, Minstrel Bks) PB.
—Festival of Esther: The Story of Purim. Silverman, Maida. (gr. 1-5). 1989. pap. 8.95 (0-671-67200-2, Little Simon) S&S Trade.
—Festival of Freedom: The Story of Passover. Silverman, Maida. (gr. 1-5). 1988. pap. 8.95 (0-671-64567-6, S&S BFYR); pap. 3.95 (0-671-66340-2, S&S BFYR) S&S Trade.
—Festival of Lights: The Story of Hanukkah. Silverman, Maida. LC 87-16076. (gr. 1-5). 1987. (Little Simon); pap. 2.95 (0-671-64376-2, Little Simon) S&S Trade.
—No Bean Sprouts, Please! Hiser, Constance. MacDonald, Patricia, ed. 64p. 1991. pap. 2.99 (0-671-72325-1, Minstrel Bks) PB.
—One-Minute Bible Stories: New Testament. Lewis, Shari & Henderson, Florence. LC 86-6401. 48p. (ps-3). 1986. PLB 10.00 (0-385-23286-1) Doubleday.
—One-Minute Bible Stories: Old Testament. Lewis, Shari. LC 86-2011. 48p. (ps-3). 1986. PLB 10.00 (0-385-19565-6); pap. 7.99 (0-385-19566-4) Doubleday.
—One-Minute Greek Myths. Lewis, Shari. 48p. (ps-3). 1987. 6.95 (0-385-23849-5); pap. 9.95 (0-385-23423-6) Doubleday.
Exact Art Design Staff. Wyoming: Courage in a Lonesome Land. Adams, Randy L. & Sodaro, Craig. Lynch, Don, ed. Fay, Keith. LC 90-82123. 313p. (ps-6). 1990. Centennial Edition. text ed. 24.95 (0-913205-12-5); special price 14.97 Grace Dangberg.
Eyolfson, Norman. Jacob Two-Two & the Dinosaur. Richler, Mordecai. Foster, Frances, ed. Rosenthal, Eileen, designed by. LC 86-20108. 96p. (gr. 1-5). 1987. 11.95 (0-394-88704-2); lib. bdg. 11.99 (0-394-98704-7) Knopf Bks Yng Read.
Ezekiel, Karen. Zoot Zoot Zaggle Splot: Or, What to Do with a Scary Dream. Ezekiel, Karen. LC 89-35425. 40p. (ps-3). 1989. 14.95 (0-943173-50-7) Harbinger AZ.

F

Faber, Gail. Pasquala: The Story of a California Indian Girl. Faber, Gail & Lasagna, Michele. 95p. (Orig.). (gr. 4-8). 1990. 12.95 (0-936480-07-6); pap. 9.95 (0-936480-06-8); tchr's. guide 8.95 (0-936480-08-4) Magpie Pubns.
Faber, Roger A. Birds on a Wire. Faber, Roger A. (ps-1). Date not set. pap. write for info. (1-880122-06-5) White Stone.
—Peter Pig Likes to Dig. Faber, Roger A. 32p. (gr. 1-2). Date not set. 12.00 (1-880122-05-7) White Stone.
Fabian, Margaret W. My Friend Luke, the Stenciller. Fabian, Margaret W. LC 83-50689. 35p. (gr. 3-4). 1987. pap. 8.95 over boards (0-931474-25-6) TBW Bks.
Fabo, J. A. Perez. Paso a Paso, Nivel 4. 3rd ed. 256p. (Orig.). (gr. 4). 1991. pap. text ed. 7.95 (1-56328-014-0) Edit Plaza Mayor.
Facklam, Paul. The Biggest Bug Book. Facklam, Margery. LC 92-24517. 1993. write for info. (0-316-27389-9) Little.
—The Brain: Magnificent Mind Machine. Facklam, Margery & Facklam, Howard. LC 81-47529. 118p. (gr. 7 up). 1982. 12.95 (0-15-211388-6, HB Juv Bks) HarBrace.
—Changes in the Wind: The Earth's Shifting Climate. Facklam, Margery & Facklam, Howard. LC 85-5475. 128p. (gr. 7 up). 1986. 14.95 (0-15-216115-5, HB Juv Bks) HarBrace.
Fadden, David K. Cave of Falling Water. Ovecka, Janice. LC 92-56713. 1992. 9.95 (0-933050-98-4) New Eng Pr VT.

Fadden, John K. Keepers of the Animals: Native American Stories & Wildlife Activities for Children. Caduto, Michael & Bruchac, Joseph. Deloria, Vine, Jr., intro. by. LC 91-71364. 288p. (gr. k-7). 1991. 19.95 (*1-55591-088-2*); tchr's. guide, 48p. 9.95 (*1-55591-107-2*) Fulcrum Pub.

Fadden, John K. & Wood, Carol. Keepers of the Earth: Native American Stories, & Environmental Activities for Children. Caduto, Michael J. & Bruchac, Joseph. Momaday, N. Scott, intro. by. LC 88-3620. 209p. (gr. 1-6). 1988. indexed 19.95 (*1-55591-027-0*) Fulcrum Pub.

Fagan, Todd. Zaccheus Meets Jesus. Stortz, Diane. 28p. (ps). 1992. 2.50 (*0-87403-958-4*, 24-03598) Standard Pub.

Fagan, Todd, et al. A King Is Born. Huff, Brenda. 20p. Date not set. 15.95 (*1-883909-01-5*) Wisdom Tree.

Fagan, Wendy. Jesus Loves Us. Odor, Ruth S. LC 91-67211. 32p. (gr. 5-7). 1992. saddle-stitched 5.99 (*0-87403-934-7*, 24-03564) Standard Pub.

Fahey, Cathy. Ming's Monster. DeBeer, Liz. LC 92-70985. 44p. (gr. k-3). 1993. 7.95 (*1-55523-521-2*) Winston-Derek.

Fahrion, Michael. The Care Bears: Try, Try Again! Kahn, Peggy. LC 85-2152. 40p. (ps-3). 1985. lib. bdg. 4.99 (*0-394-97503-0*) Random Bks Yng Read.

Fahs, Anita. Bizzy Bubbles: Santa's Littlest Elf. Jurie, Jeri. LC 77-82535. (gr. k-6). 1977. 10.95x (*0-686-01311-5*); pap. 6.95x (*0-686-01312-3*) Al Fresco.

Fahsbender, Thomas. The Bumblebee & the Ram. Rudner, Barry. LC 89-81585. 32p. (Orig.). 1989. pap. 4.95 (*0-925928-03-8*) Tiny Thought.

—The Handstand. Rudner, Barry. 32p. 1991. pap. 4.95 (*0-925928-05-4*) Tiny Thought.

—The Littlest Tall Fellow. Rudner, Barry. Carraro, J. M., ed. 28p. (gr. k-6). 1989. pap. 4.95 (*0-925928-00-3*) Tiny Thought.

—Nonsense. Rudner, Barry. (gr. k-6). 1990. write for info. (*0-925928-04-6*) Tiny Thought.

Faigin, Cecilia, jt. illus. see Traba, Henry.

Fain, Cheryl G. Lizzie - Queen of the Cattle Trails. Crawford, Ann F. 64p. (gr. 4-7). 1990. lib. bdg. 12.95 (*0-87443-091-7*) Benson.

Fair, Sylvia. The Bedspread. Fair, Sylvia. LC 81-11152. 32p. (gr. k-3). 1982. 14.95 (*0-688-00877-1*) Morrow Jr Bks.

Fairbanks, Eugene B. Earth Science: A Concise Competency Review. rev. ed. Koenig, Herbert G., et al. Gamsey, Wayne, ed. 96p. (gr. 7-12). 1991. pap. text ed. 4.11 (*0-935487-44-1*) N & N Pub Co.

—English Writing: Fifteen-Day Competency Review Text. McCabe, Ann C. & Fairbanks, Eugene B. Gamsey, Wayne H., ed. 160p. (Orig.). (gr. 7-12). 1992. pap. text ed. 4.95 (*0-935487-56-5*) N & N Pub Co.

—Global Studies: A Competency Review Text. 3rd ed. Osborne, John, et al. Gamsey, Wayne & Stich, Paul, eds. 384p. (gr. 7-12). 1992. pap. text ed. 8.33 (*0-935487-37-9*) N & N Pub Co.

—Global Studies: A Regents Review Text. 6th ed. Osborne, John, et al. Gamsey, Wayne & Stich, Paul, eds. 448p. (gr. 7-12). 1992. pap. text ed. 6.22 (*0-935487-35-2*) N & N Pub Co.

—Global Studies: Ten Day Competency Review. 2nd ed. Osborne, John, et al. Gamsey, Wayne & Stich, Paul, eds. 128p. (gr. 7-12). 1992. pap. text ed. 4.95 (*0-935487-53-0*) N & N Pub Co.

—Global Studies: Ten Day Regents Review. 2nd ed. Osborne, John, et al. Gamsey, Wayne & Stich, Paul, eds. 128p. (gr. 7-12). 1992. pap. text ed. 4.95 (*0-935487-48-4*) N & N Pub Co.

—Life Science: A Concise Competency Review. rev. ed. Koenig, Herbert G., et al. Gamsey, Wayne, ed. 96p. (gr. 7-12). 1991. pap. text ed. 4.11 (*0-935487-42-5*) N & N Pub Co.

—Physical Science: A Concise Competency Review. rev. ed. Koenig, Herbert G., et al. Gamsey, Wayne, ed. 96p. (gr. 7-12). 1991. pap. text ed. 4.11 (*0-935487-46-8*) N & N Pub Co.

—RCT Science Review. 6th ed. Koenig, Herbert G., et al. Gamsey, Wayne H., ed. 288p. (gr. 7-12). 1992. pap. text ed. 5.17 (*0-935487-09-3*) N & N Pub Co.

—United States History & Government: A Competency Review Text. 2nd ed. Stich, Paul, et al. Gamsey, Wayne, ed. 384p. (gr. 7-12). 1992. pap. text ed. 8.33 (*0-935487-20-4*) N & N Pub Co.

—United States History & Government: A Regents Review Text. 6th ed. Stich, Paul, et al. Gamsey, Wayne, ed. 416p. (gr. 7-12). 1992. pap. text ed. 6.22 (*0-935487-21-2*) N & N Pub Co.

—United States History & Government: Ten Day Competency. rev. ed. Stich, Paul, et al. Gamsey, Wayne, ed. 128p. (gr. 7-12). 1992. pap. text ed. 4.95 (*0-935487-54-9*) N & N Pub Co.

—United States History & Government: Ten Day Regents Review. rev. ed. Stich, Paul, et al. Gamsey, Wayne, ed. 128p. (gr. 7-12). 1992. pap. text ed. 4.95 (*0-935487-49-2*) N & N Pub Co.

Fairbend, Kerstin. A Car Full of Songs. Paxton, Tom & Scharrett, Darcy. 84p. (Orig.). (ps-6). 1991. 14.95 (*0-89524-632-5*) Cherry Lane.

—Tom Paxton's Children's Songbook. Paxton, Tom & Scharrett, Darcy. 68p. (Orig.). (ps-5). 1990. 12.95 (*0-89524-563-9*) Cherry Lane.

Fairbridge, John. Figaro. Barnes, Frances. LC 93-132. 1994. write for info. (*0-383-03686-0*) SRA Schl Grp.

Fairclough, Chris, photos by. Build It! Pluckrose, Henry. 32p. (gr. k-4). 1990. PLB 10.90 (*0-531-14062-8*) Watts.

—Change It! Pluckrose, Henry. LC 89-70746. 32p. (gr. k-4). 1990. PLB 10.90 (*0-531-14064-4*) Watts.

—Clay. Hull, Jeannie. LC 89-9959. 48p. (gr. 3-6). 1989. PLB 12.40 (*0-531-10757-4*) Watts.

—Clean It! Pluckrose, Henry. 32p. (gr. k-4). 1990. PLB 10.90 (*0-531-14063-6*) Watts.

—Cut It! Pluckrose, Henry. LC 89-14759. 32p. (ps-k). 1989. PLB 10.90 (*0-531-10849-X*) Watts.

—France. James, Ian. LC 88-50362. 32p. (gr. 3-6). 1989. PLB 11.90 (*0-531-10640-3*) Watts.

—Gymnastics. Wood, Tim. LC 89-50205. 32p. (gr. k-3). 1989. PLB 11.90 (*0-531-10826-0*) Watts.

—Ice Skating. Wood, Tim. 32p. (gr. k-4). 1990. PLB 11.40 (*0-531-14051-2*) Watts.

—Motor Racing. Wood, Tim. LC 89-50201. 32p. (gr. k-3). 1989. PLB 11.40 (*0-531-10828-7*) Watts.

—Mountain Biking. Wood, Tim. 32p. (gr. k-4). 1989. PLB 11.40 (*0-531-10829-5*) Watts.

—Puppets. Wright, Lyndie. 48p. (gr. 3-6). 1989. PLB 12.40 (*0-531-10635-7*) Watts.

—Wear It! Pluckrose, Henry. 32p. (gr. k-4). 1990. PLB 10.90 (*0-531-14065-2*) Watts.

Falconer, Elizabeth. The House That Jack Built. Falconer, Elizabeth. 32p. 1990. 13.95 (*0-8249-8459-5*, Ideals Child) Hambleton-Hill.

—The Owl & the Pussycat. Lear, Edward. 16p. (ps-2). 1993. pop-up bk. 12.95 (*0-8249-8571-0*, Ideals Child) Hambleton-Hill.

Falconer, Elizabeth, jt. illus. see Scruton, Clive.

Fales, et al. Wormwood. Siembieda, Kevin & Truman, Timothy. Marciniszyn, Alex, et al, eds. 152p. (Orig.). (gr. 8 up). 1993. pap. 15.95 (*0-916211-59-2*, 809) Palladium Bks.

Fales, Jim. Let's Celebrate Math. Patterson, Claire. 82p. (gr. 4-9). 1991. pap. 8.95 (*0-9623835-6-2*) Pieces of Lrning.

Fales, Kevin & Dombrowski, James. Mutants of the Yucatan. Wujcik, Erick. Marciniszyn, Alex, ed. 48p. (Orig.). (gr. 8 up). 1990. pap. 7.95 (*0-916211-44-4*, 511) Palladium Bks.

Fales, Kevin & MacDougall, Larry. Mutants in Avalon. Wallis, James & Siembieda, Kevin. Marciniszyn, Alex & Bartold, Thomas, eds. 80p. (Orig.). (gr. 8 up). 1991. pap. 9.95 (*0-916211-47-9*, 513) Palladium Bks.

Falk, Barbara. Animal Lingo. Conrad, Pam. LC 93-22163. Date not set. 15.00 (*0-06-023401-6*); PLB 14.89 (*0-06-023402-4*) HarpC Child Bks.

Falk, Barbara B. Grusha. Falk, Barbara B. LC 92-14980. 32p. (ps-3). 1993. 15.00 (*0-06-021299-3*); PLB 14.89 (*0-06-021300-0*) HarpC Child Bks.

Falla, Dominique. Goodnight. Coad, Penelope. LC 92-31960. 1993. 4.25 (*0-383-03569-4*) SRA Schl Grp.

Falter, John. Reader's Digest Best Loved Books for Young Readers: The Adventures of Huckleberry Finn. Twain, Mark. Ogburn, Jackie, ed. 192p. (gr. 4-12). 1989. 3.99 (*0-945260-30-X*) Choice Pub NY.

—Reader's Digest Best Loved Books for Young Readers: The Adventures of Tom Sawyer. Twain, Mark. Ogburn, Jackie, ed. 136p. (gr. 4-12). 1989. 3.99 (*0-945260-19-9*) Choice Pub NY.

Faltico, Mary L. Never Too Busy. Whalin, Terry. 28p. (ps-k). 1993. 4.99 (*0-7847-0038-9*, 24-03828) Standard Pub.

—Song of the Seed. Stagg, Mildred A. & Lamb, Cecile. 28p. (ps). 1992. 2.50 (*0-87403-956-8*, 24-03596) Standard Pub.

Falwell, Cathryn. Feast for Ten. Falwell, Cathryn. LC 92-35512. 32p. (ps-3). 1993. 14.95 (*0-395-62037-6*, Clarion Bks) HM.

—Nicky & Alex. Falwell, Cathryn. 32p. (ps). 1992. 5.95 (*0-395-56915-X*, Clarion Bks) HM.

—Nicky & Grandpa. Falwell, Catherine. 32p. (ps). 1991. 5.70 (*0-395-56917-6*, Clarion Bks) HM.

—Nicky Loves Daddy. Falwell, Cathryn. 32p. (ps). 1992. 5.70 (*0-395-60820-1*, Clarion Bks) HM.

—Nicky, 1-2-3. Falwell, Cathryn. Briley, Dorthy, ed. 24p. (ps). 1991. 5.70 (*0-395-56913-3*, Clarion Bks) HM.

—Nicky's Walk. Falwell, Catherine. 32p. (ps). 1991. 5.70 (*0-395-56914-1*, Clarion Bks) HM.

—Shape Space. Falwell, Cathryn. 32p. (ps-2). 1992. 13.45 (*0-395-61305-1*, Clarion Bks) HM.

—Where's Nicky? Falwell, Cathryn. Briley, Cathryn, ed. 24p. (ps). 1991. 5.70 (*0-395-56936-2*, Clarion Bks) HM.

Fancher, Lou & Johnson, Steve. Peach & Blue. Kilborne, Sarah S. LC 93-26562. 1994. write for info. (*0-679-83929-1*); PLB write for info. (*0-679-93929-6*) Knopf Bks Yng Read.

Fancher, Lou, jt. illus. see Johnson, Steve.

Fanta. The Devoted Friend. Wilde, Oscar. Batmanglij, N. Khalili, tr. from ENG. LC 87-31689. 70p. (gr. 4 up). 1988. 15.00 (*0-934211-16-7*); Bilingual Eng.-Persian. 15.00 (*0-934211-10-8*) Mage Pubs Inc.

—When the Elephants Came. Yushij, Nima. Evans, Mariam & Batmanglij, M., eds. Evans, Mariam, tr. from PER. LC 87-31690. 32p. (gr. 4 up). 1988. 18.50 (*0-934211-15-9*); English-Persian Version. 18.50 (*0-934211-09-4*) Mage Pubs Inc.

Farago, Julius. Going to Grandma's: A Sing, Color 'n Say Coloring Book Package. Paxton, Lenore & Siadi, Phillip. (ps-3). 1991. Includes cassette tape. pap. 6.95 (*1-880449-00-5*) Wrldkids Pr.

Farcot, Kimberly I. Imagine: A Journey Through the Child's Imagination. Farcot, Kimberly I. LC 92-90202. 32p. (Orig.). (gr. k-4). 1992. pap. 8.95 (*0-9632372-2-5*) Custom Artwk.

Fargo, Jerry. Special Needs: Special Answers. Pope, Lillie, et al. (gr. k-6). 1979. 19.95 (*0-87594-181-8*) Book-Lab.

Fargo, Todd. Buddy's Shadow. Becker, Shirley. 32p. (ps-2). 1992. Repr. of 1991 ed. 13.95 (*0-944727-19-0*) Jason & Nordic Pubs.

—Cookie. Kneeland, Linda C. 32p. (ps-2). 1989. pap. 6.95 (*0-944727-05-0*) Jason & Nordic Pubs.

—Cookie. Kneeland, Linda. 32p. (ps-3). 1992. Repr. of 1989 ed. 13.95 (*0-944727-16-6*) Jason & Nordic Pubs.

Farley, A. C. American Combat Vehicle Handbook. Wiseman, Loren K. 104p. (Orig.). (gr. 9-12). 1990. pap. 12.00 (*1-55878-061-0*) Game Designers.

Farley, Brendon. Lessons Learned: Students with Learning Disabilities, Ages 7-19, Share What They've Learned about Life & Learning. Fullen, Dave. 40p. (Orig.). (gr. 1 up). 1993. pap. 4.95 (*1-881650-02-2*) Mntn Bks.

—The Mountain Song. Fullen, Dave. Oremus, Earl, contrib. by. 20p. (gr. 1-6). 1992. pap. 14.95 incl. cass. (*1-881650-00-6*) Mntn Bks.

—A Nest in the Gale. Fullen, Dave. 80p. (Orig.). (gr. 2-6). 1993. incl. audio cassette 24.95 (*1-881650-03-0*); pap. 18.95 incl. audio cassette (*1-881650-01-4*) Mntn Bks.

Farley, Rick. Capturing Nature: The Writings & Art of John James Audubon. Roop, Peter & Roop, Connie, eds. LC 92-15662. 1993. 16.95 (*0-8027-8204-3*); PLB 17.85 (*0-8027-8205-1*) Walker & Co.

Farmer, Andrew. Look at Insects. rev. ed. Kirkpatrick, Rena K. LC 84-26228. 32p. (gr. 2-4). 1985. PLB 17.28 (*0-8172-2351-7*); pap. 4.95 (*0-8114-6897-6*) Raintree Steck-V.

Farmer, Andrew & Green, Robina. Brain. Mathers, Douglas. LC 90-42883. 32p. (gr. 4-6). 1992. PLB 11.89 (*0-8167-2090-8*); pap. 3.95 (*0-8167-2091-6*) Troll Assocs.

—Ears. Mathers, Douglas. LC 90-42176. 32p. (gr. 4-6). 1992. lib. bdg. 11.89 (*0-8167-2092-4*); pap. text ed. 3.95 (*0-8167-2093-2*) Troll Assocs.

—Eyes. Jedrosz, Aleksander. LC 90-42177. 32p. (gr. 4-6). 1992. lib. bdg. 11.89 (*0-8167-2094-0*); pap. text ed. 3.95 (*0-8167-2095-9*) Troll Assocs.

—Heart & Lungs. Saunderson, Jane. LC 90-42881. 32p. (gr. 4-6). 1992. PLB 11.89 (*0-8167-2096-7*); pap. text ed. 3.95 (*0-8167-2097-5*) Troll Assocs.

—Muscles & Bones. Saunderson, Jane. LC 90-42882. 32p. (gr. 4-6). 1992. lib. bdg. 11.89 (*0-8167-2088-6*); pap. text ed. 3.95 (*0-8167-2089-4*) Troll Assocs.

Farmer, Lynne. First Animal Words. 26p. 1993. 3.50 (*0-7214-1521-0*) Ladybird Bks.

Farnsworth, Bill. The Illustrated Children's Bible. LC 93-16222. (gr. 1-8). 1993. 19.95 (*0-15-232876-9*) HarBrace.

Farquhar, Kristin. Voices of the Earth: Florida's Environmental Storybook, Vol. 1: Coastal Creatures. Farquhar, Kristin. Wright, Betty & Griffin, Kimbra, eds. 48p. (Orig.). (gr. 2-3). 1992. pap. 7.95 (*0-9632864-0-4*) ECO-ALERT Pubns.

Farr, Gina. A Rime of Verdancy: Poems of Nature. White, Jesse. (Orig.). (gr. 12). Date not set. pap. 7.95 (*0-9637176-9-3*) Jesse White.

Farrar, Rick. Cantus Cunarum: English Nursery Rhymes in Latin. Barrett, Bonnie. (LAT.). 30p. (Orig.). (gr. 6-12). 1991. spiral bdg. 2.10 (*0-939507-00-5*, B707) Amer Classical.

Farre, Marie. Long Ago in a Castle. Thibault, Dominique. 40p. (gr. k-5). 1993. PLB 9.95 (*1-56674-071-1*, HTS Bks) Forest Hse.

Farris, Diane. In Dolphin Time. Farris, Diane. LC 92-42512. 32p. 1994. RSBE 14.95 (*0-02-734365-0*, Four Winds) Macmillan Child Grp.

Farris, Joseph. Louis Phillips' Loose Leaf: The Wackiest School Notebook Yet. Phillips, Louis. LC 89-28082. 48p. (gr. 5 up). 1990. SBE 11.95 (*0-689-31437-X*, Atheneum Child Bk) Macmillan Child Grp.

Farrow, T. C. The Dragon in the Cliff: A Novel Based on the Life of Mary Anning. Cole, Shelia. LC 90-40455. (gr. 4-7). 1991. 12.95 (*0-688-10196-8*) Lothrop.

Fasen, Gary, jt. illus. see Fasen, Steve.

Fasen, Steve & Fasen, Gary. All Through the Night. Boulton, Harold. (gr. 2 up). 1988. 13.95 (*0-687-01015-2*) Abingdon.

Fast, Marti. Old Mission San Luis Obispo de Tolosa: A Miniature Cut-Out & Color Model. Anderson, Kathleen. 8p. (Orig.). (gr. 4). 1990. pap. 3.95 (*0-945092-12-1*) EZ Nature.

Fast, Suellen M., photos by. America's Daughters. Fast, Sueller M. 100p. (Orig.). (gr. k up). pap. 19.00 (*0-935281-13-4*) Daughter Cult.

Faucheux, Wallace. A Cave to Share. Huffman, Marlys B. 22p. (Orig.). 1991. pap. 3.95 (*0-8198-0733-8*) St Paul Bks.

Faulkner, John. My Mom Hates Me in January. Delton, Judy. LC 77-5749. (gr. 1-3). 1977. PLB 11.95 (*0-8075-5356-5*) A Whitman.

Faulkner, Matt. The Amazing Voyage of Jackie Grace. Faulkner, Matt. 1991. pap. 3.95 (*0-590-44860-9*) Scholastic Inc.

—The Moon Clock. Faulkner, Matt. 56p. 1991. 14.95 (*0-590-41593-X*, Scholastic Hardcover) Scholastic Inc.

Faust, Jeff. Wonderpup. Macht, Debra. 40p. (gr. 4-6). 1992. 15.00 (*0-930339-03-7*) Maxrom Pr.

Favreau, Luc. Giant Works: Underground, over Water, in the Air. Barbey, Dorine. Bogard, Vicki, tr. from FRE. LC 91-48167. 38p. (gr. k-5). 1992. 4.95 (0-944589-44-8) Young Discovery Lib.
—Giant Works: Underground, over Water, in the Air. Barbey, Dorine. 40p. (gr. k-5). 1993. PLB 12.95 (1-56674-059-2, HTS Bks) Forest Hse.
—Volcano! Krafft, Maurice. Bogard, Vicki, tr. from FRE. LC 92-968. 40p. (gr. k-5). 1992. 4.95 (0-944589-41-3) Young Discovery Lib.
—Volcano! Krafft, Maurice. 40p. (gr. k-5). 1993. PLB 9.95 (1-56674-074-6, HTS Bks) Forest Hse.
Fax, Elton. Genghis Khan & the Mongol Horde. Lamb, Harold. LC 90-6328. viii, 182p. (gr. 5 up). 1990. Repr. of 1954 ed. lib. bdg. 16.50 (0-208-02287-2, Linnet) Shoe String.
Fax, Elton C. Take a Walk in Their Shoes. Turner, Glennette T. LC 89-9700. 176p. (gr. 4-8). 1989. 15.00 (0-525-65006-7, Cobblehill Bks) Dutton Child Bks.
—Take a Walk in Their Shoes: Biographies of Fourteen Outstanding African Americans - with Skits about Each to Act Out. Turner, Glennette T. LC 92-19524. 176p. (gr. 3-7). 1992. pap. 5.99 (0-14-036250-9) Puffin Bks.
Faycheux, Wallace P., Jr. The Lily Pad Four & Friends. DeLuca, June M. 32p. (gr. k-2). 1992. pap. 2.95 (0-8198-4431-4) St Paul Bks.
Fearber, Sharon, jt. illus. see Lautermilch, John.

Featherman, John. Spenser's Important Work: Introducing Your Child To Day Care. Boylan, Kristi M. 32p. (Orig.). 1993. pap. 7.99 (1-883497-00-0) Parent Track.
SPENSER'S IMPORTANT WORK is the first in a series of 32-page, four-color illustrated children's books for children who attend child care centers. Each of the five books in the series is designed to help young children become acquainted with the day to day events of child care facilities. At the back of each book is a section called Parent's Guide which presents parents with effective ways to make their child's experience at day care a positive one. SPENSER'S IMPORTANT WORK introduces children to the day care experience & helps lessen separation anxiety. Book II/SPENSER'S NEW FRIEND, teaches children how to make friends at day care. Book III/SPENSER GETS THE POX teaches children & parents about communicable diseases at day care. Book IV/LATE TO SCHOOL AGAIN teaches children the importance of being on time. Book V/SPENSER'S NEW ROOM helps children make the adjustment in changing teachers or rooms at day care. Each book retails at $7.99. Cost for ordering 5 or more books in the series is $4.00 per book. Order by sending check or money order to The Parent Track Publications, 3210 Commander Rd., Carrollton, TX 75006. Or call 214-269-2160.
Publisher Provided Annotation.

Fechner, Amrei. The Kitten Who Couldn't Purr. Titus, Eve. LC 90-13418. 32p. (ps up). 1991. Repr. 12.95 (0-688-09363-9); PLB 12.88 (0-688-09364-7, Morrow Jr Bks) Morrow Jr Bks.
Fedorov, Mikhail. The Knot in the Tracks. Plumini, Roberto. Holmes, Olivia, tr. from ITA. LC 93-20343. 32p. 1993. 14.00 (0-685-67813-X, Tambourine Bks); PLB 13.93 (0-688-11167-X, Tambourine Bks) Morrow.
Fedotousky, Alex. Dingle Dorts vs Dingle Saurs. Fedotousky, Alex. 32p. 1993. pap. text ed. 2.75 (0-9638756-0-4) Skylght Studios.
Feelings, Tom. Daydreamers. Greenfield, Eloise. (gr. k up). 1981. 13.95 (0-8037-2137-4) Dial Bks Young.
—Daydreamers. Greenfield, Eloise. LC 80-27262. (gr. k up). 1985. pap. 4.95 (0-8037-0167-5) Dial Bks Young.
—From Slave to Abolitionist: The Life of William Wells Brown. Warner, Lucille S. LC 76-2288. 144p. (gr. 6 up). 1993. 13.99 (0-8037-2743-7) Dial Bks Young.
—Jambo Means Hello: Swahili Alphabet Book. Feelings, Muriel. LC 73-15441. 56p. (gr. k-3). 1985. Repr. of 1974 ed. 15.00 (0-8037-4346-7); PLB 13.89 (0-8037-4350-5) Dial Bks Young.
—Moja Means One: A Swahili Counting Book. Feelings, Muriel. LC 76-134856. (ps-3). 1987. 13.95 (0-8037-5776-X); PLB 13.89 (0-8037-5777-8) Dial Bks Young.
—Something on My Mind. Grimes, Nikki. LC 77-86266. 32p. (gr. k up). 1986. pap. 4.95 (0-8037-0273-6) Dial Bks Young.
—To Be a Slave. Lester, Julius. LC 68-28738. (gr. 7-12). 1968. 14.95 (0-8037-8955-6) Dial Bks Young.
Feelings, Tom & Katzman, Marylyn. African Crafts. Kerina, Jane. LC 69-18916. (gr. 2-6). 1970. PLB 13.95 (0-87460-084-7) Lion Bks.
Feiffer, Jules. The Man in the Ceiling. Feiffer, Jules. LC 92-59953. 192p. (gr. 3-7). 1993. 15.00 (0-06-205035-4); PLB 14.89 (0-06-205036-2) HarpC Child Bks.
—The Phantom Tollbooth. Juster, Norton. LC 61-13202. 256p. (gr. 3-7). 1993. Repr. of 1961 ed. 3.95 (0-394-82037-1) Knopf Bks Yng Read.
Feign, Larry. Haciendome Cargo de Mi Vida: Opciones, Cambios y Yo. Harmon, Ed & Jarmin, Marge. Lerma, Olivia, tr. (SPA.). (gr. 5-12). 1993. pap. 9.95 (0-918588-26-X) Barksdale Foun.
—Taking Active Charge of Your Life: Facilitator's Manual. Harmon, Ed & Jarmin, Marge. 149p. (gr. 5-12). 1987. Repr. of 1984 ed. bk. & video or Filmstrip 175.00 (0-918588-09-X) Barksdale Foun.
—Taking Charge of My Life: Choices, Changes & Me. Harmon, Ed & Jarmin, Marge. LC 88-988. 184p. (Orig.). (gr. 5-12). 1988. pap. 9.95 (0-918588-10-3) Barksdale Foun.
Feiza, Anne. For the Love of Animals: Six Delightful Songs & a Story about How the Children Save the Animals. Rosenbaum, Cindy, et al. 24p. (Orig.). (ps-4). 1992. pap. text ed. 12.95 incl. audio tape (1-881567-00-1) Happy Kids Prods.
Felber, Michael. Insects. Tesar, Jenny. 64p. (gr. 4-8). 1993. jacketed 14.95 (1-56711-054-1) Blackbirch.
Feld, Goldie. Torah Shapes. Sebarg, R. & Zakutinsky, Adina. 12p. (ps). 1987. 4.95 (0-911643-08-7) Aura Bklyn.
Feldman, Barbara. Stephen's Frog. Feldman, Barbara. 24p. (ps-1). 1991. PLB 14.95 (1-55037-200-9, Pub. by Annick CN); pap. 4.95 (1-55037-201-7, Pub. by Annick CN) Firefly Bks Ltd.
Feldman, Lynne. Henry's Tower. Rosen, David. LC 84-61581. 36p. (gr. k-5). 1984. 10.95 (0-930905-01-6); pap. 4.95 (0-930905-00-8) Platypus Bks.
Feldman, Roper. Freeman Earns a Bike. Brumpton, Karen B. LC 84-60947. 32p. (ps-4). 1984. 10.95 (0-917487-00-1) McVie Pub.
Feldmann, Susan. Seaside Stories. Gilbert, Jeanette. Barta, Beverly, ed. 16p. (Orig.). (gr. 1-4). 1990. pap. write for info. (0-9623503-0-3) Palm Pub.
Felix, Monique. Air: My First Nature Books. Benedict, Kitty. 32p. (gr. k-2). 1993. pap. 2.95 (1-56189-167-3) Amer Educ Pub.
—All about Wool. Jobin, Claire. Matthews, Sarah, tr. from FRE. LC 87-31751. 38p. (gr. k-5). 1988. 4.95 (0-944589-18-9, 189) Young Discovery Lib.
—The Alphabet. Felix, Monique, created by. (gr. 5 up). 1992. PLB 10.95 (0-88682-563-6) Creative Ed.
—The Ant: My First Nature Books. Benedict, Kitty. 32p. (gr. k-2). 1993. pap. 2.95 (1-56189-174-6) Amer Educ Pub.
—The Colors. Felix, Monique. LC 91-4478. 32p. (gr. k-3). 1991. 8.95 (1-55670-227-2) Stewart Tabori & Chang.
—The Cow: My First Nature Books. Benedict, Kitty. 32p. (gr. k-2). 1993. pap. 2.95 (1-56189-177-0) Amer Educ Pub.
—Earth: My First Nature Books. Benedict, Kitty. 32p. (gr. k-2). 1993. pap. 2.95 (1-56189-168-1) Amer Educ Pub.
—The Earthworm: My First Nature Books. Benedict, Kitty. 32p. (gr. k-2). 1993. pap. 2.95 (1-56189-176-2) Amer Educ Pub.
—The Egg: My First Nature Books. Benedict, Kitty. 32p. (gr. k-2). 1993. pap. 2.95 (1-56189-175-4) Amer Educ Pub.
—Fire: My First Nature Books. Benedict, Kitty. 32p. (gr. k-2). 1993. pap. 2.95 (1-56189-173-8) Amer Educ Pub.
—The Gnat: My First Nature Books. Benedict, Kitty. 32p. (gr. k-2). 1993. pap. 2.95 (1-56189-171-1) Amer Educ Pub.
—Hansel & Gretel. Grimm, Jacob & Grimm, Wilhelm K. 32p. (gr. 6 up). 1983. PLB 13.95s.p. (0-87191-935-4) Creative Ed.
—The House. Felix, Monique. LC 91-281. 32p. (gr. k-3). 1991. 8.95 (1-55670-225-6) Stewart Tabori & Chang.

—Mouse Book Series, 6 bks. Felix, Monique. 32p. (Orig.). (ps-k). 1993. Set. pap. 17.70 (1-56189-077-4) Amer Educ Pub.
Almost everyone has heard of a mouse in an attic, or a mouse in a garage, but a mouse trapped in a book? Never! That is, until now. Within the wonderfully illustrated pages of the Mouse Books, Swiss illustrator Monique Felix has created six unique adventures. Each story begins with the mouse innocently eating her way into a book & from there the fun begins. Where will she go? What will she do? How will she escape? These are all the questions that only the mouse can answer. But you can be sure that no matter where the mouse goes, an exciting adventure will closely follow. So come, enter the pages of these visual escapades--there are no words--& explore the world of a little mouse trapped in a book. Titles include: Numbers, ISBN 1-56189-091-X, $2.95; Opposites, ISBN 1-56189-092-8, $2.95; Colors, ISBN 1-56189-093-6, $2.95; Alphabet, ISBN 1-56189-094-4, $2.95; Wind, ISBN 1-56189-095-2, $2.95; House, ISBN 1-56189-096-0, $2.95. *Publisher Provided Annotation.*

—The Numbers. Felix, Monique, created by. (gr. 5 up). 1992. PLB 10.95 (0-88682-562-8) Creative Ed.
—The Oak: My First Nature Books. Benedict, Kitty. 32p. (gr. k-2). 1993. pap. 2.95 (1-56189-170-3) Amer Educ Pub.
—The Opposites. LC 92-16357. (gr. 5 up). 1992. PLB 10.95 (0-88682-569-5) Creative Ed.
—The Plane. Felix, Monique. LC 92-44058. 1993. PLB 10.95s.p. (0-88682-604-7) Creative Ed.
—The Toad. Benedict, Kitty. Soutler-Perrot, Andrienne, contrib. by. LC 92-14165. (gr. 5 up). 1992. PLB 10.95 (0-88682-568-7) Creative Ed.
—The Toad: My First Nature Books. Benedict, Kitty. 32p. (gr. k-2). 1993. pap. 2.95 (1-56189-178-9) Amer Educ Pub.
—Water: My First Nature Books. Benedict, Kitty. 32p. (gr. k-2). 1993. pap. 2.95 (1-56189-169-X) Amer Educ Pub.
—The Wind. Felix, Monique. LC 91-277. 32p. (gr. k-3). 1991. 8.95 (1-55670-226-4) Stewart Tabori & Chang.
—The Wolf: My First Nature Books. Benedict, Kitty. 32p. (gr. k-2). 1993. pap. 2.95 (1-56189-172-X) Amer Educ Pub.
Felts, Shirley. Frightful Winged Creatures. Hoy, Ken. 5p. (ps-3). 1993. 12.95 (0-8249-8618-0, Ideals Publ) Hambleton-Hill.
—The Secret World of Polly Flint. Cresswell, Helen. LC 91-15531. 176p. (gr. 3-7). 1991. pap. 3.95 (0-689-71532-3, Aladdin) Macmillan Child Grp.
—Witch Words: Poems of Magic & Mystery. Fisher, Robert, ed. 80p. (gr. 3-6). 1987. laminated boards 9.95 (0-571-14559-0) Faber & Faber.
—Witch Words: Poems of Magic & Mystery. Fisher, Robert, ed. 70p. (gr. 2 up). 1991. pap. 4.95 (0-571-16319-X) Faber & Faber.
Fender, Susan. Color & Discover: A Children's Guide to the North Carolina Museum of Art. Suarez, Diana. LC 87-62986. 40p. (Orig.). (ps-6). 1987. pap. 3.50 (0-88259-956-9) NCMA.

Fenton, Mary F. & Kostecke, Nancy. Worms Eat Our Garbage: Classroom Activities for a Better Environment. Appelhof, Mary, et al. Dindal, Daniel L., pref. by. 232p. (Orig.). (gr. 4 up). 1993. Wkbk. 19.95 (0-942256-05-0) Flower Pr.
WORMS EAT OUR GARBAGE integrates earthworms with ecology, composting, natural resources, soil science, conservation, the environment, recycling, & biology in a curriculum guide & workbook designed for grades 4-8. Over 150 activities use the world of worms to help students develop science, language, math, problem-solving, & critical-thinking skills. Whether the book is used at home, in a classroom, outdoor education center, nature center or master composting program, users will find themselves drawn in & captivated by the diversity & scope of information presented. Dr. Dan Dindal, Distinguished Professor of Soil Ecology at SUNY in Syracuse, says in the preface, "Even though this book was prepared as a teaching aid for elementary & middle school grades, its potential use extends far beyond. Anyone who is fascinated & wishes to learn more about earthworms, as well

as those whose active quest is to be an exciting & creative educator, will be served well by this book." Barbara Hannaford, teacher of 6-8 grade math & science, says, "The format is appealing to both teachers & students & the content is fantastic." Teacher's guide, 400 illustrations, resources, bibliography, 16 appendices, glossary, & index. See also WORMS EAT MY GARBAGE for how to set up & maintain worm composting systems. To order: Flower Press 616-327-0108. *Publisher Provided Annotation.*

Fenton, Ronald, jt. illus. see Scruton, Clive.
Fenton, Ronald, jt. illus. see Wood, Elizabeth.
Feraris, Kathy. Good Day, Blue Goose. Mallett, Jerry J. & Ervin, Timothy S. 28p. (ps-2). 1992. 9.10 (0-7804-3992-9, 120051) Perma-Bound.
—Good Day, Blue Goose: Paper Big Book. Mallett, Jerry J. & Ervin, Timothy S. 28p. (Orig.). (ps-2). 1992. pap. 22.00 (0-7804-3994-2, 120052) Perma-Bound.
—Good Day, Blue Goose: Perma Big Book. Mallett, Jerry J. & Ervin, Timothy S. 28p. (ps-2). 1992. 47.50 (0-7804-3991-0, 120053) Perma-Bound.
Fergurson, Meg. Dog What? Njoku, Scholastica I. 49p. (gr. k up). 1989. perfect bdg. 6.95x (0-9617833-1-1) S I NJOKU.
Ferguson, Amos. Under the Sunday Tree. Greenfield, Eloise. LC 87-29373. 48p. (ps-1). 1988. PLB 14.89 (0-06-022257-3) HarpC Child Bks.
—Under the Sunday Tree. Greenfield, Eloise. LC 87-29373. 48p. (gr. 1 up). 1991. pap. 5.95 (0-06-443257-2, Trophy) HarpC Child Bks.
Ferguson, Benton. They Carried the Torch: The Story of Oklahoma's Pioneer Newspapers. Ferguson, Elva S. Griffis, Molly L., ed. Johnson, Edith, intro. by. LC 89-80349. 84p. (gr. 8 up). 1989. pap. 5.00 (0-9618634-8-X) Levite Apache.
Ferguson, Bill. The Secret of Getting Straight A's: Learn More in Less Time with Little Effort. Marshall, Brian. 182p. (Orig.). (gr. 8 up). 1993. pap. 12.95 (0-9633357-9-0) Hathaway Intl.
Ferguson, Cecil L. The Ebony Book of Black Achievement. rev. ed. Peters, Margaret W. LC 79-128544. 128p. (gr. 4-8). 1974. Repr. 8.95 (0-87485-040-1) Johnson Chi.
Ferguson, Dwayne. Afro-Bets Kids Christmas Fun: An Activity & Coloring Book. Ferguson, Dwayne. LC 92-72003. 48p. (gr. k-3). 1992. pap. 2.95 (0-940975-41-6) Just Us Bks.
—Captain Africa & the Fury of Anubis: The Graphic Novel. Ferguson, Dwayne. 96p. (gr. 4-11). 1993. 29.95 (0-86543-397-6); pap. 9.95 (0-86543-398-4) Africa World.
Ferguson, Dwayne J. Captain Africa: The Battle for Egyptica. Ferguson, Dwayne J. LC 92-78316. 156p. (gr. 7-10). 1992. 24.95 (0-86543-335-6); pap. 9.95 (0-86543-336-4) Africa World.
Ferguson, Elizabeth T. See Me Read. Price, Betty G. & Caujolle, Claude. (ps-k). 1985. pap. 19.95 (0-9614374-0-5) Prof Reading Serv.
Ferguson, Herb. Stable Girl: Working for the Family. Easton, Patricia H. 44p. (gr. 1-7). 1991. 18.95 (0-15-278340-7) HarBrace.
Ferguson, Kay. Buenas Noches, Irene. Ledbetter, H. & Lomax, John A. Pike, Raffi & Pike, D., eds. Zamora-Pearson, Marissa, tr. from ENG. (SPA.). (ps-2). 1993. pap. text ed. 15.00 (0-922053-27-8) N Edge Res.
—Goodnight Irene Big Book. Ledbetter, H. & Lomax, John A. Pike, Raffi & Pike, D., eds. (ps-2). 1988. pap. text ed. 14.00 (0-922053-08-1) N Edge Res.
Ferguson, Laurie. New Jersey: Yesterday & Today. Rabold, Ted & Fair, Phillip. 110p. (Orig.). (gr. 4). 1982. 9.95 (0-931992-41-9); pap. text ed. 4.95 (0-931992-43-5) Penns Valley.
Ferguson, Susan Y. Uncle Lester's Lemonade Lure. Ferguson, Susan Y. 15p. (Orig.). 1988. lib. bdg. write for info. (0-9621556-0-8) SYF Enter.
Fern, Eugene. Pepito's Story. Fern, Eugene. LC 90-23639. 52p. (ps-3). 1991. Repr. of 1960 ed. smythe sewn 14.95 (1-878274-04-X) Yarrow Pr.
Fernandes, Eugenie. Brush Them Bright. Quinlan, Patricia. 24p. (ps-2). 1992. 8.95 (1-56282-283-7) Hyprn Child.
—Daddies at Work. Merriam, Eve. (ps-2). 1989. pap. 5.95 (0-671-64873-X, S&S BFYR) S&S Trade.
—Daddies at Work. Merriam, Eve. 32p. (ps-2). 1991. pap. 2.50 (0-671-73276-5, Little Simon) S&S Trade.
—Don't Be Scared, Eleven. Thompson, Richard. 24p. 1993. lib. bdg. 14.95 (1-55037-286-6, Pub. by Annick CN); pap. 4.95 (1-55037-287-4, Pub. by Annick CN) Firefly Bks Ltd.
—Effie's Bath. Thompson, Richard. 1990. 14.95 (1-550370-55-3, Pub. by Annick CN); pap. 5.95 (1-550370-56-1, Pub. by Annick CN) Firefly Bks Ltd.
—Elliot Fry's Goodbye. Brimner, Larry D. 32p. (ps-3). 1994. 14.95 (1-56397-113-5) Boyds Mills Pr.
—Jesse on the Night Train. Thompson, Richard. 32p. (ps-2). 1990. 12.95 (1-55037-093-6, Pub. by Annick CN); pap. 4.95 (1-55037-094-4, Pub. by Annick CN) Firefly Bks Ltd.

—Lace Them Up. Barnes, Lilly. 36p. (ps-2). 1992. 8.95 (1-56282-282-9) Hyprn Child.
—Maggee & the Lake Minder. Thompson, Richard. 32p. (gr. k-3). 1991. PLB 14.95 (1-55037-154-1, Pub. by Annick CN); pap. 4.95 (1-55037-152-5, Pub. by Annick CN) Firefly Bks Ltd.
—Mommies at Work. Merriam, Eve. (ps-2). 1989. pap. 5.95 (0-671-64386-X, S&S BFYR) S&S Trade.
—One Light, One Sun. 32p. (ps-2). 1988. PLB 9.95 (0-517-56785-7) Crown Bks Yng Read.
—One Light, One Sun. Raffi. LC 87-22256. 32p. (ps-2). 1990. pap. 3.99 (0-517-57644-9) Crown Bks Yng Read.
—Tell Me One Good Thing: Bedtime Stories. Thompson, Richard. 48p. (ps-3). 1992. PLB 15.95 (1-55037-215-7, Pub. by Annick CN); pap. 7.95 (1-55037-212-2, Pub. by Annick CN) Firefly Bks Ltd.
Fernandes, Henry. The Very Best Christmas Present. Razzi, Jim. LC 87-83045. 24p. (Orig.). (ps-3). 1988. pap. write for info. (0-307-11711-1) Western Pub.
Fernandes, Kim. Visiting Granny. Fernandes, Kim. Lacroix, Pat, photos by. 24p. (ps-k). 1990. 12.95 (1-55037-077-4, Pub. by Annick CN); pap. 4.95 (1-55037-084-7, Pub. by Annick CN) Firefly Bks Ltd.
Fernandez, Fernando. Treasure Island. reissued ed. Stevenson, Robert Louis. Norby, Lisa, adapted by. LC 89-70039. 96p. (Orig.). (gr. 2-6). 1993. PLB 5.99 (0-679-90402-6); pap. 2.99 (0-679-80402-1) Random Bks Yng Read.
Fernandez, Laura. Different Dragons. Little, Jean. 144p. (gr. 3-7). 1989. pap. 3.95 (0-14-031998-0, Puffin) Puffin Bks.
Ferns, Ronald. Caterpillar Stew: A Feast of Animal Poems. Ewart, Gavin. 80p. (gr. 3-5). 1992. 15.95 (0-09-174097-5, Pub. by Hutchinson UK) Trafalgar.
Ferrari, Mark J. & Glockner-Ferrari, Deborah A. Humpback Whales. Patent, Dorothy H. LC 89-2026. 32p. (ps-3). 1989. reinforced 14.95 (0-8234-0779-9) Holiday.
Ferraro, Sandra. Clouds & Clocks: A Story for Children Who Soil. Galvin, Matthew R. LC 89-12278. 48p. 1989. 16.95 (0-945354-18-5); pap. 6.95 (0-945354-15-0) Magination Pr.
—Ignatius Finds Help: A Story About Psychotherapy for Children. Galvin, Matthew R. LC 87-34899. 48p. (ps-6). 1988. 16.95 (0-945354-01-0); pap. 6.95 (0-945354-00-2) Magination Pr.
—Robby Really Transforms: A Story About Grown-ups Helping Children. Galvin, Matthew R. LC 87-34883. 48p. (ps-6). 1988. lib. bdg. 16.95 (0-945354-05-3); pap. 6.95 (0-945354-02-9) Magination Pr.
Ferrer, Gabri. The Snow Angel. Boone, Debby. 32p. (ps-1). 1991. text ed. 12.99 (0-89081-871-1) Harvest Hse.
Ferrer, Gabriel. Bedtime Hugs for Little Ones. Boone, Debby. LC 87-81035. 64p. (ps-1). 1988. 11.99 (0-89081-616-6) Harvest Hse.
Ferreri, Donna, jt. illus. see Dick, Jo A.
Ferri, Giuliano. And God Created Squash: How the World Began. Hickman, Martha W. Levine, Abby, ed. LC 92-22654. 32p. (ps-3). 1993. PLB 14.95 (0-8075-0340-1) A Whitman.
—Caspar & the Star. Bosca, Francesca. 40p. (gr. 1-8). 1991. 12.95 (0-7459-2120-5) Lion USA.
Ferri, Penny J. The Snakeskin. Fiore, Carmen A. 112p. (gr. 3-7). 1991. 14.95 (0-939219-07-7) Townhouse Pub.
Ferris, Lynn B. A Classic Treasury of Christmas. 48p. 1991. 13.95 (0-8249-8524-9, Ideals Child); incl. cassette 17.95 (0-8249-7453-0) Hambleton-Hill.
—Goldilocks & the Three Bears. Ferris, Lynn B., retold by. LC 86-46154. 24p. (gr. k up). 1987. 9.95 (0-394-55882-0) Knopf Bks Yng Read.
—The Night Before Christmas. Moore, Clement C. 24p. 1991. 6.95 (0-8362-4917-8) Andrews & McMeel.
Ferris, Ron. Our Church: There's More to It Than You Think. Johnson, Gordon G. Putman, Bob, adapted by. LC 83-82990. 72p. (gr. 5-6). 1993. wkbk. 5.99 (0-935797-33-5) Harvest IL.
Ferron, Miguel, et al. Watercolor. Sanchez, Isidro. 48p. 1991. pap. 7.95 (0-8120-4717-6) Barron.
Ferron, Miquel. Galaxies. Estalella, Robert. LC 93-24596. (gr. 4-8). 1994. 12.95 (0-8120-6367-8); pap. 6.95 (0-8120-1742-0) Barron.
—Our Satellite: The Moon. Estalella, Robert. LC 93-19897. (gr. 4-8). 1994. 12.95 (0-8120-6369-4); pap. 6.95 (0-8120-1740-4) Barron.
Ferry, Kate. Maria: Goddess of the Teche. Raphael, Morris. 48p. (gr. 4-9). 1991. 13.95 (0-9608866-8-0) M Raphael.
Fetz, Ingrid. Eddie's Menagerie. Haywood, Carolyn. LC 78-6519. (gr. 4-6). 1978. PLB 12.88 (0-688-32158-5) Morrow Jr Bks.
—The Law of Gravity. Hurwitz, Johanna. LC 77-13656. 192p. (gr. 3 up). 1991. pap. 3.95 (0-688-10498-3, Pub. by Beech Tree Bks) Morrow.
—Maurice's Room. reissued ed. Fox, Paula. LC 85-7200. 64p. (gr. 2-6). 1985. SBE 13.95 (0-02-735490-3, Macmillan Child Grp) Macmillan Child Grp.
—Maurice's Room. Fox, Paula. LC 87-19504. 64p. (gr. 2-6). 1988. pap. 3.95 (0-689-71216-2, Aladdin) Macmillan Child Grp.
—Once I Was a Plum Tree. Hurwitz, Johanna. LC 79-23518. 160p. (gr. 4-6). 1980. PLB 12.88 (0-688-32223-9) Morrow Jr Bks.

—Once I Was a Plum Tree. Hurwitz, Johanna. ALC Staff, ed. LC 79-23518. 160p. (gr. 5-12). 1992. pap. 3.95 (0-688-11848-8, Pub. by Beech Tree Bks) Morrow.

The Raft. Haskell, Bess C. **(gr. 5 up). 1988. write for info. (0-933858-26-4)** Kennebec River.
The safe handling of watercraft is the first lesson children need to learn to enjoy life on the seashore, & this series provides the lessons needed, each within a story built around the characters of Dan & Muffin & their dog & cat. Handling a raft involves safety rules, just as handling a dory, or motorboat or any other craft. Author Bess Haskell trained as a teacher at the Bank Street School in New York City before moving to Tenants Harbor, Maine. THE RAFT is the first in a planned six volume series. The stories were written in the Twenties. *Publisher Provided Annotation.*

Fiammenghi, Gioia. Chucky Bellman Was So Bad. Green, Phyllis. Mathews, Judith, ed. LC 90-26823. 32p. (gr. k-3). 1991. 13.95 (0-8075-1156-0) A Whitman.
—Eagle-Eye Ernie Comes to Town. Pearson, Susan. 80p. (gr. 1-3). 1990. pap. 2.95 (0-671-70564-4, S&S BFYR); pap. 2.95 (0-671-70568-7, S&S BFYR) S&S Trade.
—The Great Soap-Bubble Ride. Poskanzer, Susan C. LC 85-14022. 48p. (Orig.). (gr. 1-3). 1986. PLB 10.59 (0-8167-0622-0); pap. text ed. 3.50 (0-8167-0623-9) Troll Assocs.
—The Green Magician Puzzle. Pearson, Susan. LC 90-22436. 1991. pap. 11.95 (0-671-74054-7, S&S BFYR); pap. 2.95 (0-671-74053-9, S&S BFYR) S&S Trade.
—A Kitten for Rosie. Frost, Erica. LC 85-14126. 48p. (Orig.). (gr. 1-3). 1986. PLB 10.59 (0-8167-0650-6); pap. text ed. 3.50 (0-8167-0651-4) Troll Assocs.
—A Koala Grows Up. Gelman, Rita G. 32p. (gr. k-3). 1986. pap. 3.95 (0-590-41869-6) Scholastic Inc.
—Little Sister for Sale. Hamilton, Morse. LC 91-8139. 32p. (ps-3). 1992. 13.00 (0-525-65078-4, Cobblehill Bks) Dutton Child Bks.
—Mike's First Haircut. Gordon, Sharon. LC 87-10911. 32p. (gr. k-2). 1988. PLB 7.89 (0-8167-1113-5); pap. text ed. 1.95 (0-8167-1114-3) Troll Assocs.
—Mr. Stumpguss Is a Third Grader. Duey, Kathleen. 80p. (Orig.). 1992. pap. 3.50 (0-380-76939-5, Camelot Young) Avon.
—My Grandma, the Witch. Robert, Adrian. LC 84-8742. 48p. (gr. 2-4). 1985. PLB 10.89 (0-8167-0422-8); pap. text ed. 3.50 (0-8167-0423-6) Troll Assocs.
—P. J. Clover, Private Eye: The Case of the Halloween Hoot. Meyers, Susan. 128p. (gr. 4-6). 1990. 13.95 (0-525-67297-4, Lodestar Bks) Dutton Child Bks.
—Second-Grade Dog. Lawlor, Laurie. Levine, Abby, ed. LC 84-22700. 40p. (gr. k-3). 1990. 13.95 (0-8075-7280-2) A Whitman.
—Secret of the Ghost Piano. Bolton, Elizabeth. LC 84-8745. 48p. (gr. 2-4). 1985. PLB 10.89 (0-8167-0410-4); pap. text ed. 3.50 (0-8167-0411-2) Troll Assocs.
—The Spooky Sleepover. Pearson, Susan. 64p. (gr. 1-3). 1991. pap. 12.00 jacketed (0-671-74070-9, S&S BFYR); pap. 3.00 (0-671-74069-5, S&S BFYR) S&S Trade.
—The Spy Code Caper. Pearson, Susan. 64p. (gr. 1-3). 1991. pap. 12.00 jacketed (0-671-74071-7, S&S BFYR); pap. 3.00 (0-671-74072-5, S&S BFYR) S&S Trade.
Fiammenghi, Giola. The Bogeyman Caper. Pearson, Susan. 80p. (gr. 1-3). 1990. pap. 11.95 (0-671-70565-2, S&S BFYR); pap. 2.95 (0-671-70569-5, S&S BFYR) S&S Trade.
—The Campfire Ghosts. Pearson, Susan. 96p. (gr. 1-3). 1990. pap. 11.95 jacketed (0-671-70567-9, S&S BFYR); pap. 2.95 (0-671-70571-7, S&S BFYR) S&S Trade.
—The Tap Dance Mystery. Pearson, Susan. 96p. (gr. 1-3). 1990. (S&S BFYR); pap. 2.95 (0-671-70570-9, S&S BFYR) S&S Trade.
Fichaux, Catherine. Brave Little Fox. Pepin, Muriel. LC 93-4238. (gr. 4 up). 1993. write for info. (0-89577-541-7, Readers Digest Kids) RD Assn.
—Little Kangaroo Finds His Way. Chottin, Ariane. Jensen, Patricia, adapted by. LC 93-4242. 1993. write for info. (0-89577-543-3, Readers Digest Kids) RD Assn.
Fiddle, Margrit. Stop-Go, Fast-Slow. McLenighan, Valjean. LC 81-17080. 32p. (ps-2). 1982. PLB 11.93 (0-516-03617-3); pap. text ed. 2.95 (0-516-43617-1) Childrens.
Field, Ann. Great Mountain. Macht, Philip. 30p. (Orig.). 1991. pap. 15.00 (0-930339-01-0) Maxrom Pr.
Field, James. Animal Homes. Pope, Joyce. LC 91-45380. 32p. (gr. 3-6). 1993. PLB 11.59 (0-8167-2775-9); pap. text ed. 3.95 (0-8167-2776-7) Troll Assocs. Postponed.

—Elephant. Blakeman, Sarah. LC 91-44728. 32p. (gr. 4-6). 1993. PLB 11.59 (0-8167-2769-4); tchr's. ed. 3.95 (0-8167-2770-8) Troll Assocs. Postponed.
Field, James, jt. illus. see Jacobs, Phil.
Field, Susan. The Sun, the Moon, & the Silver Baboon. Field, Susan. LC 92-44496. 32p. (ps-2). 1993. 14.00 (0-06-022990-X); PLB 13.89 (0-06-022991-8) HarpC Child Bks.
Fields, Don. Bible Dictionary for Young Readers. McElrath, William N. LC 65-15604. (gr. 4-6). 1965. 12.95 (0-8054-4404-1, 4244-04) Broadman.
—Elijah: Brave Prophet. Entz, Angeline J. (gr. 1-6). 1978. 5.95 (0-8054-4244-8, 4242-44) Broadman.
—Mi Primer Diccionario Biblico. McElrath, William N. McElrath, Ruth G., tr. from ENG. (SPA.). 128p. (gr. 4-6). 1991. pap. 4.50 (0-311-03656-2) Casa Bautista.
—Prophets: Preachers for God. McMinn, Tom. (gr. 1-6). 1979. 5.95 (0-8054-4250-2, 4242-50) Broadman.
Fields, Theodore. Treasure Chest: Practice Exercises for "Wee Folks Readers" Hill, Fred & Hill, Charlotte M. Young, Elaine A., ed. LC 93-71070. 90p. (Orig.). (gr. 1-3). 1993. wkbk. 6.95 (0-9620182-8-7) Charill Pubs.
—Wee Folks on Top: Adventures in Reading. Hill, Charlotte M. & Hill, Fred D. Shortridge, Cleona, ed. LC 92-90056. 66p. (Orig.). (gr. 3-5). 1992. pap. 8.95 (0-9620182-7-9) Charill Pubs.
Fields, Theodore & Jefferson, Sharon. Wee Folks Learn to Read: A Phonetic Approach to Beginning Reading. Hill, Charlotte M. Young, Elaine, et al, eds. LC 90-83256. (Orig.). (gr. k-3). 1991. pap. text ed. 7.95 (0-9620182-3-6) Charill Pubs.
Fields, Theodore, jt. illus. see Jefferson, Sharon.

Fields, Theodore, et al. Wee Folks Readers: A Phonetic Approach to Beginning Reading, 5 vols. Hill, Charlotte M. Shortridge, Cleona, ed. LC 90-832256. 70p. (Orig.). (gr. k-5). 1992. Set. pap. write for info. (0-9620182-9-5) Charill Pubs.
This five volume reading series is an eclectic approach to beginning reading. Phonics is introduced in story form, lending itself to building comprehension, skills & simultaneously, sight words to build vocabulary as well. Each sound is introduced with illustrations that represent that sound. Books One through Four teach the vowel sounds & this teaching of sounds in context allows for the immediate application of phonetic skills learned. This approach follows the principle of use & reinforcement. Book Five, "Wee Folks on Top" (Adventures in Reading), contains stories, fables & poetry with follow-up questions to improve comprehension. A bookstore owner & mother of a six year old daughter who lives in San Antonio, Texas, wrote, "My daughter was reading the first hour after I started her in Book I. I called relatives all over the country to tell them that she was reading." A director of a Prep School in Seattle, Washington, writes, "Your reading series is excellent. I am an experienced teacher & have always believed that a phonics based reading program is the best way to teach reading."
Publisher Provided Annotation.

Fieser, Stephen. The Christmas Sky. rev. ed. Branley, Franklyn M. LC 89-71210. 48p. (gr. 3-7). 1990. 14.95 (0-690-04770-3, Crowell Jr Bks); PLB 14.89 (0-690-04772-X, Crowell Jr Bks) HarpC Child Bks.
—The Christmas Sky. Branley, Franklyn M. LC 89-71210. 48p. (gr. 3-7). 1992. pap. 5.95 (0-06-446133-5, Trophy) HarpC Child Bks.
—Jesus Helps Me Grow. Corbin, Linda & Dys, Pat. 28p. (Orig.). (gr. 1-6). 1986. pap. 5.99 (0-87509-374-4) Chr Pubns.
—Jesus Lights the Way. Corbin, Linda & Dys, Pat. 30p. (Orig.). (gr. 1-6). 1987. pap. 5.99 wkbk. (0-87509-385-X) Chr Pubns.
—Jesus Teaches Me. Corbin, Linda & Dys, Pat. 35p. (gr. 1-6). 1987. wkbk. 5.99 (0-87509-389-2) Chr Pubns.
—The Silk Route. Major, John. S. LC 92-38169. 1994. 15.00 (0-06-022924-1); PLB 14.89 (0-06-022926-8) HarpC.

Figueroa, Ivelisse. La Aventura de Estudiar: Programa para Desarrollar Destrezas de Estudio e Informacion en el nivel Elemental e Intermedio. De Ponce, Blanca N. (SPA.). 100p. (Orig.). (gr. 5-9). 1984. write for info. B Ponce.
—Educate para una Mejor Condicion Fisica: Guia Basica para el Desarrollo de un Programa de Eficiencia Fisica. Ponce, Omar. (SPA.). 75p. (Orig.). 1986. write for info. B Ponce.
Figueroa, Mariano. Experience. Figueroa, Mariano. Terry, Sarah, frwd. by. 50p. (Orig.). (gr. 9-12). 1989. pap. text ed. write for info. West Side Pubns.
—Fantasia. Ortiz, Elizabeth. Iscaro, Nancy L., ed. 58p. (Orig.). (gr. 9-12). 1989. pap. text ed. write for info. West Side Pubns.
Figueroa, Mariano, et al. Pier Pleasure I. Iscaro, Nancy L., ed. 80p. (gr. 9-12). 1989. pap. text ed. write for info. West Side Pubns.
Fike, Scott. Twisted Tales: The Dripping Head & Other Gruesome Stories. Welch, R. C. 128p. (Orig.). (gr. 3-7). 1992. pap. 4.95 (1-56288-314-3) Checkerboard.
—Twisted Tales: The Slithering Corpse & Other Sinister Stories. Welch, R. C. 128p. (Orig.). (gr. 3-7). 1992. pap. 4.95 (1-56288-315-1) Checkerboard.
Filarca, Josie, jt. illus. see Kubo, Chad.
Filippo, Margaret S. Teeny-Tiny Train & Planes, 6 bks. Damashek, Sandy. (ps-k). 1992. bds. 14.95 (1-56293-241-1, Set, mini-board bks. in a tray) McClanahan Bk.
Filkins, Vanessa. Celebrate Christmas. Jones, Kathy. 144p. (gr. k-6). 1985. wkbk. 11.95 (0-86653-279-X, SS 840, Shining Star Pubns) Good Apple.
—Celebrate Easter. Riley, Kelly. 144p. (gr. k-6). 1987. pap. 11.95 (0-86653-385-0, SS 842, Shining Star Pubns) Good Apple.
—Celebrate Winter. Hartwig, Judy. 144p. (gr. k-3). 1985. wkbk. 11.95 (0-86653-266-8, SS 839, Shining Star Pubns) Good Apple.
—Chicago for Kids: Of All Ages. rev. ed. Gary Grimm & Associates Staff. 32p. (gr. k-8). Repr. of 1985 ed. wkbk. 4.00 (1-56490-001-0) G Grimm Assocs.
—Collectible Correctibles. Artman, John. 64p. (gr. 4-8). 1984. wkbk. 7.95 (0-86653-214-5, GA 559) Good Apple.
—Developing Speaking Skills. Jasper, James M. & Morgan, Edith. 64p. (gr. k-6). 1985. 7.95 (0-86653-268-4, GA 633) Good Apple.
—Faith. MacKenthun, Carole & Dwyer, Paulinus. 48p. (gr. 2-7). 1986. wkbk. 6.95 (0-86653-361-3, SS 874, Shining Star Pubns) Good Apple.
—Fun with Familiar Tunes. Warner, Laverne & Craycraft, Kenneth. 128p. (ps-3). 1987. pap. 10.95 (0-86653-414-8, GA1014) Good Apple.
—Gentleness. MacKenthun, Carole & Dwyer, Paulinus. 48p. (gr. 2 up). 1987. pap. 6.95 (0-86653-395-8, SS879, Shining Star Pubns) Good Apple.
—Goodness. MacKenthun, Carole & Dwyer, Paulinus. 48p. (gr. 2-7). 1986. wkbk. 6.95 (0-86653-363-X, SS 875, Shining Star Pubns) Good Apple.
—Joy. MacKenthun, Carole & Dwyer, Paulinus. 48p. (gr. 2-7). 1986. wkbk. 6.95 (0-86653-360-5, SS 873, Shining Star Pubns) Good Apple.
—Kindness. MacKenthun, Carole & Dwyer, Paulinus. 48p. (gr. 2 up). 1987. pap. 6.95 (0-86653-379-6, SS880, Shining Star Pubns) Good Apple.
—Let's Color Chicago. Gary Grimm & Associates Staff. 40p. (Orig.). (ps-6). 1993. wkbk. 4.00 (1-56490-000-2) G Grimm Assocs.
—Little House in the Classroom. Hackett, Christine. 112p. (gr. 3-5). 1989. wkbk. 9.95 (0-86653-444-X, GA1052) Good Apple.
—Love. MacKenthun, Carole & Dwyer, Paulinus. 48p. (gr. 2-7). 1986. wkbk. 6.95 (0-86653-359-1, SS 872, Shining Star Pubns) Good Apple.
—Patience. MacKenthun, Carole & Dwyer, Paulinus. 48p. (gr. 2-7). 1986. wkbk. 6.95 (0-86653-364-8, SS 876, Shining Star Pubns) Good Apple.
—Peace. MacKenthun, Carole & Dwyer, Paulinus. 48p. (gr. 2-7). 1986. wkbk. 6.95 (0-86653-365-6, SS 877, Shining Star Pubns) Good Apple.
—Prime Time Life Skills. Aten, Jerry. 64p. (gr. 2-5). 1983. wkbk. 7.95 (0-86653-126-2, GA 487) Good Apple.
—Prime Time Maps. Aten, Jerry. 64p. (gr. 2-5). 1983. wkbk. 7.95 (0-86653-108-4, GA 470) Good Apple.
—Prime Time Math Skills. Aten, Jerry. 64p. (gr. 2-5). 1984. wkbk. 7.95 (0-86653-155-6, GA 524) Good Apple.
—Prime Time Reading Skills. Aten, Jerry. 64p. (gr. 2-5). 1984. wkbk. 7.95 (0-86653-185-8, GA 525) Good Apple.
—Prime Time Thinking Skills. Aten, Jerry. 64p. (gr. 2-5). 1985. wkbk. 7.95 (0-86653-276-5, GA 628) Good Apple.
—Rainy Day Fun. Gleason, Karan. 112p. (gr. k-4). 1987. pap. 9.95 (0-86653-408-3, GA1002) Good Apple.
—Reading - A Novel Approach. Szabos, Janice. 112p. (gr. 4-8). 1984. wkbk. 11.95 (0-86653-186-6, GA 529) Good Apple.
—Rx for the Classroom Blahs. Embry, Lynn. 64p. (gr. 4-8). 1983. wkbk. 7.95 (0-86653-104-1, GA 462) Good Apple.
—Self-Control. MacKenthun, Carole & Dwyer, Paulinus. 48p. (gr. 2 up). 1987. pap. 6.95 (0-86653-396-6, SS878, Shining Star Pubns) Good Apple.
—The Write Stuff! Artman, John H. 64p. (gr. 4-8). 1985. wkbk. 7.95 (0-86653-273-0, GA 681) Good Apple.
Filkins, Vanessa, jt. illus. see Beebe, Mark.

Filling, Gregory. Alexander the Grape: Fruit & Vegetable Jokes. Keller, Charles. 48p. (gr. 2-6). 1985. 10.95 (0-13-021410-8); pap. 4.95 (0-13-020918-X) P-H.
—Swine Lake. Lake, Charles. 48p. (gr. 3-7). 1985. 9.95 (0-13-879743-9) P-H.
—Take Me to Your Liter: Science & Math Jokes. Keller, Charles. 40p. (gr. 2-5). 1991. PLB 13.95 (0-945912-13-7) Pippin Pr.
Fine, John C. The Hunger Road. Fine, John C. LC 87-27794. 144p. (gr. 5 up). 1988. SBE 13.95 (0-689-31361-6, Atheneum Child Bk) Macmillan Child Grp.
—Oceans in Peril. Fine, John C. LC 86-26546. 128p. (gr. 5 up). 1987. SBE 15.95 (0-689-31328-4, Atheneum Child Bk) Macmillan Child Grp.
Fink, Grace. Somedays It Feels Like It Wants to Rain. Zaslow, David. LC 76-46244. (gr. 2-6). 1976. pap. 3.95 (0-89411-001-2) Kids Matter.
Finkel, Becky, jt. illus. see Crow, James L.

Finkler, C. Etana. Kitchen Chemistry & Front Porch Physics. Hoyt, Marie A. 60p. (Orig.). (gr. 3-8). 1983. pap. 5.00 (0-914911-00-7) Educ Serv Pr. KITCHEN CHEMISTRY & FRONT PORCH PHYSICS for children ages 7-14 has instructions on how to make a SHOEBOX CHEMISTRY SET to be used in performing the 32 science experiments which demystify physics & chemistry. Its use of common materials & everyday household chemicals make the teaching of science fun, safe & in-depth. The simple understandable reading level enables students to discover science concepts by "Hands On" experience. Additionally, the glossary teacher-parent guide along with the Future Scientists of America awards make this book a science treasure to teachers, children, science group leaders & parents of both mainstream & minorities alike.
Publisher Provided Annotation.

Finley, Shawn. The Boo Baby Girl Meets the Ghost of Mable's Gable. May, Jim. LC 92-72702. 32p. (ps-5). 1992. PLB 14.95 (1-878925-03-2) Brotherstone Pubs.
Finnell, Jim. Kidding Around Washington D.C. A Young Person's Guide. 2nd ed. Pedersen, Anne. 64p. (gr. 3 up). 1993. pap. 9.95 (1-56261-093-7) John Muir.
Finney, Denise. Jungles. Catchpole, Clive. LC 83-7796. 32p. (ps-4). 1985. pap. 4.95 (0-8037-0036-9, 0481-140) Dial Bks Young.
Finney, La Rhue. Things Magical. Finney, La Rhue. 22p. (Orig.). (gr. 2-4). 1992. pap. text ed. 6.95 (0-9635276-0-6) Taffey Apple.
Finney, Pat. Austin: The Son Becomes Father. Wade, Mary D. 64p. (gr. 3-5). 1993. 10.95 (1-882539-08-7); pap. 4.95 (1-882539-09-5); tchr's. guide 5.00 (1-882539-10-9) Colophon Hse.

—**The Courage Seed. Richardson, Jean. LC 93-20182. 76p. (gr. 3-6). 1993. 14. 95 (0-89015-902-5) Eakin-Sunbelt. Mary Manygoats is a Navajo girl orphaned by a tragedy. When she comes to live with her Aunt Betsy in Houston, she faces the daunting prospect of going to a strange school where she is different from everyone else. But as Mary meets her new classmates, she quickly learns how many distinct cultures can mingle & to be proud of her own heritage. THE COURAGE SEED was inspired by the author's experiences teaching on a Navajo reservation in New Mexico & the ethnic diversity of her Houston classes. Richardson weaves traditional Navajo myths into Mary's story: the title comes from a Navajo belief that brave deeds nurture the seeds of courage planted in everyone's mind. The book includes a glossary of Navajo terms, several one-page essays on Navajo culture, & a list of books recommended for further reading. The story is illustrated by Pat Finney, a Houston artist & teacher. A good** introduction to Native American culture for young readers. Ages 8-12. Order from: Eakin Press/Sunbelt Media, P.O. Box 90159, Austin, TX 78709-0159; 512-288-1771, FAX 512-288-1513. *Publisher Provided Annotation.*

—David Crockett: Sure He Was Right. Wade, Mary D. 64p. (gr. 2-3). 1992. 11.95 (*0-89015-854-1*) Eakin-Sunbelt.

Fiore, Peter. The Adventures of Huckleberry Finn. Twain, Mark. LC 92-10194. 1992. 12.99 (*0-517-08128-8*, Child Classics) Outlet Bk Co.
—Dear Willie Rudd. Gray, Libba M. LC 92-25064. 1993. pap. 14.00 (*0-671-79774-3*, S&S BFYR) S&S Trade.
—My Country, 'tis of Thee. Hopkins, Lee B., compiled by. LC 92-24230. 1994. pap. 16.00 (*0-671-73315-X*, S&S BFYR) S&S Trade.

Fiorentinl, Al. John Fitzgerald Kennedy: America's Youngest President. Frisbee, Lucy P. LC 86-10965. 192p. (gr. 2-6). 1986. pap. 3.95 (*0-02-041990-2*, Aladdin) Macmillan Child Grp.

Fiorentino, Al. Betsy Ross: Designer of Our Flag. Weil, Ann. LC 86-10775. 192p. (gr. 2 up). 1986. pap. 3.95 (*0-02-042120-6*, Aladdin) Macmillan Child Grp.
—Martin Luther King, Jr. Young Man with a Dream. Millender, Dharathula H. LC 86-10739. 192p. (gr. 2-6). 1986. pap. 3.95 (*0-02-042010-2*, Aladdin) Macmillan Child Grp.
—Susan B. Anthony: Champion of Women's Rights. Monsell, Helen A. LC 86-10716. 192p. (gr. 2-6). 1986. pap. 3.95 (*0-02-041800-0*, Aladdin) Macmillan Child Grp.

Firmhand, Zelda. Laboratory Laughter. Alberti, Delbert & Mason, George. (Orig.). (gr. 2-9). 1974. pap. 7.95 (*0-918932-25-4*) Activity Resources.

Firmin, Charlotte. Being Bullied. Petty, Kate. 24p. (ps-2). 1991. pap. 4.95 (*0-8120-4661-7*) Barron.
—Feeling Left Out. Petty, Kate. 24p. (ps-2). 1991. pap. 4.95 (*0-8120-4658-7*) Barron.
—I'm Going on a Dragon Hunt. Jones, Maurice. LC 86-19399. 32p. (gr. k-3). 1987. SBE 13.95 (*0-02-748000-3*, Four Winds) Macmillan Child Grp.
—Making Friends. Petty, Kate. 24p. (ps-2). 1991. pap. 4.95 (*0-8120-4660-9*) Barron.
—Playing the Game. Petty, Kate. 24p. (ps-2). 1991. pap. 4.95 (*0-8120-4659-5*) Barron.

Firmin, Peter. Best Pest. Thomson, Pat. 32p. (ps-1). 1993. pap. 6.95 (*0-575-05156-6*, Pub. by Gollancz UK) Trafalgar.
—Boastful Mr. Bear. Firmin, Peter. (ps-1). 1989. 8.95 (*0-440-50083-4*) Delacorte.
—Day & Night. 16p. (ps-1). 1986. 4.50 (*0-7460-0795-7*) EDC.
—Foolish Miss Crow. Firmin, Peter. (ps-1). 1989. 8.95 (*0-440-50082-6*) Delacorte.
—Happy Miss Rat. Firmin, Peter. (ps-1). 1989. 8.95 (*0-440-50081-8*) Delacorte.
—Hungry Mr. Fox. Firmin, Peter. (ps-1). 1989. 8.95 (*0-440-50034-6*) Delacorte.
—Summer & Winter. 16p. (ps-1). 1986. 4.50 (*0-7460-0797-3*) EDC.
—Then & Now. 16p. (ps-1). 1986. 4.50 (*0-7460-0794-9*) EDC.

Firth, Barbara. Can't You Sleep, Little Bear? Waddell, Martin. LC 91-71858. 32p. (gr. up) 1992. 14.95 (*1-56402-007-X*) Candlewick Pr.
—Can't You Sleep Little Bear? Waddell, Martin. LC 91-71858. 32p. (ps up) 1993. 4.95 (*1-56402-254-4*) Candlewick Pr.
—The Grumpalump. Hayes, Sarah. 32p. (ps-2). 1991. 15. 45 (*0-89919-871-6*, Clarion Bks) HM.
—Let's Go Home, Little Bear. Waddell, Martin. LC 92-53003. 32p. (ps-3). 1993. 14.95 (*1-56402-131-9*) Candlewick Pr.
—The Park in the Dark. Waddell, Martin. Briley, D., ed. LC 88-9169. 32p. (ps-1). 1989. 11.95 (*0-688-08516-4*); PLB 11.88 (*0-688-08517-2*) Lothrop.
—The Spider. Lane, Margaret. LC 82-71354. 32p. (ps-4). 1983. 9.95 (*0-8037-8303-5*, 0339-110) Dial Bks Young.
—The Spider. Lane, Margaret. 32p. (gr. k-4). 1994. pap. 4.99 (*0-14-055277-4*, Puffin Pied Piper) Puffin Bks.
—We Love Them. Waddell, Martin. LC 89-8226. 32p. (ps-2). 1990. 12.95 (*0-688-09331-0*); lib. bdg. 12.88 (*0-688-09332-9*) Lothrop.

Firth, Barbara & Firth, Barbara. Sam Vole & His Brothers. Waddell, Martin. LC 91-58755. 32p. (ps up). 1992. 14.95 (*1-56402-082-7*) Candlewick Pr.

Firth, Barbara, et al. Amazing Air. Smith, Henry. LC 82-80991. 48p. (gr. 3-6). 1983. PLB 11.88 (*0-688-00973-5*) Lothrop.
—Amazing Air. Smith, Henry. LC 82-80991. 48p. (gr. 3-6). 1983. pap. 7.95 (*0-688-00977-8*, Pub. by Beech Tree Bks) Morrow.

Fischel, Lillian. Adventures of Simple Shmerel. Simon, Solomon. (gr. 3-7). 1942. 4.95 (*0-87441-127-0*) Behrman.

Fischer, Bruce. Arizona Is for Kids. Salts, Roberta. 32p. (gr. 1-4). 1988. pap. 2.95 (*0-685-21928-3*) Double B Pubns.

Fischer, Robert, et al. The Color Coded Alphabet: The Best Coloring Book Ever. Dulac, Glen. (gr. k-3). 1991. pap. 5.00 (*0-9628227-4-4*) Desert Bks.

Fischer, Steven. There's a Blue Dog under My Bed. Fischer, Steven. Fischer, Thomas, ed. LC 90-84006. 64p. (gr. k-6). 1991. pap. 2.95 (*0-9627367-0-8*) Blue Dog Prodns.

Fischer-Nagel, Andreas & Fischer-Nagel, Heiderose. An Ant Colony. Fischer-Nagel, Heiderose & Fischer-Nagel, Andreas. 48p. (gr. 2-5). 1989. PLB 19.95 (*0-87614-333-8*); pap. 6.95 (*0-87614-519-5*) Carolrhoda Bks.
—Life of the Honeybee. Fischer-Nagel, Andreas & Fischer-Nagel, Heiderose. 48p. (gr. 2-5). 1986. pap. 6.95 (*0-87614-470-9*) Carolrhoda Bks.
—Life of the Ladybug. Fischer-Nagel, Andreas & Fischer-Nagel, Heiderose. LC 85-25467. 48p. (gr. 2-5). 1986. lib. bdg. 19.95 (*0-87614-240-4*) Carolrhoda Bks.

Fischer-Nagel, Andreas, jt. illus. see Fischer-Nagel, Heiderose.

Fischer-Nagel, Andreas, jt. photog. see Fischer-Nagel, Heiderose.

Fischer-Nagel, Andreas, jt. photog. see Fischer-Nagel, Heidrose.

Fischer-Nagel, Heiderose & Fischer-Nagel, Andreas. The Housefly. Fischer-Nagel, Heiderose & Fischer-Nagel, Andreas. 48p. (gr. 2-5). 1990. PLB 19.95 (*0-87614-374-5*) Carolrhoda Bks.
—A Look Through the Mouse Hole. Fischer-Nagel, Heiderose & Fischer-Nagel, Andreas. 48p. (gr. 2-5). 1989. lib. bdg. 19.95 (*0-87614-326-5*) Carolrhoda Bks.

Fischer-Nagel, Heiderose, jt. illus. see Fischer-Nagel, Andreas.

Fischer-Nagel, Heiderose & Fischer-Nagel, Andreas, photos by. Life of the Butterfly. Fischer-Nagel, Heiderose & Fischer-Nagel, Andreas. Simon, Noel, tr. from GER. 48p. (gr. 2-5). 1987. lib. bdg. 19.95 (*0-87614-244-7*); pap. 6.95 (*0-87614-484-9*) Carolrhoda Bks.

Fischer-Nagel, Heidrose & Fischer-Nagel, Andreas, photos by. Fir Trees. Fischer-Nagel, Heiderose & Fischer-Nagel, Andreas. 48p. (gr. 2-5). 1989. 19.95 (*0-87614-340-0*) Carolrhoda Bks.

Fish, Richard. Haym Salomon: Liberty's Son. Milgrim, Shirley. LC 75-17349. 120p. (gr. 5-8). 1975. 7.95 (*0-8276-0073-9*) JPS Phila.

Fisher, Barbara. Car Boy. Fisher, Barbara. 29p. (Orig.). (gr. k-2). 1977. pap. 2.00 (*0-934830-02-9*) Ten Penny.
—Dan. Fisher, Barbara. 20p. (Orig.). (gr. k-5). 1981. pap. 2.00 (*0-934830-19-3*) Ten Penny.
—Harmony Hurricane Muldoon. Fisher, Barbara. 22p. (Orig.). (gr. 3-5). 1979. pap. 2.00 (*0-934830-09-6*) Ten Penny.
—Jolly Molly Molar. Fisher, Barbara. 44p. (Orig.). (gr. 1-3). 1979. pap. 2.00 (*0-934830-10-X*) Ten Penny.

Fisher, Barbara L. Getting Ready for the Guy-Girl Thing: Two Ex-Teenagers Reveal the Shocking Truth about God's Plan for Success with the Opposite Sex! Johnson, Greg & Shellenberger, Susie. Duncan, Kyle, ed. LC 91-14818. 200p. (gr. 5-9). 1991. pap. 8.99 (*0-8307-1485-5*, 5422705) Regal.

Fisher, Chris. Let's Make Magic: Over Forty Tricks You Can Do. Day, Jon. LC 92-53093. 96p. (Orig.). (gr. 2-6). 1992. 14.95 (*1-85697-834-6*); pap. 9.95 (*1-85697-806-0*) Kingfisher Bks.
—Under the Moon. French, Vivian. LC 93-877. Date not set. write for info. (*1-56402-330-3*) Candlewick Pr.

Fisher, Cynthia. Night of the Werepoodle. Hiser, Constance. LC 93-25732. 128p. (gr. 7-11). 1994. 14.95 (*0-8234-1116-8*) Holiday.
—The True Story of Harrowing Farm. Fine, Anne. LC 92-33935. 1993. 12.95 (*0-316-28316-9*, Joy St Bks) Little.

Fisher, Jon & Halpern, John. Let's Visit a Bicycle Factory. Ochoa, George. LC 89-35714. 32p. (gr. 2-4). 1990. PLB 10.79 (*0-8167-1739-7*); pap. text ed. 2.95 (*0-8167-1740-0*) Troll Assocs.

Fisher, L. E. Story of the Thirteen Colonies. Alderman, Clifford L. LC 66-11960. lib. bdg. 9.99 (*0-394-90415-X*) Random Bks Yng Read.

Fisher, Leonard E. The Alamo. Fisher, Leonard E. LC 86-46204. 64p. (gr. 3-7). 1987. reinforced bdg. 14.95 (*0-8234-0646-6*) Holiday.
—All Times, All Peoples: A World History of Slavery. Meltzer, Milton. LC 79-2810. 80p. (gr. 5-9). 1980. PLB 15.89 (*0-06-024187-X*) HarpC Child Bks.
—The American Revolution. rev. ed. Morris, Richard B. LC 85-12878. 72p. (gr. 5-10). 1985. PLB 13.50 (*0-8225-1701-9*) Lerner Pubns.
—Calendar Art: Thirteen Days, Weeks, Months, Years from Around the World. Fisher, Leonard E. LC 86-25835. 64p. (ps up). 1987. SBE 14.95 (*0-02-735350-8*, Four Winds) Macmillan Child Grp.
—Celebrations. Livingston, Myra C. LC 84-19216. 32p. (ps-3). 1985. reinforced bdg. 14.95 (*0-8234-0550-8*); pap. 5.95 (*0-8234-0654-7*) Holiday.
—A Circle of Seasons. Livingston, Myra C. LC 81-20305. 32p. (ps-3). 1982. reinforced bdg. 15.95 (*0-8234-0452-8*); pap. 5.95 (*0-8234-0656-3*) Holiday.
—The Constitution. rev. ed. Morris, Richard B. 72p. (gr. 5-10). 1985. PLB 13.50 (*0-8225-1702-7*) Lerner Pubns.
—Cyclops. Fisher, Leonard E. LC 90-29317. 32p. (ps-3). 1991. reinforced bdg. 15.95 (*0-8234-0891-4*) Holiday.
—Cyclops. Fisher, Leonard E. 1993. pap. 5.95 (*0-8234-1062-5*) Holiday.
—David & Goliath. Fisher, Leonard E., adapted by. LC 92-24063. 32p. (ps-3). 1993. reinforced bdg. 15.95 (*0-8234-0997-X*) Holiday.

—Earth Songs. Livingston, Myra C. LC 86-341. 32p. (ps-4). 1986. reinforced bdg. 14.95 (*0-8234-0615-6*) Holiday.
—Ellis Island: Gateway to the New World. Fisher, Leonard E. LC 86-2286. 64p. (gr. 3-7). 1986. reinforced 13.95 (*0-8234-0612-1*) Holiday.
—The Exploits of Xenophon. Household, Geoffrey. LC 89-12396. lx, 180p. (gr. 5-12). 1989. Repr. of 1955 ed. lib. bdg. 18.00 (*0-208-02224-4*, Linnet) Shoe String.
—Galileo. Fisher, Leonard E. LC 91-31146. 32p. (gr. 2-6). 1992. SBE 14.95 (*0-02-735235-8*, Macmillan Child Bk) Macmillan Child Grp.
—The Great Wall of China. Fisher, Leonard E. LC 85-15324. 32p. (gr. 1-5). 1986. RSBE 14.95 (*0-02-735220-X*, Macmillan Child Bk) Macmillan Child Grp.
—Gutenberg. Fisher, Leonard E. LC 92-26991. 32p. (gr. 2-6). 1993. 14.95 (*0-02-735238-2*, Macmillan Child Bk) Macmillan Child Grp.
—If You Ever Meet a Whale: Poems. Livingston, Myra C., selected by. LC 91-36265. 32p. (ps-3). 1992. reinforced bdg. 14.95 (*0-8234-0940-6*) Holiday.
—Jason & the Golden Fleece. Fisher, Leonard E. LC 89-20074. 32p. (gr. k-4). 1990. reinforced bdg. 14.95 (*0-8234-0794-2*) Holiday.
—Kinderdike. Fisher, Leonard E. LC 93-8140. 32p. (gr. k-3). 1994. RSBE 15.95 (*0-02-735365-6*, Macmillan Child Bk) Macmillan Child Grp.
—Little Frog's Song. Schertle, Alice. LC 91-10405. 32p. (ps-2). 1992. 15.00 (*0-06-020059-6*); PLB 14.89 (*0-06-020060-X*) HarpC Child Bks.
—Number Art: Thirteen 1 2 3s from Around the World. Fisher, Leonard E. LC 82-5050. 64p. (gr. 3-7). 1982. SBE 14.95 (*0-02-735240-4*, Four Winds) Macmillan Child Grp.
—Olympians: Great Gods & Goddesses of Ancient Greece. Fisher, Leonard E. LC 84-516. 32p. (gr. 1-4). 1984. reinforced bdg. 15.95 (*0-8234-0522-2*); pap. 5.95 (*0-8234-0740-3*) Holiday.
—Prince Henry the Navigator. Fisher, Leonard E. LC 89-28068. 32p. (gr. 2-6). 1990. 14.95 (*0-02-735231-5*, Macmillan Child Bk) Macmillan Child Grp.
—Pyramid of the Sun - Pyramid of the Moon. Fisher, Leonard E. LC 88-1410. 32p. (gr. 1-5). 1988. SBE 14. 95 (*0-02-735300-1*) Macmillan Child Grp.
—Sailboat Lost. Fisher, Leonard E. LC 90-21504. 32p. (ps up). 1991. 15.95 (*0-02-735351-6*, Macmillan Child Bk) Macmillan Child Grp.
—The Seven Days of Creation. Fisher, Leonard E., adapted by. LC 81-2952. 32p. (ps-3). 1981. reinforced bdg. 14.95 (*0-8234-0398-X*); pap. 5.95 (*0-8234-0757-8*) Holiday.
—Sky Songs. Livingston, Myra C. LC 83-12955. 32p. (ps-4). 1984. reinforced bdg 14.95 (*0-8234-0502-8*) Holiday.
—Space Songs. Livingston, Myra C. LC 87-19628. 32p. (ps-3). 1988. reinforced bdg. 15.95 (*0-8234-0675-X*) Holiday.
—Space Songs. Livingston, Cohn. (ps-3). 1993. pap. 5.95 (*0-8234-1029-3*) Holiday.
—The Spotted Pony: A Collection of Hanukkah Stories. Kimmel, Eric A., retold by. LC 91-24214. 72p. (gr. 2-6). 1992. 14.95 (*0-8234-0936-8*) Holiday.
—The Statue of Liberty. Fisher, Leonard E. LC 85-42878. 64p. (gr. 3-7). 1985. reinforced bdg. 14.95 (*0-8234-0586-9*) Holiday.
—Symbol Art: Thirteen Squares, Circles & Triangles from Around the World. Fisher, Leonard E. LC 85-42805. 64p. (gr. 4-6). 1986. SBE 14.95 (*0-02-735270-6*, Four Winds) Macmillan Child Grp.
—The Tanners. Fisher, Leonard E. LC 66-10136. 48p. (gr. 3 up). 1986. pap. 5.95 (*0-87923-609-4*) Godine.
—Theseus & the Minotaur. Fisher, Leonard E., retold by. LC 88-1970. 32p. (gr. 1-4). 1988. reinforced bdg. 15. 95 (*0-8234-0703-9*); pap. 5.95 (*0-8234-0954-6*) Holiday.
—The Three Princes: A Middle Eastern Tale. Kimmel, Eric A., retold by. LC 93-25862. 32p. (gr. 4-8). 1994. 15.95 (*0-8234-1115-X*) Holiday.
—The Tower of London. Fisher, Leonard E. LC 87-1629. 32p. (gr. 1-5). 1987. SBE 14.95 (*0-02-735370-2*, Macmillan Child Bk) Macmillan Child Grp.
—Up in the Air. Livingston, Myra C. LC 88-23293. 32p. (ps-3). 1989. reinforced bdg. 14.95 (*0-8234-0736-5*) Holiday.
—The Wailing Wall. Fisher, Leonard E. LC 88-27192. 32p. (gr. 1-5). 1989. SBE 15.95 (*0-02-735310-9*, Macmillan Child Bk) Macmillan Child Grp.
—The War of Eighteen Twelve. rev. ed. Morris, Richard B. 72p. (gr. 5-10). 1985. PLB 13.50 (*0-8225-1705-1*) Lerner Pubns.

Fisher, Michael, et al. Buildings, Bridges & Tunnels. Gaff, Jackie. LC 91-212. 40p. (Orig.). (gr. 2-5). 1991. pap. 3.99 (*0-679-80865-5*) Random Bks Yng Read.

Fisher, Nell F. The Christmas Crib That Zack Built. Wedeven, Carol S. LC 89-263. 1989. casebound 9.95 (*0-687-07816-4*) Abingdon.

Fisher, Richard B. The Founding of the Republic. rev. ed. Morris, Richard B. 72p. (gr. 5-10). 1985. PLB 13. 50 (*0-8225-1704-3*) Lerner Pubns.

Fisher, Steve. My Teacher Flunked the Planet. Coville, Bruce. MacDonald, Pat, ed. 176p. (Orig.). 1992. pap. 3.50 (*0-671-75081-X*, Minstrel Bks) PB.

Fishman, Tamar, jt. illus. see Wikler, Madeline.

Fitting, Brian, jt. illus. see Fitting, Devin.

Fitting, Devin & Fitting, Brian. Magical Piece of Sand. Hills, J. S. 32p. (ps-2). 1989. pap. 6.95 (*0-923889-27-2*) Inquisitors Pub.

Fittipaldi, Cica. African Animal Tales. Barbosa, Rogerio A. Guthrie, Feliz, tr. from POR. LC 92-42378. 60p. (gr. 1-3). 1993. 17.95 (0-912078-96-0) Volcano Pr.

Fitzgerald, F. A. Daffynitions. Keller, Charles, compiled by. LC 75-34280. (gr. 3 up). 1978. (Pub. by Treehouse); pap. 3.95 (0-13-196576-X) P-H.

Fitzgerald, Gerald, photos by. The Honey Festival. McAllisiter, Angela. LC 92-46079. (gr. 1-8). 1994. 13.99 (0-8037-1240-5) Dial Bks Young.

Fitzgerald, Joanne. Baby Boat. Waterton, Betty. LC 89-11173. (ps-1). 1990. PLB 11.99 (0-679-90368-2) Random Bks Yng Read.
—Dr. Kiss Says Yes. Jam, Teddy. 32p. (ps-1). 1992. 12.95 (0-88899-141-X, Pub. by Groundwood-Douglas & McIntyre CN) Firefly Bks Ltd.
—Emily's House. Scharer, Niko. 24p. 1992. pap. 4.95 (0-88899-158-4, Pub. by Groundwood-Douglas & McIntyre CN) Firefly Bks Ltd.
—Plain Noodles. Waterton, Betty. 32p. 1993. pap. 4.95 (0-88899-132-0, Pub. by Groundwood-Douglas & McIntyre CN) Firefly Bks Ltd.
—Ten Small Tales. Lottridge, Celia B. LC 92-2878. 64p. (gr. k-4). 1994. SBE 15.95 (0-689-50568-X, M K McElderry) Macmillan Child Grp.

Fitzhugh, Greg. Home Is Where Your Family Is. Kavanagh, Katie. 1994. write for info. (0-8114-4462-7) Raintree Steck-V.

Fitzhugh, Louise. Harriet the Spy. Fitzhugh, Louise. LC 64-19711. 224p. (gr. 4-7). 1964. 15.00 (0-06-021910-6); PLB 14.89 (0-06-021911-4) HarpC Child Bks.
—Harriet the Spy. large type ed. Fitzhugh, Louise. 282p. (gr. 2-6). 1987. Repr. of 1964 ed. lib. bdg. 13.95 (1-55736-012-X, Crnrstn Bks) BDD LT Grp.
—Harriet the Spy. Fitzhugh, Louise. LC 64-19711. 304p. (gr. 3-7). 1990. pap. 3.95 (0-06-440331-9, Trophy) HarpC Child Bks.
—I Am Five. Fitzhugh, Louise. LC 78-50404. (ps-2). 1978. PLB 5.47 (0-440-03953-3); pap. 5.95 (0-440-03952-5) Delacorte.
—Long Secret. Fitzhugh, Louise. LC 65-23370. (gr. 5 up). 1965. 15.00i (0-06-021410-4); PLB 14.89 (0-06-021411-2) HarpC Child Bks.
—The Long Secret. Fitzhugh, Louise. LC 65-23370. 288p. (gr. 3-7). 1990. pap. 3.95 (0-06-440332-7, Trophy) HarpC Child Bks.

Fitzsimmons, Cecilia, jt. illus. see Kuo Kang Chen.

FitzSimmons, Joy. Hide & Seek. FitzSimmons, Joy. LC 91-38246. 32p. (ps). 1992. PLB 9.95 (0-87226-467-X, Bedrick Blackie) P Bedrick Bks.

Fix, Philippe. Not So Very Long Ago: Life in a Small Country Village. Fix, Philippe. LC 93-8428. 40p. (gr. 2 up). 1994. 16.99 (0-525-44594-3, DCB) Dutton Child Bks.

Flack, Marjorie. Ask Mr. Bear. Flack, Marjorie. LC 58-8370. 32p. (ps-1). 1971. pap. 3.95 (0-02-043090-6, Aladdin) Macmillan Child Grp.
—Ask Mr. Bear. Flack, Marjorie. (ps-3). 1990. incl. cass. 19.95 (0-87499-044-0); pap. 12.95 incl. cass. (0-87499-043-2); Set; incl. 4 bks., cass., & guide. pap. 27.95 (0-87499-045-9) Live Oak Media.
—The Country Bunny & the Little Gold Shoes. Heyward, Du Bose. 48p. (gr. k-3). 1974. reinforced bdg. 13.45 (0-395-15990-3, Sandpiper); pap. 4.80 (0-395-18557-2, Sandpiper) HM.
—The Country Bunny & the Little Gold Shoes. Heyward, DuBose. (ps-3). 1989. pap. 7.70 incl. cassette (0-395-52140-8) HM.

Flanagan, Terry. The Old Ones: A Children's Book about the Anasazi Indians. Brian, J. & Freeman, Jodi L. LC 86-50383. 64p. (Orig.). (gr. k-4). 1986. pap. 2.95 (0-937871-27-3) Think Shop.

Flanagen, Romie, photos by. A Visit to the Police Station. Hannum, Dotti. LC 84-12700. 32p. (gr. k-3). 1985. PLB 15.00 (0-516-01493-5) Childrens.

Flanigan, Ruth J. The Littlest Mermaid. Stapleton, John T. 24p. (ps-2). 1992. pap. 0.99 (1-56293-109-1) McClanahan Bk.
—My First Day at School. Herman, Emmi S. 24p. (ps-2). 1992. pap. 0.99 (1-56293-106-7) McClanahan Bk.

Flashinski, Todd. Just As We Are. Flashinski, Linda. 120p. (gr. k-8). 1987. spiral bdg. 11.95 (0-9619625-0-X); lib. bdg. 14.95 (0-9619625-1-8) Lavinia Pub.

Flather, Lisa. Where the Great Bear Watches. Sage, James. 32p. (ps-3). 1993. 13.99 (0-670-84933-2) Viking Child Bks.

Flavin, Teresa. Charlie's House. Bulla, Clyde R. LC 92-23998. 96p. (gr. 3-6). 1993. 14.00 (0-679-83841-4) Knopf Bks Yng Read.
—A Haunted Year. Phillips, Ann. LC 92-45638. 144p. (gr. 4-7). 1994. SBE 14.95 (0-02-774605-4, Macmillan Child Bk) Macmillan Child Grp.

Flax, Zena. Experimenting with Batteries, Bulbs, & Wires. Ward, Alan. 48p. (gr. 2-7). 1991. lib. bdg. 12.95 (0-7910-1516-5) Chelsea Hse.
—Experimenting with Energy. Ward, Alan. 48p. (gr. 2-7). 1991. lib. bdg. 12.95 (0-7910-1510-6) Chelsea Hse.
—Experimenting with Light & Illusions. Ward, Alan. 48p. (gr. 2-7). 1991. lib. bdg. 12.95 (0-7910-1514-9) Chelsea Hse.
—Experimenting with Magnetism. Ward, ALan. 48p. (gr. 2-7). 1991. lib. bdg. 12.95 (0-7910-1509-2) Chelsea Hse.
—Experimenting with Nature Study. Ward, Alan. 48p. (gr. 2-7). 1991. lib. bdg. 12.95 (0-7910-1515-7) Chelsea Hse.
—Experimenting with Science about Yourself. Ward, Alan. 48p. (gr. 2-7). 1991. lib. bdg. 12.95 (0-7910-1512-2) Chelsea Hse.
—Experimenting with Surface Tension & Bubbles. Ward, Alan. 48p. (gr. 2-7). 1991. lib. bdg. 12.95 (0-7910-1513-0) Chelsea Hse.
—The Wind in the Willows. Grahame, Kenneth. LC 85-13538. 224p. (gr. 2 up). 1985. 12.95 (0-915361-32-9, Dist. by Watts) Modan-Adama Bks.

Fleischer, Stephanie. Messing Around with Drinking Straw Construction: A Children's Museum Activity Book. Zubrowski, Bernie. 64p. (gr. 3-7). 1981. 8.95 (0-316-98875-8); pap. 7.95 (0-685-57751-1) Little.

Fleischman, Luke T. Pony. Baber, Carolyn S. 22p. 1990. pap. 9.95 (0-9628937-0-6, TX2910777) Richmond Saddlery.

Fleishman, Seymour. Babe Ruth: One of Baseball's Greatest. Van Riper, Guernsey, Jr. LC 86-10957. 192p. (gr. 2-6). 1986. pap. 3.95 (0-02-042130-3, Aladdin) Macmillan Child Grp.
—Friends: A Handbook about Getting Along Together. Ziegler, Sandra. LC 81-17025. 112p. (gr. 2-6). 1980. PLB 21.35 (0-89565-207-2); PLB 14.95s.p. (0-685-55480-5) Childs World.
—Gus Loved His Happy Home. Thayer, Jane. LC 88-36962. 32p. (ps-2). 1989. PLB 15.00 (0-208-02249-X, Linnet) Shoe String.
—Little Old Man Who Could Not Read. Black, Irma S. LC 68-9115. (gr. k-2). 1968. PLB 11.95 (0-8075-4621-6) A Whitman.
—A Veces las Cosas Cambian (Sometimes Things Change) Eastman, Patricia. LC 83-10090. (SPA.). 32p. (ps-2). 1988. PLB 11.93 (0-516-32044-0); pap. 2.95 (0-516-52044-X) Childrens.

Fleming, Beverly A. Scott the Dot: A Self-Esteem Tale for Children. Fleming, Beverly A. LC 91-44898. 32p. (Orig.). (ps-3). 1992. pap. 3.95 (0-915166-73-9) Impact Pubs Cal.

Fleming, Denise. The Care Bears Help Santa. Kahn, Peggy. LC 84-3385. 40p. (ps-3). 1984. lib. bdg. 4.99 (0-394-96807-7, BYR) Random Bks Yng Read.
—Count! Fleming, Denise. LC 91-25686. 32p. (ps-1). 1992. 14.95 (0-8050-1595-7, Bks Young Read) H Holt & Co.
—In the Small, Small Pond. Fleming, Denise. LC 92-25770. 32p. (ps-1). 1993. PLB 15.95 (0-8050-2264-3, Bks Young Read) H Holt & Co.
—In the Tall, Tall Grass. Fleming, Denise. LC 90-26444. 32p. (ps-1). 1991. 15.95 (0-8050-1635-X, Bks Young Read) H Holt & Co.
—In the Tall, Tall Grass. Fleming, Denise. 32p. (ps-1). 1993. pap. 19.95 (0-8050-2950-8, Bks Young Read) H Holt & Co.

Fleming, Leanne. Baba Nangko. Bettison, Joan. LC 93-26225. 1994. 4.25 (0-383-03733-6) SRA Schl Grp.
—Breakfast. King, Virginia. LC 92-21391. 1993. 2.50 (0-383-03556-2) SRA Schl Grp.
—Does a Duck Eat Honey? Drew, David. LC 92-31917. 1993. 4.25 (0-383-03563-5) SRA Schl Grp.
—Getting the Mail. Anderson, Honey & Reinholtd, Bill. LC 92-34338. 1993. 3.75 (0-383-03624-0) SRA Schl Grp.
—Hands & Feet. Markham-David, Sally. LC 93-28978. 1994. 4.25 (0-383-03746-8) SRA Schl Grp.
—I Went to Visit a Friend One Day. Ferguson, Virginia & Durkin, Peter. LC 92-31926. 1993. 4.25 (0-383-03575-9) SRA Schl Grp.
—Toenails. Drew, David. LC 92-31135. 1993. 2.50 (0-383-03661-5) SRA Schl Grp.
—Waiting. Ferguson, Virginia & Durkin, Peter. LC 92-34336. 1993. 3.75 (0-383-03663-1) SRA Schl Grp.

Fleming, S., jt. illus. see Maloney, M.

Fleming, Stan & Maloney, Mary. Blue Bug's Beach Party. Poulet, Virginia. LC 74-31224. 32p. (gr. k-3). 1975. PLB 15.00 (0-516-03423-5) Childrens.

Fleming, Stan, jt. illus. see Maloney, Mary.

Flesher, Vivienne. East of the Sun, West of the Moon. MacHale, Don. LC 91-15220. 40p. (gr. k up). 1992. pap. 14.95 (0-88708-192-4, Rabbit Ears); incl. cass. 19.95 (0-88708-193-2, Rabbit Ears) Picture Bk Studio.

Fletcher, Amy. Baptism My Promise to Jesus. Clawson, Jan. 24p. (Orig.). (gr. 1-3). 1988. pap. 3.95 (0-88290-298-9) Horizon Utah.

Fletcher, Bill & Fletcher, Sally. The Universe is My Home: A Children's Adventure Story. Fletcher, Bill & Fletcher, Sally. 34p. (gr. k-5). 1993. 14.95 (0-9634622-0-2) Sci & Art Prods.

Fletcher, Claire. The Snow Angel. McAllister, Angela. LC 92-44155. 1993. write for info. (0-688-04569-3) Lothrop.

Fletcher, Sally, jt. illus. see Fletcher, Bill.

Fleuter, Craig. Kunu: Winnebago Boy Escapes. Thomasma, Kenneth. LC 89-15074. 183p. (ps-8). 1992. 10.99 (0-8010-8891-7); pap. 6.99 (0-8010-8892-5) Baker Bk.

Flick, Deborah M. When Peanut Butter Is Not Enough. Beachy, Mary D. & Wolferman, Kristie. 100p. (gr. 2-7). 1986. pap. 7.95 (0-9616883-0-0) Petit Appetit.

Flint, Ross. The Legend of Sleepy Hollow. Irving, Washington. LC 92-72020. 32p. (gr. k-4). 1992. pap. 4.95 (0-8249-8574-5, Ideals Child) Hambleton-Hill.

Flint, Russ. The Big Book of Bible Crafts & Projects. MacKenzie, Joy. 212p. (ps-4). 1981. pap. 15.99 (0-310-70151-1, 14019P) Zondervan.
—A Christmas Carol. Dickens, Charles. Kennedy, Pam, ed. 32p. (gr. k-6). 1985. pap. 2.95 (0-8249-8099-9, Ideals Child) Hambleton-Hill.
—Earl the Squirrel. Brennan, Gale. 16p. (Orig.). (gr. k-6). 1981. pap. 1.25 (0-685-02455-5) Brennan Bks.
—Henry the Hound. LaFleur, Tom & Brennan, Gale. 16p. (Orig.). (gr. k-6). 1982. pap. 1.25 (0-685-05556-6) Brennan Bks.
—The Legend of Sleepy Hollow. Irving, Washington. LC 91-72020. 32p. (gr. k-3). 1991. 12.95 (0-8249-8162-6, Ideals Child) (0-685-48861-6) Hambleton-Hill.
—My Very First Bible - New Testament. Sattgast, L. J. (Orig.). (ps-3). 1989. 16.99 (0-89081-756-1) Harvest Hse.
—Toulouse the Mouse. Brennan, Gale. 16p. (Orig.). (gr. k-6). 1981. pap. 1.25 (0-685-02458-X) Brennan Bks.

Flippin, Terry, jt. illus. see Anderson, Cindy.

Floca, Brian. City of Light, City of Dark: A Comic Book Novel. Avi. LC 93-2887. 192p. (gr. 4 up). 1993. 15.95 (0-531-06800-5); PLB 15.99 (0-531-08650-X) Orchard Bks Watts.

Floethe, Richard. The Avion My Uncle Flew. Fisher, Cyrus. 254p. (gr. 5 up). 1993. pap. 4.99 (0-14-036487-0, Puffin) Puffin Bks.
—The Dream Book: First Comes the Dream. Brown, Margaret Wise. 32p. (gr. 1-3). 1990. Repr. of 1950 ed. 9.95 (0-685-45149-6) WaterMark Inc.

Flood, William J., et al. Remember Your Relatives, Vol. 1: Yankton Sioux Images, 1851 to 1904. Sansom-Flood, Renee & Bernie, Shirley A. Bruguier, Leonard R., ed. Hoover, Herbert T., intro. by. 55p. (Orig.). (gr. 12). 1985. pap. 8.50 (0-9621936-0-7) Yankton Sioux Tribe.

Flor, Dick. Acid Rain Curriculum. Stubbs, Harriett, et al. (Orig.). (gr. 4-8). 1985. tchrs' ed. 19.95 (0-935577-00-9) Acid Rain Found.

Flora. Feathers Like a Rainbow: An Amazon Indian Tale. Flora. LC 88-26788. 32p. (gr. k-3). 1989. PLB 14.89 (0-06-021838-X) HarpC Child Bks.

Flora, James. The Fabulous Firework Family. Flora, James. LC 93-11472. (SPA.). 32p. (gr. k-4). 1994. SBE 14.95 (0-689-50596-5, M K McElderry) Macmillan Child Grp.

Florczak, Robert. The Rainbow Bridge. Wood, Audrey. LC 92-17661. 1993. write for info. (0-15-265475-5) HarBrace.

Flores, Lennie. Princess Jessica Rescues a Prince. Brooks, Jennifer. Ridley, Chas, ed. LC 93-92628. 40p. (ps-2). 1994. 15.95 (0-9636335-0-3) Nadja Pub.
In 1991, the American Association of University Women appointed a study on the emotional development of girls. The study revealed that girls have a much lower self-image & less self-confidence than boys. Strong female characters featured in quality books can provide positive role models to help improve girls' self-esteem. Little girls have always loved the popular princess stories. They adore the glamorous young women & dream of growing up to be just like them. The early impressions made by the classic fairy tales stay with us a lifetime. Considering this, a princess should be worthy of such a high regard. Rather than passively wasting her life away waiting for a Prince Charming, an admirable young princess would independently create adventures of her own. When finding herself in a dangerous situation, instead of crying helplessly, a deserving princess would exhibit courage & determination. Lastly, a princess should be beloved not merely for her physical characteristics but for all the inner qualities that constitute real beauty. Princess Jessica doesn't really care if she's considered beautiful or not. She has lots of interesting things to do. One day, three handicapped gnomes arrive at Princess Jessica's castle. They tell her of a prince far away whose singing is so beautiful that he was carried off by a lonesome sea serpent. Princess Jessica & her vain sister, Edith, set out to rescue Prince Ryan. Through her trials Princess Jessica learns about strength & love.
Publisher Provided Annotation.

Florian. King Arthur & His Knights of the Round Table. Mallory, Thomas. Lanier, Sidney & Pyle, Howard, eds. 288p. (gr. 4-6). 1950. (G&D); 13.95 (0-448-06016-7, G&D) Putnam Pub Group.

Florian, Douglas. An Auto Mechanic. Florian, Douglas. 24p. (ps up). 1994. pap. 3.95 (0-688-13104-2, Mulberry) Morrow.

—City Street. Florian, Douglas. LC 89-28694. 32p. (ps up). 1990. 12.95 (0-688-09543-7); PLB 12.88 (0-688-09544-5) Greenwillow.

—Discovering Frogs. Florian, Douglas. LC 86-6731. 32p. (ps-3). 1986. SBE 13.95 (0-684-18688-8, Scribners Young Read) Macmillan Child Grp.

—Discovering Seashells. Florian, Douglas. LC 86-11903. 32p. (ps-2). 1986. SBE 13.95 (0-684-18740-X, Scribners Young Read) Macmillan Child Grp.

—A Rumbly Tumbly Glittery Gritty Place. Ray, Mary L. LC 92-20084. 1993. 13.95 (0-15-292861-8, HB Juv Bks) HarBrace.

—Turtle Day. Florian, Douglas. LC 88-30321. 32p. (ps-2). 1989. (Crowell Jr Bks); PLB 13.89 (0-690-04745-2, Crowell Jr Bks) HarpC Child Bks.

Florman, Lisa. The Mudgrump. Greene, Jack. LC 80-68130. 56p. (Orig.). (gr. k-6). 1980. pap. text ed. 3.95 perfect binding (0-9601258-3-3) Golden Owl Pub.

Flory, Jane. The Great Bamboozlement. Flory, Jane. 160p. (gr. 5-9). 1982. 13.45 (0-395-31859-9) HM.

Floyd, Gareth. The Hallowe'en Cat. Lillington, Kenneth. 64p. (gr. 3-7). 1987. pap. 3.95 (0-571-15463-8) Faber & Faber.

—The Real Live Dinosaur & Other Stories. Lillington, Kenneth. 144p. (gr. 3-7). 1992. pap. 4.95 (0-571-16318-1) Faber & Faber.

—The Writing on the Hearth. Harnett, Cynthia. LC 83-23904. 300p. (gr. 5 up). 1984. PLB 13.50 (0-8225-0889-3) Lerner Pubns.

Fluek, Toby. Passover As I Remember It. Fluek, Toby. LC 92-9020. 40p. (gr. k-5). 1994. 14.00 (0-679-88876-7) Knopf Bks Yng Read.

Flynn, Amy. Doll Party. Herman, Gail. LC 93-12685. (ps-1). 1994. pap. write for info. (0-448-40182-7, G&D) Putnam Pub Group.

—Noah's Ark. Hayward, Linda. LC 92-64138. 22p. (ps). 1993. 3.25 (0-679-83600-4) Random Bks Yng Read.

—Teddy's Busy Night. 24p. (ps). 1993. bds. 2.95 (0-448-40557-1, G&D) Putnam Pub Group.

—Teeny Tiny Farm. Ross, Katharine. LC 91-50647. 22p. (ps). 1992. 2.95 (0-679-83388-9) Random Bks Yng Read.

Flynn, Barbara. Gildaen: The Heroic Adventures of a Most Unusual Rabbit. Buchwald, Emilie. LC 93-16255. 1993. 12.95 (0-915943-38-7) Milkweed Ed.

—Swamps & Marshes. Sabin, Francene. LC 84-2717. 32p. (gr. 3-6). 1985. PLB 9.49 (0-8167-0280-2); pap. text ed. 2.95 (0-8167-0281-0) Troll Assocs.

Flynn, Mary J. The Blue Kangaroo. Flynn, Mary J. 24p. (Orig.). (ps-k). 1992. pap. text ed. 5.95 (1-880812-03-7) S Ink WA.

—If a Seahorse Wore a Saddle. Flynn, Mary J. 48p. (Orig.). (ps-1). 1991. pap. 10.95 (0-9623072-3-8) S Ink WA.

—The Lost & Found Puppy. Flynn, Mary J. 48p. (Orig.). (gr. k-1). 1991. pap. 10.95 (0-9623072-6-2) S Ink WA.

Flynn-Stanton, Maggie. One Baby Boy. Ketteman, Helen. LC 93-23044. 1994. pap. 15.00 (0-671-87278-8, S&S BFYR) S&S Trade.

Focus on Sports-New York Staff. Football All Pro Defense. Balzer, Howard. Allison, B., intro. by. 28p. (Orig.). 1989. pap. 2.50 (0-943409-10-1) Marketcom.

—Football All Pro Offense. Balzer, Howard. Allison, B., intro. by. (Orig.). 1989. pap. 2.50 (0-943409-09-8) Marketcom.

—Football All Pro Super Stars. Balzer, Howard. Allison, B., ed. 28p. (Orig.). 1989. pap. 2.50 (0-943409-11-X) Marketcom.

Foehl, Barbara B. Trick or Treat Taffy. Foehl, Jamie L. LC 89-92436. 40p. (Orig.). (ps-6). 1989. write for info. (0-9625337-0-X); PLB write for info.; pap. write for info. B Bk Pub Co.

Fogarty, Michelle D. Divorce Happens to the Nicest Kids: A Self-Help Book For Kids (3-15) & Adults. Prokop, Michael S. Peters, Robert C., ed. LC 85-72180. 224p. (Orig.). (gr. k up). 1986. 18.95 (0-933879-25-3); pap. 6.45 Kids' Divorce Wkbk. (0-933879-26-1); kids' Divorce wkbk. 6.45 (0-933879-27-X) Alegra Hse Pubs.

Fogarty, Pat. Meet Benjamin Franklin. Scarf, Maggi. LC 88-17657. 64p. (gr. 2-4). 1989. PLB 6.99 (0-394-91961-0); pap. text ed. 2.99 (0-394-81961-6) Random Bks Yng Read.

—Meet Thomas Jefferson. Barrett, Marvin. LC 88-19069. 72p. (gr. 2-4). 1989. pap. 2.99 (0-394-81964-0) Random Bks Yng Read.

Foglio, Phil. Illegal Aliens. Pollotta, Nick & Foglio, Phil. LC 88-51727. 320p. (Orig.). 1989. pap. 3.95 (0-88038-715-7) TSR Inc.

Foleen, Chris. The Way of the Circle. Vollbracht, James. 48p. (gr. 4-8). 1993. pap. 6.95 (0-915166-76-3) Impact Pubs Cal.

Foley, Pat. Seismo & Ellie. 2nd ed. Foley, Pat. 14p. (gr. k-1). 1990. pap. 6.00 (0-9624315-1-6) Pajari Pr.

Foley, Timothy. Parables from Nature: Earthly Stories with Heavenly Meanings. 2nd ed. Reid, John C. 96p. (gr. k-4). 1991. pap. 8.99 (0-8028-4052-3) Eerdmans.

—Pink Lemonade. Schmidt, Annie. Ten Harmsel, Henrietta, tr. 64p. (ps-6). 1992. 14.99 (0-8028-4050-7) Eerdmans.

—Trash Can Review. De Jonge, Joanne. 64p. (Orig.). 1992. pap. 7.99 (0-8028-5071-5) Eerdmans.

Foley, Tom. Sakshi Gopal: A Witness for the Wedding. Greene, Joshua, retold by. 16p. (gr. 1-4). 1981. pap. 2.00 (0-89647-036-9) Bala Bks.

Folkard, Charles. Rock-a-Bye Rhymes: Miniature Nursery Rhyme Books, 4 bks. Daglish, Alice & Rhys, Ernest. (ps-3). 1993. Repr. of 1932 ed. Set, miniature bks. in rocking-horse slipcase. 16.95 (0-8118-0537-9) Chronicle Bks.

Folkens, Pieter. Exploring the World of Insects: The Equinox Guide to Insect Behavior. Forsyth, Adrian. 64p. (gr. 5 up). 1992. PLB 17.95 (0-921820-47-X, Pub. by Camden Hse CN); pap. 9.95 (0-921820-49-6, Pub. by Camden Hse CN) Firefly Bks Ltd.

—Great Whales: The Gentle Giants. Lauber, Patricia. 64p. (gr. 2-4). 1991. 14.95 (0-8050-1717-8, Redfeather BYR) H Holt & Co.

—Great Whales: The Gentle Giants. Lauber, Patricia. LC 91-692. 64p. (gr. 2-4). 1993. pap. 4.95 (0-8050-2894-3, Bks Young Read) H Holt & Co.

—Meeting the Whales: The Equinox Guide to Giants of the Deep. Hoyt, Eric. 72p. (gr. 5 up). 1991. lib. bdg. 17.95 (0-921820-25-9, Pub. by Camden Hse CN); pap. 9.95 (0-921820-23-2, Pub. by Camden Hse CN) Firefly Bks Ltd.

—Riding with the Dolphins: The Equinox Guide to Dolphins & Porpoises. Hoyt, Erich. 64p. (gr. 5 up). 1992. PLB 17.95 (0-921820-55-0, Pub. by Camden Hse CN); pap. 9.95 (0-921820-57-7, Pub. by Camden Hse CN) Firefly Bks Ltd.

Fontalvo, Nelsy. The Day the T. V. Broke. Denholtz, Roni S. LC 86-81371. 32p. (gr. k-2). 1986. PLB 7.59 (0-87386-016-0); pap. 1.95 (0-87386-012-8) Jan Prods.

—The Ghost in the New House. Denholtz, Roni S. LC 86-81369. 32p. (gr. k-2). 1986. PLB 7.59 (0-87386-017-9); pap. 1.95 (0-87386-013-6) Jan Prods.

Fontilis, Glen. Kobi the Elf, Magic & Adventure in Hawaii. Hober, David. Pickett, Timothy & Okaze, Kunio, eds. Nagaoki, Kobun, tr. (ENG & JPN.). 32p. (Orig.). (gr. 1 up). 1990. pap. 4.95 (0-9623215-0-8) Moonbeam Magic Pub.

Foord, Jo, photos by. The Book of Babies: A First Picture Book of All the Things That Babies Do. LC 90-39490. 32p. (ps). 1991. 10.95 (0-679-80955-4); PLB 12.99 (0-679-90955-9) Random Bks Yng Read.

Foott, Jeff, photos by. A Pod of Killer Whales. Leon, Vicki. 40p. (gr. 5 up). 1988. pap. 7.95 (0-918303-16-8) Blake Pub.

Forbell, Charles. Marionettes: How to Make & Work Them. Fling, Helen. (gr. 6 up). 16.50 (0-8446-4736-5) Peter Smith.

Forberg, Ati. Samurai of Gold Hill. rev. ed. Uchida, Yoshiko. LC 84-20424. 128p. (gr. 4-12). 1985. pap. 5.95 (0-916870-86-3) Creative Arts Bk.

—The Skates of Uncle Richard. Fenner, Carol. LC 78-55910. (gr. 2-5). 1978. lib. bdg. 7.99 (0-394-93553-5) Random Bks Yng Read.

Forbes, Alex. All about Divorce. Field, Mary B. Shapiro, Lawrence, intro. by. 150p. (Orig.). (gr. k-6). 1992. pap. 16.95 (1-882732-00-6) Ctr Applied Psy.

Forbes, Bart. All-Time Great World Series. Gutelle, Andrew. LC 93-35668. 1994. write for info. (0-448-40471-0, G&D) Putnam Pub Group.

Forbis, Judith E. Hoofbeats along the Tigris. Forbis, Judith E. Forbis, Donald L., intro. by. 146p. (gr. 8 up). 1990. Repr. 34.95 (0-9625644-1-9) Ansata Pubns.

Ford. The Orange Fairy Book. Lang, Andrew. (gr. 4-12). 18.75 (0-8446-4770-5) Peter Smith.

Ford, Elizabeth. If You Have a Duck... rev. ed. Kelty, Jean M. LC 82-51120. 104p. (gr. 1-9). 1982. pap. 9.95 (0-910781-00-1) G Whittell Mem.

Ford, George. Afro-Bets First Book about Africa. Ellis, Veronica F. LC 89-85157. 32p. (Orig.). (gr. 1-4). 1990. PLB 13.95 (0-940975-12-2); pap. 6.95 (0-940975-03-3) Just Us Bks.

—Baby's First Picture Book. Ford, George. LC 79-62941. (ps). 1979. 3.50 (0-394-84245-6) Random Bks Yng Read.

—The Best Time of Day. Flournoy, Valerie. LC 77-91641. 32p. (ps-1). 1992. PLB 5.99 (0-394-93799-6); 2.25 (0-394-83799-1) Random Bks Yng Read.

—Bright Eyes, Brown Skin. Hudson, Cheryl W. & Ford, Bernette G. LC 90-81648. 24p. (ps-2). 1990. 12.95 (0-940975-10-6); pap. 6.95 (0-940975-23-8) Just Us Bks.

—Ego-Tripping & Other Poems for Young People. Giovanni, Nikki. LC 73-81745. 37p. (gr. 2-7). 1974. pap. 7.95 (1-55652-062-X) L Hill Bks.

—Ego-Tripping & Other Poems for Young People. 2nd, rev. ed. Giovanni, Nikki. LC 93-29578. 72p. (gr. 5-12). 1994. 14.95 (1-55652-188-X); pap. 9.95 (1-55652-189-8) L Hill Bks.

—Good Night Baby. Hudson, Cheryl W. 1992. bds. 5.95 (0-590-45761-6, Cartwheel) Scholastic Inc.

—The Hunter Who Was King & Other African Tales. Ford, Bernette. LC 93-10278. 16p. (ps-3). 1994. 14.95 (1-56282-585-2) Hyprn Child.

—Jackie Robinson. Weinberg, Lawrence. 48p. (gr. 2-4). 1988. pap. 2.50 (0-681-40690-9) Longmeadow Pr.

—Paul Robeson. Greenfield, Eloise. LC 74-13663. 40p. (gr. 1-5). 1975. PLB 15.89 (0-690-00660-8, Crowell Jr Bks) HarpC Child Bks.

—Thomas Edison. Weinberg, Michael. 48p. (gr. 2-4). 1988. pap. 2.50 (0-681-40687-9) Longmeadow Pr.

—Willie's Wonderful Pet. Cebulash, Mel. 32p. (ps-2). 1993. pap. 2.95 (0-590-45787-X) Scholastic Inc.

Ford, H. J. Arabian Nights Entertainments. Lang, Andrew, ed. LC 69-17098. xv, 424p. (gr. k-6). 1969. pap. 6.95 (0-486-22289-6) Dover.

—The Crimson Fairy Book. Lang, Andrew. LC 67-17988. (gr. 4-8). 18.75 (0-8446-0753-3) Peter Smith.

—The Green Fairy Book. Lang, Andrew, ed. (gr. 4 up). 18.75 (0-8446-5056-0) Peter Smith.

—Lilac Fairy Book. Lang, Andrew, ed. 367p. (ps-4). 1968. pap. 6.95 (0-486-21907-0) Dover.

—Olive Fairy Book. Lang, Andrew, ed. 330p. (gr. 4-6). 1966. pap. 5.95 (0-486-21908-9) Dover.

—The Olive Fairy Book. Lang, Andrew. (gr. 2 up). 17.00 (0-8446-0754-1) Peter Smith.

—Orange Fairy Book. Lang, Andrew, ed. 358p. (gr. 1-6). 1968. pap. 6.95 (0-486-21909-7) Dover.

—The Pink Fairy Book. Lang, Andrew. (gr. 2 up). 18.75 (0-8446-0755-X) Peter Smith.

—The Violet Fairy Book. Lang, Andrew. (gr. 2 up). 18.75 (0-8446-0757-6) Peter Smith.

—The Yellow Fairy Book. Lang, Andrew. (gr. 2 up). 18. 75 (0-8446-0758-4) Peter Smith.

Ford, H. J. & Speed. The Red Fairy Book. Lang, Andrew. (gr. 2 up). 18.75 (0-8446-0756-8) Peter Smith.

Ford, Henry J. Brown Fairy Book. Lang, Andrew, ed. (gr. 1-6). pap. 6.95 (0-486-21438-9) Dover.

—Crimson Fairy Book. Lang, Andrew, ed. LC 67-17988. 371p. (gr. 4-6). 1966. pap. 6.95 (0-486-21799-X) Dover.

—Green Fairy Book. Lang, Andrew, ed. LC 34-28314. 366p. (gr. 4-6). 1965. pap. 6.95 (0-486-21439-7) Dover.

—Grey Fairy Book. Lang, Andrew, ed. LC 67-17983. 387p. (gr. 4-6). 1900. pap. 6.95 (0-486-21791-4) Dover.

—Pink Fairy Book. Lang, Andrew. 360p. (gr. 4-6). 1966. pap. 6.95 (0-486-21792-2) Dover.

—A World of Fairy Tales. Lang, Andrew & Philip, Neil, eds. LC 92-64245. 256p. 1993. 20.00 (0-8037-1250-2) Dial Bks Young.

—Yellow Fairy Book. Lang, Andrew, ed. 321p. (gr. 4-6). pap. 6.95 (0-486-21674-8) Dover.

Ford, Henry J. & Hood, G. P. Blue Fairy Book. Lang, Andrew, ed. LC 34-28315. 390p. (gr. 1-6). 1965. pap. 6.95 (0-486-21437-0) Dover.

Ford, Henry J. & Lang, H. J. Violet Fairy Book. Lang, Andrew, ed. (gr. 4-6). pap. 6.95 (0-486-21675-6) Dover.

Ford, Henry J. & Speed, Lancelot. Red Fairy Book. Lang, Andrew, ed. 367p. (gr. 4-6). pap. 6.95 (0-486-21673-X) Dover.

Ford, Jeremy. The Moon Monster. Hill, Douglas. 42p. (gr. 2-4). 1989. 3.95 (0-8120-6138-1) Barron.

Ford, John K., photos by. Killer Whales. Patent, Dorothy H. LC 92-23949. 32p. (gr. 3-7). 1993. reinforced bdg. 15.95 (0-8234-0999-6) Holiday.

Ford, Lauren. Little Book about God. Ford, Lauren. LC 81-43749. 48p. (ps-3). 1985. pap. 9.95 (0-385-17691-0) Doubleday.

Ford, Pam. Sometimes I Don't Like School. Hogan, Paula Z. Smith, David L., intro. by. LC 79-24055. 32p. (gr. k-6). 1980. PLB 17.96 (0-8172-1357-0) Raintree Steck-V.

Ford, Pamela B. Bremen Town Musicians. Grimm, Jacob & Grimm, Wilhelm K. LC 78-18064. 32p. (gr. k-3). 1979. PLB 9.79 (0-89375-133-2); pap. 1.95 (0-89375-111-1) Troll Assocs.

—Emperor's New Clothes. Andersen, Hans Christian. LC 78-18063. 32p. (gr. k-4). 1979. PLB 9.79 (0-89375-132-4); pap. 1.95 (0-89375-110-3) Troll Assocs.

Ford, Phyllis. The Twelve Powers of Animals. Dikis, Eloise. Wortman, Mary, ed. 44p. (ps-5). 1989. comb bdg. 7.95 (0-939339-06-4) AFCOM Pub.

Ford, Wayne & Robson, Eric. Lake & River Animals. Chinery, Michael. LC 92-20471. 1993. write for info. (0-679-93704-8); pap. write for info. (0-679-83704-3) Knopf Bks Yng Read.

—Questions & Answers about Freshwater Animals. Chinery, Michael. LC 93-29415. 1994. 5.95 (1-85697-962-8) Kingfisher Bks.

Ford, Wayne, et al. Questions & Answers about Seashore Animals. Chinery, Michael. LC 93-29428. 1994. 5.95 Kingfisher Bks.

Fordes, Laurence. Book. Brookfield, Karen. 64p. (gr. 5 up). 1993. 15.00 (0-679-84012-5); PLB 15.99 (0-679-94012-X) Knopf Bks Yng Read.

Fordyce, Lawrence. The Mississippi. Morgan, Nina. LC 92-39950. 48p. (gr. 5-6). 1993. PLB 22.80 (0-8114-3103-7) Raintree Steck-V.

Foreman, Michael. The Boy Who Sailed with Columbus. Foreman, Michael. 80p. (gr. 1-4). 1992. 16.95 (1-55970-178-1) Arcade Pub Inc.

—A Cat & Mouse Love Story. Newman, Nanette & Foreman, Michael. 32p. (gr. k-3). 1985. 14.95 (0-434-98045-5, Pub. by W Heinemann Ltd) Trafalgar.

—A Child's Garden of Verses. Stevenson, Robert Louis. LC 85-12766. 128p. (ps-3). 1985. 14.95 (0-385-29430-1) Delacorte.

—City of Gold. Dickinson, Peter. 192p. (gr. 5 up). 1992. pap. 13.45 (0-395-63173-4) HM.

—Edmond Went Far Away. Bax, Martin. 32p. (ps-3). 1989. 12.95 (0-15-225105-7, HB Juv Bks) HarBrace.

—Fantastic Stories. large type ed. Jones, Terry. 1993. 15. 95 (0-7451-1908-5, Galaxy Child Lrg Print) Chivers N Amer.

—Grandfather's Pencil & the Room of Stories. Foreman, Michael. LC 93-6266. 1994. 14.95 (*0-15-200061-5*) HarBrace.
—Hans Andersen: His Classic Fairy Tales. Andersen, Hans Christian. Haugaard, Erik C., tr. LC 77-74792. 196p. (gr. 1 up). 1978. 15.95 (*0-385-13364-2*) Doubleday.
—I'll Take You to Mrs. Cole! Gray, Nigel. 32p. (ps-3). 1992. 12.95 (*0-916291-39-1*) Kane-Miller Bk.
—The Jungle Book. Kipling, Rudyard. (gr. 5-9). 1987. 19.99 (*0-670-80241-7*) Viking Child Bks.
—Just So Stories. Kipling, Rudyard. (ps up). 1987. 15.00 (*0-670-80242-5*) Viking Child Bks.
—Land of the Long White Cloud: Maori Myths, Tales, & Legends. Kiri, Te Kanawa. (gr. 3 up). 1990. 16.95 (*1-55970-046-7*) Arcade Pub Inc.
—The Long Weekend. Harrison, Troon. LC 93-307. (gr. k). 1994. write for info. (*0-15-248842-1*) HarBrace.
—Michael Foreman's World of Fairy Tales. Foreman, Michael, ed. 144p. (gr. 1 up). 1991. 18.95 (*1-55970-164-1*) Arcade Pub Inc.
—Nicobobinus. Jones, Terry. LC 85-28630. 176p. (gr. k-6). 1986. 16.95 (*0-87226-065-8*) P Bedrick Bks.
—The Night Before Christmas. Moore, Clement C. LC 88-50097. (ps up). 1988. pap. 11.95 (*0-670-82388-0*) Viking Child Bks.
—One World. Foreman, Michael. 32p. (gr. 2-5). 1991. 14.95 (*1-55970-108-0*) Arcade Pub Inc.
—Over in the Meadow. 20p. (ps). 1992. pap. 13.00 casebound, pop-up (*0-671-75109-3*, S&S BFYR) S&S Trade.
—Peter Pan & Wendy. Barrie, J. M. 160p. (gr. 3-6). 1992. (Pub. by Pavilion UK); pap. 17.95 (*1-85145-449-7*, Pub. by Pavilion UK) Trafalgar.
—Saga of Erik the Viking. Jones, Terry. 144p. (ps up). 1986. pap. 9.95 (*0-14-031713-9*, Puffin) Puffin Bks.
—The Saga of Erik the Viking. Jones, Terry. 192p. (gr. 3-7). 1993. pap. 3.99 (*0-14-032261-2*, Puffin) Puffin Bks.
—The Sand Horse. Turnbull, Ann. LC 89-9. 32p. (gr. k-3). 1989. SBE 13.95 (*0-689-31581-3*, Atheneum Child Bk) Macmillan Child Grp.
—Seasons of Splendor. Jaffrey, Madhur. (ps up). pap. 7.95 (*0-317-62172-6*, Puffin) Puffin Bks.
—Seasons of Splendour: Tales, Myths & Legends of India. Jaffrey, Madhur. 128p. (gr. 4 up). 1992. pap. 16.95 (*1-85145-933-2*, Pub. by Pavilion UK) Trafalgar.
—Shakespeare Stories. Garfield, Leon. LC 85-1971. 288p. (gr. 5 up). 1991. 24.45 (*0-395-56397-6*) HM.
—The Shining Princess & Other Japanese Legends. Quayle, Eric, retold by. 112p. (gr. k-5). 1989. 15.95 (*1-55970-039-4*) Arcade Pub Inc.
—Spider the Horrible Cat. Newman, Nanette. LC 92-17242. 1993. write for info. (*0-15-277972-8*) HarBrace.
—Tales for the Telling. O'Brien, Edna. LC 87-62364. 128p. (ps up). 1988. pap. 8.95 (*0-14-032293-0*, Puffin) Puffin Bks.
—Terry Jones' Fairy Tales. Jones, Terry. 128p. (ps up). 1986. pap. 8.95 (*0-14-031642-6*, Puffin) Puffin Bks.
—Terry Jones Fairy Tales. Jones, Terry. 160p. (gr. 3-7). 1993. pap. 3.99 (*0-14-032262-0*, Puffin) Puffin Bks.
—Terry Jones' Fantastic Stories. Jones, Terry. 128p. 1993. 16.99 (*0-670-84899-9*) Viking Child Bks.
—There's a Bear in the Bath! Newman, Nanette. LC 93-12877. 1994. write for info. (*0-15-285512-2*) HarBrace.
—War Boy: A Country Childhood. Foreman, Michael. 96p. (gr. 3 up). 1990. 16.95 (*1-55970-049-1*) Arcade Pub Inc.
—Worms Wiggle. Pelham, David. (ps-1). 1989. pap. 9.95 (*0-671-67218-5*, Little Simon) S&S Trade.
Foreman, Michael, jt. illus. see Wright, Freire.
Foreman, Michael, jt. illus. see Wright, Friere.
Forest, Sandra. The Cow That Could Tap Dance. Slater, Teddy. 24p. (ps-1). 1991. 5.95 (*0-671-70412-5*); PLB 9.98 (*0-671-70408-7*) Silver Pr.
—Jan & Dan & the Super Dads. Slater, Teddy. 24p. (ps-1). 1991. 5.95 (*0-671-70414-1*); PLB 9.98 (*0-671-70410-9*) Silver Pr.
Forest, Sandra & Rankin, Laura. Is That So? Series, 4 vols. Slater, Teddy. (ps-1). 1991. Set, 24p. ea. 23.80 (*0-671-31251-0*); Set, 24p. ea. lib. bdg. 39.92 (*0-671-31249-9*) Silver Pr.
Forgeot, Claire. The Rising of the Wind: Adventures along the Beaufort Scale. Yvart, Jacques. Lazorthes, Jean, tr. from FRE. LC 83-83203. 48p. (Orig.). (gr. 7 up). 1991. 12.95 (*0-88138-031-8*, Green Tiger) S&S Trade.
Forman, Jan A. Break Dance: The Free & Easy Way! Carter, Eneida & Mikalac, Miriam. 32p. (gr. 7 up). 1984. pap. 9.95 (*0-916391-00-0*) Free & Easy Pubns.
Formaro, Rita. Daily Math Adventures. Cook, Marcy. 64p. (gr. 3-8). 1987. pap. text ed. 8.50 (*0-914040-51-0*) Cuisenaire.
—Numbers & Words: A Problem Per Day. Cook, Marcy. 64p. (gr. 3-8). 1987. pap. text ed. 8.50 (*0-914040-52-9*) Cuisenaire.
Fornari, Giuliano. The Body Atlas. Parker, Steve. LC 92-54307. 64p. (gr. 3 up). 1993. 19.95 (*1-56458-224-8*) Dorling Kindersley.
—Great Dinosaur Atlas. Lindsay, William. (gr. 3 up). 1991. 16.00 (*0-671-74480-1*, J Messner); lib. bdg. 16.98 (*0-671-74479-8*, J Messner) S&S Trade.
Forrest, Sandra. Boogie-Woogie Bugs. Cooper, Don. (ps-3). 1989. bk. & cassette 5.95 (*0-394-82950-6*) Random Bks Yng Read.

—Fanny McFancy: A Passion for Fashion. Thackray, Patricia. LC 91-16447. 40p. 1991. 12.95 (*0-671-74980-3*, Green Tiger) S&S Trade.

Forrest, Sandy. Best Kids Love the Earth Activity Book. Eyre, Sue, ed. 96p. (Orig.). (gr. 4-7). 1993. pap. 11.99 (*0-376-04010-6*) Sunset Pub.
This lively & colorful book helps kids discover the earth & develop an appreciation for the environment. The bright & whimsical illustrations & color photographs throughout highlight dozens of hands-on projects & simple experiments, from gardening to attract butterflies to making a solar snack. Nature activities ranging from special hikes to crafts projects show kids how they can help the earth through their own actions. Basic earth systems are explained simply to help kids understand how each of us affects the rest of the earth's family. Specific, positive, action-oriented suggestions inspire & empower children, giving them a feeling that "I can do it!" Also available in this kid-tested & approved series are the BEST KIDS COOK BOOK. 112p. 1992. $9.99 (0-376-02083-0), BEST KIDS GARDEN BOOK. 96p. 1992. $9.99 (0-376-03076-3), & BEST KIDS COOKIE BOOK. 112p. 1993. $11.99 (0-376-02388-0). These innovative books capture a child's imagination & give him or her a sense of accomplishment. Sunset Publishing Corporation, 80 Willow Rd., Menlo Park, CA 94025; 800-227-7346, in CA 800-321-0372. *Publisher Provided Annotation.*

Forsey, Chris. Earth, Sea & Sky. Stacy, Tom. Vestal, J., ed. LC 90-12974. 40p. (gr. 4-5). 1991. PLB 12.40 (*0-531-19106-0*) Watts.
—Earth, Sea & Sky. Stacy, Tom. LC 90-42976. 40p. (Orig.). (gr. 2-5). 1991. pap. 3.95 (*0-679-80861-2*) Random Bks Yng Read.
—Forts & Castles. Moss, Miriam. LC 93-11167. 32p. (gr. 4-6). 1993. PLB 19.97 (*0-8114-6157-2*) Raintree Steck-V.
—Fossil Detective. Pope, Joyce. LC 91-45170. 32p. (gr. 3-6). 1993. PLB 11.59 (*0-8167-2781-3*); pap. text ed. 3.95 (*0-8167-2782-1*) Troll Assocs. Postponed.
—Journey Through France. Gamgee, John, ed. LC 91-46175. 32p. (gr. 3-5). 1993. PLB 11.89 (*0-8167-2759-7*); pap. text ed. 3.95 (*0-8167-2760-0*) Troll Assocs. Postponed.
—People & Places. Butterfield, Moira. LC 91-214. 40p. (Orig.). (gr. 2-5). 1991. pap. 3.99 (*0-679-80868-X*) Random Bks Yng Read.
—The Story of Astronomy. Scott, Carole. LC 91-36604. 32p. (gr. 1-4). 1993. PLB 11.89 (*0-8167-2703-1*); pap. text ed. 3.95 (*0-8167-2704-X*) Troll Assocs. Postponed.
—The Story of Dinosaurs. Parker, Steve. LC 91-39007. 32p. (gr. 1-4). 1993. PLB 11.89 (*0-8167-2707-4*); pap. text ed. 3.95 (*0-8167-2708-2*) Troll Assocs. Postponed.
Forsey, Chris & Kenyon, Tony. I Wonder Why Stars Twinkle & Other Questions about Space: And Other Questions about Space. Maynard, Chris. LC 92-44259. 32p. (gr. k-3). 1993. 8.95 (*1-85697-881-8*) Kingfisher Bks.
Forss, Ian. But Granny Did! Wild, Margaret. LC 92-31906. 1993. 3.75 (*0-383-03559-7*) SRA Schl Grp.
—Cook with Me. Liddelow, Lorelei. 126p. (Orig.). (gr. k-3). 1989. pap. 11.95 (*0-920541-95-X*) Peguis Pubs Ltd.
—The Grasshopper. Loves, June. LC 92-34263. 1993. 4.25 (*0-383-03626-7*) SRA Schl Grp.
—In My Head. Hucklesly, Hope. LC 92-34267. 1993. 2.50 (*0-383-03634-8*) SRA Schl Grp.
—Looking after the Babysitter. Benson, Rita. LC 93-26221. 1994. 4.25 (*0-383-03760-3*) SRA Schl Grp.
—The Seesaw. Drew, David. LC 92-21394. (gr. 2 up). 1993. 2.50 (*0-685-69191-8*) SRA Schl Grp.
—Something Special for Miss Margery. Redhead, Janet S. LC 93-6632. 1994. write for info (*0-383-03673-9*) SRA Schl Grp.
—Ten Crazy Caterpillars. Tuer, Judy. LC 92-30672. 1993. 2.50 (*0-383-03658-5*) SRA Schl Grp.
Forssell, Linda. The Trouble with Secrets. Johnsen, Karen. LC 85-51803. 32p. (Orig.). (ps-3). 1986. lib. bdg. 15.95 (*0-943990-23-8*); pap. 4.95 (*0-943990-22-X*) Parenting Pr.

Forst, Sigmund. Lost Erev Shabbos in the Zoo. rev. ed. Leah, Devora. 30p. (gr. k-3). 1986. 8.95 (*0-685-18123-5*); pap. 6.95 (*0-685-18124-3*) Judaica Pr.
—The Ten Plagues of Egypt. Lepon, Shoshana. Goldstein-Alpern, Neva, ed. 32p. (gr. 4-8). 1988. 8.95 (*0-910818-77-0*); pap. 6.95 (*0-910818-76-2*) Judaica Pr.
—The Ten Tests of Abraham. Lepon, Shoshana. 32p. (Orig.). (gr. k-4). 1986. 7.95 (*0-317-52412-7*); pap. 5.95 (*0-910818-67-3*) Judaica Pr.
—Young Moses, Crown Prince of Egypt. Lehmann, Asher. Goldman, Bonnie & Goldstein-Alpern, Neva, eds. Hirschler, Gertrude, tr. 150p. (gr. 9-12). 1987. 8.95 (*0-910818-64-9*); pap. 7.95 (*0-685-18059-X*) Judaica Pr.
Forst, Sigmund. Come, Count with Me. Gruenbaum, Hannah. (ps-1). 1.50 (*0-685-86207-0*) Feldheim.
—Silent Shofar. Hubner, Carol K. (gr. 3 up). 6.95 (*0-910818-53-3*); pap. 5.95 (*0-910818-54-1*) Judaica Pr.
Fortin, David. Journey to the Interior & Other Stories. Spingarn, Lawrence P. Hansen, Joseph, intro. by. LC 92-50241. 103p. (Orig.). (gr. 4 up). 1992. pap. 9.95 (*0-912288-30-2*) Perivale Pr.
Fortnum, Peggy. Bear Called Paddington. Bond, Michael. LC 60-9096. 128p. (gr. 3-7). 1968. pap. 3.50 (*0-440-40483-5*, YB) Dell.
—Bear Called Paddington. Bond, Michael. 128p. (gr. 1-5). 1960. 13.45 (*0-395-06636-0*) HM.
—More about Paddington. Bond, Michael. (gr. 4-6). 1962. 13.45 (*0-395-06640-9*) HM.
—More about Paddington. large type ed. Bond, Michael. 176p. (gr. 8-12). 1991. 13.95 (*0-7451-1297-8*, Galaxy Child Lrg Print) Chivers N Amer.
—Paddington Abroad. Bond, Michael. 128p. (gr. 2-6). 1992. pap. 3.25 (*0-440-47352-7*, YB) Dell.
—Paddington Abroad. Bond, Michael. LC 72-2753. 128p. (gr. 1-5). 1973. 14.45 (*0-395-14331-4*) HM.
—Paddington Abroad. large type ed. Bond, Michael. 168p. 1992. 13.95 (*0-7451-1547-0*, Galaxy Child Lrg Print) Chivers N Amer.
—Paddington at Large. Bond, Michael. 128p. (gr. 3-7). 1970. pap. 2.95 (*0-440-46801-9*, YB) Dell.
—Paddington at Large. large type ed. Bond, Michael. 168p. 1993. 13.95 (*0-7451-1657-4*, Galaxy Child Lrg Print) Chivers N Amer.
—Paddington at Work. Bond, Michael. LC 67-20372. (gr. 1-5). 1967. 13.95 (*0-395-06637-9*) HM.
—Paddington Goes to Town. Bond, Michael. LC 68-28043. (gr. 1-5). 1977. 14.95 (*0-395-06635-2*) HM.
—Paddington Helps Out. Bond, Michael. 128p. (gr. 3-7). 1982. pap. 2.95 (*0-440-46802-7*, YB) Dell.
—Paddington Helps Out. Bond, Michael. (gr. 4-6). 1973. 13.45 (*0-395-06636-5*) HM.
—Paddington Marches On. large type ed. Bond, Michael. 1993. 15.95 (*0-7451-1806-2*, Galaxy Child Lrg Print) Chivers N Amer.
—Paddington on Stage. Bradley, Alfred & Bond, Michael. LC 76-62497. (gr. 2-5). 1977. 14.45 (*0-395-25155-9*) HM.
—Paddington on Top. Bond, Michael. 128p. (gr. 1-5). 1975. 13.95 (*0-395-21897-7*) HM.
—Paddington Takes the Air. Bond, Michael. LC 78-147902. (gr. 3-7). 1971. 14.45 (*0-395-10909-4*) HM.
—Paddington's Storybook. Bond, Michael. 160p. (gr. 1-5). 1984. 16.45 (*0-395-36667-4*) HM.
Foss, Debbie. Learning Power: A Student's Guide to Success. Lafferty, Jerry. Moore, Melissa, ed. LC 92-72769. 138p. (Orig.). (gr. 7-12). 1993. Incl. six audio cass. pap. 34.95 (*1-881843-29-7*) Alpha Educ Inst.
Fossey, Koen. A Tale of Two Tengu. McCoy, Karen K. LC 93-7. (gr. 1-3). 1993. 14.95 (*0-8075-7748-0*) A Whitman.
Foster, Hal. Prince Valiant: The Storytelling Game. Stafford, Greg. Dunn, Bill & Willis, Lynn, eds. 128p. (Orig.). (gr. 6 up). 1989. pap. 19.95 (*0-933635-50-8*, 2801) Chaosium.
Foster, Janet, photos by. Journey to the Top of the World. Foster, Janet. (gr. 3-7). 1988. 14.95 (*0-13-511445-4*) P-H.
Foster, Larry A. The Whales of Hawaii: Including All Species of Marine Mammals in Hawaiian & Adjacent Waters. Balcomb, Kenneth C., III & Minasian, Stanley M. Gilmartin, William, intro. by. 114p. (Orig.). (gr. 9 up). 1987. pap. 9.95 (*0-9617803-0-4*) Marine Mammal Fund.
Foster, Robert. Reader's Digest Best Loved Books for Young Readers: The Life & Strange Surprising Adventures of Robinson Crusoe. Defoe, Daniel. Ogburn, Jackie, ed. 168p. (gr. 4-12). 1989. 3.99 (*0-945260-27-X*) Choice Pub NY.
Foster, Sally, photos by. The Private World of Smith Island. Foster, Sally. LC 92-17975. (gr. 3-7). 1993. 14.99 (*0-525-65122-5*, Cobblehill Bks) Dutton Child Bks.
—Simon Says...Let's Play. Foster, Sally. LC 89-9776. 48p. (gr. 1-6). 1990. 13.95 (*0-525-65019-9*, Cobblehill Bks) Dutton Child Bks.
Foster, Sharon. Jeffrey Introduces Thirteen More Southern Ghosts. Windham, Kathryn T. LC 70-170663. 120p. (gr. 6 up). 1987. pap. 9.50t (*0-8173-0381-2*) U of Ala Pr.
Foster, Tom. Color to Read, Vol. Aleph. Foster, Tom. LuBin, L., ed. 72p. (ps-1). 1990. lib. bdg. write for info.; pap. write for info.; write for info. tchr's. ed. Lubin Pr.

—Founders. Carroll, Jeri & Wells, Candace. 64p. (ps-3). 1986. wkbk. 7.95 (*0-86653-345-1*, GA 695) Good Apple.

—Inventors. Carroll, Jeri & Wells, Candace. 64p. (gr. k-4). 1987. pap. 7.95 (*0-86653-381-8*, GA1006) Good Apple.

—Learning Centers for Little Kids. Carroll, Jeri. 64p. (ps-2). 1983. wkbk. 7.95 (*0-86653-103-3*, GA 458) Good Apple.

—Legendary Heroes. Wells, Candace & Carroll, Jeri. 64p. (gr. k-4). 1987. pap. 7.95 (*0-86653-380-X*, GA1007) Good Apple.

—Let's Learn about Magnificent Me. Carroll, Jeri. 64p. (ps-2). 1987. pap. 7.95 (*0-86653-384-2*, GA1010) Good Apple.

—Let's Learn about Safety. Courson, Diana. 64p. (ps-2). 1987. pap. 7.95 (*0-86653-382-6*, GA1011) Good Apple.

—Pathfinders. Carroll, Jeri & Wells, Candance. 64p. (gr. k-4). 1986. wkbk. 7.95 (*0-86653-357-5*, GA 696) Good Apple.

Fountain, Phil. Glad to Be Me. Boulden, Jim. 32p. (Orig.). (gr. 1-6). 1993. pap. 4.95 (*1-878076-26-4*) Boulden Pub.

—Tough Times. Boulden, Jim & Boulden, Joan. 32p. (Orig.). (gr. 1-6). 1993. pap. 4.95 (*1-878076-29-9*) Boulden Pub.

Foust, Sylvia J. Dictionary Skills. Foust, Sylvia J. 48p. (gr. 2-6). 1986. wkbk. 5.95 (*1-55734-339-X*) Tchr Create Mat.

—Parts of Speech. Foust, Sylvia J. 48p. (gr. 2-6). 1986. wkbk. 5.95 (*1-55734-337-3*) Tchr Create Mat.

Fowler, Jack. Ghost Stories of Old Texas II. Fowler, Zinita. LC 92-19263. 80p. (gr. 4-7). 1992. 10.95 (*0-89015-868-1*) Eakin-Sunbelt.

Fowler, Jim. Dolphin Adventure: A True Story. Grover, Wayne. LC 89-27226. 48p. (gr. 3 up). 1990. 12.00 (*0-688-09442-2*) Greenwillow.

—Dolphin Adventure: A True Story. Grover, Wayne. LC 92-25545. 48p. (gr. 4 up). 1993. pap. 3.95 (*0-688-12277-9*, Pub. by Beech Tree Bks) Morrow.

—Fog. Fowler, Susi G. LC 91-28509. 32p. (ps-8). 1992. 14.00 (*0-688-10593-9*); PLB 13.93 (*0-688-10594-7*) Greenwillow.

—I'll See You When the Moon Is Full. Fowler, Susi G. LC 91-47667. 24p. (ps up). 1994. write for info. (*0-688-10830-X*); PLB write for info. (*0-688-10831-8*) Greenwillow.

—When Joel Comes Home. Fowler, Susi G. LC 92-7979. 24p. (ps up). 1993. 14.00 (*0-688-11064-9*); PLB 13.93 (*0-688-11065-7*) Greenwillow.

Fowler, Richard. Let's Make It Go from Side to Side. Fowler, Richard. 8p. (ps). 1990. Repr. of 1985 ed. bds. 4.95 (*0-88335-898-0*, AT03) Milliken Pub Co.

—Let's Make It Go In & Out. Fowler, Richard. 8p. (ps). 1990. Repr. of 1984 ed. bds. 4.95 (*0-88335-737-2*, AT01) Milliken Pub Co.

—Let's Make It Go Round. Fowler, Richard. 8p. (ps). 1990. Repr. of 1984 ed. bds. 4.95 (*0-88335-738-0*, AT02) Milliken Pub Co.

—Mr. Little's Noisy Car. Fowler, Richard. LC 85-80381. 20p. (ps-1). 1986. 11.95 (*0-448-18977-1*, G&D) Putnam Pub Group.

—Mr. Little's Noisy Plane: A Lift-the-Flap Book. Fowler, Richard. 20p. (ps-1). 1988. 11.95 (*0-448-19007-9*, G&D) Putnam Pub Group.

—Mr. Little's Noisy Truck: A Life-the-Flap Book. Fowler, Richard. 20p. (ps-1). 1989. 11.95 (*0-448-19021-4*, G&D) Putnam Pub Group.

—Time Travellers. Fowler, Richard. 22p. (ps up). 1994. 10.95 (*0-8431-3594-8*) Price Stern.

Fowler, Virginia. Christmas Crafts & Customs Around the World. Fowler, Virginia. LC 84-9770. 180p. (gr. 5 up). 1988. (S&S BFYR); pap. 5.95 (*0-671-67057-3*, S&S BFYR) S&S Trade.

Fowler, Virginie. Clayworks: Colorful Crafts from Around the World. Fowler, Virginie. (gr. 5 up). 1986. 11.95 (*0-13-136417-0*) P-H.

—Folk Arts Around the World. Fowler, Virginie. 168p. (gr. 5 up). 1984. pap. 6.95 (*0-13-322975-0*) P-H.

—Paperworks: Colorful Crafts from Picture Eggs to Fish Kites. Fowler, Virginie. 162p. (Orig.). (gr. 5 up). 1982. 10.95 (*0-13-648543-X*) P-H.

Fox, David A. A Little Miracle: A Hanukah Story. Fox, Terry. LC 85-51615. 52p. (Orig.). (ps up). 1985. pap. 5.95 (*0-9615397-0-4*) Tenderfoot Pr.

Fox, Neal. A Christmas Carol. Fox, Naomi. 24p. (ps-2). 1993. pap. 9.95 (*1-882179-06-4*) Confetti Ent.

—A Difficult Kind of Christmas. Fox, Naomi. 24p. (ps-2). 1993. pap. text ed. 9.95 (*1-882179-04-8*) Confetti Ent.

—**The Frog Prince. Fox, Naomi. 24p. (ps-1). 1992. Incl. cassette. pap. 9.95 (*1-882179-11-0*) Confetti Ent.**
The Confetti Company Books & Tapes are special adaptations of well-known fairy tales which feature non-violence, happy family settings & show that children can make a difference. Narrated by Robert Guillaume, the characters come to life as a cast of children & act out the scenes. The addition of original music makes for an entertaining & magical experience. In

this fun-filled tale, children will learn responsibility, the value of friendship & the importance of keeping a promise. When Ivy loses her mother's ring, she receives the help of a lonely frog. He dives for the ring in the dark pond & Ivy promises she will continue to visit him. Busy in school & with her friends, she neglects the frog. When Ivy realizes she has not kept her promise, she enlists her friends' help. When they find the frog, Ivy excitedly kisses him on his cheek & he becomes their new friend, the Frog Prince. To order: The Confetti Entertainment Company, 15250 Ventura Blvd., Suite 800, Sherman Oaks, CA 91403. (818) 783-6253. FAX: (818) 783-6518.
Publisher Provided Annotation.

—**Hansel & Gretel. Fox, Naomi. 24p. (ps-1). 1992. Incl. cassette. pap. 9.95 (*1-882179-12-9*) Confetti Ent.**
The Confetti Company Books & Tapes are special adaptations of well-known fairy tales which feature non-violence, happy family settings & show that children can make a difference. Narrated by Robert Guillaume, the characters come to life as a cast of children act out the scenes. The addition of original music makes for an entertaining & magical experience. Desperately wanting to help their parents, Hansel & Gretel embark on an adventure in the woods to search for food. Instead they encounter an evil witch. In the end, the resourceful children manage to out-smart the witch & become heroes. In a non-violent approach, this story confirms that witches are not real people, thus leaving children with a restful night's sleep. An exciting & suspenseful story for all. To order: The Confetti Entertainment Company, 15250 Ventura Blvd., Suite 800, Sherman Oaks, CA 91403. (818) 783-6253. FAX: (818) 783-6518.
Publisher Provided Annotation.

—Little Red Riding Hood. Fox, Naomi. 24p. (ps-1). 1993. Incl. cassette. pap. 9.95 (*1-882179-14-5*) Confetti Ent.

—Rumpelstiltskin. Dixon, Doris N. 24p. (ps-2). 1993. pap. 9.95 (*1-882171-01-2*) Confetti Ent.

—**The Shoemaker & the Elves. Fox, Naomi. 24p. (ps-1). 1993. Incl. cassette. pap. 9.95 (*1-882179-15-3*) Confetti Ent.**
The Confetti Company Books & Tapes are special adaptations of well-known fairy tales, which feature non-violence, happy family settings & show that children can make a difference. Narrated by Robert Guillaume, the characters come to life as a cast of children act out the scenes. The addition of original music makes for an entertaining & magical experience. This is the magical tale of three children that save the shop of a kind-hearted shoemaker named Kwame & his loving wife Neema. Mysteriously, the children enter the shop at night & make beautifully well-crafted shoes. After discovering that their "elves" are really homeless children, Kwame & Neema offer them a new home. This warm & caring story shows children being helpful without asking for anything in return. The story ends

allowing the reader to draw their own conclusions on how the elves (children) manage to get locked into the shop. To order: The Confetti Entertainment Company, 15250 Ventura Blvd., Suite 800, Sherman Oaks, CA 91403. (818) 783-6253, FAX: (818) 783-6518.
Publisher Provided Annotation.

—**Sleeping Beauty. Fox, Naomi. 24p. (ps-1). 1992. Incl. cassette. pap. 9.95 (*1-882179-13-7*) Confetti Ent.**
The Confetti Company Books & Tapes are special adaptations of well-known fairy tales which feature non-violence, happy family endings & show that children can make a difference. Narrated by Robert Guillaume, the characters come to life as a cast of children act out the scenes. The addition of original music makes for an entertaining & magical experience. This charming adaptation of Sleeping Beauty emphasizes how good prevails over evil. Although the witch places a curse on the Princess, the good fairies use a magic spell to protect her. Though the Prince awakens Sleeping Beauty from an eternal slumber, it is the gift of a "good heart" that truly saves her life. This delightful story of love, family & friends is a favorite with children everywhere. To order: The Confetti Entertainment Company, 15250 Ventura Blvd., Suite 800, Sherman Oaks, CA 91403. (818) 783-6253. FAX: (818) 783-6518.
Publisher Provided Annotation.

Fox-Davies, Sarah. Little Beaver & the Echo. MacDonald, Amy. 32p. 1990. 14.95 (*0-399-22203-0*, Putnam) Putnam Pub Group.

—Moon Frog. Edwards, Richard. LC 92-53014. 48p. (ps-3). 1993. 16.95 (*1-56402-116-5*) Candlewick Pr.

—Tabitha. Wilson, A. N. LC 88-19820. 48p. (gr. 3 up). 1989. 14.95 (*0-531-05813-1*); PLB 14.99 (*0-531-08413-2*) Orchard Bks Watts.

Frades, Ernesto. The Happy Valley of the Elves: A Terry Turtle Adventure. Frades, Ernesto. 48p. (Orig.). (gr. k-3). 1990. pap. write for info. (*0-9624929-1-4*) Little Great Whale.

Fradon, Dana. Harold the Herald: A Book about Heraldry. Fradon, Dana. LC 89-49479. 40p. (gr. 4-7). 1990. PLB 14.95 (*0-525-44634-6*, DCB) Dutton Child Bks.

—The King's Fool: A Book about Medieval & Renaissance Fools. Fradon, Dana. LC 92-43836. 40p. (gr. 3-7). 1993. 14.99 (*0-525-45074-2*, DCB) Dutton Child Bks.

—Sir Dana - A Knight: As Told by His Trusty Armor. Fradon, Dana. LC 88-3968. 32p. (gr. 3-7). 1988. 13.95 (*0-525-44424-6*, DCB) Dutton Child Bks.

Frailey, Joy. Around the World with God's Friends: Mission Education Activity Book - Elementary Grades. Miller, Wendy. 24p. (Orig.). (gr. 1-5). 1990. pap. text ed. 1.50g (*1-877736-06-6*, Mission Focus) MB Missions.

Frame, Paul. David Glasgow Farragut: Our First Admiral. Latham, Jean L. 80p. (gr. 2-6). 1991. Repr. of 1967 ed. lib. bdg. 12.95 (*0-7910-1438-X*) Chelsea Hse.

—Escape from High Doom. Milton, Hilary. Schwartz, Betty, ed. 128p. (Orig.). (gr. 3-7). 1984. PLB 5.97 (*0-685-08595-3*) S&S Trade.

—Fun House Terrors! Milton, Hilary. 128p. (gr. 3-7). 1984. (J Messner); pap. 2.95 (*0-685-09678-5*) S&S Trade.

—The Hardy Boys: Demon's Den. Dixon, Franklin W. Barish, Wendy, ed. 208p. (gr. 3 up). 1984. 9.95 (*0-685-09177-5*) S&S Trade.

—Harry S. Truman: People's President. Collins, David R. 80p. (gr. 2-6). 1991. Repr. of 1985 ed. lib. bdg. 12.95 (*0-7910-1421-5*) Chelsea Hse.

—Helen Keller. Graff, Stewart & Graff, Polly A. 80p. (gr. 2-7). 1980. pap. 2.95 (*0-440-43566-8*, YB) Dell.

—Katie John. Calhoun, Mary. LC 60-5775. (gr. 3-6). 1960. PLB 12.89 (*0-06-020951-8*) HarpC Child Bks.

—Me & My Puppy. Diffenderfer, Terri. 24p. (Orig.). (gr. k-1). 1990. pap. 0.99 (*1-878624-41-5*) McClanahan Bk.

—Nancy Drew & the Hardy Boys. Keene, Carolyn & Dixon, Franklin W. Barish, Wendy, ed. 192p. (Orig.). (gr. 3 up). 1984. pap. 2.95 (*0-685-09176-7*) S&S Trade.

—Nancy Drew & the Hardy Boys Be a Detective Mystery Stories: Ticket to Intrigue. Keene, Carolyn & Dixon, Franklin W. Arico, Diane, ed. 128p. (Orig.). (gr. 3-7). 1985. pap. 2.95 (0-671-55735-1) S&S Trade.
—Nancy Drew & the Hardy Boys: Jungle of Evil. Keene, Carolyn & Dixon, Franklin W. Arico, Diane, ed. 128p. (Orig.). (gr. 3-7). 1985. pap. 2.95 (0-671-55734-3) S&S Trade.
—The Nancy Drew Ghost Stories. Keene, Carolyn. Schneider, Meg, ed. (gr. 3-7). 1983. 8.95 (0-685-06733-5); pap. 3.50 (0-685-42561-4) S&S Trade.
—Nancy Drew Ghost Stories. Keene, Carolyn. 160p. 1983. 8.50 (0-685-06755-6); pap. 2.85 (0-685-06756-4) S&S Trade.
—Nancy Drew: The Sinister Omen. Keene, Carolyn. 192p. (gr. 3-7). 1991. (Little Simon); pap. 3.50 (0-671-73938-7) S&S Trade.
—The Silver Cobweb. Keene, Carolyn. Schneider, Meg, ed. 192p. (Orig.). (gr. 3-7). 1983. 9.95 (0-685-06731-9) S&S Trade.
—The Silver Cobweb. Keene, Carolyn. 192p. 1983. 8.95 (0-685-06757-2); pap. 3.50 (0-685-42563-0) S&S Trade.
—Super Sleuths, No. 2. Keene, Carolyn & Dixon, Franklin W. (gr. 2-7). 1984. 3.50 (0-685-09395-6) S&S Trade.

Frammenghi, Gioia. How to Get Fabulously Rich. Rockwell, Thomas. 128p. (gr. 5-8). 1990. 13.95 (0-531-15180-8); PLB 13.90 (0-531-10877-5) Watts.
Frampton, David. Bull Run. Fleischman, Paul. LC 92-14745. 112p. (gr. 5 up). 1993. 14.00 (0-06-021446-5); PLB 13.89 (0-06-021447-3) HarpC Child Bks.
—Fresh Paint: New Poems. Merriam, Eve. LC 85-23742. 48p. (gr. 5 up). 1986. RSBE 13.95 (0-02-766860-6, Macmillan Child Bk) Macmillan Child Grp.
—Jerusalem, Shining Still. Kuskin, Karla. LC 86-25841. 32p. (ps up). 1987. 13.95 (0-06-023548-9); PLB 13.89 (0-06-023549-7) HarpC Child Bks.
—Jerusalem, Shining Still. Kuskin, Karla. LC 86-25841. 32p. (gr. 1 up). 1990. pap. 5.50 (0-06-443243-2, Trophy) HarpC Child Bks.
—Joshua in the Promised Land. Chaikin, Miriam. (gr. 3-6). 1990. pap. 6.70 (0-395-54797-0, Clarion Bks) HM.
—Just So Stories. Kipling, Rudyard. LC 90-19429. 128p. (gr. 3-7). 1991. 19.95 (0-06-023294-3); PLB 19.89 (0-06-023296-X) HarpC Child Bks.
—My Son John. Aylesworth, Jim. LC 92-27192. 1993. write for info. (0-8050-1725-9, Bks Young Read) H Holt & Co.
—Of Swords & Sorcerers: The Adventures of King Arthur & His Knights. Hodges, Margaret & Evernden, Margery. LC 91-40811. 112p. (gr. 5-7). 1993. SBE 14.95 (0-684-19437-6, Scribners Young Read) Macmillan Child Grp.
—Whaling Days. Carrick, Carol. 40p. (gr. 4-7). 1993. 15.45 (0-395-50948-3, Clarion Bks) HM.
Francetic, Karl D. & Sheehan-Burke, Julia, photos by. Synchronized Swimming Is For Me. Preston-Mauks, Susan. LC 82-17102. 48p. (gr. 2-5). 1983. PLB 13.50 (0-8225-1139-8) Lerner Pubns.
Franch, Julie. Ideas for Kids on the Go. Garee, Betty. Cheever, Raymond, intro. by. LC 84-73366. (Orig.). (ps up). 1984. pap. 6.95 (0-915708-17-5) Cheever Pub.
Francis, Irene. Storytelling with the Flannel Board, 3 Bks, Bk. 1. Anderson, Paul S. LC 21-650. 270p. (ps). 1963. 15.95 (0-513-00105-0) Denison.
Francis, John. Animals on the Move. Carwardine, Mark. Young, Richard G., ed. LC 89-32809. 45p. (gr. 3-5). 1989. PLB 14.60 (0-944483-27-5) Garrett Ed Corp.
—Hippos. Wildlife Education, Ltd. Staff. 24p. 1992. 13.95 (0-937934-79-8); pap. 2.75 (0-937934-54-2) Wildlife Educ.
—Monsters. Miller. 32p. (gr. k-6). 1977. PLB write for info. (0-86020-146-5); pap. 5.95 (0-685-42639-4) EDC.
Francis, John & Stuart, Walter. Baby Animals, Vol. 2. Wildlife Education, Ltd. Staff. 20p. 1992. 13.95 (0-937934-75-5); pap. 2.75 (0-937934-58-5) Wildlife Educ.
Francis, John, jt. illus. see Atkinson, Mike.
Francis, John, et al. Giraffes. Wildlife Education, Ltd. Staff. 20p. (gr. 5 up). 1982. pap. 2.75 (0-937934-09-7) Wildlife Educ.
Franc-Nohain, Marie M. Baby's First Year Calendar. Metropolitan Museum of Art Staff. 24p. 1984. pap. 9.95 (0-684-18258-0, Scribners Young Read) Macmillan Child Grp.
—Happy Birthday to Me! A Four-Year Record Book for Birthday Boys & Girls. Smith, Dian G. 48p. (gr. 2-5). 1989. pap. 9.95 (0-684-19046-X, Scribners Young Read) Macmillan Child Grp.
Francoeur, Janet. The Earth & You: Eating for Two. Moore, April. Stark, Elizabeth, ed. (Orig.). (gr. 8-12). 1993. write for info. (0-938443-05-4) Potomac Val Pr.
Franco-Feeney, Betsy. James Bear & the Goose Gathering. Latimer, Jim. LC 92-26190. 32p. (gr. k-2). 1994. SBE 14.95 (0-684-19526-7, Scribners Young Read) Macmillan Child Grp.
—James Bear's Pie. Latimer, Jim. LC 90-36193. 32p. (ps-2). 1992. SBE 13.95 (0-684-19226-8, Scribners Young Read) Macmillan Child Grp.
Francois, Andre. Jack & the Beanstalk. Madame d'Aulnoy's Collection Staff. 32p. (gr. 4 up). 1983. PLB 13.95s.p. (0-87191-947-8) Creative Ed.

Franczak, Brian. The Great Hunters: Meat-Eating Dinosaurs. Farlow, James O. & Molnar, Ralph E. LC 93-29844. 1994. write for info. (0-531-11180-6) Watts.
—Ornithomimids, the Fastest Dinosaur. Lessem, Don. LC 93-10264. 1993. 19.95 (0-87614-813-5) Carolrhoda Bks.
—Pterosaurs: The Flying Reptiles. Bennett, S. Christopher. LC 93-29845. 1994. write for info. (0-531-11181-4) Watts.
—Troodon, the Smartest Dinosaur. Lessem, Don. LC 92-44689. 1993. 19.95 (0-87614-798-8) Carolrhoda Bks.
Frandsen, Karen G. I'd Rather Get a Spanking Than Go to the Doctor. Frandsen, Karen G. LC 86-11735. 32p. (ps-3). 1987. pap. 3.95 (0-516-43498-5) Childrens.
—Michael's New Haircut. Frandsen, Karen G. LC 86-11696. 32p. (ps-3). 1986. pap. 3.95 (0-516-43545-0) Childrens.
Frank, Barbara. The Oldest Mommy in the Park. Grancell-Frank, Barbara. Thomas, R. David, frwd. by. 64p. (Orig.). (gr. 6-12). 1993. pap. 8.95 (1-56883-022-X) Colonial Pr AL.
Frank, Connie. Elimelech Wakes Up. Jacobs, Chana R. 32p. (ps-3). 1993. 8.95 (0-922613-54-0); pap. 6.95 (0-922613-55-9) Hachai Pubns.
Frank, Gayle. Side Saddle Riding: Four-H Manual. Bowlby, Linda A. & Thomas, Mary L. 23p. (Orig.). (gr. 9-12). 1984. pap. 5.00 (1-884011-01-2) Wrld Sidesaddle.
Frank, Lola E. Shoemaker Fooze. Pape, D. L. LC 68-56827. 48p. (gr. 2-5). 1969. PLB 10.95 (0-87783-036-3) Oddo.
Frank, Phil. Touch with Your Eyes! Atherton, Mary K., et al. 48p. (Orig.). (gr. k-8). 1982. pap. 4.50 (0-9613069-0-4) Orinda Art Coun.
Franke, Phil. Alias Diamond Jones. Salat, Cristina. (gr. 4-7). 1993. pap. 2.99 (0-553-37216-5) Bantam.
Frankel, Adrian. Hoang Breaks the Lucky Teapot. Breckler, Rosemary K. 32p. (gr. k-3). 1992. 13.45 (0-395-57031-X) HM.
Frankel, Alona. I Love You. Rennert, Maggie. (ps up). 1987. 9.95 (0-915361-71-X) Modan-Adama Bks.
Frankenberg, Robert. Cherokee Animal Tales. rev. ed. Scheer, George F., intro. by. LC 91-73537. 79p. (gr. 3-6). 1991. pap. 7.95 (0-933031-60-2) Coun Oak Bks.
Frankland, David. Brer Rabbit & the Peanut Patch. rev. ed. Dickinson, Susan. 32p. (gr. k-2). 1990. Repr. of 1985 ed. PLB 10.50 (1-878363-18-2) Forest Hse.
Franklin, Hal A., photos by. What Color Are You? Walton, Darwin. 64p. (gr. 5 up). 1973. 10.95 (0-87485-045-2) Johnson Chi.
Franta. The Patient Stone. Hedayat, Sadegh & Batmanglij, N. Batmanglij, M. & Batmanglij, N., trs. from PER. LC 86-33301. 32p. (gr. 4 up). 1987. Bilingual. 18.50 (0-934211-02-7); English. 18.50 (0-934211-07-8) Mage Pubs Inc.
—The Wonderful Story of Zaal. Batmanglij, M. & Batmanglij, N. LC 86-12665. 48p. (gr. 4 up). 1986. 18.50 (0-934211-01-9) Mage Pubs Inc.
Frascino, Edward. Count Draculations! Monster Riddles. Keller, Charles. 64p. (gr. 3-7). 1986. 10.95 (0-13-183641-2) P-H.
—Crystal's Christmas Carol. Gordon, Shirley. LC 87-33487. 40p. (gr. k-3). 1989. PLB 12.89 (0-06-022239-5) HarpC Child Bks.
—The Elephant's Child. Kipling, Rudyard. 32p. (gr. k-3). 1986. 13.95 (0-13-273640-3) P-H.
—Footsteps in the Fog. Warren, William E. 112p. (gr. 3-7). 1985. 11.95 (0-13-324807-0) P-H.
—King Henry the Ape: Animal Jokes. Keller, Charles. 40p. (gr. 2-5). 1990. PLB 13.95 (0-945912-08-0) Pippin Pr.
—Me & the Bad Guys. Gordon, Shirley. 80p. (gr. 3-7). 1984. pap. 2.25 (0-440-45520-0, YB) Dell.
—Nanny Noony & the Dust Queen. Frascino, Edward. 32p. (gr. k-3). 1990. PLB 14.95 (0-945912-09-9) Pippin Pr.
—Nanny Noony & the Magic Spell. Frascino, Edward. 32p. (gr. k-3). 1988. 14.95 (0-945912-00-5) Pippin Pr.
—Oh, Brother: And Other Family Jokes. Keller, Charles. 48p. (gr. 2-6). 1982. 8.95 (0-13-633305-2) P-H.
—Trumpet of the Swan. White, E. B. LC 72-112484. (gr. 3-6). 1970. 13.00 (0-06-026397-0); PLB 12.89 (0-06-026398-9) HarpC Child Bks.
—The Trumpet of the Swan. White, E. B. LC 72-112484. 222p. (gr. 3 up). 1973. pap. 3.95 (0-06-440048-4, Trophy) HarpC Child Bks.
—Windmill Hill. Slaughter, Hope. 64p. (gr. 2-5). 1993. 14.95 (0-945912-21-8) Pippin Pr.
Frascino, Ward. The Graveyard: And Other Not-So-Scary Stories. Warren, William E. 128p. 1984. 11.95 (0-13-363623-2) P-H.
Frasconi, Antonio. At Christmastime. Worth, Valerie. LC 92-52693. 32p. (gr. k up). 1992. 15.00 (0-06-205019-2); PLB 14.89 (0-06-205020-6) HarpC Child Bks.
—Elijah the Slave. Singer, Isaac Bashevis. LC 70-124146. 32p. (ps-3). 1970. 16.00 (0-374-32084-5) FS&G.
—Elijah the Slave. Singer, Isaac Bashevis. 32p. (ps up). 1988. pap. 4.95 (0-374-42047-5) FS&G.
—If the Owl Calls Again: A Collection of Owl Poems. Livingston, Myra C. LC 89-27659. 128p. (gr. 5 up). 1990. SBE 13.95 (0-689-50501-9, M K McElderry) Macmillan Child Grp.
—Monkey Puzzle & Other Poems. Livingston, Myra C. LC 84-3050. 64p. (gr. 6 up). 1984. SBE 12.95 (0-689-50310-5, M K McElderry) Macmillan Child Grp.

—Platero. Jimenez, Juan R., compiled by. Livingston, Myra C. & Dominguez, Joseph F., trs. LC 92-11634. (ENG & SPA.). 1993. write for info. (0-395-62365-0, Clarion Bks) HM.
Fraser, Betty. Abigail Adams: Dear Partner. Stone-Peterson, Helen. 80p. (gr. 2-6). 1991. Repr. of 1967 ed. lib. bdg. 12.95 (0-7910-1402-9) Chelsea Hse.
—The Cozy Book. Hoberman, Mary A. LC 93-10826. 1995. write for info. (0-15-276620-0, Browndeer Pr) HarBrace.
—First Things First. Fraser, Betty. LC 86-42993. 32p. (gr. k-3). 1994. pap. 4.95 (0-06-443300-5, Trophy) HarpC Child Bks.
—First Things First: An Illustrated Collection of Sayings Useful & Familiar for Children. Fraser, Betty. LC 86-42993. 32p. (gr. k-3). 1990. PLB 12.89 (0-06-021855-X) HarpC Child Bks.
—A House Is a House for Me. Hoberman, Mary Ann. LC 77-15518. (gr. k-3). 1978. pap. 14.00 (0-670-38016-4) Viking Child Bks.
—A House Is a House for Me. Hoberman, Mary Ann. (gr. k-3). 1984. incl. cassette 19.95 (0-941078-33-7); pap. 12.95 incl. cassette (0-941078-31-0); incl. 4 bks., cassette, & guide 27.95 (0-317-07117-3) Live Oak Media.
—A House Is a House for Me. Hoberman, Mary Ann. 48p. (ps-3). 1982. pap. 3.99 (0-14-050394-3, Puffin) Puffin Bks.
—A House Is a House for Me. Hoberman, Mary A. 1993. pap. 6.99 incl. cassette (0-14-095116-4, Puffin) Puffin Bks.
—Pets in a Jar: Collecting & Caring for Small Animals. Simon, Seymour. (gr. 4-8). 1979. pap. 5.99 (0-14-049186-4, Puffin) Puffin Bks.
Fraser, Douglas. David & Goliath. Metaxas, Eric. 40p. (gr. k up). 1993. incl. cass. 19.95 (0-88708-295-5, Rabbit Ears); 14.95 (0-88708-294-7, Rabbit Ears) Picture Bk Studio.
Fraser, John & Hughes, Scott. Monsters, He Mumbled. Huigin, Sean O. 28p. (ps-7). 1989. pap. 4.95 (0-88753-187-3, Pub. by Black Moss Pr CN) Firefly Bks Ltd.
Fraser, Juliette M., jt. illus. see Morgan, Rosamond S.
Fraser, Mary A. Armadillos & Other Unusual Animals. Pearce, Q. L. Steltenpohl, Jane, ed. 64p. (gr. 4-6). 1989. lib. bdg. 12.98 (0-671-68528-7, J Messner); lib. bdg. 5.95 (0-671-68645-3) S&S Trade.
—Lightning & Other Wonders of the Sky. Pearce, Q. L. Steltenpohl, Jane, ed. 64p. (gr. 4-6). 1989. lib. bdg. 12.98 (0-671-68534-1, J Messner); lib. bdg. 5.95 (0-671-68648-8) S&S Trade.
—My Favorite Dinosaur: Tyrannosaurus Rex. Pearce, Q. L. 32p. 1993. pap. 11.95 (1-56565-014-X) Lowell Hse.
—On Top of the World: The Conquest of Mount Everest. Fraser, Mary A. LC 90-48988. 40p. (gr. 2-5). 1991. 14.95 (0-8050-1578-7, Bks Young Read) H Holt & Co.
—One Giant Leap. Fraser, Mary A. LC 92-41044. 40p. (gr. 3-7). 1993. PLB 15.95 (0-8050-2295-3) H Holt & Co.
—Piranhas & Other Wonders of the Jungle. Pearce, Q. L. 64p. (gr. 4-6). 1990. lib. bdg. 12.98 (0-671-70689-6, J Messner); pap. 5.95 (0-671-70690-X) S&S Trade.
—Quicksand & Other Earthly Wonders. Pearce, Q. L. Steltenpohl, Jane, ed. 64p. (gr. 4-6). 1989. lib. bdg. 12.98 (0-671-68530-9, J Messner); lib. bdg. 5.95 (0-671-68646-1) S&S Trade.
—Ten Mile Day: The Building of the Transcontinental Railroad. Fraser, Mary A. LC 92-3007. 40p. (gr. 3-7). 1993. PLB 15.95 (0-8050-1902-2, Bks Young Read) H Holt & Co.
—Tidal Waves & Other Ocean Wonders. Pearce, Q. L. Steltenpohl, Jane, ed. 64p. (gr. 4-6). 1989. lib. bdg. 12.98 (0-671-68532-5, J Messner); lib. bdg. 5.95 (0-671-68647-X) S&S Trade.
—Tyrannosaurus Rex & Other Dinosaur Wonders. Pearce, Q. L. 64p. (gr. 4-6). 1990. lib. bdg. 12.98 (0-671-70687-X, J Messner); pap. 5.95 (0-671-70688-8) S&S Trade.
Frasier, D. The Animal that Drank up Sound. Stafford, W. 1992. 13.95 (0-15-203563-X, HB Juv Bks) HarBrace.
Frasier, Debra. On the Day You Were Born. Frasier, Debra. Johnston, Allyn, ed. 32p. (ps up). 1991. 13.95 (0-15-257995-8) HarBrace.
—We Got Here Together. Stafford, Kim R. LC 93-9814. (gr. 5 up). 1994. write for info. (0-15-294891-0) HarBrace.
Fraydas, Stan. The Magic Ring. Chitwood, Deb. LC 82-62432. 32p. (ps-3). 1983. 9.95 (0-942044-01-0) Polestar.
Frazee, Kathleen & Lumba, Eric. Ancient Europe. Frazee, Charles & Yopp, Hallie K. (gr. 6). 1990. pap. text ed. write for info. Delos Pubns.
—The Ancient World. Frazee, Charles & Yopp, Hallie K. (gr. 6). 1990. text ed. 21.08 (1-878473-51-4); tchr's. ed. 27.08 (1-878473-54-9); wkbk. 3.00 (1-878473-55-7) Delos Pubns.
—Early People & the First Civilizations. Frazee, Charles & Yopp, Hallie Kay. (gr. 6). 1990. write for info. Delos Pubns.
—Medieval & Early Modern Europe. Frazee, Charles & Yopp, Hallie K. (gr. 7). 1990. pap. text ed. 5.50 wkbk. (0-685-44932-7) Delos Pubns.
—Medieval & Early Modern Times. Frazee, Charles & Yopp, Hallie K. (gr. 7). 1990. pap. text ed. 24.77 (1-878473-56-5); tchr's. ed. 30.77 (1-878473-58-1); wkbk. 3.00 (0-685-58493-3) Delos Pubns.

Frazee, Marla. World Famous Muriel & the Magic Mystery. Alexander, Sue. LC 89-22396. 32p. (gr. k-3). 1990. (Crowell Jr Bks); PLB 12.89 (0-690-04789-4, Crowell Jr Bks) HarpC Child Bks.

Frazier, J. D. ESL Wonder Workbook, No. 1: This Is Me. Claire, Elizabeth. Flamm, Jackie, ed. 104p. (Orig.). (gr. 1-6). 1990. pap. 7.65 (1-878598-00-7) Alta Bk Co Pubs.

—ESL Wonder Workbook, No. 2: All Around Me. Claire, Elizabeth. Chapman, Charles, ed. 104p. (Orig.). (gr. 1-6). 1991. pap. write for info. (1-878598-01-5) Alta Bk Co Pubs.

Freas, Frank K. Wishing Season. Freisner, Esther M. LC 93-71527. 144p. (gr. 7 up). 1993. SBE 14.95 (0-689-31574-0, Atheneum Child Bk) Macmillan Child Grp.

Fredman, Foan. My Going to Camp Book. Felt, Freddi. 40p. (gr. 1-6). 1988. 5.95 (0-9616875-2-5) F & F Pub.

Fredman, Joan. My Going to School Book. Felt, Freddi. 48p. (gr. k-3). 1987. pap. 5.95 wkbk. (0-9616875-1-7) F & F Pub.

Free, Maya S. Fly with the Heart. Warrior, MaRaDa H. (Orig.). (gr. 4 up). 1990. pap. text ed. write for info. (0-9622031-1-4) Woman Warrior Heart.

Freeberg, Dolores. Graph Paper Art. Freeberg, Dolores. 48p. (gr. 2-6). 1986. wkbk. 5.95 (1-55734-052-8) Tchr Create Mat.

Freeberg, Dolores, jt. illus. see Freeberg, Erling.

Freeberg, Erling & Freeberg, Dolores. Challenging Graph Art. Freeberg, Erling & Freeberg, Dolores. 48p. (gr. 2-6). 1987. wkbk. 5.95 (1-55734-096-X) Tchr Create Mat.

—Holiday Graph Art. Freeberg, Erling & Freeberg, Dolores. 48p. (gr. 2-6). 1987. wkbk. 5.95 (1-55734-093-5) Tchr Create Mat.

—Patriotic Graph Art. Freeberg, Erling & Freeberg, Dolores. 48p. (gr. 2-6). 1987. wkbk. 5.95 (1-55734-094-3) Tchr Create Mat.

—Simple Graph Art. Freeberg, Erling & Freeberg, Dolores. 48p. (gr. k-1). 1987. wkbk. 5.95 (1-55734-095-1) Tchr Create Mat.

Freed, Kecia S. Annie. rev. ed. Rape & Abuse Crisis Center Staff. 21p. (ps up). 1985. pap. text ed. 2.50 (0-914633-03-1) Rape Abuse Crisis.

—Gente Bandera Roja y Gente Bandera Verde: Red Flag Green Flag People. rev. ed. Rape & Abuse Crisis Center Staff. Peterson, Francisca E., tr. from ENG. (SPA.). 36p. (gr. k-5). 1987. wkbk. 4.00 (0-914633-13-9) Rape Abuse Crisis.

—Red Flag Green Flag People. Rape & Abuse Crisis Center Staff. 28p. (gr. k up). 1985. pap. 4.00 wkbk. (0-914633-10-4) Rape Abuse Crisis.

Freedman, Russell. Rattlesnakes. Freedman, Russell. LC 84-4602. 40p. (gr. 1-4). 1984. reinforced bdg. 13.95 (0-8234-0536-2) Holiday.

—Sharks. Freedman, Russell. LC 85-42881. 40p. (gr. 1-4). 1985. reinforced bdg. 13.95 (0-8234-0582-6) Holiday.

Freedman, Russell, photos by. Indian Chiefs. Freedman, Russell. LC 86-46198. 160p. (gr. 4 up). 1987. reinforced bdg. 18.95 (0-8234-0625-3); pap. 9.95 (0-8234-0971-6) Holiday.

Freem, Elroy. If You Traveled West in a Covered Wagon. Levine, Ellen. 80p. (gr. 3-5). 1992. pap. 4.95 (0-590-45158-8) Scholastic Inc.

Freeman, Don. Quiet! There's a Canary in the Library. Freeman, Don. LC 69-15398. 48p. (gr. k-3). 1969. 15. 00 (0-516-08737-1); pap. 3.95 (0-516-48737-X) Childrens.

Freeman, Don. Beady Bear. Freeman, Don. LC 54-12295. 48p. (ps-1). 1954. 13.95 (0-670-15056-8) Viking Child Bks.

—Un Bosillo Para Corduroy: A Pocket for Corduroy. Freeman, Don. (ENG & SPA.). 32p. (ps-3). 1992. RB 13.00 (0-670-84483-7) Viking Child Bks.

—Corduroy. Freeman, Don. LC 68-16068. 32p. 1968. 12. 99 (0-670-24133-4) Viking Child Bks.

—Corduroy. Freeman, Don. (gr. k-3). 1982. incl. cass. 19. 95 (0-941078-08-6); pap. 12.95 incl. cass. (0-941078-06-X); user's guide incl. 4 pbs. & cass. 27. 95 (0-941078-07-8) Live Oak Media.

—Corduroy, Edicion Espanola. Freeman, Don. (SPA.). 32p. (ps-3). 1988. 11.95 (0-670-82265-5) Viking Child Bks.

—Corduroy: (Edicion Espanola) Freeman, Don. (SPA.). (ps-3). 1990. incl. cass. 19.95 (0-87499-212-9); pap. 12.95 incl. cass. (0-87499-213-3); Set; incl. 4 bks., guide, & cass. pap. 27.95 (0-87499-193-5) Live Oak Media.

—Dandelion. Freeman, Don. LC 64-21472. (ps-2). 1977. pap. 4.50 (0-14-050218-1, VS4, Puffin) Puffin Bks.

—Dandelion. Freeman, Don. LC 64-21472. 48p. (ps-2). 1964. pap. 14.00 (0-670-25532-7) Viking Child Bks.

—Dandelion. Freeman, Don. (gr. k-3). 1982. incl. cassette 19.95 (0-941078-11-6); pap. 12.95 incl. cassette (0-941078-09-4); user's guide incl. 4 pbs. & cassette 27.95 (0-941078-10-8) Live Oak Media.

—Mop Top. Freeman, Don. (ps-1). 1955. pap. 13.95 (0-670-48882-8) Viking Child Bks.

—Mop Top. Freeman, Don. (gr. k-3). 1982. incl. cass. 19. 95 (0-941078-14-0); pap. 12.95 incl. cass. (0-941078-12-4); user's guide incl. 6 pbs. & cass. 27.95 (0-941078-13-2) Live Oak Media.

—Norman the Doorman. Freeman, Don. (ps-3). 1989. pap. 4.99 (0-14-050288-2, Puffin) Puffin Bks.

—Norman the Doorman. Freeman, Don. (ps-2). 1959. pap. 15.95 (0-516-51515-9) Viking Child Bks.

—A Pocket for Corduroy. Freeman, Don. (gr. k-3). 1982. incl. cass. 19.95 (0-941078-17-5); pap. 12.95 incl. cass. (0-941078-15-9); user's guide incl. 4 pbs. & cass. 27.95 (0-941078-16-7) Live Oak Media.

—A Rainbow of My Own. Freeman, Don. (gr. k-3). 1982. incl. cass. 19.95 (0-941078-20-5); pap. 12.95 incl. cass. (0-941078-18-3); user's guide incl. 4 pbs. & cass. 27.95 (0-941078-19-1) Live Oak Media.

—Tilly Witch. Freeman, Don. (gr. k-3). 1969. pap. 13.95 (0-670-71303-1) Viking Child Bks.

Freeman, Tony. El Beisbol Es Nuestro Juego (Baseball's Our Game) Downing, Joan. Kratky, Lada, tr. from ENG. LC 82-4418. (SPA.). 32p. (gr. k-3). 1984. PLB 15.93 (0-516-33402-6); pap. 3.95 (0-516-53402-5) Childrens.

Freeze, Marla. Happy Birthday Songs & Games. Cooper, Don. Elkins, Stephen, contrib. by. 32p. (Orig.). (ps-3). 1988. pap. 5.95 bk. & cassette pkg. (0-394-80826-6) Random Bks Yng Read.

Freidman, Joy. Apes Find Shapes. Moncure, Jane B. LC 87-11747. 32p. (ps-2). 1987. PLB 21.35 (0-89565-364-8); PLB 14.95s.p. (0-685-55867-3) Childs World.

—One Tricky Monkey Up on Top. Moncure, Jane B. LC 87-11612. 32p. (ps-2). 1987. PLB 21.35 (0-89565-365-6); PLB 14.95s.p. (0-685-55874-6) Childs World.

Freitag, Herta. One Way Ticket: The True Story of Herta Taussig Freitag. Johnson, Mary A. 150p. (Orig.). (gr. 5 up). 1988. pap. 15.95 (0-9621465-0-1) Mary Ann Johnson.

Freitag, Jim. The Way We Feel Inside: With the Song "How I'm Made" Murphy, Mary. 28p. (gr. k-4). 1990. pap. 9.00 (0-89486-618-4) Hazelden.

Freitas, F. Bapu. Freitas, F. (gr. 1-9). 1979. Pt. I. pap. 2.50 (0-89744-173-7); Pt. II. pap. 2.50 (0-89744-174-5) Auromere.

Frem, Margie. Conversation Games: Vol. III, Solutions. Rev. ed. Freeman, Harold, Jr., intro. by. 134p. (ps-6). 1981. pap. 17.00 (0-939632-23-3) ILM.

French, Ed. The Great Forest. Springer, Jean. Peterson, Pete, ed. 169p. (gr. k-3). 1986. pap. 3.99 (0-934998-25-6) Bethel Pub.

—Peace Porridge. Douglis, Marjie. Peterson, Pete, ed. 122p. (gr. 3-6). 1986. pap. 3.99 (0-934998-22-1) Bethel Pub.

French, Larry, jt. illus. see Plunkett, Michael.

French, Marty. Bearly There at All. Krueger, Ron, et al. 26p. (ps up). 1986. Incl. cass. 7.95 (1-55578-106-3) Worlds Wonder.

—Bearly There at All. Krueger, Ron, et al. 26p. (ps up). 1988. incl. cassette 7.95 (1-55578-912-9) Worlds Wonder.

French, Marty & Christman, Michael. The Girl Who Wanted to Be Beautiful. Weber, Ane, et al. 26p. (ps up). 1986. Book & Cassette. 7.95 (1-55578-109-8) Worlds Wonder.

—The Girl Who Wanted to Be Beautiful. Weber, Ane, et al. 26p. (ps up). 1988. incl. cassette 7.95 (1-55578-915-3) Worlds Wonder.

French, Marty & Iwai, Noel. Is It Soup Yet? Weber, Ane, et al. 26p. (ps up). 1986. 7.95 (1-55578-105-5); cass. incl. Worlds Wonder.

—Is It Soup Yet? Weber, Ane, et al. 26p. (ps up). 1988. incl. cassette 7.95 (1-55578-914-5) Worlds Wonder.

—A Tailor-Made Friendship. Weber, Ane & Krueger, Ron. 26p. (ps up). 1988. incl. cassette 7.95 (1-55578-913-7) Worlds Wonder.

French, Marty & Iwia, Noel. A Tailor-Made Friendship. Weber, Ane, et al. 26p. (ps up). 1986. Book & Cassette. 7.95 (1-55578-107-1) Worlds Wonder.

French, Marty & Lamb, Jim. The Fluff Puff Farm. Graeber, Charlotte. 26p. (ps up). 1988. incl. cassette 7.95 (1-55578-917-X) Worlds Wonder.

French, Marty & Warter, Fred. The Biggest Little Girl. Christenson, Shawna, et al. 26p. (ps up). Book & Cassette. 7.95 (1-55578-108-X) Worlds Wonder.

—The Biggest Little Girl. Christenson, Shawna, et al. 26p. (ps up). 1988. incl. cassette 7.95 (1-55578-916-1) Worlds Wonder.

French, Marty, jt. illus. see Hilliard, Cindy.

French, Marty, et al. The Dog That Went Too Fast. Maddux, Bob, et al. 26p. (ps up). 1987. 7.95 (1-55578-104-7); cass. incl. Worlds Wonder.

—The Bear That Was Chicken. Weber, Ane, et al. 26p. (ps up). 1986. Book & Cassette. 7.95 (1-55578-101-2) Worlds Wonder.

—A Fence Too High. Bartelt, Jeanine, et al. 26p. (ps up). 1986. 7.95 (1-55578-103-9); cass. incl. Worlds Wonder.

—The Girl With the Pop-Up Garden. Weber, Ane, et al. 26p. (ps up). 1986. Book & Cassette. 7.95 (1-55578-102-0) Worlds Wonder.

—The Fluff Puff Farm. Graeker, Charlotte. 26p. (ps up). 1986. Book & Cassette. 7.95 (1-55578-110-1) Worlds Wonder.

French, Vanessa & French, Vanessa. Africa Brothers & Sisters. Kroll, Virginia. LC 91-20346. 32p. (ps-2). 1993. RSBE 14.95 (0-02-751166-9, Four Winds) Macmillan Child Grp.

French, Vivian, jt. illus. see Prater, John.

Frenck, Hal. Ancient China. Sabin, Louis. LC 84-2729. 32p. (gr. 3-6). 1985. PLB 9.49 (0-8167-0316-7); pap. text ed. 2.95 (0-8167-0317-5) Troll Assocs.

—Ancient Egypt. Santrey, Laurence. LC 84-2728. 32p. (gr. 3-6). 1985. PLB 9.49 (0-8167-0248-9); pap. text ed. 2.95 (0-8167-0249-7) Troll Assocs.

—Ancient Greece. Bains, Rae. LC 84-2685. 32p. (gr. 3-6). 1985. PLB 9.49 (0-8167-0244-6); pap. text ed. 2.95 (0-8167-0245-4) Troll Assocs.

—Ancient Rome. Brandt, Keith. LC 84-2684. 32p. (gr. 3-6). 1985. PLB 9.49 (0-8167-0298-5); pap. text ed. 2.95 (0-8167-0299-3) Troll Assocs.

—Babe Ruth, Home Run Hero. Brandt, Keith. LC 85-1091. 48p. (gr. 4-6). 1986. lib. bdg. 10.79 (0-8167-0553-4); pap. text ed. 3.50 (0-8167-0554-2) Troll Assocs.

—Colonial Life in America. Sabin, Louis. LC 84-2669. 32p. (gr. 3-6). 1985. PLB 9.49 (0-8167-0138-5); pap. text ed. 2.95 (0-8167-0139-3) Troll Assocs.

—George Washington. Brandt, Keith. LC 84-8624. 32p. (gr. 3-6). 1985. PLB 9.49 (0-8167-0256-X); pap. text ed. 2.95 (0-8167-0257-8) Troll Assocs.

—Harriet Tubman. Sabin, Francene. LC 84-2667. 32p. (gr. 3-6). 1985. PLB 9.49 (0-8167-0158-X); pap. text ed. 2.95 (0-8167-0159-8) Troll Assocs.

—Helen Keller. Santrey, Laurence. LC 84-2682. 32p. (gr. 3-6). 1985. PLB 9.49 (0-8167-0156-3); pap. text ed. 2.95 (0-8167-0157-1) Troll Assocs.

—James Monroe, Young Patriot. Bains, Rae. LC 85-1071. 48p. (gr. 4-6). 1986. lib. bdg. 10.79 (0-8167-0557-7); pap. text ed. 3.50 (0-8167-0558-5) Troll Assocs.

—Jesse Owens, Olympic Hero. Sabin, Francene. LC 85-1101. 48p. (gr. 4-6). 1986. lib. bdg. 10.79 (0-8167-0551-8); pap. text ed. 3.50 (0-8167-0552-6) Troll Assocs.

—Martin Luther King. Bains, Rae. LC 84-2666. 32p. (gr. 3-6). 1985. PLB 9.49 (0-8167-0160-1); pap. text ed. 2.95 (0-8167-0161-X) Troll Assocs.

—Middle Ages. Sabin, Louis. LC 84-2670. 32p. (gr. 3-6). 1985. PLB 9.49 (0-8167-0174-1); pap. text ed. 2.95 (0-8167-0175-X) Troll Assocs.

—Odysseus & the Cyclops. Homer. Richardson, I. M., adapted by. LC 83-14236. 32p. (gr. 4-8). 1984. lib. bdg. 11.79 (0-8167-0007-9); pap. text ed. 2.95 (0-8167-0008-7) Troll Assocs.

—Odysseus & the Giants. Homer. Richardson, I. M., adapted by. LC 83-14233. 32p. (gr. 4-8). 1984. PLB 11.79 (0-8167-0009-5); pap. text ed. 2.95 (0-8167-0010-9) Troll Assocs.

—Odysseus & the Great Challenge. Homer. Richardson, I. M., adapted by. LC 83-14232. 32p. (gr. 4-8). 1984. lib. bdg. 11.79 (0-8167-0013-3); pap. text ed. 2.95 (0-8167-0014-1) Troll Assocs.

—Odysseus & the Magic of Circe. Homer. Richardson, I. M., adapted by. LC 83-14237. 32p. (gr. 4-8). 1984. lib. bdg. 11.79 (0-8167-0011-7); pap. text ed. 2.95 (0-8167-0012-5) Troll Assocs.

—The Picolinis & the Haunted House. Estern, Anne G. 115p. (gr. 3-5). 1989. pap. 2.95 (0-553-15771-X, Skylark) Bantam.

—Pioneers. Sabin, Francene. LC 84-2580. 32p. (gr. 3-6). 1985. PLB 9.49 (0-8167-0120-2); pap. text ed. 2.95 (0-8167-0121-0) Troll Assocs.

—Renaissance. Sabin, Francene. LC 84-2695. 32p. (gr. 3-6). 1985. PLB 9.49 (0-8167-0246-2); pap. text ed. 2.95 (0-8167-0247-0) Troll Assocs.

—The Return of Odysseus. Homer. Richardson, I. M., adapted by. LC 83-14234. 32p. (gr. 4-8). 1984. lib. bdg. 11.79 (0-8167-0015-X); pap. text ed. 2.95 (0-8167-0016-8) Troll Assocs.

—The Tale of Benjamin Bunny. LC 87-40283. (ps up). 1990. incl. audio cassettes 6.95 (1-55782-016-3, Pub. by Warner Juvenile Bks) Little.

—The Tale of Peter Rabbit. Potter, Beatrix. LC 87-40282. 24p. (ps up). 1990. incl. audio cassettes 6.95 (1-55782-015-5, Pub. by Warner Juvenile Bks) Little.

—The Tale of Tom Kitten. Potter, Beatrix. LC 87-40285. 24p. (ps up). 1990. incl. audio cassettes 6.95 (1-55782-018-X, Pub. by Warner Juvenile Bks) Little.

—The Voyage of Odysseus. Homer. Richardson, I. M., adapted by. LC 83-14235. 32p. (gr. 4-8). 1984. lib. bdg. 11.79 (0-8167-0005-2); pap. text ed. 2.95 (0-8167-0006-0) Troll Assocs.

—The Wooden Horse. Homer. Richardson, I. M., adapted by. LC 83-18061. 32p. (gr. 4-8). 1984. PLB 11.79 (0-8167-0057-5); pap. text ed. 2.95 (0-8167-0058-3) Troll Assocs.

Freshman, Shelley. The Antcyclopedia. Rothman, Joel. 4.95 (0-685-86236-4) Pubns Devl Co TX.

Friar, Joanne H. Sarah & Puffle: A Story for Children about Diabetes. Mulder, Linnea. LC 92-25638. 32p. 1992. 16.95 (0-945354-41-X); pap. 6.95 (0-945354-42-8) Magination Pr.

Friberger, Anna. Olaf the Ship's Cat. Martin, Bengt. 32p. (ps-3). 1992. 7.95 (1-56288-266-X) Checkerboard.

Fricke, Warren. My Best Friend Martha Rodriquez: Meeting a Mexican-American Family. MacMillan, Dianne & Freeman, Dorothy. LC 86-5342. 48p. (gr. 3-6). 1986. lib. bdg. 9.98 (0-671-61973-X, J Messner) S&S Trade.

Friddle, Jacob. Jake Art. Friddle, Sue. (Orig.). (gr. k-7). 1989. pap. 5.00 (0-9623308-1-7) Anyones Pub.

Friedman, Aaron. Noah & the Rainbow. Lepon, Shoshana. LC 92-26431. 1993. write for info. (1-880582-04-X); pap. write for info. (1-880582-05-8) Judaica Pr.

—Noah's Noisy Ark. Goetz, Bracha. Zakutinsky, Ruth, ed. 32p. (gr. 1-4). 1992. PLB 6.95 (0-911643-13-3) Aura Bklyn.

—Tzvi Tells the Truth. Finkelstien, Aurohom. 64p. 1991. 10.95 (1-56062-094-3) CIS Comm.

Friedman, Arthur. The Children of Chelm. Alder, David A. (gr. 1-5). 1979. (Bonim Bks); pap. 4.50 (0-88482-773-9, Bonim Bks) Hebrew Pub.

—The Hare & the Tortoise. Aesop. LC 80-28162. 32p. (gr. k-3). 1981. PLB 9.79 (*0-89375-468-4*); pap. text ed. 1.95 (*0-89375-469-2*) Troll Assocs.
—The Three Sillies. LC 80-27636. 32p. (gr. k-4). 1981. PLB 9.79 (*0-89375-486-2*); pap. text ed. 1.95 (*0-89375-487-0*) Troll Assocs.
Friedman, Ellen. One Hundred & One Questions & Answers about Dangerous Animals. Simon, Seymour. LC 84-42975. 96p. (gr. 3-7). 1985. SBE 14.95 (*0-02-782710-0*, Macmillan Child Bk) Macmillan Child Grp.
Friedman, Howard. Rocks & Minerals. Arneson, D. J. 32p. (Orig.). 1990. pap. 2.50 (*0-942025-90-3*) Kidsbks.
Friedman, Jon. First Facts about the Solar System. Teitelbaum, Michael. 24p. 1991. 2.98 (*1-56156-085-5*) Kidsbks.
Friedman, Joy. Apes Find Shapes. Moncure, Jane. 32p. (gr. 1-3). 1993. pap. text ed. 5.95 (*1-56189-347-1*) Amer Educ Pub.
—Biggest Snowball of All. Moncure, Jane. LC 88-25600. 32p. (ps-2). 1989. PLB 21.35 (*0-89565-391-5*); PLB 14.95s.p. (*0-685-56001-5*) Childs World.
—The Biggest Snowball of All. Moncure, Jane. 32p. (gr. 1-3). 1993. pap. text ed. 5.95 (*1-56189-348-X*) Amer Educ Pub.
—Ice-Cream Cows & Mitten Sheep. Moncure, Jane B. LC 87-14603. 32p. (ps-2). 1987. PLB 21.35 (*0-89565-403-2*); PLB 14.95s.p. (*0-685-55922-X*) Childs World.
—Ice-Cream Cows & Mitten Sheep. Moncure, Jane. 32p. (gr. 1-3). 1993. pap. text ed. 5.95 (*1-56189-379-X*) Amer Educ Pub.
—Nanny Goat's Boat. Moncure, Jane B. LC 87-12839. 32p. (ps-2). 1987. PLB 21.35 (*0-89565-404-0*); PLB 14.95s.p. (*0-685-55925-4*) Childs World.
—Rain: A Great Day for Ducks. Moncure, Jane B. LC 89-24010. 32p. (ps-2). 1990. PLB 19.95 (*0-89565-553-5*); PLB 13.95s.p. (*0-685-56174-7*) Childs World.
—Snow: When Will It Fall? Riehecky, Janet. LC 89-28084. 32p. (ps-2). 1990. PLB 19.95 (*0-89565-560-8*); PLB 13.95s.p. (*0-685-56181-X*) Childs World.
—What's So Special about Me? I'm One of a Kind. McDonnell, Janet & Ziegler, Sandra. LC 88-2872. 32p. (ps-2). 1988. PLB 21.35 (*0-89565-419-9*); PLB 14.95s.p. (*0-685-55943-2*) Childs World.
—Where Is Baby Bear? Moncure, Jane B. LC 87-12840. 32p. (ps-2). 1987. PLB 21.35 (*0-89565-405-9*); PLB 14.95s.p. (*0-685-55945-9*) Childs World.
—Where Is Baby Bear? Moncure, Jane. 32p. (gr. 1-3). 1993. pap. text ed. 5.95 (*1-56189-381-1*) Amer Educ Pub.
Friedman, Judith. A Beautiful Pearl. Whitelaw, Nancy. Tucker, Kathleen, ed. LC 90-28761. 32p. (gr. 2-5). 1991. 13.95 (*0-8075-0599-4*) A Whitman.
—Cat's Got Your Tongue? A Story for Children Afraid to Speak. Schaefer, Charles E. LC 92-56869. 1993. PLB 17.26 (*0-8368-0930-0*) Gareth Stevens Inc.
—I Speak English for My Mom. Stanek, Muriel. Tucker, Kathleen, ed. LC 88-20546. 32p. (gr. 2-5). 1989. 11.95 (*0-8075-3659-8*) A Whitman.
—Tell Me a Mitzvah: Little & Big Ways to Repair the World. Siegel, Danny. 64p. (Orig.). (gr. 2-6). 1993. pap. 7.95 (*0-929371-78-X*) Kar Ben.
Friedman, Marvin. Ask Another Question: The Story & Meaning of Passover. Chaikin, Miriam. LC 84-12744. 96p. (gr. 3-6). 1985. (Clarion Bks); pap. 4.95 (*0-89919-423-0*, Clarion Bks) HM.
—Bar Mitzvah, Bat Mitzvah: How Jewish Boys & Girls Come of Age. Metter, Bert. LC 83-23230. 64p. (Orig.). (gr. 4 up). 1984. (Clarion Bks) HM.
—Dance Around the Fire. Cone, Molly. LC 74-9378. 160p. (gr. 7 up). 1974. 5.95 (*0-395-19490-3*) HM.
—Pinch. Callen, Larry. (gr. 5 up). 1976. 14.95 (*0-316-12495-8*, Joy St Bks) Little.
—Shake a Palm Branch: The Story & Meaning of Sukkot. Chaikin, Miriam. LC 84-5022. 96p. (gr. 3-6). 1984. 12. 95 (*0-89919-254-8*, Clarion Bks); pap. 4.95 (*0-89919-428-1*, Clarion Bks) HM.
Friesen, John H. Adam & Eve & Five Other Stories. Enns, Peter & Forsberg, Glen. 24p. (ps-5). 1985. book & Cassette 4.95 (*0-936215-01-1*) STL Intl.
—Daniel & the Lions & Five Other Stories. Enns, Peter & Forsberg, Glen. 24p. (ps-5). 1985. book & cassette 4.95 (*0-936215-04-6*) STL Intl.
—David & Goliath & Five Other Stories. Enns, Peter & Forsberg, Glen. 24p. (ps-5). 1985. book & Cassette 4.95 (*0-936215-03-8*) STL Intl.
—Jesus Is Alive! & Five Other Stories. Enns, Peter & Forsberg, Glen. 24p. (ps-5). 1985. book & cassette 4.95 (*0-936215-06-2*) STL Intl.
—Joseph the Dreamer & Five Other Stories. Enns, Peter & Forsberg, Glen. 24p. (ps-5). 1985. book & cassette 4.95 (*0-936215-02-X*) STL Intl.
—Six Stories of Jesus. Enns, Peter & Forsberg, Glen. 24p. (ps-5). 1985. 4.95 (*0-936215-05-4*); cassette incl. STL Intl.
—Stories That Live, 6 vols. Enns, Peter & Forsberg, Glen. 144p. (ps-5). 1985. books & cassettes 29.70 (*0-936215-00-3*) STL Intl.
Frising, Nic. Say No to Drugs Color & Learn Book. Woolley, Merle E. 20p. (gr. k-6). 1988. wkbk. 1.50 (*0-9623773-0-9*) Mapakam Inc.
—Say No to Drugs Color & Learn Book. Woolley, Merle E. Guitterez, Ruben, tr. (SPA.). 20p. (gr. k-6). 1990. 1.50 (*0-9623773-1-7*) Mapakam Inc.
Frith, Julia. Pelican Sketchbook. Frith, Julia. LC 93-29013. 1994. 4.25 (*0-383-03769-7*) SRA Schl Grp.

Frith, Michael. Autographs! I Collect Them! Frith, Michael. LC 89-63064. 48p. (gr. 1-5). 1990. pap. 4.95 (*0-679-80691-1*) Random Bks Yng Read.
—Because a Little Bug Went Ka-Choo! Stone, Rosetta. LC 75-1605. 48p. (gr. k-3). 1975. 6.95 (*0-394-83130-6*) Beginner.
Frith, Michael K. Reptiles Do the Strangest Things. Hornblow, Leonora & Hornblow, Arthur. LC 70-106500. (gr. 2-4). 1970. 6.95 (*0-394-80074-5*); lib. bdg. 8.99 (*0-394-90074-X*, 90074) Random Bks Yng Read.
Fritz, Michael, photos by. China Homecoming. Fritz, Jean. LC 84-24775. 144p. (gr. 5 up). 1985. 15.95 (*0-399-21182-9*, Putnam) Putnam Pub Group.
Fritz, Ron. Belly Laughs! Food Jokes & Riddles. Keller, Charles. LC 89-28201. 32p. (gr. k-3). 1990. pap. 13.95 jacketed (*0-671-70068-5*, S&S BFYR); pap. 5.95 (*0-671-70069-3*, S&S BFYR) S&S Trade.
—Big Bird Flies Alone. Haus, Felice. LC 88-62523. 32p. (Orig.). (ps-3). 1989. pap. 1.50 (*0-394-83932-3*) Random Bks Yng Read.
—The Care Bears & the Whale Tale. Kahn, Peggy. LC 91-53214. 32p. (Orig.). (ps-1). 1992. pap. 2.25 (*0-679-82764-1*) Random Bks Yng Read.
—Dancin' Machine. Scelsa, Greg & Millang, Steve. 24p. (ps-1). 1992. incl. cassette 9.95 (*0-679-82378-6*) Random Bks Yng Read.
—Grover's Summer Vacation. Hayward, Linda. LC 88-62524. 32p. (Orig.). (ps-3). 1989. pap. 1.50 (*0-394-83969-2*) Random Bks Yng Read.
—Songs of America. Cooper, Don, read by. 32p. (ps-3). 1990. 6.95 (*0-394-85225-7*); cass. incl. Random Bks Yng Read.
—The Three Billy Goats Gruff. Kassirer, Sue. 24p. (Orig.). (ps-k). pap. 1.50 (*0-679-84796-0*) Random Bks Yng Read.
—Tongue Twisters. Keller, Charles. LC 88-26448. (ps-4). 1989. pap. 13.95 (*0-671-67123-5*, S&S BFYR); pap. 5.95 (*0-671-67975-9*, S&S BFYR) S&S Trade.
Fritz, Ronald. Babar in the Jungle. Cristaldi, Kathryn. LC 88-63342. 32p. (Orig.). (ps-3). 1989. pap. 1.50 (*0-679-80215-0*) Random Bks Yng Read.
—Merry Christmas Songs & Games. Cooper, Don. 32p. (ps-3). 1989. pap. 5.95 incl. cassette (*0-394-82230-7*) Random Bks Yng Read.
—My Bodyworks. Schoenberg, Jane. 32p. (ps-3). 1993. pap. 2.50 (*0-590-47231-3*, Cartwheel) Scholastic Inc.
—Star Tunes. Cooper, Don, read by. 32p. (Orig.). (ps-3). 1991. pap. 6.95 incls. cassette (*0-679-81243-1*) Random Bks Yng Read.
Frohlich, Margaret, jt. illus. see Niederhauser, Hans R.
Froiland, Gary. The Bandalars. Heiderscheit, Sara M. 12p. (Orig.). (ps-4). 1988. pap. 3.50 (*0-9620385-0-4*) S Heiderscheit.
Frolich, Dany. The Magic Talisman. Blaine, John. Goodwin, Hal, afterword by. 213p. (gr. 8-12). 1989. 25.00 (*0-936414-06-5*) Manuscript Pr.
Frolich, Lorenz & Pedersen, Vilhelm. Hans Andersen's Fairy Tales: A Selection. Andersen, Hans Christian. Kingsland, L. W., tr. from DAN. Lewis, Naomi, intro. by. LC 84-7120. 1985. pap. 3.95 (*0-19-281699-3*) OUP.
Frost, A. B. A. B. Frost: American Sportsman's Artist. 2nd ed. Lanier, Henry W. 176p. (gr. 10 up). 1990. Repr. 39.95 (*1-56416-003-3*) Derrydale Pr.
Frost, Arthur B. A Tangled Tale. Carroll, Lewis. LC 87-50437. 208p. (gr. 5-12). 1987. pap. 7.95 (*0-940561-06-9*) White Rose Pr.
Froud, Brian. Are All the Giants Dead? Norton, Mary. LC 78-6622. 123p. (gr. 3-7). 1978. pap. 9.95 (*0-15-607888-0*, Voyager Bks) HarBrace.
—The Dreaming Place. Lint, Charles de. LC 90-488. 144p. (gr. 7 up). 1990. SBE 14.95 (*0-689-31571-6*, Atheneum Child Bk) Macmillan Child Grp.
Fry, W. H. Billy Whiskers: Autobiography of a Goat. Montgomery, Frances T. 159p. (gr. 2 up). 1985. pap. 4.50 (*0-486-22345-0*) Dover.
Frye, Chad. The Fun Bible Search Book...Find Rupert. Frye, Chad. 32p. 1992. 12.95 (*1-55748-309-4*) Barbour & Co.
Fuchs, Bernie. Champions: Their Glory & Beyond. Littlefield, Bill. Deford, Frank, frwd by. LC 92-31390. 1993. 21.95 (*0-316-52805-6*) Little.
—Ragtime Tumpie. Schroeder, Alan. (gr. k-4). 1989. 15. 95 (*0-316-77497-9*, Joy St Bks) Little.
Fuchs, Diane & Mohle, Flay. Getting Elected. Seib, Philip. La Freniere, Annette, ed. LC 86-14999. 69p. (Orig.). (gr. 4 up). 1986. pap. 3.95 (*0-937460-24-9*) Hendrick-Long.
Fuchs, Jeff. Ghosts Along the Bayou: Tales of Haunted Places in Southwestern Louisiana. Word, Christine. 160p. (gr. 6-12). 1988. 12.95 (*0-937614-09-2*) Acadiana Pr.
Fuchshuber, Annegert. Augsburg Story Bible. LC 92-2527. 272p. (gr. 3-7). 1992. lib. bdg. 19.99 (*0-8066-2607-0*, 9-2607, Augsburg) Augsburg Fortress.
—From Dinosaurs to Fossils. Fuchshuber, Annegert. LC 80-28596. 24p. (ps-3). 1981. PLB 10.95 (*0-87614-152-1*) Carolrhoda Bks.
—Noah's Ark. Fussenegger, Gertrud. LC 87-45153. 32p. (gr. k-3). 1987. (Lipp Jr Bks) HarpC Child Bks.
—The Pied Piper of Hamelin. Bartos-Hoppner, Barbara. LC 87-45150. 32p. (gr. k-3). 1987. (Lipp Jr Bks) HarpC Child Bks.
Fudala, Rosemary. Magic Monsters Count to Ten. Moncure, Jane B. LC 78-23634. 32p. (ps-3). 1979. PLB 21. 35 (*0-89565-058-4*); PLB 14.95s.p. (*0-685-55495-3*) Childs World.
Fudd, Richard, jt. illus. see Links, Marty.

Fuenmayor, Morella. A Bicycle for Rosaura. Barbot, Daniel. 24p. (ps-3). 1991. 9.95 (*0-916291-34-0*) Kane-Miller Bk.
Fuge, Charles. Funimals. Rogers, Paul. 32p. (ps-1). 1991. 12.95 (*0-8120-6216-7*) Barron.
Fuhr, U. & Sautai, R. Baleine. (FRE.). (ps-1). 1991. 17. 95 (*2-07-035729-5*) Schoenhof.
Fuhrman, James. Poems for Young Children. Roes, Mimi. (ps-6). 1979. pap. 1.95x (*0-89780-003-6*) NAR Pubns.
Fuhrmann, Brigita. Famous Experiments & How to Repeat Them. Filson, Brent. LC 85-22259. 64p. (gr. 4 up). 1986. lib. bdg. 12.98 (*0-671-55687-8*, J Messner) S&S Trade.
Fujikawa, Gyo. Babes of the Wild. Fujikawa, Gyo. 16p. (ps). 1989. Repr. bds. 6.95 (*1-55987-008-7*, Sunny Bks) J B Comns.
—Babies. (ps). 1963. bds. 4.95 (*0-448-03084-5*, G&D) Putnam Pub Group.
—Baby Animals. (ps). 1963. bds. 4.95 (*0-448-03083-7*, G&D) Putnam Pub Group.
—Betty Bear's Birthday. Fujikawa, Gyo. 16p. (ps). 1989. Repr. bds. 6.95 (*1-55987-011-7*, Sunny Bks) J B Comns.
—Can You Count? Fujikawa, Gyo. 16p. (ps). 1989. Repr. of 1977 ed. bds. 6.95 (*1-55987-003-6*, Sunny Bks) J B Comns.
—Good Night, Sleep Tight, Shh... 22p. (ps). 1990. bds. 2.95 (*0-679-80845-0*) Random Bks Yng Read.
—Gyo Fujikawa's Oh, What a Busy Day! Fujikawa, Gyo. 80p. 1989. 13.95 (*0-448-04304-1*, G&D) Putnam Pub Group.
—Let's Eat. Fujikawa, Gyo. 16p. (ps). 1989. Repr. of 1975 ed. bds. 6.95 (*1-55987-005-2*, Sunny Bks) J B Comns.
—Let's Grow a Garden. Fujikawa, Gyo. 16p. (ps). 1989. Repr. bds. 6.95 (*1-55987-010-9*, Sunny Bks) J B Comns.
—Let's Play. Fujikawa, Gyo. 16p. (ps). 1989. Repr. of 1975 ed. bds. 6.95 (*0-317-93045-1*, Sunny Bks) J B Comns.
—Millie's Secret. Fujikawa, Gyo. 16p. (ps). 1989. bds. 6.95 (*1-55987-006-0*, Sunny Bks) J B Comns.
—My Favorite Thing. Fujikawa, Gyo. 16p. (ps). 1989. Repr. of 1978 ed. bds. 6.95 (*1-55987-004-4*, Sunny Bks) J B Comns.
—Our Best Friends. Fujikawa, Gyo. 16p. (ps). 1989. Repr. bds. 6.95 (*1-55987-009-5*, Sunny Bks) J B Comns.
—Puppies, Pussycats & Other Friends. Fujikawa, Gyo. 16p. (ps). 1989. Repr. of 1977 ed. bds. 6.95 (*1-55987-000-1*, Sunny Bks) J B Comns.
—Sleepy Time. Fujikawa, Gyo. 16p. (ps). 1989. Repr. of 1975 ed. bds. 6.95 (*1-55987-001-X*, Sunny Bks) J B Comns.
—Sunny Books - Four-Favorite Tales, 4 bks, No. 1. Fujikawa, Gyo. (ps). 1989. Repr. of 1975 ed. Boxed set, 4 books, 16 pgs. ea. bds. write for info. (*1-55987-040-0*, Sunny Bks) J B Comns.
—Sunny Books - Four-Favorite Tales, 4 bks, No. 2. Fujikawa, Gyo. (ps). 1989. Repr. Boxed set, four bks., 16 pgs. ea. bds. write for info. (*1-55987-041-9*, Sunny Bks) J B Comns.
—Sunny Books - Four-Favorite Tales, 4 bks, No. 3. Fujikawa, Gyo. (ps). Repr. Boxed set, four bks., 16 pgs. ea. bds. write for info. (*1-55987-042-7*, Sunny Bks) J B Comns.
—Surprise! Surprise! Fujikawa, Gyo. 16p. (ps). 1989. Repr. bds. 6.95 (*1-55987-007-9*, Sunny Bks) J B Comns.
—Ten Little Babies. Fujikawa, Gyo. LC 88-60966. 24p. (ps-1). 1989. pap. 4.95 (*0-394-89033-7*) Random Bks Yng Read.
Fujishima, Kaoru, et al. Simple Science Experiments with Circles. Orii, Eijo & Orii, Masako. Knopp, Jonathan, contrib. by. LC 88-23295. 32p. (gr. 2-3). 1989. PLB 15.93 (*1-55532-857-1*) Gareth Stevens Inc.
—Simple Science Experiments with Light. Orii, Eijo & Orii, Masako. Knopp, Jonathan, contrib. by. LC 88-23306. 32p. (gr. 2-3). 1989. PLB 15.93 (*1-55532-858-X*) Gareth Stevens Inc.
—Simple Science Experiments with Marbles. Orii, Eijo & Orii, Masako. Knopp, Jonathan, contrib. by. LC 88-23297. 32p. (gr. 2-3). 1989. PLB 15.93 (*1-55532-856-3*) Gareth Stevens Inc.
—Simple Science Experiments with Ping-Pong Balls. Orii, Eijo & Orii, Masako. Knopp, Jonathan, contrib. by. LC 88-22508. 32p. (gr. 2-3). 1989. PLB 15.93 (*1-55532-852-0*) Gareth Stevens Inc.
—Simple Science Experiments with Starting & Stopping. Orii, Eijo & Orii, Masako. Knopp, Jonathan, contrib. by. LC 88-20156. 32p. (gr. 2-3). 1989. PLB 15.93 (*1-55532-855-5*) Gareth Stevens Inc.
—Simple Science Experiments with Straws. Orii, Eijo & Orii, Masako. Knopp, Jonathan, contrib. by. LC 88-23298. 32p. (gr. 2-3). 1989. PLB 15.93 (*1-55532-854-7*) Gareth Stevens Inc.
—Simple Science Experiments with Water. Orii, Eijo & Orii, Masako. Knopp, Jonathan, contrib. by. LC 88-23304. 32p. (gr. 2-3). 1989. PLB 15.93 (*1-55532-859-8*) Gareth Stevens Inc.
Fujita, Miho. Great Day for Bears. Barnes, Jill & Sueyoshi, Akiko. Rubin, Caroline, ed. Japan Foreign Rights Centre Staff, tr. from JPN. LC 90-37753. 32p. (gr. k-3). 1990. PLB 14.60 (*0-944483-84-4*) Garrett Ed Corp.

—The Little Choo-Choo: Sounds, Sights & Opposites. Green, Suzanne. 14p. (ps-k). 1988. 8.95 incl. pull toy (*0-385-24426-6*) Doubleday.

Fujiwara, Kim. Carlos Montezuma. Iverson, Peter. Viola, Herman, intro. by. 32p. (gr. 3-6). 1990. 17.96 (*0-8172-3408-X*); pap. 4.95 (*0-8114-4092-3*) Raintree Steck-V.

—Ishi. Jeffredo-Warden, Louise V. LC 92-8602. 32p. (gr. 4-5). 1992. PLB 17.96 (*0-8114-6578-0*); pap. 4.95 (*0-8114-4096-6*) Raintree Steck-V.

—Italian Portraits. Hoobler, Dorothy & Hoobler, Thomas. LC 92-13641. 96p. (gr. 7-8). 1992. PLB 22.80 (*0-8114-6377-X*) Raintree Steck-V.

—Whales. Greenberg, Judith E. & Carey, Helen H. 32p. (gr. 2-4). 1990. PLB 17.96 (*0-8172-3757-7*) Raintree Steck-V.

Fujiyama, Kakuzo. Japanese Fairy Tales. Smith, Philip, ed. LC 92-17648. 96p. (gr. k up). 1992. pap. 1.00 (*0-486-27300-8*) Dover.

Fuka. Adventures of Tom Thumb. Jacobs, Joseph. Cutts, David, adapted by. LC 87-10980. 32p. (gr. k-3). 1988. PLB 9.79 (*0-8167-1071-6*); pap. text ed. 1.95 (*0-8167-1072-4*) Troll Assocs.

Fukami, Haruo. An Orange for a Bellybutton. Fukami, Haruo. 32p. (ps-3). 1990. PLB 18.95 (*0-87614-429-6*) Carolrhoda Bks.

Fukijawa, Gyo. Gyo Fujikawa's a Child's Book of Poems. 80p. (gr. k up). 1989. 13.95 (*0-448-04302-5*, G&D) Putnam Pub Group.

Full, Roger, et al. Spacecraft. Kerrod, Robin. LC 88-17655. 24p. (Orig.). (gr. 2-5). 1989. PLB 5.99 (*0-394-99989-4*) Random Bks Yng Read.

Fullam, Sue. Great Americans. Carratello, John & Carratello, Patty. 112p. (Orig.). (gr. 2-5). 1991. 10.95 (*1-55734-112-5*) Tchr Create Mat.

—A Literature Unit: Tuck Everlasting. Nakajima, Caroline. Miriani, Patricia, ed. 48p. (Orig.). (gr. 5-8). 1992. pap. 5.95 wkbk. (*1-55734-408-6*) Tchr Create Mat.

—Penny Pinching Art. Goins, Barbara L. Goldfluss, Karen J., ed. 96p. (gr. k-6). 1993. PLB 9.95 wkbk. (*1-55734-139-7*) Tchr Create Mat.

Fullam, Sue & Vasconcelles, Keith. Literature Activities for Reluctant Readers: Primary. Carratello, John & Carratello, Patty. 112p. (gr. k-3). 1991. wkbk. 10.95 (*1-55734-353-5*) Tchr Create Mat.

—Multicultural Folk Tales: A Thematic Unit. Jeffries, David. 80p. (gr. 3-5). 1992. wkbk. 7.95 (*1-55734-230-X*) Tchr Create Mat.

—Penguins - a Thematic Unit. Willrich, Lola. 80p. (gr. 1-3). 1991. wkbk. 7.95 (*1-55734-277-6*) Tchr Create Mat.

—Using Big Books with Children. Graube, Ireta S. 80p. (ps-2). 1991. wkbk. 7.95 (*1-55734-131-1*) Tchr Create Mat.

Fullam, Sue & Wright, Theresa. Hooray for the USA! Carratello, John & Carratello, Patty. 112p. (Orig.). (gr. 2-5). 1991. 10.95 (*1-55734-113-3*) Tchr Create Mat.

Fullam, Sue, jt. illus. see Vasconcelles, Keith.

Fullam, Sue M. Word Bird's Valentine Day Words. Moncure, Jane B. 32p. (gr. k-2). 1987. PLB 21.35 (*0-89565-362-1*); PLB 14.95s.p. (*0-685-55883-5*) Childs World.

Fuller, Elizabeth. My Brown Bear Barney. Butler, Dorothy. LC 88-21199. 24p. (ps up). 1989. 14.00 (*0-688-08567-9*); PLB 13.93 (*0-688-08568-7*) Greenwillow.

—My Brown Bear Barney in Trouble. Butler, Dorothy. LC 90-24776. 24p. (ps-6). 1993. 14.00 (*0-688-10521-1*); PLB 13.93 (*0-688-10522-X*) Greenwillow.

Fuller, Glenn & Spizzirri, Peter M. Aircraft: An Educational Coloring Book. Spizzirri Publishing Co. Staff. Spizzirri, Linda, ed. 32p. (gr. 1-8). 1981. pap. 1.75 (*0-86545-033-1*) Spizzirri.

—Ships: An Educational Coloring Book. Spizzirri Publishing Co. Staff. Spizzirri, Linda, ed. 32p. (gr. 1-8). 1981. pap. 1.75 (*0-86545-035-8*) Spizzirri.

Fuller, Glenn, et al. Primates: An Educational Coloring Book. Spizzirri Publishing Co. Staff. Spizzirri, Linda, ed. 32p. (gr. 1-8). 1981. pap. 1.75 (*0-86545-030-7*) Spizzirri.

—Reptiles: An Educational Coloring Book. Spizzirri Publishing Co. Staff. Spizzirri, Linda, ed. 32p. (gr. 1-8). 1981. pap. 1.75 (*0-86545-031-5*) Spizzirri.

—Sharks: An Educational Coloring Book. Spizzirri Publishing Co. Staff. Spizzirri, Linda, ed. 32p. (gr. 1-8). 1981. pap. 1.75 (*0-86545-029-3*) Spizzirri.

—Automobiles: An Educational Coloring Book. Spizzirri Publishing Co. Staff. Spizzirri, Linda, ed. 32p. (gr. 1-8). 1981. pap. 1.75 (*0-86545-032-3*) Spizzirri.

Fuller, Sandy F. Out in the Night. Liptak, Karen. LC 89-1833. 32p. (Orig.). (gr. 3-5). 1989. pap. 8.95 (*0-943173-31-0*) Harbinger AZ.

Fuller, Tim. A Living Desert. Spencer, Guy. LC 87-3488. 32p. (gr. 3-6). 1988. PLB 10.79 (*0-8167-1169-0*); pap. text ed. 2.95 (*0-8167-1170-4*) Troll Assocs.

Fuller, Tim W. Let's Visit a Super Zoo. Irvine, Georgeanne. LC 89-34370. 32p. (gr. 2-4). 1990. lib. bdg. 10.79 (*0-8167-1745-1*); pap. text ed. 2.95 (*0-8167-1746-X*) Troll Assocs.

Fulton, Ginger A. Beautiful Attitudes Matthew 5: 3-12. Stirrup Associates, Inc. Staff. Phillips, Cheryl M. & Harvey, Bonnie C., eds. LC 84-50914. 32p. (ps). 1984. pap. 1.49 (*0-937420-17-4*) Stirrup Assoc.

—My Jesus Pocketbook of Daniel in the Lion's Den. Stirrup Associates, Inc. Staff. Harvey, Bonnie C. & Phillips, Cheryl M., eds. LC 84-50916. 32p. (Orig.). (ps-3). 1984. pap. text ed. 0.69 (*0-937420-12-3*) Stirrup Assoc.

—My Jesus Pocketbook of God's Fruit. Phillips, Cheryl & Harvey, Bonnie C., eds. LC 83-50194. 32p. (ps-3). 1983. pap. 0.69 (*0-937420-08-5*) Stirrup Assoc.

—My Jesus Pocketbook of Jonah & the Big Fish. Stirrup Associates, Inc. Staff. Harvey, Bonnie C. & Phillips, Cheryl M., eds. LC 83-51679. 32p. (ps-3). 1984. pap. 0.69 (*0-937420-09-3*) Stirrup Assoc.

—My Jesus Pocketbook of Noah & the Floating Zoo. Stirrup Associates, Inc. Staff. Harvey, Bonnie C. & Phillips, Cheryl M., eds. LC 83-51680. 32p. (ps-3). 1984. pap. 0.69 (*0-937420-10-7*) Stirrup Assoc.

—My Jesus Pocketbook of the Big Little Person: The Story of Zacchaeus. Stirrup Associates, Inc. Staff. Phillips, Cheryl M. & Harvey, Bonnie C., eds. LC 84-50917. 32p. (ps). 1984. pap. 0.69 (*0-937420-13-1*) Stirrup Assoc.

—My Jesus Pocketbook of the Lord's Prayer. Phillips, Cheryl M. & Harvey, Bonnie C., eds. LC 83-50193. 32p. (ps-3). 1983. pap. 0.69 (*0-937420-07-7*) Stirrup Assoc.

Fultz, Jim. Martin "The Hero" Merriweather. Jackson, Bobby L. & Carter, Michael C. Reuter, Janet R., frwd. by. LC 93-77056. 48p. (Orig.). (gr. 4-8). 1993. 12.95g (*0-9634932-2-1*); pap. 7.95g (*0-9634932-3-X*) Multicult Pubns.

Fulweiler, Frank. The Iron Dragon Never Sleeps. Krensky, Stephen. LC 93-31167. 1994. write for info. (*0-385-31171-0*) Delacorte.

Funai, Mamoru. Dolphin. Morris, Robert A. LC 75-6292. 64p. (gr. k-3). 1975. PLB 13.89 (*0-06-024342-2*) HarpC Child Bks.

—Dolphin. Morris, Robert A. LC 75-6292. 64p. (gr. k-3). 1983. pap. 3.50 (*0-06-444043-5*, Trophy) Irwin Prof Pubng.

—Several Tricks of Edgar Dolphin. Benchley, Nathaniel. LC 79-85038. 64p. (gr. k-3). 1970. PLB 13.89 (*0-06-020468-0*) HarpC Child Bks.

Fwhang, Duk S., jt. illus. see O'Dwyer, Chung S.

G

Gaadt, David. Happy Birthday Molly! A Springtime Story. Tripp, Valerie. Thieme, Jeanne, ed. 72p. (gr. 2-5). 1987. 12.95 (*0-937295-36-1*); PLB 12.95 (*0-937295-90-6*); pap. 5.95 (*0-937295-37-X*) Pleasant Co.

Gabby, Terry. Play Beethoven. Sage, Alison. Bunting, Janet, contrib. by. 32p. (gr. 1-4). 1988. Incl. built-in 22-note electronic keyboard. 12.95 (*0-8120-5978-6*) Barron.

—Play Mozart. Sage, Alison. Bunting, Janet, contrib. by. 32p. (gr. 1-4). 1988. Incl. built-in 22-note electronic keyboard. 12.95 (*0-8120-5924-7*) Barron.

Gaber, Susan. The Baker's Dozen: A Colonial American Tale. Forest, Heather, retold by. 28p. (ps-3). 1988. 14.95 (*0-15-200412-2*, Gulliver Bks) HarBrace.

—The Finest Horse in Town. Martin, Jacqueline B. LC 90-38596. 32p. (gr. k-5). 1992. 15.00 (*0-06-024151-9*); PLB 14.89 (*0-06-024152-7*) HarpC Child Bks.

—Good Times on Grandfather Mountain. Martin, Jacqueline B. LC 91-17058. 32p. (ps-1). 1992. 14.95 (*0-531-05977-4*); lib. bdg. 14.99 (*0-531-08577-5*) Orchard Bks Watts.

—The Princess & the Lord of Night. Bull, Emma. LC 93-19151. 1994. write for info. (*0-15-263543-2*, J Yolen Bks) HarBrace.

—The Woman Who Flummoxed the Fairies. Forest, Heather. 28p. (ps-3). 1990. 14.95 (*0-15-299150-6*) HarBrace.

Gabet, Marcia. Bulletin Boards for Holidays & Everyday. Gabet, Marcia. 64p. (gr. k-6). 1985. wkbk. 6.95 (*1-55734-060-9*) Tchr Create Mat.

—Fun with Science. Gabet, Marcia. 48p. (gr. k-3). 1985. wkbk. 5.95 (*1-55734-036-6*) Tchr Create Mat.

—Fun with Social Studies. Gabet, Marcia. 48p. (gr. k-3). 1985. wkbk. 5.95 (*1-55734-037-4*) Tchr Create Mat.

Gabler, Mirko. Brackus, Krakus. Gabler, Mirko. LC 92-25819. 32p. (ps-3). 1993. PLB 14.95 (*0-8050-1963-4*, Bks Young Read) H Holt & Co.

Gackenbach, Dick. The Adventures of Albert the Running Bear. Isenberg, Barbara & Wolf, Susan. LC 82-1311. 32p. (ps-3). 1982. (Clarion Bks); pap. 6.70 (*0-89919-125-8*, Clarion Bks) HM.

Gackenbach, Dick. The Adventures of Albert, the Running Bear. Isenberg, Barbara & Wolf, Susan. (gr. k-3). 1985. pap. 12.95 incl. cassette (*0-941078-88-4*); pap. 27.95 incl. cassette, 4 paperbacks guide (*0-941078-89-2*); PLB incl. cassette 19.95 (*0-941078-90-6*) Live Oak Media.

—Amanda & the Giggling Ghost. Kroll, Steven. LC 79-28379. 40p. (ps-3). 1980. reinforced bdg. 14.95 (*0-8234-0408-0*) Holiday.

—The Baby Blues: An Adam Joshua Story. Smith, Janice L. LC 93-14492. 1994. write for info. (*0-06-023642-6*, HarpT); PLB write for info. (*0-06-023643-4*, HarpT) HarpC.

—Beauty, Brave & Beautiful. Gackenbach, Dick. LC 89-17418. 32p. (ps-3). 1990. 14.95 (*0-395-52000-2*) HM.

—Claude Has a Picnic. Gackenbach, Dick. LC 92-8242. 32p. (ps-1). 1993. 14.95 (*0-395-61161-X*, Clarion Bks) HM.

—Claude the Dog. Gackenbach, Dick. LC 74-3403. 32p. (ps-2). 1982. pap. 4.95 (*0-89919-124-X*, Clarion Bks) HM.

—Dog for a Day. Gackenbach, Dick. LC 86-17514. 32p. (ps-1). 1987. (Clarion Bks); pap. 4.95 (*0-89919-851-1*, Clarion Bks) HM.

—Harry & the Terrible Whatzit. Gackenbach, Dick. LC 76-40205. 32p. (ps-3). 1979. 14.45 (*0-395-28795-2*, Clarion Bks) HM.

—Harry & the Terrible Whatzit. Gackenbach, Dick. LC 76-40205. 32p. (ps-3). 1984. pap. 4.95 (*0-89919-223-8*, Clarion Bks) HM.

—Harvey the Foolish Pig. Gackenbach, Dick. LC 87-15691. 32p. (gr. k-3). 1988. 13.95 (*0-89919-540-7*, Clarion Bks) HM.

—Hattie Rabbit. Gackenbach, Dick. LC 75-37018. 32p. (ps-2). 1990. pap. 2.95 (*0-06-444133-4*, Trophy) HarpC Child Bks.

—Hattie, Tom, & the Chicken Witch. Gackenbach, Dick. LC 79-2742. 64p. (gr. k-3). 1980. PLB 13.89 (*0-06-021959-9*) HarpC Child Bks.

—It's Not Easy Being George: Stories about Adam Joshua (& His Dog) Smith, Janice L. LC 88-33075. 128p. (gr. 1-4). 1989. 10.95 (*0-06-025852-7*); PLB 10.89 (*0-06-025853-5*) HarpC Child Bks.

—It's Not Easy Being George: Stories about Adam Joshua (& His Dog) Smith, Janice L. LC 88-33075. 128p. (gr. 1-4). 1991. pap. 3.50 (*0-06-440338-6*, Trophy) HarpC Child Bks.

—Jack & the Whoopee Wind. Calhoun, Mary. LC 86-1630. 32p. (ps-3). 1987. 13.95 (*0-688-06137-0*); lib. bdg. 13.88 (*0-688-06138-9*, Morrow Jr Bks) Morrow Jr Bks.

—The Kid Next Door & Other Headaches: More Stories about Adam Joshua. Smith, Janice L. LC 83-47689. 160p. (gr. 1-4). 1986. pap. 3.95 (*0-06-440182-0*, Trophy) HarpC Child Bks.

—The Kid Next Door & Other Headaches: Stories about Adam Joshua. Smith, Janice L. LC 83-47689. 160p. (gr. 1-4). 1984. PLB 12.89 (*0-06-025793-8*) HarpC Child Bks.

—Mag the Magnificent. Gackenbach, Dick. LC 85-2645. 32p. (ps-3). 1987. 12.95 (*0-89919-339-0*, Clarion Bks); pap. 4.95 (*0-89919-522-9*, Clarion Bks) HM.

—The Monster in the Third Dresser Drawer. Smith, Janice L. LC 81-47109. 96p. (gr. 1-4). 1981. 13.00 (*0-06-025734-2*); PLB 12.89 (*0-06-025739-3*) HarpC Child Bks.

—The Monster in the Third Dresser Drawer: And Other Stories about Adam Joshua. Smith, Janice L. LC 81-47109. 96p. (gr. 1-4). 1988. pap. 3.95 (*0-06-440223-1*, Trophy) HarpC Child Bks.

—My Dog & the Birthday Mystery. Adler, David A. LC 86-14269. 32p. (gr. 1-4). 1987. reinforced bdg. 13.95 (*0-8234-0632-6*); pap. 5.95 (*0-8234-0710-1*) Holiday.

—My Dog & the Green Sock Mystery. Adler, David A. LC 85-14145. 32p. (gr. 1-4). 1986. reinforced bdg. 13.95 (*0-8234-0590-7*) Holiday.

—Nelson in Love: An Adam Joshua Valentine's Day Story. Smith, Janice L. LC 91-14607. 80p. (gr. 1-4). 1992. 13.00 (*0-06-020292-0*); PLB 12.89 (*0-06-020293-9*) HarpC Child Bks.

—Poppy the Panda. Gackenbach, Dick. LC 84-4952. 32p. (ps-3). 1984. 14.45 (*0-89919-276-9*, Pub. by Clarion); pap. 4.80 (*0-89919-492-3*, Pub. by Clarion) HM.

—Roll Over, Rosie. Enell, Trinka. 32p. (ps-3). 1992. 13.45 (*0-395-59340-9*, Clarion Bks) HM.

—Serious Science: An Adam Joshua Story. Smith, Janice L. LC 91-30824. 80p. (gr. 1-4). 1993. 12.00 (*0-06-020779-5*); PLB 11.89 (*0-06-020782-5*) HarpC Child Bks.

—The Show-&-Tell War: And Other Stories about Adam Joshua. Smith, Janice L. LC 85-45842. 176p. (gr. 1-4). 1988. PLB 11.89 (*0-06-025851-9*) HarpC Child Bks.

—The Show-&-Tell War: And Other Stories about Adam Joshua. Smith, Janice L. LC 85-45842. 176p. (gr. 1-4). 1990. pap. 3.95 (*0-06-440312-2*, J312, Trophy) HarpC Child Bks.

—Supposes. Gackenbach, Dick. 103p. (ps-3). 1989. 12.95 (*0-15-200594-3*, Gulliver Bks) HarBrace.

—There's a Ghost in the Coatroom: Adam Joshua's Christmas. Smith, Janice L. LC 90-23068. 96p. (gr. 1-4). 1991. 12.95 (*0-06-022863-6*); PLB 12.89 (*0-06-022864-4*) HarpC Child Bks.

—Timid Timothy's Tongue Twisters. Gackenbach, Dick, adapted by. LC 85-30531. 32p. (ps-3). 1986. reinforced bdg. 14.95 (*0-8234-0610-5*) Holiday.

—Timid Timothy's Tongue Twisters. Gackenbach, Dick. (gr. k-3). 1989. bk. & cassette 19.95 (*0-87499-128-5*); bk. & cassette 12.95 (*0-87499-127-7*); 4 cassettes & guide 27.95 (*0-87499-129-3*) Live Oak Media.

—Tiny for a Day. Gackenbach, Dick. LC 92-37580. 1993. 14.45 (*0-395-65616-8*, Clarion Bks) HM.

—The Turkeys' Side of It. Smith, Janice L. LC 89-78419. 64p. (gr. 1-4). 1992. pap. 3.95 (*0-06-440452-8*, Trophy) HarpC Child Bks.

—The Turkeys' Side of It: Adam Joshua's Thanksgiving. Smith, Janice L. LC 89-78419. 64p. (gr. 1-4). 1990. 12.00 (*0-06-025857-8*); PLB 11.89 (*0-06-025859-4*) HarpC Child Bks.

—With Love from Gran. Gackenbach, Dick. LC 88-35248. 32p. (ps). 1989. 13.45 (*0-89919-842-2*, Clarion Bks) HM.

—The Wonderful Hay Tumble. Harris, Kathleen M. LC
87-12305. 32p. (ps-2). 1988. 12.95 (0-688-07151-1);
PLB 12.88 (0-688-07152-X, Morrow Jr Bks) Morrow
Jr Bks.
Gackenbach, Dick, photos by. When I am Eight. Nixon,
Joan Lowery. LC 93-20023. (gr. 1-3). 1994. 13.99
(0-8037-1499-8) Dial Bks Young.
Gadbois, Nick & Aschwanden, Peter. Looking Inside
Caves & Caverns. Schultz, Ron. (gr. 4-7). 1993. pap.
9.95 (1-56261-126-7) John Muir.
Gaelen, Nina. The Egyptian Star. Zakon, Miriam S. 114p.
(gr. 3-9). 1983. o. p. 6.95 (0-910818-47-9); pap. 5.95
(0-910818-48-7) Judaica Pr.
Gaes, Adam & Gaes, Tim. My Book for Kids with
Cansur: A Child's Autobiography of Hope. Gaes,
Jason. LC 90-63822. 34p. (gr. 1-8). 1991. pap. 6.95
(0-937603-09-0) Melius Pub.
Gaes, Tim, jt. illus. see Gaes, Adam.
Gaffney-Kessel, Walter. One Day in the Alpine Tundra.
George, Jean C. LC 82-45590. 48p. (gr. 5-7). 1984.
(Crowell Jr Bks); PLB 13.89 (0-690-04326-0, Crowell
Jr Bks) HarpC Child Bks.
—What's for Lunch? The Eating Habits of Seashore
Creatures. Epstein, Samuel, et al. LC 85-4964. 48p.
(gr. 1-4). 1985. RSBE 13.95 (0-02-733500-3,
Macmillan Child Bk) Macmillan Child Grp.
Gaffney-Kessel, W. The Sea Is Calling Me. Hopkins, Lee
B. LC 85-16412. 32p. (gr. 3-7). 1986. 14.95
(0-15-271155-4, HB Juv Bks) HarBrace.
Gaffney-Kessell, Walter. Bugs for Dinner? The Eating
Habits of Neighborhood Creatures. Epstein, Sam &
Epstein, Beryl. LC 88-26654. 48p. (gr. 1-5). 1989.
RSBE 13.95 (0-02-733501-1, Macmillan Child Bk)
Macmillan Child Grp.
—The Human Body: How We Evolved. Cole, Joanna. LC
86-23679. 64p. (ps-3). 1987. 12.95 (0-688-06719-0);
lib. bdg. 12.88 (0-688-06720-4, Morrow Jr Bks)
Morrow Jr Bks.
—One of the Third-Grade Thonkers. Naylor, Phyllis R.
LC 88-3130. 144p. (gr. 3-7). 1988. SBE 13.95
(0-689-31424-8, Atheneum Child Bk) Macmillan
Child Grp.
—A Sky Full of Poems. Merriam, Eve. (Orig.). (gr. k-6).
1986. pap. 3.25 (0-440-47986-X, YB) Dell.
Gag, Wanda. ABC Bunny. Gag, Wanda. LC 33-27359.
(gr. k-2). 1978. 14.95 (0-698-20000-4, Coward);
(Coward); pap. 6.95 (0-698-20683-5, Coward) Putnam
Pub Group.
—Millions of Cats. Gag, Wanda. 112p. (gr. k-3). 1977.
9.95 (0-698-20091-8, Coward) Putnam Pub Group.
Gagne, Dennis. Daring Deeds. Kelly, Terry, et al. 48p.
(gr. 5-9). 1985. pap. 5.95 (0-88625-092-7) Durkin
Hayes Pub.
Gahan, Nancy L. Learning to Control Stress. rev. ed.
Buckalew, M. W., Jr. (gr. 7-12). 1982. PLB 13.95
(0-8239-0496-2) Rosen Group.
Gainer, Cindy. Good Earth Art: Environmental Art for
Kids. Kohl, MaryAnn F. & Gainer, Cindy. 224p.
(Orig.). 1991. pap. 16.95 (0-935607-01-3)
Bright Ring.
Gal, Laszio. The Enchanted Tapestry. San Souci, Robert
D. Fogelman, Phyllis J., ed. LC 85-29283. 32p. (ps-3).
1990. pap. 4.95 (0-8037-0862-9) Dial Bks Young.
—A Flask of Sea Water. Page, P. K. 34p. (gr. 2 up) 1989.
bds. 17.00 laminated (0-19-540704-0) OUP.
Gal, Laszlo. The Enchanted Tapestry. San Souci, Robert
D. LC 85-29283. 32p. (ps-3). 1987. 11.95
(0-8037-0304-X); PLB 11.89 (0-8037-0306-6) Dial Bks
Young.
—Iduna & the Magic Apples. Mayer, Marianna. LC 88-
2494. 40p. (ps-3). 1988. RSBE 16.95
(0-02-765120-7, Macmillan Child Bk) Macmillan
Child Grp.
—Pome & Peel. Ehrlich, Amy. 32p. (ps-3). 1993. pap.
4.99 (0-14-054587-5) Puffin Bks.
—Prince Ivan & the Firebird. Gal, Laszlo. 40p. 1992. text
ed. 14.95 (0-920668-98-4) Firefly Bks Ltd.
—The Spirit of the Blue Light. Mayer, Marianna. LC 86-
12524. 40p. (gr. k-3). 1990. RSBE 15.95
(0-02-765350-1, Macmillan Child Bk) Macmillan
Child Grp.
Galas, Julie. The Will & the Grace. Westlake, Diane.
80p. (Orig.). (gr. 7 up). 1984. pap. 9.00
(0-9614438-0-4) Fen Winnie.
Galdone, Paul. Anatole & the Toy Shop. Titus, Eve.
(ps-8). 1991. pap. 4.99 (0-553-35239-3) Bantam.
—Anatole over Paris. Titus, Eve. (ps-8). 1991. pap. 4.99
(0-553-35240-7) Bantam.
—Basil in Mexico: A Basil of Baker Street Mystery.
Titus, Eve. 96p. (gr. 3-6). 1990. pap. 2.75
(0-671-64117-4, Minstrel Bks) PB.
—Because of the Sand Witches Time. Steele, Mary Q.
LC 75-5932. 192p. (gr. 3-7). 1975. 11.75
(0-688-80001-7); PLB 11.88 (0-688-84001-9)
Greenwillow.
—Cat Goes Fiddle-i-Fee. Galdone, Paul. LC 85-2686.
32p. (ps-3). 1985. 13.95 (0-89919-336-6, Clarion Bks)
HM.
—The Complete Story of the Three Blind Mice. Ivimey,
John W. LC 87-689. 32p. (ps). 1989. pap. 4.80
(0-395-51585-8, Clarion Bks) HM.
—The Elves & the Shoemaker. Galdone, Paul. LC 83-
14979. 32p. (ps-3). 1986. 13.95 (0-89919-226-2,
Clarion Bks); pap. 4.95 (0-89919-422-2, Clarion Bks)
HM.
—George Washington's Breakfast. Fritz, Jean. (gr. 2-6).
1984. (Coward); pap. 6.95 (0-698-20616-9, Coward)
Putnam Pub Group.

—The Gingerbread Boy. Galdone, Paul, retold by. LC 74-
11461. 40p. (ps-3). 1983. 14.45 (0-395-28799-5,
Clarion Bks); pap. 4.95 (0-89919-163-0, Clarion Bks) HM.
—Henny Penny. Galdone, Paul. LC 68-24735. 32p.
(ps-3). 1979. 13.45 (0-395-28800-2, Clarion Bks) HM.
—Henny Penny. Galdone, Paul. LC 68-24735. 32p.
(ps-3). 1984. pap. 4.95 (0-89919-225-4, Clarion Bks)
HM.
—How Many Teeth? Showers, Paul. 40p. (gr. k-3). 1962.
PLB 13.89 (0-690-40716-5, Crowell Jr Bks) HarpC
Child Bks.
—The Hungry Fox & the Foxy Duck. Leverich,
Kathleen. LC 78-11215. 48p. (ps-3). 1979. 5.95
(0-8193-0987-7); PLB 5.95 (0-8193-0988-5) Parents.
—It Does Not Say Meow. De Regniers, Beatrice S. LC
72-75704. 40p. (ps-3). 1979. 14.95 (0-395-28822-3,
Clarion Bks) HM.
—Jack & the Beanstalk. Galdone, Paul. 32p. (ps-3).
1982. pap. 4.95 (0-89919-085-5, Clarion Bks) HM.
—King of the Cats. Jacobs, Joseph. LC 79-16659. 32p.
(ps-3). 1980. 14.45 (0-395-29030-9, Clarion Bks) HM.
—King of the Cats: A Ghost Story. Galdone, Paul. LC
79-16659. (gr. k-3). 1985. pap. 4.95 (0-89919-400-1,
Clarion Bks) HM.
—The Lemonade Trick. Corbett, Scott. 96p. (gr. 4-6).
1988. pap. 2.95 (0-590-32197-8, Apple Paperbacks)
Scholastic Inc.
—Little Red Riding Hood. LC 74-6426. 32p. (gr. k-3).
1974. text ed. 14.95 (0-07-022732-2) McGraw.
—Little Tuppen. Galdone, Paul. LC 67-10364. 32p.
(ps-3). 1979. 14.45 (0-395-28804-5, Clarion Bks) HM.
—Little Tuppen: An Old Tale. Galdone, Paul. 32p. (ps-2).
1991. pap. 5.70 (0-395-58104-4, Clarion Bks) HM.
—The Magic Porridge Pot. Galdone, Paul. LC 76-3531.
32p. (ps-3). 1979. 13.45 (0-395-28805-3, Clarion Bks)
HM.
—Monkey & The Crocodile. Galdone, Paul. LC 78-
79939. 32p. (ps-3). 1987. 13.45 (0-395-28806-1, Pub.
by Clarion); pap. 4.80 (0-89919-524-5, Pub. by
Clarion) HM.
—The Monster & the Tailor. Galdone, Paul, retold by.
LC 82-1246. 32p. (ps-1). 1988. pap. 5.70
(0-89919-795-7, Clarion Bks) HM.
—Norma Lee I Don't Knock on Doors: Knock Knock
Jokes. Keller, Charles. LC 82-21549. 44p. (gr. 3-7).
1983. 9.95 (0-13-623587-5) P-H.
—Over in the Meadow. Galdone, Paul, adapted by.
(ps-1). 1989. (S&S BFYR); pap. 5.95 (0-671-67837-X,
S&S BFYR) S&S Trade.
—The Princess & the Pea. Andersen, Hans Christian. LC
77-12707. (ps-2). 1979. 14.45 (0-395-28807-X, Clarion
Bks) HM.
—Puss in Boots. Galdone, Paul. LC 75-25505. 32p.
(ps-4). 1979. 13.45 (0-395-28808-8, Clarion Bks) HM.
—Rumpelstiltskin. Galdone, Paul. LC 84-12741. 32p.
(ps-3). 1985. 13.95 (0-89919-266-1, Clarion Bks) HM.
—The Sword in the Tree. Bulla, Clyde R. LC 56-5699.
128p. (gr. 2-5). 1962. PLB 13.89 (0-690-79909-8,
Crowell Jr Bks) HarpC Child Bks.
—The Table, the Donkey & the Stick. Grimm, Jacob &
Grimm, Wilhelm K. (ps-3). 1976. PLB 7.95
(0-07-022701-2) McGraw.
—The Teeny Tiny Woman. Galdone, Paul. LC 84-4311.
32p. (ps-3). 1984. 14.95 (0-89919-270-X, Pub. by
Clarion); pap. 4.95 (0-89919-463-X, Pub. by Clarion)
HM.
—The Teeny-Tiny Woman. Galdone, Paul. 1993. Incl.
cassette. 7.70 (0-395-52602-7, Clarion Bks) HM.
—Three Aesop Fox Fables. Galdone, Paul. LC 79-
133061. 32p. (ps-2). 1979. 13.45 (0-395-28810-X,
Clarion Bks) HM.
—The Three Bears. Galdone, Paul, ed. LC 78-158833.
32p. (ps-3). 1979. 14.45 (0-395-28811-8, Clarion Bks)
HM.
—The Three Bears. Galdone, Paul. LC 78-158833. 32p.
(ps-3). 1985. pap. 5.95 (0-89919-401-X, Clarion Bks)
HM.
—The Three Billy Goats Gruff. Galdone, Paul. 32p.
(ps-3). 1981. pap. 4.95 (0-89919-035-9, Clarion Bks)
HM.
—The Three Billy Goats Gruff. Galdone, Paul, retold by.
LC 72-85338. 32p. (ps-3). 1979. 14.95
(0-395-28812-6, Clarion Bks) HM.
—Three Little Kittens. Galdone, Paul. LC 86-2655. 32p.
(ps-2). 1986. 13.95 (0-89919-426-5, Clarion Bks); pap.
4.95 (0-89919-796-5, Clarion Bks) HM.
—Three Little Pigs. Galdone, Paul. LC 75-123456. (ps-3).
1979. 13.45 (0-395-28813-4, Clarion Bks) HM.
—The Three Little Pigs. Galdone, Paul. LC 75-123456.
40p. (Orig.). (ps-3). 1984. pap. 4.95 (0-89919-275-0,
Clarion Bks) HM.
—The Turtle & the Monkey. Galdone, Paul. (ps-3).
1990. pap. 4.80 (0-395-54425-4, Clarion Bks) HM.
—What's in Fox's Sack? Galdone, Paul. 32p. (ps-1). 1982.
13.95 (0-89919-062-6, Clarion Bks) HM.
Galdston, Olive. Play with Puppets. rev. ed. Galdston,
Olive. 52p. (Orig.). op only). 1971. pap. 1.50x
(0-686-01100-7); pap. text ed. 1.50x (0-936426-07-1)
Play Bks.
Gale, Mark. Sunrise over the Harbor: A Story About the
Meaning. Mandrell, Louise & Collins, Ace. LC 93-
310. 1993. 12.95 (1-56530-040-8) Summit TX.
Gale, Wendy. Jack-O-Faces Big Book. (ps-2). 1988. pap.
text ed. 14.00 (0-922053-23-5) N Edge Res.
Galero, Henri. Voyage au Pays des Arbres. Le Clezio, J.
M. (FRE.). 48p. (gr. 3-7). 1990. pap. 7.95
(2-07-031187-2) Schoenhof.

Galeron, H., jt. illus. see Prunier, J.
Galeron, Henri. Chat. (FRE.). (ps-1). 1989. 8.95
(2-07-035703-1) Schoenhof
—Doigt Magique. Dahl, Roald. (FRE.). 63p. (gr. 1-5).
1989. 9.95 (2-07-031185-6) Schoenhof.
—Livre d'Automne. Ottenheimer, Laurence. (FRE.). 90p.
(gr. 4-9). 1983. 8.95 (2-07-039506-5) Schoenhof.
Galiman, Ron. Sky: All about Planets, Stars, Galaxies,
Eclipses & More. Alley, David. 32p. 1993. pap. 5.95
(1-895688-04-3, Pub. by Greey dePencier CN) Firefly
Bks Ltd.
Galinat, William. The Year Christmas Was Almost
Spoiled. Williamson, Louis. (gr. k-3). 1990. pap. 5.95
(0-533-08481-4) Vantage.
Galitzer, Channa. A Children's Treasure of Sephardic
Tales. Klein-Ehlich, Tzvia. 64p. (gr. k-10). 1985. 11.95
(0-89906-787-5); pap. 8.95 (0-89906-788-3) Mesorah
Pubns.
Gallagher, Jane. Christmas Thief. Pierce, Catherine D.
(Orig.). (ps-k). 1988. pap. text ed. 4.50
(0-9621397-0-X) C D Pierce.
Gallagher, Patrick J. Animal Stew. Roddie, Shen. 32p.
(ps). 1992. 13.45 (0-395-57582-6) HM.
Gallagher, Saelig. The Selfish Giant. Wilde, Oscar. LC
93-10393. 1994. write for info. 39-99-22448-3)
Putnam Pub Group.
Gallagher, Susan. Night of Ghosts & Hermits: Nocturnal
Life on the Seashore. Stolz, Mary. LC 84-15665. 48p.
(gr. 3-7). 1985. 12.95 (0-15-257333-X, HB Juv Bks)
HarBrace.
Gallant, Roy A. Earth's Changing Climate. Gallant, Roy
A. LC 78-22124. 240p. (gr. 7 up). 1984. SBE 14.95
(0-02-736840-8, Four Winds) Macmillan Child Grp.
Gallardo, Michelle Z. Where Does God Live? Fifty Eight
More "Something for the Kids" Children's Sermons for
Worship. Lazicki, Ted. Zapel, Arthur L. & Wray,
Rhonda, eds. LC 91-8734. 144p. (Orig.). (ps-5). 1991.
pap. 8.95 (0-916260-77-1, B189) Meriwether Pub.
Gallaz, Christophe. Stravinsky. Popov, Nicolai. LC 92-
40383. 1993. 14.95 (0-88682-605-5) Creative Ed.
Galletly, Mike. Eyes. Thomson, Ruth. FS Staff, ed. 32p.
(gr. 1-3). 1988. PLB 10.90 (0-531-10549-0) Watts.
Galli, Letitzia. The Jungle Is My Home. Fischetto,
Laura. 32p. (ps-3). 1993. pap. 4.99 (0-14-054324-4,
Puffin) Puffin Bks.
Galli, Letizia. Animals of the Bible. Ziefert, Harriet. LC
93-38568. 1995. write for info. (0-385-32084-1)
Doubleday.
—The Jungle Is My Home. Fischetto, Laura. 32p. (ps-3).
1991. 13.95 (0-670-83550-1) Viking Child Bks.
Galli, Letizia, photos by. Eeney, Meeney, Miney, Mo.
Hennessy, B. G. LC 92-23527. 1993. 3.99
(0-14-054090-3) Puffin Bks.
Galli, Stan. Reader's Digest Best Loved Books for Young
Readers: Beau Geste. Wren, Percival C. Ogburn,
Jackie, ed. 160p. (gr. 4-12). 1989. 3.99
(0-945260-33-4) Choice Pub NY.
Galloway, John B., et al. Aunt Mary, Tell Me a Story: A
Collection of Cherokee Legends & Tales. Galloway,
Mary R. & Chiltosky, Mary U. (Orig.). 1991. pap.
3.00 (0-9628630-0-9) Cherokee Comn.
Galloway, Neil. Standin' Tall Cleanliness. Brady, Janeen.
22p. (Orig.). (gr-k). 1984. pap. text ed. 1.50 activity
bk. (0-944803-54-7); cassette & bk. 8.95
(0-944803-55-5) Brite Intl.
—Standin' Tall Dependability. Brady, Janeen & Woolley,
Diane. 22p. (Orig.). (gr-k). 1984. pap. text ed. 1.50
activity bk. (0-944803-59-8); cassette & bk. 8.95
(0-944803-60-1) Brite Intl.
Galloway, Neil, jt. illus. see Wilson, Grant.
Galloway, Nixon. I'm a Jet Pilot. Williams, Geoffrey T.
32p. (gr. 1-4). 1992. 9.95 (0-8431-2928-X) Price Stern.
Galouchko, Annoucka. El Misterio De la Isla De las
Especies: The Nutmeg Princess. Keens-Douglas,
Richardo. (SPA.). 32p. (ps-2). 1992. pap. 6.95
(1-55037-260-2, Pub. by Annick Pr) Firefly Bks Ltd.
—Le Mystere d'Iles aux Epices: The Nutmeg Princess.
Keens-Douglas, Richardo. (FRE.). 32p. (ps-2). 1992.
PLB 15.95 (1-55037-249-1, Pub. by Annick Pr); pap.
6.95 (1-55037-250-5, Pub. by Annick Pr) Firefly Bks
Ltd.
—The Nutmeg Princess. Keens-Douglas, Richardo. 32p.
(ps-2). 1992. PLB 15.95 (1-55037-239-4, Pub. by
Annick Pr); pap. 5.95 (1-55037-236-X, Pub. by
Annick Pr) Firefly Bks Ltd.
Galster, Robert. The Metric System: Measures for All
Mankind. Ross, Frank, Jr. LC 74-14503. 128p. (gr. 7-
10). 1974. 27.95 (0-87599-198-X) S G Phillips.
Galvani, Maureen. A Day with Alice & Sam. Grindley,
Sally. LC 92-29124. 1993. 10.95 (1-85697-912-1)
Kingfisher Bks.
—The Story of Islam. Kamm, Anthony. 32p. (gr. 4-8).
1987. pap. 3.95 (0-317-59499-0) Cambridge U Pr.
—What Can You Series, 4 bks. Littler, Angela. 20p. (gr.
2-5). 1988. set. 15.80 (0-671-93015-X, J Messner)
S&S Trade.
Galvani, Maureen & Littler, Angela. What Can You See.
Littler, Angela. 20p. (ps-1). 1988. (J Messner); 3.95
(0-671-67228-2) S&S Trade.
Gamache, Ann. Mystery of the Midnight Visitors. Frost,
Erica. LC 78-18038. 48p. (gr. 2-4). 1979. PLB 10.89
(0-89375-094-8); pap. 3.50 (0-89375-082-4) Troll
Assocs.
Gamble, Kim. Blue Skies, Green Days. De Muth, Jillian.
48p. (gr. 1-6). 1993. 16.95 (1-86373-062-1, Pub. by
Allen & Unwin Aust Pty AT) IPG Chicago.

—The Magnificent Nose: And Other Marvels. Fienberg, Anna. (ps-3). 1992. 13.95 (0-316-28195-6, Joy Street) Little.

Gamboa, Romy & Patricio, Ernie. Twenty Thousand Leagues under the Sea. new ed. Verne, Jules. Binder, Otto, ed. LC 73-75466. 64p. (Orig.). (gr. 5-10). 1973. pap. 2.95 (0-88301-104-2); student activity bk. 1.25 (0-88301-180-8) Pendulum Pr.

Gamboli, Mario. What Else Could It Be? Gamboli, Mario. LC 91-70423. 12p. (ps-k). 1991. bds. 3.95 (1-878093-72-X) Boyds Mills Pr.

—What Is Hiding? Gamboli, Mario. LC 91-70422. 12p. (ps-k). 1991. bds. 3.95 (1-878093-92-4); Set of 3 bks. bds. 11.95 (0-685-66071-0) Boyds Mills Pr.

—What Will It Be? Gamboli, Mario. LC 91-70413. 12p. (ps-k). 1991. bds. 3.95 (1-878093-73-8) Set of 3 bks. 11.85. Boyds Mills Pr.

Gamec, Hazel S. The Disappearing ABC Game Book. Gamec, Hazel S. 12p. write for info. (0-938042-02-5) Printek.

—Looking Out of the Window. Gamec, Hazel S. 12p. 1980. write for info. (0-938042-01-7) Printek.

—The Magic Pencil Counting Book. Gamec, Hazel S. 12p. 1980. write for info. (0-938042-00-9) Printek.

Gamiello, Nina. Funtime Stencils: Animals. 16p. 1992. pap. 2.95 (1-56156-153-3) Kidsbks.

—Funtime Stencils: Cars. 16p. Date not set. pap. 2.95 (1-56156-154-1) Kidsbks.

Gamma, M. B., photos by. A Pony for Keeps. Sutton, Elizabeth H. LC 90-24435. 32p. (gr. k-3). 1991. 9.95 (0-934738-77-7) Thomasson-Grant.

Gammell, Stephen. Airmail to the Moon. Birdseye, Tom. LC 87-21199. 32p. (ps-3). 1988. reinforced bdg. 14.95 (0-8234-0683-0); pap. 5.95 (0-8234-0754-3) Holiday.

—Come a Tide. Lyon, George-Ella. LC 89-35650. 32p. (ps-2). 1990. 14.95 (0-531-05854-9); PLB 14.99 (0-531-08454-X) Orchard Bks Watts.

—Come a Tide. Lyon, George-Ella. LC 89-35650. 32p. (ps-2). 1993. pap. 5.95 (0-531-07036-0) Orchard Bks Watts.

—Dancing Teepees: Poems of American Indian Youth. Sneve, Virginia H., ed. LC 88-11075. 32p. (ps-4). 1989. reinforced bdg. 15.95 (0-8234-0724-1) Holiday.

—Dancing Teepees: Poems of American Indian Youth. Sneve, Virginia H., selected by. LC 88-11075. 32p. (ps-4). 1991. pap. 5.95 (0-8234-0879-5) Holiday.

—The Great Dimpole Oak. Lisle, Janet T. LC 87-11092. 144p. (gr. 4-6). 1987. 11.95 (0-531-05716-X); PLB 11.99 (0-531-08316-0) Orchard Bks Watts.

—Halloween Poems. Livingston, Myra C., selected by. LC 89-1741. 32p. (ps-3). 1989. reinforced bdg. 13.95 (0-8234-0762-4) Holiday.

—Monster Mama. Rosenberg, Liz. 32p. (ps-3). 1993. PLB 14.95 (0-399-21889-7) Philomel Bks) Putnam Pub Group.

—More Scary Stories to Tell in the Dark: Collected & Retold from Folklore. Schwartz, Alvin. LC 83-49494. 128p. (gr. 4-7). 1984. 14.00 (0-397-32081-7, Lipp Jr Bks); PLB 13.89 (0-397-32082-5, Lipp Jr Bks) HarpC Child Bks.

—More Scary Stories to Tell in the Dark. Schwartz, Alvin. LC 83-49494. 112p. (gr. 4 up). 1986. pap. 3.95 (0-06-440177-4, Trophy) HarpC Child Bks.

—The Old Banjo. Haseley, Dennis. LC 89-36796. 32p. (gr. 1-5). 1990. pap. 3.95 (0-689-71380-0, Aladdin) Macmillan Child Grp.

—Old Black Fly. Aylesworth, Jim. LC 91-26825. 32p. (ps-2). 1992. 15.95 (0-8050-1401-2, Bks Young Read) H Holt & Co.

—Old Henry. Blos, Joan W. LC 86-21745. 32p. (ps-4). 1987. lib. bdg. 13.95 (0-688-06399-3); 13.88 (0-688-06400-0) Morrow Jr Bks.

—Old Henry. Blos, Joan W. LC 86-21745. 32p. (ps-2). 1990. pap. 4.95 (0-688-09935-1, Mulberry) Morrow.

—Once upon MacDonald's Farm. Gammell, Stephen. LC 84-23596. 32p. (gr. k-3). 1984. Repr. of 1981 ed. RSBE 13.95 (0-02-737210-3, Four Winds) Macmillan Child Grp.

—A Regular Rolling Noah. Lyon, George E. LC 90-39984. 32p. (gr. k-3). 1991. pap. 4.95 (0-689-71449-1, Aladdin) Macmillan Child Grp.

—The Relatives Came. Rylant, Cynthia. LC 85-10929. 32p. (ps-2). 1985. RSBE 14.95 (0-02-777220-9, Bradbury Pr) Macmillan Child Grp.

—The Relatives Came. Rylant, Cynthia. LC 92-41394. 32p. (ps-2). 1993. pap. 4.95 (0-689-71738-5, Aladdin) Macmillan Child Grp.

—Scary Stories, Boxed set. Schwartz, Alvin. (gr. 4-7). 1992. pap. 11.85 (0-06-440465-X, Trophy) HarpC Child Bks.

—Scary Stories to Tell in the Dark: Collected from American folklore. Schwartz, Alvin. LC 80-8728. 128p. (gr. 5 up). 1981. 14.00 (0-397-31926-6, Lipp Jr Bks); PLB 13.89 (0-397-31927-4, Lipp Jr Bks) HarpC Child Bks.

—Scary Stories 3: More Tales to Chill Your Bones. Schwartz, Alvin. LC 90-47474. 128p. (gr. 4 up). 1991. 14.00 (0-06-021794-4); PLB 13.89 (0-06-021795-2) HarpC Child Bks.

—Scary Stories 3: More Tales to Chill Your Bones. Schwartz, Alvin. LC 90-47474. 128p. (gr. 4 up). 1991. pap. 3.95 (0-06-440418-8, Trophy) HarpC Child Bks.

—Song & Dance Man. Ackerman, Karen. LC 87-3200. 32p. (ps-2). 1988. 15.00 (0-394-89330-1); lib. bdg. 15.99 (0-394-99330-6) Knopf Bks Yng Read.

—Stonewall. Fritz, Jean. 160p. (gr. 5-9). 1989. pap. 4.99 (0-14-032937-4, Puffin) Puffin Bks.

—Terrible Things: An Allegory of the Holocaust. rev. ed. Bunting, Eve. 24p. (gr. 1-4). 1989. 11.95 (0-8276-0325-8); pap. 7.95 (0-8276-0507-2) JPS Phila.

—Thanksgiving Poems. Livingston, Myra C., ed. LC 85-762. 32p. (ps-4). 1985. reinforced bdg. 14.95 (0-8234-0570-2) Holiday.

—Thunder at Gettysburg. Gauch, Patricia L. 48p. (gr. 3-6). 1990. 14.95 (0-399-22201-4, Putnam) Putnam Pub Group.

—Waiting to Waltz: A Childhood. Rylant, Cynthia. LC 84-11030. 48p. (gr. 6-8). 1984. 12.95 (0-02-778000-7, Bradbury Pr) Macmillan Child Grp.

—Wake up, Bear...It's Christmas! Gammell, Stephen. LC 81-5019. 32p. (ps-3). 1981. PLB 12.88 (0-688-00693-0) Lothrop.

—Where the Buffaloes Begin. Baker, Olaf. LC 85-5682. 48p. (ps-4). 1989. 14.95 (0-670-82760-6); pap. 5.99 (0-14-050560-1) Viking Child Bks.

—Will's Mammoth. Martin, Rafe. 32p. (ps-1). 1993. pap. 4.95 (0-399-22603-6, Putnam) Putnam Pub Group.

—The Wing Shop. Woodruff, Elvira. LC 90-55094. 32p. (ps-3). 1991. reinforced 14.95 (0-8234-0825-6) Holiday.

Gammill, Stephen L. Who Kidnapped the Sheriff? Callen, Larry. 176p. (gr. 4 up). 1985. 14.95 (0-316-12499-0, Joy St Bks) Little.

Gamper, Ruth. The Fog's Net. Flieger, Pat. LC 93-31512. 1994. write for info. (0-395-68194-4) HM.

Gampert, John. African Portraits. Hoobler, Dorothy & Hoobler, Thomas. LC 92-17284. 96p. (gr. 7-8). 1992. PLB 22.80 (0-8114-6378-8) Raintree Steck-V.

—The Greatest Sports Stories Never Told. Nash, Bruce & Zullo, Allan. Ward, Bernie, compiled by. LC 92-15352. 1993. pap. 13.00 (0-671-79527-9); pap. 8.95 (0-671-75938-8) S&S Trade.

—The Package in Hyperspace. Asimov, Janet. (gr. 4-7). 1988. 13.95 (0-8027-6822-9); PLB 14.85 (0-8027-6823-7) Walker & Co.

Gandolfo, C. Adventures of Peter & Paul. Daughters of St. Paul. LC 84-26812. 120p. (gr. 5-9). 1984. 5.00 (0-8198-0726-5) St Paul Bks.

Gangelhoff, Gene. A Walk Through the Minnesota Zoo. Gangelhoff, Jeanne M. & Belk, Bradford. 32p. Date not set. 9.95 (0-9635006-1-9) G J & B Pub.

Ganim, Barbara. Les Champs et Les Forets. Albert, Gilbert. (FRE.). 28p. (gr. 6-8). 1986. pap. text ed. 3.95 (0-911409-46-7) Natl Mat Dev.

Gannett, Ruth. Miss Hickory. Bailey, Carolyn S. LC 46-7275. (gr. 4-7). 1977. pap. 3.99 (0-14-030956-X, Puffin) Puffin Bks.

—Miss Hickory. Bailey, Carolyn S. (gr. 4-7). 1946. pap. 14.00 (0-670-47940-3) Viking Child Bks.

—My Mother Is the Most Beautiful Woman in the World. Reyher, Becky. 40p. (gr. k-3). 1945. PLB 14.88 (0-688-51251-8) Lothrop.

Gannett, Ruth C. The Dragons of Blueland. Gannett, Ruth S. LC 86-27480. 96p. (gr. 2-5). 1963. 3.99 (0-394-89050-7) Knopf Bks Yng Read.

—Elmer & the Dragon. Gannett, Ruth S. LC 86-27479. 96p. (gr. 2-5). 1987. PLB 3.99 (0-394-89049-3) Knopf Bks Yng Read.

—My Father's Dragon. Gannett, Ruth S. LC 86-27635. 96p. (gr. 2-5). 1987. pap. 3.99 (0-394-89048-5) Knopf Bks Yng Read.

Gannett, Ruth S. My Father's Dragon. gift edition ed. Gannett, Ruth S. LC 48-6527. 88p. (gr. 2-5). 1986. 14.95 (0-394-88460-4); PLB 14.99 (0-394-91438-4) Random Bks Yng Read.

Gansen, Ed. Cribbage for Kids. Wergin, Joseph P. Corvi, Becky S., intro. by. LC 90-82436. 116p. (Orig.). (gr. 4-6). 1990. pap. 15.00 (0-9627003-0-4); Deluxe gift set. 25.00 (0-685-58857-2) Intl Gamester.

Gantner, Susan. The Insignificant Elephant. Greene, Carol. LC 84-1531. 32p. (ps-3). 1985. 13.95 (0-15-238730-7, HB Jur Bks) HarBrace.

Gantschev, Ivan. Good Morning, Good Night. Gantschev, Ivan. Clements, Andrew, tr. LC 91-3603. 28p. (gr. k up). 1991. pap. 14.95 (0-88708-183-5) Picture Bk Studio.

—Noah & the Ark & the Animals. Clements, Andrew. LC 84-9438. 28p. (gr. 1 up). 1991. pap. 14.95 (0-907234-58-5) Picture Bk Studio.

—Noah & the Ark & the Animals. Clements, Andrew. 1992. pap. 4.95 (0-590-44457-3, Blue Ribbon Bks) Scholastic Inc.

—Noah & the Ark & the Animals. Clements, Andrew. LC 90-24898. 28p. (gr. k up). 1991. pap. 4.95 (0-88708-169-X) Picture Bk Studio.

—Santa's Favorite Story. 2nd ed. Aoki, Hisako. LC 82-60895. 28p. (gr. k up). 1991. pap. 4.95 (0-88708-153-3) Picture Bk Studio.

—Santa's Favorite Story. Hisako Aoki. 24p. 1991. pap. 4.95 (0-590-44454-9, Blue Ribbon Bks) Scholastic Inc.

—Three Kings. Baumann, Kurt. Lewis, Naomi, tr. LC 89-43729. 32p. (gr. 1-3). 1990. 13.95 (1-55858-094-8) North-South Bks NYC.

—Where Is Mr. Mole? Gantschev, Ivan. Clements, Andrew, tr. LC 89-8778. 28p. (gr. k up). 1991. pap. 15.95 (0-88708-109-6) Picture Bk Studio.

Gantz, David. Davey's Hanukkah Golem. Gantz, David. LC 91-2328. 32p. (gr. k-3). 1991. 13.95 (0-8276-0380-0) JPS Phila.

—The Spookiest Day. Gantz, David. 32p. (Orig.). (gr. k-3). 1986. pap. 2.50 (0-590-40325-7) Scholastic Inc.

Gapper, Jo. Who Hides Here? Green, Janice. 12p. 1992. 4.95 (0-681-41552-5) Longmeadow Pr.

—Who Lives Here? Green, Janice. 12p. 1992. 4.95 (0-681-41551-7) Longmeadow Pr.

Gapper, Joe. Colors. 6p. (ps). 1993. bds. 5.99 (0-8431-3624-3) Price Stern.

—Mommy & Baby. 12p. (ps). 1993. bds. 5.99 (0-8431-3625-1) Price Stern.

—Opposites. 12p. (ps). 1993. bds. 5.99 (0-8431-3626-X) Price Stern.

—Togethers. 12p. (ps). 1993. bds. 5.99 (0-8431-3627-8) Price Stern.

Garafano, Marie. Ginger Goes on a Diet. Williams, S. P. LC 92-28950. 1993. 13.95 (0-395-66077-7) HM.

Garber, Barbara J. Me & Daffodil. Garber, Barbara J. LC 92-61375. 66p. 1993. page. 8.00 (1-56002-212-4, Univ Edtns) Aegina Pr.

Garber, Phyllis. The Indians & the California Missions. rev. ed. Lyngheim, Linda. LC 84-80543. 160p. (gr. 4-6). 1990. 14.95 (0-915369-00-4); pap. 10.95 (0-915369-00-1) Langtry Pubns.

Garbers, Fred. The Pappenheimers: An Animation & Vocabulary Guide. Stehr, Tamara. (gr. k-6). 1983. text ed. 12.95 (3-468-96795-0) Langenscheidt.

Garcia, Joe. Baseball Card Grand Slam Curriculum Activities. Silvani, Harold. 30p. (gr. 4-8). 1992. wkbk. 11.95 (1-878669-52-4) Crea Tea Assocs.

—FUNdamental Soccer Series. Dewazien, Karl. Maher, Alan, ed. 128p. (gr. 1 up). 1991. pap. 4.95 (0-9619139-4-0) Fun Soccer Ent.

—Kitchen, Garage & Garbage Can Science, Bks. A-C. Silvani, Harold. 35p. (gr. 1-8). 1992. wkbk. ea. 6.95 (0-685-65023-5) Bk. A (1-878669-47-8) Bk. B (1-878669-45-1) Bk. C (1-878669-46-X) Crea Tea Assocs.

—Mystery Code. Silvani, Harold. 45p. (gr. 4-8). 1989. wkbk. 7.95 (1-878669-35-4, CTA-4330) Crea Tea Assocs.

Garcia, Joseph G. Fundamental Soccer Practice. Dewazien, Karl. Lavery, Vincent J., ed. 128p. (Orig.). (gr. 6). 1985. pap. 7.95 (0-9619139-0-8) Fun Soccer Ent.

—Jump for the Apple! The Story of Lily Pond, a Soccer-Playing Frog with Long, Long Legs. Garcia, Joseph G. Day, Rhonda, ed. 28p. (gr. 4up). 1983. pap. 5.95 (0-9612350-0-4) Goal Ent.

Garcia, Manuel, jt. illus. see Gobbato, Imero.

Garcia, T. R. Ellen Ross, Private Detective. Robert, Adrian. LC 84-8744. 48p. (gr. 2-4). 1985. PLB 10.89 (0-8167-0414-7); pap. text ed. 3.50 (0-8167-0415-5) Troll Assocs.

—Water. Bains, Rae. LC 84-2718. 32p. (gr. 3-6). 1985. PLB 9.49 (0-8167-0194-6); pap. text ed. 2.95 (0-8167-0195-4) Troll Assocs.

—What's It Like to Be a Bus Driver. Stamper, Judith. LC 89-34388. 32p. (gr. k-3). 1990. lib. bdg. 10.89 (0-8167-1795-8); pap. text ed. 2.95 (0-8167-1796-6) Troll Assocs.

Garcia, T. R., jt. illus. see Weissman, Bari.

Garcia, Tom. Federiquito el Sapo. Greydanus, Rose. (SPA.). 32p. (gr. k-2). 1981. PLB 7.89 (0-89375-549-4); pap. 1.95 (0-685-04947-7) Troll Assocs.

—The Goofy Ghost. Peters, Sharon. LC 81-2573. 32p. (gr. k-2). 1981. PLB 11.59 (0-89375-533-8); pap. 2.95 (0-89375-534-6) Troll Assocs.

—Numbers. Allington, Richard L. LC 79-19200. 32p. (gr. k-3). 1985. pap. 3.95 (0-8114-8239-1) Raintree Steck-V.

—The Spelling Bee. Gordon, Sharon. LC 81-4648. 32p. (gr. k-2). 1981. PLB 11.59 (0-89375-535-4); pap. 2.95 (0-89375-536-2) Troll Assocs.

—To See or Not to See. Struble, Steve. Pohl, Kathy, ed. LC 85-15487. 32p. (gr. 2-4). 1986. PLB 17.96 (0-8172-2700-8) Raintree Steck-V.

Garcia, Veronica J. Spanish in a Taco Shell. Garcia, Yolanda P. (ENG & SPA., Orig.). (gr. 4-9). 1991. pap. 10.95 (0-935303-04-9) Victory Pub.

Gardenier, Jason C. Statistical Methods: Games & Songs. Gardenier, George E. Gardenier, T. K., ed. 99p. (gr. 3 up). 1989. 89.00 (0-685-29043-3) Teka Trends.
This series provides a unique method of teaching mathematics without fear by combining poetry, music, & three-dimensional games. It introduces principles of statistical methods to early ages, & simplifies advanced concepts used by scientists & industrial engineers. Media familiar to children are used through an experiment in planting & growth. The series consists of the following individual booklets, each accompanied by a tape of the melody, evaluation form, & optional math-manipulatives oriented game kits. OVERVIEW: FUN WITH NUMBERS (ISBN 0-685-29038-7, 0002) presents objectives & overview of terms such as "matrix," "run," & "factor." MODULE I: BRANCHING TREES (ISBN 0-685-29039-5,0003)

teaches how to use the "factorial" design & the Latin Square through an experiment in planting. MODULE II COMPUTER MODELS (ISBN 0-685-29040-9,0004) designs a "metamodel" equation & plots it in 3-D form. MODULE III: TIME (ISBN 0-685-29041-7,0005) traces changes over time & relates it to quality control concepts with examples in environmental monitoring. MODULE IV: TWO-BY-TWO (ISBN 0-685-29042-5,0006) includes templates for "stem-&-leaf" charts, an innovation in statistical histograms, & presents methods to statistically test the difference between two sets of data. The series provides a bridge between mathematics & science. Knowledge of music theory is not essential. Teamwork is emphasized by presenting dexterity oriented tasks to groups, or sets of two children. A class exercise component, which can be duplicated, has been incorporated. Options exist for purchasing individual modules with introductory overview & components of math manipulative games. Series is distributed through Pragmatica Corporation. *Publisher Provided Annotation.*

Gardenier, Turhan K. Branching Trees: Statistical Methods: Games & Songs. Kumbaraci, Turkan & Gardenier, George H. LC 89-90944. 27p. (gr. 1-8). 1989. 30.00x (*0-685-29039-5*, 0003) Teka Trends.
—Computer Models: Statistical Methods: Games & Songs. Kumbaraci, Turkan & Gardenier, George H. LC 89-90944. 19p. (gr. 1-8). 1989. Incl. manipulatives. 20.00 (*0-685-29040-9*, 0004) Teka Trends.
—Fun with Numbers: Statistical Methods: Games & Song. Kumbaraci, Turkan & Gardenier, George H. LC 89-90944. 15p. (gr. 1-8). 1989. 20.00x (*0-685-29038-7*, 0002) Teka Trends.
—Time: Statistical Methods: Games & Songs. Kumbaraci, Turkan & Gardenier, George H. LC 89-90944. 19p. (gr. 1-8). 1989. 20.00 (*0-685-29041-7*, 0005) Teka Trends.
—Two-by-Two: Statistical Methods: Games & Songs. Kumbaraci, Turkan & Gardenier, George H. LC 89-90944. 19p. (gr. 1-8). 1989. 20.00 (*0-685-29042-5*, 0006) Teka Trends.
Gardner, Beau. The Upside down Riddle Book. Phillips, Louis. LC 82-73. 32p. (gr. k up). 1982. 14.95 (*0-688-00931-X*); PLB 14.88 (*0-688-00932-8*) Lothrop.
Gardner, Charles, et al. What Makes Popcorn Pop? And Other Questions about the World Around Us. Myers, Jack. LC 90-85912. 64p. (gr. 1-5). 1991. 10.95 (*1-878093-33-9*) Boyds Mills Pr.
Gardner, Donald, jt. illus. see Timmins, Harry L.
Gardner, Earle. Snafu: The Littlest Clown. Pennington, Lillian B. LC 73-90113. 32p. (gr. 1-6). 1972. PLB 9.95 (*0-913532-00-2*); cassette 7.94x (*0-87783-225-0*) Oddo.
Gardner, Katherine W. The Robins Knew. Yost, Carolyn K. 32p. (gr. k-2). 1991. pasted 2.50 (*0-87403-817-0*, 24-03917) Standard Pub.
Gardner, Sally. The Little Nut Tree. Gardner, Sally. LC 93-26714. 32p. 1994. 14.00 (*0-688-13297-9*, Tambourine Bks); PLB write for info. (*0-688-13298-7*, Tambourine Bks) Morrow.
Garehime, Marianne. Mr. Jelly Bean, No. 1. 2nd ed. Garehime, Ed. American Red Cross Staff, tr. LC 77-82261. 64p. (ps-4). 1979. 9.95 (*0-918822-01-7*) Deem Corp.
Garibay, U. N. An Animal ABC. Edades, Jean. (gr. 3-5). 1979. pap. 3.50 (*0-686-25221-7*, Pub. by New Day Pub PI) Cellar.
Garland, Michael. Circus Girl. Garland, Michael. LC 92-22270. 32p. (ps-3). 1993. 14.99 (*0-525-45069-6*, DCB) Dutton Child Bks.
—The Legend of Sleepy Hollow. Irving, Washington. 64p. 1992. PLB 15.95 (*1-56397-027-9*) Boyds Mills Pr.
Garland, Nicholas. The River Girl. Cope, Wendy. 64p. (gr. 7 up). 1991. 16.95 (*0-571-16062-X*); pap. 7.95 (*0-571-16136-7*) Faber & Faber.
Garland, Sarah. Billy & Belle. Garland, Sarah. 32p. (ps-3). 1993. 13.00 (*0-670-84396-2*) Viking Child Bks.
Garner, David. Somebody Called Me a Retard Today - & My Heart Felt Sad. O'Shaughnessy, Ellen. LC 92-10812. 24p. 1992. 13.95 (*0-8027-8196-9*); PLB 14.85 (*0-8027-8197-7*) Walker & Co.
Garns, Allen. Gonna Sing My Head Off! Krull, Kathleen, selected by. Guthrie, Arlo, intro. by. LC 89-49562. 160p. 1992. 20.00 (*0-394-81991-8*) Knopf Bks Yng Read.

—The Winter Fox. Brutschy, Jennifer. LC 92-33467. 40p. (ps-3). 1993. 15.00 (*0-679-81524-4*); PLB 15.99 (*0-679-91524-9*) Knopf Bks Yng Read.
Garramone, Rich. Zany Knock Knocks. Cole, Ronny M. LC 92-43068. 96p. (gr. 2-7). 1993. pap. 3.95 (*0-8069-8589-5*) Sterling.
Garraty, Gail. The Farthest Shore. rev. ed. Le Guin, Ursula K. LC 72-57273. 240p. (gr. 6 up). 1990. SBE 16.95 (*0-689-31683-6*, Atheneum Child Bk) Macmillan Child Grp.
—The Tombs of Atuan. Le Guin, Ursula K. LC 70-154753. 176p. (gr. 6-9). 1971. SBE 16.95 (*0-689-31684-4*, Atheneum Child Bk) Macmillan Child Grp.
Garrick, Donald. The Wednesday Surprise. Bunting, Eve. 32p. (gr. k-3). 1989. 14.45 (*0-89919-721-3*, Clarion Bks) HM.
Garrick, Fiona. Bonnie McSmithers Is at It Again! Alderson, Sueann. 24p. (Orig.). (ps-2). 1990. pap. 0.99 (*1-55037-110-X*, Pub. by Annick CN) Firefly Bks Ltd.
—Bonnie McSmithers You're Driving Me Dithers. Alderson, Sueann. 24p. (Orig.). (ps-2). 1990. pap. 0.99 (*1-55037-108-8*, Pub. by Annick CN) Firefly Bks Ltd.
—Hurry Up, Bonnie! Alderson, Sueann. 24p. (Orig.). (ps-2). 1990. pap. 0.99 (*1-55037-109-6*, Pub. by Annick CN) Firefly Bks Ltd.
Garrick, Jacqueline. George Washington: Father of Our Country. Adler, David A. LC 88-4691. 48p. (gr. 2-5). 1988. reinforced bdg. 14.95 (*0-8234-0717-9*) Holiday.
—The Revolving Door Stops Here. Wood, Phyllis A. LC 89-23891. 192p. (gr. 6 up). 1990. 14.95 (*0-525-65022-9*, Cobblehill Bks) Dutton Child Bks.
—Thomas Jefferson: Father of Our Democracy. Adler, David A. LC 87-45336. 48p. (gr. 2-5). 1987. reinforced bdg. 14.95 (*0-8234-0667-9*) Holiday.
Garriott, Gene. Molly Pitcher: Young Patriot. Stevenson, Augusta. LC 86-10744. 192p. (gr. 2-6). 1986. pap. 3.95 (*0-02-042040-4*, Aladdin) Macmillan Child Grp.
Garris, Norma. Alexander's Praise Time Band. Stortz, Diane. LC 92-32817. 28p. (ps-k). 1993. 4.99 (*0-7847-0036-2*, 24-03826) Standard Pub.
—God Cares for Me. Stortz, Diane. 12p. (ps). 1992. deluxe ed. 4.99 (*0-87403-992-4*, 24-03112) Standard Pub.
—God Feeds the Animals. Stewart, Dana. 12p. (ps). 1992. deluxe ed. 4.99 (*0-87403-998-3*, 24-03118) Standard Pub.
Garrison, Barbara. Another Celebrated Dancing Bear. Scheffrin-Falk, Gladys. LC 89-13152. 32p. (gr. k-2). 1991. SBE 13.95 (*0-684-19164-4*, Scribners Young Read) Macmillan Child Grp.
—My First Book of Jewish Holidays. Silverman, Maida. LC 93-20370. (ps-8). 1994. 13.99 (*0-8037-1427-0*); lib. bdg. 13.89 (*0-8037-1428-9*) Dial Bks Young.
—Only One. Harshman, Marc. LC 92-11349. 32p. (ps-3). 1993. 12.99 (*0-525-65116-0*, Cobblehill Bks) Dutton Child Bks.
Garrison, Ben. Sandy of Laguna. Bell, Joseph. 72p. (Orig.). (gr. k-8). 1992. pap. 9.95 (*1-880812-01-0*) S Ink WA.
Garrison, Ron, photos by. A Day in the Life of a Test Pilot. McKeever, Michael & Irvine, Georgeanne. LC 90-37439. 32p. (gr. 4-8). 1991. lib. bdg. 11.79 (*0-8167-2224-2*); pap. text ed. 2.95 (*0-8167-2225-0*) Troll Assocs.
Garrity, Gloria J. The Magick Horn. MacLaurin, Diane. Karcher, Pamela, ed. 75p. (Orig.). (gr. 6 up). 1993. pap. write for info. (*0-934549-01-X*) Laurin Hse.
Garry-McCord, Kathi. Magic Broom. Pellowski, Michael J. LC 85-14054. 48p. (Orig.). (gr. 1-3). 1986. PLB 10.59 (*0-8167-0636-0*); pap. text ed. 3.50 (*0-8167-0637-9*) Troll Assocs.
—Wake up, Sam! Michaels, Ski. LC 85-14115. 48p. (Orig.). (gr. 1-3). 1986. PLB 10.59 (*0-8167-0580-1*); pap. text ed. 3.50 (*0-8167-0581-X*) Troll Assocs.
Garry-McCord, Kathleen. Dick Whittington. LC 80-28171. 32p. (gr. k-4). 1981. PLB 9.79 (*0-89375-482-X*); pap. text ed. 1.95 (*0-89375-483-8*) Troll Assocs.
—Zoo Worker. Stamper, Judith B. LC 88-10046. 32p. (gr. k-3). 1989. PLB 10.89 (*0-8167-1440-1*); pap. text ed. 2.95 (*0-8167-1441-X*) Troll Assocs.
Gary, N. C., jt. illus. see Acquistapace, David.
Garza, Carmen L. Family Pictures (Cuadros de familia) Lomas Garza, Carmen. LC 89-27845. (SPA & ENG.). 32p. (gr. 1-7). 1990. 13.95 (*0-89239-050-6*) Childrens Book Pr.
Gaston, Jane. Safari: A Lift-the-Flaps Adventure. Gaston, Jane. LC 92-80525. 24p. (ps-1). 1993. 7.99 (*0-679-83044-8*) Random Bks Yng Read.
Gates, Donald. Hoggle's Christmas. Shelton, Rick. LC 92-37861. 80p. (gr. 2-6). 1993. 12.99 (*0-525-65129-2*, Cobblehill Bks) Dutton Child Bks.

Gates, Donna. The Alaskan Happy Dog Trilogy: Can Dogs Talk?, Loving a Happy Dog, Secret Messages-Training a Happy Dog, 3 vols. Shields, Mary. 32p. (ps-3). 1993. Set. pap. 30.00 (*0-9618348-2-X*) Pyrola Pub. THE ALASKAN HAPPY DOG TRILOGY, $30.00, ISBN 0-9618348-2-X, CAN DOGS TALK?, $10.00, ISBN 0-9618348-1-1, with audio tape, $13.00, ISBN 0-9618348-4-6, LOVING A HAPPY DOG, $12.00, ISBN 0-9618348-3-8, SECRET MESSAGES-TRAINING A HAPPY DOG, $12.00, ISBN 0-9618348-6-2. In the first volume, CAN DOGS TALK? Rita & Ryan answer their own question with the help of an Alaskan dog musher, a book, a team of friendly huskies & a lost puppy. In the second volume, LOVING A HAPPY DOG, the kids ask Mary to give them the lost puppy, named Happy. Mary helps the kids understand the responsibilities of loving & caring for a Happy Dog, including the knowledge of a dog's life span. A pull-out puzzle is included in this book. The final volume, SECRET MESSAGES-TRAINING A HAPPY DOG unfolds as Rita, Ryan & Happy discover messages along the trail as they hike to Mary's cabin. By evening the kids have learned how to train their dog, & another important lesson-its okay to ask for help. Each volume stands on its own, but the complete trilogy gives the young reader a well-rounded introduction into enjoying the companionship of a dog. The author, Mary Shields lives in Alaska, where she raises sled dogs for companions & wilderness travelers. Donna Gates creates her fine art images of sled dogs & interior Alaskan wildlife at her home near Denali Park, Alaska. Pyrola Publishing, P.O. Box 80961, Fairbanks, AK 99708. 907-455-6469 (Alaskan time please). *Publisher Provided Annotation.*

—Can Dogs Talk, Vol. 1. Shields, Mary. 32p. (Orig.). (ps-3). 1991. pap. 10.00 (*0-9618348-1-1*); incl. tape 13.00 (*0-9618348-4-6*); write for info. Pyrola Pub.
—Loving a Happy Dog. Shields, Mary. 32p. 1992. pap. 12.00 (*0-9618348-3-8*) Pyrola Pub.
Gates, Frieda. North American Indian Masks. Gates, Frieda. 64p. (gr. 5 up). 1982. 8.95 (*0-8027-6462-2*); lib. bdg. 9.85 (*0-8027-6463-0*) Walker & Co.
Gatie, John. Strawberry Shortcake & Baby Needs a Name. Elliott, Brian. 40p. (ps-3). 1984. cancelled 5.95 (*0-910313-21-0*) Parker Bros.
Gatt, Elizabeth. Mommy & Baby in the Wild. Gibbs, Bridget. 12p. 1992. 4.95 (*0-681-41553-3*) Longmeadow Pr.
—Mommy & Baby on the Farm. Gibbs, Bridget. 12p. 1992. 4.95 (*0-681-41554-1*) Longmeadow Pr.
Gattis, L. S., III. Kites for Pathfinders: A Basic Youth Enrichment Skill Honor Packet. Gattis, L. S., III. 18p. (Orig.). (gr. 5 up). 1986. pap. 5.00 tchr's ed. (*0-936241-07-1*) Cheetah Pub.
—Leathercraft for Pathfinders: A Basic Youth Enrichment Skill Honor Packet. Gattis, L. S., III. 20p. (Orig.). (gr. 5 up). 1987. pap. 5.00 tchr's ed. (*0-936241-09-8*) Cheetah Pub.
—Leathercraft for Pathfinders: An Advanced Youth Enrichment Skill Honor Packet. Gattis, L. S., III. 20p. (Orig.). (gr. 5 up). 1987. pap. 5.00 tchr's ed. (*0-936241-10-1*) Cheetah Pub.
Gatzke, Lee. Smelling. Allington, Richard L. & Krull, Kathleen. LC 79-27147. 32p. (gr. k-3). 1985. PLB 15.33 (*0-8172-1293-0*); pap. 9.27 (*0-8172-2488-2*) Raintree Steck-V.
Gaudriault, M., jt. illus. see Rozier, J.
Gaudriault, Rozier. The Story of Birth. Prot, Viviane A. Bogard, Vicki, tr. from FRE. LC 90-50777. 38p. (gr. k-5). 1991. 4.95 (*0-944589-34-0*, 340) Young Discovery Lib.
Gaul, Randy. Coming-&-Going Men: Four Tales. Fleischman, Paul. LC 84-48336. 160p. (gr. 6 up). 1985. PLB 12.89 (*0-06-021884-3*) HarpC Child Bks.
Gaus, Helen. Script Ease: Manuscript of Calligraphy. Fellows, Marian & Parkhurst, Christine. 61p. (gr. 2-6). 1982. pap. text ed. 9.95 (*0-317-62675-2*) Kino Pubns.
Gauthier, Don. Jack & the Beanstalk: European Folk Tales. 24p. (ps-2). 1992. pap. 3.50 (*0-88625-287-3*) Durkin Hayes Pub.
Gavitt, Anne. Loving One Another. Jackson, Neta. 192p. (ps-2). 1993. 10.99 (*0-945564-66-X*, Gold & Honey) Questar Pubs.
Gawr, Rhuddlwm. The Triads: The Wisdom of the Welsh Witches. Gawr, Rhuddlwm. LC 85-73755. 140p. (Orig.). 1989. 14.95 (*0-931760-45-3*, CP 10123); pap. 10.95 (*0-931760-23-2*) Camelot GA.

Gawr, Rhuddlwm, et al. The Way: The Discovery of the Grail of Immortality. Gawr, Rhuddlwm. LC 85-73759. (Orig.). 1987. 18.95 (*0-931760-50-X*, CP 10128); pap. 15.95 (*0-931760-28-3*) Camelot GA.

Gay, Marie-Louise. Rainy Day Magic. Gay, Marie-Louise. Tucker, Kathy, ed. LC 89-5380. 32p. (ps-2). 1989. PLB 13.95 (*0-8075-6767-1*) A Whitman.

—Willy Nilly. Gay, Marie-Louise. Levine, Abby, ed. LC 90-12376. 32p. (gr. 1-3). 1990. 13.95 (*0-8075-9119-X*) A Whitman.

Gay, Michael. The Chase: A Kutenai Indian Tale. Tanaka, Beatrice. LC 91-10790. 32p. (ps-2). 1991. 14.00 (*0-517-58623-1*); lib. bdg. 14.99 (*0-517-58624-X*) Crown Bks Yng Read.

Gay, Michel. Bibi Takes Flight. Gay, Michel. LC 87-28262. 40p. (ps-1). 1988. 12.95 (*0-688-06828-6*); PLB 12.88 (*0-688-06829-4*, Morrow Jr Bks) Morrow Jr Bks.

—White Owl & Blue Mouse. Joubert, Jean. Levertov, Denise, tr. from FRE. LC 90-70710. 64p. (gr. 1-3). 1990. 13.95 (*0-944072-13-5*) Zoland Bks.

Gay, Pierre. Livre de la Langue Francaise. Rosenstiehl, Agnes. (FRE.). 93p. (gr. 4-9). 1985. 15.95 (*2-07-039524-3*) Schoenhof.

Gaydos, Michael, et al. The Collected Teenage Mutant Ninja Turtles Adventures, Vol. 1. Brown, Ryan & Clarrian, Dean. 96p. 1991. pap. 5.95 (*1-879450-03-8*) Tundra MA.

Gaydos, Tim. Tarzan of the Apes. Woods, Harold & Woods, Geraldine. LC 81-19873. 96p. (gr. 2-7). 1982. lib. bdg. 5.99 (*0-394-95089-5*); pap. 2.95 (*0-394-85089-0*, Random Juv) Random Bks Yng Read.

Gayheart, Willard. A Mountain Summer. Mashburn, William H. LC 88-11782. 140p. (Orig.). (gr. 9-12). 1990. pap. 8.95 (*0-936015-14-4*) Pocahontas Pr.

Gazsi, Edward. Kimbo's Marble. Herrick, Amy. LC 91-18988. 48p. (gr. 1-5). 1993. 16.00 (*0-06-020373-0*); PLB 15.89 (*0-06-020374-9*) HarpC Child Bks.

Gazsi, Edward S. The Seven Ravens. Geringer, Laura, retold by. LC 93-8161. Date not set. 15.00 (*0-06-023552-7*); PLB 14.89 (*0-06-023553-5*) HarpC.

Geard, David, jt. illus. see McHenry, Kitsy.

Geary, Jennifer. Best Friends Forever. Geary, Susan & Geary, Joe. 100p. (Orig.). (gr. 2-4). 1991. pap. write for info. (*0-9629760-0-8*) Bear Paw Bks.

—The Black Bear: El Oso Negro. Geary, Susan R. 100p. (Orig.). (gr. 3-4). 1991. pap. write for info. (*0-9629760-1-6*) Bear Paw Bks.

Geary, Rick. Cyberantics. Mayakovsky, Stanislaw, pseud. 56p. 1992. 14.95 (*1-878574-29-9*) Dark Horse Comics.

Gedrose, E. D. Balderdash. Cosgrove, Stephen. 32p. (gr. 3-6). 1991. 14.95 (*1-55868-045-4*) Gr Arts Ctr Pub.

GEE Studio Staff. Teenage Mutant Ninja Turtles ABC's for a Better Planet. Rosser, J. K. LC 90-53247. 32p. (Orig.). (ps-3). 1991. PLB 5.99 (*0-679-91383-1*) Random Bks Yng Read.

Geehan, Wayne. Captain Blackwell's Treasure. Geehan, Wayne. (gr. 2-6). 1993. incl. puzzle 12.95 (*0-922242-47-X*) Lombard Mktg.

—Jack London: A Life of Adventure. Bains, Rae. LC 91-3927. 48p. (gr. 4-6). 1992. PLB 10.79 (*0-8167-2513-6*); pap. text ed. 3.50 (*0-8167-2514-4*) Troll Assocs.

—A Journey to the Center of the Earth. Verne, Jules. James, Raymond, adapted by. LC 89-20560. 48p. (gr. 3-6). 1990. lib. bdg. 12.89 (*0-8167-1867-9*); pap. text ed. 3.95 (*0-8167-1868-7*) Troll Assocs.

—Men of Iron. Pyle, Howard. Hitchner, Earle, adapted by. LC 89-33926. 48p. (gr. 3-6). 1990. PLB 12.89 (*0-8167-1871-7*); pap. text ed. 3.95 (*0-8167-1872-5*) Troll Assocs.

—Twenty Thousand Leagues under the Sea. Verne, Jules. James, Raymond, adapted by. LC 89-34248. 48p. (gr. 3-6). 1990. PLB 12.89 (*0-8167-1879-2*); pap. text ed. 3.95 (*0-8167-1880-6*) Troll Assocs.

Geer, Charles. The Biggest (& Best) Flag That Ever Flew. Jones, Rebecca. LC 87-40609. 32p. (gr. k-4). 1988. 8.95 (*0-87033-381-X*) Tidewater.

Gehm, Charles. The House Without a Christmas Tree. Rock, Gail. LC 74-162. 96p. (gr. 2 up). 1974. lib. bdg. 9.99 (*0-394-92833-4*) Knopf Bks Yng Read.

—Soup. Peck, Robert N. LC 73-15117. 104p. (gr. 3 up). 1974. PLB 9.99 (*0-394-92700-1*) Knopf Bks Yng Read.

—The Thanksgiving Treasure. Rock, Gail. LC 74-163. 96p. (gr. 2 up). 1974. PLB 11.99 (*0-394-92834-2*) Knopf Bks Yng Read.

Gehr, Mary. Surprise Island. Warner, Gertrude C. LC 49-49618. (gr. 2-7). 1949. PLB 10.95 (*0-8075-7673-5*); pap. 3.50 (*0-8075-7674-3*) A Whitman.

Geiger, Paul. The Mystery of the Diamond in the Wood. Kherdian, David. LC 83-272. 128p. (gr. 3 up). 1983. lib. bdg. 9.99 (*0-394-95603-6*) Knopf Bks Yng Read.

Geis, Jacqueline. Where the Buffalo Roam. Geis, Jacqueline, adapted by. 32p. (gr. k-3). 1992. 13.95 (*0-8249-8570-2*, Ideals Child); PLB 14.00 (*0-8249-8584-2*) Hambleton-Hill.

Geisert, Arthur. Aesop & Company: With Scenes from His Legendary Life. Bader, Barbara, retold by. 64p. 1991. 16.45 (*0-395-50597-6*, Sandpiper) HM.

—The Ark. Geisert, Arthur. LC 88-15889. 48p. (ps up). 1988. 15.45 (*0-395-43078-X*) HM.

—Oink. Geisert, Arthur. LC 90-46123. 32p. 1991. 13.45 (*0-395-55329-6*) HM.

—Oink, Oink. Geisert, Arthur. LC 92-31778. 32p. (gr. k-3). 1993. 13.45 (*0-395-64048-2*) HM.

—Pa's Balloon & Other Pig Tales. Geisert, Arthur. LC 83-18552. 96p. (gr. k-3). 1984. 13.95 (*0-395-35381-5*, 5-86480) HM.

—Pigs from A to Z. Geisert, Arthur. LC 86-18542. 64p. (gr. 2 up). 1986. 16.45 (*0-395-38509-1*) HM.

—Pigs from One to Ten. Geisert, Arthur. LC 92-5097. 32p. (gr. k-3). 1992. 14.95 (*0-395-58519-8*) HM.

Geld, Goldie. Ha Shem's World of Color. Zakutinsky, Adina. 32p. (ps). 1987. PLB 4.95x (*0-911643-10-9*); board book 4.95 (*0-685-55893-2*) Aura Bklyn.

Geldart, William. The Fairy Rebel. Banks, Lynne R. LC 87-28740. 128p. (gr. 5 up). 1988. 12.95 (*0-385-24483-5*) Doubleday.

—Return of the Indian. Banks, Lynne R. LC 85-31119. 192p. (gr. 4-6). 1986. pap. 13.95 (*0-385-23497-X*) Doubleday.

—The Very Worried Sparrow. Doney, Meryl. 32p. (ps-6). 1991. 11.95 (*0-7459-1919-7*) Lion USA.

Gellman, Sim. Don't Flip, It's Only a Trip. Kaplan, Carol & Lyss, Esther. 32p. (gr. 1-4). 1993. pap. 3.99 (*0-8431-3497-6*) Price Stern.

—We're Moving. Kaplan, Carol & Lyss, Ester. 32p. (gr. 1-4). 1993. pap. 3.99 (*0-8431-3498-4*) Price Stern.

Gellos, Nancy. Personal Views. Starkman, Neal. LC 89-22302. 43p. (Orig.). (gr. 6-12). 1989. pap. 7.00 (*0-935529-12-8*) Comprehen Health Educ.

—Your Decision. Starkman, Neal. LC 88-71482. 118p. (Orig.). (gr. 9-12). 1988. pap. 13.00 (*0-935529-10-1*) Comprehen Health Educ.

Gemme, Francis R. Story of the Red Cross. Barton, Clara. (gr. 4 up). 1968. pap. 1.50 (*0-8049-0170-8*, CL-170) Airmont.

Gendusa, Sam. Carving Jack-O-Lanterns. rev. ed. Gendusa, Sam. Ruse, Arnold, ed. & intro. by. LC 89-92605. 80p. 1989. pap. 9.95x (*0-9621071-1-5*) SG Prodns.

Geneste, Marcelle. Beaver Gets Lost. Chottin, Ariane. LC 91-40651. 22p. (ps). 1992. 6.99 (*0-89577-419-4*, Readers Digest Kids) RD Assn.

—Gentle Little Lion. Clement, Claude. Jensen, Patricia, adapted by. LC 93-27047. 1994. write for info. (*0-89577-562-X*, Readers Digest Kids) RD Assn.

—The Hungry Duckling. Clement, Claude. LC 91-40648. 22p. (ps). 1992. 6.99 (*0-89577-418-6*, Readers Digest Kids) RD Assn.

—Little Bear's New Friend. Pepin, Muriel. LC 91-40652. 22p. (ps). 1992. 6.99 (*0-89577-417-8*, Readers Digest Kids) RD Assn.

—Little Puppy Saves the Day. Pepin, Muriel. LC 91-46499. 22p. (ps). 1992. 6.99 (*0-89577-426-7*, Readers Digest Kids) RD Assn.

Genet, Barbara. Ta-Poo-Ach Means Apple. Genet, Barbara. LC 85-60009. 46p. (ps-3). 1985. 8.00 (*0-86705-015-2*) A R E Pub.

Gentleman, David. Shakespeare & His Theatre. Brown, John R. LC 81-8441. 64p. (gr. 6 up). 1982. 14.95 (*0-688-00850-X*) Lothrop.

Gentry, Debra. Jeremy & the Wappo. Elwell, Sharon. 126p. (Orig.). (gr. 3-4). 1991. pap. 15.95 (*0-9626210-0-5*) Rattle OK Pubns.

Gentry, Diane. The Story of Johann: The Boy Who Longed to Come to Amerika. Lindsay, Mela M. LC 90-85324. 190p. 1991. 11.50 (*0-914222-18-X*) Am Hist Soc Ger.

Genzo, John P. A Kid's Guide to How to Stop the Violence. Terrell, Ruth H. 144p. (Orig.). 1992. pap. 2.99 (*0-380-76652-3*, Camelot) Avon.

George, Anthony & Washington, Ruby, photos by. Legacies of a Shopping Bag Lady: Poems of Life. Keel-Williams, Mildred. Holmes, Darryl, ed. Harewood, Lasana K., frwd. by. LC 84-62520. 72p. (Orig.). (gr. 7 up). 1984. pap. 6.00 (*0-9614084-1-3*) Mus Fed Ink.

George, Bob, jt. illus. see Carter, Terry.

George, Jean C. My Side of the Mountain. George, Jean C. LC 87-27556. 176p. (gr. 3-7). 1988. 15.00 (*0-525-44392-4*, 01258-370, DCB); pap. 4.95 (*0-525-44395-9*, 0481-140, DCB) Dutton Child Bks.

—The Summer of the Falcon. George, Jean C. LC 62-16543. 153p. (gr. 5 up). 1979. pap. 3.95 (*0-06-440095-6*, Trophy) HarpC Child Bks.

—Water Sky. George, Jean C. LC 86-45496. 224p. (gr. 6 up). 1987. 13.00 (*0-06-022198-4*); PLB 12.89 (*0-06-022199-2*) HarpC Child Bks.

—Water Sky. George, Jean C. LC 86-45496. 224p. (gr. 5 up). 1989. pap. 3.95 (*0-06-440202-9*, Trophy) HarpC Child Bks.

George, Lindsay B. Box Turtle at Long Pond. George, William T. LC 88-18787. 24p. (ps-1). 1989. 14.00 (*0-688-08184-3*); PLB 13.93 (*0-688-08185-1*) Greenwillow.

—Christmas at Long Pond. George, William T. LC 91-31475. 32p. (ps-8). 1992. 14.00 (*0-688-09214-4*); PLB 13.93 (*0-688-09215-2*) Greenwillow.

—Secret Places: Poems. Huck, Charlotte, selected by. LC 92-29014. 32p. (s up). 1993. 15.00 (*0-688-11669-8*); PLB 14.93 (*0-688-11670-1*) Greenwillow.

—William & Boomer. George, Lindsay B. LC 86-9789. 24p. (ps-1). 1990. 14.00 (*0-688-06640-2*); PLB 14.93 (*0-688-06641-0*) Greenwillow.

—William & Boomer. George, Lindsay B. Red Grammer Staff, narrated by. 24p. (ps-3). 1990. incl. audiocassette 19.95 (*0-924483-23-7*) Soundprints.

George, R. Jefferson, photos by. The Harper's Voices: Caves & Cowboys: Family Song Book. Harper, Jo. Boustany, Robert. (ENG & SPA.). 20p. (Orig.). (gr. 1-5). 1988. pap. 8.95 incl. cassette (*0-929932-00-5*) JCH Pr.

—Pals, Potions, & Pixies: Family Songbook. Harper, Jo. Boustany, Robert. (SPA & ENG.). 20p. (Orig.). (gr. 1-5). 1988. pap. 8.95 incl. cassette (*0-929932-01-3*) JCH Pr.

PALS, POTIONS, & PIXIES is a read-along songbook. New, original songs. Bright colors. Lively illustrations for each song. Upbeat, modern rhythms. 50 minutes of music, one side cassette vocals, one side instrumental. Educator approved. Family values. Five children in a family sing about their experiences. Companion volume to CAVES & COWBOYS, FAMILY SONGBOOK. By the author of JALAPENO HAL. *Publisher Provided Annotation.*

Geraghty, Paul. Look Out, Patrick! Geraghty, Paul. LC 89-77850. 32p. (ps-1). 1990. 13.95 (*0-02-735822-4*, Macmillan Child Bk) Macmillan Child Grp.

—Over the Steamy Swamp. Geraghty, Paul. 28p. (ps-1). 1989. 13.95 (*0-15-200561-7*, Gulliver Bks) HarBrace.

—Slobcat. Geraghty, Paul. LC 90-27577. 32p. (ps-1). 1991. 13.95 (*0-02-735825-9*, Macmillan Child Bk) Macmillan Child Grp.

—Stop That Noise! Geraghty, Paul. LC 92-6608. 32p. (ps-2). 1992. 13.95 (*0-517-59158-8*); PLB 13.99 (*0-517-59159-6*) Crown Bks Yng Read.

Geraldo, Esteban, jt. illus. see Butcher, Sam.

Gerberg, Mort. Geographunny: A Book of Global Riddles. Gerberg, Mort. 64p. (gr. 3 up). 1991. 14.45 (*0-395-52449-0*, Clarion Bks); pap. 7.70 (*0-395-60312-9*, Clarion Bks) HM.

—More Spaghetti, I Say! Gelman, Rita G. 32p. (ps-3). 1993. pap. 2.95 (*0-590-45783-7*) Scholastic Inc.

Gergely, Tibor. The Taxi That Hurried. reissued ed. Mitchell, Lucy S., et al. 24p. (ps-k). 1992. write for info. (*0-307-00144-X*, 312-09, Golden Pr) Western Pub.

—Three Best-Loved Tales: Tootle; The Happy Man & His Dump Truck; Scuffy the Tugboat. 80p. (ps-2). 1992. write for info. (*0-307-15633-8*, 15633, Golden Pr) Western Pub.

—Wheel on the Chimney. Brown, Margaret W. LC 84-48379. 32p. (ps-3). 1954. 14.00 (*0-397-30288-6*, Lipp Jr Bks); PLB 13.89 (*0-397-30296-7*) HarpC Child Bks.

—Wheel on the Chimney New. Brown, Margaret W. LC 93-29423. 1994. 15.00 (*0-06-024247-7*, Festival); PLB 14.89 (*0-06-024248-5*, Festival) HarpC Child Bks.

Gerig, Sibyl G. Ghost Town Mystery. Moore, Ruth N. LC 87-2874. 144p. (gr. 4 up). 1987. pap. 5.95 (*0-8361-3445-1*) Herald Pr.

—Mystery at Camp Ichthus. Moore, Ruth N. LC 86-25637. 128p. (Orig.). (gr. 3-9). 1986. pap. 5.95 (*0-8361-3421-4*) Herald Pr.

German Craftsmen Staff. King Winter: Treasures from the Library of Congress. 16p. 1992. Repr. of 1859 ed. saddle wired 3.95 (*1-55709-168-4*) Applewood.

Geronimi, Clyde. Amy Avocet. Pizzo, Joan E. LC 83-70739. (gr. k-6). 1983. 8.95 (*0-939126-06-0*) Back Bay.

—Chips Quips. Geronimi, Clyde. LC 83-72694. 55p. (gr. 4 up). 1983. 3.95 (*0-939126-09-5*) Back Bay.

—Little Crumb: Tales of the Back Bay. Pizzo, Joan E. 29p. (Orig.). (gr. k-6). 1980. PLB 10.95 (*0-939126-00-1*); pap. 7.95 (*0-939126-01-X*); tchr's manual, 35p 8.95 (*0-939126-03-6*) Back Bay.

—Pelican Bill. Pizzo, Joan. (gr. k-6). 1990. PLB 11.95 (*0-939126-10-9*) Back Bay.

Gerrard, Roy. The Favershams. Gerrard, Roy. 32p. (gr. 1-9). 1983. 15.00 (*0-374-32292-9*) FS&G.

—Matilda Jane. Gerrard, Jean. LC 83-48082. 32p. (ps-3). 1983. 15.00 (*0-374-34865-0*) FS&G.

Gerson, Ivan. Holiday Songs. Gerson, Trina. 84p. (ps-7). 1984. pap. text ed. write for info. (*0-9605878-2-9*) Anirt Pr.

Gerson, Janice. Holiday Crafts. Gerson, Trina. 80p. (ps-7). 1983. pap. text ed. write for info. (*0-9605878-1-0*) Anirt Pr.

—Poetic Shapes. Gerson, Trina. 52p. (ps-7). 1981. pap. text ed. 2.95 (*0-9605878-0-2*) Anirt Pr.

Gerstein, Mordecai. Frankenstein Moved in on the Fourth Floor. Levy, Elizabeth. LC 78-19830. 64p. (gr. 2-5). 1981. pap. 3.95 (*0-06-440122-7*, Trophy) HarpC Child Bks.

Gerstein, Mordicai. Arnold of the Ducks. Gerstein, Mordicai. LC 82-47735. 64p. (gr. k-3). 1983. PLB 14.89 (*0-06-022003-1*) HarpC Child Bks.

—Beauty & the Beast. Gerstein, Mordicai, retold by. 48p. (ps-2). 1989. (DCB); bk. & cassette 17.95 (*0-525-44511-0*) Dutton Child Bks.

—Dracula Is a Pain in the Neck. Levy, Elizabeth. LC 82-47707. 80p. (gr. 2-6). 1983. PLB 12.89 (*0-06-022303-2*) HarpC Child Bks.

—Dracula Is a Pain in the Neck. Levy, Elizabeth. LC 82-47707. 80p. (gr. 2-5). 1984. pap. 3.95 (*0-06-440146-4*, Trophy) HarpC Child Bks.

—Frankenstein Moved in on the Fourth Floor. Levy, Elizabeth. LC 78-19830. (gr. 1-5). 1979. PLB 12.89 (0-06-023811-9) HarpC Child Bks.
—The Mountains of Tibet. Gerstein, Mordicai. LC 85-45684. 32p. (gr. 2 up). 1987. 14.00 (0-06-022144-5) HarpC Child Bks.
—Nice Little Girls. Levy, Elizabeth. LC 73-15394. (gr. k-3). 1978. pap. 2.75 (0-440-06360-4) Delacorte.
—The Seal Mother. Gerstein, Mordicai. LC 82-29295. 32p. (ps-3). 1986. PLB 10.89 (0-8037-0303-1) Dial Bks Young.
—Something Queer at the Ball Park. Levy, Elizabeth. 48p. (gr. 1-4). 1984. pap. 2.99 (0-440-48116-3, YB) Dell.
—Something Queer at the Birthday Party. Levy, Elizabeth. 48p. (gr. 1-4). 1992. pap. 2.99 (0-440-40687-0, YB) Dell.
—Something Queer at the Haunted School. Levy, Elizabeth. LC 81-1940. 48p. (gr. 1-3). 1982. 8.95 (0-440-08349-4); pap. 9.95 (0-385-28992-8) Delacorte.
—Something Queer at the Haunted School. Levy, Elizabeth. 48p. (gr. 1-4). 1983. pap. 3.25 (0-440-48461-8, YB) Dell.
—Something Queer at the Lemonade Stand. Levy, Elizabeth. 48p. (gr. k-6). 1983. pap. 2.99 (0-440-48495-2, YB) Dell.
—Something Queer at the Library. Levy, Elizabeth. 48p. (gr. 1-4). 1989. pap. 3.25 (0-440-48120-1, YB) Dell.
—Something Queer in Outer Space. Levy, Elizabeth. LC 92-54870. 48p. (gr. 2-5). 1993. pap. 4.95 (1-56282-279-9) Hyprn Ppbks.
—Something Queer in Outer Space. Levy, Elizabeth. LC 92-54870. 48p. (gr. 2-5). 1993. 12.95 (1-56282-566-6); PLB 12.89 (1-56282-280-2) Hyprn Child.
—Something Queer in Rock N' Roll. Levy, Elizabeth. LC 86-19772. 48p. (gr. k-3). 1987. pap. 12.95 (0-385-29547-2) Delacorte.
—Something Queer in the Cafeteria. Levy, Elizabeth. LC 93-31343. 1994. write for info. (0-7868-0001-1); pap. write for info. (0-7868-1000-9) Hyprn Child.
—Something Queer Is Going On. Levy, Elizabeth. 48p. (gr. 1-4). 1982. pap. 2.99 (0-440-47974-6, YB) Dell.
—Something Queer on Vacation. Levy, Elizabeth. LC 78-72858. (gr. 1-3). 1980. 10.95 (0-440-08346-X); pap. 6.95 (0-385-28987-1) Delacorte.
—Something Queer on Vacation. Levy, Elizabeth. 48p. (gr. 1-4). 1982. pap. 2.99 (0-440-47968-1, YB) Dell.
—The Story of May. Gerstein, Mordicai. LC 90-22410. 48p. (ps-3). 1993. 16.00 (0-06-022288-3); PLB 15.89 (0-06-022289-1) HarpC Child Bks.
Gerstein, Mordicai & Harris, Susan Y. Guess What? Gerstein, Mordicai & Harris, Susan Y. LC 90-47318. 32p. (ps-2). 1991. 8.00 (0-517-58217-1) Crown Bks Yng Read.

Gertz, Susan E. Hanukkah & Christmas at My House. Gertz, Susan E. LC 91-73702. 32p. (ps-6). 1992. pap. 6.95 (0-9630934-0-1) Willow & Laurel. As seen in WORKING MOTHER & CHILD magazines. "Young children enjoy hearing tales of their parents' childhoods, & this delightful book uses a Jewish mommy's recollections of Hanukkah & a Christian daddy's memories of Christmas as the framework for presenting the stories, foods, songs, decorations, & special customs unique to each holiday. Several features which add to the value of this book are the recipes for the holiday foods, the historical background material, & the charming illustrations which can help young children visualize unfamiliar objects & events from both holidays. "Ms. Gertz has provided an EXCELLENT RESOURCE FOR FAMILIES & RELIGIOUS EDUCATION CLASSES."--District Curriculum Librarian, Unitarian Universalist Association. "For the young children for whom this book is intended, & for their parents for whom the author has provided a more detailed history & some good traditional recipes, THIS BOOK IS A MUST. It may be one of the few publications available through which to deal with a child's confusion in having a mom & dad of different religious backgrounds."--Small Press Magazine. "Potato latkes & Christmas cookies, a menorah & a Christmas angel, 'I Had a Little Dreidle' & 'Deck the Halls' all coexist in a suprisingly simple & logical manner in this extraordinary book."--All About Kids. "...A BOOK THAT ALL CHILDREN SHOULD READ, so they may better understand...families which celebrate both holidays."--B'nai Brith Messenger. Distributed by Children's Small Press Collection (800) 221-8056.** *Publisher Provided Annotation.*

Gervais, Bernadette. Voyage under the Stars. Pittau, Francisco. Pearson, Susan, ed. Packager, Belgian, tr. from FRE. LC 91-26075. 32p. (ps-3). 1992. 13.00 (0-688-11328-1); PLB 12.93 (0-688-11329-X) Lothrop.
Gervin, Joseph. Irish Fairytales. Scott, Michael. LC 89-50977. 142p. (gr. 2-5). 1989. pap. 11.95 (0-85342-866-2, Pub. by Mercier Press Ltd Eire) Dufour.
—Strange Irish Tales for Children. Lenihan, Edmund. 128p. (gr-ps-8). 1992. pap. 9.95 (0-85342-833-6, Pub. by Mercier Pr Eire) Dufour.
Gesner, Ethel & Irvine, Bonnie. The Magic Lamp. Hurd, Inis I. LC 87-30728. 140p. (gr. 4-7). 1989. PLB 14.50 (0-944517-00-5) Christian Center.
Getchell, Marianne S. The Magic Kite. Daniel, Kira. LC 85-14015. 48p. (Orig.). (gr. 1-3). 1986. PLB 10.59 (0-8167-0614-X); pap. text ed. 3.50 (0-8167-0615-8) Troll Assocs.
Geter, Tyrone. Dawn & the Round-to-It. Smalls-Hector, Irene. LC 93-19731. 1994. pap. 14.00 (0-671-87166-8, S&S BFYR) S&S Trade.
Geurts, Kelly. Bunny Butz Sings the Blues. Gaff, Sha. LC 91-67753. 70p. 1993. pap. 7.00 (1-56002-161-6, Univ Edtns) Aegina Pr.
—Farmer Brown's Friends. Parsons, Mary P. LC 90-71980. 65p. (Orig.). 1992. pap. 8.00 (1-56002-040-7) Aegina Pr.
—It's Not Alexander's Fault. Hrynko, Tamara. LC 91-67916. 96p. 1993. pap. 8.00 (1-56002-177-2, Univ Edtns) Aegina Pr.
Gewirtz, Bina. Savta Simcha & the Seven Splendid Gifts. Gauz, Yaffa. LC 87-3643. (gr. 4-7). 1987. 12.95 (0-87306-437-2) Feldheim.
—Savta Simcha, Uncle Nechemya, & the Very Strange Stone in the Garden. Ganz, Yaffa. LC 92-26165. 1992. write for info. (0-87306-618-9) Feldheim.
—Shukis Upsidedown Dream. Ganz, Yaffa. (gr. k-3). 1986. 6.95 (0-87306-384-8) Feldheim.
Gewirtz, Bina & Poppins, Jewish M. Savta Simcha & the Cinnamon Tree. Ganz, Yaffa. (gr. 6-10). 11.95 (0-87306-354-6) Feldheim.
Gholson, Virginia. Trails North - Stories of Texas Yesterdays. Baker, Charlotte. Roberts, Melissa, ed. 128p. (gr. 4-7). 1991. 10.95 Eakin-Sunbelt.
Gholson, Virginia S. Spindletop. Hancock, Sibyl. (gr. 4-7). 1981. 7.95 (0-89015-265-9, Pub. by Panda Bks) Eakin-Sunbelt.
Ghosh, R. B. Folk Tales from India. Thomas, Vernon, ed. (gr. 3-10). 1979. 14.00 (0-89744-141-9) Auromere.
Ghrist, Julie. Taelly's Counting Adventures. (ps). 1993. Gift box set of 4 bks., 12p. ea. incl. counting flash cards. bds. 14.95 (1-56828-042-4) Red Jacket Pr.
—Taelly's Counting Adventures: At Sea. 12p. (ps). 1993. 4.95 (1-56828-027-0) Red Jacket Pr.
—Taelly's Counting Adventures: Down on the Farm. 12p. (ps). 1993. 4.95 (1-56828-029-7) Red Jacket Pr.
—Taelly's Counting Adventures: In the Neighborhood. 12p. (ps). 1993. 4.95 (1-56828-030-0) Red Jacket Pr.
—Taelly's Counting Adventures: On Mars. 12p. (ps). 1993. 4.95 (1-56828-028-9) Red Jacket Pr.
Giacoia, Frank. Clara Barton: Founder of the American Red Cross. Stevenson, Augusta. LC 86-10750. 192p. (gr. 2-6). 1986. pap. 3.95 (0-02-041820-5, Aladdin) Macmillan Child Grp.
Giampa, Linda. New Testament Activity Book. Giampa, Linda. 32p. (Orig.). (gr. k-3). 1992. pap. 2.99 (0-570-04725-0) Concordia.
—Old Testament Activity Book. Giampa, Linda. 32p. (gr. k-3). 1992. pap. 2.99 (0-570-04724-2) Concordia.
Gianni, Gary. Moby Dick. Melville, Herman. Selden, Bernice, adapted by. LC 87-16788. 48p. (gr. 3-6). 1988. PLB 12.89 (0-8167-1207-7); pap. text ed. 3.95 (0-8167-1208-5) Troll Assocs.
Giannini, Enzo. Caterina the Clever Farm Girl: A Tuscan Tale. Peterson, Julienne, retold by. LC 93-15161. 1994. write for info. (0-8037-1181-6); PLB write for info. (0-8037-1182-4) Dial Bks Young.
—Milo's Toothache. Luttrell, Ida. LC 91-24315. 40p. (ps-3). 1992. 11.00 (0-8037-1034-8); PLB 10.89 (0-8037-1035-6) Dial Bks Young.
Gibbons, Gail. Baby in the Box. Asch, Frank. LC 88-16452. 32p. (ps-3). 1989. reinforced bdg. 12.95 (0-8234-0725-X) Holiday.
—Boat Book. Gibbons, Gail. LC 82-15851. 32p. (ps-3). 1983. reinforced bdg. 14.95 (0-8234-0478-1); pap. 5.95 (0-8234-0709-8) Holiday.
—Cars & How They Go. Cole, Joanna. LC 82-45575. 32p. (gr. 2-6). 1983. (Crowell Jr Bks); PLB 13.89 (0-690-04262-0, Crowell Jr Bks) HarpC Child Bks.
—Cars & How They Go. Cole, Joanna. LC 82-45575. 32p. (gr. 2-6). 1986. pap. 4.95 (0-06-446052-5, Trophy) HarpC Child Bks.
—Catch the Wind! All about Kites. Gibbons, Gail. LC 88-28820. (gr. k-3). 1989. 14.95 (0-316-30955-9) Little.
—Check It Out! The Book about Libraries. Gibbons, Gail. LC 85-5414. 32p. (ps-3). 1985. 12.95 (0-15-216400-6, HB Juv Bks) HarBrace.
—Check It Out! The Book about Libraries. Gibbons, Gail. 32p. (ps-3). 1988. pap. 3.95 (0-15-216401-4, Voyager Bks) HarBrace.
—Christmas Time. Gibbons, Gail. (gr. k-3). 1985. PLB incl. cassette 19.95 (0-941078-84-1); pap. 12.95 incl. Cassette (0-941078-82-5); PLB 27.95 incl. cassette, 4 paperbacks, guide (0-317-40160-2) Live Oak Media.
—Deadline! From News to Newspaper. Gibbons, Gail. LC 86-47654. 32p. (gr. 1-4). 1987. PLB 14.89 (0-690-04602-2, Crowell Jr Bks) HarpC Child Bks.
—Dinosaurs. Gibbons, Gail. LC 87-364. 32p. (ps-3). 1987. reinforced bdg. 14.95 (0-8234-0657-1); pap. 5.95 (0-8234-0708-X) Holiday.
—Dinosaurs, Dragonflies & Diamonds: All About Natural History Museums. Gibbons, Gail. LC 88-38831. 32p. (gr. k-3). 1988. RSBE 13.95 (0-02-737240-5, Four Winds) Macmillan Child Grp.
—Easter. Gibbons, Gail. LC 88-23292. 32p. (ps-3). 1989. reinforced bdg. 14.95 (0-8234-0737-3); pap. 5.95 (0-8234-0866-3) Holiday.
—Farming. Gibbons, Gail. LC 87-21254. 32p. (ps-3). 1988. PLB 14.95 reinforced bdg. (0-8234-0682-2); pap. 5.95 (0-8234-0797-7) Holiday.
—Fill It Up! Gibbons, Gail. LC 84-45345. 32p. (gr. k-4). 1985. (Crowell Jr Bks); PLB 14.89 (0-690-04440-2) HarpC Child Bks.
—Fire! Fire! Gibbons, Gail. LC 83-46162. 40p. (gr. k-4). 1987. pap. 5.95 (0-06-446058-4, Trophy) HarpC Child Bks.
—Flying. Gibbons, Gail. LC 85-22027. 32p. (ps-3). 1986. reinforced bdg. 14.95 (0-8234-0599-0); pap. 5.95 (0-8234-0977-5) Holiday.
—From Path to Highway: The Story of the Boston Post Road. Gibbons, Gail. LC 85-47897. 32p. (gr. 1-4). 1986. (Crowell Jr Bks); PLB 14.89 (0-690-04514-X) HarpC Child Bks.
—From Seed to Plant. Gibbons, Gail. LC 90-47037. 32p. (ps-3). 1991. reinforced bdg. 14.95 (0-8234-0872-8) Holiday.
—From Seed to Plant. Gibbons, Gail. (ps-3). 1993. pap. 5.95 (0-8234-1025-0) Holiday.
—The Great St. Lawrence Seaway. Gibbons, Gail. LC 91-9851. 40p. (gr. 1 up). 1992. 15.00 (0-688-06984-3); PLB 14.93 (0-688-06985-1) Morrow Jr Bks.
—Halloween. Gibbons, Gail. LC 84-519. 32p. (ps-3). 1984. reinforced bdg. 14.95 (0-8234-0524-9); pap. 5.95 (0-8234-0577-X) Holiday.
—Halloween. Gibbons, Gail. (gr. k-3). 1985. incl. cassette 19.95 (0-941078-87-6); pap. 12.95 incl. cassette (0-941078-85-X); incl. cassette, 4 paperbacks guide 27.95 (0-941078-86-8) Live Oak Media.
—How a House Is Built. Gibbons, Gail. LC 90-55107. 32p. (ps-3). 1990. reinforced bdg. 14.95 (0-8234-0841-8) Holiday.
—Lights! Camera! Action!: How a Movie Is Made. Gibbons, Gail. LC 85-47536. 32p. (gr. 1-4). 1985. (Crowell Jr Bks); PLB 13.89 (0-690-04477-1) HarpC Child Bks.
—Lights! Camera! Action! How a Movie Is Made. Gibbons, Gail. LC 85-47536. 32p. (gr. 1-4). 1989. pap. 4.95 (0-06-446088-6, Trophy) HarpC Child Bks.
—Marge's Diner. Gibbons, Gail. LC 88-26789. 32p. (gr. 1-4). 1989. (Crowell Jr Bks); PLB 12.89 (0-690-04606-5, Crowell Jr Bks) HarpC Child Bks.
—The Milk Makers. Gibbons, Gail. LC 86-22148. 32p. (gr. k-3). 1987. pap. 3.95 (0-689-71116-6, Aladdin) Macmillan Child Grp.
—Monarch Butterfly. Gibbons, Gail. LC 89-1880. 32p. (ps-3). 1989. reinforced bdg. 14.95 (0-8234-0773-X) Holiday.
—Monarch Butterfly. Gibbons, Gail. LC 89-1880. 32p. (ps-3). 1991. pap. 5.95 (0-8234-0909-0) Holiday.
—New Road! Gibbons, Gail. LC 82-45917. 32p. (gr. k-4). 1987. pap. 4.95 (0-06-446059-2, Trophy) HarpC Child Bks.
—Paper, Paper Everywhere. Gibbons, Gail. LC 82-3109. 32p. (gr. 1-5). 1983. 10.95 (0-15-259488-4, HB Juv Bks) HarBrace.
—Playgrounds. Gibbons, Gail. LC 84-19285. 32p. (ps-3). 1985. reinforced bdg. 14.95 (0-8234-0553-2) Holiday.
—The Post Office Book. Gibbons, Gail. LC 81-43888. 32p. (gr. k-3). 1982. (Crowell Jr Bks); PLB 14.89 (0-690-04199-3) HarpC Child Bks.
—The Post Office Book: Mail & How It Moves. Gibbons, Gail. LC 85-45397. 32p. (gr. k-4). 1986. pap. 4.95 (0-06-446029-0, Trophy) HarpC Child Bks.
—The Pottery Place. Gibbons, Gail. LC 86-32790. 32p. (ps-3). 1987. 12.95 (0-15-263265-4, HB Juv Bks) HarBrace.
—Prehistoric Animals. Gibbons, Gail. LC 88-4661. 32p. (ps-3). 1988. reinforced bdg. 14.95 (0-8234-0707-1) Holiday.
—The Puffins Are Back! Gibbons, Gail. LC 90-30525. 32p. (gr. 3-5). 1991. 14.00 (0-06-021603-4); PLB 13.89 (0-06-021604-2) HarpC Child Bks.
—Recycle! A Handbook for Kids. Gibbons, Gail. 32p. (ps-3). 1992. 14.95 (0-316-30971-0) Little.
—St. Patrick's Day. Gibbons, Gail. LC 93-29570. 32p. (gr. 4-8). 1994. 15.95 (0-8234-1119-2) Holiday.

—Say Woof! The Day of a Country Veterinarian. Gibbons, Gail. LC 91-48270. 32p. (gr. k-3). 1992. RSBE 13.95 (0-02-736781-9, Macmillan Child Bk) Macmillan Child Grp.
—Stargazers. Gibbons, Gail. LC 92-52713. 32p. (ps-3). 1992. reinforced bdg. 14.95 (0-8234-0983-X) Holiday.
—Sun up, Sun Down. Gibbons, Gail. LC 82-23420. 32p. (gr. 1-5). 1983. 14.95 (0-15-282781-1, HB Juv Bks) HarBrace.
—Sunken Treasure. Gibbons, Gail. LC 87-30114. 32p. (gr. 1-5). 1988. 14.00 (0-690-04734-7, Crowell Jr Bks); PLB 13.89 (0-690-04736-3) HarpC Child Bks.
—Sunken Treasure. Gibbons, Gail. LC 87-30114. 32p. (gr. 1-5). 1990. pap. 4.95 (0-06-446097-5, Trophy) HarpC Child Bks.
—Thanksgiving Day. Gibbons, Gail. LC 83-175. 32p. (ps-3). 1983. reinforced bdg. 14.95 (0-8234-0489-7); pap. 5.95 (0-8234-0576-1) Holiday.
—Thanksgiving Day. Gibbons, Gail. (gr. k-3). 1984. incl. cassette 19.95 (0-941078-63-9); pap. 12.95 incl. cassette (0-941078-61-2); pap. 27.95 4 bks., cassette & guide (0-941078-62-0); sound filmstrip 22.95 (0-941078-60-4) Live Oak Media.
—Tool Book. Gibbons, Gail. LC 81-13386. 32p. (ps-3). 1982. reinforced bdg. 14.95 (0-8234-0444-7); pap. 5.95 (0-8234-0694-6) Holiday.
—Trucks. Gibbons, Gail. LC 81-43039. 32p. (ps-2). 1981. (Crowell Jr Bks); PLB 14.89 (0-690-04119-5) HarpC Child Bks.
—Trucks. Gibbons, Gail. LC 81-43039. 32p. (ps-3). 1985. pap. 4.95 (0-06-443069-3, Trophy) HarpC Child Bks.
—Tunnels. Gibbons, Gail. LC 83-18589. 32p. (ps-3). 1984. reinforced bdg. 14.95 (0-8234-0507-9); pap. 5.95 (0-8234-0670-9) Holiday.
—Up Goes the Skyscraper! Gibbons, Gail. LC 85-16245. 32p. (gr. k-3). 1986. RSBE 13.95 (0-02-736780-0, Four Winds) Macmillan Child Grp.
—Up Goes the Skyscraper! Gibbons, Gail. LC 90-31777. 32p. (gr. k-3). 1990. pap. 4.95 (0-689-71411-4, Aladdin) Macmillan Child Grp.
—Valentine's Day. Gibbons, Gail. LC 85-916. 32p. (ps-3). 1986. reinforced bdg. 14.95 (0-8234-0572-9); pap. 5.95 (0-8234-0764-0) Holiday.
—Weather Forecasting. Gibbons, Gail. LC 86-7602. 32p. (gr. k-3). 1987. RSBE 13.95 (0-02-737250-2, Four Winds) Macmillan Child Grp.
—Weather Forecasting. Gibbons, Gail. LC 92-22264. 32p. (ps-3). 1993. pap. 3.95 (0-689-71683-4, Aladdin) Macmillan Child Grp.
—Weather Words & What They Mean. Gibbons, Gail. LC 89-39515. 32p. (ps-3). 14.95 (0-8234-0805-1); pap. 5.95 (0-8234-0952-X) Holiday.
—Whales. Gibbons, Gail. LC 91-4507. 32p. (ps-3). 1991. reinforced 14.95 (0-8234-0900-7) Holiday.
—Whales. Gibbons, Gail. 32p. (ps-3). 1993. pap. 5.95 (0-8234-1030-7) Holiday.
—Zoo. Gibbons, Gail. LC 87-582. 32p. (ps-3). 1987. 15.00 (0-690-04631-6, Crowell Jr Bks); PLB 14.89 (0-690-04633-2) HarpC Child Bks.
—Zoo. Gibbons, Gail. LC 87-582. 32p. (ps-3). 1991. pap. 4.95 (0-06-446096-7, Trophy) HarpC Child Bks.
Gibbons, Lee. At Your Door: A Modern-Day Campaign. Isynwill, L. N. & Keith, Herbert. Willis, Lynn & Herber, Keith, eds. 162p. (Orig.). (gr. 12 up). 1990. pap. 17.95 (0-933635-64-8, 2326) Chaosium.
Gibbons, Lee & Aulisio, Janet. Mansions of Madness: Mythos Mysteries in the Abodes of Man. Herber, Keith & Morrison, Mark. Willis, Lynn, ed. 130p. (Orig.). (gr. 12 up). 1990. pap. 17.95 (0-933635-63-X, 2327) Chaosium.
Gibbons, Lee, et al. The Cthulhu Casebook: Adventures & Atmosphere for Call of Cthulhu. Hargrave, et al. Petersen, Sandy, ed. Peterson, Sandy & Monroe, John B., eds. 130p. (Orig.). (gr. 12 up). 1990. pap. 18.95 (0-933635-67-2, 3305) Chaosium.
Gibbons, Tony. Looking at... Brachiosaurus: A Dinosaur from the Jurassic Period. Amery, Heather, et al. 24p. (gr. 2 up). 1993. PLB 17.27 (0-8368-1044-9) Gareth Stevens Inc.
—Looking at... Iguanodon: A Dinosaur from the Cretaceous Period. Amery, Heather, et al. 24p. (gr. 2 up). 1993. PLB 17.27 (0-8368-1045-7) Gareth Stevens Inc.
—Looking at... Protoceratops: A Dinosaur from the Cretaceous Period. Amery, Heather, et al. LC 93-5536. 24p. (gr. 2 up). 1993. PLB 17.27 (0-8368-1046-5) Gareth Stevens Inc.
—Looking at... Stegosaurus: A Dinosaur from the Jurassic Period. Amery, Heather, et al. LC 93-5535. 24p. (gr. 2 up). 1993. PLB 17.27 (0-8368-1047-3) Gareth Stevens Inc.
—Looking at... Triceratops: A Dinosaur from the Cretaceous Period. Amery, Heather, et al. 24p. (gr. 2 up). 1993. PLB 17.27 (0-8368-1048-1) Gareth Stevens Inc.
—Looking at... Tyrannosaurus Rex: A Dinosaur from the Cretaceous Period. Amery, Heather, et al. 24p. (gr. 2 up). 1993. PLB 17.27 (0-8368-1049-X) Gareth Stevens Inc.
—The New Dinosaur Collection, 6 titles. Amery, Heather, et al. (gr. 2 up). 1993. Set. PLB 103.60 (0-8368-1043-0) Gareth Stevens Inc.
Gibbons, Tony & Kingstone, Martin. UFOs. Wilson, Ben. LC 87-31480. 48p. (gr. 3-8). 1989. PLB 12.40 (0-531-18219-3, Pub. by Bookwright Pr) Watts.

Gibbons, Tony, et al. Aircraft Carriers. Preston, Anthony. LC 84-9669. 48p. (gr. 5 up). 1985. PLB 13.50 (0-8225-1377-3, First Ave Edns); pap. 4.95 (0-8225-9504-4, First Ave Edns) Lerner Pubns.
—Artillery. Gander, Terry. 48p. (gr. 5 up). 1987. PLB 14.95 (0-8225-1380-3, First Ave Edns); pap. 4.95 (0-8225-9541-9, First Ave Edns) Lerner Pubns.
—Bombers. Lowe, Malcolm V. 48p. (gr. 5 up). 1987. PLB 13.50 (0-8225-1381-1, First Ave Edns); pap. 4.95 (0-8225-9541-9, First Ave Edns) Lerner Pubns.
—Military Helicopters. Ladd, James D. 48p. (gr. 5 up). 1987. PLB 14.95 (0-8225-1382-X) Lerner Pubns.
—Nuclear Warfare. Martin, Laurence W. 48p. (gr. 5 up). 1989. 14.95 (0-8225-1384-6) Lerner Pubns.
—Submarines. Gibbons, Tony. 48p. (gr. 5 up). 1987. PLB 14.95 (0-8225-1383-8, First Ave Edns); pap. 4.95 (0-8225-9542-7, First Ave Edns) Lerner Pubns.
Gibson, Barbara. Desert Animals. Wolfstein, Luise. 24p. 1993. 7.95 (0-590-46006-4) Scholastic Inc.
—Forest Animals. Woelflein, Luise. 24p. 1993. 7.95 (0-590-46005-6) Scholastic Inc.
Gibson, James. Hey, God! Hurry! Gibson, Roxie C. Harvey, Paul, intro. by. LC 82-60193. 52p. (gr. 3-5). 1982. 4.95 (0-938232-08-8, 32534) Winston-Derek.
—Hey, God! Listen! Gibson, Roxie C. Harvey, Paul, intro. by. LC 81-71025. 68p. (gr. 3-5). 1982. 4.95 (0-938232-06-1, 32466) Winston-Derek.
—Hey, God! What Is America? Gibson, Roxie C. Harvey, Paul, intro. by. LC 81-71025. 52p. (gr. 3-5). 1982. 4.95 (0-938232-05-3, 32795) Winston-Derek.
—Hey, God! What Is Christmas. Gibson, Roxie C. LC 82-60192. 64p. (gr. 3-5). 1982. 4.95 (0-938232-09-6, 32752) Winston-Derek.
—Hey, God! Where Are You? Gibson, Roxie C. Harvey, Paul, intro. by. LC 82-60194. 64p. (gr. 3-5). 1982. 4.95 (0-938232-07-X, 32485) Winston-Derek.
Gibson, Judy. The Tree That Would Not Grow But Did. Duncan, Shirley E. Reid, Nancy G., ed. 1991. 12.95 (1-878647-02-4) Duncan & Duncan. Postponed.
Giddings, Noelle. Christmas with Grandma. McClanahan, Frank. 24p. (Orig.). (gr. k-1). 1990. pap. 0.99 (1-878624-46-6) McClanahan Bk.
Gider, Iskender. The Return of Rinaldo the Sly Fox. Scheffler, Ursel. James, J. Alison, tr. from GER. 32p. (gr. k-3). 1993. 12.95 (1-55858-227-4); lib. bdg. 12.88 (1-55858-228-2) North-South Bks NYC.
—Rinaldo, the Sly Fox. Scheffler, Ursel. James, J. Alison, tr. from GER. LC 92-2376. 32p. (gr. 2-3). 1992. 13.95 (1-55858-181-2); PLB 13.88 (1-55858-182-0) North-South Bks NYC.
Giesen, Rosemary, jt. illus. see Viner, Carole.
Giffard, Hannah. Fast Car. Giffard, Hannah. LC 92-62422. 12p. (ps). 1993. bds. 3.95 (0-688-12444-5, Tambourine Bks) Morrow.
—Hens Say Cluck. Giffard, Hannah. LC 92-62425. 12p. (ps). 1993. bds. 3.95 (0-688-12442-9, Tambourine Bks) Morrow.
—Red Bus. Giffard, Hannah. LC 92-62424. 12p. (ps). 1993. bds. 3.95 (0-688-12443-7, Tambourine Bks) Morrow.
—Red Fox. Giffard, Hannah. LC 90-2807. 36p. (ps-3). 1991. 12.95 (0-8037-0869-6) Dial Bks Young.
—Red Fox on the Move. Giffard, Hannah. LC 90-25646. 36p. (ps-3). 1992. 14.00 (0-8037-1057-7) Dial Bks Young.
—Striped Zebra. Giffard, Hannah. LC 92-62423. 12p. (ps). 1993. bds. 3.95 (0-688-12441-0, Tambourine Bks) Morrow.
Gifford, Kerri. Dwight & the Trilobite. Erickson, Gina C. & Foster, Kelli C. 24p. (ps-3). 1994. pap. 3.50 (0-8120-1839-7) Barron.
—Jeepers, Creepers. Erickson, Gina C. & Foster, Kelli C. 24p. (ps-3). 1994. pap. 3.50 (0-8120-1841-9) Barron.
—Tall & Small. Erickson, Gina C. & Goster, Kelli C. 24p. (ps-3). 1994. pap. 3.50 (0-8120-1840-0) Barron.
—A Valentine That Shines. Erickson, Gina C. & Foster, Kelli C. 24p. (ps-3). 1994. pap. 3.50 (0-8120-1838-9) Barron.
—What Rose Doesn't Know. Erickson, Gina C. & Foster, Kelli C. LC 93-36071. 24p. (ps-3). 1994. pap. 3.50 (0-8120-1672-6) Barron.
Gifford-Russell, Kerri. The Best Pets Yet. Erickson, Gina C. & Foster, Kelli C. 24p. (ps-2). 1992. pap. 3.50 (0-8120-4857-1) Barron.
—Bub & Chub. Erickson, Gina C. & Foster, Kelli C. 24p. (ps-2). 1992. 3.50 (0-8120-4859-8) Barron.
—Frog Knows Best. Erickson, Gina C. & Foster, Kelli C. 24p. (ps-2). 1992. 3.50 (0-8120-4855-5) Barron.
—The Tan Can. Erickson, Gina C. & Foster, Kelli C. 24p. 1992. pap. 3.50 (0-8120-4856-3) Barron.
Gilbert, Elliot. The Best-Loved Doll. Caudill, Rebecca. LC 92-898. 64p. (ps-2). 1992. 12.95 (0-8050-2103-5, Bks Young Read) H Holt & Co.
Gilbert, John. Jeffrey's Latest Thirteen: More Alabama Ghosts. Windham, Kathryn T. LC 82-50029. 152p. 1987. pap. 9.50t (0-8173-0380-4) U of Ala Pr.
Gilbert, Yvonne. Children's Bible Stories: From Genesis to Revelation. Chaikin, Miriam, retold by. LC 90-42588. 96p. (gr. 1-5). 1993. 17.99 (0-8037-0956-0); PLB 17.89 (0-8037-0990-0) Dial Bks Young.
Gilchrest, Guy. My Mom's Okay. Gilchrest, Guy. LC 91-10722. 24p. (ps-3). 1991. 5.95 (1-56288-088-8) Checkerboard.
Gilchrest, Mary. One-Two-Three Look at Me. Meltzer, Lisa. 28p. (ps). 1990. 2.95 (0-02-689486-6) Checkerboard.
Gilchrist, Cathy. I Never Win! Delton, Judy. LC 80-27618. 32p. (gr. k-4). 1981. PLB 14.95 (0-87614-139-4) Carolrhoda Bks.

—St. Patrick's Day. Kessel, Joyce K. LC 82-1254. 48p. (gr. k-4). 1982. lib. bdg. 14.95 (0-87614-193-9); pap. 3.95 (0-87614-482-2) Carolrhoda Bks.
Gilchrist, Guy. Tiny Dinos Fun at the Beach: A Book of Actions. Gilchrist, Guy. LC 87-40337. 16p. (ps-1). 1988. 4.95 (1-55782-013-9, Pub. by Warner Juvenile Bks) Little.
Gilchrist, Jan S. Aaron & Gayla's Alphabet Book. Greenfield, Eloise. 20p. 1992. 9.95 (0-86316-208-8) Writers & Readers.
—Aaron & Gayla's Counting Book. Greenfield, Eloise. 20p. 1992. 9.95 (0-86316-209-6) Writers & Readers.
—Baby. Greenfield, Eloise. Media. 14p. (ps). 1994. 4.95 (0-694-00577-0, Festival) HarpC Child Bks.
—Big Friend, Little Friend. Greenfield, Eloise. 12p. (ps-1). 1991. bds. 4.95 (0-86316-204-5) Writers & Readers.
—Children of Long Ago: Poems. Little, Lessie J. 32p. (gr. 2-5). 1988. 14.95 (0-399-21473-9, Philomel Bks) Putnam Pub Group.
—Everett Anderson's Christmas Coming. Clifton, Lucille. LC 91-2041. 32p. (ps-4). 1991. 14.95 (0-8050-1549-3, Bks Young Read) H Holt & Co.
—Everett Anderson's Christmas Coming. Clifton, Lucille. LC 91-2041. 32p. (ps-4). 1993. pap. 4.95 (0-8050-2949-4, Bks Young Read) H Holt & Co.
—First Pink Light. Greenfield, Eloise. 32p. (ps-4). 1991. 13.95 (0-86316-207-X) Writers & Readers.
—I Make Music. Greenfield, Eloise. 12p. (ps-1). 1991. bds. 4.95 (0-86316-205-3) Writers & Readers.
—Indigo & Moonlight Gold. Gilchrist, Jan S. 32p. 1992. 13.95 (0-86316-210-X) Writers & Readers.
—My Daddy & I. Greenfield, Eloise. 12p. 1991. bds. 4.95 (0-86316-203-7) Writers & Readers.
—My Doll, Keshia. Greenfield, Eloise. 12p. (ps-1). 1991. bds. 5.95 (0-86316-203-7) Writers & Readers.
—Nathaniel Talking. Greenfield, Eloise. 32p. (gr. k-5). 1988. 12.95 (0-86316-200-2) Writers & Readers.
—Shani on the Hill. Blakely, Nora B. (gr. 1). 1988. pap. 3.95 (0-88378-123-9) Third World.
—William & the Good Old Days. Greenfield, Eloise. LC 91-47030. 32p. (gr. k-3). 1993. 15.00 (0-06-021093-1); PLB 14.89 (0-06-021094-X) HarpC Child Bks.
Gildemeister, Jerry. Around the Cat's Back. Gildemeister, Jerry. 128p. (gr. 4-12). 1989. 32.50 (0-936376-06-6) Bear Wallow Pub.
Gildemeister, Jerry & Gray, Don. A Letter Home. Gildemeister, Jerry. LC 87-1151. 120p. (gr. 4-12). 1987. 24.50 (0-936376-04-X) Bear Wallow Pub.
Gildemeister, Jerry & Larson, Tim. Avian Dreamers. Gildemeister, Jerry. LC 90-85397. 9p. (gr. 9-12). 1991. 45.00 (0-936376-07-4) Bear Wallow Pub.
Giles, William B., jt. illus. see Boratynski, Katrina.
Gilfoy, Bruce. Whisper Whisper Jesse, Whisper Whisper Josh: A Story about AIDS. Pollack, Eileen. Templeman, Kristine, ed. LC 92-72471. 32p. (ps up). 1992. PLB 16.95 (0-9624828-4-6); pap. 5.95 (0-9624828-3-8) Advantage-Aurora.
Gill, Bob. What Color Is Your World. Gill, Bob. (gr. k-3). 1963. 10.95 (0-8392-3042-5) Astor-Honor.
Gill, Madelaine. Where Is the Bear at School? Nims, Bonnie L. Tucker, Kathy, ed. LC 89-37903. 24p. (ps-1). 1989. 11.95 (0-8075-8935-7) A Whitman.
—Where Is the Bear in the City? Nims, Bonnie L. Mathews, Judith, ed. LC 92-3390. 24p. (ps-1). 1992. 11.95g (0-8075-8937-3) A Whitman.
Gill, Margery. Dawn of Fear. Cooper, Susan. LC 71-115755. 157p. (gr. 5 up). 1988. 14.95 (0-15-266201-4, HB Juv Bks) HarBrace.
—Dawn of Fear. Cooper, Susan. LC 89-6820. 224p. (gr. 5 up). 1989. pap. 3.95 (0-689-71327-4, Aladdin) Macmillan Child Grp.
—Over Sea, Under Stone. Cooper, Susan. LC 66-11199. (gr. 5 up). 1966. 14.95 (0-15-259034-X, HB Juv Bks) HarBrace.
—A Search for Two Bad Mice. Clymer, Eleanor. LC 91-2453. 80p. (gr. 1-4). 1991. pap. 3.50 (0-689-71537-4, Aladdin) Macmillan Child Grp.
Gillah, Mick. Cars. Graham, Ian. LC 93-19707. 32p. (gr. 4-6). 1993. PLB 19.97 (0-8114-6162-9) Raintree Steck-V.
Gillard, Dianne & Kirkpatrick, Cindy F. The Duck & the Fox: A Metaphysical Fairy Tale. Ziegler, J. F. Butler, Sandra L., ed. LC 88-32071. 75p. (gr-9). 1988. pap. 9.00 (0-9621235-0-1) Hallelujah Pr.
Gilleece, David. Little House on Rocky Ridge. MacBride, Roger L. LC 92-39132. 368p. (gr. 3-7). 1993. 14.00 (0-06-020842-2); PLB 13.89 (0-06-020843-0) HarpC Child Bks.
—Little House on Rocky Ridge. MacBride, Roger L. LC 92-39132. 368p. (gr. 3-7). 1993. pap. 3.95 (0-06-440478-1, Trophy) HarpC Child Bks.
Gillen, Patricia B. My First Book of Sign. Baker, Pamela J. LC 86-14937. iv, 76p. (ps-3). 1986. 14.95 (0-930323-20-3, Kendall Green Pubns) Gallaudet Univ Pr.
Gilles, Pelletier. A Happy New Year's Day. Carrier, Roch. LC 91-65367. 24p. (gr. 3 up). 1991. 14.95 (0-88776-267-0) Tundra Bks.
Gillespie, Robert. Reading Experiences in Science: Apes; Bats; Bees; Beavers; Dinosaurs; Frogs; Spiders; Whales, 8 bks. Cochrane, Orin, ed. 128p. (Orig.). (gr. 2-4). 1980. Set. pap. 28.95 (1-895411-12-2) Peguis Pubs Ltd.
Gillette, Henry S. Mark Twain: Young Writer. Mason, Miriam E. LC 90-23768. 192p. (gr. 3-7). 1991. pap. 3.95 (0-689-71480-7, Aladdin) Macmillan Child Grp.

Gillham, Andrew. Discovering Earthquakes. Field, Nancy & Schepige, Adele. 40p. (Orig.). (gr. 3-6). 1994. pap. 4.95 Dog Eared Pubns.

Gilliam, Terry. The Adventures of Baron Munchausen: The Novel. Gilliam, Terry & McKeown, Charles. 192p. (Orig.). 1989. pap. 12.95 (1-55783-039-8) Applause Theatre Bk Pubs.

Gilliland, Hap, jt. illus. see Sargent, Heather.

Gillis, Paul. Goldie. Gillis, Everett A. 64p. (Orig.). (gr. 3-7). 1982. pap. 8.00 (0-938328-02-6) Pisces Pr TX.

Gillman, Alec. Confusable Creatures: And Other Look-Alikes in Nature. Graham-Barber, Lynda. LC 92-35398. 48p. (gr. k-3). 1994. RSBE 15.95 (0-02-736931-5, Four Winds) Macmillan Child Grp.
—Fast Eddie. Coleman, Janet W. LC 92-31243. 144p. (gr. 3-5). 1993. SBE 13.95 (0-02-722815-0, Four Winds) Macmillan Child Grp.

Gillman, Alec, photos by. Radio Boy. Denslow, Sharon P. LC 93-36281. 1994. write for info. (0-02-728684-3, Four Winds) Macmillan Child Grp.

Gilman, Phoebe. Jillian Jiggs. Gilman, Phoebe. 40p. (Orig.). (gr. k-3). 1988. pap. 2.50 (0-590-41340-6) Scholastic Inc.
—Once upon a Golden Apple. Little, Jean & De Vries, Maggie. 32p. (ps-3). 1991. 12.95 (0-670-82963-3) Viking Child Bks.
—Once upon a Golden Apple. Little, Jean & De Vries, Maggie. 32p. (ps-3). 1994. pap. 4.99 (0-14-054164-0) Puffin Bks.

Gilmore, Jackie, photos by. Big Birds. Casey, Denise. LC 92-17275. 48p. (gr. 1-5). 1993. 14.99 (0-525-65121-7, Cobblehill Bks) Dutton Child Bks.
—Weather Everywhere. Casey, Denise. LC 92-23239. 40p. (gr. k-4). 1993. RSBE 13.95 (0-02-717777-7, Bradbury Pr) Macmillan Child Grp.

Gilsvik, David. The Complete Book of Trapping. Gilsvik, Bob. 172p. (gr. 7). Repr. of 1976 ed. 10.95 (0-936622-29-6) A R Harding Pub.

Gimeno, J. M. Little Red Hen - La Gallina Paulina. Alonso, Fernando. (SPA & ENG.). 26p. (gr. k-2). 1989. Spanish ed. 5.25 (0-88272-467-3); English ed. 5.25 (0-88272-468-1) Santillana.
The traditional story lovingly retold. A little red hen finds a grain of wheat, but no one to share the work of planting & caring for it. Brightly colored illustrations by J.M. Gimeno brings the story to life. English & Spanish versions are available of this charming story. To order: Santillana, 901 West Walnut, Compton, CA 90220. Telephone 1-310-763-0455.
Publisher Provided Annotation.

Gimlin, Rick & Kamiya, Artie. The Perceptual-Motor Activities Book. Stillwell, Jim. 96p. (Orig.). (gr. k-6). 1990. pap. 10.00 (0-945872-05-4) Great Activities Pub Co.

Ginsberg, Daniel. Whales & Dolphins: An Educational Coloring Book. Ginsberg, Daniel. 32p. (Orig.). (gr. 1-4). 1989. pap. 2.95 (0-9623284-0-5) R Rinehart.

Ginsberg, Max. Mississippi Bridge. Taylor, Mildred D. (gr. 4-7). 1992. pap. 3.50 (0-553-15992-5, Skylark) Bantam.

Ginsburg, Max. The Friendship. Taylor, Mildred D. LC 86-29309. 56p. (gr. 2-6). 1987. 13.95 (0-8037-0417-8); PLB 13.89 (0-8037-0418-6) Dial Bks Young.

Ginsburg, Mirra. Mushroom in the Rain. Ginsburg, Mirra. LC 90-31814. 32p. (ps-1). 1990. pap. 3.95 (0-689-71441-6, Aladdin) Macmillan Child Grp.

Giotto. The Glorious Impossible. L'Engle, Madeleine. 64p. (gr. 3 up). 1990. pap. 19.95 jacketed (0-671-68690-9, Little Simon) S&S Trade.

Giovanopoulos, Paul. How Many Miles to Babylon? Fox, Paula. LC 79-25802. 128p. (gr. 5-7). 1982. SBE 13.95 (0-02-735590-X, Bradbury Pr) Macmillan Child Grp.

Giovanopoulous, Paul. Learning to Say Good-bye: When a Parent Dies. LeShan, Eda. LC 76-15155. 96p. (gr. 3 up). 1976. SBE 13.95 (0-02-756360-X, Macmillan Child Bk) Macmillan Child Grp.

Giraud, Jean M. The Blue Coats. Charlier, J. M. Starwatcher Graphics Staff, tr. from FRE. 56p. (gr. 12 up). 1990. pap. 7.95 (0-87416-093-6, Comcat Comics) Catalan Communs.
—A Yankee Named Blueberry. Charlier, J. M. Starwatcher Graphics Staff, tr. from FRE. 56p. (Orig.). (gr. 12 up). 1990. pap. 7.95 (0-87416-087-1, Comcat Comics) Catalan Communs.

Girdler, Netta & Belcher, Cynthia. Discover Ancient Egypt: Activity Book. Harrast, Tracy & Craft, Louise. 24p. (gr. 2-7). 1990. wkbk. 2.95 (0-911239-28-6) Carnegie Mus.

Girouard, Patrick. Barnaby Mouse, Detective, & the Mystery of the Big Book. Stortz, Diane. LC 93-14425. 28p. (ps). 1994. 4.99 (0-7847-0004-4, 24-03870) Standard Pub.
—The Big Big Big Boat, & Other Bible Stories about Obedience. Tanvald, Christine H. LC 93-9234. 1993. write for info. (0-7814-0926-8, Chariot Bks) Cook.

—Halloween Holiday Grab Bag. Stamper, Judith. LC 92-13224. 48p. (gr. 2-5). 1992. PLB 11.89 (0-8167-2904-2); pap. text ed. 3.95 (0-8167-2905-0) Troll Assocs.

Girst, Jack A. Renfro Would Rather Rest. Girst, Jack A. 32p. (gr. k-2). 1989. pap. 1.99 (0-87403-633-X, 3972) Standard Pub.

Githens, Elizabeth. Fun with German. Cooper, Lee. (gr. 3 up). 1972. lib. bdg. 15.95 (0-316-15588-8) Little.

Gitkin, Lisa S., photos by. The Power of Ice. Radlauer, Ruth & Gitkin, Lisa S. LC 85-5714. 48p. (gr. 3 up). 1985. pap. 4.95 (0-516-47839-7) Childrens.

Gittings, Elisa. Time & Time Again. Jenkins, Lee. Laycock, Mary, ed. 72p. (Orig.). (gr. 1-6). 1985. pap. text ed. 7.95 (0-918932-85-8) Activity Resources.

Giuliani, Alfred. The Little Engine That Could: A Story to Color. 48p. (ps-2). 1992. pap. 0.42 (0-448-40377-3, Platt & Munk Pubs) Putnam Pub Group.

Gladden, Scott. The Big Deal. Herzig, Alison C. 80p. (gr. 3-7). 1992. 13.50 (0-670-84251-6) Viking Child Bks.

Glanzman, Louis S. Noonday Friends. Stolz, Mary. LC 65-20257. 192p. (gr. 3-7). 1965. PLB 14.89 (0-06-025946-9) HarpC Child Bks.
—Pippi Goes on Board. Lindgren, Astrid. (gr. 4-6). 1957. pap. 13.00 (0-670-55677-7) Viking Child Bks.
—Pippi in the South Seas. Lindgren, Astrid. Bothmer, Gerry, tr. (gr. 4-6). 1959. pap. 13.00 (0-670-55711-0) Viking Child Bks.
—Pippi in the South Seas. Lindgren, Astrid. Bothmer, Gerry, tr. 128p. (gr. 3-7). 1977. pap. 3.99 (0-14-030958-6, Puffin) Puffin Bks.
—Pippi Longstocking. Lindgren, Astrid. Lamborn, Florence, tr. (gr. 4-6). 1950. pap. 12.95 (0-670-55745-5) Viking Child Bks.
—Pippi Longstocking. Lindgren, Astrid. Lamborn, Florence, tr. 158p. (gr. 4-6). 1977. pap. 3.99 (0-14-030957-8, Puffin) Puffin Bks.
—Reader's Digest Best Loved Books for Young Readers: Treasure Island. Stevenson, Robert Louis. Ogburn, Jackie, ed. 144p. (gr. 4-12). 1989. 3.99 (0-945260-23-7) Choice Pub NY.

Glaser, Byron, jt. illus. see Neumeier, Marty.

Glaser, Mary J. Cameras at the Zoo. Arrabito, James. 16p. (Orig.). (gr. 3-10). 1991. pap. 4.95 (0-9622596-0-8) Arraster Pub.

Glaser, Michael. Does Anyone Know Where a Hermit Crab Goes? Glaser, Michael. LC 82-84341. 32p. (Orig.). (ps-3). 1983. pap. 3.95 (0-911635-00-9) Knickerbocker.
—The Nature of the Seashore. Glaser, Michael. 16p. (Orig.). (gr. 1-6). 1986. pap. 4.95 (0-911635-02-5) Knickerbocker.

Glaseur, Willi. Belle et la Bete. De Leprince de Beaumont. (FRE.). 87p. (gr. 1-5). 1989. pap. 10.95 (2-07-031188-0) Schoenhof.
—Chat Qui Parlait Malgre Lui. Roy, Claude. (FRE.). 87p. (gr. 5-10). 1982. pap. 9.95 (2-07-033194-6) Schoenhof.
—Homme qui Plantait des Arbres. Giono, Jean. (FRE.). 71p. (Orig.). 1990. pap. 12.95 (2-07-031180-5) Schoenhof.

Glass, Andrew. The Adventures of Sherlock Holmes, Bk. 1. Doyle, Arthur Conan. Sadler, Catherine E., adapted by. 140p. (Orig.). (gr. 4-7). 1981. pap. 3.50 (0-380-78089-5, Camelot) Avon.
—The Adventures of Sherlock Holmes, Bk. 2. Doyle, Arthur Conan. Sadler, Catherine E., adapted by. 156p. (Orig.). (gr. 4-7). 1981. pap. 2.95 (0-380-78097-6, Camelot) Avon.
—The Adventures of Sherlock Holmes, Bk. 3. Doyle, Arthur Conan. Sadler, Catherine E., frwd by. 112p. (Orig.). (gr. 4-7). 1981. pap. 2.95 (0-380-78105-0, Camelot) Avon.
—The Adventures of Sherlock Holmes, Bk. 4. Doyle, Arthur Conan. Sadler, Catherine E., adapted by. 112p. (Orig.). (gr. 4-7). 1988. pap. 3.50 (0-380-78113-1, Camelot) Avon.
—The Booford Summer. Smith, Susan M. LC 93-27925. 1994. write for info. (0-395-66590-6, Clarion Bks) HM.
—Devil's Donkey. Brittain, Bill. LC 80-7907. 128p. (gr. 3-7). 1981. PLB 13.89 (0-06-020683-7) HarpC Child Bks.
—Devil's Donkey. Brittain, Bill. LC 80-7907. 128p. (gr. 3-7). 1982. pap. 3.95 (0-06-440129-4, Trophy) HarpC Child Bks.
—Dr. Dredd's Wagon of Wonders. Brittain, Bill. LC 86-45775. 208p. (gr. 3-7). 1987. PLB 13.89 (0-06-020714-0) HarpC Child Bks.
—Dr. Dredd's Wagon of Wonders. Brittain, Bill. LC 86-45775. 192p. (gr. 3-7). 1989. pap. 3.50 (0-06-440289-4, Trophy) HarpC Child Bks.
—Future Forward. Pfeffer, Susan B. (gr. 5 up). 1989. 13.95 (0-385-29740-8) Delacorte.
—The Gift. Nixon, Joan L. LC 82-17994. 96p. (gr. 4-7). 1983. SBE 13.95 (0-02-768160-2, Macmillan Child Bk) Macmillan Child Grp.
—The Gift. Nixon, Joan L. LC 87-22764. 96p. (gr. 3-7). 1988. pap. 3.95 (0-689-71217-0, Aladdin) Macmillan Child Grp.
—Graven Images. Fleischman, Paul. LC 81-48649. 96p. (gr. 6 up). 1987. pap. 3.50 (0-06-440186-3, Trophy) HarpC Child Bks.
—Gregory, Maw, & the Mean One. Gifaldi, David. 144p. (gr. 7 up). 1992. 13.45 (0-395-60821-X, Clarion Bks) HM.
—Lavender. Hesse, Karen. 64p. (gr. 2-4). 1993. PLB 14.95 (0-8050-2528-6, Bks Young Read) H Holt & Co.

—Professor Popkin's Prodigious Polish. Brittain, Bill. LC 89-78221. 160p. (gr. 3-7). 1991. pap. 3.95 (0-06-440386-6, Trophy) HarpC Child Bks.
—Professor Popkin's Prodigious Polish: A Tale of Coven Tree. Brittain, Bill. LC 89-78221. 160p. (gr. 3-7). 1991. PLB 13.89 (0-06-020727-2) HarpC Child Bks.
—She'll Be Comin' Round the Mountain. Birdseye, Tom & Birdseye, Debbie. LC 92-37641. 1994. write for info. (0-8234-1032-3) Holiday.
—Spooky & the Bad Luck Raven. Carlson, Natalie S. LC 87-15471. (ps-1). 1988. 12.95 (0-688-07650-5); lib. bdg. 12.88 (0-688-07651-3) Lothrop.
—Spooky & the Ghost Cat. Carlson, Natalie S. LC 84-17146. 32p. (ps-1). 1985. 13.00 (0-688-04316-X); lib. bdg. 12.88 (0-688-04317-8) Lothrop.
—Spooky & the Witch's Goat. Carlson, Natalie S. Stevenson, Dinah, ed. LC 88-21628. 32p. (gr. k-4). 1989. 12.95 (0-688-08540-7); PLB 12.88 (0-685-22781-2) Lothrop.
—Spooky & the Wizard's Bats. Carlson, Natalie S. LC 85-18020. 32p. (ps-1). 1986. 12.95 (0-688-06280-6); PLB 12.88 (0-688-06281-4) Lothrop.
—Spooky Night. Carlson, Natalie S. LC 82-54. 32p. (ps-3). 1982. 13.95 (0-688-00934-4); PLB 13.88 (0-688-00935-2) Lothrop.
—The Wish Giver: Three Tales of Coven Tree. Brittain, Bill. LC 82-48264. 192p. (gr. 3-7). 1983. 14.00i (0-06-020686-1); PLB 13.89 (0-06-020687-X) HarpC Child Bks.
—The Wish Giver: Three Tales of Coven Tree. Brittain, Bill. LC 82-48264. 192p. (gr. 3-7). 1986. pap. 3.95 (0-06-440168-5, Trophy) HarpC Child Bks.

Glass, Eric. President Clinton Visits Hyde Park: Story & Coloring Book. Sinnott, Trip. 52p. (Orig.). (gr. k-5). 1993. pap. 4.95 (1-883551-00-5) Attic Studio.

Glass, Roger R. The M & M's Counting Book. Barbieri-McGrath, Barbara. 1994. write for info. (0-88106-855-1); pap. write for info. (0-88106-854-3); PLB write for info. (0-88106-853-5) Charlesbridge Pub.

Glasser, Judy. The Case of the Sabotaged School Play: A Sam & Dave Mystery. Singer, Marilyn. LC 83-48437. 64p. (gr. 3-7). 1987. pap. 3.95 (0-06-440207-X, Trophy) HarpC Child Bks.
—The Guy Who Was Five Minutes Late. Grossman, Bill. LC 89-36336. 32p. (ps-3). 1990. PLB 13.89 (0-06-022269-7) HarpC Child Bks.
—The Problem with Pulcifier. Heide, Florence P. LC 81-48606. 64p. (gr. 2 up). 1992. pap. 3.95 (0-688-11570-5, Mulberry) Morrow.
—Too Much Magic. Sterman, Betsy & Sterman, Samuel. LC 85-45861. 160p. (gr. 3-7). 1994. pap. 3.95 (0-06-440404-8, Trophy) HarpC Child Bks.

Glassman, Richard, photos by. Everything You Need to Know about Teen Pregnancy. rev. ed. Hughes, Tracy. Rosen, Roger, ed. 64p. (gr. 7 up). 1992. PLB 13.95 (0-8239-1460-7) Rosen Group.

Glaubke, Robert. The Story of the Constitution. Prolman, Marilyn. LC 69-14680. 32p. (gr. 3-6). 1969. PLB 13.27 (0-516-04605-5); pap. 3.95 (0-516-44605-3) Childrens.

Gleeson, Joseph, jt. illus. see Kipling, Rudyard.

Gleeson, Joseph M. & Kipling, Rudyard. Just So Stories. Kipling, Rudyard. 244p. (gr. 2-9). 1988. 12.99 (0-517-63177-6) Outlet Bk Co.

Gleeson, Kate. Animal ABC's. Lewis-Patrick, Denise. (ps). 1990. bds. write for info. (0-307-06127-2) Western Pub.
—Baby's Book of ABC. Silverman, Maida. 12p. (ps). 1993. pap. 1.95 (0-307-06037-3, 6037, Golden Pr) Western Pub.
—How Many Animals. Lewis-Patrick, Denise. (ps). 1990. write for info. (0-307-06129-9) Western Pub.
—Taking Care of the Earth. Goodman, Billy. 24p. (ps-k). 1992. write for info. (0-307-11532-1, 11532) Western Pub.
—Too Many Jellybeans! Fulton, Mary J. 24p. (ps-k). 1993. pap. 1.45 (0-307-11539-9, 11539, Golden Pr) Western Pub.

Gleich, Shannon & Long, Lori. Puzzling about South Dakota. Burdick, Gerry & Schuett, Julie. 61p. (Orig.). (gr. 8 up). 1992. pap. 4.95 (0-9632844-0-1, 050111557) Dakota Desktop.

Gleissner, Alex & Nordgren, Steve. Means Something Else--"The Doubles" Figures of Speech Writing Book, No. 2. DeWitt, Jim. 64p. (Orig.). (gr. 6-12). 1987. wkbk. 6.00 (0-915199-51-3) Pen-Dec.

Glessner, Marc. Why Do I Daydream? Wright, Betty R. Silverman, Manuel S., intro. by. LC 80-25561. 32p. (gr. k-6). 1981. PLB 13.45 (0-8172-1371-6) Raintree Pubs Ltd.

Glick, Beth. God Must Like Cookies, Too. Snyder, Carol. LC 92-26886. 32p. (ps-3). 1993. 16.95 (0-8276-0423-8) JPS Phila.
—The Great Monarch Butterfly Chase. Prior, R. W. LC 92-7423. 32p. (ps-3). 1993. RSBE 14.95 (0-02-775145-7, Bradbury Pr) Macmillan Child Grp.

Glick, Nathan. World of the Southern Indians. Brown, Virginia P. & Owens, Laurella. LC 83-6376. 176p. (gr. 6-9). 1983. 15.95 (0-912221-00-3) Beechwood.

Glienke, Amelie. My Friend the Vampire. Sommer-Bodenburg, Angela. LC 83-23930. 160p. (gr. 3-5). 1984. PLB 9.89 (0-8037-0046-6) Dial Bks Young.
—The Vampire in Love. Sommer-Bodenburg, Angela. 128p. (gr. 2-6). 1991. 13.00 (0-8037-0905-6); lib. bdg. 12.89 (0-8037-0906-4) Dial Bks Young.

—The Vampire Moves In. Sommer-Bodenburg, Angela. (gr. 2-6). 1990. pap. 2.95 (*0-671-73698-1*, Minstrel Bks) PB.

—The Vampire Takes a Trip. Sommer-Bodenburg, Angela. LC 84-22995. 160p. (gr. 2-6). 1985. PLB 9.89 (*0-8037-0201-9*) Dial Bks Young.

Glines, Shane. Coping with Life the Principle Way: A Plain-English Common-Sense Approach to Solving the Problems of Everyday Living. rev. ed. Borden, Merritt W. 119p. (gr. 7-12). 1993. spiral bdg. 12.95 (*0-929393-11-2*) Diogenes Pub Co.

Gliori, Debi. Dulcie Dando, Soccer Star. Stops, Sue. LC 92-2259. (ps-2). 1992. 14.95 (*0-8050-2413-1*, Bks Young Read) H Holt & Co.

—Lizzie & Her Dolly. Martin, David. LC 92-54404. 24p. (ps). 1993. 6.95 (*1-56402-060-6*) Candlewick Pr.

—Lizzie & Her Friend. Martin, David. LC 92-53009. 24p. (ps). 1993. 5.95 (*1-56402-061-4*) Candlewick Pr.

—Lizzie & Her Kitty. Martin, David. LC 92-54405. (ps). 1993. 5.95 (*1-56402-058-4*) Candlewick Pr.

—Lizzie & Her Puppy. Martin, David. LC 92-53008. 24p. (ps). 1993. 5.95 (*1-56402-059-2*) Candlewick Pr.

—My Little Brother. Gliori, Debi. LC 91-58748. 32p. (ps up). 1992. 13.95 (*1-56402-079-7*) Candlewick Pr.

—New Big House. Gliori, Debi. LC 91-71829. 32p. (ps up). 1992. 13.95 (*1-56402-036-3*) Candlewick Pr.

—New Big Sister. Gliori, Debi. LC 90-49272. 32p. (ps-3). 1991. SBE 12.95 (*0-02-735995-6*, Bradbury Pr) Macmillan Child Grp.

—Oliver's Alphabets. Bruce, Lisa. LC 92-39471. 24p. (ps-1). 1993. SBE 13.95 (*0-02-735996-4*, Bradbury Pr) Macmillan Child Grp.

Glockner-Ferrari, Deborah A., jt. illus. see Ferrari, Mark J.

Glovach, Linda. Little Witch Presents a Monster Joke Book. Keller, Charles. 40p. (gr.-4). 1983. pap. 4.95 (*0-13-537811-7*, Pub. by Treehouse) P-H.

—Little Witch's Black Magic Cookbook. Glovach, Linda. (gr. 1-4). 1975. pap. 3.95 (*0-13-537936-9*, Pub. by Treehouse) P-H.

—The Little Witch's Books of Toys. Glovach, Linda. 48p. (gr. 2-5). 1986. 10.95 (*0-13-537879-6*) P-H.

—The Little Witch's Cat Book. Glovach, Linda. LC 85-6513. 48p. (gr. 1-3). 1985. 9.95 (*0-13-537697-1*) P-H.

—The Little Witch's Christmas Book. Glovach, Linda. 48p. (gr. 1-4). 1982. pap. 4.95 (*0-13-538090-1*, Pub. by Treehouse) P-H.

—Little Witch's Halloween Book. Glovach, Linda. LC 75-11713. (gr. 1-4). 1975. 7.95 (*0-13-537985-7*) P-H.

Glover, Zebrena M. Understanding Colors, Shapes, & Direction. Singletary, Helen P. & Glover, Zebrena M. 31p. (Orig.). (ps-6). 1991. pap. text ed. 20.00 (*1-880850-02-8*) Comp Trng Clinic.

Glueck. Regie's Love: A Daughter of Former Slaves Recalls. 2nd, rev. ed. Heard, Regie & Langenhahn, Bonnie. Bonjean, Marilyn, frwd. by. LC 87-61795. 168p. (gr. 8 up). 1989. pap. 9.95 (*0-9618212-1-3*) McCormick & Schilling.

Glueckselig, Leo. Mom, I Broke My Arm. Wolff, Angelika. LC 69-18646. (gr. k-3). 1969. PLB 11.95 (*0-87460-121-5*) Lion Bks.

Glugg, Professor. The Blue Skidoo Crew. Glugg, Professor. LC 92-75278. 32p. (Orig.). (ps up). 1993. pap. 3.95 (*1-881905-03-9*) Glue Bks.

—Flip & the Magic Wando Whip. Glugg, Professor. LC 92-73552. 32p. (Orig.). (ps up). 1993. pap. 3.95 (*1-881905-01-2*) Glue Bks.

—Glugg-A-Lug Bug. Glugg, Professor. LC 92-74768. 32p. (Orig.). (ps up). 1993. pap. 3.95 (*1-881905-02-0*) Glue Bks.

—Who Took Apple Frapple's Cookbook? Glugg, Professor. LC 92-73242. 32p. (Orig.). (ps up). 1992. pap. 3.95 (*1-881905-00-4*) Glue Bks.

Glutterbuck, Mary. Man Who Never Laughed. 1987. 7.95x (*0-86685-567-X*) Intl Bk Ctr.

Gobbato, Imero & Garcia, Manuel. Whisper of Glocken. Kendall, Carol. LC 85-17634. 256p. (Orig.). (gr. 3-7). 1986. pap. 4.95 (*0-15-295699-9*, Voyager Bks) HarBrace.

Gobble, Janice. Beauty for Ashes. Flores, Kathy. Cox, Gail, ed. Malvido, Lalo, photos by. 37p. (Orig.) 1990. pap. 3.98 (*0-9626862-0-4*) K Flores Min.

Goble, Paul. Adopted by the Eagles. LC 93-24247. 1994. write for info. (*0-02-736575-1*, Bradbury Pr) Macmillan Child Grp.

—Beyond the Ridge. Goble, Paul. LC 87-33113. 32p. (ps-3). 1989. RSBE 14.95 (*0-02-736581-6*, Bradbury Pr) Macmillan Child Grp.

—Beyond the Ridge. Goble, Paul. LC 92-39786. 32p. (gr. k-3). 1993. pap. 4.95 (*0-689-71731-8*, Aladdin) Macmillan Child Grp.

—Buffalo Woman. Goble, Paul. LC 86-20573. 32p. (gr. k up). 1987. pap. 4.95 (*0-689-71109-3*, Aladdin) Macmillan Child Grp.

—Crow Chief: A Plains Indian Story. Goble, Paul. LC 90-28457. 32p. (ps-2). 1992. 14.95 (*0-531-05947-2*); lib. bdg. 14.99 (*0-531-08547-3*) Orchard Bks Watts.

—Death of the Iron Horse. Goble, Paul. LC 85-28011. 32p. (gr. k-3). 1987. SBE 14.95 (*0-02-737830-6*, Bradbury Pr) Macmillan Child Grp.

—Death of the Iron Horse. Goble, Paul. LC 92-1723. 32p. (ps-3). 1993. pap. 4.95 (*0-689-71686-9*, Aladdin) Macmillan Child Grp.

—Dream Wolf. Goble, Paul. LC 89-687. 32p. (gr. 3 up). 1990. RSBE 14.95 (*0-02-736585-9*, Bradbury Pr) Macmillan Child Grp.

—The Gift of the Sacred Dog. Goble, Paul. LC 80-15843. 32p. (gr. k-2). 1982. Repr. of 1980 ed. SBE 14.95 (*0-02-736560-3*, Bradbury Pr) Macmillan Child Grp.

—The Girl Who Loved Wild Horses. Goble, Paul. LC 77-20500. 32p. (gr. k-3). 1982. SBE 14.95 (*0-02-736570-0*, Bradbury Pr) Macmillan Child Grp.

—The Girl Who Loved Wild Horses. Goble, Paul. LC 92-29560. 32p. (ps-3). 1993. pap. 4.95 (*0-689-71696-6*, Aladdin) Macmillan Child Grp.

—Her Seven Brothers. Goble, Paul. LC 92-40562. 32p. (gr. k-3). 1993. pap. 4.95 (*0-689-71730-X*, Aladdin) Macmillan Child Grp.

—I Sing for the Animals. Goble, Paul. LC 90-19812. 32p. 1991. SBE 9.95 (*0-02-737725-3*, Bradbury Pr) Macmillan Child Grp.

—Iktomi & the Berries: A Plains Indian Story. Goble, Paul, retold by. LC 88-23353. 32p. (ps-2). 1989. 14.95 (*0-531-05819-0*); PLB 14.99 (*0-531-08419-1*) Orchard Bks Watts.

—Iktomi & the Berries: A Plains Indian Story. Goble, Paul, retold by. LC 88-23353. 32p. (ps-2). 1992. pap. 5.95 (*0-531-07029-8*) Orchard Bks Watts.

—Iktomi & the Boulder: A Plains Indian Story. Goble, Paul & Jackson, Richard, eds. LC 87-35789. 32p. (ps-2). 1988. 14.95 (*0-531-05760-7*); PLB 14.99 (*0-531-08360-8*) Orchard Bks Watts.

—Iktomi & the Boulder: A Plains Indian Story. Goble, Paul, retold by. LC 87-35789. 32p. (ps-2). 1991. pap. 4.95 (*0-531-07023-9*) Orchard Bks Watts.

—Iktomi & the Buffalo Skull: A Plains Indian Story. Goble, Paul, as told by. LC 90-7716. 32p. (ps-2). 1991. 14.95 (*0-531-05911-1*); PLB 14.99 (*0-531-08511-2*) Orchard Bks Watts.

—Iktomi & the Ducks: A Plains Indian Story. Goble, Paul, retold by. LC 89-71025. 32p. (ps-1). 1990. 14.95 (*0-531-05883-2*); PLB 14.99 (*0-531-08483-3*) Orchard Bks Watts.

—Iktomi & the Ducks: A Plains Indians Story. Goble, Paul, retold by. LC 89-71025. 32p. (ps-1). 1994. pap. 5.95 (*0-531-07044-1*) Orchard Bks Watts.

—The Lost Children. Goble, Paul. LC 91-44283. 40p. (ps-12). 1993. SBE 14.95 (*0-02-736555-7*, Bradbury Pr) Macmillan Child Grp.

—The Love Flute. Goble, Paul. LC 91-19716. 32p. (ps up). 1992. SBE 14.95 (*0-02-736261-2*, Bradbury Pr) Macmillan Child Grp.

—Love Flute. Goble, Paul. (gr. k-4). 1993. 14.95 (*0-685-64813-3*); audiocassette 11.00 (*1-882869-80-X*) Read Advent.

—Red Hawk's Account of Custer's Last Battle. Goble, Paul. LC 91-231701. 64p. 1992. pap. 9.95 (*0-8032-7033-X*, Bison Books) U of Nebr Pr.

—Star Boy. Goble, Paul. LC 82-20599. 32p. (gr. k up). 1983. SBE 14.95 (*0-02-722660-3*, Bradbury Pr) Macmillan Child Grp.

—Star Boy. Goble, Paul. LC 91-8694. 32p. (gr. k-3). 1991. pap. 4.95 (*0-689-71499-8*, Aladdin) Macmillan Child Grp.

Gochnour, Luanne. Mirabelle's Country Club for Cats & Other Poems. Sadler, Norma. 48p. (gr. 2-7). 1986. pap. 9.95 (*0-9617206-0-3*) Riverstone Pr.

Godfrey, Bob. The Shutterbug. Hayward, Stan. (ps-5). 1987. pap. 2.25 (*0-671-63776-2*) S&S Trade.

Godfrey, Raymond. A Time to Love...a Time to Die. McAlister, George A. 216p. (Orig.). (gr. 10). 1988. pap. 7.95 (*0-924307-01-3*) Docutex Inc.

Goede, Don. Simply Science: Discovering the Fascinations of Our World. Brown, Dean R. 206p. (gr. 7-12). 1993. pap. text ed. 24.95 (*1-880293-02-1*) Alaken.

Goembel, Ponder. Hear the Wind Blow: American Folk Songs Retold. Sanders, Scott R. LC 85-4160. 224p. (gr. 6 up). 1985. SBE 14.95 (*0-02-778140-2*, Bradbury Pr) Macmillan Child Grp.

Goennel, Heidi. Heidi's Zoo: An Un-Alphabet Book. Goennel, Heidi. LC 92-16367. 32p. (gr. 1 up). 1993. 16.00 (*0-688-12109-8*, Tambourine Bks); PLB 15.93 (*0-688-12110-1*, Tambourine Bks) Morrow.

—It's My Birthday. Goennel, Heidi. LC 91-30231. 32p. (ps-1). 1992. 14.00 (*0-688-11421-0*, Tambourine Bks); PLB 13.93 (*0-688-11422-9*, Tambourine Bks) Morrow.

—Odds & Evens: A Numbers Book. Goennel, Heidi. LC 93-15420. 32p. 1994. 15.00 (*0-688-12918-8*, Tambourine Bks); PLB 14.93 (*0-688-12919-6*, Tambourine Bks) Morrow.

—Sometimes I Like to Be Alone. Goennel, Heidi. LC 88-30780. (gr. k-2). 1989. 14.95 (*0-316-31842-6*) Little.

—While I Am Little. Goennel, Heidi. LC 92-36795. 32p. (ps up). 1993. 14.00 (*0-688-12371-6*, Tambourine Bks); PLB 13.93 (*0-688-12372-4*, Tambourine Bks) Morrow.

Goepfert, Laura P. Re Tell Stories: From Words to Conversation with Meaning. Goepfert, Laura P. 50p. (ps-2). 1986. 16.95 (*0-937857-02-5*, 1441) Speech Bln.

Goff, O. S., jt. illus. see Remington, Frederic.

Goffe, Toni. Bat Boy. Rogers, Paul & Rogers, Emma. 96p. (gr. 5-8). 1990. pap. 6.95 (*0-460-88153-1*, Pub. by J M Dent & Sons) Trafalgar.

—A Cat Called Max: Magnificent Max. Dicks, Terrance. 64p. (gr. 3-6). 1990. pap. 2.95 (*0-8120-4427-4*) Barron.

—A Cat Called Max: Max & the Quiz Kids. Dicks, Terrance. 64p. (gr. 2-5). 1990. pap. 2.95 (*0-8120-4501-7*) Barron.

—A Cat Called Max: Max's Amazing Summer. Dicks, Terrance. 52p. (gr. 3-6). 1992. pap. 3.50 (*0-8120-4819-9*) Barron.

—Clap Your Hands: Finger Rhymes. Hayes, Sarah. LC 87-16958. (ps-1). 1988. 13.00 (*0-688-07692-0*); lib. bdg. 12.88 (*0-688-07693-9*) Lothrop.

—How to Be Rich. LC 93-9575. 1993. 5.95 (*0-85953-405-7*) Childs Play.

—In Control, Ms. Wiz? Blacker, Terence. 64p. (gr. 2-5). 1990. pap. 2.95 (*0-8120-4500-9*) Barron.

—Jesus Is Risen! Neff, LaVonne, retold by. LC 92-34972. 1993. 6.99 (*0-8423-1880-1*) Tyndale.

—The Legend of Lightning Larry. Shepard, Aaron. LC 91-43779. 32p. (gr. 1-3). 1993. SBE 14.95 (*0-684-19433-3*, Scribners Young Read) Macmillan Child Grp.

—The Monster. LC 93-21862. (ps-3). 1993. 5.95 (*0-85953-406-5*) Childs Play.

—Mother Halverson's New Cat. Aylesworth, Jim. LC 88-29279. 32p. (gr. k-3). 1989. SBE 13.95 (*0-689-31465-5*, Atheneum Child Bk) Macmillan Child Grp.

—Ms Wiz Spells Trouble. Blacker, Terence. 64p. (gr. 3-6). 1990. pap. 2.95 (*0-8120-4420-7*) Barron.

—My Little Box of Prayers, 4 bks. Henderson, Felicity. 32p. (ps-1). 1988. Set. casebound 10.95 (*0-7459-1250-8*) Lion USA.

—No Smoking: Do You Mind If I Don't Smoke? LC 92-10849. 1992. 7.95 (*0-85953-782-X*, Pub. by Child's Play UK); pap. 3.95 (*0-85953-783-8*, Pub. by Childs Play UK) Childs Play.

—President Citizen. LC 92-10848. 1992. 7.95 (*0-85953-368-9*); pap. 3.95 (*0-85953-369-7*) Childs Play.

—The Prince Who Wrote a Letter. Love, Ann. LC 92-27587. 1992. write for info. (*0-85953-398-0*, Pub. by Childs Play UK); pap. write for info. (*0-85953-399-9*, Pub. by Childs Play UK) Childs Play.

—Sid Seal, Houseman. Watkins, Will. LC 88-60095. 96p. (gr. 2-5). 1989. 14.95 (*0-531-05784-4*); PLB 14.99 (*0-531-08384-5*) Orchard Bks Watts.

—Stories Jesus Told. Neff, LaVonne, retold by. LC 92-34973. 1993. 6.99 (*0-8423-5943-5*) Tyndale.

—Treed by a Pride of Irate Lions. Zimelman, Nathan. LC 89-30344. (gr. k-3). 1990. 14.95 (*0-316-98802-2*) Little.

—You're Under Arrest, Ms. Wiz. Blacker, Terence. 64p. (gr. 2-5). 1990. pap. 2.95 (*0-8120-4499-1*) Barron.

—Zoom on a Broom: Six Fun-Filled Stories. Hindley, Judy. LC 92-53100. 72p. (gr. k-3). 1992. 10.95 (*1-85697-826-5*) Kingfisher Bks.

Goffe, Toni, photos by. The Knight Who Was Afraid to Fight. Hazen, Barbara Shook. LC 94-4608. 1994. write for info. (*0-8037-1591-9*); lib. bdg. write for info. (*0-8037-1592-7*) Dial Bks Young.

Goffin, Josse. Silent Christmas. LC 90-83430. 32p. (ps-k). 1991. 14.95 (*1-878093-08-8*) Boyds Mills Pr.

—Who Is the Boss? Goffin, Josse. (gr. k-3). 1992. 13.45 (*0-395-61192-X*, Clarion Bks) HM.

Goffstein, Brooke. An Actor. Goffstein, Brooke. LC 87-165. 32p. (gr. up). 1987. HarpC Child Bks.

Goffstein, M. B. An Artists Album. Goffstein, M. B. LC 85-42612. 48p. (ps up). 1985. HarpC Child Bks.

—Fish for Supper. Goffstein, M. B. LC 75-27598. 32p. (ps-2). 1986. pap. 3.95 (*0-8037-0284-1*) Dial Bks Young.

Goggin, Lewisa. C Is for Coyote. Stinson, Douglas. 40p. (gr. 1 up). 1993. 15.95 (*1-879244-04-7*) Windom Bks.

Gohman, Vera. My "e" Sound Box. Moncure, Jane B. LC 84-17021. 32p. (ps-2). 1984. PLB 21.35 (*0-89565-297-8*); PLB 14.95s.p. (*0-685-57951-4*) Childs World.

—My "E" Sound Box. Moncure, Jane. 32p. (gr. k-2). 1993. pap. text ed. 5.95 (*1-56189-385-4*) Amer Educ Pub.

—My "I" Sound Box. Moncure, Jane. 32p. (gr. k-2). 1993. pap. text ed. 5.95 (*1-56189-386-2*) Amer Educ Pub.

—My "O" Sound Box. Moncure, Jane B. LC 84-17023. 32p. (ps-2). 1984. PLB 21.35 (*0-89565-299-4*); PLB 14.95s.p. (*0-685-57950-6*) Childs World.

—My "O" Sound Box. Moncure, Jane. 32p. (gr. k-2). 1993. pap. text ed. 5.95 (*1-56189-387-0*) Amer Educ Pub.

—Our Thanksgiving Book. rev. ed. Moncure, Jane B. LC 85-29077. 32p. (ps-3). 1986. PLB 19.95 (*0-89565-340-0*); PLB 13.95s.p. (*0-685-55832-0*) Childs World.

—What Does Word Bird See? Moncure, Jane B. LC 81-21594. (ps-2). 1982. PLB 21.35 (*0-89565-220-X*); PLB 14.95s.p. (*0-685-55557-7*) Childs World.

—A Wish-for Dinosaur. Moncure, Jane B. LC 88-20302. 32p. (ps-2). 1989. PLB 21.35 (*0-89565-393-1*); PLB 14.95s.p. (*0-685-56000-7*) Childs World.

—Word Bird Asks: What? What? What? Moncure, Jane B. LC 83-15258. 32p. (gr. k-2). 1983. PLB 21.35 (*0-89565-258-7*); PLB 14.95s.p. (*0-685-55680-8*) Childs World.

—Word Bird Builds a City. Moncure, Jane B. LC 83-15275. 32p. (ps-2). 1983. PLB 21.35 (*0-89565-257-9*); PLB 14.95s.p. (*0-685-55677-8*) Childs World.

—Word Bird Makes Words with Dog. Moncure, Jane B. LC 83-23946. 32p. (gr. k-1). 1984. PLB 21.35 (*0-89565-263-3*); PLB 14.95s.p. (*0-685-55687-5*) Childs World.

—Word Bird's Christmas Words. Moncure, Jane B. LC 86-31666. 32p. (gr. k-2). 1987. PLB 21.35 (*0-89565-361-3*); PLB 14.95s.p. (*0-685-55879-7*) Childs World.

—Word Bird's Halloween Words. Moncure, Jane B. LC 86-31024. 32p. (gr. k-2). 1987. PLB 21.35 (*0-89565-359-1*); PLB 14.95s.p. (*0-685-55881-9*) Childs World.
—Word Bird's Hats. Moncure, Jane B. LC 81-18065. (ps-2). 1982. PLB 21.35 (*0-89565-221-8*); PLB 14. 95s.p. (*0-685-55562-3*) Childs World.
—Word Bird's Spring Words. Moncure, Jane B. LC 85-5902. 32p. (gr. k-2). 1985. PLB 21.35 (*0-89565-310-9*); PLB 14.95s.p. (*0-685-55736-7*) Childs World.
—Word Bird's Winter Words. Moncure, Jane B. LC 85-5942. 32p. (gr. k-2). 1985. PLB 21.35 (*0-89565-309-5*); PLB 14.95s.p. (*0-685-55738-3*) Childs World.
—Yes, No, Little Hippo. Moncure, Jane B. LC 87-21211. 32p. (ps-2). 1987. PLB 21.35 (*0-89565-411-3*); PLB 14.95s.p. (*0-685-55946-7*) Childs World.
Gohman, Vera K. My "I" Sound Box. Moncure, Jane B. LC 84-17022. 32p. (ps-2). 1984. PLB 21.35 (*0-89565-298-6*); PLB 14.95s.p. (*0-685-57949-2*) Childs World.
Gold, Ethel. Elizabeth Blackwell: Pioneer Woman Doctor. Latham, Jean L. 80p. (gr. 2-6). 1991. Repr. of 1975 ed. lib. bdg. 12.95 (*0-7910-1406-1*) Chelsea Hse.

—**The Kid's Club Cubs & the Search for the Treasures of the Pyramid.** Mayfield, Barbara J. 40p. (ps-2). 1994. pap. 24.95 (*1-883983-15-0*) Noteworthy Creat.
Barbara Mayfield, Registered Dietician & nutrition educator, author of KID'S CLUB: NUTRITION LEARNING ACTIVITIES FOR YOUNG CHILDREN, & NUTRITION NOTES: MUSICAL NUTRITION EDUCATION TO SING & COLOR, has written a delightful adventure story to teach young children about the new Food Guide Pyramid. The beautiful color illustrations show the Kid's Club Cubs & their friend Picky Piggy in their search for the treasures of the Pyramid, learning the difference between healthy & less-healthy foods, food groups, & the nutrient treasures they provide. The book invites participation from the reader & comes with a puzzle for the child to build their own Food Guide Pyramid & a cassette tape of the story & 11 original songs. Activity ideas for parents are included in the book as well as lyrics to the 11 songs & camera-ready artwork of the Food Guide Pyramid. The book-puzzle-tape may be ordered directly from the publisher. Noteworthy Creations, Inc., P.O. Box 335, 112 W. Main St., Delphi, IN 46923; phone 317-564-4167.
Publisher Provided Annotation.

—Let's Go to the Farm. Whitehead, Patricia. LC 84-8834. 32p. (gr-2). 1985. lib. bdg. 11.59 (*0-8167-0377-9*); pap. 2.95 (*0-8167-0378-7*) Troll Assocs.
—Safety. Santrey, Laurence. LC 84-2700. 32p. (gr. 3-6). 1985. PLB 9.49 (*0-8167-0230-6*); pap. text ed. 2.95 (*0-8167-0231-4*) Troll Assocs.
—A Very Special Friend. Levi, Dorothy. LC 88-33410. 40p. (gr. k-3). 1989. 9.95 (*0-930323-55-6*, Kendall Green Pubns) Gallaudet Univ Pr.
—A Very Special Sister. Levi, Dorothy H. 32p. (gr. k-3). 9.95 (*1-878363-24-7*) Forest Hse.
—A Very Special Sister. Levi, Dorothy H. LC 88-33410. 32p. (gr. k-3). 1992. 9.95 (*0-930323-96-3*, Pub. by K Green Pubns) Gallaudet Univ Pr.
—A Very Special Sister. Levi, Dorothy H. 36p. (gr. k-3). 1992. PLB 11.95 (*1-56674-033-9*) Forest Hse.
Goldberg, Grace. The Copper Angel of Piper's Mill & How She Saved Her Town. Cunningham, Linda. 4p. (gr. 3-5). 1989. 12.95 (*0-89272-274-6*) Down East.
—Dinosaurs. Nayer, Judy. 12p. (ps-2). 1993. bds. 6.95 (*1-56293-336-1*) McClanahan Bk.
—The Happy Little Dinosaur. Nayer, Judy. 24p. (Orig.). (gr. k-1). 1990. pap. 0.99 (*1-878624-34-2*) McClanahan Bk.
—Insects. Nayer, Judy. 12p. (ps-2). 1993. bds. 6.95 (*1-56293-335-3*) McClanahan Bk.
—Jungle Life. Nayer, Judy. 10p. (ps-2). 1992. bds. 6.95 (*1-56293-221-7*) McClanahan Bk.
—The Lost Kitten. Albee, Jo. 24p. (ps-2). 1992. pap. 0.99 (*1-56293-111-3*) McClanahan Bk.

—Mammals. Nayer, Judy. 12p. (ps-2). 1993. bds. 6.95 (*1-56293-337-X*) McClanahan Bk.
—Maxine & the Ghost Dog. Butler, Linda P. 24p. (ps-2). 1992. pap. 0.99 (*1-56293-114-8*) McClanahan Bk.
—Night Animals. Nayer, Judy. 10p. (ps-2). 1992. bds. 6.95 (*1-56293-223-3*) McClanahan Bk.
—Reptiles. Nayer, Judy. 10p. (ps-2). 1992. bds. 6.95 (*1-56293-220-9*) McClanahan Bk.
—Sea Creatures. Nayer, Judy. 10p. (ps-2). 1992. bds. 6.95 (*1-56293-222-5*) McClanahan Bk.
—Space. Nayer, Judy. 12p. (ps-2). 1993. bds. 6.95 (*1-56293-338-8*) McClanahan Bk.
Goldberg, Pat. Our Baby: A Birth & Adoption Story. Koch, Janice. LC 85-6392. 27p. (ps-2). 1985. 10.95 (*0-9609504-3-5*) Perspect Indiana.
Golden, Susan. Grandma Is Somebody Special. Goldman, Susan. Rubin, Caroline, ed. LC 76-18980. 32p. (ps-1). 1976. PLB 14.95 (*0-8075-3034-4*) A Whitman.
Goldman, Dara. Warm at Home. Schotter, Roni. LC 91-48145. 32p. (gr. k-3). 1993. RSBE 14.95 (*0-02-781295-2*, Macmillan Child Bk) Macmillan Child Grp.
Goldman, Kenneth, et al. Birds of Prey. Wildlife Education, Ltd. Staff. 20p. (Orig.). (gr. 5 up). 1980. pap. 2.75 (*0-937934-01-1*) Wildlife Educ.
Goldman, Marvin, jt. illus. see Bass, Marilyn.
Goldsborough, June. Dolphins & Porpoises. Gordon, Sharon. LC 84-8594. 32p. (gr. k-2). 1985. PLB 11.59 (*0-8167-0340-X*); pap. text ed. 2.95 (*0-8167-0443-0*) Troll Assocs.
—Hello, Farm Animals. Curran, Eileen. LC 84-8657. 32p. (gr. k-2). 1985. PLB 11.59 (*0-8167-0345-0*); pap. text ed. 2.95 (*0-8167-0346-9*) Troll Assocs.
—I Can Talk to God. Tangvald, Christine. LC 85-70217. 20p. (ps). 1985. 5.88 (*0-89191-907-4*, 59071, Chariot Bks) Cook.
—Look at a Tree. Curran, Eileen. LC 84-8843. 32p. (gr. k-2). 1985. PLB 11.59 (*0-8167-0349-3*); pap. text ed. 2.95 (*0-8167-0350-7*) Troll Assocs.
—More Prayers for Small Children: About Big & Little Things. Schreivogel, Paul A. LC 88-83018. 32p. (Orig.). (gr. 1 up). 1988. pap. 5.99 (*0-8066-2381-0*, 10-4547, Augsburg) Augsburg Fortress.
—Oceans. Sabin, Francene. LC 84-8590. 32p. (gr. 3-6). 1985. PLB 9.49 (*0-8167-0216-0*); pap. text ed. 2.95 (*0-8167-0217-9*) Troll Assocs.
—Who Taught Frogs to Hop? A Child's Book about God. Ingram, Robert D. LC 89-82552. 32p. (ps). 1990. pap. 5.99 (*0-8066-2457-4*, 9-2457) Augsburg Fortress.
Goldsmith, Melissa. In a Cat State of Mind. Goldsmith, Melissa. LC 90-403394. 120p. (Orig.). (gr. 2-11). 1990. 17.95 (*0-938921-06-1*); pap. text ed. 6.95 (*0-938921-07-X*) Tigertail Ent.
Goldstein, David. The Mouse in the Matzah Factory. Medoff, Francine. LC 82-23349. 40p. (ps-3). 1983. pap. 4.95 (*0-930494-19-9*) Kar Ben.
Goldstein, Frances. Children's Treasure Hunt Travel Guide to Italy. Goldstein, Frances. LC 79-67280. (Orig.). (gr. k-12). 1980. pap. 6.95 (*0-933334-01-X*, Dist. by Hippocrene) Paper Tiger Pap.
—Children's Treasure Hunt Travel to Belgium & France. Goldstein, Frances. LC 80-85012. 230p. (Orig.). (gr. k-12). 1981. pap. 6.95 (*0-933334-02-8*, Dist. by Hippocrene) Paper Tiger Pap.
Goldstein, Howard. Children's Yellow Pages: Orange County, 1986-87 Edition. Endo, Terry, ed. 200p. (Orig.). (gr. k up). 1986. pap. 6.95 (*0-938789-00-7*) Teruko Inc.
Goldstein, Janice G. Please Don't Cry, Mom. DenBoer, Helen. LC 93-14699. 1993. 13.50 (*0-87614-805-4*) Carolrhoda Bks.
Goldstein, Leslie. Martha Washington: America's First First Lady. Wagoner, Jean B. LC 86-10737. 192p. (gr. 2-6). 1986. pap. 3.95 (*0-02-042160-5*, Aladdin) Macmillan Child Grp.
—Mary Todd Lincoln, Girl of the Bluegrass. Wilkie, Katharine E. LC 92-9782. 192p. (gr. 3-7). 1992. pap. 3.95 (*0-689-71655-9*, Aladdin) Macmillan Child Grp.
Goldstein, Lil. The Kiddush Cup Who Hated Wine. Salop, Byrd. 32p. (gr. 1 up). 1981. pap. 5.95 (*0-8246-0265-X*) Jonathan David.
Gold-Vukson, Michael. Imagine Exploring Israel: Creative Drawing Adventures. Gold-Vukson, Marji & Gold-Vukson, Michael. 48p. (Orig.). (gr. k-4). 1993. wkbk. 3.95 (*0-929371-64-X*) Kar Ben.
Golembe, Carla. How Night Came from the Sea: A Story from Brazil. Gerson, Mary-Joan, retold by. LC 93-20054. 1992. 15.95 (*0-316-30855-2*, Joy St Bks) Little.
Golembe, Carla, photos by. The Creation: A Poem. Johnson, James Weldon. LC 92-24304. 1993. 15.95 (*0-316-46744-8*) Little.
Gollub, Mo, jt. illus. see Barks, Carl.
Golub, Nan. American Dreams. Banim, Lisa. LC 93-22573. 80p. (gr. 4-6). 1993. PLB 12.95 (*1-881889-34-3*) Silver Moon.
—East Side Story. Bader, Bonnie. 80p. (gr. 4-6). 1993. PLB 12.95 (*1-881889-22-X*) Silver Moon.
—Fire in the Valley. West, Tracey. 80p. (gr. 4-6). 1993. PLB 12.95 (*1-881889-42-4*) Silver Moon.
—Forbidden Friendship. Weber, Judith E. 80p. (gr. 4-6). 1993. PLB 12.95 (*1-881889-42-4*) Silver Moon.
Gomboli, Mario. What Are You Touching? Gomboli, Mario. 10p. (ps-k). 1992. bds. 3.95 (*1-56397-150-X*); Set of 3 bks. bds. 11.85 (*1-56397-155-0*) Boyds Mills Pr.
—What Shape Is This? Gomboli, Mario. 10p. 1992. bds. 3.95 (*1-56397-149-6*); Set of 3 bks. bds. 11.85 (*1-56397-157-7*) Boyds Mills Pr.

—What's in Disguise? Gomboli, Mario. 10p. (ps-k). 1992. bds. 3.95 (*1-56397-151-8*); Set of 3 bks. bds. 11.85 (*1-56397-156-9*) Boyds Mills Pr.
Gomez, Jose. Little Herman Meets la Llorona at the Santa Fe Fiestas: A Story-Color Book in English & Spanish. Kraul, Edward G. & Beatty, Judith. (ENG & SPA.). 24p. (gr. 3-6). 1989. story-color book 2.95 (*0-945937-03-2*) Word Process.
Gomez-Milan, Francis. Leaving Matters to God. Cantoni, Louise B. LC 92-9984. 164p. (gr. 3-8). 1984. 3.00 (*0-8198-4424-1*) St Paul Bks.
Gomi, Taro. The Big Book of Boxes. Gomi, Taro. 12p. (ps up). 1991. pap. 14.95 (*0-8118-0067-9*) Chronicle Bks.
—Bus Stops. Gomi, Taro. LC 88-10193. 32p. (ps-1). 1988. 10.95 (*0-87701-551-1*) Chronicle Bks.
—Coco Can't Wait. Gomi, Taro. (ps-1). 1985. pap. 3.95 (*0-14-050522-9*, Puffin) Puffin Bks.
—Guess What? A Peek-a-Boo Book. Gomi, Taro. Chronicle Books, tr. from JPN. 16p. (ps-k). 1992. bds. 4.95 (*0-8118-0015-6*) Chronicle Bks.
—Guess Who? A Peek-A-Boo Book. Gomi, Taro. 16p. (ps-k). 1991. bds. 4.95 (*0-8118-0021-0*) Chronicle Bks.
—There's a Mouse in the House. Gomi, Taro. Chronicle Books, tr. from JPN. 16p. (ps-k). 1991. bds. 4.95 (*0-8118-0024-5*) Chronicle Bks.
—Where's the Fish? Gomi, Taro. LC 85-15282. 32p. (ps-k). 1986. 11.95 (*0-688-06241-5*); lib. bdg. 11.88 (*0-688-06242-3*, Morrow Jr Bks) Morrow Jr Bks.
Gompper, Gail. EarlyWriter. Rothstein, Evelyn & Gess, Diane. 80p. (gr. k-1). 1989. pap. text ed. 7.95 (*0-913935-44-1*) ERA-CCR.
—Easy Writer: Student Worksheets, Level G. Bartoletti, Susan & Lisandrelli, Elaine. 38p. (Orig.). (gr. 7-9). 1986. pap. text ed. 14.95 (*0-913935-37-9*) ERA-CCR.
—Editing Writes, Blue Edition. Rothstein, Evelyn, et al. (gr. 3-4). 1990. pap. 7.95 25 or more copies (*0-913935-46-8*) ERA-CCR.
—Editing Writes, Green Edition. Rothstein, Evelyn, et al. (gr. 5-7). 1990. pap. 7.95 (*0-913935-47-6*) ERA-CCR.
—Editing Writes, Orange Edition. Rothstein, Evelyn, et al. (gr. 2-8). 1990. pap. 7.95 25 or more copies (*0-913935-48-4*) ERA-CCR.
—Editing Writes, Red Edition. Rothstein, Evelyn, et al. 110p. (gr. 4-6). 1989. pap. 7.95 (*0-913935-45-X*) ERA-CCR.
—ReWriter, Bk. I. Berliner, Larry & Berliner, Susan. 38p. (Orig.). (gr. 5 up). 1985. pap. text ed. 17.95 ea. Bk. I, gr. 5-8 & high school sp. needs (*0-913935-28-X*) Bk. II, gr. 6-9 & high school sp. needs (*0-913935-29-8*) ERA-CCR.
Gon, Adriano. Here Comes Tod! Pearce, Philippa. LC 93-20026. 1994. write for info. (*1-56402-328-1*) Candlewick Pr.
—Into the Night House. Eyles, Heather. 64p. (gr. 4-7). 1990. pap. 2.95 (*0-8120-4423-1*) Barron.
Gonzales, Joe. An Elfindale Story. Anderson, Norma R. LC 81-5977. 36p. (Orig.). (gr. 1-6). 1981. pap. 5.95 (*0-913504-64-5*) Lowell Pr.

Gonzales, Rod. To the Summit. Gonzales, Rod & Faurot, Chip. McDonald, Mike, ed. 32p. (Orig.). (gr. 5-10). 1993. pap. 3.95 (*1-882724-00-3*) Alaska Comics.
TO THE SUMMIT is the story of a 12-year-old kid who climbs Mt. McKinley. It was June 23, 1991, solstice day, that he summited, making him the youngest mountaineer to do so. Taras lives within the "shadows" of Mt. McKinley in beautiful Talkeetna, Alaska. He is the son of the late & legendary Ray Genet who perished 12 years earlier on the upper-Mt. Everest slope. It was back then that the promise was made - "...some day I'm gonna take you up Denali." That day, he was a special guest member of a guided expedition led by Fantasy Ridge Expedition, Inc. AK. Comics artist Rod Gonzalez worked closely with chief guide Chip Faurot, Taras & his mother on this project. We feel that we have produced a clean & inspirational story & are anxious to share it with you. TO THE SUMMIT is a 32-page B/W production with UV coating on the cover...printed on bookpaper (making it a great coloring book). Alaska Comics uses Capitol City Distribution, Inc., P.O. Box 8156, Madison, WI 53708. For direct contact: Max North Alaska Comics, 316 Price Street, Anchorage, AK 99508, 907/279-4913. ISBN 1-882724-00-3, $3.95.
Publisher Provided Annotation.

Gonzalez, Pepe. The Bobbsey Twins of Lakeport. Hope, Laura L. 120p. (gr. 2-5). 1989. 4.50 (*0-448-09071-6*, G&D) Putnam Pub Group.

—The Bobbsey Twins on a Houseboat. Hope, Laura L. 120p. 1990. 4.50 (*0-448-09099-6*, G&D) Putnam Pub Group.

—Mystery at Meadowbrook. Hope, Laura L. 120p. 1990. 4.50 (*0-448-09100-3*, G&D) Putnam Pub Group.

—Mystery at School. Hope, Laura L. 120p. (gr. 2-5). 1989. 5.95 (*0-448-09074-0*, G&D) Putnam Pub Group.

—The Secret at the Seashore. Hope, Laura L. 120p. (gr. 2-5). 1989. 5.95 (*0-448-09073-2*, G&D) Putnam Pub Group.

Gonzalez, Ric & Durrell, Dennis. Walt Disney's Sleeping Beauty. Singer, A. L., adapted by. LC 92-56158. 96p. 1993. 14.95 (*1-56282-366-3*); PLB 14.89 (*1-56282-367-1*) Disney Pr.

Goodale, Kit. Pas de Trois, Fun with Ballet Words. Goodale, Katherine D. Houlton, Loyce, intro. by. 25p. (Orig.). (gr. k-7). 1982. pap. 5.95 (*0-9609662-0-X*) Goodale Pub.

Goodall, John S. Great Days of a Country House. Goodall, John S. LC 91-62147. 64p. (ps up). 1992. SBE 15.95 (*0-689-50545-0*, M K McElderry) Macmillan Child Grp.

—Paddy Under Water. reissue ed. Goodall, John S. LC 83-71901. 32p. 1991. SBE 12.95 (*0-689-50297-4*, M K McElderry) Macmillan Child Grp.

—Puss in Boots. Goodall, John S. LC 90-38606. 56p. (ps-3). 1990. SBE 14.95 (*0-689-50521-3*, M K McElderry) Macmillan Child Grp.

—The Story of a Farm. Goodall, John S. LC 88-3398. (gr. 4 up). 1989. RSBE 14.95 (*0-689-50479-9*, M K McElderry) Macmillan Child Grp.

—The Story of a Main Street. Goodall, John S. LC 87-60644. 60p. 1987. SBE 14.95 (*0-689-50436-5*, M K McElderry) Macmillan Child Grp.

—The Story of an English Village. Goodall, John S. LC 78-56242. 60p. 1979. SBE 14.95 (*0-689-50125-0*, M K McElderry) Macmillan Child Grp.

Goode, Diane. Ballet Shoes. reissue ed. Streatfeild, Noel. LC 89-24390. 288p. (gr. 4-9). 1991. gift ed. 15.00 (*0-679-80105-7*); lib. bdg. 16.99 gift ed. (*0-679-90105-1*) Random Bks Yng Read.

—Ballet Shoes. Streatfeild, Noel. LC 89-24390. 288p. (gr. 4-9). 1993. pap. 3.99 (*0-679-84759-6*) Random Bks Yng Read.

—Christmas Carols. LC 82-62169. 32p. (ps up). 1988. pap. 1.25 (*0-394-81940-3*) Random Bks Yng Read.

—Cinderella. Perrault, Charles. Goode, Diane, tr. from FRE. Lange, Jessica, contrib. by. LC 87-16886. 48p. (ps up). 1989. incl. cassette 15.95 (*0-394-89600-9*) Knopf Bks Yng Read.

—The Diane Goode Book of American Folk Tales & Songs. Durell, Ann, compiled by. LC 89-1097. 64p. (ps-5). 1989. 14.95 (*0-525-44458-0*, DCB) Dutton Child Bks.

—Diane Goode's American Christmas. Goode, Diane. LC 89-25605. 80p. (ps up). 1990. 14.95 (*0-525-44620-6*, DCB) Dutton Child Bks.

—Diane Goode's Book of Scary Stories & Songs. LC 93-32610. (gr. 3 up). 1994. write for info. (*0-525-45175-7*, DCB) Dutton Child Bks.

—Diane Goode's Christmas Magic: Poems & Carols. LC 92-6366. 32p. (Orig.). (ps-3). 1992. PLB 5.99 (*0-679-92427-2*); pap. 2.25 (*0-679-82427-8*) Random Bks Yng Read.

—Diane Goode's Little Library of Christmas Classics. 32p. (gr. 1 up). 1983. boxed set 7.95 (*0-394-85229-X*) Random Bks Yng Read.

—The Dream Eater. Garrison, Christian. LC 85-26671. 32p. (ps-2). 1986. pap. 3.95 (*0-689-71058-5*, Aladdin) Macmillan Child Grp.

—The Fir Tree. Andersen, Hans Christian. Goode, Diane, adapted by. LC 82-62172. 32p. (ps up). 1988. pap. 1.25 (*0-394-81941-1*) Random Bks Yng Read.

—I Go with My Family to Grandma's. Levinson, Riki. LC 86-4490. 32p. (ps-1). 1986. 14.00 (*0-525-44261-8*, DCB); pap. 3.95 (*0-525-44557-9*, DCB) Dutton Child Bks.

—I Hear a Noise. Goode, Diane. LC 87-3060. 32p. (ps-1). 1988. 12.95 (*0-525-44353-3*, DCB) Dutton Child Bks.

—I Hear a Noise. Goode, Diane. LC 87-3060. 32p. (ps-1). 1992. pap. 3.99 (*0-525-44884-5*, Puffin) Puffin Bks.

—The Little Books of Nursery Animals: The Little Book of Cats; The Little Book of Farm Friends; The Little Book of Mice; The Little Book of Pigs. (ps). 1993. Boxed set, 24p. ea. 11.99 (*0-525-45122-6*, DCB) Dutton Child Bks.

—The Night Before Christmas. Moore, Clement C. LC 82-62171. 32p. 1988. pap. 1.25 (*0-394-81938-1*) Random Bks Yng Read.

—The Nutcracker: The Story Based on the Ballet. LC 82-62170. 32p. 1988. pap. 1.25 (*0-394-81939-X*) Random Bks Yng Read.

—Peter Pan. Barrie, James M. Frank, Josette, adapted by. LC 82-13288. 72p. (ps-4). 1983. lib. bdg. 8.99 (*0-394-95717-2*); pap. 8.95 (*0-394-85717-8*) Random Bks Yng Read.

—Peter Pan. Barrie, James M. Frank, Josette, adapted by. Redgrave, Lynn, contrib. by. 72p. (ps-5). 1987. incl. cass. 15.95 (*0-394-89226-7*) Random Bks Yng Read.

—The Random House Book of Fairy Tales. Ehrlich, Amy, adapted by. LC 83-13833. 224p. (gr. k-4). 1985. bds. 17.00 (*0-394-85693-7*); lib. bdg. 17.99 (*0-394-95693-1*) Random Bks Yng Read.

—The Story of the Nutcracker Ballet. Hautzig, Deborah. 32p. (ps-1). 1986. pap. 5.95 (*0-394-88296-2*) Random Bks Yng Read.

—The Story of the Nutcracker Ballet. Hautzig, Deborah. LC 85-30149. 32p. (ps-1). 1993. 2.25 (*0-394-88178-8*) Random Bks Yng Read.

—Two Little Christmas Classics. Moore, Clement C. 32p. (ps up). 1989. pap. 4.95 incl. cassette (*0-394-84629-X*) Random Bks Yng Read.

—Where's Our Mama? Goode, Diane. LC 91-2158. 32p. (ps-2). 1991. 13.95 (*0-525-44770-9*, DCB) Dutton Child Bks.

Goodell, Jon. Little Salt Lick & the Sun King. Armstrong, Jennifer. LC 93-18673. 1994. write for info. (*0-517-59620-2*); write for info. (*0-517-59621-0*) Crown Bks Yng Read.

Gooden, Stephen. Fables. Aesop. L'Estrange, Roger, tr. LC 92-53179. 224p. 1992. 12.95 (*0-679-41790-7*, Evrymans Lib Childs Class) Knopf.

Goodenow, Earle. Arabian Nights. Twain, Mark. (gr. 4-9). 1981. (G&D); deluxe ed. 13.95 (*0-448-06006-X*) Putnam Pub Group.

Goodfellow, Robin. Sail Away. Locke, Eleanor G., ed. 164p. (Orig.). 1987. pap. 17.00 (*0-913932-24-8*) Boosey & Hawkes.

Goodin, Sallie B. Come Comet Come Cupid. Oliver, Cookie D. LC 91-65161. 44p. (gr. k-3). 1991. 6.95 (*1-55523-426-7*) Winston-Derek.

Gooding, Beverly. Mole's Christmas. Grahame, Kenneth. 32p. (gr. k-3). 1986. pap. 4.95 (*0-13-599747-X*) P-H.

—Mole's Christmas: Or Home Sweet Home. Grahame, Kenneth. LC 82-12333. 32p. (gr. k-3). 1983. 10.95 (*0-13-599738-0*) P-H.

Goodman, Billy. Animal Homes & Societies. Goodman, Billy. 96p. (gr. 3-7). 1992. 17.95 (*0-316-32018-8*) Little.

—Natural Wonders & Disasters. Goodman, Billy. (gr. 3-7). 1991. 17.95 (*0-316-32016-1*) Little.

—The Rain Forest. Goodman, Billy. 96p. (gr. 3-7). 1992. 17.95 (*0-316-32019-6*) Little.

Goodman, Joan. Hocus Pocus, Magic Show! Greydanus, Rose. LC 81-2637. 32p. (gr. k-2). 1981. PLB 11.59 (*0-89375-539-7*); pap. text ed. 2.95 (*0-89375-540-0*) Troll Assocs.

Goodman, Joan E. Case of the Missing Rattles. Supraner, Robyn. LC 81-10378. 48p. (gr. 2-4). 1982. PLB 10.89 (*0-89375-590-7*); pap. text ed. 3.50 (*0-89375-591-5*) Troll Assocs.

—The Cat Who Wanted to Fly. Supraner, Robyn. LC 85-14119. 48p. (Orig.). (gr. 1-3). 1986. PLB 10.59 (*0-8167-0612-3*); pap. text ed. 3.50 (*0-8167-0613-1*) Troll Assocs.

—Easter Parade. Curran, Eileen. LC 84-8630. 32p. (gr. k-2). 1985. PLB 11.59 (*0-8167-0353-1*); pap. text ed. 2.95 (*0-8167-0433-3*) Troll Assocs.

—Gingerbread Boy. Cutts, David, retold by. LC 78-18069. 32p. (gr. k-2). 1979. PLB 9.79 (*0-89375-122-7*); pap. 1.95 (*0-89375-100-6*) Troll Assocs.

—The Grape Jelly Mystery. Blake, Olive. LC 78-18040. 48p. (gr. 2-4). 1979. PLB 10.89 (*0-89375-096-4*); pap. 3.50 (*0-89375-084-0*) Troll Assocs.

—Yummy, Yummy. Grey, Judith. LC 81-2360. 32p. (gr. k-2). 1981. PLB 11.59 (*0-89375-543-5*); pap. 2.95 (*0-89375-544-3*) Troll Assocs.

Goodman, John. First Day of School. Jackson, Kim. LC 84-8631. 32p. (gr. k-2). 1985. PLB 11.59 (*0-8167-0359-0*); pap. text ed. 2.95 (*0-8167-0439-2*) Troll Assocs.

Goodman, Marlene. Let's Learn English: Picture Dictionary. Passport Books Staff, ed. 72p. 1990. 9.95 (*0-8442-5453-3*, Natl Textbk) NTC Pub Grp.

—Let's Learn Italian: Picture Dictionary. Passport Books Staff, ed. 72p. 1990. 9.95 (*0-8442-8065-8*, Natl Textbk) NTC Pub Grp.

—Let's Learn Japanese Picture Dictionary: Elementary Through Junior High. (JPN.). 80p. 1993. 9.95 (*0-685-62858-2*, F8494-7, Natl Textbk); pap. 8.46 ea. 10 or more copies (F8494-7, Natl Textbk) NTC Pub Grp.

—Let's Learn Portuguese Picture Dictionary: Elementary. (POR.). 72p. 1993. 9.95 (*0-685-62862-0*, F4699-9, Natl Textbk); 10 or more copies 8.46 ea. (F4699-9, Natl Textbk) NTC Pub Grp.

—Let's Learn Spanish: Picture Dictionary. Passport Books Staff, ed. 72p. 1990. 9.95 (*0-8442-7558-1*, Natl Textbk) NTC Pub Grp.

Goodman, Marlene & Spizzirri, Peter M. Dolls: An Educational Coloring Book. Spizzirri Publishing Co. Staff. Spizzirri, Linda, ed. 32p. (gr. 1-8). 1981. pap. 1.75 (*0-86545-034-X*) Spizzirri.

Goodman, Marlene, et al. Birds: Educational Coloring Book. Spizzirri Publishing Co. Staff. Spizzirri, Linda, ed. 32p. (gr. 1-8). 1981. pap. 1.75 (*0-86545-026-9*) Spizzirri.

Goodman, Vivienne. Guess What? Fox, Mem. LC 90-4127. 28p. (ps up). 1990. 13.95 (*0-15-200452-1*, Gulliver Bks) HarBrace.

Goodnight, Paul. Irene Jennie & the Christmas Masquerade: The Johnkankus. Smalls-Hector, Irene. LC 93-7037. 1994. 15.95 (*0-316-79878-9*) Little.

Goodrich, Carter. Nutcracker. Hoffmann, E. T. Madden, Andrea C., tr. LC 86-45271. 104p. 1987. 14.95 (*0-394-55384-5*) Knopf Bks Yng Read.

Goodwill, Rita. The Life of Jesus. Savary, Louis. 43p. (ps-4). 1989. 5.59 (*0-88271-099-0*) Regina Pr.

Goodwin, Irene. Polka Dotted Pencil Pushers: Math. Goodwin, Irene & Silvers, Ruth. LC 79-63129. 156p. (Orig.). 1979. pap. 8.95 tchr's. guide (*0-932970-08-7*) Prinit Pr.

Goodwin, Judith. The Secret of Willow Castle. Cook, Lyn. 236p. (Orig.). (gr. 3-10). 1984. pap. 7.95 (*0-920656-30-7*, Pub. by Camden Hse CN) Firefly Bks Ltd.

Goor, Nancy, jt. illus. see Goor, Ron.

Goor, Ron. Heads. Goor, Ron & Goor, Nancy. LC 87-30262. 64p. (gr. 2-6). 1988. SBE 13.95 (*0-689-31400-0*, Atheneum Child Bk) Macmillan Child Grp.

Goor, Ron & Goor, Nancy. Pompeii: Exploring a Roman Ghost Town. Goor, Ron & Goor, Nancy. LC 85-47895. 128p. (gr. 5-9). 1986. 15.00 (*0-690-04515-8*, Crowell Jr Bks); PLB 14.89 (*0-690-04516-6*, Crowell Jr Bks) HarpC Child Bks.

Goor, Ron, photos by. Shadows: Here, There, & Everywhere. Goor, Ron & Goor, Nancy. LC 81-43036. 48p. (gr. k-3). 1981. PLB 13.89 (*0-690-04133-0*, Crowell Jr Bks) HarpC Child Bks.

Goor, Ronald, photos by. Backyard Insects. Selsam, Millicent E. 40p. (ps-3). 1988. pap. 2.95 (*0-590-42256-1*) Scholastic Inc.

Gooseart Publications Staff. Secrets of Life Every Teen Needs to Know. Paulson, Terry L. & Paulson, Sean D. LC 90-63405. 160p. (Orig.). (gr. 7-12). 1990. pap. 6.95 (*0-939513-42-0*) Joy Pub SJC.

Gorbachev, Valeri. What If? Just Wondering Poems. Hulme, Joy N. LC 90-60863. 32p. (ps-1). 1993. 14.95 (*1-56397-186-0*, Wordsong) Boyds Mills Pr.

Gorbaty, Norman. Baby Animals Say Hello. 12p. (ps). 1986. 3.99 (*0-394-88241-5*) Random Bks Yng Read.

—Baby at Home. 12p. (ps). 1988. 2.95 (*0-394-81924-1*) Random Bks Yng Read.

—Baby Ben's Bow-Wow Book. Ziefert, Harriet. LC 83-63539. (ps). 1984. bds. 2.95 (*0-394-86821-8*) Random Bks Yng Read.

—Baby Ben's Noisy Book. Ziefert, Harriet. LC 83-63541. (ps). 1984. bds. 2.95 (*0-394-86822-6*) Random Bks Yng Read.

—Be My Friend. Ross, Anna. LC 89-24389. 24p. (ps). 1991. 3.95 (*0-394-85496-9*) Random Bks Yng Read.

—Ducky Colors. 12p. (ps). 1991. pap. 3.95 (*0-671-74435-6*, Little Simon) S&S Trade.

—Dump Truck. Gorbaty, Norman. 12p. (ps). 1993. bds. 6.95 (*0-448-40594-6*, G&D) Putnam Pub Group.

—Fire Engine. 12p. (ps). 1993. bds. 6.95 (*0-448-40595-4*, G&D) Putnam Pub Group.

—Get up & Go, Little Dinosaur! LC 89-64282. 22p. (ps). 1990. bds. 2.95 (*0-679-80693-8*) Random Bks Yng Read.

—God's Gift. Richards, Jean, retold by. LC 92-38265. 1993. pap. 15.95 (*0-385-31092-7*, Zephyr-BFYR) Doubleday.

—I Did It! Ross, Anna. LC 89-34543. 24p. (ps). 1990. 3.95 (*0-394-86019-5*) Random Bks Yng Read.

—I Have to Go. Ross, Anna. LC 89-34542. 24p. (ps). 1990. 3.95 (*0-394-86051-9*) Random Bks Yng Read.

—Kitty in & Out. 12p. (ps). 1991. pap. 3.95 (*0-671-74437-2*, Little Simon) S&S Trade.

—Little Bert's Book of Numbers. Ross, Anna. LC 91-4921. 24p. (ps). 1992. 3.99 (*0-679-82239-9*) Random Bks Yng Read.

—Little Dinosaur. Gorbaty, Norman. LC 87-61420. 24p. (ps-1). 1988. bk. & doll pkg. 4.95 (*0-394-89575-4*) Random Bks Yng Read.

—Little Elmo's Book of Colors. Ross, Anna. LC 91-23979. 24p. (ps). 1992. 3.99 (*0-679-82238-0*) Random Bks Yng Read.

—Little Ernie's ABC's. Ross, Anna. LC 91-27823. 24p. (ps). 1992. 3.99 (*0-679-82240-2*) Random Bks Yng Read.

—Little Grover's Book of Shapes. Ross, Anna. LC 91-4920. 24p. (ps). 1992. 3.99 (*0-679-82237-2*) Random Bks Yng Read.

—Mine! A Sesame Street Book about Sharing: (Just Right for 2's & 3's) Hayward, Linda. LC 87-42810. 24p. (ps). 1988. 6.00 (*0-394-89599-1*) Random Bks Yng Read.

—Naptime. Ross, Anna. LC 89-34545. 24p. (ps). 1990. 3.95 (*0-394-85828-X*) Random Bks Yng Read.

—No More TV, Sleepy Dog. Ziefert, Harriet. LC 88-26316. 24p. (Orig.). (ps-2). 1989. 2.25 (*0-394-81996-9*) Random Bks Yng Read.

—Open the Door, Little Dinosaur. Ross, Katharine. LC 92-80950. 14p. (ps-k). 1993. bds. 3.99 (*0-679-83689-6*) Random Bks Yng Read.

—Puppy Round & Square. 12p. (ps). 1991. pap. 3.95 (*0-671-74436-4*, Little Simon) S&S Trade.

—Quiet Time. Ross, Anna. LC 89-24354. 24p. (ps). 1991. 3.95 (*0-394-85495-0*) Random Bks Yng Read.

—Say Bye-Bye. Ross, Anna. LC 90-52915. 24p. (ps). 1992. 3.95 (*0-394-85485-3*) Random Bks Yng Read.

—Say Good Night. Ross, Anna. LC 90-52914. 24p. (ps). 1992. 3.95 (*0-394-85491-8*) Random Bks Yng Read.

—Say the Magic Word, Please. Ross, Anna. LC 89-34544. 24p. (ps). 1990. 3.95 (*0-394-85857-3*) Random Bks Yng Read.

—Sleepy Dog: A Step One Book. Ziefert, Harriet. LC 84-4775. (ps-2). 1984. PLB 7.99 (*0-394-96877-8*); pap. 3.50 (*0-394-86877-3*) Random Bks Yng Read.

—Tiger Is a Scaredy Cat: A Step One Book. Phillips, Joan. LC 85-19673. 32p. (ps-1). 1986. lib. bdg. 7.99 (*0-394-98056-5*); pap. 3.50 (*0-394-88056-0*) Random Bks Yng Read.

—Time for School, Little Dinosaur. Herman, Gail. LC 89-70331. 24p. (Orig.). (ps-2). 1990. pap. 2.25 (0-679-80789-6) Random Bks Yng Read.
—Turtle Count. 12p. (ps). 1991. pap. 3.95 (0-671-74434-8, Little Simon) S&S Trade.
—What a Hungry Puppy! Herman, Gail. LC 92-24468. 32p. (ps-1). 1993. lib. bdg. 7.99 (0-448-40537-7, G&D); pap. 3.50 (0-448-40536-9, G&D) Putnam Pub Group.
—What Do You See on Sesame Street? 12p. (ps). 1988. 3.99 (0-394-80594-1) Random Bks Yng Read.
Gordillo, Henry E., photos by. Before You Were Three: How You Began to Walk, Talk, Explore & Have Feelings. Harris, Robbie & Levy, Elizabeth. LC 76-5587. 160p. (gr. 1 up). 1981. pap. 7.95 (0-440-00471-3) Delacorte.
Gordon, Ayala. Hanukah in My House. Simon, Norma. (ps-k). 1960. plastic cover 4.50 (0-8381-0705-2) United Syn Bk.
—Happy Purim Night. Simon, Norma. (ps-k). plastic cover 4.50 (0-8381-0706-0, 10-706) United Syn Bk.
—Our First Sukkah. Simon, Norma. (ps-k). 1959. plastic cover 4.50 (0-8381-0703-6) United Syn Bk.
—Purim Party. Simon, Norma. (ps-k). 1959. plastic cover 4.50 (0-8381-0707-9) United Syn Bk.
—Rosh Hashanah. Simon, Norma. (ps-k). 1961. plastic cover 4.50 (0-8381-0700-1) United Syn Bk.
—Simhat Torah. Simon, Norma. (ps-k). 1960. bds. 4.50 lam. (0-8381-0704-4) United Syn Bk.
—Yom Kippur. Simon, Norma. (ps-k). 1959. plastic cover 4.50 (0-8381-0702-8) United Syn Bk.
Gordon, Ayalah. Hasefer Alef-Beis Hametzuyar (In Color) Bachrach, Kalman. (HEB.). 67p. (gr. 1). 1960. pap. text ed. 2.50x (1-878530-01-1) K Bachrach Co.
Gordon, Christine W. Mee Glows with Health & Happiness. Gordon, Christine W. LC 87-90587. 32p. (Orig.). (ps-2). 1987. pap. 5.00 (0-9618854-1-6) Mee Enterp.
—Mee, Who Is Hardly Any Size at All. Gordon, Christine W. LC 87-90588. (Orig.). (ps-k). 1987. pap. 4.00 (0-9618854-0-8) Mee Enterp.
Gordon, Melinda. The Case of the Purloined Pork. Gustafson, Anita. 32p. (gr. 2-3). 1985. 7.95 (0-88700-004-5) Natl Live Stock.
Gordon, Mike. Mole Wins a Prize. Hunt, Rod. 32p. (ps-k). 1987. 6.95 (0-09-167520-0, Pub. by Hutchinson UK) Trafalgar.
Gordon, Richard D. Martin & the Mountaintop: An Illustrated Tribute to Dr. Martin Luther King, Jr. Gordon, Richard D. LC 88-92651. 85p. (gr. 7 up). 1988. 14.95 (0-9621308-0-X) CMark Pr.
Gore, Leonid. Jacob & the Stranger. Derby, Sally. LC 93-11022. 1994. 13.95 (0-395-66897-2) Ticknor & Fields.
Gorell, Nancy. Spindle Stories, Bk. Two: Three Units on Women's World History. Reese, Lyn. Dougherty, Mary A. & Wilkinson, Jean B., eds. 118p. (gr. 6-10). 1991. pap. text ed. 15.00 (0-9625880-1-6) Women World CRP.
—Spindle Stories: World History Units for the Middle Grades, Bk. 1. Reese, Lyn. Dougherty, Mary A. & Wilkinson, Jean B., eds. 90p. (gr. 5-9). 1990. pap. text ed. 15.00g (0-9625880-0-8) Women World CRP.
Gorey, Edward. The Adventures of Treehorn. Heide, Florence P. 128p. (gr. k-3). 1983. pap. 1.95 (0-440-40045-7, YB) Dell.
—Brer Rabbit & His Tricks. Rees, Ennis. LC 88-50415. 56p. (gr. k-5). 1994. pap. 4.95 (1-56282-577-1) Hyprn Ppbks.
—Category. LC 86-10938. (ps up). 1986. Repr. 8.95 (0-685-13444-X) Modan-Adama Bks.
—The Dark Secret of Weatherend. Bellairs, John. 208p. (gr. 5 up). 1984. 13.95 (0-8037-0072-5) Dial Bks Young.
—The House with a Clock in Its Walls. Bellairs, John. LC 92-26794. 192p. (gr. 3 up). 1993. pap. 3.50 (0-14-036336-X, Puffin) Puffin Bks.
—The Monster Den: or Look What Happened at My House - & to It. Ciardi, John. LC 90-85904. 64p. (gr. k up). 1991. Repr. 13.95 (1-878093-35-5, Wordsong) Boyds Mills Pr.
—More of Brer Rabbit's Tricks. Rees, Ennis. LC 88-50878. 56p. (gr. k-5). 1994. pap. 4.95 (1-56282-578-X) Hyprn Ppbks.
—The Revenge of the Wizard's Ghost. Bellairs, John. LC 85-4550. 160p. (gr. 5 up). 1985. 13.95 (0-8037-0170-5) Dial Bks Young.
—The Shrinking of Treehorn. Heide, Florence P. LC 78-151753. 64p. (gr. 3-6). 1971. reinforced bdg. 13.95 (0-8234-0189-8); pap. 4.95 (0-8234-0975-9) Holiday.
—Treehorn's Treasure. Heide, Florence P. LC 81-4043. 64p. (gr. 3-6). 1981. reinforced bdg. 13.95 (0-8234-0425-0) Holiday.
—Treehorn's Wish. Heide, Florence P. LC 83-6240. 64p. (gr. 3-6). 1984. reinforced bdg 8.95 (0-8234-0493-5) Holiday.
—The Vengeance of the Witch-Finder. Bellairs, John. Strickland, Brad, contrib. by. LC 93-10081. 176p. (gr. 5 up). 1993. 14.99 (0-8037-1450-5); lib. bdg. 14.89 (0-8037-1451-3) Dial Bks Young.
—The Wuggly Ump. Gorey, Edward. LC 86-11273. (ps up). 1986. 6.95 (0-915361-56-6, Dist. by Watts) Modan-Adama Bks.
—You Know Who. Ciardi, John. LC 90-85903. 48p. (gr. k up). 1991. Repr. 13.95 (1-878093-34-7, Wordsong) Boyds Mills Pr.
—You Read to Me, I'll Read to You. Ciardi, John. LC 62-16296. 64p. (gr. k-6). 1961. (Lipp Jr Bks); PLB 12.89 (0-397-30646-6) HarpC Child Bks.

—You Read to Me, I'll Read to You. Ciardi, John. LC 62-16296. 64p. (gr.-2). 1987. pap. 5.95 (0-06-446060-6, Trophy) HarpC Child Bks.
Gornari, Giuliano & Corbella, Luciano. The Earth & How It Works. Parker, Steve. LC 92-54317. 64p. (gr. 3-7). 1993. 12.95 (1-56458-235-3) Dorling Kindersley.
Gorney, Janifer & Jones, Allan. Good Math Beginnings. Christensen, Kathryn. Jones, Allan & Gorney, Janifer, eds. (Orig.). (ps). 1987. pap. 9.95 (0-9607458-5-8) Arts Pubns.
Gorski, Paul & Devito, Pam. The Tunnel under the Sea. Sargent, Ruth. Weinberger, Jane, ed. 120p. (gr. 3-6). 1993. pap. 9.95 (0-932433-11-1) Windswept Hse.
Gorsline, Douglas. Cowboys. Gorsline, Marie & Gorsline, Douglas. LC 78-1131. 32p. (ps-2). 1980. lib. bdg. 5.99 (0-394-93935-2); pap. 2.25 (0-394-83935-8) Random Bks Yng Read.
—The Night Before Christmas. Moore, Clement C. LC 75-7511. 32p. (gr. 2-6). 1975. 2.25 (0-394-83019-9) Random Bks Yng Read.
—The Night Before Christmas. Moore, Clement C. 32p. (ps-1). 1985. incl. cassette 5.95 (0-394-87658-X) Random Bks Yng Read.
—North American Indians. Gorsline, Marie & Gorsline, Douglas. LC 77-79843. 32p. (ps-2). 1978. pap. 2.25 (0-394-83702-9) Random Bks Yng Read.
—Nursery Rhymes. reissue ed. Gorsline, Marie, ed. LC 76-24168. 32p. (ps-1). 1992. pap. 2.25 (0-394-83550-6) Random Bks Yng Read.
Gorsline, Douglas, jt. illus. see Gorsline, Marie.
Gorsline, Marie & Gorsline, Douglas. The Pioneers. reissued ed. Gorsline, Marie & Gorsline, Douglas. LC 78-54960. 32p. (gr. k-4). 1982. pap. 2.25 (0-394-83905-6) Random Bks Yng Read.
Goss, Marilyn. Maggie Suzanne, Star of Christmas. Goss, Marilyn. 36p. (gr. 3 up). 1988. 15.95 (0-9620766-0-0) Art Room Pubns.
Gottlieb, Jules. Grimms' Fairy Tales. Grimm, Jacob & Grimm, Wilhelm K. (gr. 3 up). 1968. pap. 2.50 (0-8049-0168-6, CL-168) Airmont.
—Hans Christian Andersen's Fairy Tales. Andersen, Hans Christian. LC 58-6191. (gr. 3 up). 1958. pap. 1.95 (0-8049-0169-4, CL-169) Airmont.
—Stories of King Arthur. Winder, Blanche, ed. (gr. 4 up). 1968. pap. 1.95 (0-8049-0167-8, CL-167) Airmont.
Goto, Byron. Ice Magic. Christopher, Matt. (gr. 4-6). 1987. PLB 14.95 (0-316-13958-0); pap. 3.95 (0-316-13991-2) Little.
—No Arm in Left Field. Christopher, Matt. (gr. 4-6). 1987. lib. bdg. 14.95 (0-316-13964-5); pap. 3.95 (0-316-13990-4) Little.
Gottfredson, Floyd. Walt Disney's Mickey Mouse Comic Album. Gottfredson, Floyd. Blum, Geoffrey, intro. by. 48p. (Orig.). (ps up) 1987. pap. 5.95 (0-944599-03-6) Gladstone Pub.
—Walt Disney's Mickey Mouse Comic Album. Gottfredson, Floyd. Blum, Geoffrey, intro. by. 48p. (Orig.). (ps up). 1988. pap. 5.95 (0-944599-07-9) Gladstone Pub.
—Walt Disney's Mickey Mouse Comic Album. Gottfredson, Floyd. Blum, Geoff, intro. by. 48p. (Orig.). 1989. pap. 5.95 (0-944599-17-6) Gladstone Pub.
—Walt Disney's Mickey Mouse Comic Album. Gottfredson, Floyd. Blum, Geoff, intro. by. 48p. (Orig.). 1989. pap. 5.95 (0-944599-21-4) Gladstone Pub.
Gottfredson, Floyd, jt. illus. see Barks, Carl.
Gottfredson, FLoyd, jt. illus. see Barks, Carl.
Gottfredson, Floyd, jt. illus. see Barks, Carl.
Gottlieb, Dale. Big Dog. Gottlieb, Dale. LC 88-5295. 32p. (ps-1). 1989. 11.95 (0-688-07381-6); PLB 11.88 (0-688-07382-4, Morrow Jr Bks) Morrow Jr Bks.
—Christmas Carol. Teasdale, Sara. 32p. (ps-2). 1993. PLB 14.95 (0-8050-2695-9, Bks Young Read) H Holt & Co.
—My Stories by Hildy Calpurnia Rose. Gottlieb, Dale. LC 90-46096. 40p. (ps-4). 1991. 14.00 (0-679-81150-8); lib. bdg. 14.99 (0-679-91150-2) Knopf Bks Yng Read.
—Seeing Eye Willie. Gottlieb, Dale. LC 91-18606. 40p. (gr. 1-4). 1992. 15.00 (0-679-82449-9); PLB 15.99 (0-679-92449-3) Knopf Bks Yng Read.
—Taxi! Taxi! Best, Cari. LC 92-32249. 1993. 14.95 (0-316-09259-2) Little.
—Train Leaves the Station. Merriam, Eve. LC 91-28009. 32p. (ps-k). 1992. 14.95 (0-8050-1934-0, B Martin BYR) H Holt & Co.
Gottlieb, Dale, photos by. I Got a Family. Cooper, Melrose. LC 92-1689. 32p. (ps-2). 1993. PLB 14.95 (0-8050-1965-0, Bks Young Read) H Holt & Co.
Gottlieb, Jane, photos by. Garden Tales: Classic Stories from Favorite Writers. LC 89-40643. 112p. 1990. 12. 95 (0-670-83173-5, Viking Studio) Studio Bks.
Goudket, Rose. Edmund Campion: Hero of God's Underground. Gardiner, Harold C. LC 91-76073. 180p. 1992. pap. 5.95 (0-89870-387-5) Ignatius Pr.
Gould, Matt. Naomi's Road. Kogawa, Joy. 82p. (Orig.). (gr. 3 up). 1988. pap. 7.50 (0-19-540547-1) OUP.
Gould, Robert. Letters from Atlantis. Silverberg, Robert. LC 90-562. 144p. (gr. 7 up). 1990. SBE 14.95 (0-689-31570-8, Atheneum Child Bk) Macmillan Child Grp.
Goulden, Veleda. Wish & Wonder: A Manitoba Village Child. Redekopp, Elsa. 59p. (Orig.). (gr. 3-6). 1982. pap. 3.95 (0-919797-21-0) Kindred Pr.

Goulding, June. Jenny's Bear. Ratnett, Michael. 32p. (ps-3). 1992. 14.95 (0-399-22325-8, Putnam) Putnam Pub Group.
Gouldthorpe, Peter. When I Turned Six. Drew, David. LC 93-26929. 1994. 4.25 (0-383-03784-0) SRA Schl Grp.
Gourbault, Martine. My Father Is in the Navy. McKinley, Robin. LC 91-12566. 24p. (ps up). 1992. 14.00 (0-688-10639-0); PLB 13.93 (0-688-10640-4) Greenwillow.
Gourgault, Martine. Peter & the Pigeons. Zolotow, Charlotte. LC 92-29405. 24p. (ps up). 1993. 14.00 (0-688-12185-3); PLB 13.93 (0-688-12186-1) Greenwillow.
Gourlault, Martine. The Little Girl & the Dragon. Minarik, Else H. LC 90-38495. 24p. (ps up). 1991. 13. 95 (0-688-09913-0); PLB 13.88 (0-688-09914-9) Greenwillow.
Gow, Bill. Bowling Basics. Nardi, Thomas J. LC 83-22893. 48p. (gr. 3-7). 1984. PLB 10.95 (0-13-080516-5) P-H.
—Football Basics. Fox, Larry. (gr. 3-7). 1981. 9.95 (0-13-323998-5) P-H.
—Gymnastics Basics. Traetta, John & Traetta, MaryJean. 64p. (gr. 3-7). 1983. pap. 3.95 (0-13-371740-2, Pub. by Treehouse) P-H.
—Hockey Basics. MacLean, Norman. LC 83-9451. 48p. (gr. 4-6). 1983. 10.95 (0-13-392506-4) P-H.
—Ice Skating Basics. MacLean, Norman. LC 84-6933. 48p. (gr. 3-7). 1984. 9.95 (0-13-448762-1) P-H.
—Skiing Basics. Marozzi, Alfred. 48p. (gr. 3-7). 1984. pap. 4.95 (0-13-812264-4) P-H.
—Soccer Basics. Yannis, Alex. Chinaglia, George, intro. by. 48p. (gr. 3-7). 1982. 9.95 (0-13-815290-X) P-H.
—Swimming Basics. Orr, C. Rob & Tyler, Jane B. 48p. 1984. pap. 4.95 (0-13-879594-0) P-H.
—Tennis Basics. LaMarche, Bob. LC 82-21542. 48p. (gr. 3-7). 1983. 9.95 (0-13-903237-1) P-H.
Gower. Computer Controlled Robots. Potter. 48p. (gr. 5-8). 1985. PLB 10.96 (0-88110-213-X, Pub. by Usborne) EDC.
Gowing, Toby. Addie's Dakota Winter. Lawlor, Laurie. MacDonald, Patricia, ed. 160p. 1991. pap. 2.99 (0-671-70148-7, Minstrel Bks) PB.
—Addie's Long Summer. Lawlor, Laurie. Tucker, Kathleen, ed. LC 91-34877. 176p. (gr. 3-6). 1992. PLB 11.95 (0-8075-0167-0) A Whitman.
—Around the Table: Family Stories of Sholom Aleichem. Shevrin, Aliza, selected by. & tr. from YID. LC 90-49273. 96p. (gr. 5-8). 1991. SBE 12.95 (0-684-19237-3, Scribners Young Read) Macmillan Child Grp.
—George on His Own. Lawlor, Laurie. Tucker, Kathleen, ed. 144p. (gr. 3-7). 1993. 11.95g (0-8075-2823-4) A Whitman.
—The Mystery of the Turkish Tattoo. Estes, Rose. Fanelli, Jenny, ed. LC 85-62805. 128p. (gr. 4-7). 1986. pap. 2.95 (0-394-86434-4) Random Bks Yng Read.
—The Treasure Bird. Griffin, Peni R. LC 91-42773. 144p. (gr. 4-7). 1992. SBE 13.95 (0-689-50554-X, M K McElderry) Macmillan Child Grp.
Graber, E. R. Mattie Mae. Beiler, Edna. LC 67-24800. 128p. (gr. 3-7). 1967. pap. 5.95 (0-8361-1789-1) Herald Pr.
Graber, Esther R. Bittersweet Days. Hamilton, Dorothy. LC 77-18867. 128p. (gr. 4-8). 1978. pap. 3.95 (0-8361-1846-4) Herald Pr.
—The Castle. Hamilton, Dorothy. LC 75-15599. 112p. (gr. 4-8). 1975. pap. 3.95 (0-8361-1876-X) Herald Pr.
—Christmas for Holly. Hamilton, Dorothy. LC 72-141831. 112p. (gr. 4-9). 1971. pap. 3.95 (0-8361-1658-5) Herald Pr.
—Holly's New Year. Hamilton, Dorothy. LC 81-4098. 112p. (gr. 3-9). 1981. pap. 3.95 (0-8361-1961-4) Herald Pr.
—Joel's Other Mother. Hamilton, Dorothy. 120p. (gr. 3-7). 1984. pap. 3.95 (0-8361-3355-2) Herald Pr.
—Mari's Mountain. Hamilton, Dorothy. LC 78-10620. 120p. (gr. 7-10). 1978. pap. 3.95 (0-8361-1869-3) Herald Pr.
Graber, Esther Rose. Carlie's Pink Room. Hamilton, Dorothy. LC 83-26437. 88p. (gr. 7-9). 1984. pap. 3.95 (0-8361-3354-4) Herald Pr.
Graber, Jack. Reptiles Do the Strangest Things. reissued ed. Hornblow, Leonora & Hornblow, Arthur. LC 90-8598. 64p. (gr. 2-4). 1991. PLB 6.99 (0-679-91158-8); pap. 3.95 (0-679-81158-3) Random Bks Yng Read.
Grace, Alexa. When Mama Retires. Ackerman, Karen. LC 91-19139. 40p. (ps-3). 1992. 15.00 (0-679-80289-4); PLB 15.99 (0-679-90289-9) Knopf Bks Yng Read.
Grace, Eileen. Three Little Pigs. LC 80-27483. 32p. (gr. k-2). 1981. PLB 9.79 (0-89375-462-5); pap. text ed. 1.95 (0-89375-463-3) Troll Assocs.
Grace, Robert & Niles, Nancy. Changes for Samantha: A Winter Story. Tripp, Valerie. Thieme, Jeanne, ed. 72p. (Orig.). (gr. 2-5). 1988. 12.95 (0-937295-46-9); PLB 12.95 (0-937295-95-7); pap. 5.95 (0-937295-47-7) Pleasant Co.
—Happy Birthday Samantha! A Springtime Story. Tripp, Valerie. Thieme, Jeanne, ed. 72p. (gr. 2-5). 1987. 12. 95 (0-937295-34-5); PLB 12.95 (0-937295-89-2); pap. 5.95 (0-937295-35-3) Pleasant Co.
—Samantha Saves the Day: A Summer Story. Tripp, Valerie. Thieme, Jeanne, ed. 72p. (gr. 2-5). 1988. 12. 95 (0-937295-40-X); PLB 12.95 (0-937295-92-2); pap. 5.95 (0-937295-41-8) Pleasant Co.

Gracia, Fred D. The Importance of Childhood. Ortiz, Simon. 16p. (Orig.). (ps-7). 1982. pap. 3.75 (0-915347-01-6) Pueblo Acoma Pr.

Gradisher, Martha. A Class Play with Ms. Vanilla. Ehrlich, Fred. 32p. (ps-3). 1992. 9.00 (0-670-84651-1) Viking Child Bks.

—A Class Play with Ms. Vanilla. Ehrlich, Fred. 32p. (ps-3). 1992. pap. 3.50 (0-14-054580-8) Puffin Bks.

—Lunch Boxes. Ehrlich, Fred. 32p. (ps-3). 1991. 8.95 (0-670-83860-8) Viking Child Bks.

—Lunch Boxes. Ehrlich, Fred. 32p. (ps-3). 1991. pap. 3.50 (0-14-054393-7, Puffin) Puffin Bks.

—Lunch Boxes. Ehrlich, Fred. LC 93-2724. (gr. k-3). 1993. pap. 3.25 (0-14-036555-9, Puffin) Puffin Bks.

—The Princess Needs a Bath. Ziefert, Harriet. 24p. (ps-3). 1992. 3.95 (0-694-00391-3) HarpC Child Bks.

—A Valentine for Ms. Vanilla. Ehrlich, Fred. 32p. (ps-3). 1992. 8.95 (0-670-84274-5) Viking Child Bks.

—Who Spilled the Milk? Ziefert, Harriet. 24p. (ps-3). 1992. 3.95 (0-694-00390-5) HarpC Child Bks.

Grado, Janet. The Boy Who Made Dragonfly: A Zuni Myth. Hillerman, Tony. LC 86-6996. 85p. (gr. 5 up). 1986. pap. 8.95 (0-8263-0910-0) U of NM Pr.

Grady, Kitten S. Jiggsy's Necklace. Grady, Kitten S. LC 87-62211. 40p. (gr. 1-6). 1987. 5.95 (0-932433-34-0) Windswept Hse.

Graef, Renee. Anne of Green Gables. Montgomery, Lucy M. Mattern, Joanne, ed. LC 92-12703. 48p. (gr. 3-6). 1992. PLB 12.89 (0-8167-2866-6); pap. text ed. 3.95 (0-8167-2867-4) Troll Assocs.

—Changes for Kirsten: A Winter Story. Shaw, Janet. 65p. (Orig.). (gr. 2-5). 1988. 12.95 (0-937295-44-2); pap. 5.95 (0-937295-45-0) Pleasant Co.

—Changes for Kirsten: A Winter Story. Shaw, Janet. Thieme, Jeanne, ed. 72p. (gr. 2-5). 1988. PLB 12.95 (0-937295-94-9) Pleasant Co.

—Come out, Come out Wherever You Are! Sinykin, Sheri C. 32p. (Orig.). (gr. k-5). 1990. pap. 5.00 (0-89486-694-X) Hazelden.

—Dance at Grandpas. Wilder, Laura I. LC 93-24535. 1994. 15.00 (0-06-023878-X, Festival); PLB 14.89 (0-06-023879-8, Festival) HarpC Child Bks.

—Geranium Morning. Powell, E. Sandy. 40p. (gr. 1-4). 1990. PLB 13.50 (0-87614-380-X) Carolrhoda Bks.

—Going to Town. Wilder, Laura I. LC 92-46722. (gr. k-3). 1994. 15.00 (0-06-023012-6); PLB 14.89 (0-06-023013-4) HarpC Child Bks.

—Kirsten Learns a Lesson: A School Story. Shaw, Janet. Thieme, Jeanne, ed. 72p. (gr. 2-5). 1986. 12.95 (0-937295-09-4); PLB 12.95 (0-937295-82-5); pap. 5.95 (0-937295-10-8) Pleasant Co.

—Kirsten Saves the Day: A Summer Story. Shaw, Janet. Thieme, Jeanne, ed. 72p. (gr. 2-5). 1988. 12.95 (0-937295-38-8); PLB 12.95 (0-937295-91-4); pap. 5.95 (0-937295-39-6) Pleasant Co.

—Kirsten's Surprise: A Christmas Story. Shaw, Janet. Thieme, Jeanne, ed. 72p. (gr. 2-5). 1986. 12.95 (0-937295-18-3); PLB 12.95 (0-937295-85-X); pap. 5.95 (0-937295-19-1) Pleasant Co.

—Meet Kirsten: An American Girl. Shaw, Janet B. Thieme, Jeanne, ed. 72p. (gr. 2-5). 1986. 12.95 (0-937295-00-0); PLB 12.95 (0-937295-79-5); pap. 5.95 (0-937295-01-9) Pleasant Co.

—What a Wonderful World. Weiss, George D. & Thiele, Bob. 24p. 1993. 12.95 (0-7935-1840-7, 00183009) H Leonard Pub Corp.

—Winter Days in the Big Woods. Wilder, Laura I. LC 92-45883. (gr. 1-8). 1994. 15.00 (0-06-023014-2); PLB 14.89 (0-06-023022-3) HarpC Child Bks.

Graef, Renee & Lackner, Paul. Kirsten, 6 bks. Shaw, Janet. 400p. (gr. 2-5). 1991. Boxed Set. 74.95 (1-56247-012-4); Boxed Set. lib. bdg. 74.95 (1-56247-049-3); Boxed Set. pap. 34.95 (0-937295-76-0) Pleasant Co.

Graef, Renne. Happy Birthday Kirsten! A Springtime Story. Shaw, Janet. Thieme, Jeanne, ed. 72p. (gr. 2-5). 1987. 12.95 (0-937295-32-9); PLB 12.95 (0-937295-88-4); pap. 5.95 (0-937295-33-7) Pleasant Co.

Graeff, Benny, et al. Notre Langue Louisianaise: Our Louisiana Language, Bk. 1. Gelhay, Patrick & Marcantel, David E. LC 85-81018. (ENG & FRE.). 180p. (gr. 4). 1985. text ed. 14.95 (0-935085-00-9); Tchr's ed. 14.95 (0-935085-01-7); write for info. Dialogue Booklet (0-935085-03-3); Cassette Tape Set 49.95 (0-935085-02-5) Ed Francaises.

Graf, Heidi & Sturms, Aina. Apple Technic Control One Technology Pack. Barrowman, Tom, et al. Helgoe, Cathy & Lough, Tom, eds. 416p. (gr. 6-12). 1991. 575.00 (0-914831-75-5, 958) Lego Dacta.

—MS-DOS Technic Control One Technology Pack. Barrowman, Tom, et al. Helgoe, Cathy & Lough, Tom, eds. 416p. (gr. 6-12). 1991. 595.00 (0-914831-78-X, 968) Lego Dacta.

—Technic Control One Resource Guide. Barrowman, Tom, et al. Helgoe, Cathy & Lough, Tom, eds. 416p. (gr. 6-12). 1991. text ed. 75.00 (0-914831-74-7, 959) Lego Dacta.

Graham, Alastair. Down on the Funny Farm: A Step Two Book. King, P. E. LC 85-11893. 48p. (gr. 1-3). 1986. PLB 7.99 (0-394-97460-3); pap. 3.50 (0-394-87460-9) Random Bks Yng Read.

—Our Planet Earth. Wood, Tim. LC 91-26681. 32p. (ps-2). 1992. pap. 5.95 (0-689-71589-7, Aladdin) Macmillan Child Grp.

Graham, Bob. Family Car Book. Ingram, Anne & O'Donnell, Peggy. 48p. (gr. 4 up). 1992. pap. 6.95 (0-920775-43-8, Pub. by Greey dePencier CN) Firefly Bks Ltd.

—Grandad's Magic. Graham, Bob. LC 88-83007. (gr. k-2). 1989. 13.95 (0-316-32321-7) Little.

—Greetings from Sandy Beach. Graham, Bob. 32p. (ps-3). 1992. 12.95 (0-916291-40-5) Kane-Miller Bk.

—Poems for the Very Young. Rosen, Michael, ed. LC 92-45574. 80p. (gr. k-3). 1993. 15.95 (1-85697-908-3) Kingfisher Bks.

—Rose Meets Mr. Wintergarten. Graham, Bob. LC 91-71824. 32p. (ps up) 1992. 14.95 (1-56402-039-8) Candlewick Pr.

Graham, Critt. The Bloody Summer of Seventeen Forty-Two: A Colonial Boy's Journal. Blackburn, Joyce. 64p. (gr. 5-8). 1985. pap. 4.25 (0-930803-00-0) Fort Frederica.

Graham, David, photos by. The U. S. Space Camp Book of Rockets. Baird, Anne. Aldrin, Edwin E. & Buckbee, Edward O.frwd. by. LC 93-26148. 1993. write for info. (0-688-12228-0); PLB write for info. (0-688-12229-9) Morrow Jr Bks.

Graham, Florence. The Little Engine That Could & the Big Chase. Muntean, Michaela. 32p. (ps-2). 1988. pap. 1.95 (0-448-19095-8, Platt & Munk Pubs) Putnam Pub Group.

—The Tale of Peter Rabbit. Potter, Beatrix. LC 85-70809. 13p. (ps). 1986. 3.95 (0-448-10224-2, G&D) Putnam Pub Group.

—The Tale of Peter Rabbit. Potter, Beatrix. 32p. 1991. pap. 2.25 (0-448-40061-8, Platt & Munk Pubs) Putnam Pub Group.

—The Velveteen Rabbit. Williams, Margery. 32p. (ps-2). 1987. pap. 2.25 (0-448-19083-4, Platt & Munk); (Platt & Munk) Putnam Pub Group.

Graham, Jack. It Always Rains after a Dry Spell. Trimble, Marshall. 288p. (Orig.). (gr. 6 up). 1992. pap. 12.95 (0-918080-67-3) Treasure Chest.

Graham, Jennifer. Just Enough. Salem, Lynn & Stewart, Josie. 12p. (gr. 1). 1992. pap. 3.50 (1-880612-12-7) Seedling Pubns.

—My Pet. Salem, Lynn & Stewart, Josie. 8p. (gr. 1). 1992. pap. 3.50 (1-880612-11-9) Seedling Pubns.

—The Regal Beagle. Lesterson, David. Hoffman, Beverly, et al. eds. LC 93-70504. 29p. (gr. 3). Date not set. write for info. (0-9634122-3-X) Feather Fables.

Graham, Margaret B. All Falling Down. Zion, Gene. LC 51-12571. 32p. (ps-1). 1951. PLB 13.89 (0-06-026831-X) HarpC Child Bks.

—Be Nice to Spiders. Graham, Margaret B. LC 67-17101. 32p. (gr. k-3). 1967. PLB 14.89 (0-06-022073-2) HarpC Child Bks.

—Harry & the Lady Next Door. Zion, Gene. LC 60-9452. 64p. (gr. k-3). 1978. pap. 3.50 (0-06-444008-7, Trophy) HarpC Child Bks.

—Harry by the Sea. Zion, Gene. LC 65-21302. 32p. (gr. k-3). 1965. 14.00 (0-06-026855-7); PLB 14.89 (0-06-026856-5) HarpC Child Bks.

—Harry by the Sea. Zion, Gene. LC 65-21302. 32p. (ps-3). 1976. pap. 4.95 (0-06-443010-3, JP 10, Trophy) HarpC Child Bks.

—Harry the Dirty Dog. Zion, Gene. LC 56-8137. 32p. (gr. k-3). 1956. 15.00 (0-06-026865-4); PLB 14.89 (0-06-026866-2) HarpC Child Bks.

—Harry the Dirty Dog. Zion, Gene. LC 56-8137. 32p. (ps-3). 1976. pap. 4.95 (0-06-443009-X, Trophy) HarpC Child Bks.

—It's Spring! Minarik, Else H. LC 87-37202. 24p. (ps up). 1989. 11.95 (0-688-07619-X); PLB 11.88 (0-688-07620-3) Greenwillow.

—No Roses for Harry. Zion, Gene. LC 58-7752. (gr. k-3). 1958. 14.00 (0-06-026890-5); PLB 13.89 (0-06-026891-3) HarpC Child Bks.

—No Roses for Harry! Zion, Gene. LC 58-7752. 32p. (ps-3). 1976. pap. 4.95 (0-06-443011-1, Trophy) HarpC Child Bks.

—Storm Book. Zolotow, Charlotte. LC 52-7880. (gr. k-3). 1952. PLB 13.89 (0-06-027026-8) HarpC Child Bks.

—The Storm Book. Zolotow, Charlotte. LC 52-7880. 32p. (ps-3). 1989. pap. 4.95 (0-06-443194-0, Trophy) HarpC Child Bks.

Graham, Mark. Anne of the Island. Montgomery, Lucy M. 288p. (gr. 4 up). 1992. 14.95 (0-448-40311-0, G&D) Putnam Pub Group.

—Charlie Anderson. Abercrombie, Barbara. LC 89-2449. 32p. (ps-4). 1990. SBE 13.95 (0-689-50486-1, M K McElderry) Macmillan Child Grp.

—Greenbrook Farm. Pryor, Bonnie. LC 89-11573. 40p. (ps-2). 1993. pap. 4.95 (0-671-79606-2, S&S BFYR) S&S Trade.

—Home by Five. Wallace-Brodeur, Ruth. LC 90-39854. 32p. (gr. k-4). 1992. SBE 13.95 (0-689-50509-4, M K McElderry) Macmillan Child Grp.

—Louisa May Alcott: Her Girlhood Diary. Ryan, Cary, ed. LC 92-22343. 56p. (gr. 5 up). 1993. PLB 14.95 (0-8167-3139-X); pap. write for info. (0-8167-3150-0) BrdgeWater.

—Michael & the Cats. Abercrombie, Barbara. LC 92-23950. 32p. (ps-2). 1993. SBE 13.95 (0-689-50543-4, M K McElderry) Macmillan Child Grp.

—Murphy & Kate. Howard, Ellen. LC 93-26002. 1994. write for info. (0-671-79775-1, S&S BFYR) S&S Trade.

—My Father's Hands. Ryder, Joanne. LC 93-27116. 1994. write for info. (0-689-09189-X); PLB write for info. (0-688-09190-3) Morrow Jr Bks.

—Roommates Again. Galbraith, Kathryn O. LC 93-8709. 1994. write for info. (0-689-50592-2, M K McElderry) Macmillan Child Grp.

—Roommates Again. Galbraith, Kathryn O. LC 93-8709. 48p. (gr. 1-4). 1994. SBE 13.95 (0-689-50597-3, M K McElderry) Macmillan Child Grp.

—Roommates & Rachel. Galbraith, Kathryn O. LC 90-34768. 48p. (gr. 1-4). 1991. SBE 12.95 (0-689-50520-5, M K McElderry) Macmillan Child Grp.

—Shadows are About. Paul, Ann W. 32p. 1992. 13.95 (0-590-44842-0, Scholastic Hardcover) Scholastic Inc.

—Where's the Baby? Paxton, Tom. LC 92-39875. 32p. (ps up). 1993. 15.00 (0-688-10692-7); PLB 14.93 (0-688-10693-5) Morrow Jr Bks.

—Wilderness Cat. Kinsey-Warnock, Natalie. LC 90-24250. 32p. (ps-3). 1992. 14.00 (0-525-65068-7, Cobblehill Bks) Dutton Child Bks.

Graham, Thomas. Day Breaks. VerDorn, Bethea. 32p. (ps-3). 1992. 14.95 (1-55970-187-0) Arcade Pub Inc.

—Mr. Bear's Chair. Graham, Thomas. LC 86-19920. 32p. (ps-2). 1990. 10.95 (0-525-44300-2, DCB); pap. 3.95 (0-525-44651-6, DCB) Dutton Child Bks.

—Mr. McGill Goes to Town. Aylesworth, Jim. LC 89-31111. 32p. (ps-2). 1989. 13.95 (0-8050-0772-5, Owlet BYR) H Holt & Co.

—Mr. McGill Goes to Town. Aylesworth, Jim. LC 89-31111. 32p. (gr. k-2). 1992. pap. 4.95 (0-8050-2096-9, Owlet BYR) H Holt & Co.

—Moon Glows. Ver Dorn, Bethea. 32p. (ps-1). 1990. text ed. 14.95 (1-55970-073-4) Arcade Pub Inc.

Grahame-Johnstone, Anne, jt. illus. see Grahame-Johnstone, Janet.

Grahame-Johnstone, Janet & Grahame-Johnstone, Anne. The Hundred & One Dalmatians. Smith, Dodie. 208p. (gr. 1 up). 1976. pap. 2.50 (0-380-00628-6, Camelot) Avon.

Graham-Rice, Kathy. Jump with Jeremy: What Hoosiers Do on the Way to the Zoo. Thomas, Mary A. Hodge, Ellen & Poore, Luz, eds. Still, James & Escabar, URias, trs. from ENG. (SPA.). 47p. (Orig.). 1988. pap. 9.95 (0-944326-00-5) Childrens Corner.

Grainger, Sam, photos by. The First Words Picture Book. Gillham, Bill. LC 81-12452. 32p. (gr. 1-5). 1982. 7.95 (0-698-20560-X, Coward) Putnam Pub Group.

Gramatky, Hardie. Little Toot. Gramatky, Hardie. LC 78-4801. (gr. k-3). 1978. (Putnam); (Putnam); pap. 7.95 (0-399-20649-3, Putnam) Putnam Pub Group.

—Little Toot & the Loch Ness Monster. Gramatky, Hardie & Gramatky, Dorothea C. 48p. (ps-3). 1989. 13.95 (0-399-21684-7, Putnam) Putnam Pub Group.

Grammell, Stephen. A Regular Rolling Noah. Lyon, George E. LC 86-8312. 32p. (ps-3). 1986. RSBE 13.95 (0-02-761330-5, Bradbury Pr) Macmillan Child Grp.

—Will's Mammoth. Martin, Rafe. 32p. (ps-3). 1989. 15.95 (0-399-21627-8, Putnam) Putnam Pub Group.

Granderson, Eddie. The Painter Man. Johnson-Feelings, Dianne. LC 93-4063. 1993. write for info. (0-89334-220-3) Humanics Ltd.

GrandPre, Mary. Chin Yu Min & the Ginger Cat. Armstrong, Jennifer. LC 92-8658. 32p. (ps-4). 1993. 15.00 (0-517-58656-8); PLB 15.99 (0-517-58657-6) Crown Bks Yng Read.

—The Vegetables Go to Bed. King, Christopher L. LC 92-27650. 1994. write for info. (0-517-59125-1); PLB write for info. (0-517-59126-X) Crown Bks Yng Read.

Grandy, Chamie O. Ram Lam. Kyle, Louisa V. 76p. (gr. 3). 1985. 5.95 (0-927044-02-1) Four OClock Farms.

Granger, Paul. The Abominable Snowman. large type ed. Montgomery, Raymond A. 116p. (gr. 2-7). 1987. 8.95 (0-942545-02-8); PLB 9.95 (0-942545-08-7, Dist. by Grolier) Grey Castle.

—Journey under the Sea. large type ed. Montgomery, Raymond A. 117p. (gr. 3-7). 1987. Repr. of 1977 ed. 8.95 (0-942545-04-4); PLB 9.95 (0-942545-10-9, Dist. by Grolier) Grey Castle.

—Space & Beyond. large type ed. Montgomery, Raymond A. 117p. (gr. 3-7). 1987. Repr. of 1979 ed. 8.95 (0-942545-11-7); PLB 9.95 (0-942545-16-8, Dist. by Grolier) Grey Castle.

—Who Killed Harlowe Thrombey, No. 9. large type ed. Packard, Edward. 121p. (gr. 3-7). 1987. Repr. of 1981 ed. 8.95 (0-942545-13-3); PLB 9.95 (0-942545-18-4, Dist. by Grolier) Grey Castle.

—Your Code Name Is Jonah. large type ed. Packard, Edward. 114p. (gr. 3-7). 1987. Repr. of 1979 ed. 8.95 (0-942545-15-X); PLB 9.95 (0-942545-20-6, Dist. by Grolier) Grey Castle.

Grant, Donald. Airplanes & Flying Machines. (ps). 1992. bds. 10.95 (0-590-45267-3, 037, Cartwheel) Scholastic Inc.

—The Barbarians. Bombarde, Odile. LC 87-34092. 38p. (gr. k-5). 1988. 4.95 (0-944589-10-3, 103) Young Discovery Lib.

—Following Indian Trails. Grenier, Nicolas. LC 87-34597. 38p. (gr. k-5). 1988. 4.95 (0-944589-09-X, 09X) Young Discovery Lib.

—Going West: Cowboys & Pioneers. Courtault, Martine. Bogard, Vicki, tr. from FRE. LC 89-5365. 38p. (gr. k-5). 1989. 4.95 (0-944589-21-9, 021) Young Discovery Lib.

—Living with the Eskimos. Planche, Bernard. Matthews, Sarah, tr. from FRE. LC 87-31805. 38p. (gr. k-5). 1988. 4.95 (0-944589-12-X, 12X) Young Discovery Lib.

—Musical Instruments. Delafosse, Claude. 24p. (ps-2). 1994. 11.95 (0-590-47729-3, Cartwheel) Scholastic Inc.

Grant, Elaine. Critter Crafts. Grant, Elaine. 30p. (gr. 4-7). 1991. pap. 9.95 spiral bdg. (0-9632722-0-9) Arteg Creations.

Grant, Kenneth L. The Story Cloud. Edens, Cooper. LC 91-13315. 48p. (ps-1). 1991. jacketed, reinforced bdg. 16.00 (0-671-74823-8, Green Tiger) S&S Trade.

Grant, Larry & Jalbert, Marc. Unto Dust You Shall Return. Geller, Norman. 16p. (gr. 6-10). 1986. pap. 4.95 (0-915753-11-1) N Geller Pub.

Grant, Leigh. Mystery of the Runaway Sled. Frost, Erica. LC 78-60124. 48p. (gr. 2-4). 1979. PLB 10.89 (0-89375-089-1); pap. 3.50 (0-89375-077-8) Troll Assocs.

—Shoeshine Girl. Bulla, Clyde R. LC 75-8516. 64p. (gr. 2-5). 1989. pap. 3.95 (0-06-440228-2, Trophy) HarpC Child Bks.

—Wonders of the Pond. Sabin, Francene. LC 81-7407. 32p. (gr. 2-4). 1982. PLB 11.59 (0-89375-576-1); pap. text ed. 2.95 (0-89375-577-X); cassette 9.95 (0-685-04956-6) Troll Assocs.

Grant, Leslie. My First Flight. rev. ed. Moore, Kathryn C. Hutson, Ronald, ed. (ps-4). 1991. PLB 3.95 (0-9633295-0-2) K Cs Bks N Stuff. "This looks just like a real airplane!" "This is exactly what happens on an airplane trip, I know a lot of adults who need this book." "It's so easy to understand - & it's fun! These are just a few of the comments about MY FIRST FLIGHT - a children's coloring activities book. MY FIRST FLIGHT describes what goes on when you take an airplane trip from the time that you arrive at the airport until the time that you land. It is written in narrative rhyme & illustrated in coloring book style. The reader is acquainted with airline personnel, the airplane - its safety features & travel comforts & things that you can do to facilitate your own comfort (i.e. pressurization, etc.). In addition to the story there are travel related games, a flight log page, & a flight facts page. This activities book is the perfect travel companion for the unaccompanied minor. A number of parents & teachers have reviewed MY FIRST FLIGHT. They have found it to be creative, comprehensive, educational & entertaining. Welcome aboard with MY FIRST FLIGHT. Sit back enjoy the ride & have fun. Retail price $2.95. *Publisher Provided Annotation.*

Grant, Peggy. Forty Fabulous Fables of Aesop. Krill, Richard M. 90p. (gr. 3-6). 1982. 7.95 (0-942624-00-9) Promethean Arts.

Grater, Lindsay. Anna's Red Sled. Quinlan, Patricia. 24p. (ps-2). 1989. 12.95 (1-55037-073-1, Pub. by Annick CN); pap. 4.95 (1-55037-072-3, Pub. by Annick CN) Firefly Bks Ltd.

—One Hundred Shining Candles. Lunn, Janet. LC 90-8892. 32p. (gr. 2-4). 1991. SBE 13.95 (0-684-19280-2, Scribners Young Read) Macmillan Child Grp.

—Runaway Row. Grater, Lindsay. 24p. (ps-3). 1992. PLB 15.95 (1-55037-213-0, Pub. by Annick CN); pap. 5.95 (1-55037-210-6, Pub. by Annick CN) Firefly Bks Ltd.

Graves, Elizabeth. An Ancient Castle. Graves, Robert. Thomas, William D., afterword by. LC 81-17204. 72p. (gr. 7 up). 1981. 13.95 (0-935576-06-1); pap. 8.95 (0-935576-33-9) Kesend Pub Ltd.

Graves, Katheryn. Gifts of the Season: Life among the Northwest Indians. Batdorf, Carol. 24p. (Orig.). (gr. 1-6). 1990. pap. 5.95 (0-88839-246-X) Hancock House.

Graves, Keith. Clovis Crawfish & His Friends. rev. ed. Fontenot, Mary A. LC 85-16994. 32p. (ps-3). 1985. 12.95 (0-88289-479-X) Pelican.

—Clovis Crawfish & His Friends: French Edition. Fontenot, Mary A. (FRE.). 32p. (ps-3). 1994. write for info. Pelican.

—Clovis Crawfish & Petit Papillon. Fontenot, Mary A. LC 83-27325. 52p. (ps-3). 1985. Repr. 12.95 (0-88289-448-X) Pelican.

Graves, Linda, jt. illus. see Spellman, Susan.

Graves, Sharol. The People Shall Continue. Ortiz, Simon. LC 88-18929. 24p. (gr. 2-7). 1988. 13.95 (0-89239-041-7) Childrens Book Pr.

Gray, Carole. Christmas Nativity Diorama. (ps-1). 1992. pap. 13.00 case, shrinkwrapped (0-671-78513-3, S&S BFYR) S&S Trade.

Gray, Cissy. Honu. Coste, Marion. 32p. (ps-4). 1993. 9.95 (0-8248-1507-6) UH Pr.

—Nene. Coste, Marion. LC 92-36543. 32p. 1993. 9.95 (0-8248-1389-8, Kolowalu Bk) UH Pr.

—To Find the Way. Nunes, Susan. LC 91-31334. 48p. (gr. 4-8). 1992. 12.95 (0-8248-1376-6) UH Pr.

Gray, Dan, jt. illus. see Macdonald, Roland B.

Gray, Don. Children's Stories. Steber, Rick. 60p. (Orig.). 1989. pap. 4.95 (0-945134-06-1); cassette 9.95 (0-945134-56-8) Bonanza Pub.

—Cowboys. Steber, Rick. 60p. (Orig.). 1988. pap. 4.95 (0-945134-04-5); cassette 9.95 (0-945134-54-1) Bonanza Pub.

—Grandpa's Stories. Steber, Rick. 60p. (Orig.). 1991. pap. 4.95 (0-945134-10-X); cassette 9.95 (0-945134-60-6) Bonanza Pub.

—Indians. Steber, Rick. 60p. (Orig.). 1987. pap. 4.95 (0-945134-03-7); cassette 9.95 (0-945134-53-3) Bonanza Pub.

—Loggers. Steber, Rick. 60p. (Orig.). 1989. pap. 4.95 (0-945134-07-X); cassette 9.95 (0-945134-57-6) Bonanza Pub.

—Miners. Steber, Rick. 60p. (Orig.). 1990. pap. 4.95 (0-945134-09-6); cassette 9.95 (0-945134-59-2) Bonanza Pub.

—Mountain Men. Steber, Rick. 60p. (Orig.). 1990. 4.95 (0-945134-08-8); cassette 9.95 (0-945134-58-4) Bonanza Pub.

—Oregon Trail. Steber, Rick. 60p. (Orig.). 1986. pap. 4.95 (0-945134-01-0); 9.95 (0-945134-51-7) Bonanza Pub.

—Pacific Coast. Steber, Rick. 60p. (Orig.). 1987. pap. 4.95 (0-945134-02-9); cassette 9.95 (0-945134-52-5) Bonanza Pub.

—Women of the West. Steber, Rick. 60p. (Orig.). 1988. pap. 4.95 (0-945134-05-3); cassette 9.95 (0-945134-55-X) Bonanza Pub.

Gray, Don, jt. illus. see Gildemeister, Jerry.

Gray, Harold. Little Orphan Annie in the Great Depression. Gray, Harold. 58p. (Orig.). (gr. 5 up) 1979. pap. 3.95 (0-486-23737-0) Dover.

Gray, Harrel. Teacher's Guide for Uncle Noel's Fun Fables. Renshaw, Polly & Levens, Ann. 52p. (gr. 2-5). 1991. wkbk. 5.95 (0-9630734-1-9) Aesop Systs.

—Uncle Noel's Fun Fables Program. Rideau, S. Noel. 80p. (gr. 2-5). 1991. wkbk. 8.95 (0-9630734-0-0) Aesop Systs.

Gray, Heather. Beginning of the World. Goldstein-Alpern, Neva. 12p. (ps). 1987. 4.95 (0-910818-73-8) Judaica Pr.

—Ying-Ling Does Mitzvot. Goldstein-Alpern, Neva. 12p. (ps). 1987. 4.95 (0-910818-72-X) Judaica Pr.

Gray, Les. The Good-for-Something Dragon. Enderle, Judith R. & Tessler, Stephanie G. 32p. (ps-3). 1993. pap. 14.95 (1-56397-214-X) Boyds Mills Pr.

Gray, Linda. Mommy Breastfeeds Our Baby. Carroll, Teresa P. (Orig.). (ps) 1990. pap. 4.95 (0-9626614-0-6) NuBaby AL.

Gray, Rob. Riddles about Christmas. Ashley, Jill. Brook, Bonnie, ed. 32p. (ps-3). 1990. 6.95 (0-671-70554-7); PLB 10.98 (0-671-70552-0) Silver Pr.

—Riddles about Hannukah. Poskanzer, Susan. Brook, Bonnie, ed. 32p. (ps-3). 1990. 6.95 (0-671-70555-5); PLB 10.98 (0-671-70553-9) Silver Pr.

Gray, Rob, photos by. Riddles about Easter. Ashley, Jill. 32p. (ps-3). 1990. 6.95 (0-671-72727-3); PLB 10.98 (0-671-72726-5) Silver Pr.

—Riddles about Passover. Poskanzer, Susan. 32p. (ps-3). 1991. 6.95 (0-671-72725-7); PLB 10.98 (0-671-72724-9) Silver Pr.

Gray, Steve. Easily Fooled: New Insights & Techniques for Resisting Manipulation. rev. ed. Fellows, Bob. 64p. (Orig.). (gr. 7 up). 1989. pap. 5.95 (0-9622879-0-3) Mind Matters.

Grebu, Devis. Joseph Who Loved the Sabbath. Hirsh, Marilyn. 32p. (ps-3). 1988. pap. 3.95 (0-14-050670-5, Puffin Bk) Puffin Bks.

—The King's Chessboard. Birch, David. LC 87-20164. 32p. (gr. k up). 1988. PLB 10.89 (0-8037-0367-8) Dial Bks Young.

—The King's Chessboard. Birch, David. 32p. (gr. k up) 1993. pap. 4.99 (0-14-054880-7, Puffin Pied Piper) Puffin Bks.

Greder, Armin. Danny in the Toybox. Tulloch, Richard. LC 90-24637. 32p. (ps-3). 1991. 13.95 (0-688-10501-7, Tambourine Bks); PLB 13.88 (0-688-10502-5, Tambourine Bks) Morrow.

—The Great Big Scary Dog. Gleeson, Libby. LC 93-13398. 32p. (ps up). 1994. 15.00 (0-688-11293-5, Tambourine Bks); PLB 14.93 (0-688-11294-3, Tambourine Bks) Morrow.

—Uncle David. Gleeson, Libby. Greder, Armin, photos by. LC 92-18155. 32p. (ps up). 1993. 15.00 (0-688-12417-8, Tambourine Bks); PLB 14.93 (0-688-12418-6, Tambourine Bks) Morrow.

Greeley, Valerie. Field Animals. LC 83-22507. 12p. (gr. k-2). 1984. bds. 3.95 (0-911745-23-8, Bedrick Blackie) P Bedrick Bks.

—Where's My Share? Greeley, Valerie. LC 89-13299. 32p. (ps-1). 1990. SBE 12.95 (0-02-736761-4, Macmillan Child Bk) Macmillan Child Grp.

—White Is the Moon. Greeley, Valerie. LC 90-40522. 32p. (ps-1). 1991. 12.95 (0-02-736915-3, Macmillan Child Bk) Macmillan Child Grp.

Green, Andy. Jenny Giraffe & the Streetcar Party. Dartez, Cecilia C. LC 93-9924. 32p. (gr. k-3). 1993. 14.95 (0-88289-962-7) Pelican.

Green, Ann C. Castles. Smith, Beth. Rakos, Jennie, ed. LC 87-25181. 96p. (gr. 7-9). 1988. PLB 10.90 (0-531-10511-3) Watts.

Green, Anne C. Cancer. Herda, D. J. LC 89-34131. 112p. (gr. 7-10). 1989. PLB 12.90 (0-531-10803-1) Watts.

—Carbohydrates. Silverstein, Alvin, et al. LC 91-41245. 48p. (gr. 3-6). 1992. PLB 13.90 (1-56294-207-7) Millbrook Pr.

—Compromise or Confrontation: Dealing with the Adults in Your Life. Mazzenga, Isabel B. LC 89-5711. 96p. (gr. 6-10). 1989. PLB 13.40 (0-531-10805-8) Watts.

—Dating. Quiri, Patricia R. LC 89-5709. 95p. (gr. 5-10). 1989. PLB 13.40 (0-531-10806-6) Watts.

—Fats. Silverstein, Alvin, et al. LC 91-42169. 48p. (gr. 3-6). 1992. PLB 13.90 (1-56294-208-5) Millbrook Pr.

—Good Grooming for Boys. Saunders, Rubie. 96p. (gr. 5-9). 1989. PLB 12.90 (0-531-10768-X) Watts.

—Good Grooming for Girls. Saunders, Rubie. 96p. (gr. 5-9). 1989. PLB 12.90 (0-531-10769-8) Watts.

—How to Write a Letter. rev. ed. Mischel, Florence. Greenberg, Lorna, ed. LC 88-10263. 72p. (gr. 5-9). 1988. PLB 10.90 (0-531-10587-3) Watts.

—Optical Illusions. White, Lawrence B. & Brockel, Ray. LC 86-10986. (gr. 4-9). 1986. PLB 10.90 (0-531-10220-3) Watts.

—Proteins. Silverstein, Alvin, et al. LC 91-41230. 48p. (gr. 3-6). 1992. PLB 13.90 (1-56294-209-3) Millbrook Pr.

—Puberty: The Story of Growth & Change. Packer, Kenneth L. LC 89-5665. 109p. (gr. 6-9). 1989. PLB 13.40 (0-531-10810-4) Watts.

—Vitamins & Minerals. Silverstein, Alvin, et al. LC 91-41231. 48p. (gr. 3-6). 1992. PLB 13.90 (1-56294-206-9) Millbrook Pr.

Green, Barry. Dinosaur Fun File. Hopwood, Clive. (gr. 3-6). 1992. pap. 4.95 (1-56680-508-2) Mad Hatter Pub.

—Jokes, Jokes & More Jokes. Border, Rosy, ed. 48p. (gr. 3-6). 1992. pap. 2.95 (1-56680-002-1) Mad Hatter Pub.

Green, Donald A. Washington Songs & Lore. Allen, Linda & Snider, Chrystle L., eds. 200p. (gr. 1-12). 1988. pap. 15.95 (0-9616441-3-3); Abridged ed., 72 pg. comb bdg. 8.95 (0-9616441-4-1) Melior Dist.

Green, Gloria. Five Senses. Brandt, Keith. LC 84-2633. 32p. (gr. 3-6). 1985. PLB 9.49 (0-8167-0168-7); pap. text ed. 2.95 (0-8167-0169-5) Troll Assocs.

Green, Gwen. Farming. Williams, Brian. LC 92-29905. 48p. (gr. 5-8). 1993. PLB 21.34 (0-8114-4786-3) Raintree Steck-V.

Green, Hamilton. George W. Goethals: Panama Canal Engineer. Latham, Jean L. 80p. (gr. 2-6). 1991. Repr. of 1965 ed. lib. bdg. 12.95 (0-7910-1440-1) Chelsea Hse.

Green, Herb. Stupid Stories: Nonstop Nonsense for Children of All Ages. Leonard, Robert J. 108p. (Orig.). (gr. 5-10). 1989. pap. 5.95 (0-930753-05-4, Pub. by Spectacle Ln Pr) Spect Ln Pr.

Green, James, et al. Human Reproductive Systems. Newman, Matt & Lemay, Nita K. (gr. 5-8). 1980. pap. text ed. 165.00 4 filmstrips, 4 cass., 24 skill sheets, Guide (0-89290-101-2, A794-SATC) Soc for Visual.

Green, John. Operation Elephant. Bailey, Jill. LC 90-46056. 48p. (gr. 3-7). 1991. PLB 18.60 (0-8114-2706-4); pap. 4.96 (0-8114-6554-3) Raintree Steck-V.

—Operation Turtle. Bailey, Jill. LC 91-19874. 48p. (gr. 3-7). 1992. PLB 18.60 (0-8114-2713-7); pap. 4.95 (0-8114-6546-2) Raintree Steck-V.

—Polar Bear Rescue. Bailey, Jill. LC 90-4490. 48p. (gr. 3-7). 1991. PLB 18.60 (0-8114-2708-0); pap. 4.95 (0-8114-6556-X) Raintree Steck-V.

—Project Dolphin. Bailey, Jill. LC 91-16007. 48p. (gr. 3-7). 1992. PLB 18.60 (0-8114-2711-0); pap. 4.95 (0-8114-6547-0) Raintree Steck-V.

—Project Whale. Bailey, Jill. LC 90-45159. 48p. (gr. 3-7). 1991. PLB 18.60 (0-8114-2707-2); pap. 4.95 (0-8114-6555-1) Raintree Steck-V.

—Save the Snow Leopard. Bailey, Jill. LC 90-45917. 48p. (gr. 3-7). 1991. PLB 18.60 (0-8114-2709-9); pap. 4.95 (0-8114-6557-8) Raintree Steck-V.

Green, Jonathan. Father & Son. Lauture, Denize. 32p. (ps-3). 1993. 14.95 (0-399-21867-X, Philomel Bks) Putnam Pub Group.

—Noah. Gauch, Patricia Lee. LC 92-44283. 1994. write for info. (0-399-22548-X, Philomel Bks) Putnam Pub Group.

Green, Ken. Martin Luther King, Jr. Thompson-Peters, Flossie E. Behrens, Debra J. & Jeffery, Lisa E., eds. 94p. (Orig.). (gr. 3-9). 1992. pap. 7.50 (1-880784-06-8) Atlas Pr.

Green, Kenneth L. Dynamic Black Americans. Thompson-Peters, Flossie E. 32p. (gr. 1-8). 1988. pap. 4.70 (1-880784-07-6) Atlas Pr. DYNAMIC BLACK AMERICANS, a biographical series, is written by Flossie E. Thompson-Peters in lilting, rhythmic verse. Young readers find these books exciting as well as informative. Ideal as core literature, choral reading, dramatizations & read aloud books. JAN, THE SHOEMAN, Jan Matzeliger (inventor), BENJAMIN BANNEKER, 3rd ed.

(1994) (pioneer urban planner), JEAN BAPTISTE DuSABLE (founder of Chicago), New Spanish edition available 2/94, MALCOLM X, HARRIET TUBMAN (freedom fighter & Civil War heroine), & DANIEL HALE WILLIAMS (first successful open heart surgeon). Ages 7-14, Appropriate for elementary grades & selected secondary & ESL students. DYNAMIC BLACK AMERICAN SERIES. ISBN 1-880784-07-6. $4.70 per copy. $23.50 for series (5 books). Paperback. THE SHEPHERD, A BIOGRAPHY of Dr. Arthur A. Peters, by Flossie Thompson-Peters, is about a community activist, civil rights leader & Los Angeles minister who started a church in 1943 & became a great influence in the civic, spiritual & political life of the African-American community of Los Angeles. "The book is of historical significance & is of more than local interest."--L.A. Times Book Review. Photographs. General interest. Hardcover, 251 pages. $10.00. ISBN 1-880784-00-9. MARTIN LUTHER KING, JR. is a biography by Flossie Thompson-Peters in poetic, rhythmic style. Thhe life of Dr. King is chronicled from childhood, through trials & triumphs, to his tragic end, with emphasis upon his lasting influence. Ages 8 to adult. 94 pages. $7.50 ISBN 1-880784-06-8. Atlas Press, P.O. Box 56282. Jesse J. Peters, President. Los Angeles, CA 90008. (213) 295-3036.
Publisher Provided Annotation.

—El-Hajj Malik El-Shabazz: The Biography of Malcolm X. Thompson-Peters, Flossie E. Behrens, Debra J. & Jeffery, Lisa E., eds. 65p. (Orig.). (gr. 4-12). 1994. pap. 8.00 (*1-880784-08-4*) Atlas Pr.
Green, Leia A. I Am Special Too: Circle of Angels Workbook. Greene, Leia A. 99p. (gr. k-9). 1991. 18.95 (*1-880737-00-0*) Crystal Jrns.
—When the Earth Was New: An Experience in Healing Our Planet. Greene, Leia A. 20p. (gr. k-9). 1991. wkbk. 4.95 (*1-880737-02-7*) Crystal Jrns.
Green, Maureen, et al. My Magic Garden. Klipper, Ilse. 91p. (Orig.). (gr. 2-6). 1980. pap. 5.95 (*0-9605022-0-3*) Pathwys Pr CA.
Green, Michael. Miniature Velveteen Rabbit Gift Set. Williams, Margery. 88p. (ps-8). 1991. net, incl. plush bunny 2.79 (*0-89471-978-5*) Running Pr.
—The Velveteen Rabbit. Williams, Margery. LC 89-42996. 88p. (gr. 1-8). 1989. 4.95 (*0-89471-755-3*) Running Pr.
—The Velveteen Rabbit: Or How Toys Become Real. Williams, Margery. LC 81-1454. 48p. (Orig.). (gr. k-12). 1984. 9.98 (*0-89471-266-7*); Book & plush toy gift set. 22.98 (*0-89471-885-1*) Courage Bks.
Green, Mim. Honi's Circle of Trees. Gershator, Phillis. LC 93-29748. 1994. write for info. (*0-8276-0511-0*) JPS Phila.
Green, Norma. Christopher Columbus: A Step Two Book. Krensky, Stephen. LC 89-62507. 48p. (Orig.). (gr. 1-3). 1991. lib. bdg. 7.99 (*0-679-90369-0*); pap. 3.50 (*0-679-80369-6*) Random Bks Yng Read.
Green, Norman. Knights of the Round Table. Gross, Gwen. LC 85-2176. 96p. (gr. 2-6). 1993. lib. bdg. 5.99 (*0-394-97579-0*); pap. 2.99 (*0-394-87579-6*) Random Bks Yng Read.
—Wild Lion of the Sea. Reed, Don C. (gr. 5 up). 1992. 14.95 (*0-316-73661-9*) Little.
Green, Phillip M. Let's Talk about Living in a World with Violence: An Activity Book for School-Age Children. Garbarino, James. Csaszar, Sonia, tr. (SPA.). 48p. (gr. k-8). 1993. wkbk. 10.00 (*0-9639159-0-8*) Erikson Inst.
Green, Richard. Sing, Like a Hermit Thrush. Green, Richard G. Longboat, Dianne, ed. Doxtater, Michael, intro. by. 112p. (Orig.). (gr. 6). 1990. pap. 7.95x (*0-911737-01-4*) Ricara Features.
Green, Robina. Shakespeare's Stories: Histories. Birch, Beverly, retold by. LC 88-15693. 126p. (gr. 7-12). 1988. 12.95 (*0-87226-192-1*) P Bedrick Bks.
—Shakespeare's Stories: Histories. Birch, Beverley. LC 88-15693. 126p. (gr. 7-12). 1990. pap. 6.95 (*0-87226-226-X*) P Bedrick Bks.
—Shakespeare's Stories: Histories. Birch, Beverley, retold by. LC 93-13203. 1993. 6.99 (*0-517-09359-6*, Pub. by Wings Bks) Outlet Bk Co.

—What Makes Things Move? Althea. LC 90-10924. 32p. (gr. k-3). 1991. PLB 11.59 (*0-8167-2124-6*); pap. text ed. 3.95 (*0-8167-2125-4*) Troll Assocs.
Green, Robina, jt. illus. see Farmer, Andrew.
Green, Roy. Abraham. Lingo, Susan L. & Downey, Melissa C. 32p. (ps-7). 1992. wkbk. 3.99 (*0-87403-915-0*, 23-02525) Standard Pub.
—Daniel. Lingo, Susan L. & Downey, Melissa C. 32p. (ps-7). 1992. wkbk. 3.99 (*0-87403-919-3*, 23-02529) Standard Pub.
—David. Lingo, Susan L. & Downey, Melissa C. 32p. (ps-7). 1992. wkbk. 3.99 (*0-87403-918-5*, 23-02528) Standard Pub.
—Early Life of Jesus. Downey, Melissa C. & Lingo, Susan L. Hayes, Theresa, ed. 32p. (Orig.). (gr. 1-5). 1994. wkbk. 3.99 (*0-7847-0140-7*) Standard Pub.
—Joshua. Lingo, Susan L. & Downey, Melissa C. 32p. (ps-7). 1992. wkbk. 3.99 (*0-87403-917-7*, 23-02527) Standard Pub.
—Miracles of Jesus. Downey, Melissa C. & Lingo, Susan L. Hayes, Theresa, ed. 32p. (Orig.). (gr. 1-5). 1994. wkbk. 3.99 (*0-7847-0141-5*) Standard Pub.
—Moses. Lingo, Susan L. & Downey, Melissa C. 112p. (ps-7). 1992. wkbk. 3.99 (*0-87403-916-9*, 23-02526) Standard Pub.
—New Life in Jesus. Downey, Melissa C. & Lingo, Susan L. Hayes, Theresa, ed. 32p. (Orig.). (gr. 1-5). 1994. wkbk. 3.99 (*0-7847-0143-1*) Standard Pub.
—Noah. Lingo, Susan L. & Downey, Melissa C. 32p. (ps-7). 1992. wkbk. 3.99 (*0-87403-914-2*, 23-02524) Standard Pub.
—Parables of Jesus. Downey, Melissa C. & Lingo, Susan L. Hayes, Theresa, ed. 32p. (Orig.). (gr. 1-5). 1994. wkbk. 3.99 (*0-7847-0142-3*) Standard Pub.
Green, Ruby & Kenyon, Tony. I Wonder Why I Blink: And Other Questions about My Body. Avison, Brigid. LC 92-45599. 32p. (gr. k-3). 1993. 8.95 (*1-85697-875-3*) Kingfisher Bks.
Green, Timothy. Mystery of Navajo Moon. Green, Timothy. LC 91-52600. 48p. (ps-4). 1991. 14.95 (*0-87358-523-2*) Northland AZ.
Green, Victor D. & Loor, Robin. Workbook Game Sheets for Kitchen Chemistry & Front Porch Physics. Hoyt, Marie A. 44p. (Orig.). (gr. 3-8). 1983. pap. text ed. 4.00 (*0-914911-02-3*) Educ Serv Pr.
Greenaway, Elizabeth. Cat Nap. Greenaway, Elizabeth. 14p. (ps). 1994. bds. 2.99 (*0-679-83958-5*) Random Bks Yng Read.
—Rabbit Food. Greenaway, Elizabeth. 14p. (ps). 1994. bds. 2.99 (*0-679-83959-3*) Random Bks Yng Read.
Greenaway, Frank. Whale. Papastavrov, Vasilli. 64p. (gr. 5 up). 1993. 15.00 (*0-679-83884-8*); PLB 15.99 (*0-679-93884-2*) Knopf Bks Yng Read.
Greenaway, Frank, photos by. Cave Life. Gunzi, Christiane. LC 92-53490. 32p. (gr. 2-5). 1993. 9.95 (*1-56458-212-4*) Dorling Kindersley.
—River Life. Taylor, Barbara. LC 92-52822. 32p. (gr. 2-5). 1992. 9.95 (*1-56458-130-6*) Dorling Kindersley.
—Shoreline. Taylor, Barbara. LC 92-53491. 32p. (gr. 2-5). 1993. 9.95 (*1-56458-213-2*) Dorling Kindersley.
—Tide Pool. Gunzi, Christiane. LC 92-52823. 32p. (gr. 2-5). 1992. 9.95 (*1-56458-131-4*) Dorling Kindersley.
Greenaway, Frank & King, Dave, photos by. Shark. MacQuitty, Miranda. LC 92-4712. 64p. 1992. 15.00 (*0-679-81683-6*); PLB 16.99 (*0-679-91683-0*) Knopf Bks Yng Read.
Greenaway, Frank, jt. photog. see Young, Jerry.
Greenaway, Kate. Mother Goose. 12p. (ps-5). 1973. pap. 3.25 (*0-914510-04-5*) Evergreen.
—The Pied Piper of Hamelin. Browning, Robert. LC 93-767. 1993. 5.99 (*0-517-09347-2*, Pub. by Derrydale Bks) Outlet Bk Co.
Greenberg, Melanie. How to Fill an Empty Lap. Lehmann, Terry & Nobisso, Joi. 32p. (Orig.). (ps). 1980. pap. text ed. 3.00 (*0-940112-00-0*) Little Feat.
Greenberg, Melanie H. At the Beach. Greenberg, Melanie H. LC 88-29995. 24p. (ps-2). 1989. 11.95 (*0-525-44474-2*, DCB) Dutton Child Bks.
—Celebrations: Our Jewish Holidays. Greenberg, Melanie H. LC 91-12744. 32p. (ps-3). 1991. 14.95 (*0-8276-0396-7*); pap. 9.95 (*0-8276-0505-6*) JPS Phila.
—It's My Earth Too: How I Can Help the Earth Stay Alive. Krull, Kathleen. (ps-2). 1992. 13.50 (*0-385-42088-9*) Doubleday.
—My Father's Luncheonette. Greenberg, Melanie H. LC 90-44586. 32p. (ps-2). 1991. 12.95 (*0-525-44725-3*, DCB) Dutton Child Bks.
Greenblat, Rodney A. Aunt Ippy's Museum of Junk. Greenblat, Rodney A. LC 90-44939. 32p. (gr. k-4). 1991. 14.95 (*0-06-022511-4*); PLB 14.89 (*0-06-022512-2*) HarpC Child Bks.
—Uncle Wizzmo's New Used Car. Greenblat, Rodney A. LC 89-36577. 32p. (ps-3). 1990. 13.95 (*0-06-022097-X*); PLB 13.89 (*0-06-022098-8*) HarpC Child Bks.
Greene, Bruce. All about Baby-Sitting: The Essential Guide for Concerned Parents & Baby-Sitters. Schepp, Steven. Berner, Lorraine, contrib. by. LC 82-81281. 267p. (Orig.). 1982. pap. 7.95 (*0-913279-00-5*) Non Fiction Pubns.
Greene, Jeffrey. Backyard Bear. Murphy, Jim. LC 92-15479. 32p. (gr. k-3). 1993. 15.95 (*0-590-44375-5*) Scholastic Inc.
Greene, Karen, jt. illus. see Heinz, Anna M.
Greene, Leia A. The Angel Told Me to Tell You Good-Bye. Greene, Leia A. 24p. (gr. k-12). 1991. pap. text ed. 4.95 (*1-880737-06-X*) Crystal Jrns.

—The Bridge Between Two Worlds. Greene, Leia A. 36p. (gr. k-12). 1992. pap. text ed. 4.95 (*1-880737-08-6*) Crystal Jrns.
—Crystals R for Kids. Greene, Leia A. 40p. (gr. k-12). 1991. wkbk. 4.95 (*1-880737-04-3*) Crystal Jrns.
—Exploring the Chakras. Greene, Leia A. 32p. (gr. k-12). 1991. wkbk. 4.95 (*1-880737-03-5*) Crystal Jrns.
—Happy Feet: A Child's Guide to Foot Reflexology. Greene, Leia A. 38p. (gr. k-12). 1992. wkbk. 4.95 (*1-880737-10-8*) Crystal Jrns.
—Mommy! Why Is Everyone Staring at Me? Greene, Leia A. (gr. k-12). 1992. wkbk. 4.95 (*1-880737-11-6*) Crystal Jrns.
—One Red Rose. Greene, Leia A. (gr. k-12). 1992. pap. text ed. 4.95 (*1-880737-07-8*) Crystal Jrns.
—Where Is God? Greene, Leia A. 40p. (gr. k-12). 1991. pap. text ed. 4.95 (*1-880737-05-1*) Crystal Jrns.
—Who's Afraid of the Dark? Greene, Leia A. 32p. (gr. k-12). 1992. pap. text ed. 4.95 (*1-880737-09-4*) Crystal Jrns.
Greene, Nathan. The Story of the Great Depression. Stein, R. Conrad. LC 85-11039. 32p. (gr. 3-6). 1985. PLB 13.27 (*0-516-04694-2*) Childrens.
—The Story of the Montgomery Bus Boycott. Stein, R. Conrad. LC 85-31349. 32p. (gr. 3-6). 1986. PLB 13.27 (*0-516-04697-7*); pap. 3.95 (*0-516-44697-5*) Childrens.
Greene, Tom. Becoming a Christian. Odor, Harold & Odor, Ruth. 16p. (gr. 3-7). 1985. 0.99 (*0-87239-901-X*, 3301) Standard Pub.
—Sharing Your Faith. Odor, Harold & Odor, Ruth. 16p. (gr. 3-7). 1985. 0.75 (*0-87239-902-8*, 3302) Standard Pub.
Greenhatch, Betty. Hooray for Snow. Beveridge, Barbara. LC 92-27098. 1993. 3.75 (*0-383-03573-2*) SRA Schl Grp.
Greenough, Jackie & Taylor, Pamela. Know Your Wheels. Taylor, Henry T. Bylenok, Marsha, contrib. by. 51p. (gr. 4-6). 1981. pap. write for info. (*0-938956-00-0*) H T Taylor.
Greenseid, Diane. Wilson Sat Alone. Hess, Debra. LC 93-17616. 1994. pap. 15.00 (*0-671-87046-7*, S&S BFYR) S&S Trade.
Greenspun, Adele A. Daddies. Greenspun, Adele A. 48p. 1991. 15.95 (*0-399-22259-6*, Philomel Bks) Putnam Pub Group.
Greenstein, Elaine. Emily & the Crows. Greenstein, Elaine. LC 91-39917. 28p. (gr. k up). 1992. pap. 14.95 (*0-88708-238-6*) Picture Bk Studio.
—Mrs. Rose's Garden. Greenstein, Elaine. 28p. (gr. k up). 1993. 14.95 (*0-88708-264-5*) Picture Bk Studio.
Greenstein, Susan. Wash Day. Bacon, Ron. LC 92-34270. 1993. 2.50 (*0-383-03665-8*) SRA Schl Grp.
—The Wind. Holkner, Jean. LC 92-21450. 1993. 3.75 (*0-383-03668-2*) SRA Schl Grp.
Greenwald, Joe. The King's Shadow. Larranaga, Robert D. 32p. (gr. k-3). 1991. PLB 18.95 (*0-87614-688-4*) Carolrhoda Bks.
Greenwald, Sheila. Alvin Webster's Surefire Plan for Success (& How It Failed) Greenwald, Sheila. 96p. (gr. 3-6). 1987. 12.95 (*0-316-32706-9*, Joy St Bks) Little.
—Give Us a Great Big Smile, Rosy Cole. Greenwald, Sheila. 80p. (gr. 3 up). 1981. 12.95 (*0-316-32672-0*, Joy St Bks) Little.
—The Little Leftover Witch. 2nd ed. Laughlin, Florence. LC 88-10551. 96p. (gr. 2-6). 1988. pap. 3.50 (*0-689-71273-1*, Aladdin) Macmillan Child Grp.
—The Little Leftover Witch. 3rd ed. Laughlin, Florence. LC 92-41166. 96p. (gr. 1-4). 1996. pap. 3.95 (*0-689-71742-3*, Aladdin) Macmillan Child Grp.
—Mat Pit & the Tunnel Tenants. Greenwald, Sheila. 128p. (gr. k-6). 1989. pap. 2.75 (*0-440-40155-0*, YB) Dell.
—The Pink Motel. Brink, Carol R. LC 92-17953. 224p. (gr. 3-7). 1993. pap. 3.95 (*0-689-71677-X*, Aladdin) Macmillan Child Grp.
—The Remarkable Ramsey. Rinkoff, Barbara. (gr. 2-6). 15.25 (*0-8446-6195-3*) Peter Smith.
—Rosy's Romance. Greenwald, Sheila. 96p. (gr. 3-6). 1989. 12.95 (*0-316-32704-2*, Joy St Bks) Little.
—The Secret Museum. Greenwald, Sheila. 128p. (gr. k-6). 1989. pap. 2.95 (*0-440-40148-8*, YB) Dell.
—Write on, Rosy! A Young Author in Crisis. Greenwald, Sheila. 128p. (gr. 3-6). 1988. 13.95 (*0-316-32705-0*, Joy St Bks) Little.
Greer, Charles. Miss Pickerell Meets Mr. H. U. M. new ed. MacGregor, Ellen & Pantell, Dora. 160p. (gr. 2-6). 1974. o.p. (*0-07-044577-X*) McGraw.

Greer, Deborah. The Backyard Detective: A Guide for Beginning Naturalists. Wong, Herbert H. LC 92-63342. 64p. (Orig.). (gr. k-5). 1993. pap. 7.95 (*1-882489-00-4*) NatureVision. THE BACKYARD DETECTIVE provides children with a headstart in science while they have fun exploring their own environment. This book & nature kit invite children to study nature by direct observation in easily accessible environments. With this fully-illustrated guide as an outdoor companion, they use simple science

tools & basic comparison charts to investigate nature's clues & uncover their own areas of interest. Young Backyard Detectives will have the opportunity to examine, identify, measure, grow, feed, & collect organisms. They will learn how to keep their own nature journal. This book encourages children to enjoy & respect their natural environment. Dr. Herbert H. Wong, the author, is a zoologist & science educator whose children's science books have become standard favorites among children & their teachers. The ecological concepts he uses to form the framework for THE BACKYARD DETECTIVE are diversity, interrelationships, adaptations & change. THE BACKYARD DETECTIVE is available in book form only, & also with the complete exploration kit (carrying case, magnifier, observation jar, pencil & measuring tape). AVAILABLE THROUGH BOOKPEOPLE & QUALITY BOOKS. *Publisher Provided Annotation.*

Greger, C. Shana. The Boy Who Spoke Colors. Gifaldi, David. LC 92-11301. 32p. (gr. 2-5). 1993. 14.95 (*0-395-65025-9*) HM.

Gregori, Lee. A Child's Garden of Verses. Stevenson, Robert Louis. LC 85-12766. (gr. 3 up). 1969. pap. 2.25 (*0-8049-0195-3*, CL-195) Airmont.

Gregori, Lee, jt. illus. see Ward, Lynd.

Gregory, Dorothy L. All Alone with Daddy: A Young Girl Plays the Role of Mother. Fassler, Joan. LC 76-80120. 32p. (ps-3). 1975. 16.95 (*0-87705-009-0*) Human Sci Pr.

Gregory, Miriam. My Furry Bear. Piequet, Miriam. Anyone Can Read Staff, ed. 43p. (Orig.). (gr. 3-5). 1985. 15.00 (*0-914275-02-X*) Anyone Can Read Bks.

Greiner, Robert. Follow My Leader. Garfield, James B. LC 57-1611. 192p. (gr. 4-6). 1957. pap. 13.95 (*0-670-32332-2*) Viking Child Bks.

Greiner, William. Sex Respect: The Option of True Sexual Freedom: A Public Health Workbook for Students. rev. ed. Mast, Coleen K. Forrestal, Julienne, ed. 118p. (gr. 7-9). 1990. pap. text ed. 8.95 (*0-945745-05-2*) Respect Inc.

Greisman, Joan, jt. illus. see Wittles, Harriet.

Grejniec, Michael. Good Morning, Good Night. Grejniec, Michael. LC 92-23530. 32p. (gr. k-3). 1993. 14.95 (*1-55858-173-1*); lib. bdg. 14.88 (*1-55858-174-X*) North-South Bks NYC.
—Look. Grejniec, Michael. LC 93-16066. 32p. (gr. k-3). 1993. 14.95 (*1-55858-212-6*); PLB 14.88 (*1-55858-213-4*) North-South Bks NYC.
—What Do You Like? Grejniec, Michael. LC 92-3481. 32p. (gr. k). 1992. 14.95 (*1-55858-175-8*); PLB 14.88 (*1-55858-176-6*) North-South Bks NYC.

Gremard, David. The Adventure of George the Dinosaur. Blake, Doron W. Lucas, Winafred B., ed. (ps-2). Date not set. English ed. write for info. (*1-882530-04-7*); Spanish ed. write for info. (*1-882530-09-8*) Deep Forest Pr.

Gresko, Bernetta. One-a-Day Writeamins. Gresko, Bernetta. 34p. 1987. pap. 4.95 (*0-939755-15-7*) Sunset Prods.

Gresko, Bernetta. How Do You Spell...? English Only. Gresko, Bernetta. 44p. (gr. 2-8). 1987. pap. 4.95 (*0-939755-11-4*); wkbk. act sheets 4.95 (*0-939755-14-9*); wkbk. crossword puzzles 4.95 (*0-939755-06-8*) Sunset Prods.
—How Do You Spell...? English to Spanish. Gresko, Bernetta. Gresko, Bernetta, tr. 44p. (gr. 2-8). 1987. pap. 4.95 (*0-939755-12-2*); wkbk. 4.95 (*0-939755-13-0*) Sunset Prods.
—Sound It Out. Gresko, Bernetta. 75p. (gr. 2-8). 1985. pap. 8.95 (*0-939755-10-6*) Sunset Prods.
—Writing Verbs. Gresko, Bernetta. 48p. 1982. wkbk. 4.95 (*0-939755-09-2*) Sunset Prods.

Gretz, Susann. Roger Loses His Marbles! Gretz, Susanna. 32p. (ps-2). 1991. pap. 3.95 (*0-8037-0986-2*, Dial Pied Piper) Puffin Bks.

Gretz, Susanna. Duck Takes Off. Gretz, Susanna. LC 90-3846. 32p. (ps-1). 1991. RSBE 12.95 (*0-02-737472-6*, Four Winds) Macmillan Child Grp.
—Frog, Duck & Rabbit. Gretz, Susanna. LC 91-16364. 32p. (ps-1). 1992. SBE 12.95 (*0-02-737327-4*, Four Winds) Macmillan Child Grp.
—Frog in the Middle. Gretz, Susanna. LC 90-3842. 32p. (ps-1). 1991. RSBE 12.95 (*0-02-737471-8*, Four Winds) Macmillan Child Grp.
—Rabbit Rambles On. Gretz, Susanna. LC 91-17069. 32p. (ps-1). 1992. SBE 12.95 (*0-02-737325-8*, Four Winds) Macmillan Child Grp.

—Roger Loses His Marbles. Gretz, Susanna. LC 88-3753. 32p. (ps-2). 1988. 11.95 (*0-8037-0565-4*) Dial Bks Young.
—Teddy Bears ABC. Gretz, Susanna. LC 86-4742. 32p. (ps-k). 1986. RSBE 13.95 (*0-02-738130-7*, Four Winds) Macmillan Child Grp.
—Teddy Bears at the Seaside. Gretz, Susanna & Sage, Alison. LC 88-11280. 32p. (gr. k-3). 1989. SBE 12.95 (*0-02-738141-2*, Four Winds) Macmillan Child Grp.
—Teddy Bears Go Shopping. Gretz, Susanna. LC 85-4494. 32p. (gr. k-3). 1984. RSBE 13.95 (*0-02-737310-X*, Four Winds) Macmillan Child Grp.
—Teddy Bears' Moving Day. Gretz, Susanna. LC 88-10365. 32p. (gr. k-3). 1988. pap. 3.95 (*0-689-71269-3*, Aladdin) Macmillan Child Grp.
—Teddy Bears Stay Indoors. Gretz, Susanna. LC 86-19511. 32p. (gr. k-3). 1987. SBE 13.95 (*0-02-738150-1*, Four Winds) Macmillan Child Grp.
—Teddy Bears 1 to 10. Gretz, Susanna. LC 86-4795. 32p. (ps-k). 1986. RSBE 13.95 (*0-02-738140-4*, Four Winds) Macmillan Child Grp.

Greunberg, Hannah. Felix's Hat. Bancroft, Catherine & Gruenberg, Hannah C. LC 92-10868. 32p. (ps-2). 1993. RSBE 14.95 (*0-02-708325-X*, Four Winds) Macmillan Child Grp.

Greve, Andreas. Christopher's Dream Car. Greve, Andreas. 32p. (gr. 1-3). 1991. PLB 15.95 (*1-55037-169-X*, Pub. by Annick CN); pap. 5.95 (*1-55037-166-5*, Pub. by Annick CN) Firefly Bks Ltd.

Grewe, Georgeann. Calendar Companions for Fall. Grewe, Georgeann & Glover, Susanne. 128p. (gr. 1-6). 1984. wkbk. 11.95 (*0-317-43005-X*, GA 534) Good Apple.
—Calendar Companions for Spring. Grewe, Georgeann & Glover, Susanne. 128p. (gr. 1-6). 1984. wkbk. 11.95 (*0-86653-171-8*, GA 536) Good Apple.
—Calendar Companions for Winter. Grewe, Georgeann & Glover, Susanne. 128p. (gr. 1-6). 1984. wkbk. 11.95 (*0-86653-168-8*, GA 535) Good Apple.
—A Splash of Fall. Glover, Susanne & Grewe, Georgeann. 128p. (gr. 2-5). 1987. pap. 11.95 (*0-86653-410-5*, GA1024) Good Apple.
—A Splash of Spring. Glover, Susanne & Grewe, Georgeann. 128p. (gr. 2-5). 1987. pap. 11.95 (*0-86653-412-1*, GA1026) Good Apple.
—A Splash of Winter. Glover, Susanne & Grewe, Georgeann. 128p. (gr. 2-5). 1987. pap. 11.95 (*0-86653-411-3*, GA1025) Good Apple.

Griego, Tony. The Green Gourd: A North Carolina Folktale. Hunter, C. W. 32p. (ps-3). 1992. PLB 14.95 (*0-399-22278-2*, Whitebird Bks) Putnam Pub Group.

Grifalconi, Ann. Darkness & the Butterfly. Grifalconi, Ann. 32p. (ps-3). 1987. 15.95 (*0-316-32863-4*) Little.
—Everett Anderson's Friend. Clifton, Lucille. LC 92-8030. 32p. (ps-2). 1992. 14.95 (*0-8050-2246-5*, Bks Young Read) H Holt & Co.
—Everett Anderson's Goodbye. Clifton, Lucille, et al. LC 82-23426. 32p. (ps-2). 1983. 14.95 (*0-8050-0235-9*, Bks Young Read) H Holt & Co.
—Everett Anderson's Goodbye. Clifton, Lucille. LC 82-23426. 32p. (ps-2). 1988. pap. 5.95 (*0-8050-0800-4*, Bks Young Read) H Holt & Co.
—Everett Anderson's Nine Month Long. Clifton, Lucille. LC 78-2402. 32p. (ps-2). 1978. 13.95 (*0-8050-0287-1*, Bks Young Read) H Holt & Co.
—Everett Anderson's Year. rev. ed. Clifton, Lucille. LC 92-4683. 32p. (ps-2). 1992. 14.95 (*0-8050-2247-3*, Bks Young Read) H Holt & Co.
—Everett Anderson's 1-2-3. Clifton, Lucille. LC 92-8031. 32p. (ps-2). 1992. 14.95 (*0-8050-2310-0*, Bks Young Read) H Holt & Co.
—How Far, Felipe? Gray, Genevieve. LC 77-11846. 64p. (gr. k-3). 1978. PLB 11.89 (*0-06-022108-9*) HarpC Child Bks.
—The Jazz Man. 2nd ed. Weik, Mary H. LC 93-9965. 48p. (gr. 3-7). 1993. pap. 3.95 (*0-689-71767-9*, Aladdin) Macmillan Child Grp.
—Kinda Blue. Grifalconi, Ann. (ps-3). 1993. 15.95 (*0-316-32869-3*) Little.
—The Midnight Fox. Byars, Betsy C. (gr. 3-7). 1981. pap. 3.99 (*0-14-031450-4*, Puffin) Puffin Bks.
—The Midnight Fox. Byars, Betsy C. LC 68-27566. (gr. 3-7). 1968. pap. 13.95 (*0-670-47473-8*) Viking Child Bks.
—Osa's Pride, Vol. 1. Grifalconi, Ann. (ps-3). 1990. 15.95 (*0-316-32865-0*) Little.
—The Secret Soldier: The Story of Deborah Sampson. McGovern, Ann. LC 75-15819. 64p. (gr. 1-5). 1987. RSBE 13.95 (*0-02-765780-9*, Pub. by Four Winds Pr) Macmillan Child Grp.
—Village of Round & Square Houses. Grifalconi, Ann. 32p. (gr. k-3). 1986. lib. bdg. 15.95 (*0-316-32862-6*) Little.

Griffin, Charles. Discovering American History. Akinsheye, Dexter. Akinsheye, Dayo, ed. 20p. (Orig.). (gr. 2-3). 1992. pap. 4.99 (*1-877835-70-6*) TD Pub.

Griffin, David, et al. The Spirit & Vision of Notre Dame: The First 150 Years. Kaczorek, Keith. Harrow, Harriett, ed. Hesburgh, Theodore & Roberson, Kennethfrwd. by. 96p. 1992. 28.00 (*0-9623171-4-4*); pap. 18.50 (*0-9623171-5-2*); pap. text ed. 8.50 black & white ed. (*0-9623171-6-0*); write for info. coloring bk. (*0-9623171-7-9*) LBCo Pub.

Griffin, Georgene. How to Draw Fantasy Creatures. 48p. 1992. pap. 2.95 (*1-56156-144-4*) Kidsbks.

Griffin, Sandi Z. Becca Bumbum Bunny, Vol. 3: Tails with a Moral. Griffin, Sandi Z. 28p. (ps-2). 1993. write for info. (*1-883838-03-7*) S Z Griffin.

—Curly Pig, Vol. 2: Tails with a Moral. Griffin, Sandi Z. 28p. (ps-2). 1993. write for info. (*1-883838-02-9*) S Z Griffin.
—Lumpa Lou Raccoon, Vol. I: Tails with a Moral. Griffin, Sandi Z. 28p. (ps-2). 1993. write for info. S Z Griffin.

Griffin, Sandra U. Earth Circles. Griffin, Sandra U. 32p. (ps-3). 1989. 12.95 (*0-8027-6843-1*); PLB 13.85 (*0-8027-6845-8*) Walker & Co.

Griffith, Gershom. Jumping the Broom. Crump, Courtni C. LC 92-45575. 32p. (gr. 4-8). 1994. 15.95 (*0-8234-1042-0*) Holiday.
—Pearl Bailey: With a Song in Her Heart. Brandt, Keith. LC 92-20190. 48p. (gr. 4-6). 1992. PLB 10.79 (*0-8167-2921-2*); pap. text ed. 3.50 (*0-8167-2922-0*) Troll Assocs.
—A Picture Book of Sojourner Truth. Adler, David A. LC 93-7478. 32p. (gr. 4-8). 1994. 15.95 (*0-8234-1072-2*) Holiday.
—Rosa Parks: Fight for Freedom. Brandt, Keith. LC 91-34939. 48p. (gr. 4-6). 1993. lib. bdg. 10.79 (*0-8167-2831-3*); pap. text ed. 3.50 (*0-8167-2832-1*) Troll Assocs.
—Thurgood Marshall: Fight for Justice. Bains, Rae. LC 92-37302. 48p. (gr. 4-6). 1993. 10.79 (*0-8167-2827-5*); tchr's. ed. 3.50 (*0-8167-2828-3*) Troll Assocs.
—Toussaint l'Ouverture, Lover of Liberty. Santrey, Laurence. LC 93-18971. 48p. (gr. 4-6). 1993. PLB 10.79 (*0-8167-2823-2*); pap. text ed. 3.50 (*0-8167-2824-0*) Troll Assocs.

Griffith, Judith A. The Land of the Blue Flower. Hodgson-Burnett, Frances. LC 93-77029. 48p. (ps-5). 1993. Repr. of 1938 ed. 15.95 (*0-915811-46-4*) H J Kramer Inc.
Back in print for the first time since 1938. In the finest fairy-tale tradition, THE LAND OF THE BLUE FLOWER tells of the transformation of the hateful kingdom of King Mordreth into the idyllic Land of the Blue Flower. Raised in isolation by a seer known only as the Ancient One, the infant King Amor is taught by him to respect & learn from the beauty & mysteries of nature. In this process, he becomes a wise ruler who is able to restore harmony, unity & compassion to his kingdom. Using the theme of learning from & living in harmony with nature, THE LAND OF THE BLUE FLOWER tells a spectacular tale demonstrating the healing power of love. Because of the social & ecological concerns that are central to the story, as well as the spiritual values, woven throughout, the book has significance & meaning for us in the 1990s. In addition to the many exquisite full-page, full-color illustrations by artist Judith Ann Griffith, beautifully rendered blue flower borders frame each page, lending an illuminated manuscript look to the book. *Publisher Provided Annotation.*

Griffith, Linda. Exploring the Human Body. Rojany, Lisa & Strong, Stacie. Haber, Jon Z. & Smith, Rodgerconcept by. LC 92-7514. (gr. 4-7). 1992. 13.95 (*0-8120-6298-1*) Barron.

Griffith Observatory Sky & Telescope Staff. The Star that Astonished the World. Martin, Ernest L. 220p. (Orig.). (gr. 10). 1991. imp. 14.95x (*0-945657-88-9*) Acad Scriptural Knowledge.

Griffith, Sandy. An Alaskan A B C Coloring Book. Calvin, Margaret. 32p. (Orig.). (gr.-4). 1986. pap. 3.95 (*0-9615529-3-X*) Old Harbor Pr.

Grigas, Denise. Articu-ACTION. Grigas, Denise. 144p. (ps-6). 1993. tchr's. ed. 14.95 (*0-937857-37-8*, 1524) Speech Bin.

Grigni, John. Monkeyshines on How the Fifty States Were Named. Goldman, Phyllis, ed. 116p. (Orig.). 1993. pap. 11.95 (*0-9620900-4-2*) NC Learn Inst Fitness.
—Monkeyshines on Strange & Wonderful Facts. Goldman, Phyllis B. 116p. (Orig.). (ps-8). 1991. pap. 8.95 (*0-9620900-2-6*) NC Learn Inst Fitness.

Grigsby, Diane. Painting Our Way to a Better Future: An Art-Coloring Book of Contemporary Career Options for Women. Baird, Mary & Larrivee-Cohen, Donna, eds. 56p. (Orig.). (gr. 1-9). 1990. pap. 6.95 (*0-9627833-0-7*) Hard Hatted Women.

Grillis, Carla. The Mouse & the Potato. Berger, Thomas. Lawson, Polly, tr. (DUT.). 32p. (ps-2). 1990. Repr. 14. 95 (*0-86315-103-5*, Pub. by Floris Bks UK) Gryphon Hse.

Grim, Ellen & De Batuc, Alfredo. The Missions: California's Heritage, No. 1: Mission San Diego de Alcala. Boule, Mary N. 24p. (Orig.). (gr. 4-6). 1988. pap. 3.50 (*1-877599-00-X*) Merryant Pubs.
—The Missions: California's Heritage, No. 10: Mission Santa Barbara. Boule, Mary N. 24p. (Orig.). (gr. 4-6). 1988. pap. 3.50 (*1-877599-09-3*) Merryant Pubs.
—The Missions: California's Heritage, No. 11: Mission la Purisima Concepcion. Boule, Mary N. 24p. (Orig.). (gr. 4-6). 1988. pap. 3.50 (*1-877599-10-7*) Merryant Pubs.
—The Missions: California's Heritage, No. 12: Mission Santa Cruz. Boule, Mary N. 24p. (Orig.). (gr. 4-6). 1988. pap. 3.50 (*1-877599-11-5*) Merryant Pubs.
—The Missions: California's Heritage, No. 13: Mission Nuestra Senora de la Soledad. Boule, Mary N. 20p. (Orig.). (gr. 4-6). 1988. pap. 3.50 (*1-877599-12-3*) Merryant Pubs.
—The Missions: California's Heritage, No. 14: Mission San Jose. Boule, Mary N. 28p. (Orig.). (gr. 4-6). 1988. pap. 3.50 (*1-877599-13-1*) Merryant Pubs.
—The Missions: California's Heritage, No. 15: Mission San Juan Bautista. Boule, Mary N. 24p. (Orig.). (gr. 4-6). 1988. pap. 3.50 (*1-877599-14-X*) Merryant Pubs.
—The Missions: California's Heritage, No. 16: Mission San Miguel Arcangel. Boule, Mary N. 24p. (Orig.). (gr. 4-6). 1988. pap. 3.50 (*1-877599-15-8*) Merryant Pubs.
—The Missions: California's Heritage, No. 17: Mission San Fernando Rey de Espana. Boule, Mary N. 24p. (Orig.). (gr. 4-6). 1988. pap. 3.50 (*1-877599-16-6*) Merryant Pubs.
—The Missions: California's Heritage, No. 19: Mission Santa Ines. Boule, Mary N. 24p. (Orig.). (gr. 4-6). 1988. pap. 3.50 (*1-877599-18-2*) Merryant Pubs.
—The Missions: California's Heritage, No. 2: Mission San Carlos Borromeo de Carmelo. Boule, Mary N. 24p. (Orig.). (gr. 4-6). 1988. pap. 3.50 (*1-877599-01-8*) Merryant Pubs.
—The Missions: California's Heritage, No. 20: Mission San Rafael Arcangel. Boule, Mary N. 24p. (Orig.). (gr. 4-6). 1988. pap. 3.50 (*1-877599-19-0*) Merryant Pubs.
—The Missions: California's Heritage, No. 21: Mission San Francisco Solano. Boule, Mary N. 24p. (Orig.). (gr. 4-6). 1988. pap. 3.50 (*1-877599-20-4*) Merryant Pubs.
—The Missions: California's Heritage, No. 3: Mission San Antonio de Padua. Boule, Mary N. 24p. (Orig.). (gr. 4-6). 1988. pap. 3.50 (*1-877599-02-6*) Merryant Pubs.
—The Missions: California's Heritage, No. 4: Mission San Gabriel Arcangel. Boule, Mary N. 24p. (Orig.). (gr. 4-6). 1988. pap. 3.50 (*1-877599-03-4*) Merryant Pubs.
—The Missions: California's Heritage, No. 5: Mission San Luis Obispo de Tolosa. Boule, Mary N. 24p. (Orig.). (gr. 4-6). 1988. pap. 3.50 (*1-877599-04-2*) Merryant Pubs.
—The Missions: California's Heritage, No. 6: Mission San Francisco de Asis. Boule, Mary N. 24p. (Orig.). (gr. 4-6). 1988. pap. 3.50 (*1-877599-05-0*) Merryant Pubs.
—The Missions: California's Heritage, No. 7: Mission San Juan Capistrano. Boule, Mary N. 24p. (Orig.). (gr. 4-6). 1988. pap. 3.50 (*1-877599-06-9*) Merryant Pubs.
—The Missions: California's Heritage, No. 8: Mission Santa Clara de Asis. Boule, Mary N. 24p. (Orig.). (gr. 4-6). 1988. pap. 3.50 (*1-877599-07-7*) Merryant Pubs.
—The Missions: California's Heritage, No. 9: Mission San Buenaventura. Boule, Mary N. 24p. (Orig.). (gr. 4-6). 1988. pap. 3.50 (*1-877599-08-5*) Merryant Pubs.

Grim, Ellen, jt. illus. see De Batuc, Alfredo.

Grimes, Rich. Satchel Stories: Ammon's Courage. Grimes, Rich. Hiller, Annie, ed. 4p. (ps) 1992. text ed. 8.95 (*0-9623915-0-6*) Jackson Pub.
—Satchel Stories: David & Goliath. Grimes, Rich. Hiller, Annie, ed. 4p. (ps) 1992. text ed. 8.95 (*1-56713-002-X*) Jackson Pub.
—Satchel Stories: Dinosaurs. Grimes, Rich. Hiller, Annie, ed. (ps) 1992. text ed. 8.95 (*1-56713-003-8*) Jackson Pub.
—Satchel Stories: Jesus Blessing the Children. Grimes, Rich. Hiller, Annie, ed. 4p. (ps) 1992. text ed. 8.95 (*0-9623915-8-1*) Jackson Pub.
—Satchel Stories: Laban's Sword. Grimes, Rich. Hiller, Annie, ed. 4p. (ps) 1992. text ed. 8.95 (*0-9623915-8-1*) Jackson Pub.
—Satchel Stories: Nephi's Broken Bow. Grimes, Rich. Hiller, Annie, ed. 4p. (ps) 1992. text ed. 8.95 (*1-56713-000-3*) Jackson Pub.
—Satchel Stories: The Brother of Jared. Grimes, Rich. Hiller, Annie, ed. 4p. (ps) 1992. text ed. 8.95 (*0-9623915-9-X*) Jackson Pub.
—Satchel Stories: Whales. Grimes, Rich. Hiller, Annie, ed. 4p. (ps) 1992. text ed. 8.95 (*1-56713-004-6*) Jackson Pub.

Grimsley, Kent, et al. Television & the Lives of Our Children: A Manual for Teachers & Parents. DeGaetano, Gloria M. 128p. 1993. pap. text ed. 10. 95 (*0-9638737-0-9*) Train Thought. This book addresses the ways habitual viewing significantly impacts children's attention, thinking, creativity, self-concept as learners, & emotional well-being. Eight chapters cover the topics: TV Time: How Much Is Too Much?, TV Impact on Brain Development, TV & Creativity, TV & Classroom Learning, Stimulus Addiction & Video Games, Media Violence, TV & Teens, & Students & Advertising. Each chapter is divided into three sections: information, reproducible parent handouts & reproducible student activities (Grades 1-8) totaling 50 reproducible pages. Many useful ideas are given for raising & educating children in a video age - ways to protect children from the effects of media misuse & ways to educate them about wise use. This is a valuable resource for all teachers & parents. Strongly endorsed & welcomed by parent educators & experts in media literacy. Dr. Jane Healy, author of Endangered Minds, has stated, "If we want to rescue the brains of the next generation, we should pay attention to this important & practical book. Gloria doesn't mince words on the dangers of media - but she tells us how to manage it constructively. Parents & teachers, take note!" Available from the publisher, Train of Thought, P.O. Box 311, Redmond, WA 98073-0311, (206) 883-1544. *Publisher Provided Annotation.*

Gringhuis, Dirk. Mystery Ranch. Warner, Gertrude C. LC 58-9953. 128p. (gr. 2-7). 1958. PLB 10.95 (*0-8075-5390-5*); pap. 3.50 (*0-8075-5391-3*) A Whitman.
Gripe, Harald. Elvis & His Secret. Gripe, Maria. 208p. (gr. 3-7). 1979. pap. 1.50 (*0-440-42434-8*, YB) Dell.
Grishaver, Joel L. In the Beginning God Created the Alef-Bet. Gordon, Yosi. 40p. (Orig.). (gr. 3-5). 1991. pap. 3.75 wkbk. (*0-933873-61-1*) Torah Aura.
—Introduction to the Siddur: The Brakhah System. Rowe, Debi M. 96p. (gr. 4-5). 1990. wkbk. 5.50 (*0-933873-58-1*) Torah Aura.
—Introduction to the Siddur: The Shema & Its Blessings. Rowe, Debi M. 164p. (gr. 5-6). 1991. wkbk. 5.95 (*0-933873-60-3*) Torah Aura.
—When I Stood on Mt. Sinai. Grishaver, Joel L., et al. 32p. (Orig.). (gr. 6 up). 1992. pap. text ed. 2.45 (*0-933873-70-0*) Torah Aura.
—The Words Know the Way. Grishaver, Joel L. 64p. (gr. 3-4). 1990. wkbk. 4.95 (*0-933873-53-0*) Torah Aura.
Gristwood, Doreen. Enoch the Emu. Winch, Gordon. Sherwood, Rhoda, ed. LC 88-42924. 32p. (gr. 2-3). 1988. PLB 18.60 (*1-55532-908-X*) Gareth Stevens Inc.
Gristwood, Doreen, jt. illus. see Oliver, Tony.
Groat, Diane de. Tough-Luck Karen. Hurwitz, Johanna. LC 82-6443. 160p. (gr. 4-6). 1982. 12.95 (*0-688-01485-2*) Morrow Jr Bks.
Groff, Richard L. Ic Spraece Angel-Seax: A Beginning Anglo-Saxon Grammar for Children. Groff, Richard L., Jr. 36p. (Orig.). (gr. 2-6). 1991. pap. 10.98 incl. audio tape (*0-9630718-1-5*) New Dawn NY.
Grohmann, Susan. The Dust under Mrs. Merriweather's Bed. Grohmann, Susan. LC 93-21804. 1993. 13.95 (*1-879085-82-8*) Whsprng Coyote Pr.
Grooms, Red. Rembrandt Takes a Walk. Strand, Mark. (gr. 3 up). 1987. 14.95 (*0-517-56293-6*) Crown Bks Yng Read.
Gross, Lisa. The Half & Half Dog. Gross, Lisa. LC 88-9347. 26p. (gr. k-6). 1988. PLB 14.95 (*0-933849-13-3*) Landmark Edns.
Grosshandler, Henry & Grosshandler, Janet. Everyone Wins at Tee Ball. Grosshandler, Henry & Grosshandler, Janet. LC 89-7875. 32p. (gr. k-3). 1990. 12.95 (*0-525-65016-4*, Cobblehill Bks) Dutton Child Bks.
Grosshandler, Janet, jt. illus. see Grosshandler, Henry.
Grosshandler, Janet, photos by. Winning Ways in Soccer. Grosshandler, Janet. LC 90-48620. 32p. (gr. k-3). 1991. 13.95 (*0-525-65064-4*, Cobblehill Bks) Dutton Child Bks.
Grossman, Dan. Celebrate Autumn. Chupick, Carol O. 144p. (gr. k-3). 1985. wkbk. 11.95 (*0-86653-264-1*, SS 838, Shining Star Pubns) Good Apple.
—Celebrate Summer. MacKenthun, Carole. 144p. (gr. k-3). 1986. wkbk. 11.95 (*0-86653-265-X*, SS 837, Shining Star Pubns) Good Apple.
—God's ABC Zoo. McMillan, Mary. 48p. (ps-1). 1987. pap. 6.95 (*0-86653-405-9*, SS1802, Shining Star Pubns) Good Apple.

—Help for Parents of Gifted & Talented Children. Riley, Jane & Carlson, Mary. 64p. (gr. k-6). 1984. wkbk. 5.95 (*0-86653-190-4*, GA 539) Good Apple.
—King David. McMillan, Mary. 48p. (ps-1). 1987. pap. 6.95 (*0-86653-392-3*, SS 1801, Shining Star Pubns) Good Apple.
Grossman, Nancy. Did You Carry the Flag Today, Charley? Caudill, Rebecca. LC 66-11422. 96p. (gr. 2-4). 1966. reinforced bdg. 15.95 (*0-8050-1201-X*, Bks Young Read) H Holt & Co.
—Sneaker Hill. Little, Jane. LC 90-23766. 192p. (gr. 3-7). 1991. pap. 3.95 (*0-689-71477-7*, Aladdin) Macmillan Child Grp.
Grossman, Robert. The Eighteenth Emergency. Byars, Betsy C. (gr. 4-6). 1981. pap. 3.99 (*0-14-031451-2*, Puffin) Puffin Bks.
—The Eighteenth Emergency. Byars, Betsy C. LC 72-91399. 128p. (gr. 4-6). 1973. pap. 12.95 (*0-670-29055-6*) Viking Child Bks.
—What Could a Hippopotamus Be? Thaler, Mike. LC 89-77080. 40p. (ps-2). 1990. pap. 13.95 (*0-671-70847-3*, S&S BFYR) S&S Trade.
Grossmann, Dan. Baby Jesus. McMillan, Mary. 48p. (ps-1). 1986. wkbk. 6.95 (*0-86653-369-9*, SS 1800, Shining Star Pubns) Good Apple.
—Celebrate Spring. Bilyeu, Linda M. 144p. (gr. k-3). 1984. wkbk. 11.95 (*0-86653-209-9*, SS 836, Shining Star Pubns) Good Apple.
—Christmas Bulletin Boards, Walls, Windows, Doors & More. Javernick, Ellen. 96p. (gr. k-8). 1986. wkbk. 10. 95 (*0-86653-371-0*, SS 1824, Shining Star Pubns) Good Apple.
Grotke, Christopher. The Creatures Nobody Loves. Newcomb, Everett W., Jr. LC 91-66375. 48p. (gr. 4-6). 1991. pap. 3.95 (*0-9627974-3-X*) Tabby Hse Bks.
Grout, Harry. Fun & Easy Guide to San Francisco. Grout, Harry & Grout, Susan. 32p. (Orig.). (gr. 2). 1991. pap. 5.95 (*0-9626868-4-0*) Locations Plus.
Grout, Paul A. St. Louis de Montfort: The Story of Our Lady's Slave. Windeatt, Mary F. LC 90-71826. 211p. (gr. 5-9). 1991. pap. 9.00 (*0-89555-414-3*) TAN Bks Pubs.

Grove, Eric. Of Butterflies & Unicorns: And Other Wonders of the Earth. Cowden, Frances B. & Hatchett, Eve B. 52p. (gr. 7-12). 1993. pap. 7.95 (*1-884289-02-9*) Grandmother Erth. The words rich in visual & tactile imagery, sing of the need for preserving the beauty of our earth. They capture the magic of unicorns & butterflies in language suitable for middle school & high school students as well as young-at-heart adults. Both Memphis authors have taught poetry to children & young people in public schools & in workshops. Included are poems that have won prizes & have been previously published. The introduction by Patricia Garrett, principal of Lester Demonstration School, Memphis City Schools, shows how to use the book in reading lessons. Dr. Rosemary Stephens, President of the National League of American Pen Women, Chickasaw Branch in "About the Poets" gives insights into the work of the authors. The passages are illustrated with ink drawings by Memphis artist, Eric Grove. This edition is intended for all ages. However the material stresses the importance of teaching poetry to children & young people. Order directly from the publisher: Grandmother Earth Creations, 8463 Deerfield Lane, Germantown, TN 38138. *Publisher Provided Annotation.*

Grove, Jason. Barnabas Bear. Jones, Donna J. 32p. (gr. k-5). 1987. pap. 3.50 (*0-9617382-1-9*) Glacier Pub.
—Oolik: The Owl Who Couldn't Whoo. Jones, Donna J. 29p. (Orig.). (gr. k-5). 1987. pap. 3.50 (*0-9617382-0-0*) Glacier Pub.
Grove, Jeff. A Gift for Miss Milo. Wahl, Jan. 96p. 1990. 13.95 (*0-89815-339-5*) Ten Speed Pr.
Grover, Max. Miss Mabel's Table. Chandra, Deborah. LC 93-9137. (ps-2). 1993. write for info. (*0-15-276712-6*, Browndeer Pr) HarBrace.
Grover, Nina. Show a Little Love. Brady, Janeen. 48p. (gr. k-6). 1981. songbk. 6.95 (*0-944803-26-1*); cassette 7.95 (*0-944803-28-8*) Brite Intl.

Grubbs, J. Henry the Cop. Grubbs, J. & Abell, J. 50p. (Orig.). (gr. 2-5). 1993. text ed. 18.00 (*1-56611-020-3*); pap. 7.00 (*0-685-63577-5*) Jones.
—Socks, the Cat Who Moved to Washington. Grubbs, J. Abell, J., ed. 50p. (gr. 1-4). 1993. 22.00x (*1-56611-022-X*); pap. 10.00 (*0-685-63570-8*) Jones.
Grubbs, Joan. Books for Young Gentlemen. rev. ed. Grubbs, Joan J., et al. 50p. (gr. 6-8). 1993. 22.00 (*1-56611-024-6*); PLB 22.00 (*0-685-65769-8*); pap. 10.00 (*0-685-65770-1*) Jones.
—Possessive Pronouns. rev. ed. Grubbs, Joan, et al. Abell, ed. 50p. (gr. 3-6). 1993. 23.00 (*0-685-65773-6*); PLB 23.00 (*0-685-65774-4*); pap. 11.00 (*0-685-65775-2*) Jones.
Grubbs, Tab & Abell, J. Light Industrial. (gr. 1-3). 1993. pap. 7.00 spiral (*0-685-62313-0*) Jones.
Grube, Karl W. Cribbage d'Etroit. Grube, Karl W. 129p. (gr. 3 up). Date not set. 29.95 (*0-685-63059-5*); tchr's. ed. 49.95 (*0-685-63060-9*) Intl Gamester.
—Cribbage in Schools Program. Grube, Karl W. 29p. (gr. 3 up). Date not set. pap. text ed. 10.00 tchr's. guide (*0-685-63061-7*) Intl Gamester.
—Lake Huron Poker. Grube, Karl W. 124p. (gr. 3 up). Date not set. pap. text ed. 29.95 (*0-685-63062-5*); tchr's. ed. 49.95 (*0-685-63063-3*) Intl Gamester.
—Lake Michigan Poker. Grube, Karl W. 132p. (gr. 3 up). Date not set. pap. text ed. 29.95 (*0-685-63064-1*); tchr's. ed. 49.95 (*0-685-63065-X*) Intl Gamester.
Grube, Kathryn. Lake Superior Cribbage. Grube, Karl W. & Grube, Kathryn. 112p. (gr. 3 up). Date not set. pap. text ed. 29.95 (*0-685-63057-9*); tchr's. ed. 49.95 (*0-685-63058-7*) Intl Gamester.
Gruchow, Jane. Color Me Happy It's Passover. Geller, Norman. 23p. (gr. k-2). pap. 2.95 (*0-915753-14-6*) N Geller Pub.
Gruchow, Jane. Farfel, the Cat That Left Egypt. Geller, Norman. 31p. (Orig.). (gr. 3-7). 1987. pap. text ed. 6.95 (*0-915753-12-X*) N Geller Pub.
—It's Not the Jewish Christmas. Geller, Norman. 20p. (gr. 3-6). 1985. pap. 4.95 (*0-915753-09-X*) N Geller Pub.
Gruelle, Johnny. Little Treasury of Raggedy Ann & Andy. Nash, Corey. (ps-1). 1984. 5.99 (*0-517-44730-4*) Outlet Bk Co.
—The Old-Fashioned Raggedy Ann & Andy ABC Book. Kraus, Robert, et al. Kraus, Pam, ed. 32p. (ps-2). 1980. 5.95 (*0-671-42552-8*) S&S Trade.
—Raggedy Andy Stories. Gruelle, Johnny. 96p. (ps up). 1987. Repr. PLB 25.95x (*0-89966-618-3*) Buccaneer Bks.
—Raggedy Andy Stories: Introducing the Little Rag Brother of Raggedy Ann. reissued ed. Gruelle, Johnny. Gruelle, Kim, afterword by. LC 93-21967. 96p. (gr. k up). 1993. SBE 16.95 (*0-02-737586-2*, Macmillan Child Bk) Macmillan Child Grp.
—Raggedy Ann & Andy Second Giant Treasury. Dreyer, Ellen, retold by. 80p. 1989. 5.99 (*0-517-66719-3*) Outlet Bk Co.
—Raggedy Ann Stories. reissued ed. Gruelle, Johnny. Gruelle, Kim, afterword by. LC 93-630. 96p. (gr. k up). 1993. SBE 16.95 (*0-02-737585-4*, Macmillan Child Bk) Macmillan Child Grp.
Gruelle, Justin C. & Russell, Elizabeth A. Once Round the Sun. Titchenell, Elsa-Brita. LC 81-52615. iv, 57p. (gr. 1 up). 1981. Repr. of 1950 ed. 9.50 (*0-911600-61-8*) Theos U Pr.
Gruen, Chuck. Little Chief Mischief. Salter-Mathieson, Nigel. (gr. 2-7). 1962. 10.95 (*0-8392-3020-6*) Astor-Honor.
Gruettner, Diane & Black, Diane. Bugs & Critters. Holly, Brian. 32p. (gr. 3-7). 1985. pap. 3.50 (*0-88625-118-4*) Durkin Hayes Pub.

Grummer, Arnold & Rotzel, Spencer. Tin Can Papermaking: Recycle for Earth & Art. Grummer, Arnold E. 80p. (Orig.). (gr. 1 up). 1992. pap. 7.95 (*0-938251-01-5*) G Markim.
This book describes how to gather everything you need to make paper right from your own kitchen. Featuring chapters on art & decorative techniques, recycling, paper history, what paper is made of & more, this 80 page book (complete with over 60 photos) is also a small encyclopedia of paper art & science. Written by Arnold Grummer, former curator of the Dard Hunter Paper Museum housed in the Institute of Paper Chemistry, the language in this book is so simple a grade school student would have no trouble using it, yet the science discussed in the book has compelled many adults. The book also gives step-by-step instructions for making invitations, envelopes, round stationery, flower embedments, & much more using a set of tin cans & other common kitchen items. An excellent resource material or home craft guide. "... beginners will be able to create something genuinely beautiful in a short period of time..environmental information about paper & recycling is presented without preaching."-- Bloomsbury Review.
Publisher Provided Annotation.

Grundy, Lynn A. A Is for Apple. 28p. (ps). 1992. 3.50 (*0-7214-1508-3*) Ladybird Bks.
—Let's Count. 28p. (ps). 1992. 3.50 (*0-7214-1509-1*) Ladybird Bks.
Grundy, Lynn N. Shapes & Colors. Bradbury, Lynne. 28p. (ps). 1992. Series 921. 3.50 (*0-7214-1510-5*) Ladybird Bks.
—What Is the Time? Bradbury, Lynne. 28p. (ps). 1992. Series 921. 3.50 (*0-7214-1511-3*) Ladybird Bks.
Grunwald, C. Boys & Girls of Seventy-Seven. 2nd ed. Smith, Mary P. Silvester, Susan B., ed. LC 86-30607. 333p. (gr. 5 up). 1987. Repr. of 1909 ed. 17.00 (*0-913993-08-5*) Paideia MA.
Guanlao, Ernie, jt. illus. see Cruz, E. R.
Guard, Gretchen. Deirdre: A Celtic Legend. Guard, David. 120p. (gr. 4-9). 1993. pap. 8.95 (*1-883672-05-8*) Tricycle Pr.
Guarnaccia, Steven. Anansi. Gleeson, Brian. LC 91-40671. 36p. (gr. k up). 1992. pap. 14.95 (*0-88708-230-0*, Rabbit Ears); incl. cass. 19.95 (*0-88708-231-9*, Rabbit Ears) Picture Bk Studio.
—Naming the Animals. McFall, Gardner. LC 93-14532. (ps-3). 1994. PLB 13.99 (*0-670-84814-X*) Viking Child Bks.
Guell, Walt Disney's Snow White & the Seven Dwarfs. Margulies, Teddy S. 24p. (ps-3). 1993. pap. 1.95 (*0-307-12686-2*, 12686, Golden Pr) Western Pub.
Guell, Fernando. Take a Ride with Mickey. Reit, Seymour. LC 91-71336. 32p. (ps-1). 1991. 8.95 (*1-56282-060-5*) Disney Pr.
Guell, Fernando & Beelaerts, Marie. Daisy Bunny's Teatime. Karl, Linda & Siegel, Seth M. 12p. (ps-k). 1994. 3.99 (*0-679-84001-X*) Random Bks Yng Read.
—Rose Bunny's Teatime. Karl, Linda & Siegel, Seth M. 12p. (ps-k). 1994. 3.99 (*0-679-84002-8*) Random Bks Yng Read.
—Tulip Bunny's Teatime. Karl, Linda & Siegel, Seth M. 12p. (ps-k). 1994. 3.99 (*0-679-84003-6*) Random Bks Yng Read.
—Violet Bunny's Teatime. Karl, Linda & Siegel, Seth M. 12p. (ps-k). 1994. 3.99 (*0-679-84004-4*) Random Bks Yng Read.
Guelzow, Diane. Building Self-Esteem: A Workbook for Teens. Trahey, Jerome. 176p. (Orig.). (gr. 7-12). 1992. pap. 14.95 (*0-89390-231-4*) Resource Pubns.
Guenier, Emma. In the Wild: Fun.Fact.Flap. Satchell, Jonathan. 16p. (gr. 2 up). 1993. 9.95 (*0-87226-512-9*, Bedrick Blackie) P Bedrick Bks.
—On the Farm: Fun.Flap.Flaps. Satchell, Jonathan. 16p. (gr. 2 up). 1993. 9.95 (*0-87226-513-7*, Bedrick Blackie) P Bedrick Bks.
Guerin, Penny. Rainy Day Rhymes: A Collection of Chants, Forecasts & Tales. Palmer, Michele, ed. LC 84-60412. 24p. (Orig.). (gr. k up). 1984. pap. 2.95 (*0-932306-02-0*) Rocking Horse.
Guerra, Mauricio. Soo Ling: The Story of the Silkworm. Miller, Billie M. Luna, Rose Mary, tr. (SPA & ENG.). 12p. 1991. 12.00 (*1-878742-01-9*); pap. 6.00 (*1-878742-02-7*) Kidship Assoc.
Guerrero, Alex. Por Que Mi Nombre Es Marisol? Un Cuento De la Republica Dominicana. Baez, Josefina. (SPA.). 24p. (Orig.). (gr. k-3). 1993. pap. 12.95 (*1-882161-01-7*) Latinarte.
—Why Is My Name Marisol? A Dominican Children's Story. Baez, Josefina. 24p. (Orig.). (gr. k-3). 1993. pap. 12.95 (*1-882161-02-5*) Latinarte.
Guest, Mary J., jt. illus. see Bowman, Joyce.
Guevara, Susan. The Boardwalk Princess. Levine, Arthur A. LC 92-8081. 32p. (ps up). 1993. 14.00 (*0-688-10306-5*, Tambourine Bks); PLB 13.93 (*0-688-10307-3*, Tambourine Bks) Morrow.
—The Class with the Summer Birthdays. Regan, Dian C. 80p. (gr. 2-4). 1991. 13.45 (*0-8050-1657-0*, Redfeather BYR) H Holt & Co.
—The Class with the Summer Birthdays. Regan, Dian C. LC 90-19670. 80p. (gr. 2-4). 1992. pap. 4.95 (*0-8050-2327-5*, Redfeather BYR) H Holt & Co.
—Emmett's Snowball. Miller, Ned. LC 89-77787. 40p. (ps-2). 1990. 14.95 (*0-8050-1394-6*, Bks Young Read) H Holt & Co.
—I Have an Aunt on Marlborough Street. Lasky, Kathryn. LC 91-279. 32p. (gr. k-3). 1992. RSBE 13.95 (*0-02-751701-2*, Macmillan Child Bk) Macmillan Child Grp.
Gugler, Janine. Zoup Soup. Palmer, Michele. LC 78-66342. (ps-1). 1978. pap. 1.95 (*0-932306-00-4*) Rocking Horse.
Guiberson, Brenda. Salmon Story. Guiberson, Brenda Z. LC 93-1360. 64p. (gr. 2-4). 1993. PLB 14.95 (*0-8050-2754-8*, Bks Young Read) H Holt & Co.

Guida, Frank J. Shakespeare for Children: Romeo & Juliet - with a Happy Ending, Vol. 1. rev. ed. Guida, Frank J. 20p. 1991. lib. bdg. write for info. (*1-878476-00-9*) Rockmasters Intl.
This children's adaptation of William Shakespeare's classic "ROMEO & JULIET" is intended to cultivate at an early age some of the most dramatic writing in literature. Wait till you hear your youngster reading, understanding & quoting The Bard! "What a wonderful treasure you have added to the shelves of children's literature in your adaptation of Romeo & Juliet. I thank & applaud you as future generations are certain to do like-wise." --Constance F. Zimmerman, Chairperson, Norfolk Reading Council. "The presentation is superb; the art work attractive; & the text very interesting."--James Cullinan, Finnbar Books, Kent, England. "I like your story Mr. Guida because it's with a happy ending. If they're sad, I start to cry & I have bad dreams. But I wonder where you got that name wink milch?"- -Crystal (Drew School, 8 years old, Washington, D.C.). "My favorite part is when the two families become friends again & nobody got killed!"-- Brett (Drew School, 9 years old). "In a unique adaptation, Frank Guida has forged a new method of bringing great literary works to young minds."--(Julie Cimino, Educator, Wash., D.C.). "Guida's adaptation incorporates portions of the original in all capital letters, such as Juliet's famous balcony scene."--Philip Walzer (Virginian-Pilot, Norfolk, Va.).
Publisher Provided Annotation.

Guida, Liisa C. Henry & Grudge. Holland, Isabelle. 64p. (gr. 3-6). 1986. 10.95 (*0-8027-6611-0*); lib. bdg. 10.85 (*0-8027-6612-9*) Walker & Co.
Guiliani, Alfred. The Little Engine That Could: Busy Book. 48p. (ps-2). 1992. pap. 0.42 (*0-448-40378-1*, Platt & Munk Pubs) Putnam Pub Group.
Guitar, Jeremy, jt. illus. see McQueen, Lucinda.
Guiterrez, Marda L. Beginning Reading & Writing in French: A Children's French Grammar Workbook. Gutierrez, Marda L. 64p. (Orig.). (gr. k-4). 1986. 8.95 (*0-938733-03-6*) Avantage Pub.
Guitierez, Domy, jt. illus. see Trinidad, Angel.
Gullikson, Sandy. The Three Young Maniacs & the Red Rubber Boots. Nagel, Karen B. LC 91-30842. 32p. (ps-3). 1993. 15.00 (*0-06-020777-9*); PLB 14.89 (*0-06-020778-7*) HarpC Child Bks.
Gumble, Gary. When Do You Talk to God? Prayers for Small Children. McKissack, Patricia & McKissack, Fredrick. LC 86-71903. 32p. (Orig.). (gr. 3-8). 1986. pap. 5.99 (*0-8066-2239-3*, 10-7078, Augsburg) Augsburg Fortress.
Gunder Heimer, Jocelyn C. Turnabout Songs Program Complete Set: A Shortcut to Knowledge. Theo Carus Harter, Kaboblin. Smith, Betty N. & Anderson, Catherine, eds. 262p. 1993. 2 in. 3-hole ring binder, incl. 9 cass. & cass. locator guide 150.00 (*0-944528-41-4*) Child Mus Wkshop.
Gundersheimer, Karen. Colors to Know. Gundersheimer, Karen. LC 85-45390. 32p. (ps-1). 1986. HarpC Child Bks.
—Is Susan Here? Udry, Janice May. LC 90-32044. 24p. (gr. k-3). 1993. 14.00 (*0-06-026142-0*); PLB 13.89 (*0-06-026143-9*) HarpC Child Bks.
—The Merry-Go-Round Poetry Book. Larrick, Nancy, compiled by. 1989. 14.95 (*0-385-29814-5*) Delacorte.
—The Midnight Eaters. Hest, Amy. LC 88-24381. 32p. (gr. k-3). 1989. RSBE 13.95 (*0-02-743630-6*, Four Winds) Macmillan Child Grp.
—Some Things Go Together. Zolotow, Charlotte. LC 82-48694. 24p. (ps-2). 1987. pap. 4.95 (*0-06-443133-9*, Trophy) HarpC Child Bks.
—A Special Trade. Wittman, Sally. LC 77-25673. 32p. (ps-2). 1985. pap. 5.95 (*0-06-443071-5*, Trophy) HarpC Child Bks.
—What Am I? Very First Riddles. Calmenson, Stephanie. LC 87-22959. 32p. (ps-2). 1989. 11.95 (*0-06-020997-6*); PLB 11.89 (*0-06-020998-4*) HarpC Child Bks.
—What Am I? Very First Riddles. Calmenson, Stephanie. LC 87-22959. 32p. (ps-2). 1992. pap. 4.95 (*0-06-443291-2*, Trophy) HarpC Child Bks.
Gunsher, Cheryl. Danny the Dizzy Draydl. Gunsher, Cheryl. Webb, Sandra, ed. 24p. (ps). 1992. 6.00 (*1-881602-00-1*) Prism NJ.

Gunter, Annetta. Kitchen Cosmetics: Using Herbs, Fruits & Eatables in Natural Cosmetics. 2nd, rev. ed. 131p. (gr. 8 up). 1988. pap. 9.95 (*0-9620838-0-1*) Herb Studies.

Gupta, M. L. Dutta. Krishna & Sudama. Shivkumar. (gr. 1-8). 1979. pap. 2.00 (*0-89744-156-7*) Auromere.

Guravich, Dan, photos by. Arctic Summer. Matthews, Downs. LC 92-25376. 40p. (gr. 2-5). 1993. pap. 14.00 JRT (*0-671-79539-2*, S&S BFYR) S&S Trade.
—Polar Bear Cubs. Matthews, Downs. (gr. 2 up). 1989. pap. 13.95 jacketed (*0-671-66757-2*, S&S BFYR) S&S Trade.
—Polar Bear Cubs. Matthews, Downs. LC 88-10284. 32p. (gr. 2-5). 1991. pap. 4.00 (*0-671-74493-3*, S&S BFYR) S&S Trade.
—Wetlands. Matthews, Downs. LC 93-3439. 1994. pap. 14.00 (*0-671-86562-5*, S&S BFYR) S&S Trade.

Gurche, John, et al. The News about Dinosaurs. reissued ed. Lauber, Patricia. LC 88-24140. 48p. (gr. 1-5). 1989. RSBE 15.95 (*0-02-754520-2*, Bradbury Pr) Macmillan Child Grp.

Gurney, Eric. Cats & Mice. Gelman, Rita G. 48p. (gr. k-3). 1989. Big Book. 28.67 (*0-590-64644-3*); pap. 1.95 (*0-590-71593-3*) Scholastic Inc.
—Diggingest Dog. Perkins, Al. LC 67-21920. 72p. (gr. k-3). 1967. 6.95 (*0-394-80047-8*); lib. bdg. 7.99 (*0-394-90047-2*) Beginner.

Gurney, John. Hansel & Gretel. Grimm, Jacob & Grimm, Wilhelm K. Black, Fiona, retold by. 1991. 6.95 (*0-8362-4912-7*) Andrews & McMeel.
—On Our Way to Market. Dodds, Dayle A. LC 91-6436. 40p. (ps-k). 1991. pap. 13.95 jacketed (*0-671-73567-5*, S&S BFYR) S&S Trade.
—Search for Sidney's Smile. Kornblatt, Marc. LC 92-12824. 1993. pap. 13.00 JRT (*0-671-76912-X*, S&S BFYR); pap. 2.50 (*0-671-79362-4*, Little Simon) S&S Trade.
—The Worldwide Dessert Contest. Elish, Dan. LC 87-24694. 208p. (gr. 4-6). 1988. 13.95 (*0-531-05752-6*); PLB 13.99 (*0-531-08352-7*) Orchard Bks Watts.

Gurney, John S. Over the River & Through the Woods. 1992. pap. 2.50 (*0-590-45258-4*, Cartwheel) Scholastic Inc.

Gurstein, Shari. ABC Feelings: A Coloring - Learning Book. rev. ed. Delis-Abrams, Alexandra. Follendore, Joan, ed. 64p. (gr. 3-8). 1991. pap. text ed. 7.95 (*1-879889-00-5*) Adage Pubns.

Gurtzweiler, Michael & Smith, Al. Dream Catchers: Developing Career & Educational Awareness in the Intermediate Grades. Lindsay, Norene. Hall, Sara, ed. 64p. (gr. k-7). 1993. pap. 2.50 wkbk. (*1-56370-085-9*, DCP); tchr's. guide 14.95 (*1-56370-086-7*, DCTG); reproducible activity sheets 19.95 (*1-56370-087-5*, DCAS) JIST Works.

Gusman, Annie. Jokes to Read in the Dark. Corbett, Scott. LC 79-23129. 80p. (gr. 5-9). 1980. 12.95 (*0-525-32796-7*, 01063-320, DCB); (DCB) Dutton Child Bks.
—Jokes to Tell to Your Worst Enemy. Corbett, Scott. LC 83-16564. 80p. (gr. 2-6). 1984. 10.95 (*0-525-44082-8*, DCB) Dutton Child Bks.
—Teammates: Home Team Book. Perle, Ruth L. Bergstrom, Evelyn J., ed. (ps-k). 1977. pap. text ed. 3.95 (*0-89796-862-X*) New Dimens Educ.
—Teammates School Team Book. Perle, Ruth L. Bergstrom, Evelyn J., ed. (ps-k). 1977. pap. text ed. 3.95 (*0-89796-861-1*) New Dimens Educ.

Gustafson, Dana. Houdini, the Vanishing Hare. Matthews, Morgan. LC 88-1286. 48p. (Orig.). (gr. 1-4). 1989. PLB 10.59 (*0-8167-1343-X*); pap. text ed. 3.50 (*0-8167-1344-8*) Troll Assocs.
—What's It Like to Be a Dentist. Stamper, Judith. LC 89-34392. 32p. (gr. k-3). 1989. lib. bdg. 10.89 (*0-8167-1799-0*); pap. text ed. 2.95 (*0-8167-1800-8*) Troll Assocs.

Gustafson, Dru. The Illustrated I Hate School Workbook. Welch, Joyce. 88p. (Orig.). (gr. 7-9). 1979. pap. 6.95 (*0-935996-00-1*) Wibat Pubns.

Gustafson, Ronald, jt. illus. see Dibner, Ellen J.

Gustafson, Scott. The Night Before Christmas. Moore, Clement C. LC 85-40334. 32p. (ps-3). 1985. 12.95 (*0-394-54809-4*) Knopf Bks Yng Read.
—Nutcracker. Hoffman, E. T. Black, Fiona, retold by. 40p. 1991. 6.95 (*0-8362-4934-8*) Andrews & McMeel.
—Nutcracker. Hoffmann, E. T. Black, Fiona, retold by. LC 92-24140. 32p. 1992. 4.95 (*0-8362-3026-4*) Andrews & McMeel.
—Peter Pan. Barrie, J. M. 192p. 1991. 20.00 (*0-670-84180-3*) Viking Child Bks.

Gustavson, Susan. Far Walker. Leonard, Larry. LC 88-12290. 120p. (gr. 1 up). 1988. 12.95 (*0-932576-60-5*) Breitenbush Bks.

Gustovich, Michael & Dee, Jeff. Heroes Unlimited. rev. ed. Siembieda, Kevin. Marciniszyn, Alex, ed. 248p. (gr. 8 up). 1987. pap. 19.95 (*0-916211-05-3*, 500) Palladium Bks.

Gustovich, Mike & Ewell, Newton. Mutants in Orbit. Wallis, James & Sienbieda, Kevin. Marciniszyn, Alex, et al, eds. 112p. (Orig.). (gr. 8 up). 1992. pap. 11.95 (*0-916211-48-7*, 514) Palladium Bks.

Gustovich, Mike & Steranko, James. Villains Unlimited. Siembieda, Kevin & Long, Kevin. Marciniszyn, Alex & Bartold, Thomas, eds. 200p. (Orig.). (gr. 8 up). 1992. pap. 19.95 (*0-916211-49-5*, 501) Palladium Bks.

Gustovich, Mike, et al. RECON: Modern Combat. Siembieda, Kevin. Marciniszyn, Alex, et al, eds. 180p. (gr. 8 up). 1994. pap. 19.95 (*0-916211-64-9*, 614) Palladium Bks.

Gutek, Rob. All Children Create: Levels Four to Six, an Elementary Art Curriculum, Vol. II. Sefkow, Paula & Berger, Helen. LC 80-82018. 204p. (Orig.). (gr. 4-6). 1981. pap. 24.95x (*0-918452-25-2*) Learning Pubns.
—All Children Create: Levels One to Three, an Elementary Art Curriculum, Vol. I. Sefkow, Paula & Berger, Helen. LC 80-82018. 204p. (gr. 1-3). 1981. pap. 24.95 (*0-918452-24-4*) Learning Pubns.

Guthridge, Bettina. Matilda & the Dragon. Burnside, Julian. 32p. (Orig.). (gr. k-2). 1993. 14.95 (*1-86373-127-X*, Pub. by Allen & Unwin Aust Pty AT); pap. 7.95 (*1-86373-144-X*, Pub. by Allen & Unwin Aust Pty AT) IPG Chicago.

Guthrie, Kari H., jt. illus. see Nichols, Brooke.

Guthrie, Ruth. Let's Play--Right Away with Play-Along Tape, Bk. 1. Duna, Bill & Duna, Lois. 32p. (Orig.). (gr. k up). 1981. pap. 12.95 (*0-942928-00-8*) Duna Studios.
—Let's Play--Right Away with Play-Along Tape, Bk. 2. Duna, Bill & Duna, Lois. 30p. (Orig.). (gr. k-9). 1981. pap. 12.95 (*0-942928-01-6*) Duna Studios.

Guthrie, Woody. Woody's Twenty Grow Big Songs. Guthrie, Woody. LC 91-753710. 48p. (ps up). 1992. 16.00 (*0-06-020282-3*); incl. cassette 24.95 (*0-06-021033-8*); PLB 15.89 (*0-06-020283-1*) HarpC Child Bks.

Gutierrez, Ed & Michaels, Serge. Disney's Beauty & the Beast: The Beast's Story. Brooks, Laura, adapted by. 32p. (gr. k-2). 1993. pap. 3.25 (*0-307-15976-0*, 15976, Golden Pr) Western Pub.
—Disney's Beauty & the Beast: The Beast's Story, Level 2. Brooks, Laura. 40p. (gr. k-2). 1992. write for info. (*0-307-11552-6*, 11552, Golden Pr) Western Pub.

Gutierrez, M. King Pancho & the First Clock. Lopez, N. C. LC 63-16396. 32p. (gr. 2-7). 1967. PLB 9.95 (*0-87783-020-7*); pap. 3.94 deluxe ed. (*0-87783-098-3*); cassette 7.94x (*0-685-03701-0*) Oddo.

Gutierrez, Rudy. All for the Better: A Story of el Barrio. Mohr, Nicholasa. LC 92-23639. 56p. (gr. 2-5). 1992. PLB 21.34 (*0-8114-7220-5*) Raintree Steck-V.
—La Causa: The Migrant Farmworkers' Story. De Ruiz, Dana C. & Larios, Richard. LC 92-12806. 92p. (gr. 2-5). 1992. PLB 21.34 (*0-8114-7231-0*) Raintree Steck-V.

Gutman, Bessie P. I Love You: Verses & Sweet Sayings. 32p. 1994. 4.95 (*0-448-40258-0*, G&D) Putnam Pub Group.

Gutman, Nachum. Olami Sefer Shlishi, Bk. 3. Bachrach, Kalman. (HEB.). 92p. (gr. 4-6). 1936. pap. text ed. 2.00x (*1-878530-16-X*) K Bachrach Co.

Guzman, Elia. The Story of Ana: La Historia de Ana. Vasquez, Ely P., et al. (SPA & ENG.). 28p. (Orig.). (gr. 3-6). 1985. PLB 8.95 (*0-932727-15-8*); pap. 3.95 (*0-932727-01-8*) Hope Pub Hse.

Guzzi, George. The Baseball Bat. Michaels, Ski. LC 85-14065. 48p. (Orig.). (gr. 1-3). 1986. PLB 10.59 (*0-8167-0596-8*); pap. text ed. 3.50 (*0-8167-0597-6*) Troll Assocs.
—The Big Book of Real Airplanes. Ingoglia, Gina. (gr. 1-4). 1987. 7.95 (*0-448-19179-2*, G&D) Putnam Pub Group.
—Blue Feather's Vision, the Dawn of Colonial America. Knight, James E. LC 81-23082. 32p. (gr. 5-9). 1982. PLB 11.59 (*0-89375-722-5*); pap. text ed. 2.95 (*0-89375-723-3*) Troll Assocs.
—Daniel Boone & the Wilderness Road. Chambers, Catherine E. LC 83-18291. 32p. (gr. 5-9). 1984. PLB 11.59 (*0-8167-0037-0*); pap. text ed. 2.95 (*0-8167-0038-9*) Troll Assocs.
—Indian Crafts. Brandt, Keith. LC 84-2588. 32p. (gr. 3-6). 1985. lib. bdg. 9.49 (*0-8167-0132-6*); pap. text ed. 2.95 (*0-8167-0133-4*) Troll Assocs.
—Indian Festivals. Brandt, Keith. LC 84-2644. 32p. (gr. 3-6). 1985. PLB 9.49 (*0-8167-0182-2*); pap. text ed. 2.95 (*0-8167-0183-0*) Troll Assocs.
—Indian Homes. Brandt, Keith. LC 84-2650. 32p. (gr. 3-6). 1985. PLB 9.49 (*0-8167-0126-1*); pap. text ed. 2.95 (*0-8167-0127-X*) Troll Assocs.
—Indians of the West. Bains, Rae. LC 84-2600. 32p. (gr. 3-6). 1985. PLB 9.49 (*0-8167-0134-2*); pap. text ed. 2.95 (*0-8167-0135-0*) Troll Assocs.
—Journey to Monticello, Traveling in Colonial Times. Knight, James E. LC 81-23156. 32p. (gr. 5-9). 1982. PLB 11.59 (*0-89375-736-5*); pap. text ed. 2.95 (*0-89375-737-3*) Troll Assocs.
—Never Turn Back: Father Serra's Mission. Rawls, James J. LC 92-12814. 52p. (gr. 5-9). 1992. PLB 21.34 (*0-8114-7221-3*) Raintree Steck-V.
—Sailing to America, Colonists at Sea. Knight, James E. LC 81-23161. 32p. (gr. 5-9). 1982. PLB 11.59 (*0-89375-726-8*); pap. text ed. 2.95 (*0-89375-727-6*) Troll Assocs.
—Seventh & Walnut, Life in Colonial Philadelphia. Knight, James E. LC 81-24036. 32p. (gr. 5-9). 1982. PLB 11.59 (*0-89375-740-3*); pap. text ed. 2.95 (*0-89375-741-1*) Troll Assocs.
—The Winter at Valley Forge, Survival & Victory. Knight, James E. LC 81-23151. 32p. (gr. 5-9). 1982. PLB 11.59 (*0-89375-738-1*); pap. text ed. 2.95 (*0-89375-739-X*) Troll Assocs.

Gwynne, Fred. A Chocolate Moose for Dinner. Gwynne, Fred. LC 80-14150. (gr. 1-6). 1988. pap. 13.00 jacketed (*0-671-66685-1*, S&S BFYR); pap. 5.95 (*0-671-66741-6*, S&S BFYR) S&S Trade.
—The King Who Rained. Gwynne, Fred. LC 80-12939. 40p. (gr. 4 up). 1987. P-H.

—The King Who Rained. Gwynne, Fred. LC 80-12939. (gr. 1-6). 1988. pap. 14.00 jacketed (*0-671-66363-1*, S&S BFYR); pap. 5.95 (*0-671-66744-0*, S&S BFYR) S&S Trade.
—The Sixteen-Hand Horse. Gwynne, Fred. LC 79-13284. (gr. 1-5). 1987. P-H Gen Ref & Trav.
—The Sixteen Hand Horse. Gwynne, Fred. LC 79-13284. (gr. 1-6). 1987. pap. 11.95 (*0-671-66291-0*, S&S BFYR); pap. 5.95 (*0-671-66968-0*, S&S BFYR) S&S Trade.

Gynell, Donna. Always Arthur. Graham, Amanda. LC 89-4474. 32p. (gr. 2-3). 1990. PLB 18.60 (*0-8368-0096-6*) Gareth Stevens Inc.
—Educating Arthur. Graham, Amanda. LC 87-42756. 32p. (gr. 2-3). 1988. PLB 18.60 (*1-55532-411-8*) Gareth Stevens Inc.
—Who Wants Arthur? Graham, Amanda. LC 86-42812. 32p. (gr. 2-3). 1987. PLB 18.60 (*1-55532-868-7*) Gareth Stevens Inc.

H

Haas, Holly. Swept Back to a Texas Future. Freeman, Peggy P. 40p. (gr. 4-7). 1991. pap. 7.95 (*0-937460-72-9*) Hendrick-Long.

Haas, Irene. Little House of Your Own. De Regniers, Beatrice S. & Haas, Irene. LC 86-27013. 32p. (ps-3). 1955. 9.95 (*0-15-245787-9*, HB Juv Bks) HarBrace.
—The Maggie B. Haas, Irene. LC 74-18183. 32p. (ps-2). 1975. SBE 14.95 (*0-689-50021-1*, M K McElderry) Macmillan Child Grp.

Haas, Martha. Beware the Mare. Haas, Jessie. LC 92-14505. 64p. (gr. 2 up). 1993. 13.00 (*0-688-11762-7*) Greenwillow.

Haas, Shelly O. Daddy's Chair. Lanton, Sandy. LC 90-44908. 32p. (gr. k-4). 1991. 12.95 (*0-929371-51-8*) Kar Ben.
—Grandma's Soup. Karkowsky, Nancy. LC 89-30875. 32p. (gr. k-5). 1989. 10.95 (*0-930494-98-9*) Kar Ben.
—Jimmy Crack Corn. Random, Candice F. LC 93-16657. 1993. 7.00 (*0-87614-786-4*) Carolrhoda Bks.
—Listening to Crickets: A Story about Rachel Carson. Ransom, Candice F. (gr. 3-6). 1993. 14.95 (*0-87614-727-9*) Carolrhoda Bks.
—Mommy Never Went to Hebrew School. Portnoy, Mindy A. LC 89-30874. 32p. (gr. k-5). 1989. pap. 4.95 (*0-930494-97-0*) Kar Ben.
—Sophie's Name. Grode, Phyllis A. LC 90-4833. 32p. (gr. k-3). 1990. 12.95 (*0-929371-18-6*); pap. 4.95 (*0-929371-19-4*) Kar Ben.
—Thank You, God: A Jewish Child's Book of Prayers. Groner, Judyth & Wikler, Madeline. (HEB & ENG.). 32p. (ps-2). 1993. 14.95 (*0-929371-65-8*) Kar Ben.

Haberer, Robert E. Search N Shade. Cornell, Pat. Jacobs, Alan, ed. (gr. 4-9). 1979. pap. 7.50 (*0-918272-07-6*) Jacobs.
—Up with Math: Basic Skills Step by Step. McCully, Ron. Jacobs, Russell F., ed. (gr. 5-12). 1979. pap. text ed. 6.95 (*0-918272-03-3*); tchr's ed. 6.25 (*0-918272-04-1*) Jacobs.

Haber-Schaim, Navah. Look at Annette. Walter, Marion. LC 77-186592. 32p. (ps-3). 1977. 5.95 (*0-87131-071-6*) M Evans.

Haberson, Lydia. Getting to Know Jesus. Brennan-Nichols, Patricia. 68p. (Orig.). (gr. k-3). 1984. pap. 4.95 (*0-89505-130-3*, R0610) Tabor Pub.

Haberstock, Jennifer. Little Porcupine's Winter Den. Thompson-Hoffman, Susan. Thomas, Peter, narrated by. 32p. (ps-3). 1992. 11.95 (*0-924483-64-4*); incl. audiocass. tape 16.95 (*0-924483-63-6*); incl. audiocass. tape & 9" stuffed porcupine toy 39.95 (*0-924483-62-8*); incl. audiocass. tape & 7 inch stuffed porcupine toy 25.95 (*0-924483-71-7*); pap. 5.95 (*0-924483-76-8*); write for info. audiocass. tape (*0-924483-73-3*) Soundprints.

Hack, Konrad. The Odyssey. Homer. Stewart, Diana, adapted by. LC 79-24480. 48p. (gr. 4 up). 1983. PLB 18.64 (*0-8172-1654-5*) Raintree Steck-V.

Hackney, Richard. Ada, la Desordenada (Messy Bessey) McKissack, Patricia & McKissack, Fredrick. LC 87-15079. (SPA.). 32p. (ps-2). 1988. PLB 11.93 (*0-516-32083-1*); pap. 2.95 (*0-516-52083-0*) Childrens.
—I Am an Explorer. Moses, Amy. LC 90-38374. 32p. (ps-2). 1990. PLB 11.93 (*0-516-02059-5*); pap. 2.95 (*0-516-42059-3*) Childrens.
—Messy Bessey's Garden. McKissack, Patricia & McKissack, Fredrick. LC 91-15333. 32p. (ps-2). 1991. PLB 11.93 (*0-516-02008-0*); pap. 2.95 (*0-516-42008-9*) Childrens.
—What If Everybody Did That? Javernick, Ellen. LC 89-28625. 32p. (ps-3). 1990. PLB 15.00 (*0-516-03669-6*); pap. 3.95 (*0-516-43669-4*) Childrens.
—Where Does the Puppy Live? Stortz, Diane M. LC 87-62602. (ps). 1988. 1.59 (*0-87403-389-6*, 24-02019) Standard Pub.
—Where's Brooke? Javernick, Ellen. LC 92-11097. 32p. (ps-2). 1992. PLB 11.93 (*0-516-02012-9*) Childrens.
—Where's Brooke? Javernick, Ellen. LC 92-11097. 32p. (ps-2). 1993. pap. 2.95 (*0-516-42012-7*) Childrens.

Hackney, Rick. Back Home in Japan: An Activity Book. Howell, Melissa. 64p. (gr. 1-4). 1991. tchr's. ed. 1.95 (*981-3009-02-0*); wkbk. 3.95 (*981-3009-24-1*) OMF Bks.

—Messy Bessey's Closet. McKissack, Patricia C. & McKissack, Fredrick. LC 89-34667. 32p. (ps-2). 1989. PLB 11.93 (0-516-02091-9); pap. 2.95 (0-516-42091-7) Childrens.

Hackwell, W. John. Diving to the Past: Recovering Ancient Wrecks. Hackwell, W. John. LC 87-233529. 64p. (gr. 3-7). 1988. RSBE 14.95 (0-684-18918-6, Scribners Young Read) Macmillan Child Grp.

—Signs, Letters, Words: Archaeology Discovers Writing. Hackwell, W. John. LC 86-26237. 72p. (gr. 7 up). 1987. SBE 14.95 (0-684-18807-4, Scribners Young Read) Macmillan Child Grp.

Haddon, Mark. Toni & the Tomato Soup. Haddon, Mark. 21p. (ps-1). 1989. 12.95 (0-15-200610-9, Gulliver Bks) HarBrace.

Hader, Berta & Hader, Elmer. The Big Snow. 2nd ed. Hader, Berta & Hader, Elmer. LC 87-38488. 48p. (gr. k-4). 1988. pap. 4.95 (0-689-71260-X, Aladdin) Macmillan Child Grp.

—The Big Snow. 2nd ed. Hader, Berta & Hader, Elmer. LC 92-46365. 48p. (gr. k-4). 1994. pap. 4.95 (0-689-71757-1, Aladdin) Macmillan Child Grp.

—Chicken Little and Little Half Chick. LC 83-38611. 1994. pap. write for info. (0-486-27979-0) Dover.

—Humpty Dumpty and Other Mother Goose Rhymes. LC 93-38612. 1994. pap. write for info. (0-486-27488-8) Dover.

—The Little Red Hen. LC 93-33702. (gr. 2 up). 1994. pap. write for info. (0-486-27977-4) Dover.

—A Visit from St. Nicholas. Moore, Clement C. LC 93-33703. (gr. 2 up). 1994. pap. write for info. (0-486-27978-2) Dover.

Hader, Elmer, jt. illus. see Hader, Berta.

Haeffele, Deborah. Come Away Home. Smith, Alison. LC 90-41534. 112p. (gr. 3-5). 1991. SBE 12.95 (0-684-19283-7, Scribners Young Read) Macmillan Child Grp.

—The Goodbye Walk. Ryder, Joanne. LC 92-10325. 32p. (gr. k-3). 1993. 13.99 (0-525-67405-5, Lodestar Bks) Dutton Child Bks.

—Harvest Song. Hirschi, Ron. LC 90-27009. 32p. (ps-3). 1991. 13.95 (0-525-65067-9, Cobblehill Bks) Dutton Child Bks.

—Island Child. Wallis, Lisa. 32p. (gr. k-3). 1992. 14.00 (0-525-67324-5, Lodestar Bks) Dutton Child Bks.

Haeffele, Deobrah. Rosamund. Johnson, Janice. LC 92-44115. (gr. 5 up). 1994. pap. 14.00 (0-671-79923-7, S&S BFYR) S&S Trade.

Hafer, Dick. Especially for Special Children: The A-B-C's of Super Stars. Prather, Gloria M. & Prather, Alfred G. Prather, Arden C., ed. 30p. (Orig.). 1988. Picture bk. PLB write for info. (0-9619655-3-3) Academic Packs Co.

—My First Reader & Skills Book: One Hundred Words Plus. Prather, Gloria A. & Prather, Alfred G. Prather, Arden C., ed. 36p. (Orig.). (gr. 1-3). 1988. pap. write for info. (0-9619655-2-5) Academic Packs Co.

Hafer, Dick & Daley, Natalie. The Way to Go: Academic Travel Pack. Prather, Gloria M. & Prather, Alfred G. Prather, Arden C. & Smith, Ellen, eds. 48p. (gr. k-2). 1987. write for info. wkbk. (0-9619655-0-9) Academic Packs Co.

Hafner, Marylin. Bully Trouble: A Step Two Book. Cole, Joanna. LC 89-3757. 48p. (Orig.). (gr. 1-3). 1989. lib. bdg. 7.99 (0-394-94949-8); pap. 3.50 (0-394-84949-3) Random Bks Yng Read.

—Candy Witch. Kroll, Steven. (ps up). 1988. pap. 2.50 (0-590-44509-X) Scholastic Inc.

—Families. Tax, Meredith. 32p. (ps-3). 1981. 15.95 (0-316-83240-5, Pub. by Atlantic) Little.

—Germs Make Me Sick! Berger, Melvin. LC 84-45334. 32p. (ps-3). 1985. (Crowell Jr Bks); PLB 14.89 (0-690-04429-1) HarpC Child Bks.

—Happy Mother's Day. Kroll, Steven. LC 83-18498. 32p. (ps-3). 1985. reinforced bdg. 14.95 (0-8234-0504-4) Holiday.

—It's Christmas. Prelutsky, Jack. LC 81-1100. 48p. (gr. 1-3). 1981. 12.95 (0-688-00439-3); PLB 12.88 (0-688-00440-7) Greenwillow.

—It's Thanksgiving. Prelutsky, Jack. 48p. (gr. k-3). 1989. Bk.-Cassette prepack. pap. 5.95 (0-590-63169-1); pap. 2.50 (0-590-41571-9) Scholastic Inc.

—Jenny & The Tennis Nut. Schulman, Janet. 64p. (gr. 1-4). 1981. pap. 2.50 (0-440-44211-7, YB) Dell.

—The Laugh Book. Cole, Joanna & Calmenson, Stephanie. LC 85-13113. 320p. (gr. 2-6). 1986. 17.00 (0-385-18559-6) Doubleday.

—M & M & the Big Bag I Am Reading Book. Ross, Pat. LC 80-23299. 48p. (gr. 1-4). 1981. 6.95 (0-394-84340-1) Pantheon.

—M & M & the Haunted House Game. Ross, Pat. 48p. (gr. 1-3). 1981. pap. 1.25 (0-440-45544-8, YB) Dell.

—Mind Your Manners. Parish, Peggy. 56p. (gr. 1 up). Date not set. pap. 3.95 (0-688-13109-3, Mulberry) Morrow.

—The Missing Tooth. Cole, Joanna. LC 88-1903. 48p. (Orig.). (gr. 1-3). 1988. lib. bdg. 7.99 (0-394-92279-2); pap. 3.50 (0-394-89279-8) Random Bks Yng Read.

—Mrs. Gaddy & the Ghost. Gage, Wilson, pseud. LC 78-16366. 56p. (ps-3). 1991. pap. 4.95 (0-688-10996-9, Mulberry) Morrow.

—Rainy, Rainy Saturday. Prelutsky, Jack. LC 79-22217. 48p. (gr. k-3). 1980. 12.95 (0-688-80252-4); PLB 13.88 (0-688-84252-6) Greenwillow.

Hafner, Marylin. Brush, Comb, Scrub: Inventions to Keep You Clean. Cobb, Vicki. LC 88-2930. 32p. (gr. 1-4). 1993. pap. 3.95 (0-06-446107-6, Trophy) HarpC Child Bks.

—The Candy Witch. Kroll, Steven. LC 79-10141. 32p. (ps-3). 1979. reinforced bdg. 14.95 (0-8234-0359-9) Holiday.

—Chatterbox Jamie. Cooney, Nancy E. LC 92-11001. 32p. (ps-1). 1993. PLB 14.95 (0-399-22208-1, Putnam) Putnam Pub Group.

—Dinosaurs Are 568. Rogers, Jean. LC 88-5501. 96p. (gr. 3 up). 1988. 10.95 (0-688-07931-8) Greenwillow.

—The Dog Food Caper. Lexau, Joan M. LC 84-1904. 48p. (ps-3). 1985. 8.95 (0-8037-0107-1) Dial Bks Young.

—Don't Feed the Guppies. Collins, Pat L. LC 92-25336. 1994. write for info. (0-399-22530-7) Putnam Pub Group.

—An Egg & Seven Socks. Mathews, Judith. LC 91-11476. 32p. (ps-2). 1993. 14.00 (0-06-020207-6); PLB 13.89 (0-06-020208-4) HarpC Child Bks.

—Fathers, Mothers, Sisters, Brothers: A Collection of Family Poems. Hoberman, Mary A. (ps-3). 1991. 14. 95 (0-316-36736-2) Little.

—Fathers, Mothers, Sisters, Brothers: A Collection of Family Poems. Hoberman, Mary A. LC 92-26587. 1993. pap. 4.99 (0-14-054849-1, Puffin) Puffin Bks.

—Feeding Time. Cobb, Vicki. LC 88-14192. 32p. (gr. k-3). 1989. (Lipp Jr Bks); PLB 11.89 (0-397-32325-5, Lipp Jr Bks) HarpC Child Bks.

—Germs Make Me Sick! Berger, Melvin. LC 84-45334. 32p. (ps-3). 1987. (Trophy); pap. 4.50 (0-06-445053-8, Trophy) HarpC Child Bks.

—Germs Make Me Sick! Berger, Melvin. LC 93-27059. 1995. write for info. (0-06-024249-3); lib. bdg. write for info. (0-06-024250-7) HarpC Child Bks.

—Getting Dressed. Cobb, Vicki. LC 87-26097. 32p. (gr. k-3). 1989. (Lipp Jr Bks); PLB 11.89 (0-397-32143-0) HarpC Child Bks.

—Hanukkah! Schotter, Roni. (ps-3). 1990. 14.95 (0-316-77466-9, Joy St Bks) Little.

—Happy Father's Day. Kroll, Steven. LC 87-7559. 32p. (ps-3). 1988. reinforced bdg. 14.95 (0-8234-0671-7) Holiday.

—Happy Mother's Day. Kroll, Steven. LC 86-25461. 32p. (ps-3). 1987. pap. 3.99 (0-14-050730-2, Puffin) Puffin Bks.

—I'm Santa Claus & I'm Famous. Sharmat, Marjorie W. LC 90-55106. 32p. (ps-4). 1990. reinforced 14.95 (0-8234-0826-4) Holiday.

—It's Christmas. Prelutsky, Jack. 48p. (Orig.). (gr. k-3). 1986. 2.75 (0-590-44048-9); incl. cassette 5.95 (0-590-63171-3) Scholastic Inc.

—It's Halloween. Prelutsky, Jack. LC 77-2141. 56p. (gr. 1-4). 1977. 13.95 (0-688-80102-1); PLB 13.88 (0-688-84102-3) Greenwillow.

—It's Halloween. Prelutsky, Jack. 48p. (ps-3). 1987. pap. 2.50 (0-590-41536-0); Books & Cassette. 5.95 (0-590-63252-3) Scholastic Inc.

—It's Thanksgiving. Prelutsky, Jack. LC 81-1929. 48p. (gr. 1-3). 1982. 12.95 (0-688-00441-5); lib. bdg. 12.88 (0-688-00442-3) Greenwillow.

—Keeping Clean. Cobb, Vicki. LC 88-2930. 32p. (gr. k-3). 1989. 11.95 (0-397-32312-3, Lipp Jr Bks); PLB 11.89 (0-397-32313-1) HarpC Child Bks.

—Kevin & the School Nurse. Davidson, Martine. LC 91-30194. 32p. (Orig.). (ps-2). 1992. PLB 5.99 (0-679-91821-3); pap. 2.25 (0-679-81821-9) Random Bks Yng Read.

—Lunch Bunnies. Lasky, Kathryn. LC 92-31554. 1993. 13.95 (0-316-51525-6, Joy St Bks) S&S Trade.

—M & M & the Bad News Babies. Ross, Pat. 48p. (ps-3). 1985. pap. 3.95 (0-14-031851-8, Puffin) Puffin Bks.

—M & M & the Halloween Monster. Ross, Pat. LC 91-50294. 48p. (gr. 1-2). 1991. text ed. 10.95 (0-670-83003-8) Viking Child Bks.

—M & M & the Halloween Monster. Ross, Pat. LC 93-15183. 64p. (gr. 2-5). 1993. pap. 3.99 (0-14-034247-8, Puffin) Puffin Bks.

—M & M & the Mummy Mess. Ross, Pat. 48p. (gr. 1-4). 1986. pap. 3.95 (0-14-032084-9, Puffin) Puffin Bks.

—M & M & the Santa Secrets. Ross, Pat. 48p. (gr. 1-4). 2.95 (0-317-62234-X, Puffin) Puffin Bks.

—M & M & the Super Child Afternoon. Ross, Pat. 48p. (gr. 1-4). 1989. pap. 3.95 (0-14-032145-4, Puffin) Puffin Bks.

—M & M & the Superchild Afternoon. Ross, Pat. LC 86-28128. (gr. 1-4). 1987. pap. 9.95 (0-670-81208-0) Viking Child Bks.

—Maggie & the Emergency Room. Davidson, Martine. LC 91-31413. 32p. (Orig.). (ps-2). 1992. PLB 5.99 (0-679-91818-3); pap. 2.25 (0-679-81818-9) Random Bks Yng Read.

—Me Baby! Levinson, Riki. LC 90-40372. 32p. (ps-1). 1991. 13.95 (0-525-44693-1, DCB) Dutton Child Bks.

—Meet M & M. Ross, Pat. 48p. (gr. 1-4). 1988. pap. 3.95 (0-14-032651-0, Puffin) Puffin Bks.

—Mind Your Manners. Parish, Peggy. LC 77-19096. 56p. (gr. 1-3). 1978. PLB 13.88 (0-688-84157-0) Greenwillow.

—Mrs. Gaddy & the Ghost. Gage, Wilson. LC 78-16366. 56p. (gr. 1-3). 1979. 14.95 (0-688-80179-X) Greenwillow.

—My Stars, It's Mrs. Gaddy! Gage, Wilson. LC 90-478577. 96p. (gr. 1 up). 1991. 15.95 (0-688-10514-9) Greenwillow.

—Passover Magic. Schotter, Roni. LC 93-20053. (gr. 1-8). 1994. 14.95 (0-316-77468-5) Little.

—The Poison Ivy Case. Lexau, Joan M. LC 82-22123. 56p. (ps-3). 1984. Dial Bks Young.

—The Purple Turkey & Other Thanksgiving Riddles. Adler, David A. LC 86-310. 64p. (gr. 1-4). 1986. reinforced bdg. 11.95 (0-8234-0613-X) Holiday.

—Raymond's Best Summer. Rogers, Jean. LC 89-34772. 80p. (gr. 1 up). 1990. 12.95 (0-688-09391-4) Greenwillow.

—Red Day, Green Day. Kunhardt, Edith. LC 90-38490. 32p. (ps up). 1992. 14.00 (0-688-09399-X); PLB 13.93 (0-688-09400-7) Greenwillow.

—Snap, Button, Zip: Inventions to Keep Your Clothes On. Cobb, Vicki. LC 87-26097. 32p. (gr. 1-4). 1993. pap. 3.95 (0-06-446106-8, Trophy) HarpC Child Bks.

—Sports Riddles. Hafner, Everett. 48p. (gr. 1-4). 1991. pap. 3.95 (0-14-032497-6, Puffin) Puffin Bks.

—Time Flies! Heide, Florence P. LC 84-47833. 112p. (gr. 3-7). 1984. 13.95 (0-8234-0542-7) Holiday.

—The TV-Smart Book for Kids: Puzzles, Games, & Other Good Stuff. Charren, Peggy & Hulsizer, Carol. 48p. (gr. 2-7). 1986. Parent's Guide, 16 p. 6.95 (0-525-44249-9, DCB) Dutton Child Bks.

—Writing It Down. Cobb, Vicki. LC 88-14191. 32p. (gr. k-3). 1989. (Lipp Jr Bks); PLB 11.89 (0-397-32327-1, Lipp Jr Bks) HarpC Child Bks.

Hafner, Marylin, photos by. Next Year I'll Be Special. Giff, Patricia R. LC 92-20749. 1993. 13.95 (0-385-30903-1, Zephyr-BFYR) Doubleday.

Hagar, Ashley. Sitting Bull. Grey, Alan. 64p. (gr. k-6). 1993. pap. 9.95 (1-56883-015-7) Colonial Pr AL.

—Sitting Bull. Grey, Alan. 64p. Date not set. pap. 9.95 (1-56883-031-9) Colonial Pr AL.

Hagerman, Jennifer. The Helping Place. Kibbey, Marsha. 40p. (gr. 1-4). 1991. PLB 13.50 (0-87614-680-9) Carolrhoda Bks.

—Kites on the Wind: Easy-to-Make Kites that Fly Without Sticks. Kelly, Emery. 64p. (gr. 4 up). 1991. PLB 22.95 (0-8225-2400-7) Lerner Pubns.

—Say It with Music: A Story about Irving Berlin. Streissguth, Tom. LC 93-4376. (gr. 4 up). 1993. 14.95 (0-87614-810-0) Carolrhoda Bks.

Hagstrom, Amy. Strong & Free. Hagstrom, Amy. LC 87-3942. 24p. (gr. 1 up). 1987. PLB 14.95 (0-933849-15-X) Landmark Edns.

Hague, Michael. Alice's Adventures in Wonderland. Carroll, Lewis. LC 85-856. 128p. (gr. 4-6). 1985. 19.95 (0-8050-0212-X, Bks Young Read) H Holt & Co.

—Alphabears. Hague, Kathleen. (ps-2). 1985. PLB incl. cassette 19.95 (0-941078-99-X) Live Oak Media.

—Alphabears: An ABC Book. Hague, Kathleen. LC 83-26476. 32p. (ps-2). 1984. 12.95 (0-8050-0841-1, Bks Young Read) H Holt & Co.

—Alphabears: An ABC Book. Hague, Kathleen. LC 83-26476. 32p. (ps-2). 1991. pap. 4.95 (0-8050-1637-6, Bks Young Read) H Holt & Co.

—Bear Hugs. Hague, Kathleen. LC 88-28458. 32p. (ps-2). 1989. 9.95 (0-8050-0512-9, Bks Young Read) H Holt & Co.

—Bear Hugs. Hague, Kathleen. LC 88-28458. 64p. (ps-2). 1992. pap. 4.95 (0-8050-2344-5, Bks Young Read) H Holt & Co.

—Beauty & the Beast. Apy, Deborah. LC 83-4395. 80p. (gr. 2-4). 1991. 14.95 (0-8050-1448-9, Bks Young Read) H Holt & Co.

—Beauty & the Beast. Apy, Deborah, retold by. LC 83-5495. 80p. (gr. 2-4). 1988. pap. 6.95 (0-8050-0948-5, Bks Young Read) H Holt & Co.

—The Cabbage Moth & the Shamrock. Marbach, Ethel. LC 91-575. 32p. (ps-2). 1991. jacketed, reinforced bdg. 9.00 (0-671-74864-5, Green Tiger) S&S Trade.

—Cinderella: And Other Tales from Perrault. Perrault, Charles. 78p. (gr. 2-4). 1989. 18.95 (0-8050-1004-1, Bks Young Read) H Holt & Co.

—Deck the Halls. LC 90-25628. 32p. (ps up). 1991. 4.95 (0-8050-1007-6, Bks Young Read) H Holt & Co.

—Demetrius & the Golden Goblet. Bunting, Eve. LC 79-14865. 48p. (gr. 1-5). 1980. 8.95 (0-15-223186-2, HB Juv Bks) HarBrace.

—Dream Weaver. Yolen, Jane. 80p. (gr. 10 up). 1989. 15. 95 (0-399-22152-2, Philomel Bks) Putnam Pub Group.

—The Fairies. Allingham, William. LC 88-28474. 32p. (ps-2). 1988. PLB 13.95 (0-8050-1003-3, Bks Young Read) H Holt & Co.

—The Fairy Tales of Oscar Wilde. LC 92-14305. 192p. 1993. 19.95 (0-8050-1009-2, Bks Young Read) H Holt & Co.

—The Hobbit. Tolkien, J. R. R. 320p. (gr. 7 up). 1984. 24.45 (0-395-36290-3) HM.

—The Hobbit. Tolkien, J. R. R. 300p. (ps up). 1989. pap. 16.45 (0-395-52021-5, Sandpiper) HM.

—How Chipmunk Got Tiny Feet: Native American Animal Origin Stories. Hausman, Gerald & Hausman, Gerald, eds. LC 94-24186. (ps-6). 1995. 15.00 (0-06-022906-3, HarpT); PLB 14.89 (0-06-022907-1) HarpC.

—Jingle Bells. Hague, Michael. LC 90-32066. 32p. (ps up). 1990. 4.95 (0-8050-1413-6, Bks Young Read) H Holt & Co.

—The Land of Nod & Other Poems for Children. Stevenson, Robert Louis. LC 87-26533. 64p. (ps-2). 1988. 16.95 (0-8050-0746-6, Bks Young Read) H Holt & Co.

—The Legend of the Veery Bird. Hague, Kathleen. LC 84-19732. 32p. (ps up). 1985. 13.95 (0-15-243824-6, HB Juv Bks) HarBrace.

—The Lion, the Witch & the Wardrobe: Gift Edition. Lewis, C. S. LC 83-61572. 192p. (gr. 3 up). 1983. SBE 22.95 (0-02-758200-0, Macmillan Child Bk) Macmillan Child Grp.

—The Little Mermaid. Andersen, Hans Christian. LC 92-29807. 1993. write for info. (0-8050-1010-6, Bks Young Read) H Holt & Co.
—Little Women, or, Meg, Jo, Beth, & Amy. Alcott, Louisa May. LC 93-18943. 308p. (gr. 4-8). 1993. PLB 15.95 (0-8050-2767-X, Bks Young Read) H Holt & Co.
—Magic Moments: A Book of Days. 96p. 1990. 14.95 (1-55970-069-6) Arcade Pub Inc.
—The Man Who Kept House. Hague, Kathleen & Hague, Michael. LC 80-26258. 32p. (ps-3). 1981. 12.95 (0-15-251698-0, HB Juv Bks) HarBrace.
—The Man Who Kept House. Hague, Kathleen. LC 80-26258. 32p. (ps-3). 1988. pap. 3.95 (0-15-251699-9, Voyager Bks) HarBrace.
—Michael Hague's Favourite Hans Christian Andersen Fairy Tales. Andersen, Hans Christian. LC 81-47455. 168p. (ps-2). 1981. 19.95 (0-8050-0659-1, Bks Young Read) H Holt & Co.
—Mother Goose: A Collection of Classic Nursery Rhymes. LC 83-22559. 80p. (ps-2). 1984. 15.95 (0-8050-0214-6, Bks Young Read) H Holt & Co.
—The Night Before Christmas. Moore, Clement C. LC 80-84842. 12p. (gr. k up). 1981. 12.95 (0-8050-0900-0, Bks Young Read) H Holt & Co.
—Numbears: A Counting Book. Hague, Kathleen. LC 85-27006. 32p. (ps-2). 1986. 12.95 (0-8050-0309-6, Bks Young Read) H Holt & Co.
—Numbears: Alphabears. Hague, Kathleen. LC 85-27006. 32p. (ps-2). 1991. pap. 4.95 (0-8050-1679-1, Bks Young Read) H Holt & Co.
—O Christmas Tree. Hague, Kathleen. LC 90-25527. 32p. (ps up). 1991. 4.95 (0-8050-1538-8, Bks Young Read) H Holt & Co.
—Old Mother West Wind. Burgess, Thornton. LC 89-20088. 90p. (gr. 2-4). 1990. 18.95 (0-8050-1005-X, Bks Young Read) H Holt & Co.
—Out of the Nursery, into the Night. Hague, Kathleen. LC 86-14270. 32p. (ps-2). 1986. 13.95 (0-8050-0088-7, Bks Young Read) H Holt & Co.
—Peter Pan. Barrie, James M. LC 87-403. 144p. (gr. 4-6). 1987. 19.95 (0-8050-0276-6, Bks Young Read) H Holt & Co.
—The Rainbow Fairy Book. Lang, Andrew. Glassman, Peter, intro. by. LC 92-33449. 288p. 1993. 20.00 (0-688-10878-4) Morrow Jr Bks.
—Rapunzel. Grimm, Jacob & Grimm, Wilhelm K. 32p. (gr. 6 up). 1986. PLB 13.95s.p. (0-87191-936-2) Creative Ed.
—The Reluctant Dragon. Grahame, Kenneth. LC 83-209. 48p. (gr. 2-4). 1983. 14.95 (0-8050-1112-9, Bks Young Read) H Holt & Co.
—The Reluctant Dragon. Grahame, Kenneth. LC 83-209. 48p. (gr. 2-4). 1988. pap. 5.95 (0-8050-0802-0, Bks Young Read) H Holt & Co.
—Rootabaga Stories, Pt. 1. Sandburg, Carl. 192p. (gr. 3-7). 1988. 19.95 (0-15-269061-1) HarBrace.
—Rootabaga Stories, Pt. 2. Sandburg, Carl. 179p. (gr. 3-7). 1989. 19.95 (0-15-269062-X) HarBrace.
—The Secret Garden. Burnett, Frances H. LC 86-22780. 240p. (gr. 4-6). 1987. 19.95 (0-8050-0277-4, Bks Young Read) H Holt & Co.
—Sleep, Baby, Sleep: Lullabies & Night Poems. Hague, Michael, compiled by. LC 93-27119. 1994. PLB write for info. (0-688-10877-6) Morrow Jr Bks.
—Teddy Bear, Teddy Bear: A Classic Action Rhyme. LC 92-17997. 32p. (ps up). 1993. 14.00 (0-688-10671-4); PLB 13.93 (0-688-12085-7) Morrow Jr Bks.
—The Teddy Bears' Picnic. Kennedy, Jimmy. LC 91-27709. 32p. (ps-2). 1992. 16.95 (0-8050-1008-4, Bks Young Read); poster avail. H Holt & Co.
—The Unicorn Alphabet. Mayer, Marianna. 32p. (gr. 1 up). 1989. 14.95 (0-8037-0372-4); PLB 14.89 (0-8037-0373-2) Dial Bks Young.
—The Unicorn Alphabet. Mayer, Marianna. 32p. 1993. pap. 5.99 (0-14-054922-6, Puffin Pied Piper) Puffin Bks.
—The Unicorn & the Lake. Mayer, Marianna. LC 82-71356. 32p. (gr. k up). 1982. PLB 13.89 (0-8037-9338-3) Dial Bks Young.
—A Unicorn Journal. 64p. 1990. 12.95 (1-55970-068-8) Arcade Pub Inc.
—The Velveteen Rabbit: Or, How Toys Become Real. Williams, Margery. LC 82-15606. 48p. (gr. k up). 1983. 11.95 (0-8050-0209-X, Bks Young Read) H Holt & Co.
—We Wish You a Merry Christmas. LC 90-32067. 32p. (gr. k up). 1990. 4.95 (0-8050-1006-8, Bks Young Read) H Holt & Co.
—The Wizard of Oz. Baum, L. Frank. LC 82-1109. 232p. (gr. 4-6). 1982. 19.95 (0-8050-0221-9, Bks Young Read) H Holt & Co.
Hague, Michael & Krush, Joe. Prairie-Town Boy. Sandburg, Carl. 228p. (gr. 3-7). 1990. pap. 4.95 (0-15-263332-4, Odyssey) HarBrace.
Hague, Scott. Goodnight Hands: A Bedtime Adventure. Rosen, Michael J. LC 91-67933. 32p. (ps-3). 1992. pap. 14.95 (1-880444-01-1) Times to Treas.
—The Lullaby & Goodnight Sleepkit: The Gift of Sweet Dreams & Family Memories. Rosen, Michael J. 32p. (ps-3). 1992. Boxed gift set incl. cass. & parents' guide. deluxe ed. 29.95 (1-880444-00-3); Mini ed. mini ed. cass & parents' guide, Aug. 1992 14.95 (1-880444-02-X) Times to Treas.
Hahn, Deborah. The Swineherd. Andersen, Hans Christian. Hahn, Deborah, retold by. LC 90-6248. 32p. (gr. k-4). 1991. 14.95 (0-688-10052-X); PLB 14.88 (0-688-10053-8) Lothrop.

Hahn, Sylvia. A Christmas Tree from Puddin' Stone Hill. Mole, Elsie H. 36p. (ps-8). 1985. 6.95 (0-920806-74-0, Pub. by Penumbra Pr CN) U of Toronto Pr.
Haidle, David & Haidle, Helen. He Is My Shepherd: The Twenty-Third Psalm for Children. Haidle, David & Haidle, Helen. Davis, Deena, ed. LC 89-31428. 27p. (gr. 3-8). 1989. 8.99 (0-88070-278-8, Gold & Honey) Questar Pubs.
Haidle, Elizabeth. Elmer the Grump. Haidle, Elizabeth. Thatch, Nancy R., ed. Melton, David, intro. by. LC 89-31872. 26p. (gr. k-5). 1989. PLB 14.95 (0-933849-20-6) Landmark Edns.
Haidle, Helen, jt. illus. see Haidle, David.
Haight, Sandy. On the Wings of a Butterfly: A Story about Life & Death. Maple, Marilyn. Grollman, Earl, afterword by. LC 91-50854. 32p. (Orig.). (gr. 1-6). 1992. 18.95 (0-943990-69-6); pap. 9.95 (0-943990-68-8) Parenting Pr.
—Seventy-Five Fun Things to Make & Do By Yourself. Ruelle, Karen G. LC 93-5091. 80p. (gr. 2-10). 1993. 14.95 (0-8069-0331-7) Sterling.
Haines, Bill. Stories of God's Love: Creation, Noah's Ark, Christmas, Joshua & the Wall of Jericho. Barrett, John, et al. (ps-2). 1990. 9.99 (1-55513-399-1, 63990, Chariot Bks) Cook.
—Stories of People Who Loved God: Jonah, Daniel, David, Esther. Barrett, John, et al. (ps-2). 1991. 9.99 (1-55513-539-0, 65391, Chariot Bks) Cook.
Hairston, Martha. The I Hate Mathematics! Book. Burns, Marilyn. 128p. (gr. 5 up). 1975. 15.95 (0-316-11740-4); pap. 9.95 (0-316-11741-2) Little.
Hakakian, Albert. The House That Shlomo Built. Zakutinsky, Ruth. Reason, Sharon, ed. 24p. (ps-1). 1989. 9.95 (0-911643-11-7) Aura Bklyn.
Haker, Loren F. The Li'l Rascals: Tale of a Fish. Haker, Loren F. 66p. (gr. 1-8). 1984. 7.95 (0-9609964-2-7); pap. 4.95 (0-9609964-3-5) Haker Books.
Halasz, Andras & Horen, Michael. The ArtScroll Youth Pirkei Avos, 2 vols. Gold, Avie. 48p. (gr. 3-12). 1989. 15.95 ea. (0-89906-244-X); pap. 12.95 ea. (0-89906-245-8) Mesorah Pubns.
Haldane, Suzanne, photos by. Helping Hands: How Monkeys Assist People Who Are Disabled. Haldane, Suzanne. LC 90-27382. 48p. (gr. 3-7). 1991. 14.95 (0-525-44723-7, DCB) Dutton Child Bks.
Hale, Beverly M. A Rainbow Book of Song: Key of "C" 2nd ed. Hale, Beverly M. 57p. (gr. up). 1993. Blue spine bdg. pap. text ed. 13.95 (0-9634305-1-3) E-Z Keys Method.
Hale, Bruce. The Legend of the Laughing Gecko: A Hawaiian Fantasy. Hale, Bruce. Brown, Susana, concept by. 32p. (Orig.). (ps-3). 1989. pap. write for info. Geckostufs.
—Surf Gecko to the Rescue! Hale, Bruce. 32p. (ps-4). 1991. write for info. (0-9621280-1-5) Geckostufs.
Hale, Christy. The Ancestor Tree. Echewa, T. Obinkaram. Date not set. write for info. (0-525-67467-5, Lodestar Bks) Dutton Child Bks.
—The Complete Poems to Solve. Swenson, May. LC 92-26183. 128p. (gr. 3 up). 1993. SBE 13.95 (0-02-788725-1, Macmillan Child Bk) Macmillan Child Grp.
—Juan Bobo & the Pig: A Puerto Rican Folktale. Pitre, Felix, retold by. 32p. (gr. k-3). 1993. 13.99 (0-525-67429-2, Lodestar Bks) Dutton Child Bks.

Hale, Hanna. Zelda Orangutan. Hale, Hanna. 64p. (gr. 4-6). 1994. Perfect bdg. pap. 12.95 (0-9638724-0-0) Cando Pubng.

Zelda, an orphaned baby orangutan is adopted by an actress. Cathy takes her to Hollywood, where together they star in a movie. The picture is a great success, but Zelda is lonely until she makes friends with Laddie, a collie & Kat, a kitten. Together they experience amusing as well as dangerous adventures. The animals foil a kidnapping attempt. Zelda protects two children who are being bullied by older classmates. She assists a forest ranger in an effort for the preservation of a California condor egg. Because of her great strength & climbing ability, the orangutan is able to help her friends frequently. As Zelda matures, she misses her orangutan family. Cathy understands her needs & returns Zelda to Sumatra & a free life in the jungle protectorate. Ordering information: Paperback--Perfect binding--64 pages-- (c) Hanna Hale 1994--Printed in U.S. A.--All rights reserved--Price: US $12. 95/Can. $18.95. Order from: CANDO PUBLISHING CORP. 1299 Springside Drive, Ft. Lauderdale, FL

33326-2748.
Publisher Provided Annotation.

Hale, Irina. Boxman. Hale, Irina. 32p. (ps-1). 1992. 12.00 (0-670-84287-7) Viking Child Bks.
—How I Found a Friend. Hale, Irina. 32p. (ps-1). 1992. PLB 12.50 (0-670-84286-9) Viking Child Bks.
—The Naughty Crow. Hale, Irina. LC 91-39929. 32p. (gr. k-4). 1992. SBE 14.95 (0-689-50546-9, M K McElderry) Macmillan Child Grp.
Hale, James G. Barney Is Best. Carlstrom, Nancy W. LC 92-30376. 32p. (gr. k-3). 1994. 15.00 (0-06-022875-X); PLB 14.89 (0-06-022876-8) HarpC Child Bks.
—Round & Round. Skofield, James. LC 90-32831. 32p. (ps-2). 1993. 15.00 (0-06-025746-6); PLB 14.89 (0-06-025747-4) HarpC Child Bks.
—Through Moon & Stars & Night Skies. Turner, Ann. LC 87-35044. 32p. (ps-3). 1990. 13.00 (0-06-026189-7); PLB 12.89 (0-06-026190-0) HarpC Child Bks.
—Through Moon & Stars & Night Skies. Turner, Ann. LC 87-35044. 32p. (ps-3). 1992. pap. 4.95 (0-06-443308-0, Trophy) HarpC Child Bks.
Hale, Janet. Fall Think & Do Shape Books. Hale, Janet. 48p. (gr. k-2). 1989. wkbk. 5.95 (1-55734-127-3) Tchr Create Mat.
—Spring & Summer Think & Do Shape Books. Hale, Janet. 48p. (gr. k-2). 1989. wkbk. 5.95 (1-55734-129-X) Tchr Create Mat.
Hale, Kathleen. Orlando's Evening Out. Hale, Kathleen. 32p. (ps-3). 1992. 15.95 (0-7232-3652-6) Warne.
Hale, Phil & Anderson, Darrel. Hong on the Range. Wu, William F. LC 88-29329. 224p. (gr. 7 up). 1989. 17.95 (0-8027-6862-8) Walker & Co.
Halebian, Carol, photos by. Erik Is Homeless. Greenberg, Keith E. 40p. (gr. 4-8). 1992. PLB 17.50 (0-8225-2551-8) Lerner Pubns.
Haley, Amanda. It's What's Inside That Counts. McMullen, Shawn A. 32p. (ps-2). 1991. pap. text ed. 3.99 (0-87403-808-1, 24-03898) Standard Pub.
—Justin Ordinary Squirrel. McMullen, Shawn A. 32p. (ps-2). 1991. pap. text ed. 3.99 (0-87403-807-3, 24-03897) Standard Pub.
—A New Home. McMullen, Shawn. LC 91-43071. 32p. (gr. 4-8). 1992. saddle-stitched 5.99 (0-87403-976-2, 24-03866) Standard Pub.
—That's What Friends Are For. McMullen, Shawn. LC 91-43656. (gr. 4-8). 1992. saddle-stitched 5.99 (0-87403-975-4, 24-03865) Standard Pub.
Haley, Gail E. Dream Peddler. Haley, Gail E. LC 92-42074. 32p. (ps-3). 1993. 14.99 (0-525-45153-6, DCB) Dutton Child Bks.
—Jack & the Bean Tree. 48p. (gr. k-3). 1986. 13.95 (0-517-55717-7) Crown Bks Yng Read.
—Jack & the Fire Dragon. Haley, Gail E., retold by. 40p. (gr. k-4). 1988. PLB 14.95 (0-517-56814-4) Crown Bks Yng Read.
—Marguerite. Haley, Gail E. (ps-3). 1993. pap. 16.95 (0-87460-262-9) Lion Bks.
—Mountain Jack Tales. 144p. (gr. 3-8). 1992. 15.99 (0-525-44974-4, DCB) Dutton Child Bks.
—Puss in Boots. Haley, Gail E., retold by. LC 90-20629. 32p. (ps-3). 1991. 13.95 (0-525-44740-7, DCB) Dutton Child Bks.
—A Story, A Story. Haley, Gail E. LC 69-18961. 36p. (ps-3). 1970. SBE 15.95 (0-689-20511-2, Atheneum Child Bk) Macmillan Child Grp.
—A Story, a Story. Haley, Gail E. LC 87-17412. 36p. (ps-3). 1988. pap. 4.95 (0-689-71201-4, Aladdin) Macmillan Child Grp.
Haley, Gail E., et al. Altogether, One at a Time. Konigsburg, E. L. LC 70-134814. 88p. (gr. 4-7). 1971. SBE 13.95 (0-689-20638-0, Atheneum Child Bk) Macmillan Child Grp.
Haley, Gale E. Sea Tale. Haley, Gail. LC 89-34453. 32p. (ps-2). 1990. 13.95 (0-525-44567-6, DCB) Dutton Child Bks.
Haley, Laura M. The Magic Corn. Persall, Holli C. 24p. (gr. k-4). 1990. 10.95 (0-9628486-0-3) Rhyme Time.
Hall, Brenny. Old MacDonald. (ps-3). 1981. 3.50 (0-913545-04-X) Moonlight FL.
Hall, Bruce. Baby Brendon's Busy Day: A Sexuality Primer. Jennings, Donna A. Wilson, Pamela M., intro. by. 32p. (ps). 1994. 15.95 (0-9638079-0-0) Goose Pond.
Hall, Candace C. Shelley's Day: The Day of a Legally Blind Child. Hall, Candace C. 24p. (Orig.). (gr. k-6). 1980. pap. 2.95 (0-9603840-0-6) Andrew Mtn Pr.
Hall, Chris A. Let's Celebrate Kwanzaa: An Activity Book for Young Readers. Davis-Thompson, Helen. 32p. (ps-5). 1993. pap. 5.95 (0-936073-07-1) Gumbs & Thomas.
Hall, Christine, et al. Twin Talk: Vocabulary Study Writing Book, Bk. 1. DeWitt, Jim. 78p. (Orig.). (gr. 4-12). 1987. pap. 6.00 wkbk. (0-915199-25-4) Pen-Dec.
Hall, Constance. Cappy Claus. Robinson, Ann. 16p. (ps-6). 1992. pap. 4.95 (0-9633373-0-0) Chameleon FL.
Hall, Diane. The Spade Sage. Beven, Annette. 24p. (gr. 1-3). 1976. pap. 7.95 (0-913546-71-2) Dharma Pub.
Hall, Douglas & Dennison, Graham. Wild Animals. Dreyer, Ellen. LC 90-11163. 96p. (gr. 2-5). 1991. PLB 14.89 (0-8167-2242-0); pap. text ed. 6.95 (0-8167-2243-9) Troll Assocs.
Hall, Joann. On My Own: The Kids' Self Care Book. Long, Lynette. LC 84-463. 160p. (Orig.). (gr. 1-7). 1984. pap. 7.95 (0-87491-735-2) Acropolis.

Hall, Judy A. Don't Just Say No! Safety Workbook for Children. 2nd ed. Hall, Judy A. Edwards, Juanita, ed. 40p. (Orig.). (gr. k-5). 1991. pap. text ed. write for info. saddlestitch (*0-9629597-1-5*) Personal Prods.
—What Every Child Should Know & Do...for Surviving in the 90's: A Small Picture Book. Hall, Judy A. Edwards, Juanita, ed. 24p. (Orig.). (gr. k-5). 1992. saddlestitched 9.95 (*0-9629597-0-7*) Personal Prods.
Hall, Kenneth L. Joey, the Little Reindeer & the Land of Forgotten Children. LaGrange, Lynn M. 40p. (ps-6). 1990. lib. bdg. 10.95 (*1-878790-02-1*) Fables CO.
—Joey, the Little Reindeer & the Land of Forgotten Children. LaGrange, Lynn M. 40p. (ps-6). 1990. pap. 6.95 (*1-878790-05-6*) Fables CO.
—Polly & the Frog. LaGrange, Lynn M. 36p. (ps-5). 1991. 10.95 (*1-878790-08-0*); pap. 6.95 (*1-878790-09-9*) Fables Co.
—Sir Cedrick Peabody: The Royal Little Snail. LaGrange, Lynn M. 32p. (ps-5). 1991. PLB 10.95 (*1-878790-06-4*) Fables Co.
—Sir Cedrick Peabody: The Royal Little Snail. LaGrange, Lynn M. 32p. (ps-5). 1991. pap. 6.95 (*1-878790-07-2*) Fables Co.
Hall, Leo D., jt. illus. see Warnick, Kelly.
Hall, Mahji. T Is for "Terrific", Mahji's ABC's. Hall, Mahji. LC 88-62371. 32p. (Orig.). (ps-3). 1989. PLB 9.95 (*0-940880-21-0*); pap. text ed. 4.95 (*0-940880-22-9*) Open Hand.
Hall, Mary A. No Sweat! How to Use Your Learning Style to Be a Better Student. Ulrich, Cindy & Guild, Pat. Craig, Dorothy, ed. 52p. (gr. 8-12). 1986. wkbk. 5.95 (*0-317-92552-0*) Teaching Advisory.
Hall, Maureen K. Grandmother's Locket. Upham, Elizabeth. 38p. (ps-1). 1985. 12.95 (*0-940696-10-X*) Monroe County Lib.
Hall, Melanie. On the Riverbank. Temple, Charles. LC 91-43942. 32p. (ps-3). 1992. 14.45 (*0-395-61591-7*) HM.
—Shanty Boat. Temple, Charles. LC 92-46025. 1994. write for info (*0-395-66163-3*) HM.
Hall, Melanie, photos by. Weather. Hopkins, Lee B., compiled by. LC 92-14913. 64p. (gr. k-3). 1994. 14.00 (*0-06-021463-5*); PLB 13.89 (*0-06-021462-7*) HarpC Child Bks.
Hall, Melanie W. July Is a Mad Mosquito. Lewis, J. Patrick. LC 93-19743. 32p. (gr. 2-5). 1994. SBE 14.95 (*0-689-31813-8*, Atheneum Child Bk) Macmillan Child Grp.
Hall, Pat. Curious Kimo. Maness, Malia. LC 93-86143. 32p. (ps-3). 1993. 9.95 (*0-9633493-0-9*) Pacific Greetings.
—Emily's Hawaii. Tabrah, Ruth M. 191p. (gr. 4-6). 1986. pap. 6.95 (*0-916630-45-5*) Pr PaCifica.
—The Red Shark. 2nd ed. Tabrah, Ruth M. 224p. (gr. 5-10). 1991. pap. 7.95 (*0-916630-67-6*) Pr Pacifica.
Hall, Patt. The Toad That Taught Flying. Maness, Malia. LC 93-86144. 32p. (ps-3). 1993. 9.95 (*0-9633493-1-7*) Pacific Greetings.
Hall, Robyn. Daily Close-Ups for Winter. Magoldi, Mary. Russell, Bruce, ed. 96p. (gr. k-6). 1984. wkbk. 9.95 (*0-86653-256-0*, GA 562) Good Apple.
Hall, Susan. Changing Seasons. Greydanus, Rose. LC 82-19959. 32p. (gr. k-2). 1983. PLB 11.59 (*0-89375-902-3*); pap. 2.95 (*0-8167-1478-9*) Troll Assocs.
—Jonathan's Amazing Adventure. Frost, Erica. LC 85-14129. 48p. (Orig.). (gr. 1-3). 1986. PLB 10.59 (*0-8167-0662-X*); pap. text ed. 3.50 (*0-8167-0663-8*) Troll Assocs.
—Little Raccoon Who Could. Poskanzer, Susan C. LC 85-14020. 48p. (gr. 1-3). 1986. PLB 10.59 (*0-8167-0624-7*); pap. text ed. 3.50 (*0-8167-0625-5*) Troll Assocs.
—Muffy & Fluffy: The Kittens Who Didn't Agree. Craig, Janet. LC 87-16227. 32p. (gr. k-2). 1988. PLB 7.89 (*0-8167-1227-1*); pap. text ed. 1.95 (*0-8167-1228-X*) Troll Assocs.
—Oh Beans! Starring Bean Sprout. Weiss, Ellen. LC 88-19980. 32p. (gr. k-3). 1989. lib. bdg. 8.79 (*0-8167-1406-1*); pap. text ed. 1.95 (*0-8167-1407-X*) Troll Assocs.
—Oh Beans! Starring Boston Bean. Weiss, Ellen. LC 88-19981. 32p. (gr. k-3). 1989. lib. bdg. 8.79 (*0-8167-1414-2*); pap. text ed. 1.95 (*0-8167-1415-0*) Troll Assocs.
—Oh Beans! Starring Green Bean. Weiss, Ellen. LC 88-19970. 32p. (gr. k-3). 1989. lib. bdg. 8.79 (*0-8167-1398-7*); pap. text ed. 1.95 (*0-8167-1399-5*) Troll Assocs.
—Oh Beans! Starring Half-Baked Bean. Weiss, Ellen. LC 88-4901. 32p. (gr. k-3). 1989. PLB 8.79 (*0-8167-1402-9*); pap. text ed. 1.95 (*0-8167-1403-7*) Troll Assocs.
—Oh Beans! Starring Jelly Bean. Weiss, Ellen. LC 88-4904. 32p. (gr. k-3). 1989. PLB 8.79 (*0-8167-1404-5*); pap. text ed. 1.95 (*0-8167-1405-3*) Troll Assocs.
—Oh Beans! Starring Lima Bean. Weiss, Ellen. LC 88-19969. 32p. (gr. k-3). 1989. lib. bdg. 8.79 (*0-8167-1394-4*); pap. text ed. 1.95 (*0-8167-1395-2*) Troll Assocs.
—Oh Beans! Starring Mean Bean. Weiss, Ellen. LC 88-19982. 32p. (gr. k-3). 1989. lib. bdg. 8.79 (*0-8167-1400-2*); pap. text ed. 1.95 (*0-8167-1401-0*) Troll Assocs.
—Oh Beans! Starring Snap Bean. Weiss, Ellen. LC 88-4900. 32p. (gr. k-3). 1989. PLB 8.79 (*0-8167-1410-X*) Troll Assocs.

—Oh Beans! Starring String Bean. Weiss, Ellen. LC 88-4907. 32p. (gr. k-3). 1989. PLB 8.79 (*0-8167-1396-0*); pap. text ed. 1.95 (*0-8167-1397-9*) Troll Assocs.
—Oh Beans! Starring Superbean. Weiss, Ellen. LC 88-19979. 32p. (gr. k-3). 1989. lib. bdg. 8.79 (*0-8167-1416-9*); pap. text ed. 1.95 (*0-8167-1417-7*) Troll Assocs.
—Oh Beans! Starring Vanilla Bean. Weiss, Ellen. LC 88-4903. 32p. (gr. k-3). 1989. PLB 8.79 (*0-8167-1412-6*); pap. text ed. 1.95 (*0-8167-1413-4*) Troll Assocs.
—Oh Beans! Starring Wax Bean. Weiss, Ellen. LC 88-4902. 32p. (gr. k-3). 1989. PLB 8.79 (*0-8167-1408-8*); pap. text ed. 1.95 (*0-8167-1409-6*) Troll Assocs.
—Our Friend the Sun. Palazzo, Janet. LC 81-11460. 32p. (gr. k-2). 1982. PLB 11.59 (*0-89375-650-4*); pap. 2.95 (*0-89375-651-2*) Troll Assocs.
—Surprise Party. Gordon, Sharon. LC 81-4869. 32p. (gr. k-2). 1981. PLB 11.59 (*0-89375-521-4*); pap. 2.95 (*0-89375-522-2*) Troll Assocs.
—What Time Is It? Grey, Judith. LC 81-5113. 32p. (gr. k-2). 1981. PLB 11.59 (*0-89375-509-5*); pap. text ed. 2.95 (*0-89375-510-9*) Troll Assocs.
Hall, Susan T. Animals at the Zoo. Greydanus, Rose. 32p. (gr. k-2). 1980. PLB 8.79 (*0-89375-371-8*); pap. 1.95 (*0-89375-271-1*) Troll Assocs.
—Best Thanksgiving Book. Whitehead, Patricia. LC 84-8831. 32p. (gr. k-2). 1985. PLB 11.59 (*0-8167-0371-X*); pap. text ed. 2.95 (*0-8167-0372-8*) Troll Assocs.
—Noah's Ark. Hall, Susan T. 12p. (ps). 1990. pap. text ed. 5.95 (*0-927106-03-5*) Prod Concept.
—Perfect Pals. Hall, Susan T. 12p. (ps). 1989. pap. text ed. 5.95 (*0-927106-00-0*) Prod Concept.
—Pussycat Kite. Peters, Sharon. LC 84-8632. 32p. (gr. k-2). 1985. PLB 11.59 (*0-8167-0358-2*); pap. text ed. 2.95 (*0-8167-0438-4*) Troll Assocs.
—So Sleepy. Hall, Susan T. 12p. (ps). 1989. pap. text ed. 5.95 (*0-927106-01-9*) Prod Concept.
—Trick or Treat Halloween. Peters, Sharon. 32p. (gr. k-2). 1980. PLB 7.89 (*0-89375-392-0*); pap. 1.95 (*0-89375-292-4*) Troll Assocs.
Hall, Wendell E. Favorite Scary Stories of American Children. Young, Richard & Young, Judy D. 112p. (Orig.). (ps-5). 1990. pap. 8.95 (*0-87483-119-9*) August Hse.
—Favorite Scary Stories of American Children. Young, Richard & Young, Judy D. 1991. 19.95 (*0-87483-120-2*) August Hse.
Hallahan, Maureen. Zoo: First Readers. Harding, Jacqueline. 28p. (ps-k). 1992. 3.50 (*0-7214-1490-7*) Ladybird Bks.
Hallett, Joy D. Kelly Bear Activities. Davies, Leah G. LC 92-70013. 40p. (ps-3). 1992. pap. 10.95 (*0-9621054-4-9*) Kelly Bear Pr.
—Kelly Bear Drug Awareness. Davies, Leah G. 40p. (ps-3). 1993. pap. 10.95 (*0-9621054-6-5*) Kelly Bear Pr.

Hallett, Leah. Kelly Bear Beginnings, 5 bks. Davies, Leah. 176p. (ps-5). 1991. Set incl. Kelly Bear Feelings; Kelly Bear Behavior; Kelly Bear Health; Kelly Bear Activities; Kelly Bear Drug Awareness. pap. 29.95 (*0-9621054-7-3*) Kelly Bear Pr.
The KELLY BEAR books teach children important life skills such as coping positively with emotions, learning appropriate behavior, making wholesome choices & accepting responsibility for their feelings, actions & bodies. Children identify with the green bear who is a positive role model. The INTERACTION books are to be read by an adult (teacher, librarian, counselor, parent) with a child or children. Throughout the books Kelly Bear asks questions that encourage children to share their thoughts & feelings, as Kelly Bear does. When adults listen with regard, children perceive themselves as valued & their self-esteem thrives. According to Dr. Kevin Swick, Univ. of South Carolina, the KELLY BEAR books have "exemplary situations"... which "have been used successfully with parents & children from every background & cultural orientation." A teacher, stated, "The books provide invaluable insights.. .a wonderful teaching tool." The acclaimed series is being used effectively with classrooms of children, in small groups, & with individuals, include high-risk & special education

students. The KELLY BEAR books are the mainstay of an eight-week Drug Abuse Prevention Program (DAPP) $199.00. Kelly Bear Press, 4295 Co. Rd. 12, Lafayette, AL 36862. (205) 864-8991.
Publisher Provided Annotation.

Hallett, Mark. Dinosaurs. Wildlife Education, Ltd. Staff. 20p. (Orig.). (gr. k-12). 1985. pap. 2.75 (*0-937934-34-8*) Wildlife Educ.
Hallett, Mark, jt. illus. see Stuart, Walter.
Hallett, Mark, photos by. The Search for Seismosaurus. Gillette, J. Lynett. LC 92-28199. 1993. 14.99 (*0-8037-1358-4*) Dial Bks Young.
Hallin, Britta, et al. American Woman: Hidden in History, Forging the Future. 2nd & enl. ed. Hammer, Roger A. 80p. (gr. 7 up). 1993. pap. 19.95 (*0-932991-27-0*) Place in the Woods.
Hallinan, Brenda C. Mountain Massacres & Other Stories of Appalachia. Cutlip, Ralph V. 167p. (Orig.). (gr. 8 up). 1986. pap. 6.50 (*0-317-47675-0*) B Cutlip.
Hallinan, P. K. Easy Does It. Hallinan, P. K. 32p. 1992. pap. 5.00 (*0-89486-673-7*) Hazelden.
—For the Love of Our Earth. Hallinan, P. K. 24p. (gr. k-3). 1992. PLB 10.95 (*1-878363-73-5*) Forest Hse.
—How Do I Love You. Hallinan, P. K. 24p. (ps-4). 1991. PLB 10.95 (*1-878363-27-1*) Forest Hse.
—I Know I Belong. Hallinan, P. K. 28p. 1991. pap. 5.00 (*0-89486-782-2*) Hazelden.
—I Know There's a Power. Hallinan, P. K. 28p. 1991. pap. 5.00 (*0-89486-780-6*) Hazelden.
—I Know Who I Am. Hallinan, P. K. 28p. 1991. pap. 5.00 (*0-89486-781-4*) Hazelden.
—I'm Thankful Each Day! Hallinan, P. K. 24p. (gr. k-2). 1989. pap. 3.95 perfect bdg. (*0-8249-8535-4*, Ideals Child) Hambleton-Hill.
—Just Open a Book. Hallinan, P. K. LC 80-22099. 32p. (ps-3). 1981. pap. 3.95 (*0-516-43521-3*) Childrens.
—Live & Let Live. Hallinan, P. K. 32p. 1990. pap. 5.00 (*0-89486-650-8*) Hazelden.
—My First Day of School. Hallinan, P. K. 24p. (gr. k-6). 1987. perfect bdg. 3.95 (*0-8249-8533-8*, Ideals Child) Hambleton-Hill.
—My Very Best Rainy Day. Hallinan, P. K. 24p. (ps-4). 1991. PLB 10.95 (*1-878363-28-X*) Forest Hse.
—One Day At a Time. Hallinan, P. K. 28p. 1990. pap. 5.00 (*0-89486-640-0*) Hazelden.
—That's What a Friend Is. Hallinan, P. K. LC 76-27744. 32p. (gr. k-3). 1977. pap. 3.95 (*0-516-43628-7*) Childrens.
—That's What a Friend Is. Hallinan, P. K. 32p. (gr. k-2). 1985. pap. 3.95 (*0-8249-8006-9*, Ideals Child) Hambleton-Hill.
—Today Is Christmas. Hallinan, P. K. 24p. (ps-3). 1993. PLB 10.95 (*1-878363-93-X*) Forest Hse.
—Today Is Christmas! Hallinan, P. K. 24p. (ps-2). 1993. pap. 3.95 (*0-8249-8643-1*, Ideals Child) Hambleton-Hill.
—Today Is Easter! Hallinan, P. K. 24p. (Orig.). (ps-2). 1993. pap. 3.95 (*0-8249-8604-0*, Ideals Child) Hambleton-Hill.
—Today Is Easter. Hallinan, P. K. 24p. (ps-3). 1993. PLB 10.95 (*1-878363-94-8*) Forest Hse.
—Today Is Halloween! Hallinan, P. K. 24p. (ps-2). 1992. pap. text ed. 3.95 (*0-8249-8557-5*, Ideals Child) Hambleton-Hill.
—Today Is Halloween. Hallinan, P. K. 24p. (ps-3). 1992. PLB 10.95 (*1-878363-95-6*) Forest Hse.
—Today Is Thanksgiving. Hallinan, P. K. 24p. (ps-3). 1993. PLB 10.95 (*1-878363-96-4*) Forest Hse.
—Today Is Thanksgiving. Hallinan, P. K. 24p. (ps-2). 1993. pap. 3.95 (*0-8249-8637-7*, Ideals Child) Hambleton-Hill.
—Today Is Your Birthday. 24p. (ps-4). 1991. PLB 10.95 (*1-878363-29-8*) Forest Hse.
—We're Very Good Friends, My Brother & I. Hallinan, P. K. 24p. (ps-2). 1990. 3.95 (*0-8249-8469-2*, Ideals Child) Hambleton-Hill.
—We're Very Good Friends, My Father & I. Hallinan, P. K. (ps-2). 1990. pap. 3.95 perfect bdg. (*0-8249-8520-6*, Ideals Child) Hambleton-Hill.
—We're Very Good Friends, My Mother & I. Hallinan, P. K. 24p. (ps-2). 1990. pap. 3.95 perfect bdg. (*0-8249-8519-2*, Ideals Child) Hambleton-Hill.
—We're Very Good Friends, My Sister & I. Hallinan, P. K. 24p. (ps-2). 1990. 3.95 (*0-8249-8470-6*, Ideals Child) Hambleton-Hill.
Hallinan, Patrick. The Small Town Children's Easter. Hallinan, Patrick. 24p. (ps-3). 1989. pap. 2.95 (*0-8249-8319-X*, Ideals Child) Hambleton-Hill.
—We're Very Good Friends, My Grandma & I. Hallinan, Patrick. 24p. (ps-2). 1989. pap. 3.95 perfect bdg. (*0-8249-8548-6*, Ideals Child) Hambleton-Hill.
—We're Very Good Friends, My Grandpa & I. Hallinan, Patrick. 24p. (ps-2). 1989. pap. 3.95 perfect bdg. (*0-8249-8549-4*, Ideals Child) Hambleton-Hill.
Hallock, Michelle. The Land of Numm. Herron, John. 14p. 1992. pap. 9.95 (*1-881617-07-6*) Teapot Tales.
Halloway, Jan. Tales about Tails. Mack, Jacqueline. 24p. (ps-k). 1985. 10.95 (*0-88625-089-7*) Durkin Hayes Pub.
Halper, Roe. Passover Haggadah. Halper, Roe. 40p. (Orig.). 1986. pap. 5.00 (*0-916326-03-9*) Bayberry Pr.

Halperin, Wendy A. Hunting the White Cow. Seymour, Tres. LC 92-43757. 32p. (ps-2). 1993. 15.95 *(0-531-05496-9)*; PLB 15.99 *(0-531-08646-1)* Orchard Bks Watts.
—The Lampfish of Twill. Lisle, Janet T. LC 91-8279. 176p. (gr. 5 up). 1991. 15.95 *(0-531-05963-4)*; RLB 15.99 *(0-531-08563-5)* Orchard Bks Watts.
—The Lampfish of Twill. Lisle, Janet T. 176p. (gr. 3-7). 1993. pap. 2.75 *(0-590-46040-4,* Apple Paperbacks) Scholastic Inc.
Halpern, C. The Homontash That Ran Away. Halpern, C. (ps-4). 2.95 *(0-87306-995-1)* Feldheim.
Halpern, Gina. Where Is Tibet? Halpern, Gina. Jorden, Ngawang, tr. 62p. (gr. k-4). 1991. pap. 12.95 *(0-937938-93-9)* Snow Lion.
Halpern, Joan. The Carp in the Bathtub. Cohen, Barbara. 48p. (gr. 1-5). 1972. PLB 13.88 *(0-688-51627-0)* Lothrop.
Halpern, Joan, photos by. The Carp in the Bathtub. Cohen, Barbara. LC 87-80446. 32p. (gr. k-5). 1987. pap. 4.95 *(0-930494-67-9)* Kar-Ben.
Halpern, John, jt. illus. see Fisher, Jon.
Halpern, John, photos by. A Day in the Life of a Beekeeper. Michels, Penny & Tropea, Judith. LC 90-11078. 32p. (gr. 4-8). 1991. lib. bdg. 11.79 *(0-8167-2206-4)*; pap. text ed. 2.95 *(0-8167-2207-2)* Troll Assocs.
—A Day in the Life of a Museum Curator. Tropea, Judith. LC 90-11060. 32p. (gr. 4-8). 1991. lib. bdg. 11.79 *(0-8167-2212-9)*; pap. text ed. 2.95 *(0-8167-2213-7)* Troll Assocs.
—A Day in the Life of a Seeing Eye Dog Trainer. Osborn, Kevin. LC 90-11076. 32p. (gr. 4-8). 1991. lib. bdg. 11.79 *(0-8167-2218-8)*; pap. text ed. 2.95 *(0-8167-2219-6)* Troll Assocs.
Halpern, Shari. Moving from One to Ten. Halpern, Shari. LC 92-26992. 32p. (ps-1). 1993. RSBE 13.95 *(0-02-741981-9,* Macmillan Child Bk) Macmillan Child Grp.
—My River. Halpern, Shari. LC 91-33582. 32p. (gr. k-2). 1992. RSBE 13.95 *(0-02-741980-0,* Macmillan Child Bk) Macmillan Child Grp.

Halpin, Scot. Who Would Want Those Apples Anyway? Griscom, Laura & Griscom, Pam. 24p. (Orig.). (ps-5). 1993. pap. 4.95 *(0-9633705-3-7)* Share Pub CA.

WHO WOULD WANT THOSE APPLES ANYWAY? is an enchanting picture book based on three-year-old Laura Griscom's questions about agricultural pesticides, boldly illustrated by T. Scot Halpin. A bug problem in Laura's garden sends her to a commercial farm in search of advice. A friendship with a farm worker's child leads to discussions about what shoppers support with their decisions at the marketplace. Laura wonders why so many farmers & consumers make unhealthy choices. By deciding that bugs "have very TEENY little teeth," this curious child reframes a dilemma, & avoids the use of pesticides on her tiny crop, She & her sister decide that the perfect looking CONVENTIONAL produce isn't attractive after all; they want the same pear that the bug tasted, because "bugs are very smart" & "it's OK to share." From ecology to aesthetics to economics, this book is an excellent resource for parents & teachers; a non-threatening way to introduce the hidden consequences of food production to future consumers. ". ..Strikes just the right note, makes all the points & is beautifully written."-- Dr. Marion Moses. Share Publishing, 3130 Alpine Road, Suite 200-1009, Portola Valley, CA 94028. (415-851-0731) FAX: 415-854-8202.
Publisher Provided Annotation.

Halsey, Megan. Annabel. Boland, Janice. LC 91-46490. 32p. (ps-2). 1993. 12.99 *(0-8037-1254-5)*; PLB 12.89 *(0-8037-1255-3)* Dial Bks Young.
—The Darling Boys. Helldorfer, M. C. LC 91-44708. 32p. (gr. k-3). 1992. RSBE 14.95 *(0-02-743516-4,* Bradbury Pr) Macmillan Child Grp.
—Rosa & Marco and the Three Wishes. Brenner, Barbara. LC 90-26855. 32p. (gr. 1-3). 1992. RSBE 11.95 *(0-02-712315-4,* Bradbury Pr) Macmillan Child Grp.

—Stewart Stork. Madsen, Ross M. LC 92-30730. 40p. (ps-3). 1993. 11.99 *(0-8037-1325-8)*; PLB 11.89 *(0-8037-1326-6)* Dial Bks Young.
—Three Pandas Planting: Counting down to Help the Earth. Halsey, Megan. LC 93-22971. 40p. (ps-2). 1994. RSBE 14.95 *(0-02-742035-3,* Bradbury Pr) Macmillan Child Grp.
Halverson, Lydia. The Animals' Ballgame. LC 92-9416. 24p. (ps-3). 1991. PLB 16.93 *(0-685-62659-8)*; pap. 5.95 *(0-516-45139-1)* Childrens.
—Animals Can be Special Friends. Chlad, Dorothy. LC 84-23300. 32p. (ps-2). 1985. pap. 3.95 *(0-516-41978-1)* Childrens.
—Apatosaurus. Riehecky, Janet. LC 88-1694. 32p. (gr. k-4). 1988. PLB 21.35 *(0-89565-423-7)*; PLB 14.95s.p. *(0-685-55919-X)* Childs World.
—Bicycles Are Fun to Ride. Chlad, Dorothy. LC 83-23234. 32p. (ps-2). 1984. pap. 3.95 *(0-516-41975-7)* Childrens.
—Los Cerillos, los Encendedores y los Triquitraques No Son Juguetes (Matches, Lighters & Firecrackers Are Not Toys) Chlad, Dorothy. LC 81-18125. (SPA.). 32p. (ps-2). 1987. PLB 15.00 *(0-516-31982-5)*; pap. 3.95 *(0-516-51982-4)* Childrens.
—Coelophysis. Riehecky, Janet. 32p. (gr. k-4). 1990. PLB 21.35 *(0-89565-623-X)*; PLB 14.95s.p. *(0-685-56208-5)* Childs World.
—Cuando Cruzo la Calle (When I Cross the Street) Chlad, Dorothy. Kratky, Lada, tr. LC 85-31397. (SPA.). 32p. (ps-2). 1986. PLB 15.00 *(0-516-31985-X)*; pap. 3.95 *(0-516-51985-9)* Childrens.
—Cuando Hay un Incendio Sal Para Afuera (When There Is a Fire...Go Outside) Chlad, Dorothy. Kratky, Lada, tr. from ENG. LC 85-9636. (SPA.). 32p. (ps-2). 1984. PLB 15.00 *(0-516-31986-8)*; pap. 3.95 *(0-516-51986-7)* Childrens.
—Cuando viajo en auto (When I Ride in a Car) Chlad, Dorothy. LC 83-7382. (ENG & SPA.). 32p. (ps-2). 1989. PLB 15.00 *(0-516-31987-6)*; pap. 3.95 *(0-516-51987-5)* Childrens.
—Los Desconocidos (Strangers) Chlad, Dorothy. Kratky, Lada, tr. from ENG. LC 81-18109. (SPA.). 32p. (ps-2). 1984. PLB 15.00 *(0-516-31984-1)*; pap. 3.95 *(0-516-51984-0)* Childrens.
—Es Divertido Andar en Bicicleta (Bicycles Are Fun to Ride) Chlad, Dorothy. Kratky, Lada, tr. LC 85-23263. (SPA.). 32p. (ps-2). 1986. pap. 3.95 *(0-516-51975-1)* Childrens.
—In the Water...On the Water. Chlad, Dorothy. LC 88-12065. 32p. (ps-2). 1988. pap. 3.95 *(0-516-41974-9)* Childrens.
—John's Choice. Moncure, Jane B. LC 82-19897. 32p. (gr. 1-3). 1982. 19.95 *(0-89565-252-8)*; PLB 13.95 *(0-685-57930-1)* Childs World.
—Jugando en el Patio de Recreo (Playing on the Playground) Chlad, Dorothy. LC 87-5197. (SPA.). 32p. (ps-2). 1988. pap. 3.95 *(0-516-51989-1)* Childrens.
—Kwanzaa. Riehecky, Janet. LC 93-17076. (gr. 4 up). 1993. write for info. *(0-516-00686-X)* Childrens.
—Learning about Dragons. Stallman, Birdie. LC 81-4746. 48p. (gr. 2-6). 1981. pap. 4.95 *(0-516-46531-7)* Childrens.
—Martin Luther King Day. McDonnell, Janet. LC 93-13251. 1993. write for info. *(0-516-00687-8)*
—My First Presidents' Day Book. Moncure, Jane B. LC 87-10309. 32p. (ps-2). 1987. pap. 3.95 *(0-516-42910-8)* Childrens.
—Night Animals: Wake-Up, Little Owl! Moncure, Jane B. LC 89-71173. 32p. (ps-2). 1990. PLB 21.35 *(0-89565-568-3)*; PLB 14.95s.p. *(0-685-56184-4)* Childs World.
—Playing on the Playground. Chlad, Dorothy. LC 87-5197. 32p. (ps-2). 1987. pap. 3.95 *(0-516-41989-7)* Childrens.
—Playing Outdoors in the Winter. Chlad, Dorothy. LC 90-22258. 32p. (ps-2). 1991. pap. 3.95 *(0-516-41972-2)* Childrens.
—Poisons Make You Sick. Chlad, Dorothy. LC 83-24029. 32p. (ps-2). 1984. PLB 15.00 *(0-516-01976-7)*; pap. 3.95 *(0-516-41976-5)* Childrens.
—Que Semana, Luchito! Cumpiano, Ina. (SPA.). 24p. (Orig.). (gr. 1-3). 1991. pap. text ed. 29.95 big bk. *(1-56334-023-2)*; pap. text ed. 4.15 small bk. *(1-56334-037-2)* Hampton-Brown.
—Los Venenos Te Hacen Dano (Poisons Make You Sick) Chlad, Dorothy. Kratky, Lada, tr. LC 85-30738. (SPA.). 32p. (ps-2). 1986. PLB 15.00 *(0-516-31976-0)*; pap. 3.95 *(0-516-51976-X)* Childrens.
—Viajando en Autobus (Riding on a Bus) Chlad, Dorothy. LC 85-12570. (SPA.). 32p. (ps-2). 1988. PLB 15.00 *(0-516-31979-5)*; pap. 3.95 *(0-516-51979-4)* Childrens.
—The White Hare of Inaba: A Japanese Folktale. Hamada, Cheryl, retold by. LC 93-6772. 32p. (ps-3). 1993. PLB write for info. *(0-516-05147-4)* Childrens.
—Wow, What a Week! Porter, Mark. 24p. (Orig.). (gr. 1-3). 1991. pap. text ed. 29.95 big bk. *(1-56334-051-8)*; pap. text ed. 6.00 small bk. *(1-56334-057-7)* Hampton-Brown.
Halverson, Lydia & Siculan, Dan. Haunted Houses. Riehecky, Janet. LC 88-38780. 100p. (gr. 3-7). 1989. PLB 21.35 *(0-89565-454-7)*; pap. 14.95 *(0-89565-534-9)* Childs World.

Halverson, Sandy. Book of Mormon Activity Book: Creative Scripture Learning Experiences for Children 4-12. Halverson, Sandy. 80p. (gr. 3-8). 1982. pap. 5.95 *(0-88290-188-5,* 4521) Horizon Utah.
Halverson, Tom. Best of Friends. Walley, Susan. Lyall, Elizabeth, ed. 156p. (Orig.). (gr. 4-8). 1989. pap. 4.95 *(0-89084-486-0)* Bob Jones Univ Pr.
Ham, John. The Best Story about Jesus. Coleman, Sheila S. 32p. (gr. k-2). 1989. pasted 2.50 *(0-87403-602-X,* 3862) Standard Pub.
Ham, Lisa K. Rebecca: A Novel for Children. Reed, Ronald F. 37p. (Orig.). (ps-4). 1990. pap. 8.00 *(0-924303-00-X)* TX Wesleyan Coll.
Hamamaka, Sheila. Teacher's Pet. Hurwitz, Johanna. LC 87-24003. 128p. (gr. 2-5). 1988. 12.95 *(0-688-07506-1)* Morrow Jr Bks.
Hamanaka, Sheila. Chortles: New & Selected Wordplay Poems. Merriam, Eve. LC 88-29129. 64p. (gr. 3-7). 1989. 11.95 *(0-688-08152-5)*; PLB 11.88 *(0-688-08153-3,* Morrow Jr Bks) Morrow Jr Bks.
—Class Clown. Hurwitz, Johanna. LC 86-23624. 112p. (gr. 1-4). 1987. 12.95 *(0-688-06723-9)* Morrow Jr Bks.
—Class Clown. Hurwitz, Johanna. 112p. (gr. 2-5). 1988. pap. 2.75 *(0-590-41821-1,* Little Apple) Scholastic Inc.
—Class President. Hurwitz, Johanna. LC 89-28600. 96p. (gr. 2 up). 1990. 12.95 *(0-688-09114-8)* Morrow Jr Bks.
—Juliette Gordon Low: America's First Girl Scout. Kudlinski, Kathleen V. (gr. 2-6). 1988. pap. 10.95 *(0-670-82208-6)* Viking Child Bks.
—Molly the Brave & Me. O'Connor, Jane. LC 89-10864. 48p. (Orig.). (gr. 1-3). 1990. lib. bdg. 7.99 *(0-394-94175-6)*; pap. 3.50 *(0-394-84175-1)* Random Bks Yng Read.
—A Poem for a Pickle: Funnybone Verses. Merriam, Eve. LC 88-22047. 40p. (gr. k up). 1989. 12.95 *(0-688-08137-1)*; PLB 12.88 *(0-688-08138-X,* Morrow Jr Bks) Morrow Jr Bks.
—School's Out. Hurwitz, Johanna. LC 90-13446. 128p. (gr. 2 up). 1991. 12.95 *(0-688-09938-6)* Morrow Jr Bks.
—School's Out! Hurwitz, Johanna. 96p. 1992. pap. 2.75 *(0-590-45053-0,* Little Apple) Scholastic Inc.
—Screen of Frogs: An Old Tale. Hamanaka, Sheila, retold by. LC 92-24172. 32p. (ps-3). 1993. 15.95 *(0-531-05464-0)*; PLB 15.99 *(0-531-08614-3)* Orchard Bks Watts.
—Shhh! Merriam, Eve. LC 92-44110. (gr. 4 up). 1993. pap. 14.00 *(0-671-79816-2,* S&S BFYR) S&S Trade.
—Sofie's Role. Heath, Amy. LC 91-33488. 40p. (gr. k-2). 1992. RSBE 14.95 *(0-02-743505-9,* Four Winds) Macmillan Child Grp.
—The Twenty-Four Hour Lipstick Mystery. Pryor, Bonnie. 144p. (gr. 4-7). 1992. pap. 3.50 *(0-440-40736-2,* YB) Dell.
—A Visit to Amy-Claire. Mills, Claudia. LC 91-280. 32p. (gr. k-3). 1992. RSBE 14.95 *(0-02-766991-2,* Macmillan Child Bk) Macmillan Child Grp.
Hamann, Brad. The Worst Day I Ever Had. McMane, Fred & Wolf, Cathrine. (gr. 3-7). 1991. pap. 8.95 *(0-316-55354-9,* Spts Illus Kids) Little.
Hamann, Jeff. Seashore Discoveries. Farmer, Wesley M. 124p. (Orig.). (gr. 9 up). 1986. pap. text ed. 7.95x *(0-937772-01-1)* W M Farmer.
Hamberger, John. Macmillan Book of Dinosaurs & Other Prehistoric Creatures. Elting, Mary. LC 84-4372. 80p. (gr. 2-7). 1984. SBE 16.95 *(0-02-733430-9,* Macmillan Child Bk) Macmillan Child Grp.
Hamburg, Cary. The Playland Kids, Featuring Marcus Toussaint, the Recycler. Toussaint, Michael E. 24p. (Orig.). (gr. k-6). 1992. pap. 2.95 *(0-9630905-0-X)* Michael T Enter.
Hamby, Michael B. Darby the Dinosaur in Shopping with Darby. Bentley, Ray R. LC 89-51111. 24p. (ps-1). 1989. pap. 2.50 *(0-9623481-0-4)* Darby Dinosaur.
Hamel, Jean-Marie. Heart Tales: A Collection of Stories from a Child's Heart. Hamel, Jean-Marie. 40p. (ps-3). 1990. 12.95g *(0-929684-50-8)* Silver Forest Pub.
Hamel, Tom. Gruesome John Frederick: A Tale of Christmas. Clemons, Jack. LC 87-71713. 73p. (Orig.). (gr. 4-5). 1988. pap. 6.00 *(0-916383-30-X)* Aegina Pr.
Hamer, Bonnie. My Tacoma Dome. Helstrom, David C. 24p. (Orig.). (gr. 1-4). 1983. pap. 2.75 *(0-933992-29-7)* Coffee Break.
—Seattle Center. Cecotti, Loralie. 24p. (Orig.). (gr. 1-4). 1983. pap. 2.75 *(0-933992-30-0)* Coffee Break.
—Visiting Gig Harbor. Braumiller, Tanya. (Orig.). (gr. 1-4). 1983. pap. 2.75 *(0-933992-28-9)* Coffee Break.
—Visiting Tacoma. Parkhurst, Carole. 24p. (Orig.). (gr. 1-4). 1983. pap. 2.75 *(0-933992-38-6)* Coffee Break.
—Washington Wildlife. Cecotti, Loralie. 24p. (Orig.). (gr. k-5). 1984. pap. text ed. 2.75 *(0-318-04105-7)* Coffee Break.
Hamer, Bonnie, jt. illus. see Harder, Arvid.
Hamer, Sylvia. C. B. & the Pink Pointe Shoes. Hamer, Sylvia. LC 87-70557. 32p. (Orig.). (gr. 3-4). 1987. pap. 9.95 *(0-942479-00-9)* Anderson Pr.
Hamilton, Craig. Fairy Tale Rap: "Jack & the Beanstalk" & Other Stories. Leeds, Barbara. 32p. (gr. k-8). 1990. pap. 5.95 *(0-9624932-0-1)*; pap. 12.95 incl. cass. *(0-9624932-2-8)*; cassette 8.95 *(0-9624932-1-X)* Miramonte Pr.
—Fairy Tale Rap, No. 2: The Fisherman & His Wife & Other Stories. Leeds, Barbara. 40p. (Orig.). (ps-6). 1992. pap. 6.95 *(0-9624932-4-4)*; pap. 13.95 incl. audiocassette *(0-9624932-6-0)*; audiocassette 8.95 *(0-9624932-5-2)* Miramonte Pr.

Hamilton, Jack. Carla Goes to Court. Beaudry, Jo & Ketchum, Lynne. LC 82-2854. 32p. (gr. 1-5). 1982. 14.95 (*0-89885-088-6*); pap. 9.95 (*0-89885-354-0*) Human Sci Pr.

Hamilton, Linda. Staying Safe: How to Protect Yourself Against Sexual Assault. Ozer, Elizabeth M. & Toure, Nkenge. 23p. (Orig.). (gr. 2-6). 1984. pap. text ed. 3.00 (*0-318-04650-4*) Rape Crisis Ctr.

Hamilton, Sandi. Midnite & Mark. Weber, Kathryn. LC 83-8622. 64p. (Orig.). (gr. 4-6). 1983. pap. 3.95 (*0-88100-021-3*) Ranch House Pr.

Hamilton, Sharon L. Junior Capers. Ingram, Margaret L. 28p. (Orig.). (gr. 1-6). 1990. pap. text ed. 5.95 (*0-9624721-0-7*) Imagery Pubns.

Hamilton, Thomas. Swinging on a Rainbow. Perkins, Charles D. LC 91-78393. 1992. write for info. (*0-86543-286-4*); pap. write for info. (*0-86543-287-2*) Africa World.

Hamilton, Thomas A. Swinging on a Rainbow. Perkins, Charles D. LC 91-78393. 32p. (gr. k-3). 1993. 14.95 (*0-86543-386-0*); pap. 6.95 (*0-86543-385-2*) Africa World.

Hamilton, Wanda W. Peter Pelican's Pouch Problem. Hamilton, Wanda W. 22p. (Orig.). (gr. k-6). 1986. pap. 3.95 (*0-935357-01-7*) CRIC Prod.

Hamlin, Peter. Something Nice to See. Gardner, Theodroe R., II. LC 93-61121. 32p. (gr. 4 up). Date not set. 15.00 (*0-9627297-6-0*) A A Knoll Pubs.

Hammann, Brad. The Macmillan Book of How Things Work. Folsom, Michael & Folsom, Marcia. LC 86-23761. 80p. (gr. 3-7). 1987. SBE 16.95 (*0-02-735360-5*, Macmillan Child Bk) Macmillan Child Grp.

—The Macmillan Book of How Things Work. Folsom, Michael & Folsom, Marcia. LC 86-23761. 80p. (gr. 3-7). 1992. pap. 8.95 (*0-689-71139-5*, Aladdin) Macmillan Child Grp.

Hammer, Stanley. One Man's Homestead. Redding, Robert. Clark, Marvin, ed. 120p. (Orig.). 1990. pap. 10.95 (*0-937708-23-2*) Great Northwest.

Hammid, Hella. Hawaii Is a Rainbow. Feeney, Stephanie. LC 80-5462. 64p. (ps-k). 1980. 12.95 (*0-8248-1007-4*) UH Pr.

—The Sensible Book: A Celebration of Your Five Senses. rev. ed. Polland, Barbara K. 64p. 1993. pap. write for info. (*0-89087-707-6*) Celestial Arts.

Hammond, Frank. Ten Little Ducks. Hammond, Franklin. 24p. (ps). 1992. pap. 4.95 (*0-88899-153-3*, Pub. by Groundwood-Douglas & McIntyre CN) Firefly Bks Ltd.

Hammond, Janice M. When My Dad Died: A Child's View of Death. Hammond, Janice M. 48p. (Orig.). (gr. k-6). 1981. pap. 6.95 (*0-9604690-3-6*) Cranbrook Pub.

—When My Mommy Died: A Child's View of Death. Hammond, Janice M. 27p. (Orig.). (gr. ps-5). 1980. pap. 6.95 (*0-9604690-0-1*) Cranbrook Pub.

Hammond, Lee. The Jewel Folk. Frye, Tom. (Orig.). 1993. pap. 8.95 (*1-881663-17-5*) Advent Mean Pr.

Hamoy, Carol. What's Wrong? What's Wrong? Hamoy, Carol. (gr. k-3). 1965. 8.95 (*0-685-00564-X*) Astor-Honor.

Hampton, Blake. How Babies Are Made. Andry, Andrew C. & Schepp, Steven. LC 99-944003. 88p. 1984. pap. 9.95 (*0-316-04227-7*) Little.

Hampton, Cynthia V. Across-the-Curriculum Guide, Diggy Armadillo Goes to Fort Worth Stock Show & Rodeo, Bk. 1: 140 Creative Activites. Pugh, Ann. 60p. (Orig.). (gr. k-5). 1992. 10.00 (*1-879465-01-9*); Eng. & Spa. audiocassette 6.00 (*0-685-60626-0*) Diggy & Assocs.

—Diggy Armadillo Goes to the Stock Show & Rodeo. Pugh, Ann & Anderson, Joan F. Morolez-de Anda, Martha, tr. LC 90-93647. (SPA & ENG.). 62p. (Orig.). (gr. 2-5). 1992. pap. 7.95 (*1-879465-00-0*) Diggy & Assocs.

Han, Oki. Miami-Nanny Stories. Milstein, Linda B. LC 93-28680. 1994. write for info. (*0-688-11151-3*, Tambourine Bks); PLB write for info. (*0-688-11152-1*, Tambourine Bks) Morrow.

Han, Oki S. Kongi & Potgi: A Cinderella Story from Korea. Han, Oki S. & Plunkett, Stephanie H., eds. LC 93-28426. 1994. write for info. (*0-8037-1571-4*); PLB write for info. (*0-8037-1572-2*) Dial Bks Young.

—Sir Whong & the Golden Pig. Han, Oki S. & Plunkett, Stephanie H., eds. Han LC 91-43389. 32p. (ps-3). 1993. 13.99 (*0-8037-1344-4*); PLB 13.89 (*0-8037-1345-2*) Dial Bks Young.

Hanak, Mirko. Animals We Love, Bks. 1 & 2. LC 72-89571. 32p. (gr. k-4). 1973. 9.95 ea. Bk. 1 (*0-87592-005-5*) Bk. 2 (*0-87592-006-3*) Scroll Pr.

Handelman, Dorothy, jt. photog. see Hundelman, Dorothy.

Handelsman, J. B. Who's That Stepping on Plymouth Rock? Fritz, Jean. LC 74-30593. 32p. (gr. 2-6). 1975. 13.95 (*0-698-20325-9*, Coward) Putnam Pub Group.

Handford, Martin. Find Waldo Now. Handford, Martin. (ps up). 1988. 12.95 (*0-316-34292-0*) Little.

—The Great Waldo Search. Handford, Martin. (ps up). 1989. 12.95 (*0-316-34282-3*) Little.

—Where's Waldo? in Hollywood. Handford, Martin. LC 91-71819. 32p. (ps up). Nov. 1993 14.95, (*1-56402-044-4*); PLB 14.88, Jan. 1994 (*1-56402-294-3*) Candlewick Pr.

Handforth, Thomas. Mei Li. Handforth, Thomas. 48p. (gr. k-3). 1955. PLB 14.95 (*0-385-07401-8*) Doubleday.

Handville, Robert. Lord of the Sky: Zeus. Gates, Doris. (gr. 3-7). 1982. pap. 4.99 (*0-14-031532-2*, Puffin) Puffin Bks.

Haney, Elizabeth M. Now You're Cooking: A Guide to Cooking for Boys & Girls. Feig, Barbara K. LC 75-10991. 144p. (gr. 7 up). 1975. pap. 4.95 (*0-916836-01-0*) J B Pal.

Hani, Shabo. Cactus. Overbeck, Cynthia. LC 82-211. 48p. (gr. 4 up). 1982. lib. bdg. 19.95 (*0-8225-1469-9*, First Ave Edns); pap. 5.95 (*0-8225-9556-7*, First Ave Edns) Lerner Pubns.

Hani, Shabo, photos by. How Seeds Travel. Overbeck, Cynthia. 48p. (gr. 4 up). Repr. of 1982 ed. 5.95g (*0-8225-9569-9*) Lerner Pubns.

Hankins, Rod & Ray, Dan. Shoot for the Stars Basketball Handbook, Vol. 1. Woodard, Lynette & Cook, Kevin. Bunch, Lewis & Washington, Marian, eds. 60p. (gr. 9-12). 1989. text ed. write for info. Worldwide Sports.

Hankinson, John. Indian Two Feet Rides Alone. Friskey, Margaret. LC 80-12688. 32p. (gr. k-3). 1980. PLB 15.00 (*0-516-03523-1*) Childrens.

Hanna, Cheryl. An Enchanted Hair Tale. De Veaux, Alexis. LC 85-45824. 40p. (gr. k-3). 1987. 15.00 (*0-06-021623-9*); PLB 14.89 (*0-06-021624-7*) HarpC Child Bks.

—An Enchanted Hair Tale. De Veaux, Alexis. LC 85-45824. 48p. (gr. k-3). 1991. pap. 4.95 (*0-06-443271-8*, Trophy) HarpC Child Bks.

—Hard to Be Six. Adoff, Arnold. LC 89-45903. 32p. (gr. k-3). 1990. 12.95 (*0-688-09013-3*); lib. bdg. 12.88 (*0-688-09579-8*) Lothrop.

—Next Stop, Freedom: The Story of a Slave Girl. Hoobler, Dorothy & Hoobler, Thomas. 64p. (gr. 4-6). 1991. 11.95 (*0-382-24152-5*); PLB 13.98 (*0-382-24145-2*); pap. 7.95 (*0-382-24347-1*) Silver Burdett Pr.

—Phillis Wheatley, Poet. Jackson, Garnet N. LC 92-28778. 1992. 56.40 (*0-8136-5233-2*); pap. 28.50 (*0-8136-5706-7*) Modern Curr.

Hanna, Wayne. Children's Bible Basics Ser, 11 bks. Nystrom, Carolyn. (ps-2). Set. pap. 54.89 (*0-8024-5988-9*) Moody.

—Jesus Is No Secret. Nystrom, Carolyn. (ps-2). pap. 4.99 (*0-8024-6153-0*) Moody.

Hannah, Jack, jt. illus. see Barks, Carl.

Hannan, Peter. The Battle of Sillyville. Hannan, Peter. LC 90-4544. 32p. (Orig.). (ps-2). 1991. pap. 3.95 (*0-679-80286-X*) Knopf Bks Yng Read.

—Escape from Camp Wannabarf. Hannan, Peter. LC 90-33203. 32p. (Orig.). (ps-2). 1991. pap. 3.95 (*0-679-80287-8*) Knopf Bks Yng Read.

—School after Dark. Hannan, Peter. LC 90-33407. 32p. (Orig.). (ps-2). 1991. pap. 3.95 (*0-679-80288-6*) Knopf Bks Yng Read.

—Sillyville or Bust. Hannan, Peter. LC 89-35342. 32p. (Orig.). (ps-2). 1991. pap. 3.95 (*0-679-80285-1*) Knopf Bks Yng Read.

Hannant, Judith S. The Doorknob Collection of Bedtime Rhymes, Vol. 1. Hannant, Judith S. (ps). 1993. 12.95 (*0-316-34366-8*) Little.

Hannon, Holly. The Jungle Book. Kipling, Rudyard. Ashachik, Diane M., ed. LC 92-5806. 48p. (gr. 3-6). 1992. PLB 12.89 (*0-8167-2868-2*); pap. text ed. 3.95 (*0-8167-2869-0*) Troll Assocs.

—A King for Brass Cobweb. Watkins, Dawn L. Smith, Anne, ed. (Orig.). (gr. k-1). 1990. pap. write for info. (*0-89084-505-0*) Bob Jones Univ Pr.

—A Penny & Two Fried Eggs: And Other Stories. Harder, Geraldine G. LC 91-16999. 144p. (Orig.). (gr. 2-5). 1991. pap. 6.95 (*0-8361-3564-4*) Herald Pr.

Hannon, Mark. The Goodbye Painting. Berman, Linda. LC 81-20217. 32p. (gr. 3). 1982. 16.95 (*0-89885-074-6*) Human Sci Pr.

—Indians of the Eastern Woodlands. Bains, Rae. LC 84-2664. 32p. (gr. 3-6). 1985. PLB 9.49 (*0-8167-0118-0*); pap. text ed. 3.95 (*0-8167-0119-9*) Troll Assocs.

Hansen, Biruta A. The Bee. Norden, Beth. 14p. (gr. 2 up). 1991. 12.95 (*1-55670-218-3*) Stewart Tabori & Chang.

Hansen, Han H. The Magic Christmas Pony. Cooley, Regina F. LC 91-76342. 36p. (gr. 1-5). 1991. 19.95 (*1-880450-04-6*) Capstone Pub.

Hansen, Heidi. Grandma Holland's Three Tiny Bedtime Stories. Holland, Shirley. LC 91-70485. 48p. (ps-5). 1991. 12.95 (*0-89802-574-5*) Beautiful Am.

—Modern Informative Nursery Rhymes: American History, Book I. Min, Kellet I. LC 89-91719. 64p. (Orig.). (gr. 2-5). 1992. pap. 10.95 (*0-9623411-2-6*) Rhyme & Reason.

—Modern Informative Nursery Rhymes: General Science, Book I. Min, Kellet I. LC 89-91719. 64p. (Orig.). (gr. 2-5). 1993. pap. 10.95 (*0-9623411-4-2*) Rhyme & Reason.

—Modern Informative Nursery Rhymes: Values. Min, Kellet I. 32p. (Orig.). (ps-3). 1989. pap. 7.95 (*0-685-26431-9*) Rhyme & Reason.

—Modern Informative Nursery Rhymes: Values, Book I. Min, Kellet I. LC 89-91719. 32p. (ps-3). 1989. pap. 7.95 (*0-9623411-3-4*) Rhyme & Reason.

Hansen, Monica. Why Buffalo Roam. Kershen, L. Michael. Kershen, Drew L., intro. by. 32p. (gr. k-4). 1992. PLB 15.00 (*0-88045-043-6*) Stemmer Hse.

Hansen, Ron. Dinosquares: A Modern Dinosaur Book for Imaginative Children. Barlass, Gail. Hansen, Ron, ed. LC 87-62124. 24p. (ps-3). 1988. pap. 3.95 (*0-943925-07-X*) Purple Turtle Bks.

Hansen, Ronnie. Animal Squares: An Animal Picture & Rhyme Book for Imaginative Children. Henry, Gilson. Hansen, Ronnie, ed. LC 87-62123. 24p. (ps-4). 1987. pap. 3.95 (*0-943925-01-0*) Purple Turtle Bks.

—Purple Turtles Say No, No to Drugs. Henry, Gilson. Hansen, Ronnie, ed. LC 87-62124. 24p. (ps-4). 1987. pap. 3.95 (*0-943925-00-2*) Purple Turtle Bks.

Hansen, Trisha. Jibberish & Rhyme. Berg, Kevin A. 104p. (gr. 2-4). 1993. PLB 12.95 (*0-9636795-0-3*) Child Tech Bks.

Hansen-Cole, Robin. Tornado. Boelts, Maribeth. LC 92-27988. 32p. 1993. pap. 3.95 (*0-8091-6607-0*) Paulist Pr.

Hanson, Ann R. Down a Magic Stream. Hanson, Fred. 65p. (gr. 2-5). 1992. pap. 9.95 (*0-9624292-2-8*) Black Willow Pr.

—Norman. Hanson, Fred E. Hanson, Ann R., ed. LC 89-90961. 63p. (Orig.). (gr. 4-6). 1989. pap. 7.95 (*0-685-28895-1*) Black Willow Pr.

—Norman. 2nd ed. Hanson, Fred E. 64p. (gr. 3-5). 1989. pap. 7.95 (*0-9624292-0-1*) Black Willow Pr.

—Simon. Hanson, Fred E. 54p. (gr. 3-5). 1990. pap. 7.95 (*0-9624292-1-X*) Black Willow Pr.

Hanson, Eric. Ms. Cramm on Pot: The Real Story about Marijuana. Mann, Peggy & Houlton, Betsy. 21p. (gr. 6-12). 1991. pap. 1.75 (*0-89486-738-5*) Hazelden.

—Rule of the Szak King: A Smoke-Free Adventure on the Planet Quark. Engelmann, Jeanne. 23p. (gr. 5-9). 1991. pap. 1.75 (*0-89486-748-2*) Hazelden.

—The Sweet Air of Starship Orr: Rescue from the Inhalant Planet. Engelmann, Jeanne. 27p. (gr. 5-9). 1991. pap. 1.75 (*0-89486-749-0*) Hazelden.

—Tad & Me: How I Found Out about Fetal Alcohol Syndrome. Houlton, Betsy. 24p. (gr. 6-12). 1991. pap. 1.75 (*0-89486-739-3*) Hazelden.

Hanson, Joan. Can You Match This? Jokes about Unlikely Pairs. Walton, Rick & Walton, Ann. 32p. (gr. 1-4). 1989. 11.95 (*0-8225-0973-3*) Lerner Pubns.

—Can You Match This? Jokes about Unlikely Pairs. Walton, Rick & Walton, Ann. 36p. pap. 2.95 (*0-8225-9565-6*) Lerner Pubns.

—Cat's out of the Bag: Jokes about Cats. Shere, Irene & Friedman, Sharon. 32p. (gr. 1-4). 1986. 11.95 (*0-8225-0986-5*); pap. 2.95 (*0-8225-9527-3*) Lerner Pubns.

—Clowning Around! Jokes about the Circus. Walton, Rick & Walton, Ann. 32p. (gr. 1-4). 1989. 11.95 (*0-8225-0975-X*) Lerner Pubns.

—Dumb Clucks! Jokes about Chickens. Walton, Rick & Walton, Ann. 32p. (gr. 1-4). 1987. PLB 11.95 (*0-8225-0991-1*) Lerner Pubns.

—Face the Music! Jokes about Music. Peterson, Scott K. 32p. (gr. 1-4). 1988. PLB 11.95 (*0-8225-0995-4*) Lerner Pubns.

—Fossil Follies! Jokes about Dinosaurs. Walton, Rick & Walton, Ann. 32p. (gr. 1-4). 1989. 11.95 (*0-8225-0974-1*, First Ave Edns); pap. 2.95 (*0-8225-9560-5*, First Ave Edns) Lerner Pubns.

—Go Hog Wild: Jokes from down on the Farm. Roop, Peter, et al. LC 84-5662. 32p. (gr. 1-4). 1984. PLB 11.95 (*0-8225-0982-2*) Lerner Pubns.

—Hail to the Chief! Jokes about the Presidents. Burns, Diane & Burns, Clint. 32p. (gr. 1-4). 1989. 11.95 (*0-8225-0971-7*, First Ave Edns); pap. 2.95 (*0-8225-9561-3*, First Ave Edns) Lerner Pubns.

—Kiss a Frog! Jokes about Fairy Tales, Knights, & Dragons. Walton, Rick & Walton, Ann. 32p. (gr. 1-4). 1989. 11.95 (*0-8225-0970-9*) Lerner Pubns.

—Kiss a Frog! Jokes about Fairy Tales, Knights, & Dragons. Walton, Rick & Walton, Ann. 40p. (gr. 1-4). pap. 2.95g (*0-8225-9566-4*) Lerner Pubns.

—One Hundred & One Animal Jokes. Schultz, Sam. LC 81-20955. 48p. (gr. 1-4). 1982. PLB 11.95 (*0-8225-0978-4*) Lerner Pubns.

—One Hundred & One Family Jokes. Schultz, Sam. LC 81-20861. 48p. (gr. 1-4). 1982. PLB 11.95 (*0-8225-0981-4*) Lerner Pubns.

—One Hundred & One Knock-Knock Jokes. Schultz, Sam. LC 81-20954. 48p. (gr. 1-4). 1982. PLB 11.95 (*0-8225-0976-8*) Lerner Pubns.

—One Hundred & One Monster Jokes. Schultz, Sam. LC 81-20953. 48p. (gr. 1-4). 1982. PLB 11.95 (*0-8225-0977-6*) Lerner Pubns.

—One Hundred & One School Jokes. Schultz, Sam. LC 81-20912. 48p. (gr. 1-4). 1982. PLB 11.95 (*0-8225-0979-2*) Lerner Pubns.

—One Hundred & One Sports Jokes. Schultz, Sam. LC 81-20913. 48p. (gr. 1-4). 1982. PLB 11.95 (*0-8225-0980-6*) Lerner Pubns.

—Out to Lunch: Jokes about Food. Roop, Peter & Roop, Connie. LC 84-4416. 32p. (gr. 1-4). 1984. PLB 11.95 (*0-8225-0983-0*, First Ave Edns); pap. 2.95 (*0-8225-9552-4*, First Ave Edns) Lerner Pubns.

—Out to Pasture! Jokes about Cows. Bernstein, Joanne E. & Cohen, Paul. 32p. (gr. 1-4). 1988. PLB 11.95 (*0-8225-0998-9*) Lerner Pubns.

—Snakes Alive! Jokes about Snakes. Burns, Diane L. (gr. 1-4). 1988. PLB 11.95 (*0-8225-0996-2*, First Ave Edns); pap. 2.95 (*0-8225-9543-5*, First Ave Edns) Lerner Pubns.

—Space Out: Jokes about Outer Space. Roop, Peter, et al. LC 84-5650. 32p. (gr. 1-4). 1984. PLB 11.95 (*0-8225-0984-9*) Lerner Pubns.

—What a Ham! Jokes about Pigs. Walton, Rick & Walton, Ann. 32p. (gr. 1-4). 1989. 11.95 (*0-8225-0972-5*) Lerner Pubns.

—What a Ham! Jokes about Pigs. Walton, Rick & Walton, Ann. 40p. (gr. 1-4). pap. 2.95 (0-8225-9567-2) Lerner Pubns.
—What's Your Name, Again? More Jokes about Names. Walton, Rick & Walton, Ann. 32p. (gr. 1-4). 1988. PLB 11.95 (0-8225-0997-0, First Ave Edns); pap. 2.95 (0-8225-9553-2, First Ave Edns) Lerner Pubns.
—What's Your Name? Jokes about Names. Peterson, Scott K. 32p. (gr. 1-4). 1987. PLB 11.95 (0-8225-0994-6, First Ave Edns); pap. 3.95 (0-8225-9520-6, First Ave Edns) Lerner Pubns.
Hanson, L. K. Feed Your Head: Some Excellent Stuff on Being Yourself. Hipp, Earl. 137p. (gr. 6-12). 1991. pap. 10.00 perfect bdg. (0-89486-755-5, T5034) Hazelden.
Hanson, Peter. I, Columbus: My Journal - 1492. Roop, Peter & Roop, Connie, eds. 57p. (gr. 4-7). 1990. 13.95 (0-8027-6977-2); lib. bdg. 14.85 (0-8027-6978-0) Walker & Co.
—A Pocketful of Goobers: A Story about George Washington Carver. Mitchell, Barbara. 64p. (gr. 3-6). 1986. PLB 14.95 (0-87614-292-7) Carolrhoda Bks.
Hanson, Peter E. Buttons for General Washington. Roop, Peter & Roop, Connie. LC 86-6120. 48p. (gr. k-4). 1986. lib. bdg. 14.95 (0-87614-294-3); pap. 4.95 (0-87614-476-8) Carolrhoda Bks.
—Buttons for General Washington. 1987. pap. 5.95 (0-685-18657-1, First Ave Edns) Lerner Pubns.
—City Fox. Bergman, Donna. LC 90-27019. 32p. (gr. k-3). 1992. SBE 13.95 (0-689-31687-9, Atheneum Child Bk) Macmillan Child Grp.
—Keep the Lights Burning, Abbie. Roop, Peter & Roop, Connie. LC 84-27446. 40p. (gr. k-4). 1985. lib. bdg. 14.95 (0-87614-275-7); pap. 5.95 (0-87614-454-7) Carolrhoda Bks.
—Keep the Lights Burning, Abbie. Roop, Peter & Roop, Connie. (gr. 2-4). 1989. incl. cass. 19.95 (0-87499-135-8); pap. 12.95 incl. cass. (0-87499-134-X); Set; incl. 4 bks., guide, & cass. pap. 27.95 (0-87499-136-6) Live Oak Media.
—Memorial Day. Scott, Geoffrey. LC 83-1855. 48p. (gr. k-4). 1983. PLB 14.95 (0-87614-219-6) Carolrhoda Bks.
—A Pocketful of Goobers: A Story about George Washington Carver. Mitchell, Barbara. (gr. 3-6). 1987. pap. 5.95 (0-87614-474-1, First Ave Edns) Lerner Pubns.
—Unicorn Crossing. Luenn, Nancy. LC 87-995. 64p. (gr. 2-5). 1987. SBE 12.95 (0-689-31384-5, Atheneum) Macmillan Child Grp.
—Walking the Road to Freedom: A Story about Sojourner Truth. Ferris, Jeri. 64p. (gr. 3-6). 1988. lib. bdg. 14.95 (0-87614-318-4) Carolrhoda Bks.
—Walking the Road to Freedom: A Story about Sojourner Truth. Ferris, Jeri. 64p. (gr. 3-6). 1989. pap. 5.95 (0-87614-505-5, First Ave Edns) Lerner Pubns.
Hanson, Rick. Columbus Day. Liestman, Vicki. 56p. (gr. k-4). 1991. PLB 14.95 (0-87614-444-X) Carolrhoda Bks.
—Count Your Way Through Israel. Haskins, Jim. 24p. (gr. 1-4). 1990. PLB 17.50 (0-87614-415-6) Carolrhoda Bks.
—I Pledge Allegiance. Swanson, June. 40p. (gr. k-4). 1990. PLB 14.95 (0-87614-393-1) Carolrhoda Bks.
Hanson, Signe. Messing Around with Baking Chemistry: A Children's Museum Activity Book. Zubrowski, Bernie. 64p. (gr. 3-7). 1981. pap. 7.95 (0-316-98879-0) Little.

Hanson, Stephen. Picker McClikker. Johnson, Allen, Jr. (gr. k-3). 1993. 16.95 (1-878561-20-0) Seacoast AL.
Through the eyes of a small child, the world is a mighty big place often dominated by big characters, big heroes, & big events. Not so with PICKER McCLIKKER, a delightful story in which the hero is a pint-sized four year-old! Author Allen Johnson, Jr., shares the discovery of the magical talents of Joe McClikker, the youngest of six children in a sharecropper's family from Evergreen, Alabama. The youngster earns the name "Picker" due to his extraordinary speed in picking--picking anything that comes his way, beginning with the burrs on his hound dog Bone to the family's cotton harvest. Picker saves the day! In addition to its young hero, PICKER McCLIKKER features wonderfully detailed & colorful illustrations by Stephen Hanson who includes many favorite images of small children--farm animals, trains, & foreign lands. PICKER McCLIKKER, for children ages 3-8, is both fun & ennobling for the young reader. In fact, PICKER McCLIKKER just received special recognition from the Alabama Literacy Council, which will use the book in some of its programs. To order PICKER McCLIKKER, contact Southern Publishers Group by calling 1-800-628-0903. *Publisher Provided Annotation.*

Hanson, Warren. A Cup of Christmas Tea. Hegg, Tom. 46p. (gr. 4 up). 1991. 10.95 (0-931674-08-5) Waldman Hse Pr.
—The Mark of the Maker. Hegg, Tom. 46p. (gr. 4 up). 1991. 10.95 (0-931674-18-2) Waldman Hse Pr.
Hanzel, Linda & Hanzel, Linda. Abigail Adams: First Lady of Faith & Courage. Witter, Evelyn. LC 76-2416. (gr. 3-6). 1976. pap. 6.95 (0-915134-94-2) Mott Media.
Happe, Cary. Green Creatures Ten to One. Cole, Betsy. LC 88-71429. 32p. (Orig.). (gr. k-3). 1988. pap. 4.95 (0-9620606-0-7) Adventure VA.
Haqiqat, Nahid. The Tale of Ringy. Azaad, Meyer. Ghanoonparvar, Mohammad R. & Wilcox, Diane L., trs. from PER. 24p. (Orig.). (gr. 3 up). 1983. pap. 4.95 (0-686-43078-6) Mazda Pubs.
Harada, Joyce. It's the A.B.C. Book. 32p. (ps). 1982. limp 7.95 (0-89346-157-1) Heian Intl.
—It's the 0-1-2-3 Book. Harada, Joyce. 32p. (ps-3). 1985. pap. 7.95 (0-89346-252-7) Heian Intl.
Harbo, Gary. Bart Becomes a Friend: Advanced Reader. Harbo, Gary. 33p. (gr. 1-4). 1992. text ed. 8.95 (1-884149-05-7) Kutie Kari Bks.
—My New Friend: Advanced Reader. Harbo, Gary. 33p. (gr. 1-4). 1988. text ed. 8.95 (1-884149-01-4) Kutie Kari Bks.
Harbo, Gary & Wallace, Shawn. Bad Bart's Revenge: Advanced Reader. Harbo, Gary. 35p. (gr. 1-4). 1991. text ed. 8.95 (1-884149-03-0) Kutie Kari Bks.
Harbour, Jennie. My Book of Favorite Fairy Tales. LC 92-37669. 1993. 8.99 (0-517-09125-9, Pub. by Derrydale Bks) Outlet Bk Co.
Hard, Charlotte. Find Mouse in the House. Maisner, Heather. LC 93-3638. 1994. write for info. (1-56402-351-6) Candlewick Pr.
—Find Mouse in the Yard. LC 93-12825. (gr. 3 up). 1994. write for info. (1-56402-350-8) Candlewick Pr.
Harden, David G. How to Preserve Animal & Other Specimens in Clear Plastic. Harden, Cleo. 64p. (gr. 4 up). 1963. 12.95 (0-911010-47-5); pap. 4.95 (0-911010-46-7) Naturegraph.
Harden, Laurie. The Bobbsey Twins on Blueberry Island. Hope, Laura L. 1991. 4.50 (0-448-40110-X, G&D) Putnam Pub Group.
—Mystery on the Deep Blue Sea. Hope, Laura L. 1991. 4.50 (0-448-40113-4, G&D) Putnam Pub Group.
—Visit to the Great West. Hope, Laura L. 1991. 4.50 (0-448-40112-6, G&D) Putnam Pub Group.
Harder, Arvid & Hamer, Bonnie. Visiting Mt. Rainier. Helstrom, David C. 28p. (Orig.). (gr. 1-4). 1984. pap. 2.75 (0-933992-37-8) Coffee Break.
Hardgrove, Tanya. Charlie Young Bear. Van Ahnan, Katherine & Young Bear, Joan A. Gilliland, Hap, ed. 32p. (Orig.). (gr. 3-6). 1990. pap. 4.95 (0-89992-128-0) Coun India Ed.
—The Dark Side of the Moon. Gilliland, Hap & Kovach, Tom. 32p. (gr. 1-4). 1984. pap. 4.95 (0-89992-086-1) Coun India Ed.
—Kamache & the Medicine Bead: An Apache Story. Cunnyngham, Jerry. Gilliland, Hap, ed. 48p. (gr. 4-10). 1984. pap. 4.95 (0-89992-123-X) Coun India Ed.
—Keeper of Fire. Magorian, James. 78p. (Orig.). (gr. 4-12). 1984. pap. 6.95 (0-89992-088-8) Coun India Ed.
—O'kohome: The Coyote Dog. Gilliland, Hap. 47p. (Orig.). (gr. 4-9). 1989. pap. 5.95 (0-89992-102-7) Coun India Ed.
—Tul-Tok-A-Na: The Small One. Meyer, Kathleen A. 32p. (Orig.). (gr. 1-5). 1992. pap. 6.95 (0-89992-105-1) Coun India Ed.
—The Vision of the Spokane Prophet. Egbert, Rebecca A. Gilliland, Hap, ed. 36p. (Orig.). (gr. 5-10). 1989. pap. 5.95 (0-89992-118-3) Coun India Ed.
Harding, Trish T. Alphabet Soup. Anderson, Carol J. 60p. (gr. k-4). 1989. 12.95 (0-935317-26-0) Blue Heron WA.
Hardy, Sally M. The Three Bears. (ps-3). 1982. 3.50 (0-913545-08-2) Moonlight FL.
Hardy, Suzanne. The Eagle Who Thought He Was a Chicken. Khosho, Francis K. 24p. (Orig.). (gr. 7 up). 1993. pap. 8.00 (0-9619310-2-7) Khosho.
Hargraves, Roger. Little Miss Helpful. Hargraves, Roger. 32p. (ps-k). 1981. pap. 1.75 (0-8431-0897-5) Price Stern.
Hargreaves, Adam. Mr. Bump. Rojany, Lisa & Hargreaves, Adam. 5p. (gr. k-3). 1993. 5.00 (0-8431-3639-1) Price Stern.
—Mr. Funny. Rojany, Lisa & Hargreaves, Adam. 5p. (gr. k-3). 1993. 5.00 (0-8431-3637-5) Price Stern.
—Mr. Silly. Rojany, Lisa & Hargreaves, Adam. 5p. (gr. k-3). 1993. 5.00 (0-8431-3638-3) Price Stern.
Hargreaves, Angela. Penguin. Robinson, Clarie. LC 91-44727. 32p. (gr. 4-6). 1993. text ed. 11.59 (0-8167-2771-6); tchr's. ed. 3.95 (0-8167-2772-4) Troll Assocs. Postponed.

Hargreaves, Anglea & Bowring, Isabel. Birds. Gill, Peter. LC 89-20306. 32p. (gr. 3-6). 1990. PLB 11.59 (0-8167-1959-4); pap. text ed. 3.95 (0-8167-1960-8) Troll Assocs.
Hargreaves, Roger. Little Miss Bossy. Hargreaves, Roger. 32p. (ps-k). 1981. pap. 1.75 (0-8431-0893-2) Price Stern.
—Little Miss Late. Hargreaves, Roger. 32p. (ps-k). 1981. pap. 1.75 (0-8431-0896-7) Price Stern.
—Little Miss Naughty. Hargreaves, Roger. 32p. (ps-k). 1984. pap. 1.75 (0-8431-0889-4) Price Stern.
—Little Miss Neat. Hargreaves, Roger. 32p. (ps-k). 1981. pap. 1.75 (0-8431-0894-0) Price Stern.
—Little Miss Plump. Hargreaves, Roger. 32p. (ps-k). 1981. pap. 1.75 (0-8431-0895-9) Price Stern.
—Little Miss Scatterbrain. Hargreaves, Roger. 32p. (ps-k). 1981. pap. 1.75 (0-8431-0891-6) Price Stern.
—Little Miss Sunshine. Hargreaves, Roger. 32p. 1981. pap. 1.75 (0-8431-0899-1) Price Stern.
—Little Miss Tiny. Hargreaves, Roger. 32p. (ps-k). 1981. pap. 1.75 (0-8431-0892-4) Price Stern.
—Little Miss Trouble. Hargreaves, Roger. 32p. (ps-k). 1981. pap. 1.75 (0-8431-0890-8) Price Stern.
—Mr. Busy. Hargreaves, Roger. (ps-k). 1980. pap. 1.75 (0-8431-0818-5) Price Stern.
—Mr. Clever. Hargreaves, Roger. 32p. (ps-k). 1982. pap. 1.75 (0-8431-1131-3) Price Stern.
—Mr. Daydream. Hargreaves, Roger. 32p. (ps-k). 1982. pap. 1.75 (0-8431-1127-5) Price Stern.
—Mr. Dizzy. Hargreaves, Roger. 32p. (ps-k). 1982. pap. 1.75 (0-8431-1132-1) Price Stern.
—Mr. Impossible. Hargreaves, Roger. 32p. 1981. pap. 1.75 (0-8431-0819-3) Price Stern.
—Mr. Muddle. Hargreaves, Roger. 32p. (ps-k). 1981. pap. 1.75 (0-8431-0820-7) Price Stern.
—Mr. Nonsense. Hargreaves, Roger. 32p. (ps-k). 1981. pap. 1.75 (0-8431-0821-5) Price Stern.
—Mr. Small. Hargreaves, Roger. 32p. (ps-k). 1981. pap. 1.75 (0-8431-0823-1) Price Stern.
—Mr. Sneeze. Hargreaves, Roger. 32p. (ps-k). 1982. pap. 1.75 (0-8431-1125-9) Price Stern.
—Mr. Snow. Hargreaves, Roger. 32p. (ps-k). 1982. pap. 1.75 (0-8431-1133-X) Price Stern.
—Mr. Stingy. Hargreaves, Roger. 32p. (ps-k). 1982. pap. 1.75 (0-8431-1130-5) Price Stern.
—Mr. Tall. Hargreaves, Roger. 32p. (ps-k). 1982. pap. 1.75 (0-8431-1126-7) Price Stern.
Haring, Keith. The Keith Haring Coloring Book. Haring, Keith. 20p. (Orig.). (ps-5). 1992. pap. 6.95 (1-881270-51-3) FotoFolio.
—My First Coloring Book. Haring, Keith. 32p. (Orig.). (ps-5). 1993. pap. 4.95 (1-881270-61-0) FotoFolio.
Haris, Jennifer B. Jalapeno Hal. Harper, Jo. LC 92-16921. 40p. (ps-2). 1993. RSBE 14.95 (0-02-742645-9, Four Winds) Macmillan Child Grp.
Harlan, Susan. Kids & Drinking. Snyder, Anne. 47p. (gr. 3-7). 1977. pap. 4.95 (0-89638-010-6) CompCare.
Harman, Julie. The Fencerow Tails. Baker, C. David. 48p. (gr. k-5). 1991. 12.95x (0-9630669-0-0) Liberty Lines.
Harmon, Gedge. Blessed Kateri Tekakwitha. Windeatt, Mary F. 32p. (gr. 3-6). 1990. Repr. of 1954 ed. wkbk. 3.00 (0-89555-378-3) TAN Bks Pubs.
—The Brown Scapular. Windeatt, Mary F. (gr. 1-5). 1989. Repr. of 1954 ed. wkbk. 3.00 (0-89555-380-5) TAN Bks Pubs.
—Catholic Story Coloring Books. Windeatt, Mary F. 32p. (gr. 1-5). 1989. Repr. of 1954 ed. Set of 24. 48.00 (0-89555-381-3) TAN Bks Pubs.
—The Children of Fatima & Our Lady's Message to the World. Windeatt, Mary F. LC 90-71828. 161p. (gr. 5-9). 1991. pap. 6.00 (0-89555-419-4) TAN Bks Pubs.
—The Cure of Ars: The Story of Saint John Vianney, Patron Saint of Parish Priests. Windeatt, Mary F. LC 90-71827. 211p. (gr. 5-9). 1991. pap. 9.00 (0-89555-418-6) TAN Bks Pubs.
—The Little Flower: The Story of Saint Therese of the Child Jesus. Windeatt, Mary F. LC 90-71829. 167p. (gr. 5-9). 1991. pap. 7.00 (0-89555-413-5) TAN Bks Pubs.
—The Miraculous Medal: The Story of Our Lady's Appearances to Saint Catherine of Laboure. Windeatt, Mary F. LC 90-71823. 107p. (gr. 5-9). 1991. pap. 5.00 (0-89555-417-8) TAN Bks Pubs.
—Our Lady of Banneux. Windeatt, Mary F. 32p. (gr. 1-5). 1989. Repr. of 1954 ed. wkbk. 3.00 (0-89555-364-3) TAN Bks Pubs.
—Our Lady of Beauraing. Windeatt, Mary F. 32p. (gr. 1-5). 1989. Repr. of 1954 ed. wkbk. 3.00 (0-89555-363-5) TAN Bks Pubs.
—Our Lady of Fatima. Windeatt, Mary F. 32p. (gr. 1-5). 1989. Repr. of 1954 ed. wkbk. 3.00 (0-89555-357-0) TAN Bks Pubs.
—Our Lady of Guadalupe. Windeatt, Mary F. 32p. (gr. 1-5). 1989. Repr. of 1954 ed. wkbk. 3.00 (0-89555-359-7) TAN Bks Pubs.
—Our Lady of Knock. Windeatt, Mary F. 32p. (gr. 1-5). 1989. Repr. of 1954 ed. wkbk. 3.00 (0-89555-362-7) TAN Bks Pubs.
—Our Lady of la Salette. Windeatt, Mary F. 32p. (gr. 1-5). 1989. Repr. of 1954 ed. wkbk. 3.00 (0-89555-361-9) TAN Bks Pubs.
—Our Lady of Lourdes. Windeatt, Mary F. 32p. (gr. 1-5). 1989. Repr. of 1954 ed. wkbk. 3.00 (0-89555-358-9) TAN Bks Pubs.
—Our Lady of Pellevoisin. Windeatt, Mary F. 32p. (gr. 1-5). 1989. Repr. of 1954 ed. wkbk. 3.00 (0-89555-366-X) TAN Bks Pubs.

—Our Lady of Pontmain. Windeatt, Mary F. 32p. (gr. 1-5). 1989. Repr. of 1954 ed. wkbk. 3.00 (0-89555-365-1) TAN Bks Pubs.
—Our Lady of the Miraculous Medal. Windeatt, Mary F. 32p. (gr. 1-5). 1989. Repr. of 1954 ed. wkbk. 3.00 (0-89555-360-0) TAN Bks Pubs.
—Patron Saint of First Communicants: The Story of Blessed Imelda Lambertini. Windeatt, Mary F. LC 90-71824. 85p. (gr. 5-9). 1991. pap. 4.00 (0-89555-416-X) TAN Bks Pubs.
—The Rosary. Windeatt, Mary F. 32p. (gr. 1-5). 1989. Repr. of 1954 ed. wkbk. 3.00 (0-89555-379-1) TAN Bks Pubs.
—St. Anthony of Padua. Windeatt, Mary F. 32p. (gr. 1-5). 1989. Repr. of 1954 ed. wkbk. 3.00 (0-89555-369-4) TAN Bks Pubs.
—St. Christopher. Windeatt, Mary F. 32p. (gr. 1-5). 1989. Repr. of 1954 ed. wkbk. 3.00 (0-89555-376-7) TAN Bks Pubs.
—St. Dominic Savio. Windeatt, Mary F. 32p. (gr. 1-5). 1989. Repr. of 1954 ed. wkbk. 3.00 (0-89555-370-8) TAN Bks Pubs.
—St. Frances Cabrini. Windeatt, Mary F. 32p. (gr. 1-5). 1989. Repr. of 1954 ed. wkbk. 3.00 (0-89555-375-9) TAN Bks Pubs.
—St. Francis of Assisi. Windeatt, Mary F. 32p. (gr. 1-5). 1989. Repr. of 1954 ed. wkbk. 3.00 (0-89555-368-6) TAN Bks Pubs.
—St. Joan of Arc. Windeatt, Mary F. 32p. (gr. 1-5). 1989. Repr. of 1954 ed. wkbk. 3.00 (0-89555-367-8) TAN Bks Pubs.
—St. Maria Goretti. Windeatt, Mary F. 32p. (gr. 1-5). 1989. Repr. of 1954 ed. wkbk. 3.00 (0-89555-374-0) TAN Bks Pubs.
—St. Meinrad. Windeatt, Mary F. 32p. (gr. 1-5). 1989. Repr. of 1954 ed. wkbk. 3.00 (0-89555-377-5) TAN Bks Pubs.
—St. Philomena. Windeatt, Mary F. 32p. (gr. 1-5). 1989. Repr. of 1954 ed. wkbk. 3.00 (0-89555-373-2) TAN Bks Pubs.
—St. Pius X. Windeatt, Mary F. 32p. (gr. 1-5). 1989. Repr. of 1954 ed. wkbk. 3.00 (0-89555-371-6) TAN Bks Pubs.
—St. Teresa of Avila. Windeatt, Mary F. 32p. (gr. 1-5). 1989. Repr. of 1954 ed. wkbk. 3.00 (0-89555-372-4) TAN Bks Pubs.
Harms, Heather. Onion Sundaes. Adler, David A. LC 93-5878. 1994. PLB write for info. (0-679-94697-7); pap. write for info. (0-679-84697-2) Random.
Harness, Cheryl. Aaron's Shirt. Gould, Deborah. LC 88-10414. 32p. (ps-2). 1989. SBE 13.95 (0-02-736351-1, Bradbury Pr) Macmillan Child Grp.
—Fudge. Graeber, Charlotte T. LC 86-7353. 128p. (gr. 1-4). 1987. 12.95 (0-688-06735-2) Lothrop.
—Grandpa's Slide Show. Gould, Deborah. LC 86-20981. 32p. (ps-3). 1987. 13.95 (0-688-06972-X); PLB 13.88 (0-688-06973-8) Lothrop.
—The Night Before Christmas. Moore, Clement C. LC 88-35019. 40p. (ps-8). 1990. 6.99 (0-394-82698-1) Random Bks Yng Read.
—Purple Mountain Majesty. Hefley, Lynn C. Brummett, Nancy P., ed. LC 93-84708. 24p. (Orig.). (gr. 3-6). 1993. pap. text ed. write for info. (0-944943-42-X) Current Inc.
—The Queen with Bees in Her Hair. Harness, Cheryl. LC 92-14409. 32p. (ps-3). 1993. PLB 14.95 (0-8050-1715-1, Bks Young Read) H Holt & Co.
—Three Young Pilgrims. Harness, Cheryl. LC 91-7289. 40p. (gr. k-5). 1992. RSBE 15.95 (0-02-742643-2, Bradbury Pr) Macmillan Child Grp.
—The Windchild. Harness, Cheryl. LC 90-46372. 32p. (ps-4). 1991. 14.95 (0-8050-0558-7, Bks Young Read) H Holt & Co.
—Young John Quincy. Harness, Cheryl. LC 92-37266. 48p. (gr. k-5). 1994. RSBE 15.95 (0-02-742644-0, Bradbury Pr) Macmillan Child Grp.
Harnett, Cynthia. Cargo of the Madalena. Harnett, Cynthia. LC 83-24874. 240p. (gr. 5 up). 1984. 13.50 (0-8225-0890-7) Lerner Pubns.
—The Great House. Harnett, Cynthia. LC 83-24880. 180p. (gr. 5 up). 1984. 13.50 (0-8225-0893-1) Lerner Pubns.
—The Merchant's Mark. Harnett, Cynthia. LC 83-24879. 192p. (gr. 5 up). 1984. 13.50 (0-8225-0891-5) Lerner Pubns.
—The Sign of the Green Falcon. Harnett, Cynthia. LC 83-24831. 288p. (gr. 5 up). 1984. 13.50 (0-8225-0888-5) Lerner Pubns.
—Stars of Fortune. Harnett, Cynthia. LC 83-24836. 288p. (gr. 5 up). 1984. 13.50 (0-8225-0892-3) Lerner Pubns.
Harp, Dave, photos by. Swanfall: Journey of the Tundra Swans. Horton, Tom. 48p. (gr. 1-3). 1991. 15.95 (0-8027-8106-3); PLB 16.85 (0-8027-8107-1) Walker & Co.
Harper, Piers. Cabbage Moon. Chadwick, Tim. LC 93-28952. 1994. 14.95 (0-531-06827-7); lib. bdg. write for info. (0-531-08677-1) Orchard Bks Watts.
Harper, Ruth E. & Leak, Nancy M. The Kissing Hand. Penn, Audrey. LC 93-36159. 1993. 14.95 (0-87868-585-5) Child Welfare.
Harper, Steve, photos by. Artists: A Kansas Collection. Rowley, Patric. 108p. (gr. 7-12). 1989. 34.95 (0-9623079-0-4) Artists Registry.

Harper-Marinick & Kinzie, Mable B. Dine, the Navajo. Shaffer, Susan L., ed. (gr. 6). 1987. incl. 30 student bklts. & 1 tchr's. resource binder which contains poster, lesson plans, overhead transparencies, 1 realia, color slides & audio-cassette 294.43 (0-934351-15-5); tchr's. resource binder only 197.95 (0-934351-26-0); student's bklt. only 4.95 (0-934351-31-7) Heard Mus.
Harper-Marinick, Maria & Kinzie, Mable B. Inde, the Western Apache. Shaffer, Susan L., ed. (gr. 5 up). 1987. incl. 30 student bklts. & 1 tchr's. resource binder which contains poster, lesson plans, overhead transparencies, 1 realia, color slides & audio-cassette 294.43 (0-934351-11-2); tchr's. resource binder only 197.95 (0-934351-22-8); student bklt. only 4.95 (0-934351-27-9) Heard Mus.
Harrill, Sarah. The I Love the Earth Book: A Coloring Book. Harrill, Suzanne E. 12p. (ps-2). 1992. write for info. (0-9625996-4-6) Innerworks Pub.
Harriman, Marinell & Harriman, Robert. A Myriad of Minstrels. Harriman, Marinell & Harriman, Robert. 32p. (Orig.). (gr. 5-7). pap. 3.50 (0-940920-00-X) Drollery Pr.
Harriman, Robert, jt. illus. see Harriman, Marinell.
Harris, Alan, jt. illus. see Jackson, Ian.
Harris, Andrew S. Blue Eye of a Pond. Mitchell, Darby. 10p. (ps-5). 1991. 8.00 (0-9631809-0-8) Castle MI.
Harris, Dell. Canal Priests of Mars. Rowland, Marcus L. 64p. (Orig.). 1990. pap. 8.00 (1-55878-039-4) Game Designers.
—Steppelords of Mars. Theisen, John A. 64p. (Orig.). 1989. pap. 8.00 (1-55878-025-4) Game Designers.
—Twilight: Two Thousand. Chadwick, Frank A. 280p. (Orig.). 1990. pap. 20.00 (1-55878-070-X) Game Designers.
—Zork: The Cavern of Doom, No. 3. Meretzky, S. Eric. (gr. 4-6). 1984. pap. 1.95 (0-8125-7985-2, Pinnacle Bks) Tor Bks.
Harris, Denise. The Kitten Pop-up Book. Costello, Linda, contrib. by. LC 90-85726. 12p. (ps-3). 1991. 9.95 (1-878093-04-5) Boyds Mills Pr.
Harris, Denise & Cote, Nancy. The Night Before Christmas: A Pop-Up Book. Moore, Clement C. Costello, Linda, designed by. (ps-1). 1993. 9.95 (1-56397-003-1) Boyds Mills Pr.
Harris, Frank & Cheese, Bernard. Sing Hey Diddle Diddle. Harrop, Beatrice, compiled by. 96p. (ps-3). 1991. pap. 14.95 (0-317-04680-2, Pub. by A&C Black UK) Talman.
Harris, Greg. Deadly Storms in Action: An Early Reader Pop-up Book. Borgardt, Marianne. 16p. (Orig.). (ps-3). 1993. bds. 8.95 (0-689-71719-9, Aladdin) Macmillan Child Grp.
—Volcanoes & Earthquakes in Action: An Early Reader Pop-up Book. Borgardt, Marianne. 16p. (Orig.). (ps-3). 1993. bds. 8.95 (0-689-71720-2, Aladdin) Macmillan Child Grp.
Harris, Jennifer. The Day the Lifting Bridge Stuck. Yagelski, Robert. LC 90-33984. 32p. (ps-2). 1992. RSBE 14.95 (0-02-793595-7, Bradbury Pr) Macmillan Child Grp.
Harris, Jim. The Three Little Javelinas. Lowell, Susan. LC 92-14232. 32p. (ps-2). 1992. 14.95 (0-87358-542-9) Northland AZ.
—A Tree in Sprocket's Pocket: Stories about God's Green Earth. Nehemias, Paulette. LC 92-26033. 128p. (Orig.). (gr. 3-5). 1993. pap. 4.95 (0-570-04730-7) Concordia.
—Wiggler's Worms: Stories about God's Green Earth. Nehemias, Paulette. LC 92-28486. 128p. (Orig.). (gr. 3-5). 1993. pap. 4.95 (0-570-04731-5) Concordia.
Harris, Linda. Technopoly. McBurney, Jim. Kraven, Mae, ed. 96p. (gr. 4-5). 1991. text ed. 19.95 (0-9629471-0-5) J McBurney.
Harris, Nick. King Arthur & His Knights. Mockler, Anthony. 308p. 1987. jacketed 18.95 (0-19-274531-X) OUP.
Harris, Nick & Stewart, Roger. The Giant Book of the Mummy. David, Rosalie A. LC 92-22734. 14p. (gr. 2-5). 1993. 24.95 (0-525-67413-6, Lodestar Bks) Dutton Child Bks.
Harris, Susan Y., jt. illus. see Gerstein, Mordicai.
Harris, Wayne. Going Home. Wild, Margaret. LC 93-22975. 32p. (ps-3). 1994. 14.95 (0-590-47958-X) Scholastic Inc.
—Rain for Christmas. Tulloch, Richard. 32p. 1990. 10.95 (0-521-37085-X) Cambridge U Pr.
Harrison, Edith. Little Prissy & T. C. Copeland, Colene. LC 88-81916. 114p. (Orig.). (gr. 2 up). 1988. 8.95 (0-318-36004-7); pap. 3.95 (0-318-36005-5) Jordan Valley.
—Little Prissy & T. C. Copeland, Colene. LC 88-81916. 1992. 8.95 (0-939810-07-7); pap. 3.95 (0-939810-08-5) Jordan Valley.
—Mystery in the Farrowing Barn. Copeland, Colene. LC 91-62326. 150p. (Orig.). (gr. 3-7). 1991. 9.95 (0-939810-13-1); pap. 3.95 (0-939810-14-X) Jordan Valley.
—Priscilla. Copeland, Colene. LC 81-80663. 212p. (Orig.). (gr. 3 up). 1981. 8.95 (0-939810-01-8); pap. 3.95 (0-939810-02-6) Jordan Valley.
Harrison, Gaye. Advanced Projects for Children. Buxton, Marilyn. 59p. (gr. 5-7). 1984. pap. text ed. 11.95 (0-88193-105-5) Create Learn.
—Beginning Projects for Children. Buxton, Marilyn. 47p. (gr. 4-7). 1983. pap. text ed. 11.95 (0-88193-101-2) Create Learn.

—Intermediate Projects for Children. Buxton, Marilyn. 60p. (gr. 5-7). 1983. pap. text ed. 11.95 (0-88193-103-9) Create Learn.
Harrison, Judy A. Lions, Lizards & Ladybugs. Mendel, Kathleen L., ed. LC 89-51485. 80p. (gr. k-6). 1989. pap. 9.95g (0-9624384-2-1) Telstar TX.
Harrison, Marc. I Hate Lima Beans! Schweitz, Rita. LC 92-45561. (ps-3). 1993. 4.99 (0-8499-0941-4) Word Inc.
—The Incredible Bathtub Surprise. Schweitz, Rita. LC 92-45562. (ps-3). 1993. pap. 4.99 (0-8499-0943-0) Word Inc.
Harrison, Mark. Nature Hide & Seek: Oceans. Wood, John N. LC 85-73. 24p. (gr. 1-4). 1985. 13.00 (0-394-87583-4) Knopf Bks Yng Read.
Harrison, Susan. AlphaZoo Christmas. Harrison, Susan. LC 93-20351. 40p. (ps-2). 1993. 13.95 (0-8249-8623-7, Ideals Child); PLB 14.00 (0-8249-8632-6) Hambleton-Hill.
—My First Book of Christmas Carols. 24p. 1992. pap. 3.95 (0-8249-8568-0, Ideals Child) Hambleton-Hill.
—My Play a Tune Book: Christmas Songs. Wilson, Etta, ed. 26p. (gr. k up). 1987. 15.95 (0-938971-05-0) JTG Nashville.
—The Story of Esther. Pingry, Patricia. 24p. (ps-3). 1990. pap. 3.95 (0-8249-8420-X, Ideals Child) Hambleton-Hill.
—Twelve Days of Christmas. Harrison, Susan. 24p. (ps-3). 1989. pap. 2.95 (0-8249-8391-2, Ideals Child) Hambleton-Hill.
—Up on the Housetop. Hanby, Benjamin. 24p. (Orig.). (ps-2). 1991. pap. 3.95 (0-8249-8521-4, Ideals Child) Hambleton-Hill.
Harrison, Susan J. Christmas with the Bears. Harrison, Susan J. 24p. (ps up) 1987. PLB 9.95 (0-525-44329-0, 0966-290, DCB) Dutton Child Bks.
Harrison, Ted. The Cremation of Sam McGee. Service, Robert. LC 86-14971. 32p. (ps up). 1987. 15.95 (0-688-06903-7) Greenwillow.
—A Northern Alphabet. Harrison, Ted. LC 82-50244. 32p. (ps-1). 1989. 14.95 (0-88776-209-3); pap. 6.95 (0-88776-233-6) Tundra Bks.
—The Shooting of Dan McGrew. Service, Robert. LC 88-6124. (gr. 3 up). 1988. 14.95 (0-87923-748-1) Godine Pub.
Harriton, Chuck. Electricity. Brandt, Keith. LC 84-2705. 32p. (gr. 3-6). 1985. PLB 9.49 (0-8167-0198-9); pap. text ed. 2.95 (0-8167-0199-7) Troll Assocs.
—Light. Bains, Rae. LC 84-2719. 32p. (gr. 3-6). 1985. PLB 9.49 (0-8167-0202-0); pap. text ed. 2.95 (0-8167-0203-9) Troll Assocs.
—Molecules & Atoms. Bains, Rae. LC 84-2712. 32p. (gr. 3-6). 1985. PLB 9.49 (0-8167-0284-5); pap. text ed. 2.95 (0-8167-0285-3) Troll Assocs.
Harroll, Pat. Word Wizardry, Level II. Joy, Flora. 112p. (gr. 4-12). 1987. pap. 11.95 (0-86653-404-0, GA 1017) Good Apple.
—Word Wizardry, Level I. Joy, Flora. 112p. (gr. 2-8). 1987. pap. 11.95 (0-86653-403-2, GA 1016) Good Apple.
Harroun, Dorothy. Mini Walks on the Mesa. Cooper, Ursula. LC 89-4448. 32p. (Orig.). (gr. 3-6). 1989. pap. 6.95 (0-86534-133-8) Sunstone Pr.
Hart, Trish. Antarctic Diary. Hart, Trish. LC 93-110. 1994. pap. write for info. (0-383-03675-5) SRA Schl Grp.
—There Are No Polar Bears down There. Hart, Trish. LC 92-31949. 1993. 3.75 (0-383-03597-X) SRA Schl Grp.
Harte, Cheryl. Bunny Rattle. 12p. (ps). 1989. sponge-filled cloth 4.95 (0-394-89956-3) Random Bks Yng Read.
—Ducky Squeak. 12p. (ps). 1989. sponge-filled cloth 5.99 (0-394-89955-5) Random Bks Yng Read.
—Jingle Bear. Harte, Cheryl. (ps). 1991. sponge-filled 5.95 (0-679-80750-0) Random Bks Yng Read.
—My Chalkboard Book: Green Ladder Books for Kids Through 6 Years. 14p. (ps-1). 1988. bds. 6.95 (0-394-89401-4) Random Bks Yng Read.
—Push-a-Lamb. 14p. (ps). 1989. bds. 5.95 with plastic wheels (0-394-82986-7) Random Bks Yng Read.
Harte, Kathleen M. There's Lots That I Can Do. Harte, Kathleen M. LC 92-43904. 32p. (ps-k). 1993. pap. 2.25 (0-679-84798-7) Random Bks Yng Read.
Hartelius, Margaret A. Alphaboo: A Hidden Letter ABC Book. Thompson, Carol. LC 86-26925. (gr. 1 up). 1994. pap. write for info. (0-448-40213-0, G&D) Putnam Pub Group.
—The Great Carrot Top Mystery. Chardiet, Bernice. 24p. (ps-1). 1994. pap. 3.50 (0-590-33426-3, Cartwheel) Scholastic Inc.
—The Great Egg Mystery. Hartelius, Margaret A. 16p. (Orig.). (ps-2). 1994. pap. 2.95 (0-590-33427-1, Cartwheel) Scholastic Inc.
—Hide & Ghost Seek. Hartelius, Margaret. 32p. (ps-3). 1992. pap. 2.95 (0-448-40475-3, G&D) Putnam Pub Group.
—Knot Again! The Complete Lanyard Kit! Hartelius, Margaret A. 24p. (gr. 1-7). 1993. pap. 7.95 (0-448-40456-7, G&D) Putnam Pub Group.
—Over in the Meadow. 1987. pap. 6.99 incl. audiocassette (0-553-45900-7) Bantam.
—ZOOM! The Complete Paper Airplane Kit. Hartelius, Margaret A. LC 90-84671. 32p. (ps-3). 1991. 6.95 (0-448-40138-X, G&D) Putnam Pub Group.
Hartley, Al. Family Fun. Hartley, Al. (gr. 1). 1988. pap. text ed. 1.29 (1-55748-004-4) Barbour & Co.
—Flying Colors. Hartley, Al. 32p. (gr. 1). 1988. pap. text ed. 1.29 (1-55748-000-1) Barbour & Co.

—Fun in the Car. Hartley, Al. 32p. (gr. 1). 1988. pap.
text ed. 1.29 (*1-55748-001-X*) Barbour & Co.
—Fun with Friends. Hartley, Al. (gr. 1). 1988. pap. text
ed. 1.29 (*1-55748-002-8*) Barbour & Co.
—Happy Home. Hartley, Al. (gr. 1). 1988. pap. text ed.
1.29 (*1-55748-005-2*) Barbour & Co.
—School Fun. Hartley, Al. (gr. 1). 1988. pap. text ed.
1.29 (*1-55748-003-6*) Barbour & Co.
Hartman, David. What a School. Salem, Lynn & Stewart,
Josie. 16p. (gr. 1). 1992. pap. 3.50 (*1-880612-10-0*)
Seedling Pubns.
Hartman, Laura. If It Weren't for Benjamin: (I'd Always
Get to Lick the Icing Spoon) Hazen, Barbara S. LC
78-26403. 32p. (ps-3). 1979. 16.95 (*0-87705-384-7*);
pap. 9.95 (*0-89885-172-6*) Human Sci Pr.
—The Rose-Colored Glasses: Melanie Adjusts to Poor
Vision. Leggett, Linda R. & Andrews, Linda G. LC
79-12501. 32p. (gr. 3 up). 1979. 16.95
(*0-87705-408-8*) Human Sci Pr.
—Wishful Lying. Blue, Rose. LC 79-21806. 32p. (ps-3).
1980. 16.95 (*0-87705-473-8*) Human Sci Pr.
Hartman, Tim. I Can Talk about What Hurts: A Book for
Kids in Homes Where There's Chemical Dependency.
Sinberg, Janet & Daley, Dennis. 48p. (Orig.). (gr. k-5).
1991. pap. 7.00 (*0-89486-641-9*, FDO911031 A)
Hazelden.
Hartophilis, Georgene. How to Draw Dinosaurs. 32p.
(Orig.). 1990. pap. 2.95 (*0-942025-74-1*) Kidsbks.
—How to Draw Dinosaurs. 32p. 1991. 3.98
(*1-56156-022-7*) Kidsbks.
—How to Draw Endangered Animals. 32p. 1991. 3.98
(*1-56156-018-9*) Kidsbks.
—How to Draw Endangered Animals. 32p. 1991. pap.
2.95 (*1-56156-027-8*) Kidsbks.
Hartwell, Marjorie. The Poetry Book: Vol. 4. Huber,
Miriam B., et al, eds. LC 79-51968. (gr. 4). 1980.
Repr. of 1926 ed. 18.00x (*0-89609-183-X*) Roth Pub
Inc.
Hartzog, Sherri. Baskets, Beads, & Black Walnut Owls:
Creative Crafts for Ages 9-12. Healton, Sarah H. &
Whiteside, Kay H. LC 92-41247. (gr. 4-7). 1993. pap.
9.95 (*0-8306-4040-1*) TAB Bks.
Harvey, Bob & Harvey, Diane K., photos by. Fishing
with Peter: Pescando Con Pedro. Harvey, Bob, text
by. (ENG & SPA.). 48p. (ps-6). 1992. 12.95
(*0-89802-592-3*) Beautiful Am.
Harvey, Chuck. Sara Bear's Surprise. Rathbun, Carolyn
R. (Orig.). (ps). 1993. 12.95 (*0-9634808-0-4*); pap.
4.50 (*0-9634808-1-2*) Endless Love.
Harvey, Cliff, jt. illus. see Harvey, Eve S.
Harvey, Diane K., jt. photog. see Harvey, Bob.
Harvey, Eve S. & Harvey, Cliff. American Government:
The U. S. A. & West Virginia. Coffey, William E. &
Riddel, Frank S. Buckalew, Marshall, ed. 304p. (gr. 8).
1990. 25.00 (*0-914498-08-8*) WV Hist Ed Found.
—West Virginia: Our Land - Our People. Doherty,
William T. Buckalew, Marshall, ed. 320p. (gr. 8).
1990. 25.00 (*0-914498-07-X*); punched for 3-ring
binder tchr's. manual 25.00 (*0-914498-10-X*) WV Hist
Ed Found.
—West Virginia: Our State. Williams, Tony L. Buckalew,
Marshall, ed. 288p. (gr. 4). 1990. 20.00
(*0-914498-09-6*); punched for 3-ring binder tchr's.
manual 20.00 (*0-685-25544-1*) WV Hist Ed Found.
Harvey, Paul. All about Allergies. Terkel, Susan N. LC
92-17770. 64p. (gr. 2-5). 1993. 13.99 (*0-525-67410-1*,
Lodestar Bks) Dutton Child Bks.
—Animals. Marks, Burton. LC 91-3656. 24p. (gr. k-2).
1992. PLB 9.89 (*0-8167-2415-6*); pap. text ed. 2.50
(*0-8167-2416-4*) Troll Assocs.
—Animals at Night. Peters, Sharon. LC 82-19226. 32p.
(gr. k-2). 1983. lib. bdg. 11.59 (*0-89375-903-1*); pap.
2.95 (*0-8167-1477-0*) Troll Assocs.
—The Aquarium Take-Along Book. Gerstenfeld, Sheldon
L. LC 93-23059. 128p. (gr. 2-5). 1994. 14.99
(*0-670-84386-5*) Viking Child Bks.
—The Aquarium Take-along Book. Gerstenfeld, Sheldon
L. 128p. (gr. 2-5). 1994. pap. 6.99 (*0-14-036019-0*)
Puffin Bks.
—The Awful Mess Mystery. Robert, Adrian. LC 84-8724.
48p. (gr. 2-4). 1985. PLB 10.89 (*0-8167-0402-3*); pap.
text ed. 3.50 (*0-8167-0403-1*) Troll Assocs.
—Big Red Fire Engine. Greydanus, Rose. 32p. (gr. k-2).
1980. PLB 7.89 (*0-8167-0372-6*); pap. 1.95
(*0-89375-272-X*) Troll Assocs.
—Bubble Gum in the Sky. Everett, Louise. LC 86-30859.
32p. (gr. k-2). 1988. PLB 7.89 (*0-8167-0998-X*); pap.
text ed. 1.95 (*0-8167-0999-8*) Troll Assocs.
—Un Carro De Bomberos Grande y Rojo. Greydanus,
Rose. (SPA.). 32p. (gr. k-2). 1981. PLB 7.89
(*0-89375-555-9*); pap. 1.95 (*0-685-04944-2*) Troll
Assocs.
—Case of the Great Train Robbery. Bains, Rae. LC 81-
7525. 48p. (gr. 2-4). 1982. PLB 10.89
(*0-89375-588-5*); pap. text ed. 3.50 (*0-89375-589-3*)
Troll Assocs.
—Case of the Missing Chick. new ed. Frost, Erica. LC
78-18036. 48p. (gr. 2-4). 1979. PLB 10.89
(*0-89375-092-1*); pap. 3.50 (*0-89375-080-8*) Troll
Assocs.
—Case of the Wacky Cat. Bolton, Elizabeth. LC 84-8725.
48p. (gr. 2-4). 1985. PLB 10.89 (*0-8167-0400-7*); pap.
text ed. 3.50 (*0-8167-0401-5*) Troll Assocs.
—Chuck, the Unlucky Duck. Matthews, Morgan. LC 88-
1284. 48p. (Orig.). (gr. 1-4). 1989. PLB 10.59
(*0-8167-1333-2*); pap. text ed. 3.50 (*0-8167-1334-0*)
Troll Assocs.

—Colors & Numbers. Marks, Burton. LC 91-17493. 24p.
(gr. k-2). 1992. PLB 8.89 (*0-8167-2411-3*); pap. text
ed. 2.50 (*0-8167-2412-1*) Troll Assocs.
—Come on Up. Kim, Joy. LC 81-2356. 32p. (gr. k-2).
1981. PLB 11.59 (*0-89375-511-7*); pap. text ed. 2.95
(*0-89375-512-5*) Troll Assocs.
—Contento Juan. Peters, Sharon. (SPA.). 32p. (gr. k-2).
1981. PLB 7.89 (*0-89375-952-X*); pap. 1.95
(*0-685-04945-0*) Troll Assocs.
—Dinosaur in Trouble. Gordon, Sharon. 32p. (gr. k-2).
1980. PLB 7.89 (*0-89375-374-2*); pap. 1.95
(*0-89375-274-6*) Troll Assocs.
—Feliz Cumpleanos. Peters, Sharon. (SPA.). 32p. (gr.
k-2). 1981. PLB 7.89 (*0-89375-553-2*); pap. 1.95
(*0-685-04948-5*) Troll Assocs.
—Happy Birthday. Peters, Sharon. 32p. (gr. k-2). 1980.
PLB 7.89 (*0-89375-379-3*); pap. 1.95 (*0-89375-279-7*)
Troll Assocs.
—Happy Jack. Peters, Sharon. 32p. (gr. k-2). 1980. PLB
7.89 (*0-89375-380-7*); pap. 1.95 (*0-89375-280-0*) Troll
Assocs.
—How to Make a Chemical Volcano & Other Mysterious
Experiments. Kramer, Alan. 112p. (gr. 5 up). 1991.
pap. 6.95 (*0-531-15610-9*) Watts.
—Let's Go. Marks, Burton. LC 91-9986. 24p. (gr. k-2).
1992. lib. bdg. 9.89 (*0-8167-2413-X*); pap. text ed.
2.50 (*0-8167-2414-8*) Troll Assocs.
—Life in the Forest. Curran, Eileen. LC 84-16455. 32p.
(gr. k-2). 1985. PLB 11.59 (*0-8167-0446-5*); pap. text
ed. 2.95 (*0-8167-0447-3*) Troll Assocs.
—Little Danny Dinosaur. Craig, Janet. LC 87-16228.
32p. (gr. k-2). 1988. PLB 7.89 (*0-8167-1229-8*); pap.
text ed. 1.95 (*0-8167-1230-1*) Troll Assocs.
—Moosey Saves Money. Pellowski, Michael J. LC 85-
14053. 48p. (Orig.). (gr. 1-3). 1986. PLB 10.59
(*0-8167-0628-X*); pap. text ed. 3.50 (*0-8167-0629-8*)
Troll Assocs.
—Mrs. Wigglesworth's Secret. Supraner, Robyn. LC 78-
18041. 48p. (gr. 2-4). 1979. PLB 10.89 (*0-89375-097-2*);
pap. 3.50 (*0-89375-085-9*) Troll Assocs.
—My Secret Hiding Place. Greydanus, Rose. 32p. (gr.
k-2). 1980. PLB 7.89 (*0-89375-383-1*); pap. 1.95
(*0-89375-283-5*) Troll Assocs.
—Mystery of the Missing Wigs. Palazzo-Craig, Janet. LC
81-7615. 48p. (gr. 2-4). 1982. PLB 10.89
(*0-89375-592-3*); pap. text ed. 3.50 (*0-89375-593-1*)
Troll Assocs.
—Pete the Parakeet. Gordon, Sharon. 32p. (gr. k-2).
1980. PLB 7.89 (*0-89375-384-X*); pap. 1.95
(*0-89375-284-3*) Troll Assocs.
—Rainbows & Frogs: A Story about Colors. Kim, Joy. LC
81-4685. 32p. (gr. k-2). 1981. PLB 11.59
(*0-89375-505-2*); pap. text ed. 2.95 (*0-89375-506-0*)
Troll Assocs.
—Rhymes & Stories. Marks, Burton. LC 91-3663. 24p.
(gr. k-2). 1992. PLB 9.89 (*0-8167-2409-1*); pap. 2.50
(*0-8167-2410-5*) Troll Assocs.
—The Riddle King's Camp Riddles. Thaler, Mike. LC 88-
63193. 32p. (gr. 1-5). 1989. pap. 1.25 (*0-394-83995-1*)
Random Bks Yng Read.
—The Riddle King's Food Riddles. Thaler, Mike. LC 88-
63190. 32p. (gr. 1-5). 1989. pap. 1.25 (*0-394-84041-0*)
Random Bks Yng Read.
—The Riddle King's Pet Riddles. Thaler, Mike. LC 88-
63191. 32p. (gr. 1-5). 1989. pap. 1.25 (*0-394-83977-3*)
Random Bks Yng Read.
—The Riddle King's School Riddles. Thaler, Mike. LC
88-63192. 32p. (gr. 1-5). 1989. pap. 1.25
(*0-394-84004-6*) Random Bks Yng Read.
—The Rooster & the Weather Vane. Peters, Sharon. LC
86-30838. 32p. (gr. k-2). 1988. PLB 7.89
(*0-8167-0980-7*); pap. text ed. 1.95 (*0-8167-0981-5*)
Troll Assocs.
—Sporty Riddles. Bernstein, Joanne E. & Cohen, Paul.
Mathews, Judith, ed. LC 89-5294. 32p. (gr. 1-5). 1989.
PLB 8.95 (*0-8075-7590-9*) A Whitman.
—The Superduper Collector. Poskanzer, Susan C. LC 85-
14051. 48p. (Orig.). (gr. 1-3). 1986. PLB 10.59
(*0-8167-0606-9*); pap. text ed. 3.50 (*0-8167-0607-7*)
Troll Assocs.
—Three Little Chicks. Feczko, Kathy. LC 84-8629. 32p.
(gr. k-2). 1985. PLB 11.59 (*0-8167-0355-8*); pap. text
ed. 2.95 (*0-8167-0435-X*) Troll Assocs.
—What Is a Reptile? Kuchalla, Susan. LC 81-11364. 32p.
(gr. k-2). 1982. PLB 11.59 (*0-89375-672-5*); pap. 2.95
(*0-89375-673-3*) Troll Assocs.
—What Makes the Weather. Palazzo, Janet. LC 81-
11383. 32p. (gr. k-2). 1982. PLB 11.59
(*0-89375-654-7*); pap. 2.95 (*0-89375-655-5*) Troll
Assocs.
—What's under the Ocean. Craig, Janet. LC 81-11425.
32p. (gr. k-2). 1982. PLB 11.59 (*0-89375-652-0*); pap.
2.95 (*0-89375-653-9*) Troll Assocs.
Harvey, Roland. Dirty Dave. Hilton, Nette. LC 89-
35402. 32p. (ps-1). 1990. 12.95 (*0-531-05861-1*); PLB
12.99 (*0-531-08461-2*) Orchard Bks Watts.
Harvey, Roland & Levine, Joe. My Place in Space. Hirst,
Robin & Hirst, Sally. LC 89-37893. 40p. (ps-2). 1990.
13.95 (*0-531-05859-X*); PLB 13.99 (*0-531-08459-0*)
Orchard Bks Watts.
—My Place in Space. Hirst, Robin & Hirst, Sally. LC 89-
37893. 40p. (ps-2). 1992. pap. 5.95 (*0-531-07030-1*)
Orchard Bks Watts.
Harvy, Paul. Best Valentine Book. Whitehead, Patricia.
LC 84-8829. 32p. (gr. k-2). 1985. PLB 11.59
(*0-8167-0369-8*); pap. text ed. 2.95 (*0-8167-0370-1*)
Troll Assocs.

Harwood, Lynne. Honeybees at Home. Harwood, Lynne.
LC 93-33552. 40p. (gr. 3-8). 1994. 16.95
(*0-88448-119-0*) Tilbury Hse.
Hasenauer, Richard. Caravans of Mars. Andrews, Ed.
64p. (Orig.). 1989. pap. 8.00 (*1-55878-023-8*) Game
Designers.
Hashimoto, Molly. A Present for Rose. Edens, Cooper.
32p. (gr. 4 up). 1993. 15.95 (*0-912365-89-7*)
Sasquatch Bks.
Haskell, Sally. I Told My Secret: A Book for Kids Who
Were Abused. Gil, Eliana M. 16p. (Orig.). (gr. 3 up).
1986. pap. 2.00 (*0-9613205-1-6*) Launch Pr.
Haskett, Merelaine. Grandpa Haskett Presents: Original
New Christmas Stories for the Young & Young-at-
Heart. Haskett, William P. Haskett, M. R., ed. &
intro. by. 20p. (Orig.). (ps-2). 1982. pap. 3.00g
(*0-9609724-0-4*) Haskett Story.
Haskins, Francine. Things I Like about Grandma.
Haskins, Francine. 32p. (gr. 3-4). 1992. PLB 21.34
(*0-89239-107-3*) Childrens Book Pr.
Hass, E. A. Incognito Mosquito, Private Insective. Hass,
E. A. LC 82-205. 96p. (gr. 2-5). 1982. PLB 13.88
(*0-688-01434-8*) Lothrop.
Hassall, Joan. Oxford Nursery Rhyme Book. Opie, Iona
& Opie, Peter, eds. (ps-3). 1955. 29.95x
(*0-19-869112-2*) OUP.
Hassan, Hanife. Aditi & the One-Eyed Monkey.
Namjoshi, Suniti. LC 88-19058. 96p. (gr. 2-5). 1989.
lib. bdg. 10.95 (*0-8070-8314-3*); pap. 3.95
(*0-8070-8315-1*) Beacon Pr.
Hasselrie, Malthe. Tales of a Chinese Grandmother.
Carpenter, Frances. LC 72-77514. 302p. (gr. 3-8).
1972. pap. 8.95 (*0-8048-1042-7*) C E Tuttle.
Hasselriis, Else. Shen of the Sea. Chrisman, Arthur B.
(gr. 4-7). 1968. 15.00 (*0-525-39244-0*, DCB) Dutton
Child Bks.
Hassett, John. Down East Puzzles & Word Games.
Baker & Boyington. 80p. (Orig.). 1989. pap. 3.95
(*0-89272-272-X*) Down East.
—Junior - A Little Loon Tale. Hassett, John & Hassett,
Ann. 32p. (gr. 2-5). 1993. 14.95 (*0-89272-324-6*)
Down East.
—Moose on the Loose. Hassett, Ann & Hassett, John.
48p. (Orig.). (gr. 4). 1987. pap. 7.95 (*0-89272-245-2*)
Down East.
Hasting, Christine Q. Growing up with Character:
Character Building Stories for Children, Vol. 1.
Gabriel, Howard W., III. 112p. (Orig.). (gr. k-8). 1986.
pap. 7.95 (*0-936997-00-1*, 038601) M & H Enter.
Hastings, Jack. Cavalier in the Wilderness. Phares, Ross.
LC 76-1409. 290p. (gr. 6-12). 1976. 16.95
(*0-88289-128-6*); pap. 11.95 (*0-88289-127-8*) Pelican.
Hastings, Kathryn K. Fanciful Faces & Handbound
Books: Fairy Tales. Feller, Ron L. & Feller, Marsha Y.
Ennes, Phyllis L., ed. Smith, Andrew P., photos by.
LC 88-34952. 72p. (Orig.). (gr. 2-9). 1989. pap. 9.95
(*0-9615873-1-8*) Arts Factory.
—Paper Masks & Puppets for Stories, Songs & Plays.
Feller, Ron L. & Feller, Marsha Y. Joyner, Hermon,
photos by. Graves, Jan, frwd. by. LC 85-72952. 104p.
(Orig.). (gr. 2-9). 1986. pap. 14.95 (*0-9615873-0-X*)
Arts Factory.
Hasty, Patti. It's OK. 2nd ed. Crouthamel, Thomas G.,
Sr. LC 86-27694. 36p. (gr. 6 up). 1990. pap. 6.95
(*0-940701-18-9*) Keystone Pr.
Hatay, Nona. Charlie's ABC. Hatay, Nona. LC 92-72030.
32p. (ps-k). 1993. 10.95 (*1-56282-352-3*); PLB 10.89
(*1-56282-353-1*) Hyprn Child.
Hatchem, Mia. Androcles & the Lion. Michael, Emory
H. LC 87-51492. 44p. (gr. k-4). 1988. 6.95
(*1-55523-132-2*) Winston-Derek.
Hathon, Elizabeth. My Fuzzy Friends. 18p. (ps). 1993.
bds. 2.95 (*0-448-40523-7*, G&D) Putnam Pub Group.
—Sleepy Time. 18p. (ps). 1993. bds. 2.95 (*0-448-40524-5*,
G&D) Putnam Pub Group.
Hathon, Elizabeth, photos by. Ding Dong! & Other
Sounds. Dubov, Christine S. LC 90-47301. 12p. (ps).
1991. bds. 3.95 (*0-688-10162-3*, Tambourine Bks)
Morrow.
—Knock! & Other Sounds. Dubov, Christine S. LC 90-
47302. 12p. (ps). 1991. bds. 3.95 (*0-688-10161-5*,
Tambourine Bks) Morrow.
—Let's Get Together. LC 91-62668. 14p. (ps). 1992. bds.
2.99 (*0-679-82225-9*) Random Bks Yng Read.
—Oink! & Other Sounds. Dubov, Christine S. LC 90-
47303. 12p. (ps). 1991. bds. 3.95 (*0-688-10102-X*,
Tambourine Bks) Morrow.
—Sharing & Caring. LC 91-62663. 14p. (ps). 1992. bds.
2.99 (*0-679-82226-7*) Random Bks Yng Read.
Hatter, Laurie. Christmas Books & Ornaments. Greene,
George W. (ps). 1993. Gift box set of 4 bks., 12p. ea.
bds. 14.95 (*1-56828-041-6*) Red Jacket Pr.
—Gardening Storybox. Greene, George W. (ps). 1993.
Activity kit incl. 2 bks., 12p. ea. 16.95
(*1-56828-045-9*) Red Jacket Pr.
—Halloween Book & Masks. Green, George W. (ps).
1993. Gift box set of 4 bks., 12p. ea. bds. 14.95
(*1-56828-040-8*) Red Jacket Pr.
—Hamlet Trims His Tree. Greene, George W. 12p. (ps).
1993. 4.95 (*1-56828-023-8*) Red Jacket Pr.
—The Legend of Jack O'Lantern. Greene, George W.
12p. (ps). 1992. 4.95 (*1-56828-000-9*) Red Jacket Pr.
—Margaret's Christmas Stocking. Greene, George W.
12p. (ps). 1993. 4.95 (*1-56828-022-X*) Red Jacket Pr.
—Me & My Snowman. Greene, George W. (ps). 1993.
4.95 (*1-56828-020-3*) Red Jacket Pr.
—Sal's Garden Trowell. Greene, George W. 12p. (ps).
1993. 4.95 (*1-56828-031-9*) Red Jacket Pr.

—Sam's Watering Can. Greene, George W. 12p. (ps). 1993. 4.95 (1-56828-032-7) Red Jacket Pr.

—Santa's Hat. Greene, George W. 12p. (ps). 1993. 4.95 (1-56828-021-1) Red Jacket Pr.

—What Haunts Hamlet's House? Greene, George W. 12p. (ps). 1992. 4.95 (1-56828-003-3) Red Jacket Pr.

—Why Ghosts Like Halloween. Greene, George W. 12p. (ps). 1992. 4.95 (1-56828-002-5) Red Jacket Pr.

—Witch's Brew. Greene, George W. 12p. (ps). 1992. 4.95 (1-56828-001-7) Red Jacket Pr.

Haubrich, Kathy. Special Delivery. Brandt, Betty. 48p. (gr. k-4). 1988. lib. bdg. 14.95 (0-87614-312-5) Carolrhoda Bks.

—We'll Race You, Henry: A Story about Henry Ford. Mitchell, Barbara. 64p. (gr. 3-6). 1986. PLB 14.95 (0-87614-291-9) Carolrhoda Bks.

—We'll Race You, Henry: A Story about Henry Ford. Mitchell, Barbara. (gr. 3-6). 1987. pap. 5.95 (0-87614-471-7, First Ave Edns) Lerner Pubns.

Haughey, Karen. Starseed: An Introduction (for children) to the World. Bridge, Michael. 32p. 1992. 22.95 (0-944963-34-X); PLB 20.95 (0-944963-15-3); pap. 16. 95 (0-685-60191-9) Glastonbury Pr.

Hauman, Doris, jt. illus. see Hauman, George.

Hauman, George & Hauman, Doris. The Little Engine That Could: Miniature Edition. Piper, Watty. 48p. 1990. pap. 2.95 (0-448-40071-5, Platt & Munk Pubs) Putnam Pub Group.

—The Little Engine That Could: Sixtieth Anniversary Edition. Piper, Watty. 48p. 1990. 12.95 (0-448-40041-3, Platt & Munk Pubs) Putnam Pub Group.

—La Pequena Locomotora Que Si Pudo: The Little Engine That Could. Ada, Alma F., tr. (SPA.). 48p. (ps-6). 1992. 5.95 (0-448-41096-6, Platt & Munk Pubs) Putnam Pub Group.

Hausherr, Rosemary. Move over, Wheelchairs Coming Through. Roy, Ron. LC 84-14314. 96p. (gr. 4-7). 1985. 15.45 (0-89919-249-1, Clarion Bks) HM.

Hausherr, Rosemarie, photos by. Whose Hat Is That? Roy, Ron. 40p. (ps-3). 1990. pap. 5.70 (0-395-54778-4, Clarion Bks) HM.

Hausherr, Rosmarie. Children & the AIDS Virus: A Book for Children, Parents, & Teachers. Hausherr, Rosmarie. (ps up). 1989. 15.45 (0-89919-834-1, Clarion Bks); pap. 5.95 (0-395-51167-4, Clarion Bks) HM.

—The City Girl Who Went to Sea. Hausherr, Rosmarie. LC 89-27236. 80p. (gr. 3-6). 1990. SBE 14.95 (0-02-743421-4, Four Winds) Macmillan Child Grp.

—My First Kitten. Hausherr, Rosmarie. LC 85-42804. 48p. (gr. 1-4). 1985. RSBE 13.95 (0-02-743420-6, Four Winds) Macmillan Child Grp.

—My First Puppy. Hausherr, Rosmarie. LC 86-14979. 64p. (gr. 1-4). 1986. RSBE 14.95 (0-02-743410-9, Four Winds) Macmillan Child Grp.

—Whose Shoes Are These? Roy, Ron. LC 87-24279. 40p. (ps-4). 1991. pap. 5.70 (0-395-55353-9, Clarion Bks) HM.

—The Wind Warrior: The Training of a Karate Champion. Goedecke, Christopher J. LC 91-6405. 64p. (gr. 3-9). 1992. RSBE 15.95 (0-02-736262-0, Four Winds) Macmillan Child Grp.

Hausman, Sid. Ghost Walk: Native American Tales of the Spirit. Hausman, Gerald. 128p. (Orig.). 1991. pap. 9.95 (0-933553-07-2) Mariposa Print Pub.

Hausman, Suzanne. Yes, Virginia. 6.95 (0-685-86235-6) Pubns Devl Co TX.

Hautzig, David. DJs, Ratings, & Hook Tapes: Pop Music Broadcasting. Hautzig, David. LC 91-33588. 48p. (gr. 3-7). 1993. SBE 15.95 (0-02-743471-0, Macmillan Child Bk) Macmillan Child Grp.

Hautzig, David, photos by. City Within a City: How Kids Live in New York's Chinatown. Krull, Kathleen. LC 93-15846. 1994. write for info. (0-525-67437-3, Lodestar Bks) Dutton Child Bks.

—On the Air: Behind the Scenes at a TV Newscast. Hautzig, Esther. LC 91-6407. 48p. (gr. 1-4). 1991. RSBE 15.95 (0-02-743361-7, Macmillan Child Bk) Macmillan Child Grp.

—The Other Side: How Kids Live in a California Latino Neighborhood. Krull, Kathleen. LC 93-15845. (ps-6). 1994. write for info. (0-525-67438-1, Lodestar Bks) Dutton Child Bks.

Havelock, Elaine. The Crooked Angel. 2nd ed. Kavanaugh, James. LC 90-62058. 64p. (ps-3). 1990. pap. 9.95 (1-878995-02-2) S J Nash Pub.

Havens, Greg. Hey Look at Me! Here We Go. Thomasson, Merry. LC 85-62576. 20p. (ps-2). 1987. 9.95 (0-9615407-0-2) Thomasson-Grant.

Haverfield, Mary. The Adventures of Pinocchio. Collodi, Carlo. Kassirer, Sue, adapted by. LC 92-2503. 32p. (Orig.). (ps-2). 1992. pap. 2.25 (0-679-83466-4) Random Bks Yng Read.

—Tilli Comes to Texas. Oppenheimer, Evelyn. LC 86-3089. 40p. (gr. k-3). 1986. PLB 9.95 (0-937460-21-4) Hendrick-Long.

Havey, Paul. Un Dinosauro en Peligro. Gordon, Sharon. (SPA.). 32p. (gr. k-2). 1981. PLB 7.89 (0-89375-554-0); pap. 1.95 (0-685-42386-7) Troll Assocs.

Havlicek, Karel & Stuart, Walter. Koalas. Wildlife Education, Ltd. Staff. 20p. (gr. 5 up). 1983. pap. 2.75 (0-937934-13-5) Wildlife Educ.

Haw-I Publishing Co., Staff. Tales about Plants: Chinese Children's Stories, 5 vols, Vols. 6-10. Wonder Kids Publications Group Staff & Hwa-I Publishing Co., Staff. Ching, Emily, et al, eds. LC 90-60792. 140p. (gr. 3-6). 1991. Repr. of 1988 ed. Set. 39.75 (0-685-59008-9) Wonder Kids.

Hawcock, David. Whose Coat? Fields, Sadie. 10p. (ps). 1993. pap. 4.95 (0-671-79163-X, Little Simon) S&S Trade.

—Whose Home? Fields, Sadie. 10p. (ps). 1993. pap. 4.95 (0-671-79164-8, Little Simon) S&S Trade.

—Whose Nose? Fields, Sadie. 10p. (ps). 1993. pap. 4.95 (0-671-79162-1, Little Simon) S&S Trade.

Hawk, Lee. Jeffrey's Laugh. Otis, Sharon & Walker, Lois. Goldman, Howard, intro. by. (Orig.). (ps-6). 1987. wkbk. 6.50 (0-9617737-2-3) Total Lrn.

Hawkes, Kevin. Hey, Hay! A Wagonful of Funny Homonym Riddles. Terban, Marvin. Stevenson, Dinah, ed. 64p. (gr. 3-7). 1991. 14.95 (0-395-54431-9, Clarion Bks); pap. 5.70 (0-395-56183-3, Clarion Bks) HM.

—Lady Bugatti. Maxner, Joyce. LC 90-19127. 32p. (gr. k up). 1991. 13.95 (0-688-10340-5); PLB 13.88 (0-688-10341-3) Lothrop.

—Lady Bugatti. Maxner, Joyce. 32p. (ps-3). 1993. pap. 4.99 (0-14-054832-7) Puffin Bks.

—The Librarian Who Measured the Earth. Lasky, Kathryn. LC 92-42656. (gr. 4 up). 1994. 15.95 (0-316-51526-4, Joy St Bks) Little.

—The Nose. Gogol, Nicolai. Cowan, Catherine, retold by. LC 93-4975. 1995. write for info. (0-688-10464-9); PLB write for info. (0-688-10465-7) Lothrop.

—The Turnip. De La Mare, Walter. LC 92-6191. 1992. 18.95 (0-87923-934-4) Godine.

Hawkins, Beverly. A Bird of Peace Is Born in Petersburg. Beachy, J. Wayne. (Orig.). (gr. 5). 1981. pap. 2.50 (0-9608084-0-X) B Hawkins Studio.

—The Extraordinary Ordinary Christmas Matoaca, 1870. Beachy, J. Wayne. 20p. (Orig.). (gr. 5). 1984. pap. 2.50 (0-9608084-2-6) B Hawkins Studio.

—The Ghost of Rat Castle: A Story of Old Petersburg. Beachy, J. Wayne. (gr. 5). 1983. pap. 2.50 (0-9608084-1-8) B Hawkins Studio.

—Richmond Theater Fire, 1862. Beachy, J. Wayne. 24p. (Orig.). (gr. 5 up). 1987. pap. 3.00 (0-9608084-3-4) B Hawkins Studio.

Hawkins, Colin & Hawkins, Jacqui. Come for a Ride on the Ghost Train. Hawkins, Colin & Hawkins, Jacqui. Halperin, Susan, ed. LC 93-54999. 40p. (ps up). 1993. 12.95 (1-56402-236-6) Candlewick Pr.

—I Know an Old Lady Who Swallowed a Fly. Hawkins, Colin & Hawkins, Jacqui, eds. 24p. (ps-1). 1987. 12.95 (0-399-21484-4, Putnam) Putnam Pub Group.

—Knock! Knock! Hawkins, Colin & Hawkins, Jacqui. LC 91-17313. 28p. 1991. POB 10.95 (0-689-71475-0, Aladdin) Macmillan Child Grp.

—Terrible, Terrible Tiger. Hawkins, Colin & Hawkins, Jacqui. LC 87-40675. 32p. (ps-3). 1988. bds. 5.95 (1-55782-043-0, Pub. by Warner Juvenile Bks) Little.

Hawkins, Irene. Ten Candelight Tales. Uttley, Alison. 112p. (gr. k-2). 1991. pap. 3.95 (0-571-14289-3) Faber & Faber.

Hawkins, Jacqui, jt. illus. see Hawkins, Colin.

Hawkins, Linda. The Happy Girl. Heyde, Christiane. LC 89-85861. 40p. 1990. 11.95 (0-87516-618-0) DeVorss.

Hawkinson, John. Indian Two Feet & the Wolf Cubs. Friskey, Margaret. 64p. (gr. k-3). 1971. PLB 15.93 (0-516-03506-1) Childrens.

Hawksley, Gerald. At Home. Hawksley, Gerald. 10p. (ps). 1990. bds. 4.95 (1-878624-18-0) McClanahan Bk.

—Farm. Hawksley, Gerald. 10p. (ps). 1990. bds. 4.95 (1-878624-16-4) McClanahan Bk.

—First Words & Pictures. Salt, Jane. LC 92-53115. 96p. (ps-k). 1992. 9.95 (1-85697-818-4) Kingfisher Bks.

—First Words: For Babies & Toddlers. Salt, Jane. LC 90-8037. 192p. (ps-k). 1991. 9.95 (0-679-80831-0) Random Bks Yng Read.

—Monster: Stories for under Fives. Stimson, Joan. 44p. (ps-k). 1992. 3.50 (0-7214-1505-9) Ladybird Bks.

—Trucks. Hawksley, Gerald. 10p. (ps). 1990. bds. 4.95 (1-878624-17-2) McClanahan Bk.

—Zoo. Hawksley, Gerald. 10p. (ps). 1990. bds. 4.95 (1-878624-19-9) McClanahan Bk.

Hawley, Kevin. The Little Tugboat That Sneezed. Burrows, Roger. 24p. (Orig.). (gr. k-1). 1990. pap. 0.99 (1-878624-40-7) McClanahan Bk.

Hayashi, Akiko. Anna in Charge. Tsutsui, Yoriko. 32p. (ps-1). 1989. pap. 11.95 (0-670-81672-8) Viking Child Bks.

—Anna in Charge. Tsutsui, Yoriko. 32p. (ps-3). 1991. pap. 3.95 (0-14-050733-7, Puffin) Puffin Bks.

—Anna's Secret Friend. Tsutsui, Yoriko. 32p. (ps-1). 1989. pap. 3.99 (0-14-050731-0, Puffin) Puffin Bks.

—Anna's Special Present. Tsutsui, Yoriko. 32p. (ps-3). 1988. pap. 11.95 (0-670-81671-X) Viking Child Bks.

—Anna's Special Present. Tsutsui, Yoriko. 32p. (ps-3). 1990. pap. 3.95 (0-14-054219-1, Puffin) Puffin Bks.

—There's a Hippo in My Bath! Matsuoka, Kyoko. 1989. 12.95 (0-385-26188-8); PLB 12.95 (0-385-26189-6) Doubleday.

Hayashi, Nancy. Cosmic Cousin. Hayashi, Nancy. (gr. 2-5). 1990. pap. 2.95 (0-553-15841-4, Skylark) Bantam.

—Did You Lose the Car Again? Feder, Paula K. 64p. (gr. 2-5). 1991. pap. 3.50 (0-14-034800-X, Puffin) Puffin Bks.

—The Fantastic Stay-Home-from-School Day. Hayashi, Nancy. LC 91-21095. 105p. (gr. 2-5). 1992. 12.00 (0-525-44864-0, DCB) Dutton Child Bks.

Hayashi, Yoshio. Kintaro's Adventures & Other Japanese Children's Stories. Sakade, Florence. 60p. (gr. 1-5). 1958. pap. 8.95 (0-8048-0343-9) C E Tuttle.

Hayden, Marilyn, jt. illus. see Morris, Alix.

Hayes, Dan. The Easter Activity Book. 24p. (Orig.). (ps-3). 1991. pap. 4.95 (0-8249-8499-4, Ideals Child) Hambleton-Hill.

—The Thanksgiving Activity Book. 24p. (ps-3). 1992. pap. 4.95 (0-8249-8550-8, Ideals Child) Hambleton-Hill.

Hayes, Geoffrey. The Mystery of the Pirate Ghost: An Otto & Uncle Tooth Adventure. Hayes, Geoffrey. LC 84-18228. 48p. (gr. 2-3). 1985. 3.50 (0-394-87220-7) Random Bks Yng Read.

—Patrick & Ted Ride the Train: (Just Right for 4's & 5's) Hayes, Geoffrey. LC 88-3084. 32p. (Orig.). (ps-k). 1988. 4.95 (0-394-89872-9) Random Bks Yng Read.

—Patrick Goes to Bed. Hayes, Geoffrey. LC 84-6099. 40p. (ps-1). 1985. 4.95 (0-394-87264-9) Knopf Bks Yng Read.

—The Secret of Foghorn Island. Hayes, Geoffrey. LC 87-16095. 48p. (Orig.). (gr. 2-3). 1988. lib. bdg. 7.99 (0-394-99614-3); pap. 2.95 (0-394-89614-9) Random Bks Yng Read.

—The Treasure of the Lost Lagoon: A Step Three Book. Hayes, Geoffrey. LC 90-40118. 48p. (Orig.). (gr. 2-3). 1991. pap. 2.95 (0-679-81484-1); lib. bdg. 7.99 (0-679-91484-6) Random Bks Yng Read.

Hayes, James. Sucker. McCullers, Carson. LC 85-29114. 40p. (gr. 4 up). 1986. PLB 13.95s.p. (0-88682-053-7) Creative Ed.

Hayes, Michael. K Is for Kiss Good Night. Sardegna, Jill. LC 92-34404. 1994. 13.95 (0-385-31044-7) Doubleday.

Hayes, Sarah. The Cats of Tiffany Street. Hayes, Sarah. LC 91-58720. 32p. (ps up). 1992. 13.95 (1-56402-094-0) Candlewick Pr.

Hayes, Stephen. Federico Lapiz Rapido: Fast Draw Freddie. Hamsa, Bobbie. LC 83-23931. (SPA.). 32p. (ps-2). 1991. PLB 11.93 (0-516-32046-7); pap. 2.95 (0-516-52046-6) Childrens.

Hayes, Steve. Sing & Learn. Meyer, Carolyn & Pickens, Kel. 144p. (ps-3). 1989. wkbk. 11.95 (0-86653-476-8, GA1078) Good Apple.

Hayes, Steven. Pancakes, Crackers & Pizza: A Book of Shapes. Eberts, Marjorie & Gisler, Margaret. LC 84-7699. 32p. (ps-2). 1984. lib. bdg. 11.93 (0-516-02063-3); pap. 2.95 (0-516-42063-1) Childrens.

Hayes, Suzanne. Earth Tales & Bird Song. Rogers, Rick. Rogers, Rick, intro. by. 125p. (Orig.). (gr. k-9). 1991. pap. 7.50 (0-9631017-0-6) Timberdoodle.

Hayhurst, Steve. World's Weirdest "True" Ghost Stories. Beckett, John. LC 91-15408. 96p. (gr. 4 up). 1992. 12. 95 (0-8069-8410-4); pap. 3.95 (0-8069-8411-2) Sterling.

Haynes, F. Jay. Yellowstone Place Names. Whittlesey, Lee H. Manns, Timothy R., intro. by. LC 88-21610. xiii, 179p. (Orig.). (gr. 8 up). 1988. pap. 11.95 (0-917298-15-2); unabr. microfiche 8.95 (0-685-45314-6) MT Hist Soc.

Haynes, Jerry. Famous Firsts of Black Americans. Hancock, Sibyl. LC 82-612. 128p. (gr. 3-9). 1983. 11. 95 (0-88289-240-1) Pelican.

Haynes, Joyce. When the Great Canoes Came. Clifford, Mary L. LC 92-27913. 1993. 12.95 (0-88289-926-0) Pelican.

Haynes, Rebecca. Proverbs for Children. White, Kathy. Haynes, Betty B., ed. 64p. (ps-3). 1985. pap. 6.95 (0-9616130-0-9) Naftaolh Pubns.

Haynes, Richard T. The Thong Tree. Haynes, Richard T. LC 90-70508. 64p. (gr. 3-7). 1990. 11.95 (0-929146-02-6) Voyageur Pub.

Hays, Michael. Abiyoyo. Seeger, Pete. LC 93-25730. 48p. 1994. pap. 4.95 (0-689-71810-1, Aladdin) Macmillan Child Grp.

—Abiyoyo: Based on a South African Lullaby & Folk Story. Seeger, Pete. LC 85-15341. 48p. (ps-4). 1985. RSBE 15.95 (0-02-781490-4, Macmillan Child Bk) Macmillan Child Grp.

—A Birthday for Blue. Lydon, Kerry R. Levine, Abby, ed. LC 88-21697. 32p. (gr. k-3). 1989. 13.95g (0-8075-0774-1) A Whitman.

—The Gold Cadillac. Taylor, Mildred D. LC 86-11526. 48p. (gr. 2-6). 1987. 12.95 (0-8037-0342-2); PLB 12. 89 (0-8037-0343-0) Dial Bks Young.

—Hello, Tree! Ryder, Joanne. 32p. (gr. k-3). 1991. 13.95 (0-525-67310-5, Lodestar Bks) Dutton Child Bks.

—Storm. Nikola-Lisa, W. LC 92-22775. 32p. (ps-2). 1993. SBE 14.95 (0-689-31704-2, Atheneum Child Bk) Macmillan Child Grp.

—The Tin Heart. Ackerman, Karen. LC 89-6528. 32p. (gr. 1-3). 1990. SBE 13.95 (0-689-31461-2, Atheneum Child Bk) Macmillan Child Grp.

Hays, William J. Old Man: And Other Colonel Weatherford Stories. Grand, Gordon. 239p. (gr. 10 up). 1991. Repr. of 1934 ed. 40.00 (1-56416-027-0) Derrydale Pr.

Haysom, John. Children's Bible in Three Hundred Sixty-Five Stories. Batchelor, Mary. 416p. (ps up). 1987. 15. 95 (0-7459-1333-4) Lion USA.

—In the Beginning. Frank, Penny. LC 92-31617. 1992. 6.95 (0-7459-2608-8) Lion USA.

—Stefan's Secret Fear. Vann, Donna R. 32p. (gr. 4-8). 1990. 11.95 (0-7459-1307-5) Lion USA.

—The Story of Jesus. Batchelor, Mary. 192p. (gr. 1-6). 1992. 14.95 (0-7459-1884-0) Lion USA.
Haysom, John & Morris, Tony. Adam & Eve. Frank, Penny. Burow, Daniel, contrib. by. LC 92-29470. 1992. 6.95 (0-7459-2609-6) Lion USA.
—David & Goliath. Frank, Penny. Burow, Daniel, contrib. by. LC 92-20481. (gr. 5 up). 1992. 5.95 (0-7459-2606-1) RD Assn.
—The First Christmas. Frank, Penny. Burow, Daniel, contrib. by. LC 92-20479. (gr. 4 up). 1992. 5.95 (0-7459-2603-7) RD Assn.
—The First Easter. Frank, Penny. Burow, Daniel, contrib. by. LC 92-31640. 1992. 6.95 (0-7459-2607-X) Lion USA.
—Jesus on Trial. Frank, Penny. Burow, Daniel, contrib. by. LC 92-31641. 1992. 6.95 (0-7459-2610-X) RD Assn.
—Noah & the Great Flood. Frank, Penny & Burow, Daniel. 1992. 5.95 (0-7459-2605-3) RD Assn.
—When Jesus Was Young. Frank, Penny. Burow, Daniel, contrib. by. LC 92-20482. 1992. 5.95 (0-7459-2604-5) RD Assn.
Hayward, Ron. The Human Body. Gamlin, Linda. FS-Aladdin Staff, ed. LC 88-50507. 40p. (gr. 4-9). 1988. PLB 12.40 (0-531-17117-5, Gloucester Pr) Watts.
—The Human Race. Gamlin, Linda. FS-Aladdin Staff, ed. LC 88-50506. 40p. (gr. 1-6). 1988. PLB 12.40 (0-531-17118-3, Gloucester Pr) Watts.
—Life on Earth. Gamlin, Linda. FS-Aladdin Staff, ed. 40p. (gr. 4-9). 1988. PLB 12.40 (0-531-17120-5, Gloucester Pr) Watts.
—Origins of Life. Gamlin, Linda. FS-Aladdin Staff, ed. 40p. (gr. 4-9). 1988. PLB 12.40 (0-531-17119-1, Gloucester Pr) Watts.
Hayward, Ron & Khan, Aziz. Helicopters. Graham, Ian. 32p. (gr. 5-6). 1989. PLB 12.40 (0-531-17171-X, Gloucester Pr) Watts.
Hayward, Tim. Explore the World of Prehistoric Life. Dixon, Dougal. 48p. (gr. 3-7). 1992. write for info. (0-307-15607-9, 15607, Golden Pr) Western Pub.
—Rand McNally Picture Atlas of Prehistoric Life. Wood, Robert M. LC 92-5761. 1992. write for info. (0-528-83525-4) Rand McNally.
—Sea Birds. Wildlife Education, Ltd. Staff. 24p. 1992. 13.95 (0-937934-90-9); pap. 2.75 (0-937934-66-6) Wildlife Educ.
Hayward, Tim & Stuart, Walten. Sea Otters. Wildlife Education, Ltd. Staff. 1992. 13.95 (0-937934-87-9); pap. 2.75 (0-937934-70-4) Wildlife Educ.
Hayward, Tim & Stuart, Walter. Rattlesnakes. Wildlife Education, Ltd. Staff. 24p. 1992. 13.95 (0-937934-86-0); pap. 2.75 (0-937934-56-9) Wildlife Educ.
Haywood, Carolyn. B Is for Betsy. Haywood, Carolyn. LC 85-16381. 159p. (gr. 1-5). 1939. 12.95 (0-15-204975-4, HB Juv Bks) HarBrace.
—Back to School with Betsy. Haywood, Carolyn. LC 85-16380. 176p. (gr. 1-5). 1943. 12.95 (0-15-205512-6, HB Juv Bks) HarBrace.
—Betsy & Billy. Haywood, Carolyn. LC 41-51926. 119p. (gr. 1-5). 1941. 12.95 (0-15-206765-5, HB Juv Bks) HarBrace.
—Betsy's Busy Summer. Haywood, Carolyn. LC 56-7894. (gr. 3-7). 1956. PLB 13.88 (0-688-31087-7) Morrow Jr Bks.
—Betsy's Winterhouse. Haywood, Carolyn. LC 55-8453. 192p. (gr. 3-7). 1958. PLB 13.88 (0-688-31090-7) Morrow Jr Bks.
—Dot for Short. Friedman, Frieda. (gr. 5-7). 1988. pap. 3.95 (0-317-69653-X, Puffin) Puffin Bks.
—Eddie & the Fire Engine. Haywood, Carolyn. LC 49-9873. 192p. (gr. 1-5). 1949. PLB 12.88 (0-688-31252-7) Morrow Jr Bks.
—Eddie's Valuable Property. Haywood, Carolyn. LC 74-17499. 192p. (gr. 3-7). 1975. PLB 12.88 (0-688-32014-7) Morrow Jr Bks.
—Primrose Day. Haywood, Carolyn. LC 86-4620. 200p. (gr. k-3). 1986. pap. 4.95 (0-15-263510-6, Voyager Bks) HarBrace.
—Two Are Four. Haywood, Carolyn. LC 86-4619. 171p. (gr. k-3). 1986. pap. 4.95 (0-15-291771-3, Voyager Bks) HarBrace.
Haywood, Carolyn & Yakovetic, Joe. Here's a Penny. Rev. ed. Haywood, Carolyn. LC 44-7329. 150p. (gr. 1-5). 1986. pap. 4.95 (0-15-640062-6, Voyager Bks) HarBrace.
—Penny & Peter. rev. ed. Haywood, Carolyn. LC 46-21128. 160p. (gr. 1-5). 1986. pap. 4.95 (0-15-260467-7, Voyager Bks) HarBrace.
Hazlitt, Richard W. Haleakala Discovery. rev. ed. Hazlett, Richard W. 52p. (gr. 3-7). 1988. pap. 3.00 activity-color book (0-940295-08-3) HI Natural Hist.
Headley, Adriane M. The Mystery of the Pink Waterfall. Moulton, Dwayne. LC 80-84116. 192p. (gr. 3-8). 1980. 14.95 (0-9605236-0-X) Pandoras Treasures.
Heagy, William. J. R. R. Tolkien: Master of Fantasy. Collins, David R. 144p. (gr. 4-7). 1992. 21.50 (0-8225-4906-9) Lerner Pubns.
Heale, Jonathan. The Ugly Duckling. Mitchell, Adrian. LC 93-39962. (gr. 2 up). 1994. Repr. of 1994 ed. write for info (1-564585-57-3) Dorling Kindersley.
Heale, Jonathan & Heale, Jonathan. Hazel the Guinea Pig. Wilson, A. N. LC 91-71850. 96p. (gr. k-3). 1992. 13.95 (1-56402-013-4) Candlewick Pr.
Healey, Deborah. Branta & the Golden Stone. Wangerin, Walter. LC 92-34891. 1993. pap. 16.00 (0-671-79693-3, S&S BFYR) S&S Trade.

Healy, Deborah. Elisabeth & the Water-Troll. Wangerin, Walter. LC 90-4359. 64p. (gr. 3-7). 1991. HarpC Child Bks.
Heaney, Rhonda K. The Deeeeelicious Dragon. Slaughter, Hope. LC 86-652. 32p. (ps-3). 1986. pap. 4.95 (0-931093-05-8) Red Hen Pr.
Heap, Johnathan & Stower, Adam. Norse Stories. Hull, Robert. LC 93-30731. 48p. (gr. 5-9). 1993. 15.95 (1-56847-131-9) Thomson Learning.
Heap, Sue. Harry on Vacation. Sheldon, Dyan. LC 92-52999. 144p. (gr. 3-6). 1993. 13.95 (1-56402-127-0) Candlewick Pr.
—Puffin Ashore. Huddy, Delia. 32p. (ps-1). 1993. 13.95 (1-85681-171-9, Pub. by J MacRae UK) Trafalgar.
—Puffin at Sea. Huddy, Delia. 32p. (ps-1). 1993. 13.95 (1-85681-161-1, Pub. by J MacRae UK) Trafalgar.
—Splinters: A Book of Very Short Poems. Harrison, Michael, compiled by. 128p. (gr. 5 up). 1989. jacketed 10.95 (0-19-276072-6) OUP.
Heap, Sue & Heap, Sue. Harry & Chicken. Sheldon, Dyan. LC 91-71851. 80p. (gr. 3-6). 1992. 13.95 (1-56402-012-6) Candlewick Pr.
—Harry the Explorer. Sheldon, Dyan. LC 91-58734. 80p. (gr. 3-6). 1992. 13.95 (1-56402-109-2) Candlewick Pr.
Hearn, Diane D. Crane's Rebound. Jackson, Alison. LC 90-20648. 128p. (gr. 3-7). 1991. 12.95 (0-525-44722-9, DCB) Dutton Child Bks.
—Dining with Prunella. Slater, Teddy. 24p. (ps-1). 1991. 5.95 (0-671-72982-9); PLB 9.98 (0-671-72981-0) Silver Pr.
—Down Dairy Farm Road. Martin, C. L. LC 92-42848. 32p. (gr. k-3). 1994. RSBE 14.95 (0-02-762450-1, Macmillan Child Bk) Macmillan Child Grp.
—Shopping with Samantha. Slater, Teddy. 24p. (ps-1). 1991. 5.95 (0-671-72984-5); PLB 9.98 (0-671-72983-7) Silver Pr.
—Unbearable Bears. Roth, Kevin, read by. 24p. (Orig.). (ps-1). 1991. nap. 9.95 incls. cassette (0-679-81742-5) Random Bks Yng Read.
—Whinnie the Lovesick Dragon. Mayer, Mercer. LC 85-18886. 32p. (gr. k-3). 1986. RSBE 14.95 (0-02-765180-0, Macmillan Child Bk) Macmillan Child Grp.
Hearn, Diane D., jt. illus. see Alley, Robert.
Hearn, James, photos by. The Sugar Maple. Metcalf, Rosamond S. LC 82-595. 40p. (gr. 3-5). 1982. pap. 3.50x (0-914016-87-3) Phoenix Pub.
Hearne, Diane D. Happy Birthday, Hector! Kingston, Laura. 24p. (ps-k). 1992. write for info. (0-307-11522-4, 11522) Western Pub.
—Princess Horrid. Haugaard, Erik C. LC 89-8227. 48p. (gr. k-4). 1990. RSBE 14.95 (0-02-743445-1, Macmillan Child Bk) Macmillan Child Grp.
Hearne, Jack. Alfred Hitchcock & the Three Investigators in the Mystery of the Magic Circle. Carey, Mary V. LC 78-55915. (gr. 4-7). 1978. lib. bdg. 6.99 (0-394-93607-8) Random Bks Yng Read.
—Alfred Hitchcock & the Three Investigators in the Mystery of Death Trap Mine. Carey, Mary V. LC 76-8135. (gr. 4-7). 1985. pap. 3.95 (0-394-84449-1); pap. 2.95 (0-394-86424-7) Random Bks Yng Read.
Hearne, William. Alfred Hitchcock & the Three Investigators in the Mystery of the Dead Man's Riddle. Arden, William. LC 74-4934. 160p. (gr. 4-7). 1984. pap. 2.95 (0-394-86422-0) Random Bks Yng Read.
Hearue, Jack. Espanol: A Sentirlo. 4th ed. Woodford, Protase E., et al. LC 90-12. 10 up. 1977. text ed. 31.40 (0-07-071656-0, W) McGraw.
Heaston, Claudia. God Made the One & Only Me. Linville, Barbara. LC 76-8737. (ps). 1976. pap. text ed. 3.95 (0-916406-28-8, Chariot Bks) Cook.
—Let's Sing Together: Favorite Primary Songs of Members of the Church of Jesus Christ of Latter-day Saints. Perry, Frances B., ed. 96p. (ps-6). 1981. 10.98 (0-941518-00-0) Perry Enterprises.
—Let's Sing Together: Favorite Primary Songs. Perry, Frances B., ed. 96p. (ps-6). 1984. hard cover music 12.98 (0-941518-02-7) Perry Enterprises.

Heath, Dixie. My Alphabet Animals Draw Along Book: Alpahbet Animals Drawing Book. Heath, Dixie. Wexler, Terry, ed. 70p. (gr. k-5). 1993. 14.95 (0-9637484-0-8) Knight Pub WA. MY ALPHABET ANIMALS DRAW ALONG BOOK is unique because of the variety of things it does for children. This book teaches children our alphabet via big, beautiful & colorful illustrations. Writing the letters & then drawing them into animals helps you to visually remember the letters. The reading of the basic sentence also stimulates the memory of the alphabet in young minds. For example: A-Airedale-Amanda's Airedale Abode. B-Bunny-Blue Bonnie Bunny Bites, etc. The children also have draw along friends to help them through the book. Anni Alphadraw, Pencil Dude &

Paper Pals Pad take them on a learning & drawing safari. This helps the children feel it's a personal book, with friends helping which is more fun & adventurous. From beginning to end the children are involved with each step. MY ALPHABET ANIMALS DRAW ALONG BOOK also teaches awareness of our endangered animal friends. Seventeen of the animals in this book are endangered--either their lives or their habitat. There's also a glossary of words new to young minds & their meaning. I have taught this book in three different schools & the teachers & children love it - even the 6th graders. The expressions on the illustrations will leave a lasting impression for young & old to keep them coming back for more. *Publisher Provided Annotation.*

Heath, Sarah. The Classroom Dulcimer. Hornbostel, Lois. 64p. (gr. 5-8). 1991. pap. text ed. 12.95 (0-9614939-6-8) Backyard Music.
Heau, Gisela. Talking about Death: A Dialogue Between Parent & Child; With Parent's Guide & Recommended Resources. 3rd ed. Grollman, Earl A. LC 89-46061. 128p. (gr. k-4). 1990. 18.95 (0-8070-2364-7, BP531) Beacon Pr.
Hebert, Carrie. How Do You Know When You're in Acadiana. Raphael, Morris. 32p. (Orig.). (gr. 5 up). 1984. pap. 3.95 (0-9608866-3-X) M Raphael.
Hebert, Kim T. Arnie the Astronaut. Johnson, Larry D. & Mills, Jane L. LC 86-60353. 22p. (Orig.). (ps-1). 1986. pap. 4.50 (0-938155-02-4); pap. 12.00 set of 3 bks. (0-685-13517-9) Read A Bol.
—Arnie the Detective. Johnson, Larry D. & Mills, Jane L. LC 86-60364. 24p. (ps). 1986. pap. 4.50 (0-938155-06-7); pap. 12.00 set of 3 bks. (0-685-13514-4) Read A Bol.
—Arnie's Surprise. Mills, Jane L. & Johnson, Larry D. LC 86-60363. 14p. (Orig.). (ps). 1986. pap. 4.00 (0-938155-05-9); pap. 12.00 set of 3 bks. (0-685-13523-3) Read A Bol.
—Build Like Me. Mills, Jane L. & Johnson, Larry D. LC 86-60362. 13p. (Orig.). (ps). 1986. pap. 4.00 (0-938155-01-6); pap. 12.00 set of 3 bks. (0-685-13524-1) Read A Bol.
—Peek-a-Boo. Mills, Jane L. & Johnson, Larry D. LC 86-60380. 13p. (Orig.). (ps). 1986. pap. 3.50 (0-938155-04-0); pap. 12.00 set of 3 bks. (0-685-13530-6) Read A Bol.
Hechelmann, Friedrich. Ophelia's Shadow Theater. Ende, Michael. 32p. (gr. 1 up). 1989. 14.95 (0-87951-371-3) Overlook Pr.
Hecht, Muriel. Best Things about Dolls. Hecht, Joan B. 16p. (ps-3). 1987. pap. 4.95 (0-931271-08-8) Hi Plains Pr.
Heck, Ed. Shapes. Rutman, Shereen G. 16p. (ps). 1992. wkbk. 2.25 (1-56293-188-1) McClanahan Bk.
Heck, J. Parker. Growing Together: Sermons for Children. Steindam, Harold. LC 88-28718. 136p. (Orig.). 1989. pap. 9.95 (0-8298-0800-0) Pilgrim OH.
Hedden, Randall. Mister B. Lippert, Donald F. 32p. (ps). 1989. write for info. Pastel Pubns.
—Polly Popcan. Lippert, Donald F. 32p. (ps). 1989. write for info. Pastel Pubns.
—Shag & the Bouncing Ball. Lippert, Donald F. 32p. (ps). 1989. write for info. Pastel Pubns.
Hedderwick, Mairi. Brave Janet Reachfar. Duncan, Jane. LC 74-8693. 32p. (ps-3). 1975. 7.95 (0-8164-3130-2, Clarion Bks) HM.
—Janet Reachfar & the Kelpie. Duncan, Jane. LC 75-44166. 32p. (ps-3). 1976. 7.50 (0-685-02316-8, Clarion Bks) HM.
—Katie Morag & the Two Grandmothers. Hedderwick, Mairi. 32p. (gr. 3-4). 1986. picture bk. 10.95 (0-316-35400-7) Little.
—Venus Peter Saves the Whale. Rush, Christopher. LC 92-7808. 32p. (gr. 4-7). 1992. 14.95 (0-88289-928-7) Pelican.
Hedge-Cheney, Jacquelyn & Cheny, Roland J. The Little Daisy Girl & Other Poems. Hedge-Cheney, Jacquelyn & Cheney, Roland J. 48p. (Orig.). (gr. 6 up). 1989. pap. write for info (0-9621283-0-9) Lil Daisy Bks.
Hedlund, Irene. Miserable Marabou. Berliner, Franz. LC 89-30852. 23p. (gr. k-3). 1989. PLB 18.60 (0-8368-0094-X) Gareth Stevens Inc.
Hedran, Susan. At the Firehouse. Poelker, Kathy. Judge, Matt, ed. 8p. (Orig.). (ps-3). 1988. pap. text ed. 15.00 (0-929842-00-6) Hawthorne Pubs.
—One Little Drop of Sunshine. Poelker, Kathy. Judge, Matt, ed. 8p. (ps-3). 1988. pap. text ed. 15.00 (0-929842-01-4) Hawthorne Pubs.
Heffernan, Cheryl. Magic of Conflict Workshop for Young People. Crum, Thomas F. (gr. 6-12). 1989. multi-media kit 49.95 (1-877803-04-9) AIKI Works.
Heflin, Tom. The First Forest. Gile, John. LC 89-91458. 40p. (gr. k up). 1989. 13.95 (0-910941-01-7) J Gile Comm.

Hefter, Richard. Babysitter Bears. Hefter, Richard. LC 83-8205. (gr. 3-6). 1983. 5.95 (*0-911787-08-9*) Optimum Res Inc.
—Bears at Work. Hefter, Richard. LC 83-2192. 32p. (ps-1). 1983. 5.95 (*0-911787-00-3*) Optimum Res Inc.
—Bears Away from Home. Hefter, Richard. LC 83-4149. (gr. 3-6). 1983. 5.95 (*0-911787-05-4*) Optimum Res Inc.
—Fast Food. Hefter, Richard. LC 83-6734. (gr. 3-6). 1983. 5.95 (*0-911787-09-7*) Optimum Res Inc.
—Jobs for Bears. Hefter, Richard. LC 83-2197. 32p. (ps-1). 1983. 5.95 (*0-911787-02-X*) Optimum Res Inc.
—Lots of Little Bears. Hefter, Richard. LC 83-2184. 32p. (ps-1). 1983. 5.95 (*0-911787-04-6*) Optimum Res Inc.
—Neat Feet. Hefter, Richard. LC 83-8035. (gr. 3-6). 1983. 5.95 (*0-911787-07-0*) Optimum Res Inc.
—Seek & Solve: Addition No. 1 Series 1, Level 1. Perle, Ruth L. (gr. k-2). 1976. wkbk. 1.95 (*0-89796-848-4*, SSW 01) New Dimens Educ.
—Seek & Solve: Subtraction No. 1, Series 1, Level 1. Perle, Ruth L. (gr. k-2). 1976. wkbk. 1.95 (*0-89796-849-2*, SSW 02) New Dimens Educ.
—The Stickybear Book of Weather. Hefter, Richard. LC 83-2191. 32p. (ps-1). 1983. 5.95 (*0-911787-01-1*) Optimum Res Inc.
—Story Builders Activity Book. Lamport, Joan, et al. (gr. 2-3). 0.95 (*0-89796-844-1*, XTW 03) New Dimens Educ.
—Taking Tests & Relaxing Activity Book. Lamport, Joan & Perle, Ruth L. (gr. 2-3). 1976. 0.95 (*0-89796-847-6*, XTW 07) New Dimens Educ.
—Watch Out! Hefter, Richard. LC 83-2190. 32p. (ps-1). 1983. 5.95 (*0-911787-03-8*) Optimum Res Inc.
—Where Is the Bear? Hefter, Richard. LC 83-6296. 32p. (gr. 3-6). 1983. 5.95 (*0-911787-06-2*) Optimum Res Inc.
—The WordShop Activity Book. Lamport, Joan, et al. (gr. 2-3). 1976. 0.95 (*0-89796-845-X*, XTW 05) New Dimens Educ.
Hegel, Annette. Saturday Is Pattyday. Newman, Leslea. 24p. (ps-5). 1993. PLB 14.95 (*0-934678-52-9*); pap. 6.95 (*0-934678-51-0*) New Victoria Pubs.
Hegeman, Mark, et al. Our Community. Hegeman, Kathryn T. (Orig.). (gr. k-3). 1982. tchr's manual 10.00 (*0-89824-034-4*); wkbk. 4.99 (*0-89824-035-2*) Trillium Pr.
—The Animal Kingdom. Hegeman, Kathryn T. (gr. k-3). 1982. tchr's. manual 10.00 (*0-89824-031-X*); wkbk. 4.99 (*0-89824-030-1*) Trillium Pr.
Heidinger, Herbert. Annie Wilkins Mystery Series, 5 novels. Sands, AnnaMaria. 240p. (Orig.). (gr. 2-7). 1988. Set. pap. 15.00 (*0-87879-571-5*) High Noon Bks.
Heidinger, Herbert H. Connections, 5 novels. Miller, W. Wesley. Kratoville, Betty L., ed. 240p. (Orig.). (gr. 4-12). 1988. Set. pap. 15.00 (*0-87879-556-1*) High Noon Bks.
Heiges, Shawn. Jamestown Children's Activity Book. 40p. (gr. 1-6). 1992. pap. 2.00 (*0-939631-53-9*) Thomas Publications.
Heiman, Lori. Walking in God's Truth: Ten Commandments-Lord's Prayer. rev. ed. Foss, Allen J. Rinden, David, intro. by. 276p. (gr. 6-8). 1989. pap. text ed. 5.95 (*0-943167-04-3*) Faith & Fellowship Pr.
Heimlich, Hermelie. Sexually Transmitted Diseases. Landau, Elaine. Armstrong, Donald & Haundsfield, Hunterfrwd. by. LC 85-4349. 96p. (gr. 6 up). 1986. lib. bdg. 16.95 (*0-89490-115-X*) Enslow Pubs.
Heine, Helme. Friends. Heine, Helme. LC 82-49350. 32p. (ps-2). 1982. SBE 14.95 (*0-689-50256-7*, M K McElderry) Macmillan Child Grp.
—Friends. Heine, Helme. LC 86-3379. 32p. (ps-3). 1986. pap. 3.95 (*0-689-71083-6*, Aladdin) Macmillan Child Grp.
—The Most Wonderful Egg in the World. Heine, Helme. LC 82-49350. 32p. (ps-3). 1983. SBE 14.95 (*0-689-50280-X*, M K McElderry) Macmillan Child Grp.
—The Most Wonderful Egg in the World. Heine, Helme. LC 82-22251. 32p. (gr. k-3). 1987. pap. 4.95 (*0-689-71117-4*, Aladdin) Macmillan Child Grp.
—One Day in Paradise. Heine, Helme. LC 85-72492. 32p. (ps-4). 1986. SBE 14.95 (*0-689-50394-6*, M K McElderry) Macmillan Child Grp.
—The Pearl. Heine, Helme. LC 84-72404. 32p. (gr. k-4). 1985. SBE 14.95 (*0-689-50321-0*, M K McElderry) Macmillan Child Grp.
—The Pearl. Heine, Helme. LC 88-3220. 32p. (gr. k-4). 1988. pap. 3.95 (*0-689-71262-6*, Aladdin) Macmillan Child Grp.
—The Pigs' Wedding. Heine, Helme. LC 90-40996. 32p. (gr. k-3). 1991. pap. 4.95 (*0-689-71478-5*, Aladdin) Macmillan Child Grp.
Heinen, Sandy. Melissa & the Little Red Book. Sanford, Agnes. (gr. 1-6). pap. 2.25 (*0-910924-81-3*) Macalester.
Heinly, John. Tackle Twenty-Two. Foley, Louise M. 48p. (ps-3). 1981. pap. 1.75 (*0-440-48484-7*, YB) Dell.
Heinonen, Susan. Beautiful Joe. rev. & abr. ed. Currie, Quinn. Amory, Cleveland, intro. by. 72p. (gr. k-8). 1990. pap. 9.95 (*0-9623072-1-1*) S Ink WA.
—Kitty the Raccoon. 2nd ed. Stamper, John. (gr. k-10). 1989. pap. 8.95 (*0-9623072-0-3*) S Ink WA.
Heinrich, Bernd. Owl in the House. Heinrich, Bernd. Calaprice, Alice, adapted by. (gr. 5-9). 1990. 14.95 (*0-316-35456-2*, Joy St Bks) Little.
Heintze, Ty. Valley of the Eels: A Science Fiction Mystery. Heintze, Ty. LC 93-2906. 1993. 14.95 (*0-89015-904-1*) Eakin-Sunbelt.

Heinz, Anna M. & Greene, Karen. Once upon a Recipe: Delicious, Healthy Foods for Kids of all Ages. Greene, Karen. LC 92-9666. 96p. 1992. pap. 12.95 (*0-399-51784-7*, Perigee Bks) Putnam Pub Group.
Heiser, John. Abraham Lincoln's Flag: We Won't Give up a Star. Miller, Howard. 26p. (gr. 4-6). 1990. pap. text ed. 4.95 (*0-939631-19-9*) Thomas Publications.
Hejduk, John. Aesop's Fables. Aesop. LC 90-26710. 32p. 1991. 17.95 (*0-8478-1364-9*) Rizzoli Intl.
Hejndorf, Frank. Cartridge Graphics & Sound. Captain Comal's Staff. 64p. (Orig.). (gr. 6 up). 1984. pap. 6.95 (*0-928411-02-8*) Comal Users.
Helfer, Judith. Aleph Bet for You. Helfer, Judith. LC 70-88355. (ps-2). 1969. pap. 4.00 (*0-88400-024-9*) Shengold.
Helfrich, Nathan. Celebrate Halloween with Hog, Dog, & Frog. Hanson, Don & Helfrich, R. L. 64p. (Orig.). 1993. pap. 9.95 (*1-56883-018-1*) Colonial Pr AL.
—A Holiday on a Log with Hog, Dog & Frog: Greet the Easter Bunny. Hanson, Don & Helfrich, R. L. 64p. 1993. pap. 9.95 (*1-56883-020-3*) Colonial Pr AL.
Hellard, Susan. Bach. Rachlin, Ann. LC 92-9520. 1992. 5.95 (*0-8120-4991-8*) Barron.
—Brahms. Rachlin, Ann. 24p. (gr. k-3). 1993. pap. 5.95 (*0-8120-1542-8*) Barron.
—Chopin. Rachlin, Ann. 24p. (gr. k-3). 1993. pap. 5.95 (*0-8120-1543-6*) Barron.
—Dilly & the Horror Movie. Bradman, Tony. 64p. (gr. 2-5). 1991. pap. 3.95 (*0-14-032799-1*, Puffin) Puffin Bks.
—Dilly Speaks Up. Bradman, Tony. 32p. (ps-3). 1991. 11. 95 (*0-670-83680-X*) Viking Child Bks.
—Dilly the Dinosaur. Bradman, Tony. 64p. (Orig.). (gr. 2-5). 1988. pap. 3.95 (*0-14-032337-6*, Puffin) Puffin Bks.
—Handel. Rachlin, Ann. LC 92-11497. 1992. 5.95 (*0-8120-4992-6*) Barron.
—Haydn. Rachlin, Ann. LC 92-9521. 1992. 5.95 (*0-8120-4988-8*) Barron.
—It's Not Fair. Harper, Anita. LC 86-4950. 24p. (ps-k). 1986. 10.95 (*0-399-21365-1*, Philomel) Putnam Pub Group.
—Leonardo Da Vinci. Hart, Tony. LC 93-2385. 24p. (ps-3). 1994. pap. 5.95 (*0-8120-1828-1*) Barron.
—Michaelangelo. Hart, Tony. LC 93-2384. 24p. (ps-3). 1994. pap. 5.95 (*0-8120-1827-3*) Barron.
—Mozart. Rachlin, Ann. LC 92-10302. 1992. 5.95 (*0-8120-4989-6*) Barron.
—Picasso. Hart, Tony. LC 93-8750. 24p. (ps-3). 1994. pap. 5.95 (*0-8120-1826-5*) Barron.
—Schumann. Rachlin, Ann. LC 92-26965. 24p. (gr. k-3). 1993. pap. 5.95 (*0-8120-1544-4*) Barron.
—Tchaikovsky. Rachlin, Ann. 24p. (gr. k-3). 1993. pap. 5.95 (*0-8120-1545-2*) Barron.
—Toulouse-Lautrec. Hart, Tony. LC 93-22146. 24p. (ps-3). 1994. pap. 5.95 (*0-8120-1825-7*) Barron.
—Where Do You Get Your Ideas? Asher, Sandy. 96p. (gr. 5 up). 1987. 12.95 (*0-8027-6690-0*); PLB 13.85 (*0-8027-6691-9*) Walker & Co.
Hellen, Nancy. Animals of the Jungle. Hellen, Nancy. 16p. (ps). 1991. 6.95 (*0-87226-458-0*, Bedrick Blackie) P Bedrick Bks.
—Creatures of the Ocean. Hellen, Nancy. 16p. (ps). 1991. 6.95 (*0-87226-457-2*, Bedrick Blackie) P Bedrick Bks.
—Hey Riddle Riddle! Pirotta, Saviour. LC 88-34356. 32p. (gr. 2 up). 1989. PLB 9.95 (*0-87226-408-4*, Bedrick Blackie) P Bedrick Bks.
—A Visit to the Farm. Hellen, Nancy. 16p. (ps). 1991. 6.95 (*0-87226-432-7*, Bedrick Blackie) P Bedrick Bks.
—A Visit to the Zoo. Hellen, Nancy. 16p. (ps). 1990. 6.95 (*0-87226-431-9*, Bedrick Blackie) P Bedrick Bks.
Heller, Debbe. Building a Dream: Mary Bethune's School. Kelso, Richard. LC 92-18069. 46p. (gr. 2-5). 1992. PLB 21.34 (*0-8114-7217-5*) Raintree Steck-V.
—Tales from the Underground Railroad. Connell, Kate. LC 92-14415. 68p. (gr. 2-5). 1992. PLB 21.34 (*0-8114-7223-X*) Raintree Steck-V.
—To Fly with the Swallows: A Story of Old California. De Ruiz, Dana C. LC 92-14416. 53p. (gr. 2-5). 1992. PLB 21.34 (*0-8114-7204-5*) Raintree Steck-V.
Heller, Joe. Danger, Dinosaurs! A Musical Comedy about the Evolution & Extinction of the Dinosaurs. Mueller, Tobin J. (ps-8). 1990. Audio tape incl. pap. 14.95 (*1-56213-003-X*) Ctr Stage Prodns.
—To Save the Planet: A Musical Fable about the Global Environment; Performed at the United Nations for the Earth Summit. Mueller, Tobin J. 54p. (gr. 4-9). 1991. Audio tape Incl. pap. 14.95 (*1-56213-078-1*) Ctr Stage Prodns.
Heller, Joe, et al. I Want to Know! A Musical Time Line about the History of Science & Invention. Pulaski High School Drama Club Staff & Mueller, Tobin J. 55p. (gr. 4-12). 1991. 14.95 (*1-56213-059-5*) Ctr Stage Prodns.
Heller, Julek. The Enchanted Horse. Nabb, Magdalen. LC 93-18423. 96p. (gr. 3-7). 1993. 14.95 (*0-531-06805-6*); PLB 14.99 (*0-531-08655-0*) Orchard Bks Watts.
—Jack & the Beanstalk. Garner, Alan. LC 91-36717. 32p. (gr. k-3). 1992. 14.00 (*0-385-30693-8*) Doubleday.
—King Arthur & the Legends of Camelot. Perham, Molly, retold by. 176p. (gr. 1 up). 1993. 22.00 (*0-670-84990-1*) Viking Child Bks.
—The Minstrel in the Tower. Skurzynski, Gloria. LC 87-26614. 64p. (Orig.). (gr. 2-4). 1988. lib. bdg. 6.99 (*0-394-99598-8*); pap. 1.95 (*0-394-89598-3*) Random Bks Yng Read.

—The Wizards' Revenge. Wyllie, Stephen. LC 93-14494. Date not set. write for info. (*0-8037-1690-7*) Dial Bks Young.
Heller, Linda. The Castle on Hester Street. Heller, Linda. 32p. (gr. k-3). 1990. pap. 6.95t (*0-8276-0323-1*) JPS Phila.
—A Picture Book of Hanukkah. Adler, David A. LC 82-2942. 32p. (ps-3). 1982. reinforced bdg. 14.95 (*0-8234-0458-7*); pap. 5.95 (*0-8234-0574-5*) Holiday.
—A Picture Book of Jewish Holidays. Adler, David A. LC 81-2765. 32p. (ps-3). 1981. reinforced bdg. 14.95 (*0-8234-0396-3*); pap. 5.95 (*0-8234-0756-X*) Holiday.
—A Picture Book of Passover. Adler, David A. LC 81-6983. 32p. (ps-3). 1982. reinforced bdg. 14.95 (*0-8234-0439-0*); pap. 5.95 (*0-8234-0609-1*) Holiday.
Heller, Nicholas. Fish Stories. Heller, Nicholas. LC 86-14906. 24p. (gr. k-3). 1987. 11.75 (*0-688-06931-2*); PLB 11.88 (*0-688-06932-0*) Greenwillow.
—The Monster in the Cave. Heller, Nicholas. LC 86-29598. 32p. (ps-3). 1987. 11.75 (*0-688-07313-1*); lib. bdg. 11.88 (*0-688-07314-X*) Greenwillow.
Heller, Ruth. Animals Born Alive & Well. Heller, Ruth. LC 82-80872. 48p. (gr. k-2). 1982. 10.95 (*0-448-01822-5*, G&D) Putnam Pub Group.
—Blue Potatoes, Orange Tomatoes: How to Grow a Rainbow Garden. Creasy, Rosalind. LC 92-38800. (gr. 4 up). 1994. write for info. (*0-87156-576-5*) Sierra.
—Chickens Aren't the Only Ones. Heller, Ruth. LC 80-85257. 48p. (ps-1). 1981. 10.95 (*0-448-01872-1*, G&D) Putnam Pub Group.
—The Egyptian Cinderella. Climo, Shirley. LC 88-37547. 32p. (gr. k-3). 1989. 15.00 (*0-690-04822-X*, Crowell Jr Bks); PLB 14.89 (*0-690-04824-6*, Crowell Jr Bks) HarpC Child Bks.
—The Egyptian Cinderella. Climo, Shirley. LC 88-37547. 32p. (gr. k-3). 1992. pap. 4.95 (*0-06-443279-3*, Trophy) HarpC Child Bks.
—How to Hide a Butterfly. Heller, Ruth. LC 85-70287. 32p. (ps-2). 1986. 5.95 (*0-448-10478-4*, G&D) Putnam Pub Group.
—How to Hide a Butterfly: And Other Insects. Heller, Ruth. 32p. (ps-3). 1992. pap. 2.25 (*0-448-40477-X*, Platt & Munk Pubs) Putnam Pub Group.
—How to Hide a Crocodile. Heller, Ruth. 32p. (ps-2). 1986. 5.95 (*0-448-19028-1*, G&D) Putnam Pub Group.
—How to Hide a Gray Tree Frog. Heller, Ruth. 32p. (ps-2). 1986. 4.95 (*0-448-19026-5*, G&D) Putnam Pub Group.
—How to Hide a Polar Bear. Heller, Ruth. LC 85-70286. 32p. (ps-2). 1986. 5.95 (*0-448-10477-6*, G&D) Putnam Pub Group.
—How to Hide a Whippoorwill. Heller, Ruth. 32p. (ps-2). 1986. 4.95 (*0-448-19027-3*, G&D) Putnam Pub Group.
—How to Hide an Octopus. Heller, Ruth. LC 85-70288. 32p. (ps-2). 1986. pap. 5.95 (*0-448-10476-8*, G&D) Putnam Pub Group.
—How to Hide an Octopus: And Other Sea Creatures. Heller, Ruth. 32p. (ps-3). 1992. pap. 2.25 (*0-448-40478-8*, Platt & Munk Pubs) Putnam Pub Group.
—King of the Birds. Climo, Shirley. LC 87-47693. 32p. (gr. k-3). 1988. 15.00 (*0-690-04621-9*, Crowell Jr Bks); PLB 14.89 (*0-690-04623-5*) HarpC Child Bks.
—King of the Birds. Climo, Shirley. LC 87-47693. 32p. (gr. k-3). 1991. pap. 4.95 (*0-06-443273-4*, Trophy) HarpC Child Bks.
—King Solomon & the Bee. Renberg, Dalia. LC 92-30411. 1994. 15.00 (*0-06-022899-7*); PLB 14.89 (*0-06-022902-0*) HarpC Child Bks.
—Korean Cinderella. Climo, Shirley. LC 93-23268. 48p. (gr. k-3). 1993. 15.00 (*0-06-020432-X*); PLB 14.89 (*0-06-020433-8*) HarpC Child Bks.
—Many Luscious Lollipops: A Book about Adjectives. Heller, Ruth. 48p. (ps-3). 1989. 13.95 (*0-448-03151-5*, G&D) Putnam Pub Group.
—Plants That Never Ever Bloom. Heller, Ruth. 48p. (ps-2). 1984. 9.95 (*0-448-18964-X*, G&D) Putnam Pub Group.
—Plants That Never Ever Bloom. Heller, Ruth. 48p. (ps-3). 1992. pap. 5.95 (*0-448-41092-3*, Sandcastle Bks) Putnam Pub Group.
—The Reason for a Flower. Heller, Ruth. (ps-2). 1983. 9.95 (*0-448-14495-6*, G&D) Putnam Pub Group.
—The Reason for a Flower. Heller, Ruth. 48p. (ps-3). 1992. pap. 5.95 (*0-448-41091-5*, Sandcastle Bks) Putnam Pub Group.
—Up, Up & Away: A Book about Adverbs. Heller, Ruth. 48p. (gr. 1 up). 1991. 13.95 (*0-448-40249-1*, G&D) Putnam Pub Group.
—Up, up & Away: A Book about Adverbs. Heller, Ruth. 48p. (gr. 1 up). 1993. pap. 6.95 (*0-448-40159-2*, G&D) Putnam Pub Group.
Hellmuth, Jim. Learn Mishnah. Neusner, Jacob. LC 78-5482. (gr. 5-6). 1978. pap. 5.95x (*0-87441-310-9*) Behrman.
—Meet Our Sages. Neusner, Jacob. LC 80-12771. 128p. (gr. 5-8). 1980. pap. text ed. 5.95x (*0-87441-327-3*) Behrman.
Helmer, Jean. Amazing World of Night Creatures. Craig, Janet. LC 89-5002. 32p. (gr. 2-4). 1990. PLB 11.59 (*0-8167-1749-4*); pap. text ed. 2.95 (*0-8167-1750-8*) Troll Assocs.
—Amazing World of Spiders. Craig, Janet. LC 89-5005. 32p. (gr. 2-4). 1990. PLB 11.59 (*0-8167-1751-6*); pap. text ed. 2.95 (*0-8167-1752-4*) Troll Assocs.
—Star. Simon, Jo A. LC 88-38292. 64p. (Orig.). (gr. 2-4). 1989. PLB 6.99 (*0-394-92933-0*); pap. 1.95 (*0-394-82933-6*) Random Bks Yng Read.

Helmer, Jean C. Amazing World of Butterflies & Moths. Sabin, Louis. LC 81-7504. 32p. (gr. 2-4). 1982. PLB 11.59 (*0-89375-560-5*); pap. text ed. 2.95 (*0-89375-561-3*); cassette 9.95 (*0-685-04943-4*) Troll Assocs.

—Fish. Sabin, Louis. LC 84-2624. 32p. (gr. 3-6). 1985. PLB 9.49 (*0-8167-0178-4*); pap. text ed. 2.95 (*0-8167-0179-2*) Troll Assocs.

—Insects: A Close-Up Look. Seymour, Peter. 10p. (gr. 2-5). 1985. SBE 8.95 (*0-02-782120-X*), Macmillan Child Bk) Macmillan Child Grp.

—Whinny of the Wild Horses. Laundrie, Amy C. LC 88-21460. 128p. (gr. 3-6). 1990. SBE 13.95 (*0-02-754542-3*, Four Winds Press) Macmillan Child Grp.

Helmer, Katherine. The Best Peanut Butter Sandwich in the Whole World. McLean, Bill. 28p. (ps-2). 1990. pap. 4.95 (*0-88753-207-1*, Pub. by Black Moss Pr CN) Firefly Bks Ltd.

Heltshe, Mary A., photos by. Full of Hot Air: Launching, Floating High, & Landing. Paulsen, Gary. LC 92-31327. 1993. 14.95 (*0-385-30887-6*) Delacorte.

Helweg, Hans. The Complete Adventures of Olga da Polga. Boericke, Arthur, et al. LC 82-72753. 512p. (gr. 4-6). 1983. 16.95 (*0-440-00981-2*) Delacorte.

—The Tales of Olga da Polga. Bond, Michael. LC 88-31444. 128p. (gr. 3-7). 1989. Repr. of 1973 ed. SBE 13.95 (*0-02-711731-6*, Macmillan Child Bk) Macmillan Child Grp.

Hemmant, Lynette. Ace: The Very Important Pig. King-Smith, Dick. LC 90-1447. 144p. (gr. 2-7). 1990. 13.00 (*0-517-57832-8*); PLB 13.99 (*0-517-57833-6*) Crown Bks Yng Read.

—The Toby Man. King-Smith, Dick. LC 90-28443. 128p. (gr. 2-7). 1991. 14.00 (*0-517-58134-5*); lib. bdg. 14.99 (*0-517-58135-3*) Crown Bks Yng Read.

Hemmings, Tamra. There Must Be More to Life Than This. Solomon, L. Ursa. 30p. (gr. k up). 1989. spiral 6.95 (*0-9615756-2-X*) Henchanted Bks.

Hemp, Kevin. Just Hogweed. Hemp, Kevin. 128p. (Orig.). (gr. 9-12). 1988. pap. 4.95 (*0-9622059-0-7*, VA-U-105-990) Wise Guys Pub.

Hemsley, Roberta G. Grand Coulee: A Story of the Columbia River from Molten Lavas & Ice to Grand Coulee Dam. rev. ed. Baljo, Wallace, Jr. 80p. (gr. 4-6). pap. write for info. (*0-9606084-0-0*) Clipboard.

Henderson, Catherine. Alas in Blunderland. Gunning, Peter. 32p. (Orig.). (gr. 5-7). 1991. pap. 10.95 (*0-86278-271-6*, Pub. by OBrien Pr IE) Dufour.

Henderson, Dave. Family Karate. Ewing, Kathryn. 96p. (gr. 5 up). 1992. PLB 13.95 (*1-56397-117-8*) Boyds Mills Pr.

—Keep Ms. Sugarman in the Fourth Grade. Levy, Elizabeth. LC 91-22576. 96p. (gr. 3-6). 1992. 13.00 (*0-06-020426-5*); PLB 12.89 (*0-06-020427-3*) HarpC Child Bks.

Henderson, David F. The Case of the Tricky Trickster. Hope, Laura L. Greenberg, Anne, ed. 96p. (Orig.). 1992. pap. 2.99 (*0-671-73041-X*) PB.

—The Case of the Vanishing Video. Hope, Laura L. Greenberg, Ann, ed. 96p. (Orig.). 1992. pap. 2.99 (*0-671-73040-1*) PB.

—The Clue at Casper Creek. Hope, Laura L. Greenberg, Anne, ed. 96p. (Orig.). 1991. pap. 2.99 (*0-671-73038-X*, Minstrel Bks) PB.

—Fourth Grade Loser. Kahaner, Ellen. LC 90-26791. 96p. (gr. 3-5). 1992. lib. bdg. 9.89 (*0-8167-2384-2*); pap. text ed. 2.95 (*0-8167-2385-0*) Troll Assocs.

—The Terrible Truth about Third Grade. McGuire, Leslie. LC 90-26788. 96p. (gr. 2-4). 1992. lib. bdg. 9.89 (*0-8167-2382-6*); pap. text ed. 2.95 (*0-8167-2383-4*) Troll Assocs.

Henderson, Doug. Living with Dinosaurs. Lauber, Patricia. LC 90-43265. 48p. (gr. 1-5). 1991. SBE 16.95 (*0-02-754521-0*, Bradbury Pr) Macmillan Child Grp.

—Maia: A Dinosaur Grows Up. Horner, John & Gorman, James. LC 88-43384. 46p. (gr. 2 up). 1989. pap. 5.95 (*0-89471-691-3*) Running Pr.

Henderson, Doug & Nino, Alex. Search for Dinosaurs. Preiss, Byron & Bischoff, David. 144p. (Orig.). 1984. pap. 2.25 (*0-553-25399-9*) Bantam.

Hendrick, Andrea. Manure, Meadows & Milkshakes. Jorgensen, Eric, et al. Hone, Elizabeth, ed. 132p. (Orig.). (ps-8). 1986. pap. text ed. 9.95 tchrs. ed. (*0-318-20228-X*) Trust Hidden Villa.

Hendrick, Lura A. True Tales of Texas. Cox, Bertha M. LC 87-12091. 292p. (gr. 3-8). 1987. PLB 13.95 (*0-937460-28-1*); pap. 9.95 (*0-937460-77-X*) Hendrick Long.

Hendrickson, et al. The Creation Book. Dakenbing, William F. Von Braun, Wehrner. LC 75-39840. 70p. (gr. 3 up). 1976. 5.95 (*0-685-68397-4*); pap. 3.95 (*0-685-68398-2*) Triumph Pub.

Hendrickson, David. A Plantation Christmas. Peterkin, Julia. LC 72-4563. (gr. 7 up). Repr. of 1934 ed. 10.50 (*0-8369-9119-2*) Ayer.

—A Plantation Christmas. Peterkin, Julia. LC 78-22014. (gr. 6 up). 1978. pap. 2.95 (*0-89783-007-5*) Cherokee.

Hendrickson, June. Songs about the Sky. rev. ed. Russell, Hannah. 18p. 1988. pap. 4.50 (*0-9614089-2-8*) Avitar Bks.

Hendrix, Hurston H. Bunny Rabbits in Mother Gooseland. Waldrop, Ruth. LC 86-61389. (Orig.). (ps-3). 1987. pap. 4.95 (*0-317-59032-4*); cassette 4.95 (*0-317-59033-2*) RuSk Inc.

—Martha Washington. Waldrop, Ruth. LC 87-61391. 112p. (gr. 3-6). 1987. PLB 10.95 (*0-317-59028-6*); pap. 6.95 (*0-317-59029-4*) RuSk Inc.

—Santa Grows up in Mother Goose Land. Waldrop, Ruth. 34p. (ps-3). 1986. pap. 4.95 (*0-9616894-0-4*); cassette incl. RuSk Inc.

Hendry, Linda. Build It with Boxes. Irvine, Joan. LC 91-45589. 96p. (gr. 3 up). 1993. 14.00 (*0-688-12081-4*); PLB 13.93 (*0-688-11524-1*) Morrow Jr Bks.

—How to Make Super Pop-ups. Irvine, Joan. LC 92-2637. 96p. (gr. 3 up). 1992. 14.00 (*0-688-10690-0*) Morrow Jr Bks.

—Lanyard: Having Fun with Plastic Lace. Gryski, Camilla. LC 93-35992. 1994. Repr. of 1993 ed. write for info. (*0-688-13324-X*) Morrow Jr Bks.

—Let's Speak French! A First Book of Words. rev. ed. Farris, Katherine, ed. LC 92-41737. (ENG & FRE.). 48p. (ps-5). 1993. 11.99 (*0-670-85042-X*) Viking Child Bks.

—Let's Speak Spanish! A First Book of Words. Farris, Katherine, ed. 48p. (ps-5). 1993. 11.99 (*0-670-84994-4*) Viking Child Bks.

Hendryx, Brian. One Hundred One Wacky Facts about Bugs & Spiders. 96p. 1992. pap. 1.95 (*0-590-44892-7*) Scholastic Inc.

—One Hundred One Wacky Facts about Kids. 96p. 1992. pap. 1.95 (*0-590-44890-0*) Scholastic Inc.

Henebry, John, Jr. The Newspaper: Reading Skills. Gregorich, Barbara & Zack, Carol. LC 78-730963. (gr. 7-9). 1978. Incl. 4 filmstrips, 4 cass., 24 worksheets, & guide. pap. text ed. 165.00 (*0-89290-114-4*, A160) Soc for Visual.

Hengen, Nona. Monty's Pal. Small, Howard I. LC 78-73621. viii, 120p. (gr. 3-8). 1979. 6.95 (*0-931474-08-6*) TBW Bks.

Henigman, Daniel. Fruit of the Spirit. Walters, David. 44p. (Orig.). Date not set. pap. 5.95 wkbk. (*0-9629559-3-0*) Good News Min.

Henium, Marian. Blessings of Abraham Coloring Book. Tate, Susan. 12p. (gr. k-3). 1993. pap. 0.39 (*1-884395-06-6*) Clear Blue Sky.

—Bonnie Bunnie's Bicycle. Tate, Susan. 40p. (gr. k-3). 1993. pap. 3.99 (*1-884395-01-5*) Clear Blue Sky.

—Faith Coloring Book. Tate, Susan. 12p. (Orig.). (gr. k-3). 1993. pap. 0.39 (*1-884395-04-X*) Clear Blue Sky.

—George Goat's Guardian Angel. Tate, Susan. 40p. (Orig.). (gr. k-3). 1993. pap. 3.99 (*1-884395-02-3*) Clear Blue Sky.

—Larry Lion Learns To Fear Not. Tate, Susan. 40p. (gr. k-3). 1993. pap. 3.99 (*1-884395-03-1*) Clear Blue Sky.

—Ninety First Psalm Coloring Book. Tate, Susan. 12p. (gr. k-3). 1993. pap. 0.39 (*1-884395-05-8*) Clear Blue Sky.

—Petal Pals Coloring Books, 3 bks. Tate, Susan. (gr. k-3). 1993. Set. pap. 1.17 (*1-884395-08-2*) Clear Blue Sky.

Henjum, Marian. Benny Bear Believes for A Healing. Tate, Susan. (Orig.). (gr. k-3). 1993. pap. 3.99 (*1-884395-00-7*) Clear Blue Sky.

Henke, Teresa. Las Olas. Rudolph, John W. LC 87-80761. 101p. (Orig.). 1987. pap. 9.00 (*0-941611-09-4*) Shasta San Rafael.

Henkes, Kevin. Bailey Goes Camping. Henkes, Kevin. LC 84-29027. 24p. (ps-1). 1985. 14.00 (*0-688-05701-2*); lib. bdg. 13.93 (*0-688-05702-0*) Greenwillow.

—Chester's Way. Henkes, Kevin. 32p. (ps-3). 1989. pap. 3.99 (*0-14-054053-9*, Puffin) Puffin Bks.

—Clean Enough. Henkes, Kevin. LC 81-6386. 24p. (gr. k-3). 1982. PLB 10.88 (*0-688-00829-1*) Greenwillow.

—Grandpa & Bo. Henkes, Kevin. LC 85-14869. 32p. (ps-3). 1986. 14.88 (*0-688-04956-7*); PLB 14.95 (*0-688-04957-5*) Greenwillow.

—Sheila Rae, the Brave. Henkes, Kevin. LC 86-25761. 32p. (gr. k-3). 1987. 13.95 (*0-688-07155-4*); PLB 13.88 (*0-688-07156-2*) Greenwillow.

—Two under Par. Henkes, Kevin. LC 86-7556. 128p. (gr. 2-6). 1987. 10.25 (*0-688-06708-5*) Greenwillow.

—A Weekend with Wendell. Henkes, Kevin. LC 85-24822. 32p. (ps-3). 1986. 13.95 (*0-688-06325-X*); PLB 13.88 (*0-688-06326-8*) Greenwillow.

Henle, Fritz, photos by. U. S. Virgin Islands: Jewels of the Caribbean--St. Croix, St. Thomas, St. John. Bailey, Katharine R. & Bourne, Gloria. LC 86-82891. 48p. (Orig.). (gr. 7-12). 1987. pap. 6.95 (*0-88714-012-2*) KC Pubns.

Henley, Claire. At the Zoo. Henley, Claire. LC 91-25906. 32p. (ps-2). 1992. 11.95 (*1-56282-151-2*); PLB 11.89 (*1-56282-152-0*) Hyprn Child.

—The Baby in the Manger. 10p. (ps-1). 1992. bds. 6.99 (*0-7459-2181-7*) Lion USA.

—In the Ocean. Henley, Claire. LC 91-25905. 32p. (ps). 1992. 11.95 (*1-56282-153-9*); PLB 11.89 (*1-56282-154-7*) Hyprn Child.

—Stormy Day. Henley, Claire. LC 92-72025. 32p. (ps). 1993. 11.95 (*1-56282-342-6*); PLB 11.89 (*1-56282-343-4*) Hyprn Child.

—Sunny Day. Henley, Claire. LC 92-72024. 32p. (ps). 1993. 11.95 (*1-56282-340-X*); PLB 11.89 (*1-56282-341-8*) Hyprn Child.

Henley, Claire & Russell, Chris. First Atlas. Rand McNally Staff. LC 93-37528. 1994. write for info. (*0-528-83679-X*) Rand McNally.

Henley, Clark. The Night Before Christmas: Or: Account of a Visit from St. Nicholas. Moore, Clement C. Bevis, Phillip & Irwin, Colin, eds. 22p. 1984. 150.00 (*0-923980-03-2*) Arundel Pr.

Henley, Joan. The Adventures of Prince Albert & the Royal Dinosaurs. Manson, Frank A. 144p. (gr. 2-7). 1990. 11.95 (*0-918339-17-0*) Vandamere.

Henlicky, Gregg. The Captivity of Mahram. Argaman, Shmuel. LC 90-83947. 120p. (gr. 3-5). 1990. 11.95 (*1-56062-045-5*); pap. 8.95 (*0-685-46904-2*) CIS Comm.

Henneberger, Robert. Baseball Pals. Christopher, Matt. (gr. 4-6). 1990. pap. 3.95 (*0-316-14005-8*) Little.

—The Beatinest Boy. Stuart, Jesse. Miller, Jim W., et al, eds. Zornes, Rocky, contrib. by. 80p. (gr. 3-6). 1989. 10.00 (*0-945084-12-9*); pap. 5.00 (*0-945084-13-7*) J Stuart Found.

—The Rightful Owner. 2nd ed. Stuart, Jesse. Miller, Jim W., et al, eds. Zornes, Rocky, contrib. by. 95p. (gr. 3-6). 1989. 12.00 (*0-945084-14-5*); pap. 6.00 (*0-945084-15-3*) J Stuart Found.

—Stowaway to the Mushroom Planet. Cameron, Eleanor. (gr. 3-7). 1956. 14.95 (*0-316-12534-2*, Joy St Bks) Little.

—The Wonderful Flight to the Mushroom Planet. Cameron, Eleanor. (gr. 4-6). 1988. 14.95 (*0-316-12537-7*, Joy St Bks); pap. 5.95 (*0-316-12540-7*, Joy St Bks) Little.

Hennessy, Jim, jt. illus. see Christen-Pallo, Susan.

Hennessy, Jim, jt. illus. see Palto, Susan C.

Hennessy, Linda. Legend of the Ragged Boy. Magee, Wes. 32p. (ps-3). 1993. 14.95 (*1-55970-228-1*) Arcade Pub Inc.

Hennigh, Susan. Carousel Coloring Book. Hegarty, Sue & Geoghegan, Judy. 32p. (Orig.). (gr. k-8). 1989. pap. 4.50 (*0-9622526-1-1*) Freels Fndtn.

Henrich, Jean. Adventure Math, No. 2: Multiplication & Division. Henrich, Stephen & Henrich, Jean. 80p. (Orig.). (gr. 4-12). 1988. pap. write for info. (HE 700) Henrich Enter.

—Story Starters on Present Day. rev. ed. Henrich, Stephen & Henrich, Jean. 80p. (gr. 4-12). 1989. write for info. wkbk. (HE 400) Henrich Enter.

—Story Starters on the Civil War - Old West. rev. ed. Henrich, Stephen & Henrich, Jean. 80p. (gr. 4-12). 1988. write for info. wkbk. (HE 300) Henrich Enter.

—Story Starters on the Future. rev. ed. Henrich, Stephen & Henrich, Jean. 80p. (gr. 4-12). 1989. write for info. wkbk. (HE 500) Henrich Enter.

Henrich, Soren. With Hope We Can All Find Ogo Pogo: For the Child Within Us All! 100p. 1991. 5.95 (*0-9693583-1-8*, Green Tiger) S&S Trade.

Henrichsen, Ronda. Positively Mother Goose. Loomans, Diane, et al. Kramer, Linda, ed. LC 90-52634. 32p. (ps-2). 1991. 14.95 (*0-915811-24-3*) H J Kramer Inc.

Henriquez, Elsa. Contes pour Enfants pas Sages. Prevert, Jacques. (FRE.). 88p. (gr. 1-5). 1990. pap. 10.95 (*2-07-031181-3*) Schoenhof.

—The Magic Orange Tree: And Other Haitian Folktales. Wolkstein, Diane, ed. LC 79-22787. (gr. 10 up). 1987. pap. 16.00 (*0-8052-0650-7*) Schocken.

Henroit, Jean-Louis. Volcanes y Terremotos (Volcanos & Earthquakes) Chiesa, Pierre. Cobielles, Antonio, tr. (SPA.). 96p. (gr. 4 up). 1992. PLB 15.90 (*1-56294-176-3*) Millbrook Pr.

Henry, Barb. The Popples' Book of Jokes & Riddles. George, Barbara. LC 86-62222. 32p. (ps-3). 1987. pap. 1.25 (*0-394-88757-3*) Random Bks Yng Read.

Henry, Crystal A. George Mason, Father of the Bill of Rights. Henry, Carol A. 44p. (Orig.). (gr. k-5). 1991. pap. 9.95 (*0-9633634-3-3*) C A Henry. GEORGE MASON, FATHER OF THE BILL OF RIGHTS is a children's biography which contains 16 black & white full page pictures opposite each written page with easy-to-read large print. Children can learn about George Mason growing up in the Virginia & Maryland areas; how he was devoted to his family, county, state, & country; & finally why he is called "The Father of the Bill of Rights". Included are a glossary of terms; a worksheet; an answer sheet; & a copy of the Bill of Rights & The Virginia Declaration of Rights. The worksheet can be copied by teachers so students can draw lines matching parts in the Virginia Declaration of Rights, which was drafted by George Mason, to parts in the Constitution with the Bill of Rights. The illustrations are beautifully done & capture the children's interest as they read. The author is an elementary teacher who wrote the book upon requests from her students when an easy-to-read book could not be found in print. Now children can read or be "read to" & learn about this famous American who is called "The Father of the Bill of

Rights."
Publisher Provided Annotation.

Henry, James, jt. illus. see Braille International, Inc. Staff.

Henry, Marguerite & Tucker, Ezra. Marguerite Henry's Album of Horses: A Pop-up Book. 12p. (gr. k-3). 1993. bds. 14.95 (*0-689-71685-0*, Aladdin) Macmillan Child Grp.

Henry, Marie. Bunnies at Christmastime. Ehrlich, Amy. LC 86-2202. 32p. (ps-2). 1989. 11.95 (*0-8037-0321-X*) Dial Bks Young.

Henry, Marie H. Bunnies All Day Long. Ehrlich, Amy. LC 84-20031. 32p. (ps-2). 1989. (Dial Pied Piper) Puffin Bks.

—Good Night! Masurel, Claire. LC 93-30198. 1994. 12.95 (*0-8118-0644-8*) Chronicle Bks.

Henry, Matthew. The Bird, the Frog, & the Light: A Fable. Avi. LC 93-4886. 1994. write for info. (*0-531-06808-0*); PLB write for info. (*0-531-08658-5*) Orchard Bks Watts.

Henry, Paul. Does Third Grade Last Forever? Schanback, Mindy. LC 89-20603. 96p. (gr. 2-4). 1990. PLB 9.89 (*0-8167-1700-1*); pap. text ed. 2.95 (*0-8167-1701-X*) Troll Assocs.

—Fifth Grade Flop. Stine, Megan & Stine, H. William. LC 89-20624. 96p. (gr. 4-6). 1990. lib. bdg. 9.89 (*0-8167-1704-4*); pap. text ed. 2.95 (*0-8167-1705-2*) Troll Assocs.

—A Ghost of a Chance. Carris, Joan. 160p. (gr. 3-7). 1992. 14.95 (*0-316-13016-8*) Little.

—Is There Life after Sixth Grade? McGuire, Leslie. LC 89-20615. 96p. (gr. 4-6). 1990. PLB 9.89 (*0-8167-1706-0*); pap. text ed. 2.95 (*0-8167-1707-9*) Troll Assocs.

—What's So Great about Fourth Grade? Kahaner, Ellen. LC 89-20602. 96p. (gr. 3-5). 1990. PLB 9.89 (*0-8167-1702-8*); pap. text ed. 2.95 (*0-8167-1703-6*) Troll Assocs.

Henry, Ron. Experience Jerome & the Verde Valley Legends & Legacies, No. II. Bishop, James, Jr., et al. LC 90-71606. 356p. (Orig.). (gr. 8-12). 1990. pap. 12.95 (*0-9628329-1-X*) Thorne Enterprises.

Henry, Steve. Don't Just Sit There! Fifty Ways to Have a Nickelodeon Day. Burr, Daniella. LC 90-86411. 96p. (Orig.). (gr. 2-6). 1992. pap. 2.95 (*0-448-40202-5*, G&D) Putnam Pub Group.

—How Big? How Fast? How Hungry? A Book about Cats. Waverly, Barney. 24p. (ps-2). 1990. PLB 14.60 (*0-8172-3582-5*); PLB 10.95 pkg. of 3 (*0-685-58552-2*) Raintree Steck-V.

—Santa's Christmas Surprise. McIntire, Jamie. LC 93-24843. 32p. (gr. k-3). 1993. pap. text ed. 2.95 (*0-8167-3257-4*) Troll Assocs.

Henry, William. Peter Pelican-Pedro Pelicano. Roa, Annia. LC 64-22715. (SPA & ENG.). (gr. k-4). 1974. 8.95 (*0-87208-006-4*) Island Pr Pubs.

Henson, Grace. Acting for God. Jones, Kathy. 48p. (gr. 4-8). 1984. wkbk. 6.95 (*0-86653-236-6*, SS 818, Shining Star Pubns) Good Apple.

—Biblical Bulletin Boards. MacKenthun, Carole. 48p. (gr. k-4). 1984. wkbk. 6.95 (*0-86653-197-1*, SS 814, Shining Star Pubns) Good Apple.

—Seasonal Bulletin Boards That Teach. Hand, Phyllis. 48p. (gr. 1-5). 1984. wkbk. 6.95 (*0-86653-203-X*, SS 820, Shining Star Pubns) Good Apple.

Henson, Tenny, jt. illus. see Cruz, E. R.

Henstra, Friso. Cynthia & the Runaway Gazebo. Marston, Elsa. LC 91-32548. 32p. (gr. k-4). 1992. 14.00 (*0-688-10282-4*, Tambourine Bks); PLB 13.93 (*0-688-10283-2*, Tambourine Bks) Morrow.

—The Future of Yen-tzu. Morris, Winifred. LC 90-26989. 32p. (ps-3). 1992. SBE 13.95 (*0-689-31501-5*, Atheneum Child Bk) Macmillan Child Grp.

—The Last Snow of Winter. Johnston, Tony. LC 92-33862. 32p. (ps up). 1993. 14.00 (*0-688-10749-4*, Tambourine Bks); PLB 13.93 (*0-688-10750-8*, Tambourine Bks) Morrow.

—The Mouse Who Owned the Sun. Derby, Sally. LC 91-40965. 32p. (ps-3). 1993. pap. 14.95 RSBE (*0-02-766965-3*, Four Winds) Macmillan Child Grp.

—Pedro & the Padre. Aardema, Verna. LC 87-24476. 32p. (ps-3). 1991. 12.95 (*0-8037-0522-0*); PLB 12.89 (*0-8037-0523-9*) Dial Bks Young.

—Pig & Bear. Horejs, Vit. LC 88-21304. 48p. (gr. 2-4). 1989. RSBE 12.95 (*0-02-744421-X*, Four Winds) Macmillan Child Grp.

—Sophie the Circus Princess. Claesson, Stig. Stevens, Susanna, tr. from SWE. LC 93-16780. 1994. 14.00 (*0-671-87008-4*, Green Tiger) S&S Trade.

—Why Not? Hofsepian, Sylvia A. LC 89-39333. 32p. (gr. k-3). 1991. RSBE 13.95 (*0-02-743980-1*, Four Winds) Macmillan Child Grp.

Henterly, Jamichael. Fairy Went A-Marketing. Fyleman, Rose. LC 86-4468. 24p. (ps-1). 1986. 11.95 (*0-525-44258-8*, DCB) Dutton Child Bks.

—Good King Wenceslas. Neale, J. M. LC 88-3633. 24p. (ps up). 1988. 11.95 (*0-525-44420-3*, DCB) Dutton Child Bks.

—Good King Wenceslas. Neale, J. M. 24p. 1993. pap. 4.99 (*0-14-054942-0*, Puffin Unicorn) Puffin Bks.

—A Little Princess. Burnett, Frances H. 288p. (gr. 4 up). 1989. 13.95 (*0-448-09299-9*, G&D) Putnam Pub Group.

—Night Is Coming. Nikola-Lisa, W. LC 90-3806. 32p. (ps-2). 1991. 13.95 (*0-525-44687-7*, DCB) Dutton Child Bks.

Henwood, Simon. Clay Boy. Ginsburg, Mirra. 32p. (ps-3). 1993. PLB 14.95 (*0-399-21988-9*, Philomel Bks) Putnam Pub Group.

—The King Who Sneezed. McAllister, Angela. LC 88-6858. 32p. (gr. k-3). 1988. 12.95 (*0-688-08327-7*); PLB 12.88 (*0-688-08328-5*, Morrow Jr Bks) Morrow Jr Bks.

—The Postman's Palace. Henri, Adrian. LC 90-30568. 32p. (ps-2). 1990. SBE 13.95 (*0-689-31667-4*, Atheneum Child Bk) Macmillan Child Grp.

Heo, Yumi. The Rabbit's Judgment. Han, Suzanne C. LC 93-11031. 1994. write for info. (*0-8050-2674-6*) H Holt & Co.

Hepworth, Cathi. Antics! An Alphabetical Anthology. Hepworth, Cathi. 32p. (ps-6). 1992. PLB 14.95 (*0-399-21862-9*, Putnam) Putnam Pub Group.

—While You Are Asleep. Isaacs, Gwynne L. 32p. (gr. 4-8). 1991. 12.95 (*0-8027-6985-3*); lib. bdg. 13.85 (*0-8027-6986-1*) Walker & Co.

Herbert, Janet. Love Is Kind. Herbert, Janet. 32p. (ps-1). 1985. plastic comb bdg. 3.95 (*0-89191-928-7*, 59287, Chariot Bks) Cook.

—Words for the World: Including God's Word for the World. Ege, Christine. LC 91-90681. 136p. (gr. k-8). 1992. text ed. 35.00 incl. 1 8-cass. tape album (*1-884161-01-4*) Comprehen Lang.

Herbert, S. I. Teenage Mutant Ninja Turtles: A Visit to Stump Asteroid. Holm, Astrid, adapted by. LC 90-61217. 48p. (Orig.). (ps-3). 1991. pap. 1.50 (*0-679-81170-2*) Random Bks Yng Read.

—Teenage Mutant Ninja Turtles Pizza Party: A Step 1 Book - Preschool-Grade 1. Hudson, Eleanor. LC 90-53243. 32p. (Orig.). (ps-1). 1991. PLB 7.99 (*0-679-91452-8*); pap. 2.95 (*0-679-81452-3*) Random Bks Yng Read.

Herde, Tom. A Mountain Adventure. Morgan, Patricia G. LC 87-3486. 32p. (gr. 3-6). 1988. PLB 10.79 (*0-8167-1173-9*); pap. text ed. 2.95 (*0-8167-1174-7*) Troll Assocs.

Herge. Explorers on the Moon: The Adventures of Tintin. Herge. 24p. (ps-3). 1992. 16.95 (*0-316-35860-6*, Joy St Bks) Little.

Herigstad, Joni. At Grandma's House: Story Book for Young Children in Sign Language. Johnson, Sue. 28p. 1985. pap. 4.50 (*0-916708-14-4*) Modern Signs.

—I Was So Mad: Storybook for Young Children in Sign Language. Herigstad, Joni. 50p. (Orig.). (ps-4). 1986. pap. 4.95 (*0-916708-16-0*) Modern Signs.

—The Little Green Monsters. Johnson, Sue. 36p. (ps-6). 1985. pap. 4.75 (*0-916708-15-2*) Modern Signs.

—Popsicles Are Cold: Storybook for Young Children in Sign Languages. Johnson, Sue. 30p. (Orig.). (ps-3). 1984. pap. 4.75 (*0-916708-12-8*) Modern Signs.

Herkimer, Lawrence R. Go! Fight! Win! The NCA Guide for Cheerleaders. Phillips, Betty L. Shepherd, Francis, photos by. LC 79-53607. 160p. (gr. 7 up). 1981. PLB 11.80 (*0-440-02957-0*); pap. 9.95 (*0-385-29336-4*) Delacorte.

Hermoso, Elizabeth S. The Chair. Hermoso, Elizabeth S. 15p. (Orig.). (gr. k-2). 1991. pap. 3.00x (*971-10-0442-9*, Pub. by New Day Pub PI) Cellar.

—Fireworks in the Sky. Hermoso, Elizabeth S. 18p. (Orig.). (gr. k-2). 1991. pap. 3.00x (*971-10-0444-5*, Pub. by New Day Pub PI) Cellar.

—The Smartians. Hermoso, Elizabeth S. 15p. 1991. pap. 3.00x (*971-10-0443-7*, Pub. by New Day Pub PI) Cellar.

Herr, Selma E. Read for Understanding, Bk. I. new ed. Herr, Selma E. Anyone Can Read Press Staff, ed. 225p. (Orig.). (gr. 6-12). 1987. pap. 6.95 (*0-914275-04-6*) Anyone Can Read Bks.

Herrara, Velino. In My Mother's House. Clark, Ann N. 64p. (ps up). 1991. 15.95 (*0-670-83917-5*) Viking Child Bks.

—In My Mother's House. Clark, Ann N. 64p. 1992. pap. 4.99 (*0-14-054496-8*) Puffin Bks.

Herrera, Jesse, photos by. Quinceanera: A Latina's Journey to Womanhood. Lankford, Mary D. 48p. (gr. 6-9). 1994. 13.90 (*1-56294-363-4*) Millbrook Pr.

Herrera, Joe. The Bear That Turned White & Other Native Tales. Grammer, Maurine. Smith, Laurence C., frwd. by. LC 90-53590. 108p. (Orig.). (gr. 4 up). 1991. pap. 11.95 (*0-87358-515-1*) Northland AZ.

Herrick, Elizabeth T. Appreciating. McElmurry, Mary A. 64p. (gr. 2-8). 1983. wkbk. 7.95 (*0-9607366-1-1*, GA 493) Good Apple.

—Belonging. McElmurry, Mary A. 64p. (gr. 2-8). 1983. wkbk. 7.95 (*0-9607366-0-3*, GA 492) Good Apple.

Herring, Lee. Dinosaur Fossils. Granowsky, Alvin. LC 91-23407. 32p. (gr. 1-4). 1992. PLB 15.96 (*0-8114-3253-X*); pap. 3.95 (*0-8114-6228-5*) Raintree Steck-V.

Herron, Sandra & White, Kim. Beauty from the Inside Out: Becoming the Best You Can Be. Hunt, Angela E. & Calenberg, Laura K. LC 93-7132. 1993. pap. 12.99 (*0-8407-6789-7*) Nelson.

Hershkowitz, Sarah. Ketivoni Chelek Shlishi, Pt. 3. Bachrach, Kalman & Axelrod, Herman. (HEB.). 64p. (gr. 4). 1959. pap. text ed. 3.50x (*1-878530-04-6*) K Bachrach Co.

—Ketivoni Chelek Sh'Viyi, Pt. 7. Bachrach, Kalman & Axelrod, Herman. (HEB.). 64p. (gr. 8). 1974. pap. text ed. 3.50x (*1-878530-08-9*) K Bachrach Co.

Herskowitz, Sarah. Ketivoni Chelek Shishi, Pt. 6. Bachrach, Kalman & Axelrod, Herman. (HEB.). 62p. (gr. 7). 1974. pap. text ed. 3.50x (*1-878530-07-0*) K Bachrach Co.

Herz, Cary, photos by. Street Gangs in America. Gardner, Sandra. LC 92-16618. 112p. (gr. 9-12). 1992. PLB 13.40 (*0-531-11037-0*) Watts.

Herzfeld, Caryl. The Family Book of Jewish Holidays. Katz, Bobbi. LC 93-27375. 1993. 10.00 (*0-679-85820-2*) Random Bks Yng Read.

—A Family Hanukkah. Katz, Bobbi. LC 91-51093. 40p. (ps-3). 1992. 7.99 (*0-679-83240-8*); PLB 8.99 (*0-679-93240-2*) Random Bks Yng Read.

—A Family Hanukkah. Katz, Bobbi. 32p. (ps-3). 1993. incl. cass. 7.99 (*0-679-85010-4*) Random Bks Yng Read.

Hescox, Richard. Secret of the Knights. Preiss, Byron & Gasperini, Jim. 144p. (gr. 4 up). 1984. pap. 2.25 (*0-553-25368-9*) Bantam.

Hesik, Blue. The Magic King. Hillig, Chuck. LC 84-50928. 32p. (Orig.). (ps-2). 1984. 12.95 (*0-913299-07-3*, Dist. by PGW) Stillpoint.

Heslop, Michael. Greenwitch. Cooper, Susan. LC 73-85319. 148p. (gr. 4-7). 1985. SBE 14.95 (*0-689-30426-9*, M K McElderry) Macmillan Child Grp.

—The Grey King. Cooper, Susan. LC 75-8526. 224p. (gr. 4-8). 1975. SBE 14.95 (*0-689-50029-7*, M K McElderry) Macmillan Child Grp.

Hess, Dick & Eidrigewcius, Stasys. The Snow Queen. Andersen, Hans Christian. LC 83-71172. 48p. (gr. 6 up). 1984. PLB 13.95s.p. (*0-87191-950-8*) Creative Ed.

Hess, Lilo, photos by. That Snake in the Grass. Hess, Lilo. LC 86-24826. 48p. (gr. 3-6). 1987. SBE 13.95 (*0-684-18591-1*, Scribners Young Read) Macmillan Child Grp.

Hester, Ron. Early Christians: Workers for Jesus. Barrett, Marsha. (gr. 1-6). 1979. 5.95 (*0-8054-4247-2*, 4242-47) Broadman.

—God's Fall Gifts. Linam, Gail. (ps). 1992. pap. 3.95 (*0-8054-4159-X*, 4241-59) Broadman.

—God's Summer Gifts. Linam, Gail. (ps). 1992. pap. 3.95 (*0-8054-4156-5*, 4241-56) Broadman.

—Luke: Doctor-Writer. Brown, Robert. (gr. 1-6). 1977. bds. 5.95 (*0-8054-4233-2*, 4242-33) Broadman.

—Paul: The Missionary. Tucker, Iva J. (gr. 1-6). 1976. 5.95 (*0-8054-4228-6*, 4242-28) Broadman.

—Philip: Traveling Preacher. Naish, Jack. (gr. 1-6). 1978. 5.95 (*0-8054-4241-3*, 4242-41) Broadman.

Heston, Claudia. From Twisted Ear to Reverent Tear. Burgess, Allan. 96p. (gr. 7-12). 1983. 5.98 (*0-941518-25-6*) Perry Enterprises.

Hetland, David J. North Dakota: A Living Legacy. Jelliff, Theodore. 400p. (gr. 8 up). 1983. 19.50 (*0-9612140-0-7*) K K Pub Co.

Heuck, Sigrid. Pony & Bear Are Friends. Heuck, Sigrid. LC 89-77711. 32p. (ps-1). 1990. PLB 10.99 (*0-394-92311-1*) Knopf Bks Yng Read.

Heuninck, Ronald. The Little Troll. Berger, Thomas. Lawson, Polly, tr. (GER.). 32p. (gr. k-3). 1992. 14.95 (*0-86315-112-4*, Pub. by Floris Bks UK) Gryphon Hse.

—Playtime. Heuninck, Ronald. 14p. (ps). 1991. Repr. bds. 5.50 (*0-86315-124-8*) Gryphon Hse.

Hevelius, Johannes. Your Place in the Cosmos, Vol. I: A Layman's Book of Astronomy & the Mythology of the Eighty-Eight Celestial Constellations & Registry. Magee, James E. 530p. 1985. text ed. 34.45 (*0-9614354-0-2*) Mosele & Assocs.

—Your Place in the Cosmos, Vol. II: A Layman's Book of Astronomy & the Mythology of the Eighty-Eight Celestial Constellations & Registry. Magee, James E. 508p. 1988. text ed. 34.45 (*0-9614354-1-0*) Mosele & Assocs.

—Your Place in the Cosmos, Vol. III: A Layman's Book of Astronomy & the Mythology of the Eighty-Eight Celestial Constellations & Registry. Magee, James E. 388p. 1992. text ed. 49.45 (*0-9614354-2-9*) Mosele & Assocs.

Hewetson, Nicholas. The Story of the Wheel. Healey, Tim. LC 91-40417. 32p. (gr. 1-4). 1993. PLB 11.89 (*0-8167-2713-9*); pap. text ed. 3.95 (*0-8167-2714-7*) Troll Assocs. Postponed.

Hewett, Richard. The Ancient Cliff Dwellers of Mesa Verde. Arnold, Caroline. 64p. (gr. 3-6). 1992. 15.45 (*0-395-56241-4*, Clarion Bks) HM.

—Camel. Arnold, Caroline. LC 91-26805. 48p. (gr. 2 up). 1992. 15.00 (*0-688-09498-8*); PLB 14.93 (*0-688-09499-6*) Morrow Jr Bks.

—Giraffe. Arnold, Caroline. LC 87-1502. 48p. (gr. 2-5). 1987. 12.95 (*0-688-07069-8*); lib. bdg. 12.88 (*0-688-07070-1*, Morrow Jr Bks) Morrow Jr Bks.

—Hippo. Arnold, Caroline. ALC Staff, ed. LC 88-39794. 48p. (gr. 3 up). 1992. pap. 5.95 (*0-688-11697-3*, Mulberry) Morrow.

—Kangaroo. Arnold, Caroline. LC 86-18103. 48p. (gr. 2-5). 1987. 12.95 (*0-688-06480-9*); lib. bdg. 12.88 (*0-688-06481-7*, Morrow Jr Bks) Morrow Jr Bks.

—Koala. Arnold, Caroline. LC 86-18092. 48p. (gr. 2-5). 1987. 13.95 (*0-688-06478-7*); lib. bdg. 13.88 (*0-688-06479-5*, Morrow Jr Bks) Morrow Jr Bks.

—Panda. Arnold, Caroline. LC 91-33251. 48p. (gr. 2 up). 1992. 15.00 (*0-688-09496-1*); PLB 14.93 (*0-688-09497-X*) Morrow Jr Bks.

—Pets Without Homes. Arnold, Caroline. LC 83-2106. 48p. (gr. k-3). 1983. 14.95 (*0-89919-191-6*, Clarion Bks) HM.

—Zebra. Arnold, Caroline. LC 87-1503. 48p. (gr. 2-5). 1987. 13.95 (*0-688-07067-1*); lib. bdg. 13.88 (*0-688-07068-X*, Morrow Jr Bks) Morrow Jr Bks.

Hewett, Richard, photos by. Dinosaurs All Around: An Artist's View of the Prehistoric World. Arnold, Caroline. LC 92-5726. 48p. (gr. 3-6). 1993. 14.45 (0-395-62363-4, Clarion Bks) HM.
—Dinosaurs Down Under: And Other Fossils from Australia. Arnold, Caroline. 48p. (gr. 3-7). 1990. 15.45 (0-89919-814-7) HM.
—Elephant. Arnold, Caroline. LC 93-31095. 48p. (gr. 2 up). 1993. 15.00 (0-688-11342-7); PLB 14.93 (0-688-11343-5) Morrow Jr Bks.
—Flamingo. Arnold, Caroline. LC 90-19186. 48p. (gr. 2 up). 1991. 13.95 (0-688-09411-2); PLB 13.88 (0-688-09412-0) Morrow Jr Bks.
—Getting Elected: The Diary of a Campaign. Hewett, Joan. LC 88-11109. 48p. (gr. 4-7). 1989. 13.95 (0-525-67259-1, Lodestar Bks) Dutton Child Bks.
—Giraffe. Arnold, Caroline. LC 92-25550. 48p. (gr. 3 up). 1993. pap. 5.95 (0-688-12272-8, Mulberry) Morrow.
—A Guide Dog Puppy Grows Up. Arnold, Caroline. 43p. (gr. 1 up). 1991. 16.95 (0-15-232657-X) HarBrace.
—Insect Zoo. Meyers, Susan. 48p. (gr. 3-7). 1991. 16.95 (0-525-67325-3, Lodestar Bks) Dutton Child Bks.
—Kangaroo. Arnold, Caroline. LC 86-18103. (gr. 3 up). 1992. pap. 5.95 (0-688-11502-0, Mulberry) Morrow.
—Koala. Arnold, Caroline. LC 86-18092. 48p. (gr. 3 up). 1992. pap. 5.95 (0-688-11503-9, Mulberry) Morrow.
—Laura Loves Horses. Hewett, Joan. 48p. (gr. 2-5). 1990. 14.45 (0-89919-844-9) HM.
—Llama. Arnold, Caroline. LC 87-27130. 48p. (gr. 2-5). 1988. 12.95 (0-688-07540-1); PLB 12.88 (0-688-07541-X) Morrow Jr Bks.
—Look Alive: Behind the Scenes of an Animated Film. Scott, Elaine. LC 91-36220. 80p. (gr. 3 up). 1992. 14.00 (0-688-09936-X); PLB 13.93 (0-688-09937-8) Morrow Jr Bks.
—Monkey. Arnold, Caroline. LC 92-31094. 48p. (gr. 2 up). 1993. 15.00 (0-688-11344-3); PLB 14.93 (0-688-11345-1) Morrow Jr Bks.
—Orangutan. Arnold, Caroline. LC 89-38957. 48p. (gr. 2 up). 1990. 15.00 (0-688-08826-0); PLB 13.88 (0-688-08827-9, Morrow Jr Bks) Morrow Jr Bks.
—Penguin. Arnold, Caroline. LC 87-31458. 48p. (gr. 2-5). 1988. 12.95 (0-688-07706-4); PLB 12.88 (0-688-07707-2) Morrow Jr Bks.
—Public Defender: Lawyer for the People. Hewett, Joan. 48p. (gr. 4-8). 1991. 14.95 (0-525-67340-7, Lodestar Bks) Dutton Child Bks.
—Sea Lion. Arnold, Caroline. LC 93-27007. 1994. write for info. (0-688-12027-X); lib. bdg. write for info. (0-688-12028-8) Morrow Jr Bks.
—Snake. Arnold, Caroline. LC 90-22591. 48p. (gr. 2 up). 1991. 13.95 (0-688-09409-0); PLB 13.88 (0-688-09410-4) Morrow Jr Bks.
—Tiger, Tiger, Growing Up. Hewett, Joan. LC 92-9741. 32p. (ps-2). 1993. 13.95 (0-395-61583-6, Clarion Bks) HM.
—Watch out for Sharks! Arnold, Caroline. 48p. (gr. 3-6). 1991. 15.45 (0-395-57560-5, Clarion Bks) HM.
—Wild Goat. Arnold, Caroline. LC 89-38958. 48p. (gr. 2 up). 1990. 13.95 (0-688-08824-4); PLB 13.88 (0-688-08825-2, Morrow Jr Bks) Morrow Jr Bks.
—Zebra. Arnold, Caroline. LC 92-25550. 48p. (gr. 3 up). 1993. pap. 5.95 (0-688-12273-6, Mulberry) Morrow.
Hewett, Richard R. Hector Lives in the United States Now: The Story of a Mexican-American Child. Hewett, Joan. LC 89-36572. 48p. (gr. 2-5). 1990. (Lipp Jr Bks); PLB 13.89 (0-397-32278-X, Lipp Jr Bks) HarpC Child Bks.
—Ostriches & Other Flightless Birds. Arnold, Caroline. 48p. (gr. 2-5). 1990. PLB 19.95 (0-87614-377-X) Carolrhoda Bks.
Hewett, Richard R., photos by. Cats: In from the Wild. Arnold, Caroline. LC 92-32986. 1993. 19.95 (0-87614-692-2) Carolrhoda Bks.
—House Sparrows Everywhere. Arnold, Caroline. 48p. (gr. 2-5). 1992. 19.95 (0-87614-696-5) Carolrhoda Bks.
—Saving the Peregrine Falcon. Arnold, Caroline. LC 84-15576. 48p. (gr. 2-5). 1985. PLB 19.95 (0-87614-225-0); pap. 6.95 (0-87614-523-3) Carolrhoda Bks.
—Tule Elk. Arnold, Caroline. 48p. (gr. 2-5). 1989. 19.95 (0-87614-343-5) Carolrhoda Bks.
Hewitson, Jennifer. Her Story Series. Hoobler, Dorothy & Hoobler, Thomas. (gr. 4-6). 1992. 95.60 (0-382-24149-5); PLB 111.84 (0-382-24142-8); pap. 63.60 (0-382-24355-2) Silver Burdett Pr.
—A Promise at the Alamo. Hoobler, Dorothy & Hoobler, Thomas. 64p. (gr. 4-6). 1992. 13.98 (0-382-24154-1); lib. bdg. 13.98 (0-382-24147-9); pap. 7.95 (0-382-24352-8) Silver Burdett Pr.
Hewitt, Kathryn. Flower Garden. Bunting, Eve. LC 92-25766. 1994. write for info. (0-15-228776-0) HarBrace.
—King Midas & the Golden Touch. Hewitt, Kathryn. LC 86-7681. 29p. (ps-3). 1987. 12.95 (0-15-242800-3) HarBrace.
—Two by Two: The Untold Story. Hewitt, Kathryn. LC 84-4579. 32p. (ps-3). 1984. 12.95 (0-15-291801-9, HB Juv Bks) HarBrace.
—Two by Two: The Untold Story. Hewitt, Kathryn. 32p. (ps-1). 1989. pap. 3.95 (0-15-291802-7, Voyager Bks) HarBrace.
—The Worry Week. Lindbergh, Anne M. LC 84-19299. 144p. (gr. 3-7). 1985. 12.95 (0-15-299675-3, HB Juv Bks) HarBrace.

Hewitt, Kathryn & Ardizzone, Edward. The Witch Family. Estes, Eleanor. 223p. (gr. 3-7). 1990. pap. 4.95 (0-15-298572-7, Odyssey) HarBrace.
Hewitt, Margaret. Green Earrings & a Felt Hat. Newman, Jerry. LC 92-29056. 48p. (gr. 1-3). 1993. PLB 14.95 (0-8050-2392-5, Bks Young Read) H Holt & Co.
—Teddy B. Zoot. Clarke, J. LC 90-34120. 64p. (gr. 2-4). 1992. pap. 4.95 (0-8050-2210-4, Redfeather BYR) H Holt & Co.
Heyer, Carol. All Things Bright & Beautiful. Alexander, Cecil. 32p. (ps-2). 1992. 11.95 (0-8249-8544-3, Ideals Child) Hambleton-Hill.
—Beauty & the Beast. Heyer, Carol, retold by. 32p. (ps-3). 1989. 13.95 (0-8249-8359-9, Ideals Child) Hambleton-Hill.
—Beauty & the Beast. 32p. (gr. k-3). 1992. pap. 4.95 (0-8249-8579-6, Ideals Child) Hambleton-Hill.
—The Christmas Story. Heyer, Carol. LC 91-9101. 32p. (ps-1). 1991. 11.95 (0-8249-8512-5, Ideals Child) Hambleton-Hill.
—The Dream Stealer. Cosgrove, Stephen. LC 89-83843. 48p. (gr. 1-4). 1990. 16.95 (1-55868-009-8); pap. 5.95 (1-55868-021-7); pap. 12.95 incl. audio (1-55868-042-X) Gr Arts Ctr Pub.
—The Easter Story. Heyer, Carol. 32p. (ps-1). 1990. 10.95 (0-8249-8439-0, Ideals Child) Hambleton-Hill.
—Excalibur. Heyer, Carol. 32p. (gr. k-4). 1991. 14.95 (0-8249-8487-0, Ideals Child) Hambleton-Hill.
—Excalibur. Heyer, Carol, adapted by. 32p. (ps-3). 1993. pap. 4.95 (0-8249-8638-5, Ideals Child) Hambleton-Hill.
—Prancer. Cosgrove, Stephen. LC 89-83843. 32p. (gr. k-7). 1990. 14.95 (1-55868-027-9); pap. 5.95 (1-55868-020-9); pap. 12.95 incl. audio (1-55868-041-1) Gr Arts Ctr Pub.
—Rapunzel. Grimm, Jacob & Grimm, Wilhelm K. 32p. (gr. k-3). 1992. 14.95 (0-8249-8558-3, Ideals Child); PLB 15.00 (0-8249-8585-0) Hambleton-Hill.
—Robin Hood. Heyer, Carol, retold by. LC 93-18591. 32p. (ps-3). 1993. 14.95 (0-8249-8634-2, Ideals Child); PLB 15.00 (0-8249-8648-2) Hambleton-Hill.
Heyer, Marilee. Iron Hans. Grimm, Jacob & Grimm, Wilhelm K. LC 93-14662. 32p. 1993. 14.99 (0-670-81741-4) Viking Child Bks.
—The Weaving of a Dream. Heyer, Marilee. 32p. (ps-3). 1989. pap. 4.99 (0-14-050528-8, Puffin) Puffin Bks.
—The Weaving of a Dream: A Chinese Folktale. Heyer, Marilee. LC 85-20187. 32p. (gr. k-6). 1986. pap. 15.99 (0-670-80555-6) Viking Child Bks.
Heyman, Ken, photos by. Bread, Bread, Bread. Morris, Ann. LC 92-25547. 32p. (gr. k). 1993. pap. 4.95 (0-688-12275-2, Mulberry) Morrow.
—Hats, Hats, Hats. Morris, Ann. LC 92-25548. 32p. (gr. k). 1993. pap. 4.95 (0-688-12274-4, Mulberry) Morrow.
—Houses & Homes. Morris, Ann. Pearson, Susan, ed. LC 92-1365. 32p. (ps-2). 1992. 14.00 (0-688-10168-2); PLB 13.93 (0-688-10169-0) Lothrop.
—On Their Toes: A Russian Ballet School. Morris, Ann. LC 91-11903. 48p. (gr. 3-7). 1991. SBE 14.95 (0-689-31660-7, Atheneum Child Bk) Macmillan Child Grp.
—Seven Hundred Kids on Grandpa's Farm. Morris, Ann. 32p. (ps-3). 1994. 14.99 (0-525-45162-5, DCB) Dutton Child Bks.
—Tools. Morris, Ann. Pearson, Susan, ed. LC 92-3871. 32p. (ps-2). 1992. 14.00 (0-688-10170-4); PLB 13.93 (0-688-10171-2) Lothrop.

Heyne, Chris. Come in Spaceship Earth. Schmidt, Fran & Friedman, Alice. 61p. (Orig.). (gr. 4-9). 1990. Incl. poster. pap. text ed. 21.95 (1-878227-06-8) Peace Educ.
Students serve as crew members aboard Spaceship Earth. They learn to work cooperatively on a common mission - survival & improved quality of life for the human family. COME IN SPACESHIP EARTH is action-oriented as it guides students toward individual & social responsibility. The crew is challenged to tackle problems in their school, community, & world. They develop problem solving & critical thinking skills through role plays, brainstorming, & simulation games. As students plan & work together, they gain a new respect for individual differences & learn to handle conflict nonviolently. These experiences & skills help them to be responsible, capable & creative crew members now & in the future. "COME IN SPACESHIP EARTH started my students thinking about their roles as crew members in our classroom & in

their world. It is wonderful to see my students begin to act as a cohesive team, creating a positive classroom environment."--Carol Bregman, Middle School, Miami, Florida. As students plan & work together, they are guided toward individual & social responsibility.
Publisher Provided Annotation.

—Fighting Fair: Dr. Martin Luther King Jr. for Kids. Schmidt, Fran & Friedman, Alice. 40p. (Orig.). (gr. 4-9). 1986. pap. text ed. 13.95 (1-878227-01-7) Peace Educ.

—**Fighting Fair: Dr. Martin Luther King Jr. for Kids. rev. ed.** Schmidt, Fran & Friedman, Alice. (gr. 4-9). 1990. Set. pap. text ed. 74.95 69 p., incl. poster, video (1-878227-02-5); tchr's. ed., incl. poster 19.95 (1-878227-07-6); Set of 5. wkbk., 48p. 11.95 (1-878227-08-4) Peace Educ.
Challenge your students to resolve conflicts with skills - not fists - within the framework of Dr. Martin Luther King Jr.'s philosophy of nonviolence. FIGHTING FAIR: DR. MARTIN LUTHER KING, JR. FOR KIDS provides many opportunities for students to apply the skills, strategies, & values of nonviolence to their daily lives & to explore nonviolence as a method of social change. The FIGHTING FAIR program includes: A provocative eighteen-minute, award winning video which shows a coach helping a group of angry kids resolve a conflict on the basketball court. Vivid scenes of the civil rights movement are used as backdrop to help the young people understand the dynamics of nonviolence. A comprehensive teacher's guide with 43 reproducible student pages. FIGHTING FAIR involves students in brainstorming, role playing, problem solving, responsible decision making, & mediation. A colorful poster of the Rules For Fighting Fair provides students with guidelines to "fight back effectively & nonviolently. "...a valuable acquisition for school libraries, for use in guidance & social studies classes & conflict resolution workshops."--School Library Journal. "The strong man is the man who can stand up for his rights & not hit back." --Dr. Martin Luther King, Jr.
Publisher Provided Annotation.

Hezard, Pierre. Sept Contes. Tournier, Michel. (FRE.). 161p. (gr. 5-10). 1990. pap. 8.95 (2-07-033497-X) Schoenhof.
Hicks, Barbara. Ebeneezer Sneezer. Penner, Fred. 36p. (Orig.). (gr. 2-6). 1990. pap. 5.95 (0-920534-37-6, Pub. by Hyperion Pr Ltd CN) Sterling.
—Fred Penner's Sing along - Play Along. Penner, Fred. 112p. (Orig.). (ps-4). 1991. 14.95 (0-89524-625-2) Cherry Lane.
—Rollerskating. Penner, Fred. 32p. (Orig.). (gr. 2-6). 1990. pap. 5.95 (0-920534-64-3, Pub. by Hyperion Pr Ltd CN) Sterling.
Hicks, Celeste H. Let's Tour the Roanoke Valley: A Story Coloring Book. Hairston, Earnestine. 52p. (ps-4). 1987. pap. 3.95 (0-944890-00-8) Hairston & Hicks.
Hicks, Mark. Hello Arizona: The Arizona Activity Book. Tegeler, Dorothy. 32p. (Orig.). 1987. pap. 3.50 (0-943169-07-0) Fiesta Bks Inc.
Hicks, Mark A. The Most Fascinating Places on Earth. Hicks, Donna E. LC 92-41777. 128p. 1994. 14.95 (0-8069-8692-1) Sterling.
—What's It Like to Be a Postal Worker. Matthews, Morgan. LC 89-34385. 32p. (gr. k-3). 1990. lib. bdg. 10.89 (0-8167-1813-X); pap. text ed. 2.95 (0-8167-1814-8) Troll Assocs.

Hicks, Russell. Beauty & the Beast. De Beaumont, Madame. Shumate, Mark, adapted by. 26p. (ps). 1987. Packaged with pre-programmed audio cass. tape. 9.95 (0-934323-66-6) Alchemy Comms.
—One Hundred One Dalmatas: Un Libro Para Contar. Manushkin, Fran. Santacruz, Daniel M., tr. from ENG. (SPA). 32p. 1994. pap. 4.95 (1-56282-568-2) Disney Pr.
—One Hundred One Dalmatians Counting Book & Puppy. Manushkin, Fran. 32p. (ps-1). 1993. Boxed set incl. plush puppy. 16.95 (1-56282-572-0) Disney Pr.
—Walt Disney's One Hundred One Dalmatians: A Counting Book. Manushkin, Fran. LC 90-85426. 32p. (ps-k). 1991. 9.95 (1-56282-012-5); PLB 9.89 (1-56282-032-X) Disney Pr.
—Walt Disney's One Hundred One Dalmatians: A Counting Book. Mounushkin, Fran. LC 92-53493. 32p. (ps-k). 1993. pap. 4.95 (1-56282-324-8) Disney Pr.
—Winnie the Pooh & the Missing Pots. Birney, Betty. 24p. (ps-2). 1992. write for info. (0-307-12337-5, 12337) Western Pub.
Hicks, Russell, et al. The Sleeping Beauty. Hughes, Margaret A. Forsse, Ken & Becker, Mary, eds. 26p. (ps). 1986. 9.95 (0-934323-27-5) Alchemy Comms.
—Mother Goose Favorite Lullabies. Hughes, Margaret A. 26p. (ps). 1987. 9.95 (0-934323-51-8); pre-programmed audio cass. tapes avail. Alchemy Comms.
—Peter & the Wolf. Hughes, Margaret A. & Forsse, Ken, eds. 26p. (ps). 1986. packaged with preprogrammed audio cass. tape 9.95 (0-934323-33-X) Alchemy Comms.
—Quiet Please. Baron, Phil. 34p. (ps). 1987. incl. pre-programmed audio cass. 9.95 (0-934323-40-2) Alchemy Comms.
—Teddy Ruxpin Lullabies II. Forsse, Ken. 26p. (ps). 1988. 21.00 (0-934323-68-2); pre-programmed audiocassette incl. Alchemy Comms.
—Wooly & the Giant Snowzos. Baron, Phil. 34p. (ps). 1987. incl. pre-programmed audio cass. 9.95 (0-934323-42-9) Alchemy Comms.
Hidy, Lance. Losing Things at Mr. Mudd's. Coman, Carolyn. 32p. (ps-3). 1992. 14.00 (0-374-34657-7) FS&G.
Hierstein, Judith. Toby Belfer Never Had a Christmas Tree. Pushker, Gloria T. LC 91-14514. 32p. 1991. 14. 95 (0-88289-855-8) Pelican.
—Toby Belfer's Seder: A Passover Story Retold. Pushker, Gloria T. LC 93-5585. 1994. write for info. (0-88289-987-2) Pelican.
Hierstein, Judy. Celebrate Special Days. Hand, Phyllis. 144p. (gr. k-6). 1985. wkbk. 11.95 (0-86653-280-3, SS 841, Shining Star Pubns) Good Apple.
—Outstanding Women. Aten, Jerry. 64p. (gr. k-4). 1987. pap. 7.95 (0-86653-413-X, GA1008) Good Apple.
—Presidential Leaders. Aten, Jerry. 64p. (gr. k-4). 1986. wkbk. 7.95 (0-86653-347-8, GA 697) Good Apple.
—The Welcome Back to School Book. McCune, Dianne, et al. 112p. (gr. k-4). 1987. pap. 9.95 (0-86653-383-4, GA1001) Good Apple.
Hierstein-Morris, Jill. Christmas: Facts & Fun. Hierstein-Morris, Jill. 72p. (Orig.). (gr. 1 up). 1990. pap. 9.95 (1-877588-02-4) Creatively Yours.
—Halloween: Facts & Fun. Hierstein-Morris, Jill. 72p. (gr. 1 up). 1988. pap. 9.95 (1-877588-00-8) Creatively Yours.
Higashi, Sandra. The Old Demon. Buck, Pearl S. 40p. (gr. 4 up). 1982. PLB 13.95s.p. (0-87191-828-5) Creative Ed.
Higgenbottom, J. Winslow. Rats, Spiders & Love. Pryor, Bonnie. LC 85-25831. 128p. (gr. 4-6). 1986. 13.95 (0-688-05867-1) Morrow Jr Bks.
Higginbotham, David. Do It with the Sun. Shedd, Edith S. & Shedd, Alan. LC 82-81309. 208p. (Orig.). (gr. 6-9). 1982. pap. 12.95 (0-9608358-0-6) Integ Energy.
Higginbottom, J. Winslow. Lucky Chuck. Cleary, Beverly. LC 83-13386. 40p. (gr. k-3). 1984. 13.95 (0-688-02736-9); PLB 13.88 (0-688-02738-5), Morrow Jr Bks) Morrow Jr Bks.
Higgins, Susan O. The Bunny Book. 3rd ed. Higgins, Susan O. Wexner, V. I., ed. 76p. (ps-3). 1985. pap. 3.95 (0-939973-03-0) Pumpkin Pr Pub Hse.
—The Pumpkin Book. 4th ed. Higgins, Susan O. Wexner, V. I., ed. 66p. (gr. k-3). 1983. pap. 3.95 (0-939973-00-6) Pumpkin Pr Pub Hse.
—The Thanksgiving Book. 3rd ed. Higgins, Susan O. Wexner, V. I., ed. 74p. (ps-3). 1984. pap. 3.95 (0-939973-01-4) Pumpkin Pr Pub Hse.
High, David, et al. The Airship. Forsse, Ken. 26p. (ps). 1985. incl. audio-cassette 9.95 (0-934323-00-3) Alchemy Comms.
—The Do-Along Songbook. Baron, Phil. Forse, Ken, ed. 26p. (ps). 1986. 9.95 (0-934323-34-8); pre-programmed audio cass. tape incl. Alchemy Comms.
—Grundo Beach Party. Ryan, Will. Becker, Mary, ed. 26p. (ps). 1986. 9.95 (0-934323-35-6); pre-programmed audio cass. tape incl. Alchemy Comms.
—Lost in Boggley Woods. Ryan, Will. Becker, Mary, ed. 26p. (ps). 1986. 9.95 (0-934323-38-0); pre-programmed audio cass. tape incl. Alchemy Comms.
—Teddy Ruxpin's Lullabies. Forsse, Ken. 26p. (ps). 1985. incl. audio-cassette 9.95 (0-934323-01-1) Alchemy Comms.
Higham. Simple Sums. Watson. 28p. (ps-2). 1985. 2.95 (0-86020-779-X) EDC.
Higham, David. Shapes. Watson, C. 24p. (gr. k-2). 1983. 2.95 (0-86020-759-5) EDC.

—Sizes. Watson, C. 24p. (gr. k-2). 1983. 2.95 (0-86020-760-9) EDC.
Highlights for Children Staff. Action Book of Sports. Highlights for Children Staff. 32p. (gr. 3-8). 1988. pap. 2.95 (0-87534-229-9) Highlights.
—Activity Books. Highlights for Children Staff. 32p. (gr. 1-6). 1989. pap. 2.95 (0-87534-381-3) Highlights.
—Activity Books. Highlights for Children Staff. 32p. (gr. 1-6). 1989. pap. 2.95 (0-87534-382-1) Highlights.
—Activity Books. Highlights for Children Staff. 32p. (gr. 1-6). 1989. pap. 2.95 (0-87534-383-X) Highlights.
—Activity Books. Highlights for Children Staff. 32p. (gr. 1-6). 1989. pap. 2.95 (0-87534-384-8) Highlights.
—Activity Books. Highlights for Children Staff. 32p. (gr. 1-6). 1989. pap. 2.95 (0-87534-385-6) Highlights.
—Activity Books. Highlights for Children Staff. 32p. (gr. 1-6). 1989. pap. 2.95 (0-87534-386-4) Highlights.
—Activity Books. Highlights for Children Staff. 32p. (gr. 1-6). 1989. pap. 2.95 (0-87534-387-2) Highlights.
—Activity Books. Highlights for Children Staff. 32p. (gr. 1-6). 1989. pap. 2.95 (0-87534-388-0) Highlights.
—Activity Books. Highlights for Children Staff. 32p. (gr. 1-6). 1989. pap. 2.95 (0-87534-389-9) Highlights.
—Activity Books. Highlights for Children Staff. 32p. (gr. 1-6). 1989. pap. 2.95 (0-87534-390-2) Highlights.
—Basketball. Highlights for Children Staff. 48p. (gr. 3-7). 1990. pap. 2.95 (0-87534-353-8) Highlights.
—Dinosaurs: A Closer Look. Highlights for Children Staff. 32p. (gr. 3-10). 1992. pap. 3.50 (0-87534-316-3) Highlights.
—Dinosaurs: All Shapes & Sizes. Highlights for Children Staff. 32p. (gr. 3-10). 1992. pap. 3.50 (0-87534-315-5) Highlights.
—Dinosaurs: Giants of the Earth. Highlights for Children Staff. 32p. (gr. 3-10). 1992. pap. 3.50 (0-87534-313-9) Highlights.
—Dinosaurs: the Fossil Hunters. Highlights for Children Staff. 32p. (gr. 3-10). 1992. pap. 3.50 (0-87534-317-1) Highlights.
—Dinosaurs: The Real Monsters. Highlights for Children Staff. 32p. (gr. 3-10). 1992. pap. 3.50 (0-87534-314-7) Highlights.
—Hidden Pictures & Brain Bogglers. Highlights for Children Staff. 32p. (gr. 1-5). 1992. pap. 2.95 (0-87534-094-6) Highlights.
—Hidden Pictures & Brain Twisters. Highlights for Children Staff. 32p. (gr. 1-5). 1992. pap. 2.95 (0-87534-092-X) Highlights.
—Hidden Pictures & Mind Boosters. Highlights for Children Staff. 32p. (gr. 1-5). 1992. pap. 2.95 (0-87534-098-9) Highlights.
—Hidden Pictures & More Fun. Highlights for Children Staff. 32p. (gr. 1-5). 1992. pap. 2.95 (0-87534-095-4) Highlights.
—Hidden Pictures & Thinking Games. Highlights for Children Staff. 32p. (gr. 1-5). 1992. pap. 2.95 (0-87534-097-0) Highlights.
—Hidden Pictures & Tricky Teasers. Highlights for Children Staff. 32p. (gr. 1-5). 1992. pap. 2.95 (0-87534-090-3) Highlights.
—Hidden Pictures Plus Brain Bafflers. Highlights for Children Staff. 32p. (gr. 1-5). 1992. pap. 2.95 (0-87534-089-X) Highlights.
—Hidden Pictures Plus Mind Stretchers. Highlights for Children Staff. 32p. (gr. 1-5). 1992. pap. 2.95 (0-87534-093-8) Highlights.
—Hidden Pictures Plus Mind Tanglers. Highlights for Children Staff. 32p. (gr. 1-5). 1992. pap. 2.95 (0-87534-091-1) Highlights.
—Hidden Pictures Plus Other Stumpers. Highlights for Children Staff. 32p. (gr. 1-5). 1992. pap. 2.95 (0-87534-096-2) Highlights.
—One Hundred Eighteen Recyclable Crafts Kids Can Make. Highlights for Children Staff. 40p. (gr. 1-5). 1993. pap. 2.95 (0-87534-106-3) Highlights.
—One Hundred Nineteen Any Time Crafts Kids Can Make. Highlights for Children Staff. 40p. (gr. 1-5). 1993. pap. 2.95 (0-87534-108-X) Highlights.
—One Hundred Thirty-Six Party Ideas & Crafts Kids Can Make. Highlights for Children Staff. 40p. (gr. 1-5). 1993. pap. 2.95 (0-87534-110-1) Highlights.
—One Hundred Twenty-One Holiday Crafts Kids Can Make. Highlights for Children Staff. 40p. (gr. 1-5). 1993. pap. 2.95 (0-87534-109-8) Highlights.
—One Hundred Twenty-Three Gift Crafts Kids Can Make. Highlights for Children Staff. 40p. (gr. 1-5). 1993. pap. 2.95 (0-87534-107-1) Highlights.
—Preschool Headwork. Highlights for Children Staff. 32p. (ps-2). 1968. pap. 2.95 (0-87534-220-5) Highlights.
—Puzzlemania. Highlights for Children Staff. (gr. 3-7). 1989. pap. 2.98 48p. (0-87534-701-0); pap. 2.98 32p. (0-87534-801-7) Highlights.
—Puzzlemania. Highlights for Children Staff. (gr. 3-7). 1989. pap. 2.98 48p. (0-87534-702-9); pap. 2.98 32p. (0-87534-802-5) Highlights.
—Puzzlemania. Highlights for Children Staff. (gr. 3-7). 1989. pap. 2.98 48p. (0-87534-703-7); pap. 2.98 32p. (0-87534-803-3) Highlights.
—Puzzlemania. Highlights for Children Staff. (gr. 3-7). 1989. pap. 2.98 48p. (0-87534-704-5); pap. 2.98 32p. (0-87534-804-1) Highlights.
—Puzzlemania. Highlights for Children Staff. (gr. 3-7). 1989. pap. 2.98 48p. (0-87534-705-3); pap. 2.98 32p. (0-87534-805-X) Highlights.
—Puzzlemania. Highlights for Children Staff. (gr. 3-7). 1989. pap. 2.98 48p. (0-87534-706-1); pap. 2.98 32p. (0-87534-806-8) Highlights.

—Puzzlemania. Highlights for Children Staff. (gr. 3-7). 1989. pap. 2.98 48p. (0-87534-707-X); pap. 2.98 32p. (0-87534-807-6) Highlights.
—Puzzlemania. Highlights for Children Staff. (gr. 3-7). 1989. pap. 2.98 48p. (0-87534-708-8); pap. 2.98 32p. (0-87534-808-4) Highlights.
—Puzzlemania. Highlights for Children Staff. (gr. 3-7). 1989. pap. 2.98 48p. (0-87534-709-6); pap. 2.98 32p. (0-87534-809-2) Highlights.
—Puzzlemania. Highlights for Children Staff. (gr. 3-7). 1989. pap. 2.98 48p. (0-87534-710-X); pap. 2.98 32p. (0-87534-810-6) Highlights.
—Puzzlemania. Highlights for Children Staff. 48p. (gr. 3-7). 1990. pap. 2.98 (0-87534-711-8) Highlights.
—Puzzlemania. Highlights for Children Staff. 48p. (gr. 3-7). 1990. pap. 2.98 (0-87534-712-6) Highlights.
—Puzzlemania. Highlights for Children Staff. 48p. (gr. 3-7). 1990. pap. 2.98 (0-87534-713-4) Highlights.
—Puzzlemania. Highlights for Children Staff. 48p. (gr. 3-7). 1990. pap. 2.98 (0-87534-714-2) Highlights.
—Puzzlemania. Highlights for Children Staff. 48p. (gr. 3-7). 1990. pap. 2.98 (0-87534-715-0) Highlights.
—Puzzlemania. Highlights for Children Staff. 48p. (gr. 3-7). 1990. pap. 2.98 (0-87534-716-9) Highlights.
—Puzzlemania. Highlights for Children Staff. 48p. (gr. 3-7). 1990. pap. 2.98 (0-87534-717-7) Highlights.
—Puzzlemania. Highlights for Children Staff. 48p. (gr. 3-7). 1990. pap. 2.98 (0-87534-718-5) Highlights.
—Puzzlemania. Highlights for Children Staff. 48p. (gr. 3-7). 1990. pap. 2.98 (0-87534-719-3) Highlights.
—Puzzlemania. Highlights for Children Staff. 48p. (gr. 3-7). 1990. pap. 2.98 (0-87534-720-7) Highlights.
—Puzzlemania. Highlights for Children Staff. 48p. (gr. 3-7). 1990. pap. 2.98 (0-87534-721-5) Highlights.
—Puzzlemania. Highlights for Children Staff. 48p. (gr. 3-7). 1990. pap. 2.98 (0-87534-722-3) Highlights.
—Puzzlemania. Highlights for Children Staff. 48p. (gr. 3-7). 1991. pap. 2.98 (0-87534-723-1) Highlights.
—Puzzlemania. Highlights for Children Staff. 48p. (gr. 3-7). 1991. pap. 2.98 (0-87534-724-X) Highlights.
—Puzzlemania. Highlights for Children Staff. 48p. (gr. 3-7). 1991. pap. 2.98 (0-87534-725-8) Highlights.
—Puzzlemania. Highlights for Children Staff. 48p. (gr. 3-7). 1991. pap. 2.98 (0-87534-726-6) Highlights.
—Puzzlemania. Highlights for Children Staff. 48p. (gr. 3-7). 1991. pap. 2.98 (0-87534-727-4) Highlights.
—Puzzlemania. Highlights for Children Staff. 48p. (gr. 3-7). 1991. pap. 2.98 (0-87534-728-2) Highlights.
—Skills Fun: Critters. Highlights for Children Staff. (ps-3). 1991. pap. text ed. 2.95 (0-87534-192-6) Highlights.
—Skills Fun: Free Time. Highlights for Children Staff. (ps-3). 1991. pap. text ed. 2.95 (0-87534-193-4) Highlights.
—Skills Fun: Mystery. Highlights for Children Staff. (ps-3). 1991. pap. text ed. 2.95 (0-87534-194-2) Highlights.
—Skills Fun: Outdoors. Highlights for Children Staff. (ps-3). 1991. pap. text ed. 2.95 (0-87534-198-5) Highlights.
—Skills Fun: Space. Highlights for Children Staff. (ps-3). 1991. pap. text ed. 2.95 (0-87534-199-3) Highlights.
—Skills Fun: Trips. Highlights for Children Staff. (ps-3). 1991. pap. text ed. 2.95 (0-87534-200-0) Highlights.
—Summer Games. Highlights for Children Staff. 48p. (gr. 3-7). 1990. pap. 2.95 (0-87534-352-X) Highlights.
—What's Wrong & Other Mixed-up Fun. Highlights for Children Staff. 32p. (gr. k-6). 1990. pap. 2.95 (0-87534-464-X) Highlights.
—What's Wrong & Other Mixed-up Fun. Highlights for Children Staff. 32p. (gr. k-6). 1990. pap. 2.95 (0-87534-444-5) Highlights.
—What's Wrong & Other Mixed-up Fun. Highlights for Children Staff. 32p. (gr. k-6). 1990. pap. 2.95 (0-87534-449-6) Highlights.
—What's Wrong & Other Mixed-up Fun. Highlights for Children Staff. 32p. (gr. k-6). 1990. pap. 2.95 (0-87534-455-0) Highlights.
—What's Wrong & Other Mixed-up Fun. Highlights for Children Staff. 32p. (gr. k-6). 1990. pap. 2.95 (0-87534-463-1) Highlights.
—What's Wrong & Other Mixed-up Fun. Highlights for Children Staff. 32p. (gr. k-6). 1990. pap. 2.95 (0-87534-466-6) Highlights.
—Winter Sports. Highlights for Children Staff. 48p. (gr. 3-7). 1990. pap. 2.95 (0-87534-351-1) Highlights.
Highpoint Type & Graphics Staff. Esteem Builders: A Self-Esteem Curriculum for Improving Student Achievement, Behavior & School-Home Climate. Borba, Michele. Taylor-McMillan, Birah, ed. LC 88-80769. 444p. (Orig.). (gr. k-8). 1989. pap. 49.95 spiral bdg. (0-915190-53-2, JP9053-2) Jalmar Pr.
Hijkata, Shigemi, jt. illus. see Izawa, Tadasu.
Hildebrandt, Greg. Aladdin & the Magic Lamp. 48p. (ps-2). 1992. 5.95 (0-88101-266-1) Unicorn Pub.
—Alice in Wonderland. 48p. (gr. 2-5). 1991. 6.95 (0-88101-109-6) Unicorn Pub.
—Favorite Fairy Tales. 160p. (ps-7). 1985. 14.95 (0-88101-268-8) Unicorn Pub.
—Peter Cottontail's Surprise. Worth, Bonnie. LC 84-28031. 48p. (ps-2). 1985. 4.95 (0-88101-015-4) Unicorn Pub.
—Peter Pan. 48p. (gr. 2-5). 1991. 6.95 (0-88101-111-8) Unicorn Pub.
—Peter Pan. Barrie, J. M. 160p. 1987. 14.95 (0-88101-270-X) Unicorn Pub.
—Phantom of the Opera. Leroux, Gaston. (gr. 4 up). 1988. 14.95 (0-88101-082-0) Unicorn Pub.

—Phantom of the Opera. Leroux, Gaston. 208p. (gr. 7 up). 1988. 9.95 (0-88101-121-5) Unicorn Pub.
—Pinocchio. 48p. (gr. 2-5). 1992. 6.95 (0-88101-267-X) Unicorn Pub.
—Pinocchio. Collodi, Carlo. 160p. 1986. 14.95 (0-88101-271-8) Unicorn Pub.
—Robin Hood. 48p. (gr. 2-5). 1991. 6.95 (0-88101-110-X) Unicorn Pub.
—Robin Hood. McSpadden, J. Walker. 160p. 1991. 14.95 (0-88101-272-6) Unicorn Pub.
—Twas the Night Before Christmas: Includes Christmas Carols & The Nativity. 48p. 1985. 6.95 (0-88101-181-9) Unicorn Pub.
—Wizard of Oz. 48p. (gr. 2-5). 1992. 6.95 (0-88101-217-3) Unicorn Pub.
—Wizard of Oz. Baum, L. Frank. 160p. 1985. 14.95 (0-88101-273-4) Unicorn Pub.
Hildebrandt, Greg & Hildebrandt, Greg. Twas the Night Before Christmas: And Other Holiday Favorites. LC 90-10976. 48p. (gr. k-2). 1990. 4.95 (0-88101-103-7) Unicorn Pub.
Hildebrandt, Gregory. A Christmas Carol. Dickens, Charles. LC 85-15815. 128p. 1983. pap. 14.95 (0-671-45599-0, S&S BFYR) S&S Trade.
Hildebrandt, Mary. I'm a Little Teapot. 48p. (ps). 1993. 5.95 (0-88101-281-5) Unicorn Pub.
—Story of the Easter Bunny. 48p. (ps). 1993. 5.95 (0-88101-275-0) Unicorn Pub.
Hildebrandt, Tim. Shoemaker & the Christmas Elves. Hildebrandt, Tim & Laurence, Jim, eds. 1993. 6.99 (0-517-08488-0) Outlet Bk Co.
—The Unicorn Treasury: Stories, Poems & Unicorn Lore. Coville, Bruce, compiled by. LC 86-32919. 176p. (gr. 3 up). 1988. pap. 14.95 (0-385-24000-7) Doubleday.
Hildibrand. Reader's Digest Best Loved Books for Young Readers: Twenty Thousand Leagues under the Sea. Verne, Jules. Ogburn, Jackie, ed. 176p. (gr. 4-12). 1989. 3.99 (0-945260-29-6) Choice Pub NY.
Hill, Alison. Quickly, Quigley. Gravois, Jeanne M. LC 93-1990. 32p. 1994. 14.00 (0-688-13047-X, Tambourine Bks); PLB 13.93 (0-688-13048-8, Tambourine Bks) Morrow.
Hill, Darlene. Black Lizard's Startling Encounter. Hill, Chip. LC 91-16081. (gr. 4-9). 1991. 4.00 (0-915541-75-0) Star Bks Inc.
Hill, Dorothy. Mom, I Need Glasses. Wolff, Angelika. Saltzman, S. L., intro. by. LC 74-112648. (gr. k-3). 1971. PLB 12.95 (0-87460-139-8) Lion Bks.
Hill, Earl. Haiti Through Its Holidays. Telemaque, Eleanor W. LC 79-52858. 64p. (gr. 4-6). 1980. 8.50x (0-685-00779-0) Blyden Pr.
Hill, Eric. Donde Esta Spot? (Where's Spot?) Hill, Eric. (SPA.). 22p. (ps-2). 1983. 12.95 (0-399-21018-0, Putnam) Putnam Pub Group.
—Fourth Adventure of the S. S. Happiness Crew: Visit to a Magic Mountain. Dutton, June. 1983. 5.95 (0-915696-64-9) Determined Prods.
—My Very Own Spot Book: A Special Book to Fill in & Keep. Hill, Eric. 28p. (ps). 1993. 9.95 (0-399-22601-X, Putnam) Putnam Pub Group.
—La Primera Navidad de Spot. Hill, Eric. (SPA.). (ps-2). 1983. 12.95 (0-399-21024-5, Putnam) Putnam Pub Group.
—Spot at Play. Hill, Eric. LC 84-17848. 14p. (ps-1). 1985. bds. 3.95 (0-399-21228-0, Putnam) Putnam Pub Group.
—Spot at the Fair. Hill, Eric. LC 84-17849. 14p. (ps-1). 1985. 3.75 (0-399-21229-9, Putnam) Putnam Pub Group.
—Spot Counts from One to Ten. Hill, Eric. 14p. (ps-k). 1989. 3.95 (0-399-21672-3, Putnam) Putnam Pub Group.
—Spot Goes Splash! Hill, Eric. 8p. (gr. k-1). 1984. vinyl foam-filled 3.95 (0-399-21068-7, Putnam) Putnam Pub Group.
—Spot Goes to School. Hill, Eric. LC 84-42695. 22p. (ps-2). 1984. 11.95 (0-399-21073-3, Putnam) Putnam Pub Group.
—Spot Goes to the Circus. Hill, Eric. LC 85-24471. 22p. (ps). 1986. 11.95 (0-399-21317-1, Putnam) Putnam Pub Group.
—Spot Goes to the Park. Hill, Eric. 22p. 1991. 11.95 (0-399-21833-5, Putnam) Putnam Pub Group.
—Spot Learns to Count. Hill, Eric. (ps-2). 1983. 1.95 (0-399-20985-9, Putnam) Putnam Pub Group.
—Spot Looks at Colors. Hill, Eric. 14p. (ps-k). 1986. 3.95 (0-399-21349-X, Putnam) Putnam Pub Group.
—Spot Looks at Opposites. Hill, Eric. 14p. (ps-k). 1989. bds. 3.75 (0-399-21681-2, Putnam) Putnam Pub Group.
—Spot Looks at Shapes. Hill, Eric. 14p. (ps-1). 1986. 3.95 (0-399-21350-3, Putnam) Putnam Pub Group.
—Spot Looks at the Weather. Hill, Eric. 14p. (ps-k). 1989. bds. 3.75 (0-399-21673-1, Putnam) Putnam Pub Group.
—Spot on the Farm. Hill, Eric. LC 84-17850. 14p. (ps-1). 1985. 3.95 (0-399-21230-2, Putnam) Putnam Pub Group.
—Spot Va a la Circo (Spot Goes to the Circus) Hill, Eric. (SPA.). 22p. (ps). 1986. 11.95 (0-399-21318-X, Putnam) Putnam Pub Group.
—Spot's Alphabet. Hill, Eric. (ps-2). 1983. pap. 1.95 (0-399-20984-0, Putnam) Putnam Pub Group.
—Spot's Baby Sister: A Lift-the-Flap Book. Hill, Eric. 22p. (ps-k). 1989. 11.95 (0-399-21640-5, Putnam) Putnam Pub Group.

—Spot's Big Book of Words - El Libro Grande de las Palabras de Spot. Hill, Eric. (SPA & ENG.). 32p. (ps-1). 1989. 11.95 (0-399-21689-8, Putnam) Putnam Pub Group.
—Spot's Busy Year. Hill, Eric. (ps-2). 1983. pap. 1.95 (0-399-20987-5, Putnam) Putnam Pub Group.
—Spot's First Christmas. Hill, Eric. LC 82-23073. (ps-2). 1983. 11.95 (0-399-20963-8, Putnam) Putnam Pub Group.
—Spot's First Walk. Hill, Eric. 22p. (ps). 1981. 11.95 (0-399-20838-0, Putnam) Putnam Pub Group.
—Spot's First Words. Hill, Eric. 14p. 1986. 3.95 (0-399-21348-1, Putnam) Putnam Pub Group.
—Spot's Friends. Hill, Eric. 8p. (gr. k-1). 1984. vinyl foam-filled 3.95 (0-399-21066-0, Putnam) Putnam Pub Group.
—Spot's Toy Box. Hill, Eric. (ps-k). 1991. bds. 3.95 (0-399-21773-8) Putnam Pub Group.
—Spot's Toys. Hill, Eric. 8p. (gr. k-1). 1984. 3.95 (0-399-21067-9, Putnam) Putnam Pub Group.
—Spot's Walk in the Woods. Hill, Eric. 14p. (ps). 1993. 12.95 (0-399-22528-5, Philomel) Putnam Pub Group.
—Sweet Dreams, Spot! Hill, Eric. 8p. (gr. k-1). 1984. 3.95 (0-399-21069-5, Putnam) Putnam Pub Group.
—Where's Spot? A Lift-the-Flap Book Miniature Edition. Hill, Eric. 22p. (ps-k). 1990. 4.95 (0-399-21822-X, Putnam) Putnam Pub Group.
Hill, Francis. Red Wagons & White Canvas: Mollie Bailey, Circus Queen of the Southwest. Gurasich, Marjorie A. Roberts, Melissa, ed. 88p. (gr. 4-7). 1988. 10.95 (0-89015-646-8, Pub. by Panda Bks) Eakin-Sunbelt.
Hill, Frank. Rock-a-Bye Snoopy. Mendelson, Lee. 26p. (ps up). 1986. 12.95 (1-55578-011-3) Worlds Wonder.
—Snoopy & the Great Pumpkin. Mendelson, Lee. 26p. (ps up). 1986. 12.95 (1-55578-006-7) Worlds Wonder.
—Snoopy at the Dog Show. Mendelson, Lee. 26p. (ps up). 1986. 12.95 (1-55578-008-3) Worlds Wonder.
—Snoopy Goes Camping. Mendelson, Lee. 26p. (ps up). 1986. 12.95 (1-55578-002-4) Worlds Wonder.
—Snoopy Hits the Beach. Mendelson, Lee. 26p. (ps up). 1986. 12.95 (1-55578-004-0) Worlds Wonder.
—Snoopy, Spike & the Cat Next Door. Mendelson, Lee. 26p. (ps up). 1986. 12.95 (1-55578-010-5) Worlds Wonder.
—Snoopy's America. Mendelson, Lee. 26p. (ps up). 1986. 12.95 (1-55578-007-5) Worlds Wonder.
—Snoopy's Band. Mendelson, Lee. 26p. (ps up). 1986. 12.95 (1-55578-009-1) Worlds Wonder.
—Snoopy's Baseball Game. Mendelson, Lee. 26p. (ps up). 1986. 12.95 (1-55578-012-1) Worlds Wonder.
—Snoopy's Birthday Party. Mendelson, Lee. 26p. (ps up). 1986. 12.95 (1-55578-001-6) Worlds Wonder.
—Snoopy's Land of Make Believe. Mendelson, Lee. 26p. (ps up). 1986. 12.95 (1-55578-003-2) Worlds Wonder.
—Snoopy's Show & Tell. Mendelson, Lee. 26p. (ps up). 1986. 12.95 (1-55578-005-9) Worlds Wonder.
—Snoopy's Talent Show. Mendelson, Lee. 26p. (ps up). 1986. 12.95 (1-55578-000-8) Worlds Wonder.
Hill, Gerald, Jr. The Year of the Indians. Hill, Gerald N. 54p. (Orig.). (gr. 4-7). 1985. pap. 4.95 (0-912133-06-6) Hilltop Pub Co.
Hill, Jan C., jt. illus. see Hill, William E.
Hill, John. Exploring Information Technology. Hill, John. LC 92-28172. 48p. (gr. 4-8). 1992. PLB 19.92 (0-8114-2605-X) Raintree Steck-V.
Hill, Nicholas. Jane's Adventures In & Out of the Book. Gathorne-Hardy, Jonathan. LC 80-29185. 192p. (gr. 5 up). 1981. 13.95 (0-87951-122-2) Overlook Pr.
Hill, Patrick. The Black Fairy & Other Plays for Children. Perkins, Useni. LC 92-60054. 200p. (Orig.). 1993. pap. 13.95 (0-88378-077-1) Third World.
Hill, Sarah. Hopalong Purrsnickity. Beisel, Marvin. 192p. (Orig.). 1990. pap. 15.95 (0-9626309-0-X) HoppyTalk Prodns.
Hill, William E. & Hill, Jan C. Heading West: An Activity Book for Children. Hill, William E. & Hill, Jan C. 32p. (Orig.). (gr. k-4). 1992. pap. 3.95 (0-9636071-0-3) HillHouse Pub.
Hillam, Corbin. Ideas Combo Edition 37-40, 4 bks. in 1. Rice, Wayne & Thigpen, Paul, eds. 200p. (Orig.). 1990. pap. 19.95 (0-910125-34-1) Youth Special.
—Jennifer of the City. Hillam, Corbin. 32p. (ps-2). 1990. text ed. 5.00 (0-570-04183-X) Concordia.
—Jennifer of the Jungle. Hillam, Corbin. 32p. (ps-2). 1990. text ed. 5.00 (0-685-45916-0) Concordia.
Hillam, Corbin A. Sex: It's Worth Waiting For. Speck, Greg. (Orig.). 1989. pap. 6.99 (0-8024-7692-9) Moody.
Hillenbach, Patricia. Ringle & Dingle: Santa's Christmas Elves. Young, William E. 32p. (Orig.). 1991. pap. 5.95 (0-9628122-1-8) Pautuxet Pubns.
Hillenbrand, Will. Asher & the Capmakers: A Hanukkah Story. Kimmel, Eric A. LC 92-37978. 32p. (ps-3). 1993. reinforced bdg. 15.95 (0-8234-1031-5) Holiday.
—Awfully Short for the Fourth Grade. Woodruff, Elvira. LC 89-2082. 112p. (gr. 3-6). 1989. 13.95 (0-8234-0785-3) Holiday.
—Back in Action. Woodruff, Elvira. LC 91-2093. 160p. (gr. 3-7). 1991. 13.95 (0-8234-0897-3) Holiday.
—Go Ask Giorgio! Wittmann, Patricia. LC 91-2808. 32p. (gr. k-4). 1992. RSBE 14.95 (0-02-793221-4, Macmillan Child Bk) Macmillan Child Grp.
—I'm the Best. Sharmat, Marjorie W. LC 90-39176. 32p. (ps-3). 1991. reinforced 14.95 (0-8234-0859-0) Holiday.

—The King Who Tried to Fry an Egg on His Head. Ginsburg, Mirra. LC 91-10099. 32p. (gr. k-3). 1994. RSBE 14.95 (0-02-736242-6, Macmillan Child Bk) Macmillan Child Grp.
—The Magic Rocket. Kroll, Steven. LC 91-10114. 32p. (ps-3). 1992. reinforced bdg. 14.95 (0-8234-0916-3) Holiday.
—Moon Was Tired of Walking on Air. Belting, Natalia M. LC 91-20946. 48p. (gr. 4-7). 1992. 15.95 (0-395-53806-8) HM.
—Traveling to Tondo: A Tale of the Nkundo of Zaire. Aardema, Verna, retold by. LC 90-39419. 40p. (gr. k-4). 1991. 14.00 (0-679-80081-6); PLB 14.99 (0-679-90081-0) Knopf Bks Yng Read.
Hiller, Laurie L. Visions of Wonder. Hiller, Laurie L. 52p. (Orig.). (gr. 5-12). 1993. pap. text ed. 4.95 (0-9632332-0-3) Precision Pr.
Hilliard, Cindy & French, Marty. The Boy Who Wanted the Moon. Hernandez, Betsy, et al. 26p. (ps up). 1986. Book & Cassette. 7.95 (1-55578-100-4); cass. incl. Worlds Wonder.
Hilliard, Kristin. Harold, Bk. 3: You Are Special. Noffs, David & Noffs, Laurie. 24p. (Orig.). (gr. 3). 1987. wkbk. 2.50 (0-929875-04-4) Noffs Assocs.
Hilliard, Peg. Tym, the Turtle Boy. Roe, Cheryl. LC 89-51373. 40p. (Orig.). (gr. 2-5). 1990. pap. 9.95 (0-9624183-1-5) Timeless Sales.
—Tym, the Turtle Boy. Roe, Cheryl A. 52p. (Orig.). (ps-3). 1989. pap. write for info. (0-9624183-0-7) Timeless Sales.
Hillman, Carole D. It's Different Now...a New Beginning. Hillman, Carole D. 10p. (Orig.). 1990. pap. text ed. write for info. (0-9624257-1-0) Early Childhood.
—A Visit to the People Zoo. Schneider, David C. Scallon, Cheryl V., ed. LC 89-85637. 16p. (Orig.). (ps-1). 1989. pap. write for info. Early Childhood.
Hillman, Priscilla. Merry Mouse Christmas ABC. Hillman, Priscilla. LC 79-6586. 32p. (ps-1). 1980. pap. 4.95 (0-385-15596-4) Doubleday.
Hills, Alan, photos by. Bible Lands. Tubb, Jonathan. LC 91-2388. 64p. (gr. 5 up). 1991. 15.00 (0-679-81457-4); lib. bdg. 15.99 (0-679-91457-9) Knopf Bks Yng Read.
Hills, Stephen. Inspector Hare & the Black Pearls. Hills, Peter B. LC 93-28977. 1994. 4.25 (0-383-03751-4) SRA Schl Grp.
—Inspector Hare & the Locked Room. Hills, Peter B. LC 93-11734. 1994. 4.25 (0-383-03752-2) SRA Schl Grp.
Hilterbrand, Greg. Life Is Valuable. Klaus, Sandra. (gr. k-6). 1987. pap. 4.25 (1-55976-152-0) CEF Press.
Hilterbrand, Greg, jt. illus. see Butcher, Sam.
Hilty, Christi S. My Feelings. 2nd ed. Morgan, Marcia K. (ps-5). 1984. pap. text ed. 3.95 (0-930413-00-8, TX-1-361-947) Equal Just Con.
Himler, Ron. Eye Winker, Tom Tinker, Chin Chopper. Glazer, Tom. LC 72-97497. (ps-3). 1973. pap. 11.95 (0-385-08200-2, Zephyr) Doubleday.
Himler, Ronald. After the Goat Man. Byars, Betsy C. (gr. 3-7). 1982. pap. 3.95 (0-14-031533-0, Puffin) Puffin Bks.
—Animals of the Night. Banks, Merry. LC 89-6194. 32p. (ps-k). 1990. SBE 13.95 (0-684-19093-1, Scribners Young Read) Macmillan Child Grp.
—Baby, Come Out! Manushkin, Fran. LC 78-183159. 32p. (ps-3). 1984. pap. 3.95 (0-06-443050-2, Trophy) HarpC Child Bks.
—The Best Town in the World. Baylor, Byrd. LC 83-9033. 32p. (gr. 1-3). 1983. SBE 14.95 (0-684-18035-9, Scribners Young Read) Macmillan Child Grp.
—The Best Town in the World. Baylor, Byrd. LC 86-3381. 32p. (gr. 1-3). 1986. 3.95 (0-689-71086-0, Aladdin) Macmillan Child Grp.
—A Brand is Forever. Scott, Ann H. 48p. (gr. k-3). 1993. 12.95 (0-395-60118-5, Clarion Bks) HM.
—Coyote Dreams. Nunes, Susan. LC 87-30288. 32p. (ps-3). 1988. SBE 13.95 (0-689-31398-5, Atheneum Child Bk) Macmillan Child Grp.
—Coyote Dreams. Nunes, Susan. LC 93-22931. 32p. (gr. k-3). 1994. pap. 4.95 (0-689-71804-7, Aladdin) Macmillan Child Grp.
—Curly & the Wild Boar. Gipson, Fred. LC 77-25644. 96p. (gr. 5 up). 1979. HarpC Child Bks.
—Dakota Dugout. Turner, Ann. LC 85-3084. 32p. (gr. k-3). 1985. RSBE 13.95 (0-02-789700-1, Macmillan Child Bk) Macmillan Child Grp.
—Dakota Dugout. Turner, Ann. 32p. (ps-3). 1989. pap. 3.95 (0-689-71296-0, Aladdin) Macmillan Child Grp.
—Dancing on the Table. Murrow, Liza K. LC 89-46066. 128p. (gr. 3-7). 1990. 13.95 (0-8234-0808-6) Holiday.
—The Day It Rained Forever: A Story of the Johnstown Flood. Gross, Virginia T. 64p. (gr. 2-6). 1991. 11.95 (0-670-83552-8) Viking Child Bks.
—The Day It Rained Forever: The Story of the Johnstown Flood. Gross, Virginia T. LC 92-44712. 64p. (gr. 2-6). 1993. pap. 3.99 (0-14-034567-1, Puffin) Puffin Bks.
—A Day's Work. Bunting, Eve. 1995. write for info. (0-395-67321-6, Clarion Bks) HM.
—Earthquake! A Story of Old San Francisco. Kudlinski, Kathleen V. 64p. (gr. 2-6). 1993. RB 12.99 (0-670-84874-3) Viking Child Bks.
—Eli's Ghost. Hearne, Betsy G. LC 86-21096. 112p. (gr. 3-7). 1987. SBE 13.95 (0-689-50420-9, M K McElderry) Macmillan Child Grp.
—Fly Away Home. Bunting, Eve. Giblin, James, ed. 32p. (ps-2). 1991. 14.45 (0-395-55962-6, Clarion Bks) HM.
—Fly Away Home. Bunting, Eve. 32p. (gr. k-3). 1993. pap. 5.70 (0-395-66415-2, Clarion Bks) HM.

—George Washington. Hoobler, Dorothy & Hoobler, Thomas. Brook, Bonnie, ed. 32p. (gr. k-2). 1990. 6.95 (0-671-69114-7); PLB 10.98 (0-671-69108-2) Silver Pr.
—A Grass Green Gallop. Hubbell, Patricia. LC 89-36354. 48p. (gr. 4-8). 1990. SBE 14.95 (0-689-31604-6, Atheneum Child Bk) Macmillan Child Grp.
—I'm Going to Pet a Worm Today: And Other Poems. Levy, Constance. LC 91-7485. 48p. (gr. k-5). 1991. SBE 12.95 (0-689-50535-3, M K McElderry) Macmillan Child Grp.
—Janey. Zolotow, Charlotte. LC 72-9861. 24p. (ps-3). 1973. PLB 12.89 (0-06-026928-6) HarpC Child Bks.
—Joey's Way. Aver, Kate. LC 92-7830. 48p. (gr. 1-4). 1992. SBE 12.95 (0-689-50552-3, M K McElderry) Macmillan Child Grp.
—Katie's Trunk. Turner, Ann. LC 91-20409. 32p. (gr. k-3). 1992. RSBE 13.95 (0-02-789512-2, Macmillan Child Bk) Macmillan Child Grp.
—The King of Prussia & a Peanut Butter Sandwich. Fleming, Alice. LC 88-18244. 48p. (gr. 2-4). 1988. SBE 13.95 (0-684-18880-5, Scribners Young Read) Macmillan Child Grp.
—The Lily Cupboard. Oppenheim, Shulamith L. LC 90-38592. 32p. (gr. 1-3). 1992. 15.00 (0-06-024669-3); PLB 14.89 (0-06-024670-7) HarpC Child Bks.
—Lone Star: A Story of the Texas Rangers. Kudlinski, Kathleen V. 64p. (gr. 2-6). 1994. PLB 12.99 (0-670-85179-5) Viking Child Bks.
—Moon Song. Baylor, Byrd. LC 81-18427. 24p. (gr. 3-6). 1982. SBE 12.95 (0-684-17463-4, Scribners Young Read) Macmillan Child Grp.
—The Navajos: A First Americans Book. Sneve, Virginia Driving Hawk. LC 92-40330. 32p. (gr. 2-6). 1993. reinforced bdg. 15.95 (0-8234-1039-0) Holiday.
—Nettie's Trip South. Turner, Ann. LC 86-18135. 32p. (gr. 1-5). 1987. SBE 13.95 (0-02-789240-9, Macmillan Child Bk) Macmillan Child Grp.
—One Small Blue Bead. 2nd ed. Baylor, Byrd. LC 90-28160. 32p. (gr. 2-5). 1992. SBE 13.95 (0-684-19334-5, Scribners Young Read) Macmillan Child Grp.
—Pearl Harbor is Burning! A Story of World War II. Kudlinski, Kathleen V. LC 93-15135. 64p. (gr. 2-6). 1993. pap. 3.99 (0-14-034509-4, Puffin) Puffin Bks.
—Sadako & the Thousand Paper Cranes. Coerr, Eleanor B. LC 76-9872. (gr. 3-5). 1977. 14.95 (0-399-20520-9, Putnam) Putnam Pub Group.
—Sadako & the Thousand Paper Cranes. Coerr, Eleanor. 64p. (gr. 2-5). 1979. pap. 3.50 (0-440-47465-5, YB) Dell.
—The Seminoles. Sneve, Virginia D. LC 93-14316. 32p. (gr. 7-11). 1994. 15.95 (0-8234-1112-5) Holiday.
—The Sioux: A First American's Book. Sneve, Virginia D. LC 92-23946. 32p. (gr. 2-6). 1993. reinforced bdg. 15.95 (0-8234-1017-X) Holiday.
—Someday a Tree. Bunting, Eve. LC 92-24074. 32p. (gr. k-3). 1993. 14.45 (0-395-61309-4, Clarion Bks) HM.
—Someday Rider. Scott, Ann H. LC 88-35255. 32p. (ps-1). 1989. 13.45 (0-89919-792-2, Clarion Bks) HM.
—Someday Rider. Scott, Ann H. 32p. (ps-3). 1991. pap. 4.95 (0-395-58115-X, Clarion Bks) HM.
—Trouble for Lucy. Stevens, Carla. LC 79-10445. 80p. (gr. 3-6). 1987. pap. 3.95 (0-89919-523-7, Clarion Bks) HM.
—The Wall. Bunting, Eve. 32p. (ps-3). 1990. 14.45 (0-395-51588-2, Clarion Bks) HM.
—Winter Holiday Spring. Dragonwagon, Crescent. LC 88-13747. 32p. (gr. 2-5). 1990. RSBE 11.95 (0-02-733122-9, Macmillan Child Bk) Macmillan Child Grp.

Himmelman, John. Buzby. Hoban, Julia. LC 89-29408. 64p. (gr. k-3). 1990. PLB 11.89 (0-06-022398-7) HarpC Child Bks.
—Buzby. Hoban, Julia. LC 89-29408. 64p. (gr. k-3). 1992. pap. 3.50 (0-06-444152-0, Trophy) HarpC Child Bks.
—Buzby to the Rescue. Hoban, Julia. LC 91-46085. 64p. (gr. k-3). 1993. 14.00 (0-06-021025-7); PLB 13.89 (0-06-021024-9) HarpC Child Bks.
—Charlotte Shakespeare & Annie the Great. Holmes, Barbara W. LC 89-2037. 160p. (gr. 4-6). 1989. PLB 13.89 (0-06-022615-3) HarpC Child Bks.
—Charlotte Shakespeare & Annie the Great. Holmes, Barbara W. LC 89-2037. 160p. (gr. 4-6). 1991. pap. 3.95 (0-06-440385-8, Trophy) HarpC Child Bks.
—The Clover County Carrot Contest. Himmelman, John. 48p. (ps-3). 1991. PLB 8.98 (0-671-69637-8); pap. 3.95 (0-671-69641-6) Silver Pr.
—The Day-Off Machine. Himmelman, John. Brook, Bonnie, ed. 48p. (ps-3). 1990. PLB 8.98 (0-671-69635-1); pap. 3.95 (0-671-69639-4) Silver Pr.
—Fix-It Family Series, 4 vols. Himmelman, John. 192p. (ps-3). 1991. Set. PLB 35.92 (0-671-31232-4); Set. PLB 26.94x pap. (0-685-46993-X); Set. pap. 15.80 (0-671-31233-2) Silver Pr.
—Go to Sleep, Nicholas Joe. Sharmat, Marjorie W. LC 85-45689. 32p. (ps-3). 1988. PLB 11.89 (0-06-025504-8) HarpC Child Bks.
—The Great Leaf Blast-Off. Himmelman, John. Brook, Bonnie, ed. 48p. (ps-3). 1990. PLB 8.98 (0-671-69634-3); pap. 3.95 (0-671-69638-6) Silver Pr.
—A Guest Is a Guest. Himmelman, John. LC 90-43020. 32p. (ps-2). 1991. 13.95 (0-525-44720-2, DCB) Dutton Child Bks.
—Hanukkah Lights, Hanukkah Nights. Kimmelman, Leslie. LC 91-15633. 32p. (ps-k). 1992. 12.00 (0-06-020368-4); PLB 11.89 (0-06-020369-2) HarpC Child Bks.

—Rainboots for Breakfast. Leonard, Marcia. Brook, Bonnie, ed. 24p. (ps-1). 1989. 5.95 (0-671-68591-0); PLB 9.98 (0-671-68587-2) Silver Pr.
—Shopping for Snowflakes. Leonard, Marcia. Brook, Bonnie, ed. 24p. (ps-1). 1989. 5.95 (0-671-68594-5); PLB 9.98 (0-671-68590-2) Silver Pr.
—Snuggle Piggy & the Magic Blanket. Stepto, Michele. LC 86-23943. 24p. (ps-k). 1990. pap. 3.95 (0-525-44609-5, DCB) Dutton Child Bks.
—The Super Camper Caper. Himmelman, John. 48p. (ps-3). 1991. PLB 8.98 (0-671-69636-X); pap. 3.95 (0-671-69640-8) Silver Pr.
—The Ups & Downs of Simpson Snail. Himmelman, John. LC 89-30547. 48p. (ps-3). 1989. 9.95 (0-525-44542-0, DCB) Dutton Child Bks.
—Young Christopher Columbus: Discoverer of the New Worlds. Carpenter, Eric. LC 91-24975. 32p. (gr. k-2). 1992. PLB 11.59 (0-8167-2526-8); pap. text ed. 2.95 (0-8167-2527-6) Troll Assocs.
—Young George Washington: America's First President. Woods, Andrew. LC 91-26405. 32p. (gr. k-2). 1992. PLB 11.59 (0-8167-2540-3); pap. text ed. 2.95 (0-8167-2541-1) Troll Assocs.

Himmelman, John & Wallner, John. What Next, 4 bks. Leonard, Marcia. (ps-1). 1990. Set, 24p. ea. 19.80 (0-671-94102-X, J Messner); Set, 24p. ea. lib. bdg. 39. 92 (0-671-94101-1) S&S Trade.

Himmelstein, Virginia. Project Funny Bone. Fern, Tami L. 40p. (gr. 3-6). 1990. pap. 9.95 (0-936386-56-8) Creative Learning.

Hinchberger, William D. My Playbook, One, Bk. 4. Shapiro, Mary S. 12p. (ps-k). 1985. wkbk. 3.95x (0-934361-04-5) Kinder Read.

Hinchberger, William D. & Hron, Debi. Learn-to-Read. Shapiro, Mary F. 52p. (ps-k). 1986. 15.99 (0-934361-11-8) Kinder Read.

Hinds, Bill. Buzz Beamer's Radical Olympics. Hinds, Bill. 32p. (gr. 3-7). 1992. pap. 4.95 (0-316-36452-5, Spts Illus Kids) Little.

Hine, Lewis, photos by. Kids at Work: Lewis Hine & the Crusade Against Child Labor. Freedman, Russell. LC 93-5989. Date not set. write for info. (0-395-58703-4, Clarion Bks) HM.

Hiner, Stewart. I Am a Gift! Kopelman, Yvonne A. Auld-Lonie, Margaret, ed. (Orig.). (ps-k). 1993. pap. 7.95 (1-883976-00-6) I Am The Power.
—I Have the Power of Choice! Kopelman, Yvonne A. Auld-Lonie, Margaret, ed. (gr. 9-12). 1993. pap. 7.95 (1-883976-75-8) I Am The Power.

Hiner, Stuart. I Am Feeling! Kopelman, Yvonne A. Auld-Lonie, Margaret, ed. (Orig.). (gr. 1-5). 1993. pap. 7.95 (1-883976-26-X) I Am The Power.
—I Am Who I Am & I Love It! Kopelman, Yvonne A. Auld-Lonie, Margaret, ed. (Orig.). (gr. 5-8). 1993. pap. 7.95 (1-883976-50-2) I Am The Power.

Hines, Anna C. Maybe a Band-Aid Will Help. Hines, Anna C. LC 84-1533. 24p. (ps-1). 1984. 8.95 (0-525-44115-8, 0869-260, DCB) Dutton Child Bks.

Hines, Anna G. Come to the Meadow. Hines, Anna G. LC 83-14408. 32p. (ps-3). 1984. 12.95 (0-89919-227-0, Clarion Bks) Hm.
—Daddy Makes the Best Spaghetti. Hines, Anna G. LC 85-13993. (ps-1). 1986. 13.45 (0-89919-388-9, Clarion Bks) HM.
—Daddy Makes the Best Spaghetti. Hines, Anna G. LC 85-13993. (ps-1). 1988. pap. 4.95 (0-89919-794-9, Clarion Bks) HM.
—The Day of the High Climber. Hines, Gary. LC 93-12254. 32p. (ps up). 1993. write for info. (0-688-11494-6); PLB write for info. (0-688-11495-4) Greenwillow.
—Flying Firefighters. Hines, Gary. LC 92-35500. 1993. 14.95 (0-395-61197-0, Clarion Bks) HM.
—Grandma Gets Grumpy. Hines, Anna G. LC 87-17874. (ps-1). 1988. 13.95 (0-89919-529-6, Clarion Bks) HM.
—Grandma Gets Grumpy. Hines, Anna G. LC 87-17874. 32p. (ps). 1990. pap. 4.80 (0-395-52595-0) HM.
—The Greatest Picnic in the World. Hines, Anna G. Giblin, James, ed. 32p. 1991. 13.45 (0-395-55266-4, Clarion Bks) HM.
—I'll Tell You What They Say. Hines, Anna G. LC 86-4743. 24p. (ps-1). 1987. 11.75 (0-688-06486-8); PLB 11.88 (0-688-06487-6) Greenwillow.
—It's Just Me, Emily. Hines, Anna G. (ps-1). 1987. 12.95 (0-89919-487-7, Clarion Bks) HM.
—Moompa, Toby, & Bomp. Hines, Anna G. LC 92-5667. 32p. (ps-1). 1993. 14.95 (0-395-61301-9, Clarion Bks) HM.
—Moon's Wish. Hines, Anna G. 32p. (ps-1). 1992. 14.45 (0-395-58114-1, Clarion Bks) HM.
—Remember the Butterflies. Hines, Anna G. LC 90-3536. 32p. (ps-2). 1991. 12.95 (0-525-44679-6, DCB) Dutton Child Bks.
—A Ride in the Crummy. Hines, Gary. LC 90-30848. 24p. (ps up). 1991. 13.95 (0-688-09691-3); PLB 13.88 (0-688-09692-1) Greenwillow.

Hines, Bob. Samson: Last of the California Grizzlies. McClung, Robert M. LC 91-33350. 96p. (gr. 3-6). 1992. Repr. of 1973 ed. lib. bdg. 15.00 (0-208-02327-5, Pub. by Linnet) Shoe String.
—Thor, the Last of the Sperm Whales. McClung, Robert M. LC 87-26090. 64p. (gr. 3-7). 1988. Repr. of 1971 ed. PLB 15.00 (0-208-02186-8, Linnet) Shoe String.

Hinke, George. Christmas Memories: A Journal & Photographic Record Book. 48p. 1993. 17.95 (0-8249-8567-2, Ideals Child) Hambleton-Hill.

—Jolly Old Santa Claus. Ideals Staff. 24p. (gr. k-6). 1985. pap. 2.95 (0-89542-448-7, Ideals Child) Hambleton-Hill.

Hinkle, Janet W. Tail Waggings of Maggie. Baender, Margaret W. 64p. (gr. 8-10). 1982. pap. 6.00x (0-88100-012-4) Philmar Pub.

Hinklicky, G. The Captive Sultan. Teichman, Avigail. Reinman, Y. Y., ed. LC 85-72403. 128p. (gr. 7-11). 1985. 7.95 (0-935063-12-9); pap. 5.95 (0-935063-04-8) CIS Comm.
—Twilight. Gold, Avner. Reinman, Y. Y., ed. LC 85-72404. 128p. (gr. 7-11). 1985. 9.95 (0-935063-11-0); pap. 7.95 (0-935063-03-X) CIS Comm.

Hinlickey, G. A Time to Live. Rubin, Chana S. 269p. (gr. 9-12). 1988. 14.95 (0-935063-48-X) CIS Comm.

Hinlicky, G. The Dream. Gold, Avner. Reinman, Y. Y., ed. 112p. (gr. 7-11). 1983. pap. 7.95 (0-935063-01-3) CIS Comm.
—The Promised Child. Gold, Avner. Reinman, Y. Y., ed. LC 85-72493. 128p. (gr. 7-11). 1985. 9.95 (0-935063-10-2); pap. 7.95 (0-935063-00-5) CIS Comm.
—The Year of the Sword. Gold, Avner. Reinman, Y. Y., ed. 112p. (gr. 5 up). 1984. 7.95 (0-935063-02-1) CIS Comm.

Hinlicky, Gregg. The Camel Boy. Revich, S. J. 158p. (gr. 5-8). 1987. 9.95 (0-935063-44-7); pap. 7.95 (0-935063-45-5) CIS Comm.
—Ezra the Physician. Revich, S. J. 126p. (gr. 5-7). 1988. 9.95 (0-935063-63-3); pap. 7.95 (0-935063-64-1) CIS Comm.
—A Face at the Window. Gottesman, Meir U. 140p. (gr. 6-8). 1990. 10.95 (1-56062-017-X); pap. 7.95 (1-56062-018-8) CIS Comm.
—Heir to the Throne. Rothsteis, Shmuel. LC 90-83945. 224p. (gr. 5-8). 1990. 13.95 (1-56062-043-9); pap. 10.95 (1-56062-044-7) CIS Comm.
—Ibrahim the Magician. Revich, S. J. 126p. (gr. 4-7). 1987. 9.95 (0-935063-33-1); pap. 7.95 (0-935063-34-X) CIS Comm.
—The Marrano Prince. Gold, Auner. 286p. (gr. 9-12). 1988. 13.95 (0-935063-39-0); text ed. 10.95 (0-935063-40-4) CIS Comm.
—The Missing Crown. Ben-Uri, Galila. 223p. (gr. 5-7). 1988. 13.95 (0-935063-41-2); pap. 8.95 (0-935063-42-0) CIS Comm.
—The Mysterious Cargo. Ben-Uri, Galila. 285p. (gr. 5-7). 1989. 13.95 (1-56062-006-4); pap. 10.95 (1-56062-007-2) CIS Comm.
—The Poet & the Thief. Revich, S. J. 158p. (gr. 5-7). 1989. 10.95 (0-935063-71-4); pap. 7.95 (0-935063-72-2) CIS Comm.
—The Purple Ring. Gold, Auner. 191p. (gr. 9-12). 1986. 10.95 (0-935063-16-1); pap. 8.95 (0-935063-15-3) CIS Comm.

Hinman, Jim. Selections from Sharing the Season, Vol. 2. Line, Lorie. Maybery, Paul, ed. 36p. 1993. pap. text ed. 9.95 (0-9638000-0-0) Time Line Prods.

Hinter, Ronald. Edith Herself. Howard, Ellen. LC 86-10826. 144p. (gr. 3-7). 1987. SBE 13.95 (0-689-31314-4, Atheneum Child Bk) Macmillan Child Grp.

Hinton, Sam. Common Seashore Life of Southern California. Hedgpeth, Joel. 64p. (gr. 4 up). 1961. 14.95 (0-911010-63-7); pap. 6.95 (0-911010-62-9) Naturegraph.

Hirashima, Jean. Grandma's Jewelry Box. Milstein, Linda. LC 91-66738. 24p. (ps-3). 1992. 8.00 (0-679-81973-8) Random Bks Yng Read.
—The Little Noisy Book. Ross, Katharine. LC 88-62100. 28p. (ps). 1989. bds. 2.95 (0-394-82907-7) Random Bks Yng Read.
—The Little Quiet Book. Ross, Katharine. LC 88-62101. 28p. (ps). 1989. bds. 2.95 (0-394-82899-2) Random Bks Yng Read.
—The Night Before Christmas. Moore, Clement C. LC 92-27138. 32p. (ps-3). 1993. pap. 2.25 (0-448-40482-6, G&D) Putnam Pub Group.
—Wee Mouse's Peekaboo House. LC 89-64279. 14p. (ps). 1991. bds. 3.99 (0-679-80786-1) Random Bks Yng Read.

Hirokazu Miyazaki. Croc & the Baby Tree. Hirokazu Miyazaki. Clements, Andrew, adapted by. LC 91-41719. 28p. (gr. k up). 1993. Repr. of 1990 ed. 14.95 (0-88708-224-6) Picture Bk Studio.

Hirsch, Lynn A. Count With Me: One, Two, Three. 32p. (ps-k). 1992. 4.99 (0-517-07395-1, Pub. by Derrydale Bks) Outlet Bk Co.
—Do You Know Where I Am? Hirsch, Lynn. LC 92-11189. 1992. 4.99 (0-517-07394-3, Pub. by Derrydale Bks) Outlet Bk Co.
—Have You Met the Alphabet? 32p. (ps-k). 1992. 4.99 (0-517-07393-5, Pub. by Derrydale Bks) Outlet Bk Co.

Hirsh, Marilyn. Best of K'tonton. Weilerstein, Sadie R. LC 80-20177. 96p. (gr. 1 up). 1980. pap. 9.95 (0-8276-0187-5) JPS Phila.
—I Love Hanukkah. Hirsh, Marilyn. LC 84-497. 32p. (ps-3). 1984. reinforced bdg. 13.95 (0-8234-0525-7); pap. 5.95 (0-8234-0622-9) Holiday.
—I Love Hanukkah. Hirsh, Marilyn. (gr. k-3). 1989. incl. cass. 19.95 (0-87499-131-5); pap. 12.95 incl. cass. (0-87499-130-7); Set; incl. 4 bks., cass., & guide. pap. 27.95 (0-87499-132-3) Live Oak Media.
—K'tonton in the Circus: A Hanukkah Adventure. Weilerstein, Sadie R. LC 81-11765. 96p. (gr. 2 up). pap. 8.95 (0-8276-0303-7) JPS Phila.

Hiscock, Bruce. The Big Rock. Hiscock, Bruce. LC 87-31834. 32p. (gr. 1-5). 1988. RSBE 13.95 (0-689-31402-7, Atheneum Child Bk) Macmillan Child Grp.
—The Big Storm. Hiscock, Bruce. LC 92-13973. 32p. (gr. 1-5). 1993. SBE 14.95 (0-689-31770-0, Atheneum Child Bk) Macmillan Child Grp.
—The Big Tree. Hiscock, Bruce. LC 89-18286. 32p. (gr. 1-5). 1991. RSBE 13.95 (0-689-31598-8, Atheneum Child Bk) Macmillan Child Grp.
—The Big Tree. Hiscock, Bruce. LC 93-25564. 32p. (gr. 1-5). 1994. pap. 4.95 (0-689-71803-9, Aladdin) Macmillan Child Grp.
—From Quarks to Quasars: A Tour of the Universe. Jespersen, James & Fitz-Randolph, Jane. LC 86-17276. 224p. (gr. 7 up). 1987. SBE 16.95 (0-689-31270-9, Atheneum Child Bk) Macmillan Child Grp.
—Looking at the Invisible Universe. Jespersen, James & Fitz-Randolph, Jane. LC 89-14998. 160p. (gr. 7 up). 1990. SBE 13.95 (0-689-31457-4, Atheneum Child Bk) Macmillan Child Grp.
—Scavengers & Decomposers: The Cleanup Crew. Hughey, Pat. LC 83-17474. 64p. (gr. 4-6). 1984. SBE 13.95 (0-689-31032-3, Atheneum Child Bk) Macmillan Child Grp.
—Tundra: The Arctic Land. Hiscock, Bruce. LC 85-28769. 144p. (gr. 3 up). 1986. SBE 13.95 (0-689-31219-9, Atheneum Child Bk) Macmillan Child Grp.
—Understanding Radioactivity. Milne, Lorus J. & Milne, Margery. LC 88-7382. 80p. (gr. 4 up). 1989. SBE 13.95 (0-689-31362-4, Atheneum Child Bk) Macmillan Child Grp.
Hissey, Jane. Best Friends: More Old Bear Tales. Hissey, Jane. 80p. (ps-3). 1989. 16.95 (0-399-21674-X, Philomel Bks) Putnam Pub Group.
—Jane Hissey Little Bear & Book Set. Hissey, Jane. 12p. (ps). 1993. bds. 16.00 (0-679-84762-6) Random Bks Yng Read.
—Little Bear Lost. Hissey, Jane. 32p. (ps-1). 1989. 14.95 (0-399-21743-6, Philomel Bks) Putnam Pub Group.
—Little Bear's Bedtime. Hissey, Jane. 12p. (ps). 1993. bds. 3.99 (0-679-84176-8) Random Bks Yng Read.
—Little Bear's Day. Hissey, Jane. LC 92-64017. 12p. (ps). 1993. bds. 3.99 (0-679-84175-X) Random Bks Yng Read.
—Old Bear. Hissey, Jane. 32p. (ps-3). 1989. pap. 5.95 (0-399-22015-1, Sandcastle Bks, Sandcastle Bks) Putnam Pub Group.
—Old Bear Tales. Hissey, Jane. LC 88-14155. 80p. 1988. 16.95 (0-399-21642-1, Philomel Bks) Putnam Pub Group.
Hnizdovsky, Jacques. Behind the King's Kitchen Door. Smith, William J. & Ra, Carol, eds. LC 91-66056. 56p. (gr. 5 up). 1992. 18.95 (1-56397-024-4, Wordsong) Boyds Mills Pr.
—Birds & Beasts. Smith, William J. (gr. k up). 1990. 18. 95 (0-87923-865-8) Godine.
Ho, Tien. Velveteen Rabbit. Williams, Margery. Klimo, Kate, ed. 48p. 1983. pap. 8.95 (0-671-44498-0) S&S Trade.
Hoban, Brom. Hanukkah: Eight Nights, Eight Lights. Drucker, Malka. LC 80-15852. 96p. (gr. 4 up). 1980. reinforced bdg. 14.95 (0-8234-0377-7) Holiday.
—Introduction to Kings, Later Prophets & Writings, Vol. 3. Newman, Shirley. Rossel, Seymour, ed. 160p. (Orig.). (gr. 4-5). 1981. pap. text ed. 6.95x (0-87441-336-2); wkbk. by Morris Sugarman 3.95 (0-685-00733-2); tchr's ed. 14.95x (0-685-41994-0) Behrman.
Hoban, Lillian. Amy Loves the Rain. Hoban, Julia. LC 88-45851. 32p. (ps). 1989. PLB 9.89 (0-06-022358-8) HarpC Child Bks.
—Amy Loves the Rain. Hoban, Julia. LC 87-45851. 24p. (ps). 1993. pap. 3.95 (0-06-443293-9, Trophy) HarpC Child Bks.
—Amy Loves the Snow. Hoban, Julia. LC 76-45852. 24p. (ps). 1989. PLB 10.89 (0-06-022395-2) HarpC Child Bks.
—Amy Loves the Snow. Hoban, Julia. LC 87-45852. 24p. (ps). 1993. pap. 3.95 (0-06-443294-7, Trophy) HarpC Child Bks.
—Amy Loves the Wind. Hoban, Julia. LC 87-45986. 24p. (ps). 1988. PLB 9.89 (0-06-022403-7) HarpC Child Bks.
—Arthur's Camp-Out. Hoban, Lillian. LC 91-27528. 64p. (gr. k-3). 1993. 13.00 (0-06-020525-3); PLB 13.89 (0-06-020526-1) HarpC Child Bks.
—Arthur's Christmas Cookies. Hoban, Lillian. LC 72-76596. 64p. (gr. k-3). 1986. incl. cassette 5.98 (0-694-00160-0, Trophy); pap. 3.50 (0-06-444055-9, Trophy) HarpC Child Bks.
—Arthur's Funny Money. Hoban, Lillian. LC 80-7903. 64p. (gr. k-3). 1981. PLB 13.89 (0-06-022344-8) HarpC Child Bks.
—Arthur's Funny Money. Hoban, Lillian. LC 80-7903. 64p. (gr. k-3). 1987. incl. cassette 5.98 (0-694-00173-2, Trophy); pap. 3.50 (0-06-444048-6, Trophy) HarpC Child Bks.
—Arthur's Great Big Valentine. Hoban, Lillian. LC 88-21202. 64p. (gr. k-3). 1989. PLB 13.89 (0-06-022407-X) HarpC Child Bks.
—Arthur's Great Big Valentine. Hoban, Lillian. LC 88-21202. 64p. (gr. k-3). 1991. pap. 3.50 (0-06-444149-0, Trophy) HarpC Child Bks.

—Arthur's Honey Bear. Hoban, Lillian. LC 73-14325. 64p. (gr. k-3). 1974. 14.00 (0-06-022369-3); PLB 13. 89 (0-06-022370-7) HarpC Child Bks.
—Arthur's Honey Bear. Hoban, Lillian. LC 73-14324. 64p. (gr. k-3). 1986. incl. cassette 5.98 (0-694-00116-3, Trophy); pap. 3.50 (0-06-444033-8, Trophy) HarpC Child Bks.
—Arthur's Loose Tooth. Hoban, Lillian. LC 85-42611. 64p. (ps-3). 1985. PLB 13.89 (0-06-022354-5) HarpC Child Bks.
—Arthur's Loose Tooth. Hoban, Lillian. LC 85-42611. 64p. (gr. k-3). 1987. pap. 3.50 (0-06-444093-1, Trophy) HarpC Child Bks.
—Arthur's Pen Pal. Hoban, Lillian. LC 75-6289. 64p. (gr. k-3). 1976. PLB 13.89 (0-06-022372-3) HarpC Child Bks.
—Arthur's Pen Pal. Hoban, Lillian. 32p. (ps-2). 1990. pap. 6.95 (0-00-004236-6, Caedmon) HarperAudio.
—Arthur's Prize Reader. Hoban, Lillian. LC 77-25637. 64p. (ps-3). 1978. PLB 13.89 (0-06-022380-4) HarpC Child Bks.
—Attila the Angry. Sharmat, Marjorie W. LC 84-15860. 32p. (ps-3). 1985. reinforced bdg. 11.95 (0-8234-0545-1) Holiday.
—Baby Sister for Frances. newly illust. ed. Hoban, Russell. LC 92-32603. 32p. (ps-3). 1964. 15.00 (0-06-022335-9); PLB 14.89 (0-06-022336-7) HarpC Child Bks.
—A Baby Sister for Frances. newly illustrated ed. Hoban, Russell. LC 92-32603. 32p. (ps-3). 1976. pap. 4.95 (0-06-443006-5, Trophy) HarpC Child Bks.
—The Balancing Girl. Rabe, Berniece. LC 80-22100. (ps-2). 1981. 12.95 (0-525-26160-5, 0995-300, DCB) Dutton Child Bks.
—The Balancing Girl. Rabe, Berniece. LC 80-22100. 32p. (ps-2). 1988. pap. 4.99 (0-525-44364-9, 0382-120, DCB) Dutton Child Bks.
—Bargain for Frances. newly illus. ed. Hoban, Russell. LC 91-12265. 64p. (gr. k-3). 1970. 13.00 (0-06-022329-4); PLB 12.89 (0-06-022330-8) HarpC Child Bks.
—A Bargain for Frances. newly illus. ed. Hoban, Russell. LC 91-12267. 64p. (gr. k-3). 1978. pap. 3.50 (0-06-444001-X, Trophy) HarpC Child Bks.
—Bee My Valentine. Cohen, Miriam. LC 77-21950. 32p. (gr. k-3). 1978. PLB 11.88 (0-688-84129-5) Greenwillow.
—Bee My Valentine! Cohen, Miriam. (gr. k-3). 1983. pap. 2.95 (0-440-40507-6, YB) Dell.
—Best Friends. Cohen, Miriam. LC 70-146620. 32p. (ps-1). 1971. RSBE 13.95 (0-02-722800-2, Macmillan Child Bk) Macmillan Child Grp.
—Best Friends. Cohen, Miriam. 32p. (ps-1). 1989. pap. 3.95 (0-689-71334-7, Aladdin) Macmillan Child Grp.
—Best Friends for Frances. Hoban, Russell. LC 71-77935. 32p. (ps-3). 1969. 14.00 (0-06-022327-8); PLB 13.89 (0-06-022328-6) HarpC Child Bks.
—Best Friends for Frances. Hoban, Russell. LC 71-77935. 32p. (ps-3). 1976. pap. 4.95 (0-06-443008-1, Trophy) HarpC Child Bks.
—The Big Hello. Schulman, Janet. LC 91-4). 1980. pap. 1.95 (0-440-40484-3, YB) Dell.
—The Big Hello. Schulman, Janet. LC 75-33672. (gr. 1-4). 1976. 13.95 (0-688-80036-X) Greenwillow.
—Birthday for Frances. Hoban, Russell. LC 68-24321. 32p. (gr. k-3). 1968. 14.00 (0-06-022338-3); PLB 13. 89 (0-06-022339-1) HarpC Child Bks.
—A Birthday for Frances. Hoban, Russell. LC 68-24321. (ps-2). 1976. pap. 4.95 (0-06-443007-3, Trophy) HarpC Child Bks.
—Bread & Jam for Frances. newly illus. ed. Hoban, Russell. LC 92-13622. 32p. (ps-3). 1965. 15.00 (0-06-022359-6); PLB 14.89 (0-06-022360-X) HarpC Child Bks.
—Bread & Jam for Frances. newly illustrated ed. Hoban, Russell. LC 92-13622. 32p. (ps-3). 1986. pap. 4.95 (0-06-443096-0, Trophy) HarpC Child Bks.
—Bread & Jam for Frances: Big Book. Hoban, Russell. LC 92-13622. 32p. (ps-3). 1993. pap. 19.95 (0-06-443336-6, Trophy) HarpC Child Bks.
—Busybody Nora. Hurwitz, Johanna. LC 89-13649. 64p. (ps up). 1990. Repr. of 1976 ed. 12.95 (0-688-09202-3); PLB 12.88 (0-688-09093-1, Morrow Jr Bks) Morrow Jr Bks.
—Busybody Nora. Hurwitz, Johanna. 64p. (gr. 2-5). 1991. pap. 3.99 (0-14-034592-2, Puffin) Puffin Bks.
—Caps, Hats, Socks, & Mittens: A Book about the Four Seasons. Borden, Louise. 1992. pap. 3.95 (0-590-44872-2, Blue Ribbon Bks) Scholastic Inc.
—The Case of the Two Masked Robbers. Hoban, Lillian. LC 85-45819. 64p. (gr. k-3). 1988. pap. 3.50 (0-06-444121-0, Trophy) HarpC Child Bks.
—The Day the Teacher Went Bananas. Howe, James. LC 84-1536. 32p. (ps-2). 1984. 12.95 (0-525-44107-7, DCB); pap. 3.95 (0-525-44321-5, DCB) Dutton Child Bks.
—Don't Eat Too Much Turkey! Cohen, Miriam. LC 86-25660. 32p. (gr. k-3). 1987. 15.00 (0-688-07141-4); lib. bdg. 14.93 (0-688-07142-2) Greenwillow.
—E is for Elisa. Hurwitz, Johanna. LC 91-159. 80p. (ps up). 1991. 12.95 (0-688-10439-8); PLB 12.88 (0-688-10440-1) Morrow Jr Bks.
—E Is for Elisa. Hurwitz, Johanna. LC 92-26796. 96p. (gr. 2-5). 1993. pap. 3.99 (0-14-036033-6) Puffin Bks.
—The Easter Cat. DeJong, Meindert. LC 90-24407. 128p. (gr. 3-7). 1991. pap. 3.95 (0-689-71468-8, Aladdin) Macmillan Child Grp.

—Egg Thoughts & Other Frances Songs. Hoban, Russell. LC 70-183162. 32p. (ps-3). 1972. 12.95 (0-06-022331-6); PLB 12.89 (0-06-022332-4) HarpC Child Bks.
—First Grade Takes a Test. Cohen, Miriam. (gr. k-3). 1983. pap. 2.95 (0-440-42500-X, YB) Dell.
—The Great Big Dummy. Schulman, Janet. 32p. (gr. 1-3). 1961. pap. 2.50 (0-440-43072-0, YB) Dell.
—I Know Everything about John & He Knows Everything about Me. Fitzhugh, Louise. LC 92-28028. 1993. 13.95 (0-385-30802-7) Doubleday.
—I'm Gonna Tell Mama I Want an Iguana. Johnston, Tony. 32p. (ps-3). 1990. 14.95 (0-399-21934-X, Putnam) Putnam Pub Group.
—It's George! Cohen, Miriam. 24p. (ps-3). 1988. 11.95 (0-688-06812-X); lib. bdg. 11.88 (0-688-06813-8) Greenwillow.
—Jim's Dog Muffins. Cohen, Miriam. LC 83-14090. 32p. (gr. k-3). 1984. 13.95 (0-688-02564-1); PLB 13.88 (0-688-02565-X) Greenwillow.
—The Laziest Robot in Zone One. Hoban, Lillian & Hoban, Phoebe. LC 82-48613. 64p. (gr. k-3). 1983. PLB 12.89 (0-06-022352-9) HarpC Child Bks.
—The Laziest Robot in Zone One. Hoban, Lillian & Hoban, Phoebe. LC 82-48613. 64p. (gr. k-3). 1985. pap. 3.50 (0-06-444089-3, Trophy) HarpC Child Bks.
—Like Me & You. Raffi. LC 93-9840. 1994. 13.00 (0-517-59587-7, Crown); lib. bdg. 13.99 (0-517-59588-5, Crown) Crown Pub Group.
—Lost in the Museum. Cohen, Miriam. (gr. k-3). 1983. pap. 2.95 (0-440-44780-1, YB) Dell.
—Make Room for Elisa. Hurwitz, Johanna. LC 92-45864. 80p. (gr. k up). 1993. lib. bdg. 13.93 (0-688-12429-1, Pub. by Beech Tree Bks) Morrow.
—Make Room for Elisa. Hurwitz, Johanna. LC 92-45864. 80p. (gr. k up). 1993. 14.00 (0-688-12404-6) Morrow Jr Bks.
—Mouse & His Child. Hoban, Russell. LC 67-19624. (gr. 1-5). 1967. PLB 13.89 (0-06-022378-2) HarpC Child Bks.
—My Dad the Magnificent. Parker, Kristy. LC 86-24077. 32p. (ps-2). 1987. 10.95 (0-525-44314-2, DCB) Dutton Child Bks.
—My Dad the Magnificent. Parker, Kristy. LC 86-24077. 32p. (ps-2). 1990. pap. 3.95 (0-525-44607-9, DCB) Dutton Child Bks.
—The New Girl at School. Delton, Judy. LC 79-11409. (gr. k-3). 1979. 12.95 (0-525-35780-7, DCB) Dutton Child Bks.
—New Neighbors for Nora. reissued ed. Hurwitz, Johanna. LC 90-47882. 80p. (ps up). 1991. Repr. of 1979 ed. 12.95 (0-688-09947-5); PLB 12.88 (0-688-09948-3, Morrow Jr Bks) Morrow Jr Bks.
—New Neighbors for Nora. Hurwitz, Johanna. 80p. (gr. 2-5). 1991. pap. 3.99 (0-14-034594-9, Puffin) Puffin Bks.
—The New Teacher. Cohen, Miriam. LC 78-163239. 32p. (ps-1). 1989. pap. 3.95 (0-689-71332-0, Aladdin) Macmillan Child Grp.
—No Good in Art. Cohen, Miriam. LC 79-16566. 32p. (gr. k-3). 1980. PLB 14.93 (0-688-84234-8) Greenwillow.
—Nora & Mrs. Mind-Your-Own Business. reissued ed. Hurwitz, Johanna. LC 90-47997. 80p. (ps up). 1991. Repr. of 1977 ed. 12.95 (0-688-09945-9); PLB 12.88 (0-688-09946-7, Morrow Jr Bks) Morrow Jr Bks.
—Nora & Mrs. Mind-Your-Own-Business. Hurwitz, Johanna. 80p. (gr. 2-5). 1991. pap. 3.99 (0-14-034595-7, Puffin) Puffin Bks.
—Papa's Panda. Willard, Nancy. LC 78-31787. (ps-2). 1979. 5.95 (0-15-259462-0, HB Juv Bks) HarBrace.
—A Plant Called Spot. Peteraf, Nancy J. LC 92-27474. 1994. 13.95 (0-385-30885-X) Doubleday.
—Quick Chick. Hoban, Julia. LC 88-30894. 32p. (ps-2). 1989. 9.95 (0-525-44490-4, DCB) Dutton Child Bks.
—The Real-Skin Rubber Monster Mask. Cohen, Miriam. LC 89-34620. 32p. (gr. k up). 1990. 12.95 (0-688-09122-9); PLB 12.88 (0-688-09123-7) Greenwillow.
—Rip-Roaring Russell. Hurwitz, Johanna. LC 83-1019. 96p. (ps-1). 1983. 12.95 (0-688-02347-9); lib. bdg. 12. 88 (0-688-02348-7, Morrow Jr Bks) Morrow Jr Bks.
—Rip-Roarring Russell. Hurwitz, Johanna. 96p. (gr. 2-5). 1989. pap. 3.99 (0-14-032939-0, Puffin) Puffin Bks.
—Russell & Elisa. Hurwitz, Johanna. LC 88-37578. 96p. (gr. k up). 1989. 11.95 (0-688-08792-2); lib. bdg. 11.88 (0-688-08793-0, Morrow Jr Bks) Morrow Jr Bks.
—Russell Rides Again. Hurwitz, Johanna. LC 85-7287. 96p. (gr. 2-5). 1985. 12.95 (0-688-04628-2); lib. bdg. 12. 88 (0-688-04629-0, Morrow Jr Bks) Morrow Jr Bks.
—Russell Rides Again. Hurwitz, Johanna. 96p. (gr. 2-5). 1989. pap. 3.99 (0-14-032941-2, Puffin) Puffin Bks.
—Russell Sprouts. Hurwitz, Johanna. LC 87-5494. 80p. (ps-2). 1987. 12.95 (0-688-07165-1); lib. bdg. 12.88 (0-688-07166-X, Morrow Jr Bks) Morrow Jr Bks.
—Russell Sprouts. Hurwitz, Johanna. 80p. (gr. 2-5). 1989. pap. 3.99 (0-14-032942-0, Puffin) Puffin Bks.
—See You in Second Grade! Cohen, Miriam. LC 87-14869. 32p. (ps up). 1989. 13.95 (0-688-07138-4); PLB 13.88 (0-688-07139-2) Greenwillow.
—Seymour the Prince. Alexander, Sue. LC 78-31406. (gr. 2-4). 1979. 6.95 (0-685-03943-9) Pantheon.
—Silly Tilly & the Easter Bunny. Hoban, Lillian. LC 86-7682. 32p. (ps-3). 1987. 13.00 (0-06-022392-8); PLB 13.89 (0-06-022393-6) HarpC Child Bks.
—Silly Tilly & the Easter Bunny. Hoban, Lillian. LC 86-7682. 32p. (ps-2). 1989. pap. 3.50 (0-06-444127-X, Trophy) HarpC Child Bks.

—Silly Tilly's Thanksgiving Dinner. Hoban, Lillian. LC 89-29287. 64p. (gr. k-3). 1990. 14.00 (*0-06-022422-3*); PLB 13.89 (*0-06-022423-1*) HarpC Child Bks.
—Silly Tilly's Thanksgiving Dinner. Hoban, Lillian. LC 89-29287. 64p. (gr. k-3). 1991. pap. 3.50 (*0-06-444154-7*, Trophy) HarpC Child Bks.
—So What? Cohen, Miriam. LC 81-20101. 32p. (gr. k-3). 1982. PLB 15.93 (*0-688-01203-5*) Greenwillow.
—Starring First Grade. Cohen, Miriam. LC 84-5929. 32p. (gr. k-3). 1985. PLB 15.93 (*0-688-04030-6*) Greenwillow.
—The Story of Bentley Beaver. Sharmat, Marjorie W. LC 82-47715. 64p. (gr. k-3). 1984. HarpC Child Bks.
—Superduper Teddy. Hurwitz, Johanna. LC 89-13592. 80p. (gr. k-3). 1990. Repr. of 1980 ed. 12.95 (*0-688-09094-X*); PLB 12.88 (*0-688-09095-8*, Morrow Jr Bks) Morrow Jr Bks.
—Superduper Teddy. Hurwitz, Johanna. 80p. (gr. 2-5). 1991. pap. 3.95 (*0-14-034593-0*, Puffin) Puffin Bks.
—Tom & the Two Handles. Hoban, Russell. LC 65-11459. 64p. (gr. k-3). 1965. PLB 13.89 (*0-06-022431-2*) HarpC Child Bks.
—Tough Eddie. Winthrop, Elizabeth. LC 84-13664. 32p. (ps-2). 1989. pap. 3.95 (*0-525-44496-3*, DCB) Dutton Child Bks.
—Waiting for Noah. Oppenheim, Shulamith L. LC 89-35561. 32p. (ps-2). 1990. 12.95 (*0-06-024633-2*); PLB 12.89 (*0-06-024634-0*) HarpC Child Bks.
—When Will I Read? Cohen, Miriam. LC 76-28320. 32p. (ps-3). 1977. 13.95 (*0-688-80073-4*); PLB 13.88 (*0-688-84073-6*) Greenwillow.
—When Will I Read? Cohen, Miriam. (gr. k-3). 1987. pap. 3.25 (*0-440-49333-1*, YB) Dell.
—Where Does the Teacher Live? Feder, Paula K. LC 78-13157. 48p. (gr. 1-3). 1979. 12.95 (*0-525-42586-1*, DCB) Dutton Child Bks.
—Where Does the Teacher Live? Feder, Paula K. LC 78-13157. 48p. (gr. 1-3). 1992. pap. 3.99 (*0-525-44889-6*, Unicorn Pbks) Dutton Child Bks.
—Will I Have a Friend? Cohen, Miriam. LC 67-10127. 32p. (ps-1). 1967. RSBE 13.95 (*0-02-722790-1*, Macmillan Child Bk) Macmillan Child Grp.
—Will I Have a Friend? Cohen, Miriam. LC 89-31340. 32p. (ps-1). 1989. pap. 3.95 (*0-689-71333-9*, Aladdin) Macmillan Child Grp.
—Will You Be My Valentine? Kroll, Steven. 32p. (ps-3). 1993. reinforced bdg. 14.95 (*0-8234-0925-2*) Holiday.
Hoban, Tana. A Children's Zoo. Hoban, Tana. LC 84-25318. 24p. (ps-1). 1985. 15.00 (*0-688-05202-9*); lib. bdg. 14.93 (*0-688-05204-5*) Greenwillow.
—Circles, Triangles & Squares. Hoban, Tana. LC 72-93305. 32p. (ps-2). 1974. RSBE 13.95 (*0-02-744830-4*, Macmillan Child Bk) Macmillan Child Grp.
—Count & See. Hoban, Tana. LC 72-175597. 40p. (ps-2). 1972. RSBE 13.95 (*0-02-744800-2*, Macmillan Child Bk) Macmillan Child Grp.
—I Read Signs. Hoban, Tana. LC 83-1482. 32p. (ps-1). 1983. 15.00 (*0-688-02317-7*); PLB 14.93 (*0-688-02318-5*) Greenwillow.
—I Read Symbols. Hoban, Tana. LC 83-1481. 32p. (ps-1). 1983. 14.95 (*0-688-02331-2*); PLB 14.88 (*0-688-02332-0*) Greenwillow.
—I Walk & Read. Hoban, Tana. LC 83-14215. 32p. (ps-1). 1984. 14.95 (*0-688-02575-7*); PLB 14.88 (*0-688-02576-5*) Greenwillow.
—Is It Rough? Is It Smooth? Is It Shiny? Hoban, Tana. LC 83-25460. 32p. (ps-1). 1984. 15.95 (*0-688-03823-9*); PLB 15.88 (*0-688-03824-7*) Greenwillow.
—Look! Look! Look! Hoban, Tana. LC 87-25655. 40p. (ps-1). 1988. 12.95 (*0-688-07239-9*); lib. bdg. 12.88 (*0-688-07240-2*) Greenwillow.
—One, Two, Three. Hoban, Tana. LC 84-10306. 12p. (ps). 1985. bds. 4.95 (*0-688-02579-X*) Greenwillow.
—Over, Under & Through. Hoban, Tana. LC 86-20675. 32p. (ps-3). 1987. pap. 3.95 (*0-689-71111-5*, Aladdin) Macmillan Child Grp.
—Panda, Panda. Hoban, Tana. LC 86-3088. 12p. (ps). 1986. pap. 3.95 (*0-688-06564-3*) Greenwillow.
—Red, Blue, Yellow Shoe. Hoban, Tana. LC 86-3095. 12p. (ps). 1986. bds. 4.95 (*0-688-06563-5*) Greenwillow.
—Round & Round & Round. Hoban, Tana. LC 82-11984. 32p. (gr. k-3). 1983. 14.95 (*0-688-01813-0*); PLB 14.88 (*0-688-01814-9*) Greenwillow.
—Shapes & Things. LC 70-102965. 32p. (ps-2). 1970. 13.95 (*0-02-744060-5*, Macmillan Child Bk) Macmillan Child Grp.
—What Is It? Hoban, Tana. LC 84-13483. 12p. (ps). 1985. bds. 4.95 (*0-688-02577-3*) Greenwillow.
Hoban, Tana, photos by. Little Elephant. Ford, Miela. LC 93-25208. 1994. write for info. (*0-688-13140-9*); PLB write for info. (*0-688-13141-7*) Greenwillow.
—The Moon Was the Best. Zolotow, Charlotte. LC 91-47748. 32p. (ps up). 1993. 15.00 (*0-688-09940-8*); PLB 14.93 (*0-688-09941-6*) Greenwillow.
—Over, Under & Through & Other Special Concepts. Hoban, Tana. LC 72-81055. 32p. (ps-2). 1973. RSBE 13.95 (*0-02-744820-7*, Macmillan Child Bk) Macmillan Child Grp.
—Shapes, Shapes, Shapes. Hoban, Tana. LC 85-17569. 32p. (ps-3). 1986. 14.95 (*0-688-05832-9*); PLB 14.88 (*0-688-05833-7*) Greenwillow.
Hoberman, Mary Ann. Mr. & Mrs. Muddle. Hoberman, Mary Ann. LC 87-27320. 32p. (gr. k-4). 1988. 13.95 (*0-316-36735-4*, Joy St Bks) Little.

Hobson, Sally. Three Bags Full. Scamell, Ragnhild. LC 92-50882. 32p. (ps-1). 1993. 14.95 (*0-531-05486-1*) Orchard Bks Watts.
Hoburg, Maryanne R. See with Your Ears: The Creative Music Book. Kaplan, Don. LC 82-81463. 128p. (Orig.). (gr. 1-7). 1982. pap. 6.95 (*0-938530-09-7*, 09-7); tchr's guide cancelled 2.00 (*0-938530-20-8*, 20-8) Lexikos.
Hochman, Doris Z. Kid Koala's Fun Book. Hochman, Doris Z. 44p. (gr. 2-5). 1991. wkbk. 6.95 (*1-878070-00-2*) Three Elves Pr.
Hochstatter, Dan. The First Woman: Bible Stories in Rhythm & Rhyme. Haan, Sheri D. 80p. (ps-3). 1992. 6.99 (*0-8010-4368-9*) Baker Bk.
—The Time the World Drowned: Bible Stories in Rhythm & Rhyme. Haan, Sheri D. 80p. (ps-3). 1992. 6.99 (*0-8010-4369-7*) Baker Bk.
Hochstatter, Daniel J. The Big Book of All-Time Favorite Bible Stories. Beers, V. Gilbert & Beers, Ronald A. LC 92-8306. 1992. 12.99 (*0-8407-9165-8*) Oliver-Nelson.
—Sammy's Excellent Real-Life Adventures. LC 92-40532. (gr. 5 up). 1993. 9.99 (*0-8407-9675-7*) Nelson.
—Sammy's Fabulous Holy Land Travels. LC 93-34525. 1994. write for info. (*0-89528-281-X*) Oliver-Nelson.
—Sammy's Incredible Travels with Jesus & His Friends: A New Testament Adventure. LC 92-18748. 1992. 9.99 (*0-8407-9162-3*) Oliver-Nelson.
—Sammy's Tree-Mendous Christmas Adventure. LC 93-22314. 1993. 9.99 (*0-8407-9234-4*) Oliver-Nelson.
Hockerman, David. A Load of Trouble. Davoll, Barbara. 24p. 1988. pap. 6.99 (*0-89693-407-1*, Victor Books) SP Pubns.
Hockerman, Dennis. The Black Swan. Hogan, Paula Z. LC 78-27416. 32p. (gr. 1-4). 1979. PLB 17.96 (*0-8172-1254-X*) Raintree Steck-V.
—The Camping Caper. Davoll, Barbara. 24p. 1993. 6.99 (*1-56476-162-2*, Victor Books) SP Pubns.
—The Christopher Churchmouse Treasury. Davoll, Barbara. (Orig.). 1992. pap. 12.99 (*0-89693-078-5*, Victor Books) SP Pubns.
—Count Your Way Through Korea. Haskins, Jim. 24p. (gr. 1-4). 1989. 17.50 (*0-87614-348-6*); pap. 5.95 (*0-87614-516-0*) Carolrhoda Bks.
—Dusty Mole Private Eye. Davoll, Barbara. (gr. 2-6). 1992. pap. 5.99 (*0-8024-2700-6*) Moody.
—Grandpa's Secret. Davoll, Barbara. 24p. 1993. 6.99 (*1-56476-161-4*, Victor Books) SP Pubns.
—I Hate Boys-I Hate Girls. Hogan, Paula Z. McDonald, Paula & McDonald, Dickintro. by. LC 79-24056. 32p. (gr. k-6). 1980. PLB 17.96 (*0-8172-1358-9*) Raintree Steck-V.
—Little Pig's Birthday. Leonard, Marcia. 32p. 1984. pap. 2.50 (*0-553-15267-X*) Bantam.
—The Little Red Hen. McKissack, Patricia & McKissack, Fredrick. LC 85-12760. (ps-2). 1985. PLB 11.93 (*0-516-02346-3*); pap. 3.95 (*0-516-42363-0*) Childrens.
—A Pack of Lies. Davoll, Barbara. 24p. 1989. 6.99 (*0-89693-497-7*, Victor Books); cassette 9.99 (*0-89693-030-0*) SP Pubns.
—Pinta, Pinta, Gregorita (Big Book) Kratky, Lada J. (SPA.). 16p. (Orig.). (gr. k-3). 1990. pap. text ed. 29.95 (*0-917837-53-3*) Hampton-Brown.
—Pinta, Pinta, Gregorita (Small Book) Kratky, Lada J. (SPA.). 16p. (Orig.). (gr. k-3). 1992. pap. text ed. 6.00 (*1-56334-084-4*) Hampton-Brown.
—The Potluck Supper. Davoll, Barbara. 1988. 4.95 (*0-685-22774-X*); book & cassette 7.95 (*0-685-22775-8*) Zondervan.
—The Potluck Supper. Davoll, Barbara. 24p. 1988. 6.99 (*0-89693-406-3*, Victor Books); cassette 9.99 (*0-89693-617-1*) SP Pubns.
—Rainy Day Rescue. Davoll, Barbara. 24p. 1988. 6.99 (*0-89693-408-X*, Victor Books); cassette 9.99 (*0-89693-619-8*) SP Pubns.
—A Rose for Abby. Guthrie, Donna. LC 88-10577. (gr. 2 up). 1988. 11.95 (*0-687-36586-4*) Abingdon.
—Rumpelstiltskin. Grimm, Jacob & Grimm, Wilhelm K. LC 78-18079. 32p. (gr. k-3). 1979. PLB 9.79 (*0-89375-140-5*); pap. 1.95 (*0-89375-118-9*) Troll Assocs.
—The Salmon. Hogan, Paula Z. LC 78-21178. 32p. (gr. 1-4). 1979. PLB 17.96 (*0-8172-1255-8*); pap. 4.95 (*0-8114-8178-6*); pap. 9.95 incl. cassette (*0-8114-8186-7*) Raintree Steck-V.
—Saved by the Bell. Davoll, Barbara. 24p. 1988. text ed. 6.99 (*0-89693-403-9*, Victor Books); cassette 9.99 (*0-89693-614-7*) SP Pubns.
—Secret at Mossy Root Mansion. Davoll, Barbara. (gr. 2-7). 1992. 5.99 (*0-8024-2701-4*) Moody.
—The Shiny Red Sled. Davoll, Barbara. 24p. 1989. text ed. 6.99 (*0-89693-485-3*, Victor Books); cassette 9.99 (*0-89693-031-9*) SP Pubns.
—A Sticky Mystery. Davoll, Barbara. 24p. 1989. 6.99 (*0-89693-485-3*); cassette 9.99 (*0-89693-033-5*) SP Pubns.
—Summer. Allington, Richard L. & Krull, Kathleen. LC 80-25097. 32p. (gr. k-3). 1985. PLB 15.96 (*0-8172-1341-4*); pap. 3.95 (*0-8114-8241-3*) Raintree Steck-V.
—A Sunday Surprise. Davoll, Barbara. 24p. 1988. 6.99 (*0-89693-405-5*, Victor Books); cassette 9.99 (*0-89693-616-3*) SP Pubns.
—Twelve Dancing Princesses. Grimm, Jacob & Grimm, Wilhelm K. LC 78-18077. 32p. (gr. k-4). 1979. PLB 9.79 (*0-89375-139-1*); pap. 1.95 (*0-89375-117-0*) Troll Assocs.

—The White Trail. Davoll, Barbara. 24p. 1988. 6.99 (*0-89693-404-7*, Victor Books); cassette 9.99 (*0-89693-615-5*) SP Pubns.
Hodge, Anthony. Cartooning. Hodge, Anthony. Kline, Marjory, ed. LC 91-34409. 32p. (gr. 5-9). 1992. PLB 12.40 (*0-531-17322-4*, Gloucester Pr) Watts.
—Collage. Hodge, Anthony. Kline, Marjory, ed. LC 91-34408. 32p. (gr. 5-9). 1992. PLB 12.40 (*0-531-17323-2*, Gloucester Pr) Watts.
—Painting. Hodge, Anthony. Kline, M., ed. 32p. (gr. 5-9). 1991. PLB 12.40 (*0-531-17209-6*, Gloucester Pr) Watts.
Hodges, C. Walter. Silver Sword. Serraillier, Ian. LC 59-6556. (gr. 7-9). 1959. 25.95 (*0-87599-104-1*) S G Phillips.
Hodges, Carol. The Epic Adventure...Texas. 2nd ed. Hackney, Ann. Johnson, Lady Bird, intro. by. LC 85-24854. 64p. (gr. 4-7). 1985. text ed. 19.95 includes tape (*0-935077-11-1*); pap. 12.95 includes tape (*0-935077-12-X*); pap. 5.95 (*0-935077-07-3*); tchr's guide 16.95 (*0-935077-10-3*); cassette 7.95 (*0-935077-08-1*) Hist Jefferson Found.
Hodges, Del & Mavity, Dennis, photos by. Alice in Danceland. Hodges, M. Constance. Troxel, Rose. (Orig.). (gr. 3-8). 1979. PLB 5.95 (*0-934856-00-1*) Delcon.
Hoenack, Frank & Morris, Alix. Let's Sing & Play an Opera: Hansel & Gretel, Humperdinck Arr. 2nd ed. Hoenack, Peg, et al. 16p. (gr. 2-6). 1972. Student's Book in Peg Hoenack Letter Notation, with Words for Singing. pap. 4.50 (*0-913500-19-4*, L-4); Piano Accompaniment. tchr's. ed. 4.50 (*0-913500-07-0*, L-5) Peg Hoenack MusicWorks.
Hoese, H. Dickson. Things That Swim in Texas Waters Alphabetically Speaking: An and Other Coastal States of the Gulf of Mexico. Grimmer, Glenna. Eakin, Edwin M., ed. 48p. (gr. 4-6). 1989. 11.95 (*0-89015-694-8*, Pub. by Panda Bks) Eakin-Sunbelt.
Hoff, Syd. Albert the Albatross. Hoff, Syd. LC 61-5767. 32p. (gr. k-3). 1961. PLB 13.89 (*0-06-022446-0*) HarpC Child Bks.
—Barkley. Hoff, Syd. LC 75-6290. 32p. (gr. k-3). 1975. PLB 13.89 (*0-06-022448-7*) HarpC Child Bks.
—Barney's Horse. Hoff, Syd. LC 87-66. 32p. (ps-3). 1987. PLB 13.89 (*0-06-022450-9*) HarpC Child Bks.
—Barney's Horse. Hoff, Syd. LC 87-66. 32p. (ps-2). 1990. pap. 3.50 (*0-06-444142-3*, Trophy) HarpC Child Bks.
—Bernard on His Own. Hoff, Syd. LC 92-21770. 32p. (gr. k-3). 1993. 14.95 (*0-395-65226-X*, Clarion Bks) HM.
—Captain Cat. Hoff, Syd. LC 91-27518. 48p. (ps-2). 1993. 14.00 (*0-06-020527-X*); PLB 13.89 (*0-06-020528-8*) HarpC Child Bks.
—Chester. Hoff, Syd. LC 61-5768. 64p. (gr. k-3). 1961. PLB 13.89 (*0-06-022456-8*) HarpC Child Bks.
—Chester. Hoff, Syd. LC 61-5768. 64p. (gr. k-3). 1986. pap. 3.50 (*0-06-444095-8*, Trophy) HarpC Child Bks.
—Danielito y el Dinosauria. Hoff, Syd. Mlawer, Teresa, tr. from ENG. 64p. (gr. 5-7). 1991. PLB 11.95 (*0-9625162-2-8*) Lectorum Pubns.
—Danny & the Dinosaur. newly illus. ed. Hoff, Syd. LC 92-13609. 64p. (gr. k-3). 1958. 14.00 (*0-06-022465-7*); PLB 13.89 (*0-06-022466-5*) HarpC Child Bks.
—Danny & the Dinosaur. newly illustrated ed. Hoff, Syd. LC 58-7754. 64p. (gr. k-3). 1985. incl. cassette 5.98 (*0-694-00017-5*, Trophy); pap. 3.50 (*0-06-444002-8*, Trophy) HarpC Child Bks.
—Don't Be My Valentine. Lexau, Joan. LC 85-42621. 64p. (gr. k-3). 1985. PLB 13.89 (*0-06-023873-9*) HarpC Child Bks.
—Don't Be My Valentine. Lexau, Joan M. LC 85-42621. 64p. (gr. k-3). 1988. pap. 3.50 (*0-06-444115-6*, Trophy) HarpC Child Bks.
—Don't Be My Valentine. Lexau, Joan M. (gr. 1-4). 1990. incl. cass. 19.95 (*0-87499-150-1*); pap. 12.95 incl. cass. (*0-87499-149-8*); Set; incl. 4 bks., cass., & guide. pap. 27.95 (*0-685-38539-6*) Live Oak Media.
—Grizzwold. Hoff, Syd. LC 64-14366. 64p. (gr. k-3). 1963. PLB 13.89 (*0-06-022481-9*) HarpC Child Bks.
—Horse in Harry's Room. Hoff, Syd. LC 71-104753. 32p. (gr. k-3). 1970. PLB 13.89 (*0-06-022483-5*) HarpC Child Bks.
—The Horse in Harry's Room. Hoff, Syd. LC 71-104753. 32p. (ps-2). 1985. pap. 3.50 (*0-06-444073-7*, Trophy) HarpC Child Bks.
—I Saw You in the Bathtub & Other Folk Rhymes. Schwartz, Alvin, ed. LC 88-16111. 64p. (gr. k-3). 1989. 14.00 (*0-06-025298-7*); PLB 13.89 (*0-06-025299-5*) HarpC Child Bks.
—I Saw You in the Bathtub: And Other Folk Rhymes. Schwartz, Alvin. LC 88-16111. 64p. (gr. k-3). 1991. pap. 3.50 (*0-06-444151-2*, Trophy) HarpC Child Bks.
—Julius. Hoff, Syd. LC 59-8971. 64p. (gr. k-3). 1959. PLB 13.89 (*0-06-022491-6*) HarpC Child Bks.
—Little Chief. Hoff, Syd. LC 61-12098. 64p. (gr. k-3). 1961. PLB 13.89 (*0-06-022501-7*) HarpC Child Bks.
—Little Chief. Hoff, Syd. LC 61-12098. 64p. (gr. k-3). 1990. pap. 3.50 (*0-06-444135-0*, Trophy) HarpC Child Bks.
—Mrs. Brice's Mice. Hoff, Syd. LC 87-45680. 32p. (ps-2). 1988. PLB 13.89 (*0-06-022452-5*) HarpC Child Bks.
—Mrs. Brice's Mice. Hoff, Syd. LC 87-45680. 32p. (ps-2). 1991. pap. 3.50 (*0-06-444145-8*, Trophy) HarpC Child Bks.
—Oliver. Hoff, Syd. LC 60-5779. 64p. (gr. k-3). 1960. PLB 13.89 (*0-06-022516-5*) HarpC Child Bks.
—Oliver. Hoff, Syd. LC 60-5779. 64p. (gr. k-3). 1986. pap. 3.50 (*0-06-444097-4*, Trophy) HarpC Child Bks.

—Rooftop Mystery. Lexau, Joan M. LC 68-16821. 64p. (gr. k-3). 1968. PLB 13.89 (0-06-023865-8) HarpC Child Bks.
—Sammy the Seal. Hoff, Syd. LC 59-5316. 64p. (gr. k-3). 1959. PLB 13.89 (0-06-022526-2) HarpC Child Bks.
—Sammy the Seal. Hoff, Syd. LC 59-5316. 64p. (gr. k-3). 1980. pap. 3.50 (0-06-444028-1, Trophy) HarpC Child Bks.
—Stanley. newly illus. ed. Hoff, Syd. LC 91-15034. 64p. (gr. k-3). 1962. 13.00 (0-06-022535-1); PLB 12.89 (0-06-022536-X) HarpC Child Bks.
—Stanley. newly illus. ed. Hoff, Syd. LC 91-12266. 64p. (gr. k-3). 1978. pap. 3.50 (0-06-444010-9, Trophy) HarpC Child Bks.
—Syd Hoff's Animal Jokes. Hoff, Syd. LC 84-48353. 48p. (gr. k-3). 1986. (Lipp Jr Bks) HarpC Child Bks.
—Thunderhoof. Hoff, Syd. LC 75-129855. 32p. (gr. k-3). 1971. PLB 13.89 (0-685-02069-X) HarpC Child Bks.
—Who Will Be My Friends? Hoff, Syd. 32p. (gr. k-2). 1960. PLB 13.89 (0-06-022556-4) HarpC Child Bks.
—Who Will Be My Friends? Hoff, Syd. LC 60-14096. 32p. (gr. k-3). 1985. pap. 3.50 (0-06-444072-9, Trophy) HarpC Child Bks.
Hoffman, Beverly & Robinson, Michael D. A Flower for Iggey. Hoffman, Beverly & Fiorilla, Sal J. LC 92-85530. 150p. (Orig.). (gr. 3-6). 1993. 12.95 (0-9634122-1-3); cass. musical tape avail. Feather Fables.
Hoffman, Jo-Ann. Alphabet Picture Key Word Cards. Foltzer, Monica. 38p. 1987. 38 cards 4.60 (0-9607918-5-X, A 505419) St Ursula.
Hoffman, Judy. Christmas KidDoodles, Bk. 2. Wise, Beth A. 64p. (Orig.). (ps-2). 1991. pap. 0.99 activity pad (1-56293-154-7) McClanahan Bk.
Hoffman, Lee. Spaceships of the Ancients. Foley, Bernice W. LC 78-59116. (gr. 3-6). 1978. 6.95 (0-915964-04-X) Veritie Pr.

Hoffman, Nannette. The Lavender Box. Feldman, Jacqueline. LC 89-85206. 41p. (ps-6). 1992. 11.95 (0-9623903-0-5) Ellicott Pr.
A small boy disappears into a very large hat; a child silently shares poignant feelings with a chipmunk; a little girl preaches the rules of etiquette to a bee. Poems dealing with nature & the pleasures of domestic life transform childhood experiences into rhythmic images. And in the final offering, a lavender box becomes a metaphor for the entire book. Although these poems were written for children aged 3 to 11, Ms. Feldman's awareness of & wonder at the workings of a child's mind give readers of all ages an exhilarating & joyous experience. The poems are beautifully complemented by Nannette Hoffman's whimsical black & white drawings. "A resonant voice is gently in tune with the imagination of children in this poetry collection...the imagery reverberates on every page." -- SCHOOL LIBRARY JOURNAL. "In rhythmical, memorable verse, she recreates-- for children & adult readers alike-- a child's sense of wonder." -- Anne Whitehouse, poet & reviewer for THE NEW YORK TIMES. "Quite a treasure box of a book." --THE BOOK READER. THE LAVENDER BOX is now in its second printing.
Publisher Provided Annotation.

Hoffman, Rosekrans. Creepy, Crawly, Critter Riddles. Bernstein, Joanne & Cohen, Paul. Tucker, Kathleen, ed. LC 86-15911. 32p. (gr. 1-5). 1986. PLB 8.95 (0-8075-1345-8) A Whitman.
—The Horrible Holidays. Wood, Audrey. LC 87-30617. 48p. (ps-3). 1988. 9.95 (0-8037-0544-1); PLB 9.89 (0-8037-0546-8) Dial Bks Young.
—Jane Yolen's Mother Goose Songbook. Yolen, Jane, ed. Stemple, Adam, contrib. by. 96p. (ps-7). 1992. PLB 16.95 (1-878093-52-5) Boyds Mills Pr.
—Jet Black Pickup Truck. Lakin, Patricia. LC 89-71010. 32p. (ps-1). 1990. 14.95 (0-531-05885-9); PLB 14.99 (0-531-08485-X) Orchard Bks Watts.
—Three Sisters. Wood, Audrey. LC 85-29392. 48p. (ps-3). 1986. 9.95 (0-8037-0279-5); PLB 9.89 (0-8037-0280-9) Dial Bks Young.
—Three Sisters. Wood, Audrey. LC 85-29392. 48p. (ps-3). 1986. 4.95 (0-8037-0597-2) Dial Bks Young.
—The Truth about the Moon. Bess, Clayton. 48p. (gr. k-3). 1983. 13.45 (0-395-34551-0) HM.

—Where Did That Naughty Little Hamster Go? Wolcott, Patty. LC 91-12133. 32p. (ps-2). 1991. 3.50 (0-679-81924-X); PLB 6.99 (0-679-91924-4) Random Bks Yng Read.
—Where Do Little Girls Grow? Limmer, Milly J. Levine, Abby, ed. LC 92-22936. 32p. (ps-2). 1993. PLB 14.95 (0-8075-8924-1) A Whitman.
Hoffman, Sandy. Baseball Brain Teasers: Major League Puzzles. Forker, Dom. LC 85-27955. 128p. (Orig.). (gr. 5-9). 1986. pap. 4.95 (0-8069-6284-4) Sterling.
—Dinosaur Riddles. Heck, Joseph. Barish, Wendy, ed. 128p. (gr. 3-7). 1982. 9.29 (0-685-05613-9, Little Simon) S&S Trade.
—Nutty Knock Knocks! Rosenbloom, Joseph. LC 85-27626. 128p. (Orig.). (gr. 2 up). 1986. pap. 3.95 (0-8069-6304-2) Sterling.
—Rover. Mason, Margo. 32p. (ps-1). write for info. Bantam.
Hoffman, Sanford. The Craziest Riddle Book in the World. Fox, Lori M. LC 91-13209. 96p. (gr. 3-9). 1992. 12.95 (0-8069-8406-6); pap. 3.95 (0-8069-8407-4) Sterling.
—Great All-Time Excuse Book. Kushner, Maureen. LC 89-49403. 96p. (gr. 2-8). 1991. pap. 3.95 (0-8069-6965-2) Sterling.
—Great Games for Great Parties: How to Throw a Perfect Party. Campbell, Andrea. 160p. (gr. 3-10). 1992. pap. 7.95 (0-8069-8319-1) Sterling.
—Hidden Logic Puzzles. Weaver, Charles. 128p. (gr. 5 up). 1993. pap. 4.95 (0-8069-8335-3) Sterling.
—Laugh-a-Minute Joke Book. Perret, Gene. LC 90-27674. 96p. (gr. 2-10). 1991. 12.95 (0-8069-7414-1) Sterling.
—Laugh-a-Minute Joke Book. Perret, Gene. 96p. (gr. 3-9). 1991. pap. 3.95 (0-8069-7415-X) Sterling.
—The Nuttiest Riddle Book in the World. Gallant, Morrie. LC 93-7871. 96p. (gr. 2-10). 1993. 12.95 (0-8069-0420-8) Sterling.
—Oodles of Riddles. Rox, Lori M. LC 89-4549. 96p. (gr. 3-8). 1990. pap. 3.95 (0-8069-7202-5) Sterling.
—Riddlemania. Fox, Lori M. LC 90-43230. 96p. (gr. 2-7). 1991. 12.95 (0-8069-7352-8) Sterling.
—Riddlemania. Fox, Lori M. LC 90-43230. 96p. (gr. 1-7). 1992. pap. 3.95 (0-8069-7353-6) Sterling.
—Shake, Riddle & Roll. Fox, Lori M. 96p. (gr. 3-9). 1991. pap. 3.95 (0-8069-7251-3) Sterling.
—Spooky Riddles & Jokes. Rosenbloom, Joseph. LC 87-17972. 128p. (gr. 4 up). 1988. pap. 3.95 (0-8069-6736-6) Sterling.
—Super Funny School Jokes. Perret, Gene. LC 91-22501. 96p. (gr. 1-7). 1992. pap. 3.95 (0-8069-8295-0) Sterling.
—Super Sick Jokes & Riddles. Rosenbloom, Joseph. 96p. (Orig.). (gr. 2-9). 1990. pap. 3.95 (0-8069-7458-3) Sterling.
—World's Best Sports Riddles & Jokes. Rosenbloom, Joseph. LC 87-30434. 128p. (gr. 3-9). 1989. pap. 3.95 (0-8069-6848-4) Sterling.
—The World's Punniest Joke Book. Benny, Mike. LC 94-42578. 96p. 1993. 12.95 (0-8069-8544-5) Sterling.
—World's Punniest Joke Book. Benny, Mike. 96p. (gr. 2-8). 1993. pap. 3.95 (0-8069-8545-3) Sterling.
—World's Wildest Animal Jokes. Murray, Francis. 96p. (gr. 2-6). 1993. pap. 3.95 (0-8069-8539-9) Sterling.
—The Zaniest Riddle Book in the World. Rosenbloom, Joseph. LC 83-18102. 128p. (gr. 3 up). 1985. pap. 3.95 (0-8069-6252-6) Sterling.
Hoffmann, Duane. The Living Mountain: Mount St. Helens. Carson, Rob. 84p. (Orig.). (gr. k-8). 1992. pap. 10.95 (0-9623072-9-7) S Ink WA.

Hoffmann, Jo-Ann. Professor Phonics Gives Sound Advice. l2th ed. Foltzer, Monica. 1990. pap. text ed. 6.80 (0-9607918-0-9, A 505419) St Ursula.
PROFESSOR PHONICS GIVES SOUND ADVICE, the primary book, is unique in that it has the only totally organized phonics system. All of the consonant sounds are taught around four categories of vowels. It is so streamlined that all 42 basic sounds are taught on 23 pages interspersed with practice pages. Sounds arranged in more difficult spelling patterns follow. A SOUND TRACK TO READING has exactly the same format but starts with two-syllable words. All the basic sounds are taught on 14 pages. This advanced book is not geared for intermediate grades & up. Phonics is NOT reading. It is reading's only sure foundation for unlocking unknown words. The system also contains 38 PICTURE KEY WORD CARDS, MANUALS & a SPELLING WORD LIST. At the end of the year, first graders can spell 1500 words without

memorizing. Taking regular spelling first helps greatly. The ten percent of non-phonetic words then fall into place. Systematic, intensive phonics should be taught first & fast before sight words are introduced because all one does is slide sounds together. Anyone can teach another to read in this manner if one has an organized system. As Mary Pride says in her New Big Book Of Home Learning, "The program author really knows her stuff."
Publisher Provided Annotation.

Hoffmann, Mark. Eddycat & Buddy Entertain a Guest. Barnett, Ada, et al. LC 92-56883. 32p. (gr. 1 up). 1993. Repr. of 1991 ed. PLB 17.27 incl. tchr's. guide (0-8368-0946-7) Gareth Stevens Inc.
—Eddycat Attends Sunshine's Birthday Party. Barnett, Ada, et al. LC 92-56881. 1993. PLB 17.27 (0-8368-0943-2) Gareth Stevens Inc.
—Eddycat Brings Soccer to Mannersville. Barnett, Ada & Wurfer, Nicole. LC 92-56879. 1993. PLB 17.27 (0-8368-0941-6) Gareth Stevens Inc.
—Eddycat Goes Shopping with Becky Bunny. Barnett, Ada, et al. LC 93-56884. 32p. (gr. 1 up). 1993. Repr. of 1991 ed. PLB 17.27 incl. tchr's. guide (0-8368-0947-5) Gareth Stevens Inc.
—Eddycat Helps Sunshine Plan Her Party. Barnett, Ada, et al. LC 92-56880. 1993. PLB 17.27 (0-8368-0942-4) Gareth Stevens Inc.
—Eddycat Introduces Mannersville. Barnett, Ada, et al. LC 92-56877. 1993. PLB 17.27 (0-8368-0939-4) Gareth Stevens Inc.
—Eddycat Teaches Telephone Skills. Barnett, Ada, et al. LC 92-56882. 1993. PLB 17.27 (0-8368-0944-0) Gareth Stevens Inc.
—Eddycat Visits Wright Street School. Barnett, Ada, et al. LC 92-56878. 1993. PLB 17.27 (0-8368-0940-8) Gareth Stevens Inc.
—Social Skill Builders for Children: Eddycat, 6 titles. Children's Etiquette Institute Staff, et al. 32p. (gr. 1 up). 1993. Set incl. parent-tchr. guide. PLB 103.60 (0-8368-0938-6); PLB 17.27 ea. Gareth Stevens Inc.
Hoffmann, Sanford. Andy Toots His Horn. Ziefert, Harriet. (Orig.). (ps-3). 1988. pap. 3.50 (0-14-050813-9, Puffin) Puffin Bks.
Hofman, Ginnie. The Runaway Teddy Bear. Hofman, Ginnie. LC 84-23740. 32p. (ps-3). 1986. pap. 2.25 (0-394-86286-4) Random Bks Yng Read.
Hofmann, Ginnie. One Teddy Bear Is Enough! Hofmann, Ginnie. LC 88-18166. 32p. (Orig.). (ps-3). 1991. lib. bdg. 5.99 (0-394-99582-1); pap. 2.25 (0-394-89582-7) Random Bks Yng Read.
—Who Wants an Old Teddy Bear? Hofmann, Ginnie. LC 80-10445. 32p. (ps-3). 1980. lib. bdg. 5.99 (0-394-93925-5); pap. 2.25 (0-394-83925-0) Random Bks Yng Read.
Hofsinde, Robert. Indian Costumes. Hofsinde, Robert. LC 68-11895. (gr. 3-7). 1968. PLB 12.88 (0-688-31614-X) Morrow Jr Bks.
—Indian Sign Language. Hofsinde, Robert. LC 56-5178. (gr. 5 up). 1956. PLB 13.88 (0-688-31610-7) Morrow Jr Bks.
—Indian Warriors & Their Weapons. Hofsinde, Robert. LC 65-11041. (gr. 4-7). 1965. PLB 11.88 (0-688-31613-1) Morrow Jr Bks.
Hofstetter, Virginia. Nzuzi & the Spell. Shepard, Eva & Lehman, Celia. LC 92-60935. 160p. (gr. 2-8). 1992. pap. 6.95 (1-878893-22-X) Telcraft Bks.
Hofstrand, Mary. On the Stairs. Larios, Julie. LC 93-20588. Date not set. write for info. (0-689-31643-7, Atheneum) Macmillan Child Grp.
Hogan, Patricia M. Johnny Appleseed Goes a 'Planting. Jensen, Patricia A. LC 93-4811. 32p. (gr. k-2). 1993. PLB 11.59 (0-8167-3159-4); pap. text ed. 2.95 (0-8167-3160-8) Troll Assocs.
Hogan, Ryan. Double Scoop in a Day at the Babysitters. Hogan, Ryan. 18p. (ps-5). 1993. 12.95 (0-9635529-0-2) Cult Exchange.
Hogan, Wayne. Mother Goose on Wheels. Kempher, Ruth M. 30p. (Orig.). 1992. pap. 4.95 (0-934536-51-1) Rose Shell Pr.
Hogarth, William. Arctic Rovings: Or the Adventures of a New Bedford Boy on Sea & Land by Daniel Weston Hall. Beatty, Jerome. LC 91-40359. xiv, 144p. (gr. 7-10). 1992. Repr. of 1968 ed. lib. bdg. 17.50 (0-208-02324-0, Pub. by Linnet) Shoe String.
Hoggan, Pat. Armando Asked "Why?" Hulbert, Jay & Kantor, Sid. 24p. (ps-2). 1990. PLB 14.60 (0-8172-3576-0); pap. 10.95 pkg. of 3 (0-685-58548-4) Raintree Steck-V.
—Let's Sing about Animals. James, George. LC 91-763080. 32p. (gr. k-2). 1992. lib. bdg. 11.89 (0-8167-2980-8); pap. text ed. 2.95 (0-8167-2981-6) Troll Assocs.
—Treasure in the Attic. Chapman, Christina. LC 92-35814. 32p. (gr. 4-6). 1992. PLB 17.96 (0-8114-3582-2) Raintree Steck-V.

Hogrogian, Nonny. About Wise Men & Simpletons: Twelve Tales from Grimm. Grimm, Jacob & Grimm, Wilhelm K. Shub, Elizabeth, tr. LC 85-15330. 128p. (gr. 4-6). 1986. SBE 14.95 (*0-02-737450-5*, Macmillan Child Bk) Macmillan Child Grp.
—Always Room for One More. Nic Leodhas, Sorche. LC 65-12881. 32p. (ps-2). 1965. reinforced bdg. 14.95 (*0-8050-0331-2*, Bks Young Read); pap. 5.95 (Owlet Bk.) (*0-8050-0330-4*) H Holt & Co.
—Asking the River. Kherdian, David. LC 92-34912. 112p. (gr. 5 up). 1993. 14.95 (*0-531-05483-7*, Orchard Bks); PLB 14.99 (*0-531-08633-X*, Orchard Bks) Watts.
—By Myself. Kherdian, David. LC 92-44366. 32p. (ps-2). 1993. PLB 14.95 (*0-8050-2386-0*, Bks Young Read) H Holt & Co.
—Candy Floss. Godden, Rumer. 64p. (ps-3). 1991. 16.95 (*0-399-21807-6*, Philomel) Putnam Pub Group.
—The Devil with the Three Golden Hairs. Grimm, Jacob & Grimm, Wilhelm K. LC 82-12735. 40p. (gr. k-3). 1983. PLB 10.99 (*0-394-95560-9*) Knopf Bks Yng Read.
—Feathers & Tails. Kherdian, David. 96p. (gr. 1 up). 1992. PLB 19.95 (*0-399-21876-9*, Philomel Bks) Putnam Pub Group.
—I Am Eyes Ni Macho. Ward, Leila. 32p. (gr. k-3). 1987. pap. 3.95 (*0-590-40990-5*, Blue Ribbon Bks) Scholastic Inc.
—Juna's Journey. Kherdian, David. LC 92-12333. 48p. (gr. 3 up). 1993. PLB 15.95 (*0-399-22010-0*, Philomel Bks) Putnam Pub Group.
—One Fine Day. Hogrogian, Nonny. LC 75-119834. 32p. (gr. k-3). 1974. pap. 3.95 (*0-02-043620-3*, Aladdin) Macmillan Child Grp.
—A Song for Uncle Harry. Kherdian, David. 80p. (gr. 3-7). 1989. 13.95 (*0-399-21895-5*, Philomel Bks) Putnam Pub Group.
—Toad & the Green Princess. Kherdian, David. LC 92-39314. 1994. write for info. (*0-399-22539-0*, Philomel Bks) Putnam Pub Group.
Hoguet, Susan. Tidy Lady. Lindbergh, Anne. LC 88-10905. 30p. (gr. k-3). 1989. 13.95 (*0-15-287150-0*) HarBrace.
Hoguet, Susan R. Solomon Grundy. Hoguet, Susan R. LC 85-20453. 32p. (ps-3). 1986. 13.95 (*0-525-44239-1*, DCB) Dutton Child Bks.
Hoha, Linda. Helping Is Fun. Greenspan, Alice. 32p. (gr. k-2). 1990. pasted 2.50 (*0-87403-027-7*, 24-03912) Standard Pub.
Hohag, L. Ape's Adventure in Alphabet Town. McDonnell, Janet. LC 91-20539. 32p. (ps-2). 1992. 14.60 (*0-516-05401-5*) Childrens.
—Bear's Adventure in Alphabet Town. McDonnell, Janet. LC 91-20543. 32p. (ps-2). 1992. PLB 14.60 (*0-516-05402-3*) Childrens.
—Elfin's Adventure in Alphabet Town. Alden, L. LC 91-20545. 32p. (ps-2). 1992. PLB 14.60 (*0-516-05405-8*) Childrens.
—Jack & Jill's Adventure in Alphabet Town. Riehecky, J. LC 91-20541. 32p. (ps-2). 1992. PLB 14.60 (*0-516-05410-4*) Childrens.
Hohag, Linda. Away Went the Farmer's Hat. Moncure, Jane B. LC 87-11742. 32p. (ps-2). 1987. PLB 21.35 (*0-89565-367-2*); PLB 14.95s.p. (*0-685-55868-1*) Childs World.
—Baby Animals: Safe & Sound. McDonnell, Janet. LC 89-23978. 32p. (ps-2). 1990. PLB 21.35 (*0-89565-554-3*); PLB 14.95s.p. (*0-685-56175-5*) Childs World.
—Butterfly Express. Moncure, Jane B. LC 88-22944. 32p. (ps-2). 1989. PLB 21.35 (*0-89565-392-3*); PLB 14.95s.p. (*0-685-55985-8*) Childs World.
—Butterfly Express. Moncure, Jane. 32p. (gr. 1-3). 1993. pap. text ed. 5.95 (*1-56189-377-3*) Amer Educ Pub.
—A Color Clown Comes to Town. Moncure, Jane B. LC 87-11605. 32p. (ps-2). 1987. PLB 21.35 (*0-89565-369-9*); PLB 14.95s.p. (*0-685-55869-X*) Childs World.
—Dinosaurs: Back in Time. Moncure, Jane B. LC 89-38469. 32p. (ps-2). 1990. PLB 21.35 (*0-89565-550-0*) Childs World.
—A Dragon in a Wagon. Moncure, Jane B. LC 87-11755. 32p. (ps-2). 1987. PLB 21.35 (*0-89565-400-8*); PLB 14.95s.p. (*0-685-55870-3*) Childs World.
—The Easter Surprise. McDonnell, Janet. LC 93-11004. 1993. write for info. (*0-516-00683-5*) Childrens.
—Fall: A Tale of What's to Come. McDonnell, Janet. LC 93-20171. (gr. 2 up). 1993. write for info. (*0-516-00676-2*) Childrens.
—Family. Suire, Diane D., ed. LC 89-772. 32p. (gr. k-3). 1989. PLB 21.35 (*0-89565-504-7*); PLB 14.95s.p. (*0-685-56015-5*) Childs World.
—Friendship. Roberts, Sharon L. LC 86-9641. 32p. (gr. k-3). 1986. PLB 21.35 (*0-89565-350-8*) Childs World.
—God's Big Book. Hillert, Margaret. 24p. (gr. k-1). 1988. 4.99 (*0-87403-497-4*, 24-03696) Standard Pub.
—Growing Strong Inside. Moncure, Jane B. LC 85-10341. 32p. (gr. k-2). 1985. PLB 21.35 (*0-89565-333-8*); PLB 14.95s.p. (*0-685-55765-0*) Childs World.
—Happy Birthday, Word Bird. Moncure, Jane B. LC 83-15256. 32p. (gr. k-2). 1983. PLB 21.35 (*0-89565-256-0*); PLB 14.95s.p. (*0-685-55678-6*) Childs World.
—Here We Go 'Round the Year. Moncure, Jane B. LC 87-13257. 32p. (ps-2). 1987. PLB 21.35 (*0-89565-402-4*); PLB 14.95s.p. (*0-685-55920-3*) Childs World.

—Hop-skip-jump-a-roo Zoo. Moncure, Jane B. LC 87-11743. 32p. (ps-2). 1987. PLB 21.35 (*0-89565-371-0*); PLB 14.95s.p. (*0-685-55871-1*) Childs World.
—How Many Ways Can You Cut a Pie? Moncure, Jane B. LC 87-15807. 32p. (ps-2). 1987. PLB 21.35 (*0-89565-408-3*); PLB 14.95s.p. (*0-685-55921-1*) Childs World.
—Kinds of Animals: Flyers, Leapers, Crawlers, Creepers. Moncure, Jane B. LC 89-71172. 32p. (ps-2). 1990. PLB 21.35 (*0-89565-567-5*); PLB 14.95s.p. (*0-89565-596-9*) Childs World.
—Little Too-Tall. Moncure, Jane B. LC 87-11632. 32p. (ps-2). 1987. PLB 21.35 (*0-89565-374-5*); PLB 14.95s.p. (*0-685-55872-X*); pap. 6.96 (*0-89565-448-2*) Childs World.
—Love. rev. ed. Moncure, Jane B. LC 80-27479. 32p. (gr. k-3). 1981. PLB 21.35 (*0-89565-205-6*); PLB 14.95s.p. (*0-685-55492-9*) Childs World.
—The Magic Moon Machine. Moncure, Jane B. LC 87-30959. 32p. (ps-2). 1987. PLB 21.35 (*0-89565-410-5*); PLB 14.95s.p. (*0-685-55923-8*); pap. 6.96 (*0-89565-438-5*) Childs World.
—Mr. Doodle Had a Poodle. Moncure, Jane B. LC 87-15808. 32p. (ps-2). 1987. PLB 21.35 (*0-89565-409-1*); PLB 14.95s.p. (*0-685-55924-6*) Childs World.
—My Eight Book. Moncure, Jane B. LC 85-30962. 32p. (ps-2). 1986. PLB 21.35 (*0-89565-319-2*); PLB 14.95s.p. (*0-685-55823-1*) Childs World.
—My First Christmas Book. Reece, Colleen L. LC 84-9431. 32p. (ps-2). 1984. PLB 15.00 (*0-516-02901-0*); pap. 3.95 (*0-516-42901-9*) Childrens.
—My First Easter Book. Dellinger, Annetta E. LC 84-21512. 32p. (ps-2). 1985. PLB 15.00 (*0-516-02904-5*); pap. 3.95 (*0-516-42904-3*) Childrens.
—My First Fourth of July Book. Hodgson, Harriet W. LC 86-30987. 32p. (ps-2). 1987. pap. 3.95 (*0-516-42907-8*) Childrens.
—My Five Book. Moncure, Jane B. LC 85-9699. 32p. (ps-2). 1985. PLB 21.35 (*0-89565-316-8*); PLB 14.95s.p. (*0-685-55768-5*) Childs World.
—My Four Book. Moncure, Jane B. LC 85-9700. 32p. (ps-2). 1985. PLB 21.35 (*0-89565-315-X*); PLB 14.95s.p. (*0-685-55769-3*) Childs World.
—My Nine Book. Moncure, Jane B. LC 85-30959. 32p. (ps-2). 1986. PLB 21.35 (*0-89565-320-6*); PLB 14.95s.p. (*0-685-55824-X*) Childs World.
—My Seven Book. Moncure, Jane B. LC 86-2594. 32p. (ps-2). 1986. PLB 21.35 (*0-89565-318-4*); PLB 14.95s.p. (*0-685-55825-8*) Childs World.
—My Six Book. Moncure, Jane B. LC 85-30961. 32p. (ps-2). 1986. PLB 21.35 (*0-89565-317-6*); PLB 14.95s.p. (*0-685-55826-6*) Childs World.
—My Ten Book. Moncure, Jane B. LC 86-2293. 32p. (ps-2). 1986. PLB 21.35 (*0-89565-321-4*); PLB 14.95s.p. (*0-685-55827-4*) Childs World.
—My Three Book. Moncure, Jane B. LC 85-5898. 32p. (ps-2). 1985. PLB 21.35 (*0-89565-314-1*); PLB 14.95s.p. (*0-685-55770-7*) Childs World.
—Now I Am Three! Moncure, Jane B. LC 83-20892. 32p. (ps). 1984. pap. 3.95 (*0-516-41877-7*) Childrens.
—A Pocketful of Pets. Moncure, Jane B. LC 87-11748. 32p. (ps-2). 1987. PLB 21.35 (*0-89565-370-2*); PLB 14.95s.p. (*0-685-55875-4*) Childs World.
—Polka-Dot Puppy's Birthday: A Book about Colors. Suire, Diane D. LC 88-10937. 32p. (ps-2). 1988. PLB 21.35 (*0-89565-381-8*); PLB 14.95s.p. (*0-685-55927-0*) Childs World.
—Polka-Dot Puppy's New House: A Book about Counting. McDonnell, Janet. LC 88-11941. 32p. (ps-2). 1988. PLB 21.35 (*0-89565-380-X*); PLB 14.95s.p. (*0-685-55928-9*) Childs World.
—Polka-Dot Puppy's Visitor: A Book about Opposites. Riehecky, Janet. LC 88-10935. 32p. (ps-2). 1988. PLB 21.35 (*0-89565-378-8*); PLB 14.95s.p. (*0-685-55929-7*) Childs World.
—Polka-Dot Puppy's Walk: A Book about Sequences. Riehecky, Janet. LC 88-10934. 32p. (ps-2). 1988. PLB 21.35 (*0-89565-379-6*); PLB 14.95s.p. (*0-685-55930-0*) Childs World.
—Responsibility. Pemberton, Nancy & Riehecky, Janet. LC 87-37557. 32p. (ps). 1988. PLB 21.35 (*0-89565-418-0*); PLB 14.95s.p. (*0-685-55933-5*) Childs World.
—Robots: Here They Come! Riehecky, Janet. LC 90-30634. 32p. (ps-2). 1990. PLB 19.95 (*0-89565-577-2*); PLB 13.95s.p. (*0-685-56193-3*) Childs World.
—Saving the Forests: A Rabbit's Story. Riehecky, Janet. LC 89-28122. 32p. (ps-2). 1990. PLB 19.95 (*0-89565-561-6*); PLB 13.95s.p. (*0-685-56182-8*) Childs World.
—Smile, Says Little Crocodile. Moncure, Jane B. LC 87-13833. 32p. (ps-2). 1987. PLB 21.35 (*0-89565-401-6*); PLB 14.95s.p. (*0-685-55935-1*); pap. 6.96 (*0-89565-449-0*) Childs World.
—Spring: New Life Everywhere. McDonnell, Janet. LC 93-10309. 1993. write for info. (*0-516-00677-0*) Childrens.
—Step into Winter: A New Season. Moncure, Jane B. LC 90-30636. 32p. (ps-2). 1990. PLB 19.95 (*0-89565-574-8*); PLB 13.95s.p. (*0-685-56190-9*) Childs World.
—Success. McDonnell, Janet. LC 88-4348. 32p. (gr. k-3). 1988. PLB 21.35 (*0-89565-376-1*); PLB 14.95s.p. (*0-685-55936-X*) Childs World.
—Summer, a Growing Time. McDonnell, Janet. LC 93-1182. 1993. write for info. (*0-516-00678-9*) Childrens.

—Thankfulness. McDonnell, Janet. LC 88-2657. 32p. (gr. k-3). 1988. PLB 21.35 (*0-89565-375-3*); PLB 14.95s.p. (*0-685-55937-8*) Childs World.
—Umpire's Adventure in Alphabet Town. Alden, Laura. LC 92-12668. 32p. (ps-2). 1992. PLB 14.60 (*0-516-05421-X*) Childrens.
—What Can We Play Today? Moncure, Jane B. LC 87-32565. 32p. (ps-2). 1987. PLB 21.35 (*0-89565-412-1*); PLB 14.95s.p. (*0-685-55940-8*); pap. 6.96 (*0-89565-441-5*) Childs World.
—What Do You Do with a Grumpy Kangaroo? Moncure, Jane B. LC 87-11731. 32p. (ps). 1987. PLB 21.35 (*0-89565-372-9*); PLB 14.95s.p. (*0-685-55877-0*) Childs World.
—Winter: Tracks in the Snow. McDonnell, Janet. LC 93-20172. (ps-6). 1993. write for info. (*0-516-00679-7*) Childrens.
—Word Bird Makes Words with Cat. Moncure, Jane B. LC 83-23948. 32p. (gr. k-2). 1984. PLB 21.35 (*0-89565-259-5*); PLB 14.95s.p. (*0-685-55684-0*) Childs World.
—Word Bird Makes Words with Duck. Moncure, Jane B. LC 83-23943. 32p. (gr. k-2). 1984. PLB 21.35 (*0-89565-261-7*); PLB 14.95s.p. (*0-685-55686-7*) Childs World.
—Word Bird Makes Words with Hen. Moncure, Jane B. LC 83-23944. 32p. (gr. k-2). 1984. PLB 21.35 (*0-89565-260-9*); PLB 14.95s.p. (*0-685-55685-9*) Childs World.
—Word Bird's Circus Surprise. Moncure, Jane B. LC 80-29528. 32p. (gr. k-2). 1981. PLB 21.35 (*0-89565-162-9*); PLB 14.95s.p. (*0-685-55561-5*) Childs World.
—Word Bird's Dinosaur Day. Moncure, Jane B. 32p. (ps-2). 1990. PLB 21.35 (*0-89565-617-5*); PLB 14.95s.p. (*0-685-56204-2*) Childs World.
—Word Bird's Magic Wand. Moncure, Jane B. LC 90-1645. 32p. (ps-2). 1990. PLB 21.35 (*0-89565-580-2*); PLB 14.95s.p. (*0-685-56202-6*) Childs World.
—Word Bird's New Friend. Moncure, Jane B. LC 90-37002. 32p. (ps-2). 1990. PLB 21.35 (*0-89565-616-7*); PLB 14.95s.p. (*0-685-56203-4*) Childs World.
—Word Bird's Rainy-Day Dance. Moncure, Jane B. LC 90-31693. 32p. (ps-2). 1990. PLB 21.35 (*0-89565-579-9*); PLB 14.95s.p. (*0-685-56201-8*) Childs World.
—Word Bird's School Words. Moncure, Jane B. LC 89-7179. 32p. (ps-2). 1989. PLB 21.35 (*0-89565-510-1*); PLB 14.95s.p. (*0-685-56082-1*) Childs World.
—Word Bird's Shapes. Moncure, Jane B. LC 83-15255. 32p. (gr. k-2). 1983. PLB 21.35 (*0-89565-255-2*); PLB 14.95s.p. (*0-685-55679-4*) Childs World.
—Word Bird's Thanksgiving Words. Moncure, Jane B. LC 86-32639. 32p. (gr. k-2). 1987. PLB 21.35 (*0-89565-360-5*); PLB 14.95s.p. (*0-685-55882-7*) Childs World.
—An XYZ Adventure in Alphabet Town. McDonnell, Janet. LC 92-2985. 32p. (ps-2). 1992. PLB 14.60 (*0-516-05424-4*) Childrens.
Hohag, Linda & Jacobson, Lori. Here We Go 'Round the Year. Moncure, Jane. 32p. (gr. 1-3). 1993. pap. text ed. 5.95 (*1-56189-378-1*) Amer Educ Pub.
—How Many Ways Can You Cut a Pie? Moncure, Jane. 32p. (gr. 1-3). 1993. pap. text ed. 5.95 (*1-56189-349-8*) Amer Educ Pub.
—One Tricky Monkey up on Top. Moncure, Jane. 32p. (gr. 1-3). 1993. pap. text ed. 5.95 (*1-56189-376-5*) Amer Educ Pub.
—A Pocketful of Pets. Moncure, Jane. 32p. (gr. 1-3). 1993. pap. text ed. 5.95 (*1-56189-380-3*) Amer Educ Pub.
Hohag, Linda & Spoden, Dan. The Magic Moon Machine. Moncure, Jane. 32p. (gr. 1-3). 1993. pap. text ed. 5.95 (*1-56189-375-7*) Amer Educ Pub.
Hohag, Linda S. Hi, Word Bird. Moncure, Jane B. LC 80-15919. 32p. (ps-2). 1981. PLB 21.35 (*0-89565-159-9*); PLB 14.95s.p. (*0-685-55485-6*) Childs World.
—Hide-&-Seek Word Bird. Moncure, Jane B. LC 81-18068. (ps-2). 1982. PLB 21.35 (*0-89565-218-8*); PLB 14.95s.p. (*0-685-55486-4*) Childs World.
—Kindness. rev. ed. Moncure, Jane B. LC 80-39535. 32p. (gr. k-3). 1981. PLB 21.35 (*0-89565-204-8*); PLB 14.95s.p. (*0-685-55491-0*) Childs World.
—Stop! Go! Word Bird. Moncure, Jane B. LC 80-16273. 32p. (ps-2). 1981. PLB 21.35 (*0-89565-160-2*); PLB 14.95s.p. (*0-685-55552-6*) Childs World.
—Watch Out! Word Bird. Moncure, Jane B. (ps-2). 1982. PLB 21.35 (*0-89565-219-6*); PLB 14.95s.p. (*0-685-55555-0*) Childs World.
Hokanson, Lars, jt. illus. see Hokanson, Lois.
Hokanson, Lois & Hokanson, Lars. Remember Not to Forget: A Memory of the Holocaust. Finkelstein, Norman H. LC 92-24603. 32p. (gr. 2 up). 1993. pap. 4.95 (*0-688-11802-X*, Mulberry) Morrow.
Hokie. The Life & Legends of Santa Claus. Lane, Julie. Zinnott, Nicholas H., intro. by. LC 84-2741. 160p. (gr. 3-6). 1983. 10.95 (*0-917057-00-7*) Tonnis.
Hol, Coby. Bela, Etoile du Cirque. Hol, Coby. (FRE.). 32p. (gr. k-3). 1992. 14.95 (*3-314-20724-7*) North-South Bks NYC.
—Bela Wird Zirkuspony. Hol, Coby. (GER.). 32p. (gr. k-3). 1992. 14.95 (*3-314-00533-4*) North-South Bks NYC.
—La Ferme Des Tournesols. Hol, Coby. (FRE.). 32p. (gr. k-3). 1992. 13.95 (*3-85539-660-4*) North-South Bks NYC.

—Henrietta Saves the Show. Hol, Coby. Graves, Helen, tr. from GER. LC 90-47063. 32p. (ps-k). 1991. 14.95 (1-55858-102-2) North-South Bks NYC.

—Lisa & the Snowman. Hol, Coby. LC 89-42614. 32p. (gr. k-3). 1989. 13.95 (1-55858-022-0) North-South Bks NYC.

—Niki's Little Donkey. Hol, Coby. James, J. Alison, tr. from GER. LC 92-31332. 32p. (gr. k-3). 1993. 14.95 (1-55858-183-9); PLB 14.88 (1-55858-184-7) North-South Bks NYC.

—Der Sonnenhof. Hol, Coby. (GER.). 32p. (gr. k-3). 1992. 13.95 (3-85825-315-4) North-South Bks NYC.

—Tippy Bear & Little Sam. Hol, Coby. LC 91-29672. 32p. (ps-k). 1992. 11.95 (1-55858-138-3); lib. bdg. 11.88 (1-55858-149-9) North-South Bks NYC.

—Tippy Bear Goes to a Party. Hol, Coby. LC 91-8167. 32p. (ps-k). 1991. 11.95 (1-55858-129-4) North-South Bks NYC.

—Tippy Bear Hunts for Honey. Hol, Coby. LC 91-10477. 32p. (ps-k). 1991. 11.95 (1-55858-128-6) North-South Bks NYC.

—A Visit to the Farm. Hol, Coby. LC 88-25366. 32p. (gr. k-3). 1989. 13.95 (1-55858-000-X) North-South Bks NYC.

Holbrook, Clifford & LaMothe, Becky. Symbolically Speaking. Schneider, D. Douglas. Michael, ed. 85p. (ps up). 1987. pap. 5.95 (0-939169-01-0) World Peace Univ.

Holcomb, J. Paul & Holcomb, Sue A. Tex R Masaur: Down in the Dump. Holcomb, Sue A. 32p. (Orig.). (gr. k-3). Date not set. pap. 3.95 (0-9636122-2-0) Post Oak Hill.

Holcomb, Sue A. Tex R Masaur: The Beginning. Holcomb, J. Paul & Holcomb, Sue A. 32p. (Orig.). (gr. k-3). 1993. pap. 3.95 (0-9636122-1-2) Post Oak Hill.

Holcomb, Sue A., jt. illus. see Holcomb, J. Paul.

Holdcroft, Tina. Discover Dinosaurs: A Royal Ontario Museum Book. McGowan, Chris. (gr. 3-7). 1993. pap. 10.95 (1-55074-048-2) Addison-Wesley.

—Discover Dinosaurs: Become a Dinosaur Detective. McGowan, Chris. LC 92-42627. 96p. (gr. 4-7). 1993. pap. 9.95 (0-201-62267-X) Addison-Wesley.

—Scienceworks: Sixty-Five Experiments That Introduce the Fun & Wonder of Science. Ontario Science Center Staff. (gr. 2-7). 1986. pap. 8.61 (0-201-16780-8) Addison-Wesley.

Holden, Tim P. The Run According to Hawkeye. Phillips, JoAnn. Ogle, John C., intro. by. 24p. (Orig.). 1993. pap. write for info. (0-9638403-0-4) Cherokee Strip.

Holder, Elizabeth j. Tell Me a Story. Rondthaler, Katharine B. 64p. (ps-5). pap. 4.00 (1-878422-06-5) Moravian Ch in Amer.

Holder, Heidi. Aesop's Fables. 32p. (ps-3). 1993. pap. 4.99 (0-14-054872-6) Puffin Bks.

—Crows: An Old Rhyme. LC 87-45364. 32p. (ps up). 1987. 14.95 (0-374-31660-0) FS&G.

Holder, John. Dame Shirley & the Gold Rush. Rawls, Jim. LC 92-18083. (gr. 2-5). 1992. PLB 21.34 (0-8114-7222-1) Raintree Steck-V.

Holder, Stanley. No Hill Is Too High. Sealy, Adrienne V. (gr. 2-5). 1978. PLB 4.95 (0-9602670-0-X) Assn Family Living.

Holdorf, Kurt. Kenta Comes to Colorado: A Bilingual Educational Activity Book. Thomas, Carolyn S. Romer, Roy, intro. by. (ENG & JPN.). 64p. (gr. k-4). 1990. pap. 6.95 (0-913730-41-6) Robinson Pr.

Holen, Betsy L. Alaska Wildlife: A Coloring Book. Holen, Susan D. Holen, Anne M., ed. 48p. (gr. 3-8). 1988. pap. 4.95 (0-922127-00-X) Paisley Pub.

—Alaska's Wild Coast. Holen, Susan D. Holen, Anne M., ed. 48p. (Orig.). (gr. 3-8). 1994. pap. 4.95 (0-922127-02-6) Paisley Pub.

Holen, Susan D., jt. illus. see Arehart, Betsy L.

Holiday, Henry & Tenniel, John. The Snark Puzzle Book. Gardner, Martin. 124p. (gr. 3 up) 1990. Repr. of 1973 ed. PLB 14.95 (0-87975-583-0) Prometheus Bks.

Holland, Alex N. Alice's Amazing Butterfly. Holland, Alex N. 15p. (gr. 1-3). 1992. pap. 11.95 (1-56606-001-X) Bradley Mann.

—Child Art: A Book of Drawings. Holland, Alex N. Lewis, Glenn A., intro. by. 56p. (gr. 1-12). 1991. pap. text ed. 23.95 (0-9627882-2-8) Bradley Mann.

—The Children's Big Airplane. Holland, Alex N. 12p. (gr. 1-4). 1992. pap. 10.95 (1-56606-000-1) Bradley Mann.

—Harvey Learns to Drive. Holland, Alex N. 17p. (gr. k-3). 1992. pap. 10.95 (1-895583-52-7) MAYA Pubs.

—Skip. Holland, Alex N. 12p. (gr. 1-3). 1992. pap. 6.95 (1-895583-02-0) MAYA Pubs.

—Time to Learn Our ABC's. Holland, Alex N. 10p. (gr. k-3). 1992. pap. 8.95 (1-895583-14-4) MAYA Pubs.

—Time to Sing Songs. Holland, Alex N. 13p. (gr. k-3). 1992. pap. 12.95 (1-895583-10-1) MAYA Pubs.

—What It Means to Be a Bad Boy. Holland, Alex N. 13p. 1992. pap. 4.95 (1-895583-51-9) MAYA Pubs.

Holland, Audrey E. How Many More to Go, Mom? Holland, Audrey E. 15p. (gr. k-3). 1992. pap. 13.95 (1-895583-13-6) MAYA Pubs.

—When Is It My Turn. Holland, Audrey E. 15p. (gr. k-3). 1992. pap. 15.95 (1-895583-11-X) MAYA Pubs.

—When We Start Having Fun. Holland, Audrey E. 13p. 1992. pap. 10.95 (1-895583-12-8) MAYA Pubs.

Holland, Claudia P. The Worthy Wonders Lost at Sea. Linscott, Jody. LC 92-43367. 1993. pap. 15.00 (0-385-47053-3) Doubleday.

Holland, Janet. The Three Little Pigs Go to Greasy Pete's. Adams, David. 40p. (ps-3). 1993. PLB 14.95 (0-9638421-9-6); pap. 5.95 (0-9638421-8-8) Flatland Tales. SUBJECT - Our story is the tale of the Three Little Pigs before their classical encounter with a big bad wolf. This adventure finds the three young, fun loving, ornery piglets living at home with Mom & Dad. AUTHOR - With his stories, the author David Adams brings children to attentive silence at schools, churches, & family gatherings. His sense of humor & plays on words capture kids' imaginations. Parents are pleased with the way he weaves good manners into this story. ILLUSTRATION - Kids today are becoming more & more experienced working with computers. They will be intrigued to discover the illustrations for this book were created with a computer using the latest technology. Published & distributed by: Flatland Tales Publishing, P.O. Box 887, Ottawa, KS 66067-0887, specializing in quality children's books. *Publisher Provided Annotation.*

Holland, Janice. The Blue Cat of Castle Town. Coblentz, Catherine C. LC 74-14930. 124p. (gr. 3-7). 1983. pap. 8.00 (0-914378-05-8) Countryman.

Hollander, P. Scott. Herne's Promise. Hollander, P. Scott. 61p. (gr. k-4). 1992. pap. write for info. (0-9630657-2-6) Godolphin Hse.

Holleran, Betsy. Dairy Goats: Selecting, Fitting, Showing. Hall, Alice. Jackson, Robert A., frwd. by. LC 77-153203. (gr. 7 up). 1975. pap. 4.00x (0-932218-02-4) Hall Pr.

Holliday, Keaf. Frederick Douglass, Freedom Fighter. Jackson, Garnet N. LC 92-28777. 1992. 56.40 (0-8136-5229-4); pap. 28.50 (0-8136-5702-4) Modern Curr.

Holling, Holling C. Minn of the Mississippi. Holling, Holling C. (gr. 4-6). 1978. pap. 7.70 (0-395-27399-4) HM.

—Seabird. Holling, Holling C. (gr. 4-6). 1978. pap. 7.70 (0-395-26681-5) HM.

—Tree in the Trail. Holling, Holling C. 64p. (gr. 4-6). 1990. pap. 7.70 (0-395-54534-X) HM.

Holling, L. W. Pagoo. Holling, Holling C. (gr. 3-9). 1957. 16.45 (0-395-06826-6) HM.

Holling, Lucille W. Pagoo. Holling, Holling C. 96p. (gr. 4-6). 1990. pap. 7.70 (0-395-53964-1) HM.

Holmes, Bea. Child of the Silent Night: The Story of Laura Bridgman. Hunter, Edith F. 128p. (gr. 2-5). 1963. 14.45 (0-395-06835-5) HM.

Holmes, Carol. Doubleday Children's Picture Dictionary. Law, Felicia. LC 86-16216. 192p. (gr. k-6). 1987. pap. 16.00 (0-385-23711-1) Doubleday.

Holmes, Dave & Kenyon, Sue. A Visit to the Fire Station. Hannum, Dotti. LC 84-12155. 32p. (gr. k-3). 1985. PLB 15.00 (0-516-01491-9); pap. 3.95 (0-516-41491-7) Childrens.

Holmes, Dave, photos by. A Visit to the Post Office. Ziegler, Sandra. LC 89-35061. 32p. (ps-3). 1989. PLB 15.00 (0-516-01487-0); pap. 3.95 (0-516-41487-9) Childrens.

Holmes, David & Robinson, Bernard. Rainforest Animals. Chinery, Michael. LC 91-53143. 40p. (Orig.). (gr. 2-5). 1992. PLB 8.99 (0-679-92047-1); pap. 4.99 (0-679-82047-7) Random Bks Yng Read.

Holmes, David, et al. Nature Search: Underwater. Starry, Paul & Cleave, Andrew. 32p. (gr. 4-7). 1992. 14.00 (0-89577-449-6) RD Assn.

Holmes, Dawn. Out of Step: The Twins Were So Alike... but So Different. Richardson, Jean. LC 92-39666. 28p. (ps-3). 1993. 12.95 (0-8120-5790-2); pap. 5.95 (0-8120-1553-3) Barron.

—Thomas's Sitter. Richardson, Jean. LC 90-13799. 32p. (ps-1). 1991. SBE 13.95 (0-02-776146-0, Four Winds) Macmillan Child Grp.

Holmes, Gerald. Alkali County Tales. Erickson, John R. 100p. (Orig.). (gr. 3up). 1984. 9.95 (0-916941-06-X); pap. 5.95 (0-9608612-8-9) Maverick Bks.

—Hank the Cowdog: Let Sleeping Dogs Lie. Erickson, John R. 19p. (gr. 3 up). 1986. 9.95 (0-916941-15-9); pap. 6.95 (0-916941-14-0); talking book 13.95 (0-916941-16-7) Maverick Bks.

—Hank the Cowdog, Vol. 19: The Case of the Midnight Rustler. Erickson, John R. 116p. (Orig.). (gr. 4-6). 1992. 11.95 (0-87719-219-7); pap. 6.95 (0-87719-218-9); tape 15.95 (0-87719-220-0) Gulf Pub.

Holmes, Gerald L. Cowboys Are Partly Human. Erickson, John R. 110p. (Orig.). (gr. 3 up). 1983. 9.95 (0-9608612-6-2); pap. 5.95 (0-9608612-4-6) Maverick Bks.

—The Further Adventures of Hank the Cowdog. Erickson, John R. 93p. (Orig.). (gr. 3). 1983. 9.95 (0-9608612-7-0); pap. 6.95 (0-9608612-5-4); tape 13.95 (0-916941-02-7) Maverick Bks.

—Hank the Cowdog: Murder in the Middle Pasture. Erickson, John R. 91p. (Orig.). (gr. 3 up). 1985. 9.95 (0-916941-08-6); pap. 6.95 (0-916941-07-8); talking book 13.95 (0-916941-09-4) Maverick Bks.

Holmes, Louis F. Color Me Brown. rev. ed. Giles, Lucille. 47p. (gr. k-6). 1974. pap. 5.00 (0-87485-017-7) Johnson Chi.

Holmes, Sally. The Complete Fairy Tales of Charles Perrault. Philip, Neil & Simborowski, Nicoletta, trs. Philip, Neil & Philip, Neil intro. by. LC 92-17781. 1993. 18.45 (0-395-57002-6, Clarion Bks) HM.

Holmes, Stephen & Kenyon, Tony. I Wonder Why Camels Have Humps & Other Questions about Animals: And Other Questions about Animals. Ganeri, Anita. LC 92-44260. 32p. (gr. k-3). 1993. 8.95 (1-85697-873-7) Kingfisher Bks.

Holmgren, George E. Small Prayers for Small Children. Schreivogel, Paul A. LC 76-135226. 32p. (gr. k-4). 1980. pap. 5.99 (0-8066-1804-3, 10-5836, Augsburg) Augsburg Fortress.

Holt, Cather C. Miss Circo Comes Apart at the Seams. Thompson, Frances M. 18p. (Orig.). (gr. k-3). 1986. pap. 3.95 (0-9616207-0-6) Bks By Brooks.

Holt, Shirley. Mike Goes to the North Pole. Holt, S. Marie. 28p. (gr. k-5). 1993. 21.95x (0-9613476-6-X) Shirlee.

—Mike Moves to the City. Holt, S. Marie. 28p. (gr. k-5). 1992. 21.95x (0-9613476-5-1) Shirlee.

—Mother Goose Nursery Rhymes, Vol. II. Holt, Shirley. 28p. (gr. k-3). 1990. 19.95x (0-9613476-3-5) Shirlee.

—Mother Goose Nursery Rhymes, Vol. II. (gr. k-3). 1991. 19.95x (0-9613476-4-3) Shirlee.

—The Night Before Christmas. Moore, Clement C. 28p. 16.95 (0-9613476-2-7) Shirlee.

—Sophie's Surprise. 2nd ed. Richardson, Lee. 28p. (gr. 3-8). 1984. 16.95 (0-9613476-0-0) Shirlee.

Holtan, Gene. Black & Blue Magic. Snyder, Zilpha K. LC 66-12850. 192p. (gr. 3-7). 1972. Spartan ed. 5.95 (0-689-30075-1, Atheneum) Macmillan Child Grp.

Holtman, Noel. Life's Changes. Maguire, Arlene. LC 91-9353. 32p. (Orig.). (ps-5). 1991. 6.95 (0-941992-26-8) Los Arboles Pub.

Holtzman, Yehudit. Why the Moon Only Glows. Rosenfeld, Dina. 32p. (ps-1). 1992. 8.95 (0-922613-00-1); pap. 6.95 (0-922613-01-X) Hachai Pubns.

Holub, Joan. American Heart Association Kids' Cookbook. American Heart Association Staff & Moller, James. LC 92-56800. 128p. (gr. 4 up). 1993. pap. 15.00 (0-8129-1930-0, Times Bks) Random.

—The Fortune Teller & other Tales, No. 3. Razzi, Jim. LC 90-85300. 64p. (Orig.). (gr. 2-5). 1991. pap. 2.95 (0-448-41082-6, G&D) Putnam Pub Group.

—The Over-the-Hill Ghost. Calif, Ruth. LC 87-30523. 160p. (gr. 3-8). 1988. 10.95 (0-88289-667-9) Pelican.

—The Over-the-Hill Witch. Calif, Ruth. LC 89-35371. 144p. (gr. 5). 1990. 10.95 (0-88289-754-3) Pelican.

—The World Is a Rainbow. Scelsa, Greg & Millang, Steve. 24p. (ps-1). 1992. incl. cassette 9.95 (0-679-81979-7) Random Bks Yng Read.

Holub, Joan, jt. illus. see Rogers, Jacqueline.

Hom, Nancy. The Little Weaver of Thai-Yen Village. Tran-Khan-Tuyet. LC 86-17186. (ENG & VIE.). 24p. (gr. 2-9). 1987. 13.95 (0-89239-030-1) Childrens Book Pr.

Hone, Michael J. Jack's Amazing Magic Bed. Bennett, Helen S. 32p. (gr. 2). 1993. pap. 9.95 (0-9638747-0-5) Tomac Pubng.

Honey, Elizabeth. Dream Time. Gascoigne, Toss, et al, eds. 192p. 1991. 13.45 (0-395-57434-X, Sandpiper) HM.

Honeywood, Varnette P. & Joysmith, Brenda. Shake It to the One That You Love the Best: Play Songs & Lullabies from Black Musical Traditions. Mattox, Cheryl W., ed. (Orig.). (ps-6). 1990. pap. 7.95 (0-9623381-0-9) Warren-Mattox.

Hong, Lily T. How the Ox Star Fell from Heaven. Hong, Lily T. Fay, Ann, ed. LC 90-38978. 32p. (gr. k-3). 1991. 14.95 (0-8075-3428-5) A Whitman.

—Two of Everything. Lily Toy Hong. Mathews, Judith, ed. LC 92-29880. 32p. (gr. k-3). 1993. PLB 14.95 (0-8075-8157-7) A Whitman.

Honore, Paul. Tales from Silver Lands. Finger, Charles J. 225p. (gr. 7 up). 1965. 16.95 (0-685-00496-7) Doubleday.

Hood, G. P., jt. illus. see Ford, Henry J.

Hood, Philip. Androcles and the Lion. Shaw, George Bernard. Storr, Catherine, ed. LC 86-6665. 32p. (gr. 2-5). 1986. PLB 17.96 (0-8172-2625-7) Raintree Steck-V.

Hoofnagle, Keith L. Hawaii Volcanoes Coloring Book. Hoofnagle, Keith L. 32p. (ps-3). 1979. pap. 1.50 coloring book (0-940295-07-5) HI Natural Hist.

Hook, Frances. A Day of Surprises. Tester, Sylvia R. LC 78-23263. 25p. (ps-3). 1979. PLB 21.35 (0-89565-022-3); PLB 14.95s.p. (0-685-55479-1) Childs World.

—Frances Hook Picture Book. Hayes, Wanda. (gr. k-2). 1989. 10.99 (0-87239-243-0, 3548) Standard Pub.

—I Never Say I'm Thankful, But I Am. Moncure, Jane B. LC 78-21577. (ps-3). 1979. PLB 21.35 (*0-89565-023-1*); PLB 14.95s.p. (*0-685-55488-0*) Childs World.
—Jesus Makes Me Happy. Hayes, Wanda. 32p. (gr. k-2). 1990. pasted 2.50 (*0-87403-705-0*, 24-03905) Standard Pub.
—My Baby Brother Needs a Friend. Moncure, Jane B. LC 78-21935. (ps-3). 1979. PLB 21.35 (*0-89565-019-3*) Childs World.
—Saying Thank You Makes Me Happy. Hayes, Wanda. 32p. (gr. k-2). 1990. pasted 2.50 (*0-87403-708-5*, 24-03908) Standard Pub.
—Sometimes I'm Afraid. Tester, Sylvia R. LC 78-23262. (ps-3). 1979. PLB 21.35 (*0-89565-021-5*); PLB 14. 95s.p. (*0-685-55549-6*) Childs World.
—To Be Me. Hazen, Barbara S. LC 75-12960. (ps-2). 1975. PLB 21.35 (*0-913778-09-5*); PLB 14.95s.p. (*0-685-55554-2*) Childs World.
—We Laughed a Lot, My First Day of School. Tester, Sylvia R. LC 78-10900. (ps-3). 1979. PLB 21.35 (*0-89565-020-7*); PLB 14.95s.p. (*0-685-55556-9*) Childs World.
—Wishes, Whispers & Secrets. Moncure, Jane B. LC 78-31295. 1979. PLB 21.35 (*0-89565-024-X*); PLB 14.95s.p. (*0-685-55560-7*) Childs World.
Hook, Frances, jt. illus. see Hook, Richard.
Hook, Frances, jt. illus. see Hook, Robert.
Hook, Richard. The Age of Leif Eriksson. Humble, Richard. LC 89-8867. 32p. (gr. 5-8). 1989. PLB 12.40 (*0-531-10741-8*) Watts.
—Growing up in Ancient China. Teague, Ken. LC 91-14879. 32p. (gr. 3-5). 1993. PLB 11.89 (*0-8167-2715-5*); pap. text ed. 3.95 (*0-8167-2716-3*) Troll Assocs. Postponed.
—Growing up in Aztec Times. Wood, Marion. LC 91-39444. 32p. (gr. 3-5). 1993. PLB 11.89 (*0-8167-2723-6*); pap. text ed. 3.95 (*0-8167-2724-4*) Troll Assocs. Postponed.
—Harald Hardrada & the Vikings. Speed, Peter. LC 92-5818. 63p. (gr. 6-7). 1992. PLB 24.26 (*0-8114-3353-6*) Raintree Steck-V.
—The Voyages of Columbus. Humble, Richard. 32p. (gr. 5-8). 1991. PLB 12.40 (*0-531-14189-6*) Watts.
Hook, Richard & Danforth, Liz. Perils on the Sea of Rhun. Feild, William B., Jr. & Stassun, Peter G. Ney, Jessica, ed. 32p. (Orig.). (gr. 12). 1989. pap. 6.00 (*0-685-37962-0*, 8110) Iron Crown Ent Inc.
Hook, Richard & Hook, Frances. The Big Picture Book about Jesus. D. C. Cook Editors. LC 77-72722. (gr. 3-7). 1977. 13.95 (*0-89191-077-8*, 08292, Chariot Bks) Cook.
—McGee's Favorite Bible Stories. Taylor, Kenneth N. LC 92-20265. 1992. 15.99 (*0-8423-4142-0*) Tyndale.
—The One Year Bible Story Book. Muir, Virginia J. 384p. (gr. 5). 1988. 12.99 (*0-8423-2631-6*) Tyndale.
Hook, Robert & Hook, Frances. My First Bible Stories in Pictures. Taylor, Kenneth N., ed. Lockwood, Robert P., intro. by. 272p. (gr. k-5). 1990. 14.95 (*0-87973-245-8*, 245); 10.95 (*0-87973-246-6*, 246) Our Sunday Visitor.
Hooker, Irene H. & Brindle, Susan A. The Caterpillar That Came to Church - la Oruga Que Fue a Misa: A Story of the Eucharist - Un Cuento de la Eucaristia. Hooker, Irene H. & Brindle, Susan A. Lademan, Miriam A., ed. Houtman, Jane F. & De Martinez, Luz M., trs. LC 92-63219. (ENG & SPA.). 64p. (Orig.). 1993. 9.95 (*0-87973-874-X*, 874); pap. 6.95 (*0-87973-875-8*, 875) Our Sunday Visitor.
Hooker, Russel. Tales of Dunsworth P. Dragon: The Dragon Who Eats Marshmallows. Hooker, Russel. 64p. (ps-3). Date not set. pap. 9.95 (*1-56883-005-X*) Colonial Pr AL.
Hooker, Saralinda & Ragus, Christopher. The Art of Construction: Projects & Principles for Beginning Engineers & Architects. 3rd ed. Salvadori, Mario. LC 89-49406. 144p. (gr. 5 up). 1990. pap. 9.95 (*1-55652-080-8*) Chicago Review.
Hoopes, Barbara. Alligators & Crocodiles. Wildlife Education, Ltd. Staff. 20p. (Orig.). (gr. 5 up). 1984. pap. 2.75 (*0-937934-25-9*) Wildlife Educ.
—Sharks. Wildlife Education, Ltd. Staff. 20p. (gr. 5 up). 1983. pap. 2.75 (*0-937934-15-1*) Wildlife Educ.
—Wild Horses. Wildlife Education, Ltd. Staff. 20p. (Orig.). (gr. 5 up). 1982. pap. 2.75 (*0-937934-08-9*) Wildlife Educ.
Hoopes, Barbara & Oden, Dick. Snakes. Wildlife Education, Ltd. Staff. 20p. (Orig.). (gr. 5 up). 1981. pap. 2.75 (*0-937934-05-4*) Wildlife Educ.
Hoopes, Barbara, et al. Elephants. Wildlife Education, Ltd. Staff. 20p. (Orig.). (gr. 5 up). 1980. pap. 2.75 (*0-937934-00-3*) Wildlife Educ.
Hope, Muriel. Rudy Visits the North. Lang, Aubrey. LC 91-75423. 40p. (ps-2). 1992. 14.95 (*1-56282-182-2*); PLB 14.89 (*1-56282-208-X*) Hyprn Child.
Hopkins, Catherine. A Boy's Best Friend. Alden, Joan. LC 92-8061. 32p. (ps-2). 1992. 12.95 (*1-55583-203-2*, Alyson Wonderland) Alyson Pubns.
Horen, Michael. Alef To Tav. Ganz, Yaffa. 48p. (gr. 1-6). 1989. 11.95 (*0-89906-962-2*); pap. 7.95 (*0-89906-963-0*) Mesorah Pubns.
—The Artscroll Youth Megillah: Fully Illustrated with the Complete Text, Simplified Translation & Comments. Scherman, Nosson & Zlotowitz, Meir. Gold, Avie, ed. 48p. (gr. 3-12). 1988. 15.95 (*0-89906-067-6*); pap. 12.95 (*0-89906-068-4*) Mesorah Pubns.

—My Blessings for Food: Birchas Hamozon. Zlotowitz, M. 32p. (gr. 1-6). 7.95 (*0-89906-799-9*) Mesorah Pubns.
Horen, Michael, jt. illus. see Dershowitz, Yosef.
Horen, Michael, jt. illus. see Halasz, Andras.
Horen, Michael, jt. illus. see Snowden, Linda.
Horenstein, Henry. Sam Goes Trucking. Horenstein, Henry. (ps-3). 1989. 14.45 (*0-395-44313-X*) HM.
Horenstein, Henry, photos by. Hoops: Behind the Scenes with the Boston Celtics. Boyd, Brendan, text by. 128p. (gr. 3-7). 1989. (Spts Illus Kids); pap. 8.95 (*0-316-37309-5*) Little.
—Mike Goes Trucking. 1988. write for info. HM.
—That's a Wrap: How Movies Are Made. Dowd, Ned. Mamet, David, frwd. by. LC 91-6435. 64p. (gr. 3-7). 1991. pap. 15.00 jacketed (*0-671-70972-0*, S&S BFYR) S&S Trade.

Horine, Billie & Seitz, Connie. Kidworks Series, No. 1. Smith, J. C. & McLean, J. (ps-5). 1993. Set. PLB 32.65g (*1-882627-17-2*) KTS Pub. New Educational Activity-Coloring Books for children ages 10 & under. The series includes ALPHAPICS, SHAPEPICS, WORDINATIONS, EASY DRAW & TEACHPAKS. A fun way to learn, provides hours of learning fun in the basics. Teaches eye-hand coordination, counting, number & letter recognition, easy reading, shapes. Brightly colored covers. ALPHAPICS uses ABCs & fun pictures with tracing paper & alliterations to teach ages 5 & under letters. SHAPEPICS teaches counting, numbers & shapes with tracing paper & pictures created with shapes. Very basic. WORDINATIONS - five titles- FUNTIME, MAMAS & BABIES, AROUND TOWN, SEASONS & HOLIDAYS & BIBLE STORIES. Word find puzzles with pictures, rebus stories & writing pages. Ages 9 & under. TEACHPAKS variations of ALPHAPICS & WORDINATIONS. Pages provided for copying for use by educators. EASY DRAW develops eye-hand coordination while tracing & coloring pictures.
Publisher Provided Annotation.

Hormann, Toni. Young Amelia Earhart: A Dream to Fly. Alcott, Sarah. LC 91-24974. 32p. (gr. k-2). 1992. text ed. 11.59 (*0-8167-2528-4*); pap. text ed. 2.95 (*0-8167-2529-2*) Troll Assocs.
Horn, Donna. Party & Holiday Decorations: A Handbook of Wafer Fun. Horn, Donna. LC 87-50697. 88p. (Orig.). (gr. 4-12). 1988. pap. 14.95 (*0-935009-97-3*) Wafer Mache.
Horne, Daniel. The Phantom of the Northern Marches. Staplehurst, Graham. Fenlon, Peter, ed. 32p. (Orig.). (gr. 10-12). 1986. pap. 6.00 (*0-915795-47-7*, 8102) Iron Crown Ent Inc.
—Raiders of Cardolan. McKeage, Jeff. Charlton, Coleman, ed. 32p. (Orig.). (gr. 10-12). 1988. pap. 6.00 (*1-55806-005-7*, 8108) Iron Crown Ent Inc.
Horning, Robert. My Pop-up Photo Book. Costello, Linda, contrib. by. LC 90-85727. 8p. (ps-1). 1991. 10. 95 (*1-878093-05-3*) Boyds Mills Pr.
Hornsby, Sarah. At the Name of Jesus. Hornsby, Sarah. 256p. 1986. 12.99 (*0-8007-9078-2*) Chosen Bks.
Horosko, Marina M. I Can't Wait. Crary, Elizabeth. LC 82-6277. 32p. (Orig.). (ps-2). 1982. PLB 15.95 (*0-9602862-6-8*); pap. 4.95 (*0-9602862-3-3*) Parenting Pr.
—I Want It. Crary, Elizabeth. LC 82-2129. 32p. (Orig.). (ps-2). 1982. PLB 15.95 (*0-9602862-5-X*); pap. 4.95 (*0-9602862-2-5*) Parenting Pr.
—I Want to Play. Crary, Elizabeth. LC 82-3610. 32p. (Orig.). (ps-2). 1982. PLB 15.95 (*0-9602862-7-6*); pap. 4.95 (*0-9602862-4-1*) Parenting Pr.
—My Name Is Not Dummy. Crary, Elizabeth. LC 83-24983. 32p. (Orig.). (ps-2). 1983. PLB 15.95 (*0-9602862-9-2*); pap. 4.95 (*0-9602862-8-4*) Parenting Pr.
Horstman, Lisa. Fast Friends: A Tail & Tongue Tale. Horstman, Lisa. LC 93-28630. 1994. 13.00 (*0-679-85404-5*); PLB 13.99 (*0-679-95404-X*) Knopf Bks Yng Read.
Horton, Terri, jt. illus. see Sherentz, Michael.

Horton, Verne. Battleborn Nevada: Its People, History & Stories. Lynch, Don & Thompson, David. Bean, James H., ed. LC 93-79470. 360p. (gr. 6 up). 1994. 31.00 (*0-913205-20-6*) Grace Dangberg.
A colorful montage by a Nevada artist leads off each of the eight chapters in this 260-page hard cover book. Pictures of characters, places, events, & maps, over 275 illustrations in all, guide the reader through Nevada from prehistoric Indians through statehood during the Civil War & on to modern Nevada with its diverse ethnic & cultural population. The chapters: 1) The Indians, 2) Trailblazers & Emigrants, 3) Railroads, Cities, & Travel, 4) Mining, 5) Agriculture, 6) Government, 7) Business, & 8) The People of Nevada portray Nevada through the use of the land. The book tells of the importance of mining to the state of the nation, the coming of the railroad, & the beginning of Nevada cities. Also told is the development of gambling in Nevada as a natural heritage of the mining boom towns, & how gaming & tourism developed the communities of Nevada. The reader will see how the geographical influence of the Great Basin & the social & economic influence of gaming as an industry make Nevada different from any other state.
Publisher Provided Annotation.

Horton, Vicki M. My Book of Zoo Rhymes. Graham, Bill. 18p. (ps). 1991. 9.95 (*1-879680-10-6*) About You.
Horvat, Karl J. Owlbert. Harris, Nicholas. LC 89-4445. 32p. (gr. 2-3). 1989. PLB 18.60 (*0-8368-0110-5*) Gareth Stevens Inc.
Horvat, Laurel M. Lancelot the Ocelot. Bechtel, Beverly. 32p. (gr. k-3). 1991. PLB 18.95 (*0-87614-687-6*) Carolrhoda Bks.
Horwitz, Joshua. Night Markets: Bringing Food to a City. Horwitz, Joshua. LC 85-45401. 96p. (gr. 2-6). 1986. pap. 6.95 (*0-06-446046-0*, Trophy) HarpC Child Bks.
Hosack, Leona H. Willie & the Number Three Door & Other Adventures. Reeves, Adrienne E. 120p. (Orig.). (gr. 1-3). 1991. pap. 8.95 (*0-87743-703-3*) Bahai.
Hosking-Smith, Jan. Click! A Story about George Eastman. Mitchell, Barbara. 64p. (gr. 3-6). 1986. PLB 14.95 (*0-87614-289-7*) Carolrhoda Bks.
Hosten, James. The Original Freddie Ackerman. Irwin, Hadley. LC 91-43145. 192p. (gr. 5 up). 1992. SBE 14. 95 (*0-689-50562-0*, M K McElderry) Macmillan Child Grp.
Hotshots. Cabbage Patch Kids Adventure. 24p. (gr. 1-5). 1984. 5.95 (*0-910313-31-8*) Parker Bros.
Houbre, Gilbert. Carotte. (FRE.). (ps-1). 1989. 14.95 (*2-07-035711-2*) Schoenhof.
Houget, Susan R. I Unpacked My Grandmother's Trunk. Hoguet, Susan R. LC 83-1701. 58p. (ps-3). 1983. 13. 95 (*0-525-44069-0*, DCB) Dutton Child Bks.
Hough, Bonnie J. & Cook, Allen. Milas, the Innkeeper of Harvest Tree. Dela Pena, Alba. 28p. 1993. saddle stitched 8.95 (*1-56167-119-3*) Am Literary Pr.
Hough, Judith. Mary Mack - A Paper Doll Circa 1895: Color Decorate Authentic Fashions & Ethnic Costumes. Hough, Judith. 26p. (gr. 2-6). 1992. pap. 7.95 (*0-9633769-1-8*) Touch The Sky.
—My School Days Memories: Grades K-6. Hough, Judith M. 40p. (gr. k-6). 1992. pap. 7.95 (*0-9633769-0-X*) Touch The Sky.
Houghes, jt. illus. see Wheelhouse, A. V.
Houghton, Diane. The Quiet Hero - A Baseball Story. Lonborg, Rosemary. 32p. (gr. 2-6). 1993. perfect bound 7.95 (*0-8283-1958-8*) Branden Pub Co.
Houk, Randy. Bentley & Blueberry. Houk, Randy. 32p. (gr. k-3). 1993. 14.95 (*1-882728-00-9*); read-along cass. 7.95 (*1-882728-03-3*) Benefactory.
—Jasmine. Houk, Randy. 32p. (gr. k-3). 1993. 14.95 (*1-882728-01-7*); read-along cass. 7.95 (*1-882728-04-1*) Benefactory.
—Ruffle, Coo & Hoo Doo. Houk, Randy. 32p. (gr. k-3). 1993. 14.95 (*1-882728-02-5*); read-along cass. 7.95 (*1-882728-05-X*) Benefactory.

Houle, Tim. Be the Best You Can Be. Puckett, Kirby. 40p. 1993. 14.95 (*0-931674-20-4*) Waldman Hse Pr. Baseball superstar Kirby Puckett shares with kids his life story & the many values & lessons he has learned both on & off the field. Kirby tells about growing up in the south side of Chicago, his love & respect for his family, & his amazing baseball career. BE THE BEST YOU CAN BE inspires kids to reach for excellence in whatever they do. "...the book is a solid piece of inspirational biography that portrays both the man & the baseball player. It will be a useful purchase for school & public libraries."-- BOOKLIST. Filled with four-color illustrations & photographs. Hardcover, $14.95. 40pp. ISBN 0-931674-20-4. *Publisher Provided Annotation.*

House, David J. Loving Memories from Dog to Dog. Gabriel, Howard W., III. 32p. (Orig.). (gr. k-6). 1987. pap. 2.95 (0-936997-01-X) M & H Enter.
Houser, Allan C. Runner in the Sun. McNickle, D'Arcy. LC 87-5986. 260p. 1987. pap. 11.95 (0-8263-0974-7) U of NM Pr.
Houston, Dick, photos by. Safari Adventure. Houston, Dick. LC 91-8038. 160p. (gr. 6 up). 1991. 15.95 (0-525-65051-2, Cobblehill Bks) Dutton Child Bks.
Houston, James. Drifting Snow: An Arctic Search. Houston, James. LC 91-42674. 160p. (gr. 5 up). 1992. SBE 13.95 (0-689-50563-9, M K McElderry) Macmillan Child Grp.
—First Came the Indians. Wheeler, M. J. LC 82-13916. 32p. (gr. 1-5). 1983. SBE 12.95 (0-689-50258-3, M K McElderry) Macmillan Child Grp.
—Frozen Fire: A Tale of Courage. Houston, James. LC 77-6366. 160p. (gr. 7 up). 1977. SBE 13.95 (0-689-50083-1, M K McElderry) Macmillan Child Grp.
—Frozen Fire: A Tale of Courage. 2nd ed. Houston, James. LC 91-46062. 160p. (gr. 3-7). 1992. pap. 4.95 (0-689-71612-5, Aladdin) Macmillan Child Grp.
—The Incredible Eskimo. Coccola, Raymond de & King, Paul. Cameron, J., ed. 435p. (Orig.). (gr. 9). 1986. pap. 16.95 (0-88839-189-7) Hancock House.
Hovland, Gary. Krindlekrax: Or How Ruskin Splinter Battled a Horrible Monster & Saved His Entire Neighborhood. Ridley, Philip. LC 91-23374. 144p. (gr. 3-7). 1992. 15.00 (0-679-81764-6); PLB 15.99 (0-679-91764-0) Knopf Bks Yng Read.
Howard, Alan. The Faber Book of Magical Tales. Lines, Kathleen, ed. LC 85-4437. 176p. (gr. 5-9). 1985. pap. 7.95 (0-571-13648-6) Faber & Faber.
Howard, Arthur. Mr. Putter & Tabby Pour the Tea. Rylant, Cynthia. LC 93-21470. (ps-6). 1994. write for info. (0-15-256255-9) HarBrace.
—Mr. Putter & Tabby Walk the Dog. Rylant, Cynthia. LC 93-21467. (ps-6). 1994. write for info. (0-15-256259-1) HarBrace.
Howard, Cecelia, jt. illus. see Murchison, Leon.
Howard, Cecelia, et al. Henry Box Brown; Struggle for Freedom; Wildfire. 2nd ed. Pruitt, Pamela, et al. McCluskey, John A., ed. (Orig.). (gr. 4-7). 1993. pap. 3.00 (0-913678-25-2) New Day Pr.
Howard, Jean G. Half a Cage. Howard, Jean G. LC 78-62962. 319p. (gr. 4-12). 1978. 5.50 (0-930954-07-6) Tidal Pr.
—Of Mice & Mice. limited ed. Howard, Jean G. LC 78-50486. (gr. k-4). 1978. 5.50 (0-930954-03-3); deluxe ed. 35.00 deluxe ed. (0-930954-04-1) Tidal Pr.

Howard, Kim. Lovables in the Kingdom of Self-Esteem. Loomans, Diane. Carleton, Nancy, ed. LC 90-52633. 32p. **(ps-5). 1991. 14.95 (0-915811-25-1)** H J Kramer Inc.
THE LOVABLES illuminates the heart of self-esteem! An absolute must for teachers & parents.--Dr. Andrew Mecca, former chairman, California Task Force to Promote Self-Esteem & Personal & Social Responsibility. "A truly outstanding self-esteem book for children. The most beautiful I've seen!" --LeRoy Foster, Executive Director, National Council for Self-Esteem. "I am lovable!" is the magic phrase that opens the gates to the Kingdom of Self-Esteem. Blending an imaginative narrative, charming illustrations, & important lessons in living, this book conducts young readers to the enchanted realm where twenty-four remarkable animals--the Lovables-- await them. Each member of the Lovable Team has a special gift to share that gives the child a way of

identifying with & creating qualities that make up a positive self-image. 60,000 copies in print. ENDORSED BY THE NEW YORK BOARD OF EDUCATION FOR USE IN ALL SCHOOLS. *Publisher Provided Annotation.*

—The Other Side of the Wall. Woychuk, Denis. LC 90-49415. 32p. (ps up). 1991. 13.95 (0-688-09894-0); PLB 13.88 (0-688-09895-9) Lothrop.
Howard, Linda. I Have a Song for You, Vol. 3: About Animals. Brady, Janeen. 50p. (ps-4). 1988. pap. text ed. 6.95 activity bk. (0-944803-08-3); Ed. by Ted Brady, Illus. by Phyllis & Warren Luch, 1979, 42pgs. songbook 6.95 (0-944803-06-7); cassette 7.95 (0-944803-07-5) Brite Intl.
Howard, Paul. Rosie's Fishing Expedition. Hest, Amy. LC 93-28543. 1994. write for info. (1-56402-296-X) Candlewick Pr.
Howard, Richard. The Call of the Running Tide: A Portrait of an Island Family. Graff, Nancy P. (gr. 3-7). 1991. 16.95 (0-316-32278-4) Little.
—The Strength of the Hills: A Portrait of a Family Farm, Vol. 1. Graff, Nancy Price. 1989. 14.95 (0-316-32277-6) Little.
Howard, Richard, photos by. Where the River Runs: A Portrait of a Refugee Family. Graff, Nancy P. LC 92-24184. 1993. 16.95 (0-316-32287-3) Little.
Howard, Susie. Katharine Lee Bates: Author of "America the Beautiful" Glover, Janice. (Orig.). (gr. 3-7). 1993. pap. 7.95 (1-883613-00-0) Byte Size.
Howard, Wayne. The Friendly Forest. Howard, Wayne. Perle, Ruth L., ed. (gr. k-1). 1977. pap. text ed. 0.60 (0-89796-855-7) New Dimens Educ.
—Heat Wave. Howard, Wayne. Perle, Ruth L., ed. (gr. k-1). 1977. pap. text ed. 0.60 (0-89796-856-5) New Dimens Educ.
—The Well. Howard, Wayne. Perle, Ruth L., ed. (gr. k-1). 1977. pap. text ed. 0.60 (0-89796-859-X) New Dimens Educ.
Howatson, Melody. I'm Always in Trouble. Cummings, Carol. 24p. (Orig.). (ps-3). 1991. pap. 3.99 (0-9614574-5-7) Teaching WA.
—Sticks & Stones. Cummings, Carol. 24p. (Orig.). (ps-3). 1992. pap. 4.99 (0-9614574-8-1) Teaching WA.
—Tattlin' Madeline. Cummings, Carol. 24p. (Orig.). (ps-3). 1991. pap. 3.99 (0-9614574-4-9) Teaching WA.
—Win-Win Day. Cummings, Carol. 24p. (Orig.). (ps-3). 1991. pap. 3.99 (0-9614574-6-5) Teaching WA.
Howe, Caroline W., jt. illus. see Mariana.
Howe, John. The Fisherman & His Wife. Grimm, Jacob & Grimm, Wilhelm K. 32p. (gr. 6 up). 1983. PLB 13.95s.p. (0-87191-937-0) Creative Ed.
—The Knight with the Lion: The Story of Yvain. Howe, John, retold by. LC 92-25940. 1993. 14.95 (0-316-37583-7) Little.
—The Man Who Lit the Stars. Clement, Claude. (ps-3). 1992. 15.95 (0-316-14741-5) Little.
—Rip Van Winkle. Irving, Washington. Howe, John, retold by. (ps-3). 1988. 14.95 (0-316-37578-0) Little.
—Rip Van Winkle. Irving, Washington. Howe, John, retold by. (ps-3). 1991. pap. 5.95 (0-316-37584-5) Little.
Howell, Dean. The Story of Chinaman's Hat. Howell, Dean. 36p. (ps-4). 1990. 7.95 (0-89610-149-5) Island Heritage.
Howell, Frank. Many Winters. Wood, Nancy. LC 74-3554. 80p. (gr. 6 up). 1974. pap. 14.95 (0-385-02226-3) Doubleday.
—Many Winters. Wood, Nancy. LC 74-3554. 80p. (gr. 7 up). 1974. pap. 10.00 (0-385-30865-5) Doubleday.
—Spirit Walker: Poems. Wood, Nancy. LC 92-29376. 1993. pap. 19.95 (0-385-30927-9) Doubleday.
Howell, Kathleen C. Dog Days. Rodowsky, Colby. 96p. (gr. 2-6). 1990. 14.00 (0-374-36342-0) FS&G.
—Garage Sale Fever. Myers, Laurie. LC 92-40342. 80p. (gr. 1-5). 1993. 13.00 (0-06-022905-5); PLB 12.89 (0-06-022908-X) HarpC.
—How I Found Myself at the Fair. Mauser, Pat R. LC 90-30630. 64p. (gr. 1-4). 1990. pap. 2.95 (0-689-71414-9, Aladdin) Macmillan Child Grp.
—The Singing Green: New & Selected Poems for All Seasons. Merriam, Eve. LC 91-31205. 112p. (gr. 3 up). 1992. 14.00 (0-688-11025-8) Morrow Jr Bks.
Howell, Troy. Birds. Adoff, Arnold. LC 81-47753. 64p. (gr. k-5). 1982. (Lipp Jr Bks) HarpC Child Bks.
—The Comeback Dog. Thomas, Jane R. 64p. (gr. 2-6). 1981. 13.45 (0-395-29432-0, Clarion Bks) HM.
—Favorite Greek Myths. Osborne, Mary P. (gr. 2-6). 1989. pap. 15.95 (0-590-41338-4) Scholastic Inc.
—Fox in a Trap. Thomas, Jane R. LC 86-17412. 96p. (gr. 3-6). 1987. 13.95 (0-89919-473-7, Clarion Bks) HM.
—Fox in a Trap. Thomas, Jane R. LC 86-17412. 96p. (gr. 2-5). 1990. pap. 3.95 (0-395-54426-2, Clarion Bks) HM.
—Friend Dog. Adoff, Arnold. LC 80-7773. 48p. (gr. k-5). 1980. PLB 11.89 (0-685-02080-0, Lipp Jr Bks) HarpC Child Bks.
—Lucy's Winter Tale. Ehrlich, Amy. LC 88-25740. 32p. (gr. k). 1992. 14.00 (0-8037-0659-6); PLB 13.89 (0-8037-0661-8) Dial Bks Young.
—The Night Swimmers. Byars, Betsy. LC 79-53597. 160p. (gr. 4-6). 1980. 9.95 (0-685-01397-9); pap. 11.95 (0-385-28709-7) Delacorte.

—The Night Swimmers. Byars, Betsy. 144p. (gr. 5-9). 1983. pap. 3.50 (0-440-45857-9, YB) Dell.
—The Old-Fashioned Storybook. Schwartz, Betty, ed. 144p. (gr. k-6). 1985. 12.95 (0-685-10340-4) S&S Trade.
—Peter & the North Wind. Littledale, Freya. 32p. (gr. k-3). 1989. pap. 2.50 (0-590-40629-9) Scholastic Inc.
—The Secret Garden. Burnett, Frances H. 288p. (gr. k-6). 12.99 (0-517-63225-X) Outlet Bk Co.
—The Ugly Duckling. Andersen, Hans Christian. Howell, Troy, retold by. 40p. 1990. 15.95 (0-399-22158-1, Putnam) Putnam Pub Group.
Howes, Janice. A Classroom Presents the Constitution of the United States: A Story for Elementary School Children. Howes, Janice. LC 87-50078. 35p. (Orig.). (gr. k-5). 1987. pap. 7.00 (0-942431-00-6) Teachers Pub Hse.
Howett, Andrew & Davidson, Gordon. Farm Through the Ages. Steele, Philip. LC 91-37819. 32p. (gr. 3-6). 1993. PLB 11.89 (0-8167-2731-7); pap. text ed. 3.95 (0-8167-2732-5) Troll Assocs. Postponed.
—House Through the Ages. Steele, Philip. LC 91-36481. 32p. (gr. 3-6). 1993. PLB 11.89 (0-8167-2733-3); pap. text ed. 3.95 (0-8167-2734-1) Troll Assocs. Postponed.
—Road Through the Ages. Steele, Philip. LC 91-35878. 32p. (gr. 3-6). 1993. PLB 11.89 (0-8167-2737-6); pap. text ed. 3.95 (0-8167-2738-4) Troll Assocs. Postponed.
Howland, Deborah. After Columbus: The Horse's Return to America. Viola, Herman J. Thomas, Peter, narrated by. 32p. (gr. 2-5). 1992. 11.95 (0-924483-61-X); incl. audiocass. tape 16.95 (0-924483-60-1); incl. audiocass. tape & 13" stuffed mustang toy 39.95 (0-924483-58-X); incl. audiocass. tape & 9" stuffed mustang toy 25.95 (0-924483-59-8); audiocassette (0-924483-74-1) Soundprints.
—Prairie Dog Town. Rogers, Bettye. Komicar, Alexi, narrated by. 32p. (gr. k-3). 1993. 11.95 (1-56899-005-7); incl. audiocassette 16.95 (1-56899-004-9); incl. audiocassette, 11 in. plush toy 39.95 (1-56899-002-2); incl. audiocassette, 8 in. plush toy 25.95 (1-56899-003-0) Soundprints.
Howland, Thomas. Fundamental Skills of Mathematics. Thompson, Denisse & Van Loy, Merrie. Howland, Joe & Savige, Katherine, eds. LC 87-50098. 536p. (gr. 9-12). 1987. text ed. 19.95 (0-943202-16-7) H & H Pub.
Howsepian, Brenda. Historical Connections in Mathematics: Resources for Using History of Mathematics in the Classroom. Reimer, Wilbert & Reimer, Luetta. 103p. (Orig.). (gr. 4-9). 1992. pap. text ed. 14.95 (1-881431-35-5, 2002) AIMS Educ Fnd.
Hoy, Joanne H. Me Plus Math Equals Headache. Wardlaw, Lee. LC 86-20305. (Orig.). (gr. 1-3). 1986. pap. 3.50 (0-931093-07-4) Red Hen Pr.
Hoys, James. Jug of Silver. Capote, Truman. LC 86-4230. 48p. (gr. 4 up). 1986. PLB 13.95s.p. (0-88682-076-6) Creative Ed.
—Let Me Fall Before I Fly. Wersba, Barbara. LC 86-2686. 48p. (gr. 6 up). 1986. PLB 13.95s.p. (0-88682-057-X) Creative Ed.
Hrivnak, James R., jt. illus. see Hrivnak, Suzette.
Hrivnak, Suzette & Hrivnak, James R. Mealtime at the Zoo. Bornstein, Harry. 48p. (ps-2). 1973. pap. 5.95 (0-913580-11-2) Gallaudet Univ Pr.
Hron, Debi. Red, Green, Yellow. Shapiro, Mary S. 12p. (ps-k). 1985. 3.95 (0-934361-01-0); Set. write for info. Kinder Read.
—Stop, Start. Shapiro, Mary S. 14p. (ps-k). 1985. 3.95 (0-934361-03-7); Set. write for info. (0-934361-00-2) Kinder Read.
Hron, Debi, jt. illus. see Hinchberger, William D.
Hsu, Serena. Colorful Kansas City. Branton, Leslie B. LC 90-50125. 64p. (Orig.). (gr. 2 up). 1990. pap. 4.95 (0-933701-47-0) Westport Pubs.
Hsu-Flanders, Lillian. Dumpling Soup. Rattigan, Jama K. (gr. 4-8). 1993. 15.95 (0-316-73445-4) Little.
Hu, Ying-Hwa. Dressing up Like Mommy. French, Susan M. 24p. (Orig.). (gr. k-1). 1990. pap. 0.99 (1-878624-35-0) McClanahan Bk.
—The Story of Jonah. Schorsch, Laurence, retold by. 24p. (ps-3). 1992. 4.95 (1-56288-222-8) Checkerboard.
Huang, Benrei. Boo! Guess Who? LC 89-61374. 14p. (ps). 1990. bds. 3.99 (0-679-80278-9) Random Bks Yng Read.
—Let's Go Riding in Our Strollers. Manushkin, Fran. LC 92-72935. 32p. (ps-k). 1993. 13.95 (1-56282-390-6); PLB 13.89 (1-56282-391-4) Hyprn Child.
—Pop-up Merry Christmas. 14p. (ps-1). 1992. 3.95 (0-448-40253-X, G&D) Putnam Pub Group.
—Pop-up Monster Party. 14p. (ps-1). 1992. 3.95 (0-448-40255-6, G&D) Putnam Pub Group.
—Pop-up Santa's Workshop. 14p. (ps-1). 1992. 3.95 (0-448-40252-1, G&D) Putnam Pub Group.
—Pop-up Spooky Night. 14p. (ps-1). 1992. 3.95 (0-448-40254-8, G&D) Putnam Pub Group.
—The Teeny Tiny Woman. 18p. (ps). 1993. bds. 3.95 (0-448-40176-2, G&D) Putnam Pub Group.
—What Can a Giant Do? Cuneo, Mary L. LC 92-8307. 32p. (ps-2). 1994. 14.00 (0-06-021214-4); PLB 13.89 (0-06-021217-9) HarpC Child Bks.
Hubbard, Woodleigh. C Is for Curious: An ABC of Feelings. Hubbard, Woodleigh. 40p. (ps-1). 1990. 12.95 (0-87701-679-8) Chronicle Bks.
—Four Fur Feet. Brown, Margaret W. LC 93-31523. 1994. write for info. (0-7868-0002-X); PLB write for info. (0-7868-2000-4) Hyprn Child.
—Hip Cat. London, Jonathan. LC 93-1179. 1993. 13.95 (0-8118-0315-5) Chronicle Bks.

—The Moles & the Mireuk: A Korean Folktale. Kwon, Holly H., retold by. LC 92-437. 32p. (gr. k-3). 1993. 14.95 (*0-395-64347-3*) HM.
—Two Is for Dancing: A One, Two, Three of Actions. Hubbard, Woodleigh. 32p. (ps-1). 1991. 13.95 (*0-87701-895-2*) Chronicle Bks.
Hubbi, Mona. Grandma's Garden. Kezzeiz, Ediba. 21p. (Orig.). 1991. pap. 3.50 (*0-89259-113-7*) Am Trust Pubns.
Huber, Carrie. Cinco de Mayo: An Historical Play. Bradley, Mignon L. LC 81-8341. (ENG & SPA.). 60p. (Orig.). (gr. 4 up). 1981. pap. 6.95 (*0-939584-00-X*) LUISA Prods.
Huber, Nancy D. Forget-Me-Not. Falk, Bonnie H. LC 84-90501. 192p. (gr. 4-8). 1984. pap. 7.95 (*0-9614108-0-9*) BHF Memories.
Huberman, Caryn & Wetzel, JoAnne, photos by. Onstage Backstage. Huberman, Caryn & Wetzel, JoAnne. 56p. (gr. 2-5). 1987. PLB 21.50 (*0-87614-307-9*) Carolrhoda Bks.
Hubley, Faith. Enter Life. Hubley, Faith & Towe, Kenneth M. LC 82-71680. 32p. (gr. 4 up). pap. 9.95 (*0-440-02357-2*, E Friede) Delacorte.
Hubrich, Dan. The Canterbury Tales. Chaucer, Geoffrey. Stewart, Diana, adapted by. LC 80-22141. 48p. (gr. 4 up). 1983. PLB 18.64 (*0-8172-1666-9*) Raintree Steck-V.
Huculak, Greg, jt. illus. see Tisserand, Rose-Ann.
Hudd, Stacy. Just Mole. Tripp, C. J. LC 87-71721. 137p. (Orig.). (gr. 4-6). 1989. pap. 7.00 (*0-916383-39-3*) Aegina Pr.
Hudgins, Paul. Cedar Fever: Story of a German-Texan Girl During World War I. Martinello, Marian L. LC 92-73295. 212p. (gr. 7-9). 1992. 15.95 (*0-931722-90-X*); pap. 7.95 (*0-931722-95-0*) Corona Pub.
Hudnut, R. Digging Down to China. Frost, Lesley. 64p. (gr. 1-4). 1968. 9.95 (*0-8159-5306-2*) Devin.
Hudson, Carol. Folk Tales Told Around the World. Pasamanick, Judith & Thoms, Judith J. LC 92-47128. 48p. (gr. 4-6). 1993. PLB 13.98 (*0-382-24363-3*); 11. 98 (*0-382-24372-2*) Silver Burdett Pr.
Hudson, Cheryl W. Afro-Bets A B C Book. Hudson, Cheryl W. LC 87-81580. 24p. (ps-3). 1987. pap. 3.95 (*0-940975-00-9*) Just Us Bks.
—Afro-Bets 1 2 3 Book. Hudson, Cheryl W. LC 87-82952. 24p. (ps-3). 1988. pap. 3.95 (*0-940975-01-7*) Just Us Bks.
Hudson, Mark. The Bell Reef. Kendall, Sarita. 144p. (gr. 5-9). 1990. 13.45 (*0-395-53354-6*) HM.
Hudson, Thomas. Garrett Morgan, Inventor. Jackson, Garnet N. LC 92-28801. 1992. write for info. (*0-8136-5231-6*); pap. write for info. (*0-8136-5704-0*) Modern Curr.
Huehnergarth, John. Words in the News: A Student's Dictionary of American Government & Politics. Silberdick, Barbara F. LC 93-19373. 144p. 1993. PLB 13.40 (*0-531-11164-4*) Watts.
Huens, Jean L. Reader's Digest Best Loved Books for Young Readers: The Merry Adventures of Robin Hood. Pyle, Howard. Ogburn, Jackie, ed. 136p. (gr. 4-12). 1989. 3.99 (*0-945260-20-2*) Choice Pub NY.
Huerta, Catherine. The Nightingale. Andersen, Hans Christian. 32p. (ps-3). 1992. 6.95 (*0-8362-4927-5*) Andrews & McMeel.
—Stories to Tell a Cat. Schwartz, Alvin. LC 91-37257. 80p. (gr. 4 up). 1992. 15.00 (*0-06-020850-3*); PLB 14. 89 (*0-06-020851-1*) HarpC Child Bks.
Huff, Laura. Copycat Sam: Developing Ties with a Special Child. Stefanik, Alfred. LC 81-20212. 32p. (gr. k-5). 1982. 16.95 (*0-89885-058-4*) Human Sci Pr.
Huffman, Elise, jt. illus. see Kramer, Stephen.
Huffman, Tom. Alcohol-What It Is, What It Does. Seixas, Judith S. LC 76-43344. 56p. (gr. 1-4). 1977. o.s.i 8.50 (*0-688-80080-7*, Mulberry); PLB 11.88 (*0-688-84080-9*, Mulberry) Morrow.
—Allergies--What They Are, What They Do. Seixas, Judith. LC 90-30753. 56p. (gr. 1 up). 1991. 12.95 (*0-688-09638-7*); PLB 12.88 (*0-688-08877-5*) Greenwillow.
—Be a Perfect Person in Just Three Days! Manes, Stephen. 64p. (gr. 3-6). 1982. 13.45 (*0-89919-064-2*, Clarion Bks) HM.
—Cards for Kids: Games, Tricks & Amazing Facts. McCoy, Elin. LC 91-11373. 160p. (gr. 1-7). 1991. SBE 13.95 (*0-02-765461-3*, Macmillan Child Bk) Macmillan Child Grp.
—The Dove Dove: Funny Homograph Riddles. Terban, Marvin. LC 88-2611. 64p. (gr. 4-7). 1988. 12.95 (*0-89919-723-X*, Clarion Bks) pap. 6.95 (*0-89919-810-4*, Clarion Bks) HM.
—Drugs--What They Are, What They Do. Seixas, Judith S. LC 86-33624. 48p. (gr. 1-4). 1987. 12.95 (*0-688-07399-9*); lib. bdg. 12.88 (*0-688-07400-6*) Greenwillow.
—Drugs: What They Are, What They Do. Seixas, Judith S. LC 86-33624. 48p. 1991. pap. 4.95 (*0-688-10487-8*, Mulberry) Morrow.
—Junk Food--What It Is, What It Does. Seixas, Judith S. LC 83-14135. 48p. (gr. 1-3). 1984. 12.95 (*0-688-02559-5*); PLB 12.88 (*0-688-02560-9*) Greenwillow.
—Pot: What It Is, What It Does. Tobias, Ann. LC 78-10817. 48p. (gr. 3-4). 1979. PLB 12.88 (*0-688-84200-3*) Greenwillow.
—Pot: What It Is, What It Does. Tobias, Ann. LC 78-10817. 48p. (ps-3). 1991. pap. 4.95 (*0-688-00463-6*, Mulberry) Morrow.

—Punching the Clock: Funny Action Idioms. Terban, Marvin. 64p. (gr. 3-7). 1990. pap. 4.80 (*0-89919-865-1*) HM.
—Robots - What They Are, What They Do. Berger, Fredericka. LC 91-14128. 48p. (gr. 1 up). 1992. 14.00 (*0-688-09863-0*); PLB 13.93 (*0-688-09864-9*) Greenwillow.
—Small Plays for Special Days. Alexander, Sue. LC 76-28424. 64p. (ps-1). 1988. pap. 4.95 (*0-89919-798-1*, Clarion Bks) HM.
—Tobacco: What It Is, What It Does. Seixas, Judith S. LC 81-837. 56p. (gr. 1-3). 1981. 12.95 (*0-685-42145-7*, Mulberry); (Mulberry) Morrow.
—Water- What It Is, What It Does. Seixas, Judith S. LC 86-14926. 56p. (gr. 1-4). 1987. 12.95 (*0-688-06607-0*); lib. bdg. 12.88 (*0-688-06608-9*) Greenwillow.
—Whatever Happened to Uncle Albert? Alexander, Sue. 128p. (gr. 3-6). 1980. 13.45 (*0-395-29104-6*, Clarion Bks) HM.
Hughes, jt. illus. see Stratton, Helen.
Hughes, Arthur. At the Back of the North Wind. MacDonald, George. 378p. 1992. Repr. of 1886 ed. 16.00 (*1-881084-07-8*) Johannesen.
—The Light Princess. MacDonald, George. LC 93-561. 160p. 1993. 6.00 (*1-56957-903-2*) Shambhala Pubns.
—Sing Song: A Nursery Rhyme Book. Rossetti, Christina G. LC 68-55822. x, 130p. (gr. 3-7). 1969. pap. 4.50 (*0-486-22107-5*) Dover.
Hughes, Arthur & Willie, Gutta P. The Wise Woman - Gutta Percha Willie, (Duplex) MacDonald, George. 442p. (gr. 5 up). 1993. Repr. of 1901 ed. 16.00 (*1-881084-17-5*) Johannesen.
Hughes, Darryl. I Like Gym Shoe Soup. Deloch-Hughes, Edye. 16p. (gr. k-3). 1991. 10.25 (*0-941484-11-4*) Urban Res Pr.
Hughes, George. The Dastardly Murder of Dirty Pete. Clifford, Eth. 128p. (gr. 2-5). 1981. 13.45 (*0-395-31671-5*) HM.
—Just Tell Me When We're Dead! Clifford, Eth. LC 83-10865. 144p. (gr. 2-5). 1983. 13.45 (*0-395-33071-8*) HM.
—Never Hit a Ghost with a Baseball Bat. Clifford, Eth. LC 92-8347. 128p. (gr. 3-5). 1993. 13.95 (*0-395-61587-9*) HM.
—Scared Silly. Clifford, Eth. LC 87-30694. 128p. (gr. 3-7). 1988. 13.45 (*0-395-46845-0*) HM.
Hughes, Jan. Noah & the Ark. Hughes, Jan. 28p. (Orig.). (gr. 1 up). 1988. 9.95 (*0-914544-97-7*); pap. 6.95 (*0-914544-98-5*) Living Flame Pr.
Hughes, Janet. Life Story of TV Star & Celebrity Herman the Worm. Sroda, George. 189p. (gr. k-7). 1979. 4.95 (*0-9604486-2-4*); pap. 3.95 (*0-685-01814-8*) G Sroda.
—No Angle Left Unturned: Facts About Nightcrawlers. Sroda, George. 111p. (gr. 10 up). 1975. pap. 4.95 (*0-9604486-0-8*) G Sroda.
Hughes, Jenny. Exploring Earth in Space. Stephenson, Robert & Browne, Roger. LC 91-44198. 48p. (gr. 4-8). 1992. PLB 19.92 (*0-8114-2603-3*) Raintree Steck-V.
—Exploring Habitats. Peacock, Graham & Hudson, Terry. LC 92-29907. 48p. (gr. 4-8). 1992. PLB 19.92 (*0-8114-2608-4*) Raintree Steck-V.
—Exploring Humans & the Environment. Baines, John. LC 92-24734. 48p. (gr. 4-8). 1992. PLB 19.92 (*0-8114-2604-1*) Raintree Steck-V.
Hughes, Mark. Amazing Adventures. Donev, Stef. 48p. (gr. 5-9). 1985. pap. 5.95 (*0-88625-093-5*) Durkin Hayes Pub.
—Space Tour. Mackie, Dan. 32p. (gr. 5-9). 1985. pap. 5.95 (*0-88625-103-6*) Durkin Hayes Pub.
Hughes, Neal. Marvin Redpost: Kidnapped at Birth? Sachar, Louis. LC 91-51105. 80p. (Orig.). (gr. 1-4). 1992. PLB 9.99 (*0-679-91946-5*); pap. 2.99 (*0-679-81946-0*) Random Bks Yng Read.
—Marvin Redpost: Why Pick on Me? Sachar, Louis. LC 92-12858. 80p. (Orig.). (gr. 1-4). 1993. PLB 9.99 (*0-679-91947-3*); pap. 2.99 (*0-679-81947-9*) Random Bks Yng Read.
Hughes, Scott, jt. illus. see Fraser, John.
Hughes, Shirley. Alfie Gets in First. Hughes, Shirley. LC 81-8427. 32p. (ps-1). 1982. 13.95 (*0-688-00848-8*); PLB 13.88 (*0-688-00849-6*) Lothrop.
—Alfie Gives a Hand. Hughes, Shirley. LC 83-14883. 32p. (ps-1). 1984. 12.95 (*0-688-02386-X*); PLB 14.88 (*0-688-02387-8*) Lothrop.
—Alfie's Feet. Hughes, Shirley. LC 82-13012. 32p. (ps-1). 1983. 14.95 (*0-688-01658-8*); PLB 14.88 (*0-688-01660-X*) Lothrop.
—Another Helping of Chips. Hughes, Shirley. LC 86-20958. 64p. (gr. 2-4). 1987. 11.95 (*0-688-06871-5*); PLB 11.88 (*0-688-06872-3*) Lothrop.
—The Big Concrete Lorry: A Tale of Trotter Street. Hughes, Shirley. LC 89-8051. 32p. (ps-1). 1990. 13.95 (*0-688-08534-2*); lib. bdg. 13.88 (*0-688-08535-0*) Lothrop.
—Bouncing. Hughes, Shirley. LC 92-56300. 24p. (ps). 1993. 12.95 (*1-56402-128-9*) Candlewick Pr.
—Dogger. Hughes, Shirley. LC 87-33787. 32p. (ps-2). 1988. 11.95 (*0-688-07980-6*); PLB 11.88 (*0-688-07981-4*) Lothrop.
—An Evening at Alfie's. Hughes, Shirley. LC 84-11297. 32p. (ps-1). 1985. 14.95 (*0-688-04122-1*); PLB 14.88 (*0-688-04123-X*) Lothrop.
—The Girl with the Green Ear: Stories about Magic in Nature. Mahy, Margaret. LC 91-14992. 112p. (gr. 3-7). 1992. 15.00 (*0-679-82231-3*); PLB 15.99 (*0-679-92231-8*) Knopf Bks Yng Read.

—The Girl with the Green Ear: Stories about Magic in Nature. Mahy, Margaret. LC 91-14992. 112p. (gr. 3-7). 1993. pap. 3.25 (*0-679-84000-1*, Bullseye Bks) Knopf Bks Yng Read.
—Giving. Hughes, Shirley. LC 92-53002. 24p. (ps). 1993. 12.95 (*1-56402-129-7*) Candlewick Pr.
—Here Comes Charlie Moon. Hughes, Shirley. LC 85-24125. 128p. (gr. 2-5). 1986. Repr. of 1980 ed. 11.95 (*0-688-06401-9*) Lothrop.
—The Little Cat That Could Not Sleep. Fox, Frances M. LC 72-89335. 32p. (gr. k-4). 1973. 7.95 (*0-87592-030-6*) Scroll Pr.
—Lucy & Tom's Day. Hughes, Shirley. 32p. (ps-1). 1986. pap. 3.50 (*0-14-050068-5*, Puffin) Puffin Bks.
—Moving Molly. Hughes, Shirley. 32p. (ps-2). 1982. pap. 3.95 (*0-13-604579-0*, Pub. by Treehouse) P-H.
—Moving Molly. Hughes, Shirley. LC 87-34250. 32p. (ps-2). 1988. 11.95 (*0-688-07982-2*); PLB 11.88 (*0-688-07984-9*) Lothrop.
—My Naughty Little Sister & Bad Harry's Rabbit. Edwards, Dorothy. (ps-2). 1981. 8.95x (*0-13-608935-6*) P-H.
—The Secret Garden. Burnett, Frances H. 240p. (gr. 5 up). 1989. pap. 18.95 (*0-670-82571-9*) Viking Child Bks.
—Stories for Eight-Year-Olds. Corrin, Sara & Corrin, Stephen, eds. 192p. (gr. 2-4). 1984. pap. 9.95 (*0-571-12969-2*) Faber & Faber.
—Stories for Nine-Year-Olds. Corrin, Sara & Corrin, Stephen, eds. LC 79-670371. 160p. (gr. 2-5). 1979. pap. 10.95 (*0-571-12931-5*) Faber & Faber.
—Stories for Seven-Year-Olds. Corrin, Sara & Corrin, Stephen, eds. 188p. (gr. 1-3). 1982. pap. 9.95 (*0-571-12910-2*) Faber & Faber.
—Stories for Six-Year-Olds. Corrin, Sara & Corrin, Stephen, eds. 198p. (gr. k-2). 1984. pap. 9.95 (*0-571-12959-5*) Faber & Faber.
—Stories for Under-Fives. Corrin, Sara, et al, eds. 158p. (ps-5). 1974. pap. 9.95 (*0-571-12920-X*) Faber & Faber.
Hukill, Marilyn. Letter City & the Alphabet Winds. Kimmel, Larry. LC 91-65466. 32p. (ps-2). 1991. text ed. 12.95 (*0-9628129-4-3*) Sagebrush Bks.
Hulbert, Elizabeth M. I Love to Ski. Hulbert, Elizabeth M. LC 87-51331. 64p. (Orig.). (gr. 1-3). 1986. pap. 4.95 (*0-932433-25-1*) Windswept Hse.
—The Memory Quilt. Hulbert, Elizabeth M. LC 87-51331. 64p. (gr. 1-4). 1989. pap. 5.95 (*0-932433-42-1*) Windswept Hse.
Hulet, Grant, jt. illus. see Perry, Scott.
Hull, Biz. My Sister Katie: How She Sees God's World. Wright, Christine. LC 90-81702. 32p. 1990. text ed. 7.99 (*0-8066-2497-3*, 9-2497) Augsburg Fortress.
Hull, Jim. Casey at the Bat. Thayer, Ernest L. Gardner, Martin, intro. by. 17.25 (*0-8446-5613-5*) Peter Smith.
Hull, John. Prehistoric Mammals. Keen, Martin L. (gr. 4-6). pap. 2.95 (*0-8431-4255-3*) Wonder.
Hull, Nancy & Williams, Michele. Fat Dog's First Visit: A Child's View of the Hospital. Krall, Charlotte B. & Jim, Judith M. Hull, Nancy, ed. LC 87-2745. 28p. (Orig.). (ps-3). 1987. pap. text ed. 4.00 (*0-939838-23-0*) Pritchett & Hull.
Hull, Richard. The Alphabet from Z to A: With Much Confusion on the Way. Viorst, Judith. LC 91-39338. 32p. (gr. 2-5). 1994. SBE 14.95 (*0-689-31768-9*, Atheneum Child Bk) Macmillan Child Grp.
—The Cat & the Fiddle & More. Aylesworth, Jim. LC 91-30956. 32p. (ps-1). 1992. SBE 13.95 (*0-689-31715-8*, Atheneum Child Bk) Macmillan Child Grp.
—The Living World. Parker, Steve. 48p. (gr. 3-6). 1992. pap. 2.95 (*1-56680-011-0*) Mad Hatter Pub.
Hulser, Andrea. Henry in the Caribbean. Hulser, Andrea. 40p. 1993. pap. 14.95 (*0-89825-007-2*) Pub Resces PR.
Hulsmann, Eva. The Gray Kangaroo at Home. Rau, Margaret. LC 77-14942. 32p. (gr. 5-8). 1978. lib. bdg. 6.99 (*0-394-93451-2*) Knopf Bks Yng Read.
—The Snow Monkey at Home. Rau, Margaret. LC 78-31550. 32p. (gr. 4-7). 1979. lib. bdg. 6.99 (*0-394-93976-X*) Knopf Bks Yng Read.
Hulteng, Lee. From Tent Town to City: A Chronological History of Billings, Montana 1882-1935. Cooper, Myrtle E. Von Vogt, Janice, ed. Wright, Kathryn, intro. by. 79p. (Orig.). (gr. 6-8). 1982. pap. 5.95 (*0-9613224-0-3*) Parmly Lib.
Hultgren, Ken, jt. illus. see Crawford, Mel.
Hummel, Berta. The Hummel. Hummel, Berta. 1972. 17. 00 (*0-88431-129-5*) IBD Ltd.
Humphrey, Brian, jt. illus. see Rivoche, Paul.
Humphrey, Maud. The Light Princess & Other Fairy Tales. MacDonald, George. 305p. (gr. 5 up). 1993. Repr. of 1893 ed. 16.00 (*1-881084-16-7*) Johannesen.
Humphrey, Maude. Nursery Rhymes. Humphrey. LC 92-13790. 1992. 4.99 (*0-517-08274-8*, Pub. by Derrydale Bks) Outlet Bk Co.
Humphries, Tudor. Doom of the Gods. Harrison, Michael. 80p. (gr. 3 up). 1987. 18.95 (*0-19-274128-4*) OUP.
—Eagle. Allen, Judy. LC 93-28541. 1994. write for info. reinforced bdg. (*1-56402-143-2*) Candlewick Pr.
—Elephant. Allen, Judy. LC 92-54407. 32p. (ps up). 1993. 14.95 (*1-56402-069-X*) Candlewick Pr.
—Panda. Allen, Judy. LC 92-54411. 32p. (ps up). 1993. 14.95 (*1-56402-142-4*) Candlewick Pr.
—Seal. Allen, Judy. LC 93-3642. 1994. write for info. (*1-56402-145-9*) Candlewick Pr.
—Whale. Allen, Judy. LC 92-53019. 32p. (gr. 1-3). 1993. 14.95 (*1-56402-160-2*) Candlewick Pr.

Humphries, Tudor & Humphries, Tudor. Tiger. Allen, Judy. LC 91-58760. 32p. (ps up). 1992. 14.95 (1-56402-083-5) Candlewick Pr.

Hundelman, Dorothy & Handelman, Dorothy, photos by. Disney Babies Look at Babies. Edwards, Lisa. LC 91-71346. 24p. (ps). 1991. 6.95 (1-56282-053-2) Disney Pr.

Hundley, Eunice. Naya Nuki: Shoshoni Girl Who Ran. 2nd ed. Thomasma, Kenneth. LC 89-143272. 175p. (Orig.). 1992. 10.99 (0-8010-8869-0); pap. 6.99 (0-8010-8868-2) Baker Bk.

Hung, Gil. Science Dictionary of the Human Body. Richardson, James. LC 91-19162. 48p. (gr. 3-7). 1992. lib. bdg. 11.59 (0-8167-2523-3); pap. 3.95 (0-8167-2442-3) Troll Assocs.

Hungerford, La Farne G. Memories of Me Baby, 18 vols. Dickman, Chareleen. (ps). Date not set. pap. text ed. 34.95 (1-882237-01-3) Life Time Pubs.

Hunkel, Cary. Discovering Wolves. Field, Nancy & Karasov, Corliss. 40p. (Orig.). (gr. 3-6). 1991. pap. 4.95 (0-941042-10-3) Dog Eared Pubns.

Hunn, Diane. The Elves of Bellaire Drive. Janssen, James S. Dietrich, Helen R., ed. Roniger, Mary S., frwd. by. 66p. (Orig.). 1989. pap. 5.95 (0-944784-02-X) Habersham.

—Further Adventures of the Elves of Bellaire Drive. Janssen, James S. Roiniger, Mary Sue, intro. by. (ps-5). 1991. pap. 5.95 (0-9619160-1-X) W S Nelson & Co.

—**More Fun with the Elves of Bellaire Drive.** Janssen, James S., Mary S., intro. by. 66p. (gr. 2-10). 1992. pap. text ed. 5.95 (0-9619160-2-8) W S Nelson & Co.
This is the third book of short stories about the three elves, Ajax, Brice, & Calvin, who live in the big hollow oak tree in the backyard of the Little White Cottage on Bellaire Drive. The first book, THE ELVES OF BELLAIRE DRIVE, appeared in 1989. Since it was well received, the author, James S. Janssen, wrote a second volume, FURTHER ADVENTURES OF THE ELVES OF BELLAIRE DRIVE, which was published in 1991. It also went well, so it was decided to write & publish a third book, MORE FUN WITH THE ELVES OF BELLAIRE DRIVE. The elves continue to maintain pleasant & amicable relations with the children of the neighborhood. Although these children never get to see the elves, they do visit the hollow tree, knock on the little red door, sing to the elves & speak aloud to them, hoping that their voices & messages are being heard by their unseen wee friends. In the silence of the night, the elves perform kind deeds for the neighborhood, especially for the children, the animals & even for the fairies who occasionally visit the area. They set many good examples for the children. This book, as the previous two, is illustrated with drawings by Diane Hunn, a local artist. *Publisher Provided Annotation.*

Hunnam, Lucinda. The Giant. Clayton, Sandra. LC 93-28992. 1994. 4.25 (0-383-03745-X) SRA Schl Grp.

—Mr. Clutterbus. Matthews, Cecily. LC 92-34257. 1993. 4.25 (0-383-03642-9) SRA Schl Grp.

—Up the Stairs. Odgers, Sally F. LC 92-21395. 1993. 4.25 (0-383-03601-1) SRA Schl Grp.

—You're So Clever. Scarffe, Bronwen. LC 92-34339. 1993. 3.75 (0-383-03669-0) SRA Schl Grp.

Hunnum, Cindy. Talk with Me. Liddelow, Lorelei. 101p. (Orig.). (gr-k). 1984. pap. 11.95 (0-920541-97-6) Peguis Pubs Ltd.

Hunt, Jonathan. Illuminations. Hunt, Jonathan. LC 88-38967. 40p. 1989. RSBE 16.95 (0-02-745770-2, Bradbury Pr) Macmillan Child Grp.

—Illuminations. Hunt, Jonathan. LC 92-23542. 40p. (ps-12). 1993. pap. 5.95 (0-689-71700-8, Aladdin) Macmillan Child Grp.

—Jumbo. Blumberg, Rhoda. LC 91-34789. 48p. (gr-k-5). 1992. RSBE 15.95 (0-02-711683-2, Bradbury Pr) Macmillan Child Grp.

—The Mapmaker's Daughter. Helldorfer, M. C. LC 89-39330. 40p. (ps-3). 1991. RSBE 15.95 (0-02-743515-6, Bradbury Pr) Macmillan Child Grp.

—Moon Trouble. Helldorfer, M. C. LC 92-22233. 32p. (gr. k-4). 1994. RSBE 16.95 (0-02-743517-2, Bradbury Pr) Macmillan Child Grp.

—A Tale of Tulips, a Tale of Onions. Birchman, David. LC 92-31240. 40p. (gr. 1-4). 1994. RSBE 15.95 (0-02-710112-6, Four Winds) Macmillan Child Grp.

Hunt, Joseph. Science Dictionary of Space. Richardson, James. LC 91-16551. 48p. (gr. 3-7). 1992. lib. bdg. 11.59 (0-8167-2524-1); pap. 3.95 (0-8167-2443-1) Troll Assocs.

Hunt, Lynn B. American Big Game Fishing. Connett, Eugene V., intro. by. 251p. (gr. 10 up). 1993. Repr. of 1935 ed. 50.00 (1-56416-070-X) Derrydale Pr.

—An Artist Game Bag. 2nd ed. Hunt, Lynn B. 106p. (gr. 10 up). 1990. Repr. of 1936 ed. 39.95 (0-381-20045-0) Derrydale Pr.

—Grouse Feathers. 2nd ed. Spiller, Burton L. 207p. (gr. 10 up). 1989. Repr. 35.00 (1-56416-008-4) Derrydale Pr.

—More Grouse Feathers. 2nd ed. Spiller, Burton L. 238p. (gr. 10 up). 1990. Repr. of 1938 ed. 35.00 (1-56416-009-2) Derrydale Pr.

—Thoroughbred. 2nd ed. Spiller, Burton L. 200p. (gr. 10 up). 1989. Repr. of 1936 ed. 35.00 (1-56416-010-6) Derrydale Pr.

Hunter, Karen. Millions & Illions. Riddlebaugh, Mary Jane. (gr. 4-8). 1990. pap. 11.95 (1-878347-16-0) NL Assocs.

Hunter, Llyn. Allosaurus. Riehecky, Janet. LC 88-1693. 32p. (gr. k-4). 1988. PLB 21.35 (0-89565-421-0); PLB 14.95s.p. (0-685-55918-1) Childs World.

—Deinonychus. Riehecky, Janet. 32p. (gr. k-4). 1990. PLB 21.35 (0-89565-625-6); PLB 14.95s.p. (0-685-56210-7) Childs World.

—Monster Jokes. Suire, Diane, compiled by. LC 88-17487. 48p. (gr. 1-5). 1988. pap. 3.95 (0-516-41866-1) Childrens.

—Pachycephalosaurus. Riehecky, Janet. 32p. (gr. k-4). 1990. PLB 21.35 (0-89565-632-9); PLB 14.95s.p. (0-685-56217-4) Childs World.

Hunter, Marjorie B. & Williams, Mark. M. E. Beverly Hunter Great Masterpiece: Beverly Entertaining & Interesting Thoughts & Beverly Entertaining Melody. Hunter, Marjorie B. (Orig.). (gr. 5 up). 1986. pap. text ed. 30.00 (0-317-93273-X); tape 10.00 (0-317-93274-8) MH & Pr.

Hunter, Mel. More Science Projects You Can Do. Stone, George K. (gr. 5 up). 1981. pap. 3.95 (0-13-600916-6, Pub. by Treehouse) P-H.

Hunter, Stan. Anne of Avonlea. Montgomery, Lucy M. LC 92-10199. 1992. 12.99 (0-517-08127-X, Child Classics) Outlet Bk Co.

Hunter, Susan. Merlin the Wizard. Lawrence, Ann. 32p. (gr. 2-5). 1986. PLB 17.96 (0-8172-2628-1) Raintree Steck-V.

—The Sword in the Stone. Storr, Catherine. LC 84-18293. 32p. (gr. 2-5). 1985. PLB 17.96 (0-8172-2113-1) Raintree Steck-V.

Huntington, Seiko. Japanese "ABCs" Hiragana Learning Cards. Huntington, Seiko. 128p. (Orig.). (gr. 1 up). 1988. pap. 16.95 (0-936845-05-8) Sakura Press.

Huntley, Chris. The Beast in the Bathroom. Huntley, Chris. 32p. (ps). 1991. write for info. Smythe bdg. (0-9616679-2-3) Aquarelle Pr.

Huntoon, Cathy, jt. illus. see Lindsay, Warren.

Hurd, Clement. Come & Have Fun. Hurd, Edith T. LC 62-13324. 32p. (gr. k-3). 1962. PLB 13.89 (0-06-022681-1) HarpC Child Bks.

—Day the Sun Danced. Hurd, Edith T. LC 64-16641. 32p. (gr. k-3). 1966. PLB 13.89 (0-06-022692-7) HarpC Child Bks.

—Goodnight Moon. Brown, Margaret W. LC 47-30762. 36p. (ps-1). 1947. 13.00 (0-06-020705-1); PLB 12.89 (0-06-020706-X) HarpC Child Bks.

—Goodnight Moon. Brown, Margaret W. LC 47-30762. (ps-2). 1977. pap. 3.95 (0-06-443017-0, Trophy) HarpC Child Bks.

—Goodnight Moon Bedtime Box. Brown, Margaret W. 32p. (ps-3). 1992. incl. bunny 19.95 (0-694-00373-5) HarpC Child Bks.

—Goodnight Moon Board Book. Brown, Margaret W. LC 47-30762. 34p. (ps). 1991. 6.95 (0-694-00361-1) HarpC Child Bks.

—The Goodnight Moon Room: A Pop-Up Book. Brown, Margaret W. LC 83-48169. 10p. (ps-1). 1985. 10.95 (0-694-00003-5) HarpC Child Bks.

—Johnny Lion's Book. Hurd, Edith T. LC 65-14490. 64p. (gr. k-3). 1965. PLB 13.89 (0-06-022706-0) HarpC Child Bks.

—Johnny Lion's Book. Hurd, Edith T. LC 65-14490. 64p. (gr. k-3). 1985. pap. 3.50 (0-06-444074-5, Trophy) HarpC Child Bks.

—Johnny Lion's Rubber Boots. Hurd, Edith T. LC 70-183165. 64p. (gr. k-3). 1972. PLB 13.89 (0-06-022710-9) HarpC Child Bks.

—Last One Home Is a Green Pig. Hurd, Edith T. LC 59-8972. 64p. (gr. k-3). 1959. PLB 11.89 (0-06-022716-8) HarpC Child Bks.

—The Runaway Bunny. Brown, Margaret W. LC 71-183168. 40p. (ps-2). 1942. 13.00 (0-06-020765-5); PLB 12.89 (0-06-020766-3) HarpC Child Bks.

—The Runaway Bunny. Brown, Margaret W. LC 71-183168. 40p. (ps-2). 1977. pap. 3.95 (0-06-443018-9, Trophy) HarpC Child Bks.

—The Runaway Bunny. Brown, Margaret W. (gr. k-3). 1985. incl. cassette 19.95 (0-941078-78-7); tape 12.95 incl. cassette (0-941078-76-0); cassette, 4 paperbacks & guide 27.95 (0-941078-77-9) Live Oak Media.

—The Runaway Bunny Board Book. Brown, Margaret W. LC 71-183168. 32p. (ps). 1991. pap. 6.95 (0-06-107429-2) HarpC Child Bks.

—Stop Stop. Hurd, Edith T. LC 61-12095. 64p. (gr. k-3). 1961. PLB 13.89 (0-06-022704-4) HarpC Child Bks.

—The World Is Round. limited ed. Stein, Gertrude. Hurd, Margaret T., intro. by. (gr. 3 up). 1985. 200.00 (0-910457-16-6) Arion Pr.

Hurd, Thacher. Axle the Freeway Cat. Hurd, Thacher. LC 80-8432. 32p. (ps-3). 1988. pap. 3.95 (0-06-443173-8, Trophy) HarpC Child Bks.

—Dinosaur Chase. Otto, Carolyn. LC 90-2021. 32p. (ps-1). 1991. 15.00 (0-06-021613-1); PLB 14.89 (0-06-021614-X) HarpC Child Bks.

—Dinosaur Chase. Otto, Carolyn. LC 90-2021. 32p. (ps-1). 1993. pap. 4.95 (0-06-443330-7, Trophy) HarpC Child Bks.

—Fritzi Fox Flew in from Florida. Komaiko, Leah. LC 93-4754. 1994. 15.00 (0-06-021506-2); PLB 14.89 (0-06-021507-0) HarpC Child Bks.

—Little Mouse's Big Valentine. Hurd, Thacher. LC 89-34515. 32p. (ps-1). 1990. 13.00 (0-06-026192-7); PLB 12.89 (0-06-026193-5) HarpC Child Bks.

—Little Mouse's Big Valentine. Hurd, Thacher. LC 89-34515. 32p. (ps-1). 1992. pap. 3.95 (0-06-443281-5, Trophy) HarpC Child Bks.

—Little Mouse's Birthday Cake. Hurd, Thacher. LC 91-11919. 32p. (ps-1). 1992. 15.00 (0-06-020215-7); PLB 14.89 (0-06-020216-5) HarpC Child Bks.

—Little Mouse's Birthday Cake. Hurd, Thacher. LC 91-11919. 32p. (ps-1). 1994. pap. 4.95 (0-06-443353-6, Trophy) HarpC Child Bks.

—Mama Don't Allow. Hurd, Thacher. LC 83-47703. 40p. (ps-3). 1985. pap. 4.95 (0-06-443078-2, Trophy) HarpC Child Bks.

—Mystery on the Docks. Hurd, Thacher. LC 82-48261. 32p. (ps-3). 1983. 13.00 (0-06-022701-X); PLB 14.89 (0-06-022702-8) HarpC Child Bks.

—Mystery on the Docks. Hurd, Thacher. LC 82-48261. 32p. (gr. k-3). 1984. pap. 4.95 (0-06-443058-8, Trophy) HarpC Child Bks.

—Tomato Soup. Hurd, Thacher. LC 90-21421. 40p. (ps-3). 1992. 15.00 (0-517-58237-6); PLB 15.99 (0-517-58238-4) Crown Bks Yng Read.

—Wheel Away! Dodds, Dayle A. LC 87-27091. 32p. (ps-1). 1989. PLB 13.89 (0-06-021689-1) HarpC Child Bks.

—Wheel Away! Dodds, Dayle A. LC 87-27091. 32p. (ps-1). 1991. pap. 4.95 (0-06-443267-X, Trophy) HarpC Child Bks.

Hurford, John. Another Happy Tale. Butler, Dorothy. LC 91-23133. 32p. (ps-3). 1991. 12.95 (0-940793-88-1, Crocodile Bks) Interlink Pub.

—A Happy Tale. Butler, Dorothy. LC 90-34500. 32p. (ps-5). 1990. 11.95 (0-940793-61-X, Crocodile Bks) Interlink Pub.

—Mr. Cat. Corrin, Ruth. LC 91-20236. 32p. (ps-3). 1991. 13.95 (0-940793-89-X, Crocodile Bks) Interlink Pub.

—Son-of-Thunder. Holmas, Stig. Born, Anne, tr. from NOR. LC 93-4211. 128p. (gr. 7 up). 1993. 16.95 (0-943173-88-4); pap. 10.95 (0-943173-87-6) Harbinger AZ.

Hurst, Maragaret. The Last Days of the Dinosaurs: Text Editions. Gabriele, Joseph. 32p. (Orig.). (gr. 1-3). 1985. pap. 1.95 (0-911211-57-8, Pub. by Know & Show Bks) Penny Lane Pubns.

—Prehistoric Reptiles of the Sea & Air: Text Editions. Gabriele, Joseph. 32p. (gr. 1-3). 1985. pap. 1.95 (0-911211-58-6, Pub. by Know & Show Bks) Penny Lane Pubns.

Hurst, Maragaret. The First Days of the Dinosaurs: Text Edition. Gabriele, Joseph. 32p. (Orig.). (gr. 1-3). pap. 1.95 (0-911211-55-1, Pub. by Know & Show Bks) Penny Lane Pubns.

Hurst, Margaret. The Great Age of the Dinosaurs. Gabriele, Joseph. 32p. (Orig.). (gr. 1-3). 1985. pap. text ed. 1.95 (0-911211-56-X, Pub. by Know & Show Bks) Penny Lane Pubns.

Hurt-Newton, Tania. Love, Your Bear, Pete. Sheldon, Dyan. LC 93-2883. 1994. write for info. (1-56402-332-X) Candlewick Pr.

Hussey, Lorna. Animaze! A Collection of Amazing Nature Mazes. Madgwick, Wendy. LC 91-46892. 40p. (ps-3). 1992. 13.00 (0-679-82665-3); PLB 13.99 (0-679-92665-8) Knopf Bks Yng Read.

Huston, Joan. Hail Mary. Hutson, Joan. 28p. (ps). 1987. 3.95 (0-8198-3324-X) St Paul Bks.

Huszar, Susan. Hermanas - Sisters. Bailey, Debbie. (SPA). 14p. 1993. 4.95 (1-55037-307-2, Pub. by Annick CN) Firefly Bks Ltd.

—Hermanos - Brothers. Bailey, Debbie. (SPA). 14p. 1993. 4.95 (1-55037-308-0, Pub. by Annick CN) Firefly Bks Ltd.

—Sisters. Bailey, Debbie. 14p. 1993. text ed. 4.95 (1-55037-275-0, Pub. by Annick CN) Firefly Bks Ltd.

Huszar, Susan, photos by. Brothers. Bailey, Debbie. 14p. 1993. text ed. 4.95 (1-55037-274-2, Pub. by Annick CN) Firefly Bks Ltd.

—The Talk-about-Books Series, 6 vols. Bailey, Debbie. 14p. (ps-k). 1991. bds. 4.95 ea. (Pub. by Annick CN) Toys (1-55037-165-7) Hats (1-55037-159-2) Shoes (1-55037-161-4) Clothes (1-55037-167-3) My Mom (1-55037-163-0) My Dad. 4.95 (1-55037-164-9) Firefly Bks Ltd.

Hutcherson, Matthew, III. How Many Vehicles Can You Name? I Can Name These Objects! Can You? What Animals Do You See, 3 vols. Middlebrooks-Hutcherson, Gracie. Clowney, Earle D., tr. (SPA & ENG., Orig.). 1992. Set. 25.00 (*1-882485-05-X*); Set. pap. 12.00 (*1-882485-07-6*); write for info. cass. tape (*1-882485-06-8*) Enhance Your Chlds.

Hutchings, Richard, photos by. Firehouse Dog. Hutchings, Amy & Hutchings, Richard. 32p. (ps-2). 1993. pap. 2.50 (*0-590-46846-4*, Cartwheel) Scholastic Inc.

Hutchings, Tony. Little Fluffy Duckling. Hutchings, Tony. 12p. (ps-1). 1990. 4.95 (*1-878624-14-8*, 1553800014) McClanahan Bk.
—Little Pink Piglet. Hutchings, Tony. 12p. (ps-1). 1990. 4.95 (*1-878624-15-6*, 1553800015) McClanahan Bk.
—Little Spotted Calf. Hutchings, Tony. 12p. (ps-1). 1990. 4.95 (*1-878624-12-1*, 1553800012) McClanahan Bk.
—Little Woolly Lamb. Hutchings, Tony. 12p. (ps-1). 1990. 4.95 (*1-878624-13-X*, 1553800013) McClanahan Bk.

Hutchins, Laurence. Follow That Bus! Hutchins, Pat. LC 76-21822. 112p. (gr. 3-7). 1988. pap. 2.95 (*0-394-80792-8*) Knopf Bks Yng Read.

Hutchins, Lawrence. The House That Sailed Away. Hutchins, Pat. LC 74-9823. 192p. (gr. 2-6). 1975. PLB 11.88 (*0-688-84013-2*) Greenwillow.

Hutchins, Pat. Changes, Changes. Hutchins, Pat. LC 70-123133. 32p. (ps-k). 1971. RSBE 13.95 (*0-02-745870-9*, Aladdin) Macmillan Child Grp.
—Changes, Changes. Hutchins, Pat. LC 86-22331. 32p. (ps-1). 1987. pap. 4.95 (*0-689-71137-9*, Aladdin) Macmillan Child Grp.
—Clocks & More Clocks. Hutchins, Pat. LC 93-11208. 32p. (gr-3). 1994. pap. 4.95 (*0-689-71769-5*, Aladdin) Macmillan Child Grp.
—Clocks & More Clocks. reissued ed. Hutchins, Pat. 32p. (ps-3). 1994. RSBE 13.95 (*0-02-745921-7*, Macmillan Child Bk) Macmillan Child Grp.
—The Doorbell Rang. Hutchins, Pat. LC 85-12615. 24p. (ps-3). 1986. 15.00 (*0-688-05251-7*); PLB 14.93 (*0-688-05252-5*) Greenwillow.
—Doorbell Rang. Hutchins, Pat. LC 85-12615. (ps-3). 1989. pap. 3.95 (*0-688-09234-9*, Mulberry) Morrow.
—Good-Night, Owl! Hutchins, Pat. LC 72-186355. 32p. (ps-2). 1972. RSBE 13.95 (*0-02-745900-4*, Macmillan Child Bk) Macmillan Child Grp.
—Good-Night, Owl! Hutchins, Pat. LC 91-8172. 36p. (gr. k-3). 1991. pap. 16.95 big book ed. (*0-689-71541-2*, Aladdin) Macmillan Child Grp.
—One-Eyed Jake. Hutchins, Pat. 32p. (ps up) 1994. pap. 3.95 (*0-688-13113-1*, Mulberry) Morrow.
—One Hunter. Hutchins, Pat. LC 81-6352. 24p. (ps-1). 1982. 15.00 (*0-688-00614-0*); PLB 14.93 (*0-688-00615-9*) Greenwillow.
—Rosie's Walk. Hutchins, Pat. LC 68-12090. 32p. (ps-1). 1968. RSBE 14.95 (*0-02-745850-4*, Macmillan Child Bk) Macmillan Child Grp.
—Rosie's Walk. Hutchins, Pat. LC 87-17550. 32p. (ps-k). 1971. pap. 3.95 (*0-02-043750-1*, Aladdin) Macmillan Child Grp.
—The Surprise Party. Hutchins, Pat. LC 91-10599. 32p. (gr. k-3). 1991. big bk. 16.95 (*0-689-71542-0*, Aladdin); 3.95 (*0-689-71543-9*, Aladdin) Macmillan Child Grp.
—Titch. Hutchins, Pat. LC 77-146622. 32p. (ps-1). 1971. RSBE 13.95 (*0-02-745880-6*, Macmillan Child Bk) Macmillan Child Grp.
—Titch. Hutchins, Pat. LC 92-1642. 40p. (ps-1). 1993. pap. 4.95 (*0-689-71688-5*, Aladdin) Macmillan Child Grp.
—The Very Worst Monster. Hutchins, Pat. LC 84-5928. 32p. (gr. k-3). 1985. 11.75 (*0-688-04010-1*); PLB 11.88 (*0-688-04011-X*) Greenwillow.
—Where's The Baby? Hutchins, Pat. LC 86-33566. 32p. (ps-3). 1988. 11.95 (*0-688-05933-3*); lib. bdg. 11.88 (*0-688-05934-1*) Greenwillow.
—The Wind Blew. Hutchins, Pat. 32p. (ps-1). 1986. pap. 3.99 (*0-14-050236-X*, Puffin) Puffin Bks.
—The Wind Blew. Hutchins, Pat. LC 92-44903. 32p. (ps-1). 1993. pap. 4.95 (*0-689-71744-X*, Aladdin) Macmillan Child Grp.
—You'll Soon Grow into Them, Titch. Hutchins, Pat. LC 82-11755. 32p. (gr. k-3). 1983. 14.95 (*0-688-01770-3*); PLB 14.88 (*0-688-01771-1*) Greenwillow.
—You'll Soon Grow into Them, Titch. Hutchins, Pat. LC 82-11755. 32p. (ps up). 1992. pap. 4.95 (*0-688-11507-1*, Mulberry) Morrow.

Hutchins, William. The Ringling Brothers: Circus Family. Glendinning, Richard & Glendinning, Sally. 80p. (gr. 2-6). 1991. Repr. of 1972 ed. lib. bdg. 12.95 (*0-7910-1468-1*) Chelsea Hse.

Hutchinson, William M., jt. illus. see Lattimore, Deborah N.

Hutson, Joan. I Think... I Know... a Poster Book about God. Hutson, Joan. 32p. (Orig.). (gr. 2-4). 1979. pap. 1.95 (*0-87793-186-0*) Ave Maria.
—I'm Glad I Am: Christian Affirmations for Children. Hutson, Joan. LC 92-10627. 48p. (Orig.). (gr. 1-4). 1992. pap. 3.95 (*0-8198-3623-0*) St Paul Bks.
—It's Important. Hutson, Joan. 48p. (ps). 1987. 3.95 (*0-8198-3615-X*) St Paul Bks.
—Legend of the Nine Talents. Hutson, Joan. LC 92-26957. 1992. 4.95 (*0-8198-4468-3*) St Paul Bks.
—My Happy Ones. Hutson, Joan. 32p. (ps). 1987. 3.95 (*0-8198-4723-2*) St Paul Bks.
—Who? Hutson, Joan. LC 92-31811. 32p. (ps-2). 1992. 3.50 (*0-8198-8266-6*) St Paul Bks.

Hutton, Katherine. Chris Gets Ear Tubes. Pace, Betty. LC 87-26759. 48p. (ps-2). 1987. 5.95 (*0-930323-36-X*, Kendall Green Pubns) Gallaudet Univ Pr.

Hutton, Kathryn. Carefulness. Reihecky, Janet. LC 89-71195. 32p. (gr. k-3). 1990. PLB 13.95.s.p. (*0-89565-564-0*); PLB 13.95.s.p. (*0-685-58727-4*) Childs World.
—Cooperation. Reihecky, Janet. LC 89-48284. 32p. (gr. k-3). 1990. PLB 21.35 (*0-89565-565-9*); PLB 14.95s.p. (*0-685-56199-2*) Childs World.
—Feeling Angry. Barsuhn, Rochelle N. LC 82-19911. 32p. (gr. 1-2). 1983. PLB 21.35 (*0-89565-244-7*); PLB 14.95s.p. (*0-685-55659-X*) Childs World.
—Look, I'm Growing Up. Kneopfel, Marilyn & Farber, Betty. 32p. (gr. k-2). 1991. pasted 2.50 (*0-87403-819-7*, 24-03919) Standard Pub.
—Manners. Ziegler, Sandra. LC 88-15013. 32p. (gr. k-3). 1986. PLB 21.35 (*0-89565-377-X*); PLB 14.95s.p. (*0-685-55992-0*) Childs World.
—My First Book. Moncure, Jane B. LC 84-17455. 32p. (ps-2). 1984. PLB 21.35 (*0-89565-271-4*); PLB 14.95s.p. (*0-685-57948-4*) Childs World.
—Now I Am Four! Moncure, Jane B. LC 83-25270. 32p. (ps-2). 1984. pap. 3.95 (*0-516-41878-5*) Childrens.
—Now I Am Two! Moncure, Jane B. LC 83-20891. 32p. (ps). 1984. pap. 3.95 (*0-516-41878-5*) Childrens.
—One Tiny Baby. Taylor, Mark A. 32p. (gr. k-2). 1989. 2.50 (*0-87403-599-6*, 3859) Standard Pub.
—Respect. Fiday, Beverly & Crowdy, Deborah. LC 87-36981. 32p. (gr. k-3). 1988. PLB 21.35 (*0-89565-417-2*); PLB 14.95s.p. (*0-685-55932-7*) Childs World.
—Self-Control. Gambill, Henrietta. LC 82-1201. 32p. (gr. k-3). 1982. PLB 21.35 (*0-89565-225-0*); PLB 14.95s.p. (*0-685-55648-4*) Childs World.

Hutton, Warwick. Adam & Eve: The Bible Story. Hutton, Warwick. LC 86-27690. 32p. 1987. SBE 14.95 (*0-689-50433-0*, M K McElderry) Macmillan Child Grp.
—Beauty & the Beast. Hutton, Warwick. LC 84-48441. 32p. 1985. SBE 14.95 (*0-689-50316-4*, M K McElderry) Macmillan Child Grp.
—The Cricket Warrior. Chang, Margaret & Chang, Raymond. LC 93-35395. (gr. 3 up) 1994. write for info. (*0-689-50605-8*, Atheneum Child Bk) MacMillan.
—Moses in the Bulrushes. Hutton, Warwick. LC 85-72261. 32p. 1986. SBE 13.95 (*0-689-50393-8*, M K McElderry) Macmillan Child Grp.
—Moses in the Bulrushes. Hutton, Warwick, retold by. LC 91-13971. 32p. (gr. k-3). 1992. pap. 4.95 (*0-689-71553-6*, Aladdin) Macmillan Child Grp.
—Persephone. Hutton, Warwick. LC 93-20590. 32p. (gr. 2 up). 1994. SBE 14.95 (*0-689-50600-7*, M K McElderry) Macmillan Child Grp.
—Perseus. Hutton, Warwick. LC 92-7639. 32p. (gr. 2 up). 1993. SBE 14.95 (*0-689-50565-5*, M K McElderry) Macmillan Child Grp.
—The Selkie Girl. Cooper, Susan. LC 90-39982. 32p. 1991. pap. 4.95 (*0-689-71467-X*, Aladdin) Macmillan Child Grp.
—The Silver Cow: A Welsh Tale. Cooper, Susan. LC 82-13928. 32p. (gr. k-4). 1983. SBE 14.95 (*0-689-50236-2*, M K McElderry) Macmillan Child Grp.
—The Silver Cow: A Welsh Tale. Cooper, Susan. LC 91-234. 32p. (gr. k-3). 1991. pap. 4.95 (*0-689-71512-9*, Aladdin) Macmillan Child Grp.
—Tam Lin. Cooper, Susan, retold by. LC 90-5571. 32p. (gr. k-4). 1991. SBE 14.95 (*0-689-50505-1*, M K McElderry) Macmillan Child Grp.
—Theseus & the Minotaur. Hutton, Warwick. LC 88-26875. 32p. (gr. 1-5). 1989. SBE 14.95 (*0-689-50473-X*, M K McElderry) Macmillan Child Grp.
—The Tinderbox. Andersen, Hans Christian. Moser, Barry, adapted by. LC 88-9206. 32p. (gr. 1 up). 1988. SBE 14.95 (*0-689-50458-6*, M K McElderry) Macmillan Child Grp.
—To Sleep. Sage, James. LC 89-36931. 32p. (ps-3). 1990. SBE 13.95 (*0-689-50497-7*, M K McElderry) Macmillan Child Grp.
—The Trojan Horse. Hutton, Warwick, retold by. LC 91-21590. 32p. (gr. 2 up). 1992. SBE 14.95 (*0-689-50542-6*, M K McElderry) Macmillan Child Grp.

Huxley, Dee H. Mr. Nick's Knitting. Wild, Margaret. 28p. (ps-3). 1989. 12.95 (*0-15-200518-8*, Gulliver Bks) HarBrace.

Hwa-I Publishing Co., Staff. Animal Tales: Chinese Children's Stories, Vols. 11-15. Wonder Kids Publications Group Staff (USA) & Hwa-I Publishing Co., Staff. Ching, Emily, et al, eds. Wonder Kids Publication Staff, tr. from CHI. LC 90-60793. 28p. (gr. 3-6). 1991. Repr. of 1988 ed. Five vol. set, 28p. ea. bk. 39.75 (*0-685-58702-9*) Wonder Kids.
—The Blind Man & the Cripple - Orchard Village: Folklore: English - Spanish Version. Wonder Kids Publications Group Staff. Ching, Emily, et al, eds. Wonder Kids Publications Staff, tr. from CHI. 28p. (gr. 3-6). 1992. Repr. of 1988 ed. 12.95 (*1-56162-126-9*) Wonder Kids.
—The Blind Man & the Cripple - Orchard Village: Folklore: English - Cambodian Version. Wonder Kids Publications Group Staff. Ching, Emily, et al, eds. Wonder Kids Publications Staff, tr. from CHI. 28p. (gr. 3-6). 1992. Repr. of 1988 ed. 12.95 (*1-56162-128-5*) Wonder Kids.

—The Blind Man & the Cripple - Orchard Village: Folklore: English - Vietnamese Version. Wonder Kids Publications Group Staff. Ching, Emily, et al, eds. Wonder Kids Publications Staff, tr. from CHI. 28p. (gr. 3-6). 1992. Repr. of 1988 ed. 12.95 (*1-56162-127-7*) Wonder Kids.
—Brother Cat & Brother Rat - The Rooster's Antlers: Twelve Beasts & the Years: English - Spanish Version. Wonder Kids Publications Group Staff. Ching, Emily, et al, eds. Wonder Kids Publications Staff, tr. from CHI. 28p. (gr. 3-6). 1992. Repr. of 1988 ed. 12.95 (*1-56162-121-8*) Wonder Kids.
—Brother Cat & Brother Rat - The Rooster's Antlers: Twelve Beasts & the Years: English - Cambodian Version. Wonder Kids Publications Group Staff. Ching, Emily, et al, eds. Wonder Kids Publications Staff, tr. from CHI. 28p. (gr. 3-6). 1992. Repr. of 1988 ed. 12.95 (*1-56162-123-4*) Wonder Kids.
—Brother Cat & Brother Rat - The Rooster's Antlers: Twelve Beasts & the Years: English - Vietnamese Version. Wonder Kids Publications Group Staff. Ching, Emily, et al, eds. Wonder Kids Publications Staff, tr. from CHI. 28p. (gr. 3-6). 1992. Repr. of 1988 ed. 12.95 (*1-56162-122-6*) Wonder Kids.
—Celebrating New Year - Miss Yuan-Shiau: Festivals: English - Cambodian Version. Wonder Kids Publications Group Staff. Ching, Emily, et al, eds. Wonder Kids Publications Staff, tr. from CHI. 28p. (gr. 3-6). 1992. Repr. of 1988 ed. 12.95 (*1-56162-133-1*) Wonder Kids.
—Celebrating New Year - Miss Yuan-Shiau: Festivals: English - Spanish Version. Wonder Kids Publications Group Staff. Ching, Emily, et al, eds. Wonder Kids Publications Staff, tr. from CHI. 28p. (gr. 3-6). 1992. Repr. of 1988 ed. 12.95 (*1-56162-131-5*) Wonder Kids.
—Celebrating New Year - Miss Yuan-Shiau: Festivals: English - Vietnamese Version. Wonder Kids Publications Group Staff. Ching, Emily, et al, eds. Wonder Kids Publications Staff, tr. from CHI. 28p. (gr. 3-6). 1992. Repr. of 1988 ed. 12.95 (*1-56162-132-3*) Wonder Kids.
—Chinese Children's Stories, Vol. 10: The Money Tree, The Coxcomb. Hwa-I Publishing Co., Staff. Ching, Emily, et al, eds. Wonder Kids Publications Staff, tr. from CHI. LC 90-60792. 28p. (gr. 3-6). 1991. Repr. of 1988 ed. 7.95x (*1-56162-010-6*) Wonder Kids.
—Chinese Children's Stories, Vol. 100: From Rice into Flowers, The Shy Rainbow. Hwa-I Publishing Co., Staff. Ching, Emily, et al, eds. Wonder Kids Publications Staff, tr. from CHI. LC 90-60811. 28p. (gr. 3-6). 1991. Repr. of 1988 ed. 7.95x (*1-56162-100-5*) Wonder Kids.
—Chinese Children's Stories, Vol. 12: The Snail & the Ox, Sparrows Can't Walk. Hwa-I Publishing Co., Staff. Ching, Emily, et al, eds. Wonder Kids Publications Staff, tr. from CHI. LC 90-60793. 28p. (gr. 3-6). 1991. Repr. of 1988 ed. 7.95x (*1-56162-012-2*) Wonder Kids.
—Chinese Children's Stories, Vol. 13: Rooster Summons the Sun, The White-Haired Bird. Hwa-I Publishing Co., Staff. Ching, Emily, et al, eds. Wonder Kids Publications Staff, tr. from CHI. LC 90-60793. 28p. (gr. 3-6). 1991. Repr. of 1988 ed. 7.95x (*1-56162-013-0*) Wonder Kids.
—Chinese Children's Stories, Vol. 14: Weasel Steals the Chickens, Why is the Crow Black? Hwa-I Publishing Co., Staff. Ching, Emily, et al, eds. Wonder Kids Publications Staff, tr. from CHI. LC 90-60793. 28p. (gr. 3-6). 1991. Repr. of 1988 ed. 7.95x (*1-56162-014-9*) Wonder Kids.
—Chinese Children's Stories, Vol. 15: Jiggle in the Wind, The Bat Can't See the Sun. Hwa-I Publishing Co., Staff. Ching, Emily, et al, eds. Wonder Kids Publications Staff, tr. from CHI. LC 90-60793. 28p. (gr. 3-6). 1991. Repr. of 1988 ed. 7.95x (*1-56162-015-7*) Wonder Kids.
—Chinese Children's Stories, Vol. 17: The Monkey & the Fire, Lazy Wife & the Bread Ring. Hwa-I Publishing Co., Staff. Ching, Emily, et al, eds. Wonder Kids Publications Staff, tr. from CHI. LC 90-60794. 28p. (gr. 3-6). 1991. Repr. of 1988 ed. 7.95x (*1-56162-017-3*) Wonder Kids.
—Chinese Children's Stories, Vol. 18: The Little Bamboo Pole, The Wise Old Man. Hwa-I Publishing Co., Staff. Ching, Emily, et al, eds. Wonder Kids Publications Staff, tr. from CHI. LC 90-60794. 28p. (gr. 3-6). 1991. Repr. of 1988 ed. 7.95x (*1-56162-018-1*) Wonder Kids.
—Chinese Children's Stories, Vol. 19: Crow Moves Away, Baby Lion & Baby Rhino. Hwa-I Publishing Co., Staff. Ching, Emily, et al, eds. Wonder Kids Publications Staff, tr. from CHI. LC 90-60794. 28p. (gr. 3-6). 1991. Repr. of 1988 ed. 7.95x (*1-56162-019-X*) Wonder Kids.
—Chinese Children's Stories, Vol. 20: Ah-Liu Picks Corn, Cuckoo's Winter. Hwa-I Publishing Co., Staff. Ching, Emily, et al, eds. Wonder Kids Publications Staff, tr. from CHI. LC 90-60794. 28p. (gr. 3-6). 1991. Repr. of 1988 ed. 7.95x (*1-56162-020-3*) Wonder Kids.
—Chinese Children's Stories, Vol. 22: The Steal a Bell, The Dropout. Hwa-I Publishing Co., Staff. Ching, Emily, et al, eds. Wonder Kids Publications Staff, tr. from CHI. LC 90-60796. 28p. (gr. 3-6). 1991. Repr. of 1988 ed. 7.95x (*1-56162-022-X*) Wonder Kids.

—Chinese Children's Stories, Vol. 23: Dummy Afa, The Fox in a Tiger's Suit. Hwa-I Publishing Co., Staff. Ching, Emily, et al, eds. Wonder Kids Publications Staff, tr. from CHI. LC 90-60796. 28p. (gr. 3-6). 1991. Repr. of 1988 ed. 7.95x (*1-56162-023-8*) Wonder Kids.

—Chinese Children's Stories, Vol. 24: Running Fifty vs. One-Hundred Strides, Atu Yanks the Rice Seedlings. Hwa-I Publishing Co., Staff. Ching, Emily, et al, eds. Wonder Kids Publications Staff, tr. from CHI. LC 90-60796. 28p. (gr. 3-6). 1991. Repr. of 1988 ed. 7.95x (*1-56162-024-6*) Wonder Kids.

—Chinese Children's Stories, Vol. 25: The Blindmen & the Elephant, Little Frog in the Well. Hwa-I Publishing Co., Staff. Ching, Emily, et al, eds. Wonder Kids Publications Staff, tr. from CHI. LC 90-60796. 28p. (gr. 3-6). 1991. Repr. of 1988 ed. 7.95x (*1-56162-025-4*) Wonder Kids.

—Chinese Children's Stories, Vol. 27: Sky-Mending Festival, Decorative Paper for Graves. Hwa-I Publishing Co., Staff. Ching, Emily, et al, eds. Wonder Kids Publications Staff, tr. from CHI. LC 90-60797. 28p. (gr. 3-6). 1991. Repr. of 1988 ed. 7.95x (*1-56162-027-0*) Wonder Kids.

—Chinese Children's Stories, Vol. 28: Mih-Ro River, The Herder & the Seamstress. Hwa-I Publishing Co., Staff. Ching, Emily, et al, eds. Wonder Kids Publications Staff, tr. from CHI. LC 90-60797. 28p. (gr. 3-6). 1991. Repr. of 1988 ed. 7.95x (*1-56162-028-9*) Wonder Kids.

—Chinese Children's Stories, Vol. 29: Moon Cake, Fei's Adventure. Hwa-I Publishing Co., Staff. Ching, Emily, et al, eds. Wonder Kids Publications Staff, tr. from CHI. LC 90-60797. 28p. (gr. 3-6). 1991. Repr. of 1988 ed. 7.95x (*1-56162-029-7*) Wonder Kids.

—Chinese Children's Stories, Vol. 30: La-Ba Porridge, The Stove God. Hwa-I Publishing Co., Staff. Ching, Emily, et al, eds. Wonder Kids Publications Staff, tr. from CHI. LC 90-60797. 28p. (gr. 3-6). 1991. Repr. of 1988 ed. 7.95x (*1-56162-030-0*) Wonder Kids.

—Chinese Children's Stories, Vol. 32: Dumplings, Ham. Hwa-I Publishing Co., Staff. Ching, Emily, et al, eds. Wonder Kids Publications Staff, tr. from CHI. LC 90-60798. 28p. (gr. 3-6). 1991. Repr. of 1988 ed. 7.95x (*1-56162-032-7*) Wonder Kids.

—Chinese Children's Stories, Vol. 33: Noodles over the Bridge, Steamed Bread. Hwa-I Publishing Co., Staff. Ching, Emily, et al, eds. Wonder Kids Publications Staff, tr. from CHI. LC 90-60798. 28p. (gr. 3-6). 1991. Repr. of 1988 ed. 7.95x (*1-56162-033-5*) Wonder Kids.

—Chinese Children's Stories, Vol. 34: The Stuffed Steamed Bao, Miss Freckle's Tofu. Hwa-I Publishing Co., Staff. Ching, Emily, et al, eds. Wonder Kids Publications Staff, tr. from CHI. LC 90-60798. 28p. (gr. 3-6). 1991. Repr. of 1988 ed. 7.95x (*1-56162-034-3*) Wonder Kids.

—Chinese Children's Stories, Vol. 35: Monks' Beef Stew, Yue's Tofu Store. Hwa-I Publishing Co., Staff. Ching, Emily, et al, eds. Wonder Kids Publications Staff, tr. from CHI. LC 90-60798. 28p. (gr. 3-6). 1991. Repr. of 1988 ed. 7.95x (*1-56162-035-1*) Wonder Kids.

—Chinese Children's Stories, Vol. 37: Confucius' Bookkeeping, The Scissors Shop. Hwa-I Publishing Co., Staff. Ching, Emily, et al, eds. Wonder Kids Publications Staff, tr. from CHI. LC 90-60799. 28p. (gr. 3-6). 1991. Repr. of 1988 ed. 7.95x (*1-56162-037-8*) Wonder Kids.

—Chinese Children's Stories, Vol. 38: The Peace Drum, Comb. Hwa-I Publishing Co., Staff. Ching, Emily, et al, eds. Wonder Kids Publications Staff, tr. from CHI. LC 90-60799. 28p. (gr. 3-6). 1991. Repr. of 1988 ed. 7.95x (*1-56162-038-6*) Wonder Kids.

—Chinese Children's Stories, Vol. 39: Brush Pen, Duan's Ink-Slab. Hwa-I Publishing Co., Staff. Ching, Emily, et al, eds. Wonder Kids Publications Staff, tr. from CHI. LC 90-6079. 28p. (gr. 3-6). 1991. Repr. of 1988 ed. 7. 95x (*1-56162-039-4*) Wonder Kids.

—Chinese Children's Stories, Vol. 40: The Ink-Stick, Shiuan Paper. Hwa-I Publishing Co., Staff. Ching, Emily, et al, eds. Wonder Kids Publications Staff, tr. from CHI. LC 90-60799. 28p. (gr. 3-6). 1991. Repr. of 1988 ed. 7.95x (*1-56162-040-8*) Wonder Kids.

—Chinese Children's Stories, Vol. 42: Tiger Seeks a Master, Why Are Cats Afraid of Dogs? Hwa-I Publishing Co., Staff. Ching, Emily, et al, eds. Wonder Kids Publications Staff, tr. from CHI. LC 90-60800. 28p. (gr. 3-6). 1991. Repr. of 1988 ed. 7.95x (*1-56162-042-4*) Wonder Kids.

—Chinese Children's Stories, Vol. 43: The Bunny's Tail, Fox, Monkey, Rabbit & Horse. Hwa-I Publishing Co., Staff. Ching, Emily, et al, eds. Wonder Kids Publications Staff, tr. from CHI. LC 90-60800. 28p. (gr. 3-6). 1991. Repr. of 1988 ed. 7.95x (*1-56162-043-2*) Wonder Kids.

—Chinese Children's Stories, Vol. 44: Snake's Lost Drum, Ox & Buffalo Change Clothes. Hwa-I Publishing Co., Staff. Ching, Emily, et al, eds. Wonder Kids Publications Staff, tr. from CHI. LC 90-60800. 28p. (gr. 3-6). 1991. Repr. of 1988 ed. 7.95x (*1-56162-044-0*) Wonder Kids.

—Chinese Children's Stories, Vol. 45: The Goat & the Camel, The Wolf & the Pig. Hwa-I Publishing Co., Staff. Ching, Emily, et al, eds. Wonder Kids Publications Staff, tr. from CHI. LC 90-60800. 28p. (gr. 3-6). 1991. Repr. of 1988 ed. 7.95x (*1-56162-045-9*) Wonder Kids.

—Chinese Children's Stories, Vol. 47: The Crane-Riding Immortal, Lyu Dungbin & Guanyin. Hwa-I Publishing Co., Staff. Ching, Emily, et al, eds. Wonder Kids Publications Staff, tr. from CHI. LC 90-60801. 28p. (gr. 3-6). 1991. Repr. of 1988 ed. 7.95x (*1-56162-047-5*) Wonder Kids.

—Chinese Children's Stories, Vol. 48: Sir Thunder & Lady Lightning, The Door Guards. Hwa-I Publishing Co., Staff. Ching, Emily, et al, eds. Wonder Kids Publications Staff, tr. from CHI. LC 90-60801. 28p. (gr. 3-6). 1991. Repr. of 1988 ed. 7.95x (*1-56162-048-3*) Wonder Kids.

—Chinese Children's Stories, Vol. 49: The Slippery Nose Deity, Under the Moonlight. Hwa-I Publishing Co., Staff. Ching, Emily, et al, eds. Wonder Kids Publications Staff, tr. from CHI. LC 90-60801. 28p. (gr. 3-6). 1991. Repr. of 1988 ed. 7.95x (*1-56162-049-1*) Wonder Kids.

—Chinese Children's Stories, Vol. 50: Zung Kuei & the Little Ghost, Earth God & Earth Goddess. Hwa-I Publishing Co., Staff. Ching, Emily, et al, eds. Wonder Kids Publications Staff, tr. from CHI. LC 90-60801. 28p. (gr. 3-6). 1991. Repr. of 1988 ed. 7.95x (*1-56162-050-5*) Wonder Kids.

—Chinese Children's Stories, Vol. 52: Joining the Army, Beating up the Tiger. Hwa-I Publishing Co., Staff. Ching, Emily, et al, eds. Wonder Kids Publications Staff, tr. from CHI. LC 90-60802. 28p. (gr. 3-6). 1991. Repr. of 1988 ed. 7.95x (*1-56162-052-1*) Wonder Kids.

—Chinese Children's Stories, Vol. 53: Meeting an Angel, The Child in the Deer Skin. Hwa-I Publishing Co., Staff. Ching, Emily, et al, eds. Wonder Kids Publications Staff, tr. from CHI. LC 90-60802. 28p. (gr. 3-6). 1991. Repr. of 1988 ed. 7.95x (*1-56162-053-X*) Wonder Kids.

—Chinese Children's Stories, Vol. 54: The Story of Shun, Village of Filial Piety. Hwa-I Publishing Co., Staff. Ching, Emily, et al, eds. Wonder Kids Publications Staff, tr. from CHI. LC 90-60802. 28p. (gr. 3-6). 1991. Repr. of 1988 ed. 7.95x (*1-56162-054-8*) Wonder Kids.

—Chinese Children's Stories, Vol. 55: Two Baskets of Mulberries, Trun's Little Daughter. Hwa-I Publishing Co., Staff. Ching, Emily, et al, eds. Wonder Kids Publications Staff, tr. from CHI. LC 90-60802. 28p. (gr. 3-6). 1991. Repr. of 1988 ed. 7.95x (*1-56162-055-6*) Wonder Kids.

—Chinese Children's Stories, Vol. 57: The Little-Boy God, A Rooster's Egg. Hwa-I Publishing Co., Staff. Ching, Emily, et al, eds. Wonder Kids Publications Staff, tr. from CHI. LC 90-60803. 28p. (gr. 3-6). 1991. Repr. of 1988 ed. 7.95x (*1-56162-057-2*) Wonder Kids.

—Chinese Children's Stories, Vol. 58: Three Princes & the Firewood, Wang's Memory. Hwa-I Publishing Co., Staff. Ching, Emily, et al, eds. Wonder Kids Publications Staff, tr. from CHI. LC 90-60803. 28p. (gr. 3-6). 1991. Repr. of 1988 ed. 7.95x (*1-56162-058-0*) Wonder Kids.

—Chinese Children's Stories, Vol. 59: A Tankful of Water, The Little Hero. Hwa-I Publishing Co., Staff. Ching, Emily, et al, eds. Wonder Kids Publications Staff, tr. from CHI. LC 90-60803. 28p. (gr. 3-6). 1991. Repr. of 1988 ed. 7.95x (*1-56162-059-9*) Wonder Kids.

—Chinese Children's Stories, Vol. 60: Weighing an Elephant, The Distant Homeland. Hwa-I Publishing Co., Staff. Ching, Emily, et al, eds. Wonder Kids Publications Staff, tr. from CHI. LC 90-60803. 28p. (gr. 3-6). 1991. Repr. of 1988 ed. 7.95x (*1-56162-060-2*) Wonder Kids.

—Chinese Children's Stories, Vol. 62: To Catch the Suns, Two Quarrelsome Brothers. Hwa-I Publishing Co., Staff. Ching, Emily, et al, eds. Wonder Kids Publications Staff, tr. from CHI. LC 90-60804. 28p. (gr. 3-6). 1991. Repr. of 1988 ed. 7.95x (*1-56162-062-9*) Wonder Kids.

—Chinese Children's Stories, Vol. 63: To Speak or Not, The Dark Village. Hwa-I Publishing Co., Staff. Ching, Emily, et al, eds. Wonder Kids Publications Staff, tr. from CHI. LC 90-60804. 28p. (gr. 3-6). 1991. Repr. of 1988 ed. 7.95x (*1-56162-063-7*) Wonder Kids.

—Chinese Children's Stories, Vol. 64: Why Is the Sky So High?, Turning into Stone. Hwa-I Publishing Co., Staff. Ching, Emily, et al, eds. Wonder Kids Publications Staff, tr. from CHI. LC 90-60804. 28p. (gr. 3-6). 1991. Repr. of 1988 ed. 7.95x (*1-56162-064-5*) Wonder Kids.

—Chinese Children's Stories, Vol. 65: Lugging Mountains, What's a Life Span? Hwa-I Publishing Co., Staff. Ching, Emily, et al, eds. Wonder Kids Publications Staff, tr. from CHI. LC 90-60804. 28p. (gr. 3-6). 1991. Repr. of 1988 ed. 7.95x (*1-56162-065-3*) Wonder Kids.

—Chinese Children's Stories, Vol. 67: The After-Meal Bell, Passing the Three Gorges. Hwa-I Publishing Co., Staff. Ching, Emily, et al, eds. Wonder Kids Publications Staff, tr. from CHI. LC 90-60805. 28p. (gr. 3-6). 1991. Repr. of 1988 ed. 7.95x (*1-56162-067-X*) Wonder Kids.

—Chinese Children's Stories, Vol. 68: The Donkey-Riding Poet, The Backyard Song. Hwa-I Publishing Co., Staff. Ching, Emily, et al, eds. Wonder Kids Publications Staff, tr. from CHI. LC 90-60805. 28p. (gr. 3-6). 1991. Repr. of 1988 ed. 7.95x (*1-56162-068-8*) Wonder Kids.

—Chinese Children's Stories, Vol. 69: The Young Family, Tsuei's Beautiful Bride. Hwa-I Publishing Co., Staff. Ching, Emily, et al, eds. Wonder Kids Publications Staff, tr. from CHI. LC 90-60805. 28p. (gr. 3-6). 1991. Repr. of 1988 ed. 7.95x (*1-56162-069-6*) Wonder Kids.

—Chinese Children's Stories, Vol. 7: Dragon Eye & Cassia Circle, The Conceited Barber. Hwa-I Publishing Co., Staff. Ching, Emily, et al, eds. Wonder Kids Publications Staff, tr. from CHI. LC 90-60792. 28p. (gr. 3-6). 1991. Repr. of 1988 ed. 7.95x (*1-56162-007-6*) Wonder Kids.

—Chinese Children's Stories, Vol. 70: Ji's Jokes, The Scrooge. Hwa-I Publishing Co., Staff. Ching, Emily, et al, eds. Wonder Kids Publications Staff, tr. from CHI. LC 90-60805. 28p. (gr. 3-6). 1991. Repr. of 1988 ed. 7.95x (*1-56162-070-X*) Wonder Kids.

—Chinese Children's Stories, Vol. 72: The Lotus Child, The Ghost in the Basin. Hwa-I Publishing Co., Staff. Ching, Emily, et al, eds. Wonder Kids Publications Staff, tr. from CHI. LC 90-60806. 28p. (gr. 3-6). 1991. Repr. of 1988 ed. 7.95x (*1-56162-072-6*) Wonder Kids.

—Chinese Children's Stories, Vol. 73: Walking through Walls, Who Is the Real Lord Ji? Hwa-I Publishing Co., Staff. Ching, Emily, et al, eds. Wonder Kids Publications Staff, tr. from CHI. LC 90-60806. 28p. (gr. 3-6). 1991. Repr. of 1988 ed. 7.95x (*1-56162-073-4*) Wonder Kids.

—Chinese Children's Stories, Vol. 74: Chaos in the Heavenly Palace, Eating the Ginseng Fruit. Hwa-I Publishing Co., Staff. Ching, Emily, et al, eds. Wonder Kids Publications Staff, tr. from CHI. LC 90-60806. 28p. (gr. 3-6). 1991. Repr. of 1988 ed. 7.95x (*1-56162-074-2*) Wonder Kids.

—Chinese Children's Stories, Vol. 75: Tang's Strange Journey, Dwarfs & Giants. Hwa-I Publishing Co., Staff. Ching, Emily, et al, eds. Wonder Kids Publications Staff, tr. from CHI. LC 90-60806. 28p. (gr. 3-6). 1991. Repr. of 1988 ed. 7.95x (*1-56162-075-0*) Wonder Kids.

—Chinese Children's Stories, Vol. 77: Sir Guan's Big Red Face, Turning Cranes into Words. Hwa-I Publishing Co., Staff. Ching, Emily, et al, eds. Wonder Kids Publications Staff, tr. from CHI. LC 90-60807. 28p. (gr. 3-6). 1991. Repr. of 1988 ed. 7.95x (*1-56162-077-7*) Wonder Kids.

—Chinese Children's Stories, Vol. 78: Tang Buohu's Drawings, The General & the Water Tank. Hwa-I Publishing Co., Staff. Ching, Emily, et al, eds. Wonder Kids Publications Staff, tr. from CHI. LC 90-60807. 28p. (gr. 3-6). 1991. Repr. of 1988 ed. 7.95x (*1-56162-078-5*) Wonder Kids.

—Chinese Children's Stories, Vol. 79: Black-Faced Sir Bao, Doctor Hwa-Tuo. Hwa-I Publishing Co., Staff. Ching, Emily, et al, eds. Wonder Kids Publications Staff, tr. from CHI. LC 90-60807. 28p. (gr. 3-6). 1991. Repr. of 1988 ed. 7.95x (*1-56162-079-3*) Wonder Kids.

—Chinese Children's Stories, Vol. 8: The Millets Won't Go Home, The Immortal Palm. Hwa-I Publishing Co., Staff. Ching, Emily, et al, eds. Wonder Kids Publications Staff, tr. from CHI. LC 90-60792. 28p. (gr. 3-6). 1991. Repr. of 1988 ed. 7.95x (*1-56162-008-4*) Wonder Kids.

—Chinese Children's Stories, Vol. 80: The Dwarf Minister, The Fabulous Chimera's Gift. Hwa-I Publishing Co., Staff. Ching, Emily, et al, eds. Wonder Kids Publications Staff, tr. from CHI. LC 90-60807. 28p. (gr. 3-6). 1991. Repr. of 1988 ed. 7.95x (*1-56162-080-7*) Wonder Kids.

—Chinese Children's Stories, Vol. 82: The Fish Minister, The Hidden Sword. Hwa-I Publishing Co., Staff. Ching, Emily, et al, eds. Wonder Kids Publications Staff, tr. from CHI. LC 90-60808. 28p. (gr. 3-6). 1991. Repr. of 1988 ed. 7.95x (*1-56162-082-3*) Wonder Kids.

—Chinese Children's Stories, Vol. 83: The Revenge of Chao's Orphan, Tien's Wonderful Strategies. Hwa-I Publishing Co., Staff. Ching, Emily, et al, eds. Wonder Kids Publications Staff, tr. from CHI. LC 90-60808. 28p. (gr. 3-6). 1991. Repr. of 1988 ed. 7.95x (*1-56162-083-1*) Wonder Kids.

—Chinese Children's Stories, Vol. 84: Who Is the Real Liu Bong?, Kong Borrows the East Wind. Hwa-I Publishing Co., Staff. Ching, Emily, et al, eds. Wonder Kids Publications Staff, tr. from CHI. LC 90-60808. 28p. (gr. 3-6). 1991. Repr. of 1988 ed. 7.95x (*1-56162-084-X*) Wonder Kids.

—Chinese Children's Stories, Vol. 85: The Battle of the Fei River, The Princess' Engagement. Hwa-I Publishing Co., Staff. Ching, Emily, et al, eds. Wonder Kids Publications Staff, tr. from CHI. LC 90-60808. 28p. (gr. 3-6). 1991. Repr. of 1988 ed. 7.95x (*1-56162-085-8*) Wonder Kids.

—Chinese Children's Stories, Vol. 87: Fan Bridge & Escape Alley, The Stream of Flowers. Hwa-I Publishing Co., Staff. Ching, Emily, et al, eds. Wonder Kids Publications Staff, tr. from CHI. LC 90-60809. 28p. (gr. 3-6). 1991. Repr. of 1988 ed. 7.95x (*1-56162-087-4*) Wonder Kids.

—Chinese Children's Stories, Vol. 88: Five Stone Goats, Six-Foot Street. Hwa-I Publishing Co., Staff. Ching, Emily, et al, eds. Wonder Kids Publications Staff, tr. from CHI. LC 90-60809. 28p. (gr. 3-6). 1991. Repr. of 1988 ed. 7.95x (*1-56162-088-2*) Wonder Kids.

—Chinese Children's Stories, Vol. 89: Peach Blossom Cave, Mt. Lee. Hwa-I Publishing Co., Staff. Ching, Emily, et al, eds. Wonder Kids Publications Staff, tr. from CHI. LC 90-60809. 28p. (gr. 3-6). 1991. Repr. of 1988 ed. 7.95x (*1-56162-089-0*) Wonder Kids.
—Chinese Children's Stories, Vol. 9: The Story of Rice, The Cows & the Trumpet. Hwa-I Publishing Co., Staff. Ching, Emily, et al, eds. Wonder Kids Publications Staff, tr. from CHI. LC 90-60792. 28p. (gr. 3-6). 1991. Repr. of 1988 ed. 7.95x (*1-56162-009-2*) Wonder Kids.
—Chinese Children's Stories, Vol. 90: The Dragon Who Puts out Fires, The Golden Hairpin Well. Hwa-I Publishing Co., Staff. Ching, Emily, et al, eds. Wonder Kids Publications Staff, tr. from CHI. LC 90-60809. 28p. (gr. 3-6). 1991. Repr. of 1988 ed. 7.95x (*1-56162-090-4*) Wonder Kids.
—Chinese Children's Stories, Vol. 92: White-Rice Magic Cave, Sun-Moon Lake. Hwa-I Publishing Co., Staff. Ching, Emily, et al, eds. Wonder Kids Publications Staff, tr. from CHI. LC 90-60810. 28p. (gr. 3-6). 1991. Repr. of 1988 ed. 7.95x (*1-56162-092-0*) Wonder Kids.
—Chinese Children's Stories, Vol. 93: Mt. Anvil & the Sword Well, Two Waters. Hwa-I Publishing Co., Staff. Ching, Emily, et al, eds. Wonder Kids Publications Staff, tr. from CHI. LC 90-60810. 28p. (gr. 3-6). 1991. Repr. of 1988 ed. 7.95x (*1-56162-093-9*) Wonder Kids.
—Chinese Children's Stories, Vol. 94: Muddy Water Stream, Sister Lakes & Brother Trees. Hwa-I Publishing Co., Staff. Ching, Emily, et al, eds. Wonder Kids Publications Staff, tr. from CHI. LC 90-60810. 28p. (gr. 3-6). 1991. Repr. of 1988 ed. 7.95x (*1-56162-094-7*) Wonder Kids.
—Chinese Children's Stories, Vol. 95: Half-Shield Mountain, The Adopted Daughter Lake. Hwa-I Publishing Co., Staff. Ching, Emily, et al, eds. Wonder Kids Publications Staff, tr. from CHI. LC 90-60810. 28p. (gr. 3-6). 1991. Repr. of 1988 ed. 7.95x (*1-56162-095-5*) Wonder Kids.
—Chinese Children's Stories, Vol. 97: Tiger Aunty, Ah-Long & Ah-Hwa. Hwa-I Publishing Co., Staff. Ching, Emily, et al, eds. Wonder Kids Publications Staff, tr. from CHI. LC 90-60811. 28p. (gr. 3-6). 1991. Repr. of 1988 ed. 7.95x (*1-56162-097-1*) Wonder Kids.
—Chinese Children's Stories, Vol. 98: Ai-Yu Jello, Granny & the Fox. Hwa-I Publishing Co., Staff. Ching, Emily, et al, eds. Wonder Kids Publications Staff, tr. from CHI. LC 90-60811. 28p. (gr. 3-6). 1991. Repr. of 1988 ed. 7.95x (*1-56162-098-X*) Wonder Kids.
—Chinese Children's Stories, Vol. 99: The Underground People, Half-Street Lai. Hwa-I Publishing Co., Staff. Ching, Emily, et al, eds. Wonder Kids Publications Staff, tr. from CHI. LC 90-60811. 28p. (gr. 3-6). 1991. Repr. of 1988 ed. 7.95x (*1-56162-099-8*) Wonder Kids.
—Chinese Sites: Chinese Children's Stories, Vols. 86-90. Wonder Kids Publications Group Staff (USA) & Hwa-I Publishing Co., Staff. Ching, Emily, et al, eds. Wonder Kids Publications Staff, tr. from CHI. LC 90-60809. (gr. 3-6). 1991. Repr. of 1988 ed. Five vol. set, 28p. ea. bk. 39.75 (*0-685-58717-7*) Wonder Kids.
—Fables: Chinese Children's Stories, Vols. 16-20. Wonder Kids Publications Group Staff (USA) & Hwa-I Publishing Co., Staff. Ching, Emily & Ching, Ko-Shee, eds. Wonder Kids Publications Staff, tr. from CHI. LC 90-60794. (gr. 3-6). 1991. Repr. of 1988 ed. Five vol. set, 28p. ea. bk. 39.75 (*0-685-58703-7*) Wonder Kids.
—Fairy Tales: Chinese Children's Stories, Vols. 46-50. Wonder Kids Publications Group Staff (USA) & Hwa-I Publishing Co., Staff. Ching, Emily, et al, eds. Wonder Kids Publications Staff, tr. from CHI. LC 90-60801. (gr. 3-6). 1991. Repr. of 1988 ed. Five vol. set, 28p. ea. bk. 39.75 (*0-685-58709-6*) Wonder Kids.
—Festivals: Chinese Children's Stories, Vols. 26-30. Wonder Kids Publications Group Staff (USA) & Hwa-I Publishing Co., Staff. Ching, Emily, et al, eds. Wonder Kids Publications Staff, tr. from CHI. LC 90-60797. (gr. 3-6). 1991. Repr. of 1988 ed. Five vol. set, 28p. ea. bk. 39.75 (*0-685-58705-3*) Wonder Kids.
—Filial Piety: Chinese Children's Stories, Vols. 51-55. Wonder Kids Publications Group Staff (USA) & Hwa-I Publishing Co., Staff. Ching, Emily, et al, eds. Wonder Kids Publications Staff, tr. from CHI. LC 90-60802. (gr. 3-6). 1991. Repr. of 1988 ed. Five vol. set, 28p. ea. bk. 39.75 (*0-685-58710-X*) Wonder Kids.
—Folklore: Chinese Children's Stories, Vols. 1-5. Wonder Kids Publications Group Staff (USA) & Hwa-I Publishing Co., Staff. Ching, Emily, et al, eds. Wonder Kids Publications Staff, tr. from CHI. LC 90-60791. 28p. (gr. 3-6). 1991. Repr. of 1988 ed. Set, 28p. ea. bk. 39.75 (*0-685-58701-0*); Set (100 vols.) 795.00 (*1-56162-120-X*) Wonder Kids.
—Heroes: Chinese Children's Stories, Vols. 76-80. Wonder Kids Publications Group Staff (USA) & Hwa-I Publishing Co., Staff. Ching, Emily, et al, eds. Wonder Kids Publications Staff, tr. from CHI. LC 90-60807. (gr. 3-6). 1991. Repr. of 1988 ed. Five vol. set, 28p. ea. bk. 39.75 (*0-685-58715-0*) Wonder Kids.
—Historical Accounts: Chinese Children's Stories, Vols. 81-85. Wonder Kids Publications Group Staff (USA) & Hwa-I Publishing Co., Staff. Ching, Emily, et al, eds. Wonder Kids Publications Staff, tr. from CHI. LC 90-60808. (gr. 3-6). 1991. Repr. of 1988 ed. Five vol. set, 28p. ea. bk. 39.75 (*0-685-58716-9*) Wonder Kids.

—Idioms: Chinese Children's Stories, Vols. 21-25. Wonder Kids Publications Group Staff (USA) & Hwa-I Publishing Co., Staff. Ching, Emily, et al, eds. Wonder Kids Publications Staff, tr. from CHI. LC 90-60796. (gr. 3-6). 1991. Repr. of 1988 ed. Five vol. set, 28p. ea. bk. 39.75 (*0-685-58704-5*) Wonder Kids.
—Inventions: Chinese Children's Stories, Vols. 36-40. Wonder Kids Publications Group Staff (USA) & Hwa-I Publishing Co., Staff. Ching, Emily, et al, eds. Wonder Kids Publications Staff, tr. from CHI. LC 90-60799. (gr. 3-6). 1991. Repr. of 1988 ed. Five vol. set, 28p. ea. bk. 39.75 (*0-685-58707-X*) Wonder Kids.
—Literature: Chinese Children's Stories, Vols. 66-70. Wonder Kids Publications Group Staff (USA) & Hwa-I Publishing Co., Staff. Ching, Emily, et al, eds. Wonder Kids Publications Staff, tr. from CHI. LC 90-60805. (gr. 3-6). 1991. Repr. of 1988 ed. Five vol. set, 28p. ea. bk. 39.75 (*0-685-58713-4*) Wonder Kids.
—Mythology: Chinese Children's Stories, Vols. 61-65. Wonder Kids Publications Group Staff (USA) & Hwa-I Publishing Co., Staff. Ching, Emily, et al, eds. Wonder Kids Publications Staff, tr. from CHI. LC 90-60804. (gr. 3-6). 1991. Repr. of 1988 ed. Five vol. set, 28p. ea. bk. 39.75 (*0-685-58712-6*) Wonder Kids.
—Popular Narratives: Chinese Children's Stories, Vols. 71-75. Wonder Kids Publications Group Staff (USA) & Hwa-I Publishing Co., Staff. Ching, Emily, et al, eds. Wonder Kids Publications Staff, tr. from CHI. LC 90-60806. (gr. 3-6). 1991. Repr. of 1988 ed. Five vol. set, 28p. ea. bk. 39.75 (*0-685-58714-2*) Wonder Kids.
—Taiwanese Folklore: Chinese Children's Stories, Vols. 96-100. Wonder Kids Publications Group Staff (USA) & Hwa-I Publishing Co., Staff. Ching, Emily, et al, eds. Wonder Kids Publication Staff, tr. from CHI. LC 90-60811. (gr. 3-6). 1991. Repr. of 1988 ed. Five vol. set, 28p. ea. bk. 39.75 (*0-685-58719-3*) Wonder Kids.
—Taiwanese Sites: Chinese Children's Stories, Vols. 91-95. Wonder Kids Publications Group Staff (USA) & Hwa-I Publishing Co., Staff. Ching, Emily, et al, eds. Wonder Kids Publications Staff, tr. from CHI. LC 90-60810. (gr. 3-6). 1991. Repr. of 1988 ed. Five vol. set, 28p. ea. bk. 39.75 (*0-685-58718-5*) Wonder Kids.
—Tales about Food: Chinese Children's Stories, Vols. 31-35. Wonder Kids Publications Group Staff (USA) & Hwa-I Publishing Co., Staff. Ching, Emily, et al, eds. Wonder Kids Publications Staff, tr. from CHI. LC 90-60798. (gr. 3-6). 1991. Repr. of 1988 ed. Five vol. set, 28p. ea. bk. 39.75 (*0-685-58706-1*) Wonder Kids.
—Twelve Beasts & the Years: Chinese Children's Stories, Vols. 41-45. Wonder Kids Publications Group Staff (USA) & Hwa-I Publishing Co., Staff. Ching, Emily, et al, eds. Wonder Kids Publications Staff, tr. from CHI. LC 90-60800. (gr. 3-6). 1991. Repr. of 1988 ed. Five vol. set, 28p. ea. bk. 39.75 (*0-685-58708-8*) Wonder Kids.
—Wonder Kids: Chinese Children's Stories, Vols. 56-60. Wonder Kids Publications Group Staff (USA) & Hwa-I Publishing Co., Staff. Ching, Emily, et al, eds. Wonder Kids Publications Staff, tr. from CHI. LC 90-60803. (gr. 3-6). 1991. Repr. of 1988 ed. Five vol. set, 28p. ea. bk. 39.75 (*0-685-58711-8*) Wonder Kids.
Hyde, Maureen. A Christmas Fable. Karlins, Mark. LC 89-29321. 32p. (gr. 1-5). 1990. SBE 13.95 (*0-689-31480-9*, Atheneum Child Bk) Macmillan Child Grp.
—Grandpa Loved. Nobisso, Josephine. 32p. 1991. 12.95 (*0-88138-119-5*, Green Tiger) S&S Trade.
—Shh! The Whale Is Smiling. Nobisso, Josephine. LC 91-21521. 40p. (ps-1). 1992. 14.00 (*0-671-74908-0*, Green Tiger) S&S Trade.
Hygaard, Elizabeth. What Was It Before It Was Bread? Moncure, Jane B. LC 85-11402. 32p. (ps-2). 1985. PLB 21.35 (*0-89565-323-0*); PLB 14.95x.p. (*0-685-55775-8*) Childs World.
Hyman, Pat. A Carousel of Limericks. Roehl, Harvey N. LC 85-22538. 60p. (Orig.). (gr. 4-8). 1986. pap. 7.95 (*0-911572-47-3*) Vestal.
Hyman, Schart. The Kitchen Knight: A Tale of King Arthur. Hodges, Margaret. 1993. pap. 5.95 (*0-8234-1063-3*) Holiday.
Hyman, Trina S. Among the Dolls. Sleator, William. (gr. 2-5). 1975. 12.50 (*0-525-25563-X*, DCB) Dutton Child Bks.
—The Bad Times of Irma Baumlein. 2nd ed. Brink, Carol R. LC 91-13976. 144p. (gr. 3-7). 1991. pap. 3.95 (*0-689-71513-7*, Aladdin) Macmillan Child Grp.
—Caddie Woodlawn. Brink, Carol R. LC 73-588. 288p. (gr. 4-6). 1973. SBE 14.95 (*0-02-713670-1*, Macmillan Child Bk) Macmillan Child Grp.
—Canterbury Tales. Chaucer, Geoffrey. Cohen, Barbara, adapted by. LC 86-21045. 96p. (gr. 5 up). 1988. 17.95 (*0-688-06201-6*) Lothrop.
—The Castle in the Attic. Winthrop, Elizabeth. LC 85-5607. 192p. (gr. 4-7). 1985. 14.95 (*0-8234-0579-6*) Holiday.
—Cat Poems. Livingston, Myra C., compiled by. LC 86-14810. 32p. (ps-3). 1987. reinforced bdg. 13.95 (*0-8234-0631-8*) Holiday.
—A Child's Christmas in Wales. Thomas, Dylan. LC 85-766. 48p. (gr. 4-6). 1985. reinforced bdg. 14.95 (*0-8234-0565-6*) Holiday.
—A Christmas Carol. Dickens, Charles. LC 85-15815. 128p. (gr. 4-6). 1983. 16.95 (*0-8234-0486-2*) Holiday.
—Christmas Poems. Livingston, Myra C., selected by. LC 83-18559. 32p. (ps-3). 1984. reinforced bdg. 14.95 (*0-8234-0508-7*) Holiday.

—A Connecticut Yankee in King Arthur's Court. Twain, Mark. LC 87-62879. 384p. (gr. 5 up). 1988. 19.95 (*0-688-06346-2*); signed ltd. ed. 100.00 (*0-688-08258-0*, Morrow Jr Bks) Morrow Jr Bks.
—Fairy Poems. Wallace, Daisy, ed. LC 79-18763. 32p. (ps-3). 1980. reinforced bdg. 13.95 (*0-8234-0371-8*) Holiday.
—The Fairy Tale Life of Hans Christian Andersen. Moore, Eva. 80p. 1992. pap. 2.75 (*0-590-45225-8*, Apple Paperbacks) Scholastic Inc.
—Hershel & the Hanukkah Goblins. Kimmel, Eric A. LC 89-1954. 32p. (ps-3). 1989. reinforced bdg. 15.95 (*0-8234-0769-1*) Holiday.
—How Does It Feel to Be Old? Farber, Norma. LC 79-11516. 32p. (ps-3). 1988. (DCB); pap. 4.99 (*0-525-44367-3*, DCB) Dutton Child Bks.
—How Six Found Christmas. Hyman, Trina S. LC 91-70462. 32p. (ps-3). 1991. reinforced bdg. 13.95 (*0-8234-0914-7*) Holiday.
—The Kitchen Knight. Hodges, Margaret, retold by. LC 89-11215. 32p. (gr. 1-4). 1990. reinforced bdg. 15.95 (*0-8234-0787-X*) Holiday.
—Let's Steal the Moon. Serwer-Bernstein, Blanche. 96p. (gr. 7 up). 1987. pap. 6.95 (*0-933503-27-X*) Shapolsky Pubs.
—A Little Alphabet. Hyman, Trina S. LC 92-29692. 40p. 1993. Repr. of 1980 ed. 5.95 (*0-688-12034-2*); PLB 14.93 (*0-688-12035-0*) Morrow Jr Bks.
—Little Red Riding Hood. Grimm, Jacob & Grimm, Wilhelm K. Hyman, Trina S., retold by. LC 82-7700. 32p. (ps-3). 1983. reinforced bdg. 15.95 (*0-8234-0470-6*); pap. 5.95 (*0-8234-0653-9*) Holiday.
—Magic in the Mist. Kimmel, Margaret M. LC 74-18186. 32p. (gr. k-4). 1975. SBE 13.95 (*0-689-50026-2*, M K McElderry) Macmillan Child Grp.
—The Night Journey. Lasky, Kathryn. 152p. (gr. 5-9). 1986. pap. 4.99 (*0-14-032048-2*, Puffin) Puffin Bks.
—Rapunzel. Grimm, Jacob & Grimm, Wilhelm K. Rogasky, Barbara, retold by. LC 81-6419. 32p. (ps-3). 1982. Reinforced bdg. 14.95 (*0-8234-0454-4*); pap. 5.95 (*0-8234-0652-0*) Holiday.
—A Room Made of Windows. Cameron, Eleanor. 288p. (gr. 4 up). 1990. pap. 4.95 (*0-14-034156-0*, Puffin) Puffin Bks.
—St. George & the Dragon. Hodges, Margaret, adapted by. LC 83-19980. (gr. 6-8). 1984. 15.95 (*0-316-36789-3*) Little.
—Self-Portrait: Trina Schart Hyman. Hyman, Trina S. LC 80-26662. 32p. (gr. 4-7). 1989. PLB 14.89 (*0-06-022766-4*) HarpC Child Bks.
—The Sleeping Beauty. Hyman, Trina S., ed. LC 75-43769. (gr. 1 up). 1983. 15.95 (*0-316-38702-9*); pap. 6.95 (*0-316-38708-8*) Little.
—Snow White. Grimm, Jacob & Grimm, Wilhelm K. Heins, Paul, tr. (ps-3). 1979. lib. bdg. 14.95 (*0-316-35450-3*, Joy St Bks); pap. 6.95 (*0-316-35451-1*, Joy St Bks) Little.
—Star Mother's Youngest Child. Moeri, Louise. 48p. (ps-2). 1980. 14.45 (*0-395-21406-8*, Sandpiper); pap. 4.95 (*0-395-29929-2*) HM.
—Swan Lake. Fonteyn, Margot. 1991. incl. cassette 19.95 (*0-15-200602-8*, HB Juv Bks) HarBrace.
—Tiempos Duros: Tight Times. Hazen, Shook. 32p. (ps-3). 1993. PLB 12.99 (*0-670-84841-7*) Viking Child Bks.
—Tight Times. Hazen, Barbara S. LC 78-31867. (gr. k-3). 1979. pap. 12.95 (*0-670-71287-6*) Viking Child Bks.
—Tight Times. Hazen, Barbara S. 32p. (ps-3). 1983. pap. 3.99 (*0-14-050442-7*, Puffin) Puffin Bks.
—The Water of Life. Rogasky, Barbara, retold by. LC 84-19226. 40p. (gr. k-3). 1986. reinforced bdg. 15.95 (*0-8234-0552-4*); pap. 5.95 (*0-8234-0907-4*) Holiday.
—Why Don't You Get a Horse, Sam Adams? Fritz, Jean. 48p. (gr. 2-6). 1982. 13.95 (*0-698-20292-9*, Coward); pap. 6.95 (*0-698-20545-6*, Coward) Putnam Pub Group.
—Will You Sign Here, John Hancock? Fritz, Jean. LC 75-33243. 48p. (gr. 2-6). 1982. 13.95 (*0-698-20308-9*, Coward); pap. 6.95 (*0-698-20539-1*, Coward) Putnam Pub Group.
—Witch Poems. Wallace, Daisy, ed. LC 76-9036. 32p. (ps-3). 1976. reinforced bdg. 13.95 (*0-8234-0281-9*); pap. 4.95 (*0-8234-0850-7*) Holiday.
Hyndman, Kathryn. Bible Crosswords. Krein, Linda. 48p. (gr. 3 up). 1986. wkbk. 6.95 (*0-86653-366-4*, SS 881, Shining Star Pubns) Good Apple.
—Bible Word Fun. Layton, Karen & Layton, Ron. 48p. (gr. 3 up). 1986. wkbk. 6.95 (*0-86653-367-2*, SS 882, Shining Star Pubns) Good Apple.
—Explorers. Artman, John. 64p. (gr. 4 up). 1986. 7.95 (*0-86653-340-0*, GA 796) Good Apple.
—Our Living Constitution - Then & Now. Aten, Jerry. 168p. (gr. 5 up). 1986. wkbk. 12.95 (*0-86653-386-9*, GA 1000) Good Apple.
—Parties for Home & School: A Piece of Cake. Lamb, Sandra & Bellows, Dena. 144p. (ps-4). 1985. wkbk. 11.95 (*0-86653-328-1*, GA 647) Good Apple.
—Pioneers. Artman, John. 64p. (gr. 4 up). 1987. pap. 7.95 (*0-86653-401-6*, GA 1027) Good Apple.
—Presidents. Aten, Jerry. 176p. (gr. 4 up). 1985. wkbk. 12.95 (*0-86653-281-1*, GA 627) Good Apple.
—Thursday Think Time. Palumbo, Thomas J. 64p. (gr. 3-8). 1985. wkbk. 7.95 (*0-86653-311-7*, GA 650) Good Apple.
—Tuesday Timely Teasers. Palumbo, Thomas J. 64p. (gr. 3-8). 1985. wkbk. 7.95 (*0-86653-309-5*, GA 648) Good Apple.

—Wednesday Midweek Winners. Palumbo, Thomas J. 64p. (gr. 3-8). 1985. wkbk. 7.95 (0-86653-310-9, GA 649) Good Apple.
—Women in History. Aten, Jerry. 144p. (gr. 4 up). 1986. wkbk. 11.95 (0-86653-344-3, GA 692) Good Apple.
Hynes, Robert, et al. Apes. Wildlife Education, Ltd. Staff. 20p. (Orig.). (gr. 5 up). 1981. pap. 2.75 (0-937934-03-8) Wildlife Educ.

I

Iarsen, Barbara. Lyndy. Kallstrom, Theresa. York, Sherri, ed. LC 87-50259. 44p. (Orig.). (gr. 3 up). 1987. pap. 3.95 (1-55523-081-4) Winston-Derek.
Ichikawa, Satomi. Bravo, Tanya. Gauch, Patricia L. 40p. (ps-3). 1992. PLB 14.95 (0-399-22145-X, Philomel Bks) Putnam Pub Group.
—Dance, Tanya. Gauch, Patricia L. 32p. (ps-3). 1989. 13.95 (0-399-21521-2, Philomel Bks) Putnam Pub Group.
—Fickle Barbara. Ichikawa, Satomi. LC 92-23200. 40p. (ps-3). 1993. 14.95 (0-399-22020-8, Philomel Bks) Putnam Pub Group.
—Here a Little Child I Stand: Poems of Prayer & Praise for Children. Mitchell, Cynthia, ed. LC 85-3450. 32p. (gr. k-3). 1985. 12.95 (0-399-21244-2, Philomel) Putnam Pub Group.
—Keep Running, Allen! Bulla, Clyde R. LC 77-23311. (gr. k-2). 1978. PLB 14.89 (0-690-01375-2, Crowell Jr Bks) HarpC Child Bks.
—Nora's Castle. Ichikawa, Satomi. LC 85-17293. 32p. (gr. 1-3). 1986. 15.95 (0-399-21302-3, Putnam) Putnam Pub Group.
—Nora's Duck. Ichikawa, Satomi. 40p. (ps-3). 1991. 14.95 (0-399-21805-X, Philomel) Putnam Pub Group.
—Nora's Stars. Ichikawa, Satomi. 32p. (ps-3). 1989. 14.95 (0-399-21616-2, Philomel Bks) Putnam Pub Group.
—Tanya & Emily in a Pas De Deux. Gauch, Patricia L. LC 93-5354. 1994. write for info. (0-399-22688-5, Philomel Bks) Putnam Pub Group.
Ida, Gerald, et al. The Kaua'i Guide to Beaches & Water Activities with Safety Tips. rev. ed. Durkin, Pat. 80p. pap. 2.50 (0-942255-08-9, G4-2) Magic Fishes Pr.
Idalia, Rosario. Idalia's Project ABC-Proyecto ABC: An Urban Alphabet Book in English & Spanish. Rosario, Idalia. LC 80-21013. (ps-2). 1981. (Bks Young Read); pap. 5.95 (0-8050-0296-0) H Holt & Co.
Ieff, Tova. Read Me the Haggadah. Freund, Chavie. (ps-2). 1990. 10.95 (1-56062-021-8) CIS Comm.
Iguchi, Bunshu. The Old Man Who Made the Trees Bloom. Shibano, Tamizo. Ooka, D. T., tr. from JPN. 32p. 1985. 11.95 (0-89346-247-0) Heian Intl.
—The Tiny Sheep. Iguchi, Bunshu. 24p. (ps up). 1986. 10.00 (0-8170-1108-0) Judson.
Ikegami, Ryoichi. Crying Freeman, Vol. 1. Koike, Kazuo. Horibuchi, Seiji, ed. Fujii, Satoru, et al, trs. from JPN. 64p. (Orig.). (gr. 12 up). 1989. pap. text ed. 3.50 (0-929279-50-6) Viz Comms Inc.
—Crying Freeman, Vol. 2. Koike, Kazuo. Horibuchi, Seiji, ed. Fujii, Satoru, et al, trs. from JPN. 64p. (Orig.). (gr. 12 up). 1989. pap. text ed. 3.50 (0-929279-51-4) Viz Comms Inc.
—Crying Freeman, Vol. 3. Koike, Kazuo. Horibuchi, Seiji, ed. Fujii, Satoru, et al, trs. from JPN. 64p. (Orig.). (gr. 12 up). 1989. pap. text ed. 3.50 (0-929279-52-2) Viz Comms Inc.
—Crying Freeman, Vol. 4. Koike, Kazuo. Horibuchi, Seiji, ed. Fujii, Satoru, et al, trs. from JPN. 64p. (Orig.). (gr. 12 up). 1990. pap. text ed. 3.50 (0-929279-53-0) Viz Comms Inc.
—Crying Freeman, Vol. 5. Koike, Kazuo. Horibuchi, Seiji, ed. Fujii, Satoru, et al, trs. from JPN. 64p. (Orig.). (gr. 12 up). 1990. pap. text ed. 3.50 (0-929279-54-9) Viz Comms Inc.
—Crying Freeman, Vol. 6. Koike, Kazuo. Horibuchi, Seiji, ed. Fujii, Satoru, et al, trs. from JPN. 64p. (Orig.). (gr. 12 up). 1990. pap. text ed. 3.50 (0-929279-55-7) Viz Comms Inc.
—Crying Freeman, Vol. 7. Koike, Kazuo. Horibuchi, Seiji, ed. Fujii, Satoru, et al, trs. from JPN. 64p. (Orig.). (gr. 12 up). 1990. pap. text ed. 3.50 (0-929279-56-5) Viz Comms Inc.
—Crying Freeman, Vol. 8. Koike, Kazuo. Horibuchi, Seiji, ed. Fugii, Satoru, et al, trs. from JPN. 64p. (Orig.). (gr. 12 up). 1990. pap. text ed. 3.50 (0-929279-57-3) Viz Comms Inc.
—Crying Freeman, Pt. II, Vol. 9. Koike, Kazuo. Horibuchi, Seiji, ed. Fujii, Satoru, et al, trs. from JPN. 72p. (Orig.). (gr. 12 up). 1991. pap. text ed. 3.75 (0-929279-37-9) Viz Comms Inc.
—Shades of Death, Pt. 1: Crying Freeman Graphic Novel. Koike, Kazuo. Horibuchi, Seiji, ed. Fujii, Satoru, tr. from JPN. 212p. (Orig.). (gr. 12 up). 1991. pap. 14.95 (0-929279-75-1) Viz Commns Inc.
—Shades of Death, Pt. 2: Crying Freeman Graphic Novel. Koike, Kazuo. Horibuchi, Seiji, ed. Fujii, Satoru, tr. from JPN. 212p. (Orig.). (gr. 12 up). 1992. pap. 14.95 (0-929279-76-X) Viz Commns Inc.
—Shades of Death, Pt. 3: Crying Freeman Graphic Novel. Koike, Kazuo. Horibuchi, Seiji, ed. Fujii, Satoru, tr. from JPN. 212p. (gr. 12 up). 1992. pap. 14.95 (0-929279-77-8) Viz Commns Inc.
Imershein, Betsy. Animal Doctor. Imershein, Betsy. LC 87-20266. 32p. (gr. 1-5). 1988. (J Messner); lib. bdg. 4.95 (0-671-65862-X) S&S Trade.

Imershein, Betsy, photos by. Finding Red Finding Yellow. Imershein, Betsy. LC 88-35808. 32p. (ps). 1989. 10.95 (0-15-200453-X, Gulliver Bks) HarBrace.
Imler, Kathryn A. Lucy's Feet. Stein, Stephanie. LC 92-4602. 32p. (ps-3). 1992. 12.95 (0-944934-05-6) Perspect Indiana.
Imrick, Ann T. Allergy. Dees, Susan C. Head, J. J., ed. LC 86-72199. 16p. (Orig.). (gr. 10 up). 1988. pap. text ed. 2.75 (0-89278-169-6, 45-9769) Carolina Biological.
—The Human Kidney. Blythe, William B. Head, J. J., ed. LC 86-72196. 16p. (Orig.). (gr. 10 up). 1991. pap. text ed. 2.75 (0-89278-167-X, 45-9767) Carolina Biological.
—The Nerve Cell. Ralston, Diane D. & Ralston, Henry J., III. Head, J. J., ed. LC 84-45836. 16p. (Orig.). (gr. 10 up). 1988. pap. text ed. 2.75 (0-89278-357-5, 45-9757) Carolina Biological.
—Viruses. Flint, S. Jane. Head, J. J., ed. LC 87-70987. 16p. (Orig.). (gr. 10 up). 1988. pap. text ed. 2.75 (0-89278-094-0, 45-9794) Carolina Biological.
Imsand, Marcel. A Christmas Carol. Dickens, Charles. LC 85-15815. 78p. (gr. 4 up). 1984. PLB 13.95.s.p. (0-87191-955-9) Creative Ed.
Imsand, Marcel & Marshall, Rita. The Fir Tree. Andersen, Hans Christian. 40p. (gr. 6 up). 1983. PLB 13.95.s.p. (0-87191-949-4) Creative Ed.
Incisa, Monica. The Forgetful Wishing Well: Poems for Young People. Kennedy, X. J. LC 84-45977. 96p. (gr. 4 up). 1985. SBE 12.95 (0-689-50317-2, M K McElderry) Macmillan Child Grp.
—Whiff, Sniff, Nibble, & Chew: The Gingerbread Boy Retold. Pomerantz, Charlotte. LC 83-14179. 24p. (gr. k-3). 1984. PLB 8.59 (0-688-02552-8) Greenwillow.
Incrocci, Rick. My Very First Book of Bible Heroes. Hollingsworth, Mary. LC 93-7292. 1993. 4.99 (0-8407-9230-1) Nelson.
—My Very First Book of Prayers. Hollingsworth, Mary. LC 93-7291. 1993. 4.99 (0-8407-9229-8) Nelson.
Indereiden, Nancy. Frustrated. Tester, Sylvia R. LC 79-23804. (ps-2). 1980. PLB 18.50 (0-89565-110-6); PLB 12.95s.p. (0-685-55481-3) Childs World.
—Glad. Odor, Ruth S. LC 79-26076. (ps-2). 1980. PLB 18.50 (0-89565-114-9); PLB 12.95s.p. (0-685-55483-X) Childs World.
—Jealous. Tester, Sylvia R. LC 79-24042. (ps-2). 1980. PLB 18.50 (0-89565-111-4); PLB 12.95s.p. (0-685-55490-2) Childs World.
—Please. Odor, Ruth S. LC 79-25319. (ps-2). 1980. PLB 18.50 (0-89565-115-7); PLB 12.95s.p. (0-685-55538-0) Childs World.
—Sad. Tester, Sylvia R. LC 79-26252. (ps-2). 1980. PLB 18.50 (0-89565-112-2); PLB 12.95s.p. (0-685-55541-0) Childs World.
—Thanks. Odor, Ruth S. LC 79-23926. (ps-2). 1980. PLB 18.50 (0-89565-113-0); PLB 12.95s.p. (0-685-55553-4) Childs World.
Indereiden, Nancy. Saying Please. Moncure, Jane B. LC 82-19927. 32p. (ps-2). 1981. PLB 21.35 (0-89565-248-X); PLB 14.95s.p. (0-685-55661-1) Childs World.
Ingersoll, Norm. Fire Fighters. Seymour, Peter. 12p. (gr. k-3). 1990. 12.95 (0-525-67295-8, Lodestar Bks) Dutton Child Bks.
—Pilots. Seymour, Peter. 12p. (gr. k-3). 1992. 13.00 (0-525-67372-5, Lodestar Bks) Dutton Child Bks.
Ingpen, Robert. The Age of Acorns. Ingpen, Robert. LC 90-433. 28p. (gr. k-3). 1990. PLB 14.95 (0-87226-436-X, Bedrick Blackie) P Bedrick Bks.
—Generals Who Changed the World. Wilkinson, Philip & Pollard, Michael. LC 93-31358. 1994. write for info. (0-7910-2761-9); pap. write for info. (0-7910-2786-4) Chelsea Hse.
—The Great Deeds of Heroic Women. Saxby, Maurice. LC 91-11211. 152p. (gr. 4 up). 1992. 18.95 (0-87226-348-7) P Bedrick Bks.
—The Great Deeds of Superheroes. Saxby, Maurice. 184p. (gr. 4 up). 1990. 24.95 (0-87226-342-8) P Bedrick Bks.
—The Great Deeds of Superheroes. Saxby, Maurice. 184p. (gr. 4 up). 1993. pap. 14.95 sewn (0-87226-260-X) P Bedrick Bks.
—The Idle Bear. Ingpen, Robert. LC 87-1187. 32p. (gr. k-3). 1987. PLB 14.95 (0-87226-159-X, Bedrick Blackie) P Bedrick Bks.
—Peace Begins with You. Scholes, Katherine. 40p. (gr. 1-5). 1990. 12.95 (0-316-77436-7) Sierra.
—People Who Changed the World. Wilkinson, Philip & Dineen, Jacqueline. LC 93-31357. 1994. write for info. (0-7910-2764-3); pap. write for info. (0-7910-2789-9) Chelsea Hse.
—River Through the Ages. Steele, Philip. LC 91-33279. 32p. (gr. 3-6). 1993. PLB 11.89 (0-8167-2735-X); pap. text ed. 3.95 (0-8167-2736-8) Troll Assocs. Postponed.
—Treasure Island. Stevenson, Robert Louis. 176p. 1992. 20.00 (0-670-84685-6) Viking Child Bks.
Ingraham, Erick. The Animals' Lullaby. Paxton, Tom. LC 92-18841. 40p. (ps up). 1993. 15.00 (0-688-10468-1); PLB 14.93 (0-688-10469-X) Morrow Jr Bks.
—Henry the Sailor Cat. Calhoun, Mary. LC 92-29794. 1994. write for info. (0-688-10840-7); lib. bdg. write for info. (0-688-10841-5) Morrow Jr Bks.
—High-Wire Henry. Calhoun, Mary. LC 89-35642. 40p. (gr. k up). 1991. 13.95 (0-688-08983-6); PLB 13.88 (0-688-08984-4, Morrow Jr Bks) Morrow Jr Bks.

—Little Daylight. MacDonald, George. Ingraham, Erick, adapted by. LC 85-29769. 40p. (gr. 2 up). 1988. 12.95 (0-688-06300-4); PLB 12.88 (0-688-06301-2, Morrow Jr Bks) Morrow Jr Bks.
—Mazemaker. Dexter, Catherine. LC 88-32349. 224p. (gr. 5-9). 1989. 11.95 (0-688-07383-2) Morrow Jr Bks.
Ingram, Fred & Jennings, Elkay. The Dinkywinkies & Snickity Snackety Snort. Rasbach, Hubert H. LC 79-89378. (ps-4). 1982. 6.95 (0-934822-05-0) Plus One Pub.
Ingram, Jay. Real Live Science: Top Scientists Present Amazing Activities Any Kid Can Do. Ingram, Jay. 48p. (gr. 4 up). 1992. text ed. 16.95 (1-895688-00-0, Pub. by Greey de Pencier CN); pap. 8.95 (0-920775-87-X, Pub. by Greey de Pencier CN) Firefly Bks Ltd.
Inis, Ninabeth R. The Fairy of Masara. Fuentes, Vilma M. 24p. (Orig.). 1984. pap. 3.50 (971-10-0211-6, Pub by New Day Philippines) Cellar.
—Kimod & the Swan Maiden. Fuentes, Vilma M. 36p. (Orig.). (gr. k-3). 1984. pap. 3.50 (971-10-0135-7, Pub. by New Day Pub PI) Cellar.
—Manggob & His Golden Top. Fuentes, Vilma M. 48p. (Orig.). (gr. k-3). 1985. pap. 4.00 (971-10-0218-3, Pub. by New Day Pub PI) Cellar.
Inkpen, Mick. If I Had a Pig. Inkpen, Mick. (ps). 1988. 7.95 (0-316-41887-0) Little.
—If I Had a Sheep. Inkpen, Mick. (ps). 1988. 7.95 (0-316-41888-9) Little.
—Jasper's Beanstalk. Butterworth, Nick & Inkpen, Mich. LC 92-14886. 32p. (ps-1). 1993. SBE 13.95 (0-02-747811-3, Bradbury Pr) Macmillan Child Grp.
Inkpen, Mick, jt. illus. see Butterworth, Nick.
Innes, George C. What Was I Like? Childhood Memory Book Series, 6 bks, Set 1. Harris, Jennifer. (ps). 1992. Set. slipcased 49.95 (1-879956-12-8) Tintern Abbey.
—What Was I Like? Childhood Memory Book Series, 5 bks, Set 2. Harris, Jennifer. (gr. k-4). 1992. Set. slipcased 49.95 (1-879956-13-6) Tintern Abbey.
Innes, Nancy. The Weather Cock & Other Tales. Uttley, Alison. 111p. (gr. k-3). 1991. pap. 2.95 (0-571-14174-9) Faber & Faber.
Innocenti, Roberto. The Adventures of Pinocchio. Collodi, Carlo. Harden, E., tr. from ITA. LC 88-8918. 144p. (ps up). 1988. 18.95 (0-394-82110-6) Knopf Bks Yng Read.
—The Adventures of Pinocchio. Collodi, Carlo. 144p. (gr. 1-12). Date not set. lib. bdg. 19.95 RLB smythe-sewn (0-8211-0394-6, 97080-098) Creative Ed.
—A Christmas Carol. Dickens, Charles. LC 90-1335. 152p. 1990. 30.00 (1-55670-161-6) Stewart Tabori & Chang.
—A Christmas Carol. Dickens, Charles. 152p. (gr. 1-12). Date not set. lib. bdg. 25.00 RLB smythe-sewn (0-88682-327-7, 97200-098) Creative Ed.
Inns, Kenneth. Egermeier's Picture-Story Life of Jesus. Egermeier, Elsie E. (gr. k-6). 1969. 7.95 (0-87162-008-1, D2015) Warner Pr.
Inouye, Carol. Dinosaur Babies. Silverman, Maida. LC 88-4690. 1990. pap. 4.95 (0-671-69438-3, Little Simon) S&S Trade.
—Hungry Dinosaurs. Granowsky, Alvin. LC 91-23405. 32p. (gr. 1-4). 1992. PLB 15.96 (0-8114-3252-1); pap. 3.95 (0-8114-6226-9) Raintree Steck-V.
—Kids' Cooking Without a Stove: A Cookbook for Young Children. rev. ed. Paul, Aileen. LC 84-22230. 64p. 1985. pap. 7.95 (0-86534-060-9) Sunstone Pr.
—The Luminous Pearl: A Chinese Folktale. Torre, Betty L., retold by. LC 89-70999. 32p. (ps-3). 1990. 14.95 (0-531-05890-5); PLB 14.99 (0-531-08490-6) Orchard Bks Watts.
—Meat-Eating Dinosaurs. Granowsky, Alvin. LC 91-23406. 32p. (gr. 1-4). 1992. PLB 15.96 (0-8114-3254-8); pap. 3.95 (0-8114-6227-7) Raintree Steck-V.
Intervisual Staff. Ernest Nister's Book of Christmas. Nister, Ernest. 12p. 1991. 12.95 (0-399-21799-1, Philomel) Putnam Pub Group.
—Farmyard Friends. Nister, Ernest. 10p. (ps up). 1991. 4.95 (0-399-22110-7, Philomel) Putnam Pub Group.
—Little Dolls. Nister, Ernest. 10p. (ps up). 1991. 4.95 (0-399-22107-7, Philomel) Putnam Pub Group.
—My Little Pets. Nister, Ernest. 10p. (ps up). 1991. 4.95 (0-399-22109-3, Philomel) Putnam Pub Group.
—Tiny Tots. Nister, Ernest. 10p. (ps up). 1991. 4.95 (0-399-22108-5, Philomel) Putnam Pub Group.
Iosa, Ann. The Boy Who Wouldn't Eat Breakfast. Coco, Eugene. 24p. (ps-2). 1993. pap. text ed. 0.99 (1-56293-349-3) McClanahan Bk.
—Clipper's Crazy Race. Kingsriter, Debbie & Kingsriter, Doug. LC 92-12327. 32p. 1992. 7.99 (0-8499-0921-X) Word Pub.
—Finny's Big Break. Kingsriter, Debbie & Kingsriter, Doug. LC 92-12325. 32p. (ps-2). 1992. 7.99 (0-8499-0920-1) Word Pub.
—Gilroy's Goof. Kingsriter, Debbie & Kingsriter, Doug. LC 92-12580. 32p. (ps-2). 1992. 7.99 (0-8499-0922-8) Word Pub.
—Real Bears & Alligators. Robinson, Fay. LC 92-10755. 32p. (ps-2). 1993. pap. 3.95 (0-516-42374-6) Childrens.
—Thanksgiving Holiday Grab Bag. Stamper, Judith. LC 92-13420. 48p. (gr. 2-5). 1992. PLB 11.89 (0-8167-2906-9); pap. text ed. 3.95 (0-8167-2907-7) Troll Assocs.

—What Was the Wicked Witch's Real Name? & Other Character Riddles. Bernstein, Joanne E. & Cohen, Paul. LC 86-1648. 32p. (gr. 1-5). 1986. 8.95 (0-8075-8854-7) A Whitman.
—When Nicki Went Away. Robinson, Fay. LC 92-13835. 32p. (ps). 1993. pap. 3.95 (0-516-42376-2) Childrens.
Iosa, Ann W. A Ghost in the Toy Box. Robinson, Fay. LC 92-10758. 32p. (ps-2). 1993. PLB 15.00 (0-516-02371-3); pap. 3.95 (0-516-42371-1) Childrens.
—Laura Jean the Yard Sale Queen. Leonard, Marcia. Brook, Bonnie, ed. LC 89-70304. 24p. (ps-1). 1990. 5.95 (0-671-70405-2); PLB 9.98 (0-671-70401-X) Silver Pr.
—Old MacDonald Had a Farm. Robinson, Fay. LC 92-10757. 32p. (ps-2). 1993. PLB 15.00 (0-516-02372-1) Childrens. Postponed.
—Pizza Soup. Robinson, Fay. LC 92-10756. 32p. (ps-2). 1993. PLB 15.00 (0-516-02373-X); pap. 3.95 (0-516-42373-8) Childrens.
—Real Bears & Alligators. Robinson, Fay. LC 92-10755. 32p. (ps-2). 1992. PLB 15.00 (0-516-02374-8) Childrens.
—Rhymes We Like. Robinson, Fay. LC 92-10754. 32p. (ps-2). 1993. PLB 15.00 (0-516-02375-6) Childrens. Postponed.
—What's It Like to Be an Airline Pilot. Bauer, Judith. LC 89-34397. 32p. (gr. k-3). 1990. PLB 10.89 (0-8167-1791-5); pap. text ed. 2.95 (0-8167-1792-3) Troll Assocs.
—When Nicki Went Away. Robinson, Fay. LC 92-13835. 32p. (ps). 1992. PLB 15.00 (0-516-02376-4) Childrens.
Iosa, Ann W., jt. illus. see Chambliss, Maxie.
Ipina, David. Ishi: America's Last Stone Age Indian. Burrill, Richard L. 50p. 1990. pap. 8.95 (1-878464-01-9) Anthro CO.
Ipina, David, jt. illus. see Waters, Robyn.
Ireland, Joe, et al. Las Cruces: An Illustrated History. Harris, Linda B. Priestley, Lee, intro. by. LC 93-22913. 144p. 1993. 29.95 (0-9623682-5-3) Arroyo Pr.
Ireland, Shep. Merry Christmas. Ireland, Shep. 1992. 4.75 (0-8378-3799-5) Gibson.
—Wesley & Wendell: At Home. Ireland, Shep. 40p. (gr. 1). 1991. lib. bdg. 4.75 (0-8378-0330-6) Gibson.
—Wesley & Wendell: Happy Birthday. Ireland, Shep. 40p. (gr. 1). 1991. lib. bdg. 4.75 (0-8378-0333-0) Gibson.
—Wesley & Wendell: In the Garden. Ireland, Shep. 40p. (gr. 1). 1991. lib. bdg. 4.75 (0-8378-0331-4) Gibson.
—Wesley & Wendell: Vacation. Ireland, Shep. 40p. (gr. 1). 1991. lib. bdg. 4.75 (0-8378-0332-2) Gibson.
Irvine, Bonnie, jt. illus. see Gesner, Ethel.
Irvine, Rex J. The Ayyam-i Ha Camel. Holt-Fortin, Cher. 40p. (Orig.). (gr. 2-6). 1989. 9.95 (0-933770-73-1) Kalimat.
—The Cornerstone: A Story About 'Abdu'l-Baha in America. Lee, Anthony A. 24p. (Orig.). (gr. k-5). 1979. pap. 3.00 (0-933770-01-4) Kalimat.
Irvine, Rex John. The Unfriendly Governor. Lee, Anthony A. 24p. (gr. k-5). 1980. pap. 3.00 (0-933770-02-2) Kalimat.
Irving, James G. Birds. Zim, Herbert S. & Gabrielson, Ira N. (gr. 7 up). 1956. PLB write for info. (0-307-24053-3); pap. write for info. (Golden Pr) Western Pub.
—Dinosaurs. Zim, Herbert S. LC 54-5080. 64p. (gr. 3-7). 1954. PLB 11.88 (0-688-31239-X) Morrow Jr Bks.
—Insects. Cottam, Clarence & Zim, Herbert S. 160p. 1987. pap. write for info. (0-307-24055-X, Pub. by Golden Bks) Western Pub.
—Snakes. Zim, Herbert S. LC 49-10266. 64p. (gr. 3-7). 1949. PLB 12.88 (0-688-31549-6) Morrow Jr Bks.
—Stars. rev. ed. Zim, Herbert S. & Baker, Robert H. (gr. 6 up). 1985. pap. write for info. (0-307-24493-8, Golden Pr) Western Pub.
Isaac, Barbara K. One Sad Day. Kohn, Bernice. LC 78-169153. 48p. 1972. 11.95 (0-89388-026-4) Okpaku Communications.
—Third World Voices for Children. McDowell, Robert E. & Lavitt, Edward, eds. LC 71-169091. 156p. (gr. 5-9). 1981. 7.95 (0-89388-020-5, Odarkai) Okpaku Communications.
Isaacs, Jean & Tourtillotte, Barb. Huff & Puff on Halloween. Warren, Jean. Cubley, Kathleen, ed. LC 92-62824. 32p. (Orig.). (ps-2). 1993. 12.95 (0-911019-68-5); pap. text ed. 5.95 (0-911019-69-3) Warren Pub Hse.
Isaacson, Phillip M. Round Buildings, Square Buildings & Buildings That Wiggle Like a Fish. Isaacson, Phillip M. LC 87-16967. 128p. (gr. 5 up). 1990. 14.95 (0-394-89382-4); lib. bdg. 16.99 (0-394-99382-9); pap. 10.95 (0-679-80649-0) Knopf Bks Yng Read.
Isadora, Rachel. At the Crossroads. Isadora, Rachel. 32p. (ps up). Date not set. pap. 4.95 (0-688-13103-4, Mulberry) Morrow.
—Ben's Trumpet. Isadora, Rachel. LC 78-12885. 32p. (gr. k-3). 1979. 14.00 (0-688-80194-3) Greenwillow.
—City Seen from A to Z. Isadora, Rachel. LC 82-11966. 32p. (gr. k-3). 1983. PLB 11.88 (0-688-01803-3) Greenwillow.
—Cutlass in the Snow. Shub, Elizabeth. LC 85-5442. 48p. (gr. 1-4). 1986. 11.95 (0-688-05927-9); PLB 11.88 (0-688-05928-7) Greenwillow.
—Flossie & the Fox. McKissack, Patricia C. LC 86-2024. 32p. (ps-3). 1986. 14.00 (0-8037-0250-7); PLB 13.89 (0-8037-0251-5) Dial Bks Young.

—Golden Bear. Young, Ruth. 32p. (ps-1). 1992. PLB 14.00 (0-670-82577-8) Viking Child Bks.
—Golden Bear. Young, Ruth. 32p. (ps-1). 1994. pap. 4.99 (0-14-050959-3) Puffin Bks.
—Grandfather's Lovesong. Lindbergh, Reeve. LC 92-22112. 32p. 1993. 14.99 (0-670-84842-5) Viking Child Bks.
—I Hear. Isadora, Rachel. LC 84-6103. 32p. (ps). 1985. 15.00 (0-688-04061-6); PLB 14.93 (0-688-04062-4) Greenwillow.
—I See. Isadora, Rachel. LC 84-6104. 32p. (ps). 1985. 15.00 (0-688-04059-4); PLB 14.93 (0-688-04060-8) Greenwillow.
—I Touch. Isadora, Rachel. LC 84-13673. 32p. (ps). 1985. 15.00 (0-688-04255-4); lib. bdg. 14.93 (0-688-04256-2) Greenwillow.
—Lili at Ballet. Isadora, Rachel. LC 92-8429. 32p. (ps-3). 1993. PLB 14.95 (0-399-22423-8, Putnam) Putnam Pub Group.
—The Little Match Girl. Andersen, Hans Christian. 32p. (ps-3). 1990. 14.95 (0-399-21336-8, Sandcastle Bks); pap. 5.95 (0-399-22007-0, Sandcastle Bks) Putnam Pub Group.
—Max. Isadora, Rachel. LC 76-9088. 32p. (gr. k-3). 1976. RSBE 13.95 (0-02-747450-X, Macmillan Child Bk) Macmillan Child Grp.
—Prayers, Praises, & Thanksgivings. Stoddard, Sandol, compiled by. LC 86-32822. 160p. 1992. 18.50 (0-8037-0421-6) Dial Bks Young.
—The White Stallion. Shub, Elizabeth. LC 81-20308. 56p. (gr. 1-3). 1982. 15.95 (0-688-01210-8); PLB 15.88 (0-688-01211-6) Greenwillow.
—The White Stallion. Shub, Elizabeth. 64p. (gr. 1-4). 1984. pap. 2.50 (0-553-15244-0, Skylark) Bantam.
Isaksen, Patricia. Captain Flounder, His Sole Brothers & Friends. Bozanich, Tony L. Isaksen, Lisa A., ed. 16p. (ps-4). 1984. pap. 4.95 (0-930655-00-1) Antarctic Pr.
Isami, Ikuyo. The Fox's Egg. Isami, Ikuyo. 40p. (ps-2). 1989. 18.95 (0-87614-339-7) Carolrhoda Bks.
Isen, Harold. Alfred Hitchcock's Spellbinders in Suspense. Hitchcock, Alfred. (gr. 7-11). 1982. 4.99 (0-394-84900-0) Random Bks Yng Read.
Ishikawa, Eiko. Mother Goose. 16p. (ps). 1992. pap. 4.95 (0-671-77012-8, Little Simon) S&S Trade.
—What's Inside? 16p. (ps). 1992. pap. 4.95 (0-671-77017-9, Little Simon) S&S Trade.
—Where Is Kitty? 16p. (ps). 1992. pap. 4.95 (0-671-77018-7, Little Simon) S&S Trade.
—Who Lives Here? 16p. (ps). 1992. pap. 4.95 (0-671-77023-3, Little Simon) S&S Trade.
Ishikawa, Yoko. Rainbow Collection, 1987: Stories & Poetry by Young People. Janger, Kathie, ed. Johnson, Rafer, intro. by. 160p. (gr. 1-8). 1987. pap. text ed. 6.00 (0-929889-02-9) Young Writers Contest Found.
Ishinabe, Fusako. Spring Snowman. Barnes, Jill & Ishinabe, Fusako. Rubin, Caroline, ed. Japan Foreign Rights Centre Staff, tr. from JPN. LC 90-37748. 32p. (gr. k-3). 1990. PLB 14.60 (0-944483-83-6) Garrett Ed Corp.
Iskowitz, Joel. A Candle for Grandpa: A Guide to the Jewish Funeral for Children & Parents. Techner, David & Hirt-Manheimer, Judith. (gr. k-3). 1993. 10.95 (0-8074-0507-8, 123070) UAHC.
—Emma Ansky-Levine & Her Mitzvah Machine. Bush, Lawrence. (gr. k-6). 1991. pap. 7.95 (0-8074-0458-6, 123933) UAHC.
—Emma's Turn. Weyn, Suzanne. LC 89-31348. 96p. (gr. 3-5). 1990. lib. bdg. 9.89 (0-8167-1623-4); pap. text ed. 2.95 (0-8167-1624-2) Troll Assocs.
—Joshua's Dream: A Journey to the Land of Israel. Segal, Sheila F. LC 91-45513. (gr. k-3). 1992. 10.95 (0-8074-0476-4, 101062) UAHC.
—Pointing Toward Trouble. Weyn, Suzanne. LC 89-34549. 96p. (gr. 3-5). 1990. PLB 9.89 (0-8167-1653-6); pap. text ed. 2.95 (0-8167-1654-4) Troll Assocs.
—Stage Fright. Weyn, Suzanne. LC 89-31349. 96p. (gr. 3-5). 1990. lib. bdg. 9.89 (0-8167-1651-X); pap. text ed. 2.95 (0-8167-1652-8) Troll Assocs.
—Stepping Out. Weyn, Suzanne. LC 89-30586. 96p. (gr. 3-5). 1990. PLB 9.89 (0-8167-1619-6); pap. text ed. 2.95 (0-8167-1620-X) Troll Assocs.
—Three for the Show. Weyn, Suzanne. LC 89-34547. 96p. (gr. 3-5). 1990. PLB 9.89 (0-8167-1655-2); pap. text ed. 2.95 (0-8167-1656-0) Troll Assocs.
—A Twist of Fate. Weyn, Suzanne. LC 89-30585. 96p. (gr. 3-5). 1990. PLB 9.89 (0-8167-1621-8); pap. text ed. 2.95 (0-8167-1622-6) Troll Assocs.
Ito, Joel. Human Skin. Montagna, William. Head, J. J., ed. LC 84-45831. 16p. (Orig.). (gr. 10 up). 1986. pap. text ed. 2.75 (0-89278-159-9, 45-9759) Carolina Biological.
Ito, Yoriko. Lily & the Wooden Bowl: A Japanese Folktale. Schroeder, Alan, adapted by. LC 93-17900. Date not set. write for info. (0-385-31073-0) Dial Bks Young.
Itoko Maeno. Mother Nature Nursery Rhymes. Stryker & Bingham. Paine, ed. 32p. (ps-6). 1990. 14.95 (0-911655-01-8) Advocacy Pr.
Iverson, Diane. Buttons: The Foster Bunny. Grover, Teddi. Martone, Frederick M., intro. by. 48p. (Orig.). (ps-5). 1992. pap. 8.95 (0-9623349-3-6) MS Pub.
—Where Are the Babies? Iverson, Diane. 48p. (Orig.). (ps). 1992. 14.95 (0-9623349-1-X); pap. 8.95 (0-9623349-2-8) MS Pub.

Ives, Michael. The Arizona Alphabet Book. Schmid-Belk, Donna D. Belk, Gordon G., ed. 32p. (Orig.). (ps-8). 1989. pap. text ed. 7.95 (0-685-28841-2) Donna Dee Bks.
Ives, Penny. The Bedtime Book. Henderson, Kathy, selected by. LC 92-9413. (ps-3). 1992. 14.95 (0-8120-6295-7) Barron.
—Goldilocks & the Three Bears: A Peek-Through-the-Window Book. (ps-1). 1992. 14.95 (0-399-22121-2, Putnam) Putnam Pub Group.
—The Nest. Baines, Chris. LC 89-77653. 24p. (ps-3). 1990. 7.95 (0-940793-55-5, Crocodile Bks) Interlink Pub.
—The Night Before Christmas: A Revolving Picture & Lift-the-Flap Book. Moore, Clement C. 14p. 1988. 14.95 (0-399-21544-1, Putnam) Putnam Pub Group.
—On Christmas Eve. Sadie Fields Productions Staff. 14p. 1992. 16.95 (0-399-22148-4, Putnam) Putnam Pub Group.
—The Picnic. Baines, Chris. LC 89-77746. 24p. (ps-3). 1990. 7.95 (0-940793-54-7, Crocodile Bks) Interlink Pub.
Ivins, Dorothy & Strait, Barbara. Forget the ABC's until after Your Child Has Learned to Read. Cordell, Rose. 211p. (Orig.). 1993. 17.95x (0-940047-00-4); PLB 25.95 (0-940047-01-2); text ed. 17.95 (0-940047-02-0); pap. 14.95 (0-940047-03-9); tchr's guide for 6 yr. old 31.95 (0-940047-04-7); wkbk. level 1 words 7.00 (0-940047-05-5); tchr's guide for 5 yr. old (0-940047-06-3) Child Alphabet.
Ivory, Lesley A. Cats in the Sun. Ivory, Lesley A. LC 90-43068. 32p. (ps up). 1991. 14.95 (0-8037-0955-2) Dial Bks Young.
—Cats Know Best. Eisler, Colin. LC 87-15653. 32p. (ps up). 1988. 13.95 (0-8037-0503-4); PLB 13.89 (0-8037-0560-3) Dial Bks Young.
—Little Angels. Van der Meer, Ron & Ivory, Lesley A. LC 92-70261. 12p. 1992. Mini pop-up bk. in gift box. 10.00 (0-679-83472-9) Knopf Bks Yng Read.
Ivory, Leslie A. The Birthday Cat. Ivory, Leslie A. LC 93-129. 32p. (ps-3). 1993. 15.00 (0-8037-1622-2) Dial Bks Young.
Iwai, Noel, jt. illus. see French, Marty.
Iwamura, Kazuo. The Fourteen Forest Mice & the Harvest Moon Watch. Iwamura, Kazuo. Knowlton, Mary L., tr. from JPN. LC 90-50706. 32p. (gr. k-3). 1991. PLB 17.27 (0-8368-0497-X) Gareth Stevens Inc.
—The Fourteen Forest Mice & the Spring Meadow Picnic. Iwamura, Kazuo. Knowlton, Mary L., tr. from JPN. LC 90-50704. 32p. (gr. k-3). 1991. PLB 17.27 (0-8368-0498-8) Gareth Stevens Inc.
—The Fourteen Forest Mice & the Summer Laundry Day. Iwamura, Kazuo. Knowlton, Mary L., tr. from JPN. LC 90-50705. 32p. (gr. k-3). 1991. PLB 17.27 (0-8368-0576-3) Gareth Stevens Inc.
—The Fourteen Forest Mice & the Winter Sledding Day. Iwamura, Kazuo. Knowlton, Mary L., tr. from JPN. LC 90-50707. 32p. (gr. k-3). 1991. PLB 17.27 (0-8368-0499-6) Gareth Stevens Inc.
Iwanowski, Elka. The Story of Cape Cod. Shortsleeve, Kevin. Shortsleeve, Brian F., ed. 64p. (gr. k-3). 1993. pap. 9.75 (0-9622782-1-1) Cape Cod Life Mag.
Iwasaki, Chihiro. The Little Mermaid. Andersen, Hans Christian. LC 84-9490. 32p. (gr. 2 up). 1991. pap. 15.95 (0-907234-59-3) Picture Bk Studio.
—The Little Mermaid. Andersen, Hans Christian. 1991. pap. 3.95 (0-590-44456-5) Scholastic Inc.
—The Red Shoes. Andersen, Hans Christian. LC 82-61836. 36p. (gr. 3 up). 1991. pap. 15.95 (0-907234-26-7) Picture Bk Studio.
—Snow White & the Seven Dwarfs. Grimm, Jacob & Grimm, Wilhelm K. LC 85-12158. 40p. (gr. 1 up). 1991. pap. 15.95 (0-88708-012-X) Picture Bk Studio.
—Swan Lake. Bell, Anthea. LC 86-9509. 28p. (gr. 1 up). 1991. pap. 15.95 (0-88708-028-6) Picture Bk Studio.
Iwia, Noel, jt. illus. see French, Marty.
Izaguirre, Oscar. Sing a Rainbow Big Book. Hamilton, Arthur. (ps-2). 1988. pap. text ed. 14.00 (0-922053-21-9) N Edge Res.
Izawa, Masana. Mosses. Johnson, Sylvia A. LC 83-17488. 48p. (gr. 4 up). 1983. PLB 19.95 (0-8225-1482-6) Lerner Pubns.
—Mushrooms. Johnson, Sylvia A. LC 82-212. 48p. (gr. 4 up). 1982. PLB 19.95 (0-8225-1473-7) Lerner Pubns.
Izawa, Masana, photos by. Mosses. Johnson, Sylvia. 48p. (gr. 4 up). 1983. pap. 5.95g (0-8225-9563-X) Lerner Pubns.
Izawa, Tadasu & Hijkata, Shigemi. What Time Is It? 18p. (gr. k-2). 1981. (G&D). PLB 3.95 (0-448-03701-7, G&D) Putnam Pub Group.
Izawa, Yohji. One Christmas. Funakoshi, Canna. LC 90-7445. 40p. (gr. k up). 1991. pap. 12.95 (0-88708-140-1) Picture Bk Studio.
—One Evening. Funakoshi, Canna. LC 87-29243. (ps up). 1991. pap. 11.95 (0-88708-063-4) Picture Bk Studio.

J

Ja, Andrea. Wings for Lai Ho. Lim, Genny. Lew, Gordon, tr. 48p. (Orig.). (gr. 5-8). 1982. pap. 5.95 (0-934788-01-4) E-W Pub Co.
Jabar, Cynthia. How Many, How Many, How Many. Walton, Rick. LC 92-54408. 32p. (ps up). 1993. 14.95 (1-56402-062-2) Candlewick Pr.
—A Koala for Katie. London, Jonathan. LC 93-16085. 1993. write for info. (0-8075-4209-1) A Whitman.

—Party Day! Jabar, Cynthia. (ps-1). 1987. 11.95 (0-316-43456-6, Joy St Bks) Little.
—Shimmy Shake Earthquake: Don't Forget to Dance Poems. Jabar, Cynthia, compiled by. 32p. (ps-3). 1992. 14.95 (0-316-43459-0, Joy St Bks) Little.
Jackson, Al. Our Family Table: Recipes & Food Memories from African-American Life Models. Williams, Thelma. Cellino, Maria E. & Rolfes, Ellen, eds. Cosby, Camille O., intro. by. 96p. (gr. 7 up). 1993. 14.95 (1-879958-14-7); PLB 14.95 (1-879958-16-3) Tradery Hse.
Jackson, Gregory A. Fire & Firecrackers. 3rd ed. Brown, Lynn. Walker, Granville, Jr., ed. 14p. (Orig.). (ps-6). 1982. pap. 2.97x (0-9608466-1-1) Fun Reading.
—Ms. Worm. 3rd ed. Brown, Lynn. Walker, Granville, Jr., ed. (Orig.). (ps-6). 1982. pap. 2.95x (0-9608466-0-3) Fun Reading.
Jackson, I. & Suttie, A. Rocks & Fossils. Cork, B. & Bramwell, M. 32p. (gr. 5-8). 1983. PLB 13.96 (0-88110-159-1); pap. 6.95 (0-86020-765-X) EDC.
Jackson, Ian. Plant Life. Cork, Barbara. 32p. (gr. 6up). 1984. PLB 13.96 (0-88110-169-9); pap. 5.95 (0-86020-755-2) EDC.
Jackson, Ian & Harris, Alan. Insect Life. Owen, Jennifer. 32p. (gr. 4-7). 1985. PLB 13.96 (0-88110-173-7, Pub. by Usborne). pap. 5.95 (0-86020-843-5) EDC.
Jackson, Ian & Quinn, David. Mysteries & Marvels of Nature. Cork, Barbara & Morris, R. 192p. (gr. 3-6). 1983. 19.95 (0-7460-0421-4) EDC.
Jackson, Ian & Shields, Chris. Small Pets. Hill. Cork, Barbara, ed. (gr. 3-6). pap. 4.50 (0-86020-648-3, 15122); lib. bdg. 11.96 (0-88110-087-0) EDC.
Jackson, Ian, et al. Ocean Life. Morris, R. 32p. (gr. 3-6). 1983. (Usborne-Haynes); PLB 13.96 (0-88110-149-4, Usborne-Haynes); pap. 5.95 (0-86020-753-6, Usborne-Haynes) EDC.
Jackson, Jeff. Righteous Rhymes, Vol. 1. Lash, Jamie S. 24p. (gr. 2-7). 1983. pap. 2.95 (0-915775-00-X, Dist. by Stardust) Love Song Mess Assn.
—Righteous Rhymes, Vol. 2. Lash, Jamie S., ed. 24p. (Orig.). 1987. pap. 2.95 (0-915775-01-8) Love Song Mess Assn.
Jackson, Jett & Arnoff, Julie. The Cinnamon Bear: The Missing Star. Heisch, Glan & Heisch, Elisabeth. Bishop, Kathryn, ed. & intro. by. 32p. 1992. PLB 13. 95 (1-880623-01-3); pap. 8.95 (1-880623-02-1) Stiles-Bishop.
Jackson, Julian. Kidnapped by River Rats. Jackson, Dave & Jackson, Neta. 144p. (Orig.). (gr. 3-7). 1991. pap. 4.99 (1-55661-220-6) Bethany Hse.
—The Queen's Smuggler. Jackson, Dave & Jackson, Neta. 144p. (Orig.). (gr. 3-7). 1991. pap. 4.99 (1-55661-221-4) Bethany Hse.
Jackson, Lori. Look up Look Down Look All Around Chaco Culture National Historical Park. Hallett, Bill & Hallett, Jane. 32p. (Orig.). (gr. 3-8). 1989. pap. 3.45 activity bk. (0-685-26277-4) Look & See.
—Look up Look down Look All Around East African Safari. Hallett, Bill & Hallett, Jane. 32p. (Orig.). (gr. 3-8). 1990. pap. 2.95 activity bk. (1-877827-01-0) Look & See.
Jackson, Nathan, jt. illus. see Osawa, Yasu.
Jackson, Paul. Fold Your Own Dinosaurs. Morris, Campbell. LC 92-32894. 48p. (Orig.). 1993. pap. 7.95 (0-399-51794-4, Perigee Bks) Putnam Pub Group.
—Paper Pandas & Jumping Frogs. Temko, Florence. Petersen, Richard, et al, photos by. LC 86-70960. 135p. (gr. 3-6). 1986. pap. 11.95 (0-8351-1770-7) China Bks.
Jackson, Russ. Mission Adventures in Many Lands. Driskill, J. Lawrence. LC 92-15689. (gr. 3-6). 1992. PLB 17.95 (0-932727-57-3); pap. 11.95 (0-932727-56-5) Hope Pub Hse.
Jackson, Sarah & Patterson, Mary Ann. A Child's History of Texas. Jackson, Sarah & Patterson, Mary Ann. (gr. 1-6). 1972. 5.95 (0-89015-056-7, Pub. by Panda Bks) Eakin-Sunbelt.
Jackson, Shelley. Do You Know Me. Farmer, Nancy. LC 92-34068. 112p. (gr. 3-5). 1993. 15.95 (0-531-05474-8); PLB 15.99 (0-531-08624-0) Orchard Bks Watts.
Jackson, Tim. AIDS: Just the Facts Jack. Jackson, Tim. (Orig.). (gr. 5 up). 1988. pap. 1.95 (0-942675-06-1, 6) Creative License.
—The Case of: The Great Graffiti. Jackson, Tim. 19p. (Orig.). (gr. 5-8). 1987. pap. 1.95 (0-942675-04-5) Creative License.
—Friends & Choices. Jackson, Tim. Jackson, Tim & Peterson, Jeannein. intro. by. 24p. (Orig.). (gr. 6-12). 1987. pap. 1.95 (0-942675-05-3) Creative License.
—Friends Are For, Being Different. Jackson, Tim. Jackson, Tim, intro. by. 18p. (gr. 5-9). 1985. pap. 1.95 (0-942675-01-0) Creative License.
—Just Like a Happy Family. Jackson, Tim. 17p. (gr. 4 up). 1985. pap. 1.95 (0-942675-00-2) Creative License.
—That's All They're Good For. Jackson, Tim. Jackson, Tim, intro. by. 20p. (gr. 5-9). 1986. pap. 1.95 (0-942675-02-9) Creative License.
—What Are Friends For? HIV Safe Coloring Book. Jackson, Tim. 32p. (Orig.). (gr. 3-6). 1990. pap. write for info. (0-942675-08-8, 0942675088) Creative License.
Jacob, Murv. How Rabbit Tricked Otter & Other Cherokee Trickster Stories. Ross, Gayle. LC 93-3637. 1994. 15.00 (0-06-021285-3, HarpT); PLB 14.89 (0-06-021286-1) HarpC.

Jacobi, Kathy. The Half-a-Moon Inn. Fleischman, Paul. LC 79-2010. 96p. (gr. 4-7). 1980. PLB 12.89 (0-06-021918-1) HarpC Child Bks.
—The Half-a-Moon Inn. Fleischman, Paul. LC 79-2010. 96p. (gr. 3-7). 1991. 96p. pap. 3.95 (0-06-440364-5, Trophy) HarpC Child Bks.
—Rose of Mother-of-Pearl. Olujic, Grozdana. Kessler, Jascha, tr. LC 83-18254. (SER & CRO.). 19p. (Orig.). (gr. 4 up). 1983. pap. 6.00 (0-915124-90-4, Pub. by Toothpaste) Coffee Hse.
—Tomorrow's Wizard. MacLachlan, Patricia. LC 81-47733. 96p. (gr. 3-6). 1982. 12.95 (0-06-024073-3); PLB 12.89 (0-06-024074-1) HarpC Child Bks.
Jacobs, Arnold. Hiawatha: Messenger of Peace. Fradin, Dennis B. LC 90-26312. 48p. (gr. 2-6). 1992. SBE 14. 95 (0-689-50519-1, M K McElderry) Macmillan Child Grp.
Jacobs, Edgar P. The Time Trap. Jacobs, Edgar P. Surbeck, Jean-Jacques, tr. from FRE. 49p. (Orig.). (gr. 12 up). 1989. pap. 8.95 (0-87416-066-9, Comcat Comics) Catalan Communs.
Jacobs, Elizabeth. Two More. Drew, David. LC 92-31957. 1993. 3.75 (0-383-03600-3) SRA Schl Grp.
Jacobs, Lou, Jr. A Place of Your Own. James, Elizabeth & Barkin, Carol. 96p. (gr. 9 up). 1981. (Dutton); pap. o.p. (0-525-37099-4) NAL-Dutton.
Jacobs, Phil. The Power Pop-up Book: Our Planet's Energy Resources: Production, Consumption, Conservation, & Innovation. Vita-Finzi, Claudio. Wilgress, Paul, contrib. by. 10p. (gr. 3 up). 1991. pap. 13.95 casebound pop-up (0-671-73535-7, S&S BFYR) S&S Trade.
Jacobs, Phil & Field, James. A Pop-Up Book of North American Cities. Pierce, Pat. 20p. (gr. 2-6). 1991. 12. 95 (0-8249-8517-6, Ideals Child) Hambleton-Hill.
Jacobs, Philip. The Weather Pop-Up Book. Wilson, Francis. Wilgrass, Paul, contrib. by. (gr. 5 up). 1987. pap. 15.00 (0-671-63699-5, S&S BFYR) S&S Trade.
Jacobs, Philip & Peterkin, Mike. The Pop-up Atlas of the World. Rowland-Entwistle, Theodore. 18p. (gr. 3 up). 1988. pap. 12.95 (0-671-65898-0, S&S BFYR) S&S Trade.
Jacobsen, Alice. Something Special Within. 2nd ed. Richter, Betts. 48p. (ps-5). 1982. pap. 6.95 (0-87516-488-9) DeVorss.
Jacobsen, Walter. The Good Samaritan. Benda, Andreas. 10p. (gr. k-2). 1993. puzzle bk. 6.99 (0-8028-5083-9) Eerdmans.
—The Good Shepherd. Benda, Andreas. 10p. (gr. k-2). 1993. puzzle bk. 6.99 (0-8028-5084-7) Eerdmans.
Jacobson, David. The Big, Red Blanket. Ziefert, Harriet. 24p. (ps-3). 1992. 3.95 (0-694-00393-X) HarpC Child Bks.
—Later, Rover. Ziefert, Harriet & Nicklaus, Carol. 32p. (ps-3). 1992. 8.95 (0-670-83863-2) Viking Child Bks.
—Three Wishes. Ziefert, Harriet. 32p. (ps-3). 1993. 9.00 (0-670-84569-8) Viking Child Bks.
—Three Wishes. Ziefert, Harriet. 32p. (ps-3). 1993. pap. 3.50 (0-14-054556-5) Puffin Bks.
Jacobson, Julie. The Non-Reader's Telephone Directory. Skowronski, Deborah. LC 82-61510. 36p. 1982. pap. text ed. 2.25 (0-9609618-0-1) Sunburst.
Jacobson, Lori, jt. illus. see Hohag, Linda.
Jacobson, Mary M. Phonics: A Tool for Better Reading & Spelling, Bk. II. Baggiani, J. M. & Tewell, V. M. (gr. 3-6). 1967. pap. 3.50 (0-934329-02-8); wkbk. 2.00 (0-934329-03-6) Baggiani-Tewell.
Jacobson, Mary M. & Davis, Mary I. Phonics: A Tool for Better Reading & Spelling, Bk. III. Baggiani, J. M. & Tewell, V. M. (gr. 5-12). 1984. pap. 5.75 (0-934329-04-4); wkbk. 4.00 (0-934329-05-2) Baggiani-Tewell.
Jacques, Benoit. Tomorrow's Earth: A Squeaky-Green Guide. Bellamy, David. LC 91-58652. 68p. (gr. 3 up). 1992. Repr. of 1991 ed. 9.98 (1-56138-124-1) Courage Bks.
Jacques, Faith. Charlie et le Grand Ascenseur de Verre. Dahl, Roald. (FRE.). 151p. (gr. 5-10). 1978. pap. 7.95 (2-07-033065-6) Schoenhof.
—The Faber Book of Greek Legends. Lines, Kathleen, ed. 268p. (gr. 4 up). 1986. pap. 11.95 (0-571-13920-5) Faber & Faber.
Jacques, Laura. Sweet Magnolia. Kroll, Virginia. LC 93-11966. 32p. (ps-4). 1994. 14.95 (0-88106-415-7); PLB 15.00 (0-88106-416-5); pap. 6.95 (0-88106-414-9) Charlesbridge Pub.
Jacquet, Jean-Pierre & Mathieu, Joe. Big Bird's Copycat Day: A Step 1 Book. Lerner, Sharon. LC 84-6869. 32p. (ps-2). 1984. lib. bdg. 7.99 (0-394-96912-X); pap. 3.50 (0-394-86912-5) Random Bks Yng Read.
Jael, jt. illus. see Ward, Lynd.
Jainschigg, Nicholas. The Wizard's Apprentice. Somtow, S. P. 144p. (gr. 7 up). 1993. SBE 14.95 (0-689-31576-7, Atheneum Child Bk) Macmillan Child Grp.
Jakoben, Kathy. Johnny Appleseed. Lindbergh, Reeve. (ps-4). 1990. 14.95 (0-316-52618-5, Joy St Bks) Little.
Jakubiszyn, Audrey. The Puppet Book: How to Make & Operate Puppets & Stage a Puppet-Play. Buchwald, Claire. LC 90-38080. 134p. (Orig.). 1990. pap. 13.95 (0-8238-0293-0) Plays.
Jalbert, Marc, jt. illus. see Grant, Larry.
Jambor, Louis, jt. illus. see Magagna, Anna M.
James, Ann. Dial-a-Croc. Dumbleton, Mike. LC 90-25385. 32p. (ps-2). 1991. 14.95 (0-531-05945-6); RLB 14.99 (0-531-08545-7) Orchard Bks Watts.
—Dog in, Cat Out. Rubinstein, Gillian. LC 92-39785. 1993. 13.45 (0-395-66596-5) Ticknor & Fields.

—Penny Pollard in Print. Klein, Robin. 64p. (gr. 4 up). 1988. bds. 10.95 (0-19-554638-5) OUP.
—Penny Pollard's Diary. Klein, Robin. 56p. (ps-6). 1987. pap. 7.00 (0-19-554649-0) OUP.
—Penny Pollard's Letters. Klein, Robin. 64p. (ps-6). 1987. 10.95 (0-19-554575-3) OUP.
—Penny Pollard's Passport. Klein, Robin. 74p. (gr. 6 up). 1990. bds. 10.95 (0-19-554868-X) OUP.
—Prince Lachlan. Hilton, Nette. LC 89-22846. 32p. (ps-1). 1990. 13.95 (0-531-05863-8); PLB 13.99 (0-531-08463-9) Orchard Bks Watts.
—Tangles. Broome, Errol. LC 93-30637. 1994. 13.00 (0-679-85713-3) Knopf Bks Yng Read.
—Wiggy & Boa. Feinberg, Anna. 112p. (gr. 3-7). 1990. 13.95 (0-395-53704-5) HM.
James, Betsy. The Fireplug Is First Base. Petersen, P. J. LC 92-18956. 64p. (gr. 2-5). 1992. pap. 3.99 (0-14-036165-0) Puffin Bks.
—Mary Ann. James, Betsy. LC 93-13364. 32p. (ps-3). 1994. 13.99 (0-525-45077-7) Dutton Child Bks.
James, Claire. First Science: Practice at Home Science Activity. Harker, Jillian. 24p. (gr. k-2). 1992. pap. 2.95 wkbk. (0-7214-3244-1) Ladybird Bks.
James, Derek. Who Stole the Wizard of Oz? Avi. LC 81-884. 128p. (gr. 3-6). 1990. Repr. of 1981 ed. 3.99 (0-394-84992-2) Random Bks Yng Read.
James, Elden & Baerg, Harry. Life, Man & Time. 2nd ed. Marsh, Frank L. LC 66-21121. (gr. 7 up). 1967. 8.95 (0-911080-15-5) Outdoor Pict.
James, J. Alison & Bhend, Kathi. Rabbit Spring. Michaels, Tilde. LC 87-18107. 85p. (gr. 2-6). 1989. 11.95 (0-15-200568-4, Gulliver Bks) HarBrace.
James, J. Alison, jt. illus. see Schmid, Eleonore.
James, John. Life in the Time of Pericles & the Ancient Greeks. Poulton, Michael. LC 92-5817. 63p. (gr. 6-7). 1992. PLB 24.26 (0-8114-3352-8) Raintree Steck-V.
—A Medieval Cathedral. MacDonald, Fiona. 48p. (gr. 5 up). 1991. 17.95 (0-87226-350-9) P Bedrick Bks.
—A Nineteenth Century Railway Station: Inside Story. MacDonald, Fiona. 48p. (gr. 5 up). 1990. 17.95 (0-87226-341-X) P Bedrick Bks.
—The Story of Boats. Hutchinson, Gillian. LC 91-39010. 32p. (gr. 1-4). 1993. PLB 11.89 (0-8167-2705-8); pap. text ed. 3.95 (0-8167-2706-6) Troll Assocs. Postponed.
James, John, jt. illus. see Bergin, Mark.
James, Lillie. Good Luck, Bad Luck. Ziefert, Harriet. 32p. (ps-3). 1992. 8.95 (0-670-84275-3) Viking Child Bks.
—Halloween Parade. Ziefert, Harriet. 32p. (ps-3). 1992. 9.00 (0-670-84568-X) Viking Child Bks.
—Halloween Parade. Ziefert, Harriet. 32p. (ps-3). 1992. pap. 3.50 (0-14-054555-7) Puffin Bks.
—What is Easter? 16p. (ps). 1994. 5.95 (0-694-00480-4, Festival) HarpC Child Bks.
—What Is Passover? Ziefert, Harriet. 16p. (ps). 1994. 5.95 (0-694-00482-0, Festival) HarpC Child Bks.

James, Linda & Corpening, Gene S. I Love to Hear the Cold Wind Howl. Corpening, Gene S. 40p. (Orig.). (gr. 1 up). 1993. pap. 7.95g (0-9636775-9-4) Alice Pub.
A children's fairy tale that captures the wonderment of childhood in both verse & unforgettable illustrations. Told through the eyes of a little boy, it is the story of Dirty Ann (a reputed witch) & Farmer Plucket. Snuggle down into bed & pull the covers 'round your head, as you read about the strange doings of Dirty Ann & her disagreement with Plucket in a bygone time. Sixteen four-color illustrations. Volume discounts available from publisher--Alice Publishing, P.O. Box 257, Granite Falls, NC 28630; 704-396-7094.
Publisher Provided Annotation.

James, Nancy D. The Strawberry Fox. Daves, Prentiss V. Quintahlen, Patrique, ed. LC 91-62065. 54p. (Orig.). 1992. pap. 3.95 (0-9615560-9-9) Scotjia Pub Co.
James, Nancy V. Musical Wisdom: Songs & Drawings for the Child in Us All. Robson, Tom. 88p. (Orig.). (gr. k-6). 1992. pap. 16.95 (0-9633332-0-8) Laughing Cat.
James, Raymond. Adventures of Tom Sawyer. Twain, Mark, pseud. Gise, Joanne, adapted by. LC 89-20559. 48p. (gr. 3-6). 1990. lib. bdg. 12.89 (0-8167-1859-8); pap. text ed. 3.95 (0-8167-1860-1) Troll Assocs.
James, Rhian N. A New Dress for Maya. Blackman, Malorie. LC 91-50337. 32p. (ps-3). 1993. PLB 17.27 (0-8368-0713-8); PLB 17.27 s.p. (0-685-61500-6) Gareth Stevens Inc.
James, Robin. Buttermilk. Cosgrove, Stephen. 32p. (gr. 5-9). 1986. pap. 2.95 (0-8431-1565-3) Price Stern.
—Buttermilk-Bear. Cosgrove, Stephen. 32p. (gr. 1-4). 1987. pap. 2.95 (0-8431-1908-X) Price Stern.
—Butterwings. James, Robin. 32p. (gr. 1-6). 1993. pap. 2.95 (0-8431-3494-1) Price Stern.
—Catundra. Cosgrove, Stephen. 32p. (gr. 1-4). 1978. pap. 2.95 (0-8431-0571-2) Price Stern.

—Crabby Gabby. Cosgrove, Stephen. LC 85-14351. 32p. (Orig.). (gr. 1-4). 1985. pap. 2.95 (*0-8431-1441-X*) Price Stern.
—Creole's Clever Collection of Puzzles. 48p. (gr. 2-6). 1983. Repr. wkbk. 2.95 (*0-8431-1403-7*) Price Stern.
—Crickle-Crack. Cosgrove, Stephen. 32p. (gr. 1-4). 1987. pap. 2.95 (*0-8431-1909-8*) Price Stern.
—Dragolin. Cosgrove, Stephen. LC 85-14400. (Orig.). (gr. k-5). 1978. pap. 2.95 (*0-8431-1165-8*) Price Stern.
—The Dream Tree. Cosgrove, Stephen. (gr. 1-6). 1974. pap. 2.95 (*0-8431-0553-4*) Price Stern.
—Fanny. Cosgrove, Stephen. 32p. (gr. 5-9). 1986. pap. 2.95 (*0-8431-1460-6*) Price Stern.
—Feather Fin. Cosgrove, Stephen. LC 84-15057. 32p. (Orig.). (gr. k-4). 1983. pap. 2.95 (*0-8431-0593-3*) Price Stern.
—Flutterby Fly. Cosgrove, Stephen. LC 85-14353. (Orig.). (gr. k-4). 1984. pap. 2.95 (*0-8431-1162-3*) Price Stern.
—Gigglesnitcher. Cosgrove, Stephen E. 48p. (gr. k-9). 1991. 12.95 (*1-55868-034-9*) Gr Arts Ctr Pub.
—Glitterby Baby. Cosgrove, Stephen. LC 85-14354. 32p. (Orig.). (gr. 1-4). 1978. pap. 2.95 (*0-8431-1166-6*) Price Stern.
—Gnome from Nome. Cosgrove, Stephen. 32p. (gr. 1-6). 1974. pap. 2.95 (*0-8431-0555-0*) Price Stern.
—Grampa-Lop. Cosgrove, Stephen. LC 84-15078. 32p. (Orig.). (gr. k-4). 1981. pap. 2.95 (*0-8431-0586-0*) Price Stern.
—Jingle Bear. Cosgrove, Stephen. 32p. (Orig.). (gr. 1-4). 1985. pap. 2.95 (*0-8431-1440-1*) Price Stern.
—Kartusch. Cosgrove, Stephen. (gr. k-4). 1978. pap. 2.95 (*0-8431-0568-2*) Price Stern.
—Kyomi. Cosgrove, Stephen. (Orig.). (gr. k-4). 1984. pap. 2.95 (*0-8431-1164-X*) Price Stern.
—Leo the Lop: Tail Three. Cosgrove, Stephen. 32p. (gr. k-4). 1978. pap. 2.95 (*0-8431-0577-1*) Price Stern.
—Leo the Lop: Tail Two. Cosgrove, Stephen. 32p. (Orig.). (gr. k-6). 1978. pap. 2.95 (*0-8431-0572-0*) Price Stern.
—Little Mouse. Cosgrove, Stephen. 32p. (gr. 1-4). 1978. pap. 2.95 (*0-8431-0569-0*) Price Stern.
—Maui-Maui. Cosgrove, Stephen. 32p. (gr. k-6). 1979. pap. 2.95 (*0-8431-0561-5*) Price Stern.
—Maui Maui's Mindbogglers. 48p. (gr. 2-6). 1983. Repr. wkbk. 2.95 (*0-8431-1402-9*) Price Stern.
—Maynard's Mermaid. James, Robin. 32p. (gr. 1-6). 1993. pap. 2.95 (*0-8431-3495-X*) Price Stern.
—Ming Ling. Cosgrove, Stephen. 32p. (Orig.). (gr. k-4). 1978. pap. 2.95 (*0-8431-0592-5*) Price Stern.
—Minikin. Cosgrove, Stephen. (Orig.). (gr. k-4). 1984. pap. 2.95 (*0-8431-1163-1*) Price Stern.
—Morgan Morning. Cosgrove, Stephen. 32p. (gr. 1-6). 1982. pap. 2.95 (*0-8431-0591-7*) Price Stern.
—Muffin Muncher. Cosgrove, Stephen. 32p. (gr. 1-6). 1975. pap. 2.95 (*0-8431-0561-5*) Price Stern.
—Mumkin. Cosgrove, Stephen. 32p. (gr. 5-9). 1986. pap. 2.95 (*0-8431-1431-2*) Price Stern.
—Napolean's Rainbow. James, Robin. 32p. (Orig.). (gr. 4-6). 1993. pap. 2.95 (*0-8431-3610-3*) Price Stern.
—Nitter Pitter. Cosgrove, Stephen. 32p. (gr. 1-4). 1978. pap. 2.95 (*0-8431-0570-4*) Price Stern.
—Persnickety. Cosgrove, Stephen. (gr. k-4). 1988. pap. 2.95 (*0-8431-2303-6*) Price Stern.
—Pish-Posh. Cosgrove, Stephen. 32p. (gr. 5-9). 1986. pap. 2.95 (*0-8431-1449-5*) Price Stern.
—Raz-Ma-Taz. Cosgrove, Stephen. 32p. (gr. 1-6). 1982. pap. 2.95 (*0-8431-0588-7*) Price Stern.
—Raz Ma Taz' Dazzling Dot-to-Dot. (gr. 2-6). 1983. wkbk. 2.95 (*0-8431-1404-5*) Price Stern.
—Rhubarb. Cosgrove, Stephen. 32p. (gr. k-4). 1988. pap. 2.95 (*0-8431-2300-1*) Price Stern.
—Sadie. James, Robin. 32p. (gr. 4-6). 1994. pap. 2.95 (*0-8431-3611-1*) Price Stern.
—Sassafras. Cosgrove, Stephen. (gr. k-4). 1988. pap. 2.95 (*0-8431-2302-8*) Price Stern.
—Sniffles. Cosgrove, Stephen. 32p. (gr. k-4). 1988. pap. 2.95 (*0-8431-2301-X*) Price Stern.
—Squeakers. Cosgrove, Stephen. 32p. (Orig.). (gr. 1-4). 1985. pap. 2.95 (*0-8431-1442-8*) Price Stern.
—Trapper. Cosgrove, Stephen. 32p. (gr. k-4). 1982. pap. 2.95 (*0-8431-0587-9*) Price Stern.

James, Simon. Dear Mr. Blueberry. James, Simon. LC 90-50815. 32p. (ps-2). 1991. SBE 13.95 (*0-689-50529-9*, M K McElderry) Macmillan Child Grp.
—Sally & the Limpet. James, Simon. LC 90-40088. 32p. (ps-3). 1991. SBE 13.95 (*0-689-50528-0*, M K McElderry) Macmillan Child Grp.
—The Wild Woods. James, Simon. LC 92-54582. 32p. (ps up). 1993. 13.95 (*1-56402-219-6*) Candlewick Pr.

James, Will. Smoky the Cow Horse. 2nd ed. James, Will. LC 92-28753. 324p. (gr. 3-7). 1993. pap. 3.95 (*0-689-71682-6*, Aladdin) Macmillan Child Grp.

Jamieson, Lindsey, jt. illus. see Meade, Javier.

Jamieson, Myles. Felt Fun, Flannel Board Stories. Jamieson, Rita. (ps-8). 1990. pap. text ed. 5.00 (*0-9622329-1-2*) R Jamieson.

Jammer, Cornelius C., Jr. Honey Brown in Search of Her Identity, Vol. 1. Campbell, Tammie L. Moon, Felicia, intro. by. 24p. (Orig.). (gr. k-5). 1990. pap. 4.95 (*0-9623947-0-X*) T L Campbell.

Jangl, Alda M. Ancient Legends of the Twelve Birthflowers. Jangl, Alda M. & Jangl, James F. 40p. (gr. 9-12). 1987. pap. 3.95 (*0-942647-01-7*) Prisma Pr.

Jangl, Alda M. & Jangl, James F. Birthstone Coloring Book: Birthstone Legends & Other Gem Folklore. Jangl, James F. 32p. (gr. k up). 1987. pap. 3.50 (*0-942647-03-3*) Prisma Pr.

Jangl, James F., jt. illus. see Jangl, Alda M.

Jann, Gayle. A Day in the Life of a Ballet Dancer. Martin, John H. LC 84-2424. 32p. (gr. 4-8). 1985. PLB 11.79 (*0-8167-0089-3*); pap. text ed. 2.95 (*0-8167-0090-7*) Troll Assocs.
—A Day in the Life of a Chef. Bourne, Miriam A. LC 87-13762. 32p. (gr. 4-8). 1988. PLB 11.79 (*0-8167-1115-1*); pap. text ed. 2.95 (*0-8167-1116-X*) Troll Assocs.
—A Day in the Life of a Construction Foreman. Jann, Gayle. LC 87-13761. 32p. (gr. 4-8). 1988. PLB 11.79 (*0-8167-1121-6*); pap. text ed. 2.95 (*0-8167-1122-4*) Troll Assocs.
—A Day in the Life of a Cross-Country Trucker. Bourne, Miriam A. LC 87-13582. 32p. (gr. 4-8). 1988. PLB 11.79 (*0-8167-1117-8*); pap. text ed. 2.95 (*0-8167-1118-6*) Troll Assocs.
—A Day in the Life of a Disc Jockey. Wong, Michael A. LC 87-10943. 32p. (gr. 4-8). 1988. PLB 11.79 (*0-8167-1125-9*); pap. text ed. 2.95 (*0-8167-1126-7*) Troll Assocs.
—A Day in the Life of a Fashion Designer. Hodgman, Ann. LC 87-13394. 32p. (gr. 4-8). 1988. PLB 11.79 (*0-8167-1119-4*); pap. text ed. 2.95 (*0-8167-1120-8*) Troll Assocs.
—A Day in the Life of a High-Iron Worker. Martin, John H. LC 84-2449. 32p. (gr. 4-8). 1985. PLB 11.79 (*0-8167-0107-5*); pap. text ed. 2.95 (*0-8167-0108-3*) Troll Assocs.
—A Day in the Life of a Horse Trainer. Freeman, Charlotte M. LC 87-10681. 32p. (gr. 4-8). 1988. PLB 11.79 (*0-8167-1111-9*); pap. text ed. 2.95 (*0-8167-1112-7*) Troll Assocs.
—A Day in the Life of a Photographer. Jann, Gayle. LC 87-13751. 32p. (gr. 4-8). 1988. PLB 11.79 (*0-8167-1123-2*); pap. text ed. 2.95 (*0-8167-1124-0*) Troll Assocs.
—A Day in the Life of a Police Cadet. Martin, John H. LC 84-2578. 32p. (gr. 4-8). 1985. PLB 11.79 (*0-8167-0103-2*); pap. text ed. 2.95 (*0-8167-0104-0*) Troll Assocs.
—A Day in the Life of a Theater Set Designer. Hodgman, Ann. LC 87-10951. 32p. (gr. 4-8). 1988. PLB 11.79 (*0-8167-1127-5*); pap. text ed. 2.95 (*0-8167-1128-3*) Troll Assocs.

Janosch. Animal Antics. Bell, Anthea. 128p. (gr. k-2). 1987. 17.95 (*0-86264-033-4*, Pub. by Anderson Pr UK) Trafalgar.
—The Cricket & the Mole. Janosch. Bell, Anthea, tr. 70p. (ps-1). 1987. 8.95 (*0-86264-043-1*, Pub. by Anderson Pr UK) Trafalgar.
—I'll Make You Well, Tiger, Said the Bear. Janosch. LC 86-11274. 48p. (ps up). 1987. 9.95 (*0-915361-42-6*) Modan-Adama Bks.

Janovitz, Marilyn. America's First Elephant. McClung, Robert M. LC 89-13764. 40p. (gr. k up). 1991. 14.95 (*0-688-08358-7*); PLB 14.88 (*0-688-08359-5*) Morrow Jr Bks.
—Baa Baa Black Sheep. Janovitz, Marilyn, adapted by. LC 91-71384. 32p. (ps-1). 1991. 6.95 (*1-56282-085-0*); PLB 6.89 (*1-56282-086-9*) Hyprn Child.
—Hey Diddle Diddle. Janovitz, Marilyn, adapted by. LC 91-26483. 32p. (ps-k). 1992. 6.95 (*1-56282-168-7*); PLB 6.89 (*1-56282-169-5*) Hyprn Child.
—Hickory Dickory Dock. Janovitz, Marilyn, adapted by. LC 91-71378. 32p. (ps-k). 1991. 6.95 (*1-56282-083-4*); PLB 6.89 (*1-56282-084-2*) Hyprn Child.
—Just Like Me. Schlein, Miriam. LC 91-40019. 32p. (ps-2). 1993. 12.95 (*1-56282-233-0*); PLB 12.89 (*1-56282-234-9*) Hyprn Child.
—Pat-a-Cake. Janovitz, Marilyn, adapted by. & adapted by. LC 91-26950. 32p. (ps-k). 1992. 6.95 (*1-56282-170-9*); PLB 6.89 (*1-56282-171-7*) Hyprn Child.

Janssen, Beverly B. Green Lake Tales & Trails. Janssen, Lawrence H. LC 84-71073. 96p. (gr. ps-6). 1984. pap. 4.95 (*0-917575-00-8*) Cedars WI.

Janssen, Lawrence H. Earth Care a Mandate: Nature Study Guide Keyed to the Black Hills. Janssen, Lawrence H. LC 85-73644. 80p. (Orig.). (gr. 7-12). 1985. pap. 3.95 (*0-917575-03-2*) Cedars WI.
—Horsethief Lake Old Baldy Trail Guides. Janssen, Lawrence H. (Orig.). (gr. 7-12). 1986. pap. 1.00 (*0-917575-04-0*) Cedars WI.

Jantzen, Franz. A Day in the Life of an FBI Agent-in-Training. Smith, Carter. LC 90-11150. 32p. (gr. 4-8). 1991. PLB 11.79 (*0-8167-2210-2*); pap. text ed. 2.95 (*0-8167-2211-0*) Troll Assocs.

Janums, Aija. My Family History. Burgeson, Nancy. LC 92-3086. 32p. (gr. 3-6). 1992. pap. text ed. 1.95 (*0-8167-2794-5*) Troll Assocs.

Janus, Donna. Remember the Light. Fisher, Mary P. 32p. (Orig.). (gr. k-4). 1986. pap. 4.50 (*0-9615149-7-3*) Fenton Valley Pr.

Jaquays, Paul, jt. illus. see Martin, David.

Jaquays, Paul, jt. illus. see Roberts, Tony.

Jaques, Faith. The Box of Delights: Or, When the Wolves Were Running. Masefield, John. Crampton, Patricia, abridged by. 176p. (gr. k up). 1984. pap. 2.95 (*0-440-40853-9*, YB) Dell.
—Old Peter's Russian Tales. Ransome, Arthur. 256p. (gr. 5-9). 1975. pap. 3.50 (*0-14-030696-X*) Viking Child Bks.

—The Orchard Book of Nursery Rhymes. Sutherland, Zena, selected by. LC 89-71002. 96p. 1990. 21.95 (*0-531-05903-0*) Orchard Bks Watts.

Jardine, Thomas. The Butterfly & the Stone. Fisher, Lucretia. LC 80-29260. 48p. (Orig.). (ps up). 1981. pap. 3.95 (*0-916144-69-0*) Stemmer Hse.
—Two Monsters: A Fable. Fisher, Lucretia. LC 76-21684. 48p. (ps up). 1976. pap. 3.95 (*0-916144-08-9*) Stemmer Hse.

Jarka, Jeff. Cat Man. Rutman, Shereen. 16p. (ps). 1993. wkbk. 2.25 (*1-56293-327-2*) McClanahan Bk.
—Jokes & Riddles. Coco, Eugene. 24p. (ps-2). 1993. pap. text ed. 0.99 (*1-56293-290-X*) McClanahan Bk.
—The Very Busy Baker. 12p. (ps-k). 1993. bds. 2.50 (*1-56293-308-6*) McClanahan Bk.
—The Very Busy Farmer. 12p. (ps-k). 1993. bds. 2.50 (*1-56293-305-1*) McClanahan Bk.
—The Very Busy Toymaker. 12p. (ps-k). 1993. bds. 2.50 (*1-56293-306-X*) McClanahan Bk.
—The Very Busy Zookeeper. 12p. (ps-k). 1993. bds. 2.50 (*1-56293-307-8*) McClanahan Bk.

Jarlov, Christian. Fanfou dans les Bayous: The Adventures of a Bilingual Elephant in Louisiana. Perales, Andre P. LC 82-15148. 40p. (gr. 1-7). 1982. pap. 5.95 (*0-88289-378-5*); cassette 11.95 (*0-88289-410-2*) Pelican.

Jarrett, Judy. Sunday Morning. Ramshaw, Gail. 46p. (gr. k-3). 1993. 15.95 (*1-56854-005-1*, SUN/AM) Liturgy Tr Pubns.

Jarrett, Lauren. A Child's Look at the Twenty-Third Psalm. Keller, W. Phillip. LC 84-13718. 96p. (gr. 3 up). 1985. pap. 7.95 (*0-385-15457-7*, Galilee) Doubleday.

Jarvis, David. Suzanne's African Adventure: A Visit to Cucu's Land. Muchene, Barbara S. & Muchene, Munene. Wagner, Shirley L., ed. LC 92-75821. 90p. (Orig.). (gr. 3-6). 1993. pap. 9.95 (*1-878398-18-0*) Blue Note Pubns.

Jaspers, Kate. One Special Star. McFadzean, Anita. LC 90-21485. 32p. (ps-k). 1991. pap. 11.95 jacketed (*0-671-74023-7*, S&S BFYR); pap. 3.95 (*0-671-74024-5*, Little Simon) S&S Trade.

Jaspersohn, William. Cookies. Jaspersohn, William. LC 91-45023. 48p. (gr. 3-6). 1993. RSBE 14.95 (*0-02-747822-X*, Macmillan Child Bk) Macmillan Child Grp.

Javan, Yousef J. The Tale of the Little Black Fish: Mahi Siah Kuchulu. Behrangi, Samad. Amuzegar, Hooshang, tr. LC 91-73480. (PER & ENG.). 72p. (Orig.). 1992. pap. 6.95 (*0-936347-20-1*) Iran Bks.

Jean, Priscilla. Pattie Round & Wally Square. Jean, Priscilla. (gr. k-3). 1965. 8.95 (*0-8392-3048-6*) Astor-Honor.

Jeanie And Joanie And Judy, photos by. Sing Through the Day: Ninety Songs for Younger Children. 3rd ed. Swinger, Marlys. Society of Brothers Staff, ed. LC 68-9673. 144p. (gr. 5 up). 1968. 17.00 (*0-87486-005-9*); cassette 7.00 (*0-87486-047-4*) Plough.

Jean-Jacques, Tony. Pour Mieux t'Aimer. Jean-Jacques, Tony. (FRE & CRP.). 128p. (gr. 6-12). 1993. text ed. 10.00x (*0-938534-01-7*) Soup Nuts Pr.

Jeffares, Jeanne. An Around-the-World Alphabet. Jeffares, Jeanne. LC 89-32135. 36p. 1989. 14.95 (*0-87226-324-X*) P Bedrick Bks.

Jeffers, Susan. Benjamin's Barn. Lindbergh, Reeve. 32p. (ps-3). 1990. 13.95 (*0-8037-0613-8*); PLB 13.89 (*0-8037-0614-6*) Dial Bks Young.
—Black Beauty. Sewell, Anna. Vance, Eleanor G., ed. LC 84-27575. 72p. (ps-5). 1986. 15.00 (*0-394-86575-8*); lib. bdg. 12.99 (*0-394-96575-2*) Random Bks Yng Read.
—Black Beauty. Sewell, Anna. McKinley, Robin, adapted by. Kingsley, Ben, contrib. by. 72p. (ps-5). 1987. incl. cass. 17.95 (*0-394-89228-3*) Random Bks Yng Read.
—Brother Eagle, Sister Sky: A Message from Chief Seattle. LC 90-27713. 32p. 1991. 16.00 (*0-8037-0969-2*); PLB 14.89 (*0-8037-0963-3*) Dial Bks Young.
—Cinderella. Perrault, Charles. Ehrlich, Amy, retold by. LC 85-1685. 32p. (ps-3). 1985. 14.00 (*0-8037-0205-1*); PLB 12.89 (*0-8037-0206-X*) Dial Bks Young.
—Close Your Eyes. Marzollo, Jean. LC 76-42935. (ps-2). 1978. PLB 12.89 (*0-8037-1610-9*) Dial Bks Young.
—Close Your Eyes. Marzollo, Jean. (ps-k). 1981. 4.95 (*0-8037-1617-6*) Dial Bks Young.
—Hansel & Gretel. Grimm, Jacob & Grimm, Wilhelm K. LC 80-15079. 32p. (gr. k up). 1980. 16.00 (*0-8037-3492-1*); PLB 14.89 (*0-8037-3491-3*) Dial Bks Young.
—Hansel & Gretel. Grimm, Jacob & Grimm, Wilhelm K. LC 80-15079. 32p. (gr. k up). 1986. pap. 4.95 (*0-8037-0318-X*) Dial Bks Young.
—Hiawatha. Longfellow, Henry Wadsworth. 32p. (gr. k up). 1983. 15.00 (*0-8037-0013-X*); PLB 14.89 (*0-8037-0014-8*) Dial Bks Young.
—If Wishes Were Horses: Mother Goose Rhymes. Jeffers, Susan. LC 79-9986. 32p. (ps-3). 1979. 13.95 (*0-525-32531-X*, DCB) Dutton Child Bks.
—The Midnight Farm. Lindbergh, Reeve. LC 86-1722. 32p. (ps-2). 1987. 14.95 (*0-8037-0331-7*); PLB 14.89 (*0-8037-0333-3*) Dial Bks Young.
—Silent Night. Mohr, Joseph. LC 84-8113. 32p. (ps up). 1984. 14.95 (*0-525-44144-1*, DCB); pap. 4.95 (*0-8037-4443-9*, DCB) Dutton Child Bks.
—The Snow Queen. Andersen, Hans Christian. LC 82-70199. 40p. (gr. k up). 1982. 15.95 (*0-8037-8011-7*); PLB 12.89 (*0-8037-8029-X*); pap. 4.95 (*0-8037-0692-8*) Dial Bks Young.

—Stopping by Woods on a Snowy Evening. Frost, Robert. LC 78-8134. (ps up). 1978. 13.00 (*0-525-40115-6*, 01063-320, DCB) Dutton Child Bks.

—The Three Jovial Huntsmen. Jeffers, Susan. LC 88-32708. 32p. (ps-2). 1989. pap. 3.95 (*0-689-71309-6*, Aladdin) Macmillan Child Grp.

—Thumbelina. Andersen, Hans Christian. LC 79-50146. (ps-3). 1979. PLB 14.89 (*0-8037-8814-2*) Dial Bks Young.

—Thumbelina. Andersen, Hans Christian. LC 79-50146. 32p. (ps-3). 1985. pap. 5.95 (*0-8037-0232-9*) Dial Bks Young.

—Waiting for the Evening Star. Wells, Rosemary. LC 92-30492. 40p. (gr. k-3). 1993. 15.00 (*0-8037-1398-3*); PLB 14.89 (*0-8037-1399-1*) Dial Bks Young.

—Wild Robin. Jeffers, Susan. LC 76-21343. 40p. (ps-3). 1986. pap. 4.95 (*0-525-44244-8*, DCB) Dutton Child Bks.

—The Wild Swans. Andersen, Hans Christian. Ehrlich, Amy, retold by. LC 81-65843. 40p. (gr. k up). 1976. 15.95 (*0-8037-9381-2*) Dial Bks Young.

—Wild Swans. Andersen, Hans Christian. LC 81-65843. 40p. (gr. k up). 1987. pap. 5.95 (*0-8037-0451-8*) Dial Bks Young.

—Wynken, Blynken & Nod. Field, Eugene. LC 82-2434. 32p. (ps-1). 1982. 13.50 (*0-525-44022-4*, DCB) Dutton Child Bks.

Jefferson, Lisa E., jt. illus. see Sansome, Constance J.

Jefferson, Sharon & Fields, Theodore. Wee Folks Moving Up: A Phonetic Approach to Beginning Reading. Hill, Charlotte M. Shortridge, Cleona, intro. by. LC 91-70303. (Orig.). (gr. k-3). 1991. pap. text ed. 7.95 (*0-9620182-5-2*) Charill Pubs.

Jefferson, Sharon, jt. illus. see Fields, Theodore.

Jeffery, Megan E. Journey to a Magic Castle. Kaufman, Gershen. LC 91-78278. 30p. (gr. 5-8). 1993. pap. write for info. incl. worksheets (*0-916634-14-0*) Double M Pr.

—Old Lop-Ear Wolf. Holland, Royce Q. Gilliland, Hap, ed. (gr. 4-10). 1991. pap. 6.95 (*0-89992-129-9*) Coun India Ed.

Jelinek, Lucy. Everyone Knows Gato Pinto: More Tales from Spanish New Mexico. Hayes, Joe. Mowrey, Joe, ed. 80p. (Orig.). (gr. 2-12). 1993. pap. 9.95 (*0-933553-09-9*) Mariposa Print Pub.

—Mariposa, Mariposa. Hayes, Joe. (SPA & ENG.). 32p. (Orig.). (gr. k-5). 1988. pap. 3.95 (*0-939729-08-3*); Bk. & cass. pkg. 7.95 (*0-939729-09-1*) Trails West Pub.

—Monday, Tuesday, Wednesday, Oh! Lunes, Martes, Miercoles, O! Hayes, Joe. 32p. (Orig.). (gr. 2-5). 1987. pap. 3.95 (*0-939729-04-0*); bk. & cassette 7.95, (*0-939729-05-9*) Trails West Pub.

—No Way, Jose! De Ninguna Manera, Jose! Hayes, Joe. 32p. (ps-3). 1986. pap. 3.95 (*0-939729-00-8*); cassette & bk. pkg. 7.95 (*0-939729-01-6*) Trails West Pub.

—The Terrible Tragadabas: El Terrible Tragadabas. Hayes, Joe. 32p. (Orig.). (gr.-4). 1987. pap. 3.95 (*0-939729-02-4*); bk. & cassette 7.95, (*0-939729-03-2*) Trails West Pub.

—The Wise Little Burro. Hayes, Joe. 48p. (Orig.). (gr. k-6). 1991. pap. 5.95 (*0-939729-20-2*) Trails West Pub.

Jelinek, Otakar. Listen, Kids... Czech Fairy Tales. Erben, Karel J. Ciuffreda, Lillian, ed. Kalnoky, Julius, tr. LC 87-83652. 65p. (gr. 3-8). 1988. 13.95 (*0-9619982-0-2*) Kalnoky Pr.

Jenkin-Pearce, Susie. Nesta, the Little Witch. McAllister, Angela. 32p. (ps-3). 1993. pap. 4.99 (*0-14-054266-3*, Puffin) Puffin Bks.

—One Breeze-Scented, Sun-Sparkling Morning. McAllister, Angela. 32p. (ps-1). 1993. 17.95 (*0-09-176363-0*, Pub. by Hutchinson UK) Trafalgar.

—Wriggly Pig. Blake, Jon. LC 91-24171. 32p. (ps-3). 1992. 14.00 (*0-688-11295-1*, Tambourine Bks); PLB 13.93 (*0-688-11296-X*, Tambourine Bks) Morrow.

Jenkins, Debra R. I Wanted to Know All about God. Kroll, Virginia L. LC 93-37382. 1993. write for info. (*0-8028-5078-2*) Eerdmans.

Jenkins, Jean. The Inside-Out Stomach: An Introduction to Animals without Backbones. Loewer, Peter. LC 89-6499. 64p. (gr. 2 up). 1990. SBE 13.95 (*0-689-31432-9*, Atheneum Child Bk) Macmillan Child Grp.

—Pond Water Zoo: An Introduction to Microscopic Life. Loewer, Peter. LC 93-18468. (gr. 1-8). 1995. text ed. 13.95 (*0-689-31736-0*, Atheneum) Macmillan.

—Today's Special: Z. A. P. & Zoe. Lord, Athena V. LC 84-9661. 160p. (gr. 4-7). 1984. SBE 13.95 (*0-02-761440-9*, Macmillan Child Bk) Macmillan Child Grp.

Jenkins, Leonard. Mayfield Crossing. Nelson, Vaunda M. LC 92-10564. 96p. (gr. 3-7). 1993. 14.95 (*0-399-22331-2*, Putnam) Putnam Pub Group.

Jenkins, Maurice M. Here Comes Niya. rev. ed. Davenport-Powell, Maurice. LC 87-410800. 22p. (Orig.). (ps-3). 1988. incl. cassette 12.95 (*0-945203-00-4*) Hi-Hopes Pub.

Jenkins, Steve. Cock-a-Doodle Doo! What Does It Sound Like to You? Robinson, Marc. LC 92-30961. 32p. 1993. 12.95 (*1-55670-267-1*) Stewart Tabori & Chang.

—My Dad. Horowitz, Janet & Faggella, Kathy. 48p. 1991. 9.95 (*1-55670-174-8*) Stewart Tabori & Chang.

—My Mom. Horowitz, Janet & Faggella, Kathy. 48p. 1991. 9.95 (*1-55670-173-X*) Stewart Tabori & Chang.

—My Pet: A Photolog Book. Horowitz, Janet & Faggella, kathy. 48p. 1992. bds. 9.95 (*1-55670-268-X*) Stewart Tabori & Chang.

—My School. Horowitz, Janet & Faggella, Kathy. 48p. 1991. 9.95 (*1-55670-176-4*) Stewart Tabori & Chang.

—My Town. Horowitz, Janet & Faggella, Kathy. 48p. 1991. 9.95 (*1-55670-175-6*) Stewart Tabori & Chang.

Jenkins, Todd. Daniel: A Melodrama. Jenkins, Lee. Greeno, Ron, frwd. by. 32p. (Orig.). (ps-3). 1993. pap. 6.95 (*1-883952-02-6*) Hse of Steno.

Jenness, Aylette. In Two Worlds: A Yup'ik Eskimo Family. Jenness, Aylette & Rivers, Alice. (gr. 6 up). 1989. 13.45 (*0-395-42797-5*) HM.

Jenney, David. Sawtooth Mountain Fun. Ferguson, Jane & Ferguson, Gary. 24p. (ps-6). 1982. pap. 1.98 (*0-9624846-0-1*) J & G Ferguson.

Jennings, Ann, jt. illus. see Lord, Anne.

Jennings, Elkay, jt. illus. see Ingram, Fred.

Jennis, Paul. The Case of the Close Encounter. Hope, Laura L. 96p. (gr. 2-3). 1988. pap. 2.95 (*0-671-62656-6*, Minstrel Bks) PB.

—Mystery on the Mississippi. Hope, Laura L. 96p. (Orig.). (gr. 2-4). 1988. pap. 2.95 (*0-671-62657-4*, Minstrel Bks) PB.

—The Phantom of the Opera. Leroux, Gaston. McMullan, Kate, adapted by. LC 88-34079. 96p. (Orig.). (gr. 3-7). 1993. lib. bdg. 5.99 (*0-394-93847-X*); pap. 2.99 (*0-394-83847-5*) Random Bks Yng Read.

Jensen, Debbie, jt. illus. see Bock, William S.

Jensen, Robert. Canten Navidad. MacArthur, Barbara. (ENG & SPA). 15p. (Orig.). (ps-12). 1993. pap. 12.95 incl. cass. (*1-881120-09-0*) Frog Pr WI.

—Chantez Noel. MacArthur, Barbara. (ENG & FRE.). 14p. (ps-12). 1993. pap. 12.95 incl. cass. (*1-881120-10-4*) Frog Pr WI.

—Sing, Dance, Laugh & Eat Cheeseburgers. MacArthur, Barbara. 35p. (ps-9). 1992. pap. text ed. 17.95 (*1-881120-06-6*) Frog Pr WI.

—Sing, Dance, Laugh & Eat Quiche. rev. ed. MacArthur, Barbara. (FRE.). 35p. (ps-9). 1990. pap. text ed. 17.95 (*1-881120-00-7*) Frog Pr WI.

—Sing, Dance, Laugh & Eat Quiche 2. MacArthur, Barbara. (Orig.). 35p. (ps-9). 1989. pap. text ed. 17.95 incl. cass. (*1-881120-01-5*) Frog Pr WI.

—Sing, Dance, Laugh, & Eat Quiche 3. MacArthur, Barbara. (FRE.). 35p. (Orig.). (ps-12). 1992. pap. 17.95 (*1-881120-07-4*) Frog Pr WI.

—Sing, Dance, Laugh & Eat Tacos. MacArthur, Barbara. (SPA.). 35p. (Orig.). (ps-9). 1990. pap. text ed. 17.95 incl. cass. (*1-881120-04-X*) Frog Pr WI.

—Sing, Dance, Laugh & Eat Tacos 2. MacArthur, Barbara. (SPA.). 36p. (Orig.). (ps-9). 1991. pap. text ed. 17.95 incl. cass. (*1-881120-05-8*) Frog Pr WI.

—Sing, Dance, Laugh & Learn German. MacArthur, Barbara. (ENG & GER.). 18p. (Orig.). (ps-8). 1993. pap. 12.95 incl. cass. (*1-881120-11-2*) Frog Pr WI.

—Sing, Dance, Laugh & Learn Spanish. MacArthur, Barbara. 18p. (Orig.). (ps-4). 1993. pap. 12.95 (*1-881120-08-2*) Frog Pr WI.

—Singen Weihnachten. MacArthur, Barbara. (GER.). 14p. (ps-12). 1993. pap. 12.95 (*1-881120-12-0*) Frog Pr WI.

Jensen, Shirlee, jt. illus. see Bejna, Barbara.

Jeram, Anita. All Pigs Are Beautiful. King-Smith, Dick. LC 92-53136. 32p. (ps-3). 1993. 14.95 (*1-56402-148-3*) Candlewick Pr.

—My Hen is Dancing: Read & Wonder Bks. Wallace, Karen. LC 93-930. (ps-3). 1994. 14.95 (*1-56402-303-6*) Candlewick Pr.

Jermy, Paul, jt. illus. see McBride, Angus.

Jernigan, E. Wesley. Agave Blooms Just Once. Jernigan, Gisela. LC 89-35428. 32p. (Orig.). (ps-1). 1989. pap. 8.95 (*0-943173-44-2*) Harbinger AZ.

—One Green Mesquite Tree. 2nd ed. Jernigan, Gisela. LC 88-2294. 24p. (Orig.). (ps-1). 1989. 12.95 (*0-943173-35-3*); pap. 8.95 (*0-943173-39-6*) Harbinger AZ.

—Sonoran Seasons: A Year in the Desert. Jernigan, Gisela. 32p. (Orig.). (ps-2). 1994. pap. 8.95 (*0-943173-91-4*) Harbinger AZ.

Jerome, Debra P. A Tail of a Different Color. Anderson, Myra. 32p. (gr. k-4). 1992. 13.95 (*0-9625620-3-3*) DOT Garnet.

Jerome, Karen A. The Shiniest Rock of All. Patterson, Nancy R. 80p. (gr. 3 up). 1991. 11.95 (*0-374-36805-8*) FS&G.

—The Valentine's Day Mystery. Markham, Marion M. LC 92-8391. 48p. (gr. 2-5). 1992. 13.45 (*0-395-61589-5*) HM.

Jeschke, Susan. Busybody Nora. Hurwitz, Johanna. 64p. (gr. 1-5). 1982. pap. 1.50 (*0-440-41019-3*, YB) Dell.

—Into the Great Forest: A Story for Children Away from Parents for the First Time. Marcus, Irene W. & Marcus, Paul. LC 92-56871. 1993. PLB 17.26 (*0-8368-0932-7*) Gareth Stevens Inc.

—New Neighbors for Nora. Hurwitz, Johanna. LC 78-12631. 80p. (gr. k-3). 1979. 11.95 (*0-688-22173-4*) Morrow Jr Bks.

—Nora & Mrs. Mind-Your-Own-Business. Hurwitz, Johanna. LC 76-54283. 64p. (gr. k-3). 1982. 11.95 (*0-688-22097-5*) Morrow Jr Bks.

—Perfect the Pig. Jeschke, Susan. LC 80-39998. 48p. (ps-2). 1981. 14.95 (*0-8050-0704-0*, Bks Young Read) H Holt & Co.

—Perfect the Pig. Jeschke, Susan. 40p. (gr. k-3). 1985. pap. 3.50 (*0-590-43710-0*) Scholastic Inc.

—Scary Night Visitors: A Story for Children with Bedtime Fears. Marcus, Irene W. & Marcus, Paul. LC 90-41919. 32p. (ps-2). 1990. 16.95 (*0-945354-26-6*); pap. 6.95 (*0-945354-25-8*) Magination Pr.

—Scary Night Visitors: A Story for Children with Bedtime Fears. Marcus, Irene W. & Marcus, Paul. LC 92-56874. 1993. PLB 17.26 (*0-8368-0935-1*) Gareth Stevens Inc.

Jesionowski, Mary & Schnickel, Jacob. A Big House, a Little Girl & a Few Things That Made Them Laugh. Bee, Cindy. 20p. (Orig.). (ps-5). 1990. pap. 2.75 (*0-9616308-1-7*) Hearthstn Inn.

Jessel, Camilla. The Kitten Book. Jessel, Camilla. LC 91-71841. 32p. (ps up). 1992. 14.95 (*1-56402-020-7*) Candlewick Pr.

—Life at the Royal Ballet School. Jessel, Camilla. LC 79-12162. 143p. (gr. 4 up). 1979. 15.95 (*0-416-30191-6*, NO. 0137) Routledge Chapman & Hall.

—The Puppy Book. Jessel, Camilla. LC 91-71825. 32p. (ps up). 1992. 14.95 (*1-56402-021-5*) Candlewick Pr.

Jessie. Please Tell. Jessie. 33p. 1991. pap. 8.00 (*0-89486-776-8*) Hazelden.

Jew, Flora. Super Santa of All Space & Beyond Assisted by His Galaxy Elves. Obergfoll, Michael. 38p. (gr. 2-12). 1988. 2.95 (*0-929052-00-5*) Super Santa Prodns.

Jewell, Jack. The Story of Warple. Robinson, Jan. 32p. (ps). 1990. 12.95 (*0-89334-137-1*) Humanics Ltd.

Jezierski, Chet. New Friends in a New Land: A Thanksgiving Story. Stamper, Judith B. LC 92-18072. 32p. (gr. 2-5). 1992. PLB 21.34 (*0-8114-7213-2*) Raintree Steck-V.

Ji, Li. Why Snails Have Shells: Minority & Han Folktales of China. Han, Carolyn, retold by. Han, Jay, tr. 1993. 14.95 (*0-685-65268-8*, Kolowalu Bk) UH Pr.

—Why Snails Have Shells: Minority & Han Folktales of China. Han, Carolyn, ed. Han, Jay, tr. from CHI. 80p. (gr. 3-8). 1993. 14.95 (*0-8248-1505-X*) UH Pr.

Jimco, Janet. I Would If I Could: A Teenager's Guide to ADHD-Hyperactivity. Gordon, Michael. 34p. (Orig.). (gr. 6-12). 1992. pap. 12.50 (*0-9627701-3-2*) GSI Pubns.

Job, Heather H. Those Mysterious Dinosaurs: A Biblical Approach for Children, Their Parents & Their Teachers. 2nd ed. Whitcomb, Norma A. Wyrtzen, Jack, frwd. by. 125p. (gr. 4 up). 1993. Spiral bdg. pap. 7.20x (*0-685-67781-8*); pap. text ed. 11.99 (*0-9635049-0-8*) Whitcomb Minist. Dino Mania has hit again! Children need to know that there is an alternative to the evolutionary, millions-of-years theory with which they are being bombarded. The pictures are designed to capture children's eyes & minds while the understandable text is substantiated with, "Thus said the Lord." Adults will be impacted & fascinated, as well, as they interpret captivating Biblical & scientific truths to curious young ones. Where did the dinosaurs come from? When were they here? Why aren't they around anymore? These are only a few of the baffling questions the book answers from God's Word. "Well researched & of scholarly excellence. A must for every school library, classroom, home." --Dr. Henry Morris, Pres., Institute for Creation Research. "An intriguing glimpse of those fascinating creatures from the creation-science point of view. ..well written."--Ellen Linduall, author. Also available in the set: A Christian video for children: DINOSAURS. To order contact: Whitcomb Ministries, Inc., BO, P.O. Box 277, Winona Lake, IN 46590-0277. *Publisher Provided Annotation.*

Johannsen, Rob, jt. illus. see Anderian, Kaffi.

John, Helen. All-of-a-Kind Family. Taylor, Sydney. 192p. (gr. k-6). 1980. pap. 3.50 (*0-440-40059-7*, YB) Dell.

—All-of-a-Kind Family. Taylor, Sydney. 189p. (gr. 3-6). 1988. Repr. of 1951 ed. 11.95 (*0-929093-00-3*) Taylor Prodns.

John, Joseph, Jr. The Very Best Me: Growing up Drug Free. Weikel, Ann T. Christian, Cora L., contrib. by. 60p. (Orig.). (gr. k-3). 1991. pap. 3.95 (*0-935357-11-4*) CRIC Prod.

John, Joyce. Come Sing God's Song. Thigpen, Thomas P. LC 86-24197. (ps-1). 1987. 8.99 (*1-55513-052-6*, Chariot Bks) Cook.

—God Cares for Me. Woody, Marilyn J. 14p. (ps). 1988. bds. 6.99 (*1-55513-319-3*, Chariot Bks) Cook.

—God Made My World. Woody, Marilyn. 14p. (ps). 1988. bds. 6.99 (*1-55513-320-7*, Chariot Bks) Cook.

—High Chair Devotions: God Gave Me a Gift. Woody, Marilyn J. 14p. (ps). 1989. bds. 6.99 spiral bdg. (1-55513-729-6, 37325, Chariot Bks) Cook.
—High Chair Devotions: God Is My Friend. Woody, Marilyn J. 14p. (ps). 1989. bds. 6.99 spiral bdg. (1-55513-728-8, 37283, Chariot Bks) Cook.
—My Friend Goes Left. Gregorich, Barbara. Hoffman, Joan, ed. 16p. (Orig.). (gr. k-2). 1984. pap. 2.25 (0-88743-008-2, 06008) Sch Zone Pub Co.
—Sue Likes Blue. Gregorich, Barbara. Hoffman, Joan, ed. 16p. (Orig.). (gr. k-2). 1984. pap. 2.25 (0-88743-011-2, 06011) Sch Zone Pub Co.
John-Petrie, Sandi. Side Saddle Riding: Four-H Manual. 2nd, rev. ed. Bowlby, Linda A. & Thomas, Mary L. 24p. (gr. 9-12). 1993. pap. 5.00 (1-884011-06-3) Wrld Sidesaddle.
Johnson, Amy. To the Point: A Story about E. B. White. Collins, David R. 56p. (gr. 3-6). 1989. 14.95 (0-87614-345-1); pap. 5.95 (0-87614-508-X) Carolrhoda Bks.
—What Are You Figuring Now? A Story about Benjamin Banneker. Ferris, Jeri. LC 88-7267. 56p. (gr. 3-6). 1988. PLB 14.95 (0-87614-331-1); pap. 4.95 (0-685-19616-X) Carolrhoda Bks.
—What Are You Figuring Now? A Story about Benjamin Banneker. Ferris, Jeri. 64p. (gr. 3-6). Repr. of 1988 ed. 4.95 (0-87614-521-7) Carolrhoda Bks.
Johnson, Anne. Sam Predicts a Storm. Davis, Marion M. 35p. (Orig.). 1991. pap. 6.95 (0-9622221-1-9) Starboard Cove.
Johnson, Arden. Katie & the Night Noises. Sweeney, Jacqueline. LC 93-22198. 32p. (ps-2). 1993. PLB 14.95 (0-8167-3014-8); pap. text ed. write for info. (0-8167-3015-6) BrdgeWater.
—The Sleepytime Book. Wahl, Jan. LC 91-10176. 32p. (ps-3). 1992. 15.00 (0-688-10275-1, Tambourine Bks); PLB 14.93 (0-688-10276-X, Tambourine Bks) Morrow.
Johnson, Audean. A to Z: Look & See. 32p. (Orig.). 1989. pap. 2.25 (0-394-86127-2) Random Bks Yng Read.
—Fuzzy As a Puppy. Johnson, Audean. LC 92-80353. 14p. (ps). 1993. 8.00 (0-679-83239-4) Random Bks Yng Read.
—Soft as a Kitten. 14p. (ps). 1982. bds. 8.00 (0-394-85517-5) Random Bks Yng Read.
Johnson, Bruce. I Once Knew an Indian Woman. Cutler, Ebbitt. 72p. (gr. 5 up). 1985. (Dist. by U of Toronto Pr); pap. 6.95 (0-88776-068-6) Tundra Bks.
Johnson, Carol. A Journey of Hope: Una Jornada de Esperanza. Harvey, Bob & Harvey, Diane K. LC 91-4556. (ENG & SPA.). 48p. (gr. k-6). 1991. 12.95 (0-89802-603-2) Beautiful Am.
Johnson, Cathy. A Rainy Day. Markle, Sandra. LC 91-17059. 32p. (ps-2). 1993. 14.95 (0-531-05976-6); PLB 14.99 (0-531-08576-7) Orchard Bks Watts.
Johnson, Cliff. Judges & Kings: God's Chosen Leaders. McElrath, William E. (gr. 1-6). 1979. 5.99 (0-8054-4249-9, 4242-49) Broadman.
Johnson, Colleen C. Just for Kids. Avis, Jen & Ward, Kathy. 166p. 1990. spiral bdg. 12.95 (0-9628683-1-0) Avis & Ward.
Johnson, Crockett. Carrot Seed. Krauss, Ruth. LC 45-4530. 24p. (gr. k-3). 1945. 13.00 (0-06-023350-8); PLB 12.89 (0-06-023351-6) HarpC Child Bks.
—The Carrot Seed. Krauss, Ruth. LC 45-4530. 32p. (ps-1). 1989. pap. 3.95 (0-06-443210-6, Trophy) HarpC Child Bks.
—The Carrot Seed. Krauss, Ruth. (ps-3). 1990. incl. cass. 19.95 (0-87499-177-3); pap. 12.95 incl. cass. (0-87499-176-5); Set: incl. 4 bks., guide, & cass. pap. 27.95 (0-685-38538-8) Live Oak Media.
—Carrot Seed Board Book. Krauss, Ruth. LC 45-4530. 24p. (ps-1). 1993. 4.95 (0-694-00492-8, Festival) HarpC Child Bks.
—Frowning Prince. Johnson, Crockett. (gr. 1-4). 1974. Repr. 15.00 (0-912846-09-7) Bookstore Pr.
—Harold & the Purple Crayon. Johnson, Crockett. LC 55-7683. (gr. k-3). 1958. 12.00 (0-06-022935-7); PLB 11.89 (0-06-022936-5) HarpC Child Bks.
—Harold & the Purple Crayon. Johnson, Crockett. LC 55-7683. 64p. (ps-3). 1981. pap. 3.95 (0-06-443022-7, Trophy) HarpC Child Bks.
—Harold's ABC. Johnson, Crockett. LC 63-14444. 64p. (ps-3). 1981. pap. 3.95 (0-06-443023-5, Trophy) HarpC Child Bks.
—Harold's Circus. Johnson, Crockett. LC 59-5318. 64p. (ps-3). 1981. pap. 3.95 (0-06-443024-3, Trophy) HarpC Child Bks.
—Harold's Fairy Tale. Johnson, Crockett. LC 56-8147. 64p. (gr up). 1994. 12.89 (0-06-022975-6) HarpC Child Bks.
—Harold's Fairy Tale. Johnson, Crockett. LC 56-8147. 64p. (ps-1). 1994. pap. 4.95 (0-06-443347-1, Trophy) HarpC Child Bks.
—Harold's Trip to the Sky. Johnson, Crockett. LC 57-9262. (gr. k-3). 1957. PLB 11.89 (0-06-022986-1) HarpC Child Bks.
—Harold's Trip to the Sky. Johnson, Crockett. LC 57-9262. 64p. (ps-3). 1981. pap. 3.95 (0-06-443025-1, Trophy) HarpC Child Bks.
—Picture for Harold's Room. Johnson, Crockett. LC 60-6372. (gr. k-3). 1960. PLB 13.89 (0-06-023006-1) HarpC Child Bks.
—A Picture for Harold's Room. Johnson, Crockett. LC 60-6372. 64p. (ps-3). 1985. pap. 3.50 (0-06-444085-0, Trophy) HarpC Child Bks.

—Will Spring Be Early or Will Spring Be Late? Johnson, Crockett. LC 59-9424. 48p. (gr. k-3). 1961. PLB 13.89 (0-690-89423-6, Crowell Jr Bks) HarpC Child Bks.
—Will Spring Be Early? or Will Spring Be Late? Johnson, Crockett. LC 59-9424. 48p. (gr. k-3). 1990. pap. 3.95 (0-06-443224-6, Trophy) HarpC Child Bks.
Johnson, Dagny. Cats in My Life from Granny to Ginger. Johnson, Esther G. 103p. (gr. 9-12). 1990. pap. 7.95 (0-9629143-0-4) Skyehill Pubns.
Johnson, David. The Boy Who Drew Cats. Johnson, David. 40p. (gr. k up). 1991. pap. 14.95 (0-88708-194-0, Rabbit Ears); incls. cassette 19.95 (0-88708-195-9, Rabbit Ears) Picture Bk Studio.
—Thumbelina. Andersen, Hans Christian. Roberts, Tom, adapted by. LC 89-8484. 32p. (gr. 1 up). 1991. pap. 14.95 (0-88708-113-4, Rabbit Ears); incl. cassette 19.95 (0-88708-114-2, Rabbit Ears) Picture Bk Studio.
—Thumbelina. Andersen, Hans Christian. McGillis, Kelly, read by. Isham, Mark, contrib. by. 32p. (ps up). 1992. pap. write for info. slipcase pkg., incl. cassette (0-307-14331-7, 14331, Golden Pr) Western Pub.
—Thumbelina. Andersen, Hans Christian. 64p. 1992. Repr. of 1989 ed. Mini-bk. incl. cass. 9.95 (0-88708-256-4, Rabbit Ears) Picture Bk Studio.
Johnson, David, photos by. Meet Shaquille O'Neal. St. Pierre, Stephanie. LC 93-1678. 112p. (gr. 3-5). 1993. pap. 2.99 (0-679-85444-4) Random Bks Yng Read.
—My First Cookbook. Wilkes, Angela. LC 88-13798. 48p. (gr. 3-7). 1989. 13.00 (0-394-80427-9) Knopf Bks Yng Read.
Johnson, Delores. Jenny. Wilson, Beth P. LC 89-8135. 32p. (gr. k-3). 1990. SBE 13.95 (0-02-793120-X, Macmillan Child Bk) Macmillan Child Grp.
Johnson, Diane. Arizona Alphabet. Penland, Violet & Johnson, Diane. (Orig.). 1989. pap. text ed. write for info. Bellwether UT.
Johnson, Dolores. The Best Bug to Be. Johnson, Dolores. LC 90-22231. 32p. (gr. k-3). 1992. SBE 13.95 (0-02-747842-4, Macmillan Child Bk) Macmillan Child Grp.
—Calvin's Christmas Wish. Miles, Calvin. 32p. (ps-3). 1993. 13.99 (0-670-84295-8) Viking Child Bks.
—Now Let Me Fly: The Story of a Slave Family. Johnson, Dolores. LC 92-33683. 32p. (gr. k-10). 1993. RSBE 14.95 (0-02-747699-5, Macmillan Child Bk) Macmillan Child Grp.
—Papa's Stories. Johnson, Dolores. LC 93-17534. 32p. (gr. k-3). 1994. RSBE 14.95 (0-02-747847-5, Macmillan Child Bk) Macmillan Child Grp.
—What Will Mommy Do When I'm at School? Johnson, Dolores. LC 90-5559. 32p. (ps-1). 1990. RSBE 13.95 (0-02-747845-9, Macmillan Child Bk) Macmillan Child Grp.
—Your Dad Was Just Like You. Johnson, Dolores. LC 92-6347. 32p. (gr. k-3). 1993. RSBE 13.95 (0-02-747838-6, Macmillan Child Bk) Macmillan Child Grp.
Johnson, E. Harper. Clara Barton: Soldier of Mercy. Rose, Mary C. 80p. (gr. 2-6). 1991. Repr. of 1960 ed. lib. bdg. 12.95 (0-7910-1403-7) Chelsea Hse.
—Daniel Boone: Taming the Wilds. Wilkie, Katharine E. 72p. (gr. 2-6). 1991. Repr. of 1960 ed. PLB 12.95 (0-7910-1407-X) Chelsea Hse.
Johnson, George C. Baby's First Words. 20p. (ps-1). 1986. bds. 4.95 (0-448-03093-4, G&D) Putnam Pub Group.
Johnson, Gillian. Sahara-Sara: Saranohair. Johnson, Gillian. (FRE.). 56p. 1992. 12.95 (1-55037-258-0, Pub. by Annick Pr) Firefly Bks Ltd.
Johnson, Gillian K. Saranohair. Johnson, Gillian K. 56p. 1992. 12.95 (1-55037-211-4, Pub. by Annick Pr) Firefly Bks Ltd.
Johnson, Gloria, jt. illus. see Clark, Melissa.
Johnson, Hilda S. A Child's Diary - the 1930's. Johnson, Hilda S. LC 88-51304. 64p. (Orig.). (gr. 3-8). 1988. pap. 3.95 (0-931563-02-X) Wishing Am.
Johnson, James, jt. photog. see Maudlsley, Toby.
Johnson, James H., Jr. They Walked the Earth. Johnson, James H., Jr. 112p. (Orig.). (gr. 1-6). 1992. pap. 12.95 (0-9632717-0-9) P Q Pubns.
Johnson, Jane. From Me to You. Rogers, Paul. LC 87-7943. 32p. (ps-2). 1988. 12.95 (0-531-05732-1); PLB 12.99 (0-531-08332-2) Orchard Bks Watts.
—Grandma's Bill. Waddell, Martin. LC 90-43014. 32p. (ps-2). 1991. 12.95 (0-531-05923-5); PLB 12.99 (0-531-08523-6) Orchard Bks Watts.
Johnson, Jean, photos by. Firefighters: A to Z. Johnson, Jean. LC 85-5348. 39p. (gr. 1-3). 1985. 11.95 (0-8027-6589-0); PLB 11.85 (0-8027-6590-4) Walker & Co.
—Librarians A to Z. Johnson, Jean. Johnson, Jean. 48p. (gr. 1-3). 1989. 11.95 (0-8027-6841-5); lib. bdg. 12.85 (0-8027-6842-3) Walker & Co.
Johnson, John E. Here Comes the Bus. 14p. (gr. 2-5). 1985. 3.99 (0-394-87544-3) Random Bks Yng Read.
—Here Comes the Circus. 14p. (gr. 2-5). 1985. 3.99 (0-394-87543-5) Random Bks Yng Read.
—Here Comes the Farmer. 14p. (ps-3). 1985. 3.99 (0-394-87552-4) Random Bks Yng Read.
—Here Comes the Train. 14p. (gr. 2-5). 1985. 3.99 (0-394-87551-6) Random Bks Yng Read.
—The Me Book. Johnson, John E. LC 79-62042. (ps). 1979. 3.50 (0-394-84243-X) Random Bks Yng Read.
—My First Book of Things. LC 78-64609. (ps). 1979. 3.95 (0-394-84128-X) Random Bks Yng Read.
Johnson, Karen. Crocodiles & Alligators. Petty, Kate. 1990. pap. 3.95 (0-531-15153-0) Watts.

Johnson, Larry. Football Fugitive. Christopher, Matt. 128p. (gr. 4-6). 1988. 14.95 (0-316-13971-8); pap. 3.95 (0-316-14064-3) Little.
—Knoxville, Tennessee. Giovanni, Nikki. LC 93-8877. 32p. 1994. 14.95 (0-590-47074-4) Scholastic Inc.
—Soccer Halfback. Christopher, Matt. (gr. 4-6). 1985. 14. 95 (0-316-13946-7); pap. 3.95 (0-316-13981-5) Little.
—When Jo Louis Won the Title. Rochelle, Belinda. LC 93-34317. (gr. 4 up). 1994. write for info. (0-395-66614-7) HM.
Johnson, Lary. The Fox Steals Home. Christopher, Matt. LC 78-17526. (gr. 4-6). 1985. 14.95 (0-316-13976-9); pap. 3.95 (0-316-13986-6) Little.
Johnson, Laurie K. Clouds of Terror. Welch, Catherine A. LC 93-18416. (gr. 4 up). 1993. 10.95 (0-87614-771-6) Carolrhoda Bks.
Johnson, Leonard J. Mae C. Jemison: First Black Female Astronaut. Ceasor, Ebraska D. Durant, Charlotte & Pye, Ethel, eds. 40p. (Orig.). (ps-1). 1992. pap. 4.00 (0-913678-22-8) New Day Pr.
Johnson, Lewis. Air, Air, Air. Jefferies, Lawrence. LC 82-15808. 32p. (gr. 3-6). 1983. PLB 10.59 (0-89375-880-9); pap. text ed. 2.95 (0-89375-881-7) Troll Assocs.
—All about Sound. Knight, David C. LC 82-17387. 32p. (gr. 3-6). 1983. PLB 10.59 (0-89375-878-7); pap. text ed. 2.95 (0-89375-879-5) Troll Assocs.
—Wonders of Energy. Adler, David. LC 82-20042. 32p. (gr. 3-6). 1983. PLB 10.59 (0-89375-884-1); pap. text ed. 2.95 (0-89375-885-X) Troll Assocs.
Johnson, Linda. The Reiss Rules for Two-Hour Monopoly: Fun, Fast, Unofficial Way to Play America's Favorite Board Game. Reiss, Stephen. LC 93-85455. 64p. (Orig.). (gr. 1-12). 1994. pap. 6.95 (0-9637853-3-8) Prosprty Prtnrs.
Johnson, Lois. Brush up Hair Care. Phillips, Betty L. LC 82-60643. 64p. (gr. 9-12). 1983. lib. bdg. 9.29 (0-671-44932-2, J Messner) S&S Trade.
Johnson, Lonni S. Mother Earth's Counting Book. Clements, Andrew. LC 90-7343. 44p. (gr. k up). 1992. pap. 15.95 (0-88708-138-X) Picture Bk Studio.
—A Snake Is Totally Tail. Barrett, Judi. LC 83-2657. 32p. (ps-1). 1983. SBE 13.95 (0-689-30979-1, Atheneum Child Bk) Macmillan Child Grp.
—A Snake Is Totally Tail. Barrett, Judith. LC 87-1123. 32p. (ps-1). 1987. pap. 3.95 (0-689-71148-4, Aladdin) Macmillan Child Grp.
Johnson, Lonnie S. Be Nice to Marilyn. Luttrell, Ida. LC 91-15695. 32p. (ps-3). 1992. SBE 13.95 (0-689-31716-6, Atheneum Child Bk) Macmillan Child Grp.
—Pickles Have Pimples: And Other Silly Statements. Barrett, Judi. LC 85-20073. 32p. (ps-2). 1986. SBE 13. 95 (0-689-31187-7, Atheneum Child Bk) Macmillan Child Grp.
—The Story of Z. Modesitt, Jeanne. LC 89-3923. 28p. (ps up). 1991. pap. 14.95 (0-88708-105-3) Picture Bk Studio.
—The Story of Z. Modesitt, Jeanne. LC 92-6626. 28p. 1992. pap. 4.95 (0-88708-278-5) Picture Bk Studio.
Johnson, Mackenzie. Harry's Grandpa Takes a Mysterious Journey. Brackett, Rona N. LC 86-1233. 55p. (Orig.). (gr. 3-6). 1986. text ed. 12.50 (0-916955-04-4); pap. 6.75 (0-916955-05-2) Arcus Pub.
Johnson, Marc, jt. illus. see Ranno, Jim.
Johnson, Marc, jt. illus. see Round, Jim.
Johnson, Mark. Campfire Favorites: A Songbook for Balance-Control Karaoke. Johnson, Mark. 24p. (Orig.). (gr. k-12). Date not set. pap. 2.49 (1-883988-08-X); pap. 8.99 incl. cassette (1-883988-02-0) RSV Prods.
—The Complete Bugler: Practice & Performance Aid for the Young Bugler. Johnson, Mark. 24p. (Orig.). (gr. 4-12). 1993. pap. 2.95 (1-883988-10-1); pap. 8.95 incl. cassette (1-883988-04-7) RSV Prods.
—Cowboy Classics: A Songbook for Balance-Control Karaoke. Johnson, Mark. 24p. (Orig.). (gr. k-12). 1993. pap. 2.49 (1-883988-06-3); pap. 8.99 incl. cassette (1-883988-00-4) RSV Prods.
—Fun-to-Sing: A Songbook for Balance-Control Karaoke. Johnson, Mark. 24p. (Orig.). (gr. k-12). 1993. pap. 2.49 (1-883988-07-1); pap. 8.99 incl. cassette (1-883988-01-2) RSV Prods.
—Good 'n Gross: A Songbook for Balance-Control Karaoke. Johnson, Mark. 24p. (Orig.). (gr. k-12). 1993. pap. 2.49 (1-883988-09-8); pap. 8.99 incl. cassette (1-883988-03-9) RSV Prods.
Johnson, Meredith. Alfred MacDuff Is Afraid of War. Skoglund, Elizabeth R. 48p. (ps-2). 1991. pap. 3.99 (0-8423-0032-5) Tyndale.
—All Tutus Should Be Pink. Brownrigg, Sheri. 32p. 1992. pap. 2.95 (0-590-43904-9, Cartwheel) Scholastic Inc.
—The Bathwater Gang. Spinelli, Jerry. 64p. (gr. 2-4). 1992. pap. 3.95 (0-316-80779-6) Little.
—Best Friends Wear Pink Tutus. Brownrigg, Sheri. LC 92-27569. 1993. write for info. (0-590-46437-X) Scholastic Inc.
—Brothers Don't Know Everything. Maifair, Linda Lee. LC 93-4605. 1993. 3.99 (0-8066-2635-6, Augsburg) Augsburg Fortress.
—The Children's Macbeth. (gr. 5-9). 1993. pap. 3.95 (0-88388-186-1) Bellerophon Bks.
—Mountain Bikes & Garbanzo Beans. Lewis, Beverly. LC 93-4606. 1993. pap. 3.99 (0-8066-2663-1, Augsburg) Augsburg Fortress.
—N-O Spells No! Slater, Teddy. LC 92-21422. 32p. (ps-2). 1993. pap. 2.95 (0-590-44186-8) Scholastic Inc.

—The Six-Hour Mystery. Lewis, Beverley. LC 93-35020. (gr. 4 up). 1993. 3.99 (0-8066-2666-6) Augsburg Fortress.
—Soccer Shock. Napoli, Donna J. LC 91-20706. 192p. (gr. 4-7). 1991. 13.95 (0-525-44827-6, DCB) Dutton Child Bks.
—Soccer Shock. Napoli, Donna J. LC 93-7483. 192p. (gr. 3-7). 1993. pap. 3.99 (0-14-036482-X, Puffin) Puffin Bks.
—The Sub. Petersen, P. J. LC 92-22269. (gr. 2-5). 1993. 12.99 (0-525-45059-9, DCB) Dutton Child Bks.
Johnson, Mike. Sign Language Made Simple. Lawrence, Edgar D. LC 79-10417. 240p. (gr. k up). 1975. text ed. 13.95 (0-88243-604-X, 02-0604); Video tape. 49.95 (0-685-57733-3); Set, incl. video tape. 58.90 (0-685-57734-1) Gospel Pub.
Johnson, Milton. Black Pearl. O'Dell, Scott. LC 67-23311. 160p. (gr. 7 up). 1967. 13.45 (0-395-06961-0) HM.
—Lives of Famous Romans. Coolidge, Olivia. LC 91-40360. 248p. (gr. 8-12). 1992. Repr. of 1965 ed. lib. bdg. 19.50 (0-208-02333-X, Pub. by Linnet) Shoe String.
Johnson, Nancy D., photos by. Jane Long: A Child's Pictorial History. Morgan, Elizabeth D. Richards, Ann, intro. by. LC 92-17739. 96p. (gr. 4-7). 1992. 12.95 (0-89015-861-4) Eakin-Sunbelt.
Johnson, Neil. The Battle of Gettysburg. Johnson, Neil. LC 88-30414. 64p. (gr. 5 up). 1989. SBE 14.95 (0-02-747831-9, Four Winds) Macmillan Child Grp.
—Step into China. Johnson, Neil. LC 87-20266. 32p. (gr. 3-6). 1988. lib. bdg. 9.98 (0-671-64338-X, J Messner); pap. 5.95 (0-671-65852-2) S&S Trade.
Johnson, Neil, photos by. The Battle of Lexington & Concord. Johnson, Neil. LC 91-22790. 40p. (gr. 4 up). 1992. RSBE 15.95 (0-02-747841-6, Four Winds) Macmillan Child Grp.
—How Puppies Grow. Selsam, Millicent E. 32p. (ps-3). 1990. pap. 2.50 (0-590-42736-9) Scholastic Inc.
—Jack Creek Cowboy. Johnson, Neil. LC 92-921. 32p. (gr. 2-5). 1993. 14.99 (0-8037-1228-6); PLB 14.89 (0-8037-1229-4) Dial Bks Young.
Johnson, Nola. Good Planets Are Hard to Find: An Environmental Information Guide for Kids. Dehr, Roma & Bazar, Ronald. 40p. (Orig.). (gr. 4 up). 1990. pap. 4.95 (0-919597-09-2) Firefly Bks Ltd.
Johnson, Pamela. And Then There Was One: The Mysteries of Extinction. Facklam, Margery. 45p. (gr. 3-6). 1992. 6.95 (0-316-25982-9) Sierra.
—Bees Dance & Whales Sing: The Mysteries of Animal Communication. Facklam, Margery. 48p. (gr. 3-6). 1992. 14.95 (0-87156-573-0) Sierra.
—Birds. Santrey, Laurence. LC 84-2731. 32p. (gr. 3-6). 1985. PLB 9.49 (0-8167-0192-X); pap. text ed. 2.95 (0-8167-0193-8) Troll Assocs.
—Birds Nests. Curran, Eileen. LC 84-8658. 32p. (gr. k-2). 1985. PLB 11.59 (0-8167-0341-8); pap. text ed. 2.95 (0-8167-0342-6) Troll Assocs.
—Cuckoo Clock. Stolz, Mary. LC 86-45538. 112p. 1986. 13.95 (0-87923-653-1) Godine.
—Deputy Shep. Stolz, Mary. LC 90-38664. 96p. (gr. 2-5). 1991. 12.95 (0-06-026039-4) HarpC Child Bks.
—Discovering Reptiles & Amphibians. Caitlin, Stephen. LC 89-4972. 32p. (gr. 2-4). 1990. PLB 11.59 (0-8167-1753-2); pap. text ed. 2.95 (0-8167-1754-0) Troll Assocs.
—Discovering Whales & Dolphins. Craig, Janet. LC 89-5004. 32p. (gr. 2-4). 1990. PLB 11.59 (0-8167-1759-1); pap. text ed. 2.95 (0-8167-1760-5) Troll Assocs.
—Do Not Disturb: The Mysteries of Animal Hibernation & Sleep. Facklam, Margery. LC 88-10921. 48p. (gr. 3-6). 1989. 15.95 (0-316-27379-1) Little.
—Fireflies. Arnold, Caroline. LC 93-30439. 1994. write for info. (0-590-46944-4) Scholastic Inc.
—Next Spring an Oriole. Whelan, Gloria. LC 87-4910. 64p. (gr. 2-4). 1987. lib. bdg. 6.99 (0-394-99125-7); pap. 1.95 (0-394-89125-2) Random Bks Yng Read.
—Pangur Ban. Stolz, Mary. LC 87-35049. 196p. (gr. 7 up). 1988. PLB 13.89 (0-06-025862-4) HarpC Child Bks.
—Partners for Life: The Mysteries of Animal Symbiosis. Facklam, Margery. 48p. (gr. 3-6). 1989. 12.95 (0-316-25983-7) Sierra.
—Quentin Corn. Stolz, Mary. LC 84-48321. 128p. (gr. 1-7). 1985. 14.95 (0-87923-553-5) Godine.
—The Rabbi's Girls. Hurwitz, Johanna. LC 82-2102. 192p. (gr. 4-6). 1982. 11.95 (0-688-01089-X) Morrow Jr Bks.
—The Rabbi's Girls. Hurwitz, Johanna. 160p. (gr. 3-7). 1989. pap. 3.95 (0-14-032951-X, Puffin) Puffin Bks.
—Reindeer. Arnold, Caroline. LC 93-12981. (gr. 4-7). 1993. pap. 3.95 (0-590-46943-6) Scholastic Inc.
—Robert Louis Stevenson: Young Storyteller. Sabin, Francene. LC 91-3924. 48p. (gr. 4-6). 1992. PLB 10.79 (0-8167-2507-1); pap. text ed. 3.50 (0-8167-2508-X) Troll Assocs.
—Song of the Giraffe. Jacobs, Shannon K. (gr. 2-4). 1991. 11.95 (0-316-45555-5) Little.
—The Story of the First Christmas. LC 90-23154. 24p. (ps up). 1991. 2.95 (0-694-00364-6) HarpC Child Bks.
—Tales at the Mousehole. Stolz, Mary. LC 88-46130. 96p. (gr. 2-4). 1992. 15.95 (0-87923-789-9) Godine.
—Whales & Dolphins. Sabin, Francene. LC 84-2709. 32p. (gr. 3-6). 1985. PLB 9.49 (0-8167-0286-1); pap. text ed. 2.95 (0-8167-0287-X) Troll Assocs.

—What Does the Crow Know? The Mysteries of Animal Intelligence. Facklam, Margery. LC 93-17811. 48p. (gr. 3-6). 1993. 14.95 (0-87156-544-7) Sierra.
Johnson, Pamela F. Prehistoric Animals. Cohen, Daniel. LC 86-19666. 48p. (gr. k-3). 1988. 9.95 (0-385-23416-3) Doubleday.
Johnson, Patricia & Steffen, Ann T. Human Hormones. Villee, Claude A., Jr. Head, J. J., ed. LC 86-72197. 16p. (Orig.). (gr. 10 up). 1987. pap. text ed. 2.75 (0-89278-371-0, 45-9771) Carolina Biological.
Johnson, Paul. Amazon Rainforest. Butterfield, Moira. 16p. (gr. k-5). 1992. pap. 6.95 (0-8249-8566-4, Ideals Child) Hambleton-Hill.
—Bird. Butterfield, Moira. 24p. (ps-1). 1992. pap. 3.95 (0-671-75892-6, Little Simon) S&S Trade.
—Butterfly. Butterfield, Moira. 24p. (ps-1). 1992. pap. 3.95 (0-671-75894-2, Little Simon) S&S Trade.
—Christmas Prayers. 16p. (ps). 1993. bds. 2.98 (0-8317-4277-1) Smithmark.
—Edd the Duck in Storyland. MacKay-Robinson, Christina & Faulkner, Keith. 32p. (gr. k-3). 1992. 12.95 (0-563-36046-1, BBC-Parkwest) Parkwest Pubns.
—Edd's Ghost Story. MacKay-Robinson, Christina. 32p. (gr. k-3). 1992. pap. 4.95 (0-563-36063-1, BBC-Parkwest) Parkwest Pubns.
—Family Prayers. 16p. (ps). 1993. bds. 2.98 (0-8317-4278-X) Smithmark.
—Flower. Butterfield, Moira. 24p. (ps-1). 1992. pap. 3.95 (0-671-75891-8, Little Simon) S&S Trade.
—Frog. Butterfield, Moira. 24p. (ps-1). 1992. pap. 3.95 (0-671-75893-4, Little Simon) S&S Trade.
—My First Phrases in Spanish & English. Faulkner, Keith. 14p. (ps-4). 1993. pap. 11.00 casebound (0-671-86595-1, S&S BFYR) S&S Trade.
—Playdays Colours & Shapes. Boyle, Alison. 32p. (ps-2). 1992. pap. 2.95 (0-563-20887-2, BBC-Parkwest) Parkwest Pubns.
—Playdays Letters & Words. Boyle, Alison. 32p. (ps-2). 1992. pap. 2.95 (0-563-20890-2, BBC-Parkwest) Parkwest Pubns.
—Playdays Numbers. Boyle, Alison. 32p. (ps-2). 1992. pap. 2.95 (0-563-20889-9, BBC-Parkwest) Parkwest Pubns.
—Playdays Out & About. Boyle, Alison. 32p. (ps-2). 1992. pap. 2.95 (0-563-20888-0, BBC-Parkwest) Parkwest Pubns.
—Undersea World. Butterfield, Moira. 16p. (gr. 1-5). 1992. pap. 6.95 (0-8249-8589-3, Ideals Child) Hambleton-Hill.
Johnson, Paul, jt. illus. see Bull, Peter.
Johnson, Paul B. Saint Patrick & the Peddler. Hodges, Margaret. LC 92-44522. 40p. (gr. k-3). 1993. 15.95 (0-531-05489-6); PLB 15.99 (0-531-08639-9) Orchard Bks Watts.
Johnson, Pete. Busy Being Me: Fitness, Fun & Fundamentals. Dowell, Ruth I. 40p. (Orig.). (ps-3). 1988. pap. 6.00 (0-945842-07-4) Pollyanna Prodns.
—Jiggle on the Doorknob. Dowell, Ruth I. 70p. (Orig.). (gr. 2-6). 1984. pap. 4.00 (0-945842-01-5) Pollyanna Prodns.
—Think about It! Dowell, Ruth I. 36p. (Orig.). (ps-6). 1987. pap. 3.00 (0-945842-04-X) Pollyanna Prodns.
—Watch Out, Pollyanna! Dowell, Ruth I. 40p. (gr. 2-6). 1986. pap. 4.00 (0-945842-02-3) Pollyanna Prodns.
Johnson, Phyllis. Exploring the Lives of Gifted People-The Sciences. Balsamo, Kathy. 80p. (gr. 4 up). 1987. pap. 8.95 (0-86653-417-2, GA 1038) Good Apple.
—Exploring the Lives of Gifted People-The Arts. Balsamo, Kathy. 80p. (gr. 4 up). 1987. pap. 8.95 (0-86653-406-7, GA1037) Good Apple.
Johnson, Priscilla M. Oliver. Wickstrom, Lois. (gr. k-6). 1978. pap. 2.00 (0-916176-03-7) Sproing.
Johnson, Priscilla M., jt. illus. see Mion, Francie.
Johnson, Saundra L. Listen to Your Mother. Brunner, Robert F., et al. LC 90-92041. 70p. (Orig.). (ps-3). 1991. PLB write for info. (1-879209-00-4); pap. text ed. write for info.; tchr's. ed. avail. Saundras Story Bks.
—When You Feel Like Your Out of Luck. Brunner, Robert F., et al. LC 90-92036. 58p. (Orig.). (ps-3). 1991. PLB 24.95 (1-879209-01-2); pap. text ed. write for info.; tchr's. ed. avail. Saundras Story Bks.
Johnson, Stephen T. The Nutcracker Ballet. Hayden, Melissa, retold by. LC 92-20654. 32p. 1992. 14.95 (0-8362-4501-6) Andrews & McMeel.
—The Samurai's Daughter. San Souci, Robert D. LC 91-15585. 32p. (ps-3). 1992. 15.00 (0-8037-1135-2); PLB 14.89 (0-8037-1136-0) Dial Bks Young.
—The Snow Wife. San Souci, Robert D., retold by. LC 92-28966. 32p. (ps-3). 1993. 14.99 (0-8037-1409-2); PLB 14.89 (0-8037-1410-6) Dial Bks Young.
—When Solomon Was King. MacGill-Callahan, Sheila. LC 93-28058. 1995. write for info. (0-8037-1589-7); PLB write for info. (0-8037-1590-0) Dial Bks Young.
Johnson, Steve. The Frog Prince, Continued. Scieszka, Jon. 32p. (ps-3). 1991. 14.95 (0-670-83421-1) Viking Child Bks.
—No Star Nights. Smucker, Anna E. LC 88-2782. 48p. (ps-3). 1989. 12.95 (0-394-89925-3); lib. bdg. 13.99 (0-394-99925-8) Knopf Bks Yng Read.
—The Salamander Room. Mazer, Anne. LC 90-33301. 32p. (ps-3). 1991. 14.00 (0-394-82945-X); PLB 14.99 (0-394-92945-4) Knopf Bks Yng Read.
Johnson, Steve & Fancher, Lou. The First Night. Hennessy, B. G. LC 93-9659. 32p. (ps-3). 1993. 13.99 (0-670-83026-7) Viking Child Bks.
Johnson, Steve, jt. illus. see Fancher, Lou.

Johnson, Tani B. The Magical Adventures of Sun Beams. Mack, Karen. 32p. (ps-4). 1992. pap. 5.95 (0-9631644-0-6) Shooting Star.
Johnson, V. C. Bride Comes to Yellow Sky. Crane, Stephen. 40p. (gr. 6 up). 1982. PLB 13.95s.p. (0-87191-827-7) Creative Ed.
—The Open Boat. Crane, Stephen. 64p. (gr. 6 up). 1982. PLB 13.95s.p. (0-87191-826-9) Creative Ed.
Johnson, W. Cameron. Boy on a Bus. Johnson, W. Cameron. McKay, Dermot, contrib. by. (gr. 3-7). 1991. pap. 3.50 (0-91269-009-3) Grosvenor USA.
—Chico the Street Boy. Puig, Evelyn. 85p. (gr. 4-8). 1991. 3.95 (0-901269-79-4) Grosvenor USA.
—Return of the Indian Spirit. Brown, Vinson. LC 81-65887. 64p. (gr. 5 up). 1982. pap. 7.95 (0-89087-401-8) Celestial Arts.
Johnson, William H. Li'l Sis & Uncle Willie: A Story Based on the Life & Paintings of William H. Johnson. Everett, Gwen & National Museum of American Art Staff. LC 91-14800. 32p. (ps-3). 1992. Repr. of 1991 ed. 13.95 (0-8478-1462-9) Rizzoli Intl.
Johnson, William R. Dinosaurs & Other Prehistorics. Johnson, William R. Johnson, Pauline D., ed. 48p. (gr. 3-6). 1986. pap. 4.95 (0-936917-02-4, B606) Blip Prods.
—Kids of the World: Cursive. Johnson, William R. Johnson, Pauline D., ed. 48p. (gr. 3-6). 1986. pap. 4.95 (0-936917-01-6, B604) Blip Prods.
—Kids of the World: Manuscript. Johnson, William R. Johnson, Pauline D., ed. 48p. (Orig.). (ps-2). 1986. pap. 4.95 (0-936917-00-8, B603) Blip Prods.
—Numbers One to Twenty: The Circus & the Bees. Johnson, William R. Johnson, Pauline D., ed. 48p. (ps-2). 1986. pap. 4.95 (0-936917-03-2, B605) Blip Prods.
Johnston, Anne. Sam the Royal Cat, No. 1. Davis, Marion M. Starboard Cove Publishing Staff, ed. 35p. (Orig.). 1989. pap. 5.95x (0-9622221-0-0) Starboard Cove.
Johnston, Cliff. Isaiah: Messenger for God. Heifner, Fred. (gr. 1-6). 1978. 5.95 (0-8054-4243-X, 4242-43) Broadman.
Johnston, Clinton. Elevator. Mallett, Jerry J. & Ervin, Timothy S. 23p. (ps-2). 1992. 9.10 (0-7804-3989-9, 088542) Perma-Bound.
—Elevator: Paper Big Book. Mallett, Jerry J. & Ervin, Timothy S. 23p. (Orig.). (ps-2). 1992. pap. 22.00 (0-7804-3988-0, 088544) Perma-Bound.
—Elevator: Perma Big Book. Mallett, Jerry J. & Ervin, Timothy S. 23p. (ps-2). 1992. 47.50 (0-7804-3987-2, 088543) Perma-Bound.
Johnston, Dirk & Bright, Mark. RDF Accelerated Training Program. Reed, Gary. Marciniszyn, Alex & Cartier, Randi, eds. 56p. (Orig.). (gr. 8 up). 1988. pap. 7.95 (0-916211-32-0, 555) Palladium Bks.
Johnston, Joe. The Adventures of Teebo: A Tale of Magic & Suspense. Star Wars. LC 83-24686. 48p. (gr. 2-7). 1984. lib. bdg. 5.99 (0-394-96568-X) Random Bks Yng Read.
Johnston, Lynn. Is This "One of Those Days," Daddy? Johnston, Lynn. LC 82-72417. 128p. (gr. 5 up). 1982. pap. 8.95 (0-8362-1197-9) Andrews & McMeel.
Joiner, Eddie, jt. illus. see Devi-Doolin, Daya.
Joles, Michael, jt. illus. see Joles, Richard.
Joles, Richard & Joles, Michael. Signs of Survival. McKinley, Nancy L. (gr. 5-12). 1986. Box 30 4x6 cards. 12.00 (0-930599-10-1) Thinking Pubns.
—Signs of Survival. McKinley, Nancy L. (gr. 5-12). 1987. Box 30 4x6 cards. 12.00 (0-930599-15-2) Thinking Pubns.
Joliffe, Dale. Fair Game: How to Play Impartial Combinatorial Games. Guy, Richard K. Malkevitch, Joseph, ed. 113p. (Orig.). (gr. 5-12). Pap. text ed. 12.95 (0-912843-16-0) COMAP Inc.
Jolly, Cheryl. Jackie. Lewis, Luevester. (gr. k-5). 1970. pap. 1.00 (0-685-42384-0) Third World.
Jomra, J. Some Indian Saints. Talwalker, Gopinath. 64p. (Orig.). (gr. 5 up). 1980. pap. 2.50 (0-89744-208-3, Pub. by Natl Bk Trust IA) Auromere.
Jonas, Ann. Holes & Peeks. Jonas, Ann. LC 83-14128. 24p. (ps-1). 1984. 15.95 (0-688-02537-4); PLB 15.88 (0-688-02538-2) Greenwillow.
—Now We Can Go. Jonas, Ann. LC 85-12614. 24p. (ps-1). 1986. 11.75 (0-688-04802-1); PLB 11.88 (0-688-04803-X) Greenwillow.
—The Quilt. Jonas, Ann. LC 83-25385. 32p. (ps-1). 1984. 16.00 (0-688-03825-5); PLB 15.93 (0-688-03826-3) Greenwillow.
—Round Trip. Jonas, Ann. LC 82-12026. 32p. (gr. k-3). 1983. 16.00 (0-688-01772-X); PLB 15.93 (0-688-01781-9) Greenwillow.
—The Trek. Jonas, Ann. LC 84-25962. 32p. (gr. k-3). 1985. 14.95 (0-688-04799-8); lib. bdg. 14.88 (0-688-04800-5) Greenwillow.
—Two Bear Cubs. Jonas, Ann. LC 82-2860. 24p. (gr. k-3). 1982. PLB 14.88 (0-688-01408-9) Greenwillow.
—When You Were a Baby. Jonas, Ann. LC 81-12800. 24p. (ps-1). 1982. 15.00 (0-688-00863-1); PLB 14.93 (0-688-00864-X) Greenwillow.
—Where Can It Be? Jonas, Ann. LC 86-304. 32p. (ps-1). 1986. 14.95 (0-688-05169-3); PLB 14.88 (0-688-05246-0) Greenwillow.
Jonas, Dieter. Origami for Children. Kneissler, Irmgard. LC 92-453. 64p. (ps up). 1992. PLB 19.93 (0-516-09261-8) Childrens.
—Origami for Children. Kneissler, Irmgard. LC 92-453. 64p. (ps up). 1993. pap. 8.95 (0-516-49261-6) Childrens.

Jones, Allan, jt. illus. see Gorney, Janifer.

Jones, Amy. Abracadabra. Jones, Amy. Thatch, Nancy R., ed. Melton, David, intro. by. LC 93-13421. 29p. (gr. 3-5). 1993. PLB 14.95 (*0-933849-46-X*) Landmark Edns.

Jones, Bob. Danny Dorfman's Dream Band, No. 3: The Case of the Missing Case. Kidd, Ronald. LC 92-17208. 80p. (gr. 2-6). 1992. pap. 2.99 (*0-14-034988-X*) Puffin Bks.
—Danny Dorfman's Dream Band, No. 4: Rapunzel, Sort Of. Kidd, Ronald. LC 92-16495. 80p. (gr. 2-6). 1992. pap. 3.50 (*0-14-034987-1*) Puffin Bks.
—Jelly Belly. Smith, Robert K. LC 80-23898. 160p. (gr. 4-6). 1981. pap. 13.95 (*0-385-28477-2*) Delacorte.
—A Legend in His Own Mind. Kidd, Ronald. 80p. (gr. 3-6). 1992. pap. 2.99 (*0-14-034986-3*, Puffin) Puffin Bks.
—Teddy Teaburry's Fabulous Facts. Asher, Sandy. 110p. (Orig.). (gr. 4-5). 1985. pap. 2.50 (*0-440-48576-2*, YB) Dell.

Jones, Carol. The Cat Sat on the Mat. LC 93-14341. 1994. write for info. (*0-395-68392-0*) HM.
—Drummond: The Search for Sarah. Odgers, Sally F. LC 90-55198. 112p. (gr. 2-6). 1990. reinforced 16.95 (*0-8234-0851-5*) Holiday.
—Hickory Dickory Dock. 48p. (gr. k-3). 1992. 10.70 (*0-395-60834-1*) HM.
—Old MacDonald Had a Farm. (ps-3). 1989. 12.70 (*0-395-49212-2*) HM.
—This Old Man. Jones, Carol. 48p. (gr. k-3). 1990. 13.45 (*0-395-54699-0*) HM.

Jones, Ceri, jt. illus. see Adams, Pam.

Jones, Dan. The Secret Life of the Underwear Champ. Miles, Betty. LC 80-15651. (gr. 3-7). 1981. PLB 8.99 256p. (*0-394-94563-8*); pap. 3.50 128p. (*0-394-84563-3*) Knopf Bks Yng Read.

Jones, Dennis. Come to Jesus: Jesus Blesses the Children. Simon, Mary M. 24p. (Orig.). (ps-1). 1992. pap. 2.39 (*0-570-04707-2*) Concordia.
—Daniel & the Tattletales: Daniel 6: Daniel in the Lions' Den. Simon, Mary M. LC 92-31887. 32p. (Orig.). (gr. 1-3). 1993. pap. 3.99 (*0-570-04733-1*) Concordia.
—The First Christmas: Luke 2: The Birth of Jesus. Simon, Mary M. LC 92-21372. 32p. (Orig.). (gr. 1-3). 1993. pap. 3.99 (*0-570-04741-2*) Concordia.
—Follow That Star. Simon, Mary M. 24p. (ps-1). 1990. pap. 2.39 (*0-570-04177-5*) Concordia.
—The Hide-&-Seek Prince: Second Kings 11-12: 16: Joash. Simon, Mary M. LC 93-35606. 1994. write for info. (*0-570-04740-4*) Concordia.
—Hide the Baby: The Birth of Moses. Simon, Mary M. 24p. (Orig.). (ps-1). 1991. pap. 2.39 (*0-570-04702-1*) Concordia.
—Hurray for the Lord's Army! Judges 6: 11 - 7: 22 (Gideon) Simon, Mary M. LC 93-35604. 1994. write for info. (*0-570-04739-0*) Concordia.
—Jibber-Jabber: The Tower of Babel. Simon, Mary M. 24p. (Orig.). (ps-1). 1992. pap. 2.39 (*0-570-04705-6*) Concordia.
—The No-Go King: Exodus 5-15: The Exodus. Simon, Mary M. LC 92-31888. 32p. (Orig.). (gr. 1-3). 1993. pap. 3.99 (*0-570-04732-3*) Concordia.
—Row the Boat. Simon, Mary M. 24p. (ps-1). 1990. pap. 2.39 (*0-570-04186-4*, 56-1645) Concordia.
—Send a Baby: Birth of John the Baptist. Simon, Mary M. 24p. (Orig.). (ps-1). 1992. pap. 2.39 (*0-570-04706-4*) Concordia.
—Sit Down! Mary & Martha. Simon, Mary M. 24p. (Orig.). (ps-1). 1991. pap. 2.39 (*0-570-04701-3*) Concordia.
—Thank you, Jesus: Luke 17: 11-19; Jesus Heals Ten Men with Leprosy. Simon, Mary M. LC 93-36192. 1994. write for info. (*0-570-04762-5*) Concordia.
—Through the Roof. Simon, Mary M. LC 93-36193. 1994. write for info. (*0-570-04734-X*) Concordia.
—Too Tall, Too Small. Simon, Mary M. 24p. (ps-1). 1990. pap. 2.39 (*0-570-04185-6*) Concordia.
—Toot! Toot! Simon, Mary M. 24p. (ps-1). 1990. pap. 2.39 (*0-570-04184-8*) Concordia.
—A Walk on the Waves: Matthew 14: 13-32: Jesus Walks on the Water. Simon, Mary M. LC 92-21374. 32p. (Orig.). (gr. 1-3). 1993. pap. 3.99 (*0-570-04735-8*) Concordia.
—Where Is Jesus? Easter. Simon, Mary M. 24p. (ps-1). 1991. pap. 2.39 (*0-570-04703-X*) Concordia.
—Whoops! Jonah. Simon, Mary M. 24p. (Orig.). (ps-1). 1992. pap. 2.39 (*0-570-04704-8*) Concordia.

Jones, Don. What You Can See, You Can Be! Anderson, David A. 48p. (Orig.). (gr. 3-8). 1988. 11.95 (*0-87516-603-2*) DeVorss.

Jones, Elizabeth O. Prayer for a Child. Field, Rachel. LC 44-47191. 32p. (ps-1). 1968. SBE 11.95 (*0-02-735190-4*, Macmillan Child Bk) Macmillan Child Grp.
—Prayer for a Child. Field, Rachel. LC 84-70991. 32p. (ps-k). 1984. pap. 3.95 (*0-02-043070-1*, Aladdin) Macmillan Child Grp.

Jones, Eric. The Great Quarterback Switch. Christopher, Matt. LC 83-25628. (gr. 4-6). 1984. 14.95 (*0-316-13903-3*) Little.

Jones, Harold. Lavender's Blue. Lines, Kathleen. 180p. (ps-7). 1990. pap. 12.00 (*0-19-272208-5*) OUP.
—Lavender's Blue: A Book of Nursery Rhymes. Lines, Kathleen, ed. 180p. 1987. 22.00 (*0-19-279537-6*) OUP.
—The Voyage of QV66. large type ed. Lively, Penelope. 280p. 1992. 13.95 (*0-7451-1548-9*, Galaxy Child Lrg Print) Chivers N Amer.

Jones, Holly. The Story of Hanukkah: A Lift-the-Flap Rebus Book. Rojany, Lisa. 16p. (ps-3). 1993. 12.95 (*1-56282-420-1*) Hyprn Child.

Jones, J. Wallace, et al. Black Guard. Barrett, Kevin. Charlton, S. Coleman, ed. 40p. (Orig.). (gr. 12). 1990. pap. 8.00 (*1-55806-115-0*, 7012) Iron Crown Ent Inc.

Jones, Jan N. Make a Wish, Molly. Cohen, Barbara. LC 93-17901. 1994. 14.95 (*0-385-31079-X*) Delacorte.
—These Lands Are Ours: Tecumseh's Fight for the Old Northwest. Connell, Kate. LC 92-14417. 96p. (gr. 2-5). 1992. PLB 21.34 (*0-8114-7227-2*) Raintree Steck-V.
—We Want Jobs! A Story of the Great Depression. Norrell, Robert J. LC 92-18082. 40p. (gr. 2-5). 1992. PLB 21.34 (*0-8114-7229-9*) Raintree Steck-V.

Jones, Jean. Youth Poems. Amos, Winsom. 24p. (Orig.). (gr. 6-12). 1983. pap. 1.75x (*0-932510-00-0*) Soma Pr.

Jones, Jerry D. Patrick the Pelaganty. Watkins, Tracy D. Herbrechtsmeier, Keith, ed. LC 93-83730. 40p. (ps-3). 1993. 8.99 (*1-883261-00-7*) Pelaganty.

Jones, John. Clouds. Wandelmaier, Roy. LC 84-8643. 32p. (gr. k-2). 1985. PLB 11.59 (*0-8167-0338-8*); pap. text ed. 2.95 (*0-8167-0441-4*) Troll Assocs.
—Earth. Brandt, Keith. LC 84-8444. 32p. (gr. 3-6). 1985. PLB 9.49 (*0-8167-0250-0*); pap. text ed. 2.95 (*0-8167-0251-9*) Troll Assocs.
—Earthquakes & Volcanoes. Santrey, Laurence. LC 84-2676. 32p. (gr. 3-6). 1985. PLB 9.49 (*0-8167-0212-8*); pap. text ed. 2.95 (*0-8167-0213-6*) Troll Assocs.
—Flying Carrots. Cornell, S. A. LC 85-14093. 48p. (Orig.). (gr. 1-3). 1986. PLB 10.59 (*0-8167-0640-9*); pap. text ed. 3.50 (*0-8167-0641-7*) Troll Assocs.
—The Great Bunny Race. Feczko, Kathy. LC 84-8634. 32p. (gr. k-2). 1985. PLB 11.59 (*0-8167-0357-4*); pap. text ed. 2.95 (*0-8167-0437-6*) Troll Assocs.
—Little Eagle Learns to Fly. Cornell, S. A. LC 85-14086. 48p. (Orig.). (gr. 1-3). 1986. lib. bdg. 10.59 (*0-8167-0618-2*); pap. text ed. 3.50 (*0-8167-0619-0*) Troll Assocs.
—No Fleas, Please! Pellowski, Michael J. LC 85-14066. 48p. (Orig.). (gr. 1-3). 1986. PLB 10.59 (*0-8167-0608-5*); pap. text ed. 3.50 (*0-8167-0609-3*) Troll Assocs.
—Rita Goes to the Hospital. Davidson, Martine. LC 91-43293. 32p. (Orig.). (ps-2). 1992. PLB 5.99 (*0-679-91820-5*); pap. 2.25 (*0-679-81820-0*) Random Bks Yng Read.
—The Sorcerer's Apprentice. Eastman, David. LC 87-13767. 32p. (gr. k-4). 1988. PLB 9.79 (*0-8167-1067-8*); pap. text ed. 1.95 (*0-8167-1068-6*) Troll Assocs.

Jones, John R. Amazing True Stories. Wulffson, Don L. LC 90-28105. 128p. (gr. 4-9). 1991. 13.95 (*0-525-65070-9*, Cobblehill Bks) Dutton Child Bks.
—Dinosaur Hunters. McMullan, Kate. LC 88-30742. 48p. (Orig.). (gr. 2-4). 1989. PLB 7.99 (*0-394-91150-4*); 3.50 (*0-394-81150-X*) Random Bks Yng Read.
—Discovering Earthquakes & Volcanoes. Damon, Laura. LC 89-4974. 32p. (gr. 2-4). 1990. PLB 11.59 (*0-8167-1757-5*); pap. text ed. 2.95 (*0-8167-1758-3*) Troll Assocs.
—Willie Mays, Young Superstar. Sabin, Louis. LC 89-33979. 48p. (gr. 4-6). 1990. PLB 10.79 (*0-8167-1775-3*); pap. text ed. 3.50 (*0-8167-1776-1*) Troll Assocs.

Jones, Judy. Apple Jack & the Big Storm: A Brave Horse to the Rescue. Zeplin, Zeno & Jones, Judy. Ebersapacher, Margy, ed. 48p. (gr. k-3). 1991. lib. bdg. 9.95 (*1-877740-10-1*); pap. text ed. 5.50 (*1-877740-11-X*) Nel-Mar Pub.
—The Cross-Eyed Ghost. Zeplin, Zeno. 154p. (gr. 3-6). 1991. PLB 14.95 casebound (*0-9615760-05-5*); pap. text ed. 7.95 (*1-877740-06-3*) Nel-Mar Pub.
—Discovery on Dusty Creek. Zeplin, Zeno. 112p. (gr. 3-6). 1994. 14.95 (*1-877740-23-3*); pap. 7.95 (*1-877740-24-1*) Nel-Mar Pub.
—Great Texas Christmas Legends. 2nd ed. Zeplin, Zeno. 156p. (gr. 4 up). 1987. 15.95 (*0-9615760-2-2*); pap. 7.95 (*0-9615760-3-0*) Nel-Mar Pub.
—The Haunted Classroom. Zeplin, Zeno. 136p. (gr. 4-7). 1989. text ed. 14.95 (*0-9615760-8-1*); pap. text ed. 7.95 (*0-9615760-9-X*) Nel-Mar Pub.
—Popcorn Is Missing: A Katy & Beth Mystery. Zeplin, Zeno. 48p. (gr. 2-4). 1990. lib. bdg. 7.95 casebound (*1-877740-01-2*); pap. text ed. 5.50 (*1-877740-02-0*) Nel-Mar Pub.
—Secret Magic. Zeplin, Zeno. 56p. (gr. 3-6). 1990. lib. bdg. 9.95 casebound (*1-877740-03-9*); pap. text ed. 5.50g (*1-877740-04-7*) Nel-Mar Pub.

Jones, Julienne. Makimba's Animal World. Jackson, Bobby L. Gordon, April, ed. LC 93-79595. 32p. (Orig.). (gr. k-4). 1994. 12.95 (*0-9634932-9-9*); pap. 7.95 (*0-9634932-8-0*) Multicult Pubns.

Jones, Kathy. Our World. Bittinger, Gayle. McKinnon, Elizabeth, ed. LC 89-52145. 80p. (ps-1). 1990. pap. 8.95 (*0-911019-30-8*) Warren Pub Hse.

Jones, Ken & Thompson, Quentin. A Real Winner. McKissack, Patricia & McKissack, Fredrick. LC 88-61637. 32p. (gr. 1-3). 1987. text ed. 8.95 (*0-88335-732-1*); pap. text ed. 4.95 (*0-88335-752-6*) Milliken Pub Co.

Jones, Kert. I Am This & More, Bk. 1. Jones, Kathleen I. 12p. (ps-5). 1989. write for info. (*0-9624790-0-4*) Kindle Bks.
—I Am This & More, Bk. 2. Jones, Kathy. 12p. (ps-5). 1990. write for info. (*0-9624790-1-2*) Kindle Bks.

Jones, Lois M. Negro Art, Music, & Rhyme. Whiting, Helen A. (gr. 2). 1990. 4.25 (*0-87498-005-4*) Assoc Pubs DC.
—Negro Folk Tales. Whiting, Helen A. (gr. 1). 1990. 4.25 (*0-87498-006-2*) Assoc Pubs DC.
—Picture Poetry Book. McBrown, Gertrude P. 1990. 4.25 (*0-87498-007-0*) Assoc Pubs DC.
—Pioneers of Long Ago. Roy, Jessie H. & Turner, Geneva C. 1990. 12.95 (*0-87498-008-9*) Assoc Pubs DC.

Jones, MariaElena G. Rosalia, Be Proud. Jones, Jay S. 41p. (gr. k-6). 1992. 14.95 (*0-9632040-0-9*); PLB 14.95 (*0-9632040-1-7*) Integrity Inst.

Jones, Mary E. I Am: Memory Book for Pre-Schoolers. Woychuk, N. A. 33p. (Orig.). (ps). 1988. pap. 7.95 (*1-880960-10-9*) Script Memory Fl.

Jones, Michael R., jt. illus. see Bailey-Jones, Suzanne.

Jones, Randy. Cookie Monster, Where Are You? Sesame Street Staff. LC 75-39342. (ps-3). 1976. 8.99 (*0-394-83257-4*) Random Bks Yng Read.
—The Sesame Street Mother Goose. Sesame Street Staff. LC 75-39341. (ps-3). 1976. 8.95 (*0-394-83256-6*) Random Bks Yng Read.

Jones, Renata S. Tabitha Jones. 2nd ed. Weinberger, Jane. 40p. (Orig.). (ps-4). 1985. pap. 3.95 (*0-932433-07-3*) Windswept Hse.

Jones, Ronald. Famous Firsts of Black Women. Plowden, Martha W. 112p. (gr. 4-8). 1993. 11.95 (*0-88289-973-2*) Pelican.

Jones, S. Max. Naming Game: Storybook to Color. Thornton, Claire & Thomas, Thornton. 22p. (Orig.). (gr. k-3). 1988. pap. 3.95 (*0-317-92517-2*) Sparky Star Pr.
—Naming Game: Storybook to Color by Grandpa T. Thomas, Claire & Thomas, Thornton, eds. 18p. (Orig.). (gr. k-3). 1988. 2.95x (*0-9621616-0-8*) Sparky Star Pr.

Jones, Scott. Activities for the Children's Dictionary of Occupations. rev. ed. Parramore, Barbara & Hopke, Bill. 20p. (gr. 3-4). 1992. wkbk. 12.95 (*1-56191-191-7*) Meridian Educ.
—Activities for the Children's Dictionary of Occupations. rev. ed. Parramore, Barbara & Hopke, Bill. 20p. (gr. 5-6). 1992. wkbk. 12.95 (*1-56191-192-5*) Meridian Educ.
—The Children's Dictionary of Occupations. rev. ed. Parramore, Barbara & Hopke, Bill. 130p. (gr. 3-8). 1992. pap. text ed. 12.95 (*1-56191-190-9*) Meridian Educ.

Jones, Shari. Swim Free. Sanborn, Laura & Eberhardt, Lorraine. 32p. (gr. 6-12). 1982. pap. 6.95x (*0-910715-00-9*) Search Public.

Jones, Tim, photos by. Wild Critters. Walker, Tom, text by. Sturgis, Kent, ed. Newman, Leslie. LC 91-7308. 48p. (Orig.). 1992. 15.95x (*0-945397-10-0*); pap. 7.95, Feb. 1993 (*0-945397-25-9*) Epicenter Pr.

Jones, Yochanan. The Hostage Torah. Winkler, Gershon. (gr. 7 up). 1981. pap. 5.95 (*0-910818-34-7*) Judaica Pr.

Jonsson, Deborah. *Our Little Flower Girl: A Child Has Her First Experience Participating in a Wedding.* Thomas, Charlotte E. LC 92-72538. 32p. (ps-3). 1992. PLB 16.95 singer-sewn (*0-9633607-0-1*) Golden Rings. *Finally, the first storybook written specifically to help little girls selected to be a flower girl in a wedding ceremony. While informing them of what their role will entail, it also entertains them with a delightful story. The tale begins with her invitation to join the bridal party & proceeds through the many preparations & customs leading up to THE BIG DAY. Her finery is chosen & she discovers it must be ordered, which is a new experience for her. She solicits her friends & their toys to help her practice for her exciting role. The meanings of rehearsal & reception are also made known to her. A very apprehensive child in the beginning of the story, she ends up eagerly anticipating becoming a bride herself someday. This must have book is beautifully illustrated in full color & contains a page for signatures of the wedding party & special friends making it a true KEEPSAKE.* **Publisher Provided Annotation.**

Joos, Frederic. The Golden Snowflake. Joos, Francoise. (ps-3). 1991. 14.95 (*0-316-47328-6*) Little.
—Sorry, Miss Folio! Furtado, Jo. 32p. (ps-3). 1988. 10.95 (*0-916291-18-9*) Kane-Miller Bk.
—Sorry, Miss Folio! Furtado, Jo. (ps-3). 1992. pap. 6.95 (*0-916291-41-3*) Kane-Miller Bk.

Joos, Louis. Oregon's Journey. LC 93-11796. 40p. (gr. k-4). 1993. PLB 15.95 (*0-8167-3305-8*); pap. text ed. 3.95 (*0-8167-3306-6*) Troll Assocs.

Jordan, Debra. A Visit to the Eagles' Nest. Jordan, Tina. 20p. (gr. 3-5). 1980. PLB 2.25 (*0-938574-00-0*) Cherubim.

Jordan, Jael. My Grandmother's Stories: A Collection of Jewish Folk Tales. Geras, Adele. LC 90-4309. 96p. (gr. 3-7). 1990. 17.95 (*0-679-80910-4*); PLB 18.99 (*0-679-90910-9*) Knopf Bks Yng Read.

Jordan, Martin. Journey of the Red-Eyed Tree Frog. Jordan, Tanis. LC 91-29526. 40p. (ps-3). 1992. 16.00 (*0-671-76903-0*, Green Tiger) S&S Trade.

Jordan, Polly. All about Me. Rutman, Shereen G. 32p. (ps). 1992. wkbk. 1.95 (*1-56293-174-1*) McClanahan Bk.

—Follow Directions. Wise, Beth A. 32p. (ps). 1992. wkbk. 1.95 (*1-56293-169-5*) McClanahan Bk.

—In the Jungle. 24p. (ps-2). 1993. pap. text ed. 2.95 (*1-56293-320-5*) McClanahan Bk.

—In the Ocean. 24p. (ps-2). 1993. pap. text ed. 2.95 (*1-56293-319-1*) McClanahan Bk.

—One Hundred Birds & Ten Bugs. 10p. (ps-1). 1992. bds. 2.95 (*1-56293-253-5*) McClanahan Bk.

—One Hundred Cats & Ten Mice. 10p. (ps-1). 1992. bds. 2.95 (*1-56293-251-9*) McClanahan Bk.

—One Hundred Fish & Ten Worms. 10p. (ps-1). 1992. bds. 2.95 (*1-56293-254-3*) McClanahan Bk.

—One Hundred Frogs & Ten Flies. 10p. (ps-1). 1992. bds. 2.95 (*1-56293-252-7*) McClanahan Bk.

Jorfald, Ivind S. The Rebellious Alphabet. Diaz, Jorge. Fox, Geoffrey, tr. LC 93-12697. 32p. (gr. 7 up). 1993. PLB 14.95 (*0-8050-2765-3*, Bks Young Read) H Holt & Co.

Jorgensen, David. The Tailor of Gloucester. Potter, Beatrix. LC 88-11510. 44p. (ps up). 1991. pap. 14.95 (*0-88708-080-4*, Rabbit Ears); bk. & cass. pkg. 19.95 (*0-88708-085-5*, Rabbit Ears) Picture Bk Studio.

—The Tale of Mr. Jeremy Fisher. Potter, Beatrix. LC 88-34668. 32p. (ps up). 1991. pap. 14.95 (*0-88708-094-4*, Rabbit Ears); incl. cassette 19.95 (*0-88708-095-2*, Rabbit Ears) Picture Bk Studio.

—The Tale of Mr. Jeremy Fisher. Potter, Beatrix. LC 92-22584. 64p. 1992. Repr. of 1989 ed. 5.95 (*0-88708-253-X*, Rabbit Ears); Mini-bk. incl. cassette 9.95 (*0-88708-252-1*, Rabbit Ears) Picture Bk Studio.

—The Tale of Peter Rabbit. Potter, Beatrix. LC 88-11509. 36p. (ps up). 1991. 14.95 (*0-317-89758-6*, Rabbit Ears); bk. & cass. pkg. 19.95 (*0-88708-084-7*, Rabbit Ears) Picture Bk Studio.

—The Tale of Peter Rabbit. Potter, Beatrix. Streep, Meryl, read by. Mays, Lyle, contrib. by. 32p (ps up). 1992. pap. write for info. slipcase pkg., incl. cassette (*0-307-14328-7*, 14328, Golden Pr) Western Pub.

—The Tale of Peter Rabbit. Potter, Beatrix. LC 92-36655. 64p. 1993. Repr. of 1988 ed. 4.95 (*0-88708-296-3*, Rabbit Ears); incl. cassette 9.95 (*0-88708-297-1*) Picture Bk Studio.

—The Three Billy Goats Gruff. Roberts, Tom. LC 89-32138. 32p. (gr. 1 up). 1991. pap. 14.95 (*0-88708-117-7*, Rabbit Ears); incl. cassette 19.95 (*0-88708-118-5*, Rabbit Ears) Picture Bk Studio.

—The Three Billy Goats Gruff. Roberts, Tom & Hunter, Holly, eds. Lande, Art, contrib. by. 32p. (ps up). 1993. pap. write for info. slipcase pkg., incl. cassette (*0-307-14329-5*, 14329, Golden Pr) Western Pub.

—The Three Billy Goats Gruff. minibook ed. Roberts, Tom. LC 93-6678. (ps-6). 1993. 9.95 (*0-88708-319-6*, Dist. by S&S Trade) Picture Bk Studio.

—The Three Little Pigs. Roberts, Tom. LC 89-70097. 32p. (ps up). 1991. pap. 14.95 (*0-88708-132-0*, Rabbit Ears); pap. 19.95 incl. cass. (*0-88708-133-9*, Rabbit Ears) Picture Bk Studio.

—The Three Little Pigs. Roberts, Tom & Hunter, Holly, eds. Lande, Art, contrib. by. 32p. (ps up). 1993. pap. write for info. (*0-307-14327-9*, 14327, Golden Pr) Western Pub.

—The Three Little Pigs. Roberts, Tom. 64p. 1993. Repr. of 1990 ed. incl. cass. 9.95 (*0-88708-299-8*, Rabbit Ears) Picture Bk Studio.

—The Three Little Pigs. Roberts, Tom, adapted by. LC 92-36277. 1993. 4.95 (*0-88708-298-X*, Rabbit Ears) Picture Bk Studio.

—The Velveteen Rabbit. Williams, Margery. 48p. (ps up). 1985. with cassette 15.95 (*0-394-87712-8*); 11.95 (*0-394-87711-X*) Knopf Bks Yng Read.

—The Velveteen Rabbit. Williams, Margery. LC 85-4257. 48p. (ps-2). 1990. pap. 3.95 (*0-679-80333-5*) Knopf Bks Yng Read.

—The Velveteen Rabbit: A Board Book. Williams, Margery. LC 89-63161. 10p. (ps). 1990. bds. 3.95 (*0-679-80644-X*) Random Bks Yng Read.

Jorgenson, Anders. The Experiment. Myers, Bill. 160p. (Orig.). (gr. 3 up). 1991. pap. 5.99 (*1-55661-214-1*) Bethany Hse.

—The Portal. Myers, Bill. 160p. (Orig.). (gr. 3 up). 1991. pap. 5.99 (*1-55661-163-3*) Bethany Hse.

—The Tablet. Myers, Bill. LC 92-34301. 160p. (Orig.). (gr. 3 up). 1992. pap. 5.99 (*1-55661-299-0*) Bethany Hse.

Joshi, Jagadish. Sonali's Friend. Shankar, Alaka. 16p. (Orig.). (gr. k-3). 1980. pap. 2.50 (*0-89744-218-0*, Pub. by Childrens Bk Trust IA) Auromere.

Joshi, Jagdish. King Kamel. Ramakrishnan, Prema. 24p. (Orig.). (gr. k-3). 1980. pap. 2.50 (*0-89744-210-5*, Pub. by Childrens Bk Trust IA) Auromere.

Jossem, Carol. Keaka & the Liliko'i Vine. Laird, Donivee M. LC 82-72452. 42p. (gr. k-3). 1982. 7.95x (*0-940350-10-6*) Barnaby Bks.

—The Three Little Hawaiian Pigs & the Magic Shark. Laird, Donivee. LC 81-67047. 40p. (ps-3). 1981. 7.95x (*0-940350-19-X*) Barnaby Bks.

—Will Wai Kula & the Three Mongooses. Laird, Donivee M. LC 83-8805. 44p. (gr. k-3). 1983. 7.95x (*0-940350-13-0*) Barnaby Bks.

Jouannigot, Loic. Beechwood Bunny Tales Series. Huriet, Genevieve. (gr. k-2). 1991. Set. PLB 120.89 (*0-8368-0524-0*) Gareth Stevens Inc.

—Dandelion's Vanishing Vegetable Garden. Huriet, Genevieve. LC 90-4857. 32p. (gr. k-2). 1991. lib. bdg. 17.27 (*0-8368-0526-7*) Gareth Stevens Inc.

—Mistletoe & the Baobab Tree. Huriet, Genevieve. LC 90-4856. 32p. (gr. k-2). 1991. PLB 17.27 (*0-8368-0525-9*) Gareth Stevens Inc.

—Perriwinkle at the Full Moon Ball. Huriet, Genevieve. LC 90-4859. 32p. (gr. k-2). 1991. lib. bdg. 17.27 (*0-8368-0527-5*) Gareth Stevens Inc.

—Poppy's Dance. Huriet, Genevieve. LC 90-4858. 32p. (gr. k-2). 1991. PLB 17.27 (*0-8368-0528-3*) Gareth Stevens Inc.

Joudrey, Ken. Trees. Pine, Jonathan. LC 93-3136. 1994. 13.00 (*0-06-021468-6*); PLB 12.89 (*0-06-021469-4*) HarpC Child Bks.

Jouve, Paul. Reader's Digest Best Loved Books for Young Readers: The Jungle Books. Kipling, Rudyard. Ogburn, Jackie, ed. 160p. (gr. 4-12). 1989. 3.99 (*0-945260-26-1*) Choice Pub NY.

Joy, Carol. B. J. & the Language of the Woodland. Deibert, Alvin N. LC 82-24422. 48p. (Orig.). (gr. 2-6). 1983. pap. 7.50 (*0-87743-701-7*, 353-019, Pub. by Bellwood Pr) Bahai.

Joyce, William. Bently & Egg. Joyce, William. LC 91-55499. 32p. (ps-3). 1992. 15.00 (*0-06-020385-4*); PLB 14.89 (*0-06-020386-2*) HarpC Child Bks.

—A Day with Wilbur Robixson. Joyce, William. LC 90-4066. 32p. (ps-3). 1993. pap. 5.95 (*0-06-443339-0*, Trophy) HarpC Child Bks.

—A Day with Wilbur Robinson. Joyce, William. LC 90-4066. 32p. (ps-3). 1990. 13.95 (*0-06-022967-5*); PLB 14.89 (*0-06-022968-3*) HarpC Child Bks.

—Dinosaur Bob: And His Adventures with the Family Lazardo. Joyce, William. LC 87-30796. 32p. (ps-3). 1988. 15.00 (*0-06-023047-9*); PLB 14.89 (*0-06-023048-7*) HarpC Child Bks.

—George Shrinks. Joyce, William. LC 83-47697. 32p. (ps-2). 1985. 14.00 (*0-06-023070-3*); PLB 13.89 (*0-06-023071-1*) HarpC Child Bks.

—George Shrinks. Joyce, William. LC 83-47697. 32p. (ps-2). 1987. pap. 3.95 (*0-06-443129-0*, Trophy) HarpC Child Bks.

—George Shrinks. miniature ed. Joyce, William. LC 90-46285. 32p. (ps-2). 1991. 3.95 (*0-06-023299-4*) HarpC Child Bks.

—Humphrey's Bear. Wahl, Jan. LC 85-5541. 32p. (ps-2). 1987. 13.95 (*0-8050-0332-0*, Bks Young Read) H Holt & Co.

—Humphrey's Bear. Wahl, Jan. LC 85-5541. 32p. (ps-2). 1989. pap. 5.95 (*0-8050-1169-2*, Bks Young Read) H Holt & Co.

—My First Book of Nursery Tales: Five Favorite Bedtime Tales. reissue ed. Mayer, Marianna. Mayer, Marianna, retold by. LC 82-20452. 48p. (ps-1). 1992. text ed. 10.00 (*0-394-85396-2*) Random Bks Yng Read.

—Nicholas Cricket. Maxner, Joyce. LC 88-33076. 32p. (gr. k-3). 1989. 14.00 (*0-06-024216-7*); PLB 13.89 (*0-06-024222-1*) HarpC Child Bks.

—Nicholas Cricket. Maxner, Joyce. LC 88-33076. 28p. (gr. k-3). 1991. pap. 4.95 (*0-06-443275-0*, Trophy) HarpC Child Bks.

—Santa Calls. Joyce, William. LC 92-52691. 40p. (ps up). 1993. 18.00 (*0-06-021133-4*); PLB 17.89 (*0-06-021134-2*); ltd. ed. 125.00 (*0-06-023355-9*) HarpC Child Bks.

—Shoes. Winthrop, Elizabeth. LC 85-45841. 32p. (ps-2). 1986. 14.00 (*0-06-026591-4*); PLB 13.89 (*0-06-026592-2*) HarpC Child Bks.

—Shoes. Winthrop, Elizabeth. LC 85-45841. 32p. (ps-3). 1988. pap. 4.95 (*0-06-443171-1*, Trophy) HarpC Child Bks.

—Shoes. Winthrop, Elizabeth. (ps-1). 1988. bk. & cassette 19.95 (*0-87499-113-7*); bk. & cassette 12.95 (*0-87499-112-9*); 4 cassettes & guide 27.95 (*0-87499-114-5*) Live Oak Media.

—Shoes Big Book. Winthrop, Elizabeth. LC 85-45841. 24p. (ps-3). 1993. pap. 19.95 (*0-06-443320-X*, Trophy) HarpC Child Bks.

—Some of the Adventures of Rhode Island Red. Manes, Stephen. LC 89-35397. 128p. (gr. 3-7). 1990. (Lipp Jr Bks); PLB 10.89 (*0-397-32348-4*, Lipp Jr Bks) HarpC Child Bks.

—Some of the Adventures of Rhode Island Red. Manes, Stephen. LC 89-35397. 128p. (gr. 3-7). 1993. pap. 3.95 (*0-06-440358-0*, Trophy) HarpC Child Bks.

—Tammy & the Gigantic Fish. Gray, Catherine & Gray, James. LC 82-47732. 32p. (ps-1). 1991. pap. 3.95 (*0-06-443263-7*, Trophy) HarpC Child Bks.

—Waiting-for-Spring Stories. Roberts, Bethany. LC 83-49486. 32p. (ps-3). 1984. PLB 14.89 (*0-06-025062-3*) HarpC Child Bks.

Joyner, Jerry. My First Cookbook. Coyle, Rena. LC 84-40683. 128p. (Orig.). (gr. 1-5). 1985. pap. 8.95 (*0-89480-846-X*, 846) Workman Pub.

—My First Gamebook. Dobbs, Katy. LC 85-40524. (ps-2). 1986. 6 bds. 5.95 (*0-89480-945-8*, 945) Workman Pub.

Joysmith, Brenda. From a Child's Heart. Grimes, Nikki. LC 93-79000. 32p. (gr. 2-6). 1993. 15.95 (*0-940975-44-0*); pap. 7.95 (*0-940975-43-2*) Just Us Bks.

Joysmith, Brenda, jt. illus. see Honeywood, Varnette P.

Judice, Van. T-Boy the Little Cajun. Edler, Timothy J. 36p. (gr. k-8). 1978. pap. 6.00 (*0-931108-01-2*) Little Cajun Bks.

Judkis, Jim. Going to the Doctor. Rogers, Fred. 32p. (ps-2). 1986. 12.95 (*0-399-21298-1*, Putnam) (Putnam) Putnam Pub Group.

—Going to the Potty. Rogers, Fred. 32p. (ps-2). 1986. 14.95 (*0-399-21296-5*, Putnam); pap. 5.95 (*0-399-21297-3*, Putnam) Putnam Pub Group.

Judkis, Jim, photos by. Going to the Dentist. Rogers, Fred. 32p. (Orig.). (ps-2). 1989. (Putnam); pap. 5.95 (*0-399-21634-0*, Putnam) Putnam Pub Group.

—Going to the Hospital. Rogers, Fred. 32p. (ps-4). 1988. 14.95 (*0-399-21503-4*, Putnam); pap. 5.95 (*0-399-21530-1*, Putnam) Putnam Pub Group.

—Making Friends. Rogers, Fred. (ps-1). 1987. 12.95 (*0-399-21382-1*, Putnam); pap. 5.95 (*0-399-21385-6*, Putnam) Putnam Pub Group.

—The New Baby. Rogers, Fred. LC 84-26210. 32p. (gr. k-2). 1985. 12.95 (*0-399-21236-1*, Putnam); pap. 5.95 (*0-399-21238-8*, Putnam) Putnam Pub Group.

—When a Pet Dies. Rogers, Fred. 32p. (ps-4). 1988. (Putnam); pap. 5.95 (*0-399-21529-8*, Putnam) Putnam Pub Group.

Judson, Thomas. Color Me Cleveland: A Cleveland Coloring Book. Johnston, Christopher, text by. 32p. 1993. pap. 4.95 (*0-9631738-2-0*) Gray & Co Pubs.

Judy, Ann F. Wros-tonne & Other Stories of Science Fantasy. Schuller, Mary Ann. LC 87-90482. 134p. (Orig.). (gr. 3-8). 1987. pap. 4.95 (*0-9617889-0-9*) Sweet Koala Pr.

Juffman, Tom. Vitamins - What They Are, What They Do. Seixas, Judith S. LC 85-17761. 56p. (gr. 1-4). 1986. 12.95 (*0-688-06065-X*); PLB 12.93 (*0-688-06066-8*) Greenwillow.

Ju-Hong Chen. The Fourth Question: A Chinese Folktale. Wang, Rosalind C., retold by. LC 90-43536. 32p. (ps-3). 1991. reinforced 14.95 (*0-8234-0855-8*) Holiday.

—A Song of Stars. Birdseye, Tom. LC 89-20066. 32p. (gr. 4-8). 1990. reinforced bdg. 14.95 (*0-8234-0790-X*) Holiday.

Julian-Ottie, Vanessa. The Caravan Puppets. Bond, Michael. LC 85-109047. 130p.(gr. 3 up). 1983. write for info. (*0-00-184135-1*) Harper SF.

—Fuzzy Rabbit Saves Christmas. Billam, Rosemary. LC 89-77934. 32p. (Orig.). (ps-3). 1991. pap. 2.25 (*0-679-80460-9*) Random Bks Yng Read.

—Go Away, Bad Dreams. Hill, Susan. Lerner, Sharon, ed. LC 84-17759. 32p. (ps-2). 1985. pap. 2.25 (*0-394-87222-3*) Random Bks Yng Read.

—More Stories for Under-Fives. Corrin, Sara & Corrin, Stephen, eds. 116p. (ps). 1990. pap. 9.95 (*0-571-12921-8*) Faber & Faber.

—Patrick in Person. Clarke, Norman. 130p. (gr. 3 up). 1992. bds. 16.95 laminated (*0-571-16225-8*) Faber & Faber.

—Whiskers & Paws. Waters, Fiona, ed. LC 89-77349. 32p. 1990. 9.95 (*0-940793-51-2*, Pub. by Crocodile Bks) Interlink Pub.

Julien, Claudia. The Magic of Johnny Readingseed. Bloom, Daniel H. 48p. (gr. 5-9). 1990. 9.95 (*0-944007-60-0*) Shapolsky Pubs.

Julien, Terry. Uncle Alphonso & the Frosty, Fibbing Dinosaurs. Pearson, Jack. LC 92-39373. 1993. write for info. (*0-7814-0100-3*, Chariot Bks) Cook.

Junco, Janet H. My Brother's a World-Class Pain: A Sibling's Guide to ADHD-Hyperactivity. Gordon, Michael. Thomas, Sandra F., intro. by. 40p. (gr. 4 up). 1992. pap. 11.00 (*0-9627701-2-4*) GSI Pubns.

Jung, Mary. Candle, a Story of Love & Faith. Smith, Sally Ann. Luther, Luana, ed. LC 91-72745. 32p. (gr. 3-6). 1991. pap. 9.95 (*0-944875-22-X*) Doral Pub.

Jung, Tom, photos by. Base Ten Mathematics. Laycock, Mary. Moray, Joe, intro. by. (gr. 1-9). 1976. pap. 7.95 (*0-918932-03-3*) Activity Resources.

Junkasem, Rochana. Scientists Around the World. DeBruin, Jerry. 160p. (gr. 4-12). 1987. pap. 12.95 (*0-86653-416-4*, GA1005) Good Apple.

Jurgens, Steve. Trek for Trivia. Minn, Loretta B. 48p. (gr. 3-8). 1985. wkbk. 6.95 (*0-86653-291-9*, GA 646) Good Apple.

Justice, Bill, jt. illus. see Dempster, Al.

K

Kabel Pub Staff. Fairy Tales from Czechoslovakia, Vol. I. Nemcova, B. Velinsky, L., tr. Absolon, Karel B., intro. by. (CZE.). 305p. (Orig.). (gr. 4 up). 1987. pap. 39.50 (*0-685-19314-4*) KABEL Pubs.

Kaetler, Sarah. More Stories from Grandpa's Rocking Chair. Kaetler, Sarah. 73p. (gr. 3-6). 1991. pap. 4.95 (*0-919797-75-X*) Kindred Pr.

Kaghan, Joan. Beaver Ball at the Bug Club. Craver, Mike. 32p. (ps-3). 1992. bds. 12.00 (*0-374-30662-1*) FS&G.

Kahalewai, Marilyn. Hawaiian Myths of Earth, Sea, & Sky. Thompson, Vivian L. LC 88-1325. 88p. (gr. 3-8). 1988. pap. 8.50 (0-8248-1171-2, Kolowalu Bk) UH Pr.
—Whose Slippers Are Those? Kahalewai, Marilyn. LC 87-92272. 16p. (ps-6). 1988. 7.95 (0-935848-58-4) Bess Pr.
Kahalewai, Marilyn & Poepoe, Karen. Too Many Curls. Kahalewai, Marilyn & Poepoe, Karen. LC 89-82131. 16p. (ps-2). 1992. 12.95 (0-935848-83-5); pap. 5.95 (1-880188-20-1) Bess Pr.
Kahla, Robert. Mr. X from Planet X: And Other Animules. Kahla, Robert. 64p. Date not set. pap. 8.95 (1-882820-00-2) Cracked Egg.
Kahler, Carole. Sea Life at the Ocean's Edge. Corbett, Julia. Warren, Hank & Moore, Shirley, eds. 24p. (gr. 4-6). 1984. pap. text ed. 3.95 (0-685-34734-6) NW Interpretive.
Kahn, Jonathan. Patulous: The Prairie Rattlesnake. Kahn, Jonathan. Thatch, Nancy R., ed. Melton, David, intro. by. LC 91-13652. 26p. (gr. k-4). 1991. PLB 14.95 (0-933849-36-2) Landmark Edns.
Kahn, Katherine. Introduction to Jewish History. Rossel, Seymour. Kozodoy, Neil, ed. 128p. (gr. 4-5). 1981. pap. text ed. 6.95 (0-87441-335-4); By Lenore C. Kipper. tchr's guide 12.50x (0-87441-378-8); Malkah L. Avrami. student's activity bk. 4.25 (0-87441-363-X) Behrman.
—Our Holidays. Schlein, Miriam. 128p. (gr. k-3). 1983. pap. text ed. 7.95x (0-87441-382-6) Behrman.
—The Shofar Calls to Us. LC 91-60592. 12p. (ps). 1991. bds. 4.95 (0-929371-61-5) Kar Ben.
—The Whole Megillah. Silberman, Shoshana. LC 90-5137. 40p. (gr. k-6). 1991. pap. 3.95 (0-929371-23-2) Kar Ben.
Kahn, Katherine J. Alef Is One: A Hebrew Alphabet & Counting Book. Kahn, Katherine J. LC 89-24428. 48p. (ps-4). 1989. 12.95 (0-929371-05-4); pap. 7.95 (0-929371-04-6) Kar Ben.
—Hanukkah Fun: For Little Hands. Groner, Judye & Wikler, Madeline. 32p. (ps-2). 1992. pap. 3.95 (0-929371-62-3) Kar Ben.
—Israel Is... Topek, Susan R. LC 88-83569. 12p. (ps). 1989. bds. 4.95 (0-930494-92-X) Kar Ben.
—It's Rosh-Hashanah. Gellman, Ellie. LC 85-80783. 12p. (ps). 1985. bds. 4.95 (0-930494-50-4) Kar Ben.
—Judah Who Always Said, "No!" Feder, Harriet K. LC 90-4854. 32p. (gr. k-3). 1990. 12.95 (0-929371-13-5); pap. 4.95 (0-929371-14-3) Kar Ben.
—Let's Build a Sukkah. Groner, Judyth & Wikler, Madeine. LC 86-81717. 12p. (ps). 1986. bds. 4.95 (0-930494-58-X) Kar Ben.
—The Magic Faucet. Lev, M. LC 90-85473. 32p. (gr. 1-3). 1991. 12.95 (1-877-65604-6) Antroll Pub.
—The Odd Potato. Sherman, Eileen B. LC 84-17186. 32p. (gr. k-5). 1984. pap. 4.95 (0-930494-37-7) Kar-Ben.
—Passover Fun: For Little Hands. Kahn, Katherine J. 32p. (ps-2). 1991. wkbk. 3.95 (0-929371-56-9) Kar Ben.
—The Passover Parrot. Zusman, Evelyn. LC 83-22182. 40p. (ps-3). 1984. pap. 4.95 (0-930494-30-X) Kar Ben.
—The Purim Parade. Saypol, Judyth R. & Wikler, Madeline. LC 86-71816. 12p. (ps). 1986. bds. 4.95 (0-930494-60-1) Kar Ben.
—Rainbow Candles: A Chanukah Counting Book. Shostak, Myra. LC 86-81718. 12p. (ps). 1986. bds. 4.95 (0-930494-59-8) Kar Ben.
—Rosh Hashanah - A Family Service. Abrams, Judith Z. LC 90-4855. 32p. (Orig.). (ps-4). 1990. pap. 3.95 (0-929371-16-X) Kar Ben.
—A Rosh Hashanah Walk. Levin, Carol. LC 87-3106. (ps-3). 1987. 4.95 (0-930494-70-9) Kar Ben.
—Sammy Spider's First Hanukkah. Rouss, Sylvia A. LC 92-39639. 1993. 13.95 (0-929371-45-3); pap. 5.95 (0-929371-46-1) Kar Ben.
—Selichot - A Family Service. Abrams, Judith Z. LC 90-4863. 24p. (ps-4). 1990. pap. 3.95 (0-929371-15-1) Kar Ben.
—Shabbat: A Family Service. Abrams, Judith Z. LC 91-31640. 24p. (Orig.). (gr. k-3). 1992. pap. text ed. 3.95 (0-929371-29-1) Kar Ben.
—Sukkot: A Family Seder. Abrams, Judith. 24p. (ps-6). 1993. pap. 3.95 (0-929371-75-5) Kar Ben.
—Tamar's Sukkah. Gellman, Ellie. LC 88-23388. 32p. (ps-2). 1988. pap. 4.95 (0-930494-79-2) Kar Ben.
—Yom Kippur - A Family Service. Abrams, Judith Z. LC 90-4862. 22p. (Orig.). (ps-4). 1990. pap. 3.95 (0-929371-17-8) Kar Ben.
Kahn, Katherine J., photos by. Dayenu - Enough! How Uncle Murray Saved the Seder. Schilder, Rosalind. LC 88-1238. (Orig.). (ps-3). 1988. pap. 4.95 (0-930494-76-8) Kar Ben.
Kahn, Katherine Janus. Jewish Holiday Crafts for Little Hands. Brinn, Ruth Esrig. LC 92-39638. (gr. k up). 1993. pap. 10.95 (0-929371-47-X) Kar Ben.
Kahoun, Cindy. The Woodland Gang & the Ghost Cat. Schultz, Irene. 128p. (gr. 3 up). 1988. pap. 4.95 (0-201-50054-X) Addison-Wesley.
—The Woodland Gang & the Indian Cave. Schultz, Irene. 128p. (gr. 3 up). 1988. pap. 4.95 (0-201-50055-8) Addison-Wesley.
—The Woodland Gang & the Museum Robbery. Schultz, Irene. 128p. (Orig.). (gr. 3 up). 1988. pap. 4.95 (0-201-50053-1) Addison-Wesley.
—The Woodland Gang & the Mystery Quilt. Schultz, Irene. 128p. (gr. 3 up). 1988. pap. 4.95 (0-201-50051-5) Addison-Wesley.

Kaicher, Sally & Dolan, Tom. Pond Life. Reid, George K. Zim, Herbert S., ed. (gr. 7 up). 1967. pap. write for info. (0-307-24017-7, Golden Pr) Western Pub.
Kaila, Kaarina. Thumbelina. abr. ed. Andersen, Hans Christian. Hautzig, Deborah, adapted by. Collins, Judy, contrib. by. 32p. (ps-5). 1990. Incl. 30 min. cassette. slipcased 15.95 (0-679-80810-8) Knopf Bks Yng Read.
—Thumbelina. abr. ed. Andersen, Hans Christian. Hautzig, Deborah, adapted by. LC 89-29700. 32p. (ps-3). 1990. PLB 10.99 (0-679-90667-3) Knopf Bks Yng Read.
—The Wild Swans. Andersen, Hans Christian. Hautzig, Deborah, adapted by. LC 91-47879. 32p. (gr. k-3). 1992. 12.00 (0-679-83446-X); PLB 12.99 (0-679-93446-4) Knopf Bks Yng Read.
Kaiulani. Children's Hulas from Hawaii, Bk. 5. Roes, Carol. 13p. (gr. 8). 1966. pap. 5.50 (0-930932-10-2); record incl. M Loke.
Kaizuki, Kiyonori. A Calf Is Born. Kaizuki, Kiyonori. Hirano, Cathy, tr. LC 89-23091. (JPN.). 40p. (ps-2). 1990. 13.95 (0-531-05862-X); PLB 13.99 (0-531-08462-0) Orchard Bks Watts.
Kakkak, Dale, photos by. Ininatig's Gift of Sugar: Traditional Native Sugarmaking. Wittstock, Laura W. Dorris, Michael, frwd. by. LC 92-37980. 1993. 19.95 (0-8225-2653-0) Lerner Pubns.
—The Sacred Harvest: Ojibway Wild Rice Gathering. Regguinti, Gordon. 48p. (gr. 3-6). 1992. PLB 19.95 (0-8225-2650-6) Lerner Pubns.
Kalas, Sybille. The Wild Horse Family Book. Kalas, Sybille. Crampton, Patricia, tr. LC 89-3929. (ps up). 1991. pap. 15.95 (0-88708-110-X) Picture Bk Studio.
Kalina, Amy. Falasha No More: An Ethiopian Jewish Child Comes Home. Kushner, Arlene. 58p. (gr. 1-5). 1986. 9.95 (0-933503-43-1) Shapolsky Pubs.
Kalish, Lionel. Count the Days of Hanukkah. Herman, Gail. LC 92-30914. 16p. (ps-3). 1993. 3.95 (0-590-47081-7, Cartwheel) Scholastic Inc.
—Magic...Naturally: Science Entertainments & Amusements. new ed. Cobb, Vicki. LC 90-21829. 160p. (gr. 4 up). 1993. pap. 4.95 (0-06-446031-2, Trophy) HarpC Child Bks.
—Magic...Naturally! Science Entertainments & Amusements. Cobb, Vicki. LC 90-21829. 160p. (gr. 4 up). 1993. 15.00 (0-06-022474-6); PLB 14.89 (0-06-022475-4) HarpC Child Bks.
—When Daddy Had the Chicken Pox. Ziefert, Harriet. LC 90-43559. 32p. (ps-3). 1991. PLB 13.89 (0-06-026907-3) HarpC Child Bks.
Kalish, Lionel & Weissman, Bari. Trick-or-Treat Books, 4 vol. set. Doyle, Tara. 16p. (ps-1). 1993. pap. 2.75 (0-590-66583-9, Cartwheel) Scholastic Inc.
Kalman, Maira. Chicken Soup, Boots. Kalman, Maira. 40p. 1993. reinforced bdg. 14.99 (0-670-85201-5) Viking Child Bks.
—Max in Hollywood, Baby. Kalman, Maira. 32p. 1992. 15.00 (0-670-84479-9) Viking Child Bks.
—Sayonara, Mrs. Kackleman. Kalman, Maira. 40p. (ps-5). 1989. pap. 14.95 (0-670-82945-5) Viking Child Bks.
—Stay up Late. Byrne, David. LC 87-10399. (ps up). 1987. pap. 14.95 (0-670-81895-X) Viking Child Bks.
Kalmenoff, Matthew. How Did We Find Out About Electricity? Asimov, Isaac. Selsam, Millicent E., ed. LC 72-81380. 64p. (gr. 5-8). 1973. PLB 10.85 (0-8027-6124-0) Walker & Co.
—How Did We Find Out the Earth Is Round? Asimov, Isaac. Selsam, Millicent E., ed. LC 72-81378. 64p. (gr. 5-8). 1972. PLB 5.85 (0-8027-6122-4) Walker & Co.
Kalow, Gisela. The Wonderful Bedmobile. Broger, Achim. 28p. (ps-2). 1991. smythe sewn reinforced bdg. 9.95 (1-56182-033-4) Atomium Bks.
Kalthoff, Sandra C. All My Toys Are on the Floor. Blocksma, Mary. LC 85-27000. 24p. (ps-2). 1986. PLB 12.33 (0-516-01579-6); pap. 3.95 (0-516-41579-4) Childrens.
—Apple Tree! Apple Tree! Blocksma, Mary. LC 82-19852. 24p. (ps-2). 1983. PLB 12.33 (0-516-01584-2); pap. 3.95 (0-516-41584-0) Childrens.
—Baby Koala Finds a Home. Tripp, Valerie. LC 87-6325. 24p. (ps-2). 1987. pap. 3.95 (0-516-41577-8) Childrens.
—The Best-Dressed Bear. Blocksma, Mary. LC 84-9565. 24p. (ps-2). 1984. lib. bdg. 12.33 (0-516-01585-0); pap. text ed. 3.95 (0-516-41585-9) Childrens.
—Chirrinchinchina Que Hay en la Tina? Kratky, Lada J. (SPA.). 24p. (Orig.). (gr. k-3). 1989. pap. text ed. 29. 95 big bk. (0-917837-11-8) Hampton-Brown.
—Chirrinchinchina Que Hay en la Tina? Kratky, Lada J. (SPA.). 24p. (Orig.). (gr. k-3). 1989. pap. text ed. 6.00 small bk. (0-917837-13-4) Hampton-Brown.
—Chirrinchinchina Que Hay en la Tina? Kratky, Lada J. (SPA.). 24p. (Orig.). (gr. k-3). 1989. Six-Pack Set. pap. text ed. 36.00 (0-917837-44-4) Hampton-Brown.
—Grandma Dragon's Birthday. Blocksma, Mary. LC 82-19851. 24p. (ps-2). 1983. pap. 3.95 (0-516-41582-4) Childrens.
—Manzano, Manzano! Ada, Alma F. 24p. (Orig.). (gr. k-3). 1989. Six-Pack Set. pap. text ed. 36.00 (0-917837-46-0) Hampton-Brown.
—Manzano, Manzano! (Big Book) Ada, Alma F. (SPA.). 24p. (Orig.). (gr. k-3). 1989. pap. text ed. 29.95 (0-917837-09-6) Hampton-Brown.
—El Oso Mas Elegante. Ada, Alma F. 24p. (Orig.). (gr. k-3). 1989. Six-Pack Set. pap. text ed. 36.00 (0-917837-43-6) Hampton-Brown.

—El Oso Mas Elegante (Big Book) Ada, Alma F. (SPA.). 24p. (Orig.). (gr. k-3). 1989. pap. text ed. 29.95 (0-917837-10-X) Hampton-Brown.
—Pequeno Coala Busca Casa. Kratky, Lada J. (SPA.). 24p. (Orig.). (gr. k-3). 1989. pap. text ed. 6.00 (0-917837-14-2) Hampton-Brown.
—Pequeno Coala Busca Casa. Kratky, Lada J. (SPA.). 24p. (Orig.). (gr. k-3). 1989. Six-Pack Set. pap. text ed. 36.00 (0-917837-45-2) Hampton-Brown.
—Pequeno Coala Busca Casa (Baby Koala Finds a Home) Tripp, Valerie. LC 87-6325. (SPA & ENG.). 24p. (ps-2). 1989. PLB 12.33 (0-516-31577-3); pap. 3.95 (0-516-51577-2); pap. 30.60 big bk. (0-516-59515-6) Childrens.
—Pequeno Coala Busca Casa (Big Book) Kratky, Lada J. (SPA.). 24p. (Orig.). (gr. k-3). 1989. pap. text ed. 29. 95 (0-917837-12-6) Hampton-Brown.
—The Pup Went Up. Blocksma, Mary. LC 82-19862. 24p. (ps-2). 1983. PLB 12.33 (0-516-01583-4) Childrens.
—Rub-a-Dub-Dub - What's in the Tub? Blocksma, Mary. LC 84-12139. 24p. (ps-2). 1984. lib. bdg. 12.33 (0-516-01586-9); pap. 3.95 (0-516-41586-7) Childrens.
—Todos Mis Juquetes (All My Toys Are on the Floor) Blocksma, Mary. LC 85-27000. (SPA.). 24p. (ps-2). 1989. pap. 3.95 (0-516-51579-9) Childrens.
Kaluza, Mary K. & Carreiro, Bob. Marty the Marathon Bear. Wood, Bill. Kauffman, Helen, photos by. 136p. (Orig.). (gr. 3-7). 1988. pap. text ed. 6.95 (0-317-93376-0) Rallysport Video Prodns.
Kamen, Gloria. Charlie Chaplin. Kamen, Gloria. LC 82-1674. 96p. (gr. 2-6). 1982. SBE 13.95 (0-689-30925-2, Atheneum Child Bk) Macmillan Child Grp.
—Lisa & Her Soundless World. Levine, Edna S. (gr. 1-5). 1984. 14.95 (0-87705-104-6); pap. 9.95 (0-89885-204-8) Human Sci Pr.
—Paddle, Said the Swan. Kamen, Gloria. LC 88-16749. 32p. (ps-1). 1989. SBE 13.95 (0-689-31330-6, Atheneum Child Bk) Macmillan Child Grp.
—The Ringdoves: From the Fables of Bidpai. Kamen, Gloria. LC 87-17404. 32p. (gr. k-3). 1988. SBE 13.95 (0-689-31312-8, Atheneum Child Bk) Macmillan Child Grp.
—Second-Hand Cat. Kamen, Gloria. LC 91-250. 32p. (gr. k-3). 1992. SBE 13.95 (0-689-31631-3, Atheneum Child Bk) Macmillan Child Grp.
—Siggy's Spaghetti Works. Thomson, Peggy. LC 92-13186. 32p. (gr. 1 up). 1993. 14.00 (0-688-11373-7, Tambourine Bks); PLB 13.93 (0-688-11374-5, Tambourine Bks) Morrow.
Kamiya, Artie, jt. illus. see Gimlin, Rick.
Kamstra, Angela. Teach Me More German. Mahoney, Judy. (GER.). 20p. (ps-6). 1990. pap. 13.95 incl. audiocassette (0-934633-23-1); tchr's ed. 6.95 (0-934633-34-7) Teach Me.
—Teach Me More Japanese. Mahoney, Judy. Satoh, Naomi, tr. (JPN.). 20p. (ps-6). 1991. pap. 13.95 incl. audiocassette (0-934633-20-7); tchr's ed. 6.95 (0-934633-36-3) Teach Me.
Kandell, Alice. Ben's ABC Day. Berger, Terry. LC 81-13754. 32p. (gr. k-3). 1982. PLB 14.88 (0-688-00882-8) Lothrop.
Kandoian, Ellen. Molly's Seasons. Kandoian, Ellen. LC 91-8039. 32p. (ps-3). 1992. 13.00 (0-525-65076-8, Cobblehill Bks) Dutton Child Bks.
—Rainy Day Rhymes. Radley, Gail, selected by. 48p. (gr. 2-5). 1992. 13.45 (0-395-59967-9) HM.
Kane, Bob, et al. Batman: The Sunday Classics. Finger, Bill & Schwartz, Alvin. Kitchen, Dennis, ed. Schwartz, Alvin, intro. by. 208p. (Orig.). 1991. pap. 19.95 (0-930289-95-1) DC Comics.
Kane, Harry. Alfred Hitchcock & the Three Investigators in the Mystery of the Talking Skull. Arthur, Robert. Hitchcock, Alfred, ed. LC 69-20274. (gr. 4-7). 1984. pap. 3.95 (0-394-86411-5) Random Bks Yng Read.
—Alfred Hitchcock & the Three Investigators in the Mystery of the Vanishing Treasure. Arthur, Robert. Hitchcock, Alfred, ed. (gr. 4-8). 1985. lib. bdg. 6.99 (0-394-91550-X); pap. 3.95 (0-394-86405-0) Random Bks Yng Read.
—Alfred Hitchcock & the Three Investigators in the Mystery of the Fiery Eye. Arthur, Robert. LC 77-28860. (gr. 4-8). 1984. pap. 3.95 (0-394-86407-7) Random Bks Yng Read.
—Alfred Hitchcock & the Three Investigators in the Mystery of the Silver Spider. Arthur, Robert. (gr. 4-8). 1985. pap. 2.95 (0-394-86408-5) Random Bks Yng Read.
—Alfred Hitchcock & the Three Investigators in the Secret of Skeleton Island. Arthur, Robert. Hitchcock, Alfred, ed. (gr. 4-9). 1985. pap. 3.95 (0-394-86406-9) Random Bks Yng Read.
Kane, Henry B. For Me to Say. McCord, David. (gr. 5 up). 1970. 12.95 (0-316-55511-8) Little.
—One at a Time. McCord, David. (gr. 4 up). 1986. 18.95 (0-316-55516-9) Little.
—Take Sky. McCord, David. (gr. 4 up). 1962. 12.95 (0-316-55509-6) Little.
Kang, Mi-Sun. The Lazy Man. Vorhees, Duance & Mueller, Mark. 46p. (gr. 2-5). 1991. PLB 9.95x (0-930878-73-6) Hollym Intl.
—The Snail Lady: The Magic Vase. Vorhees, Duance & Mueller, Mark. 46p. (gr. 2-5). 1990. PLB 9.95x (0-930878-89-2) Hollym Intl.
Kang, Mi-Sun & Kim, Yon-Kyong. The Faithful Daughter Shim Ch'ong: The Little Frog Who Never Listened. Vorhees, Duance & Mueller, Mark. 46p. (gr. 2-5). 1990. PLB 9.95x (0-930878-92-2) Hollym Intl.

Kang, Mi-Sun & Kim, Yong-Kyong. Brave Hong Kil-Dong: The Man Who Bought the Shade of a Tree. Kim, Yong-Kol. 46p. (gr. 2-5). 1990. PLB 9.95x (0-930878-91-4) Hollym Intl.

Kang, Mi-Sun, jt. illus. see Kim, Yon-Kyong.

Kangas, Juli. Fluffy Bunny's Friend. Kangas, Juli. LC 90-84676. 12p. (ps). 1992. 2.95 (0-448-40140-1, G&D) Putnam Pub Group.

—Ginger Kitten's Surprise. Kangas, Juli. LC 90-84675. 12p. (ps). 1992. 2.95 (0-448-40139-8, G&D) Putnam Pub Group.

—Hello, Honey Bear. Kangas, Juli. LC 90-84672. 12p. (ps). 1992. 2.95 (0-448-40141-X, G&D) Putnam Pub Group.

—Say Thank You, Theodore. Lewison, Wendy. 32p. (ps-3). 1992. pap. 2.25 (0-448-40476-1, G&D) Putnam Pub Group.

Kanner, Catherine. Fun with Ballet. 1992. incl. cass. 16.95 (0-8362-4214-9) Andrews & McMeel.

Kapelman, Helen H. Nini's Way, Bk. 1. Kapelman, Helen H. (gr. k-2). 1988. 4.95 (0-9621807-0-X) H H Kapelman.

Kaplan, Boche, jt. illus. see Abisch, Roz.

Kaplan, Mark. Earth Words: A Dictionary of Ecology & Pollution. Simon, Seymour. LC 92-34005. 48p. (gr. 2-5). 1994. 15.00 (0-06-020233-5); PLB 14.89 (0-06-020234-3) HarpC Child Bks.

Karas, Brian. Arnold Plays Baseball. Whitehead, Patricia. LC 84-8827. 32p. (gr. k-2). 1985. PLB 11.59 (0-8167-0367-1); pap. text ed. 2.95 (0-8167-0368-X) Troll Assocs.

—Eek! Stories to Make You Shriek. O'Connor, Jane. 48p. (gr. 1-3). 1992. (G&D); pap. 3.50 (0-448-40382-X, G&D) Putnam Pub Group.

—Martin & the Teacher's Pet. Chardiet, Bernice & Maccarone, Grace. 48p. 1992. pap. 2.50 (0-590-44931-1) Scholastic Inc.

—One Hundred & One Questions & Answers about Pets & People. Squire, Ann. LC 87-34657. 96p. (gr. 3-7). 1988. SBE 13.95 (0-02-786580-0, Macmillan Child Bk) Macmillan Child Grp.

—The Scoop on Ice Cream. Cobb, Vicki. 48p. (gr. 4 up). 1985. Little.

—Squeaky Shoes. Matthews, Morgan. LC 85-14014. 48p. (Orig.). (gr. 1-3). 1986. PLB 10.59 (0-8167-0642-5); pap. text ed. 3.50 (0-8167-0643-3) Troll Assocs.

Karas, G. Brian. We Scream for Ice Cream. Chardiet, Bernice & Maccarone, Grace. 48p. (ps-3). 1992. pap. 2.50 (0-590-44934-6) Scholastic Inc.

Karas, G. Brian. The Best Teacher in the World. Chardiet, Bernice & Maccarone, Grace. 32p. (ps-2). 1991. Repr. 2.50 (0-590-43307-5) Scholastic Inc.

—Cinder-Elly. Minters, Frances. LC 93-14533. 32p. (ps-3). 1994. PLB 13.99 (0-670-84417-9) Viking Child Bks.

—Don't Read This Book Whatever You Do! More Poems about School. Dakos, Kalli. LC 92-23236. 64p. (gr. 2-6). 1993. RSBE 13.95 (0-02-725582-4, Four Winds) Macmillan Child Grp.

—The Forever Secret. Starkman, Neal. LC 91-14799. 50p. (Orig.). (gr. 5). 1991. pap. 9.00 (0-935529-28-4) Comprehen Health Educ.

—Good Luck, Bad Luck. Schlachter, Rita. LC 85-14069. 48p. (Orig.). (gr. 1-3). 1986. PLB 10.59 (0-8167-0572-0); pap. text ed. 3.50 (0-8167-0573-9) Troll Assocs.

—Here Comes Hungry Albert. Whitehead, Patricia. LC 84-8835. 32p. (gr. k-2). 1985. PLB 11.59 (0-8167-0379-5); pap. text ed. 2.95 (0-8167-0380-9) Troll Assocs.

—Here Comes Winter. Craig, Janet. LC 87-13738. 32p. (gr. k-2). 1988. PLB 7.89 (0-8167-1225-5); pap. text ed. 1.95 (0-8167-1226-3) Troll Assocs.

—The Holiday Handwriting School. Pulver, Robin. LC 89-77085. 32p. (gr. k-3). 1991. RSBE 12.95 (0-02-775455-3, Four Winds) Macmillan Child Grp.

—Home for a Dinosaur. Curran, Eileen. LC 84-8627. 32p. (gr. k-2). 1985. lib. bdg. 11.59 (0-8167-0351-5); pap. text ed. 2.95 (0-8167-0431-7) Troll Assocs.

—If You're Not Here, Please Raise Your Hand: Poems about School. Dakos, Kalli. LC 89-71530. 64p. (gr. 2-6). 1990. SBE 12.95 (0-02-725581-6, Four Winds) Macmillan Child Grp.

—Into This Night We Are Rising. London, Jonathan. LC 92-27471. (ps-3). 1993. 13.99 (0-670-84905-7) Viking Child Bks.

—Madison Moves to the Country. Martin, Melanie. LC 88-1313. 48p. (Orig.). (gr. 1-4). 1989. PLB 10.59 (0-8167-1345-6); pap. text ed. 3.50 (0-8167-1346-4) Troll Assocs.

—Martin & the Tooth Fairy. Maccarone, Grace & Chardiet, Bernice. 32p. 1991. pap. 2.50 (0-590-43305-9) Scholastic Inc.

—Merry Christmas, What's Your Name School Friends. Chardiet, Bernice & Maccarone, Grace. 32p. (ps-2). 1991. 2.50 (0-590-43306-7) Scholastic Inc.

—Nobody's Mother Is in Second Grade. Pulver, Robin. LC 91-16395. 32p. (gr. k-3). 1992. 13.50 (0-8037-1210-3); PLB 13.89 (0-8037-1211-1) Dial Bks Young.

—Not-Too-Sweet Trick or Treat. Buck, Nola. 16p. (ps-3). 1993. 4.95 (0-694-00489-8, Festival) HarpC Child Bks.

—Odds 'N Ends Alvy. Frank, John. LC 92-27151. 32p. (gr. k-4). 1993. RSBE 14.95 (0-02-735675-2, Four Winds) Macmillan Child Grp.

—Playground Fun. Gordon, Sharon. LC 86-30854. 32p. (gr. k-2). 1988. lib. bdg. 7.89 (0-8167-0990-4); pap. text ed. 1.95 (0-8167-0991-2) Troll Assocs.

—Truman's Aunt Farm. Rattigan, Jama K. LC 93-4860. 1994. write for info. (0-395-65661-3) HM.

—Westward Ho, Ho, Ho. Hartman, Victoria. 48p. (gr. 2-6). 1994. pap. 3.99 (0-14-036851-5) Puffin Bks.

—Westward Ho Ho! Jokes from the Wild West. Hartman, Victoria. 48p. (gr. 2-6). 1992. PLB 11.00 (0-670-84040-8) Viking Child Bks.

Karch, Pat. Fifty-Two Elementary Patterns. Vonk, Idalee W. 48p. (Orig.). (gr. 1-6). 1979. pap. 6.99 (0-87239-340-2, 3366) Standard Pub.

—Julie's New Home. Moncure, Jane B. LC 82-19900. 32p. (gr. 3-4). 1983. lib. bdg. 8.45 (0-89565-254-4) Childs World.

—El Nino Jesus. Shely, Patricia. Granberry, Nola, tr. (SPA.). 16p. (gr. 1-3). 1987. pap. 1.40 (0-311-38563-X) Casa Bautista.

—The Very Special Night. Odor, Ruth S. 32p. (gr. k-2). 1990. pasted 2.50 (0-87403-709-3, 24-03909) Standard Pub.

Karch, Paul. Baby Jesus. Bennett, Marian, ed. 10p. (ps). 1985. 4.99 (0-87239-907-9, 2747) Standard Pub.

—David: Shepherd, Musician, & King. Hollaway, Lee. (gr. 1-6). 1977. bds. 5.95 (0-8054-4230-8, 4242-30) Broadman.

—Honesty. rev. ed. Moncure, Jane B. LC 80-39571. 32p. (gr. k-3). 1981. PLB 21.35 (0-89565-203-X); PLB 14.95s.p. (0-685-55487-2) Childs World.

—Marty Finds a Treasure. Richards, Dorothy F. LC 82-19906. 32p. (gr. 3-4). 1983. lib. bdg. 8.45 (0-89565-251-X) Childs World.

—Peter: The Prince of Apostles. Blackwell, Muriel. (gr. 1-6). 1978. 5.95 (0-8054-4227-8, 4242-27) Broadman.

—Timothy: Young Pastor. Caldwell, Louise. (gr. 1-6). 1978. 5.95 (0-8054-4239-1, 4242-39) Broadman.

—Women in the Bible: Helpful Friends. Latham, Judy. (gr. 1-6). 1979. 5.95 (0-8054-4248-0, 4242-48) Broadman.

Kardas, Alek. Stormy. Weinberger, Jane. LC 85-62021. 54p. (gr. 1-6). 1985. 5.95 (0-932433-13-8) Windswept Hse.

Kariuki, Emmanuel. Njamba Nene & the Flying Bus. Ngugi wa Thiong'o. Wangui wa Goro, tr. LC 88-70433. 34p. (gr. 2-7). 1989. 12.95 (0-86543-079-9); pap. 5.95 (0-86543-080-2) Africa World.

—Njamba Nene's Pistol. Ngugi wa Thiong'o. Wangui wa Goro, tr. LC 88-70432. 32p. (gr. 2-7). 1989. 12.95 (0-86543-081-0); pap. 5.95 (0-86543-082-9) Africa World.

Karl, Dan & Shefelman, Tom. Willow Creek Home. Shefelman, Janice. 128p. (gr. 5-7). 1985. 10.95 (0-89015-535-6, Pub. by Panda Bks) Eakin-Sunbelt.

Karle, Carol, jt. illus. see Mueller, Virginia.

Karlin, Bernie. Night Ride. Karlin, Bernie & Karlin, Mati. (ps-2). 1988. pap. 12.95 jacketed (0-671-66733-5, S&S BFYR) S&S Trade.

—Twelve Ways to Get to Eleven. Merriam, Eve. LC 92-25810. 40p. (ps-1). 1993. pap. 14.00 JRT (0-671-75544-7, S&S BFYR) S&S Trade.

Karlin, Eugene. Adventure in the Desert. Kaufmann, Herbert. (gr. 7 up). 1961. 10.95 (0-8392-3000-1) Astor-Honor.

Karlin, Nurit. The April Rabbits. Cleveland, David. 32p. (gr. k-3). 1986. pap. 2.95 (0-590-42369-X) Scholastic Inc.

—Little Big Mouse. Karlin, Nurit. LC 90-36192. 32p. (ps-1). 1991. PLB 13.89 (0-06-021608-5) HarpC Child Bks.

—The Tooth Witch. Karlin, Nurit. LC 84-62553. 32p. (ps-2). 1985. pap. 4.95 (0-06-443079-0, Trophy) HarpC Child Bks.

Karlsson, Kris. Laura's Gift. Jacobs, Dee. 64p. (Orig.). (gr. 6-12). 1980. PLB 15.95 (0-938628-00-3); pap. 9.95 (0-938628-01-1) Oriel Pr.

Karoi, Ken. Buster & the Dandelions. Madokoro, Hisako. LC 90-47926. 24p. (gr. k-2). 1991. PLB 14.60 (0-8368-0491-0) Gareth Stevens Inc.

Karpen, Florence B. Brothers in Arms. Huntington, Lee P. 72p. (gr. 3-8). 1991. pap. 8.00 (0-88150-214-6) Countryman.

Karpin, Florence B. Tree Spirits: The Story of a Boy Who Loved Trees. Karpin, Florence B. 32p. (Orig.). (ps-3). 1992. PLB 14.00 (0-88150-248-0) Countryman.

Karpinski, John E. Everything Is Beautiful. Stevens, Ray. 24p. 1992. 12.95 (0-7935-1856-3, 00183011) H Leonard Pub Corp.

—Laurie Tells. Lowery, Linda. LC 93-9786. (gr. 4 up). 1994. 18.95 (0-87614-790-2) Carolrhoda Bks.

Karpinski, Rick. Space. Greenberg, Judith E. & Carey, Helen H. 32p. (gr. 2-4). 1990. 17.96 (0-8172-3754-2) Raintree Steck-V.

Karsky, A. K. Dreams of Cycling. Wojcieshowska, Maia. 52p. 1994. 14.50 (1-883740-13-4) Pebble Bch CA.

—Dreams of Fashion. Wojcieshowska, Maia. 52p. 1994. 14.50 (1-883740-05-3) Pebble Bch CA.

—Dreams of Ice Dancing. Wojcieshowska, Maia. 52p. 1994. 14.50 (1-883740-08-8) Pebble Bch CA.

—Dreams of Soccer. Wojcieshowska, Maia. 52p. 1994. 14.50 (1-883740-06-1) Pebble Bch CA.

—Dreams of Super Bowl. Wojcieshowska, Maia. 52p. 1993. 14.50 (1-883740-03-7) Pebble Bch CA.

—Dreams of the Deep. Wojcieshowska, Maia. 52p. 1994. 14.50 (1-883740-12-6) Pebble Bch CA.

—Dreams of the Hoop. Wojcieshowska, Maia. 52p. 1994. 14.50 (1-883740-10-X) Pebble Bch CA.

—Dreams of the Indy Five Hundred. Wojcieshowska, Maia. 52p. 1994. 14.50 (1-883740-11-8) Pebble Bch CA.

—Dreams of the Kentucky Derby. Wojcieshowska, Maia. 52p. 1994. 14.50 (1-883740-07-X) Pebble Bch CA.

—Dreams of the World Series. Wojcieshowska, Maia. 52p. 1994. 14.50 (1-883740-09-6) Pebble Bch CA.

—Dreams of Wimbledon. Wojcieshowska, Maia. 52p. 1993. 14.50 (1-883740-02-9) Pebble Bch CA.

—Dreams of Winter Gold. Wojcieshowska, Maia. 52p. 1993. 14.50 (1-883740-04-5) Pebble Bch CA.

Kasamatsu, Shiro. Grandfather Cherry Blossom. McCarthy, Ralph F., et al, eds. LC 93-18301. 48p. 1993. 13.00 (4-7700-1759-6) Kodansha.

—The Inch-High Samurai. McCarthy, Ralph F., et al, eds. LC 93-16310. 48p. 1993. 13.00 (4-7700-1758-8) Kodansha.

Kasamatsu, Shiro & Oda, Kancho. The Moon Princess. McCarthy, Ralph F., et al, eds. LC 93-18300. 48p. 1993. 13.00 (4-7700-1756-1) Kodansha.

Kaser, Robert. Remember Pearl Harbor. Hamilton, Elizabeth L. 29p. (gr. 3). 1981. pap. 2.95 (0-685-63557-0) AZ Mem Mus.

Kasl, Janette. Chief Stephen's Parky: One Year in the Life of An Athapascan Girl. 2nd ed. Chandonnet, Ann. LC 92-61910. 80p. (gr. 4-6). 1993. pap. 7.95 (1-879373-39-4) R Rinehart.

Kassian, Elena. Eastern Cougar. Funston, Sylvia. 32p. (gr. 1-5). 1992. 4.95 (0-920775-95-0, Pub. by Greey de Pencier CN) Firefly Bks Ltd.

Kassian, Olena. Leatherback Turtle. Funston, Sylvia. 32p. (gr. 1-5). 1992. 4.95 (0-920775-97-7, Pub. by Greey de Pencier CN) Firefly Bks Ltd.

—Peregrine Falcon. Funston, Sylvia. Owl Magazine Staff, ed. 32p. (gr. 1 up). 1992. 4.95 (0-920775-99-3, Pub. by Greey de Pencier CN) Firefly Bks Ltd.

—A Place for Owls. McKeever, Catherine. 96p. (gr. 3 up). 1992. pap. 7.95 (0-920775-24-1, Pub. by Greey de Pencier CN) Firefly Bks Ltd.

—St. Lawrence Beluga. Funston, Sylvia. 32p. (gr. 1-5). 1992. 4.95 (0-920775-93-4, Pub. by Greey de Pencier CN) Firefly Bks Ltd.

—The Wilds of Whip-Poor-Will-Farm. Foster, Janet. 112p. (gr. 3 up). 1992. pap. 7.95 (0-919872-79-4, Pub. by Greey de Pencier CN) Firefly Bks Ltd.

Kastner, Jill. Aurora Means Dawn. Sanders, Scott R. LC 88-24127. 32p. (gr. 1-5). 1989. 13.95 (0-02-778270-0, Bradbury Pr) Macmillan Child Grp.

—Down at Angel's. Chmielarz, Sharon. LC 93-11020. 1994. for info. 14.95 (0-395-65993-0) Ticknor & Fields.

—I Want to Go Home. McLerran, Alice. LC 91-9599. 32p. (ps-3). 1992. 15.00 (0-688-10144-5, Tambourine Bks); PLB 14.93 (0-688-10145-3, Tambourine Bks) Morrow.

—Naomi Knows It's Springtime. Kroll, Virginia L. LC 92-71267. 32p. (ps-3). 1993. reinforced 14.95 (1-56397-006-6) Boyds Mills Pr.

—Night Owls. Denslow, Sharon P. LC 89-33937. 32p. (ps-2). 1990. RSBE 12.95 (0-02-728681-9, Bradbury Pr) Macmillan Child Grp.

—Sarah's Surprise. Alexander, Sally. LC 89-36780. 32p. (gr. k-3). 1990. RSBE 13.95 (0-02-700391-4, Macmillan Child Bk) Macmillan Child Grp.

—The Shepherd Boy: El Nino Pastor. Franklin, Kristine L. Ada, Alma F., tr. (ENG & SPA.). 40p. (ps-1). 1994. English ed. SBE 14.95 (0-689-31809-X, Atheneum Child Bk); Spanish ed. SBE 14.95 (0-689-31918-5, Atheneum Child Bk) Macmillan Child Grp.

—Snake Hunt. Kastner, Jill. LC 92-32601. 32p. (ps-2). 1993. RSBE 14.95 (0-02-749395-4, Four Winds) Macmillan Child Grp.

—Song for the Ancient Forest. Luenn, Nancy. LC 91-17187. 32p. (gr. k-3). 1993. SBE 14.95 (0-689-31719-0, Atheneum Child Bk) Macmillan Child Grp.

—True Stories about Abraham Lincoln. Gross, Ruth B. LC 89-45899. 48p. (gr. k-3). 1989. 12.95 (0-688-08797-3); lib. bdg. 12.88 (0-688-08798-1) Lothrop.

—With a Name Like Lulu, Who Needs More Trouble? Springstubb, Tricia. (gr. 5-9). 1989. 14.95 (0-385-29823-4) Delacorte.

—You're My Nikki. Eisenberg, Phyllis R. LC 91-2670. 32p. (ps-3). 1992. 14.00 (0-8037-1127-1); PLB 13.89 (0-8037-1129-8) Dial Bks Young.

Kastner, John. Martin Luther King, Jr. A Biography for Young Children. Schlank, Carol H. & Metzger, Barbara. 24p. (ps-3). 1989. pap. 3.95 (0-9613271-2-X) RAEYC.

—Martin Luther King, Jr. A Biography for Young Children. rev. ed. Schlank, Carol H. & Metzger, Barbara. 32p. (ps-k). 1990. PLB 14.95 (0-87659-123-3); pap. 6.95 (0-87659-122-5) Gryphon Hse.

Kastro, Carlos. London, Vol. 1: Bloodline. Barker, Clive & Niles, Steve. Skulan, Tom, ed. 48p. (Orig.). 1993. pap. 5.95 (0-938782-25-8) Fantaco.

—London, Vol. 2: End of the Line. Barker, Clive & Niles, Steve. Skulan, Tom, ed. 48p. 1993. pap. 5.95 (0-938782-26-6) Fantaco.

Kasza, Keiko. A Mother for Choco. Kasza, Keiko. 32p. (ps-1). 1992. PLB 14.95 (0-399-21841-6, Putnam) Putnam Pub Group.

—The Pigs' Picnic. Kasza, Keiko. 32p. (ps-1). 1988. PLB 13.95 (0-399-21543-3, Putnam) Putnam Pub Group.

—The Pigs' Picnic. Kasza, Keiko. 32p. (ps-3). 1992. pap. 5.95 (*0-399-21883-1*, Sandcastle Bks) Putnam Pub Group.
—When the Elephant Walks. Kasza, Keiko. 32p. (ps-1). 1990. 13.95 (*0-399-21755-X*, Putnam) Putnam Pub Group.
—The Wolf's Chicken Stew. Kasza, Keiko. (gr. k-3). 1987. 13.95 (*0-399-21400-3*, Putnam) Putnam Pub Group.
Katan, Norma J. Hieroglyphs: The Writing of Ancient Egypt. Katan, Norma J. & Mintz, Barbara. LC 80-13576. 96p. (gr. 4-7). 1981. SBE 13.95 (*0-689-50176-5*, M K McElderry) Macmillan Child Grp.
Katayama, Mits. What Next? Nelson, JoAnne. LC 91-35731. 24p. (Orig.). (gr. k-2). 1993. pap. 5.95 (*0-935529-19-5*) Comprehen Health Educ.
Katchamakoff, Atanas. Dobry. Shannon, Monica. LC 92-31442. 176p. (gr. 5 up). 1993. pap. 4.99 (*0-14-036334-3*) Puffin Bks.
Kate, David A. You Can Be a Woman Marine Biologist. McAlarv, Florence & Cohen, Judith L. 40p. (Orig.). (gr. 4-7). 1992. pap. 6.00 (*1-880599-06-6*) Cascade Pass.
Kato, Setsvo, photos by. Children of the World: England. O'Brien, John & Taylor-Boyd, Susan, eds. LC 89-4462. 64p. (gr. 5-6). 1989. PLB 19.93 (*1-55532-211-5*) Gareth Stevens Inc.
Katona, Robert. Walk When the Moon Is Full. Hamerstrom, Frances. LC 75-33878. 64p. (gr. 3-8). 1975. 15.95 (*0-912278-69-2*); pap. 6.95 (*0-912278-84-6*) Crossing Pr.
Katsma, Candi. Isaiah Fifty-Three: An Illustrated Bible Chapter for Young Children. Meyer, David & Meyer, Alice, eds. LC 91-90827. 40p. (Orig.). (ps-4). 1991. 12.95. pap. 11.95 incl. cassette (*1-879099-06-3*) Thy Word.
—The Lord's Prayer: An Illustrated Bible Passage for Young Children. Meyer, David & Meyer, Alice, eds. LC 91-90826. 32p. (Orig.). (ps-4). 1991. pap. 10.95 incl. cassette (*1-879099-05-5*) Thy Word.
—Psalm Twenty-Three: An Illustrated Bible Chapter for Young Children. Meyer, David & Meyer, Alice, eds. 32p. (Orig.). (ps-4). 1990. pap. 9.95 incl. cassette (*1-879099-00-4*) Thy Word.
—The Ten Commandments: An Illustrated Bible Passage for Young Children. Meyer, David & Meyer, Alice. LC 90-71557. 40p. (Orig.). (ps-4). 1991. pap. 11.95 incl. cassette (*1-879099-02-0*) Thy Word.
Katsma, Candi, jt. illus. see DeWind, June.
Katz, Avner. Tortoise Solves a Problem. Katz, Avner. LC 91-32503. 40p. (gr. k-3). 1993. 13.00 (*0-06-020798-1*); PLB 12.89 (*0-06-020799-X*) HarpC Child Bks.
Katz, David. To Puedes Ser una Paleontologa. Gabriel, Diane & Cohen, Judith. Yanez, Juan, tr. from ENG. (SPA.). 40p. (gr. 3-7). 1993. pap. text ed. 6.00 (*1-880599-13-9*) Cascade Pass.
—Tu Puedes Ser una Egiptologa. Bryan, Betsy & Cohen, Judith. Yanez, Juan, tr. from ENG. (SPA.). 40p. (gr. 4-7). 1993. pap. 6.00 (*1-880599-11-2*) Cascade Pass.
—Tu Puedes Ser una Zoologa. Cohen, Judith L. & Thompson, Valerie. Yanez, Juan, tr. (SPA.). 40p. (gr. 4-7). 1993. pap. 6.00 (*1-880599-09-0*) Cascade Pass.
—You Can Be a Woman Egyptologist. Bryan, Betsy & Cohen, Judith. LC 93-1267. 40p. (Orig.). (gr. 3-6). 1993. pap. 6.00 (*1-880599-10-4*) Cascade Pass.
—You Can Be a Woman Paleontologist. Gabriel, Diane & Cohen, Judith. LC 93-21349. 40p. (gr. 3-6). 1993. pap. 6.00 (*1-880599-12-0*) Cascade Pass.
—You Can Be a Woman Zoologist. Cohen, Judith L. & Thompson, Valerie. LC 93-1092. 40p. (Orig.). (gr. 3-7). 1992. pap. 6.00 (*1-880599-08-2*) Cascade Pass.
Katz, David A. Tu Puedes Ser una Arquitecta. Cohen, Judith L. & Siegel, Margot. Yanez, Juan, tr. from ENG. (SPA.). 40p. (gr. 4-7). 1992. pap. 6.00 (*1-880599-05-8*) Cascade Pass.
—Tu Puedes Ser una Ingeniera. Cohen, Judith L. Yanez, Juan, tr. from ENG. (SPA.). 40p. (Orig.). (gr. 4-7). 1992. pap. 6.00 (*1-880599-03-1*) Cascade Pass.
—You Can Be a Woman Architect. Cohen, Judith L. & Siegel, Margot. 40p. (Orig.). 1992. pap. 6.00 (*1-880599-04-X*) Cascade Pass.
Katz, David A. & Yanez, Juan. Tu Puedes Ser Biologa Marina. McAlary, Florence & Cohen, Judith L. (SPA.). 40p. (gr. 4-7). 1992. pap. 6.00 (*1-880599-07-4*) Cascade Pass.
Katz, Deborah. Mr. Luckypennys Magic Book. Firestone, Allan L. LC 77-71450. 32p. (gr. 2-7). 1977. pap. 4.95 (*0-934682-01-1*) Emmett.
Katz, Kathleen. Angel, Devils, Mermaids & Monsters. Duffy, Karen & Lokenvitz, Judith. 1989. pap. 4.95 (*0-89013-187-2*) Museum NM Pr.
Katz, Richard. The Puppet in the Big Black Box. Chaney, Steve. 32p. (gr. k-5). 1989. write for info. Stiff Lip.
Katz, Shmuel. The Fifth Wheel. rev. ed. Shamir, Moshe. Hodes, Aubrey, tr. from HEB. 115p. (gr. 8 up). 1986. pap. 8.95 (*0-917883-02-0*) Benmir Bks.
Katzen, Mollie. Pretend Soup: And Other Real Recipes. Katzen, Mollie & Henderson, Ann. 96p. (ps). 1993. 14.95 (*1-883672-06-6*) Tricycle Pr.
Katzman, Marylyn, jt. illus. see Feelings, Tom.
Kauai County Planning Dept. Staff. The Kaua'i Guide to Beaches, Water Activities & Safety. Durkin, Pat. 64p. (Orig.). 1988. 2.50 (*0-942255-05-4*, G4) Magic Fishes Pr.
Kaufman, Jeff. Is Somewhere Always Far Away? Poems about Home. Jacobs, Leland B. 32p. (gr. k-3). 1993. PLB 14.95 (*0-8050-2677-0*, Bks Young Read) H Holt & Co.

—Just Around the Corner: Poems about the Seasons. Jacobs, Leland B. LC 93-18342. 32p. (gr. k-3). 1993. PLB 14.95 (*0-8050-2676-2*, Bks Young Read) H Holt & Co.
Kaufman, Richard. How to Haunt a House for Halloween. Friedhoffer & Brown, Harriet. White, Timothy, photos by. 96p. (gr. 3 up). 1989. pap. 6.95 (*0-531-15122-0*) Watts.
—More Magic Tricks, Science Facts. Friedhoffer. White, Timothy, photos by. 128p. (gr. 5-8). 1990. PLB 12.90 (*0-531-10969-0*) Watts.
Kaufman, Richard & Eisenberg, Linda. Forces, Motion, & Energy. Friedhoffer, Robert. White, Timothy, photos by. LC 92-16625. 112p. (gr. 5-8). 1992. PLB 13.40 (*0-531-11052-4*) Watts.
—Light. Friedhoffer, Robert. White, Timothy, photos by. LC 92-19522. (gr. 5-8). 1992. PLB 13.40 (*0-531-11082-6*) Watts.
—Magnetism & Electricity. Friedhoffer, Robert. White, Timothy, photos by. LC 92-16623. (gr. 5-8). 1992. PLB 13.40 (*0-531-11084-2*) Watts.
—Matter & Energy. Friedhoffer, Robert. White, Timothy, photos by. LC 92-16623. (gr. 5-8). 1992. PLB 13.40 (*0-531-11051-6*) Watts.
—Molecules & Heat. Friedhoffer, Robert. White, Timothy, photos by. LC 92-16960. (gr. 5-8). 1992. PLB 13.40 (*0-531-11053-2*) Watts.
—Sound. Friedhoffer, Robert. White, Timothy, photos by. LC 92-16961. (gr. 5-8). 1992. PLB 13.90 (*0-531-11083-4*) Watts.
Kaufman, Richard, jt. illus. see Mateu, Franc.
Kaufman, Robert. Count-a-Saurus. Blumenthal, Nancy. LC 88-21320. 24p. (ps-3). 1989. RSBE 12.95 (*0-02-749391-1*, Four Winds) Macmillan Child Grp.
Kaufman, Robert J. Count-A-Saurus. Blumenthal, Nancy. LC 91-41250. 24p. (gr. k-3). 1992. pap. 3.95 (*0-689-71633-8*, Aladdin) Macmillan Child Grp.
Kaulbach, Kathy. Shivers in Your Nightshirt: Eerie Stories to Read in Bed. Children's Writers' Workshop Staff. 106p. 1991. pap. 6.95 (*0-920852-94-7*, Pub. by Nimbus Publishing Ltd CN) Chelsea Green Pub.
Kawashima, Kazunari. Hermit Crabs. Johnson, Sylvia A. 48p. (gr. 4 up). 1989. PLB 19.95 (*0-8225-1488-5*) Lerner Pubns.
Kay, Gene. Speedy O'Hare's Sun Valley Race. Kay, Gene. 36p. (ps-7). 1987. pap. 8.95 (*0-945222-24-6*) Gazelle Prodns.
Kazuko. Cuckoobush Farm. King-Smith, David. LC 87-14871. 32p. (ps-1). 1988. 11.95 (*0-688-07680-7*); lib. bdg. 11.88 (*0-688-07681-5*) Greenwillow.
Keane, Marie. Touch of Spring. Smith, Viola B. Michel, Sandra S., ed. 64p. (gr. 5 up). 1976. pap. 4.00 (*0-917178-02-5*) Lenape Pub.

Kear, Suzanne. Pamela & the Revolution. Prowense, Mary J. Schatz, Molly, ed. 130p. (gr. 7 up). 1993. 12.95 (*0-9635107-2-X*) Marc Anthony. Nominated for the Golden Kite Award for 1993, this book is highly recommended by teachers & parents for delightful reading while learning history 'firsthand.' Beautifully illustrated with 15 line drawings, this is how The Book Reader, Fall Issue described PAMELA & THE REVOLUTION. 'A time warp that uses some familiar historical figures to construct an engaging novel. A contemporary California teenager, Pamela visits Paris where she had lived as a youngster, excited at the memories of her family's long French ancestry. Her heritage would play a part more intimate than she could ever imagine, for upon leaving the ladies' room in her hotel, she hears strange voices. "The Americans will not be the only ones who will win their War of Independence! France will be next." It's not a movie set. Lafayette & Thomas Paine had not just come from wardrobe. Indeed, Pamela has been swooped back two centuries to the age of Marie Antoinette! She meets a mystic named Cazotte who relishes the chance acquaintance of a fellow-seer, & the chance to perhaps re-write history, & spare some of the bloodshed recounted in the Reign of Terror. He gives her a golden ring: "In my plan you will wear this ring. It will enable you to remember who you are." Pamela would become Marie Antoinette & move throughout the courts of her new time, adorned with new identity, & power & grace. She meets & puzzles Lafayette with her knowledge of future events, & she gets caught up in the gossip involving Madame DuBarry. And just when her hopes with Louis XVI seem the brightest, she twists her golden ring a special way, & returns to present time. A spell binding, delightful tale which enlivens history & does justice to the memory of Marie Antoinette.' PAMELA & THE REVOLUTION is destined to become a classic in children's literature. Be one of the first to get this charming way to learn about history while experiencing adventure. Marc Anthony Publications, P.O. Box 5610, Blue Jay, CA 92317. *Publisher Provided Annotation.*

Kearney, Paul. Accountants Visit School. Halbur, Donna K. 24p. (gr. 3-5). 1979. pap. 3.00 (*0-686-25249-7*) Halbur.
Keates, Colin. Dinosaur. Norman, David & Miller, Angela. LC 88-27167. 64p. (gr. 5 up). 1989. 15.00 (*0-394-82253-6*); PLB 15.99 (*0-394-92253-0*) Knopf Bks Yng Read.
Keates, Colin, photos by. Crystal & Gem. Symes, R. F. & Harding, Roger. LC 90-4930. 64p. (gr. 5 up). 1991. 15.00 (*0-679-80781-0*); PLB 15.99 (*0-679-90781-5*) Knopf Bks Yng Read.
—Fossil. Taylor, Paul. LC 89-36444. 64p. (gr. 5 up). 1990. 15.00 (*0-679-80440-4*); PLB 15.99 (*0-679-90440-9*) Random Bks Yng Read.
Keates, Colin & Arnold, Nick, photos by. Reptile. McCarthy, Colin & Arnold, Nick. LC 90-4890. 64p. (gr. 5 up). 1991. 15.00 (*0-679-80783-7*); PLB 15.99 (*0-679-90783-1*) Knopf Bks Yng Read.
Keates, Colin & Einsiedel, Andreas, photos by. Rocks & Minerals. Natural History Museum Staff. LC 87-26514. 64p. (gr. 5 up). 1988. 15.00 (*0-394-89621-1*); lib. bdg. 15.99 (*0-394-99621-6*) Knopf Bks Yng Read.
Keates, Colin, jt. photog. see King, Dave.
Keates, Colin, et al, photos by. Insect. Mound, Laurence. LC 89-15603. 64p. (gr. 5 up). 1990. 15.00 (*0-679-80441-2*); PLB 15.99 (*0-679-90441-7*) Knopf Bks Yng Read.
—Butterfly & Moth. Whalley, Paul. LC 88-1574. 64p. (gr. 5 up). 1988. 15.00 (*0-394-89618-1*); lib. bdg. 15.99 (*0-394-99618-6*) Knopf Bks Yng Read.
Keating, Edward. How to Drive an Indy Race Car. Rubel, David. 48p. (Orig.). (gr. 3 up). 1992. pap. 9.95 (*1-56261-062-7*) John Muir.
—How to Fly a 747. Paulson, Tim. 48p. (Orig.). (gr. 3 up). 1992. pap. 9.95 (*1-56261-061-9*) John Muir.
Keating, Edward, photos by. How to Fly the Space Shuttle. Shorto, Russell. 48p. (Orig.). (gr. 4-7). 1992. pap. 9.95 (*1-56261-063-5*) John Muir.
Keating, Elizabeth A. Saints of the Americas Coloring Book. Daughters of St. Paul Staff. Flanagan, Anne J., ed. 18p. (-1-4). 1993. pap. 0.95 (*0-8198-4768-2*) St Paul Bks.
Keating, Pam. Who Will Miss Me If I Don't Go to Church? O'Keefe, Susan H. LC 92-28347. 32p. 1993. pap. 3.95 (*0-8091-6592-9*) Paulist Pr.
Keating, Pamela T. A Season for Giving. O'Keefe, Susan H. 1990. 2.95 (*0-8091-6592-9*) Paulist Pr.
Keats, Ezra. The Trip. Keats, Ezra. LC 77-24907. 32p. (gr. k-3). 1978. PLB 15.93 (*0-688-84123-6*) Greenwillow.
Keats, Ezra J. Goggles! Keats, Ezra J. LC 86-28718. 40p. (gr. k-3). 1987. pap. 4.95 (*0-689-71157-3*, Aladdin) Macmillan Child Grp.
—Hi, Cat! 2nd ed. Keats, Ezra J. LC 87-37433. 40p. (gr. k-4). 1988. pap. 4.95 (*0-689-71258-8*, Aladdin) Macmillan Child Grp.
—In a Spring Garden. Lewis, Richard, ed. LC 65-23965. 32p. (ps-3). 1989. Repr. of 1965 ed. 13.95 (*0-8037-4024-7*) Dial Bks Young.
—In a Spring Garden. Lewis, Richard, ed. 32p. (ps up). 1989. pap. 4.95 (*0-8037-4033-6*, Dial Pied Piper) Puffin Bks.
—Jennie's Hat. Keats, Ezra J. LC 66-15683. 32p. (gr. k-3). 1966. 15.00i (*0-06-023113-0*); PLB 14.89 (*0-06-023114-9*) HarpC Child Bks.
—Jennie's Hat. Keats, Ezra J. LC 66-15683. 32p. (ps-3). 1985. pap. 5.95 (*0-06-443072-3*, Trophy) HarpC Child Bks.
—King's Fountain. Alexander, Lloyd. LC 72-13310. 32p. (ps-3). 1989. (DCB); pap. 4.95 (*0-525-44537-4*, DCB) Dutton Child Bks.
—Kitten for a Day. Keats, Ezra J. LC 81-69518. 32p. (ps-3). 1984. RSBE 14.95 (*0-02-749630-9*, Four Winds) Macmillan Child Grp.
—Kitten for a Day. Keats, Ezra J. LC 92-40563. 32p. (ps-1). 1993. pap. 4.95 (*0-689-71737-7*, Aladdin) Macmillan Child Grp.
—Letter to Amy. Keats, Ezra J. LC 68-24329. (gr. k-3). 1968. 15.00 (*0-06-023108-4*); PLB 14.89 (*0-06-023109-2*) HarpC Child Bks.

—The Little Drummer Boy. Keats, Ezra J. LC 68-25714. 32p. (gr. k-3). 1987. pap. 3.95 (0-689-71158-1, Aladdin) Macmillan Child Grp.
—Louie. Keats, Ezra J. LC 75-6766. 32p. (gr. k-3). 1983. PLB 14.88 (0-688-02383-5) Greenwillow.
—Louie's Search. Keats, Ezra J. LC 80-10176. 40p. (gr. k-3). 1980. RSBE 13.95 (0-02-749700-3, Four Winds) Macmillan Child Grp.
—Louie's Search. Keats, Ezra J. LC 89-15128. 32p. (gr. k-3). 1989. pap. 4.95 (0-689-71354-1, Aladdin) Macmillan Child Grp.
—Maggie & the Pirate. Keats, Ezra J. LC 85-29347. 32p. (gr. k-3). 1987. Repr. of 1979 ed. RSBE 13.95 (0-02-749710-0, Four Winds) Macmillan Child Grp.
—Over in the Meadow. Wadsworth, Olive A. (gr. k-3). 1985. 3.95 (0-590-44848-X) Scholastic Inc.
—Pet Show! Keats, Ezra J. LC 86-17225. 40p. (gr. k-3). 1987. pap. 4.95 (0-689-71159-X, Aladdin) Macmillan Child Grp.
—Peter's Chair. Keats, Ezra J. LC 67-4816. (gr. k-3). 1967. 15.00i (0-06-023111-4); PLB 14.89 (0-06-023112-2) HarpC Child Bks.
—Peter's Chair Big Book. Keats, Ezra J. LC 67-4816. 32p. (ps-3). 1993. pap. 19.95 (0-06-443325-0, Trophy) HarpC Child Bks.
—Regards to the Man in the Moon. Keats, Ezra J. LC 86-28774. 32p. (gr. k-3). 1987. 3.95 (0-689-71160-3, Aladdin Bks) Macmillan Child Grp.
—The Snowy Day. Keats, Ezra J. LC 62-15441. 40p. (ps-1). 1962. 13.00 (0-670-65400-0) Viking Child Bks.
—Two Tickets to Freedom: The True Story of Ellen & William Craft, Fugitive Slaves. Freedman, Florence B. 96p. (gr. 4 up). 1989. 12.95 (0-87226-330-4); pap. 5.95 (0-87226-221-9) P Bedrick Bks.
—Whistle for Willie. Keats, Ezra J. LC 64-13595. (ps-1). 1977. pap. 4.50 (0-14-050202-5, Puffin) Puffin Bks.
—Whistle for Willie. Keats, Ezra J. (ps-1). 1964. pap. 14.00 (0-670-76240-7) Viking Child Bks.
Keavney, Pamela. Matzoh Mouse. Wohl, Lauren L. LC 90-31976. 32p. (gr. k-3). 1991. 14.00 (0-06-026580-9) HarpC Child Bks.
—Matzoh Mouse. Wohl, Lauren L. LC 90-31976. 32p. (gr. k-3). 1993. pap. 4.95 (0-06-443323-4, Trophy) HarpC Child Bks.
Keebler, Charlie. Advanced Squad Leader: WWII Tactical Warfare. Greenwood, Donald J. 200p. (gr. 9 up). 1989. 45.00 (0-911605-50-9) Avalon Hill.
Keefe, Betty. Fingerpuppet ABC. Keefe, Betty. Champlin, John, ed. 100p. (ps-2). 1988. pap. 17.95 (0-938594-10-9) Spec Lit Pr.
Keegan, Marcia. Moonsong Lullaby. Highwater, Jamake. LC 81-1909. 32p. (ps-3). 1981. 14.95 (0-688-00427-X) Lothrop.
Keegan, Marcia, photos by. Pueblo Boy: Growing up in Two Worlds. Keegan, Marcia. LC 90-45187. 48p. (gr. 2-6). 1991. 15.00 (0-525-65060-1, Cobblehill Bks) Dutton Child Bks.
Keeler, Patricia. Secrets of the Universe: Discovering the Universal Laws of Science. Fleisher, Paul. LC 86-14001. 224p. (gr. 5-9). 1987. SBE 17.95 (0-689-31266-0, Atheneum Child Bk) Macmillan Child Grp.

Keenan, Joy D. Are You My Friend? Derby, Janice. 32p. (ps-3). 1993. 11.95 (0-8361-3609-8) Herald Pr.
The expressive watercolors of Joy Dunn Keenan dance across these pages as a boy & his grandfather spend a day at the park. Throughout the day they meet many people & the boy observes how they are different from him. He also notices that they are like him in the things they enjoy seeing & doing. He asks each one, "Are you my friend?" At the end, all the friends gather at the carousel. This book written by Janice Derby allows children to acknowledge characteristics such as language, skin color, being physically or mentally challenged, or having a different economic status that can separate us. By observing that others enjoy the same kinds of activities, children learn that the differences are minor compared to the many similarities we share. For children ages 4-to-8 & the adults who love them.
Publisher Provided Annotation.

—**Why Are Your Fingers Cold? McKaughan, Larry. LC 92-16549. 32p. (Orig.). (ps-1). 1992. 14.95 (0-8361-3604-7) Herald Pr.**
Childlike questions & reassuring

answers are complemented by exquisite illustrations. Several family groupings including African American & Caucasian people appear, as children & adults interact. This delightful picture book helps children to become more sensitive to the needs of others. It fosters a strong sense of extended family & community. For children ages 2 to 6 & the adults that love them.
Publisher Provided Annotation.

Keeping, Charles. Beowulf. Sutcliff, Rosemary. (gr. 5-9). 1984. 22.00 (0-8446-6165-1) Peter Smith.
—Beowulf. Crossley-Holland, Kevin. 48p. (gr. 5 up). 1988. 16.00 (0-19-279770-0); pap. 7.50 (0-19-272184-4) OUP.
—Black Beauty. Sewell, Anna. 216p. (gr. 5 up). 1990. 19.95 (0-374-30776-8) FS&G.
—A Break in the Sun. Ashley, Bernard. 186p. (gr. 6 up). 1980. 21.95 (0-87599-230-7) S G Phillips.
—Friend Monkey. Travers, Pamela L. LC 70-161389. (ps up). 1971. 6.95 (0-15-229555-0, HB Juv Bks) HarBrace.
—The Highwayman. Noyes, Alfred. 32p. 1987. 16.00 (0-19-279748-4); pap. 7.50 (0-19-272133-X) OUP.
—A Kind of Wild Justice. Ashley, Bernard. LC 78-10899. (gr. 7 up). 1979. 21.95 (0-87599-229-3) S G Phillips.
—The Lady of Shalott. Tennyson, Alfred. 36p. 1987. 16.00 (0-19-276057-2) OUP.
—The Lady of Shalott. Tennyson, Alfred. 32p. (gr. 1 up). 1990. pap. 7.50 (0-19-272211-5) OUP.
—The Tale of Sir Gawain. Philip, Neil, as told by. 112p. (gr. 5 up). 1987. 13.95 (0-399-21488-7, Philomel) Putnam Pub Group.
—Terry on the Fence. Ashley, Bernard. LC 76-39898. (gr. 5-9). 1977. 21.95 (0-87599-222-6) S G Phillips.
—The Wedding Ghost. Garfield, Leon. 66p. (gr. 6 up). 1987. bds. 16.00 laminated (0-19-279779-4) OUP.
—The Wedding Ghost. Garfield, Leon. 64p. (gr. 4 up). 1992. pap. 6.95 (0-19-272246-8) OUP.
—Weland: Smith of the Gods. Synge, Ursula. LC 73-5945. 94p. (gr. 7 up). 1973. 21.95 (0-87599-200-5) S G Phillips.

Keetle, Lisbeth. The Christmas Tree Express. Johnson, Allen, Jr. (gr. 4-8). Date not set. 12.95 (1-878561-21-9) Seacoast AL.
Twin school bullies threaten to disrupt the peaceful, rural Vermont world of teen T.J. Flint at the beginning of Allen Johnson, Jr.'s new novel for intermediate readers, THE CHRISTMAS TREE EXPRESS. This tension sets the stage for a summer of adventure for T.J. & his best friend Sally. From their rescue of sled-dog Silver to a train ride with T.J.'s grandfather, a retired train engineer, to the rescue of the bullies themselves in a real cliff-hanger, to working alongside Dad on a real Christmas tree farm, T.J. & Sally's experiences define the depth of their rural life. Neither rich or privileged materially, T.J.'s prevailing thought on Christmas Eve is to count his blessings. At a glance, this book is a fun adventure story that offers a view of rural New England life. More importantly, at its depth, THE CHRISTMAS TREE EXPRESS is an invitation--to a place where family & community values not only still exist, but are shown to provide happiness, success & meaning to the lives of ALL of the characters. To order THE CHRISTMAS TREE EXPRESS, contact Southern Publishers Group by calling 1-800-628-0903.
Publisher Provided Annotation.

Kehn, Regina. The Night of Wishes. Ende, Michael. Schwarzbauer, Heike & Takvorian, Rick, trs. 244p. (gr. 5 up). 1992. 16.00 (0-374-19594-3) FS&G.
Keith, Doug. Nose to Toes. Nelson, JoAnne. LC 91-34706. 24p. (Orig.). (gr. k-2). 1993. pap. 5.95 (0-935529-16-0) Comprehen Health Educ.
—A Place for Grace. Okimoto, Jean D. 32p. (gr. 1 up). 1993. 14.95 (0-912365-73-0) Sasquatch Bks.

—When I'm Sick. Nelson, JoAnne. LC 93-9348. 1994. 5.95 (0-935529-61-6) Comprehen Health Educ.
Keith, Eros. The House of Dies Drear. reissued ed. Hamilton, Virginia. LC 68-23059. 256p. (gr. 6-9). 1984. SBE 15.95 (0-02-742500-2, Macmillan Child Bk); pap. 3.95 (0-02-043520-7, Collier) Macmillan Child Grp.
Keith, Hal. More Wires & Watts: Understanding & Using Electricity. Math, Irwin. LC 88-15767. 96p. (gr. 7 up). 1988. SBE 14.95 (0-684-18914-3, Scribners Young Read) Macmillan Child Grp.
—Tomorrow's Technology: Experimenting with the Science of the Future. Math, Irwin. LC 91-32341. 80p. (gr. 7 up). 1992. SBE 13.95 (0-684-19294-2, Scribners Young Read) Macmillan Child Grp.
—Wires & Watts: Understanding & Using Electricity. Math, Irwin. LC 88-15767. 96p. (gr. 7 up). 1981. RSBE 15.95 (0-684-16854-5, Scribners Young Read) Macmillan Child Grp.
Keitz, Roderick. My Very Own Stories. Taylor, Alice K. 16p. (gr. 2-8). 1993. PLB 11.95 (0-9638873-0-0) J Taylor Ltd.
Keitz, Roderick K. The Christmas Eve Tradition. Thompson, R. W., Jr. 16p. (ps-3). 1993. PLB 8.95 (0-9636442-1-1) N Pole Chron.
Kelleher, Kathie. Bears. Kuchalla, Susan. LC 81-11368. 32p. (gr. k-2). 1982. PLB 11.59 (0-89375-674-1); pap. 2.95 (0-89375-675-X) Troll Assocs.
—Turtles. Craig, Janet. LC 81-11448. 32p. (gr. k-2). 1982. PLB 11.59 (0-89375-664-4); pap. 2.95 (0-89375-665-2) Troll Assocs.
Keller, Dick. The Thingumajig Book of Manners. Keller, Irene. 32p. (ps-3). 1989. pap. 3.95 (0-8249-8346-7, Ideals Child) Hambleton-Hill.
Keller, Holly. Air Is All Around You. Rev. ed. Branley, Franklyn M. LC 85-47884. 32p. (gr. k-3). 1986. (Crowell Jr Bks); PLB 13.89 (0-690-04503-4) HarpC Child Bks.
—Air Is All Around You. Branley, Franklyn M. LC 85-45405. 32p. (gr. k-3). 1987. incl. cassette 7.95 (0-694-00202-X, Trophy); pap. 4.50 (0-06-445048-1, Trophy) HarpC Child Bks.
—Be a Friend to Trees. Lauber, Patricia. LC 92-24082. 32p. (gr. k-4). 1994. 15.00 (0-06-021528-3); PLB 14.89 (0-06-021529-1) HarpC Child Bks.
—Be a Friend to Trees. Lauber, Patricia. LC 92-24082. 32p. (gr. k-4). 1994. pap. 4.95 (0-06-445120-8, Trophy) HarpC Child Bks.
—A Bear for Christmas. Keller, Holly. LC 85-12645. 32p. (ps-3). 1986. 11.75 (0-688-05988-0); PLB 11.88 (0-688-05989-9) Greenwillow.
—Cromwell's Glasses. Keller, Holly. LC 81-6644. 32p. (gr. k-3). 1982. 14.95 (0-688-00834-8) Greenwillow.
—Ears Are for Hearing. Showers, Paul. LC 89-17479. 32p. (gr. k-4). 1990. (Crowell Jr Bks); PLB 14.89 (0-690-04720-7, Crowell Jr Bks) HarpC Child Bks.
—Ears Are for Hearing. Showers, Paul. LC 89-17479. 32p. (gr. k-4). 1993. pap. 4.50 (0-06-445112-7, Trophy) HarpC Child Bks.
—Frogs & Tadpoles. Pfeffer, Wendy. LC 93-3135. (gr. 3 up). 1994. 14.00 (0-06-023044-4); PLB 13.89 (0-06-023117-3) HarpC Child Bks.
—Geraldine's Blanket. Keller, Holly. LC 83-14062. 32p. (ps-1). 1984. 13.95 (0-688-02539-0); PLB 13.88 (0-688-02540-4) Greenwillow.
—Goodbye, Max. Keller, Holly. LC 86-4680. 32p. (ps-3). 1987. 12.95 (0-688-06561-9); PLB 12.88 (0-688-06562-7) Greenwillow.
—An Octopus Is Amazing. Lauber, Patricia. LC 89-29300. 32p. (ps-1). 1990. 14.00 (0-690-04801-7, Crowell Jr Bks); PLB 13.89 (0-690-04803-3, Crowell Jr Bks) HarpC Child Bks.
—Rock Collecting. 2nd ed. Gans, Roma. LC 83-46170. 32p. (gr. k-3). 1984. PLB 13.89 (0-690-04266-3, Crowell Jr Bks) HarpC Child Bks.
—Rock Collecting. Gans, Roma. LC 83-46170. 32p. (ps-3). 1987. pap. 4.50 (0-06-445063-5, Trophy) HarpC Child Bks.
—Shooting Stars. Branley, Franklyn M. LC 88-14190. 32p. (ps-1). 1989. 13.95 (0-690-04701-0, Crowell Jr Bks); PLB 13.89 (0-690-04703-7, Crowell Jr Bks) HarpC Child Bks.
—Shooting Stars. Branley, Franklyn M. LC 88-14190. 32p. (ps-1). 1991. pap. 4.50 (0-06-445103-8, Trophy) HarpC Child Bks.
—Snakes Are Hunters. Lauber, Patricia. LC 87-47695. 32p. (ps-3). 1988. (Crowell Jr Bks); PLB 13.89 (0-690-04630-8, Crowell Jr Bks) HarpC Child Bks.
—Snow Is Falling. rev. ed. Branley, Franklyn M. LC 85-48256. 32p. (ps-3). 1986. pap. 4.50 (0-06-445058-9, Trophy) HarpC Child Bks.
—Snow Is Falling. rev. ed. Branley, Franklyn M. LC 85-48256. 32p. (gr. k-3). 1986. (Crowell Jr Bks); PLB 14.89 (0-690-04548-4, Crowell Jr Bks) HarpC Child Bks.
—Sponges Are Skeletons. Esbensen, Barbara J. LC 92-9740. 32p. (gr. k-4). 1993. 15.00 (0-06-021034-6); PLB 14.89 (0-06-021037-0) HarpC Child Bks.
—Ten Sleepy Sheep. Keller, Holly. LC 83-1477. 32p. (gr. k-3). 1983. 10.25 (0-688-02306-1); PLB 13.93 (0-688-02307-X) Greenwillow.
—Who Eats What. Lauber, Patricia. LC 93-10609. (ps-6). 1995. 15.00 (0-06-022981-0); PLB 14.89 (0-06-022982-9) HarpC Child Bks.
—Why I Cough, Sneeze, Shiver, Hiccup, & Yawn. Berger, Melvin. LC 82-45587. 40p. (gr. k-3). 1983. PLB 13.89 (0-690-04254-X, Crowell Jr Bks) HarpC Child Bks.

Keller, Katie. Seven Loaves of Bread. Wolff, Ferida. LC 92-34313. 32p. (ps up). 1993. 14.00 *(0-688-11101-7,* Tambourine Bks); PLB 13.93 *(0-688-11112-2,* Tambourine Bks) Morrow.

Keller, Ronald. Edna St. Vincent Millay's Poems Selected for Young People. Millay, Edna St. Vincent. LC 77-25671. 120p. (gr. 7 up). 1979. 14.00 *(0-06-024218-3)* HarpC Child Bks.

Kelley, Cathy. The Red Letter Alphabet Book. Gould, Ellen. 29p. (gr. k up). 1983. pap. 7.00 *(0-938017-00-4)* Learn Tools.

Kelley, Colleen. Kids' Stuff: Simple Science & Nature Projects for Children. Kelley, Colleen. 96p. (gr. k-6). 1989. pap. text ed. 4.95 *(0-9618052-2-6)* Daily Hampshire.

Kelley, Colleen M. The Wiggly Tooth Book. Pohl, Linda. 16p. (ps-2). 1991. 3.95 *(0-9625453-1-7)* L P Pohl.

Kelley, Elizabeth A. Mystic Monkey. Baba Hari Dass. LC 81-51051. 64p. (Orig.). (gr. 4-8). 1984. pap. 9.95 *(0-918100-05-4)* Sri Rama.

Kelley, Gary. The Christmas of the Reddle Moon. Lewis, J. Patrick. LC 93-28049. 1994. write for info. *(0-8037-1566-8)*; PLB write for info. *(0-8037-1567-6)* Dial Bks Young.

—The Foghorn. Bradbury, Ray. 32p. 1987. PLB 13.95s.p. *(0-88682-107-X)* Creative Ed.

—Frankenstein. Shelley, Mary Wollstonecraft. Stewart, Diana, adapted by. LC 81-5216. 48p. (gr. 4 up). 1983. PLB 18.64 *(0-8172-1674-X)* Raintree Steck-V.

—The Legend of Sleepy Hollow. Irving, Washington. (gr. 4-12). Date not set. lib. bdg. 19.95 RLB smythe-sewn *(0-88682-328-5,* 97206-098) Creative Ed.

—The Necklace. De Maupassant, Guy. (gr. 5 up). 1992. PLB 19.95 *(0-88682-489-3)* Creative Ed.

—Rip Van Winkle. Irving, Washington. LC 93-17093. 1993. PLB 21.95s.p. *(0-88682-631-4)* Creative Ed.

—Rip Van Winkle. Irving, Washington. 64p. 1993. 21.95 *(1-56846-082-1)* Creat Editions.

Kelley, Midorie. The Beestys' Journey, 20 Vols, Vol. 1. Salazar, Yolanda L. 36p. (gr. 3 up). 1989. write for info. ADAPT Pub Co.

—The Beestys' What Color Is... Salazar, Yolanda L. 10p. (ps). 1989. 7.95 *(0-317-94002-3)* ADAPT Pub Co.

—The Beesty's What Shape Is... Salazar, Yolanda L. 10p. (ps). 1989. 7.95 *(0-317-94001-5)* ADAPT Pub Co.

—The Beestys' What Time Is... Salazar, Yolanda L. 10p. (ps). 1989. 7.95 *(0-317-94003-1)* ADAPT Pub Co.

Kelley, Patte. Dippy Diplodocus: Story & Gameboard. Carnegie Museum of Natural History, Division of Education Staff. 16p. (Orig.). (ps-2). 1988. pap. 5.95 *(0-911239-23-5)* Carnegie Mus.

Kelley, Rosemary S. Seavy Seagull & the Friendship Sloop Race. 2nd ed. Kelley, Rosemary S. 39p. (ps-k). 1985. pap. 5.95 *(0-9616905-0-X)* R S Kelley.

Kelley, True. All Around the World. Donnelly, Judy. 1991. 13.95 *(0-448-40137-1,* G&D) Putnam Pub Group.

—Baby's Peek-a-Boo Album. Meryl, Debra. 24p. (ps) 1989. 11.95 *(0-448-15375-0,* G&D) Putnam Pub Group.

—Clara Joins the Circus. Pellowski, Michael. LC 80-25602. 48p. (ps-3). 1981. 5.95 *(0-8193-1057-3);* PLB 5.95 *(0-8193-1058-1)* Parents.

—Cuts, Breaks, Bruises & Burns: How Your Body Heals. Cole, Joanna. LC 84-45335. 48p. (gr. 2-6). 1985. (Crowell Jr Bks); PLB 13.89 *(0-690-04438-0)* HarpC Child Bks.

—Dinostory. Morgan, Michaela. LC 90-44935. 32p. (ps-4). 1991. 13.95 *(0-525-44726-1,* DCB) Dutton Child Bks.

—Get Ready for Robots. Lauber, Patricia. LC 85-48255. 32p. (ps-3). 1987. PLB 13.89i *(0-690-04578-6,* Crowell Jr Bks) HarpC Child Bks.

—Guess Where You're Going, Guess What You'll Do. Bauman, A. F. 32p. (ps-k). 1989. 13.45 *(0-395-50211-X)* HM.

—How Many Teeth? rev. ed. Showers, Paul. LC 89-71731. 32p. (ps-1). 1991. pap. 4.95 *(0-06-445098-8,* Trophy) HarpC Child Bks.

—How Many Teeth? rev. ed. Showers, Paul. LC 89-13995. 32p. (ps-1). 1991. 14.00 *(0-06-021633-6);* PLB 13.89 *(0-06-021634-4)* HarpC Child Bks.

—How to Catch a Flying Saucer. Deem, James M. LC 90-4931. 192p. (gr. 5-9). 1991. 16.45 *(0-395-51958-6)* HM.

—How to Catch a Flying Saucer. Deem, James M. 192p. 1993. pap. 3.50 *(0-380-71898-7,* Camelot) Avon.

—How to Find a Ghost. Deem, James M. 144p. (gr. 5-9). 1988. 13.45 *(0-395-46846-9)* HM.

—How to Hunt Buried Treasure. Deem, James M. LC 91-21749. 192p. (gr. 3-7). 1992. 15.45 *(0-395-58799-9)* HM.

—How to Read Your Mother's Mind. Deem, James M. LC 92-41351. 1994. write for info. *(0-395-62426-6)* HM.

—I Really Want a Dog. Breslow, Susan & Blakemore, Sally. 40p. (ps-3). 1993. pap. 4.99 *(0-14-054941-2,* Puffin Unicorn) Puffin Bks.

—I Saw a Purple Cow & 100 Other Recipes for Learning. Cole, Ann, et al. 96p. (gr. k up). 1972. 8.95 *(0-316-15175-0)* Little.

—It's Raining Cats & Dogs: All Kinds of Weather & Why We Have It. Branley, Franklyn M. LC 86-27546. 128p. (gr. k-3). 1987. 14.45 *(0-395-33070-X)* HM.

—I've Got Chicken Pox. Kelley, True. LC 93-11685. 1994. write for info. *(0-525-45185-4)* Dutton Child Bks.

—Let's Eat. Kelley, True. LC 88-25699. 32p. (ps-1). 1989. 11.95 *(0-525-44482-3,* DCB) Dutton Child Bks.

—Look at Your Eyes. rev. ed. Showers, Paul. LC 91-10167. 32p. (ps-1). 1992. 14.00 *(0-06-020188-6);* PLB 13.89 *(0-06-020189-4)* HarpC Child Bks.

—Look at Your Eyes. rev. ed. Showers, Paul. LC 91-10168. 32p. (ps-1). 1992. pap. 4.50 *(0-06-445108-9,* Trophy) HarpC Child Bks.

—Look Baby! Listen Baby! Do Baby! Kelley, True. LC 87-6800. 32p. (ps). 1987. 9.95 *(0-525-44320-7,* DCB) Dutton Child Bks.

—Mixed-Up Magic. Cole, Joanna. Donnelly, Judy, ed. LC 87-14965. 32p. (gr. k-3). 1987. 8.95 *(0-8038-9298-5)* Hastings.

—The Skeleton Inside You. rev. ed. Balestrino, Philip. LC 88-23672. 32p. (gr. k-3). 1989. 14.00 *(0-690-04731-2,* Crowell Jr Bks); PLB 13.89 *(0-690-04733-9)* HarpC Child Bks.

—The Skeleton Inside You. rev. ed. Balestrino, Philip. LC 88-24600. 32p. (gr. k-3). 1989. pap. 4.50 *(0-06-445087-2,* Trophy) HarpC Child Bks.

—A Valentine for Fuzzboom. Kelley, True. LC 80-24284. 24p. (gr. k-3). 1982. HM.

—What the Moon Is Like. rev. ed. Branley, Franklyn M. LC 85-47904. 32p. (ps-3). 1986. PLB 14.89 *(0-690-04512-3,* Crowell Jr Bks) HarpC Child Bks.

—What the Moon Is Like. Branley, Franklyn M. LC 85-45400. 32p. (gr. k-3). 1987. Book & Cassette Set. 7.95 *(0-694-00205-4,* Trophy); pap. 4.50 *(0-06-445052-X,* Trophy) HarpC Child Bks.

Kelley, True & Lindblom, Steve. Fossil Factory: A Kid's Guide to Digging up Dinosaurs, Exploring Evolution & Finding Fossils. Eldredge, Niles, et al. 111p. (gr. 2-7). 1989. pap. 8.61 *(0-201-18599-7)* Addison-Wesley.

Kelley, True, jt. illus. see Raffi.

Kellner, Ron. Baptism. Todd, Richard E., ed. 16p. (Orig.). (gr. 1-6). 1980. pap. 0.50 *(0-9605324-0-4)* Crosswalk Res.

Kellner, Ron, jt. illus. see Miller, Alma E.

Kellog, Steven. Come Here, Cat. Nodset, Joan L. LC 92-39005. (ps-3). 1973. 10.00 *(0-06-024557-3);* PLB 9.89 *(0-06-024558-1)* HarpC Child Bks.

—Jimmy's Boa & the Big Splash Birthday Bash. Noble, Trinka H. LC 88-10933. 32p. (ps-3). 1989. 13.95 *(0-8037-0539-5);* PLB 13.89 *(0-8037-0540-9)* Dial Bks Young.

—Jimmy's Boa Bounces Back. Noble, Trinka H. LC 83-14289. 32p. (ps-3). 1984. 13.95 *(0-8037-0049-0);* PLB 13.89 *(0-8037-0050-4)* Dial Bks Young.

Kellogg, Steven. A, My Name Is Alice. Bayer, Jane. LC 84-7059. (gr. k-3). 1984. 15.00 *(0-8037-0123-3);* PLB 14.89 *(0-8037-0124-1)* Dial Bks Young.

—A, My Name Is Alice. Bayer, Jane. LC 84-7059. 32p. (ps-2). 1987. pap. 4.95 *(0-8037-0130-6)* Dial Bks Young.

—Abby. Caines, Jeannette. LC 73-5480. 32p. (ps-3). 1973. PLB 12.89 *(0-06-020922-4)* HarpC Child Bks.

—Abby. Caines, Jeannette. LC 73-5480. 32p. (ps-3). 1984. 4.95 *(0-06-443049-9,* Trophy) HarpC Child Bks.

—Adventures of Huckleberry Finn. Twain, Mark. Glassman, Peter, afterword by. LC 92-27398. 1993. write for info. *(0-688-10656-0)* Morrow Jr Bks.

—Appeard & Liverwurst. Mayer, Mercer. LC 89-13803. 40p. (gr. k up). 1990. 13.95 *(0-688-09659-X);* PLB 13.88 *(0-688-09660-3,* Morrow Jr Bks) Morrow Jr Bks.

—Aster Aardvark's Alphabet Adventures. Kellogg, Steven. LC 87-5715. 40p. (gr. k up). 1987. 13.95 *(0-688-07256-9);* lib. bdg. 13.88 *(0-688-07257-7,* Morrow Jr Bks) Morrow Jr Bks.

—Barney Bipple's Magic Dandelions. Chapman, Carol. LC 77-5747. 32p. (gr. k-3). 1988. 13.95 *(0-525-44449-1,* DCB) Dutton Child Bks.

—Barney Bipple's Magic Dandelions. Chapman, Carol. LC 77-14852. 32p. (gr. k-3). 1992. pap. 3.99 *(0-14-054540-9,* Puffin Unicorn) Puffin Bks.

—Best Friends. Kellogg, Steven. LC 85-15971. 32p. (ps-3). 1986. 13.95 *(0-8037-0099-7);* PLB 13.89 *(0-8037-0101-2)* Dial Bks Young.

—Best Friends. Kellogg, Steven. Fogelman, Phyllis J., ed. LC 85-15971. 32p. (ps-3). 1990. pap. 4.99 *(0-8037-0829-7)* Dial Bks Young.

—Boy Who Was Followed Home. Mahy, Margaret. LC 75-2866. 32p. (ps-3). 1986. 13.95 *(0-8037-0286-8)* Dial Bks Young.

—The Boy Who Was Followed Home. Mahy, Margaret. 32p. (ps-3). 1983. pap. 4.95 *(0-8037-0903-X)* Dial Bks Young.

—Can I Keep Him? Kellogg, Steven. LC 72-142453. (ps-3). 1971. 13.99 *(0-8037-0988-9);* PLB 12.89 *(0-8037-0989-7)* Dial Bks Young.

—The Christmas Witch. Kellogg, Steven. LC 91-32688. 40p. (gr. k-3). 1992. 15.00 *(0-8037-1268-5);* PLB 14.89 *(0-8037-1269-3)* Dial Bks Young.

—The Day Jimmy's Boa Ate the Wash. Noble, Trinka H. LC 80-15098. 32p. (ps-3). 1980. 13.95 *(0-8037-1723-7);* PLB 13.89 *(0-8037-1724-5);* pap. 4.95 *(0-8037-0094-6)* Dial Bks Young.

—The Day Jimmy's Boa Ate the Wash. Noble, Trinka H. 32p. (ps-3). 1992. pap. 4.99 *(0-14-054623-5,* Puffin Pied Piper) Puffin Bks.

—Day the Goose Got Loose. Lindbergh, Reeve. LC 87-28959. 32p. (ps-3). 1990. 12.95 *(0-8037-0408-9);* PLB 12.89 *(0-8037-0409-7)* Dial Bks Young.

—Engelbert the Elephant. Paxton, Tom. LC 89-9376. 32p. (ps up). 1990. 14.95 *(0-688-08935-6);* PLB 14.88 *(0-688-08936-4,* Morrow Jr Bks) Morrow Jr Bks.

—The Great Christmas Kidnapping Caper. Van Leeuwen, Jean. LC 75-9201. 144p. (gr. 2-6). 1975. 12.95 *(0-685-01454-1)* Dial Bks Young.

—The Great Christmas Kidnapping Caper. Van Leeuwen, Jean. 172p. (gr. 3 up). 1990. pap. 3.99 *(0-14-034287-7,* Puffin) Puffin Bks.

—How Much Is a Million? Schwartz, David M. LC 84-5736. 40p. (gr. k-5). 1985. PLB 14.88 *(0-688-04050-0);* 15.00 *(0-688-04049-7)* Lothrop.

—How Much Is a Million? Schwartz, David M. 40p. (gr. k-3). 1992. Big Book. 28.67 *(0-590-71767-7)* Scholastic Inc.

—How Much Is a Million? Schwartz, David M. 40p. (gr. 1-4). 1986. pap. 3.95 *(0-590-43614-7)* Scholastic Inc.

—How Much Is a Million? Schwartz, David M. 40p. (gr. k up). 1993. pap. 4.95 *(0-688-09933-5,* Mulberry) Morrow.

—Is Your Mama a Llama? Guarino, Deborah. 1991. pap. 3.95 *(0-590-44725-4,* Blue Ribbon Bks) Scholastic Inc.

—The Island of the Skog. Kellogg, Steven. LC 73-6019. 32p. (ps-3). 1973. 15.00 *(0-8037-3842-0);* PLB 13.89 *(0-8037-3840-4)* Dial Bks Young.

—Iva Dunnit & the Big Wind. Purdy, Carol. LC 84-17441. 32p. (ps-3). 1985. 12.95 *(0-8037-0183-7)* Dial Bks Young.

—Iva Dunnit & the Big Wind. Purdy, Carol. LC 84-17441. 32p. (ps-3). 1988. pap. 4.99 *(0-8037-0493-3)* Dial Bks Young.

—Jack & the Beanstalk. Kellogg, Steven, retold by. LC 90-45990. 48p. 1991. 14.95 *(0-688-10250-6);* PLB 14.88 *(0-688-10251-4)* Morrow Jr Bks.

—Jimmy's Boa & the Big Splash Birthday Bash. Noble, Trinka H. 32p. (ps-3). 1993. pap. 4.99 *(0-14-054921-8,* Puffin Pied Piper) Puffin Bks.

—Jimmy's Boa Bounces Back. Noble, Trinka H. 32p. (ps-3). 1993. pap. 4.99 *(0-14-054654-5,* Puffin Pied Piper) Puffin Bks.

—Johnny Appleseed. Kellogg, Steven. LC 87-27317. 48p. (gr. 2 up). 1988. 14.95 *(0-688-06417-5);* PLB 14.88 *(0-688-06418-3,* Morrow Jr Bks) Morrow Jr Bks.

—Leo, Zack & Emmie. Ehrlich, Amy. LC 81-2604. 64p. (ps-3). 1981. PLB 9.89 *(0-8037-4761-6)* Dial Bks Young.

—Leo, Zack & Emmie. Ehrlich, Amy. 64p. (ps-3). 1981. pap. 4.95 *(0-8037-4760-8,* Dial Easy to Read) Puffin Bks.

—Liverwurst Is Missing. Mayer, Mercer. LC 90-5435. 32p. (gr. k up). 1990. 13.95 *(0-688-09657-3);* lib. bdg. 13.88 *(0-688-09658-1,* Morrow Jr Bks) Morrow Jr Bks.

—Matilda Who Told Lies. Belloc, Hilaire. LC 78-121812. 32p. (gr. k up). 1992. 13.00 *(0-8037-1101-8)* Dial Bks Young.

—Matilda Who Told Lies. Belloc, Hilaire. LC 78-121812. 32p. (gr. k up). 1992. pap. 3.99 *(0-14-054547-6,* Puffin Pied Piper) Puffin Bks.

—Mike Fink. Kellogg, Steven, retold by. LC 91-46014. 48p. 1992. 15.00 *(0-688-07003-5);* PLB 14.93 *(0-688-07004-3)* Morrow Jr Bks.

—Much Bigger Than Martin. Kellogg, Steven. LC 75-2799. 32p. (ps-3). 1976. 12.95 *(0-8037-5809-X);* PLB 11.89 *(0-8037-5810-3)* Dial Bks Young.

—Much Bigger Than Martin. Kellogg, Steven. LC 75-27599. 32p. (ps-3). 1976. pap. 3.95 *(0-8037-5811-1)* Dial Bks Young.

—The Mysterious Tadpole. Kellogg, Steven. LC 77-71517. 32p. 1979. pap. 4.95 *(0-8037-6244-5)* Dial Bks Young.

—The Mystery of the Flying Orange Pumpkin. Kellogg, Steven. LC 80-11748. 32p. (ps-2). 1983. pap. 3.50 *(0-8037-0019-9)* Dial Bks Young.

—The Mystery of the Stolen Blue Paint. Kellogg, Steven. LC 81-15314. 32p. (ps-2). 1982. PLB 8.89 *(0-8037-5659-3)* Dial Bks Young.

—Mystery of the Stolen Blue Paint. Kellogg, Steven. LC 81-15314. 32p. (ps-2). 1986. pap. 3.95 *(0-8037-0285-X)* Dial Bks Young.

—Parents in the Pub, Pigs in the Tub. Ehrlich, Amy. LC 91-15601. 40p. (ps-3). 1993. 14.99 *(0-8037-0933-1);* lib. bdg. 14.89 *(0-8037-0928-5)* Dial Bks Young.

—Paul Bunyan. rev. ed. Kellogg, Steven. 48p. (ps up). 1993. pap. 18.95 *(0-688-12610-3,* Mulberry) Morrow.

—Paul Bunyan. Kellogg, Steven. Marcuse, Aida, tr. from ENG. (SPA.). 48p. (gr. k up). 1994. pap. 5.95 *(0-688-13202-2,* Mulberry) Morrow.

—Pecos Bill. Kellogg, Steven. LC 86-784. 32p. (ps up). 1986. 15.95 *(0-688-05871-X);* lib. bdg. 15.88 *(0-688-05872-8,* Morrow Jr Bks) Morrow Jr Bks.

—Pinkerton, Behave! Kellogg, Steven. LC 78-31794. (ps-2). 1979. 13.95 *(0-8037-6573-8);* PLB 13.89 *(0-8037-6575-4)* Dial Bks Young.

—Pinkerton, Behave! Kellogg, Steven. (gr. k-3). 1982. 4.95 *(0-8037-7250-5)* Dial Bks Young.

—Prehistoric Pinkerton. Kellogg, Steven. LC 86-2201. 32p. (ps-3). 1987. 12.95 *(0-8037-0322-8);* PLB 12.89 *(0-8037-0323-6)* Dial Bks Young.

—Ralph's Secret Weapon. Kellogg, Steven. LC 82-22115. (ps-3). 1983. 13.95 *(0-8037-7086-3);* PLB 13.89 *(0-8037-7087-1);* pap. 3.95 *(0-8037-0307-4)* Dial Bks Young.

—Ralph's Secret Weapon. Kellogg, Steven. LC 82-22115. 32p. (ps-3). 1986. pap. 4.95 *(0-8037-0024-5)* Dial Bks Young.

—The Rattlebang Picnic. Mahy, Margaret. LC 93-36294. (gr. 3 up). 1994. write for info. *(0-8037-1318-5);* PLB write for info. *(0-8037-1319-3)* Dial Bks Young.

—A Rose for Pinkerton. Kellogg, Steven. LC 81-65848. 32p. (ps-3). 1981. 14.00 (0-8037-7502-4); PLB 12.89 (0-8037-7503-2) Dial Bks Young.
—Tallyho, Pinkerton! Kellogg, Steven. LC 82-70198. 32p. (ps-3). 1983. 14.95 (0-8037-8731-6) Dial Bks Young.
—Tallyho, Pinkerton! Kellogg, Steven. LC 82-2341. 32p. (ps-3). 1985. 4.95 (0-8037-0166-7) Dial Bks Young.
—Uproar on Holler Cat Hill. Marzollo, Jean. LC 79-22201. 1981. Dial Bks Young.
—The Wizard Next Door. Glassman, Peter. LC 92-21562. 40p. (gr. k up). 1993. 15.00 (0-688-10645-5); PLB 14.93 (0-688-10646-3) Morrow Jr Bks.
—Yankee Doodle. Bangs, Edward. LC 80-17024. 40p. (ps-3). 1989. SBE 13.95 (0-02-749800-X, Four Winds) Macmillan Child Grp.
Kells, Valerie A. One Earth, a Multitude of Creatures. Roop, Peter & Roop, Connie. LC 92-14057. 32p. 1992. 14.95 (0-8027-8192-6); lib. bdg. 15.85 (0-8027-8193-4) Walker & Co.
Kelly, Andy. Your Move: A Chess Adventure for Young Beginners. Fitzpatrick, Michael. 64p. (gr. 3-6). 1990. 12.95 (0-86278-196-5, Pub. by OBrien Pr IE) Dufour.
Kelly, Cathy. The Blue Number Counting Book. Gould, Ellen. 13p. (ps-2). pap. 6.00 (0-938017-01-2) Learn Tools.
Kelly, Douglas, jt. illus. see Nelson, Ray, Jr.
Kelly, Geoff. Playtime. Worland, Denyse. LC 92-31077. 1993. 4.25 (0-383-03590-2) SRA Schl Grp.
—The Sparrows & the Circus. Bernardson, Derek. 96p. (Orig.). (gr. 1-3). 1993. pap. 6.95 (1-86373-061-3, Pub. by Allen & Unwin Aust Pty AT) IPG Chicago.
—The Sparrows & the Spies. Bernardson, Derek. 96p. (Orig.). (gr. 1-3). 1993. pap. 6.95 (1-86373-042-7, Pub. by Allen & Unwin Aust Pty AT) IPG Chicago.
—Traffic Jam. Scarffe, Bronwen. LC 92-31956. 1993. 3.75 (0-383-03599-6) SRA Schl Grp.
—Who's He & Who's Out. Hope, Cathy. LC 92-21396. 1993. 4.25 (0-383-03607-0) SRA Schl Grp.
Kelly, George. I Like Me. Smith, Vanessa. 32p. (Orig.). (gr. 1-2). Date not set. pap. write for info. (0-9634122-4-8) Feather Fables.
Kelly, Kathleen M. One Ghost Too Many: A Sarah Capshaw Mystery. Stevenson, Drew. LC 90-47361. 128p. (gr. 4-6). 1991. 13.95 (0-525-65052-0, Cobblehill Bks) Dutton Child Bks.
—Sisters, Long Ago. Kehret, Peg. LC 89-38677. 160p. (gr. 5 up). 1990. 14.95 (0-525-65021-0, Cobblehill Bks) Dutton Child Bks.
Kelly, Kathryn. God Loves Me: Three Psalms for Little Children. Walters, Julie & Kelly, Kathryn. 96p. (gr. k-2). 1977. pap. 2.95 (0-87793-138-0) Ave Maria.
Kelly, Laura. The Flower of Sheba. Orgel, Doris & Schecter, Ellen. LC 92-33477. 1994. pap. 3.50 (0-553-37235-1, Little Rooster, Little Rooster) Bantam.
—The Gypsies' Tale. Pochocki, Ethel. LC 93-3320. (gr. 4 up). 1994. pap. 14.00 (0-671-79934-7, S&S BFYR) S&S Trade.
—Old Bet & the Start of the American Circus. McClung, Robert. LC 92-11020. 32p. (gr. k up). 1993. 15.00 (0-688-10642-0); PLB 14.93 (0-688-10643-9) Morrow Jr Bks.
Kelly, Susan & Kelly, Thomas. Fishes of Hawaii Coloring Book. Kelly, Susan & Kelly, Thomas. 32p. (ps-2). 1992. 3.95 (1-880188-32-5) Bess Pr.
Kelly, Thomas, jt. illus. see Kelly, Susan.

Kelsch, Gregg B. A World of Dinosaurs Series. Kelsch, Gregg B. 1993. write for info. (1-883736-01-3) Acorn Pub UT.

What did Dinosaurs look like? What did they eat? Gregg B. Kelsch has been intrigued with Dinosaurs & has asked these same questions too. He then set out to study Dinosaurs & what scientists have discovered about them, & found that ideas vary greatly. His interest in Dinosaurs & his love of drawing came together as Gregg expressed his own ideas of what Dinosaurs were like. Being an artist, Gregg knows the importance of imagination & creativity; so he decided to make a coloring book for Dinosaur lovers everywhere to use their skill & imagination in coloring these magnificent animals. Four volumes are available in A WORLD OF DINOSAURS: Volume 1 is on a pre-school level, Volume 2 is for lower elementary school ages, Volume 3 is for upper-elementary & junior high school ages, & Volume 4 is upper level young adult to adult. Volumes 1 through 3 are created in a cartoon effect with Volume 4 being more

intricate in design & true to life. Available from Acorn Publishing at 250 West 2855 South, Salt Lake City, UT 84115. You may also phone us at (801) 485-2424 or FAX us at (801) 484-6961 for volume pricing information. *Publisher Provided Annotation.*

Kelso, Mary J. Abducted! Kelso, Mary J. 144p. (Orig.). (gr. 6 up). 1987. pap. 6.95 (0-9621406-0-0) MarKel Pr.
—Goodbye, Bodie. Kelso, Mary J. 120p. (Orig.). (gr. 6 up). 1989. pap. 6.95 (0-9621406-1-9) MarKel Pr.
—Sierra Summer. Kelso, Mary J. 120p. (Orig.). (gr. 6 up). 1992. pap. 6.95 (0-9621406-3-5) Markel Pr.
Keltz, Martha. The Wayfaring Princes: A Tale of Questing & Adventure. Lawrence, Edith. 106p. (Orig.). (gr. 4-7). 1987. pap. 8.00 (0-936132-86-8) Merc Pr NY.
Kemp, Moira. Baa, Baa, Black Sheep. 10p. (ps). 1991. bds. 4.95 (0-525-67331-8, Lodestar Bks) Dutton Child Bks.
—Baa, Baa, Black Sheep. LC 93-18703. 12p. (ps). 1994. 2.99 (0-525-67443-8, Lodestar Bks) Dutton Child Bks.
—Helpful Betty to the Rescue. Morgan, Michaela. LC 93-39885. 1994. 18.95 (0-87614-831-3) Carolrhoda Bks.
—Hey Diddle Diddle. 10p. (ps). 1991. bds. 4.95 (0-525-67329-6, Lodestar Bks) Dutton Child Bks.
—Hey Diddle Diddle. LC 93-18702. 12p. (ps). 1994. 2.99 (0-525-67445-4, Lodestar Bks) Dutton Child Bks.
—Hickory, Dickory, Dock. 10p. (ps). 1991. bds. 4.95 (0-525-67328-8, Lodestar Bks) Dutton Child Bks.
—Hickory, Dickory, Dock. LC 93-18704. 12p. (ps). 1994. 2.99 (0-525-67444-6, Lodestar Bks) Dutton Child Bks.
—I'm a Little Teapot. 12p. (ps). 1992. bds. 2.50 (0-525-67394-6, Lodestar Bks) Dutton Child Bks.
—Knock at the Door. 12p. (ps). 1992. bds. 2.50 (0-525-67396-2, Lodestar Bks) Dutton Child Bks.
—Pat-a-Cake. 12p. (ps). 1992. bds. 2.50 (0-525-67393-8, Lodestar Bks) Dutton Child Bks.
—La Ropa (Clothes) Price, Mathew. Mlawer, Teresa, tr. 1993. 4.99 (0-553-09560-9) Bantam.
—Round & Round the Garden. 12p. (ps). 1992. bds. 2.50 (0-525-67395-4, Lodestar Bks) Dutton Child Bks.
—Tales from the Enchanted World. Williams-Ellis, Anabel. (gr. 3-7). 1988. 17.95 (0-316-94133-6) Little.
—This Little Piggy. 10p. (ps). 1991. bds. 4.95 (0-525-67330-X, Lodestar Bks) Dutton Child Bks.
—This Little Piggy. LC 93-18683. 12p. (ps). 1994. 2.99 (0-525-67446-2, Lodestar Bks) Dutton Child Bks.
Kendall, Benjamin. Alien Invasions. Kendall, Benjamin. Thatch, Nancy R., ed. Melton, David, intro. by. LC 93-13423. 29p. (gr. 2-4). 1993. PLB 14.95 (0-933849-42-7) Landmark Edns.
Kendall, Jane. Miranda & the Movies. Kendall, Jane. LC 89-1515. 224p. (gr. 6 up). 1989. PLB 14.99 (0-517-57357-1) Crown Bks Yng Read.
Kendall, Jane F. Charles Dickens' A Christmas Carol. Dickens, Charles. Richardson, I. M., ed. LC 87-11270. 32p. (gr. 2-6). 1988. PLB 9.79 (0-8167-1053-8); pap. text ed. 1.95 (0-8167-1054-6) Troll Assocs.
—Petrouchka: A Ballet Cut-Out Book. Marcus, Leonard S. 16p. (gr. 3-6). 1983. pap. 12.95 cutout bk. (0-87923-469-5) Godine.
Kendall, Robert. Mike's Kite. MacDonald, Elizabeth. LC 90-6912. 32p. (ps-3). 1990. 13.95 (0-531-05876-X); PLB 13.99 (0-531-08476-0) Orchard Bks Watts.
Kendall, Russ, photos by. Samuel Eaton's Day: A Day in the Life of a Pilgrim Boy. Waters, Kate. LC 92-32325. (gr. 4 up). 1993. 14.95 (0-590-46311-X) Scholastic Inc.
—Sarah Morton's Day: A Day in the Life of a Pilgrim Girl. Waters, Kate. LC 88-35581. 32p. (gr. k-4). 1989. pap. 14.95 (0-590-42634-6) Scholastic Inc.
—Sarah Morton's Day: A Day in the Life of a Pilgrim Girl. Waters, Kate. 32p. 1991. pap. 4.95 (0-590-44871-4, Blue Ribbon Bks) Scholastic Inc.
Kendrick, Dennis. The Fox with Cold Feet. Singer, Bill. LC 80-10288. 48p. (ps-3). 1980. 5.95 (0-8193-1021-2); PLB 5.95 (0-8193-1022-0) Parents.
—Instant Paper Toys to Pop, Spin, Whirl & Fly. Churchill, E. Richard. LC 85-26229. 112p. (gr. 1-8). 1987. pap. 7.95 (0-8069-6278-X) Sterling.
—Know about Smoking. rev. ed. Hyde, Margaret O. (gr. 3-7). 1990. 12.95 (0-8027-6924-1); lib. bdg. 13.85 (0-8027-6926-8) Walker & Co.
—Scarlet Monster Lives Here. Sharmat, Marjorie W. LC 78-19484. 64p. (gr. k-3). 1979. PLB 11.89 (0-06-025527-7) HarpC Child Bks.
—Scarlet Monster Lives Here. Sharmat, Marjorie W. LC 78-19484. 64p. (gr. k-3). 1986. pap. 3.50 (0-06-444098-2, Trophy) HarpC Child Bks.
—Six Hundred Ninety-Six Silly School Jokes & Riddles. Rosenbloom, Joseph. 128p. (gr. 2 up). 1987. pap. 3.95 (0-8069-6392-1) Sterling.
—Stories about Rosie. Voigt, Cynthia. LC 86-3640. 48p. (gr. 1-4). 1986. SBE 13.95 (0-689-31296-2, Atheneum Child Bk) Macmillan Child Grp.
—Tall & Small: A Book about Height. Phifer, Kate G. LC 86-32401. 96p. (gr. 5 up). 1987. 11.95 (0-8027-6684-6); PLB 12.85 (0-8027-6685-4) Walker & Co.
—Wild Words & How to Tame Them. Asher, Sandy. 96p. (gr. 5 up). 1989. 13.95 (0-8027-6887-3); PLB 14.85 (0-8027-6888-1) Walker & Co.

—World's Toughest Tongue Twisters. Rosenbloom, Joseph. LC 86-5983. 128p. (gr. 2-8). 1987. pap. 3.95 (0-8069-6596-7) Sterling.
Kendrick, John. Guide to the Use of Street-Folk-Musical Games in the Classroom: Song Games. Hillery, Mable & Simmons, Patricia M. 71p. (gr.-6). 1974. pap. 12.00 (0-939632-01-2) ILM.
Kendrick, John & May, Warren. A Guide to the Use of Street-Folk-Musical Games in the Classroom: Chanting Games. rev. ed. Hillery, Mable & Hall, Patricia. Freeman, Harold, Jr., intro. by. 77p. (gr.-6). 1982. pap. 12.00 (0-939632-05-5) ILM.
Kennaley, Lucinda H. My Mom Is Pregnant! Kennaley, Lucinda H. 60p. (Orig.). (gr.). 1990. pap. text ed. 9.95 (0-9628067-0-6) Thoth MO.
Kennan, Elaine & Ward, Fredrick. Dog & Puppies. Hill. Goaman, Karen, ed. (gr. 2-5). 1983. pap. 4.50 (0-86020-646-7); lib. bdg. 11.96 (0-88110-086-2) EDC.
Kennaway, Adrienne. Baby Baboon. Hadithi, Mwenye. LC 92-56397. 1993. 15.95 (0-316-33729-3) Little.
—Crafty Chameleon. Hadithi, Mwenye. 32p. (ps-3). 1987. 15.95 (0-316-33723-4) Little.
—Greedy Zebra. 1984 ed. Hadithi, Mwenye. (ps-3). 1984. 15.95 (0-316-33721-8) Little.
—Hot Hippo. Hadithi, Mwenye. (ps-3). 1986. lib. bdg. 14.95 (0-316-33722-6) Little.
—Little Elephant's Walk. Kennaway, Adrienne. LC 91-19727. 32p. (ps-2). 1992. 13.95 (0-06-020377-3); PLB 13.89 (0-06-020378-1) HarpC Child Bks.
—Tricky Tortoise. Hadithi, Mwenye. (ps-3). 1988. 15.95 (0-316-33724-2) Little.
Kennaway, Adrienne, jt. illus. see Kennaway, Mwalimu.
Kennaway, Mwalimu & Kennaway, Adrienne. Awful Aardvark. Kennaway, Mwalimu & Kennaway, Adrienne. LC 89-80028. (ps-2). 1989. 14.95 (0-316-59218-8) Little.
Kennedy. Mortimer Visits Santa Claus. Mora, Emma. (ps-1). 1987. 3.95 (0-8120-5808-9) Barron.
Kennedy, Anne. Colors & Shapes. 6p. (ps). 1992. bds. 3.95 (1-56293-185-7) McClanahan Bk.
—Funny Fingers, Funny Toes. Damon, Laura. LC 87-10915. 32p. (gr. k-2). 1988. PLB 11.59 (0-8167-1089-9); pap. text ed. 2.95 (0-8167-1090-2) Troll Assocs.
—Maxwell Finds a Friend. Pellowski, Michael J. LC 85-14085. 48p. (Orig.). (gr. 1-3). 1986. PLB 10.59 (0-8167-0586-0); pap. text ed. 3.50 (0-8167-0587-9) Troll Assocs.
—Secret Valentine. Damon, Laura. LC 87-13736. 32p. (gr. k-2). 1988. PLB 11.59 (0-8167-1101-1); pap. text ed. 2.95 (0-8167-1102-X) Troll Assocs.
—What's It Like to Be a Farmer. Matthews, Morgan. LC 89-34386. 32p. (gr. k-3). 1990. lib. bdg. 10.89 (0-8167-1803-2); pap. text ed. 2.95 (0-8167-1804-0) Troll Assocs.
Kennedy, Anne & Wilson, Ann. Subtraction. Evans, Karen. Nayer, Judith E., ed. 32p. (gr. k-1). 1991. wkbk. 1.95 (1-878624-58-X) McClanahan Bk.
Kennedy, Faye W. Please Don't Step on Me. George, Elly-Kree. 20p. (gr. 1-3). 1981. 3.50 (0-935741-07-0) Cherokee Pubns.
Kennedy, Kara, jt. illus. see Knapp, William.
Kennedy, Maureen. A Is for Alligator. Love, Hallie. 64p. (gr. 1 up). 1993. 15.95 (1-879244-02-0) Windom Bks.
Kennedy, Paul. Adventures of Ricky & Chub. Shay, Myrtle. (gr. 4-8). PLB 7.19 (0-685-02937-9) Lantern.

Kennedy, Philip R. Get a Move on, Neuron! Kennedy, Philip R. LC 92-97171. 42p. (Orig.). (gr. 5-8). 1992. pap. text ed. 10.00 (0-9635701-0-2); Tchr's. ed. 12.00 (0-9635701-1-0) Your Chlds Neuro.

This fun book succeeds in stimulating the child's imagination about how the brain works. It takes the child on a walk through the special places in the brain as he or she performs a familiar routine. Each place is described along with its connections to other places, its function, & lack of function after an injury. Each chapter ends with an activity that the child can do with parents or teachers. A revision quiz follows each chapter. (ISBN 0-9635701-0-2, $10.00 plus $2.00 s/h). Praise from fellow neuroscientists, who write: "This is terrific. From the homey, accurate description to the philosophical aside at the end. Good work!" "My wife is a third grade teacher & has been in search of materials such as your book for a long time!" "Wonderful!" "Excellent place to start." The teacher's manual (0-9635701-1-0, $12.00 plus $2.00 s/h) is an expanded book with extra activities.

The fun play (0-9635701-2-9) is based on the book & adds an interactive learning program for over 20 pupils. Volume discounts available from the publisher: Your Child's NEUROscience Press, 3932 Sidney Lanier Blvd., Duluth, GA 30136, (404) 894-4257. *Publisher Provided Annotation.*

Kennedy-Smith, Kristin. Simply Funtastic! Creative Play Ideas from Current (R) Cliff, Donna, ed. 32p. (gr. 1 up). 1993. pap. 6.10 (0-944943-31-4, CODE 21165-7) Current Inc.

Kent, Jack. The Biggest Shadow in the Zoo. Kent, Jack. LC 80-25517. 48p. (ps-3) 1981. 5.95 (0-8193-1047-6); PLB 5.95 (0-8193-1048-4) Parents.

—The Bremen-Town Musicians. Gross, Ruth B. 32p. (Orig.). 1985. pap. 2.50 (0-590-42364-9) Scholastic Inc.

—Easy As Pie: A Guessing Game of Sayings. Folsom, Marcia & Folsom, Michael. LC 84-14978. 64p. (ps-3). 1985. 13.95 (0-89919-303-X, Clarion Bks); pap. 5.95 (0-89919-351-X, Clarion Bks) HM.

—The Emperor's New Clothes. Gross, Ruth B. 32p. (Orig.). 1991. pap. 2.50 (0-590-43267-2) Scholastic Inc.

—Grime Doesn't Pay: Law & Order Jokes. Keller, Charles. 64p. 1984. 9.95 (0-13-365503-2) P-H.

—Little Peep. Kent, Jack. 32p. (gr up). 1989. pap. 12.95 jacketed (0-671-67051-4, S&S BFYR); pap. 5.95 (0-671-67052-2, S&S BFYR) S&S Trade.

—Q Is for Duck. Elting, Mary & Folsom, Michael. LC 80-13854. 64p. (ps-3). 1980. 13.95 (0-395-29437-1, Clarion Bks); pap. 5.95 (0-395-30062-2) HM.

—Round Robin. Kent, Jack. (ps up). 1989. pap. 12.95 jacketed (0-671-66698-3, S&S BFYR); pap. 5.95 (0-671-66969-9, S&S BFYR) S&S Trade.

—Silly Goose. Kent, Jack. LC 82-21441. 32p. (ps-3). 1986. 10.95 (0-13-809947-2); pap. 5.95 (0-13-810177-9) P-H.

—Socks for Supper. Kent, Jack. LC 78-6224. 40p. (ps-3). 1978. 5.95 (0-8193-0964-8); PLB 5.95 (0-8193-0965-6) Parents.

—The Wizard. rev. ed. Kent, Jack. 32p. (gr. k-3). 1989. pap. 5.95 (0-927370-00-X) WW Pr.

Kent, Rockwell. Paul Bunyan. Shephard, Esther. LC 85-5448. 233p. (gr. 7 up). 1985. 12.95 (0-15-259749-2, HB Juv Bks) HarBrace.

Kenyon, Mark. Teddies to the Rescue. Kurland, Alexandra. 56p. (gr. k-4). 1986. 11.95 (0-938209-27-2) Bear Hollow Pr.

Kenyon, Tony. Becky Garcia. Murphy, Elspeth C. LC 86-8877. 108p. (gr. 3-7). 1986. pap. 4.49 (1-55513-029-1, Chariot Bks) Cook.

—Coping with—Food Trash. Bonar, Veronica & Daniel, Jamie, eds. LC 93-32478. 1994. write for info. (0-8368-1056-2) Gareth Stevens Inc.

—Curtis Anderson. Murphy, Elspeth C. LC 86-8819. 120p. (gr. 3-7). 1986. pap. 4.49 (1-55513-027-5, Chariot Bks) Cook.

—Kailia & the King's Horse. McLane, Gretel B. 96p. (gr. 4-6). 1982. 7.95 (0-916630-28-5) Pr Pacifica.

Kenyon, Tony, jt. illus. see Forsey, Chris.

Kenyon, Tony, jt. illus. see Green, Ruby.

Kenyon, Tony, jt. illus. see Holmes, Stephen.

Kepes, Juliet. Cock-A-Doodle-Doo. Kepes, Juliet. LC 76-44433. (ps-2). 1978. 6.95 (0-394-83867-X) Pantheon.

—Frogs Merry. Kepes, Juliet. (ps-2). 1963. lib. bdg. 6.99 (0-394-91176-8) Pantheon.

Kerins, Anthony. Tat Rabbit's Treasure. Kerins, Anthony. LC 92-32600. 32p. (ps-1). 1993. SBE 14.95 (0-689-50553-1, M K McElderry) Macmillan Child Grp.

Kerins, Tony. Look...What Do You See? Rye, Jennifer. LC 90-40231. 32p. (gr. k-3). 1991. lib. bdg. 11.59 (0-8167-2122-X); pap. text ed. 3.95 (0-8167-2123-8) Troll Assocs.

—Shakespeare's Stories: Tragedies. Birch, Beverly, retold by. LC 88-18112. 126p. (gr. 7-12). 1988. 12.95 (0-87226-193-X) P Bedrick Bks.

—Shakespeare's Stories: Tragedies. Birch, Beverley. LC 88-18112. 126p. (gr. 7-12). 1990. pap. 6.95 (0-87226-227-8) P Bedrick Bks.

—Shakespeare's Stories: Tragedies. Birch, Beverley, retold by. LC 93-13199. 1993. 6.99 (0-517-09360-X, Pub. by Wings Bks) Outlet Bk Co.

Kern, Donna. From Apple to Zipper. Cohen, Nora. LC 92-43691. 32p. (ps-1). 1993. POB 8.95 (0-689-71708-3, Aladdin) Macmillan Child Grp.

Kern, Phyllis F. Bumble Cat: How She Came to Be. Kern, Phyllis F. 32p. (gr. k-3). 1985. HM.

Kerns, Aaron. I Like Me, Vol. I. Gaston, Blanche P. 24p. (Orig.). (gr. k-3). 1982. 6.95x (0-9608516-0-7); pap. 4. 95x (0-9608516-1-5) I Like Me Pub.

Kerr, Angela. Fun with Numbers. Richards, Elspeth & Fernyhough, Frances. (gr. k-3). 1987. pap. 2.95 (0-385-23844-4, Zephyr-BFYR) Doubleday.

Kerr, Elizabeth. Making Presents. Bawden, Juliet. LC 92-18649. 48p. (gr. 1-5). 1994. 6.99 (0-679-83495-8); PLB 9.99 (0-679-93495-2) Random Bks Yng Read.

Kerr, Elizabeth, jt. illus. see Venus, Joanna.

Kerr, Judith. Look Out, Mog! Kerr, Judith. LC 90-62202. 24p. (ps-1). 1991. 7.95 (0-679-81067-6) Random Bks Yng Read.

—Mog & Bunny. Kerr, Judith. LC 88-16899. 40p. (ps-1). 1989. 8.95 (0-394-82249-8) Knopf Bks Yng Read.

Kerr, Kathleen. One Hundred Excuses for Kids. Joyer, Mike & Roberts, Zack. Black, Cynthia, ed. 96p. (Orig.). 1990. pap. 4.95 (0-941831-48-5) Beyond Words Pub.

Kerr, Rita. The Ghost of Panna Maria. Kerr, Rita. Eakin, Ed, ed. 96p. (gr. 2-4). 1990. 10.95 (0-89015-791-X); pap. 3.95 (0-89015-803-7) Eakin-Sunbelt.

—Texas Cavalier: The Story of James Butler Bonham. Kerr, Rita. Roberts, Melissa, ed. 64p. (gr. 4-7). 1989. 10.95 (0-89015-714-6, Pub. by Panda Bks) Eakin-Sunbelt.

—Texas Rebel. Kerr, Rita. Eakin, Edwin M., ed. 80p. (gr. 4-6). 1989. 10.95 (0-89015-695-6) Eakin-Sunbelt.

—Texas Rebel. Kerr, Rita. Roberts, M., ed. 80p. (gr. 5-7). 1989. 10.95 (0-685-50916-8) Eakin-Sunbelt.

—A Wee Bit of Texas. Kerr, Rita. 80p. (gr. 1-4). 1991. 10.95 (0-89015-809-6) Eakin-Sunbelt.

Kerr, Tom. On My Own: Helping Kids Help Themselves. Navarra, Tova. 128p. (gr. 2-8). 1993. pap. 6.95 (0-8120-1563-0) Barron.

—Playing It Smart: What to Do When You're on Your Own. Navarra, Tova. 128p. (gr. 2-8). 1989. 12.95 (0-8120-6131-4) Barron.

Kerrod, Robin, et al. The Random House Book of One Thousand-One Wonders of Science. Williams, Brenda & Williams, Brian. LC 89-3954. 160p. 1990. PLB 11. 99 (0-679-90080-2); pap. 13.00 (0-679-80080-8) Random Bks Yng Read.

Kerry, Jill, jt. illus. see Drucklieb, Herman L.

Kerstetter, J. Harriet Tubman: They Called Me Moses. Meyer, Linda D. LC 87-43308. 32p. (Orig.). (ps-4). 1988. lib. bdg. 16.95 (0-943990-33-5); pap. 5.95 (0-943990-32-7) Parenting Pr.

Kerstetter, Judy. Elizabeth Blackwell: The Story of the First Woman Doctor. Steelsmith, Shari. LC 86-62434. 32p. (Orig.). (gr. 4-7). 1987. lib. bdg. 16.95 (0-943990-31-9); pap. 5.95 (0-943990-30-0) Parenting Pr.

Kessler, Leonard. Are There Seals in the Sandbox? Kessler, Ethel & Kessler, Leonard. 24p. (ps). 1990. pap. 4.95 casebound, padded cover (0-671-70539-3, Little Simon) S&S Trade.

—Be Ready at Eight. Parish, Peggy. LC 87-1040. 64p. (gr. 1-4). 1987. pap. 3.95 (0-689-71163-8, Aladdin) Macmillan Child Grp.

—The Big Mile Race. Kessler, Leonard. LC 82-9274. 48p. (gr. 1-3). 1983. 9.00 (0-688-01420-8) Greenwillow.

—Binky Brothers, Detectives. Lawrence, James. LC 68-10374. (gr. k-3). 1978. pap. 3.50 (0-06-444003-6, Trophy) HarpC Child Bks.

—Binky Brothers, Detectives. Lawrence, James. LC 68-10374. 64p. (ps-3). 1985. incl. cassette 5.98 (0-694-00018-3, Trophy) HarpC Child Bks.

—Ducks Don't Get Wet. rev. ed. Goldin, Augusta. LC 88-18073. 32p. (ps-3). 1989. (Crowell Jr Bks); PLB 13. 89 (0-690-04782-7, Crowell Jr Bks) HarpC Child Bks.

—Ducks Don't Get Wet. rev. ed. Goldin, Augusta. LC 88-18073. 32p. (ps-3). 1989. pap. 4.95 (0-06-445082-1, Trophy) HarpC Child Bks.

—The Family under the Moon. Jewell, Nancy. LC 76-2344. (ps-3). 1976. PLB 14.89i (0-06-022827-X) HarpC Child Bks.

—Here Comes the Strikeout. newly illus. ed. Kessler, Leonard. LC 91-14717. 64p. (gr. k-3). 1965. 13.00 (0-06-023155-6); PLB 12.89 (0-06-023156-4) HarpC Child Bks.

—Here Comes the Strikeout. newly illus. ed. Kessler, Leonard. LC 91-14720. 64p. (gr. k-3). 1978. pap. 3.50 (0-06-444011-7, Trophy) HarpC Child Bks.

—Here Comes the Strikeout. Kessler, Leonard. LC 65-10728. 64p. (gr. k-3). 1987. incl. cassette 5.98 (0-694-00174-0, Trophy) HarpC Child Bks.

—Illustrated Baseball Dictionary for Young People. Walker, Henry. (gr. 4 up). 1978. pap. 2.50 (0-13-450924-2, Pub. by Treehouse) P-H.

—Is There a Horse in Your House? Kessler, Ethel & Kessler, Leonard. 32p. (ps). 1990. casebound with padded cov 4.95 (0-671-70540-7, Little Simon) S&S Trade.

—Kick, Pass, & Run. Kessler, Leonard. LC 66-18656. 64p. (ps-3). 1966. PLB 13.89 (0-06-023160-2) HarpC Child Bks.

—Kick, Pass & Run. Kessler, Leonard. LC 66-18656. (gr. k-3). 1978. pap. 3.50 (0-06-444012-5, Trophy) HarpC Child Bks.

—Last One in Is a Rotten Egg. Kessler, Leonard. LC 69-10209. 64p. (gr. k-3). 1969. PLB 13.89 (0-06-023158-0) HarpC Child Bks.

—Last One in Is a Rotten Egg. Kessler, Leonard. LC 69-10209. 64p. (gr. k-3). 1989. pap. 3.50 (0-06-444118-0, Trophy) HarpC Child Bks.

—Lend Me Your Ears: Telephone Jokes. Keller, Charles, compiled by. 40p. (gr. 2-5). 1993. PLB 13.95 (0-945912-23-4) Pippin Pr.

—Old Turtle's Baseball Stories. Kessler, Leonard. LC 81-6390. 56p. (gr. 1-3). 1982. 13.95 (0-688-00723-6); PLB 13.88 (0-688-00724-4) Greenwillow.

—Old Turtle's Riddle & Joke Book. Kessler, Leonard. LC 85-12565. 48p. (gr. 1-4). 1986. 12.95 (0-688-05953-8); PLB 12.88 (0-688-05954-6) Greenwillow.

—Pesah Is Coming. Chanover, Hyman & Chanover, Alice. (gr. k-2). 1956. 5.95 (0-8381-0713-3, 10-713) United Syn Bk.

—Pesah Is Here. Chanover, Hyman & Chanover, Alice. (gr. k-2). 1956. 5.95 (0-8381-0714-1) United Syn Bk.

—Stan the Hot Dog Man. Kessler, Ethel & Kessler, Leonard. LC 89-34474. 64p. (gr. k-3). 1990. PLB 13. 89 (0-06-023280-3) HarpC Child Bks.

—Sukkah & the Big Wind. Edelman, Lily. (gr. k-2). 1956. 5.95 (0-8381-0716-8) United Syn Bk.

—What's up, Doc? Doctor & Dentist Jokes. Keller, Charles. LC 84-6821. 64p. (gr. 3-7). 1984. 9.95 (0-13-954967-6) P-H.

—The Worst Team Ever. Kessler, Leonard. LC 84-25883. 47p. (gr. 1-3). 1985. 10.25 (0-688-04234-1); lib. bdg. 10.88 (0-688-04235-X) Greenwillow.

Kest, Kristin. Bees, Wasps, & Ants. Fichter, George S. 36p. (gr. k-3). 1993. 4.95 (0-307-11434-1, 11434, Golden Pr) Western Pub.

—Butterflies & Moths. Fichter, George S. 36p. (gr. k-3). 1993. 4.95 (0-307-11435-X, 11435, Golden Pr) Western Pub.

Kesteven, Peter. The Saga of Sammy-Cat. Mannin, Ethel. (gr. 1-3). 1969. Repr. of 1969 ed. 2.59 (0-08-013397-5) Pergamon.

—The Vikings. Stainer, Tom & Sutton, Harry. 32p. (gr. 4-6). 1992. pap. 4.95 (0-563-21356-6, BBC-Parkwest) Parkwest Pubns.

Kettle, Peter. African Stories. Hull, Robert. LC 92-40632. 48p. (gr. 5-9). 1993. 15.95 (1-56847-004-5) Thomson Lrning.

Kettner, Christine. An Ordinary Cat. Kettner, Christine. LC 90-19441. 32p. (ps-3). 1991. PLB 13.89 (0-06-023173-4) HarpC Child Bks.

Kew, Katinka. Little Monster. Wade, Barrie. LC 89-37277. 32p. (ps-2). 1990. 13.95 (0-688-09596-8); lib. bdg. 13.88 (0-688-09597-6) Lothrop.

—When Granfather's Parrot Inherited Kennington Court. Allen, Linda. (gr. 3-7). 1990. 12.95 (0-316-03413-4, Joy St Bks) Little.

Kew, Tony. Princess Finola: The Battle for Moytura. Vard, Colin. 67p. (Orig.). (gr. 3-6). 1993. pap. 11.95 (1-897973-00-4, Pub. by Celtpress ER) Irish Bks Media.

Kezer, Karel. The Call of the Wild. London, Jack. LC 63-14831. 144p. (gr. 6 up). 1970. 13.95 (0-02-759510-2, Macmillan Child Bk) Macmillan Child Grp.

Kezys, Algimantas, photos by. Caged-In. Sodeika, Zita. 94p. (Orig.). 1992. dug. 15.00 (0-685-59569-2) Galerija.

Khalsa, Dayal K. Cowboy Dreams. Khalsa, Dayal K. LC 89-22782. 32p. (gr. k-4). 1990. 16.00 (0-517-57490-X, Clarkson Potter); PLB 16.99 (0-517-57491-8, Clarkson Potter) Crown Bks Yng Read.

—How Pizza Came to Our Town. Khalsa, Dayal K. 32p. (gr. k-8). 1989. 14.95 (0-88776-231-X) Tundra Bks.

—How Pizza Came to Queens. Khalsa, Dayal K. (gr. 1 up). 1989. PLB 13.95 (0-517-57126-9, Clarkson Potter) Crown Bks Yng Read.

—Julian. Khalsa, Dayal K. 24p. (gr. k-8). 1989. 17.95 (0-88776-237-9) Tundra Bks.

—My Family Vacation. Khalsa, Dayal K. (gr. 1-3). 1988. PLB 13.95 (0-517-56697-4, Clarkson Potter) Crown Bks Yng Read.

—My Family Vacation. Khalsa, Dayal K. (gr. k-8). 1988. 14.95 (0-88776-226-3) Tundra Bks.

—The Snow Cat. Khalsa, Dayal K. LC 92-8988. 32p. (ps-2). 1992. 14.00 (0-517-59183-9, Clarkson Potter) Crown Bks Yng Read.

Khalsa, Mahan K. Seventy-Two Stories of God, Good, & Goods. Bhajan, Yogi. Khalsa, Tej K., ed. 28p. (Orig.). (gr. 10). 1989. pap. 9.95 (0-685-29452-8) Harimander Pub.

Khan, Aziz. Birds & Mammals. Bender, Lionel. Franklin Watts Ltd., ed. 40p. (gr. 7-9). 1988. PLB 12.40 (0-531-17091-8, Gloucester Pr) Watts.

—Fish to Reptiles. Bender, Lionel. Franklin Watts Ltd., ed. 40p. (gr. 7-9). 1988. PLB 12.40 (0-531-17093-4, Gloucester Pr) Watts.

—Invertebrates. Bender, Lionel. 40p. (gr. 1). 1988. 12.40 (0-531-17092-6) Watts.

Khan, Aziz, jt. illus. see Hayward, Ron.

Khanna, Krishna. As They Saw India. Khanna, K. (gr. 1-9). 1979. pap. 2.50 (0-89744-172-9) Auromere.

Khemraj, P. Story of Swarajya: Part II. Prakash, Sumangal. (gr. 1-10). 1979. pap. 2.50 (0-89744-186-9) Auromere.

—Tales for All Times. Rungachary, Santha. (gr. 1-9). 1979. pap. 2.50 (0-89744-187-7) Auromere.

Khoury, Diana. Human Biological Rhythms. Palmer, J. D. Head, J. J., ed. LC 81-67983. 16p. (gr. 10 up). 1983. pap. 2.75 (0-89278-304-4, 45-9704) Carolina Biological.

Kidd, Nina. June Mountain Secret. Kidd, Nina. LC 90-31574. 32p. (gr. 1-9). 1991. 15.00 (0-06-023167-X); PLB 14.89 (0-06-023168-8) HarpC Child Bks.

Kiddell-Monroe, Joan. African Myths & Legends. Arnott, Kathleen. 224p. (gr. 4 up). 1990. pap. 10.95 (0-19-274143-8) OUP.

—Chinese Myths & Fantasies. Birch, Cyril, ed. 144p. 1993. 10.95 (0-19-274152-7) OUP.

—French Legends, Tales & Fairy Stories. Picard, Barbara L. 216p. (gr. 4 up). 1992. pap. 10.95 (0-19-274149-7) OUP.

—The Iliad of Homer. Picard, Barbara L. 224p. (gr. 4 up). 1991. pap. 10.95 (0-19-274147-0) OUP.

—Odyssey by Homer. Picard, Barbara L. 288p. (gr. 4 up). 1991. pap. 10.95 (0-19-274146-2) OUP.

—Russian Tales & Legends. Downing, Charles. 224p. (gr. 4 up). 1990. pap. 10.95 (0-19-274144-6) OUP.

—Scandinavian Legends & Folk-Tales. Jones, Gwyn, retold by. 192p. (gr. 4 up). 1992. pap. 10.95 (0-19-274150-0) OUP.

—Scottish Folk-Tales & Legends. Wilson, Barbara K. 224p. (ps-7). 1990. pap. 10.95 (*0-19-274141-1*) OUP.
—Sirga. Guillot, Rene. LC 59-12198. (gr. 6-9). 1959. 21. 95 (*0-87599-046-0*) S G Phillips.
—West Indian Folk Tales. Sherlock, Philip M. 151p. (gr. 3 up). 1988. pap. 10.95 (*0-19-274127-6*) OUP.
Kidder, Christine. Clovis Crawfish & the Curious Crapaud. Fontenot, Mary A. LC 86-4997. 32p. (ps-3). 1986. 12.95 (*0-88289-610-5*) Pelican.
Kidder, Harvey. Catch That Pass, Vol. 1. Christopher, Matt. LC 77-77442. (gr. 4-6). 1989. lib. bdg. 14.95 (*0-316-13932-7*); pap. 3.95 (*0-316-13924-6*) Little.
—Johnny Long Legs. Christopher, Matt. 144p. (gr. 3-6). 1988. pap. 3.95 (*0-316-14065-1*) Little.
—The Kid Who Only Hit Homers. Christopher, Matt. (gr. 4-6). 1972. lib. bdg. 14.95 (*0-316-13918-1*) Little.
—The Kid Who Only Hit Homers. Christopher, Matt. 160p. (gr. 4 up). 1986. pap. 3.95 (*0-316-13987-4*) Little.
—Look Who's Playing First Base. Christopher, Matt. (gr. 4-6). 1987. pap. 3.95 (*0-316-13989-0*) Little.
—Shortstop from Tokyo. Christopher, Matt. (gr. 3-6). 1988. pap. 3.95 (*0-316-13992-0*) Little.
—Tough to Tackle. Christopher, Matt. 152p. (gr. 4-6). 1987. pap. 3.95 (*0-316-14058-9*) Little.
Kidship Associates Staff. Lluvia de Palabras. Kidship Associates Staff. (SPA.). 109p. (gr. 1-3). 1988. pap. text ed. 2.00 (*1-878742-00-0*) Kidship Assoc.
Kiedrowski, Priscilla. Christmas around the World. Kelley, Emily. 48p. (gr. k-4). 1986. lib. bdg. 14.95 (*0-87614-249-8*) Carolrhoda Bks.
—Christmas Around the World. Kelley, Emily. 48p. (ps-4). 1986. pap. 5.95 (*0-87614-453-9*, First Ave Edns) Lerner Pubns.
—Happy New Year. Kelley, Emily. 48p. (gr. k-4). 1984. PLB 14.95 (*0-87614-269-2*) Carolrhoda Bks.
—Happy New Year. Kelley, Emily. (gr. k-4). 1987. pap. 3.95 (*0-87614-469-5*, First Ave Edns) Lerner Pubns.
—My First Hanukkah Book. Fisher, Aileen L. LC 84-21510. 32p. (ps-2). 1985. PLB 15.00 (*0-516-02905-3*); pap. 3.95 (*0-516-42905-1*) Childrens.
Kiefer, Christa. Priscilla Alden & the Story of the First Thanksgiving. Boynton, Alice B. Brook, Bonnie, ed. 32p. (gr. k-2). 1990. 6.95 (*0-671-69111-2*); PLB 10.98 (*0-671-69105-8*) Silver Pr.
Kiefer, Jill. The Adventures of Pinto Bean & Chapulin. Hayes, Frederick & Hayes, Jean. 20p. (Orig.). (gr. 1-8). 1988. pap. text ed. 6.95 (*0-317-93098-2*) Pinto Pub.
Kiefer, Scott. The Children's Organizer: A Calendar System of Daily Tasks for Children. Pighetti, Toni. 32p. (Orig.). (gr. k-8). 1983. pap. 7.95 (*0-913005-03-7*) TAM Assoc.
Kieffer, Christa. The Lemon Drop Jar. Widman, Christine. LC 91-11209. 32p. (gr. k-3). 1992. RSBE 14.95 (*0-02-792759-8*, Macmillan Child Bk) Macmillan Child Grp.
—Mary Baker Eddy, a Special Friend. Sass, Karin. LC 83-72002. 32p. (gr. k-3). 1983. 8.95 (*0-87510-165-8*) Christian Sci.
Kiefhaber, Jan. Off to Camp! Pravda, Myra & Weiland, Jeanne. 72p. (Orig.). (gr. 2-7). 1989. pap. 4.95 perfect bdg. (*0-9622328-0-7*) JSP Pub.
Kielesinski, Chris, jt. illus. see VanRoon, Terry.

Kifer, Kathy. Caring for Young Children: Signing for Day Care Providers & Sitters. Collins, S. Harold. 32p. (Orig.). (gr. 1-8). 1993. pap. text ed. 2.95 (*0-931993-58-X*, GP-058) Garlic Pr OR.
CARING FOR YOUNG CHILDREN is one of four books in the Beginning Sign Language Series. This book is geared to those who work with or care for young hearing impaired children. CAN I HELP? (ISBN 0-931993-57-1, 32p., $2.95) presents signs, sentences & information to help a beginning signer of any age communicate with a hearing impaired person who may need help. The FINGER ALPHABET BOOK (ISBN 0-931993-46-6, 32p., $2.95) teaches alphabet signs & starts you on your way to TALKING with your hands. Its companion book, SIGNING AT SCHOOL, (ISBN 0-931993-47-4, 32p., $2.95) presents signs, sentences & vocabulary to enable a beginning signer to ask questions, get information, give greetings, & give directions. These wonderful books with glossy durable covers provide easy-to-follow illustrations & activities to make sign language fascinating & fun for both children & adults.
Publisher Provided Annotation.

Kifer, Kathy & Solar, Dahna. Addition & Subtraction: No Regrouping. Lawrence, H. S. (ENG & SPA.). 30p. (Orig.). (gr. 1-6). 1992. pap. 3.95 wkbk. (*0-931993-51-2*, GP-051) Garlic Pr OR.
—Addition: No Regrouping. Lawrence, H. S. (ENG & SPA.). 30p. (Orig.). (gr. 1-6). 1992. pap. 3.95 wkbk. (*0-931993-49-0*, GP-049) Garlic Pr OR.
—Multiplication: Factors 1-12. Lawrence, H. S. (ENG & SPA.). 30p. (Orig.). (gr. 3-6). 1992. pap. 3.95 wkbk. (*0-931993-52-0*, GP-052) Garlic Pr OR.
—Subtraction: No Regrouping. Lawrence, H. S. (ENG & SPA.). 30p. (Orig.). (gr. 1-6). 1992. pap. 3.95 wkbk. (*0-931993-50-4*, GP-050) Garlic Pr OR.
Kight, Joshua. Jeremy Firefly: Oh to Glow. Howard, Diane W. 48p. (Orig.). (gr. k-3). 1991. PLB 13.95 (*0-9623524-2-X*) Hunt Hse Pub.
Kightley, Rosalinda. Bear Facts: Sounds. Bennett, David. (ps-k). 1989. 3.95 (*0-553-05494-5*, Little Rooster) Bantam.
—Bear Facts: Water. Bennett, David. 1989. pap. 3.95 (*0-553-05811-8*) Bantam.
—Day & Night. Bennett, David. 32p. (ps up). 1988. pap. 3.95 (*0-553-05479-1*) Bantam.
—Earth. Bennett, David. 32p. (ps-12). 1988. pap. 3.95 (*0-553-05481-3*) Bantam.
—The Farmer. Kightley, Rosalinda. LC 88-19431. 32p. (ps-2). 1989. pap. 3.95 (*0-689-71222-7*, Aladdin) Macmillan Child Grp.
—Fire. Bennett, David. 1989. 3.95 (*0-553-05813-4*) Bantam.
—Seasons. Bennett, David. 32p. (ps up). 1988. pap. 3.95 (*0-553-05480-5*) Bantam.
Kightly, Rosalinda, et al. My First Book: Words & Pictures for the Very Young. Kightley, Rosalinda, et al. LC 91-71831. 64p. (ps). 1992. 14.95 (*1-56402-034-7*) Candlewick Pr.
Kikuchi, Isao. Bluejay in the Desert. Shigekawa, Marlene. LC 92-35424. 36p. (gr. k-4). 1993. 12.95 (*1-879965-04-6*) Polychrome Pub.
Kilgore, Julia. Three Monkey Saves the Day. Ryder, Virginia P. 21p. (Orig.). (gr. k-12). 1991. pap. 8.95 (*0-935098-04-6*) Amigo Pr.
Kilgore, Susie. Vilma Martinez. Codye, Corinn. De Varona, Frank, intro. by. (ENG & SPA.). 32p. (gr. 3-6). 1990. PLB 15.96 (*0-8172-3382-2*); pap. 4.95 (*0-8114-6762-7*) Raintree Steck-V.
Killeen, Leah R. At the Park. Killeen, Leah R. 32p. (ps-2). Date not set. 11.95 (*1-56065-154-7*) Capstone Pr. Postponed.
—Rainbow Fruit Salad. Killeen, Leah R. 32p. (ps-2). Date not set. 11.95 (*1-56065-155-5*) Capstone Pr. Postponed.
Killgrew, John. I Can Read About Pecos Bill. Anderson, J. I. LC 76-54575. (gr. 2-5). 1977. pap. 1.95 (*0-89375-042-5*) Troll Assocs.
Kills Two & Amos Bad Heart Bull. These Were the Sioux. Sandoz, Mari. LC 85-8914. 118p. (gr. 6-12). 1985. pap. 5.95 (*0-8032-9151-5*, Bison Books) U of Nebr Pr.
Kim, Holly C. The Iroko-Man: A Yoruba Folktale. Gershator, Phyllis, retold by. LC 93-4888. 32p. (ps-2). 1994. 14.95 (*0-531-06810-2*); PLB 14.99 (*0-531-08660-7*) Orchard Bks Watts.
Kim, Jody. Habari Gani? What's the News? Morninghouse, Sundaira. 32p. (gr. k-4). 1992. 14.95 (*0-940880-39-3*) Open Hand.
—The Man Who Founded a Town. Mumford, Esther H. 32p. (Orig.). (gr. 2-5). 1990. 8.95 (*0-9605670-2-X*); pap. 4.95 (*0-9605670-3-8*) Ananse Pr.
—Nightfeathers: Black Goose Rhymes. Morninghouse, Sundaira. LC 89-63264. 32p. (gr. 1-4). 1989. 9.95 (*0-940880-27-X*); pap. text ed. 4.95 (*0-940880-28-8*) Open Hand.
Kim, Yun-Kyong. Mr. Moon & Miss Sun. Vorhees, Duance & Mueller, Mark, eds. 45p. (gr. 2-5). 1990. PLB 9.95x (*0-930878-72-8*) Hollym Intl.
—The Ogres' Magic Clubs. Vorhees, Duance & Mueller, Mark. 46p. (gr. 2-5). 1991. PLB 9.95x (*0-930878-88-4*) Hollym Intl.
—The Woodcutter & the Heavenly Maiden. Vorhees, Duance & Mueller, Mark, eds. 45p. (gr. 2-5). 1990. PLB 9.95x (*0-930878-71-X*) Hollym Intl.
Kim, Yon-Kyong & Kang, Mi-Sun. The Son of the Cinnamon Tree: The Donkey's Egg. Vorhees, Duance & Mueller, Mark. 46p. (gr. 2-5). 1990. PLB 9.95x (*0-930878-93-0*) Hollym Intl.
Kim, Yon-Kyong, jt. illus. see Kang, Mi-Sun.
Kim, Yon-Kyong, jt. illus. see Pak, Mi-Son.
Kim, Yong-Kyong, jt. illus. see Kang, Mi-Sun.
Kimball, Katherine. The Wonderful Counting Clock. Edens, Cooper. LC 93-14404. 1994. 14.00 (*0-671-88334-8*, Green Tiger) S&S Trade.
Kimball, Linda H. Science Projects & Activities. Challand, Helen J. LC 84-23252. 93p. (gr. 5-8). 1985. PLB 17.27 (*0-516-00569-3*) Childrens.
Kimber, Julianne S. I Love America, Pt. 1: Teacher's Resource Kit. Kimber, Julianne S. 313p. (gr. k-2). 1986. wkbk. 14.95 (*0-88080-018-6*) Natl Ctr Constitutional.
Kimber, William. Night Time. Pettigrew, Eileen. 24p. (ps-1). 1992. PLB 14.95 (*1-55037-235-1*, Pub. by Annick Pr); pap. 4.95 (*1-55037-242-4*, Pub. by Annick Pr) Firefly Bks Ltd.
—The Pathfinder's Adventure Kit. Kennedy, Christine & Smith, Mark. LC 92-34711. 56p. (Orig.). (gr. 4-7). 1993. pap. 15.00 (*0-679-83491-5*) Random Bks Yng Read.

Kimberling, Bryce. One Elephant Went Out to Play Big Book. (ps-2). 1988. pap. text ed. 14.00 (*0-922053-16-2*) N Edge Res.
Kim Chee, Wendy. I Like Poems & Poems Like Me. Pagliaro, Penny, ed. LC 76-50343. (gr. 1-6). 1977. PLB 8.95 (*0-916630-03-X*) Pr Pacifica.
Kimmel, Joan. Piggyback Songs to Sign. Warren, Jean & Shroyer, Susan. LC 85-50433. 96p. 1992. 8.95 (*0-911019-53-7*, WPH 029) Warren Pub Hse.
Kimmel, Joan G. ABC - Sign with Me. Shroyer, Susan P. & Kimmel, Joan G. 32p. (Orig.). (ps-2). 1987. pap. 4.95 (*0-939849-00-3*) Sugar Sign Pr.
Kimmel, Nita. Young Man's Guide to Autos: Basics, Operation, Safety & Maintenance. Bouquet, Jeff S. 80p. 1991. 55.00x (*1-56216-017-6*); pap. 25.00x (*1-56216-018-4*) Systems Co.
Kimura, Hideo M. How to Pick & Strum the Ukulele, Bk. II. rev. ed. Kimura, Hideo M. 44p. (gr. 7 up). 1988. pap. text ed. write for info. (*0-917822-18-8*) Heedays.
Kincade, Nancy. Even If I Did Something Awful? Hazen, Barbara S. LC 81-1907. 36p. (ps-2). 1981. SBE 13.95 (*0-689-30843-4*, Atheneum Child Bk) Macmillan Child Grp.
—Even If I Did Something Awful? Hazen, Barbara S. LC 91-23143. 32p. (ps-2). 1992. pap. 3.95 (*0-689-71600-1*, Aladdin) Macmillan Child Grp.
—My Mother Is the Smartest Woman in the World. Clymer, Eleanor. LC 82-1685. 96p. (gr. 4-6). 1982. SBE 12.95 (*0-689-30916-3*, Atheneum Child Bk) Macmillan Child Grp.
Kindberg, Sally. Pet Poems. Fisher, Robert, ed. 96p. (gr. 1 up). 1993. pap. 4.95 (*0-571-16830-2*) Faber & Faber.
Kindberg, Sally, jt. illus. see Dann, Penny.
Kindersley, Dorling. Birds. Kindersley, Dorling. LC 92-8601. 24p. (ps-k). 1992. POB 7.95 (*0-689-71644-3*, Aladdin) Macmillan Child Grp.
Kinens, Janis J. The Old Woodcutter. Kinens, Janis J. LC 88-81904. 32p. (gr. k-12). 1988. PLB 12.95 (*0-9620999-0-2*); 12.95 (*0-9620999-1-0*) Guzzy Pr.
Kiner, K. C. I Can't Sleep with Those Elves Watching Me. Cavanaugh, Kate. 25p. (ps-8). 1990. pap. text ed. 4.95 (*0-9622353-1-8*) KAC.
—Pete & His Elves Series. Cavanaugh, Kate. 28p. 1992. Set. pap. write for info. (*0-9622353-4-2*) KAC.
—Pete Goes to Grand Island. Cavanaugh, Kate. 24p. 1992. pap. 5.95 (*0-9622353-3-4*) KAC.
—Pete's Lost. Cavanaugh, Kate. 24p. (Orig.). 1991. pap. 4.95 (*0-9622353-2-6*) KAC.
King, Barbara L. Daniel Forbes: A Pioneer Boy. Hamilton, Dorothy. (Orig.). (ps-4). 1980. pap. 3.95 (*0-686-32860-4*) Barnwood Pr.
King, Celia. Seven Modern Wonders of the World: A Pop-up Book. King, Celia. 7p. (gr. 3 up). 1992. 9.95 (*0-8118-0159-4*) Chronicle Bks.
—The Seven Natural Wonders of the World: A Pop-up Book. King, Celia. 7p. (ps up). 1991. 8.95 (*0-8118-0001-6*) Chronicle Bks.
King, Charles S., Jr. Dreams, Things & I Remember When. King, Charles S., Jr. 64p. (Orig.). 1989. 9.95 (*0-685-25964-1*) Swan Sea Music.
King, Colin. Birthday Time: Toddler's World. Griffey, Harriet. 28p. (ps-1). 1992. 3.50 (*0-7214-1479-6*, 928-2) Ladybird Bks.
—Chemistry Experiments. Johnson, May. 64p. (gr. 3-6). 1983. lib. bdg. 11.96 (*0-88110-161-3*); pap. 4.95 (*0-86020-527-4*) EDC.
—Children's Encyclopedia. Elliot, J. 128p. (gr. 3-6). 1987. PLB 12.95 (*0-88110-265-2*); pap. 12.95 (*0-7460-0000-6*) EDC.
—Flight & Floating. Ward, Alan. 64p. (gr. 3-6). 1983. pap. 4.95 (*0-86020-529-0*); lib. bdg. 11.96 (*0-88110-162-1*) EDc.
—My First Atlas, Vol. 1. Petty, Kate. (gr. k-8). 1991. 9.95 (*1-55782-361-8*, Pub. by Warner Juvenile Bks) Little.
—My Lift the Flap Car Book. Royston, Angela. 90-8615. 1991. 14.95 (*0-399-22006-2*, Putnam) Putnam Pub Group.
—My Lift-the-Flap Plane Book. Royston, Angela. LC 92-38631. 18p. (ps-1). 1993. 14.95 (*0-399-22533-1*, Putnam) Putnam Pub Group.
King, Dave. Seashore. Parker, Steve. LC 88-27173. 64p. (gr. 5 up). 1989. 15.00 (*0-394-82254-4*); PLB 15.99 (*0-394-92254-9*) Knopf Bks Yng Read.
King, Dave, photos by. Amazing Bears. Greenaway, Theresa. LC 92-910. 32p. (Orig.). (gr. 1-5). 1992. PLB 9.99 (*0-679-92769-7*); pap. 7.99 (*0-679-82769-2*) Knopf Bks Yng Read.
—Amazing Cars. Lord, Trevor. LC 91-53138. 32p. (Orig.). (gr. 1-5). 1992. PLB 9.99 (*0-679-92766-2*); pap. 6.95 (*0-679-82766-8*) Knopf Bks Yng Read.
—Arms & Armor. Byam, Michele. LC 87-26449. 64p. (gr. 5 up). 1988. 15.00 (*0-394-89622-X*); lib. bdg. 15. 99 (*0-394-99622-4*) Knopf Bks Yng Read.
—Cat. Clutton-Brock, Juliet. LC 91-9399. 64p. (gr. 5 up). 1991. 15.00 (*0-679-81458-2*); lib. bdg. 15.99 (*0-679-91458-7*) Knopf Bks Yng Read.
—Early Humans. Merriman, Nick. LC 88-13431. 64p. (gr. 5 up). 1989. 15.00 (*0-394-82257-9*); lib. bdg. 15.99 (*0-394-92257-3*) Knopf Bks Yng Read.
—Film. Platt, Richard. LC 91-53133. 64p. (gr. 5 up). 1992. 15.00 (*0-679-81679-8*); PLB 15.99 (*0-679-91679-2*) Knopf Bks Yng Read.
—Invention. Bender, Lionel. LC 90-4888. 64p. (gr. 5 up). 1991. 15.00 (*0-679-80782-9*); PLB 15.99 (*0-679-90782-6*) Knopf Bks Yng Read.
—My First Garden Book. Wilkes, Angela. LC 90-40332. 48p. (gr. 2-5). 1992. 13.00 (*0-679-81412-4*); PLB 13. 99 (*0-679-91412-9*) Knopf Bks Yng Read.

—Sports. Hammond, Tim. LC 88-1573. 64p. (gr. 5 up). 1988. 15.00 (0-394-89616-5); lib. bdg. 15.99 (0-394-99616-X) Knopf Bks Yng Read.

King, Dave & Keates, Colin, photos by. Fish. Parker, Steve. LC 89-36445. 64p. (gr. 5 up). 1990. 15.00 (0-679-80439-0); PLB 15.99 (0-679-90439-5) Random Bks Yng Read.

King, Dave, jt. photog. see Burton, Jane.

King, Dave, jt. photog. see Greenaway, Frank.

King, Dave, et al. Plant & Flower. Burnie, David. LC 88-27172. 64p. (gr. 5 up). 1989. 15.00 (0-394-82252-8); PLB 15.99 (0-394-92252-2) Knopf Bks Yng Read.

King, Dave, et al, photos by. Music. Ardley, Neil. LC 88-13394. 64p. (gr. 5 up). 1989. 15.00 (0-394-82259-5); lib. bdg. 15.99 (0-394-92259-X) Knopf Bks Yng Read.

—Flying Machine. Nahum, Andrew. LC 90-4007. 64p. (gr. 5 up). 1990. 15.00 (0-679-80744-6); PLB 15.99 (0-679-90744-0) Knopf Bks Yng Read.

King, Debbie. Look at Seeds & Weeds. rev. ed. Kirkpatrick, Rena K. LC 84-26226. 32p. (gr. 2-4). 1985. PLB 17.28 (0-8172-2357-6); pap. 4.95 (0-8114-6903-4) Raintree Steck-V.

King, Deborah. Custer: The Story of a Horse. King, Deborah. 32p. (ps-3). 1992. PLB 14.95 (0-399-22147-6, Philomel Bks) Putnam Pub Group.

King, Ed. Encuentralo con Elena. Foreman, Mary M., tr. from ENG. (SPA.). 24p. 1992. pap. 3.95 (1-56288-238-4) Checkerboard.

—Gus Is Gone. LC 90-28634. 24p. (ps up). 1991. pap. 3.95 (1-56288-008-X) Checkerboard.

—Investigalo con Ines. Foreman, Mary M., tr. from ENG. (SPA.). 24p. 1992. pap. 3.95 (1-56288-239-2) Checkerboard.

—Lucy is Lost. LC 90-27675. 24p. 1991. pap. 3.95 (1-56288-009-8) Checkerboard.

—Paseate con Paco. Foreman, Mary M., tr. from ENG. (SPA.). 24p. 1929. pap. 3.95 (1-56288-240-6) Checkerboard.

—Viaja con Victor. Foreman, Mary M., tr. from ENG. (SPA.). 24p. 1992. pap. 3.95 (1-56288-237-6) Checkerboard.

—William Wanders Off. LC 90-27677. 24p. 1991. pap. 3.95 (1-56288-011-X) Checkerboard.

King, Elizabeth, photos by. Backyard Sunflower. King, Elizabeth. LC 92-31002. (ps-3). 1993. 13.99 (0-525-45082-3, DCB) Dutton Child Bks.

King, Gordon. Enciclopedia de Historias Biblicas. Robertson, Jenny. LaValle, Maria T., tr. (SPA.). 272p. (gr. 3-5). 1984. 17.00 (0-311-03671-6) Casa Bautista.

—Jesus: Historias de su Vida. Ralph, Margaret. LaValle, Teresa, tr. 28p. (gr. 4). 1979. 2.75 (0-311-38536-2, Edit Mundo) Casa Bautista.

King, Helen B. Sandy. King, Helen B. 18p. (ps up). 1985. pap. 4.95 (0-9615366-4-0) King ME.

King, James B. Haiku Is... a Feeling. Leivis, Edith M. Leivis, Edith M., intro. by. LC 89-64144. 64p. (Orig.). (gr. 1-3). 1990. pap. 5.95 (0-9624993-0-7) Pippin Bks.

King, Jesse J., Sr. You Can Say No to Drugs. King, Jesse J., Sr. King, Linda L., ed. 24p. (Orig.). (gr. k-5). 1989. pap. text ed. 1.25 (0-685-25956-0) J Lynn Pub.

—You Can Say No to Drugs: For Fifth Grade. King, Jesse J., Sr. King, Linda L., ed. 24p. (Orig.). (gr. 5). 1990. pap. text ed. 1.25 (0-685-25962-5) J Lynn Pub.

—You Can Say No to Drugs: For First Grade. King, Jesse J., Sr. King, Linda L., ed. 24p. (Orig.). (gr. 1). 1989. pap. text ed. 1.25 (0-685-25958-7) J Lynn Pub.

—You Can Say No to Drugs: For Fourth Grade. King, Jesse J., Sr. King, Linda L., ed. 24p. (Orig.). (gr. 4). 1990. pap. text ed. 1.25 (0-685-25961-7) J Lynn Pub.

—You Can Say No to Drugs: For Kindergarten. King, Jesse J., Sr. King, Linda L., ed. 24p. (Orig.). (gr. k). 1989. pap. text ed. 1.25 (0-685-25957-9) J Lynn Pub.

—You Can Say No to Drugs: For Second Grade. King, Jesse J., Sr. King, Linda L., ed. 24p. (Orig.). (gr. 2). 1989. pap. text ed. 1.25 (0-685-25959-5) J Lynn Pub.

—You Can Say No to Drugs: For Third Grade. King, Jesse J., Sr. King, Linda L., ed. 24p. (Orig.). (gr. 3). 1990. pap. text ed. 1.25 (0-685-25960-9) J Lynn Pub.

King, Kevin. Boon the Raccoon & Easel the Weasel: A Fable by Bobby L. Jackson. Jackson, Bobby L. Reuter, Janet R., frwd. by. LC 92-62211. 32p. (gr. 2-3). 1993. 9.95 (0-9634932-0-5, Dist. by Baker & Taylor Bks.); pap. 5.95 (0-9634932-1-3) Multicult Pubns.

—The Gift of the Magi. O. Henry. 32p. (gr. 5 up). 1988. pap. 12.95 (0-671-64706-7, Little Simon) S&S Trade.

Kingman, Dong. Effect of Gamma Rays on Man-in-the-Moon Marigolds. Zindel, Paul. (gr. 9 up). 1984. pap. 3.95 (0-553-28028-7) Bantam.

—Effect of Gamma Rays on Man-in-the-Moon Marigolds. Zindel, Paul. LC 79-135772. 128p. (gr. 7 up). 1971. 18.00 (0-06-026829-8) HarpC Child Bks.

Kingshead Corporation Staff. Cut, Color & Create: Make Your Own: Alphabet Blocks. Kingshead Corporation Staff. 24p. (ps-3). 1987. pap. 2.97 (1-55941-005-1) Kingshead Corp.

—Cut, Color & Create: Make Your Own: Alphabet Friends. Kingshead Corporation Staff. 24p. (ps-3). 1987. pap. 2.97 (1-55941-003-5) Kingshead Corp.

—Cut, Color & Create: Make Your Own: Beach. Kingshead Corporation Staff. 24p. (ps-4). 1987. pap. 2.97 (1-55941-011-6) Kingshead Corp.

—Cut-Color-&-Create: Make Your Own: Box Magic. Kingshead Corporation Staff. 24p. (ps-1). 1989. pap. 2.97 (1-55941-039-6) Kingshead Corp.

—Cut-Color-&-Create: Make Your Own: Box Magic. Kingshead Corporation Staff. 24p. (ps-1). 1989. pap. 2.97 (1-55941-038-8) Kingshead Corp.

—Cut, Color & Create: Make Your Own: Christmas Cards. Kingshead Corporation Staff. 24p. (gr. k-4). 1987. pap. 2.97 (1-55941-021-3) Kingshead Corp.

—Cut, Color & Create: Make Your Own: Christmas Garland. Kingshead Corporation Staff. 24p. (ps-2). 1987. pap. 2.97 (1-55941-020-5) Kingshead Corp.

—Cut, Color & Create: Make Your Own: Circus. Kingshead Corporation Staff. 24p. (ps-4). 1987. pap. 2.97 (1-55941-008-6) Kingshead Corp.

—Cut, Color & Create: Make Your Own: Christmas Ornaments. Kingshead Corporation Staff. 24p. (gr. 2 up). 1987. pap. 2.97 (1-55941-018-3) Kingshead Corp.

—Cut, Color & Create: Make Your Own: Christmas Snowflakes. Kingshead Corporation Staff. 24p. (gr. k-3). 1987. pap. 2.97 (1-55941-017-5) Kingshead Corp.

—Cut, Color & Create: Make Your Own: Christmas Snowflakes. Kingshead Corporation Staff. 24p. (gr. 3 up). 1987. pap. 2.97 (1-55941-019-1) Kingshead Corp.

—Cut, Color & Create: Make Your Own: Doll's Christmas. Kingshead Corporation Staff. 24p. 1987. pap. 2.97 (1-55941-013-2) Kingshead Corp.

—Cut-Color-&-Create: Make Your Own: Easter Fun. Kingshead Corporation Staff. 24p. (ps-1). 1989. pap. 2.97 (1-55941-022-1) Kingshead Corp.

—Cut-Color-&-Create: Make Your Own: Easter Fun. Kingshead Corporation Staff. 24p. (ps-1). 1989. pap. 2.97 (1-55941-023-X) Kingshead Corp.

—Cut-Color-&-Create: Make Your Own: Easter Fun. Kingshead Corporation Staff. 24p. (ps-1). 1989. pap. 2.97 (1-55941-024-8) Kingshead Corp.

—Cut, Color & Create: Make Your Own: Easy Christmas Ornaments. Kingshead Corporation Staff. 24p. (ps-2). 1987. pap. 2.97 (1-55941-016-7) Kingshead Corp.

—Cut, Color & Create: Make Your Own: Farm. Kingshead Corporation Staff. 24p. (ps-4). 1987. pap. 2.97 (1-55941-007-8) Kingshead Corp.

—Cut, Color & Create: Make Your Own: Masks. Kingshead Corporation Staff. 24p. (ps-4). 1988. pap. 2.97 (0-685-22520-8) Kingshead Corp.

—Cut, Color & Create: Make Your Own: Number People. Kingshead Corporation Staff. 24p. (ps-3). 1987. pap. 2.97 (1-55941-004-3) Kingshead Corp.

—Cut, Color & Create: Make Your Own: Number Blocks. Kingshead Corporation Staff. 24p. (ps-3). 1987. pap. 2.97 (1-55941-006-X) Kingshead Corp.

—Cut, Color & Create: Make Your Own: Places to Go. Kingshead Corporation Staff. 24p. (ps-4). 1987. pap. 2.97 (1-55941-012-4) Kingshead Corp.

—Cut, Color & Create: Make Your Own: Paperplate Puppets. Kingshead Corporation Staff. 24p. (ps-3). 1987. pap. 2.97 (1-55941-002-7) Kingshead Corp.

—Cut, Color & Create: Make Your Own: Paperbag Puppets. Kingshead Corporation Staff. 24p. (ps-3). 1987. pap. 2.97 (1-55941-001-9) Kingshead Corp.

—Cut-Color-&-Create: Make Your Own: Pumpkin Magic. Kingshead Corporation Staff. 24p. (ps-1). 1988. pap. 2.97 (1-55941-037-X) Kingshead Corp.

—Cut, Color & Create: Make Your Own: Safari. Kingshead Corporation Staff. 24p. (ps-4). 1987. pap. 2.97 (1-55941-010-8) Kingshead Corp.

—Cut, Color & Create: Make Your Own: Valentine Fun. Kingshead Corporation Staff. 24p. (gr. k-3). 1987. pap. 2.97 (1-55941-015-9) Kingshead Corp.

—Cut, Color & Create: Make Your Own: Valentines. Kingshead Corporation Staff. 24p. (gr. k-3). 1987. pap. 2.97 (1-55941-014-0) Kingshead Corp.

—Cut, Color & Create: Make Your Own: Zoo. Kingshead Corporation Staff. 24p. (ps-4). 1987. pap. 2.97 (1-55941-009-4) Kingshead Corp.

Kingston, Arlene. The Bagels Are Coming. Kingston, Arlene. 40p. (ps up). 1988. pap. 5.95 (0-929934-00-8) Child Time Pubs.

Kingstone, Martin, jt. illus. see Gibbons, Tony.

Kinne, Kathy. Once upon a Cook Book. Kaplan, Lisa. 80p. (Orig.). (gr. k-3). pap. 4.00 (0-937730-01-7) Good Sign.

Kinneavy, Janice. Great Answer Book. Pansini, Anna, ed. LC 90-44452. 48p. (gr. 3-6). 1991. PLB 10.89 (0-8167-2308-7); pap. text ed. 2.95 (0-8167-2309-5) Troll Assocs.

—Let's Celebrate Thanksgiving: A Book of Drawing Fun. Kinneay, Janice. LC 87-61373. 32p. (gr. 2-6). 1988. PLB 10.65 (0-8167-1131-3); pap. text ed. 1.95 (0-8167-1132-1) Troll Assocs.

—Meet the Real Me. Gavin, Peggy, compiled by. LC 92-21644. 32p. (gr. 2-8). 1992. pap. text ed. 2.50 (0-8167-2939-5) Troll Assocs.

—A Picture Book of Animal Opposites. Mabie, Grace. LC 91-33596. 24p. (gr. 1-4). 1992. text ed. 9.59 (0-8167-2438-5); 2.50 (0-8167-2439-3) Troll Assocs.

—A Picture Book of Dinosaurs. Nemes, Claire. LC 89-37331. 24p. (gr. 1-4). 1990. lib. bdg. 9.59 (0-8167-1900-4); pap. text ed. 2.50 (0-8167-1901-2) Troll Assocs.

—A Picture Book of Insects. Mattern, Joanne. LC 90-11211. 24p. (gr. 1-4). 1991. PLB 9.59 (0-8167-2154-8); pap. 2.50 (0-8167-2155-6) Troll Assocs.

—A Picture Book of Night-Time Animals. Mabie, Grace. LC 91-33597. 24p. (gr. 1-4). 1992. PLB 9.59 (0-8167-2432-6); pap. 2.50 (0-8167-2433-4) Troll Assocs.

Kinnelay, Janice. A Picture Book of Reptiles & Amphibians. Scott, Mary. LC 92-19054. 24p. (gr. 1-4). 1992. lib. bdg. 9.59 (0-8167-2838-0); pap. text ed. 2.50 (0-8167-2839-9) Troll Assocs.

Kinnell, Shannon. Alligator & the Toothfairy. Roberts, Jo-Anna. 56p. (ps-2). 1991. 11.50g (1-879212-00-5) Desert Star Intl.

Kinney, Pamela. The Magic of Marionettes. Masson, A. 88p. (gr. 6 up). 1989. pap. 9.95 (1-55037-042-1, Pub. by Annick CN) Firefly Bks Ltd.

Kinzer, Kaaren. Fifty-Two Things to Do on Sabbath. Robinson, Glen. Wheeler, Gerald, ed. (Orig.). 1983. pap. 2.95 (0-8280-0199-5) Review & Herald.

Kinzie, Mable B., jt. illus. see Harper-Marinick.

Kinzie, Mable B., jt. illus. see Harper-Marinick, Maria.

Kipling, Rudyard. Just So Stories. Kipling, Rudyard. LC 92-53177. 192p. 1992. 12.95 (0-679-41797-4, Evrymans Lib Childs Class) Knopf.

Kipling, Rudyard & Gleeson, Joseph. How the Leopard Got Its Spots: And Other Just So Stories. Kipling, Rudyard. LC 93-540. 184p. 1993. 6.00 (1-56957-902-4) Shambhala Pubns.

Kipling, Rudyard, jt. illus. see Gleeson, Joseph M.

Kirby, Keith. Literature Cross-A-Word Book I: Crossword Learning Experiences with Animal Stories, Modern Fantasy, & Space & Time. Bell, Irene W. 96p. 1982. pap. 14.75 (0-89774-062-9) Oryx Pr.

Kirby, Thomas. The Clear Red Stone: A Myth & the Meaning of Menstruation. Kolkmeyer, Alexandra. Goldstein, Lynn, ed. LC 82-2956. 64p. (gr. 3-12). 1982. text ed. 9.50 (0-942524-01-2) In Sight Pr NM.

Kirchhoff, Art. Stephen's Bag. Singerman, Ellen. McKissack, Patricia & McKissack, Fredrick, eds. LC 87-61642. 32p. (Orig.). (gr. 1-3). 1987. pap. 8.95 (0-88335-729-1); pap. text ed. 4.95 (0-88335-749-6) Milliken Pub Co.

Kirchoff, Art, jt. illus. see Agnew, Tim.

Kirehoff, Dan. Sal T. Dog. Clough, Fred. 48p. (gr. 1-3). 1990. 12.95 (0-89272-281-9) Down East.

Kirk, Barbara, photos by. Joey's Story: Straight Talk about Drugs. Berger, Gilda. 64p. (gr. 7 up). 1991. PLB 12.90 (1-56294-003-1) Millbrook Pr.

—Patty's Story: Straight Talk about Drugs. Berger, Gilda. 64p. (gr. 7 up). 1991. PLB 12.90 (1-878841-04-1) Millbrook Pr.

Kirk, Tim. The Goat Parade. Kroll, Steven. LC 82-10604. 48p. (ps-3). 1983. 5.50 (0-8193-1099-9); PLB 5.95 (0-8193-1100-6) Parents.

—Pigs in the House. Kroll, Steven. LC 83-13310. 48p. (ps-3). 1983. 5.95 (0-8193-1111-1) Parents.

—The Tale of Benjamin Bunny. Potter, Beatrix. LC 80-27468. 32p. (gr. k-3). 1981. PLB 9.79 (0-89375-484-6); pap. text ed. 1.95 (0-89375-485-4) Troll Assocs.

Kirkeeide, Debi. Circle of Seasons. Linker, Corinne. 32p. (ps-2). Date not set. 11.95 (1-56065-157-1) Capstone Pr. Postponed.

Kirkeeide, Deborah. Narrow Gauge Fun. Ferguson, Jane & Ferguson, Gary. 24p. (ps-6). 1987. pap. 1.98 (0-9624846-1-X) J & G Ferguson.

—Noon to Night. Kuebler, Sharon. 32p. (ps-2). Date not set. 11.95 (1-56065-161-X) Capstone Pr. Postponed.

Kirkpatrick, Cindy F., jt. illus. see Gillard, Dianne.

Kirkpatrick, Joey. Plowie. Kirkpatrick, Patricia. LC 93-13712. Date not set. write for info. (0-15-262802-9) HarBrace.

Kirmse, Marguerite. Lassie Come Home. Knight, Eric M. LC 78-3570. 265p. (gr. 4-6). 1978. 16.95 (0-8050-0721-0, Bks Young Read) H Holt & Co.

Kirschbaum, John. I Read You Loud & Clear: A Kid's Thesaurus of Colorful Phrases. Sommer, Elyse. 128p. 1990. text ed. 10.95 (0-88687-575-7, World Almanac) F&W Inc NJ.

Kirschner, Robert. Nosey Notes. Kirschner, Frances & Sorrentino, Joanna. 60p. (Orig.). (gr. 3-9). 1983. pap. 3.00 (0-9612696-0-X) Frantasy Wkshp.

Kish, Ely. The Thiny Perfect Dinosaur Book, Bones, Egg, & Poster: Presenting Tyrannosaurus Rex. Russell, Dale A. & Acorn, John. 32p. 1993. 12.95 incl. poster & toy (0-8362-4216-5) Andrews & McMeel.

—The Tiny Perfect Dinosaur Book, Bones, Egg & Poster: Presenting Leptoceratops. Russell, Dale A. & Acorn, John. 32p. (Orig.). 1991. pap. 10.95 (0-8362-4213-0) Andrews & McMeel.

Kishida, Isao. Beetles. Johnson, Sylvia A. LC 82-7230. 48p. (gr. 4 up). 1982. lib. bdg. 19.95 (0-8225-1476-1) Lerner Pubns.

—Silkworms. Johnson, Sylvia A. LC 82-250. 48p. (gr. 4 up). 1982. PLB 19.95 (0-8225-1478-8, First Ave Edns); pap. 5.95 (0-8225-9557-5, First Ave Edns) Lerner Pubns.

Kisvet, Fran. Lojor's Letters: A Space-Age Story about a Boy & a Gnome & Learning Italic Handwriting. Svaren, Jacqueline. Reynolds, Lloyd J., intro. by. LC 78-60185. 72p. (Orig.). (gr. 1 up). 1981. pap. 10.00 (0-931474-04-3) TBW Bks.

Kita, Helen M. Grandma's Cookies. Buak, Karen. 40p. (Orig.). 1992. pap. text ed. 6.95 chapbk. (1-56315-055-7) Guyasuta Pubs.

Kitamura, Satoshi. Angry Arthur. Oram, Hiawyn. LC 88-31695. 32p. (ps-1). 1989. (DCB). pap. 3.95 (0-525-44472-6) Dutton Child Bks.

—In the Attic. Oram, Hiawyn. LC 84-15570. 32p. (ps-2). 1985. 13.95 (0-8050-0779-2, Bks Young Read) H Holt & Co.

—In the Attic. Oram, Hiawyn. LC 84-15570. 32p. (Orig.). (ps-2). 1988. pap. 4.95 (0-8050-0780-6, Bks Young Read) H Holt & Co.

—My Friend Mr. Morris. LC 87-542. (gr. k-2). 1988. pap. 2.50 (0-317-69489-8) Delacorte.

—Ned & the Joybaloo. Oram, Hiawyn. 28p. (ps up). 1989. 11.95 (0-374-35501-0) FS&G.

—What's Inside? Kitamura, Satoshi. 32p. (ps up). 1987. pap. 4.95 (0-374-48324-8) FS&G.
—What's Inside: The Alphabet Book. Kitamura, Satoshi. LC 84-73117. 32p. (ps up). 1985. 14.00 (0-374-38306-5) FS&G.
Kitchen, Bert. And So They Build. Kitchen, Bert. LC 92-54403. 32p. (ps up). 1993. 15.95 (1-56402-217-X) Candlewick Pr.
—Animal Alphabet. Kitchen, Bert. LC 83-23929. 32p. (ps up). 1984. 13.95 (0-8037-0117-9) Dial Bks Young.
—Animal Alphabet. Kitchen, Bert. LC 83-23929. 32p. (Orig.). (ps up). 1988. pap. 4.95 (0-8037-0431-3, Dial Pied Piper) Puffin Bks.
—Gorilla-Chinchilla: And Other Animal Rhymes. Kitchen, Bert. Fogelman, Phyllis J., ed. LC 89-16851. 32p. (ps up). 1990. 13.95 (0-8037-0770-3); PLB 13.89 (0-8037-0771-1) Dial Bks Young.
—Pig in a Barrow. Kitchen, Bert. LC 90-43413. 32p. (ps-3). 1991. 13.95 (0-8037-0943-9) Dial Bks Young.
—Somewhere Today. Kitchen, Bert. LC 91-58754. 32p. (ps up). 1992. 15.95 (1-56402-074-6) Candlewick Pr.
—Tenrec's Twigs. Kitchen, Bert. 32p. (gr. k-4). 1989. 14. 95 (0-399-21720-7, Philomel Bks) Putnam Pub Group.
Kittredge, Sonya, photos by. Chickadee Rescue. Kittredge, Sonya. Weinberger, Jane, ed. 32p. (Orig.). (ps-3). 1993. pap. 7.95 (0-932433-78-2) Windswept Hse.
Kiuchi, Tatsuro. The Seasons & Someone. Kroll, Virginia. LC 93-11123. Date not set. write for info. (0-15-271233-X) HarBrace.
—The Twilight of Magic. Lofting, Hugh. LC 92-15766. 1993. pap. 15.00 (0-671-78358-0, S&S BFYR) S&S Trade.
Kiwak, Barbara. They Shall Be Heard: The Story of Susan B. Anthony & Elizabeth Cady Stanton. Connell, Kate. LC 92-18088. 85p. (gr. 2-5). 1992. PLB 21.34 (0-8114-7228-0) Raintree Steck-V.
Kiyabu, Walter H. The Bossy Hawaiian Moon. Ehlers, Sabine. 32p. (ps-1). 1980. pap. 2.95 (0-930492-15-3) Hawaiian Serv.
Klages, Simone. The Blue Boy. Auer, Martin. LC 91-39130. 32p. (gr. 2 up). 1992. POB 11.95 (0-02-707610-5, Macmillan Child Bk) Macmillan Child Grp.
Klassen, Grace & Nachtigall, Kelly. Brain Drain, 2 bks. Ranucci, Ernest R. & Rollins, Wilma E. 70p. (gr. 6-12). Bks. A & B. write for info. incl. tchr's ed. (1-878669-09-5, 4301); wkbk., tchr's ed. 7.50 ea. Bk. A, 1975 (1-878669-10-9, 4301) Bk. B, 1978 (4420) Crea Tea Assocs.
Klassen, Neil. Stories from Grandpa's Rocking Chair. Kaetler, Sarah. 64p. (Orig.). (gr. 1-5). 1984. pap. 3.95 (0-919797-11-3) Kindred Pr.
Klein, Arthur. Yoga Is for Me. Terkel, Susan N. LC 81-18623. 48p. (gr. 2-5). 1982. PLB 13.50 (0-8225-1098-7) Lerner Pubns.
Klein, Bill. A Kids' Guide to Building Forts. Birdseye, Tom. LC 92-45908. 64p. (Orig.). (gr. 3-9). 1993. pap. 8.95 (0-943173-69-8) Harbinger AZ.
Klein, Debby. Kid-Ish Yiddish. Markowitz, Endel. 44p. 1993. PLB 16.95 (0-933910-05-3) Haymark.
Klein, Erika. Varya & Her Greenfinch. Tolstoy, Leo. (ps-2). 1988. 7.95 (0-86315-043-8, 20238) Gryphon Hse.
Klein, John F. A Day in the Life of a Circus Clown. Gaskin, Carol. LC 87-10954. 32p. (gr. 4-8). 1988. PLB 11.79 (0-8167-1107-0); pap. text ed. 2.95 (0-8167-1108-9) Troll Assocs.
—A Day in the Life of a Commercial Fisherman. Klein, John F. & Gaskin, Carol. LC 87-10949. 32p. (gr. 4-8). 1988. PLB 11.79 (0-8167-1109-7); pap. text ed. 2.95 (0-8167-1110-0) Troll Assocs.
—A Day in the Life of a Racing Car Mechanic. Gaskin, Carol. LC 84-2430. 32p. (gr. 4-8). 1985. PLB 11.79 (0-8167-0091-5); pap. 2.95 (0-8167-0092-3) Troll Assocs.
Klein, Nancy. King Cole's Party. Beall, Pamela C. & Nipp, Susan H. (ps-2). 1987. 19.95 (0-8431-4714-8); incl. audiocassette soundtrack 24.95 (0-8431-4715-6) Price Stern.
—Wee Sing America. Beall, Pamela C. & Nipp, Susan H. 64p. (ps-2). 1987. pap. 2.95 (0-8431-4702-4); incl. cass. 9.95 (0-8431-1983-7) Price Stern.
—Wee Sing Bible Songs. Beall, Pamela C. & Nipp, Susan H. 64p. (ps-2). 1986. pap. 2.95 (0-8431-1566-1); bk. & cass. 9.95 (0-8431-1780-X) Price Stern.
Klein, Susan. Let's Celebrate Easter: A Book of Drawing Fun. Brook, Bonnie. LC 87-50428. 32p. (gr. 2-6). 1988. PLB 10.65 (0-8167-1051-1); pap. text ed. 1.95 (0-8167-1052-X) Troll Assocs.
Kleinert, Enno. Ships! Come Aboard. Aust, Siegfried. LC 92-12761. 1993. 18.95 (0-8225-2156-3) Lerner Pubns.
Kleven, Elisa. Abuela. Dorros, Arthur. LC 90-21459. 40p. (ps-2). 1991. 14.00 (0-525-44750-4, DCB) Dutton Child Bks.
—B Is for Bethlehem: A Christmas Alphabet. Wilner, Isabel. LC 89-49481. 32p. (ps up). 1990. 13.95 (0-525-44622-2, DCB) Dutton Child Bks.
—The City by the Bay: A Magical Journey Around San Francisco. Junior League of San Francisco Staff & Brown, Tricia. LC 92-32104. 1993. 12.95 (0-8118-0233-7) Chronicle Bks.
—Ernst. Kleven, Elisa. LC 89-1634. 32p. (ps-3). 1989. 11. 95 (0-525-44515-3, DCB) Dutton Child Bks.
—Snowsong Whistling. Lotz, Karen E. LC 92-47117. 32p. (ps-2). 1993. 14.99 (0-525-44516-1, DCB) Dutton Child Bks.

Klimo, Joan F. What Can I Do Today? A Treasury of Crafts for Children. Klimo, Joan F. LC 73-15110. 64p. (gr. k-3). 1974. pap. 2.95 (0-394-82809-7) Pantheon.
Kline, Dick. Outdoor Games. Buskin, David. Thompson, Morton, intro. by. (gr. k-4). 1966. PLB 12.95 (0-87460-090-1) Lion Bks.
Kline, Gail. Courage: An Anthology of Short Stories, Articles & Poems. Davenport, May, ed. LC 79-26261. (Orig.). (gr. 6-9). 1979. pap. text ed. 3.50x (0-9603118-3-1) Davenport.
Kline, Jane. Colorado Businesses. Thumhart, Suzanne, compiled by. 48p. (gr. 4-7). 1984. 11.95x (0-939650-21-5) R H Pub.
—Colorado Chronicles Index. Ayer, Eleanor H., compiled by. 48p. (gr. 4-7). 1986. pap. 6.95x (0-939650-26-6) R H Pub.
—Colorado Wonders. Thumhart, Suzanne. Ayer, Eleanor H., ed. 48p. (gr. 4-7). 1986. pap. 6.95x (0-939650-16-9) R H Pub.
—Hispanic Colorado. Ayer, Eleanor H. 48p. (gr. 4-7). 1982. 11.95x (0-939650-11-8); pap. 6.95x (0-939650-10-X) R H Pub.
Klineman, Harvey. Follow the Moon: A Journey Through the Jewish Year. Ganz, Yaffa. (gr. k-4). 1984. 8.95 (0-87306-369-4) Feldheim.
—Sharing a Sunshine Umbrella: A Mimmy & Simmy Story. Ganz, Yaffa. 1989. 9.95 (0-87306-496-8) Feldheim.
—Who Knows One? A Book of Jewish Numbers. Ganz, Yaffa. (gr. k-4). 1981. 10.95 (0-87306-285-X) Feldheim.

Kling, Fred. The Tree Frog Sings. Kling, Imogene. Gibbs, Jeanne, ed. 32p. (gr. k-2). 1993. PLB 14.95X (0-932762-19-0) Ctr Source Pubns. This is a delightful book for children, ages 4 to 8, but with a symbolic message for readers of any age. Four-color illustrations express the magical beauty of the fine garden in which Buffy, the tree frog lives. The story tells us that... Buffy is a one inch long tree frog who is tired of having three cats, a dog, many birds, large toads & bigger frogs frighten him away from the beautiful garden. More than anything he longs for his own quiet time beside the fountain. One day he decides he will not hide anymore, but will do something different. He climbs the garden wall, & to everyone's surprise finds an exciting magical way to sound bigger than he ever has been before. The whimsical story will appeal to anyone who has ever felt too small or insignificant in the midst of larger noisy creatures...& who also may have longed for the space to sing his or her own song in a quiet garden at sunset. Volume discounts available from Publisher: Center Source Publications, 805 Tesconi Circle, Santa Rosa, CA 95401, Phone: 707-577-8233. *Publisher Provided Annotation.*

Kliros, Thea. Aladdin & Other Favorite Arabian Nights Stories. Smith, Philip, ed. LC 93-22073. 96p. (gr. 3 up). 1993. pap. 1.00 (0-486-27571-X) Dover.
—Black Beauty. abr. ed. Sewell, Anna. LC 93-244. 96p. (gr. 1-9). 1993. pap. 1.00 (0-486-27570-1) Dover.
—A Child's Garden of Verses. unabr. ed. Stevenson, Robert Louis. LC 92-25818. 96p. 1992. pap. 1.00 (0-486-27301-6) Dover.
—How the Leopard Got His Spots & Other Just So Stories. Kipling, Rudyard. LC 92-20780. 96p. 1992. pap. text ed. 1.00 (0-486-27297-4) Dover.
—Irish Fairy Tales. Smith, Philip, ed. LC 93-243. 96p. 1993. pap. 1.00 (0-486-27572-8) Dover.
—The Little Mermaid & Other Fairy Tales. Andersen, Hans Christian. LC 93-14418. 96p. 1993. pap. 1.00 (0-486-27816-6) Dover.
Kliros, Thea, jt. illus. see Cady, Harrison.
Klofkorn, Lisa. Convection: A Current Event. Gould, Alan. Bergman, Lincoln & Fairwell, Kay, eds. Hoyt, Richard, photos by. 38p. (Orig.). (gr. 6-9). 1988. pap. 8.50 (0-912511-15-X) Lawrence Science.
—Discovering Density. Buegler, Marion E. Bergman, Lincoln & Fairwell, Kay, eds. Hoyt, Richard, photos by. 49p. (Orig.). (gr. 6-10). 1988. pap. 8.50 (0-912511-17-6) Lawrence Science.
—Fingerprinting. Ahouse, Jeremy J. Bergman, Lincoln & Fairwell, Kay, eds. Hoyt, Richard, photos by. 38p. (Orig.). (gr. 4-8). 1987. pap. 8.50 (0-912511-21-4) Lawrence Science.

—Height-O-Meters. Sneider, Cary & Gould, Alan. Bergman, Lincoln & Fairwell, Kay, eds. Hoyt, Richard. 60p. (gr. 6-10). 1989. pap. 8.50 (0-912511-22-2) Lawrence Science.
—Liquid Explorations. Agler, Leigh. Bergman, Lincoln & Fairwell, Kay, eds. Hoyt, Richard, photos by. 67p. (Orig.). (gr. 1-3). 1987. pap. 8.50 (0-912511-51-6) Lawrence Science.
—Quadice. Cossey, Ruth, et al. Bergman, Lincoln & Fairwell, Kay, eds. Hoyt, Richard, photos by. 44p. (Orig.). (gr. 4-8). 1987. pap. 8.50 (0-912511-66-4) Lawrence Science.
Klofkorn, Lisa & Craig, Rose. Global Warming & the Greenhouse Effect. Hocking, Colin, et al. Bergman, Lincoln & Fairwell, Kay, eds. Hoyt, Richard, photos by. 168p. (gr. 7-10). 1990. pap. 12.00 (0-912511-75-3) Lawrence Science.
Klofkorn, Lisa, jt. illus. see Baker, Lisa H.
Klofkorn, Lisa, jt. illus. see Bevilacqua, Carol.
Klugman, Micha. My Own Pesah Story. Stuhlman, Daniel D. (Orig.). (gr. 1-6). 1981. Personalized Version. pap. 3.95x (0-934402-09-4); Trade Version. pap. 3.00 (0-934402-10-8); Seder cards 1.50 (0-934402-11-6) BYLS Pr.
Kmiecik, Anne. Beni the Bashful Beaver. Grandma Marian, pseud. LC 87-71490. 32p. 1988. 6.95 (0-9614989-1-9) Banmar Inc.
Knapp, William & Kennedy, Kara. Introduction to Computing, Bk. 1. Kennedy, Sandra. Schroeder, Bonnie, ed. (gr. 2). 1989. wkbk. 5.95 (1-56177-101-5, 491-1) CES Compu-Tech.
Knapp, William, jt. illus. see Anastasia, Karyn.
Knecker, Don. The First Christmas According to Luke. 32p. (ps-4). 1993. incl. dust jacket 15.99 (0-570-04753-6) Concordia.
Kneen, Maggie. Who's Getting Ready for Christmas? Kneen, Maggie. LC 93-11061. (gr. 4-7). 1993. 13.95 (0-8118-0470-4) Chronicle Bks.
Knezevich, Joyce. Sillas Especiales. Zollars, Jean A. Montano, Macrina C., ed. Millar, Alejandra, tr. (SPA.). 95p. (Orig.). 1993. pap. 20.00 (1-882632-02-8); pap. 10.00 Third World Countries Nonprofits (1-882632-04-4) PAX Pr.
—Special Seating. Zollars, Jean A. 95p. (Orig.). 1993. pap. 20.00 (1-882632-01-X); pap. 10.00 Third World Countries Nonprofits (1-882632-05-2) PAX Pr.
Kniffke, Sophie. From Oil to Plastic. Brice, Raphaelle. Matthews, Sarah, tr. from FRE. LC 87-31753. 38p. (gr. k-5). 1988. 4.95 (0-944589-17-0, 170) Young Discovery Lib.
—The Sunny Hours. Usher, Alice. 40p. (Orig.). (ps-2). 1991. pap. 3.95 (0-671-75281-2, Green Tiger) S&S Trade.
—Weather. De Bourgoing, Pascale. 24p. 1991. pap. 10.95 (0-590-45234-7, Cartwheel) Scholastic Inc.
Knight, Ann. Look at Magnets. rev. ed. Kirkpatrick, Rena K. LC 84-26252. 32p. (gr. 2-4). 1985. PLB 17.28 (0-8172-2354-1); pap. 4.95 (0-8114-6900-X) Raintree Steck-V.
Knight, Ann, jt. illus. see Worth, Jo.
Knight, Anne R. Elizabeth Cady Stanton. Kendall, Martha E. LC 88-81556. 72p. (gr. 3-5). 1987. text ed. 10.95 (0-945783-03-5); pap. 5.95 (0-945783-02-7) Highland Pub Group.
Knight, C. W., jt. illus. see Rungius, Carl.
Knight, Christopher. Surtsey: The Newest Place on Earth. Lasky, Kathryn. LC 92-52990. 64p. (gr. 3-7). 1992. 15.95 (1-56282-300-0); PLB 15.89 (1-56282-301-9) Hyprn Child.
Knight, Christopher, photos by. Monarchs. Lasky, Kathryn, text by. LC 92-33972. 1993. 16.95 (0-15-255296-0); pap. 8.95 (0-15-255297-9) HarBrace.
Knight, Christopher G. A Baby for Max. Lasky, Kathryn. LC 86-22131. 48p. (ps-2). 1987. pap. 4.95 (0-689-71118-2, Aladdin) Macmillan Child Grp.
—Sugaring Time. Lasky, Kathryn. Knight, Christopher G., photos by. LC 82-23928. 64p. (gr. 3-7). 1983. RSBE 13.95 (0-02-751680-6, Macmillan Child Bk) Macmillan Child Grp.
Knight, Christopher G., photos by. Dinosaur Dig. Lasky, Kathryn. LC 89-13212. 64p. (gr. 3 up). 1990. 13.95 (0-688-08574-1); PLB 13.88 (0-688-08575-X, Morrow Jr Bks) Morrow Jr Bks.
—Searching for Laura Ingalls: A Reader's Journey. Lasky, Kathryn & Knight, Meribah. LC 92-26188. 48p. (gr. 2-6). 1993. RSBE 15.95 (0-02-751666-0, Macmillan Child Bk) Macmillan Child Grp.
—Sugaring Time. Lasky, Kathryn. LC 86-3468. 64p. (gr. 3-7). 1986. pap. 4.95 (0-689-71081-X, Aladdin) Macmillan Child Grp.
Knight, Christopher G. & Swedberg, Jack, photos by. Think Like an Eagle: At Work with a Wildlife Photographer. Lasky, Kathryn. 48p. (gr. 3 up). 1992. 15.95 (0-316-51519-1, Joy St Bks) Little.
Knight, Ginny. Jessie Helps a Wish. Knight, Ginny. 1991. 3.00 (0-940248-82-4) Guild Pr.
—Postcard from Heaven. Sloan, Phyllis J. 1990. 3.00 (0-940248-81-6) Guild Pr.
—Trembling with Wonder. Sloan, Phyllis J., et al. (gr. 4 up). 1990. 3.00 (0-940248-80-8) Guild Pr.
Knight, Hilary. The Animal Garden. Nash, Ogden. LC 65-21772. 48p. (gr. 10 up). 1988. pap. 5.95 (0-87131-568-8) M Evans.
—Beauty & the Beast. Leprince de Beaumont's, Marie. Howard, Richard, tr. Cocteau, Jean. 48p. (gr. 1-5). 1990. pap. 14.95 jacketed (0-671-70720-5, S&S BFYR) S&S Trade.

—The Best Little Monkeys in the World. Standiford, Natalie. LC 86-15425. 48p. (gr. 1-3). 1987. lib. bdg. 7.99 (0-394-98616-4); 3.50 (0-394-88616-X) Random Bks Yng Read.
—Cinderella. Knight, Hilary. LC 80-18660. 32p. (ps-2). 1982. lib. bdg. 5.99 (0-394-93759-7) Random Bks Yng Read.
—Eloise. Thompson, Kay. LC 55-11039. (gr. k-6). 1969. pap. 15.95 jacketed (0-671-22350-X, S&S BFYR) S&S Trade.
—The Golden Picture Dictionary. Ogle, Lucille & Thoburn, Tina. (ps-3). 1989. write for info. (0-307-17861-7, Pub. by Golden Bks) Western Pub.
—Happy Birthday. Hopkins, Lee B., selected by. 40p. (ps-2). 1991. pap. 11.95 jacketed (0-671-70973-9, S&S BFYR) S&S Trade.
—Happy Birthday. Hopkins, Lee B. LC 90-10086. 40p. (ps-2). 1993. pap. 5.95 (0-671-79851-0, S&S BYR) S&S Trade.
—Hello, Mrs. Piggle-Wiggle. MacDonald, Betty. LC 57-5613. (gr. k-3). 1957. 14.00 (0-397-31715-8, Lipp Jr Bks) HarpC Child Bks.
—Hilary Knight's the Twelve Days of Christmas. Knight, Hilary. LC 87-1137. 34p. (ps up). 1987. pap. 4.95 (0-689-71150-6, Aladdin) Macmillan Child Grp.
—Mrs. Piggle-Wiggle. rev. ed. MacDonald, Betty. LC 47-1876. (gr. k-3). 1957. 14.00 (0-397-31712-3, Lipp Jr Bks) HarpC Child Bks.
—Mrs. Piggle-Wiggle's Magic. new ed. MacDonald, Betty. LC 49-11124. (gr. k-3). 1957. 14.00 (0-397-31714-X, Lipp Jr Bks) HarpC Child Bks.
—Side by Side: Poems to Read Together. Hopkins, Lee B., ed. LC 87-33025. 96p. (gr. 1 up). 1988. pap. 14.95 (0-671-63579-4, S&S BFYR) S&S Trade.
—Sunday Morning. 2nd ed. Viorst, Judith. LC 92-16928. 40p. (ps-3). 1992. RSBE 13.95 (0-689-31794-8, Atheneum Child Bk) Macmillan Child Grp.
—Sunday Morning. 2nd ed. Viorst, Judith. LC 92-29561. 32p. (gr. k-3). 1993. pap. 3.95 (0-689-71702-4, Aladdin) Macmillan Child Grp.
—Telephone Time: A First Book of Telephone Do's & Don'ts. Weiss, Ellen. LC 86-42560. 32p. (gr. k-3). 1986. lib. bdg. 5.99 (0-394-98252-5); pap. 1.95 (0-394-88252-0) Random Bks Yng Read.
—Ten Tall Soldiers. Robison, Nancy. LC 87-32090. 32p. (ps-2). 1991. 13.95 (0-8050-0768-7, Bks Young Read) H Holt & Co.
—When I Have a Little Boy. Zolotow, Charlotte. LC 67-14072. 32p. (ps-3). 1988. pap. 3.95 (0-06-443176-2, Trophy) HarpC Child Bks.
—When I Have a Little Girl. Zolotow, Charlotte. LC 65-24656. 32p. (gr. k-3). 1965. 13.00 (0-06-027045-4) HarpC Child Bks.
—When I Have a Little Girl. Zolotow, Charlotte. LC 65-24656. 32p. (ps-3). 1988. pap. 3.95 (0-06-443175-4, Trophy) HarpC Child Bks.
—Where's Wallace? Knight, Hilary. LC 64-19717. (ps-3). 1964. 15.00 (0-06-023170-X); PLB 14.89 (0-06-023171-8) HarpC Child Bks.
—Where's Wallace? Knight, Hilary. LC 64-19717. 48p. (ps-3). 1986. pap. 5.95 (0-06-443094-4, Trophy) HarpC Child Bks.

Knight, Rosalinda. Rain, No. 1. Bennett, David. 32p. (Orig.). 1988. pap. 3.95 (0-553-05474-0) Bantam.
Knipper, Sue. The Bears Upstairs. Moncure, Jane B. LC 87-11715. 32p. (ps-2). 1987. PLB 21.35 (0-89565-373-7); PLB 14.95s.p. (0-685-55876-2) Childs World.
Knoles, David. Spooky Magic Tricks. Knoles, David. LC 93-1642. 128p. (gr. 3-10). 1993. 12.95 (0-8069-0418-6) Sterling.
Knoop, Gayle. Things to Do in the Car. Hodgdon, Linda Q. 32p. (Orig.). pap. write for info. (0-9616786-0-7) Young Ideas.
Knotts, Howard. The Big Red Barn. Bunting, Eve. LC 78-12186. 32p. (gr. k-3). 1979. pap. 6.95 (0-15-611938-2, Voyager Bks) HarBrace.
—Winter's Coming. Bunting, Eve. LC 76-28321. 32p. (ps-3). 1990. pap. 3.95 (0-15-298037-7) HarBrace.
Knotts, Richard. Life's Battles. Williams, Selver B. Lundberg, Louise, ed. 220p. (gr. 8 up). 1991. pap. 10. 95 (0-9626633-0-1) Taliaferro IN.
Knowles, Tizzie. A Treasury of Stories for Six Year Olds. Blishen, Edward & Blishen, Nancy, eds. LC 92-53108. 160p. (Orig.). (gr. k-5). 1992. pap. 5.95 (1-85697-828-1) Kingfisher Bks.
Knowlton, Barbara W. At Babci's Knee. Lehman, Patricia J. & Padzik, Alicja, eds. Zurawiecka, Aska, tr. LC 85-51371. (ENG & POL). 165p. (Orig.). 1985. pap. 25.00 (0-935003-01-0); cassette incl. (0-935003-00-2) Talent Ed.
Knox, Jolyne. Desperate for a Dog. Impey, Rose. 64p. (gr. 2-5). 1991. pap. 3.50 (0-14-034798-4, Puffin) Puffin Bks.
—No-Name Dog. Impey, Rose. LC 92-18957. 64p. (gr. 2-5). 1992. pap. 3.99 (0-14-036164-2) Puffin Bks.
Knox, Robert. Going for a Walk. newly illus ed. De Regniers, Beatrice S. LC 91-43177. 32p. (ps-1). 1993. 15.00 (0-06-022954-3); PLB 14.89 (0-06-022957-8) HarpC Child Bks.
Knuckey, Cam. The Cat's Whiskers. Marshall, Val & Tester, Bronwyn. LC 93-11737. 1994. 4.25 SRA Schl Grp.
Knuppel, Helga. Christabel Crocodile's Birthday Egg. Knuppel, Helga. LC 92-24360. 32p. (ps-3). 1993. 13. 95 (1-56656-113-2, Crocodile Bks) Interlink Pub.

Knutson, Barbara. Count Your Way Through Africa. Haskins, Jim. 24p. (gr. 1-3). 1989. 17.50 (0-87614-347-8); pap. 5.95 (0-87614-514-4) Carolrhoda Bks.
—From Heaven Above: The Story of Christmas Proclaimed by the Angels. McKissack, Patricia & McKissack, Fredrick. LC 92-70385. 32p. (ps-2). 1992. pap. 4.99 (0-8066-2609-7, 9-2609, Augsburg) Augsburg Fortress.
—Hanna's Cold Winter. Marx, Trish. LC 92-27143. 1993. 18.95 (0-87614-772-4) Carolrhoda Bks.
—How the Guinea Fowl Got Her Spots: A Swahili Tale of Friendship. Knutson, Barbara. 24p. (ps-4). 1990. PLB 18.95 (0-87614-416-4) Carolrhoda Bks.
—Sungura & Leopard: A Swahili TricksterTale. Knutson, Barbara, retold by. LC 92-31905. 1993. 15.95 (0-316-50010-0) Little.
Knutson, Dana & Nelson, Jim. The Rigger Black Book: A Shadowrun Sourcebook. McGregor, Philip. Ippolito, Donna & Mulvihill, Sharon T., eds. 136p. (Orig.). (gr. 7 up). 1991. pap. 15.00 (1-55560-169-3) FASA Corp.
Knutson, Dana, jt. illus. see Venters, Steve.
Knutson, Kimberley. Ska-Tat! Knutson, Kimberly. LC 92-38072. 32p. (ps-1). 1993. RSBE 14.95 (0-02-750846-3, Macmillan Child Bk) Macmillan Child Grp.
Kobayashi, Robert. Maria Mazaretti Loves Spaghetti. Kobayashi, Robert. LC 90-20015. 40p. (ps-2). 1991. 14.00 (0-679-81659-3); lib. bdg. 14.99 (0-679-91659-8) Knopf Bks Yng Read.
Kobeh, Ana G., jt. illus. see Kurtycz, Marcos.

Koch, Barry. Friends - Amigos. Ada, Alma F. (SPA & ENG.). 26p. (gr. k-2). 1989. Spanish ed. 5.25 (0-88272-501-7); English ed. 5.25 (0-88272-500-9) Santillana.
Prejudice & tolerance are treated in a sensitive & easy-to-understand manner in this story. The main characters are geometric shapes who are not allowed to play or talk to each other. Then one day they inadvertently discover that friends can come in many different forms. English & Spanish versions are available of this entertaining & instructive story. To order: Santillana, 901 West Walnut, Compton, CA 90220. Telephone 1-310-763-0455.
Publisher Provided Annotation.

Koch, Richard L. San Diego, California: The Travel Guide for Kids. Stacke, Mary E. 32p. (gr. k-4). 1991. pap. 4.95 (0-945600-06-2) Colormore Inc.
Koch, Sis. The Cloud's Journey. Heuck, Sigrid. 28p. (ps-2). 1991. pap. 9.95 smythe sewn reinforced bdg. (1-56182-021-0) Atomium Bks.
Koch, Susan C. Colormore Travels - Austin, Texas: The Travel Guide for Kids. Koch, Susan C. 32p. (Orig.). (gr. k-4). 1988. pap. 4.50 (0-945600-00-3) Colormore Inc.
—Colormore Travels - Ft. Worth, Texas: The Travel Guide for Kids. Koch, Susan C. (Orig.). (gr. k-4). 1989. pap. 4.50 (0-945600-02-X) Colormore Inc.
—Colormore Travels - San Antonio, Texas: The Travel Guide for Kids. Koch, Susan C. 32p. (Orig.). (gr. k-4). 1990. pap. 4.50 (0-945600-05-4) Colormore Inc.
—Honolulu, Hawaii: The Travel Guide for Kids. Aka, Karen Y. 32p. (gr. k-4). 1992. pap. 4.95 (0-945600-08-9) Colormore Inc.
Koci, Marta. Nick Ribbeck of Ribbeck of Havelland. Fontane, Theodor. Bell, Anthea, tr. from GER. LC 90-7164. 32p. (gr. k-4). 1991. pap. 14.95 (0-88708-149-5) Picture Bk Studio.
Kocjak, Gordon. Rhythm, Rhyme & Read: States & Capitals. Thompson, Kim M. & Hilderbrand, Karen M. 48p. (gr. 3-6). 1992. 6.99 (0-9632249-5-6); audio cass. 8.39 (0-9632249-6-4) Twin Sisters.
Kock, Carl. Fudge Dream Supreme. Graham, Tether. LC 73-16815. (ps-2). 1975. 6.95 (0-87955-109-7); PLB 5.95 (0-686-57941-0) O'Hara.
—Kibby & the Red Elephant. Corddry, Thomas. LC 72-13771. (gr. 3-6). 1973. 6.95 (0-87955-106-2) O'Hara.
Koda-Callan, Elizabeth. The Magic Locket. Koda-Callan, Elizabeth. LC 88-5508. 40p. (ps-3). 1988. 12.95 (0-89480-602-5, 1602) Workman Pub.
Koechel & Peterson. Today I Feel Like a Warm Fuzzy. Coleman, William L. LC 80-19708. 126p. (Orig.). (ps-2). 1980. pap. 6.99 (0-87123-565-X) Bethany Hse.
Koehler, Ed. Animals of the Bible Activity Book. Stohs, Anita R. 32p. (Orig.). (ps-2). 1992. pap. 2.99 (0-570-04712-9) Concordia.
—I'm in Junior High, but It's Not My Fault. Elmshauser, John, ed. 127p. (Orig.). (gr. 7-9). 1992. pap. 6.99 (0-570-04723-4) Concordia.
—The Legend of Fredbird. Kveton, Steven. 16p. (ps-up). 1986. pap. text ed. 2.95 (0-9616799-0-5) Water St Missouri.
Koehler, Phoebe. Making Room. Koehler, Phoebe. LC 91-41356. 48p. (ps-3). 1993. SBE 14.95 (0-02-750875-7, Bradbury Pr) Macmillan Child Grp.
Koehn, Sara. Lost in the Corn. Pond, Joyce. 31p. (Orig.). (gr. 6). 1992. pap. 6.95 (0-9635877-0-6) JBP Press.

Koeller, Neena. Beginning Reading Four. Forman-Hitt, Kathy & Young, Janet. Wheeler, Sharon, ed. (ps). 1986. wkbk. 1.95 (0-916119-21-1) Creat Teach Pr.
—Beginning Reading Three. Forman-Hitt, Kathy & YOung, Janet. Wheeler, Sharon, ed. (ps). 1986. wkbk. 1.95 (0-916119-20-3) Creat Teach Pr.
Koeller, Neena C. Alphabet. Wheeler, Sharon, ed. (ps). 1984. wkbk 1.95 (0-916119-02-5) Creat Teach Pr.
—Colors. Wheeler, Sharon, ed. (ps). 1984. wkbk. 1.95 (0-916119-01-7) Creat Teach Pr.
—Life Skills. Wheeler, Sharon, ed. (ps). 1984. wkbk 1.95 (0-916119-11-4) Creat Teach Pr.
Koeller, Nina C. Same-Different. Wheeler, Sharon, ed. (ps). 1984. wkbk 1.95 (0-916119-07-6) Creat Teach Pr.
Koelsch, Michael. Garden Hose Trumpet: and 5 Other Musical Instruments You Can Make. Oates, Eddie. LC 92-20060. 32p. (gr. 2-5). 1995. 14.00 (0-06-021478-3); PLB 13.89 (0-06-021479-1) HarpC Child Bks.
Koeppen, Peter. Pedro's Journal: A Voyage with Christopher Columbus. Conrad, Pam. LC 90-85723. 96p. (gr. 3-7). 1991. 13.95 (1-878093-17-7) Boyds Mills Pr.
—A Swinger of Birches: Poems of Robert Frost for Young People. Frost, Robert. Fadiman, Clifton, intro. by. LC 82-5517. 80p. (gr. 4 up). 1982. 21.95 (0-916144-92-5); pap. 14.95 (0-916144-93-3); cass. & bk. 23.90 (0-685-05629-5, 102-5); cassette only 8.95 (0-88045-099-1) Stemmer Hse.
Koff, Deborah. Follow the Blue Butterfly. Andersdatter, Karla M. (gr. 4-8). 1980. 6.00 (0-935430-00-8) In Between.
Kogan, Deborah. The Seven Good Years & Other Stories of I. L. Peretz. Hautzig, Esther, tr. from YID. 96p. (gr. 3-6). 1984. 10.95 (0-8276-0244-8) JPS Phila.
Kogan, Mark. Mother, Father, Big Sopha & Me. Kogan, Mark. Chotianovsky, Olga, ed. 104p. (Orig.). 1991. pap. text ed. 6.00 (0-9624922-2-1) Hazar NY.
—Zabavi Nasmeshlivoi Zvezdi. Kogan, Mark. Chotianovsky, Olga, ed. 129p. (Orig.). 1991. pap. text ed. 9.00 (0-9624922-3-X) Hazar NY.
Kohl, Joe. The Best Joke Book for Kids, No. 2. Eckstein, Joan & Gleit, Joyce. 64p. (gr. 3 up). 1987. pap. 2.99 (0-380-75209-3, Camelot) Avon.
Kohler, Keith. Animals Do the Strangest Things. Hornblow, Leonora & Hornblow, Arthur. LC 88-37710. 64p. (gr. 2-4). 1990. lib. bdg. 6.99 (0-394-94308-2); pap. 3.95 (0-394-84308-8) Random Bks Yng Read.
—The Titanic: Lost...& Found. Donnelly, Judy. LC 86-20402. 48p. (gr. 1-3). 1987. lib. bdg. 7.99 (0-394-98669-5); pap. 3.50 (0-394-88669-0) Random Bks Yng Read.
Kohn, Arnie. Dinosaurs: An Educational Coloring Book. Spizzirri Publishing Co. Staff. Spizzirri, Linda, ed. 32p. (gr. 1-8). 1981. pap. 1.75 (0-86545-019-6) Spizzirri.
—Prehistoric Sea Life: An Educational Coloring Book. Spizzirri Publishing Co. Staff. Spizzirri, Linda, ed. 32p. (gr. 1-8). 1981. pap. 1.75 (0-86545-020-X) Spizzirri.
Koide, Yasuko. May We Sleep Here Tonight? Koide, Tan. LC 82-72247. 32p. (ps-3). 1983. SBE 12.95 (0-689-50261-3, M K McElderry) Macmillan Child Grp.
Koike, Hiro. Apple Trees. Johnson, Sylvia A. LC 83-16230. 48p. (gr. 4 up). 1983. PLB 19.95 (0-8225-1479-6) Lerner Pubns.
Kojoyian, Armen. A Drop of Honey. Bider, Djemma. (ps-4). 1989. pap. 14.95 jacketed (0-671-66265-1, S&S BFYR) S&S Trade.
Koken, Tom, et al. AAA Travel Activity Book: The Official AAA Fun Book for Kids. Koken, Tom, et al. 144p. 1990. pap. 4.95 (1-56288-071-3) Checkerboard.
Kokino, Olga. Little Jollys Find a Home. Hannah, Valerie. Herrick, George H., ed. 36p. (Orig.). (gr. k-3). 1991. pap. 5.95 (0-941281-79-5) V H Pub.
Kolanovic, Dubravka. A Special Day. Kolanovic, Dubravka. Thatch, Nancy R., ed. Melton, David, intro. by. LC 93-13419. 29p. (gr. k-2). 1993. PLB 14. 95 (0-933849-45-1) Landmark Edns.
Kolding, Max. Johnny Thumbs. Hartman, Bob. 48p. (Orig.). (gr. 1-3). 1993. pap. 3.99 (0-7847-0093-1, 24-03943) Standard Pub.
Kolding, Richard. The Care Bears & the Big Clean-Up. Katz, Bobbi. LC 91-52705. 40p. (ps-4). 1991. 4.99 (0-679-82367-0) Random Bks Yng Read.
Kolding, Richard M. Show & Tell. Gordon, Sharon. LC 86-30855. 32p. (gr-2). 1988. PLB 7.89 (0-8167-0994-7); pap. text ed. 1.95 (0-8167-0995-5) Troll Assocs.
—Silly Sidney. Matthews, Morgan. LC 85-14063. 48p. (Orig.). (gr. 1-3). 1986. PLB 10.59 (0-8167-0610-7); pap. text ed. 3.50 (0-8167-0611-5) Troll Assocs.
—Skating on Thin Ice. Everett, Louise. LC 86-30857. 32p. (gr. k-2). 1988. PLB 7.89 (0-8167-0992-0); pap. text ed. 1.95 (0-8167-0993-9) Troll Assocs.
—What's It Like to Be a Newspaper Reporter. Craig, Janet. LC 89-34384. 32p. (gr. k-3). 1989. lib. bdg. 10. 89 (0-8167-1807-5); pap. text ed. 2.95 (0-8167-1808-3) Troll Assocs.
—Whoo's Too Tired? Matthews, Morgan. LC 88-1285. 48p. (Orig.). (gr. 1-4). 1988. PLB 10.59 (0-8167-1331-6); pap. text ed. 3.50 (0-8167-1332-4) Troll Assocs.

Kolino, Olga. Three Jolly Stories Include: Three Jollys, Jollys Visit L. A., Jolly Gets Mugged: An ESL Adult-Child Reader. Weisberg, Valerie H. 76p. (Orig.). (gr. 4 up). 1985. pap. text ed. 6.95x (*0-9610912-4-X*) V H Pub.

Komatsu, Yoshio, photos by. Egypt. Weber, Valerie & Rateliff, John D., eds. LC 87-42579. 64p. (gr. 5-6). 1991. PLB 19.93 (*1-55532-209-3*) Gareth Stevens Inc.

Komisarow, Don. More Captain Whopper Tales. Miller, Albert G. (gr. 3-7). 1968. 10.95 (*0-8392-3060-5*) Astor-Honor.

Komisarow, Donald. Captain Whopper. Miller, Albert G. (gr. 3-7). 1968. 10.95 (*0-8392-3058-3*) Astor-Honor.

Komoda, Beverly. The Winter Day. Komoda, Beverly. LC 91-104. 32p. (ps-1). 1991. PLB 13.89 (*0-06-023302-8*) HarpC Child Bks.

Komoda, Kiyo. Catch a Sunbeam: A Book of Solar Study & Experiments. Adams, Florence. LC 78-52820. (gr. 3-7). 1978. 10.95 (*0-15-215197-4*, HB Juv Bks) HarBrace.

Komoto, Sachiko. Chessie, the Long Island Squirrel. Komoto, Sachiko. LC 90-46860. 64p. (gr. 1-3). 1993. PLB 19.93 (*0-8368-0198-9*); PLB 19.93 s.p. (*0-685-58720-7*) Gareth Stevens Inc.

Kondo, Yuki. Bitty's Halloween Surprise. Brook, Ruth. LC 86-30730. 32p. (gr. k-3). 1988. PLB 11.89 (*0-8167-0916-5*); pap. text ed. 2.95 (*0-8167-0917-3*) Troll Assocs.

—Good for You, Lolly. Brook, Ruth. LC 86-30733. 32p. (gr. k-3). 1988. PLB 11.89 (*0-8167-0914-9*); pap. text ed. 2.95 (*0-8167-0915-7*) Troll Assocs.

—Happy Birthday, Baby. Brook, Ruth. LC 86-30750. 32p. (gr. k-3). 1988. PLB 11.89 (*0-8167-0912-2*); pap. text ed. 2.95 (*0-8167-0913-0*) Troll Assocs.

—Jingle's Big Race. Brook, Ruth. LC 86-30729. 32p. (gr. k-3). 1988. PLB 11.89 (*0-8167-0902-5*); pap. text ed. 2.95 (*0-8167-0903-3*) Troll Assocs.

—Jump for Joy, Betty. Brook, Ruth. LC 86-30731. 32p. (gr. k-3). 1988. PLB 11.89 (*0-8167-0908-4*); pap. text ed. 2.95 (*0-8167-0909-2*) Troll Assocs.

—Play It Again, Rosie! Brook, Ruth. LC 86-30749. 32p. (gr. k-3). 1988. PLB 11.89 (*0-8167-0904-1*); pap. text ed. 2.95 (*0-8167-0905-X*) Troll Assocs.

—Sweet Hearts for Dolly. Brook, Ruth. LC 86-30732. 32p. (gr. k-3). 1988. PLB 11.89 (*0-8167-0906-8*); pap. text ed. 2.95 (*0-8167-0907-6*) Troll Assocs.

—Toony & the Midnight Monster. Brook, Ruth. LC 86-30739. 32p. (gr. k-3). 1988. lib. bdg. 11.89 (*0-8167-0910-6*); pap. text ed. 2.95 (*0-8167-0911-4*) Troll Assocs.

Konemund, Gisela. Grow It! An Indoor - Outdoor Gardening Guide for Kids. Markmann, Erika. LC 90-45043. 48p. (gr. 2-7). 1991. PLB 11.99 (*0-679-91528-1*); pap. 6.95 (*0-679-81528-7*) Random Bks Yng Read.

Kong, Emilie. The Huddles Jumbo Activity & Coloring Book. Nathan, Beverly & Bizer, Linda. 128p. (ps-8). pap. write for info (*0-910313-78-4*) Parker Bros.

—A Hug for a New Friend. Anderson, Janet. 40p. (ps). 4.00 (*0-910313-88-1*) Parker Bros.

—A Hug Is for Happiness. 12p. (ps). 1985. 2.65 (*0-317-18485-7*) Parker Bros.

—A Hugga Bunch Hello. Cowell, Phyllis. 40p. (ps). 1985. 4.00 (*0-910313-87-3*) Parker Bros.

—Huggins & Kisses. Creighton, Susan. 40p. (ps). 1985. 4.00 (*0-910313-94-6*) Parker Bros.

—One-Two-Three Hug. 12p. (ps). 1985. 2.65 (*0-910313-93-8*) Parker Bros.

—The Trolls & the Shoemaker. Snyder, Margaret, adapted by. 24p. (ps-4). 1992. 20.00 (*0-307-74027-7*, 64027, Golden Pr) Western Pub.

—Twenty Thousand Leaks under the Sea. Carney, Charles. 24p. (ps-4). 1993. 20.00 (*0-307-74030-7*, 64030, Golden Pr) Western Pub.

Kong, Emilie, jt. illus. see Paris, Pat.

Konigsburg, E. L. About the B'nai Bagels. Konigsburg, E. L. LC 69-13529. 176p. (gr. 4-6). 1971. SBE 14.95 (*0-689-20631-3*, Atheneum Child Grp) Macmillan Child Grp.

—About the B'nai Bagels. Konigsburg, E. L. 176p. (gr. 4-7). 1985. pap. 3.50 (*0-440-40034-1*, YB) Dell.

—Amy Elizabeth Explores Bloomingdale's. Konigsburg, E. L. LC 91-40132. 32p. (ps-3). 1992. SBE 14.95 (*0-689-31766-2*, Atheneum Child Bk) Macmillan Child Grp.

—From the Mixed-Up Files of Mrs. Basil E. Frankweiler. Konigsburg, E. L. LC 67-18988. 168p. (gr. 3-7). 1970. SBE 13.95 (*0-689-20586-4*, Atheneum Child Bk) Macmillan Child Grp.

—Jennifer, Hecate, Macbeth, William McKinley & Me, Elizabeth. Konigsburg, E. L. LC 67-10458. 128p. (gr. 3-5). 1971. SBE 12.95 (*0-689-30007-7*, Atheneum Child Bk) Macmillan Child Grp.

—A Proud Taste for Scarlet & Miniver. Konigsburg, E. L. LC 73-76320. 208p. (gr. 5-9). 1973. SBE 14.95 (*0-689-30111-1*, Atheneum Child Bk) Macmillan Child Grp.

—Samuel Todd's Book of Great Colors. Konigsburg, E. L. LC 89-6640. 32p. (ps-k). 1990. SBE 13.95 (*0-689-31593-7*, Atheneum Child Bk) Macmillan Child Grp.

—Samuel Todd's Book of Great Inventions. Konigsburg, E. L. LC 90-23688. 32p. (ps-2). 1991. SBE 13.95 (*0-689-31680-1*, Atheneum Child Bk) Macmillan Child Grp.

Konsterile, Paul. Jesus Comes: the Story of Jesus' Birth for Children. Klug, Ron & Klug, Lyn. LC 86-81808. 32p. (Orig.). (gr. 3-8). 1986. pap. 5.99 saddlestitch (*0-8066-2234-2*, 10-3497, Augsburg) Augsburg Fortress.

—Jesus Loves: Stories about Jesus for Children. Klug, Ron & Klug, Lyn. LC 86-81807. 32p. (Orig.). (gr. 3-8). 1986. saddlestitch 5.99 (*0-8066-2235-0*, 10-3526, Augsburg) Augsburg Fortress.

Kontoyianraki, Elizabeth. The Adventures of Millie. Kontoyiannaki, Elizabeth. 15p. (gr. 1-3). 1992. pap. 10.95 (*1-56606-012-5*) Bradley Mann.

—Bozo Is a Dog. Kontoyiannaki, Elizabeth. 17p. (gr. k-3). 1992. pap. 8.95 (*1-895583-44-6*) MAYA Pubs.

—Dad, Play Chess with Me. Kontoyiannaki, Elizabeth. 13p. (gr. k-3). 1993. pap. 12.95 (*1-56606-015-X*) Bradley Mann.

—I Can Count. Kontoyiannaki, Elizabeth. 16p. (gr. k-3). 1992. pap. 12.95 (*1-895583-41-1*) MAYA Pubs.

—An Island Called Samos. Kontoyiannaki, Elizabeth. 14p. (gr. k-3). 1992. pap. 9.95 (*1-895583-42-X*) MAYA Pubs.

—Leo & His Friends. Kontoyiannaki, Elizabeth. 12p. (gr. 1-4). 1992. pap. 12.95 (*1-56606-011-7*) Bradley Mann.

—Plants Grow in Gardens. Kontoyiannaki, Elizabeth. 18p. (gr. k-3). 1992. pap. 10.95 (*1-895583-43-8*) MAYA Pubs.

—Run, Don't Walk. Kontoyiannaki, Elizabeth. 14p. (gr. k-3). Date not set. pap. 13.95 (*1-56606-016-8*) Bradley Mann.

—Where Does the World End? Kontoyiannaki, Elizabeth. 14p. (gr. k-3). 1992. pap. 12.95 (*1-895583-45-4*) MAYA Pubs.

Kontoyiannaki, Kosta. Agean Fun. Kontoyiannaki, Kosta. 16p. (gr. k-3). 1992. pap. 12.95 (*1-895583-23-3*) MAYA Pubs.

—Can You Find Greece on the Map? Kontoyiannaki, Kosta. 14p. (gr. k-3). 1992. pap. 14.95 (*1-895583-20-9*) MAYA Pubs.

—Frankie Bear's Birthday Cake. Kontoyiannaki, Kosta. 14p. (gr. 1-6). 1992. pap. 13.95 (*1-56606-004-4*) Bradley Mann.

—Horse Rides for Homer. Kontoyiannaki, Kosta. 15p. (gr. k-3). 1992. pap. 12.95 (*1-895583-21-7*) MAYA Pubs.

—Ralph Takes a Train Ride. Kontoyiannaki, Kosta. 18p. (gr. k-3). 1992. pap. 13.95 (*1-895583-24-1*) MAYA Pubs.

—Time. Kontoyiannaki, Kosta. 12p. (gr. k-3). 1992. pap. 10.95 (*1-895583-22-5*) MAYA Pubs.

Kool, Jonna. The Little Person. Haley, Patrick. LC 81-65114. 64p. (gr. 2-3). 1981. PLB 9.00 (*0-9605738-0-1*) East Eagle.

—Wildflower & the Big Voice in the Sky. Haley, Patrick. LC 82-82990. 44p. (gr. 3-4). 1982. 9.00 (*0-9605738-1-X*) East Eagle.

—The Woodpecker & the Oak Tree. Haley, Patrick. LC 82-91740. 64p. (gr. 3-4). 1982. 9.00 (*0-9605738-2-8*) East Eagle.

Koontz, Robin M. Addition & Subtraction: First Grade. Gregorich, Barbara. Hoffman, Joan, ed. 32p. (gr. 1). 1990. wkbk. 2.29 (*0-88743-182-8*) Sch Zone Pub Co.

—Addition & Subtraction: Second Grade. Gregorich, Barbara. Hoffman, Joan, ed. 32p. (gr. 2). 1990. wkbk. 2.29 (*0-88743-188-7*) Sch Zone Pub Co.

—Alike-Not Alike & Go-Togethers: Kindergarten. Gregorich, Barbara. Hoffman, Joan, ed. 32p. (gr. k). 1990. wkbk. 2.29 (*0-88743-176-3*) Sch Zone Pub Co.

—Alphabet Skills: Kindergarten. Gregorich, Barbara. Hoffman, Joan, ed. 32p. (gr. k). 1990. wkbk. 2.29 (*0-88743-177-1*) Sch Zone Pub Co.

—Basic Math: First Grade. Gregorich, Barbara. Hoffman, Joan, ed. 32p. (gr. 1). 1990. wkbk. 2.29 (*0-88743-181-X*) Sch Zone Pub Co.

—Basic Math: Second Grade. Gregorich, Barbara. Hoffman, Joan, ed. 32p. (gr. 2). 1990. wkbk. 2.29 (*0-88743-187-9*) Sch Zone Pub Co.

—Chicago & the Cat. Koontz, Robin M. LC 91-34863. 32p. (gr. k-3). 1993. 12.00 (*0-525-65097-0*, Cobblehill Bks) Dutton Child Bks.

—Chicago & the Cat: The Camping Trip. Koontz, Robin M. LC 92-46685. 32p. (gr. k-3). 1994. 12.99 (*0-525-65137-3*, Cobblehill Bks) Dutton Child Bks.

—Chicago & the Cat: The Halloween Party. Koontz, Robin M. LC 93-27043. 1994. write for info. (*0-525-65138-1*, Cobblehill Bks) Dutton Child Bks.

—I See Something You Don't See: A Riddle-Me Picture Book. Koontz, Robin M. LC 91-8025. 32p. (ps-3). 1992. 13.00 (*0-525-65077-6*, Cobblehill Bks) Dutton Child Bks.

—In a Cabin in a Wood. McNally, Darcie, adapted by. LC 89-25192. 32p. (ps-3). 1991. 12.95 (*0-525-65035-0*, Cobblehill Bks) Dutton Child Bks.

—Letters & Words: Kindergarten. Gregorich, Barbara. Hoffman, Joan, ed. 32p. (gr. k). 1990. wkbk. 2.29 (*0-88743-179-8*) Sch Zone Pub Co.

—Music in the Night. Wilson, Etta. LC 92-11575. (ps-2). 1993. 12.99 (*0-525-65113-6*, Cobblehill Bks) Dutton Child Bks.

—Positional Words & Opposite Words: Kindergarten. Gregorich, Barbara. Hoffman, Joan, ed. 32p. (gr. k). 1990. wkbk. 2.29 (*0-88743-180-1*) Sch Zone Pub Co.

—Reading: First Grade. Gregorich, Barbara. Hoffman, Joan, ed. 32p. (gr. 1). 1990. wkbk. 2.29 (*0-88743-183-6*) Sch Zone Pub Co.

—Reading: Second Grade. Gregorich, Barbara. Hoffman, Joan, ed. 32p. (gr. 2). 1990. wkbk. 2.29 (*0-88743-189-5*) Sch Zone Pub Co.

—Victoria Flies High. Ayres, Becky. LC 89-694. 32p. (ps-3). 1990. 12.95 (*0-525-65014-8*, Cobblehill Bks) Dutton Child Bks.

—Word Skills: First Grade. Gregorich, Barbara. Hoffman, Joan, ed. 32p. (gr. 1). 1990. wkbk. 2.29 (*0-88743-184-4*) Sch Zone Pub Co.

—Word Skills: Second Grade. Gregorich, Barbara. Hoffman, Joan, ed. 32p. (gr. 2). 1990. wkbk. 2.29 (*0-88743-190-9*) Sch Zone Pub Co.

Koop, Christie. Patrick & Patty Go to Time Out. Buchanan-Hedman, Pat. 24p. (Orig.). (ps-5). 1991. 8.95 (*1-880121-50-6*) Three Cs Ent.

—A Stepfather Named Buddy. Buchanan-Hedman, Pat & Kingsbury, Kenneth. (Orig.). (ps-5). 1991. write for info. (*1-880121-25-5*) Three Cs Ent.

—Stepmothers & Moonkisses. Buchanan-Hedman, Pat. 23p. (Orig.). (ps-5). 1991. 8.95 (*1-880121-00-X*) Three Cs Ent.

—Tracy & the Lavender Piece of Paper: A Realistic Story to Help Children Cope with Painful & Bitter Divorces. Buchanan-Hedman, Pat. (Orig.). (gr. 1-6). 1991. write for info. (*1-880121-75-1*) Three Cs Ent.

Koopmans, Loek. The Woodcutter's Mitten: An Old Tale. Koopmans, Loek. LC 90-2545. 32p. (ps-2). 1990. 13.95 (*0-940793-67-9*, Crocodile Bks) Interlink Pub.

Koosak, Tara. Boy Girl Daze Craze. Koosak, Tara. LC 91-91469. 60p. (Orig.). (gr. 4-8). 1992. pap. 3.50 (*0-934426-44-9*) NAPSAC Reprods.

Kopald, Suanne K. Serina's First Flight: A Tooth Fairy's Tale. Kopald, Suanne K. LC 91-12783. 32p. (gr. k-3). 1992. 13.95 (*0-934738-88-2*) Thomasson-Grant.

Kopari, Catherine. Ghostly Tales of Lake Superior. Schumacher, Claire W. LC 87-91292. 94p. (Orig.). (gr. 9). 1987. PLB 6.95 (*0-917378-06-7*) Zenith City.

Kopecky, Robert. Curveballs Strikes Again: More Wacky Facts to Bat Around. Rolfe, John. 32p. (gr. 3-7). 1992. pap. 4.95 (*0-316-75460-9*, Spts Illus Kids) Little.

Kopen, Pamela A. Grandpa's Magic Drawer. Kopen, Pamela A. Kopen, Dan F., intro. by. LC 91-91475. 32p. (ps-3). 1992. 14.95 (*0-9628914-1-X*) Padakami Pr.

—The Trillium Trail. Kopen, Pamela A. & Kopen, Dan F. LC 93-28228. 32p. (ps-12). 1993. pap. 9.95 (*0-9628914-3-6*) Padakami Pr.

Kopper, Lisa. The Disappearing Granny. Lavelle, Sheila. 42p. (gr. 2-4). 1989. 3.95 (*0-8120-6134-9*) Barron.

—Happy Birthday! 18p. (ps). 1992. bds. 4.95 (*0-448-41088-5*, G&D) Putnam Pub Group.

—Hush-a-Bye Baby. 18p. (ps). 1992. bds. 4.95 (*0-448-40266-1*, G&D) Putnam Pub Group.

—I Can Play Soccer. Fraser, Sheila. 24p. (ps-3). 1991. 5.95 (*0-8120-6225-6*) Barron.

—I Can Ride a Bike. Fraser, Sheila. 24p. (ps-3). 1991. 5.95 (*0-8120-6227-2*) Barron.

—I Can Roller Skate. Fraser, Sheila. 24p. (ps-3). 1991. 5.95 (*0-8120-6228-0*) Barron.

—I Can Swim. Fraser, Sheila. 24p. (ps-3). 1991. 5.95 (*0-8120-6226-4*) Barron.

—Jafta. Lewin, Hugh. (ps-3). 1989. pap. 4.95 (*0-87614-494-6*, First Ave Edns) Lerner Pubns.

—Jafta & the Wedding. Lewin, Hugh. LC 82-12836. 24p. (ps-3). 1983. pap. 4.95 (*0-87614-497-0*) Carolrhoda Bks.

—Jafta: The Homecoming. Lewin, Hugh. LC 93-12945. 32p. (ps-2). 1994. 8.99 (*0-87614-481-X*); PLB 9.99 (*0-679-94722-1*) Knopf Bks Yng Read.

—Jafta: The Journey. Lewin, Hugh. LC 84-4326. 24p. (ps-3). 1984. PLB 15.95 (*0-87614-265-X*) Carolrhoda Bks.

—Jafta: The Town. Lewin, Hugh. LC 84-4950. 24p. (ps-3). 1984. PLB 15.95 (*0-87614-266-8*) Carolrhoda Bks.

—Jafta's Father. Lewin, Hugh. 24p. (ps-3). 1989. pap. 4.95 (*0-87614-496-2*, First Ave Edns) Lerner Pubns.

—Jafta's Father. Lewin, Hugh. 24p. (ps-3). 1983. 4.95 (*0-87614-209-9*) Carolrhoda Bks.

—Jafta's Mother. Lewin, Hugh. 24p. (ps-3). 1989. pap. 4.95 (*0-87614-495-4*, First Ave Edns) Lerner Pubns.

—Lost in Town. Bonnici, Peter. 32p. (gr. k-2). 1990. 11.95 (*0-340-48612-0*, Pub. by Hodder & Stoughton UK) Trafalgar.

—Merry Christmas! Richards, Kelly F. LC 90-83243. 24p. (ps-3). 1991. 2.50 (*0-448-40125-8*, G&D) Putnam Pub Group.

—Peek-a-Boo Baby. 12p. (ps). 1993. bds. 3.95 (*0-448-40197-5*, G&D) Putnam Pub Group.

—Peek-a-Boo Kitty. 12p. (ps). 1993. bds. 3.95 (*0-448-40196-7*, G&D) Putnam Pub Group.

—Peek-a-Boo Teddy. 12p. (ps). 1993. bds. 3.95 (*0-448-40195-9*, G&D) Putnam Pub Group.

—The Special Event. Bonnici, Peter. 32p. (gr. k-2). 1990. 11.95 (*0-340-48609-0*, Pub. by Hodder & Stoughton UK) Trafalgar.

—Ten Little Babies. Lewin, Hugh. LC 89-49478. 24p. (ps-3). 1990. 9.95 (*0-525-44643-5*, DCB) Dutton Child Bks.

—The Village Show. Bonnici, Peter. 32p. (gr. k-2). 1990. 11.95 (*0-340-48610-4*, Pub. by Hodder & Stoughton UK) Trafalgar.

Korach, Mimi. The Old Witch & the Wizard. DeLage, Ida. 48p. (gr. k-4). 1991. Repr. of 1974 ed. lib. bdg. 12.95 (*0-7910-1480-0*) Chelsea Hse.

—The Old Witch's Party. DeLage, Ida. 48p. (gr. k-4). 1991. Repr. of 1976 ed. lib. bdg. 12.95 (*0-7910-1484-3*) Chelsea Hse.

Koren, Edward. Art Ventures: A Guide for Families to Ten Works of Art in the Carnegie Museum of Art. Judson, Bay, et al. LC 87-858. 24p. (Orig.). (gr. 4-6). 1987. pap. text ed. 5.95 (0-88039-014-X) Mus Art Carnegie.

Korner, David. Come out & Play. Korner, David. LC 86-2811. 56p. (gr. 1-5). 1987. pap. 9.95 (0-939827-00-X) Korn Kompany.

Koropp, Robert, photos by. Space Camp: The Great Adventures for NASA Hopefuls. Baird, Anne. Shepard, Alan B. & Buckbee, Edward O.frwd. by. LC 91-21587. 48p. (gr. 3 up). 1992. 14.00 (0-688-10227-1); PLB 13.93 (0-688-10228-X) Morrow Jr Bks.

Kors, Erika. How Did We Find about Microwaves? Asimov, Isaac. 64p. (gr. 1-4). 1989. 11.95 (0-8027-6837-7); PLB 12.85 (0-8027-6838-5) Walker & Co.

—How Did We Find Out about Lasers? Asimov, Isaac. (gr. 5 up). 1990. 12.95 (0-8027-6935-7); lib. bdg. 13.85 (0-8027-6936-5) Walker & Co.

—How Did We Find Out about Neptune? Asimov, Isaac. 64p. (gr. 5 up). 1990. 12.95 (0-8027-6981-0); lib. bdg. 13.85 (0-8027-6982-9) Walker & Co.

—How Did We Find Out about Photosynthesis. Asimov, Isaac. 32p. (gr. 1-4). 1989. 11.95 (0-8027-6899-7); PLB 12.85 (0-8027-6886-5) Walker & Co.

—How Did We Find Out about Pluto? Asimov, Isaac. 64p. (gr. 5 up). 1991. 12.95 (0-8027-6991-8); PLB 13.85 (0-8027-6992-6) Walker & Co.

—Two Orphan Cubs. Brenner, Barbara & Garelick, May. (ps-1). 1989. 12.95 (0-8027-6868-7); PLB 13.85 (0-8027-6869-5) Walker & Co.

Kortekaas, Kelly. The Beginning of the River: Herman's Quest. Drake, John. 48p. (gr. k-5). 1992. 16.95 (0-9633574-0-9) Little Turtle.

Korth-Sander, Irmtraut. Will You Be My Friend? Korth-Sander, Irmtraut. Lanning, Rosemary, tr. from GER. LC 86-60485. 32p. (gr. k-2). 1986. 14.95 (1-55858-071-9) North-South Bks NYC.

Koscielniak, Bruce. Bear & Bunny Grow Tomatoes. Koscielniak, Bruce. LC 92-10065. 40p. (ps-2). 1993. 8.99 (0-679-83667-X); PLB 9.99 (0-679-93687-4) Knopf Bks Yng Read.

—Hector & Prudence. Koscielniak, Bruce. LC 88-31359. 40p. (ps-2). 1990. 12.95 (0-394-84514-5); lib. bdg. 14.99 (0-394-94514-X) Knopf Bks Yng Read.

—Hector & Prudence - All Aboard! Koscielniak, Bruce. LC 89-2008. 40p. (ps-2). 1990. PLB 13.99 (0-679-90486-7) Knopf Bks Yng Read.

Koshkin, Alexander. Say Something. rev. & newly illus. ed. Stolz, Mary. LC 92-8317. 32p. (ps-3). 1993. 15.00 (0-06-021158-X); PLB 14.89 (0-06-021159-8) HarpC Child Bks.

—Stolen Thunder: A Norse Myth. Climo, Shirley. LC 93-24627. 1994. write for info. (0-395-64368-6, Clarion Bks) HM.

—Vasilissa the Beautiful. Winthrop, Elizabeth. LC 89-26903. 40p. (gr. 1-5). 1994. pap. 5.95 (0-06-443345-5, Trophy) HarpC Child Bks.

—Vasilissa the Beautiful: A Russian Folktale. Winthrop, Elizabeth, adapted by. LC 89-26903. 40p. (gr. 1-5). 1991. 16.00 (0-06-021662-X); PLB 15.89 (0-06-021663-8) HarpC Child Bks.

Koslowski, Richard K. Milo's Friends in the Dark. Ploetz, Craig T. 32p. (ps-4). 1992. PLB 11.95 (1-882172-00-0) Milo Prods.

Kossin, Sandy. The Easy Baseball Book. Kalb, Jonah. LC 75-44085. 64p. (gr. 2-5). 1976. 14.45 (0-395-24385-8) HM.

Kossin, Sanford. Mystery of the Lost Letter. Blake, Olive. LC 78-18037. 48p. (gr. 2-4). 1979. PLB 10.89 (0-89375-093-X); pap. 3.50 (0-89375-081-6) Troll Assocs.

Kostal, Pavel. Science Can Be Fun. Wicks, Keith. 32p. (gr. 4-7). 1988. PLB 14.95 (0-8225-0896-6, First Ave Edns); pap. 4.95 (0-8225-9559-1, First Ave Edns) Lerner Pubns.

Kostecke, Nancy, jt. illus. see Fenton, Mary F.

Kostrina, I. D. Volk u Telonok: Wolf & Calf. Lipskerov, M. F. (RUS.). 18p. (Orig.). 1989. pap. 14.95 (0-934393-15-X) Rector Pr.

Kostrina, Irina. Samy Malenky Gnom (a Very Small Gnome) Lipskerov, M. F. (RUS.). 18p. (Orig.). 1991. pap. 14.95 (0-934393-22-0) Rector Pr.

Kostrko, Zofia. Bert. Skulavik, Mary A. 32p. (ps-3). 1990. 13.95 (0-8027-6962-4); lib. bdg. 14.85 (0-8027-6963-2) Walker & Co.

Kotomaimoce, Kathy. Our Selves. Bittinger, Gayle. LC 91-67076. 80p. 1992. 8.95 (0-911019-51-0, WPH 1202) Warren Pub Hse.

Koury, Jennifer. Where Was George Washington? Heymsfeld, Carla. LC 92-17341. 1992. 14.95 (0-931917-20-4); pap. write for info. (0-931917-21-2) Mt Vernon Ladies.

Kovach, Gay H. Ghost in the Capitol. Bodie, Idella. 116p. (gr. 5-9). 1986. pap. 6.95 (0-87844-072-0) Sandlapper Pub Co.

Kovalski, Mary A. Sharon, Lois & Bram's Mother Goose Songs, Finger Rhymes, Tickling Verses, Games & More. Sharon, et al. 92p. (ps-2). 1986. 16.95i (0-316-78281-5, 782815); pap. 9.95i (0-316-78282-3) Little.

Kovalski, Maryann. The Big Storm. Tregebov, Rhea. LC 92-55040. 32p. (ps-3). 1993. 13.95 (1-56282-461-9); PLB 13.89 (1-56282-462-7) Hyprn Child.

—The Cake That Mack Ate. Robart, Rose. LC 86-47709. (ps-3). 1987. 14.95 (0-316-74890-0) Little.

—The Cake That Mack Ate. Robart, Rose. (ps-3). 1991. pap. 4.95 (0-316-74891-9) Little.

—Doctor Knickerbocker & Other Rhymes. Booth, David, compiled by. LC 92-46266. (ps). 1993. 16.45 (0-395-67168-X) Ticknor & Fields.

—I Went to the Zoo. Gelman, Rita G. LC 92-27671. 1993. 14.95 (0-590-45882-5) Scholastic Inc.

—Jingle Bells. Kovalski, Maryann. 32p. (ps-2). 1988. 12.95 (0-316-50258-8) Little.

—Pizza for Breakfast. Kovalski, Maryann. LC 90-46078. 32p. (gr. k up). 1991. Repr. of 1990 ed. 13.95 (0-688-10409-6); PLB 13.88 (0-688-10410-X, Morrow Jr Bks) Morrow Jr Bks.

—The Wheels on the Bus. Kovalski, Maryann. 32p. (ps-k). 1987. 14.95 (0-316-50256-1, Joy St Bks) Little.

Kovick, Kris. How Would You Feel If Your Dad Was Gay? Heron, Ann & Maran, Meredith. 48p. (gr. 1-5). 1994. pap. 6.95 (1-55583-243-1) Alyson Pubns.

Kozjak, Goran. A Little Rhythm, Rhyme & Read: Colors & Shapes. Thompson, Kim M. & Hilderbrand, Karen M. 28p. (ps-1). 1993. Wkbk., incl. audio cass. 9.98 (1-882331-16-8) Twin Sisters. Twin Sisters Productions, Inc. is introducing the second title in their Early Childhood Education Series: A LITTLE "RHYTHM, RHYME & READ" COLORS & SHAPES. A LITTLE "RHYTHM, RHYME & READ" COLORS & SHAPES is a deluxe 28 page activity book filled with easy-to-read sheet music & lyrics for sing-along fun. The book contains developmentally appropriate activities, creative art projects, simple coloring pages, & easy-to-follow lesson plans. Children are encouraged to learn about their strengths & individuality as they complete an "I Am Special Activity." Animated characters help children remember concepts as they sing about "Sammy Sue," a friendly shark with triangular teeth & circular eyes, who loves to eat square lunch boxes! Vivid sound effects enhance the many musical genres from the jazzy "Betty Bunny" to the multicultural "All The Children Of The World." All products are teacher written & classroom tested. Call 1-800-248-TWIN to place an order or to find out about the many other fine quality Twin Sisters Productions' products. Twin Sisters Productions, Inc., 488 Graham Rd., Cuyahoga Falls, OH 44221. *Publisher Provided Annotation.*

—A Little Rhythm, Rhyme & Read: Letters & Numbers. Thompson, Kim M. & Hilderbrand, Karen M. 28p. (ps-1). 1993. Wkbk., incl. audio cass. 9.98 (1-882331-15-X) Twin Sisters. Twin Sisters Productions, Inc. is introducing the first title in their Early Childhood Educational Series: A LITTLE "RHYTHM, RHYME & READ" LETTERS & NUMBERS. A LITTLE "RHYTHM, RHYME & READ" LETTERS & NUMBERS is a deluxe 28 page activity book filled with easy-to-read sheet music & lyrics for sing-along fun. The book contains developmentally appropriate activities, creative art projects, simple coloring pages, & easy-to-follow lesson plans. Children are encouraged to make letters out of pretzel dough, take an alphabet hike & learn basic addition with jelly beans. Vivid sound effects & easy-to-sing melodies make learning numerical sequences, letter names & basic addition fun. A variety of original & familiar melodies combines fun & educational learning. All products are

teacher written & clasroom tested. Call 1-800-248-TWIN to place an order to find out about the many other fine quality Twin Sisters Productions' products. Twin Sisters Productions, Inc., 488 Graham Rd., Cuyahoga Falls, OH 44221. *Publisher Provided Annotation.*

Kozlina, Yvonne. Fingerplays & Action Chants: Animals, Vol. 1. Weimer, Tonja E. 42p. (Orig.). (gr. k-1). 1986. pap. text ed. 8.95 (0-936823-00-3); cassette 8.95 (0-936823-01-1) Pearce Evetts.

—Fingerplays & Action Chants: Family & Friends, Vol. 2. Weimer, Tonja E. 44p. (Orig.). (ps-1). 1986. pap. text ed. 8.95 (0-936823-02-X); cassette 8.95 (0-936823-03-8) Pearce Evetts.

—Space Songs for Children: Fun Songs & Activities about Outer Space. Weimer, Tonja E. 100p. (Orig.). (ps-3). 1993. 13.98 (0-936823-11-9); cassette 9.95 (0-936823-12-7) Pearce Evetts.

Krahenbuhl, Eddy. The Cathedral Builders. Perdrizet, Marie-Pierre. Raycraft, Mary B., tr. from FRE. LC 91-24233. 64p. (gr. 4-6). 1992. PLB 14.90 (1-56294-162-3) Millbrook Pr.

Krahn, Fernando. Amanda & the Mysterious Carpet. Krahn, Fernando. LC 84-14201. 32p. (ps-3). 1985. 13.45 (0-89919-258-0, Clarion Bks) HM.

—Mooga Mega Mekki. Wahl, Jahn. LC 73-16818. 48p. (gr. 2-4). 1974. 7.95 (0-87955-111-9) O'Hara.

—They've Discovered a Head in the Box for the Bread & Other Laughable Limericks. Brewton, John E. & Blackburn, Lorraine A., eds. LC 77-26598. 144p. (gr. 3-7). 1978. PLB 13.89 (0-690-03883-6, Crowell Jr Bks) HarpC Child Bks.

Kramer, Anthony. The Great Condominium Rebellion. Snyder, Carol. LC 81-65491. 128p. (gr. 4-6). 1981. PLB 11.95 (0-385-28352-0) Delacorte.

—Have You Seen Hyacinth Macaw? Giff, Patricia R. (gr. 4-6). 1981. 11.95 (0-385-28389-X); pap. 12.95 (0-385-28390-3) Delacorte.

—Have You Seen Hyacinth Macaw: A Mystery. Giff, Patricia R. LC 80-68729. 128p. (gr. 4-7). 1981. 9.95 (0-440-03467-1); PLB 9.89 (0-440-03472-8) Delacorte.

—Loretta P. Sweeny, Where Are You? Giff, Patricia R. 144p. (gr. 4-8). 1990. pap. 3.25 (0-440-44926-X, YB) Dell.

—The Magic of Sound. Rev. ed. Kettelkamp, Larry. LC 82-6510. 96p. (gr. 4-6). 1982. lib. bdg. 12.88 (0-688-01493-3) Morrow Jr Bks.

—Omega Station. Slote, Alfred. LC 85-45395. 160p. (gr. 2-5). 1986. pap. 3.95 (0-06-440167-7, Trophy) HarpC Child Bks.

—The Search for Champ. Gilligan, Shannon. 50p. (gr. 4). 1983. pap. 2.25 (0-553-15442-7) Bantam.

—The Skyscraper Book. Giblin, James C. Anderson, David, photos by. LC 81-43038. 96p. (gr. 3-6). 1981. (Crowell Jr Bks); PLB 14.89 (0-690-04155-1, Crowell Jr Bks) HarpC Child Bks.

—Tootsie Tanner, Why Don't You Talk? An Abby Jones, Junior Detective, Mystery. Giff, Patricia R. LC 86-32910. 144p. (gr. 4-6). 1987. pap. 13.95 (0-385-29579-0) Delacorte.

Kramer, Devorah. The Haunted Shul. Hubner, Carol K. (gr. 3-8). 1979. 6.95 (0-910818-14-2) Judaica Pr.

—The Tattered Tallis. Hubner, Carol K. 128p. (gr. 3-8). 1979. 6.95 (0-910818-19-3) Judaica Pr.

—The Whispering Mezuzah. Hubner, Carol K. (gr. 3-9). 1979. 6.95 (0-910818-18-5) Judaica Pr.

Kramer, Frank. The Magical Mimics in Oz. Snow, Jack. 240p. (gr. 3 up). 1991. 24.95 (0-929605-08-X); pap. 11.95 (0-929605-09-8) Books Wonder.

—The Shaggy Man of Oz. Snow, Jack. 256p. (gr. 3 up). 1991. 24.95 (0-929605-11-X); pap. 11.95 (0-929605-11-X) Books Wonder.

Kramer, Gary. Music for Little People. Feierabend, John. 74p. (Orig.). (ps). 1989. pap. 11.95 (0-913932-46-9); pap. 14.95 incl. tape (0-913932-48-5) Boosey & Hawkes.

Kramer, Gary M. Music for Very Little People. Feierabend, John M. 74p. (ps). 1986. pap. 14.95 (0-685-14607-3); pap. write for info. incl. tape (0-913932-13-2); cassette avail. Boosey & Hawkes.

Kramer, Remi. The Legend of LoneStar Bear, Bk. One: How LoneStar Got His Name. Kramer, Remi. 64p. 1988. PLB 12.95 (0-945887-01-9) Northwind Pr.

—The Legend of LoneStar Bear, Bk. Two: Soaring with Eagles. Kramer, Remi. 72p. 1989. 14.95 (0-945887-02-7) Northwind Pr.

Kramer, Robin. Baby's First Body Book. Silverman, Maida. (ps-1). 1987. 3.95 (0-448-10554-3, G&D) Putnam Pub Group.

—Daisy's Crazy Thanksgiving. Cuyler, Margery. LC 90-4323. 32p. (ps-2). 1990. 14.95 (0-8050-0559-5, Owlet BYR) H Holt & Co.

—Daisy's Crazy Thanksgiving. Cuyler, Margery. LC 90-4323. 32p. (ps-2). 1992. pap. 4.95 (0-8050-2348-8, Owlet BYR) H Holt & Co.

—Hide-&-Seek on the Farm. Damon, Laura. LC 87-13737. 32p. (gr. k-2). 1988. PLB 7.89 (0-8167-1231-X); pap. text ed. 1.95 (0-8167-1232-8) Troll Assocs.

—One, Two, Three Thanksgiving! Nikola-Lisa, W. Levine, Abby, ed. LC 90-26838. 32p. (ps-1). 1991. 13.95 (0-8075-6109-6) A Whitman.

—The Two O'Clock Secret. Roberts, Bethany. Grant, Christy, ed. LC 92-6405. 32p. (ps-2). 1993. 13.95g (*0-8075-8159-3*) A Whitman.
—Why Worms? rev. ed. Davies, Gillian. 32p. (gr. k-2). 1990. Repr. of 1989 ed. PLB 10.50 (*1-878363-07-7*) Forest Hse.

Kramer, Stephen & Huffman, Elise. Cows Are Vegetarians! A Book for Vegetarian Kids. Bradley, Ann. 24p. (gr. 2-8). 1992. pap. 7.95 (*0-9630893-0-7*) Healthways.

Kranz, Ellen. Busy Fingers, Growing Minds: Finger Plays, Verses & Activities for Whole Language Learning. Redleaf, Rhoda. Nelson, Eileen, ed. Galle, Lynn, intro. by. LC 93-39636. 164p. (Orig.). (ps). 1993. pap. 18.95 (*0-934140-79-0*) Redleaf Pr.

Kranz, Stewart. Don't Worry Dear. Fassler, Joan. LC 74-147124. 32p. (ps-3). 1971. 16.95 (*0-87705-055-4*) Human Sci Pr.
—My Grandpa Died Today. Fassler, Joan. LC 71-147126. 32p. (ps-3). 1983. 14.95 (*0-87705-053-8*); pap. 9.95 (*0-89885-174-2*) Human Sci Pr.

Krasnoborski, William. I Can Read About Johnny Appleseed. Anderson, J. I. LC 76-54445. (gr. 2-5). 1977. pap. 1.95 (*0-89375-037-9*) Troll Assocs.
—I Can Read About the Sun & Other Stars. Harris, Richard. LC 76-54577. (gr. 2-4). 1977. pap. 1.95 (*0-89375-044-1*) Troll Assocs.

Kraulis, J. A. Ottawa: A Kid's Eye View. Aziz, Laurel & Edwards, Frank B. 72p. 1993. text ed. 19.95 (*0-921285-27-2*, Pub. by Bungalo Bks CN); pap. 9.95 (*0-921285-26-4*, Pub. by Bungalo Bks CN) Firefly Bks Ltd.

Kraus, Robert. The Adventures of Wise Old Owl. Kraus, Robert. LC 92-20436. 32p. (ps-3). 1992. PLB 10.89 (*0-8167-2943-3*); pap. text ed. 2.95 (*0-8167-2944-1*) Troll Assocs.
—Buggy Bear Cleans Up. Kraus, Robert. Brook, Bonnie, ed. 48p. (ps-3). 1989. PLB 8.98 (*0-671-68608-9*); pap. 3.95 (*0-671-68612-7*) Silver Pr.
—Daddy Long Ears. Kraus, Robert. (ps-1). 1989. 4.95 (*0-671-67415-3*, Little Simon) S&S Trade.
—Ella the Bad Speller. Kraus, Robert. Brook, Bonnie, ed. 48p. (ps-3). 1989. PLB 8.98 (*0-671-68606-2*); pap. 3.95 (*0-671-68610-0*) Silver Pr.
—Good Morning, Miss Gator. Kraus, Robert. Brook, Bonnie, ed. 48p. (ps-3). 1989. PLB 8.98 (*0-671-68605-4*); pap. 3.95 (*0-671-68609-7*) Silver Pr.
—Here Comes Tardy Toad. Kraus, Robert. Brook, Bonnie, ed. 48p. (ps-3). 1989. PLB 8.98 (*0-671-68607-0*); pap. 3.95 (*0-671-68611-9*) Silver Pr.
—How Spider Saved Easter. Kraus, Robert. 32p. (ps-2). 1991. 12.95 (*0-8038-9331-0*) Hastings.
—How Spider Saved Halloween. Kraus, Robert. 32p. (ps-3). 1988. pap. 2.25 (*0-671-66889-7*, Little Simon) S&S Trade.
—How Spider Saved Valentine's Day. Kraus, Robert. 32p. (Orig.). (ps-1). 1986. pap. 2.50 (*0-590-42514-5*) Scholastic Inc.
—Klunky Monkey, New Kid in Class. Kraus, Robert. Brook, Bonnie, ed. 48p. (ps-3). 1990. lib. bdg. 8.98 (*0-671-70853-8*); pap. 3.95 (*0-671-70854-6*) Silver Pr.
—Miss Gator's School House, 6 bks. Kraus, Robert. (gr. k-3). 1989. Set, 48p. ea. lib. bdg. 53.88 (*0-671-94105-4*, J Messner); Set, 48p. ea. pap. 21.00 (*0-671-94106-2*) S&S Trade.
—Squirmy's Big Secret. Kraus, Robert & Brook, Bonnie. 48p. (ps-3). 1990. lib. bdg. 8.98 (*0-671-70851-1*); pap. 3.95 (*0-671-70852-X*) Silver Pr.
—Wise Old Owl's Canoe Trip Adventure. Kraus, Robert, ed. LC 91-39014. 32p. (ps-3). 1993. text ed. 10.89 (*0-8167-2947-6*); pap. text ed. 2.95 (*0-8167-2948-4*) Troll Assocs.

Krause, Brad. SSS: Social Skill Strategies, Book B: A Curriculum for Adolescents. Mayo, Patty & Gajewski, Nancy. 350p. (Orig.). (gr. 5-12). 1989. pap. text ed. 33.00x (*0-930599-52-7*) Thinking Pubns.

Krause, Robert, jt. illus. see Sibley, Norman.

Krause, Ute. Ottie Slockett. Luttrell, Ida. Fogelman, Phyllis J., ed. LC 88-30884. 40p. (ps-3). 1990. 9.95 (*0-8037-0709-6*); PLB 9.89 (*0-8037-0711-8*) Dial Bks Young.
—A Package for Miss Marshwater. Donnelly, Elfie. (gr. 2-5). 1987. Dial Bks Young.
—Pig Surprise. Krause, Ute. LC 88-31108. 32p. (ps-3). 1989. 11.95 (*0-8037-0714-2*) Dial Bks Young.
—The Santa Clauses. Broger, Achim, retold by. LC 86-2147. 28p. (ps-3). 1986. 11.95 (*0-8037-0266-3*) Dial Bks Young.
—The Santa Clauses. Broger, Achim, retold by. LC 86-2147. 28p. (ps-3). 1988. pap. 3.95 (*0-8037-0557-3*) Dial Bks Young.

Krause, William. Human Anatomy for Children. Goldsmith, Ilse. (gr. 5-8). 1969. pap. 2.95 (*0-486-22355-8*) Dover.

Krauss, Ruth. This Breast Gothic. Krauss, Ruth. 48p. (gr. 7 up). 1973. pap. 8.00 (*0-912846-02-5*) Bookstore Pr.

Kray, Robert. Mammals. Tesar, Jenny. 64p. (gr. 4-8). 1993. jacketed 14.95 (*1-56711-055-X*) Blackbirch.

Kredel, Fritz. Adventures of Pinocchio. Collodi, Carlo. (gr. 4-6). 1982. 12.95 (*0-448-06001-9*, G&D) Putnam Pub Group.
—Aesop's Fables. Aesop. LC 33-31662. (gr. 4-6). 1963. (G&D); deluxe ed. 12.95 (*0-448-06003-5*); Companion Library. companion lib. o.p. 2.95 (*0-448-05453-1*); pap. ed (IJL) o.p. 4.95 (*0-686-76870-1*) Putnam Pub Group.

Kreffel, Mike. Career Preparation: Getting the Most from Training & Education. Christophersen, Susan & Farr, J. Michael. Croy, Greg, ed. 64p. (gr. 9-12). 1990. pap. 6.95 (*0-942784-59-6*, CP) JIST Works.
—I Am (Already) Successful: Getting Motivated, Being Me. Hooker, Dennis. Holcomb, Ann, ed. 156p. (gr. 7-12). 1990. pap. 6.95 (*0-942784-41-3*, AM); instr's. manual, 32p. 12.95 (*0-942784-42-1*, AMIG) JIST Works.
—Knowing Yourself: Learning about Your Skills, Values & Planning Your Life. Christophersen, Susan & Farr, J. Michael. Croy, Greg, ed. 64p. (gr. 9-12). 1990. pap. 6.95 (*0-942784-58-8*, KM) JIST Works.
—Your Career: Thinking about Jobs & Careers. Christophersen, Susan & Farr, J. Michael. Croy, Greg, ed. 64p. (gr. 9-12). 1990. pap. 6.95 (*0-942784-60-X*, MC) JIST Works.

Kreiswirth, Kinny. The Lunch Book & Bag: A Fit Kid's Guide to Making Delicious (& Nutritious) Lunches. Bodily, Jolene & Kreiswirth, Kinny. LC 92-2815. 56p. (gr. 2-6). 1992. pap. 12.95 (*0-688-11624-8*, Tambourine Bks) Morrow.

Kreloff, Elliot. Kitten. (ps-k). 1993. Set, lg. bk. 12p., small bk. 6p. bds. 4.95 (*1-56293-360-4*) McClanahan Bk.
—Puppy. (ps-k). 1993. Set, lg. bk. 12p., small bk. 6p. bds. 4.95 (*1-56293-359-0*) McClanahan Bk.
—Train. (ps-k). 1993. Set, lg. bk. 12p., small bk. 6p. bds. 4.95 (*1-56293-357-4*) McClanahan Bk.
—Truck. (ps-k). 1993. Set, lg. bk. 12p., small bk. 6p. bds. 4.95 (*1-56293-358-2*) McClanahan Bk.

Krementz, Jill. How It Feels to Fight for Your Life. Krementz, Jill. 1989. 15.95 (*0-316-50364-9*, Joy St Bks) Little.
—A Storyteller's Story. Martin, Rafe. 32p. (gr. 2-5). 1992. 12.95 (*0-913461-03-2*) R Owen Pubs.

Krementz, Jill, photos by. Jack Goes to the Beach. Krementz, Jill. 32p. (ps-k). 1986. bds. 3.95 (*0-394-88001-3*) Random Bks Yng Read.
—A Very Young Gardener. Krementz, Jill. LC 92-2766. 40p. (gr-3). 1991. 13.95 (*0-8037-0874-2*) Dial Bks Young.
—A Very Young Musician. Krementz, Jill. 48p. (gr. 3-7). 1991. pap. 14.95 jacketed (*0-671-72687-0*, S&S BFYR) S&S Trade.

Krenkel, Roy. The Wonderful Wizard of Oz. Baum, L. Frank. (gr. 4 up). 1965. pap. 1.75 (*0-8049-0069-8*, CL-69) Airmont.

Krensky, Stephen, jt. illus. see Brown, Marc.

Krenzke, Chris. The Write Source: A Student Handbook. Sebranek, Patrick, et al. 304p. (gr. 4-8). 1987. 8.95 (*0-939045-02-8*); text ed. 8.95 (*0-685-18820-5*); pap. text ed. 7.95 (*0-939045-03-6*) Write Source.
—Write Source Two Thousand: A Guide to Writing, Thinking, & Learning. Sebranek, et al. 400p. (Orig.). (gr. 4-9). 1990. text ed. 11.95 (*0-939045-34-6*); pap. text ed. 9.95 (*0-939045-33-8*); tchr's. ed., 116p. 9.95 (*0-939045-52-4*) Write Source.
—Writers Inc: A Guide to Writing, Thinking, & Learning. 2nd ed. Sebranek, et al. 360p. (gr. 9 up). 1990. text ed. 10.95 (*0-939045-49-4*); pap. text ed. 8.95 (*0-939045-48-6*); Inc Sights, 94p. tchr's. ed. 7.95 (*0-939045-32-X*) Write Source.

Krestjanoff. Martin & Tommy. Poltarness, Weller. LC 93-13609. (gr. 4 up). 1994. 14.00 (*0-671-88067-5*, Green Tiger Pr) S&S Trade.

Kretschmann, Karin. Creature Feature: And Other Tales of Horror. Razzi, Jim. 64p. 1990. (G&D); pap. 2.95 (*0-448-40066-9*, G&D) Putnam Pub Group.
—The Ghost in the Mirror: And Other Ghost Stories. Razzi, Jim. 64p. 1990. (G&D); pap. 2.95 (*0-448-40058-8*, G&D) Putnam Pub Group.

Kretschmar, Sonia. Pasquale's Gift. Lukic, Marie. LC 93-29002. 1994. 4.25 (*0-383-03768-9*) SRA Schl Grp.

Krevitsky, Nik. It Happened in Chelm: A Story of the Legendary Town of Fools. Freeman, Florence B. 64p. (gr. 3-8). 1990. pap. text ed. 9.95 (*0-933503-22-9*) Shapolsky Pubs.

Kricher, John & Morrison, Gordon. A Field Guide to Tropical Forests Coloring Book. Kricher, John & Morrison, Gordon. 64p. 1991. pap. 4.80 (*0-395-57321-1*) HM.

Kricher, John C. & Morrison, Gordon. Peterson First Guide to Seashores. Kricher, John C. & Morrison, Gordon. 128p. (5 up). 1992. pap. 4.80 (*0-395-61901-7*) HM.

Krinard, Sue, et al. Pendragon: Roleplaying in King Arthur's Britain. 3rd ed. Stafford, Greg & Dunn, Bill. 208p. (gr. 9 up). 1990. pap. 21.95 (*0-933635-59-1*, 2) Chaosium.

Krings, Antoon. Oliver's Bicycle. Krings, Antoon. LC 91-25030. 32p. (ps-k). 1992. 6.95 (*1-56282-164-4*); PLB 6.89 (*1-56282-165-2*) Hyprn Child.
—Oliver's Pool. Krings, Antoon. LC 91-24589. 32p. (ps-k). 1992. 6.95 (*1-56282-160-1*); PLB 6.89 (*1-56282-161-X*) Hyprn Child.
—Oliver's Strawberry Patch. Krings, Antoon. LC 91-27022. 32p. (ps-k). 1992. 6.95 (*1-56282-162-8*); PLB 6.89 (*1-56282-163-6*) Hyprn Child.

Kritchman-Knuteson, Joan. Bingo the Bear. LaFleur, Tom & Brennan, Gale. 16p. (Orig.). (gr. k-6). 1981. pap. 1.25 (*0-685-02454-7*) Brennan Bks.

Kromer, Christiane. The Children Who Lived in a Tree. White, Carolyn. LC 92-46428. 1994. pap. 14.00 (*0-671-79818-9*, S&S BFYR) S&S Trade.

Krone, Mike & Panek, Judy. Fun Food to Tickle Your Mood: A Cookbook for Children Who Cherish the Earth. Ellinger, Marko. 96p. (Orig.). (gr. 2-6). 1992. pap. 9.95 (*0-9630147-5-7*) Piccadilly TX.

Kronz, Leslie S. Grey Neck. Mamin-Sibiryak, D. N. Rudolph, Marguerita, adapted by. LC 88-2100. 32p. (gr. k-3). 1988. 13.95 (*0-88045-068-1*) Stemmer Hse.

Kropa, Susan. Famous Fables for Little Troupers. Lipson, Greta. 168p. (gr. k-6). 1984. 12.95 (*0-86653-202-1*, GA 554) Good Apple.
—Romeo & Juliet: Plainspoken. Lipson, Greta & Solomon, Susan. 256p. (gr. 7-12). 1985. 15.95 (*0-86653-283-8*, GA 659) Good Apple.
—Sky Blue, Grass Green. Kropa, Susan. 128p. (gr. 1-3). 1986. wkbk. 11.95 (*0-86653-355-9*, GA 698) Good Apple.

Kropa, Susie. Faces, Legs, & Belly Buttons. Kropa, Susie. 80p. (ps). 1984. wkbk. 8.95 (*0-86653-239-0*, GA 564) Good Apple.

Kroupa, Melanie. A Little Touch of Monster. Lampert, Emily. LC 85-26847. 32p. (ps-3). 1986. lib. bdg. 12.95 (*0-316-51287-7*, 512877, Joy St Bks) Little.

Krovatin, Dan. A Matter of Conscience: The Trial of Anne Hutchinson. Nichols, Joan K. LC 92-18087. 101p. (gr. 2-5). 1992. PLB 21.34 (*0-8114-7233-7*) Raintree Steck-V.

Kruck, Gerry. Developing the Early Learner: Level 1. rev. ed. Bibeau, Simone. 64p. (ps-2). 1983. pap. text ed. 4.95 (*0-940406-01-2*) Perception Pubns.
—Developing the Early Learner: Level 2. rev. ed. Bibeau, Simone. 64p. (ps-2). 1983. pap. text ed. 4.95 (*0-940406-02-0*) Perception Pubns.
—Developing the Early Learner: Level 3. rev. ed. Bibeau, Simone. 64p. (ps-2). 1983. pap. text ed. 4.95 (*0-940406-03-9*) Perception Pubns.
—IQ Booster Kit: Developing the Early Learner Levels 1-4. Bibeau, Simone. 256p. (ps-2). 1983. pap. text ed. 85.00 (bks. & cassettes) (*0-940406-05-5*) Perception Pubns.
—Writing Poetry. Hardt, Elaine. 32p. (Orig.). (gr. 1-9). 1983. pap. 1.95 (*0-940406-09-8*) Perception Pubns.
—Writing the Advanced Short Story. Bibeau, Simone. 32p. (gr. 1-12). 1983. pap. text ed. 1.95 (*0-940406-07-1*) Perception Pubns.
—Writing the Beginning Short Story. Bibeau, Simone. 32p. (Orig.). (gr. 1-9). 1983. pap. text ed. 1.95 (*0-940406-06-3*) Perception Pubns.
—Writing the Fantasy Story. Bibeau, Simone. 32p. (Orig.). (gr. 1-9). 1983. pap. text ed. 1.95 (*0-940406-08-X*) Perception Pubns.

Krudop, Walter. Blue Claws. Krudop, Walter L. LC 92-9922. 36p. (gr. 1-3). 1993. SBE 14.95 (*0-689-31787-5*, Atheneum Child Bk) Macmillan Child Grp.

Krudop, Walter L. The Good-Night Kiss. Aylesworth, Jim. LC 91-40952. 32p. (ps-3). 1993. SBE 14.95 (*0-689-31515-5*, Atheneum Child Bk) Macmillan Child Grp.
—One Rainy Night. Gove, Doris. LC 93-13900. 32p. (gr. 2-5). 1994. SBE 14.95 (*0-689-31800-6*, Atheneum Child Bk) Macmillan Child Grp.
—What I'll Remember When I Am a Grownup. Willner-Pardo, Gina. LC 92-42148. 1994. write for info. (*0-395-63310-9*, Clarion Bks) HM.

Krug, Ken. The Beanstalk Bandit: The Giant's Version of "Jack & the Beanstalk" Lomsky, Gerry. 30p. (gr. 2-7). 1993. pap. 4.95 (*1-883499-00-3*); Story cass. 6.95 (*1-883499-01-1*) Princess NJ.
For years now, GIANTS, like many other minority groups, have been the target of literary malignment & discrimination. This TRUE story describes the GIANT'S quest for peace & tranquility in a castle in the clouds, his peaceful relationship with his pet hen & his love of harp music. One day, the GIANT'S peaceful life changes as a strange weed sprouts in his garden. Mysterious events confuse the harmless GIANT -- strange noises, footprints in the house, & coins missing from his Gramps' collection. The GIANT experiences true loneliness after his magical friend is "harp-napped." In the exciting climax, the GIANT pursues Jack to regain his stolen pet hen, Cuddles, only to fall off the beanstalk, damaging Jack's house & ending up in jail. The reader is encouraged to be the judge & render the verdict on the GIANT, who is charged with assaulting Jack, stealing coins, pet abuse & house destruction! The reader is also encouraged to join many others who have written to Princess Publishing in

support of the GIANT'S case. To order call 609-596-9146. Story cassette also available for $6.95. *Publisher Provided Annotation.*

Krukman, Tsvi. Hasefer Chelek Sheini, Pt. 2. Bachrach, Kalman. (HEB.). 91p. (gr. 2). 1942. pap. text ed. 2.25x (*1-878530-09-7*) K Bachrach Co.
—Hasefer Chelek Shlishi, Pt. 3. Bachrach, Kalman. (HEB.). 74p. (gr. 3). 1947. pap. text ed. 2.25x (*1-878530-10-0*) K Bachrach Co.
—Ketivoni Chelek Rishon, Pt. 1. Bachrach, Kalman & Axelrod, Herman. (HEB.). 72p. (gr. 2). 1957. pap. text ed. 3.50x (*1-878530-02-X*) K Bachrach Co.
—Ketivoni Chelek Sheni, Pt. 2. Bachrach, Kalman & Axelrod, Herman. (HEB.). 62p. (gr. 3). 1958. pap. text ed. 3.50x (*1-878530-03-8*) K Bachrach Co.
—Olami Sefer Rishon, Bk. 1. rev. ed. Bachrach, Kalman. (HEB.). 59p. (gr. 2). 1943. pap. text ed. 2.00x (*1-878530-14-3*) K Bachrach Co.
—Olami Sefer Sheini, Bk. 2. rev. ed. Bachrach, Kalman. (HEB.). 71p. (gr. 3-4). 1950. pap. text ed. 2.00x (*1-878530-15-1*) K Bachrach Co.
Krum, Ronda. Ted Bear's Magic Swing. Baker, Dianne. LC 91-65819. 32p. (gr. 1-3). 1992. 12.95 (*0-87159-162-6*) Unity Bks.
Krupinski, Loretta. Dear Rebecca, Winter Is Here. George, Jean C. LC 92-9515. 32p. (ps-3). 1993. 15.00 (*0-06-021139-3*); PLB 14.89 (*0-06-021140-7*) HarpC Child Bks.
—How a Seed Grows. rev. ed. Jordan, Helene J. LC 91-10166. 32p. (ps-1). 1992. 14.00 (*0-06-020104-5*); PLB 13.89 (*0-06-020185-1*) HarpC Child Bks.
—How a Seed Grows. rev. ed. Jordan, Helene J. LC 91-10165. 32p. (ps-1). 1992. pap. 4.50 (*0-06-445107-0*, Trophy) HarpC Child Bks.
—I Can Read. Wise, Beth A. & Levin, Amy. Naver, Judith E., ed. 32p. (gr. k-1). 1991. wkbk. 1.95 (*1-878624-63-6*) McClanahan Bk.
—Leaves Change Color. Maestro, Betsy. LC 93-9611. (gr. k-3). 1994. 14.00 (*0-06-022873-3*); PLB 13.89 (*0-06-022874-1*) HarpC Child Bks.
—Lost in the Fog. Bacheller, Irving. Krupinski, Loretta, adapted by. LC 88-25923. (gr. k-3). 1990. 14.95 (*0-316-07462-4*) Little.
—The Old Ladies Who Liked Cats. Greene, Carol. LC 90-4443. 32p. (gr. k-3). 1991. 15.00 (*0-06-022104-6*); PLB 14.89 (*0-06-022105-4*) HarpC Child Bks.
—The Old Ladies Who Liked Cats. Greene, Carol. LC 90-4443. 32p. (gr. k-3). 1994. pap. 4.95 (*0-06-443354-4*, Trophy) HarpC Child Bks.
—Sailing to the Sea. Helldorfer, Mary C. 32p. (ps-3). 1991. 13.95 (*0-670-83520-X*) Viking Child Bks.
—Sailing to the Sea. Helldorfer, Mary C. 32p. (ps-3). 1993. pap. 4.99 (*0-14-054317-1*, Puffin) Puffin Bks.
—Wonderful Worms. Glaser, Linda. LC 91-38752. 32p. (gr. k-3). 1992. 14.95 (*1-56294-703-6*); PLB 14.90 (*1-56294-062-7*) Millbrook Pr.
Krupinsky, Lisa, jt. illus. see Arbuckle, Jane.
Krupp, Marion. Jim Beckwourth: Adventures of a Mountain Man. Sabin, Louis. LC 92-8717. 48p. (gr. 4-6). 1992. PLB 10.79 (*0-8167-2819-4*); pap. text ed. 3.50 (*0-8167-2820-8*) Troll Assocs.
Krupp, Robin R. Big Dipper & You. Krupp, E. C. LC 88-1501. 48p. (gr. 2 up). 1989. 13.95 (*0-688-07191-0*); PLB 13.88 (*0-688-07192-9*, Morrow Jr Bks) Morrow Jr Bks.
—The Comet & You. Krupp, Edwin C. LC 84-20152. 48p. (gr. 1-4). 1985. RSBE 13.95 (*0-02-751250-9*, Macmillan Child Bk) Macmillan Child Grp.
—Get Set to Wreck! Krupp, Robin R. LC 86-19956. 32p. (gr. 1-3). 1988. RSBE 14.95 (*0-02-751140-5*, Pub. by Four Winds Pr) Macmillan Child Grp.
—Let's Go Traveling. Krupp, Robin R. LC 91-21845. 40p. (gr. 2 up). 1992. 15.00 (*0-688-08989-5*); PLB 14.93 (*0-688-08990-9*) Morrow Jr Bks.
—The Moon & You. Krupp, E. C. LC 92-16231. 48p. (gr. k-4). 1993. RSBE 13.95 (*0-02-751142-1*, Macmillan Child Bk) Macmillan Child Grp.
Krush, Beth. The Shoe Bird. Welty, Eudora. 88p. (gr. 4-6). 1993. 14.95 (*0-87805-668-8*) U Pr of Miss.
Krush, Beth & Krush, Joe. All-of-a-Kind Family Downtown. Taylor, Sydney. 187p. 1988. Repr. of 1972 ed. 11.95 (*0-929093-01-1*) Taylor Prodns.
—Borrowers. Norton, Mary. LC 53-7870. 180p. (gr. 3 up). 1953. 13.95 (*0-15-209987-5*, HB Juv Bks) HarBrace.
—The Borrowers. Norton, Mary. 200p. (gr. 3-7). 1989. pap. 4.95 (*0-15-209990-5*, Odyssey) HarBrace.
—Borrowers Afield. Norton, Mary. LC 55-11011. 215p. (gr. 3 up). 1955. 13.95 (*0-15-210166-7*, HB Juv Bks) HarBrace.
—Borrowers Afloat. Norton, Mary. LC 59-5630. 191p. (gr. 3 up). 1959. 12.95 (*0-15-210345-7*, HB Juv Bks) HarBrace.
—Borrowers Aloft. Norton, Mary. LC 61-11751. 192p. (gr. 3 up). 1961. 12.95 (*0-15-210524-7*, HB Juv Bks) HarBrace.
—The Borrowers Aloft. Norton, Mary. 196p. (gr. 3-7). 1990. pap. 4.95 (*0-15-210533-6*, Odyssey) HarBrace.
—Jean & Johnny. Cleary, Beverly. LC 59-7806. 288p. (gr. 6-9). 1959. 12.95 (*0-688-21740-0*); PLB 12.88 (*0-688-31740-5*, Morrow Jr Bks) Morrow Jr Bks.
—Joseph & His Brothers. Berg, Jean H. 32p. (Orig.). (gr. k-3). 1976. pap. 9.95 incl. audiocassette (*0-87510-104-6*) Christian Sci.
—Plain Girl. Sorensen, Virginia. 151p. (gr. 3-7). 1988. pap. 5.95 (*0-15-262437-6*, Voyager Bks) HarBrace.
—Poor Stainless. Norton, Mary. LC 70-140781. 32p. (gr. 3 up). 1985. 7.95 (*0-15-263221-2*, HB Juv Bks) HarBrace.
—Sister of the Bride. Cleary, Beverly. LC 63-8802. 256p. (gr. 7 up). 1963. PLB 13.88 (*0-688-31742-1*) Morrow Jr Bks.
—The Story of Jesus. Berg, Jean H. 40p. (Orig.). (gr. k-3). 1977. pap. 9.95 incl. audiocassette (*0-87510-185-2*) Christian Sci.
Krush, Beth, jt. illus. see Dyer, Jane.
Krush, Beth, jt. illus. see Krush, Joe.
Krush, Joe & Krush, Beth. Emily's Runaway Imagination. Cleary, Beverly. LC 61-10939. 224p. (gr. 3-7). 1961. 12.95 (*0-688-21267-0*); PLB 12.88 (*0-688-31267-5*, Morrow Jr Bks) Morrow Jr Bks.
—Fifteen. Cleary, Beverly. LC 56-7509. 256p. (gr. 6-9). 1956. 12.95 (*0-688-21285-9*); PLB 12.88 (*0-688-31285-3*, Morrow Jr Bks) Morrow Jr Bks.
Krush, Joe, jt. illus. see Hague, Michael.
Krush, joe, jt. illus. see Krush, Beth.
Krush, Joe, jt. illus. see Krush, Beth.
Krych, Duane. Batboy. Cebulash, Mel. (gr. 1-8). 1992. PLB 8.95 (*0-89565-882-8*); Resale. 12.75 (*0-685-60975-8*) Childs World.
—Flippers Boy. Cebulash, Mel. (gr. 1-8). 1992. PLB 8.95 (*0-89565-881-X*); Resale. 12.75 (*0-685-60974-X*) Childs World.
—Muscle-Bound. Cebulash, Mel. (gr. 1-8). 1992. PLB 8.95 (*0-89565-883-6*); Resale. 12.75 (*0-685-60976-6*) Childs World.
Krykorka, Vladyana. Baseball Bats for Christmas. Kusugak, Michael A. 24p. (gr. k-3). 1990. 15.95 (*1-55037-145-2*, Pub. by Annick CN); pap. 5.95 (*1-55037-144-4*, Pub. by Annick CN) Firefly Bks Ltd.
—Hide-&-Sneak. Kusugak, Michael. 32p. (ps-3). 1992. PLB 14.95 (*1-55037-229-7*, Pub. by Annick CN); pap. 4.95 (*1-55037-228-9*, Pub. by Annick CN) Firefly Bks Ltd.
—Planting Seeds. Quinlan, Patricia. 24p. (ps-2). 1988. 12.95 (*1-55037-007-3*, Pub. by Annick CN); pap. 4.95 (*1-55037-006-5*, Pub. by Annick CN) Firefly Bks Ltd.
—A Promise Is a Promise. Munsch, Robert & Kusugak, M. 32p. (gr. k-3). 1988. PLB 14.95 (*1-550370-09-X*, Pub. by Annick CN); pap. 4.95 (*1-550370-08-1*, Pub. by Annick CN) Firefly Bks Ltd.
—Whump. Chislett, Gail. (ps-1). 1992. 0.99 (*1-55037-253-X*, Pub. by Annick Pr) Firefly Bks Ltd.
Kubick, Dana. Pop-Up Ballerina Bear. Kubick, Dana. 16p. (ps up). 1993. Incl. 4 1/2" doll. 12.95 (*0-590-46753-0*, Cartwheel) Scholastic Inc.
Kubinyi, Laszio. Red Riding Hood. Roberts, Tom, adapted by. LC 90-25377. 32p. (gr. k up). 1991. pap. 14.95 (*0-88708-162-2*, Rabbit Ears); pap. 19.95 incl. cassette (*0-88708-163-0*, Rabbit Ears) Picture Bk Studio.
Kubinyi, Laszlo. El Color de la Luz. Joval, Nomi. (SPA.). 16p. (ps-4). 1993. PLB 13.95 (*1-879567-20-2*, Valeria Bks) Wonder Well.
—Color of Light. Joval, Nomi. 16p. (ps-4). 1993. PLB 13.95 (*1-879567-19-9*, Valeria Bks) Wonder Well.
—Goldilocks. Roberts, Tom & Ryan, Meg, eds. Lande, Art, contrib. by. 32p. (ps up). 1992. pap. write for info. slipcase pkg., incl. cassette (*0-307-14332-5*, 14332, Golden Pr) Western Pub.
—Goldilocks. Roberts, Tom. LC 93-6679. (ps-6). 1993. Incl. cassette. 9.95 (*0-88708-322-6*, Dist. by S&S Trade) Picture Bk Studio.
—Goldilocks & the Three Bears. Roberts, Tom. 32p. (gr. k up). 1991. pap. 14.95 (*0-88708-146-0*, Rabbit Ears); pap. 19.95 incl. cass. (*0-88708-147-9*, Rabbit Ears) Picture Bk Studio.
—La Lupa Maravillosa. Joval, Nomi. (SPA.). 24p. (ps-4). 1993. PLB 13.95 (*1-879567-22-9*, Valeria Bks) Wonder Well.
—Power of Glass. Joval, Nomi. 16p. (ps-4). 1993. PLB 13.95 (*1-879567-21-0*, Valeria Bks) Wonder Well.
—Red Riding Hood. minibook ed. Roberts, Tom. LC 93-12152. (ps-6). 1993. Incl. cassette. 9.95 (*0-88708-320-X*, Rabbit Ears) Picture Bk Studio.
—Room of Mirrors. Joval, Nomi. 16p. (gr. k-4). 1991. PLB 13.95 (*1-879567-06-7*, Valeria Bks) Wonder Well.
—Salon de Espejos. Joval, Nomi. (SPA.). 16p. (gr. k-4). 1992. PLB 13.95 (*1-879567-07-5*, Valeria Bks) Wonder Well.
—Who'd Believe John Colter? Christian, Mary B. LC 92-33822. 64p. (gr. 2-6). 1993. SBE 13.95 (*0-02-718477-3*, Macmillan Child Bk) Macmillan Child Grp.
—The Wizard in the Tree. Alexander, Lloyd. 144p. (gr. 4-7). 1974. 14.95 (*0-525-43128-4*, DCB) Dutton Child Bks.
Kubo, Chad & Filarca, Josie. Favorite Menus. Cavanagh, Mary. 13p. (gr. 3-5). 1980. pap. 3.95 (*0-8431-2573-X*) Enrich.
Kubota, Kenji. Tales of a Japanese Grandmother, 5 Vols. Hashimoto, Yasuko & Edades, Jean. (Orig.). (gr. k-3). 1982. Set. pap. 12.50 (*0-686-37564-5*, Pub. by New Day Pub PI) Cellar.
Kucharski, Michael. The Palladium RPG Book II: Old Ones. Siembieda, Kevin. Marciniszyn, Alex, ed. 210p. (Orig.). (gr. 8 up). 1984. pap. 14.95 (*0-916211-09-6*, 453) Palladium Bks.
Kucharski, Micheal. The Palladium Role-Playing Game. rev. ed. Siembieda, Kevin. Leasure, Paula, ed. 274p. (gr. 8 up). 1983. pap. 19.95 (*0-916211-04-5*, 450) Palladium Bks.
Kuchera, John & Margolis, Al. What Every Kid Should Know. Kalb, Jonah & Viscott, David. 128p. (gr. 4-7). 1992. pap. 4.80 (*0-395-62983-7*, Sandpiper) HM.
Kuchera, Kathleen. The Rooster Who Went to His Uncle's Wedding: A Latin American Folktale. Ada, Alma F., retold by. LC 92-14087. 32p. (ps-3). 1992. PLB 14.95 (*0-399-22412-2*, Putnam) Putnam Pub Group.
—Your Skin & Mine. rev. ed. Showers, Paul. LC 90-37430. 32p. (gr. k-4). 1991. 13.95 (*0-06-022522-X*); PLB 13.89 (*0-06-022523-8*) HarpC Child Bks.
—Your Skin & Mine. rev. ed. Showers, Paul. LC 90-37429. 32p. (gr. k-4). 1991. pap. 4.50 (*0-06-445102-X*, Trophy) HarpC Child Bks.
Kuchukian, J. Angele. The Photograph. Couch, Donna E. 40p. (gr. 1-6). 1992. 10.00g (*0-9634359-0-6*) Seabright Pr.
Kudrna, C. Imbiore. To Bathe a Boa. Kudrna, C. Imbior. 32p. (ps-4). 1986. PLB 18.50 (*0-87614-306-0*); pap. 5.95 (*0-87614-490-3*) Carolrhoda Bks.
Kuehn, Christopher. The Adventures of Rondy. Schwartz, Frederick J. Olson, Wayne, ed. 148p. (gr. k-7). 1985. 7.95 (*0-9616638-0-4*) Rondy Pubns.
Kueker, Don. My Stories about God's People. Fletcher, Sarah. 32p. (ps-3). 1974. pap. 2.89 (*0-570-03426-4*, 56-1181) Concordia.
—My Stories about Jesus. Fletcher, Sarah. 32p. (ps-3). 1974. pap. 2.89 (*0-570-03427-2*, 56-1182) Concordia.
—Prayers for Little People. Fletcher, Sarah. 32p. (gr. 3-7). 1974. pap. 2.89 (*0-570-03429-9*, 56-1184) Concordia.
Kuester, Robert. Mexican Portraits. Hoobler, Dorothy & Hoobler, Thomas. LC 92-13642. 96p. (gr. 7-8). 1992. PLB 22.80 (*0-8114-6376-1*) Raintree Steck-V.
Kugler, Lisa. A New Baby for Us: Sibling Preparation & Activity Book for Big Brothers & Sisters. Kugler, Lisa. 32p. (Orig.). (ps-1). 1990. pap. 5.95 (*0-944782-03-5*) Glover Pr.
Kuhn, Bob. Big Red. Kjelgaard, Jim. 254p. (gr. 6 up). 1956. 15.95 (*0-8234-0007-7*) Holiday.
Kuhn, Dwight, photos by. The Hidden Life of the Forest. Schwartz, David M., text by. 40p. (gr. 1 up). 1988. PLB 15.00 (*0-517-57058-0*) Crown Bks Yng Read.
—The Hidden Life of the Meadow. Schwartz, David M., text by. 40p. (gr. 1 up). 1988. PLB 12.95 (*0-517-57059-9*) Crown Bks Yng Read.
—The Hidden Life of the Pond. Schwartz, David M., text by. 40p. (gr. 1 up). 1988. PLB 15.00 (*0-517-57060-2*) Crown Bks Yng Read.
—How Ducklings Grow. Molleson, Diane. 32p. (ps-2). 1993. pap. 2.50 (*0-590-45201-0*) Scholastic Inc.
—Hungry Little Frog. Hirschi, Ron, text by. 32p. (ps-2). 1992. 9.95 (*0-525-65109-8*, Cobblehill Bks) Dutton Child Bks.
—More Than Just a...Series, 2 vols. Kuhn, Dwight. 80p. (gr. 2 up). 1990. Set. 27.90 (*0-671-94439-8*); Set. PLB 31.96 (*0-671-94438-X*) Silver Pr.
Kuklin, Susan. Going to My Ballet Class. Kuklin, Susan. LC 88-37556. 32p. (ps-3). 1989. RSBE 13.95 (*0-02-751235-5*, Bradbury Pr) Macmillan Child Grp.
—Going to My Gymnastics Class. Kuklin, Susan. LC 90-20206. 40p. (ps-1). 1991. RSBE 13.95 (*0-02-751236-3*, Bradbury Pr) Macmillan Child Grp.
—Going to My Nursery School. Kuklin, Susan. LC 89-37077. 40p. (ps-k). 1990. RSBE 13.95 (*0-02-751237-1*, Bradbury Pr) Macmillan Child Grp.
—How My Family Lives in America. Kuklin, Susan. LC 91-22949. 40p. (ps-3). 1992. RSBE 13.95 (*0-02-751239-8*, Bradbury Pr) Macmillan Child Grp.
—Outside & Inside You. Markle, Sandra. LC 90-37791. 40p. (ps-3). 1991. RSBE 14.95 (*0-02-762311-4*, Bradbury Pr) Macmillan Child Grp.
—Reaching for Dreams: A Ballet from Rehearsal to Opening Night. Kuklin, Susan. LC 86-15356. (gr. 4-9). 1987. 12.95 (*0-688-06316-0*) Lothrop.
—Taking My Cat to the Vet. Kuklin, Susan. LC 88-5052. 32p. (ps-k). 1988. RSBE 13.95 (*0-02-751233-9*, Bradbury Pr) Macmillan Child Grp.
—Taking My Dog to the Vet. Kuklin, Susan. LC 88-5047. 32p. (ps-k). 1988. RSBE 13.95 (*0-02-751234-7*, Bradbury Pr) Macmillan Child Grp.
Kula, Elsa. Magic Animals of Japan. Pratt, Davis. LC 67-17483. (gr. 1-4). 1967. (Pub. by Parnassus); PLB 5.88 (*0-87466-020-3*) HM.
Kuller, Alison M., jt. illus. see Stewart, Thomas R.
Kulman, Andrew. Red Light Stop, Green Light Go. Kulman, Andrew. LC 92-14228. (ps). 1993. pap. 15.00 JRT (*0-671-79493-0*, S&S BFYR) S&S Trade.
Kummer, Mary. The Christmas Collie. Paul, Ted. LC 89-17994. 42p. (ps-7). 1989. 12.95 (*0-89802-548-6*) Beautiful Am.
Kunda, Shmuel. Mitzvos We Can Do. Rosenthal, Yaffa. 32p. (gr. 1-8). 1982. 10.95 (*0-89906-775-1*); pap. 7.95 (*0-89906-776-X*) Mesorah Pubns.
—Oh, Zalmy! or, the Tale of the Tooth: Book 2. Kleinbard, Gitel. (gr. k-3). 1977. 5.95 (*0-917274-02-4*); pap. 3.95 (*0-917274-03-2*) Mah Tov Pubns.
—Thank You Hashem. Rosenthal, Yaffa. 32p. (gr. 1-8). 1983. 10.95 (*0-89906-777-8*); pap. 7.95 (*0-89906-778-6*) Mesorah Pubns.
Kunhardt, Dorothy. Pat the Bunny. Kunhardt, Dorothy. (ps). 1942. write for info. (*0-307-12000-7*, Golden Bks) Western Pub.

—Pat the Bunny. Kunhardt, Dorothy. (ps). 1988. Includes Touch & Feel Book with Plush Doll. pap. write for info. (0-307-14000-8, Pub. by Golden Bks) Western Pub.

—Pudding Is Nice. Kunhardt, Dorothy. LC 75-19948. 64p. (gr. 1 up). 1975. 15.00 (0-912846-18-6); pap. 8.00 (0-912846-12-7) Bookstore Pr.

Kunhardt, Edith. Pat the Cat. Kunhardt, Edith. LC 83-83106. (ps-3). 1984. write for info. comb. bdg. (0-307-12001-5, 12001, Golden Bks) Western Pub.

Kunstler, Mort. Dinosaur Story. Cole, Joanna. LC 74-5931. 32p. (gr. k-3). 1974. PLB 13.88 (0-688-31826-6) Morrow Jr Bks.

Kunz, Anita. The Toynbee Convector. Bradbury, Ray. 32p. (gr. 7-9). 1992. 10.95 (1-878685-15-5) Turner Pub GA.

Kuo Kang Chen. Observing Minibeasts. Harlow, Rosie & Morgan, Gareth. 40p. (gr. 5-8). 1991. PLB 12.90 (0-531-19125-7, Warwick) Watts.

Kuo Kang Chen & Bull, Peter. One Hundred Seventy-Five More Science Experiments to Amuse & Amaze Your Friends. Casn, Terry & Taylor, Barbara. LC 90-39250. 176p. (Orig.). (gr. 4-7). 1991. pap. 12.00 (0-679-80390-4) Random Bks Yng Read.

—One Hundred Seventy-Five Science Experiments to Amuse & Amaze Your Friends. Walpole, Brenda. LC 88-4526. 176p. (Orig.). (gr. 4-7). 1988. pap. 12.00 (0-394-89991-1) Random Bks Yng Read.

Kuo Kang Chen & Fitzsimmons, Cecilia. Energy & Growth. Harlow, Rosie & Morgan, Gareth. 40p. (gr. 5-8). 1991. PLB 12.90 (0-531-19124-9, Warwick) Watts.

Kuo Kang Chen, et al. One Hundred Seventy-Five Amazing Nature Experiments. Harlow, Rosie & Morgan, Gareth. LC 91-21113. 176p. (Orig.). (gr. 4-7). 1992. pap. 12.00 (0-679-82043-4) Random Bks Yng Read.

Kuper, Rachel. Runaway Bear. Freeman, Chester D. & McGuire, John E. LC 93-16893. 32p. (gr. k-3). 1993. 14.95 (0-88289-956-2); ltd. boxed signed ed. 29.95 (1-56554-016-6) Pelican.

Kuppersmith-Krause, Molly B. My Own Hanukah Story. Stuhlman, Daniel D. (Orig.). (ps-5). 1980. pap. 3.95 personalized version (0-934402-07-8); decorations 1.00 (0-934402-08-6); trade version 2.50 (0-934402-12-4) BYLS Pr.

Kurelek, William. A Northern Nativity. Kurelek, William. (gr. 4 up). 1976. 14.95 (0-88776-099-6); pap. 7.95 (0-685-04960-4) Tundra Bks.

—A Prairie Boy's Summer. Kurelek, William. 48p. (gr. 5 up). 1975. 14.95 (0-88776-058-9); pap. 6.95 (0-88776-116-X) Tundra Bks.

—A Prairie Boy's Winter. Kurelek, William. LC 73-8913. 48p. (gr. k-3). 1984. 14.45 (0-395-17708-1); pap. 6.70 (0-395-36609-7) HM.

Kuribayashi, Satoshi. Fireflies. Johnson, Sylvia A. 48p. (gr. 4 up) 1986. PLB 19.95 (0-8225-1485-0) Lerner Pubns.

Kuroi, Ken. The Adventures of Buster the Puppy, 6 vols. Madokoro, Hisako. 96p. (gr. k-2). 1991. Set. PLB 87. 60 (0-8368-0488-0) Gareth Stevens Inc.

—Buster & the Little Kitten. Madokoro, Hisako. LC 90-47947. 24p. (gr. k-2). 1991. PLB 14.60 (0-8368-0490-2) Gareth Stevens Inc.

—Buster Catches a Cold. Madokoro, Hisako. LC 90-47948. 24p. (gr. k-2). 1991. PLB 14.60 (0-8368-0494-5) Gareth Stevens Inc.

—Buster's Blustery Day. Madokoro, Hisako. LC 90-47927. 24p. (gr. k-2). 1991. PLB 14.60 (0-8368-0493-7) Gareth Stevens Inc.

—Buster's First Snow. Madokoro, Hisako. LC 90-47946. 24p. (gr. k-2). 1991. PLB 14.60 (0-8368-0492-9) Gareth Stevens Inc.

—Buster's First Thunderstorm. Madokoro, Hisako. LC 90-47869. 24p. (gr. k-2). 1991. PLB 14.60 (0-8368-0493-7) Gareth Stevens Inc.

—Little Bunny's Christmas Present. Yazaki, Setsuo. Ooka, D. T., tr. from JPN. 32p. (ps-8). 1983. 11.95 (0-89346-225-X) Heian Intl.

Kurokawa, Mitsuhiro. Dinosaur Valley. Kurokawa, Mitsuhiro. LC 92-10788. 48p. (gr. 1-5). 1992. 14.95 (0-8118-0257-4) Chronicle Bks.

—The Great Big Book of Dinosaurs. Kurokawa, Mitsuhiro. Obata, Ikuo, contrib. by. LC 88-24779. 32p. (gr. 4-5). 1989. PLB 21.26 (0-8368-0000-1) Gareth Stevens Inc.

Kurosaki, Yoshio. Japanese Children's Favorite Stories. Sakade, Florence. LC 58-11620. 120p. (gr. 2-6). 1958. bds. 16.95 (0-8048-0284-X) C E Tuttle.

Kurosaki, Yoshisuke. Peach Boy & Other Japanese Children's Favorite Stories. Sakade, Florence. 58p. (gr. 1-5). 1958. pap. 8.95 (0-8048-0469-9) C E Tuttle.

Kurtycz, Marcos & Kobeh, Ana G. Tigers & Opossums: Animal Legends. Kurtycz, Marcos & Kobeh, Ana G. LC 82-17949. (gr. k-3). 1984. 12.95 (0-316-50718-0) Little.

Kurtz, John. Disney's the Little Mermaid: Sebastian's Story. Colby, J. 24p. (ps-k). 1992. write for info. (0-307-10020-0, 10020) Western Pub.

—The Jungle Book. Kidd, Ronald, adapted by. 24p. (ps-4). 1993. 20.00 (0-307-74028-5, 64028, Golden Pr) Western Pub.

—Walt Disney's Pinocchio: Fun with Shapes & Sizes. Gave, Marc. 24p. (ps-k). 1992. bds. write for info. (0-307-12332-4, 12332, Golden Pr) Western Pub.

—Walt Disney's Winnie the Pooh & the Honey Tree. Campbell, Janet, adapted by. LC 92-53442. 48p. (ps-4). 1993. 12.95 (1-56282-379-5) Disney Pr.

Kurtz, John, jt. illus. see Marderosian, Mark.

Kurz, Ann. Cranberries from A to Z: An Educational Picture Book. Kurz, Ann. LC 89-61059. 32p. (gr. k-8). 1989. PLB 13.95 (0-9622784-0-8) Cranberry Origs.

Kuska, George, jt. illus. see Clark, Cindy.

Kuskin, Karla. Any Me I Want to Be. Kuskin, Karla. LC 77-105485. 64p. (gr. 1-4). 1972. PLB 11.89 (0-06-023616-7) HarpC Child Bks.

—Dogs & Dragons, Trees & Dreams. Kuskin, Karla. LC 79-2814. 96p. (gr. k-3). 1992. pap. 4.95 (0-06-446212-X, Trophy) HarpC Child Bks.

—Dogs & Dragons, Trees & Dreams: A Collection of Poems. Kuskin, Karla. LC 79-2814. 96p. (gr. 1-6). 1980. PLB 13.89 (0-06-023544-6) HarpC Child Bks.

—Near the Window Tree: Poems & Notes. Kuskin, Karla. LC 74-20394. 64p. (gr. 2-6). 1975. PLB 13.89 (0-06-023540-3) HarpC Child Bks.

—Roar & More. rev. ed. Kuskin, Karla. LC 89-15650. 48p. (ps-1). 1990. PLB 13.89 (0-06-023619-1) HarpC Child Bks.

—Roar & More. rev. ed. Kuskin, Karla. LC 89-15650. 48p. (ps-1). 1990. pap. 4.95 (0-06-443244-0, Trophy) HarpC Child Bks.

—Soap Soup: And Other Verses. Kuskin, Karla. LC 91-22947. 64p. (gr. k-3). 1992. 14.00 (0-06-023571-3); PLB 13.89 (0-06-023572-1) HarpC Child Bks.

—Soap Soup: and Other Verses. Kuskin, Karla. LC 90-27357. 32p. (gr. k-4). 1994. pap. 3.50 (0-06-444174-1, Trophy) HarpC Child Bks.

—Something Sleeping in the Hall. Kuskin, Karla. LC 82-47721. 64p. (gr. k-3). 1985. PLB 13.89 (0-06-023634-5) HarpC Child Bks.

Kusmierz, James P. Real Ghosts Don't Wear Sheets. Farrant, Don W. 80p. (Orig.). 1985. pap. 7.00 (0-935604-02-2) Ivystone.

Kuykendall, John M., photos by. Let's Grow! Seventy-Two Gardening Adventures with Children. Tilgner, Linda. Burns, Deborah, ed. LC 87-45581. 216p. (Orig.). (ps up). 1988. 21.95 (0-88266-471-9, Garden Way Pub); pap. 10.95 (0-88266-470-0, Garden Way Pub) Storey Comm Inc.

Kuzjak, Goran. Addition. Thompson, Kim M. & Hilderbrand, Karen M. 24p. (gr. 1-4). 1993. wkbk. 9.98 (1-882331-20-6, TWIN 402) Twin Sisters.

—Addition: Twinset. Thompson, Kim M. & Hilderbrand, Karen M. 48p. (gr. 1-4). 1993. wkbk. 14.99 (1-882331-04-8, TWIN 300) Twin Sisters.

—Division. Thompson, Kim M. & Hilderbrand, Karen M. 24p. (gr. 3-6). 1993. wkbk. 9.98 (1-882331-22-2, TWIN 404) Twin Sisters.

—Division: Twinset. Thompson, Kim M. & Hilderbrand, Karen M. 48p. 1993. wkbk. 14.99 (1-882331-06-0, TWIN 304) Twin Sisters.

—Multiplication. Thompson, Kim M. & Hilderbrand, Karen M. 24p. (gr. 2-6). 1993. wkbk. 9.98 (1-882331-19-2, TWIN 401) Twin Sisters.

—Multiplication: Twinset. Thompson, Kim M. & Hilderbrand, Karen M. 48p. (gr. 2-6). 1993. wkbk. 14. 99 (1-882331-03-6, TWIN 301) Twin Sisters.

—Phonics. Thompson, Kim M. & Hilderbrand, Karen M. 24p. (gr. 3-5). 1993. wkbk. 9.98 (1-882331-23-0, TWIN 405) Twin Sisters.

—Phonics: Twinset. Thompson, Kim M. & Hilderbrand, Karen M. 64p. (gr. 3-5). 1993. wkbk. 14.99 (1-882331-07-9, TWIN 305) Twin Sisters.

—States & Capitals. Thompson, Kim M. & Hilderbrand, Karen M. 24p. (gr. 2-6). 1993. wkbk. 9.98 (1-882331-24-9, TWIN 406) Twin Sisters.

—States & Capitals: Twinset. Thompson, Kim M. & Hilderbrand, Karen M. 48p. (gr. 2-6). 1993. wkbk. 14. 99 (1-882331-08-7, TWIN 306) Twin Sisters.

—Subtraction. Thompson, Kim M. & Hilderbrand, Karen M. 24p. 1993. wkbk. 9.98 (1-882331-21-4, TWIN 403) Twin Sisters.

—Subtraction: Twinset. Thompson, Kim M. & Hilderbrand, Karen M. 48p. (gr. 1-4). 1993. wkbk. 14. 99 (1-882331-05-2, TWIN 303) Twin Sisters.

Kuzma, Steve. Sports Pages. Adoff, Arnold. LC 85-45169. 80p. (gr. 3-7). 1986. (Lipp Jr Bks); PLB 14.89 (0-397-32103-1, Lipp Jr Bks) HarpC Child Bks.

—Sports Pages. Adoff, Arnold. LC 85-45169. 80p. (gr. 3 up). 1990. pap. 5.95 (0-06-446098-3, Trophy) HarpC Child Bks.

Kuznetsov, Eugene, jt. illus. see Squillace, Albert.

Kvarnes, Davette L. A Sunnybrook Garden Tale. Davis, Rebecca J. LC 92-97014. 32p. (gr. 3-5). 1993. PLB 12.00 (0-9634032-0-6) R J Davis. **Filled with bright, colorful language & accompanied by vivid illustrations A SUNNYBROOK GARDEN TALE thoughtfully addresses the consequences of irresponsible use of pesticides through two unlikely, but very effective characters. By personifying a bad beetle--Buster Beetle, & a very insecure thistle-- Missile Thistle, the story conveys the message that all living beings must live harmoniously if our planet & all that live on it are to remain healthy. Review**

Quotes: "All the wonderful characters, human & otherwise, weave a story that can enter a child's imagination & find a home there."--Donna Aquaviva, writer. "It carries a gentle environmental message that children should hear when they're very young."--Bob Naylor, editor. "A very pleasant story from an interesting point of view, & the scale of the story makes ecology more approachable for children."--Anita Trout, librarian. "A SUNNYBROOK GARDEN TALE has brought back the goodness that children need to read about."--JoAnn Overington, teacher. "Delightful, charming--fun for all ages." --Felicia Cogan, professor. "With exquisite illustrations & charming personifications of thistles, beetles & other plants & creatures the story delivers an ecological message."--Rana Harmon, The Shepherdstown Chronicle (5/28/93). "Award-winner, Children's Literature, 1991 Shenandoah Valley Writers' Guild Creative Writing Conference."--Author. Rebecca J. Davis, P.O. Box 144, Route 1/13, Summit Point, WV 25446-0144, (304) 725-1609. *Publisher Provided Annotation.*

Kyzer, Martha. Bucky for Beginners. Laycock, Mary. 64p. (Orig.). (gr. 4-12). 1984. pap. text ed. 7.95 (0-918932-82-3) Activity Resources.

—Focus on Calculator Math. Lund, Charles & Smart, Margaret. Laycock, Mary, intro. by. (gr. 4-12). 1979. pap. text ed. 8.50 (0-918932-66-1) Activity Resources.

—Skateboard Practice: Addition & Subtraction. new ed. Laycock, Mary, et al. (gr. 1-2). 1978. pap. text ed. 7.95 (0-918932-55-6) Activity Resources.

Kyzer, Martha, jt. illus. see Kyzer, Walter.

Kyzer, Walter & Kyzer, Martha. Create a Cube. Smart, Margaret A. & Laycock, Mary. 64p. (Orig.). (gr. 4-12). 1985. pap. text ed. 7.95 (0-918932-84-X) Activity Resources.

L

Labastida, Aurora. Nine Days to Christmas. Ets, Marie H. 48p. (ps-3). 1991. 4.95 (0-14-054442-9, Puffin) Puffin Bks.

—Nueve Dias Para Navidad. Ets, Marie H. 48p. (ps-3). 1991. 4.95 (0-14-054441-0, Puffin) Puffin Bks.

Labby, Sherman. The Famous Hooper Brothers. Evans, David. 101p. (Orig.). 1988. pap. 15.95 (0-929422-00-7) Jonah Pr.

La Belle, Susan. Baby's Book. Jacobsen, Mark & Kozlovski, Jane. Jacobsen, Judith, ed. 1989. 24.95 (0-9623800-0-8) Me Two Pubns.

—Baby's First Year. Jacobsen, Mark & Kozlovski, Jane. Jacobsen, Judith, ed. 1989. pap. 9.95 (0-9623800-1-6) Me Two Pubns.

Labinski, Gail. Mommy & Daddy Are Fighting: A Book for Children about Family Violence. Paris, Susan. LC 85-22193. 24p. (Orig.). (ps-4). 1986. pap. 8.95 (0-931188-33-4) Seal Pr Feminist.

Lacapa, Michael. Antelope Woman: An Apache Folktale. Lacapa, Michael. LC 92-41598. 48p. (gr. 3 up). 1992. 14.95 (0-87358-543-7) Northland AZ.

—The Flute Player: An Apache Folktale. Lacapa, Michael. LC 89-63749. 48p. (gr. 1-3). 1990. 14.95 (0-87358-500-3) Northland AZ.

—The Mouse Couple. Malotki, Ekkehart, retold by. LC 88-60916. 64p. (gr. 2-7). 1988. 14.95 (0-87358-473-2) Northland AZ.

Lace, Lynn. The Shyest 'Kid in the 'Patch. Daly, Kathleen N. 40p. (gr. 1-5). 1984. 5.95 (0-910313-30-X) Parker Bros.

Lacey, Carol. The Bear on the Moon. Ryder, Joanne. LC 89-13133. 32p. (gr. 1 up). 1991. 14.95 (0-688-08109-6); PLB 14.88 (0-688-08110-X) Morrow Jr Bks.

Lackner, Paul, jt. illus. see Graef, Renee.

Lacome, Julie. Funny Business. Lacome, Julie. LC 90-36258. (ps up). 1991. 11.95 (0-688-10159-3, Tambourine Bks) Morrow.

—Guess Where? Ayres, Pam. LC 93-24336. 1994. write for info. (1-56402-314-1) Candlewick Pr.

—Guess Why. Ayres, Pam. LC 93-24337. 1994. write for info. (1-56402-315-X) Candlewick Pr.

—Hocus Pocus. Lacome, Julie. LC 90-36257. (ps up). 1991. 11.95 (0-688-10158-5, Tambourine Bks) Morrow.

—Walking Through the Jungle. Lacome, Julie. LC 92-53018. 32p. (ps). 1993. 13.95 (*1-56402-137-8*) Candlewick Pr.

Lacome, Julie & Lacome, Julie. A Was Once an Apple Pie. Lear, Edward. LC 91-71865. 32p. (ps). 1992. 13.95 (*1-56402-000-2*) Candlewick Pr.

Lacroix, Dana. Nana's Adoption Farm: The Story of Little Rachell. Horn, Tryntje. 40p. (gr. k-6). 1992. 16.95 (*0-9617426-8-2*) J N Townsend.

La Farge, Margaret. Pack, Band & Colony: The World of Social Animals. Kohl, Judith & Kohl, Herbert. LC 82-20951. 114p. (gr. 6 up). 1983. 13.95 (*0-374-35694-7*) FS&G.

LaFave, Kim. Duck Cakes for Sale. Lunn, Janet. 32p. (ps-2). 1991. 13.95 (*0-88899-094-4*, Pub. by Groundwood-Douglas & McIntyre CN); pap. 4.95 (*0-88899-157-6*) Firefly Bks Ltd.

—Goldie & the Sea. Saltman, Judith. 32p. (ps-2). 1991. 4.95 (*0-88899-133-9*, Pub. by Groundwood-Douglas & McIntyre CN) Firefly Bks Ltd.

La Fave, Kim. The Mare's Egg. Spray, Carole. Atwood, Margaret, afterword by. 56p. (Orig). (gr. k-7). 1981. (Pub. by Camden Hse CN); pap. 9.95 (*0-920656-07-2*, Pub. by Camden Hse CN) Firefly Bks Ltd.

LaFave, Kim. Pumpkin Time. Andrews, Jan. 32p. (ps-3). 1991. 12.95 (*0-88899-112-6*, Pub. by Groundwood-Douglas & McIntyre CN) Firefly Bks Ltd.

—Sharon, Lois & Bram Sing A to Z. Sharon & Lois. 91-18990. 64p. (Orig). (ps-4). 1992. 9.99 (*0-517-58723-8*) Crown Bks Yng Read.

Laffolay, Anne. Busy Little Squirrel. Ikhlef, Anne. 10p. (ps). 1991. bds. 4.99 (*0-679-81612-7*) Random Bks Yng Read.

—Fuzzy Little Bear. Ikhlef, Anne. 10p. (ps). 1991. bds. 4.99 (*0-679-81613-5*) Random Bks Yng Read.

—Happy Little Dolphin. Ikhlef, Anne. 10p. (ps). 1991. bds. 4.99 (*0-679-81615-1*) Random Bks Yng Read.

—Woolly Little Lamb. Ikhlef, Anne. 10p. (ps). 1991. bds. 4.99 (*0-679-81614-3*) Random Bks Yng Read.

La Framboise, Karin. Rotary Roundup. Hopkins, Judy, et al. LC 93-27838. 96p. (Orig). 1994. pap. write for info. (*1-56477-028-1*, B164) That Patchwork.

Lagana, Giuseppe. The Planet Putipoo. Sclavi, Tiziano. 16p. 1989. 8.95 (*0-8120-5997-2*) Barron.

Laimgruber, Monika. Cats' Carnival. Schreiber-Wicke, Edith. LC 85-45964. 24p. 1986. 13.95 (*0-87923-627-2*) Godine.

—Little Red Cap: A Fairy Tale. Grimm, Jacob & Grimm, Wilhelm K. Bell, Anthea, tr. from GER. LC 93-19923. 32p. (gr. k-3). 1993. 14.95 (*1-55858-167-7*); PLB 14.88 (*1-55858-168-5*) North-South Bks NYC.

Laing, Jennifer. Aspen High Country: The Geology, a Pictorial Guide to Roads & Trails. Laing, David & Lampiris, Nicholas. 144p. (Orig). (gr. 9-12). 1980. pap. write for info. (*0-9604274-0-6*) Thunder River.

Laird, Peter. After the Bomb. Wujcik, Erick & Balent, Matthew. Marciniszyn, Alex & Siembieda, Kevin, eds. 48p. (Orig). (gr. 8 up). 1986. pap. 7.95 (*0-916211-15-0*, 503) Palladium Bks.

Laird, Peter & Eastman, Kevin. The Teenage Mutant Ninja Turtles Adventures. Wujcik, Erick. Marciniszyn, Alex, ed. 48p. (Orig). (gr. 8 up). 1986. pap. 7.95 (*0-916211-16-9*, 504) Palladium Bks.

Laird, Peter, jt. illus. see Eastman, Kevin.

Laitin, Lindy. Playing Soccer. Laitin, Ken & Laitin, Steve. LC 79-63980. (gr. 2-7). 1979. pap. 9.95 (*0-916802-22-1*) Soccer for Am.

Lalo. Bye, Bye Boogieman. Rev. ed. Rae, Judy. Timm, Stephen A., intro. by. LC 83-70412. 42p. (Orig). (ps-3). 1984. pap. 3.95 (*0-939728-09-5*) Steppingstone Ent.

—The Dragon & the Mouse: The Dream. Timm, Stephen A. 45p. 1982. 12.95 (*0-939728-05-2*); pap. 4.95 (*0-939728-06-0*) Steppingstone Ent.

—The Dragon & the Mouse: Together Again. Timm, Stephen A. LC 81-90230. 46p. (ps-8). 1981. 12.95 (*0-939728-03-6*); pap. 4.95 (*0-939728-04-4*) Steppingstone Ent.

Lam, Fahn. Haiku Animal World. Fields, Richard L. 80p. (Orig). (gr. 6-12). 1989. pap. 7.95 (*0-927256-00-2*) ELF Assocs.

LaMac, Liz. The Story of Dummyland: Little King Joe & the Witch's Maze. LaMac, Liz. 130p. (gr. 4-5). 1990. 9.95 (*0-927278-03-0*) L LaMac Productions.

LaMarche, Jim. Mandy. Booth, Barbara D. LC 90-19989. 32p. (gr. 1 up). 1991. 14.95 (*0-688-10338-3*); PLB 14.88 (*0-688-10339-1*) Lothrop.

—A Matter of Pride. Crofford, Emily. LC 81-387. 48p. (gr. 2-6). 1991. Repr. of 1981 ed. PLB 17.50 (*0-87614-171-8*, AACR2) Carolrhoda Bks.

—The Rainbabies. Melmed, Laura. Pearson, Susan, ed. LC 91-16877. 32p. (gr. 1 up). 1992. 15.00 (*0-688-10755-9*); PLB 14.93 (*0-688-10756-7*) Lothrop.

—Two Places to Sleep. Schuchman, Joan. LC 79-88201. 32p. (gr. 1-4). 1979. PLB 13.50 (*0-87614-108-4*) Carolrhoda Bks.

—The Walloping Window-Blind. Carryl, Charles E. LC 92-40338. (gr. k-5). 1993. write for info. (*0-688-12517-4*); lib. bdg. write for info. (*0-688-12518-2*) Lothrop.

Lamb, Jim. Discussion Manual for Student Discipleship, Vol. 1. McAllister, Dawson & Webster, Dan. (gr. 5-12). 1975. pap. 8.50 (*0-923417-15-X*) Shepherd Minst.

—Discussion Manual for Student Discipleship, Vol. 2. McAllister, Dawson & Miller, John. (gr. 5-12). 1978. pap. 8.50 (*0-923417-16-8*) Shepherd Minst.

—Discussion Manual for Student Relationships, Vol. 1. McAllister, Dawson & Webster, Dan. (gr. 5-12). 1975. pap. 8.75 (*0-923417-06-0*) Shepherd Minst.

—Discussion Manual for Student Relationships, Vol. 2. McAllister, Dawson. (gr. 5-12). 1976. pap. 8.75 (*0-923417-07-9*) Shepherd Minst.

—Discussion Manual for Student Relationships, Vol. 3. McAllister, Dawson. (gr. 5-12). 1978. pap. 8.75 (*0-923417-08-7*) Shepherd Minst.

—Self Esteem & Loneliness. McAllister, Dawson. (gr. 5-12). 1989. pap. 3.95 (*0-923417-02-8*) Shepherd Minst.

—Student Conference Follow-Up Manual. McAllister, Dawson. (gr. 5-12). 1989. pap. 2.95 (*0-923417-10-9*) Shepherd Minst.

Lamb, Jim, jt. illus. see French, Marty.

Lamb, Susan C. Best Enemies. Leverich, Kathleen. LC 88-19150. (gr. 1 up). 1989. 10.95 (*0-688-08316-1*) Greenwillow.

—Best Enemies. Leverich, Kathleen. LC 88-19150. 80p. (gr. 1-4). 1990. pap. 2.95 (*0-679-80156-1*) Knopf Bks Yng Read.

—Caitlin's Holiday. Griffith, Helen V. LC 89-27228. 96p. (gr. 1 up). 1990. 12.95 (*0-688-09470-8*) Greenwillow.

—Doll Trouble. Griffith, Helen V. LC 92-31510. 128p. (gr. 3 up). 1993. 13.00 (*0-688-12421-6*) Greenwillow.

—Emily & the Enchanted Frog. Griffith, Helen V. LC 88-16511. 32p. (gr. 1 up). 1989. 12.95 (*0-688-08483-4*); PLB 12.88 (*0-688-08484-2*) Greenwillow.

—My Great-Aunt Arizona. Houston, Gloria. LC 90-44112. 32p. (gr. 1-4). 1992. 15.00 (*0-06-022606-4*); PLB 14.89 (*0-06-022607-2*) HarpC Child Bks.

Lambert, Eileen. The Story of Tahoe Tessie: The Original Lake Tahoe Monster. 5th, rev. ed. McCormick, Bob. (gr. 1-4). 1990. pap. 5.95 (*0-9626792-6-7*) Tahoe Tourist.

Lambert, J. K. Brothers Lionheart. Lindgren, Astrid. Tate, Joan, tr. LC 85-573. 184p. (gr. 4-6). 1985. pap. 4.95 (*0-14-031955-7*, Puffin) Puffin Bks.

Lambert, Jonathan. Boastful Bullfrog. Faulkner, Keith. 22p. (gr. 1-3). 1991. 5.95 (*0-681-41051-5*) Longmeadow Pr.

—Butterfly. Faulkner, Keith. 12p. (ps-2). 1993. 4.95 (*0-694-00463-4*, Festival) HarpC Child Bks.

—Colors. 18p. (ps-1). 1992. bds. 1.95 (*0-681-41562-2*) Longmeadow Pr.

—David Dreaming of Dinosaurs. Faulkner, Keith. (ps-3). 1992. 13.00 (*1-56021-182-2*) W J Fantasy.

—Dracula. Faulkner, Keith. 16p. (ps-2). 1993. 10.95 (*0-694-00559-2*, Festival) HarpC Child Bks.

—Elephant & the Rainbow. Faulkner, Keith. 22p. (gr. 1-3). 1990. 5.95 (*0-681-40977-0*) Longmeadow Pr.

—Frog. Faulkner, Keith. 12p. (ps-2). 1993. 4.95 (*0-694-00464-2*, Festival) HarpC Child Bks.

—Giant Jungle Pop-up Book: Animals of the Endangered Rain Forest. Lambert, Jonathan. (ps-3). 1992. 28.00 (*1-56021-183-0*) W J Fantasy.

—Good Night, Tom. Faulkner, Keith. LC 92-82912. 20p. (ps). 1993. 4.95 (*0-590-46924-X*, Cartwheel) Scholastic Inc.

—My New Neighbors. Faulkner, Keith. 24p. (ps-2). 1992. 9.95 (*0-694-00426-X*, Festival) HarpC Child Bks.

—Numbers. 18p. (ps-1). 1992. bds. 1.95 (*0-681-41563-0*) Longmeadow Pr.

—Oh No! A Giant Flap Book. Faulkner, Keith. 16p. (ps-1). 1991. pap. 14.95 (*0-671-74747-9*, S&S BFYR) S&S Trade.

—Opposites. 18p. (ps-1). 1992. bds. 1.95 (*0-681-41565-7*) Longmeadow Pr.

—Runaway Whale. Faulkner, Keith. 22p. (gr. 1-3). 1990. 5.95 (*0-681-41014-0*) Longmeadow Pr.

—Shapes. 18p. (ps-1). 1992. bds. 1.95 (*0-681-41564-9*) Longmeadow Pr.

—This Is Me. Faulkner, Keith. 10p. (ps-k). 1987. 5.95 (*0-312-00967-4*) St Martin.

—Tom's Friends. Faulkner, Keith. LC 92-82910. 20p. (ps). 1993. 4.95 (*0-590-46949-5*, Cartwheel) Scholastic Inc.

—Tom's Picnic. Faulkner, Keith. LC 92-82911. 20p. (ps). 1993. 4.95 (*0-590-46947-9*, Cartwheel) Scholastic Inc.

—Tom's School Day. Faulkner, Keith. LC 92-82909. 20p. (ps). 1993. 4.95 (*0-590-46948-7*, Cartwheel) Scholastic Inc.

Lambert, Mary. Kidding Around Paris: A Young Person's Guide to the City. Clay, Rebecca. 64p. (Orig). (gr. 3 up). 1991. pap. 9.95 (*0-945465-82-3*) John Muir.

—Kidding Around San Diego: A Young Person's Guide to the City. Luhrs, Ruth J. 64p. (Orig). (gr. 3 up). 1991. pap. 9.95 (*1-56261-010-4*) John Muir.

Lambert, Paulette L. Quest for Courage. Rodolph, Stormy. 112p. (gr. 4-6). 1993. pap. 8.95x (*1-879373-57-2*) R Rinehart.

Lambert, Saul. Portrait of Ivan. reissue ed. Fox, Paula. LC 74-93085. 144p. (gr. 5-7). 1985. SBE 13.95 (*0-02-735510-1*, Bradbury Pr) Macmillan Child Grp.

—Portrait of Ivan. Fox, Paula. LC 87-1109. 144p. (gr. 6-8). 1987. pap. 3.95 (*0-689-71167-0*, Aladdin) Macmillan Child Grp.

—Spies & More Spies. Arthur, Robert, ed. (gr. 7-11). 1972. lib. bdg. 5.39 (*0-394-91673-5*) Random Bks Yng Read.

Lambert, Stephen. Fly by Night. Crebbin, June. LC 92-53140. 32p. (ps-3). 1993. 14.95 (*1-56402-149-1*) Candlewick Pr.

—What Is the Sun? Lindbergh, Reeve. LC 93-3557. 1994. write for info. (*1-56402-146-7*) Candlewick Pr.

Lambert, Tony. Monster in My Bathroom. Faulkner, Keith. 16p. (gr. 1-4). 1993. text ed. 4.99 (*0-8431-3482-8*) Price Stern.

—Monster in My Toybox. Faulkner, Keith. 16p. (gr. 1-4). 1993. text ed. 4.99 (*0-8431-3481-X*) Price Stern.

—Two by Two. Faulkner, Keith. 16p. (gr. 1-4). 1993. 12.99 (*0-8431-3477-1*) Incline Pr.

Lamont, Pricilla. Our Mammoth Goes to School. Lamont, Pricilla. 32p. (ps-3). 1988. 11.95 (*0-15-258837-X*, HB Juv Bks) HarBrace.

Lamont, Priscilla. Our House. Rogers, Paul & Rogers, Emma. LC 92-53015. 40p. (gr. k-3). 1993. 14.95 (*1-56402-134-3*) Candlewick Pr.

—Our Mammoth. Mitchell, Adrian. (ps-3). 1987. 11.95 (*0-15-258838-8*) HarBrace.

—Ring-a-Round-a Rosy: Nursery Rhymes, Action Rhymes & Lullabies. Lamont, Priscilla. (ps). 1990. 15.95 (*0-316-51292-3*, Joy St Bks) Little.

—Where's My Mom? Rosselson, Leon. LC 93-32383. 1994. write for info. (*1-56402-392-3*) Candlewick Pr.

La Mont, Violet. The Prize in the Packard. Hammond, Pearle L. 100p. (Orig). (gr. 5-8). 1990. pap. 8.95 (*0-9615161-6-X*) Incline Pr.

Lamorisse, Albert, photos by. Red Balloon. Lamorisse, Albert. LC 57-9229. 45p. (gr. 3-7). 1967. 13.95 (*0-685-01494-0*) Doubleday.

LaMorte, Kathy. Ecology Green Pages for Students & Teachers. LaMorte, Kathy & Lewis, Sharen. Keeling, Jan, ed. 64p. (Orig). 1993. pap. text ed. 7.95 (*0-86530-269-3*) Incentive Pubns.

—U. S. Social Studies Yellow Pages for Students & Teachers. LaMorte, Kathy & Lewis, Sharen. Keeling, Jan, ed. 64p. (Orig). 1993. pap. text ed. 7.95 (*0-86530-267-7*) Incentive Pubns.

—World Social Studies Yellow Pages for Students & Teachers. LaMorte, Kathy & Lewis, Sharen. Newton, Rebecca, ed. 64p. (Orig). 1993. pap. text ed. 7.95 (*0-86530-268-5*) Incentive Pubns.

LaMothe, Becky, jt. illus. see Holbrook, Clifford.

Lanawn-Shee Studios Staff. Leif the Lucky. Dandola, John. 24p. (Orig). (gr. k up). 1991. pap. 3.95 (*1-878452-05-3*) Tory Corner Editions.

—Lifestyles of Colonial America. Quincannon, Alan, ed. 24p. (Orig). (gr. k-6). 1992. pap. 3.95 (*1-878452-10-X*) Tory Corner Editions.

—More Soldiers of Colonial America. Quincannon, Alan, ed. 24p. (Orig). (gr. k-6). 1992. pap. 3.95 (*1-878452-12-6*) Tory Corner Editions.

—People of Colonial America. Quincannon, Alan, ed. 20p. (Orig). (gr. k-6). 1992. pap. 3.95 (*1-878452-09-6*) Tory Corner Editions.

—Robin Hood. Brice, Donald. 28p. (Orig). (gr. k up). 1991. pap. 3.95 (*1-878452-04-5*) Tory Corner Editions.

—Soldiers of Colonial America. Quincannon, Alan, ed. 24p. (Orig). (gr. k-6). 1992. pap. 3.95 (*1-878452-11-8*) Tory Corner Editions.

Lancaster, Derek. Picture America: States & Capitals. Lancaster, Derek. Anderson, Stevens, ed. 136p. (gr. 5). 1992. pap. 4.95 (*1-880184-02-8*) Compact Classics.

Landa, Peter. The Man of the House. Fassler, Joan. LC 73-80122. 32p. (ps-3). 1975. 16.95 (*0-87705-010-4*) Human Sci Pr.

—The Sign of the Chrysanthemum. Paterson, Katherine. LC 72-7553. 128p. (gr. 6 up). 1988. pap. 3.95 (*0-06-440232-0*, Trophy) HarpC Child Bks.

Landgraff, Michael. Los Ninos de la Biblia. Bourgeois, Jean-Francois. Maecha, Alberto, ed. (SPA). 40p. (gr. 3-5). 1984. pap. write for info. (*0-942504-11-9*) Overcomer Pr.

Landis, Frederick. The Emperors New Clothes. (LAT). 52p. (gr. 9-12). 3.55 (*0-939507-04-8*, B710) Amer Classical.

Landman, Rodney G. I'm Special: An Experiential Workbook for the Child in Us All. Landsman, Sandra G. (gr. k up). 1986. pap. 6.95 (*0-935571-02-7*) Treehouse.

Landon, Linda L. Earth Angel Child: You May Be One. Landon, Linda L. (Orig). (gr. 3 up). 1992. pap. 8.80 (*0-9633759-0-3*) Harmony Hill.

Landon, Lucinda. Meg MacKintosh & the Case of the Curious Whale Watch. Landon, Lucinda. 48p. (gr. 2-5). 1987. 13.95 (*0-316-51362-8*, Joy St Bks) Little.

—Meg MacKintosh & the Case of the Missing Babe Ruth Baseball: A Solve-It-Yourself Mystery. Landon, Lucinda. LC 85-20055. 48p. (gr. 2-5). 1986. 13.95 (*0-316-51318-0*, 513180, Joy St Bks) Little.

—Meg MacKintosh & the Mystery at the Medieval Castle. Landon, Lucinda. 64p. (gr. 2-5). 1989. 13.95 (*0-316-51363-6*, Joy St Bks) Little.

—The Young Detective's Handbook. Butler, William V. (gr. 3-7). 1986. (Pub. by Atlantic Monthly Pr); pap. 6.95 (*0-316-11889-3*) Little.

Landstrom, Olof. Olson's Meat Pies. Cohen, Peter. Fisher, Richard E., tr. (gr. k-4). 1989. 12.95 (*91-29-59180-5*, Pub. by R & S Bks) FS&G.

—Shorty Takes Off. Lindgren, Barbro. Fisher, Richard E., tr. 28p. (ps-3). 1990. 13.95 (*91-29-59770-6*, Pub. by R & S Bks) FS&G.

Lane, Dan. The Cherry Migration. Balan, Bruce. 32p. 1991. 12.95 (*0-88138-098-9*, Green Tiger) S&S Trade.

—Valerie & the Silver Pear. Darling, Benjamin. LC 90-24945. 32p. (gr. k-3). 1992. RSBE 14.95 (*0-02-726100-X*, Four Winds) Macmillan Child Grp.

Lane, Daniel. Santa Cow Island Vacation. Edens, Cooper. LC 93-30899. 1994. write for info. (*0-671-88319-4*, Green Tiger) S&S Trade.

—Santa Cows. Edens, Cooper. LC 91-57. 40p. (gr. 2 up). 1991. jacketed, reinforced bdg. 14.00 (0-671-74863-7, Green Tiger) S&S Trade.
Lane, John. The Case of the Nervous Newsboy. Hildick, E. W. 112p. (gr. 3-6). 1991. pap. 2.95 (0-88741-807-4, 01304) Sundance Pubs.
—The Kids' World Almanac of Animals & Pets. Felder, Deborah G. 1990. 14.95 (0-88687-556-0, World Almanac); pap. 6.95 (0-88687-555-2, World Almanac) F&W Inc NJ.
—The Kids' World Almanac of Baseball. Aylesworth, Thomas G. Hershiser, Orel, intro. by. 288p. 1990. text ed. 14.95 (0-88687-463-7, World Almanac); pap. 6.95 (0-88687-563-3, World Almanac) F&W Inc NJ.
—The Kids' World Almanac of History. Felder, Deborah G. 288p. (Orig.). 1991. 14.95 (0-88687-496-3, World Almanac); pap. 6.95 (0-88687-495-5, World Almanac) F&W Inc NJ.
—The Kids' World Almanac of Music: From Rock to Bach & Back Again. Sommer, Elyse. 288p. (Orig.). 1992. 14.95 (0-88687-522-6, World Almanac); pap. 7.95 (0-88687-521-8, World Almanac) F&W Inc NJ.
Lane, Sandy. God's Little Dreamer. Kiemel Anderson, Ann. LC 90-33475. 32p. (ps-8). 1990. 10.99 (0-89081-785-5) Harvest Hse.
Lanfredi, Judy. Sheep Dreams. Levine, Arthur A. LC 91-44929. 32p. (ps-3). 1993. 13.99 (0-8037-1194-8); PLB 13.89 (0-8037-1195-6) Dial Bks Young.
—The Year You Were Born, 1983. Martinet, Jeanne. LC 91-31605. 56p. 1992. PLB 13.93 (0-688-11078-9, Tambourine Bks); pap. 7.95 (0-688-11077-0, Tambourine Bks) Morrow.
—The Year You Were Born, 1985. Martinet, Jeanne. LC 91-37439. 56p. 1992. PLB 13.93 (0-688-11082-7, Tambourine Bks); pap. 7.95 (0-688-11081-9, Tambourine Bks) Morrow.
—The Year You Were Born, 1986. Martinet, Jeanne. 56p. (gr. 2 up). 1993. PLB 13.93 (0-688-11969-7, Tambourine Bks); pap. 7.95 (0-688-11968-9, Tambourine Bks) Morrow.
—The Year You Were Born, 1987. Martinet, Jeanne. 56p. (gr. 2 up). 1993. PLB 13.93 (0-688-11971-9, Tambourine Bks); pap. 7.95 (0-688-11970-0, Tambourine Bks) Morrow.
Lanfredi, Judy & Lanfredi, Judy. The Year You Were Born, 1984. Martinet, Jeanne. LC 91-34577. 56p. 1992. PLB 13.93 (0-688-11080-0, Tambourine Bks); pap. 7.95 (0-688-11079-7, Tambourine Bks) Morrow.
Lang, Aubrey, photos by. Bears. Stirling, Ian. 64p. (gr. 3-6). 1992. 14.95 (0-87156-574-9) Sierra.
Lang, Cecily. A Birthday Basket for Tia. Mora, Pat. LC 91-15753. 32p. (ps-1). 1992. RSBE 13.95 (0-02-767400-2, Macmillan Child Bk) Macmillan Child Grp.
—A Birthday Basket for Tia. Mora, Pat. (gr. k-4). 1993. 13.95 (0-685-64816-8); audio cass. 11.00 (1-882869-78-8) Read Advent.
Lang, Charles, et al. Demons & Deviants. Barker, Clive, et al. Brown, Mike, ed. 62p. (Orig.). 1993. pap. 4.95 (0-938782-24-5) Fantaco.
Lang, H. J., jt. illus. see Ford, Henry J.
Lang, Irene. Daniel Scott & the Monster. Evelyn-Marie. ES-13369. 32p. (gr. k-3). 1985. 7.95 (0-9614746-1-0); PLB 9.95 (0-9614746-2-9); bk. & cassette 11.95 (0-9614746-0-2); pap. 3.00 (0-9614746-4-5) Berry Bks.
Langcaon, Jeff. Where's Kimo? Langcaon, Jeff. 24p. (gr. k-2). 1993. pap. 5.95 (1-880188-65-1) Bess Pr.
Langenfass, Hansjorg, jt. illus. see Rettich, Rolf.
Langevin, Isabelle. Ce Si Papa se Perd au Zoo? Lamont-Clarke, Ginette & Stevens, Florence. LC 91-65364. (FRE.). (gr. 2-5). 1991. 12.95 (0-88776-266-2); pap. 6.95 (0-88776-273-5) Tundra Bks.
—What If Dad Gets Lost at the Zoo? Stevens, Florence & Lamont-Clarke, Ginette. LC 91-65365. 24p. (ps-2). 1991. 12.95 (0-88776-265-4); pap. 6.95 (0-685-48807-1) Tundra Bks.
Langford, Alton. Caribou Country: From an Original Article Which Appeared in Ranger Rick Magazine, Copyright National Wildlife Federation. Boyle, Doe & Thomas, Peter, eds. Luther, Sallie, contrib. by. 20p. (gr. k-3). 1992. 6.95 (0-924483-53-9); incl. audiocass. tape & 13" toy 35.95 (0-924483-50-4); incl. 9" toy 21.95 (0-924483-51-2); incl. audiocass. tape 9.95 (0-924483-52-0); write for info. audiocass. tape (0-924483-80-6) Soundprints.
—Deputy Scarlett: From an Original Article Which Appeared in Ranger Rick Magazine, copyright National Wildlife Federation. Boyle, Doe & Thomas, Peter, eds. Luther, Sallie, contrib. by. 20p. (gr. k-3). 1992. 6.95 (0-924483-49-0); incl. audiocass. tape & 11" toy 35.95 (0-924483-46-6); incl. 8" toy 21.95 (0-924483-47-4); incl. audiocass. tape 9.95 (0-924483-48-2); write for info. audiocass. tape (0-924483-79-2) Soundprints.
—Rick's First Adventure: From an Original Article Which Appeared in Ranger Rick Magazine, Copyright National Wildlife Federation. Boyle, Doe & Thomas, Peter, eds. Luter, Sallie, contrib. by. 20p. (gr. k-3). 1992. 6.95 (0-924483-45-8); incl. audiocass. tape & 13" toy 35.95 (0-924483-42-3); incl. 9" toy 21.95 (0-924483-43-1); incl. audiocass. tape 9.95 (0-924483-44-X); write for info. audiocass. tape (0-924483-78-9) Soundprints.
—Whales: The Gentle Giants. Milton, Joyce. LC 88-15616. 48p. (Orig.). (gr. k-3). 1989. lib. bdg. 7.99 (0-394-99809-X); pap. 3.50 (0-394-89809-5) Random Bks Yng Read.

Langley, Bill & Dias, Ron. Walt Disney's Lady & the Tramp. Slater, Teddy, adapted by. 24p. (ps-3). 1993. 3.50 (0-307-12367-7, 12367, Golden Pr) Western Pub.
—Walt Disney's One Hundred One Dalmatians. (ps-2). 1991. write for info. (0-307-12346-4, Golden Pr) Western Pub.
Langley, Bill & Wakeman, Diana. Disney's Winnie the Pooh's A to Zzzz. Ferguson, Don. LC 91-73812. 32p. 1992. 12.95 (1-56282-015-X) Disney Pr.
—Disney's Winnie the Pooh's Easter. Talkington, Bruce. LC 92-53441. 32p. (ps-4). 1993. 10.95 (1-56282-377-9) Disney Pr.
—Walt Disney Bambi's Game. Phillips, Joan. 32p. (ps-1). 1992. pap. write for info. (0-307-15968-X, 15968) Western Pub.
—Walt Disney's Bambi's Game. Phillips, Joan. (ps-1). 1991. write for info. (0-307-11599-2, Golden Pr) Western Pub.
—Walt Disney's Winnie the Pooh & the Very Big Bear. Phillips, Joan. 32p. (ps-1). 1992. pap. write for info. (0-307-15969-8, 15969) Western Pub.
—Winnie the Pooh & the Blustery Day. Slater, Teddy. LC 92-55130. 48p. (ps-k). 1993. 12.95 (1-56282-488-0) Disney Pr.
Langley, Bill & Wakeraw, Diana. Walt Disney's Bambi: Count to Five. Muldron, Diane. (ps-k). 1991. bds. write for info. (0-307-06114-0, Golden Pr) Western Pub.
Langley, Bill, et al. Disney's Two-Minute Good Night Stories. Packard, Mary. LC 87-83200. 36p. (ps-1). 1988. write for info. (0-307-12181-X) Western Pub.
Langley, Jonathan. Goldilocks & the Three Bears. Langley, Jonathan. LC 93-13155. 32p. (gr. k-3). 1993. 11.00 (0-06-020814-7); PLB 10.89 (0-06-020815-5) HarpC Child Bks.
—My First Dictionary. Leyton, Lawrence & Root, Betty. LC 93-20145. 96p. (gr. k-4). 1993. 16.95 (1-56458-277-9) Dorling Kindersley.
—Potty Time. Civardi, Anne. 24p. (ps). 1988. 6.95 (0-671-65896-4, Little Simon) S&S Trade.
—Potty Time. Civardi, Anne. LC 87-21910. 24p. (ps). 1993. pap. 3.95 (0-671-79618-6, S&S BYR) S&S Trade.
—Rain, Rain, Go Away! A Book of Nursery Rhymes. LC 89-34594. 96p. (ps-k). 1991. 12.95 (0-8037-0762-2) Dial Bks Young.
—Rumpelstiltskin. Langley, Jonathan, retold by. LC 91-11133. 32p. (ps-3). 1992. 14.95 (0-06-020198-3); PLB 14.89 (0-06-020199-1) HarpC Child Bks.
—The Three Billy Goats Gruff. Langley, Jonathan. LC 92-4842. 32p. (ps-3). 1994. 15.00 (0-06-021224-1); PLB 14.89 (0-06-021474-0) HarpC Child Bks.
Langley, Marilynn. Christmas in Vermont: Three Stories. Carty, Margaret F. LC 83-62750. 48p. (Orig.). (gr. 5 up). 1983. pap. 2.95 (0-933050-21-6) New Eng Pr VT.

Langley, William A. Tales of a Nuf in the Land of Doon. MacKay, Judy F. 84p. (Orig.). (gr. 4-7). 1992. pap. 9.95 perfect bdg. (1-882748-00-X) MacKay-Langley.
McKay-Langley Publishing is dedicated to producing children's books that educate, enlighten & provoke laughter. TALES OF A NUF IN THE LAND OF DOON is their Premier Edition. The six-color cover introduces the reader to the Land of Doon: a land filled with love & light, & just a hint of darkness in the form of chocolate-eating Murcs & their leader Tsol Eno. The story begins with a struggling, cantankerous Nuf (Htrim) who has been sent to find a boy, a creature unknown to him. As the story unfolds, Htrim & the boy (Anthony) discover that their destinies are intertwined. With great difficulty Anthony succeeds in adjusting to Htrim: who turns his ears off & on at will so that he can "go within"; who is not an elf; who turns the color of whatever vegetable he is eating. With the help of Xela the Dream Merchant, Uncle Twinkle, Htrim's mentor & the colorful Nam Wobniar, a prophecy is fulfilled; a Nuf learns what love is; a boy learns what inner peace is; & the reader learns that children's literature can be non-violent, & still be an adventure in reading. *Publisher Provided Annotation.*

Langoulant, Allan. Everybody's Different. Langoulant, Allan. LC 90-36811. 32p. (gr. 2-3). 1990. PLB 18.60 (0-8368-0435-X) Gareth Stevens Inc.

—A Prize for Percival. Langoulant, Allan. Sherwood, Rhoda, ed. LC 88-42912. 32p. (gr. 2-3). 1988. PLB 18.60 (1-55532-931-4) Gareth Stevens Inc.
Lanier, Frances. Thirteen Georgia Ghosts & Jeffrey. Windham, Kathryn T. LC 73-87004. 160p. (gr. 6 up). 1987. pap. 9.50t (0-8173-0377-4) U of Ala Pr.
Lankford, Robert D. Dream Weaver: Survive until Dawn, Vol. 1, Issue 1. Lankford, Robert D. 24p. (gr. 11 up). 1987. pap. 1.95 (0-9621811-0-2) Lankford Comics.
Lanos, H. En Famille, Tome 2. Malot, Hector. (FRE.). 221p. (gr. 5-10). 1980. pap. 8.95 (2-07-033132-6) Schoenhof.
Lanot, H. En Famille, Tome 1. Malot, Hector. (FRE.). 220p. (gr. 5-10). 1980. pap. 8.95 (2-07-033131-8) Schoenhof.
Lansdale, Paul. Teacher's Guide to Pearl Makers. Willis, Doris. 64p. (Orig.). 1989. pap. 5.95 (0-377-00194-5) Friendship Pr.
Lanting, Frans. Albatrosses of Midway Island. Johnson, Sylvia A. 48p. (gr. 2-5). 1990. PLB 19.95 (0-87614-391-5) Carolrhoda Bks.
Lanting, Frans, photos by. Elephant Seals. Johnson, Sylvia A. LC 88-12924. 48p. (gr. 4 up). 1989. PLB 19.95 (0-8225-1487-7) Lerner Pubns.
Lantz, Carol. Fairy Tale Jewels. rev. & expanded ed. Farha, Mary N. 110p. (gr. 2-10). 1991. 10.95 (1-55914-522-6); pap. 8.95 (1-55914-523-4) ABBE Pubs Assn.
Lantz, Paul. Blue Willow. Gates, Doris. LC 40-32435. (gr. 4-6). 1976. pap. 3.99 (0-14-030924-1, VS30, Puffin) Puffin Bks.
—Blue Willow. Gates, Doris. LC 40-32435. 176p. (gr. 4-7). 1940. pap. 14.00 (0-670-17557-9) Viking Child Bks.
Lanza, Barbara. Good Night, Baby. Patrick, Denise L. 24p. (ps). 1993. bds. 3.50 (0-307-06144-2, 6144, Golden Pr) Western Pub.
—Hopscotch, the Tiny Bunny. Colmenson, Stephenie. (ps-3). 1991. pap. 1.75 (0-307-12617-X, Golden Pr) Western Pub.
—Rags. Scarry, Patricia. 32p. (ps-1). 1991. write for info. (0-307-15702-4, Golden Pr) Western Pub.
Lanza, Barbara, jt. illus. see Lundell, Margo.
La Padula, Thomas. To the Top! Climbing the World's Highest Mountain. Kramer, S. A. LC 92-22164. 48p. (Orig.). (gr. 2-4). 1993. PLB 7.99 (0-679-93885-0); pap. 3.50 (0-679-83885-6) Random Bks Yng Read.
—True-Life Treasure Hunts. Donnelly, Judy. 48p. (Orig.). (gr. 2-4). 1993. PLB 7.99 (0-679-93980-6); pap. 3.50 (0-679-83980-1) Random Bks Yng Read.
La Padula, Tom. Black Beauty. Sewell, Anna. Simpson, Anne, ed. LC 92-5805. 48p. (gr. 3-6). 1992. PLB 12.89 (0-8167-2860-7); pap. text ed. 3.95 (0-8167-2861-5) Troll Assocs.
LaPadula, Tom. The Golden Book of Space Exploration. Moche, Dinah. (ps-7). 1990. write for info. (0-307-15855-1, Pub. by Golden Bks) Western Pub.
—The Golden Book of Stars & Planets. Heidt, Judith. 48p. (gr. 3-7). 1988. write for info. (0-307-15572-2) Western Pub.
—Space Machines. Abernathy, Susan. (gr. 3-6). 1991. 8.50 (0-307-17872-2, Golden Pr) Western Pub.
—The Truck Book. Gere, Bill. 24p. (ps-k). 1987. pap. write for info. (0-307-10051-0, Pub. by Golden Bks) Western Pub.

La Pierre, Keith C. The Wanna Beezzz. La Pierre, Keith C. LC 93-78057. 34p. (ps-3). 1993. 8.95 (0-9631513-1-2); PLB write for info. (0-9631513-2-0) Lee Pub NY.
THE WANNA BEEZZZ is a comically illustrated picture book in which an imaginative swarm of bees try desperately to educate a bewildered bear cub in the ways of make-believe. The story begins when the bear cub finds a bee hive in an old tree, but what he finds is not honey. What he does find is five whimsical bees. Each bee tries in vain to teach the cub how to play make-believe, to use his imagination. The story comes alive as the author uses rhyme & verse to guide the young reader through the make believe world of the Wanna Beezzz. Keith La Pierre's writing style adds excitement & energy to an already spirited plot. Teachers & librarians alike will find this title to be a welcome edition to their Children's book collection. ISBN: 0-9631513-1-2, 34 pages, $8.95. Lee Publishing, P.O. Box 726, Glenwood Landing, NY 11547. Tel. 516-358-0785. *Publisher Provided Annotation.*

Laplaca, Michael. How to Draw Boats, Trains, & Planes. LaPlaca, Michael. LC 81-52123. 32p. (gr. 2-6). 1982. PLB 10.65 *(0-89375-682-2)*; pap. text ed. 1.95 *(0-89375-497-8)* Troll Assocs.
—How to Draw Cars & Trucks. LaPlaca, Michael. LC 81-52122. 32p. (gr. 2-6). 1982. PLB 10.65 *(0-89375-681-4)*; pap. text ed. 1.95 *(0-89375-498-6)* Troll Assocs.
—How to Draw Dinosaurs. LaPlaca, Michael. LC 81-52118. 32p. (gr. 2-6). 1982. PLB 10.65 *(0-89375-683-0)*; pap. text ed. 1.95 *(0-89375-496-X)* Troll Assocs.
Lapointe, Claude. Aventures de Tom Sawyer. Twain, Mark, pseud. (FRE.). 296p. (gr. 5-10). 1987. pap. 10. 95 *(2-07-033449-X)* Schoenhof.
—Grabuge et l'Indomptable Amelie. De Brissac, Elvire. (FRE.). 144p. (gr. 3-7). 1990. pap. 11.95 *(2-07-031212-7)* Schoenhof.
Lapointe, Claudine. Du Commerce de la Souris. Serres, Alain. (FRE.). 55p. (gr. 1-5). 1989. pap. 8.95 *(2-07-031195-3)* Schoenhof.
Laporte, Michele. Child Star: When Talkies Came to Hollywood. Weaver, Lydia. 64p. (gr. 2-6). 1992. PLB 12.00 *(0-670-84039-4)* Viking Child Bks.
—Edith Wilson: The Woman Who Ran the United States. Giblin, James C. 64p. (gr. 2-6). 1992. RB 11.00 *(0-670-83005-4)* Viking Child Bks.
—Edith Wilson: The Woman Who Ran the United States. Giblin, James C. LC 93-15139. 64p. (gr. 2-5). 1993. pap. 3.99 *(0-14-034249-4,* Puffin) Puffin Bks.
—Touch Choices: A Story of the Vietnam War. Antle, Nancy. 64p. (gr. 2-6). 1993. reinforced bdg. 12.99 *(0-670-84879-4)* Viking Child Bks.
Laporte, Michelle. Diana: Twentieth-Century Princess. Giff, Patricia R. 64p. (gr. 3-5). 1992. pap. 3.99 *(0-14-034707-0,* Puffin) Puffin Bks.
Lapper, Ivan, jt. illus. see Batchelor, John.
Lapper, Ivan, et al. City Through the Ages. Steele, Philip. LC 91-37350. 32p. (gr. 3-6). 1993. PLB 11.89 *(0-8167-2727-9)*; pap. text ed. 3.95 *(0-8167-2728-7)* Troll Assocs. Postponed.
—Factory Through the Ages. Steele, Philip. LC 91-33262. 32p. (gr. 3-6). 1993. PLB 11.89 *(0-8167-2729-5)*; pap. text ed. 3.95 *(0-8167-2730-9)* Troll Assocs. Postponed.
Lardner, Kym. Arnold the Prickly Teddy. Lardner, Kym. LC 92-31919. 1993. 14.00 *(0-383-03552-X)* SRA Schl Grp.
Large, Annabel. Beauty & the Beast. Daniels, Patricia. LC 79-28433. 24p. (gr. k-5). 1980. PLB 14.64 *(0-8393-0258-4)* Raintree Steck-V.
Large, Hazel. Fly Beyond the Mountain. Eastman, Elizabeth. ii, 18p. (Orig.). (gr. k-4). 1985. pap. 1.49 *(0-9615959-0-6)* JAARS Inc.
Larimer, Donna. Mama, Daddy, Baby & Me. Gewing, Lisa. 30p. (ps) 1989. 12.95 *(0-944296-04-1)* Spirit Pr.
Larke, Karol. The Bullfrog & the Grasshopper & Other "Tails" Larke, Joe. 72p. (gr. k-6). 1987. 10.00 *(0-9620112-0-7)* Grin A Bit.
—Can't Reach the Itch. Larke, Joe. 72p. (gr. 1-6). 1988. 10.00x *(0-9620112-1-5)* Grin A Bit.
—Dopie Dope Goes to the Fair. Larke, Joe. 49p. (gr. k-5). 1992. 13.95 *(0-9620112-7-4)* Grin A Bit.
—Dopie Dope Grin A Bit Poetry Series. Larke, Joe. (gr. k-6). 1992. write for info. *(0-9620112-9-0)* Grin A Bit.
Larkin, Bob. Merc: Two Thousand. Wiseman, Loren K. 120p. (Orig.). (gr. 9-12). 1990. pap. 16.00 *(1-55878-072-6)* Game Designers.
Larkin, Catherine. Dinosaur Diary: My Triassic Homeland. Gillette, Lynett. 32p. (gr. 4). 1988. pap. 2.95 *(0-945695-00-4)* Petrified Forest Mus Assn.
Laroche, Giles. The Color Box. Dodds, Dayle A. 32p. (ps-1). 1992. 12.95 *(0-316-18820-4)* Little.
—General Store. Field, Rachel. LC 87-37218. (ps-3). 1988. 15.95 *(0-316-28163-8)* Little.
Laroche, Giles, photos by. Sing a Song of People. Lenski, Lois. (ps-3). 1987. pap. 15.95 *(0-316-52074-8)* Little.
LaRochelle, David. The Stingy Baker. Greeson, Janet. 32p. (ps-3). 1989. PLB 18.95 *(0-87614-378-8)* Carolrhoda Bks.
Larocque, Jean-Paul. Numbers Time. Larocque, Jean-Paul. 17p. (gr. k-3). 1993. pap. 11.95 *(1-895583-62-4)* MAYA Pubs.
—What Is Two Plus Two. Larocque, Jean-Paul. 12p. (gr. k-3). 1993. pap. 10.95 *(1-895583-63-2)* MAYA Pubs.
—Wille Wacka Land. Larocque, Jean-Paul. 12p. (gr. 1-3). 1992. pap. 6.95 *(1-895583-04-7)* MAYA Pubs.
Larrecq, John M. Broderick. Ormondroyd, Edward. LC 77-83752. (gr. k-3). 1969. (Pub. by Parnassus); PLB 4.77 *(0-686-86580-4)* HM.
—Broderick. Ormondroyd, Edward. LC 77-83752. 40p. (ps-3). 1984. pap. 4.95 *(0-395-36170-2,* 4-92538) HM.
—Green Christmas. Kroeber, Theodora. LC 67-26304. (gr. k-2). 1967. 6.95 *(0-87466-047-5,* Pub. by Parnassus) HM.
—A Single Speckled Egg. Levitin, Sonia. LC 75-4189. 40p. (ps-3). 1976. 6.95 *(0-87466-074-2,* Pub. by Parnassus) HM.
—Theodore. Ormondroyd, Edward. LC 66-10352. 40p. (ps-3). 1984. pap. 5.95 *(0-395-36610-0)* HM.
—Theodore's Rival. Ormondroyd, Edward. LC 76-156876. 40p. (gr. k-3). 1971. (Pub. by Parnassus); PLB 4.59 *(0-87466-001-7)* HM.
—Theodore's Rival. Ormondroyd, Edward. (gr. 4-8). 1986. pap. 3.80 *(0-395-41669-8,* Sandpiper) HM.
—Wonders, Inc. Kilian, Crawford. (gr. 1 up). 1968. 6.95 *(0-87466-058-0,* Pub. by Parnassus) HM.

Larsen, Rob. Packing for Heaven. Delp, Debra. Zoglio, Suzanne, ed. 32p. (Orig.). (gr. k-5). 1991. pap. text ed. 8.95 *(0-941668-03-7)* Tower Hill Pr.
Larsen, Suzanne K. Spook. Little, Jane. LC 90-31296. 128p. (gr. 2-5). 1990. pap. 3.95 *(0-689-71417-3,* Aladdin) Macmillan Child Grp.
Larson, Dorothy W. Bright Shadows. Larson, Dorothy W. LC 92-81679. 96p. (gr. 4-6). 1992. 14.95 *(0-9621779-0-3)* Sandstone Pub.
Larson, Leonard. Mother Goose in the Space Age. Jensen, Lillian. (gr. 5-9). 1985. 7.95 *(0-933494-28-9)* Earthwise Pubns.
Larson, Lynn. The Child of Two Mothers. Rosholt, Malcolm & Rosholt, Margaret. LC 83-63177. 108p. (gr. 4 up). 1983. PLB 9.95x *(0-910417-03-2)* Rosholt Hse.
Larson, Tim, jt. illus. see Gildemeister, Jerry.
Larsson, Karl. The Mother Ditch. LaFarge, Oliver. Ortego, Pedro R., tr. LC 82-10712. (ENG & SPA.). 64p. (gr. 1-12). 1983. pap. 8.95 *(0-86534-009-9)* Sunstone Pr.
La Rue, Doug, et al. The Littlest Aggie. Henderson, Shelia & George, Bonnie S. Darr, S. C., ed. Williams, Clayton, Jr., frwd. by. 56p. 1990. 18.95 *(0-9623171-2-8)*; coloring bk. 4.95 *(0-9623171-3-6)* LBCo Pub.
Larvor, Yves. Water. Michel, Francois. LC 92-9715. 1993. write for info. *(0-688-11427-X)* Lothrop.
Lascom, Adrian. What Is a Fish? Snedden, Robert. Oxford Scientific Films Staff, photos by. LC 93-6495. 1993. write for info. *(0-87156-545-5)* Sierra.
—What Is an Amphibian? Snedden, Robert. Oxford Scientific Films Staff, photos by. LC 93-11619. 1994. write for info. *(0-87156-469-6)* Sierra.
Lasker, Je. The Pilgrim's First Thanksgiving. McGovern, Ann. 48p. (gr. k-5). 1984. pap. 2.50 *(0-590-40617-5)* Scholastic Inc.
Lasker, Joe. All Kinds of Families. Simon, Norma. Rubin, Caroline, ed. LC 75-42283. 40p. (gr. k-2). 1976. PLB 13.95 *(0-8075-0282-0)* A Whitman.
—Christopher Columbus: Admiral of the Ocean Sea. Haskins, Jim. 64p. (gr. 2-5). 1991. pap. 2.95 *(0-590-42396-7)* Scholastic Inc.
—Cobweb Christmas. Climo, Shirley. LC 81-43879. 32p. (ps-3). 1982. 15.00 *(0-690-04215-9,* Crowell Jr Bks); PLB 14.89 *(0-690-04216-7)* HarpC Child Bks.
—The Cobweb Christmas. Climo, Shirley. LC 81-43879. 32p. (ps-3). 1986. pap. 4.50 *(0-06-443110-X,* Trophy) HarpC Child Bks.
—He's My Brother. Lasker, Joe. LC 73-7318. 40p. (gr. 1-3). 1974. PLB 13.95 *(0-8075-3218-5)* A Whitman.
—How Do I Feel? Simon, Norma. LC 77-126430. (ps-2). 1970. PLB 13.95 *(0-8075-3414-5)* A Whitman.
—Howie Helps Himself. Fassler, Joan. LC 74-12284. 32p. (gr. 1-3). 1975. PLB 13.95 *(0-8075-3422-6)* A Whitman.
—Merry Ever After. Lasker, Joe. (gr. 1-3). 1978. pap. 4.95 *(0-14-050280-7,* Puffin) Puffin Bks.
—Mothers Can Do Anything. Lasker, Joe. LC 72-83684. 40p. (gr. k-2). 1972. PLB 13.95 *(0-8075-5287-9)* A Whitman.
—Nick Joins In. Lasker, Joe. Tucker, Kathleen, ed. LC 79-29637. 32p. (gr. 1-3). 1980. PLB 13.95 *(0-8075-5612-2)* A Whitman.
—Tournament of Knights. Lasker, Joe. LC 85-48075. 32p. (gr. 3 up). 1986. (Crowell Jr Bks); PLB 13.89 *(0-690-04542-5,* Crowell Jr Bks) HarpC Child Bks.
—A Tournament of Knights. Lasker, Joe. LC 85-48075. 32p. (gr. 3 up). 1989. pap. 5.95 *(0-06-443192-4,* Trophy) HarpC Child Bks.
—Way Mothers Are. Schlein, Miriam. LC 63-13332. (ps-2). 1963. PLB 13.95 *(0-8075-8692-7)* A Whitman.
—The Way Mothers Are: Thirtieth Anniversary Edition. rev. ed. Schlein, Miriam. Tucker, Kathy, ed. LC 92-21516. 32p. (ps-k). 1993. PLB 13.95 *(0-8075-8691-9)* A Whitman.
—What Do I Do: English - Spanish Edition. Simon, Norma. LC 74-79544. 40p. (ps-2). 1969. PLB 13.95 *(0-8075-8823-7)* A Whitman.
—What Do I Say. Simon, Norma. LC 67-17420. (ENG & SPA.). (ps-2). 1967. 13.95 *(0-8075-8828-8)*; PLB 13.95 *(0-8075-8826-1)* A Whitman.
Lasky, Mark. Sharing. Pincus, Debbie. 80p. (gr. 4-8). 1983. wkbk. 8.95 *(0-86653-117-3,* GA 468) Good Apple.
Lasley, Susan K., jt. illus. see Belding, Pam.
Lassell, A. One Eyed Poacher of Privilege. 2nd ed. Smith, Edmund W. 187p. (gr. 10 up). 1991. Repr. of 1941 ed. 35.00 *(1-56416-019-X)* Derrydale Pr.
Lassen, Cary P. Big Busy Building. Reasoner, Chuck. 5p. (gr. k-3). 1993. bds. 9.95 *(0-8431-3659-6)* Price Stern.
Latella, Lisa. A Song for the Prince. Latella, Lisa. 36p. (Orig.). (gr. k up). 1984. pap. write for info. *(0-9608592-1-7)* Gallery Arts.
Lathrop, Dorothy. Animals of the Bible. Lathrop, Dorothy B. Fish, Helen D., selected by. LC 86-46118. 68p. (ps-up). 1937. 16.00 *(0-397-31536-8,* Lipp Jr Bks); PLB 15.89 *(0-397-30047-6)* HarpC Child Bks.
Lathrop, Dorothy P. Hitty: Her First Hundred Years. Field, Rachel. LC 29-22704. 220p. (gr. 4-6). 1969. SBE 14.95 *(0-02-734840-7,* Macmillan Child Bk) Macmillan Child Grp.
Lathwell, Alan. Where Have All the Colours Gone? Courtney, Jane. 1990. 29.00x *(0-85439-407-9,* Pub. by St Paul Pubns UK) St Mut.

Latterman, Terry. Little Joe, a Hopi Indian Boy, Learns a Hopi Indian Secret. Latterman, Terry. Hawkins, Mary E., ed. LC 85-61836. 32p. (gr. 4-12). 1985. 12.95 *(0-934739-01-3)* Pussywillow Pub.
Lattermen, Terry. The Watermelon Treat. Latterman, Terry. Hawkins, Mary E., ed. LC 85-63266. 48p. (gr. 1-4). 1987. 8.95 *(0-934739-03-X)*; pap. 5.95 *(0-934739-04-8)* Pussywillow Pub.
Lattimer, Evan. Be Kind to Animals! Duffy, James. LC 88-80281. 24p. (gr. k-3). 1988. *(0-307-10285-8)* Western Pub.
Lattimore, Deborah L. Dragon's Robe. Lattimore, Deborah N. LC 89-34512. 32p. (gr. 1-5). 1993. pap. 4.95 *(0-06-443321-8,* Trophy) HarpC Child Bks.
Lattimore, Deborah N. The Dragon's Robe. Lattimore, Deborah N. LC 89-34512. 32p. (gr. 1-5). 1990. 15.00 *(0-06-023719-8)*; PLB 14.89 *(0-06-023723-6)* HarpC Child Bks.
—The Flame of Peace: A Tale of the Aztecs. Lattimore, Deborah N. LC 86-26934. 48p. (gr. k-3). 1987. PLB 12.89 *(0-06-023709-0)* HarpC Child Bks.
—The Flame of Peace: A Tale of the Aztecs. Lattimore, Deborah N. LC 86-26934. 48p. (ps-3). 1991. pap. 5.95 *(0-06-443272-6,* Trophy) HarpC Child Bks.
—The Prince & the Golden Ax: A Minoan Tale. Lattimore, Deborah N. LC 87-121193. 40p. (gr. k-3). 1988. PLB 12.89 *(0-06-023716-3)* HarpC Child Bks.
—The Sailor Who Captured the Sea. Lattimore, Deborah N. LC 89-26937. 40p. (gr. 2-5). 1993. pap. 5.95 *(0-06-443342-0,* Trophy) HarpC Child Bks.
—The Sailor Who Captured the Sea: A Story of the Book of Kells. Lattimore, Deborah N. LC 89-26937. 40p. (gr. 2-5). 1991. 16.00 *(0-06-023710-4)*; PLB 15.89 *(0-06-023711-2)* HarpC Child Bks.
—Why There Is No Arguing in Heaven: A Mayan Myth. Lattimore, Deborah N. LC 87-35045. 40p. (gr. 1-5). 1989. PLB 13.89 *(0-06-023718-X)* HarpC Child Bks.
—The Winged Cat: A Tale of Ancient Egypt. Lattimore, Deborah N. LC 90-38441. 40p. (gr. 2-5). 1992. 15.00 *(0-06-023635-3)*; PLB 14.89 *(0-06-023636-1)* HarpC Child Bks.
—Zekmet the Stone Carver: A Tale of Ancient Egypt. Stolz, Mary. LC 86-22931. 32p. (gr. 2-5). 1988. 14.95 *(0-15-299961-2)* HarBrace.
Lattimore, Deborah N. & Hutchinson, William M. Castaways in Lilliput. Winterfeld, Henry. 220p. (gr. 3-7). 1990. pap. 4.95 *(0-15-214822-1,* Odyssey) HarBrace.
—Trouble at Timpetill. Winterfeld, Henry. 199p. (gr. 3-7). 1990. pap. 4.95 *(0-15-290786-6,* Odyssey) HarBrace.
Lattimore, Eleanor F. Little Pear. Lattimore, Eleanor F. LC 31-22069. (gr. 2-5). 1968. pap. 3.95 *(0-15-652799-5,* Voyager Bks) HarBrace.
Laubenstein, Jeff & Bradstreet, Tim. Native American Nations: A Shadowrun Sourcebook, Vol. 1. Findley, Nigel D. Ippolito, Donna & Mulvihill, Sharon T., eds. 136p. (gr. 7 up). 1991. pap. 12.00 *(1-55560-130-8,* 7202) FASA Corp.
Lauck, Dawn. Mountains, Meadows, & More: A Book about Places God Has Made. Gunn, Robin J. LC 93-9990. 1994. write for info. *(0-7814-0101-1,* Chariot Bks) Cook.
Laufer, Diana. Hide & Seek. Laufer, Diana. 12p. (gr. 1-4). 1994. lift-a-flap 9.95 *(0-8431-3591-3)* Price Stern.
Laughlin, Christopher. The Building Blocks of Self-Esteem. Shapiro, Lawrence E. 108p. (Orig.). (gr. k-4). 1993. pap. 9.95 *(1-882732-08-1)* Ctr Applied Psy.
Laughlin, Denise D. The Little Pine Tree's Christmas Dream. Thomson, Clarence. LC 93-5301. 32p. (Orig.). (gr. 1-6). 1993. pap. 4.95 *(0-8091-6614-3)* Paulist Pr.
Laughlin, Mary J. ABCs of Texas Wildflowers. Grimmer, Glenna. Roberts, M, ed. 64p. (gr. 2-5). 1982. 9.95 *(0-89015-358-2)* Eakin-Sunbelt.
Launching Pad Studio, Inc. Staff. Alphabet Pal. Buschemeyer, Robin Q. 64p. (Orig.). (ps-3). 1986. pap. 2.99 *(0-935609-01-6)* Eduplay.
—Word Pal. Buschemeyer, Robin Q. 40p. (Orig.). (ps-3). 1986. pap. 2.99 *(0-935609-00-8)* Eduplay.
Launching Pad Studio Inc. Staff. Number Pal. Buschemeyer, Robin Q. 40p. (Orig.). (ps-3). 1986. pap. 2.99 *(0-935609-02-4)* Eduplay.
Laur, Calvin. My Mom, the Sailor. Taylor, Norra. 1992. 12.95 *(0-533-10302-9)* Vantage.
Laurent, Richard. A Different Tune. Witty, Bruce. Hoffman, Joan, ed. 32p. (gr. k-2). 1987. wkbk. 1.99 *(0-88743-103-8,* 02603) Sch Zone Pub Co.
Laurent, Richard & Pape, Richard. The Fox, the Goose & the Corn: Reading Workbook. Gregorich, Barbara. Hoffman, Joan, ed. 32p. (Orig.). (gr. k-2). 1988. 1.99 *(0-88743-107-0)* Sch Zone Pub Co.
Lauter, Richard. The Fourth-Grade Dinosaur Club. Bograd, Larry. LC 88-22876. (gr. 3 up). 1989. 13.95 *(0-440-50128-8)* Delacorte.
—The War with Grandpa. Smith, Robert K. LC 83-14366. 128p. (gr. 4-8). 1984. pap. 12.95 *(0-385-29314-3)* Delacorte.
—The War with Grandpa. Smith, Robert K. 128p. (gr. 5-9). 1984. pap. 3.99 *(0-440-49276-9,* YB) Dell.
Lautermilch, John. B-I-B-L-E That's the Book for Me! Lynn, Claire. 18p. (Orig.). (ps-1). 1981. pap. 1.00 *(0-89323-013-8)* Bible Memory.
—The Bible ABCs: A Memory Book for Boys & Girls ages 3-5. BMA Staff. 54p. (ps). 1980. pap. text ed. 4.95 *(0-89323-051-0)* Bible Memory.
—Bible Animal Stories, Bk. 1. Wolf, Bob. 86p. (gr. 2-7). 1983. pap. 2.00 *(0-89323-044-8)* Bible Memory.
—Bible Bees. Ellis, Joyce & Lynn, Claire. 36p. (gr. k). 1981. 2.95 *(0-89323-049-9)* Bible Memory.

—David Livingstone, Missionary to Africa. Bostrom, Alice. 32p. (Orig.). 1982. pap. 1.30 (*0-89323-027-8*) Bible Memory.
—Knowing Christ Song. Montgomery, Dorothy. 19p. (gr. k-6). 1981. visualized song 2.99 (*3-90117-025-1*) CEF Press.
—Tommy Learns about Time & Eternity. Buck, Peggy J. 68p. (Orig.). (gr. 1-3). 1980. pap. 1.25 (*0-89323-006-5, 023*) Bible Memory.
—Uncle Bob's Bible Stories. Wolf, Bob. 108p. (Orig.). (gr. 4-8). 1982. pap. 1.50 (*0-89323-028-6*) Bible Memory.
Lautermilch, John & Fearber, Sharon. Build on the Rock. Lynn, Claire, compiled by. 52p. (Orig.). (ps-7). 1979. pap. 1.25 (*0-89323-000-6, 707*) Bible Memory.
Lavallee, Barbara. Mama, Do You Love Me? Joosse, Barbara M. 32p. (ps-1). 1991. 13.95 (*0-87701-759-X*) Chronicle Bks.
—This Place Is Cold. Cobb, Vicki. (gr. 2-4). 1989. 14.95 (*0-8027-6852-0*); PLB 13.85 (*0-8027-6853-9*) Walker & Co.
—This Place Is Cold. Cobb, Vicki. 32p. (gr. 2-5). 1990. pap. 7.95 (*0-8027-7340-0*) Walker & Co.
—This Place Is Dry. Cobb, Vicki. (gr. 2-4). 1989. 12.95 (*0-8027-6854-7*); PLB 13.85 (*0-8027-6855-5*) Walker & Co.
—This Place Is Dry. Cobb, Vicki. 32p. (Orig.). (gr. 2-5). 1993. pap. 6.95 (*0-8027-7400-8*) Walker & Co.
—This Place Is High. Cobb, Vicki. 32p. (gr. 2-4). 1989. 12.95 (*0-8027-6882-2*); PLB 13.85 (*0-8027-6883-0*) Walker & Co.
—This Place Is Lonely. Cobb, Vicki. 32p. (gr. 7-8). 1991. 13.95 (*0-8027-6959-4*); lib. bdg. 14.85 (*0-8027-6960-8*) Walker & Co.
—This Place Is Wet. Cobb, Vicki. 32p. (gr. 2-4). 1989. 12.95 (*0-8027-6880-6*); PLB 13.85 (*0-8027-6881-4*) Walker & Co.
—This Place Is Wet. Cobb, Vicki. 32p. (Orig.). (gr. 2-5). 1993. pap. 6.95 (*0-8027-7399-0*) Walker & Co.
Lavallee, Barbara & Shtainmets, Leon. The Snow Child. Littledale, Freya. 32p. (gr. 2-5). 1989. pap. 2.50 (*0-590-42141-7*) Scholastic Inc.
Lavarello, Jose M. Aladdin's Lamp: A Classic Tale. Jose, Eduard, adapted by. Suire, Diane D., tr. from SPA. LC 88-35312. 32p. (gr. 1-4). 1988. PLB 19.95 (*0-89565-481-4*); PLB 13.95s.p. (*0-685-56030-9*) Childs World.
—The Emperor's Nightingale: A Classic Tale. Andersen, Hans Christian. Jose, Eduard, adapted by. Moncure, Jane B., tr. from SPA. LC 88-35209. 32p. (gr. 1-4). 1988. PLB 19.95 (*0-89565-484-9*); PLB 13.95s.p. (*0-685-56034-1*) Childs World.
—Fearless John: A Classic Tale. Jose, Eduard, adapted by. Moncure, Jane B., tr. LC 88-35215. 32p. (gr. 1-4). 1988. PLB 19.95 (*0-89565-470-9*); PLB 13.95s.p. (*0-685-56038-4*) Childs World.
—Goldilocks & the Three Bears: A Classic Tale. Jose, Eduard, adapted by. McDonnell, Janet, tr. LC 88-36870. 32p. (gr. 1-4). 1988. PLB 19.95 (*0-89565-465-2*); PLB 13.95s.p. (*0-685-56047-3*) Childs World.
—The Little Mermaid: A Classic Tale. Andersen, Hans Christian. Jose, Eduard, adapted by. Moncure, Jane B., tr. LC 88-36869. 32p. (gr. 1-4). 1988. PLB 19.95 (*0-89565-477-6*); PLB 13.95s.p. (*0-685-56045-7*) Childs World.
—Little Red Riding Hood: A Classic Tale. Perrault, Charles. Jose, Eduard, ed. Moncure, Jane B., tr. LC 88-37088. 32p. (gr. 1-4). 1988. PLB 19.95 (*0-89565-457-1*); PLB 13.95s.p. (*0-685-56027-9*) Childs World.
—Ricky the Tuft: A Classic Tale. Perrault, Charles. Jose, Eduard, adapted by. Moncure, Jane B., tr. from SPA. LC 88-36792. 32p. (gr. 1-4). 1988. PLB 19.95 (*0-89565-473-3*); PLB 13.95s.p. (*0-685-56041-4*) Childs World.
Lavie, Arlette. Who Cares about Animal Rights? Twinn, M. LC 92-10852. 1992. 7.95 (*0-85953-358-1*, Pub. by Childs Play UK) Childs Play.
Lavies, Bianca. Compost Critters. Lavies, Bianca. LC 92-35651. 32p. (gr. 2-6). 1993. 14.99 (*0-525-44763-6*, DCB) Dutton Child Bks.
Lavies, Bianca, photos by. The Atlantic Salmon. Lavies, Bianca. LC 91-27990. 32p. (gr. 2-5). 1992. 14.50 (*0-525-44860-8*, DCB) Dutton Child Bks.
—A Gathering of Garter Snakes. Lavies, Bianca. 32p. (gr. 3 up). 1993. reinforced bdg. 14.99 (*0-525-45099-8*, DCB) Dutton Child Bks.
—Lily Pad Pond. Lavies, Bianca. LC 88-31697. 32p. (ps-2). 1989. 14.00 (*0-525-44483-1*, DCB) Dutton Child Bks.
—Mangrove Wilderness: Nature's Nursery. Lavies, Bianca. 32p. (gr. 4 up). 1994. 15.99 (*0-525-45186-2*, DCB) Dutton Child Bks.
—Tree Trunk Traffic. Lavies, Bianca. LC 88-30001. 32p. (ps-2). 1989. 14.95 (*0-525-44495-5*, DCB) Dutton Child Bks.
—Wasps at Home. Lavies, Bianca. LC 90-27338. 32p. (gr. 2-5). 1991. 13.95 (*0-525-44704-0*, DCB) Dutton Child Bks.
LaVigne, Daniel. Outer Space & All That Junk. Gilden, Mel. LC 88-37110. 176p. (gr. 5-9). 1989. (Lipp Jr Bks); PLB 12.89 (*0-397-32307-7*, Lipp Jr Bks) HarpC Child Bks.
Lavis, Stephen. One Thousand & One Arabian Nights. McCaughrean, Geraldine. 260p. 1987. 18.95 (*0-19-274530-1*) OUP.

Lawhead, Steve. Howard Had a Hot Air Ballon. Lawhead, Steve. 32p. (gr. k-3). 1988. 7.99 (*0-7459-1268-0*) Lion USA.
—Howard Had a Shrinking Machine. Lawhead, Steve. 32p. (gr. k-3). 1988. 7.99 (*0-7459-1316-4*) Lion USA.
Lawler, Dan. Amazing Magnets. Adler, David. LC 82-17377. 32p. (gr. 3-6). 1983. PLB 10.59 (*0-89375-894-9*); pap. text ed. 2.95 (*0-89375-895-7*) Troll Assocs.
—Rocks & Minerals. Marcus, Elizabeth. LC 82-17424. 32p. (gr. 3-6). 1983. PLB 10.59 (*0-89375-876-0*); pap. text ed. 2.95 (*0-89375-877-9*) Troll Assocs.
Lawn, John. Daniel Boone: Frontier Adventures. Brandt, Keith. LC 82-15915. 48p. (gr. 4-6). 1983. PLB 10.79 (*0-89375-843-4*); pap. text ed. 3.50 (*0-89375-844-2*) Troll Assocs.
—Fire Fighter. Pellowski, Michael J. LC 88-10353. 32p. (gr. 1-3). 1989. PLB 10.89 (*0-8167-1428-2*); pap. text ed. 2.95 (*0-8167-1429-0*) Troll Assocs.
—Flatboats on the Ohio: Westward Bound. Chambers, Catherine E. LC 83-18278. 32p. (gr. 5-9). 1984. PLB 11.59 (*0-8167-0049-4*); pap. text ed. 2.95 (*0-8167-0050-8*) Troll Assocs.
—Indiana Days: Life in a Frontier Town. Chambers, Catherine E. LC 83-18283. 32p. (gr. 5-9). 1984. PLB 11.59 (*0-8167-0055-9*); pap. text ed. 2.95 (*0-8167-0056-7*) Troll Assocs.
—Lewis & Clark. Sabin, Francene. LC 84-2642. 32p. (gr. 3-6). 1985. PLB 9.49 (*0-8167-0224-1*); pap. text ed. 2.95 (*0-8167-0225-X*) Troll Assocs.
—Lou Gehrig, Pride of the Yankees. Brandt, Keith. LC 85-1075. 48p. (gr. 4-6). 1986. lib. bdg. 10.79 (*0-8167-0549-6*); pap. text ed. 3.50 (*0-8167-0550-X*) Troll Assocs.
—The Masque of the Red Death. Poe, Edgar Allan. Cutts, David E., adapted by. LC 81-15959. 32p. (gr. 5-10). 1982. PLB 10.79 (*0-89375-620-2*); pap. text ed. 2.95 (*0-89375-621-0*); cassettes avail. Troll Assocs.
—The Monkey's Paw. Jacobs, W. W. Richardson, I. M., adapted by. LC 81-19824. 32p. (gr. 5-10). 1982. PLB 10.79 (*0-89375-628-8*); pap. text ed. 2.95 (*0-89375-629-6*) Troll Assocs.
—Robert E. Lee. Brandt, Keith. LC 84-2687. 32p. (gr. 3-6). 1985. PLB 9.49 (*0-8167-0278-0*); pap. text ed. 2.95 (*0-8167-0279-9*) Troll Assocs.
—Texas Roundup: Life on the Range. Chambers, Catherine E. LC 83-18281. 32p. (gr. 5-9). 1984. PLB 11.59 (*0-8167-0047-8*); pap. text ed. 2.95 (*0-8167-0048-6*) Troll Assocs.
—Wilbur & Orville Wright: The Flight to Adventure. Sabin, Louis. LC 82-15879. 48p. (gr. 4-6). 1983. PLB 10.79 (*0-89375-851-5*); pap. text ed. 3.50 (*0-89375-852-3*) Troll Assocs.
—Young Queen Elizabeth. Sabin, Francene. LC 89-33941. 48p. (gr. 4-6). 1990. PLB 10.79 (*0-8167-1785-0*); pap. text ed. 3.50 (*0-8167-1786-9*) Troll Assocs.
Lawrence, George, et al. Best Short Stories, Middle Level. Harris, Raymond. (gr. 6-10). 1983. text ed. 16.50 (*0-89061-322-2*, 793H); pap. text ed. 12.95 (*0-89061-321-4*, 793) Jamestown Pubs.
Lawrence, Grace. Poetry with a Purpose. Malley, Barbara & Allen, Frances. 128p. (gr. 4-7). 1987. pap. 10.95 (*0-86653-415-6*, GA 1018) Good Apple.

Lawrence, Jacob. John Brown: One Man Against Slavery. Everett, Gwen. LC 92-41973. 32p. (gr. 5 up). 1993. 15.95 (*0-8478-1702-4*) Rizzoli Intl.
JOHN BROWN is the story of the famous abolitionist told from the viewpoint of his young daughter, Annie. John Brown's legendary fight against slavery electrified the nation & moved it closer to Civil War on the night of October 16, 1859, when he led a raid on the U.S. Government Arsenal in Harper's Ferry, Virginia. Gwen Everett, author of award winning LI'L SIS & UNCLE WILLIE (Rizzoli, 1992), recounts Brown's sincere conviction that all people are equal, regardless of skin color. By capturing the events through Annie's eyes, Everett allows young readers to explore contemporary issues & to examine questions of might versus morality. Was it right for one man to seek a positive change through murder & bloodshed? Were there alternatives? Can one person fight a corrupt system? A stunning series of gouache paintings created in 1941 by renowned African-American artist Jacob Lawrence illustrates this valuable new book. Throughout his career, he has often worked in series dealing with historical

& social issues, recording the triumphs & tragedies of African-Americans. The JOHN BROWN sequence is featured here for the first time in book format. His dramatic compositions radiate with the intensity & intrigue of this riveting chapter in American history. "A powerful presentation...the gouaches are captivating."--Kirkus Reviews (Pointer.)
Publisher Provided Annotation.

Lawrence, John. Christmas on Exeter Street. Hendry, Diana. LC 89-45256. 32p. (gr. k-3). 1989. PLB 13.99 (*0-679-90134-5*) Knopf Bks Yng Read.
—Emily's Own Elephant. Pearce, Philippa. LC 87-14039. 32p. (gr. k-3). 1988. 11.95 (*0-688-07678-5*); lib. bdg. 11.88 (*0-688-07679-3*) Greenwillow.
—King of Kings. Hill, Susan. LC 92-54624. 32p. (ps up). 1993. 14.95 (*1-56402-210-2*) Candlewick Pr.
—Poems for the Young. Philip, Neil, compiled by. LC 92-344. 96p. 1992. 19.95 (*1-55670-262-0*) Stewart Tabori & Chang.
—Shades of Green. Harvey, Anne. LC 91-15234. 192p. 1992. 18.00 (*0-688-10890-3*) Greenwillow.
—The Word Party. Edwards, Richard. LC 91-26919. 80p. (gr. k-3). 1992. 13.50 (*0-385-30620-2*) Delacorte.
Lawrence, Terry. Tales of a Nebraska Country Girl. Rystrom, Zella R. 48p. (Orig.). (gr. 6-12). 1988. pap. 4.95 (*0-936015-18-7*) Pocahontas Pr.
Lawrie, Robin. See How It Works: Cars. Potter, Tony. 28p. (ps-3). 1989. Repr. of 1989 ed. POB 7.95 (*0-689-71303-7*, Aladdin) Macmillan Child Grp.
—See How It Works: Earth Movers. Potter, Tony. 28p. (ps-3). 1989. Repr. of 1989 ed. POB 7.95 (*0-689-71302-9*, Aladdin) Macmillan Child Grp.
—See How It Works: Planes. Potter, Tony. 28p. (ps-3). 1989. Repr. of 1989 ed. POB 7.95 (*0-689-71304-5*, Aladdin) Macmillan Child Grp.
—See How It Works: Trucks. Potter, Tony. 28p. (ps-3). 1989. Repr. of 1989 ed. POB 7.95 (*0-689-71301-0*, Aladdin) Macmillan Child Grp.
Lawson, Jim. Teenage Mutant Ninja Turtles: The Secret of the Ooze - Movie Adaptation. Clarrain, Dean & Lawson, Jim. 64p. (Orig.). 1991. pap. 5.95 (*1-879450-08-9*) Tundra MA.
Lawson, Jim & Burger, Dan. Teenage Mutant Ninja Turtles Totally Awesome Activity Book. Greene, Shelley. 96p. (gr. 1-5). 1990. pap. 3.95 (*0-679-81108-7*) Random Bks Yng Read.
Lawson, Laura. Beary, Beary, Quite Contrary. Graf, Rosanna & Graf, Virginia. Date not set. pap. 9.50 (*1-882788-02-8*) VanGar Pubs.
Lawson, Robert. Adam of the Road. Gray, Elizabeth J. 320p. (gr. 4-8). 1942. pap. 15.95 (*0-670-10435-3*) Viking Child Bks.
—Adam of the Road. Gray, Elizabeth J. (gr. 3-7). 1987. pap. 4.99 (*0-14-032464-X*, Puffin) Puffin Bks.
—Ben & Me. Lawson, Robert. 1939p. (gr. 7-10). 1988. 15.95 (*0-316-51732-1*); pap. 5.95 (*0-316-51730-5*) Little.
—El Cuento de Ferdinando. Leaf, Munro. Belpre, Pura, tr. (SPA.). 72p. (ps-3). 1962. pap. 13.00 (*0-670-25065-1*) Viking Child Bks.
—El Cuento de Ferdinando: The Story of Ferdinand. Leaf, Munro. Belpre, Pura, tr. (SPA.). 72p. (ps-3). 1990. pap. 4.50 (*0-14-054253-1*, Puffin) Puffin Bks.
—El Cuento de Ferdinando: (The Story of Ferdinand) Leaf, Munro. Belpre, Pura, tr. (gr. k-3). 1990. Set; incl. 4 bks., guide, & cass. incl. cass. 19.95 (*0-87499-189-7*); pap. 12.95 incl. cass. (*0-87499-188-9*); pap. 27.95 (*0-87499-191-9*) Live Oak Media.
—The Great Wheel. Lawson, Robert. 180p. 1993. pap. 7.95 (*0-8027-7392-3*) Walker & Co.
—Mr. Popper's Penguins. Atwater, Richard & Atwater, Florence. (gr. 3 up) 1938. 14.95 (*0-316-05842-4*) Little.
—Mr. Revere & I. Lawson, Robert. (gr. 7-10). 1953. 16.95 (*0-316-51739-9*) Little.
—Mr. Revere & I. Lawson, Robert. 152p. (gr. 3-6). 1988. pap. 5.95 (*0-316-51729-1*) Little.
—Rabbit Hill. Lawson, Robert. (gr. 4-6). 1944. pap. 14.00 (*0-670-58675-7*) Viking Child Bks.
—Robbut: A Tale of Tails. Lawson, Robert. LC 89-32367. 94p. (gr. 4-6). 1989. Repr. of 1948 ed. lib. bdg. 16.00 (*0-208-02236-8*, Linnet) Shoe String.
—The Story of Ferdinand. Leaf, Munro. LC 36-19452. (gr. k-3). 1936. 13.00 (*0-670-67424-9*) Viking Child Bks.
—The Story of Ferdinand. Leaf, Munro. (ps-3). 1988. pap. 9.95 (*0-14-095075-3*, Puffin); bk. & t-shirt 9.95 (*0-318-37105-7*, Puffin); bk. & cassette 6.95 (*0-318-37106-5*, Puffin) Puffin Bks.
—The Story of Ferdinand. Leaf, Munro. 1993. pap. 6.99 incl. cassette (*0-14-095115-6*, Puffin) Puffin Bks.
—The Story of Simpson & Sampson. Leaf, Munro. LC 88-39014. 64p. (gr. 1-3). 1989. Repr. of 1941 ed. lib. bdg. 16.50 (*0-208-02244-9*, Pub. by Linnet) Shoe String.
—They Were Strong & Good. Lawson, Robert. (gr. 4-6). 1940. pap. 14.00 (*0-670-69949-7*) Viking Child Bks.
—The Tough Winter. Lawson, Robert. (gr. 3-7). 1979. pap. 3.95 (*0-14-031215-3*, Puffin) Puffin Bks.

Laycock, Mary, et al. Geoblocks & Geojackets: Metric Version. rev., 2nd ed. Laycock, Mary, et al. 96p. (Orig.). (gr. 3-10). 1988. pap. 8.95 (*0-918932-91-2*) Activity Resources.

Layerfeld, Karl. The Emperor's New Clothes. Andersen, Hans Christian. 1992. 40.00 (*0-87113-527-2*) Grove-Atltic.

Lazare, Jerry. Home from Far. Little, Jean. (gr. 5 up). 1989. 14.95 (*0-316-52792-0*); pap. 4.95 (*0-316-52802-1*) Little.

Lazarevich, Mila. Do Your Ears Hang Low? Glazer, Tom. LC 78-20072. 96p. (gr. 1-3). 1980. 12.95 (*0-385-12602-6*) Doubleday.

Lazor-Bahr, Beverly. An American Tail: The Illustrated Story. Dubowski, Cathy E. LC 91-70104. 48p. (ps-3). 1991. 9.95 (*0-448-40211-4*, G&D) Putnam Pub Group.
—Fievel Saves the Day. LC 90-85174. 14p. (ps). 1991. 5.95 (*0-448-41075-3*, G&D) Putnam Pub Group.
—Fievel the Hero. LC 90-85299. 14p. (ps). 1991. 4.95 (*0-448-41080-X*, G&D) Putnam Pub Group.
—Fievel's Big Showdown. Herman, Gail. Kirschner, David, created by. 32p. (ps-3). 1992. pap. 3.50 (*0-448-40392-7*, G&D) Putnam Pub Group.
—We're Back! The Illustrated Story. Korman, Justine. 48p. (ps-3). 1993. 9.95 (*0-448-40444-3*, G&D) Putnam Pub Group.
—Westward, Ho! LC 90-85298. 14p. (ps). 1991. 4.95 (*0-448-41081-8*, G&D) Putnam Pub Group.

Lazzarino, Luciano. Los Apache. McCall, Barbara A. Marcuse, Aida E., tr. from SPA. LC 92-12177. 1992. 17.26 (*0-86625-454-4*); 12.95s.p. (*0-685-59386-X*) Rourke Pubns.

Lazzarino, Luciano & Palacios, Argentina. Hans Christian Andersen, Vida de Cuento de Hadas. Cote, Elizabeth. LC 92-9534. (SPA.). 1992. PLB 14.60 (*0-86593-186-0*); 10.95s.p. (*0-685-59299-5*) Rourke Corp.

Lazzaro, Victor. The Narrowest Bar Mitzvah. Schnur, Steven. 48p. (Orig.). (gr. 4-6). 1986. pap. text ed. 6.95 (*0-8074-0316-4*, 123923) UAHC.
—The Return of Morris Schumsky. Schnur, Steven. 48p. (gr. 4-6). 1987. pap. 6.95 (*0-8074-0358-X*, 123927) UAHC.

Leach, Carol. Just for Kids: The New England Guide & Activity Book for Young Travelers. Frost, Ed & Frost, Roon. 150p. (Orig.). (ps-5). 1989. pap. 7.95 (*0-9618806-2-7*) Glove Compart Bks.
—The Kids' Holiday Book: Activities Through the Seasons. Frost, Ed & Frost, Roon. 176p. (Orig.). (ps-7). 1990. pap. 11.95 (*0-9618806-3-5*) Glove Compart Bks.

Leaf, Munro. Manners Can Be Fun. 2nd, rev. ed. Leaf, Munro. LC 84-48459. 48p. (gr. k-3). 1985. pap. 4.95 (*0-06-443053-7*, Trophy) HarpC Child Bks.

Leaf, Richard, jt. illus. see Esquivel, Jim.

Leak, Nancy M., jt. illus. see Harper, Ruth E.

Leake, Don. A Moment in Time. Rothman, Joel. LC 72-90693. 32p. (ps-2). 1973. 7.95 (*0-87592-034-9*) Scroll Pr.

Leamon, Tom. Poli - a Mexican Boy in Early Texas. Neugeboren, Jay. LC 88-64094. 120p. (gr. 7 up). 1992. pap. 7.95 (*0-931722-74-8*) Corona Pub.

Lear, Edward. A Book of Nonsense. Lear, Edward. LC 92-53176. 240p. 1992. 12.95 (*0-679-41798-2*, Evrymans Lib Childs Class) Knopf.
—The Complete Nonsense of Edward Lear. Lear, Edward. Jackson, H., intro. by. xxix, 287p. (gr. 4-6). pap. 5.95 (*0-486-20167-8*) Dover.
—Edward Lear: King of Nonsense. Kamen, Gloria. LC 89-28023. 80p. (gr. 2-7). 1990. SBE 13.95 (*0-689-31419-1*, Atheneum Child Bk) Macmillan Child Grp.

Learner, Vicki M. The Missing Snowman. Albee, Jo. 24p. (Orig.). (gr. k-1). 1990. pap. 0.99 (*1-878624-47-4*) McClanahan Bk.

Learner, Vickie. The Dress-up Parade. Herman, Emmi S. 24p. (ps-2). 1992. pap. 0.99 (*1-56293-112-1*) McClanahan Bk.

Learner, Vickie M. Hundred Million Reasons for Owning an Elephant: Or at Least a Dozen That I Can Think of Right Now. Grambling, Lois G. 32p. (ps). 1990. 6.95 (*0-8120-6189-6*) Barron.
—Willoughby Wallaby. 1987. pap. 6.99 incl. audiocassette (*0-553-45903-1*) Bantam.

Leary, Lory B. An Alaskan Child's Garden of Verse. Leary, Lory B. 40p. (Orig.). (gr. 6 up). 1989. pap. 6. 95 (*0-924663-02-2*) Alaskan Viewpoint.

Leatham, Moyra. The Three Hundred Ninety-Seventh White Elephant. Guillot, Rene. (gr. 3-7). 1957. 20.95 (*0-87599-043-6*) S G Phillips.

Leavitt, Fred. Lies (People Believe) about Animals. Sussman, Susan & James, Robert. Tucker, Kathleen, ed. LC 86-15949. 48p. (gr. 2-7). 1987. PLB 11.95 (*0-8075-4530-9*) A Whitman.

LeBaudour, RoseMarie. The True Story of Christmas. Cavendish, Mark P. 56p. (Orig.). (gr. 4 up). 1991. pap. 15.00 (*0-9628016-2-3*) Gentian Servs.

Lebenson, Richard. Merlin's Mistake. Newman, Robert. (gr. 5-9). 15.75 (*0-8446-6187-2*) Peter Smith.

LeBlanc, Andre. Parasaurolophus. Riehecky, Janet. 32p. (gr. k-4). 1990. PLB 21.35 (*0-89565-633-7*); PLB 14.95s.p. (*0-685-56218-2*) Childs World.

Le Blanc, L. Adrift on a Raft. Olsen, E. A. LC 68-16397. 48p. (gr. 3 up). 1970. PLB 10.95 (*0-87783-000-2*); pap. 3.94 deluxe ed. (*0-87783-078-9*); cassette 10.60x (*0-87783-176-9*) Oddo.
—Horny. Emery, C. F. LC 68-17304. 48p. (gr. 2 up). 1967. PLB 9.26 (*0-87783-017-7*) Oddo.

—Killer in the Trap. Olsen, E. A. LC 68-16399. 48p. (gr. 3 up). 1970. PLB 10.95 (*0-87783-019-3*); pap. 3.94 deluxe ed. (*0-87783-097-5*); cassette 10.60x (*0-87783-190-4*) Oddo.
—Little Frog Learns to Sing. Le Blanc, L. LC 68-16394. 32p. (ps-2). 1967. PLB 9.95 (*0-87783-022-3*) cassette 7.94x (*0-87783-191-2*) Oddo.
—Where Is Duckling Three? Green, I. LC 68-16402. 32p. (gr. 1-2). 1967. PLB 9.95 (*0-87783-048-7*) Oddo.

LeBlanc, Lorraine. Bernard et Bridget: a la cabane a sucre. Gaudreau, Carmen. (FRE.). 40p. (gr. k-1). 1979. pap. text ed. 1.50 (*0-91409-47-5*); of 53 2x2 slides 13.25 set (*0-686-42727-0*) Natl Mat Dev.

Le Cain, Erro. The Lotus & the Grail: Legends from East to East. Harris, Rosemary. 272p. (gr. 7 up). 1985. pap. 7.95 (*0-571-13536-6*) Faber & Faber.

Le Cain, Errol. Aladdin. Keene, Andrew. 32p. (gr. k-3). 1983. pap. 4.95 (*0-14-050389-7*, Puffin) Puffin Bks.
—Alfi & the Dark. Meiles, Sally. LC 88-1043. 32p. (ps-1). 1988. 13.95 (*0-87701-527-9*) Chronicle Bks.
—Child in the Bamboo Grove. Harris, Rosemary. LC 72-4064. (gr. 1-3). 1972. 21.95 (*0-87599-194-7*) S G Phillips.
—Cinderella; or, The Little Glass Slipper. Perrault, Charles. (gr. 1 up). 1977. pap. 3.95 (*0-14-050137-1*, Puffin) Puffin Bks.
—Growltiger's Last Stand & Other Poems. Eliot, T. S. 32p. (ps up). 1987. 14.00 (*0-374-32809-9*, Co-pub. by HarBraceJ) FS&G.
—Growltigers Last Stand & Other Poems. Eliot, T. S. (ps up). 1990. pap. 4.95 (*0-374-42811-5*) FS&G.
—Hiawatha's Childhood. Longfellow, Henry Wadsworth. 32p. (gr. k up). 1984. 15.00 (*0-374-33065-4*) FS&G.

LeCain, Errol. Hiawatha's Childhood. Longfellow, Henry Wadsworth. (ps-3). 1987. pap. 3.99 (*0-14-050562-8*, Puffin) Puffin Bks.

Le Cain, Errol. Mr. Mistoffelees with Mungojerrie & Rumpelteazer. Eliot, T. S. Howton, Louise, ed. 32p. (ps up). 1991. 13.95 (*0-15-256230-3*) HarBrace.
—The Pied Piper of Hamelin. Corrin, Stephen & Corrin, Sara, eds. 32p. (ps-5). 1989. 14.95 (*0-15-261596-2*, HB Juv Bks) HarBrace.
—The Snow Queen. Andersen, Hans Christian. Lewis, Naomi, adapted by. (ps-3). 1982. pap. 3.95 (*0-14-050294-7*, Puffin) Puffin Bks.

LeDee, Kim. Children's Bible Stories with Questions. Matthews, Graham P., Jr. LC 93-19623. (gr. 3 up). 1993. write for info. (*0-910683-18-2*) Townsnd Pr.

Leder, Dora. Day Care ABC. Phillips, Tamara. Levine, Abby, ed. LC 88-33911. (ps-2). 1989. PLB 13.95 (*0-8075-1483-7*) A Whitman.
—Don't Touch! Kline, Suzy. Tucker, Kathleen, ed. LC 85-612. 32p. (ps-1). 1985. 13.95 (*0-8075-1707-0*) A Whitman.
—Don't Touch! Kline, Suzy. 32p. (gr. 2-6). 1988. pap. 3.95 (*0-14-050861-9*, Puffin) Puffin Bks.
—God's Gifts. Beringer, Joan E. LC 81-82908. 32p. (gr. k-3). 1984. 8.95 (*0-87510-160-7*) Christian Sci.
—I Know What I Like. Simon, Norma. LC 76-165822. (ps-2). 1971. PLB 11.95 (*0-8075-3507-9*) A Whitman.
—I'm Busy, Too. Simon, Norma. Tucker, Kathleen, ed. LC 79-18374. (ps-1). 1980. PLB 11.95 (*0-8075-3464-1*) A Whitman.
—Julian's Glorious Summer. Cameron, Ann. LC 86-33828. 64p. (gr. 2-4). 1987. lib. bdg. 6.99 (*0-394-99117-6*); 2.50 (*0-394-89117-1*) Random Bks Yng Read.
—Let's Peek in Santa's Pack. LC 89-61375. 14p. (ps). 1990. bds. 2.95 (*0-679-80277-0*) Random Bks Yng Read.
—Mama Cat's Year. Simon, Norma. Tucker, Kathleen, ed. LC 90-26825. 32p. (ps-3). 1991. 14.95 (*0-8075-4958-4*) A Whitman.
—Nobody's Perfect, Not Even My Mother. Simon, Norma. Tucker, Kathleen, ed. LC 81-520. 32p. (gr. k-3). 1981. PLB 11.95 (*0-8075-5707-2*) A Whitman.
—Oh, That Cat! Simon, Norma. LC 85-15546. 32p. (ps-4). 1986. 11.95 (*0-8075-5919-9*) A Whitman.
—Ooops! Kline, Suzy. Fay, Ann, ed. LC 87-25429. 32p. (ps-2). 1988. PLB 13.95 (*0-8075-6122-3*) A Whitman.
—Ooops! Kline, Suzy. 32p. (ps). 1989. pap. 3.95 (*0-14-050986-0*, Puffin) Puffin Bks.
—The Plum Tree War. Pryor, Bonnie. LC 88-32426. 128p. (gr. 3-6). 1989. 11.95 (*0-688-08142-8*) Morrow Jr Bks.
—The Plum Tree War. Pryor, Bonnie. (gr. 4-7). 1992. pap. 3.25 (*0-440-40619-6*, Pub. by Yearling Classics) Dell.
—Why Am I Different? Simon, Norma. Rubin, Caroline, ed. LC 76-41172. 32p. (gr. k-2). 1976. PLB 11.95 (*0-8075-9074-6*) A Whitman.
—Will Dad Ever Move Back Home? Hogan, Paula Z. Muir, Martha F., intro. by. LC 79-24058. 32p. (gr. k-6). 1980. PLB 17.96 (*0-8172-1356-2*) Raintree Steck-V.

Lederer, Ilene W. Kind Little Rivka. Rosenfeld, Dina. 32p. (ps-1). 1991. 8.95 (*0-922613-44-3*); pap. 6.95 (*0-922613-45-1*) Hachai Pubns.
—A Little Boy Named Avram. Rosenfeld, Dina. 32p. (ps-1). 1989. 8.95 (*0-922613-08-7*); pap. 6.95 (*0-922613-09-5*) Hachai Pubns.

Lederman, Diana. Make-Me-a-Match. 1992. spiral bdg. 4.95 (*965-229-025-4*, Pub. by Gefen Pub Hse IS) Gefen Bks.

Ledet, Billy. Grandma Was a Sailmaker: Tales of the Cajun Wetlands. Pitre, Verne. 160p. (Orig.). (gr. 9). 1991. pap. 12.95 (*0-9621724-5-6*) Blue Heron LA.

Lee, Alan. Black Ships Before Troy. Sutcliff, Rosemary. LC 92-38782. (gr. 4 up). 1993. 19.95 (*0-385-31069-2*) Delacorte.
—Merlin Dreams. Dickinson, Peter. LC 88-3985. 160p. (gr. k-12). 1988. 19.95 (*0-440-50067-2*) Delacorte.
—Puppet Show. Peters, Sharon. 32p. (gr. k-2). 1980. PLB 7.89 (*0-89375-385-8*); pap. 1.95 (*0-89375-286-X*) Troll Assocs.

Lee, Alana. Una Funcion De Titeres. Peters, Sharon. (SPA.). 32p. (gr. k-2). 1981. PLB 7.89 (*0-89375-551-6*); pap. 1.95 (*0-685-42387-5*) Troll Assocs.

Lee, Brian. Ghost Train: A Spooky Hologram Book. Wyllie, Stephen. LC 91-15719. 24p. (gr. k). 1992. 18.00 (*0-8037-1163-8*) Dial Bks Young.

Lee, Connell. Ducks. Gaw, Robyn. LC 92-31915. 1993. 4.25 (*0-383-03567-8*) SRA Schl Grp.

Lee, Dom. Baseball Saved Us. Mochizuki, Ken. LC 92-73215. 32p. (gr. k-8). 1993. 14.95 (*1-880000-01-6*) Lee & Low Bks.

Lee, Jan. Angel Island Prisoner. Chetin, Helen. Harvey, Catherine, tr. LC 82-51170. (CHI & ENG.). (gr. 3 up). 1982. 7.95 (*0-938678-09-4*) New Seed.

Lee, Jared. The Bully Brothers: Gobblin' Halloween. Thaler, Mike. LC 92-34197. 32p. (ps-3). 1993. pap. 2.25 (*0-448-40158-4*, G&D) Putnam Pub Group.
—The Bully Brothers Trick the Tooth Fairy. Thaler, Mike. LC 92-72834. 32p. (ps-3). 1993. pap. 2.25 (*0-448-40519-9*, G&D) Putnam Pub Group.
—Camp Rottentime. Thaler, Mike. LC 92-3231. 32p. (ps-3). 1993. PLB 9.79 (*0-8167-3024-5*); pap. 2.95 (*0-8167-3025-3*) Troll Assocs.
—Cannon the Librarian. Thaler, Mike. 32p. (Orig.). 1993. pap. 3.50 (*0-380-76964-6*, Camelot Young) Avon.
—Fang the Dentist. Thaler, Mike. LC 92-18594. 32p. (ps-3). 1993. PLB 9.79 (*0-8167-3020-2*); pap. 2.95 (*0-8167-3021-0*) Troll Assocs.
—A Hippopotamus Ate the Teacher. Thaler, Mike. 32p. 1981. pap. 2.95 (*0-380-78048-8*, Camelot) Avon.
—My Cat Is Going to the Dogs. Thaler, Mike. LC 92-18596. 32p. (ps-3). 1993. PLB 9.79 (*0-8167-3022-9*); pap. 2.95 (*0-8167-3023-7*) Troll Assocs.

Lee, Jeanne M. Ba-Nam. Lee, Jeanne M. LC 86-27127. 32p. (ps-2). 1987. 13.95 (*0-8050-0169-7*, Bks Young Read) H Holt & Co.
—Legend of the Li River: An Ancient Chinese Tale. Lee, Jeanne M. LC 83-79. 32p. (ps-2). 1983. 11.95 (*0-03-063523-3*, Bks Young Read) H Holt & Co.
—The Legend of the Milky Way. Lee, Jeanne M., retold by. LC 81-6906. 32p. (ps-2). 1982. 14.95 (*0-8050-0217-0*, Bks Young Read) H Holt & Co.
—Legend of the Milky Way. Lee, Jeanne M. LC 81-6906. 32p. (ps-2). 1990. pap. 5.95 (*0-8050-1361-X*, Owlet BYR) H Holt & Co.
—Toad Is the Uncle of Heaven. Lee, Jeanne M., retold by. LC 85-5639. 32p. (ps-2). 1985. 13.95 (*0-8050-1146-3*, Bks Young Read) H Holt & Co.
—Toad Is the Uncle of Heaven: A Vietnamese Folk Tale. Lee, Jeanne M., retold by. LC 85-5639. 32p. (ps-2). 1989. pap. 5.95 (*0-8050-1147-1*, Owlet BYR) H Holt & Co.

Lee, Jeff. And the Winner Is... A Book about Inner Beauty. Mitchell, Lorayne. 32p. (ps-4). 1987. PLB 12.95 (*0-943491-00-2*) Valued Pubns.
—Beautiful Feathers: A Book about Selflessness. Mitchell, Lorayne. 32p. (ps-4). 1987. PLB 12.95 (*0-943491-01-0*) Valued Pubns.
—The Shadow in the Window: A Book about Caring. Mitchell, Lorayne. 32p. (ps-4). 1987. PLB 12.95 (*0-943491-02-9*) Valued Pubns.

Lee, Jody. Anne of Green Gables. Montgomery, L. M. (gr. 4 up). 1983. deluxe ed. 13.95 (*0-448-06030-2*, G&D) Putnam Pub Group.

Lee, Katie. Black Bear Cub. Lind, Alan. LC 93-13130. 1994. 11.95 (*1-56899-030-8*) Soundprints.
—Puffin's Homecoming: The Story of an Atlantic Puffin. Bailer, Darice. Thomas, Peter, narrated by. LC 92-43762. 32p. (ps-3). 1993. 11.95 (*0-924483-90-3*); incl. audiocassette tape 16.95 (*0-924483-91-1*); incl. audiocassette tape & 7" toy 25.95 (*0-924483-92-X*); incl. audiocassette tape & 11" toy 39.95 (*0-924483-93-8*); audiocassette tape only avail. (*0-924483-94-6*) Soundprints.

Lee, Marlene K. Visit to the Attic. Welty, Harry R. LC 92-90838. 250p. (Orig.). (gr. 6-8). 1992. pap. 6.95 (*0-9632953-0-6*) Welty Pr.

Lee, Michael S. The Night Before Christmas in Hawaii. Moore, Clement C. 32p. 1991. text ed. write for info. (*0-9627294-2-6*) Hawaiian Resources.

Lee, Nancy. A Child's Life of Christ. Peterson, Esther A. 44p. (gr. 3-8). 1987. 6.95 (*1-55523-045-8*) Winston-Derek.
—From Africa to the Arctic: Five Explorers. Mumford, Donald & Mumford, Esther. 48p. (gr. 1-3). 1992. 9.95 (*0-9605670-6-2*) Ananse Pr.

Lee, Penny. Color Us Rational. Waters, Virginia. LC 78-71011. 73p. 1979. pap. 3.00 (*0-917476-15-8*) Inst Rational-Emotive.

Lee, Robert J. The Magic Pumpkin. Martin, Bill, Jr. & Archambault, John. LC 89-11162. 32p. (ps-2). 1989. 14.95 (*0-8050-1134-X*, Bks Young Read) H Holt & Co.
—The Wind in the Willows. Grahame, Kenneth. 256p. (gr. 1 up). 1969. pap. 3.25 (*0-440-49555-5*, YB) Dell.

Lee, Tommy. Modeling & You! Lee, Anna. 117p. (Orig.). (gr. 6-12). 1991. pap. 12.95 (*0-9629647-0-0*) CUE Pubns.

Lee, Vincent B., jt. photog. see Dunn, Phoebe.

Lee, Wendy K. One Small Girl. Chan, Jennifer L. LC 92-35423. 32p. (gr. k-2). 1993. 12.95 (*1-879965-05-4*) Polychrome Pub.

Leech, Dorothy. Stardust Otel. Janeczko, Paul B. LC 92-44514. 64p. (gr. 7 up). 1993. 14.95 (*0-531-05498-5*); lib. bdg. 14.99 (*0-531-08648-8*) Orchard Bks Watts.

Leedom, Valerie. Bible Trivia. Schlegl, William. 48p. (gr. 3 up). 1986. wkbk. 6.95 (*0-86653-368-0*, SS 883, Shining Star Pubns) Good Apple.

Leedy, Loreen. Big, Small, Short, Tall. Leedy, Loreen. LC 86-46203. 32p. (ps-3). 1987. reinforced bdg. 12.95 (*0-8234-0645-8*) Holiday.

—Blast off to Earth! A Look at Geography. Leedy, Loreen. LC 92-2567. 32p. (ps-3). 1992. reinforced bdg. 14.95 (*0-8234-0973-2*) Holiday.

—The Bunny Play. Leedy, Loreen. LC 87-17793. 32p. (ps-3). 1988. reinforced bdg. 12.95 (*0-8234-0679-2*) Holiday.

—The Dinosaur Princess & Other Prehistoric Riddles. Adler, David A. LC 87-25121. 64p. (gr. 1-4). 1988. reinforced bdg. 12.95 (*0-8234-0686-5*) Holiday.

—The Dragon ABC Hunt. Leedy, Loreen. LC 85-21907. 36p. (ps-1). 1986. reinforced bdg. 14.95 (*0-8234-0596-6*) Holiday.

—A Dragon Christmas: Things to Make & Do. Leedy, Loreen. LC 88-4635. 32p. (ps-3). 1988. reinforced bdg. 13.95 (*0-8234-0716-0*) Holiday.

—The Dragon Halloween Party. Leedy, Loreen. LC 86-286. 32p. (ps-3). 1986. reinforced bdg. 14.95 (*0-8234-0611-3*); pap. 5.95 (*0-8234-0765-9*) Holiday.

—The Dragon Thanksgiving Feast: Things to Make & Do. Leedy, Loreen. LC 90-55110. 32p. (ps-3). 1990. reinforced 14.95 (*0-8234-0828-0*) Holiday.

—Fraction Action. Leedy, Loreen. LC 93-22800. 32p. (gr. 4-8). 1994. 15.95 (*0-8234-1109-5*) Holiday.

—The Furry News - How to Create a Newspaper: A Reading Rainbow Feature Book. Leedy, Loreen. (ps-3). 1993. pap. 5.95 (*0-8234-1026-9*) Holiday.

—The Furry News: How to Make a Newspaper. Leedy, Loreen. LC 89-20094. 32p. (ps-3). 1990. reinforced bdg. 13.95 (*0-8234-0793-4*) Holiday.

—The Great Trash Bash. Leedy, Loreen. LC 90-46554. 32p. (ps-3). 1991. reinforced 14.95 (*0-8234-0869-8*) Holiday.

—Messages in the Mailbox: How to Write a Letter. Leedy, Loreen. LC 91-8718. 32p. (ps-3). 1991. reinforced 14.95 (*0-8234-0889-2*) Holiday.

—The Monster Money Book. Leedy, Loreen. LC 91-18168. 32p. (ps-3). 1992. reinforced bdg. 14.95 (*0-8234-0922-8*) Holiday.

—A Number of Dragons. Leedy, Loreen. LC 85-730. 32p. (ps-1). 1985. reinforced bdg. 14.95 (*0-8234-0568-0*) Holiday.

—Pingo the Plaid Panda. Leedy, Loreen. LC 88-17005. 32p. (ps-3). 1989. reinforced bdg. 13.95 (*0-8234-0727-6*) Holiday.

—The Potato Party & Other Troll Tales. Leedy, Loreen. LC 89-1746. 32p. (ps-3). 1989. reinforced 14.95 (*0-8234-0761-6*) Holiday.

—Waiting for Baby. Birdseye, Tom. LC 90-29076. 32p. (ps-3). 1991. reinforced 14.95 (*0-8234-0892-2*) Holiday.

Leeflang-Oudenarden, C. Tina's Island Home. Walsum-Quispel, J. van. LC 71-99920. 36p. (gr. k-5). 7.95 (*0-87592-053-5*) Scroll Pr.

Leek, Kenny. How to Be a Human Bean. Markels, Bobby. 24p. (gr. 3 up). 1989. pap. 3.50 (*1-880991-01-2*) Stone Pub.

Leeman, Michael. Morningtown Ride. Reynolds, Malvina. 20p. (ps-4). 1984. 10.95 (*0-931793-00-9*) Turn the Page.

Leer, Rebecca. And Now a Word from Our Sponsor. Hoobler, Dorothy & Hoobler, Thomas. 64p. (gr. 4-6). 1992. 11.95 (*0-382-24153-3*); PLB 13.98 (*0-382-24146-0*); pap. 7.95 (*0-382-24350-1*) Silver Burdett Pr.

—No Boys Allowed. Levinson, Marilyn. LC 93-22335. 128p. (gr. 5-8). 1993. PLB 13.95 (*0-8167-3135-7*); pap. write for info. (*0-8167-3136-5*) BrdgeWater.

Leeson, Pat, jt. illus. see Leeson, Tom.

Leeson, Pat, jt. photog. see Leeson, Tom.

Leeson, Tom & Leeson, Pat. Bears. Mattern, Joanne. LC 92-20176. 24p. (gr. 4-7). 1992. (Pub. by Watermill Pr); pap. 1.95 (*0-8167-2952-2*, Pub. by Watermill Pr) Troll Assocs.

Leeson, Tom & Leeson, Pat, photos by. The Wonder of Bald Eagles. Foran, Eileen, adapted by. LC 92-16943. 1992. PLB 18.60 (*0-8368-0854-1*) Gareth Stevens Inc.

Le Fever, Bill, et al. The Oxford Children's Dictionary. 3rd ed. Weston, John & Spooner, Alan, eds. LC 93-17585. 1993. 7.99 (*0-19-861297-4*) OUP.

Leff, Tora. Read Me Berashis. Feund, Chanie. LC 90-83948. 32p. (ps-2). 1990. 9.95 (*0-685-46905-0*) CIS Comm.

Leff, Tova. Special Days Are Wonderful: A Guessing Game Book. Elias, Miriam L. 32p. (ps). 1993. English ed. 9.95 (*0-922613-46-X*); Russian ed. 9.95 (*0-922613-49-4*) Hachai Pubns.

—A Very Special Gift. Gettinger, Shifrah. 32p. (ps-3). 1993. 8.95 (*0-922613-52-4*); pap. text ed. 6.95 (*0-922613-53-2*) Hachai Pubns.

Leggat, Bonnie-Alise. Punt, Pass & Point! Leggat, Bonnie-Alise. Thatch, Nancy R., ed. Melton, David, intro. by. LC 92-17598. 26p. (gr. 3-5). 1992. PLB 14.95 (*0-933849-39-7*) Landmark Edns.

Legman, Linda C. Ladybug. Scherer, Catharine D. LC 83-70738. 10p. (gr. 6-11). 1983. 2.95 (*0-9611024-0-3*) Drum Assocs.

Legros, Ivor L. Instant Centers - Holidays. rev. ed. LeGros, Lucy C. 51p. (gr. k-2). 1988. tchr's ed. 5.95 (*0-317-65724-0*) Creat Res NC.

—Instant Centers - Numbers 10-20. LeGros, Lucy C. 33p. (gr. k-2). 1988. tchr's ed. 5.95 (*0-937306-07-X*) Creat Res NC.

Lehan, Daniel. This Is Not a Book about Dodos. Lehan, Daniel. LC 91-794. 32p. (gr. k-3). 1992. 14.00 (*0-525-44878-0*, DCB) Dutton Child Bks.

—Wipe Your Feet! Lehan, Daniel. LC 91-44145. 32p. (gr. k-3). 1993. 14.00 (*0-525-44992-2*, DCB) Dutton Child Bks.

LeHew, Ron. Animal Craft Fun: Indoor & Outdoor Activities & Projects. Murray, Beth, ed. 32p. (gr. k-5). 1994. pap. 3.95 (*1-56397-314-6*) Boyds Mills Pr.

—Crafts from Recyclables: Great Ideas from Throwaways. Van Blaricom, Colleen, ed. LC 91-72872. 48p. (gr. 1-5). 1992. pap. 4.95 (*1-56397-015-5*) Boyds Mills Pr.

—Indoor Sunshine: Great Things to Make & Do on Rainy Days. Cherkerzian, Diane. LC 92-73628. 32p. (gr. 2-7). 1993. Set of 3 bks. 11.85 (*1-56397-169-0*); pap. 3.95 (*1-56397-163-1*) Boyds Mills Pr.

—Outdoor Fun: Great Things to Make & Do on Sunny Days. Cherkerzian, Diane. LC 92-74583. 32p. (gr. 2-7). 1993. Set of 3 bks. 11.85 (*1-56397-168-2*); pap. 3.95 (*1-56397-162-3*) Boyds Mills Pr.

LeHew, Ronald. The Marfan Syndrome: A Booklet for Teenagers. Bernhardt, Barbara A., et al. 20p. 1988. pap. 1.00 (*0-918335-03-5*) Natl Marfan Foun.

Lehman, Barbara. Abracadabra to Zigzag: An Alphabet Book. Lecourt, Nancy. LC 92-12503. 32p. (ps-3). 1992. pap. 4.99 (*0-14-054470-4*) Puffin Bks.

Leigh, Nila K. Learning to Swim in Swaziland: A Child's Eye-View of a Southern African Country. Leigh, Nila K. LC 92-13223. 48p. (gr. k-3). 1993. 15.95 (*0-590-45938-4*) Scholastic Inc.

Leigh, Tom. Babysitting with Big Bird. Alexander, Liza. 24p. (ps-4). 1993. 20.00 (*0-307-74029-3*, 64029, Golden Pr) Western Pub.

—Big Bird Can Share. Anastasio, Dina. 32p. (ps-k). 1985. write for info. (*0-307-12016-3*, Pub. by Golden Bks) Western Pub.

—Don't Cry, Big Bird. Roberts, Sarah. LC 81-4075. 40p. (gr. k-2). 1981. 4.95 (*0-394-84868-3*) Random Bks Yng Read.

—Don't Cry, Big Bird. Roberts, Sarah. LC 81-4075. 40p. (ps-3). 1993. pap. 2.99 (*0-679-83950-X*) Random Bks Yng Read.

—Grover's Ten Terrific Ways to Help Our Wonderful World. Ross, Anna. LC 91-11095. 32p. (Orig.). (ps-3). 1992. PLB 5.99 (*0-679-91384-X*); pap. 2.25 (*0-679-81384-5*) Random Bks Yng Read.

—It's a Secret! Hautzig, Deborah. LC 87-20542. 40p. (ps-3). 1988. 4.95 (*0-394-89672-6*); lib. bdg. 6.99 (*0-394-99672-0*) Random Bks Yng Read.

—It's Not Fair. Hautzig, Deborah. LC 85-30154. 40p. (ps-3). 1986. 4.95 (*0-394-88151-6*) Random Bks Yng Read.

—It's Not Fair! Hautzig, Deborah. LC 85-30154. 40p. (ps-3). 1993. pap. 2.99 (*0-679-83951-8*) Random Bks Yng Read.

—Muppet Kids in Help! We're Lost! Gikow, Louise. (ps-3). 1991. pap. 1.95 (*0-307-12659-5*, Golden Pr) Western Pub.

—Sesame Street: Ernie & His Merry Monsters & Other Good-Night Stories. Muntean, Michaela. 24p. (ps-3). 1992. write for info. (*0-307-12336-7*, 12336, Golden Pr) Western Pub.

—The Sesame Street Word Book. 72p. (ps). 1983. write for info. (*0-307-15549-8*, 15818, Golden Bks) Western Pub.

—TV or Not TV. Brown, Ann. 24p. (ps-3). 1992. 1.95 (*0-307-12652-8*, 12652, Golden Pr) Western Pub.

—A Visit to the Sesame Street Zoo. Weiss, Ellen. LC 88-3201. 32p. (Orig.). (ps-1). 1988. lib. bdg. 5.99 (*0-394-90447-8*); pap. 2.25 (*0-394-80447-3*, Random Juv) Random Bks Yng Read.

Leight, Edward. The Boy Apprenticed to an Enchanter. Colum, Padraic. (gr. 3-7). 1991. 20.00 (*0-8446-6482-0*) Peter Smith.

Leighton, Clare. Imagination's Other Place: Poems of Science & Mathematics. Reissue. ed. Plotz, Helen. LC 55-9216. 200p. (gr. 7 up). 1987. PLB 12.89 (*0-690-04700-2*, Crowell Jr Bks) HarpC Child Bks.

Leiner, Alan. Poems That Sing to You. Strickland, Michael, ed. 64p. (gr. 5 up). 1993. 13.95 (*1-56397-178-X*, Wordsong) Boyds Mills Pr.

Leipzig, Arthur, photos by. All in My Jewish Family. Roseman, Kenneth. 32p. (gr. k-3). 1984. pap. 5.00 wkbk. (*0-8074-0266-4*, 103800) UAHC.

Leisner, Kurt. God Answers Prayers. Odor, Ruth S. LC 91-67209. 32p. (gr. 5-7). 1992. saddle-stitch 5.99 (*0-87403-932-0*, 24-03562) Standard Pub.

Leissner, John, Jr. Let's Slice the Ice: A Collection of Black Children's Ring Games & Chants. Fulton, Eleanor & Smith, Pat. 56p. (ps-k). 1978. pap. 7.95 (*0-918812-02-X*) MMB Music.

Leitz, Pierr M. Kindergarten Cooks. Edge, Nellie. LC 76-48558. 165p. (gr. k-6). 1975. pap. 9.95 (*0-918146-00-3*) Peninsula WA.

LeJeune, Shonda. God Is. LeJeune, Shonda. 32p. (Orig.). (gr. 3-8). 1993. pap. 8.95 (*0-87516-659-8*) DeVorss.

Leloup, Roger. Vulcan's Forge. Leloup, Roger. Surbeck, Jean-Jacques, tr. from FRE. 49p. (Orig.). (gr. 12 up). 1989. pap. 6.95 (*0-87416-065-0*, Comcat Comics) Catalan Communs.

LeMair, Henriette W. Baby's Diary. 112p. (ps up). 1987. 12.95 (*0-399-21454-2*, Philomel Bks) Putnam Pub Group.

Lemaitre, Pascal. Emily the Giraffe. Lemaitre, Pascal. LC 92-85508. 32p. (ps-2). 1993. 13.95 (*1-56282-403-1*); PLB 13.89 (*1-56282-404-X*) Hyprn Child.

—Zelda's Secret. Lemaitre, Pascal. LC 93-28448. (ps-3). 1993. PLB 13.95 (*0-8167-3309-0*); pap. 3.95t (*0-8167-3310-4*) Troll Assocs.

Leman, Martin. Sleepy Kittens. Leman, Jill. LC 93-24232. 32p. 1994. 14.00 (*0-688-13288-X*, Tambourine Bks); PLB 13.93 (*0-688-13289-8*, Tambourine Bks) Morrow.

Lemeiux, Margo. Mean Words. Milios, Rita. LC 92-10837. 32p. (ps-2). Date not set. 11.95 (*1-56065-163-6*) Capstone Pr. Postponed.

Lemelman, Martin. Bible Work & Play, Vol. 3. rev. ed. Fochman, Joyce. 80p. 1986. pap. 5.00 wkbk. (*0-8074-0305-9*, 103640) UAHC.

—Jewish Holiday Book. 10p. 1989. bds. 4.95 (*0-8074-0431-4*, 102004) UAHC.

—My Jewish Home. Lemelman, Martin. 10p. (ps-k). 1988. pap. 3.95 boardbk. (*0-8074-0415-2*, 102002) UAHC.

Lemerise, Bruce. Sheldon's Lunch. Lemerise, Bruce. LC 80-10449. 32p. (ps-3). 1980. 5.95 (*0-8193-1025-5*) Parents.

Lemieux, Margo. Zachary's New Home: A Story for Foster & Adopted Children. Blomquist, Geraldine M. & Blomquist, Paul B. LC 90-41914. 32p. (ps-2). 1990. 16.95 (*0-945354-28-2*); pap. 6.95 (*0-945354-27-4*) Magination Pr.

—Zachary's New Home: A Story for Foster & Adopted Children. Blomquist, Geraldine M. & Blomquist, Paul B. LC 92-56876. 1993. PLB 17.26 (*0-8368-0937-8*) Gareth Stevens Inc.

Lemieux, Michele. Amahl & the Night Visitors. Menotti, Gian-Carlo. LC 84-27196. 64p. (ps up). 1986. 15.00 (*0-688-05426-9*); lib. bdg. 14.88 (*0-688-05427-7*, Morrow Jr Bks) Morrow Jr Bks.

—A Gift from Saint Francis: The First Creche. Cole, Joanna. LC 88-22048. 40p. 1989. 13.95 (*0-688-06502-3*); PLB 13.88 (*0-688-06503-1*, Morrow Jr Bks) Morrow Jr Bks.

—The Pied Piper of Hamelin. Lemieux, Michele. LC 92-21338. 32p. 1993. 15.00 (*0-688-09848-7*); PLB 14.93 (*0-688-09849-5*) Morrow Jr Bks.

—Voices on the Wind: Poems for All Seasons. Booth, David, ed. LC 90-5566. 48p. (ps up). 1990. 13.95 (*0-688-09554-2*); PLB 13.88 (*0-688-09555-0*, Morrow Jr Bks) Morrow Jr Bks.

—What's That Noise? Lemieux, Michele. LC 84-16631. 32p. (ps-1). 1985. 11.95 (*0-688-04139-6*); PLB 11.88 (*0-688-04140-X*, Morrow Jr Bks) Morrow Jr Bks.

—Winter Magic. Hasler, Eveline. LC 85-2944. 32p. (ps-3). 1985. lib. bdg. 12.88 (*0-688-05258-4*) Morrow Jr Bks.

Leming, Ron, jt. illus. see Sullivan, Tom.

Lemke, Horst. Around the World in Eighty Dishes. Van der Linde, Polly & Van der Linde, Tasha. LC 71-160447. 88p. (gr. k-7). 10.95 (*0-87592-007-1*) Scroll Pr.

—Places & Faces. LC 78-160446. 32p. (ps-k). 8.95 (*0-87592-041-1*) Scroll Pr.

—Ride with Me Through ABC. Bond, Susan. LC 67-19376. 32p. (ps-k). 6.95 (*0-87592-043-8*) Scroll Pr.

Lemoine, Charles A. Louisiana's Cypress Bayou Elves: Pontain the Trapper. Lemoine, Charles A. 40p. (Orig.). (gr. 1-12). 1986. pap. 5.00 (*0-941327-01-9*) Charles A Lemoine.

—Santa Clawfish. Lemoine, Charles A. 32p. (Orig.). 1986. pap. 3.20 (*0-941327-00-0*) Charles A Lemoine.

Lemoine, Georges. Barbedor. Tournier, Michel. (FRE.). 48p. (gr. 3-7). 1990. pap. 8.95 (*2-07-031172-4*) Schoenhof.

—The Book of Creation. Beaude, Pierre-Marie. Clements, Andrew, tr. LC 90-35418. 56p. (gr. 5 up). 1991. pap. 16.95 (*0-88708-141-X*) Picture Bk Studio.

—Celui Qui N'Avait Jamais vu la Mer. Le Clezio, J. M. (FRE.). 107p. (gr. 5-10). 1988. pap. 6.95 (*2-07-033492-9*) Schoenhof.

—The Christmas Story According to St. Luke. 32p. 1978. PLB 13.95s.p. (*0-87191-957-5*) Creative Ed.

—Comment Wang-Fo Fut Sauve. Yourcenar, Marguerite. (FRE.). 48p. (gr. 3-7). 1990. pap. 7.95 (*2-07-031178-3*) Schoenhof.

—Lullaby. Le Clezio, J. M. (FRE.). (gr. 5-10). 1995. pap. 6.95 (*2-07-033448-1*) Schoenhof.

—Maison Qui S'Envole. Roy, Claude. (FRE.). 90p. (gr. 5-10). 1977. pap. 6.95 (*2-07-033001-X*) Schoenhof.

—Pied. (FRE.). (ps-1). 1989. 14.95 (*2-07-035701-5*) Schoenhof.

—Rossignol de l'Empereur de Chine. Andersen, Hans Christian. (FRE.). 56p. (gr. 3-7). 1990. pap. 8.95 (*0-685-60280-X*) Schoenhof.

—The Steadfast Tin Soldier. Andersen, Hans Christian. 32p. 1983. PLB 13.95s.p. (*0-87191-948-6*) Creative Ed.

—Vendredi ou la Vie Sauvage. Tournier, Michel. (FRE.). 191p. (gr. 5-10). 1987. pap. 7.95 (*2-07-033445-7*) Schoenhof.

—Villa Aurore. Le Clezio, J. M. (FRE.). 112p. (gr. 5-10). 1990. pap. 6.95 (*2-07-033603-4*) Schoenhof.

LeMonnier, Joe. Tornadoes. Armbruster, Ann & Taylor, Elizabeth A. LC 89-31827. 64p. (gr. 4-7). 1989. PLB 12.90 (*0-531-10755-8*) Watts.

Lenchner, George. Mathematical Olympiad Contest Problems for Children (Also for Teachers, Parents, & Other Adults) Lenchner, George. LC 90-83825. 176p. (Orig.). (gr. 3-8). 1990. pap. 18.95 (0-9626662-0-3) Glenwood Pubns.

Lennox, Elsie & Lennox, Elsie. Little Obie & the Flood. Waddell, Martin. LC 91-58741. 80p. (gr. 3-6). 1992. 13.95 (1-56402-106-8) Candlewick Pr.

Lenski, Lois. Betsy & Tacy Go Downtown. reissue ed. Lovelace, Maud H. LC 43-51264. 192p. (gr. 2-5). 1979. pap. 3.95 (0-06-440098-0, Trophy) HarpC Child Bks.

—Betsy & Tacy Go Downtown. Lovelace, Maud H. LC 43-51264. 192p. (gr. 2-5). 1966. PLB 14.89 (0-690-13450-9, Crowell Jr Bks) HarpC Child Bks.

—Betsy & Tacy Go over the Big Hill. reissue ed. Lovelace, Maud H. LC 42-23557. 176p. (gr. 2-5). 1979. pap. 3.95 (0-06-440099-9, Trophy) HarpC Child Bks.

—Betsy & Tacy Go over the Big Hill. Lovelace, Maud H. LC 42-23557. 176p. (gr. 2-5). 1966. PLB 14.89 (0-690-13521-1, Crowell Jr Bks) HarpC Child Bks.

—Betsy-Tacy. Lovelace, Maud H. LC 40-30965. 128p. (gr. 2-5). 1979. pap. 3.95 (0-06-440096-4, Trophy) HarpC Child Bks.

—Betsy-Tacy. Lovelace, Maud H. LC 40-30965. 128p. (gr. 2-5). 1966. PLB 14.89 (0-690-13805-9, Crowell Jr Bks) HarpC Child Bks.

—Betsy-Tacy & Tib. reissue ed. Lovelace, Maud H. LC 41-18714. 144p. (gr. 2-5). 1979. pap. 3.95 (0-06-440097-2, Trophy) HarpC Child Bks.

—Betsy-Tacy & Tib. Lovelace, Maud H. LC 41-18714. 144p. (gr. 2-5). 1966. PLB 14.89 (0-690-13876-8, Crowell Jr Bks) HarpC Child Bks.

—Chimney Corner Stories: Tales for Little Children. Hutchinson, Veronia S., ed. LC 92-10760. 140p. (ps-3). 1992. lib. bdg. 22.50 (0-208-02339-9, Pub. by Linnet); (Pub. by Linnet) Shoe String.

—Little Airplane. Lenski, Lois. LC 59-12487. (gr. k-3). 1980. 5.25 (0-8098-1004-2) McKay.

—Little Auto. Lenski, Lois. LC 58-14239. (gr. k-3). 1980. 5.25 (0-8098-1001-8) McKay.

—Little Farm. Lenski, Lois. LC 58-12902. (gr. k-3). 1980. 5.25 (0-8098-1009-3) McKay.

—Strawberry Girl. Lenski, Lois. 208p. (gr. k-6). 1987. pap. 3.50 (0-440-48347-6, YB) Dell.

—Strawberry Girl. Lenski, Lois. LC 45-7609. 192p. (gr. 4-6). 1945. 16.00 (0-397-30109-X, Lipp Jr Bks); PLB 15.89 (0-397-30110-3, Lipp Jr Bks) HarpC Child Bks.

Lenski, Lois L. Read-to-Me Storybook. Child Study Association of America Staff. LC 47-31488. (ps-1). 1947. 16.95i (0-690-68832-6, Crowell Jr Bks) HarpC Child Bks.

Lent, Blair. Baba Yaga. Small, Ernest & Lent, Blair. 48p. (gr. k-3). 1992. pap. 5.70 (0-395-63037-1, Sandpiper) HM.

—Bayberry Bluff. Lent, Blair. 32p. (gr. k-3). 1992. pap. 4.80 (0-395-62984-5, Sandpiper) HM.

—The Funny Little Woman. Mosel, Arlene. LC 75-179046. 40p. (ps-4). 1972. 16.00 (0-525-30265-4, 01258-370, DCB); pap. 4.95 (0-525-45036-X, DCB) Dutton Child Bks.

—Little Match Girl. Andersen, Hans Christian. LC 68-28050. (gr. k-3). 1975. pap. 1.95 (0-685-02294-3) HM.

—Molasses Flood. Lent, Blair. LC 92-1125. 32p. (ps-3). 1992. 14.45 (0-395-45314-3) HM.

—Tikki Tikki Tembo. Mosel, Arlene. LC 68-11839. 32p. (ps-2). 1968. 14.95 (0-8050-0662-1, Bks Young Read) H Holt & Co.

—Tikki Tikki Tembo. Mosel, Arlene, retold by. LC 68-11839. 32p. (ps-2). 1989. pap. 5.95 (0-8050-1166-8, Bks Young Read) H Holt & Co.

—Tikki Tikki Tembo: Big Book. Mosel, Arlene. LC 68-11839. 32p. (ps-2). 1990. pap. 18.95 (0-8050-2345-3, Bks Young Read) H Holt & Co.

—Wave. Hodges, Margaret. (gr. k-3). 1964. 3.50 (0-395-06817-7) HM.

—Why the Sun & Moon Live in the Sky. Dayrell, Elphinstone. 32p. (gr. k-3). 1990. pap. 4.80 (0-395-53963-3) HM.

Lenzen, Diane. Being with God: Advent Devotions. Ward, Elaine M. 32p. (Orig.). (gr. 1-6). 1988. pap. 4.50 (0-940754-66-5) Ed Ministries.

Leon, Linda. Barnaby Bear. Leon, Margaret. 32p. (ps-8). 1983. 7.95 (0-920806-42-2, Pub. by Penumbra Pr CN) U of Toronto Pr.

—The Cedar Glen Secret. Maitland, Sandra M. 24p. (ps-8). 1983. 6.95 (0-920806-44-9, Pub. by Penumbra Pr CN) U of Toronto Pr.

Leon, Yael. Why Jonathan Doesn't Cry. Modan, Shula. (ps-2). 1988. 7.95 (1-55774-022-4, Dist. by Watts) Modan-Adama Bks.

Leonard, Alain. Theodore's Superheroes. Leonard, Alain. Tambourine Books Staff, tr. from FRE. LC 92-82140. 32p. (ps-8). 1993. 15.00 (0-688-12766-5, Tambourine Bks); PLB 14.93 (0-688-12767-3, Tambourine Bks) Morrow.

Leonard, Pamela. Touchstone. Regan, Peter. 208p. (gr. 4-7). 1989. 13.95 (0-947962-44-1, Pub. by Childrens Pr) Irish Bks Media.

Leonard, Richard. Buffalo Soldiers. Miller, Robert. 104p. (gr. 4-7). 1992. PLB 13.98 (0-382-24080-4); pap. 7.95 (0-382-24085-5) (0-685-47034-2) Silver Burdett Pr.

—Cowboys. Miller, Robert. 104p. (gr. 4-7). 1992. PLB 13.98 (0-382-24079-0); pap. 7.95 (0-382-24084-7) Silver Burdett Pr.

—I Am Not Afraid! Based on a Masai Tale. Mann, Kenny. LC 92-13811. 1993. 9.99 (0-553-09119-0, Little Rooster); 3.50 (0-553-37108-8, Little Rooster) Bantam.

—Mountain Men. Miller, Robert. 104p. (gr. 4-7). 1991. PLB 13.98 (0-382-24082-0); pap. 7.95 (0-382-24087-1) Silver Burdett Pr.

—Pioneers. Miller, Robert. 104p. (gr. 4-7). 1991. PLB 13.98 (0-382-24081-2); pap. 7.95 (0-382-24086-3) Silver Burdett Pr.

—Reflections of a Black Cowboy Series, 4 vols. Miller, Robert. 416p. (gr. 4-7). 1991. Set. PLB 55.92 (0-382-24078-2); Set. pap. 31.80 (0-382-24083-9) Silver Burdett Pr.

Leonard, Tom. Under the Sun & Moon: And Other Poems. Brown, Margaret W. 40p. (ps-2). 1993. 14.95 (1-56282-354-X); PLB 14.89 (1-56282-355-8) Hyprn Child.

Leone, S. Littlest Angel. Tazewell, Charles. 32p. (gr. 1 up). 1946. PLB 15.00 (0-516-03533-9) Childrens.

Leonidez, Nestor & Redondo, Nestor. Madame Curie - Albert Einstein. Farr, Naunerle. (gr. 4-12). 1979. pap. text ed. 2.95 (0-88301-356-8); wkbk. 1.25 (0-88301-380-0) Pendulum Pr.

Lepagnol, Cyril. The Blue Planet: Seas & Oceans. De Beauregard, Diane C. Bogard, Vicki, tr. from FRE. LC 89-8912. 38p. (gr. k-5). 1989. 4.95 (0-944589-22-7, 022) Young Discovery Lib.

Lerer, Mark. Hebrew, Holidays, & Heroes: The Jewish Fun Book. Kasakove, David P. & Olitzky, Kerry M. (gr. 4-6). 1992. pap. 7.00 (0-8074-0478-0, 123937) UAHC.

Lerner, Carol. Cactus. Lerner, Carol. LC 91-35678. 32p. 1992. 15.00 (0-688-09636-0); PLB 14.93 (0-688-09637-9) Morrow Jr Bks.

—A Desert Year. Lerner, Carol. LC 90-44643. 48p. 1991. 13.95 (0-688-09382-5); PLB 13.88 (0-688-09383-3) Morrow Jr Bks.

—Dumb Cane & Daffodils: Poisonous Plants in the House & Garden. Lerner, Carol. LC 89-33622. 32p. 1990. 13.95 (0-688-08791-4); PLB 13.88 (0-688-08796-5, Morrow Jr Bks) Morrow Jr Bks.

—A Forest Year. Lerner, Carol. LC 86-9741. 48p. (ps up). 1987. 12.95 (0-688-06413-2); lib. bdg. 12.88 (0-688-06414-0, Morrow Jr Bks) Morrow Jr Bks.

—Plant Families. Lerner, Carol. LC 88-26653. 32p. (gr. 4 up). 1989. 12.95 (0-688-07881-8); PLB 12.88 (0-688-07882-6, Morrow Jr Bks) Morrow Jr Bks.

—Plants That Make You Sniffle & Sneeze. Lerner, Carol. LC 92-21561. 32p. 1993. 15.00 (0-688-11489-X); PLB 14.93 (0-688-11490-3) Morrow Jr Bks.

—Tree Flowers. Selsam, Millicent E. LC 83-17353. 32p. (gr. 4 up). 1984. PLB 12.88 (0-688-02769-5) Morrow Jr Bks.

Lerner, Sharon. The Fish Book. Overbeck, Cynthia. LC 78-7205. 32p. (gr. k-3). 1978. PLB 10.95 (0-8225-1110-X) Lerner Pubns.

—The Flower Book. Orange, Anne. LC 74-12743. 32p. (gr. k-3). 1975. PLB 10.95 (0-8225-0294-1) Lerner Pubns.

—The Fruit Book. Overbeck, Cynthia. LC 74-12744. 32p. (gr. k-3). 1975. PLB 10.95 (0-8225-0295-X) Lerner Pubns.

—The Leaf Book. Orange, Anne. LC 74-12745. 32p. (gr. k-3). 1975. PLB 10.95 (0-8225-0296-8) Lerner Pubns.

—The Vegetable Book. Overbeck, Cynthia. LC 74-12746. 32p. (gr. k-3). 1975. PLB 10.95 (0-8225-0297-6) Lerner Pubns.

Le Saux, Alain. Daddy Shaves. Le Saux, Alain. 28p. (ps). 1992. 6.95 (0-8050-2194-9, Bks Young Read) H Holt & Co.

—King Daddy. Le Saux, Alain. 28p. (ps). 1992. 6.95 (0-8050-2193-0, Bks Young Read) H Holt & Co.

Lescanff, Jacques. Gospel for Young Christians. Winstone, Harold. 192p. (gr. 3-6). 1985. 3.95 (0-225-27392-6) Harper SF.

Lesch, Christiane. In Bethlehem Long Ago. Lesch, Christiane. Lawson, Polly, tr. from GER. 28p. (ps-2). Repr. of 1988 ed. 14.95 (0-86315-076-4, Pub. by Floris Bks UK) Gryphon Hse.

—Ivan Korovavich: The Son of a Cow. Afanasiev, A. N. 28p. (gr. k-4). 1990. 14.95 (0-903540-57-6, 625, Pub. by Floris Bks UK) Anthroposophic.

Leslie, Amanda. Play Kitten Play: Ten Animal Fingerwiggles. Leslie, Amanda. LC 91-58752. 10p. (ps up). 1992. 6.95 (1-56402-088-6) Candlewick Pr.

—Play Puppy Play: Ten Animal Fingerwiggles. Leslie, Amanda. LC 91-58753. 10p. (ps up). 1992. 6.95 (1-56402-087-8) Candlewick Pr.

Leslie, Donna. Alitji in Dreamland: Alitjinya Ngura Tjukurmankuntjala: An Aboriginal Version of Lewis Carroll's Alice's Adventures in Wonderland. Sheppard, Nancy, adapted by. LC 92-17640. 104p. (gr. 6 up). 1992. 16.95 (0-89815-478-2) Ten Speed Pr.

Lessac, Frane. Caribbean Alphabet. Lessac, Frane. LC 93-15833. 32p. 1994. 15.00 (0-688-12952-8, Tambourine Bks); PLB 14.93 (0-688-12953-6, Tambourine Bks) Morrow.

—Caribbean Carnival: Songs of the West Indies. Burgie, Irving. Guy, Rosa, intro. by. LC 91-760838. 32p. (gr. 1 up). 1992. 15.00 (0-688-10779-6, Tambourine Bks); PLB 14.93 (0-688-10780-X, Tambourine Bks) Morrow.

—The Chalk Doll. Pomerantz, Charlotte. LC 88-872. 32p. (gr. k-3). 1989. 15.00 (0-397-32318-2, Lipp Jr Bks); PLB 14.89 (0-397-32319-0) HarpC Child Bks.

—Chalk Doll. Pomerantz, Charlotte. LC 88-872. 32p. (ps-3). 1993. pap. 4.95 (0-06-443333-1, Trophy) HarpC Child Bks.

—The Fire Children: A West African Creation Tale. Maddern, Eric, retold by. LC 92-34685. (ps-3). 1993. 14.50 (0-8037-1477-7) Dial Bks Young.

—Little Gray One. Wahl, Jan. LC 92-33776. 32p. (ps up). 1993. 15.00 (0-688-12037-7, Tambourine Bks); PLB 14.93 (0-688-12038-5, Tambourine Bks) Morrow.

—My Little Island. Lessac, Frane. LC 84-48355. 48p. (gr. 1-4). 1985. 14.00 (0-397-32114-7, Lipp Jr Bks); PLB 13.89 (0-397-32115-5) HarpC Child Bks.

—My Little Island. Lessac, Frane. LC 84-48355. 48p. (ps-3). 1987. pap. 4.95 (0-06-443146-0, Trophy) HarpC Child Bks.

—Nine O'Clock Lullaby. Singer, Marilyn. LC 90-32116. 32p. (ps-3). 1991. PLB 14.89 (0-06-025648-6) HarpC Child Bks.

—Nine O'Clock Lullaby. Singer, Marilyn. LC 90-32116. 32p. (ps-3). 1993. pap. 4.95 (0-06-443319-6, Trophy) HarpC Child Bks.

—Not a Copper Penny in Me House: Poems from the Caribbean. Gunning, Monica. 32p. 1993. 14.95 (1-56397-050-3, Wordsong) Boyds Mills Pr.

—The Wonderful Towers of Watts. Zelver, Patricia. LC 93-20344. 32p. 1994. 15.00 (0-688-12649-9, Tambourine Bks); PLB 14.93 (0-688-12650-2, Tambourine Bks) Morrow.

Lester, Alison. Imagine. Lester, Alison. 32p. (gr. k-3). 1990. 13.45 (0-395-53753-3) HM.

—Isabella's Bed. Lester, Alison. LC 92-22935. 32p. (gr. k-3). 1993. Repr. of 1991 ed. 14.95 (0-395-65565-X) HM.

—The Journey Home. Lester, Alison. LC 89-28355. 32p. (gr. k-3). 1991. 13.45 (0-395-53355-4) HM.

—Magic Beach. Lester, Alison. 32p. (ps-3). 1992. 13.95 (0-316-52177-9, Joy St Bks) Little.

—Rosie Sips Spiders. Lester, Alison. 32p. (ps-k). 1989. 13.45 (0-395-51526-2) HM.

—Tessa Snaps Snakes. Lester, Alison. 32p. (ps-k). 1991. 13.45 (0-395-59505-3) HM.

—Tessa Snaps Snakes. Lester, Alison. LC 91-2665. 32p. (ps-k). 1991. pap. 13.95 (0-685-52551-1, Sandpiper) HM.

Lester, Mike. Santa's New Suit. Rojany, Lisa. 11p. (gr. 1-4). 1993. 7.95 (0-8431-3587-5) Price Stern.

Le-Tan, Pierre. Puss in Boots. Metaxas, Eric. LC 92-7789. 40p. 1992. pap. 14.95 (0-88708-285-8, Rabbit Ears); pap. 19.95 incl. cass. (0-88708-286-6, Rabbit Ears) Picture Bk Studio.

Le Tord, Bijou. The Deep Blue Sea. Le Tord, Bijou. LC 89-16314. 32p. 1990. 13.95 (0-531-05853-0); PLB 13.99 (0-531-08453-1) Orchard Bks Watts.

Letwenko, Ed. What's a Body to Do? Odor, Ruth S. LC 81-17031. 112p. (gr. 2-6). 1980. PLB 21.35 (0-89565-209-9); PLB 14.95s.p. (0-685-55559-3) Childs World.

Leung, Paul. One Thousand Plus Picture Dictionary: One Hundred One Activities. Freifeld, Art. 90p. (Orig.). (gr. 5 up). 1988. pap. text ed. 6.95 (0-916177-06-8); tchr's. ed. 1.45 (0-916177-24-6) Am Eng Pubns.

Levers, John. The Time & Space of Uncle Albert. large type ed. Stannard, Russell. 176p. 1993. 13.95 (0-7451-1660-4, Galaxy Child Lrg Print) Chivers N Amer.

Levert, Mireille. Jeremiah & Mrs. Ming. Jennings, Sharon. 24p. (ps). 1990. PLB 15.95 (1-55037-079-0, Pub. by Annick CN); pap. 5.95 (1-55037-078-2, Pub. by Annick CN) Firefly Bks Ltd.

—Une Journee avec Jeremie et Mme. Ming: When Jeremiah Found Mrs. Ming. Jennings, Sharon. (FRE). 24p. (ps). 1992. PLB 15.95 (1-55037-247-5, Pub. by Annick Pr); pap. 6.95 (1-55037-248-3, Pub. by Annick Pr) Firefly Bks Ltd.

—When Jeremiah Found Mrs. Ming. Jennings, Sharon. 24p. (ps). 1992. PLB 15.95 (1-55037-237-8, Pub. by Annick Pr); pap. 5.95 (1-55037-234-3, Pub. by Annick Pr) Firefly Bks Ltd.

Levin, Arnie. The Gigantic Baby. Gerstein, Mordicai. LC 90-35537. 32p. (gr. k-3). 1991. PLB 14.89 (0-06-022106-2) HarpC Child Bks.

—Homer & the House Next Door. Pulver, Robin. LC 93-4377. Date not set. write for info. (0-02-775457-X, Four Winds) Macmillan Child Grp.

Levin, Betsy. Kitten in Trouble. Polushkin, Maria. LC 85-5753. 32p. (ps-k). 1988. RSBE 13.95 (0-02-774740-9, Bradbury Pr) Macmillan Child Grp.

Levin, Debra K. The Day the Sky Split. Lev, M. LC 91-71188. 32p. (gr. 1-3). 1991. 12.95 (1-877-65607-0) Antroll Pub.

Levine, David. The Fables of Aesop. Levine, David, selected by. Gregory, Patrick & Gregory, Justina, trs. LC 84-12894. 108p. (gr. 8). 1984. 13.95 (0-87645-074-5, Pub. by Gambit); pap. 8.95 (0-87645-116-4) Harvard Common Pr.

Levine, Joe, jt. illus. see Harvey, Roland.

Levine, Lisa. Book Factory. Suid, Murray & Lincoln, Wanda. 64p. (gr. 2-6). 1988. pap. 6.95 (0-912107-72-3) Monday Morning Bks.

Levine, Marge. The Glass Menorah & Other Stories for Jewish Holidays. Silverman, Maida. LC 91-13890. 64p. (gr. 1-4). 1992. RSBE 14.95 (0-02-782682-1, Four Winds) Macmillan Child Grp.

Levitt, Sidney. Bingo, the Best Dog in the World. Siracusa, Catherine. LC 90-44400. 64p. (gr. k-3). 1991. 11.95 (0-06-025812-8); PLB 11.89 (0-06-025813-6) HarpC Child Bks.

—Carrot Delight. Mangas, Brian. 32p. (ps-1). 1991. pap. 2.25 (0-671-73278-1, Little Simon) S&S Trade.
—The Mighty Movers. Levitt, Sidney. 48p. (gr. k-3). 1994. 10.95 (1-56282-421-X); PLB 10.89 (1-56282-422-8) Hyprn Child.
—A Nice Surprise for Father Rabbit. Mangas, Brian. 32p. (ps-1). 1991. pap. 2.25 (0-671-73277-3, Little Simon) S&S Trade.
—You Don't Get a Carrot Unless You're a Bunny. Mangas, Brian. 1989. pap. 5.95 (0-671-67201-0, Little Simon) S&S Trade.
—You Don't Get a Carrot Unless You're a Bunny. Mangas, Brian. LC 88-19763. 32p. (ps-k). 1991. pap. 2.25 (0-671-74200-0, Little Simon) S&S Trade.
Levrin, Nora. Ship That Flew. Lewis, Hilda. LC 58-5903. (gr. 3-7). 1958. 25.95 (0-87599-067-3) S G Phillips.
Levy, Pam. Amazing Mark. Supraner, Robyn. LC 85-14070. 48p. (Orig.). 1986. 7.95 (0-8167-0644-1); pap. text ed. 3.50 (0-8167-0645-X) Troll Assocs.
Levy, Ruth. Space. Morris, Ting & Morris, Neil. LC 93-24435. 1994. write for info. (0-531-14282-5) Watts.
Lewer, Bridget. Naturewatch. Katz, Adrienne. (ps up). 1986. pap. 8.61 (0-201-10457-1) Addison-Wesley.
Lewin, Betsy. Araminta's Paint Box. Ackerman, Karen. LC 88-35033. 32p. (gr. 1-3). 1990. SBE 13.95 (0-689-31462-0, Atheneum Child Bk) Macmillan Child Grp.
—The Detective Stars & the Case of the Super Soccer Team. Levine, Caroline. LC 92-28600. 48p. (gr. 1-4). 1994. 11.99 (0-525-65134-9, Cobblehill Bks) Dutton Child Bks.
—Doodle Dandy! The Complete Book of Independence Day Words. Graham-Barber, Lynda. LC 91-19409. 128p. (gr. 4-10). 1992. SBE 13.95 (0-02-736675-8, Bradbury Pr) Macmillan Child Grp.
—Eddie & the Fire Engine. Haywood, Carolyn. ALC Staff, ed. 192p. (gr. 2-8). 1992. pap. 4.95 (0-688-11498-9, Pub. by Beech Tree Bks) Morrow.
—First Grade Elves. Ryder, Joanne. LC 93-25543. 32p. (ps-2). 1993. PLB 9.89 (0-8167-3010-5); pap. text ed. 2.95 (0-8167-3011-3) Troll Assocs.
—First Grade Ladybugs. Ryder, Joanne. LC 92-43528. 32p. (ps-2). 1993. PLB 9.79 (0-8167-3006-7); pap. text ed. 2.95 (0-8167-3007-5) Troll Assocs.
—First Grade Valentines. Rider, Joanne. LC 91-35388. 32p. (gr. k-2). 1992. PLB 9.79 (0-8167-3004-0); pap. text ed. 2.95 (0-8167-3005-9) Troll Assocs.
—Fraidy Cats. Krensky, Stephen. LC 92-35360. (gr. 3 up). 1993. 2.95 (0-590-46438-8) Scholastic Inc.
—Furlie Cat. Freschet, Bernice. LC 85-11656. 32p. (ps-3). 1986. 12.95 (0-688-05917-1) Lothrop.
—Gobble! The Complete Book of Thanksgiving Words. Graham-Barber, Lynda. LC 90-22770. 128p. (gr. 4-10). 1991. SBE 13.95 (0-02-708332-2, Bradbury Pr) Macmillan Child Grp.
—The Great Ape Trick. Gregorich, Barbara. Hoffman, Joan, ed. 32p. (gr. k-2). 1987. wkbk. 1.99 (0-88743-105-4, 02605) Sch Zone Pub Co.
—Greens. Adoff, Arnold. LC 85-16631. (gr. 1-5). 1988. 12.95 (0-688-04276-7); lib. bdg. 12.88 (0-688-04277-5) Lothrop.
—Hello, First Grade. Ryder, Joanne. LC 93-9041. 32p. (ps-2). 1993. PLB 9.89 (0-8167-3008-3); pap. text ed. 2.95 (0-8167-3009-1) Troll Assocs.
—Ho! Ho! Ho! The Complete Book of Christmas Words. Graham-Barber, Lynda. LC 92-6715. 128p. (gr. 4-7). 1993. pap. 14.95 SBE (0-02-736933-1, Bradbury Pr) Macmillan Child Grp.
—Itchy, Itchy Chickenpox. Maccarone, Grace. 32p. 1992. pap. 2.95 (0-590-44948-6) Scholastic Inc.
—Jim Hedgehog & the Lonesome Tower. Hoban, Russell. 48p. (gr. 1-4). 1992. 12.95 (0-395-59760-9, Clarion Bks) HM.
—Jim Hedgehog's Supernatural Christmas. Hoban, Russell. 48p. (gr. 2-5). 1992. 12.70 (0-395-56240-6, Clarion Bks) HM.
—Mattie's Little Possum Pet. Luttrell, Ida. LC 91-47709. 40p. (ps-3). 1993. SBE 14.95 (0-689-31786-7, Atheneum Child Bk) Macmillan Child Grp.
—Mushy! The Complete Book of Valentine Words. Graham-Barber, Lynda. LC 89-33047. 128p. (gr. 4-10). 1990. 13.95 (0-02-736941-2, Bradbury Pr) Macmillan Child Grp.
—Weird! The Complete Book of Halloween Words. Limburg, Peter R. LC 88-38678. 128p. (gr. 4-10). 1989. SBE 13.95 (0-02-759050-X, Bradbury Pr) Macmillan Child Grp.
—What If the Shark Wears Tennis Shoes? Morris, Winifred. LC 89-38150. 32p. (gr. k-3). 1990. SBE 13. 95 (0-689-31587-2, Atheneum Child Bk) Macmillan Child Grp.
—Yo, Hungry Wolf! A Nursery Rap. Vozar, David. LC 91-46264. (gr. 1-4). 1993. 15.00 (0-385-30452-8) Doubleday.
Lewin, Janetta. Look at Weather. rev. ed. Kirkpatrick, Rena K. LC 84-26251. 32p. (gr. 2-4). 1985. PLB 17.28 (0-8172-2360-6); pap. 4.95 (0-8114-6906-9) Raintree Steck-V.
Lewin, T. Matthew's Meadow. Demas-Bliss, C. 1992. 14. 95 (0-15-200759-8, HB Juv Bks) HarBrace.
Lewin, Ted. Ali, Child of the Desert. London, Jonathan. LC 92-44164. (gr. 3 up). 1995. write for info. (0-688-12560-3); PLB write for info. (0-688-12561-1) Lothrop.
—The Always Prayer Shawl. Oberman, Sheldon. 32p. (gr. 2 up). 1994. 14.95 (1-878093-22-3) Boyds Mills Pr.

—Amazon Boy. Lewin, Ted. LC 92-15798. 32p. (gr. k-3). 1993. RSBE 14.95 (0-02-757383-4, Macmillan Child Bk) Macmillan Child Grp.
—Babe Didrikson: Athlete of the Century. Knudson, R. R. 64p. (gr. 2-6). 1986. pap. 3.95 (0-14-032095-4, Puffin) Puffin Bks.
—Bird Watch. Yolen, Jane. 48p. 1990. 15.95 (0-399-21612-X, Philomel Bks) Putnam Pub Group.
—Brother Francis & the Friendly Beasts. Hodges, Margaret. LC 90-33026. 32p. (gr. 1-3). 1991. SBE 13. 95 (0-684-19173-3, Scribners Young Read) Macmillan Child Grp.
—A Brown Bird Singing. Wosmek, Frances. LC 85-24002. 160p. (gr. 5-10). 1985. 11.95 (0-688-06251-2) Lothrop.
—A Brown Bird Singing. Wosmek, Frances. LC 92-43784. 128p. (gr. 5 up). 1993. pap. 4.95 (0-688-04596-0, Pub. by Beech Tree Bks) Morrow.
—Faithful Elephants. Tsuchiya, Yukio. Dykes, Tomoko T., tr. from JPN. 32p. (ps up). 1988. 13.45 (0-395-46555-9) HM.
—The Great Pumpkin Switch. McDonald, Megan. LC 91-39660. 32p. (ps-2). 1992. 14.95 (0-531-05450-0); PLB 14.99 (0-531-08600-3) Orchard Bks Watts.
—Herds of Thunder, Manes of Gold: A Collection of Horse Stories & Poems. Coville, Bruce. LC 88-34651. 176p. (gr. 5-10). 1989. 15.95 (0-385-24642-0) Doubleday.
—The Horse in the Attic. Clymer, Eleanor. LC 83-6377. 96p. (gr. 3-6). 1983. SBE 12.95 (0-02-719040-4, Bradbury Pr) Macmillan Child Grp.
—I Was a Teenage Professional Wrestler. Lewin, Ted. LC 92-31523. 128p. (gr. 6-12). 1993. 16.95 (0-531-05477-2); RLB 16.99 (0-531-08627-5) Orchard Bks Watts.
—Island of the Blue Dolphins. O'Dell, Scott. 192p. (gr. 5 up). 1990. 18.45 (0-395-53680-4) HM.
—Margaret Mead: The World Was Her Family. Saunders, Susan. (Orig.). (gr. 2-6). 1988. pap. 3.99 (0-14-032063-6) Viking Child Bks.
—Matthew Wheelock's Wall. Weller, Frances W. LC 91-9608. 40p. (gr. k-3). 1992. RSBE 14.95 (0-02-792612-5, Macmillan Child Bk) Macmillan Child Grp.
—Months: A Book of Poems for Children. Otten, Charlotte. LC 92-44159. 1995. write for info. (0-688-12556-5); PLB write for info. (0-688-12557-3) Lothrop.
—Mother Teresa: A Sister to the Poor. Giff, Patricia R. LC 85-40885. 64p. (gr. 2-6). 1986. pap. 10.95 (0-670-81096-7) Viking Child Bks.
—Mother Teresa: Sister to the Poor. Giff, Patricia R. (gr. 2-6). 1987. pap. 4.50 (0-14-032225-6, Puffin) Puffin Bks.
—National Velvet. Bagnold, Enid. LC 85-2982. 207p. (gr. 3 up). 1985. 15.95 (0-688-05788-8) Morrow Jr Bks.
—The Potato Man. McDonald, Megan. LC 90-7758. 32p. (ps-2). 1991. 14.95 (0-531-05914-6); PLB 14.99 (0-531-08514-7) Orchard Bks Watts.
—Puffin, Bird of the Open Seas. Martin, Lynne. LC 76-3486. (gr. 3-7). 1976. PLB 12.88 (0-688-32074-0) Morrow Jr Bks.
—Rachel Carson: Pioneer of Ecology. Kudlinski, Kathleen V. 64p. (gr. 2-7). 1988. pap. 10.95 (0-670-81488-1) Viking Child Bks.
—Rachel Carson: Pioneer of Ecology. Kudlinski, Kathleen V. 64p. (gr. 2-6). 1989. pap. 3.99 (0-14-032242-6, Puffin) Puffin Bks.
—The Reindeer People. Lewin, Ted. LC 93-19252. 1994. write for info. (0-02-757390-7) Macmillan Child Grp.
—Sami & the Time of the Troubles. Heide, Florence P. & Gilliland, Judith H. 32p. (gr. k-4). 1992. 13.45 (0-395-55964-2, Clarion Bks) HM.
—The Serpent Never Sleeps: A Novel of Jamestown & Pocahontas. O'Dell, Scott. 240p. (gr. 5 up). 1987. 16. 95 (0-395-44242-7) HM.
—Soup for President. Peck, Robert N. LC 77-3548. (gr. 6 up). 1978. PLB 10.99 (0-394-93675-2) Knopf Bks Yng Read.
—Tiger Trek. Lewin, Ted. LC 89-12710. 40p. (gr. 1-5). 1990. RSBE 14.95 (0-02-757381-8, Macmillan Child Bk) Macmillan Child Grp.
—Young Nick & Jubilee. Garfield, Leon. (gr. 1-2). 1989. 13.95 (0-385-29777-7) Delacorte.
—Zia. O'Dell, Scott. LC 75-44156. 224p. (gr. 4-8). 1976. 14.95 (0-395-24393-9) HM.
Lewin, Ted, photos by. Cowboy Country. Scott, Ann H. LC 92-24499. 1993. 14.45 (0-395-57561-3, Clarion Bks) HM.
Lewis, Allen. Calico Bush. reissued ed. Field, Rachel. LC 66-19095. 224p. (gr. 5-9). 1987. SBE 14.95 (0-02-734610-2, Macmillan Child Bk) Macmillan Child Grp.
Lewis, Anthony. Mozart's Story. Willson, Robina B. 48p. (gr. 3 up). 1991. 14.95 (0-7136-3311-5, Pub. by A&C Black UK) Talman.
—My Five Disguises. Sinnett, Kate. LC 90-44374. 28p. (gr. 4-8). 1991. PLB 12.95 (0-87226-444-0, Bedrick Blackie) P Bedrick Bks.
Lewis, Charlotte. The Magic Quilts. Fager, Charles. 100p. (gr. 3-6). 1990. pap. 12.95 (0-945177-03-8) Kimo Pr.
Lewis, Cynthia Y. Country Spunky Gets Lost. Jones, Sheila B. LC 92-56938. 40p. (gr. k-3). 1993. 6.95 (1-55523-582-4) Winston-Derek.

Lewis, Dallas. The Planet Yes. Lewis, Dallas & Lewis, Lisa. 32p. (Orig.). (gr. 3). 1994. 13.95x (0-9634087-1-2); pap. 6.95x (0-9634087-2-0) Silly Billys Bks.
Lewis, Earl B. The New King: A Madagascan Legend. Rappaport, Doreen, adapted by. LC 93-28561. 1995. write for info. (0-8037-1460-2); PLB write for info. (0-8037-1461-0) Dial Bks Young.
Lewis, Glenn A. Dinner at Mario's. Lewis, Glenn A. 19p. (gr. k-3). 1992. pap. 5.95 (1-895583-53-5) MAYA Pubs.
—Funny Things. Lewis, Glenn A. 15p. (gr. k-3). 1992. pap. 4.95 (1-895583-54-3) MAYA Pubs.
Lewis, Jan. Orla's Upside Down Day. rev. ed. Smith, Mary M. 32p. (gr. k-2). 1990. Repr. of 1989 ed. PLB 10.50 (1-878363-05-0) Forest Hse.
Lewis, Karen. Sylvia Stark: A Pioneer. Scott, Victoria & Jones, Ernest. 64p. (Orig.). (gr. 4-12). 1992. PLB 12. 95 (0-940880-37-7); pap. 6.95 (0-940880-38-5) Open Hand.
Lewis, Kim. Emma's Lamb. Lewis, Kim. LC 90-3863. 32p. (ps-1). 1991. SBE 13.95 (0-02-758821-1, Four Winds) Macmillan Child Grp.
—First Snow. Lewis, Kim. LC 92-54413. 32p. (ps up). 1993. 14.95 (1-56402-194-7) Candlewick Pr.
—The Shepherd Boy. Lewis, Kim. LC 89-23679. 32p. (ps-1). 1990. SBE 13.95 (0-02-758581-6, Four Winds) Macmillan Child Grp.
Lewis, Patrick. Big As Texas: The A to Z Tour of Texas Cities & Places. Michael, Linda. Lowdermilk, Karen, ed. LC 87-36793. 64p. (gr. k-3). 1988. pap. 6.95 (0-937460-34-6) Hendrick-Long.
Lewis, Paul. Who Are You, Jesus? McAllister, Dawson. (gr. 5-12). 1986. pap. 7.95 (0-923417-05-2) Shepherd Minst.
Lewis, Paul O. Ever Wondered. Lewis, Paul O. 36p. (gr. 3-6). 1991. pap. 4.95 (0-941831-67-1) Beyond Words Pub.
—Grasper: A Young Crab's Discovery out of His Shell. Lewis, Paul O. Roehm, Michelle, ed. 36p. 1993. 13.95 (0-941831-85-X) Beyond Words Pub.
Lewis, Robin B. Big or Little. Stinson, Kathy. 24p. (ps-1). 1987. pap. 0.99 (0-920303-19-6, Pub. by Annick CN) Firefly Bks Ltd.
—Red Is Best. Stinson, Kathy. (ps-1). 1992. 0.99 (1-55037-252-1, Pub. by Annick CN) Firefly Bks Ltd.
—Steven's Baseball Mitt: A Book about Being Adopted. Stinson, Kathy. 32p. (ps-4). 1992. PLB 14.95 (1-55037-233-5, Pub. by Annick CN); pap. 4.95 (1-55037-232-7, Pub. by Annick CN) Firefly Bks Ltd.
Lewis, Sarah, photos by. A Day in the Life of an Emergency Room Nurse. Witty, Margot. LC 78-68842. 32p. (gr. 4-8). 1980. PLB 11.79 (0-89375-226-6); pap. 2.95 (0-89375-230-4); cassettes avail. Troll Assocs.
Lewis, T. Cinderella & Cinderella's Stepsister. Shorto, Russell. (ps-2). 1990. 12.95 (0-685-38933-2, Birch Ln Pr) Carol Pub Group.
—Peter Pan. Barrie, J. M. Shebar, Susan, ed. LC 87-15480. 48p. (gr. 2-6). 1988. PLB 12.89 (0-8167-1199-2); pap. text ed. 3.95 (0-8167-1200-X) Troll Assocs.
—The Untold Story of Cinderella. Shorto, Russell. 1992. pap. 8.95 (0-8065-1298-9, Citadel Pr) Carol Pub Group.
Lewis, William B. Carlin School, A History Book: The Story of a School in Ravenna, Ohio, U. S. A. Lewis, Lois F. 28p. (Orig.). (gr. 5). 1989. pap. text ed. write for info. (0-9620136-3-3) L F Lewis.
—Tappan School, a History Book: The Story of a School in Ravenna, Ohio, U. S. A. Lewis, Lois F. 28p. (Orig.). (gr. 5). 1989. pap. text ed. write for info. (0-9620136-1-7) L F Lewis.
—West Main School, a History Book: The Story of a School in Ravenna, Ohio, U. S. A. Lewis, Lois F. (Orig.). (gr. 5). 1988. pap. text ed. 2.00 (0-9620136-0-9) L F Lewis.
Lewison, Terry. Into the High Branches. Malone, P. M. 196p. (Orig.). (gr. 1-8). 1992. pap. text ed. 11.95 (0-9631957-1-9) Raspberry Hill.
—Out of the Nest. Malone, P. M. 198p. (Orig.). (gr. 1-8). 1991. pap. text ed. 11.95 (0-9631957-0-0) Raspberry Hill.
—To Find a Way Home. Malone, P. M. 200p. (Orig.). (gr. 1-8). 1993. pap. text ed. 11.95 (0-9631957-2-7) Raspberry Hill.
Lexa, Susan. Do I Have To? Quigley, Stacy. Silverman, Manuel, intro. by. LC 85-24350. 32p. (gr. k-6). 1980. PLB 17.96 (0-8172-1352-X) Raintree Steck-V.
—Our Mother's Day Book. Rev. ed. Moncure, Jane B. LC 86-29980. (ps-3). 1987. PLB 19.95 (0-89565-346-X); PLB 13.95s.p. (0-685-55537-2) Childs World.
—What Was It Before It Was Orange Juice? Moncure, Jane B. LC 85-11396. 32p. (ps-2). 1985. PLB 21.35 (0-89565-322-2); PLB 14.95s.p. (0-685-55779-0) Childs World.
—Will I Ever Be Older? Grant, Eva. Hollingsworth, Charles E., intro. by. LC 80-24782. (gr. k-6). 1981. PLB 17.96 (0-8172-1363-5) Raintree Steck-V.
Lexa-Senning, Susan. Compsognathus. Riehecky, Janet. 32p. (gr. k-4). 1990. PLB 21.35 (0-89565-624-8); PLB 14.95s.p. (0-685-58729-0) Childs World.
—Life Cycles: The Singing Mailbox. Moncure, Jane B. LC 89-24000. 32p. (ps-2). 1990. PLB 21.35 (0-89565-552-7); PLB 14.95s.p. (0-685-56173-9) Childs World.

—Step into Fall: A New Season. Moncure, Jane B. LC 90-30637. 32p. (ps-2). 1990. PLB 19.95 (*0-89565-573-X*); PLB 13.95s.pp. (*0-685-56189-5*) Childs World.

Leyden, Richard. Simulators. Smith, Norman F. & Smith, Douglas W. LC 89-9083. 126p. (gr. 6-9). 1989. PLB 12.90 (*0-531-10812-0*) Watts.

—Sometimes I Like to Cry. Stanton, Elizabeth & Stanton, Henry. Rubin, Caroline, ed. LC 77-19131. 32p. (ps-2). 1978. PLB 13.95 (*0-8075-7537-2*) A Whitman.

Liberatore, Michael. Pattern Animals: Puzzles for Pattern Blocks. Mogensen & Magarian-Gold. 48p. (gr. 1-4). 1986. pap. text ed. 7.95 (*0-914040-46-4*) Cuisenaire.

Liberman, Jane. Mommy Doesn't Live Here Anymore. Duggan, Maureen H. 48p. (Orig.). (ps-7). 1987. pap. 8.95 (*0-944453-01-5*) B Brae. MOMMY DOESN'T LIVE HERE ANYMORE - a sensitive chronicle of a mother's alcoholism & how it affected her children. It has successfully captured the essence of life within an alcoholic family: the stresses, tensions, pressures & pains. Most importantly, it has done so from the vantage point of the child, as the child reflects upon the total experience. No other work has presented such a realistic portrayal of the magnitude of suffering, emotional pain & psychic turmoil of young children within alcoholic families. It reveals the thoughts, reasoning, feelings & behaviors of children in alcoholic homes, & yet, accomplishes such spirit of understanding & sympathy within an overall message of hope & help for our children. MOMMY DOESN'T LIVE HERE ANYMORE is an inspirational work, revealing that the tragedies of familial alcoholism & tragic consequences for our youth need to be dealt with in a personal & delicate manner. "Maureen Duggan has always been regarded highly for her thoughtful & gentle manner, compassionate understanding, & her acute sensitivity towards alcoholics & family needs. Her own serenity & spirituality are guides for many seeking their own honesty & fulfillment."--Nelson C. Acquilano, Executive Director, Council on Alcoholism of The Finger Lakes, N.Y. *Publisher Provided Annotation.*

Lichtner, Schomer. Alphabet Drawings. Lichtner, Schomer. 88p. (Orig.). (gr. k up). 1973. pap. 4.50 (*0-686-97176-0*) Lichtner.

Lidberg, Rolf. A Troll Wedding: The Troll Children's Search for the Magic Wedding Flower. Arpi, Erik. Engen, Kari & Gracey, Kirsten, trs. from SWE. LC 92-60297. 30p. (ps-5). 1992. 12.95 (*1-881278-00-X*) M S Pr.

Liddell, Dan. The California Native American Tribes. Boule, Mary N. (gr. 1-8). 1991. pap. 85.00 boxed ed. (*1-877599-23-9*) Merryant Pubs.

Liddell, Daniel. California's Native American Tribes, No. 1: Achumawi Tride. Boule, Mary N. 40p. (Orig.). (gr. 2-3). 1992. pap. 4.50 (*1-877599-25-5*) Merryant Pubs.

—California's Native American Tribes, No. 11: Coast Miwok. Boule, Mary N. 40p. (Orig.). (gr. 2-4). 1992. pap. 4.50 (*1-877599-35-2*) Merryant Pubs.

—California's Native American Tribes, No. 17: East & S. E. Pomo Tribe. Boule, Mary N. 40p. (Orig.). (gr. 3-4). 1992. pap. 4.50 (*1-877599-40-9*) Merryant Pubs.

—California's Native American Tribes, No. 12: Eastern Miwok Tribe. Boule, Mary N. 40p. (Orig.). (gr. 3-5). 1992. pap. 4.50 (*1-877599-36-0*) Merryant Pubs.

—California's Native American Tribes, No. 13: Lake Miwok Tribe. Boule, Mary N. 40p. (Orig.). (gr. 3-5). 1992. pap. 4.50 (*1-877599-37-9*) Merryant Pubs.

—California's Native American Tribes, No. 10: Maidu-KonKow Tribe. Boule, Mary N. 40p. (Orig.). (gr. 4-5). 1992. pap. 4.50 (*1-877599-34-4*) Merryant Pubs.

—California's Native American Tribes, No. 14: Ohlone Tribe. Boule, Mary N. 40p. (Orig.). (gr. 4-5). 1992. pap. 4.50 (*1-877599-38-7*) Merryant Pubs.

—California's Native American Tribes, No. 15: Patwin Tribe. Boule, Mary N. 60p. (Orig.). (gr. 3-5). 1992. pap. text ed. 4.50 (*1-877599-49-2*) Merryant Pubs.

—California's Native American Tribes, No. 18: Salinan Tribe. Boule, Mary N. 40p. (Orig.). (gr. 4-5). 1992. pap. 4.50 (*1-877599-41-7*) Merryant Pubs.

—California's Native American Tribes, No. 19: Shasta Tribe. Boule, Mary N. 40p. (Orig.). (gr. 2-4). 1992. pap. 4.50 (*1-877599-42-5*) Merryant Pubs.

—California's Native American Tribes, No. 16: Western & N. E. Pomo Tribe. Boule, Mary N. 40p. (Orig.). (gr. 2-3). 1992. pap. 4.50 (*1-877599-39-5*) Merryant Pubs.

—California's Native American Tribes, No. 2: Atsugewi Tribe. Boule, Mary N. 40p. (Orig.). (gr. 2-3). 1992. pap. 4.50 (*1-877599-26-3*) Merryant Pubs.

—California's Native American Tribes, No. 24: Foothill Yokuts Tribe. Boule, Mary N. 40p. (Orig.). (gr. 3-5). 1992. pap. 4.50 (*1-877599-46-8*) Merryant Pubs.

—California's Native American Tribes, No. 20: Tolowa Tribe. Boule, Mary N. 40p. (Orig.). (gr. 2-3). 1992. pap. 4.50 (*1-877599-43-3*) Merryant Pubs.

—California's Native American Tribes, No. 21: Tubatulabal Tribe. Boule, Mary N. 60p. (gr. 2-4). 1992. pap. 4.50 (*1-877599-24-7*) Merryant Pubs.

—California's Native American Tribes, No. 23: Valley Yokuts Tribe. Boule, Mary N. 40p. (Orig.). (gr. 4-5). 1992. pap. 4.50 (*1-877599-45-X*) Merryant Pubs.

—California's Native American Tribes, No. 22: Wintu Tribe. Boule, Mary N. 40p. (Orig.). (gr. 4-5). 1992. pap. 4.50 (*1-877599-44-1*) Merryant Pubs.

—California's Native American Tribes, No. 25: Yuki Tribe. Boule, Mary N. 40p. (Orig.). (gr. 2-3). 1992. pap. 4.50 (*1-877599-47-6*) Merryant Pubs.

—California's Native American Tribes, No. 26: Yurok Tribe. Boule, Mary N. 40p. (Orig.). (gr. 2-4). 1992. pap. 4.50 (*1-877599-48-4*) Merryant Pubs.

—California's Native American Tribes, No. 3: Cahuilla Tribe. Boule, Mary N. 40p. (Orig.). (gr. 2-4). 1992. pap. 4.50 (*1-877599-27-1*) Merryant Pubs.

—California's Native American Tribes, No. 4: Chumash Tribe. Boule, Mary N. 40p. (Orig.). (gr. 3-5). 1992. pap. 4.50 (*1-877599-28-X*) Merryant Pubs.

—California's Native American Tribes, No. 5: Diegueno (Ipai-Tipai) Boule, Mary N. 40p. (Orig.). (gr. 2-4). 1992. pap. 4.50 (*1-877599-29-8*) Merryant Pubs.

—California's Native American Tribes, No. 6: Gabrielino Tribe. Boule, Mary N. 40p. (Orig.). (gr. 4-5). 1992. pap. 4.50 (*1-877599-30-1*) Merryant Pubs.

—California's Native American Tribes, No. 7: Hupa Tribe. Boule, Mary N. 40p. (Orig.). (gr. 2-4). 1992. pap. 4.50 (*1-877599-31-X*) Merryant Pubs.

—California's Native American Tribes, No. 8: Karok Tribe. Boule, Mary N. 40p. (Orig.). (gr. 2-3). 1992. pap. 4.50 (*1-877599-32-8*) Merryant Pubs.

—California's Native American Tribes, No. 9: Luiseno Tribe. Boule, Mary N. 40p. (Orig.). (gr. 4-5). 1992. pap. 4.50 (*1-877599-33-6*) Merryant Pubs.

Lie, Eula. Aladdin & the Magic Lamp. Dolan, Ellen M. & Bolinske, Janet L., eds. LC 87-61661. 32p. (Orig.). (gr. 1-3). 1987. text ed. 8.95 (*0-88335-564-7*); pap. text ed. 4.95 (*0-88335-584-1*) Milliken Pub Co.

—Henny Penny. Dolan, Ellen M. & Bolinske, Janet L., eds. LC 87-61674. 32p. (Orig.). (gr. 1-3). 1987. spiral bdg. 14.95 (*0-88335-541-8*); text ed. 8.95 (*0-88335-551-5*); pap. text ed. 4.95 (*0-88335-571-X*) Milliken Pub Co.

—The Legend of Sleepy Hollow. Dolan, Ellen M. & Bolinske, Janet L., eds. LC 87-61665. 32p. (Orig.). (gr. 1-3). 1987. text ed. 8.95 (*0-88335-560-4*); pap. text ed. 4.95 (*0-88335-580-9*) Milliken Pub Co.

—The Nightingale. Dolan, Ellen M. & Bolinske, Janet L., eds. LC 87-61666. 32p. (Orig.). (gr. 1-3). 1987. text ed. 8.95 (*0-88335-559-0*); pap. text ed. 4.95 (*0-88335-579-5*) Milliken Pub Co.

—Peter Rabbit. Dolan, Ellen M. & Bolinske, Janet L., eds. LC 87-61672. 32p. (Orig.). (gr. 1-3). 1987. spiral bdg. 14.95 (*0-88335-552-3*); text ed. 8.95 (*0-88335-572-8*) Milliken Pub Co.

—The Ugly Duckling. Dolan, Ellen M. & Bolinske, Janet L., eds. LC 87-61671. 32p. (Orig.). (gr. 1-3). 1987. spiral bdg. 14.95 (*0-88335-544-2*); text ed. 8.95 (*0-88335-554-X*); pap. text ed. 4.95 (*0-88335-574-4*) Milliken Pub Co.

Liebman, Oscar. Reader's Digest Best Loved Books for Young Readers: Tales of Poe, Edgar Allan. Ogburn, Jackie, ed. 152p. (gr. 4-12). 1989. 3.99 (*0-945260-24-5*) Choice Pub NY.

Liedahl, Brian. I Speak for the Women: A Story about Lucy Stone. McPherson, Stephanie S. LC 92-13786. 1992. 14.95 (*0-87614-740-6*) Carolrhoda Bks.

Lies, Brian. Flatfoot Fox & the Case of the Missing Eye. Clifford, Eth. 48p. (gr. 2-5). 1990. 12.70 (*0-395-51945-4*) HM.

—Flatfoot Fox & the Case of the Missing Whoooo. Clifford, Eth. LC 92-21903. 1993. 13.95 (*0-395-65364-9*) HM.

—Flatfoot Fox & the Case of the Nosy Otter. Clifford, Eth. LC 91-26930. 48p. (gr. 2-5). 1992. 13.45 (*0-395-60289-0*) HM.

—George & the Dragon Word. Snyder, Dianne. 56p. (gr. 2-4). 1991. 13.45 (*0-395-55129-3*, Sandpiper) HM.

Life, Kay. Poppy's Chair. Hesse, Karen. LC 91-47708. 32p. (gr. k-3). 1993. RSBE 14.95 (*0-02-743705-1*, Macmillan Child Bk) Macmillan Child Grp.

Lighburn, Ron. Eagle Dreams. McFarlane, Sheryl. LC 93-21232. 1994. write for info. (*0-399-22695-8*, Philomel Bks) Putnam Pub Group.

Lightbown, Meredith. Three Wishes. Perrault, Charles. LC 78-18060. 32p. (gr. k-3). 1979. PLB 9.79 (*0-89375-129-4*); pap. 1.95 (*0-89375-107-3*) Troll Assocs.

Lightburn, Ron. Waiting for the Whales. McFarlane, Sheryl. LC 92-25117. 32p. (ps-3). 1993. PLB 14.95 (*0-399-22515-3*, Philomel Bks) Putnam Pub Group.

Lightfoot, Marge. Cartooning for Kids. Lightfoot, Marge. 64p. 1993. 16.95 (*1-895688-03-5*, Pub. by Greey dePencier CN); pap. 8.95 (*0-920775-84-5*, Pub. by Greey dePencier CN) Firefly Bks Ltd. All kids love cartoons. CARTOONING FOR KIDS helps them draw their very own! British Columbia cartoonist & cartooning teacher Marge Lightfoot shows kids how to create cartoons like a pro in this easy to follow & delightfully illustrated book. With fun, simple steps & helpful diagrams featuring a cast of colourful characters, Lightfoot answers any questions a budding Charles Schulz or Lynn Johnson might have. Beginners will discover what materials they'll need & how to put them to work drawing animals & people. Other pointers include how to vary facial expressions & show bodies in different positions & how to create wardrobes, fill in backgrounds & work in colour. Lightfoot also shares techniques for coming up with bright ideas, splitting stories into frames, creating captions or speech balloons & developing funny punch lines. And kids can extend their newfound skills by making greeting cards, posters, flip books & other wacky creations. There are hours of fun in CARTOONING FOR KIDS-- the perfect book for every kid who loves cartoons. *Publisher Provided Annotation.*

Lightfoot, Patricia. It's Fun to Read Coloring, Vol. 1. Spirit, Bonnie. 10p. (Orig.). (ps up). 1988. pap. text ed. 3.95 (*0-9614089-1-X*) Avitar Bks.

—Pink Rose Bush. Spirit, Bonnie. 64p. (ps up). 1985. text ed. 9.95 (*0-9614089-0-1*) Avitar Bks.

Light-Waller, Sara. Patarick Packrat & His Very Old House. Campbell, Martha S. 32p. (Orig.). (gr. 1-5). 1993. pap. 6.95 (*0-918080-68-1*) Treasure Chest.

Lightwood, Jeannette. The Story of an Arabian Foal. Jesseau, Patricia. 32p. (gr. 8). 1985. 6.95 (*0-920806-70-8*, Pub. by Penumbra Pr CN) U of Toronto Pr.

Ligon, Terry. God Is Good. Enns, Peter. 24p. (ps-5). 1985. 4.95 (*0-936215-21-6*); cassette incl. STL Intl.

—Jesus Loves Me. Enns, Peter. 24p. (ps-5). 1985. 4.95 (*0-936215-23-2*); cassette incl. STL Intl.

—Special Friends. Enns, Peter. 24p. (ps-5). 4.95 (*0-936215-22-4*); cassette incl. STL Intl.

—Stories to Remember: David, God's Champion. Enns, Peter. 32p. (ps-5). 1987. pap. 2.98 (*0-943593-04-2*); cassette 5.98 (*0-943593-06-9*); coloring bk. 0.98 (*0-943593-05-0*) Kids Intl Inc.

—Stories to Remember: Here Comes Jesus. Enns, Peter. 32p. (ps-5). 1987. pap. 2.98 (*0-943593-12-3*); coloring bk. 0.98 (*0-943593-13-1*); cassette 5.98 (*0-943593-14-X*) Kids Intl Inc.

—Stories to Remember: Walking with Jesus. Enns, Peter. 32p. (ps-5). 1987. pap. 2.98 (*0-943593-08-5*); coloring bk. 0.98 (*0-943593-09-3*) Kids Intl Inc.

Likht, Marina. Sing Along with Me. DiSilvestro, Frank. 52p. (gr. 8-10). 1985. pap. 7.95 (*0-934591-00-8*) Songs & Stories.

Lilly, Charles. Escape from Slavery: Five Journeys to Freedom. Rappaport, Doreen. LC 90-38170. 128p. (gr. 4-7). 1991. 13.00 (*0-06-021631-X*); PLB 12.89 (*0-06-021632-8*) HarpC Child Bks.

—The Legends of Marco. Willis, Meredith S. LC 93-14491. 1994. write for info. (*0-06-023558-6*); PLB write for info. (*0-06-023559-4*) HarpC Child Bks.

—Philip Hall Likes Me, I Reckon, Maybe. Greene, Bette. 144p. 1975. pap. 3.50 (*0-440-45755-6*, YB) Dell.

—Runaway to Freedom. Smucker, Barbara. LC 77-11834. 160p. (gr. 4-8). 1979. pap. 3.95 (*0-06-440106-5*, Trophy) HarpC Child Bks.

—Soup & Me. Peck, Robert N. LC 75-9514. 112p. (gr. 3-6). 1975. PLB 10.99 (*0-394-93157-2*) Knopf Bks Yng Read.

—When the Nightingale Sings. Thomas, Carol. LC 92-6045. 160p. (gr. 7 up). 1994. pap. 3.95 (*0-06-440524-9*, Trophy) HarpC Child Bks.

Lilly, Isabel. The Thames. Rogers, Daniel. LC 92-44702. 48p. (gr. 5-6). 1993. PLB 22.80 (*0-8114-3104-5*) Raintree Steck-V.

Lilly, Kenneth. The Animal Atlas. Taylor, Barbara. LC 91-53142. 64p. (gr. 3-7). 1992. 20.00 (0-679-80501-X); PLB 21.99 (0-679-90501-4) Knopf Bks Yng Read.
—Colorful Animals. Wilkes, Angela. LC 92-52799. 24p. (ps-1). 1992. 3.95 (1-56458-103-9) Dorling Kindersley.
—Come, Come to My Corner. William, Mayne. 32p. (ps-3). 1987. 9.95 (0-13-152497-6) P-H.
—Daytime Animals. Cole, Joanna. LC 85-4301. 32p. (ps-2). 1985. PLB 12.99 (0-394-97188-4) Knopf Bks Yng Read.
—Feathery Animals. Wilkes, Angela. LC 92-52800. 24p. (ps-1). 1992. 3.95 (1-56458-104-7) Dorling Kindersley.
—A Field Full of Horses. Hansard, Peter. LC 92-45830. 1994. write for info. (1-56402-302-8) Candlewick Pr.
—Furry Animals. Wilkes, Angela. LC 92-52801. 24p. (ps-1). 1992. 3.95 (1-56458-105-5) Dorling Kindersley.
—Kenneth Lilly's Animals. Pope, Joyce. LC 87-31147. 96p. (gr. 3 up). 1988. 16.95 (0-688-07696-3) Lothrop.
—Large As Life Animals in Beautiful Life-Size Paintings. Cole, Joanna. LC 89-15391. 56p. (ps-5). 1990. 14.95 (0-679-80459-5) Knopf Bks Yng Read.
—Prickly Animals. Wilkes, Angela. LC 92-52802. 24p. (ps-1). 1992. 3.95 (1-56458-106-3) Dorling Kindersley.
—Scaly Animals. Wilkes, Angela. LC 92-52803. 24p. (ps-1). 1992. 3.95 (1-56458-107-1) Dorling Kindersley.
—Spotty Animals. Wilkes, Angela. LC 92-52804. 24p. (ps-1). 1992. 3.95 (1-56458-108-X) Dorling Kindersley.
—The Squirrel. Lane, Margaret. LC 81-1229. 32p. (gr. k-4). 1993. 13.99 (0-8037-8230-6) Dial Bks Young.
—The Squirrel. Lane, Margaret. 32p. (gr. k-4). 1993. pap. 4.99 (0-14-054926-4, Puffin Pied Piper) Puffin Bks.
—Stripey Animals. Wilkes, Angela. LC 92-52805. 24p. (ps-1). 1992. 3.95 (1-56458-109-8) Dorling Kindersley.
—Wrinkly Animals. Wilkes, Angela. LC 92-52806. 24p. (ps-1). 1992. 3.95 (1-56458-110-1) Dorling Kindersley.
Lim, Ron. Ex-Mutants Graphic Novel: The Saga Begins, Vol. 1. Lawrence, David. 88p. 1988. pap. 6.95 (0-944735-03-7) Malibu Graphics.
—Ex-Mutants Graphic Novel, Vol. 2: Gods or Men. Lawrence, David. 100p. 1988. pap. 7.95 (0-944735-05-3) Malibu Graphics.
Lin, Lesley. The Mouse Bride: A Chinese Folktale. Chang, Monica. LC 91-44296. 32p. (gr. k-4). 1992. 14.95 (0-87358-533-X) Northland AZ.
Lincoln, Patricia H. An Actor's Life for Me! Gish, Lillian & Lanes, Selma. 64p. (gr. 2-5). 1987. pap. 15.00 (0-670-80416-9) Viking Child Bks.
—Camp Kickapoo. Gondosch, Linda. LC 92-28060. 128p. (gr. 4-6). 1993. 13.99 (0-525-67373-3, Lodestar Bks) Dutton Child Bks.
Lind, Jenny. Navajo Coyote Tales. Morgan, William. Thompson, Hildegard, ed. & tr. LC 88-72048. 50p. (gr. 1-3). 1988. pap. 8.95 (0-941270-52-1) Ancient City Pr.
Lind, Naomi. La Historia de Maria Wanna: O Como te Dana la Marihuana. Mann, Peggy. Ramirez, Gloria & Gatti, Maria N., trs. from ENG. (SPA.). 44p. (Orig.). (gr. 1-6). 1990. pap. text ed. 3.95 (0-942493-15-X) Woodmere Press.
—The Mary Wanna Student Activity Book. Moran, Bill. Mann, Peggy, intro. by. 23p. (gr. 4-6). 1989. pap. 2.50 (0-942493-10-9) Woodmere Press.
—The Mary Wanna Student Activity Book: Based Upon: The Sad Story of Mary Wanna Or How Marijuana Harms You. rev. ed. Moran, Bill & Mann, Peggy. 26p. (gr. 4-6). 1990. pap. text ed. 2.95 (0-942493-11-7) Woodmere Press.
Lindamood, Phyllis. Vanilla Vocabulary: Visualized-Verbalized Vocabulary Book. Bell, Nanci & Lindamood, Phyllis. 200p. (gr. 4-7). Date not set. pap. 19.00 (0-945856-03-2) Acad Reading.
Lindberg, Dean. Can You Hitch a Ride on a Comet? Rosen, Sidney. LC 92-16808. 1993. 19.95 (0-87614-719-8) Carolrhoda Bks.
—How Far Is a Star? Rosen, Sidney. 40p. (gr. k-2). 1992. 19.95 (0-87614-684-1) Carolrhoda Bks.
Lindberg, Jeffrey. A Mom by Magic. Dillon, Barbara. LC 89-29410. 144p. (gr. 3-7). 1990. (Lipp Jr Bks); PLB 13.89 (0-397-32449-9, Lipp Jr Bks) HarpC Child Bks.
—Twenty Ways to Lose Your Best Friend. Singer, Marilyn. LC 89-36576. 128p. (gr. 2-5). 1990. PLB 14.89 (0-06-025643-5) HarpC Child Bks.
—Twenty Ways to Lose Your Best Friend. Singer, Marilyn. LC 89-36576. 128p. (gr. 2-5). 1993. pap. 3.95 (0-06-440353-X, Trophy) HarpC Child Bks.
Lindblom, Steve. Messing Around with Water Pumps & Siphons: A Children's Museum Activity Book. Zubrowski, Bernie. 64p. (gr. 3-7). 1981. pap. 7.95 (0-316-98877-4) Little.
Lindblom, Steve, jt. illus. see Kelley, True.
Lindbloom, Nancy. Make the Morning. Lindbloom, James A. (gr. 3-8). 1977. pap. 3.00 (0-89409-007-0) Childrens Art.
Linden, Madelaine G. All Small. McCord, David. (gr. 6-8). 1986. lib. bdg. 12.95 (0-316-55519-3); pap. 4.95 (0-316-55520-7) Little.
—Bunny Rabbit Rebus. Adler, David A. LC 82-45574. 40p. (gr. 1-4). 1983. (Crowell Jr Bks); (Crowell Jr Bks) HarpC Child Bks.
—Bunny Rabbit Rebus. Adler, David A. (ps-3). 1987. pap. 3.95 (0-14-050775-2, Puffin) Puffin Bks.
Linder, Elizabeth. God Is My Best Friend. Burgess, Beverly C. 32p. (Orig.). (gr. 1-3). 1986. pap. 1.98 (0-89274-293-3) Harrison Hse.
—God Is Never to Busy to Listen. Burgess, Beverly C. (Orig.). (gr. 1-3). 1987. pap. 1.98 (0-89274-457-X) Harrison Hse.

Lindquist, Barbara. Something Happened to Me. Sweet, Phyllis. LC 81-83422. (gr. 2-5). 1985. pap. 4.95 (0-941300-00-5) Mother Courage.
Lindsay, Warren & Huntoon, Cathy. Christmas Time of Year: A Sing, Color, 'n Say Fun Book-Tape Package. Paxton, Lenore & Siadi, Phillip. 32p. (ps-3). 1992. pap. 6.95 (1-880449-04-8) Wrldkids Pr.
—Happy B-I-R-T-H-DAY: A Sing, Color, 'n Say Fun Book-Tape Package. Paxton, Lenore & Siadi, Phillip. 32p. (ps-3). 1992. pap. 6.95 incl. tape (1-880449-02-1) Wrldkids Pr.
Lindstrom, Eric C. Invisible Bugs & Other Creepy Creatures That Live with You. Lang, Susan S. LC 91-43712. 96p. 1992. 12.95 (0-8069-8208-X) Sterling.
—Invisible Bugs & Other Creepy Creatures That Live with You. Lang, Susan S. 96p. (gr. 4-10). 1993. pap. 4.95 (0-8069-8209-8) Sterling.
Lindstrom, Jack. Help for Kids: Understanding Your Feelings about Moving. Gesme, Carole & Peterson, Larry. Schmoker, Lisa, ed. 64p. (gr. 1-12). 1992. spiral bound wkbk. 12.95 (0-9633761-0-1); spiral bound 8.95 (0-9633761-1-X) Pine Tr Pr MN.
—I Bet You Didn't Know That Fish Sleep with Their Eyes Open & Other Facts & Curiosities. Iverson, Carol. 32p. (gr. 3-6). 1990. PLB 10.95 (0-8225-2277-2) Lerner Pubns.
—I Bet You Didn't Know That Hummingbirds Can Fly Backwards & Other Facts & Curiosities. Iverson, Carol. 32p. (gr. 3-6). 1990. PLB 10.95 (0-8225-2276-4) Lerner Pubns.
—I Bet You Didn't Know That There Are Golf Balls on the Moon & Other Facts & Curiosities. Iverson, Carol. 32p. (gr. 3-6). 1990. PLB 10.95 (0-8225-2275-6) Lerner Pubns.
—I Bet You Didn't Know That You Can't Sink in the Dead Sea & Other Facts & Curiosities. Iverson, Carol. 32p. (gr. 3-6). 1990. PLB 10.95 (0-8225-2278-0) Lerner Pubns.
Lindy, Heidi. The Ant & the Dove. Resnick, Jane P. 1992. bds. 3.25 (0-8378-2523-7) Gibson.
—The Fox & the Crow. Resnick, Jane P. 1992. bds. 3.25 (0-8378-2525-3) Gibson.
—The Lion & the Mouse. Resnick, Jane P. 1992. bds. 3.25 (0-8378-2526-1) Gibson.
—The Tortoise & the Hare. Resnick, Jane P. 1992. bds. 3.25 (0-8378-2524-5) Gibson.
Linehan, Maxene M. The Just for Kids Cookbook. Potter, Betty M. 180p. (Orig.). (gr. 1-6). 1985. pap. 9.95 comb. bdg. (0-913703-06-0) Branches.
Ling, Bill, photos by. Pig. Ling, Mary. LC 92-53487. 24p. (ps-1). 1993. 7.95 (1-56458-204-3) Dorling Kindersley.
Lingenfelter, Rosemary E. Dear Kids of Alcoholics. Hall, Lindsey & Cohn, Leigh. 96p. (gr. 3-10). 1988. pap. 6.95 (0-936077-18-2) Gurze Bks.
Lingle, Bea, jt. illus. see Mosley, Rob.
Lings, Steve. Be a Dinosaur Detective. Dixon, Dougal. 36p. (gr. k-4). 1988. 18.95 (0-8225-0894-X); pap. 4.95 (0-8225-9538-9) Lerner Pubns.
Lings, Steve & Weston, Steve. Jungle Birds. Ganeri, Anita. LC 93-19869. 32p. (gr. 4-6). 1993. PLB 19.97 (0-8114-6160-2) Raintree Steck-V.
Links, Marty & Clark, Cindy. Love the Earth. Linse, Barbara & Knight, Marilyn. Dresser, Ginny, ed. 32p. 1991. pap. write for info. Arts Pubns.
Links, Marty & Fudd, Richard. Yes I Can: Yes I Did. Links, Marty. Lins, Barbara, ed. Knight, Marilyn, intro. by. 32p. (Orig.). (ps). 1990. pap. write for info. (1-878079-00-X) Arts Pubns.
Lionni, Leo. Alexander & the Wind-up Mouse. Lionni, Leo. LC 74-2088. 32p. (ps-3). 1974. pap. 4.99 (0-394-82911-5) Pantheon.
—Alexander & the Wind-up Mouse. reissue ed. Lionni, Leo. LC 76-77423. 32p. (ps-2). 1969. 15.00 (0-394-80914-9); lib. bdg. 15.99 (0-394-90914-3) Knopf Bks Yng Read.
—Biggest House in the World. Lionni, Leo. LC 68-12646. (gr. k-3). 1968. lib. bdg. 14.99 (0-394-90944-5) Pantheon.
—A Color of His Own. Lionni, Leo. LC 75-28456. 40p. (ps-k). 1993. 8.99 (0-679-84197-0); PLB 9.99 (0-679-94197-5) Knopf Bks Yng Read.
—Fish Is Fish. Lionni, Leo. LC 78-117452. (gr. k-3). 1970. lib. bdg. 13.99 (0-394-90440-0) Pantheon.
—Frederick. Lionni, Leo. LC 66-10355. 40p. (ps-2). 1967. 16.00 (0-394-81040-6); PLB 16.99 (0-394-91040-0) Knopf Bks Yng Read.
—Frederick. Lionni, Leo. LC 66-10355. 32p. (gr. k-3). 1973. pap. 4.99 (0-394-82614-0) Knopf Bks Yng Read.
—Frederick & His Friends. Lionni, Leo. (ps-2). 1989. bk. & cassette 14.95 (0-394-82784-8) Knopf Bks Yng Read.
—Frederick's Fables: A Leo Lionni Treasury of Favorite Stories. reissued ed. Lionni, Leo. Bettelheim, Bruno, intro. by. LC 85-5186. 144p. (ps-3). 1993. 20.00 (0-394-87710-1) Knopf Bks Yng Read.
—It's Mine. Lionni, Leo. LC 85-190. 32p. (ps-1). 1986. 15.00 (0-394-87000-X); lib. bdg. 15.99 (0-394-97000-4) Knopf Bks Yng Read.
—Let's Play. Lionni, Leo. 28p. (ps). 1993. 3.25 (0-679-84030-3) Random Bks Yng Read.
—Matthew's Dream. Lionni, Leo. LC 90-34243. 32p. (ps-3). 1991. 15.00 (0-679-81075-7); PLB 15.99 (0-679-91075-1) Knopf Bks Yng Read.
—Mr. McMouse. Lionni, Leo. LC 92-8963. 40p. (ps-1). 1992. 15.00 (0-679-83890-2); PLB 15.99 (0-679-93890-7) Knopf Bks Yng Read.

—Swimmy. reissued ed. Lionni, Leo. LC 63-8504. 40p. (ps-2). 1963. 14.95 (0-394-81713-3); lib. bdg. 15.99 (0-394-91713-8) Knopf Bks Yng Read.
—Tillie & the Wall. Lionni, Leo. LC 88-9316. 32p. (ps-2). 1989. 12.95 (0-394-82155-6); lib. bdg. 13.99 (0-394-92155-0) Knopf Bks Yng Read.
Lipczenko, Susan D. When I Was Little Like You. Porett, Jane. LC 93-13974. 1993. 12.95 (0-87868-530-8) Child Welfare.
Lipking, Ron, jt. illus. see Paris, Pat.
Lipney, Stephanie & Moore, Dick. Teenage Survival Manual: How to Reach '20' in One Piece (& Enjoy Every Step of the Journey) 4th, rev. ed. Coombs, H. Samm. 235p. (gr. 9-12). 1993. pap. 9.95 (0-925258-08-3) DB Inc CA.
Lippie, Jane, jt. illus. see Lippie, Joel.
Lippie, Joel & Lippie, Jane. Eastside Historic Coloring Book. Johnston, Helen & Elvidge, Vivian, eds. McClelland, John M., Jr. 32p. (Orig.). (gr. 1-4). 1985. pap. 2.00 (0-685-28865-X) Marymoor Mus.
Lippincott, G. Jennifer Murdley's Toad. Coville, Bruce. 1992. 16.95 (0-15-200745-8, HB Juv Bks) HarBrace.
Lippincott, Gary. The Fisherman & His Wife. Grimm, Jacob & Grimm, Wilhelm K. Richardson, I. M., ed. LC 87-10902. 32p. (gr. k-4). 1988. PLB 9.79 (0-8167-1075-9); pap. text ed. 1.95 (0-8167-1076-7) Troll Assocs.
—Jeremy Thatcher, Dragon Hatcher. Coville, Bruce. Yolen, Jane, ed. 148p. (gr. 3-7). 1991. 16.95 (0-15-200748-2, J Yolen Bks) HarBrace.
—With Love, at Christmas. Fox, Mem. LC 88-6332. (gr. 2 up). 1988. 12.95 (0-87445863-3) Abingdon.
Lippincott, Gary A. Ancient Egypt. Cohen, Daniel. 48p. (gr. 2-6). 1990. 10.95 (0-385-24586-6, Zephyr-BFYR); (Zephyr-BFYR) Doubleday.
—Jennifer Murdley's Toad. Coville, Bruce. MacDonald, Pat, ed. 176p. 1993. pap. 3.50 (0-671-79401-9, Minstrel Bks) PB.
Lippincott, Laurene. My First Birthday Book. Bellamy, H. A. & Shaw, Joan. 32p. 1991. write for info. (0-9629039-0-6) Happy Rainbow.
Lippman, Peter. Busy Trains. Lippman, Peter. LC 77-86145. 32p. (ps-3). 1981. lib. bdg. 5.99 (0-394-93748-1); pap. 2.25 (0-394-83748-7) Random Bks Yng Read.
—From Here to There. Lippman, Peter. LC 75-19947. 48p. (gr. 1 up). 1975. pap. 5.00 (0-912846-11-9) Bookstore Pr.
—The Pigs' Book of World Records. Stine, Bob. LC 79-5239. 96p. (gr. 3 up). 1980. pap. 4.99 (0-394-94402-X) Random Bks Yng Read.
—Science Experiments You Can Eat. Cobb, Vicki. LC 71-151474. 127p. (gr. 5-8). 1972. PLB 14.89 (0-397-31487-6, Lipp Jr Bks) HarpC Child Bks.
Lipstein, Morissa G. The Never-Be-Bored Book: Quick Things to Make When There's Nothing to Do. Lehne, Judith L. LC 92-16529. 128p. 1992. 17.95 (0-8069-1254-5) Sterling.
Lisenby, Foy & Poole, Jerry D. Adventure Tales of Arkansas: A Cartoon History of a Spirited People. Williams, C. Fred. Clinton, Bill & Jonsson, Phillip R. intro. by. x, 38p. (Orig.). (gr. 5-7). 1986. pap. 5.95 (0-9616677-0-2); tchr's. ed. 3.50 (0-9616677-1-0) Signal Media.
Lisi, Victoria. March of the Wooden Soldiers. 48p. (ps-2). 1992. 5.95 (0-88101-261-0) Unicorn Pub.
—One-Minute Teddy Bear Stories. Lewis, Shari & O'Kun, Lan. LC 92-23033. 1993. pap. 12.95 (0-385-30909-0) Doubleday.
—Rapunzel. Grimm, Jacob & Grimm, Wilhelm K. Black, Fiona, retold by. LC 92-14259. 32p. 1992. 6.95 (0-8362-4924-0) Andrews & McMeel.
—Snowbear Whittington. Hooks, William H. LC 93-8691. 1994. write for info. (0-02-744355-8) Macmillan.
—A Visit to Christmasland: A Storybook with a Real Charm Bracelet. Eisen, Armand. 32p. 1993. incl. bracelet 12.95 (0-8362-4506-7) Andrews & McMeel.
Lisi, Victoria & Lisi, Victoria. Babes in Toyland. McDonald, Mandi. 72p. (gr. 3-7). 1990. 11.95 (0-88101-100-2) Unicorn Pub.
Lisker, Sonia O. Freckle Juice. Blume, Judy. LC 85-280. 48p. (gr. 1-3). 1978. pap. 3.50 (0-440-42813-0, YB) Dell.
—Freckle Juice. Blume, Judy. LC 85-280. 40p. (gr. 1-3). 1984. Repr. of 1971 ed. 12.95 (0-02-711690-5, Four Winds) Macmillan Child Grp.
—Leonard Bernstein: A Passion for Music. Hurwitz, Johanna. 80p. (gr. 4 up). 1993. 12.95 (0-8276-0501-3) JPS Phila.
Litchfield, Marion. The Littlest Lighthouse. Sargent, Ruth. LC 81-66268. 32p. (Orig.). (ps-1). 1981. pap. 4.50 (0-89272-119-7) Down East.
Little, Debbie. The Battle of Galveston. Townsend, Tom. Eakin, Edwin M., ed. 80p. (gr. 9-11). 1989. 10.95 (0-89015-685-9, Pub. by Panda Bks). 5.95 (0-89015-713-8) Eakin-Sunbelt.
—The Potluck Adventures of Mrs. Marmalade: A Children's Cookbook. Swendson, Patsy. Roberts, Melissa, ed. 32p. (gr. k-3). 1989. 10.95 (0-89015-718-9, Pub. by Panda Bks) Eakin-Sunbelt.
Little, Lessie J. Childtimes: A Three-Generation Memoir. Greenfield, Eloise. LC 77-26581. 192p. (gr. 4-6). 1993. pap. 5.95 (0-06-446134-3, Trophy) HarpC Child Bks.
Little, Nan K. Li'l Ol' Charlie. Wayne, Kyra P. LC 39-438. 88p. (Orig.). 1989. pap. 8.95 (0-931866-41-3) Alpine Pubns.

Littlejohn, Claire. Aesop's Fables: A Pull-the-Tab-Pop-Up-Book. LC 87-24478. 14p. (ps up). 1988. 13.95 (0-8037-0487-9) Dial Bks Young.

Littlejohn, Clare. The Owl & the Pussycat. Lear, Edward. LC 86-46115. 14p. (ps-3). 1987. 6.95 (0-694-00193-7) HarpC Child Bks.

Littler, Angela, jt. illus. see Galvani, Maureen.

Littlewood, Barbara S. The Adventures of the Black Hand Gang. Hansjurgen Press & Littlewood, Barbara S. 128p. (gr. 3-7). 1983. pap. 6.95 (0-13-013938-6, Pub. by Treehouse); pap. 4.95 (0-13-014035-X) P-H.

Littlewood, Karin. Gemma & the Baby Chick. Barber, Antonia. 32p. (ps-3). 1993. 14.95 (0-590-45479-X) Scholastic Inc.

—How Does It Feel? Landa, Norbert. LC 92-39238. 26p. 1993. 14.95 (1-56566-032-3) Thomasson-Grant.

—Science Fiction Stories. Blishen, Edward, selected by. LC 92-26453. 256p. (gr. 4-9). 1993. 6.95 (1-85697-889-3) Kingfisher Bks.

Littlewood, Valerie. Fu-Dog. Godden, Rumer. 64p. (ps-2). 1990. pap. 14.95 (0-670-82300-7) Viking Child Bks.

—Goliath & the Burglar. Dicks, Terrance. 64p. (gr. k-4). 1987. 7.95 (0-8120-5823-2); pap. 3.50 (0-8120-3820-7) Barron.

—Goliath & the Buried Treasure. Dicks, Terrance. (gr. k-4). 1987. 7.95 (0-8120-5822-4); pap. 2.95 (0-8120-3819-3) Barron.

—Goliath & the Cub Scouts. Dicks, Terrance. 64p. (gr. 2-4). 1990. pap. 2.95 (0-8120-4493-2) Barron.

—Goliath at the Dog Show. Dicks, Terrance. 64p. (gr. k-4). 1987. 7.95 (0-8120-5821-6); pap. 3.50 (0-8120-3818-5) Barron.

—Goliath at the Seaside. Dicks, Terrance. 52p. (gr. 2-4). 1989. pap. 2.95 (0-8120-4209-3) Barron.

—Goliath Goes to Summer School. Dicks, Terrance. 52p. (gr. 2-4). 1989. pap. 2.95 (0-8120-4210-7) Barron.

—Goliath on Vacation. Dicks, Terrance. 64p. (gr. k-4). 1987. 7.95 (0-8120-5824-0); pap. 3.50 (0-8120-3821-5) Barron.

—Goliath's Birthday. Dicks, Terrance. 52p. (gr. 2-5). 1992. pap. 3.50 (0-8120-4821-0) Barron.

—Goliath's Christmas. Dicks, Terrance. 64p. (gr. 2-4). 1987. PLB 7.95 (0-8120-5843-7); pap. 2.95 (0-8120-3878-9) Barron.

—Great Grandfather's House. Godden, Rumer. LC 91-48030. 80p. (gr. 1 up). 1993. 18.00 (0-688-11319-2) Greenwillow.

—On Their Own. Dicks, Terrance. 64p. (gr. 2-5). 1993. pap. 3.50 (0-8120-1675-0) Barron.

—Teacher's Pet. Dicks, Terrance. 52p. (gr. 2-5). 1992. pap. 3.50 (0-8120-4820-2) Barron.

Littlewood, Valerie & Littlewood, Valerie. Glass Angels. Hill, Susan. LC 91-58731. 96p. (gr. 3-6). 1992. 16.95 (1-56402-111-4) Candlewick Pr.

Litzinger, Rosanne. The Biggest Birthday Cake in the World. Spurr, Elizabeth. Grove, Karen, ed. LC 89-19001. 32p. (ps-3). 1991. 14.95 (0-15-207150-4) HarBrace.

—Left & Right. Oppenheim, Joanne. LC 87-22939. 153p. (ps-3). 1989. 13.95 (0-15-200505-6, Gulliver Bks) HarBrace.

—The Story Book Prince. Oppenheim, Joanne. LC 85-31745. 32p. (ps-3). 1987. 12.95 (0-15-200590-0, Gulliver Bks) HarBrace.

Litzinger, Roseanne. John Henry & His Mighty Hammer. Jensen, Patricia A. LC 93-4810. 32p. (gr. k-2). 1993. PLB 11.59 (0-8167-3156-X); pap. text ed. 2.95 (0-8167-3157-8) Troll Assocs.

—The Treasure Trap. Masterman-Smith, Virginia. LC 91-45217. 208p. (gr. 3-7). 1992. pap. 3.95 (0-689-71578-1, Aladdin) Macmillan Child Grp.

Liu, Monica. Kao & the Golden Fish: A Folktale from Thailand. Hamada, Cheryl, retold by. LC 93-298. 32p. (ps-3). 1993. PLB write for info. (0-516-05145-8) Childrens.

Liu, Sam, et al. Cyberpunk. Pondsmith, Michael. Fisk, Colin, contrib. by. 98p. (gr. 10-12). 1988. game bk. 10. 00 (0-937279-05-6, CP 3001) R Talsorian.

Livanova, Elena. The Tempest. Garfield, Leon, abridged by. LC 92-14526. 48p. (gr. 5 up). 1993. PLB 11.99 (0-679-93873-7); pap. 6.99 (0-679-83873-2) Knopf Bks Yng Read.

Lively, Penelope. Dragon Trouble. Lively, Penelope. 42p. (gr. 2-4). 1989. 3.95 (0-8120-6136-5) Barron.

Livesley, Lorna. Tall Timber Tales: More Paul Bunyan Stories. McCormick, Dell J. LC 39-20778. (gr. 4-6). 1939. 11.95 (0-87004-094-4) Caxton.

Livingston, Francis. Davy Crockett: Young Pioneer. Santrey, Laurence. LC 82-16040. 48p. (gr. 4-6). 1983. PLB 10.79 (0-89375-847-7); pap. text ed. 3.50 (0-89375-848-5) Troll Assocs.

—Kamal's Quest. Proflet, Cynthia. 40p. (gr. 5-6). 1993. 15.95 (0-9637735-0-X) Sterling Pr MS.

—Oregon Trail. Santrey, Laurence. LC 84-2643. 32p. (gr. 3-6). 1985. PLB 9.49 (0-8167-0196-2); pap. text ed. 2.95 (0-8167-0197-0) Troll Assocs.

Livingston, Malcolm. How Many Birds? 16p. (ps). 1986. 3.95 (0-86020-962-8) EDC.

—How Many Monkeys? 16p. (ps). 1986. 3.95 (0-86020-961-X) EDC.

—How Many Monsters? 16p. (ps). 1986. 3.95 (0-86020-960-1) EDC.

Livingston, Richard, jt. illus. see Bastien, Charles.

Livingstone, Malcolm. Reptiles. Brennan, Frank. LC 91-26684. 32p. (Orig.). (ps-2). 1992. pap. 5.95 (0-689-71587-0, Aladdin) Macmillan Child Grp.

—Under the Sea. Wood, Jenny. LC 91-7484. 32p. (gr. k-3). 1991. pap. 5.95 (0-689-71488-2, Aladdin) Macmillan Child Grp.

Livington, Janice. How Anansi Obtained the Sky God's Stories. Skivington, Janice. LC 91-7581. 48p. (ps-3). 1991. PLB 19.00 (0-516-05134-2); pap. 6.95 (0-516-45134-0) Childrens.

Lloyd, Errol. Shawn Goes to School. Breinburg, Petronella. LC 73-8003. 32p. (ps-2). 1974. PLB 14.89 (0-690-00277-7, Crowell Jr Bks) HarpC Child Bks.

Lloyd, Frances. The Super Science Book of Sound. Glover, David. 32p. 1994. 14.95 (1-56847-156-4) Thomson Lrning.

—The Super Science Book of Space. Wellington, Jerry. LC 93-24405. 32p. (gr. 4-8). 1993. 14.95 (1-56847-129-7) Thomson Lrning.

—The Super Science Book of the Environment. Morgan, Sally. 32p. (gr. 4-8). 1994. 14.95 (1-56847-095-9) Thomson Lrning.

—The Super Science Book of Time. Davies, Kay & Oldfield, Wendy. LC 92-42131. 32p. (gr. 4-8). 1993. 14.95g (1-56847-020-7) Thomson Lrning.

—The Super Science Book of Weather. Davies, Kay & Oldfield, Wendy. LC 92-43298. 32p. (gr. 4-8). 1993. 14.95 (1-56847-021-5) Thomson Lrning.

Lloyd, John R. Saints G'Lore: Our Shining Examples. Dumelle, Graci. 32p. (Orig.). (gr. k-6). 1992. pap. 5.95 (0-937739-12-X) Roman IL.

Lloyd, Megan. Baba Yaga: A Russian Folktale. Kimmel, Eric A., retold by. LC 90-39215. 32p. (ps-3). 1991. reinforced bdg. 14.95 (0-8234-0854-X) Holiday.

—Baba Yaga: A Russian Folktale. Kimmel, Eric A. Date not set. pap. 5.95 (0-8234-1060-9) Holiday.

—Cactus Hotel. Guiberson, Brenda Z. LC 90-41748. 32p. (ps-2). 1991. 15.95 (0-8050-1333-4, Bks Young Read) H Holt & Co.

—Cactus Hotel. Guiberson, Brenda Z. LC 90-41748. 32p. (ps-3). 1993. pap. 4.95 (0-8050-2960-5, Bks Young Read) H Holt & Co.

—The Christmas Tree Ride. Neville, Mary. LC 91-28853. 32p. (ps-3). 1992. reinforced bdg. 14.95 (0-8234-0956-2) Holiday.

—The Gingerbread Man. Kimmel, Eric A., retold by. 32p. (ps-3). 1993. reinforced bdg. 14.95 (0-8234-0824-8) Holiday.

—How We Learned the Earth Is Round. Lauber, Patricia. LC 89-49650. 32p. (gr. k-4). 1990. 14.00 (0-690-04860-2, Crowell Jr Bks); PLB 13.89 (0-690-04862-9, Crowell Jr Bks) HarpC Child Bks.

—How We Learned the Earth Is Round. Lauber, Patricia. LC 89-49650. 32p. (gr. k-4). 1992. pap. 4.50 (0-06-445109-7, Trophy) HarpC Child Bks.

—How You Talk. rev. ed. Showers, Paul. LC 90-1484. 32p. (gr. k-4). 1992. 14.00 (0-06-022767-2); PLB 13. 89 (0-06-022768-0) HarpC Child Bks.

—How You Talk. rev. ed. Showers, Paul. LC 90-4056. 32p. (gr. k-4). 1992. pap. 4.50 (0-06-445099-6, Trophy) HarpC Child Bks.

—The Little Old Lady Who Was Not Afraid of Anything. Williams, Linda. LC 85-48250. 32p. (ps-2). 1986. 14.00 (0-690-04584-0, Crowell Jr Bks); PLB 13. 89 (0-690-04586-7) HarpC Child Bks.

—The Little Old Lady Who Was Not Afraid of Anything. Williams, Linda. LC 85-48250. 32p. (ps-2). 1988. pap. 4.95 (0-06-443183-5, Trophy) HarpC Child Bks.

—Lobster Boat. Guiberson, Brenda Z. LC 92-4055. 32p. (ps-3). 1993. PLB 14.95 (0-8050-1756-9, Bks Young Read) H Holt & Co.

—Look Out for Turtles! Berger, Melvin. LC 90-36894. 32p. (gr. k-4). 1992. 15.00 (0-06-022539-4); PLB 14. 89 (0-06-022540-8) HarpC Child Bks.

—More Surprises. Hopkins, Lee B., ed. LC 86-45335. 64p. (gr. k-3). 1987. PLB 13.89 (0-06-022605-6) HarpC Child Bks.

—Spoonbill Swamp. Guiberson, Brenda Z. LC 91-8555. 32p. (ps-3). 1992. 14.95 (0-8050-1583-3, Bks Young Read) H Holt & Co.

—Super Cluck. O'Connor, Jane & O'Connor, Robert. LC 90-32832. 64p. (ps-3). 1991. 11.95 (0-06-024594-8); PLB 11.89 (0-06-024595-6) HarpC Child Bks.

—Super Cluck. O'Connor, Jane & O'Connor, Robert. LC 90-32832. 64p. (gr. k-3). 1993. pap. 3.50 (0-06-444162-8, Trophy) HarpC Child Bks.

—Surprises. Hopkins, Lee B. LC 83-47712. 64p. (gr. k-3). 1986. pap. 3.50 (0-06-444105-9, Trophy) HarpC Child Bks.

—That Sky, That Rain. Otto, Carolyn. LC 89-36582. 32p. (ps-3). 1990. (Crowell Jr Bks); PLB 12.89 (0-690-04765-7, Crowell Jr Bks) HarpC Child Bks.

—That Sky, That Rain. Otto, Carolyn. LC 89-36582. 32p. (ps-3). 1992. pap. 4.95 (0-06-443290-4, Trophy) HarpC Child Bks.

Lo-An. House in the Bend of Bourbon Street. Flettrich, Terry. (gr. 1-6). 1974. pap. 2.95 (0-88289-015-8) Pelican.

Loates, Glen. Forest Mammals. Kalman, Bobbie. 56p. (gr. 3-4). 1987. 15.95 (0-86505-165-8); pap. 7.95 (0-86505-185-2) Crabtree Pub Co.

—Owls. Kalman, Bobbie. 56p. (gr. 3-4). 1987. 15.95 (0-86505-164-X); pap. 7.95 (0-86505-184-4) Crabtree Pub Co.

Loates, Mick & Male, Alan. Ponds & Streams. Stidworthy, John. LC 89-20331. 32p. (gr. 3-6). 1990. PLB 11.59 (0-8167-1963-2); pap. text ed. 3.95 (0-8167-1964-0) Troll Assocs.

Loback, Tom, jt. illus. see Martin, David.

Lobato, Arcadio. The Greatest Treasure. Lobato, Arcadio. LC 89-3612. 28p. (ps up). 1991. pap. 14.95 (0-88708-093-6) Picture Bk Studio.

—Just One Wish. Lobato, Arcadio. Clements, Andrew, tr. from GER. LC 89-49263. 32p. (ps up). 1991. pap. 14. 95 (0-88708-134-7) Picture Bk Studio.

Lobban, John. More Fun with Science: Practice at Home. Dwyer, Derek & Corby, Jill. 24p. (Orig.). (gr. 3-5). 1992. pap. 2.95 wkbk. (0-7214-3240-9, S9115-3) Ladybird Bks.

—Paddington at the Circus. Bond, Michael. LC 91-44210. 32p. (ps-2). 1992. 8.95 (0-694-00415-4, Festival) HarpC Child Bks.

—Paddington at the Seashore. Bond, Michael. 28p. (ps). 1992. 2.95 (0-694-00397-2) HarpC Child Bks.

—Paddington Bear. Bond, Michael. LC 91-29781. 32p. (ps-3). 1992. 8.95 (0-694-00394-8) HarpC Child Bks.

—Paddington Goes Shopping. Bond, Michael. 28p. (ps). 1992. 2.95 (0-694-00395-6) HarpC Child Bks.

—Paddington in the Kitchen. Bond, Michael. 28p. (ps). 1992. 2.95 (0-694-00396-4) HarpC Child Bks.

—Paddington Meets the Queen. Bond, Michael. LC 92-24938. 32p. (ps-3). 1993. 3.95 (0-694-00460-X, Festival) HarpC Child Bks.

—Paddington Rides On! Bond, Michael. LC 92-24937. 32p. (ps-3). 1993. 3.95 (0-694-00461-8, Festival) HarpC Child Bks.

—Paddington Takes a Bath. Bond, Michael. 28p. (ps). 1992. 2.95 (0-694-00398-0) HarpC Child Bks.

—Paddington's Colors. Bond, Michael. 32p. (ps-1). 1991. 10.99 (0-670-84102-1) Viking Child Bks.

—Paddington's Garden. Bond, Michael. LC 92-24527. 32p. (ps-3). 1993. 8.95 (0-694-00462-6, Festival) HarpC Child Bks.

—Paddington's Magical Christmas. Bond, Michael. 32p. (ps-3). 1993. 8.95 (0-694-00503-7, Festival) HarpC Child Bks.

Lobel, Anita. The Dwarf Giant. Lobel, Anita. LC 90-39214. 32p. (ps-3). 1991. reinforced 14.95 (0-8234-0852-3) Holiday.

—Indian Summer. Monjo, F. N. LC 78-20264. 192p. (gr. k-3). 1968. PLB 13.89 (0-06-024328-7) HarpC Child Bks.

—Looking for Daniela: A Romantic Adventure. Kroll, Steven. LC 87-29071. 32p. (ps-3). 1988. reinforced bdg. 14.95 (0-8234-0695-4) Holiday.

—A New Coat for Anna. Ziefert, Harriet. LC 86-2722. 40p. (ps-3). 1986. PLB 11.99 (0-394-97426-3) Knopf Bks Yng Read.

—A New Coat for Anna. Ziefert, Harriet. LC 86-2722. 40p. (ps-3). 1988. pap. 4.95 (0-394-89861-3) Knopf Bks Yng Read.

—The Night Before Christmas. Moore, Clement C. LC 84-4342. 32p. (ps-5). 1984. 12.00 (0-394-86863-3); lib. bdg. 12.99 (0-394-96863-8) Knopf Bks Yng Read.

—On Market Street. Lobel, Arnold. LC 80-21418. 40p. (gr. k-3). 1981. 14.00 (0-688-80309-1); PLB 13.93 (0-688-84309-3); Greenwillow.

—On Market Street. Lobel, Arnold. LC 80-21418. (ps up). 1989. pap. 4.95 (0-688-08745-0, Mulberry) Morrow.

—Once: A Lullaby. Nichol, B. P. LC 85-9942. 24p. (ps-1). 1986. 11.95 (0-688-04284-8); PLB 11.88 (0-688-04285-6) Greenwillow.

—Once: A Lullaby. Nichol, B. P. LC 85-9942. 24p. (ps up). 1992. pap. 4.95 (0-688-04286-4, Mulberry) Morrow.

—Princess Furball. Huck, Charlotte. LC 88-18780. 40p. (ps up). 1989. 13.95 (0-688-07837-0); PLB 13.88 (0-688-07838-9) Greenwillow.

—Princess Furball. Huck, Charlotte. 40p. (ps up). 1994. pap. 4.95 (0-688-13107-7, Mulberry) Morrow.

—The Rose in My Garden. Lobel, Arnold. LC 83-14097. 40p. (gr. k-3). 1984. 16.00 (0-688-02586-2); PLB 15. 93 (0-688-02587-0) Greenwillow.

—The Rose in My Garden. Lobel, Arnold. 32p. (ps-2). 1985. pap. 3.95 (0-590-41530-1) Scholastic Inc.

—The Rose in My Garden. Lobel, Arnold. LC 92-24588. 40p. (ps). 1993. pap. 4.95 (0-688-12265-5, Mulberry) Morrow.

—Singing Bee! A Collection of Favorite Children's Songs. Hart, Jane, ed. LC 82-15296. 160p. 1989. Repr. of 1982 ed. 17.95 (0-688-41975-5) Lothrop.

—Singing Bee! A Collection of Favorite Children's Songs. Hart, Jane, ed. LC 82-15296. 160p. 1991. pap. 12.00 (0-688-09113-X, Mulberry) Morrow.

—This Quiet Lady. Zolotow, Charlotte. LC 90-38485. 24p. (ps up). 1992. 14.00 (0-688-09305-1); PLB 13.93 (0-688-09306-X) Greenwillow.

—A Treeful of Pigs. Lobel, Arnold. 32p. (gr. k-3). 1988. pap. 3.95 (0-590-41280-9, Blue Ribbon Bks) Scholastic Inc.

Lobel, Arnold. As I Was Crossing Boston Common. Farber, Norma. LC 75-6520. 32p. (ps-2). 1991. Repr. 14.95 (0-525-25960-0, DCB) Dutton Child Bks.

—As I Was Crossing Boston Common. Farber, Norma. LC 75-6520. 32p. (ps-2). 1991. pap. 3.95 (0-525-44781-4, Puffin) Puffin Bks.

—The Book of Pigericks. Lobel, Arnold. LC 82-47730. 48p. (gr. k-3). 1983. PLB 14.89 (0-06-023983-2) HarpC Child Bks.

—The Book of Pigericks (Pig Limericks) Lobel, Arnold. LC 82-47730. 48p. (ps up). 1988. pap. 5.95 (0-06-443163-0, Trophy) HarpC Child Bks.

—Circus! Prelutsky, Jack. 32p. (ps-2). 1989. pap. 3.95 (0-689-70806-8, Aladdin) Macmillan Child Grp.

—Days with Frog & Toad. Lobel, Arnold. LC 78-21786. 64p. (ps-3). 1985. (Trophy); pap. 3.50 (0-06-444058-3, Trophy) HarpC Child Bks.
—The Devil & Mother Crump. Carey, Valerie S. LC 87-64. 40p. (gr. k-3). 1987. HarpC Child Bks.
—The Devil & Mother Crump. Carey, Valerie S. LC 87-64. 40p. (gr. 2-5). 1992. pap. 4.95 (0-06-443278-5, Trophy) HarpC Child Bks.
—Dinosaur Time. Parish, Peggy. LC 73-14331. 32p. (gr. k-3). 1974. 14.00 (0-06-024653-7); PLB 13.89 (0-06-024654-5) HarpC Child Bks.
—Dinosaur Time. Parish, Peggy. LC 73-14331. 32p. (ps-2). 1983. pap. 3.50 (0-06-444037-0, Trophy) HarpC Child Bks.
—Fables. Lobel, Arnold. LC 79-2004. 48p. (gr. 1-4). 1980. 15.00 (0-06-023973-5); PLB 14.89 (0-06-023974-3) HarpC Child Bks.
—Frog & Toad All Year. Lobel, Arnold. LC 76-2343. 64p. (gr. k-3). 1985. (Trophy); pap. 3.50 (0-06-444059-1, Trophy) HarpC Child Bks.
—Frog & Toad Are Friends. Lobel, Arnold. LC 73-105492. 64p. (gr. k-3). 1970. 14.00 (0-06-023957-3); PLB 13.89 (0-06-023958-1) HarpC Child Bks.
—Frog & Toad Are Friends. Lobel, Arnold. LC 73-105492. 64p. (gr. k-3). 1985. (Trophy); pap. 3.50 (0-06-444020-6, Trophy) HarpC Child Bks.
—Frog & Toad Boxed Set, 4 bks. Lobel, Arnold. (gr. k-3). 1994. pap. 14.00 64p. ea. (0-06-444167-9, Trophy) HarpC Child Bks.
—The Frog & Toad Pop-Up Book. Lobel, Arnold. LC 85-45373. 12p. (ps-3). 1986. 9.95i (0-06-023986-7) HarpC Child Bks.
—Frog & Toad Together. Lobel, Arnold. LC 73-183163. 64p. (gr. k-3). 1972. 14.00 (0-06-023959-X); PLB 13.89 (0-06-023960-3) HarpC Child Bks.
—Frog & Toad Together. Lobel, Arnold. LC 73-183163. 64p. (ps-3). 1985. (Trophy); pap. 3.50 (0-06-444021-4, Trophy) HarpC Child Bks.
—Giant John. Lobel, Arnold. LC 64-16639. 32p. (gr. k-3). 1964. PLB 14.89 (0-06-022946-2) HarpC Child Bks.
—Grasshopper on the Road. Lobel, Arnold. LC 77-25653. 64p. (gr. k-3). 1978. 14.00 (0-06-023961-1); PLB 13.89 (0-06-023962-X) HarpC Child Bks.
—Grasshopper on the Road. Lobel, Arnold. LC 77-25653. 64p. (gr. k-3). 1986. pap. 3.50 (0-06-444094-X, Trophy) HarpC Child Bks.
—Great Blueness & Other Predicaments. Lobel, Arnold. LC 68-24323. 32p. (ps-3). 1994. pap. 5.95 (0-06-443316-1, Trophy) HarpC Child Bks.
—Greg's Microscope. Selsam, Millicent E. LC 63-8002. 64p. (gr. k-3). 1963. PLB 13.89 (0-06-025296-0) HarpC Child Bks.
—Greg's Microscope. Selsam, Millicent E. LC 63-8002. 64p. (gr. k-3). 1990. pap. 3.50 (0-06-444144-X, Trophy) HarpC Child Bks.
—The Headless Horseman Rides Tonight. Prelutsky, Jack. LC 80-10372. 40p. (gr. 1-4). 1980. 13.95 (0-688-80273-7); PLB 13.88 (0-688-84273-9) Greenwillow.
—The Headless Horseman Rides Tonight. Prelutsky, Jack. ALC Staff, ed. LC 80-10372. 40p. (gr. 1 up). 1992. pap. 4.95 (0-688-11705-8, Mulberry) Morrow.
—Hildilid's Night. reissued ed. Ryan, Cheli D. LC 86-5294. 32p. (ps-2). 1986. RSBE 13.95 (0-02-777260-8, Macmillan Child Bk) Macmillan Child Grp.
—Holiday for Mister Muster. Lobel, Arnold. LC 63-15323. 32p. (gr. k-3). 1963. PLB 12.89 (0-06-023956-5) HarpC Child Bks.
—I'll Fix Anthony. Viorst, Judith. LC 78-77942. (ps-3). 1969. 14.00i (0-06-026306-7); PLB 13.89 (0-06-026307-5) HarpC Child Bks.
—I'll Fix Anthony. Viorst, Judith. LC 87-18725. 32p. (gr. k-4). 1988. pap. 3.95 (0-689-71202-2, Aladdin) Macmillan Child Grp.
—Junk Day on Easy Street & Other Easy-To-Read Stories. Moore, Lilian. (gr. 1-4). 1991. pap. 2.75 (0-553-15627-6, Skylark) Bantam.
—The Just Right Mother Goose: Just Right for 3's & 4's. LC 88-43156. 32p. (ps). 1989. PLB 5.99 (0-394-92860-1) Random Bks Yng Read.
—Little Runner of the Longhouse. Baker, Betty. LC 62-8040. 64p. (gr. k-3). 1962. PLB 13.89 (0-06-020341-2) HarpC Child Bks.
—Little Runner of the Longhouse. Baker, Betty. LC 62-8040. 64p. (gr. k-3). 1989. pap. 3.50 (0-06-444122-9, Trophy) HarpC Child Bks.
—The Magic Spectacles & Other Easy-to-Read Stories. Moore, Lilian. 1992. pap. 2.99 (0-553-48026-X) Bantam.
—Martha the Movie Mouse. Lobel, Arnold. LC 66-18654. 32p. (ps-3). 1993. pap. 4.95 (0-06-443318-8, Trophy) HarpC Child Bks.
—The Mean Old Mean Hyena. Prelutsky, Jack. LC 78-2300. 32p. (gr. k-3). 1978. PLB 11.88 (0-688-84163-5) Greenwillow.
—The Microscope. Kumin, Maxine. LC 82-47728. 32p. (ps-3). 1984. PLB 12.89 (0-06-023524-1) HarpC Child Bks.
—Ming Lo Moves the Mountain. Lobel, Arnold. LC 81-13327. 32p. (gr. k-3). 1982. PLB 14.93 (0-688-00611-6) Greenwillow.
—Ming Lo Moves the Mountain. Lobel, Arnold. (gr. k-4). 1993. 14.95 (0-685-64815-X); audio cass. 11.00 (1-882869-76-1) Read Advent.

—Miss Suzy's Easter Surprise. Young, Miriam. LC 80-16966. 48p. (ps-3). 1984. Repr. of 1972 ed. RSBE 13.95 (0-02-793680-5, Four Winds) Macmillan Child Grp.
—More Tales of Oliver Pig. Van Leeuwen, Jean. LC 80-23289. (ps-3). 1981. PLB 9.89 (0-8037-8714-6); pap. 4.95 (0-8037-8713-8) Dial Bks Young.
—More Tales of Oliver Pig. Van Leeuwen, Jean. (gr. k-3). 1993. pap. 3.25 (0-14-036554-0, Puffin) Puffin Bks.
—Mouse Soup. Lobel, Arnold. LC 76-41517. 64p. (gr. k-3). 1977. 14.00 (0-06-023967-0); PLB 13.89 (0-06-023968-9) HarpC Child Bks.
—Mouse Soup. Lobel, Arnold. LC 76-41517. 64p. (gr. k-3). 1986. (Trophy); pap. 3.50 (0-06-444041-9, Trophy) HarpC Child Bks.
—Mouse Tales. Lobel, Arnold. LC 66-18654. 64p. (gr. k-3). 1972. 14.00 (0-06-023941-7); PLB 13.89 (0-06-023942-5) HarpC Child Bks.
—Mouse Tales. Lobel, Arnold. LC 72-76511. 64p. (ps-3). 1978. pap. 3.50 (0-06-444013-3, Trophy) HarpC Child Bks.
—Nightmares: Poems to Trouble Your Sleep. Prelutsky, Jack. 40p. 1993. pap. 4.95 (0-688-04589-8, Mulberry) Morrow.
—On the Day Peter Stuyvesant Sailed into Town. Lobel, Arnold. LC 75-148420. 48p. (ps-3). 1987. pap. 4.95 (0-06-443144-4, Trophy) HarpC Child Bks.
—Oscar Otter. Benchley, Nathaniel. LC 66-11499. 64p. (gr. k-3). 1966. PLB 13.89 (0-06-020472-9) HarpC Child Bks.
—Oscar Otter. Benchley, Nathaniel. LC 66-11499. 64p. (gr. k-3). 1980. pap. 3.50 (0-06-444025-7, Trophy) HarpC Child Bks.
—Owl at Home. Lobel, Arnold. LC 74-2630. 64p. (gr. k-3). 1975. PLB 13.89 (0-06-023949-2) HarpC Child Bks.
—Owl at Home. Lobel, Arnold. LC 74-2630. 64p. (gr. k-3). 1987. incl. cassette 5.98 (0-694-00176-7, Trophy); pap. 3.50 (0-06-444034-6, Trophy) HarpC Child Bks.
—Prince Bertram the Bad. Lobel, Arnold. LC 63-8741. 32p. (gr. k-3). 1963. PLB 13.89 (0-06-023976-X) HarpC Child Bks.
—The Quarreling Book. Zolotow, Charlotte. LC 63-14445. 32p. (gr. k-3). 1963. 13.00 (0-06-026975-8); PLB 12.89 (0-06-026976-6) HarpC Child Bks.
—The Quarreling Book. Zolotow, Charlotte. LC 63-14445. 32p. (gr. k-3). 1982. pap. 3.95 (0-06-443034-0, Trophy) HarpC Child Bks.
—The Random House Book of Mother Goose: A Treasury of 306 Timeless Nursery Rhymes. Lobel, Arnold, selected by. LC 86-47532. 176p. (gr. 2-6). 1986. 16.00 (0-394-86799-8); lib. bdg. 16.99 (0-394-96799-2, Random Juv) Random Bks Yng Read.
—The Random House Book of Poetry for Children. Prelutsky, Jack. LC 81-85940. 248p. (gr. 1-5). 1983. 17.00 (0-394-85010-6); lib. bdg. 17.99 (0-394-95010-0) Random Bks Yng Read.
—Red Fox & His Canoe. Benchley, Nathaniel. LC 64-16650. 64p. (gr. k-3). 1964. PLB 13.89 (0-06-020476-1) HarpC Child Bks.
—Red Fox & His Canoe. Benchley, Nathaniel. LC 64-16650. 64p. (gr. k-3). 1985. pap. 3.50 (0-06-444075-3, Trophy) HarpC Child Bks.
—Red Tag Comes Back. Phleger, Frederick B. LC 61-11452. 64p. (gr. k-3). 1961. PLB 13.89 (0-06-024706-1) HarpC Child Bks.
—Sam the Minuteman. Benchley, Nathaniel. LC 68-10211. 64p. (gr. k-3). 1969. PLB 13.89 (0-06-020480-X) HarpC Child Bks.
—Sam the Minuteman. Benchley, Nathaniel. LC 68-10211. 64p. (gr. k-3). 1987. pap. 3.50 (0-06-444107-5, Trophy) HarpC Child Bks.
—Secret Three. Myrick, Mildred. LC 63-13323. 64p. (gr. k-3). 1963. PLB 13.89 (0-06-024356-2) HarpC Child Bks.
—Small Pig. Lobel, Arnold. LC 69-10213. 64p. (gr. k-3). 1969. PLB 13.89 (0-06-023932-8) HarpC Child Bks.
—Small Pig. Lobel, Arnold. LC 69-10213. 64p. (gr. k-3). 1988. pap. 3.50 (0-06-444120-2, Trophy) HarpC Child Bks.
—Someday. Zolotow, Charlotte. LC 64-16654. 32p. (gr. k-3). 1965. PLB 12.89 (0-06-027016-0) HarpC Child Bks.
—Strange Disappearance of Arthur Cluck. Benchley, Nathaniel. LC 67-4151. 64p. (gr. k-3). 1967. PLB 13.89 (0-06-020478-8) HarpC Child Bks.
—The Tale of Meshka the Kvetch. Chapman, Carol. LC 80-11225. 32p. (gr. k-3). 1980. 13.95 (0-525-40745-6, DCB) Dutton Child Bks.
—The Tale of Meshka the Kvetch. Chapman, Carol. LC 80-11225. 32p. (gr. k-3). 1989. pap. 3.95 (0-525-44494-7, DCB) Dutton Child Bks.
—Tales of Oliver Pig. Van Leeuwen, Jean. LC 79-4276. 64p. (ps-3). 1979. PLB 9.89 (0-8037-8736-7); pap. 4.95 (0-8037-8737-5) Dial Bks Young.
—Tales of Oliver Pig. Van Leeuwen, Jean. (gr. k-3). 1993. pap. 3.25 (0-14-036549-4, Puffin) Puffin Bks.
—The Terrible Tiger. Prelutsky, Jack. LC 88-7901. 32p. (ps-2). 1989. pap. 3.95 (0-689-71300-2, Aladdin) Macmillan Child Grp.
—Terry & the Caterpillars. Selsam, Millicent E. LC 62-13309. 64p. (gr. k-3). 1962. PLB 11.89 (0-06-025406-8) HarpC Child Bks.
—A Three Hat Day. Geringer, Laura. LC 85-42640. 32p. (ps-3). 1985. PLB 14.89 (0-06-021989-0) HarpC Child Bks.

—A Three Hat Day. Geringer, Laura. LC 85-42640. 32p. (ps-3). 1987. pap. 4.95 (0-06-443157-6, Trophy) HarpC Child Bks.
—The Turnaround Wind. Lobel, Arnold. LC 87-45293. 32p. (ps-3). 1988. PLB 12.89 (0-06-023988-3) HarpC Child Bks.
—Tyrannosaurus Was a Beast. Prelutsky, Jack. LC 87-25131. 32p. (ps up). 1992. pap. 4.95 (0-688-11569-1, Mulberry) Morrow.
—Tyrannosaurus Was a Beast. enl. ed. Prelutsky, Jack. 32p. (ps up). 1993. pap. 18.95 (0-688-12613-8, Mulberry) Morrow.
—Uncle Elephant. Lobel, Arnold. LC 80-8944. 64p. (gr. k-3). 1981. 14.00 (0-06-023979-4); PLB 13.89 (0-06-023980-8) HarpC Child Bks.
—Whiskers & Rhymes. Lobel, Arnold. LC 83-25424. 48p. (gr. k-3). 1985. 13.00 (0-688-03835-2); lib. bdg. 12.88 (0-688-03836-0) Greenwillow.

Lobley, Robert E. Hannah Hummingbird. Hall, Sarabel. LC 88-30357. 16p. (Orig.). (gr. 1-3). 1989. pap. 6.95 (0-86534-131-1) Sunstone Pr.

LoBue, Elisa M. Big Foot, Little Foot. Kimball, Kathleen M. LC 78-68822. (ps). 1979. 6.95 (0-933308-00-0) West Village.

Loccisano, Karen. Midnight in the Dollhouse. Stover, Marjorie. Levine, Abby, ed. LC 89-37904. 160p. (gr. 3-6). 1990. 11.95 (0-8075-5124-4) A Whitman.
—The Teddy Bear Who Couldn't Do Anything. Anastasio, Dina. 24p. 1993. 2.95 (0-7214-3511-4) Ladybird Bks.
—When the Dolls Woke. Stover, Marjorie. Levine, Abby, ed. LC 85-3154. 128p. (gr. 3-6). 1985. PLB 10.95 (0-8075-8882-2) A Whitman.

Locke, Barbara K. What's So Special about Nantucket? Miles, Mary. LC 98-71418. 36p. (ps up). 1993. PLB 17.00 (0-9636885-0-2) Faraway Pub. This is the story of "Tuck," traveling by ferry with his mother to Nantucket Island where he was born. They will spend the summer with his Gram there while Mom writes a book. Tuck doesn't remember the island at all, but people have told him that he'll love it because "there's something so special about Nantucket." As he visits famous scenic, & historic island sites with his Gram he keeps wondering if THIS or THAT is the special thing. Is it the peppermint-striped lighthouse? Is it bubble-blowing at sunset at Steps Beach? Is it band concerts with balloons & tubas & dancing kids & ice cream cones? Tuck scarcely realizes that he's learning a lot about the history & environment of Nantucket as he enjoys day after day of exploring with Gram & her dog Emma. But finally he discovers the answer to the big question: it's not only boats & lighthouses, flowers & birds & cobblestones & scallops that make the island special--it's seeing your Dad arriving on the ferry as it rounds Brant Point & suddenly knowing that the most special thing of all is sharing the Nantucket Island with the people you love. To order: Faraway Publishing Group, Box 792, Nantucket, MA 02554. *Publisher Provided Annotation.*

Locke, Lafe. Clown Skits for Everyone. Happy Jack Feder. Zapel, Arthur, ed. LC 90-29297. 176p. (gr. 9 up). 1990. pap. 9.95 (0-916260-75-5, B147) Meriwether Pub.

Locker, Thomas. The Boy Who Held Back the Sea. Hort, Lenny. LC 86-32893. 1987. 15.00 (0-8037-0406-2); PLB 14.89 (0-8037-0407-0) Dial Bks Young.
—Calico & Tin Horns. Christiansen, Candace. LC 91-3706. 32p. 1992. 16.00 (0-8037-1179-4); PLB 15.89 (0-8037-1180-8) Dial Bks Young.
—Catskill Eagle. Melville, Herman. 32p. (gr-3). 1991. 15.95 (0-399-21857-2, Philomel) Putnam Pub Group.
—Family Farm. Locker, Thomas. LC 87-19645. 32p. (ps up). 1988. 16.99 (0-8037-0489-5); PLB 14.89 (0-8037-0490-9) Dial Bks Young.
—First Thanksgiving. George, Jean C. LC 91-46643. 32p. (ps up). 1993. PLB 15.95 (0-399-21991-9, Philomel Bks) Putnam Pub Group.
—The Ice Horse. Christiansen, Candace. LC 92-28964. 1993. PLB write for info. Dial Bks Young.

—The Land of Gray Wolf. Locker, Thomas. LC 90-3915. 32p. (ps up). 1991. 15.95 (0-8037-0936-6); lib. bdg. 15.89 (0-8037-0937-4) Dial Bks Young.
—The Mare on the Hill. Locker, Thomas. LC 85-1684. 32p. (gr. k-12). 1985. 15.95 (0-8037-0207-8); PLB 15.89 (0-8037-0208-6) Dial Bks Young.
—Rip Van Winkle. Locker, Thomas, adapted by. LC 87-24448. 32p. (ps up). 1988. 15.95 (0-8037-0520-4); PLB 15.89 (0-8037-0521-2) Dial Bks Young.
—Sailing with the Wind. Locker, Thomas. LC 85-23381. 32p. (ps up). 1986. 15.00 (0-8037-0311-2); PLB 14.89 (0-8037-0312-0) Dial Bks Young.
—Snow Toward Evening, a Year in a River Valley. Frank, Josette, selected by. LC 89-48307. 32p. 1990. 16.00 (0-8037-0810-6); PLB 15.89 (0-8037-0811-4) Dial Bks Young.
—Thirteen Moons on Turtle's Back: A Native American Year of Moons. Bruchac, Joseph & London, Jonathan, eds. 32p. (ps-8). 1992. PLB 15.95 (0-399-22141-7, Philomel Bks) Putnam Pub Group.
—The Ugly Duckling. Andersen, Hans Christian. Mayer, Marianna, retold by. LC 85-23869. 40p. (ps up). 1987. RSBE 16.95 (0-02-765130-4, Macmillan Child Bk) Macmillan Child Grp.
Lockhart, Lynne. Christmas Tall Books, 3 bks. Lockhart, Barbara. 36p. (ps). 1993. Set, incl. snowman. bds. 14.95 (1-56828-044-0) Red Jacket Pr.
—The Christmas Tree. Lockhart, Barbara. 12p. (ps). 1993. 4.95 (1-56828-025-4) Red Jacket Pr.
—Once a Pony Time at Chincoteague. Lockhart, Barbara & Lockhart, Lynne. 30p. (gr. k-5). 1992. 8.95 (0-87033-436-0) Tidewater.
—Santa. Lockhart, Barbara. 12p. 1993. 4.95 (1-56828-026-2) Red Jacket Pr.
—The Snowman. Lockhart, Barbara. 12p. (ps). 1993. 4.95 (1-56828-024-6) Red Jacket Pr.
Lockman, Vic. Cartooning for Young Children, Bk. II. Lockman, Vic. 48p. (ps-8). 1992. stapled bdg. 6.95 (0-936175-23-0) V Lockman.
—God's Law for Modern Man: Cartoon Illustrated. Lockman, Vic. 60p. 1993. stapled 6.00 (0-936175-25-7) V Lockman.
—Machines. Lockman, Vic. 48p. (Orig.). (gr. 8 up) 1992. pap. 5.95 stapled (0-936175-20-6) V Lockman.
—Miracle Art: Trick Cartoons. Lockman, Vic. 48p. (Orig.). (gr. 8 up). 1992. pap. 5.95 stapled (0-936175-19-2) V Lockman.
—Reading & Understanding the Bible. Lockman, Vic. 56p. (gr. 6). 1992. stapled 5.95 (0-936175-18-4) V Lockman.
—Super Bug Leads Tim Burr to the Gospel in the Woods. Lockman, Vic. 24p. (Orig.). (gr. 8 up). 1991. pap. 2.95 (0-936175-14-1) V Lockman.
Lodge, Bernard. Prince Ivan & the Firebird: A Russian Folk Tale. Bernard, Lodge, retold by. LC 93-12343. (ps-12). 1993. smythe sewn reinforced 14.95 (1-879085-86-0) Whsprng Coyote Pr.
—There Was an Old Woman Who Lived in a Glove: A Picture Book. Lodge, Bernard. LC 92-12967. 32p. (ps-12). 1992. smythe sewn reinforced 14.95 (1-879085-55-0) Whsprng Coyote Pr.
Loestoeter, Lori. How the Leopard Got His Spots. Kipling, Rudyard. LC 89-31374. (ps up). 1991. pap. 14.95 (0-88708-111-8, Rabbit Ears); book & cassette package 19.95 (0-88708-112-6, Rabbit Ears) Picture Bk Studio.
Loewen, Janelle. Eight of a Kind & More Than Empty Dreams. Hockett, Betty M. (gr. 3-8). 1988. Set. pap. 13.95 (0-913342-66-1) Barclay Pr.
—Keeping Them All in Stitches: The Life-Story of Geraldine Custer. Hockett, Betty M. 80p. (Orig.). (gr. 3-6). 1990. pap. 3.50 (0-943701-18-X) George Fox Pr.
—More Than Empty Dreams. Hockett, Betty M. LC 88-71327. 140p. (Orig.). (gr. 3-8). 1988. pap. 7.50 (0-913342-65-3) Barclay Pr.
—Mud on Their Wheels: The Life-Story of Vern & Lois Ellis. Hockett, Betty M. 81p. (Orig.). (gr. 3-6). 1988. pap. 3.50 (0-943701-14-7) George Fox Pr.
—No Time Out: The Life-Story of George & Dorothy Thomas. Hockett, Betty M. 80p. (Orig.). (gr. 3-6). 1991. pap. 3.95 (0-943701-19-8) George Fox Pr.
—Outside Doctor on Call: The Life-Story of Dr. Ezra & Frances DeVol. Hockett, Betty M. 80p. (Orig.). (gr. 3-6). 1992. pap. 4.95 (0-943701-20-1) George Fox Pr.
—Whistling Bombs & Bumpy Trains: The Life-Story of Anna Nixon. Hockett, Betty M. LC 89-84572. 80p. (Orig.). (gr. 3-6). 1989. pap. 3.50 (0-943701-15-5) George Fox Pr.
LoFamia, Jun, jt. illus. see Redondo, Nestor.
Lofgren, Ulf. Alvin the Zookeeper. Lofgren, Ulf. 32p. (ps-3). 1991. PLB 18.95 (0-87614-689-2) Carolrhoda Bks.
Loftin, Beth. Leaves in the Wind. Meinders, LaDonna K. Wheeler, J. Clyde, intro. LC 89-81374. 152p. 1989. 15.95 (0-934188-31-9) Evans Pubns.
Lofting, Hugh. Doctor Dolittle & the Green Canary. Lofting, Hugh. (gr. 4 up) 1989. 14.95 (0-318-41607-7) Delacorte.
Lofts, Pamela. Wombat Stew. Vaughan, Marcia K. LC 85-63492. 32p. (ps-3). 1985. 8.95 (0-382-09211-2); s.p. 6.71 (0-382-24356-0) Silver Burdett Pr.
Loftus, Barbara & Bateman, Noel. Egyptian Stories. Hull, Robert. LC 93-35684. 48p. (gr. 5-9). 1994. 15.95 (1-56847-155-6) Thomson Lrning.
Logan, Ann, jt. illus. see Barker, Melissa.
Logan, Ann, jt. illus. see Berker, Melissa.

Logvinoff, Anne. Cats, Big & Little. Fontanel, Beatrice. Bogard, Vicki, tr. from FRE. LC 90-50772. 38p. (gr. k-5). 1991. 4.95 (0-944589-27-8, 278) Young Discovery Lib.
Loh, Carolyn. Best Jokes & Riddles. Pansini, Anna, ed. LC 89-20324. 48p. (gr. 2-6). 1990. PLB 8.59 (0-8167-1917-9); pap. text ed. 2.50 (0-8167-1918-7) Troll Assocs.
—Christmas KidDoodles, No. 6. Herman, Emmi. 64p. (ps-2). 1992. pap. 0.99 (1-56293-271-3) McClanahan Bk.
—Christmas KidDoodles, No. 8. Herman, Emmi. 64p. (ps-2). 1992. pap. 0.99 (1-56293-272-1) McClanahan Bk.
—Great Riddles, Giggles & Jokes. Pansini, Anna, ed. LC 89-5200. 48p. (gr. 2-6). 1990. PLB 8.59 (0-8167-1915-2); pap. text ed. 2.50 (0-8167-1916-0) Troll Assocs.
—Let's Celebrate Valentine's Day: A Book of Things to Draw. Loh, Carolyn. LC 87-50429. 32p. (gr. 2-6). 1988. PLB 10.65 (0-8167-1035-X); pap. text ed. 1.95 (0-8167-1036-8) Troll Assocs.
—My Book of Opposites. Rutman, Shereen G. 32p. (ps). 1992. wkbk. 1.95 (1-56293-171-7) McClanahan Bk.
—Numbers. Rutman, Shereen G. 16p. (ps). 1992. wkbk. 2.25 (1-56293-191-1) McClanahan Bk.
—Santa's Cookie Surprise. Craig, Janet. LC 88-19997. 32p. (gr. k-2). 1989. lib. bdg. 7.89 (0-8167-1538-6); pap. text ed. 1.95 (0-8167-1539-4) Troll Assocs.
—Sizes. Wise, Beth A. 16p. (ps). 1992. wkbk. 2.25 (1-56293-187-3) McClanahan Bk.
—Teeny Witch & Christmas Magic. Matthews, Liz. LC 90-11206. 48p. (gr. k-1). 1991. PLB 11.89 (0-8167-2270-6); pap. 3.50 (0-8167-2271-4) Troll Assocs.
—Teeny Witch & the Great Halloween Ride. Matthews, Liz. LC 90-11207. 48p. (gr. k-1). 1991. PLB 11.89 (0-8167-2274-9); pap. text ed. 3.50 (0-8167-2275-7) Troll Assocs.
—Teeny Witch & the Perfect Valentine. Matthews, Liz. LC 90-11204. 48p. (gr. k-1). 1991. PLB 11.89 (0-8167-2280-3); pap. text ed. 3.50 (0-8167-2281-1) Troll Assocs.
—Teeny Witch & the Terrible Twins. Matthews, Liz. LC 90-11139. 48p. (gr. k-1). 1991. PLB 11.89 (0-8167-2266-8); pap. text ed. 3.50 (0-8167-2267-6) Troll Assocs.
—Teeny Witch & the Tricky Easter Bunny. Matthews, Liz. LC 90-11205. 48p. (gr. k-1). 1991. PLB 11.89 (0-8167-2272-2); pap. text ed. 3.50 (0-8167-2273-0) Troll Assocs.
—Teeny Witch Goes on Vacation. Matthews, Liz. LC 90-11141. 48p. (gr. k-1). 1991. lib. bdg. 11.89 (0-8167-2278-1); pap. text ed. 3.50 (0-8167-2279-X) Troll Assocs.
—Teeny Witch Goes to School. Matthews, Liz. LC 90-11208. 48p. (gr. k-1). 1991. PLB 11.89 (0-8167-2276-5); pap. 3.50 (0-8167-2277-3) Troll Assocs.
—Teeny Witch Goes to the Library. Matthews, Liz. LC 90-11140. 48p. (gr. k-1). 1991. PLB 11.89 (0-8167-2268-4); pap. 3.50 (0-8167-2269-2) Troll Assocs.
—Thinking. Wise, Beth A. 16p. (ps). 1992. wkbk. 2.25 (1-56293-190-3) McClanahan Bk.
Lohstoeter, Lori. How the Leopard Got His Spots. Kipling, Rudyard. Glover, Danny, read by. 32p. (ps up). 1992. pap. write for info. slipcase pkg., incl. cassette (0-307-14330-9, 14330, Golden Pr) Western Pub.
—How the Leopard Got His Spots. Kipling, Rudyard. 64p. 1993. Repr. of 1989 ed. incl. cass. 9.95 (0-88708-301-3, Rabbit Ears) Picture Bk Studio.
—Noah & the Ark. Guernsey, Paul. 40p. (gr. k up). 1993. incl. cass. 19.95 (0-88708-293-9, Rabbit Ears); 14.95 (0-88708-292-0, Rabbit Ears) Picture Bk Studio.
Lohstoeter, Lori, photos by. A Christmas Surprise for Chabelita. Palacios, Argentina. LC 93-22336. 32p. (gr. 5-9). 1993. PLB 14.95 (0-8167-3131-4); pap. write for info. (0-8167-3132-2) Brdgewater.
Lo-Koon-Chiu. Favorite Children's Stories from China & Tibet. Hume, Lotta C. LC 61-6219. 120p. (gr. 1-4). 1962. pap. 14.95 (0-8048-1605-0) C E Tuttle.
Loman, Roberta K. All about Hands. 28p. (ps). 1992. 2.50 (0-87403-951-7, 24-03591) Standard Pub.
—Billions of Bugs. Mishica, Clare. 28p. (ps). 1993. 4.99 (0-7847-0039-7, 24-03829) Standard Pub.
—Busy Feet. Watson, Elaine. 28p. (ps). 1992. 2.50 (0-87403-952-5, 24-03592) Standard Pub.
—What God Did for Zeke the Fuzzy Caterpillar. O'Rourke, Robert. 32p. (gr. k-2). 1991. pasted 2.50 (0-87403-824-3, 24-03924) Standard Pub.
Lomax, James. Turtles. Perkins, Anne T. 8p. (ps-k). 1993. 12.00 (1-884204-00-7) Teach Nxt Door.
Lombard, Lynette. Horizons Never End. Pudaite, Rochunga. 20p. (gr. k-6). 1988. pap. text ed. 4.25 (1-55976-144-X) CEF Press.
—I Dare. Dick, Lois H. 42p. (gr. k-6). 1971. pap. text ed. 9.45 (1-55976-034-6) CEF Press.
Lonette, Reisie. The Fireball Mystery. Adrian, Mary. LC 77-17151. (gr. 2-6). 1977. 8.95 (0-8038-2325-8) Hastings.
Long, Bernard & Robson, Eric. Questions & Answers about Forest Animals. Chinery, Michael. LC 93-29427. 1994. 5.95 (1-85697-963-6) Kingfisher Bks.

Long, C. Mayapriya, et al. North Carolina: Our People, Places & Past. Charlet, James D., et al. 320p. (gr. 4 up). 1987. lib. bdg. 22.95 (0-89089-319-5) Carolina Acad Pr.
Long, Kevin. The REF Field Guide. Siembieda, Kevin. Marciniszyn, Alex, et al. 144p. (Orig.). (gr. 8 up). 1989. pap. 15.95 (0-916211-36-3, 558) Palladium Bks.
—Rifts Sourcebook. Siembieda, Kevin. Marciniszyn, Alex & Bartold, Thomas, eds. 120p. (Orig.). (gr. 8 up). 1991. pap. 11.95 (0-916211-51-7, 801) Palladium Bks.
—Turtles Go Hollywood. Greenberg, Daniel & Siembieda, Kevin. Marciniszyn, Alex, ed. 48p. (Orig.). (gr. 8 up). 1990. pap. 7.95 (0-916211-46-0, 510) Palladium Bks.
—The Vampire Kingdoms. Siembieda, Kevin. Marciniszyn, Alex & Bartold, Thomas, eds. 176p. (Orig.). (gr. 8 up). 1991. pap. 15.95 (0-916211-52-5, 802) Palladium Bks.
Long, Kevin & Beauvais, Denis. Boxed Nightmares. Siembieda, Kevin & Long, Kevin. Marciniszyn, Alex & Bartold, Thomas, eds. 80p. (Orig.). (gr. 8 up) 1990. pap. 11.95 (0-916211-49-5) Palladium Bks.
Long, Kevin & Parkinson, Keith. Atlantis. Siembieda, Kevin. Marciniszyn, Alex & Bartold, Thomas, eds. 160p. (Orig.). (gr. 8 up) 1992. pap. 15.95 (0-916211-54-1, 804) Palladium Bks.
—Rifts Role-Playing Game. Siembieda, Kevin. Marciniszyn, Alex & Bartold, Thomas, eds. 256p. (Orig.). (gr. 8 up) 1990. pap. 24.95 (0-916211-50-9, 800) Palladium Bks.
Long, Kevin & Siembieda, Kevin. Triax & the NGR. Siembieda, Kevin & Long, Kevin. Marciniszyn, Alex, et al, eds. 176p. (Orig.). (gr. 8 up). 1994. pap. 19.95 (0-916211-60-6, 810) Palladium Bks.
Long, Kevin, et al. Rifts Conversion Book. Siembieda, Kevin. Marciniszyn, Alex & Bartold, Thomas, eds. 224p. (Orig.). (gr. 8 up) 1991. pap. 19.95 (0-916211-53-3, 803) Palladium Bks.
—Macross II: The Role-Playing Game. Siembieda, Kevin. Marciniszyn, Alex, et al, eds. 112p. (Orig.). (gr. 8 up). 1993. pap. 11.95 (0-916211-62-2, 590) Palladium Bks.
—The Mechanoids. Siembieda, Kevin. Marciniszyn, Alex, et al, eds. 112p. (Orig.). (gr. 8 up). 1992. pap. 11.95 (0-916211-55-X, 805) Palladium Bks.
—The U. N. Spacy. Siembieda, Kevin. Marciniszyn, Alex, et al, eds. 64p. (Orig.). (gr. 8 up). 1993. pap. 9.95 (0-916211-63-0, 591) Palladium Bks.
Long, Laurel. American Adventures: True Stories from America's Past, 1770-1870. Greenberg, Morrie. LC 90-2652. 96p. (Orig.). (gr. 4-9). 1991. pap. text ed. 9.95 (0-9622652-1-7) Brooke-Richards.
Long, Laurie. Little Toot. Gramatky, Hardie. 12p. (ps). 1993. bds. 4.95 (0-448-40585-7, G&D) Putnam Pub Group.
Long, Laurie S. Amy's (Not So) Great Camp-Out. O'Connor, Jane. LC 92-45881. 64p. (gr. 1-4). 1993. 7.99 (0-448-40167-3, G&D); pap. 3.95 (0-448-40166-5, G&D) Putnam Pub Group.
—Corrie's Secret Pal. O'Connor, Jane. LC 92-35602. 64p. (gr. 1-4). 1993. 7.99 (0-448-40161-4, G&D); pap. 3.95 (0-448-40160-6, G&D) Putnam Pub Group.
—Make up Your Mind, Marsha! O'Connor, Jane. LC 92-45880. 64p. (gr. 1-4). 1993. 7.99 (0-448-40165-7, G&D); pap. 3.95 (0-448-40164-9, G&D) Putnam Pub Group.
—Sarah's Incredible Idea. O'Connor, Jane. LC 92-36803. 64p. (gr. 1-4). 1993. 7.99g (0-448-40163-0, G&D); pap. 3.95 (0-448-40162-2, G&D) Putnam Pub Group.
Long, Lori, jt. illus. see Gleich, Shannon.
Long, Olivia. The Dandelion Queen. Long, Olivia. 32p. (ps-4). Date not set. 9.95 (1-880042-08-8, SL12461) Shelf-Life Bks.
—Diary of a Dog. Long, Olivia. 32p. (ps-4). Date not set. 9.95 (1-880042-06-1, SL12456) Shelf-Life Bks.
—A Horse of a Different Color. Long, Olivia. 32p. (ps-4). Date not set. 9.95 (1-880042-01-0, SL12451) Shelf-Life Bks.
Long, Rachel L. I Is for Island - 1 Para Isla. Cuyler, Juliana & Walsh, Moira. (MAP & ENG.). 108p. (Orig.). (ps-2). 1992. 10.00 (0-9635260-0-6) Alphabet.
Long, Sylvia. Alejandro's Gift. Albert, Richard E. LC 93-30199. 1994. 13.95 (0-8118-0436-4) Chronicle Bks.
—Fire Race: A Karuk Coyote Tale about How Fire Came to the People. London, Jonathan & Pinola, Lanny. Lang, Julian, afterword by. LC 92-32352. 1993. 13.95 (0-8118-0241-8) Chronicle Bks.
—The Most Timid in the Land: A Bunny Romance. Herford, Oliver. 32p. (ps-1). 1992. 12.95 (0-87701-862-6) Chronicle Bks.
—Ten Little Rabbits. Grossman, Virginia. 32p. (ps-3). 1991. 12.95 (0-87701-552-X) Chronicle Bks.
Long, Teddy C. Fun with Paper Bags & Cardboard Tubes. Walter, F. Virginia. LC 92-14944. 80p. (gr. 5 up). 1992. 17.95 (1-89556-908-7) Sterling.

Long, Woodie. The Story of Lucy What's-Her-Name! And Your Name Too! Blount, Lucy D. 48p. 1992. Spiral bdg. pap. 12.00 (0-9630017-2-8) Light-Bearer.
Author Lucy Blount has created an uplifting children's story peppered with special hints & clues to help little ones uncover the secret name God has

chosen for each of His children. Through THE STORY OF LUCY WHAT'S-HER-NAME (AND YOUR NAME TOO!), Mrs. Blount has woven a comforting tapestry of love, self-confidence, reassurance & joy. The book is designed to lift the spirits of children, build their self-esteem, & help them discover their individuality. "...because each one of us has received God's loving light differently, so each one of us gives His Light off differently. We are all to shine, like our God's created stars in the night, but each of us twinkles differently." Illustrated with honesty & simplicity by Alabama folk artist Woodie Long, whose work is featured in art galleries across the nation. Spiral-bound, with blank pages for little artists to create their own special illustrations. *Publisher Provided Annotation.*

Longe, Bob. Nutty Challenges & Zany Dares. Longe, Bob. LC 93-32391. 1994. write for info. (*0-8069-0454-2*) Sterling.

Long Soldier, Daniel. A Legend from Crazy Horse Clan. Crow, Moses N. Flood, Renee S., ed. 36p. (Orig.). (gr. 3 up). 1987. pap. 4.95 (*1-877976-03-2, 406-0010*) Tipi Pr.
A LEGEND FROM CRAZY HORSE CLAN is a story for children of all ages. Beautiful illustrations by Daniel Long Soldier keep the legend alive in the reader's eye. The historian or student of Indian ways will enjoy the book as much as the child of seven, in whose imagination the baby raccoon Mesu embodies all that is faithful & loving in a small furry pet. Listen carefully to the words of Tashia. The symbolic role of man & woman is evident throughout the legend. Although the story essentially describes the life of a girl, the narrator is male. Clearly, the legend describes the male viewpoint of manhood, religion, courtship, aging & death. The characters are gentle, yet there is a strong underlying theme of tribal identity. Without a doubt, we are looking at life through the eyes of a warrior. Indian oral narration is spoken American literature in its finest form. When Lakota children of the 1990s become grandparents themselves, they will tell the legends again. Thanks to Moses Big Crow, one of those legends may well be A LEGEND FROM CRAZY HORSE CLAN. *Publisher Provided Annotation.*

Longstreet, Stephen. Magic Trumpets: The Story of Jazz for Young People. Longstreet, Stephen. (Orig.). (gr. 6-12). 1989. pap. 16.95 (*0-913705-42-X*) Zephyr Pr AZ.
Longworth, Mark. Adventure Programs. Tyler, J. & Hawarth, L. 48p. (gr. 6 up). 1983. lib. bdg. 10.96 (*0-88110-143-5*); pap. 3.95 (*0-86020-741-2*) EDC.
Looney, Barbara. Wynken, Blynken & Nod. Field, Eugene. 32p. 1991. Repr. of 1964 ed. 9.95 (*0-8038-9333-7*) Hastings.
Loor, Robin, jt. illus. see Green, Victor D.
Lopez, Angelo. Two Moms, the Zark, & Me. Valentine, Johnny. 48p. (gr. k-3). 1993. 12.95 (*1-55583-236-9*) Alyson Pubns.
Lopez, Graciela C. How We Came to the Fifth World (Como Vinimos al Quinto Mundo) Rohmer, Harriet & Anchondo, Mary. LC 76-7240. (ENG & SPA.). 24p. (gr. 2-6). 1988. 13.95 (*0-89239-024-7*) Childrens Book Pr.
Lopez, Judith. Dancers in the Garden. Ryder, Joanne. LC 89-10555. 32p. (gr. k-4). 1992. 15.95 (*0-87156-578-1*) Sierra.

Lopez, Mercedes. Cuba. Cummins, Ronald. LC 89-43170. 64p. (gr. 5-6). 1991. PLB 19.93 (*0-8368-0219-5*) Gareth Stevens Inc.
Lopez, Mercedes, photos by. Cuba Is My Home. Holland, Gini, adapted by. LC 92-17725. 1992. PLB 18.60 (*0-8368-0848-7*) Gareth Stevens Inc.
Lopez, Paul. Crystals. Bell, Robert A. 24p. (gr. k-5). 1992. pap. write for info. blister pk., incl. 3 crystal specimens & magnifying glass (*0-307-12856-3,* 12856, Golden Pr) Western Pub.
—The Dinosaurs' Last Days. Granowsky, Alvin. LC 91-23408. 32p. (gr. 1-4). 1992. PLB 15.96 (*0-8114-3250-5*); pap. 3.95 (*0-8114-6225-0*) Raintree Steck-V.
—Dinosaurs of All Sizes. Granowsky, Alvin. LC 91-22343. 32p. (gr. 1-4). 1992. PLB 15.96 (*0-8114-3251-3*); pap. 3.95 (*0-8114-6229-3*) Raintree Steck-V.
Lopez, Ruth K. A Child's Garden Diary: Coloring & Activity Book. Lopez, Ruth K. 56p. (Orig.). (gr. k-6). 1992. pap. 5.95 (*0-9627463-4-7*) Gardens Growing People.
Lopez, Stella. If You Squint at a Rhinoceros... Dunn, Cynthia T. LC 90-30384. 32p. (gr. 2-5). 1990. 12.95 (*0-943173-67-1*) Harbinger AZ.
LoPrete, Tere. My Head Is Red & Other Riddle Rhymes. Livingston, Myra C. LC 89-24528. 32p. (ps-3). 1990. reinforced bdg. 12.95 (*0-8234-0806-X*) Holiday.
Lopshire, Robert. ABC Games. Lopshire, Robert. LC 85-47883. 64p. (ps-1). 1986. (Crowell Jr Bks) HarpC Child Bks.
—Big Max. newly illus. ed. Platt, Kin. LC 91-14743. (gr. k-3). 1978. pap. 3.50 (*0-06-444006-0*, Trophy) HarpC Child Bks.
—Big Max. newly illus. ed. Platt, Kin. LC 91-14742. 64p. (gr. k-3). 1965. 13.00 (*0-06-024750-9*); PLB 12.89 (*0-06-024751-7*) HarpC Child Bks.
—I Want to Be Somebody New. Lopshire, Robert. LC 85-43098. 48p. (gr. k-3). 1986. 6.95 (*0-394-87616-4*); lib. bdg. 7.99 (*0-394-97616-9*) Beginner.
Lord, Anne & Jennings, Ann. Keeping a Head in School: A Student's Book about Learning Abilities & Learning Disorders. rev. ed. Levine, Mel. 312p. (gr. 4-10). 1991. pap. text ed. 19.35 (*0-8388-2069-7*, 2069); 6 cassettes 24.50 (*0-8388-2070-0*, 2070) Ed Pub Serv.
Lord, John V. The Giant Jam Sandwich. Lord, John V. & Burroway, Janet. LC 72-13578. 32p. (gr. k-3). 1987. 15.45 (*0-395-16033-2*); pap. 4.80 (*0-395-44237-0*) HM.
Lord Baden-Powell. Rovering to Success: A Guide for Young Manhood. Lord Baden-Powell. 247p. (Orig.). 1992. pap. 16.95 (*0-9632054-3-9*) Stevens Pub.
Lorenz, Albert. Landmarks: Eighteen Wonders of the New York World. Diamonstein, Barbaralee. 160p. 1992. 35.00 (*0-8109-3565-1*) Abrams.
Lorenz, Lee. Big Gus & Little Gus. Lorenz, Lee. 32p. (gr. k-3). 1984. pap. 5.95 (*0-13-078122-3*) P-H.
—Driving Me Crazy: Fun on Wheels Jokes. Keller, Charles. 40p. (gr. 2-5). 1989. 13.95 (*0-945912-05-6*) Pippin Pr.
—Hugo & the Spacedog. Lorenz, Lee. LC 82-22960. 30p. (ps-3). 1986. 10.95 (*0-13-444497-3*); pap. 5.95 (*0-13-444480-9*) P-H.
—Mr. Munday & the Space Creatures. Pryor, Bonnie. (ps-3). 1989. pap. 13.95 (*0-671-67114-6*) S&S Trade.
—Remember the a Mode! Riddles & Puns. Keller, Charles, ed. LC 83-13832. 64p. (gr. 3-5). 1983. 10.95 (*0-13-773358-5*) P-H.
—Remember the Ala Mode: Riddles & Puns. Keller, Charles. Keller, Charles, compiled by. 64p. (gr. 3-7). 1986. pap. 5.95 (*0-13-773342-9*) P-H.
—Scornful Simkin. Lorenz, Lee. 30p. (Orig.). (gr. k-3). 1982. pap. 3.95 (*0-13-796730-6*, Pub. by Treehouse) P-H.
—Seven Times Eight. Updike, David. 40p. (gr. 2-5). 1990. PLB 14.95 (*0-945912-10-2*) Pippin Pr.
—Smokey the Shark: And Other Fishy Stories. Keller, Charles. (gr. 2-6). 1981. 8.95 (*0-13-814707-8*) P-H.
—Sylvester Bear Overslept. Wahl, Jan. LC 79-4095. 48p. (ps-3). 1979. 5.95 (*0-8193-1003-4*); PLB 5.95 (*0-8193-1004-2*) Parents.
—Sylvester Bear Overslept. Wahl, Jan. LC 93-13039. write for info. (*0-8368-0977-7*) Gareth Stevens Inc.
—Waiter, There's a Fly in My Soup. Keller, Charles. LC 86-12222. 64p. (gr. 3-7). 1986. 10.95 (*0-13-944182-4*) P-H.
—A Weekend in the City. Lorenz, Lee. 32p. (gr. k-3). 1991. 14.95 (*0-945912-15-3*) Pippin Pr.
—A Weekend in the Country. Lorenz, Lee. 32p. (gr. k-3). 1985. 11.95 (*0-13-947961-9*) P-H.
Lorraine, Walter. Best Enemies Again. Leverich, Kathleen. LC 90-30303. 96p. (gr. 2 up). 1991. 12.95 (*0-688-09440-6*) Greenwillow.
—Hilary & the Troublemakers. Leverich, Kathleen. LC 91-15234. 1992. 13.00 (*0-688-10857-1*) Greenwillow.
—Hilary & the Troublemakers. Leverich, Kathleen. LC 91-13762. 144p. (Orig.). (gr. 3-7). 1993. pap. 3.99 (*0-679-84716*) Random Bks Yng Read.
Lorraine, Walter H. McBroom & the Big Wind. Fleischman, Sid. 48p. (gr. 3 up). 1982. (Pub. by Atlantic Monthly Pr); pap. 3.95 (*0-316-28544-7*) Little.
—McBroom & the Great Race. Fleischman, Sid. 64p. (gr. 3-7). 1980. 13.95 (*0-316-28568-4*, Joy St Bks) Little.
—McBroom Tells the Truth. Fleischman, Sid. LC 81-1035. 48p. (gr. 3-7). 1981. 12.45i (*0-316-28550-1*, Pub. by Atlantic Pr) Little.

—McBroom's Almanac. Fleischman, Sid. (gr. 3-7). 1984. 14.95 (*0-316-26009-6*, Joy St Bks) Little.
Lorseyedi, Barb. Frontier American Activity Book: Art, Crafts, Ccooking. Milliken, Linda. (gr. k-6). 1990. pap. text ed. 5.95 (*1-56472-017-9*) Edupress.
Lotfren, Ulf. Alvin the Pirate. Lofgren, Ulf. 32p. (ps-3). 1990. PLB 18.95 (*0-87614-402-4*) Carolrhoda Bks.
Loturco, Laura. Huskings, Quiltings, & Barn Raisings: Work-Play Parties in Early America. Sherrow, Victoria. LC 92-8725. 78p. 1992. 13.95 (*0-8027-8186-1*); PLB 14.85 (*0-8027-8188-8*) Walker & Co.
—Shaker Villages. Bolick, Nancy O. & Randolph, Sallie G. LC 92-34587. 96p. (gr. 5 up). 1993. 12.95 (*0-8027-8209-4*); PLB 13.85 (*0-8027-8210-8*) Walker & Co.
Loubet, Dennis. Mythic Greece: Age of Heroes. Allston, Aaron. Charlton, Coleman, ed. 160p. (Orig.). (gr. 10-12). 1988. pap. 12.00 (*1-55806-002-2*, 1020) Iron Crown Ent Inc.
Louden, Claire & Louden, George, Jr. The Defender. Kalashnikoff, Nicholas. LC 92-33560. 144p. (gr. 3-7). 1993. pap. 6.95 (*0-8027-7397-4*) Walker & Co.
Louden, George, Jr., jt. illus. see Louden, Claire.
Lougheed, Robert. Mustang, Wild Spirit of the West. Henry, Marguerite. LC 91-25187. 224p. (gr. 3-7). 1992. pap. 3.95 (*0-689-71601-X*, Aladdin) Macmillan Child Grp.
—San Domingo: The Medicine Hat Stallion. Henry, Marguerite. LC 91-46020. 240p. (gr. 3-7). 1992. pap. 3.95 (*0-689-71631-1*, Aladdin) Macmillan Child Grp.
Loughran, Donna. The Ghost at the Old Stone Fort. Jones, Martha T. LaFreniere, Annette, ed. LC 90-4087. 104p. (gr. 4 up). 1991. 90. lib. bdg. 11.95 (*0-937460-61-3*); pap. 6.95 (*0-937460-87-7*) Hendrick-Long.
—The Mystery of Y'Barbo's Tunnel. Jones, Martha T. LaFreniere, Annette, ed. LC 91-2980. 152p. (gr. 3-7). 1991. 14.95 (*0-937460-68-0*) Hendrick-Long.
Loui, Jill. The All Gone Book. Stodden, Norma J. & McCormick, Linda. Levy, Gail, ed. 18p. (ps). 1988. bds. 3.95 (*0-943693-05-5*) TRI Pubns.
—The Love Book. Stodden, Norma J. & McCormick, Linda. Levy, Gail, ed. 18p. (ps). 1988. bds. 3.95 (*0-943693-04-7*) TRI Pubns.
—The More Book. Stodden, Norma J. & McCormick, Linda. Levy, Gail, ed. 18p. (ps). 1988. bds. 3.95 (*0-943693-03-9*) TRI Pubns.
Louie, Bo-Kim. Two Dozen Dinosaurs: A First Book of Dinosaur Facts & Mysteries, Games & Fun. Ripley, Catherine. 32p. (gr. k up). 1992. pap. 9.95 (*0-920775-55-1*, Pub. by Greey dePencier CN) Firefly Bks Ltd.
Louise, Anita. Christmas Crafts: Merry Things to Make. Van Blaricom, Colleen, ed. 32p. (Orig.). (ps-5). 1993. pap. 3.95 (*1-56397-083-X*) Boyds Mills Pr.
Louisiana Students. Ascending. Louisiana School Students. Thornton, Don, intro. by. 302p. (Orig.). (gr. 1-12). Date not set. pap. 25.00 (*1-882913-00-0*) Thornton LA.
Love, David, photos by. Buns Travels Across America. Cottonpaw. 48p. (gr. k-5). 1992. pap. 7.95 (*1-881274-01-2*) Cotton Tale.
Love, Judith D. Honey, My Rabbit. Beveridge, Barbara. LC 92-34272. 1993. 2.50 (*0-383-03630-5*) SRA Schl Grp.
—Leapin Lizzie. Squier, Karl. LC 84-27784. 32p. (gr. k-5). 1985. pap. 12.95 incl. cassette (*0-931905-00-1*); pap. 7.95 (*0-931905-01-X*); cassette 7.95 (*0-931905-02-8*) Lady Lake Learn.
Love, Judy. There's a Duck in My Closet. Trent, John T. LC 93-15707. (gr. k-5). 1993. 12.99 (*0-8499-1037-4*) Word Pub.
Love, Kenna, photos by. Exposures, Women & Their Art. Brown, Betty A. & Raven, Arlene. Comini, Alessandra, intro. by. 128p. (gr. 9 up). 1989. 39.95 (*0-939165-10-4*); ltd. ed. 60.00 (*0-939165-13-9*); pap. 24.95 (*0-939165-11-2*) NewSage Press.
Lovejoy, Lois. Nature's Tricksters: Animals & Plants That Aren't What They Seem. Batten, Mary. (gr. 3-6). 1992. 14.95 (*0-316-08371-2*) Little.
Loveless, Liz. One, Two, Buckle My Shoe. Loveless, Liz. LC 92-40947. 32p. (ps). 1993. 13.95 (*1-56282-477-5*); PLB 13.89 (*1-56282-478-3*) Hyprn Child.
Lovell, Craig, photos by. La Familia Villarreal. Kratky, Lada J. (SPA.). 24p. (Orig.). (gr. 1-3). 1991. pap. text ed. 29.95 big bk. (*1-56334-022-4*); pap. text ed. 4.15 small bk. (*1-56334-036-4*) Hampton-Brown.
—Meet the Villarreals. Kratky, Lada J. 24p. (Orig.). (gr. 1-3). 1991. pap. text ed. 29.95 big bk. (*1-56334-050-X*); pap. text ed. 4.15 small bk. (*1-56334-056-9*) Hampton-Brown.
Loverseed, Amanda. The Thunder King: A Peruvian Tale. Loverseed, Amanda. 32p. (gr. k-3). 1991. PLB 14.95 (*0-87226-450-5*, Bedrick Blackie) P Bedrick Bks.
—Tikkatoo's Journey: An Eskimo Folk Tale. Loverseed, Amanda. LC 89-17840. 32p. (gr. k-3). 1990. PLB 14.95 (*0-87226-420-3*, Bedrick Blackie) P Bedrick Bks.
Loving, Judy V. No Bones about Driftiss. Penn, Audrey. LC 89-13326. viii, 146p. (gr. 2-6). 1989. lib. bdg. 14.95 (*0-939923-11-4*); pap. 7.95 (*0-939923-12-2*) M & W Pub Co.
Low, Joseph. Alex & the Cat. Griffith, Helen V. LC 81-11608. 64p. (gr. 1-3). 1982. 13.95 (*0-688-00420-2*); PLB 13.88 (*0-688-00421-0*) Greenwillow.
—Hear Your Heart. Showers, Paul. LC 68-11067. 40p. (gr. k-3). 1968. PLB 13.89 (*0-690-37379-1*, Crowell Jr Bks) HarpC Child Bks.

—How a Seed Grows. Jordan, Helene J. LC 60-11541. 33p. (gr. k-3). 1972. pap. 4.95 *(0-690-40646-0, Crowell Jr Bks)* HarpC Child Bks.

Low, William. The King, the Princess, & the Tinker. McKenzie, Ellen K. LC 91-31316. 80p. (gr. 2-4). 1992. 14.95 *(0-8050-1773-9, Redfeather BYR)* H Holt & Co.

—The King, the Princess, & the Tinker. McKenzie, Ellen K. LC 91-31316. 64p. (gr. 2-4). 1993. pap. 4.95 *(0-8050-2951-6, Bks Young Read)* H Holt & Co.

—Lily. Thomas, Abagail. LC 93-14199. (gr. 5 up). 1994. write for info. *(0-8050-2690-8)* H Holt & Co.

—Stargone John. McKenzie, Ellen K. LC 90-34119. 80p. (gr. 2-4). 1990. 13.95 *(0-8050-1451-9, Redfeather BYR)* H Holt & Co.

—Stargone John. McKenzie, Ellen K. LC 90-34119. 64p. (gr. 2-4). 1992. pap. 4.95 *(0-8050-2069-1, Redfeather BYR)* H Holt & Co.

—Summer Stories. Thacker, Nola. LC 87-45880. 160p. (gr. 3-7). 1988. (Lipp Jr Bks); (Lipp Jr Bks) HarpC Child Bks.

—Summer Stories. Thacker, Nola. (gr. 3-7). 1989. pap. 2.75 *(0-590-42191-3, Apple Paperbacks)* Scholastic Inc.

—Wake up, Wilson Street. Thomas, Abigail. LC 92-10873. 32p. (gr. 5 up). 1993. 15.95 *(0-8050-2006-3, Bks Young Read)* H Holt & Co.

Lowe, Dave. The Great ABC Search. Johannson, Anna T. 48p. (gr. ps-k). 1993. pap. 5.95 *(1-56565-059-X)* Lowell Hse.

—The Great One Two Three Search. Johannson, Anna T. 48p. Date not set. pap. text ed. 5.95 *(1-56565-066-2)* Lowell Hse.

Lowe, Vicky. Waiting for Amos. Kulling, Monica. LC 92-19550. 32p. (ps-2). 1993. SBE 13.95 *(0-02-751245-2, Bradbury Pr)* Macmillan Child Grp.

Lowenheim, Al. Dr. Gardner's Modern Fairy Tales. Gardner, Richard A. LC 83-40149. 106p. (gr. 2-6). Repr. 14.95 *(0-933812-09-4)* Creative Therapeutics.

—The Girls & Boys Book about Good & Bad Behavior. Gardner, Richard A. LC 90-31241. 221p. (gr. 2-6). 1990. 17.00 *(0-933812-21-3)* Creative Therapeutics.

Lowenheim, Alfred. The Boys & Girls Book about Stepfamilies. Gardner, Richard A. 180p. (gr. 3-10). 1985. pap. 4.99 *(0-933812-13-2)* Creative Therapeutics.

—Dr. Gardner's Fairy Tales for Today's Children. Gardner, Richard A. LC 80-16187. 96p. (gr. 1-6). 1978. Repr. of 1974 ed. PLB 14.95 *(0-933812-02-7)* Creative Therapeutics.

—Dr. Gardner's Stories About the Real World, Vol. I. Gardner, Richard A. LC 80-16542. 127p. (gr. k-6). 1980. Repr. of 1972 ed. PLB 14.95 *(0-933812-04-3)* Creative Therapeutics.

Lowenstein, Bernice. The Luck of Pokey Bloom. Conford, Ellen. 144p. (gr. 4-6). 1975. 14.95 *(0-316-15305-2)* Little.

Lowery, Carol. Bound for Boston. Hughes, Richard. Wheeler, Jill, ed. LC 88-71730. 48p. (gr. 4). 1989. lib. bdg. 10.95 *(0-939179-44-X)* Abdo & Dghtrs.

—Lost in London. Hughes, Richard. Wheeler, Jill, ed. LC 88-71732. 48p. (gr. 4). 1988. lib. bdg. 10.95 *(0-939179-47-4)* Abdo & Dghtrs.

Lowmiller, Cathie. Bizagolaa; Apache Cut & Color Book. Mike, Jan & Lowmiller, Cathie. 32p. (Orig.). (gr. k-6). 1989. 3.95 *(0-918080-46-0)* Treasure Chest.

—Dezbah & the Dancing Tumbleweeds. Garaway, Margaret K. 175p. (Orig.). (gr. 3-5). 1990. pap. 7.95 *(0-918080-50-9)* Treasure Chest.

—Dolii; a Navajo Girl: Historical Paper Doll Book to Read, Color & Cut. Mike, Jan M. 32p. (gr. k-6). 1990. pap. 3.95 *(0-918080-54-1)* Treasure Chest.

—Kachi; a Hopi Girl: Historical Paper Doll Book to Read, Color & Cut. Mike, Jan M. 32p. (gr. k-6). 1989. pap. 3.95 *(0-918080-47-9)* Treasure Chest.

—New Mexico, Land of Enchantment Alphabet Book. Mike, Jan. 32p. (Orig.). (gr. k-5). 1993. pap. 7.95 *(0-918080-55-X)* Treasure Chest.

Lowmiller, Cathy. Chana, An Anasazi Girl: Historical Paperdoll Books to Read, Color & Cut. Mike, Jan. 32p. (Orig.). (gr. k-4). 1991. pap. 3.95 *(0-918080-61-4)* Treasure Chest.

Lowry, Patrick. The Amazing Adventures of Teddy Tum Tum. Breese, Gillian & Langham, Tony. 32p. (ps-3). 1992. 11.95 *(1-55970-185-4)* Arcade Pub Inc.

Lowry-Elks, C. The Arabic Alphabet. Girgis, Nazih. (ENG & ARA.). 57p. (gr. k-12). 1983. pap. 15.00 incl. cass. *(0-86685-340-5)* Intl Bk Ctr.

Lowther, Marilyn. With Domingo Leal in San Antonio, 1734. Martinello, Marian L. & Nesmith, Samuel P. Institute of Texan Cultures Staff, ed. 78p. (Orig.). (gr. 5-8). 1980. pap. 6.95 *(0-933164-40-8)* U of Tex Inst Tex Culture.

Loyd, Megan. A Regular Flood of Mishap. Birdseye, Tom. LC 93-9888. 32p. (gr. 4-8). 1994. 15.95 *(0-8234-1070-6)* Holiday.

Lubach, Peter. Harry & the Singing Fish. Lubach, Peter. LC 91-73824. 32p. (gr. k-4). 1992. 12.95 *(1-56282-158-X)*; PLB 12.89 *(1-56282-159-8)* Hyprn Child.

Lubin, Leonard. Aladdin & His Wonderful Lamp. Lubin, Leonard. adapted by Burton, Richard F., tr. from ARA. LC 82-70308. 48p. (gr. 1-4). 1982. 10.95 *(0-440-00302-4)*; PLB 10.89 *(0-440-00304-0)* Delacorte.

—Aladdin & His Wonderful Lamp. Lubin, Leonard. Burton, Richard T., tr. from ARA. LC 82-70308. 48p. (ps-3). 1982. 12.95 *(0-385-28033-5)* Delacorte.

—My Little Book of Mother Goose Rhymes. Muldrow, Diane, selected by. 24p. (ps-k). 1992. pap. write for info. *(0-307-11756-1, 11756, Pub. by Golden Bks)* Western Pub.

—R-T, Margaret, & the Rats of NIMH. Conly, Jane L. LC 89-19968. 288p. (gr. 4-7). 1990. 14.00 *(0-06-021363-9)*; PLB 13.89 *(0-06-021364-7)* HarpC Child Bks.

—R-T, Margaret, & the Rats of NIMH. Conly, Jane L. LC 89-19968. 272p. (gr. 4-7). 1991. pap. 3.95 *(0-06-440387-4, Trophy)* HarpC Child Bks.

—Racso & the Rats of NIMH. Conly, Jane L. LC 85-42634. 288p. (gr. 4-7). 1988. pap. 3.95 *(0-06-440245-2, Trophy)* HarpC Child Bks.

—Rasco & the Rats of NIMH. Conly, Jane L. LC 85-42634. 288p. (gr. 4-7). 1986. 13.00 *(0-06-021361-2)*; PLB 12.89 *(0-06-021362-0)* HarpC Child Bks.

Lucas, Margeaux. Twin Monkeys. Lucas, Sally. 32p. (ps-2). Date not set. 11.95 *(1-56065-156-3)* Capstone Pr. Postponed.

Lucas, Patti L. Many Children: Religions Around the World. Thomas, M. Angele & Ramey, Mary L. LC 87-91771. 70p. (Orig.). (gr. 2-6). 1987. pap. text ed. 6.95 *(0-9619293-0-8)* M A Thomas.

Lucas, Sheila. The Terrible, Horrible, Awful, Deplorable, Lovable, Little Troll. Meservy, Jay. LC 91-41387. 32p. (ps-2). 1992. pap. 6.95 *(0-89802-586-9)* Beautiful Am.

Lucero, Ruth. Quest for Courage. Rodolph, Stormy. 102p. (Orig.). (gr. 5-12). 1984. pap. 8.95 *(0-89992-092-6)* Coun India Ed.

Lucht, Irmgard. In This Night... Lucht, Irmgard. LC 92-54620. 32p. (ps-3). 1993. 13.95 *(1-56282-408-2)* Hyprn Child.

Lucia, Virginia. Danny & the Merry-Go-Round. Holcomb, Nan. 32p. (Orig.). 1988. pap. 6.95 *(0-944727-00-X)* Jason & Nordic Pubs.

—Danny & the Merry-Go-Round. Holcomb, Nan. 32p. (ps-2). 1992. Repr. of 1988 ed. 13.95 *(0-944727-11-5)* Jason & Nordic Pubs.

Luck, Oliver W. Music Is Math. Luck, Oliver W. (Orig.). (gr. 4-12). 1987. pap. 7.00 *(0-9626686-0-5)* Owl Pub CA.

Ludlow, Keren. Big Pig's Hat. Smax, Willy. LC 92-19442. (ps-3). 1993. 13.95 *(0-8037-1476-9)* Dial Bks Young.

Ludlow, Patricia. A Treasury of Stories for Seven Year Olds. Blishen, Edward & Blishen, Nancy, eds. LC 92-53109. 160p. (Orig.). (gr. k-5). 1992. pap. 5.95 *(1-85697-829-X)* Kingfisher Bks.

Ludlow, Patricia D. Dear Santa. Luck LC 93-28618. 1993. 11.95 *(0-85953-778-1)* Childs Play.

Ludwig, Lyndell. The Little White Dragon. Ludwig, Lyndell. 23p. (gr. 5 up). 1989. pap. 4.95 *(0-9621782-0-9)* Star Dust Bks.

THE LITTLE WHITE DRAGON - This timeless, well-loved tale from ancient China takes you into the world of a wonderful little dragon intent on exploring everything both inside & outside of his realm. At one point he even changes himself into a little fish so he can dive into the waters of the deep sea. However, after numerous adventures, including a miraculous escape, he decides that, after all, it is much better just to be the dragon he really is, with untold worlds yet to discover. The third in a series of authentic Chinese tales in picture book form, delightfully told & illustrated by the author who is well qualified both as an illustrator & in her knowledge of the Chinese language. ("Like the tales of Rudyard Kipling 'these stories' transport children to another time & a different, fascinating world."--Creative Arts). Children are important! As the world changes cultures are blending. And stories from distant lands such as China are enormously valuable in broadening the scope for growth & understanding. They are also fun to read. TS'AO CHUNG WEIGHS AN ELEPHANT ("...splendid, vibrantly colored paintings..."--Publishers Weekly) & THE SHOEMAKER'S GIFT are also available from Star Dust Books at $4.95 each.
Publisher Provided Annotation.

Ludwig, Warren. The Cowboy & the Blackeyed Pea. Johnston, Tony. 32p. (ps-3). 1992. 14.95 *(0-399-22330-4, Putnam)* Putnam Pub Group.

Luedecke, Bev. Love Is... Swaby, Barbara. Rayburn, Cherie, ed. LC 93-72093. 16p. (gr. k-1). 1994. pap. text ed. 16.20 *(0-944943-34-9)* Current Inc.

Luering, Jacqueline M. Scarlet Arena 30303. Moore, Silas. Oddo, Genevieve, ed. LC 74-190272. 196p. (gr. 8-12). 1972. PLB 3.95 *(0-87783-063-0)* Oddo.

Lujan, Tonita. Little Boy with Three Names: Stories of Taos Pueblo. reformatted ed. Clark, Ann N. LC 89-81747. 50p. (gr. 1-5). 1990. pap. 8.95 *(0-941270-59-9)* Ancient City Pr.

Luks, Peggy. The How: Making the Best of a Mistake. Boyd, Selma & Boyd, Pauline. LC 80-13513. 32p. (ps-3). 1981. 16.95 *(0-87705-176-3)* Human Sci Pr.

—Me & Einstein: Breaking Through the Reading Barrier. Blue, Rose. (gr. 3 up). 1984. 14.95 *(0-87705-388-X)*; pap. 9.95 *(0-89885-185-8)* Human Sci Pr.

—Two Homes to Live In: A Child's-Eye View of Divorce. Hazen, Barbara S. LC 77-21849. 32p. (ps-3). 1978. 16.95 *(0-87705-313-8)*; pap. 9.95 *(0-89885-173-4)* Human Sci Pr.

Lumba, Eric, jt. illus. see Frazee, Kathleen.

Lumetta, Lawrence. The Four Seasons. Annable, Toni & Kaspar, Maria H. Viola, Amy, tr. 80p. (Orig.). (gr. 5 up). 1992. Set. pap. text ed. 8.95 *(1-882828-09-7)* Vol. 1: English-Spanish, Las Cuatro Estaciones. Vol. 2: English-French, Les Quatre Saisons. Kasan Imprints.

What does it mean when the leaves turn red? How does the snow know when to stop falling? What is the dormouse looking for & where do baby birds go to school? Four children discover the joys of seasonal changes. Contains charming poems for each season. Beautifully illustrated. An original dual language book for children grades 5-6. Features our easy line-by-line, side-by-side format. Series contains one each English-Spanish & English-French. 40 pages each. Quantity discounts available. To order: contact: KIP Children's Books, 1239 Nile Dr., Suite 3, Corpus Christi, TX 78412. 1-800-982-5298.
Publisher Provided Annotation.

—The Four Seasons: Las Cuatro Estaciones. Annable, Toni & Kaspar, Maria H. Viola, Amy, tr. 40p. (Orig.). (gr. 5 up). 1992. pap. 4.95 *(1-882828-02-X)* Kasan Imprints.

—The Four Seasons: Les Quatre Saisons. Annable, Toni & Kaspar, Maria H. 40p. (Orig.). (gr. 5 up). 1992. pap. 4.95 *(1-882828-03-8)* Kasan Imprints.

—Sherm the Worm: Lozano El Gusano. Annable, Toni & Kaspar, Maria H. Viola, Amy, tr. 40p. (Orig.). (gr. k up). 1992. 4.95 *(1-882828-00-3)* Kasan Imprints.

—Sherm the Worm: Valere le ver. Annable, Toni & Kaspar, Maria H. 48p. (Orig.). (gr. k up). 1992. pap. 4.95 *(1-882828-01-1)* Kasan Imprints.

—The Silver Tree: El Arbol de Plata. Annable, Toni & Kaspar, Maria H. Viola, Amy, tr. 40p. (Orig.). (gr. 6 up). 1992. 4.95 *(1-882828-06-2)* Kasan Imprints.

—The Silver Tree: L'Arbre Argente. Annble, Toni & Kaspar, Maria H. 40p. (Orig.). (gr. 6 up). 1992. 4.95 *(1-882828-07-0)* Kasan Imprints.

Lund, Gary. Coyote Stories for Children. Strauss, Susan. Norman, Howard, ed. 50p. (gr. 1-6). 1991. 10.95 *(0-941831-61-2)*; pap. 6.95 *(0-941831-62-0)* Beyond Words Pub.

—Wolf Stories: Myths & True Life Tales from Around the World. Sollie, Eddie C. Livingston, Julie, ed. 48p. (Orig.). (gr. 1-6). 1993. 11.95 *(0-941831-84-1)*; pap. 7.95 *(0-941831-83-3)* Beyond Words Pub.

Lundell, Margo & Lanza, Barbara. Dearest Baby. Muldrow, Diane. 14p. (ps). 1993. bds. 3.95 *(0-307-12394-4, 12394, Golden Pr)* Western Pub.

Luongo, Aldo. The Flower Princess. Davis, Michael. 32p. (gr. k-12). 1989. write for info.; PLB write for info. R Bane Ltd.

Lurie, Leon, photos by. Bubby, Me & Memories. Pomerantz, Barbara. LC 83-191743. 32p. (ps up). 1983. 7.95 *(0-8074-0253-2, 14025)* UAHC.

Lusk, Nancy M, jt. illus. see Niles, Nancy.
Lusk, Nancy N, jt. illus. see Niles, Nancy.

Lustig, Loretta. Get Rich Mitch! Sharmat, Marjorie W. LC 85-8799. 160p. (gr. 3-7). 1985. 13.95 *(0-688-05790-X)* Morrow Jr Bks.

—The Pop-Up Book of the Circus. LC 78-68789. (ps-3). 1979. 8.99 *(0-394-84134-4)* Random Bks Yng Read.

—The Pop-up Book of Trucks. LC 73-19318. (ps-2). 1974. 8.99 *(0-394-82826-7)* Random Bks Yng Read.

—Skip to My Lou. 1994. bk. & cassette 6.99 *(0-553-45908-2)* Bantam.

—The Three Billy Goats Gruff. Greenway, Jennifer, retold by. 1991. 6.95 *(0-8362-4913-5)* Andrews & McMeel.

Lustig, Loretta, jt. illus. see Sims, Deborah.
Lustig, Michael. Willy Whyner, Cloud Designer. Lustig, Michael & Lustig, Esther. LC 93-21957. 40p. (gr. k-4). 1994. RSBE 14.95 (0-02-761365-8, Four Winds) Macmillan Child Grp.
Luttrell, Chuck. Everything's Going Wrong. 74p. (Orig.). (gr. 3-6). 1986. pap. 6.95 (0-9617609-0-7) Shade Tree NV.
—Winning Isn't Everything. Luttrell, Jean. 76p. (Orig.). (gr. 3-5). 1990. pap. 6.95 (0-9617609-2-3) Shade Tree NV.
Lu Wang. The Stone Lion & Other Chinese Detective Stories: The Wisdom of Lord Bau. Yin-lien C. Chin & Center, Y. LC 91-46520. 192p. (gr. 8-12). 1992. 24.95 (0-87332-634-2); pap. 13.95 (0-87332-635-0) M E Sharpe.
Lux, Don. A Man from the Past. 2nd ed. Higby, Roy C. McLoughlin, William G., intro. by. (gr. 5-12). pap. 8.00 (0-914692-02-X) Big Moose.
Luzak, Dennis. Our Home Is the Sea. Levinson, Riki. LC 87-36419. 32p. (gr. k-3). 1988. pap. 13.95 (0-525-44406-8, DCB) Dutton Child Bks.
—Our Home Is the Sea. Levinson, Riki. 32p. (gr. k-3). 1992. pap. 4.99 (0-14-054552-2, Puffin Unicorn) Puffin Bks.
Luzatti, Lele. Chichibo & the Crane. Boccaccio, Giovanni. (gr. 1-6). 1961. 8.95 (0-8392-3004-4) Astor-Honor.
Lyall, Dennis. Baseball Tips. Hughes, Dean & Hughes, Tom. LC 92-13406. 96p. (gr. 2-6). 1993. RLB 9.99 (0-679-93642-4); pap. 5.99 (0-679-83642-X) Random Bks Yng Read.
—Big Base Hit. Hughes, Dean. LC 89-37875. 96p. (Orig.). (gr. 2-6). 1993. PLB 6.99 (0-679-90427-1); pap. 2.95 (0-679-80427-7) Knopf Bks Yng Read.
—Quick Moves. Hughes, Dean. LC 92-44933. 112p. (Orig.). (gr. 2-6). 1993. pap. 3.50 (0-679-84358-2, Bullseye Bks) Random Bks Yng Read.
Lydbury, Jane, et al. Earth, Air, Fire & Water. Heslewood, Juliet. 182p. (gr. 4-8). 1989. jacketed 15.95 (0-19-278107-3) OUP.
Lydecker, Laura. Dragonsong. McCaffrey, Anne. LC 75-30530. 224p. (gr. 5-9). 1976. 16.95 (0-689-30507-9, Atheneum Child Bk) Macmillan Child Grp.
—Mouse in the House. Baehr, Patricia. LC 93-4068. (ps-3). 1994. write for info. (0-8234-1102-8) Holiday.
—The Tooth Fairy Book. Kovacs, Deborah. LC 92-53679. 32p. 1992. 9.95 (1-56138-147-0) Running Pr.
—The Wind in the Willows. Grahame, Kenneth. Ashachik, Diane M., retold by. LC 92-13203. 48p. (gr. 3-6). 1992. PLB 12.89 (0-8167-2870-4); pap. text ed. 3.95 (0-8167-2871-2) Troll Assocs.
Lyerly, Elaine M. Mister Cookie Breakfast Cookbook. Neely, Cynthia H. & Lyerly, Elaine M. LC 86-2386. 32p. (gr. k-4). 1986. pap. 2.95 (0-88289-493-5) Pelican.
Lyle, Tom. Target: Hero. Matalon, David. Bell, Robert, ed. 32p. (Orig.). (gr. 10-12). 1988. pap. 6.00 (1-55806-004-9, 34) Iron Crown Ent Inc.
Lynch, P. J. The Candlewick Book of Fairy Tales. Hayes, Sarah, ed. LC 92-54961. 96p. (ps up). 1993. 16.95 (1-56402-260-9) Candlewick Pr.
—East o' the Sun & West o' the Moon. Dasent, George W., tr. LC 91-58727. 48p. (ps up). 1992. 15.95 (1-56402-049-5) Candlewick Pr.
—Fairy Tales of Ireland. Yeats, William Butler. Philip, Neil, selected by. & intro. by. 1990. 16.95 (0-385-30249-5) Delacorte.
—Stories for Children. Wilde, Oscar. LC 90-38854. 96p. (gr. 3 up). 1991. 14.95 (0-02-792765-2, Macmillan Child Bk) Macmillan Child Grp.
Lynch, Patrick J. A Bag of Moonshine. Garner, Alan. LC 86-13362. 160p. (gr. k-5). 1986. pap. 15.95 (0-385-29517-0) Delacorte.
Lynch, Patti. Kid's Stuff: Good & Healthy Stuff That's Fun to Cook & Eat. Lynch, Patti. 1993. pap. 12.95 (0-9620469-2-2) Sweet Inspirations.
Lynch, Reg. The Daily Harold, Bk. 6. Noffs, David & Noffs, Laurie. 24p. (Orig.). (gr. 6). 1987. wkbk. 2.50 (0-929875-07-9) Noffs Assocs.
Lyness, Katy. The Littlest Piggy. Jerris, Tony. 20p. (Orig.). (ps up). 1992. pap. 9.95 (0-9630107-2-7) Little Spruce.
Lynn, David. Phone Call from a Ghost: Strange Tales from Modern America. Cohen, Daniel. MacDonald, Patricia, ed. 112p. (gr. 5-7). 1990. pap. 3.50 (0-671-68242-3, Minstrel) PB.
Lynn, Patricia. The World of Young Andrew Jackson. Hilton, Suzanne. (gr. 5-8). 1988. 12.95 (0-8027-6814-8); PLB 13.85 (0-8027-6815-6) Walker & Co.
Lynn, Patty. The Magic Train. French, Susan M. 24p. (Orig.). (gr. k-1). 1990. pap. 0.99 (1-878624-33-4) McClanahan Bk.
—The Mouse's Christmas. Schorsch, Kit. 24p. (Orig.). (gr. k-1). 1990. pap. 0.99 (1-878624-45-8) McClanahan Bk.
Lynn, Ruth. Ester: The Story of a Small Ghost. Lynn, Ruth. Wagner, R. M., ed. LC 81-69693. 28p. (gr. 5 up). 1981. 12.95 (0-941674-00-2) Woodcock Pr.
Lynn, Sara. Clothes. Lynn, Sara. 14p. (ps). 1986. bds. 2.95 (0-689-71095-X, Aladdin Bks) Macmillan Child Grp.
—Toys. Lynn, Sara. 14p. (ps). 1986. bds. 2.95 (0-689-71096-8, Aladdin) Macmillan Child Grp.
Lynn, Sara, photos by. Playing with Paint. James, Diane. 24p. (ps-1). 1992. pap. 3.95 (0-590-45739-X, Cartwheel) Scholastic Inc.

—Playing with Paper. James, Diane. 24p. (ps-1). 1992. pap. 3.95 (0-590-45738-1, Cartwheel) Scholastic Inc.
Lynn, Susan K. The Cat Who Was Named Twice. Wareing, Eleanor J. 141p. (gr. 3-6). 1990. pap. 6.95 (0-9629175-0-8) E J Wareing.
Lyon, Lucinda. How to Break into Politics on a Shoestring. DeBiase, Louis A. 61p. (Orig.). (gr. 9-12). 1981. pap. 4.95 (0-686-31571-5) Louvin Pub.
Lyons, Oren. When Thunders Spoke. Sneve, Virginia D. LC 93-10953. 96p. (gr. 5 up). 1993. pap. 7.95 (0-8032-9220-1, Bison Books) U of Nebr Pr.
Lysaker, Gene. Peter's Pockets. Morgan, Lenore. (gr. k-2). 1978. pap. 1.25 (0-89508-063-X) Rainbow Bks.
—The Tale of Theodore Bear. Green, Cecile. (gr. 1-2). 1978. pap. 1.25 (0-89508-060-5) Rainbow Bks.
Lysne, Mary E. New Testament Match Up. Lysne, Mary. 32p. 1991. pap. 1.99 saddle stitch (0-87403-876-6, 25-02506) Standard Pub.
—Old Testament Match Up. Lysne, Mary. 32p. 1991. pap. 1.99 saddle stitch (0-87403-875-8, 25-02505) Standard Pub.
—Read the Pictures: Fun from the New Testament, Bk. 1. Lysne, Mary. 32p. (gr. k-3). 1991. pap. 1.99 saddle stitch (0-87403-879-0, 23-02509) Standard Pub.
—Read the Pictures: Fun from the Old Testament, Bk. 1. Lysne, Mary. 32p. (gr. k-3). 1991. pap. 1.99 saddle stitch (0-87403-877-4, 23-02507) Standard Pub.
—Read the Pictures: More Fun from the New Testament, Bk. 2. Lysne, Mary. 32p. (gr. k-3). 1991. pap. 1.99 saddle stitch (0-87403-880-4, 23-02510) Standard Pub.
—Read the Pictures: More Fun from the Old Testament, Bk. 2. Lysne, Mary. 32p. (gr. k-3). 1991. pap. 1.99 saddle stitch (0-87403-878-2, 23-02508) Standard Pub.
Lyttle, Kirk. Twenty-Two Splendid Tales to Tell from Around the World, Vol. 1. 2nd ed. DeSpain, Pleasant L. LC 90-62095. 96p. (gr. 1-6). 1990. pap. 10.95x (0-9627239-0-8) Merrill Ct Pr.
—Twenty-Two Splendid Tales to Tell from Around the World, Vol. 2. 2nd ed. DeSpain, Pleasant L. LC 90-62095. 96p. (gr. 1-6). 1990. pap. 10.95x (0-9627239-1-6) Merrill Ct Pr.

M

M. J. Art Concepts Staff. Rolf & the Rainbow Christmas. Wedell, Robert F. LC 89-91971. 133p. (Orig.). 1989. pap. 5.00 (0-9625221-1-2) Milrob Pr.
Ma, Wenhai. The Painted Fan. Singer, Marilyn. LC 92-29796. 1994. write for info. (0-688-11742-2); lib. bdg. write for info. (0-688-11743-0) Morrow Jr Bks.
—Red Means Good Fortune: A Story of San Francisco's Chinatown. Goldin, Barbara D. 64p. (gr. 2-6). 1994. PLB 12.99 (0-670-85352-6) Viking Child Bks.
Maas, Katherine. Gifted Kids Have Feelings Too: And Other Not-So-Fictitious Stories for & about Teenagers. Rimm, Sylvia B. & Priest, Christine. LC 90-81442. 162p. (Orig.). (gr. 6-12). 1990. pap. text ed. 15.00 (0-937891-06-1); pap. text ed. 15.00 discussion book (0-937891-07-X) Apple Pub Wisc.
Maas, Mieke. The Dictionary. Beebe, Brooke M. & Rosenblatt, Ruth Y. LC 77-730283. (gr. 3-5). 1977. pap. text ed. 165.00 4 filmstrips, 4 cass., 24 skill sheets, Guide (0-89290-121-7, A151-SATC) Soc for Visual.
Maas, Robert, photos by. Fire Fighters. Maas, Robert. 32p. (gr. k-3). 1989. pap. 12.95 (0-590-41459-3) Scholastic Inc.
Maass, Robert, photos by. When Autumn Comes. Maass, Robert. LC 90-53045. 32p. (ps-2). 1990. 15.95 (0-8050-1259-1, Owlet BYR) H Holt & Co.
McAllan, Marina. Moggy the Mouser. Lawton, Helen. LC 93-6571. 1994. write for info. (0-383-03702-6) SRA Schl Grp.
McAllister, Angela. The Battle of Sir Cob & Sir Filbert. McAllister, Angela. LC 91-19023. 32p. (ps-2). 1992. 15.00 (0-517-58730-0) Crown Bks Yng Read.
McAllister, David. Animals in Danger. Amos, Janine. LC 92-16336. 32p. (gr. 2-3). 1992. PLB 18.99 (0-8114-3404-4) Raintree Steck-V.
—Bear. Down, Mike. LC 91-44726. 32p. (gr. 4-6). 1993. text ed. 11.59 (0-8167-2765-1); tchr's. ed. 3.95 (0-8167-2766-X) Troll Assocs. Postponed.
McAllister, Mimi & Becker, Richard. Christmas at Gump's. McAllister, Mimi. LC 90-60435. 48p. 1990. 16.95 (0-9624887-4-7) C Salway Pr.
McAllister, Stephen. Tooth Fairy Legend. McAllister, Frank. LC 90-28136. 40p. (gr. k-6). 1992. 12.95 (0-915677-54-7) Roundtable Pub.
McAllister-Stammen, Joellen. The Crimson Ribbon. Hippely, Hilary H. LC 92-43066. 1994. write for info. (0-399-22542-0, Putnam) Putnam Pub Group.
Macari, Mario. Bein' Green. Raposo, Joe. 24p. 1993. 12.95 (0-7935-1680-3, 00183008) H Leonard Pub Corp.
Macaro, Catherine A. Suzy & the Mouse King. Wahl, Jan. 78p. 1992. lib. bdg. 12.95 (0-940696-34-7) Monroe County Lib.
Macarther-Onslow, Annette. The Man from Snowy River. Paterson, A. B. 32p. (gr. k-3). 1991. pap. 7.95 (0-7322-7234-3, Pub. by Angus & Robertson AT) HarpC.
McArthur, Kenny, photos by. Thomas Gets Tricked & Other Stories: Based on the Railway Series. Awdry, W. LC 89-8502. 32p. (ps-3). 1989. PLB 5.99 (0-679-90100-0); pap. 2.25 (0-679-80100-6) Random Bks Yng Read.

—Thomas the Tank Engine ABC: (Just Right for 2's & 3's) Awdry, W. LC 89-10605. 24p. (ps). 1990. 5.99 (0-679-80362-9) Random Bks Yng Read.
—Trouble for Thomas & Other Stories: Based on the Railway Series. Awdry, W. LC 89-8503. 32p. (ps-3). 1989. pap. 2.25 (0-679-80101-4) Random Bks Yng Read.
McArthur, Kenny, et al. Meet Thomas the Tank Engine & His Friends. Awdry, W. LC 89-32299. 32p. (ps-1). 1989. 6.95 (0-679-80102-2) Random Bks Yng Read.
McArthur, Kenny, et al, photos by. Thomas Gets Tricked & Other Stories. Awdry, W. Starr, Ringo, contrib. by. 32p. (Orig.). (ps-3). 1991. pap. 5.95 incl. 20-min. cassette (0-679-80108-1) Random Bks Yng Read.
—Thomas the Tank Engine Take-along Library, 5 bks. Awdry, W. (ps-3). 1992. Boxed set incls. A Cow on the Line & Other Stories, Thomas Gets Tricked & Other Stories, Diesel's Devious Deed & Other Stories, Trouble for Thomas & Other Stories, & Catch Me! Catch Me!, 32p. ea. 11.50 (0-679-83840-6) Random Bks Yng Read.
—Trouble for Thomas & Other Stories. reissue ed. Awdry, W. Starr, Ringo, contrib. by. 32p. (ps-2). 1991. incl. 20-min. cassette 5.95 (0-679-80106-5) Random Bks Yng Read.
Macaulay, David. Black & White. Macaulay, David. 32p. 1990. 14.45 (0-395-52151-3) HM.
—Castle. Macaulay, David. LC 77-7159. 80p. (gr. 1 up). 1982. 14.45 (0-395-25784-0); pap. 7.70 (0-395-32920-5) HM.
—City: A Story of Roman Planning & Construction. Macaulay, David. 112p. (gr. 6 up). 1974. 15.95 (0-395-19492-X); pap. 7.95 (0-395-34922-2) HM.
—Mill. Macaulay, David. 128p. (gr. 6 up) 1983. 15.45 (0-395-34830-7) HM.
—Pyramid. Macaulay, David. 80p. (gr. 7 up) 1975. 14.95 (0-395-21407-6) HM.
—Pyramid PA. Macaulay, David. (gr. 5 up). 1982. pap. 7.70 (0-395-32121-2) HM.
—Unbuilding. Macaulay, David. LC 80-15491. 128p. (gr. 5 up). 1987. pap. 6.95 (0-395-45360-7) HM.
—Underground. Macaulay, David. (gr. 1 up). 1976. 16.95 (0-395-24739-X); pap. 8.70 (0-395-34065-9) HM.
—The Way Things Work. Macaulay, David. 400p. (ps up). 1988. 29.45 (0-395-42857-2) HM.
Macaulay, Kitty. I Feel Orange Today. Godwin, Patricia. 24p. 1993. lib. bdg. 14.95 (1-55037-284-X, Pub. by Annick CN); pap. 4.95 (1-55037-285-8, Pub. by Annick CN) Firefly Bks Ltd.
McAulay, Liz, photos by. Costume. Rowland-Warne, L. LC 91-53135. 64p. (gr. 5 up). 1992. 15.00 (0-679-81680-1); PLB 15.99 (0-679-91680-6) Knopf Bks Yng Read.
McAulay, Robert. Budgerigars. Vrbova, Zuza. 48p. (gr. 2 up). 1990. PLB 9.95 (0-86622-556-0, J-006) TFH Pubns.
—Guinea Pigs. Vrbova, Zuza. 48p. 1990. PLB 9.95 (0-86622-555-2, J-005) TFH Pubns.
—Junior Pet Care Koi for Ponds. Vrbova, Zuza. 48p. (gr. 1-6). 1990. PLB 9.95 (0-685-45484-3, J-008) TFH Pubns.
—Kittens. Vrbova, Zuza. 48p. (gr. 2 up). 1990. PLB 9.95 (0-86622-553-6, J-003) TFH Pubns.
—Puppies. Vrbova, Zuza. 48p. (gr. 2 up). 1990. PLB 9.95 (0-86622-552-8, J-002) TFH Pubns.
—Rabbits. Vrbova, Zuza. 48p. 1990. PLB 9.95 (0-86622-550-1, J-001) TFH Pubns.
—Snakes. Vrbova, Zuza. 48p. 1990. PLB 9.95 (0-86622-557-9, J-007) TFH Pubns.
—Turtles. Vrbova, Zuza. 48p. 1990. PLB 9.95 (0-86622-559-5, J-009) TFH Pubns.
McAvinn, Douglas. Effective Language Arts Techniques for Middle Grades (4-8) An Integrated Approach. Opie, Brenda & McAvinn, Douglas. 84p. (gr. 4-8). 1989. pap. text ed. 7.95 (0-685-26803-9) Masterminds Pubns.
Macbain, Carol. Summer Talk: Phrase-a-Day French for Families. White, Judith. 27p. (ps-6). 1986. wkbk. 6.25 (0-937531-01-4) Fgn Lang Young Child.
McBarnet, Gill. Fountain of Fire. McBarnet, Gill. 32p. (gr. k-2). 1987. 7.95 (0-9615102-3-4) Ruwanga Trad.
—Gecko Hide & Seek. McBarnet, Gill. 24p. (ps-2). Date not set. 7.95 (0-9615102-7-7) Ruwanga Trad.
—The Shark Who Learned a Lesson. McBarnet, Gill. 32p. (ps-2). 1990. 7.95 (0-9615102-5-0) Ruwanga Trad.
—The Whale Who Wanted to Be Small. McBarnet, Gill. 32p. (gr. k-2). 1985. 7.95 (0-9615102-0-X) Ruwanga Trad.
—A Whale's Tale. McBarnet, Gill. 32p. (ps-2). 1988. 6.95 (0-9615102-4-2) Ruwanga Trad.
—The Wonderful Journey. McBarnet, Gill. 32p. (gr. k-2). 1986. 7.95 (0-9615102-2-6) Ruwanga Trad.
McBarnett, Gill. The Pink Parrot. McBarnet, Gill. 40p. (gr. k-2). 1986. 7.95 (0-9615102-1-8) Ruwanga Trad.
McBee, Jane. All about Seeds. Kuchalla, Susan. LC 81-11480. 32p. (gr. k-2). 1982. lib. bdg. 10.89 (0-89375-658-X); pap. 2.95 (0-89375-659-8) Troll Assocs.
McBoon, Linda. Platy: The Child in Us. Brittain, Grady B. LC 81-6503. 53p. (Orig.). (ps-8). 1981. pap. 2.00 (0-86663-761-3) Ide Hse.
McBride, Angus. Assassins of Dol Amroth. Crutchfield, Charlie. Fenlon, Peter C., Jr., ed. (Orig.). (gr. 10-12). 1987. pap. 6.00 (0-915795-98-1, 8106) Iron Crown Ent Inc.

—Brigands of Mirkwood. Crutchfield, Charles. Fenlon, Peter C., Jr., ed. 32p. (Orig.). (gr. 10-12). 1987. pap. 7.00 (0-915795-85-X, 8090) Iron Crown Ent Inc.

—Ents of Fangorn. Doty, Randall. Fenlon, Peter C., Jr., ed. 60p. (Orig.). (gr. 10-12). 1987. pap. 12.00 (0-915795-84-1, 3500) Iron Crown Ent Inc.

—Far Harad, the Scorched Land. Crutchfield, Charles. Charlton, Coleman, ed. 64p. (gr. 10-12). 1988. pap. 12.00 (1-55806-007-3, 3800) Iron Crown Ent Inc.

—Gates of Mordor. Staplehurst, Graham. Fenlon, Peter C., Jr., ed. 32p. (Orig.). (gr. 10-12). 1987. pap. 6.00 (0-915795-81-7, 8105, Dist. by Berkley Pub Group) Iron Crown Ent Inc.

—Growing up in Ancient Egypt. David, Rosalie. LC 91-40264. 32p. (gr. 3-5). 1993. PLB 11.89 (0-8167-2717-1); pap. text ed. 3.95 (0-8167-2718-X) Troll Assocs. Postponed.

—Growing up in Viking Times. Tweddle, Dominic. LC 91-41396. 32p. (gr. 3-5). 1993. PLB 11.89 (0-8167-2725-2); pap. text ed. 3.95 (0-8167-2726-0) Troll Assocs. Postponed.

—Havens of Gondor, Land of Belfalas. Willner, Carl. Fenlon, Peter, ed. 64p. (Orig.). (gr. 10-12). 1987. pap. 12.00 (0-915795-25-6, 3300) Iron Crown Ent Inc.

—Lords of Middle-Earth, Vol 1. Fenlon, Peter C. & Colborn, Mark. 96p. (Orig.). 1986. pap. 12.00 (0-915795-26-4, 8002) Iron Crown Ent Inc.

—Lords of Middle-Earth, Vol. 2: The Mannish Races. Fenlon, Peter C., Jr., ed. 112p. (Orig.). (gr. 10-12). 1987. pap. 12.00 (0-915795-32-9, 8003) Iron Crown Ent Inc.

—Minas Tirith. Staplehurst, Graham. Fenlon, Peter C., Jr., ed. 192p. (gr. 10-12). 1988. 18.00 (1-55806-001-4, 8301) Iron Crown Ent Inc.

—Moctezuma & the Aztecs. Burell, Roy. LC 92-5823. 63p. (gr. 6-7). 1992. PLB 24.26 (0-8114-3351-X) Raintree Steck-V.

—Pirates of Pelargir. Sochard, Ruth. Fenlon, Peter, ed. 32p. (Orig.). (gr. 10-12). 1987. pap. 6.00 (0-915795-44-2, 8104) Iron Crown Ent Inc.

—Rivendell, the House of Elrond. Amthor, Terry K. 36p. (Orig.). (gr. 10-12). 1987. pap. 7.00 (0-915795-87-6, 8080) Iron Crown Ent Inc.

—Robin Hood. Staplehurst, Graham. Fenlon, Peter & Charlton, S. Coleman, eds. 160p. (Orig.). (gr. 10-12). 1987. pap. 15.00 (0-915795-28-0, 1010) Iron Crown Ent Inc.

—Rolemaster Companion. Colborn, Mark. Charlton, S. C., ed. 96p. (gr. 10-12). 1986. pap. 12.00 (0-915795-12-4, 1500) Iron Crown Ent Inc.

—Sea-Lords of Gondor. Morin, John B. Fenlon, Peter C., Jr., ed. 64p. (Orig.). (gr. 10-12). 1987. pap. 12.00 (0-915795-88-4, 3400) Iron Crown Ent Inc.

—Woses of the Black Wood. McKeage, Jeff & Fenlon, Peter C., Jr. 32p. (gr. 10-12). 1987. pap. 6.00 (0-915795-99-X, 8107) Iron Crown Ent Inc.

McBride, Angus & Danforth, Liz. Dark Mage of Rhudaur. McKeage, Jeffrey. Ney, Jessica, ed. 40p. (Orig.). (gr. 12). 1989. pap. 7.00 (1-55806-072-3, 8013) Iron Crown Ent Inc.

—Denizens of the Dark Wood. Birkner, Malthias & Birkner, Karen. Ney, Jessica, ed. 32p. (Orig.). (gr. 12). 1989. pap. 6.00 (1-55806-081-2, 8111) Iron Crown Ent Inc.

—Forest of Tears. Crutchfield, Charles. Ney, Jessica, ed. 40p. (Orig.). (gr. 12). 1989. pap. 7.00 (1-55806-084-7, 8015) Iron Crown Ent Inc.

—Ghost Warriors. Ferrone, John M. Ney, Jessica, ed. 48p. (Orig.). (gr. 12). 1990. pap. 10.00 (1-55806-107-X, 8016) Iron Crown Ent Inc.

—Hazards of the Harod Wood. Crowdis, John. Ney, Jessica, ed. 32p. (Orig.). (gr. 12). 1990. pap. 6.00 (1-55806-096-0, 8112) Iron Crown Ent Inc.

McBride, Angus & Jermy, Paul. Rogues of the Borderlands. Crowdis, John. Ney, Jessica, ed. 40p. (Orig.). (gr. 12). 1990. pap. 7.00 (1-55806-083-9, 8014) Iron Crown Ent Inc.

McBride, Angus & Midgette, Darrell. Ghosts of the Southern Arduin. Crowdis, John. Ney, Jessica & Fenlon, Peter C., Jr., eds. 32p. (Orig.). (gr. 12). 1989. pap. 6.00 (1-55806-030-8, 8109) Iron Crown Ent Inc.

McBride, Angus & Robin, Jeremy. Warlords of the Desert. Crutchfield, Charles. Ney, Jessica, ed. 40p. (Orig.). (gr. 12). 1989. pap. 7.00 (1-55806-058-8, 8012) Iron Crown Ent Inc.

McBride, Angus, jt. illus. see Sharp, Shawn.

McBride, Michael. Some Gentle Moving Thing. 2nd ed. Floyd, James C. LC 82-60198. 70p. (gr. 7-9). 1982. 6.95 (0-938232-11-8) Winston-Derek.

—Watch Out for the Golly Whompers. Corrigan, Dorothy D. LC 88-50754. 35p. (gr. k-3). 1988. 6.95 (1-55523-149-7) Winston-Derek.

McBride, Molly J. Sing a Song of Halloween: With Communication, Arts & Nutrition Activities. Strand, Julie & Boggs, Juanita. 133p. 1982. pap. text ed. 10.95 (0-910817-00-6) Collaborative Learn.

McBride, Shawn. Mordechai. Haalman, Perry. 36p. (gr. 4 up). 1990. pap. 8.00 (0-9624155-2-9) Cottage Wordsmiths.

Maccabe, Richard. Conservation & Pollution. Santrey, Laurence. LC 84-2703. 32p. (gr. 3-6). 1985. PLB 9.49 (0-8167-0260-8); pap. text ed. 2.95 (0-8167-0261-6) Troll Assocs.

—Fossils. Sabin, Louis. LC 84-2716. 32p. (gr. 3-6). 1985. PLB 9.49 (0-8167-0228-4); pap. text ed. 2.95 (0-8167-0229-2) Troll Assocs.

—Rockets & Satellites. Sabin, Francene. LC 84-2738. 32p. (gr. 3-6). 1985. PLB 9.49 (0-8167-0288-8); pap. text ed. 2.95 (0-8167-0289-6) Troll Assocs.

—Rocks & Minerals. Bains, Rae. LC 84-8644. 32p. (gr. 3-6). 1985. PLB 9.49 (0-8167-0186-5); pap. text ed. 2.95 (0-8167-0187-3) Troll Assocs.

McCaffery, Janet. The Witch of Hissing Hill. Calhoun, Mary. LC 64-15475. (gr. k-3). 1964. PLB 13.88 (0-688-31762-6) Morrow Jr Bks.

McCaffrey, Kevin. Adventures of Fionn & the Fianna. 40p. (gr. 4 up). 1989. 9.95 (1-871423-05-8) Irish Bks Media.

McCaig, Iaian. Dragon's Plunder. Strickland, Brad. LC 91-45664. 160p. (gr. 7 up). 1992. SBE 14.95 (0-689-31573-2, Atheneum Child Bk) Macmillan Child Grp.

McCaig, Rob. Roman Times. Chisholm, Jan. 24p. (gr. 3-6). 1982. PLB 11.96 (0-88110-105-2); pap. 4.50 (0-86020-619-X); lib. bdg. 11.96 (0-685-57844-5) EDC.

McCaig, Rob & Ashman, Iain. Castle Times. Gee, Robyn, ed. 24p. (gr. 3-6). 1982. lib. bdg. 11.96 (0-88110-106-0); pap. 4.50 (0-86020-621-1) EDC.

McCaig, Ron, jt. illus. see Stitt, Sue.

McCall, Jeff. Edna Eagle. Costello, Gwen. Kendzia, Mary C., ed. 32p. (Orig.). 1992. pap. 4.95 (0-89622-528-3) Twenty-Third.

McCallum, J. Cat's Adventure in Alphabet Town. Alden, L. LC 91-3605. 32p. (ps-2). 1992. PLB 14.60 (0-516-05403-1) Childrens.

—Fox's Adventure in Alphabet Town. McDonnell, Janet. LC 91-20546. 32p. (ps-2). 1992. PLB 14.60 (0-516-05406-6) Childrens.

—Kangaroo's Adventure in Alphabet Town. McDonnell, Janet. LC 91-20540. 32p. (ps-2). 1992. PLB 14.60 (0-516-05411-2) Childrens.

—Little Lady's Adventure in Alphabet Town. Riehecky, J. LC 91-20542. 32p. (ps-2). 1992. PLB 14.60 (0-516-05412-0) Childrens.

McCallum, Joanne. A Child's Book of Manners. Odor, Ruth S. 32p. (gr. k-2). 1990. pasted 2.50 (0-87403-701-8, 24-03901) Standard Pub.

—Christy's Pouting Again. Linville, Barbara. McCallum, Joanne, created by. 32p. (gr. k-2). 1989. 2.99 (0-87403-627-5, 3891) Standard Pub.

—Joey's Too Much TV. Linville, Barbara. McCallum, Joanne, created by. 32p. (gr. k-2). 1989. 2.99 (0-87403-628-3, 3892) Standard Pub.

—Susie's Afraid of the Dark. Linville, Barbara. McCallum, Joanne, created by. 32p. (gr. k-2). 1989. 2.99 (0-87403-629-1, 3893) Standard Pub.

—Tommy's Afraid to Try. Linville, Barbara. McCallum, Joanne, created by. 32p. (gr. k-2). 1989. 2.99 (0-87403-630-5) Standard Pub.

McCallum, Joanne V. Devotions for Little Boys & Girls: New Testament. Webb, Joan C. 112p. (ps-k). 1992. pap. 5.99 (0-87403-682-8, 12-02822) Standard Pub.

—Devotions for Little Boys & Girls: Old Testament. Webb, Joan C. 112p. (Orig.). (ps-k). 1992. pap. 5.99 (0-87403-681-X, 12-02821) Standard Pub.

McCallum, Jodi. Play with A & T. Moncure, Jane B. LC 89-774. 32p. (gr. k-2). 1989. PLB 21.35 (0-89565-505-5); PLB 14.95s.p. (0-685-56019-8) Childs World.

McCallum, Jodie. Caring for My Body. Moncure, Jane B. 32p. (ps-2). 1990. PLB 18.50 (0-89565-668-X); PLB 12.95s.p. (0-685-58737-1) Childs World.

—Children Around the World Celebrate Christmas! Osborn, Susan T. & Tangvald, Christine H. LC 93-6683. (gr. 4 up). 1993. 10.00 (0-87403-799-9, 24-03664) Standard Pub.

—Halloween. Alden, Laura. LC 93-7633. (gr. 4 up). 1993. write for info. (0-516-00684-3) Childrens.

—The Happy Times Players Present - The Story of Creation. Stewart, Dana. 12p. (ps). 1993. 4.99 (0-7847-0127-X, 23-02219) Standard Pub.

—The Happy Times Players Present - The Story of Noah's Ark. Stewart, Dana. 12p. (ps). 1993. 4.99 (0-7847-0128-8, 23-02220) Standard Pub.

—Nightingale's Adventure in Alphabet Town. Alden, Laura. LC 92-1069. 32p. (ps-2). 1992. PLB 14.60 (0-516-05414-7) Childrens.

—Owl's Adventure in Alphabet Town. Alden, Laura. LC 92-4091. 32p. (ps-2). 1992. PLB 14.60 (0-516-05415-5) Childrens.

—Pride. Crowdy, Deborah. LC 89-48107. 32p. (gr. k-3). 1990. PLB 21.35 (0-89565-566-7); PLB 14.95s.p. (0-685-56200-X) Childs World.

—Quarterback's Adventure in Alphabet Town. McDonnell, Janet. LC 92-1067. 32p. (ps-2). 1992. PLB 14.60 (0-516-05417-1) Childrens.

—Step into Summer: A New Season. Moncure, Jane B. LC 90-30456. 32p. (ps-2). 1990. PLB 19.95 (0-89565-572-1); PLB 13.95s.p. (0-685-56188-7) Childs World.

McCarthy, Bobette. Happy Hiding Hippos. McCarthy, Bobette. LC 92-32599. 32p. (ps-1). 1994. RSBE 13.95 (0-02-765446-X, Bradbury Pr) Macmillan Child Grp.

—The Solo. Lasky, Kathryn. LC 92-44456. 32p. (ps-2). 1994. RSBE 14.95 (0-02-751664-4, Macmillan Child Bk) Macmillan Child Grp.

—The Tantrum. Lasky, Kathryn. LC 92-3701. 32p. (ps-1). 1993. RSBE 13.95 (0-02-751661-X, Macmillan Child Bk) Macmillan Child Grp.

—Ten Little Hippos: A Counting Book. McCarthy, Bobette. LC 91-17175. 32p. (ps-2). 1992. SBE 13.95 (0-02-765445-1, Bradbury Pr) Macmillan Child Grp.

McCarthy, Carole H. Tales of Tutu Nene & Nele. Bates, Gale. 36p. (ps-4). 1991. 7.95 (0-89610-193-2) Island Heritage.

McCarthy, Donald W. Fun with Math-E-Magic. McCarthy, Donald. Cooper, William H., ed. 65p. (gr. 4-9). 1984. pap. 2.60 (0-914127-01-2) Univ Class.

McCarthy, Kathleen. Beginning to Subtract. Evans, Karen. Nayer, Judith E., ed. 32p. (gr. k-1). 1991. wkbk. 1.95 (1-878624-56-3) McClanahan Bk.

MacCarthy, Patricia. Herds of Words. MacCarthy, Patricia. LC 90-31537. 32p. (ps-3). 1991. 11.95 (0-8037-0892-0) Dial Bks Young.

—The Horrendous Hullabaloo. Mahy, Margaret. 32p. (ps-3). 1992. 13.00 (0-670-84547-7) Viking Child Bks.

—Seventeen Kings & Forty-Two Elephants. Mahy, Margaret. LC 87-5311. 32p. (ps-3). 1987. 13.99 (0-8037-0458-5) Dial Bks Young.

—Seventeen Kings & Forty-Two Elephants. Mahy, Margaret. Fogelman, Phyllis J., ed. LC 87-5311. 32p. (ps-3). 1990. pap. 4.95 (0-8037-0781-9) Dial Bks Young.

McCaul, Laura. I Can Sign My ABC's. Chaplin, Susan. LC 86-22890. 56p. (ps-1). 1986. 9.95 (0-930323-19-X, Kendall Green Pubns) Gallaudet Univ Pr.

McCay, Winsor. The Complete Little Nemo in Slumberland: In the Land of Wonderful Dreams, Part 2 - 1913-1914, Vol. VI. McCay, Winsor. Marschall, Richard, ed. 96p. (gr. 6 up). 1992. 34.95 (0-924359-36-6) Remco Wrldserv Bks.

McClelland, Linda. This Is the Book That I Borrowed. Loves, June. LC 92-31955. 1993. 4.25 (0-383-03598-8) SRA Schl Grp.

—Walking to School. Gleeson, Libby. LC 92-31945. 1993. 2.50 (0-383-03602-X) SRA Schl Grp.

—What Angela Needs. Benson, Rita. LC 92-34266. 1993. 14.00 (0-383-03666-6) SRA Schl Grp.

McCloskey, Patty. Find the Real Mother Goose. 32p. (ps-1). 1993. pap. 5.95 (1-56565-054-9) Lowell Hse.

McCloskey, Patty, et al. The Real Mother Goose: Book of American Rhymes. Slier, Debby, ed. 128p. (ps-5). 1993. 12.95 (1-56288-399-2) Checkerboard.

McCloskey, Robert. Blueberries for Sal. McCloskey, Robert. LC 48-4955. (ps-1). 1976. pap. 3.99 (0-14-050169-X, Puffin) Puffin Bks.

—Blueberries for Sal. McCloskey, Robert. LC 48-4955. 56p. (ps-1). 1948. pap. 14.95 (0-670-17591-9) Viking Child Bks.

—Burt Dow: Deep-Water Man. McCloskey, Robert. LC 68-364. 64p. (gr. 4-6). 1963. pap. 15.95 (0-670-19748-3) Viking Child Bks.

—Centurburg Tales. McCloskey, Robert. LC 51-10675. 192p. (gr. 4-6). 1951. pap. 14.95 (0-670-20977-5) Viking Child Bks.

—Henry Reed, Inc. Robertson, Keith. (gr. 4-6). 1958. pap. 14.95 (0-670-36796-6) Viking Child Bks.

—Henry Reed, Inc. Robertson, Keith. 240p. (gr. 4-6). 1989. pap. 4.99 (0-14-034114-7, Puffin) Puffin Bks.

—Henry Reed's Baby-Sitting Service. Robertson, Keith. (gr. 5-8). 1966. pap. 14.95 (0-670-36825-3) Viking Child Bks.

—Henry Reed's Baby-Sitting Service. Robertson, Keith. 208p. (gr. 4-6). 1989. pap. 3.99 (0-14-034146-3, Puffin) Puffin Bks.

—Henry Reed's Big Show. Robertson, Keith. (gr. 4-6). 1970. pap. 14.95 (0-670-36839-3) Viking Child Bks.

—Henry Reed's Big Show. Robertson, Keith. 208p. (gr. 4-7). 1978. pap. 2.50 (0-440-43570-6, YB) Dell.

—Henry Reed's Journey. Robertson, Keith. 224p. (gr. 4-6). 1989. pap. 4.99 (0-14-034145-5, Puffin) Puffin Bks.

—Homer Price. McCloskey, Robert. (gr. 4-6). 1943. pap. 14.00 (0-670-37729-5) Viking Child Bks.

—Lentil. McCloskey, Robert. (gr. k-3). 1940. pap. 14.95 (0-670-42357-2) Viking Child Bks.

—Make Way for Ducklings. McCloskey, Robert. (gr. k-3). 1941. pap. 13.99 (0-670-45149-5) Viking Child Bks.

—One Morning in Maine. McCloskey, Robert. (gr. k-3). 1952. pap. 14.00 (0-670-52627-4) Viking Child Bks.

—Time of Wonder. McCloskey, Robert. 64p. (gr. k-3). 1989. pap. 4.99 (0-14-050201-7, Puffin) Puffin Bks.

—Time of Wonder. McCloskey, Robert. (gr. k-3). 1957. pap. 16.00 (0-670-71512-3) Viking Child Bks.

McCloskey-Padgett, Patty. The Real Mother Goose ABC's. McCloskey-Padgett, Patty. 1993. pap. 5.95 (1-56565-090-5) Lowell Hse.

McCloud, Scott. Understanding Comics. 2nd ed. McCloud, Scott. Martin, Mark, ed. 224p. (gr. 4 up). 1993. 27.95 (0-87816-244-5); ltd. signed ed. 34.95 (0-87816-245-3); pap. 19.95 (0-87816-243-7) Kitchen Sink.

McClun, Rhonda. The Tale of Dan De Lion. Disch, Thomas M. 32p. (up. up). 1986. 9.95 (0-918273-30-7) Coffee Hse.

McClung, Robert M. Major: The Story of a Black Bear. McClung, Robert M. LC 87-26126. 64p. (gr. 9-12). 1988. Repr. of 1956 ed. lib. bdg. 15.00 (0-208-02201-5, Linnet) Shoe String.

McClure, Gillian. Tog the Ribber: Or Granny's Tales. Coltman, Paul. LC 84-82555. 32p. (ps-5). 1985. 15.00 (0-374-37630-1) FS&G.

McClure, Nancee. Bible Teacher Time Savers. Daniel, Rebecca. 48p. (gr. k-5). 1984. wkbk. 6.95 (0-86653-235-8, SS 817, Shining Star Pubns) Good Apple.

—Book I-His Birth. Daniel, Rebecca. 32p. (gr. 2-7). 1984. wkbk. 5.95 (0-86653-213-7, SS 824, Shining Star Pubns) Good Apple.

—Book II-His Boyhood. Daniel, Rebecca. 32p. (gr. 2-7). 1984. wkbk. 5.95 (0-86653-223-4, SS 825, Shining Star Pubns) Good Apple.
—Book III-Gathering His Disciples. Daniel, Rebecca. 32p. (gr. 2-7). 1984. wkbk. 5.95 (0-86653-224-2, SS 826, Shining Star Pubns) Good Apple.
—Book IV-the Teacher. Daniel, Rebecca. 32p. (gr. 2-7). 1984. wkbk. 5.95 (0-86653-225-0, SS 827, Shining Star Pubns) Good Apple.
—Book V-The Healer. Daniel, Rebecca. 32p. (gr. 2-7). 1984. wkbk. 5.95 (0-86653-226-9, SS 828, Shining Star Pubns) Good Apple.
—Book VI-His Miracles. Daniel, Rebecca. 32p. (gr. 2-7). 1984. wkbk. 5.95 (0-86653-227-7, SS 829, Shining Star Pubns) Good Apple.
—Book VII-His Parables. Daniel, Rebecca. 32p. (gr. 2-7). 1984. wkbk. 5.95 (0-86653-228-5, SS 830, Shining Star Pubns) Good Apple.
—Book VIII-More Parables. Daniel, Rebecca. 32p. (gr. 2-7). 1984. wkbk. 5.95 (0-86653-229-3, SS 831, Shining Star Pubns) Good Apple.
—Book X-His Last Days. Daniel, Rebecca. 32p. (gr. 2-7). 1984. wkbk. 5.95 (0-86653-231-5, SS 833, Shining Star Pubns) Good Apple.
—Book XI-His Last Hours. Daniel, Rebecca. 32p. (gr. 2-7). 1984. wkbk. 5.95 (0-86653-232-3, SS 834, Shining Star Pubns) Good Apple.
—Book XII-His Resurrection. Daniel, Rebecca. 32p. (gr. 2-7). 1984. wkbk. 5.95 (0-86653-233-1, SS 835, Shining Star Pubns) Good Apple.
—Breaking into Bible Games. Hand, Phyllis. 48p. (gr. 3-6). 1984. wkbk. 6.95 (0-86653-181-5, SS 819, Shining Star Pubns) Good Apple.
—Creative Egg Carton Crafts. McClure, Nancee. 64p. (ps-2). 1989. wkbk. 7.95 (0-86653-471-7, GA1077) Good Apple.
—Daily Close-Ups for Spring. Magoldi, Mary. Russell, Bruce, ed. 96p. (gr. k-6). 1984. wkbk. 9.95 (0-86653-255-2, GA 563) Good Apple.
—Scientific Encounters of the Curious Kind. Embry, Lynn. 64p. (gr. 4-7). 1984. wkbk. 7.95 (0-86653-176-9, GA 550) Good Apple.
—Scientific Encounters of the Endangered Kind. Embry, Lynn. 64p. (gr. 4-7). 1986. wkbk. 7.95 (0-86653-353-2, GA 694) Good Apple.
—Scientific Encounters of the Mysterious Sea. Embry, Lynn. 64p. (gr. 4-7). 1987. pap. 7.95 (0-86653-407-5, GA1013) Good Apple.
McClure, Tim. Father Miguel Hidalgo: A Cry for Freedom. Perlin, D. E. LC 90-27375. (ENG & SPA.). 32p. (gr. k-4). 1991. pap. 5.95 (0-937460-67-2) Hendrick-Long.
McCoig, Rich, photos by. Chris Has An Accident. Kirby, Jackie M. McCormack, Nancy, ed. 52p. (Orig.). (gr. 3-4). 1987. pap. 5.95 (0-942459-00-8) McCormack Co.
McColgan, Susie. The Special Princess. Luth, Sophie A. 36p. 1990. glossy cover 5.95 (0-9626153-0-7) Luth & Assocs.
McCollin, Russ. Three Little Africans. Alhaji Obaba Abdullahi Muhammad. 36p. (Orig.). (gr. k-4). 1978. pap. 2.50 (0-916157-00-8) African Islam Miss Pubns.
MacCombie, Turi. Awesome Animals. Ingoglia, Gina. 48p. (gr. 2-4). 1992. pap. write for info. (0-307-11472-4, 11472, Golden Pr) Western Pub.
—Hush, Little Baby. 1994. pap. 6.99 (0-553-45907-4) Bantam.
—My First Book of Animals from A to Z: More Than 150 Animals Every Child Should Know. LC 92-19284. 64p. (ps-2). 1994. 12.95 (0-590-46305-5, Cartwheel) Scholastic Inc.
—Stegosaurs: The Solar-Powered Dinosaurs. Sattler, Helen R. Pearson, Susan, ed. LC 91-4542. 32p. (gr. 1 up). 1992. 15.00 (0-688-10055-4); PLB 14.93 (0-688-10056-2) Lothrop.
—Velveteen Rabbit. 48p. (ps-3). 1991. 9.95 (0-88101-114-2) Unicorn Pub.
—Velveteen Rabbit. 48p. (ps-3). 1992. 12.95 (0-88101-236-X) Unicorn Pub.
McCombs, Toni. English Is Fun. Barrier, Jean & Kennedy, Alice. Barrier, Jean & Kennedy, Aliceintro. by. 96p. (gr. k-5). 1981. pap. 6.00 (0-911743-01-4) Barrier & Kennedy.
—English Is Fun Books. Barrier, Jean & Kennedy, Alice. 192p. (gr. k-8). 1991. pap. text ed. 12.00 (0-911743-07-3) Barrier & Kennedy.
—English Is Fun II. Barrier, Jean & Kennedy, Alice. Catoe, Kaye, et al, eds. 96p. (gr. 2-8). 1985. pap. text ed. 6.00 (0-911743-04-9); tchr's ed. 8.00 (0-911743-06-5) Barrier & Kennedy.
McConnell, Keith. The ReptAlphabet Encyclopedia. McConnell, Keith. 48p. (Orig.). (gr. 4 up). 1984. pap. 5.95 (0-88045-045-2) Stemmer Hse.
—The SeAlphabet Encyclopedia. McConnell, Keith. 48p. (gr. 4 up). 1982. pap. 5.95 (0-88045-016-9) Stemmer Hse.
McConnell, Keith A. The AnimAlphabet Encyclopedia. McConnell, Keith. 48p. (gr. 4 up). 1982. pap. 5.95 (0-916144-97-6) Stemmer Hse.
McConnell, Mary. A Quilt for Elizabeth. Tiffault, Benette W. 32p. (Orig.). (gr. 2-5). 1992. pap. 8.95x (1-56123-034-0) Centering Corp.
—The Secret Places: The Story of a Child's Adventure with Grief. Campbell, James A. 45p. (Orig.). (gr. 4-9). 1992. pap. 5.25 (1-56123-051-0) Centering Corp.
McCord, Kathi. That's Me in Here. Darby, Jean. 43p. (Orig.). (gr. 1-2). 1989. pap. 4.95 (0-8198-7345-4) St Paul Bks.

McCord, Kathleen. Don't Be Afraid, Amanda. Moore, Lilian. LC 91-19661. 64p. (gr. 2-5). 1992. SBE 12.95 (0-689-31725-5, Atheneum Child Bk) Macmillan Child Grp.
McCord, Kathleen G. Adam Mouse's Book of Poems. Moore, Lilian. LC 91-42223. 64p. (ps-5). 1992. SBE 11.95 (0-689-31765-4, Atheneum Child Bk) Macmillan Child Grp.
—Crackle Creek. Monsell, Mary E. LC 89-15105. 64p. (gr. 2-4). 1990. SBE 12.95 (0-689-31564-3, Atheneum Child Bk) Macmillan Child Grp.
—The Pudgy Noisy Book. Shine, Deborah. 18p. (ps) 1988. bds. 2.95 (0-448-19055-9, G&D) Putnam Pub Group.
McCormick, Dell J. Paul Bunyan Swings His Axe. McCormick, Dell J. LC 36-33409. (gr. 4-6). 1936. 11. 95 (0-87004-093-6) Caxton.
McCormick, J. Shane. Schaefer, Jack. (gr. 7 up) 1954. 15.95 (0-395-07090-2) HM.
McCormick, Keith & Abrahamson, Evy. Celebrating Sacraments. rev. ed. Stoutzenberger, Joseph. Allaire, Barbara, ed. 304p. (gr. 10-). 1993. pap. text ed. 13.70 (0-88489-279-4); tchr's. ed., 290p. 18.95 (0-88489-280-8) St Marys.
McCoy, Beverly. Jimmy Coon Story Book, No. 1. Deitz, Lawrence. 34p. (Orig.). 1985. pap. 2.95 (0-934750-79-3) Mntn Memories Bks.
—Jimmy Coon Story Book, No. 2. Deitz, Lawrence. 37p. 1985. pap. 2.95 (0-934750-42-4) Mntn Memories Bks.
—Jimmy Coon Story Book, No. 4. Deitz, Lawrence. 30p. 1986. pap. 2.95 (0-934750-14-9) Mntn Memories Bks.
McCoy, Judy. Scribble Cookies & Other Independent Creative Art Experiences for Children. Kohl, MaryAnn F. LC 87-8220. 144p. (ps-6). 1985. pap. 12.95 (0-935607-10-2) Bright Ring.
McCoy, William M. Wally Koala & Friends. Mazzola, Toni & Guten, Mimi. Cohen, Keri, ed. LC 93-94001. 24p. (ps-3). 1993. saddlestitch bdg. incl. cassette 9.95 (1-883747-00-7) WK Prods.
—Wally Koala & the Little Green Peach. Mazzola, Toni & Guten, Mimi. Cohen, Keri, ed. 24p. (ps-3). 1993. saddlestitch bdg. incl. cassette 9.95 (1-883747-02-3) WK Prods.
McCracken, Bill. Benjy's New Home. Scherer, Bonnie. LC 89-60806. 7p. 1989. pap. 1.50 (0-9622421-0-1) B Scherer.
McCracken, Steve. Willie Pearl: Under the Mountain. Green, Michelle Y. Green, Oliver W., contrib. by. (Orig.). (gr. 4-6). 1992. pap. 9.95 (0-9627697-1-1) W Ruth Co.
McCrady, Lady. My Mother the Mail Carrier - Mi Mama la Cartera. Maury, Inez. Alemany, Norah, tr. LC 76-14275. (ENG & SPA.). 32p. (Orig.). (gr. k-4). 1976. 7.95 (0-935312-23-4) Feminist Pr.
McCreary, Jane, jt. illus. see Cleaveland, C. A.
McCue, Lisa. Baby Elephant's Bedtime. McCue, Dick. 24p. (ps). 1985. pap. 2.95 (0-671-55853-6, Little Simon) S&S Trade.
—Bunnies Love. LC 90-61307. 24p. (ps-1). 1991. 4.95 (0-679-80385-8) Random Bks Yng Read.
—Bunny's Numbers. McCue, Dick. 24p. (ps). 1984. pap. 2.95 (0-671-50944-6, Little Simon) S&S Trade.
—Corduroy's Busy Street & Corduroy Goes to the Doctor, 2 bks. Freeman, Don. (ps-k). 1989. Repr. of 1987 ed. bds. 12.95 incl. cass. (0-87499-133-1) Live Oak Media.
—Corduroy's Christmas. Freeman, Don & Hennessy, B. G.concept by. 16p. (ps-1). 1992. 10.95 (0-670-84477-2) Viking Child Bks.
—Corduroy's Day. Freeman, Lydia. LC 84-40477. 14p. (ps). 1985. pap. 3.99 (0-670-80521-1) Viking Child Bks.
—Corduroy's Party. Freeman, Lydia. LC 84-40476. 14p. (ps). 1985. pap. 3.99 (0-670-80520-3) Viking Child Bks.
—Corduroy's Toys. Freeman, Lydia. LC 84-40478. 24p. 1985. pap. 3.99 (0-670-80522-X) Viking Child Bks.
—Ducklings Love. LC 90-61308. 24p. (ps-1). 1991. 4.95 (0-679-80386-6) Random Bks Yng Read.
—Ducky's Seasons. 24p. (ps). 1983. pap. 2.95 (0-671-45491-9, Little Simon) S&S Trade.
—Fairest of All. Packard, Mary. LC 93-11056. (gr. 5 up). 1993. write for info. (0-516-00826-9) Childrens.
—Fox under First Base. Latimer, Jim. LC 89-27576. 32p. (gr. k-2). 1991. SBE 13.95 (0-684-19053-2, Scribners Young Read) Macmillan Child Grp.
—Froggie's Treasure. (ps-2). 1983. 2.95 (0-671-45488-9, Little Simon) S&S Trade.
—Fuzzy Kitten. Ross, Katharine. LC 92-62262. 22p. (ps-3). 1993. 3.50 (0-679-84644-1) Random Bks Yng Read.
—Fuzzy Teddy. Ross, Katharine. LC 92-62263. 22p. (ps). 1993. 3.50 (0-679-84643-3) Random Bks Yng Read.
—Fuzzytail Bunny. McCue, Lisa. 22p. (ps). 1992. bds. 2.95 (0-679-84721-2) Random Bks Yng Read.
—The Fuzzytail Friends' Great Egg Hunt. Ross, Katherine. LC 87-50812. 14p. (ps). 1988. bds. 2.95 (0-394-89475-8) Random Bks Yng Read.
—Fuzzytail Lamb. McCue, Lisa. 22p. (ps). 1992. bds. 2.95 (0-679-81720-4) Random Bks Yng Read.
—Fuzzytail Bunny Book & Bunny Set. McCue, Lisa. 22p. (ps). 1994. incl. stuffed animal 10.00 (0-679-85103-8) Random Bks Yng Read.
—Hedgehog for Breakfast. Turner, Ann. LC 88-8228. 32p. (ps-2). 1989. RSBE 13.95 (0-02-789241-7, Macmillan Child Bk) Macmillan Child Grp.

—Hired Help for Rabbit. Delton, Judy. LC 91-15551. 32p. (gr. k-3). 1992. pap. 4.50 (0-689-71522-6, Aladdin) Macmillan Child Grp.
—Kitten's Christmas. 1985. pap. 2.95 (0-671-55851-X, Little Simon) S&S Trade.
—Kittens Love. McCue, Lisa. LC 89-61137. 24p. (ps-1). 1990. 4.95 (0-394-82876-3) Random Bks Yng Read.
—Kitty's Colors. (ps-2). 1983. pap. 2.95 (0-671-45489-7, Little Simon) S&S Trade.
—The Little Chick. McCue, Lisa. LC 85-63658. 7p. (ps). 1993. bds. 3.95 (0-394-88017-X) Random Bks Yng Read.
—Nighty-Night, Little One. McCue, Lisa. LC 87-42786. 28p. (ps). 1988. bds. 2.95 (0-394-89476-6) Random Bks Yng Read.
—Norman Fools the Tooth Fairy. Carrick, Carol. 32p. 1992. 13.95 (0-590-42240-5, Scholastic Hardcover) Scholastic Inc.
—Panda's Playtime. McCue, Dick. 12p. (ps). 1985. 2.95 (0-671-55850-1, Little Simon) S&S Trade.
—The Perfect Christmas Gift. Delton, Judy. LC 91-6549. 32p. (gr. k-3). 1992. RSBE 13.95 (0-02-728471-9, Macmillan Child Bk) Macmillan Child Grp.
—Playing by the Rules. Packard, Mary. LC 94-4423. 1993. write for info. (0-516-00827-7) Childrens.
—Popcorn Dragon. Thayer, Jane. LC 88-39855. 32p. (ps up). 1989. 12.95 (0-688-08340-4); PLB 12.88 (0-688-08876-7, Morrow Jr Bks) Morrow Jr Bks.
—Puppies Love. McCue, Lisa. LC 89-61140. 24p. (ps-1). 1990. 4.95 (0-394-82875-5) Random Bks Yng Read.
—Puppy Peek-a-Boo. LC 88-60759. 14p. (ps). 1989. bds. 3.99 (0-394-81950-0) Random Bks Yng Read.
—The Puppy Who Wanted a Boy. rev. ed. Thayer, Jane. LC 85-15465. 48p. (ps-1). 1986. 12.95 (0-688-05944-9); PLB 12.88 (0-688-05945-7, Morrow Jr Bks); pap. 4.95 (0-685-43017-0, Mulberry Bks) Morrow Jr Bks.
—The Puppy Who Wanted a Boy. Thayer, Jane. LC 85-15465. (ps-3). 1988. pap. 4.95 (0-688-08293-9, Mulberry) Morrow.
—Raccoon's Hide & Seek. McCue, Dick. 12p. (ps). 1985. 2.95 (0-671-55854-4, Little Simon) S&S Trade.
—Safe & Sound. Packard, Mary. LC 93-11058. 1993. write for info. (0-516-00828-5) Childrens.
—Save the Swamp. Packard, Mary. LC 93-11059. 1993. write for info. (0-516-00829-3) Childrens.
—Sebastian (Super Sleuth) & the Baffling Bigfoot. Christian, Mary B. LC 89-13049. 64p. (gr. 2-6). 1990. SBE 10.95 (0-02-718215-0, Macmillan Child Bk) Macmillan Child Grp.
—Sebastian (Super Sleuth) & the Bone to Pick Mystery. Christian, Mary B. LC 83-5406. 64p. (gr. 2-5). 1983. RSBE 11.95 (0-02-718440-4, Macmillan Child Bk) Macmillan Child Grp.
—Sebastian (Super Sleuth) & the Clumsy Cowboy. Christian, Mary B. LC 84-21758. 64p. (gr. 2-5). 1985. RSBE 11.95 (0-02-718480-3, Macmillan Child Bk) Macmillan Child Grp.
—Sebastian (Super Sleuth) & the Copycat Crime. Christian, Mary B. 64p. (gr. 4-7). 1993. SBE 11.95 (0-02-718211-8, Macmillan Child Bk) Macmillan Child Grp.
—Sebastian (Super Sleuth) & the Crummy Yummies Caper. Christian, Mary B. LC 82-20861. 64p. (gr. 2-5). 1983. RSBE 10.95 (0-02-718430-7, Macmillan Child Bk) Macmillan Child Grp.
—Sebastian (Super Sleuth) & the Egyptian Connection. Christian, Mary B. LC 87-34986. 64p. (gr. 2-5). 1988. RSBE 10.95 (0-02-718560-9, Macmillan Child Bk) Macmillan Child Grp.
—Sebastian (Super Sleuth) & the Egyptian Connection. Christian, Mary B. 64p. (gr. 3-7). 1991. pap. 3.95 (0-689-71514-5, Aladdin) Macmillan Child Grp.
—Sebastian (Super Sleuth) & the Hair of the Dog Mystery. Christian, Mary B. LC 82-10066. 64p. (gr. 2-5). 1982. RSBE 10.95 (0-02-718260-6, Macmillan Child Bk) Macmillan Child Grp.
—Sebastian (Super Sleuth) & the Impossible Crime. Christian, Mary B. LC 91-28633. 64p. (gr. 2-6). 1992. SBE 11.95 (0-02-718435-8, Macmillan Child Bk) Macmillan Child Grp.
—Sebastian (Super Sleuth) & the Mystery Patient. Christian, Mary B. No 40-45092. 64p. (gr. 2-6). 1991. SBE 10.95 (0-02-718571-0, Macmillan Child Bk) Macmillan Child Grp.
—Sebastian (Super Sleuth) & the Purloined Sirloin. Christian, Mary B. LC 85-15238. 64p. (gr. 2-5). 1986. RSBE 10.95 (0-02-718210-X, Macmillan Child Bk) Macmillan Child Grp.
—Sebastian (Super Sleuth) & the Secret of the Skewered Skier. Christian, Mary B. LC 83-19569. 64p. (gr. 2-5). 1984. RSBE 10.95 (0-02-718450-1, Macmillan Child Bk) Macmillan Child Grp.
—Sebastian (Super Sleuth) & the Stars-In-His-Eyes Mystery. Christian, Mary B. LC 86-21771. 64p. (gr. 2-5). 1987. RSBE 10.95 (0-02-718540-0, Macmillan Child Bk) Macmillan Child Grp.
—Sebastian (Super Sleuth) & the Time Capsule Caper. Christian, Mary B. LC 88-29295. 64p. (gr. 2-6). 1989. SBE 10.95 (0-02-718570-2, Macmillan Child Bk) Macmillan Child Grp.
—Snot Stew. Wallace, Bill. LC 83-31976. 96p. (gr. 3-7). 1989. 13.95 (0-8234-0745-4) Holiday.
—Snot Stew. Wallace, Bill. 96p. 1990. pap. 2.99 (0-671-69335-2, Minstrel Bks) PB.

—Spike & Mike & the Treasure Hunt. Packard, Mary. LC 92-50295. 1993. write for info. (0-679-93936-9); lib. bdg. write for info. (0-679-83936-4) Knopf Bks Yng Read.

—Teddy Dresses. 1983. 2.95 (0-671-45490-0, Little Simon) S&S Trade.

—Ten Little Puppy Dogs. LC 86-63577. 28p. (ps). 1987. 2.95 (0-394-89149-X) Random Bks Yng Read.

McCue, Lisa & Scribner, Toni. Starting Over. Packard, Mary. LC 93-11060. 1993. write for info. (0-516-00831-5) Childrens.

McCulloch, Jerry. David, the Trash Cop: A Child's Guide to Recycling. Allison, John P. & Allison, Lee A. 21p. (Orig.). (gr. 1-6). 1992. pap. 6.95 (0-9632789-2-4) RMC Pub Grp.

McCully, Emily. Amzat & His Brothers: Three Italian Folktales. Fox, Paula. LC 92-19494. 80p. (gr. 3-5). 1993. 15.95 (0-531-05462-4); PLB 15.99 (0-531-08612-7) Orchard Bks Watts.

—Gertrude's Pocket. Miles, Miska. (gr. 2-5). 1984. 15.25 (0-8446-6164-3) Peter Smith.

—The Highest Hit. Willard, Nancy. LC 77-88970. (gr. 4-7). 1978. 6.95 (0-15-234278-8, HB Juv Bks) HarBrace.

—How to Eat Fried Worms. Rockwell, Thomas. LC 73-4262. (gr. 4-6). 1973. PLB 13.90 (0-531-02631-0) Watts.

—It Always Happens to Leona. Havill, Juanita. (gr. 2 up). 1989. LC 87-57227-3) Crown Bks Yng Read.

—Leona & Ike. Havill, Juanita. LC 90-40411. 128p. (gr. 2-6). 1991. 13.95 (0-517-57687-2); PLB 14.99 (0-517-57688-0) Crown Bks Yng Read.

McCully, Emily A. The Amazing Felix. McCully, Emily A. 32p. (ps-3). 1993. 14.95 (0-685-65234-3, Putnam) Putnam Pub Group.

—Annie Flies the Birthday Bike. Dragonwagon, Crescent. LC 90-42861. 32p. (gr. k-3). 1993. RSBE 14.95 (0-02-733155-5, Macmillan Child Bk) Macmillan Child Grp.

—The Bed Book. Plath, Sylvia. LC 76-3825. 40p. (ps-3). 1989. pap. 6.95 (0-06-443184-3, Trophy) HarpC Child Bks.

—Best Friend Insurance. Gormley, Beatrice. LC 83-5713. 160p. (gr. 3-6). 1983. 10.95 (0-525-44066-6, DCB) Dutton Child Bks.

—Best Friend Insurance. Gormley, Beatrice. 160p. (gr. 3-7). 1985. pap. 2.50 (0-380-69854-4, Camelot) Avon.

—Black Is Brown Is Tan. Adoff, Arnold. LC 73-9855. 32p. (ps-3). 1973. 15.00i (0-06-020083-9); PLB 14.89 (0-06-020084-7) HarpC Child Bks.

—Black Is Brown Is Tan. Adoff, Arnold. LC 73-9855. 32p. (ps-3). 1992. pap. 3.95 (0-06-443269-6, Trophy) HarpC Child Bks.

—The Boston Coffee Party. Rappaport, Doreen. LC 87-45301. 64p. (gr. k-3). 1988. PLB 13.89 (0-06-024825-4) HarpC Child Bks.

—The Boston Coffee Party. Rappaport, Doreen. LC 87-45301. 64p. (gr. k-3). 1990. pap. 3.50 (0-06-444141-5, Trophy) HarpC Child Bks.

—The Butterfly Birthday. Herold, Ann B. LC 90-6628. 48p. (gr. 1-5). 1991. RSBE 12.95 (0-02-743691-8, Macmillan Child Bk) Macmillan Child Grp.

—The Christmas Gift. McCully, Emily A. LC 87-45758. 32p. (ps-3). 1988. PLB 12.89 (0-06-024212-4) HarpC Child Bks.

—The Christmas Present Mystery. Markham, Marion M. LC 84-4557. 48p. (gr. 2-5). 13.45 (0-395-36383-7) HM.

—The Christmas Present Mystery. Markham, Marion M. 64p. 1990. pap. 2.95 (0-380-70966-X, Camelot) Avon.

—Dinah's Mad, Bad Wishes. Joosse, Barbara M. LC 88-884. 32p. (gr. k-3). 1989. PLB 12.89 (0-06-023099-1) HarpC Child Bks.

—The Evil Spell. McCully, Emily A. LC 89-24536. 32p. (gr. k-3). 1990. PLB 13.89 (0-06-024154-3) HarpC Child Bks.

—The Explorer of Barkham Street. Stolz, Mary. LC 84-48339. 192p. (gr. 4-6). 1985. 15.00 (0-06-025976-0); PLB 14.89 (0-06-025977-9) HarpC Child Bks.

—The Explorer of Barkham Street. Stolz, Mary. LC 84-48339. 192p. (gr. 3-7). 1987. pap. 3.95 (0-06-440210-X, Trophy) HarpC Child Bks.

—Fifth Grade Magic. Gormley, Beatrice. 128p. (gr. 3-7). 1984. pap. 3.50 (0-380-67439-4, Camelot) Avon.

—First Snow. McCully, Emily A. LC 84-43244. 32p. (ps-1). 1985. PLB 13.89 (0-06-024129-2) HarpC Child Bks.

—First Snow. McCully, Emily A. LC 84-43244. 32p. (ps-1). 1988. pap. 4.95 (0-06-443181-9, Trophy) HarpC Child Bks.

—Fourth of July. Joosse, Barbara M. LC 82-17301. 48p. (ps-2). 1985. PLB 11.99 (0-394-95195-6) Knopf Bks Yng Read.

—Friday Night Is Papa Night. Sonneborn, Ruth. 32p. (ps-2). 1987. pap. 4.99 (0-14-050754-X, Puffin) Puffin Bks.

—Go & Hush the Baby. Byars, Betsy C. (ps-3). 1982. pap. 4.99 (0-14-050396-X, Puffin) Puffin Bks.

—The Grandma Mix-Up. McCully, Emily A. LC 87-29378. 64p. (gr. k-3). 1988. PLB 13.89 (0-06-024240-7) HarpC Child Bks.

—The Grandma Mix-Up. McCully, Emily A. LC 87-29378. 64p. (gr. k-3). 1991. pap. 3.50 (0-06-444150-4, Trophy) HarpC Child Bks.

—Grandmas at Bat. McCully, Emily A. LC 92-8318. 64p. (gr. k-3). 1993. 13.00 (0-06-021031-1); PLB 12.89 (0-06-021032-X) HarpC Child Bks.

—Grandmas at the Lake. McCully, Emily A. LC 89-26590. 64p. (gr. k-3). 1990. PLB 10.89 (0-06-024127-6) HarpC Child Bks.

—The Grandpa Days. Blos, Joan W. LC 88-19801. 32p. (ps). 1989. pap. 8.95 jacketed (0-671-64640-0, Little Simon) S&S Trade.

—The Halloween Candy Mystery. Markham, Marion M. LC 82-6059. 48p. (gr. 2-5). 1982. 9.95 (0-395-32437-8) HM.

—I & Sproggy. Greene, Constance C. 144p. (gr. 5 up). 1981. pap. 1.95 (0-440-43986-8, YB) Dell.

—I Dance in My Red Pajamas. Hurd, Edith T. LC 81-47721. 32p. (gr. 1-3). 1982. PLB 14.89 (0-06-022700-1) HarpC Child Bks.

—In My Tent. Singer, Marilyn. LC 91-16115. 32p. (gr. k-3). 1992. RSBE 14.95 (0-02-782701-1, Macmillan Child Bk) Macmillan Child Grp.

—Jam Day. Joosse, Barbara M. LC 86-46117. 32p. (gr. k-3). 1987. HarpC Child Bks.

—The Jingle Bells Jam. Giff, Patricia R. 80p. (Orig.). (gr. 1-4). 1992. pap. 3.25 (0-440-40534-3, YB) Dell.

—Lulu & the Witch Baby. O'Connor, Jane. LC 85-45832. 64p. (gr. k-3). 1986. PLB 13.89 (0-06-024627-8) HarpC Child Bks.

—Lulu Goes to Witch School. O'Connor, Jane. LC 87-37. 64p. (gr. k-3). 1987. HarpC Child Bks.

—Lulu Goes to Witch School. O'Connor, Jane. LC 87-37. 64p. (gr. k-3). 1990. pap. 3.50 (0-06-444138-5, Trophy) HarpC Child Bks.

—The Magic Mean Machine. Gormley, Beatrice. 128p. (Orig.). (gr. 5 up). 1989. pap. 2.95 (0-380-75519-X, Camelot) Avon.

—Mail-Order Wings. Gormley, Beatrice. 164p. (gr. 3-7). 1984. pap. 2.95 (0-380-67421-1, Camelot) Avon.

—Meet the Lincoln Lions Band. Giff, Patricia R. 80p. (Orig.). (gr. 1-4). 1992. pap. 3.25 (0-440-40516-5, YB) Dell.

—Mitzi & the Terrible Tyrannosaurus Rex. Williams, Barbara. 112p. (gr. 3-7). 1983. pap. 1.95 (0-440-45673-8, YB) Dell.

—Molly. Radlauer, Ruth S. (ps-2). 1987. 10.95 (0-13-599762-3) P-H.

—Molly Goes Hiking. Radlauer, Ruth S. LC 86-18761. 32p. (ps-3). 1987. pap. 10.95 (0-671-66860-9) S&S Trade.

—New Baby. McCully, Emily A. LC 87-45294. 32p. (ps-1). 1988. HarpC Child Bks.

—One Very Best Valentine's Day. Blos, Joan W. 32p. (ps-2). 1992. pap. 2.25 (0-671-75297-9, Little Simon) S&S Trade.

—Picnic. McCully, Emily A. LC 83-47913. 32p. (ps-1). 1989. pap. 3.95 (0-06-443199-1, Trophy) HarpC Child Bks.

—School. McCully, Emily A. LC 87-156. 32p. (ps-2). 1987. PLB 13.89 (0-06-024133-0) HarpC Child Bks.

—School. McCully, Emily A. LC 87-156. 32p. (ps-1). 1990. pap. 4.95 (0-06-443233-5, Trophy) HarpC Child Bks.

—Sky Guys to White Cat. Gormley, Beatrice. LC 91-364. 144p. (gr. 3-6). 1991. 12.95 (0-525-44743-1, DCB) Dutton Child Bks.

—Speak up, Blanche! McCully, Emily A. LC 90-36945. 32p. (gr. k-3). 1991. 15.00 (0-06-024227-2); PLB 14.89 (0-06-024228-0) HarpC Child Bks.

—Stepbrother Sabotage. Wittman, Sally. LC 89-26804. 80p. (gr. 2-5). 1990. 13.00 (0-06-026561-2); PLB 12.89 (0-06-026562-0) HarpC Child Bks.

—Stepbrother Sabotage. Wittman, Sally. LC 89-26804. 80p. (gr. 2-5). 1991. 3.95 (0-06-440408-0, Trophy) HarpC Child Bks.

—The Take-Along Dog. Porte, Barbara A. LC 88-18775. 40p. (gr. 1 up). 1989. 11.95 (0-688-08053-7); PLB 11.88 (0-688-08054-5) Greenwillow.

—Wheels. Thomas, Jane R. LC 85-13291. 32p. (ps-3). 1986. 14.95 (0-89919-410-9, Clarion Bks) HM.

—Yankee Doodle Drumsticks. Giff, Patricia R. 80p. (Orig.). (gr. 1-4). 1992. pap. 3.25 (0-440-40518-1, YB) Dell.

McCurdy, Bruce S. Hawaii: The Aloha State. rev. ed. Bauer, Helen. Rayson, Ann, rev. by. LC 82-72319. 192p. (gr. 4-7). 1982. 25.95 (0-935848-13-4); pap. 16.95 (0-935848-15-0); wkbk. 5.95 (0-935848-34-7); tchr's. manual 5.00 (1-880188-46-5) Bess Pr.

McCurdy, Michael. American Tall Tales. Osborne, Mary P. LC 89-37235. 128p. (gr. 1 up). 1991. 18.00 (0-679-80089-1); lib. bdg. 18.99 (0-679-90089-6) Knopf Bks Yng Read.

—The Beasts of Bethlehem. Kennedy, X. J. LC 91-38417. 48p. (gr. 1 up). 1992. SBE 13.95 (0-689-50561-2, M K McElderry) Macmillan Child Grp.

—The Devils Who Learned to Be Good. McCurdy, Michael. 32p. (gr. 2-5). 1987. 13.95 (0-316-55527-4, Joy St Bks) Little.

—Escape from Slavery: The Boyhood of Frederick Douglass in His Own Words. Douglass, Frederick. McCurdy, Michael, ed. King, Coretta S., intro. by. LC 93-19239. 64p. (gr. 4 up). 1994. 15.00 (0-679-84652-2); pap. 5.99 (0-679-84651-4) Knopf Bks Yng Read.

—Giants in the Land. Appelbaum, Diana. LC 92-26526. 1993. 14.95 (0-395-64720-7) HM.

—Hannah's Farm: Seasons on an Early American Homestead. McCurdy, Michael. LC 87-29631. 32p. (ps-4). 1988. reinforced bdg. 12.95 (0-8234-0700-4) Holiday.

—Lucy's Summer. Hall, Donald. LC 93-17130. 1995. write for info. (0-15-276873-4, HB Juv Bks) HarBrace.

—An Old-Fashioned Thanksgiving. Alcott, Louisa May. LC 89-1908. 32p. (gr. 3-7). 1989. reinforced 14.95 (0-8234-0772-1) Holiday.

—The Old Man & the Fiddle. McCurdy, Michael. 32p. (ps-3). 1992. PLB 14.95 (0-399-21812-2, Putnam) Putnam Pub Group.

McDaniel, Diane. My Very Own Special Body Book. 4th ed. Bassett, Kerry. Wooley, Marilyn J., intro. by. 18p. (ps-2). 1987. pap. 3.25 (0-9620154-0-7) Hawthorne Pr.

McDaniel, Jerry. A Bird's Eye View of the Statue of Liberty: As Seen by Lorenzo the Parrot. Wolf, D. M. 32p. (gr. 3-4). 1988. pap. 4.95 (0-9617057-2-8) Storyviews Pub.

—We the People: Bits, Bytes & Highlights of the U. S. Constitution & Bill of Rights from Honey Bees Tye & Sy. Wolf, D. M. 32p. (ps-3). 1987. pap. 4.95 (0-9617057-1-X) Storyviews Pub.

McDermott, Dennis. The Listening Silence. Root, Phyllis. LC 90-37425. 128p. (gr. 3-7). 1992. 14.00 (0-06-025092-5); PLB 13.89 (0-06-025093-3) HarpC Child Bks.

—Oom Razoom or Go I Know Not Where, Bring Back I Know Not What. Wolkstein, Diane. LC 91-6308. 32p. (gr. k up). 1991. 14.95 (0-688-09416-3); PLB 14.88 (0-688-09417-1) Morrow Jr Bks.

McDermott, Gerald. Anansi the Spider: A Tale from the Ashanti. McDermott, Gerald, retold by. LC 76-150028. 48p. (ps-2). 1972. reinforced bdg. 15.95 (0-8050-0310-X, Bks Young Read); pap. 5.95 (0-8050-0311-8) H Holt & Co.

—Arrow to the Sun: A Pueblo Indian Tale. McDermott, Gerald. (gr. 1 up). 1977. pap. 4.99 (0-14-050211-4, Puffin) Puffin Bks.

—Coyote: A Trickster Tale from the Southwest. McDermott, Gerald, as told by. LC 92-32979. 1992. write for info. (0-15-220724-4) HarBrace.

—Daniel O'Rourke. McDermott, Gerald. LC 85-20188. 32p. (ps-3). 1986. pap. 12.95 (0-670-80924-1) Viking Child Bks.

—Daughter of Earth: A Roman Myth. McDermott, Gerald. LC 82-23585. 32p. (ps-3). 1984. pap. 15.00 (0-385-29294-5) Delacorte.

—Flecha al Sol: Un Cuento do Los Indios Pueblo. McDermott, Gerald. (SPA.). 48p. (ps-3). 1991. pap. 4.99 (0-14-054364-3, Puffin) Puffin Bks.

—Marcel the Pastry Chef. Mayer, Marianna. 32p. (ps-3). 1991. 14.95 (0-553-05192-X) Bantam.

—Tim O'Toole & the Wee Folk. McDermott, Gerald. 32p. (ps-3). 1992. pap. 3.99 (0-14-050675-6) Puffin Bks.

McDermott, Michael. Three Good Blankets. Luttrell, Ida. LC 89-36353. 32p. (ps-2). 1990. SBE 13.95 (0-689-31586-4, Atheneum Child Bk) Macmillan Child Grp.

—The Truth about Unicorns. Giblin, James C. LC 90-47233. 128p. (gr. 3-7). 1991. 15.00 (0-06-022478-9); PLB 14.89 (0-06-022479-7) HarpC Child Bks.

McDill, Layl. What's for Dinner? Salem, Lynn & Stewart, Josie. 12p. (gr. 1). 1992. pap. 3.50 (1-880612-09-7) Seedling Pubns.

MacDonald, Hugh. The Ugly Christmas Tree. Scott, Bob. LC 92-93614. 24p. (Orig.). (gr. 3-8). 1993. 7.95 (0-9621201-1-1); pap. 4.95 (0-9621201-2-X) B Scott Bks.

Macdonald, Judith L. Stagecoach Santa. Reinstedt, Randall A. Bergez, John, ed. LC 86-81735. 48p. (gr. 3-6). 1986. case 11.95 (0-933818-20-3); pap. 7.95 (0-933818-75-0) Ghost Town.

MacDonald, Karen. Fanny & Sarah. 2nd ed. Weinberger, Jane. LC 84-51987. 40p. (gr. k-4). 1986. pap. 3.95 (0-932433-02-2) Windswept Hse.

MacDonald, Roland B. & Gray, Dan. Baking Projects for Children: Fun Foods to Make with Children from 4 to 10. Stephens, Fran. 128p. (gr. k-5). 1991. pap. 9.95 (1-878767-10-0) Murdoch Bks.

—Birthday Parties for Children: Activities, Games, Cakes & Fun for Children from 4-10. Jenny, Gerri. 128p. (gr. k-5). 1991. pap. 9.95 (1-878767-15-1) Murdoch Bks.

—Let's Make a Present! Easy to Make Gifts for Friends & Relatives of Any Age. Cheng, Andrea. 128p. (gr. k-5). 1991. pap. 9.95 (1-878767-16-X) Murdoch Bks.

MacDonald, Suse. Alphabatics. MacDonald, Suse. LC 91-38497. 56p. (ps-1). 1992. pap. 6.95 (0-689-71625-7, Aladdin) Macmillan Child Grp.

MacDonald, Thoreau. A Canadian ABC: An Alphabet Book for Kids. Cook, Lynn. 60p. 1990. pap. 8.95 (0-921254-24-5, Pub. by Penumbra Pr CN) U of Toronto Pr.

McDonnell, J. Hippo's Adventure in Alphabet Town. McDonnell, Janet. LC 91-20549. 32p. (ps-2). 1992. PLB 14.60 (0-516-05408-2) Childrens.

McDonnell, Janet. Turtle's Adventure in Alphabet Town. McDonnell, Janet. LC 92-2984. 32p. (ps-2). 1992. PLB 14.60 (0-516-05420-1) Childrens.

McDonough, Chris. Mother Goose Monsters ABC's Sticker Book. 24p. (ps-2). 1992. pap. 2.95 (1-56293-246-2) McClanahan Bk.

—Mother Goose Monsters Counting Sticker Book. 24p. (ps-2). 1992. pap. 2.95 (1-56293-247-0) McClanahan Bk.

—My First Words. Wise, Beth A. 32p. (ps). 1992. wkbk. 1.95 (1-56293-176-8) McClanahan Bk.

MacDougall, Larry. Further Adventures in the Northern Wilderness. Siembieda, Kevin. Marciniszyn, Alex, ed. 48p. (Orig.). (gr. 8 up). 1990. pap. 7.95 (0-916211-40-1, 457) Palladium Bks.

MacDougall, Larry, jt. illus. see Fales, Kevin.

MacDougall, Rob. Disaster in Room One Hundred One. Mooser, Stephen. LC 93-24055. 80p. (gr. 2-4). 1993. PLB 9.89 (0-8167-3278-7); pap. text ed. 2.95 (0-8167-3279-5) Troll Assocs.

McElrath-Eslick, Lori. Does God Know How to Tie Shoes? Carlstrom, Nancy W. 40p. (ps-3). 1993. 14.99 (0-8028-5074-X) Eerdmans.

—The Lark Who Had No Song. Nystrom, Carolyn. 32p. (ps-6). 1991. 11.95 (0-7459-1879-4) Lion USA.

McEwan, Chris. First Songs & Action Rhymes. Wood, Jenny. LC 90-44773. 64p. (ps-k). 1991. POB 6.95 (0-689-71472-6, Aladdin) Macmillan Child Grp.

McEwan, Joe. Archaeology. Cork, Barbara. 32p. (gr. 5-8). 1985. PLB 13.96 (0-88110-220-2, Pub. by Usborne); pap. 6.95 (0-86020-865-6) EDC.

McEwan, Joseph. Cathedrals. Stainer, Tom & Sutton, Harry. 32p. (gr. 4-6). 1992. pap. 4.95 (0-563-34161-0, BBC-Parkwest) Parkwest Pubns.

—The Greeks. Stainer, Tom & Sutton, Harry. 25p. (gr. 4-6). 1992. pap. 4.95 (0-563-21174-1, BBC-Parkwest) Parkwest Pubns.

Macey, Barry. Paddington on Screen. Bond, Michael. (gr. 2-5). 1982. 14.45 (0-395-32950-7) HM.

McFadden, Eliza. Sky Watchers of Ages Past. Weiss, Malcolm E. (gr. 5-9). 1982. 14.45 (0-395-29525-4) HM.

McGaffrey, Janet. Hey-How for Halloween! Hopkins, Lee B., ed. LC 74-5601. 32p. (gr. 1-5). 1974. 12.95 (0-15-233900-0, HB Juv Bks) HarBrace.

McGarry, Steve. Jerry Rice. Rolfe, John. 1993. pap. 3.99 (0-553-48157-6) Bantam.

—Shaquille O'Neal. Cohen, Neil. (gr. 8 up). 1993. pap. 3.99 (0-553-48158-4) Bantam.

McGee, Barbara. Counting Sheep. McGee, Barbara. 24p. (gr. k-3). 1991. 12.95 (1-55037-157-6, Pub. by Annick CN); pap. 4.95 (1-55037-160-6, Pub. by Annick CN) Firefly Bks Ltd.

McGee, E. Alan. Georgia to Georgia: Making Friends in the U. S. S. R. Dolphin, Laurie. LC 90-47494. 40p. (gr. 2 up). 1991. 13.95 (0-688-09896-7, Tambourine Bks); PLB 13.88 (0-688-09897-5, Tambourine Bks) Morrow.

McGee, Martin. Plants & Flowers. Holly, Brian. 32p. (gr. 3-7). 1985. pap. 3.50 (0-88625-114-1) Durkin Hayes Pub.

McGee, Shelagh. A Joke-a-Day Book. Brandreth, Gyles. 96p. 1992. Repr. of 1979 ed. 3.99 (0-517-07766-3, Pub. by Wings Bks) Outlet Bk Co.

McGinley-Nally, Sharon. First Snow, Magic Snow. Cech, John. LC 91-42988. 40p. (gr. k-2). 1992. RSBE 14.95 (0-02-717971-0, Four Winds) Macmillan Child Grp.

—Hazel's Circle. Denslow, Sharon P. LC 91-18182. 32p. (ps-2). 1992. RSBE 14.95 (0-02-728683-5, Four Winds) Macmillan Child Grp.

—My Grandmother's Journey. Cech, John. LC 90-35731. 40p. (ps-4). 1991. RSBE 14.95 (0-02-718135-9, Bradbury Pr) Macmillan Child Grp.

—Pigs Will Be Pigs. Axelrod, Amy. LC 93-7640. 40p. (gr. k-3). 1994. RSBE 14.95 (0-02-765415-X, Four Winds) Macmillan Child Grp.

McGinnis, Susan. Tanya's Big Green Dream. Glaser, Linda. LC 93-9968. 48p. (gr. 1-5). 1994. RSBE 13.95 (0-02-735994-8, Macmillan Child Bk) MacMillan Child Grp.

McGinnity, Molly. Using Cereal Boxes. Gill, Nancy. 13p. (gr. 4-6). 1980. pap. 3.95 (0-8431-2574-8) Enrich.

McGlophlin, David. Barney Goes to the Zoo. Dowdy, Linda. Hartley, Linda, ed. 20p. (ps-k). 1993. 4.95 (0-7829-0371-1) Barney Pub.

McGovern, Ann, et al. Down Under, Down Under: Diving Adventures on the Great Barrier Reef. McGovern, Ann. LC 88-30530. 48p. (gr. 2-6). 1989. SBE 14.95 (0-02-765770-1, Macmillan Child Bk) Macmillan Child Grp.

McGovern, Brian. The Challenger. Biel, Timothy L. LC 90-6255. 64p. (gr. 5-8). 1990. PLB 11.95 (1-56006-013-1) Lucent Bks.

—Chernobyl. Nardo, Don. LC 90-33567. 64p. (gr. 5-8). 1990. PLB 11.95 (1-56006-008-5) Lucent Bks.

—The Hindenburg. Stacey, Tom. LC 90-6256. 64p. (gr. 5-8). 1990. PLB 11.95 (1-56006-010-7) Lucent Bks.

—Hiroshima. Farris, John. LC 90-34064. 64p. (gr. 5-8). 1990. PLB 11.95 (1-56006-015-8) Lucent Bks.

—The Irish Potato Famine. Nardo, Don. LC 90-6246. 64p. (gr. 5-8). 1990. PLB 11.95 (1-56006-012-3) Lucent Bks.

—Krakatoa. Nardo, Don. LC 90-6003. 64p. (gr. 5-8). 1990. PLB 11.95 (1-56006-011-5) Lucent Bks.

McGrath, Meggan. My Grapes. McGrath, Meggan. LC 93-24057. 48p. (Orig.). 1994. pap. 16.95 (0-938586-99-8) Pfeifer-Hamilton.

McGraw, Deloss. Fish Story. Andres, Katherine. LC 92-14677. 1993. pap. 15.00 (0-671-79270-9) S&S Trade.

—Hippity Hop, Frog on Top. Wing, Natasha. LC 93-11473. 1994. write for info. (0-671-87045-9, S&S BFYR) S&S Trade.

Mcgraw, Sheila. Love You Forever. Munsch, Robert. 32p. (gr. 4-10). 1986. 12.95 (0-920668-36-4); pap. 4.95 (0-920668-37-2) Firefly Bks Ltd.

—My Father's Hands. McGraw, Sheila & Cline, Paul. 32p. 1992. 6.95 (0-9625261-6-9, Green Tiger) S&S Trade.

—Siempre Te Querre (Love You Forever) Munsch, Robert. 32p. 1992. pap. 4.95 (1-895565-01-4) Firefly Bks Ltd.

McGregor, Barbara. Purple Delicious Blackberry Jam. Peters, Lisa W. 32p. (ps-3). 1992. 14.95 (1-55970-167-6) Arcade Pub Inc.

McGregor, Doug. MacGregor's Editorial Cartoons: A Collection of Cartoons Published in the Norwich Bulletin. MacGregor, Doug. 192p. (Orig.). (gr. 6-8). 1988. pap. write for info. Norwich Bulletin.

McGregor, Douglas. A Collection of MacGregor Editorial Cartoons from the Norwich Bulletin. MacGregor, Douglas. Dodd, Christopher J., intro. by. LC 88-92529. 196p. (Orig.). (gr. 6-8). 1988. pap. text ed. 10.00 (0-9621270-0-0) Norwich Bulletin.

McGregor, Malcolm, jt. illus. see Ovendon, Dennis.

MacGregor, Marilyn. Helen & the Great Quiet. Fitzgerald, Rick. LC 88-5095. 32p. (ps-2). 1989. 13.95 (0-688-07723-4); PLB 13.88 (0-688-07724-2, Morrow Jr Bks) Morrow Jr Bks.

—On Top. MacGregor, Marilyn. LC 87-12481. 32p. (ps-7). 1988. 7.95 (0-688-07490-1); PLB 7.88 (0-688-07491-X, Morrow Jr Bks) Morrow Jr Bks.

McGrew, Michelle. Breathe on Me Butterflies. Trott, Betty. LC 93-60232. 44p. (gr. k-3). 1994. pap. 8.95 (1-55523-603-0) Winston-Derek.

McGuiness, Doreen. Secrets of the Deep. Selberg, Ingrid. Fogelman, Phyllis J., ed. 12p. (gr. 1-5). 1990. 14.95 (0-8037-0766-5) Dial Bks Young.

McGuinness, Doreen. Secrets of the Pond. Selberg, Ingrid. Rapoport, Roger, ed. 12p. (gr. 1-6). 1993. text ed. 16.95g (0-9636161-0-2, Wetlands) RDR Bks.

M'Guinness, Jim. Kids Gardening: A Kid's Guide to Messing Around in the Dirt. Raferty, Kim G. & Raftery, Kevin. 84p. (Orig.). 1989. pap. 12.95 incl. 15 varieties of seeds (0-932592-25-2) Klutz Pr.

—Kid's Songs: A Holler along Handbook. Cassidy, Nancy & Cassidy, John. 86p. (Orig.). 1986. pap. 10.95 incl. 48 min. stereo cassette (0-932592-13-9) Klutz Pr.

—Kids Songs Two: Another Holler-along Handbook. Cassidy, John & Cassidy, Nancy. 70p. (Orig.). 1989. pap. 10.95 incl. 48-min. stereo cassette (0-932592-20-1) Klutz Pr.

McGuire, Leslie. This Farm Is a Mess. McGuire, Leslie. LC 80-25811. 48p. (ps-3). 1981. 5.95 (0-8193-1045-X); pap. 3.95 (0-8193-1046-8) Parents.

Mcguire, Michael. The Birthday of a King. Hartman, Bob. 24p. (ps-2). 1993. 7.99 (1-56476-043-X, Victor Books) SP Pubns.

—The Edge of the River. Hartman, Bob. 24p. (ps-2). 1993. 7.99 (1-56476-041-3, Victor Books) SP Pubns.

—The Middle of the Night. Hartman, Bob. 24p. (ps-2). 1993. 7.99 (1-56476-042-1, Victor Books) SP Pubns.

—The Morning of the World. Hartman, Bob. 24p. (ps-2). 1993. 7.99 (1-56476-040-5, Victor Books) SP Pubns.

Machat, Mike. Top Secret Bird: The Luftwaffe's ME-163 Comet. Spate, Wolfgang. LC 88-90967. 276p. (Orig.). (gr. 8-12). 1989. pap. text ed. 11.95 (0-929521-08-0) Pictorial Hist.

McHenry, Ellen J. Inside a Freight Train. McHenry, Ellen J. LC 92-23225. (ps-3). 1993. 9.99 (0-525-65099-7, Cobblehill Bks) Dutton Child Bks.

McHenry, Kitsy & Geard, David. In the Light of a Child: Fifty-Two Verses for Children & the Child in Every Human Being. Burton, Michael H. 62p. (Orig.). (gr. 4). 1989. pap. text ed. 12.95 (0-932776-17-5) Adonis Pr.

Machlin, Mikki. Love Is Always There. Kent, Lisa. LC 93-20412. 32p. 1993. pap. 4.95 (0-8091-6611-9) Paulist Pr.

—Maria's Secret. Toretta-Fuentes, June. LC 92-9866. 32p. 1992. pap. 3.95 (0-8091-6606-2) Paulist Pr.

Machlis, Sally. Discovering Crater Lake. Field, Nancy & Machlis, Sally. 32p. (Orig.). (gr. 1-6). 1989. pap. 3.50 (0-941042-08-1) Dog Eared Pubns.

—Discovering Mount Rainier. Field, Nancy & Machlis, Sally. 28p. (Orig.). (gr. 1-6). 1980. pap. 3.50 (0-941042-02-2) Dog Eared Pubns.

—Discovering Northwest Volcanoes. rev. ed. Field, Nancy & Machlis, Sally. 32p. (Orig.). (gr. 2-6). 1980. pap. 3.50 (0-941042-03-0) Dog Eared Pubns.

—Discovering Salmon. Field, Nancy & Machlis, Sally. 32p. (Orig.). (gr. k-6). 1984. 3.50 (0-941042-05-7) Dog Eared Pubns.

—Discovery Book for the Seattle Aquarium. rev. & abr. ed. Field, Nancy & Machlis, Sally. 32p. (gr. 1-6). 1987. pap. 3.50 (0-941042-07-3) Dog Eared Pubns.

Machlis, Sally & Torvik, Sharon. Nature Discovery Library. Field, Nancy, et al. (gr. 3-6). 1990. Set. pap. text ed. 42.50 (0-941042-15-4) Dog Eared Pubns.

Machotka, Hana. Magic Ring: A Year With The Big Apple Circus. Machotka, Hana. Binder, Paul, intro. by. LC 87-28230. 80p. (gr. 3 up). 1988. 13.95 (0-688-07449-9); pap. 8.95 (0-688-08222-X, Pub. by Beech Tree Bks) Morrow.

—Pasta Factory. Machotka, Hana. LC 92-4333. 32p. (ps-3). 1992. 14.45 (0-395-60197-5) HM.

Machotka, Hana, photos by. Breathtaking Noses. Machotka, Hana. LC 91-12252. 32p. (gr. k up). 1992. 15.00 (0-688-09526-7); PLB 14.93 (0-688-09527-5) Morrow Jr Bks.

—What Do You Do at a Petting Zoo? Machotka, Hana. LC 89-34478. 32p. (gr. k up). 1990. 13.95 (0-688-08737-X); PLB 13.88 (0-688-08738-8, Morrow Jr Bks) Morrow Jr Bks.

—What Neat Feet! Machotka, Hana. LC 90-40886. 32p. (gr. k up). 1991. 13.95 (0-688-09474-0); PLB 13.88 (0-688-09475-9, Morrow Jr Bks) Morrow Jr Bks.

McHugh, Paula. Better Than Money: Tales to Treasure for a Lifetime. McHugh, Joe. LC 91-70909. 125p. (gr. 1-8). 1991. 11.95g (0-9619943-1-2) Catalpa Pr.

---

appreciation for wholesome & clean riddles. In addition, this witty book can be used in children's activities & programs & young people can also incorporate it in their social activities. Parents can also share it as a gift to their children, knowing satisfactorily that the riddles are children oriented. This Bible riddle indeed is for all ages & ages to come. Family of God Publishing House, P.O. Box 758, Vista, CA 92083-0758. (619) 598-3629, FAX (619) 966-0312. *Publisher Provided Annotation.*

Macie, Edward. Commodore Perry & Other Paper Dolls of the Flagship Niagara. Erie Art Museum Staff. 10p. (Orig.). (gr. 1-3). 1988. pap. 6.00 (0-9616623-4-4) Erie Art Mus.

McIlrath, James. Before You Were Born. Nixon, Joan L. LC 79-91741. 32p. (ps up). 1980. pap. 5.95 (0-87973-343-8) Our Sunday Visitor.
—God Sends the Seasons. Meyer, Kathleen A. LC 81-80712. 32p. (ps-2). 1981. 7.50 (0-87973-668-2, 668) Our Sunday Visitor.
—A Saint for Your Name: Saints for Boys. Nevins, Albert J. LC 79-92504. 120p. (gr. 4-7). 1980. pap. 5.95 (0-87973-320-9, 320) Our Sunday Visitor.
—A Saint for Your Name: Saints for Girls. Nevins, Albert J. LC 79-92502. 104p. (gr. 4-7). 1980. pap. 5.95 (0-87973-321-7, 321) Our Sunday Visitor.
McIntosh, Carolyn. Niddy Noddy the Noodlemaker. Maas, Virginia. (ps-2). 1981. pap. 2.75 (0-933992-15-7) Coffee Break.
McIntyre, Brian. Deserts. Catchpole, Clive. LC 83-7757. 32p. (ps-4). 1985. pap. 4.95 (0-8037-0037-7, 0481-140) Dial Bks Young.
—Mountains. Catchpole, Clive. LC 83-25273. 32p. (gr. k-4). 1985. pap. 4.95 (0-8037-0087-3, 0481-140) Dial Bks Young.
McIntyre, Brian, jt. illus. see Butler, John.
Mack, Stan. The King's Cat Is Coming. Mack, Stan. (ps-1). 1976. lib. bdg. 4.99 (0-394-93302-8) Pantheon.
—Ten Bears in My Bed: A Goodnight Countdown. Mack, Stan. LC 74-151. 32p. (ps-1). 1974. lib. bdg. 11.99 (0-394-92902-0) Pantheon.
MacKain, Bonnie. One Hundred Hungry Ants. Pinczes, Elinor J. 32p. (gr. k-3). 1993. 13.95 (0-395-63116-5) HM.
McKay, Ardis. American Indians. Kindle, Patricia & Finney, Susan. 64p. (gr. 4-8). 1985. wkbk. 7.95 (0-86653-290-0, GA 673) Good Apple.
—Fantasy & Fairy Tales. Kindle, Patricia & Finney, Susan. 64p. (gr. 4-8). 1985. wkbk. 7.95 (0-86653-317-6, GA 669) Good Apple.
—Russia to the Revolution. Kindle, Pat & Finney, Susan. 64p. (gr. 4-8). 1987. pap. 7.95 (0-86653-398-2, GA 1020) Good Apple.
McKay, Bob. How to Draw Funny People. McKay, Bob. LC 81-69658. 32p. (gr. 2-6). 1981. PLB 10.65 (0-89375-688-1); pap. text ed. 1.95 (0-89375-408-0) Troll Assocs.
McKay, Donald & Polseno, Jo. Adventures of Huckleberry Finn. Twain, Mark. LC 85-9576. 448p. (gr. 4-6). 1981. 14.95 (0-448-06000-0, G&D); (G&D) Putnam Pub Group.
—Adventures of Tom Sawyer. Twain, Mark. LC 62-19420. (gr. 4-6). 1981. 13.95 (0-448-06002-7, G&D); (G&D) Putnam Pub Group.
Mackay, Donald A. The Stone-Faced Boy. Fox, Paula. LC 68-9053. 112p. (gr. 4-6). 1982. SBE 13.95 (0-02-735570-5, Bradbury Pr) Macmillan Child Grp.
McKay, Robert. Grandfather's Day. Tomey, Ingrid. 64p. (gr. 3-7). 1992. PLB 12.95 (1-56397-022-8) Boyds Mills Pr.
McKay, Suzanne. The Miracle of a Christmas Doll. Njoku, Scholastica J. 29p. (gr. k up). 1986. perfect bdg. 5.95x (0-9617833-0-3) S I NJOKU.
McKeating, Eileen. Amelia Earhart: Courage in the Sky. Kerby, Mona. LC 92-19520. 64p. (gr. 3-5). 1992. pap. 3.99 (0-14-034263-X) Puffin Bks.
—The Exiles. McKay, Hilary. LC 91-38220. 208p. (gr. 4-7). 1992. SBE 14.95 (0-689-50555-8, M K McElderry) Macmillan Child Grp.
—Laura Ingalls Wilder: Growing Up in the Little House. Giff, Patricia R. (gr. 2-6). 1987. pap. 10.95 (0-670-81072-X) Viking Child Bks.
—Nightmare Mountain. Kehret, Peg. LC 89-1535. 176p. (gr. 5 up). 1989. 13.95 (0-525-65008-3, Cobblehill Bks) Dutton Child Bks.
—Roz & Ozzie. Hurwitz, Johanna. LC 91-42338. 128p. (gr. 2 up). 1992. 13.00 (0-688-10945-4) Morrow Jr Bks.
McKee, D. Who's a Clever Baby? McKee, David. Briley, D., ed. LC 88-22966. 32p. (gr. 1-3). 1989. 12.95 (0-688-08595-4); PLB 12.88 (0-688-08596-2) Lothrop.
McKee, David. Marvelous Land of Oz. Baum, L. Frank. 192p. (gr. 4-6). 1985. pap. 2.25 (0-14-035041-1, Puffin) Puffin Bks.
—Out of the Blue: Poems about Color. Oram, Hiawyn. LC 92-55044. 64p. (gr. 1-5). 1993. 18.95 (1-56282-469-4); PLB 18.89 (1-56282-470-8) Hyprn Child.

—Two Can Toucan. McKee, David. 32p. (gr. k-3). 1987. 15.95 (0-86264-094-6, Pub. by Anderson Pr UK) Trafalgar.
McKee, Karen A. How to Draw Airplanes. 32p. (Orig.). 1990. pap. 2.95 (0-942025-73-3) Kidsbks.
—How to Draw Airplanes. 32p. 1991. 3.98 (1-56156-021-9) Kidsbks.
—How to Draw Cars. 32p. 1991. 3.98 (1-56156-017-0) Kidsbks.
—How to Draw Cars. 32p. 1991. pap. 2.95 (1-56156-026-X) Kidsbks.
—How to Draw Trucks. 48p. 1992. pap. 2.95 (1-56156-145-2) Kidsbks.
McKee, Mary. Do You Have a Secret? How to Get Help for Scary Secrets. Russell, Pamela & Stone, Beth. LC 85-27986. 36p. (Orig.). (ps-2). 1986. pap. 6.95 (0-89638-098-X) CompCare.
McKee, Mary M. Tutoring: Learning by Helping: A Student Handbook for Training Peer & Cross Age Tutors. rev. ed. Foster, Elizabeth S. LC 92-71011. 140p. (gr. 8-12). 1992. pap. text ed. 12.95x (0-932796-44-3) Ed Media Corp.
Mckee, Vici. How Can I Please You, God? Burgess, Beverly C. 32p. (ps-5). 1991. Repr. of 1989 ed. 3.98 (1-879470-00-4) Burgess Pub.
—Seedtime Stories: Bedtime Stories with Poems & Devotionals. Burgess, Beverly C. (Orig.). (gr. 2-6). 1991. pap. 4.95 (1-879470-01-2) Burgess Pub.
McKee, Vicki. How Can I Please You God? Burgess, Beverly Capps. 29p. (Orig.). 1989. pap. text ed. 4.00 (0-9618975-1-1) Annette Capps.
MacKeen, Leslie A. Who Can Fix It? MacKeen, Leslie A. Thatch, Nancy R., ed. Melton, David, intro. by. LC 89-31819. 26p. (gr. k-3). 1989. PLB 14.95 (0-933849-19-2) Landmark Edns.
McKelvey, David. Maverick the Lucky Longhorn. McKelvey, David. 32p. (gr. k-3). 1986. lib. bdg. 10.95 (0-931722-48-9); pap. 3.95 (0-931722-47-0) Corona Pub.
McKelvey, Robbie. A Frog on a Log. McKelvey, Robbie. 22p. (Orig.). (gr. k-4). 1993. pap. 3.95 plastic laminate (1-884525-00-8) Whimsical Pubns.
McKenna, Terry. Seven Eggs. reissued ed. Hooper, Meredith. 24p. (ps-1). 1986. 5.95 (0-694-00144-9, Festival) HarpC Child Bks.
McKeown, Gloria. I Can Read About Spiders. Merrians, Deborah. LC 76-54576. (gr. 2-5). 1977. pap. 1.95 (0-89375-043-3) Troll Assocs.
—I Can Read About Synonyms & Antonyms. Supraner, Robyn. LC 76-54441. (gr. 2-5). 1977. pap. 1.95 (0-89375-035-2) Troll Assocs.
—I Can Read About the First Thanksgiving. Anderson, J. I. LC 76-54400. (gr. 2-5). 1977. pap. 1.95 (0-89375-034-4) Troll Assocs.
McKeveny, Tom. The High Voyage: The Final Crossing of Christopher Columbus. Litowinsky, Olga. 160p. (gr. 5-9). 1992. pap. 3.50 (0-440-40703-6, YB) Dell.
—A Sending of Dragons. Yolen, Jane. LC 87-6689. 240p. (gr. 7 up). 1987. pap. 14.95 (0-385-29587-1) Delacorte.
McKie, Angus. Tales from Deep Space. Foley, Tod. Amthor, Terry K., ed. 32p. (Orig.). (gr. 10-12). 1988. pap. 6.00 (1-55806-006-5, 9103) Iron Crown Ent Inc.
McKie, Roy. The Alphabet Block Book. McKie, Roy. LC 79-63611. (ps-1). 1979. 3.95 (0-394-84269-3) Random Bks Yng Read.
—Eye Book. Le Sieg, Theodore. (ps-1). 1968. 6.95 (0-394-81094-5, BE2); lib. bdg. 7.99 (0-394-91094-X, BE2) Random Bks Yng Read.
—Guess a Rhyme: Poems to Complete! Riddles to Solve! reissued ed. Weinburg, Larry. LC 81-15689. 32p. (ps-1). 1993. 2.25 (0-394-85062-9) Random Bks Yng Read.
—I Can Write! A Book by Me, Myself. LeSieg, Theo. 32p. (ps-1). 1993. pap. 2.99 (0-679-84700-6) Random Bks Yng Read.
—I Wish That I Had Duck Feet. LeSieg, Theo. 64p. (ps-1). 1988. bk. & cassette pkg. 6.95 (0-394-89777-3) Random Bks Yng Read.
—The Joke Book. McKie, Roy. LC 78-62699. (ps-3). 1979. pap. 2.25 (0-394-84077-1) Random Bks Yng Read.
—Mr. Wizard's Supermarket Science. Herbert, Don. LC 79-27217. 96p. (gr. 4-7). 1980. lib. bdg. 9.99 (0-394-93800-3); pap. 9.00 (0-394-83800-9) Random Bks Yng Read.
—Nose Book. Perkins, Al. LC 71-117540. (ps-1). 1970. 6.95 (0-394-80623-9); lib. bdg. 7.99 (0-394-90623-3) Random Bks Yng Read.
—The Pop-up Mice of Mr. Brice. LeSieg, Theo. LC 89-60507. 20p. (ps-3). 1989. 10.00 (0-679-80132-4) Random Bks Yng Read.
—The Tooth Book. Le Sieg, Theodore. LC 80-28320. 48p. (ps-1). 1981. 6.95 (0-394-84825-X, XBYR); lib. bdg. 7.99 (0-394-94825-4) Random Bks Yng Read.
—Who Will Be My Pet? Tusan, Stan. 40p. (ps-1). 1992. write for info. (0-307-11582-8, 11582) Western Pub.
—Who Will Be My Pet? Tusan, Stan. 32p. (ps-1). 1993. pap. 3.25 (0-307-15972-8, 15972, Golden Pr) Western Pub.
Mc Kig, Susan. Let's Praise & Play: Children's Christian Mini-Piano Book. Advance Cal-Tech Inc. Kung, Edward, ed. Childe, Laura, intro. by. 36p. (ps-6). text ed. write for info. (0-943759-00-5) Advance Cal Tech.
McKinley, John. The Great Gerbil Roundup. Manes, Stephen. 105p. (gr. 3-7). 1988. 13.95 (0-15-232490-9, HB Juv Bks) HarBrace.

—The Great Gerbil Roundup. Manes, Stephen. LC 88-2266. 112p. (gr. 3-7). 1991. pap. 3.50 (0-06-440375-0, Trophy) HarpC Child Bks.
McKinley, Robin & Treherne, Katie T. The Light Princess. McDonald, George. LC 86-33636. 44p. (ps up). 1988. 13.95 (0-15-245300-8, HB Juv Bks) HarBrace.
McKinnell, Michael. Feeling Fit, That's It! Nelson, JoAnne. LC 92-37719. 1994. pap. 5.95 (0-935529-58-6) Comprehen Health Educ.
McKinstry-Peterson, Laurel. Can You Come with Me? McKinstry, Anne P. 44p. (gr. 4-8). 1986. 5.95 (1-55523-034-2) Winston-Derek.
McKissack, Vern. How Does It Work? rev. ed. Long, Jack. 32p. (gr. 2-4). 1990. Repr. of 1988 ed. PLB 9.95 (1-878363-17-4) Forest Hse.
—Why Is the Sky Blue? Long, Jack. 32p. (gr. 2-4). 1990. Repr. of 1988 ed. PLB 9.95 (1-878363-15-8) Forest Hse.
McKissack, Vernon. The Mouse in the Manger. Gentile, Gennaro L. LC 78-72944. 80p. (gr. k-4). 1978. pap. 5.95 (0-87793-165-8) Ave Maria.
Mcknight, C. D. Christina & the Little Red Bird. Peterson, Elizabeth J. 23p. (Orig.). (ps-1). pap. 5.95 (0-938911-02-3) Indiv Music Syst.
McKnight, Fred. Grandpa Beaver: His Amazing Tales. Weiss, Clarence B. Easson, Roger, ed. LC 87-20457. 98p. (Orig.). (gr. 5-12). 1987. pap. 6.95 (0-942179-01-3) Shelby Hse.
McKowen, K. D. Wildlife Activity & Coloring Book. rev. ed. McKowen, K. D. 32p. (gr. 2-6). 1987. workbook 1.50 (0-913635-02-2) Aspen Prods.
McLachlan, Edward. Henrietta the Clumsy Hippo. Greaves, John. (ps-3). 1988. 7.95 (0-8120-6090-3) Barron.
McLane, Lois. Mystery on Mackinac Island. Hale, Anna. LC 89-35484. 184p. (gr. 3-5). 1989. pap. 9.95 (0-943173-34-5) Harbinger AZ.
McLaughlin, Dorthy. Color Me...Cuddly! Owens, Carolyn. 32p. (ps-4). 1982. pap. 1.19 (0-87123-695-8) Bethany Hse.
Maclean & Tuminell. Psychology for Kids: Forty Fun Tests That Help You Learn about Yourself. Kincher, Jonni. Bach, Julie, ed. Elliott, Thomas, frwd. by. LC 90-47742. 160p. (Orig.). (gr. 4 up). 1990. pap. 11.95 (0-915793-23-7) Free Spirit Pub.
McLean, Andrew. Fire-Engine Lil. McLean, Janet. 32p. (Orig.). (gr. k-2). 1993. pap. 6.95 (0-04-928067-8, Pub. by Allen & Unwin Aust Pty AT) IPG Chicago.
—Hector & Maggie. McLean, Janet. 32p. (Orig.). (gr. k-2). 1993. 16.95 (0-04-442162-1, Pub. by Allen & Unwin Aust Pty AT); pap. 6.95 (0-04-442245-8, Pub. by Allen & Unwin Aust Pty AT) IPG Chicago.
—Oh, Kipper! McLean, Janet. 32p. (Orig.). (gr. k-2). 1993. 16.95 (1-86373-013-3, Pub. by Allen & Unwin Aust Pty AT); pap. 6.95 (1-86373-080-X, Pub. by Allen & Unwin Aust Pty AT) IPG Chicago.
McLean, Chari. Shai's Shabbat Walk. Gellman, Ellie. LC 85-80780. 12p. (ps). 1985. bds. 4.95 (0-930494-49-0) Kar Ben.
McLean, Chari P. Matzah Meals: A Passover Cookbook for Kids. Tabs, Judy & Steinberg, Barbara. LC 85-40. 72p. (ps up). 1985. pap. 6.95 spiral bd. (0-930494-44-X) Kar-Ben.
McLean, Chari R. A Seder for Tu B'Shevat. Appleman, Harlene & Shapiro, Jane. 32p. (ps up). 1984. pap. 2.95 (0-930494-39-3) Kar Ben.
McLean, Colin & Maclean, Moira. Animals: Stories for under Fives. Stimson, Joan. 44p. (ps-k). 1992. 3.50 (0-7214-1484-2) Ladybird Bks.
—King Cole's Castle. Maclean, Colin & Maclean, Moira. LC 92-53098. 24p. (ps-1). 1992. 9.95 (1-85697-819-2) Kingfisher Bks.
—Mother Goose Rhymes. LC 92-26443. 32p. (ps-1). 1993. 9.95 (1-85697-898-2) Kingfisher Bks.
—Nursery Rhyme Songbook: With Easy Music to Play for Piano & Guitar. Emerson, Sally. LC 92-53106. 72p. (ps-k). 1992. 16.95 (1-85697-823-0) Kingfisher Bks.
—Peter's Pumpkin House. Maclean, Colin & Maclean, Moira. LC 92-53099. 24p. (ps-1). 1992. 9.95 (1-85697-820-6) Kingfisher Bks.
—The Young Child's Busy Book: Of Playing, Learning, Stories & Rhymes. Carter, Margaret. LC 92-53094. 96p. (ps-k). 1992. 14.95 (1-85697-822-2) Kingfisher Bks.
Maclean, Colin, jt. illus. see Maclean, Moira.
McLean, Dee, et al. Deserts. Stephen, Richard. LC 89-20300. 32p. (gr. 4-6). 1990. PLB 11.59 (0-8167-1969-1); pap. text ed. 3.95 (0-8167-1970-5) Troll Assocs.
McLean, Meg. Laughing All the Way. Shannon, George. LC 91-41135. 32p. (ps-3). 1992. 13.45 (0-395-62473-8) HM.
McLean, Mina G. The Mystery at Misty Falls. Gezi, Kal & Bradford, Ann. LC 80-15708. 32p. (gr. k-4). 1980. PLB 18.50 (0-89565-147-9); PLB 12.95s.p. (0-685-55525-9) Childs World.
—The Mystery at the Tree House. Bradford, Ann & Gezi, Kal. LC 80-15654. 32p. (gr. k-4). 1980. PLB 18.50 (0-89565-148-3); PLB 12.95s.p. (0-685-55526-7) Childs World.
—The Mystery in the Secret Club House. Gezi, Kal & Bradford, Ann. LC 78-6418. 32p. (gr. k-3). 1978. PLB 18.50 (0-89565-027-4); PLB 12.95s.p. (0-685-55527-5) Childs World.

—The Mystery of the Blind Writer. Gezi, Kal & Bradford, Ann. LC 80-12395. 32p. (gr. k-4). 1980. PLB 18.50 (0-89565-145-9); PLB 12.95s.p. (0-685-55528-3) Childs World.
—The Mystery of the Live Ghosts. Gezi, Kal & Bradford, Ann. LC 78-8142. (gr. k-3). 1978. PLB 18.50 (0-89565-026-6); PLB 12.95s.p. (0-685-55529-1) Childs World.
—The Mystery of the Midget Clown. Bradford, Ann & Gezi, Kal. LC 80-72513. 32p. (gr. k-4). 1980. PLB 18. 50 (0-89565-146-7); PLB 12.95s.p. (0-685-55530-5) Childs World.
—The Mystery of the Missing Dogs. Bradford, Ann & Gezi, Kal. LC 80-10436. 32p. (gr. k-4). 1980. PLB 18. 50 (0-89565-143-2); PLB 12.95s.p. (0-685-55531-3) Childs World.
—The Mystery of the Square Footprints. Gezi, Kal & Bradford, Ann. LC 80-10437. 32p. (gr. k-4). 1980. PLB 18.50 (0-89565-144-0); PLB 12.95s.p. (0-685-55532-1) Childs World.
—Our Valentine's Day Book. Rev. ed. Moncure, Jane B. LC 86-28387. 32p. (ps-3). 1987. PLB 19.95 (0-89565-343-5); PLB 13.95s.p. (0-685-55852-5) Childs World.
—What Was It Before It Was My Chair? Schreckhise, Roseva. LC 85-13238. 32p. (ps-2). 1985. PLB 21.35 (0-89565-326-5); PLB 14.95s.p. (0-685-55777-4) Childs World.
Maclean, Moira & Maclean, Colin. Action Rhymes. Emerson, Sally & Corbett, Pie, eds. LC 92-26445. 32p. (ps-k). 1993. pap. 4.95 (1-85697-900-8) Kingfisher Bks.
—Baby Games & Lullabies. Emerson, Sally, selected by. LC 92-27488. 1993. 4.95 (1-85697-901-6) Kingfisher Bks.
—Dancing & Singing Games. Corbett, Pie & Emerson, Sally, eds. LC 92-28425. 1993. 4.95 (1-85697-902-4) Kingfisher Bks.
—Jack & the Beanstalk & Other Stories. Price, Susan, retold by. LC 92-26442. 1993. 4.95 (1-85697-903-2) Kingfisher Bks.
—Little Red Riding Hood & Other Stories. Price, Susan, retold by. LC 92-26448. 1993. 5.95 (1-85697-904-0) Kingfisher Bks.
—Nursery Rhymes. Emerson, Sally, compiled by. LC 92-26446. 32p. (ps-k). 1993. pap. 4.95 (1-85697-905-9) Kingfisher Bks.
—The Nursery Treasury: A Collection of Rhymes, Poems, Lullabies & Games. Emerson, Sally, compiled by. 128p. 1988. pap. 17.95 (0-385-24650-1) Doubleday.
—The Three Bears & Other Stories. Price, Susan, retold by. LC 92-26450. 24p. (ps-1). 1993. 4.95 (1-85697-906-7) Kingfisher Bks.
Maclean, Moira, jt. illus. see Maclean, Colin.
MacLean, Robert. Potluck: Exploring American Foods & Meals. Clark, Raymond C. 128p. (Orig.). (gr. 5 up). 1985. text ed. 9.50x (0-86647-012-3) Pro Lingua.
—Vermont, the State with the Storybook Past. rev. ed. Cheney, Cora. Muller, H. N., III, intro. by. LC 86-60341. 272p. (gr. 5-9). 1986. pap. 14.95 (0-933050-36-4) New Eng Pr VT.
MacLean, Robert & Sempe, Jean J. Grammar Exercises Part One: Elementary-Intermediate ESL. 2nd, rev. ed. Burrows, Arthur A. Clark, Raymond C., ed. 256p. (Orig.). (gr. 8 up). 1992. pap. text ed. 10.95x (0-86647-011-5) Pro Lingua.
McLean-Carr, Carol. Tiny Timothy Turtle. Leditschke, Anna. 32p. (ps-k). 1991. PLB 17.27 (0-8368-0667-0) Gareth Stevens Inc.
Macleod, Andi. ScienceArts: Discovering Science Through Art Experiences. Kohl, MaryAnn & Potter, Jean. 144p. (Orig.). (ps-4). Date not set. pap. text ed. 15.95 (0-935607-04-8) Bright Ring.
McLeod, Chum. Come to Your Senses. Tytla, Milan. 96p. 1993. pap. 9.95 (1-55037-292-0) Firefly Bks Ltd.
—Henry & the Cow Problem. Whishaw, Iona. (ps-1). 1992. 0.99 (1-55037-254-8, Pub. by Annick CN) Firefly Bks Ltd.
McLoughlin, Mary. Those Green Things. Stinson, Kathy. 24p. (gr. k-3). 1985. 12.95 (0-920303-40-4, Pub. by Annick CN) pap. 4.95 (0-920303-41-2, Pub. by Annick CN) Firefly Bks Ltd.
McLoughlin, Wayne. Voices of the Wild. London, Jonathan. LC 92-27651. 32p. (ps up). 1993. 15.00 (0-517-59217-7); PLB 15.99 (0-517-59218-5) Crown Bks Yng Read.
McLusky, John. The Illustrated James Bond, 007. Schenkman, Richard, ed. 90p. (Orig.). (gr. 5 up). 1981. pap. 6.95 (0-9605838-0-7) Bond Double-O Seven.
McMahan, Dean. Ajuna's Star. rev. ed. McMahan, Dean & Rose, Willi. LC 90-80841. 24p. (ps-2). 1990. pap. 4.95 (0-9626254-1-8); write for info. audio-cassette (0-9626254-2-6) Ajuna Unlimited.
McMahan, Kelly. More Phonics Fun: Crossword Puzzles. Cron, Mary. 48p. (Orig.). (gr. k-2). 1989. pap. 2.95 incl. chipboard (0-8431-2358-3) Price Stern.
McMahon, W. Franklin. We Came from Vietnam. Stanek, Muriel. Fay, Ann, ed. LC 84-29927. 48p. (gr. 1-6). 1985. PLB 10.50 (0-8075-8699-4) A Whitman.
McManus, Joseph F. & Reynolds, Kevin. Time to Read: Short Stories for Young People. McHenry, Martha J. McManus, Joseph F., ed. 96p. 1991. 12.50 (0-929443-06-3) Quali-Type.
McManus, Michael. Song of Sirius. McManus, Dorothy. Myhre, M., ed. 155p. (Orig.). 1990. pap. 8.00 (0-929686-01-2) Temple Golden Pubns.

McMaster, Jack. Father Goose & His Goslings. Lishman, Bill. 72p. (Orig.). (gr. k-8). 1992. pap. 9.95 (0-9623072-8-9) S Ink WA.
McMillan, Bruce. Beach Ball - Left, Right. McMillan, Bruce. LC 91-32802. 32p. (ps-3). 1992. reinforced bdg. 14.95 (0-8234-0946-5) Holiday.
—A Beach for the Birds. McMillan, Bruce. LC 92-10920. 32p. (gr. 2-5). 1993. 15.45 (0-395-64050-4) HM.
—Everything Grows. Raffi. LC 88-37162. 32p. (ps-2). 1989. 9.95 (0-517-57387-3) Crown Bks Yng Read.
—Everything Grows. Raffi. LC 88-37162. 32p. (ps-2). 1993. pap. 3.99 (0-517-88098-9) Crown Bks Yng Read.
—Kitten Can...a Concept Book. McMillan, Bruce. LC 83-19539. 32p. (ps-1). 1984. 12.95 (0-688-02668-0); PLB 12.88 (0-688-02669-9) Lothrop.
—One Sun: A Book of Terse Verse. Mcmillan, Bruce. LC 89-24625. 32p. (ps-3). reinforced bdg. 15.95 (0-8234-0810-8); pap. 5.95 (0-8234-0951-1) Holiday.
—Penguins at Home: Gentoos of Antarctica. McMillan, Bruce. LC 92-34769. 1993. 15.95 (0-395-66560-4) HM.
—Play Day: A Book of Terse Verse. McMillan, Bruce. LC 90-29077. 32p. (ps-3). 1991. reinforced 14.95 (0-8234-0894-9) Holiday.
—Puniddles. McMillan, Bruce & McMillan, Brett. (gr. 2 up). 1982. pap. 4.80 (0-395-32076-3) HM.
—Step by Step. McMillan, Bruce. LC 87-4195. 32p. (ps-1). 1987. 13.95 (0-688-07233-X) Lothrop.
—Super, Super, Superwords. McMillan, Bruce. Briley, D., ed. LC 88-9342. 32p. (ps-2). 1989. 12.95 (0-688-08098-7); PLB 12.88 (0-688-08099-5) Lothrop.
McMillan, Bruce, photos by. Fire Engine Shapes. McMillan, Bruce. LC 87-38145. 32p. (ps-2). 1988. 12. 95 (0-688-07842-7); PLB 12.88 (0-688-07843-5) Lothrop.
—Growing Colors. McMillan, Bruce. LC 88-2767. 40p. (ps-2). 1988. 13.95 (0-688-07844-3); PLB 13.88 (0-688-07845-1) Lothrop.
—Growing Colors. McMillan, Bruce. 32p. (ps up). 1994. pap. 4.95 (0-688-13112-3, Mulberry) Morrow.
—Here a Chick, There a Chick. McMillan, Bruce. LC 82-20348. 32p. (ps-1). 1983. 15.95 (0-688-02000-3); PLB 15.88 (0-688-02001-1) Lothrop.
—Sense Suspense. McMillan, Bruce. LC 93-30272. 1994. 14.95 (0-590-47904-0) Scholastic Inc.
MacMillan, Marilyn, jt. illus. see Wren, James E.
McMullan, Jim. Nutcracker Noel. McMullan, Kate. LC 93-77115. 32p. (ps up). 1993. 15.00 (0-06-205039-7); PLB 14.89 (0-06-205040-0) HarpC Child Bks.
McMurdy, Michael. Lucy's Cristmas. Hall, Donald. LC 92-46292. (gr. 1 up). 1994. write for info. (0-15-276870-X, Browndeer Pr) HarBrace.
McMurray, Chuck. Moosewhopper: A Juicy, Moosey Min-Min-Minnesota Burger Tale. 3rd ed. Blair, Al. LC 83-61092. 32p. (gr. 3). 1983. pap. 3.95 (0-930366-04-2) Northcountry Pub.
McNally, Bruce. For Every Child, a Better World. Gikow, Louise & Weiss, Ellen. 48p. (gr. k-4). 1993. 9.95 (0-307-15628-1, 15628, Golden Pr) Western Pub.
—Kermit's Garden of Verses. Prelutsky, Jack. LC 82-480. 64p. (gr. 4-6). 1982. lib. bdg. 5.99 (0-394-95410-6) Random Bks Yng Read.
—The Sesame Street Book of Poetry. Moss, Jeff. LC 90-8994. 48p. (ps-3). 1992. 10.00 (0-679-80774-8); PLB 10.99 (0-679-90774-2) Random Bks Yng Read.
McNatt, Richard. Terrybrook Dragon. Cosgrove, Stephen E. 32p. (gr. k-7). 1990. 14.95 (1-55868-036-5) Gr Arts Ctr Pub.
McNaught, Harry. Astronomy Today: Planets, Stars, Space Exploration. Moche, Dinah. LC 82-5211. 96p. (gr. 5 up). 1982. lib. bdg. 12.99 (0-394-94423-2); pap. 12.00 (0-394-84423-8) Random Bks Yng Read.
—Baby Animals. McNaught, Harry. LC 75-36462. 14p. (ps-1). 1976. Repr. of 1976 ed. bds. 3.95 (0-394-83241-8) Random Bks Yng Read.
—Los Camiones. McNaught, Harry. (SPA). 32p. (ps-3). 1993. 2.25 (0-394-85220-6) Random Bks Yng Read.
—Cinco Ciento Palabras Nuevas Para Ti. De Cuenca, Pilar. Alvarez, Ines, tr. LC 81-13766. 32p. (ps-3). 1982. lib. bdg. 5.99 (0-394-95145-X); pap. 2.25 (0-394-85145-5) Random Bks Yng Read.
—Do You Know? One Hundred Fascinating Facts. Ford, B. G. LC 78-62132. (ps-1). 1979. pap. 2.25 (0-394-84070-4) Random Bks Yng Read.
—Exploring the Sea: Oceanography Today. Blair, Carvel. Rimson, Ole & Luke, Melinda, eds. LC 85-43336. 96p. (gr. 5 up). 1986. pap. 8.95 (0-394-85927-8) Random Bks Yng Read.
—Muppets in My Neighborhood. McNaught, Harry. LC 77-74472. (ps-k). 1977. bds. 3.95 (0-394-83593-X) Random Bks Yng Read.
—The Sesame Street ABC Book of Words. Sesame Street Editors. LC 86-62405. 48p. (ps-k). 1988. pap. 11.00 (0-394-88880-4) Random Bks Yng Read.
—Trucks. McNaught, Harry. LC 75-36463. 14p. (ps-1). 1976. Repr. of 1976 ed. bds. 3.95 (0-394-83240-X) Random Bks Yng Read.
—Trucks. Loehr, Mallory. LC 91-75344. 22p. (ps). 1992. 2.95 (0-679-83061-8) Random Bks Yng Read.
—Words to Grow On. LC 84-6880. 24p. (ps-1). 1984. 3.95 (0-394-86103-5); lib. bdg. 4.99 (0-394-96103-X) Random Bks Yng Read.
McNaughton, Colin. Captain Abdul's Pirate School. McNaughton, Colin. LC 93-21293. 1994. write for info. (1-56402-429-6) Candlewick Pr.

—Guess Who's Just Moved in Next Door? McNaughton, Colin. 32p. (ps-2). 1991. 15.00 (0-679-81802-2) Random Bks Yng Read.
—If Dinosaurs Were Cats & Dogs. rev. ed. McNaughton, Colin. LC 90-22870. 32p. (ps-3). 1991. SBE 13.95 (0-02-765785-X, Four Winds) Macmillan Child Grp.
—Treasure Island. Stevenson, Robert Louis. LC 93-18941. 272p. (gr. 4-8). 1993. PLB 15.95 (0-8050-2773-4, Bks Young Read) H Holt & Co.
—Walk Rabbit Walk. McNaughton, Colin. LC 91-32608. 32p. (ps-3). 1992. Repr. of 1977 ed. 13.00 (0-688-11410-5, Tambourine Bks) Morrow.
—Who's That Banging on the Ceiling? McNaughton, Colin. LC 91-58768. 32p. (ps up). 1992. 13.95 (1-56402-105-X) Candlewick Pr.
Macneil, Melanie F. Calbert & His Adventures. Henney, Carolee W. LC 90-83140. 104p. (Orig.). (gr. 2-5). 1990. collector's first ed., numbered, signed by author, with dust jacket, sim. gold imprint title-author on spine 24.95 (0-9626580-1-4); pap. 9.95 (0-9626580-0-6) Aton Pr.
McNicholas, Shelagh. Five Hundred French Words & Phrases for Children. Watson, Carol & De Saulles, Janet. 32p. (gr. 1-2). 1994. 8.95 (0-7818-0267-9) Hippocrene Bks.
—Five Hundred Spanish Words & Phrases for Children. Watson, Carol & De Saulles, Janet. (SPA & ENG.). 32p. (gr. 1-2). 1994. 8.95 (0-7818-0262-8) Hippocrene Bks.
McNichols, William H. Feliz Navidad, Pablo. Martini, Teri. (gr. 4 up). 1990. 2.95 (0-8091-6597-X) Paulist Pr.
McNutt, Mary M. Little Red Hiding Wolf. Holbrook, Janet M. 35p. (gr. k-12). 1992. pap. 8.95 (0-9636203-0-4) Holbrook Dogwds.
Macombi, Turi. Little Bunny's Magic Nose. Teitelbaum, Michael, retold by. (ps-2). 1991. 5.25 (0-307-15701-6, Golden Pr) Western Pub.
McPeek, Ellen. Flags in the History of Texas. Veazey, Steve & Porter, John D., Jr. 40p. (gr. 4 up). 1991. pap. 6.95 (0-937460-73-7) Hendrick-Long.
McPhail, David. Andrew's Bath. McPhail, David. (ps-3). 1984. 13.95 (0-316-56319-6, Joy St Bks) Little.
—The Bear's Bicycle. McLeod, Emilie W. 32p. (gr. k-3). 1986. (Joy St Bks); pap. 5.95 (0-316-56206-8, Joy St Bks) Little.
—The Bear's Bicycle. McLeod, Emilie W. (gr. 1-3). 1986. incl. cassette 19.95 (0-87499-025-4); pap. 12.95 incl. cassette (0-87499-023-8); 4 paperbacks, cassette & guide 27.95 (0-87499-024-6) Live Oak Media.
—The Bear's Toothache. McPhail, David. (gr. k-2). 1986. incl. cassette 19.95 (0-87499-081-5); pap. 12.95 incl. cassette (0-87499-080-7); 4 paperbacks, cassette & guide 27.95 (0-87499-082-3) Live Oak Media.
—The Bear's Toothache. McPhail, David. (ps-3). 1988. pap. 5.95 (0-316-56325-0, Joy St Bks) Little.
—A Big Fat Enormous Lie. Sharmat, Marjorie W. LC 77-15645. (ps-2). 1978. 13.00 (0-525-26510-4, DCB) Dutton Child Bks.
—A Big Fat Enormous Lie. Sharmat, Marjorie W. LC 77-15645. 32p. (ps-2). 1986. pap. 3.99 (0-525-44242-1, DCB) Dutton Child Bks.
—El Cuento de Pedrito Conejo. Potter, Beatrix. Marcuse, Aida, tr. from ENG. (SPA.). (gr. k-4). 1993. pap. 2.95 (0-590-46475-2) Scholastic Inc.
—The Dream Child. McPhail, David. LC 84-18755. 32p. (ps-3). 1988. pap. 4.95 (0-525-44366-5, 0383-120, DCB) Dutton Child Bks.
—Emma's Pet. McPhail, David. (ps-2). 1988. bk. & cassette 19.95 (0-87499-107-2); bk. & cassette 12.95 (0-87499-106-4); 4 cassettes & guide 27.95 (0-87499-108-0) Live Oak Media.
—Emma's Pet. McPhail, David. LC 85-4414. 24p. (ps-k). 1988. pap. 3.95 (0-525-44430-0, DCB) Dutton Child Bks.
—Emma's Vacation. McPhail, David. LC 86-24066. 24p. (ps-k). 1987. 7.95 (0-525-44315-0, DCB) Dutton Child Bks.
—Farm Boy's Year. McPhail, David. LC 91-4982. 32p. (gr. k-3). 1992. SBE 13.95 (0-689-31679-8, Atheneum Child Bk) Macmillan Child Grp.
—Farm Morning. McPhail, David. LC 84-19167. 32p. (ps-3). 1985. 15.95 (0-15-227299-2, HB Juv Bks) HarBrace.
—First Flight. McPhail, David. LC 86-28804. (ps-3). 1987. 14.95i (0-316-56323-4, Joy St Bks) Little.
—Fix-It. McPhail, David. LC 83-16459. 24p. (ps-k). 1984. 11.00 (0-525-44093-3, DCB) Dutton Child Bks.
—Fix-It. McPhail, David. (gr. k-3). 1988. bk. & cassette 19.95 (0-87499-084-X); bk. & cassette 12.95 (0-87499-083-1); 4 cassettes & guide 27.95 (0-87499-085-8) Live Oak Media.
—Fix-It. McPhail, David. LC 83-16459. 24p. (ps-k). 1987. pap. 3.95 (0-525-44323-1, 0383-120, DCB) Dutton Child Bks.
—Henry Bear's Park. McPhail, David. 48p. (gr. 1-3). 1976. lib. bdg. 14.95 (0-316-56315-3, Joy St Bks) Little.
—Night Sounds. Wells, Rosemary. LC 93-31815. 1994. write for info. (0-8037-1301-0); PLB write for info. (0-8037-1302-9) Dial Bks Young.
—The Nightgown of the Sullen Moon. Willard, Nancy. LC 83-8472. (ps-3). 1983. 14.95 (0-15-257429-8, HB Juv Bks) HarBrace.
—The Nightgown of the Sullen Moon. Willard, Nancy. LC 83-8472. 32p. (Orig.). (ps-3). 1987. pap. 4.95 (0-15-257430-1, Voyager Bks) HarBrace.

—On a Starry Night. Kinsey-Warnock, Natalie. LC 93-4878. 1994. write for info. (0-531-06820-X); PLB write for info. (0-531-08670-4) Orchard Bks Watts.
—Pig Pig & the Magic Photo Album. McPhail, David. LC 85-20459. 24p. (ps-3). 1986. 10.95 (0-525-44238-3, DCB) Dutton Child Bks.
—Pig Pig Goes to Camp. McPhail, David. LC 83-1412. 24p. (ps-3). 1987. pap. 3.95 (0-525-44302-9, DCB) Dutton Child Bks.
—Pig Pig Grows Up. McPhail, David. (ps-2). 1985. pap. 12.95 incl. cassette (0-941078-94-9); incl. cassette 19.95 (0-941078-96-5); incl. cassette 4 paperbacks guide 27.95 (0-941078-95-7) Live Oak Media.
—Pig Pig Rides. McPhail, David. LC 82-9777. 24p. (ps-3). 1982. 14.00 (0-525-44024-0, DCB) Dutton Child Bks.
—Pig Pig Rides. McPhail, David. (gr. 1-3). 1988. bk. & cassette 19.95 (0-87499-090-4); bk. & cassette 12.95 (0-87499-089-0); 4 cassettes & guide 27.95 (0-87499-091-2) Live Oak Media.
—Pig Pig Rides. McPhail, David. LC 82-9777. 24p. (ps-3). 1985. pap. 3.95 (0-525-44222-7, DCB) Dutton Child Bks.
—Sailing to Cythera. Willard, Nancy. LC 74-5602. 72p. (gr. 5 up). 1985. pap. 5.95 (0-15-269961-9, Voyager Bks) HarBrace.
—Snow Lion. McPhail, David. LC 82-8119. 48p. (ps-3). 1987. 5.95 (0-8193-1097-2); PLB 5.95 (0-8193-1098-0) Parents.
—Snow Lion. McPhail, David. 48p. (gr. 3-7). 1990. pap. 2.95 (0-448-04335-1, G&D) Putnam Pub Group.
—Something Special. McPhail, David. 32p. (ps-3). 1988. 12.95 (0-316-56324-2) Little.
—The Tale of Peter Rabbit. Potter, Beatrix. 32p. (Orig.). (gr. k-3). 1986. pap. 2.50 (0-590-41101-2); incl. cassette 5.95 (0-590-63091-1) Scholastic Inc.
—Those Terrible Toy-Breakers. McPhail, David. LC 80-10450. 48p. (ps-3). 1980. 5.95 (0-8193-1019-0); PLB 5.95 (0-8193-1020-4) Parents.
—Those Terrible Toy Breakers. McPhail, David. 48p. (ps-2). 1990. pap. 2.95 (0-448-04343-2, G&D) Putnam Pub Group.
—Uncle Terrible: More Adventures of Anatole. Willard, Nancy. LC 82-47940. 120p. (gr. 5 up). 1985. pap. 5.95 (0-15-292794-8, HB Juv Bks) HarBrace.
McPhail, David M. Why a Disguise? Numeroff, Laura. LC 93-19025. 1994. pap. 14.00 (0-671-87006-8, S&S BFYR) S&S Trade.
McPheeters, Neal. The Adventures of Grover in Outer Space. Roberts, Sarah. LC 84-60188. 32p. (ps-3). 1984. pap. 1.25 (0-394-86300-3) Random Bks Yng Read.
McPheeters, William. John: Beloved Apostle. Laux, Dorothy. (gr. 1-6). 1977. bds. 5.95 (0-8054-4234-0, 4242-34) Broadman.
McPheeters, William N. Old Testament Friends: Men of Courage. Fulbright, Robert G. (gr. 1-6). 1979. 5.95 (0-8054-4251-0, 4242-51) Broadman.
Macpherson, Elaine. Dope Deal. Kropp, Paul. LC 81-9766. 96p. (gr. 7-12). 1982. pap. 4.50 (0-88436-818-1, 35272); wkbk. 1.20 (0-88436-927-7, 35685); read-along cassette 10.00 (0-88436-951-X, 35106) EMC.
McQueen, Don. How Billy Joe Bobtail Met Texas Slim. May, Robert E. 32p. (gr. k-7). 1987. lib. bdg. 11.89 (0-87397-303-8); pap. 5.95 (0-87397-300-3) Strode.
—Poppa & Elizabeth: A Bobtail Romance. May, Robert E. 32p. (Orig.). (ps-3). 1988. PLB 11.89 (0-87397-314-3); pap. 5.95 (0-87397-313-5) Strode.
McQueen, Lucinda. Coloring Bears. LC 90-53242. 24p. (ps). 1991. 2.50 (0-448-40126-6, G&D) Putnam Pub Group.
—The Just-Right Family. Callen, Larry. 40p. 1984. 5.95 (0-910313-31-9) Parker Bros.
—The Little Red Hen. 32p. (Orig.). (gr. k-2). 1985. Big book. 19.95 (0-590-71718-9); pap. 2.50 (0-590-41145-4) Scholastic Inc.
—Pudgy Face Babies. 16p. 1989. bds. 2.95 (0-448-02256-7, G&D) Putnam Pub Group.
—The Water of Life. Williams, Jay & Williams, Victoria. 40p. (gr. k-12). 1980. 15.00 (0-89486-721-0, T5129) Hazelden.
—The Wee Kitten Who Sucked Her Thumb. Tufts, Mary L. 32p. (ps-2). 1986. pap. 1.95 (0-448-19076-1, G&D) Putnam Pub Group.
—The Wee Mouse Who Was Afraid of the Dark. Lundell, Margo. 32p. 1991. pap. 1.95 (0-448-40060-X, Platt & Munk Pubs) Putnam Pub Group.
—The Wee Puppy Who Wet His Bed. Lundell, Margo. 32p. (ps-2). 1989. pap. 2.25 (0-448-19114-8, Platt & Munk Pubs) Putnam Pub Group.
—Xavier's Fantastic Discovery. LC 83-20446. 1984. incl. cassette 7.95 (0-910313-60-1); 5.95 (0-910313-25-3) Parker Bros.
McQueen, Lucinda & Guitar, Jeremy. Otis Lee. 12p. (gr. 1-5). 1984. 4.00 (0-910313-33-4) Parker Bros.
—Sybil Sadie. 12p. (gr. 1-5). 1984. 4.00 (0-910313-32-6) Parker Bros.
McRae, Patrick. The Americas: A Sticker Atlas of Exploration & Discovery. Crouch, Robin. 16p. (Orig.). (gr. 1-3). 1993. pap. 5.95 (0-8249-8556-7, Ideals Child) Hambleton-Hill.
—Let's Build a Car. Schaefer, Margaret A. 32p. (gr. k-5). 1992. pap. 4.95 (0-8249-8536-2, Ideals Child) Hambleton-Hill.
—Peter Cottontail. 24p. (Orig.). (gr. k-6). 1986. pap. 2.95 (0-8249-8106-5, Ideals Child) Hambleton-Hill.

McRae, Rodney. Crazy Alphabet. Cox, Lynn. LC 91-3734. 32p. (ps-1). 1992. 13.95 (0-531-05966-9); lib. bdg. 13.99 (0-531-08566-X) Orchard Bks Watts.
Macsolis. Baile de Luna: Dance Moon. Macsolis. (SPA.). 25p. (ps-2). 1991. 12.95 (84-261-2583-2) Donars.
McSweeney, Terry. Great Gift & the Wish-Fulfilling Gem. Tulku, Tarthang, intro. by. LC 86-19767. 32p. (gr. k-5). 1987. PLB 14.95 (0-89800-157-9); pap. 7.95 (0-89800-143-9) Dharma Pub.
McTaggart, David. Ben at the Beach. MacDonald, Maryann. 32p. (ps-3). 1991. 14.95 (0-670-83920-5) Viking Child Bks.
McWhirter, Kore L. Growing Through Grief: A K-Twelve Curriculum to Help Young People Through All Kinds of Loss. rev. ed. O'Toole, Donna R. 392p. (gr. k-12). 1989. pap. 59.95 3-ring bdr. (1-878321-00-5, Mntn Rainbow) Rainbow NC.
McWhirter, Mary Lou. Aarvy Aardvark Finds Hope: A Read-Aloud Story for People of All Ages. O'Toole, Donna. 80p. (Orig.). (ps up). 1989. pap. 9.95 (1-878321-25-0, Mntn Rainbow); tchr's guide 6.95 (1-878321-26-9, Mntn Rainbow); audio tape 9.95 (0-685-20985-7, Mntn Rainbow) Rainbow NC.
Madama, John, photos by. Clambake: A Wampanoag Tradition. Peters, Russell M. 48p. (gr. 3-6). 1992. PLB 19.95 (0-8225-2651-4) Lerner Pubns.
Maddem, Don. Is There Life in Outer Space? Branley, Franklyn M. LC 85-45057. 32p. (gr. k-3). 1986. pap. 4.50 (0-06-445049-X, Trophy) HarpC Child Bks.
Madden, Don. Center. Sullivan, George. LC 85-48245. 64p. (gr. 3-7). 1988. (Crowell Jr Bks); (Crowell Jr Bks) HarpC Child Bks.
—Drop of Blood. Showers, Paul. LC 67-23672. (gr. k-3). 1967. PLB 12.89 (0-690-24526-2, Crowell Jr Bks) HarpC Child Bks.
—A Drop of Blood. rev. ed. Showers, Paul. LC 88-3623. 32p. (gr. k-4). 1989. (Crowell Jr Bks); PLB 13.89 (0-690-04717-7, Crowell Jr Bks) HarpC Child Bks.
—Gravity Is a Mystery. rev. ed. Branley, Franklyn M. LC 85-48247. 32p. (gr. k-3). 1986. (Crowell Jr Bks); PLB 14.89 (0-690-04527-1) HarpC Child Bks.
—How to Play Better Soccer. Jackson, C. Paul. LC 76-51450. (gr. 3-7). 1978. 8.95 (0-690-01363-9, Crowell Jr Bks); (Crowell Jr Bks) HarpC Child Bks.
—Is There Life in Outer Space? Branley, Franklyn M. LC 83-45057. 32p. (ps-3). 1984. (Crowell Jr Bks); PLB 14.89 (0-690-04375-9) HarpC Child Bks.
—Nehemiah Builds the Wall. Berg, Jean H. 32p. (Orig.). (gr. k-3). 1978. pap. 9.95 incl. audiocassette (0-87510-114-3) Christian Sci.
—Noah & the Ark. Berg, Jean H. 32p. (Orig.). (gr. k-3). 1974. pap. 9.95 incl. audiocassette (0-87510-180-1) Christian Sci.
—The Planets in Our Solar System. rev. ed. Branley, Franklyn M. LC 86-47530. 32p. (ps-3). 1987. 15.00 (0-690-04579-4, Crowell Jr Bks); PLB 14.89 (0-690-04581-6) HarpC Child Bks.
—The Planets in Our Solar System. rev. ed. Branley, Franklyn M. LC 86-45171. 32p. (ps-3). 1987. pap. 4.50 (0-06-445064-3) HarpC Child Bks.
—Sherlick Hound & the Valentine Mystery. Goldman, Kelly & Davidson, Ronnie. Levine, Abby, ed. LC 88-20561. 32p. (gr. 1-4). 1989. 8.95 (0-8075-7335-3) A Whitman.
—The Sun: Our Nearest Star. rev. ed. Branley, Franklyn M. LC 87-47764. 32p. (ps-3). 1988. (Crowell Jr Bks); PLB 13.89 (0-690-04678-2) HarpC Child Bks.
—Telephones, Televisions, & Toilets: How They Work & What Can Go Wrong. Berger, Melvin & Berger, Gilda. LC 92-18198. (gr. k-3). 1993. 12.00 (0-8249-8645-8, Ideals Child); pap. 3.95 (0-8249-8608-3) Hambleton-Hill.
Madden, Paul. A Drop of Blood. rev. ed. Showers, Paul. LC 85-43021. 32p. (gr. k-4). 1989. pap. 4.50 (0-06-445090-2, Trophy) HarpC Child Bks.
Maddison, Kevin, jt. illus. see Channell, Jim.
Madinaveitia, Horacio. La Gran Aventura de Don Roberto. Madinaveitia, Horacio. (SPA.). 32p. (gr. k-4). 1992. PLB 13.95 (1-879567-02-4, Valeria Bks) Wonder Well.
—Sir Robert's Little Outing. Madinaveitia, Horacio. 32p. (gr. k-4). 1991. PLB 13.95 (1-879567-01-6, Valeria Bks); pap. text ed. 7.95 (1-879567-00-8) Wonder Well.
Madsen, Kris. Communicate Junior. Mayo, Patty, et al. 60p. (gr. 1-4). 1991. incl. game board 35.00 (0-930599-68-3) Thinking Pubns.
—Study Smart. Mayo, Patty, et al. 59p. (gr. 5-12). 1990. bd. game 39.00 (0-930599-64-0) Thinking Pubns.
—Super Speech Adventures. Samuelson, Rita. 96p. (gr. k-4). 1991. pap. text ed. 10.00 (0-930599-65-9) Thinking Pubns.
Maehlis, Sally. Discovering Mount Rainier. rev. ed. Field, Nancy & Maehlis, Sally. 32p. (gr. 1-6). 1992. pap. 3.95 (0-941042-13-8) Dog Eared Pubns.
Maendel, Maria. Behold That Star: A Christmas Anthology: A Collection of Fifteen Christmas Stories. 3rd ed. Society of Brothers Staff, ed. LC 67-25968. 368p. (gr. 4 up). 1966. 17.00 (0-87486-003-2) Plough.
Maendel, Maria A. & Maendel, Maria M. Shepherd's Pipe Songs from the Holy Night: A Christmas Cantata for Children's Voices or Youth Choir. Choral ed. Gick, Georg J. & Swinger, Marlys. Clement, J. T., intro. by. LC 71-85805. 64p. (gr. k-4). 1969. pap. 3.50 (0-87486-011-3); cassette 7.00 (0-87486-049-0) Plough.
Maendel, Maria M., jt. illus. see Maendel, Maria A.

Maeno, Itoko. Berta Benz & the Motorwagen. Bingham, Mindy. 48p. (gr. 1-6). 1992. with dust jacket 14.95 (0-911655-38-7) Advocacy Pr.
—Clarissa. Talley, Carol. LC 91-29958. 32p. (gr. 1-4). 1992. 16.95 (1-55942-014-6, 7650) Marshfilm.
—Gumbo Goes Downtown. Talley, Carol. LC 93-3551. 32p. (gr. 1-4). 1993. 16.95 (1-55942-042-1, 7654) Marshfilm.
—Hana's Year. Talley, Carol. LC 92-19290. 32p. (gr. 1-4). 1992. 16.95 (1-55942-034-0, 7652); incl. video & tchr's. guide 79.95 (1-55942-037-5, 9371) Marshfilm.
—Kylie's Concert. Sheehan, Patty. 32p. 1993. 16.95 (1-55942-046-4, 7655); incl. video & tchr's. guide 79.95 (1-55942-049-9, 9374) Marshfilm.
—Minou. Bingham, Mindy. LC 86-26539. 64p. (gr. k-6). 1987. 14.95 (0-911655-36-0) Advocacy Pr.
—My Way Sally. Paine, Penelope C. & Bingham, Mindy. LC 88-2653. 48p. (ps-6). 1988. 14.95 (0-911655-27-1) Advocacy Pr.
—Nature's Wonderful World in Rhyme. Sheehan, William. LC 93-15247. 1993. 14.95 (0-911655-47-6) Advocacy Pr.
—Papa Piccolo. Talley, Carol. LC 92-4319. 32p. (gr. 1-4). 1992. 16.95 (1-55942-028-6, 7651) Marshfilm.
—Pequena the Burro. Parkison, Jami. LC 93-30377. 32p. (gr. 1-4). 1994. 16.95 (1-55942-055-3, 7657); video, tchr's. guide & storybook 79.95 (1-55942-058-8, 9376) Marshfilm.
Maeno, Itoko, et al. Career Choices: A Guide for Teens & Young Adults: Who Am I? What Do I Want? How Do I Get It? Bingham, Mindy & Stryker, Sandy. Shafer, Robert, ed. LC 90-81785. 288p. (Orig.). (gr. 9 up). 1990. pap. 19.95 (1-878787-02-0) Able Pub.
Maes, Dominique. Too Little, Too Big: Trop Petite, Trop Grande. Hellings, Colette. 40p. (ps-3). 1993. 10.95 (0-8118-0530-1) Chronicle Bks.
Maestas, Ken. Earth's Children. Venino, Suzanne. 64p. (Orig.). (gr. 4-6). 1991. pap. 5.95 (1-877731-50-1) Earthbooks Inc.
Maestis, Ken. National Wildlife Federation's Book of Endangered Species. Earthbooks, Inc Staff. 64p. (Orig.). (gr. 4-6). 1991. pap. 5.95 (1-877731-17-X) Earthbooks Inc.
Maestro, Betsy & Maestro, Giulio. Traffic: A Book of Opposites. reissued ed. Maestro, Betsy & Maestro, Giulio. LC 80-29641. 32p. (ps-1). 1991. 16.00 (0-517-54427-X) Crown Bks Yng Read.
Maestro, Giulio. All Aboard Overnight: A Book of Compound Words. Maestro, Betsy. 32p. (ps-2). 1992. 14.45 (0-395-51120-8, Clarion Bks) HM.
—The Beginning of the Earth. rev. ed. Branley, Franklyn M. LC 87-47765. 32p. (ps-3). 1988. (Crowell Jr Bks); PLB 13.89 (0-690-04654-5, Crowell Jr Bks) HarpC Child Bks.
—The Beginning of the Earth. rev. ed. Branley, Franklyn M. LC 87-45677. 32p. (ps-3). 1988. pap. 4.50 (0-06-445074-0, Trophy) HarpC Child Bks.
—Big City Port. Maestro, Betsy & DelVecchio, Ellen. LC 85-4339. 32p. (gr. k-3). 1984. RSBE 14.95 (0-02-762110-3, Four Winds) Macmillan Child Grp.
—Big City Port. Maestro, Betsy & DelVecchio, Ellen. 32p. (gr. k-3). 1984. pap. 3.95 (0-590-41577-8) Scholastic Inc.
—Bike Trip. Maestro, Betsy. LC 90-35935. 32p. (gr. k-4). 1992. 16.00 (0-06-022731-1); PLB 15.89 (0-06-022732-X) HarpC Child Bks.
—Caves. Gans, Roma. LC 76-4881. 40p. (gr. k-3). 1962. PLB 14.89 (0-690-01070-2, Crowell Jr Bks) HarpC Child Bks.
—Comets. rev. ed. Branley, Franklyn M. LC 83-46161. 32p. (gr. k-3). 1984. (Crowell Jr Bks); PLB 13.89 (0-690-04415-1) HarpC Child Bks.
—Comets. Branley, Franklyn M. LC 83-46161. 32p. (ps-3). 1989. 7.95 (0-694-00199-6, Trophy); pap. 4.50 (0-06-445088-0, Trophy) HarpC Child Bks.
—Delivery Van: Words for Town & Country. Maestro, Betsy. 32p. (ps-2). 1990. 14.45 (0-395-51119-4, Clarion Bks) HM.
—The Dinosaur Is the Biggest Animal That Ever Lived & Other Wrong Ideas You Thought Were True. Simon, Seymour. LC 83-48960. 64p. (gr. 2-5). 1984. (Lipp Jr Bks); PLB 12.89 (0-397-32076-0, Lipp Jr Bks) HarpC Child Bks.
—The Dinosaur Is the Biggest Animal That Ever Lived, & Other Wrong Ideas You Thought Were True. Simon, Seymour. LC 83-48960. 64p. (gr. 2-5). 1986. pap. 4.95 (0-06-446053-3, Trophy) HarpC Child Bks.
—Eight Ate: A Feast of Homonym Riddles. Terban, Marvin. LC 81-12203. 64p. (gr. 1-3). 1982. 13.45 (0-89919-067-7, Clarion Bks); pap. 5.95 (0-89919-086-3, Clarion Bks) HM.
—Ferryboat. Maestro, Betsy. LC 85-47887. 32p. (ps-3). 1986. (Crowell Jr Bks); PLB 14.89 (0-690-04520-4) HarpC Child Bks.
—Fish Facts & Bird Brains: Animal Intelligence. Sattler, Helen R. LC 83-20805. 128p. (gr. 5-9). 1984. 13.95 (0-525-66915-9, Lodestar Bks) Dutton Child Bks.
—Guppies in Tuxedos: Funny Eponyms. Terban, Marvin. LC 87-32630. 64p. (gr. 4-7). 1988. (Clarion Bks); pap. 5.95 (0-89919-770-1, Clarion Bks) HM.
—Halloween Howls: Riddles That Are a Scream. Maestro, Giulio. LC 83-1419. 64p. (gr. 3-7). 1983. 10.95 (0-525-44059-3, DCB) Dutton Child Bks.
—How Do Apples Grow? Maestro, Betsy. LC 91-9468. 32p. (gr. k-4). 1992. 14.00 (0-06-020055-3); PLB 13.89 (0-06-020056-1) HarpC Child Bks.

—How Do Apples Grow? Maestro, Betsy. LC 91-9468. 32p. (ps-2). 1993. pap. 4.95 (0-06-445117-8, Trophy) HarpC Child Bks.
—Hurricane Watch. Branley, Franklyn M. LC 85-47534. 32p. (ps-3). 1985. PLB 13.89 (0-690-04471-2, Crowell Jr Bks) HarpC Child Bks.
—Hurricane Watch. Branley, Franklyn M. LC 85-47534. 32p. (gr. k-3). 1987. pap. 4.50 (0-06-445062-7, Trophy) HarpC Child Bks.
—I Think I Thought & Other Tricky Verbs. Terban, Marvin. LC 83-19034. 64p. (Orig.). (ps-4). 1984. (Clarion Bks); pap. 5.70 (0-89919-290-4, Clarion Bks) HM.
—In a Pickle & other Funny Idioms. Terban, Marvin. LC 82-9585. 64p. (gr. 1-4). 1983. (Clarion Bks); pap. 4.95 (0-89919-164-9, Clarion Bks) HM.
—Mad As a Wet Hen & Other Funny Idioms. Terban, Marvin. LC 86-17575. (gr. 3-6). 1987. (Clarion Bks); pap. 4.95 (0-89919-479-6, Clarion Bks) HM.
—A More Perfect Union: The Story of Our Constitution. Maestro, Betsy. LC 87-4083. 48p. (gr. 1-5). 1987. 15. 95 (0-688-06839-1); PLB 15.88 (0-688-06840-5) Lothrop.
—More Science Experiments You Can Eat. Cobb, Vicki. LC 78-12732. (gr. 5 up). 1979. 13.00 (0-397-31828-6, Lipp Jr Bks); PLB 14.89 (0-397-31878-2, Lipp Jr Bks) HarpC Child Bks.
—Razzle-Dazzle Riddles. Maestro, Giulio. LC 85-3785. 64p. (Orig.). (gr. 2-5). 1985. 11.95 (0-89919-382-X, Clarion Bks); pap. 5.95 (0-89919-405-2, Clarion Bks) HM.
—Riddle Roundup: A Wild Bunch to Beef up Your Word Power. Maestro, Giulio. LC 86-33404. 64p. (gr. 2-5). 1989. (Clarion Bks); pap. 5.70 (0-89919-537-7, Clarion Bks) HM.
—Rockets & Satellites. rev. ed. Branley, Franklyn M. LC 86-27047. 32p. (ps-3). 1987. pap. 4.50 (0-06-445061-9, Trophy) HarpC Child Bks.
—The Silly Kid Joke Book. Levine, Caroline A. LC 82-17727. 64p. (gr. 1-3). 1983. 10.95 (0-525-44039-9, DCB) Dutton Child Bks.
—The Story of Money. Maestro, Betsy. 48p. (gr. 4-7). 1993. 15.45 (0-395-56242-2, Clarion Bks) HM.
—The Story of the Statue of Liberty. Maestro, Betsy. LC 85-11324. 40p. (ps-3). 1986. PLB 12.88 (0-688-05774-8) Lothrop.
—Sunshine Makes the Seasons. rev. ed. Branley, Franklyn M. LC 85-47540. 32p. (ps-3). 1985. PLB 14. 89 (0-690-04482-8, Crowell Jr Bks) HarpC Child Bks.
—Sunshine Makes the Seasons. rev. ed. Branley, Franklyn M. LC 85-42750. 32p. (ps-3). 1988. incl. cassette 7.95 (0-694-00203-8, Trophy); pap. 4.50 (0-06-445019-8, Trophy) HarpC Child Bks.
—Superdupers: Really Funny Real Words. Terban, Marvin. LC 88-38325. 63p. (gr. 4-8). 1989. 13.45 (0-89919-804-X, Clarion Bks); pap. 4.80 (0-395-51123-2, Clarion Bks) HM.
—Taxi: A Book of City Words. Maestro, Betsy. LC 88-22867. (ps-2). 1989. 13.95 (0-89919-528-8, Clarion Bks) HM.
—Taxi: A Book of City Words. Maestro, Betsy. LC 88-22867. (ps-3). 1990. pap. 5.70 (0-395-54811-X, Clarion Bks) HM.
—Too Hot to Hoot: Funny Palindrome Riddles. Terban, Marvin. LC 84-14942. 64p. (gr. 2-5). 1985. 13.95 (0-89919-319-6, Clarion Bks); pap. 6.95 (0-89919-320-X, Clarion Bks) HM.
—Tornado Alert. Branley, Franklyn M. LC 87-29379. 32p. (ps-3). 1988. (Crowell Jr Bks); PLB 13.89 (0-690-04688-X) HarpC Child Bks.
—Tornado Alert. Branley, Franklyn M. LC 87-29379. 32p. (gr. k-4). 1990. pap. 4.95 (0-06-445094-5, Trophy) HarpC Child Bks.
—What's a Frank Frank? Tasty Homograph Riddles. Maestro, Giulio. LC 84-5021. 64p. (gr. 2-5). 1984. 13. 95 (0-89919-297-1, Clarion Bks); pap. 5.95 (0-89919-317-X, Clarion Bks) HM.
—What's Mite Might? Homophone Riddles to Boost Your Word Power! Maestro, Giulio. LC 86-2665. 64p. (gr. 2-5). 1986. 11.95 (0-89919-434-6, Clarion Bks); pap. 4.95 (0-89919-435-4, Clarion Bks) HM.
—Where Is My Friend? A Word Concept Book. Maestro, Betsy. LC 75-15902. 32p. (ps-1). 1986. PLB 12.95 (0-517-52436-8) Crown Bks Yng Read.
—Your Foot's on My Feet: And Other Tricky Nouns. Terban, Marvin. LC 85-19561. (gr. 2-5). 1986. pap. 11.95 (0-89919-411-7, Clarion Bks); pap. 4.95 (0-89919-413-3, Clarion Bks) HM.
Maestro, Giulio, jt. illus. see Maestro, Betsy.
Maestro, Guilio. The Discovery of the Americas Activities Book. Maestro, Betsy. Bodnar, Judit Z., ed. 92p. (gr. 1-6). 1992. pap. 7.95 (0-688-08590-3) Lothrop.
—It Figures! Fun Figures of Speech. Terban, Marvin. LC 92-35529. 1993. 13.95 (0-395-61584-4, Clarion Bks) HM.
Maez, Frances. Come See What God Made. Maez, Frances. 16p. (gr. k). 1991. pap. text ed. 3.95 (1-880047-02-0) Creative Des.
Magagna, Anna M. & Jambor, Louis. Little Women. Alcott, Louisa May. (gr. 4-6). 1981. (G&D); deluxe ed. 15.95 (0-448-06019-1) Putnam Pub Group.
Magaril, Mikhail. The Feather Merchants & Other Tales of the Fools of Chelm. Sanfield, Steve. LC 90-29273. 112p. (gr. 3 up). 1991. 15.99 (0-531-05958-8); RLB 15.99 (0-531-08558-9) Orchard Bks Watts.

—The Feather Merchants & Other Tales of the Fools of Chelm. Sanfield, Steve. LC 92-43767. 96p. (gr. 5 up). 1993. pap. 3.95 (0-688-12568-9, Pub. by Beech Tree Bks) Morrow.
Magellan, Mauro. Cambio Chameleon. Magellan, Mauro. LC 89-19995. 32p. 1990. 12.95 (0-89334-118-5) Humanics Ltd.
—Home at Last. Magellan, Mauro. LC 89-19994. 32p. 1989. 12.95 (0-89334-119-3) Humanics Ltd.
—Max, the Apartment Cat. Magellan, Mauro. LC 88-32067. 32p. 1989. 12.95 (0-89334-117-7) Humanics Ltd.
—Son of an Earl...Sold for a Slave. Weems, David B. LC 92-27917. 112p. (gr. 5 up). 1992. 11.95 (0-88289-921-X) Pelican.
—The South Carolina Lizard Man. Rhyne, Nancy. LC 92-17289. 128p. (gr. 5-9). 1992. pap. 7.95 (0-88289-907-4) Pelican.
Magers, Pat. Sing with Me Animal Songs. (ps-1). 1987. incl. cassette 5.95 (0-394-88809-X) Random Bks Yng Read.
Magill, Ann. Jessie's Journey. McAllister, Angela. LC 92-313. 32p. (ps-3). 1992. SBE 13.95 (0-02-765366-8, Macmillan Child Bk) Macmillan Child Grp.
Magine, John. Birthday Surprise. Sabin, Louis. LC 81-2632. 32p. (gr. k-2). 1981. PLB 11.59 (0-89375-527-3); pap. text ed. 2.95 (0-89375-528-1) Troll Assocs.
—Christmas Surprise. Gordon, Sharon. 32p. (gr. k-2). 1980. PLB 7.89 (0-89375-373-4); pap. 1.95 (0-89375-273-8) Troll Assocs.
—Friendly Snowman. Gordon, Sharon. 32p. (gr. k-2). 1980. PLB 7.89 (0-89375-377-7); pap. 1.95 (0-89375-277-0) Troll Assocs.
—Magic Monsters Learn about Safety. Tester, Sylvia R. LC 78-24365. (ps-3). 1979. PLB 21.35 (0-89565-060-6); PLB 14.95s.p. (0-685-57683-3) Childs World.
Magine, Sharon. Easter Bunny's Lost Egg. Gordon, Sharon. 32p. (gr. k-2). 1980. PLB 7.89 (0-89375-375-0); pap. 1.95 (0-89375-275-4) Troll Assocs.
Magnus, Erica. Around Me. Magnus, Erica. Pearson, Susan, ed. LC 90-26459. 32p. (ps-3). 1992. 13.00 (0-688-09756-1); PLB 12.93 (0-688-09753-7) Lothrop.
Magnuson, Diana. Anatosaurus. Riehecky, Janet. 32p. (gr. k-4). 1989. PLB 21.35 (0-89565-545-4); PLB 14. 95s.p. (0-685-56086-4) Childs World.
—Animal Camouflage: Hide & Seek Animals. McDonnell, Janet. LC 89-28083. 32p. (ps-2). 1990. PLB 21.35 (0-89565-562-4); PLB 14.95s.p. (0-685-56183-6) Childs World.
—Ankylosaurus. Riehecky, Janet. 32p. (gr. k-4). 1990. PLB 21.35 (0-89565-621-3); PLB 14.95s.p. (0-685-58728-2) Childs World.
—Bigfoot. Odor, Ruth S. LC 88-7882. 100p. (gr. 3-7). 1989. PLB 21.35 (0-89565-455-5); PLB 14.95s.p. (0-685-55994-7) Childs World.
—Dinosaur Jokes. Alden, Laura, compiled by. LC 88-17489. 48p. (gr. 1-5). 1988. lib. bdg. 13.27 (0-516-01865-5); pap. 3.95 (0-516-41865-3) Childrens.
—Dinosaur Relatives. Riehecky, Janet. 32p. (gr. k-4). 1990. PLB 21.35 (0-89565-626-4); PLB 14.95s.p. (0-685-56211-5) Childs World.
—Dream Rooms, Decorating with Flair. Sherrow, Victoria. LC 90-48241. 128p. (gr. 5-9). 1991. lib. bdg. 10.89 (0-8167-2293-5); pap. text ed. 2.95 (0-8167-2294-3) Troll Assocs.
—Great Parties, How to Plan Them. Wallach, Susan. LC 90-46879. 128p. (gr. 5-9). 1991. PLB 10.89 (0-8167-2291-9); pap. text ed. 2.95 (0-8167-2292-7) Troll Assocs.
—How to Make & Keep Friends. Karlsberg, Elizabeth. LC 90-48252. 128p. (gr. 5-9). 1991. lib. bdg. 10.89 (0-8167-2295-1); pap. text ed. 2.95 (0-8167-2296-X) Troll Assocs.
—Iguanodon. Riehecky, Janet. LC 89-15850. 32p. (gr. k-4). 1989. PLB 21.35 (0-89565-544-6); PLB 14.95s.p. (0-685-56087-2) Childs World.
—It's up to Me! Nelson, JoAnne. LC 93-9349. 1994. 5.95 (0-935529-63-2) Comprehen Health Educ.
—Jokes & More Jokes. Ziegler, Sandra K. LC 82-19742. 48p. (gr. 1-5). 1983. PLB 13.27 (0-516-01871-X) Childrens.
—Knock-Knocks, Limericks, & Other Silly Sayings. Ziegler, Sandra K. LC 82-19764. 48p. (gr. 1-5). 1983. pap. 3.95 (0-516-41872-6) Childrens.
—The Land of No. Anderson, Jill. Blackwelder, Kathy, ed. LC 87-51628. 40p. (gr. 1-4). 1990. PLB 14.95 (0-9608284-5-1) Timberline Pr.
—Magic Monsters Look for Colors. Moncure, Jane B. LC 78-23792. (ps-3). 1979. PLB 21.35 (0-89565-056-8); PLB 14.95s.p. (0-685-55502-X) Childs World.
—Magic Monsters Look for Shapes. Moncure, Jane B. LC 78-21529. (ps-3). 1979. PLB 21.35 (0-89565-057-6); PLB 14.95s.p. (0-685-55503-8) Childs World.
—Maiasaura. Riehecky, Janet. LC 89-22076. 32p. (gr. k-4). 1989. PLB 21.35 (0-89565-543-8); PLB 14.95s.p. (0-685-56085-6) Childs World.
—Megalosaurus. Alden, Laura. 32p. (gr. k-4). 1990. PLB 21.35 (0-89565-629-9); PLB 14.95s.p. (0-685-56214-X) Childs World.
—Oviraptor. Riehecky, Janet. 32p. (gr. k-4). 1990. PLB 21.35 (0-89565-631-0); PLB 14.95s.p. (0-685-56216-6) Childs World.

—Protoceratops. Riehecky, Janet. 32p. (gr. k-4). 1990. PLB 21.35 (0-89565-634-5); PLB 14.95s.p. (0-685-56219-0) Childs World.
—Riddles & More Riddles. Shannon, J. Michael. LC 82-19765. 48p. (gr. 1-5). 1983. PLB 13.27 (0-516-01873-6); pap. 3.95 (0-516-41873-4) Childrens.
—Stegosaurus. Riehecky, Janet. LC 88-15347. 32p. (gr. k-4). 1988. PLB 21.35 (0-89565-385-0); PLB 14.95s.p. (0-685-67670-6) Childs World.
—Still More Jokes. Shannon, J. Michael. LC 85-27971. 48p. (gr. 1-5). 1986. lib. bdg. 13.27 (0-516-01867-1); pap. 3.95 (0-516-41867-X) Childrens.
—Still More Riddles. Shannon, J. Michael. LC 85-29065. 48p. (gr. 1-5). 1986. pap. 3.95 (0-516-41869-6) Childrens.
—Triceratops. Riehecky, Janet. LC 88-508. 32p. (gr. k-4). 1988. PLB 21.35 (0-89565-422-9); PLB 14.95s.p. (0-685-55938-6) Childs World.
—Walrus' Adventure in Alphabet Town. Riehecky, Janet. LC 92-1330. 32p. (ps-2). 1992. PLB 14.60 (0-516-05423-6) Childrens.
—What Is a Monster? Tester, Sylvia R. LC 78-23642. (ps-3). 1979. PLB 21.35 (0-89565-055-X); PLB 14. 95s.p. (0-685-55558-5) Childs World.
Magnuson, Diana L. Tyrannosaurus. Riehecky, Janet. LC 88-1692. 32p. (gr. k-4). 1988. PLB 21.35 (0-89565-424-5); PLB 14.95s.p. (0-685-55939-4) Childs World.
Maguire, Kerry. Of Things Natural, Wild, & Free: A Story about Aldo Leopold. Lorbiecki, Marybeth. LC 92-44049. 1993. 14.95 (0-87614-797-X) Carolrhoda Bks.
Magurn, Susan. Singing Sam. Bulla, Clyde R. LC 88-19758. 48p. (Orig.). (gr. 1-3). 1989. PLB 7.99 (0-394-91977-7); pap. 3.50 (0-394-81977-2) Random Bks Yng Read.
—The Winning of Miss Lynn Ryan. Cooper, Ilene. LC 87-15233. 128p. (gr. 3-6). 1987. 11.95 (0-688-07231-3) Morrow Jr Bks.
Mah, Ronald. Predator Prey Puppets & Toys: Eight Paper Animal Projects to Make. Mah, Ronald. 32p. (ps-3). 1986. pap. 3.95 (0-9615903-1-9) Symbiosis Bks.
Mahan, Ben. Addition. Silliman, Emery & Jonson, Liz. Nayer, Judith E., ed. 32p. (gr. k-1). 1991. wkbk. 1.95 (1-878624-57-1) McClanahan Bk.
—Addition. 6p. (gr. k-1). 1992. bds. 3.95 (1-56293-183-0) McClanahan Bk.
—All Around. 12p. (ps-k). 1993. bds. 2.50 (1-56293-316-7) McClanahan Bk.
—Busy Bunnies. Caitlin, Stephen. LC 87-10912. 32p. (gr. k-2). 1988. PLB 11.59 (0-8167-1083-X); pap. text ed. 2.95 (0-8167-1084-8) Troll Assocs.
—Counting. 12p. (ps-k). 1993. bds. 2.50 (1-56293-313-2) McClanahan Bk.
—Felix, the Funny Fox. Michaels, Ski. LC 85-14097. 48p. (Orig.). (gr. 1-3). 1986. PLB 10.59 (0-8167-0590-9); pap. text ed. 3.50 (0-8167-0591-7) Troll Assocs.
—Homer the Beachcomber. Craig, Janet. LC 87-10913. 32p. (gr. k-2). 1988. PLB 11.59 (0-8167-1085-6); pap. text ed. 2.95 (0-8167-1086-4) Troll Assocs.
—The Land of Peek-A-Boo. Rosenbluth, Rosalyn. 24p. (ps-2). 1993. pap. text ed. 0.99 (1-56293-344-2) McClanahan Bk.
—Little Bits. 12p. (ps-k). 1993. bds. 2.50 (1-56293-315-9) McClanahan Bk.
—Maxie the Mutt. Peters, Sharon. LC 87-10914. 32p. (gr. k-2). 1988. PLB 11.59 (0-8167-1087-2); pap. text ed. 2.95 (0-8167-1088-0) Troll Assocs.
—My ABC's Uppercase. Wise, Beth A. Nayer, Judith E., ed. 32p. (ps). 1991. wkbk. 1.95 (1-56293-165-2) McClanahan Bk.
—My Wet Hen. Rutman, Shereen. 16p. (ps). 1993. wkbk. 2.25 (1-56293-324-8) McClanahan Bk.
—One-Minute Favorite Fairy Tales. Lewis, Shari. LC 84-25968. 48p. (ps-3). 1985. pap. 8.95 (0-385-19322-X) Doubleday.
—Peanut Butter, Apple Butter, Cinnamon Toast: Food Riddles for You to Guess. Palacios, Argentina. 24p. (ps-2). 1990. PLB 14.60 (0-8172-3584-1); PLB 10.95 pkg. of 3 (0-685-58553-0) Raintree Steck-V.
—See a Circle. 10p. (ps-k). 1992. bds. 1.95 (1-56293-206-3) McClanahan Bk.
—See a Square. 10p. (ps-k). 1992. bds. 1.95 (1-56293-207-1) McClanahan Bk.
—See a Star. 10p. (ps-k). 1992. bds. 1.95 (1-56293-208-X) McClanahan Bk.
—See a Triangle. 10p. (ps-k). 1992. bds. 1.95 (1-56293-209-8) McClanahan Bk.
—Shapes. 12p. (ps-k). 1993. bds. 2.50 (1-56293-314-0) McClanahan Bk.
—The Thin Pig. Rutman, Shereen. 16p. (ps). 1993. wkbk. 2.25 (1-56293-325-6) McClanahan Bk.
—Tricky Alex. Matthews, Morgan. LC 85-14018. 48p. (Orig.). (gr. 1-3). 1986. PLB 10.59 (0-8167-0598-4); pap. text ed. 3.50 (0-8167-0599-2) Troll Assocs.
Mahan, Benton. Goldilocks & the Three Bears. LC 80-27631. 32p. (gr. k-2). 1981. PLB 9.79 (0-89375-470-6); pap. text ed. 1.95 (0-89375-471-4) Troll Assocs.
—Little Red Riding Hood. Grimm, Jacob & Grimm, Wilhelm K. LC 80-27684. 32p. (gr. k-3). 1981. PLB 9.79 (0-89375-488-9); pap. 1.95 (0-89375-489-7) Troll Assocs.
—My Play a Tune Book: Twelve Favorite Bible Songs. Wilson, Etta, ed. 26p. (ps up). 1988. 12.95 (0-687-27554-7) JTG Nashville.

—Pecos Bill, the Roughest, Toughest Best. Jensen, Patricia A. LC 93-2217. 32p. (gr. k-2). 1993. PLB 11. 59 (0-8167-3165-9); pap. text ed. 2.95 (0-8167-3166-7) Troll Assocs.

Mahler, Joseph. The Itch Book. Dragonwagon, Crescent. LC 89-2695. 32p. (gr. k-3). 1990. RSBE 13.95 (0-02-733121-0). Macmillan Child Bk) Macmillan Child Grp.

Mahoney, Ellen. Button Tales: Fluffy Gets Dressed. Mahoney, Ellen. 8p. (ps). 1993. 6.99 (0-8431-3543-3) Price Stern.

—Pocketales: In My Pocket. Mahoney, Ellen. 8p. (ps). 1993. 6.99 (0-8431-3544-1) Price Stern.

Mahoney, Ellen V. Animals. Mahoney, Ellen V. 8p. (ps). 1993. vinyl 4.99 (0-8431-3545-X) Price Stern.

—Food. Mahoney, Ellen V. 8p. (ps). 1993. vinyl 4.99 (0-8431-3546-8) Price Stern.

—The Sea. Mahoney, Ellen V. 8p. (ps). 1993. vinyl 4.99 (0-8431-3547-6) Price Stern.

—Toys. Mahoney, Ellen V. 8p. (ps). 1993. vinyl 4.99 (0-8431-3548-4) Price Stern.

Mahy, Margaret. Bubble Trouble: And Other Poems & Stories. Mahy, Margaret. LC 92-3540. 80p. (gr. 3-7). 1992. SBE 13.95 (0-689-50557-4, M K McElderry) Macmillan Child Grp.

Maidenberg, E. Den Meda: Annie's Day. Vahnina, Galya. (RUS.). (Illus.). 1987. pap. 14.95 (0-934393-16-8) Rector Pr.

Maidoff, Jules. Hatznea Lechet: Walk Humbly. Shumsky, Abraham & Shumsky, Adaia. Spiro, Jack D., ed. (gr. 4). 1971. text ed. 6.00 (0-8074-0181-1, 405307); tchrs'. guide 3.50 (0-8074-0182-X, 205308); wkbk. 6.00 (0-8074-0183-8, 405306) UAHC.

Main, Katy. Baby Animals of the North. Main, Katy. 36p. (ps-k). 1992. bds. 12.95 (0-88240-395-8) Alaska Northwest.

Mair, Jacqui. Merry-Go-Round. Philip, Ned, compiled by. LC 93-32620. (gr. 2 up). 1994. write for info. (0-688-13367-3) Lothrop.

Maitland, Anthony. The Ghost of Thomas Kempe. Lively, Penelope. LC 73-77456. 192p. (gr. 3-6). 1973. 14.95 (0-525-30495-9, DCB) Dutton Child Bks.

Majesty, Paul. Creative Child Care: You Can Make a Difference. Spaulding, Janet. 140p. (Orig.). 1992. pap. 18.00 spiral bdg. (0-9634214-0-9) MARV Pubns.
CREATIVE CHILD CARE: YOU CAN MAKE A DIFFERENCE was written for moms who are home with their young children & for people with home child-care businesses. This book was created to give ideas about various activities to help keep children away from the television. At the same time it offers over 150 activities with step-by-step instructions to stimulate young minds. There are guidelines for discipline, social skills, coping with children's fears & lies, potty training, safety precautions, how to make homemade baby food, ways to deal with infant colic, giving children choices, & dealing with various age levels. The book has sample certificates, a health chart, behavior chart, curriculum, & contracts. The author has included suggestions on how to use the newest terminology in order to replace phrases such as, 'Good Boy', 'Be Careful' etc. The new terminology helps instill positive self-esteem & promotes higher level thinking skills. To order contact: MARV Publications, 402A West Taylor Ave. Ste. 183, Round Rock, TX 78664.
Publisher Provided Annotation.

Majewski, Chuck. The Tator Tales: A Guide to Substance Abuse Prevention for Youth & Adults. Gibson, Christine R. & Hargrave, J. Michael. (Orig.). (gr. 4-8). 1989. write for info. Tator Enterprises.

—The Tator Tales: A Story & Activity Book on Handling Peer Pressure. Gibson, Christine R. & Hargrave, J. Michael. 51p. (gr. 3-5). 1988. pap. 6.95 (0-9624285-0-7) Tator Enterprises.

—The Tator Tales: Cool Spuds Avoid Drugs, a Story & Activity Book on Substance Abuse Prevention. Hargrave, J. Michael & Gibson, Christine R. 96p. (Orig.). (gr. 4-8). 1990. pap. 8.95 (0-9624285-1-5) Tator Enterprises.

Majewski, Dawn & Cozzolino, Sandra. King Midas. Newby, Robert. 64p. (gr. 1-6). 1990. PLB 15.95 (1-878363-25-5) Forest Hse.

—King Midas: With Selected Sentences in American Sign Language. Newby, Robert. LC 90-4908. 64p. (gr. 1-5). 1990. 14.95 (0-930323-75-0, Pub. by K Green Pubns); incl. video 38.20 (0-930323-77-7, Pub. by K Green Pubns); video 29.95 (0-930323-71-8) Gallaudet Univ Pr.

Majewski, Maria. A Friend for Oscar Mouse. Majewski, Joe. LC 87-5365. 32p. (ps-2). 1991. pap. 3.99 (0-8037-0913-7, Dial Pied Piper) Puffin Bks.

Mak, Kam. The Moon of the Monarch Butterflies. George, Jean C. LC 91-33152. 48p. (gr. 3-7). 1993. 15.00 (0-06-020816-3); PLB 14.89 (0-06-020817-1) HarpC Child Bks.

—The Year of the Panda. Schlein, Miriam. LC 89-71307. 96p. (gr. 3-7). 1990. (Crowell Jr Bks); PLB 13.89 (0-690-04866-1, Crowell Jr Bks) HarpC Child Bks.

—The Year of the Panda. Schlein, Miriam. LC 89-71307. 96p. (gr. 2-5). 1992. pap. 3.95 (0-06-440366-1, Trophy) HarpC Child Bks.

Makarov, Igor. Romeo & Juliet. Garfield, Leon, abridged by. LC 92-14523. 48p. (gr. 5 up). 1993. PLB 11.99 (0-679-93874-5); pap. 6.99 (0-679-83874-0) Knopf Bks Yng Read.

Makela, Constance E. Iron Mining Fun Book for Children: Featuring Orville Ore. Makela, Constance E. 44p. (Orig.). (gr. k-6). 1982. pap. 2.00x (0-9608686-0-7) Happy Thoughts & Rainbow.

Male, Alan. Insects & Other Small Creatures. Althea. LC 89-20307. 32p. (gr. k-6). 1990. PLB 11.59 (0-8167-1961-6); pap. text ed. 3.95 (0-8167-1962-4) Troll Assocs.

—Spider. Chinery, Michael. Watts, Barrie, photos by. LC 90-10941. 32p. (gr. 4-6). 1991. lib. bdg. 11.59 (0-8167-2108-4); pap. text ed. 3.95 (0-8167-2109-2) Troll Assocs.

Male, Alan, jt. illus. see Loates, Mick.

Malecki, Maryann. Mom & Dad & I Are Having a Baby! Malecki, Maryann. LC 82-81707. 70p. (Orig.). (ps-3). 1982. pap. 6.95 (0-937604-03-8) Pennypress.

Maley, Matthew & Benjamin, Ann. Proud That I'm Still Me. Messina, Kathlyn & Dacquino, Vinny. LC 92-70002. 21p. (Orig.). (ps-5). 1992. pap. 7.95 shrinkwrapped (0-910569-05-3) Hampton Court Pub.

Malin, Edward. Ah Mo: Indian Legends from Washington State. Griffin, Arthur E., ed. 75p. (Orig.). (gr. 2-5). 1989. pap. write for info. Bainbridge Pr.

—The Legend of Tom Pepper & Other Stories. Griffin, Arthur E., ed. 100p. (Orig.). (gr. 2-5). 1989. pap. write for info. Bainbridge Pr.

—Spelyi & Other Indian Legends. Griffin, Arthur E., ed. (gr. 2-5). 1989. write for info. Bainbridge Pr.

Malley, Sarah H. Observa-Story: Portland to Cut & Color. Lightbody, Nancy K. & Malley, Sarah H. LC 76-54460. (gr. 1-4). 1976. pap. 1.25 (0-9600612-5-8) Greater Portland.

Mallord, Lauri. Princess Pickle Head. Dreizler, Loch A. LC 88-80123. 42p. (Orig.). (ps-4). 1988. pap. 2.95 (0-9620053-0-4) LAD Redondo Beach.

Mallout, Christine. The Earth. Pearce, Q. L. 48p. (ps-2). 1991. wkbk. 2.95 (0-8431-2913-1) Price Stern.

Malone, Nola L. Earrings! Viorst, Judith. LC 89-17846. 32p. (gr. 1-4). 1990. SBE 13.95 (0-689-31615-1, Atheneum Child Bk) Macmillan Child Grp.

—Earrings! Viorst, Judith. LC 92-42984. 32p. (gr. 1-5). 1993. pap. 4.95 (0-689-71669-9, Aladdin) Macmillan Child Grp.

—King of the Playground. Naylor, Phyllis R. 32p. (ps-3). 1991. SBE 13.95 (0-689-31558-9, Atheneum Child Bk) Macmillan Child Grp.

—The King of the Playground. Naylor, Phyllis R. LC 93-25125. 32p. (gr. k-3). 1994. pap. 4.95 (0-689-71802-0, Aladdin) Macmillan Child Grp.

—Pot Luck. Tobias, Tobi. LC 92-27678. 1993. write for info. (0-688-09824-X) Lothrop.

—A Small, Elderly Dragon. Keller, Beverly. LC 83-13632. 144p. (gr. 5 up). 1984. 12.95 (0-688-02553-6) Lothrop.

Maloney, M. & Fleming, S. El Tesoro de Azulin (Blue Bug's Treasure) Poulet, Virginia. LC 75-40352. (SPA.). 32p. (ps-2). 1988. pap. 3.95 (0-516-53424-6) Childrens.

Maloney, Mary & Fleming, Stan. Blue Bug Finds a Friend. Poulet, Virginia. LC 76-30369. 32p. (ps-3). 1977. PLB 15.00 (0-516-03426-X) Childrens.

—Blue Bug's Surprise. Poulet, Virginia. LC 76-50670. 32p. (gr. k-3). 1977. PLB 15.00 (0-516-03427-8) Childrens.

Maloney, Mary, jt. illus. see Fleming, Stan.

Malowicky, Sinai. A Basic Guide to the Mishkan. rev. ed. Teitelbaum, Eli. Malowicky, Sinai. ed. 16p. (gr. 7-12). 1992. pap. text ed. write for info. (1-878895-01-X, A320) Torah Umesorah.

Malvern, Corinne. Doctor Dan the Bandage Man. reissued ed. Gaspard, Helen. 24p. (ps-k). 1992. write for info. (0-307-00142-3, 312-07, Golden Pr) Western Pub.

Malzeke-McDonald, Karen. Barney's Farm Animals. Kearns, Kimberly & O'Brien, Marie. Hartley, Linda, ed. 24p. (ps). 1993. 3.95 (0-7829-0370-3) Barney Pub.

Manchee, Bruce N. I'm Rattle-Me-Bones III, Esquire. Metoyer, Patrick G. LC 87-90349. 24p. (Orig.). (gr. 1-6). 1988. pap. 3.95 (0-944523-02-1) Western Slope Pubns.

—No Bones! No Bones! Metoyer, Patrick G. LC 87-90350. 24p. (gr. k-2). 1988. pap. 3.95 (0-944523-03-X) Western Slope Pubns.

Mancini, Rob. Bad Dog, George! George, Sally. LC 92-34258. 1993. 4.25 (0-383-03616-X) SRA Schl Grp.

—Hello, Puppet. King, Virginia. LC 92-21392. 1993. 2.50 (0-383-03572-4) SRA Schl Grp.

—Over the Marble Mountain. Beveridge, Barbara. LC 92-27097. (gr. 4 up). 1993. 2.50 (0-383-03589-9) SRA Schl Grp.

—Putting on a Concert: The Television News. Hall, Roger. LC 92-24557. (gr. 4 up). 1994. 4.25 (0-383-03770-0) SRA Schl Grp.

Mandel, Harris. A Chanukah Story for Night Number Three. Rosenfeld, Dina. Pape, David S., ed. 32p. (ps-1). 1989. 9.95 (0-922613-16-8); pap. 7.95 (0-922613-17-6) Hachai Pubns.

Mandel, Jille. All Feelings Are Ok - It's What You Do with Them That Counts. Shapiro, Lawrence E. Shose, Hennie M., ed. 100p. (Orig.). (gr. k-4). 1993. 14.95 (1-882732-04-9) Ctr Applied Psy.

Mandel, Suzy. Dr. Cat. Ziefert, Harriet. LC 88-62152. 32p. (ps-3). 1989. pap. 3.50 (0-14-050985-2, Puffin) Puffin Bks.

—Make Your Own Calendar, 1994. Mandel, Suzy. (gr. 1-5). 1993. 5.95 (0-316-54559-7) Little.

—Tim & Jim Take Off. Ziefert, Harriet. 32p. (ps-3). 1990. pap. 3.50 (0-14-054222-1, Puffin) Puffin Bks.

—Under the Water. Ziefert, Harriet. 32p. (ps-3). 1990. pap. 3.50 (0-14-054221-3, Puffin) Puffin Bks.

—Under the Water. Ziefert, Harriet. 32p. (gr. k-3). 1993. pap. 3.25 (0-14-036535-4, Puffin) Puffin Bks.

Manderfield, Diane. George Washington: Man of Courage & Prayer. Camp, Norma C. LC 76-3084. (gr. 3-6). 1977. pap. 6.95 (0-915134-25-X) Mott Media.

Mangelsen, Thomas D., photos by. Fall. Hirschi, Ron. LC 90-19595. 32p. (ps-3). 1991. 14.00 (0-525-65053-9, Cobblehill Bks) Dutton Child Bks.

—Summer. Hirschi, Ron. LC 90-19596. 32p. (ps-3). 1991. 13.95 (0-525-65054-7, Cobblehill Bks) Dutton Child Bks.

—A Time for Babies. Hirschi, Ron. LC 92-21409. 32p. (ps-3). 1993. 13.99 (0-525-65095-4, Cobblehill Bks) Dutton Child Bks.

—A Time for Sleeping. Hirschi, Ron. LC 92-21408. 32p. (ps-3). 1993. 13.99 (0-525-65128-4, Cobblehill Bks) Dutton Child Bks.

Mangelsen, Tom, photos by. The Eagle & the River. Craighead, Charles. LC 92-23240. (gr. 1-5). 1994. RSBE 14.95 (0-02-762265-7, Macmillan Child Bk) Macmillan Child Grp.

Mangiat, Jeff. Fright Party. Zindel, Paul. (gr. 4-7). 1993. pap. 3.50 (0-553-48082-0) Bantam.

Mangold, Paul. Tracks in the Snow. Horneck, Heribert. Young, Richard G., ed. LC 89-11890. 24p. (gr. 1-3). 1989. PLB 14.60 (0-944483-53-4) Garrett Ed Corp.

Manierre, Betsy. When the Zebras Came for Lunch. Van Curen, Barbara. 64p. (ps-2). 1989. pap. text ed. 5.95 (0-922510-01-6) Lucky Bks.

Maniscalco, Joe. Daniel & the Big Cats: Level One. Linde, Lavaun & Quishenberry, Mary. 32p. (gr. 1). 1986. pap. text ed. 4.99 (0-945107-04-8) Bradshaw Pubs.

—God Adds Oil: Level Two. Linde, Lavaun & Quishenberry, Mary. 32p. (Orig.). (gr. 1). 1988. pap. text ed. 4.99 (0-945107-05-6) Bradshaw Pubs.

—I Will Help: Level One. Linde, Lavaun & Quishenberry, Mary. 32p. (Orig.). (gr. 1). 1986. pap. text ed. 4.99 (0-945107-01-3) Bradshaw Pubs.

—Jonah's Ride: Level Two. Linde, Lavaun & Quishenberry, Mary. 32p. (Orig.). (gr. 1). 1988. pap. text ed. 4.99 (0-945107-09-9) Bradshaw Pubs.

—The Lad's Bag: Level One. Linde, Lavaun & Quishenberry, Mary. 32p. (gr. 1). 1986. pap. text ed. 4.99 (0-945107-03-X) Bradshaw Pubs.

—Mom & the Lad: Level One. Linde, Lavaun & Quishenberry, Mary. 32p. (gr. 1). 1986. pap. text ed. 4.99 (0-945107-02-1) Bradshaw Pubs.

—Not a Bed: Level One. Linde, Lavaun & Quishenberry, Mary. 32p. (gr. 1). 1986. pap. text ed. 4.99 (0-945107-00-5) Bradshaw Pubs.

—Seven Dips: Level Two. Linde, Lavaun & Quishenberry, Mary. 32p. (Orig.). (gr. 1). 1988. pap. text ed. 4.99 (0-945107-08-0) Bradshaw Pubs.

—Three Brave Men: Level Two. Linde, Lavaun & Quishenberry, Mary. 32p. (Orig.). (gr. 1). 1988. pap. text ed. 4.99 (0-945107-07-2) Bradshaw Pubs.

—Zacchaeus' Cash Bag: Level Two. Linde, Lavaun & Quishenberry, Mary. 32p. (Orig.). (gr. 1). 1988. pap. text ed. 4.99 (0-945107-06-4) Bradshaw Pubs.

Mann, Brenda. A Cote of Many Colors. Oke, Janette. 128p. (Orig.). (gr. 3 up). 1987. pap. 4.99 (0-934998-27-2) Bethel Pub.

—Ducktails. Oke, Janette. 132p. (gr. 3 up). 1985. pap. 4.99 (0-934998-20-5) Bethel Pub.

—The Impatient Turtle. Oke, Janette. Peterson, Pete, ed. 110p. (Orig.). (gr. 3-6). 1986. pap. 4.99 (0-934998-24-8) Bethel Pub.

—Maury Had a Little Lamb. Oke, Janette. 137p. (Orig.). (gr. 3 up). 1989. pap. 4.99 (0-934998-34-5) Bethel Pub.

—New Kid in Town. Oke, Janette. 125p. (Orig.). (gr. 3 up). 1983. pap. 4.99 (0-934998-16-7) Bethel Pub.

—Pordy's Prickly Problem. Oke, Janette. 1993. pap. 4.99 (0-934998-50-7) Bethel Pub.

—Prairie Dog Town. Oke, Janette. 140p. (gr. 3 up). 1988. pap. 4.99 (0-934998-31-0) Bethel Pub.

—This Little Pig. Oke, Janette. 145p. (Orig.). (gr. 1-6). 1991. pap. 4.99 (0-934998-43-4) Bethel Pub.

—Trouble in a Fur Coat. Oke, Janette. 152p. (Orig.). (gr. 1-6). 1990. pap. 4.99 (0-934998-38-8) Bethel Pub.

Mann, Marek. Annie's City Adventures. Mann, Marek. Max, Jill, ed. Verlag, Mangold, tr. from GER. LC 91-21302. 24p. (gr. k-3). 1991. PLB 14.60 (*1-56074-031-0*) Garrett Ed Corp.
—Annie's High Sea Adventure. Mann, Marek. Max, Jill & Bradford, Elizabeth, eds. Verlag, Mangold, tr. from GER. LC 91-21305. 24p. (gr. k-3). 1991. PLB 14.60 (*1-56074-027-2*) Garrett Ed Corp.
—Dino, the Star Keeper. Mann, Marek. Max, Jill, ed. Verlag, Mangold, tr. from GER. LC 91-21304. 24p. (gr. k-3). 1991. PLB 14.60 (*1-56074-028-0*) Garrett Ed Corp.
Mann, Paul. Boys Who Became Prophets. Cory, Lynda. LC 92-29812. 1992. 8.95 (*0-87579-664-8*) Deseret Bk.
Mannerberg, Patricia A. More Literature Puzzles for Elementary & Middle Schools. Veitch, Carol J. & Crawford, Jane. LC 86-7161. xiii, 90p. (gr. 1-7). 1986. pap. text ed. 15.50 (*0-87287-518-0*) Libs Unl.
Mannetti, William. Dinosaurs in Your Backyard. Mannetti, William. LC 81-7998. 160p. (gr. 4-7). 1982. SBE 13.95 (*0-689-30906-6*, Atheneum Child Bk) Macmillan Child Grp.
Manning, Garrian. This Is Rhythm. Jenkins, Ella. 1993. pap. 14.95 (*1-881322-02-5*) Sing Out Corp.
Manning, Janet. Does That Goal Count? Rowan, Barbara C. LC 89-61850. 23p. (Orig.). (gr. 4-7). 1989. pap. 4.50 (*9-9622863-1-1*) Bristlecone Pubns.
Manning, Maurie J. The Night Before Christmas Hidden Picture Book. Moore, Clement C. 32p. 1992. bds. 7.95 (*1-56397-116-X*) Boyds Mills Pr.
Manning, Mick. Think of a Beaver. Wallace, Karen. LC 92-53132. 32p. (gr. k-4). 1993. 14.95 (*1-56402-179-3*) Candlewick Pr.
Mannino, Angelica L. La Cola Magico De Marjorie. Mannino, Marc P. & Mannino, Angelica L. Norman-Grumbley, Patricia, tr. from ENG. LC 93-86116. (SPA.). 32p. (Orig.). (gr. k-3). 1993. pap. 7.95 (*0-9638340-1-0*) Sugar Sand.
Manry, Douglas. The Land the Cleves Built. Manry, Douglas. Sloan, Stephen, ed. 32p. (gr. 2-5). 1989. write for info. (*0-9622316-0-6*) Sloan Manry Pubs.
Mansell, Dom. Creepy Crawlies. Thomson, Ruth. LC 91-7482. 32p. (gr. k-3). 1991. pap. 5.95 (*0-689-71489-0*, Aladdin) Macmillan Child Grp.
—My Old Teddy. Mansell, Dom. LC 91-71830. 32p. (ps). 1992. 12.95 (*1-56402-035-5*) Candlewick Pr.
—The Selfish Giant. Wilde, Oscar. LC 86-9356. 32p. (gr. 1-4). 1986. 10.95 (*0-13-803586-5*) P-H.
—The Selfish Giant. Wilde, Oscar. 1986. pap. 10.95 (*0-671-66847-1*) S&S Trade.
Mansfield, Carol. A Handful of Colors. Schwartz, Jeanne. 32p. 1981. 4.25 (*0-9604538-2-2*) CBH Pub.
Mansfield, Renee. Thomas Knew There Were Pirates Living in the Bathroom. Parker, Beth. 28p. (ps-3). 1990. (*0-88753-224-1*, Pub. by Black Moss Pr CN); pap. 4.95 (*0-88753-201-2*, Pub. by Black Moss Pr CN) Firefly Bks Ltd.
Mansfield, Renee & Pawczuk, Eugene. Fun with Fitness. Roberts, Alison J. Hayes, Dympna, ed. 32p. (gr. 2). 1987. PLB 14.97 (*0-88625-167-2*); pap. 2.95 (*0-88625-157-5*) Durkin Hayes Pub.
Manso, Leo. St. Isaac & the Indians. 2nd, rev. ed. Lomask, Milton. LC 90-85767. 170p. (gr. 6-8). 1991. pap. 9.95 (*0-89870-355-7*) Ignatius Pr.
Manson, Christopher. The Crab Prince. Manson, Christopher. LC 90-26626. 32p. (gr. k-3). 1991. 14.95 (*0-8050-1215-X*, Bks Young Read) H Holt & Co.
—A Farmyard Song. Manson, Christopher. LC 91-46238. 32p. (gr. k). 1992. 14.95 (*1-55858-169-3*); PLB 14.88 (*1-55858-170-7*) North-South Bks NYC.
—The Marvellous Blue Mouse. Manson, Christopher. LC 91-29131. 32p. (gr. k-3). 1992. 15.95 (*0-8050-1622-8*, Bks Young Read) H Holt & Co.
—Over the River & Through the Wood. Child, Lydia M. 32p. (gr. k-3). 1993. 14.95 (*1-55858-210-X*); lib. bdg. 14.88 (*1-55858-211-8*) North-South Bks NYC.
—The Tree in the Wood: An Old Nursery Song. Manson, Christopher, adapted by. LC 92-23524. 32p. (gr. k-3). 1993. 14.95 (*1-55858-192-8*); PLB 14.88 (*1-55858-193-6*) North-South Bks NYC.
Mantinband, Gerda. Three Clever Mice. Mantinband, Gerda, retold by. LC 91-48171. 32p. (gr. k up). 1993. 14.00 (*0-688-11369-9*); PLB 13.93 (*0-688-11370-2*) Greenwillow.
Manwaring, Kerry. Fifty Nifty Science Fair Projects. Amato, Carol & Ladizinsky, Eric. 64p. (Orig.). (gr. 3-7). 1993. pap. 3.95 (*1-56565-053-0*) Lowell Hse.
—Fifty Nifty Ways to Earn Money. Urton, Andrea. 80p. Date not set. pap. 4.95 (*0-685-66755-3*) Lowell Hse.
—Hoppin' Magic: My First Card & Coin Magic Tricks. Johnson, Stephanie. 32p. 1993. pap. 5.95 (*1-56565-089-1*) Lowell Hse.
Manyum, Wallop. Mr. Munday & the Rustlers. Pryor, Bonnie. LC 87-17539. 32p. (ps-3). 1987. PLB 12.95 (*0-13-604737-8*) P-H.
Marantz, Robbie. What Is God? Boritzer, Etan. 32p. (Orig.). (gr. 1-7). 1990. 14.95 (*0-920668-89-5*); pap. 5.95 (*0-920668-88-7*) Firefly Bks Ltd.
—What Is Love? Boritzer, Etan. LC 93-94066. 32p. (gr. k-5). 1994. 14.95 (*0-9637597-2-8*); pap. 5.95 (*0-9637597-3-6*) V Lane Bks.
Marasco, Pam. Act It Out: Original Plays Plus Crafts for Costumes & Scenery. Molyneux, Lynn & Gordner, Brad. 192p. (gr. 2-6). 1986. spiral bdg. 12.95 (*0-685-29139-1*) Trellis Bks Inc.
Maraslis, Demetra, jt. illus. see Charlip, Remy.

Marcel Socias Studio Staff. The Fascinating World of Ants. Julivert, Maria A. Arridondo, F. 32p. (gr. 3-7). 1991. 11.95 (*0-8120-6281-7*) Barron.
—The Fascinating World of Butterflies & Moths. Julivert, Maria A. Arridondo, F. 32p. (gr. 3-7). 11.95 (*0-8120-6282-5*) Barron.
—The Fascinating World of Frogs & Toads. Julivert, Maria A. Arridondo, F. 32p. (gr. 3-7). 1993. 11.95 (*0-8120-6345-7*); pap. 7.95 (*0-8120-1565-7*) Barron.
—The Fascinating World of Snakes. Julivert, Maria A. Arridondo, F. 32p. (gr. 3-7). 1993. 11.95 (*0-8120-6346-5*); pap. 7.95 (*0-8120-1564-9*) Barron.
Marcellino, Fred. Dragondrums. McCaffrey, Anne. LC 78-11318. 256p. (gr. 6 up). 1979. SBE 15.95 (*0-689-30685-7*, Atheneum Child Bk) Macmillan Child Grp.
—El Gato Con Botas: (Puss in Boots) Perrault, Charles. Marcuse, Aida, tr. (SPA.). 32p. 1991. 16.00 (*0-374-36158-4*) FS&G.
—Puss in Boots. Perrault, Charles. Arthur, Malcolm, tr. 32p. 1990. 16.00 (*0-374-36160-6*) FS&G.
—A Rat's Tale. Seidler, Tor. 187p. (gr. 1-8). 1986. 16.00 (*0-374-36185-1*) FS&G.
—The Steadfast Tin Soldier. Andersen, Hans Christian. Seidler, Tor, retold by. LC 92-52690. 32p. (ps-3). 1992. 15.00 (*0-06-205000-1*); PLB 14.89 (*0-06-205001-X*) HarpC Child Bks.
—The Wainscott Weasel. Seidler, Tor. LC 92-54526. 200p. (gr. 2 up). 1993. 20.00 (*0-06-205032-X*); PLB 19.89 (*0-06-205033-8*) HarpC Child Bks.
Marchesi, Stephen. The Power Twins. Follett, Ken. LC 90-35367. 96p. (gr. 5 up). 1990. 12.95g (*0-688-08723-X*) Morrow Jr Bks.
Marchesi, Stephen. Betty Friedan: A Voice for Women's Rights. Meltzer, Milton. LC 85-40441. 57p. (gr. 5 up). 1985. 10.95 (*0-670-80786-9*) Viking Child Bks.
—Don Quixote & Sancho Panza. Hodges, Margaret, adapted by. LC 90-24098. 80p. (gr. 6 up). 1992. SBE 16.95 (*0-684-19235-7*, Scribners Young Read) Macmillan Child Grp.
—Gamebuster. Johnson, Annabel & Johnson, Edgar. LC 90-1330. 192p. (gr. 7 up). 1990. 14.95 (*0-525-65033-4*, Cobblehill Bks) Dutton Child Bks.
—The Glow-in-the-Dark Night Sky Book. Hatchett, Clint. LC 87-61531. 24p. (gr. 3-7). 1988. 12.00 (*0-394-89113-9*) Random Bks Yng Read.
—The Glow-in-the-Dark Zodiac Storybook. Ross, Katharine. LC 92-61555. 24p. (gr. 3-7). 1993. 14.00 (*0-679-82470-7*) Random Bks Yng Read.
—Living Monsters: The World's Most Dangerous Animals. Tomb, Howard. 48p. (gr. 3-7). 1990. pap. 9.95 (*0-671-69017-5*, S&S BFYR) S&S Trade.
—Mama. Hopkins, Lee B. LC 91-24712. 112p. (gr. 2-8). 1992. pap. 13.00 jacketed, 3-pc. bdg. (*0-671-74985-4*, S&S BFYR) S&S Trade.
—Mama & Her Boys. Hopkins, Lee B. LC 91-23399. 176p. (gr. 5 up). 1993. pap. 13.00 JRT (*0-671-74986-2*, S&S BFYR) S&S Trade.
—Mary McCleod Bethune. Meltzer, Milton. (gr. 2-6). 1988. pap. 3.50 (*0-317-69647-5*, Puffin) Puffin Bks.
—Mary McLeod Bethune: Voice of Black Hope. Meltzer, Milton. LC 86-15923. (gr. 2-6). 1987. pap. 11.95 (*0-670-80744-3*) Viking Child Bks.
—Meet Abraham Lincoln. Cary, Barbara. LC 88-19066. 72p. (gr. 2-4). 1989. PLB 6.99 (*0-394-91966-1*); pap. 2.99 (*0-394-81966-7*) Random Bks Yng Read.
—Meet George Washington. Hellbroner, Joan. LC 88-19067. 72p. (gr. 2-4). 1989. PLB 6.99 (*0-394-91965-3*); pap. 2.99 (*0-394-81965-9*) Random Bks Yng Read.
—The Mysterious Rays of Dr. Roentgen. Gherman, Beverly. LC 92-38966. 32p. (gr. 2-5). 1994. SBE 14.95 (*0-689-31839-1*, Atheneum Child Bk) Macmillan Child Grp.
—Railway Ghosts & Highway Horrors. Cohen, Daniel. LC 91-11161. 112p. (gr. 4 up). 1991. 13.95 (*0-525-65071-7*, Cobblehill Bks) Dutton Child Bks.
—Silver. Whelan, Gloria. LC 87-26612. 64p. (Orig.). (gr. 2-4). 1988. lib. bdg. 5.99 (*0-394-99611-9*); 2.50 (*0-394-89611-4*) Random Bks Yng Read.
—Winnie Mandela: The Soul of South Africa. Meltzer, Milton. LC 86-5531. 64p. (gr. 2-6). 1986. pap. 10.95 (*0-670-81249-8*) Viking Child Bks.
—Winnie Mandela: The Soul of South Africa. Meltzer, Milton. (gr. 2-6). 1987. pap. 3.99 (*0-14-032181-0*, Puffin) Puffin Bks.
—With the Wind. Damrell, Liz. LC 89-48942. 32p. (ps-2). 1991. 14.95 (*0-531-05882-4*); PLB 14.99 (*0-531-08482-5*) Orchard Bks Watts.
Marchiori, Roberto. Humages. Mariotti, Mario. (Orig.). 1991. pap. 8.95 (*0-671-75233-2*, Green Tiger) S&S Trade.
Marchiori, Roberto, jt. illus. see Mariotti, Mario.
Marchiori, Roberto, photos by. Humands. Mariotti, Mario. 1991. pap. 8.95 (*0-671-75235-9*, Green Tiger) S&S Trade.
Marcil, Beth, jt. illus. see America, Alexis.
Marcroft, Renee. Fulbert Firefly. Marcroft, Karen. LC 85-90463. 48p. (gr. 3-8). 1986. 14.95 (*0-935849-00-9*) Marcroft Prods.
Marcus, Audrey F. Conversations. Hatcher, John. 208p. (gr. 8-10). 1988. 0.00; pap. 12.95 (*0-85398-275-9*) G Ronald Pub.
Marden, Carol K. Autumn. Callinan, Karen. 32p. (ps-2). Date not set. 11.95 (*1-56065-153-9*) Capstone Pr. Postponed.
—Circles. Callinan, Karen. 32p. (ps-2). Date not set. 11.95 (*1-56065-151-2*) Capstone Pr. Postponed.

—Green. Callinan, Karen. 32p. (ps-2). 1992. 11.95 (*1-56065-152-0*) Capstone Pr.
—O'Clock. Callinan, Karen. 32p. (ps-2). Date not set. 11.95 (*1-56065-149-0*) Capstone Pr. Postponed.
—Rectangles. Callinan, Karen. 32p. (ps-2). Date not set. 11.95 (*1-56065-150-4*) Capstone Pr. Postponed.
Marderosian, Mark. Slow Moe. Pedicini, John G. Serino, John, ed. 32p. (gr. k-2). 1991. 9.95 (*0-9627436-7-4*) Je Suis Derby.
Marderosian, Mark & Kurtz, John. Disney's Aladdin: The Genie's Tale. Kreider, Karen. 24p. (ps). 1993. pap. 1.95 (*0-307-10019-7*, 10019, Golden Pr) Western Pub.
Marella, Maria P. Seven Kisses in a Row. MacLachlan, Patricia. LC 82-47718. 64p. (gr. 2-5). 1983. 13.00 (*0-06-024083-0*); PLB 12.89 (*0-06-024084-9*) HarpC Child Bks.
Marffy, Janos. Projects for Christmas. Green, Mary A. Young, Richard G., ed. LC 89-35285. 32p. (gr. 3-5). 1989. PLB 15.93 (*0-944483-43-7*) Garrett Ed Corp.
Margit Studio. That's What Counts. Weinberger, Jane. LC 87-50549. 40p. (gr. k-4). 1988. pap. 5.95 (*0-932433-33-2*) Windswept Hse.
Margodo, Dick. The Magic Words. Murad, Maria B. 40p. (ps-3). 1984. 5.95 (*0-910313-17-2*) Parker Bros.
Margolies, Barbara. Kanu of Kathmandu: A Journey to Nepal. Margolies, Barbara A. LC 92-12482. 40p. (gr. 1-4). 1992. RSBE 14.95 (*0-02-762282-7*, Four Winds) Macmillan Child Grp.
—Warriors, Wigmen, & Crocodile People: Journeys in Papua New Guinea. Margolies, Barbara A. LC 92-27475. 40p. (gr. 1-5). 1993. RSBE 14.95 (*0-02-762283-5*, Four Winds) Macmillan Child Grp.
Margolies, Barbara A. Olbalbal: A Day in Maasailand. Margolies, Barbara A. LC 93-19744. 32p. (gr. 1-4). 1994. RSBE 15.95 (*0-02-762284-3*, Four Winds) Macmillan Child Grp.
Margolis, Al, jt. illus. see Kuchera, John.
Margolis, Ezrachi. The Third Beis Hamikdash: The Third Temple. Steinberg, Shalom D. Miller, Moshe L., tr. from HEB. 240p. (gr. 11-12). 1993. 15.95 (*0-940118-80-7*) Moznaim.
Mariana. Little Bear Marches in the Saint Patrick's Day Parade. Janice. LC 67-15712. 40p. (gr. k-3). PLB 11.88 (*0-688-51075-2*) Lothrop.
—Little Bear's Christmas. Janice. LC 64-21191. (gr. k-3). 1964. PLB 12.88 (*0-688-51076-0*) Lothrop.
—Little Bear's Thanksgiving. Janice. LC 67-22593. 32p. (gr. k-3). 1967. PLB 12.88 (*0-688-51078-7*) Lothrop.
—Miss Flora McFlimsey's Birthday. rev. ed. Mariana. LC 86-15269. 40p. (ps-2). 1987. 11.95 (*0-688-04537-5*) Lothrop.
—Miss Flora McFlimsey's Easter Bonnet. rev. ed. Mariana. LC 86-15268. 40p. (gr. k-3). 1987. 9.95 (*0-688-04535-9*); PLB 8.88 (*0-688-04536-7*) Lothrop.
—Miss Flora McFlimsey's Halloween. rev. ed. Mariana. LC 86-15270. 40p. (ps-2). 1987. 11.95 (*0-688-04549-9*) Lothrop.
—Miss Flora McFlimsey's May Day. rev. ed. Mariana. LC 86-15252. 40p. (ps-2). 1987. 9.95 (*0-688-04545-6*) Lothrop.
—Miss Flora McFlimsey's Valentine. rev. ed. Mariana. LC 86-15254. 40p. (gr. k-3). 1987. 9.95 (*0-688-04547-2*) Lothrop.
Mariana & Howe, Caroline W. Miss Flora McFlimsey & the Baby New Year. rev ed ed. Mariana. LC 86-15339. 40p. (ps-2). 1988. 11.95 (*0-688-04533-2*); PLB 11.88 (*0-688-04534-0*) Lothrop.
—Miss Flora McFlimsey's Christmas Eve. rev ed ed. Mariana. LC 86-15259. 40p. (ps-2). 1988. 11.95 (*0-688-04282-1*); PLB 11.88 (*0-688-04283-X*) Lothrop.
Marichal, Poli. Adios Falcon. Deliz, Wenceslao S. LC 85-1116. (SPA.). 15p. (ps-3). 1985. pap. 2.00 (*0-8477-3530-3*) U of PR Pr.
Maril, Herman. Me, Molly Midnight, the Artist's Cat. Maril, Nadja. LC 77-22708. 40p. (gr. k up). 1977. 9.95 (*0-916144-15-1*); pap. 3.95 (*0-916144-16-X*) Stemmer Hse.
—Runaway Molly Midnight, the Artist's Cat. Maril, Nadja. LC 80-17097. 40p. (gr. k up). 1980. 9.95 (*0-916144-62-3*) Stemmer Hse.
Marilue. Bobby Bear & Uncle Sam's Riddle. Mountain, Lee. 32p. (ps-1). 1988. PLB 11.45 (*0-87783-221-8*) Oddo.
—Bobby Bear at the Circus. Marilue. LC 89-62708. 32p. (ps-2). 1990. PLB 12.95 (*0-87783-252-8*) Oddo.
—Bobby Bear's Birthday. Oetting, Rae. LC 87-62508. 32p. (ps-1). 1988. PLB 11.45 (*0-87783-220-X*) Oddo.
—Bobby Bear's Kite Contest. Marilue. LC 87-62507. 32p. (ps-1). 1988. PLB 11.45 (*0-87783-219-6*) Oddo.
—Bobby Bear's Magic Show. Marilue. LC 89-62707. 32p. (ps-2). 1990. PLB 12.95 (*0-87783-253-6*) Oddo.
—Orderly Cricket. Oetting, R. LC 68-16395. 32p. (gr. 2-3). 1967. PLB 9.95 (*0-87783-028-2*) Oddo.
—When Jesus Was a Lad. Otting, Rae. (gr. 1-2). 1978. pap. 1.25 (*0-89508-055-9*) Rainbow Bks.
Marinin, Sally. Danny D Books, 4 vols. Briscoe, Stuart & Briscoe, Jill. 12p. (gr. 2-5). 1993. Set. pap. 9.99 (*0-8010-1061-6*) Baker Bk.
—How Much Does God Know? Briscoe, Stuart & Briscoe, Jill. 12p. 1993. pap. 2.99 (*0-8010-1040-3*) Baker Bk.
—How Strong Is God? Briscoe, Stuart & Briscoe, Jill. 12p. (Orig.). (gr. 4 up). 1993. pap. 2.99 (*0-8010-1037-3*) Baker Bk.
—Is God Ever Naughty? Briscoe, Stuart & Briscoe, Jill. 12p. 1993. pap. 2.99 (*0-8010-1041-1*) Baker Bk.
—Where Is God? Briscoe, Stuart & Briscoe, Jill. 12p. 1993. pap. 2.99 (*0-8010-1038-1*) Baker Bk.

Mariotti, Mario & Marchiori, Roberto. Hanimals. 40p. (Orig.). (gr. 4 up). 1991. pap. 8.95 (0-671-75232-4, Green Tiger) S&S Trade.

Maris, Ron. Are You There, Bear? Maris, Ron. 32p. (ps-1). 1986. pap. 3.50 (0-14-050524-5, Puffin) Puffin Bks.
—Ducks Quack. Maris, Ron. LC 91-58726. 14p. (ps). 1992. 4.95 (1-56402-080-0) Candlewick Pr.
—Frogs Jump. Maris, Ron. LC 91-58730. 14p. (ps). 1992. 4.95 (1-56402-081-9) Candlewick Pr.
—Is Anyone Home? Maris, Ron. LC 85-5436. 32p. (ps-2). 1986. 16.00 (0-688-05899-X) Greenwillow.
—My Book. Maris, Ron. 32p. (ps-1). 1986. pap. 3.95 (0-14-050523-7, Puffin) Puffin Bks.
Maritz, Nicolaas. Somewhere in Africa. Mennen, Ingrid & Daly, Niki. LC 91-19379. 32p. (ps-3). 1992. 13.00 (0-525-44848-9, DCB) Dutton Child Bks.
Mark, Joan G., et al. Gurus & Griots. Bathersfield, Arnold, et al. Gibbs, C. Jeanean, ed. LC 87-90523. 108p. (gr. 7 up). 1987. pap. 6.00 (0-9618755-0-X) Palm Tree Ent.
Mark, Joseph. I Hear the Day. Johnston, Catherine D. (gr. 2-3). 1977. 9.00 (0-914562-04-5); wkbk 3.00 (0-914562-05-3) Merriam-Eddy.
Mark, Steve. Grumble Day. Green, Kate. (gr. 1-8). 1992. PLB 15.95 (0-89565-870-4); Resale. 22.75 (0-685-60968-5) Childs World.
—Just about Perfect. Green, Kate. (gr. 1-8). 1992. PLB 15.95 (0-89565-871-2); Resale. 22.75 (0-685-60967-7) Childs World.
—The Mouse & the Lion. Varnai, Gyorgy. LC 92-43693. (gr. 3 up). Date not set. write for info. (1-56766-091-6) Childs World. Postponed.
—Three Blind Mice. Ivemey, John W. LC 92-41175. (gr. 2 up). Date not set. write for info. (1-56766-090-8) Childs World. Postponed.
Markle, Sandra. Exploring Autumn: A Season of Science Activities, Puzzlers, & Games. Markle, Sandra. LC 90-24209. 160p. (gr. 3-7). 1991. SBE 14.95 (0-689-31620-8, Atheneum Child Bk) Macmillan Child Grp.
—Exploring Summer: A Season of Science Activities, Puzzlers, & Games. Markle, Sandra. LC 86-17322. 176p. (gr. 3-7). 1987. SBE 14.95 (0-689-31212-1, Atheneum Child Bk) Macmillan Child Grp.
—Exploring Winter. Markle, Sandra. LC 84-3049. 160p. (gr. 3-7). 1984. SBE 14.95 (0-689-31065-X, Atheneum Child Bk) Macmillan Child Grp.
—The Kids' Earth Handbook. Markle, Sandra. LC 90-27478. 48p. (gr. 3-7). 1991. SBE 13.95 (0-689-31707-7, Atheneum Child Bk) Macmillan Child Grp.
—Math Mini-Mysteries. Markle, Sandra. LC 92-11217. 64p. (gr. 3-7). 1993. SBE 14.95 (0-689-31700-X, Atheneum Child Bk) Macmillan Child Grp.
—Outside & Inside Spiders. Markle, Sandra. LC 93-22643. 40p. (ps-3). 1994. SBE 15.95 (0-02-762314-9, Bradbury Pr) Macmillan Child Grp.
Marklew, Gilly. City Cat, Country Cat. Cleveland-Peck, Patricia. LC 91-42402. 32p. (ps). 1992. 14.00 (0-688-11644-2); PLB 13.93 (0-688-11645-0) Morrow Jr Bks.
—The Little Book of Poems. Walsh, Caroline, selected by. LC 92-29126. 1993. 7.95 (1-85697-887-7) Kingfisher Bks.
Marks, Alan. The Fisherman & His Wife. Grimm, Jacob & Grimm, Wilhelm K. Bell, Anthea, tr. LC 88-15165. 28p. (ps up). 1991. pap. 14.95 (0-88708-072-3) Picture Bk Studio.
—Nowhere to be Found. Marks, Alan. LC 87-32729. 28p. (ps up). 1991. pap. 14.95 (0-88708-062-6) Picture Bk Studio.
—Ring-a-Ring o' Roses & a Ding, Dong Bell: A Collection of Nursery Rhymes. Marks, Alan, ed. LC 91-15222. 96p. (gr. k up). 1991. pap. 19.95 (0-88708-187-8) Picture Bk Studio.
—The Ugly Duckling. Andersen, Hans Christian. Bell, Anthea, tr. LC 89-3975. 42p. (gr. k up). 1991. pap. 14.95 (0-88708-116-9) Picture Bk Studio.
Marks, Theresa. Close at Hand. Gregory, Kim. LC 91-93065. 36p. (Orig.). (ps-3). 1992. pap. text ed. 10.98 incl. wristband with interchangeable snap-on theme lids (0-9630898-0-3) K T Kids.
Marksbury, Tina. Nighty-Night, Teddy Beddy Bear. 12p. (ps). 1986. 4.99 (0-394-88244-X) Random Bks Yng Read.
Markson, Sue, jt. illus. see Holmes, Dave.
Marlette, Doug. The Before & After Book. Marlette, Doug. 48p. (ps-8). 1992. pap. 5.70 (0-395-60905-4) HM.
Marlow, Eric. Rosa Parks. Greenfield, Eloise. LC 72-83782. 40p. (gr. 1-5). 1973. PLB 14.89 (0-690-71211-1, Crowell Jr Bks) HarpC Child Bks.
Marquardt, Marsha. Little Ghost Goes to School. Marquardt, Marsha. 12p. (Orig.). (gr. 1). 1993. pap. text ed. write for info. (1-882225-12-0) Tott Pubns.
Marrella, Maria P. Seven Kisses in a Row. MacLachlan, Patricia. LC 82-47718. 64p. (gr. 2-5). 1988. pap. 3.95 (0-06-440231-2, Trophy) HarpC Child Bks.
Marriott, Pat. The Wolves of Willoughby Chase. Aiken, Joan. LC 63-18034. 168p. (gr. 4-6). 1989. pap. 13.95 (0-385-03594-2) Doubleday.
Marrone, Russell. The Wizard's Quest. Marrone, Russell. LC 87-50268. 102p. (gr. 3-5). 1987. 7.95 (1-55523-078-4) Winston-Derek.
Marrs, Greg. Pet Cobwebs. Marrs, Carol R. 112p. (gr. 1 up). 1988. 12.95 (0-9621234-0-4) Funny Farm Pr.

Mars, W. T. Running Out of Time. Levy, Elizabeth. LC 79-28064. 128p. (gr. 3-6). 1980. lib. bdg. 4.99 (0-394-94422-4) Knopf Bks Yng Read.
Mars, Witold T. The Adventures of Greek Heroes. McLean, Mollie & Wiseman, Anne. LC 61-10628. 192p. (ps-3). 1973. 15.45 (0-395-06913-0, Sandpiper); pap. 5.95 (0-685-42189-9, Sandpiper) HM.
—Calico Captive. Speare, Elizabeth G. 288p. (gr. 7-9). 1957. 15.45 (0-395-07112-7) HM.
Marschall, Ken. Westward with Columbus. Dyson, John. Christopher, Peter, photos by. LC 90-15566. 64p. (gr. 4-7). 1991. 6.95 (0-590-43847-X) Scholastic Inc.
Marsden, Helen. Big Book of Time. Edmonds, William. LC 93-35709. 1994. write for info. (0-89577-579-4) RD Assn.
Marsh, Carol. Mystery of the World's Fair. Marsh, Carole. (Orig.). (gr. 3-9). 1982. pap. 14.95 (0-935326-04-9) Gallopade Pub Group.
Marsh, Carole. Autumn: Silly Trivia. Marsh, Carole. (Orig.). (gr. 2-9). 1986. 24.95 (1-55609-274-1); pap. 14.95 (0-685-14606-5) Gallopade Pub Group.
—Halloween: Silly Trivia. Marsh, Carole. (Orig.). (gr. 2-9). 1986. PLB 24.95 (1-55609-169-9); pap. 14.95 (0-685-14605-7) Gallopade Pub Group.
—The Haunt of Hope Plantation. Marsh, Carole. (Orig.). (gr. 3-9). 1982. 24.95 (1-55609-170-2); pap. 14.95 (0-935326-03-0) Gallopade Pub Group.
—World's Fair Fun Trivia Book. Marsh, Carole. (Orig.). (gr. 4 up). 1982. pap. 4.95 (0-935326-06-5) Gallopade Pub Group.
Marsh, Dilleen. All Kinds of Answers. Porter, Barbara. LC 92-6976. 29p. (gr. 1-3). 1992. 11.95 (0-87579-538-2) Deseret Bk.
—Grandpa & Me & the Wishing Star. Porter, Barbara J. LC 90-81831. 32p. (ps). 1990. 10.95 (0-87579-269-3) Deseret Bk.
Marsh, Susan. Jack & the Beanstalk; with an Inflatable Beanstalk. Morgan, Hal & Tucker, Kerry. 10p. (ps-3). 1987. pap. 4.95 (0-942820-21-5) Steam Pr MA.
—The Kids' Bathtub Rhyme Book. Tucker, Kerry & Morgan, Hal, eds. 12p. (Orig.). (ps-1). 1988. pap. 4.95 (0-942820-25-8) Steam Pr MA.
—The Kids' Bathtub Songbook. Tucker, Kerry & Morgan, Hal, eds. 10p. (Orig.). (ps-3). 1985. pap. 4.95 (0-942820-14-2) Steam Pr MA.
Marsh, T. F. Little Book of Questions & Answers: Animals. Jones, Teri C. 32p. (gr. k-3). 1992. PLB 10.95 (1-56674-012-6, HTS Bks) Forest Hse.
—Little Book of Questions & Answers: My Home. Jones, Teri C. 32p. (gr. k-3). 1992. PLB 10.95 (1-56674-013-4, HTS Bks) Forest Hse.
—Little Book of Questions & Answers: Nature. Jones, Teri C. 32p. (gr. k-3). 1992. PLB 10.95 (1-56674-014-2, HTS Bks) Forest Hse.
—Little Book of Questions & Answers: Things That Go. Jones, Teri C. 32p. (gr. k-3). 1992. PLB 10.95 (1-56674-015-0, HTS Bks) Forest Hse.
Marsh, T. F., et al. Tom Kitten. Potter, Beatrix, created by. 24p. (gr. 2). 1992. PLB 10.95 (1-56674-010-X, HTS Bks) Forest Hse.
—Two Bad Mice. Potter, Beatrix, created by. 24p. (gr. 2-4). 1992. PLB 10.95 (1-56674-011-8, HTS Bks) Forest Hse.
Marshall, David. You Mean I Have to Stand Up & Say Something? Detz, Joan. LC 86-3611. 96p. (gr. 5-9). 1986. SBE 13.95 (0-689-31221-0, Atheneum Child Bk) Macmillan Child Grp.
Marshall, James. The Adventures of Isabel. Nash, Ogden. (ps-3). 1991. 14.95 (0-316-59874-7) Little.
—All the Way Home. Segal, Lore. 32p. (ps up). 1988. pap. 3.95 (0-374-40355-4) FS&G.
—Bumps in the Night. Allard, Harry. 48p. (gr. 1-4). 1984. pap. 2.25 (0-553-15284-X, Skylark) Bantam.
—Bumps in the Night. Allard, Harry. (gr. k-3). 1984. 2.99 (0-553-15711-6, Skylark) Bantam.
—Cinderella. Karlin, Barbara, retold by. 32p. (ps-3). 1992. pap. 4.95 (0-316-48303-6) Little.
—The Cut-Ups. Marshall, James. 32p. (ps-3). 1986. pap. 3.95 (0-14-050637-3, Puffin) Puffin Bks.
—Dinner at Alberta's. Hoban, Russell. 48p. (gr. k-6). 1980. pap. 2.95 (0-440-41864-X, YB) Dell.
—Dinner at Alberta's. Hoban, Russell. LC 73-94796. 40p. (gr. 1-3). 1975. PLB 12.89 (0-690-23993-9, Crowell Jr Bks) HarpC Child Bks.
—The Exploding Frog: & Other Fables from Aesop. McFarland, John. (gr. 3 up). 1981. pap. 8.70i (0-685-03085-7, Pub. by Atlantic Pr) (0-316-55577-0) Little.
—Four on the Shore. Marshall, Edward. LC 84-1708. 48p. (ps-3). 1985. 9.95 (0-8037-0155-1); PLB 9.89 (0-8037-0142-X) Dial Bks Young.
—Fox All Week. Marshall, Edward. LC 84-1708. (ps-3). 1984. 10.95 (0-8037-0062-8) Dial Bks Young.
—Fox All Week. Marshall, Edward. LC 84-1708. (ps-3). 1987. pap. 4.95 (0-8037-0008-3) Dial Bks Young.
—Fox & His Friends. Marshall, Edward. LC 81-68769. 56p. (ps-3). 1982. PLB 10.89 (0-8037-2669-4); pap. 4.95 (0-8037-2668-6) Dial Bks Young.
—Fox at School. Marshall, Edward. LC 82-45506. 48p. (ps-3). 1983. PLB 9.89 (0-8037-2675-9); pap. 4.95 (0-8037-2674-0) Dial Bks Young.
—Fox at School. Marshall, Edward. LC 93-2721. (gr. 1-4). 1993. pap. 3.25 (0-14-036544-3, Puffin) Puffin Bks.

—Fox Be Nimble. Marshall, James. Fogelman, Phyllis J., ed. LC 89-7933. 48p. (ps-3). 1990. 10.95 (0-8037-0760-6); PLB 10.89 (0-8037-0761-4) Dial Bks Young.
—Fox in Love. Marshall, Edward. LC 82-70190. 56p. (ps-3). 1982. PLB 10.89 (0-8037-2433-0) Dial Bks Young.
—Fox on Stage. Marshall, James. LC 91-46740. 48p. (ps-3). 1993. 10.99 (0-8037-1356-8); PLB 10.89 (0-8037-1357-6) Dial Bks Young.
—Fox on the Job. Marshall, James. LC 87-15589. 48p. (gr. k-3). 1988. 10.99 (0-8037-0350-3); PLB 9.89 (0-8037-0351-1) Dial Bks Young.
—Fox on Wheels. Marshall, Edward. LC 83-5254. 48p. (ps-3). 1983. PLB 10.89 (0-8037-0002-4) Dial Bks Young.
—Fox on Wheels. Marshall, Edward. (gr. 1-4). 1993. pap. 3.25 (0-14-036541-9, Puffin) Puffin Bks.
—Fox Outfoxed. Marshall, James. LC 91-21815. 48p. (ps-3). 1992. 11.00 (0-8037-1036-4); PLB 10.89 (0-8037-1037-2) Dial Bks Young.
—The Frog Prince. Tarcov, Edith H., retold by. 32p. (Orig.). (ps-2). 1987. pap. 2.50 (0-590-43132-3) Scholastic Inc.
—The Frog Prince. Tarcov, Edith H., retold by. LC 92-25167. 32p. (ps-2). 1993. pap. 2.95 (0-590-46571-6) Scholastic Inc.
—George & Martha. Marshall, James. LC 74-184250. 48p. (gr. k-3). 1972. 13.45 (0-395-16619-5) HM.
—George & Martha Back in Town. Marshall, James. LC 83-22842. 32p. (gr. k-3). 1984. 14.45 (0-395-35386-6, 5-90939); pap. 3.95 (0-685-07886-8) HM.
—George & Martha One Fine Day. Marshall, James. 48p. (gr. k-3). 1978. 14.45 (0-395-27154-1); pap. 4.80 (0-395-32921-3) HM.
—George & Martha Rise & Shine. Marshall, James. (gr. k-3). 1979. 13.45 (0-395-24738-1); pap. 4.80 (0-395-28006-0) HM.
—George & Martha Round & Round. Marshall, James. LC 88-14739. 48p. (gr. k-3). 1988. 13.45 (0-395-46763-2) HM.
—Goldilocks & the Three Bears. Marshall, James. LC 87-32983. 32p. (ps-3). 1988. 14.00 (0-8037-0542-5); PLB 13.89 (0-8037-0543-3) Dial Bks Young.
—Haunted House Jokes. Phillips, Louis. 64p. (gr. 2-5). 1988. pap. 3.95 (0-14-032062-8, Puffin) Puffin Bks.
—How Beastly! A Menagerie of Nonsense Poems. Yolen, Jane. 48p. (gr. 2-6). 1994. 14.95 (1-56397-086-4) Boyds Mills Pr.
—James Marshall's Mother Goose. Marshall, James. LC 79-2574. 40p. (ps-3). 1979. 15.00 (0-374-33653-9) FS&G.
—James Marshall's Mother Goose. Marshall, James. LC 79-2574. 40p. (ps-6). 1986. pap. 5.95 (0-374-43723-8) FS&G.
—Mary Alice Returns. Allen, Jeffrey. (ps-3). 1986. lib. bdg. 13.95i (0-316-03429-0) Little.
—Merry Christmas, Space Case. Marshall, James. LC 85-1664. 32p. (ps-3). 1986. 11.95 (0-8037-0215-9) Dial Bks Young.
—Miss Nelson Has a Field Day. Allard, Harry. LC 84-27791. 32p. (gr. k-3). 1985. 13.45 (0-395-36690-9) HM.
—Miss Nelson Has a Field Day. Allard, Harry. 32p. (gr. k-3). 1988. pap. 4.80 (0-395-48654-8, Sandpiper) HM.
—Miss Nelson Has a Field Day. Allard, Harry. (ps-3). 1989. pap. 7.70 incl. cassette (0-395-52138-6) HM.
—Miss Nelson Is Back. Allard, Harry. 1988. pap. 7.70 incl. cass. (0-395-48872-9) HM.
—Miss Nelson Is Missing! Allard, Harry & Marshall, James. (gr. k-3). 1985. reinforced bdg. 13.45 (0-395-25296-2); pap. 3.80 (0-395-40146-1) HM.
—The Night Before Christmas. Moore, Clement C. 32p. (ps-3). 1989. pap. 5.95 incl. cass. (0-590-63489-5); pap. 2.50 (0-590-42758-X) Scholastic Inc.
—The Night Before Christmas. Moore, Clement C. 32p. 1991. 13.95 (0-590-45075-1, Scholastic Hardcover) Scholastic Inc.
—Nosey Mrs. Rat. Allen, Jeffery. LC 84-19618. 32p. (ps-3). 1985. pap. 11.95 (0-670-80880-6) Viking Child Bks.
—Nosey Mrs. Rat. Allen, Jeffery. LC 86-25462. 32p. (ps-3). 1987. pap. 3.95 (0-14-050665-9, Puffin) Puffin Bks.
—La Pandilla en la Orilla - Four on the Shore. Marshall, Edward. (SPA). 52p. (gr. 2-4). 1990. pap. write for info. (84-204-4678-5) Santillana.
—The Piggy in the Puddle. Pomerantz, Charlotte. LC 73-6047. 32p. (ps-1). 1974. RSBE 14.95 (0-02-774900-2, Macmillan Child Bk) Macmillan Child Grp.
—The Piggy in the Puddle. Pomerantz, Charlotte. LC 88-8368. 32p. (ps-1). 1989. pap. 3.95 (0-689-71293-6, Aladdin) Macmillan Child Grp.
—Pocketful of Nonsense. Marshall, James, compiled by. LC 93-18297. 1993. 12.95 (0-307-17552-9, Golden Pr) Western Pub.
—Rats on the Roof: And Other Stories. Marshall, James. LC 90-44084. 80p. (gr. 1-5). 1991. 13.00 (0-8037-0834-3); lib. bdg. (0-8037-0835-1) Dial Bks Young.
—Roger's Umbrella. Pinkwater, Daniel. LC 81-2294. 32p. (gr. 1-3). 1982. 11.95 (0-525-38555-X, DCB) Dutton Child Bks.
—Roger's Umbrella. Pinkwater, Daniel. LC 81-2294. 32p. (gr. 1-3). 1985. pap. 3.95 (0-525-44223-5, DCB) Dutton Child Bks.
—Space Case. Marshall, Edward. LC 80-13369. 32p. (ps-3). 1980. 14.00 (0-8037-8005-2); PLB 12.89 (0-8037-8007-9) Dial Bks Young.

—Space Case. Marshall, Edward. 40p. (gr. k-3). 1982. pap. 4.99 (0-8037-8431-7) Dial Bks Young.
—The Stupids Have a Ball. Allard, Harry. LC 77-27660. (gr. k-3). 1984. 13.45 (0-395-26497-9); pap. 4.80 (0-395-36169-9) HM.
—The Stupids Step Out. Allard, Harry. LC 73-21698. 32p. (gr. k-3). 1974. 14.95 (0-395-18513-0); pap. 4.80 (0-395-25377-2) HM.
—The Stupids Step Out. Allard, Harry. (ps-3). 1993. pap. 7.95 incl. cassette (0-395-52139-4) HM.
—The Stupids Take Off. Allard, Harry. 32p. (gr. k-3). 1993. pap. 4.95 (0-395-65743-1) HM.
—Three by the Sea. Marshall, Edward. 48p. (ps-3). 1981. PLB 10.89 (0-8037-8687-5) Dial Bks Young.
—The Three Little Pigs. Marshall, James, retold by. LC 88-33411. (ps-3). 1989. 12.95 (0-8037-0591-3); PLB 12.89 (0-8037-0594-8) Dial Bks Young.
—Three up a Tree. Marshall, James. LC 86-2163. 48p. (ps-3). 1986. 9.95 (0-8037-0328-7); PLB 9.89 (0-685-13452-0) Dial Bks Young.
—Tres en un Arbol - Three up a Tree. Marshall, James. Baro, Ana B., tr. (SPA.). 48p. (gr. 2-4). 1990. pap. write for info. (84-204-4637-8) Santillana.
—Troll Country. Marshall, Edward. LC 79-19324. 56p. (ps-3). 1980. pap. 4.95 (0-8037-6210-0) Dial Bks Young.
—What's the Matter with Carruthers? Marshall, James. LC 72-75607. 32p. (gr. k-3). 1972. 16.95 (0-395-13895-7) HM.
—Willis. Marshall, James. LC 74-5259. (gr. k-3). 1974. 13.95 (0-395-19494-6) HM.
—Willis. Marshall, James. (ps-3). 1989. pap. 4.95 (0-395-51008-2, Sandpiper) HM.
—Yummers! Marshall, James. LC 72-5400. 32p. (gr. k-3). 1973. 13.45 (0-395-14757-3) HM.
—Yummers Too. Marshall, James. LC 86-10667. 32p. (gr. k-3). 1986. 12.95 (0-395-38990-9) HM.
—Yummers Too: The Second Course. Marshall, James. 32p. (gr. k-3). 1990. pap. 4.95 (0-395-53967-6) HM.
Marshall, James, jt. illus. see Allard, Harry.
Marshall, Janet. Talkaty Talker. Manley, Molly. 24p. (ps-1). 1994. prepub. 9.95 (1-56397-195-X) Boyds Mills Pr.
Marshall, Janet P. Barnyard Tracks. Duffy, Deborah. LC 91-72973. 32p. (ps up). 1992. 12.95 (1-878093-66-5) Boyds Mills Pr.
—My Camera: At the Zoo. Marshall, Janet P. 32p. (ps-2). 1989. 12.95 (0-316-54687-9) Little.
—Ohmygosh My Pocket. Marshall, Janet P. 24p. (ps-k). 1992. bds. 7.95 (1-56397-044-9) Boyds Mills Pr.
Marshall, Laura. The Girl Who Changed Her Fate. Marshall, Laura. LC 91-23137. 32p. (ps-3). 1992. SBE 14.95 (0-689-31742-5, Atheneum Child Bk) Macmillan Child Grp.
Marshall, Linda D., et al. What Is a Step? Marshall, Linda D. LC 91-67511. 48p. (Orig.). (ps-5). 1992. pap. 10.00 (1-879289-00-8) Native Sun Pubs.
Marshall, Ray & Bradley, John. The Car: Watch It Work by Operating the Moving Diagrams! Marshall, Ray & Bradley, John. LC 83-40569. 10p. 1984. pap. 14.95 (0-670-20371-8) Viking Child Bks.
—The Train: Watch It Work. Marshall, Ray & Bradley, John. 1986. pap. 13.95 (0-670-81134-3) Viking Child Bks.
Marshall, Richard, photos by. T-Ball Is Our Game. Gemme, Leila B. LC 77-17173. 32p. (gr. k-3). 1978. PLB 15.93 (0-516-03630-0) Childrens.
Marshall, Rita. The Gift of the Magi: A Special Christmas Edition. rev. ed. O. Henry. 32p. (gr. 4 up). 1984. PLB 13.95 s.p. (0-87191-954-0) Creative Ed.
Marshall, Rita, jt. illus. see Imsand, Marcel.
Marshall, Victoria. Alice in Bibleland Storybooks: Prayers & Graces. Davidson, Alice J. 32p. (gr. 3 up). 1986. 5.50 (0-8378-5078-9) Gibson.
—Alice in Bibleland Storybooks: Psalms & Proverbs. Davidson, Alice J. 32p. (gr. 3 up). 1984. 5.50 (0-8378-5069-X) Gibson.
—Alice in Bibleland Storybooks: Story of David & Goliath. Davidson, Alice J. 32p. (gr. 3 up). 1985. 5.50 (0-8378-5070-3) Gibson.
—Alice in Bibleland Storybooks: Story of Daniel & the Lions. Davidson, Alice J. 32p. (gr. 3 up). 1986. 5.50 (0-8378-5079-7) Gibson.
—Alice in Bibleland Storybooks: Story of Baby Jesus. Davidson, Alice J. 32p. (gr. 3 up). 1985. 5.50 (0-8378-5072-X) Gibson.
—Alice in Bibleland Storybooks: Story of Baby Moses. Davidson, Alice J. 32p. (gr. 3 up). 1985. 5.50 (0-8378-5071-1) Gibson.
—Alice in Bibleland Storybooks: Story of Creation. Davidson, Alice J. 32p. (gr. 3 up). 1984. 5.50 (0-8378-5066-5) Gibson.
—Alice in Bibleland Storybooks: Story of Easter. Davidson, Alice J. 32p. (gr. 3 up). 1988. 5.50 (0-8378-1839-7) Gibson.
—Alice in Bibleland Storybooks: Story of Jonah. Davidson, Alice J. 32p. (gr. 3 up). 1984. 5.50 (0-8378-5068-1) Gibson.
—Alice in Bibleland Storybooks: Story of Noah. Davidson, Alice J. 32p. (gr. 3 up). 1984. 5.50 (0-8378-5067-3) Gibson.
—Alice in Bibleland Storybooks: Story of the Loaves & Fishes. Davidson, Alice J. 32p. (ps-3). 1985. 5.50 (0-8378-5073-8) Gibson.
Marson, Peg. Animal Survival. Balick, Don. Marson, Ron, ed. 80p. (gr. 5-10). 1986. 13.95 (0-941008-37-1) Tops Learning.

—Electricity. Marson, Ron. LC 81-90444. 80p. (gr. 5-10). 1983. 13.95 (0-941008-32-0) Tops Learning.
—Green Thumbs: Corn & Beans. Marson, Ron. 80p. (gr. 5-10). 1989. tchr's ed. 13.95 (0-941008-39-8) Tops Learning.
—Green Thumbs: Radishes. Marson, Ron. 80p. (gr. 5-10). 1986. tchr's ed. 13.95 (0-941008-38-X) Tops Learning.
—Intermediate Aphabet Soup: A Curriculum for Your First Week of School. Fellers, Pat & Gritzmacher, Kathy. Marson, Ron, ed. 112p. (gr. 3-8). 1985. tchr's. ed. 13.95 (0-941008-62-2) Tops Learning.
—Magnetism. Marson, Ron. LC 81-90445. 78p. (gr. 5-10). 1984. 13.95 (0-941008-33-9) Tops Learning.
—Metric Measuring. Marson, Ron. LC 81-90446. 80p. (gr. 5-10). 1984. 13.95 (0-941008-35-5) Tops Learning.
—Pendulums. Marson, Ron. LC 81-90447. 80p. (gr. 5-10). 1983. 13.95 (0-941008-34-7) Tops Learning.
—Rocks & Minerals. Metcalf, Doris & Marson, Ron. 88p. (gr. 7-12). 1989. tchr's. ed. 15.70 (0-941008-23-1) Tops Learning.
Marstall, Bob. Fire in the Forest. Pringle, Laurence. LC 92-32257. 32p. (gr. 2-4). 1993. 15.95 (0-02-775215-1, Macmillan Child Bk) Macmillan Child Grp.
—Johnny May Grows Up. Branscum, Robbie. LC 86-45780. 128p. (gr. 4-8). 1987. HarpC Child Bks.
—The Lady & the Spider. McNulty, Faith. LC 85-5427. 48p. (gr. 1-4). 1986. PLB 14.89 (0-06-024192-6) HarpC Child Bks.
—The Lady & the Spider. McNulty, Faith. LC 85-5427. 48p. (gr. 1-4). 1987. pap. 4.95 (0-06-443152-5, Trophy) HarpC Child Bks.
—Mitch & Amy. reissued ed. Cleary, Beverly. LC 67-10041. 224p. (gr. 2 up). 1991. 13.95 (0-688-10806-7); PLB 13.88 (0-688-10807-5) Morrow Jr Bks.
—My Best Friend Mee-Yung Kim: Meeting a Korean-American Family. MacMillan, Dianne & Freeman, Dorothy. Steltenpohl, Jane, ed. 48p. (gr. 3-5). 1989. lib. bdg. 9.98 (0-671-65691-0, J Messner) S&S Trade.
—One Day in the Prairie. George, Jean C. LC 85-48254. 48p. (gr. 5-7). 1986. PLB 13.89 (0-690-04566-2, Crowell Jr Bks) HarpC Child Bks.
Martchenko, Michael. Agu, Agu, Agu: Murmel, Murmel, Murmel. Munsch, Robert. (SPA.). 32p. (ps-2). 1991. pap. 5.95 (1-55037-095-2, Pub. by Annick CN) Firefly Bks Ltd.
—Angela's Airplane. Munsch, Robert. 24p. (gr. k-3). 1988. PLB 14.95 (1-550370-27-8, Pub. by Annick CN); pap. 4.95 (1-550370-26-X, Pub. by Annick CN) Firefly Bks Ltd.
—Angela's Airplane. Munsch, Robert. 24p. (ps-1). 1986. pap. 0.99 (0-920236-75-8, Pub. by Annick CN) Firefly Bks Ltd.
—El Avion de Angela: (Angela's Airplane) Munsch, Robert. Langer, Shirley, tr. (SPA.). 32p. 1991. pap. 5.95 (1-55037-189-4, Pub. by Annick CN) Firefly Bks Ltd.
—Bird Feeder Banquet. Martchenko, Michael. 24p. (Orig.). (gr. k-3). 1990. 14.95 (1-55037-147-9, Pub. by Annick CN); pap. 4.95 (1-55037-146-0, Pub. by Annick CN) Firefly Bks Ltd.
—Boy in the Drawer. Munsch, Robert. 32p. (gr. k-3). 1982. 12.95 (0-920236-34-0, Pub. by Annick CN); pap. 4.95 (0-920236-36-7, Pub. by Annick CN) Firefly Bks Ltd.
—The Boy in the Drawer. Munsch, Robert. 24p. (ps-1). 1987. pap. 0.99 (0-920303-50-1, Pub. by Annick CN) Firefly Bks Ltd.
—Los Cochinos: (Pigs) Munsch, Robert. Langer, Shirley, tr. (SPA.). 32p. 1991. pap. 5.95 (1-55037-191-6, Pub. by Annick CN) Firefly Bks Ltd.
—El Cumpleanos de Mariela: Moira's Birthday. Munsch, Robert. (SPA.). 32p. (ps-1). 1992. pap. 5.95 (1-55037-269-6, Pub. by Annick CN) Firefly Bks Ltd.
—David's Father. Munsch, Robert. 32p. (gr. k-3). 1983. PLB 14.95 (0-920236-62-6, Pub. by Annick CN); pap. 4.95 (0-920236-64-2, Pub. by Annick CN) Firefly Bks Ltd.
—David's Father. Munsch, Robert. 24p. (Orig.). (ps-2). 1989. pap. 0.99 (1-55037-011-1, Pub. by Annick CN) Firefly Bks Ltd.
—La Estacion de Bomberos: The Fire Station. Munsch, Robert. (SPA.). 32p. (ps-1). 1992. pap. 5.95 (1-55037-268-8, Pub. by Annick CN) Firefly Bks Ltd.
—Fifty Below Zero. Munsch, Robert. 24p. (gr. k-3). 1986. PLB 14.95 (0-920236-86-3, Pub. by Annick CN); pap. 4.95 (0-920236-91-X, Pub. by Annick CN) Firefly Bks Ltd.
—The Fire Station. Munsch, Robert. 24p. (Orig.). (gr. k-3). 1991. PLB 14.95 (1-55037-170-3, Pub. by Annick CN); pap. 4.95 (1-55037-171-1, Pub. by Annick CN) Firefly Bks Ltd.
—The Fire Station. Munsch, Robert. 24p. (ps-1). 1986. pap. 0.99 (0-920236-77-4, Pub. by Annick CN) Firefly Bks Ltd.
—I Have to Go! Munsch, Robert. 24p. (gr. k-2). 1987. PLB 14.95 (0-920303-77-3, Pub. by Annick CN); pap. 4.95 (0-920303-74-9, Pub. by Annick CN) Firefly Bks Ltd.
—I Have to Go! Munsch, Robert. 24p. (ps-1). 1987. pap. 0.99 (0-920303-51-X, Pub. by Annick CN) Firefly Bks Ltd.
—Il N'y a Pas de Fumee - Where There's Smoke. Munsil, Janet. (ENG & FRE.). 24p. 1993. PLB 14.95 (1-55037-291-2, Pub. by Annick CN); French ed. pap. 4.95 (1-55037-311-0, Pub. by Annick CN); English ed. pap. 4.95 (1-55037-290-4, Pub. by Annick CN) Firefly Bks Ltd.

—Jeremy's Decision. Brott, Ardyth. 32p. (ps-3). 1990. 12.95 (0-916291-31-6) Kane-Miller Bk.
—Jonathan Cleaned Up. Munsch, Robert. 24p. (ps-1). 1986. pap. 0.99 (0-920236-21-9, Pub. by Annick CN) Firefly Bks Ltd.
—Jonathan Cleaned-up: Then He Heard a Sound. Munsch, Robert. 32p. (gr. 4-7). 1981. PLB 14.95 (0-920236-22-7, Pub. by Annick CN); pap. 4.95 (0-920236-20-0, Pub. by Annick CN) Firefly Bks Ltd.
—Mateo y la Grua de Medianoche: (Matthew & the Midnight Tow Truck) Munsch, Robert. Langer, Shirley, tr. (SPA.). 32p. 1991. pap. 5.95 (1-55037-190-8, Pub. by Annick CN) Firefly Bks Ltd.
—Mateo y los Pavos de Medianoche: (Matthew & the Midnight Turkeys) Morgan, Allen. Langer, Shirley, tr. (SPA.). 32p. 1991. pap. 5.95 (1-55037-188-6, Pub. by Annick CN) Firefly Bks Ltd.
—Matthew & the Midnight Money Van. Morgan, Allen. 24p. (ps-2). 1991. pap. 0.99 (1-55037-194-0, Pub. by Annick CN) Firefly Bks Ltd.
—Matthew & the Midnight Tow Truck. Morgan, Allen. 24p. (ps-2). 1991. pap. 0.99 (1-55037-192-4, Pub. by Annick CN) Firefly Bks Ltd.
—Matthew & the Midnight Turkeys. Morgan, Allen. 24p. (ps-2). 1991. pap. 0.99 (1-55037-193-2, Pub. by Annick CN) Firefly Bks Ltd.
—Moira's Birthday. Munsch, Robert. 32p. (gr. k-3). 1987. 12.95 (0-920303-85-4, Pub. by Annick CN); pap. 4.95 (0-920303-83-8, Pub. by Annick CN) Firefly Bks Ltd.
—Mortimer. Munsch, Robert. 24p. (gr. k-3). 1985. PLB 14.95 (0-920303-12-9, Pub. by Annick CN); pap. 4.95 (0-920303-11-0, Pub. by Annick CN) Firefly Bks Ltd.
—Mortimer. Munsch, Robert. 24p. (ps-1). 1986. pap. 0.99 (0-920236-68-5, Pub. by Annick CN) Firefly Bks Ltd.
—El Muchacho en la Gaveta: The Boy in the Drawer. Munsch, Robert. (SPA.). 32p. (ps-2). 1989. pap. 5.95 (1-55037-097-9, Pub. by Annick CN) Firefly Bks Ltd.
—Murmel, Murmel, Murmel. Munsch, Robert. 32p. (gr. k-3). 1982. PLB 14.95 (0-920236-29-4, Pub. by Annick CN); pap. 4.95 (0-920236-31-6, Pub. by Annick CN) Firefly Bks Ltd.
—Murmel, Murmel, Murmel. Munsch, Robert. 24p. (Orig.). (ps-2). 1989. pap. 0.99 (1-55037-012-X, Pub. by Annick CN) Firefly Bks Ltd.
—El Papa de David: David's Father. Munsch, Robert. (SPA.). 32p. (ps-2). 1991. pap. 5.95 (1-55037-096-0, Pub. by Annick CN) Firefly Bks Ltd.
—Paper Bag Princess. Munsch, Robert. 32p. (gr. k-3). 1980. PLB 14.95 (0-920236-82-0, Pub. by Annick CN); pap. 4.95 (0-920236-16-2, Pub. by Annick CN) Firefly Bks Ltd.
—The Paper Bag Princess. Munsch, Robert. 24p. (ps-1). 1986. pap. 0.99 (0-920236-25-1, Pub. by Annick CN) Firefly Bks Ltd.
—Pigs. Munsch, Robert. 24p. (gr. k-2). 1989. 12.95 (1-550370-39-1, Pub. by Annick CN); pap. 4.95 (1-550370-38-3, Pub. by Annick CN) Firefly Bks Ltd.
—La Princesa Vestida Con Una Bolsa De Papel: The Paperbag Princess. Munsch, Robert. (SPA.). 32p. (ps-2). 1991. pap. 5.95 (1-55037-098-7, Pub. by Annick CN) Firefly Bks Ltd.
—Something Good. Munsch, Robert. 24p. (ps-2). 1990. PLB 14.95 (1-55037-099-5, Pub. by Annick CN); pap. 4.95 (1-55037-100-2, Pub. by Annick CN) Firefly Bks Ltd.
—Thomas' Snowsuit. Munsch, Robert. 24p. (gr. k-3). 1985. PLB 14.95 (0-920303-32-3, Pub. by Annick CN); pap. 4.95 (0-920303-33-1, Pub. by Annick CN) Firefly Bks Ltd.
—Zoomerang a Boomerang: Poems to Make Your Belly Laugh. Parry, Caroline, compiled by. LC 92-26589. 32p. (ps-3). 1993. pap. 4.99 (0-14-054869-6) Puffin Bks.
Martell, Ralph. Aesop's Fables in Song. Martell, Ralph. 21p. (gr. k-5). 1987. bk. & cassette 9.95 (0-941977-00-5, RTB-1) Ralmar Enter.
Marten, Charles E. Island Winter. Martin, Charles E. LC 83-14098. 32p. (gr. k-3). 1984. 13.95 (0-688-02590-0); PLB 13.88 (0-688-02592-7) Greenwillow.
Martens, Ray. Take the Pizza & Run: And Other Stories for Children about Stewardship. DeGrote, Barbara. 32p. 1992. pap. 5.99 (0-8066-2599-6, 10-25996) Augsburg Fortress.
Martin, Alice, et al. When Two Saints Meet. Hunger, Bill. Ripley, Jill. ed. 100p. (Orig.). (gr. 6-12). pap. 9.95 (0-9625782-0-7) Two Saints Pub.
Martin, Annie-Claude. The Ancient Greeks: In the Land of the Gods. Descamps-Lequime, Sophie & Vernerey, Denise. LaRose, Mary K., tr. from FRE. LC 91-35941. 64p. (gr. 4-6). 1992. PLB 14.90 (1-56294-069-4) Millbrook Pr.
—The Romans: Life in the Empire. Guittard, Charles. LaRose, Mary K., tr. from FRE. LC 92-9467. 64p. (gr. 4-6). 1992. PLB 14.90 (1-56294-200-X) Millbrook Pr.
Martin, B. Jay. Conundrum, Vol. 1: A Cartoon Collection of Concepts, College, & Confounded Connotations. Martin, B. Jay. Lillard, Ross E., intro. by. 160p. (Orig.). (gr. 12 up). 1988. pap. 5.95 (0-922073-00-7) Thought Wave Pr.
Martin, Bob. My Grandpa Henry. Swaby, Barbara. Rayburn, Cherie, ed. LC 93-72092. 16p. (gr. k-3). 1994. pap. text ed. 16.20 (0-944943-28-4, 91675-3) Current Inc.
Martin, Charles E. El Arca de Noe. Lorimer, Lawrence. (SPA.). 32p. (ps-3). 1993. pap. 2.25 (0-394-85129-3) Random Bks Yng Read.

—For Rent. Martin, Charles E. LC 85-864. 32p. (gr. k-3). 1986. 11.75 (0-688-05716-0); PLB 11.88 (0-688-05717-9) Greenwillow.

—Island Rescue. Martin, Charles E. LC 84-13672. 32p. (gr. k-3). 1985. 11.75 (0-688-04257-0); PLB 11.88 (0-688-04258-9) Greenwillow.

—Noah's Ark. Lorimer, Lawrence T. & Lerner, Sharon, eds. LC 77-92377. (ps-2). 1978. lib. bdg. 5.99 (0-394-93861-5); pap. 2.25 (0-394-83861-0) Random Bks Yng Read.

—Sams Saves the Day. Martin, Charles E. LC 86-19594. 32p. (gr. k-3). 1987. 11.75 (0-688-06814-6); lib. bdg. 11.88 (0-688-06815-4) Greenwillow.

—Summer Business. Martin, Charles E. LC 83-25422. 32p. (gr. k-3). 1984. PLB 14.88 (0-688-03864-6) Greenwillow.

Martin, Clovis. Bicycles Are Fun. Chlad, Dorothy. LC 92-12193. 32p. (ps-2). 1992. PLB 15.00 (0-516-01971-6) Childrens.

—Bonk! Goes the Ball. Stevens, Philippa J. LC 89-48561. 32p. (ps-2). 1990. PLB 11.93 (0-516-02061-7); pap. 2.95 (0-516-42061-5) Childrens.

—Bugs! McKissack, Patricia & McKissack, Fredrick. LC 88-22875. 32p. (ps-2). 1988. PLB 11.93 (0-516-02088-9); pap. 2.95 (0-516-42088-7) Childrens.

—Caring for My Baby Sister. Moncure, Jane B. 32p. (ps-2). 1990. PLB 18.50 (0-89565-669-8); PLB 12.95s.p. (0-685-58738-X) Childs World.

—Donde Esta Pedro? Sneaky Pete. Milios, Rita. LC 89-34666. (SPA.). 32p. (ps-2). 1991. PLB 11.93 (0-516-32092-0); pap. 2.95 (0-516-52092-X) Childrens.

—Dulces Suenos: Sweet Dreams. Neasi, Barbara J. LC 87-15083. (SPA.). 32p. (ps-2). 1991. PLB 11.93 (0-516-32084-X); pap. 2.95 (0-516-52084-9) Childrens.

—I Am. Milios, Rita. LC 87-5163. 32p. (ps-2). 1987. PLB 11.93 (0-516-02081-1); pap. 2.95 (0-516-42081-X) Childrens.

—Just a Little Different. Dobkin, Bonnie. LC 93-13024. 1993. write for info. (0-516-02018-8) Childrens.

—Larry & the Cookie. McDaniel, Becky B. LC 92-37871. 32p. (ps-2). 1993. PLB 11.93 (0-516-02014-5); pap. 2.95 (0-516-42014-3) Childrens.

—A Minute Is a Minute. Neasi, Barbara J. 32p. (ps-3). 1988. pap. 3.95 (0-516-43491-8) Childrens.

—Miss Apple's Hats. Greene, Carol. McKissack, Patricia & McKissack, Fredrick, eds. LC 88-60395. 32p. (Orig.). (gr. 1-3). 1988. text ed. 8.95 (0-88335-779-8); pap. text ed. 4.95 (0-88335-791-7) Milliken Pub Co.

—Un Murmullo Es Silencioso: A Whisper Is Quiet. Lunn, Carolyn. LC 88-11968. (SPA.). 32p. (ps-2). 1991. PLB 11.93 (0-516-32087-4); pap. 2.95 (0-516-52087-3) Childrens.

—Oh No, Otis! Frankel, Julie E. LC 91-15328. 32p. (ps-2). 1991. PLB 11.93 (0-516-02009-9); pap. 2.95 (0-516-42009-7) Childrens.

—Quien Viene? (Who Is Coming?) McKissack, Patricia. LC 86-11805. (SPA & ENG.). 32p. (ps-2). 1989. PLB 11.93 (0-516-32073-4); pap. 2.95 (0-516-52073-3) Childrens.

—Sneaky Pete. Milios, Rita. LC 89-34666. 32p. (ps-2). 1989. PLB 11.93 (0-516-02092-7); pap. 2.95 (0-516-42092-5) Childrens.

—Sweet Dreams. Neasi, Barbara. LC 87-15083. 32p. (ps-2). 1987. PLB 11.93 (0-516-02084-6); pap. 2.95 (0-516-42084-4) Childrens.

—Where Is Mittens? Boivin, Kelly. LC 90-2220. 32p. (ps-2). 1990. PLB 11.93 (0-516-02060-9); pap. 2.95 (0-516-42060-7) Childrens.

—A Whisper Is Quiet. Lunn, Carolyn. LC 88-11968. 32p. (ps-2). 1988. PLB 11.93 (0-516-02087-0); pap. 2.95 (0-516-42087-9) Childrens.

—Who Is Coming? McKissack, Patricia. LC 86-11805. 32p. (ps-3). 1990. PLB 11.93 (0-516-02073-0); pap. 2.95 (0-516-42073-9); pap. 30.60 big bk. (0-516-49458-9) Childrens.

—The Winter Duckling. Polette, Keith. McKissack, Patricia & McKissack, Fredrick, eds. LC 88-60393. 32p. (Orig.). (gr. 1-3). 1990. text ed. 8.95 (0-88335-777-1); pap. text ed. 4.95 (0-88335-789-5) Milliken Pub Co.

—Yo Soy (I Am) Milios, Rita. LC 87-5163. (SPA.). 32p. (ps-2). 1990. PLB 11.93 (0-516-32081-5); pap. 2.95 (0-516-52081-4) Childrens.

Martin, David & Jaquays, Paul. The Orgillion Horror. Taylor, Timothy. Ruemmler, John D., ed. 32p. (Orig.). (gr. 12). 1989. pap. 6.00 (1-55806-029-4, 6006) Iron Crown Ent Inc.

—Tales of the Loremasters, Book 2. Kane, Tom. Ruemmler, John D., ed. 32p. (Orig.). (gr. 12). 1989. pap. 6.00 (1-55806-034-0, 6008) Iron Crown Ent Inc.

Martin, David & Loback, Tom. Halls of the Elven-King. Loback, Tom. Ruemmler, John D., ed. 32p. (Orig.). (gr. 12). 1988. pap. 6.00 (1-55806-015-4, 8204) Iron Crown Ent Inc.

Martin, David & Martin, Elissa. Teeth of Mordor. Amthor, Terry K. Fenlon, Peter C., Jr., ed. 32p. (gr. 10-12). 1988. pap. 6.00 (0-915795-96-5, 8202) Iron Crown Ent Inc.

—Weathertop, the Tower of the Wind. Sochard, Ruth. Fenlon, Peter C., Jr., ed. 32p. (Orig.). (gr. 12). 1987. 6.00 (0-915795-89-2, 8201) Iron Crown Ent Inc.

Martin, David, jt. illus. see Danforth, Liz.

Martin, David, et al. Calenhad: A Beacon of Gondor. Cooke, Tim. Ney, Jessica, ed. 48p. (Orig.). (gr. 12). 1990. pap. 9.00 (1-55806-097-9, 8203) Iron Crown Ent Inc.

Martin, David S. The Holocaust: A History of Courage & Resistance. Stadtler, Bea. Bial, Morrison D., ed. Bauer, Yehuda, intro. by. LC 74-11469. 210p. (gr. 5-7). 1975. pap. text ed. 5.95x (0-87441-231-5); Discussion Guide: By Nancy Karkowsky. pap. text ed. 6.95 (0-87441-257-9) Behrman.

Martin, Diane. My Best Book: A Year-Long Record of "Personal Bests" Martin, Claire & Martin, Steve. 40p. (Orig.). (gr. 3-5). 1988. pap. 7.95 (0-929545-00-1) Black Birch Bks.

Martin, Dick. The Macmillan Book of Fascinating Facts: An Almanac for Kids. Elwood, Ann & Madigan, Carol O. LC 88-22844. 448p. (gr. 4 up). 1989. SBE 16.95 (0-02-733461-9, Macmillan Child Bk) Macmillan Child Grp.

—Merry Go Round in Oz. Jarvis McGraw, Eloise & McGraw, Lauren. 303p. (gr. 3-6). 1989. 24.95 (0-929605-06-3) Books Wonder.

Martin, Elissa, jt. illus. see Martin, David.

Martin, Ellisa, jt. illus. see Velez, Waller.

Martin, Francesca. Lottie's Cats. Cecil, Mirabel. LC 89-29038. 32p. (ps-3). 1990. 12.95 (0-517-57707-0) Crown Bks Yng Read.

Martin, J. V. Nosey Rides the Train. Martin, Lillian. 22p. (ps-4). 1992. pap. 3.95 (1-881079-04-X) Antex Corp.

Martin, Joan S. A to Z with Quincy. Healy, Therese. 50p. (Orig.). (ps-1). 1986. pap. text ed. 8.95 spiral bdg. (0-9617581-0-4) T Healy.

Martin, Josephine. The Evolution of the World: A Revolving Picture Book. Saville, David. LC 91-71383. 12p. 1991. 13.95 (1-56282-095-8) Hyprn Child.

Martin, Judith. Dandelion. Martin, Judith. (Orig.). (gr. 1-5). 1978. pap. 4.50 (0-9606662-0-6) Paper Bag.

Martin, Kerry. Walt Disney's Dumbo. LC 91-71354. 12p. 1991. 9.95 (1-56282-056-7) Disney Pr.

—Walt Disney's One Hundred One Dalmatians Play Hide-&-Seek. LC 92-52972. 18p. (ps-1). 1992. 9.95 (1-56282-270-5) Disney Pr.

Martin, Kerry & Marvin, Fred. Disney's The Little Mermaid. Birney, Betty, adapted by. 28p. (ps). 1992. bds. write for info. (0-307-12534-3, 12534, Golden Pr) Western Pub.

Martin, Kerry & Wakeman, Diana. Walt Disney's Sleeping Beauty. 32p. (ps-k). 1993. 11.95 (1-56282-369-8) Disney Pr.

Martin, Lisi. Lisi & the Kittens. Green, Krister. Coughlin, Ramona, tr. from SWE. 28p. (gr. 3-5). 1990. 12.95g (0-940607-07-7) Pictura NJ.

Martin, Lyn. The Cat at the Door: And Other Stories to Live By. Mather, Anne D. & Weldon, Louise B. 192p. (ps-2). 1991. pap. 12.00 perfect bdg. (0-89486-758-X, T5131) Hazelden.

Martin, Rene. The Sun, the Moon, & the Stars. rev. ed. Freeman, Mae B. & Freeman, Ira M. LC 78-64604. (gr. 2-4). 1979. 8.95 (0-394-80110-5); lib. bdg. 5.99 (0-394-90110-X) Random Bks Yng Read.

—Your Stomach & Digestive Tract. Zim, Herbert S. LC 72-6734. 64p. (gr. 3-7). 1973. PLB 12.88 (0-688-31838-X, Morrow Jr Bks) Morrow Jr Bks.

Martin, Richard E. The Cat Who Wore a Pot on Her Head. Seidler, Ann & Slepian, Jan. 32p. (gr. k-3). 1987. pap. 3.95 (0-590-43708-9) Scholastic Inc.

—The Hungry Thing. Slepian, Jan & Siedler, Ann. 32p. (ps-3). 1988. pap. 3.95 (0-590-42292-8) Scholastic Inc.

—The Hungry Thing Returns. Slepian, Jan & Seidler, Ann. LC 89-6350. (ps-3). 1990. pap. 11.95 (0-590-42890-X) Scholastic Inc.

Martin, Rick. Incredible Fishing Stories for Kids. Morey, Shaun. LC 93-77082. 96p. (Orig.). 1993. pap. 11.95 (0-9633691-1-3) Incrdble Fish.

Martin, Sandra K. Chirrinchinchina - Que Hay en la Tina? (Rub-a-Dub-Dub - What's in the Tub?) Blocksma, Mary. LC 84-12139. (SPA.). 24p. (ps-2). 1988. PLB 12.33 (0-516-31586-2); pap. 3.95 (0-516-51586-1) Childrens.

—Donde Esta el Pato? - Where's That Duck? Blocksma, Mary. LC 85-15001. (SPA.). 24p. (ps-2). 1990. PLB 12.33 (0-516-31587-0); pap. 3.95 (0-516-51587-X) Childrens.

—Happy, Happy Mother's Day! Tripp, Valerie. LC 89-35757. 24p. (ps-2). 1989. pap. 3.95 (0-516-41521-2) Childrens.

—El Perro Cantor (The Singing Dog) Tripp, Valerie. LC 86-14797. (SPA.). 24p. (ps-2). 1990. PLB 12.33 (0-516-31578-1); pap. 3.95 (0-516-51578-0) Childrens.

—Los Pinguinos Se Ponen a Pintar (The Penguins Paint) Tripp, Valerie. LC 87-14081. (SPA.). 24p. (ps-2). 1990. PLB 12.33 (0-516-31567-6); pap. 3.95 (0-516-51567-5) Childrens.

—Sillyhen's Big Surprise. Tripp, Valerie. LC 89-35758. 24p. (ps-2). 1989. pap. 3.95 (0-516-41522-0) Childrens.

—La Sorpresa de Gallinita (Sillyhen's Big Surprise) Tripp, Valerie. LC 89-35758. (SPA.). 24p. (ps-2). 1990. pap. 3.95 (0-516-51522-5) Childrens.

—Squirrel's Thanksgiving Surprise. Tripp, Valerie. LC 87-35518. 24p. (gr. k-2). 1988. PLB 12.33 (0-516-01568-0); pap. 3.95 (0-516-41568-9) Childrens.

Martin, Sandy. Who Is Uncle Sam? Jones, Taffy. LC 91-52615. 64p. (Orig.). 1991. pap. 6.95 (0-917882-32-6) MD Hist Pr.

Martin, Shawna. Forty-Seven Alligators. McMahon, James. Little, Carl. ed. 48p. (Orig.). (ps-3). 1993. pap. 10.95 (0-932433-95-2) Windswept Hse.

Martinez, Ed. Too Many Tamales. Soto, Gary. 32p. (ps-3). 1993. 14.95 (0-399-22146-8, Putnam) Putnam Pub Group.

Martinez, Francesc, jt. illus. see Ballestar, Vincenc.

Martinez, Jesse. The Day Happy E. Bunny Lost His Cotton Tail. Miller, Sherry. 16p. (Orig.). (gr. k-5). 1983. pap. 0.49 saddle-stitched (0-685-43303-X) Double M Pub.

—Lost in the Arctic with Pal Bear. Miller, Sherry. 32p. (Orig.). (gr. k-5). 1984. pap. 1.95 saddle-stitched (0-913379-01-8) Double M Pub.

—Santa's Helper. Miller, Sherry. LC 83-72493. 32p. (Orig.). (gr. k-5). 1983. pap. 1.95 saddle-stitched (0-913379-00-X) Double M Pub.

—Snowharry Takes a Vacation (with Arctic Friends) Miller, Sherry. 32p. (gr. k-5). 1985. pap. write for info. saddle-stitched (0-913379-03-4) Double M Pub.

—Snowskate Goes for Gold. Miller, Sherry. 32p. (Orig.). (gr. k-5). 1984. pap. 1.95 saddle-stitched (0-913379-02-6) Double M Pub.

Martinez, Leovigildo. The Moon Was at a Fiesta. Gollub, Matthew. LC 93-14750. 32p. 1994. 15.00 (0-688-11637-X, Tambourine Bks); PLB 14.93 (0-688-11638-8) Morrow.

—The Twenty-Five Mixtec Cats. Gollub, Matthew. LC 92-13585. 32p. (gr. 1 up). 1993. 14.00 (0-688-11639-6, Tambourine Bks); PLB 13.93 (0-688-11640-X, Tambourine Bks) Morrow.

Martinez, Sergio. Cabeza de Vaca: New World Explorer. Brandt, Keith. LC 92-36960. 48p. (gr. 4-6). 1993. lib. bdg. 10.79 (0-8167-2829-1); 3.50 (0-8167-2830-5) Troll Assocs.

Martinez, Sergio & Paget, Sidney. The Hound of the Baskervilles. Doyle, Arthur Conan. 272p. (gr. 4 up). 1992. 12.99 (0-517-07770-1, Child Classics) Outlet Bk Co.

Martins, George. How Would You Feel If Your Dad Was Gay? Heron, Ann & Maran, Meredith. 32p. (gr. 1-5). 1991. text ed. 9.95 (1-55583-188-5) Alyson Pubns.

—Spin a Soft Black Song. rev. ed. Giovanni, Nikki. LC 84-19287. 64p. (gr. 2 up). 1985. 11.95 (0-8090-8796-0) Hill & Wang.

—Spin a Soft Black Song. rev. ed. Giovanni, Nikki. (gr. k up). 1987. pap. 3.95 (0-374-46469-3, Sunburst) FS&G.

Martishuis, Walter & Nino, Alex. American Revolutionary. Cover, Arthur B. 144p. (gr. 7-12). 1985. pap. 2.50 (0-553-26773-6) Bantam.

Martland, Elizabeth. Solo Plus One. Scamell, Ragnhild. 32p. (ps-3). 1992. 13.95 (0-316-77242-9) Little.

Marton, Jirina. Amelia's Celebration. Marton, Jirina. 24p. (ps-3). 1992. PLB 15.95 (1-55037-221-1, Pub. by Annick CN); pap. 5.95 (1-55037-220-3, Pub. by Annick CN) Firefly Bks Ltd.

—Emma's Sea Journey. Quinlan, Patricia. 24p. (ps-3). 1991. PLB 15.95 (1-55037-179-7, Pub. by Annick CN); pap. 5.95 (1-55037-177-0, Pub. by Annick CN) Firefly Bks Ltd.

—Flowers for Mom. Marton, Jirina. 24p. (ps-3). 1991. PLB 15.95 (1-55037-155-X, Pub. by Annick CN); pap. 5.95 (1-55037-158-4, Pub. by Annick CN) Firefly Bks Ltd.

—I'll Do It Myself. Marton, Jirina. 1990. 14.95 (1-550370-63-4, Pub. by Annick CN); pap. 5.95 (1-550370-62-6, Pub. by Annick CN) Firefly Bks Ltd.

—Setting Wonder Free. Barnes, Maryke. 24p. 1993. lib. bdg. 14.95 (1-55037-241-6, Pub. by Annick CN); pap. 4.95 (1-55037-238-6, Pub. by Annick CN) Firefly Bks Ltd.

Martz, Susan. Gittel & the Bell. Goldshlag-Cooks, Roberta. LC 87-2828. (gr. k-4). 1987. 10.95 (0-930494-68-7) Kar Ben.

Maruki, Toshi. Hiroshima No Pika. Maruki, Toshi. LC 82-15365. 48p. (gr. 7 up). 1982. 14.95 (0-688-01297-3) Lothrop.

Marvin, Fred. Bambi: The New Prince. LC 93-71377. 10p. (ps-k). 1994. 4.95 (1-56282-601-8) Disney Pr.

—The Little Mermaid Novels. (gr. 1-4). 1993. Boxed set incl. Green-Eyed Pearl, Nefazia Visits the Palace, Reflections of Arsulu & The Same Old Song. 15.80 (1-56282-562-3) Disney Pr.

—Pinocchio: Geppetto's Surprise. Lampl, Cathy, ed. LC 92-54877. 10p. (ps-k). 1993. 4.95 (1-56282-397-3) Disney Pr.

—Snow White & the Seven Dwarfs: Suppertime. LC 93-71376. 10p. (gr. 2-5). 1994. 4.95 (1-56282-600-X) Disney Pr.

—Walt Disney's Pinocchio. Muldrow, Diane, adapted by. 28p. (ps). 1992. bds. write for info. (0-307-12532-7, 12532, Golden Pr) Western Pub.

—Walt Disney's Snow White & the Seven Dwarfs. Razzi, Jim. LC 92-53430. 96p. 1993. 14.95 (1-56282-362-0); PLB 14.89 (1-56282-363-9) Disney Pr.

Marvin, Fred, jt. illus. see Martin, Kerry.

Marvin, Frederic. Grover. Cleaver, Vera & Cleaver, Bill. LC 69-12001. 128p. (gr. 4-7). 1970. 13.00 (0-397-31118-4, Lipp Jr Bks) HarpC Child Bks.

—How Big Is a Brachiosaurus? Carroll, Susan. 32p. (ps-2). 1986. pap. 1.95 (0-448-19077-X, G&D) Putnam Pub Group.

—A Little Princess. Burnett, Frances H. Adorjan, Carol M., adapted by. LC 87-15485. 48p. (gr. 3-6). 1988. PLB 12.89 (0-8167-1201-8); pap. text ed. 3.95 (0-8167-1202-6) Troll Assocs.

Mary Loretta. Catholic Truth for Youth. Fox, Robert J. Luther, Ben, intro. by. LC 78-104309. 448p. (gr. 5-12). 1978. pap. 5.95 (0-911988-05-X) AMI Pr.

Marzilli, Roanne O. Return of the Nighthawks. Marzilli, Vincent, II. 56p. (Orig.). (gr. k-6). 1987. pap. 7.95 (0-9617809-1-6) Vincent Marzilli.

Masaomi Kanzaki. Xenon, Vol. 2: Heavy Metal Warrior. Masaomi Kanzaki. Seiji Horibuchi, ed. Satoru Fujii, tr. from JPN. 192p. 1991. pap. 14.95 (0-929279-41-7) Viz Commns Inc.
—Xenon, Vol. 4: Heavy Metal Warrior. Masaomi Kanzaki. Seiji Horibuchi, ed. Satoru Fujii, tr. from JPN. 176p. 1992. pap. 14.95 (0-929279-47-6) Viz Commns Inc.
Masheris, Bob. Luis W. Alvarez. Codye, Corinn. De Varona, Frank, intro. by. (SPA & ENG.). 32p. (gr. 3-6). 1990. PLB 15.96 (0-8172-3376-8); pap. 4.95 (0-8114-6750-3) Raintree Steck-V.
—The Rain Forest. Greenberg, Judith E. & Carey, Helen H. 32p. (gr. 2-4). 1990. PLB 17.96 (0-8172-3753-4) Raintree Steck-V.
Masheris, Robert. The Dreams of Hummingbirds: Poems from Nature. Coleman, Mary A. Mathews, Judith, ed. LC 92-28169. 32p. (gr. 3-7). 1993. PLB 14.95 (0-8075-1720-8) A Whitman.
—The Fox on the Box. Gregorich, Barbara. Hoffman, Joan, ed. 16p. (Orig.). (gr. k-2). 1984. pap. 2.25 (0-88743-005-8, 06005) Sch Zone Pub Co.
—Sandra Day O'Connor: Justice for All. Gherman, Beverly. LC 92-42464. 64p. (gr. 2-6). 1993. pap. 3.99 (0-14-034100-5, Puffin) Puffin Bks.
—Up Went the Goat. Gregorich, Barbara. Hoffman, Joan, ed. 16p. (Orig.). (gr. k-2). 1984. pap. 2.25 (0-88743-002-3, 06202) Sch Zone Pub Co.
Masiello, Ralph. The Extinct Alphabet Book. Pallotta, Jerry. LC 93-1512. 1993. 14.95 (0-88106-471-8); PLB 15.00 (0-88106-486-6); pap. 6.95 (0-88106-470-X) Charlesbridge Pub.
—The Frog Alphabet Book. Pallotta, Jerry. 32p. (Orig.). (ps-4). 1990. 14.95 (0-88106-463-7); pap. 6.95 (0-88106-462-9) Charlesbridge Pub.
—The Icky Bug Alphabet Book. Palotta, Jerry. 32p. (ps-3). 1989. 14.95 (0-88106-456-4); pap. 6.95 (0-88106-450-5) Charlesbridge Pub.
Masihlall, Kamala. Drug Card. Masihlall, Kamala. 13p. (gr. k-3). 1993. pap. 12.95 (1-895583-61-6) MAYA Pubs.
—Rozan with Personnel. Masihlall, Kamala. 16p. (gr. k-3). 1993. pap. 9.95 (1-895583-60-8) MAYA Pubs.
Maslen, John R. Bob Books, Even More for Young Readers, 8 bks, Set III. Maslen, Bobby L. 144p. 1987. pap. 14.95 incl. teaching guide (0-9612104-2-7) Bob Bks.
—Bob Books, More for Young Readers, Set II. Maslen, Bobby L. 144p. 1987. Set of 8 books & teaching guide. 13.95 (0-9612104-1-9) Bob Bks.
Mason, Charles, photos by. Friendship Across Arctic Waters: Alaskan Cub Scouts Visit Their Soviet Neighbors. Murphy, Claire R. 48p. (gr. 3-8). 1991. 15.95 (0-525-67348-2, Lodestar Bks) Dutton Child Bks.
Mason, Debbie. Walking with Clara Belle. Ackerman, Karen. 40p. (gr. k-3). 1993. 9.95 (0-8198-8243-7) St Paul Bks.
Mason, Eric. The Blackstone Book of Magic & Illusion. Blackstone, Harry, Jr., et al. Bradbury, Ray, frwd. by. LC 84-29486. 248p. (gr. 7 up). 1985. 22.95 (0-937858-45-5) Newmarket.
Mason, Gwen. The Smallest Koala. Broome, Errol. (ps-1). 1988. 11.95 (0-949447-65-X) Terra Nova.
Mason, MacAdam L. Muffin, The Maine Puffin. Campbell, Louise A. & Bowers, Grace A. 40p. (Orig.). (gr. k-3). 1988. pap. 9.95 (0-9621949-0-5) Muffin Enter.
Mass, Ronald, photos by. Inside the Synagogue. rev. ed. Freeman, Grace & Sugarman, Joan. 64p. (gr. 1-3). 1984. pap. 6.00 (0-8074-0268-0, 301785) UAHC.
Massed, Cal. Black Shogun of Japan - Sophonisa: Wife of Two Warring Kings & Other Stories from Antiquity. Hyman, Mark. 120p. (Orig.). (gr. 9-12). 1989. pap. 11.00 (0-915515-01-6) The Way Pub.
Massey, Cal. I Love My Family. Hudson, Wade. 32p. (ps-2). 1993. 10.95 (0-590-45763-2) Scholastic Inc.
Massey, Cal, et al. Grio "The Praise Singer" The 1987 Chronicle of Afro-American Heritage, Vol. III. Sutton, Charyn, ed. 80p. (Orig.). (gr. k-12). 1988. pap. text ed. 9.95 (0-936509-00-7); 183.25 (0-936509-01-5) Enteracom Inc.
Massie, Diane R. Chameleon Was a Spy. Massie, Diane R. LC 78-19510. (gr. 2-6). 1979. (Crowell Jr Bks) HarpC Child Bks.
Massingill, Susan. Bake a Snake: How to Survive by Your Own Cooking. Hunter, Gerald R. & Hoffmann, Peggy. LC 81-10293. 68p. (Orig.). (gr. 1-7). 1981. 9.00 (0-939710-10-2); pap. 4.75 (0-939710-09-9) Meridional Pubns.

Massmann, Jane H. Come Follow Me. Wilson, Jean A. 26p. (ps-3). 1989. 12.95 (0-911586-01-6) Wahr.

Jean Wilson's second book of verses for children 3-7, follows the children through the seasons for discovery, learning & questioning. The children go to a supermarket; slide down a hill; ride a bike; go to a band concert; feel a live rabbit; & a horse; see their shadows; wonder about frost; leaves & snowmen, play jacks; go to a birthday party; wonder about raindrops & go to bed (but, according to the last verse, not without washing their feet). Reality based, vivid illustrations, accurate animal drawings & musical instruments. Again Wilson, adds another dimension to her whimsical verses through thoughtful questions posed by the child narrator. *Publisher Provided Annotation.*

Mastrangelo, Judy & Mastrangelo, Judy. The Sandman: And Other Sleepy-Time Rhymes. LC 90-34513. 48p. (ps-2). 1990. 4.95 (0-88101-105-3) Unicorn Pub.
Masuda, Modoki. Bats. Johnson, Sylvia A. LC 85-15999. 48p. (gr. 4 up). 1985. PLB 19.95 (0-8225-1461-3, First Ave Edns); pap. 5.95 (0-8225-9500-1, First Ave Edns) Lerner Pubns.
—Snails. Johnson, Sylvia A. LC 82-10086. 48p. (gr. 4 up). 1982. PLB 19.95 (0-8225-1475-3, First Ave Edns); pap. 5.95 (0-8225-9544-3, First Ave Edns) Lerner Pubns.
—Tree Frogs. Johnson, Sylvia A. LC 86-2721. 48p. (gr. 4 up). 1986. PLB 19.95 (0-8225-1467-2) Lerner Pubns.
—Water Insects. Johnson, Sylvia A. 48p. (gr. 4 up). 1989. PLB 19.95 (0-8225-1489-3) Lerner Pubns.
Masuda, Modoki, photos by. Snakes. Johnson, Sylvia A. LC 87-7162. 48p. (gr. 4 up). 1986. PLB 19.95 (0-8225-1484-2, First Ave Edns); pap. 5.95 (0-8225-9503-6, First Ave Edns) Lerner Pubns.
Mataya, David. Earthwise at Play: A Guide to the Care & Feeding of Your Planet. Lorbiecki, Marybeth & Lowery, Linda. 92-9870. 1993. 19.95 (0-87614-729-5) Carolrhoda Bks.
—Tales for Hard Times: A Story about Charles Dickens. Collins, David R. 64p. (gr. 3-6). 1990. PLB 14.95 (0-87614-433-4) Carolrhoda Bks.
Maten, Franc. Walt Disney's Alice in Wonderland. Slater, Teddy, adapted by. (ps-2). 1991. write for info. (0-307-12341-3, Golden Pr) Western Pub.
Maten, Frenc. Walt Disney Pictures Presents the Little Mermaid. Calmenson, Stephanie, adapted by. (ps-k). 1991. pap. write for info. (0-307-10027-8, Golden Pr) Western Pub.
Matens, Margaret H. Mandy & the Kookalocka. Matens, Margaret H. 93-77130. 32p. (gr. k-5). 1993. 14.95 (1-882959-53-1) Foxglove TN.
—So You're off to Summer Camp: A Trunk Load of Tips for a Fun-Filled Camp Adventure. Queen, Margaret M. LC 93-77129. 136p. (gr. 2-12). 1993. 14.95 (1-882959-55-8); perfect bdg. 6.95 (1-882959-50-7) Foxglove TN.
—Wuzzy the Witch. Matens, Margaret H. LC 93-77128. 42p. (gr. k-5). 1993. 14.95 (1-882959-54-X) Foxglove TN.
Mateo, Franc. Walt Disney's Snow White & the Seven Dwarfs. Lampl, C., ed. LC 92-53432. 12p. (ps-k). 1993. 11.95 (1-56282-365-5) Disney Pr.
Mateu. Disney's Aladdin. Kidd, Ronald, adapted by. 24p. (ps-4). 1992. 20.00 (0-307-74026-9, 64026, Golden Pr) Western Pub.
—The Easy-to-Read Little Engine That Could. Piper, Watty. Retan, Walter, adapted by. (ps-2). 1990. pap. 4.95 (0-448-34344-4, Platt & Munk Pubs) Putnam Pub Group.
—Snow White & the Seven Dwarfs. Kidd, Ronald, adapted by. 24p. (ps up) 1991. write for info. (0-307-74018-8, 64018) Western Pub.
Mateu, Franc. Lady & the Tramp: Illustrated Classic. Strasser, Todd, adapted by. LC 93-71378. 96p. 1994. 14.95 (1-56282-613-1); PLB 14.89 (1-56282-615-8) Disney Pr.
—Minnie 'n Me: What Will I Wear? Calder, Lyn. 32p. (ps-1). 1992. pap. write for info. (0-307-15967-1, 15967) Western Pub.
—Teenage Mutant Ninja Turtles: School Daze. Holm, Astrid. LC 90-61185. 32p. (Orig.). (ps-3). 1991. pap. 1.50 (0-679-81169-9) Random Bks Yng Read.
—Walt Disney Pictures Presents the Little Mermaid: Ariel above the Sea. Colmenson, Stephanie. (gr. k-2). 1991. 4.25 (0-307-11697-2, Golden Pr) Western Pub.
—Walt Disney's The Little Mermaid: Ariel above the Sea. Calder, Lyn. 32p. (ps-2). 1992. pap. write for info. (0-307-15965-5, 15965) Western Pub.
Mateu, Franc & Kaufman, Richard. Walt Disney's Sorcerer's Apprentice Storybook & Magic Tricks. Friedhoffer, Bob. Slater, Teddy, retold by. LC 91-73813. 64p. (gr. 1-7). 1993. 12.95 (1-56282-144-X) Disney Pr.
Mateus. The Easy-to-Read-Little Engine That Could. Piper, Watty. Retan, Walter, adapted by. 32p. (ps-2). 1986. pap. 2.25 (0-448-19078-8, G&D); incl. cassette 5.95 (0-448-19088-5) Putnam Pub Group.
Math, Irwin. Wires & Watts: Using & Understanding Electricity. Math, Irwin. LC 81-2255. 96p. (gr. 7 up). 1989. pap. 4.95 (0-689-71298-7, Aladdin) Macmillan Child Grp.
Matheis, Shelley. The Bookmonster. Minsberg, David. 32p. (ps-k). 1981. 7.50 (0-940674-00-9); incl. bookmonster doll 27.95 (0-685-03087-3) Littlebee.
—Josie's Troubles. Naylor, Phyllis R. LC 90-47641. 128p. (gr. 3-7). 1992. SBE 12.95 (0-689-31659-3, Atheneum Child Bk) Macmillan Child Grp.

Mathers, Dawn. Christmas Gifts That Didn't Need Wrapping. Mackall, Dandi D. 32p. (ps-2). 1990. pap. 5.99 (0-8066-2466-3, 9-2466) Augsburg Fortress.
—Kay's Birthday Surprise. Mackall, Dandi D. LC 89-82554. 32p. (ps-2). 1990. pap. 5.99 (0-8066-2467-1, 9-2467) Augsburg Fortress.
Mathers, Peter. Borreguita & the Coyote: A Tale from Ayutla, Mexico. Aardema, Verna, retold by. & tr. LC 90-39419. 40p. (ps-3). 1991. 15.00 (0-679-80921-X); lib. bdg. 15.99 (0-679-90921-4) Knopf Bks Yng Read.
Mathers, Petra. Aunt Elaine Does the Dance from Spain. Komaiko, Leah. LC 91-45474. 32p. (ps-3). 1992. 15.00 (0-385-30674-1) Doubleday.
—The Block Book. Couture, Susan A. LC 89-34504. 32p. (ps-3). 1990. HarpC Child Bks.
—Frannie's Fruits. Kimmelman, Leslie. LC 88-17637. 32p. (ps-3). 1989. PLB 13.89 (0-06-023164-5) HarpC Child Bks.
—I'm Flying! Wade, Alan. LC 88-31360. 40p. (gr. k-4). 1990. 13.95 (0-394-84510-2) Knopf Bks Yng Read.
—Little Love Song. Kennedy, Richard. LC 91-2053. 32p. 1992. 8.00 (0-679-81177-X) Knopf Bks Yng Read.
—Maria Theresa. Mathers, Petra. LC 84-48346. 32p. (ps-3). 1985. PLB 13.89 (0-06-024112-8) HarpC Child Bks.
—Maria Theresa. Mathers, Petra. LC 84-48346. 32p. (gr. k-3). 1992. pap. 4.95 (0-06-443282-3, Trophy) HarpC Child Bks.
—Molly's New Washing Machine. Geringer, Laura. LC 85-45839. 32p. (gr. k-3). 1986. HarpC Child Bks.
—Mrs. Merriwether's Musical Cat. Purdy, Carol. LC 92-43934. Write for info. (0-399-22543-9, Putnam) Putnam Pub Group.
—Patchwork Island. Kuskin, Karla. LC 92-10344. 1994. 14.00 (0-06-021242-X, HarpT); PLB 13.89 (0-06-021284-5, HarpT) HarpC.
—Sophie & Lou. Mathers, Petra. LC 90-37562. 32p. (ps-3). 1991. 15.00 (0-06-024071-7); PLB 14.89 (0-06-024072-5) HarpC Child Bks.
—Victor & Christabel. Mathers, Petra. LC 92-33468. 40p. (ps-3). 1993. 15.00 (0-679-83060-X); PLB 15.99 (0-679-93060-4) Knopf Bks Yng Read.
—When It Snowed That Night. Farber, Norma. LC 92-27414. 40p. (gr. k up). 1993. 16.00 (0-06-021707-3); PLB 15.89 (0-06-021708-1) HarpC Child Bks.
Matheson, Hedda. Granny Boy & the Puny Warbler. Cartwright, Hal V. LC 92-71096. 48p. (Orig.). (gr. 4). 1992. pap. 8.50 (0-923687-16-5) Celo Valley Bks.
Mathews, Jenny, photos by. Adventure Holiday. Brearley, Sue. 28p. (gr. 1-4). 1991. 12.95 (0-7136-3382-4, Pub. by A&C Black UK) Talman.
Mathews, Sally S. The Sad Night: The Story of an Aztec Victory & a Spanish Loss. Mathews, Sally S. LC 92-25119. 1993. write for info. (0-395-63035-5, Clarion Bks) HM.

Mathewson, Mel. North America's ENDANGERED Species. Sanger, David. Lynch, Don, ed. 97p. (Orig.). (ps-8). 1992. pap. text ed. 4.00 (0-913205-17-6); special price 2.40 Grace Dangberg.

This exciting book for young people contains 97 pages of 44 selected endangered wildlife representing nine categories. The 9" x 11 1/2" paperback book includes maps showing locations of the endangered wildlife, a summary of information about each selection, & a full-page black & white drawing of each wildlife which can be colored. Young people will enjoy the original art work by Mel Mathewson & learn of the endangered from it. Published by The Grace Dangberg Foundation, Inc. in 1992, the book is celebrated by a 20" x 30" color poster of the endangered wildlife represented in the book. The poster is now available from the Foundation. *Publisher Provided Annotation.*

Mathieo, Joe. Grover & the Everything in the Whole Wide World Museum. Stiles, Norman & Wilcox, Daniel. LC 73-18736. 32p. 1974. pap. 2.25 (0-394-82707-4) Random Bks Yng Read.
Mathieu, Agnes. Animals in Winter. De Sairigne, Catherine. Matthews, Sarah, tr. from FRE. LC 87-34086. 38p. (gr. k-5). 1988. 4.95 (0-944589-05-7, 057) Young Discovery Lib.
—Arthur Sets Sail. Schaffer, Libor. LC 87-1594. 32p. (gr. k-3). 1987. 14.95 (1-55858-059-X) North-South Bks NYC.
—The Easter Bunny. Wolf, Winifred. LC 85-10115. 24p. (ps-3). 1991. pap. 3.99 (0-8037-0912-9, Dial Pied Piper) Puffin Bks.
—The Easter Bunny. Wolf, Winfried. LC 85-10115. 32p. (ps-3). 1987. 8.95 (0-8037-0239-6) Dial Bks Young.

—Jonathan Mouse & the Baby Bird. Ostheeren, Ingrid. Lanning, Rosemary, tr. from GER. LC 91-6614. 32p. (gr. k-3). 1991. 14.95 (1-55858-108-1) North-South Bks NYC.
—Jonathan Mouse & the Magic Box. Ostheeren, Ingrid. Lanning, Rosemary, tr. from GER. LC 89-43248. 32p. (gr. k-3). 1990. 13.95 (1-55858-087-5) North-South Bks NYC.
—Jonathan Mouse at the Circus. Ostheeren, Ingrid. Lanning, Rosemary, tr. from GER. LC 87-42980. 32p. (gr. k-3). 1988. 12.95 (1-55858-055-7) North-South Bks NYC.
—Jonathan Mouse, Detective. Ostheeren, Ingrid. Lanning, Rosemary, tr. from GER. LC 92-29023. 32p. (gr. k-3). 1993. 14.95 (1-55858-164-2); pap. 14.95 (1-55858-141-3) North-South Bks NYC.
Mathieu, Joe. A, My Name Is Alice: A Sesame Street Alphabet Book. Holt, Virginia. LC 88-18520. 32p. (Orig.). (ps). 1989. lib. bdg. 5.99 (0-394-92241-7); pap. 2.25 (0-394-82241-2) Random Bks Yng Read.
—Bert & the Missing Mop Mix-Up. Roberts, Sarah. LC 82-22971. 40p. (gr. k-2). 1983. 4.95 (0-394-85752-6) Random Bks Yng Read.
—Big Bird Plays the Violin. Hautzig, Deborah. LC 90-8967. 40p. (ps-3). 1991. 4.95 (0-679-81675-5); PLB 6.99 (0-679-91675-X) Random Bks Yng Read.
—Big Bird Visits the Dodos. Hautzig, Deborah, adapted by. LC 84-43051. 32p. (ps-3). 1985. lib. bdg. 5.99 (0-394-97373-9) Random Bks Yng Read.
—Big Bird's Big Book. Mathieu, Joe. 12p. (ps-1). 1987. 29.95 (0-394-89128-7) Random Bks Yng Read.
—Big Dan's Moving Van. McGuire, Leslie. LC 90-4417. 32p. (Orig.). (ps-1). 1993. pap. 2.25 (0-679-80565-6) Random Bks Yng Read.
—The Book of the Unknown. Woods, Harold & Woods, Geraldine. LC 82-3683. 72p. (gr. 4-7). 1982. lib. bdg. 5.99 (0-394-95233-2) Random Bks Yng Read.
—Brewster's Courage. Kovacs, Deborah. LC 91-21481. 112p. (gr. 2-6). 1992. pap. 14.00 jacketed, 3-pc. bdg. (0-671-74016-4, S&S BFYR) S&S Trade.
—Christmas Eve on Sesame Street. Stone, Jon & Bailey, Joe. LC 81-50247. 64p. (ps-2). 1981. 7.95 (0-394-84733-4); lib. bdg. 6.99 (0-394-94733-9, Random Juv) Random Bks Yng Read.
—Dogs Don't Wear Sneakers. Numeroff, Laura. LC 92-27007. 1993. pap. 14.00 (0-671-79525-2, S&S BFYR) S&S Trade.
—Elmo Wants a Bath. Mathieu, Joe. 10p. (ps). 1992. vinyl 3.95 (0-679-83066-9) Random Bks Yng Read.
—Elmo's Big Lift-&-Look Book. Ross, Anna. 12p. (ps-k). 1994. 8.00 (0-679-84468-6) Random Bks Yng Read.
—Ernie & Bert's New Kitten. Hautzig, Deborah. LC 89-10583. 40p. (ps-3). 1990. 4.95 (0-679-80420-X); PLB 6.99 (0-679-90420-4) Random Bks Yng Read.
—Ernie & Bert's New Kitten. Hautzig, Deborah. LC 89-10583. 40p. (ps-3). 1993. pap. 2.99 (0-679-83954-2) Random Bks Yng Read.
—Ernie's Big Mess. Roberts, Sarah. LC 81-2464. 40p. (ps-3). 1992. pap. 2.99 (0-679-82398-0) Random Bks Yng Read.
—Ernie's Little Lie. Elliott, Dan. LC 82-7574. 40p. (ps-3). 1992. 4.95 (0-394-85440-3); pap. 2.99 (0-679-82401-4) Random Bks Yng Read.
—Get Well, Granny Bird. Hautzig, Deborah. LC 88-18446. 40p. (ps-3). 1989. PLB 6.99 (0-394-92247-6) Random Bks Yng Read.
—The Giant Book of More Strange but True Sports Stories. Liss, Howard. LC 82-13236. 160p. (gr. 5-10). 1983. pap. 8.95 (0-394-85633-3) Random Bks Yng Read.
—The Giant Book of Strange but True Sports Stories. Liss, Howard. LC 76-8132. (gr. 5-9). 1976. 9.00 (0-394-83287-6) Random Bks Yng Read.
—Grover's Bad Dream. Hautzig, Deborah. LC 90-32085. 40p. (ps-3). 1990. 4.95 (0-679-80898-1); lib. bdg. 6.99 (0-679-90898-6) Random Bks Yng Read.
—I Want to Go Home. Roberts, Sarah. LC 84-11725. 40p. (ps-3). 1985. 4.95 (0-394-87027-1) Random Bks Yng Read.
—It's Easy! Hautzig, Deborah. LC 88-6441. 40p. (ps-3). 1988. 4.95 (0-394-81376-6) Random Bks Yng Read.
—My Doll Is Lost! Elliott, Dan. LC 83-11211. 40p. (ps-3). 1993. pap. 2.99 (0-679-83953-4) Random Bks Yng Read.
—Nobody Cares about Me! Roberts, Sarah. LC 81-15913. 40p. (ps-3). 1992. pap. 2.99 (0-679-82399-9) Random Bks Yng Read.
—The Olden Days. Mathieu, Joe. 32p. (ps-3). 1981. lib. bdg. 4.99 (0-394-94085-7) Random Bks Yng Read.
—Plants Do Amazing Things. Nussbaum, Hedda. LC 75-36471. 72p. (gr. 2-3). 1977. 9.95 (0-394-83232-9); lib. bdg. 9.99 (0-394-93232-3) Random Bks Yng Read.
—Pop Goes the Santa! A Sesame Street Thumb Fun Book. LC 91-68546. 48p. (ps). 1992. pap. 2.50 (0-679-83065-0) Random Bks Yng Read.
—Rocking Reindeer: A Sesame Street Thumb Fun Book. LC 91-68545. 48p. (Orig.). (ps). 1992. pap. 2.50 (0-679-83064-2) Random Bks Yng Read.
—The Sesame Street Dictionary. Sesame Street Staff & Hayward, Linda. LC 80-11644. 256p. (ps-3). 1980. bds. 15.95 (0-394-84007-0); PLB 17.99 (0-394-94007-5) Random Bks Yng Read.
—Sesame Street Fire Trucks. 14p. (ps-k). 1988. bds. 3.99 (0-394-89952-0) Random Bks Yng Read.
—Sesame Street One Two Three: A Counting Book from 1 to 100. Mathieu, Joe. LC 91-1992. 32p. (ps-1). 1991. 9.00 (0-679-81230-X); lib. bdg. 10.99 (0-679-91230-4) Random Bks Yng Read.

—Sesame Street, the Ernie & Bert Book. Stiles, Norman. 24p. (ps-k). 1977. pap. write for info. (0-307-10072-3, Pub. by Golden Bks) Western Pub.
—The Superkids & the Singing Dog. West, Cindy. LC 81-50042. 48p. (gr. 1-4). 1982. lib. bdg. 4.99 (0-394-94924-2) Random Bks Yng Read.
—Susan & Gordon Adopt a Baby. Freudberg, Judy & Geiss, Tony. LC 86-2951. 24p. (ps-2). 1992. 5.99 (0-394-88341-1) Random Bks Yng Read.
—Trucks in Your Neighborhood. 14p. (ps-k). 1988. bds. 3.99 (0-394-89951-2) Random Bks Yng Read.
—Two Wheels for Grover. Elliott, Dan. LC 84-4732. 40p. (ps-3). 1984. 4.95 (0-394-86586-3); lib. bdg. 6.99 (0-394-96586-8) Random Bks Yng Read.
—A Visit to the Sesame Street Firehouse. Elliott, Dan. LC 83-4606. 32p. (ps-3). 1983. lib. bdg. 5.99 (0-394-96029-7); pap. 2.25 (0-394-86029-2) Random Bks Yng Read.
—A Visit to the Sesame Street Hospital. Hantzig, Deborah. LC 84-17852. 32p. (ps-4). 1985. lib. bdg. 5.99 (0-394-97062-4); pap. 2.25 (0-394-87062-X) Random Bks Yng Read.
—A Visit to the Sesame Street Library. Hautzig, Deborah. LC 85-18312. 32p. (ps-1). 1986. 2.25 (0-394-87744-6); lib. bdg. 5.99 (0-394-97744-0) Random Bks Yng Read.
—Una Visita a la Biblioteca De Sesame Street. Hautzig, Deborah. Saunders, Paola B., tr. LC 92-16609. (SPA.). 32p. (ps-3). 1993. pap. 2.25 (0-679-83943-7) Random Bks Yng Read.
—Una Visita a la Estacion de Bomberos de Sesame Street. Elliott, Dan. Miro, Norma S. & Saunders, Paola B., trs. from ENG. LC 92-3814. (SPA.). 32p. (ps-3). 1992. pap. 2.25 (0-679-83499-0) Random Bks Yng Read.
—Una Visita Al Hospital De Sesame Street. Hautzig, Deborah. Saunders, Paola B., tr. LC 92-16610. (SPA.). 32p. (ps-3). 1993. pap. 2.25 (0-679-83944-5) Random Bks Yng Read.
—Wait for Me! Cross, Molly. LC 87-12926. 40p. (ps-3). 1987. 4.95 (0-394-89135-X) Random Bks Yng Read.
—Wait for Me! Cross, Molly. LC 87-12926. 40p. (ps-3). 1993. pap. 2.99 (0-679-83952-6) Random Bks Yng Read.
—We're Different, We're the Same. Kates, Bobbi J. LC 91-38545. 32p. (Orig.). (ps-3). 1992. pap. 2.25 (0-679-83227-0) Random Bks Yng Read.
Mathieu, Joe, jt. illus. see Jacquet, Jean-Pierre.
Mathieu, Joseph. Big Joe's Trailer Truck. reissued ed. Mathieu, Joseph. LC 74-2538. 32p. (Orig.). (ps-1). 1993. pap. 2.95 (0-394-82925-5) Random Bks Yng Read.
Mathiew, Joe. A Visit to the Sesame Street Museum. Alexander, Liza. LC 87-1685. 32p. (gr. 3-6). 1987. lib. bdg. 5.99 (0-394-98715-2); pap. 2.25 (0-394-88715-8) Random Bks Yng Read.
Mathis, Melissa B. Great Gravity the Cat. rev. ed. Johnston, Johanna & Johnston, Abigail. LC 88-13351. 64p. (gr. 3-7). 1989. lib. bdg. 15.00 (0-208-02223-6, Linnet) Shoe String.
—The Turtle & the Moon. Turner, Charles. LC 90-43841. 32p. (ps-2). 1991. 14.00 (0-525-44659-1, DCB) Dutton Child Bks.
—What a Wonderful Day to Be a Cow. Lesser, Carolyn. LC 93-13211. 1995. 15.00 (0-679-82430-8); PLB 15.99 (0-679-92430-2) Knopf.
Matinez, Antonielena C. Brother Tree. Szekely, Edmond B. 32p. 1977. 3.50 (0-89564-074-0) IBS Intl.
Matisse, Henri. Henri Matisse. Raboff, Ernest. LC 87-17701. 32p. (gr. 1 up). 1988. pap. 7.95 (0-06-446080-0, Trophy) HarpC Child Bks.
Matsick, Anni. Mirror Magic. Simon, Seymour. LC 90-85921. 32p. (ps-3). 1991. Repr. 9.95 (1-878093-07-X) Boyds Mills Pr.
—Thanksgiving Fun: A Bountiful Harvest of Crafts, Recipes, & Games. Murray, Beth. 32p. (Orig.). (gr. 2-7). 1993. pap. 3.95 (1-56397-280-8) Boyds Mills Pr.
Matsuda, S. Physics Experiments for Children. Mandell, Muriel. LC 68-9308. (gr. 3-10). 1968. pap. 2.95 (0-486-22033-8) Dover.
Matsumoto, Allen. Herschel's Special Dream. Gay, Kristin. 40p. (Orig.). 1986. pap. 5.95 (0-945265-08-5) Accord Comm.
Matte, L'Enc. Strange Partners: The Story of Symbiosis. Dean, Anabel. LC 75-38479. 96p. (gr. 3-6). 1976. lib. bdg. 9.50 (0-8225-1100-2) Lerner Pubns.
Matthews, Anne. Kim Meets Santa Claus. Stimson, Joan. 28p. (ps-1). 1991. 3.95 (0-7214-9615-6, S808-24 SER.) Ladybird Bks.
—Picture Dictionary. Murray, William. 28p. (ps-2). 1991. 3.50 (0-7214-1416-8, 9112-1) Ladybird Bks.
Matthews, Bethan. Lizzie's List. Harrison, Maggie. LC 92-54580. 32p. (gr. 3-6). 1993. 14.95 (1-56402-197-1) Candlewick Pr.
Matthews, Bonnie J. The Teacher from Outer Space. Korman, Justine H. LC 93-24846. 32p. (gr. 1-4). 1993. PLB 9.59 (0-8167-3180-2); pap. text ed. 2.95 (0-8167-3181-0) Troll Assocs.
Matthews, Morgan. One Hundred Two Out of This World Jokes. Matthews, Morgan. LC 91-45021. 64p. (gr. 2-6). 1992. pap. text ed. 2.95 (0-8167-2789-9) Troll Assocs.
Matthews, Mozelle. See How I Grow. Alpine Partners Staff. Mitchell, Suzanne, ed. 32p. Date not set. 39.95 (0-9637894-0-6) Video Moments.

Matthews, Sam. Understanding the Alphabets. Singletary, Helen P. & Glover, Zebrena M. 59p. (Orig.). (ps-6). 1991. pap. text ed. 20.00 (1-880850-03-6) Comp Trng Clinic.
Mattos, D. Mommy Moon & the Rainbow Children. Heitz, True. 13p. (Orig.). (ps-2). 1982. pap. 3.00 (0-686-37664-1) True Heitz.
Mattotti, Lorenzo. Pinocchio. Collodi, Carlo. LC 92-44161. (ENG.). (gr. 2 up). 1993. write for info. (0-688-12450-X); lib. bdg. write for info. (0-688-12451-8) Lothrop.
Mattozzi, Patricia R. Eastertime. Mattozzi, Patricia R. 1992. 3.95 (0-8378-2459-1) Gibson.
Mattson, George. Tuna & Billfish: Fish Without a Country. 2nd ed. Joseph, James, et al. Revelle, Roger, intro. by. LC 80-81889. 53p. (Orig.). (gr. 7-12). 1980. pap. 7.95 (0-9603078-1-8) Inter-Am Tropical.
Maudsley, Toby & Johnson, James, photos by. Design. James, Diane. Bulloch, Ivan, designed by. LC 93-35626. 48p. (gr. 3-7). 1994. 16.95 (1-56847-148-3) Thomson Lrning.
Maudsley, Keith. Leslie: Maybe I'll Be. Flowers, Sandra H. Allred, David & Leonard, Camille, eds. 24p. (Orig.). (gr. 1-4). Date not set. pap. 1.00 (0-9630029-4-5) Community Comm.
Maul, Bill. The Baseball Hall of Shame's Funtastic Trivia & Sticker Book. Nash, Bruce & Zullo, Allan. 24p. (gr. 1 up). 1992. pap. 3.95 (0-671-74439-9, Little Simon) S&S Trade.
—The Sports Hall of Shame's Funtastic Trivia & Sticker Book. Nash, Bruce & Zullo, Allan. 24p. (gr. 1 up). 1992. pap. 3.95 incl. 24 stickers (0-671-74438-0, Little Simon) S&S Trade.
Mauney, Michael. A Day in the Life of a Zoo Veterinarian. Paige, David. LC 84-6538. 32p. (gr. 4-8). 1985. PLB 11.79 (0-8167-0095-8); pap. text ed. 2.95 (0-8167-0096-6) Troll Assocs.
Mauney, Michael, photos by. A Day in the Life of a Forest Ranger. Paige, David. LC 78-68809. 32p. (gr. 4-8). 1980. PLB 11.79 (0-89375-227-4); pap. 2.95 (0-89375-231-2) Troll Assocs.
Maurer, Jason F. Forever in My Heart: A Story to Help Children Participate in Life As a Parent Dies. Levine, Jennifer. LC 92-50678. 32p. (Orig.). (gr. 1-6). 1992. pap. 6.95 (1-878321-08-0) Rainbow NC.
Maus, Jim. Am I Still a Sister? 3th ed. Sims, Alicia M. Sims, Darcie D., intro. by. LC 87-71613. 48p. (gr. k-9). 1993. pap. 5.00 (0-9618995-0-6) Big A NM.
Mavity, Dennis, jt. photog. see Hodges, Del.
Mavor, Sally. Come to My Party. Richardson, Judith B. LC 91-16320. 32p. (ps-1). 1993. RSBE 13.95 (0-02-776147-9, Macmillan Child Bk) Macmillan Child Grp.
—The Way Home. Richardson, Judith B. LC 88-35951. 32p. (ps-1). 1991. RSBE 13.95 (0-02-776145-2, Macmillan Child Bk) Macmillan Child Grp.
—The Way Home. Richardson, Judith B. LC 93-25729. 32p. (gr. k-3). 1994. pap. 3.95 (0-689-71790-3, Aladdin) Macmillan Child Grp.
Mavor, Sally. The Way Home. Richardson, Judith B. (gr. k). 13.95 (0-685-41406-X) Macmillan.
Mawicke, Tran. Robert Fulton: Steamboat Builder. Landers-Henry, Joanne. 80p. (gr. 6). 1991. Repr. of 1975 ed. lib. bdg. 12.95 (0-7910-1411-8) Chelsea Hse.
Mawolski, Stanley M. Lisa & the Magic Doll: Russian & Ukrainian Fairy Tales. Dolson, Gina, ed. Mandeville, Jerry & Brodsky, Anna, trs. from RUS & UKR. 56p. (Orig.). (gr. 4-10). 1986. pap. 4.50x (0-914265-07-5) New Eng Pub MA.
Maxwell, Barbara. The Wolf. Hogan, Paula Z. LC 79-13309. 32p. (gr. 1-4). 1979. PLB 17.96 (0-8172-1507-7) Raintree Steck-V.
Maxwell, Cassandra. Bright Star, Bright Star, What Do You See? Maxwell, Cassandra. LC 89-82551. 32p. (ps-k). 1990. write. 5.99 (0-8066-2462-0, 9-2462) Augsburg Fortress.
—Meet the Alphabuddies. Weaver, Jill. LC 89-14599. 30p. (ps-4). 1990. 10.95 (0-8192-1518-X) Morehouse Pub.
—Yosef's Gift of Many Colors: An Easter Story. Maxwell, Cassandra. LC 92-44189. 32p. (ps-3). 1993. 14.99 (0-8066-2627-5, 9-2627) Augsburg Fortress.
May, Darcy. The Good Stepmother. Zakhoder's, Boris. Rudolph, Marguerita, retold by. LC 90-10063. 40p. (ps-2). 1992. pap. 14.00 jacketed (0-671-68270-9, S&S BFYR) S&S Trade.
—The Little Mermaid: A Step Three Book. Andersen, Hans Christian. Hautzig, Deborah, adapted by. LC 91-6632. 48p. (Orig.). (gr. 2-3). 1991. lib. bdg. 7.99 (0-679-92241-5); pap. 3.50 (0-679-82241-0) Random Bks Yng Read.
—Snow White & the Seven Dwarfs. Grimm, Jacob & Grimm, Wilhelm K. Kassier, Sue, retold by. LC 92-44516. (gr. 2 up). 1993. pap. 2.25 (0-679-84347-7) Random Bks Yng Read.
May, Lawrence. Catechism Lessons: Pupil's Book. Fehlauer, Adolph. Grunze, Richard, ed. 336p. (gr. 5-6). 1981. 6.95 (0-938272-09-8) WELS Board.
May, Lawrence & Steele, Lawrence. Reaching Tender Hearts, 3 vols. Groth, Lynn. Grunze, R., ed. (Orig.). (ps-k). 1988. Set. pap. text ed. write for info. (0-938272-45-4) WELS Board.
May, Lawrence & Steele, Loren. Reaching Tender Hearts, Vol. 1. Groth, Lynn. Grunze, Richard, ed. 157p. (ps-k). 1987. pap. 7.95 (0-938272-42-X) WELS Board.

—Reaching Tender Hearts, Vol. 2. Groth, Lynn. Grunze, Richard, ed. 176p. (ps-k). 1988. pap. 8.95 (*0-938272-43-8*) WELS Board.

May, Warren, jt. illus. see Kendrick, John.

Mayabb, Darrell. Sound the Charge. Weingardt, Richard. LC 78-59321. 184p. (gr. 6-12). 9.95 (*0-932446-00-0*); pap. 4.95 (*0-932446-01-9*) Jacqueline Enter.

Mayer & Mercer. All By Myself. Mayer, Mercer. 24p. (ps-3). 1985. pap. write for info. (*0-307-11938-6*, Pub. by Golden Bks) Western Pub.

Mayer, Bill. Brer Rabbit & Boss Lion. Kessler, Brad. 40p. (gr. k up). 1993. incl. cass. 19.95 (*0-88708-274-2*, Rabbit Ears); 14.95 (*0-88708-273-4*, Rabbit Ears) Picture Bk Studio.

Mayer, Larry. Fire! in Yellowstone. Ekey, Robert. LC 89-43156. 32p. (gr. 2-4). 1989. PLB 15.93 (*0-8368-0226-8*) Gareth Stevens Inc.

Mayer, Marianna. Beauty & the Beast. Mayer, Marianna. LC 78-54679. 48p. (gr. k up). 1984. SBE 15.95 (*0-02-765270-X*, Four Winds) Macmillan Child Grp.

Mayer, Maxine. Gamble for God. Daughters of St. Paul. LC 83-10087. 132p. (gr. 3-8). 1984. 3.00 (*0-8198-3033-X*) St Paul Bks.

Mayer, Mercer. Baby Sister Says No. Mayer, Mercer. LC 86-82368. 24p. (gr. 4-8). 1987. pap. write for info. (*0-307-11949-1*, Pub. by Golden Bks) Western Pub.

—Beauty & the Beast. Mayer, Marianna. LC 87-1095. 48p. (ps up). 1987. pap. 5.95 (*0-689-71151-4*, Aladdin) Macmillan Child Grp.

—A Boy, a Dog & a Frog. Mayer, Mercer. LC 67-22254. 32p. (ps-2). 1985. pap. 3.50 (*0-8037-0769-X*) Dial Bks Young.

—Bubble Bubble. rev. ed. Mayer, Mercer. 48p. 1992. pap. 5.95 (*1-879920-03-4*) Rain Bird Prods.

—A Christmas Carol: Being a Ghost Story of Christmas. Mayer, Mercer, abridged by. LC 86-12651. 48p. (ps up). 1986. SBE 16.95 (*0-02-730310-1*, Macmillan Child Bk) Macmillan Child Grp.

—East of the Sun & West of the Moon. Mayer, Mercer. LC 80-11496. 48p. (gr. k up). 1984. SBE 15.95 (*0-02-765190-8*, Four Winds) Macmillan Child Grp.

—Everyone Knows What a Dragon Looks Like. Williams, Jay. LC 84-29589. 32p. (gr. k-3). 1984. RSBE 14.95 (*0-02-793090-4*, Four Winds) Macmillan Child Grp.

—The Figure in the Shadows. Bellairs, John. LC 74-2885. 168p. (gr. 4-7). 1975. Dial Bks Young.

—The Figure in the Shadows. Bellairs, John. LC 92-31362. 160p. (gr. 3 up). 1993. pap. 3.50 (*0-14-036337-8*) Puffin Bks.

—Frog Goes to Dinner. Mayer, Mercer. LC 74-2881. 32p. (ps-2). 1974. 8.95 (*0-8037-3386-0*); PLB 8.89 (*0-8037-3381-X*) Dial Bks Young.

—Frog Goes to Dinner. Mayer, Mercer. (gr. k-2). 1977. pap. 2.95 (*0-8037-2733-X*) Dial Bks Young.

—Frog on His Own. Mayer, Mercer. LC 73-6018. 32p. (ps-2). 1973. 8.95 (*0-8037-2701-1*); PLB 8.89 (*0-8037-2695-2*) Dial Bks Young.

—Frog on His Own. Mayer, Mercer. LC 73-6018. 32p. (ps-2). 1980. pap. 2.95 (*0-8037-2716-X*) Dial Bks Young.

—Frog, Where Are You? Mayer, Mercer. LC 72-85544. 32p. (ps-2). 1969. 9.95 (*0-8037-2737-2*); PLB 9.89 (*0-8037-2732-1*) Dial Bks Young.

—Frog, Where Are You? Mayer, Mercer. LC 72-85544. 32p. (ps-2). 1980. pap. 2.95 (*0-8037-2729-1*) Dial Bks Young.

—The Gillygoofang. Mendoza, George. 32p. (ps-2). 1982. Dial Bks Young.

—The Great Brain. Fitzgerald, John D. LC 67-22252. (gr. 4-8). 1985. 12.95 (*0-8037-3074-8*); PLB 11.89 (*0-8037-3076-4*) Dial Bks Young.

—The Great Brain at the Academy. Fitzgerald, John D. LC 72-712. 176p. (gr. 4-7). 1985. 12.95 (*0-8037-3039-X*); PLB 11.89 (*0-8037-3040-3*) Dial Bks Young.

—The Great Brain Does It Again. Fitzgerald, John D. LC 74-18600. (gr. 4-7). 1975. PLB 11.89 (*0-8037-5066-8*) Dial Bks Young.

—Happy Easter, Little Critter. Mayer, Mercer. LC 87-81759. 24p. (ps-3). 1988. pap. write for info. (*0-307-11723-5*, Pub. by Golden Bks) Western Pub.

—I Just Forgot. Mayer, Mercer. LC 87-81779. 24p. (Orig.). (ps-3). 1988. pap. write for info. (*0-307-11975-0*) Western Pub.

—Just a Mess. Mayer, Mercer. LC 86-82369. 24p. (gr. 4-8). 1987. pap. write for info. (*0-307-11948-3*, Pub. by Golden Bks) Western Pub.

—Just for You. Mayer, Mercer. 24p. (ps-3). 1975. pap. write for info. (*0-307-11838-X*, Golden Bks.) Western Pub.

—Just Go to Bed. rev. ed. Mayer, Mercer. 24p. (ps-3). 1985. pap. write for info. (*0-307-11940-8*, 11940, Pub. by Golden Bks) Western Pub.

—Just Grandpa & Me. Mayer, Mercer. 24p. (ps-3). 1985. pap. write for info. (*0-307-11936-X*, Pub. by Golden Bks) Western Pub.

—Just Me & My Babysitter. Mayer, Mercer. 24p. (Orig.). (ps-3). 1986. pap. write for info. (*0-307-11945-9*, Pub. by Golden Bks) Western Pub.

—Just Me & My Cousin. Mayer, Mercer. 24p. (ps-3). 1992. pap. write for info. (*0-307-12688-9*, 12688, Golden Pr) Western Pub.

—Just Me & My Little Sister. Mayer, Mercer. 24p. (Orig.). (ps-3). 1986. pap. write for info. (*0-307-11946-7*, Pub. by Golden Bks) Western Pub.

—Just Me & My Puppy. Mayer, Mercer. 24p. (ps-3). 1985. pap. write for info. (*0-307-11937-8*, Pub. by Golden Bks) Western Pub.

—Just My Friend & Me. Mayer, Mercer. 1988. write for info. (*0-307-11947-5*, 11947, Pub. by Golden Bks) Western Pub.

—Liza Lou & the Yeller Belly Swamp. Mayer, Mercer. LC 80-16605. 48p. (gr. k-3). 1980. Repr. of 1976 ed. RSBE 14.95 (*0-02-765220-3*, Four Winds) Macmillan Child Grp.

—Me & My Little Brain. Fitzgerald, John D. LC 71-153732. (gr. 4-7). 1985. PLB 11.89 (*0-8037-5532-5*) Dial Bks Young.

—Me Too! Mayer, Mercer. 24p. (ps-3). 1985. pap. write for info. (*0-307-11941-6*, Pub. by Golden Bks) Western Pub.

—Merry Christmas Mom & Dad. Mayer, Mercer. 24p. (ps-3). 1982. pap. write for info. (*0-307-11886-X*, Golden Bks.) Western Pub.

—More Adventures of the Great Brain. Fitzgerald, John D. LC 73-85547. (gr. 4-8). 1985. 12.95 (*0-8037-5819-7*, 01160-350) Dial Bks Young.

—The New Baby. Mayer, Mercer. 24p. (ps-3). 1985. pap. write for info. (*0-307-11942-4*, Pub. by Golden Bks) Western Pub.

—One Frog Too Many. Mayer, Mercer & Mayer, Marianna. LC 75-6325. 32p. (ps-2). 1985. 9.95 (*0-8037-4838-8*); PLB 9.89 (*0-8037-4858-2*) Dial Bks Young.

—The Pied Piper of Hamlin. Mayer, Mercer. LC 87-1607. 48p. (gr. k up). 1987. RSBE 16.95 (*0-02-765361-7*, Macmillan Child Bk) Macmillan Child Grp.

—Professor Wormbog in Search for the Zipperump-a-Zoo. Mayer, Mercer. 48p. (ps up). 1992. pap. 5.95 (*1-879920-04-2*) Rain Bird Prods.

—The Return of the Great Brain. Fitzgerald, John D. LC 73-15443. 176p. (gr. 4-7). 1985. 12.95 (*0-8037-7403-6*) Dial Bks Young.

—A Silly Story: Nothing Less Nothing More. Mayer, Mercer. 48p. 1992. pap. 5.95 (*1-879920-02-6*) Rain Bird Prods.

—Staying Overnight. Mayer, Mercer. LC 87-83014. 40p. (gr. k-2). 1988. write for info. (*0-307-11662-X*) Western Pub.

—Terrible Troll. Mayer, Mercer. LC 68-28730. (gr. k-3). 1968. Dial Bks Young.

—There's a Nightmare in My Closet. giant ed. Mayer, Mercer. LC 68-15250. (ps-3). 1985. 12.95 (*0-8037-8682-4*); PLB 12.89 (*0-8037-8683-2*); pap. 4.95 (*0-8037-8574-7*); guide 17.99 (*0-8037-0843-2*) Dial Bks Young.

—There's Something in My Attic. Mayer, Mercer. LC 86-32875. 32p. (ps-3). 1988. 11.95 (*0-8037-0414-3*); PLB 11.89 (*0-8037-0415-1*) Dial Bks Young.

—There's Something in My Attic. Mayer, Mercer. 32p. (ps-3). 1992. pap. 3.99 (*0-14-054813-0*, Puffin) Puffin Bks.

—These Are My Pets. Mayer, Mercer. LC 87-83016. 40p. (gr. k-2). 1988. write for info. (*0-307-11664-6*) Western Pub.

—These Are My Pets, Level 2. Mayer, Mercer. 32p. (gr. 1-2). 1992. pap. 3.00 (*0-307-15962-0*, 15962, Golden Pr) Western Pub.

—This Is My House. Mayer, Mercer. LC 87-116603. 40p. (gr. k-2). 1988. write for info. (*0-307-11660-3*) Western Pub.

—The Trip. Mayer, Mercer. LC 87-83013. 40p. (gr. k-2). 1988. write for info. (*0-307-11661-1*) Western Pub.

—When I Get Bigger. Mayer, Mercer. 24p. (ps-3). 1985. pap. write for info. (*0-307-11943-2*, Pub. by Golden Bks) Western Pub.

—The Wizard Comes to Town. Mayer, Mercer. 40p. 1991. pap. 5.95 (*1-879920-00-X*) Rain Bird Prods.

—You're the Scaredy-Cat. Mayer, Mercer. 40p. 1991. pap. 5.95 (*1-879920-01-8*) Rain Bird Prods.

Mayer, Mercer, et al. Altogether, One at a Time. 2nd ed. Konigsburg, E. L. 96p. (gr. 3-7). 1989. pap. 2.95 (*0-689-71290-1*, Aladdin) Macmillan Child Grp.

Mayers, Diane. Blew & the Death of the Mag. Lichtman, Wendy. 74p. (gr. 3-9). 1975. 5.00 (*0-913512-53-2*) Freestone Pub Co.

Mayfield, Ana M. God Loves Us. Josef, Marion. 32p. (Orig.). (ps-1). 1993. pap. 3.95 (*0-8198-3037-2*) St Paul Bks.

—We Thank God. Josef, Marion. 28p. (Orig.). (gr. k-4). 1993. pap. 0.95 (*0-8198-8267-4*) St Paul Bks.

Mayhew, James. Katie & the Dinosaurs. Mayhew, James. (ps-3). 1992. 15.00 (*0-553-08129-2*, Little Rooster) Bantam.

Mayo, Frank. Dracula, Go Home. Platt, Kin. 96p. (gr. 7 up). 1981. pap. 1.25 (*0-440-92022-1*, LE) Dell.

Mayo, Gretchen. Change: Getting to Know about Ebb & Flow. Greene, Laura. LC 80-81081. 32p. (gr. k-3). 1981. 16.95 (*0-87705-401-0*) Human Sci Pr.

—Help: Getting to Know about Needing & Giving. Greene, Laura. LC 80-81082. 32p. (ps-3). 1981. 16.95 (*0-87705-402-9*) Human Sci Pr.

—I Hate My Name. Grant, Eva. Hollingsworth, Charles, intro. by. LC 80-14428. 32p. (gr. k-6). 1980. PLB 17.96 (*0-8172-1362-7*) Raintree Steck-V.

—The Kangaroo. Hogan, Paula Z. LC 79-13660. (gr. 1-4). 1979. PLB 17.96 (*0-8172-1504-2*); pap. 4.95 (*0-8114-8181-6*); pap. 9.95 incl. cassette (*0-8114-8189-1*) Raintree Steck-V.

Mayo, Gretchen W. Anna & the Cat Lady. Joosse, Barbara M. LC 91-12510. 176p. (gr. 3-7). 1992. 14.00 (*0-06-020242-4*); PLB 13.89 (*0-06-020243-2*) HarpC Child Bks.

—Anna, the One & Only. Joosse, Barbara M. LC 88-890. 144p. (gr. 3-7). 1988. (Lipp Jr Bks); PLB 11.89 (*0-397-32323-9*, Lipp Jr Bks) HarpC Child Bks.

—Anna, the One & Only. Joosse, Barbara M. LC 88-890. 144p. (gr. 2-6). 1990. pap. 3.50 (*0-06-440345-9*, Trophy) HarpC Child Bks.

—Earthmaker's Tales: North American Indian Stories about Earth Happenings. Mayo, Gretchen W. LC 88-20515. 96p. (gr. 5 up). 1989. 12.95 (*0-8027-6839-3*); PLB 13.85 (*0-8027-6840-7*) Walker & Co.

—North American Indian Stories, 4 vols. Mayo, Gretchen W. 256p. (gr. 5 up). 1990. Set. pap. 23.80 (*0-8027-7341-9*) Walker & Co.

—North American Indian Stories: Earthmaker's Tales. Mayo, Gretchen W. 48p. (gr. 5 up). 1990. pap. 5.95 (*0-8027-7343-5*) Walker & Co.

—North American Indian Stories: More Earthmaker's Tales. Mayo, Gretchen W. 48p. (gr. 5 up). 1990. pap. 5.95 (*0-8027-7344-3*) Walker & Co.

—North American Indian Stories: More Star Tales. Mayo, Gretchen W. 48p. (gr. 5 up). 1990. pap. 5.95 (*0-8027-7347-8*) Walker & Co.

—North American Indian Stories: Star Tales. Mayo, Gretchen W. 48p. (gr. 5 up). 1990. pap. 5.95 (*0-8027-7345-1*) Walker & Co.

—Whale Brother. Steiner, Barbara. (ps-3). 1988. 12.95 (*0-8027-6804-0*); PLB 13.85 (*0-8027-6805-9*) Walker & Co.

Mayo, Steve, jt. illus. see Runestrand, Meredith.

Mayorga, Dolores. David Plays Hide-&-Seek in Celebrations: David Juega Al Escondite y Celebra. Mayorga, Dolores. (ENG & SPA.). 24p. (gr. 2-5). 1992. PLB 18.95 (*0-8225-2001-X*) Lerner Pubns.

—David Plays Hide-&-Seek in Folktales: David Juega Al Escondite En Cuentos Folkloricos. Mayorga, Dolores. (ENG & SPA.). 24p. (gr. 2-5). 1992. PLB 18.95 (*0-8225-2003-6*) Lerner Pubns.

—David Plays Hide-&-Seek in the City: David Juega Al Escondite En la Ciudad. Mayorga, Dolores. (ENG & SPA.). 24p. (gr. 2-5). 1992. PLB 18.95 (*0-8225-2002-8*) Lerner Pubns.

—David Plays Hide-&-Seek on Vacation: David Juega Al Escondite En Vacaciones. Mayorga, Dolores. (ENG & SPA.). 24p. (gr. 2-5). 1992. PLB 18.95 (*0-8225-2004-4*) Lerner Pubns.

Mayr-Pletschen, Heide. A Christmas Carol Book. (gr. 3 up). 2.75 (*0-685-24603-5*) Merry Thoughts.

Mays, Victor. Charles Lindbergh: Hero Pilot. Collins, David R. 80p. (gr. 2-6). 1991. Repr. of 1978 ed. lib. bdg. 12.95 (*0-7910-1417-7*) Chelsea Hse.

Mazal, Chanan. The Mystery of the Missing Pushke. Gevirtz, Eliezer. 200p. (gr. 5-7). 1982. 8.95 (*0-87306-291-4*); pap. 6.95 (*0-685-07004-2*) Feldheim.

Maze, Deborah. Anna Marie's Blanket. Barkan, Joanne. 32p. 1990. 12.95 (*0-8120-6124-1*) Barron.

—Elephant & Mouse Celebrate Halloween. Grambling, Lois. (ps-1). 1991. 12.95 (*0-8120-6186-1*); pap. 5.95 (*0-8120-4761-3*) Barron.

—Elephant & Mouse Get Ready for Christmas. Grambling, Lois G. 32p. 1990. with dust jacket 12.95 (*0-8120-6185-3*) Barron.

Maze, Debrah. Elephant & Mouse Get Ready for Easter. Grambling, Lois G. 32p. (ps-3). 1991. 12.95 (*0-8120-6200-0*) Barron.

Mazer, Susan. Together Forever: An Adoption Story Coloring Book. Barris, Sara L. & Seltzer, Doryle P. 32p. 1992. pap. 3.95 (*0-9632023-0-8*) Shoot Star Pr.

Mazzarella, James, jt. illus. see Mazzarella, Mimi.

Mazzarella, Mimi & Mazzarella, James. Alphabatty Animals & Funny Foods. Mazzarella, Mimi. LC 83-81449. 96p. (Orig.). (gr. k-3). 1984. pap. 5.95 (*0-89709-045-4*) Liberty Pub.

Mazzola, Frank, Jr. The Ocean Alphabet Book. Pallotta, Jerry. 32p. (ps-3). 1989. 14.95 (*0-88106-458-0*); pap. 6.95 (*0-88106-452-1*) Charlesbridge Pub.

Mazzu, Kenneth. True Texas Tales. Brown, William F. LC 92-93887. 64p. (Orig.). (gr. 7 up). 1992. pap. 8.75 perfect bdg. (*1-881936-14-7*) WFB Ent.

Mbengue, Demba. Aesop: Tales of Aethiop the African, Vol. 1. 64p. (gr. 2-9). 1991. 6.95 (*1-877610-03-8*); cass. 6.95 (*0-685-50185-X*) Sea Island.

Meade, Holly. Rata-Pata-Scata-Fata: A Caribbean Story. Gershator, Phillis. LC 92-40695. 1993. 14.95 (*0-316-30470-0*, Joy St Bks) Little.

Meade, Javier & Jamieson, Lindsey. What Happened to Sherlock Holmes? as Set to Rest In... The Legend of Wilson-The Amazing Athlete. White, Terence. Blackburn, Francis, et al, eds. Barton, Hill, intro. by. LC 83-51870. 102p. 1984. 9.95 (*0-9612698-0-4*) Seagull Pub Co.

Means, Gary & Cook, Beth A. Footsteps of Faith. Mapstone, Edna. 32p. (Orig.). (gr. 1-5). 1993. wkbk. 2.99 (*0-87509-528-3*) Chr Pubns.

Mear, Roger & Ward, Rebecca, photos by. Destination: Antarctica. Swan, Robert. 48p. (gr. 2-7). 1989. pap. 5.95 (*0-590-41286-8*) Scholastic Inc.

Mecklenberg, Jan. Alphabet Animals. Mecklenberg, Jan. LC 93-35479. 1994. write for info. (*0-7852-8218-1*) Oliver-Nelson.

—Counting God's Creatures. Mecklenberg, Jan. LC 93-36019. 1994. write for info. (*0-7852-8217-3*) Nelson.

Meddaugh, Susan. Amanda's Perfect Hair. Milstein, Linda B. LC 92-34314. 32p. (ps up). 1993. 14.00 (*0-688-11153-X*, Tambourine Bks); PLB 13.93 (*0-688-11154-8*, Tambourine Bks) Morrow.

—Beast. Meddaugh, Susan. 32p. (gr. k-3). 1985. 13.95 (*0-395-30349-4*); pap. 3.95 (*0-317-18511-X*) HM.

—The Best Halloween of All. Wojciechowski, Susan. LC 91-9369. 32p. (ps-2). 1992. 10.00 (*0-517-57765-8*); PLB 10.99 (*0-517-57835-2*) Crown Bks Yng Read.
—Bimwili & the Zimwi. Aardema, Verna. LC 85-4449. 32p. (ps-3). 1985. 14.99 (*0-8037-0212-4*); PLB 12.89 (*0-8037-0213-2*) Dial Bks Young.
—Bimwili & the Zimwi. Aardema, Verna. LC 85-4449. 32p. (Orig.). (ps-3). 1988. pap. 4.95 (*0-8037-0553-0*) Dial Bks Young.
—In the Haunted House. Bunting, Eve. LC 89-77663. 32p. (ps-3). 1990. 13.45 (*0-395-51589-0*, Clarion Bks) HM.
—Martha Speaks. Meddaugh, Susan. LC 91-48455. 32p. (ps-3). 1992. 13.45 (*0-395-63313-3*) HM.
—No Nap. Bunting, Eve. LC 88-35256. 32p. (ps-k). 1989. 15.45 (*0-89919-813-9*, Clarion Bks) HM.
—A Perfect Father's Day. Bunting, Eve. Giblin, James, ed. 32p. (ps-1). 1991. 13.95 (*0-395-52590-X*, Clarion Bks) HM.
—A Perfect Father's Day. Bunting, Eve. 32p. (gr. k-3). 1993. pap. 5.70 (*0-395-66416-0*, Clarion Bks) HM.
—Ruthie's Rude Friends. Marzollo, Jean & Marzollo, Claudio. LC 84-1707. (ps-3). 1984. Dial Bks Young.
—Ruthie's Rude Friends. Marzollo, Jean & Marzollo, Claudio. LC 84-1707. 48p. (ps-3). 1987. pap. 4.95 (*0-8037-0378-3*) Dial Bks Young.
—That Terrible Baby. Armstrong, Jennifer. LC 93-14727. 32p. 1994. 14.00 (*0-688-11832-1*, Tambourine Bks); PLB 13.93 (*0-688-11833-X*, Tambourine Bks) Morrow.
—Tree of Birds. Meddaugh, Susan. 32p. (gr. k-3). 1990. 13.45 (*0-395-53147-0*) HM.
—Two Ways to Count to Ten. Dee, Ruby. LC 86-33513. 32p. (ps-2). 1990. pap. 5.95 (*0-8050-1314-8*, Owlet BYR) H Holt & Co.
—The Way I Feel... Sometimes. De Regniers, Beatrice S. LC 87-18245. 48p. (gr. 1-4). 1988. 13.95 (*0-89919-647-0*, Clarion Bks) HM.
—The Way I Feel...Sometimes. Schenk de Regniers, Beatrice. (gr. 1-4). 1988. 13.95 (*0-318-35052-1*, Clarion Bks) HM.
—The Witches' Supermarket. Meddaugh, Susan. 32p. (gr. k-3). 1991. 13.95 (*0-395-57034-4*, Sandpiper) HM.
Mediawerks Staff. Giving & Growing: A Student's Guide for Service Projects. O'Connell, Frances H. Stamschror, Robert P., ed. 79p. (Orig.). (gr. 7-12). 1990. text ed. 3.50 stitched (*0-88489-224-7*); tchr's. ed. 3.95 (*0-88489-225-5*) St Marys.
Medina, Mary L. Catability. Rodriguez, Agatha A. 20p. (Orig.). 1990. pap. text ed. 7.95g (*0-933196-04-0*) Bilingue Pubns.
—Paracaidas, Paracaidas. Rodriguez, Agatha A. (SPA.). 20p. (Orig.). 1992. pap. 5.00 (*0-933196-05-9*) Bilingue Pubns.
Medley, Linda. Really Scared Stiff: Three Creepy Tales. Efron, Marshall & Olsen, Alfa-Betty. 48p. (gr. 2-4). 1992. pap. write for info. (*0-307-11469-4*, 11469, Golden Pr) Western Pub.
Medlock, Scott. Extra Innings: Baseball Poems. Hopkins, Lee B., selected by. LC 92-13013. (gr. 4 up). 1993. write for info. (*0-15-226833-2*) HarBrace.
Medrano, JoAnn. Who is Santa? Morris, Dixie G. Robinson, Deborah L., intro. by. 25p. (Orig.). (ps-3). 1988. spiral bdg. 7.50 (*0-929946-04-9*) L P T C.
Meek, Barbara. Cyril Squirrel & Sheryl: An Ecological Tale. Hannah, Valerie. Herrick, George H., ed. 46p. (Orig.). (gr. k-3). 1991. pap. 6.95 (*0-941281-78-7*) V H Pub.
Meeks, Catherine F. The Ant & the Duck. Garside, Alice H. 30p. (Orig.). (gr. k-2). 1990. pap. 2.10 (*1-882063-07-4*) Cottage Pr MA.
—The Dog & the Bone. Garside, Alice H. 20p. (Orig.). (gr. k-2). 1990. pap. 2.10 (*1-882063-11-2*) Cottage Pr MA.
—The Dog & the Wolf. Garside, Alice H. 20p. (Orig.). (gr. k-2). 1990. pap. 2.10 (*1-882063-08-2*) Cottage Pr MA.
—The Fox & the Stork. Garside, Alice H. 40p. (Orig.). (gr. k-2). 1990. pap. 2.10 (*1-882063-10-4*) Cottage Pr MA.
—The Fox & the Thrush. Garside, Alice H. 20p. (Orig.). (gr. k-2). 1990. pap. 2.10 (*1-882063-09-0*) Cottage Pr MA.
—The Garside Readers, 6 vols. Garside, Alice H. 1990. Set. pap. 6.25 (*1-882063-18-X*) Cottage Pr MA.
—The Man, the Fox & the Skunk. Garside, Alice H. 24p. (Orig.). (gr. k-2). 1989. pap. text ed. 2.10 (*1-882063-06-6*) Cottage Pr MA.
Meents, Len, jt. illus. see Wahl, Richard.
Meents, Len W. The Story of the Spirit of St. Louis. Stein, R. Conrad. LC 83-23174. 32p. (gr. 3-6). 1984. pap. 3.95 (*0-516-44667-3*) Childrens.
Megale, Marina. Dial Zero for Help: A Story of Parental Kidnapping. Jance, Judy. Meyer, Linda D. & Lyons, Carole, eds. 30p. (Orig.). (gr. k-4). 1985. lib. bdg. 9.00 (*0-932091-06-7*); pap. 3.95 (*0-932091-07-5*) Franklin Pr WA.
—Help Yourself to Safety: A Guide to Avoiding Dangerous Situations with Strangers & Friends. Hubbard, Kate & Berlin, Evelyn. Meyer, Linda D., ed. Walsh, John & Walsh, Whiteintro. by. Lyons, Carole, ed. LC 84-82541. 48p. (Orig.). (gr. 4-6). 1985. lib. bdg. 9.00 (*0-932091-00-8*); pap. 3.95 (*0-932091-01-6*) Franklin Pr WA.
—I'm Lost. Crary, Elizabeth. LC 84-62128. 32p. (Orig.). (ps-2). 1985. PLB 15.95 (*0-943990-08-4*); pap. 4.95 (*0-943990-09-2*) Parenting Pr.

—Kids to the Rescue! First-Aid Techniques for Kids. Boelts, Maribeth & Boelts, Darwin. LC 91-50666. 80p. (Orig.). (ps-6). 1992. PLB 17.95 (*0-943990-83-1*); pap. 7.95 (*0-943990-82-3*) Parenting Pr.
—Mommy Don't Go. Crary, Elizabeth. LC 85-63759. 32p. (Orig.). (ps-2). 1986. lib. bdg. 15.95 (*0-943990-27-0*); pap. 4.95 (*0-943990-26-2*) Parenting Pr.
—Something Is Wrong at My House. Davis, Diane. LC 84-62129. 40p. (Orig.). (ps-6). 1985. PLB 15.95 (*0-943990-11-4*); pap. 4.95 (*0-943990-10-6*) Parenting Pr.
—Strangers Don't Look Like the Big Bad Wolf! Buschman, Janis & Hunley, Debbie. Lyons, Carole & Meyer, Linda D., eds. McMorris, Sharon, intro. by. LC 85-80513. 38p. (Orig.). (gr. 2-4). 1985. lib. bdg. 9.00 (*0-932091-04-0*); pap. 3.95 (*0-932091-05-9*) Franklin Pr WA.
Megale, Marina & Schumacher, Sharon. A Horse's Tale: Ten Adventures in One Hundred Years. Luenn, Nancy, ed. LC 88-61152. 96p. (Orig.). (gr. 2-6). 1988. lib. bdg. 16.95 (*0-943990-51-3*); pap. 7.95 (*0-943990-50-5*) Parenting Pr.
Megale, Mauna. It's Not Your Fault. Jance, Judy. Meyer, Linda D. & Lyons, Carole R., eds. LC 85-70434. 32p. (gr. k-4). 1985. lib. bdg. 9.00 (*0-932091-03-2*) Franklin Pr Wa.
Meggendorfer, Lothar. The Doll's House: A Reproduction of the Antique Pop-up Book. Meggendorfer, Lothar. Shiller, Justin G., notes by. LC 79-5072. (gr. k-3). 1989. pap. 8.95 (*0-670-27761-4*) Viking Child Bks.
Meiczinger, John. How to Draw Indian Arts & Crafts. Meiczinger, John. LC 88-50807. 32p. (gr. 2-6). 1989. lib. bdg. 10.65 (*0-8167-1537-8*, Pub. by Watermill Pr); pap. text ed. 1.95 (*0-8167-1515-7*, Pub. by Watermill Pr) Troll Assocs.
Meier, David S. Ellsworth & Millicent. Alexander, Sue. LC 92-7705. 28p. (gr. k up). 1993. 14.95 (*0-88708-247-5*) Picture Bk Studio.
—Jeremy Quacks. Balan, Bruce. LC 89-31372. 32p. (ps up). 1991. pap. 14.95 (*0-88708-104-5*) Picture Bk Studio.
Meier, Max, photos by. Amazing Spiders. Schnieper, Claudia. 48p. (gr. 2-5). 1989. 19.95 (*0-87614-342-7*); pap. 6.95 (*0-87614-518-7*) Carolrhoda Bks.
—Chameleons. Schnieper, Claudia. 48p. (gr. 2-5). 1989. 19.95 (*0-87614-341-9*); pap. 6.95 (*0-87614-520-9*) Carolrhoda Bks.
Meier, Melissa. Kidding Around Seattle: A Young Person's Guide to the City. Steves, Rick. 64p. (Orig.). (gr. 3 up). 1991. pap. 9.95 (*0-945465-84-X*) John Muir.
—Play It Safe. Nelson, JoAnne. LC 93-12173. 1994. 5.95 (*0-935529-62-4*) Comprehen Health Educ.
Meighan, Don. Blue Bug & the Bullies. Poulet, Virginia. LC 79-159789. 32p. (ps-3). 1971. PLB 15.00 (*0-516-03418-9*) Childrens.
Meilo So. The Emperor & the Nightingale. So, Meilo. LC 91-40693. 32p. (ps-2). 1992. SBE 13.95 (*0-02-786045-0*, Bradbury Pr) Macmillan Child Grp.
Meirer, Max. Lizards. Schnieper, Claudia. 48p. (gr. 2-6). 1990. PLB 19.95 (*0-87614-405-9*) Carolrhoda Bks.
Meisel, Paul. Busy Buzzing Bumblebees & Other Tongue Twisters. newly illus. ed. Schwartz, Alvin. LC 91-4799. 64p. (gr. k-3). 1982. 13.00 (*0-06-025268-5*); PLB 12.89 (*0-06-025269-3*) HarpC Child Bks.
—Busy Buzzing Bumblebees & Other Tongue Twisters. newly illus. ed. Schwartz, Alvin. LC 91-4800. 64p. (gr. k-3). 1982. pap. 3.50 (*0-06-444036-2*, Trophy) HarpC Child Bks.
—The Cow Buzzed. Zimmerman, Andrea & Clemesha, David. LC 91-31905. 32p. (ps-1). 1993. 15.00 (*0-06-020808-2*); PLB 14.89 (*0-06-020809-0*) HarpC Child Bks.
—I Am Really a Princess. Shields, Carol D. LC 92-37161. 32p. (ps-3). 1993. 13.99 (*0-525-45138-2*, DCB) Dutton Child Bks.
—Mr. Bubble Gum: Level 3. Hooks, William H. 1989. 9.99 (*0-553-05834-7*) Bantam.
—Mr. Dinosaur. Hooks, William H. LC 92-33476. 1994. 10.95 (*0-553-09042-9*, Little Rooster); pap. 3.50 (*0-553-37234-3*, Little Rooster) Bantam.
—Mr. Monster, Level 3. Hooks, William H. 1990. PLB 9.99 (*0-553-05897-5*, Little Rooster); pap. 3.50 (*0-553-34927-9*, Little Rooster) Bantam.
—Monkey-Monkey's Trick. McKissack, Patricia. LC 88-3072. 48p. (Orig.). (gr. 1-3). 1988. lib. bdg. 7.99 (*0-394-99173-7*); pap. 3.50 (*0-394-89173-2*) Random Bks Yng Read.
—Wizard & Wart. Smith, Janice L. LC 92-41170. 1994. 13.00 (*0-06-022960-8*, HarpT); PLB 12.89 (*0-06-022961-6*, HarpT) HarpC.
—Your Insides. Cole, Joanna. 40p. (ps-1). 1992. 14.95 (*0-399-22123-9*, Putnam) Putnam Pub Group.
Mejia, Roger. A Handful of Magic. Fabian, Stella. 125p. (gr. 2-6). 1988. pap. 3.25 (*0-922434-36-0*) Brighton & Lloyd.
Melcher, Mary. Peekaboo Bunny. Capucilli, Alyssa S. 24p. (ps-1). 1994. 6.95 (*0-590-46754-9*, Cartwheel) Scholastic Inc.
Melendez, Francisco. The Mermaid & the Major: or, the True Story of the Invention of the Submarine. Melendez, Francisco. April. 1991. 24.95 (*0-8109-3619-4*) Abrams.
Mellen, Stephanie. The Crystal Rabbit. Mellen, Stephanie. 52p. (gr. k-12). 1993. pap. 5.95 (*0-9637414-0-3*) Meltec.

—The Teeny Tiny Voice. Polakiewicz, David M. & Mellen, Stephanie. 52p. (gr. k-12). 1992. pap. 5.95 (*1-878040-08-1*) Personal Growth.
Meller, Eric. Rabbit Who Overcame Fear: A Jataka Tale. Cook, Elizabeth, adapted by. Tulku, Tarthang, intro. by. 32p. (Orig.). (gr. k-4). 1991. 14.95 (*0-89800-212-5*); pap. 7.95 (*0-89800-211-7*) Dharma Pub.
Mello, Marsha. The Friendship of Hesper & Rani. Solomon, L. Ursa. 60p. (gr. 1 up). 1985. spiral bdg. 7.95 (*0-9615756-1-1*) Henchanted Bks.
—Pioneer California: Tales of Explorers, Indians, & Settlers. Roberts, Margaret. Bancroft Library. LC 81-22543. 296p. (gr. 6 up). 1982. 12.95 (*0-914598-42-2*); pap. text ed. cancelled (*0-914598-43-0*) Bear Flag Bks.
Melnyczuk, Peter. Follow That Cat! Pirotta, Saviour. LC 92-38287. 32p. (gr. k-3). 1993. 13.99 (*0-525-45125-0*, DCB) Dutton Child Bks.
—Red Fox. Wallace, Karen. LC 93-32381. 1994. write for info. (*1-56402-422-9*) Candlewick Pr.
—While Shepherds Watched. Fleetwood, Jenni. Pearson, Susan, ed. LC 91-38779. 32p. (gr. k-3). 1992. 14.00 (*0-688-11598-5*); PLB 13.93 (*0-688-11599-3*) Lothrop.
Meloni, Maria T. Old Father Christmas: Based on a Story by Juliana Horatia Ewing. Ewing, Juliana H. Doherty, Berlie, retold by. LC 92-43820. 42p. (ps-3). 1993. 12.95 (*0-8120-6354-6*) Barron.
Melton, Dana D. Hooked on Games. Melton, Dana D. & Ledbetter, Frances M. 150p. (Orig.). (gr. k-8). 1989. pap. 9.95 (*0-685-29409-9*) Hooked Games.
Melton, David. Don't Feed the Monster on Tuesdays! The Children's Self-Esteem Book. Moser, Adolph. Thatch, Nancy R., ed. Moser, Adolph, intro. by. LC 91-12941. 55p. (gr. k-12). 1991. PLB 14.95 (*0-933849-38-9*) Landmark Edns.
—Goodbye, Mommy. Doman, Bruce K. LC 77-79632. 86p. (ps-2). 1982. 8.95 (*0-936676-00-0*) Better Baby.
—Images of Greatness: A Celebration of Life. LC 87-26300. 64p. (gr. 4 up). 1987. 15.95 (*0-933849-11-7*) Landmark Edns.
—The One & Only Autobiography of Ralph Miller: The Dog Who Knew He Was a Boy. Melton, David. LC 86-27551. 104p. (gr. 2-6). 1986. pap. 5.95 (*0-933849-05-2*) Landmark Edns.
—The One & Only Second Autobiography of Ralph Miller: The Dog Who Knew He Was a Boy. Melton, David. LC 86-27556. 128p. (gr. 2-6). 1986. pap. 5.95 (*0-933849-06-0*) Landmark Edns.
Melton, Gerald. Musical Mysteries. Ferguson, Kathleen M. 144p. (gr. 4-8). 1985. wkbk. 11.95 (*0-86653-282-X*, GA 684) Good Apple.
—Research Workout. Martin, Susan & Green, Harriet. 144p. (gr. 4-9). 1984. wkbk. 11.95 (*0-86653-194-7*, GA 551) Good Apple.
Melton, Todd. A Boy Called Hopeless. Melton, David. LC 86-27557. 232p. (gr. 4 up). 1986. pap. 5.95 (*0-933849-07-9*) Landmark Edns.
—A Boy Called Hopeless. Melton, David. LC 86-27557. 231p. (gr. 4 up). 1986. Repr. of 1976 ed. PLB 13.95 (*0-933849-32-X*) Landmark Edns.
Meltzer, Dave. Orangutans. Wildlife Education, Ltd. Staff. 20p. (Orig.). (gr. 5 up). 1980. pap. 2.75 (*0-937934-02-X*) Wildlife Educ.
Meltzer, Dave, et al. Big Cats. Wildlife Education, Ltd. Staff. 20p. (Orig.). (gr. 5 up). 1981. pap. 2.75 (*0-937934-04-6*) Wildlife Educ.
Meltzer, Davis & Ripper, Chuck. Butterflies. Wildlife Education, Ltd. Staff. 20p. 1992. 13.95 (*0-937934-76-3*); pap. 2.75 (*0-937934-65-8*) Wildlife Educ.
Melvin, James. Billy Bluefish: A Tale of Big Blues. Tate, Suzanne. LC 88-92517. 28p. (Orig.). (gr. k-3). 1988. pap. 3.95 (*0-9616344-4-8*) Nags Head Art.
—Crabby & Nabby: A Tale of Two Blue Crabs. Tate, Suzanne. LC 88-61096. 28p. (Orig.). (gr. k-3). 1988. pap. 3.95 (*0-9616344-3-X*) Nags Head Art.
—Crabby's Water Wish: A Tale of Saving Sea Life. Tate, Suzanne. LC 91-60262. 28p. (Orig.). (gr. k-3). 1991. pap. 3.95 (*1-878405-04-7*) Nags Head Art.
—Danny & Daisy: A Tale of a Dolphin Duo. Tate, Suzanne. LC 92-93915. 28p. (Orig.). (gr. k-3). 1992. pap. 3.95 (*1-878405-07-1*) Nags Head Art.
—Flossie Flounder: A Tale of Flat Fish. Tate, Suzanne. LC 88-92679. 28p. (Orig.). (gr. k-3). 1989. pap. 3.95 (*0-9616344-5-6*) Nags Head Art.
—Harry Horseshoe Crab: A Tale of Crawly Creatures. Tate, Suzanne. LC 91-61375. 28p. (Orig.). (gr. k-9). 1991. pap. 3.95 (*1-878405-03-9*) Nags Head Art.
—Lucky Lookdown: A Tale of a Funny Fish. Tate, Suzanne. LC 89-92221. 28p. (Orig.). (gr. k-3). 1989. pap. 3.95 (*0-9616344-8-0*) Nags Head Art.
—Mary Manatee: A Tale of Sea Cows. Tate, Suzanne. LC 90-60102. 28p. (Orig.). (gr. k-3). 1990. pap. 3.95 (*0-9616344-9-9*) Nags Head Art.
—Old Reddy Drum: A Tale of Redfish. Tate, Suzanne. LC 93-83435. 28p. (Orig.). (gr. k-3). 1993. pap. 3.95 (*1-878405-08-X*) Nags Head Art.
—Pearlie Oyster: A Tale of an Amazing Oyster. Tate, Suzanne. LC 89-92226. 28p. (Orig.). (gr. k-3). 1989. pap. 3.95 (*0-9616344-7-2*) Nags Head Art.
—Salty Seagull: A Tale of an Old Salt. Tate, Suzanne. LC 92-60375. 28p. (Orig.). (gr. k-3). 1992. pap. 3.95 (*1-878405-06-3*) Nags Head Art.
—Sammy Shrimp: A Tale of a Little Shrimp. Tate, Suzanne. LC 90-61002. 28p. (Orig.). (gr. k-3). 1990. pap. 3.95 (*1-878405-00-4*) Nags Head Art.

—Spunky Spot: A Tale of One Smart Fish. Tate, Suzanne. LC 88-63784. 28p. (Orig.). (gr. k-3). 1989. pap. 3.95 (0-9616344-6-4) Nags Head Art.
—Stevie B. Sea Horse: A Tale of a Proud Papa. Tate, Suzanne. 28p. (Orig.). (gr. k-3). 1991. pap. 3.95 (1-878405-09-8) Nags Head Art.
—Tammy Turtle: A Tale of Saving Sea Turtles. Tate, Suzanne. LC 91-67275. 28p. (Orig.). (gr. k-3). 1991. PLB 3.95 (1-878405-05-5) Nags Head Art.
Menck, Kevin. Stories That End with a Hug. Elkins, Stephen. 32p. (gr. k-8). 1993. 12.98 (1-56919-002-X) Wonder Wkshop.
—-Stories That End with a Prayer. Elkins, Stephen. 32p. (gr. k-8). Date not set. 12.98 (1-56919-003-8) Wonder Wkshop.
—Stories That End with a Song. Elkins, Stephen. 32p. (gr. k-8). Date not set. 12.98 (0-685-68095-9) Wonder Wkshop.
Mendelson, S. T. Stupid Emilien. Mendelson, S. T. LC 90-28780. 32p. (gr. k-3). 1991. 14.95 (1-55670-213-2) Stewart Tabori & Chang.
Mendelson, Steve. The Emperor's New Clothes. Mendelson, Steve, retold by. LC 91-42606. 32p. 1992. 14.95 (1-55670-232-9) Stewart Tabori & Chang.
Mendez, Consuelo. Friends from the Other Side: Amigos del otro lado. Anzaldua, Gloria. LC 92-34384. 32p. (gr. 2-7). 1993. 13.95 (0-89239-113-8) Childrens Book Pr.
Mendez, Gerardo. Love for Priscilla. Moriwaki, Glenda. 28p. (Orig.). (ps-3). 1991. pap. 4.95 (0-9627956-7-4) Meadora Pub.
Mendez, Phil, et al. Happiness. Kaplan, Marcia P. & Kaplan, David E. 96p. (Orig.). (gr. 1 up). 1986. 5.95 (0-9617744-3-6) Cheers.
Mendez, Raymond A., jt. photog. see Wexler, Jerome.
Menefee, Paige & Smith, Patti. The Battle for the Worlds. Bullock, Harold B. Anderson, Jean, ed. 1990. 14.95 (0-9626219-4-3) Summit TX.

Menicucci, Gina. El Conejo y el Coyote. Kohen, Clarita. (SPA.). 16p. (Orig.). (gr. k-5). 1993. PLB 7.50x (1-56492-100-X) Laredo.
A humorous rhyme adaptation of a traditional Mexican tale of the rabbit & the coyote. When the coyote wants to trick the rabbit, the rabbit surprises him & proves to be more clever. Vividly illustrated with simple text for early readers. In Spanish.
Publisher Provided Annotation.

Mennella, Roxanna, jt. illus. see Wilkins, Sarah.
Menzel, Marian. Engineer from the Comanche Nation, Nancy Wallace. Verheyden-Hilliard, Mary E. LC 84-25935. 32p. (Orig.). (gr. 1-4). 1985. pap. 5.00 (0-932469-10-8) Equity Inst.
—Scientist & Administrator, Antoinette Rodez Schiesler. Verheyden-Hilliard, Mary E. LC 84-25978. 32p. (Orig.). (gr. 1-4). 1985. pap. 5.00 (0-932469-08-6) Equity Inst.
—Scientist & Astronaut, Sally Ride. Verheyden-Hilliard, Mary E. LC 84-25940. 32p. (Orig.). (gr. 1-4). 1985. pap. 5.00 (0-932469-07-8) Equity Inst.
—Scientist & Governor, Dixy Lee Ray. Verheyden-Hilliard, Mary E. LC 84-25986. 32p. (Orig.). (gr. 1-4). 1985. pap. 5.00 (0-932469-06-X) Equity Inst.
—Scientist from the Santa Clara Pueblo, Agnes Naranjo Stroud-Lee. Verheyden-Hilliard, Mary E. LC 84-25959. 32p. (Orig.). (gr. 1-4). 1985. pap. 5.00 (0-932469-09-4) Equity Inst.
—Scientist with Determination, Elma Gonzalez. Verheyden-Hilliard, Mary E. LC 84-25981. 32p. (Orig.). (gr. 1-4). 1985. pap. 5.00 (0-932469-01-9) Equity Inst.
Menzel, Mary. Scientist & Puzzle Solver, Constance Tom Noguchi. Verheyden-Hilliard, Mary E. LC 84-25924. 32p. (Orig.). (gr. 1-4). 1985. pap. 5.00 (0-932469-05-1) Equity Inst.
Mercer, jt. illus. see Mayer.
Mercer, Mayer. East of the Sun & West of the Moon. Mayer, Mercer. LC 86-20578. 48p. (ps-3). 1987. pap. 5.95 (0-689-71113-1, Aladdin) Macmillan Child Grp.
Mercier, Sheryl. The Budding Botanist: Investigations with Plants. Hoover, Evalyn, et al. Winkleman, Gretchen & Hillen, Judith, eds. 109p. (Orig.). (gr. 3-6). 1993. pap. text ed. 14.95 (1-881431-40-1, 1213) AIMS Educ Fnd.
Meredith Corporation, Better Homes & Gardens Staff. At the Zoo. Meredith Corporation, Better Homes & Gardens Staff. 32p. (gr. p-12). 1991. Repr. of 1989 ed. PLB 10.95 (1-878363-30-1) Forest Hse.
—Bird Buddies. Meredith Corporation, Better Homes & Gardens Staff. 32p. (gr. p-12). 1991. Repr. of 1989 ed. PLB 10.95 (1-878363-31-X) Forest Hse.
—Make Believe. Meredith Corporation, Better Homes & Gardens Staff. 32p. (gr. p-12). 1991. Repr. of 1989 ed. PLB 10.95 (1-878363-32-8) Forest Hse.
—On the Farm. Meredith Corporation, Better Homes & Gardens Staff. 32p. (gr. p-12). 1991. Repr. of 1989 ed. PLB 10.95 (1-878363-33-6) Forest Hse.
Meredith, Marianne, jt. illus. see Anderson, John.

Meredith, Susan H. Nature Walk. 2nd ed. Meredith, Susan H. 25p. 1993. pap. text ed. 4.95 (1-880666-09-X) Oughten Hse.
—Wonder Walk. Meredith, Susan H. 25p. (Orig.). 1993. pap. text ed. 4.95 (1-880666-02-2) Oughten Hse.
Merrell, David. Hooray for Oklahoma (1889) Kirschstein, Carolyn V. 48p. (gr. k-4). 1989. write for info. B C Pub Inc.
Merriam, Robert L. Abigail Chamberlain the Telephone Company. Merriam, Robert L. 8p. (Orig.). (ps-6). 1972. pap. 1.50x (0-686-32483-8) R L Merriam.
Merrick, Paul. Coin Stamp Mathematics. Jenkins, Lee. (Orig.). (gr. k-4). 1977. pap. 7.95 (0-918932-05-X) Activity Resources.
—Number Triangles. Bureloff, Morris, et al. Laycock, Mary & Merrick, Paul, eds. (Orig.). (gr. 5-12). 1977. pap. 7.95 (0-918932-36-X) Activity Resources.
—Tangram Geometry in Metric. Brownlee, Juanita. (Orig.). (gr. 5-10). 1976. pap. 7.95 (0-918932-43-2, 0140701407) Activity Resources.
Merrilees, Rebecca. Trees of North America. Brockman, C. Frank. Zim, Herbert S. & Fichter, George S., eds. (gr. 9 up). 1968. pap. write for info (0-307-13658-2, Golden Pr) Western Pub.
Merrill, Christine, photos by. Famous Animals. George, Jean C. LC 92-28326. 1994. 15.00 (0-06-021543-7); PLB 14.89 (0-06-021544-5) HarpC Child Bks.
Merrill, Frank, jt. illus. see Smith, Jessie W.
Merrill, John N. Legends of Derbyshire. 2nd ed. Merrill, John N. 71p. (Orig.). (gr. 6 up). 1975. pap. 3.00 (0-913714-15-1) Legacy Bks.
Merrill, Reed. My Bible ABC Book. McKissack, Patricia & McKissack, Frederick. LC 87-70473. 32p. (Orig.). (ps-3). 1987. pap. 5.99 (0-8066-2271-7, 10-4588, Augsburg) Augsburg Fortress.
—Those Mean Nasty Dirty Downright Disgusting but... Invisible Germs. Rice, Judith A. Gwaltney, Jack M., Jr. LC 89-34091. 32p. (Orig.). (ps-3). 1989. pap. 7.95 (0-934140-46-4) Redleaf Pr.
Mertins, Lisa. The SillyOZbul of OZ & Toto. Baum, Roger S. 1992. 15.95 (0-9630101-1-5) Yellow Brick Rd.
—The SillyOZbuls of OZ. Baum, Roger S. LC 91-66003. 1991. 15.95 (0-9630101-0-7) Yellow Brick Rd.
Merveille, David. Ms. Blanche, the Spotless Cow. Zidrou. LC 92-28673. 32p. (ps-k). 1993. PLB 14.95 (0-8050-2550-2, Bks Young Read) H Holt & Co.
—Thomas the Circus Boy. Merveille, David. 32p. (ps-1). 1993. PLB 14.95 (0-8050-2953-2, Bks Young Read) H Holt & Co.
Meshi, Ita. A Child's Picture English-Hebrew Dictionary. Sheheen, Dennis, ed. (gr. 1-3). 1987. 9.95 (0-915361-75-2) Modan-Adama Bks.
Mesqali, Farshid. Uncle Noruz (Uncle New Year) Farjam, Farideh & Azaad, Meyer. Jabbari, Ahmad, ed. & tr. from PER. LC 83-60450. 24p. (Orig.). (gr. k up). 1983. pap. 4.95 (0-939214-14-8) Mazda Pubs.
Messenger, Jannat. Child's Garden of Verses. Stevenson, Robert Louis. 12p. (ps-6). 1992. 13.95 (0-525-44997-3, DCB) Dutton Child Bks.
—Lullaby & Goodnight: A Bedtime Book with Music. Messenger, Jannat. 12p. (ps-1). 1988. POB 10.95 (0-689-71268-5, Aladdin) Macmillan Child Grp.
—Twinkle Twinkle Little Star: A Lullaby Book with Lights & Music. Messenger, Jannat. 12p. (ps-1). 1987. bds. 10.95 (0-689-71136-0, Aladdin) Macmillan Child Grp.
Messenger, Norman. Once upon a Time. Garner, Alan, retold by. LC 93-9686. 32p. (gr. 2-6). 1993. 12.95 (1-56458-380-5) Dorling Kindersley.
—Once upon a Time. Garner, Alan. LC 93-9686. 32p. (gr. k-4). 1993. 12.95 (1-56458-381-3) Dorling Kindersley.
Messent, Jan, et al. Every Kind of Smocking. Pyman, Kit, ed. 126p. (Orig.). 1989. pap. 17.95 (0-85532-632-8, Pub. by Search Pr UK) A Schwartz & Co.
Messer, Cathy. Proud to Be Me, Peewee Platypus. Anderson, Lisa. 40p. (ps-4). 1990. pap. 12.95 (0-9628323-0-8) Ridge Enter.
Mesturini, Cristina. The Cat. Mantegazza, Giovanna. LC 91-73872. 12p. (ps-1). 1992. 6.95 (1-56397-032-5) Boyds Mills Pr.
—The Hippopotamus. Mantegazza, Giovanna. LC 91-73871. 12p. (ps-1). 1992. 6.95 (1-56397-033-3) Boyds Mills Pr.
Metayer, Phil. The Many Voices of Paws: A Workbook for Young Stutterers. Reville, Julie D. 64p. (ps-3). 1989. 25.00 (0-937857-11-4, 1568) Speech Bin.
Metrejean, Nikki N. Diddle Diddle Red Hot Fiddle. Powell, Patricia. 32p. (gr. 1-8). 1990. pap. text ed. 6.95 (0-944512-01-1) Radiant LA.
Metropolitan Museum of Art Staff. We Wish You a Merry Christmas: Songs of the Season for Young People. Fox, Dan. 80p. 1989. 16.95 (1-55970-043-2) Arcade Pub Inc.
Mets, Marilyn. Chalk Around the Block: A Somerville House Book. McKay, Sharon & MacLeod, David. LC 92-41495. 48p. 1993. incl. 5 pieces of sidewalk chalk 8.95 (0-8362-4502-4) Andrews & McMeel.
—Splat! O'Connor, Jane. LC 93-34127. (gr. 3 up). 1994. 3.50 (0-448-40220-3, G&D); pap. write for info. (0-448-40219-X) Putnam Pub Group.
Mettler, Rene. Birds. Jeunesse, Gallimard, et al. LC 92-15956. 1993. 10.95 (0-590-46367-5) Scholastic Inc.

—Elephants: Big, Strong & Wise. Pfeffer, Pierre. Matthews, Sarah, tr. from FRE. LC 87-33995. 38p. (gr. k-5). 1988. 4.95 (0-944589-04-9, 049) Young Discovery Lib.
—Flowers. Jeunesse, Gallimard, created by. LC 92-15957. 1993. 10.95 (0-590-46383-7) Scholastic Inc.

Meyer, George. Endangered Species Coloring-Learning Books Adventure Series. Meyer, Nancy. (ps-3). 1993. write for info. (1-883408-05-9) Meyer Pub FL.
ENDANGERED SPECIES COLORING/LEARNING BOOKS... ADVENTURE SERIES teaches children the importance of protecting our endangered species. Each adventure story is factorial & details the dangers the animal faces, not only from man, but from nature, & what are we doing to help protect the animal from extinction. The stories are action packed & recommended for preschoolers to age eight. The pictures are large & fun to color challenging children's creative ability & continuing to make learning fun. The book includes 16 pages plus a colorful cover which depicts the endangered species in its natural habitat. The series is written so that our children will grow up with an insight into the plight of our wildlife giving them a concern & caring nature for all living things. Titles include: The Adventures of Mortie the Manatee (1-883408-00-8), The Adventures of Susie the Green Sea Turtle (1-883408-01-6), The Adventures of Wally the Right Whale (1-883408-02-4), The Adventures of Dimples the Dolphin (1-883408-03-2), The Adventures of Peter the Florida Panther (1-883408-04-0). Retail Price $4.50 each. Order from: Meyer Publishing, Inc., 10991-55 San Jose Blvd., Suite 149, Jacksonville, FL 32223.
Publisher Provided Annotation.

Meyer, Jacque S. Ellie the Elephant. Broker, Loretta. 28p. (Orig.). (ps-k). 1990. pap. 2.95 (0-916109-09-7) Summers Pub.
Meyer, Lydia V., jt. illus. see Spangler, Melissa.
Meyer, Mary A. Paco Pumpkin. Haas, James. Kendzia, Mary C., ed. 32p. (Orig.). 1992. pap. 4.95 (0-89622-529-1) Twenty-Third.
Meyer, Monty Dale. My Kaleidoscope of Poetry & Stories. Hurst, Ida Olivia. LC 91-92380. 96p. (Orig.). 1992. pap. 11.95 (0-9632521-0-0) Gemstone OR.
Meyer, Rita. Captain Noah. Thompson, Don. 32p. (gr. 3-5). 1991. pap. 1.19 (0-87123-696-6) Bethany Hse.
Meyer-Brauer, Lydia. Where Freedom Begins. Pitts, Teresa A. 27p. (Orig.). (gr. 5 up). 1990. pap. 10.00 (0-9618600-1-4) T A Pitts.
Meyerowitz, Rick. Joshua & Bigtooth. Childress, Mark. 32p. (ps-3). 1992. 14.95 (0-316-14011-2) Little.
—Paul Bunyan. Gleeson, Brian. LC 90-8558. 32p. (gr. k up). 1991. pap. 14.95 (0-88708-142-8, Rabbit Ears); pap. 19.95 incl. cass. (0-88708-143-6, Rabbit Ears) Picture Bk Studio.
—Paul Bunyan. Gleeson, Brian & Winters, Jonathan, eds. Kottke, Leo, contrib. 8p. (3 up). 1992. pap. write for info. slipcase pkg., incl. cassette (0-307-14325-2, 14325, Golden Pr) Western Pub.
—Paul Bunyan. Gleeson, Brian. 64p. 1993. Repr. of 1990 ed. incl. cass. 9.95 (0-88708-303-X, Rabbit Ears); 5.95 (0-88708-302-1, Rabbit Ears) Picture Bk Studio.
Meyerriecks, William & Ronan, Frank. All about Our Fifty States. rev. ed. Ronan, Margaret. LC 78-16658. (gr. 5-9). 1978. 11.00 (0-394-80244-6) Random Bks Yng Read.
Meyers, William. Moses: God's Helper. Young, William E. (gr. 1-6). 1976. 5.95 (0-8054-4225-1, 4242-25) Broadman.
Micallef, Mary. Floods & Droughts. Micallef, Mary. 48p. (gr. 4-8). 1985. wkbk. 6.95 (0-86653-323-0, GA 632) Good Apple.
—Listening: The Basic Connection. Micallef, Mary. 96p. (gr. 3-8). 1984. wkbk. 9.95 (0-86653-188-2, GA 555) Good Apple.
—Storms & Blizzards. Micallef, Mary. 48p. (gr. 4-8). 1985. wkbk. 6.95 (0-86653-321-4, GA 683) Good Apple.

—Tornadoes & Hurricanes. Deery, Ruth. 48p. (gr. 4-8). 1985. wkbk. 6.95 *(0-86653-318-4, GA 631)* Good Apple.

Michael, Linda. Dishes. Perry, Marion. Walsh, Joy, ed. 25p. 1988. pap. 5.00 *(0-938838-29-6)* Textile Bridge.

Michaels, Elizabeth. Patty Reed's Doll: The Story of the Donner Party. Laurgaard, Rachel K. 144p. (gr. 3-6). 1989. pap. 7.95 *(0-9617357-2-4)* Tomato Enter.

Michaels, James. Fabulous Paper Airplanes. Churchill, E. Richard. LC 91-10490. 128p. (gr. 5 up). 1992. pap. 7.95 *(0-8069-8343-4)* Sterling.

—Fast & Funny Paper Toys You Can Make. Churchill, E. Richard. LC 89-32411. 128p. (gr. 4-10). 1991. pap. 7.95 *(0-8069-5771-9)* Sterling.

—Holiday Paper Projects. Churchill, E. Richard. LC 92-12100. 128p. (gr. 3-9). 1992. 14.95 *(0-8069-8512-7)* Sterling.

—Holiday Paper Projects. Churchill, E. Richard. 128p. (gr. 6 up). 1993. pap. 7.95 *(0-8069-8513-5)* Sterling.

—Instant Paper Airplanes. Churchill, E. Richard. LC 88-12325. 128p. (gr. 3 up). 1988. 14.95 *(0-8069-6796-X)* Sterling.

—Paper Action Toys. Churchill, E. Richard. LC 93-23860. 128p. (gr. 6 up). 1993. 14.95 *(0-8069-0368-6)* Sterling.

—Paper Science Toys. Churchill, E. Richard. LC 90-9891. 128p. (gr. 4-11). 1991. pap. 7.95 *(0-8069-5835-9)* Sterling.

—Paper Toys That Fly, Soar, Zoom & Whistle. Churchill, E. Richard. LC 88-30311. 192p. (gr. 10-12). 1989. 14. 95 *(0-8069-6840-0)* Sterling.

—Paper Tricks & Toys. Churchill, E. Richard. 128p. (gr. 2-8). 1993. pap. 7.95 *(0-8069-8417-1)* Sterling.

Michaels, Serge, jt. illus. see Gutierrez, Ed.

Michaels, Serge, jt. illus. see Ortiz, Phil.

Michaels, Ski. One Hundred Two Creepy, Crawly Bug Jokes. Michaels, Ski. LC 91-42737. 64p. (gr. 2-6). 1992. pap. text ed. 2.95 *(0-8167-2745-7)* Troll Assocs.

Michaels, Steve. Count Your Way Through Canada. Haskins, Jim. 24p. (gr. 1-4). 1989. 17.50 *(0-87614-350-8)*; pap. 5.95 *(0-87614-515-2)* Carolrhoda Bks.

—Pioneer Plowmaker: A Story about John Deere. Collins, David R. 64p. (gr. 3-6). 1990. PLB 14.95 *(0-87614-424-5)* Carolrhoda Bks.

—What Do You Mean? A Story about Noah Webster. Ferris, Jeri. 56p. (gr. 3-6). 1988. PLB 14.95 *(0-87614-330-3)* Carolrhoda Bks.

Michaels, William. Clare & Her Shadow. Michaels, William. LC 90-8487. 32p. (ps-k). 1991. lib. bdg. 15.00 *(0-208-02301-1,* Linnet) Shoe String.

Michel, Robin. String Figures from Around the World. Dewitt, Morena. 32p. (gr. 2-6). 1992. pap. 4.95 *(0-89346-356-6)* Heian Intl.

Michelini, Carlo A. The Falling Star. Spires, Elizabeth. LC 84-80288. 24p. (ps-k). 1989. 9.95 *(0-448-21026-6,* G&D) Putnam Pub Group.

—The Horse. Bussolati, Emanuela. LC 92-72118. 10p. (ps). 1993. 6.95 *(1-56397-201-8)* Boyds Mills Pr.

—What Animal Is It? Sclavi, Tiziano. 10p. (ps). 1994. prepub. 4.95 *(1-56397-345-6)* Boyds Mills Pr.

—What's on the Other Side? Sclavi, Tiziano. 10p. (ps). 1994. prepub. 4.95 *(1-56397-333-7)* Boyds Mills Pr.

Michels, Tilde. Sophie the Rag Picker. Michels, Tilde. (gr. k-1). 1962. 10.95 *(0-8392-3036-2)* Astor-Honor.

Michl, Reinhard. At the Frog Pond. Michels, Tilde. Ignatowicz, Nina, tr. from GER. LC 88-37835. 32p. (ps-4). 1989. (Lipp Jr Bks) HarpC Child Bks.

—The Foundling Fox. Korschunow, Irina. Skofield, James, tr. from GER. LC 84-47631. 48p. (gr. k-3). 1984. HarpC Child Bks.

—Small Fur. Korschunow, Irina. Skofield, James, tr. from GER. LC 87-45289. 80p. (gr. 1-4). 1988. HarpC Child Bks.

—Who's That Knocking at My Door? Michels, Tilde. 28p. (ps-3). 1986. 10.95 *(0-8120-5732-5)* Barron.

—Who's That Knocking at My Door? Michels, Tilde. 28p. (ps-3). 1992. pap. 4.95 *(0-8120-1486-3)* Barron.

Micich, Paul. The Littlest Angel. Tazewell, Charles. LC 91-2442. 32p. (ps). 1991. 15.95 *(0-8249-8516-8,* Ideals Child) Hambleton-Hill.

Mickie, Roy. Big Ball of String. 2nd ed. Holland, Marion. LC 92-16355. 72p. (gr. 1-2). 1993. 6.95 *(0-394-80005-2)*; PLB 7.99 *(0-394-90005-7)* Random Bks Yng Read.

Micucci, Charles. A Little Night Music. Micucci, Charles. LC 88-505. 32p. (ps-3). 1989. 10.95 *(0-688-07900-8)*; PLB 10.88 *(0-688-07901-6,* Morrow Jr Bks) Morrow Jr Bks.

Middendorf, Frances. What about Me? When Brothers & Sisters Get Sick. Peterkin, Allan. LC 92-20035. 32p. 1992. 16.95 *(0-945354-48-7)*; pap. 6.95 *(0-945354-49-5)* Magination Pr.

Middendorf, Nancy. The Four Daughters of Yusuf the Dairy Farmer. Simpson, Juwairiah J. 40p. (Orig.). (gr. 1-4). 1894. pap. 3.75 *(0-89259-056-4)* Am Trust Pubns.

Middleton, Michael. Luke Has Asthma, Too. Rogers, Alison. Plaut, Thomas F., frwd. by. LC 87-40053. 32p. (Orig.). (ps-2). 1987. pap. 6.95 *(0-914525-06-9)* Waterfront Bks.

Midgette, Darrell, jt. illus. see McBride, Angus.

Midgette, Darrell, jt. illus. see Ridge, Jeff.

Mierzejewska, Anna. Ode to Madonna & Other Poems. Paine, Alan. 160p. (Orig.). (gr. 4 up). 1992. pap. 12.95 *(0-9632582-1-4)* Diogenes Pr.

Miesen, Christine. Let's Go Fishing. Wilson, Trevor. LC 93-26220. 1994. 4.25 *(0-383-03758-1)* SRA Schl Grp.

Mietzelfeld, Mary. A Hundred Scoops of Ice Cream: Tiny Tales. Josefowitz, Natasha. 64p. (gr. 1 up). 1988. bds. 7.95x *(0-312-01444-9)* St Martin.

Migale, Lawrence, photos by. Celebrating Kwanzaa. Hoyt-Goldsmith, Diane. LC 93-16799. 32p. (gr. 3-7). 1993. reinforced bdg. 15.95 *(0-8234-1048-X)* Holiday.

Migdale, Lawrence. Arctic Hunter. Hoyt-Goldsmith, Diane. LC 92-2563. 32p. (gr. 3-7). 1992. reinforced bdg. 15.95 *(0-8234-0972-4)* Holiday.

—Pueblo Storyteller. Hoyt-Goldsmith, Diane. LC 90-46405. 32p. (gr. 3-7). 1991. reinforced bdg. 15.95 *(0-8234-0864-7)* Holiday.

—Totem Pole. Hoyt-Goldsmith, Diane. LC 89-26720. 32p. (gr. 3-7). 1990. reinforced bdg. 15.95 *(0-8234-0809-4)* Holiday.

Migdale, Lawrence, photos by. Cherokee Summer. Hoyt-Goldsmith, Diane. LC 92-54416. 32p. (gr. 3-7). 1993. reinforced bdg. 15.95 *(0-8234-0995-3)* Holiday.

—Hoang Anh: A Vietnamese-American Boy. Hoyt-Goldsmith, Diane. LC 91-28880. 32p. (gr. 3-7). 1992. reinforced bdg. 14.95 *(0-8234-0948-1)* Holiday.

Migliore, Ron. BASIC. Mackie, Dean & Mackie, David. 48p. (gr. 1-5). 1985. pap. 3.95 *(0-88625-085-4)* Durkin Hayes Pub.

—Birds. McKean, Barb. 32p. (gr. 3-7). 1985. pap. 3.50 *(0-88625-116-8)* Durkin Hayes Pub.

—Computer Play. Lear, Peter. 48p. (gr. 1-5). 1985. pap. 4.95 *(0-88625-087-0)* Durkin Hayes Pub.

Mignard, Phyllis D. Quiet One. Clark, Della R. 64p. (ps-5). 1992. 15.00 *(0-9631252-0-6)* Desert Rose.

Migron, Hagit. How the Rosh Hashanah Challah Became Round. Epstein, Sylvia. 28p. 1993. 8.95 *(965-229-095-5,* Pub. by Gefen Pub Hse IS) Gefen Bks.

Mijares, David P. Modern Samurai Training. Mijares, David P. 100p. (Orig.). 1989. pap. 9.95 *(0-9623400-0-6)* Group M Probelications.

Mike, Samuel A. Desert Seasons. Mike, Jan M. 32p. (gr. k-8). 1991. pap. 7.95 *(0-918080-49-5)* Treasure Chest.

Mikolayack, Charles. A Fair Wind for Troy. Gates, Doris. 96p. (gr. 4-6). 1984. pap. 4.95 *(0-14-031718-X,* Puffin) Puffin Bks.

—Peter & the Wolf. Prokofiev, Sergei. Carlson, Maria, tr. 32p. (ps-3). 1986. pap. 4.99 *(0-14-050633-0,* Puffin) Puffin Bks.

Mikolaycak, Charles. Babushka: An Old Russian Folktale. Mikolaycak, Charles. LC 84-500. 32p. (ps-3). 1984. reinforced bdg. 15.95 *(0-8234-0520-6)*; pap. 5.95 *(0-8234-0712-8)* Holiday.

—Bearhead: A Russian Folktale. Kimmel, Eric A., adapted by. LC 91-55026. 32p. (ps-3). 1991. reinforced 15.95 *(0-8234-0902-3)* Holiday.

—The Changing Maze. Snyder, Zilpha K. LC 91-45323. 32p. (gr. k-3). 1992. pap. 4.95 *(0-689-71618-4,* Aladdin) Macmillan Child Grp.

—Exodus. Chaikin, Miriam. LC 85-27361. 32p. (gr. 1-4). 1987. reinforced bdg. 15.95 *(0-8234-0607-5)* Holiday.

—A Gift from Saint Nicholas. Kismaric, Carole, adapted by. LC 87-8797. 32p. (ps-3). 1988. reinforced bdg. 15. 95 *(0-8234-0674-1)* Holiday.

—He Is Risen: The Easter Story. Winthrop, Elizabeth, adapted by. LC 84-15869. 32p. (gr. 4-6). 1985. reinforced bdg. 15.95 *(0-8234-0547-8)* Holiday.

—The Highwayman. Noyes, Alfred. LC 83-725. 40p. (gr. 5 up). 1983. 11.95 *(0-688-02117-4)* Lothrop.

—Juma & the Magic Jinn. Anderson, Joy. LC 85-23815. 40p. (gr. 1-3). 1986. 12.95 *(0-688-05443-9)*; PLB 12. 88 *(0-688-05444-7)* Lothrop.

—The Legend of the Christmas Rose. Lagerlof, Selma. Greene, Ellin, retold by. LC 89-77511. 32p. (ps up). 1990. reinforced 15.95 *(0-8234-0821-3)* Holiday.

—The Lullaby Songbook. Yolen, Jane. LC 85-752885. 32p. (ps up). 1986. 13.95 *(0-15-249903-2,* HB Juv Bks) HarBrace.

—The Man Who Could Call Down Owls. Bunting, Eve. LC 83-17568. 32p. (gr. k-3). 1984. RSBE 13.95 *(0-02-715380-0,* Macmillan Child Bk) Macmillan Child Grp.

—Perfect Crane. Laurin, Anne. LC 80-7912. 32p. (gr. 1-4). 1981. PLB 13.89 *(0-06-023744-9)* HarpC Child Bks.

—Perfect Crane. Laurin, Anne. LC 80-7912. 32p. (gr. 1-4). 1987. pap. 4.95 *(0-06-443154-1,* Trophy) HarpC Child Bks.

—Peter & the Wolf. Prokofiev, Sergei. Carlson, Maria, tr. (gr. 2-5). 1987. incl. cassette 19.95 *(0-87499-074-2)*; pap. 12.95 incl. cassette *(0-87499-073-4)*; 4 paperbacks, cassette & guide 27.95 *(0-87499-075-0)* Live Oak Media.

—The Rumor of Pavel & Paali: A Ukrainian Folktale. Kismaric, Carole, adapted by. LC 87-19958. 32p. (gr. 1-3). 1988. HarpC Child Bks.

—Tam Lin. Yolen, Jane. LC 88-2280. 24p. (gr. 1-7). 1990. 14.95 *(0-15-284261-8)* HarBrace.

Mikolaycak, Charles, photos by. A Child Is Born: The Christmas Story. Winthrop, Elizabeth. LC 82-11728. 32p. (ps-3). 1983. reinforced bdg. 15.95 *(0-8234-0472-2)* Holiday.

Milam, Harris. Tales of the Texians. Sinclair, Dorothy T. LC 85-90411. 104p. (Orig.). (gr. 4-7). 1986. 12.95 *(0-9615311-0-X)*; pap. 7.95 *(0-9615311-1-8)* Sinclair Ent.

Milam, Larry. Before the Lark. Brown, Irene B. 180p. (gr. 4 up). 1992. pap. 7.95 *(0-936085-22-3)* Blue Heron OR.

—Morning Glory Afternoon. Brown, Irene B. 224p. (gr. 7 up). 1991. pap. 8.95 *(0-936085-20-7)* Blue Heron OR.

—Skitterbrain. Brown, Irene B. LC 78-18349. 128p. (gr. 4 up). 1992. pap. 6.95 *(0-936085-21-5)* Blue Heron OR.

Milanowski, Stephanie. Who Am I? Paterson, Katherine. 96p. (Orig.). 1992. pap. 8.99 *(0-8028-5072-3)* Eerdmans.

Miles, Elizabeth. Fisherman & His Wife. Grimm, Jacob & Grimm, Wilhelm K. 32p. (ps-3). 1992. 6.95 *(0-8362-4930-5)* Andrews & McMeel.

—Goldilocks & the Three Bears. Greenway, Jennifer, retold by. 1991. 6.95 *(0-8362-4900-3)* Andrews & McMeel.

—Velveteen Rabbit. Williams, Margery. (ps-3). 1990. pap. 2.50 *(0-590-42805-5)* Scholastic Inc.

Milhous, Katherine. The Egg Tree. Milhous, Katherine. LC 50-6817. 32p. (gr. 1-4). 1971. RSBE 13.95 *(0-684-12716-4,* Scribners Young Read) Macmillan Child Grp.

—The Silver Pencil. Dalgliesh, Alice. 248p. (gr. 7 up). 1991. pap. 4.99 *(0-14-034792-5,* Puffin) Puffin Bks.

Mill, Eleanor. A Button in Her Ear. Litchfield, Ada B. Rubin, Caroline, ed. LC 75-28390. 32p. (gr. 2-4). 1976. PLB 13.95 *(0-8075-0987-6)* A Whitman.

—A Cane in Her Hand. Litchfield, Ada B. Rubin, Caroline, ed. LC 77-14255. (gr. 1-3). 1977. PLB 13.95 *(0-8075-1056-4)* A Whitman.

—I Won't Go Without a Father. Stanek, Muriel. LC 78-188435. 32p. (gr. 1-3). 1972. PLB 11.95 *(0-8075-3524-9)* A Whitman.

—What Mary Jo Shared. Udry, Janice M. LC 66-16082. 40p. (gr. k-2). 1966. PLB 13.95 *(0-8075-8842-3)* A Whitman.

Millar, H. R. Five Children & It. Nesbit, Edith. 224p. (gr. 4-6). 1985. pap. 2.95 *(0-14-035061-6,* Puffin) Puffin Bks.

—Phoenix & the Carpet. Nesbit, Edith. (gr. 4-6). 1985. pap. 2.25 *(0-14-035062-4,* Puffin) Puffin Bks.

Millar, H. R. & Shepperson, Claude. Whereyouwantogoto: And Other Unlikely Tales. Nesbit, E. LC 93-18685. 224p. 1993. 6.00 *(1-56957-904-0)* Shambhala Pubns.

Millard, Carolyn. Stolen Princess: A Northwest Indian Legend. Morss, Willard N. & Herren, Janet M. LC 83-82920. 79p. (Orig.). (gr. 4-8). 1983. pap. 8.95 *(0-9613025-0-X)* J M Herren.

Miller, Alma E. & Kellner, Ron. Baptism. rev. ed. Todd, Richard E. 26p. (gr. 2-6). 1993. wkbk. 2.45 *(0-9605324-1-2)* Crosswalk Res.

—Church. Todd, Richard E. 26p. (gr. 2-6). 1993. wkbk. 2.45 *(0-9605324-4-7)* Crosswalk Res.

—Communion. rev. ed. Todd, Richard E. 26p. (gr. 2-6). 1993. wkbk. 2.45 *(0-9605324-3-9)* Crosswalk Res.

—Salvation. rev. ed. Todd, Richard E. 26p. (gr. 2-6). 1993. wkbk. 2.45 *(0-9605324-6-3)* Crosswalk Res.

Miller, Andrew. Nature's Hidden World. Selberg, Ingrid. 14p. (gr. k-2). 1984. 13.95 *(0-399-20973-5,* Philomel) Putnam Pub Group.

—Our Changing World: A Moving Parts Book. Selberg, Ingrid. 12p. (ps-8). 1992. 12.95 *(0-399-20869-0,* Philomel Bks) Putnam Pub Group.

Miller, Benjamin S. RAPmetic, the Arithmetic Rap. Musson, Gloria J. & Musson, Cyril D. 48p. (Orig.). (gr. 3 up). 1988. pap. text ed. 3.50 *(0-9619321-0-4)*; cass. 6.50 *(0-9619321-1-2)* Sq One Pubns.

Miller, Bob. Blossom Bird Falls in Love. Paul, Sherry. 32p. (Orig.). (ps-2). 1981. pap. 14.10 Bks. only *(0-685-01192-5)*; pap. 16.20 bks & Skill Masters *(0-685-01193-3)* CPI Pub.

—Blossom Bird Finds a Family. Paul, Sherry. 32p. (Orig.). (ps-2). 1981. pap. 14.10 set *(0-686-31343-7)*; Bks. & Skill Masters Set 16.20 *(0-685-01194-1)* CPI Pub.

—Blossom Bird Goes South. Paul, Sherry. 32p. (Orig.). (ps-2). 1981. pap. 14.10 set *(0-675-01080-2)*; Bks. & Skillmasters set 16.20 *(0-685-01195-X)* CPI Pub.

—Finn the Foolish Fish: Trouble with Bubbles. Paul, Sherry. 32p. (Orig.). (ps-2). 1981. pap. 14.10 set *(0-675-01084-5)*; Bks. & Skillmasters set 16.20 *(0-685-01196-8)* CPI Pub.

Miller, Cliff. In Search of the Hidden Statue. Foley, Louise M. (gr. 2-6). 1993. incl. puzzle 12.95 *(0-922242-46-1)* Lombard Mktg.

Miller, David. The Pact of Pasaquine. Schnurr, Carl. McGlothlen, Ken, et al, eds. 96p. (Orig.). (gr. 11 up). 1991. pap. 12.95 *(0-9627790-8-3)* White Wolf.

Miller, Dennis. Ten Stories for Children. Hardegrove, Nelle A. 10p. (Orig.). (gr. 1-5). 1987. pap. text ed. 7.95 *(0-9619227-3-7)* N A Hardegrove.

Miller, Edna. Mousekin Finds a Friend. Miller, Edna. (ps-3). 1971. (Pub. by Treehouse) P-H.

—Mousekin's Birth. Miller, Edna. 32p. (gr. k-3). 1982. pap. 2.50 *(0-13-604132-9,* Pub. by Treehouse) P-H.

—Mousekin's Christmas Eve. Miller, Edna. (gr. k-3). 1972. 11.95 *(0-13-604044-6,* Pub. by Treehouse) P-H.

—Mousekin's Close Call. Miller, Edna. LC 77-27571. (gr. k-3). 1980. 9.95 *(0-13-604207-4,* Pub. by Treehouse); pap. 3.95 *(0-13-604199-X)* P-H.

—Mousekin's Easter Basket. Miller, Edna. LC 86-22511. 32p. (gr. k-3). 1989. pap. 12.95 jacketed *(0-671-66803-X,* S&S BFYR); pap. 5.95 *(0-671-67439-0,* S&S BFYR) S&S Trade.

—Mousekin's Fables. Miller, Edna. 28p. (ps-3). 1982. 11. 95 *(0-13-604165-5)* P-H.

—Mousekin's Family. Miller, Edna. (gr. k-3). 1972. PLB 9.95x *(0-13-604462-X,* Pub. by Treehouse); pap. 5.95 *(0-13-604157-4)* P-H.

—Mousekin's Golden House. Miller, Edna. (gr. k-3). 1971. PLB 9.95x *(0-13-604421-2,* Pub. by Treehouse) P-H.

—Mousekin's Thanksgiving. Miller, Edna. 32p. (ps-3). 1988. pap. 5.95 (*0-671-66859-5*, S&S BFYR) S&S Trade.
—Patches Finds a New Home. Miller, Edna. (ps-4). 1989. pap. 12.95 jacketed (*0-671-66266-X*, S&S BFYR) S&S Trade.
—Scamper: A Gray Tree Squirrel. Miller, Edna. 32p. (gr. k-3). 1991. PLB 14.95 (*0-945912-12-9*) Pippin Pr.
Miller, J. P. A Birthday Present for Mama: A Step Two Book. Lorian, Nicole. LC 83-26849. (ps-2). 1984. pap. 3.50 (*0-394-86755-6*) Random Bks Yng Read.
—The Cow Says Moo. (ps). 1979. 3.50 (*0-394-84131-X*) Random Bks Yng Read.
—Do You Know Colors? Howard, Katherine. LC 78-1133. (ps-1). 1979. lib. bdg. 5.99 (*0-394-93957-3*); 2.25 (*0-394-83957-9*) Random Bks Yng Read.
—Farmer John's Animals. Miller, J. P. LC 79-63900. (ps-1). 1979. 3.95 (*0-394-84270-7*) Random Bks Yng Read.
—Good Night, Little Rabbit. Miller, J. P. LC 85-62017. 7p. (ps). 1993. bds. 3.95 (*0-394-87992-9*) Random Bks Yng Read.
—Learn about Colors with Little Rabbit. Miller, J. P. LC 84-6943. (ps-1). 1984. 3.95 (*0-394-86671-1*); lib. bdg. 4.99 (*0-394-96671-6*) Random Bks Yng Read.
—Little Bunny Follows His Nose. Howard, Katherine. 32p. (ps-2). 1971. write for info. (*0-307-13536-5*, Golden Bks.) Western Pub.
—Little Rabbit Takes a Walk. Miller, J. P. LC 86-61525. 24p.(ps-1). 1987. pap. 5.95 bk. & doll pkg. (*0-394-88667-4*) Random Bks Yng Read.
—Lucky Bear. Phillips, Joan. LC 85-14467. 32p. (ps-1). 1986. lib. bdg. 7.99 (*0-394-97987-7*); pap. 3.50 (*0-394-87987-2*) Random Bks Yng Read.
—Sweet Smell of Christmas. Scarry, Patricia M. 32p. (ps-2). 1970. write for info. (*0-307-13527-6*, Golden Bks) Western Pub.
—Yoo-Hoo Little Rabbit. Miller, J. P. LC 85-61529. (ps). 1986. 3.99 (*0-394-87884-1*) Random Bks Yng Read.
Miller, Jackie. Fireman Fred's, Fire Safety Coloring Book. Franklin, Herb. 8p. (gr. 1-5). 1990. pap. 0.50 (*0-945145-02-0*) Miller Family Pubns.
Miller, Jane. The Farm Alphabet Book. Miller, Jane. 32p. (ps-2). 1987. pap. 2.50 (*0-590-31991-4*) Scholastic Inc.
—Farm Counting Book. Miller, Jane. 24p. (ps-3). 1986. 8.95 (*0-13-304790-3*); pap. 4.95 (*0-13-304809-8*) P-H.
—Seasons on the Farm. Miller, Jane. 32p. (gr. k-3). 1986. 10.95 (*0-13-797275-X*) P-H.
Miller, Jane, photos by. Farm Noises. Miller, Jane. (ps-3). 1989. pap. 8.95 (*0-671-67450-1*, Little Simon) S&S Trade.
Miller, Jayna. Too Much Trick or Treat. Miller, Jayne. Thatch, Nancy R., ed. Melton, David, intro. by. LC 91-14930. 26p. (gr. k-4). 1991. PLB 14.95 (*0-933849-37-0*) Landmark Edns.
Miller, Jon. The Fox Busters. King-Smith, Dick. LC 87-37409. 128p. (gr. 4-7). 1988. 13.95 (*0-440-50064-8*) Delacorte.
Miller, L. Dennis. The Enchanted Raisin. Balcells, Jacqueline. Miller, Elizabeth G., tr. from SPA. LC 88-28587. 104p. (gr. 3-7). 1989. pap. 11.00 (*0-935480-38-2*) Lat Am Lit Rev Pr.
Miller, Lyle. Abraham Lincoln. Barkan, Joanne. Brook, Bonnie, ed. 32p. (gr. k-2). 1990. 6.95 (*0-671-69113-9*); PLB 10.98 (*0-671-69107-4*) Silver Pr.
—Benjamin Franklin: Printer, Inventor, Statesman. Adler, David A. LC 91-28816. 48p. (gr. 2-5). 1992. reinforced bdg. 14.95 (*0-8234-0929-5*) Holiday.
—Boomer's Kids. Tolliver, Ruby C. 128p. (gr. 4 up). 1992. 14.95 (*0-937460-69-9*) Hendrick-Long.
—Christopher Columbus: Great Explorer. Adler, David A. LC 90-28668. 48p. (gr. 2-5). 1991. reinforced bdg. 14.95 (*0-8234-0895-7*) Holiday.
—Hats for Watering Horses: Why the Cowboy Dressed That Way. Christain, Mary B. 64p. (gr. 2 up). 1994. write for info. (*0-937460-89-3*); pap. write for info. (*0-937460-95-8*) Hendrick-Long.
—Thomas Alva Edison: Great Inventor. Adler, David A. LC 89-77507. 48p. (gr. 2-5). 1990. reinforced bdg. 14.95 (*0-8234-0820-5*) Holiday.
—Uncle Carmello. Zucker, David. LC 91-15258. 32p. (ps-4). 1993. RSBE 14.95 (*0-02-793760-7*, Macmillan Child Bk) Macmillan Child Grp.
Miller, Lyle L. Blind Bess, Buddy, & Me. Tolliver, Ruby C. Welch, Karen, ed. 104p. (gr. 4 up). 1990. lib. bdg. 12.95 (*0-937460-63-X*) Hendrick-Long.
—Shipwrecked on Padre Island. Marvin, Isabel R. 160p. (gr. 4 up). 1993. 14.95 (*0-937460-83-4*) Hendrick-Long.
Miller, Margaret. More First Words: My Birthday. Miller, Margaret. LC 89-82635. 14p. (ps). 1991. 3.95 (*0-694-00302-6*) HarpC Child Bks.
—Rat-a-Tat, Pitter Pat. Benjamin, Alan. LC 87-568. 40p. (ps-k). 1987. (Crowell Jr Bks); PLB 11.89 (*0-690-04611-1*) HarpC Child Bks.
Miller, Margaret, photos by. Funny Papers: Behind the Scenes of the Comics. Scott, Elaine. LC 92-46727. 96p. (gr. 3 up). 1993. 14.95 (*0-688-11575-6*); PLB 14.93 (*0-688-11576-4*) Morrow Jr Bks.
—How You Were Born. rev. ed. Cole, Joanna. 48p. (ps up). 1994. pap. 4.95 (*0-688-12061-X*, Mulberry) Morrow.
—How You Were Born: Illustrated with Photographs. rev. ed. Cole, Joanna. LC 92-23970. 48p. (ps up). 1993. 15.00 (*0-688-12059-8*); PLB 14.93 (*0-688-12060-1*) Morrow Jr Bks.

—My Puppy Is Born. rev. ed. Cole, Joanna. LC 90-42011. 48p. (ps up) 1991. pap. 4.95 (*0-688-10198-4*, Mulberry) Morrow.
—My Puppy Is Born. rev. ed. Cole, Joanna. LC 90-42011. 48p. (ps up) 1991. 13.95 (*0-688-09770-7*); PLB 13.88 (*0-688-09771-5*, Morrow Jr Bks) Morrow Jr Bks.
—Ramona: Behind the Scenes of a Television Show. Scott, Elaine. LC 87-33313. 96p. (gr. 3-7). 1988. 14.95 (*0-688-06818-9*); PLB 14.88 (*0-688-06819-7*, Morrow Jr Bks) Morrow Jr Bks.
—Safe in the Spotlight: The Dawn Animal Agency & the Sanctuary for Animals. Scott, Elaine. LC 90-49677. 80p. (gr. 3 up). 1991. 12.95 (*0-688-08177-0*); PLB 12.88 (*0-688-08178-9*, Morrow Jr Bks) Morrow Jr Bks.
Miller, Marianne M. Too Busy: A Days of the Week Story. Miller, Marianne M. Wray, Rhonda, ed. LC 93-11657. 36p. (Orig.). (gr. k-3). 1993. pap. 8.95 (*0-916260-96-8*, B114) Meriwether Pub.
Miller, Myron. Brain Bafflers. Steinwachs, Robert. 128p. (gr. 10-12). 1993. pap. 4.95 (*0-8069-8787-1*) Sterling.
—Challenging Lateral Thinking Puzzles. Sloane, Paul & MacHale, Des. 96p. (gr. 10-12). 1993. pap. 4.95 (*0-8069-8671-9*) Sterling.
—Logical Thinking Puzzles. Sloane, Paul & MacHale, Des. LC 92-19095. 96p. (gr. 5 up). 1992. 12.95 (*0-8069-8670-0*) Sterling.
—Witty Words: A Hilarious Collection of Outrageous Quotations for Every Day of the Year. Mason, Eileen. LC 92-25145. 224p. (gr. 10-12). 1992. 18.95 (*0-8069-8604-2*) Sterling.
Miller, Ralph R. Don't Be a Grumpy Bear: A Coloring Book about Manners in Signed English. Bornstein, Harry, et al. 32p. (ps-2). 1986. pap. 3.95 (*0-930323-26-2*, Pub. by K Green Pubns) Gallaudet Univ Pr.
—The Tale of Peter Rabbit: A Coloring Book in Signed English. Potter, Beatrix. Roy, Howard L., et al. 64p. (ps-2). 1986. pap. 3.95 (*0-930323-29-7*, Pub. by K Green Pubns) Gallaudet Univ Pr.
Miller, Ralph R., Sr. The Signed English Starter. Bornstein, Harry & Saulnier, Karen L. LC 84-4042. 232p. (ps-6). 1984. pap. text ed. 13.95 (*0-913580-82-1*, Clerc Bks) Gallaudet Univ Pr.
Miller, Robert H. Reflections of a Black Cowboy. Miller, Robert H. 9p. (Orig.). (gr. 5-7). 1988. pap. text ed. 9.95x (*0-929592-01-8*) Waterlinc Prodns.
Miller, Robert W. Moss, a Border Collie. Nordmark, Magdalene L. Miller, Janus W., prologue by. 37p. (Orig.). 1988. pap. 7.00 (*0-685-21901-1*) Willow Run UT.
Miller, Ron, et al. The Macmillan Book of Astronomy. Gallant, Roy A. LC 86-24158. 80p. (gr. 3-7). 1986. pap. 8.95 (*0-02-042330-5*, Aladdin) Macmillan Child Grp.
Miller, Susan. Fish for Supper. Matthews, Morgan. LC 85-14056. 48p. (Orig.). (gr. 1-3). 1986. PLB 10.59 (*0-8167-0588-7*); pap. text ed. 3.50 (*0-8167-0589-5*) Troll Assocs.
—Joey the Jack-O'-Lantern. Craig, Janet. LC 87-10845. 32p. (gr. k-2). 1988. PLB 11.59 (*0-8167-1105-4*); pap. text ed. 2.95 (*0-8167-1106-2*) Troll Assocs.
—Little Christmas Star. Craig, Janet. LC 87-10936. 32p. (gr. k-2). 1988. PLB 11.59 (*0-8167-1097-X*); pap. text ed. 2.95 (*0-8167-1098-8*) Troll Assocs.
—Which Way, Hannah? Matthews, Morgan. LC 85-14132. 48p. (Orig.). (gr. 1-3). 1986. PLB 10.59 (*0-8167-0648-4*); pap. text ed. 3.50 (*0-8167-0649-2*) Troll Assocs.
Miller, Susan L. Rescue the Reef! A Coloring-Activities Book. Earthbound Environmental Creations, Inc. Staff. Stec, Ruth E., intro. by. 40p. (ps-4). 1993. pap. text ed. write for info. (*0-9632284-3-9*) R M S Pub.
Miller, Ted. Jesse James. Ernst, John. LC 76-10206. (gr. 4-7). 1976. 9.95 (*0-13-509695-2*) P-H.
Miller, Tom. This Path of Scattered Glass: A Collection of Poems. Miller, Tom. LC 92-84067. 96p. (Orig.). (gr. 7 up). 1993. pap. 6.95 (*1-878893-39-4*) Telcraft Bks.
Miller, Virginia. Go to Bed! Miller, Virginia. LC 92-54958. 32p. (ps up) 1993. 14.95 (*1-56402-244-7*) Candlewick Pr.
Miller, Virginia, jt. illus. see Austin, Virginia.
Miller, Warren. Young Santa. Greenburg, Dan. 80p. 1991. 13.95 (*0-670-83905-1*) Viking Child Bks.
—Young Santa. Greenburg, Dan. LC 93-7482. 80p. 1993. pap. 4.99 (*0-14-034773-9*, Puffin) Puffin Bks.
Miller, Wynn. Kids in Motion Creative Movement & Song Book. Weissman, Julie, et al. Schiff, Ronny S., ed. 102p. (ps-4). 1987. pap. text ed. 14.95 (*0-88284-356-7*, 2337) Alfred Pub.
Miller-Ray, Sue E. Earthquakes & Volcanoes. Deery, Ruth. 48p. (gr. 4-8). 1985. wkbk. 6.95 (*0-86653-272-2*, GA 630) Good Apple.
Millet, C. & Millet, D. Castles. Jeunesse, Gallimard, et al. LC 92-15955. 1993. 10.95 (*0-590-46377-2*) Scholastic Inc.
Millet, Claude & Millet, Denise. Music! Laurencin, Genevieve. Bogard, Vicki, tr. from FRE. LC 89-8892. (gr. k-5). 1989. 4.95 (*0-944589-25-1*, 025) Young Discovery Lib.
Millet, D., jt. illus. see Millet, C.
Millet, Denise, jt. illus. see Millet, Claude.
Milligan, John. I Can Read About Basketball. Harris, Richard. LC 76-54397. (gr. 2-5). 1977. 1.95 (*0-89375-032-8*) Troll Assocs.
—I Can Read About Football. Harris, Richard. LC 76-54398. (gr. 2-5). 1977. 1.95 (*0-89375-033-6*) Troll Assocs.

Mills, Elaine. One Winter's Night. Lockwood, Primrose. LC 90-22891. 32p. (ps-1). 1991. SBE 13.95 (*0-02-759235-9*, Macmillan Child Bk) Macmillan Child Grp.
Mills, Jackie. Sirena of Salado. Mills, Jackie. 32p. (gr. 2-7). 1991. 10.95 (*0-9629284-0-2*) Indian Trail.
Mills, Janie. Jennie Barnes: Right Now Forever. Saban, Vera. LC 90-39763. 130p. (Orig.). (gr. 4-6). 1990. pap. 6.95 (*0-914565-34-6*, Timbertrails) Capstan Pubns.
Mills, Lauren. Anne of Green Gables Address Book. Montgomery, L. M. 1990. 8.95 (*0-7704-2363-9*) Bantam.
—Anne of Green Gables Birthday Book. Montgomery, L. M. 1990. 8.95 (*0-7704-2362-0*) Bantam.
—At the Back of the North Wind. MacDonald, George. LC 87-45455. 320p. 1988. 18.95 (*0-87923-703-1*) Godine.
—Elfabet: An ABC of Elves. Yolen, Jane. (ps-3). 1990. 14.95 (*0-316-96900-1*) Little.
—The Tsar's Promise. SanSouci, Robert. 32p. (ps up). 1992. 14.95 (*0-399-21581-6*, Philomel Bks) Putnam Pub Group.
Mills, Michael. The Winner's Edge: What Every Young Person Should Know Before Experimenting with Life. Page, Roland. Pickett, Christine, ed. 176p. (Orig.). (gr. 6-12). 1990. pap. 10.00 (*0-9626244-0-3*) New Impres UT.
Mills, Patricia. Until the Cows Come Home. Mills, Patricia. LC 92-31049. 32p. (gr. k-3). 1993. 14.95 (*1-55858-190-1*); PLB 14.88 (*1-55858-191-X*) North-South Bks NYC.
Mills, Peter. Jonah's Adventure with the Big Fish: Bible Adventures. Mills, Peter. 1991. bds. 8.99 with flaps (*0-8007-7121-4*) Revell.

Mills, Tiffany. Melvin Howard's Fireside Chats. Krieger, Michael T. 149p. (Orig.). (gr. 7 up). 1992. pap. 9.00 (*0-9634329-0-7*) M T Krieger. **Day-dreaming Martin Hovrick, a shy, under-confident teenager, is having trouble growing up. He has many questions about life, girls, friendship, & the future. But, all of his burdens start to become surprisingly easier to carry after his accidental introduction to Melvin Howard, a grandfatherly man, who provides young Martin with guidance & friendship at a critical time in both characters' lives. Set in Northwest Ohio, the book exemplifies finding adventure & worthwhile living in common "everyday" life. As well as being a reflection of the people akin to this area of the Midwest, MELVIN HOWARD'S FIRESIDE CHATS also takes readers, through Melvin's memories, to many places, like a photo safari in the Congo & a deep sea fishing trip just off the Bahamas. But, mostly this novel is a nostalgic journey through time that takes readers back to a simpler, yet more vulnerable period. Melvin Howard's memories, as they are told to Martin, touch many emotions, & supply wise advice to curing traditional woes that have plagued the young throughout time. Each tale that Melvin weaves subtly conveys a poignant life lesson. Since the stories are pulled from all points in Melvin's past, the emphasis indicates that growing up never really stops. Martin listens to Melvin's stories intently at first as entertainment, but then later he realizes the bigger picture: life is a non-stop growing experience. Martin finds that everyone occasionally lacks self-confidence, & knowing that he is not alone in this effort is a comfort that helps Martin begin to grow within himself, for himself. To order copies, call 419-666-1380.** *Publisher Provided Annotation.*

Mills, Yaroslava. Mitten. Tresselt, Alvin R. LC 64-14436. 30p. (gr. k-3). 1964. PLB 12.88 (*0-688-51053-1*) Lothrop.
—The Mitten. Tresselt, Alvin. LC 64-14436. 30p. (ps-3). 1989. pap. 4.95 (*0-688-09238-1*, Mulberry) Morrow.

—Rosachok: A Russian Story. Zakhoder, Boris. LC 72-10148. (gr. k-3). 1970. PLB 12.88 (*0-688-51113-9*) Lothrop.
Millsap, Darrel. Kangaroos. Wildlife Education, Ltd. Staff. 24p. 1992. 13.95 (*0-937934-80-1*); pap. 2.25 (*0-937934-63-1*) Wildlife Educ.
Milne, Annabel & Stebbing, Peter. Look at Flowers. rev. ed. Kirkpatrick, Rena K. LC 84-26227. 32p. (gr. 2-4). 1985. PLB 17.28 (*0-8172-2352-5*); pap. 4.95 (*0-8114-6898-4*) Raintree Steck-V.
—Look at Leaves. rev. ed. Kirkpatrick, Rena K. LC 84-26360. 32p. (gr. 2-4). 1985. PLB 17.28 (*0-8172-2353-3*); pap. 4.95 (*0-8114-6899-2*) Raintree Steck-V.
—Look at Pond Life. rev. ed. Kirkpatrick, Rena K. LC 84-26249. 32p. (gr. 2-4). 1985. PLB 17.28 (*0-8172-2355-X*); pap. 4.95 (*0-8114-6901-8*) Raintree Steck-V.
—Look at Shore Life. rev. ed. Kirkpatrick, Rena K. LC 84-26249. 32p. (gr. 2-4). 1985. PLB 17.28 (*0-8172-2358-4*); pap. 4.95 (*0-8114-6904-2*) Raintree Steck-V.
Milne, James A. Shambala Warriors: Non-Violent Fighters for Peace. Milne, Teddy. LC 86-64054. 150p. (Orig.). (gr. 4 up). 1987. pap. 7.95 (*0-938875-07-8*) Pittenbruach Pr.
Milne, Terry. The Cat, the Crow, & the Banyan Tree. Lively, Penelope. LC 93-22355. (ps-3). write for info. (*1-56402-325-7*) Candlewick Pr.
—The Polka Dot Horse. Thiel, Elizabeth. LC 92-10221. 1993. pap. 14.00 (*0-671-79419-1*, S&S BYR) S&S Trade.
Milne, Terry A. & Milne, Terry A. The Toymaker. Waddell, Martin. LC 91-58762. 32p. (ps up). 1992. 13.95 (*1-56402-103-3*) Candlewick Pr.
Milone, Karen. Ali Baba Bernstein, Lost & Found. Hurwitz, Johanna. LC 92-4774. 96p. (gr. 3-7). 1992. 14.00 (*0-688-11454-7*); PLB 13.93 (*0-688-11455-5*) Morrow Jr Bks.
—Amelia Earhart: Adventure in the Sky. Sabin, Francene. LC 82-15987. 48p. (gr. 4-6). 1983. PLB 10.79 (*0-89375-839-6*); pap. text ed. 3.50 (*0-89375-840-X*) Troll Assocs.
—Are You Flying, Charlie Duncan? O'Donnell, Elizabeth L. LC 92-39876. 96p. (gr. 4 up). 1993. 14.00 (*0-688-09027-3*) Morrow Jr Bks.
—Beauty & the Beast. Rand. LC 81-612. 32p. (gr. k-4). 1981. PLB 9.79 (*0-89375-464-1*); pap. text ed. 1.95 (*0-89375-465-X*) Troll Assocs.
—The Farm, Life in Colonial Pennsylvania. Knight, James E. LC 81-23083. 32p. (gr. 5-9). 1982. PLB 11.59 (*0-89375-730-6*); pap. text ed. 2.95 (*0-89375-731-4*) Troll Assocs.
—Hopscotch Around the World. Lankford, Mary D. LC 91-17152. 48p. (gr. 4 up). 1992. 15.00 (*0-688-08419-2*); PLB 14.93 (*0-688-08420-6*) Morrow Jr Bks.
—Ice Cream. Neimark, Jill. LC 84-10915. (gr. 2-6). 1986. 11.95 (*0-8038-3440-3*); pap. 11.95 (*0-8038-9290-X*) Hastings.
—The Louisa May Alcott Cookbook. Anderson, Gretchen, ed. 96p. (gr. 3 up). 1985. 12.95 (*0-316-03951-9*) Little.
—Marcy Hooper & the Greatest Treasure in the World. Tolan, Stephanie S. LC 91-12176. 64p. (gr. 2 up). 1991. 12.95 (*0-688-10078-3*) Morrow Jr Bks.
—Marie Curie: Brave Scientist. Brandt, Keith. LC 82-16092. 48p. (gr. 4-6). 1983. PLB 10.79 (*0-89375-855-8*); pap. text ed. 3.50 (*0-89375-856-6*) Troll Assocs.
—A Second Thought. Cormier, Michael J. LC 91-41619. 32p. (gr. 2-6). 1992. PLB 17.96 (*0-8114-3578-4*) Raintree Steck-V.
—Shooting Star Summer. Ransom, Candice F. 32p. (ps-3). 1992. PLB 14.95 (*1-56397-005-8*) Boyds Mills Pr.
—Still As a Star: A Book of Nighttime Poems. Hopkins, Lee B., selected by. 32p. (ps-3). 1989. 14.95 (*0-316-37272-2*) Little.
—The Wild Swans. Andersen, Hans Christian. LC 80-27685. 32p. (gr. k-4). 1981. PLB 9.79 (*0-89375-480-3*); pap. text ed. 1.95 (*0-89375-481-1*) Troll Assocs.
Milord, Susan. Adventures in Art: Art & Crafts Experiences for 7- to 14-Year Olds. Milord, Susan. Williamson, Susan, ed. LC 90-39031. 160p. (Orig.). (gr. 2-8). 1990. pap. 12.95 (*0-913589-54-3*) Williamson Pub Co.
Miluck, Nancy C. Nevada History Coloring Books: Nevada's Native Americans. Miluck, Nancy C. 48p. (gr. k-5). 1992. pap. text ed. 3.50 (*0-9606382-4-5*) Dragon Ent.
—Nevada History Coloring Books: The First Settlers. Miluck, Nancy C. 48p. (gr. k-6). 1993. pap. 3.50 (*0-9606382-5-3*) Dragon Ent. Postponed.
—Nevada History Coloring Books: The 20th Century. Miluck, Nancy C. 48p. (Orig.). (gr. k-5). 1992. pap. text ed. 3.50 (*0-9606382-3-7*) Dragon Ent.
Miner, Julia. The Shepherd's Song: The Twenty-Third Psalm. LC 91-31067. 32p. 1993. 14.99 (*0-8037-1196-4*) Dial Bks Young.
Mines, Bob. Lost Wild America: The Story of Our Extinct & Vanishing Wildlife. rev., enl. & updated ed. McClung, Robert M. LC 93-15657. 312p. (gr. 6-12). 1993. PLB 25.00 (*0-208-02359-3*, Pub. by Linnet) Shoe String.

Ming-Yi, Yang. The Shell Woman & the King: A Chinese Folktale. Yep, Laurence, retold by. LC 92-9583. 32p. (gr. k-3). 1993. 13.99 (*0-8037-1394-0*); PLB 13.89 (*0-8037-1395-9*) Dial Bks Young.
Minks, Leah, jt. illus. see Minks, Louise.
Minks, Louise & Minks, Leah. Memorial Hall Coloring Book. 24p. (Orig.). (gr. 3-4). 1989. pap. 2.95 (*0-9612876-7-5*) Pocumtuck Valley Mem.
Minnick, Molly A. Divorce Illustrated: Workbook. Minnick, Molly A. 60p. (Orig.). (gr. 4). 1990. pap. 5.00 (*1-878526-03-0*) Pineapple MI.
Minor, Wendell. The Everglades. George, Jean C. LC 92-9517. 1992. 15.00 (*0-06-021228-4*); PLB 14.89 (*0-06-021229-2*) HarpC Child Bks. Postponed.
—Heartland. Siebert, Diane. LC 87-29380. 32p. (ps-3). 1989. 16.00 (*0-690-04730-4*, Crowell Jr Bks); PLB 15.89 (*0-690-04732-0*) HarpC Child Bks.
—Heartland. Siebert, Diane. LC 87-29380. 32p. (gr. 2 up). 1992. pap. 5.95 (*0-06-443287-4*, Trophy) HarpC Child Bks.
—Julie's Choice. George, Jean C. LC 93-27738. 1994. write for info. (*0-06-023528-4*); lib. bdg. write for info. (*0-06-023529-2*) HarpC Child Bks.
—Mojave. Siebert, Diane. LC 86-24329. 32p. (ps up) 1988. 15.00 (*0-690-04567-0*, Crowell Jr Bks); PLB 14.89 (*0-690-04569-7*, Crowell Jr Bks) HarpC Child Bks.
—Mojave. Siebert, Diane. LC 86-24329. 32p. (gr. k-3). 1992. pap. 4.95 (*0-06-443283-1*, Trophy) HarpC Child Bks.
—The Moon of the Owls. George, Jean C. LC 91-2735. 48p. (gr. 3-7). 1993. 15.00 (*0-06-020192-4*); PLB 14.89 (*0-06-020193-2*) HarpC Child Bks.
—The Seashore Book. Zolotow, Charlotte. LC 91-22783. 32p. (ps-3). 1992. 15.00 (*0-06-020213-0*); PLB 14.89 (*0-06-020214-9*) HarpC Child Bks.
—Sierra. Siebert, Diane. LC 90-30522. 32p. (ps-3). 1991. 16.00 (*0-06-021639-5*); PLB 15.89 (*0-06-021640-9*) HarpC Child Bks.
Minson, Grant L. The First Snowflake. McArthur, Dalton R. 32p. (Orig.). (gr. ps-4). 1991. pap. 4.95x (*0-9626111-0-7*) McArthur UT.
Minter, Daniel. The Footwarmer & the Black Crow. Coleman, Evelyn. LC 92-38352. (gr. 3 up). 1994. text ed. 14.95 (*0-02-722816-9*) MacMillan.
Minton, Barbara. Texas Star. Cole, Barbara H. LC 88-25205. 32p. (ps-2). 1990. 14.95 (*0-531-05820-4*); PLB 14.99 (*0-531-08420-5*) Orchard Bks Watts.
Minvielle, Chestee H. The Battle in the Bayou Country. Raphael, Morris. 199p. (gr. 5-12). 1976. 12.95 (*0-9608866-0-5*) M Raphael.
Mion, Francie & Johnson, Priscilla M. Ladybugs for Loretta. Wickstrom, Lois. (gr. k-6). 1978. pap. 2.00 (*0-916176-04-5*) Sproing.
Mir, Anjum. Inside & Under the World of Wonder. Kezzeiz, Ediba. 38p. (Orig.). (ps). 1992. pap. text ed. 4.00 (*0-89259-112-9*) Am Trust Pubns.
Miracle, Ric. Word Bird's Fall Words. Moncure, Jane B. LC 85-5935. 32p. (gr. k-2). 1985. PLB 21.35 (*0-89565-308-7*); PLB 14.95s.p. (*0-685-55735-9*) Childs World.
—Word Bird's Summer Words. Moncure, Jane B. LC 85-5930. 32p. (gr. k-2). 1985. PLB 21.35 (*0-89565-311-7*); PLB 14.95s.p. (*0-685-55737-5*) Childs World.
Miralles, Jose. Little Sure Shot: The Story of Annie Oakley. Spinner, Stephanie. LC 92-17014. 48p. (Orig.). (gr. 2-3). 1993. PLB 7.99 (*0-679-93432-4*); pap. 3.50 (*0-679-83432-X*) Random Bks Yng Read.
Miranda, Anne. Night Songs. Miranda, Anne. LC 92-251. 32p. (ps-1). 1993. RSBE 13.95 (*0-02-767250-6*, Bradbury Pr) Macmillan Child Grp.
Miret, Gil. The Farmer & the Witch. DaLage, Ida. 48p. (gr. k-4). 1991. Repr. of 1966 ed. PLB 12.95 (*0-7910-1474-6*) Chelsea Hse.
—The Old Witch & the Snores. DeLage, Ida. 48p. (gr. k-4). 1991. Repr. of 1970 ed. lib. bdg. 12.95 (*0-7910-1479-7*) Chelsea Hse.
Mirocha, Kay. My Changing Body. Kino Learning Center Staff, et al. 64p. (gr. 5-9). 1987. pap. 7.95 (*0-86653-420-2*, GA1030) Good Apple.
—My Choices & Decisions. Kino Learning Center Staff & Sanders, Corinne. 64p. (gr. 5-9). 1987. pap. 7.95 (*0-86653-421-0*, GA1031) Good Apple.
—My Journal of Personal Growth. Kino Learning Center Staff, et al. 64p. (gr. 5-9). 1987. pap. 7.95 (*0-86653-418-0*, GA 1028) Good Apple.
—My Relationships with Others. Kino Learning Center Staff, et al. 64p. (gr. 5-9). 1987. pap. 7.95 (*0-86653-419-9*, GA 1029) Good Apple.
—Saints Alive! Bisignano, Judith & Sanders, Corine. LC 86-63988. 64p. (gr. 5-7). 1987. wkbk. 7.95 (*1-55612-038-9*) Sheed & Ward MO.
Mirocha, Paul. Awesome Animal Actions. Compass Productions Staff. 10p. (gr. k-4). 1992. 5.95 (*0-694-00409-X*, Festival) HarpC Child Bks.
—Baffling Bird Behavior. Compass Productions Staff. 10p. (gr. k-4). 1992. 5.95 (*0-694-00410-3*, Festival) HarpC Child Bks.
—Freaky Fish Facts. Compass Productions Staff. 10p. (gr. k-4). 1992. 5.95 (*0-694-00411-1*, Festival) HarpC Child Bks.
—I Am Lavina Cummings. Lowell, Susan. 200p. (gr. 2-6). 1993. 14.95 (*0-915943-39-5*); pap. 6.95 (*0-915943-77-8*) Milkweed Ed.
—Incredible Insect Instincts. Compass Productions Staff. 10p. (gr. k-4). 1992. 5.95 (*0-694-00412-X*, Festival) HarpC Child Bks.

—The Moon of the Wild Pigs. George, Jean C. LC 91-3495. 48p. (gr. 3-7). 1992. 15.00 (*0-06-020263-7*); PLB 14.89 (*0-06-020264-5*) HarpC Child Bks.
—Oil Spill! Berger, Melvin. LC 92-34779. 1994. 14.00 (*0-06-022909-8*); PLB 13.89 (*0-06-022912-8*) HarpC Child Bks.
Misla, Victor M. Little Anabo from Boriken. Misla, Victor M. 28p. (Orig.). (gr. 6-7). 1987. pap. 5.00 (*0-9626870-0-6*) NW Monarch Pr.
—The Treasure of Camuy's Cave. Misla, Victor M. 30p. (Orig.). (gr. 6-7). 1987. pap. 5.00 (*0-9626870-1-4*) NW Monarch Pr.

Miss Lori. Shapeless & the Magic Box, Bk. 1. Miss Lori. White, Lori G., ed. 18p. (Orig.). (ps-1). 1990. pap. 11.99 (*0-9623368-3-1*) Shapeless Enterprises. It is the intention of Shapeless Enterprises to develop, design & produce top quality early childhood literature through various media outlets. Individual stories feature texts, videos, & sound recordings. Each storyline represents an educational concept as well as a valuable moral stepping stone for personal success. We are striving to provide a service to the youth of our communities by nurturing their most positive attributes. By captivating the senses of sight, sound & imagination we facilitate a positive, nonviolent image. SHAPELESS & THE MAGIC BOX, Book 1, ISBN 0-9623368-3-1. This exciting, full color, fictional children's text is rendered in poetic verse. Its educational basis features self-image, shapes & colors. Cassette available. JUVENILE 2-7. SHAPE UP THE EARTH/LOVE IS SHAPELESS, ISBN 0-923368-4-X. What a fun way to remember how important earth conservation is. Our poster is filled with smiles & poetic phrases to soften every global heart. BEE SAFE'S SWAT THE DRUG BUG POSTER, ISBN 0-9623368-1-5. Help your little champions become a success with our newest hero Bee Safe. This attractive full color delight is a must for your little poster bug. Shapless Enterprises, P.O. Box 297, Harbor City, CA 90710. *Publisher Provided Annotation.*

—Shapeless & the Magic Box, Bk. 2. Miss Lori. White, Lori G., ed. 18p. (Orig.). (ps-1). 1991. pap. 11.99 (*0-9623368-8-2*) Shapeless Enterprises.
Mitchell, Anastasia. A Cold Is Nothing to Sneeze At. Perry, Susan. (gr. 1-8). 1992. PLB 14.95 (*0-89565-819-4*); Resale. 21.35 (*0-685-60979-0*) Childs World.
—Moose on the Loose. Ochs, Carol P. 32p. (ps-4). 1991. PLB 18.95 (*0-87614-448-2*) Carolrhoda Bks.
—No Time for Christmas. Delton, Judy. 48p. (gr. k-4). 1988. PLB 14.95 (*0-87614-327-3*) Carolrhoda Bks.
—No Time for Christmas. Delton, Judy. 48p. (gr. k-4). 1989. pap. 5.95 (*0-87614-503-9*, First Ave Edns) Lerner Pubns.
—Professor Solomon Snickerdoodle Looks at Water. Murray, Peter. LC 93-1322. 1993. write for info. (*1-56766-081-9*) Childs World.
Mitchell, Hetty. Helping Skills for Middle School Students. Myrick, Robert D. & Sorenson, Don L. LC 92-70820. 160p. (Orig.). (gr. 6-8). 1992. pap. text ed. 7.95x (*0-932796-40-0*) Ed Media Corp.
—Martin Luther King Day. Lowery, Linda. 56p. (gr. k-4). 1987. lib. bdg. 14.95 (*0-87614-299-4*) Carolrhoda Bks.
—Martin Luther King Day. Lowery, Linda. (gr. 3-5). 1987. incl. cassette 19.95 (*0-87499-071-8*); pap. 12.95 incl. cassette (*0-87499-070-X*); 4 paperbacks, cassette & guide 27.95 (*0-87499-072-6*) Live Oak Media.
—Martin Luther King Day. Lowery, Linda. 56p. (gr. k-4). 1987. pap. 5.95 (*0-87614-468-7*, First Ave Edns) Lerner Pubns.
—Raggin' A Story about Scott Joplin. Mitchell, Barbara. 64p. (gr. 3-6). 1987. PLB 14.95 (*0-87614-310-9*) Carolrhoda Bks.
—Rooftop Astronomer: A Story about Maria Mitchell. McPherson, Stephanie. 32p. (gr. 3-6). 1990. PLB 14.95 (*0-87614-410-5*) Carolrhoda Bks.
—Shoes for Everyone: A Story about Jan Matzeliger. Mitchell, Barbara. 64p. (gr. 3-6). 1986. PLB 14.95 (*0-87614-290-0*) Carolrhoda Bks.

—Shoes for Everyone: A Story about Jan Matzeliger. Mitchell, Barbara. (gr. 3-6). 1987. pap. 5.95 (0-87614-473-3, First Ave Edns) Lerner Pubns.
—The Wizard of Sound: A Story about Thomas Edison. Mitchell, Barbara. 64p. (gr. 3-6). 1991. PLB 14.95 (0-87614-445-8) Carolrhoda Bks.
Mitchell, Joanie. Is a Mountain Just a Rock. Uba, Gregory. LC 83-61882. 260p. (gr. 6-9). 1984. pap. 3.95 (0-942610-03-2) Mina Pr.
Mitchell, Judith. A Dragon in the Family. Koller, Jackie F. LC 93-7028. 1993. 12.95 (0-316-50151-4) Little.
Mitchell, Judy. The City by the Sea. Doyle, Debra & Macdonald, James. LC 89-5213. 144p. (gr. 5-9). 1990. PLB 9.89 (0-8167-1830-X); pap. text ed. 2.95 (0-8167-1831-8) Troll Assocs.
—The Prince's Players. Doyle, Debra & Macdonald, James. LC 89-5244. 144p. (gr. 5-9). 1990. PLB 9.89 (0-8167-1832-6); pap. text ed. 2.95 (0-8167-1833-4) Troll Assocs.
—School of Wizardry. Doyle, Debra & Macdonald, James. LC 89-33882. 144p. (gr. 5-9). 1990. PLB 9.89 (0-8167-1826-1); pap. text ed. 2.95 (0-8167-1827-X) Troll Assocs.
—Tournament & Tower. Doyle, Debra & Macdonald, James. LC 89-33881. 144p. (gr. 5-9). 1990. PLB 9.89 (0-8167-1828-8); pap. text ed. 2.95 (0-8167-1829-6) Troll Assocs.
Mitchell, Kathy. Aladdin & the Magic Lamp. Hautzig, Deborah. LC 92-1608. 48p. (Orig.). (gr. 2-3). 1993. PLB 7.99 (0-679-93241-0); pap. 3.50 (0-679-83241-6) Random Bks Yng Read.
—Jane Eyre. Bronte, Charlotte. (gr. 4 up). 1983. deluxe ed. 15.95 (0-448-06031-0, G&D) Putnam Pub Group.
—The Secret Garden. Burnett, Frances H. 320p. (gr. 4 up). 1987. 13.95 (0-448-06029-9, G&D) Putnam Pub Group.
—Silent Night: A Christmas Book with Lights & Music. Mitchell, Kathy. 12p. (ps-3). 1989. bds. 10.95 (0-689-71330-4, Aladdin) Macmillan Child Grp.
Mitchell, Lyn. Animals. 10p. (ps). 1992. 4.95 (0-448-40304-8, G&D) Putnam Pub Group.
—Clothes. 10p. (ps). 1992. 4.95 (0-448-40307-2, G&D) Putnam Pub Group.
—Doctor. Slater, Helen. 24p. 1992. 2.98 (0-8317-9508-5) Smithmark.
—Eating. 10p. (ps). 1992. 4.95 (0-448-40305-6, G&D) Putnam Pub Group.
—Playing. 10p. (ps). 1992. 4.95 (0-448-40306-4, G&D) Putnam Pub Group.
Mitchell, Mark. Elizabeth Bayley Seton: An American Saint. Stone, Elaine M. LC 92-42020. 96p. 1993. pap. 4.95 (0-8091-6609-7) Paulist Pr.
—First Bible Stories. Waddy, Lawrence, ed. LC 93-34710. 194p. 1994. pap. 4.95 (0-8091-6613-5) Paulist Pr.
—The Mustang Professor: The Story of J. Frank Dobie. Mitchell, Mark. 96p. (gr. 4-7). 1993. 12.95 (0-89015-823-1) Eakin-Sunbelt.
—Nanny's Special Gift. Potaracke, Rochelle. LC 93-26093. 1994. pap. 3.95 (0-8091-6615-1) Paulist Pr.
Mitchell, Vic. Great Miracles of Jesus. Svensson, Borje. 10p. (ps-2). 1985. 9.99 (0-89191-940-6, 59402, Chariot Bks) Cook.
—Great Stories from the Bible. Svensson, Borje. 10p. (ps-2). 1985. 9.99 (0-89191-939-2, 59394, Chariot Bks) Cook.
Mitchell, Victor. Birds. Mitchell, Victor. 16p. (gr. k up). 1988. pap. 1.99 (0-7459-1467-5) Lion USA.
—Fish. Mitchell, Victor. 16p. (gr. k up). 1988. pap. 1.99 (0-7459-1468-3) Lion USA.
—Flowers. Mitchell, Victor. 16p. (gr. k up). 1988. pap. 1.99 (0-7459-1470-5) Lion USA.
—Jungles. Mitchell, Victor. 16p. (gr. k up). 1988. pap. 1.99 (0-7459-1473-X) Lion USA.
—Pets. Mitchell, Victor. 16p. (gr. k up). 1988. pap. 1.99 (0-7459-1469-1) Lion USA.
—Seashore. Mitchell, Victor. 16p. (gr. k up). 1988. pap. 1.99 (0-7459-1471-3) Lion USA.
—Woodlands. Mitchell, Victor. 16p. (gr. k up). 1988. pap. 1.99 (0-7459-1472-1) Lion USA.
Mitchinson, Shelia. A Thanksgiving Story in Vermont - 1852. Barth, Jeff. 60p. (Orig.). (gr. 3-8). 1989. pap. write for info. (0-9624067-0-8) Parable Pub.
Mitchroney, Ken, et al. The Collected Teenage Mutant Ninja Turtles Adventures, Vol. 2. Brown, Ryan & Clarrian, Dean. 88p. 1991. pap. 5.95 (1-879450-04-6) Tundra MA.
—The Collected Teenage Mutant Ninja Turtles Adventures, Vol. 4. Clarrain, Dean & Brown, Ryan. 88p. 1991. pap. 5.95 (1-879450-06-2) Tundra MA.
Mitgutsch, Ali. From Blossom to Honey. Mitgutsch, Ali. 24p. (ps-3). 1981. PLB 10.95 (0-87614-146-7) Carolrhoda Bks.
—From Cacao Bean to Chocolate: Translation of Vom Kakao Zur Schokolade. Mitgutsch, Ali. LC 80-29588. 24p. (ps-3). 1981. PLB 10.95 (0-87614-147-5) Carolrhoda Bks.
—From Cement to Bridge. Mitgutsch, Ali. LC 81-334. 24p. (ps-3). 1981. PLB 10.95 (0-87614-148-3) Carolrhoda Bks.
—From Clay to Bricks. Mitgutsch, Ali. LC 80-29567. 24p. (ps-3). 1981. PLB 10.95 (0-87614-149-1) Carolrhoda Bks.
—From Cotton to Pants. Mitgutsch, Ali. LC 80-29552. 24p. (ps-3). 1981. PLB 10.95 (0-87614-150-5) Carolrhoda Bks.
—From Fruit to Jam. Mitgutsch, Ali. LC 81-58. 24p. (ps-3). 1981. PLB 10.95 (0-87614-154-8) Carolrhoda Bks.

—From Gold to Money. Mitgutsch, Ali. LC 84-17488. 24p. (ps-3). 1985. PLB 10.95 (0-87614-230-7) Carolrhoda Bks.
—From Grain to Bread. Mitgutsch, Ali. LC 80-28592. 24p. (ps-3). 1981. PLB 10.95 (0-87614-155-6) Carolrhoda Bks.
—From Graphite to Pencil. Mitgutsch, Ali. LC 84-17469. 24p. (ps-3). 1985. PLB 10.95 (0-87614-231-5) Carolrhoda Bks.
—From Grass to Butter. Mitgutsch, Ali. LC 80-28588. 24p. (ps-3). 1981. PLB 10.95 (0-87614-156-4) Carolrhoda Bks.
—From Milk to Ice Cream. Mitgutsch, Ali. LC 81-81. 24p. (ps-3). 1981. PLB 10.95 (0-87614-158-0) Carolrhoda Bks.
—From Oil to Gasoline. Mitgutsch, Ali. LC 80-29562. 24p. (ps-3). 1981. PLB 10.95 (0-87614-160-2) Carolrhoda Bks.
—From Ore to Spoon. Mitgutsch, Ali. LC 80-28862. 24p. (ps-3). 1981. PLB 10.95 (0-87614-161-0) Carolrhoda Bks.
—From Rubber Tree to Tire. Mitgutsch, Ali. Lerner, Mark, tr. from GER. 24p. (ps-3). 1986. lib. bdg. 10.95 (0-87614-297-8) Carolrhoda Bks.
—From Sand to Glass. Mitgutsch, Ali. LC 80-29572. 24p. (ps-3). 1981. PLB 10.95 (0-87614-162-9) Carolrhoda Bks.
—From Sea to Salt. Mitgutsch, Ali. LC 84-17466. 24p. (ps-3). 1985. PLB 10.95 (0-87614-232-3) Carolrhoda Bks.
—From Seed to Pear. Mitgutsch, Ali. LC 81-83. 24p. (ps-3). 1981. PLB 10.95 (0-87614-163-7) Carolrhoda Bks.
—From Sheep to Scarf. Mitgutsch, Ali. LC 80-29557. 24p. (ps-3). 1981. PLB 10.95 (0-87614-164-5) Carolrhoda Bks.
—From Swamp to Coal. Mitgutsch, Ali. LC 84-17465. 24p. (ps-3). 1985. PLB 10.95 (0-87614-233-1) Carolrhoda Bks.
—From Tree to Table. Mitgutsch, Ali. LC 81-672. 24p. (ps-3). 1981. PLB 10.95 (0-87614-165-3) Carolrhoda Bks.
—From Wood to Paper. Mitgutsch, Ali. Lerner, Mark, tr. from GER. 24p. (ps-3). 1986. lib. bdg. 10.95 (0-87614-296-X) Carolrhoda Bks.
—A Knight's Book. Mitgutsch, Ali. Crawford, Elizabeth D., tr. 40p. (gr. 2-5). 1991. 16.45 (0-395-58103-6, Clarion Bks) HM.
Mitra, Annie. Penguin Moon. Mitra, Annie. LC 88-32797. 32p. (ps-1). 1989. reinforced bdg. 13.95 (0-8234-0749-7) Holiday.
—Tusk! Tusk! Mitra, Annie. LC 89-77508. 32p. (ps-2). 1990. reinforced 13.95 (0-8234-0819-1) Holiday.
Mitsui, Eiichi. Joji & the Dragon. Lifton, Betty J. LC 88-8434. 64p. (gr. 1-3). 1989. Repr. of 1957 ed. lib. bdg. 16.00 (0-208-02245-7, Pub. by Linnet) Shoe String.
Mitsumasa Anno. The Animals: Selected Poems. Mado, Michio. HRM the Empress of Japan, tr. LC 92-10356. (ENG & JPN). 48p. (ps up). 1992. SBE 16.95 (0-689-50574-4, M K McElderry) Macmillan Child Grp.
Mitter, Kathryn. Jesus Calms the Storm: Matthew 8, 23-27 & Mark 4, 35-41 for the Beginning Reader. Gangwer, Rosalie M. LC 93-17472. 32p. (ps-3). 1993. 6.50 (0-8198-3955-8) St Paul Bks.
Mitter, Kathy. The Big Secret: The Good News Kids Learn about Gentleness. Mock, Dorothy K. LC 93-6865. 32p. (Orig.). (ps-2). 1993. pap. 5.99 (0-570-04744-7) Concordia.
—God Is Everywhere: The Good News Kids Learn about Self-Control. Mock, Dorothy K. LC 93-22311. 32p. (Orig.). (ps-2). 1993. pap. 5.99 (0-570-04745-5) Concordia.
—Holiday Plays. Kaplan, Carol B. 37p. (ps). 1989. tchr's. ed. 16.95 (0-88734-410-0) Players Pr.
—One Big Family: The Good News Kids Learn about Kindness. Mock, Dorothy. LC 92-27012. 32p. (Orig.). (ps-2). 1993. pap. 5.99 (0-570-04737-4) Concordia.
—Springtime Special: The Good News Kids Learn about Patience. Mock, Dorothy. LC 92-27010. 32p. (Orig.). (ps-2). 1993. pap. 5.99 (0-570-04736-6) Concordia.
—Tall Phil & Small Bill. McKissack, Patricia & McKissack, Fredrick. LC 87-61644. 32p. (Orig.). (gr. 1-3). 1987. text ed. 8.95 (0-88335-727-5); pap. text ed. 4.95 (0-88335-747-X) Milliken Pub Co.
—The Thanksgiving Parade: The Good News Kids Learn about Faithfulness. Mock, Dorothy K. LC 93-2988. 32p. (Orig.). (ps-2). 1993. pap. 5.99 (0-570-04743-9) Concordia.
—Three Nanny Goats Gruff. Kaplan, Carol & Becker, Sandi. 33p. (ps). 1989. tchr's. ed. 16.95 (0-88734-409-7) Players Pr.
—Tikki Tikki Tembo. Kaplan, Carol B. 32p. (ps). 1989. 16.95 (0-88734-406-2) Players Pr.
—The Trouble with Trevor: The Good News Kids Learn about Goodness. Mock, Dorothy. LC 92-27013. 32p. (Orig.). (ps-2). 1993. pap. 5.99 (0-570-04738-2) Concordia.
—What's the Matter with Miss Taylor. Witter, Evelyn. McKissack, Patricia & McKissack, Fredrick, eds. LC 87-61643. 32p. (Orig.). (gr. 1-3). 1987. text ed. 8.95 (0-88335-728-3); pap. text ed. 4.95 (0-88335-748-8) Milliken Pub Co.
Mitton, David & Permane, Terry. Thomas, Percy, & the Post Train. Awdry, W. 1994. write for info. (0-679-86046-0) Random Bks Yng Read.

Mitton, David & Permane, Terry, photos by. A Cow on the Line & Other Thomas the Tank Engine Stories. Awdry, W. LC 91-21706. 32p. (Orig.). (ps-3). 1992. PLB 5.99 (0-679-91977-5); pap. 2.25 (0-679-81977-0) Random Bks Yng Read.
—A Cow on the Line & Other Thomas the Tank Engine Stories. reissue ed. Awdry, W. Starr, Ringo, narrated by. 32p. (ps-3). 1992. pap. 5.95 incl. cass. (0-679-83476-1) Random Bks Yng Read.
—Diesel's Devious Deed & Other Thomas the Tank Engine Stories. Awdry, W. LC 91-21133. 32p. (Orig.). (ps-3). 1992. PLB 5.99 (0-679-91976-7); pap. 2.25 (0-679-81976-2) Random Bks Yng Read.
—Diesel's Devious Deed & Other Thomas the Tank Engine Stories. reissue ed. Awdry, W. Starr, Ringo, narrated by. 32p. (ps-3). 1992. pap. 5.95 incl. cass. (0-679-83474-5) Random Bks Yng Read.
—Duck Takes Charge. Awdry, W. LC 92-45564. 32p. (ps-2). 1993. 3.50 (0-679-84763-4) Random Bks Yng Read.
—Edward's Exploit. LC 92-23189. 32p. (ps-3). 1993. pap. 2.25 (0-679-83896-1) Random Bks Yng Read.
—Gordon and the Famous Visitor. Awdry, W. LC 92-45569. 32p. (ps-3). 1993. 3.50 (0-679-84764-2) Random Bks Yng Read.
—Percy's Promise. Awdry, W. LC 92-43773. 32p. (ps-2). 1993. 3.50 (0-679-84765-0) Random Bks Yng Read.
—Thomas & Trevor. Awdry, W. LC 92-43774. 32p. (ps-2). 1993. 3.50 (0-679-84766-9) Random Bks Yng Read.
—Thomas the Tank Engine Storybook. Awdry, W., created by. LC 92-35915. 1993. 8.00 (0-679-84465-1) Random Bks Yng Read.
Mitton, David, et al, photos by. James in a Mess & Other Thomas the Tank Engine Stories. LC 92-25654. 32p. (ps-3). 1993. pap. 2.25 (0-679-83895-3) Random Bks Yng Read.
Miyajina, Yasuhiko, photos by. U. S. R. R. Taylor-Boyd, Susan & Brown, Julie, eds. LC 88-42891. 64p. (gr. 5-6). 1989. PLB 19.93 (1-55532-215-8) Gareth Stevens Inc.
Miyake, Yoshi. Ahyoka & the Talking Leaves. Roop, Peter & Roop, Connie. LC 91-3036. (gr. 1 up). 1992. text ed. 12.00 (0-688-10697-8) Lothrop.
—Annie Oakley. Gleiter, Jan & Thompson, Kathleen. 32p. (gr. 2-5). 1986. PLB 17.96 (0-8172-2641-9) Raintree Steck-V.
—The Beaver. Hogan, Paula Z. LC 79-13305. 32p. (gr. 1-4). 1979. PLB 17.96 (0-8172-1502-6) Raintree Steck-V.
—Caves. Greenberg, Judith E. & Carey, Helen H. 32p. (gr. 2-4). 1990. PLB 17.96 (0-8172-3750-X) Raintree Steck-V.
—Mozart, Young Music Genius. Sabin, Francene. LC 89-33980. 48p. (gr. 4-6). 1990. lib. bdg. 10.79 (0-8167-1773-7); pap. text ed. 3.50 (0-8167-1774-5) Troll Assocs.
—Osceola. Viola, Herman J. LC 92-5683. 32p. (gr. 4-5). 1992. PLB 17.96 (0-8114-6575-6); pap. 4.95 (0-8114-4098-2) Raintree Steck-V.
—Plenty Coups. Doss, Michael P. Viola, Herman, intro. by. 32p. (gr. 3-6). 1990. PLB 17.96 (0-8172-3409-8); pap. 4.95 (0-8114-4089-3) Raintree Steck-V.
—Rachel Carson: Friend of the Earth. Sabin, Francene. LC 92-5825. 48p. (gr. 4-6). 1992. PLB 10.79 (0-8167-2821-6); pap. text ed. 3.50 (0-8167-2822-4) Troll Assocs.
—Sacagawea. Gleiter, Jan & Thompson, Kathleen. 32p. (gr. 2-5). 1987. PLB 17.96 (0-8172-2651-6) Raintree Steck-V.
—What Makes It Rain? Brandt, Keith. LC 81-7495. 32p. (gr. 2-4). 1982. PLB 11.59 (0-89375-582-6); pap. text ed. 2.95 (0-89375-583-4) Troll Assocs.
—Wonders of Rivers. Bains, Rae. LC 81-7423. 32p. (gr. 2-4). 1982. PLB 11.59 (0-89375-570-2); pap. text ed. 2.95 (0-89375-571-0) Troll Assocs.
—Young Abigail Adams. Sabin, Francene. LC 91-17112. 48p. (gr. 4-6). 1992. PLB 10.79 (0-8167-2503-9); pap. text ed. 3.50 (0-8167-2504-7) Troll Assocs.
Miyaki, Yoshi. Wonders of Plants & Flowers. Damon, Laura. LC 89-5003. 32p. (gr. 2-4). 1990. PLB 11.59 (0-8167-1761-3); pap. text ed. 2.95 (0-8167-1762-1) Troll Assocs.
Miyazaki, Hayao. Tokuma's Magical Adventure Series. Miyazaki, Hayao. Zimmerman, Maureen, ed. Saburi, Eugene, tr. from JPN. 132p. (gr. 3-6). 1992. PLB 44.85 (4-19-086974-0) Tokuma Pub.
Mizobuti, Masaru. Picture Purrfect Kitten. Tatihara, Erika. 32p. (ps-2). 1993. 12.95 (0-8120-6359-7); pap. 5.95 (0-8120-1712-9) Barron.
Mock, Paul D. Red-Hot Hightops. Christopher, Matt. 128p. (gr. 4-6). 1987. 14.95 (0-316-14056-2) Little.
Modarressi, Mitra. Tumble Tower. Tyler, Anne. LC 92-44524. 32p. (ps-2). 1993. 14.95 (0-531-05497-7); PLB 14.99 (0-531-08647-X) Orchard Bks Watts.
Modell, Frank. Look Out, It's April Fools' Day. Modell, Frank. LC 84-4138. 24p. (ps up). 1985. 13.00 (0-688-04016-0); PLB 12.88 (0-688-04017-9) Greenwillow.
—Mr. Hacker. Stevenson, James. LC 89-30479. 32p. (gr. k up). 1990. 12.95 (0-688-09216-0); PLB 12.88 (0-688-09217-9) Greenwillow.
Moehlman, Patricia D., photos by. Jackal Woman: Exploring the World of Jackals. Pringle, Laurence. LC 92-28207. 48p. (gr. 4-6). 1993. SBE 14.95 (0-684-19435-X, Scribners Young Read) Macmillan Child Grp.

Moerbeek, Kees. Hi Mom, I'm Home. Moerbeek, Kees. 20p. 1992. 9.95 (*0-8431-3393-7*) Price Stern.
—New at the Zoo: A Mix-&-Match Pop-up Book. Moerbeek, Kees. LC 89-60077. 10p. (ps-1). 1989. bds. 8.99 (*0-679-80076-X*) Random Bks Yng Read.
—New at the Zoo Two: A Mix-&-Match Pop-up Book. Moerbeek, Kees. LC 92-60763. 10p. (ps-1). 1993. 8.99 (*0-679-83711-6*) Random Bks Yng Read.
Moffatt, Judith. Bats! Creatures of the Night. Milton, Joyce. LC 92-43198. 48p. (ps-1). 1993. 7.99g (*0-448-40194-0*, G&D); pap. 3.50 (*0-448-40193-2*, G&D) Putnam Pub Group.
—Crocodile! Crocodile! And Other Folktales. Baumgartner, Barbara, retold by. LC 93-28027. 1994. write for info. (*1-56458-463-1*) Dorling Kindersley.
—Snakes! Smith, Patricia. LC 92-24466. 48p. (gr. 1-3). 1993. lib. bdg. 7.99 (*0-448-40514-8*, G&D); pap. 3.50 (*0-448-40513-X*, G&D) Putnam Pub Group.
Moffatt, Judy. KidDoodles, Bk. 2. Wise, Beth A. 64p. (Orig.). 1991. pap. 0.99 activity pad (*1-878624-51-2*) McClanahan Bk.
Moffett, Eileen. Korean Ways. Moffett, Eileen. 55p. (gr. k up). 1986. 10.95 (*0-8048-7013-6*, Pub. by Seoul Intl Tourist SK) C E Tuttle.
Mogensen, Jan. The Elephant's Child. Kipling, Rudyard. LC 89-7787. 48p. 1989. 13.95 (*0-940793-41-5*, Pub. by Crocodile Bks) Interlink Pub.
—The Elephant's Child. Kipling, Rudyard. LC 89-7787. 48p. 1991. pap. 6.95 (*0-940793-77-6*, Crocodile Bks) Interlink Pub.
—El Hijo del Elefante: The Elephant's Child. Kipling, Rudyard. Martinez, Lourdes, tr. from GER. (SPA.). 42p. (gr. k-4). 1990. 13.95 (*87-14-18825-2*) Hispanic Bk Dist.
—The Land of the Big. Mogensen, Jan. LC 92-18302. 32p. (gr-5). 1993. 14.95 (*1-56656-111-6*, Crocodile Bks) Interlink Pub.
—Teddy Runs Away. Mogensen, Jan. LC 90-36069. 32p. (gr. 3-4). 1990. PLB 18.60 (*0-8368-0371-X*) Gareth Stevens Inc.
—Teddy's Birthday Bugle. Mogensen, Jan. LC 90-10071. 32p. (gr. 3-4). 1990. PLB 18.60 (*0-8368-0372-8*) Gareth Stevens Inc.
Mohle, Flay, jt. illus. see Fuchs, Diane.
Mohler, Sarah. Celebrate the Christian Family. Javernick, Ellen. 144p. (gr. k-6). 1987. pap. 11.95 (*0-86653-391-5*, SS 844, Shining Star Pubns) Good Apple.
Mohrann, Gary. Exploring Sand & the Desert: And the Desert. Bittinger, Gayle. Harrison, Brenda M., ed. LC 92-62463. 96p. (Orig.). (ps-1). 1993. pap. 8.95 (*0-911019-58-8*) Warren Pub Hse.
—Exploring Water & the Ocean: And the Ocean. Bittinger, Gayle. Harrison, Brenda M., ed. LC 92-62462. 96p. (Orig.). (ps-1). 1993. pap. 8.95 (*0-911019-59-6*) Warren Pub Hse.
—Exploring Wood & the Forest: And the Forest. Bittinger, Gayle. Harrison, Brenda M., ed. LC 92-62464. 96p. (Orig.). (ps-1). 1993. pap. 8.95 (*0-911019-60-X*) Warren Pub Hse.
Mohrman, Janet S. Pa Pong: A Siamese Kitty. Snyder, Phillip C. 28p. (ps-1). 1981. pap. text ed. 3.95 (*0-940560-03-8*) Custom Hse.
—Poochie. Snyder, Phillip C. 28p. (Orig.). (ps). 1982. pap. 3.95 (*0-940560-04-6*) Custom Hse.
Mohrmann, Gary. Alphabet Theme-a-Saurus: The Great Big Book of Letter Recognition. Warren, Jean, et al, eds. LC 90-71272. 280p. (ps-1). 1991. pap. text ed. 19.95 (*0-911019-38-3*) Warren Pub Hse.
—Animal Patterns. Warren, Jean. Bittinger, Gayle, ed. 240p. (Orig.). (ps-1). 1990. pap. text ed. 16.95 (*0-911019-31-6*) Warren Pub Hse.
—Chemistry Magic. Palder, Edward. 153p. (gr. 5 up). 1987. pap. 12.95 (*0-933149-25-5*) Woodbine House.
—Easy-to-Make Puppets: Step-by-Step Instructions. Duch, Mabel. LC 93-15320. 64p. (gr. 3-8). 1993. pap. 8.95 (*0-8238-0300-7*) Plays.
—Everyday Patterns: Multi-Sized Patterns for Making Cut-Outs, Puppets & Learning Games. Warren, Jean. Bittinger, Gayle, ed. 240p. (Orig.). (ps-1). 1990. pap. text ed. 16.95 (*0-911019-35-9*) Warren Pub Hse.
—Holiday Patterns: Multi-Sized Patterns for Making Cut-Outs, Puppets & Learning Games. Warren, Jean & Bittinger, Gayle, eds. 240p. (Orig.). (ps-1). 1991. pap. text ed. 16.95 (*0-911019-45-6*) Warren Pub Hse.
—Nature Patterns: Multi-Sized Patterns for Making Cut-Outs, Puppets & Learning Games. Warren, Jean. Bittinger, Gayle, ed. 240p. (Orig.). (ps-1). 1990. pap. text ed. 16.95 (*0-911019-36-7*) Warren Pub Hse.
—Play & Learn with Magnets. Bittinger, Gayle. Warren, Jean, ed. LC 93-61084. 64p. (Orig.). 1994. pap. text ed. 7.95 (*0-911019-92-8*) Warren Pub Hse.
—Play & Learn with Rubber Stamps. McKinnon, Elizabeth. Warren, Jean, ed. LC 93-61083. 64p. (Orig.). 1994. pap. text ed. 7.95 (*0-911019-93-6*) Warren Pub Hse.
Moiles, Holly B. The Golden Flower: A Taino Myth from Puerto Rico. Jaffe, Nina, adapted by. & tr. LC 92-42364. 32p. (ps-3). 1994. RSBE 15.95 (*0-02-747585-9*, Macmillan Child Bk) Macmillan Child Grp.
Molan, Chris. Explorers & Mapmakers. Ryan, Peter. LC 89-31824. 48p. (gr. 4-7). 1990. 14.95 (*0-525-67285-0*, Lodestar Bks) Dutton Child Bks.
—The First Easter: Retold by Catherine Storr. 32p. (gr. k-4). 1984. 14.65 (*0-8172-1987-0*, Raintree Childrens Books Belitha Press Ltd. - London) Raintree Steck-V.
—Growing up in Ancient Greece. Chelepi, Chris. LC 91-14852. 32p. (gr. 3-5). 1993. PLB 11.89 (*0-8167-2719-8*); pap. text ed. 3.95 (*0-8167-2720-1*) Troll Assocs. Postponed.
—Growing up in Ancient Rome. Corbishley, Mike. LC 91-14851. 32p. (gr. 3-5). 1993. PLB 11.89 (*0-8167-2721-X*); pap. text ed. 3.95 (*0-8167-2722-8*) Troll Assocs. Postponed.
—Heidi. rev. & abr. ed. Spyri, Johanna. De Graaf, Anne, ed. 96p. (gr. 1-5). 1991. 8.95 (*0-89107-600-X*) Good News.
—Joseph the Dream Teller: Retold by Catererine Storr. 32p. (gr. k-4). 1984. 14.65 (*0-8172-1989-7*, Raintree Children's Books Belitha Press Ltd. - London) Raintree Steck-V.
—Mummies, Masks, & Mourners. Berrill, Margaret. LC 89-31822. 48p. (gr. 4-7). 1990. 14.95 (*0-525-67282-6*, Lodestar Bks) Dutton Child Bks.
Molan, Christine. Augustus & the Ancient Romans. Poulton, Michael. LC 92-5824. 63p. (gr. 6-7). 1992. PLB 24.26 (*0-8114-3350-1*) Raintree Steck-V.
—Miracles by the Sea. Storr, Catherine, retold by. LC 82-23022. 32p. (gr. k-4). 1983. PLB 14.65 (*0-8172-1983-8*) Raintree Steck-V.
Moldoff, Kirk. The Macmillan Book of the Human Body. Elting, Mary. LC 85-24204. 80p. (gr. 3-7). 1986. pap. 8.95 (*0-02-043080-9*, Aladdin) Macmillan Child Grp.
Moler, Kathy. Olive, Char, Lizzie & Izzie: A Sea Otter Story. Van Gorden, Charles L. 24p. (Orig.). (gr. 1-4). 1991. pap. 4.95 saddle-stitched (*1-56167-050-2*) Am Literary Pr.
Moles, Danna. Marijuana: A Dangerous "High" Way. rev. ed. Leahy, Barbara H. Farrell, Lee & Jensen, Rosemary D., eds. LC 82-62440. 173p. (Orig.). (gr. 4-9). 1983. pap. 6.95 (*0-9610312-1-2*) B Leahy.
Molk, Laurel. Grandpappy. Carlstrom, Nancy W. (ps-3). 1990. 14.95 (*0-316-12855-4*) Little.
—On the Farm: Poems. Hopkins, Lee B. (ps-3). 1991. 14.95 (*0-316-37274-9*) Little.
Moller, Johanna. Fit for Pigs. Hammar, Asa. 40p. (gr. k-3). 1992. 9.95 (*1-56288-265-1*) Checkerboard.
Moller, Ray, jt. photog. see Dunning, Mike.
Molloy, Eideen. Kara: The Lonely Falcon. Girzone, Joseph F. LC 78-63393. 52p. (gr. 2 up). 1985. Repr. of 1979 ed. 8.95 (*0-911519-05-X*) Richelieu Court.
Molyneux, Lisa. Shakespeare for Children: The Story of Romeo & Juliet. Foster, Cass. LC 89-80371. 105p. (gr. 2 up). 1989. pap. 9.95 (*0-9619853-3-X*) Five Star AZ.
Monceaux, Morgan. Jazz. Monceaux, Morgan. LC 93-38177. 1994. write for info. (*0-679-86518-7*); PLB write for info. (*0-679-96518-1*) Knopf Bks Yng Read.
Moncus, Stephen. Oyen Ninos, Listen Children. Hofer, Grace & Day, Rachel. Day, Rachel, tr. 96p. (gr. 4-7). 1993. 12.95 (*0-89015-865-7*) Eakin-Sunbelt.
Moneli, jt. illus. see Biene, Susanna.
Mones. The Big Book of Real Fire Trucks. Slater, Teddy. 48p. (gr. 1-4). 1987. 7.95 (*0-448-19176-8*, G&D) Putnam Pub Group.
—Walt Disney's Bambi. Patrick, Denise L., adapted by. 28p. (ps). 1992. bds. write for info. (*0-307-12535-1*, 12535, Golden Pr) Western Pub.
—Walt Disney's Cinderella. Balducci, Rita, adapted by. 28p. (ps). 1992. bds. write for info. (*0-307-12530-0*, 12530, Golden Pr) Western Pub.
—Walt Disney's Snow White & the Seven Dwarfs. Patrick, Denise L., adapted by. 28p. (ps). 1992. bds. write for info. (*0-307-12531-9*, 12531, Golden Pr) Western Pub.
—The Young Indiana Jones Chronicles: The Mummy's Curse. Smith, Parker. 24p. (ps-3). 1992. pap. write for info. (*0-307-12689-7*, 12689, Golden Pr) Western Pub.
Mones, Isidre. A Big Day for Brum. Hickle, Victoria. LC 92-45105. 32p. (ps-1). 1993. pap. 2.25 (*0-679-84494-5*) Random Bks Yng Read.
—Brum. Holm, Astrid. LC 92-61952. 22p. (ps). 1993. 3.25 (*0-679-84493-7*) Random Bks Yng Read.
—Out & about with Brum. Hickle, Victoria. 14p. (ps-k). 1993. 4.99 (*0-679-84470-8*) Random Bks Yng Read.
—Teenage Mutant Ninja Turtles Don't Do Drugs! A Rap Song. Katz, Bobbi. LC 90-53244. 32p. (Orig.). (ps-3). 1991. PLB 5.99 (*0-679-91485-4*); pap. 2.25 (*0-679-81485-X*) Random Bks Yng Read.
—Tire Trouble for Brum. Hickle, Victoria. 24p. (Orig.). (ps-k). 1993. pap. 1.50 (*0-679-84495-3*) Random Bks Yng Read.
Monesson, Harry S. The World's Biggest Tummy. Monesson, Harry S. LC 92-96830. 40p. (Orig.). (gr. k-3). 1992. pap. 6.95 (*0-9633735-0-1*) H S Monesson.
Monroe, Betsy. My Visit to My Doctor: A Coloring Book for Kids. Monroe, Betsy. 24p. (Orig.). (gr. k-4). 1989. pap. write for info. (*1-878083-01-5*) Color Me Well.
—My Visit to the Emergency Room: A Coloring Book for Kids. Monroe, Betsy. (SPA.). 32p. (gr. k-4). 1990. pap. write for info. (*1-878083-03-1*) Color Me Well.
—My Visit to the Hospital: A Coloring Book for Kids. Monroe, Betsy. 32p. (Orig.). (gr. k-4). 1986. pap. write for info. (*1-878083-02-3*) Color Me Well.
—My Visit to the Outpatient Department: A Coloring Book for Kids. Monroe, Betsy. 24p. (gr. k-4). 1986. pap. write for info. (*1-878083-04-X*) Color Me Well.
—Sibling Scrapbook: An Activity Book for the New Big Brother & Big Sister. Monroe, Betsy. 24p. (Orig.). (gr. k-4). 1989. pap. write for info. (*1-878083-00-7*) Color Me Well.
Monroe, John. What Happened to Milly? Faber, Roger A. (gr. 3 up). Date not set. pap. write for info. (*1-880122-07-3*) White Stone.
Monse, Keith. Power Words SAT Cartoon Flashcards. Sennet, Carole L. & Sennet, Edith. (gr. 7 up). 1991. 301 2-sided cards plus thesaurus 21.95 (*1-879871-01-5*) Sennet & Sarnoff.
Montague, William A., jt. illus. see Payne, Maxine.
Montanari, Donata. Look Around the City. Malfatti, Patrizia, tr. 16p. (ps-3). 1993. bds. 11.95 (*0-448-40187-8*, G&D) Putnam Pub Group.
Monteith, Jay. ABC's African Art Coloring Book. Monteith, Jay. 32p. (ps-3). 1992. pap. text ed. 6.95 (*0-9627366-3-5*) Arts & Comns NY.
Montenegro, Laura N. One Stuck Drawer. Montenegro, Laura N. LC 90-46139. 32p. (gr. k-3). 1991. 14.45 (*0-395-57319-X*) HM.
Montero, Miguel. Aprende a Leer a Traves de Musica, Juegos y Ritmos. Ronnholm, Ursala O. Deliz, Osdila O., ed. (SPA.). 42p. (gr. k up). 1986. text ed. 20.00 incl. cassette (*0-941911-01-2*) Two Way Bilingual.
—Aprende a Leer a Trave's de Musica, Juegos y Ritmos. rev. ed. Ronnholm, Ursula O. Rabell, Edda, ed. & tr. (SPA.). 42p. (gr. k-2). 1989. pap. text ed. 20.00 incl. cass. (*0-941911-07-1*) Two Way Bilingual.
—Mi Libro de Escritura. Ronnholm, Ursula O. (SPA.). 74p. (gr. k-3). 1986. 4.00 (*0-941911-05-5*) Two Way Bilingual.
—Mi Libro de Palabras, Oraciones y Cuentos. Ronnholm, Ursula O. Deliz, Osdila O., ed. 100p. (gr. k-6). pap. text ed. 7.00 (*0-941911-02-0*) Two Way Bilingual.
—Mi Libro de Palabras: Oraciones y Cuentos. rev. ed. Ronnholm, Ursula O. Rabell, Edda, ed. & tr. (SPA.). 100p. (gr. k-6). 1989. pap. 7.00 (*0-941911-08-X*) Two Way Bilingual.
Montes, Jesus. Raices y Alas (Poesias Para Ninos y Jovenes) Del Rosario Marquez, Nieves. LC 81-65415. (Orig.). (gr. 6). 1981. pap. 5.00 (*0-89729-289-8*) Ediciones.
Montezinos, Nina. Joe Joe. Serfozo, Mary. LC 92-30133. 32p. (ps-k). 1993. SBE 15.95 (*0-689-50578-7*, M K McElderry) Macmillan Child Grp.
—Look! Snow! Galbraith, Kathryn O. LC 91-28250. 32p. (gr. k-3). 1992. SBE 13.95 (*0-689-50551-5*, M K McElderry) Macmillan Child Grp.
Montgomery, Charlotte B. The Reindeer's Shoe & Other Stories. Wilson, Karle B. Montgomery, Charlotte B., intro. by. LC 88-2292. 112p. (ps-12). 1988. casebound 17.95 (*0-936650-07-9*) E C Temple.
Montgomery, Lucy. The Great Egg Bust. Harrell, Janice. Ashby, Ruth, ed. 112p. (Orig.). 1993. pap. 2.99 (*0-671-72861-X*, Minstrel Bks) PB.
—Onion Tears. Kidd, Diana. LC 90-43011. 72p. (gr. 2-5). 1991. 12.95 (*0-531-05870-0*); PLB 12.99 (*0-531-08470-1*) Orchard Bks Watts.
—Onion Tears. Kidd, Diana. LC 92-46601. 80p. (gr. 5 up). 1993. pap. 3.95 (*0-688-11862-3*, Pub. by Beech Tree Bks) Morrow.
Montgomery, Michael. The Steadfast Tin Soldier. Andersen, Hans Christian. Easton, Samantha, retold by. 1991. 6.95 (*0-8362-4929-1*) Andrews & McMeel.
Montrell, Dan. B. G., Vol. 1: The Little Drummer Girl Who Drums for the Sun. Lowe, George L. 21p. (Orig.). (ps). 1988. PLB 5.00x (*0-685-22681-6*) G L Lowe.
Montresor, Beni. Belling the Tiger. Stolz, Mary. LC 61-5776. 64p. (gr. 2-5). 1990. PLB 12.89 (*0-06-025863-2*) HarpC Child Bks.
—May I Bring a Friend? De Regniers, Beatrice S. LC 64-19562. 48p. (ps-2). 1971. RSBE 14.95 (*0-689-20615-1*, Atheneum Child Bk) Macmillan Child Grp.
—May I Bring a Friend? De Regniers, Beatrice S. LC 89-15087. 48p. (gr. k-3). 1989. pap. 4.95 (*0-689-71353-3*, Aladdin) Macmillan Child Grp.
Montroll, John. African Animals in Origami. Montroll, John. LC 91-76400. 160p. (Orig.). 1993. pap. 9.95 (*1-877656-09-7*) Antroll Pub.
—Origami Inside-Out. Montroll, John. LC 95-90214. 120p. (Orig.). 1993. pap. 9.95 (*1-877656-08-9*) Antroll Pub.
—Origami Sculptures. 2nd ed. Montroll, John. Montroll, Andrew, ed. 144p. 1990. pap. text ed. 9.95 (*1-877656-02-X*) Antroll Pub.
Moon, Ivan. And I'm Stuck with Joseph. Sommer, Susan. LC 84-611. 120p. (gr. 7-9). 1984. pap. 3.95 (*0-8361-3356-0*) Herald Pr.
—Anita's Choice. Hamilton, Dorothy. LC 70-131535. 96p. (gr. 4-9). 1971. pap. 3.95 (*0-8361-1741-7*) Herald Pr.
Moon, Sarah, photos by. Little Red Riding Hood. Perrault, Charles. 32p. (gr. 9 up). 1983. PLB 13.95s.p. (*0-87191-943-5*) Creative Ed.
Mooney, Ann J., photos by. The Sock Animals: Tiger's New Friends. Mooney, Ann J. LC 91-76359. 32p. (Orig.). (ps-2). 1992. pap. 7.95 (*0-9631035-0-4*) Jamondas Pr.
Mooney, David. Where Dinosaurs Still Rule: A Guide to Dinosaur Areas of the West. Tewell, Debbie & Shirley, Gayle C. 48p. (Orig.). 1993. pap. 6.95 (*1-56044-177-1*) Falcon Pr MT.
Moorbeek, Kees. Boo Whoo: Pop-up Book. Moorbeek, Kees. 10p. 1993. 9.99 (*0-8431-3623-5*) Price Stern.
—Museum of Unnatural History. Moorbeek, Kees. 6p. (gr-4). 1993. 14.99 (*0-8431-3541-7*) Price Stern.
Moore, Abd A. The Car Theft Kidnapping. Hutchinson, Haji U. Siddiqui, Zeba, ed. 152p. (gr. 6-12). 1992. pap. 6.00 (*0-89259-123-4*) Am Trust Pubns.
—The Mystery of the Missing Pearls. Hutchinson, Haji U. Siddiqui, Zeba, ed. 131p. (gr. 6-12). 1993. pap. 6.00 (*0-89259-124-2*) Am Trust Pubns.

Moore, Beverly. Echo's Song. Moore, Beverly. 40p. (gr. k-3). 1993. PLB 13.95g (*0-9637288-7-3*) River Walker Bks. The setting & characters in ECHO'S SONG are all real. This beautifully illustrated children's story is told through the daily adventures of ECHO, a tropical bird who happens to live in the Colorado Rocky Mountains between the high-country & the meadow. He lives contentedly in a log home with a ferret named TWIRP, a girl named TRACY, & TYLER, a big, yellow dog. This lovely story is as simple & safe as the woodland meadow where they live & play. ECHO sings his own unique song to express his love for the life he lives & to joyfully communicate that love to the broader world around him. The events described in this book are recorded & interpreted by artist Beverly Moore. A native of the Colorado mountain country, Beverly Moore lives & works in the Roaring Fork Valley near Aspen. For many years a professional artist, she has won awards for graphic design & illustration, & as an art director & magazine publisher. Her paintings, drawings, & sculpture have been widely exhibited. ECHO'S SONG is dedicated to the extraordinary creatures who live among us as our friends & teachers, & are commonly referred to as "pets." Volume discounts available from publisher--River Walker Books, 3334 Wyandot St., Denver, CO 80211; 303-480-5009.
Publisher Provided Annotation.

Moore, Cyd. Jane Yolen's Songs of Summer. Yolen, Jane, ed. Stemple, Adam, designed by. LC 92-85034. 32p. 1993. 12.95 (*1-56397-110-0*, Wordsong) Boyds Mills Pr.

Moore, Cyd, photos by. A Frog Inside My Hat. Robinson, Fay. LC 93-22200. 64p. (ps-3). 1993. PLB 16.95 (*0-8167-3129-2*); pap. write for info. (*0-8167-3130-6*) BrdgeWater.

Moore, Daniel. The Ocean's Call. Stonecipher, A. D. LC 91-62027. 16p. (ps-4). 1992. lib. bdg. 9.95 (*0-9621759-2-7*) Rochester Pub Lib Dist.

Moore, Daryl J. Snow White. Shearer, Marilyn J. LC 90-60396. 16p. (Orig.). (ps-6). 1990. 19.95 (*0-685-33066-4*); pap. 10.95 (*1-878389-00-9*) L Ashley & Joshua.

Moore, Dick, jt. illus. see Lipney, Stephanie.

Moore, Ella. The Wise Woman. Strichartz, Naomi. 43p. (Orig.). (gr. 2-6). 1986. pap. 3.50 (*0-9618182-0-4*) Cranehill Pr.

—The Wise Woman's Sacred Wheel of the Year. Strichartz, Naomi. (Orig.). (gr. 2-6). 1988. pap. 3.50 (*0-9618182-1-2*) Cranehill Pr.

Moore, Erin C. From London to Appalachia. Breeding, Robert L. 200p. (gr. 4-7). 1991. pap. 9.95 (*1-880258-03-X*) Thriftecon.

Moore, Eugenia. Kidnapped by an Angel. Moore, Eugenia. Leiper, Esther M., ed. 32p. (Orig.). (gr. 3-4). 1988. pap. 3.95x (*0-9617284-4-2*) Sand & Silk.

Moore, Inga. The Little Book of Prayers. Walsh, Caroline. LC 92-30860. 1993. 7.95 (*1-85697-888-5*) Kingfisher Bks.

—Little Dog Lost. Moore, Inga. LC 90-24483. 32p. (ps-3). 1991. SBE 14.95 (*0-02-767648-X*, Macmillan Child Bk) Macmillan Child Grp.

—Oh, Little Jack. Moore, Inga. LC 91-71827. 32p. (ps up). 1992. 14.95 (*1-56402-028-2*) Candlewick Pr.

—The Sorcerer's Apprentice. Moore, Inga. LC 88-27195. 32p. (gr. k-3). 1989. SBE 14.95 (*0-02-767645-5*, Macmillan Child Bk) Macmillan Child Grp.

Moore, Jim, photos by. Be a Mime! Stolzenberg, Mark. LC 91-18171. 128p. (gr. 4-12). 1991. pap. 10.95 (*0-8069-8394-9*) Sterling.

—Nothing's Impossible: Stunts to Entertain & Amaze. Sheridan, Jeff. LC 81-20780. 64p. (gr. 5 up). 1982. 12.95 (*0-688-01169-1*) Lothrop.

Moore, Larry. The Grasshopper & the Ants. Brown, Margaret W. LC 93-70938. 32p. 1993. 12.95 (*1-56282-534-8*); PLB 12.89 (*1-56282-535-6*) Disney Pr.

—That Tickles! The Disney Book of Senses. West, Cindy. LC 92-53444. 32p. (ps-k). 1993. 9.95 (*1-56282-383-3*) Disney Pr.

Moore, Peggy S. My Very First book of Poetry & Other Things. Moore, Peggy S. 16p. (gr. 3-5). 1982. pap. 1.98 (*0-9613078-0-3*) Detroit Black.

Moore, Stanley B. Ornamental Horticulture As a Vocation. 2nd ed. Moore, Stanley B. 1988. text ed. 11.95x (*0-912178-01-9*) Mor-Mac.

Moore, Stephen. Faster Than the Bull. Braun, Lutz. LC 92-37947. 32p. (gr. 4-6). 1992. PLB 17.96 (*0-8114-3580-6*) Raintree Steck-V.

Moore, Susan J. I Love You, Charles Henry: Cats & Dogs in My Life. Roach, Margaret J. Moore, Susan & Craft, Page, eds. (gr. 1-6). 1994. pap. 13.50 (*1-882666-02-X*) M Roach & Assocs.
This book is actually about not only Charles Henry, her latest year old puppy. It is a collection of stories, true ones, about each of her dogs & cats in her lifetime. Laddie, the cat & Lindy, the dog belong to her 10 year old era; Charles Henry belongs to her 70's era. In the years in between there have been purebreds & pets of questionable ancestry. The author has loved each with intensity & loyal possession, with much love. Cats have always come from friends with too many kittens, the humane society, or from friends moving from a house to a "NO PET" apartment. Each pet has added a new dimension into her life by their individual expressions of love. Her cats she never possessed; they possessed her. Her dogs have given & received enough love for all their lives & hers. Perhaps she has learned gentleness from her pets & how to love unconditionally. Order from: Margaret Jo Roach, 4515 NW Big Oak Place, #10, Corvallis, OR 97330, (503) 752-3396.
Publisher Provided Annotation.

—Mac & His Dog, Sir John. Roach, Margaret J. (Orig.). (gr. k-8). 1993. Spanish ed., Mac y Su Perro, Don Juan. pap. 13.50 (*1-882666-01-1*); English ed. pap. 13.50 (*1-882666-00-3*) M Roach & Assocs.
Sir John, the hero in the book, MAC & HIS DOG, SIR JOHN, was (in real life) CANIM HANIM which means in Turkish, "My dear Lady." I got her as a very young puppy when I was stationed in Okinawa with the USO... 1963-65. Mac, the sergeant of the USAF Sentry Dog School near Kadena Air Base, believed that no woman knew how to take care of a precious German shepherd. Much against his wishes, I got the shepherd. It was fun to prove him wrong. After Mac found out I did know how to take care of a German shepherd, Canim Hanim was invited to join the obedience training for sentry dogs. She proved to be an able student except for her fear of the dark, two-barrel tunnel. He had watched Sir John, the young sergeant German shepherd, go part way through the two-barrel tunnel & then stop. No urging commands could make the dog move through the tunnel. When all failed, Mac decided to take his willful pup off the training field for a walk around the Air Base on Okinawa. The ending is a delightful surprise, & proves there is really nothing to be afraid of in the dark. "Jo's story gives us characters we can admire: the kind & patient trainer,

the beautiful courageous dog. Three cheers for Sir John!"--Anne Warren Smith, Writing teacher & author of young adult novels. Illustrated by Susan J. Moore. Volume discounts available from the publisher. Margaret Jo Roach, P.O. Box 213, Philomath, OR 97370. 503/752-4478.
Publisher Provided Annotation.

Moore, Trisha. Chester...the Imperfect All Star. Peckinpah, Sandra L. LC 92-74057. (gr. 1-5). 1993. PLB 15.95 (*0-9627806-1-8*); pap. text ed. 8.95 (*0-9627806-2-6*) Dasan Prodns.

—Rosey...the Imperfect Angel. Peckinpah, Sandra L. LC 90-63058. 32p. (ps-4). 1991. 15.95 (*0-9627806-0-X*) Dasan Prodns.

Moore, Yvette. A Prairie Alphabet. Bannatyne-Cugnet, Jo. LC 92-80414. 32p. (gr. k up). 1992. 19.95 (*0-88776-292-1*) Tundra Bks.

Moores, Ian. Aircraft. Munro, Bob. LC 93-19868. 32p. (gr. 4-6). 1993. PLB 19.97 (*0-8114-6161-0*) Raintree Steck-V.

Moores, Ian, jt. illus. see Bull, Peter.

Moores, Jeff. The Helping Hands Handbook. Adams, Patricia & Marzollo, Jean. LC 91-42947. 96p. (Orig.). (gr. 3 up). 1992. PLB 11.99 (*0-679-92816-2*); pap. 4.99 (*0-679-82816-8*) Random Bks Yng Read.

Moorhead, Carol A. Colorado's Backyard Wildlife. Moorhead, Carol A. 96p. (Orig.). (gr. 6-8). 1992. pap. 10.95 (*1-879373-08-4*) R Rinehart.

Moorhouse, Bob, photos by. A Day in the Life of a Cowboy. Davis, Alvin G. LC 90-11130. 32p. (gr. 4-8). 1991. PLB 11.79 (*0-8167-2208-0*); pap. text ed. 2.95 (*0-8167-2209-9*) Troll Assocs.

Mora, Francisco X. La Gran Fiesta. Mora, Francisco X. LC 92-44365. 32p. (ps-k). 1993. PLB 19.00 (*0-917846-19-2*, 95518) Highsmith Pr.

—Juan Tuza & the Magic Pouch. Mora, Francisco X. 32p. (ps-1). 1993. PLB 19.00 (*0-917846-24-9*, 95563) Highsmith Pr.

—The Legend of the Two Moons. Mora, Francisco X. LC 92-31552. 32p. (ps-k). 1993. PLB 19.00 (*0-917846-15-X*, 95517) Highsmith Pr.

—Listen to the Desert - Que Dice el Desierto? Mora, Pat. LC 93-31463. (ENG & SPA.). 1994. write for info. (*0-395-67292-9*, Clarion Bks) HM.

—Pablo's Tree. Mora, Pat. LC 92-27145. 32p. (ps-1). 1993. RSBE 13.95 (*0-02-767401-0*, Macmillan Child Bk) Macmillan Child Grp.

—The Tiger & the Rabbit: A Puerto Rican Folk Tale. Mora, Francisco X. LC 91-3500. 32p. (ps-3). 1991. PLB 16.93 (*0-516-05137-7*); pap. 5.95 (*0-516-45137-5*) Childrens.

Moral, Jean D. Cheerleading Is for Me. Hawkins, Jim W. LC 81-3719. (gr. 2-5). 1981. PLB 13.50 (*0-8225-1127-4*, AACRZ) Lerner Pubns.

Morales, Cuitlahuac. Forest Friends Help Each Other. Dobson, Danae. 32p. (ps-k). 1993. 7.99 (*0-8499-0986-4*) Word Inc.

—Forest Friends Learn to Be Kind. Dobson, Danae. 32p. 1993. 7.99 (*0-8499-1016-1*) Word Inc.

—Forest Friends Learn to Share. Dobson, Danae. 32p. (ps-k). 1993. 7.99 (*0-8499-0985-6*) Word Inc.

—Forest Friends Play Fair. Dobson, Danae. 32p. (ps-k). Date not set. 7.99 (*0-8499-0987-2*) Word Inc.

Morales, Sioux N. The Boy Who Loved to Dance. Appelt, Kathi A. 48p. (ps-3). 1986. PLB 11.95 (*0-938169-00-9*); pap. 6.95 (*0-938169-01-7*) Pecan Tree Pr.

Moran, J. Douglas. Painting the Fire. Farrington, Liz & Sherwood, Jonathan. Farrington, Liz, created by. LC 92-76022. 40p. (gr. k-4). 1993. 14.95 (*1-56844-001-4*) Enchante Pub.

Moran, Michael. Mystery on the Mississippi. Loredo, Betsy. 80p. (gr. 4-6). 1994. PLB 12.95 (*1-881889-35-1*) Silver Moon.

Moran, Patrick & Sempe, Jean J. The Grammar Handbook Part One: Elementary-Intermediate ESL. 2nd, rev. ed. Clair, Nancy. Clark, Raymond C., ed. LC 84-11548. 176p. (gr. 6 up). 1991. pap. text ed. 9.95x (*0-86647-042-5*) Pro Lingua.

Moran, Patrick R. Index Card Games for ESL. 2nd, rev. ed. Clark, Raymond C. & Brown, Ruthanne. LC 82-9786. 80p. (Orig.). (gr. 3 up). 1992. pap. 9.50x (*0-86647-002-6*) Pro Lingua.

Morbiim. Agate Eyes. Jackson, Cherry R. 1978. pap. text ed. 4.00 (*0-9605208-1-3*) Sea Urchin.

Mordechai, Tova. Good Night My Friend Aleph. Mordechai, Tova. 32p. (ps-1). 1989. 9.95 (*0-922613-12-5*); pap. 7.95 (*0-922613-13-3*) Hachai Pubns.

Mordvinoff, Nicolas. Finders Keepers. Will & Nicolas. LC 51-12326. 32p. (gr. k-4). 1989. pap. 3.95 (*0-15-630950-5*, Voyager Bks) HarBrace.

More, David & Allen, Graham. Trees & Leaves. Althea. LC 89-20308. 32p. (gr. 3-6). 1990. PLB 11.59 (*0-8167-1967-5*); pap. text ed. 3.95 (*0-8167-1968-3*) Troll Assocs.

Morehead, Arlene. Muffin's Book, Bk. II. Homes, Patricia. 40p. Date not set. pap. 8.95 (*0-9618379-6-9*) Parkside Pubns.

Morehead, Ruth J. A Christmas Countdown with Ruth J. Morehead's Holly Babes. LC 90-61905. 22p. (ps). 1991. bds. 2.95 (0-679-81417-5) Random Bks Yng Read.

—Christmas Is Coming with Ruth J. Morehead's Holly Babes: A Book of Poems & Songs. LC 89-3717. 32p. (Orig.). (ps-1). 1990. pap. 2.25 (0-679-80075-1) Random Bks Yng Read.

—The Christmas Story with Holly Babies. Morehead, Ruth J. LC 85-32305. 32p. (ps-1). 1987. 2.25 (0-394-88051-X); cassette pkg. 5.95 (0-394-89058-2) Random Bks Yng Read.

Moreno, Rene K. The Pocket Book. Aldridge, Josephine H. LC 93-1939. 1994. pap. 14.00 (0-671-87128-5, S&S BFYR) S&S Trade.

Moreton, Ann. Spiders. Hopf, Alice L. LC 89-9716. 64p. (gr. 5 up). 1990. 13.95 (0-525-65017-2, Cobblehill Bks) Dutton Child Bks.

Morey, Jean. Seven Diving Ducks. Friskey, Margaret. LC 65-20889. 32p. (gr. k-3). 1965. PLB 15.00 (0-516-03605-X) Childrens.

Morford, Pam P. Pregnant Too Soon: Adoption Is an Option. rev. ed. Lindsay, Jeanne W. Monserrat, Catherine, frwd. by. LC 87-22042. 224p. (gr. 7-12). 1987. pap. 9.95 (0-930934-27-X); tchr's. guide 2.50 (0-930934-27-X) Morning Glory.

Morgado, Richard. Colors, Shapes, & Sizes. Wise, Beth A. 32p. (ps). 1992. wkbk. 1.95 (1-56293-168-7) McClanahan Bk.

—My First Math Book. Wise, Beth A. 32p. (ps). 1992. wkbk. 1.95 (1-56293-172-5) McClanahan Bk.

—My Phonics Word Book. Hollander, Cass. 64p. 1993. pap. 5.95 (1-56293-321-3) McClanahan Bk.

—My Sticker Dictionary. Osterink, Carol. 64p. (ps-2). 1992. pap. 5.95 (1-56293-250-0) McClanahan Bk.

—Rhyming Words. Rutman, Shereen G. 32p. (ps). 1992. wkbk. 1.95 (1-56293-170-9) McClanahan Bk.

—What Belongs? Rutman, Shereen G. 32p. (ps). 1992. wkbk. 1.95 (1-56293-175-X) McClanahan Bk.

Morgan. Europe in the Middle Ages. Sabbagh, Antoine. Ridett, Anthea, tr. from FRE. 77p. (gr. 7 up). 1988. 17.98 (0-382-09484-0) Silver Burdett Pr.

—Kouk & the Ice Bear. Rocard, Ann. 38p. (ps-1). 1991. smythe sewn reinforced bdg. 9.95 (1-56182-029-6) Atomium Bks.

Morgan, Cheryl K. The Everglades. Morgan, Cheryl K. LC 89-5175. 32p. (gr.-3-6). 1990. PLB 10.79 (0-8167-1733-8); pap. text ed. 2.95 (0-8167-1734-6) Troll Assocs.

Morgan, Connie. Ben. Buckman, Mary. 32p. (gr. k-5). 1992. pap. 8.95 (1-879414-09-0) Mary Bee Creat.

Morgan, Mary. All Things Bright & Beautiful. Alexander, Cecil F. 32p. (Orig.). (ps-2). 1989. pap. 1.95 (0-448-34304-5, Platt & Munk Pubs) Putnam Pub Group.

—Animal Tracks & Traces. Kudlinski, Kathleen V. 32p. (gr. 1 up). 1991. 12.95 (0-531-15185-9); PLB 12.90 (0-531-10742-6) Watts.

—Asleep in a Heap. Winthrop, Elizabeth. LC 92-11310. 32p. (ps-3). 1993. reinforced bdg. 15.95 (0-8234-0992-9) Holiday.

—Baby's First Mother Goose. Lewison, Wendy, compiled by. 24p. (ps). 1993. bds. 3.50 (0-307-06143-4, 6143, Golden Pr) Western Pub.

—Benjamin's Bugs. Morgan, Mary. LC 93-22911. 44p. (ps-1). 1994. RSBE 12.95 (0-02-767450-9, Bradbury Pr) Macmillan Child Grp.

—Bloomers! Blumberg, Rhoda. LC 92-27154. 40p. (gr. k-5). 1993. RSBE 14.95 (0-02-711684-0, Bradbury Pr) Macmillan Child Grp.

—Boo! Peekaboo! Lewison, Wendy. LC 90-83244. 24p. (ps). 1991. 2.50 (0-448-40133-9, G&D) Putnam Pub Group.

—Buba Leah & Her Paper Children. Ross, Lillian H. 32p. (gr. k-3). 1991. 16.95 (0-8276-0375-4) JPS Phila.

—Christmas Cookies. Lewison, Wendy. 24p. (ps). 1993. bds. 2.95 (0-448-40554-7, G&D) Putnam Pub Group.

—Guess Who I Love? 18p. (ps). 1992. bds. 2.95 (0-448-40313-7) Putnam Pub Group.

—Hannah & Jack. Nethery, Mary. LC 93-4651. 1995. write for info. (0-02-768125-4, Bradbury Pr) Macmillan Child Grp.

—Happy Thanksgiving! Lewison, Wendy. 24p. (ps). 1993. bds. 2.95 (0-448-40552-0, G&D) Putnam Pub Group.

—Hugs. McLerran, Alice. 32p. (ps-3). 1993. 4.95 (0-590-44637-1) Scholastic Inc.

—I'm the Boss! Winthrop, Elizabeth. LC 93-9029. 32p. (gr. 3-8). 1994. 15.95 (0-8234-1113-3) Holiday.

—Jake Baked the Cake. Hennessy, B. G. 32p. (ps-3). 1990. pap. 12.95 (0-670-82237-X) Viking Child Bks.

—Jake Baked the Cake. Hennessy, B. G. 32p. (ps-3). 1992. pap. 3.99 (0-14-050882-1) Puffin Bks.

—Kisses. McLerran, Alice. 32p. (ps-3). 1993. 4.95 (0-590-44711-4) Scholastic Inc.

—Let's Trade. Ziefert, Harriet. LC 88-62150. 32p. (ps-3). 1989. pap. 3.50 (0-14-050982-8, Puffin) Puffin Bks.

—Molly's Monsters. Slater, Teddy. 32p. (ps). 1992. PLB 2.25 (0-448-19099-0, Platt & Munk Pubs) Putnam Pub Group.

—Puddle Wonderful: Poems to Welcome Spring. Katz, Bobbi, ed. LC 91-8066. 32p. (Orig.). (ps-1). 1992. PLB 5.99 (0-679-91493-5); pap. 2.25 (0-679-81493-0) Random Bks Yng Read.

—The Pudgy Merry Christmas Book. 16p. 1989. bds. 2.95 (0-448-09222-1, G&D) Putnam Pub Group.

—Singing Birds & Flashing Fireflies: How Animals Talk to Each Other. Patent, Dorothy H. LC 89-9081. 32p. (gr. 1-3). 1989. PLB 12.90 (0-531-10717-5) Watts.

—Sleepy Time. LC 89-63997. 14p. (ps). 1990. bds. 3.95 (0-679-80753-5) Random Bks Yng Read.

—Surprise! Ziefert, Harriet. LC 87-26217. 32p. (ps-3). 1988. pap. 8.95 (0-670-82036-9) Viking Child Bks.

—What Can Baby Do? Ariev, Lauren. 24p. (ps). 1992. bds. write for info. (0-307-06140-X, 6140) Western Pub.

—Who Are Baby's Friends? Ariev, Lauren. 24p. (ps). 1992. bds. write for info. (0-307-06142-6, 6142, Golden Pr) Western Pub.

Morgan, Pierr. Adventures Beyond the Solar System Plentron & Me. Williams, Geoffrey T. 64p. (gr. 2-7). 1988. 9.95 (0-8431-2298-6) Price Stern.

—The Bells of Santa Lucia. Cazzola, Gus. 32p. (ps-3). 1991. 14.95 (0-399-21804-1, Philomel) Putnam Pub Group.

—The Turnip: An Old Russian Folktale. Milhous, Katherine & Dalgiesh, Alice. 32p. (ps-3). 1990. 14.95 (0-399-22229-4, Philomel Bks) Putnam Pub Group.

Morgan, Rosamond S. & Fraser, Juliette M. The Hawaiians: An Island People. Pratt, Helen G. 210p. (gr. 6 up). 1991. pap. 9.95 (0-8048-1709-X) C E Tuttle.

Morgan, Sally. The Flying Emu & Other Australian Stories. Morgan, Sally. LC 92-37880. 128p. (gr. k-7). 1993. 18.00 (0-679-84705-7) Knopf Bks Yng Read.

Morice, David. Now We'll Make the Rafters Ring: Classic & Contemporary Rounds for Everyone. Finckel, Edwin A. LC 92-43866. 144p. (Orig.). (gr. k-12). 1993. pap. 11.95 (1-55652-186-3) A Cappella Bks.

Morin, Paul. The Dragon's Pearl. Lawson, Julie. 32p. (gr. k-3). 1993. 15.45 (0-395-63623-X, Clarion Bks) HM.

—Fox Song. Bruchac, Joseph. LC 92-24815. 32p. (ps). 1993. 14.95 (0-399-22346-0, Philomel Bks) Putnam Pub Group.

—The Mud Family. James, Betsy. LC 92-43537. 1994. write for info. (0-399-22549-8, Putnam) Putnam Pub Group.

—Orphan Boy. Mollel, Tololwa M. 32p. (gr. k-3). 1991. 15.45 (0-89919-985-2, Clarion Bks) HM.

—The Orphan Boy. Mollel, Tololwa M. 1991. 14.95 (0-685-53587-8) HM.

Morissette, Oliver. Prey. Morissette, Oliver, et al. (Orig.). Date not set. pap. 19.95 (0-938782-29-0) Fantaco.

Moriya, Noboru. Rice. Johnson, Sylvia A. 48p. (gr. 4 up). 1985. PLB 19.95 (0-8225-1466-4) Lerner Pubns.

Morley, Carol. Buck. Benjamin, Alan. LC 93-17090. 1994. write for info. (0-06-023454-7); PLB write for info. (0-06-023459-8) HarpC Child Bks.

—Buck. Benjamin, Alan. LC 93-31161. 1994. write for info. (0-671-88718-1, S&S BFYR) S&S Trade.

—Dots & Spots. Morley, Carol. LC 92-24526. 32p. (ps-3). 1993. 14.00 (0-06-021526-7); PLB 13.89 (0-06-021527-5) HarpC Child Bks.

—The Tapestry Cats. Turnbull, Ann. 1992. 14.95 (0-316-85626-6) Little.

Moroney, Tracey. Toothless Albert. Taylor, Carol. LC 93-28937. 1994. 4.25 (0-383-03780-8) SRA Schl Grp.

Morozumi, Atsuko. One Gorilla: A Counting Book. Morozumi, Atsuko. 26p. (ps-1). 1990. 15.00 (0-374-35644-0) FS&G.

Morril, Leslie. The Bell Witch. Schoder, Judith & Shebar, Sharon S. LC 82-42873. 64p. (gr. 7 up). 1983. (J Messner); PLB 9.29 (0-671-44005-5) S&S Trade.

Morrill, Les. The Wind in the Willows. Grahame, Kenneth. Sale, Roger, intro. by. 256p. (gr. 4-12). 1983. pap. 1.95 (0-553-21129-3, Bantam Classics) Bantam.

—The Wind in the Willows. Grahame, Kenneth. Sale, Roger, intro. by. 256p. 1983. pap. 2.95 (0-553-21368-7, Bantam Classics Spectra) Bantam.

Morrill, Leslie. America's Own Holidays: Mas de Fiesta de los Estados Unidos. Alexander, Sue. FS Staff, ed. (ENG & SPA). 48p. 1988. PLB 11.40 (0-531-10293-9) Watts.

—Angel in Charge. Delton, Judy. LC 84-27862. 152p. (gr. 2-5). 1985. 13.45 (0-395-37488-X) HM.

—Back Yard Angel. Delton, Judy. 112p. (gr. 2-5). 1983. 14.45 (0-395-33883-2) HM.

—Back Yard Angel. Delton, Judy. 112p. (gr. k up). 1990. pap. 3.25 (0-440-40445-2, YB) Dell.

—The Big Bicycle Race. Robinson, Marileta. 1984. incl. cassette 7.95 (0-685-42663-7); 5.95 (0-910313-29-6) Parker Bros.

—A Boy in the Doghouse. Duffey, Betsy. LC 90-47751. 96p. (gr. 2-6). 1993. pap. 2.95 (0-671-86698-2, Half Moon Bks) S&S Trade.

—The Case of the Slippery Sharks. Mooser, Stephen. LC 87-3490. 96p. (gr. 3-6). 1988. PLB 9.89 (0-8167-1177-1); pap. text ed. 2.95 (0-8167-1178-X) Troll Assocs.

—The Celery Stalks at Midnight. Howe, James. LC 83-2665. 128p. (gr. 4-6). 1983. SBE 12.95 (0-689-30987-2, Atheneum Child Bk) Macmillan Child Grp.

—Creepy-Crawly Birthday. Howe, James. LC 90-35370. 48p. (gr. k up). 1991. 13.95 (0-688-09687-5); PLB 13.88 (0-688-09688-3) Morrow Jr Bks.

—Dinosaurs & Their Young. Freedman, Russell. LC 83-6160. 32p. (gr. 1-4). 1983. reinforced bdg. 13.95 (0-8234-0496-X) Holiday.

—Dog Poems. Livingston, Myra C., ed. LC 89-2061. 32p. (ps-3). 1990. reinforced 12.95 (0-8234-0776-4) Holiday.

—Eddie & the Fairy Godpuppy. Roberts, Willo D. LC 83-15678. 136p. (gr. 3-5). 1984. SBE 12.95 (0-689-31021-8, Atheneum Child Bk) Macmillan Child Grp.

—Eddie & the Fairy Godpuppy. Roberts, Willo D. LC 91-28003. 128p. (gr. 3-7). 1992. pap. 3.95 (0-689-71602-8, Aladdin) Macmillan Child Grp.

—Fang. Hazen, Barbara S. LC 86-28697. 32p. (gr-2). 1987. SBE 13.95 (0-689-31307-1, Atheneum Child Bk) Macmillan Child Grp.

—Fourth Grade Celebrity. Giff, Patricia R. 128p. (gr. 4-6). 1984. 8.95 (0-385-28308-3) Delacorte.

—Fourth Grade Celebrity. Giff, Patricia R. LC 79-50678. (gr. 4-6). 1979. 8.95 (0-440-02725-X); PLB 8.89 (0-440-02726-8) Delacorte.

—Freddy the Politician. Brooks, Walter R. LC 85-14713. 264p. (gr. 3-7). 1986. pap. 3.95 (0-394-87600-8) Knopf Bks Yng Read.

—The Fright Before Christmas. Howe, James. LC 87-26280. 48p. (gr. k-3). 1988. 13.95 (0-688-07664-5); PLB 13.88 (0-688-07665-3, Morrow Jr Bks) Morrow Jr Bks.

—The Girl Who Knew It All. Giff, Patricia R. (gr. 4-6). 1984. 6.95 (0-385-28362-8); PLB 6.95 (0-385-28363-6) Delacorte.

—The Girl Who Knew It All. Giff, Patricia R. LC 79-50677. (gr. 4-6). 1979. 6.95 (0-440-03137-0); PLB 6.89 (0-440-03138-9) Delacorte.

—Hardy Boys: The Submarine Caper. Dixon, Franklin W. 192p. (Orig.). (gr. 3-7). 1981. S&S Trade.

—Hot Fudge. Howe, James. LC 89-13468. 48p. (gr. k up). 1990. 13.95 (0-688-08237-8); PLB 13.88 (0-688-09701-4, Morrow Jr Bks) Morrow Jr Bks.

—I Hate My Sister Maggie. Dragonwagon, Crescent. LC 88-8197. 32p. (gr. k-3). 1989. RSBE 12.95 (0-02-733150-4, Macmillan Child Bk) Macmillan Child Grp.

—Judge Benjamin: The Superdog Gift. McInerney, Judith W. 128p. (gr. 2-4). 1987. pap. 2.95 (0-8167-1043-0) Troll Assocs.

—Judge Benjamin: The Superdog Rescue. McInerney, Judith W. (gr. 4-6). pap. 2.75 (0-317-66178-7, Minstrel Bks) PB.

—Left-Handed Shortstop. Giff, Patricia R. 128p. (gr. k-6). 1989. pap. 2.95 (0-440-44672-4, YB) Dell.

—Left-Handed Shortstop. Giff, Patricia R. 1980. pap. 11.95 (0-385-28533-7); pap. 11.95 (0-385-28534-5) Delacorte.

—Love, from the Fifth-Grade Celebrity. Giff, Patricia R. LC 85-46075. 144p. (gr. 4-6). 1986. 13.95 (0-385-29486-7) Delacorte.

—Lucky on the Loose. Duffey, Betsy. LC 92-21421. 1993. pap. 13.00 (0-671-86424-6, S&S BFYR) S&S Trade.

—Morgan's Zoo. Howe, James. LC 84-6325. 192p. (gr. 3-6). 1984. SBE 13.95 (0-689-31046-3, Atheneum Child Bk) Macmillan Child Grp.

—The Mummy's Secret. Mooser, Stephen. LC 87-16152. 96p. (gr. 3-6). 1988. PLB 9.89 (0-8167-1181-X); pap. text ed. 2.95 (0-8167-1182-8) Troll Assocs.

—Nighty-Nightmare. Howe, James. LC 86-22334. 128p. (gr. 3-7). 1987. SBE 12.95 (0-689-31207-5, Atheneum Child Bk) Macmillan Child Grp.

—Rat Teeth. Giff, Patricia R. LC 83-16601. 144p. (gr. 4-6). 1984. 12.95 (0-385-29339-9); PLB 12.95 (0-385-29309-7) Delacorte.

—Scared Silly: A Halloween Treat. Howe, James. LC 88-7837. 48p. (gr. k up). 1989. 13.95 (0-688-07666-1); PLB 13.88 (0-688-07667-X, Morrow Jr Bks) Morrow Jr Bks.

—The Secret Gold Mine. Mooser, Stephen. LC 87-16151. 96p. (gr. 3-6). 1988. PLB 9.89 (0-8167-1179-8); pap. text ed. 2.95 (0-8167-1180-1) Troll Assocs.

—Secret in the Old Mansion. Mooser, Stephen. LC 87-15456. 96p. (gr. 3-6). 1988. PLB 9.89 (0-8167-1175-5); pap. text ed. 2.95 (0-8167-1176-3) Troll Assocs.

—Squeak Saves the Day & Other Tooley Tales. Snyder, Zilpha K. LC 87-31010. 192p. (gr. 2-5). 1988. pap. 14.95 (0-385-29661-4) Delacorte.

—Totally Disgusting! Wallace, Bill. LC 90-47561. 112p. (gr. 3-7). 1991. 13.95 (0-8234-0873-6) Holiday.

—Tough Beans. Bates, Betty. 96p. (gr. 3-7). 1992. pap. 3.50 (0-440-40689-7, YB) Dell.

—Watch the House. Whayne, Susanne S. LC 91-28071. 80p. (gr. k-3). 1992. pap. 12.00 jacketed (0-671-75886-1, S&S BFYR) S&S Trade.

—Watch the House. Whayne, Susanne S. LC 91-28071. 80p. (gr. k-3). 1993. pap. 2.95 (0-671-86700-8, Half Moon Bks) S&S Trade.

—The Winter Worm Business. Giff, Patricia R. 144p. (gr. k-6). 1983. pap. 3.50 (0-440-49259-9, YB) Dell.

—The Winter Worm Business. Giff, Patricia R. (gr. 4-6). 1981. pap. 8.95 (0-385-29152-3); pap. 8.89 (0-385-29154-X) Delacorte.

Morrill, Leslie & Wiese, Kurt. Freddy & the Men from Mars. Brooks, Walter R. LC 86-40421. 256p. (gr. 3-7). 1987. pap. 3.95 (0-394-88887-1) Knopf Bks Yng Read.

—Freddy & the Perilous Adventure. Brooks, Walter R. LC 85-14653. 256p. (gr. 3-7). 1986. lib. bdg. 9.99 (0-394-97601-0) Knopf Bks Yng Read.

—Freddy Goes Camping. Brooks, Walter R. LC 48-8629. 264p. (gr. 3-7). 1986. lib. bdg. 9.99 (0-394-97602-9); pap. 4.95 (0-394-87602-4) Knopf Bks Yng Read.

Morrill, Leslie H. The Byte Brothers Input an Investigation. McCoy, Lois, et al. 1983. pap. 2.25 (0-380-85571-2, 85571, Camelot) Avon.

—The Celery Stalks at Midnight. Howe, James. 128p. (gr. 3-7). 1984. pap. 3.99 (0-380-69054-2, Camelot) Avon.

—Fang. Hazen, Barbara S. LC 91-1966. 32p. (gr. k-2). 1991. pap. 4.95 (0-689-71501-3, Aladdin) Macmillan Child Grp.

—The Fright Before Christmas. Howe, James. 48p. 1989. pap. 5.95 (0-380-70445-5, Camelot) Avon.
—Jesse Builds a Road. Pringle, Laurence. LC 88-29297. 32p. (ps-1). 1989. RSBE 14.95 (0-02-775311-5, Macmillan Child Bk) Macmillan Child Grp.
Morris, Aaron. A Day in the Life of the Monarch Butterfly. Zappler, Liz. Eakin, Ed, ed. 48p. (gr. 2-6). 1989. 8.85 (0-89015-616-6) Eakin-Sunbelt.
—The Deathless White Stallion & Other Tales. Ferguson, Joe. Sky Rivers & Eakin, Edwin M., eds. 64p. (gr. 4-6). 1989. 10.95 (0-89015-702-2, Pub. by Panda Bks); pap. 3.95 (0-89015-712-X) Eakin-Sunbelt.
—Dinosaur Days in Texas. Allen, Tom, et al. LC 88-37237. 64p. (gr. 3 up). 1989. lib. bdg. 14.95 (0-937460-30-3) Hendrick-Long.
Morris, Alix & Hayden, Marilyn. Let's Sing & Play Carols & Holiday Songs: Thanksgiving, Hanukkah, Christmas, New Year's: Easy-to-Read Letter Notation for Recorder, "Flutes," Piano, any Melody Instrument. 2nd ed. Hoenack, Peg & Jones, Kay. 48p. (gr. 2-7). 1978. pap. text ed. 4.95 (0-913500-18-6, L-3) Peg Hoenack MusicWorks.
—Let's Sing & Play: Easy-to-Learn Letter Notation Method for Recorder, "Flutes," Keyboard. 4th ed. Hoenack, Peg. 64p. (gr. 2-7). 1991. student easel book, wire binding 5.50 (0-913500-43-7, L-1); Set 1, for teaching 32 songs. transparencies for overhead projector 64.00 (0-913500-40-2, L-8) Peg Hoenack MusicWorks.
—Let's Sing & Play While Learning Rhythm Notation, Bk. 2-R: Easy Transition from Letter Notes to Rhythm Symbols. 2nd ed. Hoenack, Peg & Jones, Kay. 32p. (gr. 2-7). 1992. A-frame easel book with wire binding 5.50 (0-913500-44-5, L-2R) Peg Hoenack MusicWorks.
—Songs I Can Play: Easy-to-Learn Numeral Notation Method for 8-Bar Xylophone, Resonator Bells, Piano. 5th ed. Hoenack, Peg, et al. 40p. (ps-2). 1983. Repr. of 1972 ed. Little Book - Child's Size. A-frame easel, wirebound 4.75 (0-913500-21-6, S-1); write for info. braille; Big Book - Classrom Size. wirebound, standup covers 46.00 (0-913500-17-8, S-3) Peg Hoenack MusicWorks.
Morris, Alix, jt. illus. see Hoenack, Frank.
Morris, Douglas. A New Look at the Pilgrims: Why They Came to America. Siegel, Beatrice. LC 76-57060. 82p. (gr. 3-7). 1987. Repr. of 1977 ed. 13.85 (0-8027-6292-1) Walker & Co.
Morris, Susan S. The Jesus Tree. Dellinger, Annetta. 32p. (ps-2). 1991. 7.99 (0-570-04191-0) Concordia.
Morris, Tony. Mining. Williams, Brian. LC 92-29906. 48p. (gr. 5-8). 1993. PLB 21.34 (0-8114-4789-8) Raintree Steck-V.
—Papa Panov's Special Day. 2nd ed. Tolstoy, Leo. Molder, Mig, retold by. 32p. 1988. 11.95 (0-7459-1358-X) Lion USA.
—A Song at Christmas. Absolon, Mary. 64p. (gr. 3-8). 1991. 9.99 (0-7459-1951-0) Lion USA.
Morris, Tony, jt. illus. see Haysom, John.
Morris, Tony, et al. A Baby Called John. Frank, Penny. 24p. (ps-3). 3.99 (0-85648-756-2) Lion USA.
—Come Down, Zacchaeus! Frank, Penny. 24p. (ps-3). 3.99 (0-85648-768-6) Lion USA.
—Elijah Asks for Bread. Frank, Penny. 24p. (ps-3). 3.99 (0-85648-746-5) Lion USA.
—God Speaks to Samuel. Frank, Penny. 24p. (ps-3). 3.99 (0-85648-741-4) Lion USA.
—Good News for Everyone. Frank, Penny. 24p. (ps-3). 3.99 (0-85648-774-0) Lion USA.
—Isaac Finds a Wife. Frank, Penny. 24p. (ps-3). 3.99 (0-85648-730-9) Lion USA.
—Jesus' Special Friends. Frank, Penny. 24p. (ps-3). 3.99 (0-85648-759-7) Lion USA.
—Joseph & the King of Egypt. Frank, Penny. 24p. (ps-3). 3.99 (0-85648-733-3) Lion USA.
—Joseph the Dreamer. Frank, Penny. 24p. (ps-3). 3.99 (0-85648-732-5) Lion USA.
—A King for Israel. Frank, Penny. 24p. (ps-3). 3.99 (0-85648-742-2) Lion USA.
—King Nebuchadnezzar's Golden Statue. Frank, Penny. 24p. (ps-3). 3.99 (0-85648-751-1) Lion USA.
—Let My People Go! Frank, Penny. 24p. (ps-3). 3.99 (0-85648-735-X) Lion USA.
—People Jesus Met. Frank, Penny. 24p. (ps-3). 3.99 (0-85648-770-8) Lion USA.
—Queen Esther Saves Her People. Frank, Penny. 24p. (ps-3). 3.99 (0-85648-753-8) Lion USA.
—Ruth's New Family. Frank, Penny. 24p. (ps-3). 3.99 (0-85648-740-6) Lion USA.
—The Story of the Great Feast. Frank, Penny. 24p. (ps-3). 3.99 (0-85648-766-X) Lion USA.
—The Story of the Lost Sheep. Frank, Penny. 24p. (ps-3). 3.99 (0-85648-767-8) Lion USA.
—The Story of the Sower. Frank, Penny. 24p. (ps-3). 3.99 (0-85648-764-3) Lion USA.
Morriseau, Brent. The Fish Skin. Oliviero, Jamie. LC 92-85509. 40p. (ps-2). 1993. 14.95 (1-56282-401-5); PLB 14.89 (1-56282-402-3) Hyprn Child.
Morrison, Bill. The Easy Hockey Book. Kalb, Jonah. 64p. (gr-5). 1977. 13.95 (0-395-25842-1) HM.
—How to Be a Space Scientist in Your Own Home. Simon, Seymour. LC 81-47759. (gr. 4-7). 1982. (Lipp Jr Bks); (Lipp Jr Bks) HarpC Child Bks.
—The Secret Life of Hardware: A Science Experiment Book. Cobb, Vicki. LC 81-48607. 96p. (gr. 5 up). 1982. (Lipp Jr Bks); (Lipp Jr Bks) HarpC Child Bks.

—The Secret Life of School Supplies. Cobb, Vicki. LC 81-47108. 96p. (gr. 5 up). 1981. PLB 13.89 (0-397-31925-8, Lipp Jr Bks) HarpC Child Bks.
—Squeeze a Sneeze. Morrison, Bill. LC 76-62503. (gr. k-3). 1987. pap. 3.80 (0-395-44238-9) HM.
Morrison, Gordon. Peterson First Guide to Dinosaurs. Kricher, John C. Peterson, Roger T., frwd. by. 128p. 1990. pap. 4.80 (0-395-52440-7) HM.
Morrison, Gordon, jt. illus. see Kricher, John.
Morrison, Gordon, jt. illus. see Kricher, John C.
Morrison, Gordon, jt. illus. see Walton, Richard K.
Morrison, Penelope. Snorkels for Tadpoles. Morrison, Rob & Morrison, Penelope. LC 93-28967. 1994. 4.25 (0-383-03775-1) SRA Schl Grp.
Morrison, William. Now You See It: Easy Magic for Beginners. Broekel, Ray & White, Laurence. (gr. 1-3). 1979. 13.95 (0-316-93595-6) Little.
Morrow, Barbara. Edward's Portrait. Morrow, Barbara. LC 90-45008. 32p. (ps-3). 1991. RSBE 13.95 (0-02-767591-2, Macmillan Child Bk) Macmillan Child Grp.
—Help for Mr. Peale. Morrow, Barbara. LC 89-39273. 32p. (gr. k-3). 1990. RSBE 13.95 (0-02-767590-4, Macmillan Child Bk) Macmillan Child Grp.
Morrow, Gray. Crispus Attucks: Black Leader of Colonial Patriots. Millender, Dharathula H. LC 86-10779. 192p. (gr. 2-6). 1986. pap. 3.95 (0-02-041810-8, Aladdin) Macmillan Child Grp.
—Jim Thorpe: Olympic Champion. Van Riper, Guernsey, Jr. LC 86-3478. 192p. (gr. 2-6). 1986. pap. 3.95 (0-02-042140-0, Aladdin) Macmillan Child Grp.
—Teddy Roosevelt: Young Rough Rider. Parks, Edd W. LC 89-37819. 192p. (gr. 2-6). 1989. pap. 3.95 (0-689-71349-5, Aladdin) Macmillan Child Grp.
Morrow, Gray, jt. illus. see Arthur, James.
Morrow, Skip. Awesome Facts to Blow Your Mind. Clark, Judith F. 48p. (gr. 2 up). 1993. pap. 4.99 (0-8431-3577-8) Price Stern.
—Gross Facts to Blow Your Mind. Clark, Judith F. LC 93-12250. 48p. 1993. pap. 4.99 (0-8431-3578-6) Price Stern.
—Scary Facts to Blow Your Mind. Clark, Judith F. 48p. (gr. 2 up). 1993. pap. 4.99 (0-8431-3580-8) Price Stern.
—Weird Facts to Blow Your Mind. Clark, Judith F. 48p. (gr. 2 up). 1993. pap. 4.99 (0-8431-3579-4) Price Stern.
Morse, Debby. Valentine's Day Mess. Craig, Janet A. LC 93-2211. 32p. (gr. k-2). 1993. PLB 11.59 (0-8167-3254-X); pap. text ed. 2.95 (0-8167-3255-8) Troll Assocs.
Mortenson, Bob. All Kinds of Separation. Cunningham, Carolyn. 24p. (gr. k-6). 1988. wkbk. 3.95 (0-685-20040-X, 0494) Kidsrights.
—Steps to Healthy Touching. MacFarlane, Kee & Cunningham, Carolyn. 144p. (Orig.). (gr. k-7). 1988. wkbk. 19.95 (0-685-20041-8, 1400) Kidsrights.

Mortenson, Denis. What Would Jesus Do? Thomas, Mack. 253p. (ps-2). 1991. 12.99 (0-945564-05-8, Gold & Honey) Questar Pubs.
Almost a century ago, a new novel revolutionized the concept of Christian discipleship. The book was Charles M. Sheldon's In His Steps. Conservative estimates place the book's sales at more than 25 million copies--ranking it behind only the Bible in popularity among Christian readers in this century. And now, In His Steps has been retold for children, with its timeless message as clear & powerful as ever. As both a book & audio cassette, WHAT WOULD JESUS DO? presents the stirring call of following Christ in a way that young children can easily understand & embrace. The delightful text is written in short, simple sentences, & is set in a clear typeface especially recommended for early readers. Each short chapter focuses in a fresh way on the book's core concept--learning to ask throughout the day, What would Jesus do? Discussion questions for each chapter help parents & teachers highlight this truth for children. Enhancing the text are full-color illustrations on more than 200 pages. Detailed & charming, they capture the book's flavor as a work that transcends time & cultures. Order from Questar Publications, P.O. Box 1720, Sisters,

OR 97759, 503-549-1144.
Publisher Provided Annotation.

Morter, Peter. The Great Atlas of Discovery. Grant, Neil. LC 91-29668. 64p. 1992. 20.00 (0-679-81660-7); PLB 21.99 (0-679-91660-1) Knopf Bks Yng Read.
Mortimer, Anne. Tosca's Christmas. Sturgis, Matthew. 1989. 11.95 (0-8037-0722-3) Dial Bks Young.
—Tosca's Christmas. Sturgis, Matthew. 32p. (ps-3). 1992. pap. 3.99 (0-14-054840-8, Puffin Pied Piper) Puffin Bks.
—Tosca's Surprise. Sturgis, Matthew. LC 90-38731. 32p. (ps-3). 1991. 11.95 (0-8037-0946-3) Dial Bks Young.
—Tosca's Surprise. Stufgis, Matthew. 32p. (ps-3). 1994. pap. 4.50 (0-14-055270-7, Puffin Pied Piper) Puffin Bks.
Morton, Robert. Explore the World of Exotic Rainforests. Ganeri, Anita. 48p. (gr. 3-7). 1992. write for info. (0-307-15606-0, 15606, Golden Pr) Western Pub.
Morton, Tom. Freddy & Betty, Vol. 1. Michaels, Scott, ed. (gr. 1-6). 1989. tchr's ed. 2.50 (0-317-93682-4) S Michaels Pub.
Moseley, Dudley, jt. illus. see Everitt-Stewart, Andy.
Moser, B. Beauty & the Beast. Willard, N. 1992. 19.95 (0-15-206052-9, HB Juv Bks) HarBrace.
Moser, Barry. The Adventures of Sherlock Holmes. Doyle, Arthur Conan. Glassman, Peter, afterword by. LC 91-39632. 352p. 1992. 20.00 (0-688-10782-6) Morrow Jr Bks.
—Ariadne, Awake! Orgel, Doris. LC 93-24123. 80p. (ps-3). 1994. PLB 15.99 (0-670-85158-2) Viking Child Bks.
—The Ballad of Biddy Early. Willard, Nancy. LC 88-29187. 48p. (gr. 5 up). 1989. lib. bdg. 14.99 (0-394-98414-5) Knopf Bks Yng Read.
—Big Mistreatin' Bittersweet'n' Blues. Olswanger, Anna. LC 92-24430. 1994. write for info. (0-553-09184-0) Bantam.
—The Call of the Wild. London, Jack. Paulsen, Gary, intro. by. LC 93-18409. 1994. text ed. 19.95 (0-02-759455-6) Macmillan.
—Casey at the Bat: A Centennial Edition. Thayer, Ernest L. Hall, Donald, afterword by. LC 88-45285. 32p. (gr. 1 up). 1988. 14.95 (0-87923-722-8) Godine.
—The Centaur. Swenson, May. LC 92-14897. 32p. (gr. k-3). 1994. RSBE 14.95 (0-02-788726-X, Macmillan Child Bk) Macmillan Child Grp.
—The Dreamer. Rylant, Cynthia. LC 93-19915. 32p. (ps-6). 1993. 14.95 (0-590-47341-7) Scholastic Inc.
—East of the Sun & West of the Moon: A Play. Willard, Nancy. 64p. (gr. 3 up). 1989. 14.95 (0-15-224750-5) HarBrace.
—Fly! A Brief History of Flight Illustrated. Moser, Barry. LC 92-30960. 56p. (gr. 1 up). 1993. 16.00 (0-06-022893-8); PLB 15.89 (0-06-022894-6) HarpC Child Bks.
—The Ghost Horse of the Mounties. O'Huigin, Sean. LC 87-46287. (gr. 4-6). 1991. 14.95 (0-87923-721-X) Godine.
—Grass Songs: Poems. Turner, Ann. LC 92-11684. (gr. 4 up). 1993. write for info. (0-15-136788-4) HarBrace.
—I Am the Dog, I Am the Cat. Hall, Donald. LC 93-28060. 1994. write for info. (0-8037-1504-8); PLB write for info. (0-8037-1505-6) Dial Bks Young.
—In the Beginning: Creation Stories from Around the World. Hamilton, Virginia. 161p. (ps up). 1988. 22.95 (0-15-238740-4) HarBrace.
—Jump Again! More Adventures of Brer Rabbit. Harris, Joel C. Moser, Barry, adapted by. 40p. (ps-3). 1987. 16.95 (0-15-241352-9, HB Juv Bks) HarBrace.
—Kashtanka. Chekhov, Anton. Pevear, Richard, tr. from RUS. LC 89-10866. 1991. 16.95 (0-399-21905-6, Putnam) Putnam Pub Group.
—Little Tricker the Squirrel Meets Big Double the Bear. Kesey, Ken. 1990. 14.95 (0-670-81136-X) Viking Child Bks.
—Little Trickster the Squirrel Meets Big Double the Bear. Kesey, Ken. LC 92-10605. (gr. 4 up). 1992. 4.99 (0-14-050623-3) Puffin Bks.
—The Magic Hare. Banks, Lynne R. LC 92-10585. 64p. 1993. 15.00 (0-688-10895-4); PLB 14.93 (0-688-10896-2) Morrow Jr Bks.
—The Magic Wood. Treece, Henry. LC 91-29547. 32p. (gr. 1 up). 1992. 16.00 (0-06-020802-3); PLB 15.89 (0-06-020803-1) HarpC Child Bks.
—Noah's Cats & the Devil's Fire. Olson, Arielle N. LC 91-17408. 32p. (ps-3). 1992. 14.95 (0-531-05984-7); lib. bdg. 14.99 (0-531-08584-8) Orchard Bks Watts.
—The Other Wise Man. Wells, Ruth & Van Dyke, Henry, eds. LC 93-16259. (ps-8). 1993. 16.95 (0-88708-329-3) Picture Bk Studio.
—Polly Vaughn: A Traditional British Ballad. Moser, Barry, retold by. 32p. (gr. 2 up). 1992. 15.95 (0-316-58541-6) Little.
—Prayers from the Ark: Selected Poems. Bernos de Gasztold, Carmen. Godden, Rumer, tr. 32p. 1992. 16.00 (0-670-84496-9) Viking Child Bks.
—St. Jerome & the Lion. Hodges, Margaret, retold by. LC 90-22142. 32p. (ps-3). 1991. 14.95 (0-531-05938-3); RLB 14.99 (0-531-08538-4) Orchard Bks Watts.
—Sky Dogs. Yolen, Jane. LC 89-26960. 32p. (ps-3). 1990. 15.95 (0-15-275480-6); limited ed., numbered & s 100.00 (0-15-275481-4) HarBrace.

—Summer of 1944. Hall, Donald. LC 92-38613. 32p. 1994. 13.99 (0-8037-1501-3); PLB 13.89 (0-8037-1502-1) Dial Bks Young.

—The Wonderful Wizard of Oz. Baum, L. Frank. 1986. 29.95 (0-520-05822-4) U CA Pr.

Moser, Barry & Moser, Cara. Turtle Island ABC: A Gathering of Native American Symbols. Hausman, Gerald. LC 92-14982. 32p. (gr. ps-2). Date not set. 15.00 (0-06-021307-8); PLB 14.89 (0-06-021308-6) HarpC Child Bks. Postponed.

Moser, Cara, jt. illus. see Moser, Barry.

Moser, Erwin. The Crow in the Snow & Other Bedtime Stories. Moser, Erwin. Agee, Joel, tr. from GER. LC 86-10740. 48p. (ps up). 1986. 10.95 (0-915361-49-3) Modan-Adama Bks.

Moser, Jeanie W. The Great Farm Adventure. McConnell, Em. (gr. k-3). Bk. & cassette 4.95 (0-932715-07-9) Evans FL.

—Strange Sounds. McConnell, Em. (gr. k-3). Bk. & cassette 4.95 (0-932715-09-5) Evans FL.

—The Yellow Star Sticker. Stanton, P. (gr. k-3). Bk. & cassette 4.95 (0-932715-08-7) Evans FL.

Moses, Grandma. The Grandma Moses Night before Christmas. 2nd ed. Moore, Clement C. LC 90-24145. 32p. 1991. 15.00 (0-679-81526-0); lib. bdg. 15.99 (0-679-91526-5) Random Bks Yng Read.

Moses, Grandma, jt. illus. see Ruff, Donna.

Moskowitz, Stewart. Patchwork Fish Tale. Moskowitz, Stewart. Klimo, Kate, ed. 32p. 1982. 4.95 (0-671-45327-0) S&S Trade.

Mosley, Keith. Animals in Danger: A Pop-up Book. McCay, William. (gr. 1-7). 1990. pap. 12.95 (0-689-71408-4), Aladdin Macmillan Child Grp.

Mosley, Rob & Lingle, Bea. Dachshund Tails North. Mosley, Marilyn C. LC 82-90167. 50p. (Orig.). (gr. 5). 1982. 4.95 (0-9614850-0-0) M C Mosley.

Moss, Barbara. If Hurricanes Were Candy Canes. Bonilla, Jayne. 16p. (Orig.). (gr. k-6). 1992. pap. 4.95 (0-9635105-0-9) J R Bonilla.

Moss, David. Here, There & Everywhere: A Find & Name Picture Word Book. Clempner, Jane. 32p. (ps). 1993. 6.95 (0-8249-8590-7, Ideals Child) Hambleton-Hill.

Moss, Marissa. But Not Kate. Moss, Marissa. Donovan, Melanie, ed. LC 90-25751. 32p. (ps-3). 1992. 14.00 (0-688-10600-5); PLB 13.93 (0-688-10601-3) Lothrop.

—In America. Moss, Marissa. LC 93-26885. 1994. write for info. (0-525-45152-8, DCB) Dutton Child Bks.

—Knick Knack Paddywack. Moss, Marissa. 32p. (ps-3). 1992. 13.45 (0-395-54701-6) HM.

—Mother Goose & More: Classic Nursery Rhymes with Added Lines. Hickey. 48p. (ps-3). 1990. 7.77 (0-9623940-0-9); lib. bdg. 7.00 (0-685-45370-7); text ed. 12.95 (0-685-45371-5); tchr's. ed. 9.00 (0-685-45372-3) Additions Pr.

—One, Two, Three & Four: No More? Gray, Catherine. 32p. (gr. k-3). 1988. 13.45 (0-395-48293-3) HM.

—Regina's Big Mistake. Moss, Marissa. 32p. (gr. k-3). 1990. 13.45 (0-395-55330-X) HM.

—Want to Play? Moss, Marissa. 32p. (ps-3). 1990. 13.45 (0-395-52022-3) HM.

—Who Was It? Moss, Marissa. (gr. k-3). 1989. 13.45 (0-395-49699-3) HM.

Moss, P. Buckley. Reuben & the Fire. Good, Merle. LC 93-1798. 32p. (ps-3). 1993. PLB 14.95 (1-56148-091-6) Good Bks Pa.

Mosse, Richard. Bun-Bun's Brook Trout. Mosse, Richard. Sonstegard, Jeff, ed. 32p. (gr. 6-10). 1992. 9.95 (0-9630328-1-X) SDPI.

Most, Andee. Peter Can't Wait. Plum, Carol T. 32p. (gr. k-3). 1991. 9.95 (0-87973-006-4, 6); pap. 5.95 (0-87973-007-2, 7) Our Sunday Visitor.

Most, Bernard. A Dinosaur Named after Me. Most, Bernard. D'Andrade, Diane, ed. 32p. (ps-3). 1991. 12.95 (0-15-223494-2) HarBrace.

—Four & Twenty Dinosaurs. Most, Bernard. LC 89-34472. 40p. (ps-2). 1990. PLB 13.89 (0-06-024377-5) HarpC Child Bks.

—If the Dinosaurs Came Back. Most, Bernard. LC 77-23911. (ps-2). 1978. 13.95 (0-15-238020-5, HB Juv Bks) HarBrace.

—If the Dinosaurs Came Back. Most, Bernard. LC 77-23911. 32p. (ps-2). 1984. pap. 4.95 (0-15-238021-3, Voyager Bks) HarBrace.

—If the Dinosaurs Came Back. Most, Bernard. 32p. (ps-2). 1991. pap. 19.95 (0-15-238022-1) HarBrace.

—The Littlest Dinosaurs. Most, Bernard. 30p. (ps-3). 1989. 13.95 (0-15-248125-7) HarBrace.

—There's an Ant in Anthony. Most, Bernard. LC 79-23089. 32p. (gr. k-3). 1980. PLB 12.88 (0-688-32226-3) Morrow Jr Bks.

—Whatever Happened to the Dinosaurs? Most, Bernard. LC 84-3779. 30p. (ps-3). 1984. 13.95 (0-15-295295-0, HB Juv Bks) HarBrace.

Most, Richard. Searching in God's Word-New Testament. Grunze, Richard. 142p. (gr. 5-6). 1986. 4.95 (0-938272-41-1) WELS Board.

—Searching in God's Word-Old Testament. Grunze, Richard. 140p. (gr. 5-6). 1986. 4.95 (0-938272-40-3) WELS Board.

—Where the Big River Runs. Plum, Carol T. 32p. (gr. k-3). 1991. 9.95 (0-87973-011-0, 11); pap. 5.95 (0-87973-010-2, 10) Our Sunday Visitor.

Mosteller, Rosella. The Very Special Place. Shirley, Joseph. 32p. (Orig.). (gr. k-4). 1992. pap. 10.95 incl. cass. (0-9632816-0-7) NISIS.

Mostyn, David. Freaky Frank's Cut Out Fun Book. Bradley, Susannah. (gr. 3-6). 1992. pap. 3.95 (1-56680-506-6) Mad Hatter Pub.

—How Things Work. Bramwell, Martyn. 38p. (ps-3). 1985. PLB 10.95 (0-86020-847-8, Pub. by Usborne) EDC.

—Spring-Heeled Jack. Pullman, Philip. LC 90-5151. 112p. (Orig.). (gr. 4-6). 1991. lib. bdg. 9.99 (0-679-91057-3); pap. 8.00 (0-679-81057-9) Knopf Bks Yng Read.

Mother Goof. The Sheep Who Was Allergic to Wool. Mother Goof. LC 92-60096. 32p. (gr. 3 up). 1992. 8.95 (0-9623184-1-8) Sunflower Hill.

Mott, Evelyn C. Balloon Ride. Mott, Evelyn C. 32p. (ps-1). 1991. 13.95 (0-8027-8124-1); PLB 14.85 (0-8027-8126-8) Walker & Co.

Mou-sien Tseng, jt. illus. see Tseng, Jean.

Moutoussamy-Ashe, Jeanne, photos by. Daddy & Me. Moutoussamy-Ashe, Jeanne. LC 93-11513. 40p. (ps-3). 1993. 12.00 (0-679-85096-1); PLB 13.99 (0-679-95096-6) Knopf Bks Yng Read.

Mow, Kathy. The Sparrow. 4th ed. Clement, Jane T. Hutterian Brethren Staff, ed. Moody, Ruby, intro. by. LC 68-21133. 212p. (gr. 4 up). 1992. pap. 10.00 (0-87486-009-1) Plough.

Mowrer, Sheri L. The Doggonest Vacation. Stack, Richard L. 1991. write for info. (0-9628262-0-0) Windmill MD.

Moxley, Sheila. The Christmas Story: A Lift-the-Flap Advent Calendar. LC 92-29520. 24p. 1993. 15.99 (0-8037-1351-7) Dial Bks Young.

Moya, Patricia. The Adventures of Gilly, the Guitar, Bk. 1. Ellis, Cathy. 40p. (ps-2). 1991. wkbk. incl. audiotape 15.95 (1-879542-04-8) Ellis Family Mus.

—More Adventures with Gilly, the Guitar, Bk. 2. Ellis, Cathy. 48p. (ps-2). 1992. wkbk. 12.95 (1-879542-08-0); audiotape 14.95 (1-879542-14-5) Ellis Family Mus.

Moyer, Barry. The Magic Word. Joseph, Joel. 12p. (Orig.). (ps-2). 1986. pap. 9.95 (0-915765-31-4) Natl Pr Bks.

Moyer, Barry S. Planet of Trash. Poppel, George. 32p. (ps-3). 1987. 9.95 (0-915765-42-X, Pub. by Panda Monium Bks.) Natl Pr Bks.

Moyers, William. Black Jupiter. MacDougall, Mary-Katherine. Gruver, Kate E., ed. 181p. (gr. 5 up). 1983. 8.95 (0-940175-01-0) Now Comns.
"It was late for the horses to be so high in the mountains. By this time in other years they had already found winter quarters in a lower area. But this fall they were waiting for a colt." That colt was Black Jupiter. Snow came. The horses had to leave through the rock gateway the black mare could not yet get through. The stallion stayed with her. The next dawn the colt came but did not move or make a sound. The horses left the newborn colt alone in the snow. Jim Peters, a prospector, living alone in his cabin, was sensitive to wildlife. He felt something was wrong when he heard two horses leaving a day after the herd. He found Black Jupiter alive but not strong. He took him to his cabin. There are Gregg & Jenine Jordan, children of a mining engineer, a threat to Jim & his mining plans. In turn, Jim is suspected of stealing from the surveying crew. Black Jupiter, set in the Rocky Mountains with a factual copper mining background, is a mystery story of distrust & misunderstanding, healed by love & a colt. There is a happy Christmas chapter. Black & white illustrations.
Publisher Provided Annotation.

Moyes, Lesley. Annie & Moon. Smith, Miriam. Sherwood, Rhoda, ed. Mahuika, A. T., tr. LC 88-42909. 32p. (gr. 3-4). 1988. PLB 18.60 (1-55532-928-4) Gareth Stevens Inc.

—Charlie Best. Corrin, Ruth. LC 93-9229. 1994. write for info. (0-383-03681-X) SRA Schl Grp.

Moyes, Liz. The Multiplying Glass. Phillips, Ann. 158p. 1987. 15.00 (0-19-271455-4) OUP.

Moylan, Holly. Lakes & Ponds. Santrey, Laurence. LC 84-2653. 32p. (gr. 3-6). 1985. PLB 9.49 (0-8167-0206-3); pap. text ed. 2.95 (0-8167-0207-1) Troll Assocs.

—Plants, Seeds & Flowers. Sabin, Louis. LC 84-2720. 32p. (gr. 3-6). 1985. PLB 9.49 (0-8167-0226-8); pap. text ed. 2.95 (0-8167-0227-6) Troll Assocs.

—Space Exploration & Travel. Sabin, Louis. LC 84-2698. 32p. (gr. 3-6). 1985. PLB 9.49 (0-8167-0258-6); pap. text ed. 2.95 (0-8167-0259-4) Troll Assocs.

Mozzini, Lisa. Simple Computer Maintenance & Repair. Wang, Wally & Millard, Scott. Collier, Cynthia & Lingham, Gretchen, eds. 60p. (Orig.). (gr. 9 up). 1990. pap. 2.95 (0-945776-10-1) Comptr Pub Enterprises.

Mrviein, Mark. Conversational Spanish: Quick & Easy. Saloom, Barbara B. Cogger, Virginia & Ricardo-Gil, Jose, eds. 120p. (Orig.). 1988. pap. text ed. 12.95 (0-9627755-0-9) B B Saloom.

Mucci, Tina. Poe. Loewen, Nancy. 64p. 1993. 16.95 (1-56846-084-8) Creat Editions.

Mucci, Tina, photos by. Poe. Loewen, Nancy. LC 93-17095. 1993. PLB 16.95 (0-88682-509-1) Creative Ed.

Muelken, Mary. What Is God Like? Rohwer, Lee O. 64p. (Orig.). (gr. k-4). 1986. pap. 5.95 (0-9617788-0-6) Damon Pub.

—What Is God Like? 2nd, rev. ed. Rohwer, Lee O. 68p. (Orig.). (gr. 8 up). 1989. pap. 7.95 (0-9617788-1-4) Damon Pub.

Mueller, Marge, jt. illus. see Diamond, Lynnell.

Mueller, Peggy. The Storybook: An Adult Book for Teens. Pokeberry, P. J. Urie, Luanna, frwd. by. 96p. (Orig.). (gr. 5 up). 1993. pap. 6.50 (0-943962-02-1) Viewpoint Pr.

Mueller, Virginia & Karle, Carol. The Children's Arkansas Puzzle Book. Pape, Donna L. 28p. (gr. k up). 1984. pap. 2.00 (0-914546-55-4) Rose Pub.

Mugnaini, Joseph. The Halloween Tree. Bradbury, Ray. LC 72-2433. 160p. (gr. 6 up). 1988. Repr. of 1972 ed. 15.00 (0-394-82409-1); PLB 13.99 (0-394-92409-6) Knopf Bks Yng Read.

Muir, Michael. The Magic Garden & Other Stories. Larson, Greg. LC 88-18879. 95p. (gr. 3-6). 1988. 7.95 (0-87579-141-7) Deseret Bk.

Mukerji, Debrabrata. Legends from Indian History. Ghosh, A. (gr. 1-8). 1979. pap. 3.00 (0-89744-157-5); 4.50 (0-685-00594-1) Auromere.

—Stories from Panchatantra: Book III. Shivkumar. (gr. 1-9). 1979. 4.50 (0-89744-164-8); pap. 3.00 (0-685-57663-9) Auromere.

—Treasury of Indian Tales: Book I. Shankar. (gr. 8-12). 1979. 4.95 (0-89744-170-2) Auromere.

Mukhida, Zul, photos by. Block Printing. O'Reilly, Susie. LC 92-43263. 32p. (gr. 4-6). 1993. 14.95 (1-56847-065-7) Thomson Lrning.

—Modeling. O'Reilly, Susie. LC 93-7517. 32p. (gr. 4-6). 1993. 14.95 (1-56847-066-5) Thomson Lrning.

—Weaving. O'Reilly, Susie. LC 93-18935. 32p. (gr. 4-6). 1993. 14.95 (1-56847-067-3) Thomson Lrning.

Mulkey, Kim. Adventure in the Lost World. Stroh, R. W. LC 85-2530. 96p. (gr. 3-6). 1985. lib. bdg. 9.49 (0-8167-0535-6); pap. text ed. 2.95 (0-8167-0536-4) Troll Assocs.

—The Lobster & Ivy Feelings. Buss, Nancy. LC 91-72868. 64p. (gr. 3-7). 1992. 13.95 (1-56397-011-2) Boyds Mills Pr.

—Mystery at Loch Ness. Wandelmaier, Roy. LC 85-2532. 112p. (gr. 3-6). 1985. lib. bdg. 9.49 (0-8167-0529-1) Troll Assocs.

Mull, Christ, et al. Uncle Arthur's Storytime, Vol. 2. Maxwell, Arthur S. & Holloway, Cheryl W. 128p. 1989. PLB 29.90 (1-877773-02-6) Family Media.

Mull, Christy, et al. Uncle Arthur's Storytime. Maxwell, Arthur S. & Holloway, Cheryl W. 128p. 1989. 29.90 (1-877773-03-4) Family Media.

Mullen, Don. The Inside Story: Living & Learning Through Life's Storms. Ryder, Donald G. LC 85-27780. 56p. (gr. 7 up). 1985. 14.95 (0-935973-38-9) Ryder Pub Co.

—The Story of Old Abe Wisconsin's Civil War Hero. Rosholt, Malcolm & Rosholt, Margaret. 110p. (gr. 4-12). 1987. 14.95 (0-910417-09-1) Rosholt Hse.

Muller, Anna-Hermine. Little Lights in the Darkness: Stories & Activities for Advent & Christmas. Wever, Hinke B. Vilain, Frederic, tr. from GER. LC 90-42800. 99p. (Orig.). 1990. pap. 9.95 (0-8198-4444-6) St Paul Bks.

—On the Way to Bethlehem. De Vries, C. M. Vilain, Frederic, tr. from DUT. LC 90-43765. 16p. (Orig.). 1990. pap. 1.50 (0-8198-5415-8) St Paul Bks.

Muller, Brenda, jt. illus. see Muller, Carrel.

Muller, Carrel. Dinosaur Discovery. Muller, Carrel & Jacques, Ethel M. 32p. (gr. 4-6). 1987. wkbk. 3.75 (0-915785-02-1) Bonjour Books.

Muller, Carrel & Muller, Brenda. Louisiana Indians. Muller, Carrel & Muller, Brenda. 64p. (gr. 3 up). 1985. 7.50 (0-915785-01-3) Bonjour Books.

Muller, Gerda. The Adventures of Tom Thumb. 48p. (gr. 2-6). 1991. 2.99 (0-517-02418-1) Outlet Bk Co.

—The Garden in the City. Muller, Gerda. 40p. (gr. k-5). 1992. 13.50 (0-525-44697-4, DCB) Dutton Child Bks.

—Jack & the Beanstalk. 48p. (gr. 2-6). 1991. 2.99 (0-517-02421-7) Outlet Bk Co.

—The Ugly Duckling. 48p. (gr. 2-6). 1991. 2.99 (0-517-02422-5) Outlet Bk Co.

Muller, Jorg. The Animals' Rebellion. Steiner, Jorge. 32p. 1991. smythe sewn reinforced bdg. 15.95 (1-56182-025-3) Atomium Bks.

—The Changing City. Muller, Jorg. LC 76-46646. 8p. (gr. 4 up). 1977. portfolio 18.95 (0-689-50084-X, M K McElderly) Macmillan Child Grp.

Mullin, Buddy. Stephen F. Austin: The Father of Texas. Flynn, Jean. 64p. (gr. 4-7). 1981. 10.95 (0-89015-285-3) Eakin-Sunbelt.

Mullins, Frank, jt. illus. see Schoenherr, John.

Mullins, Patricia. Crocodile Beat. Jorgensen, Gail. LC 89-578. 32p. (ps-1). 1989. RSBE 14.95 (0-02-748010-0, Bradbury Pr) Macmillan Child Grp.
—Dinosaur Encore. Mullins, Patricia. LC 92-19848. 32p. (ps-2). 1993. 15.00 (0-06-021069-9); PLB 14.89 (0-06-021073-7) HarpC Child Bks.
—Hattie & the Fox. Fox, Mem. LC 86-18849. 32p. (ps-2). 1988. RSBE 13.95 (0-02-735470-9, Bradbury Pr); pap. 16.95 big book (0-02-735471-7) Macmillan Child Grp.
—Hattie & the Fox. Fox, Mem. LC 91-41727. 32p. (ps-2). 1992. pap. 4.95 (0-689-71611-7, Aladdin) Macmillan Child Grp.
—Shoes from Grandpa. Fox, Mem. LC 89-35401. 32p. (ps-1). 1990. 13.95 (0-531-05848-4); PLB 13.99 (0-531-08448-5) Orchard Bks Watts.
—Shoes from Grandpa. Fox, Mem. LC 89-35401. 32p. (ps-1). 1992. pap. 4.95 (0-531-07031-X) Orchard Bks Watts.

Mulvey, Glen. Super Snacks. Warren, Jean. 48p. 1992. 6.95 (0-911019-49-9, WPH 1601) Warren Pub Hse.

Mulvihill, Patricia. An American Army of Two. Greeson, Janet. 48p. (gr. k-4). 1991. PLB 14.95 (0-87614-664-7) Carolrhoda Bks.
—The Cellar. Howard, Ellen. LC 90-23190. 64p. (gr. 2-4). 1992. SBE 11.95 (0-689-31724-7, Atheneum Child Bk) Macmillan Child Grp.

Mumford, Claire. The Nile. 32p. (gr. 3-5). 1983. 7.95x (0-86685-447-9) Intl Bk Ctr.

Munching, Paul V. The Vampire. Polidori, John. Martin, Les, adapted by. LC 88-34078. 96p. (Orig.). (gr. 3-7). 1989. lib. bdg. 5.99 (0-394-93844-5); pap. 2.95 (0-394-83844-0) Random Bks Yng Read.

Munger, Nancy. An A-B-C Christmas. Houts, Amy. 28p. (ps-k). 1993. 4.99 (0-7847-0063-X, 24-03843) Standard Pub.
—Jesus Grew. Bennett, Marian & Stortz, Diane. 12p. (ps). 1992. deluxe ed. 4.99 (0-87403-995-9, 24-01115) Standard Pub.
—A One-Two-Three Christmas. Stortz, Diane. 28p. (ps-k). 1993. 4.99 (0-7847-0064-8, 24-03844) Standard Pub.

Munoz, Alison. African-American Firsts: Famous, Little-Known, & Unsung Triumphs of Blacks in America. Potter, Joan & Clayton, Constance. LC 93-84716. 352p. (Orig.). (gr. 7 up). 1994. pap. 14.95 (0-9632476-1-1) Pinto Pr.

Munoz, Claudio. Come Back, Grandma. Limb, Sue. LC 92-43534. 32p. (ps-2). 1994. 13.00 (0-679-84720-0) Knopf Bks Yng Read.
—Doris. Cutler, Ivor. LC 92-5923. 32p. (gr. k-3). 1992. PLB 14.00 (0-688-11939-5, Tambourine Bks) Morrow.

Munoz, Rie. Andy: An Alaskan Tale. Welsh-Smith, Susan. 24p. 1988. 13.95 (0-521-35535-4) Cambridge U Pr.
—Goodbye, My Island. Rogers, Jean. LC 82-15816. 96p. (gr. 5-7). 1983. 12.95 (0-688-01964-1); PLB 12.88 (0-688-01965-X) Greenwillow.
—King Island Christmas. Rogers, Jean. LC 84-25865. 32p. (gr. k-3). 1985. 13.00 (0-688-04236-8); lib. bdg. 12.93 (0-688-04237-6) Greenwillow.
—Runaway Mittens. Rogers, Jean. LC 87-12024. 24p. (ps-3). 1988. 15.00 (0-688-07053-1); lib. bdg. 14.93 (0-688-07054-X) Greenwillow.

Munoz, William. Deer & Elk. Patent, Dorothy H. LC 93-25894. 1994. write for info. (0-395-52003-7, Clarion Bks) HM.
—Inside the Zoo Nursery. Smith, Roland. LC 92-3344. 64p. (gr. 5 up). 1993. 15.00 (0-525-65084-9, Cobblehill Bks) Dutton Child Bks.
—Nutrition: What's in the Food We Eat. Patent, Dorothy H. LC 92-3665. 40p. (gr. 3-7). 1992. reinforced bdg. 14.95 (0-8234-0968-6) Holiday.
—Pelicans. Patent, Dorothy H. 64p. (gr. 4-7). 1992. 14.45 (0-395-57224-X, Clarion Bks) HM.
—Places of Refuge: Our National Wildlife Refuge System. Patent, Dorothy H. 80p. (gr. 4-9). 1992. 15.95 (0-89919-846-5, Clarion Bks) HM.
—Primates in the Zoo. Smith, Roland. LC 91-46968. 64p. (gr. 3-6). 1992. PLB 13.90 (1-56294-210-7) Millbrook Pr.
—Snakes in the Zoo. Smith, Roland. LC 91-45588. 64p. (gr. 3-6). 1992. PLB 13.90 (1-56294-211-5) Millbrook Pr.
—Where Food Comes From. Patent, Dorothy H. LC 90-49833. 40p. (gr. 3-7). 1991. reinforced 14.95 (0-8234-0877-9) Holiday.
—Where the Bald Eagles Gather. Patent, Dorothy H. LC 83-20852. 64p. (gr. 3-6). 1984. 15.45 (0-89919-230-0, Clarion Bks) HM.
—Wild Turkey, Tame Turkey. Patent, Dorothy H. LC 89-613. 64p. (gr. 3-6). 1989. 14.45 (0-89919-704-3, Clarion Bks) HM.

Munoz, William, photos by. Appaloosa Horses. Patent, Dorothy H. LC 88-4470. 80p. (gr. 3-7). 1988. reinforced bdg. 14.95 (0-8234-0706-3) Holiday.
—An Apple a Day: From Orchard to You. Patent, Dorothy H. LC 89-33504. 64p. (gr. 3-7). 1990. 13.95 (0-525-65020-2, Cobblehill Bks) Dutton Child Bks.
—Baby Horses. Patent, Dorothy H. 56p. (gr-1). 1991. PLB 17.50 (0-87614-690-6) Carolrhoda Bks.
—Cattle. Patent, Dorothy H. LC 92-32987. 1993. 19.95 (0-87614-765-1) Carolrhoda Bks.
—Dogs: The Wolf Within. Patent, Dorothy H. LC 92-12334. 1992. 19.95 (0-87614-691-4) Carolrhoda Bks.
—A Family Goes Hunting. Patent, Dorothy H. 64p. (gr. 4-9). 1991. 14.45 (0-395-52004-5, Clarion Bks) HM.

—Feathers. Patent, Dorothy H. 64p. (gr. 5 up). 1992. 15.00 (0-525-65081-4, Cobblehill Bks) Dutton Child Bks.
—Flowers for Everyone. Patent, Dorothy H. LC 89-23937. 64p. (gr. 5 up). 1990. 14.95 (0-525-65025-3, Cobblehill Bks) Dutton Child Bks.
—Gray Wolf, Red Wolf. Patent, Dorothy H. 64p. (gr. 4 up). 1990. 15.95 (0-89919-863-5, Clarion Bks) HM.
—Horses. Patent, Dorothy H. LC 93-12329. 1993. 14.95 (0-87614-766-X) Carolrhoda Bks.
—Hugger to the Rescue. Patent, Dorothy H. LC 93-32031. 1994. write for info. (0-525-65161-6, Cobblehill Bks) Dutton Child Bks.
—Miniature Horses. Patent, Dorothy H. LC 90-38641. 48p. (gr. 3-7). 1991. 14.95 (0-525-65049-0, Cobblehill Bks) Dutton Child Bks.
—Osprey. Patent, Dorothy H. LC 92-30103. 64p. (gr. 4-9). 1993. 14.45 (0-395-63391-5, Clarion Bks) HM.
—Prairie Dogs. Patent, Dorothy H. LC 92-34724. 1993. 15.45 (0-395-56572-3, Clarion Bks) HM.
—The Way of the Grizzly. Patent, Dorothy H. LC 86-17562. 64p. (gr. 4 up). 1993. 12.95 (0-89919-383-8, Clarion Bks); pap. 6.95 (0-395-58112-5, Clarion Bks) HM.
—Whales, Dolphins, & Porpoises in the Zoo. Smith, Roland. LC 93-35425. 1994. lib. bdg. write for info. (1-56294-318-9) Millbrook Pr.
—What Good Is a Tail? Patent, Dorothy H. LC 92-45639. 32p. (gr. 1-5). 1994. 13.99 (0-525-65148-9, Cobblehill Bks) Dutton Child Bks.
—Where the Bald Eagles Gather. Patent, Dorothy H. 56p. (gr. 3-7). 1990. pap. 5.95 (0-395-52598-5) HM.
—The Whooping Crane: A Comeback Story. Patent, Dorothy H. LC 88-2871. 96p. (gr. 4 up) 1988. 14.95 (0-89919-455-9, Clarion Bks) HM.

Munoz, William, et al. Yellowstone Fires: Flames & Rebirth. Patent, Dorothy H. LC 89-24544. 40p. (gr. 3-7). 1990. reinforced bdg. 14.95 (0-8234-0807-8) Holiday.

Munro, Roxie. Architects Make Zigzags: Looking at Architecture from A to Z. Maddex, Diane, contrib. by. LC 84-9679. 64p. (Orig.). (gr. 3 up) 1986. pap. 8.95 (0-89133-121-2) Preservation Pr.
—Blimps. Munro, Roxie. LC 88-18138. 32p. (gr. 2-7). 1988. 12.95 (0-525-44441-6, DCB) Dutton Child Bks.
—The Great American Landmarks Adventure. Weeks, Kay, created by. LC 92-31806. 1992. 3.25 (0-16-038003-0) USGPO.
—The Inside-Outside Book of Paris. Munro, Roxie. LC 91-29318. 48p. (ps up) 1992. 15.00 (0-525-44863-2, DCB) Dutton Child Bks.
—Inside Outside Book of Washington D.C. Munro, Roxie. LC 86-24267. 48p. (ps up). 1987. 13.95 (0-525-44298-7, DCB) Dutton Child Bks.

Munsinger, Lynn. An Arkful of Animals: Poems for the Very Young. Cole, William E., ed. 128p. (gr. 3-7). 1978. 13.45 (0-395-27205-X) HM.
—Babysitting for Benjamin. Gregory, Valiska. LC 92-18373. 32p. (ps-3). 1993. 13.95 (0-316-32785-9) Little.
—Bedtime for Bear. Stoddard, Sandol. LC 85-5259. 32p. (gr. k-3). 1985. pap. 4.80 (0-395-47949-5) HM.
—Boris & the Monsters. Willoughby, Elaine M. 32p. (gr. k-3). 1986. 13.45 (0-395-29067-8); pap. 4.80 (0-395-42649-9) HM.
—Don't Call Me Names! (Just Right for 4's & 5's) Cole, Joanna. LC 89-35412. 32p. (ps). 1990. 4.95 (0-679-80258-4); PLB 5.99 (0-679-90258-9) Random Bks Yng Read.
—Group Soup. Brenner, Barbara. 32p. (ps-3). 1992. PLB 12.50 (0-670-82867-X) Viking Child Bks.
—A Halloween Mask for Monster. Mueller, Virginia. Fay, Ann, ed. LC 86-1569. 24p. (ps-1). 1986. 11.95 (0-8075-3134-0) A Whitman.
—A Halloween Mask for Monster. Mueller, Virginia. (ps-1). 1988. pap. 3.95 (0-14-050879-1, Puffin) Puffin Bks.
—Hello, House! Hayward, Linda. LC 86-22080. 32p. (Orig.). (ps-1). 1988. lib. bdg. 6.99 (0-394-98864-7); pap. 3.50 (0-394-88864-2) Random Bks Yng Read.
—Ho for a Hat! Smith, William J. LC 88-39864. (ps-1). 1989. 14.95 (0-316-80120-8, Joy St Bks) Little.
—How the Alligator Missed Breakfast. Kinnell, Galway. 32p. (gr. k-3). 1992. 85.99 (0-395-32436-X) HM.
—Howliday Inn. Howe, James. LC 81-10886. 208p. (gr. 4-6). 1982. SBE 13.95 (0-689-30846-9, Atheneum Child Bk) Macmillan Child Grp.
—Howliday Inn. Howe, James. 200p. 1983. pap. 3.99 (0-380-64543-2, Camelot) Avon.
—Hugh Pine. Van de Wetering, Janwillem. ALC Staff, ed. LC 80-13652. 88p. (gr. 2-8). 1992. pap. 3.95 (0-688-11799-6, Pub. by Beech Tree Bks) Morrow.
—Hugh Pine & Something Else. Van de Wetering, Janwillem. 96p. (gr. 3 up). 1989. 13.45 (0-395-49216-9) HM.
—Hugh Pine & Something Else. Van de Wetering, Janwillem. ALC Staff, ed. LC 88-35801. 80p. (gr. 2-8). 1992. pap. 3.95 (0-688-11800-3, Pub. by Beech Tree Bks) Morrow.
—Hugh Pine & the Good Place. Van De Wetering, Janwillem. LC 84-3108. 80p. (gr. 3 up). 1986. 13.95 (0-395-40147-X) HM.
—Hugh Pine & the Good Place. Van de Wetering, Janwillem. ALC Staff, ed. LC 86-3108. 72p. 1992. pap. 3.95 (0-688-11801-1, Pub. by Beech Tree Bks) Morrow.
—It Wasn't My Fault. Lester, Helen. LC 84-19212. 32p. (gr. k-3). 1985. 14.45 (0-395-35629-6) HM.
—It Wasn't My Fault. Lester, Helen. (ps-3). 1989. pap. 5.70 (0-395-51007-4, Sandpiper) HM.

—Just a Little Bit. Tompert, Ann. LC 92-31857. 1993. 14.95 (0-395-51527-0) HM.
—Me First. Lester, Helen. LC 91-45808. 32p. (gr up) 1992. 13.45 (0-395-58706-9) HM.
—Monster & the Baby. Mueller, Virginia. Fay, Ann, ed. LC 85-3127. 24p. (ps-1). 1985. PLB 11.95 (0-8075-5253-4) A Whitman.
—Monster & the Baby. Mueller, Virginia. (ps-1). 1988. pap. 3.95 (0-14-050880-5, Puffin) Puffin Bks.
—Monster Can't Sleep. Mueller, Virginia. Fay, Ann, ed. LC 86-1568. 24p. (ps-1). 1986. PLB 11.95 (0-8075-5261-5) A Whitman.
—Monster Can't Sleep. Mueller, Virginia. (ps-1). 1988. pap. 3.95 (0-14-050878-3, Puffin) Puffin Bks.
—Monster Goes to School. Mueller, Virginia. Levine, Abby, ed. LC 90-29873. 24p. (ps-1). 1991. 11.95 (0-8075-5264-X) A Whitman.
—Monster's Birthday Hiccups. Mueller, Virginia. Levine, Abby, ed. LC 91-2118. 24p. (ps-1). 1991. 11.95 (0-8075-5267-4) A Whitman.
—My Mother Never Listens to Me. Sharmat, Marjorie. Tucker, Kathleen, ed. LC 84-17201. 32p. (ps-3). 1984. 11.95 (0-8075-5347-6) A Whitman.
—My New Boy. Phillips, Joan. LC 85-30129. 32p. (ps-1). 1986. lib. bdg. 7.99 (0-394-98277-0); 3.50 (0-394-88277-6) Random Bks Yng Read.
—Norma Jean, Jumping Bean. Cole, Joann. LC 86-15588. 48p. (gr. 1-3). 1987. lib. bdg. 7.99 (0-394-98668-7); 3.50 (0-394-88668-2) Random Bks Yng Read.
—Nothing Sticks Like a Shadow. Tompert, Ann. LC 83-18554. 32p. (gr. k-3). 1988. 14.45 (0-395-35391-2, 5-97100); pap. 4.80 (0-395-47950-9) HM.
—Ollie Knows Everything. Levine, Abby. LC 93-29600. 1994. write for info. (0-8075-6020-0) A Whitman.
—One Hungry Monster: A Counting Book in Rhyme. O'Keefe, Susan H. 32p. (ps-3). 1989. 12.95 (0-316-63385-2, Joy St Bks) Little.
—One Hungry Monster: A Counting Book in Rhyme. O'Keefe, Susan H. 32p. (ps-3). 1992. pap. 4.95 (0-316-63388-7, Joy St Bks) Little.
—A Playhouse for Monster. Mueller, Virginia. Fay, Ann, ed. LC 85-3144. 24p. (ps-1). 1985. PLB 11.95 (0-8075-6541-5) A Whitman.
—A Playhouse for Monster. Mueller, Virginia. (ps-1). 1988. pap. 3.95 (0-14-050877-5, Puffin) Puffin Bks.
—Pookins Gets Her Way. Lester, Helen. (ps-3). 1987. 13.95 (0-395-42636-7); pap. 4.80 (0-395-53965-X) HM.
—The Rainbow Ribbon. Hooks, William H. & Boegehold, Betty. LC 93-27706. 1994. write for info. (0-14-054092-X) Puffin Bks.
—The Revenge of the Magic Chicken. Lester, Helen. 32p. (gr. k-3). 1990. 13.45 (0-395-50929-7) HM.
—Rough Tough Rowdy. Hooks, William H. 32p. (ps-3). 1992. PLB 12.50 (0-670-82868-8) Viking Child Bks.
—Silly School Riddles & Other Classroom Crack-Ups. Levine, Caroline. Levine, Abby, ed. LC 84-17300. 32p. (gr. 1-5). 1984. 8.95 (0-8075-7359-0) A Whitman.
—Spiffen: A Tale of a Tidy Pig. Schwartz, Mary A. Levine, Abby, ed. LC 88-15. 32p. (ps-3). 1988. PLB 13.95 (0-8075-7580-1) A Whitman.
—Tacky the Penguin. Lester, Helen. LC 87-30684. 32p. (ps-3). 1988. 13.45 (0-395-45536-7) HM.
—Tacky the Penguin. Lester, Helen. 32p. (gr. k-3). 1990. pap. 4.80 (0-395-56233-3) HM.
—This Little Pig Had a Riddle. Latta, Richard. Fay, Anne, ed. LC 83-26112. 32p. (gr. 1-5). 1984. PLB 8.95 (0-8075-7893-2) A Whitman.
—Three Cheers for Tacky. Lester, Helen. LC 93-14342. 1994. write for info. (0-395-66841-7) HM.
—Tomorrow, up & Away. Collins, Pat L. 32p. (gr. k-3). 1990. 13.45 (0-395-51524-6) HM.
—Underwear! Monsell, Mary E. Levine, Abby, ed. LC 87-25419. 24p. (ps-2). 1988. PLB 11.95 (0-8075-8308-1) A Whitman.
—A Very Mice Joke Book. Gounaud, Karen J. (gr. 2-5). 1981. HM.
—A Week of Raccoons. Whelan, Gloria. LC 87-16800. 40p. (ps-1). 1988. PLB 12.99 (0-394-98396-3) Knopf Bks Yng Read.
—The Wizard, the Fairy, & the Magic Chicken. Lester, Helen. LC 82-21302. 32p. (gr. k-3). 1988. pap. 5.70 (0-395-47945-2) HM.
—A Zooful of Animals. Cole, William, selected by. 96p. (ps-8). 1992. 17.45 (0-395-52278-1) HM.

Murakami, Koichi. The Fisherman & the Grateful Turtle. Okawa, Essei. Ooka, D. T., tr. from JPN. 32p. (gr. k-6). 1985. PLB 11.95 (0-89346-257-8) Heian Intl.

Murakami, Tsutomu. Elephant Rescue. Barnes, Jill & Teramura, Terua. Rubin, Caroline, ed. Japan Foreign Rights Centre Staff, tr. from JPN. LC 90-37750. 40p. (gr. k-3). 1990. PLB 15.93 (0-944483-85-2) Garrett Ed Corp.
—The Monkey & the Crab. Horio, Seishi. Ooka, D. T., tr. from JPN. 32p. 1985. 11.95 (0-89346-246-2) Heian Intl.

Murakami, Yukuo. The Fox. Morton, Leith D. LC 91-43003. (ENG & JPN.). 32p. (ps-6). 1992. 14.95 (0-87358-534-8) Northland AZ.

Murchison, Leon & Howard, Cecelia. Struggle for Freedom & Henry Box Brown. Johnston, Brenda A. & Pruitt, Pamela. McCluskey, John A., ed. 22p. (gr. 2-4). 1987. pap. 4.00 incl. audiocassette (0-913678-16-3) New Day Pr.

Murchison, Leon, jt. illus. see Smith, Ron.

Murdocca, Sal. But Why? Reading Workbook. Lewison, Wendy C., et al. Pape, Richard, designed by. 32p. (Orig.). (gr. k-2). 1988. wkbk. 1.99 (0-88743-109-7) Sch Zone Pub Co.
—Dinosaurs Before Dark. Osborne, Mary P. LC 91-51106. 80p. (Orig.). (gr. 1-4). 1992. PLB 9.99 (0-679-92411-6); pap. 2.99 (0-679-82411-1) Random Bks Yng Read.
—Encyclopedia Brown's Record Book of Weird & Wonderful Facts. Sobol, Donald J. LC 78-72857. (gr. 3 up). 1979. PLB 9.89 (0-440-02330-0) Delacorte.
—Encyclopedia Brown's Third Record Book of Weird & Wonderful Facts. Sobol, Donald J. LC 85-11613. 144p. (gr. 3-7). 1985. 11.95 (0-688-05705-5) Morrow Jr Bks.
—Eureka! It's a Telephone! Bendick, Jeanne. LC 92-5085. 48p. (gr. 2-6). 1993. PLB 14.90 (1-56294-215-8) Millbrook Pr.
—Eureka! It's an Airplane! Bendick, Jeanne. LC 91-34791. 48p. (gr. 2-6). 1992. PLB 14.90 (1-56294-058-9) Millbrook Pr.
—Eureka! It's an Automobile! Bendick, Jeanne. LC 91-34790. 48p. (gr. 2-6). 1992. PLB 14.90 (1-56294-057-0) Millbrook Pr.
—Eureka! It's Television! Bendick, Jeanne & Bendick, Robert. Murdocca, Sal, designed by. LC 92-15652. 48p. (gr. 2-6). 1993. PLB 14.90 (1-56294-214-X) Millbrook Pr.
—Everything You Need to Survive: Money Problems. Stine, Jane & Stine, Jovial B. LC 82-23117. 96p. (gr. 5-9). 1983. pap. 1.95 (0-394-85247-8) Random Bks Yng Read.
—Freddie the Fly. Grodin, Charles. LC 92-5234. 32p. (ps-2). 1993. 12.00 (0-679-83847-3) Random Bks Yng Read.
—The Knight at Dawn. Osborne, Mary P. LC 92-13075. 80p. (Orig.). (gr. 1-4). 1993. PLB 9.99 (0-679-92412-4); pap. 2.99 (0-679-82412-X) Random Bks Yng Read.
—Mummies in the Morning. Osborne, Mary P. 1993. PLB 9.99 (0-679-92424-8); pap. 2.99 (0-679-82424-3) Random Bks Yng Read.
—Pan, Pan, Gran Pan (Big Book) Cumpiano, Ina. (SPA.). 16p. (Orig.). (gr. k-3). 1990. pap. text ed. 29.95 (0-917837-52-5) Hampton-Brown.
—Pan, Pan, Gran Pan (Small Book) Cumpiano, Ina. (SPA.). 16p. (Orig.). (gr. k-3). 1992. pap. text ed. 6.00 (1-56334-085-2) Hampton-Brown.
—A Pig Tale. Newton-John, Olivia & Hurst, Brian S. LC 92-44116. 1993. pap. 12.00 (0-671-78778-0, S&S BFYR) S&S Trade.
—Pirates Past Noon. Osborne, Mary P. LC 93-2039. Date not set. PLB write for info. (0-679-92425-6); pap. write for info. (0-679-82425-1) Random.
—Tom the TV Cat: A Step Two Book. Heilbroner, Joan. LC 83-24600. 48p. (ps-2). 1984. lib. bdg. 7.99 (0-394-96708-9); pap. 2.95 (0-394-86708-4) Random Bks Yng Read.
—Words Around the Year. Doty, Roy. LC 92-19312. 1994. pap. 11.00 (0-671-77836-6, S&S BFYR) S&S Trade.
Murdocca, Sal & Pape, Richard. Trouble Again: Reading Workbook. Gregorich, Barbara. Hoffman, Joan, ed. 32p. (Orig.). (gr. k-2). 1988. 1.99 (0-88743-110-0) Sch Zone Pub Co.
Muren, Nancy L. More Parables for Little People. Castagnola, Larry. LC 87-62532. 88p. (Orig.). (gr. 4-5). 1987. pap. 8.95 (0-89390-095-8) Resource Pubns.
Muren, Nancy L., jt. illus. see Somerville, Sheila.
Muren, Nancy LaBerge. Parables for Little People. Castagnola, Lawrence. Quinn, Francis A. LC 86-60029. 104p. (Orig.). (gr. 4 up). 1982. pap. 7.95 (0-89390-034-6) Resource Pubns.
Murez, Steve. A Day on the Boat with Captain Betty. Murez, Diane. LC 92-11428. 32p. (gr. 2 up). 1993. RSBE 14.95 (0-02-767430-4, Macmillan Child Bk) Macmillan Child Grp.
Murie, Olaus J. Those of the Forest. Grange, Wallace B. Petrie, Chuck, ed. Johnson, Dan, intro. by. 336p. (gr. 6 up). 1989. Repr. of 1953 ed. 19.50 (0-932558-49-6) Willow Creek Pr.
Murphy, Albert, jt. illus. see Murphy, Rowan B.
Murphy, Anne. Mommy in the Sky. Derrig, Leslie A. & Westdyk, Roxanne H. LC 83-73248. 32p. (Orig.). (gr. k-5). 1983. pap. 6.95 (0-915479-68-0) Cottage Pub Co.
Murphy, Bob. Two-B & the Rock 'n' Roll Band. Paul, Sherry. 32p. (Orig.). (ps-2). pap. 14.10 set (0-675-01082-9); Bks & Skillmasters set 16.20 (0-685-01197-6) CPI Pub.
—Two-B & the Space Visitor. Paul, Sherry. 32p. (Orig.). (ps-2). pap. 14.10 bks. only (0-685-01198-4); pap. 16.20 Bks. & Skill Masters (0-685-01199-2) CPI Pub.
Murphy, Chuck. The Pop-up Book of Big Trucks. Seymour, Peter. (ps-3). 1989. 11.95 (0-316-78197-5) Little.
Murphy, Emmy L. A Child's Shining Pathway. Eavey, Louise. (ps-1). 1976. pap. 1.95 (0-915374-08-0, 08-0) Rapids Christian.
—Happiness Rhymes for Children. Eavey, Louise. (ps-1). 1969. pap. 1.95 (0-915374-09-9, 09-0) Rapids Christian.
Murphy, Jill. A Bad Spell for the Worst Witch. large type ed. Murphy, Jill. 1993. 15.95 (0-7451-1809-7, Galaxy Child Lrg Print) Chivers N Amer.
—Five Minutes' Peace: Miniature Edition. Murphy, Jill. 32p. (ps-3). 1989. 4.95 (0-399-21938-2, Putnam) Putnam Pub Group.

—Jeffrey Strangeways. Murphy, Jill. LC 91-71844. 144p. (gr. 3-6). 1992. 14.95 (1-56402-018-5) Candlewick Pr.
—Peace at Last. Murphy, Jill. LC 80-66743. 32p. (ps-2). 1980. 13.95 (0-8037-6757-9) Dial Bks Young.
—Peace at Last. Murphy, Jill. LC 80-66743. 32p. (ps-2). 1982. pap. 3.95 (0-8037-6964-4) Dial Bks Young.
—What Next, Baby Bear! Murphy, Jill. LC 83-7316. 32p. (ps-2). 1984. 13.95 (0-8037-0027-X) Dial Bks Young.
—What Next, Baby Bear! Murphy, Jill. LC 83-7316. 32p. (ps-2). 1986. pap. 3.95 (0-685-37306-1) Dial Bks Young.
—The Worst Witch. large type ed. Murphy, Jill. 96p. 1992. 13.95 (0-7451-1549-7, Galaxy Child Lrg Print) Chivers N Amer.
—The Worst Witch Strikes Again. large type ed. Murphy, Jill. 96p. 1993. 13.95 (0-7451-1672-8, Galaxy Child Lrg Print) Chivers N Amer.
Murphy, Marty. Learning English Book: A TV-Video Standard Program. Howard, Lati, et al. McLaughlin, Michael & Schneider, Amy, eds. 240p. (Orig.). 1992. pap. text ed. 10.95 (0-937354-76-7) Delta Systems.
Murphy, Rowan B. The Bluebeards: Adventure on Skull Island. Bradman, Tony. 64p. (gr. 3-6). 1990. pap. 2.95 (0-8120-4421-5) Barron.
—The Bluebeards: Mystery at Musket Bay. Bradman, Tony. 64p. (gr. 3-6). 1990. pap. 2.95 (0-8120-4422-3) Barron.
—The Bluebeards: Peril at the Pirate School. Bradman, Tony. 64p. (gr. 2-5). 1990. pap. 2.95 (0-8120-4502-5) Barron.
—The Bluebeards: Revenge at Ryan's Reef. Bradman, Tony. 52p. (ps-3). 1992. pap. 3.50 (0-8120-4903-9) Barron.
Murphy, Rowan B. & Murphy, Albert. The Great Book of Optical Illusions. Brandreth, Gyles. LC 85-9898. 96p. (Orig.). (gr. 2 up). 1985. pap. 4.95 (0-8069-6258-5) Sterling.
Murray, Cleitus O. Stories of the Southern Mountains & Swamps. Murray, Cleitus O. 192p. (Orig.). 1992. pap. 9.95 (0-9632132-0-2) Murray Pubns.
Murray, Eleanor H. Bend Like the Bamboo. Murray, Eleanor H. 91p. (Orig.). (gr. 9-12). 1982. pap. 8.95 (1-879313-02-2) Murrays Leprechaun Bks.
Murray, Hubert, photos by. Cherokee County Summer. Murray, Eleanor B. 48p. (Orig.). (gr. 9-12). 1981. pap. 3.98 (1-879313-01-4) Murrays Leprechaun Bks.
Murray, Jim. Mickey Mantle. Wolff, Rick. 64p. (gr. 3 up). 1991. lib. bdg. 14.95 (0-7910-1181-X) Chelsea Hse.
Murray, Joe. Kidvid: Fun-Damentals of Video Instruction. Black, Kaye. 112p. (Orig.). (gr. 4-8). 1989. pap. 15.95 (0-913705-44-6) Zephyr Pr AZ.
Murray, Peggy. Free & Inexpensive Teaching Tools to Make & Use. Learning Exchange Staff. 112p. (gr. 2-6). 1986. wkbk. 9.95 (0-86653-388-5, GA 1004) Good Apple.
Murray, Ruth E. The True Confessions of Charlotte Doyle. Avi. LC 90-30624. 224p. (gr. 6-8). 1990. 15.95 (0-531-05893-X); PLB 15.99 (0-531-08493-0) Orchard Bks Watts.
Murtagh, Betty. Spunky the Monkey. LaFleur, Tom & Brennan, Gale. 16p. (Orig.). (gr. k-6). 1981. pap. 1.25 (0-685-02457-1) Brennan Bks.
—Together at Mass. Cronin, Gaynell B. & Bellina, Joan. LC 87-70417. 32p. (Orig.). (ps-2). 1987. pap. 2.95 (0-87793-357-X) Ave Maria.
—Tuffy the Tiger. LaFleur, Tom & Brennan, Gale. 16p. (gr. k-6). 1982. pap. 1.25 (0-685-05557-4) Brennan Bks.
Murtagh, Mark, jt. illus. see Wyeth, N. C.
Musio, Nino. Saint for the Family: The Story of St. John Bosco. Schmidt, Elizabeth. 34p. (Orig.). (gr. 4-8). 1987. 9.95 (0-89944-088-6, Don Bosco Pubns) Don Bosco Multimedia.
Musser, Rebecca F. Charlotte. Edwards, Archibald C. LC 90-63680. 112p. (Orig.). (gr. 7 up). 1990. pap. 11.95 (0-9626413-0-8) Rosedale Pr.
Mussino, Attilio. The Adventures of Pinocchio. reissued ed. Collodi, C. Chiesa, Carol D., tr. from ITA. LC 88-26684. 320p. (gr. 3 up). 1989. SBE 24.95 (0-02-722821-5, Macmillan Child Bk) Macmillan Child Grp.
Mutchroney, Ken, et al. Collected Teenage Mutant Ninja Turtles Adventures, Vol. 3. Clarrain, Dean & Brown, Ryan. 88p. 1991. pap. 5.95 (1-879450-05-4) Tundra MA.
Mutimer, Ray, jt. illus. see Everitt-Stewart, Andy.
Myers, Amy. Sale El Oso (Big Book) Ada, Alma F. (SPA.). 16p. (Orig.). (gr. k-3). 1988. pap. text ed. 29.95 (0-917837-03-7) Hampton-Brown.
—Sale el Oso (Small Book) Ada, Alma F. (SPA.). 16p. (Orig.). (gr. k-3). 1992. pap. text ed. 6.00 (1-56334-079-8) Hampton-Brown.
Myers, Bernice. Cry Baby. Myers, Bernice. LC 89-12342. 32p. (ps-2). 1990. 12.95 (0-688-09083-4); lib. bdg. 12.88 (0-688-09084-2) Lothrop.
—How Joe the Bear & Sam the Mouse Got Together. De Regniers, Beatrice S. LC 89-12110. 32p. (ps-2). 1990. 12.95 (0-688-09079-6); lib. bdg. 12.88 (0-688-09080-X) Lothrop.
—Sidney Rella & the Glass Sneaker. Myers, Bernice. LC 85-3044. 32p. (gr. k-3). 1985. RSBE 14.95 (0-02-767790-7, Macmillan Child Bk) Macmillan Child Grp.
Myers, Bob. Johnny Texas. Hoff, Carol. 150p. (gr. 4 up). 1992. lib. bdg. 15.95 (0-937460-80-X); pap. 9.95 (0-937460-81-8) Hendrick-Long.

Myers, Glenn. We Believe: Jr. High. rev. ed. Case, Riley B. & Keysor, Charles W. Heidinger, James V., II, et al, eds. 60p. (gr. 6-9). 1988. wkbk. 4.35 (0-917851-20-X) Bristol Hse.
Myers, Mary B. Sam in Flight: Further Adventures of Bad Sam. Autry, Raz. LC 92-496. 64p. (Orig.). (gr. 1-6). 1992. pap. 5.95 (1-56474-029-3) Fithian Pr.
Myers, Robert. Dr. Gardner's Fables for Our Times. Gardner, Richard A. LC 80-26098. 125p. (gr. k-6). 1981. 14.95 (0-933812-06-X) Creative Therapeutics.
—Dr. Gardner's Stories About the Real World, Vol. II. Gardner, Richard A. LC 80-16592. 95p. (gr. k-6). 1983. 14.95 (0-933812-05-1) Creative Therapeutics.
Myers, William. Daniel: Faithful Captive. Heath, Lou. (gr. 1-6). 1977. bds. 5.95 (0-8054-4231-6, 4242-31) Broadman.
Myler, Terry. Con's Fabulous Journey to the Land of Gobel O'Glug. rev. ed. O'Shaughnessy, Peter. 104p. (gr. 6-10). 1992. pap. 5.95 (0-947962-68-9, Pub. by Anvil Bks Ltd ER) Irish Bks Media.
—Cornelius in Charge. Flynn, Mary. (Orig.). (gr. 1-6). 1990. 10.95 (0-947962-53-0, Pub. by Anvil Bks Ltd Ireland); pap. 7.95 (0-947962-54-9, Pub. by Anvil Bks Ltd Ireland) Irish Bks Media.
—Fionuala the Glendalough Goat. Pettigrew, Vera. 112p. (Orig.). (gr. 1-8). 1990. 10.95 (0-947962-42-5, Pub. by Anvil Bks Ltd Ireland); pap. 7.95 (0-947962-43-3, Pub. by Anvil Bks Ltd Ireland) Irish Bks Media.
—Martha & the Ruby Ring. MacGrory, Yvonne. 192p. (Orig.). (gr. 4-8). 1993. pap. 7.95 (0-947962-77-8) Irish Bks Media.
—Save the Unicorns. Jones, Shelagh. 140p. (gr. 4-7). 1989. 11.95 (0-947962-48-4, Pub. by Childrens Pr) Irish Bks Media.
—The Secret of the Ruby Ring. MacGrory, Yvonne. 160p. (Orig.). 1991. pap. 7.95 (0-947962-64-6, Pub. by Childrens Pr ER) Irish Bks Media.
—The Silent Sea. McCaughren, Tom. 111p. (Orig.). 1988. pap. 7.95 (0-947962-20-4, Pub. by Children's Pr) Irish Bks Media.
My Ly, Ha. Vietnamese Word Book. Nguyen, Kim-Anh. LC 93-73560. (VIE & ENG.). 144p. (gr. k-6). 1994. 15.95 (1-880188-70-8); pap. 11.95 (1-880188-51-1) Bess Pr.

N

Naava. My Cat Ginger. Wahl, Jan. LC 91-31883. 32p. (ps-2). 1992. 14.00 (0-688-10722-2, Tambourine Bks); PLB 13.93 (0-688-10723-0, Tambourine Bks) Morrow.
Nachreiner, Tom. The Crocodile. Hogan, Paula Z. LC 79-13699. 32p. (gr. 1-4). 1979. PLB 17.96 (0-8172-1503-4) Raintree Steck-V.
—The Tiger. Hogan, Paula Z. LC 79-13604. (gr. 1-4). 1979. PLB 17.96 (0-8172-1506-9) Raintree Steck-V.
Nacht, Merle. Doodle Soup. Ciardi, John. LC 85-814. 64p. (gr. 2-5). 1985. 13.45 (0-395-38395-1) HM.
—On Home Ground. Lelchuk, Alan. LC 87-8496. 72p. (gr. 5 up). 1987. 9.95 (0-15-200560-9, Gulliver Bks) HarBrace.
Nachtigall, Kelly, jt. illus. see Klassen, Grace.
Nadel, Marc. Searchin' Safari: Looking for Camouflaged Creatures. O'Hare, Jeff. LC 91-72974. 32p. (ps-3). 1992. 8.95 (1-56397-016-3) Boyds Mills Pr.
Nagata, Thomas. The One & Only Original Sanibel-Captiva Alphabet Coloring Book. Montgomery, Monty. 32p. (Orig.). (gr. 7 up). 1988. pap. 6.95 (0-945026-00-5) SME Pr.
Nagle, I. The Secret of the Doo Dah House. Aba, Adam. LC 91-89270. 192p. (gr. 4-7). 1992. pap. 16.95 (1-878756-51-6) YCP Pubns.
Nakamura, Haruko, photos by. Tanzania. Pelnar, Tom & Weber, Valerie, eds. LC 88-42890. 64p. (gr. 5-6). 1989. PLB 19.93 (1-55532-210-7) Gareth Stevens Inc.
Nakanishi, Nadine. Snorkeling for Kids. 2nd ed. Jennet, Judith. 56p. (ps-9). 1992. pap. text ed. 5.95 (0-916974-50-2, 212) NAUI.
Nakano, Dokuihtei. Easy Origami. Nakano, Dokuihtei. Kenneway, Eric, tr. LC 85-40644. 64p. (gr. k-12). 1986. pap. 13.00 (0-670-80382-0) Viking Child Bks.
Nalerio, Claudio. Handstands in the Sand. Zamost, Barbara. 48p. (ps-6). 1992. 12.95 (1-881970-00-0) Saras Prints.
Nance, John. Lobo of the Tasaday: A Stone Age Boy Meets the Modern World. Nance, John. LC 81-14113. 56p. (gr. 3-7). 1982. 9.95 (0-394-85077-7) Pantheon.
Nannie, pseud. The Lord's Prayer for Children. Lucy, Reda, pseud. 24p. (Orig.). (ps-3). 1981. pap. 2.25 (0-87516-437-4) DeVorss.
Nannini, Roger. Josephine's Toy Shop: A Look-&-Play Book with a Special Fold-Out Toy Shop. (ps-2). 1991. 15.95 (0-8037-1004-6) Dial Bks Young.
Napoli, Lizzi. A Child's Life of Jesus. Bomer, John M., tr. from FRE. LC 89-81355. 40p. (Orig.). (ps-2). 1990. 8.95 (0-87793-415-0) Ave Maria.
Nappi, Rudi. The Great Director. Gorman, Carol. LC 93-20228. 60p. (Orig.). (gr. 2-4). 1993. pap. 3.99 (0-570-04746-3) Concordia.
Nappi, Rudy. Nobody's Friend. Gorman, Carol. LC 92-24936. 60p. (Orig.). (gr. 1-4). 1993. pap. 3.99 (0-570-04729-3) Concordia.
—The Richest Kid in the World. Gorman, Carol. LC 92-24935. 60p. (Orig.). (gr. 1-4). 1993. pap. 3.99 (0-570-04728-5) Concordia.

—Skin Deep. Gorman, Carol. LC 93-20230. 60p. (gr. 2-4). 1993. pap. 3.99 (0-570-04747-1) Concordia.

Naprstek, Joel. Reading. Allington, Richard L. & Krull, Kathleen. LC 80-16547. 32p. (ps-2). 1985. pap. 3.95 (0-8114-8235-9) Raintree Steck-V.

—Tom Sawyer. Twain, Mark. Edwards, June, adapted by. LC 80-22095. 48p. (gr. 4 up). 1983. PLB 18.64 (0-8172-1665-0) Raintree Steck-V.

Narahashi, Keiko. I Have a Friend. Narahashi, Keiko. LC 86-27628. 32p. (ps-3). 1987. SBE 13.95 (0-689-50432-2, M K McElderry) Macmillan Child Grp.

—The Little Band. Sage, James. LC 90-40089. 32p. (ps-3). 1991. SBE 13.95 (0-689-50516-7, M K McElderry) Macmillan Child Grp.

—The Magic Purse. Uchida, Yoshiko. LC 92-30132. 32p. (gr. 1-4). 1993. SBE 15.95 (0-689-50559-0, M K McElderry) Macmillan Child Grp.

—My Grandfather's Hat. Scheller, Melanie. LC 91-12486. 32p. (ps-3). 1992. SBE 13.95 (0-689-50540-X, M K McElderry) Macmillan Child Grp.

—Rain Talk. Serfozo, Mary. LC 89-12178. 32p. (ps-3). 1990. SBE 13.95 (0-689-50496-9, M K McElderry) Macmillan Child Grp.

—Rain Talk. Serfozo, Mary. LC 92-29562. 32p. (gr. k-3). 1993. pap. 4.95 (0-689-71699-0, Aladdin) Macmillan Child Grp.

—Who Said Red? Serfozo, Mary. LC 88-9345. 32p. (ps-1). 1988. RSBE 13.95 (0-689-50455-1, M K McElderry) Macmillan Child Grp.

—Who Said Red? Serfozo, Mary. LC 91-21160. 32p. (ps-1). 1992. pap. 4.95 (0-689-71592-7, Aladdin); pap. 18.95 big bk. (0-689-71651-6, Aladdin) Macmillan Child Grp.

—Who Wants One? Serfozo, Mary. LC 88-26614. 32p. (ps-1). 1989. SBE 13.95 (0-689-50474-8, M K McElderry) Macmillan Child Grp.

—Who Wants One? Serfozo, Mary. LC 92-4341. 32p. (ps-1). 1992. pap. 4.95 (0-689-71642-7, Aladdin); pap. 18.95 Big bk. (0-689-71652-4, Aladdin) Macmillan Child Grp.

Nardi, James B. Once upon a Tree: Life from Treetop to Root Tips. Nardi, James B. LC 92-36444. 104p. (gr. 5-10). 1993. 16.95x (0-8138-0917-7) Iowa St U Pr.

NASA Staff. Journey to the Planets. 2nd, rev. ed. Lauber, Patricia. LC 90-33102. 1990. PLB 16.99 (0-517-58125-6) Crown Bks Yng Read.

NASA Staff, photos by. The NOVA Space Explorer's Guide: Where to Go & What to See. Maurer, Richard. LC 90-20074. 128p. (gr. 3-7). 1991. 20.00 (0-517-57758-5, Clarkson Potter) Crown Bks Yng Read.

—Voyager: An Adventure to the Edge of the Solar System. Ride, Sally. LC 91-32495. 36p. (gr. 2-6). 1992. 14.00 (0-517-58157-4); PLB 14.99 (0-517-58158-2) Crown Bks Yng Read.

Nash, Linell. Custard the Dragon. Nash, Ogden. (gr. k-3). 1973. lib. bdg. 14.95 (0-316-59841-0) Little.

Nast, Thomas, jt. illus. see Obering, Kay.

Nasta, Vincent. The Moon of the Winter Bird. George, Jean C. LC 91-15237. 48p. (gr. 3-7). 1992. 15.00 (0-06-020267-X); PLB 14.89 (0-06-020268-8) HarpC Child Bks.

—Plane Song. Siebert, Diane. LC 92-17359. 32p. (ps-3). 1993. 15.00 (0-06-021464-3); PLB 14.89 (0-06-021467-8) HarpC Child Bks.

Natchev, Alexi. The Hobyahs. San Souci, Robert D. LC 92-28655. 1994. 14.95 (0-385-30934-1) Doubleday.

—Matreshka. Ayres, Becky H. LC 91-36359. 32p. (gr. k-3). 1992. pap. 15.00 (0-385-30657-1) Doubleday.

—Nathaniel Willy, Scared Silly. Matthews, Judith & Robinson, Fay. LC 92-4052. 32p. (ps-3). 1994. RSBE 14.95 (0-02-765285-8, Bradbury Pr) Macmillan Child Grp.

Natchev, Alexi, photos by. Forri the Baker. Myers, Edward. LC 93-2468. 1994. write for info. (0-8037-1396-7); PLB write for info. (0-8037-1397-5) Dial Bks Young.

Nation, Tate. Yo! Millard Fillmore: And All Those Other Presidents You Never Heard Of. Cleveland, Will & Alvarez, Mark. 112p. (gr. 5). 1992. pap. 7.95 (0-9632778-0-4) Goodwood Pr.

—Yo, Millard Fillmore! And All Those Other Presidents You Never Heard Of. 2nd, rev. ed. Cleveland, Will & Alvarez, Mark. 112p. (Orig.). (gr. 5). 1993. pap. write for info. (0-9632778-1-2) Goodwood Pr.

Natti, Susanna. The Almost Awful Play. Giff, Patricia R. LC 84-17922. 32p. (ps-3). 1985. pap. 3.95 (0-14-050530-X, Puffin) Puffin Bks.

—The Almost Awful Play. Giff, Patricia R. (gr. 2-4). 1989. bk. & cassette 19.95 (0-87499-116-1); bk. & cassette 12.95 (0-87499-115-3); pap. 27.95 4 cassettes & guide (0-87499-117-X) Live Oak Media.

—Cam Jansen & the Mystery at the Haunted House. Adler, David A. 64p. (gr. 2-5). 1992. PLB 11.00 (0-670-83419-X) Viking Child Bks.

—Cam Jansen & the Mystery at the Monkey House. Adler, David A. LC 85-40043. 56p. (gr. 2-4). 1985. pap. 10.95 (0-670-80782-6) Viking Child Bks.

—Cam Jansen & the Mystery at the Monkey House. Adler, David. LC 93-13047. 64p. (gr. 2-5). 1993. pap. 3.99 (0-14-036023-9, Puffin) Puffin Bks.

—Cam Jansen & the Mystery Corn Popper. Adler, David A. 64p. (gr. 2-5). 1986. pap. 10.95 (0-670-81118-1) Viking Child Bks.

—Cam Jansen & the Mystery Monster Movie. Adler, David A. LC 83-16693. 64p. (gr. 2-5). 1984. pap. 10. 95 (0-670-20035-2) Viking Child Bks.

—Cam Jansen & the Mystery of Flight 54. Adler, David A. 64p. (gr. 2-5). 1989. pap. 10.95 (0-670-81841-0) Viking Child Bks.

—Cam Jansen & the Mystery of Flight 54. Adler, David A. 64p. (gr. 2-5). 1992. pap. 3.99 (0-14-036104-9, Puffin) Puffin Bks.

—Cam Jansen & the Mystery of the Babe Ruth Baseball. Adler, David A. LC 82-2621. 64p. (gr. 2-5). 1982. pap. 11.00 (0-670-20037-9) Viking Child Bks.

—Cam Jansen & the Mystery of the Babe Ruth Baseball. Adler, David A. (gr. 1-4). 1984. pap. 2.75 (0-440-41020-7, YB) Dell.

—Cam Jansen & the Mystery of the Carnival Prize. Adler, David A. 64p. (gr. 2-5). 1992. pap. 3.99 (0-14-036022-0) Puffin Bks.

—Cam Jansen & the Mystery of the Chocolate Fudge Sale. Adler, David A. 64p. (gr. 2-5). 1993. reinforced bdg. 11.99 (0-670-84968-5) Viking Child Bks.

—Cam Jansen & the Mystery of the Circus Clown. Adler, David A. LC 82-50363. 64p. (gr. 2-4). 1983. pap. 10. 95 (0-670-20036-0) Viking Child Bks.

—Cam Jansen & the Mystery of the Circus Clown. Adler, David A. 64p. (gr. 1-4). 1985. pap. 2.75 (0-440-41021-5, YB) Dell.

—Cam Jansen & the Mystery of the Dinosaur Bones. Adler, David A. LC 80-25132. 64p. (gr. 2-5). 1981. pap. 11.99 (0-670-20040-9) Viking Child Bks.

—Cam Jansen & the Mystery of the Dinosaur Bones. Adler, David A. (gr. 1-4). 1983. pap. 2.75 (0-440-41199-8, YB) Dell.

—Cam Jansen & the Mystery of the Dinosaur Bones. Adler, David A. 64p. (gr. 2-5). 1991. pap. 3.99 (0-14-034674-0, Puffin) Puffin Bks.

—Cam Jansen & the Mystery of the Gold Coins. Adler, David A. LC 81-16158. 64p. (gr. 2-5). 1982. pap. 10. 95 (0-670-20038-7) Viking Child Bks.

—Cam Jansen & the Mystery of the Gold Coins. Adler, David A. 64p. (gr. k-6). 1984. pap. 2.75 (0-440-40996-9, YB) Dell.

—Cam Jansen & the Mystery of the Haunted House, No. 13. Adler, David A. 64p. (gr. 2-5). 1994. pap. 3.99 (0-14-034478-0) Puffin Bks.

—Cam Jansen & the Mystery of the Monster Movie. Adler, David A. 64p. (gr. 2-5). 1992. pap. 3.99 (0-14-036021-2) Puffin Bks.

—Cam Jansen & the Mystery of the Stolen Corn Popper. Adler, David A. 64p. (gr. 2-5). 1992. pap. 3.99 (0-14-036103-0, Puffin) Puffin Bks.

—Cam Jansen & the Mystery of the Stolen Diamonds. Adler, David A. LC 79-20695. 64p. (gr. 2-5). 1980. pap. 10.95 (0-670-20039-5) Viking Child Bks.

—Cam Jansen & the Mystery of the Stolen Diamonds. Adler, David A. (gr. 1-4). 1982. pap. 2.75 (0-440-41111-4, YB) Dell.

—Cam Jansen & the Mystery of the Stolen Diamonds. Adler, David A. 64p. (gr. 2-5). 1991. pap. 3.99 (0-14-034670-8, Puffin) Puffin Bks.

—Cam Jansen & the Mystery of the Television Dog. Adler, David A. LC 81-2207. 64p. (gr. 2-5). 1981. pap. 10.95 (0-670-20042-5) Viking Child Bks.

—Cam Jansen & the Mystery of the Television Dog. Adler, David A. (gr. 1-4). 1983. pap. 2.75 (0-440-41196-3, YB) Dell.

—Cam Jansen & the Mystery of the Television Dog. Adler, David A. 64p. (gr. 2-5). 1991. pap. 3.99 (0-14-034676-7, Puffin) Puffin Bks.

—Cam Jansen & the Mystery of the U. F. O. Adler, David A. LC 80-15580. 64p. (gr. 7-10). 1980. pap. 10. 95 (0-670-20041-7) Viking Child Bks.

—Cam Jansen & the Mystery of the U. F. O. Adler, David A. 64p. (gr. 2-5). 1991. pap. 3.99 (0-14-034672-4, Puffin) Puffin Bks.

—The Cam Jansen Fun Book. Adler, David A. 32p. (gr. 2-5). 1992. pap. 3.99 (0-14-034490-X, Puffin) Puffin Bks.

—Happy Birthday, Ronald Morgan! Giff, Patricia R. LC 85-32303. 32p. (ps-4). 1986. pap. 10.95 (0-670-80741-9) Viking Child Bks.

—Happy Birthday, Ronald Morgan! Giff, Patricia R. 32p. (Orig.). (ps-3). 1988. pap. 4.99 (0-14-050668-3, Puffin) Puffin Bks.

—Happy Birthday, Ronald Morgan. Giff, Patricia R. (gr. 2-4). 1989. bk. & cassette 19.95 (0-87499-122-6); bk. & cassette 12.95 (0-87499-121-8); 4 cassettes & guide 27.95 (0-87499-123-4) Live Oak Media.

—It's My Money: A Kid's Guide to the Green Stuff. Banks, Ann. 32p. (gr. 2-6). 1993. pap. 3.99 (0-14-036086-7, Puffin) Puffin Bks.

—It's My Money: A Kid's Guide to the Green Stuff. Banks, Ann. LC 93-12618. (gr. 3-7). 1993. 3.99 (0-670-36086-4) Puffin Bks.

—Lionel at Large. Krensky, Stephen. LC 85-1450. 56p. (ps-3). 1986. 9.95 (0-8037-0240-X) Dial Bks Young.

—Lionel at Large. Krensky, Stephen. LC 85-15930. 56p. (ps-3). 1988. pap. 4.95 (0-8037-0556-5) Dial Bks Young.

—Lionel at Large. Krensky, Stephen. (gr. 1-4). 1993. pap. 3.25 (0-14-036542-7, Puffin) Puffin Bks.

—Lionel in the Fall. Krensky, Stephen. LC 86-32876. 48p. (ps-3). 1987. 9.95 (0-8037-0384-8); PLB 9.89 (0-8037-0385-6) Dial Bks Young.

—Lionel in the Fall. Krensky, Stephen. (gr. 1-4). 1993. pap. 3.25 (0-14-036545-1, Puffin) Puffin Bks.

—Lionel in the Spring. Krensky, Stephen. LC 88-30885. 48p. (ps-3). 1992. pap. 3.99 (0-14-036117-0, Dial Easy to Read) Puffin Bks.

—Lionel in Winter. Krensky, Stephen. LC 92-36121. 1994. write for info. (0-8037-1333-9); PLB write for info. (0-8037-1334-7) Dial Bks Young.

—Puppy Love. Duffey, Betsy. LC 92-12705. 64p. (gr. 2-6). 1992. 13.00 (0-670-84346-6) Viking Child Bks.

—Ronald Morgan Goes to Bat. Giff, Patricia R. 32p. (gr. k-4). 1988. pap. 10.95 (0-670-81457-1) Viking Child Bks.

—Ronald Morgan Goes to Bat. Giff, Patricia R. 32p. (ps-3). 1990. pap. 3.99 (0-14-050669-1, Puffin) Puffin Bks.

—Throw-Away Pets. Duffey, Betsy. 80p. (gr. 2-6). 1993. 12.99 (0-670-84348-2) Viking Child Bks.

—Today Was a Terrible Day. Giff, Patricia R. 1980. 11. 95 (0-670-71830-0) Viking Child Bks.

—Today Was a Terrible Day. Giff, Patricia R. 32p. (ps-k). 1984. pap. 3.99 (0-14-050453-2) Viking Child Bks.

—Today Was a Terrible Day. Giff, Patricia R. 32p. (ps-k). 1984. pap. 3.95 incl. cassette (0-685-54175-4, Penguin Bks) Viking Penguin.

—Today Was a Terrible Day. Giff, Patricia R. 1993. pap. 6.99 incl. cassette (0-14-095119-9, Puffin) Puffin Bks.

—Watch Out, Ronald Morgan. Giff, Patricia R. LC 84-19623. 24p. (gr. k-3). 1985. pap. 10.95 (0-670-80433-9) Viking Child Bks.

—Watch Out, Ronald Morgan. Giff, Patricia R. 32p. (gr. k-4). 1986. pap. 4.99 (0-14-050638-1, Puffin) Puffin Bks.

—The Wild Things. Duffey, Betsy. LC 92-25938. 80p. (gr. 2-6). 1993. 12.99 (0-670-84347-4) Viking Child Bks.

Natti, Susanna, photos by. Catch the Baby! Kingman, Lee. LC 92-26588. 1993. pap. 4.99 (0-14-050762-0) Puffin Bks.

Natti, Sussanns. I Am Three. Fitzhugh, Louise. LC 81-15218. 48p. (ps). 1982. 8.95 (0-440-04035-3); PLB 8.89 (0-440-04039-6) Delacorte.

Natti, Suzanna. Today Was a Terrible Day. Giff, Patricia R. (gr. k-3). 1984. incl. cassette 19.95 (0-941078-50-7); pap. 12.95 incl. cassette (0-941078-48-5); pap. 27.95 4 bks, cassette, & guide (0-941078-49-3); sound fimlstrip 22.95 (0-941078-47-7) Live Oak Media.

Nau, Pat, photos by. State Patrol. Nau, Patrick. LC 83-2716. 32p. (gr. k-4). 1984. PLB 13.50 (0-87614-264-1) Carolrhoda Bks.

Naumenko, Maria. The Life of Saint Seraphim Wonderworkerof Sarov. Naumenko, Maria. 22p. (Orig.). (gr. 5-10). 1992. pap. 3.00 (0-88465-049-9) Holy Trinity.

—The Life of Saint Seraphim Wonderworkerof Sarov: (Zhitie Prepodobnovo Serpahima, Sarovskovo Chudotvortsa) Naumenko, Maria. (RUS.). 22p. (Orig.). (gr. 5-10). 1992. pap. 3.00 (0-88465-052-9) Holy Trinity.

Naylor, Raymon. Hunting the Hard Way. Hill, Howard. St. Charles, Glenn, frwd. by. 318p. (gr. 10 up). 1993. Repr. of 1953 ed. 39.95 (1-56416-095-5) Derrydale Pr.

Nazar, Steve. The Instant Bulletin Board Book: December Holidays. Sevaly, Karen & Sevaly, Richard. 96p. (Orig.). (gr. 2-6). 1993. pap. 9.95 tchr's. ed. (0-943263-36-0, TF1904) Teachers Friend Pubns.

—The Instant Bulletin Board Book: Winter Playtime. Sevaly, Karen & Sevaly, Richard. 96p. (Orig.). (gr. 2-6). 1993. pap. 9.95 tchr's. ed. (0-943263-37-9, TF1905) Teachers Friend Pubns.

Neal, Jo A. The Real Texas Coloring Book: (For "Real" Texans) Roberts, Pamela J. 38p. (ps-3). 1992. pap. 3.95 (1-881345-00-9) Penzance Co.

Neary, Bryan. The Turbulent Triangle. Bradley, Susannah. 48p. (gr. 3-6). 1992. pap. 2.95 (1-56680-001-3) Mad Hatter Pub.

Neary, D., jt. illus. see Conkle, Nancy.

Neavill, Michelle. How Wise Is an Owl? The Strange Things People Say about Animals in the Woods. Dennard, Deborah. LC 92-10354. 1992. 19.95 (0-87614-721-X) Carolrhoda Bks.

—**Pink Stars & Angel Wings. Ekberg, Susan. LC 91-91216. 32p. (ps up). 1992. 16.95 (0-9630419-0-8) Spiritseeker. "Wish, whoosh, Kari swooshed through the window..." Kari's magical journey to her special star reveals much about herself & the world. Through a delightful tale of faith & love, we share Kari's adventure, her hopes & joy as she learns that she will never be alone in this big world -- we all have someone protecting us, watching us, & loving us. This is a story for children of all ages, about peace found through self-awareness & trust in the universe. This book focuses on children's spirituality, & deals with issues about God, guardian angels, our inner voice, & believing in things we can't always see with our eyes. "The gentle guidance & reassurance that Kate gives Kari is so healing & nurturing to a child's** questioning mind...this story is a delightful trail to the heart...it is indeed a journey to one's inner voice of love & self-acceptance...so needed in these days of rapid change & growth..." Illustrated by Michelle Neavill. Published by: Spiritseeker Publishing, Inc. PO Box 2441, Fargo, ND, 58108-2441; 1-800-538-6415. T-shirts, posters, buttons & stickers also available. Call or write for brochure. *Publisher Provided Annotation.*

Neaville, Michelle. Places to Sleep. Collins, Nancy. LC 92-14392. 32p. (ps-2). Date not set. 11.95 (1-56065-165-2) Capstone Pr. Postponed.
Nebeker, Kinde. My Birthday Memories. Green, Laurel & Beck, Trudy. (ps-12). 1985. 5.00 (0-9613079-1-9) Greenbeck.
Nebel, Gustave E. The Old Witch Goes to the Ball. DeLage, Ida. 48p. (gr. k-4). 1991. Repr. of 1969 ed. lib. bdg. 12.95 (0-7910-1483-5) Chelsea Hse.
Nebres, Rudy. Black Beauty. new ed. Sewell, Anna. Farr, Naunerle, ed. LC 59-12495. 64p. (Orig.). (gr. 5-10). 1973. pap. 2.95 (0-88301-094-1) Pendulum Pr.
Nechodom, Kerry. The Rainbow Bridge: A Chumash Legend. Nechodom, Kerry, adapted by. 32p. (Orig.). (gr. k-3). 1992. pap. 6.95 (0-944627-36-6) Sand River Pr.
Nedobeck, Don. Nedobecks Twelve Days of Christmas. (gr. 1-8). 1988. Repr. lib. bdg. 9.95 (0-944314-02-3) New Wrinkle.
—Your Uvula Is Showing: Names to Call Your Sister or Brother. Carlson, Lisa. (Orig.). (gr. 3 up). Date not set. pap. write for info. (0-942679-11-3) Upper Access.
Needham, James. Black Beauty. Sewell, Anna. 220p. 1992. 24.95 (0-88363-200-4) H L Levin.
—Peter Set Free. Truitt, Gloria. 24p. (gr. k-4). 1991. pap. 1.89 (0-570-09027-X) Concordia.
—Zwort's Nature Report: Forest Trail. Pitts, Paul. 36p. (ps-4). 1991. pap. 4.95 incl. audiocassette (1-55999-152-6) LinguiSystems.
—Zwort's Nature Report: Ocean Dive. Pitts, Paul. 36p. (ps-4). 1991. pap. 4.95 incl. audiocassette (1-55999-153-4) LinguiSystems.
—Zwort's Nature Report: Safari Adventure. Pitts, Paul. 36p.(ps-4). 1991. pap. 4.95 incl. audiocassette (1-55999-154-2) LinguiSystems.
Needler, Jerry. The Blue Caboose. Hamilton, Dorothy. LC 72-5474. 135p. (gr. 3-6). 1973. pap. 3.95 (0-8361-1696-8) Herald Pr.
Neel, Jennifer & Williams, Roger. The Magic Hole in the Sky. Derman, Karen. 48p. (Orig.). 1992. pap. 14. 95 (0-9630026-0-0) Childlight Pr.
Neely, Heather. Six Silly Puppet Plays, Vol. I. Mister Tom. Neely, David, ed. LC 89-50784. 44p. (Orig.). (gr. 4-6). 1989. spiral bdg. 6.95 (0-925237-05-1) Ten Pubns.
—Six Silly Puppet Plays, Vol. 2. Mister Tom. Neely, David, ed. 32p. (Orig.). (gr. k-3). 1989. pap. 6.95 spiral bdg. (0-925237-06-X) Ten Pubns.
Neely, Keith. The Story of the Erie Canal. Stein, R. Conrad. LC 84-28525. 32p. (gr. 3-6). 1985. PLB 13.27 (0-516-04682-9); pap. 3.95 (0-516-44682-7) Childrens.
—The Story of the Powers of Congress. Stein, R. Conrad. LC 85-10943. 32p. (gr. 3-6). 1985. PLB 13.27 (0-516-04695-0); pap. 3.95 (0-516-44695-9) Childrens.
Neely, Keith R. Peace Be with You. Lehn, Cornelia. Regier, Harold R. & Schwartzentruber, Hubertintro. by. LC 80-70190. 126p. (gr. k-5). 1981. 12.95 (0-87303-061-3) Faith & Life.
Neeper, William. Good Morning, Sun. McPartland, Suzy. 12p. (ps-k). 1994. bds. 4.95 (0-689-71747-4, Aladdin) Macmillan Child Grp.
—Sleepy-Time Moon. McPartland, Suzy. 12p. (ps-k). 1994. bds. 4.95 (0-689-71748-2, Aladdin) Macmillan Child Grp.
—Toy-Shop Surprise. McPartland, Suzy. 12p. (ps-k). 1994. bds. 4.95 (0-689-71749-0, Aladdin) Macmillan Child Grp.
—Zoom, Car, Zoom. McPartland, Suzy. 12p. (ps-k). 1994. bds. 4.95 (0-689-71750-4, Aladdin) Macmillan Child Grp.
Neeves, D'Reen. God Cares for Me. 12p. (ps-2). 1991. bds. 6.99 (0-7459-2059-4) Lion USA.
—God Cares for the Earth. 12p. (ps-2). 1991. bds. 6.99 (0-7459-2060-8) Lion USA.
Negri, Rocco. Journey Outside. Steele, Mary Q. (gr. 3-7). 1979. pap. 3.95 (0-14-030588-2, Puffin) Puffin Bks.
—The One Bad Thing about Father. Monjo, F. N. LC 71-85036. 64p. (gr. k-3). 1987. pap. 3.50 (0-06-444110-5, Trophy) HarpC Child Bks.
—Renfroe's Christmas: A Novel by Robert Burch. Burch, Robert. LC 92-44773. 56p. (gr. 4-6). 1993. Repr. of 1971 ed. 14.95 (0-8203-1553-2) U of Ga Pr.
—Trouble River. Byars, Betsy. (gr. 3-7). 1969. pap. 13. 95 (0-670-73257-5) Viking Child Bks.
—Trouble River. Byars, Betsy C. 160p. (gr. 3-7). 1989. pap. 3.99 (0-14-034243-5, Puffin) Puffin Bks.
Negrini, Wendy. Eeeeaaassy Party Planning. Jackson, Sonia. 80p. 1988. pap. 6.95 (0-9619056-0-3) Entrtnmnt Enter.

Negron, Bill. The Cardinal's Snuffbox. Roseman, Kenneth. 128p. (gr. 4-6). 1982. pap. text ed. 7.95 (0-8074-0059-9, 140060) UAHC.
Neidigh, Sherry. Creatures at My Feet. Davis, Charles E. LC 92-81235. 32p. (ps). 1993. 14.95 (0-87358-560-7) Northland AZ.
—The Floor That Said "No More" Timm, Stephen A. LC 86-60276. 48p. 1986. pap. 5.95 (0-939728-12-5) Steppingstone Ent.
—Huckleberry Finn. Twain, Mark. Stewart, Diana, adapted by. LC 79-24312. 48p. (gr. 4 up). 1983. PLB 18.64 (0-8172-1651-0) Raintree Steck-V.
—Shalom at Last. Dyck, Peter J. 128p. (Orig.). 1992. pap. 5.95 (0-8361-3615-2) Herald Pr.
—Top Hog. Rutman, Shereen. 16p. (ps). 1993. wkbk. 2.25 (1-56293-322-1) McClanahan Bk.
Neill, Eileen M. Out the Door. Matthias, Catherine. LC 81-17060. 32p. (ps-2). 1982. PLB 11.93 (0-516-03560-6); pap. 2.95 (0-516-43560-4) Childrens.
—Sal y Entra (Out the Door) Matthias, Catherine. LC 81-17060. (SPA.). 32p. (ps-2). 1989. PLB 11.93 (0-516-33560-X); pap. 2.95 (0-516-53560-9) Childrens.
Neill, Eileen M., jt. illus. see Deal, L. Kate.
Neill, John R. Dorothy & the Wizard in Oz. Baum, L. Frank. 256p. (gr. 5-10). 1984. pap. 5.95 (0-486-24714-7) Dover.
—Dorothy & the Wizard in Oz. facsimile ed. Baum, L. Frank. Glassman, Peter, afterword by. LC 90-592. 272p. (ps up). 1990. Repr. 19.95g (0-688-09826-6) Morrow Jr Bks.
—The Emerald City of Oz. Baum, L. Frank. Glassman, Peter, afterword by. LC 92-61765. 304p. 1993. 20.00 (0-688-11558-6) Morrow Jr Bks.
—Marvelous Land of Oz. Baum, L. Frank. Gardner, M., intro. by. xvii, 287p. (gr. 4-6). 1969. pap. 5.95 (0-486-20692-0) Dover.
—The Marvelous Land of Oz. Baum, L. Frank. LC 85-4856. 288p. (gr. 4-6). 1985. 15.00 (0-688-05439-0) Morrow Jr Bks.
—Ozma of Oz. Baum, L. Frank. LC 88-63291. 288p. 1989. 19.95 (0-688-06632-1) Morrow Jr Bks.
—The Road to Oz. Baum, L. Frank. Glassman, Peter, afterword by. LC 90-48349. 272p. 1991. Repr. of 1909 ed. 16.95 (0-688-09997-1) Morrow Jr Bks.
—The Scalawagons in Oz. Neill, John R. 309p. (gr. 3 up). 1991. 24.95 (0-929605-12-8) Books Wonder.
—The Sea Fairies. Baum, L. Frank. 240p. 1987. 19.95 (0-929605-03-9); pap. 11.95 (0-929605-00-4) Books Wonder.
—Sky Island. Baum, L. Frank. 288p. (gr. 3 up). 1988. 19. 95 (0-929605-02-0); pap. 11.95 (0-929605-01-2) Books Wonder.
—The Wonder City of Oz. Neill, John R. 318p. (gr. 2 up). 1990. text ed. 24.95 (0-929605-07-1) Books Wonder.
Neilson, Gena. Dinosaurs. (ps-1). 1986. spiral bdg. 9.95 (0-937763-00-4) Lauri Inc.
—It's Your Birthday. (ps-1). 1986. spiral bdg. 9.95 (0-937763-03-9) Lauri Inc.
—Noah's Ark. (ps-1). 1986. spiral bdg. 9.95 (0-937763-01-2) Lauri Inc.
Neilson, Harry B., et al. A. B. C. of Fashionable Animals. Poltarnees, Welleran, et al, eds. 64p. 1991. 12.95 (0-88138-122-5, Green Tiger) S&S Trade.
Neis, Kevin A. From Sorceress to Scientist: Biographies of Women Physical Scientists. Nies, Kevin A. 95p. (Orig.). (gr. 8 up). 1991. 30.00 (1-880211-00-9); pap. 14.99 (1-880211-01-7); tchr's. ed. 14.99 (1-880211-02-5) Calif Video.
Nellist, Cassandra L. Child's First Book about Hawaii. Nellist, Cassandra L. 24p. (ps). 1987. 7.95 (0-916630-58-7) Pr Pacifica.
Nelsen, Jeffrey S. The Case of the Anteater's Missing Lunch. Binnamin, Vivian. Brook, Bonnie, ed. 32p. (gr. k-3). 1990. PLB 6.98 (0-671-68816-2); pap. 2.95 (0-671-68820-0) Silver Pr.
—The Case of the Mysterious Mermaid. Binnamin, Vivian. Brook, Bonnie, ed. 32p. (gr. k-3). 1990. PLB 6.98 (0-671-68817-0); pap. 2.95 (0-671-68821-9) Silver Pr.
—The Case of the Planetarium Puzzle. Binnamin, Vivian. Brook, Bonnie, ed. 32p. (gr. k-3). 1990. PLB 6.98 (0-671-68819-7); pap. 2.95 (0-671-68823-5) Silver Pr.
—The Case of the Snoring Stegosaurus. Binnamin, Vivian. Brook, Bonnie, ed. 32p. (gr. k-3). 1990. PLB 6.98 (0-671-68818-9); pap. 2.95 (0-671-68822-7) Silver Pr.
—Field Trip Mysteries Series, 4 vols. Binnamin, Vivian. 128p. (gr. k-3). 1990. Set. PLB 27.92 (0-671-94436-3) Set. pap. 11.80 (0-671-94437-1) Silver Pr.
Nelson, Andy. The Impressionists Coloring Book. Nelson, Andy. 96p. (Orig.). (gr. 1-6). 1990. pap. 5.95 (0-929636-06-6) Culpepper Pr.
Nelson, Anita. Loon & Deer Were Traveling: A Story of the Upper Skagit. Hilbert, Vi, as told by. LC 92-5450. 24p. (ps-3). 1992. PLB 16.93 (0-516-05140-7); pap. 5.95 (0-516-45140-5) Childrens.
—Spanish Memory Book: A New Approach to Vocabulary Building. Harrison, William F. & Welker, Dorothy W. LC 93-12717. 96p. (Orig.). (gr. 7-12). 1993. text ed. 22.50x (0-292-73079-9); pap. 8.95 (0-292-73081-0) U of Tex Pr.
Nelson, Anita, jt. illus. see Schoonover, Pat.
Nelson, Anita, jt. illus. see Schoonover, pat.
Nelson, Anita, jt. illus. see Schoonover, Pat.
Nelson, Anita, jt. illus. see Thiewes, Sam.
Nelson, Donna. The Bible Is for Me. Tangvald, Christine H. 24p. (ps-1). 1988. pap. 3.49 (1-55513-706-7, Chariot Bks) Cook.

—Christmas Is for Me. Tangvald, Christine H. 24p. (ps-1). 1988. pap. 3.49 (1-55513-705-9, Chariot Bks) Cook.
Nelson, Donna K. The One & Only Delgado Cheese: A Tale of Talent, Fame, & Friendship. Hartman, Bob. LC 92-29059. 40p. (gr. k-3). 1993. 13.95 (0-7459-2405-0) Lion USA.
Nelson, Eloise, jt. illus. see Twede, Evan.
Nelson, Gladys T. War Drums at Eden Prairie. Nelson, Gladys T. (gr. 5-9). 1977. 5.95 (0-87839-023-5) North Star.
Nelson, Jane. Everybody, Shout Hallelujah! Murphy, Elspeth C. LC 81-65525. 24p. (ps-2). 1981. pap. 2.99 (0-89191-369-6, 53694, Chariot Bks) Cook.
—I'm Listening, God. Murphy, Elspeth C. LC 81-71813. (ps-2). 1983. misc. format 2.99 (0-89191-583-4, Chariot Bks) Cook.
—It's My Birthday, God: Psalm 90. Murphy, Elspeth C. (ps-2). 1983. misc. format 2.99 (0-89191-580-X, Chariot Bks) Cook.
—Make Way for the King: Psalm 145 & 24. Murphy, Elspeth C. (ps-2). 1983. 2.99 (0-89191-581-8, Chariot Bks) Cook.
—Sometimes I Get Lonely. Murphy, Elspeth C. LC 80-70251. 24p. (ps-2). 1981. pap. 2.99 (0-89191-367-X, 53678, Chariot Bks) Cook.
—Sometimes I Have to Cry. Murphy, Elspeth C. (ps-2). 1981. pap. 2.99 (0-89191-494-3, 54940, Chariot Bks) Cook.
—Sometimes I'm Good, Sometimes I'm Bad. Murphy, Elspeth C. 24p. (ps-2). 1981. pap. 2.99 (0-89191-368-8, 53686, Chariot Bks) Cook.
Nelson, Jane E. The Barefoot Ballerina. Heinzerling, Doris M. 24p. (gr. k-1). 1993. write for info. (1-879094-40-1) Avonstoke Pr.
—Sometimes I Get Scared. Murphy, Elspeth C. (ps-2). 1980. pap. 2.99 (0-89191-275-4, 52753, Chariot Bks) Cook.
—What Can I Say to You, God? Murphy, Elspeth C. (ps-2). 1980. pap. 2.99 (0-89191-276-2, Chariot Bks) Cook.
—Where Are You, God? Murphy, Elspeth C. (ps-2). 1980. pap. 2.99 (0-89191-274-6, Chariot Bks) Cook.
Nelson, Jeffrey S. Animal Jokes & Riddles. Nelson, Jeffrey S. LC 90-27676. 24p. (gr. 3 up). 1991. pap. 1.95 (1-56288-016-0) Checkerboard.
—Family Jokes & Riddles. Nelson, Jeffrey S. 24p. (gr. 3 up). 1991. pap. 1.95 (1-56288-015-2) Checkerboard.
—Jungle Jokes & Riddles. Nelson, Jeffrey S. 24p. (gr. 3 up). 1991. pap. 1.95 (1-56288-017-9) Checkerboard.
—Yucky Jokes & Riddles. Nelson, Jeffrey S. 24p. (gr. 3 up). 1991. pap. 1.95 (1-56288-014-4) Checkerboard.
Nelson, Jennie A. Pieces of Eight. Engler, Johnson, Charles. 110p. (gr. 3-6). 1989. 9.95 (0-944770-00-2) Discovery GA.
Nelson, Jim & Biske, Joel. Virtual Realities: A Shadowrun Sourcebook. Dowd, Tom & Kubasik, Chris. Ippolito, Donna & Mulvihill, Sharon T., eds. 160p. (gr. 7 up). 1991. pap. 15.00 (1-55560-144-8, 7107) FASA Corp.
Nelson, Jim, jt. illus. see Knutson, Dana.
Nelson, John. Christopher Columbus, Who Sailed on! Richards, Dorothy F. LC 78-7664. (gr. k-4). 1978. PLB 19.95 (0-89565-032-0); PLB 13.95s.p. (0-685-55476-7) Childs World.
—George Washington, a Talk with His Grandchildren. Richards, Dorothy F. LC 78-8564. (gr. k-4). 1978. PLB 19.95 (0-89565-034-7); PLB 13.95s.p. (0-685-55482-1) Childs World.
—Pocahontas, Child-Princess. Richards, Dorothy F. LC 78-7719. (gr. k-4). 1978. PLB 19.95 (0-89565-035-5); PLB 13.95s.p. (0-685-57685-X) Childs World.
Nelson, Kelly, jt. illus. see Price, Susan.
Nelson, Linda K. Teddy Bear's Easter Picnic. Wolf, Jill. 24p. (gr. 3-7). 1985. pap. 2.50 (0-89549-424-X) Antioch Pub Co.
Nelson, Lois, jt. illus. see Eichorn, Chris.
Nelson, Mary F. Sexual Abuse! What Is It? An Informational Book for the Hearing Impaired. LaBarre, Alice, et al. LC 92-80161. 80p. (gr. 1-6). 1992. pap. 9.00 (0-9629302-1-0) Liberty.
Nelson, Mike. The Kid's Cookbook. rev. ed. Barrett-Dragan, Patricia & Dalton, Rosemary. 192p. (gr. 2-8). 1992. pap. 8.95 (1-55867-043-2, Nitty Gritty Ckbks) Bristol Pub Ent CA.
Nelson, Ray, Jr. & Kelly, Douglas. Greetings from America: Postcards from Donovan Willoughby. Nelson, Ray, Jr. LC 92-14819. 48p. (gr. k-4). 1992. 12. 95 (0-89802-590-7) Beautiful Am.

Nelson, Scott. Winning Checkers for Kids of All Ages. Pike, Robert W. 64p. (Orig.). (gr. 3-8). 1992. pap. 9.95 (0-9635300-0-3) C&M Pub MA. WINNING CHECKERS FOR KIDS OF ALL AGES is the ONLY available primer written for children on this subject. Well illustrated with cartoon characters & checkerboard graphics, WINNING CHECKERS FOR KIDS OF ALL AGES is a "straightforward" easily digested guide that explains the basic rules of the game & offers strategies for competitive play."--The Landmark Press, Holden, Massachusetts. Tactics that give the reader an edge are described & reinforced with clear annotated checkerboard illustrations. The player learns how to control the center of the board, protect the back row & spot enough double & triple opportunities to crown more than their fair share of Kings. Children can clip out a numbered checkerboard on the last page & use pennies & dimes as checkers pieces if they don't have their own game set. "With so many requests, the absence of any substantive material on this most popular of lifetime board games for children has always been frustrating. Well written & engagingly illustrated, WINNING CHECKERS FOR CHILDREN OF ALL AGES fills a definite void in a most enjoyable & easy to follow way - our kids love it."--Jane Dutton, Children's Librarian, Holden, Massachusetts. *Publisher Provided Annotation.*

Nelson, Trish. A Stress Management Guide for Young People. 6th ed. Youngs, Bettie B. 88p. (gr. 6-12). 1986. pap. text ed. 9.95x (*0-940221-00-4*) Lrng Tools-Bilicki Pubns.
Nenninger, J. D. Rufus. Montgomery, Rutherford G. LC 78-150819. (Orig.). (gr. 4-8). 1973. 4.95 (*0-87004-227-0*) Caxton.
Nenninger, Jerome D. Pekan the Shadow. Montgomery, Rutherford G. LC 78-84779. (gr. 8-12). 1970. 3.95 (*0-87004-132-0*) Caxton.
Neri, Susan. Gold! Gold! A Beginner's Handbook & Recreational Guide: How & Where to Prospect for Gold. 5th, rev. ed. Petralia, Joseph F. Applegate, Jill, ed. LC 81-126200. 144p. 1992. pap. 9.95 (*0-9605890-5-8*, AB92) Sierra Trading.
Nerlove, Meriam. Thanksgiving. Nerlove, Miriam. Mathews, Judith, ed. LC 89-49363. 24p. (ps-1). 1990. PLB 11.95 (*0-8075-7818-5*) A Whitman.
Nerlove, Miriam. Christmas. Nerlove, Miriam. Tucker, Kathy, ed. LC 89-70737. 24p. (ps-1). 1990. 11.95 (*0-8075-1148-X*) A Whitman.
—Easter. Nerlove, Miriam. Mathews, Judith, ed. LC 89-35394. 24p. (ps-1). 1989. 11.95 (*0-8075-1871-9*); pap. 4.95 (*0-8075-1872-7*) A Whitman.
—Halloween. Nerlove, Miriam. Levine, Abby, ed. LC 88-36858. 24p. (ps-1). 1989. PLB 11.95 (*0-8075-3131-6*); pap. 4.95 (*0-8075-3130-8*) A Whitman.
—Hanukkah. Nerlove, Miriam. Levine, Abby, ed. LC 88-36648. 24p. (ps-1). 1989. PLB 11.95 (*0-8075-3143-X*); pap. 4.95 (*0-8075-3142-1*) A Whitman.
—I Can! Can You? rev. ed. Adorjan, Carol. Levine, Abby, ed. LC 90-37665. 24p. (ps). 1990. 11.95 (*0-8075-3491-9*) A Whitman.
—I Made a Mistake. Nerlove, Miriam. LC 85-6018. 32p. (ps-2). 1985. SBE 13.95 (*0-689-50327-X*, M K McElderry) Macmillan Child Grp.
—If All the World Were Paper. Nerlove, Miriam. Tucker, Kathy, ed. LC 90-39217. 32p. (gr. k-3). 1991. 13.95 (*0-8075-3535-4*) A Whitman.
—Just One Tooth. Nerlove, Miriam. LC 88-19488. 32p. (ps-3). 1989. SBE 13.95 (*0-689-50465-9*, M K McElderry) Macmillan Child Grp.
—Passover. Nerlove, Miriam. Levine, Abby, ed. LC 89-35393. 24p. (ps-1). 1989. 11.95 (*0-8075-6360-9*); pap. 4.95 (*0-8075-6361-7*) A Whitman.
—Purim. Nerlove, Miriam. Levine, Abby, ed. LC 91-19516. 24p. (ps-1). 1992. PLB 11.95 (*0-8075-6682-9*) A Whitman.
—Valentine's Day. Nerlove, Miriam. Mathews, Judith, ed. LC 91-19289. 24p. (ps-1). 1992. PLB 11.95 (*0-8075-8454-1*) A Whitman.
—Why Does It Always Rain on Sukkot? Youdovin, Susan S. Levine, Abby, ed. LC 90-11923. 32p. (ps-3). 1990. PLB 13.95 (*0-8075-9079-7*) A Whitman.
Nerlove, Miriam & Pape, Richard. Noise in the Night: Reading Workbook. Witty, Bruce & Gregorich, Barbara. Hoffman, Joan, ed. 32p. (Orig.). (gr. k-2). 1988. 1.99 (*0-88743-106-2*) Sch Zone Pub Co.
Nesbitt, Jan. The Serpent Shell. Greaves, Margaret. 32p. (ps-3). 1993. 13.95 (*0-8120-6350-3*) Barron.
—A Tall Story & Other Tales. Mahy, Margaret. LC 91-62222. 96p. (gr. 3-7). 1992. SBE 15.95 (*0-689-50547-7*, M K McElderry) Macmillan Child Grp.
—Trouble at Mrs. Portwine's. Wood, John. 96p. (gr. 5-9). 1990. 14.95x (*0-86327-147-2*, Pub. by Wolfhound Pr EIRE); pap. 8.95 (*0-86327-148-0*, Pub. by Wolfhound Pr EIRE) Dufour.
Ness, Evaline. The Hand-Me-Down Doll. Kroll, Steven. LC 83-4394. 32p. (ps-3). 1983. reinforced bdg. 12.95 (*0-8234-0495-1*) Holiday.

—A Pocketful of Cricket. Caudill, Rebecca. LC 64-12617. 48p. (gr. k-2). 1964. reinforced bdg. 7.95 (*0-03-089752-1*, Bks Young Read); pap. 5.95 (*0-8050-1275-3*) H Holt & Co.
—Sam, Bangs & Moonshine. Ness, Evaline. LC 66-10113. 48p. (ps-2). 1966. 14.95 (*0-8050-0314-2*, Bks Young Read); pap. 5.95 (*0-8050-0315-0*) H Holt & Co.
—The Sherwood Ring. Pope, Elizabeth M. 272p. (gr. 7 up). 1992. pap. 3.99 (*0-14-034911-1*, Puffin) Puffin Bks.
—Some of the Days of Everett Anderson. Clifton, Lucille. LC 78-98922. 32p. (ps-2). 1988. 13.95 (*0-8050-0290-1*, Bks Young Read) H Holt & Co.
Netherton, John, jt. photog. see Baker, Howard.
Nethery, Susan. Christmas KidDoodles, Bk. 3. Tuchman, Gail. 64p. (Orig.). (ps-2). 1991. pap. 0.99 activity pad (*1-56293-155-5*) McClanahan Bk.
—KidDoodles, Bk. 4. Wise, Beth A. 64p. (Orig.). (ps-2). 1991. pap. 0.99 activity pad (*1-878624-53-9*) McClanahan Bk.
Neuhaus, David. Focus on Alcohol. O'Neill, Catherine. 56p. (gr. 2-4). 1990. PLB 14.95 (*0-941477-96-7*) TFC Bks NY.
Neubacher, Gerda. Tales from the Beechy Woods: Fluff's Birthday. Neubacher, Gerda. 32p. (ps-k). 1983. 10.95 (*0-88625-044-7*) Durkin Hayes Pub.
—Tales of the Amazon. Elbl, Martin. 32p. (gr. k-3). 1985. 10.95 (*0-88625-127-3*) Durkin Hayes Pub.
Neugebauer, Michael. The Chimpanzee Family Book. Goodall, Jane. LC 88-33359. 72p. (ps up). 1991. pap. 17.95 (*0-88708-090-1*) Picture Bk Studio.
Neuhaus, David. Alerta a la Marihuana: Focus on Marijuana. Zeller, Paula K. (SPA.). 56p. (gr. 3-7). 1991. PLB 21.27 (*0-516-37354-4*) Childrens.
—Focus on Cocaine & Crack. Shulman, Jeffrey. 56p. (gr. 2-4). 1990. PLB 14.95 (*0-941477-98-3*) TFC Bks NY.
—Focus on Drugs & the Brain. Friedman, David. 64p. (gr. 2-4). 1990. PLB 14.95 (*0-941477-95-9*) TFC Bks NY.
—I Can Save the Earth: A Kid's Handbook for Keeping Earth Healthy & Green. Holmes, Anita. LC 91-30611. 96p. (gr. 2-5). 1993. lib. bdg. 13.98 (*0-671-74544-1*, J Messner); lib. bdg. 7.95 (*0-671-74545-X*, J Messner) S&S Trade.
Neuhaus, Roy. My Dad's Definitely Not a Drunk! Carbone, Elisa L. Weber, Susan B., ed. LC 92-53883. 116p. (Orig.). (gr. 4-9). 1992. text ed. 11.95 (*0-914525-21-2*); pap. text ed. 7.95 (*0-914525-22-0*) Waterfront Bks.
Neuhouse, David. The Halloween Grab Bag: A Book of Tricks & Treats. Wolff, Ferida & Kozielski, Dolores. 96p. (gr. 2-5). 1993. pap. 5.95 (*0-06-446148-3*, Trophy) HarpC Child Bks.
Neulinger, Karen. The Little Bird. Sobel, Barbara. LC 86-81462. 32p. (gr. k-2). 1986. PLB 7.59 (*0-87386-018-7*); pap. 1.95 (*0-87386-014-4*) Jan Prods.
Neumann, Ann. Smell, the Subtle Sense. Silverstein, Alvin, et al. LC 91-21745. 96p. (gr. 3 up). 1992. 14.00 (*0-688-09396-5*); PLB 13.93 (*0-688-09397-3*) Morrow Jr Bks.
Neumeier, Marty. An Occurrence at Owl Creek Bridge. Bierce, Ambrose. 40p. (gr. 6 up). 1980. PLB 13.95.s.p. (*0-87191-770-X*) Creative Ed.
—To Build a Fire. London, Jack. 48p. (gr. 6 up). 1980. PLB 13.95.s.p. (*0-87191-769-6*) Creative Ed.
Neumeier, Marty & Glaser, Byron. Action Alphabet. Neumeier, Marty & Glaser, Byron. LC 84-25322. 56p. (ps-1). 1985. 14.00 (*0-688-05703-9*); lib. bdg. 13.93 (*0-688-05704-7*) Greenwillow.
Neville, Vera. Betsy & Joe. Lovelace, Maud H. LC 48-8096. 256p. (gr. 5 up). 1948. 14.95 (*0-690-13378-2*, Crowell Jr Bks) HarpC Child Bks.
—Betsy in Spite of Herself. Lovelace, Maud H. LC 46-11995. 272p. (gr. 4-7). 1980. pap. 3.95 (*0-06-440111-1*, Trophy) HarpC Child Bks.
—Betsy Was a Junior. Lovelace, Maud H. LC 46-11995. 248p. (gr. 5 up). 1947. 14.95 (*0-690-13946-2*, Crowell Jr Bks) HarpC Child Bks.
—Betsy's Wedding. Lovelace, Maud H. LC 55-11108. 241p. (gr. 5 up). 1955. 14.95 (*0-690-13733-8*, Crowell Jr Bks) HarpC Child Bks.
—Heaven to Betsy. Lovelace, Maud H. LC 45-9806. 268p. (gr. 4-7). 1980. pap. 3.50 (*0-06-440110-3*, Trophy) HarpC Child Bks.
Nevins, Dan. Silly Goofy Jokes. Perkins, Gary. LC 92-20779. 64p. (gr. 2-6). 1992. pap. text ed. 1.50 (*0-8167-2965-4*, Pub. by Watermill Pr) Troll Assocs.
—Silly Haunted Jokes. Perkins, Gary. LC 92-20760. 64p. (gr. 2-6). 1992. pap. text ed. 1.50 (*0-8167-2963-8*, Pub. by Watermill Pr) Troll Assocs.
—Silly School Jokes. Perkins, Gary. LC 92-20437. 64p. (gr. 2-6). 1992. pap. text ed. 1.50 (*0-8167-2964-6*, Pub. by Watermill Pr) Troll Assocs.
New, Dwight. The College Matchmaker. Blaker, Charles W. LC 80-67604. 56p. (Orig.). (gr. 11-12). 1980. pap. text ed. 3.50 (*0-9604614-0-X*) Rekalb Pr.
New England Aquarium Staff, photos by. Dive to the Coral Reefs. New England Aquarium Staff. LC 86-4565. 36p. (gr. k up). 1990. pap. 4.95 (*0-517-58210-4*) Crown Bks Yng Read.
New South Press Staff. Poetry of Love: Baby Boomers. Carey, Becca. 72p. (Orig.). (gr. 6 up). 1987. pap. 5.95 (*0-9617859-0-X*) Careys Pub Co.
New Vrindaban Community Artists. Lila in the Land of Illusion: A Re-Telling of Lewis Carroll's Alice in Wonderland. Bhaktipada, Swami. LC 87-18626. 127p. (gr. 3-8). 1987. 12.95 (*0-932215-22-X*); pap. text ed. 7.95 (*0-932215-19-X*) Palace Pub.

Newberry, Clare T. April's Kittens. Newberry, Clare T. LC 40-32442. 32p. (gr. 1). 1940. 17.00 (*0-06-024400-3*); PLB 16.89 (*0-06-024401-1*) HarpC Child Bks.
Newcomer, Carolyn. Murphy Wants to Be Famous. Hasty, Kathy N. 27p. (Orig.). (ps-2). 1991. pap. 3.99 (*0-9631480-0-1*) Story Time Pubns.
Newell, Peter. The Rocket Book. Newell, Peter. LC 69-12080. 52p. (gr. k-4). 1969. Repr. of 1912 ed. 14.95 (*0-8048-0505-9*) C E Tuttle.
—The Slant Book. Newell, Peter. LC 67-12304. 50p. (gr. k-4). 1967. Repr. of 1910 ed. 16.95 (*0-8048-0532-6*) C E Tuttle.
Newhouse, Dora. Homonyms Plus. (gr. 6-12). 1979. wkbk 6.95 (*0-918050-41-3*); tchr's guide 6.95 (*0-918050-43-X*); activity cards 4.95 (*0-918050-44-8*) Newhouse Pr.
Newlin, Lana S. Surviving Sixth Grade. Newlin, Lana S. Morey, Cathy, ed. 90p. (gr. 5-7). 1990. 16.95 (*0-9625413-0-3*); pap. 9.95 (*0-9625413-1-1*) Christmans.
Newman, Beth, jt. illus. see Battles-Herron, Linda.
Newman, Chris. Phillip's Dream World: A Coloring Book. Newman, Chris. 52p. (Orig.). 1992. pap. 5.95 (*0-9635004-3-0*) Flying Heart.
Newman, Ed. Hot Air & Gas: The Basics of Balloons. Newman, Ed. LC 92-70713. 52p. (Orig.). (gr. 4-12). 1992. pap. 6.95 (*0-9632038-0-0*) Greenway Pub.
Newman, Jack. The Tiger & the Millionaire. Hall, Roger. LC 93-28932. 1994. 4.25 (*0-383-03786-7*) SRA Schl Grp.
Newman, Penny. Nibbly Mouse. Drew, David. LC 92-21397. 1993. 4.25 (*0-383-03587-2*) SRA Schl Grp.
Newman, Sheila. All the Way Around Green Lake. Backus, Mary L. 24p. (Orig.). (ps). 1984. pap. write for info. (*0-9613400-0-2*) Grnwillow End.
Newsom, Carol. Alien Alert! Hess, Debra. LC 93-528. 128p. (gr. 3-6). 1993. pap. 3.50 (*1-56282-567-4*) Hyprn Ppbks.
—Billy & Ben: The Terrible Two. Quin-Harken, Janet. 1992. pap. 3.50 (*0-553-48022-7*) Bantam.
—Do You Like Cats? Oppenheim, Joanne. LC 92-14113. 1993. 9.99 (*0-553-09116-6*, Little Rooster); pap. 3.50 (*0-553-37107-X*, Little Rooster) Bantam.
—An Edward Lear Alphabet. Lear, Edward. LC 82-10037. 32p. (gr. k-3). 1983. PLB 11.88 (*0-688-00965-4*) Lothrop.
—An Edward Lear Alphabet. Lear, Edward. LC 82-10037. (ps-3). 1986. 4.95 (*0-688-06523-6*, Mulberry) Morrow.
—Escape from Earth. Hess, Debra. 1994. write for info. (*1-56282-682-4*) Hyprn Child.
—The Greatest Idea Ever. Carris, Joan. LC 89-34516. 176p. (gr. 3-7). 1990. (Lipp Jr Bks); PLB 13.89 (*0-397-32379-4*, Lipp Jr Bks) HarpC Child Bks.
—Imp for Always. Koller, Jackie F. 64p. (gr. 2-4). 1989. 9.95 (*0-316-50147-6*) Little.
—Kevin Corbett Eats Flies. Hermes, Patricia. LC 85-27086. 160p. (gr. 3-7). 1986. 13.95 (*0-15-242290-0*, HB Juv Bks) HarBrace.
—A Memory for Tino. Buscaglia, Leo F. 50p. (ps up). 1988. 12.95 (*0-688-07482-0*) SLACK Inc.
—Midnight Soup & a Witch's Hat. Orgel, Doris. (gr. 2-5). 1987. pap. 10.95 (*0-670-81440-7*) Viking Child Bks.
—My Horrible Secret. Roos, Stephen. 128p. (Orig.). (gr. 4-7). 1991. pap. 3.25 (*0-440-43956-6*, YB) Dell.
—My Horrible Secret. Roos, Stephen. LC 82-14954. 128p. (gr. 4-6). 1983. pap. 10.95 (*0-385-29246-5*) Delacorte.
—My Secret Admirer. Roos, Stephen. LC 84-5010. 112p. (gr. 4-6). 1984. 14.95 (*0-385-29342-9*); PLB 13.95 (*0-385-29343-7*) Delacorte.
—Spies Incorporated, Vol. 4: The Spy from Outer Space. Hess, Debra. 1994. pap. write for info. (*1-56282-683-2*) Hyprn Child.
—The Terrible Truth: Secrets of a Sixth-Grader. Roos, Stephen. LC 83-5253. 128p. (gr. 4-6). 1983. 12.95 (*0-385-29306-2*) Delacorte.
—The Terrible Truth: Secrets of a Sixth-Grader. Roos, Stephen. 128p. (gr. 4-7). 1991. pap. 3.25 (*0-440-48578-9*, YB) Dell.
—Too Many Spies. Hess, Debra. 128p. (gr. 3-6). 1993. pap. 3.95 (*1-56282-569-0*) Hyprn Ppbks.
—Whiskers, Once & Always. Orgel, Doris. 96p. (gr. 2-5). 1989. pap. 3.95 (*0-14-032038-5*, Puffin) Puffin Bks.
Newsom, Carol, jt. illus. see Newsom, Tom.
Newsom, Tom. How I Survived My Summer Vacation. Coville, Bruce. 96p. (Orig.). (gr. 3-5). 1988. pap. 2.99 (*0-671-68176-1*, Minstrel Bks) PB.
—I Sailed with Columbus. Schlein, Miriam. LC 90-24532. 144p. (gr. 3-6). 1991. 14.00 (*0-06-022513-0*); PLB 13.89 (*0-06-022514-9*) HarpC Child Bks.
—I Sailed with Columbus. Schlein, Miriam. LC 90-24532. 144p. (gr. 3-6). 1992. pap. 3.95 (*0-06-440423-4*, Trophy) HarpC Child Bks.
—Make-Believe Ball Player. Slote, Alfred. LC 89-30598. 112p. (gr. 2-5). 1989. 13.00 (*0-397-32285-2*, Lipp Jr Bks); PLB 12.89 (*0-397-32286-0*, Lipp Jr Bks) HarpC Child Bks.
—The Mystery of the Cupboard. Banks, Lynne R. LC 92-39295. 256p. (gr. 5 up). 1993. 13.95 (*0-688-12138-1*); PLB 13.88 (*0-688-12635-9*) Morrow Jr Bks.
—Seven Stories of Christmas Love. Buscaglia, Leo F. 110p. 1987. 12.95 (*0-688-07521-5*) SLACK Inc.
—The Wonderful Wizard of Oz. Baum, L. Frank. Mabie, Grace, ed. LC 92-12704. 48p. (gr. 3-6). 1992. PLB 12.89 (*0-8167-2864-X*); pap. text ed. 3.95 (*0-8167-2865-8*) Troll Assocs.

Newsom, Tom & Newsom, Carol. Olympia Odette Presents: Annie Oakley's Star Studded Stunt. Littke, Lael. 36p. (ps-3). 1991. pap. 4.95 incl. audiocassette (1-55999-155-0) LinguiSystems.
—Olympia Odette Presents: Betsy Ross's Shag-a-Ragged Rainbow. Littke, Lael. 36p. (ps-3). 1991. pap. 4.95 incl. audiocassette (1-55999-148-8) LinguiSystems.
—Olympia Odette Presents: Davy Crockett's Bear-ly Believable. Littke, Lael. 36p. (ps-3). 1990. pap. 4.95 incl. audiocassette (1-55999-130-5) LinguiSystems.
—Olympia Odette Presents: Nails, Rails, & Donkey Tails. Littke, Lael. 36p. (ps-3). 1991. pap. 4.95 incl. audiocassette (1-55999-147-X) LinguiSystems.
—Olympia Odette Presents: Nellie Bly's "In-a-Jam" Telegram. Littke, Lael. 36p. (ps-3). 1990. pap. 4.95 incl. audiocassette (1-55999-131-3) LinguiSystems.
—Olympia Odette Presents: Paul Bunyan's Blue Ox Blues. Littke, Lael. 36p. (ps-3). 1990. pap. 4.95 incl. audiocassette (1-55999-129-1) LinguiSystems.
Newsome, Carol. Heads, I Win. Hermes, Patricia. LC 87-19249. 132p. (gr. 3-7). 1988. 12.95 (0-15-233659-1, HB Juv Bks) HarBrace.
Newson, Carol. Little Owl Leaves the Nest. Leonard, Marcia. 32p. 1984. pap. 2.75 (0-553-15460-5) Bantam.
Newton, Jill. Keeping Up with Cheetah. Camp, Lindsay. LC 92-44162. (gr. k-4). 1993. write for info. (0-688-12655-3) Lothrop.
—Matepo. McAllister, Angela. LC 90-33113. 32p. (ps-3). 1991. 12.95 (0-8037-0838-6) Dial Bks Young.
Newton, Laurie. The Hole Book. Kline, Suzy. 24p. (ps-k). 1989. 9.95 (0-399-21719-3, Putnam) Putnam Pub Group.
Newton, Martin. Computer Jargon. Stockley, C. & Watts, L. 48p. (gr. 6 up). 1983. lib. bdg. 10.96 (0-88110-141-9); pap. 3.95 (0-86020-737-4) EDC.
Newton, Martin & Andrews, Jane. Electronics. Beasant, Pam & Findly, Ian. 48p. (gr. 5-8). 1985. (Pub. by Usborne); pap. 6.95 (0-86020-809-5) EDC.
Newton, Michael. Walking for Freedom: The Montgomery Bus Boycott. Kelso, Richard. LC 92-18080. 52p. (gr. 2-5). 1992. PLB 21.34 (0-8114-7218-3) Raintree Steck-V.
Newton, Pam. The Stonecutter: An Indian Folktale. Newton, Pam, retold by. 32p. (ps-3). 1990. 14.95 (0-399-22187-5, Putnam-Whitebird) Putnam Pub Group.
Newton-King, Laurie. Howie Hugemouth. Hunt, Angela E. 28p. (ps-k). 1993. 4.99 (0-7847-0066-4, 24-03846) Standard Pub.
Nex, Anthony. I Love Pets. Ostarch, Judy. 10p. (ps). 1993. bds. 4.99 (0-8431-3656-1) Price Stern.
—Let's Get Dressed. Ostarch, Judy. 10p. (ps). 1993. bds. 4.99 (0-8431-3654-5) Price Stern.
—My Family. Ostarch, Judy. 10p. (ps). 1993. bds. 4.99 (0-8431-3655-3) Price Stern.
—Playtime. Ostarch, Judy. 10p. (ps). 1993. bds. 4.99 (0-8431-3657-X) Price Stern.
Neyndorff, Mark. The Conception Connection: The Journey into Creation. rev. ed. Katz, Ellie. 100p. (gr. k-12). 1991. pap. 12.95 (1-880806-00-2) Playology Hlth.
Nez, John. Where in America's Past Is Carmen Sandiego? Peel, John. Vaccarello, Paul, contrib. by. 96p. (gr. 3-7). 1992. pap. 2.95 (0-307-22205-5, 22205, Golden Pr) Western Pub.
—Where in Time Is Carmen Sandiego, Pt. II. Peel, John. 96p. (gr. 3-7). 1993. pap. 3.25 (0-307-22206-3, 22206-00, Golden Pr) Western Pub.
Ng, Simon. Tales from Gold Mountain: Stories of the Chinese in the New World. Yee, Paul. LC 89-12643. 64p. (ps up). 1990. RSBE 15.95 (0-02-793621-X, Macmillan Child Bk) Macmillan Child Grp.
Nguyen, Peter, jt. illus. see Conway, Robin.
Nichol, Bee. The Coming of the Sun. Dolan, Ellen M. & Bolinske, Janet L., eds. LC 87-61659. 32p. (Orig.). (gr. 1-3). 1987. text ed. 8.95 (0-88335-566-3); pap. text ed. 4.95 (0-88335-586-8) Milliken Pub Co.
—Hansel & Gretel. Dolan, Ellen M. & Bolinske, Janet L., eds. LC 87-61670. 32p. (Orig.). (gr. 1-3). 1987. text ed. 8.95 (0-88335-555-8); 4.95 (0-88335-545-0); pap. text ed. 3.95 (0-88335-575-2) Milliken Pub Co.
—The Leaves of Autumn. Dolan, Ellen M. & Bolinske, Janet L., eds. LC 87-61658. 32p. (Orig.). (gr. 1-3). 1987. text ed. 8.95 (0-88335-567-1); pap. text ed. 4.95 (0-88335-587-6) Milliken Pub Co.
—The Robin's Red Breast. Dolan, Ellen M. & Bolinske, Janet L., eds. LC 87-61657. 32p. (Orig.). (gr. 1-3). 1987. text ed. 8.95 (0-88335-568-X); pap. text ed. 4.95 (0-88335-588-4) Milliken Pub Co.
—Why the Loon Calls. Dolan, Ellen M. & Bolinske, Janet L., eds. LC 87-61660. 32p. (Orig.). (gr. 1-3). 1987. text ed. 8.95 (0-88335-565-5); pap. text ed. 4.95 (0-88335-585-X) Milliken Pub Co.
Nicholas. New Illustrated Just So Stories. Kipling, Rudyard. (gr. 1-7). 1952. PLB o.p. (0-385-02180-1) Doubleday.
Nicholas, Charles. Banner in the Sky. Gifford, Mary, adapted by. (gr. 4-12). 1978. pap. text ed. 2.25 (0-88301-301-0) Pendulum Pr.
—God Is My Co-Pilot. Cadrain, Linda A., adapted by. LC 78-50959. (gr. 4-12). 1978. pap. text ed. 2.25 (0-88301-302-9) Pendulum Pr.
—Hiroshima. Cadrain, Linda A., adapted by. LC 78-50861. (gr. 4-12). 1978. pap. text ed. 2.25 (0-88301-304-5) Pendulum Pr.
—Hot Rod. Cadrain, Linda A., adapted by. LC 78-50957. (gr. 4-12). 1978. pap. text ed. 2.25 (0-88301-305-3) Pendulum Pr.
—Just Dial a Number. Gifford, Mary, adapted by. LC 78-50860. (gr. 4-12). 1978. pap. text ed. 2.25 (0-88301-306-1) Pendulum Pr.
—Lost Horizon. Wichterman, Catherine, adapted by. 32p. (Orig.). (gr. 3-5). 1979. pap. text ed. 2.25 (0-88301-309-6) Pendulum Pr.
Nicholas, Frank. Paul Revere: Boston Patriot. Stevenson, Augusta. LC 86-10743. 192p. (gr. 2-6). 1986. pap. 3.95 (0-02-042090-0, Aladdin) Macmillan Child Grp.
Nicholls, Nick, photos by. Ancient Greece. Pearson, Anne. LC 92-4713. 64p. (gr. 5 up). 1992. 15.00 (0-679-81682-8); PLB 16.99 (0-679-91682-2) Knopf Bks Yng Read.
Nichols, Brooke & Guthrie, Kari H. National Anthems, Bk. 1. Guthrie, Kari H. Guthrie, Kari H., intro. by. 36p. (Orig.). (gr. 2-8). 1992. pap. 6.95 (0-9631333-0-6) Hi I Que Pub.
Nichols, Fran. Sarah: A Story of Love & Adoption. Nichols, Kathie. 32p. (Orig.). (gr. 2-4). 1992. pap. 6.95 (0-943861-21-7) Lone Tree.
Nichols, Frank. Circles. (Orig.). (ps-2). 1976. pap. 2.95 (0-85953-047-7) Childs Play.
Nichols, K. Sticker Atlas of the United States. Bloch, Carol Z. (Orig.). 1990. pap. 3.95 (1-879424-10-X) Nickel Pr.
Nichols, Michael. How Mountain Gorillas Live. Harrison, Virginia. LC 91-2022. 32p. (gr. 2-3). 1991. PLB 15.93 (0-8368-0446-5) Gareth Stevens Inc.
—Mountain Gorillas & Their Young. Harrison, Virginia. LC 91-7600. 32p. (gr. 2-3). 1991. PLB 15.93 (0-8368-0445-7) Gareth Stevens Inc.
Nichols, Michael, photos by. Mountain Gorillas in Danger. Ritchie, Rita. LC 91-10831. 32p. (gr. 2-3). 1991. PLB 15.93 (0-8368-0447-3) Gareth Stevens Inc.
Nicholson, John. Amabel Abroad: More Amazing Adventures. Prior, Natalie J. (Orig.). (gr. 6 up). 1993. pap. 7.95 (1-86373-130-X, Pub. by Allen & Unwin Aust Pty AT) IPG Chicago.
—The Amazing Adventures of Amabel. Prior, Natalie J. 112p. (Orig.). (gr. 6 up). 1993. pap. 7.95 (0-04-442163-X, Pub. by Allen & Unwin Aust Pty AT) IPG Chicago.
Nicholson, Larry. Pearl Harbor Child: A Child's View of Pearl Harbor-From Attack to Peace. Nicholson, Dorinda M. 60p. 1993. pap. write for info. (0-9631388-6-3) AZ Mem Mus.
Nicholson, William. Velveteen Rabbit. Williams, Margery. 47p. (gr. 3-5). 1991. PLB (0-385-07748-3); pap. 9.95 (0-385-07725-4); pap. 15.95 slipcased (0-385-00913-5) Doubleday.
—The Velveteen Rabbit. Williams, Margery. 40p. (gr. k up). 1994. pap. 2.99 (0-380-00255-8, Camelot) Avon.
—The Velveteen Rabbit. Williams, Margery. 48p. (gr. k-4). 1992. 4.99 (0-440-40722-2, YB) Dell.
Nick, Christopher. The Shape of Good Nutrition. Francis, Lynnrae & Francis, Steven. Birch, Gail, intro. by. 20p. (Orig.). 1993. saddlestitched 2.50 (0-9638754-0-X) Providers Pr.
Nickell, Joe. Wonderworkers! How They Perform the Impossible. Nickell, Joe. 80p. (Orig.). 1991. pap. 11.95 (0-87975-688-8) Prometheus Bks.
Nickens, Linda. Senefer: A Young Genius in Old Egypt. Lumpkin, Beatrice. LC 92-71026. 32p. (gr. 2-5). 1992. 16.95 (0-86543-244-9); pap. 8.95 (0-86543-245-7) Africa World.
Nickiens, Linda. Imani & the Flying Africans. Liddell, Janice. 32p. (gr. 3-8). 1993. 14.95 (0-685-65590-3); pap. 6.95 (0-86543-366-6) Africa World.
Nicklaus, Carol. Where's My Blankie? Dickson, Anna H. LC 83-83278. 32p. (ps). 1984. write for info. (0-307-12013-9, 12013, Golden Bks) Western Pub.
Nicklaus, Carol. Bathtubs, Slides, Roller Coaster Rails: Simple Machines That Are Really Inclined Planes. Lampton, Christopher. 32p. (gr. 2-4). 1991. PLB 12.40 (1-878841-23-8) Millbrook Pr.
—Big Bird at the Beach. Hautzig, Deborah. LC 89-61613. 32p. (ps-3). 1990. pap. 1.50 (0-679-80159-6) Random Bks Yng Read.
—Big Bird Visits Granny Bird. Herman, Gail. LC 90-60822. 32p. (Orig.). 1991. pap. 1.50 (0-679-81050-1) Random Bks Yng Read.
—Bunny Shines. LC 91-68458. 48p. (Orig.). (ps up) 1993. pap. 2.50 (0-679-83449-4) Random Bks Yng Read.
—Come Dance with Me. Nicklaus, Carol. 32p. (ps-1). 1991. PLB 8.98 (0-671-73503-9); pap. 9.98 (0-671-73507-1) Silver Pr.
—A Dozen Dogs: A Read-&-Count Story. Ziefert, Harriet. LC 84-17797. 32p. (ps-1). 1985. lib. bdg. 6.99 (0-394-96935-9); 3.50 (0-394-86935-4) Random Bks Yng Read.
—Eggs-O-Poppin' Art. LC 91-68547. 48p. (Orig.). (ps up) 1993. pap. 2.50 (0-679-83448-6) Random Bks Yng Read.
—Elmo Goes to Day Camp. Hayward, Linda. LC 89-61614. 32p. (Orig.). 1990. pap. 1.25 (0-679-80158-8) Random Bks Yng Read.
—Ernie & Bert's Summer Project. Hayward, Linda. LC 90-60821. 32p. (Orig.). 1991. pap. 1.50 (0-679-81051-X) Random Bks Yng Read.
—The Go Club. Nicklaus, Carol. 32p. (ps-1). 1991. PLB 8.98 (0-671-73500-4); pap. 3.95 (0-671-73505-5) Silver Pr.
—Happy Birthday, Cookie Monster! A Step One Book. Haus, Felice. LC 85-25639. 32p. (ps-1). 1986. lib. bdg. 7.99 (0-394-98182-0); pap. 3.50 (0-394-88182-6) Random Bks Yng Read.
—The Haunted House: Book & Puzzle Set. Herman, Gail. 24p. (ps-1). 1989. 5.95 (0-394-82717-1) Random Bks Yng Read.
—Marbles, Roller Skates, Doorknobs: Simple Machines That Are Really Wheels. Lampton, Christopher. LC 92-34332. 32p. (gr. 2-4). 1991. PLB 12.40 (1-878841-24-6) Millbrook Pr.
—Seesaws, Nutcrackers, Brooms: Simple Machines That Are Really Levers. Lampton, Christopher. 32p. (gr. 2-4). 1991. PLB 12.40 (1-878841-22-X) Millbrook Pr.
—Silver Sports Series, 4 vols. Nicklaus, Carol. (ps-1). 1991. Set, 32p. ea. lib. bdg. 35.92 (0-671-31271-5); Set, 32p. ea. pap. 15.80 (0-671-31272-3) Silver Pr.
—So Hungry! Ziefert, Harriet. LC 87-4763. 32p. (ps-1). 1987. lib. bdg. 7.99 (0-394-99127-3); 3.50 (0-394-89127-9) Random Bks Yng Read.
—So Sick. Ziefert, Harriet. LC 85-1957. 32p. (ps-1). 1985. pap. 2.95 (0-394-87580-X) Random Bks Yng Read.
—Sometimes I Share. Ziefert, Harriet. 24p. (ps-1). 1991. pap. 3.95 (0-06-107425-X) HarpC Child Bks.
—Tick Tock, Let's Read the Clock: Green Ladder Books for Kids Through 6 Years. Katz, Bobbi. 16p. (ps-1). 1988. incl. clock 7.99 (0-394-89399-9) Random Bks Yng Read.
Nickless, Will. Further Adventures of Robinson Crusoe. Treece, Henry. LC 58-9623. (gr. 7-11). 1958. 21.95 (0-87599-116-5) S G Phillips.
Nicklin, Flip. Whale Magic for Kids. Wolpert, Tom. LC 90-50718. 48p. (gr. 3-4). 1991. PLB 18.60 (0-8368-0660-3) Gareth Stevens Inc.
Nicklin, Flip, photos by. The Wonder of Whales. Weber, Valerie, adapted by. LC 92-16946. 1992. PLB 18.60 (0-8368-0857-6) Gareth Stevens Inc.
Niclaus, Carol. How to Be a Reasonably Thin Teenage Girl (Without Starving, Losing Your Friends, or Running Away from Home) Lukes, Bonnie L. LC 86-3347. 96p. (gr. 6 up). 1986. SBE 13.95 (0-689-31269-5, Atheneum) Macmillan Child Grp.
Nicolas. Finders Keepers. Will & Nicolas. LC 51-12326. 32p. (gr. k-4). 1951. 14.95 (0-15-227529-0, HB Juv Bks) HarBrace.
Niederhauser, Hans R. & Frohlich, Margaret. Form Drawing. Niederhauser, Hans R. & Frohlich, Margaret. 57p. (Orig.). 1974. pap. 10.00 (0-318-41110-5) Merc Pr NY.
Nielsen, Deborah B. God Is So Great. Worrall, Joyce. 19p. (gr. k-6). 1985. pap. text ed. 4.25 (1-55976-132-6) CEF Press.
Nielsen-McLellan, Karen L. Ginger Bear's Christmas Cookie Mystery. Nielsen-McLellan, Karen L. 32p. (ps-1). 1992. 12.95 (0-9634851-0-5) Scand Descent.
Nielson, Deborah. Stolen Ice Cream Bar. London, Carolyn. 12p. (gr. k-6). 1981. pap. text ed. 4.25 (1-55976-151-2) CEF Press.
Nielson, Mike, jt. illus. see Biske, Joel.
Niemann, Gail. Rabbits, Rabbits. Fisher, Aileen. LC 82-48849. 32p. (gr. k-3). 1983. 12.95i (0-06-021896-7) HarpC Child Bks.
Nienhaus, Laura L. Eye on Nature: The Snake Dictionary. Gustafson, Sarah. 48p. 1993. pap. 5.95 (1-56565-070-0) Lowell Hse.

Nierman, Lewis G. Lefty's Place. Nierman, Lewis G. 32p. (gr. 1-4). 1994. 18.95g (0-9636820-0-8) Kindness Pubns.
LEFTY'S PLACE; a factual & inspiring story of a young child's hard work to give an injured wild animal a chance at life. EXPLORES a loving relationship & the rewards of kindness & courage. SHOWS how the child, from this experience, will never again look at animals without thinking & caring more about their lives & feelings. FOSTERS in children a greater tolerance & appreciation for all living things. HELPS develop a greater ability to face the challenges of injury, illness, or hardship in their own lives. SHOWS how every single child & every act of kindness can make a difference. Uniquely illustrated in artwork combined with original photography for dramatic impact. ORDER FROM KINDNESS PUBLICATIONS, INC., 1859 North Pine Island Rd., Suite # 135, Plantation, FL 33322. (305) 424-9323; FAX (305) 721-0910. From KINDNESS: Children's reading to educate, entertain & inspire a more sensitive & caring future generation of adults. *Publisher Provided Annotation.*

Nieves, Ernesto R. Juan Bobo: Four Silly Tales from Puerto Rico. Bernier-Grand, Carmen. LC 93-12936. Date not set. 14.00 (0-06-023389-3); PLB 13.89 (0-06-023390-7) HarpC.

Nightingale, Sandy. Cat's Knees & Bee's Whiskers. Nightingale, Sandy. LC 92-39811. 1993. 14.95 (0-15-215364-0) HarBrace.

—Rumpelstiltskin. Daniels, Patricia. LC 79-27140. 24p. (gr. k-5). 1980. PLB 14.64 (0-8393-0252-5) Raintree Steck-V.

Nightingale, Sandy A. Hansel & Gretel. LC 85-2222. 24p. (ps-1). 1985. lib. bdg. 4.99 (0-394-97022-5) Random Bks Yng Read.

Nigoghossian, Christine W. Discovering Trees. Brandt, Keith. LC 81-7522. 32p. (gr. 2-4). 1982. PLB 11.59 (0-89375-566-4); pap. text ed. 2.95 (0-89375-567-2) Troll Assocs.

—Thumbelina. Andersen, Hans Christian. LC 78-18080. 32p. (gr. k-4). 1979. PLB 9.79 (0-89375-141-3); pap. 1.95 (0-89375-119-7) Troll Assocs.

Nii-owoo, Ife. A Is for Africa: Looking at Africa Through the Alphabet. Nii-owoo, Ife. LC 90-81575. 32p. (gr. k-5). 1992. 12.95 (0-86543-182-5); pap. 5.95 (0-86543-183-3) Africa World.

Nikly, Michelle. Japan: Land of Samurai & Robots. Ottenheimer, Laurence. LC 87-34524. 38p. (gr. k-5). 1988. 4.95 (0-944589-11-1, 111) Young Discovery Lib.

Niland, Deborah. Families Are Funny. Hunt, Nan. LC 91-15628. 32p. (ps-1). 1992. 13.95 (0-531-05969-3); lib. bdg. 13.99 (0-531-08569-4) Orchard Bks Watts.

Niland, Kilmeny. My Brother John. Church, Kristine. LC 90-25868. 32p. (ps-3). 1991. 12.95 (0-688-10800-8, Tambourine Bks); PLB 12.88 (0-688-10801-6, Tambourine Bks) Morrow.

Niles, Nancy & Lusk, Nancy M. Meet Samantha: An American Girl. Adler, Susan S. Thieme, Jeanne, ed. 72p. (gr. 2-5). 1986. 12.95 (0-937295-03-5); PLB 12.95 (0-937295-80-9); pap. 5.95 (0-937295-04-3) Pleasant Co.

Niles, Nancy & Lusk, Nancy N. Samantha Learns a Lesson: A School Story. Adler, Susan S. Thieme, Jeanne, ed. 72p. (gr. 2-5). 1986. 12.95 (0-937295-12-4); PLB 12.95 (0-937295-83-3); pap. 5.95 (0-937295-13-2) Pleasant Co.

—Samantha's Surprise: A Christmas Story. Schur, Maxine R. Thieme, Jeanne, ed. 72p. (gr. 2-5). 1986. 12.95 (0-937295-21-3); PLB 12.95 (0-937295-86-8); pap. 5.95 (0-937295-22-1) Pleasant Co.

Niles, Nancy, jt. illus. see Grace, Robert.

Niles, Nancy, et al. Samantha, 6 bks. Adler, Susan S, et al. 432p. (gr. 2-5). 1991. Boxed Set. 74.95 (1-56247-013-2); Boxed Set. lib. bdg. 74.95 (1-56247-050-7); Boxed Set. pap. 34.95 (0-937295-77-9) Pleasant Co.

Nilles, Burgandy & Thiewes, Sam. Beauty & the Beast. Jerrard, Jane, adapted by. 24p. 1993. PLB 10.95 (1-56674-061-4, HTS Bks) Forest Hse.

—Goldilocks & the Three Bears. Jerrard, Jane, adapted by. 24p. (gr. k-4). 1993. PLB 10.95 (1-56674-063-0, HTS Bks) Forest Hse.

Nilsson, Lennart. Being Born. Kitzinger, Sheila. 64p. (gr. 2-5). 1986. 17.95 (0-448-18990-9, G&D) Putnam Pub Group.

—Being Born. Kitzinger, Sheila. (ps-1). 1992. pap. 11.95 (0-399-22225-1, Putnam) Putnam Pub Group.

Nino, Alex. The Invisible Man: Student Activity Book. Sohl, Marcia & Dackerman, Gerald. (gr. 4-10). 1976. wkbk 1.25 (0-88301-190-5) Pendulum Pr.

—Moby Dick. new ed. Melville, Herman. Shapiro, Irwin, ed. LC 73-75458. 64p. (Orig.). (gr. 5-10). 1973. pap. 2.95 (0-88301-099-2) Pendulum Pr.

—Moby Dick Student Activity Book. Sohl, Marcia & Dackerman, Gerald. (gr. 4-10). 1976. pap. 1.25 (0-88301-181-6) Pendulum Pr.

—The Three Musketeers: Student Activity Book. Sohl, Marcia & Dackerman, Gerald. (gr. 4-10). 1976. wkbk 1.25 (0-88301-197-2) Pendulum Pr.

—The Time Machine. Wells, H. G. Binder, Otto, ed. LC 73-75467. 64p. (Orig.). (gr. 5-10). 1973. pap. 2.95 (0-88301-102-6) Pendulum Pr.

—The War of the Worlds: Student Activity Book. Sohl, Marcia & Dackerman, Gerald. (gr. 4-10). 1976. wkbk 1.25 (0-88301-198-0) Pendulum Pr.

Nino, Alex, jt. illus. see Henderson, Doug.

Nino, Alex, jt. illus. see Martishuis, Walter.

Nino, Alex, jt. illus. see Pierard, John.

Nintendo. My Play a Tune Book: Nintendo. Ellis, Toni. 26p. 1989. 15.95 (0-939871-21-2) JTG Nashville.

Nintendo Staff. Super Mario Bros. Adventures. Nintendo Staff. 32p. (Orig.). (gr. 1-7). 1991. pap. 6.95 incl. cassette (0-679-81822-7) Random Bks Yng Read.

Nisbet, Richard C., jt. illus. see Plesissner, Ogden M.

Nishimura, Chris. When I Visit Yosemite. Arrigo, Mary & Hargreaves, Connie. 43p. (Orig.). pap. 2.95 (0-318-21253-6) Arrigo CA.

Nister, Ernest. The Children's Picture Book. Nister, Ernest. LC 80-7613. 18p. (ps-3). 1980. pop-up bk. 9.95 (0-385-28173-0) Delacorte.

—Golden Tales from Long Ago, 3 vols. Nister, Ernest. LC 80-7614. (24p. ea.). 1980. Set. 6.95 (0-440-03015-3) Delacorte.

—The Great Panorama Picture Book. Nister, Ernest. LC 82-70305. 18p. (ps-3). 1982. pop-up bk. 8.95 (0-385-28327-X) Delacorte.

—Land of Sweet Surprises: An Antique Revolving Picture Books. Nister, Ernest. (gr. k up). 1983. 12.95 (0-399-20993-X, Philomel) Putnam Pub Group.

—Moving Pictures: An Antique Picture Book. 12p. (ps up). 1985. 11.95 (0-399-21272-8, Philomel) Putnam Pub Group.

—Our Farmyard: A Pop-up Book with Punch-out Play Figures. Nister, Ernest. 12p. (ps-3). 1991. 13.95 (0-525-44689-3, DCB) Dutton Child Bks.

—Playtime Delights. 26p. 1993. 15.95 (0-685-66598-4, Philomel Bks) Putnam Pub Group.

—Special Days. Nister, Ernest. (gr. k up). 1989. 5.95 (0-399-21694-4, Philomel Bks) Putnam Pub Group.

—Visiting Grandma. Nister, Ernest. (gr. k up). 1989. 5.95 (0-399-21695-2, Philomel Bks) Putnam Pub Group.

—We Visit the Farm. Nister, Ernest. (gr. k up). 1989. 13.95 (0-399-21724-X, Philomel Bks) Putnam Pub Group.

Nivens, Chuck. Johnny Lynch. Hogan, Stephen. 165p. (gr. 5-6). 1991. PLB 13.00x (0-945253-07-9) Thornsbury Bailey Brown.

Nix, Harriet. Secret Passageway. Coleman, Mary A. 48p. (Orig.). (gr. 1-6). 1989. pap. 8.50 (0-685-28398-4) Agee Pub.

Noakes, Polly. Leon's Lucky Lunch-Break. Hoffman, Mary. 32p. (ps-k). 1993. 14.95 (0-460-88021-7, Pub. by J M Dent & Sons) Trafalgar.

—A Treasury of Stories for Five Year Olds. Blishen, Edward & Blishen, Nancy, eds. LC 92-53107. 160p. (Orig.). (gr. k-5). 1992. pap. 5.95 (1-85697-827-3) Kingfisher Bks.

Nobens, C. A. Montgomery's Time Zone. Nobens, C. A. 32p. (ps-4). 1990. PLB 18.95 (0-87614-398-2) Carolrhoda Bks.

—Stories from the Blue Road. Crofford, Emily. LC 81-21229. 168p. (gr. 4-8). 1981. PLB 13.50 (0-87614-189-0) Carolrhoda Bks.

Nobens, Cheryl A. April Fool's Day. Kelley, Emily. LC 82-23559. 48p. (gr. k-4). 1983. PLB 14.95 (0-87614-218-8); pap. 3.95 (0-87614-481-4) Carolrhoda Bks.

Nobis, Kevin. P. E. Curriculum Guide. Ortwerth, John & Nicks, Mel J. 160p. (gr. 1-6). 1984. wkbk. 12.95 (0-86653-262-5, GA 599) Good Apple.

Noble, Constance. Andy Bear: A Polar Cub Grows Up at the Zoo. Johnston, Ginny & Cutchins, Judy. LC 85-3095. 64p. (gr. 2-5). 1985. 13.00 (0-688-05627-X); lib. bdg. 12.88 (0-688-05628-8, Morrow Jr Bks) Morrow Jr Bks.

Noble, Marty. By Day & by Night. Pandell, Karen. Kramer, Linda, ed. LC 90-52635. 32p. (ps-2). 1991. 14.95 (0-915811-26-8) H J Kramer Inc.

Noble, Trinka H. Apple Tree Christmas. Noble, Trinka H. LC 84-1901. 32p. (ps-2). 1988. 13.50 (0-8037-0102-0); PLB 12.89 (0-8037-0103-9) Dial Bks Young.

—Hansy's Mermaid. Noble, Trinka H. LC 82-45509. 32p. (ps-2). 1983. PLB 10.89 (0-8037-3606-1) Dial Bks Young.

—Karin's Christmas Walk. Pearson, Susan. LC 80-11739. 32p. (ps-3). 1980. Dial Bks Young.

—Karin's Christmas Walk. Pearson, Susan. LC 80-11739. 32p. (ps-3). 1983. 4.95 (0-8037-0020-2) Dial Bks Young.

Nobleman, Louis R. Second Dreams. Nobleman, Louis R. (gr. k-6). 1993. pap. 9.95 (1-56883-010-6) Colonial Pr AL.

Nobles, Henry, Jr. The Kingdom of the South: The Long Journey. Wampamba, Mazzi. (gr. 1-4). 1992. pap. 3.95 (1-56411-045-1) Untd Brothers.

Nockels, David. The Beaver. Lane, Margaret. LC 81-67074. 32p. (gr. k-4). 1993. 13.99 (0-8037-0624-3) Dial Bks Young.

—The Beaver. Lane, Margaret. 32p. (gr. k-4). 1993. pap. 4.99 (0-14-054925-0, Puffin Pied Piper) Puffin Bks.

Nodel, Norman. Birds. Weinboreir, Messody. Satat, Noah, photos by. (gr. 3-8). 1990. 10.95 (0-922613-33-8); pap. 8.95 (0-922613-34-6) Hachai Pubns.

—Flying Dragons, Ancient Reptiles That Ruled the Air. Eldridge, David. LC 79-87965. 32p. (gr. 3-6). 1980. PLB 10.79 (0-89375-241-X); pap. 2.95 (0-89375-245-2) Troll Assocs.

—The Giant Dinosaurs, Ancient Reptiles That Ruled the Land. Eldridge, David. LC 79-87967. 32p. (gr. 3-6). 1980. PLB 10.79 (0-89375-242-8); pap. 2.95 (0-89375-246-0) Troll Assocs.

—I Can Read About Fossils. Howard, John. LC 76-54446. (gr. 2-5). 1977. pap. 1.95 (0-89375-038-7) Troll Assocs.

—I Can Read About Insects. Merrians, Deborah. LC 76-54493. (gr. 2-5). 1977. pap. 1.95 (0-89375-040-9) Troll Assocs.

—I Can Read About Prehistoric Animals. Eastman, David. LC 76-54492. (gr. 2-4). 1977. pap. 1.95 (0-89375-039-5) Troll Assocs.

—Kaleidoscope. Kornbluth, Adina F. 160p. (gr. 6-10). 1992. 10.95 (0-922613-31-1); pap. 8.95 (0-922613-32-X) Hachai Pubns.

—Labels for Laibel. Rosenfeld, Dina. 32p. (ps-1). 1990. 8.95 (0-922613-35-4); pap. 6.95 (0-922613-36-2) Hachai Pubns.

—Last of the Dinosaurs, the End of an Age. Eldridge, David. LC 79-64636. 32p. (gr. 3-6). 1980. PLB 10.79 (0-89375-243-6); pap. 2.95 (0-89375-247-9) Troll Assocs.

—Moral or Less: An Adventure in Addition & Subtraction. Nodel, Maxine. 32p. (ps-3). 1990. 8.95 (0-922613-25-7); pap. 6.95 (0-922613-26-5); 4.95 (0-922613-27-3); cass. 9.00 (0-922613-28-1) Hachai Pubns.

—Nicanor Knew the Secret. Goetz, Bracha. Zakutinsky, Ruth, ed. 32p. (gr. 3). 1992. PLB 6.95 (0-911643-14-1) Aura Bklyn.

—Rambam: The Story of Rabbi Moshe Ben Maimon. Yaffe, Rochel. 220p. (gr. 8 up). 1992. 10.95 (0-922613-14-1); pap. 8.95 (0-922613-15-X) Hachai Pubns.

—Sea Monsters, Ancient Reptiles That Ruled the Sea. Eldridge, David. LC 79-87964. 32p. (gr. 3-6). 1980. PLB 10.79 (0-89375-240-1); pap. 2.95 (0-89375-244-4) Troll Assocs.

—The Torah for Children. Falk, Aaron. LC 92-28623. 1992. write for info. (1-880582-06-6); pap. write for info. (1-880582-07-4) Judaica Pr.

—Yossi & Laibel Hot on the Trail. Rosenfeld, Dina. 32p. (ps-1). 1991. 8.95 (0-922613-47-8); pap. 6.95 (0-922613-48-6) Hachai Pubns.

Noel, Arlene. A Visit to the Haunted House. Walley, Dean & Ingle, Annie. 14p. (ps-3). 1992. 7.99 (0-679-82450-2) Random Bks Yng Read.

Noffs, Lauri. The Daily Harold, Bk. 8. Noffs, David & Noffs, Laurie. 24p. (Orig.). (gr. 8). 1991. wkbk. 2.50 (0-929875-09-5) Noffs Assocs.

Noffs, Lauri A. Harold Magazine, Bk. 4: Let's Be Friends. Noffs, David & Noffs, Laurie. 24p. (Orig.). (gr. 4). 1987. wkbk. 2.50 (0-929875-05-2) Noffs Assocs.

—Harold Magazine, Bk. 5: Watching the Stars at Night. Noffs, David & Noffs, Laurie. 24p. (Orig.). (gr. 5). 1987. wkbk. 2.50 (0-929875-06-0) Noffs Assocs.

Noffs, Laurie. Day of the Dinosaur. Noffs, David & Noffs, Laurie. 24p. (Orig.). (gr. 4-8). 1989. wkbk. 2.50 (0-929875-12-5) Noffs Assocs.

—The Happy Healthy Harold, Bk. 1. Noffs, David & Noffs, Laurie. 24p. (Orig.). (gr. 1). 1987. wkbk. 2.50 (0-929875-02-8) Noffs Assocs.

—A Happy Healthy Harold, Bk. 2. Noffs, David & Noffs, Laurie. 24p. (Orig.). (gr. 2). 1987. wkbk. 2.50 (0-929875-03-6) Noffs Assocs.

—Harold: Revista. rev. ed. Noffs, David & Noffs, Laurie. (SPA.). 24p. 1991. wkbk. 2.50 (0-929875-11-7) Noffs Assocs.

—Kindergarten - Introductory, Bk. K: The Happy Healthy Harold. Noffs, David & Noffs, Laurie. 24p. (Orig.). (gr. k). 1987. wkbk. 2.50 (0-929875-01-X) Noffs Assocs.

Nofsiger, Edward. Los Tres Osos: The Three Bears. Hutchinson, Hanna. (SPA.). 22p. (gr. k-2). 1990. pap. 2.95 (0-922852-06-5) AIMS Intl.

Nofziger, Edward. Chuyen Ba Con Gau: The Three Bears. Hutchinson, Hanna. Vu, Christine, tr. from ENG. (VIE.). 22p. (Orig.). (gr. k-2). 1990. pap. 2.95 (0-922852-10-3) AIMS Intl.

—Dame Renard et Dame Cigogne - Mrs. Fox & Mrs. Stork. 2nd ed. De la Fontaine, Jean. Calamaro, Emanuel, adapted by. (FRE.). 19p. (gr. k-12). 1993. pap. 2.95 (0-922852-20-0) AIMS Intl.

—Dona Zorra y Dona Ciguena - Mrs. Fox & Mrs. Stork. 2nd ed. La Fonatine, Jean de. Elgorriaga, Jose A., adapted by. (SPA.). 19p. (gr. k-12). 1993. pap. 2.95 (0-922852-19-7) AIMS Intl.

—Drei Baren: The Three Bears. Hutchinson, Hanna. Proffitt, Bettina, tr. from ENG. (GER.). 22p. (Orig.). (gr. k-2). 1990. pap. 2.95 (0-922852-08-1) AIMS Intl.

—Mrs. Fox & Mrs. Stork. La Fonatine, Jean de. Ko, Tonya, tr. from ENG. (KOR.). 19p. (Orig.). (gr. k-12). 1993. pap. 2.95 (0-922852-24-3) AIMS Intl.

—Mrs. Fox & Mrs. Stork. La Fonatine, Jean de. Suwa, Naomi, tr. from ENG. (JPN.). 19p. (Orig.). (gr. k-12). 1993. pap. 2.95 (0-922852-23-5) AIMS Intl.

—Mrs. Fox & Mrs. Stork. La Fonatine, Jean de. 19p. (Orig.). (gr. k-12). 1993. pap. 2.95 (0-922852-21-9) AIMS Intl.

—Mrs. Fox & Mrs. Stork. La Fonatine, Jean de. Do, Le, tr. from ENG. (VIE.). 19p. (Orig.). (gr. k-12). 1993. pap. 2.95 (0-922852-25-1) AIMS Intl.

—Mrs. Fox & Mrs. Stork. La Fonatine, Jean de. Wang, May S., tr. from ENG. (CHI.). 19p. (Orig.). (gr. k-12). 1993. pap. 2.95 (0-922852-22-7) AIMS Intl.

—I Tre Orsi: The Three Bears. Hutchinson, Hanna. Amico, Victoria, tr. from ENG. (ITA.). 22p. (Orig.). (gr. k-2). 1990. pap. 2.95 (0-922852-09-X) AIMS Intl.

—Les Trois Ours: The Three Bears. rev. ed. Calamaro, Emanuel. (FRE.). 22p. (gr. k-2). 1990. pap. 2.95 (0-922852-07-3) AIMS Intl.

Nofziger, Harold H. And It Was Good. 36p. (ps up). 1993. 12.95 (0-8361-3634-9) Herald Pr.

Nojoomi, Nikzad. The Crystal Flower & the Sun. new & rev. ed. Farjam, Farideh. Jabbari, Ahmad, ed. & tr. from PER. LC 83-60453. 24p. (Orig.). (gr. k up). 1983. pap. 4.95 (0-939214-16-4) Mazda Pubs.

Nolan, Denis. The Legend of the White Doe. Hooks, William H. LC 87-11176. 48p. (gr. 3 up). 1988. RSBE 13.95 (0-02-744350-7, Macmillan Child Bk) Macmillan Child Grp.

Nolan, Dennis. The Castle Builder. Nolan, Dennis. LC 86-23784. 32p. (gr. k-3). 1987. RSBE 13.95 (0-02-768240-4, Macmillan Child Bk) Macmillan Child Grp.

—The Castle Builder. Nolan, Dennis. LC 92-29563. 32p. (gr. k-3). 1993. pap. 4.95 (0-689-71703-2, Aladdin) Macmillan Child Grp.

—Dinosaur Dream. Nolan, Dennis. LC 89-78208. 32p. (ps-2). 1990. RSBE 14.95 (0-02-768145-9, Macmillan Child Bk) Macmillan Child Grp.

—Dove Isabeau. Yolen, Jane. 32p. (gr. 3-7). 1989. 13.95 (0-15-224131-0) HarBrace.

—An Ellis Island Christmas. Leighton, Maxinne R. 32p. (gr. 1-4). 1992. 15.00 (0-670-83182-4) Viking Child Bks.
—The Gentleman & the Kitchen Maid. Stanley, Diane. LC 93-157. 1994. 13.99 (0-8037-1320-7); lib. bdg. 13.89 (0-8037-1321-5) Dial Bks Young.
—Julie & Jackie & the Calendar: The Music Book (with Song Lyrics, Complete Narration & Cassette) Carey, Karla. LC 88-12894. 61p. 1990. pap. 9.95 complete pkg. (1-55768-200-3); pap. 9.95 book only (1-55768-175-9); cass. 9.95 (0-317-67817-5) LC Pub.
—Julie & Jackie & the Calendar: The Play & Musical Play (with Music Book, Story-&-Song Cassette & Piano Cassette) Carey, Karla. LC 88-12894. 61p. 1990. pap. 35.00 complete pkg. (1-55768-150-3); pap. 25.00 book only (0-317-89494-3); story-&-song or piano cass. 8.00 (0-317-89495-1) LC Pub.
—Julie & Jackie at Christmas-Time: The Narration & Music Book. Carey, Karla. 69p. 1990. pap. 18.95 complete pkg. (0-685-35761-9); pap. 9.95 (1-55768-201-1); cassette 9.95 (0-685-35762-7) LC Pub.
—Julie & Jackie at Christmas-Time: The Play & Musical Play (with Music Book, Story-&-Song Cassette & Piano Cassette) Carey, Karla. LC 88-12909. 39p. 1990. pap. 35.00 complete pkg. (1-55768-151-1); pap. 25.00 book only (1-55768-026-4); story-&-song or piano cass. 8.00 (0-685-19710-7) LC Pub.
—Julie & Jackie at the Circus: The Narration & Music Book. Carey, Karla. 57p. 1990. pap. 18.95 complete pkg. (0-685-35759-7); pap. 9.95 (1-55768-202-X); cassette 9.95 (0-685-35760-0) LC Pub.
—Julie & Jackie at the Circus: The Play & Musical Play (with Music Book, Story-&-Song Cassette & Piano Cassette) Carey, Karla. LC 88-12910. 44p. 1990. pap. 35.00 complete pkg. (1-55768-152-X); pap. 25.00 book only (1-55768-177-5); story-&-song or piano cass. 8.00 (1-55768-027-2) LC Pub.
—Julie & Jackie Go a'Journeying: The Narration & Music Book. Carey, Karla. 76p. 1990. pap. 18.95 complete pkg. (0-685-35755-4); pap. 9.95 (1-55768-203-8); cassette 9.95 (0-685-35756-2) LC Pub.
—Julie & Jackie Go a'Journeying: The Play & Musical Play (with Music Book, Story-&-Song Cassette & Piano Cassette) Carey, Karla. LC 88-9171. 73p. 1990. pap. 35.00 complete pkg. (1-55768-153-8); pap. 25.00 book only (1-55768-028-0); story-&-song or piano cass. 8.00 (0-685-19711-5) LC Pub.
—Julie & Jackie on the Ranch: The Narration & Music Book. Carey, Karla. 91p. 1990. pap. 18.95 complete pkg. (0-685-35757-0); pap. 9.95 (1-55768-204-6); cassette 9.95 (0-685-35758-9) LC Pub.
—Julie & Jackie on the Ranch: The Play & Musical Play (with Music Book, Story-&-Song Cassette & Piano Cassette) Carey, Karla. LC 88-12911. 46p. 1990. pap. 35.00 complete pkg. (1-55768-154-6); pap. 25.00 book only (1-55768-029-9); story-&-song or piano cass. 8.00 (0-685-19712-3) LC Pub.
—Mockingbird Morning. Ryder, Joanne. LC 88-21305. 32p. (gr. k-3). 1989. RSBE 14.95 (0-02-777961-0, Four Winds) Macmillan Child Grp.
—No Nap for Benjamin Badger. Carlstrom, Nancy W. LC 90-42564. 32p. (ps-1). 1991. RSBE 13.95 (0-02-717285-6, Macmillan Child Bk) Macmillan Child Grp.
—Savina, the Gypsy Dancer. Tompert, Ann. LC 90-5902. 32p. (gr. k-3). 1991. RSBE 13.95 (0-02-789205-0, Macmillan Child Bk) Macmillan Child Grp.
—Step into the Night. Ryder, Joanne. LC 87-37982. 32p. (gr. k-3). 1988. RSBE 14.95 (0-02-777951-3, Four Winds) Macmillan Child Grp.
—The Sword in the Stone. White, Terence H. LC 92-24808. 256p. 1993. 18.95 (0-399-22502-1, Philomel Bks) Putnam Pub Group.
—Under Your Feet. Ryder, Joanne. LC 89-33897. 32p. (gr. k-3). 1990. RSBE 14.95 (0-02-777955-6, Four Winds) Macmillan Child Grp.
—Wolf Child. Nolan, Dennis. LC 88-35955. 40p. (gr. 1-5). 1989. RSBE 13.95 (0-02-768141-6, Macmillan Child Bk) Macmillan Child Grp.
Nolan, Gary. Three Wise Birds. Stamler, Suzanne. (gr. 1-6). 1976. pap. 7.95 (0-913546-68-2) Dharma Pub.
Noland, Mimi. Elephant in the Living Room: The Children's Book. Hastings, Jill M. & Typpo, Marion H. LC 84-70189. 88p. (Orig.). (gr. 3-8). 1984. wkbk. 9.95 (0-89638-071-8) CompCare.
Noll, Cheryl K. The Girl Who Wouldn't See. Lanton, Sandy. LC 93-14390. 32p. (ps-2). Date not set. 11.95 (1-56065-140-7) Capstone Pr. Postponed.
—Morgan's Whistle. Londner, Renee. LC 92-14390. 32p. (ps-2). Date not set. 11.95 (1-56065-162-8) Capstone Pr. Postponed.
—That's Not the Way Mommy Does It. Lanton, Sandy. 32p. (ps-2). Date not set. 11.95 (1-56065-142-3) Capstone Pr. Postponed.
Noll, Sally. Jiggle Wiggle Prance. Noll, Sally. LC 86-18322. 24p. (ps-1). 1987. 11.75 (0-688-06760-3); PLB 11.88 (0-688-06761-1) Greenwillow.
Noll, Sally, jt. illus. see Craig, Rose.
Nolt, Marilyn P. The Biggest Popcorn Party Ever in Center County. Peifer, Jane. LC 86-27063. 32p. (Orig.). (ps-1). 1987. pap. 4.95 (0-8361-3435-4) Herald Pr.
Nolte, Larry. ABCs of the Sacraments...for Children. O'Connor, Francine M. 32p. (gr. k-3). 1989. pap. 2.95 (0-89243-298-5) Liguori Pubns.

—Animal Behavior. Walker, Dava J. 48p. (gr. 3-6). Date not set. PLB 12.95 (1-56065-116-4) Capstone Pr. Postponed.
—Astronomy. Wroble, Lisa. 48p. (gr. 3-6). Date not set. PLB 12.95 (1-56065-110-5) Capstone Pr. Postponed.
—Computers. Chaffin, Ken. 48p. (gr. 3-6). Date not set. PLB 12.95 (1-56065-115-6) Capstone Pr. Postponed.
—Ecology. Perry, Susan. 48p. (gr. 3-6). Date not set. PLB 12.95 (1-56065-117-2) Capstone Pr. Postponed.
—Fifty Nifty Ways to Paint Your Face. Monroe, Lucy. LC 92-549. 1992. pap. 3.95 (1-56565-029-8) Lowell Hse.
—The Golden Circle. 2nd ed. Collins, David R. & Witter, Evelyn. LC 91-67503. 105p. (gr. 4-8). 1992. pap. 6.95 (1-55523-492-5) Winston-Derek.
—Mathematics. Walker, Dava J. 48p. (gr. 3-6). Date not set. PLB 12.95 (1-56065-113-X) Capstone Pr. Postponed.
—Natural Science. Wroble, Lisa. 48p. (gr. 3-6). Date not set. PLB 12.95 (1-56065-112-1) Capstone Pr. Postponed.
—Ride a Red Dinosaur. Collins, David R. McKissack, Patricia & McKissack, Fredrick, eds. LC 87-61645. 32p. (Orig.). (gr. 1-3). 1987. text ed. 8.95 (0-88335-726-7); pap. text ed. 4.95 (0-88335-746-1) Milliken Pub Co.
—Space Science. Wroble, Lisa. 48p. (gr. 3-6). Date not set. PLB 12.95 (1-56065-114-8) Capstone Pr. Postponed.
—Zoology. Perry, Susan. 48p. (gr. 3-6). Date not set. PLB 12.95 (1-56065-111-3) Capstone Pr. Postponed.
Nomes, Eric J. Sugar Blue. Cleaver, Vera. LC 83-19910. 160p. (gr. 5 up). 1984. 13.00 (0-688-02720-2) Lothrop.
Nones, Eric J. Dog Crazy. Feldman, Eve B. LC 91-11083. 112p. (gr. 2 up). 1992. 13.00 (0-688-10819-9, Tambourine Bks) Morrow.
—The Great Quarterback Switch. Christopher, Matt. (gr. 3-6). 1991. pap. 3.95 (0-316-14077-5) Little.
Nonnast, Marie. Fourth of July Story. Dalgliesh, Alice. LC 56-6138. 32p. (ps-3). 1972. RSBE 13.95 (0-684-13164-1, Scribners Young Read); (Scribner) Macmillan Child Grp.
—The Fourth of July Story. Dalgliesh, Alice. LC 86-20662. 32p. (gr. k-4). 1987. pap. 3.95 (0-689-71115-8, Aladdin) Macmillan Child Grp.
Noonan, Julia. Sweetwater. Yep, Laurence. LC 72-9867. 224p. (gr. 5 up). 1983. pap. 3.50 (0-06-440135-9, Trophy) HarpC Child Bks.
—Twinkle, Twinkle, Little Star. Taylor, Jane. (ps-3). 1993. pap. 4.95 (0-590-45928-7, Cartwheel) Scholastic Inc.
Noonan, W. Bigfoot & other Legendary Creatures. Walker, P. 1992. 15.95 (0-15-207147-4, HB Juv Bks) HarBrace.
Norberg, Jon. Academic Sportfolio. Norberg, Jon. Gallup, Beth, ed. 1200p. (gr. 3-6). 1987. 495.00 (0-685-24265-X) Acad Sportfolio.
—Academic Sportfolio: Excuse Notes Are No Excuse. Norberg, Jon. Pranzo, Donard, ed. (gr. 3-6). 1987. portfolio ser. 50.00 (0-924086-00-9) Acad Sportfolio.

Nordensten, Ellen H. Hamel the Camel: A Different Mammal. Perinchief, Robert. 21p. (ps-5). 1993. 12.95 (1-882809-00-9) Perry Pubns. HAMEL THE CAMEL is unlike any other camel. Because he is different (on the outside) from his cousin-dromedaries, he is teased, laughed at & abused. At last he meets someone who looks past his different appearance, & sees something special. In the end, we discover that because of HAMEL'S special nature, he plays a very important role in a story told & retold for centuries. We are reminded throughout the book & song that..." THOSE WHO ARE DIFFERENT DON'T NEED OUR ABUSE... THOSE WHO ARE DIFFERENT CAN BE OF GOOD USE." HAMEL was first a poem, then a song, & finally a book-with-cassette. He is an irresistible, lovable character with an inner beauty & purpose which eventually allows people to look past his feature which for so long was the subject of jeering. HAMEL has proven to be especially meaningful to children & youths with special needs, & those with latent doubts about their own self-esteem. It deals profoundly with the issue of the worthiness of everyone. In an age of stressing diversity, this book is essential. To order: Send check to Perry Publications, P.O. Box 204,

Whitewater, WI 53190; or call 1-800-527-2966. $12.95 plus $3.00 S&H. *Publisher Provided Annotation.*

Nordgren, Steve, jt. illus. see Gleissner, Alex.
Nordqvist, Sven. Festus & Mercury: Ruckus in the Garden. Nordquist, Sven. 24p. (ps-3). 1991. PLB 18.95 (0-87614-678-7) Carolrhoda Bks.
—Festus & Mercury: Wishing to Go Fishing. Nordquist, Sven. 24p. (ps-3). 1991. PLB 18.95 (0-87614-658-2) Carolrhoda Bks.
—Tomten's Christmas Porridge. Nordquist, Sven. Haug, Arden, tr. from SWE. 26p. (ps-3). 1991. 14.95 (0-9615394-2-9) Skandisk.
Nordqvist, Sven. The Fox Hunt. Nordquist, Sven. LC 87-28197. 32p. (ps-2). 1988. 12.95 (0-688-06881-2); PLB 12.88 (0-688-06882-0, Morrow Jr Bks) Morrow Jr Bks.
Noren, Catherine & Camhi, Morrie. The Hispanic Americans. Meltzer, Milton. LC 81-43314. 160p. (gr. 5 up). 1982. 15.00 (0-690-04110-1, Crowell Jr Bks); PLB 14.89 (0-690-04111-X, Crowell Jr Bks) HarpC Child Bks.
Noren, Catherine, photos by. A Day in the Life of a Firefighter. Smith, Betsy. LC 80-54099. 32p. (gr. 4-8). 1981. PLB 11.79 (0-89375-444-7); cassettes avail. Troll Assocs.
Norieka, Robert. A Moon for Seasons. Turner, Ann. LC 92-36857. 40p. (gr. 1-5). 1994. RSBE 14.95 (0-02-789513-0, Macmillan Child Bk) Macmillan Child Grp.
Norman, Floyd. Afro-Classic Folk Tales, Bk. 1: A Rattlesnake Tale. Norman, Floyd E. Stewart, Lyn, ed. Sullivan, Leo, intro. by. 28p. (Orig.). (gr. 4-7). 1992. pap. 9.95 (1-881368-00-9) Vignette.
—Afro-Classic Folk Tales, Bk. 2: Anancy & the Tiger. Sullivan, Leo. Stewart, Lyn, ed. 28p. (Orig.). (gr. 4-7). 1992. pap. 9.95 (1-881368-19-X) Vignette.
Norman, Philip R. The Carrot War. Norman, Philip R. 32p. (ps-3). 1992. 13.95 (0-316-61200-6) Little.
Norris, Carolyn. In Our House: Story for Young Children in Sign Language. Norris, Carolyn. 32p. (Orig.). (ps-3). 1984. 4.95 (0-916708-11-X) Modern Signs.
—Jeans Christmas Stocking. Norris, Carolyn. 24p. (Orig.). (ps-4). 1982. pap. 3.95 (0-916708-10-1) Modern Signs.
—Music in Motion: Twenty Two Songs in Signing Exact English, for Children. Wojcio, Michael D. & Gustason, Gerilee. 112p. (Orig.). 1982. 12.95 (0-916708-07-1) Modern Signs.
Norsgaard, Campbell, photos by. How to Raise Butterflies. Norsgaard, Jaediker E. 48p. (gr. 2-5). 1988. 11.99 (0-396-09144-X, Putnam) Putnam Pub Group.
—Nature's Great Balancing Act: In Our Own Backyard. Norsgaard, E. Jaediker. LC 89-38589. 64p. (gr. 4 up). 1990. 14.95 (0-525-65028-8, Cobblehill Bks) Dutton Child Bks.
Northcote, James. Colonel Hawker's Shooting Diaries. 2nd ed. Parker, Eric. 300p. (gr. 10 up). 1990. Repr. of 1931 ed. 35.00 (1-56416-000-9) Derrydale Pr.
Northway, Jennifer. Carry Go Bring Come. Samuels, Vyanne. LC 89-1528. 32p. (ps-2). 1989. SBE 13.95 (0-02-778121-6, Four Winds) Macmillan Child Grp.
—Nancy No-Size. Hoffman, Mary. 32p. (gr. k-3). 1987. 9.95 (0-19-520596-0) OUP.
Norton, Andrea. Ernest the Fierce Mouse. rev. ed. Rowe, Amy & Rowe, Philip. 32p. (gr. k-2). 1990. Repr. of 1985 ed. PLB 10.50 (1-878363-08-5) Forest Hse.
Norwood, David, et al. Children's Tour of Red Stick City. 32p. (gr. 1-6). 1980. pap. text ed. 2.00 (0-9608282-2-2) YWCO.
Nouvelle, Catherine. Go to Sleep, Little Groundhog. Clement, Claude. LC 91-46234. 22p. (ps). 1992. 6.99 (0-89577-424-0, Readers Digest Kids) RD Assn.
Novack, Kevin. Junipero Serra: God's Pioneer. Martin, Teri. 64p. (gr. 7-9). 1990. pap. 4.95 (0-8091-6589-9) Paulist Pr.
Novak, Justin. Discover It Yourself: Where in the World Are You? Cooper, Kay. 96p. 1993. pap. 3.50 (0-380-71299-7, Camelot) Avon.
—The Kid's Money Book. Godfrey, Neale S. 128p. (gr. 3 up). 1991. 12.95 (1-56288-002-0) Checkerboard.
—Where in the World Are You? Cooper, Kay. 80p. (gr. 3-7). 1990. 13.95 (0-8027-6912-8); lib. bdg. 14.85 (0-8027-6913-6) Walker & Co.
Novak, Matt. It's about Time. Hopkins, Lee B., compiled by. LC 92-12128. (ps-3). 1993. pap. 14.00 JRT (0-671-78512-5, S&S BFYR) S&S Trade.
—The Last Christmas Present. Novak, Matt. LC 92-44513. 32p. (ps-1). 1993. 14.95 (0-531-05495-0); PLB 14.99 (0-531-08645-3) Orchard Bks Watts.
—Who Does This Job? Upton, Pat. LC 90-85722. 32p. (ps-1). 1991. 7.95 (1-878093-20-7) Boyds Mills Pr.
Novakshonoff, V. Innokenty of Alaska. Puhalo, Lazar. 86p. (Orig.). (gr. 8 up). 1986. pap. 5.00 (0-913026-86-7) Synaxis Pr.
Nover, Teri. Chanukah A-Z. Sidi, Smadar S. (ps-2). 1988. 9.95 (1-55774-041-0) Modan-Adama Bks.
Novit, R. Z., Graphic Design Staff. Counting by Tens & Fives. Novit, Renee Z. 16p. (ps-k). Date not set. pap. 7.95 (1-883371-02-3) Kidz & Katz.
—Counting One to Twenty. Novit, Renee Z. 16p. (ps-k). Date not set. pap. 7.95 (1-883371-01-5) Kidz & Katz.

Noyce, Robert. Watch Me Sing, Vol. 1. Brady, Janeen. 31p. (ps-2). 1977. pap. text ed. 5.95 songbk. (*0-944803-09-1*); cassette 7.95 (*0-944803-10-5*) Brite Intl.

Noyes, Beppie. Wigglesworth. Noyes, Beppie. LC 85-62022. 74p. (gr. k-4). 1985. pap. 5.95 (*0-932433-08-1*) Windswept Hse.

Noyes, Leslie. You Can Carve Fantastic Jack-O-Lanterns. Hart, Rhonda M. Foster, Kim, ed. LC 90-55042. 112p. 1990. pap. 6.95 (*0-88266-580-4*) Storey Comm Inc.

Nudd, Stacy. The Adventures of Jozedek. Bishop & Leechman. LC 86-72946. 62p. (Orig.). (gr. 4-5). 1987. pap. 6.00 (*0-916383-23-7*) Aegina Pr.

Nuemeier, Marty. The Outcasts of Poker Flat. Harte, Bret. 48p. (gr. 6 up) 1980. PLB 13.95s.p. (*0-87191-768-8*) Creative Ed.

Nusbaum, Linda. Sounds Around Us. Wittner, Seth H. 32p. (ps). 1988. Incl. audio-cassette. pap. 9.95 (*0-9619269-8-8*) Sound World Record.

Nutt, Ken. I Am Phoenix: Poems for Two Voices. Fleischman, Paul. LC 85-42615. 64p. (gr. 3-8). 1985. 12.00 (*0-06-021881-9*); PLB 11.89 (*0-06-021882-7*) HarpC Child Bks.

Nyborg, Randy. Cinderella & the Prince: A Colorful Pictorial Recount of the Cinderella Story. Perrault, Charles. 27p. (gr. k-10). 1992. 12.95 (*1-87776-766-2*); PLB 19.95 (*1-87776-767-0*) Regal Pubns.

—Oliver Twist. Dickens, Charles. 373p. 1992. Repr. PLB 29.95 (*1-87776-769-7*) Regal Pubns.

Nygaard, Elizabeth. Celebrate God & Country. Hand, Phyllis. 144p. (gr. k-6). 1987. pap. 11.95 (*0-86653-390-7*, SS 843, Shining Star Pubns) Good Apple.

Nygren, Tord. Grandfathers Laika. Wahl, Mats. 32p. (gr. k-4). 1990. PLB 18.95 (*0-87614-434-2*) Carolrhoda Bks.

—Sugaring Season: Making Maple Syrup. Burns, Diane. 32p. (gr. k-4). 1990. PLB 19.95 (*0-87614-420-2*) Carolrhoda Bks.

Nyman, Elisabeth. The Top & the Ball. Andersen, Hans Christian. 32p. (gr. k-3). 1992. 14.95 (*0-8249-8547-8*, Ideals Child); PLB 15.00 (*0-8249-8583-4*) Hambleton-Hill.

Nyncke, Helge. Lenses! Take a Closer Look. Aust, Siegfried. 32p. (gr. 2-5). 1991. PLB 18.95 (*0-8225-2151-2*) Lerner Pubns.

—Light! A Bright Idea. Aust, Siegfried. LC 92-9704. 1992. 18.95 (*0-8225-2155-5*) Lerner Pubns.

O

Oakes, Terry. A Pull-the-Tab Pop-Up Book of Classic Tales of Horror. Marshall, Ray, designed by. 10p. (ps up). 1988. 13.95 (*0-525-44418-1*, DCB) Dutton Child Bks.

Oakeshott, R. Ewart. Knight & His Castle. Oakeshott, R. Ewart. 108p. 1992. 16.95 (*0-8023-1294-2*) Dufour.

Oakley, Graham. The Church Mice & the Moon. Oakley, Graham. LC 74-75569. 40p. (gr. k-3). 1974. SBE 13.95 (*0-689-30437-4*, Atheneum Childrens Bks) Macmillan Child Grp.

—The Church Mice & the Ring. Oakley, Graham. LC 91-45273. 32p. (ps up). 1992. SBE 14.95 (*0-689-31790-5*, Atheneum Child Bk) Macmillan Child Grp.

—The Church Mice Spread Their Wings. Oakley, Graham. LC 75-15102. 40p. (gr. k-3). 1976. SBE 13.95 (*0-689-30496-X*, Atheneum Child Bk) Macmillan Child Grp.

—The Church Mouse. Oakley, Graham. LC 72-75276. 40p. (gr. k-3). 1972. SBE 13.95 (*0-689-30058-1*, Atheneum Child Bk) Macmillan Child Grp.

—Hetty & Harriet. Oakley, Graham. LC 81-8024. 32p. (gr. k-3). 1982. SBE 13.95 (*0-689-30888-4*, Atheneum Child Bk) Macmillan Child Grp.

Oakley, John. A Friend for Zacchaeus. Hunter, Elrose. 10p. (ps). 1993. 5.95 (*0-687-47215-6*) Abingdon.

—The Good Neighbor. Hunter, Elrose. 10p. (ps). 1993. 5.95 (*0-687-15525-8*) Abingdon.

—Joseph the Dreamer. Hunter, Elrose. 10p. (ps). 1993. 5.95 (*0-687-20544-1*) Abingdon.

—Moses the Leader. Hunter, Elrose. 10p. (ps). 1993. 5.95 (*0-687-27266-7*) Abingdon.

Oak-Rhind, Mary & Dennison, Graham. Treasury of Animal Stories. Miles, John C., ed. LC 90-11158. 96p. (gr. 2-5). 1991. lib. bdg. 14.89 (*0-8167-2240-4*); pap. text ed. 6.95 (*0-8167-2241-2*) Troll Assocs.

Ober, Carol. How Music Came into the World. Ober, Hal, retold by. LC 93-11330. Date not set. write for info. (*0-395-67523-5*) HM.

Oberdieck, Bernhard. The Lost Princess: A Double Story. MacDonald, George. Sadler, Glenn E., ed. 144p. 1992. text ed. 19.99 (*0-8028-5070-7*) Eerdmans.

Obergfoll, Michael. Super Santa of All Space & Beyond Assisted by His Galaxy Elves: Coloring Activity Book. Obergfoll, Michael. LC 72-847. 34p. (gr. 2-12). 1988. 10.95 (*0-929052-01-3*) Super Santa Prodns.

Obering, Kay & Nast, Thomas. A Child's Christmas Cookbook. Chancellor, Betty. 40p. (Orig.). (gr. 1-8). 1969. pap. 4.00 (*0-914510-00-2*) Evergreen.

Oberlander, Gerhard. Piebald Pup. Korschunow, Irina. (gr. k-3). 1959. 9.95 (*0-8392-3026-5*) Astor-Honor.

Oberste, Kenneth, jt. illus. see Van Ronzelen, George.

Obligado, Lilian. One Terrific Thanksgiving. Sharmat, Marjorie W. LC 85-726. 32p. (ps-3). 1985. reinforced bdg. 14.95 (*0-8234-0569-9*) Holiday.

O'Boyle, Rick. Student Thesaurus. Ryan, Elizabeth A. LC 89-20305. 160p. (gr. 2-8). 1990. PLB 14.89 (*0-8167-1914-4*); pap. text ed. 6.95 (*0-8167-1856-3*) Troll Assocs.

O'Brian, Bill. Ear Book. Perkins, Al. LC 68-28464. (ps-1). 1968. 6.95 (*0-394-81199-2*); lib. bdg. 7.99 (*0-394-91199-7*) Random Bks Yng Read.

O'Brien, Ann S. Double-Dip Feelings: A Book to Help Children Understand Emotions. Cain, Barbara S. LC 89-49382. 32p. 1990. 16.95 (*0-945354-23-1*); pap. 8.95 (*0-945354-20-7*) Magination Pr.

O'Brien, Anne S. I Don't Want to Go. O'Brien, Anne S. LC 85-82108. 14p. (ps-2). 1986. bds. 3.95 (*0-8050-0051-8*, Bks Young Read) H Holt & Co.

—Jamaica & Brianna. Havill, Juanita. LC 92-36508. 1993. 13.95 (*0-395-64489-5*) HM.

—Jamaica Tag-Along. Havill, Juanita. (ps-3). 1989. 13.45 (*0-395-49602-0*) HM.

—Jamaica Tag-Along. Havill, Juanita. 1990. pap. 4.80 (*0-395-54949-3*) HM.

—Jamaica's Find. Havill, Juanita. (ps-3). 1986. 13.45 (*0-395-39376-0*) HM.

—Jamaica's Find. Havill, Juanita. LC 85-14542. 32p. (gr. 4-8). 1987. pap. 4.80 (*0-395-45357-7*) HM.

—The Mystery of the Haunted Cabin. Delton, Judy. LC 86-7723. 128p. (gr. 2-5). 1986. 13.45 (*0-395-41917-4*) HM.

—Talking Walls. Knight, Margy B. LC 91-67867. 40p. (gr. k-8). 1992. 17.95 (*0-88448-102-6*) Tilbury Hse.

—Who Belongs Here? An American Story. Knight, Margy B. 40p. (gr. 3-8). 1993. 16.95 (*0-88448-110-7*) Tilbury Hse.

O'Brien, John. Brother Billy Bronto's Bygone Blues Band. Birchman, David F. LC 90-2611. (ps-3). 1992. 14.00 (*0-688-10423-1*); PLB 13.93 (*0-688-10424-X*) Lothrop.

—The Curious Adventures of Jimmy McGee. Estes, Eleanor. LC 86-31793. 160p. (gr. 3-7). 1987. 14.95 (*0-15-221075-X*, HB Juv Bks) HarBrace.

—Daffy Down Dillies: Silly Limericks. Lear, Edward. LC 91-72986. 32p. 1992. 14.95 (*1-56397-007-4*) Boyds Mills Pr.

—Favorite Tales of Monsters & Trolls. Jonsen, George. Lerner, Sharon, ed. LC 76-24182. (ps-2). 1977. lib. bdg. 5.99 (*0-394-93477-6*) Random Bks Yng Read.

—Flapdoodle: Pure Nonsense from American Folklore. Schwartz, Alvin. LC 79-9618. 128p. (gr. 5 up) 1980. PLB 13.89 (*0-397-31920-7*, Lipp Jr Bks) HarpC Child Bks.

—Funny You Should Ask: How to Make up Jokes & Riddles with Wordplay. Terban, Marvin. 64p. (gr. 4-7). 1992. 13.95 (*0-395-60556-3*, Clarion Bks); pap. 5.95 (*0-395-58113-3*, Clarion Bks) HM.

—The Irish Piper. Latimer, Jim. LC 90-34550. 32p. (gr. 1-3). 1991. SBE 13.95 (*0-684-19130-X*, Scribners Young Read) Macmillan Child Grp.

—The Saracen Maid. Garfield, Leon. LC 93-6612. 1994. pap. 13.00 (*0-671-86646-X*, S&S BFYR) S&S Trade.

—Sir Small & the Dragonfly. O'Connor, Jane. LC 87-35309. 32p. (Orig.). (ps-1). 1988. lib. bdg. 7.99 (*0-394-99625-9*); 3.50 (*0-394-89625-4*, Random Juv) Random Bks Yng Read.

—Six Creepy Sheep. Enderle, Judith R. & Tessler, Stephanie G. 24p. (ps-1). 1992. PLB 12.95 (*1-56397-092-9*) Boyds Mills Pr.

—Six Creepy Sheep. Enderle, Judith R. & Tessler, Stephanie G. LC 93-7140. 26p. (ps-1). 1993. pap. 4.99 (*0-14-054994-3*, Puffin) Puffin Bks.

—Six Sleepy Sheep. Gordon, Jeffie R. LC 90-85728. 24p. (ps-1). 1991. 12.95 (*1-878093-06-1*) Boyds Mills Pr.

—Six Sleepy Sheep. Gordon, Jeffie R. 24p. (ps-1). 1993. pap. 4.99 (*0-14-054848-3*, Puffin) Puffin Bks.

—What His Father Did. Greene, Jacqueline D. 32p. (gr. k-3). 1992. 13.45 (*0-395-55042-4*) HM.

O'Brien, John, photos by. This Is Baseball. Blackstone, Margaret. LC 92-22921. 32p. (ps-k). 1993. 14.95 (*0-8050-2390-9*, Bks Young Read) H Holt & Co.

O'Brien, Michael, photos by. Chi-Hoon: A Korean Girl. McMahon, Patricia. LC 92-81331. 48p. (gr. 4-7). 1993. 16.95 (*1-56397-026-0*) Boyds Mills Pr.

O'Brien, Teresa. Henry's Wild Morning. Greaves, Margaret. LC 90-3554. 40p. (ps-3). 1991. 13.95 (*0-8037-0907-2*) Dial Bks Young.

Obrist, Jurg. Harold's Hideaway Thumb. Sonnenschein, Harriet. 32p. (ps-k). 1993. pap. 2.25 (*0-671-79602-X*, Little Simon) S&S Trade.

—Harold's Hideway Thumb. Sonnenschein, Harriet. LC 91-6486. 40p. (ps-k). 1991. pap. 12.95 jacketed (*0-671-73568-3*, S&S BFYR) S&S Trade.

—Harold's Runaway Nose. Sonnenschein, Harriet. LC 91-6486. 40p. (ps). 1989. pap. 12.95 jacketed (*0-671-66912-5*, Little Simon) S&S Trade.

Ockenga, Starr, photos by. The Ark in the Attic: An Alphabet Adventure. Doolittle, Eileen. LC 86-45534. (ps up). 1987. 19.95 (*0-87923-684-1*) Godine.

O'Cleary, Michael. Cruncher Sparrow's Flying School. Snell, Gordon. 76p. (Orig.). (gr. 2-6). 1991. pap. 6.95 (*1-85371-163-2*, Pub. by Poolbeg Pr ER) Dufour.

O'Connell, Jennifer B. A Garden of Whales. Davis, Maggie S. LC 92-34411. 32p. 1993. 16.95 (*0-944475-36-1*); pap. 6.95 (*0-944475-35-3*) Camden Hse Pub.

O'Connell, Ruth. Guess, Guess. Hillert, Margaret. 24p. (gr. k-1). 1988. 4.99 (*0-87403-456-6*, 24-03695) Standard Pub.

—The Little Lost Sheep. Lindsey, Marilyn L. LC 87-91993. (gr. k-2). 1988. 2.50 (*0-87403-398-5*, 24-03808) Standard Pub.

O'Connell, Ruth A. A Surprise for Miss Van. Frederick, Ruth. 32p. (gr. 1-2). 1991. pap. 3.99 (*0-87403-805-7*, 24-03895) Standard Pub.

—Where's Tommy? Frederick, Ruth. 32p. (gr. 1-2). 1991. pap. 3.99 saddle stitch (*0-87403-806-5*, 24-03896) Standard Pub.

O'Connor, Barbara. The Menehune & the Nene. Yamashita, Susan. LC 84-3290. (gr. 3-6). 1984. 7.95 (*0-916630-42-0*) Pr Pacifica.

O'Connor, Claiborne. Little Brown Roadrunner: Who Did It Herself. Wender, Leon. 24p. (Orig.). (gr. 1-3). 1992. pap. text ed. 4.00 (*0-938513-14-1*) Amador Pubs.

O'Connor, David & Sibbick, John. Gods & Pharaohs from Egyptian Mythology. Harris, Geraldine. LC 90-23455. 132p. (gr. 6 up). 1992. 22.50 (*0-87226-907-8*) P Bedrick Bks.

—Gods & Pharoahs from Egyptian Mythology. Harris, Geraldine. 128p. (gr. 6 up). 1993. pap. 14.95 sewn (*0-87226-908-6*) P Bedrick Bks.

O'Connor, Jane. Coaching Ms. Parker. Heymsfeld, Carla. LC 91-28484. 96p. (gr. 3-5). 1992. SBE 12.95 (*0-02-743715-9*, Bradbury Pr) Macmillan Child Grp.

O'Connor, Thom, et al. Space: 34-24-34: The Exciting Adventures of the Nova Girls. Nicieza, Mariano. 64p. (Orig.). (gr. 9). 1989. write for info. MN DPPD Inc.

O'Connor, Tim. My Bedtime Anytime Storybook. Beers, V. Gilbert. LC 92-8376. 1992. 12.99 (*0-8407-9166-6*) Oliver-Nelson.

—My Sunny Day, & Day Nursery Rhyme Book. Beers, V. Gilbert. LC 93-17261. 1993. 12.99 (*0-8407-9253-0*) Nelson.

Oda, Kancho, jt. illus. see Kasamatsu, Shiro.

O'Daniel, Thurman B. Blacker the Berry. Thurman, Wallace. Larson, Charles R., ed. (gr. 11 up). 1970. pap. 7.00 (*0-02-054750-1*, Collier Young Ad) Macmillan Child Grp.

Oddie, Alan, photos by. Gymnastics Is for Me. Washington, Rosemary G. LC 79-4496. 48p. (gr. 2-5). 1979. PLB 13.50 (*0-8225-1078-2*) Lerner Pubns.

Odell, Dave. Being a Christian. Walters, David. 40p. (Orig.). (gr. 2-10). Date not set. write for info. wkbk. (*0-9629559-2-2*) Good News Min.

O'Dell, Scott. Carlota. O'Dell, Scott. LC 77-9468. 176p. (gr. 5-9). 1977. 13.45 (*0-395-25487-6*) HM.

Oden, Dick, jt. illus. see Hoopes, Barbara.

Oden, Ron. Grandfather's Stories. Roland, Donna. (Orig.). (gr. k-3). 1993. pap. 4.95 (*0-941996-00-X*); Tchr's. ed. 5.50 (*0-685-42442-1*); Flannelboard set. 12.00; Video cass. 32.00; Audio cass., per culture. 5.95 Open My World. This is a series which provides students with both cultural information as well as a strong sense of personal & social values. The series portrays families living in the U.S., but through the eyes of Grandfather the grandchildren learn about their cultural heritage. Cultures presently available are: Cambodia, Germany, Mexico, the Philippines, & Viet Nam. Each culture is represented by two books: GRANDFATHER'S STORIES, which introduces the culture by means of sharing about its history & social customs. In the first book Grandfather also shares what values he would most want to pass on to his grandchildren, MORE OF GRANDFATHER'S STORIES continues to emphasize values. This time Grandfather actually tells a folktale which illustrates the values shared in the first book. The teacher's guide & activity book offers numerous suggestions & additional information which enhances & expands the storyline. Although written on a 2nd grade reading level the format & illustrations lend themselves to older grades as well, especially when the teacher's guide is used in conjunction with the student books. The student books are available in both paperback as well as hardcover versions. Video cassette, flannelboard sets & cassettes also available. Published by Open My World Publishing, San Diego, CA. Distributed by: Paperback versions, Multicultural Publishing, 800 N. Grand Ave., Covina CA 91724, Weiser

Educational, 30085 Comercio, Ranchos Santa Margarita, CA 92688, Shen's Books & Supplies, 821 S. First Ave., Arcadia, CA 91724, Yellow Book Road, 8315 La Mesa Blvd., La Mesa, CA 91941. Hardcover versions: Econo-Clad, 2101 N. Topeka Blvd., Topeka, KS 66608, Hertzberg-New Method (Perma Bound) 617 E. Vandalla Rd., Jacksonville, IL 62650-3599. Flannelboard Sets: Elfs, 22916 Styles St., Woodland Hills, CA 91367, Open My World Publishing, P.O. Box 15011, San Diego, CA 92175. *Publisher Provided Annotation.*

—More of Grandfather's Stories. Roland, Donna. 25p. (Orig.). (gr. k-3). 1993. pap. 4.95 (*0-941996-02-6*); tchr's ed. 5.50 (*0-941996-13-1*) Open My World.

O'Donnell, Peter. Carnegie's Excuse. O'Donnell, Peter. LC 92-17617. 32p. (ps-3). 1993. 14.95 (*0-590-46435-3*) Scholastic Inc.

O'Dwyer, Chung S. & Fwhang, Duk S. Mi Jun's Difficult Decision. Burkholder, Ruth C. LC 83-20494. 14p. (Orig.). (gr. 4-6). 1984. pap. 4.95 (*0-377-00139-2*) Friendship Pr.

—Won Gil's Secret Diary. Burkholder, Ruth C. LC 83-16529. 14p. (Orig.). (gr. 1-3). 1984. pap. 4.95 (*0-377-00138-4*) Friendship Pr.

Oechsli, K. More of the Songs We Sing. Coopersmith, Harry, ed. (ENG & HEB.). 288p. (gr. 4-10). 1970. 9. 50x (*0-8381-0217-4*) United Syn Bk.

Oechsli, Kelli. Weeny Witch. DeLage, Ida. 48p. (gr. k-4). 1991. Repr. of 1966 ed. lib. bdg. 12.95 (*0-7910-1485-1*) Chelsea Hse.

Oechsli, Kelly. In My Garden: A Child's Gardening Book. Oechsli, Helen & Oechsli, Kelly. LC 84-21285. 32p. (ps-2). 1985. RSBE 12.95 (*0-02-768510-1*, Macmillan Child Bk) Macmillan Child Grp.

—Mice at Bat. Oechsli, Kelly. LC 85-45266. 64p. (gr. 1-3). 1986. HarpC Child Bks.

—Mice at Bat. Oechsli, Kelly. LC 85-45266. 64p. (gr. k-3). 1990. pap. 3.50 (*0-06-444139-3*, Trophy) HarpC Child Bks.

—One Minute Stories of Brothers & Sisters. Lewis, Shari. LC 87-20056. 48p. (ps-3). 1988. pap. 7.95 (*0-385-23425-2*) Doubleday.

—Scruffy. Parish, Peggy. LC 87-45564. 64p. (gr. k-3). 1988. 14.00 (*0-06-024659-6*); PLB 13.89 (*0-06-024660-X*) HarpC Child Bks.

—Scruffy. Parish, Peggy. LC 87-45564. 64p. (gr. k-3). 1990. pap. 3.50 (*0-06-444137-7*, Trophy) HarpC Child Bks.

Offen, Hilda. Beauty & the Beast & Other Stories. Carter, Margaret, retold by. LC 93-5772. 1994. 3.95 (*1-85697-967-9*) Kingfisher Bks.

—Cinderella & Other Stories. Carter, Margaret, retold by. LC 93-5770. 1994. 3.95 (*1-85697-968-7*) Kingfisher Bks.

—Elephant Pie. Offen, Hilda. 32p. (ps-2). 1993. 13.99 (*0-525-45123-4*, DCB) Dutton Child Bks.

—Goldilocks & Other Stories. Carter, Margaret, retold by. LC 93-5771. 1994. 3.95 (*1-85697-969-5*) Kingfisher Bks.

—Little Red Riding Hood & Other Stories. Carter, Margaret, retold by. LC 93-5768. 1994. 3.95 (*1-85697-970-9*) Kingfisher Bks.

—My Favorite Nursery Rhymes. (ps-1). 1987. pap. 12.95 (*0-671-64705-9*, S&S BFYR) S&S Trade.

—The Sheep Made a Leap. Offen, Hilda. 32p. (ps-2). 1994. 10.99 (*0-525-45124-9*, DCB) Dutton Child Bks.

—Sleeping Beauty & Other Stories. Carter, Margaret, retold by. LC 93-5769. 1994. 3.95 (*1-85697-971-7*) Kingfisher Bks.

—Snow White & Other Stories. Carter, Margaret, retold by. LC 93-5767. 1994. 3.95 (*1-85697-972-5*) Kingfisher Bks.

—The Three Little Pigs & Other Stories. Carter, Margaret, retold by. LC 93-11741. 1994. 3.95 (*1-85697-973-3*) Kingfisher Bks.

—A Treasury of Bedtime Stories. Yeatman, Linda, compiled by. 160p. (ps-3). 1981. pap. 13.00 (*0-671-44463-8*, S&S BFYR) S&S Trade.

—A Treasury of Mother Goose. (gr. k up). 1984. pap. 13. 00 (*0-671-50118-6*, S&S BFYR) S&S Trade.

—The Ugly Duckling & Other Stories. Carter, Margaret, retold by. LC 93-5766. 1994. 3.95 (*1-85697-974-1*) Kingfisher Bks.

Officer, Robyn. The Little Mermaid. Andersen, Hans Christian. 32p. (ps). 1992. 6.95 (*0-8362-4918-6*) Andrews & McMeel.

—Mother Goose's Nursery Rhymes. 32p. (ps-3). 1992. 6.95 (*0-8362-4907-0*) Andrews & McMeel.

—A Real Little Bunny: A Sequel to The Velveteen Rabbit. Greenway, Jennifer. LC 92-37149. 40p. 1993. 14.95 (*0-8362-4936-4*) Andrews & McMeel.

—Santa's Christmas Ride: A Storybook with Real Presents. Egan, Louise B. 52p. 1993. incl. gifts 16.95 (*0-8362-4505-9*) Andrews & McMeel.

—The Story of the Easter Bunny. Black, Sheila. LC 87-81934. 32p. (ps-1). 1988. write for info. (*0-307-10415-X*, Pub. by Golden Bks) Western Pub.

—A Tale of Peter Rabbit. Potter, Beatrix. 1991. 6.95 (*0-8362-4908-9*) Andrews & McMeel.

—Thumbelina. Andersen, Hans Christian. 32p. (ps-3). 1992. 6.95 (*0-8362-4926-7*) Andrews & McMeel.

—Ugly Duckling. Andersen, Hans Christian. 32p. (ps-3). 1992. 6.95 (*0-8362-4911-9*) Andrews & McMeel.

—The Velveteen Rabbit. Williams, Margery. 40p. 1991. 6.95 (*0-8362-4910-0*) Andrews & McMeel.

Ogawa, Hiroshi. Wasps. Johnson, Sylvia A. LC 83-23847. 48p. (gr. 4 up). 1984. PLB 19.95 (*0-8225-1460-5*) Lerner Pubns.

Ogden, Betina. Clouds. Hessell, Jenny. LC 92-27099. 1993. 3.75 (*0-383-03561-9*) SRA Schl Grp.

—Farm Babies. Bergen, Lara R. LC 93-26192. 1994. pap. write for info. (*0-448-40212-2*, G&D) Putnam Pub Group.

—The Puppy Who Went to School. Herman, Gail. 32p. (ps-3). 1992. pap. 2.25 (*0-448-40481-8*, G&D) Putnam Pub Group.

—The Ugly Duckling. 18p. (ps). 1994. bds. 3.95 (*0-448-40184-3*, G&D) Putnam Pub Group.

Ogden, Bill. The Dog That Called the Signals. Christopher, Matt. LC 82-15234. 48p. (gr. 3-5). 1982. 12.95 (*0-316-13980-7*) Little.

—The Dog That Stole Football Plays. Christopher, Matt. 48p. (gr. 3-5). 1980. 13.95 (*0-316-13978-5*) Little.

—More Power to You! Cobb, Vicki. 64p. (gr. 3-5). 1986. lib. bdg. 11.95 (*0-316-14899-7*) Little.

Ogden, Ethel F. The Medibears Guide to the Doctor's Exam: For Children & Parents. Ogden, John A. (gr. k-5). 1991. 10.95 (*0-8130-1082-9*) U Press Fla.

O'Grady-Steinberg, Chrissy. His-Her, The Shy Serpent. Eisemann, Henry. (Orig.). (gr. k-6). 1992. pap. 6.95 (*0-938129-05-8*) Emprise Pubns.

O'Halloran, Tim. Know Your Numbers. O'Halloran, Tim. 38p. (ps-1). 1983. 10.95 (*0-88625-045-5*) Durkin Hayes Pub.

—Let's Go on Safari. King, Vivienne, et al. 32p. (ps-3). 1985. pap. 3.95 (*0-88625-107-9*) Durkin Hayes Pub.

—Words Around Us. O'Halloran, Tim. 48p. (ps-k). 1985. 10.95 (*0-88625-124-9*) Durkin Hayes Pub.

—Words Around Us in French. O'Halloran, Tim. (FRE.). 48p. (ps-k). 1985. 10.95 (*0-88625-125-7*) Durkin Hayes Pub.

O'Halloran, Tim, jt. illus. see Williams, Harland.

Ohi, Ruth. Aa-Choo! Orr, Wendy. 32p. (ps-3). 1992. PLB 14.95 (*1-55037-209-2*, Pub. by Annick CN); pap. 4.95 (*1-55037-208-4*, Pub. by Annick CN) Firefly Bks Ltd.

—Amanda's Book. Westell, Kerry. 24p. (ps-1). 1991. PLB 15.95 (*1-55037-185-1*, Pub. by Annick CN); pap. 5.95 (*1-55037-182-7*, Pub. by Annick CN) Firefly Bks Ltd.

—And You Can Be the Cat. Hutchins, Hazel. 24p. (ps-3). 1992. PLB 14.95 (*1-55037-219-X*, Pub. by Annick CN); pap. 4.95 (*1-55037-216-5*, Pub. by Annick CN) Firefly Bks Ltd.

—Anniranni & Mollymishi the Wild-Haired Doll. Lamm, C. Drew. 24p. (ps-2). 1990. 14.95 (*1-55037-105-3*, Pub. by Annick CN); pap. 5.95 (*1-55037-106-1*, Pub. by Annick CN) Firefly Bks Ltd.

—Nicholas at the Library. Hutchins, Hazel. 24p. (ps-2). 1990. 14.95 (*1-55037-134-7*, Pub. by Annick CN); pap. 5.95 (*1-55037-132-0*, Pub. by Annick CN) Firefly Bks Ltd.

—Pegasus & Ooloo-Moo-loo. Orr, Wendy. 32p. 1993. lib. bdg. 14.95 (*1-55037-278-5*, Pub. by Annick CN); pap. 4.95 (*1-55037-279-3*, Pub. by Annick CN) Firefly Bks Ltd.

Ohlsson, Ib. Alphabet of Girls. rev. ed. Jacobs, Leland. LC 93-8328. 1994. write for info. (*0-8050-3018-2*) H Holt & Co.

—Celebration: The Story of American Holidays. Penner, Lucille R. LC 92-25871. 80p. (gr. 1 up). 1993. SBE 15.95 (*0-02-770903-5*, Macmillan Child Bk) Macmillan Child Grp.

—Encyclopedia Brown Carries On. Sobol, Donald J. LC 79-6340. 80p. (gr. 3-7). 1984. SBE 12.95 (*0-02-786190-2*, Four Winds) Macmillan Child Grp.

—Encyclopedia Brown Sets the Pace. Sobol, Donald J. LC 81-69511. 96p. (gr. 3-7). 1984. SBE 12.95 (*0-02-786200-3*, Four Winds) Macmillan Child Grp.

—Encyclopedia Brown Takes the Cake! A Cook & Case Book. Sobol, Donald J. & Andrews, Glenn. LC 82-84250. 128p. (gr. 3-7). 1983. SBE 12.95 (*0-02-786210-0*, Four Winds) Macmillan Child Grp.

—Hats off to John Stetson. Christian, Mary B. LC 91-34272. 64p. (gr. 2-6). 1992. SBE 13.95 (*0-02-718465-X*, Macmillan Child Bk) Macmillan Child Grp.

—It Happened in America: True Stories from the Fifty States. Perl, Lila. 302p. (gr. 4-6). 1992. 21.95 (*0-8050-1719-4*, Bks Young Read) H Holt & Co.

—A Moon in Your Lunch Box: Poems. Spooner, Michael. LC 92-32662. 64p. (gr. 2-6). 1993. PLB 14.95 (*0-8050-2209-0*, Bks Young Read) H Holt & Co.

—Timmy Green's Blue Lake. Bergman, Donna. LC 91-30232. 32p. (ps up). 1992. 14.00 (*0-688-10747-8*, Tambourine Bks); PLB 13.93 (*0-688-10748-6*, Tambourine Bks) Morrow.

Ohtomo, Yasuo. How Do I Put It on? Watanabe, Shigeo. LC 79-12714. 12p. (gr. 2-4). 1984. (Philomel); pap. 5.95 (*0-399-21040-7*, Philomel) Putnam Pub Group.

—I Can Take a Walk! Watanabe, Shigeo. 32p. 1991. (Philomel Bks); pap. 4.95 (*0-399-21847-5*, Philomel Bks) Putnam Pub Group.

—Let's Go Swimming. Watanabe, Shigeo. 32p. (ps-2). 1990. 10.95 (*0-399-21896-3*, Philomel Bks) Putnam Pub Group.

Oido, Yukio. Me & Alves: A Japanese Journey. Akio, Terumasa. Matsui, Susan, tr. 24p. 1993. lib. bdg. 14.95 (*1-55037-223-8*, Pub. by Annick CN); pap. 4.95 (*1-55037-222-X*, Pub. by Annick CN) Firefly Bks Ltd.

O'Keefe, Maureen. How the Children Stopped the Wars. Wahl, Jan. LC 93-2479. 96p. 1993. Repr. of 1969 ed. 15.95 (*1-883672-00-7*) Tricycle Pr.

O'Kelley, Mattie L. A Winter Place. Radin, Ruth Y. LC 82-15349. 32p. (gr. 3 up). 1982. 15.95 (*0-316-73218-4*, Joy St Bks) Little.

Oldfield, Margaret J. Fat Cat & Ebenezer Geezer: The Teeny Tiny Mouse. 2nd ed. Oldfield, Margaret J. (gr. k-2). 1980. pap. 3.00 (*0-934876-13-4*) Creative Storytime.

—Tell & Draw Paper Bag Puppet Book. 2nd ed. Oldfield, Margaret J. (gr. k-2). 1981. pap. 5.95 (*0-934876-16-9*) Creative Storytime.

—Tell & Draw Paper Cut-Outs. Oldfield, Margaret J. (Orig.). (gr. k-2). 1988. pap. 3.50 (*0-934876-23-1*, 23) Creative Storytime.

Olds, Tom, jt. illus. see Tolley, Lynn.

O'Leary, Patrick, photos by. Lessons from the Eastern Warriors. Neff, Fred. 96p. (gr. 5-12). 1992. PLB 14.95 (*0-8225-1166-5*) Lerner Pubns.

—Lessons from the Fighting Commandos. Neff, Fred. 96p. (gr. 5-12). 1992. PLB 14.95 (*0-8225-1165-7*) Lerner Pubns.

—Lessons from the Japanese Masters. Neff, Fred. 96p. (gr. 5-12). 1992. PLB 14.95 (*0-8225-1164-9*) Lerner Pubns.

Olguin, John. Whalewatch! Behrens, June. LC 78-7338. 32p. (gr. k-4). 1978. PLB 13.67 (*0-516-08873-4*, Golden Gate); pap. 3.95 (*0-516-48873-2*) Childrens.

Oling, Tom. Smarts: A Study Skills Resource Guide. rev. ed. Custer, Susan, et al. (gr. 5-7). 1991. tchr's ed. 11. 95 (*0-944584-27-6*) Sopris.

Oliver, Bryan. Snowflake Come Home: A Wolf's Story. Giegling, John. 124p. (gr. 7-9). 1992. pap. 4.95 (*0-912661-12-7*) Woodsong Graph.

Oliver, Jenni. Free. Warburg, Sandol S. LC 75-40013. 48p. (gr. 1 up). 1976. PLB 5.95 (*0-395-24210-X*) HM.

—A Summer to Die. Lowry, Lois. (gr. 3-7). 1977. 13.45 (*0-395-25338-1*) HM.

Oliver, Maria F. The Night of the Stars. Gutierrez, Douglas. Dearden, Carmen D., tr. from SPA. 24p. (ps-1). 1988. 9.95 (*0-916291-17-0*) Kane-Miller Bk.

Oliver, Stephen, photos by. Clothes. LC 90-23999. 24p. (ps-k). 1991. 7.00 (*0-679-81806-5*) Random Bks Yng Read.

—Counting. LC 90-8577. 24p. (ps-k). 1991. 6.95 (*0-679-81163-X*) Random Bks Yng Read.

—Home. LC 89-63092. 24p. (ps-k). 1990. 6.95 (*0-679-80602-5*) Random Bks Yng Read.

—My First Look at Colors. LC 89-63091. 24p. (ps-k). 1990. 7.00 (*0-679-80535-4*) Random Bks Yng Read.

—My First Look at Numbers. LC 89-63088. 24p. (ps-k). 1990. 7.00 (*0-679-80533-8*) Random Bks Yng Read.

—My First Look at Shapes. LC 89-63087. 24p. (ps-k). 1990. 7.00 (*0-679-80534-6*) Random Bks Yng Read.

—My First Look at Sizes. LC 89-63086. 24p. (ps-k). 1990. 7.00 (*0-679-80532-X*) Random Bks Yng Read.

—Nature. LC 90-23568. 24p. (ps-k). 1991. 7.00 (*0-679-81805-7*) Random Bks Yng Read.

—Noises. LC 90-8587. 24p. (ps-k). 1991. 6.95 (*0-679-81161-3*) Random Bks Yng Read.

—Opposites. LC 89-63093. 24p. (ps-k). 1990. 6.95 (*0-679-80620-2*) Random Bks Yng Read.

—Seasons. LC 89-63094. 24p. (ps-k). 1990. 6.95 (*0-679-80621-0*) Random Bks Yng Read.

—Shopping. LC 90-23567. 24p. (ps-k). 1991. 7.00 (*0-679-81803-0*) Random Bks Yng Read.

—Sorting. LC 90-8575. 24p. (ps-k). 1991. 6.95 (*0-679-81162-1*) Random Bks Yng Read.

—Things That Go. LC 90-23562. 24p. (ps-k). 1991. 7.00 (*0-679-81804-9*) Random Bks Yng Read.

—Time. LC 90-8576. 24p. (ps-k). 1991. 6.95 (*0-679-81164-8*) Random Bks Yng Read.

—Touch. LC 89-63095. (ps-k). 1990. 6.95 (*0-679-80623-7*) Random Bks Yng Read.

Oliver, Tony & Gristwood, Doreen. Partly True Tales, 2 vols. Winch, Gordon. 64p. (gr. 2-3). 1988. Set. PLB 37.20 (*1-55532-938-1*) Gareth Stevens Inc.

Oliviera, Gerry. My Family & Friends. Bennett, Marian & Stortz, Diane. 12p. (ps). 1992. deluxe ed. 4.99 (*0-87403-994-0*, 24-03114) Standard Pub.

Ollive, Richard. It's Fun to Speak Spanish with ZoZo. Scibor, Teresa. 32p. (ps-3). 1993. pap. 12.95 incl. cassette (*0-8120-8107-2*) Barron.

Olliver, Tony. Possum in the House. Jensen, Kiersten. Sherwood, Rhoda, ed. LC 88-42910. 32p. (gr. 1-2). 1988. PLB 18.60 (*1-55532-933-0*) Gareth Stevens Inc.

—Samantha Seagull's Sandals. Winch, Gordon. Sherwood, Rhoda, ed. LC 88-42923. 32p. (gr. 2-3). 1988. PLB 13.95 (*1-55532-909-8*) Gareth Stevens Inc.

Olofsdotter, Marie. Sofia & the Heartmender. Olofsdotter, Marie. LC 92-46200. 32p. (gr. k up). 1993. 14.95 (*0-915793-50-4*) Free Spirit Pub.

O'Loughlin, Sue. The Queen's Holiday. Wild, Margaret. LC 91-14004. 32p. (ps-1). 1992. 13.95 (*0-531-05973-1*); PLB 13.99 (*0-531-08573-2*) Orchard Bks Watts.

—The Strongest Man in Gundiwallanup. Tulloch, Richard. 32p. 1990. 10.95 (*0-521-36651-8*) Cambridge U Pr.

Olsen, Karen. My Father Raped Me: Frances Ann Speaks Out. 2nd ed. Chetin, Helen. 20p. (gr. 5 up). 1977. pap. 4.95 (*0-938678-05-1*) New Seed.

Olsen, Shirley. Gail's Paint Pail. Carratello, Patty. Spivak, Darlene, ed. 16p. (gr. k-2). 1988. wkbk. 1.95 (*1-55734-385-3*) Tchr Create Mat.
—Holidays on Parade. Sterling, Mary E. 64p. (gr. k-2). 1988. wkbk. 6.95 (*1-55734-377-2*) Tchr Create Mat.
—My Favorite Things. Spivak, Darlene. 48p. (gr. k-2). 1988. wkbk. 5.95 (*1-55734-375-6*) Tchr Create Mat.
—Will Bill? Carratello, Patty. Spivak, Darlene, ed. 16p. (gr. k-2). 1988. wkbk. 1.95 (*1-55734-388-8*) Tchr Create Mat.
Olson, Gordon. Scuffy the Tugboat. Crampton, Gertrude. 24p. (ps-k). 1993. 9.00 (*0-307-74813-8*, 64813, Golden Pr) Western Pub.
Olson, Margaret J. Aloysious Alligator. 2nd ed. Olson, Margaret J. (gr. k-2). 1980. pap. 3.00 (*0-934876-14-2*) Creative Storytime.
Olubo, Joseph. Spiderman Anancy. Berry, James. LC 89-33418. 148p. (gr. 4-6). 1989. 13.95 (*0-8050-1207-9*, Bks Young Read) H Holt & Co.
Olugebefola, Ademola & Sherman, Ed. It's a New Day: Poems for Young Brothas & Sistuhs. Sanchez, Sonia. LC 72-155311. (gr. 5 up). 1971. pap. 3.00 (*0-910296-60-X*) Broadside Pr.
Omalade, Kip. Hello! My Name Is Mr. ImGonChop. Sculfield, Byron. 1993. pap. 5.95 (*0-88378-097-6*) Third World.
O'Malley, Kevin. The Box. O'Malley, Kevin. LC 92-25153. 32p. 1993. 8.95 (*1-55670-275-2*) Stewart Tabori & Chang.
—Cinder Edna. Jackson, Ellen. LC 92-44160. (gr. 3 up). 1994. write for info. (*0-688-12322-8*); lib. bdg. write for info. (*0-688-12323-6*) Lothrop.
—Froggy Went A-Courtin' O'Malley, Kevin. LC 91-41449. 32p. 1992. 14.95 (*1-55670-260-4*) Stewart Tabori & Chang.
—Let's Sing about America. Belling, Andrew. LC 92-763081. 32p. (gr. k-2). 1992. PLB 11.89 (*0-8167-2982-4*); pap. text ed. 3.95 (*0-8167-2983-2*) Troll Assocs.
—Row, Row, Row Your Boat. Oppenheim, Joanne. LC 92-29015. 1993. 9.99 (*0-553-09498-X*) Bantam.
O'Meara, Michael. Kids' Guide to Common Alaska Critters. O'Meara, Jan. 32p. (Orig.). 1993. pap. text ed. 7.95 (*0-9621543-3-4*) Wizard Works.
Omerod, Jan. The Frog Prince. Ormerod, Jan & LLoyd, David. LC 89-12977. 32p. (ps-3). 1990. 12.95 (*0-688-09568-2*); lib. bdg. 12.88 (*0-688-09569-0*) Lothrop.
Omodt, Mary. The Chronicles of Caroltune: Scherzo Finds a Home. Omodt, Jimm. Omodt, Mary, ed. 40p. (Orig.). (gr. 3-8). 1993. pap. text ed. 10.00 (*1-881026-05-1*) Scherzo Pub.
—The Huge Hairy Horse Comes Back with Twenty-Six More. Omodt, Jimm A. Omodt, Mary, ed. 40p. (Orig.). (gr. ps-5). 1993. pap. text ed. 10.00 (*1-881026-03-5*); pap. text ed. 20.00 incl. cassette (*1-881026-02-7*) Scherzo Pub.
Omolade, Kip. Grandma Jackson's Poetry. Hyman, Ramona. 32p. 1992. 16.95 (*0-685-60764-X*); pap. 8.95 (*0-685-60765-8*) Third World.
Omoleye, Amoke. Yoruba Children's Tales. Omoleye, Amoke. 33p. (Orig.). (gr. k-8). 1990. pap. 5.95 (*0-9625699-1-7*) Amoke Omoleye Pub.
Omoto, Larry. Boomerang: A One-Act Play for Grades 7-9. Schuyler, Royce. Kester, Ellen S., ed. 50p. (Orig.). 1989. pap. text ed. 6.95 (*0-685-26284-7*) Pickwick Pubs.
—Boomerang: Drama for Study & Performance. Schuyler, Royce. Kester, Ellen S., ed. 100p. (Orig.). 1989. pap. text ed. 35.00 (*0-685-26285-5*) Pickwick Pubs.
O'Neal, Lauren. Oregon Firsts: Oregon's Trailblazing Past & Present. Long, James A. 224p. (Orig.). 1993. pap. 24.95 (*1-8826350-0-0*) Pumpkin Ridge.
O'Neal, Marian. Piney the Tiny Christmas Tree. Richards, Jack & Richards, John. 21p. (gr. k-5). 1993. 4.95 (*1-883025-00-1*, Piney Pubns); pap. 9.95 talking bk. cass. (*1-883025-01-X*, Piney Pubns); pap. 12.95 cass. & bk. (*1-883025-02-8*); pap. 14.95 video (*1-883025-03-6*); pap. 24.95 video, cass. & bk. (*1-883025-04-4*) Piney Prods.
O'Neil, Sharron. Y Tu, Donde Vives? Cumpiano, Ina. (SPA.). 24p. (Orig.). (gr. 1-3). 1992. pap. text ed. 29.95 big bk. (*1-56334-019-4*); pap. text ed. 6.00 small bk. (*1-56334-045-3*) Hampton-Brown.
O'Neill, Catharine. Fish Fry Tonight. Koller, Jackie F. LC 89-49369. 32p. (ps-3). 1992. 13.00 (*0-517-57814-X*); PLB 13.99 (*0-517-57815-8*) Crown Bks Yng Read.
—Mrs. McDockerty's Knitting. Martinez, Ruth. 32p. (ps-3). 1990. 13.45 (*0-395-51591-2*) HM.
O'Neill, Catherine. J. B. Wigglebottom & the Parade of Pets. Sathre, Vivian. LC 92-17375. 96p. (gr. 2-6). 1993. SBE 12.95 (*0-689-31811-1*, Atheneum Bk) Macmillan Child Grp.
O'Neill, Pablo M. & Robare, Lorie. Descubre Aves. Weidensaul, Scott. University of Mexico City Staff, tr. from SPA. 48p. (gr. 3-8). 1993. PLB 16.95 (*1-56674-047-9*, HTS Bks) Forest Hse.
—Descubre Dinosaurios. Arem, Joel E. University of Mexico City Staff, tr. from SPA. 48p. (gr. 3-8). 1993. PLB 16.95 (*1-56674-049-5*, HTS Bks) Forest Hse.
—Descubre Estrellas y Planetas. Eugene, Toni. University of Mexico City Staff, tr. from SPA. 48p. (gr. 3-8). 1993. PLB 16.95 (*1-56674-052-5*, HTS Bks) Forest Hse.

—Descubre La Vida En el Oceano. Jablonsky, Alice. University of Mexico City Staff, tr. from SPA. 48p. (gr. 3-8). 1993. PLB 16.95 (*1-56674-050-9*, HTS Bks) Forest Hse.
—Descubre Mariposas. Dunn, Gary. University of Mexico City Staff, tr. from SPA. 48p. (gr. 3-8). 1993. PLB 16.95 (*1-56674-048-7*, HTS Bks) Forest Hse.
—Descubre Rocas y Minerales. Arem, Joel E. University of Mexico City Staff, tr. from SPA. 48p. (gr. 3-8). 1993. PLB 16.95 (*1-56674-051-7*, HTS Bks) Forest Hse.
O'Neill, Steven. Dinosaur Do's & Don'ts. Polhamus, Jean B. LC 75-11743. (gr. 1-3). 1975. (Pub. by Treehouse); pap. 2.50 (*0-13-214668-1*) P-H.
Ong, Christina. Animal Car. Barkan, Joanne. 12p. (ps). 1993. bds. 3.50 (*0-689-71676-1*, Aladdin) Macmillan Child Grp.
—Circus Locomotive. Barkan, Joanne. 12p. (ps). 1993. bds. 3.50 (*0-689-71674-5*, Aladdin) Macmillan Child Grp.
—Clown Caboose. Barkan, Joanne. 12p. (ps). 1993. bds. 3.50 (*0-689-71675-3*, Aladdin) Macmillan Child Grp.
—The Little Engine That Could Pudgy Word Book. Shine, Deborah. 18p. (ps). 1988. bds. 2.95 (*0-448-19054-0*, G&D) Putnam Pub Group.
—Performers' Car. Barkan, Joanne. 12p. (ps). 1993. bds. 3.50 (*0-689-71673-7*, Aladdin) Macmillan Child Grp.
Ong, Cristina. The Little Engine That Could ABC. 20p. (ps-3). 1994. bds. 2.95 (*0-448-40262-9*, Platt & Munk Pubs) Putnam Pub Group.
—The Little Engine That Could Colors. 20p. (ps-3). 1994. bds. 2.95 (*0-448-40264-5*, Platt & Munk Pubs) Putnam Pub Group.
—The Little Engine That Could Let's Count 123. Piper, Watty. LC 90-83240. 24p. (ps). 1991. 9.95 (*0-448-40131-2*, G&D) Putnam Pub Group.
—The Little Engine That Could: Let's Sing ABC. 24p. (ps). 1993. 9.95 (*0-448-40509-1*, Platt & Munk Pubs) Putnam Pub Group.
—The Little Engine That Could: Little Library, 3 bks. (Set incls. Colors, ABC & Numbers, 20 pgs. ea. bk.). (ps). 1992. bds. 9.95 slipcased (*0-448-40261-0*, Platt & Munk Pubs) Putnam Pub Group.
—The Little Engine That Could Numbers. 20p. (ps-3). 1994. bds. 2.95 (*0-448-40263-7*, Platt & Munk Pubs) Putnam Pub Group.
—The Little Mermaid. Korman, Justine. 32p. (ps-1). 1993. pap. 2.50 (*0-590-46448-5*, Cartwheel) Scholastic Inc.
—Three's a Crowd. Horowitz, Jordan. 32p. (ps-3). 1992. pap. 2.50 (*0-590-45459-5*) Scholastic Inc.
Ong, Helen. Amal & the Letter from the King: Adapted from a Play by Rabindranath Tagore. Gajadin, Chitra & Tagore, Rabindranath, eds. 40p. 1992. PLB 14.95 (*1-56397-120-8*) Boyds Mills Pr.
Ontal, Carlo. Best Wishes. Rylant, Cynthia. 32p. (gr. 2-5). 1992. 12.95 (*1-878450-20-4*) R Owen Pubs.
Onyefulu, Ifeoma, photos by. A Is for Africa. Onyefulu, Ifeoma. LC 92-39964. 32p. (ps-3). 1993. 14.99 (*0-525-65147-0*, Cobblehill Bks) Dutton Child Bks.
Oomen, Francine. Come Outside. Oomen, Francine. 8p. (ps). 1993. 4.99 (*0-8431-3535-2*) Price Stern.
—I Can Do It, Too! Oomen, Francine. 8p. (ps). 1993. 4.99 (*0-8431-3534-4*) Price Stern.
—Moo, Says the Cow. Oomen, Francine. 8p. (ps). 1993. 4.99 (*0-8431-3532-8*) Price Stern.
—My Day! Oomen, Francine. 8p. (ps). 1993. 4.99 (*0-8431-3533-6*) Price Stern.
Opgenoorth, Winifried. The Snowman Who Went for a Walk. Lobe, Mira. LC 83-27298. 32p. (ps-2). 1984. 11.95 (*0-688-03865-4*); PLB 11.88 (*0-688-03866-2*) Morrow Jr Bks.
Oppenheimer, Jennie. A Pocket Book of Manners for Young People. Hammond, Elizabeth. LC 90-90325. 96p. (Orig.). (gr. 4-8). 1990. pap. 5.95 (*0-9627061-0-8*) Trotwood Press.
Oppermann-Dimow, Christina. My Old Grandad. Harranth, Wolf. Carter, Peter, tr. 30p. (ps-6). 1987. 11.95 (*0-19-279787-5*) OUP.
Opsahl, Gail K. Sea Otters, River Otters: A Story & Activity Book. Robinson, Sandra C. LC 92-62078. 64p. (Orig.). (gr. 1-6). 1993. pap. 7.95 (*1-879373-41-6*) R Rinehart.
—The Wonder of Wolves: A Story & Activity Book. Robinson, Sandra C. (gr. 1-6). 1989. pap. 7.95 (*0-911797-65-3*) R Rinehart.
Ordonez, Maria A. Actividades y Asignaciones: Cuaderno del Estudiante. Resnik, Hank, et al. Callejas, Juan, et al, eds. Luobriel, Marta B., et al, trs. from ENG. (SPA., Orig.). (gr. 6-8). 1991. wkbk. 4.85 (*1-56095-022-6*) Quest Intl.
Ordonez, Maria A. & Espada, Frank. Cambios: Descubriendo lo Mejor Que Hay en Ti. Cosby, Bill, et al. Callejas, Juan, et al, eds. Trevant, Pierre, tr. from ENG. (SPA.). 192p. (Orig.). (gr. 6-8). 1987. pap. text ed. 6.85 (*0-933419-21-X*) Quest Intl.
—Universal Spanish--Cambios: Descubriendo lo Mejor Que Hay en Ti. Cosby, Bill, et al. Callejas, Juan, et al, eds. Trevant, Pierre, tr. from ENG. (SPA.). 181p. (Orig.). (gr. 6-8). 1988. pap. text ed. 6.85 (*0-933419-44-9*) Quest Intl.
Orecchia, Giulia. Nighty-Night. Lewison, Wendy. 24p. (ps). 1992. spiral bdg. 9.95 (*0-448-40391-9*, G&D) Putnam Pub Group.
Orehek, Don. One Hundred & One Wacky Kid Jokes. Stine, Bob. 96p. 1988. pap. 1.95 (*0-590-41399-6*) Scholastic Inc.

—One Hundred One Fast Funny Food Jokes. Hirsh, Phil. 96p. (Orig.). (gr. 4-6). 1987. pap. 1.95 (*0-590-32421-7*) Scholastic Inc.
—One Hundred One Ghost Jokes. Eisenberg, Lisa & Hall, Katy. (ps up). 1988. pap. 1.95 (*0-590-41811-4*) Scholastic Inc.
—One Hundred One School Jokes. Hall, Katy & Eisenberg, Lisa. 96p. (gr. 4-7). 1987. pap. 1.95 (*0-590-41182-9*) Scholastic Inc.
—The Silly Joke Book. Hartman, Victoria G. 96p. (gr. 4-6). 1987. pap. 1.95 (*0-590-33846-3*) Scholastic Inc.
Oremerod, Jan. Peter Pan. Barrie, James M. (FRE.). 239p. (gr. 5-10). 1988. pap. 9.95 (*2-07-033411-2*) Schoenhof.
Orloff, Denis. New Providence: A Changing Cityscape. Von Tscharner, Renata & Fleming, Ronald L. 26p. (ps up). 1987. 10.95 (*0-15-200540-4*, Gulliver Bks) HarBrace.
—New Providence: A Changing Cityscape. Von Tscharner, Renata & Fleming, Ronald L. 32p. (gr. k-4). 1992. pap. 9.95 (*0-89133-191-3*) Preservation Pr.
Orlova, Natalia, et al. Hamlet. Garfield, Leon, abridged by. LC 92-14525. 48p. (gr. 5 up). 1993. PLB 11.99 (*0-679-93871-0*); pap. 6.99 (*0-679-83871-6*) Knopf Bks Yng Read.
Orlowski, Dennis. I Have a Stepfamily but... Kirkland, Dianna K. 40p. (Orig.). (ps-5). 1981. pap. 6.50 (*0-685-00148-2*); counseling activity guide-stepfamilies 6.50 (*0-686-96649-X*) Aid-U Pub.
—Last Year I Failed...but. Kirkland, Dianna C. 32p. (Orig.). (ps-5). 1981. pap. 6.50 (*0-940370-04-2*); counseling activity guide-failure 6.50 (*0-940370-07-7*) Aid-U Pub.
—My Dad Is Unemployed... But. Morris-Vann, Artie M. 40p. (Orig.). (ps-5). 1981. pap. 6.50 (*0-940370-01-8*); counseling activity guide-unemployed families 6.50 (*0-685-00149-0*) Aid-U Pub.
—My Mom Keeps Hitting Me...But. Morris-Vann, Artie M. 32p. (Orig.). (ps-5). 1981. pap. 6.50x (*0-940370-02-6*); counseling activity guide-abused children 6.50 (*0-940370-06-9*) Aid-U Pub.
Ormai, Stella. Bet You Can! Science Possibilities to Fool You. Cobb, Vicki & Darling, Kathy. 112p. (gr. 3-7). 1983. pap. 3.50 (*0-380-82180-X*, Camelot) Avon.
—Bizzy Bones & Uncle Ezra. Martin, Jacqueline B. LC 83-25618. 32p. (ps-2). 1984. PLB 12.88 (*0-688-03782-8*) Lothrop.
—Creatures. Hopkins, Lee B., ed. LC 84-15698. 32p. (ps-3). 1985. 14.95 (*0-15-220875-5*, HB Juv Bks) HarBrace.
—Mole & Shrew. Koller, Jackie F. LC 90-609. 32p. (ps-3). 1991. SBE 12.95 (*0-689-31611-9*, Atheneum Child Bk) Macmillan Child Grp.
—Mole & Shrew Step Out. Koller, Jackie F. LC 91-20531. 32p. (ps-3). 1992. SBE 13.95 (*0-689-31713-1*, Atheneum Child Bk) Macmillan Child Grp.
—The Moon Came Too. Carlstrom, Nancy W. LC 86-18046. 32p. (ps-1). 1987. SBE 13.95 (*0-02-717380-1*, Macmillan Child Bk) Macmillan Child Grp.
—Scrawny, the Classroom Duck. Clymer, Susan. 96p. (gr. 2-5). 1991. pap. 2.50 (*0-590-43729-1*) Scholastic Inc.
—Shadow Magic. Simon, Seymour. LC 84-4433. 48p. (ps-3). 1985. PLB 13.88 (*0-688-02682-6*) Lothrop.
—Soap Bubble Magic. Simon, Seymour. LC 84-4432. 48p. (ps-3). 1985. PLB 13.88 (*0-688-02685-0*) Lothrop.
Ormerod, Jan. The Chewing-Gum Rescue & Other Stories. Mahy, Margaret. 142p. (gr. 3-7). 1991. 12.95 (*0-87951-424-8*) Overlook Pr.
—Come Back, Kittens: A Hide & Seek Book with See-Through Pages. Ormerod, Jan. Pearson, Susan, ed. LC 91-30426. 32p. (ps up). 1992. 13.00 (*0-688-09134-2*) Lothrop.
—Come Back, Puppies: A Hide & Seek Book with See-Through Pages. Ormerod, Jan. Pearson, Susan, ed. LC 91-30424. 32p. (ps up). 1992. 13.00 (*0-688-09135-0*) Lothrop.
—Grandfather & I. Buckley, Helen E. LC 93-22936. 1994. write for info. (*0-688-12533-6*); PLB write for info. (*0-688-12534-4*) Lothrop.
—Grandmother & I. Buckley, Helen E. LC 93-22937. (gr. 3 up). 1994. write for info. (*0-688-12531-X*); PLB write for info. (*0-688-12532-8*) Lothrop.
—Happy Christmas, Gemma. Hayes, Sarah. LC 85-23674. 32p. (ps-1). 1986. 13.95 (*0-688-06508-2*) Lothrop.
—Happy Christmas, Gemma. Hayes, Sarah. ALC Staff, ed. LC 85-23674. 32p. (ps up). 1992. pap. 4.95 (*0-688-11702-3*, Mulberry) Morrow.
—The Magic Skateboard. Richemont, Enid. LC 92-53010. 80p. (gr. 3-6). 1993. 13.95 (*1-56402-132-7*) Candlewick Pr.
—Midnight Pillow Fight. Ormerod, Jan. LC 92-53011. 32p. (ps-3). 1993. 14.95 (*1-56402-169-6*) Candlewick Pr.
—Mom's Home. Ormerod, Jan. LC 87-2712. 24p. (ps). 1987. 5.95 (*0-688-07274-7*) Lothrop.
—Moonlight. Ormerod, Jan. LC 81-8290. 32p. (ps-1). 1982. 14.95 (*0-688-00846-1*); PLB 14.88 (*0-688-00847-X*) Lothrop.
—One Ballerina Two. French, Vivian. LC 90-45969. 32p. (ps up). 1991. 13.95 (*0-688-10333-2*); PLB 13.88 (*0-688-10334-0*) Lothrop.
—One Hundred One Things to Do with a Baby. Ormerod, Jan. 32p. (ps-3). 1986. pap. 3.50 (*0-14-050447-8*, Puffin) Puffin Bks.
—Peter Pan. Barrie, J. M. 208p. (gr. 5 up). 1993. pap. 3.99 (*0-14-032007-5*) Puffin Bks.

—The Saucepan Game. Ormerod, Jan. Briley, D., ed. LC 88-12893. 32p. (ps). 1989. 10.95 (0-688-08518-0); PLB 10.88 (0-688-08519-9) Lothrop.

—The Story of Chicken Licken. Ormerod, Jan. LC 85-7911. 32p. (ps-1). 1986. 13.00 (0-688-06058-7) Lothrop.

—Sunflakes: Poems for Children. Moore, Lilian, selected by. 96p. (ps-3). 1992. 18.45 (0-395-58833-2, Clarion Bks) HM.

—This Little Nose. Ormerod, Jan. LC 87-2605. 24p. (ps). 1987. 5.95 (0-688-07276-3) Lothrop.

Ormsby, Lawrence. America's Mountains. Turbak, Gary. 32p. (gr. 1 up). 1994. 14.95 (0-87358-573-9) Northland AZ.

—America's Oceans. Turbak, Gary. 32p. (gr. 1 up). 1994. 14.95 (0-87358-574-7) Northland AZ.

O'Rourke, Dawn. My Number Word Book. Krampe, Leesa. Ehrlich, Doris, ed. 100p. (Orig.). (ps-1). 1987. pap. text ed. 3.95 (0-932957-94-3) Natl School.

O'Rourke, Dawn M. Animal Alphabet. 2nd ed. Ehrlich, Doris. 36p. (ps-k). 1988. pap. text ed. 80.00 classroom pack (0-932957-90-0); tchr's. ed. 4.50 (0-932957-91-9); wkbk. 3.90 (0-932957-89-7); wall posters 17.50 (0-932957-96-X) Natl School.

O'Rourke, Michael E., photos by. The Highest School in California: A Story of Bodie, California. O'Rourke, Everett V. 32p. (Orig.). (gr. 1-4). 1978. 4.00 (0-685-22567-4) E ORourke.

O'Rourke, Page. Rub-a-Dub-Dub. 9p. (ps-1). 1993. bds. 4.95 (0-448-40521-0, G&D) Putnam Pub Group.

O'Rourke, Page E. See & Say: A Book of First Words. 12p. (ps). 1993. bds. 4.95 (0-448-40540-7, G&D) Putnam Pub Group.

Orr, Chris, et al. A First Poetry Book. Foster, John, compiled by. 128p. (gr. 1-3). 1980. 11.95 (0-19-918113-6); pap. 5.95 (0-19-918112-8) OUP.

Orr, Chris, Illustration Staff. Mysterious Microbes. Parker, Steve. Savage, Ann. LC 94-6476. 1994. write for info. (0-8114-2344-1) Raintree Steck-V.

Orr, Katherine. The Coral Reef Coloring Book. Orr, Katherine. 48p. (gr. 2 up). 1988. pap. 5.95 (0-88045-090-8) Stemmer Hse.

—The Hawaiian Coral Reef Coloring Book. Orr, Katherine. 48p. (Orig.). (gr. 1-6). 1992. pap. 5.95 (0-88045-122-X) Stemmer Hse.

—My Grandpa & the Sea. Orr, Katherine. LC 89-23876. 32p. (gr. 1-4). 1990. PLB 18.95 (0-87614-409-1) Carolrhoda Bks.

—Story of a Dolphin. Orr, Katherine. LC 92-28656. 1993. 18.95 (0-87614-777-5) Carolrhoda Bks.

Orr, Kathy. A Christmas Garland. Mitchell, Julie, compiled by. 40p. 1991. lib. bdg. 8.95 (0-8378-2069-3) Gibson.

Orr, Richarad. The Bird Atlas. Orr, Richard. LC 93-18225. 64p. (gr. 4 up). 1993. 19.95 (1-56458-327-9) Dorling Kindersley.

Orr, Richard. Camels. Wildlife Education, Ltd. Staff. 20p. (gr. 5 up). 1984. pap. 2.75 (0-937934-24-0) Wildlife Educ.

—Lions. Wildlife Education, Ltd. Staff. 24p. 1992. 13.95 (0-937934-81-X); pap. 2.75 (0-937934-42-9) Wildlife Educ.

—Old World Monkeys. Wildlife Education, Ltd. Staff. 24p. 1992. 13.95 (0-937934-92-5); pap. 2.75 (0-937934-69-0) Wildlife Educ.

—Zebras. Wildlife Education, Ltd. Staff. 24p. 1992. 13.95 (0-937934-91-7); pap. 2.75 (0-937934-57-7) Wildlife Educ.

Orr, Richard & Stuart, Walter. Gorillas. Wildlife Education, Ltd. Staff. 24p. 1992. 13.95 (0-937934-78-X) Wildlife Educ.

—Little Cats. Wildlife Education, Ltd. Staff. 200p. (gr. 5 up). 1983. pap. 2.75 (0-937934-16-X) Wildlife Educ.

—Little Cats. Wildlife Education, Ltd. Staff. 24p. 1992. 13.95 (0-937934-82-8) Wildlife Educ.

Orr, Richard, et al. Gorillas. Wildlife Education, Ltd. Staff. 20p. (Orig.). (gr. 1-8). 1984. pap. 2.75 (0-937934-28-3) WildLife Educ.

—Tigers. Wildlife Education, Ltd. Staff. 20p. (Orig.). (gr. k-12). 1985. pap. 2.75 (0-937934-35-6) Wildlife Educ.

Orrin, Mary. A Shaker Sampler: Coloring Book. 24p. Moriarty, Kathleen M. 30p. (gr. k-6). 1991. pap. 4.95 (0-915836-15-7) United Soc Shakers.

Ortega, Jennifer. A Heart for God in India. Richardson, Arleta. Payne, Peggy & Yoder, Tamra, eds. 52p. (Orig.). (gr. 4-6). 1989. pap. 4.00 (0-89367-144-4) Light & Life.

Ortega, Jose. Fiesta! Zapater, Beatriz M. 32p. (gr. 2-5). 1993. pap. 4.95 (0-671-79842-1, S&S BYR) S&S Trade.

—Where Angels Glide at Dawn: New Stories from Latin America. Carlson, Lori M. & Ventura, Cynthia L., eds. LC 90-6697. 128p. (gr. 5 up). 1990. 14.00 (0-397-32424-1, Lipp Jr Bks) 1990; PLB 13.89 (0-397-32425-1, Lipp Jr Bks) HarpC Child Bks.

Ortega, Pat. A Place of Silver Silence. Mayhar, Ardath. (gr. 7 up). 1988. 15.95 (0-8027-6825-3) Walker & Co.

Ortiz, Fran, photos by. Chinese New Year. Brown, Tricia. LC 87-8532. 48p. (gr. 2-5). 1987. 14.95 (0-8050-0497-1, Bks Young Read) H Holt & Co.

—Hello, Amigos! Brown, Tricia. LC 86-9882. 48p. (ps-2). 1992. 15.95 (0-8050-1891-3, Owlet BYR); pap. 5.95 (0-8050-0090-9) H Holt & Co.

Ortiz, Gloria. A World of Children's Songs. Walker, Mary L., ed. LC 93-709103. 192p. (gr. 1-6). 1993. pap. 19.95 (0-377-00260-7) Friendship Pr.

—A World of Children's Stories. Pellowski, Anne, ed. LC 93-13509. 192p. (Orig.). (gr. 3-6). 1993. pap. 19.95 (0-377-00259-3) Friendship Pr.

Ortiz, Gloria C. Most Ministers Wear Sneakers. Poling, Nancy W. LC 91-15116. 32p. (gr. 4-8). 1991. 6.95 (0-8298-0907-4, P-0907-4); pap. 6.95 (0-8298-0901-5, P-0901-5) Pilgrim OH.

Ortiz, Juan & Bliss, Phil. Hello World. Manushkin, Fran. LC 91-71337. 32p. (ps-1). 1991. 8.95 (1-56282-059-1) Disney Pr.

Ortiz, Phil & Michaels, Serge. Disney's Aladdin. Braybrooks, Ann. 24p. (ps-3). 1992. pap. write for info. (0-307-12692-7, 12692, Golden Pr) Western Pub.

Ortiz, Phil & Wakeman, Diana. Walt Disney's Dumbo. Balducci, Rita, adapted by. 28p. (ps). 1992. bds. write for info. (0-307-12533-5, 12533, Golden Pr) Western Pub.

—Walt Disney's Pinocchio & the Whale. Ingoglia, Gina. 40p. (ps-1). 1992. write for info. (0-307-11583-6, 11583, Golden Pr) Western Pub.

—Walt Disney's Pinocchio & the Whale. Ingoglia, Gina. 32p. (ps-1). 1993. pap. 3.25 (0-307-15975-2, 15975, Golden Pr) Western Pub.

Ortland, Stephen. The Adventures of Boo: The Journey Begins. Cox, Julie. LC 90-62757. 32p. 1990. write for info. (0-9627586-0-4); write for info. audio cassette (0-9627586-1-2) Mango Entrps.

—The Adventures of Boo, Vol. 2: Circus. Cox, Julia. 32p. 1992. write for info. (0-9627586-2-0) Mango Entrps.

Osawa, Yasu. The Return of the Comet. Schatz, Dennis & Osawa, Yasu. 42p. (gr. 4-9). 1985. pap. 7.95 (0-935051-00-7) Pacific Sci Ctr.

Osawa, Yasu & Dawson, Nancy. The Button Blanket. 2nd ed. McNutt, Nan. 44p. (gr. k-3). 1989. pap. 7.95 (0-9614534-1-9) N McNutt Assocs.

Osawa, Yasu & Jackson, Nathan. The Bentwood Box. 3rd ed. McNutt, Nan. 36p. (Orig.). (gr. 3-8). 1989. pap. text ed. 9.95 (0-9614534-0-0) N McNutt Assocs.

Osborn, Kathy. The Emperor's Garden. Wolff, Ferida. LC 93-14751. 1994. write for info. (0-688-11651-5, Tambourine Bks); PLB write for info. (0-688-11652-3) Morrow.

—The Joke's on George. Tunnell, Michael O. LC 92-33312. 32p. (gr. k up). 1993. 14.00 (0-688-11758-9, Tambourine Bks); PLB 13.93 (0-688-11759-7, Tambourine Bks) Morrow.

Osborn, Stephen. Bending Light: An Exploratorium Toolbook. Murphy, Pat, et al. LC 92-20336. 1993. 15.95 (0-316-25851-2) Little.

Osborne, Gretchen. Magic Journey. Klipper, Ilse. 83p. (Orig.). (gr. k-5). 1983. pap. 5.95 (0-9605022-1-3) Pathwys Pr CA.

Osborne, John, photos by. My Teacher Said Goodbye Today: Planning for the End of the School Year. 2nd ed. Osborne, Judy. 39p. (ps-6). 1987. pap. text ed. 9.95 (0-9618303-8-7) Emijo Pubns.

Osborne, John T. Miracles. Osborne, John T. 90p. 1988. pap. text ed. 5.75 (0-929918-00-2) Midstates Pub.

Osborne, Mitchel. Mardi Gras! Coil, Suzanne M. LC 92-21166. 48p. (gr. 2 up). 1994. RSBE 15.95 (0-02-722805-3, Macmillan Child Bk) Macmillan Child Grp.

Osborn-Smith, Jane. Were You a Wild Duck, Where Would You Go? Mendoza, George. LC 89-28596. 32p. 1990. PLB 14.95 (1-55670-136-5) Stewart Tabori & Chang.

Oseki, Iku. Big Annie: An American Tall Tale. Robbins, Sandra. 32p. (gr. k-4). 1991. pap. text ed. 3.99 (1-882601-09-2); pap. text ed. 9.98 incl. cass. (1-882601-03-3) See-Mores Wrkshop.

—The Growing Rock: A Southwest Native American Tale. Robbins, Sandra. 32p. (Orig.). (ps-4). 1993. pap. 9.98 incl. cass. (1-882601-15-7) See Mores Wrkshop.

—How the Turtle Got Its Shell: An African Tale. Robbins, Sandra. 32p. (gr. k-6). 1991. pap. text ed. 3.99 (1-882601-10-6); pap. text ed. 9.98 incl. cass. (1-882601-04-1) See-Mores Wrkshop.

—Ring Around a Rainbow. Robbins, Sandra. 32p. (gr. k-6). 1991. pap. text ed. 3.99 (1-882601-08-4); pap. text ed. 9.98 incl. cass. (1-882601-05-X) See-Mores Wrkshop.

O'Shea, Bronwyn C. The Black Cat Inn. O'Shea, Brandy. LC 91-67920. Date not set. pap. 8.00 (1-56002-180-2, Univ Edtns) Aegina Pr.

Oskow, Craig. We Tell It to Our Children: The Story of Passover: A Haggadah for Seders with Young Children. Wark, MaryAnn E. Lerner, Leigh D., frwd. by. LC 87-63604. 150p. (Orig.). (ps-6). 1988. Leader's Edition with Puppets. pap. 11.95 wire-o bdg. (0-9619880-9-6) Mensch Makers Pr. Children's active participatory Haggadah makes the Passover story into an engaging drama of the Exodus story. A complete guide, including multi-national recipes, for putting on the traditional Seder meal for Passover. Text is a musical puppet show with Judaically-meaningful lyrics set to simple American folk tunes.

Everyone participates in singing throughout the service. This Leader's edition has 9 cut out puppets who are the "guests" from the past, who in a "you-are-there" style tell the story of the Exodus. Parts for non-readers & early readers. Guest edition - no puppets with full text also available. Endorsed by rabbis, religious educators (Jewish & Christian), children's book store owners, preschool teachers, parents & grandparents nationwide. For home or model seders. Authentically Jewish; easy for non-Jews. Developmentally appropriate for children. Downright fun for adults. Other unique features include the Passover food symbols, like matzah, explained at the appropriate time in the story; special sections to personalize & teach about world Jewry. Difficult concepts like slavery are taught through action, songs, & pictures. Lyrics respond to children's thinking while tackling complicated issues surrounding freedom. Plentiful, detailed drawings emphasize immediacy of ideas & illustrate every idea & ceremonial symbol. *Publisher Provided Annotation.*

—We Tell It to Our Children: The Story of Passover: A Haggadah for Seders with Young Children. 2nd ed. Wark, Mary A. Lerner, Leigh D., frwd. by. LC 88-92282. 126p. (Orig.). (ps-6). 1988. pap. 5.95 wire bdg. (0-9619880-8-8) Mensch Makers Pr.

Ostberg, Marie & Ostberg, Nils. Sports & Games the Indians Gave Us. Whitney, Alex. (gr. 7 up). 1977. 7.95 (0-679-20391-5) McKay.

Ostberg, Nils, jt. illus. see Ostberg, Marie.

Ostendorf, Ned. Carter G. Woodson: The Father of Black History. McKissack, Patricia & McKissack, Fredrick. LC 91-8813. 32p. (gr. 1-4). 1991. lib. bdg. 12.95 (0-89490-309-8) Enslow Pubs.

—Frederick Douglass: Leader Against Slavery. McKissack, Patricia & McKissack, Fredrick. LC 91-3084. 32p. (gr. 1-4). 1991. lib. bdg. 12.95 (0-89490-306-3) Enslow Pubs.

—George Washington Carver: The Peanut Scientist. McKissack, Patricia & McKissack, Fredrick. LC 91-8814. 32p. (gr. 1-4). 1991. lib. bdg. 12.95 (0-89490-308-X) Enslow Pubs.

—Ida B. Wells-Barnett: A Voice Against Violence. McKissack, Patricia & McKissack, Fredrick. LC 90-49848. 32p. (gr. 1-4). 1991. lib. bdg. 12.95 (0-89490-301-2) Enslow Pubs.

—Louis Armstrong: Jazz Musician. McKissack, Patricia & McKissack, Fredrick. LC 91-12420. 32p. (gr. 1-4). 1991. lib. bdg. 12.95 (0-89490-307-1) Enslow Pubs.

—Marian Anderson: A Great Singer. McKissack, Patricia & McKissack, Fredrick. LC 90-19163. 32p. (gr. 1-4). 1991. lib. bdg. 12.95 (0-89490-303-9) Enslow Pubs.

—Martin Luther King, Jr. Man of Peace. McKissack, Patricia & McKissack, Fredrick. LC 90-19156. 32p. (gr. 1-4). 1991. lib. bdg. 12.95 (0-89490-302-0) Enslow Pubs.

—Mary Church Terrell: Leader for Equality. McKissack, Patricia & McKissack, Fredrick. LC 91-3083. 32p. (gr. 1-4). 1991. lib. bdg. 12.95 (0-89490-305-5) Enslow Pubs.

—Mary McLeod Bethune: A Great Teacher. McKissack, Patricia & McKissack, Fredrick. LC 91-8818. 32p. (gr. 1-4). 1991. lib. bdg. 12.95 (0-89490-304-7) Enslow Pubs.

—Ralph J. Bunche: Peacemaker. McKissack, Patricia & McKissack, Fredrick. LC 90-49849. 32p. (gr. 1-4). 1991. lib. bdg. 12.95 (0-89490-300-4) Enslow Pubs.

Ostermayer, Sharon. The Ah-Chooo Book. Pohl, Linda. 20p. (ps-2). 1990. 3.95 (0-9625453-0-9) L P Pohl.

Ostovar, Terry. Tablet of the Heart: God & Me. Abdu'l-Baha. Fisher, Betty J. & Lundberg, Leslie, eds. Oldziey, Pepper P., contrib. by. (ps-2). 1987. PLB 15.95 (0-87743-207-4) Bahai.

Ostroff, Lanny. Backyard Scientist, Series Four. Hoffman, Jane. 54p. (ps-7). 1992. pap. text ed. 8.50 (0-9618663-4-9) Backyard Scientist. THE BACKYARD SCIENTIST SERIES provides the young scientist with excitement & fun to do hands-on science experiments & projects covering chemistry, physics & the life sciences (biology, entomology, physiology) & more. Experiments use materials usually found in most homes. Each experiment carries a sprightly illustration, & has a list of supplies needed for the experiment, step-by-step instructions & questions that lead the children through the observation process. The questions are designed to improve critical thinking skills. An explanation of the experiment & the scientific principles at work are given after each experiment. Experiments are meant to develop the young scientist's curiosity to do further exploration of the scientific concepts, thus further developing conceptual thought processes. The format makes the book easy to use for teachers, parents & students. Little advance preparation is required & with tight budgets, the inexpensive supplies required by the experiments allow for more science instruction. While all this learning takes place, the author has not forgotten to make the learning experience fun for student & teacher or parent. Author Jane Hoffman has appeared at prestigious museums throughout the country. Jane also lectures & conducts workshops for educators & parent groups throughout the nation. *Publisher Provided Annotation.*

—Backyard Scientist: Series One. Hoffman, Jane. 52p. (Orig.). (gr. k-6). 1987. pap. text ed. 8.50 (0-9618663-0-6) Backyard Scientist.
—The Original Backyard Scientist. Hoffman, Jane. 58p. (Orig.). (gr. k-6). 1987. text ed. 8.50 (0-9618663-1-4) Backyard Scientist.
Ostrove, Karen. Fins & Scales: A Kosher Tale. Miller, Deborah & Ostrove, Karen. LC 90-24388. 32p. (gr. 1-3). 1992. 12.95 (0-929371-25-9); pap. 5.95 (0-929371-26-7) Kar Ben.
Ostrovsky, Alexsandr. Birthday (Den Rosdenia) Ostrovsky, Alexsandr. (RUS.). 16p. (Orig.). 1982. pap. 14.95 (0-934393-17-6) Rector Pr.
—Clouds (Oblaka) Ostrovsky, Alexsandr. (RUS.). 16p. (Orig.). 1984. pap. 14.95 (0-934393-20-6) Rector Pr.
—Paper Kite (Bumazhni Emei) Ostrovsky, Alexsandr. (RUS.). 30p. (Orig.). 1987. pap. 14.95 (0-934393-18-4) Rector Pr.
O'Sullivan, Tom. A Royal Ball. Springer, Margaret. 32p. (gr. k-3). 1992. bds. 9.95 (1-878093-64-9) Boyds Mills Pr.
Otani, June. Oh Snow. Mayper, Monica. LC 90-42088. 32p. (ps-1). 1991. PLB 14.89 (0-06-024204-3) HarpC Child Bks.
—Peach Boy. Hooks, William H. (ps-3). 1992. pap. 3.50 (0-553-35429-9, Little Rooster) Bantam.
—The Poodle Who Barked at the Wind. Zolotow, Charlotte. LC 86-42992. 32p. (ps-3). 1987. HarpC Child Bks.
—What Makes a Shadow? rev. ed. Bulla, Clyde R. LC 92-36350. 32p. (ps-1). 1994. 15.00 (0-06-022915-2); PLB 14.89 (0-06-022916-0) HarpC Child Bks.
—What Makes a Shadow? Bulla, Clyde R. LC 92-36350. 32p. (ps-1). 1994. pap. 4.95 (0-06-445118-6, Trophy) HarpC Child Bks.
Otera, Ben. The Headless Haunt & Other African-American Ghost Stories. Haskins, James. LC 93-26223. 1994. write for info. (0-06-022994-2); PLB write for info. (0-06-022997-7) HarpC Child Bks.
O'Toole, Tim, jt. illus. see Beck, Connie.
O'Toole, Tom. The Witch Who Couldn't. Henry, Terry H. 96p. (gr. 5). 1988. 10.95 (0-947962-39-5, Pub. by Anvil Bks Ltd Ireland) Irish Bks Media.
Ottensien, Claire & Cogbill, Catherine. Catch a Whiffle-Poofle! Ottenstein, Claire. 64p. (Orig.). 1991. lib. bdg. 8.95 (1-878149-03-2) Counterpoint Pub.
Otto, Svend. Ling & the Little Devils. Tate, Joan. (ps-3). 9.95 (0-317-61896-2) Viking Child Bks.
Oubrerie, Clement. The Kooken. Lebentritt, Julia & Ploetz, Richard. LC 91-26826. 32p. (gr. 1-3). 1992. 14.95 (0-8050-1749-6, Bks Young Read) H Holt & Co.
Oubrerie, Clement, photos by. It's Hard to Read a Map with a Beagle on Your Lap. Singer, Marilyn. LC 92-26166. 32p. (gr. 1-4). 1993. PLB 15.95 (0-8050-2201-5, Bks Young Read) H Holt & Co.
Ouellet, Odile. Et Si L'Autobus Nous Oublie? Stevens, Florence & Lamont-Clarke, Ginette. LC 90-70136. 24p. (ps-2). 1990. 12.95 (0-88776-252-2); pap. 6.95 (0-88776-260-3) Tundra Bks.

—What If the Bus Doesn't Come? Stevens, Florence & Lamont-Clarke, Ginette. LC 90-70135. 24p. (ps-2). 1990. 12.95 (0-88776-251-4); pap. 6.95 (0-88776-259-X) Tundra Bks.
Ouellet, Pauline A. The Hanukah Tooth. Greene, Jacqueline D. LC 81-90033. 28p. (ps-2). 1981. pap. 3.00 (0-938836-02-1) Pascal Pubs.
Ovenden, Denys. Snake. Chinery, Michael. Watts, Barrie, photos by. LC 90-10951. 32p. (gr. 4-6). 1991. PLB 11.59 (0-8167-2106-8); pap. text ed. 3.95 (0-8167-2107-6) Troll Assocs.
Ovendon, Dennis & McGregor, Malcolm. Sea Mammals. Ganeri, Anita. LC 93-19706. 32p. (gr. 4-6). 1993. PLB 19.97 (0-8114-6159-9) Raintree Steck-V.
Overlie, George. The Adventure of the Dancing Men: The Three Garridebs. Shaw, Murray, adapted by. LC 92-21787. 1993. PLB 14.95 (0-87614-716-3); pap. 4.95 (0-87614-555-1) Carolrhoda Bks.
—The Adventures of Black Peter & The 'Gloria Scott', Vol. I. Shaw, Murray, adapted by. (gr. 4-6). 1990. PLB 14.95 (0-87614-385-0) Carolrhoda Bks.
—The Adventures of the Cardboard Box & Scandal in Bohemia, Vol. II. Shaw, Murray, adapted by. (gr. 4-6). 1990. PLB 14.95 (0-87614-386-9) Carolrhoda Bks.
—Adventures of the Copper Beeches & The Redheaded League, Vol. IV. Shaw, Murray, adapted by. (gr. 4-6). 1990. PLB 14.95 (0-87614-388-5) Carolrhoda Bks.
—Adventures of the Six Napoleons & the Blue Carbuncle, Vol. III. Shaw, Murray, adapted by. (gr. 4-6). 1990. PLB 14.95 (0-87614-387-7) Carolrhoda Bks.
—April Fools' Day Magic. Baker, James W. 48p. (gr. 2-5). 1989. 11.95 (0-8225-2230-6) Lerner Pubns.
—Birthday Magic. Baker, James W. LC 88-2717. 48p. (gr. 2-5). 1988. lib. bdg. 11.95 (0-8225-2226-8, First Ave Edns); pap. 3.95 (0-8225-9536-2, First Ave Edns) Lerner Pubns.
—Christmas Magic. Baker, James W. 48p. (gr. 2-5). 1988. lib. bdg. 11.95 (0-8225-2227-6); pap. 3.95 (0-8225-9537-0) Lerner Pubns.
—Halloween Magic. Baker, James W. 48p. (gr. 2-5). 1988. lib. bdg. 11.95 (0-8225-2228-4, First Ave Edns); pap. 3.95 (0-8225-9551-6, First Ave Edns) Lerner Pubns.
—Independence Day Magic. Baker, James W. 48p. (gr. 2-5). 1989. 11.95 (0-8225-2236-5) Lerner Pubns.
—Match Wits with Sherlock Holmes, Vol. V: "The Adventure of the Speckled Bird" & "The Sussex Vampire" Shaw, Murray, adapted by. 64p. (gr. 4-6). 1991. PLB 14.95 (0-87614-665-5) Carolrhoda Bks.
—Match Wits with Sherlock Holmes, Vol. VI: "The Adventure of Abbey Grange" & "The Boscombe Valley Mystery" Shaw, Murray, adapted by. 64p. (gr. 4-6). 1991. PLB 14.95 (0-87614-666-3) Carolrhoda Bks.
—Merry-Go-Rounds. Thomas, Art. LC 81-3825. 48p. (gr. k-4). 1981. PLB 14.95 (0-87614-168-8) Carolrhoda Bks.
—Presidents' Day Magic. Baker, James W. 48p. (gr. 2-5). 1989. 11.95 (0-8225-2232-2) Lerner Pubns.
—St. Patrick's Day Magic. Baker, James W. 48p. (gr. 2-5). 1989. 11.95 (0-8225-2234-9) Lerner Pubns.
—Thanksgiving Magic. Baker, James W. 48p. (gr. 2-5). 1989. 11.95 (0-8225-2233-0) Lerner Pubns.
—Valentine Magic. Baker, James W. LC 88-2710. 48p. (gr. 2-5). 1988. lib. bdg. 11.95 (0-8225-2229-2, First Ave Edns); pap. 3.95 (0-8225-9550-8, First Ave Edns) Lerner Pubns.
Overlie, Goerge. New Year's Magic. Baker, James W. 48p. (gr. 2-5). 1989. 11.95 (0-8225-2231-4) Lerner Pubns.
Overstreet, Charles. Indian & Mountain Man Crafts: Cuttin' & Stitchin' Overstreet, Charles. Smith, Monte, ed. 106p. (Orig.). (gr. 8-12). 1994. pap. 10.95 perfect bdg. (0-943604-41-9) Eagles View.
Overton, Amy. Freddie the Frog. DeCremer, Shirley. LC 92-33094. 16p. Date not set. 14.95 (0-935343-03-2) Peartree.
Owen, C. Tales of Mystery & Imagination, Retold by Henniker-Major. Poe, Edgar Allan. (gr. 3 up). 1975. pap. text ed. 4.95x (0-19-580511-9) OUP.
Owen, Gail. Hot & Cold Summer. Hurwitz, Johanna. LC 83-19336. 176p. (gr. 3-5). 1984. 12.95 (0-688-02746-6) Morrow Jr Bks.
Owen, Mary B. The Man Who Sang in the Dark. Clifford, Eth. 96p. (gr. 2-5). 1987. 13.95 (0-395-43664-8) HM.
Owens, Gail. Addie Across the Prairie. Lawlor, Laurie. MacDonald, Patricia, ed. 128p. 1991. pap. 2.99 (0-671-70147-9, Minstrel Bks) PB.
—Amy, Ben, & Catalpa the Cat: A Fanciful Story of This & That. Coon, Alma S. 40p. (ps-2). 1990. 7.95 (0-87935-079-2) Williamsburg.
—Annabelle's Un-Birthday. Kroll, Steven. LC 90-24316. 40p. (gr. 1-5). 1991. RSBE 13.95 (0-02-751171-5, Macmillan Child Bk) Macmillan Child Grp.
—Benjy the Football Hero. Van Leeuwen, Jean. LC 84-21459. 192p. (gr. 2-6). 1985. PLB 11.89 (0-8037-0190-X) Dial Bks Young.
—A Bundle of Sticks. Mauser, Pat R. LC 87-1074. 176p. (gr. 3-6). 1987. pap. 3.95 (0-689-71169-7, Aladdin) Macmillan Child Grp.
—The Cat Next Door. Wright, Betty R. LC 90-29080. 32p. (ps-3). 1991. reinforced 14.95 (0-8234-0896-5) Holiday.
—The Cybil War. Byars, Betsy C. LC 80-26912. 144p. (gr. 8-12). 1981. pap. 12.95 (0-670-25248-4) Viking Child Bks.

—The Cybil War. Byars, Betsy C. 144p. (gr. 3 up). 1990. pap. 3.99 (0-14-034356-3, Puffin) Puffin Bks.
—The Daring Rescue of Marlon the Swimming Pig. Saunders, Susan. LC 87-4633. 64p. (gr. 2-4). 1987. lib. bdg. 6.99 (0-394-98293-2); pap. 1.95 (0-394-88293-8, Random Juv) Random Bks Yng Read.
—Encyclopedia Brown & the Case of the Disgusting Sneakers. Sobol, Donald J. LC 89-13939. 96p. (gr. 3 up). 1990. 12.95g (0-688-09012-5) Morrow Jr Bks.
—Encyclopedia Brown & the Case of the Mysterious Handprints. Sobol, Donald J. LC 85-8798. 96p. (gr. 3-7). 1985. 12.95 (0-688-04626-6) Morrow Jr Bks.
—Encyclopedia Brown & the Case of the Treasure Hunt. Sobol, Donald J. LC 87-22048. 96p. (gr. 3-7). 1988. 12.95 (0-688-06955-X) Morrow Jr Bks.
—Going Places: The Young Traveler's Guide & Activity Book. Webster, Harriet. LC 90-41234. 112p. (gr. 3-7). 1991. pap. 4.95 (0-689-71288-X, Aladdin) Macmillan Child Grp.
—Going Places: The Young Traveler's Guide & Activity Book. Webster, Harriet. LC 89-24201. 112p. (gr. 4-7). 1991. SBE 13.95 (0-684-19078-8, Scribners Young Read) Macmillan Child Grp.
—Good-Bye, Sammy. Murrow, Liza K. LC 88-17011. 32p. (ps-3). 1989. reinforced bdg. 13.95 (0-8234-0726-8) Holiday.
—Great-Grandma Tells of Threshing Day. Cross, Verda. Tucker, Kathleen, ed. LC 90-28442. 40p. (gr. 1-6). 1992. 15.95 (0-8075-3042-5) A Whitman.
—Hail, Hail Camp Timberwood. Conford, Ellen. LC 78-18715. (gr. 3-7). 1978. 14.95 (0-316-15291-9) Little.
—Hurray for Ali Baba Bernstein. Hurwitz, Johanna. LC 88-19107. 112p. (gr. 3-7). 1989. 11.95 (0-688-08241-6); PLB 11.88 (0-688-08242-4, Morrow Jr Bks) Morrow Jr Bks.
—I Had a Friend Named Peter: Talking to Children about the Death of a Friend. Cohn, Janice. LC 86-31150. 32p. (ps-2). 1987. 13.00 (0-688-06685-2); lib. bdg. 13.88 (0-688-06686-0, Morrow Jr Bks) Morrow Jr Bks.
—I'm the Big Sister Now. Emmert, Michelle. Levine, Abby, ed. LC 89-5584. 32p. (gr. 2-6). 1989. PLB 13.95 (0-8075-3458-7) A Whitman.
—Julia & the Hand of God. Cameron, Eleanor. LC 77-4507. (gr. 4-7). 1977. 12.95 (0-525-32910-2, DCB) Dutton Child Bks.
—Julia & the Hand of God. Cameron, Eleanor. 176p. (gr. 3-7). 1989. pap. 3.95 (0-14-034042-4, Puffin) Puffin Bks.
—Julia's Magic. Cameron, Eleanor. LC 84-8118. 144p. (gr. 2-5). 1984. 13.95 (0-525-44114-X, DCB) Dutton Child Bks.
—Julia's Magic. Cameron, Eleanor. 176p. (gr. 3-7). 1989. pap. 3.95 (0-14-034040-8, Puffin) Puffin Bks.
—Mr. Adams's Mistake. Parish, Peggy. LC 81-17221. 64p. (gr. 1-4). 1982. SBE 11.95 (0-02-769800-9) Macmillan Child Grp.
—Poison Ivy & Eyebrow Wigs. Pryor, Bonnie. LC 92-38881. 176p. (gr. 3 up). 1993. 14.00 (0-688-11200-5) Morrow Jr Bks.
—That Julia Redfern. Cameron, Eleanor. LC 82-2405. 144p. (gr. 2-5). 1982. 12.95 (0-525-44015-1, DCB) Dutton Child Bks.
—That Julia Redfern. Cameron, Eleanor. 144p. (gr. 3-7). 1989. pap. 3.95 (0-14-034041-6, Puffin) Puffin Bks.
—The Up & Down Spring. Hurwitz, Johanna. LC 92-21337. 112p. (gr. 3 up). 1993. 14.00 (0-688-11922-0) Morrow Jr Bks.
—Vinegar Pancakes & Vanishing Cream. Pryor, Bonnie. LC 86-31085. 128p. (gr. 2-5). 1987. 12.95 (0-688-06728-X) Morrow Jr Bks.
—Why Did It Happen? Helping Young Children Cope with the Existence of Violence. Cohn, Janice I. LC 93-1573. 1994. write for info. (0-688-12312-0); PLB write for info. (0-688-12313-9) Morrow Jr Bks.
Owens, Gay. All Alone after School. Stanek, Muriel. Fay, Ann, ed. LC 84-17243. 32p. (gr. 1-4). 1985. PLB 11.95 (0-8075-0278-2) A Whitman.
Owens, Mary B. Animals Don't Wear Pajamas: A Book about Sleeping. Feldman, Eve B. LC 91-25192. 32p. (ps-3). 1992. 14.95 (0-8050-1710-0, Bks Young Read) H Holt & Co.
—Prize in the Snow. Easterling, Bill. LC 92-23411. 1993. 15.95 (0-316-22489-8) Little.
—Rosebud & Red Flannel. Pochocki, Ethel. LC 90-4933. 32p. (ps-3). 1991. 14.95 (0-8050-1213-3, Bks Young Read) H Holt & Co.
—The Summer of the Dancing Horse. Clifford, Eth. LC 90-4939. 112p. (gr. 3-7). 1991. 13.45 (0-395-50066-4) HM.
Owens, Nate. Jesus for Jews. Rosen, Ruth, ed. LC 87-20343. 336p. (Orig.). (gr. 12). 1987. 13.95 (0-9616148-3-8); pap. 7.95 (0-9616148-4-6); pap. 4.95 mass market (0-9616148-2-X) Purple Pomegranate.
Owens, Nubia. My Lives & How I Lost Them. Cat, Christopher & Cullen, Countee. Strickland, Dorothy, frwd. by. LC 92-46738. 174p. (gr. 3-5). 1993. PLB 14.98 (0-382-24360-9); 12.95 (0-382-24369-2) Silver Burdett Pr.
Oxenbury, Helen. All Fall Down. Oxenbury, Helen. 10p. (ps-k). 1987. bds. 5.95 (0-02-769040-7, Aladdin) Macmillan Child Grp.
—The Car Trip. Oxenbury, Helen. (gr. 1). 1983. 3.95 (0-8037-0009-1, 0383-120) Dial Bks Young.
—Clap Hands. Oxenbury, Helen. 10p. (ps). 1987. bds. 5.95 (0-02-769030-X, Aladdin) Macmillan Child Grp.

—The Dancing Class. Oxenbury, Helen. LC 82-19791. 24p. (ps-1). 1983. 5.95 (0-8037-1651-6, 0383-120) Dial Bks Young.

—Dressing. Oxenbury, Helen. 14p. (ps-k). 1981. 3.95 (0-671-42113-1, Little Simon) S&S Trade.

—Friends. Oxenbury, Helen. 14p. (ps-k). 1981. 3.95 (0-671-42111-5, Little Simon) S&S Trade.

—Helen Oxebury's Numbers of Things. Oxenbury, Helen. LC 83-5263. 32p. (ps-3). 1992. write for info. (0-385-29288-0); pap. 9.95 (0-385-29289-9) Delacorte.

—Helen Oxenbury's ABC of Things. Oxenbury, Helen. LC 83-5263. 56p. (ps-3). 1983. PLB 13.95 (0-385-29291-0); pap. 12.95 (0-385-29290-2) Delacorte.

—Helen Oxenbury's ABC of Things. Oxenbury, Helen. 28p. (ps). 1993. Repr. bds. 3.95 (0-689-71761-X, Aladdin) Macmillan Child Grp.

—Helen Oxenbury's First Nursery Stories. Oxenbury, Helen. 32p. (ps-k). 1994. bds. 3.95 (0-689-71825-X, Aladdin) Macmillan Child Grp.

—I Hear. Oxenbury, Helen. LC 85-61367. 14p. (ps). 1986. 3.95 (0-394-87481-1) Random Bks Yng Read.

—I See. Oxenbury, Helen. LC 85-61365. 14p. (ps). 1986. Repr. of 1986 ed. bds. 3.95 (0-394-87479-X) Random Bks Yng Read.

—Pippo Gets Lost. Oxenbury, Helen. LC 89-340. 14p. (ps-k). 1989. bds. 5.95 (0-689-71336-3, Aladdin) Macmillan Child Grp.

—Playing. Oxenbury, Helen. 14p. (ps-k). 1981. 3.95 (0-671-42109-3, Little Simon) S&S Trade.

—Say Goodnight. Oxenbury, Helen. 10p. (ps). 1987. bds. 5.95 (0-02-769010-5, Aladdin) Macmillan Child Grp.

—The Three Little Wolves & the Big Bad Pig. Trivizas, Eugene. LC 92-24829. 32p. (gr. k-5). 1993. SBE 15.95 (0-689-50569-8, M K McElderry) Macmillan Child Grp.

—Tickle, Tickle. Oxenbury, Helen. 10p. (ps). 1987. bds. 5.95 (0-02-769020-2, Aladdin) Macmillan Child Grp.

—Tiny Tim. Bennett, Jill, selected by. LC 81-68916. 32p. (ps-3). 1982. PLB 10.95 (0-685-01402-9); pap. 10.95 (0-385-29055-1) Delacorte.

—Tom & Pippo & the Dog. Oxenbury, Helen. LC 89-341. 14p. (ps-k). 1989. bds. 5.95 (0-689-71338-X, Aladdin) Macmillan Child Grp.

—Tom & Pippo & the Washing Machine. Oxenbury, Helen. LC 89-37431. 14p. (ps-k). 1988. bds. 5.95 (0-689-71255-3, Aladdin) Macmillan Child Grp.

—Tom & Pippo Go for a Walk. Oxenbury, Helen. LC 87-37432. 14p. (ps-k). 1988. bds. 5.95 (0-689-71254-5, Aladdin) Macmillan Child Grp.

—Tom & Pippo Go Shopping. Oxenbury, Helen. LC 88-10497. 14p. (ps-1). 1989. Repr. of 1989 ed. bds. 5.95 (0-689-71278-2, Aladdin) Macmillan Child Grp.

—Tom & Pippo in the Garden. Oxenbury, Helen. LC 88-9145. 14p. (ps-1). 1989. Repr. of 1989 ed. bds. 5.95 (0-689-71275-8, Aladdin) Macmillan Child Grp.

—Tom & Pippo in the Snow. Oxenbury, Helen. LC 89-336. 14p. (ps-k). 1989. bds. 5.95 (0-689-71337-1, Aladdin) Macmillan Child Grp.

—Tom & Pippo Make a Friend. Oxenbury, Helen. LC 89-337. 14p. (ps-k). 1989. bds. 5.95 (0-689-71339-8, Aladdin) Macmillan Child Grp.

—Tom & Pippo Make a Mess. Oxenbury, Helen. LC 87-37437. 14p. (ps-k). 1988. bds. 5.95 (0-689-71253-7, Aladdin) Macmillan Child Grp.

—Tom & Pippo on the Beach. Oxenbury, Helen. LC 92-53130. 24p. (ps). 1993. 5.95 (1-56402-181-5) Candlewick Pr.

—Tom & Pippo Read a Story. Oxenbury, Helen. LC 87-37438. 14p. (ps-k). 1988. bds. 5.95 (0-689-71252-9, Aladdin) Macmillan Child Grp.

—Tom & Pippo See the Moon. Oxenbury, Helen. 14p. (ps-1). 1989. Repr. of 1989 ed. bds. 5.95 (0-689-71277-4, Aladdin) Macmillan Child Grp.

—Tom & Pippo's Day. Oxenbury, Helen. 14p. (ps-1). 1989. Repr. of 1989 ed. bds. 5.95 (0-689-71276-6, Aladdin) Macmillan Child Grp.

—We're Going on a Bear Hunt. Rosen, Michael. LC 88-13338. 40p. (ps-4). 1989. SBE 15.95 (0-689-50476-4, M K McElderry) Macmillan Child Grp.

—Working. Oxenbury, Helen. 7p. (ps). 1981. 3.95 (0-671-42112-3, Little Simon) S&S Trade.

Oxenbury, Helen & Oxenbury, Helen. Farmer Duck. Waddell, Martin. LC 91-71855. 40p. (ps up). 1992. 15.95 (1-56402-009-6) Candlewick Pr.

Oxford Illustrators Staff, et al. Mind Twisters. Hall, Godfrey. LC 91-27688. 96p. (Orig.). (gr. 3-7). 1992. PLB 13.99 (0-679-92038-2); pap. 10.00 (0-679-82038-8) Random Bks Yng Read.

Oxford Scientific Film Staff. The Deer in the Forest. Gamlin, Linda. LC 87-9916. 32p. (gr. 4-6). 1987. PLB 15.93 (1-55532-273-5) Gareth Stevens Inc.

—The Owl in the Tree. Coldrey, Jennifer. LC 87-9915. 32p. (gr. 4-6). 1987. PLB 15.93 (1-55532-272-7) Gareth Stevens Inc.

—The Penguin in the Snow. Allen, Douglas. LC 87-9968. 32p. (gr. 4-6). 1987. PLB 15.93 (1-55532-270-0) Gareth Stevens Inc.

—The Seal on the Rocks. Allan, Doug. LC 87-9950. 32p. (gr. 4-6). 1988. PLB 15.93 (1-55532-271-9) Gareth Stevens Inc.

Oxford Scientific Films, photos by. The Dragonfly over the Water. O'Toole, Christopher. LC 87-42613. 32p. (gr. 4-6). 1988. PLB 15.93 (1-55532-306-5) Gareth Stevens Inc.

—The Falcon over the Town. Birkhead, Mike. LC 87-42615. 32p. (gr. 4-6). 1988. PLB 15.93 (1-55532-304-9) Gareth Stevens Inc.

—How Big Am I? Greenway, Shirley. LC 93-18593. 32p. (ps-1). 1993. PLB 11.00 (0-8249-8625-3, Ideals Child); pap. 3.95 (0-8249-8601-6) Hambleton-Hill.

—The Lizard in the Jungle. Linley, Mike. LC 87-42612. 32p. (gr. 4-6). 1988. PLB 15.93 (1-55532-303-0) Gareth Stevens Inc.

—The Mouse in the Barn. Burton, Robert. LC 87-42614. 32p. (gr. 4-6). 1988. PLB 15.93 (1-55532-305-7) Gareth Stevens Inc.

—What Is a Bird? Snedden, Robert. 32p. (gr. 2-5). 1993. 13.95 (0-87156-539-0) Sierra.

—What Is an Insect? Snedden, Robert. LC 92-35060. 32p. (gr. 2-5). 1993. 13.95 (0-87156-540-4) Sierra.

Oxford Scientific Films Ser., photos by. The Hummingbird among the Flowers. Foster, Susan Q. LC 89-31912. 32p. (gr. 4-6). 1989. PLB 15.93 (0-8368-0115-6) Gareth Stevens Inc.

Oxford Scientific Films Staff. The World of Deer. Saintsing, David. LC 87-6539. 32p. (gr. 2-3). 1987. PLB 15.93 (1-55532-302-2) Gareth Stevens Inc.

—The World of Dragonflies. Harrison, Virginia. LC 87-42610. 32p. (gr. 2-3). 1988. PLB 15.93 (1-55532-310-3) Gareth Stevens Inc.

—The World of Owls. Saintsing, David. LC 87-6537. 32p. (gr. 2-3). 1987. PLB 15.93 (1-55532-301-4) Gareth Stevens Inc.

—The World of Penguins. Saintsing, David. LC 87-6536. 32p. (gr. 2-3). 1987. PLB 15.93 (1-55532-274-3) Gareth Stevens Inc.

Oxford Scientific Films Staff, photos by. The Ant on the Ground. Losito, Linda. LC 89-4460. 32p. (gr. 4-6). 1989. PLB 15.93 (0-8368-0111-3) Gareth Stevens Inc.

—The Bat in the Cave. Riley, Helen. LC 89-4469. 32p. (gr. 4-6). 1989. PLB 15.93 (0-8368-0112-1) Gareth Stevens Inc.

—Color Me Bright. Greenway, Shirley. 16p. (ps-k). 1992. bds. 3.95 (1-879085-53-4) Whsprng Coyote Pr.

—The Elephant in the Bush. Redmond, Ian. LC 89-11297. 32p. (gr. 4-6). 1989. PLB 15.95 (0-8368-0116-4) Gareth Stevens Inc.

—Here's Ears. Greenway, Shirley. 16p. (ps-k). 1992. bds. 3.95 (1-879085-50-X) Whsprng Coyote Pr.

—The Honeybee in the Meadow. O'Toole, Christopher. LC 89-33935. 32p. (gr. 4-6). 1989. PLB 15.93 (0-8368-0117-2) Gareth Stevens Inc.

—Legs & All. Greenway, Shirley. 16p. (ps-k). 1992. bds. 3.95 (1-879085-52-6) Whsprng Coyote Pr.

—The Polar Bear on the Ice. Banks, Martin. LC 89-4472. 32p. (gr. 4-6). 1989. PLB 15.93 (0-8368-0114-8) Gareth Stevens Inc.

—The Snake in the Grass. Linley, Mike. LC 89-4621. 32p. (gr. 4-6). 1989. PLB 15.93 (0-8368-0118-0) Gareth Stevens Inc.

—A Tale of Tails. Greenway, Shirley. 16p. (ps-k6). 1992. bds. 3.95 (1-879085-51-8) Whsprng Coyote Pr.

—What Do I Eat? Greenway, Shirley. LC 93-18592. 32p. (ps). 1993. PLB 11.00 (0-8249-8627-X, Ideals Child); pap. 3.95 (0-8249-8602-4) Hambleton-Hill.

—The World of a Falcon. Harrison, Virginia. LC 87-42611. 32p. (gr. 2-3). 1988. PLB 15.93 (1-55532-308-1) Gareth Stevens Inc.

—The World of Elephants. Harrison, Virginia. LC 89-11547. 32p. (gr. 2-3). 1989. PLB 15.93 (0-8368-0141-5) Gareth Stevens Inc.

—The World of Honeybees. Harrison, Virginia. LC 89-33936. 32p. (gr. 2-3). 1989. PLB 15.93 (0-8368-0142-3) Gareth Stevens Inc.

—The World of Hummingbirds. Harrison, Virginia. LC 89-31913. 32p. (gr. 2-3). 1989. PLB 15.93 (0-8368-0140-7) Gareth Stevens Inc.

—The World of Lizards. Harrison, Virginia. LC 87-42608. 32p. (gr. 2-3). 1988. PLB 15.93 (1-55532-307-3) Gareth Stevens Inc.

—The World of Mice. Harrison, Virginia. LC 87-42609. 32p. (gr. 2-3). 1988. PLB 15.93 (1-55532-309-X) Gareth Stevens Inc.

—The World of Snakes. Harrison, Virginia. LC 89-4634. 32p. (gr. 2-3). 1989. PLB 15.93 (0-8368-0143-1) Gareth Stevens Inc.

O'Young, Leoung, photos by. Lost & Found. Little, Jean. (gr. 2-5). 1988. pap. 3.95 (0-14-031997-2, Puffin) Puffin Bks.

Oz, Robin. Me & My Aunts. Newton, Laura. Fay, Ann, ed. LC 86-15950. 32p. (gr. 2-5). 1986. PLB 13.95 (0-8075-5029-9) A Whitman.

P

Pace, Anne. Silver Ships-Green Fields. Juengst, Sara C. 52p. (Orig.). (gr. 1-6). 1986. pap. 5.95 (0-377-00161-9) Friendship Pr.

Pace, David. Emily & the Werewolf. Brennan, Herbie. 96p. (ps-3). 1993. SBE 16.95g (0-689-50593-0, M K McElderry) Macmillan Child Grp.

Pace Studios. Palmer Method Cursive, Consumable. King, Fred M. (gr. 5). 1979. wkbk. 3.96 (0-914268-66-X, 79-5C); tchr's. ed. 5.60 (0-914268-67-8, 79-5CTE) A N Palmer.

—Palmer Method Cursive, Non-Consumable. King, Fred M. (gr. 6). 1979. wkbk. 4.24 (0-914268-82-1, N79-6C); tchr's. ed. 5.60 (0-914268-83-X, N79-6CTE) A N Palmer.

—Palmer Method Cursive, Non-Consumable. King, Fred M. (ps-8). 1979. tchr's. ed. 5.60 (0-914268-81-3, N79-5CTE); wkbk. 4.24 (0-914268-80-5, N79-5C) A N Palmer.

Pache, Jocelyne. The Egg. Benedict, Kitty. Soutter-Perrot, Andrienne, concept by. LC 92-15014. (gr. 5 up). 1992. PLB 10.95 (0-88682-565-2) Creative Ed.

Pacheco, Dave & Wakeman, Diana. Disney's Peek-a-Boo Bambi. Patrick, Denise L. 14p. (ps-k). 1992. write for info. (0-307-12392-8, 12392) Western Pub.

Pacheco, David & Clay, Jesse. Walt Disney's Bambi. Ryder, Joanne, adapted by. LC 92-54876. 96p. 1993. 14.95 (1-56282-442-2); PLB 14.89 (1-56282-443-0) Disney Pr.

Pacheco, David & Wakeman, Diana. Bambi's Snowy Day. Birney, Betty. 32p. (ps-k). 1992. write for info. (0-307-15704-0, 15704, Golden Pr) Western Pub.

—Walt Disney's Bambi: Thumper's Book of Opposites. Balducci, Rita. 12p. (ps). 1993. bds. 1.95 (0-307-06124-8, 6124, Golden Pr) Western Pub.

Pacinelli, Donna. Heidi. 48p. (gr. 2-5). 1991. 6.95 (0-88101-112-6) Unicorn Pub.

Pacovska, Kveta. One, Five, Many. Pacovska, Kveta. 30p. (gr. k-3). 1990. 16.45 (0-395-54997-3, Clarion Bks) HM.

Padgett, James. Apostles: Jesus' Special Helpers. Rowell, Edmon L., Jr. (gr. 1-6). 1979. 5.99 (0-8054-4246-4, 4242-46) Broadman.

—Jesus: God's Son, Saviour, Lord. Chamberlain, Eugene. (gr. 1-6). 1976. pap. 5.95 (0-8054-4226-X, 4242-26) Broadman.

—John the Baptist: Forerunner of Jesus. Human, Johnnie. (gr. 1-6). 1978. 5.95 (0-8054-4240-5, 4242-40) Broadman.

Padgett, James R. Mary: Mother of Jesus. Hintze, Barbara. (gr. 1-6). 1977. bds. 5.95 (0-8054-4232-4, 4242-32) Broadman.

Padmavasan. Ramayana for Children. Swami Raghaveshananda. 44p. (Orig.). (gr. 3-6). 1989. pap. 3.95 (81-7120-102-4, Pub. by Ramakrishna Math Madras India) Vedanta Pr.

—Story of Sri Krishna for Children, Pt. I. Swami Raghaveshananda. 60p. (gr. 4). 1990. 3.95 (81-7120-140-7, Pub. by Ramakrishna Math Madras India) Vedanta Pr.

Paek, Min. Aekyung's Dream. Paek, Min. LC 88-18928. (ENG & KOR.). 24p. (gr. 2-7). 1988. 13.95 (0-89239-042-5) Childrens Book Pr.

Paerry, Anna. Riders Ready! A Book about BMX...with Advice from the Experts. Perry, Anne. LC 85-50294. 130p. (Orig.). (gr. 5-8). pap. 8.95 (0-9615253-0-4); perma-bound 12.05 (0-8479-9930-0) Tadpole.

Paff, Mike. Steps to Inner Freedom. Horie, Michiaki & Horie, Hildegard. Huff, Dawn, tr. from GER. 120p. (Orig.). (gr. 7 up). 1987. pap. 5.95 (0-939925-06-0) R C Law & Co.

Pagaard, Tim. One Hundred Ten Tips, Time-Savers & Tricks of the Trade for Youth Workers. Rice, Wayne, ed. 72p. (Orig.). 1984. pap. 5.95 (0-910125-04-X) Youth Special.

Page, Don. Drip Drop. Gordon, Sharon. LC 81-5112. 32p. (gr. k-2). 1981. PLB 11.59 (0-89375-507-9); pap. 2.95 (0-89375-508-7) Troll Assocs.

—Little Christmas Elf. Curran, Eileen. LC 84-8628. 32p. (gr. k-2). 1985. PLB 11.59 (0-8167-0352-3); pap. text ed. 2.95 (0-8167-0432-5) Troll Assocs.

—Play Ball, Kate! Gordon, Sharon. LC 81-4855. 32p. (gr. k-2). 1981. pap. text ed. 11.59 (0-89375-525-7); pap. 2.95 (0-89375-526-5) Troll Assocs.

—Trouble in Space. Greydanus, Rose. LC 81-5114. 32p. (gr. k-2). 1981. PLB 11.59 (0-89375-517-6); pap. text ed. 2.95 (0-89375-518-4) Troll Assocs.

—Valentine's Day Grump. Greydanus, Rose. LC 81-4712. 32p. (gr. k-2). 1981. PLB 11.59 (0-89375-515-X); pap. text ed. 2.95 (0-89375-516-8) Troll Assocs.

—What a Funny Bunny. Whitehead, Patricia. LC 84-8833. 32p. (gr. k-2). 1985. PLB 11.59 (0-8167-0361-2); pap. text ed. 2.95 (0-8167-0362-0) Troll Assocs.

Page, Jean R. From Hoof to Wheel. Page, Jean R. 75p. (Orig.). (gr. 7-12). 1992. pap. 7.95 (0-9632755-0-X) Jean Page.

Page, Ken. Shoes Like Miss Alice's. Johnson, Angela. LC 93-4872. 1994. write for info. (0-531-06814-5); PLB write for info. (0-531-08664-X) Orchard Bks Watts.

Paget, Sidney, jt. illus. see Martinez, Sergio.

Pagnoni, Roberta. What Does Baby See? Lundell, Margo. 24p. (ps-k). 1990. bds. 9.95 (0-448-19098-2, G&D) Putnam Pub Group.

Pagnucci, Susan. I Never Had a Pet. Pagnucci, Franco. Pagnucci, Gian, ed. 32p. (Orig.). (gr. 1-5). 1992. pap. 5.95 (0-929326-09-1) Bur Oak Pr Inc.

Paiss, Jana. Alef-Bet of Jewish Values: Code Words of Jewish Life. Kipper, Lenore & Bogot, Howard. 64p. (gr. 4-6). 1985. pap. text ed. 6.00 (0-8074-0267-2, 101087) UAHC.

—I Can Read Hebrew. Strauss, Ruby G. & Schuller, Ahuva. 64p. (gr. k-2). 1982. pap. text ed. 4.25x (0-87441-358-3) Behrman.

—My Haggadah. Cherney, Ila. 66p. (gr. 4-7). 1985. pap. text ed. 4.25 (0-317-60058-3) Behrman.

—My Siddur. Miller, Deborah U. 35p. (gr. k-2). 1984. pap. text ed. 4.25 (0-87441-389-3) Behrman.

Pak, Mi-Son. The Seven Brothers & the Big Dipper. Vorhees, Duance & Mueller, Mark. 46p. (gr. 2-5). 1991. PLB 9.95x (0-930878-74-4) Hollym Intl.

Pak, Mi-Son & Kim, Yon-Kyong. The Greedy Princess: The Rabbit & the Tiger. Vorhees, Duance & Mueller, Mark. 46p. (gr. 2-5). 1990. PLB 9.95x (0-930878-90-6) Hollym Intl.
Pakarnyk, Alan. Julie Gerond & the Polka Dot Pony. Penner, Fred & Oberman, Sheldon. 32p. (gr. 2-6). 1990. pap. 5.95 (0-920534-70-8, Pub. by Hyperion Pr Ltd CN) Sterling.
Palacios, Argentina, jt. illus. see Lazzarino, Luciano.
Palagonia, Peter. Flit, Flutter, Fly! Poems about Bugs & Other Crawly Creatures. Hopkins, Lee B., compiled by. LC 91-12441. 32p. (gr. k-4). 1992. pap. 14.00 (0-385-41468-4) Doubleday.
—The Magic House. Eversole, Robyn H. LC 91-17824. 32p. (ps-2). 1992. 13.95 (0-531-05924-3); lib. bdg. 13.99 (0-531-08524-4) Orchard Bks Watts.
—No Babies Asleep. Nikola-Lisa, W. LC 93-20589. Date not set. write for info. (0-689-31841-3, Atheneum) Macmillan Child Grp.
Palan, R. Michael. Cat & Dog Mysteries: Fourteen Exciting Mini-Mysteries with Hidden Pictures. O'Hare, Jeff, ed. 32p. (Orig.). (gr. 2-7). 1993. pap. 4.95 (1-56397-291-3) Boyds Mills Pr.
—Halloween Craft Book: Spooky & Fun Things to Make. Van Blaricom, Colleen, ed. 32p. (gr. 2-5). 1992. Set of 3 bks. age. 11.85 (1-56397-165-8); pap. 3.95 (1-56397-119-4) Boyds Mills Pr.
Palazzo, Tony. The Biggest & the Littlest Animals. Palazzo, Tony. LC 77-112374. 40p. (gr. k-3). 1973. PLB 13.95 (0-87460-225-4) Lion Bks.
—Magic Crayon. Palazzo, Tony. (gr. k-2). 1967. PLB 10.95 (0-87460-089-8) Lion Bks.
Palecek, Josef. Bremen Town Musicians. Grimm, Jacob & Grimm, Wilhelm K. Bell, Anthea, tr. LC 88-15179. 32p. (ps up). 1991. pap. 13.95 (0-88708-071-5) Picture Bk Studio.
—Die Nachtigall. Andersen, Hans Christian. (GER.). 40p. (gr. k-3). 1992. 13.95 (3-314-00521-0) North-South Bks NYC.
—The Nightingale. Andersen, Hans Christian. Lewis, Naomi, tr. LC 89-43723. 40p. (gr. k-3). 1990. 13.95 (1-55858-090-5) North-South Bks NYC.
—Peter & the Wolf. Prokofiev, Sergei. Crampton, Patricia, tr. LC 87-13915. (ps up). 1991. pap. 13.95 (0-88708-049-9) Picture Bk Studio.
—Le Rossignol. Andersen, Hans Christian. (FRE.). 40p. (gr. k-3). 1992. 13.95 (3-314-20707-7) North-South Bks NYC.
Palencar, John. Tinker vs. Des Moines: Student Rights on Trial. Rappaport, Doreen. LC 92-25019. 160p. (gr. 5 up). 1993. 15.00 (0-06-025117-4); PLB 14.89 (0-06-025118-2) HarpC Child Bks.
Palencar, John J. Nightmare Island: And Other Real-Life Mysteries. Razzi, Jim. LC 92-32638. 96p. (gr. 3-7). 1993. pap. 3.95 (0-06-440426-9, Trophy) HarpC Child Bks.
—The Restless Dead: More Strange Real-Life Mysteries. Razzi, Jim. LC 93-34745. (gr. 6 up). 1994. pap. write for info. (0-06-440427-7, Trophy) HarpC Child Bks.
Paley, Nina. Ellie's Birthday. ETR Associates Staff. LC 92-8358. 1992. write for info. (1-56071-106-X) ETR Assocs.
—A Family That Fits. ETR Associates Staff. LC 92-8361. 1992. write for info. (1-56071-103-5) ETR Assocs.
—The Golden Treasure. ETR Associates Staff. LC 92-8360. 1992. write for info. (1-56071-104-3) ETR Assocs.
—A Helmet for Harry. ETR Associates Staff. LC 92-8357. 1992. write for info. (1-56071-102-7) ETR Assocs.
—In My Shoes. ETR Associates Staff. LC 92-8359. 1992. write for info. (1-56071-105-1) ETR Assocs.
—Messages from the Zoo. ETR Associates Staff. LC 93-16477. 1993. write for info. ETR Assocs.
—No, No, Annette. ETR Associates. LC 93-16478. (gr. 5 up). 1993. write for info. ETR Assocs.
—Who Likes That Stuff? ETR Associates Staff. LC 92-8356. 1992. write for info. (1-56071-101-9) ETR Assocs.
Palin, Nicki. Owls & Pussycats: Nonsense Verse. Lear, Edward & Carroll, Lewis. LC 93-2714. 64p. (gr. 3 up). 1993. 16.95 (0-87226-366-5) P Bedrick Bks.
Palladini, David. The Eyes of the Dragon. King, Stephen. 336p. 1987. pap. 21.95 (0-670-81458-X) Viking Child Bks.
—The Girl Who Cried Flowers & Other Tales. Yolen, Jane. LC 73-8903. 64p. (gr. 3-6). 1974. 12.95 (0-690-00216-5, Crowell Jr Bks); (Crowell Jr Bks) HarpC Child Bks.
Palm, Felix. Pirates & Privateers. McCall, Edith. LC 63-15637. 128p. (gr. 3-10). 1980. PLB 15.00 (0-516-03360-3) Childrens.
—The Story of Peter. Berg, Jean H., retold by. 40p. (Orig.). (gr. k-3). 1990. pap. 9.95 incl. audiocassette (0-87510-216-6) Christian Sci.
Palm, Felix & Crouch, Ellen. The Story of Ruth. Berg, Jean H., adapted by. 32p. pap. 9.95 (0-87510-273-5, G81244) Christian Sci.
Palmer, Jan. Happy Hanukkah Rebus. Adler, David A. 32p. (ps-3). 1989. pap. 11.95 (0-670-82419-4) Viking Child Bks.
—Happy Hanukkah Rebus. Adler, David A. 32p. (ps-3). 1991. 3.99 (0-14-050915-1, Puffin) Puffin Bks.
—One Minute Christmas Stories. Lewis, Shari. Matthews, Gerry, contrib. by. LC 86-29146. 48p. (gr. k-3). 1987. pap. 7.95 (0-385-23424-4) Doubleday.

—Something New to Do. Michaels, Ski. LC 85-14021. 48p. (Orig.). (gr. 1-3). 1986. PLB 10.59 (0-8167-0634-4); pap. text ed. 3.50 (0-8167-0635-2) Troll Assocs.
—The Toothpaste Millionaire. Merrill, Jean. LC 73-22055. 96p. (gr. 2-5). 1974. 13.95 (0-395-18511-4) HM.
—The Village, Life in Colonial Times. Knight, James E. LC 81-23084. 32p. (gr. 5-9). 1982. PLB 11.59 (0-89375-728-4); pap. text ed. 2.95 (0-89375-729-2); cassette avail. Troll Assocs.
Palmer, Kate S. Octopus Hug. Pringle, Laurence. 32p. (ps-3). 1993. 14.95 (1-56397-034-1) Boyds Mills Pr.
Palmer, Norman D. The Spaceship Earth. Nord, Barry M. 64p. (Orig.). (gr. 6 up). pap. 9.95 (0-935656-09-X) Nords Studio.
Palmisciano, Diane. Can Do, Jenny Archer. Conford, Ellen. (gr. 2-4). 1991. 11.95 (0-316-15356-7) Little.
—A Case for Jenny Archer. Conford, Ellen. LC 88-14169. (gr. 2-4). 1988. 10.95 (0-316-15266-8) Little.
—Chase That Pig. Leonard, Marcia. 24p. (ps up). 1988. pap. write for info. (0-553-05476-7) Bantam.
—Counting Kangaroos, A Book about Numbers. Leonard, Marcia. LC 89-4960. 24p. (gr. k-2). 1990. PLB 9.59 (0-8167-1722-2); pap. text ed. 1.95 (0-8167-1723-0) Troll Assocs.
—Jenny Archer, Author. Conford, Ellen. 64p. (gr. 2-4). 1989. 10.95 (0-316-15255-2) Little.
—Nibble, Nibble, Jenny Archer. Conford, Ellen. LC 92-34306. 1993. 12.95 (0-316-15371-0) Little.
—Paintbox Penguins, A Book about Colors. Leonard, Marcia. LC 89-4979. 24p. (gr. k-2). 1990. lib. bdg. 9.59 (0-8167-1716-8); pap. text ed. 1.95 (0-8167-1717-6) Troll Assocs.
—Patti's Pet Gorilla. Mauser, Patricia R. LC 86-20546. 64p. (gr. 2-4). 1987. SBE 11.95 (0-689-31279-2, Atheneum Child Bk) Macmillan Child Grp.
—What's Cooking, Jenny Archer? Conford, Ellen. (gr. 2-4). 1989. 12.95 (0-316-15254-4) Little.
Palsa, Soozee. Tommy the Toothbrush. Miller, Robert D. 16p. (gr. 2-4). 1982. write for info Miller OH.
Palto, Susan C. & Hennessy, Jim. Please Put Me: Simple Spatial Concepts. Toomey, Marilyn M. 48p. (ps-8). 1989. 16 cards & 32 worksheets 17.95 (0-923573-12-7) Circuit Pubns.
Paltrow, Robert. National Park Service: Activities & Adventures for Kids. Hallett, Bill & Hallett, Jane. 32p. (Orig.). (gr. 3-8). 1991. activity bk. 3.95 (1-877827-07-X) Look & See.
Panek, Dennis. A Rhinoceros Wakes Me up in the Morning. Goodspeed, Peter. 32p. (ps-k). 1984. pap. 3.95 (0-14-050455-9, Puffin) Puffin Bks.
—Splash, Splash. Sheppard, Jeff. LC 92-26163. 40p. (ps-k). 1994. RSBE 14.95 (0-02-782455-1, Macmillan Child Bk) Macmillan Child Grp.
Panek, Judy, jt. illus. see Krone, Mike.
Pang, Alex. One Hundred One Science Surprises: Exciting Experiments with Everyday Materials. Richards, Roy. LC 92-32491. 104p. 1993. 14.95 (0-8069-8822-3) Sterling.
—One Hundred One Things to Make: Fun Craft Projects with Everyday Materials. Bawden, Juliet. LC 93-29633. 1994. write for info. (0-8069-0596-4) Sterling.
Pangrazio, Micheal. Glim the Glorious or How the Little Folk Bested the Gubgoblins. Middleton, Gayle. LC 86-2978. 64p. (gr. k-5). 1987. 12.95 (0-394-88081-1) Knopf Bks Yng Read.
Pantheon Books Staff. The Further Adventures of Nils. rev. ed. Lagerlof, Selma. Johnson, Nancy, ed. Howard, Velma S., tr. from SWE. 250p. (gr. 2 up). 1992. pap. 12.95x (0-9615394-4-5) Skandisk.
—The Wonderful Adventures of Nils, Bk. 1. Lagerlof, Selma. Johnson, Nancy, intro. by. Howard, Velma S., tr. from SWE. 250p. (gr. 2 up). 1991. pap. 12.95 (0-9615394-3-7) Skandisk.
Panton, Doug. The Violin-Maker's Gift. large type ed. Kushner, Donn. 88p. (gr. 5-6). Repr. of 1981 ed. 17.16 (0-317-01960-0, 4-27120-00) Am Printing Hse.
Pantry, Stuart. Plants & Flowers. Pope, Joyce. LC 91-45378. 32p. (gr. 3-6). 1993. PLB 11.59 (0-8167-2779-1); pap. text ed. 3.95 (0-8167-2780-5) Troll Assocs. Postponed.
Paolillo, Ronald G. Red Wings of Christmas. Eure, Wesley. LC 92-5457. 160p. (gr. 3-7). 1992. 19.95 (0-88289-902-3) Pelican.
Paparone, Pam. Fire Fighters. Simon, Norma. LC 93-4439. 1994. pap. 14.00 (0-671-87282-6) S&S Trade.
Paparone, Pamela. Two Legged, Four-Legged, No-Legged Rhymes. Lewis, J. Patrick. LC 90-20651. 40p. (ps-3). 1991. 13.00 (0-679-80771-3); lib. bdg. 13.99 (0-679-90771-8) Knopf Bks Yng Read.
Papas, William. Armenian Folk-Tales & Fables. Downing, Charles. 240p. 1993. pap. 10.95 (0-19-274155-1) OUP.
Pape, Richard. Adjectives & Adverbs. Gregorich, Barbara. 24p. (gr. 3-4). 1980. wkbk. 2.95 (0-89403-596-7) EDC.
—El Alfabeto: Minusculas: Alphabet: Lowercase. Gregorich, Barbara. Hoffman, Joan, ed. Shepherd-Bartram, tr. from ENG. (SPA.). 32p. (Orig.). (ps). 1987. wkbk. 1.99 (0-938256-76-9) Sch Zone Pub Co.
—Alphabet: Lowercase. Gregorich, Barbara. Hoffman, Joan, ed. 32p. (ps). 1983. wkbk. 1.99 (0-938256-66-1) Sch Zone Pub Co.
—Alphabet: Uppercase. Gregorich, Barbara. Hoffman, Joan, ed. 32p. (ps). 1983. wkbk. 1.99 (0-938256-65-3) Sch Zone Pub Co.

—Apostrophe, Colon, Hyphen. Gregorich, Barbara. 24p. (gr. 3-4). 1980. wkbk. 2.95 (0-89403-593-2) EDC.
—Beginning Sounds. Gregorich, Barbara. Hoffman, Joan, ed. 32p. (ps). 1983. wkbk. 1.99 (0-938256-54-8) Sch Zone Pub Co.
—Capital Letters. Gregorich, Barbara. 24p. (gr. 3-4). 1980. wkbk. 2.95 (0-89403-604-1) EDC.
—Los Colores. Gregorich, Barbara. Hoffman, Joan, ed. Shepherd-Bartram, tr. from ENG. (SPA.). 32p. (Orig.). (ps). 1987. wkbk. 1.99 (0-938256-78-5) Sch Zone Pub Co.
—Colors. Gregorich, Barbara. Hoffman, Joan, ed. 32p. (ps). 1983. wkbk. 1.99 (0-938256-64-5) Sch Zone Pub Co.
—Comma. Gregorich, Barbara. 24p. (gr. 3-4). 1980. wkbk. 2.95 (0-89403-595-9) EDC.
—Connect the Dots. Gregorich, Barbara. Hoffman, Joan, ed. 32p. (ps). 1983. wkbk. 1.99 (0-938256-58-0) Sch Zone Pub Co.
—Contando del 1 al 10: Counting 1 to 10. Gregorich, Barbara. Hoffman, Joan, ed. Shepherd-Bartram, tr. from ENG. (SPA.). 32p. (Orig.). 1987. wkbk. 1.99 (0-938256-79-3) Sch Zone Pub Co.
—Context Clues. Gregorich, Barbara. 24p. (gr. 3-4). 1980. wkbk. 2.95 (0-89403-602-5) EDC.
—Counting One to Ten. Gregorich, Barbara. Hoffman, Joan, ed. 32p. (ps). 1983. wkbk. 1.99 (0-938256-56-4) Sch Zone Pub Co.
—Dictionary Skills. Gregorich, Barbara. 24p. (gr. 3-4). 1980. wkbk. 2.95 (0-89403-605-X) EDC.
—Does It Belong? Gregorich, Barbara. Hoffman, Joan, ed. 32p. (ps). 1983. wkbk. 1.99 (0-938256-59-9) Sch Zone Pub Co.
—El Alfabeto: Mayusculas: Alphabet: Uppercase. Gregorich, Barbara. Hoffman, Joan, ed. Shepherd-Bartram, tr. from ENG. (SPA.). 32p. (Orig.). (ps). 1987. wkbk. 1.99 (0-938256-75-0) Sch Zone Pub Co.
—Figures of Speech. Gregorich, Barbara. 24p. (gr. 3-4). 1980. wkbk. 2.95 (0-89403-601-7) EDC.
—Following Directions. Gregorich, Barbara. Hoffman, Joan, ed. 32p. (ps). 1983. wkbk. 1.99 (0-938256-62-9) Sch Zone Pub Co.
—Hidden Pictures. Gregorich, Barbara. Hoffman, Joan, ed. 32p. (Orig.). (ps). 1983. wkbk. 1.99 (0-938256-50-5) Sch Zone Pub Co.
—Igual O Diferente: Same or Different. Gregorich, Barbara. Hoffman, Joan, ed. Shepherd-Bartram, tr. from ENG. (SPA.). 32p. (Orig.). (ps). 1987. wkbk. 1.99 (0-938256-80-7) Sch Zone Pub Co.
—It's Magic. Gregorich, Barbara. Hoffman, Joan, ed. 32p. (gr. k-2). 1987. 1.99 (0-88743-104-6, 02604) Sch Zone Pub Co.
—Mazes. Gregorich, Barbara. Hoffman, Joan, ed. 32p. (ps). 1983. wkbk. 1.99 (0-938256-57-2) Sch Zone Pub Co.
—Nouns & Pronouns. Tilkin, Sheldon L. 24p. (gr. 3-4). 1980. wkbk. 2.95 (0-89403-599-1) EDC.
—Paragraph & Topic Sentence. Tilkin, Sheldon. 24p. (gr. 3-4). 1980. wkbk. 2.95 (0-89403-606-8) EDC.
—Period, Question Mark, Exclamation Mark. Gregorich, Barbara. 24p. (gr. 3-4). 1980. wkbk. 2.95 (0-89403-592-4) EDC.
—Prefixes, Bases, & Suffixes. Gregorich, Barbara. 24p. (gr. 3-4). 1980. wkbk. 2.95 (0-89403-600-9) EDC.
—Prepositions & Conjunctions. Gregorich, Barbara. 24p. (gr. 3-4). 1980. wkbk. 2.95 (0-89403-597-5) EDC.
—Quotation Marks & Underlining. Tilkin, Sheldon. 24p. (gr. 3-4). 1980. 2.95 (0-89403-594-0) EDC.
—Rhyming Pictures. Gregorich, Barbara. Hoffman, Joan, ed. 32p. (ps). 1983. wkbk. 1.99 (0-938256-53-X) Sch Zone Pub Co.
—Same or Different. Gregorich, Barbara. Hoffman, Joan, ed. 32p. (ps). 1983. wkbk. 1.99 (0-938256-52-1) Sch Zone Pub Co.
—School Time Fun. Gregorich, Barbara. Hoffman, Joan, ed. 32p. (ps). 1983. wkbk. 1.99 (0-938256-67-X) Sch Zone Pub Co.
—Shapes. Gregorich, Barbara. Hoffman, Joan, ed. 32p. (ps). 1983. wkbk. 1.99 (0-938256-63-7) Sch Zone Pub Co.
—Los Sonidos para Empezar: Beginning Sounds. Gregorich, Barbara. Hoffman, Joan, ed. Shepherd-Bartram, tr. from ENG. (SPA.). 32p. (Orig.). (ps). 1987. wkbk. 1.99 (0-938256-77-7, 02077) Sch Zone Pub Co.
—Synonyms, Antonyms, Homonyms. Tilkin, Sheldon. 24p. (gr. 3-4). 1980. wkbk. 2.95 (0-89403-603-3) EDC.
—Verbs. Tilkin, Sheldon. 24p. (gr. 3-4). 1980. wkbk. 2.95 (0-89403-598-3) EDC.
Pape, Richard, jt. illus. see Laurent, Richard.
Pape, Richard, jt. illus. see Murdocca, Sal.
Pape, Richard, jt. illus. see Nerlove, Miriam.
Pape, Richard, jt. illus. see Sandford, John.
Parado, Arturo H. Sameer's Journey. Lubcker, Donna H. 40p. (Orig.). (gr. 3-5). 1992. pap. 10.00 (0-9633803-3-8) Jasmine Studios.
Paraskevas, Michael. Junior Kroll. Paraskevas, Betty. LC 92-14207. (gr. k up). 1993. 13.95 (0-15-241497-5) HarBrace.
—Junior Kroll & Company. Paraskevas, Betty. LC 93-9138. (ps-6). 1994. write for info. (0-15-292855-3) HarBrace.
—On the Edge of the Sea. Paraskevas, Betty. LC 91-31489. 32p. 1992. 14.00 (0-8037-1130-1); PLB 13.89 (0-8037-1263-4) Dial Bks Young.
—Shamlanders. Paraskevas, Betty. LC 92-32980. 1993. 13.95 (0-15-292854-5) HarBrace.

—The Strawberry Dog. Paraskevas, Betty. LC 92-18216. (ps-3). 1993. 13.99 (*0-8037-1367-3*); PLB 13.89 (*0-8037-1368-1*) Dial Bks Young.

Pardew, Les. Let's Learn about Tithing. Clawson, Jan. 24p. (gr. k-6). 1988. pap. 3.95 (*0-88290-339-X*) Horizon Utah.

Pardew, Louise. Bible Heroes: Stories for Children Ages One to Six. Randall, Louise A. LC 87-82112. 56p. (ps). 1988. pap. 4.95 (*0-88290-316-0*) Horizon Utah.

Pare, Roger. L' Alphabet: A Child's Introduction to the Letters & Sounds of French. Pare, Roger. 32p. 1990. 7.95 (*0-8442-1395-0*, Natl Textbk) NTC Pub Grp.
—Animal Capers. Pare, Roger. 24p. 1992. PLB 14.95 (*1-55037-243-2*, Pub. by Annick Pr); pap. 4.95 (*1-55037-244-0*, Pub. by Annick Pr) Firefly Bks Ltd.
—The Annick ABC. Pare, Roger. 24p. (ps-2). 1989. pap. 0.99 (*0-920303-78-1*, Pub. by Annick CN) Firefly Bks Ltd.
—A Friend Like You. Pare, Roger. 24p. (ps-2). 1989. pap. 0.99 (*0-920303-80-3*, Pub. by Annick CN) Firefly Bks Ltd.
—Winter Games. Pare, Roger. 24p. 1991. PLB 14.95 (*1-55037-187-8*, Pub. by Annick CN); pap. 4.95 (*1-55037-184-3*, Pub. by Annick CN) Firefly Bks Ltd.

Parent, Laurence E., photos by. Capulin Volcano National Monument. Parent, Laurence E. Priehs, T. J. & Jorgen, Randolph, eds. LC 91-60463. 16p. (Orig.). 1991. pap. 2.95 (*0-911408-94-0*) SW Pks Mnmts.
—Gila Cliff Dwellings National Monument. Parent, Laurence E. Priehs, T. J. & Jorgen, Randolph, eds. LC 91-60461. 16p. (Orig.). 1992. pap. 2.95 (*0-911408-96-7*) SW Pks Mnmts.

Paris, Pat. Bear Cubs. 10p. (ps). 1989. 4.95 (*0-8120-5987-5*) Barron.
—Bunnies. 10p. (ps). 1989. 4.95 (*0-8120-5990-5*) Barron.
—Kittens. 10p. (ps). 1989. 4.95 (*0-8120-5989-1*) Barron.
—The Old Witch Finds a New House. DeLage, Ida. 48p. (gr. k-4). 1991. Repr. of 1979 ed. lib. bdg. 12.95 (*0-7910-1481-9*) Chelsea Hse.
—Puppies. 10p. (ps). 1989. 4.95 (*0-8120-5988-3*) Barron.
—Rose-Petal & the Evil Weeds. Buss, Nancy. 1984. incl. cassette 7.95 (*0-685-08159-1*) Parker Bros.
—Where Does Our Garbage Go? Bowden, Joan. (gr. 1-5). 1992. pap. 10.00 (*0-385-30652-0*) Doubleday.
—Who's in the Box, Bobby? 28p. (ps). 1987. 9.95 (*0-8431-1906-3*) Price Stern.

Paris, Pat & All, Wendy. Rose-Petal. 12p. (ps-3). 1984. cancelled 4.00 (*0-910313-53-9*) Parker Bros.
—Sunny Sunflower. 14p. (ps-3). 1984. cancelled 4.00 (*0-910313-55-5*) Parker Bros.

Paris, Pat & Kong, Emilie. King Size Coloring & Activity Book. Nathan, Beverly & Bizer, Linda. 128p. (ps-8). 1984. pap. 2.50 (*0-910313-57-1*) Parker Bros.

Paris, Pat & Lipking, Ron. A Garden of Love to Share: A Panorama. (ps-3). 1984. 4.00 (*0-910313-56-3*) Parker Bros.

Paris, Pat & Posey, Pam. A Garden of Love to Share. Keller, Beverly. 40p. (ps-3). 1984. 5.95 (*0-910313-49-0*) Parker Bros.

Paris, Pat & Shackelford, Jeane. The Fantastic Fashion Show. Foslien, Dagmar. 40p. (ps-3). 1984. 5.95 (*0-910313-50-4*) Parker Bros.

Paris, Pat & Thornley, Jean. A Matter of Music. Gehrt, Vicky E. 1984. incl. cassette 7.95 (*0-910313-64-4*) Parker Bros.

Paris, Pat & Williams, Karin. A Garden of Love to Share. Foslien, Dagmar. 1984. incl. cassette 7.95 (*0-910313-63-6*) Parker Bros.

Park, Dong-Il. Korea's Favorite Tales & Lyrics. Hyun, Peter, ed. 124p. 1986. 12.95 (*0-318-32535-7*, Pub. by Seoul Intl Tourist SK) C E Tuttle.

Park, Julie. Three Cheers for Big Ears. Pearson, Mary Rose. 48p. (gr. 2). 1992. pap. 2.99 (*0-8423-1043-6*) Tyndale.

Park, Rosemary. Active Learning for Young Children. Molyneux, Lynn. 228p. (ps-3). 1989. 19.95 (*0-685-29143-X*) Trellis Bks Inc.

Parker, Carolyn. Dottie, the Unfoolish Mule. Baily, Jane B. LC 90-93258. 32p. (Orig.). (gr. k-3). 1990. pap. 6.95 (*0-9626642-1-9*) J B Baily.

Parker, Ed. Jack & the Beanstalk. LC 78-18072. 32p. (gr. k-4). 1979. PLB 9.79 (*0-89375-125-1*); pap. 1.95 (*0-89375-103-0*) Troll Assocs.
—Mystery of the Lost Pearl. Blake, Olive. LC 78-60121. 48p. (gr. 2-4). 1979. PLB 10.89 (*0-89375-086-7*); pap. 3.50 (*0-89375-074-3*) Troll Assocs.
—Three Billy Goats Gruff. LC 78-18068. 32p. (gr. k-3). 1979. PLB 9.79 (*0-89375-121-9*); pap. 1.95 (*0-89375-099-9*); cassette 9.95 (*0-685-04953-1*) Troll Assocs.

Parker, Edward, photos by. Antonio's Rain Forest. Lewington, Anna. 48p. (gr. 2-5). 1993. 21.50 (*0-87614-749-X*) Carolrhoda Bks.

Parker, James W. Let's Visit a Chocolate Factory. O'Neill, Catherine. LC 87-3460. 32p. (gr. 2-4). 1988. PLB 10.79 (*0-8167-1161-5*); pap. text ed. 2.95 (*0-8167-1162-3*) Troll Assocs.
—Let's Visit a Printing Plant. O'Neill, Catherine. LC 87-3484. 32p. (gr. 2-4). 1988. PLB 10.79 (*0-8167-1163-1*); pap. text ed. 2.95 (*0-8167-1164-X*) Troll Assocs.

Parker, Lewis. Mine for Keeps. Little, Jean. (gr. 3-7). 1988. pap. 4.95 (*0-316-52800-5*) Little.

Parker, Nancy W. Aren't You Coming Too? Rice, Eve. LC 86-33506. 32p. (ps-3). 1988. 11.95 (*0-688-06446-9*); lib. bdg. 11.88 (*0-688-06447-7*) Greenwillow.

—Barbara Frietchie. Whittier, John Greenleaf. LC 90-41755. 32p. (gr. 1 up). 1992. 14.00 (*0-688-09829-0*); PLB 13.93 (*0-688-09830-4*) Greenwillow.
—Black Crow, Black Crow. Guy, Ginger F. LC 89-34619. 24p. (ps up). 1991. 13.95 (*0-688-08956-9*); PLB 13.88 (*0-688-08957-7*) Greenwillow.
—Bugs. Parker, Nancy W. & Wright, Joan R. LC 86-29387. (ps-3). 1988. pap. 4.95 (*0-688-08296-3*, Mulberry) Morrow.
—The Dress I'll Wear to the Party. Neitzel, Shirley. LC 91-30906. 32p. (ps-4). 1992. 14.00 (*0-688-09959-9*); PLB 13.93 (*0-688-09960-2*) Greenwillow.
—General Store. Field, Rachel. LC 87-21641. 24p. (ps-1). 1988. 11.95 (*0-688-07353-0*); lib. bdg. 11.88 (*0-688-07354-9*) Greenwillow.
—The Goat in the Rug. Blood, Charles L. & Link, Martin. LC 80-17315. 40p. (ps-3). 1984. Repr. of 1976 ed. RSBE 14.95 (*0-02-710920-8*, Four Winds) Macmillan Child Grp.
—The Goat in the Rug. Blood, Charles L. & Link, Martin. LC 89-77701. 40p. (ps-3). 1990. pap. 4.95 (*0-689-71418-1*, Aladdin) Macmillan Child Grp.
—Here Comes Henny. Pomerantz, Charlotte. LC 93-5480. 1994. write for info. (*0-688-12355-4*); PLB write for info. (*0-688-12356-2*) Greenwillow.
—My Mom Travels a Lot. Bauer, Caroline Feller. (gr. k-3). 1982. incl. cassette 19.95 (*0-941078-23-X*); pap. 12.95 incl. cassette (*0-941078-21-3*); pap. 27.95 4 bks., cassette & guide (*0-941078-22-1*); sound filmstrip 22. 95 (*0-941078-24-8*) Live Oak Media.
—Oh, A-Hunting We Will Go. Langstaff, John. LC 74-76274. 32p. (ps-3). 1974. SBE 14.95 (*0-689-50007-6*, M K McElderry) Macmillan Child Grp.
—Oh, A-Hunting We Will Go. Langstaff, John. LC 91-1987. 32p. (gr. k-3). 1991. pap. 4.95 (*0-689-71503-X*, Aladdin) Macmillan Child Grp.
—Paul Revere's Ride. Longfellow, Henry Wadsworth. LC 84-4139. 48p. (gr. 1 up). 1985. 14.95 (*0-688-04014-4*); PLB 14.88 (*0-688-04015-2*) Greenwillow.
—Paul Revere's Ride. Longfellow, Henry Wadsworth. LC 92-23319. 48p. (gr. 1 up). 1993. pap. 4.95 (*0-688-12387-2*, Mulberry) Morrow.
—Peter's Pockets. Rice, Eve. LC 87-15640. 32p. (ps up). 1989. 16.95 (*0-688-07241-0*); PLB 14.88 (*0-688-07242-9*) Greenwillow.
—The President's Cabinet & How It Grew. Parker, Nancy W. LC 89-70851. 40p. (gr. 3-5). 1991. PLB 14. 89 (*0-06-021618-2*) HarpC Child Bks.
—Sheridan's Ride. Read, Thomas B. LC 92-16225. 32p. 1993. 14.00 (*0-688-10873-3*); PLB 13.93 (*0-688-10874-1*) Greenwillow.
—When the Rooster Crowed. Lillie, Patricia. LC 90-30783. 32p. (ps up). 1991. 13.95 (*0-688-09378-7*); PLB 13.88 (*0-688-09379-5*) Greenwillow.
—Willy Bear. Kantrowitz, Mildred. LC 89-31868. 32p. (ps-1). 1989. pap. 3.95 (*0-689-71345-2*, Aladdin) Macmillan Child Grp.

Parker, Nancy W., photos by. The Jacket I Wear in the Snow. Neitzel, Shirley. LC 92-43789. Date not set. write for info. (*0-688-04587-1*, Mulberry) Morrow. Postponed.

Parker, Patricia. Muscles, the Moose Calf. DeVries, Douglas. LC 89-84651. 32p. (Orig.). (ps-3). 1989. 8.00 (*1-877721-00-X*) Jade Ram Pub.
—Muscles Visits Anchorage. DeVries, Douglas. LC 90-61154. 32p. (Orig.). (ps-3). 1990. pap. text ed. 8.00 (*1-877721-01-8*) Jade Ram Pub.

Parker, Robert A. An Autumn Tale. Updike, David. 40p. (gr. 2 up). 1988. 14.95 (*0-945912-02-1*) Pippin Pr.
—The Black Swans (a Russian Folktale). Weinerman, Eli, tr. & retold by. 32p. (gr. k-3). 1994. 14.95 (*0-945912-19-6*) Pippin Pr.
—Circus of the Wolves. Bushnell, Jack. LC 93-8092. 1994. write for info. (*0-688-12554-9*); lib. bdg. write for info. (*0-688-12555-7*) Lothrop.
—Father Time & the Day Boxes. Lyon, George E. LC 93-25201. 32p. (gr. k-3). 1994. pap. 4.95 (*0-689-71792-X*, Aladdin) Macmillan Child Grp.
—The Fox & the Kingfisher. Mellecker, Judith. LC 89-27180. 48p. (gr. k-4). 1990. 14.95 (*0-679-80539-7*); lib. bdg. 15.99 (*0-679-90539-1*) Knopf Bks Yng Read.
—Full Worm Moon. Lemieux, Margo. LC 93-14728. 32p. 1994. 15.00 (*0-688-12105-5*, Tambourine Bks); PLB 14.93 (*0-688-12106-3*, Tambourine Bks) Morrow.
—Grandfather Tang's Story. Tompert, Ann. LC 89-22205. 32p. (ps-2). 1990. 15.00 (*0-517-57487-X*); PLB 15.99 (*0-517-57272-9*) Crown Bks Yng Read.
—A Great Miracle Happened There: A Chanukah Story. Kuskin, Karla. LC 92-17909. 32p. (gr. k-3). 1993. 15. 00 (*0-06-023617-5*); PLB 14.89 (*0-06-023618-3*) HarpC Child Bks.
—Guess Who My Favorite Person Is. Baylor, Byrd. LC 77-7151. 32p. (gr. 1-5). 1985. pap. 4.95 (*0-689-71052-6*, Aladdin) Macmillan Child Grp.
—Guess Who My Favorite Person Is. reissued ed. Baylor, Byrd. LC 77-7151. 32p. (gr. 1-4). 1992. RSBE 14.95 (*0-684-19514-3*, Scribners Young Read) Macmillan Child Grp.
—Gunga Din. Kipling, Rudyard. LC 86-19388. 28p. (gr. 1 up). 1987. 12.95 (*0-15-200456-4*, Gulliver Bks) HarBrace.
—The Magic Wings: A Tale from China. Wolkstein, Diane. LC 83-1611. 32p. (gr. 2-4). 1983. (DCB) pap. 4.95 (*0-525-44275-8*, DCB) Dutton Child Bks.
—The Magician's Visit: A Passover Tale. Goldin, Barbara D. LC 92-22903. 34p. 1993. 14.99 (*0-670-84840-9*) Viking Child Bks.

—The Monkey's Haircut: And Other Stories Told by the Maya. Bierhorst, John, ed. LC 85-28471. 160p. (gr. 5 up). 1986. 13.00 (*0-688-04269-4*) Morrow Jr Bks.
—The Sounds of Summer. Updike, David. 40p. (gr. 2-5). 1993. 14.95 (*0-945912-20-X*) Pippin Pr.
—A Spring Story. Updike, David. 40p. (gr. 2 up). 1989. PLB 14.95 (*0-945912-06-4*) Pippin Pr.
—The Trees Stand Shining: Poetry of the North American Indians. reissue ed. Jones, Hettie. LC 79-142452. 32p. (gr. k up). 1993. 13.99 (*0-8037-9083-X*); PLB 13.89 (*0-8037-9084-8*) Dial Bks Young.
—The Woman Who Fell from the Sky: The Iroquois Story of Creation. Bierhorst, John, retold by. LC 92-5591. 32p. (gr. k up). 1993. 15.00 (*0-688-10680-3*); PLB 14.93 (*0-688-10681-1*) Morrow Jr Bks.
—The Year of No More Corn. Ketteman, Helen. LC 90-29092. 32p. (ps-2). 1993. 14.95 (*0-531-05950-2*); PLB 14.99 (*0-531-08550-3*) Orchard Bks Watts.
—Zeek Silver Moon. Ehrlich, Amy. LC 70-181787. 32p. (ps-3). 1972. Dial Bks Young.

Parker, Robert Andrew. The Dancing Skeleton. DeFelice, Cynthia C. LC 88-30245. 32p. (gr. k-3). 1989. RSBE 13.95 (*0-02-726452-1*, Macmillan Child Bk) Macmillan Child Grp.

Parker, Ron. The Moon of the Bears. George, Jean C. LC 91-22557. 48p. (gr. 3-7). 1993. 15.00 (*0-06-022791-5*); PLB 14.89 (*0-06-022792-3*) HarpC Child Bks.
—The Moon of the Mountain Lions. new ed. George, Jean C. LC 90-39451. 48p. (gr. 3-7). 1991. 15.00 (*0-06-022429-0*); PLB 14.89 (*0-06-022438-X*) HarpC Child Bks.

Parker, Sherry. Dinosaurs Don't Wear Diapers. Moser, Cindy & Hummel, Nancy. 16p. (Orig.). (ps). 1990. pap. text ed. 9.95 (*0-9628204-0-7*) Stopher.

Parker, Steve. Beaches Are for Kids! An Activity Book for Kids. Salts, Bobbi. 32p. (gr. 1-6). 1990. pap. 2.95 (*0-929526-09-0*) Double B Pubns.
—California Is for Kids! An Activity Book. Salts, Bobbi, ed. 32p. (gr. 1-6). 1990. pap. 2.95 (*0-929526-04-X*) Double B Pubns.
—Charles Darwin & Evolution. Parker, Steve. LC 91-30272. 32p. (gr. 3-7). 1992. 14.00 (*0-06-020733-7*) HarpC Child Bks.
—Color Sedona. Salts, Bobbi. 32p. (Orig.). (ps-6). 1991. pap. 2.95 (*0-929526-10-4*) Double B Pubns.
—Colorado Is for Kids! An Activity Book for Kids! Fischer, Lee, ed. 32p. (gr. 1-6). 1990. pap. 2.95 (*0-929526-05-8*) Double B Pubns.
—Death Valley Discovery! Salts, Bobbi. 32p. (Orig.). (gr. k-6). 1991. pap. 3.95 (*1-878900-19-6*) DVNH Assn.
—Desert Discovery: An Activity Book for Kids. Salts, Bobbi. 32p. (gr. 1-6). 1989. pap. text ed. 2.95 (*0-929526-01-5*) Double B Pubns.
—Discover Grand Teton National Park. Salts, Bobbi. NPS Staff, ed. 32p. 1992. pap. 3.95 (*0-931895-22-7*) Grand Teton NHA.
—Discover the Oregon Trail. Salts, Bobbi. 32p. (Orig.). (gr. 4-6). 1992. pap. 3.95 (*0-931056-06-3*) Jefferson Natl.
—Discover Westward Expansion. Salts, Bobbi. 32p. (Orig.). (gr. 4-6). 1992. pap. text ed. 3.95 (*0-931056-03-9*) Jefferson Natl.
—Draw Partner: How to Draw Wild West Cartoons for Kids. Parker, Steve. 32p. (gr. 1-6). 1990. pap. 2.95 (*0-929526-08-2*) Double B Pubns.
—Galileo & the Universe. Parker, Steve. LC 91-28315. 32p. (gr. 3-7). 1992. 14.00 (*0-06-020735-3*) HarpC Child Bks.
—Marie Curie & Radium. Parker, Steve. LC 92-3616. 32p. (gr. 3-7). 1992. pap. 5.95 (*0-06-446143-2*, Trophy) HarpC Child Bks.
—New Mexico Is for Kids! An Activity Book. Salts, Bobbi. 32p. (gr. 1-6). 1989. pap. 2.95 (*0-929526-02-3*) Double B Pubns.
—Sequoia & Kings Canyon Discovery. Salts, Bobbi. 36p. (Orig.). (gr. 1-6). 1992. pap. 3.95 (*1-878441-05-1*) Sequoia Nat Hist Assn.
—Southwestern American Indian Discovery. Salts, Bobbi. (gr. 2-8). 1991. pap. 3.95 (*0-929526-11-2*) Double B Pubns.
—Thomas Edison & Electricity. Parker, Steve. LC 92-6805. 32p. (gr. 3-7). 1992. pap. 5.95 (*0-06-446144-0*, Trophy) HarpC Child Bks.
—Utah Is for Kids! Salts, Bobbi. 32p. (Orig.). (gr. 1-6). 1991. pap. 3.95 (*0-929526-06-6*) Double B Pubns.

Parker, Tom. A B Cedar: An Alphabet of Trees. Lyon, George-Ella. LC 88-22797. 32p. (ps-1). 1989. 14.95 (*0-531-05795-X*); PLB 14.99 (*0-531-08395-0*) Orchard Bks Watts.

Parkin, Rex. The Red Carpet. Parkin, Rex. LC 92-19912. 48p. (gr. k-3). 1993. pap. 4.95 (*0-689-71678-8*, Aladdin) Macmillan Child Grp.

Parkins, David. Dodos are Forever. large type ed. King-Smith, Dick. 112p. 1993. 13.95 (*0-7451-1682-5*, Galaxy Child Lrg Print) Chivers N Amer.
—No Problem. Browne, Eileen. LC 92-53134. 40p. (gr. k-3). 1993. bk. ed. 14.95 (*1-56402-176-9*); bk. & kit ed. 14.99 (*1-56402-200-5*) Candlewick Pr.
—Paddy's Pot of Gold. King-Smith, Dick. LC 91-24586. 128p. (gr. 2-7). 1992. 14.00 (*0-517-58136-1*); PLB 14. 99 (*0-517-58137-X*) Crown Bks Yng Read.
—Sophie in the Saddle. King-Smith, Dick. LC 93-26723. 1994. write for info. (*1-56402-329-X*) Candlewick Pr.
—Tick-Tock. Browne, Eileen. LC 93-927. 1994. write for info. (*1-56402-300-1*) Candlewick Pr.

—The Water Horse. large type ed. King-Smith, Dick. 124p. PLB 13.95 (0-7451-1610-8, Lythway Large Print) Hall.
Parkins, David & Parkins, David. Sophie's Tom. King-Smith, Dick. LC 91-58756. 112p. (gr. k-4). 1992. 14.95 (1-56402-107-6) Candlewick Pr.
Parkinson, Kathy. Dry Days, Wet Nights. Boelts, Maribeth. LC 93-28674. 1994. write for info. (0-8075-1723-2) A Whitman.
—The Enormous Turnip. LC 85-14432. 32p. (ps-1). 1985. 13.95 (0-8075-2062-4) A Whitman.
—The Farmer in the Dell. LC 87-25322. 32p. (ps-2). 1988. PLB 13.95 (0-8075-2271-6) A Whitman.
—Too Much Mush! Levine, Abby. Tucker, Kathy, ed. LC 88-33906. 32p. (ps-2). 1989. PLB 13.95 (0-8075-8025-2) A Whitman.
Parkinson, Keith, jt. illus. see Long, Kevin.
Parkinson, Keith, et al. Africa. Siembieda, Kevin. Marciniszyn, Alex, et al, eds. 160p. (Orig.). (gr. 8 up). 1993. pap. 15.95 (0-916211-58-4, 808) Palladium Bks.
—England. Siembieda, Kevin. Marciniszyn, Alex, et al, eds. 152p. (Orig.). (gr. 8 up). 1993. pap. 15.95 (0-916211-57-6, 807) Palladium Bks.
Parks, Gordon, photos by. J. T. Wagner, Jane. 128p. (gr. 3-8). 1972. pap. 3.50 (0-440-44275-3, YB) Dell.
Parks, Kathy. Just Like Everybody Else. Pierson, Jim. Tada, Joni A., intro. by. 32p. (ps-3). 1993. 10.99 (0-87403-842-1, 24-03661) Standard Pub.
Parmenter, Wayne. The Frog Prince. Grimm, Jacob & Grimm, Wilhelm K. Black, Fiona, retold by. 1991. 6.95 (0-8362-4920-8) Andrews & McMeel.
—If Your Name Was Changed at Ellis Island. Levine, Ellen. LC 92-27940. 80p. (gr. 2-5). 1993. 15.95 (0-590-46134-6) Scholastic Inc.
Parnall, Peter. Annie & the Old One. Miles, Miska. (gr. 1-3). 1972. lib. bdg. 14.95i (0-316-57117-2, Joy St Bks) Little.
—Annie & the Old One. Miles, Miska. (gr. 1-3). 1985. pap. 6.95 (0-316-57120-2) Little.
—Apple Tree. Parnall, Peter. LC 86-23730. 32p. (gr. k-3). 1988. RSBE 14.95 (0-02-770160-3, Macmillan Child Bk) Macmillan Child Grp.
—Become a Bird & Fly! Ross, Michael E. LC 91-36562. 32p. (gr. k up). 1992. PLB 14.90 (1-56294-074-0) Millbrook Pr.
—Cats from Away. Parnall, Peter. LC 88-30532. 32p. (ps up). 1989. RSBE 14.95 (0-02-770150-6, Macmillan Child Bk) Macmillan Child Grp.
—The Desert Is Theirs. Baylor, Byrd. LC 74-24417. 32p. (ps-3). 1975. SBE 14.95 (0-684-14266-X, Scribners Young Read) Macmillan Child Grp.
—The Desert Is Theirs. Baylor, Byrd. LC 86-17323. 32p. (gr. 1-5). 1987. pap. 4.95 (0-689-71105-0, Aladdin) Macmillan Child Grp.
—Desert Voices. Baylor, Byrd. LC 80-17061. 32p. (ps-3). 1981. SBE 14.95 (0-684-16712-3, Scribners Young Read) Macmillan Child Grp.
—Everybody Needs a Rock. Baylor, Byrd. LC 74-9163. 32p. (ps-3). 1974. RSBE 14.95 (0-684-13899-9, Scribners Young Read) Macmillan Child Grp.
—Everybody Needs a Rock. Baylor, Byrd. LC 74-9163. 32p. (gr. k-3). 1985. pap. 4.95 (0-689-71051-8, Aladdin) Macmillan Child Grp.
—Feet! Parnall, Peter. LC 88-5272. 32p. (ps-1). 1988. RSBE 14.95 (0-02-770110-7, Macmillan Child Bk) Macmillan Child Grp.
—Hawk, I'm Your Brother. Baylor, Byrd. LC 75-39296. 48p. (ps-3). 1976. SBE 14.95 (0-684-14571-5, Scribners Young Read) Macmillan Child Grp.
—Hawk, I'm Your Brother. reissued ed. Baylor, Byrd. LC 86-10742. 48p. (gr. 1-5). 1986. pap. 3.95 (0-689-71102-6, Aladdin) Macmillan Child Grp.
—If You Are a Hunter of Fossils. Baylor, Byrd. LC 79-17926. 32p. (ps-3). 1980. SBE 14.95 (0-684-16419-1, Scribners Young Read) Macmillan Child Grp.
—If You Are a Hunter of Fossils. Baylor, Byrd. LC 79-17926. 32p. (gr. 3-6). 1984. pap. 4.95 (0-689-70773-8, Aladdin) Macmillan Child Grp.
—I'm in Charge of Celebrations. Baylor, Byrd. LC 85-19633. 32p. (gr. 1-4). 1986. SBE 14.95 (0-684-18579-2, Scribners Young Read) Macmillan Child Grp.
—Kavik, the Wolf Dog. Morey, Walt. LC 68-24727. (gr. 5-9). 1977. 14.95 (0-525-33093-3, DCB) Dutton Child Bks.
—Marsh Cat. Parnall, Peter. LC 90-25733. 128p. (gr. 3 up). 1991. SBE 13.95 (0-02-770120-4, Macmillan Child Bk) Macmillan Child Grp.
—The Other Way to Listen. Baylor, Byrd. LC 78-23430. 32p. (ps-3). 1978. SBE 14.95 (0-684-16017-X, Scribners Young Read) Macmillan Child Grp.
—The Rock. Parnall, Peter. LC 90-6021. 32p. (gr. k-3). 1991. RSBE 14.95 (0-02-770181-6, Macmillan Child Bk) Macmillan Child Grp.
—Stuffer. Parnall, Peter. LC 90-26997. 32p. (gr. k-4). 1992. RSBE 14.95 (0-02-770152-2, Macmillan Child Bk) Macmillan Child Grp.
—The Table Where Rich People Sit. Baylor, Byrd. LC 93-1251. 1994. text ed. 14.95 (0-684-19653-0, Scribner) Macmillan.
—Water Pup. Parnall, Peter. LC 92-40850. 144p. (gr. 3 up). 1993. SBE 13.95 (0-02-770151-4, Macmillan Child Bk) Macmillan Child Grp.
—The Way to Start a Day. Baylor, Byrd. LC 78-113. 32p. (ps-3). 1978. SBE 14.95 (0-684-15651-2, Scribners Young Read) Macmillan Child Grp.

—The Way to Start a Day. Baylor, Byrd. LC 85-28802. 32p. (gr. 1-4). 1986. pap. 3.95 (0-689-71054-2, Aladdin) Macmillan Child Grp.
—Woodpile. Parnall, Peter. LC 89-29322. 32p. (gr. k-3). 1990. RSBE 14.95 (0-02-770155-7, Macmillan Child Bk) Macmillan Child Grp.
Parnell, Peter. Desert Voices. Baylor, Byrd. LC 92-24475. 32p. (gr. 1-5). 1993. pap. 3.95 (0-689-71691-5, Aladdin) Macmillan Child Grp.
—Knee-Deep in Thunder. Moon, Sheila. LC 86-19534. 307p. (gr. 8-12). 1986. pap. 8.95 (0-917479-08-4) Guild Psy.
Parr, John. Baby Animals. Parr, John. LC 79-62943. (ps) 1979. 3.50 (0-394-84244-8) Random Bks Yng Read.
Parrish, George I., Jr. Jim Bridger: Man of the Mountains. Luce, Willard & Luce, Celia. 80p. (gr. 2-6). 1991. Repr. of 1966 ed. lib. bdg. 12.95 (0-7910-1454-1) Chelsea Hse.
Parrish, Maxfield. The Arabian Nights: Their Best-Known Tales. Wiggin, Kate D. & Smith, Nora A., eds. LC 92-38552. 368p. 1993. ltd. ed. 75.00 (0-684-19588-7, Scribners Young Read); text ed. 25.00 (0-684-19589-5, Scribners Young Read) Macmillan Child Grp.
—Dream Days. Grahame, Kenneth. LC 92-44589. 1993. 18.95 (0-89815-546-0) Ten Speed Pr.
—The Golden Age. Grahame, Kenneth. LC 92-44992. 1993. 18.95 (0-89815-545-2) Ten Speed Pr.
Parrotte, Timothy. Sometimes I Drive My Mom Crazy, but I Know She's Crazy about Me: A Self-Esteem Book for Overactive & Impulsive Children. Shapiro, Lawrence E. Shore, Hennie M., ed. 80p. (gr. k-6). 1993. 9.95 (1-882732-03-0) Ctr Applied Psy.
Parry, Alan. Baby Jesus. Parry, Alan & Parry, Linda. 24p. (ps). 1990. pap. 0.99 (0-8066-2478-7, 9-2478) Augsburg Fortress.
—Baby Moses. Parry, Alan & Parry, Linda. 24p. (ps). 1990. pap. 0.99 (0-8066-2477-9, 9-2477) Augsburg Fortress.
—The Farmer & the Seed. Parry, Alan & Parry, Linda. 24p. (ps). 1990. pap. 0.99 (0-8066-2474-4, 9-2474) Augsburg Fortress.
—Jesus is Alive! Parry, Alan & Parry, Linda. 24p. (ps) 1990. pap. 0.99 (0-8066-2479-5, 9-2479) Augsburg Fortress.
—Joseph & His Coat. Parry, Alan & Parry, Linda. 24p. (ps). 1990. pap. 0.99 (0-8066-2476-0, 9-2476) Augsburg Fortress.
—Noah & the Ark. Parry, Alan & Parry, Linda. 24p. (ps). 1990. pap. 0.99 (0-8066-2475-2, 9-2475) Augsburg Fortress.
—Paul Meets Jesus. Parry, Alan & Parry, Linda. 24p. (ps). 1990. pap. 0.99 (0-8066-2480-9, 9-2480) Augsburg Fortress.
Parry, Alan & Parry, Linda. Bruno Helps Out. Parry, Alan & Parry, Linda. LC 91-70401. 16p. (ps-k). 1991. bds. 1.49 (0-8066-2528-7, 9-2528, Augsburg) Augsburg Fortress.
—Bruno Is Sorry. Parry, Alan & Parry, Linda. LC 91-70402. 16p. (ps-k). 1991. bds. 1.49 (0-8066-2529-5, 9-2529, Augsburg) Augsburg Fortress.
—Bruno Makes Friends. Parry, Alan & Parry, Linda. LC 91-70402. 16p. (ps-k). 1991. bds. 1.49 (0-685-59565-X, 9-2530, Augsburg) Augsburg Fortress.
—Bruno Says Thanks. Parry, Alan & Parry, Linda. LC 91-70404. 16p. (ps-k). 1991. bds. 1.49 (0-8066-2531-7, 9-2531, Augsburg) Augsburg Fortress.
Parry, Alan, jt. illus. see Parry, Linda.
Parry, Linda & Parry, Alan. Jacob & Esau. Parry, Linda & Parry, Alan. LC 90-80555. 24p. (Orig.). (ps-2). 1990. pap. 1.99 (0-8066-2490-6, 9-2490, Augsburg) Augsburg Fortress.
—Jesus & You. Parry, Linda & Parry, Alan. LC 91-71033. 10p. (ps-k). 1991. 3.99 (0-8066-2557-0, 9-2557, Augsburg) Augsburg Fortress.
—Jesus Loves You. Parry, Linda & Parry, Alan. LC 91-71034. 10p. 1991. 5.99 (0-8066-2558-9, 9-2558, Augsburg) Augsburg Fortress.
—Joseph & His Brothers. Parry, Linda & Parry, Alan. LC 90-80557. 24p. (Orig.). (ps-2). 1990. pap. 1.99 (0-8066-2488-4, 9-2488, Augsburg) Augsburg Fortress.
—Martha & Mary. Parry, Linda & Parry, Alan. LC 90-80558. 24p. (Orig.). (ps-2). 1990. pap. 1.99 (0-8066-2487-6, 9-2487, Augsburg) Augsburg Fortress.
—Miriam & Moses. Parry, Linda & Parry, Alan. LC 90-80556. 24p. (Orig.). (ps-2). 1990. pap. 1.95 (0-8066-2489-2, 9-2489, Augsburg) Augsburg Fortress.
Parry, Linda, jt. illus. see Parry, Alan.
Parry, Marian. City Mouse - Country Mouse & Two More Mouse Tales from Aesop. (gr. 2-3). 1989. big bk. 28.67 (0-590-65228-1) Scholastic Inc.
Parsons, Brian. From Mountain to Mountain: Stories about Baha'u'llah. Garst, Hitjo. McKinley, Olive, tr. from DUT. 138p. (gr. 3-4). 1988. 20.95 (0-85398-265-1) G Ronald Pub.
Partin, Robin C. Daydreams & Sunbeams: An Album of Framable Word Pictures. Partin, Charlotte C. 18p. (Orig.). (gr. 7 up). 1987. pap. 4.00 (0-9619816-0-1) C Partin.
Parton, Steve. In the Shogun's Shadow: Understanding a Changing Japan. Langone, John. LC 93-23999. 1994. 15.95 (0-316-51409-8) Little.
—Kidnapped. Stevenson, Robert Louis. Mattern, Joanne, retold by. LC 92-5803. 48p. (gr. 3-6). 1992. PLB 12.89 (0-8167-2862-3); pap. text ed. 3.95 (0-8167-2863-1) Troll Assocs.

Parton, Steven. Who Harnessed the Horse? The Story of Animal Domestication. Facklam, Margery. 176p. (gr. 2-5). 1992. 15.95 (0-316-27381-3) Little.
Partridge, Sherri. Trail of Apple Blossoms. Hunt, Irene. LC 92-46739. 64p. (gr. 4-6). 1993. PLB 13.98 (0-382-24359-5); 11.98 (0-382-24368-4) Silver Burdett Pr.
Pascal, Robin. Little Donkey Learns to Help. Clement, Claude. Jensen, Patricia, adapted by. LC 93-2952. 1993. write for info. (0-89577-502-6, Readers Digest Kids) RD Assn.
Pascarella, Sam. That's Life, 13 vols. Cleveland, David. (gr. k-8). 1986. Each individual grade level; k-12. tchrs ed. 65.00 (1-56117-028-3); Eng. wkbk. 3.50 (0-685-29914-7); Span. wkbk. 3.95 (0-685-58484-4); preschool 35.00 (0-685-58485-2); complete k-12 curriculum set 795.00 (0-685-58486-0) Telesis CA.
Pasco, Duane. The Prince & the Salmon People. Murphy, Claire R., retold by. LC 92-38394. 48p. 1993. 19.95 (0-8478-1662-1) Rizzoli Intl.
Pashuk, Lauren. Fun with Colors. Pashuk, Lauren. 32p. (ps-k). 1985. pap. 2.95 (0-88625-106-0) Durkin Hayes Pub.
Pashuk, Lauren, jt. illus. see Winik, J. T.
Pasifull, Linda. My Book of Favorite Prayers. Newman, Marjorie, ed. LC 89-82555. 28p. (ps-2). 1990. pap. 9.99 (0-8066-2469-8, 9-2469) Augsburg Fortress.
Passen, Lisa. Fat, Fat Rose Marie. Passen, Lisa. LC 90-21112. 32p. (ps-3). 1991. 14.95 (0-8050-1653-8, Bks Young Read) H Holt & Co.
Pastor, Terry. Big Machines. Royston, Angela. LC 93-16019. (gr. 3 up). 1994. 12.95 (0-316-76070-6) Little.
Pate, Dorothy. The Black Hawk War, Why? Efflandt, Lloyd H. 25p. pap. 1.25 (0-9617938-0-5, 5M) Rock Isl Arsenal Hist Soc.
Pate, Rodney. Benjamin Banneker, Scientist. Joshua, Garnet N. LC 92-28799. 1992. write for info. (0-8136-5226-6); pap. write for info. (0-8136-5701-6) Modern Curr.
—Dolly Parton: Country Goin' to Town. Saunders, Susan. 64p. (gr. 2-6). 1986. pap. 3.95 (0-14-032162-4, Puffin) Puffin Bks.
—Efan the Great. Schotter, Roni. LC 84-25070. 32p. (gr. 2-5). 1986. 12.95 (0-688-04986-9); PLB 12.88 (0-688-04987-7) Lothrop.
—Me, Mop, & the Moondance Kid. Myers, Walter D. LC 88-6503. 128p. (gr. 3-7). 1988. 13.95 (0-440-50065-6) Delacorte.
Patel, Mickey. Stories from Bapu's Life. Joshi, Uma. (gr. 1-9). 1979. pap. 2.50 (0-89744-180-X) Auromere.
Patent, Dorothy H. Looking at Ants. Patent, Dorothy H. LC 89-1943. 48p. (gr-4). 1989. reinforced 12.95 (0-8234-0771-3) Holiday.
—Whales: Giants of the Deep. Patent, Dorothy H. LC 84-729. 96p. (gr. 3-7). 1984. reinforced bdg. 15.95 (0-8234-0530-3) Holiday.
Paterson, Bettina. Baby's ABC. 18p. 1992. bds. 4.95 (0-448-40130-4, G&D) Putnam Pub Group.
—Baby's 1, 2, 3. 18p. (ps). 1992. bds. 4.95 (0-448-40265-3, G&D) Putnam Pub Group.
—Jolly Snowman. 12p. (ps). 1992. bds. 2.50 (0-448-40575-X, G&D) Putnam Pub Group.
—Joy to the World! Anastasio, Dina. 32p. (ps-3). 1992. (G&D); pap. 2.25 (0-448-40479-6, G&D) Putnam Pub Group.
—Merry ABC. 24p. (ps). 1993. bds. 2.95 (0-448-40553-9, G&D) Putnam Pub Group.
—Merry Christmas, Santa! 12p. (ps). 1992. bds. 2.50 (0-448-40576-8, G&D) Putnam Pub Group.
—My First Wild Animals. Paterson, Bettina. LC 89-17305. 32p. (ps-k). 1991. 8.95 (0-690-04771-1, Crowell Jr Bks); (Crowell Jr Bks) HarpC Child Bks.
—Potty Time. 12p. (ps). 1993. bds. 4.95 (0-448-40539-3, G&D) Putnam Pub Group.
Paterson, Bettine. Busy Witch. 12p. (ps). 1993. bds. 2.50 (0-448-40573-3, G&D) Putnam Pub Group.
Paterson, Brian. The Foxwood Kidnap. Paterson, Cynthia. 32p. (ps-3). 1986. 6.95 (0-8120-5771-6) Barron.
Paterson, Diane. Abuelita's Paradise. Nodar, Carmen M. Mathews, Judith, ed. LC 91-42330. 32p. (gr. k-3). 1992. 13.95g (0-8075-0129-8) A Whitman.
—Abuelita's Paradise. Nodar, Carmen S. (gr. k-4). 1993. 13.95 (0-685-66422-8); audio. casa. 11.00 (1-882869-79-6) Read Advent.
—The Big Surprise. Michaels, Ski. LC 85-14017. 48p. (gr. 1-3). 1986. PLB 10.59 (0-8167-0576-3); pap. text ed. 3.50 (0-8167-0577-1) Troll Assocs.
—Camping in the Temple of the Sun. Gould, Deborah. LC 91-16358. 32p. (gr. k-5). 1992. RSBE 13.95 (0-02-736355-4, Bradbury Pr) Macmillan Child Grp.
—Champ on Ice. Peters, Sharon. LC 87-10908. 32p. (gr. k-2). 1988. PLB 11.59 (0-8167-1093-7); pap. text ed. 2.95 (0-8167-1094-5) Troll Assocs.
—The Duck Who Loved Puddles. Pellowski, Michael J. LC 85-14058. 48p. (Orig.). (gr. 1-3). 1986. PLB 10.59 (0-8167-0578-X); pap. text ed. 3.50 (0-8167-0579-8) Troll Assocs.
—Fun in the Snow. Damon, Laura. LC 87-10843. 32p. (gr. k-2). 1988. PLB 11.59 (0-8167-1081-3); pap. text ed. 2.95 (0-8167-1082-1) Troll Assocs.
—Fun in the Sun. Michaels, Ski. LC 85-14055. 48p. (Orig.). (gr. 1-3). 1986. PLB 10.59 (0-8167-0568-2); pap. text ed. 3.50 (0-8167-0569-0) Troll Assocs.
—The Golden Goose. Grimm, Jacob & Grimm, Wilhelm K. LC 80-29207. 32p. (gr. k-3). 1981. PLB 9.79 (0-89375-476-5); pap. 1.95 (0-89375-477-3) Troll Assocs.

—Kitty: A Cat's Diary. Supraner, Robyn. LC 85-14023. 48p. (Orig). (gr. 1-3). 1986. PLB 10.59 (0-8167-0574-7); pap. text ed. 3.50 (0-8167-0575-5) Troll Assocs.

—Let Me Do It! Gibala-Broxholm, Janice. LC 92-12856. 32p. (ps-k). 1994. RSBE 14.95 (0-02-735827-5, Bradbury Pr) Macmillan Child Grp.

—The Littlest Pig. Frost, Erica. LC 85-14121. 48p. (Orig). (gr. 1-3). 1986. PLB 10.59 (0-8167-0654-9); pap. text ed. 3.50 (0-8167-0655-7) Troll Assocs.

—The Messy Monster. Pellowski, Michael J. LC 85-14064. 48p. (Orig). (gr. 1-3). 1986. PLB 10.59 (0-8167-0570-4); pap. text ed. 3.50 (0-8167-0571-2) Troll Assocs.

—Monnie Hates Lydia. Pearson, Susan. LC 75-9198. 32p. (ps-3). 1985. Dial Bks Young.

—El Paraiso de Abuelita. Nodar, Carmen M. Mathews, Judith, ed. Mlawer, Teresa, tr. LC 92-3767. (SPA.). 32p. (gr. k-3). 1992. 13.95g (0-8075-6346-3) A Whitman.

—Puppeteer. Poskanzer, Susan C. LC 88-10042. 32p. (gr. 1-3). 1989. PLB 10.89 (0-8167-1432-0); pap. text ed. 2.95 (0-8167-1433-9) Troll Assocs.

—Someday. Paterson, Diane. LC 92-11401. 40p. (gr. 1-3). 1993. SBE 12.95 (0-02-770565-X, Bradbury Pr) Macmillan Child Grp.

—Stone Soup. LC 80-27947. 32p. (gr. 1-4). 1981. PLB 9.79 (0-89375-478-1); pap. text ed. 1.95 (0-89375-479-X) Troll Assocs.

—Teacher. Daniel, Kira. LC 88-10041. 32p. (gr. k-3). 1989. PLB 10.89 (0-8167-1430-4); pap. text ed. 2.95 (0-8167-1431-2) Troll Assocs.

—Thumbs Up, Rico! Testa, Maria. 1994. write for info. (0-8075-7906-8) A Whitman.

—Thump, Bump. Craig, Janet. LC 87-10933. 32p. (gr. k-2). 1988. PLB 11.59 (0-8167-1077-5); pap. text ed. 2.95 (0-8167-1078-3) Troll Assocs.

—You Breathe In, You Breathe Out: All about Your Lungs. Adler, David A. Roxas, Reni, ed. 32p. (gr. 1-4). 1991. PLB 12.90 (0-531-10700-0) Watts.

Paterson, Jim. Get on to Your Hormones: Straight Talk on Sex, Love & Dating. Hadland, Beverly J. 192p. (Orig). 1992. pap. 4.95x (0-919225-38-1) Life Cycle Bks.

Patience, John. Roarasaurus. Patience, John. 12p. (ps up). 1994. pop-up 14.95 (0-8431-3686-3) Price Stern.

—Who's Afraid of Tigers. Patience, John. 6p. (gr. k-4). 1993. 14.99 (0-8431-3542-5) Price Stern.

Patkau, Karen. In the Sea. Patkau, Karen. 24p. (ps). 1990. 15.95 (1-55037-067-7, Pub. by Annick CN); pap. 5.95 (1-55037-066-9, Pub. by Annick CN) Firefly Bks Ltd.

—One Watermelon Seed. Lottridge, Celia B. 24p. (ps up). 1990. pap. 6.95 (0-19-540735-0) OUP.

Patkins, David. Sophie Hits Six. 1st U.S. ed. King-Smith, Dick. LC 92-54692. (gr. k-4). 1993. 14.95 (1-56402-216-1) Candlewick Pr.

Paton, David, jt. illus. see Paton, Sandy.

Paton, Jane. Twins of Ceylon. Williams, Harry. LC 65-12044. (gr. 6-9). 1965. 12.95 (0-8023-1108-3) Dufour.

Paton, Sandy & Paton, David. I've Got a Song! A Collection of Songs for Youngsters. 2nd ed. Paton, Sandy & Paton, Caroline. 40p. (Orig). (gr. k-4). 1989. pap. 10.98 (0-938702-05-X) Folk-Legacy.

Patric. The Cry of the Conch. Roop, Peter. LC 84-4232. (gr. 3-5). 1984. 8.95 (0-916630-39-0) Pr Pacifica.

Patricio, Ernie, jt. illus. see Gamboa, Romy.

Patros, Ann & Patros, Dan, photos by. Say Yes! to Life: A Musical Drama about the Dangers Drugs Pose to the Joys of Living. Mueller, Tobin J. (gr. 4-up). 1990. Audio tape incl. pap. 14.95 (1-56213-045-5) Ctr Stage Prodns.

Patros, Dan, jt. photog. see Patros, Ann.

Patterson, Anne. Double-Dip Feelings: Stories to Help Children Understand Emotions. Cain, Barbara S. LC 92-56870. 1993. Repr. of 1990 ed. PLB 17.26 (0-8368-0931-9) Gareth Stevens Inc.

Patterson, Bob. Jokes for Children. Young, Frederica & Kohl, Marguerite. 128p. (gr. 2 up). 1983. pap. 4.95 (0-374-43832-3, Sunburst) FS&G.

—More Jokes for Children. Young, Frederica & Kohl, Marguerite. (gr. 2-5). 1984. pap. 4.95 (0-374-45360-8, Sunburst) FS&G.

Patterson, Don, photos by. Ski Vacation. Patterson, Don. 40p. (gr. k-6). 1991. 13.95 (0-9629093-3-5) MyndSeye.

Patterson, Ippy. No Bones: A Key to Bugs & Slugs, Worms, & Ticks, Spiders & Centipedes, & Other Creepy Crawlies. Shepherd, Elizabeth. LC 87-1549. 96p. (gr. 2-5). 1988. SBE 13.95 (0-02-782880-8, Macmillan Child Bk) Macmillan Child Grp.

Patterson, Karen T. Alphabet of Bible Creatures. McKenzie, Marni S. 56p. (ps-8). 1993. 14.95 (1-882630-00-9) Mercy Pr.

Patterson, Kathleen. Come & See. Lysne, Mary E. Gambill, Henrietta, ed. 24p. (ps-3). 1993. wkbk. 2.39 (0-7847-0104-0, 23-02584) Standard Pub.

—Five Minutes 'til Bedtime: Twelve Quick-As-a-Wink Bible Stories. Rector, Andy. 32p. (Orig). 1993. pap. 5.99 (0-87401-110-8, 24-03670) Standard Pub.

—Five Minutes 'til Bedtime: Twelve Quick-As-a-Wink Bible Stories. Rector, Andy. LC 93-7339. 1993. 5.99 (0-7847-0110-5) Standard Pub.

—Mary & Elizabeth. Lysne, Mary E. Gambill, Henrietta, ed. 24p. (ps-3). 1993. wkbk. 2.39 (0-7847-0101-6, 23-02581) Standard Pub.

—Parables of Jesus. Lysne, Mary E. Gambill, Henrietta, ed. 24p. (ps-3). 1993. wkbk. 2.39 (0-7847-0102-4, 23-02582) Standard Pub.

—Paul. Lysne, Mary E. Gambill, Henrietta, ed. 24p. (ps-3). 1993. wkbk. 2.39 (0-7847-0106-7, 23-02586) Standard Pub.

—Peter. Lysne, Mary E. Gambill, Henrietta, ed. 24p. (ps-3). 1993. wkbk. 2.39 (0-7847-0105-9, 23-02585) Standard Pub.

—Quick-As-a-Wink New Testament Bedtime Stories. Rector, Andy. 12p. (ps). 1993. bds. 4.99 (0-7847-0112-1, 24-03102) Standard Pub.

—Quick-As-a-Wink Old Testament Bedtime Bible Stories. Rector, Andy. 12p. (ps). 1993. bds. 4.99 (0-7847-0111-3, 24-03101) Standard Pub.

—What Happened? Lysne, Mary E. Gambill, Henrietta, ed. 24p. (ps-3). 1993. wkbk. 2.39 (0-7847-0103-2, 23-02583) Standard Pub.

Patterson, Mary Ann, jt. illus. see Jackson, Sarah.

Patterson, Ron. Los Animales Del Arca. Shely, Patricia. Cranberry, Nola, tr. from ENG. (SPA.). 16p. (gr. 1-3). 1987. pap. 1.99 (0-311-38561-3, X1982) Casa Bautista.

Patti, Joyce. The Night Before Christmas. Moore, Clement C. LC 92-9084. 6p. 1992. 10.95 (1-55670-274-4) Stewart Tabori & Chang.

Patz, Nancy. The Family Treasury of Jewish Holidays. Drucker, Malka. LC 93-7549. Date not set. 21.95 (0-316-19343-7) Little.

—Moses Supposes His Toeses Are Roses: And Seven Other Silly Old Rhymes. Patz, Nancy. LC 82-3099. 32p. (ps-3). 1983. 13.95 (0-15-255690-7, HB Juv Bks) HarBrace.

—No Thumping No Bumping No Rumpus Tonight! Patz, Nancy. LC 88-7717. 32p. (gr. k-3). 1990. RSBE 13.95 (0-689-31510-4, Atheneum Child Bk) Macmillan Child Grp.

—Sarah Bear & Sweet Sidney. Patz, Nancy. LC 88-21300. 32p. (ps-2). 1989. RSBE 13.95 (0-02-770270-7, Four Winds) Macmillan Child Grp.

—To Annabella Pelican from Thomas Hippopotamus. Patz, Nancy. LC 90-30038. 32p. (ps-3). 1991. RSBE 13.95 (0-02-770280-4, Four Winds) Macmillan Child Grp.

Paul, Corky. Dragon Poems. Foster, John, ed. 32p. (gr. 1 up). 1992. bds. 12.95 laminated (0-19-276096-3); pap. 2.95 (0-19-916425-8) OUP.

Paul, F. A. A Basic Course in American Sign Language. Humphries, Tom, et al. 280p. (gr. 9 up). 1980. pap. text ed. 26.95 spiral bdg. (0-932666-24-8, 013S) T J Pubs.

Paul, Frank A., jt. illus. see Castillo, Romulo.

Paul, Korky. The Fish Who Could Wish. Bush, John. 32p. (ps-3). 1991. 13.95 (0-916291-35-9) Kane-Miller Bk.

—The Fish Who Could Wish. Bush, John. 32p. 1994. pap. 6.95 (0-916291-48-0) Kane-Miller Bk.

—Mrs. Wolf: A Three-Dimensional Picture Book. Roddie, Shen. LC 92-1202. 24p. (gr. k-3). 1993. 13.99 (0-8037-1300-2) Dial Bks Young.

—Never Say Boo to a Ghost. Foster, John. 96p. 1991. pap. 2.75 (0-590-45127-8) Scholastic Inc.

—Professor Puffendorf's Secret Potions. Tzannes, Robin. 40p. (ps-5). 1992. 16.95 (1-56288-267-8) Checkerboard.

—Winnie the Witch. Thomas, Valerie. 32p. (ps-3). 1987. 13.95 (0-916291-13-8) Kane-Miller Bk.

—Winnie the Witch. Thomas, Valerie. 32p. (ps-3). 1990. pap. 6.95 (0-916291-32-4) Kane-Miller Bk.

Pauley, Lynn. In the Children's Garden. Schaefer, Carole L. LC 93-15980. 1994. write for info. (0-8050-1958-8) H Holt & Co.

Pauley, Paige. Lone Hunter & the Cheyennes. Worcester, Donald. LC 85-4746. 78p. (gr. 4 up). 1985. Repr. of 1957 ed. 10.95 (0-87565-018-X) Tex Christian.

—Lone Hunter's Gray Pony. Worcester, Donald. LC 84-16157. 70p. (gr. 4 up). 1985. 10.95 (0-87565-001-5) Tex Christian.

—War Pony. Worcester, Donald E. LC 83-40486. 96p. (gr. 4 up). 1984. Repr. of 1961 ed. 10.95 (0-912646-85-3) Tex Christian.

Paull, Grace. Secret Valley. Bulla, Clyde R. LC 49-10917. 112p. (gr. 2-5). 1993. pap. 3.95 (0-06-440456-0, Trophy) HarpC Child Bks.

Paulsen, Ruth W. Woodsong. Paulsen, Gary. LC 89-70835. 160p. (gr. 7 up). 1990. SBE 14.95 (0-02-770221-9, Bradbury Pr) Macmillan Child Grp.

Pavia, Cathy. The Magic Clown. Coco, Eugene. 24p. (ps-2). 1992. pap. text ed. 0.99 (1-56293-348-5) McClanahan Bk.

Pawczuk, Eugene. Robin Hood. Pawczuk, Eugene. Pronk, Mary, ed. 32p. (Orig). (gr. 1-6). 1992. PLB 15.55 (0-88625-266-0); pap. 5.95 (0-88625-264-4) Durkin Hayes Pub.

—Tattercoats: European Folk Tales. 24p. (ps-2). 1992. pap. 3.50 (0-88625-285-7) Durkin Hayes Pub.

Pawczuk, Eugene, jt. illus. see Mansfield, Renee.

Payevsky, Robert. Birds of a Feather: And Other Aesop's Fables. Paxton, Tom. LC 92-2909. 40p. (ps up). 1993. 15.00 (0-688-10400-2); PLB 14.93 (0-688-10401-0) Morrow Jr Bks.

—Our King Has Horns! Pevear, Richard. LC 86-23525. 32p. (gr. k-3). 1987. RSBE 14.95 (0-02-773920-1, Macmillan Child Bk) Macmillan Child Grp.

Payne, Brian. Animals Alive! An Ecological Guide to Animal Activities. Holley, Dennis. 300p. (gr. 5-12). 1993. pap. text ed. 24.95 (1-879373-58-0) R Rinehart.

Payne, C. F. Meet Molly: An American Girl. Tripp, Valerie. Thieme, Jeanne, ed. 72p. (gr. 2-5). 1986. 12.95 (0-937295-06-X); PLB 12.95 (0-937295-81-7); pap. 5.95 (0-937295-07-8) Pleasant Co.

—Molly Learns a Lesson: A School Story. Tripp, Valerie. Thieme, Jeanne, ed. 72p. (gr. 2-5). 1986. 12.95 (0-937295-15-9); PLB 12.95 (0-937295-84-1); pap. 5.95 (0-937295-16-7) Pleasant Co.

—Molly's Surprise: A Christmas Story. Tripp, Valerie. Thieme, Jeanne, ed. 72p. (gr. 2-5). 1986. 12.95 (0-937295-24-8); PLB 12.95 (0-937295-87-6); pap. 5.95 (0-937295-25-6) Pleasant Co.

Payne, Katharine, photos by. Elephants Calling. Payne, Katharine. LC 91-34547. 36p. (gr. 2-6). 1992. 14.00 (0-517-58175-2); PLB 14.99 (0-517-58176-0) Crown Bks Yng Read.

Payne, Maxine & Montague, William A. Little Mouse: The Mouse Who Lived with Henry David Thoreau at Walden Pond. Montague, William A. Roof, Christopher, ed. LC 93-73231. 56p. (Orig.). (gr. 2-4). 1993. pap. text ed. 7.95 (0-9638644-0-8) Concord MouseTrap.
The book introduces young people to one of America's great figures, Henry David Thoreau! The story is based on the little mouse that Thoreau describes in Walden, under "Brute Neighbors." It follows Walden chronologically along with the detail building of his little house, skating, showshoeing, planting beans, writing in his journal, & translates some of his more complex statements into "Mouse Talk." After Walden, Thoreau moves into Emerson house & takes Little Mouse along, & meets the Emerson children, Ellen, Edith & Edward. She sleeps in the doll house that you can see today. The book includes a map of Thoreau's house site, where the story took place at Walden Pond. A guide map, to find The Emerson House, to see the doll house. The Concord Museums, to see Thoreau's actual furniture & the Thoreau Lyceum, for information on Thoreau.
Publisher Provided Annotation.

Payne, Roger. Julius Caesar: Shakespeare for Everyone. Mulherin, Jennifer. LC 90-476. 32p. (gr. 3-7). 1990. 12.95 (0-87226-338-X) P Bedrick Bks.

—Over Nine Hundred Years Ago: With the Vikings. Martell, Hazel M. LC 93-2647. 32p. (gr. 6 up). 1993. RSBE 13.95 (0-02-726325-8, New Discovery Bks) Macmillan Child Grp.

Payor, Terry. Magic of Music - Children's Song: Piano - Vocal. Okun, Milton & Sosin, Donald, eds. 80p. (Orig). 1988. pap. text ed. 9.95 (0-89524-372-5) Cherry Lane.

Payson, Dale. The Lucky Stone. Clifton, Lucille. LC 78-72862. 64p. (gr. 4-6). 1979. pap. 6.46 (0-385-28600-7) Delacorte.

—Lucky Stone. Clifton, Lucille. (gr. 2-5). 1986. pap. 2.99 (0-440-45110-8, YB) Dell.

Pazzaglia, Nadia. The Land of Colors. Lundell, Margaretta. LC 88-81410. 24p. (gr. k-3). 1989. 9.95 (0-448-21028-2, G&D) Putnam Pub Group.

Peabody, Paul. Blackberry Hollow. Peabody, Paul. LC 92-8968. 160p. (gr. 3-7). 1993. 15.95 (0-399-22500-5, Philomel Bks) Putnam Pub Group.

Peacock, Irvine. Navigation: A Three-Dimensional Exploration. Blanchard, Anne. LC 92-80434. 12p. (gr. 2-6). 1992. 15.95 (0-531-05455-1) Orchard Bks Watts.

Peacock, Joe. Catch a Winner. Eytcheson, Pat. Eakin, Edwin M., ed. 48p. (gr. 2-3). 1989. 10.95 (0-89015-704-9, Pub. by Panda Bks) Eakin-Sunbelt.

Peak, Jan. Trash to Treasure Crafts: From Recyclable Materials. Peak, Jan & Hennig, Anna. 80p. (gr. 3 up). 1992. wkbk. 8.99 (0-87403-890-1, 14-02146) Standard Pub.

Peake, Mervyn. Treasure Island. Stevenson, Robert Louis. LC 92-53174. 240p. 1992. 12.95 (0-679-41800-8, Evrymans Lib Childs Class) Knopf.

Peaker, Denelle. I Take Good Care of Me! I Take Good Care of Us! Meyer, Linda D. Meyer, Linda D., intro. by. 64p. (Orig). (gr. k-4). 1987. pap. 2.95 (0-9603516-9-8) Franklin Pr Wa.

Pearce, Molly. Barney's Joy. Waterston, Ellen. 32p. 1991. Repr. of 1990 ed. text ed. 14.95 (0-9628129-2-7) Sagebrush Bks.

—Big Cat the Proud. Pearce, Molly. LC 91-65488. 32p. (gr. k-2). 1991. pap. 4.95 (0-9628129-7-8) Sagebrush Bks.

—Jimmy the Beet Truck. Pearce, Molly. LC 91-65464. 32p. (gr. k-2). 1991. pap. 4.95 (*0-9628129-9-4*) Sagebrush Bks.

—Tale of Three Tractors. Pearce, Molly. LC 91-65489. 32p. (gr. k-2). 1991. pap. 4.95 (*0-9628129-8-6*) Sagebrush Bks.

Pearce, Susie J. That's Not a Fish. Bradman, Tony. (ps-k). 1993. 15.95 (*0-460-88039-X*, Pub. by J M Dent & Sons) Trafalgar.

Pearson, Allison K. The Adventures of Tusky & His Friends: A Christmas Mystery. Greenberg, Kenneth R. 63p. (gr. k-3). 1991. PLB 14.95 (*1-879100-01-0*) Tusky Enterprises.

—The Adventures of Tusky & His Friends, Bk. 1: A Jungle Adventure. Greenberg, Kenneth R. 51p. (gr. k-3). 1991. 13.95 (*1-879100-00-2*) Tusky Enterprises.

—The Adventures of Tusky & His Friends, Bk. 3: Tusky Gets Mad at Tusky. Greenberg, Kenneth R. 52p. (gr. k-4). 1992. 15.50 (*1-879100-02-9*) Tusky Enterprises.

—The Adventures of Tusky & His Friends Series, Bk. I. Greenberg, Kenneth R. (gr. k-3). 1992. PLB write for info. (*1-879100-49-5*) Tusky Enterprises.

THE ADVENTURES OF TUSKY & HIS FRIENDS. Book I. A JUNGLE ADVENTURE. ISBN 1-879100-00-2 $13.95. The introductory book of an educational "Snuggle-Up" & read-along series of picture story books for ages 6-8 that encourages interaction between child & reader. Tusky & his friend Packy meet Hooty, an owl, who becomes their mentor. Negative & positive thinking, reacting to "labels" people give us, showing sensitivity & thinking ahead are discussed. A CHRISTMAS MYSTERY: A HOLIDAY SPECIAL ISBN 1-879100-01-0 $14.95. While the animals are decorating the jungle for Christmas, someone poisons the elephant herd. Hooty solves the mystery & Santa Claus calls Tusky & his friends heroes for saving the herd. Book 2: TUSKY MEETS THE GREEN-EYED MONSTER ISBN 1-879100-03-7 (Approx. $15.50). Tusky is jealous of Ellie, his sister. In anger, he runs away from home. He talks to a stranger & is kidnapped. Hooty devises a plan to free him & later explains jealousy & how to overcome it. Tusky returns home & gets a big surprise. Book 3: TUSKY GETS MAD AT TUSKY. ISBN 1-879100-02-9 (Approx. $15.50). Tusky is mad at himself because there are too many things he can't do. Hooty helps him feel better about himself. There is a thunder & lightning storm & when Tusky saves the life of a doe, his self-concept is improved. Discussion questions have been prepared for each story.
Publisher Provided Annotation.

—The Adventures of Tusky & His Friends, Vol. 2: Tusky Meets the Green-Eyed Monster. Greenberg, Kenneth R. 66p. (gr. k-4). 1992. 15.95 (*1-879100-03-7*) Tusky Enterprises.

Pearson, C. Adventures on Library Shelves. Ringstad, M. LC 68-16398. 48p. (gr. 2 up). 1967. PLB 12.35 prebound (*0-87783-001-0*) Oddo.

Pearson, David. Earth: All about Earthquakes, Volacnoes, Glaciers, Oceans & More. Allen, Carol. 32p. 1993. pap. 5.95 (*1-895688-06-X*, Pub. by Greey dePencier CN) Firefly Bks Ltd.

Pearson, Justin. Davy Crockett: Young Rifleman. Parks, Aileen W. LC 86-10781. 192p. (gr. 2-6). 1986. pap. 3.95 (*0-02-041840-X*, Aladdin) Macmillan Child Grp.

Pearson, Sue. The Haunted School. Pearson, Sue. (gr. 3-6). 1992. pap. 7.95 (*1-56680-509-0*) Mad Hatter Pub.

Pearson, Tracey. Fat Chance Claude. Nixon, Joan L. (ps-3). 1987. 11.95 (*0-670-81459-8*) Viking Child Bks.

Pearson, Tracey C. Beats Me, Claude. Nixon, Joan L. LC 86-5465. 32p. (ps-3). 1986. 11.95 (*0-670-80781-8*) Viking Child Bks.

—Beats Me, Claude. Nixon, Joan L. (ps-3). 1988. pap. 3.95 (*0-14-050847-3*, Puffin) Puffin Bks.

—Fat Chance, Claude. Nixon, Joan L. 32p. (ps-3). 1989. pap. 4.95 (*0-14-050679-9*, Puffin) Puffin Bks.

—The Missing Tarts. Hennessy, B. G. 32p. (ps-3). 1989. pap. 12.95 (*0-670-82039-3*) Viking Child Bks.

—The Missing Tarts. Hennessy, B. G. 32p. (ps-3). 1991. pap. 3.95 (*0-14-050815-5*, Puffin) Puffin Bks.

—Old MacDonald Had a Farm. LC 83-18815. 32p. (ps-2). 1984. 11.95 (*0-8037-0068-7*) Dial Bks Young.

—Old MacDonald Had a Farm. Pearson, Tracey C. LC 83-18815. 32p. (ps-2). 1986. pap. 4.95 (*0-8037-0274-4*) Dial Bks Young.

—School Days. Hennessy, B. G. LC 92-12008. (gr. 4 up). 1992. pap. 3.99 (*0-14-054179-9*, Puffin) Puffin Bks.

—Sing a Song of Sixpence. Pearson, Tracey C. LC 84-14206. 32p. (ps-2). 1988. Dial Bks Young.

—That's the Spirit, Claude. Nixon, Joan L. 32p. (ps-3). 1992. 13.00 (*0-670-83434-3*) Viking Child Bks.

—There's a Cow in the Road! Lindbergh, Reeve. LC 92-34883. 32p. (ps-2). 1993. 13.99 (*0-8037-1335-5*); PLB 13.89 (*0-8037-1336-3*) Dial Bks Young.

—We Wish You a Merry Christmas. LC 82-22224. 32p. (ps up) 1983. 8.95 (*0-8037-9368-5*); pap. 3.95 (*0-8037-0310-4*) Dial Bks Young.

—You Bet Your Britches, Claude. Nixon, Joan L. 32p. (ps-3). 1989. pap. 11.95 (*0-670-82310-4*) Viking Child Bks.

—You Bet Your Britches, Claude. Nixon, Joan L. 32p. (ps-3). 1991. pap. 3.95 (*0-14-050900-3*, Puffin) Puffin Bks.

Pearson, Tracy C. Grandpa Putter & Granny Hoe. Fakih, Kimberly O. 128p. (gr. 2-5). 1992. 13.00 (*0-374-32762-9*) FS&G.

Pearson-Cooper, Michelle. Fairies & Friends. Hart, Tom. 120p. 1981. 8.95 (*0-685-01043-0*, Pub. by Quartet England) Charles River Bks.

Peattie, Gary. Christmas Time in the Mountains. Luton, Mildred. 44p. (Orig.). (gr. 1-6). 1981. pap. 5.00 (*0-87516-434-X*) DeVorss.

Peaver, Walt. The Witchy Broom. DeLage, Ida. 48p. (gr. k-4). 1991. Repr. of 1969 ed. lib. bdg. 12.95 (*0-7910-1487-8*) Chelsea Hse.

Peck, Beth. The Ballad of the Harp Weaver. Millay, Edna St. Vincent. 32p. (ps-3). 1991. 14.95 (*0-399-21611-1*, Philomel) Putnam Pub Group.

—A Christmas Memory. Capote, Truman. LC 88-36452. 48p. (gr. 2 up). 1989. 16.00 (*0-679-80040-9*) Knopf Bks Yng Read.

—Day Before Christmas. Bunting, Eve. 32p. (ps-3). 1992. 14.95 (*0-89919-866-X*, Clarion Bks) HM.

—Dear Levi: Letters from the Overland Trail. Woodruff, Elvira. LC 93-5315. 1994. 13.00 (*0-679-84641-7*); PLB 13.99 (*0-679-94641-1*) Knopf.

—Grandmother & the Runaway Shadow. Rosenberg, Liz. LC 92-42349. 1994. write for info. (*0-399-22545-5*, Philomel Bks) Putnam Pub Group.

—The House on Maple Street. Pryor, Bonnie. LC 86-12648. 32p. (gr. k-3). 1987. 15.95 (*0-688-06380-2*); lib. bdg. 14.88 (*0-688-06381-0*) Morrow Jr Bks.

—The House on Maple Street. Pryor, Bonnie. ALC Staff, ed. LC 86-14628. 32p. (gr. k up) 1992. pap. 4.95 (*0-688-12031-8*, Mulberry) Morrow.

—How Many Days to America? A Thanksgiving Story. Bunting, Eve. LC 88-2590. 32p. (gr. k-4). 1988. 15.45 (*0-89919-521-0*, Clarion Bks) HM.

—Matthew & Tilly. Jones, Rebecca C. LC 90-3730. 32p. (ps-3). 1991. 13.95 (*0-525-44684-2*, DCB) Dutton Child Bks.

—Night Outside. Wrightson, Patricia. LC 85-7529. 64p. (gr. 4-7). 1985. SBE 13.95 (*0-689-50363-6*, M K McElderry) Macmillan Child Grp.

—The Silver Whistle. Tompert, Ann. LC 88-1446. 32p. (gr. k-3). 1988. RSBE 14.95 (*0-02-789160-7*, Macmillan Child Bk) Macmillan Child Grp.

—The Snow Goose. 50th anniversary ed. Gallico, Paul. LC 90-46880. 48p. 1992. 16.00 (*0-679-80683-0*); PLB 16.99 (*0-679-90683-5*) Knopf Bks Yng Read.

—Sweet Notes, Sour Notes. Levinson, Nancy S. LC 92-19549. 64p. (gr. 2-5). 1993. 12.99 (*0-525-67379-2*, Lodestar Bks) NAL-Dutton.

Peck, Bill. Star Patrol: The Adventures Begin. Simmons, Herbert R. & Boyice, Lester L. 56p. (ps-7). 1987. lib. bdg. 8.95 (*0-930355-05-9*) ELRAMCO Enter.

Peck, Christopher S. The Friendly Snowflake: A Fable of Faith, Love & Family. Peck, M. Scott. 40p. (gr. 3 up). 14.95 (*1-878685-28-7*) Turner Pub GA.

Peck, Marshall. Pretty Polly. King-Smith, Dick. LC 91-42449. 128p. (gr. 2-7). 1992. 14.00 (*0-517-58606-1*); PLB 14.99 (*0-517-58607-X*) Crown Bks Yng Read.

—Sea Turtles. Arnold, Caroline. LC 93-6353. 1994. 3.95 (*0-590-46945-2*) Scholastic Inc.

Peck, Marshall H., III. Amazing Rescues. Shea, George. LC 90-53221. 48p. (gr. 2-3). 1992. PLB 7.99 (*0-679-91107-3*); pap. 3.50 (*0-679-81107-9*) Random Bks Yng Read.

—Heavy-Duty Trucks. 14p. (ps-k). 1992. bds. 3.99 (*0-679-83244-0*) Random Bks Yng Read.

Peck, Marshall, III. Blast Off! A Space Counting Book. Cole, Norma. LC 93-28794. 32p. (ps-4). 1994. 14.95 (*0-88106-499-8*); PLB 15.00 (*0-88106-493-9*); pap. 6.95 (*0-88106-498-X*) Charlesbridge Pub.

Peck, Stephen R. Science Projects You Can Do. Stone, George K. 101p. (gr. 7-9). 1963. (Pub. by Treehouse). pap. 4.95 (*0-13-795328-3*) P-H.

Peck, Virginia. Secrets of the Best Choice. Johnson, Lois W. LC 88-60475. 192p. (Orig.). 1988. pap. 7.00 (*0-89109-232-3*) NavPress.

—Thanks for Being My Friend. Johnson, Lois W. LC 88-60473. 180p. (Orig.). 1988. pap. 7.00 (*0-89109-234-X*) NavPress.

—You Are Wonderfully Made! Johnson, Lois W. LC 88-60474. 192p. (Orig.). 1988. pap. 7.00 (*0-89109-235-8*) NavPress.

—You're Worth More Than You Think! Johnson, Lois W. LC 88-60476. 180p. (Orig.). 1988. pap. 7.00 (*0-89109-233-1*) NavPress.

Pedersen, Judy. On the Road of Stars: Native American Night Poems & Sleep Charms. Bierhorst, John, selected by. LC 92-20001. 32p. (gr. 1). 1994. RSBE 14.95 (*0-02-709735-8*, Macmillan Child Bk) Macmillan Child Grp.

—Out in the Country. Pedersen, Judy. LC 90-40032. 40p. (ps-2). 1991. PLB 14.99 (*0-679-90630-4*) Knopf Bks Yng Read.

—The Tiny Patient. Pedersen, Judy. LC 88-21806. 40p. (ps-2). 1989. PLB 13.99 (*0-394-90170-3*) Knopf Bks Yng Read.

Pedersen, Vilhelm, jt. illus. see Frolich, Lorenz.

Peduzzi, Carolyn. Exploring the Forest with Grandforest Tree. Dennee, JoAnne. 275p. (Orig.). (gr. 1-4). 1993. pap. write for info. (*1-884430-03-1*) Food Works.

—Exploring the Secrets of the Meadow-Thicket. DeNee, JoAnne & Hand, Julia. 275p. (Orig.). (gr. 1-4). 1993. pap. write for info. (*1-884430-02-3*) Food Works.

—The Wonderful World of Wigglers: The Mysteries & Magic of the Mighty Earthworm. Hand, Julia. 181p. (Orig.). (gr. 1-6). 1993. pap. write for info. (*1-884430-00-7*) Food Works.

Peek, Merle. Mary Wore Her Red Dress, & Henry Wore His Green Sneakers. Peek, Merle. LC 84-12733. 32p. (ps-2). 1985. 14.95 (*0-89919-324-2*, Clarion Bks) HM.

—Mary Wore Her Red Dress & Henry Wore His Green Sneakers. Peek, Merle. 1993. Incl. cassette. 7.70 (*0-395-61577-1*, Clarion Bks) HM.

—Roll Over! A Counting Song. Peek, Merle. 32p. (ps-2). 1981. 14.95 (*0-395-29438-X*, Clarion Bks) HM.

—Roll Over! A Counting Song. Peek, Merle. 32p. (ps). 1993. pap. 4.80 (*0-395-58105-2*, Clarion Bks); pap. 7.95 incl. cassette (*0-395-60117-7*, Clarion Bks) HM.

Peet, Bill. The Ant & the Elephant. Peet, Bill. LC 74-179918. 48p. (gr. k-3). 1980. 13.95 (*0-395-16963-1*); pap. 7.95 (*0-395-29205-0*) HM.

—Big Bad Bruce. Peet, Bill. LC 76-62502. (gr. k-3). 1982. 13.95 (*0-395-25150-8*); pap. 5.95 (*0-395-32922-1*) HM.

—Bill Peet: An Autobiography. Peet, Bill. (gr. 3 up). 1989. 16.45 (*0-395-50932-7*) HM.

—Caboose Who Got Loose. Peet, Bill. LC 79-155554. 48p. (gr. k-3). 1980. 13.95 (*0-395-14805-7*); pap. 4.80 (*0-395-28715-4*) HM.

—Chester the Worldly Pig. Peet, Bill. (gr. k-3). 1978. pap. 4.80 (*0-395-27271-8*) HM.

—Cock-a-Doodle Dudley. Peet, Bill. 48p. (gr. k-3). 1990. 14.45 (*0-395-55331-8*) HM.

—Cock-A-Doodle Dudley. Peet, Bill. 48p. (gr. k-3). 1993. pap. 4.80 (*0-395-65745-8*) HM.

—Countdown to Christmas. Peet, Bill. LC 72-78394. 48p. (gr. k-8). 1972. (Golden Gate); PLB 15.93 (*0-516-08716-9*) Childrens.

—Eli. Peet, Bill. LC 77-17500. 48p. (gr. k-3). 1978. 13.45 (*0-395-26454-5*) HM.

—Eli. Peet, Bill. LC 77-17500. 48p. (gr. k-3). 1984. pap. 4.95 (*0-395-36611-9*) HM.

—Ella. Peet, Bill. 48p. (gr. k-3). 1978. pap. 4.80 (*0-395-27269-6*) HM.

—Encore for Eleanor. Peet, Bill. 48p. (gr. k-3). 1981. 13.45 (*0-395-29860-1*); pap. 3.95 (*0-317-18520-9*) HM.

—Farewell to Shady Glade. Peet, Bill. 48p. (gr. k-3). 1981. 13.45 (*0-395-18975-6*); pap. 5.70 incl. cassette (*0-395-60166-5*) HM.

—Fly Homer Fly. Peet, Bill. (gr. k-3). 1979. 13.45 (*0-395-24536-2*); pap. 4.80 (*0-395-28005-2*) HM.

—The Gnats of Knotty Pine. Peet, Bill. LC 75-17024. 48p. (gr. k-3). 1984. 13.45 (*0-395-21405-X*); pap. 4.80 (*0-395-36612-7*) HM.

—How Droofus the Dragon Lost His Head. Peet, Bill. LC 75-135136. 48p. (gr. k-3). 1983. 13.45 (*0-395-15085-X*); pap. 4.80 (*0-395-34066-7*) HM.

—Huge Harold. Peet, Bill. (gr. k-3). 1982. pap. 4.80 (*0-395-32923-X*) HM.

—Jennifer & Josephine. Peet, Bill. (gr. k-3). 1980. 13.95 (*0-395-18225-5*); pap. 4.80 (*0-395-29608-0*) HM.

—The Kweeks of Kookatumdee. Peet, Bill. LC 84-22379. 32p. (gr. k-3). 1985. 13.95 (*0-395-37902-4*) HM.

—The Kweeks of Kookatumdee. Peet, Bill. 32p. (gr. k-3). 1988. pap. 4.80 (*0-395-48656-4*, Sandpiper) HM.

—The Luckiest One of All. Peet, Bill. (gr. k-3). 1982. 14.95 (*0-395-31863-7*); pap. 4.80 (*0-395-39593-3*) HM.

—Merle the High Flying Squirrel. Peet, Bill. LC 73-18371. 32p. (gr. k-3). 1974. reinforced bdg. 13.45 (*0-395-18452-5*) HM.

—Merle the High Flying Squirrel. Peet, Bill. 30p. (gr. k-3). 1983. pap. 5.70 (*0-395-34923-0*) HM.

—No Such Things. Peet, Bill. LC 82-23234. 32p. (gr. k-3). 1983. 13.95 (*0-395-33888-3*); pap. 4.80 (*0-395-39594-1*) HM.

—Pamela Camel. Peet, Bill. LC 83-18594. 32p. (gr. k-3). 1984. 14.45 (*0-395-35975-9*, 5-93025) HM.

—Smokey. Peet, Bill. 48p. (gr. k-3). 1983. pap. 3.80 (*0-395-34924-9*) HM.

—The Spooky Tail of Prewitt Peacock. Peet, Bill. LC 72-7930. 32p. (gr. k-3). 1973. 13.95 (*0-395-15494-4*) HM.

—Whingdingdilly. Peet, Bill. LC 71-98521. (gr. k-3). 1977. 14.45 (*0-395-24729-2*); pap. 4.80 (*0-395-31381-3*) HM.

—Wump World. Peet, Bill. LC 72-124999. (gr. 3-5). 1974. 14.95 (0-395-19841-0); pap. 4.80 (0-395-31129-2) HM.
—The Wump World. Peet, Bill. 1991. incl. cass. 7.70 (0-395-58412-4) HM.
Pef. Oukele la Tele. Morgenstern, Susie. (FRE.). 54p. (gr. 1-5). 1991. pap. 9.95 (2-07-031190-2) Schoenhof.
Pegoda, Dan & Wilson, Craig. Ideas Combo Edition 9-12, 4 bks. in 1. Rice, Wayne & Yaconelli, Mike, eds. 180p. (Orig.). 1980. pap. 19.95 (0-910125-27-9) Youth Special.
Peinkowski, Jan. Road Hog. Peinkowski, Jan. 5p. (gr. k-3). 1993. 13.99 (0-8431-3586-7) Price Stern.
Pelham, David. Sam's Sandwich. Pelham, David. 22p. (ps-4). 1991. 8.99 (0-525-44751-2, DCB) Dutton Child Bks.
Pelham, Richard. By Hook or by Crook: My Autograph Book. Zola, Meguido. 48p. (gr. 1 up). 1987. 9.95 (0-88776-201-8) Tundra Bks.
Pelizzoli, Francesca. Kings, Gods & Spirits from African Mythology. Knappert, Jan. LC 93-12903. 88p. (gr. 6 up). 1993. 22.50 (0-87226-916-7); pap. 12.95 sewn (0-87226-917-5) P Bedrick Bks.
Pellaton, Karen E. Habits of Rabbits. Daniel, Kira. LC 85-14122. 48p. (Orig.). (gr. 1-3). 1986. PLB 10.59 (0-8167-0632-8); pap. text ed. 3.50 (0-8167-0633-6) Troll Assocs.
—What's It Like to Be a Chef. Poskanzer, Susan C. LC 89-34390. 32p. (gr. k-3). 1990. lib. bdg. 10.89 (0-8167-1797-4); pap. text ed. 2.95 (0-8167-1798-2) Troll Assocs.
—What's It Like to Be a Nurse. Bauer, Judith. LC 89-34387. 32p. (gr. k-3). 1990. lib. bdg. 10.89 (0-8167-1809-1); pap. text ed. 2.95 (0-8167-1810-5) Troll Assocs.
Pellegrini, Nina. Families Are Different. Pellegrini, Nina. LC 90-22876. 32p. (ps-3). 1991. reinforced 14.95 (0-8234-0887-6) Holiday.
Pelletier, Gilles. Un Bonne et Heureuse Annee. Carrier, Roch. LC 91-65366. (FRE.). 24p. (gr. 3 up). 1991. 14.95 (0-88776-268-9) Tundra Bks.
—The Sugaring-off Party. London, Jonathan. LC 93-21911. 1994. write for info. (0-525-45187-0, DCB) Dutton Child Bks.
Pellowski, Michael. One Hundred Two School Jokes. Pellowski, Michael J. LC 91-20702. 64p. (gr. 2-6). 1991. pap. 2.95 (0-8167-2579-9) Troll Assocs.
Pels, Winslow. Noble-Hearted Kate. Mayer, Marianna. (gr. 3 up). 1990. 14.95 (0-553-07049-5, Skylark) Bantam.
—Turandot. Mayer, Marianna. LC 93-27033. Date not set. write for info. (0-688-09073-7); lib. bdg. write for info. (0-688-09074-5) Morrow.
Pels, Winslow P. Beauty & the Beast. Osborne, Mary P., retold by. 40p. (gr. 1-4). 1988. pap. 3.95 (0-590-40166-1) Scholastic Inc.
—The Magic Fish. Littledale, Freya. 32p. (Orig.). (gr. k-3). 1986. pap. 2.50 (0-590-41100-4) Scholastic Inc.
—Stone Soup. McGovern, Ann. 32p. (Orig.). (gr. k-2). 1986. pap. 2.50 (0-590-41602-2) Scholastic Inc.
Peltier, P. Ichabod's Adventure in Alphabet Town. McDonnell, Janet. LC 91-20547. 32p. (ps-2). 1992. PLB 14.60 (0-516-05409-0) Childrens.
Peltier, Pam. Mi Primer Libro de el Dia de las Brujas: My First Halloween Book. Reece, Colleen L. Kratky, Lada, tr. LC 85-31396. (SPA.). 32p. (ps-3). 1986. PLB 15.00 (0-516-32902-2); pap. 3.95 (0-516-52902-1) Childrens.
—My "a" Sound Box. Moncure, Jane B. LC 84-17024. 32p. (ps-2). 1984. PLB 21.35 (0-89565-296-X); PLB 14.95s.p. (0-685-55767-7) Childs World.
—My First Halloween Book. Reece, Colleen L. LC 84-9431. 32p. (ps-2). 1984. pap. 3.95 (0-516-42902-7) Childrens.
—My One Book. Moncure, Jane B. LC 85-5897. 32p. (ps-2). 1985. PLB 21.35 (0-89565-312-5); PLB 14.95s.p. (0-685-55770-7) Childs World.
—My Two Book. Moncure, Jane B. LC 85-7885. 32p. (ps-2). 1985. PLB 21.35 (0-89565-313-3); PLB 14.95s.p. (0-685-55772-3) Childs World.
—My "u" Sound Box. Moncure, Jane B. LC 84-17012. 32p. (ps-2). 1984. PLB 21.35 (0-89565-300-1); PLB 14.95s.p. (0-685-55773-1) Childs World.
—Our Halloween Book. rev. ed. Moncure, Jane B. LC 85-30868. 32p. (ps-3). 1986. PLB 19.95 (0-89565-348-6); PLB 13.95s.p. (0-685-55830-4) Childs World.
—Rabbits' Habits. Moncure, Jane B. LC 87-12841. 32p. (ps-2). 1987. PLB 21.35 (0-89565-406-7); PLB 14.95s.p. (0-685-55931-9) Childs World.
—Victor's Adventure in Alphabet Town. McDonnell, Janet. LC 92-4036. 32p. (ps-2). 1992. PLB 14.60 (0-516-05422-8) Childrens.
Pelton, Fawn. Folks I Wish I'd Known. Pelton, Jeanette. Pelton, Dan, ed. 75p. (gr. 5-8). 1993. pap. 4.00 (1-879564-05-X) Long Acre Pub.
—Kids Grow in My Garden. Pelton, Jeanette. LC 91-90004. 88p. (gr. 4-6). 1991. pap. 3.50 (1-879564-01-7, GWG1) Long Acre Pub.
—Natural Morning. Pelton, Jeanette. Pelton, Dan, ed. 100p. (Orig.). (gr. 5-7). 1993. pap. 6.00 (1-879564-06-8) Long Acre Pub.
Pelzel, Kelly C. The Story of Orange. Pelzel, Vernise E. Monk, Lenore, ed. 48p. (gr. 3-12). 1987. pap. 6.95 (0-944131-01-8) HPL Pub.
Pence, Nedra. Literature Activities for Young Children. Sullivan, Dianna. 96p. (ps-1). 1989. wkbk. 9.95 (1-55734-300-4) Tchr Create Mat.

—Literature Activities for Young Children. Sullivan, Dianna. 96p. (ps-1). 1989. wkbk. 9.95 (1-55734-301-2) Tchr Create Mat.
—Literature Activities for Young Children. Sullivan, Dianna. 96p. (ps-1). 1989. wkbk. 9.95 (1-55734-302-0) Tchr Create Mat.
—Literature Activities for Young Children. Sullivan, Dianna. 96p. (ps-1). 1989. wkbk. 9.95 (1-55734-303-9) Tchr Create Mat.
Pence, Nedra L. Literature Activities for Young Children. Sullivan, Dianna. 96p. (ps-1). 1990. wkbk. 9.95 (1-55734-305-5) Tchr Create Mat.
—Literature Activities for Young Children. Sullivan, Dianna. 96p. (ps-1). 1990. wkbk. 9.95 (1-55734-306-3) Tchr Create Mat.
—Literature Activities for Young Children. Sullivan, Dianna. 96p. (ps-1). 1990. wkbk. 9.95 (1-55734-307-1) Tchr Create Mat.
Pendergast, Holly. Taking Care of Rosie. Salem, Lynn & Stewart, Josie. 8p. (gr. 1). 1992. pap. 3.50 (1-880612-05-4) Seedling Pubns.
Pene du Boid, William. My Grandson Lew. Zolotow, Charlotte. LC 73-1433. 32p. (ps-3). 1985. pap. 3.95 (0-06-443066-9, Trophy) HarpC Child Bks.
—William's Doll. Zolotow, Charlotte. LC 70-183173. 32p. (ps-3). 1985. pap. 4.95 (0-06-443067-7, Trophy) HarpC Child Bks.
Pene du Bois, William. Bear in Mind: A Book of Bear Poems. Goldstein, Bobbye S., compiled by. 32p. (ps-3). 1991. pap. 3.95 (0-14-050799-X, Puffin) Puffin Bks.
Pene du Bois, William. Magic Finger. Dahl, Roald. LC 66-18657. 46p. (gr. 3-6). 1966. 15.00 (0-06-021381-7); PLB 14.89 (0-06-021382-5) HarpC Child Bks.
Pene du Bois, William. Twenty & Ten. Bishop, Claire H. (gr. 3-7). 1978. pap. 3.99 (0-14-031076-2, Puffin) Puffin Bks.
—Twenty & Ten. Bishop, Claire H. (gr. 5-9). 1984. 16.75 (0-8446-6168-6) Peter Smith.
—Twenty-One Balloons. Pene Du Bois, William. 192p. (gr. 4-8). 1982. pap. 2.75 (0-440-49183-5, YB) Dell.
—The Twenty-One Balloons. Pene Du Bois, William. (gr. 5-9). 1947. pap. 15.00 (0-670-73441-1) Viking Child Bks.
—William's Doll. Zolotow, Charlotte. LC 70-183173. 32p. (ps-3). 1992. 14.00 (0-06-027047-0); PLB 13.89 (0-06-027048-9) HarpC Child Bks.
Pennanen, Judi. Little Stitch. Edwards, Margaret B. 24p. (ps-8). 1986. 7.95 (0-920806-69-4, Pub. by Penumbra Pr CN) U of Toronto Pr.
—The Secret Code of DNA. Razzell, Mary. 36p. (ps-8). 1986. 7.95 (0-920806-83-X, Pub. by Penumbra Pr CN) U of Toronto Pr.
Penner, Kathy. Adam & Andrea Learn & Grow: Understanding Church Words from a Kid's Viewpoint. Martens, Sheri. 80p. (ps-5). 1989. pap. 7.95 (0-919797-81-4) Kindred Pr.
—Bears for Breakfast: The Thiessen Family Adventures. Doerksen, Nan. 34p. (ps-k). 1983. pap. 2.50 (0-919797-07-5) Kindred Pr.
Pennie, Dawn. Scents of Place: Season of the St. Croix Valley. Gustavson, Cynthia B. (Orig.). (gr. 9-12). 1987. pap. 8.95 (0-317-91094-9) Country Messenger Inc.
Pennington, Eunice. Perry, the Pet Pig. Pennington, Eunice. (gr. 4-7). 1966. 3.00 (0-685-19374-8, 911120-06-8); pap. 1.00 (0-685-19375-6) Pennington.
Penton, Ben. The Light of the Pentecost: A Unique Historical Account of the New Testament Church. Huston, David A. (gr. 7 up). 1989. pap. 5.95 (0-932345-03-4) Antioch Publishes.
Peperell, Liz. Cycles & Seasons. Harlow, Rosie & Morgan, Gareth. LC 91-2567. 40p. (gr. 5-8). 1991. PLB 12.90 (0-531-19123-0, Warwick) Watts.
—Trees & Leaves. Harlow, Rosie & Morgan, Gareth. 40p. (gr. 5-8). 1991. PLB 12.90 (0-531-19126-5, Warwick) Watts.
Peppe, Rodney. Circus Numbers. Peppe, Rodney. LC 75-86381. (ps-3). 1969. 5.95 (0-440-01288-0); pap. 3.69 (0-440-01289-9) Delacorte.
—The Color Catalog. Peppe, Rodney. 24p. (gr. k-2). 1992. 9.95 (0-87226-472-6, Bedrick Blackie) P Bedrick Bks.
—The House That Jack Built. Peppe, Rodney. 32p. (ps-3). 1985. pap. 4.95 (0-385-28430-6) Delacorte.
—Huxley Pig's Airplane. Peppe, Rodney. (ps-2). 1990. 8.95 (0-385-30038-7) Doubleday.
—Run Rabbit, Run! A Pop-Up Book. Peppe, Rodney. LC 82-70307. 12p. (ps-3). 1982. pap. 8.95 (0-385-28851-4) Delacorte.
—The Shapes Finder. Peppe, Rodney. 24p. (ps) 1991. bds. 9.95 (0-87226-462-9, Bedrick Blackie) P Bedrick Bks.
—Thumbprint Circus. Peppe, Rodney. (ps-1). 1989. 12.95 (0-440-50154-7) Delacorte.
—Thumbprint Circus. Peppe, Rodney. 32p. (ps-1). 1992. pap. 3.99 (0-440-40692-7, YB) Dell.
Pepperell, Liz, et al. Flowers, Trees & Other Plants. Stidworthy, John. LC 91-215. 40p. (Orig.). (gr. 2-5). 1991. pap. 3.99 (0-679-80867-1) Random Bks Yng Read.
Peraza, Michael. An Under-the-Sea Christmas: A Holiday Songbook. Luck 93-70939. 48p. 1993. 9.95 (1-56282-504-6) Disney Pr.
Percels, Beth. Love from the Sea. Cutburth, Ronald W. Naumann, Cynthia E., ed. 27p. (Orig.). (gr. 4-7). 1990. pap. 3.50 (1-878291-01-7) Love From Sea.

Perceval, Don. The Iroquois Trail: Dickon among the Onondagas & Senecas. Harrington, M. R. 215p. 1991. pap. 9.95 (0-8135-0480-5) Rutgers U Pr.
—Owl in the Cedar Tree. Momaday, Natachee S. LC 91-41866. viii, 117p. 1992. pap. 9.95 (0-8032-8184-6, Bison) U of Nebr Pr.
Percival, Keith, jt. photog. see Shone, Karl.
Percy, Graham. City Mouse & Country Mouse, Heron & the Fish, Crow & the Fox, Lion & the Mouse, 4 bks. Percy, Graham. 32p. (ps-2). 1993. PLB 19.95 (0-8050-2563-4, Bks Young Read) H Holt & Co.
—The Cock, the Mouse, & the Little Red Hen. LC 91-71857. 32p. (ps up). 1992. 14.95 (1-56402-008-8) Candlewick Pr.
—Elephants Never Forget: Classic Nursery Rhymes. 48p. (ps-1). 1992. 12.95 (0-8118-0239-6) Chronicle Bks.
—The Fantastic Dinosaur Adventure. Durrell, Gerald. LC 89-49099. 96p. (gr. 2-5). 1990. pap. 16.95 (0-671-70871-6) S&S Trade.
—Meg & the Great Race. Percy, Graham. LC 92-44851. 1993. write for info. (1-56766-077-0) Childs World.
—Reynard the Fox. Hastings, Selina, retold by. LC 90-11105. 80p. (gr. 2-4). 1991. 16.95 (0-688-09949-1, Tambourine Bks); PLB 16.88 (0-688-10156-9, Tambourine Bks) Morrow.
—Thirty-Six Strange Little Animals Waiting to Eat: With Simple Little Recipes to Make. Denny, Roz. LC 92-358. 32p. 1992. 12.95 (1-55670-272-8) Stewart Tabori & Chang.
—The Tortoise & the Hare: And Other Favorite Fables, 4 bks. Percy, Graham, retold by. (ps-2). 1993. Set, 32p. eac. bk. boxed 19.95 (0-8050-2556-1) H Holt & Co.
—The Wind in the Willows. Grahame, Kenneth. 192p. (gr. 3-6). 1992. 24.95 (1-85145-603-1, Pub. by Pavilion UK) Trafalgar.
—Woodland Gospels: According to Captain Beaky & His Band. Lloyd, Jeremy. LC 83-20790. 63p. (gr. k up). 1984. pap. 4.95 (0-571-14285-0) Faber & Faber.
Percy, Graham, photos by. Pigasus. Murphy, Pat. LC 93-32214. (gr. 3 up). 1995. write for info. (0-8037-1587-0); lib. bdg. write for info. (0-8037-1588-9) Dial Bks Young.
Pereira, Ernesto. In Quest of the Zohar. Fasco, Rudolph. Frades, Ernesto, ed. 275p. (Orig.). 1990. pap. write for info. (0-9624929-0-6) Little Great Whale.
Perenyi, Constance. Growing Wild: Inviting Wildlife into Your Yard. Perenyi, Constance. 40p. (gr. 1-3). 1991. 14.95 (0-941831-60-4); pap. 9.95 (0-941831-63-9) Beyond Words Pub.
Perez, George & Sutherland, Jackie. The Olympians. Dershem, Kurt. Bell, Rob, ed. 48p. (Orig.). (gr. 12). 1990. pap. 9.00 (1-55806-114-2, 414) Iron Crown Ent Inc.
Peris, Carme, jt. illus. see Rius, Maria.
Perkins, Lani, jt. illus. see Perkins, William C.
Perkins, Lori L., jt. illus. see Perkins, William C.
Perkins, William C. & Perkins, Lani. Bored Betty's Wish. Perkins, Myrna. 32p. (Orig.). (gr. 2-5). 1986. pap. 5.95 (0-937729-02-7) Markins Enter.
Perkins, William C. & Perkins, Lori L. What Does A Spider Do? Perkins, Myrna. 20p. (Orig.). (ps-3). 1985. pap. 3.95 (0-937729-00-0) Markins Enter.
—What Is This? Perkins, Myrna. 36p. (Orig.). (ps-3). 1986. pap. 4.95 (0-937729-01-9) Markins Enter.
—What Makes Honey? Perkins, Myrna. 32p. (Orig.). (ps-3). pap. 3.95 (0-937729-03-5) Markins Enter.
Perl, Susan. Jumbo the Boy & Arnold the Elephant. Greenburg, Dan. LC 87-24931. 48p. (gr. 2-4). 1989. Repr. of 1969 ed. HarpC Child Bks.
—So That's How I Was Born. Brooks, Robert. LC 81-20859. 48p. (ps-2). 1993. pap. 4.95 (0-671-78344-0, S&S BYR) S&S Trade.
—Where Is Daddy? The Story of a Divorce. Goff, Beth. LC 69-14608. 32p. (ps-k). 1969. pap. 4.95 (0-8070-2305-1, BP 694) Beacon Pr.
Perlman, Raymond. Fossils. Rhodes, Frank H., et al. (gr. 6 up). 1962. PLB write for info. (0-307-63515-5); pap. write for info. (0-307-24411-3, Golden Pr) Western Pub.
—Fossils: A Golden Guide. rev. ed. Rhodes, Frank H., et al. 1990. pap. write for info. (Golden Pr) Western Pub.
—Rocks & Minerals. Zim, Herbert S. & Shaffer, Paul R. (gr. 6 up). 1957. pap. write for info. (0-307-24499-7, Golden Pr) Western Pub.
Perlstein, Rivky. The Mentchkins Make Shabbos. Rothstein, Chaya L. (ps-2). 1986. pap. 2.95 (0-317-42728-8) Feldheim.
Permane, Terry, jt. illus. see Mitton, David.
Permane, Terry, jt. photog. see Mitton, David.
Perna, Debi. The Birthday Book: Stickers to Stick & Cards to Create for Every Month of the Year. Perna, Debi. 36p. (ps up). 1992. 6.95 (0-920775-57-8, Pub. by Greey de Pencier CN) Firefly Bks Ltd.
—The Chickadee Book of Puzzles & Fun. Chickadee Magazine Editors. Perna, Debi, ed. 32p. (ps up). 1992. pap. 4.95 (0-920775-82-9, Pub. by Greey de Pencier CN) Firefly Bks Ltd.
Perols, S., jt. illus. see Valat, P. M.
Perols, Sylvaine. Grains of Salt. Joly, Dominique. LC 87-34534. 38p. (gr. k-5). 1988. 4.95 (0-944589-20-0, 200) Young Discovery Lib.
—Nature's Timekeeper - The Tree. Morel, Gaud. Bogard, Vicki, tr. from FRE. LC 92-2710. 38p. (gr. k-5). 1992. 4.95 (0-944589-43-X) Young Discovery Lib.
—Nature's Timekeeper: The Tree. Morel, Gaud. 40p. (gr. k-5). 1993. PLB 9.95 (1-56674-072-X, HTS Bks) Forest Hse.

Perols, Sylvie. Ladybug & Other Insects. De Bourgoing, Pascale. 24p. 1991. pap. 10.95 (0-590-45235-5, Cartwheel) Scholastic Inc.
Perols, Sylvie, jt. illus. see Valat, P. M.
Perret, Paul. The Goose Girl. Grimm, Jacob & Grimm, Wilhelm K. 32p. (gr. 4 up). 1984. PLB 13.95s.p. (0-87191-934-6) Creative Ed.
Perrin, Sandra. Unicorns & Dreams. Waller, Wanda W. Lopez, Ron, ed. 39p. (Orig.). (gr. k-6). 1985. pap. 4.95 (0-930825-00-4) Lola Library.
Perrone, Donna. The Mermaid's Twin Sister: More Stories from Trinidad. Joseph, Lynn. LC 93-28436. 1994. write for info. (0-395-64365-1, Clarion Bks) HM.
Perrot, Catherine. How the Ocelots Got Their Spots. Wicker, Ireene. 32p. (gr. 2-4). 1976. 6.95 (0-8184-0231-8) Carol Pub Group.
Perry, Alfred. My Weekly Reader Picture Word Book. Holl, Adelaide. 128p. (ps-k). 1981. pap. 5.95 (0-671-42542-0) S&S Trade.
Perry, Craig P. Heritage Kids Volume Set: George Washington Carver: Bessie Coleman: Harriet Tubman: Jean Baptiste DuSable. Johnson, LaVerne C. LC 92-35256. 1992. 3.95 (0-922162-90-5); Set. write for info. (0-922162-99-9) Empak Pub.
Perry, Craig R. Bessie Coleman: Writer. Johnson, LaVerne C. LC 92-35255. 1992. 3.95 (0-922162-95-6) Empak Pub.
—George Washington Carver: Writer. Johnson, LaVerne C. LC 93-35254. (gr. 6-9). 1992. pap. 3.95 (0-922162-91-3) Empak Pub.
—Harriet Tubman: Writer. Johnson, LaVerne C. LC 92-35251. 1992. 3.95 (0-922162-92-1) Empak Pub.
—Jean Baptiste DuSable: Writer. Johnson, LaVerne C. LC 92-35252. 1992. 3.95 (0-922162-93-X) Empak Pub.
Perry, David. The Peace & Quiet Diner. Maguire, Gregory. LC 87-36865. 48p. (ps-3). 1988. 5.95 (0-8193-1176-6) Parents.
—The Peace-&-Quiet Diner. Maguire, Gregory. LC 93-7770. 1994. PLB 13.27 (0-8368-0971-8) Gareth Stevens Inc.
Perry, Jill. The Ocean: Consider the Connections. Center for Environmental Education Staff. Maraniss, Linda & Bierce, Rose, eds. Asimov, Isaac, frwd. by. 104p. (Orig.). (gr. 2-6). 1985. pap. 8.95 wkbk. (0-9615294-0-7) Ctr Env Educ.
Perry, Lucille R. Alphabet Talk: Gospel Rhymes for Each Letter of the Alphabet. Larsen, Rayola C. LC 89-83429. 32p. (Orig.). (gr. k-3). 1989. pap. 4.95 (0-88290-147-8) Horizon Utah.
—Growing up in the Church: Gospel Principles & Practices for Children. rev. ed. Crowther, Jean D. LC 67-25433. 84p. (gr. 2-6). 1973. Repr. of 1965 ed. 7.95 (0-88290-024-2) Horizon Utah.
Perry, Rebecca. Lots of Limericks. Livingston, Myra C., selected by. LC 91-329. 144p. (gr. 3 up). 1991. SBE 13.95 (0-689-50531-0, M K McElderry) Macmillan Child Grp.
—Riddle-Me Rhymes. Livingston, Myra C., selected by. LC 93-25179. 96p. (gr. 3-7). 1994. SBE 13.95 (0-689-50602-3, M K McElderry) Macmillan Child Grp.
Perry, Scott & Hulet, Grant. Take Your Hat Off When the Flag Goes By. Brady, Janeen. 22p. (Orig.). (gr. k-6). 1987. activity bk. 2.25 (0-944803-31-8); Set of 20. wkbk. 12.00 (0-944803-34-2); cassette & bk. 9.95 (0-944803-32-6); dialogue bk. 1.25 (0-944803-33-4); songbk. 7.95 (0-944803-29-6) Brite Intl.
Perry, Steve. Sword of the Samurai. Reaves, Michael. 144p. (gr. 4 up). 1984. pap. 2.75 (0-553-26427-3) Bantam.
Persels, Beth. Love from the Sea. Cutburth, Ronald W. Naumann, Cynthia E., ed. Witt, Hannelore, tr. (GER.). 27p. (gr. 5-8). 1989. pap. write for info. (1-878291-03-3) Love From Sea.
—Love from the Sea. Cutburth, Ronald W. Naumann, Cynthia E., ed. Witt, Hannelore, tr. (FRE.). 27p. (gr. 5-8). 1989. pap. write for info (1-878291-07-6) Love From Sea.
—Love from the Sea. Cutburth, Ronald W. Naumann, Cynthia E., ed. Lander, Kerstin, tr. (SWE.). 27p. (gr. 5-8). 1989. pap. write for info. (1-878291-06-8) Love From Sea.
—Love from the Sea. Cutburth, Ronald W. Naumann, Cynthia E., ed. Tostado, Rocio G., tr. (SPA.). 27p. (gr. 5-8). 1990. pap. write for info. (1-878291-09-2) Love From Sea.
—Love from the Sea. Cutburth, Ronald W. Naumann, Cynthia E., ed. West, Bobbie, tr. (CHI.). 27p. (gr. 5-8). 1990. pap. write for info (1-878291-11-4) Love From Sea.
Persico, F. S. First Facts about Flying Machines. Teitelbaum, Michael. 24p. 1991. 2.98 (1-56156-086-3) Kidsbks.
—First Facts about Giant Sea Creatures. Phillips, Gina. 24p. 1991. 2.98 (1-56156-084-7) Kidsbks.
—First Facts about Giant Sea Creatures. Phillips, Gina. 24p. 1992. pap. 2.50 (1-56156-156-8) Kidsbks.
—First Facts about Prehistoric Animals. Phillips, Gina. 24p. 1991. 2.98 (1-56156-083-9) Kidsbks.
—First Facts about Prehistoric Animals. Phillips, Gina. 24p. 1992. pap. 2.50 (1-56156-157-6) Kidsbks.
—First Facts about Snakes & Reptiles. Phillips, Gina. 24p. (Orig.). 1991. pap. 2.50 (1-56156-037-5) Kidsbks.
—First Facts about Snakes & Reptiles. Phillips, Gina. 24p. 1991. write for info. (1-56156-060-X) Kidsbks.

—First Facts about Wild Animals. Phillips, Gina. 24p. (Orig.). 1991. pap. 2.50 (1-56156-038-3) Kidsbks.
—First Facts about Wild Animals. Phillips, Gina. 24p. 1991. write for info. (1-56156-061-8) Kidsbks.
—Three Minute Aesop's Fables. Phillips, Gina, ed. 24p. 1991. 2.98 (1-56156-088-X) Kidsbks.
—Three Minute Bedtime Stories. Phillips, Gina, ed. 24p. 1991. 2.98 (1-56156-087-1) Kidsbks.
Pertzoff, Alexander. Three Names. MacLachlan, Patricia. LC 90-4444. 32p. (gr. k-4). 1991. 14.95 (0-06-024035-0); PLB 14.89 (0-06-024036-9) HarpC Child Bks.
Pesiri, Evelyn. All Aboard with Bulletin Boards. Spizman, Robyn. 96p. (gr. k-8). 1983. wkbk. 9.95 (0-86653-105-X, GA 467) Good Apple.
—Bulletin Boards: For Reading, Spelling & Language Skills. Spizman, Robyn. 64p. (gr. k-6). 1984. wkbk. 7.95 (0-86653-210-2, GA 574) Good Apple.
—Bulletin Boards: Ideas for Holidays & Special Days. Spizman, Robyn. 64p. (gr. k-6). 1984. wkbk. 7.95 (0-86653-211-0, GA 567) Good Apple.
—Bulletin Boards: Seasonal Ideas & Activities. Spizman, Robyn. 64p. (gr. k-6). 1984. wkbk. 7.95 (0-86653-218-8, GA 568) Good Apple.
—Bulletin Boards to Promote Good Study Skills & Positive Self-Concept. Spizman, Robyn. 48p. (gr. k-6). 1984. wkbk. 6.95 (0-86653-261-7, GA 575) Good Apple.
—Bulletin Boards: To Reinforce Basic Math Skills. Spizman, Robyn. 64p. (gr. k-6). 1984. wkbk. 7.95 (0-86653-208-0, GA 573) Good Apple.
—Learn to Hear. Pesiri, Evelyn. 64p. (gr. k-3). 1986. wkbk. 7.95 (0-86653-337-0, GA 675) Good Apple.
—Learn to See. Pesiri, Evelyn. 64p. (gr. k-3). 1985. wkbk. 7.95 (0-86653-286-2, GA 674) Good Apple.
—Learn to Think. Pesiri, Evelyn. 64p. (gr. k-3). 1986. wkbk. 7.95 (0-86653-343-5, GA 676) Good Apple.
—Learn to Write. Pesiri, Evelyn. ed. 64p. (gr. k-3). 1986. wkbk. 7.95 (0-86653-342-7, GA 791) Good Apple.
Petach, Heidi. Air, Air All Around. Barkan, Joanne. Brook, Bonnie, ed. 32p. (ps-1). 1990. 5.95 (0-671-68659-3); PLB 9.98 (0-671-68655-0) Silver Pr.
—Fire, Fire Burning Bright. Barkan, Joanne. Brook, Bonnie, ed. 32p. (ps-1). 1990. 5.95 (0-671-68658-5); PLB 9.98 (0-671-68654-2) Silver Pr.
—Grandpa Told Me So. Deverell, Catherine. LC 87-62600. 20p. (ps). 1988. pap. 1.59 (0-87403-387-X, 24-02017) Standard Pub.
—Jonah: The Inside Story. Petach, Heidi. 32p. (gr. k-2). 1989. 2.50 (0-87403-594-5, 3854) Standard Pub.
—The Monster That Glowed in the Dark. Ingle, Annie. LC 92-30144. 16p. (ps-1). 1993. pap. 4.99 (0-679-84194-6) Random Bks Yng Read.
—Rainbow Babies. Ross, Katharine. LC 91-66659. 28p. (ps). 1992. 2.95 (0-679-83068-5) Random Bks Yng Read.
—Rocks, Rocks Big & Small. Barkan, Joanne. Brook, Bonnie, ed. 32p. (ps-1). 1990. 5.95 (0-671-68660-7); PLB 9.98 (0-671-68656-9) Silver Pr.
—Sing a Happy Song. Rosen, Gary & Shontz, Bill. 24p. (ps-1). 1990. pap. 9.95 incl. cassette (0-679-80805-1) Random Bks Yng Read.
—Water, Water Everywhere. Barkan, Joanne. Brook, Bonnie, ed. 32p. (ps-1). 1990. 5.95 (0-671-68657-7); PLB 9.98 (0-671-68653-4) Silver Pr.
Peterkin, Mike. Three Little Pigs: Pop-up Book. LC 93-70940. 10p. (ps-3). 1993. 11.95 (1-56282-513-5) Disney Pr.
Peterkin, Mike, jt. illus. see Jacobs, Philip.
Peters, David. Giants of Land, Sea & Air - Past & Present: A Science Club Book Series. Peters, David. LC 86-2719. 64p. (gr. 3 up). 1986. PLB 15.99 (0-394-97805-6) Knopf Bks Yng Read.
—Strange Creatures. Peters, David. LC 91-36205. 48p. (gr. 3 up). 1992. 16.00 (0-688-10154-2); PLB 15.93 (0-688-10155-0) Morrow Jr Bks.
Peters, Patricia & Tom, Linda. Nursery Rhymes from Mother Goose: Told in Signed English. Bornstein, Harry & Saulnier, Karen L. 48p. (ps-2). 1992. 14.95 (0-930323-99-8, Pub. by K Green Pubns) Gallaudet Univ Pr.
Peters, Patricia & Tom, Linda C. Mother Goose: Nursery Rhymes. Bornstein, Harry & Saulnier, Karen L. 48p. (gr. k-3). 1992. PLB 15.95 (1-56674-034-7) Forest Hse.
Peters, Robert. Doodles, Diddles, Puzzles, Quizzies & Fun Stuff, Vol. 2. Donaldson, Judith E. 144p. (Orig.). (gr. 2 up). 1981. pap. 2.25 (0-939942-00-3) Larkspur.
Peters, Shirley. Rainy Day Book. Ingram, Anne & O'Donnell, Peggy. 48p. (gr. 3 up). 1992. pap. 6.95 (0-920775-44-6, Pub. by Greey dePencier CN) Firefly Bks Ltd.

Peters, Terry. The Wet Hat: And Other Stories from Beyond the Black Stump. Loder, Ann. 102p. (Orig.). (gr. 4 up). 1993. pap. write for info. (0-9636643-0-1) A L Loder. THE WET HAT, & OTHER STORIES FROM BEYOND THE BLACK STUMP is a collection of Australian short stories taken from the author's childhood & family album growing up on an Australian sheep ranch. The stories concern family pets; a gutsy pony, two heroic dogs; a kookaburra, (a native Australian bird), a chicken, & a tale about a tiny silkworm. There is a mystery story about a lost ring. Lastly, there is a humorous one. Each story is based on fact & is suitable for children from fourth to eighth grade, up. A dog is featured on the full color cover & there is a black & white illustration with each story. Order from: American Business Communications, 251 Michelle Ct., South San Francisco, CA 94080. FAX: (415) 952-3716 (att: Noel Loder). 415-952-8700. *Publisher Provided Annotation.*

Peters, Thea. Degas, the Ballet, & Me. Van Beek, Tom. 48p. (gr. 2-7). 1993. 12.95 (1-56288-424-7) Checkerboard.
Petersen, R. F. Weird & Wonderful Ants. Poole, Lynn & Poole, Gray. (gr. 5 up). 1961. 8.95 (0-8392-3041-9) Astor-Honor.
Petersham, Maud & Petersham, Miska. Circus Baby. Petersham, Maud & Petersham, Miska. LC 50-9295. 32p. (ps-1). 1968. RSBE 13.95 (0-02-771670-8, Macmillan Child Bk) Macmillan Child Grp.
—The Circus Baby. Petersham, Maud & Petersham, Miska. LC 88-7369. 32p. (ps-1). 1989. pap. 3.95 (0-689-71295-2, Aladdin) Macmillan Child Grp.
—The Rooster Crows: A Book of American Rhymes & Jingles. Petersham, Maud & Petersham, Miska. LC 46-446. 64p. (ps-2). 1969. RSBE 13.95 (0-02-773100-6, Macmillan Child Bk) Macmillan Child Grp.
—The Rooster Crows: A Book of American Rhymes & Jingles. Petersham, Maud & Petersham, Miska. LC 87-1138. 64p. (ps-3). 1987. pap. 4.95 (0-689-71153-0, Aladdin) Macmillan Child Grp.
Petersham, Miska, jt. illus. see Petersham, Maud.
Peterson, jt. illus. see Koechel.
Peterson, Adria, jt. illus. see Baker, Lisa H.
Peterson, Betty F. The Bunny Who Found Easter. Zolotow, Charlotte. 32p. (gr. k-3). 1983. 14.45 (0-395-27677-2); pap. 5.70 (0-395-34068-3) HM.
Peterson, Bryan. Splish Splash. Darin, Bobby & Murray, Jean. 24p. 1993. 12.95 (0-7935-1841-5, 00183010) H Leonard Pub Corp.
Peterson, Dawn. Baxter Bear & Moses Moose. Bernier, Evariste. LC 90-61408. 48p. (gr. 1-4). 1990. 12.95 (0-89272-287-8) Down East.
—Ellie Bear & the Fly-Away Fly. Rowinski, Kate. LC 93-25260. 32p. (gr. 1-4). 1993. 14.95 (0-89272-335-1) Down East.
—L. L. Bear's Island Adventure. Rowinski, Kate. LC 92-71972. 32p. (gr. 4). 1992. 14.95 (0-89272-320-3) Down East.
Peterson, George. Stuck in the Mud, Vol. 1. Peterson, George C. 208p. (Orig.). (gr. 9-12). 1988. pap. write for info. (0-9621320-0-4) G Peterson.
Peterson, Mary J. Call Me Jonathan for Short. Godreau, Cecile. 64p. (gr. 4-5). 1991. pap. 2.95 (0-8198-1463-6) St Paul Bks.
Peterson, Nancy G. Dino, the Ding Bat Cat. Richardson, Jean. LC 92-17736. 48p. (gr. 1-3). 1992. 12.95 (0-89015-869-X) Eakin-Sunbelt.
Peterson, Nancy M. Anthony Mouse Goes Swimming. Powhida, Elizabeth C. 40p. (ps-5). 1993. pap. write for info. (0-9625842-1-5, TXU538146) Kinderhook Pubs.
Peterson, Russell F. Dinosaurs & Other Prehistoric Animals. Gela, Darlene. 108p. (gr. 3-8). 1982. 9.95 (0-448-02882-4, G&D) Putnam Pub Group.
Peterson, Sherry, et al. The Mound People: An Earth Parable. ltd. ed. James, Mark. Lambert, Cindy & Kozar, Elaine, eds. 80p. (Orig.). (gr. 5-12). 1985. pap. 6.95 (0-943806-03-8) Neahtawanta Pr.
Petie, Haris. Both Ends of the Leash: Selecting & Training Your Dog. Unkelbach, Kurt. (gr. 3-7). 1968. P-H.
—Job Well Done. Alexander, Linda. (gr. 1-4). PLB 7.19 (0-8313-0002-7) Lantern.
—Tiger in the Lake. Kurkul, Edward. LC 68-11183. (gr. 1-3). 1968. write for info. (0-8313-0076-0); PLB 7.19 (0-685-42237-2) Lantern.
—Tommy's Big Problem. Chaffin, Lillie D. (ps-2). PLB 7.19 (0-8313-0016-7) Lantern.
—Trouble with Tikki. Carr, Jo. LC 71-115459. (gr. k-2). 1970. 7.19 (0-8313-0013-2) Lantern.
Petrone, Valeria. Gallop off & Go! rev. ed. Wilmer, Diane. 32p. (gr. k-2). 1989. Repr. of 1989 ed. lib. bdg. 10.50 (1-878363-01-8) Forest Hse.
Petronella, Michael. Photography Basics: An Introduction for Young People. Owens-Knudsen, Vic. LC 83-9775. 48p. (gr. 5-9). 1983. 9.95 (0-13-664995-5) P-H.
—Robotics Basics. Liptak, Karen. 48p. (gr. 3-7). 1984. 10. 95 (0-13-782087-9) P-H.
—Water Sports Basics. Wallace, Don. LC 84-22294. 48p. (gr. 3-7). 1985. 9.95 (0-13-945957-X) P-H.

—Word Processing Basics: An Introduction for Young People. Dudley, Art. LC 84-22315. 48p. (gr. 4-9). 1985. 9.95 (0-13-963513-0) P-H.

Petruccio, Steven. Dolphin's First Day. Zoehfeld, Kathleen W. LC 93-27270. 1994. 14.95 (1-56899-024-3); pap. 4.95 (1-56899-025-1) Soundprints.

—Puddles & Ponds. Wyler, Rose. 32p. (gr. k-2). 1990. lib. bdg. 11.98 (0-671-66348-8, J Messner) S&S Trade.

—Raindrops & Rainbows. Wyler, Rose. Steltenpohl, Jane, ed. 32p. (gr. k-2). 1989. (J Messner); lib. bdg. 4.95 (0-671-66350-X) S&S Trade.

—A Service Dog Goes to School: The Story of a Dog Trained to Help the Disabled. Smith, Elizabeth S. LC 88-17598. 64p. (gr. 1-4). 1988. 12.95 (0-688-07648-3); PLB 12.88 (0-688-07649-1, Morrow Jr Bks) Morrow Jr Bks.

—The Starry Sky. Wyler, Rose. Steltenpohl, Jane, ed. 32p. (gr. k-2). 1989. lib. bdg. 11.98 (0-671-66345-3, J Messner); lib. bdg. 4.95 (0-671-66349-6) S&S Trade.

—Wonderful Woods. Wyler, Rose. 32p. (gr. k-3). 1990. (J Messner); lib. bdg. 4.95 (0-671-69166-X) S&S Trade.

Petruccio, Steven J. Giants of the Deep. Pearce, Q. L. 48p. (gr. 3-7). 1993. pap. 5.95 (1-56565-042-5) Lowell Hse.

Petterson, Jay. Giants, Witches & Dragons Three-D Coloring Book. 32p. (Orig.). 1990. pap. 3.95 (0-942025-81-4) Kidsbks.

Petty, Melissa. Creative Food Box Crafts. Giles, Nancy. 64p. (ps-2). 1989. wkbk. 7.95 (0-86653-475-X, GA1076) Good Apple.

—Creative Milk Carton Crafts. Giles, Nancy. 64p. (ps-2). 1989. wkbk. 7.95 (0-86653-462-8, GA1075) Good Apple.

Pevenyi, Constance. Wild Wild West: Wildlife Habitats of Western North America. Perenyi, Constance. LC 92-46995. 32p. (gr. 1 up). 1993. text ed. 14.95 (0-912365-82-X); pap. 8.95 (0-912365-90-0) Sasquatch Bks.

Peyo. Romeo & Smurfette & Twelve Other Smurfy Stories. Delporte, pseud. LC 82-60258. 48p. (gr. 4-7). 1983. 2.95 (0-394-85618-X) Random Bks Yng Read.

Peyton, John L. Voices from the Ice. Peyton, John L. 56p. (gr. k-4). 1990. pap. 7.95 (0-939923-15-7) M & W Pub Co.

Pfeiffer, Cyndi. Creative Fabric Frames. Paul, Sally. 32p. (gr. 7-12). 1981. pap. 6.00 (0-932946-06-2) Burdett Ca.

Pfeiffer, Werner. Dante's Inferno. Tusiani, Joseph. (gr. 5 up). 1965. 9.95 (0-8392-3046-X) Astor-Honor.

Pfister, Marcus. The Christmas Star. Pfister, Marcus. James, J. Alison, tr. from GER. 32p. (gr. k-3). 1993. 16.95 (1-55858-203-7); lib. bdg. 16.88 (1-55858-204-5) North-South Bks NYC.

—Four Candles for Simon. Scheidl, Gerda M. LC 86-33199. 32p. (gr. k-3). 1987. 13.95 (1-55858-065-4) North-South Bks NYC.

—Hopper. Pfister, Marcus. LC 90-47065. 32p. (ps-k). 1991. 14.95 (1-55858-106-5) North-South Bks NYC.

—Hopper Hunts for Spring. Pfister, Marcus. Lanning, Rosemary, tr. from GER. LC 91-29671. 32p. (gr. k-3). 1992. 14.95 (1-55858-139-1); lib. bdg. 14.88 (1-55858-140-5) North-South Bks NYC.

—Hopper's Easter Surprise. Siegenthaler, Kathrin & Pfister, Marcus. Lanning, Rosemary, tr. from GER. LC 92-29117. 32p. (gr. k-3). 1993. 14.95 (1-55858-199-5); PLB 14.88 (1-55858-200-2) North-South Bks NYC.

—I See the Moon: Good-Night Poems & Lullabies. Pfister, Marcus, selected by. LC 91-10841. 32p. (ps-k). 1991. 14.95 (1-55858-119-7) North-South Bks NYC.

—My Penguin Pete Address Book. 1991. 7.95 (1-55858-126-X) North-South Bks NYC.

—My Penguin Pete Birthday Book. 1991. 7.95 (1-55858-127-8) North-South Bks NYC.

—Les Nouveaux Amis De Pit. Pfister, Marcus. (FRE.). 32p. (gr. k-3). 1992. 13.95 (3-85539-632-9) North-South Bks NYC.

—Penguin Pete. Pfister, Marcus. LC 87-1627. 32p. (gr. k-3). 1987. 13.95 (1-55858-018-2) North-South Bks NYC.

—Penguin Pete, Ahoy! Pfister, Marcus. Lanning, Rosemary, tr. from GER. LC 93-19921. 32p. (gr. k-3). 1993. 14.95 (1-55858-220-7); PLB 14.88 (1-55858-221-5) North-South Bks NYC.

—Penguin Pete & Pat. Pfister, Marcus. Bell, Anthea, tr. from GER. LC 88-25296. 32p. (gr. k-3). 1989. 14.95 (1-55858-003-4) North-South Bks NYC.

—Penguin Pete's New Friends. Pfister, Marcus. LC 87-72037. 32p. (gr. k-3). 1988. 13.95 (1-55858-025-5) North-South Bks NYC.

—Pinguin Pit. Pfister, Marcus. (GER.). 32p. (gr. k-3). 1992. 13.95 (3-314-00297-1) North-South Bks NYC.

—Pit et Pat. Pfister, Marcus. (FRE.). 32p. (gr. k-3). 1992. 13.95 (3-85539-657-4) North-South Bks NYC.

—Pit, le Petit Pingouin. Pfister, Marcus. (FRE.). 32p. (gr. k-3). 1992. 13.95 (3-314-20627-5) North-South Bks NYC.

—Pit und Pat. Pfister, Marcus. (GER.). 32p. (gr. k-3). 1992. 13.95 (3-314-00327-7) North-South Bks NYC.

—Pit's Neue Freunde. Pfister, Marcus. (GER.). 32p. (gr. k-3). 1992. 13.95 (3-85825-301-4) North-South Bks NYC.

—Rainbow Fish. Pfister, Marcus. James, J. Alison, tr. from GER. LC 91-42158. 32p. (gr. k-3). 1992. 16.95 (1-55858-009-3); PLB 16.88 (1-55858-010-7) North-South Bks NYC.

—Santa Claus & the Woodcutter. Siegenthaler, Kathrin. Crawford, Elizabeth, tr. LC 87-32203. 32p. (gr. k-3). 1988. 13.95 (1-55858-027-1) North-South Bks NYC.

—Santa Claus & the Woodcutter. Siegenthaler, Kathrin. Crawford, Elizabeth, tr. from GER. 32p. (gr. k-3). 1989. pap. 2.95 (1-55858-032-8) North-South Bks NYC.

Pfloog, Jan. Asi Son los Gatitos! (Kittens are Like That) Pfloog, Jan. Saunders, Paola B., tr. LC 93-19920. 32p. (ps-3). 1993. pap. 2.25 (0-679-84719-7) Random Bks Yng Read.

—Asi Son los Perritos! Pfloog, Jan. (SPA.). 32p. (ps-3). 1993. pap. 2.25 (0-394-85064-5) Random Bks Yng Read.

—Kittens Are Like That. Pfloog, Jan. LC 75-36469. 32p. (ps-1). 1976. 2.25 (0-394-83243-4) Random Bks Yng Read.

—Puppies Are Like That. Pfloog, Jan. LC 74-2542. 32p. (Orig.). (ps-1). 1975. pap. 2.25 (0-394-82923-9) Random Bks Yng Read.

Pflug, Kathy. Pulling Together. Watkins, Dawn L. Cooper, Carolyn, ed. 135p. (Orig.). (gr. 2-4). 1992. pap. 4.95 (0-89084-609-X) Bob Jones Univ Pr.

Phelps, Cheryl. I Like Colors. Swaby, Barbara. Rayburn, Cherie, ed. LC 93-72094. 19p. (gr. k-3). 1994. pap. text ed. 16.20 (0-944943-35-7, 91677-1) Current Inc.

Pheris, William E., IV. Falklands Fiasco. Albertson, Jon. Hooper, Anne, ed. 284p. (gr. 12). 1989. 16.95 (0-9621448-1-9) Aeolus Bks.

Philbrook, Diana. Dating: What to Do...What Not to Do. Eager, George B. 29p. (Orig.). (gr. 6-12). 1993. pap. 3. 00x (1-879224-09-7) Mailbox.

—Love, Dating & Sex: What Teens Want to Know. Eager, George B. 208p. (gr. 7-12). 1989. PLB 14.95 (0-9603752-9-5); pap. text ed. 9.95 (0-9603752-8-7) Mailbox.

—Peer Pressure: How to Handle It. Eager, George B. 29p. (Orig.). 1993. 3.00x (1-879224-10-0) Mailbox.

—Relationships: How to be a Winner! Eager, George B. (Orig.). (gr. 6-12). 1993. pap. 3.00x (1-879224-08-9) Mailbox.

—Save Sex. 2nd ed. Eager, George B. 29p. (gr. 6-12). 1993. pap. 3.00x (1-879224-97-6) Mailbox.

—Understanding Your Sex Drive. Eager, George B. 29p. (Orig.). (gr. 6-12). 1993. pap. 3.00x (1-879224-05-4) Mailbox.

—Understanding Your Sex Drive. rev. ed. Eager, George B. 96p. (gr. 6-12). 1993. pap. 5.95 (1-879224-12-7) Mailbox.

—What Is Real Love? Eager, George B. (Orig.). (gr. 6-12). 1993. pap. 3.00x (1-879224-06-2) Mailbox.

Phillipps, Julie. Mom, I Don't Want to Get My Hair Washed: And Other Poems. McBrayer, Brenda. 43p. (Orig.). (gr. 2 up). 1992. pap. 7.95 (0-910303-40-1) Writers Pub Serv.

Phillips, Bobby, photos by. Through My Picture Window. Phillips, Robert B. LC 88-90639. 256p. (gr. 9-12). 1988. 9.95 (0-9620577-1-1) R B Phillips Pub.

Phillips, Dave. Hidden Treasure Maze Book. 48p. (Orig.). (gr. 2 up) 1984. pap. 2.95 (0-486-24566-7) Dover.

Phillips, George. Not Better... Not Worse... Just Different. Scott, Sharon & Nicholas. 118p. (Orig.). (gr. k-5). 1992. pap. 7.95 (0-87425-195-8) Human Res Dev Pr.

When children are VERY young, they will usually make friends with anyone & everyone. This includes other children, adults of all ages, animals & even stuffed toys! They do not discriminate because of age, sex, race, intelligence, physical difference, or brand labels worn. Somewhere along the way, however, they learn that people are different & that society places higher value on certain physical traits. This can cause children to be unkind to one another, stare at differences, & tease unmercifully. NOT BETTER... NOT WORSE... JUST DIFFERENT is a beautifully illustrated, skills-based book that teaches children ages 5 to 10 to be kind to one another! Using his animal friends, Nicholas, the Cocker Spaniel co-author, presents specific steps for accepting all types of differences. Children will learn how to respect & accept one another regardless of learning or physical differences, race, or sex. To reinforce the learning, the last chapter contains real-life examples & practice sessions. This provides a

safe environment for children to integrate these important skills that will further their development in becoming sensitive, kind individuals. *Publisher Provided Annotation.*

—Too Smart for Trouble. Scott, Sharon. 112p. (Orig.). (gr. k-5). 1990. pap. 7.95 (0-87425-121-4) Human Res Dev Pr.

Phillips, Jane B. Big Book of Fun: Creative Learning Activities for Home & School. Haas, Carolyn B. LC 87-20325. 288p. (Orig.). (ps-7). 1987. pap. 9.95 (1-55652-020-4) Chicago Review.

—Look at Me: Creative Learning Activities for Babies & Toddlers. Haas, Carolyn B. LC 87-20288. 230p. (Orig.). 1987. pap. 9.95 (1-55652-021-2) Chicago Review.

Phillips, Jennifer. The Puzzled Pumpkin. Kaslow, Florence R. LC 91-60798. 24p. (Orig.). (gr. k-4). 1991. pap. 4.95 (0-9628321-0-3) Pumpkin Patch Pubs.

Phillips, Joe & Dunn, Ben. Day of the Destroyer. Bennie, Scott. Bell, Rob, ed. 32p. (Orig.). (gr. 12). 1990. pap. 7.00 (1-55806-101-0, 408) Iron Crown Ent Inc.

Phillips, Ted, Jr. Little David Had No Fear. Still, Judith A. (Orig.). (gr. 6-8). 1990. write for info. (1-877873-03-9); pap. write for info. Master-Player Lib.

Philpot, Graham. Yes, Dear. Jones, Diana W. LC 91-17733. 32p. (ps-6). 1992. 14.00 (0-688-11195-5) Greenwillow.

Phipps, Weston & Deyhle, Karen. A Wing & a Prayer. Hostetler, Paul. Pierce, Glen, ed. LC 92-75502. 159p. (Orig.). 1993. pap. 7.95 (0-916035-58-1) Evangel Indiana.

Picasso, Pablo. Pierre Auguste Renoir. Raboff, Ernest. LC 87-45147. 32p. (gr. 1 up). 1987. pap. 7.95 (0-06-446068-1, Trophy) HarpC Child Bks.

Piccirilli, Charles. No Need to Be Afraid...First Pelvic Exam: A Handbook for Young Women & Their Mothers. Curro, Ellen. 80p. (gr. 9-12). 1991. pap. text ed. 4.95 (0-9629417-1-9) Linking Ed Med.

Picha, Amy. McDurfee: Billy's Special Pal. Klas, Nell. 20p. (Orig.). (gr. k-3). 1991. pap. 4.00 (0-9628560-0-2) N Klas.

Pickett, Robert, photos by. Eggs. Moss, Miriam. Stefoff, Rebecca, ed. LC 91-18186. 32p. (gr. 3-5). 1991. PLB 15.93 (1-56074-005-1) Garrett Ed Corp.

Pickett, Stacy. The Story of Elijah. Colburn, Rhonda. 24p. (ps-3). 1990. pap. 3.95 (0-8249-8419-6, Ideals Child) Hambleton-Hill.

Pickney, Jerry. The Sunday Outing. Pickney, Gloria J. LC 93-25383. 1994. 14.99 (0-8037-1198-0); PLB 14. 89 (0-8037-1199-9) Dial Bks Young.

Pidgeon, Jean. Friends Afloat. Rosenbaum, Eliza. LC 92-39029. 24p. (gr. 2-3). 1992. PLB 17.96 (0-8114-3584-9) Raintree Steck-V.

Pidgeon, Jean L. Paul Bunyan & His Blue Ox. Jensen, Patricia A. LC 93-24802. 32p. (gr. k-2). 1993. PLB 11. 59 (0-8167-3162-4); pap. text ed. 2.95 (0-8167-3163-2) Troll Assocs.

Piemme, P. I. Karuk Tales. Holsinger, Rosemary. 70p. (gr. 4-8). 1992. pap. 7.95 (1-880922-00-2) Bell Bks CA.

Pienkowski, Jan. ABC Pienkowski, Jan. (ps). 1989. 2.95 (0-671-68133-8, Little Simon) S&S Trade.

—ABC Dinosaurs: And Other Prehistoric Creatures. 10p. (ps-k). 1993. 18.99 (0-525-67468-3, Lodestar Bks) Dutton Child Bks.

—Christmas. LC 84-5719. 32p. (ps-8). 1989. pap. 9.95 (0-394-82609-4) Knopf Bks Yng Read.

—Christmas. miniature ed. 32p. 1991. 6.95 (0-679-81442-6) Knopf Bks Yng Read.

—Colors. Pienkowski, Jan. 14p. (ps). 1989. 2.95 (0-671-68134-6, Little Simon) S&S Trade.

—Easter. 32p. 1992. 6.99 (0-679-82670-X) Knopf Bks Yng Read.

—Faces. Pienkowski, Jan. 24p. (ps-k). 1991. pap. 2.95 (0-671-72846-6, Little Simon) S&S Trade.

—Food. Pienkowski, Jan. 24p. (ps-k). 1991. pap. 2.95 (0-671-72845-8, Little Simon) S&S Trade.

—A Foot in the Grave. Aiken, Joan. 128p. (gr. 5 up). 1992. 15.95 (0-670-84169-2) Viking Child Bks.

—Jan Pienkowski Fairy Tale Library, 4 bks. Grimm, Jacob, et al. Walser, David, tr. 48p. 1992. Slipcase set incls. miniature eds. of Cinderella, Puss-in-Boots, The Sleeping Beauty, & Snow White. 15.00 (0-679-82270-4) Knopf Bks Yng Read.

—One Two Three. Pienkowski, Jan. 14p. (ps). 1989. 2.95 (0-671-68136-2) S&S Trade.

—Past Eight O'Clock. Aiken, Joan. 128p. (gr. 2-6). 1991. pap. 4.95 (0-14-032355-4, Puffin) Puffin Bks.

—Pets. Pienkowski, Jan. 24p. (ps). 1992. pap. 2.95 (0-671-74518-2, Little Simon) S&S Trade.

—Robot. Pienkowski, Jan. 12p. (gr. 1 up). 1981. 9.95 (0-440-07459-2) Delacorte.

—Sally Go Round the Moon & Other Revels Songs & Singing Games for Young Children. Langstaff, Nancy & Langstaff, John. LC 86-90535. 127p. (ps-1). 1986. pap. 12.95 (0-9618334-0-8) Revels Pubns.

—Shapes. Pienkowski, Jan. (ps). 1989. 2.95 (0-671-68135-4, Little Simon) S&S Trade.

—Sizes. Pienkowski, Jan. 24p. (ps-k). 1991. pap. 2.95 (0-671-72844-X, Little Simon) S&S Trade.

—Stop Go. Pienkowski, Jan. 24p. (ps). 1992. pap. 2.95 (0-671-74519-0, Little Simon) S&S Trade.

—Time. Pienkowski, Jan. 24p. (ps-k). 1991. pap. 2.95 (0-671-72847-4, Little Simon) S&S Trade.

—Wheels. Pienkowski, Jan. 24p. (ps). 1992. pap. 2.95 (0-671-74517-4, Little Simon) S&S Trade.

—Yes No. Pienkowski, Jan. 24p. (ps). 1992. pap. 2.95 (0-671-74520-4, Little Simon) S&S Trade.

—Zoo. Pienkowski, Jan. 32p. (ps-1). 1985. 13.95 (0-434-95652-X, Pub. by W Heinemann Ltd) Trafalgar.

Piequet, Miriam. Yesterday in the Nineteen Twenties. Naylor, Bob. LC 83-61988. 62p. (Orig.). 1983. pap. 6.95 (0-914275-00-3) Anyone Can Read Bks.

Pierard, John. The Dinosaur That Followed Me Home. Coville, Bruce. 160p. (Orig.). (gr. 3-6). 1990. pap. 2.99 (0-671-64750-4, Minstrel Bks) PB.

—My Babysitter Bites Again. Hodgman, Ann. Ashby, Ruth, ed. 144p. (Orig.). (gr. 3-6). 1993. pap. 2.99 (0-671-79378-0, Minstrel Bks) PB.

—My Babysitter Has Fangs. Hodgeman, Ann. Ashby, Ruth, ed. 128p. (Orig.). 1992. pap. 2.99 (0-671-75868-3, Minstrel Bks) PB.

—My Babysitter Is a Vampire. Hodgman, Ann. Ashby, Ruth, ed. (Orig.). 1991. pap. 2.99 (0-671-64751-2, Minstrel Bks) PB.

—My Teacher Glows in the Dark. Coville, Bruce. MacDonald, Patricia, ed. 144p. (Orig.). 1991. pap. 3.50 (0-671-72709-5, Minstrel Bks) PB.

—There's a Bat Wing in My Lunchbox. Hodgman, Ann. 96p. 1988. pap. 2.95 (0-380-75426-6, Camelot) Avon.

Pierard, John & Nino, Alex. Sail with Pirates. Gasperini, Jim. 144p. (gr. 4 up). 1984. pap. 2.50 (0-553-26497-4) Bantam.

Pierce, Brenda H. Creative Art Picture Starters: General Subjects - Level II. Pierce, Brenda H. 32p. (gr. 4-6). 1988. tchr's. ed. 3.95 (0-922694-03-6) Moons Creat Prods.

Pierpoint, Marsha W. A Turtle on Her Toe. Glines, Edna L. LC 83-17870. 66p. (ps up). 1984. 9.95 (0-9612160-0-X) Tumbleweed Pub Co.

Pierre, Philippe, photos by. France. Tolan, Sally & Sherwood, Rhoda I., eds. LC 88-42889. 64p. (gr. 5-6). 1990. PLB 19.93 (1-55532-212-3) Gareth Stevens Inc.

Piette, Nadine. Mi Primer ABC. (SPA.). 60p. (ps-k). 1993. Repr. of 1991 ed. 3.95 (970-607-186-5) CKG Pubs.

—Mis Primeras Palabras En Ingles. (SPA.). 60p. (ps-k). 1993. Repr. of 1991 ed. 3.95 (970-607-187-3) CKG Pubs.

—Mis Primeros Conocimentos. (SPA.). 60p. (ps-k). 1993. Repr. of 1993 ed. 3.95 (970-607-188-1) CKG Pubs.

Pileggi, Steve. Move with Me One Two Three. Schade, Charlene. Ziebarth, Pat, ed. Senter, Sheri, intro. by. 58p. (Orig.). (ps-1). 1988. Includes audio cassette. 16.90 (0-924860-00-6) Exer Fun Pub.

Pilgrim, Millie W. Jason's Adventures with the Tuskegee Airmen. rev. ed. Pilgrim, Millie W. 54p. (gr. 3 up). 1992. pap. text ed. 8.00 (0-685-60294-X, 133-720); tchr's. guide 2.00 (0-685-60295-8) H&M Ent.

Pilkey, Dav. Don't Pop Your Cork on Mondays! The Children's Anti-Stress Book. Moser, Adolph J. LC 88-13912. 48p. (gr. k up). 1988. PLB 14.95 (0-933849-18-4) Landmark Edns.

—The Dumb Bunnies. Denim, Sue. LC 93-2255. 32p. (ps-3). 1994. 12.95 (0-590-47708-0, Blue Sky Press) Scholastic Inc.

—The Place Where Nobody Stopped. Segal, Jerry. LC 90-43016. 160p. (gr. 6-8). 1991. 14.95 (0-531-05897-2); PLB 14.99 (0-531-08497-3) Orchard Bks Watts.

—Twas the Night Before Thanksgiving. Pilkey, Dav. LC 89-48941. 32p. (ps-2). 1990. 14.95 (0-531-05905-7); PLB 14.99 (0-531-08505-8) Orchard Bks Watts.

—World War Won. Pilkey, Dav. LC 87-2711. 32p. (gr. 1 up). 1987. PLB 14.95 (0-933849-22-2) Landmark Edns.

Pilkey, Dav, photos by. Julius. Johnson, Angela. LC 92-24175. 32p. (ps-1). 1993. 14.95 (0-531-05465-9); PLB 14.99 (0-531-08615-1) Orchard Bks Watts.

Pilkington, Brian. Flumbra: An Icelandic Folktale. Helgadottir, Gudrun. Sanders, Christopher, tr. from ICE. LC 86-6173. 32p. (gr. 1-6). 1986. lib. bdg. 18.95 (0-87614-243-9) Carolrhoda Bks.

—Grandpa Claus. Pilkington, Brian. 28p. (ps-3). 1990. PLB 19.95 (0-87614-436-9) Carolrhoda Bks.

Pillar, Marjorie. Join the Band! Pillar, Marjorie. LC 90-23261. 32p. (gr. 1-3). 1992. 15.00 (0-06-021834-7); PLB 14.89 (0-06-021829-0) HarpC Child Bks.

—Squirrel Watching. Schlein, Miriam. LC 91-6481. 64p. (gr. 2-6). 1992. 15.00 (0-06-022753-2); PLB 14.89 (0-06-022754-0) HarpC Child Bks.

Pilorget, Bruno. Livre de la Jungle. Kipling, Rudyard. (FRE.). 254p. (gr. 5-10). 1987. pap. 9.95 (2-07-033456-2) Schoenhof.

Pilot Productions Staff, photos by. A Visit to the Bakery. Ziegler, Sandra. LC 86-32647. 32p. (ps-3). 1987. PLB 15.00 (0-516-01495-1) Childrens.

Pilot Productions Staff, et al, photos by. A Visit to the Zoo. Tester, Sylvia R. LC 84-12697. 32p. (ps-3). 1987. PLB 15.00 (0-516-01494-3) Childrens.

Pinckney, Jerry. The Tales of Uncle Remus: The Adventures of Brer Rabbit, Vol. I. Lester, Julius. LC 85-20449. (ps up). 1987. 16.95 (0-8037-0271-X); PLB 16.89 (0-8037-0272-8) Dial Bks Young.

Pincus, Harriet. Tell Me a Mitzi. Segal, Lore. LC 69-14980. 40p. (ps-3). 1982. 17.00 (0-374-37392-2) FS&G.

—The Wedding Procession of the Rag Doll & the Broom Handle & Who Was in It. Sandburg, Carl. LC 67-10211. 32p. (ps-3). 1978. pap. 3.95 (0-15-695487-7, Voyager Bks) HarBrace.

Pinder, Polly. Polly Pinder's Chocolate Cookbook. Pinder, Polly. Search Studios Staff, photos by. 144p. (gr. 7 up). 1988. 24.95 (0-85532-603-4, Pub. by Search Pr UK) Pathway Bk Serv.

Pini, Wendy & Schultz, Carolyn. Elfquest: The Official Roleplaying Game. 2nd ed. Perrin, Steve. Chodak, Yurek, ed. Pini, Richard, intro. by. 192p. (gr. 9 up). 1989. pap. 19.95 (0-933635-54-0, 2605) Chaosium.

Pinkerton, Susan. Me & My World. Cohen, Lynn. 64p. 1986. 6.95x (0-912107-46-4, Dist. by Good Apple) Monday Morning Bks.

Pinkey, Jerry. The Patchwork Quilt. Flournoy, Valerie. LC 84-1711. (gr. 4-8). 1985. 14.00 (0-8037-0097-0); PLB 13.89 (0-8037-0098-9) Dial Bks Young.

—Turtle in July. Singer, Marilyn. LC 93-14430. 32p. (gr. 3-7). 1994. pap. 4.95 (0-689-71805-5, Aladdin) Macmillan Child Grp.

Pinkney, Brian. Alvin Ailey. Davis Pinkney, Andrea. LC 92-54865. 32p. (gr. 1-4). 1993. 13.95 (1-56282-413-9); PLB 13.89 (1-56282-414-7) Hyprn Child.

—The Ballad of Belle Dorcas. Hooks, William H. LC 89-2715. 48p. (gr. 2-7). 1990. 13.95 (0-394-84645-1); lib. bdg. 14.99 (0-394-94645-6) Knopf Bks Yng Read.

—Cut from the Same Cloth. San Souci, Robert. 144p. (gr. 5 up). 1993. 16.95 (0-399-21987-0, Philomel Bks) Putnam Pub Group.

—The Dark-Thirty: Southern Tales of the Supernatural. McKissack, Patricia. LC 92-3021. 128p. (gr. 3-7). 1992. 15.00 (0-679-81863-4); PLB 15.99 (0-679-91863-9) Knopf Bks Yng Read.

—Day of Delight: A Jewish Sabbath in Ethiopia. Schur, Maxine R. LC 93-31451. 1994. write for info. (0-8037-1413-0); PLB write for info. (0-8037-1414-9) Dial Bks Young.

—Dear Benjamin Banneker. Pinkney, Andrea D. LC 93-31162. 1994. write for info. (0-15-200417-3, Gulliver Bks) HarBrace.

—The Dream Keeper: And Other Poems. Hughes, Langston. 96p. 1994. 12.00 (0-679-84421-X); PLB 12.99 (0-679-94421-4) Knopf Bks Yng Read.

—The Elephant's Wrestling Match. Sierra, Judy. 32p. (gr. k-3). 1992. 14.00 (0-525-67366-0, Lodestar Bks) Dutton Child Bks.

—Harriet Tubman. Carter, Polly. Brook, Bonnie, ed. 32p. (gr. k-2). 1990. 6.95 (0-671-69115-5); PLB 10.98 (0-671-69109-0) Silver Pr.

—Lost Zoo. Cat, Christopher & Cullen, Countee. 96p. (gr. 3-5). 1991. PLB 14.98 (0-382-24255-6); 12.95 (0-382-24256-4) Silver Burdett Pr.

—Seven Candles for Kwanzaa. Pinkney, Andrea D. LC 92-3698. 32p. (gr. k up). 1993. 14.99 (0-8037-1292-8); lib. bdg. 14.89 (0-8037-1293-6) Dial Bks Young.

—Sukey & the Mermaid. San Souci, Robert D. LC 90-24559. 32p. (gr. k-3). 1992. RSBE 14.95 (0-02-778141-0, Four Winds) Macmillan Child Grp.

—A Time to Talk: Poems of Friendship. Livingston, Myra C. LC 91-42234. 128p. (gr. 7 up). 1992. SBE 12.95 (0-689-50558-2, M K McElderry) Macmillan Child Grp.

—Wave in Her Pocket: Stories from Trinidad. Joseph, Lynn. Stevenson, Dinah, ed. 64p. (gr. 3-7). 1991. 13.95 (0-395-54432-7, Clarion Bks) HM.

—Where Does the Trail Lead? Albert, Burton. LC 90-21450. 40p. (ps-3). 1993. pap. 5.95 (0-671-79617-8, S&S BFYR) S&S Trade.

Pinkney, J. Drylongso. Hamilton, V. 1992. write for info. (0-15-224241-4, HB Juv Bks) HarBrace.

Pinkney, J. Brian. The Boy & the Ghost. San Souci, Robert. (ps-3). 1989. pap. 13.95 jacketed (0-671-67176-6, S&S BFYR) S&S Trade.

—Feliz Cumpleanos, Martin Luther King: Happy Birthday, Martin Luther King. Marzollo, Jean. Romo, Alberto, tr. from English. (SPA.). (gr. 3-7). 1994. pap. 4.95 (0-590-47507-X) Scholastic Inc.

—Happy Birthday, Martin Luther King. Marzollo, Jean. LC 91-42137. 32p. (gr. 3-7). 1993. 14.95 (0-590-44065-9) Scholastic Inc.

Pinkney, Jeny. Song of the Trees. Taylor, Mildred. LC 74-18598. 56p. (gr. 2-5). 1975. 13.50 (0-8037-5452-3); PLB 11.89 (0-8037-5453-1) Dial Bks Young.

Pinkney, Jerry. The Adventures of Spider: West African Folk Tales. Arkhurst, Joyce C., retold by. LC 92-444. 1992. 6.95 (0-316-05107-1) Little.

—Back Home. Pinkney, Gloria J. LC 91-22610. 40p. (gr. k-4). 1992. 15.00 (0-8037-1168-9); PLB 14.89 (0-8037-1169-7) Dial Bks Young.

—Childtimes: A Three-Generation Memoir. Greenfield, Eloise & Little, Lessie J. LC 77-26581. 160p. (gr. 5 up). 1979. (Crowell Jr Bks); PLB 13.89 (0-690-03875-5, Crowell Jr Bks) HarpC Child Bks.

—Count on Your Fingers African Style. Zaslavsky, Claudia. LC 77-26586. 32p. (gr. k-3). 1980. (Crowell Jr Bks); (Crowell Jr Bks) HarpC Child Bks.

—David's Songs: His Psalms & Their Story. Eisler, Colin, compiled by. Eisler, Bolin, intro. by. Np-25459. 64p. 1992. 17.00 (0-8037-1058-5); PLB 16.89 (0-8037-1059-3) Dial Bks Young.

—Fever Dream. Yolen, Jane. LC 93-10070. (gr. 4 up). Date not set. 14.00 (0-06-021482-1); PLB 13.89 (0-06-021483-X) Harpc Child Bks.

—Further Tales of Uncle Remus: The Misadventures of Brer Rabbit, Brer Fox, Brer Wolf, the Doodang, & All the Other Creatures. Lester, Julius & Fogelman, Phyllis J., eds. LC 88-20223. 160p. (ps up). 1990. 15.00 (0-8037-0610-3); PLB 14.89 (0-8037-0611-1) Dial Bks Young.

—The Green Lion of Zion Street. Fields, Julia. LC 87-15519. 32p. (gr. k-4). 1988. SBE 14.95 (0-689-50414-4, M K McElderry) Macmillan Child Grp.

—The Green Lion of Zion Street. Fields, Julia. LC 92-24571. 32p. (gr. k-3). 1993. pap. 4.95 (0-689-71693-1, Aladdin) Macmillan Child Grp.

—Half a Moon & One Whole Star. Dragonwagon, Crescent. LC 85-13818. 32p. (gr. k-3). 1986. RSBE 14.95 (0-02-733120-2, Macmillan Child Bk) Macmillan Child Grp.

—Half a Moon & One Whole Star. Dragonwagon, Crescent. LC 89-18643. 32p. (gr. k-3). 1990. pap. 3.95 (0-689-71415-7, Aladdin) Macmillan Child Grp.

—Home Place. Dragonwagon, Crescent. LC 89-32911. 40p. (gr. k-3). 1990. SBE 14.95 (0-02-733190-3, Macmillan Child Bk) Macmillan Child Grp.

—Home Place. Dragonwagon, Crescent. LC 92-46366. 40p. (gr. k-3). 1993. pap. 4.95 (0-689-71758-X, Aladdin) Macmillan Child Grp.

—I Want to Be. Moss, Thylias. LC 92-28965. 32p. (ps-3). 1993. 14.99 (0-8037-1286-3); PLB 14.89 (0-8037-1287-1) Dial Bks Young.

—In for Winter, Out for Spring. Adoff, Arnold. Ingber, Bonnie V., ed. 43p. (ps-3). 1991. 14.95 (0-15-238637-8) HarBrace.

—The Last Tales of Uncle Remus. Lester, Julius, as told by. LC 93-7531. (ps-4). 1994. 16.99 (0-8037-1303-7); PLB 16.89 (0-8037-1304-5) Dial Bks Young.

—Man Who Kept His Heart in a Bucket. Levitin, Sonia. (ps-3). 1991. 14.95 (0-8037-1029-1); PLB 14.89 (0-8037-1030-5) Dial Bks Young.

—Mary McLeod Bethune. Greenfield, Eloise. LC 76-11522. 40p. (gr. 2-5). 1977. PLB 14.89 (0-690-01129-6, Crowell Jr Bks) HarpC Child Bks.

—Mirandy & Brother Wind. McKissack, Patricia C. LC 87-349. 32p. (ps-3). 1988. 15.00 (0-394-88765-4); lib. bdg. 15.99 (0-394-98765-9) Knopf Bks Yng Read.

—Mirandy & Brother Wind. McKissack, Patricia C. Tyson, Cicely, narrated by. LC 87-349. 32p. (ps up). 1992. incl. cassette 17.00 (0-679-82668-8) Knopf Bks Yng Read.

—More Tales of Uncle Remus: Further Adventures of Brer Rabbit, His Friends, Enemies & Others. Lester, Julius, as told by. LC 86-32890. 160p. (ps up). 1988. 15.95 (0-8037-0419-4); PLB 15.89 (0-8037-0420-8) Dial Bks Young.

—New Shoes for Silvia. Hurwitz, Johanna. LC 92-40868. 32p. (ps up). 1993. 15.00 (0-688-05286-X); PLB 14.93 (0-688-05287-8) Morrow Jr Bks.

—Pretend You're a Cat. Marzollo, Jean. Fogelman, Phyllis J., ed. LC 89-34546. 32p. (ps-3). 1990. PLB 12.89 (0-8037-0774-6) Dial Bks Young.

—Rabbit Makes a Monkey of Lion. Aardema, Verna. LC 86-11523. 32p. (ps-3). 1989. 11.95 (0-8037-0297-3); PLB 11.89 (0-8037-0298-1) Dial Bks Young.

—Rabbit Makes a Monkey of Lion: A Swahili Tale. Aardema, Verna, retold by. 32p. (ps-3). 1993. pap. 4.99 (0-14-054593-X) Puffin Bks.

—Roll of Thunder, Hear My Cry. Taylor, Mildred D. LC 76-2287. (gr. 6 up). 1976. 15.00 (0-8037-7473-7) Dial Bks Young.

—The Talking Eggs. San Souci, Robert D. (ps-3). 1989. 15.00 (0-8037-0619-7) Dial Bks Young.

—Turtle in July. Singer, Marilyn. LC 89-2745. 32p. (gr. k-3). 1989. RSBE 14.95 (0-02-782881-6, Macmillan Child Bk) Macmillan Child Grp.

—Wild Wild Sunflower Child Anna. Carlstrom, Nancy W. LC 86-18226. 32p. (ps-1). 1987. RSBE 14.95 (0-02-717360-7, Macmillan Child Bk) Macmillan Child Grp.

—Wild Wild Sunflower Child Anna. Carlstrom, Nancy W. LC 90-40679. 32p. (ps-1). 1991. pap. 4.95 (0-689-71445-9, Aladdin) Macmillan Child Grp.

Pinkney, Jerry, photos by. The Planet of Junior Brown. Hamilton, Virginia. LC 85-16651. 224p. (gr. 5-9). 1986. pap. 3.95 (0-02-043540-1, Collier Young Ad) Macmillan Child Grp.

Pinkney, Nathaniel. Conversation Games: Vol. I-People Times. 87p. (Orig.). (gr. k-6). 1978. pap. 15.00 (0-939632-17-9) ILM.

—Conversation Games: Vol. II-Experiences. 87p. (Orig.). (gr. k-6). 1978. pap. 15.00 (0-939632-20-9) ILM.

Pinkwater, D. Manus. Fat Men from Space. Pinkwater, D. Manus. 64p. (gr. 4-6). 1980. pap. 3.25 (0-440-44542-6, YB) Dell.

Pinkwater, Daniel. Aunt Lulu. Pinkwater, Daniel. LC 88-1736. 32p. (gr. k-3). 1988. RSBE 12.95 (0-02-774661-5, Macmillan Child Bk) Macmillan Child Grp.

—Aunt Lulu. Pinkwater, Daniel. LC 90-39981. 32p. (gr. k-3). 1991. pap. 3.95 (0-689-71413-0, Aladdin) Macmillan Child Grp.

—Author's Day. Pinkwater, Daniel. LC 92-18154. 32p. (gr. k-3). 1993. SBE 13.95 (0-02-774642-9, Macmillan Child Bk) Macmillan Child Grp.

—Doodle Flute. Pinkwater, Daniel. LC 90-6622. 32p. (gr. k-3). 1991. RSBE 13.95 (0-02-774635-6, Macmillan Child Bk) Macmillan Child Grp.

—Guys from Space. Pinkwater, Daniel. LC 88-13485. 32p. (gr. k-3). 1989. RSBE 13.95 (0-02-774672-0, Macmillan Child Bk) Macmillan Child Grp.

—Guys from Space. Pinkwater, Daniel. LC 91-20100. 32p. (gr. k-3). 1992. pap. 3.95 (0-689-71590-0, Aladdin) Macmillan Child Grp.

—I Was a Second Grade Werewolf. Pinkwater, Daniel. (gr. 1-3). 1986. incl. cassette 19.95 (0-87499-010-6); pap. 12.95 incl. cassette (0-87499-008-4); incl. cassette, 4 paperbacks guide 27.95 (0-87499-009-2) Live Oak Media.

—I Was a Second Grade Werewolf. Pinkwater, Daniel. LC 82-17715. 32p. (ps-2). 1985. pap. 3.95 (0-525-44194-8, DCB) Dutton Child Bks.

—Spaceburger: A Kevin Spoon & Mason Mintz Story. Pinkwater, Daniel. LC 93-6658. 32p. (gr. k-3). 1993. RSBE 13.95 (0-02-774643-7, Macmillan Child Bk) Macmillan Child Grp.

—Tooth-Gnasher Superflash. Pinkwater, Daniel. LC 89-18207. 32p. (gr. k-3). 1990. Repr. of 1981 ed. RSBE 13.95 (0-02-774655-0, Macmillan Child Bk) Macmillan Child Grp.

—Wempires. Pinkwater, Daniel. LC 90-46925. 32p. (gr. k-3). 1991. RSBE 13.95 (0-02-774411-6, Macmillan Child Bk) Macmillan Child Grp.

Pinkwater, Daniel M. Blue Moose, & Return of the Moose. Pinkwater, Daniel M. LC 93-22614. 112p. (Orig.). (gr. 2-7). 1993. pap. 3.99 (0-679-84717-0) Random Bks Yng Read.

Pinto, Ralph. The Knee-High Man & Other Tales. Lester, Julius. LC 72-181785. 32p. (ps-3). 1985. 12.95 (0-8037-4593-1) Dial Bks Young.

—The Knee-High Man & Other Tales. Lester, Julius. LC 72-181785. 32p. (ps-3). 1985. pap. 3.95 (0-8037-0234-5, 0383-120, Dial Pied Piper) Puffin Bks.

Pio. Be Careful, Little Antelope. Clement, Claude. Jensen, Patricia, adapted by. LC 93-2950. 1993. write for info. (0-89577-504-2, Readers Digest Kids) RD Assn.

—Worried Little Lamb. Guidoux, Valerie. Jensen, Patricia, adapted by. LC 93-27048. 1994. write for info. (0-89577-563-8, Readers Digest Kids) RD Assn.

Piper, Molly & Ekberg, Marion. Huff & Puff Around the World: A Totline Teaching Tale. Warren, Jean. Cubley, Kathleen, LC 93-5490. 32p. (Orig.). (ps-2). 1994. 12.95 (0-911019-81-2); pap. 5.95 (0-911019-80-4) Warren Pub Hse.

—Huff & Puff Go to School. Warren, Jean. 1993. 12.95; pap. 5.95 (0-911019-94-4) Warren Pub Hse.

—Huff & Puff on Thanksgiving: A Totline Teaching Tale. Warren, Jean. Cubley, Kathleen, ed. LC 93-13545. 32p. (Orig.). (ps-2). 1993. 12.95 (0-911019-71-5); pap. 5.95 (0-911019-70-7) Warren Pub Hse.

—Huff & Puff's April Showers: A Totline Teaching Tale. Warren, Jean. Cubley, Kathleen, ed. LC 93-5489. 32p. (Orig.). (ps-2). 1994. 12.95 (0-911019-79-0); pap. 5.95 (0-911019-78-2) Warren Pub Hse.

Pistolesi, Roseanna. Let's Celebrate Christmas: A Book of Drawing Fun. Pistolesi, Roseanna. LC 87-61376. 32p. (gr. 2-6). 1988. PLB 10.65 (0-8167-1133-X); pap. text ed. 1.95 (0-8167-1134-8) Troll Assocs.

—Let's Celebrate Halloween: A Book of Drawing Fun. Pistolesi, Roseanna. LC 87-50426. 32p. (gr. 2-6). 1988. PLB 10.65 (0-8167-1002-3); pap. text ed. 1.95 (0-8167-1003-1) Troll Assocs.

—A Picture Book of Baby Animals. Mabie, Grace. LC 92-26264. 24p. (gr. 1-4). 1992. PLB 9.59 (0-8167-2468-7); pap. text ed. 2.50 (0-8167-2469-5) Troll Assocs.

—A Picture Book of Birds. Gise, Joanne. LC 89-37328. 24p. (gr. 1-4). 1990. PLB 9.59 (0-8167-1898-9); pap. text ed. 2.50 (0-8167-1899-7) Troll Assocs.

—A Picture Book of Butterflies & Moths. Mattern, Joanne. LC 92-5225. 24p. (gr. 1-4). 1992. PLB 9.59 (0-8167-2796-1); pap. 2.50 (0-8167-2797-X) Troll Assocs.

—Picture Book of Cats. Mattern, Joanne. LC 90-42548. 24p. (gr. 1-4). 1991. PLB 9.59 (0-8167-2146-7); pap. 2.50 (0-8167-2147-5) Troll Assocs.

—A Picture Book of Desert Animals. Gise, Joanne. LC 90-40436. 24p. (gr. 1-4). 1991. lib. bdg. 9.59 (0-8167-2148-3); pap. text ed. 2.50 (0-8167-2149-1) Troll Assocs.

—A Picture Book of Dogs. Gise, Joanne. LC 89-39430. 24p. (gr. 1-4). 1990. PLB 9.59 (0-8167-1902-0); pap. text ed. 2.50 (0-8167-1903-9) Troll Assocs.

—A Picture Book of Flowers. Grace, Theresa. LC 92-8716. 24p. (gr. 1-4). 1992. PLB 9.59 (0-8167-2836-4); pap. text ed. 2.50 (0-8167-2837-2) Troll Assocs.

—A Picture Book of Forest Animals. Gise, Joanne. LC 89-37329. 24p. (gr. 1-4). 1990. lib. bdg. 9.59 (0-8167-1904-7); pap. text ed. 2.50 (0-8167-1905-5) Troll Assocs.

—A Picture Book of Horses. Gise, Joanne. LC 90-40437. 24p. (gr. 1-4). 1991. lib. bdg. 9.59 (0-8167-2152-1); pap. text ed. 2.50 (0-8167-2153-X) Troll Assocs.

—A Picture Book of Swamp & Marsh Animals. Grace, Theresa. LC 91-16034. 24p. (gr. 1-4). 1992. lib. bdg. 9.59 (0-8167-2434-2); pap. text ed. 2.50 (0-8167-2435-0) Troll Assocs.

—A Picture Book of Underwater Life. Grace, Theresa. LC 89-37330. 24p. (gr. 1-4). 1990. lib. bdg. 9.59 (0-8167-1906-3); pap. text ed. 2.50 (0-8167-1907-1) Troll Assocs.

—A Picture Book of Water Birds. Mabie, Grace. LC 91-34129. 24p. (gr. 1-4). 1992. PLB 9.59 (0-8167-2436-9); pap. text ed. 2.50 (0-8167-2437-7) Troll Assocs.

—A Picture Book of Wild Animals. Gise, Joanne. LC 89-37334. 24p. (gr. 1-4). 1990. lib. bdg. 9.59 (0-8167-1908-X); pap. text ed. 2.50 (0-8167-1909-8) Troll Assocs.

—A Picture Book of Wild Cats. Scott, Mary. LC 91-16500. 24p. (gr. 1-4). 1992. PLB 9.59 (0-8167-2430-X); pap. 2.50 (0-8167-2431-8) Troll Assocs.

Pistone, Nancy. Friends of God. Jones, Sally L. 10p. (ps-3). 1993. text ed. 10.99 (0-7847-0047-8, 24-03657) Standard Pub.

—In the Beginning. Jones, Sally L. 10p. (ps-3). 1993. text ed. 10.99 (0-7847-0046-X, 24-03656) Standard Pub.

—Jesus & the Children. Tester, Sylvia. 12p. (ps). 1992. deluxe ed. 4.99 (0-87403-993-2, 24-03113) Standard Pub.

Pitkanen, Matti A. The Children of China. Harkonen, Reijo. 40p. (gr. 3-6). 1990. PLB 19.95 (0-87614-394-X) Carolrhoda Bks.

—The Children of Nepal. Harkonen, Reijo. 48p. (gr. 3-6). 1990. PLB 19.95 (0-87614-395-8) Carolrhoda Bks.

Pitkanen, Matti A., photos by. The Children of Egypt. Harkonen, Reijo. 40p. (gr. 3-6). 1991. PLB 19.95 (0-87614-396-6) Carolrhoda Bks.

—The Grandchildren of the Incas. Harkonen, Reijo. 40p. (gr. 3-6). 1991. PLB 19.95 (0-87614-397-4) Carolrhoda Bks.

Pittenger, Shari. Listen, Color & Learn: A Coloring Book for Family Devotions, Vol. I, Psalm 1-30. Pittenger, Shari. Harris, Gregg, intro. by. 35p. (Orig.). (ps-6). 1989. pap. text ed. 4.95 (0-923463-49-6) Noble Pub Assocs.

Pittman, Dockery. Little Airplane. Durham, Jamie A. 32p. (ps). 1989. write for info. Magpie AL.

Pittman, Helena C. A Dinosaur for Gerald. Pittman, Helena C. 32p. (gr. k-3). 1990. PLB 18.95 (0-87614-431-8) Carolrhoda Bks.

—The Gift of the Willows. Pittman, Helena C. 32p. (gr. k-4). 1988. 18.95 (0-87614-354-0) Carolrhoda Bks.

—Miss Hindy's Cats. Pittman, Helena C. LC 89-22214. 32p. (ps-3). 1990. pap. 18.95 (0-87614-368-0) Carolrhoda Bks.

—Where Will You Swim Tonight? Limmer, Milly J. Fay, Ann, ed. LC 90-38938. 32p. (ps-1). 1991. 14.95 (0-8075-8949-7) A Whitman.

Pittman, Jackie. Kids' Cuisine. Goldstein, Helen H. Bolch, Judy, ed. LC 83-60306. 64p. (Orig.). (gr. k-7). 1983. pap. 19.95 (0-935400-09-5) News & Observer.

Pitz, Henry & Sousa, Joseph. A Patriot Lad of Old Cape Cod. Carter, Russell G. LC 75-5092. 224p. (gr. 6-8). 1975. 4.95 (0-88492-007-0); pap. 1.95 (0-88492-008-9) W S Sullwold.

Pizer, Abigail. It's a Perfect Day. Pizer, Abigail. LC 89-37937. 32p. (ps-3). 1992. pap. 4.95 (0-06-443302-1, Trophy) HarpC Child Bks.

—The Unicorn of the West: El Unicornio del Oeste. Ada, Alma F. Zubizarreta, Rosa, tr. LC 92-7425. (ENG & SPA.). 40p. (gr. 1-3). 1994. English ed. SBE 14.95 (0-689-31778-6, Atheneum Child Bk); Spanish ed. SBE 14.95 (0-689-31916-9, Atheneum Child Bk) Macmillan Child Grp.

Place, Francois. Living in Ancient Rome. Bombarde, Odile & Moatti, Claude. Matthews, Sarah, tr. from FRE. LC 87-37113. 38p. (gr. k-5). 1988. 4.95 (0-944589-08-1, 081) Young Discovery Lib.

—Living in Ancient Rome. Bombarde, Odile & Moatti, Claude. 40p. (gr. k-5). 1993. PLB 9.95 (1-56674-060-6, HTS Bks) Forest Hse.

Plank, George. The Hedgehog. Doolittle, Hilda. Schaffner, Perdita, intro. by. LC 88-3927. 96p. 1988. 12.95 (0-8112-1069-3) New Directions.

Plant, Andrew. Drawing Is Easy. Plant, Andrew. LC 93-16116. 1994. pap. write for info. (0-383-03692-5) SRA Schl Grp.

Plasencia, Peter P. Photography: A Manual for Shutterbugs. Kohn, Eugene. Noa, Pedro A., photos by. (gr. 3-7). 1965. pap. 1.25 (0-685-03891-2) P-H.

Pleasance, Geoff. How It Works. Parker, Steve. 48p. (gr. 3-6). 1992. pap. 2.95 (1-56680-010-2) Mad Hatter Pub.

Plecas, Jennifer. I Found Mouse. Greenwood, Pamela D. LC 93-46427. (ps). 1994. write for info. (0-395-64548-5, Clarion Bks) HM.

—The Outside Dog. Pomerantz, Charlotte. LC 91-6351. 64p. (gr. k-3). 1993. 14.00 (0-06-024782-7); PLB 13.89 (0-06-024783-5) HarpC Child Bks.

—Rattlebone Rock. Andrews, Sylvia. LC 93-4426. Date not set. 15.00 (0-06-023451-2); PLB 14.89 (0-06-023452-0) HarpC.

Plesissner, Ogden M. & Nisbet, Richard C. Atlantic Salmon Fishing. Phair, Charles. Hunt, Richard C., intro. by. 193p. (gr. 10 up). 1993. Repr. of 1937 ed. 50.00 (1-56416-049-1) Derrydale Pr.

Plewes, Andrew. Bee Hives & Bat Caves: Amazing Animal Homes. Owl Magazine Editors. 48p. (gr. 1 up). 1992. pap. 6.95 (0-920775-46-2, Pub. by Greey dePencier CN) Firefly Bks Ltd.

Pliskin, Jacqueline J. The Bible Story Activity Book. Pliskin, Jacqueline J. 96p. (gr. 1-4). 1990. pap. 5.95 (0-944007-67-8) Shapolsky Pubs.

Plomer, Martin & Shone, Karl. Flag. Crampton, William. LC 88-27174. 64p. (gr. 5 up). 1989. 15.00 (0-394-82255-2); PLB 15.99 (0-394-92255-7) Knopf Bks Yng Read.

Ploog, Mike. The Life & Adventures of Santa Claus. Baum, L. Frank. 96p. 1992. text ed. 24.95 (1-879450-76-3) Tundra MA.

Ploss, Douglas A. The Tweens at Deep Lake: An Original American Fantasy. Ploss, Douglas A. LC 79-90996. 88p. (gr. 3 up). 1979. PLB 13.50 (0-9603632-0-3); pap. 8.50 (0-9603632-1-1) OPC.

Plowitz, Kurt. Asot Mishpat. Shumsky, Abraham & Shumsky, Adaia. (gr. 4-6). 1969. text ed. 6.00 (0-8074-0178-1, 405301); tchrs'. guide 3.50 (0-8074-0179-X, 205302); wkbk. 6.00 (0-8074-0180-3, 405300) UAHC.

Plum, K. D. The Hayloft. Peters, Lisa W. LC 93-18718. Date not set. write for info. (0-8037-1490-4); lib. bdg. write for info. (0-8037-1491-2) Dial Bks Young.

Plume, Ilse. The Bremen-Town Musicians. Plume, Ilse. LC 86-42990. 32p. (ps-3). 1987. pap. 5.95 (0-06-443141-X, Trophy) HarpC Child Bks.

—The Christmas Witch. Plume, Ilse. LC 91-71380. 32p. (gr. k-4). 1991. 13.95 (1-56282-077-X); PLB 13.89 (1-56282-078-8) Hyprn Child.

—The Christmas Witch. Plume, Ilse. LC 91-71380. 32p. (gr. k-3). 1993. pap. 4.95 (1-56282-524-0) Hyprn Ppbks.

—Night Story. Willard, Nancy. LC 85-17677. 32p. (ps-3). 1986. 13.95 (0-15-257348-8, HB Juv Bks) HarBrace.

—Salt: A Russian Folktale. Langton, Jane, retold by. Plume, Alice, tr. from RUS. LC 91-74007. 48p. (gr. k-3). 1992. 14.95 (1-56282-178-4); PLB 14.89 (1-56282-179-2) Hyprn Child.

—Sleepy Book. Zolotow, Charlotte. LC 87-45861. 32p. (ps-1). 1988. PLB 12.89 (0-06-026968-5) HarpC Child Bks.

—Sleepy Book. Zolotow, Charlotte. LC 87-45861. 32p. (ps-1). 1990. pap. 5.95 (0-06-443239-4, Trophy) HarpC Child Bks.

—The Twelve Days of Christmas. Plume, Ilse. LC 89-49063. 32p. (gr. 1-4). 1990. PLB 16.89 (0-06-024738-X) HarpC Child Bks.

—The Velveteen Rabbit: Or How Toys Become Real. Williams, Margery. LC 86-33544. 32p. (ps-3). 1987. 10.95 (0-15-293500-2) HarBrace.

Plunkett, Kathleen. C. T. the Living Christmas Tree. Dewoody, Darrel W. & Dewoody, Betty N. (gr. k-6). 1989. write for info. Old Amer Pr.

Plunkett, Michael. Let's Visit a Space Camp. Alston, Edith. LC 89-34373. 32p. (gr. 2-4). 1990. lib. bdg. 10.79 (0-8167-1743-5); pap. text ed. 2.95 (0-8167-1744-3) Troll Assocs.

Plunkett, Michael, photos by. A Day in the Life of a Major League Baseball Player. Monteleone, John. LC 90-36052. 32p. (gr. 4-8). 1991. PLB 11.79 (0-8167-2216-1); pap. text ed. 2.95 (0-8167-2217-X) Troll Assocs.

Plunkett, Michael & French, Larry, photos by. A Day in the Life of a Newspaper Reporter. Wickenden, Martha. LC 90-37547. 32p. (gr. 4-8). 1991. lib. bdg. 11.79 (0-8167-2214-5); pap. text ed. 2.95 (0-8167-2215-3) Troll Assocs.

Plunkett, Michael. Let's Visit a Toy Factory. Bourne, Miriam A. LC 87-3489. 32p. (gr. 2-4). 1988. PLB 10.79 (0-8167-1159-3); pap. text ed. 2.95 (0-8167-1160-7) Troll Assocs.

—A River Adventure. Morgan, Patricia G. LC 87-3485. 32p. (gr. 3-6). 1988. PLB 10.79 (0-8167-1171-2); pap. text ed. 2.95 (0-8167-1172-0) Troll Assocs.

Pocick, Margo. It's Okay to Paint a Purple Turtle. Bedford, Viola & Richtel, Anne. 24p. (Orig.). (gr. k-8). 1991. 8.95 (0-938911-07-4) Indiv Educ Syst.

Pocock, R. A Jewish Holiday ABC. Drucker, M. 1992. 13.95 (0-15-200482-3, HB Juv Bks) HarBrace.

Podgorski, Mary E., jt. illus. see Cullinan, Dorothy K.

Poe, Janice. Boat Ride. Gillespie, Bill. 24p. 1988. pap. 3.50 (0-940859-05-X) Snd Dollar Pub.

—Butterflies' Wings & Beautiful Things. Gillespie, Bill. 24p. 1986. pap. 3.50 (0-940859-02-5) Snd Dollar Pub.

—Giraffes. Gillespie, Bill. 12p. (Orig.). 1985. pap. 3.00 (0-940859-00-9) Snd Dollar Pub.

—Peter Potter Teeter Totter. Gillespie, Bill. 22p. (Orig.). 1987. pap. 3.50 (0-940859-06-8) Snd Dollar Pub.

—Spotty Spotty Jones. Gillespie, Bill. 22p. (Orig.). 1986. pap. 3.50 (0-940859-03-3) Snd Dollar Pub.

Poepoe, Karen, jt. illus. see Kahalewai, Marilyn.

Pogany, Willy. The Children of Odin: The Book of Northern Myths. reissued ed. Colum, Padraic. LC 83-20368. 280p. (gr. 5up). 1984. SBE 15.95 (0-02-722890-8, Collier Young Ad); pap. 8.95 (0-02-042100-1, Collier Young Ad) Macmillan Child Grp.

—The Children's Homer: The Adventures of Odysseus & the Tale of Troy. Colum, Padraic. LC 82-12643. 256p. (gr. 5 up). 1982. pap. 7.95 (0-02-042520-1, Collier Young Ad) Macmillan Child Grp.

—The Golden Fleece: And the Heroes Who Lived Before Achilles. reissued ed. Colum, Padraic. LC 82-21667. 320p. (gr. 5 up). 1983. SBE 15.95 (0-02-723620-X, Macmillan Child Bk); pap. 7.95 (0-02-042260-1, Collier Young Ad) Macmillan Child Grp.

Pohrt, Tom. Crow & Weasel. Lopez, Barry. LC 90-31500. 64p. (gr. 5 up). 1990. 16.95 (0-86547-439-7, North Pt Pr) FSG.

—Miko: Little Hunter of the North. Donehower, Bruce. (gr. 2-7). 1990. 12.95 (0-374-34970-3) FS&G.

Poindexter, Cathlene & Brouwer, Jack. Om-Kas-Toe of the Blackfeet: Blackfeet Twin Captures an Elkdog. Thomasma, Kenneth. LC 89-14879. 215p. (gr. 4-8). 1992. 10.99 (0-8010-8883-6); pap. 6.99 (0-8010-8884-4) Baker Bk.

Points, Maureen. The Adventures of Pepe the Poodle & Other Stories. Points, Maureen. 1978. pap. 3.50 (0-9601594-1-X) Maureen Points.

Poirier, Kathleen. Now He Knows. Salem, Lynn & Stewart, Josie. 12p. (gr. 1). 1993. pap. 3.50 (1-880612-06-2) Seedling Pubns.

Poissenot, Jean-Marie. Living in the Heart of Africa. Henry-Biabaud, Chantal. Bogard, Vicki, tr. from FRE. LC 90-50774. 38p. (gr. k-5). 1991. 4.95 (0-944589-29-4, 294) Young Discovery Lib.

Polacco, Patricia. Appelemando's Dreams. Polacco, Patricia. 32p. (ps-3). 1991. 14.95 (0-399-21800-9, Philomel) Putnam Pub Group.

—Casey at the Bat. Thayer, Ernest L. 32p. (ps-3). 1992. pap. 5.95 (0-399-21884-X, Sandcastle Bks) Putnam Pub Group.

—Chicken Sunday. Polacco, Patricia. 32p. (ps-3). 1992. PLB 14.95 (0-399-22133-6, Philomel Bks) Putnam Pub Group.

—Just Plain Fancy. Polacco, Patricia. 32p. (ps-3). 1990. 14.95 (0-553-05884-3, Little Rooster); PLB 15.99 (0-553-07062-2, Little Rooster) Bantam.

—The Keeping Quilt. Polacco, Patricia. 32p. (ps-3). 1988. pap. 14.95 3-pc. bdg. (0-671-64963-9, S&S BFYR) S&S Trade.

—The Keeping Quilt. Polacco, Patricia. (gr. k-4). 1993. 14.95 (0-685-64811-7); audiocassette 11.00 (1-882869-82-6) Read Advent.

—Meteor! Polacco, Patricia. 32p. (gr. k-3). 1987. 14.95 (0-399-21699-5, Putnam) Putnam Pub Group.

—My Rotten, Redheaded, Older Brother. Polacco, Patricia. 1994. pap. 15.00 (0-671-72751-6, S&S BFYR) S&S Trade.

—Rechenka's Eggs. Polacco, Patricia. 32p. (ps-3). 1988. 14.95 (0-399-21501-8, Philomel Bks) Putnam Pub Group.

—Uncle Vova's Tree. Polacco, Patricia. 32p. (ps-3). 1989. 14.95 (0-399-21617-0, Philomel Bks) Putnam Pub Group.

Polgreen, John. Sky Observer's Guide. rev. ed. Mayall, R. Newton, et al. (gr. 9 up). 1985. pap. write for info. (0-307-24009-6, Golden Pr) Western Pub.

Polis, Gary A., photos by Scorpion Man: Exploring the World of Scorpions. Pringle, Laurence. LC 93-34936. (gr. 4 up). 1994. write for info. (0-684-19560-7, Scribner) MacMillan.

Politi, L. Lorenzo the Naughty Parrot. Johnston, T. 1992. write for info. (0-15-249350-6, HB Juv Bks) HarBrace.

Politi, Leo. Song of the Swallows. Politi, Leo. 32p. (gr. k-3). 1987. pap. 4.95 (0-689-71140-9, Aladdin) Macmillan Child Grp.

—Three Stalks of Corn. reissue ed. Politi, Leo. LC 75-35009. 32p. (gr. k-3). 1993. RSBE 14.95 (0-684-19538-0, Scribners Young Read) Macmillan Child Grp.

—Three Stalks of Corn. Politi, Leo. LC 93-19737. 32p. (gr. k-3). 1994. pap. 4.95 (0-689-71782-2, Aladdin) Macmillan Child Grp.

Pollard, Jean A. The Ice Ladder. Pollard, Jean A. Weinberger, Jane, ed. LC 87-62209. 58p. (Orig.). (gr. 4-8). 1988. pap. 5.00 (0-932433-31-6) Windswept Hse.

Pollard, Nan. The Christmas Santa Almost Missed. Dubowski, Cathy E. 24p. (Orig.). (gr. k-1). 1990. pap. 0.99 (1-878624-48-2) McClanahan Bk.

—Friends Together. Pollard, Nan. 32p. (ps-3). 1990. 4.95 (1-56288-048-9) Checkerboard.

—Grandma's Visit. Schorsh, Laurence. (ps-3). 1990. 4.95 (1-56288-049-7) Checkerboard.

—The Littlest Angel. Dubowski, Cathy E. 24p. (ps-2). 1991. pap. 0.99 (1-56293-116-4) McClanahan Bk.

—The Night Before Christmas. Moore, Clement C. 24p. (Orig.). (gr. k-1). 1990. pap. 0.99 (1-878624-49-0) McClanahan Bk.

—The Night the Toys Came Alive. Hollander, Cass. 24p. (Orig.). (gr. k-1). 1990. pap. 0.99 (1-878624-42-3) McClanahan Bk.

Pollock, Dean. Many Horses. Wood, Elizabeth L. (gr. 5-11). 1953. 7.95 (0-8323-0175-2) Binford Mort.

Polseno, Jo, jt. illus. see McKay, Donald.

Pomeroy, Bradley O. Little Red Riding Hood. Bornstein, Harry & Saulnier, Karen. 48p. (gr. 1-6). 1990. PLB 15.95 (1-878363-26-3) Forest Hse.

—Little Red Riding Hood: Told in Signed English. Bornstein, Harry & Saulnier, Karen L. LC 90-3477. 48p. (ps-2). 1990. 14.95 (0-930323-63-7, Pub. by K Green Pubns) Gallaudet Univ Pr.

Pons, Bernadette. Little Squirrel's Special Nest. Clement, Claude. LC 93-4243. (gr. 4 up). 1993. write for info. (0-89577-542-5, Reader's Digest Kids) RD Assn.

Ponte, Douglas J. Tree Man. Deedy, Carmen A. LC 93-1667. 1993. 16.95 (1-56145-077-4) Peachtree Pubs.

Ponter, James. The Bedford Adventure. Leeson, Muriel. LC 87-11943. 136p. (Orig.). (gr. 4-9). 1987. pap. 4.50 (0-8361-3448-6) Herald Pr.

—Busboys at Big Bend. Hamilton, Dorothy. LC 74-8689. 112p. (gr. 8-12). 1974. o. p. 4.95 (0-8361-1744-1); pap. 3.95 (0-8361-1745-X) Herald Pr.

—Tree Tall & the Horse Race. Evans, Shirlee. LC 86-7659. 136p. (Orig.). (gr. 3-8). 1986. pap. 3.95 (0-8361-3414-1) Herald Pr.

—Tree Tall to the Rescue. Evans, Shirlee. LC 87-8615. 144p. (Orig.). (gr. 4-9). 1987. pap. 4.50 (0-8361-3444-3) Herald Pr.

Pontet, Daniel G. Washington Irving's Pilgrim of Love: From the Tales of the Alhambra. 2nd ed. Calderon, Frank, ed. 64p. (gr. 4 up). 1990. text ed. 19.95 (0-939193-20-5) Edit Concepts.

Poole, Ann. The Hunky Dory. Haskell, Bess C. 48p. (Orig.). (gr. 3-8). 1992. pap. 10.95 (0-9626857-2-0) Coastwise Pr.

THE HUNKY DORY is the second in the six-volume WIND, WAVES & AWAY! SERIES written by Bess C. Haskell of Tenants Harbor, Maine. Bess, who was born September 9, 1896, wrote these books in the early '20s to read to her own children. Bess & her husband, Henry Haskell, both taught school for many years & co-founded the first interracial summer camp for children in Maine in the '40s. In 1936, while teaching in a private school, Henry read the books to his students, who loved them. Each of the six books centers around the adventures of two children & a different water craft. The children, Dan & Margaret Currier, learn the proper handling of each boat--raft, dory, sailboat, canoe, motorboat & schooner--through a series of misadventures. Their pet dog & cat always join, & sometimes, cause the fun. From their parents, the children also learn the essential family values prevalent at the turn of the century. After 1936, these stories were lost for many years. When they resurfaced in the early '80s, Bess revised them for publication. The first book, THE RAFT, was published in 1988. Every page of THE HUNKY DORY is beautifully illustrated with line drawings.
Publisher Provided Annotation.

Poole, Ann M. Sailing to Pint Pot. Haskell, Bess C. 72p. (Orig.). (gr. 4 up). 1993. pap. 10.95 (0-9626857-4-7) Coastwise Pr.
SAILING TO PINT POT takes the Currier family sailing to a Maine island. After a fun-filled day of picnicking & discovering natural wonders, they encounter danger when they go off course on the way home. PINT POT is the third book in the six-part WIND, WAVES & AWAY! series written by Bess C. Haskell of Tenants Harbor, Maine. Each book in the series illustrates proper handling of a different water craft through the adventures of Margaret & Dan Currier, their mom & dad, & sometimes their pet cat & dog. The old-fashioned but universal tales engage & delight all young children while teaching valuable but non-preachy lessons. All books in the series are beautifully illustrated with line drawings that capture the rocky, spruce-dotted coast of Maine.
Publisher Provided Annotation.

Poole, Jerry D., jt. illus. see Lisenby, Foy.

Poole, Valerie. Hey Look at Me! I Can Be. Thomasson, Merry. LC 87-90455. 20p. (ps-2). 1987. 9.95 (0-9615407-1-0) Thomasson-Grant.

—Hey Look at Me! I Like to Dream. Thomasson, Merry. LC 87-90547. 20p. (ps-2). 1987. 9.95 (0-9615407-2-9) Thomasson-Grant.

Pooley, Sarah. Air, Air Everywhere. Johnston, Tom. LC 87-42752. 32p. (gr. 4-6). 1988. PLB 15.93 (1-55532-406-1) Gareth Stevens Inc.

—Electricity Turns the World On! Johnston, Tom. LC 87-42655. 32p. (gr. 4-6). 1987. PLB 15.93 (1-55532-410-X) Gareth Stevens Inc.

—Energy: Making It Work. Johnston, Tom. LC 87-42751. 32p. (gr. 4-6). 1987. PLB 15.93 (1-55532-405-3) Gareth Stevens Inc.

—The Forces with You! Johnston, Tom. LC 87-42753. 32p. (gr. 4-6). 1987. PLB 15.93 (1-55532-408-8) Gareth Stevens Inc.

—It's Raining, It's Pouring: A Book for Rainy Days. Pooley, Sarah, compiled by. LC 92-16859. (ps up). 1993. 18.00 (0-688-11803-8) Greenwillow.

—Light! Color! Action! Johnston, Tom. LC 87-42754. 32p. (gr. 4-6). 1988. PLB 15.93 (1-55532-409-6) Gareth Stevens Inc.

—My Giant Word & Number Book. Salt, Jane. LC 92-31508. 1993. 9.95 (1-85697-861-3) Kingfisher Bks.

—Science in Action, 6 vols. Johnston, Tom. 32p. (gr. 4-6). 1987. Set. PLB 95.58 (1-55532-412-6) Gareth Stevens Inc.

—Water, Water! Johnston, Tom. LC 87-42750. 32p. (gr. 4-6). 1988. PLB 15.93 (1-55532-407-X) Gareth Stevens Inc.

Poore, Clara. Weaving with Wheat: A Manual for Beginning Wheat Weavers, No. 1. 2nd ed. Poore, Clara. 16p. (gr. 2-6). 1984. pap. 4.00 (0-9613993-1-7) Wheat'N Flower.

Pope, Connie J. Juliette Gordon Low: Founder of the Girl Scouts. Steelsmith, Shari. LC 89-62673. 32p. (Orig.). (ps-4). 1990. lib. bdg. 16.95 (0-943990-37-8); pap. 5.95 (0-943990-36-X) Parenting Pr.

Poppel, Hans. Benny's Hat. Walbrecker, Dirk. 28p. (ps-1). 1991. smythe sewn reinforced bdg. 9.95 (1-56182-028-8) Atomium Bks.

—Clocks! How Time Flies. Aust, Siegfried. 32p. (gr. 2-5). 1991. PLB 18.95 (0-8225-2154-7) Lerner Pubns.

—Flight! Free As a Bird. Aust, Siegfried. 32p. (gr. 2-5). 1991. PLB 18.95 (0-8225-2150-4) Lerner Pubns.

—Miss Eva & the Red Balloon. Glennon, Karen M. LC 89-32515. 32p. (ps-3). 1990. pap. 13.95 jacketed (0-671-68854-5, S&S BFYR) S&S Trade.

—Que Ruido! What Noise! Brodmann, Aliana. Krohn, Hildegard M., tr. from GER. (SPA.). 26p. (gr. 3 up). 1990. 13.95 (968-6465-08-1) Hispanic Bk Dist.

—Salmon Moon. Karlins, Mark. LC 92-15702. 1993. pap. 14.00 (0-671-73624-8, S&S BFYR) S&S Trade.

—A Seed, a Flower, a Minute, an Hour. Blos, Joan W. LC 91-4992. 40p. (ps-2). 1992. pap. 14.00 jacketed, 3-pc. bdg. (0-671-73214-5, S&S BFYR) S&S Trade.

—Such a Noise! Brodmann, Aliana. Fillingham, David, tr. from GER. 32p. (gr. k-3). 1989. 11.95 (0-916291-25-1) Kane-Miller Bk.

Poppins, Jewish M., jt. illus. see Gewirtz, Bina.

Poppler, Susan. The Swan: A Storybook for Adults & Other Children. Smock, Jerri. 21p. (gr. 7 up). 1989. incl. cassette 13.95g (0-944586-00-7) WIN Pub.

Porfirio, Guy. The Raggly, Scraggly, No-Soap, No-Scrub Girl. Birchman, David F. LC 92-40339. (gr. 3 up). 1995. write for info. (0-688-11060-6); PLB write for info. (0-688-11061-4) Lothrop.

Portadino, Norma. Complete Classroom Kit. rev. ed. Dickson, Sue. 7968p. (gr. k-3). 1984. pap. 533.00 (1-55574-000-6, KC 510) CBN Publishing.

—Phonetic Storybook Readers, 17 vols. rev. ed. Dickson, Sue. 960p. (gr. k-3). 1984. pap. 48.00 (1-55574-003-0, SR-310) CBN Publishing.

—Raceway. rev. ed. Dickson, Sue. 96p. (gr. k-3). 1984. pap. 4.97 (1-55574-002-2, WB-140) CBN Publishing.

Porter, Bruce. Bill & the Burning Bush. Porter, Bruce. 40p. (Orig.). (gr. 1 up). 1987. pap. 3.95 (0-939925-12-5) R C Law & Co.

—Butch & the Bad Baloney. Porter, Bruce. 40p. (Orig.). (gr. 1 up). 1987. pap. 3.95 (0-939925-15-X) R C Law & Co.

—Jonah Gets the Jitters. Porter, Bruce. 40p. (Orig.). (gr. 3 up). 1987. pap. 3.95 (0-939925-14-1) R C Law & Co.

—The Parable of Pa Diggle's Son. Porter, Bruce. 40p. (Orig.). (gr. 3 up). 1987. pap. 3.95 (0-939925-11-7) R C Law & Co.

—Samuel & the Strange Sound. Porter, Bruce. 40p. (Orig.). (gr. 3 up). 1987. pap. 3.95 (0-939925-13-3) R C Law & Co.

—Squirt & the Super Soldier. Porter, Bruce. 40p. (Orig.). (gr. 3 up). 1987. pap. 3.95 (0-939925-16-8) R C Law & Co.

Porter, Coni, jt. illus. see Zarins, Joyce A.

Porter, Debbie. Tammy's Smile. Otis, Sharon & Walker, Lois. Goldman, Howard, pref. by. (Orig.). (ps-7). 1985. wkbk. 6.00 (0-9617737-0-7) Total Lrn.

Porter, Frederick. A Place Called Heartbreak: A Story of Vietnam. Myers, Walter D. LC 92-14428. 71p. (gr. 2-5). 1992. PLB 21.34 (0-8114-7237-X) Raintree Steck-V.

Porter, George. Mitch & Amy. Cleary, Beverly. LC 67-10041. 224p. (gr. 3-7). 1967. 15.95 (0-688-21688-9); PLB 15.88 (0-688-31688-3, Morrow Jr Bks) Morrow Jr Bks.

Porter, James A. Talking Animals. Hambly, Wilfrid D. 1990. 7.95 (0-87498-025-9) Assoc Pubs DC.

Porter, Janice L. Allen Jay & the Underground Railroad. Brill, Marlene T. LC 92-25279. 1993. 14.95 (0-87614-776-7); pap. write for info. (0-87614-605-1) Carolrhoda Bks.

Porter, Malcolm. The Dillon Press Children's Atlas. 96p. (gr. 5 up). 1993. lib. bdg. 17.95 RSBE (0-87518-606-8, Dillon) Macmillan Child Grp.

—The Kingfisher Reference Atlas: An A-Z Guide to Countries of the World. Williams, Brian. LC 92-54829. 216p. (gr. 5 up). 1993. 19.95 (1-85697-838-9) Kingfisher Bks.

Porter, Mary D. Springboard to French: Introduction to the French Language. rev. ed. Criminale, Ulrike & The Language School of the American

Cultural Exchange Staff. 32p. (gr. k-4). 1991. Incl. cassettes. 19.95 (*1-880770-00-8*) ACE Pub. SPRINGBOARD is a set of easy, encouraging foreign language lessons for young children ages 4-8. This popular series features two 90-minute cassettes on which a native speaker of the foreign language leads the child in short, playful sessions through a variety of actions by repeating simple commands in both the foreign language & in English. The child is not required to read or write the language. Instead, the language is absorbed almost effortlessly as the child enjoys a progression of music, games & activities. The program emphasizes well-planned lessons for the adult leader & can be enjoyed by anyone in the home setting as well as in class. Because the cassettes guide the activity, the adult is not required to know the language, but instead simply participates with the child. The accompanying Springboard books provide attractive illustrations & a word-for-word transcript of the cassettes along with a comprehensive Vocabulary Chart for review & an Activities Supplement with suggestions for further learning. The Series is available in French, German & Spanish, & will soon be available in Japanese. *Publisher Provided Annotation.*

—Springboard to German: Introduction to the German Language. Criminale, Ulrike & The Langauge School of the American Cultural Exchange. 32p. (gr. k-4). 1991. Incl. cassettes. 19.95 (*1-880770-01-6*) ACE Pub. SPRINGBOARD is a set of easy, encouraging foreign language lessons for young children ages 4-8. This popular series features two 90-minute cassette tapes on which a native speaker of the foreign language leads the child in short, playful sessions through a variety of actions by repeating simple commands both in the foreign language & in English. The child is not required to read or write the language. Instead, the language is absorbed almost effortlessly as the child enjoys a progression of music, games & activities. The program emphasizes well-planned lessons for the adult leader & can be enjoyed by anyone in the home setting as well as in class. Because the cassettes guide the activity, the adult is not required to know the language, but instead simply participates with the child. The accompanying Springboard books provide attractive illustrations & a word-for-word transcript of the cassettes along with a comprehensive Vocabulary Chart for review & an Activities Supplement with suggestions for further learning. The Series is available in French, German & Spanish, & will soon be available in Japanese. *Publisher Provided Annotation.*

—Springboard to Spanish: Introduction to the Spanish Language. rev. ed. Criminale, Ulrike & The Language School of the American Cultural Exchange Staff. (gr. k-4). 1991. Incl. cassettes. 19.95 (*1-880770-02-4*) ACE Pub. SPRINGBOARD is a set of easy, encouraging foreign language lessons for young children ages 4-8. This popular series features two 90-minute cassette tapes on which a native speaker of the foreign language leads the child in short, playful sessions through a variety of actions by repeating simple commands in both the foreign langauge & in English. The child is not required to read or write the language. Instead, the language is absorbed almost effortlessly as the child enjoys a progression of music, games & activities. The program emphasizes well-planned lessons for the adult leader & can be enjoyed by anyone in the home setting as well as in class. Because the cassettes guide the activity, the adult is not required to know the language, but instead simply participates with the child. The accompanying Springboard books provide attractive illustrations & a word-for-word transcript of the cassettes along with a comprehensive Vocabulary Chart for review & an Activities Supplement with suggestions for further learning. The Series is available in French, German & Spanish &, will soon be available in Japanese. *Publisher Provided Annotation.*

Porter, Pat. Happy Burpday, Maggie McDougal! Gregory, Valiska. 64p. (gr. 2-4). 1992. 11.95 (*0-316-32777-8*) Little.
—Slime Time. O'Connor, Jim & O'Connor, Jane. LC 89-77324. 64p. (Orig.). (gr. 2-4). 1990. PLB 6.99 (*0-679-90714-9*); pap. 2.50 (*0-679-80714-4*) Random Bks Yng Read.
Porter, Pat G. Luke's Bully. Winthrop, Elizabeth. 64p. (gr. 2-5). 1990. pap. 11.95 (*0-670-83103-4*) Viking Child Bks.
—Luke's Bully. Winthrop, Elizabeth. 64p. (gr. 2-5). 1992. pap. 3.99 (*0-14-034329-6*, Puffin) Puffin Bks.

Porter, Robin A. Season Science 1: Seasonal Mystery of Animal Coat Change. Darneille, Diane D. 32p. (Orig.). (gr. k-5). 1992. pap. 13.95 (*0-9634246-1-0*) Sci Passport. A National Literacy Foundation "Highly Recommended" Book. This non-fiction, early reader science book relates a child's experience changing his own coat to the seasonal coat changes animals make. Memorable verse & lifelike watercolor illustrations of children & animals fill the pages of SEASON SCIENCE (TM) 1. A rabbit ("showshoe hare") changes coat colors. A horse ("mustang") sheds its heavy coat for a lighter one. A reindeer (" barren-ground caribou") adds a fat lining to its coat for warmth & grows antlers for air conditioning. There's even a mystery to solve -- the way scientists do -- that leads to the discovery of a link between seasons & the earth's tilt relative to the sun. Included art activities, games & cards reinforce the learning in fun, age appropriate ways. *Publisher Provided Annotation.*

Porter, Sharon H. Wonderful, Wonder-Full Donkey. Cossi, Olga. LC 89-50142. 54p. (ps-4). 1989. pap. 10. 95 (*0-932413-55-3*) Windswept Hse.
Porter, Sue. Mary's Tiger. Harley, Rex. LC 89-49009. 23p. (ps-2). 1990. 13.95 (*0-15-200524-2*, Gulliver Bks) HarBrace.

Portlock, Rob. Buster the Biker Sheep. Portlock, Rob. 32p. (Orig.). 1993. pap. 4.99 (*0-8308-1904-5*, 1904) InterVarsity.
—My Dad Ran over a Frog. Portlock, Rob. LC 92-11584. 32p. (Orig.). (ps-1). 1992. pap. 4.99 (*0-8308-1901-0*, 1901) InterVarsity.
—Noon on the Moon. Portlock, Rob. 32p. (Orig.). (ps-2). 1993. pap. 4.99 (*0-8308-1903-7*, 1903) InterVarsity.
—Someone's Trying to Cut off My Head. Portlock, Rob. LC 92-12483. 32p. (Orig.). (ps-1). 1992. pap. 4.99 (*0-8308-1902-9*, 1902) InterVarsity.
Portugal, Jan. ABC Sillies. Portugal, Jan. LC 83-10291. 56p. (Orig.). (ps-1). 1983. pap. 3.00 (*0-937148-13-X*) Wild Horses.
Portwood, Andrew. Dragon Scales & Willow Leaves. Givens, Terryl. LC 93-665. Date not set. write for info. (*0-399-22619-2*, Putnam) Putnam Pub Group.
Posey, Pam. Alfred. Scarffe, Bronwen. LC 92-21442. 1993. 3.75 (*0-383-03612-7*) SRA Schl Grp.
—Barnaby's Birthday. Fitzgerald, John & Fitzgerald, Lyn. LC 92-34275. 1993. 14.00 (*0-383-03618-6*) SRA Schl Grp.
—How Long Is a Piece of String? Atkins, Kirsten. LC 93-18062. 1994. write for info. (*0-383-03672-0*) SRA Schl Grp.
—Manners in God's House. Uhrich, Ethel. Hayes, Theresa, ed. 16p. (gr. 3-6). 1992. wkbk. 7.99 (*0-87403-929-0*, 14-03501) Standard Pub.
—Thomas the Tank Engine - Colors. Awdry, W., contrib. by. 12p. (ps). 1993. bds. 2.29 (*0-679-81646-1*) Random Bks Yng Read.
—Thomas the Tank Engine: Coming & Going -- A Book of Opposites. Awdry, W., contrib. by. 14p. (ps). 1991. pap. 2.29 (*0-679-81645-3*) McKay.
Posey, Pam, jt. illus. see Paris, Pat.
Posner, Marcia. Hinkl & Other Shlemiel Stories. Chaikin, Miriam. LC 86-29755. 96p. (Orig.). (gr. 7 up). 1987. pap. 6.95 (*0-933503-37-7*) Shapolsky Pubs.
Post, Doug. The Race to the South Pole. Matthews, Rupert. LC 88-7534. 32p. (gr. 5-8). 1989. PLB 11.90 (*0-531-18273-8*, Pub. by Bookwright Pr) Watts.
Post, Mance. The Secret of Thut-Mouse III: or Basil Beaudesert's Revenge. Kirby, Mansfield. LC 85-47588. 64p. (ps up). 1985. 14.00 (*0-374-36677-2*) FS&G.
Postgate, Oliver. Columbus: The Triumphant Failure. Postgate, Oliver & Linnell, Naomi. 44p. (gr. 5-8). 1992. 14.95 (*0-531-15240-5*) Watts.
Postma, Lidia. The Stolen Mirror. Postma, Lidia. LC 75-43888. 32p. (ps-3). 1976. McGraw.
—The Twelve Dancing Princesses & Other Tales from Grimm. Lewis, Naomi, ed. LC 85-6964. 100p. (ps up). 1986. 14.95 (*0-8037-0237-X*) Dial Bks Young.
Potter, Beatrix. Baby's First Year: A Beatrix Potter Gift Set. 32p. 1990. 16.95 (*0-7232-3763-8*) Warne.
—The Complete Adventures of Peter Rabbit. Potter, Beatrix. 96p. (ps-3). 1987. 12.95 (*0-7232-2951-1*) Warne.
—The Complete Tales of Beatrix Potter. Potter, Beatrix. 384p. (ps-6). 1989. 35.00 (*0-7232-3618-6*) Viking Child Bks.
—Gardening with Peter Rabbit. Walters, Jennie. 48p. (gr. k-4). 1992. 9.00 (*0-7232-3998-3*) Warne.
—Gardening with Peter Rabbit: A Gardening Kit. Walters, Jennie. 48p. (gr. k-4). 1992. pap. 14.50 (*0-7232-4024-8*) Warne.
—Little Treasury of Peter Rabbit, 6 vols. Nash, Corey, retold by. (ps). 1983. 5.99 (*0-517-41069-9*, Chatham River Pr) Outlet Bk Co.
—Meet Hunca Munca. Potter, Beatrix. 12p. (ps). 1986. bds. 2.95 (*0-7232-3421-3*) Warne.
—Meet Jemima Puddle-Duck. Potter, Beatrix. 12p. (ps). 1986. bds. 3.50 (*0-7232-3420-5*) Warne.
—Meet Peter Rabbit. Potter, Beatrix. 12p. (ps). 1986. bds. 3.50 (*0-7232-3418-3*) Warne.
—Meet Tom Kitten. Potter, Beatrix. 12p. (ps). 1986. bds. 3.50 (*0-7232-3419-1*) Warne.
—My Peter Rabbit Keepsake: A Photograph Album. 32p. 1994. 9.99 (*0-7232-4121-X*) Warne.
—The Original Peter Rabbit Miniature Collection, No. I. Potter, Beatrix. (ps-3). 1991. pap. 5.95 (*0-7232-3982-7*) Warne.
—Panache Petitgris. Potter, Beatrix. (FRE.). 60p. 1990. 9.95 (*0-7859-3713-7*) Fr & Eur.
—Peter Rabbit & Eleven Other Favorite Tales. Potter, Beatrix. Stewart, Pat, adapted by. LC 93-14417. 96p. 1994. pap. 1.00t (*0-486-27845-X*) Dover.
—The Peter Rabbit Make-&-Play Book. 32p. (ps-5). 1992. pap. 6.99 (*0-7232-3991-6*) Warne.
—The Peter Rabbit Sticker Book. rev. ed. 20p. (ps-3). 1991. pap. 6.99 (*0-7232-3979-7*) Warne.
—Peter Rabbit's ABC. Potter, Beatrix. 48p. (ps-2). 1987. 6.95 (*0-7232-3423-X*) Warne.
—So I Shall Tell You a Story: The Magic World of Beatrix Potter. Taylor, Judy, ed. Sendak, Maurice, et al. 224p. 1993. 24.95 (*0-7232-4025-6*) Warne.
—The Stories of Beatrix Potter, Vol. 1. Potter, Beatrix. 96p. (ps-2). 1991. 4 bks. & 2 audio cassettes 16.98 (*1-55886-063-0*) Smarty Pants.
—The Stories of Beatrix Potter, Vol. 2. Potter, Beatrix. 96p. (ps-2). 1992. 4 bks. & 2 audio cassettes 16.98 (*1-55886-067-3*) Smarty Pants.
—The Tale of Jemima Puddle-Duck. Potter, Beatrix. 24p. (ps-2). 1991. incl. cassette 5.98 (*1-55886-057-6*) Smarty Pants.
—The Tale of Mrs. Tiggy-Winkle. Potter, Beatrix. 24p. (ps-2). 1991. incl. cassette 5.98 (*1-55886-058-4*) Smarty Pants.

—The Tale of Peter Rabbit. Potter, Beatrix. 24p. (ps-2). 1991. incl. cassette 5.98 (*1-55886-055-X*) Smarty Pants.
—Tales from Beatrix Potter. Potter, Beatrix. 228p. (ps-3). 1986. 8.95 (*0-7232-3971-1*) Warne.
—The Two Bad Mice Pop-Up Book. Potter, Beatrix. (ps-3). 1986. 11.95 (*0-7232-3360-8*) Warne.
Potter, D. J. The Happy Garden. Potter, Jamie & Powers, Janet. 52p. (Orig.). (ps-4). 1985. pap. 5.95 (*0-936511-00-1*) Gopher.
Potter, John. Battle of the Little Bighorn. Henckel, Mark. 32p. (Orig.). (gr. 3-7). 1992. pap. 5.95 (*1-56044-042-2*) Falcon Pr MT.
—Colter's Run. Edwards, Judith. 32p. (Orig.). 1993. pap. 5.95 (*1-56044-178-X*) Falcon Pr MT.
—Outdoors Just for Kids. Henckel, Mark. 128p. (Orig.). (gr. 1-8). 1992. pap. 8.95 spiral bdg. (*0-9627618-3-4*) Billings Gazette.
Potts, Evangela, jt. illus. see Potts, Leanna K.
Potts, Leanna K. & Potts, Evangela. Thyme for Kids. Potts, Leanna K. & Potts, Evangela. 84p. (gr-p8). 1990. pap. 7.95 (*0-935069-24-0*) White Oak Pr.
Poulin, Stephane. As-Tu Vu Josephine? Poulin, Stephane. LC 86-51044. (FRE.). 24p. (gr. k-4). 1988. 12.95 (*0-88776-188-7*); pap. 6.95 (*0-88776-224-7*) Tundra Bks.
—Benjamin & the Pillow Saga. Poulin, Stephane. 1990. 14.95 (*1-550370-69-3*, Pub. by Annick CN); pap. 9.95 (*1-550370-68-5*, Pub. by Annick CN) Firefly Bks Ltd.
—Can You Catch Josephine? Poulin, Stephane. LC 87-50374. 24p. (gr-k4). 1988. 12.95 (*0-88776-198-4*); pap. 6.95 (*0-88776-214-X*) Tundra Bks.
—Have You Seen Josephine? Poulin, Stephane. LC 86-51043. (gr. k-4). 1988. 12.95 (*0-88776-180-1*); pap. 6.95 (*0-88776-215-8*) Tundra Bks.
—My Mother's Love. Poulin, Stephane. 32p. (ps-1). 1990. 15.95 (*1-55037-149-5*, Pub. by Annick CN); pap. 6.95 (*1-55037-148-7*, Pub. by Annick CN) Firefly Bks Ltd.
—Teddy Rabbit. Stinson, Kathy. 32p. (gr. k-3). 1988. 12. 95 (*1-550370-17-0*, Pub. by Annick CN); pap. 4.95 (*1-550370-16-2*, Pub. by Annick CN) Firefly Bks Ltd.
—Travels for Two: Stories & Lies from My Childhood. Poulin, Stephane. 32p. (ps-2). 1991. PLB 15.95 (*1-55037-205-X*, Pub. by Annick CN); pap. 5.95 (*1-55037-204-1*, Pub. by Annick CN) Firefly Bks Ltd.
Pound, Claire. Finished Being Four. Wilkins, Verna A. LC 93-12120. 1993. 7.95 (*1-870516-10-9*) Childs Play.
Pound, Garry. Hey, Look at Me! Merry Manners: Merry Manors. Thomasson, Merry F. Date not set. write for info. (*1-882607-06-6*) Merrybooks VA.
Powell, Ann, et al. California's Chumash Indians. rev. ed. Santa Barbara Museum of Natural History. 72p. (ps-4). 1988. pap. 5.95 (*0-945092-00-8*) EZ Nature.
Powell, Ivan. The Time Machine. Wells, H. G. Wright, Betty R., adapted by. LC 81-4097. 48p. (gr. 4 up). 1983. PLB 18.64 (*0-8172-1675-8*) Raintree Steck-V.
Powell, Michelle. Denial of Rights. Rowan, Barbara. LC 90-84008. 153p. (Orig.). (gr. 8 up). 1991. pap. 8.00 (*0-9622863-4-6*) Bristlecone Pubns.
—Igor & Mom. Rowan, Barbara. LC 90-84009. 43p. (Orig.). (gr. k-4). 1991. pap. 7.50 (*0-9622863-2-X*) Bristlecone Pubns.
Powell, Terry. Jason & the Mischievous Mongoose. Sheppard, Nancy D. LC 91-40480. 48p. (Orig.). 1991. pap. text ed. 3.95 (*0-87227-172-2*) Reg Baptist.
—What Christmas Means to Me. Snyder, J. L. 43p. (gr. 8-12). 1989. pap. text ed. 2.50 (*0-87227-134-X*) Reg Baptist.
Power, Margaret. The Leaf Raker. Caisley, Raewyn. LC 93-26218. 1994. 4.25 (*0-383-03756-5*) SRA Schl Grp.
—The Long Red Scarf. Hilton, Nette. 32p. (ps-3). 1990. PLB 18.95 (*0-87614-399-0*) Carolrhoda Bks.
—The Name. Epstein, June. LC 92-34161. 1993. 3.75 (*0-383-03643-7*) SRA Schl Grp.
—Ssh, Don't Wake the Baby! Wiener, Yvonne. LC 92-34160. 1993. 3.75 (*0-383-03655-0*) SRA Schl Grp.
Powers, Christine. Young Pocahontas: Indian Princess. Benjamin, Anne. LC 91-32654. 32p. (gr. k-2). 1992. PLB 11.59 (*0-8167-2534-9*); pap. text ed. 2.95 (*0-8167-2535-7*) Troll Assocs.
Powers, Daniel. Tuti, Blue Horse, & the Nipnope Man. Mathews, Judith. LC 93-1. 1993. write for info. (*0-8075-8130-5*) A Whitman.
Powers, Mary E. Our Teacher's in a Wheelchair. Powers, Mary E. Tucker, Kathleen, ed. LC 86-1623. 32p. (ps-3). 1986. 11.95 (*0-8075-6240-8*) A Whitman.
Powers, Richard M. American Tall Tales. Stoutenburg, Adrien. (gr. 3-7). 1976. pap. 3.99 (*0-14-030928-4*, Puffin) Puffin Bks.
Powers, Tom. The Table & the Chair. Lear, Edward. LC 91-45538. 32p. (ps-3). 1993. 15.00 (*0-06-020804-X*); PLB 14.89 (*0-06-020805-8*) HarpC Child Bks.
Powzyk, Joyce. Animal Camouflage: A Closer Look. Powzyk, Joyce. LC 89-9848. 40p. (gr. 2-9). 1990. SBE 15.95 (*0-02-774980-0*, Bradbury Pr) Macmillan Child Grp.
—A Child's Book of Wildflowers. Kelly, M. A. LC 91-30368. 32p. (gr. k-4). 1992. RSBE 15.95 (*0-02-750142-6*, Four Winds) Macmillan Child Grp.
—Crow Moon, Worm Moon. Skofield, James. LC 89-1370. 32p. (gr. k-3). 1990. RSBE 13.95 (*0-02-782915-4*, Four Winds) Macmillan Child Grp.
—Henry. Bawden, Nina. LC 87-29339. (gr. 3 up). 1988. PLB 13.95 (*0-688-07894-X*) Lothrop.
—The New Illustrated Dinosaur Dictionary. Sattler, Helen R. 1990. 24.95 (*0-688-08462-1*) Lothrop.

—The New Illustrated Dinosaur Dictionary. Sattler, Helen R. LC 90-3313. 352p. 1990. pap. 14.95 (*0-688-10043-0*, Pub. by Beech Tree Bks) Morrow.
—Tasmania: A Wildlife Journey. Powzyk, Joyce. LC 86-7288. 32p. (gr. 3-6). 1987. 12.95 (*0-688-06459-0*) Lothrop.
Poydar, Nancy. At the Laundromat. Loomis, Christine. LC 93-10884. 1993. 14.95 (*0-590-72830-X*); pap. 4.95 (*0-590-49488-0*) Scholastic Inc.
—At the Library. Loomis, Christine. LC 93-10882. 1994. 14.95 (*0-590-72831-8*); pap. 4.95 (*0-590-49489-9*) Scholastic Inc.
—At the Mall. Loomis, Christine. 1994. 14.95 (*0-590-72832-6*); pap. 4.95 (*0-590-49490-2*) Scholastic Inc.
—Chelsea Martin Turns Green. Lindberg, Becky T. Tucker, Kathy, ed. LC 92-31613. 144p. (gr. 2-4). 1993. PLB 11.95 (*0-8075-1134-X*) A Whitman.
—Dirty Kurt. Serfozo, Mary. LC 90-29065. 32p. (ps-3). 1992. SBE 13.95 (*0-689-50537-X*, M K McElderry) Macmillan Child Grp.
—In the Diner. Loomis, Christine. 32p. (ps-3). 1994. 14. 95 (*0-590-46716-6*, Scholastic Hardcover) Scholastic Inc.
—Rachel Parker, Kindergarten Show-Off. Martin, Ann M. LC 91-25793. 40p. (ps-3). 1992. reinforced bdg. 15.95 (*0-8234-0935-X*) Holiday.
—Rachel Parker Kingergarten Show-Off. Martin, Ann. 1993. pap. 6.95 (*0-8234-1067-6*) Holiday.
—Scrabble Creek. Wittmann, Patricia. LC 92-10810. 32p. (gr. k-3). 1993. RSBE 14.95 (*0-02-793225-7*, Macmillan Child Bk) Macmillan Child Grp.
—Second Grade Pig Pals. Larson, Kirby. LC 93-16061. (gr. 1-5). 1994. write for info. (*0-8234-1107-9*) Holiday.
—Speak up, Chelsea Martin! Lindberg, Becky T. Tucker, Kathleen, ed. LC 93-3318. 128p. (gr. 2-4). 1991. 11.95 (*0-8075-7552-6*) A Whitman.
—When the Water Closes over My Head. Napoli, Donna J. LC 93-14486. 60p. (gr. 3-5). 1994. 13.99 (*0-525-45083-1*) Dutton Child Bks.
—Will There Be a Lap for Me? Corey, Dorothy. Levine, Abby, ed. LC 91-20324. 24p. (ps-1). 1992. PLB 11.95 (*0-8075-9109-2*) A Whitman.
Poyser, Victoria. The Summer the Flowers Had No Scent. 3rd ed. Nicolai, D. Miles. 28p. (gr. 3-5). 1977. pap. 2.75 (*0-933992-19-X*) Coffee Break.
Pragoff, Fiona. Autumn. Pragoff, Fiona. 20p. (ps). 1993. spiral bdg. 5.95 (*0-689-71705-9*, Aladdin) Macmillan Child Grp.
—It's Fun to Be One. Pragoff, Fiona. 24p. (ps). 1994. bds. 6.95 (*0-689-71813-6*, Aladdin) Macmillan Child Grp.
—It's Great to Be Two. Pragoff, Fiona. 24p. (ps). 1994. bds. 6.95 (*0-689-71814-4*, Aladdin) Macmillan Child Grp.
—Let's Find Teddy. Pragoff, Fiona. LC 92-2765. 32p. (ps). 1992. 10.00 (*0-679-83501-6*) Random Bks Yng Read.
—Winter. Pragoff, Fiona. 20p. (ps). 1993. Repr. spiral bdg. 5.95 (*0-689-71704-0*, Aladdin) Macmillan Child Grp.
Prater, John. The Gift. Prater, John. 32p. (ps-3). 1986. pap. 9.95 (*0-670-80952-7*) Viking Child Bks.
—Little Ghost. Catt, Louis. LC 93-29804. 1994. write for info. (*1-56402-394-X*) Candlewick Pr.
—No! Said Joe. Prater, John. LC 91-71828. 32p. (ps up). 1992. 14.95 (*1-56402-037-1*) Candlewick Pr.
—Tim & the Blanket Thief: Timid Tim & the Cuggy Thief. Prater, John. LC 93-6563. 32p. (ps-3). 1993. SBE 14.95 (*0-689-31881-2*, Atheneum Child Bk) Macmillan Child Grp.
Prater, John & French, Vivian. Once upon a Time. LC 92-53139. 32p. (ps). 1993. 14.95 (*1-56402-177-7*) Candlewick Pr.
Prato, Rodica. King Midas & the Golden Touch. Metaxas, Eric. LC 91-40670. 40p. (gr. k up). 1992. pap. 14.95 (*0-88708-234-3*, Rabbit Ears); incl. cass. 19. 95 (*0-88708-235-1*, Rabbit Ears) Picture Bk Studio.
Pratt, George. Enemy Ace: War Idyll. Pratt, George. Helfer, Andrew, ed. Kubert, Joe, intro. by. 128p. (Orig.). 1991. pap. 14.95 (*0-930289-78-1*) DC Comics.
Pratt, Kristin J. Un Paseo Por el Bosque Lluvioso: A Walk in the Rainforest. Pratt, Kristin. (SPA & ENG.). 32p. (ps-5). 1993. pap. 6.95 (*1-883220-02-5*) Dawn CA.
—A Swim Through the Sea. Pratt, Kristin J. 44p. (Orig.). (ps-5). 1994. 14.95 (*1-883220-03-3*); pap. 6.95 (*1-883220-04-1*) Dawn CA.
Pratt, Pierre. Follow that Hat! Pratt, Pierre. 32p. (ps-2). 1992. PLB 15.95 (*1-55037-261-0*, Pub. by Annick Pr); pap. 5.95 (*1-55037-259-9*, Pub. by Annick Pr) Firefly Bks Ltd.
—Leon sans Son Chapeau: Follow That Hat! Pratt, Pierre. (FRE.). 32p. (ps-2). 1992. 15.95 (*1-55037-263-7*, Pub. by Annick Pr); pap. 6.95 (*1-55037-262-9*, Pub. by Annick Pr) Firefly Bks Ltd.
—Uncle Henry's Dinner Guests. Froissart, Benedicte. 32p. (ps-2). 1990. 14.95 (*1-55037-141-X*, Pub. by Annick CN); pap. 4.95 (*1-55037-140-1*, Pub. by Annick CN) Firefly Bks Ltd.
Pre, Karen G. Misty's Twilight. Henry, Marguerite. LC 91-42582. 144p. (gr. 3-7). 1992. SBE 13.95 (*0-02-743623-3*, Macmillan Child Bk) Macmillan Child Grp.
Prebenna, David. Babar the Boy King. Herman, Gail. LC 88-63343. 32p. (Orig.). (ps-3). 1989. pap. text ed. 1.50 (*0-394-84533-1*) Random Bks Yng Read.

—Baby Kermit's Playtime ABC. Jones, Lily. 24p. (ps-k). 1992. pap. 1.79 laminated covers (*0-307-10024-3*, 10024, Golden Pr) Western Pub.
—Best Friends. Davis, Allison. 32p. (ps-k). 1992. write for info. (*0-307-12008-2*, 12008) Western Pub.
—A Car Trip for Mole & Mouse. Ziefert, Harriet. 32p. (ps-3). 1991. 8.95 (*0-670-83858-6*) Viking Child Bks.
—A Car Trip for Mole & Mouse. Ziefert, Harriet. 32p. (ps-3). 1991. pap. 3.50 (*0-14-054392-9*, Puffin) Puffin Bks.
—A Clean House for Mole & Mouse. Ziefert, Harriet. (Orig.). (ps-3). 1988. pap. 3.50 (*0-14-050810-4*, Puffin) Puffin Bks.
—A Clean House for Mole & Mouse. Ziefert, Harriet. LC 87-25420. 32p. (ps-3). 1988. pap. 8.95 (*0-670-82032-6*) Viking Child Bks.
—Go Away, Crows! Mason, Margo. 32p. (ps-1). 1989. 3.50 (*0-553-34725-X*) Bantam.
—A New House for Mole & Mouse. Ziefert, Harriet. LC 86-46222. 32p. (ps-3). 1987. pap. 3.50 (*0-14-050745-0*, Puffin) Puffin Bks.
—New House for Mouse & Mole. Ziefert, Harriet. (ps-3). 1987. pap. 8.95 (*0-670-81720-1*) Viking Child Bks.
—Piggety Pig Books, 6 of ea. title. Ziefert, Harriet. 96p. (ps-k). 1988. 2.95 (*0-316-98758-1*) Little.
—Sesame Street: Sleep Tight! Allen, Constance. (ps-k). 1991. pap. write for info. (*0-307-10026-X*, Golden Pr) Western Pub.
Prechtel, Martin. Grandmother Sweat Bath: A Story of the Tzutujil Mana. Prechtel, Martin. Rodney, Janet, ed. 39p. (Orig.). (gr. 6 up). 1990. write for info. Weaselsleeves Pr.
Preis, Donna, jt. photog. see Siede, George.
Preiss, Leah P. Chocolate Chip Cookies. Wagner, Karen. 32p. (ps-2). 1990. 14.95 (*0-8050-1268-0*, Bks Young Read) H Holt & Co.
Premo, Steve. Dear Santa, Make Me a Star. Roos, Stephen. 96p. (gr. 2-6). 1991. pap. 3.50 perfect bdg. (*0-89486-764-4*, T5174) Hazelden.
—Leave It to Augie. Roos, Stephen. 96p. (gr. 2-6). 1991. pap. 3.50 perfect bdg. (*0-89486-774-1*, T5172) Hazelden.
—My Blue Tongue. Roos, Stephen. 96p. (gr. 2-6). 1991. pap. 3.50 perfect bdg. (*0-89486-784-9*, T5173) Hazelden.
—Silver Secrets: Maple Street Kids Ser. Roos, Stephen. 96p. (gr. 2-6). 1991. pap. 3.50 perfect bdg. (*0-89486-777-6*, T5171) Hazelden.
Present, David, jt. illus. see Dessereau, April.
Press, Jenny. Christmas Bear. Russell, Georgina. 28p. (ps-2). 1991. 8.95 (*0-7214-5331-7*, S808) Ladybird Bks.
—Christmas Bear (Miniature) Russell, Georgina. 28p. (gr. 3-4). 1992. 2.95 (*0-7214-3506-8*) Ladybird Bks.
—Noah's Story. Backhouse, Halcyon. LC 92-952. 1992. 7.99 (*0-8407-3417-9*) Oliver-Nelson.
—Samson the Strong Man. Pipe, Rhona. LC 92-13326. (gr. 1 up). 1993. 7.99 (*0-8407-3421-2*) Oliver-Nelson.
—When Time Began. Pipe, Rhona. LC 92-13321. 1993. 7.99 (*0-8407-3419-0*) Oliver-Nelson.
Pressley, Ann. The Captain, the Gypsy & the Giant Bird. Cormier, Larry. Bruni, Mary-Ann S., ed. 48p. (gr. k-8). 1986. 12.95 (*0-935857-07-9*); pap. write for info. (*0-935857-08-7*) Texart.
Preston, Heather. Remember the Secret. Kubler-Ross, Elisabeth. LC 81-68454. 32p. (ps up). 1988. pap. 9.95 (*0-89087-524-3*) Celestial Arts.
Preston, Judy J. The Outer Banks Story. Preston, Judy J. 117p. (Orig.). (gr. 5 up). 1985. pap. 3.49 (*0-9613824-0-6*) Seabright.
Preston-Mauks, Susan & Sheehan-Burke, Julia. Field Hockey Is for Me. Preston-Mauks, Susan. LC 83-11268. 48p. (gr. 2-5). 1983. PLB 13.50 (*0-8225-1141-X*) Lerner Pubns.
Presutto, Josephine. Come, Walk in the Woods with Me. Hilton, Kathlyn G. LC 92-72704. 32p. (gr. 7-9). 1993. 12.95 (*1-880851-04-0*) Greene Bark Pr.
Pretro, Korinna. The Star Counters. Luttrell, Ida. LC 93-20342. 32p. 1994. 15.00 (*0-688-12149-7*, Tambourine Bks); PLB 14.93 (*0-688-12150-0*, Tambourine Bks) Morrow.
Price, C. Viking's Dawn. Treece, Henry. LC 56-9962. (gr. 7-9). 1956. 21.95 (*0-87599-117-3*) S G Phillips.
Price, Caroline. Amish Adventure. Smucker, Barbara. LC 83-80892. 144p. (gr. 6-9). 1983. pap. 6.95 (*0-8361-3339-0*) Herald Pr.
Price, Christine. Men of the Hills. Treece, Henry. LC 58-5448. (gr. 6-9). 1958. 21.95 (*0-87599-115-7*) S G Phillips.
—Ride into Danger. Treece, Henry. LC 59-12203. (gr. 7-10). 1959. 21.95 (*0-87599-113-0*) S G Phillips.
—Road to Miklagard. Treece, Henry. LC 57-12280. (gr. 6-10). 1957. 21.95 (*0-87599-114-9*) S G Phillips.
Price, David. Birds & Beasts. Roberts, Sheena, compiled by. 80p. (gr. 1-6). 12.95 (*0-7136-5653-0*, Pub. by A&C Black UK) Talman.
Price, Gerry. Fun Math Flip Book Series, 4 bks. (gr. 7-9). 1994. No. 1: I Can Add! pap. 7.99 (*0-553-09564-1*); No. 2: I Can Subtract! pap. 7.99 (*0-553-09565-X*); No. 3: I Can Multiply! pap. 7.99 (*0-553-09566-8*); No. 4: I Can Divide! pap. 7.99 (*0-553-09567-6*) Bantam.
Price, Hattie L. Rose in Bloom. Alcott, Louisa May. (gr. 7 up). 1976. 19.95 (*0-316-03098-8*) Little.
Price, Nick. Magical Animals. Watson, Carol. (gr. k-4). 1982. (Usborne-Hayes); PLB 11.96 (*0-88110-095-1*); pap. 4.50 (*0-86020-670-X*) EDC.

Price, Norman & Van Swearingen, E. C. Three Musketeers. Dumas, Alexandre. (gr. 4-6). 1953-59. (G&D); deluxe ed. 13.95 (0-448-06024-8) Putnam Pub Group.

Price, Susan & Nelson, Kelly. Pioneers of Forest & City. Stapler, Harry. Blanchard, James J. & Austin, Richard H.intro. by. LC 85-62817. 227p. (gr. 4-8). 1985. 12.00 (0-935719-00-8) MI Dept Hist.

Price, T. Alexander. The Forbidden Towers. Gaskin, Carol. LC 84-16219. 128p. (gr. 3-7). 1985. lib. bdg. 9.49 (0-8167-0324-8) Troll Assocs.

—The Magician's Ring. Gaskin, Carol. LC 84-8499. 128p. (gr. 3-7). 1985. PLB 9.49 (0-8167-0320-5); pap. text ed. 2.95 (0-8167-0321-3) Troll Assocs.

—Master of Mazes. Gaskin, Carol. LC 84-24015. 128p. (gr. 3-7). 1985. PLB 9.49 (0-8167-0322-1) Troll Assocs.

—The War of the Wizards. Gaskin, Carol. LC 84-2663. 128p. (gr. 3-7). 1985. PLB 9.49 (0-8167-0318-3); pap. text ed. 2.95 (0-8167-0319-1) Troll Assocs.

Priceman, Marjorie. For Laughing Out Loud: Poems to Tickle Your Funnybone. Prelutsky, Jack, compiled by. LC 90-33010. 96p. (gr. 2-7). 1991. 14.95 (0-394-82144-0); PLB 15.99 (0-394-92144-5) Knopf Bks Yng Read.

—Friend or Frog. Priceman, Marjorie. (ps-3). 1989. 13.45 (0-395-44523-X) HM.

—Friend or Frog. Priceman, Marjorie. 32p. (gr. k-3). 1991. pap. 4.80 (0-395-60286-6, Sandpiper) HM.

—A Mouse in My House. Van Laan, Nancy. LC 89-15591. 32p. (ps-3). 1990. 9.95 (0-679-80043-3); PLB 10.99 (0-679-90043-8) Knopf Bks Yng Read.

—A Nonny Mouse Writes Again! Prelutsky, Jack. LC 92-5214. 40p. (ps-5). 1993. 13.00 (0-679-83715-9); PLB 13.99 (0-679-93715-3) Knopf Bks Yng Read.

—Rachel Fister's Blister. MacDonald, Amy. 32p. (ps-3). 1990. 13.45 (0-395-52152-1) HM.

—Rachel Fister's Blister. MacDonald, Amy. 32p. (gr. k-3). 1993. pap. 4.80 (0-395-65744-X) HM.

—The Tiny, Tiny Boy & the Big, Big Cow. Van Laan, Nancy. LC 91-33738. 40p. (ps-2). 1993. 8.99 (0-679-82078-7); PLB 9.99 (0-679-92078-1) Knopf Bks Yng Read.

Priddy, R. Robotics. Potter, T. & Guild, I. 48p. (gr. 6 up). 1983. PLB 13.96 (0-88110-152-4); pap. 6.95 (0-86020-724-2) EDC.

Pride, Alexis, et al. Once upon a Ryme Tyme for Growing Minds. Ali-El, Yusuf. LC 83-90101. 90p. (gr. k-5). 1983. pap. 9.95 (0-912475-09-9) Natl Res Unltd.

Priebe, Vel. Wendy's Gift. Priebe, Vel. 24p. (Orig.). (ps-2). 1988. pap. 1.50 (0-919797-67-9) Kindred Pr.

Priestley, Alice. Out on the Ice in the Middle of the Bay. Cunning, Peter. 32p. 1993. lib. bdg. 15.95 (1-55037-276-9, Pub. by Annick CN); pap. 5.95 (1-55037-277-7, Pub. by Annick CN) Firefly Bks Ltd.

Primavera, Elise. Best Witches. Yolen, Jane. 48p. (gr. k-4). 1989. 14.95 (0-399-21539-5, Putnam) Putnam Pub Group.

—C. K. & the Time She Quit the Family. Gauch, Patricia L. 32p. (ps-3). 1992. pap. 5.95 (0-399-22405-X, Putnam) Putnam Pub Group.

—Christina Katerina & the Great Bear Train. Gauch, Patricia L. 32p. 1990. 14.95 (0-399-21623-5, Putnam) Putnam Pub Group.

—Christina Katerina & the Time She Quit the Family. Gauch, Patricia L. 32p. (ps-3). 1987. 14.95 (0-399-21408-9, Putnam) Putnam Pub Group.

—Double Dare Dog. Gilson, Jamie. LC 87-37855. 126p. (gr. 3-5). 1988. 12.95 (0-688-07969-5) Lothrop.

—Grandma's House. Moore, Elaine. LC 84-11233. 32p. (gr. k up). 1985. PLB 14.88 (0-688-04116-7); 14.95 (0-688-04115-9) Lothrop.

—Grandma's Promise. Moore, Elaine. LC 86-33762. (gr. k-3). 1988. 14.95 (0-688-06740-9); lib. bdg. 14.88 (0-688-06741-7) Lothrop.

—Hobie Hanson, You're Weird. Gilson, Jamie. MacDonald, Pat, ed. 176p. (gr. 3-6). 1988. pap. 2.99 (0-671-73752-X, Minstrel Bks) PB.

—Make Way for Sam Houston. Fritz, Jean. LC 85-25601. 109p. (gr. 4-6). 1986. 13.95 (0-399-21303-1, Putnam); pap. 6.95 (0-399-21304-X) Putnam Pub Group.

—Moe the Dog in Tropical Paradise. Stanley, Diane. 32p. (ps-3). 1992. 14.95 (0-399-22127-1, Putnam) Putnam Pub Group.

—The Three Dots. Primavera, Elise. LC 92-12979. 40p. (ps-3). 1993. 14.95 (0-399-22429-7, Putnam) Putnam Pub Group.

—WOWO, the Radio Dog. McCloskey, Kevin. LC 92-44165. (gr. 3 up). 1994. write for info. (0-688-12657-X); PLB write for info. (0-688-12658-8) Lothrop.

Prince, Jane. A New Baby at Koko Bear's House. reissued ed. Lansky, Vicki. 32p. (Orig.). 1991. pap. 4.95 (0-916773-22-1) Book Peddlers.

Prince, Jane L. Koko Bear's New Potty, No. 1. Lansky, Vicki. 32p. 1986. pap. 3.50 (0-553-34243-6) Bantam.

Prittie, Edwin J. Black Beauty. Sewell, Anna. 298p. 1993. Repr. 29.95 (1-877767-86-7) Regal Pubns.

Probst, Emile. The Life of St. Martin. Smith, Verena. (gr. 2-5). 1993. pap. write for info. (0-913026-43-3) St Nectarios.

Pronin, Anatolii. Ipostas' - Poems: Chetvertaia Kniga Stikhotvorenii, 1968-1988. Jupp, Michael. LC 88-6090. (RUS.). 164p. (gr. 9-12). 1991. 30.00 (0-911971-30-0) Effect Pub.

Proof Positive-Farrowlyne Associates, Inc. Staff. Celebrating the Eucharist. Nelson, Yvette. 73p. (Orig.). (gr. 7-8). 1992. pap. text ed. 2.80 (0-88489-269-7); tchr's ed. 6.00 (0-88489-270-0) St Marys.

—Making Decisions. Brown, Maggie W. 61p. (Orig.). 1990. text ed. 2.80 stitched (0-88489-200-X); tchr's ed. 6.00 (0-88489-201-8) St Marys.

Prorokova, Elena. A Midsummer Night's Dream. Garfield, Leon, abridged by. LC 92-14522. 48p. (gr. 5 up). 1993. PLB 11.99 (0-679-93870-2); pap. 6.99 (0-679-83870-8) Knopf Bks Yng Read.

Prosser, Donna. The Education of Character: Lesson for Beginners. Keim, Will S. Pittman, Bruce, intro. by. 96p. 1992. 14.95 (0-9631834-0-0) Viaticum Pr.

Prosser, Les. What You Should Know about the American Flag. rev. ed. Williams, Earl P., Jr. Sheads, Scott S., frwd. by. 68p. (gr. 4-6). 1989. pap. text ed. 4.95 (0-939631-10-5) Thomas Publications.

Provensen, Alice. The Buck Stops Here: The Presidents of the United States. Provensen, Alice. LC 88-35036. 56p. (gr. 2 up). 1990. 18.00 (0-06-024786-X); PLB 17.89 (0-06-024787-8) HarpC Child Bks.

Provensen, Alice & Provensen, Martin. A Book of Seasons. Provensen, Alice & Provensen, Martin. LC 75-36470. 32p. (ps-1). 1976. pap. 2.25 (0-394-83242-6) Random Bks Yng Read.

—The Mother Goose Book. reissue ed. Provensen, Alice & Provensen, Martin. LC 76-8548. 64p. (gr. 1 up). 1976. 10.00 (0-394-82122-X) Random Bks Yng Read.

—Old Mother Hubbard. Provensen, Alice & Provensen, Martin. LC 76-24176. 32p. (ps-1). 1992. pap. 2.25 (0-394-83460-7) Random Bks Yng Read.

—Our Animal Friends at Maple Hill Farm. reissue ed. Provensen, Alice & Provensen, Martin. LC 74-828. 64p. (ps-3). 1992. 10.00 (0-394-82123-8) Random Bks Yng Read.

—A Peaceable Kingdom: The Shaker Abecedarius. Barsam, Richard M., afterword by. (gr. k-3). 1981. pap. 5.99 (0-14-050370-6, Puffin) Puffin Bks.

—A Peaceable Kingdom: The Shaker Abecedarius. Barsam, Richard M., afterword by. LC 78-125. 42p. (gr. k-2). 1978. pap. 16.00 (0-670-54500-7) Viking Child Bks.

—A Visit to William Blake's Inn: Poems for Innocent & Experienced Travelers. Willard, Nancy. LC 80-27403. 44p. (ps-3). 1981. 14.95 (0-15-293822-2, HB Juv Bks) HarBrace.

—The Year at Maple Hill Farm. Provensen, Alice & Provensen, Martin. LC 88-10367. 32p. (ps-2). 1988. pap. 3.95 (0-689-71270-7, Aladdin) Macmillan Child Grp.

Provensen, Alice, jt. illus. see Provensen, Martin.

Provensen, Martin & Provensen, Alice. The Voyage of the Ludgate Hill: A Journey with Robert Louis Stevenson. Willard, Nancy, et al. LC 86-19502. 32p. (gr. k-3). 1987. 14.95 (0-15-294464-8) HarBrace.

Provensen, Martin, jt. illus. see Provensen, Alice.

Provensen, Martin, jt. illus. see Provensen, Nancy.

Provensen, Nancy & Provensen, Martin. A Visit to William Blake's Inn. Willard, Nancy. LC 80-27403. 44p. (ps-3). 1982. pap. 5.95 (0-15-293823-0, Voyager Bks) HarBrace.

Provincial, Bernard W. Hoksila & the Red Buffalo. Crow, Moses N. 40p. (Orig.). (gr. 3 up). 1991. pap. 5.95 (1-877976-02-4, 406-0017) Tipi Pr. Among the Lakota, this legend is called, Enya-hoksei. It is told differently by every story-teller of every clan. The outline of the legend remains the same as it travels with time. The whole story changes with the changing of times. The significance of it, as it goes through the ages, is that it has no horses in it. The story has to be very old. But like all legends, it keeps in tune with the passing of time. When Hoksila the young warrior begins his long journey, his hunt to rescue his wife & to rid his tribe of the red buffalo with the ugly black spots. Then he could free all the young maidens. This is a story of the battle of good & evil, & how it's been handed down by the Lakota. An engaging story for the young & those not so young. *Publisher Provided Annotation.*

Prunier, J. & Galeron, H. Dinosaure. (FRE.). (ps-1). 1991. 17.95 (2-07-056642-0) Schoenhof.

Prunier, James. Metals: Born of Earth & Fire. Reymond, Jean-Pierre. LC 87-34596. 38p. (gr. k-5). 1988. 4.95 (0-944589-19-7, 197) Young Discovery Lib.

Pryor, Ainslie. The Baby Blue Cat Who Said No. Pryor, Ainslie. LC 87-21026. 32p. (ps-k). 1988. 11.95 (0-670-81780-5) Viking Child Bks.

Pryor, Ernest, et al. Can You Count?; Carpetbaggers in Action; Mr. Impossible. 2nd ed. Ceasor, Frank, Sr. & Gaines, Edith. McCluskey, John A., ed. (gr. 4-7). 1993. pap. 3.00 (0-913678-27-9) New Day Pr.

Prytkova, Ksenia. Twelfth Night. Garfield, Leon, abridged by. LC 92-14524. 48p. (gr. 5 up). 1993. PLB 11.99 (0-679-93872-9); pap. 6.99 (0-679-83872-4) Knopf Bks Yng Read.

Puccetti, Patricia I. Following Christ. DiCarlo, Joseph, Jr. 142p. (Orig.). (gr. 6). 1985. pap. 6.80 (0-89870-065-5) Ignatius Pr.

Pucmer, Inka. Rampion. Pucmer, Inka. 25p. (gr. 2-4). 1982. 19.95 (0-88010-064-8, Pub. by Walter Keller Pr) Anthroposophic.

Pugh, Anna. Copycats & Artifacts. Post, Marianne. LC 86-45532. 96p. 1986. pap. 9.95 (0-87923-645-0) Godine.

Pugh, Kayleen. Stand Tall. Erickson, P. C. (Orig.). (gr. 4-8). 1978. pap. 2.95 (0-89036-111-8) Hawkes Pub Inc.

Puglisi, Lou. My First Health & Nutrition Coloring Book: Mr. Carrots Coloring Book. Greenbaum, David & Wasser, Edward. 40p. (Orig.). (gr. 2). 1988. pap. 0.99 (0-9621833-0-X) D Greenbaum.

Pullen, Pip. The Little Girl Who Grew up to be Governor: Stories from the Life of Martha Layne Collins. Smith, Frances. LC 91-73725. 64p. (gr. 2-4). 1991. 13.95 (0-9630135-0-5) Denham Pub.

Pullig, Louis. Charlie Churchmouse Finds a Home. Hollier, Jo. Kichejian, Janet, ed. 16p. 1989. 14.95 (0-685-29440-4) Silver Pubns.

Pulver, Harry. Find It! The Inside Story at Your Library. McInerney, Claire. 56p. (gr. 4-6). 1989. PLB 14.95 (0-8225-2425-2) Lerner Pubns.

—Tracking the Facts: How to Develop Research Skills. McInerney, Claire. 64p. (gr. 4 up). 1990. PLB 14.95 (0-8225-2426-0) Lerner Pubns.

Pulver, Harry, Jr. Bringing up Parents: The Teenager's Handbook. Packer, Alex J. Espeland, Pamela, ed. LC 92-36625. 272p. (gr. 7 up). 1993. pap. 12.95 (0-915793-48-2) Free Spirit Pub.

Punches, Laurie C. How to Simply Cut Hair. Punches, Laurie C. Martinez, Carla, et al, eds. LC 88-92443. 109p. (Orig.). (gr. 11 up). 1989. pap. 8.95 (0-929883-06-3); VHS & Beta. video 29.95 (0-929883-07-1) Punches Prodns.

—How to Simply Cut Hair Even Better: Advanced Haircutting. Punches, Laurie C. LC 88-92468. 129p. (Orig.). (gr. 11 up). 1989. pap. 9.95 (0-929883-08-X) Punches Prodns.

—How to Simply Highlight Hair. Punches, Laurie C. LC 88-92469. 79p. (Orig.). (gr. 11 up). 1989. pap. 6.95 (0-929883-02-0); VHS & Beta. video 19.95 (0-929883-03-9) Punches Prodns.

—How to Simply Perm Hair. Punches, Laurie C. LC 88-92467. 74p. (Orig.). (gr. 11 up). 1989. pap. 6.95 (0-929883-04-7); VHS & Beta. video 19.95 (0-929883-05-5) Punches Prodns.

Purcell, Gordon & Villagran, Ricardo. The Best of Star Trek. Barr, Mike, et al. Greenberger, Bob & Hill, Michael, eds. 240p. (Orig.). 1991. pap. 19.95 (1-56389-009-7) DC Comics.

Puricelli, Luigi, jt. illus. see Cristini, Ermanno.

Pusterla, Fred. My First Magnifier Book. Pusterla, Fred. 12p. (ps-1). 1993. bds. 9.95 (1-56293-140-7) McClanahan Bk.

Putman, Brian. The How-to Book of Teen Self Discovery: Helping Teens Find Balance, Security & Esteem. 2nd ed. Childre, Doc L. Cryer, Bruce & Rozman, Deborah, eds. (SPA.). 128p. 1992. pap. 8.95 (1-879052-18-0) Planetary Pubns.

Puulton, Yvonne. Ancient China. Burland, Cottie A. (gr. 4-8). 1974. Repr. of 1960 ed. 10.95 (0-7175-0018-7) Dufour.

Pye, Trevor. It Always Rains for Jackie. Corrin, Ruth. 32p. (ps-2). 1990. bds. 8.95 (0-19-558205-5) OUP.

Pyle, Howard. Last of the Mohicans - Robin Hood. Holder, Glenn, ed. 384p. 1993. Repr. of 1952 ed. 29.95 (1-877767-82-4) Regal Pubns.

—The Merry Adventures of Robin Hood. Pyle, Howard. LC 68-55820. xxii, 296p. (gr. 3-6). 1968. pap. 6.95 (0-486-22043-5) Dover.

—The Merry Adventures of Robin Hood. Pyle, Howard. (gr. 4-8). 18.75 (0-8446-2765-8) Peter Smith.

—Otto of the Silver Hand. Pyle, Howard. xv, 173p. (gr. 5-9). 1967. pap. 5.95 (0-486-21784-1) Dover.

—The Story of King Arthur & His Knights. Pyle, Howard. xviii, 313p. (gr. 7 up). pap. 6.95 (0-486-21445-1) Dover.

—The Story of the Champions of the Round Table. Pyle, Howard. xviii, 329p. (ps-4). 1968. pap. 7.95 (0-486-21883-X) Dover.

—The Story of the Grail & the Passing of Arthur. Pyle, Howard. LC 85-40302. 340p. (gr. 7 up). 1985. SBE 19.95 (0-684-18483-4, Scribners Young Read) Macmillan Child Grp.

Q

Qrmai, Stella. Bizzy Bones & the Lost Quilt. Martin, Jacqueline B. LC 87-13577. (ps-3). 1988. 12.95 (0-688-07407-3); PLB 12.88 (0-688-07408-1) Lothrop.

Quackenbush, Marcia. The Kids' First Book about Sex. Blank, Joani. LC 89-14800. 48p. (Orig.). (ps-3). 1983. pap. 5.50 (0-940208-07-5, Yes Pr) Down There Pr.

—Period. updated ed. Gardner-Loulan, JoAnn, et al. LC 90-46065. 95p. (gr. 4-8). 1991. pap. 9.95 incl. removable parents' guide (0-912078-88-X) Volcano Pr.
Quackenbush, Robert. Benjamin Franklin & His Friends. Quackenbush, Robert. 32p. (gr. 2-5). 1991. 14.95 (0-945912-14-5) Pippin Pr.
—Bicycle to Treachery. Quackenbush, Robert. 48p. (gr. 1-5). 1985. pap. 4.95 (0-13-076258-X) P-H.
—Cable Car to Catastrophe. Quackenbush, Robert. 48p. (gr. 1-5). 1985. pap. 4.95 (0-13-110032-7) P-H.
—Danger in Tibet: A Miss Mallard Mystery. Quackenbush, Robert. 32p. (gr. 1-4). 1989. 14.95 (0-945912-03-X) Pippin Pr.
—Evil Under the Sea: A Miss Mallard Mystery. Quackenbush, Robert. 32p. (gr. 1-4). 1992. 14.95 (0-945912-16-1) Pippin Pr.
—First Grade Jitters. Quackenbush, Robert. LC 81-47757. 32p. (gr. k-2). 1982. PLB 11.89 (0-397-31981-9, Lipp Jr Bks) HarpC Child Bks.
—Henry Babysits. Quackenbush, Robert. LC 83-2247. 48p. (gr. ps-3). 1983. 5.95 (0-8193-1107-3); lib. bdg. 5.95 (0-8193-1108-1) Parents.
—Henry Babysits. Quackenbush, Robert. 48p. (ps-2). 1990. pap. 2.95 (0-448-04338-6, G&D) Putnam Pub Group.
—Henry's Awful Mistake. Quackenbush, Robert. LC 80-20327. 48p. (ps-3). 1981. 5.95 (0-8193-1039-5); PLB 5.95 (0-8193-1040-9) Parents.
—Henry's Important Date. Quackenbush, Robert. LC 81-5026. 48p. (ps-3). 1982. 5.95 (0-8193-1067-0); PLB 5.95 (0-8193-1068-9) Parents.
—Henry's World Tour. Quackenbush, Robert. LC 91-31257. 48p. (ps-3). 1992. pap. 14.00 (0-385-42010-2) Doubleday.
—I Did It with My Hatchet: A Story of George Washington. Quackenbush, Robert. 32p. (gr. 2-6). 1989. 14.95 (0-945912-04-8) Pippin Pr.
—It's Raining Cats & Dogs: Cat & Dog Jokes. Keller, Charles. 40p. (gr. 2-6). 1988. 13.95 (0-945912-01-3) Pippin Pr.
—James Madison & Dolly Madison & Their Times. Quackenbush, Robert. 40p. (gr. 2-5). 1992. 14.95 (0-945912-18-8) Pippin Pr.
—John Adams & Abigail Adams & Their Times. Quackenbush, Robert. 40p. (gr. 2-5). 1994. 14.95 (0-945912-24-2) Pippin Pr.
—Lost in the Amazon: A Miss Mallard Mystery. Quackenbush, Robert. 32p. (gr. 1-4). 1990. PLB 14.95 (0-945912-11-0) Pippin Pr.
—Mouse Feathers. Quackenbush, Robert. LC 87-15690. 40p. (gr. k-3). 1988. 12.95 (0-89919-527-X, Clarion Bks) HM.
—Old Silver Leg Takes Over: A Story of Peter Stuyvesant. Quackenbush, Robert. 40p. (gr. 1-5). 1986. 10.95 (0-13-633934-4) P-H.
—Pass the Quill; I'll Write a Draft: A Story of Thomas Jefferson. Quackenbush, Robert. 32p. (gr. 2-6). 1989. PLB 14.95 (0-945912-07-2) Pippin Pr.
—Quick, Annie, Give Me a Catchy Line! Quackenbush, Robert. 32p. (gr. 3-7). 1983. 10.95 (0-13-749762-8) P-H.
—Sheriff Sally Gopher & the Thanksgiving Caper. Quackenbush, Robert. LC 82-135. 32p. (gr. 1-3). 1982. PLB 13.88 (0-688-01293-0) Lothrop.
—Sherlock Chick & the Case of the Night Noises. Quackenbush, Robert. LC 89-70984. 48p. (ps-3). 1990. 5.95 (0-8193-1194-4) Parents.
—Sherlock Chick & the Giant Egg Mystery. Quackenbush, Robert. LC 88-4093. (ps-3). 1989. 5.95 (0-8193-1178-2) Parents.
—Sherlock Chick & the Peekaboo Mystery. Quackenbush, Robert. LC 87-3591. 48p. (ps-3). 1987. 5.95 (0-8193-1149-9) Parents.
—Sherlock Chick & the Peekaboo Mystery. Quackenbush, Robert. 48p. (gr. 3-7). 1990. pap. 2.95 (0-448-04343-3, G&D) Putnam Pub Group.
—Sherlock Chick's First Case. Quackenbush, Robert. LC 86-9398. 48p. (ps-3). 1986. 5.95 (0-8193-1148-0) Parents.
—The Spinster's Daughter. Littlesugar, Amy. 40p. (gr. 1-4). 1993. PLB 14.95 (0-945912-22-6) Pippin Pr.
—Stage Door to Terror. Quackenbush, Robert. LC 84-22295. 48p. (gr. 1-5). 1985. 11.95 (0-13-840364-3) P-H.
—Stairway to Down. Quackenbush, Robert. 48p. (gr. 1-5). 1986. pap. 5.95 (0-13-840604-9) P-H.
—Surfboard to Peril: A Miss Mallard Mystery. Quackenbush, Robert. 48p. (gr. 1-5). 1986. 11.95 (0-13-877986-4) P-H.
—Taxi to Intrigue. Quackenbush, Robert. LC 84-4691. 48p. (gr. 1-5). 1984. 10.95 (0-13-886813-1) P-H.
—Texas Trail to Calamity. Quackenbush, Robert. 48p. (gr. 1-5). 1986. 11.95 (0-13-912544-2) P-H.
—Watt Got You Started, Mr. Fulton? Quackenbush, Robert. 39p. (gr. 1-4). 1982. 7.95 (0-13-944397-5) P-H.
—Where Did Your Family Come From? A Book about Immigrants. Berger, Melvin & Berger, Gilda. LC 92-28626. (gr. k-3). 1993. 12.00 (0-8249-8647-4, Ideals Child); pap. 3.95 (0-8249-8610-5) Hambleton-Hill.
—The Whole World in Your Hands: Looking at Maps. Berger, Melvin & Berger, Gilda. LC 92-18199. (gr. k-3). 1993. 12.00 (0-8249-8646-6, Ideals Child); pap. 3.95 (0-8249-8609-1) Hambleton-Hill.
Quay, M. J. Bellybuttons Are Navels. Schoen, Mark. Calderone, Mary, intro. by. 40p. (ps-3). 1990. Repr. 16.95 (0-87975-585-7) Prometheus Bks.

Quayle, Greg. Jose' el Diablo: The World's Most Traveled Dog. Quayle, Thomas E., ed. 95p. (Orig.). 1985. pap. 3.00 (0-9623144-0-4) Vilate Pub.
Quenell, Midge. Animal Tales Big Book Package, 6 bks. Kaplan, Carol B. Bolinske, Janet L., ed. 144p. (ps-k). 1988. Set of 6 bks., 24 pgs. ea. bk. 100.00 (0-88335-759-3) Milliken Pub Co.
—The Brown Bear Who Wasn't. Kaplan, Carol B. Bolinske, Janet L., ed. LC 87-63000. (ps-k). 1988. 17.95 (0-88335-753-4); pap. 4.95 (0-88335-076-9) Milliken Pub Co.
—The Haunted Picnic. Kaplan, Carcl B. Bolinske, Janet L., ed. LC 87-62999. 24p. (Orig.). (ps-k). 1988. 17.95 (0-88335-754-2); pap. write for info. (0-88335-077-7) Milliken Pub Co.
—The Not-So-Fast Rabbit. Kaplan, Carol B. Bolinske, Janet L., ed. LC 87-62997. 24p. (Orig.). (ps-k). 1988. 17.95 (0-88335-755-0); pap. 4.95 (0-88335-079-3) Milliken Pub Co.
—The Picky Pig. Kaplan, Carol B. Bolinske, Janet L., ed. LC 87-62998. 24p. (Orig.). (ps-k). 1988. spiral bdg. 17.95 (0-88335-756-9); pap. 4.95 (0-88335-078-5) Milliken Pub Co.
—The Underground Tea Party. Kaplan, Carol B. Bolinske, Janet L., ed. LC 87-62996. 24p. (Orig.). (ps-k). 1988. spiral-bound Big Book 17.95 (0-88335-758-5); pap. 4.95 (0-88335-080-7) Milliken Pub Co.
—Wicker's Wishes. Kaplan, Carol B. Bolinske, Janet L., ed. LC 87-63001. 24p. (Orig.). (ps-k). 1988. 17.95 (0-88335-757-7); pap. 4.95 (0-88335-075-0) Milliken Pub Co.
Quentin, Laurence. Behind the Wall of China. Busuttil, Joelle. Bogard, Vicki, tr. from FRE. LC 92-969. (gr. k-5). 1992. 4.95 (0-944589-42-1) Young Discovery Lib.
—Behind the Wall of China. Busuttil, Joelle. 40p. (gr. k-5). 1993. PLB 9.95 (1-56674-057-6, HTS Bks) Forest Hse.
Quigley, Ed. She's Gone. Caldwell, E. S. LC 75-43158. 128p. (Orig.). (gr. 8-11). 1976. pap. 2.95 (0-88243-893-X, 02-0893); tchr's. guide 4.50 (0-88243-167-6, 32-0167) Gospel Pub.
Quigley, Ray. Benjamin Franklin: Young Printer. Stevenson, Augusta. LC 86-10786. 192p. (gr. 2-6). 1986. pap. 3.95 (0-02-041920-1, Aladdin) Macmillan Child Grp.
Quigley, Sebastian. Explore the World of Mighty Oceans. Wells, Susan. 48p. (gr. 3-7). 1992. write for info. (0-307-15609-5, 15609, Golden Pr) Western Pub.
—Explore the World of Space & the Universe. Nicolson, Iain. 48p. (gr. 3-7). 1992. write for info. (0-307-15608-7, 15608, Golden Pr) Western Pub.
—I Wonder Why Planes Have Wings & Other Questions about Transport. Maynard, Chris. LC 92-43373. 32p. (gr. k-3). 1993. 8.95 (1-85697-877-X) Kingfisher Bks.
Quiles, Esther. The Faceless Pumpkin. Lugo, Norma. Mankowitz, Sonia, intro. by. 32p. (Orig.). (gr. k-2). 1989. pap. text ed. write for info. West Side Pubns.
Quinlivan, Mary & Snyder, Deborah. Presenting Jessica Lyn in King Purple. Linsenman-Schuh, Norma. 32p. (Orig.). 1993. pap. 5.95 (1-884073-04-2); pap. 24.95 incl. doll (1-884073-01-8) Esteem Intl.
Quinn, Annie. My Big Box. Foley, Diane. LC 92-31910. 1993. 3.75 (0-383-03584-8) SRA Schl Grp.
—Sand. King, Virginia. LC 92-31959. 1993. 2.50 (0-383-03591-0) SRA Schl Grp.
Quinn, David. Animal World. Goaman. 32p. (gr. 6up). 1984. 13.96 (0-88110-168-0); PLB 5.95 (0-86020-751-X) EDC.
—Reptile World. Spellerberg, Ian & McKerchar, Marit. 32p. (gr. 4-7). 1985. PLB 13.96 (0-88110-174-5, Pub. by Usborne); pap. 5.95 (0-86020-845-1) EDC.
Quinn, David, jt. illus. see Jackson, Ian.
Quinn, David, et al. Bird Life. Wallace, Ian, et al. 32p. (gr. 4-7). 1985. lib. bdg. 13.96 (0-88110-172-9); pap. 5.95 (0-86020-841-9) EDC.
Quinn, Kay. Dinosaurs & Prehistoric Animals. Quinn, Kay. 64p. (gr. 2-10). 1990. 4.99 (0-517-03566-9) Outlet Bk Co.
Quinn, Kaye. Cities. 48p. (ps-2). 1988. pap. 2.95 (0-8431-2250-1) Price Stern.
—Inventive Inventions. Quinn, Kaye. 40p. (gr. 2-6). 1986. pap. 2.95 (0-8431-1893-8) Price Stern.
—Mission: Space. Quinn, Kaye. 40p. (gr. 2-6). 1986. pap. 2.95 (0-8431-1894-6) Price Stern.
—Pets. 48p. (ps-2). 1988. pap. 2.95 (0-8431-2252-8) Price Stern.
—Playground. 48p. (ps-2). 1988. pap. 2.95 (0-8431-2249-8) Price Stern.
—Reptiles. Quinn, Kaye. 40p. (gr. 2-6). 1987. pap. 2.95 (0-8431-1892-X) Price Stern.
—Science Dictionary of Animals. Richardson, James. LC 91-18826. 48p. (gr. 3-7). 1992. lib. bdg. 11.59 (0-8167-2521-7); pap. 3.95 (0-8167-2440-7) Troll Assocs.
—Science Dictionary of Dinosaurs. Richardson, James. LC 91-4110. 48p. (gr. 3-7). 1992. lib. bdg. 11.59 (0-8167-2522-5); pap. 3.95 (0-8167-2441-5) Troll Assocs.
—Telephone Power. Cavanagh, Mary. 13p. (gr. 3-5). 1980. pap. 3.95 (0-8431-2572-1) Enrich.
—Toys. 48p. (ps-2). 1988. pap. 2.95 (0-8431-2251-X) Price Stern.
—World of the Dinosaurs. Quinn, Kaye. 40p. (gr. 2-4). 1987. pap. 2.95 (0-8431-1890-3) Price Stern.

Quinn, Patrick. Matthew Pinkowski's Special Summer. Quinn, Patrick. LC 91-10982. 188p. (Orig.). (gr. 5-8). 1991. pap. 5.95 (0-930323-82-3, Pub. by K Green Pubns) Gallaudet Univ Pr.
Quinn, Sidney. Sara's Trek. Schloneger, Florence E. 100p. (gr. 7 up). 1982. pap. 4.95 (0-87303-071-0) Faith & Life.
Quinn, Stephen C. What Color Is That Dinosaur? Questions, Answers, & Mysteries. Dingus, Lowell. LC 93-10664. 72p. (gr. 4-6). 1994. PLB 14.90 (1-56294-365-0) Millbrook Pr.
Quintero, Nora. Del Nacimiento de la Isla de Boriken. Barsy, Kalman. LC 82-83288. (SPA.). 76p. (gr. 6). 1982. pap. 7.50 (0-940238-01-2) Ediciones Huracan.

R

R. Z. Novit Graphic Design Staff. Alphabet Aa to Zz. Novit, Renee Z. 16p. (ps-k). Date not set. pap. 7.95 (1-883371-00-7) Kidz & Katz.
Ra, Ruth. Many Lands, Many Stories: Asian Folk Tales for Children. Conger, David, retold by. LC 87-50167. 94p. 1987. 12.95 (0-8048-1527-5) C E Tuttle.
Raap, Cynthia. Overeating: Let's Talk about It. Sanchez, Gail J. & Gerbino, Mary. LC 85-25388. 120p. (gr. 4 up). 1987. RSBE 9.95 (0-87518-371-9, Dillon) Macmillan Child Grp.
Raber, Rhonda. Big Promises for Little People. Rutan, Debbie. (gr. 1-3). 1991. pap. 3.95 (0-9624777-2-9) Green & White Pub.
Rabinowitz, Sandy. The Black Stallion: An Easy-to-Read Adaptation. Farley, Walter. LC 85-19927. 48p. (ps-3). 1986. lib. bdg. 7.99 (0-394-96876-X) Random Bks Yng Read.
—The Something-Special Horse. Hall, Lynn. LC 84-23636. 112p. (gr. 4-7). 1985. SBE 13.95 (0-684-18343-9, Scribners Young Read) Macmillan Child Grp.
Raboff, Ernest. Raphael Sanzio. Raboff, Ernest. LC 87-45299. 32p. (gr. 1 up). 1988. pap. 7.95 (0-06-446075-4, Trophy) HarpC Child Bks.
Rachford, Mary A., et al. Beyond the Doors. Rosenkranz, Shirley A., ed. Konoske, Kathryn, intro. by. LC 88-72070. 240p. (gr. 5-12). 1988. pap. 5.95 (0-9620953-3-8) A Class Act.
Rackham, Arthur. Aesop's Fables. (gr. 2-9). 1992. 7.99 (0-517-17198-8) Outlet Bk Co.
—The Arthur Rackham Fairy Book. 271p. (gr. 2-10). 1991. 3.99 (0-517-24213-3) Outlet Bk Co.
—Fairy Tales. Grimm, Jacob & Grimm, Wilhelm K. LC 92-53180. 224p. 1992. 12.95 (0-679-41796-6, Evrymans Lib Childs Class) Knopf.
—Gulliver's Travels. Swift, Jonathan. LC 47-31082. 3.98 (0-517-46611-2) Outlet Bk Co.
—The Legend of Sleepy Hollow. facsimile ed. Irving, Washington. Glassman, Peter, afterword by. LC 90-591. 112p. (ps up). 1990. Repr. of 1928 ed. 16.95 (0-688-05276-2) Morrow Jr Bks.
—Rip Van Winkle. Irving, Washington. LC 92-9843. 128p. (gr. 1). 1992. 19.00 (0-8037-1264-2) Dial Bks Young.
—Sixty Fairy Tales of the Brothers Grimm. (gr. 2-7). 8.98 (0-517-28525-8) Outlet Bk Co.
—Sleeping Beauty. Rackham, Arthur. 110p. (gr. k-4). 1920. pap. 3.95 (0-486-22756-1) Dover.
Rackham, Arthur, et al. Favorite Fairy Tales: A Classic Illustrated Edition. Edens, Cooper & Darling, Harold, eds. 128p. (ps up). 1991. 16.95 (0-87701-848-0) Chronicle Bks.
Rader, Laura. Bigger Than a Baby. Ziefert, Harriet. LC 90-20287. 32p. (ps-3). 1991. 13.95 (0-06-026902-2); PLB 13.89 (0-06-026903-0) HarpC Child Bks.
—Getting Ready for New Baby. Ziefert, Harriet. LC 90-32197. 36p. (ps-3). 1990. PLB 13.89 (0-06-026897-2) HarpC Child Bks.
—Goody New Shoes. Ziefert, Harriet. 32p. (ps-3). 1991. 8.95 (0-670-83859-4) Viking Child Bks.
—Goody New Shoes. 32p. (ps-3). 1991. pap. 3.50 (0-14-054391-0, Puffin) Puffin Bks.
—I Hate Boots! Ziefert, Harriet. 24p. (ps-3). 1991. pap. 3.95 (0-06-107423-3) HarpC Child Bks.
—A Letter to Santa. Craig, Janet A. LC 93-22214. 32p. (gr. k-2). 1993. PLB 11.59 (0-8167-3252-3); pap. text ed. 2.95 (0-8167-3253-1) Troll Assocs.
—Mother Hubbard's Cupboard: A Mother Goose Surprise Book. Rader, Laura. LC 92-45103. 48p. (ps up). 1993. 12.95 (0-688-12562-X, Tambourine Bks) Morrow.
—Move Over! Ziefert, Harriet. 24p. (ps-3). 1991. pap. 3.95 (0-06-107421-7) HarpC Child Bks.
—Music Lessons. Ziefert, Harriet. 24p. (ps-3). 1992. 3.95 (0-694-00392-1) HarpC Child Bks.
—My Apple Tree. Ziefert, Harriet. 24p. (ps-3). 1991. pap. 3.95 (0-06-107420-9) HarpC Child Bks.
—My Camera. Ziefert, Harriet. 14p. (ps). 1993. 4.50 (0-694-00417-0, Festival) HarpC Child Bks.
—My Cassette Player. Ziefert, Harriet. 14p. (ps). 1993. 4.50 (0-694-00418-9, Festival) HarpC Child Bks.
—My Telephone. Ziefert, Harriet. 14p. (ps). 1993. 4.50 (0-694-00419-7, Festival) HarpC Child Bks.
—My Television. Ziefert, Harriet. 14p. (ps). 1993. 4.50 (0-694-00420-0, Festival) HarpC Child Bks.
—Penny Goes to the Movies. Ziefert, Harriet. 32p. (ps-3). 1990. pap. 3.50 (0-14-054225-6, Puffin) Puffin Bks.
—The Pudgy Where Is Your Nose? Book. 16p. 1989. bds. 2.95 (0-448-02258-3, G&D) Putnam Pub Group.

—See What I Can Do! Linehan, Patricia. 24p. (ps). 1990. bds. 2.50 (*0-448-02259-1*, G&D) Putnam Pub Group.

—Where's Bobo? Ziefert, Harriet. LC 92-24495. 24p. (ps up). 1993. 10.95 (*0-688-12327-9*, Tambourine Bks) Morrow.

Rader, Marjie. No-Gluten Solution: Children's Cookbook. Redjou, Pat C. (gr. 4 up). 1991. pap. 22.00 (*0-9626052-2-0*) Rae Pub.

Radford, Derek. Building Machines & What They Do. Radford, Derek. LC 91-71860. 32p. (ps up). 1992. 8.95 (*1-56402-006-1*) Candlewick Pr.

—Cargo Machines & What They Do. Radford, Derek. LC 91-71823. 32p. (ps up). 1992. 8.95 (*1-56402-005-3*) Candlewick Pr.

—Harry at the Airport. Radford, Derek. LC 91-16116. 32p. (gr. k-3). 1991. POB 10.95 (*0-689-71504-8*, Aladdin) Macmillan Child Grp.

—Let's Look Inside a Bus, Train, Ferry, & Plane. Radford, Derek. LC 92-41487. 20p. (ps). 1993. 9.99 (*0-525-67459-4*, Lodestar Bks) Dutton Child Bks.

Radford, Stephan. Mutazoids. Whitman, Ken & Wilkey, Chris. Sumner, Robert, ed. 98p. (Orig.). (gr. 10-12). 1989. pap. text ed. 12.95 (*0-685-29088-3*) Whit Prodns.

Radin, Chari. Miracle Meals: Eight Nights of Chanukah Food & Fun. Wikler, Madeline & Groner, Judye. LC 87-17325. 48p. (gr. k up). 1987. spiral bd. 6.95 (*0-930494-71-7*) Kar Ben.

Radin, Chari M. I Have Four Questions. Wikler, Madeline & Groner, Judye. LC 88-83570. 12p. (ps). 1989. bds. 4.95 (*0-930494-90-3*) Kar Ben.

Radinowitz, Sandy. Amigo Means Friend. Everett, Louise. LC 87-11274. 32p. (gr. k-2). 1988. PLB 7.89 (*0-8167-1000-7*); pap. text ed. 1.95 (*0-8167-1001-5*) Troll Assocs.

Radlauer, Ed. Mammoth Cave National Park. updated ed. Radlauer, Ruth. LC 77-26764. 48p. (gr. 3 up). 1987. (Elk Grove Bks); pap. 4.95 (*0-516-47496-0*) Childrens.

Radlauer, Ed & Radlauer, Ruth. Acadia National Park. Radlauer, Ruth. LC 77-18056. 48p. (gr. 3 up). 1978. PLB 17.27 (*0-516-07495-4*, Elk Grove Bks); pap. 4.95 (*0-516-47495-2*) Childrens.

—Bryce Canyon National Park. updated ed. Radlauer, Ruth. LC 79-22722. 48p. (gr. 3 up). 1987. PLB 17.27 (*0-516-07484-9*, Elk Grove Bks.); pap. 4.95 (*0-516-47484-7*) Childrens.

—Hawaii Volcanoes National Park. updated ed. Radlauer, Ruth. LC 78-19718. 48p. (gr. 3 up). 1987. PLB 17.27 (*0-516-07498-9*, Elk Grove Bks); pap. 4.95 (*0-516-47498-7*) Childrens.

Radlauer Productions Staff. Bears, Bears & More Bears. Radlauer, Ed. 32p. (ps-4). 1991. PLB 9.95 (*1-878363-34-4*) Forest Hse.

—Cats, Cats, & More Cats. Radlauer, Ed. 32p. 1991. PLB 9.95 (*1-878363-35-2*) Forest Hse.

—Wheels, Wheels, & More Wheels. Radlauer, Ed. 32p. 1991. PLB 9.95 (*1-878363-36-0*) Forest Hse.

Radlauer, Ruth, jt. illus. see Radlauer, Ed.

Radrigan, Roberto. Thinking Tools. Stevens, Lawrence A. 73p. (Orig.). (gr. 5-10). 1984. pap. text ed. 6.50 (*0-89550-223-2*) Stevens & Shea.

Radtke, Becky. Christmas KidDoodles, No. 5. Herman, Emmi. 64p. (ps-2). 1992. pap. 0.99 (*1-56293-270-5*) McClanahan Bk.

—Christmas KidDoodles, No. 7. Herman, Emmi. 64p. (ps-2). 1992. pap. 0.99 (*1-56293-269-1*) McClanahan Bk.

—Halloween KidDoodles, No. 2. Tuchman, Gail. 64p. (ps-2). 1992. pap. 0.99 (*1-56293-260-8*) McClanahan Bk.

Radtke, Bruce. Blue Ribbon Winner's Bakebook. Kruglak, Fredlyn. 320p. (Orig.). (gr. 6-12). 1980. pap. 7.95 (*0-9606686-0-8*) Bakebks & Cookbks.

Radunsky, Vladimir. Hail to Mail. Marshak, Samuel. Pevear, Richard, tr. from RUS. LC 89-7605. 32p. (ps-2). 1990. 14.95 (*0-8050-1132-3*, Bks Young Read) H Holt & Co.

—The Pup Grew Up! Marshak, Samuel. Pevear, Richard, tr. from RUS. LC 88-28428. 32p. (ps-2). 1989. 13.95 (*0-8050-0952-3*, Bks Young Read) H Holt & Co.

—The Story of a Boy Named Will, Who Went Sledding Down the Hill. Kharms, Daniil. Gambrell, Jamey, tr. from RUS. 32p. (gr. k-3). 1993. 14.95 (*1-55858-214-2*); lib. bdg. 14.88 (*1-55858-215-0*) North-South Bks NYC.

Radzinski, Kandy. The Twelve Cats of Christmas. 32p. 1992. 9.95 (*0-8118-0102-0*) Chronicle Bks.

Rae, Mary M. The Farmer in the Dell: A Singing Game. 32p. (ps-1). 1990. pap. 3.95 (*0-14-050788-4*, Puffin) Puffin Bks.

—Over in the Meadow. Wadsworth, Olive A. (gr. 1-5). 1986. pap. 3.99 (*0-14-050606-3*, Puffin) Puffin Bks.

Rafferty, Trisha. I Wouldn't Thank You for a Valentine: Poems for Young Feminists. Duffy, Carol A. 112p. (gr. 7 up). 1994. PLB 14.95 (*0-8050-2756-4*, Bks Young Read) H Holt & Co.

—I Wouldn't Thank You for a Valentine: Poems for Young Feminists. Duffy, Carol A., ed. LC 93-3172. 1993. write for info. H Holt & Co.

Raffi & Kelley, True. The Spider on the Floor. LC 92-33442. 32p. (ps-3). 1993. 13.00 (*0-517-59381-5*); PLB 13.99 (*0-517-59464-1*) Crown Bks Yng Read.

Ragland, Teresa. A Child's Gift of Bedtime Stories. Chaffin, Gary & Burnsed, Linda. LC 93-17766. 44p. (ps-6). 1993. 13.95 (*1-56566-044-7*) Thomasson-Grant.

—A Child's Gift of Bedtime Stories, Vol. 1. Burnsed, Linda & Chaffin, Garry. Brown, J. Aaron, ed. 28p. (gr. 1-4). 1993. incl. cass. 12.95 (*0-927945-07-X*) Someday Baby.

—**God's Mustard Seed, Vol. 1. Kile, Joan.** 32p. (ps-5). 1993. PLB 15.00 (*0-9636314-0-3*) Musty the Mustard. GOD'S MUSTARD SEED is the first in a series of Musty the Mustard Seed Books. Geared to children 3-10 yrs. of age, it is a book that encourages children to pray, read the Bible & love Jesus. Musty the Mustard Seed, the little character, inspires children to have faith as a grain of mustard seed. Musty leads the reader through the pages of the Bible. Books are written from scripts of the Mustard Seed Gospel Radio Program, narrated by Joan Kile. Many children who participated in the radio programs drew picture ideas for the illustrations of Musty the Mustard Seed Books. The colorful illustrations came from the hearts of children. The MMSB have been used with great success during Joan Kile's 21 years of teaching. The children have enthusiastically responded to GOD'S MUSTARD SEED by saying, "Read it again!" Order from SPRING ARBOR, BAKER & TAYLOR or Musty the MustardSeed Books, 104 Stable Court, Franklin, TN 37064, 615-790-1996. *Publisher Provided Annotation.*

Ragland, Teresa B. Cooking in the Kitchen with Santa. 24p. 1992. pap. 4.95 (*0-8249-3096-7*, Ideals Child) Hambleton-Hill.

—Cooking in the Kitchen with Santa. 32p. (ps up). 1992. PLB 11.95 (*1-56674-028-2*) Forest Hse.

Raglin, Tim. Deputy Dan & the Bank Robbers. Rosenbloom, Joseph. LC 84-159969. 48p. (gr. 2-3). 1985. lib. bdg. 7.99 (*0-394-97045-4*); 3.50 (*0-394-87045-X*) Random Bks Yng Read.

—Deputy Dan Gets His Man. Rosenbloom, Joseph. 48p. (gr. 2-3). 1985. pap. 2.95 (*0-394-87250-9*) Random Bks Yng Read.

—The Elephant's Child. Kipling, Rudyard. LC 86-377. 48p. (gr. k up). 1986. incl. cassette 14.95 (*0-394-88300-4*) Knopf Bks Yng Read.

—Five Funny Frights. Stamper, Judith. LC 92-44538. (gr. 4 up). 1993. pap. 2.95 (*0-590-46416-7*) Scholastic Inc.

—How the Camel Got His Hump. Kipling, Rudyard. LC 88-33366. 32p. (ps up). 1991. pap. 14.95 (*0-88708-090-0*, Rabbit Ears); incl. cassette 19.95 (*0-88708-097-9*, Rabbit Ears) Picture Bk Studio.

—How the Rhinoceros Got His Skin. Kipling, Rudyard. LC 88-11439. 28p. (ps up). 1991. pap. 14.95 (*0-88708-078-2*, Rabbit Ears); bk. & cass. pkg. 19.95 (*0-88708-083-9*, Rabbit Ears) Picture Bk Studio.

—How the Rhinoceros Got His Skin. Kipling, Rudyard. LC 92-22119. 64p. 1992. Repr. of 1988 ed. 5.95 (*0-88708-255-6*, Rabbit Ears); Mini-bk. incl. cass. 9.95 (*0-88708-254-8*, Rabbit Ears) Picture Bk Studio.

—Pecos Bill. Gleeson, Brian, as told by. LC 88-11581. 36p. (ps up). 1991. pap. 14.95 (*0-88708-081-2*, Rabbit Ears); bk. & cass. pkg. 19.95 (*0-88708-086-3*, Rabbit Ears) Picture Bk Studio.

Raglund, Teresa. Baby Days & Lullabye Nights. 48p. 1993. 17.95 (*0-8249-8619-9*, Ideals Child); gift box incl. cass. 24.95 (*0-8249-7629-0*) Hambleton-Hill.

Ragus, Christopher, jt. illus. see Hooker, Saralinda.

Raham, R. Gary. Sillysaurs: Dinosaurs That Could Have Been. Raham, R. Gary. 16p. (Orig.). (gr. k-4). 1990. write for info. saddle-stitched (*0-9626301-0-1*) Biostration.

Rahmas, Sigrid. Mother Sun & Her Planet Children. Rahmas, Sigrid. 32p. (Orig.). (ps-3). 1991. 6.25 (*0-87157-099-8*); pap. 5.95 (*0-87157-599-X*) Story Hse Corp.

Rahn, Dee. Spring. Allington, Richard L. & Krull, Kathleen. LC 80-25093. 32p. (gr. k-3). 1985. PLB 15. 96 (*0-8172-1342-2*); pap. 3.95 (*0-8114-8244-8*) Raintree Steck-V.

Rahn, Joan E. Animals That Changed History. Rahn, Joan E. LC 86-3635. 128p. (gr. 4-8). 1986. SBE 13.95 (*0-689-31137-0*, Atheneum Child Bk) Macmillan Child Grp.

Raible, Alton. The Egypt Game. Snyder, Zilpha K. LC 67-10467. 224p. (gr. 4-6). 1967. SBE 14.95 (*0-689-30006-9*, Atheneum Child Bk) Macmillan Child Grp.

—The Headless Cupid. Snyder, Zilpha K. LC 78-154763. 208p. (gr. 4-6). 1971. SBE 14.95 (*0-689-20687-9*, Atheneum Child Bk) Macmillan Child Grp.

—The Headless Cupid. Snyder, Zilpha K. (gr. 3-7). 1985. pap. 3.50 (*0-440-43507-2*, YB) Dell.

—The Witches of Worm. Snyder, Zilpha K. LC 72-75283. 192p. (gr. 4-8). 1972. SBE 14.95 (*0-689-30066-2*, Atheneum Child Bk) Macmillan Child Grp.

Raichert, Lane. D.C. Hopper, the First Starbunny. Raichert, Lane. LC 91-23055. 32p. (gr. 2-6). 1992. 15. 95 (*1-880009-81-1*, DC-P1) Blue Zero Pub.

Raine, Patricia. Orange Cheeks. O'Callahan, Jay. LC 92-43509. 40p. (ps-3). 1983. 15.95 (*1-56145-073-1*) Peachtree Pubs.

Rainis, Kenneth G. Nature Projects for Young Scientists. Rainis, Kenneth G. LC 89-5662. 142p. (gr. 6 up). 1989. PLB 13.90 (*0-531-10789-2*) Watts.

Rajpar, Shamin & Wolf, Gerald. A Book about Anna: For Children & Their Parents. Wolf, Aline D. LC 80-84874. 56p. (Orig.). (ps-k). 1980. 9.95x (*0-685-03953-6*); pap. 5.95x (*0-9601016-4-0*) Parent-Child Pr.

Ram, Govinder. Rama & Sita: A Folk Tale from India. Ram, Govinder. LC 87-14333. 32p. (gr. k-3). 1988. PLB 14.95 (*0-87226-171-9*, Bedrick Blackie) P Bedrick Bks.

Ramel, Charlotte. My Sister Lotta & Me. Dahlback, Helena. Lesser, Rika, tr. from SWE. 32p. (gr. k-3). 1993. PLB 15.95 (*0-8050-2558-8*, Bks Young Read) H Holt & Co.

Ramirez-Walker, Linda J. Patches, the Blessed Beast of Burden. Barnes, Joyce B. 36p. 1990. 15.00 (*0-9628493-0-8*) J B Barnes.

Ramon, Estelle. Smooth As Silk. 2nd ed. Philipps, Myra. (gr. 3 up). 1979. 1.95 (*0-686-10960-0*) Basin Pub.

Ramsay, Marjorie B. Nyra. Ramsay, Marjorie B. (gr. 4-7). 1979. 4.95 (*0-917182-10-3*) Triumph Pub.

Ramsey, Marcy. Buffy's Orange Leash. Golder, Stephen & Memling, Lise. 32p. (gr. k-3). 9.95 (*1-878363-23-9*) Forest Hse.

—Caroline Zucker & the Birthday Disaster. Bradford, Jan. LC 90-11159. 96p. (gr. 2-5). 1991. lib. bdg. 9.89 (*0-8167-2021-5*); pap. text ed. 2.95 (*0-8167-2022-3*) Troll Assocs.

—Caroline Zucker Helps Out. Bradford, Jan. LC 90-11156. 96p. (gr. 2-5). 1991. PLB 9.89 (*0-8167-2025-8*); pap. text ed. 2.95 (*0-8167-2026-6*) Troll Assocs.

—Caroline Zucker Makes a Big Mistake. Bradford, Jan. LC 90-11160. 96p. (gr. 2-5). 1991. PLB 9.89 (*0-8167-2023-1*); pap. text ed. 2.95 (*0-8167-2024-X*) Troll Assocs.

—Challenge at Second Base. Christopher, Matt. 144p. (gr. 3-6). 1992. pap. 3.95 (*0-316-14249-2*) Little.

—Jackie Robinson: A Life of Courage. Brandt, Keith. LC 91-17852. 48p. (gr. 4-6). 1992. PLB 10.79 (*0-8167-2505-5*); pap. text ed. 3.50 (*0-8167-2506-3*) Troll Assocs.

—Little Lefty. Christopher, Matt. (gr. 4-7). 1993. pap. 3.95 (*0-316-14100-3*) Little.

—The Missing Doll. Hiser, Constance. (gr. 4-7). 1993. 13. 95 (*0-8234-1046-3*) Holiday.

—One Dog Day. Lewis, J. Patrick. LC 92-24573. 64p. (gr. 2-5). 1993. SBE 12.95 (*0-689-31808-1*, Atheneum Child Bk) Macmillan Child Grp.

—The Submarine Pitch. Christopher, Matt. 144p. (gr. 3-6). 1992. pap. 3.95 (*0-316-14250-6*) Little.

Ramsey, Marcy D. Boy on the Beach. Meacham, Margaret. 144p. (gr. 4-8). 1992. pap. 8.95 (*0-87033-441-7*) Tidewater.

—Caroline Zucker Gets Even. Bradford, Jan. LC 89-20630. 96p. (gr. 2-5). 1991. lib. bdg. 9.89 (*0-8167-2015-0*); pap. text ed. 2.95 (*0-8167-2016-9*) Troll Assocs.

—Caroline Zucker Gets Her Wish. Bradford, Jan. LC 90-31549. 96p. (gr. 2-5). 1991. PLB 9.89 (*0-8167-2019-3*); pap. text ed. 2.95 (*0-8167-2020-7*) Troll Assocs.

—Caroline Zucker Meets Her Match. Bradford, Jan. LC 90-10813. 96p. (gr. 2-5). 1991. lib. bdg. 9.89 (*0-8167-2017-7*); pap. text ed. 2.95 (*0-8167-2018-5*) Troll Assocs.

—Chessie, the Sea Monster That Ate Annapolis. Holland, Jeffrey. 32p. (gr. k-4). 1990. 8.95 (*0-9618461-0-0*) BaySailor Bks.

—It's up to You, Griffin! Pickford, Susan T. 32p. (gr. k-4). 1993. bds. 10.95 (*0-87033-446-8*) Tidewater.

—Santa & the Skipjack. Meneely, Janie. 32p. (gr. k-6). 1991. write for info. (*0-9618461-1-9*) BaySailor Bks.

—The Story of Laura Ingalls Wilder. Stine, Megan. 112p. (Orig.). (gr. 2-5). 1992. pap. 3.50 (*0-440-40578-5*, YB) Dell.

—Toying with Danger: A Sarah Capshaw Mystery. Stevenson, Drew. LC 92-19325. (gr. 4-6). 1993. 14.00 (*0-525-65115-2*, Cobblehill Bks) Dutton Child Bks.

—What's It Like to Be a Grocer. Wilks, Shelley. LC 89-34394. 32p. (gr. k-3). 1990. lib. bdg. 10.89 (*0-8167-1805-9*); pap. text ed. 2.95 (*0-8167-1806-7*) Troll Assocs.

—What's It Like to Be a Veterinarian. Stamper, Judith. LC 89-34391. 32p. (gr. k-3). 1990. lib. bdg. 10.89 (*0-8167-1817-2*); pap. text ed. 2.95 (*0-8167-1818-0*) Troll Assocs.

—When the Frost Is Gone. Bat-Ami, Miriam. LC 92-26181. 64p. (gr. 4 up). 1994. SBE 14.95 (*0-02-708497-3*, Macmillan Child Bk) Macmillan Child Grp.

—Young Eleanor Roosevelt. Sabin, Francene. LC 89-33939. 48p. (gr. 4-6). 1990. PLB 10.79 (*0-8167-1779-6*); pap. text ed. 3.50 (*0-8167-1780-X*) Troll Assocs.

Ramsey, Mercy. The Rosenbergs. Larsen, Anita. LC 91-22311. 48p. (gr. 5 up). 1992. RSBE 11.95 (0-89686-612-2, Crestwood Hse) Macmillan Child Grp.

Rancan, Janet. How to Draw Cats. Rancan, Janet. LC 81-52121. 32p. (gr. 2-6). 1982. PLB 10.65 (0-89375-679-2); pap. text ed. 1.95 (0-89375-680-6) Troll Assocs.

Rand, Ted. Barn Dance! Martin, Bill, Jr. & Archambault, John. LC 86-14225. 32p. (ps-2). 1986. 13.95 (0-8050-0089-5, Bks Young Read); pap. 4.95 (0-8050-0799-7) H Holt & Co.

—The Bear That Heard Crying. Kinsey-Warnock, Natalie & Kinsey, Helen. 32p. (ps-3). 1993. reinforced bdg. 13.99 (0-525-65103-9, Cobblehill Bks) Dutton Child Bks.

—The Cabin Key. Rand, Gloria. LC 93-10398. 1994. write for info. (0-15-213884-6) HarBrace.

—Can I Be Good? Taylor, Livingston & Taylor, Maggie. LC 92-23193. 1993. 14.95 (0-15-200436-X) HarBrace.

—Christmas Trees. Frost, Robert. LC 89-48899. 32p. (gr. 2-4). 1990. 14.95 (0-8050-1208-7, Bks Young Read) H Holt & Co.

—Country Crossing. Aylesworth, Jim. LC 89-78184. 32p. (ps-2). 1991. SBE 13.95 (0-689-31580-5, Atheneum Child Bk) Macmillan Child Grp.

—Don't Forget. Lakin, Patricia. LC 93-20341. 32p. 1994. 14.00 (0-688-12075-X, Tambourine Bks); PLB 13.93 (0-688-12076-8, Tambourine Bks) Morrow.

—The Ghost-Eye Tree. Martin, Bill, Jr. & Archambault, John. LC 85-8422. 32p. (Orig.). 1985. 13.95 (0-8050-0208-1, Bks Young Read); pap. 5.95 (0-8050-0947-7) H Holt & Co.

—Grandma According to Me. Beil, Karen M. LC 91-10624. 32p. (ps-3). 1992. pap. 15.00 (0-385-41484-6) Doubleday.

—Here Are My Hands. Martin, Bill, Jr. & Archambault, John. LC 86-25842. 32p. (ps-2). 1987. 14.95 (0-8050-0328-2, Bks Young Read) H Holt & Co.

—Here Are My Hands. Martin, Bill, Jr. & Archambault, John. LC 86-25842. 32p. (ps-2). 1989. pap. 5.95 (0-8050-1168-4, Owlet BYR) H Holt & Co.

—Knots on a Counting Rope. Martin, Bill, Jr. & Archambault, John. LC 87-14832. 32p. (ps-2). 1987. 14.95 (0-8050-0571-4, Bks Young Read) H Holt & Co.

—Knots on a Counting Rope. Martin, Bill. 32p. (gr. k-3). 1993. pap. 19.95 (0-8050-2955-9, Bks Young Read) H Holt & Co.

—My Buddy. Osofsky, Audrey. LC 92-3028. 32p. (gr. k-3). 1992. 14.95 (0-8050-1747-X, Bks Young Read) H Holt & Co.

—My Shadow. Stevenson, Robert Louis. 32p. 1990. 14.95 (0-399-22216-2, Putnam) Putnam Pub Group.

—Once When I Was Scared. Pittman, Helena C. LC 88-3598. 32p. (gr. k-3). 1988. 14.00 (0-525-44407-6, DCB) Dutton Child Bks.

—Once When I Was Scared. Pittman, Helena C. 36p. (ps-3). 1993. pap. 4.99 (0-14-054932-3, Puffin Unicorn) Puffin Bks.

—The Owl Who Became the Moon. London, Jonathan. LC 92-14699. (ps-2). 1993. 13.99 (0-525-45054-8, DCB) Dutton Child Bks.

—Paul Revere's Ride. Longfellow, Henry Wadsworth. LC 89-25630. 40p. (gr. k-4). 1990. 14.95 (0-525-44610-9, DCB) Dutton Child Bks.

—Prince William. Rand, Gloria. LC 91-25180. 32p. (gr. 1-3). 1992. 14.95 (0-8050-1841-7, Bks Young Read) H Holt & Co.

—Salt Hands. Aragon, Jane Chelsea. LC 88-38470. 24p. (ps-2). 1989. 12.95 (0-525-44489-0, DCB) Dutton Child Bks.

—Salt Hands. Aragon, Jane C. 24p. (ps-2). 1994. pap. 4.99 (0-14-050321-8, Puffin Unicorn) Puffin Bks.

—Salty Dog. Rand, Gloria. LC 88-13453. 32p. (ps-2). 1989. 13.95 (0-8050-0837-3, Bks Young Read) H Holt & Co.

—Salty Dog. Rand, Gloria. LC 88-13453. 32p. (ps-2). 1991. pap. 4.95 (0-8050-1847-6, Bks Young Read) H Holt & Co.

—Salty Sails North. Rand, Gloria. LC 89-39063. 32p. (ps-2). 1990. 14.95 (0-8050-1160-9, Owlet BYR) H Holt & Co.

—Salty Sails North. Rand, Gloria. LC 89-39063. 32p. (ps-3). 1992. pap. 4.95 (0-8050-2188-4, Owlet BYR) H Holt & Co.

—Salty Takes Off. Rand, Gloria. LC 90-46371. 32p. (ps-2). 1991. PLB 14.95 (0-8050-1159-5, Bks Young Read) H Holt & Co.

—A Snake in the House. McNulty, Faith. LC 92-27939. 32p. (ps-3). 1994. 14.95 (0-590-44758-0) Scholastic Inc.

—The Sun, the Wind & the Rain. Peters, Lisa W. LC 87-23808. 48p. (ps-2). 1988. 13.95 (0-8050-0699-0, Bks Young Read) H Holt & Co.

—The Sun, the Wind & the Rain. Peters, Lisa W. LC 87-23808. 48p. (ps-2). 1990. pap. 4.95 (0-8050-1481-0, Owlet BYR) H Holt & Co.

—Up & down on the Merry-Go-Round. Martin, Bill, Jr. & Archambault, John. LC 87-28836. 32p. (ps-2). 1988. 12.95 (0-8050-0681-8, Bks Young Read) H Holt & Co.

—Up & Down on the Merry-Go-Round. Martin, Bill, Jr. & Archambault, John. LC 87-28836. 32p. (ps-2). 1991. pap. 4.95 (0-8050-1638-4, Bks Young Read) H Holt & Co.

—The Walloping Window Blind. Carryl, Charles. 32p. (ps-3). 1992. 14.95 (1-55970-154-4) Arcade Pub Inc.

—Water's Way. Peters, Lisa. 32p. (ps-2). 1991. 14.95 (1-55970-062-9) Arcade Pub Inc.

—White Dynamite & Curly Kidd. Martin, Bill, Jr. & Archambault, John. LC 85-27214. 48p. (ps-2). 1986. 12.95 (0-8050-0658-3, Bks Young Read) H Holt & Co.

—White Dynamite & Curly Kidd. Martin, Bill, Jr. & Archambault, John. LC 85-27214. 48p. (ps-2). 1989. pap. 5.95 (0-8050-1018-1, Bks Young Read) H Holt & Co.

—The Wizard's Promise. Marshak, Suzanna. LC 92-36507. 1994. pap. 15.00 (0-671-78431-5, S&S BFYR) S&S Trade.

Randquist, Thomas J. Horse Is Boss Drug Culture Education & Prevention Game. 2nd ed. Rundquist, Thomas J. & Parent, Frederick. 42p. (Orig.). (gr. 7-12). 1988. pap. text ed. 30.50x (0-9618567-1-8) Nova Media.

Raney, Ken. Invitation to Life: Student Work Sheets. Bauman, Kenneth. LC 86-81531. 27p. (gr. 9-12). 1986. P. 27. student wkbk. 7.95 (0-87303-102-4); P. 45. Leader's Guide 5.95 (0-87303-121-0) Faith & Life.

Rankin, Laura. The Fabulous Fish from Lake Wiggawalla. Slater, Teddy. 24p. (ps-1). 1991. 5.95 (0-671-70413-3); PLB 9.98 (0-671-70409-5) Silver Pr.

—Why Buster Beasley Was Late for Lunch. Slater, Teddy. 24p. (ps-1). 1991. 5.95 (0-671-70415-X); PLB 9.98 (0-671-70411-7) Silver Pr.

Rankin, Laura, jt. illus. see Forest, Sandra.

Rankin, Rich, jt. illus. see Wagner, Matt.

Ranno, Jim & Johnson, Marc. Kirins: The Flight of the Ain. Priest, James D. LC 91-9111_0. 336p. (Orig.). (gr. 6-12). 1992. pap. 11.95 (0-9626225-5-9) Yellow Pr MN.

Ransom, Robert. Serena's Secret. Strong, Bryan & DeVault, Christine. Nelson, Mary, ed. (gr. 5-8). 1987. pap. 3.95 (0-941816-32-X) ETR Assocs.

Ransom, Robert D. Alcohol-The Real Story. Stronck, David. Nelson, Mary & Clark, Kay, eds. 30p. (gr. 5-8). 1987. pap. text ed. 2.95 (0-941816-35-4) ETR Assocs.

—Christy's Chance. Strong, Bryan & DeVault, Christine. Nelson, Mary, ed. 72p. (gr. 5-8). 1987. pap. text ed. 3.95 (0-941816-33-8) ETR Assocs.

—Danny's Dilemma. Strong, Bryan & DeVault, Christine. Nelson, Mary, ed. (gr. 5-8). 1987. pap. 3.95 (0-941816-31-1) ETR Assocs.

—Marijuana - The Real Story. Stronck, David. Nelson, Mary & Clark, Kay, eds. 30p. (gr. 5-8). 1987. pap. text ed. 2.95 (0-941816-36-2) ETR Assocs.

—Tobacco - The Real Story. Stronck, David. Nelson, Mary & Clark, Kay, eds. 30p. (gr. 5-8). 1987. pap. text ed. 2.95 (0-941816-34-6) ETR Assocs.

Ransom, Stefan P. Ah...To Be A Kid: Three Dozen Aikido Games for Children of All Ages. Friedl, Michael. 82p. (Orig.). 1994. pap. 9.95 (0-9638530-1-5, Castle Capers) Magical Michael.

AH...TO BE A KID is a must for those of you teaching children or adults about conflict resolution. This book introduces a variety of games which teach people how to harmonize with each other & to interact in a noncompetitive manner. Using movement principles of Aikido, the author explains the importance of blending & redirecting movement instead of competing with it. As children (& adults) actually play the games described, they gain skills that help them to assess situations & react quickly, to think clearly, & to remain relaxed. One teacher sums it up this way: "Noncompetitive games are important tools for teaching children how to cooperate & succeed. This book provides educators with several ideas for helping children learn harmony among themselves & with their environment." Whether you are four years old or forty, if you enjoy the "kid" in you, then these games will create laughter, giggles & a joy for physical interaction. AH...TO BE A KID is an excellent resource for teaching conflict resolution skills in a fun & interactive manner.
Publisher Provided Annotation.

Ransome, James. All the Lights in the Night. Levine, Arthur A. LC 90-47496. 32p. (ps-3). 1991. 14.95 (0-688-10107-0, Tambourine Bks); PLB 14.88 (0-688-10108-9, Tambourine Bks) Morrow.

—Aunt Flossie's Hats (& Crab Cakes Later) Howard, Elizabeth F. 32p. (ps-1). 1991. 14.95 (0-395-54682-6, Clarion Bks) HM.

—Bonesy & Isabel. Rosen, Michael J. LC 93-7892. 1994. write for info. (0-15-209813-5) HarBrace.

—The Creation. Johnson, James Weldon. LC 93-3207. 32p. (gr. 4-8). 1994. 15.95 (0-8234-1069-2) Holiday.

—Do Like Kyla. Johnson, Angela. LC 89-16229. 32p. (ps-2). 1990. 14.95 (0-531-05852-2); PLB 14.99 (0-531-08452-3) Orchard Bks Watts.

—Freedom's Fruit. Hooks, William H. LC 93-235. 1995. 15.00 (0-679-82438-3); lib. bdg. 15.95 (0-679-92438-8) Knopf.

—How Many Stars in the Sky. Hort, Lenny. LC 90-36044. 32p. (ps-3). 1991. 13.95 (0-688-10103-8, Tambourine Bks); PLB 13.88 (0-688-10104-6, Tambourine Bks) Morrow.

—The Hummingbird Garden. Widman, Christine. LC 91-27338. 32p. (ps-3). 1993. RSBE 14.95 (0-02-792761-X, Macmillan Child Bk) Macmillan Child Grp.

—Sweet Clara & the Freedom Quilt. Harris, Deborah. LC 91-11601. 40p. (gr. k-5). 1993. 15.00 (0-679-82311-5) Knopf Bks Yng Read.

Ransome, James E. Do Like Kyla. Johnson, Angela. LC 89-16229. 32p. (ps-2). 1993. pap. 5.95 (0-531-07040-9) Orchard Bks Watts.

—The Girl Who Wore Snakes. Johnson, Angela. LC 92-44521. 32p. (ps-2). 1993. 14.95 (0-531-05491-8); PLB 14.99 (0-531-08641-0) Orchard Bks Watts.

—My Best Shoes. Burton, Marilee R. LC 92-33863. 32p. 1994. 15.00 (0-688-11756-2, Tambourine Bks); PLB 14.93 (0-688-11757-0, Tambourine Bks) Morrow.

—Red Dancing Shoes. Patrick, Denise L. LC 91-32666. 32p. (ps up). 1993. 14.00 (0-688-10392-8, Tambourine Bks); PLB 13.93 (0-688-10393-6, Tambourine Bks) Morrow.

Ranson, Peggy. J & J Language Readers: Level I. Greene, Jane F. & Woods, Judy F. (gr. 2-3). 1992. Set of 18 units, 45p. ea. pap. text ed. 49.00 (0-944584-86-1) Sopris.

—J & J Language Readers: Level II. Greene, Jane F. & Woods, Judy F. (gr. 2-4). 1992. Set of 18 units, 45p. ea. pap. text ed. 49.00 (0-944584-87-X) Sopris.

—J & J Language Readers: Level III. Greene, Jane F. & Woods, Judy F. (gr. 3-5). 1992. Set of 18 units, 45p. ea. pap. text ed. 49.00 (0-944584-88-8) Sopris.

Rao, Anthony. The Cow in the Kitchen. Johnson, Evelyne, retold by. LC 90-85905. 24p. (ps-2). 1991. Repr. 8.95 (1-878093-45-2) Boyds Mills Pr.

—Dinosaurs of North America. Sattler, Helen R. Ostrom, John H., intro. by. LC 80-27411. 160p. (gr. 2 up). 1981. 17.95 (0-688-51952-0) Lothrop.

—Halloween Masks. 24p. (ps-3). 1984. pap. 3.99 saddle-stitched (0-394-86126-4) Random Bks Yng Read.

—Nursery Rhymes. LC 90-85900. 32p. (ps-1). 1991. Repr. 8.95 (1-878093-24-X) Boyds Mills Pr.

—The Smallest Dinosaurs. Simon, Seymour. (gr. k-3). 1988. 4.95 (0-517-56550-1) Crown Bks Yng Read.

—The Three Investigator's Book of Mystery Puzzles. McCall, Barbara. 64p. (gr. 3-7). 1982. pap. 1.50 (0-394-85107-2) Random Bks Yng Read.

Rao, Tony. Getting Ready for Baby. Tannenbaum, D. Leb. Bahr, Amy C., ed. 64p. 1982. pap. 3.95 (0-671-45324-6) S&S Trade.

Raphael, Elaine & Bolognese, Don. Drawing History: Ancient Greece. Raphael, Elaine & Bolognese, Don. 32p. (gr. 5-6). 1989. PLB 13.40 (0-531-10738-8) Watts.

Raphael, Elaine, jt. illus. see Bolognese, Don.

Raqchwerger, Lisa, et al. Bet Man. Wise, Ira J. 96p. (gr. 1-2). 1991. 4.95 (0-933873-55-7) Torah Aura.

Raquois, Olivier. The Curious Little Dolphin. Chottin, Ariane. LC 91-46500. 22p. (ps). 1992. 6.99 (0-89577-425-9, Readers Digest Kids) RD Assn.

—Kitty's Special Job. Clement, Claude. LC 91-46233. 22p. (ps). 1992. 6.99 (0-89577-427-5, Readers Digest Kids) RD Assn.

Rarey, D. Postcards from Europe Series, 5 bks. Mullin. Kratoville, B. L., ed. 48p. (gr. 6-10). 1994. pap. text ed. 15. 00 (0-87879-976-1) Acad Therapy. Four multi-cultural junior high students & their teacher are treated to a trip to Europe by an anonymous benefactor. The four young travelers never stop learning as facts about the historical & cultural treasures of each country are woven into the fast-paced, exciting stories: THE LONDON CONNECTION, The kids climb on board a double-decker bus to see the sights: Buckingham Palace, Westminster Abbey, the Tower of London, & more. PASSPORT TO PARIS, The history of the Arc de Triomphe & the Eiffel Tower, fine art at the Louvre, & folklore & facts about Notre Dame are all part of this whirlwind tour. RIDDLES IN ROME,

The kids roam through the ruins at the Forum & the Coliseum, marvel at Michaelangelo's Pieta & Sistine Chapel at Vatican City, & enjoy gelato. THE CLUES TO MADRID, In Madrid, the kids are dazzled by the Prado Museum, Picasso's Guernica, & the Plaza Mayor, & end up at the bullfights. SECRETS OF THE MATTERHORN, A fondue dinner & a hike to a Swiss hut on the slopes of the Matterhorn are only a part of this entertaining excursion. *Publisher Provided Annotation.*

Rarey, Damon. Postcards from America Series: The White House Mystery, High Time in New York, Windy City Whirl, Trouble in the Black Hills, San Francisco Adventure. Mullin, Penn. Kratoville, B. L., ed. (Orig.). (gr. 4-12). 1992. pap. 15.00 (*0-87879-957-5*, 957-5) High Noon Bks.
Lisa, Juan, Amy & Justin could hardly believe that they won the national essay contest that awarded them a three-week trip across America. At each spot they visit, the group manages to encounter an adventure that adds considerable spice to these high-interest novels. Sites seen include: The White House Mystery-the White House, Washington Monument & the Lincoln Memorial; High Time in New York-the Statue of Liberty & Ellis Island; Windy City Whirl-Sears Tower & Wrigley Field; Trouble in the Black Hills-Mount Rushmore & the site of an ancient Indian reservation; & San Francisco Adventure-Chinatown & Fisherman's Wharf, among other locales. A multicultural mix of central characters (African-American, Mexican-American, Asian-American & Caucasian) is featured. For recreational reading, these books offer a great mix of reading for fun & knowledge at a comfortable (2nd grade) reading level. Because these captivating fictional accounts are filled with interesting facts about each location, the novels also are a great way for classroom teachers to engage student interest in elements of American history for further study. Each adult-size paperback book in the five title series features a full-color & full-page illustrations of the sites. *Publisher Provided Annotation.*

Raschka, Christopher. The Owl & the Tuba. Lehman, James H. LC 91-73880. 32p. 1991. 13.95 (*1-878925-02-4*) Brotherstone Pubs.
—The Saga of Shakespeare Pintlewood & the Great Silver Fountain Pen. Lehman, James H. LC 90-82303. 32p. (gr. k-3). 1990. PLB 13.95 (*1-878925-00-8*) Brotherstone Pubs.

Rasher, Steven. Soddy Bear: The Persian Gulf War. Toussant, Eliza. 76p. (Orig.). (gr. 4 up). 1991. pap. 17.95 (*0-9630583-0-4*) E Toussant.
Eliza Toussant has put a new twist in the Persian Gulf War. Devastated by the war herself & seeing the fear & concerns of children, she decided to write the Bear facts about the DESERT STORM WAR from August 2, 1990 to February 27, 1991. It's not your average story by any means. The names have been changed, as has the natural resource. This story was written to help children understand the war, adding a little humor to take away some of the hostility felt during & after the war. The characters are as follows: 1) President Bush is portrayed as---President Tush. 2) Sadam Hussein is portrayed as---Soddy Bear. 3) General Norman Schwarzkopf as---Stormy Duke Bear. In her well illustrated book, Eliza Toussant placed killer bees in scud missiles & planted deadly scorpions across the fields of Kuwait. She spilled millions of gallons of honey into the Persian Gulf, she used bears as soldiers. This book is a learning tool for educators, parents, community workers, as well as children. Although SODDY BEAR, THE PERSIAN GULF WAR is listed as fiction, it is also non fiction, there was a Gulf War & the true facts are there. SODDY BEAR, THE PERSIAN GULF WAR is history. *Publisher Provided Annotation.*

Raskin, Betty. Houdini. Alden, Laura. LC 88-34126. 100p. (gr. 3-7). 1989. PLB 21.35 (*0-89565-456-3*); PLB 14.95s.p. (*0-685-55993-9*) Childs World.
—My First Columbus Day Book. Lillegard, Dee. LC 87-10304. 32p. (ps-2). 1987. PLB 15.00 (*0-516-02909-6*); pap. 3.95 (*0-516-42909-4*) Childrens.
—Saltasaurus. Riehecky, Janet. 32p. (gr. k-4). 1990. PLB 21.35 (*0-89565-635-3*); PLB 14.95s.p. (*0-685-58730-4*) Childs World.
Raskin, Ellen. Ellen Grae. Cleaver, Vera. LC 67-10623. 96p. 1967. PLB 12.89 (*0-397-30938-4*, Lipp Jr Bks) HarpC Child Bks.
—Figgs & Phantoms. Raskin, Ellen. LC 73-17309. 160p. (gr. 4 up). 1977. pap. 15.95 (*0-525-29680-8*, 01063-320, DCB); (DCB) Dutton Child Bks.
—Nothing Ever Happens on My Block. Raskin, Ellen. LC 89-31342. 32p. (gr. k-4). 1989. pap. 3.95 (*0-689-71335-5*, Aladdin) Macmillan Child Grp.
—Piping Down the Valleys Wild. Larrick, Nancy, intro. by. LC 68-27742. 256p. (ps-3). 1985. 14.95 (*0-385-29429-8*) Delacorte.
—Spectacles. 2nd ed. Raskin, Ellen. LC 88-10363. 48p. (gr. k-4). 1988. pap. 4.50 (*0-689-71271-5*, Aladdin) Macmillan Child Grp.
—The Westing Game. Raskin, Ellen. 192p. (gr. 7 up). 1984. pap. 3.50 (*0-380-67991-4*, Flare) Avon.
Rasmussen, George L. Discover Michigan. McConnell, David B. LC 81-6722. 144p. (gr. 4). 1989. text ed. 17.45x (*0-910726-07-8*); tchr's. guide 7.45x (*0-910726-33-7*) Hillsdale Educ.
—Explore Michigan A to Z. McConnell, David B. McConnell, Stella M., ed. LC 93-17430. 48p. (Orig.). (gr. 3-4). 1993. pap. 7.95 (*0-910726-55-8*) Hillsdale Educ.
Rasmussee-Frerichs, Cyndy. Colorado Springs History A to Z: For Children. Skolout, Patricia F. 37p. (gr. k-6). 1990. Repr. of 1989 ed. activity bk. 3.95 (*0-9625712-0-2*) P F Skolout.
Ratcliffe, Annelle W. Window of Time. Weinburg, Karen. LC 90-20856. (gr. 2-4). 1991. pap. 9.95 (*0-942597-18-4*) White Mane Pub.
Rathman, Peggy. Bootsie Barker Bites. Bottner, Barbara. 32p. (ps-3). 1992. 14.95 (*0-399-22125-5*, Putnam) Putnam Pub Group.
Ratz de Tagyos, Paul. A Coney Tale. Ratz de Tagyos, Paul. 32p. (gr. k-3). 1992. 14.45 (*0-395-58834-0*, Clarion Bks) HM.
Ratzlaff, Lynette. Learning from God's Animals. Jay, Ruth J. 36p. (Orig.). (ps-k). 1981. pap. 2.99 (*0-934998-04-3*) Bethel Pub.
—Learning from God's Birds. Jay, Ruth J. 34p. (Orig.). (ps-k). 1981. pap. 2.99 (*0-934998-05-1*) Bethel Pub.
Rauchwerger, Lisa. A Mouse in Our Jewish House. Zeldin, Florence. LC 89-40362. 32p. (ps). 1990. 11.95 (*0-933873-43-3*) Torah Aura.
Rauh, Herb. Our Brat Cat. Punnett, Dick. LC 84-23027. 32p. (gr. k-3). 1985. PLB 19.95 (*0-89565-303-6*); PLB 13.95s.p. (*0-685-55733-2*) Childs World.
Rauzon, Mark, photos by. Water, Water Everywhere. Rauzon, Mark & Bix, Cynthia O. LC 92-34521. 1993. write for info. (*0-87156-598-6*) Sierra.
Rauzon, Mark J. Catch a Comet by the Tail. Rauzon, Mark J. 48p. (gr. 5-10). 1985. pap. 6.95 (*0-935181-00-8*) Marine Endeavors.
Ravielli, Anthony. Entertaining Science Experiments with Everyday Objects. Gardner, Martin. (gr. 5 up). 16.50 (*0-8446-5888-X*) Peter Smith.
Ravilious, Robin. The Story Tree. Bradman, Tony. 32p. (gr. 1-3). 1993. 17.95 (*0-460-88093-4*, Pub. by J M Dent & Sons) Trafalgar.
Rawley-Whitaker, Jena. Fairy Tea. Ullrich, Annie. 52p. (ps up). 1992. 16.95g (*1-879244-35-7*) Windom Bks.
Rawlings, Janet. The Hollow Land. Gardam, Jane. LC 81-6620. 160p. (gr. 5-9). 1982. 10.25 (*0-688-00873-9*) Greenwillow.

Rawlins, Donna. Fast Forward. Pausacker, Jenny. (gr. 4-7). 1991. 12.95 (*0-688-10195-X*) Lothrop.
—Jeremy's Tail. Ball, Duncan. LC 90-28952. 32p. (ps-1). 1991. 14.95 (*0-531-05951-0*); RLB 14.99 (*0-531-08551-1*) Orchard Bks Watts.
—My Dearest Dinosaur. Wild, Margaret. LC 91-46166. 32p. (ps-2). 1992. 14.95 (*0-531-05453-5*); PLB 14.99 (*0-531-08603-8*) Orchard Bks Watts.
—My Place. Wheatley, Nadia. LC 92-9006. 24p. (gr. 3 up). 1992. 14.95 (*0-916291-42-1*) Kane-Miller Bk.
—Tucking Mommy In. Loh, Morag. LC 87-16740. 40p. (ps-2). 1988. 13.95 (*0-531-05740-2*); PLB 13.99 (*0-531-08340-3*) Orchard Bks Watts.
Ray, Dan, jt. illus. see Hankins, Rod.
Ray, David. The Banshee. Ackerman, Karen. 32p. (ps-3). 1990. 14.95 (*0-399-21924-2*, Philomel Bks) Putnam Pub Group.
—Night of the Whippoorwill. Larrick, Nancy, ed. 72p. (ps up). 1992. 19.95 (*0-399-21874-2*, Philomel Bks) Putnam Pub Group.
—Pumpkin Light. Ray, David. LC 92-25118. 32p. (ps-3). 1993. 14.95 (*0-399-22028-3*, Philomel Bks) Putnam Pub Group.
—Silver at Night. Bartoletti, Susan C. (gr. 4 up). 1994. 15.00 (*0-517-59426-9*); PLB 15.99 (*0-517-59427-7*) Crown Bks Yng Read.
Ray, Deborah. I Have a Sister, My Sister Is Deaf. Peterson, Jeanne W. LC 76-24306. (gr. k-3). 1977. PLB 13.89 (*0-06-024702-9*) HarpC Child Bks.
—I Have a Sister, My Sister Is Deaf. Peterson, Jeanne W. LC 76-24306. 32p. (ps-3). 1984. pap. 4.95 (*0-06-443059-6*, Trophy) HarpC Child Bks.
—Through Grandpa's Eyes. MacLachlan, Patricia. LC 79-2019. 48p. (gr. 2-4). 1971. PLB 13.89 (*0-06-022560-2*) HarpC Child Bks.
—Through Grandpa's Eyes. MacLachlan, Patricia. LC 79-2019. 48p. (gr. k-3). 1983. pap. 4.95 (*0-06-443041-3*, Trophy) HarpC Child Bks.
—Winter Picnic. Welber, Robert. LC 77-77418. (gr. 7 up). 1970. lib. bdg. 5.99 (*0-394-90444-3*) Pantheon.
—The Winter Picnic. Welber, Robert. (ps-3). 1973. pap. 0.95 (*0-394-82621-3*) Pantheon.
Ray, Deborah K. All Joseph Wanted. Radin, Ruth Y. LC 91-12643. 80p. (gr. 3-7). 1991. SBE 12.95 (*0-02-775641-6*, Macmillan Child Bk) Macmillan Child Grp.
—Apple Picking Time. Slawson, Michele B. LC 92-23400. 1994. write for info.; PLB write for info. (*0-517-58976-1*) Crown Bks Yng Read.
—Cassie's Journey: Going West in the 1860s. Harvey, Brett. LC 87-23599. 40p. (gr. 1-4). 1988. reinforced bdg. 13.95 (*0-8234-0684-9*) Holiday.
—Chang's Paper Pony. Coerr, Eleanor. LC 87-45679. 64p. (gr. k-3). 1988. 14.00 (*0-06-021328-0*); PLB 13.89 (*0-06-021329-9*) HarpC Child Bks.
—Fat Chance! Borton, Lady. 32p. (ps-3). 1993. 14.95 (*0-399-21963-3*, Philomel) Putnam Pub Group.
—Ghosts & Goose Bumps: Poems to Chill Your Bones. Katz, Bobbi. LC 89-37134. 32p. (Orig.). (ps-3). 1991. lib. bdg. 9.99 (*0-679-90372-0*); pap. 2.25 (*0-679-80372-6*) Random Bks Yng Read.
—Ghosts & Goose Bumps: Poems to Chill Your Bones. Katz, Bobbi, ed. 32p. (ps-1). 1993. incl. cass. 5.95 (*0-679-84799-5*) Random Bks Yng Read.
—Hist Whist. Cummings, e. e. LC 89-596. 24p. (gr. k-4). 1989. 10.95 (*0-517-57360-1*) Crown Bks Yng Read.
—The Hokey-Pokey Man. Kroll, Steven. LC 88-17012. 32p. (ps-3). 1989. reinforced bdg. 14.95 (*0-8234-0728-4*) Holiday.
—How Does the Wind Walk? Carlstrom, Nancy W. LC 90-25958. 32p. (ps-3). 1993. RSBE 14.95 (*0-02-717275-9*, Macmillan Child Bk) Macmillan Child Grp.
—Hubknuckles. Herman, Emily. LC 84-21355. 32p. (gr. 1-4). 1985. 9.95 (*0-517-55646-4*) Crown Bks Yng Read.
—I Know a Place. Ackerman, Karen. 32p. (ps-3). 1992. 13.45 (*0-395-53932-3*) HM.
—Immigrant Girl: Becky of Eldridge Street. Harvey, Brett. LC 86-15038. 40p. (gr. 1-4). 1987. reinforced bdg. 13.95 (*0-8234-0638-5*) Holiday.
—Little Tree. Cummings, e. e. LC 86-30940. 32p. (gr. k-4). 1988. PLB 10.95 (*0-517-56598-6*) Crown Bks Yng Read.
—Maggie's Whopper. Alexander, Sally H. LC 91-7726. 32p. (gr. k-3). 1992. RSBE 14.95 (*0-02-700201-2*, Macmillan Child Bk) Macmillan Child Grp.
—My Daddy Was a Soldier: A World War Two Story. Ray, Deborah K. LC 89-20056. 40p. (ps-4). 1990. reinforced bdg. 12.95 (*0-8234-0795-0*) Holiday.
—My Dog, Trip. Ray, Deborah K. LC 87-401. 48p. (ps-4). 1987. reinforced bdg. 12.95 (*0-8234-0662-8*) Holiday.
—My Prairie Christmas. Harvey, Brett. LC 90-55104. 32p. (ps-3). 1990. reinforced 14.95 (*0-8234-0827-2*) Holiday.
—My Prairie Christmas. Harvey, Brett. 1993. pap. 5.95 (*0-8243-1064-0*) Holiday.
—My Prairie Year. Harvey, Brett. (ps-3). 1993. pap. 4.95 (*0-8234-1028-5*) Holiday.
—My Prairie Year: Based on the Diary of Elenore Plaisted. Harvey, Brett. LC 85-27177. 40p. (gr. 1-4). 1986. reinforced bdg. 13.95 (*0-8234-0604-0*) Holiday.
—On Grandma's Roof. Silverman, Erica. LC 99-31255. 32p. (ps-2). 1990. RSBE 13.95 (*0-02-782681-3*, Macmillan Child Bk) Macmillan Child Grp.
—Other Bells for Us to Ring. Cormier, Robert. 144p. (gr. 4-7). 1992. pap. 3.50 (*0-440-40717-6*, YB) Dell.

—Poems for Mothers. Livingston, Myra C. LC 87-19629. 32p. (ps-3). 1988. reinforced bdg. 13.95 (0-8234-0678-4) Holiday.
—Sky Words. Singer, Marilyn. LC 92-3765. 32p. (gr. k-3). 1994. RSBE 14.95 (0-02-782882-4, Macmillan Child Bk) Macmillan Child Grp.
—Some of the Pieces. Madenski, Melissa. (ps-3). 1991. 15.95 (0-316-54324-1) Little.
—Stargazing Sky. Ray, Deborah K. LC 90-36775. 32p. (ps-2). 1991. 13.95 (0-517-57816-6); PLB 14.99 (0-517-57838-7) Crown Bks Yng Read.
—Uncle Magic. Gauch, Patricia. LC 91-22356. 32p. (ps-3). 1992. reinforced bdg. 14.95 (0-8234-0937-6) Holiday.
Ray, Deborah K., jt. illus. see Croll, Carolyn.
Ray, Jane. A Balloon for Grandad. Gray, Nigel. LC 87-27867. 32p. (ps-2). 1988. 13.95 (0-531-05755-0); PLB 13.99 (0-531-08355-1) Orchard Bks Watts.
—La Historia de Navidad. LC 91-578. (SPA.). 32p. (ps up). 1991. 16.00 (0-525-44830-6, DCB) Dutton Child Bks.
—Magical Tales from Many Lands. Mayo, Margaret, retold by. LC 93-12164. 128p. 1993. 19.99 (0-525-45017-3, DCB) Dutton Child Bks.
—Mother Gave a Shout: Poems by Women & Girls. Steele, Susanna & Styles, Morag, eds. LC 90-12938. 128p. (gr. 3-8). 1991. 14.95 (0-912078-90-1) Volcano Pr.
—The Story of Christmas: Words from the Gospels of Matthew & Luke. LC 91-11357. 32p. (ps up). 1991. 15.95 (0-525-44768-7, DCB) Dutton Child Bks.
Ray, Jane, photos by. The Story of the Creation: Words from Genesis. LC 92-20862. 32p. (gr. 1 up). 1993. 16.00 (0-525-44946-9, DCB); Spanish ed. 16.00 (0-525-45055-6, DCB) Dutton Child Bks.
Rayevsky, Robert. Aesop's Fables. Aesop. Paxton, Tom, retold by. LC 88-1652. 40p. (ps-2). 1988. 13.95 (0-688-07360-3); PLB 13.88 (0-688-07361-1, Morrow Jr Bks) Morrow Jr Bks.
—Androcles & the Lion: And Other Aesop's Fables. Paxton, Tom, retold by. LC 90-19173. 40p. (ps up). 1991. 13.95 (0-688-09682-4); PLB 13.88 (0-688-09683-2) Morrow Jr Bks.
—Angels, Angels All Around. Hartman, Bob. 96p. (gr. 1-5). 1993. 15.95 (0-7459-2623-1) Lion USA.
—Belling the Cat: And Other Aesop's Fables. Paxton, Tom. LC 89-39851. 40p. (ps up). 1990. 13.95 (0-688-08158-4); PLB 13.88 (0-688-08159-2, Morrow Jr Bks) Morrow Jr Bks.
—The Dragon Nanny. Martin, C. L. LC 87-7674. 32p. (gr. k-3). 1988. RSBE 14.95 (0-02-762440-4, Macmillan Child Bk) Macmillan Child Grp.
—The Dragon Nanny. Martin, C. L. LC 90-39985. 32p. (gr. k-3). 1991. pap. 3.95 (0-689-71451-3, Aladdin) Macmillan Child Grp.
—The Golden Heart of Winter. Singer, Marilyn. LC 90-35346. 40p. (gr. 1 up). 1991. 13.95 (0-688-07717-X); PLB 13.88 (0-688-07718-8) Morrow Jr Bks.
—Three Sacks of Truth: A Story from France. Kimmel, Eric A., adapted by. 32p. (ps-3). 1993. reinforced bdg. 15.95 (0-8234-0921-X) Holiday.
—The Tzar's Bird. Tompert, Ann. LC 89-31376. 32p. (gr. k-3). 1990. RSBE 14.95 (0-02-789401-0, Macmillan Child Bk) Macmillan Child Grp.
—A Word to the Wise: And Other Proverbs. Hurwitz, Johanna, compiled by. LC 93-26836. 1993. write for info. (0-688-12065-2); PLB write for info. (0-688-12066-0) Morrow Jr Bks.
Rayher, Ed. Alice's Flip Book. Rayher, Ed. 38p. 1982. pap. 1.75 perfect bdg. (0-934714-19-3) Swamp Pr.
Rayl, Eleanor. Barber, Barber, Shave a Pig. Howard, Nina. 16p. (ps-k). 1981. tchr's ed. 4.95 (0-917206-13-4) Children Learn Ctr.
—Classroom Chefs. Howard, Nina. 96p. (gr. 2). 1981. 7.95 (0-917206-14-2) Children Learning Ctr.
Raymo, Chet. Geologic & Topographic Profile of the United States along Interstate 80. Raymo, Chet. 21p. (Orig.). (gr. 6-12). 1982. pap. text ed. 7.50 (0-8331-1714-9, 473) Hubbard Sci.
Raymond, Alex. Scuttle Watch. Ryder, Marion C. LC 79-91988. 286p. (gr. 4-12). 1979. pap. 4.95 (0-88492-034-8) W S Sullwold.
Raymond, Charlene T. Finding a Way Home. Twohy, Patrick J. LC 83-90797. 296p. 1990. pap. text ed. 12.00 (0-9623418-0-0) P J Twohy.
Raymond, Larry. Chico Mendes: Fight for the Forest. DeStefano, Susan. 76p. (gr. 4-7). 1992. PLB 14.95 (0-8050-2887-0) TFC Bks NY.
—Drugs & Crime. Shulman, Jeffrey. 88p. (gr. 5-8). 1991. PLB 14.95 (0-941477-60-6) TFC Bks NY.
—Drugs & Sports. Talmadge, Katherine S. 88p. (gr. 5-8). 1991. PLB 14.95 (0-941477-59-2) TFC Bks NY.
—Drugs & the Family. DeStefano, Susan. 88p. (gr. 5-8). 1991. PLB 14.95 (0-941477-61-4) TFC Bks NY.
—Gaylord Nelson: A Day for the Earth. Shulman, Jeffrey & Rogers, Teresa. 68p. (gr. 4-7). 1992. PLB 14.95 (0-941477-40-1) TFC Bks NY.
—George Washington Carver: Nature's Trailblazer. Rogers, Teresa. 72p. (gr. 4-7). 1992. PLB 14.95 (0-8050-2115-9) TFC Bks NY.
—Henry David Thoreau: A Neighbor to Nature. Reef, Catherine. 72p. (gr. 4-7). 1992. PLB 14.95 (0-941477-39-8) TFC Bks NY.
—It's Only Goodbye: An Immigrant Story. Gross, Virginia T. LC 92-18959. 64p. (gr. 2-6). 1992. pap. 3.99 (0-14-034409-8) Puffin Bks.

—Jacques Cousteau: Champion of the Sea. Reef, Catherine. 72p. (gr. 4-7). 1992. PLB 14.95 (0-8050-2114-0) TFC Bks NY.
—Marjory Stoneman Douglas: Voice of the Everglades. Bryant, Jennifer. 72p. (gr. 4-7). 1992. PLB 14.95 (0-8050-2113-2) TFC Bks NY.
—Rachel Carson: The Wonder of Nature. Reef, Catherine. 68p. (gr. 4-7). 1992. PLB 14.95 (0-941477-38-X) TFC Bks NY.
—When Andy's Father Went to Prison. rev. ed. Hickman, Martha W. Levine, Abby, ed. LC 89-77318. 40p. (gr. 2-5). 1990. PLB 11.95 (0-8075-8874-1) A Whitman.
Raymond, Thomas. The Creek Captives: And Other Alabama Stories. Blackshear, Helen F. 112p. (Orig.). (gr. 4-9). 1990. pap. 9.95 (0-9622815-2-2) Black Belt Pr.
Rayner, Mary. Babe: The Gallant Pig. reissued ed. King-Smith, Dick. LC 91-11429. 176p. (gr. 3-6). 1993. 13.00 (0-517-55556-5) Crown Bks Yng Read.
—Garth Pig Steals the Show. Rayner, Mary. LC 92-24508. (ps-3). 1993. 13.99 (0-525-45023-8, DCB) Dutton Child Bks.
—Mr. & Mrs. Pig's Evening Out. Rayner, Mary. LC 76-4476. 32p. (gr. k-3). 1976. SBE 13.95 (0-689-30530-3, Atheneum Child Bk) Macmillan Child Grp.
—Mrs. Pig Gets Cross & Other Stories. Rayner, Mary. LC 86-13433. 64p. (ps-3). 1987. 11.95 (0-525-44280-4, DCB) Dutton Child Bks.
—Mrs. Pig's Bulk Buy. Rayner, Mary. LC 80-19875. 32p. (gr. k-3). 1981. SBE 13.95 (0-689-30831-0, Atheneum Child Bk) Macmillan Child Grp.
—Oh, Paul! Rayner, Mary. 42p. (gr. 2-4). 1989. 3.95 (0-8120-6145-4) Barron.
—Rug. rev. ed. Rayner, Mary. 32p. (gr. k-2). 1989. Repr. of 1989 ed. lib. bdg. 10.50 (1-878363-03-4) Forest Hse.
Rayner, Shoo. Cat in a Flap. Rayner, Shoo. 18p. 1992. 12.95 (0-87226-501-3, Bedrick Blackie) P Bedrick Bks.
Raynor, Mary. Thank You for the Tadpole. LC 87-474. (gr. k-2). 1988. pap. 2.50 (0-317-69488-X) Delacorte.
Read, Jacqueline P., jt. illus. see Ertmann, Caren L.
Read, Maggie. Cinderella. Bunless, Patricia. LC 79-28526. 24p. (gr. k-5). 1980. PLB 29.28 incl. cassette (0-8393-1834-0); PLB 14.64 (0-8393-0253-3) Raintree Steck-V.
Read, Maryann. My Beginning Mass Book. Angers, JoAnn M. 48p. (Orig.). (gr. 1-4). 1978. pap. 1.95 (0-89622-082-6) Twenty-Third.
—Praying & Doing the Stations of the Cross with Children. Abajian, Diane. 24p. (gr. 1-3). 1980. pap. 1.95 (0-89622-118-0) Twenty-Third.
—Priscilla Tadpole. Costello, Gwen. Kendzia, Mary C., ed. 32p. (Orig.). 1992. pap. 4.95 (0-89622-527-5) Twenty-Third.
Reade, Deborah, jt. illus. see Dewey, Jennifer O.
Reader, Dennis. Butterfingers. Reader, Dennis. LC 90-46124. 32p. (gr. k-3). 1991. 13.45 (0-395-57581-8) HM.
Reader, Spring D., photos by. Exploring Careers: The World of Work & You. Farr, J. Michael & Amore, JoAnn. 32p. (gr. 6-12). 1989. wkbk. 1.95 (0-942784-28-6, EXPAB) JIST Works.
Reading, Bryan. Rotten Riddles & Goofy Gags. Danby, Mary, compiled by. LC 89-48859. 96p. (gr. 2-8). 1991. pap. 3.95 (0-8069-7310-2) Sterling.
Reams, Ron. American History in Verse: Special Bicentennial Edition. Southworth, John V. LC 76-590. 120p. (gr. 7 up). 1976. pap. 10.00 (0-912760-20-6) Valkyrie Pub Hse.
Reasoner, Charles. First Words. 6p. (ps). 1992. bds. 3.95 (1-56293-182-2) McClanahan Bk.
—Gift of the Nile: An Ancient Egyptian Legend. Mike, Jan M. LC 92-5826. 32p. (gr. 2-5). 1992. PLB 11.89 (0-8167-2813-5); pap. text ed. 3.95 (0-8167-2814-3) Troll Assocs.
—Llama's Secret: A Peruvian Legend. Palacios, Argentina. LC 92-21436. 32p. (gr. 2-5). 1993. lib. bdg. 11.89 (0-8167-3049-0); pap. text ed. 3.95 (0-8167-3050-4) Troll Assocs.
—My First Calculator Book. 10p. (ps-2). 1991. bds. 10.95 (1-56293-101-6) McClanahan Bk.
—My First Musical Piggy Bank Book. 6p. (ps-2). 1992. bds. 9.95 (1-56293-139-3) McClanahan Bk.
—My First Phone Book. 10p. (ps-2). 1991. bds. 9.95 (1-56293-100-8) McClanahan Bk.
—My First Time Book. 10p. (ps-2). 1991. bds. 10.95 (1-56293-102-4) McClanahan Bk.
—Number Munch. Reasoner, Charles. 36p. (ps). 1993. bds. 9.95 (0-8431-3674-X) Price Stern.
—Opossum & the Great Firemaker A Mexican Legend. Mike, Jan M. LC 92-36459. 32p. (gr. 2-5). 1993. lib. bdg. 11.89 (0-8167-3055-5); tchr's. ed. 3.95 (0-8167-3056-3) Troll Assocs.
—The Princess Who Lost Her Hair: An Akamba Legend. Mollel, Tololwa M., retold by. LC 92-13273. 32p. (gr. 2-5). 1992. lib. bdg. 11.89 (0-8167-2815-1); pap. 3.95 (0-8167-2816-X) Troll Assocs.
—Read Aloud Topsy-Turvy Library, 26 vols. Cosgrove, Stephen. (ps-3). 1988. Set. 155.48 (0-87475-600-6) Stuttman.
—Santa's Super Christmas, 22 bks. (ps-3). 1988. bds. 19.95 (1-56293-138-5, Set, mini-board bks. in a tray) McClanahan Bk.
Reasoner, Charles E. Wee Sing over in the Meadow. Beall, Pamela C., et al. 64p. (ps). 10.95 (0-8431-1949-7); incl. cass. 14.95 (0-8431-1978-0) Price Stern.

Reasoner, Chuck. Bees Buzz. Mann, P. Z. 14p. (ps-1). 1992. bds. 1.95 (1-56293-203-9) McClanahan Bk.
—A Big Alphabet Book. Reasoner, Chuck. 23p. (ps). 1993. bds. 9.99 (0-8431-3552-2) Price Stern.
—Chomp, Crunch, Chew! Reasoner, Chuck. 6p. (ps). 1993. bds. 3.99 (0-8431-3549-2) Price Stern.
—Frogs Fiddle. Mann, P. Z. 14p. (ps-2). 1992. bds. 1.95 (1-56293-202-0) McClanahan Bk.
—One Big Counting Book. Reasoner, Chuck. 23p. (ps). 1993. bds. 9.99 (0-8431-3551-4) Price Stern.
—Spiders Spin. Mann, P. Z. 14p. (ps-1). 1992. bds. 1.95 (1-56293-205-5) McClanahan Bk.
—Turtles Tiptoe. Mann, P. Z. 14p. (ps-2). 1992. bds. 1.95 (1-56293-204-7) McClanahan Bk.
—Who's Peeking. Reasoner, Chuck. 6p. (ps-1). 1993. text ed. 9.99 (0-8431-3478-X) Price Stern.
—Who's There. Reasoner, Chuck. 6p. (ps-1). 1993. text ed. 9.99 (0-8431-3479-8) Price Stern.
Reccardi, Chris. Pat the Stimpy: A Nitty Gritty Touchy Smelly Book. Hill, Tom & Friedman, Donna. 14p. (gr. 3 up). 1993. 9.95 (0-448-40199-1, G&D) Putnam Pub Group.
Recht, Ruth. Grandfather's Rock. Strangis, Joel. LC 92-26525. 1993. 14.95 (0-395-65367-3) HM.
Reczuch, Karen. The Auction. Andrews, Jan. LC 90-41378. 32p. (ps-3). 1991. RSBE 13.95 (0-02-705535-3, Macmillan Child Bk) Macmillan Child Grp.
Redenbaugh, Vicki J. Pug, Slug, & Doug the Thug. Saller, Carol. LC 92-44340. 1993. 13.95 (0-87614-803-8) Carolrhoda Bks.
Redford, Jim L. World of the Heart. Island, John. 48p. (ps-6). Date not set. text ed. 14.95 (0-9637712-0-5) Island Flowers.
Redman, Tom. Bernardo De Galvez. De Varona, Frank. (SPA & ENG.). 32p. 1993. PLB 15.96 (0-8172-3379-2) Raintree Steck-V.
Redmond, Marilyn. Henry Hamilton, Graduate Ghost. Redmond, Marilyn. LC 81-22693. 159p. (gr. 6 up). 1982. 11.95 (0-88289-303-3) Pelican.
Redondo, Francisco. Around the World in Eighty Days. new & abr. ed. Verne, Jules. Calhoun, D'Ann, ed. (gr. 4-12). 1977. pap. text ed. 2.95 (0-88301-261-8) Pendulum Pr.
—A Connecticut Yankee in King Arthur's Court. new & abr. ed. Twain, Mark. Fago, John N., ed. LC 83-9162. (gr. 4-12). 1977. pap. text ed. 2.95 (0-88301-263-4) Pendulum Pr.
—Huckleberry Finn. Clemens, Samuel. Farr, Naunerle, ed. LC 73-75468. 64p. (Orig.). (gr. 5-10). 1973. pap. 2.95 (0-88301-098-4) Pendulum Pr.
Redondo, Frank. Americans Move Westward, 1800-1850. Farr, Naunerle. Calhoun, D'Ann & Bloch, Lawrence W., eds. (gr. 4-12). 1977. pap. text ed. 2.95 (0-88301-227-8); wkbk. 1.25 (0-88301-239-1) Pendulum Pr.
—Kidnapped: Student Activity Book. Sohl, Marcia & Dackerman, Gerald. (gr. 4-10). 1976. wkbk. 1.25 (0-88301-192-1) Pendulum Pr.
Redondo, Frank & Carrillo, Fred. Jim Thorpe - Althea Gibson. Fago, John N. & Farr, Naunerle C. (gr. 4-12). 1979. pap. text ed. 2.95 (0-88301-360-6); wkbk. 1.25 (0-88301-384-3) Pendulum Pr.
Redondo, Nestor. Dr. Jekyll & Mr. Hyde. new ed. Stevenson, Robert Louis. Platt, Kin, ed. LC 73-75457. 64p. (Orig.). (gr. 5-10). 1973. pap. 2.95 (0-88301-096-8); student activity bk. 1.25 (0-88301-176-X) Pendulum Pr.
—Dracula. Stoker, Bram. Farr, Naunerle, ed. LC 83-5471. 64p. (Orig.). (gr. 5-10). 1973. pap. 2.95 (0-88301-100-X); student activity bk. 1.25 (0-88301-175-1) Pendulum Pr.
Redondo, Nestor & LoFamia, Jun. Abraham Lincoln - Franklin D. Roosevelt. Farr, Naunerle C. (gr. 4-12). 1979. pap. text ed. 2.95 (0-88301-354-1); wkbk. 1.25 (0-88301-378-9) Pendulum Pr.
Redondo, Nestor, jt. illus. see Carrillo, Fred.
Redondo, Nestor, jt. illus. see Leonidez, Nestor.
Redondo, Virgilio. The Scarlet Letter: Student Activity Book. Sohl, Marcia & Dackerman, Gerald. (gr. 4-10). 1976. wkbk. 1.25 (0-88301-194-8) Pendulum Pr.
Reed, Allison. The Story of Jonah. Baumann, Kurt, retold by. LC 86-62522. 32p. (gr. k-3). 1987. 13.95 (1-55858-050-6) North-South Bks NYC.
Reed, J. Take a Whistler's Walk. Reed, Joyce G. 77p. (gr. 4-9). 1988. 12.95 (0-943487-08-0); pap. 4.95 (0-943487-07-2) Sevgo Pr.
Reed, Libby, jt. illus. see Ambriz, Don.
Reed, Naomi. Practice Your BASIC. Cutler, C. 48p. (gr. 6 up). 1983. PLB 10.96 (0-88110-142-7); pap. 3.95 (0-86020-743-9) EDC.
Reed, Tom. Criterion Referenced Test Kit: Math. Craig, Linda & Praytor, Phyllis. 54p. (gr. 4). 1978. write for info. (0-936394-01-3) Education Serv.
Reeder, Bill. Where & Why. Swartz, Susan S. 24p. (Orig.). (ps-6). 1987. pap. 4.50 wkbk. (0-943901-00-6) Creare Pubns.
Reeder, Colin. The Day Patch Stood Guard. Laird, Elizabeth. LC 90-11153. 32p. (gr. k up). 1991. 11.95 (0-688-10239-5, Tambourine Bks) PLB 11.88 (0-688-10240-9, Tambourine Bks) Morrow.
—The Day Sidney Ran Off. Laird, Elizabeth. LC 90-11154. 32p. (gr. k up). 1991. 11.95 (0-688-10241-7, Tambourine Bks) PLB 11.88 (0-688-10242-5, Tambourine Bks) Morrow.
—The Day the Ducks Went Skating. Laird, Elizabeth. LC 90-25899. 32p. (gr. k up). 1991. 11.95 (0-688-10246-8, Tambourine Bks) PLB 11.88 (0-688-10247-6, Tambourine Bks) Morrow.

—The Day Veronica Was Nosy. Laird, Elizabeth. LC 90-24063. 32p. (gr. k up). 1991. 11.95 (*0-688-10248-4*, Tambourine Bks); PLB 11.88 (*0-688-10249-2*, Tambourine Bks) Morrow.

Reepen, Ronald. Lefty Meets Hefty. Reepen, Ronald. 40p. (gr. 2-7). 1987. 6.95 (*0-930905-02-4*) Platypus Bks.

Rees, Claudia. The Bird with the Word Talks about Self-Control. Rees, Claudia. (Orig.). (gr. 1-3). 1987. pap. 0.98 (*0-89274-451-0*) Harrison Hse.

Rees, Gary. The Trouble with Josh. Nystrom, Carolyn. 48p. (gr. 6-12). 1989. text ed. 7.99 (*0-7459-1621-X*) Lion USA.

Rees, Mary. Mine! Oram, Hiawyn. 16p. (ps-k). 1992. with dust jacket 12.95 (*0-8120-6303-1*); pap. 5.95 (*0-8120-4905-5*) Barron.

—Spooky Poems. Cummings, e. e., et al. Bennett, Jill, compiled by. (ps-3). 1989. 14.95 (*0-316-08987-7*, Joy St Bks) Little.

—Ten in a Bed. Rees, Mary, adapted by. (ps-1). 1988. 13.95 (*0-316-73708-9*, Joy St Bks) Little.

Reese, Bob. ABCs. Reese, Bob. LC 92-12188. 24p. (ps-2). 1992. PLB 12.33 (*0-516-05577-1*) Childrens.

—Abert & Kaibab. Reese, Bob. (gr. k-6). 1987. 7.95 (*0-89868-226-6*); pap. 2.95 (*0-89868-227-4*) ARO Pub.

—Abert & Kaibab. Reese, Bob. (gr. k-6). 1987. pap. 20.00 (*0-685-50872-2*) ARO Pub.

—Ape Escape. Reese, Bob. 1983. 7.95 (*0-89868-147-2*); pap. 2.95 (*0-89868-146-4*) ARO Pub.

—The Ape Team. Reese, Bob. 1983. 7.95 (*0-89868-145-6*); pap. 2.95 (*0-89868-144-8*) ARO Pub.

—Apricot Ape. Reese, Bob. 1983. 7.95 (*0-89868-141-3*); pap. 2.95 (*0-89868-140-5*) ARO Pub.

—Art. Reese, Bob. LC 92-12187. 24p. (ps-2). 1992. PLB 12.33 (*0-516-05578-X*) Childrens.

—Bags the Lamb. Kanno, Wendy. (gr. k-2). 1984. 7.95 (*0-89868-165-0*); pap. 2.95 (*0-89868-166-9*) ARO Pub.

—Big Big Book Series, 7 bks. Reese, Bob, et al. (gr. k-6). 1987. pap. 140.00 (*0-89868-244-4*) ARO Pub.

—Bubba Bear. Reese, Bob. (gr. k-6). 1986. 7.95 (*0-89868-173-1*); pap. 2.95 (*0-89868-174-X*) ARO Pub.

—Bubba Bear. Reese, Bob. (gr. k-6). 1986. pap. 20.00 (*0-685-50871-4*) ARO Pub.

—Buffa Buffalo. Reese, Bob. (gr. k-6). 1986. 7.95 (*0-89868-175-8*); pap. 2.95 (*0-89868-176-6*) ARO Pub.

—Bugle Elk & Little Toot. Reese, Bob. (gr. k-6). 1986. 7.95 (*0-89868-177-4*); pap. 2.95 (*0-89868-178-2*) ARO Pub.

—Camper Critters. Reese, Bob. (gr. k-6). 1986. 7.95 (*0-89868-169-3*); pap. 2.95 (*0-89868-170-7*) ARO Pub.

—Christopher Columbus. Murphy, Carol. (gr. k-6). 1991. 11.95 (*0-89868-228-2*) ARO Pub.

—Christopher Columbus. Murphy, Carol. (gr. k-6). 1991. pap. 20.00 (*0-89868-229-0*) ARO Pub.

—Cocos Berry Party. Reese, Bob. (gr. k-6). 1987. 7.95 (*0-89868-193-6*); pap. 2.95 (*0-89868-194-4*) ARO Pub.

—Elmo Pig. Kanno, Wendy. (gr. k-2). 1984. 7.95 (*0-89868-161-8*); pap. 2.95 (*0-89868-162-6*) ARO Pub.

—Elmo Pig. Kanno, Wendy. (gr. k-3). 1984. pap. 20.00 (*0-685-50870-6*) ARO Pub.

—Field Trip. Reese, Bob. LC 92-12186. 24p. (ps-2). 1992. PLB 12.33 (*0-516-05579-8*) Childrens.

—Fire Drill. Cox, Mike, et al. Wasserman, Dan, ed. (gr. k-1). 1979. 7.95 (*0-89868-071-9*); pap. 2.95 (*0-89868-082-4*) ARO Pub.

—Flowers. Cox, Mike & Cox, Kris. Wasserman, Dan, ed. 1979. 7.95 (*0-89868-076-X*); pap. 2.95 (*0-89868-087-5*) ARO Pub.

—Forty Word Yellowstone Series, 6 bks. Reese, Bob. (gr. k-6). 1986. Set. 47.70 (*0-89868-239-8*); Set. pap. 29.50 (*0-89868-238-X*) ARO Pub.

—Funny Bunny. Schoder, Judy. Wasserman, Dan, ed. (gr. k-1). 1979. 7.95 (*0-89868-069-7*); pap. 2.95 (*0-89868-080-8*) ARO Pub.

—The Funny Farm House. Kanno, Wendy. (gr. k-2). 1984. 7.95 (*0-89868-155-3*); pap. 2.95 (*0-89868-156-1*) ARO Pub.

—Glasses. Reese, Bob. LC 92-12185. 24p. (ps-2). 1992. PLB 12.33 (*0-516-05580-1*) Childrens.

—Going Bananas. Reese, Bob. 1983. 7.95 (*0-89868-143-X*); pap. 2.95 (*0-89868-142-1*) ARO Pub.

—Holy Moley Cow. Kanno, Wendy. (gr. k-2). 1984. 7.95 (*0-89868-159-6*); pap. 2.95 (*0-89868-160-X*) ARO Pub.

—Honest Ape. Reese, Bob. 1983. 7.95 (*0-89868-149-9*); pap. 2.95 (*0-89868-148-0*) ARO Pub.

—The Jungle Train. Reese, Bob. 1983. 7.95 (*0-89868-151-0*); pap. 2.95 (*0-89868-150-2*) ARO Pub.

—Jungle Train. Reese, Bob. (gr. k-3). 1983. pap. 20.00 (*0-685-50868-4*) ARO Pub.

—Little Dinosaur. Reese, Bob. Wasserman, Dan, ed. (gr. k-1). 1979. 7.95 (*0-89868-070-0*); pap. 2.95 (*0-89868-081-6*) ARO Pub.

—Martin Luther King, Jr. Murphy, Carol. (gr. k-6). 1991. 11.95 (*0-89868-230-4*) ARO Pub.

—Martin Luther King, Jr. Murphy, Carol. (gr. k-6). 1991. pap. 20.00 (*0-89868-231-2*) ARO Pub.

—Mickey Moose. Reese, Bob. (gr. k-6). 1986. 7.95 (*0-89868-171-5*); pap. 2.95 (*0-89868-172-3*) ARO Pub.

—Milk. Shebar, Sharon. Wasserman, Dan, ed. (gr. k-1). 1979. 7.95 (*0-89868-067-0*); pap. 2.95 (*0-89868-078-6*) ARO Pub.

—My Dolly. Willoughby, Alana. Wasserman, Dan, ed. (gr. k-1). 1979. 7.95 (*0-89868-075-1*); pap. 2.95 (*0-89868-086-7*) ARO Pub.

—My First Animal Ride. Allen, Julia. (gr. k-3). 1987. 7.95 (*0-89868-179-0*); pap. 2.95 (*0-89868-180-4*) ARO Pub.

—My First Camping Trip. Allen, Julia. (gr. k-3). 1987. 7.95 (*0-89868-181-2*); pap. 2.95 (*0-685-50867-6*) ARO Pub.

—My First Camping Trip. Allen, Julia. (gr. k-3). 1987. pap. 20.00 (*0-89868-182-0*) ARO Pub.

—My First Dentist Visit. Allen, Julia. (gr. k-3). 1987. 7.95 (*0-89868-185-5*); pap. 2.95 (*0-89868-186-3*) ARO Pub.

—My First Doctor Visit. Allen, Julia. (gr. k-3). 1987. 7.95 (*0-89868-187-1*); pap. 2.95 (*0-89868-188-X*) ARO Pub.

—My First Job. Allen, Julia. (gr. k-3). 1987. 7.95 (*0-89868-184-7*); pap. 2.95 (*0-89868-183-9*) ARO Pub.

—My First Phone Call. Allen, Julia. (gr. k-3). 1987. 7.95 (*0-89868-189-8*); pap. 2.95 (*0-89868-190-1*) ARO Pub.

—Night Monsters. Shebar, Sharon. (gr. k-3). 1979. pap. 20.00 (*0-685-50869-2*) ARO Pub.

—Nightmonsters. Shebar, Sharon. Wasserman, Dan, ed. (gr. k-1). 1979. 7.95 (*0-89868-068-9*); pap. 2.95 (*0-89868-079-4*) ARO Pub.

—Old Faithful. Reese, Bob. (gr. k-6). 1986. 7.95 (*0-89868-167-7*); pap. 2.95 (*0-89868-168-5*) ARO Pub.

—Pamba & the Bink. Reese, Bob. (gr. k-6). 1984. 11.95 (*0-89868-152-9*) ARO Pub.

—Raven's Roost. Reese, Bob. (gr. k-6). 1987. 7.95 (*0-89868-195-2*); pap. 2.95 (*0-89868-196-0*) ARO Pub.

—Recess. Reese, Bob. LC 92-12184. 24p. (ps-2). 1992. PLB 12.33 (*0-516-05581-X*) Childrens.

—Sack Lunch. Reese, Bob. LC 92-12183. 24p. (ps-2). 1992. PLB 12.33 (*0-516-05582-8*) Childrens.

—Sampson Horse. Kanno, Wendy. (gr. k-2). 1984. 7.95 (*0-89868-163-4*); pap. 2.95 (*0-89868-164-2*) ARO Pub.

—Sixty Word Grand Canyon Series, 6 bks. Reese, Bob. (gr. k-6). 1987. Set. 47.70 (*0-89868-241-X*); Set. pap. 29.50 (*0-89868-240-1*) ARO Pub.

—Slitherfoot Snake. Reese, Bob. (gr. k-6). 1987. 7.95 (*0-89868-191-X*); pap. 2.95 (*0-89868-192-8*) ARO Pub.

—Sunshine. Reese, Bob. Wasserman, Dan, ed. (gr. k-1). 1979. 7.95 (*0-89868-073-5*); pap. 2.95 (*0-89868-084-0*) ARO Pub.

—Surefoot Mule. Reese, Bob. (gr. k-6). 1987. 7.95 (*0-89868-197-9*); pap. 2.95 (*0-89868-198-7*) ARO Pub.

—Ten Word Book Series, 10 bks. Reese, Bob. Wasserman, Dan, ed. (gr. k-1). 1979. Set. write for info. (*0-89868-077-8*) ARO Pub.

—Thirty Word My First Series, 6 bks. Allen, Julia. (gr. k-3). 1987. Set. 47.70 (*0-89868-237-1*); Set. pap. 29.50 (*0-89868-236-3*) ARO Pub.

—Twenty Word Funny Farm Series, 6 bks. Kanno, Wendy. (gr. k-2). 1984. Set. 47.70 (*0-685-50866-8*); Set. pap. 29.50 (*0-89868-154-5*) ARO Pub.

—Waldo Duck. Kanno, Wendy. (gr. k-2). 1984. 7.95 (*0-89868-157-X*); pap. 2.95 (*0-89868-158-8*) ARO Pub.

—Who's New at the Zoo? Winder, Jack. Wasserman, Dan, ed. (gr. k-1). 1979. 7.95 (*0-89868-074-3*); pap. 2.95 (*0-89868-085-9*) ARO Pub.

—Wild Turkey Run. Reese, Bob. (gr. k-6). 1987. 7.95 (*0-89868-199-5*); pap. 2.95 (*0-89868-225-8*) ARO Pub.

—Zero Word Going Ape Series, 6 bks. Reese, Bob. 1983. Set. 47.70 (*0-89868-139-1*); Set. pap. 29.50 (*0-89868-138-3*) ARO Pub.

Reese, Dan. Crab Apple. Reese, Bob. Wasserman, Dan, ed. (gr. k-1). 1979. 7.95 (*0-89868-072-7*); pap. 2.95 (*0-89868-083-2*) ARO Pub.

Reese, Jeff, photos by. A Is for Aloha. Feeney, Stephanie. LC 85-50569. 64p. (ps-3). 1985. 8.95 (*0-8248-0722-7*) UH Pr.

Reese, Ralph. Grand Slam. Montgomery, Robert. LC 89-5198. 176p. (gr. 5-8). 1991. PLB 9.89 (*0-8167-1988-8*); pap. text ed. 2.95 (*0-8167-1989-6*) Troll Assocs.

—Hitting Streak. Montgomery, Robert. LC 90-10968. 176p. (gr. 5-8). 1991. PLB 9.89 (*0-8167-1982-9*); pap. text ed. 2.95 (*0-8167-1983-7*) Troll Assocs.

—Home Run! Montgomery, Robert. LC 89-5190. 176p. (gr. 5-8). 1991. PLB 9.89 (*0-8167-1986-1*); pap. text ed. 2.95 (*0-8167-1987-X*) Troll Assocs.

—Joe Gunn. De Haven, Tom. (gr. 7 up). 1988. 15.95 (*0-8027-6824-5*) Walker & Co.

—MVP. Montgomery, Robert. LC 89-20180. 176p. (gr. 5-8). 1991. lib. bdg. 9.89 (*0-8167-1992-6*); pap. text ed. 2.95 (*0-8167-1993-4*) Troll Assocs.

—Prisoner of the Ant People. Montgomery, Raymond A. 115p. (gr. 4). 1983. pap. 2.25 (*0-553-25763-3*) Bantam.

—The Show! Montgomery, Robert. LC 90-20586. 176p. (gr. 5-8). 1991. PLB 9.89 (*0-8167-1984-5*); pap. text ed. 2.95 (*0-8167-1985-3*) Troll Assocs.

—Triple Play. Montgomery, Robert. LC 89-20179. 176p. (gr. 5-8). 1991. lib. bdg. 9.89 (*0-8167-1990-X*); pap. text ed. 2.95 (*0-8167-1991-8*) Troll Assocs.

—Trouble on Planet Earth. Montgomery, Raymond A. (Orig.). (gr. 4). 1984. pap. text ed. 2.25 (*0-553-26308-0*) Bantam.

Reeves, Eira. Doing Things. LC 91-76214. 12p. (ps). 1992. bds. 3.99 bds. (*0-8066-2590-2*, 9-2590, Augsburg) Augsburg Fortress.

—Going Places. LC 91-76215. 12p. (ps). 1992. 3.99 (*0-8066-2589-9*, 9-2589) Augsburg Fortress.

—Helping. LC 91-76216. 12p. (ps). 1992. bds. 3.99 (*0-8066-2588-0*, 9-2588, Augsburg) Augsburg Fortress.

—Playing. LC 91-76217. 12p. (ps). 1992. bds. 3.99 (*0-8066-2587-2*, 9-2587, Augsburg) Augsburg Fortress.

Regan, Dana. Baby Boo! 12p. (ps). 1992. 5.99 (*0-679-81544-9*) Random Bks Yng Read.

—Christmas Holiday Grab Bag. Stamper, Judith. LC 92-13226. 48p. (gr. 2-5). 1992. PLB 11.89 (*0-8167-2908-5*); pap. text ed. 3.95 (*0-8167-2909-3*) Troll Assocs.

—I'm the Greatest Me There Could Ever Be! Kuyper, Vicki J. Gress, Jonna, ed. LC 92-72843. 14p. (Orig.). (ps-3). 1992. pap. 5.40 (*0-944943-30-6*, CODE 21175-5) Current Inc.

—It's Christmas, Baby-Boo. Leonard, Marcia. 1992. bds. 3.25 (*0-8378-3798-7*) Gibson.

—The Night Before Christmas. Moore, Clement C. LC 90-22388. 24p. (ps up). 1991. 2.95 (*0-694-00365-4*) HarpC Child Bks.

—The Night Before Christmas. Moore, Clement C. LC 91-46766. 26p. (ps). 1992. 4.95 (*0-694-00424-3*, Festival) HarpC Child Bks.

—Teacher's Pet Projects: A Pet Education Program. Arkow, Phil. Gress, Jonna, ed. 14p. (Orig.). 1993. pap. 16.20 incl. tchr's. guide, stickers, board game, bulletin board decos, & 5 reproducibles (*0-944943-22-5*, 20554-8) Current Inc.

Regan, Dana & DeMarco, Susanne. Letters & Sounds. Wise, Beth A. Nayer, Judith E., ed. 32p. (gr. k-1). 1991. wkbk. 1.95 (*1-878624-60-1*) McClanahan Bk.

Regan, Laura. Welcome to the Greenhouse. Yolen, Jane. 32p. (ps-3). 1993. PLB 14.95 (*0-399-22335-5*, Putnam) Putnam Pub Group.

Regan, Rick. The Farmer, the Buffalo, & the Tiger: A Folktale from Vietnam. Hamada, Cheryl, retold by. LC 93-21725. 32p. (ps-3). 1993. PLB write for info. (*0-516-05143-1*) Childrens.

—The Naughty Little Rabbit & Old Man Coyote: A Tewa Story from San Juan Pueblo. Martinez, Estefanita, as told by. LC 92-8992. 24p. (ps-3). 1992. PLB 15.53 (*0-516-05141-5*); pap. 4.95 (*0-516-45141-3*) Childrens.

Regier, Robert. The Sun & the Wind. Lehn, Cornelia. 32p. (gr. k-5). 1983. 7.95 (*0-87303-072-9*) Faith & Life.

Regier, Robert W. The Sun & the Wind. Lehn, Cornelia. LC 32-+010. 32p. 1987. 7.95 (*0-8361-3466-4*) Herald Pr.

Rego, Paul. Computer Encounters...of the Fourth Kind: "What the Beginner Should Know When Exploring the Apple II" Rego, Paul. 139p. (Orig.). (ps up). 1988. pap. 29.95 (*0-945876-03-3*) Insight Data.

Rehnman, Mats. The Clay Flute. Rehnman, Mats. Bibb, Eric, tr. (ps-4). 1989. 12.95 (*91-29-59184-8*, Pub. by R & S Bks) FS&G.

Reichel, Cara. A Stone Promise. Reichel, Cara. Thatch, Nancy R., ed. Melton, David, intro. by. LC 91-15059. 26p. (gr. 5 up). 1991. PLB 14.95 (*0-933849-35-4*) Landmark Edns.

Reichley, David. Jasper & Sam. Reichley, David. (gr. 4-6). 1992. 14.95 (*1-879260-04-2*) Evanston Pub.

Reichmann, Naczinski & Associates. The Parts of Speech. Lutgendorf, Philip & James, Shirley M. LC 77-730079. (gr. 7-9). 1976. pap. text ed. 219.00 6 filmstrips, 6 cass., 30 skill sheets, Guide (*0-89290-118-7*, A134-SATC) Soc for Visual.

Reichmeier, Betty. Potty Time! Yellow Ladder Books for Toddlers Through 4 Years. 10p. 1988. vinyl 7.00 (*0-394-89403-0*) Random Bks Yng Read.

—Sing with Me Play-along & Counting Songs. (ps-1). 1987. incl. cassette 5.95 (*0-394-88810-3*) Random Bks Yng Read.

—Teddy Beddy Bear's Bedtime Adventure. Slier, Debby. LC 85-60215. 28p. (ps). 1985. bds. 2.95 (*0-394-87535-4*) Random Bks Yng Read.

Reid, Ace. Cowpokes Comin' Yore Way. 5th ed. Reid, Ace. 64p. (gr. k up). 1985. pap. 5.95 (*0-917207-05-X*) Reid Ent.

—Cowpokes Cookbook & Cartoons. 12th ed. Reid, Ace. 64p. (gr. 5 up). pap. 5.95 (*0-917207-06-8*) Reid Ent.

—Cowpokes Cow Country Cartoons. 14th ed. Reid, Ace. Barker, S. Omar, intro. by. 56p. (gr. 5 up). pap. 5.95 (*0-917207-00-9*) Reid Ent.

—Cowpokes Home Remedies. 7th ed. Reid, Ace. 56p. (gr. k-5). pap. 5.95 (*0-917207-07-6*) Reid Ent.

—Cowpokes Rarin' to Go. 2nd ed. Reid, Ace. 74p. (gr. 5 up). pap. 5.95 (*0-917207-09-2*) Reid Ent.

—Cowpokes Ride Again. 4th ed. Reid, Ace. 64p. (gr. k up). 1985. pap. 5.95 (*0-917207-08-4*) Reid Ent.

—Cowpokes Tales & Cartoons. 2nd ed. Reid, Ace. Pickens, Slim, intro. by. 64p. (gr. 5 up). pap. 5.95 (*0-917207-10-6*) Reid Ent.

—Cowpokes Wanted. 12th ed. Reid, Ace. Gipson, Fred, intro. by. 62p. (gr. 5 up). pap. 5.95 (*0-917207-02-5*) Reid Ent.

—Draggin' S Ranch Cowpokes. 14th ed. Reid, Ace. 65p. (gr. 5 up). pap. 5.95 (*0-917207-04-1*) Reid Ent.

—More Cowpokes. 14th ed. Reid, Ace. Robertson, FrankC., intro. by. 60p. (gr. 5 up). pap. 5.95 (*0-917207-01-7*) Reid Ent.

Reid, Barbara. Effie. Allinson, Beverley. 32p. (ps-1). 1991. 11.95 (*0-590-44045-4*, Scholastic Hardcover) Scholastic Inc.

—Have You Seen Birds? Oppenheim, Joanne. (ps-2). 1988. 2.95 (*0-590-40890-9*) Scholastic Inc.

Reid, Diana S. Big Enough. Anderson, Myra. 32p. (gr. k-3). 1991. 12.95 (*0-9625620-0-9*) DOT Garnet.

Reid, James. Basic Karate Method. Neff, Fred. LC 75-38471. 56p. (gr. 5 up). 1976. PLB 14.95 (*0-8225-1150-9*) Lerner Pubns.

—Basic Self-Defense Manual. Neff, Fred. LC 75-38473. 56p. (gr. 5 up). 1976. PLB 14.95 (0-8225-1152-5) Lerner Pubns.
—Foot-Fighting Manual for Self-Defense & Sport Karate. Neff, Fred. LC 75-38474. 56p. (gr. 5 up). 1977. PLB 14.95 (0-8225-1153-3) Lerner Pubns.
—The Great Drama of Jesus: A Life of Christ for Teens Who Want to Be Challenged. Galeone, Victor. 207p. (Orig.). (gr. 7-8). 1979. pap. 7.95 (0-913382-31-0, 101-28) Prow Bks-Franciscan.
—Hand-Fighting Manual for Self-Defense & Sport Karate. Neff, Fred. LC 75-38475. 56p. (gr. 5 up). 1977. PLB 11.95 (0-8225-1154-1) Lerner Pubns.
—Keeping Fit Handbook for Physical Conditioning & Better Health. Neff, Fred. LC 75-38478. 56p. (gr. 5 up). 1977. PLB 14.95 (0-8225-1157-6) Lerner Pubns.
—Manual of Throws for Sport Judo & Self-Defense. Neff, Fred. LC 75-38476. 56p. (gr. 5 up). 1976. PLB 14.95 (0-8225-1155-X) Lerner Pubns.
—Self-Protection Guide-Book for Girls & Women. Neff, Fred. LC 75-38477. 56p. (gr. 5 up). 1977. PLB 11.95 (0-8225-1156-8) Lerner Pubns.
Reid, James E. Running Is for Me. Neff, Fred. LC 79-16789. 48p. (gr. 2-5). 1980. PLB 13.50 (0-8225-1093-6) Lerner Pubns.
Reid, James E., photos by. Karate Is for Me. Neff, Fred. LC 79-16900. 48p. (gr. 2-5). 1980. PLB 13.50 (0-8225-1090-1) Lerner Pubns.

Reid, William K., Jr. A Funny Feeling. Kimball, Richard S. LC 87-32155. 64p. (Orig.). (gr. 3 up). 1988. pap. 7.95 (0-944443-00-1) Green Timber. This collection of 41 cleverly illustrated poems explores common feelings & sayings about them for entertainment & enlightenment of youngsters aged eight & above. Eight-year olds will identify with Reginald Botts who was "tied up in knots & couldn't get his thoughts undone." Ten-year olds will enjoy the image of Louise being made small by the weight of the grudge she carries. Twelve-year olds will sympathize with Annie who has reached the age "when staying in means being left out" & "going out means being in." Everybody will be delighted by "tongue tied" Sid & by the many other characters & poems. With humor, this book allows readers & listeners to think about their own funny feelings & can open the way for discussion with parents, teachers, counselors, church groups, & friends. Paperback, $7.95.
Publisher Provided Annotation.

Reidel, Marlene. From Egg to Bird. Reidel, Marlene. 24p. (ps-3). 1981. PLB 10.95 (0-87614-159-5) Carolrhoda Bks.
—From Egg to Butterfly. Reidel, Marlene. LC 81-204. 24p. (ps-3). 1981. PLB 10.95 (0-87614-153-X) Carolrhoda Bks.
—From Ice to Rain. Reidel, Marlene. 24p. (ps-3). 1981. PLB 10.95 (0-87614-157-2) Carolrhoda Bks.
Reilly, Kathy. The Lion & the Boy. Lyne, Sandy. 48p. (gr. 4-7). 1988. 12.95 (0-933905-04-1); pap. 9.95 (0-933905-15-7) Claycomb Pr.
Reilly, Nicholas. Freddie's Spaghetti. Doyle, Charlotte. LC 90-61003. 24p. (Orig.). (ps-2). 1991. pap. 2.25 (0-679-81160-5) Random Bks Yng Read.
Reilly, Veronica. Always Alvin. Van Allen, Diane. (Orig.). (ps). 1984. pap. 3.95 (0-939332-11-6) J Pohl Assocs.
Reiner, John. Howard Huge Comes to Stay. Hoest, Bunny. LC 91-23629. 32p. (Orig.). (gr. 1). 1992. pap. 2.25 (0-679-82033-7) Random Bks Yng Read.
Reiner, Traudl, jt. illus. see Reiner, Walter.
Reiner, Walter & Reiner, Traudl. Me & Clara & Casimir the Cat. Inkiow, Dimiter. LC 78-31316. (gr. 1-4). 1979. 2.95 (0-394-84124-7) Pantheon.
Reinert, Rick. The Nutcracker. Kidd, Ron. 48p. (gr. k-6). 1985. 6.95 (0-8249-8095-6, Ideals Child) Hambleton-Hill.
Reinertson, Barbara. Christopher. Koff, Richard M. Kelly, Orly, ed. LC 81-65885. 128p. (gr. 7 up). 1981. 8.95 (0-89742-050-0) Celestial Arts.
—Grandma & Grandpa Are Special People. Polland, Barbara K. LC 84-66961. 80p. (gr. k-3). 1984. pap. 7.95 (0-89087-343-7) Celestial Arts.
Reingold, Michael. The Common Cold & Influenza. Stedman, Nancy. LC 86-8387. 72p. (gr. 4-8). 1986. lib. 11.98 (0-671-60022-2, J Messner) S&S Trade.
—Diabetes. Tiger, Steven. LC 86-23498. 72p. (gr. 4-8). 1987. lib. bdg. 13.98 (0-671-63273-6, J Messner) S&S Trade.

Reingold-Reiss, Debra, photos by. Kitten Care & Critters, Too! Petersen-Fleming, Judy & Fleming, Bill. LC 93-24200. 40p. (ps-3). 1994. 15.00 (0-688-12563-8, Tambourine Bks); PLB 14.93 (0-688-12564-5, Tambourine Bks) Morrow.
Reinhard, Michl. The Redheaded Woman. Eustis, Helen. LC 84-145828. 36p. (Orig.). (gr. 7 up). 1991. pap. 2.95 (0-88138-013-X, Green Tiger) S&S Trade.
Reisberg, Mira. Leaving for America. Bresnick-Perry, Roslyn. LC 92-8450. 32p. (ps-7). 1992. PLB 13.95 (0-89239-105-7) Childrens Book Pr.
Reisberg, Veg. Elinda Who Danced in the Sky: An Eastern European Folktale from Estonia. Moroney, Lynn, adapted by. LC 99-2247. 32p. (gr. 1-7). 1990. 13.95 (0-89239-066-2) Childrens Book Pr.
—Uncle Nacho's Hat (El Sombrero de Tio Nacho) Rohmer, Harriet, adapted by. Flor Ada, Alma & Zubizarreta, Rosalma, trs. LC 88-37090. (ENG & SPA.). 32p. (ps-5). 1989. 13.95 (0-89239-043-3) Childrens Book Pr.
Reisenauer, Cindy. How to Draw Creepy Creatures. 32p. 1991. 3.98 (1-56156-019-7); pap. 2.95 (1-56156-064-2) Kidsbks.
Reiss, John. Statistics. Srivastava, Jane J. LC 72-7559. (gr. 1-5). 1973. PLB 12.89 (0-690-77300-5, Crowell Jr Bks) HarpC Child Bks.
Reiss, John J. Colors. Reiss, John J. LC 69-13653. 32p. (ps-2). 1982. RSBE 13.95 (0-02-776130-4, Bradbury Pr) Macmillan Child Grp.
—Colors. Reiss, John J. LC 86-22189. 32p. (ps-2). 1987. pap. 3.95 (0-689-71119-0, Aladdin) Macmillan Child Grp.
—Numbers. Reiss, John J. LC 76-151313. 32p. (ps-2). 1982. RSBE 13.95 (0-02-776150-9, Bradbury Pr) Macmillan Child Grp.
—Numbers. Reiss, John J. LC 86-22243. 32p. (ps-2). 1987. pap. 3.95 (0-689-71120-4, Aladdin) Macmillan Child Grp.
—Shapes. Reiss, John J. LC 86-22164. 32p. (ps-2). 1987. pap. 3.95 (0-689-71121-2, Aladdin) Macmillan Child Grp.
Rembrandt. Rembrandt. Raboff, Ernest. LC 87-45148. 32p. (gr. 1 up). 1987. pap. 7.95 (0-06-446072-X, Trophy) HarpC Child Bks.
Remington, Barbara. Really, Not Really. Frost, Lesley. 64p. (ps-3). 1966. 10.00 (0-8155-6702-0) Devin.
Remington, Frederic. First Three Wagon Trains. Bidwell, John, et al. 118p. (gr. 7-9). 1993. pap. 11.95 (0-8323-0504-9) Binford Mort.
—Frederic Remington. Raboff, Ernest. LC 87-17698. 32p. (gr. 1 up). 1988. pap. 7.95 (0-06-446079-7, Trophy) HarpC Child Bks.
Remington, Frederic & Goff, O. S. The Indian As a Soldier at Fort Custer, Montana 1890-1895: Lieutenant Samuel C. Robertson's First Cavalry Crow Indian Contingent. Upton, Richard. LC 83-80826. 147p. (gr. 7-12). 1983. 27.50 (0-912783-00-1) Upton Sons.
Remkiewecz, Frank. Horrible Harry & the Christmas Surprise. Kline, Suzy. 64p. (gr. 2-5). 1991. 10.95 (0-670-83357-6) Viking Child Bks.
—Horrible Harry & the Green Slime. Kline, Suzy. 64p. (gr. 2-5). 1991. pap. 2.99 (0-14-032913-7, Puffin) Puffin Bks.
Remkiewicz, Frank. Ants Can't Dance. Jackson, Ellen. LC 90-5942. 32p. (gr. k-3). 1991. RSBE 12.95 (0-02-747661-8, Macmillan Child Bk) Macmillan Child Grp.
—El Chivo en la Huerta (Big Book) Kratky, Lada J. (SPA.). 16p. (gr. k-3). 1988. pap. text ed. 29.95 (0-917837-04-5) Hampton-Brown.
—El Chivo en la Huerta (Small Book) Kratky, Lada J. (SPA.). 16p. (Orig.). (gr. k-3). 1992. pap. text ed. 6.00 (1-56334-080-1) Hampton-Brown.
—Froggy Gets Dressed. London, Jonathan. 32p. (ps-1). 1992. 13.00 (0-670-84249-4) Viking Child Bks.
—The Great Mosquito, Bull, & Coffin Caper. Lamb, Nancy. Pearson, Susan, ed. LC 91-31125. 160p. (gr. 3 up). 1992. reinforced bdg. 12.00 (0-688-10933-0) Lothrop.
—The Great Mosquito, Bull, & Coffin Caper. Lamb, Nancy. 128p. (gr. 5 up). 1994. pap. 3.95 (0-688-12944-7, Pub. by Beech Tree Bks) Morrow.
—Horrible Harry & the Ant Invasion. Kline, Suzy. 64p. (gr. 2-5). 1989. pap. 11.00 (0-670-82649-9) Viking Child Bks.
—Horrible Harry & the Ant Invasion. Kline, Suzy. 64p. (gr. 2-5). 1991. 2.95 (0-14-032914-5) Puffin Bks.
—Horrible Harry & the Christmas Surprise. Kline, Suzy. LC 93-15137. 64p. (gr. 2-5). 1993. pap. 2.99 (0-14-034452-7, Puffin) Puffin Bks.
—Horrible Harry & the Green Slime. Kline, Susan. 64p. (gr. 2-5). 1989. pap. 10.95 (0-670-82468-2) Viking Child Bks.
—Horrible Harry & the Kickball Wedding. Kline, Suzy. LC 92-5827. 64p. (gr. 2-5). 1992. 11.00 (0-670-83358-4) Viking Child Bks.
—Horrible Harry in Room 2B. Kline, Suzy. (gr. 2-5). 1988. pap. 10.95 (0-670-82176-4) Viking Child Bks.
—Horrible Harry in Room 2B. Kline, Suzy. 64p. (gr. 2-5). 1990. pap. 2.99 (0-14-032825-4, Puffin) Puffin Bks.
—Horrible Harry's Secret. Kline, Suzy. 64p. (gr. 2-5). 1992. pap. 2.99 (0-14-032915-3) Puffin Bks.
—I Hate Camping. Petersen, P. J. LC 90-39650. 80p. (gr. 4-7). 1991. 13.00 (0-525-44673-7, DCB) Dutton Child Bks.
—I Hate Camping. Petersen, P. J. 96p. (gr. 2-5). 1993. pap. 3.99 (0-14-036446-3, Puffin) Puffin Bks.

—I Love Saturday. Giff, Patricia R. 32p. (ps-3). 1991. pap. 3.99 (0-14-050653-5) Puffin Bks.
—Let's Go, Froggy! London, Jonathan. LC 93-24059. 32p. (ps-3). 1994. PLB 12.99 (0-670-85055-1) Viking Child Bks.
—No Carrots for Harry! Langerman, Jean. LC 89-3373. (ps-3). 1989. 5.95 (0-8193-1190-1) Parents.
—No Carrots for Harry! Langerman, Jean. 48p. (ps-2). 1992. pap. 2.95 (0-448-40320-X, G&D) Putnam Pub Group.
—Una Semilla Nada Mas (Big Book) Ada, Alma F. (SPA.). 16p. (Orig.). (gr. k-3). 1990. pap. text ed. 29.95 (0-917837-56-8) Hampton-Brown.
—Una Semilla Nada Mas (Small Book) Ada, Alma F. (SPA.). 16p. (gr. k-3). 1992. pap. text ed. 6.00 (1-56334-083-6) Hampton-Brown.
—Song Lee in Room Two B. Kline, Suzy. 64p. (gr. 2-5). 1993. RB 10.99 (0-670-84772-0) Viking Child Bks.
Renard, Jan. Classy Christmas Concerts. Ogilvy, Carol & Tinkham, Trudy. 112p. (gr. k-7). 1986. wkbk. 9.95 (0-86653-349-4, GA 795) Good Apple.
—Hand-Shaped Art. Bonica, Diane. 112p. (ps-2). 1989. wkbk. 9.95 (0-86653-474-1, GA1079) Good Apple.
Rendal, Camille. Crystal Kids: PLAYBook. Singer, Marcia. LC 89-90988. 64p. (Orig.). 1989. pap. 9.95 (0-9622543-0-4) PLAY House.
—Eating for a Fresh Start: A P.L.A.Y. Book. Singer, Marcia. LC 90-91969. 64p. (Orig.). (gr. 1-7). 1990. pap. write for info. (0-9622543-1-2) PLAY House.

—**Love Me, Love My Planet P.L.A.Y. Book: An Environmental Guide.** Singer, Marcia. LC 91-91308. 64p. (Orig.). (gr. 1-7). 1991. pap. 7.95 (0-9622543-2-0) PLAY House. LOVE ME, LOVE MY PLANET: P. L.A.Y. BOOK. Teacher's/Family's environmental awareness guide, stressing interconnectedness of all living things & value of everyone's contributions. Scientific facts, terms, planet-saving 'do' ideas, edu-P.L.A.Y.-tional activities. Adorable, colorable illustrations. "An engaging educational tool for our most important budding environmentalists - our children."--Daphne Loysham, Editor, Greenpeace Magazine. "A really good book,"--Melissa Poe, KidsF.A.C.E. Also recommended by Whole Life Times, Mother-to-Mother Newsletter, LA Outdoor Science School. CRYSTAL KIDS: P.L.A.Y. BOOK. (ISBN 0-9622543-0-4) Metaphysics, meditations, healing arts, crystal fun for beginners. Feast of enchanting, colorable illustraP.L.A.Ytions, storyline, songs. Stimulates imagination, creativity. Recommended by Psychic Research Institute (Marsel Vogel) newsletter, Whole Life Times, & authors Dael Walker, Katrina Raphaell, Frank Alper, Terry Cole-Whittaker, Wabun Wind, & Hay House's Laura Wilson. EATING FOR A FRESH START: P. L.A.Y.BOOK (ISBN 0-9622543-1-2). Teacher's/Family's guide to beginning vegetarianism & ecologically sound eating habits. Easy instructions for sprouting, food combining, good digestion practices. Yummy, simple recipes. Features scientific definitions, charmer, illustrations, activities, "rap" style verse. Promotes physical, emotional, mental health. "Balances sound nutritional principles with games & activities."--Marilyn Diamond, Fit For Life. "Helps children be more aware & healthy." John Robbins, Diet for A New America. Also recommended by Garbage Magazine, L.A. Weekly, L.A. County Office of Education, Vegetarian Society, author Gabriel Cousens, Earth Save & Earthtrust Foundations.
Publisher Provided Annotation.

Renfrew, Susan. Deepest Roots. Moon, Sheila. LC 86-19578. 240p. (gr. 8-12). 1986. pap. 8.95 (0-917479-10-6) Guild Psy.
—Hunt down the Prize. Moon, Sheila. LC 86-19576. 245p. (gr. 8-12). 1986. pap. 8.95 (0-917479-09-2) Guild Psy.

Renfro, Nancy. Pocketful of Puppets: Poems for Church School. Irving, Lynn. Keller, Merily H., ed. 48p. (Orig.). (ps-3). 1982. pap. 9.95 (0-931044-05-7) Renfro Studios.
—Pocketful of Puppets: Three Plump Fish & Other Short Stories. Winer, Yvonne. Keller, Merily H., ed. 48p. (Orig.). (ps-4). 1982. pap. 9.95 (0-931044-08-1) Renfro Studios.
—Puppet Shows Made Easy! Renfro, Nancy. Cromack, Celeste, ed. 96p. (Orig.). (gr. 2-12). pap. 14.95 (0-931044-13-8) Renfro Studios.

Renfroe, Dan. Jeraboam & the Amazing Spaghetti Mountain. Hurlbut, Phillip R., Jr. LC 79-90933. 123p. (Orig.). (gr. 3 up). 1979. pap. 2.95 (0-936086-00-9) Entertainment Factory.

Resch, Barbara. A Place for Everyone. Resch, Barbara. 28p. (ps-3). 1991. smythe sewn reinforced bdg. 9.95 (1-56182-022-9) Atomium Bks.

Resnick, Sandi W. Apple Valley Year. Turner, Ann. LC 90-37733. 32p. (ps-3). 1993. RSBE 14.95 (0-02-789281-6, Macmillan Child Bk) Macmillan Child Grp.

Ressler, William. Giving, Christian Stewardship: Teaching Bks. Price, Brena. 14p. (gr. 1-8). 1971. pap. text ed. 3.95 (0-86508-154-9) BCM Pubn.

Rethi, Lili. St. Philip of the Joyous Heart. Connolly, Francis X. LC 92-74761. 189p. (gr. 5-8). 1993. pap. 9.95 (0-89870-431-6) Ignatius Pr.

Rettich, Rolf. The Castle of the Red Gorillas. Ecke, Wolfgang. LC 82-23122. 120p. (gr. 5-9). 1983. 9.95 (0-13-120360-6) P-H.
—The Castle of the Red Gorillas. Ecke, Wolfgang. 120p. (gr. 5-9). 1986. pap. 5.95 (0-13-120387-8) P-H.
—The Midnight Chess Game. Ecke, Wolfgang. LC 84-26564. 144p. (gr. 5 up). 1985. 10.95 (0-13-582826-0) P-H.

Rettich, Rolf & Langenfass, Hansjorg. The Bank Holdup. Ecke, Wolfgang. 144p. (gr. 3-7). 1985. pap. 5.95 (0-13-056474-5) P-H.

Rettmer, Georgia M. The Greatest Gift of All. Rinehart, Kimberly R. 70p. 1987. 12.95 (0-942865-02-2) It Takes Two.

Rey, H. A. Cecily G. & the Nine Monkeys. Rey, H. A. 32p. (gr. 1-3). 1974. 14.45 (0-395-18430-4) HM.
—Cecily G. & the Nine Monkeys. Rey, H. A. (ps-3). 1989. pap. 3.80 (0-395-50651-4, Sandpiper) HM.
—Curious George. Rey, H. A. 48p. (gr. k-3). 1973. pap. 4.80 (0-395-15023-X, Sandpiper) HM.
—Curious George Flies a Kite. Rey, Margaret & Rey, H. A. (gr. k-3). 1977. pap. 4.80 (0-395-25937-1) HM.
—Curious George Gets a Medal. Rey, H. A. LC 57-7206. 48p. (gr. k-3). 1974. pap. 4.80 (0-395-18559-9, Sandpiper) HM.
—Curious George Learns the Alphabet. Rey, H. A. LC 62-12261. 72p. (gr. k-3). 1973. pap. 4.80 (0-395-13718-7, Sandpiper) HM.
—Curious George Takes a Job. Rey, H. A. 48p. (gr. k-3). 1974. pap. 4.80 (0-395-18649-8, Sandpiper) HM.
—Don't Frighten the Lion! Brown, Margaret W. 32p. (ps-2). 1993. pap. 4.95 (0-06-443262-9, Trophy) HarpC Child Bks.
—Elizabite: Adventures of a Carnivorous Plant. Rey, H. A. LC 90-4834. 32p. (ps-3). 1990. Never of 1942 ed. lib. bdg. 17.00 (0-208-02288-0, Linnet) Shoe String.
—Find the Constellations. rev. ed. Rey, H. A. 72p. (gr. 3-7). 1976. pap. 8.70 (0-395-24418-8, Sandpiper) HM.
—Katy No-Pocket. Payne, Emmy. 32p. (gr. k-3). 1973. pap. 5.70 (0-395-13717-9, Sandpiper) HM.
—Katy No-Pocket. Payne, Emmy. (ps-3). 1989. pap. 8.70 incl. cassette (0-395-52141-6) HM.
—Park Book. Zolotow, Charlotte. LC 44-9471. 32p. (ps-1). 1986. PLB 13.89 (0-06-026973-1) HarpC Child Bks.

Reyes, Augustine. Windows of a Heart. Uhing, Mary J. Lauer, Alphonse, ed. 72p. 1993. pap. 5.00 (1-56788-013-4, 20-002) BMH Pubns.

Reyes, Eric S. Food for Wet Fingers. Hines, Sharon R. & Hecht, Joyce C. 28p. (gr. 7-12). 1981. pap. 3.00 (0-941904-02-4) Hot Water Pubs.

Reyes, Roger I., jt. illus. see Cherin, Robin.

Reynolds, Carol. I'd Like to Hear a Flower Grow. Halloran, Phyllis. LC 89-60979. 56p. (gr. k-8). 1989. 12.95 (0-943867-02-9) Reading Inc.
—Red Is My Favorite Color. Halloran, Phyllis. LC 88-60132. (Orig.). (gr. k up). 1988. 12.95 (0-943867-01-0) Reading Inc.

Reynolds, Kevin, jt. illus. see McManus, Joseph F.

Reynolds, Nancy L. Mom & Dad Don't Live Together Anymore. Stinson, Kathy. 32p. (gr. k-3). 1984. PLB 14.95 (0-920236-92-8, Pub. by Annick CN); pap. 4.95 (0-920236-87-1, Pub. by Annick CN) Firefly Bks Ltd.

Reynolds, Pat. All the Better to See You With. Wild, Margaret. Tucker, Kathy, ed. LC 92-39127. 32p. (gr. 1-3). 1993. PLB 13.95 (0-8075-0284-7) A Whitman.
—The Band. King, Virginia. LC 92-21390. 1993. 2.50 (0-383-03553-8) SRA Schl Grp.
—Little Ho & the Golden Kites. Scott, Mavis. 32p. (Orig.). (gr. k-3). 1993. pap. 6.95 (0-04-442242-3, Pub. by Allen & Unwin Aust Pty AT) IPG Chicago.
—The Python Caught the Eagle. Drew, David. LC 92-31134. 1993. 2.50 (0-383-03648-8) SRA Schl Grp.

Reynolds, Patrick M. Texas Lore, Vols. 1, 2, 3, & 4. Reynolds, Patrick M. 228p. (Orig.). (gr. 8-12). 1992. pap. 12.95 (0-932514-27-8) Red Rose Studio.

Reynolds-Strauss, Karen. Romanian Fairy Tales. Reynolds-Strauss, Karen & Gligor, Adrian. 85p. (Orig.). (ps-6). 1992. pap. text ed. 11.95 (0-9634797-0-9) K Strauss & A Gligor.

Rhead, Louis & Wheelwright, Rowland. King Arthur & His Knights. Knowles, James, compiled by. 416p. 1986. 12.99 (0-517-61885-0) Outlet Bk Co.

Rhie, Schi-Zhin. Soon-Hee in America. Rhie, Schi-Zhin. LC 77-81780. 36p. (gr. k-3). 1977. PLB 6.50x (0-930878-00-0) Hollym Intl.

Rhinelander, Mary F. Hanukkah Fun: Crafts & Games. Weiss, Andrea. 32p. (gr. k-5). 1992. Set of 3 bks. pap. 14.85 (1-56397-170-4); pap. 4.95 (1-56397-059-7) Boyds Mills Pr.

Rhiney, Sharon. Christopher & Cumulus Cloud. Hill, Fred D. Young, Elaine & Hill, Charlotte, eds. LC 90-80285. 31p. (Orig.). (gr. k-4). 1990. pap. 5.95 (0-9620182-1-X) Charill Pubs.

Rhodes, Priscilla. Clemson Football Mystery. Longmeyer, Carole M. (Orig.). (gr. 3 up). 1983. PLB 24.95 (1-55609-164-8); pap. 14.95 (0-935326-28-6) Gallopade Pub Group.
—Deadly Duke Football Mystery. Longmeyer, Carole M. (Orig.). (gr. 3 up). pap. 14.95 (0-935326-31-6) Gallopade Pub Group.
—Georgia Tech Football Mystery. Longmeyer, Carole M. (Orig.). (gr. 3 up). 1983. pap. 14.95 (0-935326-30-8) Gallopade Pub Group.
—The Lost Colony Activity Book. Longmeyer, Carole M. (Orig.). (gr. 3 up). 1983. pap. 14.95 (0-935326-41-3) Gallopade Pub Group.
—The Lost Colony Storybook. Longmeyer, Carole M. (gr. 4 up). 1983. pap. 14.95 (0-935326-38-3) Gallopade Pub Group.
—Maryland Football Mystery. Longmeyer, Carole M. 80p. (Orig.). (gr. 3 up). pap. 14.95 (0-935326-32-4) Gallopade Pub Group.
—NC State Football Mystery. Longmeyer, Carole M. (Orig.). (gr. 3 up). pap. 14.95 (0-935326-33-2) Gallopade Pub Group.
—Those Whose Names Were Terrible. Marsh, Carole. (Orig.). (gr. 4-8). 1983. pap. 14.95 (0-935326-48-0) Gallopade Pub Group.
—Virginia Football Mystery. Longmeyer, Carole M. 80p. (Orig.). (gr. 3 up). pap. 24.95 (0-935326-35-9) Gallopade Pub Group.
—Wake Forest Football Mystery. Longmeyer, Carole M. (Orig.). (gr. 3 up). pap. 14.95 (0-935326-34-0) Gallopade Pub Group.
—What Did You Sayeth? Longmeyer, Carole M. (Orig.). (gr. 4 up). 1983. pap. 14.95 (0-935326-45-6) Gallopade Pub Group.

Ricci, Regolo. The Nightingale. Bedard, Michael. (gr. k-4). 1992. 14.95 (0-395-60735-3, Clarion Bks) HM.

Riccio, Frank. Bob, Son of Battle. Ollivant, Alfred. Hinkle, Don, ed. LC 87-15477. 48p. (gr. 3-6). 1988. PLB 12.89 (0-8167-1211-5); pap. text ed. 3.95 (0-8167-1212-3) Troll Assocs.

Rice, Eve. Oh, Lewis! Rice, Eve. LC 92-24584. 32p. 1993. pap. 4.95 (0-688-11790-2, Mulberry) Morrow.
—Once in a Wood: Ten Tales from Aesop. Rice, Eve, adapted by. LC 92-24605. 64p. (gr. 1 up). 1993. pap. 4.95 (0-688-12268-X, Mulberry) Morrow.

Rice, Eve, jt. illus. see Tafuri, Nancy.

Rice, James. Cajun Columbus. rev. ed. Hughes, Alice D. LC 91-16783. 40p. 1991. 12.95 (0-88289-875-2) Pelican.
—A Cajun Night Before Christmas. Trosclair. Jacobs, Howard, ed. LC 74-151725. 48p. (gr. 6-12). 1973. 12.95 (0-88289-002-6) Pelican.
—Cajun Night Before Christmas: Full-Color Edition. Trosclair. Jacobs, Howard, ed. LC 92-8375. 48p. (gr. k-3). 1992. 14.95 (0-88289-940-6); ltd. boxed signed ed. 25.00 (0-88289-947-3); audio 9.95 (0-88289-914-7) Pelican.
—A Christmas Carol. Dickens, Charles. Rice, James, retold by. 48p. (gr. k-3). (0-88289-812-4) Pelican.
—Cowboy Alphabet. 40p. (gr. k-4). 1983. 10.95 (0-88289-427-7) Pelican.
—Cowboy Rodeo. Rice, James. LC 91-34924. 32p. 1992. 14.95 (0-88289-903-1) Pelican.
—Flags of Texas. Gilbert, Charles E., Jr. LC 88-34511. 96p. (gr. 6 up). 1989. 14.95 (0-88289-721-7) Pelican.
—Gaston Drills an Offshore Oil Well. Rice, James. LC 82-11240. 48p. (gr. 1-6). 1982. Pelican.
—Gaston Goes to Nashville. Rice, James. LC 85-6605. 32p. (gr. 1-6). 1985. 12.95 (0-88289-477-3) Pelican.
—Gaston Goes to Texas. Rice, James. LC 78-12490. 32p. (gr. 1-6). 1978. 12.95 (0-88289-204-5) Pelican.
—Gaston the Green-Nosed Alligator Coloring Book. Rice, James. 32p. (Orig.). (gr. 1-6). 1976. pap. 2.75 (0-88289-139-1) Pelican.
—Hillbilly Night Afore Christmas. Turner, Thomas N. LC 83-4120. 32p. (gr. 1-6). 1983. 12.95 (0-88289-367-X) Pelican.
—Jefferson Davis Coloring Book. Caldeira, Ernesto. 32p. (Orig.). (gr. 1-6). 1982. pap. 2.95 (0-88289-256-8) Pelican.
—Lyn & the Fuzzy. Rice, James. LC 75-19096. 40p. (gr. 2-6). 1975. 12.95 (0-88289-087-5) Pelican.
—A Medal for Murphy. Odom, Melissa. LC 86-25369. 32p. (gr. 1-6). 1987. 12.95 (0-88289-635-0) Pelican.
—The Night Before Christmas. Moore, Clement C. LC 89-34789. 32p. 1990. 14.95 (0-88289-755-1) Pelican.

—No Regard Beauregard & the Golden Rule. Odom, Melissa W. LC 87-36118. 132p. (gr. k-6). 1988. 12.95 (0-88289-686-5) Pelican.
—La Nochebuena South of the Border. Rice, James. Smith, Ana, tr. LC 93-13002. (ENG & SPA.). 32p. (gr. k-3). 1993. 14.95 (0-88289-966-X) Pelican.
—Southern Love for Christmas. Bernardini, Robert. 32p. (gr. k-3). 1993. 14.95 (0-88289-974-0) Pelican.
—A Southern Time Christmas. Bernardini, Robert. LC 91-12467. 32p. 1991. 14.95 (0-88289-828-0) Pelican.
—Texas Alphabet. Rice, James. LC 87-31159. 132p. (gr. k-5). 1988. 12.95 (0-88289-692-X) Pelican.
—Texas Jack at the Alamo. Rice, James. LC 88-31691. 40p. 1989. 12.95 (0-88289-725-X) Pelican.
—Texas Night Before Christmas. Rice, James. LC 86-9445. 32p. (gr. 1-6). 1986. 12.95 (0-88289-603-2) Pelican.
—Texas Night Before Christmas Coloring Book. Rice, James. 1989. pap. 2.75 (0-88289-727-6) Pelican.

Rice, Kendrick. I'm Black & I'm Beautiful. Felder, Pamela T. Slade, John, ed. 14p. (Orig.). 1993. pap. 3.50 (0-9638310-0-3) Pams Unique.

Rich, Andrea. Cat & Sparrow. Dass, Baba H. LC 81-51915. 32p. (gr. k-3). 1982. 6.95 (0-918100-06-2) Sri Rama.

Rich, Anna. Joshua's Masai Mask. Hru, Dakari. LC 92-73219. 32p. (gr. k-4). 1993. 14.95 (1-880000-02-4) Lee & Low Bks.
—Saturday at The New You. Barber, Barbara E. LC 93-5165. 1994. 14.95 (1-880000-06-7) Lee & Low Bks.

Rich, Beverly. The Nutcracker. Whitehead, Pat. LC 87-10916. 32p. (gr. k-4). 1988. PLB 9.79 (0-8167-1063-5); pap. text ed. 1.95 (0-8167-1064-3) Troll Assocs.

Richa, Anna. Annie's Gifts. Medearis, Angela S. LC 92-71998. 32p. (gr. 1-4). 1993. 14.95 (0-940975-30-0); pap. 6.95 (0-940975-31-9) Just Us Bks.

Richards, Linda. The Enchantment of Beaver Creek. Boynton, LaVerne L. 248p. 1988. 12.95 (0-685-44325-6) Starlite Pub.

Richardson, David, jt. illus. see Cunningham, Imogen.

Richardson, Frederick. Great Children's Stories: Classic Volland Edition. Hunt, Irene, intro. by. LC 72-83891. 160p. (ps-3). 1938. 12.95 (1-56288-040-3) Checkerboard.
—Mother Goose. Classic Volland ed. Grover, Eulalie O., intro. by. LC 72-161577. 160p. (ps-4). 1915. 12.95 (1-56288-254-6) Checkerboard.
—Mother Goose: The Original Volland Edition. 128p. (gr. k up). 1985. 8.99 (0-517-43619-1) Outlet Bk Co.
—Queen Zixi of Ix: Or, the Story of the Magic Cloak. Baum, L. Frank. Gardner, M., intro. by. 231p. (gr. 1-3). 1971. pap. 4.95 (0-486-22691-3) Dover.

Richardson, John. The Adventures of Budgie. Duchess of York. LC 92-11218. 1992. ltd. ed. 60.00 (0-685-59711-3, S&S BFYR); incls. cassettes 20.00 (0-685-59712-1) S&S Trade.
—Budgie at Bendick's Point. Duchess of York. (ps-1). 1989. pap. 11.95 jacketed (0-671-67684-9, S&S BFYR) S&S Trade.
—Budgie the Little Helicopter. Duchess of York. (ps-1). 1989. pap. 11.95 jacketed (0-671-67683-0, S&S BFYR) S&S Trade.
—The Hiding Beast. Richardson, John. (ps-3). 1989. 13.45 (0-395-49213-0) HM.
—Ten Bears in a Bed. Richardson, John. LC 91-26501. 22p. (ps-k). 1992. 13.95 (1-56282-157-1) Hyprn Child.
—Where's Jack? A Christmas Pop-up Book. Richardson, John. 24p. (ps-2). 1993. bds. 12.95 POB (0-689-71713-X, Aladdin) Macmillan Child Grp.

Richardson, Joyce. When the Spirit Says Sing: A Read-along, Sing-along, Coloring Book. Paton, Sandy & Paton, Caroline. Wood, Chip, intro. by. 40p. (Orig.). (gr. k-8). 1989. pap. 13.98 (0-938702-06-8) Folk-Legacy.

Richardson, Mark. The Secret Elephant of Harlan Kooter. Harvey, Dean. LC 91-45955. 160p. (gr. 2-5). 1992. 13.95 (0-395-62523-8) HM.

Richardson, Nichole. Jimmy & the Sun Drop. Reece, June E. Reece, June E., intro. by. (Orig.). (ps-3). 1992. pap. 3.50 (0-9631934-0-6) Sun Drop.

Richardson, Peter. Grimm's Fairy Tales. Grimm, Jacob & Grimm, Wilhelm N. Carter, Peter, ed. & tr. 238p. (ps-6). 1987. 18.95 (0-19-274529-8) OUP.

Richardson, Ruth. Window, Mirror, Moon. Rosenberg, Liz. LC 89-26971. 32p. (ps-3). 1990. HarpC Child Bks.

Riches, Judith. The Dollhouse. Karas, Jacqueline. LC 92-32262. 32p. (ps up). 1993. 15.00 (0-688-12480-1, Tambourine Bks); PLB 14.93 (0-688-12481-X, Tambourine Bks) Morrow.
—Rooster Crows. Scamell, Rajnhild. LC 93-31348. 1994. write for info. (0-688-13290-1, Tambourine Bks); PLB write for info. (0-688-13291-X, Tambourine Bks) Morrow.
—Sam's Worries. Macdonald, Maryann. LC 91-71379. 32p. (ps-3). 1991. 13.95 (1-56282-081-8); PLB 13.89 (1-56282-082-6) Hyprn Child.
—Sam's Worries. Macdonald, Maryann. 32p. (ps-2). 1994. pap. write for info. (1-56282-522-4) Hyprn Ppbks.
—Tigers. Edwards, Roland. LC 91-40098. 32p. (ps-2). 1992. 15.00 (0-688-11685-X, Tambourine Bks); PLB 14.93 (0-688-11686-8, Tambourine Bks) Morrow.

Richesson, Robin. Beginning Reading Five. Forman-Hitt, Kathy & Young, Janet. Wheeler, Sharon, ed. (ps). 1986. wkbk. 1.95 (0-916119-22-X) Creat Teach Pr.

—Beginning Reading One. Forman-Hitt, Kathy & Young, Janet. Wheeler, Sharon, ed. (ps) 1986. wkbk. 1.95 (0-916119-18-1) Creat Teach Pr.
—Beginning Reading Six. Forman-Hitt, Kathy & Young, Janet. Wheeler, Sharon, ed. (ps). 1986. wkbk. 1.95 (0-916119-23-8) Creat Teach Pr.
—Beginning Reading Two. Forman-Hitt, Kathy & Young, Janet. Wheeler, Sharon, ed. (ps). 1986. wkbk. 1.95 (0-916119-19-X) Creat Teach Pr.
—Classification. Wheeler, Sharon, ed. (ps). 1984. wkbk 1.95 (0-916119-06-8) Creat Teach Pr.
—I'm Growing Up. Garafalo, Lorraine. Wheeler, Sharon, ed. (ps). 1985. wkbk. 1.95 (0-916119-16-5) Creat Teach Pr.
—I'm Starting School. Garafalo, Lorraine. Wheeler, Sharon, ed. (ps). 1985. wkbk. 1.95 (0-916119-15-7) Creat Teach Pr.
—I'm Staying Healthy. Garafalo, Lorraine. Wheeler, Sharon, ed. (ps). 1985. wkbk. 1.95 (0-916119-17-3) Creat Teach Pr.
—Making Friends. Garafalo, Lorraine. Wheeler, Sharon, ed. (ps). 1985. wkbk. 1.95 (0-916119-13-0) Creat Teach Pr.
—My Family & Me. Garafalo, Lorraine. Wheeler, Sharon, ed. (ps). 1985. pap. 1.95 wkbk. (0-916119-12-2) Creat Teach Pr.
—My Own Feelings. Garafalo, Lorraine. Wheeler, Sharon, ed. (ps). 1985. pap. 1.95 wkbk. (0-916119-14-9) Creat Teach Pr.
—Number Skills. Wheeler, Sharon, ed. (ps). 1984. wkbk 1.95 (0-916119-04-1) Creat Teach Pr.
—Opposites. Wheeler, Sharon. (ps). 1984. wkbk 1.95 (0-916119-05-X) Creat Teach Pr.
—Sequencing. Wheeler, Sharon. (ps). 1984. wkbk 1.95 (0-916119-10-6) Creat Teach Pr.
—Shapes. Wheeler, Sharon. (ps). 1984. wkbk 1.95 (0-916119-00-9) Creat Teach Pr.
—Visual Skills. Wheeler, Sharon, ed. (ps). 1984. wkbk. 1.95 (0-916119-08-4) Creat Teach Pr.
Richey, Donald. Feeling Fit. Martinez, Alicia. LC 90-10864. 128p. (gr. 5-9). 1991. PLB 10.89 (0-8167-2140-8); pap. text ed. 2.95 (0-8167-2141-6) Troll Assocs.
—Finishing Touches, Manners with Style. David, Jo. LC 90-10888. 128p. (gr. 5-9). 1991. lib. bdg. 10.89 (0-8167-2179-3); pap. text ed. 2.95 (0-8167-2180-7) Troll Assocs.
—Looking Good. Sloate, Susan. LC 89-28019. 128p. (gr. 5-9). 1991. lib. bdg. 10.89 (0-8167-1999-3); pap. text ed. 2.95 (0-8167-2000-2) Troll Assocs.
—Now You're Talking. Havens, Ami. LC 90-10764. 128p. (gr. 5-9). 1991. lib. bdg. 10.89 (0-8167-2142-4); pap. text ed. 2.95 (0-8167-2143-2) Troll Assocs.
Richmond, Frank. Dorothy & the Lizard of Oz. Gardner, Richard A. LC 80-12787. 108p. (gr. 1-6). 1980. 14.95 (0-933812-03-5) Creative Therapeutics.
Richmond, Robin. Animals in Art. Richmond, Robin. 48p. (gr. 2-5). 1993. PLB 16.00 (0-8249-8626-1, Ideals Child); text ed. 15.95 (0-8249-8613-X) Hambleton-Hill.
—Children in Art: The Story in a Picture. Richmond, Robin. 48p. (gr. 2-5). 1992. 15.95 (0-8249-8552-4, Ideals Child); PLB 16.00 (0-8249-8588-5) Hambleton-Hill.
Richter, Mischa. A Book about Names. Meltzer, Milton. LC 83-45241. 128p. (gr. 7 up). 1984. (Crowell Jr Bks); PLB 13.89 (0-690-04381-3, Crowell Jr Bks) HarpC Child Bks.
—The Marvelous Music Machine: A Story of the Piano. Blocksma, Mary. LC 84-4892. 64p. (gr. 3-7). 1984. 10.95 (0-13-559410-3) P-H.
—Planet of the Grapes: Show Biz Jokes & Riddles. Keller, Charles. 40p. (gr. 3-7). 1992. 13.95 (0-945912-17-X) Pippin Pr.
Rickels, Robert E. North Country Spring. Kouhi, Elizabeth. 54p. (ps-8). 1980. 6.95 (0-920806-10-4, Pub. by Penumbra Pr CN) U of Toronto Pr.
Ricklen, Neil. My Clothes: Mi Ropa. LC 93-27162. (ENG & SPA.). 14p. (ps-k). 1994. bds. 3.95 (0-689-71773-3, Aladdin) Macmillan Child Grp.
—My Colors: Mis Colores. LC 93-27195. (ENG & SPA.). 14p. (ps-k). 1994. bds. 3.95 (0-689-71772-5, Aladdin) Macmillan Child Grp.
—My Family: Mi Familia. LC 93-30661. (ENG & SPA.). 14p. (ps-k). 1994. bds. 3.95 (0-689-71771-7, Aladdin) Macmillan Child Grp.
—My Numbers: Mis Numeros. LC 93-27165. (ENG & SPA.). 14p. (ps-k). 1994. bds. 3.95 (0-689-71770-9, Aladdin) Macmillan Child Grp.
Ricklen, Neil, photos by. Baby Inside. 24p. (ps). 1991. pap. 4.95 casebound, padded cover (0-671-73878-X, Little Simon) S&S Trade.
—Baby Outside. 24p. (ps). 1991. pap. 4.95 casebound, padded cover (0-671-73879-8, Little Simon) S&S Trade.
—Baby's ABC. 24p. 1990. casebound, padded cover 4.95 (0-671-69540-1, Little Simon) S&S Trade.
—Baby's Birthday. 24p. (ps). 1991. pap. 4.95 casebound, padded cover (0-671-73880-1, Little Simon) S&S Trade.
—Baby's Christmas. 24p. (ps). 1991. pap. 4.95 casebound, padded cover (0-671-73881-X, Little Simon) S&S Trade.
Ricklen, Neil, photos by. Daddy & Me. 28p. (ps). 1988. 4.95 (0-671-64537-4, Little Simon) S&S Trade.
—Grandma & Me. 28p. (ps-k). 1988. 4.95 (0-671-64540-4, S&S BFYR) S&S Trade.

—Grandpa & Me. 28p. (ps-k). 1988. 4.95 (0-671-64539-0, S&S BFYR) S&S Trade.
—Mommy & Me. 28p. (ps-k). 1988. 4.95 (0-671-64538-2, Little Simon) S&S Trade.
Rickman, David. Jorinda & Joringel. Grimm, Jacob & Grimm, Wilhelm K. Cutts, David, ed. LC 87-10937. 32p. (gr. k-4). 1988. PLB 9.79 (0-8167-1065-1); pap. text ed. 1.95 (0-8167-1066-X) Troll Assocs.
Rickman, Philip. British & American Game Birds. Pollard, H. B. & Barclay-Smith. Phyllis. 48p. (gr. 10 up). Date not set. 50.00 (1-56416-071-8) Derrydale Pr.
Ricks, Thom. Rosita's Christmas Wish. Bruni, Mary A. LC 85-52040. 48p. (gr. k-8). 1985. 13.95 (0-935857-00-1); ltd. ed. 125.00 (0-935857-03-6); write for info. (0-935857-09-5); pap. write for info. (0-935857-01-X); pap. write for info. (0-935857-10-9) Texart.
—El Sueno de Rosita. Bruni, Mary-Ann S. De Castro, Rogelio, tr. from ENG. (SPA.). 48p. (gr. k-8). 1987. 13.95 (0-935857-04-4) (0-935857-11-7) (0-935857-12-5) Texart.
Ricks, Thorn. Who Are the Chinese Texans? Martinello, Marian & Field, William T., Jr. 84p. (Orig.). (gr. 5-8). 8.95 (0-933164-34-5); pap. 5.95 (0-933164-46-7) U of Tex Inst Tex Culture.
Rico, Armando B. Hay Roca en Tu Coca. Rico, Armando B. (SPA.). 47p. (Orig.). 1992. pap. 2.75 (1-879219-05-0) Veracruz Pubs.
Riddell, Chris. The Abradizil. Gibson, Andrew. 164p. (gr. 3-7). 1992. pap. 4.95 (0-571-16508-7) Faber & Faber.
—Dracula's Daughter. Hoffman, Mary. 42p. (gr. 2-4). 1989. 3.95 (0-8120-6135-7) Barron.
—Ellis & the Hummick. Gibson, Andrew. 132p. (gr. 3-6). 1990. pap. 3.95 (0-571-14412-8) Faber & Faber.
—Jemima, Grandma & the Great Lost Zone. Gibson, Andrew. 128p. (gr. 3-7). 1992. 15.95 (0-571-16455-2) Faber & Faber.
—Jemima, Grandma & the Great Lost Zone. Gibson, Andrew. 128p. (gr. 3-7). 1992. pap. 6.95 (0-571-16737-3) Faber & Faber.
—Lizzie Dripping & the Witch. large type ed. Cresswell, Helen. 160p. 1993. 13.95 (0-7451-1681-7, Galaxy Child Lrg Print) Chivers N Amer.
—Out for the Count. Cave, Kathryn. LC 91-22096. 32p. (ps-3). 1992. pap. 14.00 jacketed (0-671-75591-9, S&S BFYR) S&S Trade.
—The Trouble with Elephants. Riddell, Chris. LC 87-24963. 32p. (ps-3). 1990. pap. 5.95 (0-06-443170-3, Trophy) HarpC Child Bks.
—When the Walrus Comes: The Screenplay. Riddell, Chris. LC 89-31718. 1990. 13.95 (0-385-29858-7) Doubleday.
Riddell, Edwina. See How You Grow. Pearse, Patricia. LC 87-33268. 32p. (gr. 1-4). 1988. 13.95 (0-8120-5936-0) Barron.
—The Senses. Royston, Angela. LC 92-25715. 24p. (ps-3). 1993. 13.95 (0-8120-6272-8) Barron.
Riddell, Russ. Won't You Ever Listen. Cummings, Carol. 24p. (Orig.). (ps-3). 1992. pap. 5.99 (0-9614574-7-3) Teaching WA.
Ridge, Jeff & Midgette, Darrell. Disaster on Adonis Three. Crowdis, John. LaDell, Leo, ed. 32p. (Orig.). (gr. 12). 1989. pap. 6.00 (1-55806-039-1, 9107) Iron Crown Ent Inc.
Ridge, Jeff & Waltrip, Jason. Legacy of the Ancients. LaDell, Leo. Amthor, Terry K., ed. 32p. (Orig.). (gr. 12). 1989. pap. 6.00 (1-55806-035-9, 9106) Iron Crown Ent Inc.
Ridgeway, Jo A. Going Fishing. Mitchell, Greg. LC 92-14449. 1993. 3.75 (0-383-03625-9) SRA Schl Grp.
—Our Playhouse. Mitchell, Greg. LC 92-21451. 1993. 3.75 (0-383-03647-X) SRA Schl Grp.
—Simply Sam. Mitchell, Greg. LC 92-21452. 1993. 3.75 (0-383-03652-6) SRA Schl Grp.
Riegel, Martin P. The Ships of the Orange Coast. Riegel, Martin P. LC 88-92522. 40p. (Orig.). (gr. 9 up). 1988. PLB 11.00 (0-944871-08-9); pap. 4.75 (0-944871-09-7) Riegel Pub.
Rieger, Shay. The Secret of the Sabbath Fish. Aronin, Ben. LC 78-63437. (gr. k-4). 1979. 8.95 (0-8276-0110-7) JPS Phila.
Rigby, Rodney. Hello, This Is Your Penguin Speaking. Rigby, Rodney. LC 91-39501. 32p. (ps-2). 1992. 13.95 (1-56282-231-4); PLB 13.89 (1-56282-232-2) Hyprn Child.
—The Night the Moon Fell Asleep. Rigby, Rodney. LC 92-45928. 32p. (ps-3). 1993. 13.95 (1-56282-334-5); PLB 13.89 (1-56282-335-3) Hyprn Child.
—There's a Building on Sixth Avenue. Rigby, Rodney. LC 91-23097. 32p. (ps-3). 1992. 13.95 (1-56282-155-5); PLB 13.89 (1-56282-156-3) Hyprn Child.
Riger, Robert. Wren. Killilea, Marie. (gr. 3-7). 1981. pap. 0.95 (0-440-49704-3, YB) Dell.
Rigg, Lucy. Goldilocks & the Three Bears. Jensen, Karen. 32p. (ps up). 1987. 9.95 (0-910079-05-6) Lucy & Co.
Riggio, Anita. Coal Mine Peaches. Dionetti, Michelle. LC 90-28693. 32p. (ps-2). 1991. 14.95 (0-531-05948-0); RLB 14.99 (0-531-08548-1) Orchard Bks Watts.
—Dad Gummit & Ma Foot. Waggoner, Karen. LC 89-70983. 32p. (ps-3). 1990. 14.95 (0-531-05891-3); PLB 14.99 (0-531-08491-4) Orchard Bks Watts.
—Easter Crafts. Van Blaricom, Colleen, ed. LC 91-72873. 32p. (ps-3). 1992. pap. 3.95 (1-56397-014-7) Boyds Mills Pr.

—Hobie Hanson, Greatest Hero of the Mall. Gilson, Jamie. 160p. (gr. 3-6). 1990. pap. 2.95 (0-671-70646-2, Minstrel Bks) PB.
—I Eat Dinner. Facklam, Margery. LC 91-76020. 6p. (ps). 1992. bds. 3.95 (1-56397-031-7); Set of 3 bks. bds. 11.85 (1-56397-077-5) Boyds Mills Pr.
—I Go to Sleep. Facklam, Margery. LC 91-76018. 6p. (ps). 1992. bds. 3.95 (1-56397-030-9); Set of 3 bks. bds. 11.85 (1-56397-076-7) Boyds Mills Pr.
—Jumping Jenny. Pryor, Bonnie. 192p. (gr. 2 up). 1992. 14.00 (0-688-09684-0) Morrow Jr Bks.
—A Moon in My Teacup. Riggio, Anita. 32p. (ps-3). 1993. PLB 14.95 smythe sewn (1-56397-008-2) Boyds Mills Pr. Postponed.
Rigie, Mitch. The Great Genghis Khan Look-Alike Contest. Sharmat, Marjorie W. 80p. (Orig.). (gr. 1-4). 1993. PLB 9.99 (0-679-95002-8); pap. 2.99 (0-679-85002-3) Random House Yng Read.
Rigo, Christina. Caring for My Kitty. Moncure, Jane B. 32p. (ps-2). 1990. PLB 18.50 (0-89565-666-3); PLB 12.95s.p. (0-685-56167-4) Childs World.
—Sharing. Riehecky, Janet. LC 87-26811. 32p. (gr. k-3). 1988. PLB 21.35 (0-89565-416-4); PLB 14.95s.p. (0-685-55934-3) Childs World.
—What I Like Best about Christmas. Cassat, Julie. 14p. (gr. 4-7). 1989. pap. text ed. 5.95 (0-927106-02-7) Prod Concept.
Rigo, Christina L. Patience. Fiday, Beverly. LC 86-12984. 32p. (gr. k-3). 1986. PLB 21.35 (0-89565-358-3); PLB 14.95s.p. (0-685-55833-9) Childs World.
Rigo, Cristina. Good Sportsmanship. Riehecky, Janet. LC 89-29663. 32p. (gr. k-3). 1990. PLB 21.35 (0-89565-563-2); PLB 14.95s.p. (0-685-56197-6) Childs World.
Rigo, R. Dinosaur's Adventure in Alphabet Town. Cook, D. LC 91-20544. 32p. (ps-2). 1992. PLB 14.60 (0-516-05404-X) Childrens.
Rigo, Russell. Object Talks from A to Z. DeWolf, Carol. 64p. (gr. k-4). 1987. 7.99 (0-87403-237-7, 2867) Standard Pub.
—Space Jokes. Shannon, Michael, compiled by. LC 88-17488. 48p. (gr. 1-5). 1988. pap. 3.95 (0-516-41874-2) Childrens.
Riley, Cyd. Twelve. Kittredge, Elaine. 84p. 1989. pap. 9.95 (0-9611266-1-2); audiotape, 80 mins. 9.95 (0-9611266-2-0) Optext.
Riley, Terry. I, Houdini: The Autobiography of a Self-Educated Hamster. Banks, Lynne R. LC 87-22284. 128p. (gr. 5 up). 1988. pap. 12.95 (0-385-24482-7) Doubleday.
Rinciari, Ken. Whistle in the Graveyard: Folktales to Chill Your Bones. Leach, Maria. (gr. 3-7). 1982. pap. 4.95 (0-14-031529-2, Puffin) Puffin Bks.
Rinek, Susan. Sea Scapes: In Kairos Time. Hollenbeck, Joan W. Banks, Doris, ed. 96p. (gr. 10 up). 1993. pap. 14.95x (0-936822-01-5) Peppertree.
Ringgold, Faith. Aunt Harriet's Underground in the Sky. Ringgold, Faith. LC 92-00072. 32p. (ps-4). 1993. 16.00 (0-517-58767-X, Clarkson Potter); lib. bdg. 17.99 (0-517-58768-8, Clarkson Potter) Crown Bks Yng Read.
—Dinner at Aunt Connie's House. Ringgold, Faith. LC 92-54871. 32p. (gr. 1-4). 1993. 14.95 (1-56282-425-2); PLB 14.89 (1-56282-426-0) Hyprn Child.
—Tar Beach. Ringgold, Faith. LC 90-40410. 32p. (ps-3). 1991. 16.00 (0-517-58030-6); lib. bdg. 16.99 (0-517-58031-4) Crown Bks Yng Read.
Ringgold-Reiss, Debra, photos by. Puppy Care & Critters, Too! Petersen-Fleming, Judy & Fleming, Bill. LC 93-23129. 40p. 1993. 15.00 (0-688-12565-4, Tambourine Bks); PLB 14.93 (0-688-12566-2, Tambourine Bks) Morrow.
Ringston, Ray. Where's the Green Pea? Greene, Michael. LC 91-91536. 32p. (ps-1). 1992. PLB 19.95 incl. audiocassette (1-881134-00-8) Tues Child.
Riojas, Edward. The First Rainbow: Favorite Bible Stories to Learn From. Reid, John C. 248p. (Orig.). 1991. pap. 12.99 (0-8028-4056-6) Eerdmans.
Ripley, Edward, jt. illus. see Bushe, Claire.
Ripley, Elizabeth. Eenie-Meenie-Minie-Mo & Other Counting-Out Rhymes. Withers, Carl. 44p. (ps up). 1970. pap. 2.50 (0-486-22414-7) Dover.
Ripper, Chuck, jt. illus. see Meltzer, Davis.
Ripper, Peter. Hullo Sun. Hodgson, Joan. (ps-3). 1972. 6.95 (0-85487-019-9) DeVorss.
—Our Father. Hodgson, Joan. (ps-3). 1977. pap. 2.95 (0-85487-040-7) DeVorss.
Riquier, Aline. The Cotton in Your T-Shirt. Riquier, Aline. Bogard, Vicki, tr. from FRE. LC 91-45786. 38p. (gr. k-5). 1992. 4.95 (0-944589-40-5) Young Discovery Lib.
—The Cotton in Your T-Shirt. Riquier, Aline. 40p. (gr. k-5). 1993. PLB 9.95 (1-56674-058-4, HTS Bks) Forest Hse.
—Living in India. Singh, Anne. Matthews, Sarah, tr. from FRE. LC 87-31803. 38p. (gr. k-5). 1988. 4.95 (0-944589-14-6, 146) Young Discovery Lib.
—Rice: The Little Grain That Feeds the World. Brice, Raphaelle. Bogard, Vicki, tr. from FRE. LC 90-50775. 38p. (gr. k-5). 1991. 4.95 (0-944589-30-8, 308) Young Discovery Lib.
Riswold, Gilbert. The Grizzly. Johnson, Annabel & Johnson, Edgar. LC 64-11831. 194p. (gr. 5-9). 1973. pap. 3.95 (0-06-440036-0, Trophy) HarpC Child Bks.

Ritchie, Fern. Fingertip Phonics. Piequet, Miriam. Anyone Can Read Staff, ed. Piequet, M., intro. by. 290p. (Orig.). (gr. 1-12). 1985. 19.95 (0-914275-05-4) Anyone Can Read Bks.

Ritchie, Scot. The Bears We Know. Silsbe, Brenda. 24p. (Orig.). (ps-2). 1989. pap. 0.99 (1-55037-048-0, Pub. by Annick CN) Firefly Bks Ltd.

—Dinner at Auntie Rose's. Munsil, Janet. 24p. (Orig.). (ps-2). 1989. pap. 0.99 (1-55037-047-2, Pub. by Annick CN) Firefly Bks Ltd.

—Dinosaur Dreams. Westell, Kerry. 24p. (Orig.). (ps-2). 1989. pap. 0.99 (1-55037-049-9, Pub. by Annick CN) Firefly Bks Ltd.

Ritner, Wanda. Totally Trusting. Lee, Chas. 222p. (gr. 4-10). 1992. 19.95 (1-878044-09-5) Mayhaven Pub.

Ritz, Karen. Between Two Worlds: A Story about Pearl Buck. Mitchell, Barbara. 56p. (gr. 3-6). 1988. PLB 14.95 (0-87614-332-X) Carolrhoda Bks.

—Boys Here - Girls There. Levinson, Riki. LC 92-5321. 1993. 13.00 (0-525-67374-1, Lodestar Bks) Dutton Child Bks.

—Cory Coleman, Grade Two. Brimner, Larry D. 80p. (gr. 2-4). 1990. 12.95 (0-8050-1312-1, Bks Young Read) H Holt & Co.

—Cory Coleman, Grade 2. Brimner, Larry D. LC 89-24694. 80p. (gr. 2-4). 1991. pap. 4.95 (0-8050-1844-1, Bks Young Read) H Holt & Co.

—A Family That Fights. Bernstein, Sharon C. Levine, Abby, ed. LC 90-29889. 32p. (gr. k-4). 1991. 11.95 (0-8075-2248-1) A Whitman.

—Frontier Surgeons: A Story about the Mayo Brothers. Crofford, Emily. 64p. (gr. 3-6). 1989. PLB 14.95 (0-87614-381-8) Carolrhoda Bks.

—The Ghost of Popcorn Hill. Wright, Betty R. LC 92-16391. 96p. (gr. 3-7). 1993. 13.95 (0-8234-1009-9) Holiday.

—Go Free or Die: A Story about Harriet Tubman. Ferris, Jeri. 64p. (gr. 3-6). 1988. lib. bdg. 14.95 (0-87614-317-6) Carolrhoda Bks.

—Go Free or Die: A Story about Harriet Tubman. Ferris, Jeri. 64p. (gr. 3-6). 1989. pap. 5.95 (0-87614-504-7, First Ave Edns) Lerner Pubns.

—Healing Warrior: A Story about Sister Elizabeth Kenny. Crofford, Emily. 64p. (gr. 3-6). 1989. PLB 14.95 (0-87614-382-6) Carolrhoda Bks.

—Kate Shelley & the Midnight Express. Wetterer, Margaret. 48p. (gr. k-4). 1990. PLB 14.95 (0-87614-425-3) Carolrhoda Bks.

—My Grammy. Kibbey, Marsha. 32p. (gr. 1-4). 1988. PLB 13.50 (0-87614-328-1) Carolrhoda Bks.

—A Picture Book of Anne Frank. Adler, David A. LC 92-17283. 32p. (ps-3). 1993. reinforced bdg. 14.95 (0-8234-1003-X) Holiday.

—Taxi Cat & Huey. LeRoy, Gen. LC 90-27383. 144p. (gr. 3-7). 1992. 14.00 (0-06-021768-5); PLB 13.89 (0-06-021769-3) HarpC Child Bks.

—Tell Me Your Best Thing. Hines, Anna G. LC 91-7833. 124p. (gr. 2-4). 1991. 13.95 (0-525-44734-2, DCB) Dutton Child Bks.

—Tell Me Your Best Thing. Hines, Anna G. 128p. (gr. 2-5). 1994. pap. 3.99 (0-14-036447-1) Puffin Bks.

—Valentine's Day. Kessel, Joyce K. LC 81-3842. 48p. (gr. k-4). 1981. PLB 14.95 (0-87614-166-1) Carolrhoda Bks.

—Valentine's Day. Kessel, Joyce K. 48p. (gr. k-4). 1988. pap. 5.95 (0-87614-502-0, First Ave Edns) Lerner Pubns.

Rius, Maria. Hearing. Parramon, J. M. & Puig, J. J. 32p. (Orig.). (ps). 1985. pap. 5.95 ea.; pap. 6.95 (0-8120-3563-1) Span. ed (0-8120-3606-9) Barron.

—Prehistory to Egypt. Verges, Gloria & Verges, Oriol. (SPA & ENG.). 32p. (gr. 2-4). 1988. pap. 4.95 (0-8120-3390-6); La Prehistoria y el Antiguo Egipto. pap. 6.95 (0-8120-3391-4) Barron.

—Sight. Parramon, J. M. & Puig, J. J. 32p. (Orig.). (ps). 1985. pap. 5.95 (0-8120-3564-X); pap. 6.95 Spanish ed. (0-8120-3605-0) Barron.

—Smell. Parramon, J. M. & Puig, J. J. 32p. (ps). 1985. pap. 5.95 (0-8120-3565-8); pap. 6.95 (0-8120-3607-7) Span. ed. Barron.

—Taste. Parramon, J. M. & Puig, J. J. 32p. (ps). 1985. pap. 5.95 (0-8120-3566-6); Span. ed. pap. 6.95 (0-8120-3608-5) Barron.

—Touch. Parramon, J. M. & Puig, J. J. 32p. (Orig.). (ps). 1985. pap. 5.95 (0-8120-3567-4); Span. ed. pap. 6.95 (0-8120-3609-3) Barron.

Rius, Maria & Peris, Carme. The Contemporary Age (Nineteenth & Twentieth Century) Verges, Gloria & Verges, Oriol. (ENG & SPA.). 32p. (gr. 2-4). 1988. pap. 4.50 (0-8120-3394-9); La Edad Contemporanea. pap. 6.95 (0-8120-3395-7) Barron.

—The Greek & Roman Eras. Verges, Gloria & Verges, Oriol. (ENG & SPA.). 32p. (gr. 2-4). 1988. pap. 6.95 (0-8120-3388-4); La Edad Antigua. pap. 6.95 (0-8120-3389-2) Barron.

—The Middle Ages. Verges, Gloria & Verges, Oriol. 32p. (gr. 2-4). 1988. pap. 6.95 (0-8120-3386-8); La Edad Media. pap. 6.95 (0-8120-3387-6) Barron.

—Modern Times (Seventeenth & Eighteenth Century) Verges, Gloria & Verges, Oriol. 32p. (gr. 2-4). 1988. pap. 4.50 (0-8120-3392-2); La Edad Moderna. pap. 6.95 (0-8120-3393-0) Barron.

—The Renaissance. Verges, Gloria & Verges, Oriol. 32p. (gr. 2-4). 1988. pap. 6.95 (0-8120-3396-5); El Renacimiento. pap. 6.95 (0-8120-3397-3) Barron.

Rivera, Doreen, et al. Writing & Cooperative Learning: Writing & Cooperative Learning. Brown, Marzella. 48p. (gr. 2-5). 1990. wkbk. 5.95 (1-55734-110-9) Tchr Create Mat.

—Great Games for Cooperative Learning. Brown, Marzella. 48p. (gr. 2-5). 1990. wkbk. 5.95 (1-55734-108-7) Tchr Create Mat.

—Activities for Cooperative Learning. Brown, Marzella. 48p. (gr. 2-5). 1990. wkbk. 5.95 (1-55734-109-5) Tchr Create Mat.

Rivlin, Lilly. When Will the Fighting Stop? A Child's View of Jerusalem. Morris, Ann. LC 88-34181. 64p. (gr. 3-7). 1989. SBE 13.95 (0-689-31508-2, Atheneum Child Bk) Macmillan Child Grp.

Rivoche, Paul & Humphrey, Brian. Skystalker. Nevfield, Len. 128p. (Orig.). 1985. pap. 1.95 (0-553-24894-4) Bantam.

Rizzuto, Joe, jt. illus. see Tully, Carol.

RKB Studios Staff. The New Testament in Everyday American English. rev. ed. Anderson, Julian G. x, 886p. (gr. 10 up). 1989. pap. 4.95 (0-685-27817-4) Anderson Bks.

Robain, Armando O. El Grillo Grunon: Cuentos para Chicos y Grandes. Arroyo, Anita. LC 84-13199. (SPA.). 122p. (Orig.). (gr. 1-6). 1984. pap. 5.50 (0-8477-3527-3) U of PR Pr.

Robare, Lorie, jt. illus. see O'Neill, Pablo M.

Robbin, Jodi. Tweedles & Foodles for Young Noodles. Reynolds, Malvina. LC 73-80670. 42p. (gr. k-4). 1961. pap. 5.75 (0-915620-08-1) Schroder Music.

Robbins, Arthur & Walter, Paul. Where Did I Come From. Mayle, Peter. 48p. (gr. 3 up). 1973. 12.00 (0-8184-0161-3); pap. 6.95 (0-8184-0253-9) Carol Pub Group.

Robbins, Ken. A Flower Grows. Robbins, Ken. (gr. k up). 1990. 12.95 (0-8037-0764-9); PLB 12.89 (0-8037-0765-7) Dial Bks Young.

—A Horse Named Paris. Sonberg, Lynn. LC 86-6886. 48p. (gr. 2-4). 1986. SBE 15.95 (0-02-786260-7, Bradbury Pr) Macmillan Child Grp.

Robbins, Ken, photos by. Power Machines. Robbins, Ken, text by. LC 92-30649. 32p. (gr. k-3). 1993. 15.95 (0-8050-1410-1, Bks Young Read) H Holt & Co.

Robbins, Michael. Tobias Turkey. Robbins, Sandra. 32p. (ps-3). 1991. pap. text ed. 3.99 (1-882601-07-6); pap. text ed. 9.98 incl. cass. (1-882601-06-8) See-Mores Wrkshop.

Robbins, Ruth. The Beautiful Christmas Tree. Zolotow, Charlotte. 16p. (gr. k-3). 1983. 13.95 (0-395-27676-4); pap. 4.95 (0-395-34925-7) HM.

—Ishi: Last of His Tribe. Kroeber, Theodora. 208p. 1964. PLB 14.45 (0-395-27644-6) HM.

Robbins-Ptak, Elizabeth. Look Who's Drivin' the Bus. Rubly-Burggraff, Roberta. 150p. (Orig.). (gr. 9 up). 1993. pap. 29.95 (0-937997-25-0) Hi-Time Pub.

—Magnum Opus: An Affirmation Journal. Rubly-Burggraff, Roberta. 72p. (Orig.). (gr. 7-12). 1989. pap. 5.95 (0-937997-14-5) Hi-Time Pub.

Robert, Luc. The Legend of Greenmantle. Villeneuve, Jocelyne. 80p. (ps-8). 1988. 9.95 (0-920806-95-3, Pub. by Penumbra Pr CN) U of Toronto Pr.

—Nanna Bijou: The Legend of the Sleeping Giant. Villeneuve, Jocelyne. 46p. (ps-8). 1984. 6.95 (0-920806-26-0, Pub. by Penumbra Pr CN) U of Toronto Pr.

Roberts, Bruce, photos by. Ghosts & Specters of the Old South. Roberts, Nancy. LC 73-20909. 93p. (gr. 4-12). 1984. pap. 7.95 (0-87844-058-5) Sandlapper Pub Co.

—Once There Was a Stream. Rothman, Joel. LC 72-90692. 32p. (gr. k-4). 1973. 8.95 (0-87592-038-1) Scroll Pr.

Roberts, John. Sound Friendships: The Story of Willa & Her Hearing Dog. Yates, Elizabeth. Leaman, Christine, ed. O'Brien, Sheila, frwd by. 113p. (Orig.). (gr. 7-12). 1992. pap. 4.95 (0-89084-650-2) Bob Jones Univ Pr.

—The Spelling Window. Watkins, Dawn L. LC 92-47049. 1993. write for info. (0-89084-677-4) Bob Jones Univ Pr.

Roberts, Ken G. Paper Airplanes from Around the World, Vol. I. 3rd, rev. & enl. ed. Roberts, Ray. 240p. (gr. 6 up). 1992. Repr. of 1988 ed. lib. bdg. 19.95 (0-929995-00-7) AIR Burbank.

Roberts, Tom. The Adventures of Curious Eric: Learning Concepts. Shearer, Marilyn J. LC 90-60397. 16p. (ps-6). 1990. 19.95 (0-685-33064-8); pap. 10.95 (1-878389-01-7) L Ashley & Joshua.

—I Like to Play. Shearer, Marilyn J. 16p. (Orig.). (ps-6). 1989. 19.95 (0-685-30097-8); pap. 10.95 (0-685-30098-6) L Ashley & Joshua.

Roberts, Tony. The Cygnus Conspiracy. Lindsay, A. Brook, III. Amthor, Terry, ed. 32p. (Orig.). (gr. 10-12). 1987. pap. 12.00 (0-915795-92-2, 9102) Iron Crown Ent Inc.

Roberts, Tony & Jaquays, Paul. Cyclops Vale & Other Tales. Taylor, Tim. Ruemmler, John D., ed. 32p. (Orig.). (gr. 12). 1989. pap. 6.00 (1-55806-042-1, 6009) Iron Crown Ent Inc.

—Tales of the Loremasters. Kane, Thomas. Amthor, Terry K. & Ruemmler, John D., ed. 32p. (Orig.). (gr. 12). 1989. pap. 6.00 (1-55806-073-1, 6004) Iron Crown Ent Inc.

Roberts, William. Santa Claus' Snack. Merriam, Robert L. 14p. (ps-6). 1970. pap. 2.00x (0-686-32491-9) R L Merriam.

Robertson, Graham. Looking at Penguins. Patent, Dorothy H. LC 92-37673. 40p. (ps-4). 1993. reinforced bdg. 15.95 (0-8234-1037-4) Holiday.

Robertson, Ian. Make a Salad Face. Drew, David. LC 92-34335. 1993. 2.50 (0-383-03640-2) SRA Schl Grp.

Robertson, James. My Backyard History Book. Weitzman, David. 128p. (gr. 4 up). 1975. 15.95 (0-316-92901-8); pap. 9.95 (0-316-92902-6) Little.

Robertson, Jeanne L. Illustrated Guide to Fishes in Kansas. Cross, Frank B. & Collins, Joseph T. 14p. (gr. 4-6). 1976. pap. 1.00 (0-89338-000-8) U of KS Mus Nat Hist.

Robey, Adele. The Jones Family. Cochrane, Shirley G. & Townsend, Betsy B. 50p. (Orig.). 1992. pap. 10.00 (0-9609062-2-3) WA Expatriates Pr.

Robin. Our Library Lives in a Bus. Enerson, Laura. LC 77-11462. (gr. 3-5). 1977. 3.50 (0-930480-01-5) R H Barnes.

Robin, Jeremy, jt. illus. see McBride, Angus.

Robins, Arthur. Little Rabbit Foo Foo. Rosen, Michael. LC 90-9598. 32p. (ps-1). 1993. pap. 3.95 (0-671-79604-6, Little Simon) S&S Trade.

—The Same but Different. Dahl, Tessa. 32p. (ps-3). 1993. pap. 3.99 (0-14-054823-8) Puffin Bks.

—Sweet Dreams & Monsters: A Beginner's Guide to Dreams & Nightmares & Things That Go Bump under the Bed. Mayle, Peter. (gr. k up). 1986. 9.95 (0-517-55997-2, Harmony) Crown Pub Group.

—Why Are We Getting a Divorce? Mayle, Peter. LC 87-12105. 32p. (gr. k-3). 1988. 15.00 (0-517-56527-7, Harmony) Crown Pub Group.

—Why Do I Have to Wear Glasses? Stuart, Sandra L. 48p. 1989. 12.00 (0-8184-0477-9) Carol Pub Group.

—Why Was I Adopted? Livingston, Carole. (gr. 1 up). 1978. text ed. 12.00 (0-8184-0257-1) Carol Pub Group.

Robins, Arthur, jt. illus. see Walter, Paul.

Robinson. Soup on Wheels. Peck, Robert N. LC 80-17661. 128p. (gr. 4 up). 1981. PLB 11.99 (0-394-94581-6) Knopf Bks Yng Read.

Robinson, A. Elijah's Angel. Rosen, Michael J. 1992. 13.95 (0-15-225394-7, HB Juv Bks) HarBrace.

Robinson, Alan J. Here Is the Arctic Winter. Dunphy, Madeleine. LC 92-72022. 32p. (ps-3). 1993. 14.95 (1-56282-336-1); PLB 14.89 (0-685-59361-4) Hyprn Child.

Robinson, Bernard. Fishing. Williams, Brian. LC 92-21389. 48p. (gr. 5-8). 1992. PLB 21.34 (0-8114-4788-X) Raintree Steck-V.

—Trading. Williams, Brian. LC 92-27031. 48p. (gr. 5-8). 1993. PLB 21.34 (0-8114-4787-1) Raintree Steck-V.

Robinson, Bernard, jt. illus. see Holmes, David.

Robinson, Charles. All the Money in the World. Brittain, Bill. LC 77-25635. 160p. (gr. 4-7). 1982. pap. 3.95 (0-06-440128-6, Trophy) HarpC Child Bks.

—A Child's Garden of Verses. Stevenson, Robert Louis. (gr. 1 up). 1976. pap. 9.95 (0-85967-313-8, Pub. by Scolar Pr UK) Ashgate Pub Co.

—A Child's Garden of Verses. Stevenson, Robert Louis. LC 92-53175. 128p. 1992. 12.95 (0-679-41799-0, Evrymans Lib Childs Class) Knopf.

—A Child's Garden of Verses. Stevenson, Robert Louis. LC 93-41101. 1994. 6.00 (1-56957-926-1) Barefoot Bks.

—A Clearing in the Forest: A Story about a Real Settler Boy. Henry, Joanne L. LC 91-18554. 64p. (gr. 3-6). 1992. RSBE 14.95 (0-02-743671-3, Four Winds) Macmillan Child Grp.

—The Daybreakers. Curry, Jane L. (gr. 3-7). 1991. 20.50 (0-8446-6474-X) Peter Smith.

—The Happy Prince & Other Stories. Wilde, Oscar. Glassman, Peter, afterword by. LC 90-48353. 144p. 1991. Repr. of 1913 ed. 16.95 (0-688-10390-1) Morrow Jr Bks.

—The House on Parchment Street. McKillip, Patricia. LC 90-27119. 192p. (gr. 3-7). 1991. pap. 3.95 (0-689-71471-8, Aladdin) Macmillan Child Grp.

—Ike & Mama & the Once-a-Year Suit. Snyder, Carol. LC 92-9201. 48p. (gr. 2-5). 1992. pap. 9.95 (0-8276-0418-1) JPS Phila.

—Journey Home. Uchida, Yoshiko. LC 78-8792. 144p. (gr. 5-7). 1978. SBE 13.95 (0-689-50126-9, M K McElderry) Macmillan Child Grp.

—Journey Home. 2nd ed. Uchida, Yoshiko. LC 91-40149. 144p. (gr. 3-7). 1992. pap. 3.95 (0-689-71641-9, Aladdin) Macmillan Child Grp.

—Journey to America. Levitin, Sonia. LC 86-22234. 160p. (gr. 3-6). 1987. pap. 3.95 (0-689-71130-1, Aladdin) Macmillan Child Grp.

—Just a Few Words, Mr. Lincoln: The Story of the Gettysburg Address. Fritz, Jean. LC 92-35319. 48p. (gr. 2-3). 1993. 7.99 (0-448-40171-1, G&D); pap. 3.50 (0-448-40170-3, G&D) Putnam Pub Group.

—Little Soup's Turkey. Peck, Robert N. 80p. (Orig.). (gr. 1-4). 1992. pap. 2.99 (0-440-40724-9, YB) Dell.

—My Grandma's in a Nursing Home. Delton, Judy & Tucker, Dorothy. Tucker, Kathleen, ed. LC 86-1640. 32p. (gr. 2-5). 1986. PLB 11.95 (0-8075-5333-6) A Whitman.

—Pioneer Cat. Hooks, William J. LC 88-4708. 64p. (Orig.). (gr. 2-4). 1988. lib. bdg. 6.99 (0-394-92038-4); 2.50 (0-394-82038-X) Knopf Bks Yng Read.

—The Rock Star, the Rooster, &. Me, the Reporter. Shalant, Phyllis. 169p. (gr. 3-7). 1991. pap. 3.95 (0-14-034596-5, Puffin) Puffin Bks.

—Soup Ahoy. Peck, Robert N. LC 93-14097. 1994. write for info. (0-679-84978-5); PLB write for info. (0-679-94978-X) Knopf.

—Soup in the Saddle. Peck, Robert N. LC 82-14010. 96p. (gr. 3-6). 1983. PLB 11.99 (0-394-95294-4) Knopf Bks Yng Read.

—Soup on Fire. Peck, Robert N. LC 87-5261. 112p. (gr. 4-7). 1987. pap. 13.95 (0-385-29580-4) Delacorte.
—Soup on Ice. Peck, Robert N. LC 85-218. 128p. (gr. 3-7). 1985. PLB 10.99 (0-394-97613-4) Knopf Bks Yng Read.
—Soup's Drum. Peck, Robert N. LC 79-17982. 128p. (gr. 3-6). 1980. PLB 10.99 (0-394-94251-5) Knopf Bks Yng Read.
—Soup's Goat. Peck, Robert N. LC 83-16245. 112p. (gr. 4-6). 1984. lib. bdg. 12.99 (0-394-96322-9) Knopf Bks Yng Read.
—Soup's Uncle. Peck, Robert N. LC 87-37538. 112p. (gr. 4-7). 1988. 13.95 (0-440-50062-1) Delacorte.
—A Taste of Blackberries. Smith, Doris B. LC 72-7558. 64p. (gr. 3-6). 1973. PLB 12.89 (0-690-80512-8, Crowell Jr Bks) HarpC Child Bks.
—The Terrible Wave: Memorial Edition. Dahlstedt, Marden A. LC 72-76687. 125p. (gr. 7 up). 1988. pap. 5.00 (0-9621827-0-2) R R Dahlstedt.
Robinson, Claire, jt. illus. see Stower, Adam.
Robinson, Colin. Sunrise. Robinson, Colin. LC 91-40988. 32p. (ps-1). 1992. PLB 12.95 (0-87226-468-8, Bedrick Blackie) P Bedrick Bks.
Robinson, Don. Saving Our Planet. Ferraro, Bonita. 40p. (gr. 3). 1991. wkbk. 3.95 (1-561894-03-6) Amer Educ Pub.
—Saving Our Planet. Ferraro, Bonita. 40p. (gr. 2). 1991. wkbk. 3.95 (1-561894-02-8) Amer Educ Pub.
—Saving Our Planet. Ferraro, Bonita. 40p. (gr. 1). 1991. wkbk. 3.95 (1-561894-01-X) Amer Educ Pub.
Robinson, Famous. Brandon's First Baseball Game. Banks, Joann. LC 90-63290. 37p. (Orig.). (gr.-6). 1990. pap. text ed. 5.00 (0-9627951-0-0) JRBB Pubs.
Robinson, Jane. The Whale in Lowell's Cove. Robinson, Jane. LC 91-77670. 48p. (gr. 1-4). 1992. 14.95 (0-89272-308-4) Down East.
Robinson, Jerry. Abraham Lincoln: The Great Emancipator. Stevenson, Augusta. 192p. (gr. 2-6). 1986. pap. 3.95 (0-02-042030-7, Aladdin) Macmillan Child Grp.
—Lou Gehrig: One of Baseball's Greatest. Van Riper, Guernsey, Jr. LC 86-10951. 192p. (gr. 2-6). 1986. pap. 3.95 (0-02-041930-9, Aladdin) Macmillan Child Grp.
Robinson, Jerry, et al. Batman Archives, Vol. 2. Kane, Bob, et al. Gold, Mike, ed. Marschall, Rick, intro. by. 288p. 1991. text ed. 39.95 (1-56389-000-3) DC Comics.
Robinson, Jessie B. Beautiful Garden & Other Bible Tales. Levinger, Elma E. (gr. 3-5). 6.95 (0-8197-0253-6) Bloch.
—Mother Goose Rhymes for Jewish Children. Levy, Sara G. (ps-2). 1979. pap. 8.95 (0-8197-0254-4) Bloch.
Robinson, Keith. Fortune Telling. Green, Carl R. & Sanford, William R. LC 93-12029. 48p. (gr. 4-10). 1993. lib. bdg. 14.95 (0-89490-456-6) Enslow Pubs.
—Mysterious Mind Powers. Green, Carl R. & Sanford, William R. LC 92-44678. 48p. (gr. 4-10). 1993. PLB 14.95 (0-89490-455-8) Enslow Pubs.
—Recalling Past Lives. Green, Carl R. & Sanford, William R. 48p. (gr. 4-10). 1993. lib. bdg. 14.95 (0-89490-458-2) Enslow Pubs.
—Seeing the Unseen. Green, Carl R. & Sanford, William R. LC 92-44677. 48p. (gr. 4-10). 1993. lib. bdg. 14.95 (0-89490-454-X) Enslow Pubs.
Robinson, Lafayette. Penmanship from A to Z. Robinson, Lafayette. 72p. (gr. 3-4). 1988. wkbk. 7.95 (0-9621081-1-1) Educ Graphics.
Robinson, Marilyn. More Sewing Machine Fun. Smith, Nancy J. & Milligan, Lynda. Holmes, Sharon, ed. 72p. (gr. 2-8). 1993. pap. 15.95 plastic comb. (1-880972-05-0) Pssblts Denver.
—Sewing Machine Fun. Smith, Nancy & Milligan, Lynda. Holmes, Sharon, ed. 72p. (gr. 1-12). 1993. pap. 15.95 GBC bdg. (1-880972-04-2, DreamSpinners) Pssblts Denver.
—Sewing Machine Fun: Activity Kit. Smith, Nancy & Milligan, Lynda. Holmes, Sharon, ed. 72p. (gr. 1-12). 1993. pap. 29.95 (1-880972-10-7, DreamSpinners) Pssblts Denver.
—Step Into Patchwork. Smith, Nancy & Milligan, Lynda. Holmes, Sharon, ed. 72p. (gr. 1-12). 1994. pap. 15.95 plastic comb bdg. (1-880972-09-3, DreamSpinners) Pssblts Denver.
Robinson, Michael. Anytime Stories. Sawicki, Leo. 64p. (ps-8). 1988. 7.95 (0-920806-78-3, Pub. by Penumbra Pr CN) U of Toronto Pr.
Robinson, Michael D., jt. illus. see Hoffman, Beverly.
Robinson, Robbie. Heavy Stuff Student Workbook. Shivens, Frank. (Orig.). (gr. 7-12). 1991. 5.95 (1-8781270-1-2) F Shivers Evangelistic.
Robinson, Susan. The Christmas Invitation: A Child's Christmas in the South. Jones, Margaret W. Easson, Roger R., ed. LC 85-2035. 48p. (gr. 5 up). 1985. 9.95 (0-918518-42-3) St Lukes Pr.
Robinson, Susan, jt. illus. see Cheairs, Nancy.
Robinson, W. Heath, jt. illus. see Thomas, Charles.
Robinsunne. Nannee. Robinsunne. 36p. (ps). 1993. 15.95 (0-9636986-0-5) Robinsunne Pstcrd.
Robison, Bill. The Puppy Nobody Wanted. Pellowski, Michael J. 24p. (ps-3). 1988. 1.95 (0-87406-338-8) Willowisp Pr.
Robison, Deborah. Your Turn, Doctor. Robison, Deborah & Perez, Carla. LC 81-68778. 32p. (ps-2). 1982. Dial Bks Young.
Robison, Don. Activities & Assignments: Student Workbook. rev. ed. Resnik, Hank. Barr, Linda, ed. 178p. (gr. 6-8). 1988. wkbk. 4.85 (0-933419-26-0) Quest Intl.

—Colors & Shapes. Ferarro, Bonita. 32p. (Orig.). (ps). 1993. wkbk. 1.99 (1-56189-058-8) Amer Educ Pub.
—English. 2nd ed. Gerber, Carole, ed. 40p. (gr. 2). 1992. wkbk. 1.99 (1-56189-082-0) Amer Educ Pub.
—English. Gerber, Carole, ed. 40p. (gr. 3). 1992. wkbk. 1.99 (1-56189-083-9) Amer Educ Pub.
—English & Phonics. Gerber, Carole, ed. 32p. (gr. k). 1992. wkbk. 1.99 (1-56189-080-4) Amer Educ Pub.
—English & Phonics. Gerber, Carole, ed. 40p. (gr. 1). 1992. wkbk. 1.99 (1-56189-081-2) Amer Educ Pub.
—Letters & Sounds. Ferarro, Bonita. 32p. (Orig.). (ps). 1993. wkbk. 1.99 (1-56189-059-6) Amer Educ Pub.
—Math. Douglas, Vincent. 48p. (Orig.). (gr. 4). 1993. wkbk. 1.99 (1-56189-074-X) Amer Educ Pub.
—Math. Douglas, Vincent. 48p. (Orig.). (gr. 5). 1993. wkbk. 1.99 (1-56189-075-8) Amer Educ Pub.
—Math. Douglas, Vincent. 48p. (Orig.). (gr. 6). 1993. wkbk. 1.99 (1-56189-076-6) Amer Educ Pub.
—Numbers & Counting. Ferarro, Bonita. 32p. (Orig.). (ps). 1993. wkbk. 1.99 (1-56189-057-X) Amer Educ Pub.
Robison, Don, et al. Changes: Becoming the Best You Can Be. rev. ed. Cosby, Bill, et al. Barr, Linda & Wojcicki, Marba, eds. 196p. (gr. 6-8). 1988. pap. text ed. 6.85 (0-933419-24-4) Quest Intl.
—Brighter Child Software: Math. Douglas, Vincent & Way, Voldi. 32p. (gr. 1). 1993. wkbk., incl. software 9.95 (1-561894-15-X) Amer Educ Pub.
—Brighter Child Software: Math. Douglas, Vincent & Way, Voldi. 32p. (gr. 3). 1993. wkbk., incl. software 9.95 (1-561894-17-6) Amer Educ Pub.
—Brighter Child Software: Math. Douglas, Vincent & Way, Voldi. 32p. (gr. 2). 1993. wkbk., incl. software 9.95 (1-561894-16-8) Amer Educ Pub.
—Brighter Child Software: Reading. Douglas, Vincent & Way, Voldi. 32p. (gr. 1). 1993. wkbk., incl. software 9.95 (1-561894-11-7) Amer Educ Pub.
—Brighter Child Software: Reading. Douglas, Vincent & Way, Voldi. 32p. (gr. 2). 1993. wkbk., incl. software 9.95 (1-561894-12-5) Amer Educ Pub.
—Brighter Child Software: Reading. Douglas, Vincent & Way, Voldi. 32p. (gr. 3). 1993. wkbk., incl. software 9.95 (1-561894-13-3) Amer Educ Pub.
Robson, Eric. Ocean Animals. Chinery, Michael. LC 91-53144. 40p. (Orig.). (gr. 2-5). 1992. PLB 8.99 (0-679-92046-3); pap. 4.99 (0-679-82046-9) Random Bks Yng Read.
—The World of Animals. Stacy, Tom. LC 90-42619. 40p. (Orig.). (gr. 2-5). 1991. pap. 3.95 (0-679-80864-7) Random Bks Yng Read.
Robson, Eric, jt. illus. see Ford, Wayne.
Robson, Eric, jt. illus. see Long, Bernard.
Robson, Pat. Oil. 32p. (gr. 3-5). 1935. 7.95x (0-86685-449-5) Intl Bk Ctr.
—Rain. 32p. (gr. 3-5). 1985. 7.95x (0-86685-451-7) Intl Bk Ctr.
Rocco, John. Alice. Goldberg, Whoopi. LC 92-15935. 48p. 1992. 15.00 (0-553-08990-0) Bantam.
Rocco, John, photos by. The Krazees. Swope, Sam. LC 92-24435. 32p. (ps-1). Date not set. 15.00 (0-06-021541-0); PLB 14.89 (0-06-021542-9) HarpC Child Bks.
Roch, J. Rosie: The Oldest Horse in St. Augustine. Gilbert, Miriam. LC 67-30409. (FRE, SPA & ENG.). (gr. k-6). 1974. 6.95 (0-87208-105-2); pap. 5.95 (0-87208-007-2) Island Pr Pubs.
Roche, P. K. At Christmas Be Merry. Roche, P. K., selected by. 32p. (ps-1). 1989. pap. 3.95 (0-14-050680-2, Puffin) Puffin Bks.
—Webster & Arnold & the Giant Box. Roche, P. K. LC 80-11595. 56p. (gr. ps-3). 1980. Dial Bks Young.
Rocklen, Margot. Molly's Special Wish. Supraner, Robyn. LC 85-14087. 48p. (Orig.). (gr. 1-3). 1986. PLB 10.59 (0-8167-0660-3); pap. text ed. 3.50 (0-8167-0661-1) Troll Assocs.
Rockwell, Ann. Bikes. Rockwell, Anne. LC 86-19923. 24p. (ps-1). 1987. 11.95 (0-525-44287-1, DCB) Dutton Child Bks.
Rockwell, Anne. Big Wheels. Rockwell, Anne. LC 85-16248. 24p. (ps-1). 1986. 12.95 (0-525-44226-X, DCB) Dutton Child Bks.
—Boats. Rockwell, Anne. LC 82-2420. 24p. (ps). 1985. 12.95 (0-525-44004-6, DCB); (DCB) Dutton Child Bks.
—Cars. Rockwell, Anne. LC 83-14080. 24p. (ps-1). 1984. 12.95 (0-525-44079-8, DCB) Dutton Child Bks.
—Cars. Rockwell, Anne. LC 83-14080. 24p. (ps-1). 1986. pap. 3.95 (0-525-44241-3, DCB) Dutton Child Bks.
—Come to Town. Rockwell, Anne. LC 86-6217. 32p. (ps-1). 1987. (Crowell Jr Bks) HarpC Child Bks.
—First Comes Spring. Rockwell, Anne. LC 84-45331. 32p. (ps-1). 1991. pap. 4.95 (0-06-107412-8) HarpC Child Bks.
—Hugo at the Park. Rockwell, Anne. LC 89-2417. 32p. (ps-k). 1990. RSBE 13.95 (0-02-777301-9, Macmillan Child Bk) Macmillan Child Grp.
—Hugo at the Window. Rockwell, Anne. LC 87-11058. 32p. (ps-k). 1988. SBE 13.95 (0-02-777330-2, Macmillan Child Bk) Macmillan Child Grp.
—In the Morning. Rockwell, Anne. LC 85-47742. 15p. (ps). 1986. 2.50 (0-694-00078-7, Crowell Jr Bks) HarpC Child Bks.
—Mr. Panda's Painting. Rockwell, Anne. LC 92-9220. 32p. (ps-3). 1993. RSBE 14.95 (0-02-777451-1, Macmillan Child Bk) Macmillan Child Grp.
—On Our Vacation. Rockwell, Anne. LC 88-29996. 32p. (ps-1). 1989. 12.95 (0-525-44487-4, DCB) Dutton Child Bks.

—Planes. Rockwell, Anne. LC 84-13732. 24p. (ps-1). 1985. 12.95 (0-525-44159-X, DCB) Dutton Child Bks.
—Puss in Boots & Other Stories. Rockwell, Anne, as told by. LC 87-14976. 96p. (gr. k-4). 1988. SBE 15.95 (0-02-777781-2, Macmillan Child Bk) Macmillan Child Grp.
—Things That Go. Rockwell, Anne. LC 86-6199. 24p. (ps-1). 1986. 10.95 (0-525-44266-9, DCB) Dutton Child Bks.
—Things to Play With. Rockwell, Anne. LC 87-33399. 24p. (ps-1). 1988. 11.95 (0-525-44409-2, DCB) Dutton Child Bks.
—Three Sillies & Ten Other Stories. Rockwell, Anne. LC 85-45404. 96p. (ps-3). 1986. pap. 8.95 flexi-bind (0-06-443093-6, Trophy) HarpC Child Bks.
—Trains. Rockwell, Anne. LC 87-22180. 24p. (ps-1). 1988. 13.00 (0-525-44377-0, 01063-320, DCB) Dutton Child Bks.
—Trucks. Rockwell, Anne. LC 84-1556. 24p. (ps-1). 1984. 11.95 (0-525-44147-6, DCB) Dutton Child Bks.
—Trucks. Rockwell, Anne. LC 84-1556. 24p. (ps-1). 1988. pap. 3.95 (0-525-44432-7, DCB) Dutton Child Bks.
—The Turtle & the Two Ducks: Animal Fables Retold from La Fontaine. Plante, Patricia & Bergman, David. LC 81-47409. 32p. (ps-2). 1981. (Crowell Jr Bks) HarpC Child Bks.
—The Way to Captain Yankee's. Rockwell, Anne. LC 92-44644. 32p. (ps-2). 1994. RSBE 13.95 (0-02-777271-3, Macmillan Child Bk) Macmillan Child Grp.
—What Happens to a Hamburger? rev. ed. Showers, Paul. LC 84-45343. 32p. (ps-3). 1985. (Crowell Jr Bks); PLB 14.89 (0-690-04427-5, Crowell Jr Bks) HarpC Child Bks.
—What Happens to a Hamburger? rev. ed. Showers, Paul. LC 84-48784. 32p. (gr. k-3). 1985. pap. 4.50 (0-06-445013-9, Trophy) HarpC Child Bks.
—What We Like. Rockwell, Anne. LC 91-4990. 24p. (ps-1). 1992. RSBE 13.95 (0-02-777274-8, Macmillan Child Bk) Macmillan Child Grp.
—When We Grow Up. Rockwell, Anne. LC 80-21768. (ps-1). 1981. 10.95 (0-525-42575-6, Dutton) NAL-Dutton.
—Willy Can Count. Rockwell, Anne. 32p. (ps). 1989. 13.95 (1-55970-013-0) Arcade Pub Inc.
Rockwell, Anne & Rockwell, Harlow. Happy Birthday to Me. Rockwell, Anne & Rockwell, Harlow. LC 81-3738. 24p. (ps-k). 1981. RSBE 9.95 (0-02-777680-8, Macmillan Child Bk) Macmillan Child Grp.
—I Play in My Room. Rockwell, Anne & Rockwell, Harlow. LC 81-2634. 24p. (ps-k). 1981. RSBE 9.95 (0-02-777670-0, Macmillan Child Bk) Macmillan Child Grp.
—Sick in Bed. Rockwell, Anne & Rockwell, Harlow. LC 81-15637. 24p. (ps-k). 1982. RSBE 9.95 (0-02-777730-8, Macmillan Child Bk) Macmillan Child Grp.
Rockwell, Gail. Dreams of Victory. Conford, Ellen. 144p. (gr. 4-6). 1973. 14.95 (0-316-15294-3) Little.
Rockwell, Harlow. At the Beach. Rockwell, Anne. LC 86-2943. 24p. (ps-1). 1987. RSBE 13.95 (0-02-777940-8, Macmillan Child Bk) Macmillan Child Grp.
—At the Beach. Rockwell, Anne. LC 90-45620. 24p. (ps-1). 1991. pap. 3.95 (0-689-71494-7, Aladdin) Macmillan Child Grp.
—The Emergency Room. Rockwell, Anne. LC 84-20161. 24p. (ps-2). 1985. RSBE 13.95 (0-02-777300-0, Macmillan Child Bk) Macmillan Child Grp.
—The First Snowfall. Rockwell, Anne & Rockwell, Harlow. LC 91-41247. 24p. (ps-1). 1992. pap. 3.95 (0-689-71614-1, Aladdin) Macmillan Child Grp.
—Look at This. Rockwell, Harlow. LC 87-1033. 64p. (gr. 1-4). 1987. pap. 3.95 (0-689-71165-4, Aladdin) Macmillan Child Grp.
—My Doctor. Rockwell, Harlow. LC 72-92442. 24p. (ps-1). 1973. SBE 13.95 (0-02-777480-5, Macmillan Child Bk) Macmillan Child Grp.
—My Doctor. Rockwell, Harlow. LC 91-27163. 24p. (ps-2). 1992. pap. 3.95 (0-689-71606-0, Aladdin) Macmillan Child Grp.
—Our Garage Sale. Rockwell, Anne. LC 80-16704. 24p. (ps-1). 1984. 10.25 (0-688-80278-8); PLB 10.88 (0-688-84278-X) Greenwillow.
—Touch Me Book. Witte, Eve & Witte, Pat. (ps). 1961. write for info (0-307-12146-1, Golden Bks) Western Pub.
Rockwell, Harlow & Rockwell, Lizzy. My Spring Robin. Rockwell, Anne. LC 88-13333. 24p. (ps-1). 1989. RSBE 13.95 (0-02-777611-5, Macmillan Child Bk) Macmillan Child Grp.
Rockwell, Harlow, jt. illus. see Rockwell, Anne.
Rockwell, Lizzie. A Sort-of Sailor. Hest, Amy. LC 89-38252. 32p. (gr. k-3). 1990. RSBE 13.95 (0-02-743641-1, Four Winds) Macmillan Child Grp.
Rockwell, Lizzy. Apples & Pumpkins. Rockwell, Anne. LC 88-22628. 24p. (ps-1). 1989. RSBE 13.95 (0-02-777270-5, Macmillan Child Bk) Macmillan Child Grp.
—Ducklings & Polliwogs. Rockwell, Anne. LC 93-16600. (gr. 3 up). 1994. write for info. (0-02-777452-X) Macmillan Child Grp.
—Our Yard Is Full of Birds. Rockwell, Anne. LC 90-30436. 32p. (ps-2). 1992. RSBE 13.95 (0-02-777273-X, Macmillan Child Bk) Macmillan Child Grp.

—Pots & Pans. Rockwell, Anne. LC 91-4976. 32p. (ps-1). 1993. RSBE 13.95 (0-02-777631-X, Macmillan Child Bk) Macmillan Child Grp.

Rockwell, Lizzy, jt. illus. see Rockwell, Harlow.

Rockwell, Norman. Home for Christmas: An Advent Book. 1993. 13.99 (0-525-44894-2, DCB) Dutton Child Bks.

Rodanas, Kristina. Dragonfly's Tale. Rodanas, Kristina, retold by. 32p. (gr. k-3). 1992. 14.45 (0-395-57003-4, Clarion Bks) HM.

—Rocking - Horse Land. Housman, Laurence. LC 89-45902. 32p. (gr. k-3). 1990. 13.95 (0-688-09014-1); lib. bdg. 13.88 (0-688-09015-X) Lothrop.

—The Story of Wali Dad. Rodanas, Kristina. LC 86-34423. 32p. (gr. k-3). 1988. 13.95 (0-688-07262-3); PLB 13.88 (0-688-07263-1) Lothrop.

Rodegast, Roland. Double Trouble. Greydanus, Rose. LC 81-2358. 32p. (gr. k-2). 1981. PLB 11.59 (0-89375-529-X); pap. 2.95 (0-89375-530-3) Troll Assocs.

Rodell, Don. The Moon of the Chickarees. new ed. George, Jean C. LC 90-22409. 48p. (gr. 3-7). 1992. 15.00 (0-06-022507-6); PLB 14.89 (0-06-022508-4) HarpC Child Bks.

Rodgers, Frank. Mr. Majeika. large type ed. Carpenter, Humphrey. 96p. (gr. 1-8). 1992. 13.95 (0-7451-1582-9, Galaxy Child Lrg Print) Chivers N Amer.

—Who's Afraid of the Ghost Train? Rodgers, Frank. 23p. (ps-1). 1989. 12.95 (0-15-200642-7, Gulliver Bks) HarBrace.

Rodgers, Gregg. Life in a Forest. Mason, Helen. 32p. (Orig.). (gr. 3-6). 1992. pap. 3.50 (0-88625-260-1) Durkin Hayes Pub.

—Life in a Pond. Mason, Helen. 32p. (Orig.). (gr. 3-6). 1992. pap. 3.50 (0-88625-255-5) Durkin Hayes Pub.

—Musicians of Bremen: European Folk Tales. Grimm, Jacob & Grimm, Wilhelm K. 24p. 1992. pap. 3.50 (0-88625-286-5) Durkin Hayes Pub.

Rodrigue, George. The Loup-Garou of Cote Gelee. Raphael, Morris. 48p. (gr. 3-9). 1990. 12.95 (0-9608866-7-2) M Raphael.

Rodrigues, Anita. Aunt Martha & the Golden Coin. Rodriguez, Anita. LC 92-7316. 32p. (ps-2). 1993. 14. 00 (0-517-59337-8, Clarkson Potter); PLB 14.99 (0-517-59338-6, Clarkson Potter) Crown Bks Yng Read.

Rodriguez, Anita. Jamal & the Angel. Rodriguez, Anita. LC 91-11636. 32p. (ps-2). 1992. 14.00 (0-517-58601-0); PLB 15.99 (0-517-59115-4) Crown Bks Yng Read.

Rodriguez, Carlos. Silly Ghost Riddles. Salinas, Roger. 32p. (Orig.). (gr. 3-5). 1987. pap. 2.95 (0-942673-00-X) Salinas Salinas & Matthews.

Rodriguez, Jose L. Diccionario Geografico Universal. 3rd, rev. ed. Alvarez del Real, Maria E., ed. (SPA.). 876p. (Orig.). 1992. pap. 5.95 (1-56259-020-0) Editorial Amer.

Roe, Richard. Baby Animals. Roe, Richard. LC 85-2223. 24p. (ps-1). 1985. 3.95 (0-394-86956-7) Random Bks Yng Read.

—Dinosaur Days. Milton, Joyce. LC 84-17861. 48p. (gr. k-3). 1985. lib. bdg. 7.99 (0-394-97023-3); pap. 3.50 (0-394-87023-9) Random Bks Yng Read.

—Dinosaur Days. Milton, Joyce. 48p. (gr. k-3). 1988. pap. 5.95 bk. & cassette pkg. (0-394-89774-9) Random Bks Yng Read.

Roennfeldt, Robert. The Paddock: A Story in Praise of the Earth. Norman, Lilith. LC 92-15013. 32p. (ps-3). 1993. 12.00 (0-679-83887-2) Knopf Bks Yng Read.

—Something Silver, Something Blue. Drew, David. LC 92-34256. 1993. 4.25 (0-383-03654-2) SRA Schl Grp.

—What's That Noise? Roennfeldt, Mary. LC 91-16215. 32p. (ps-1). 1992. 13.95 (0-531-05972-3); lib. bdg. 13. 99 (0-531-08572-4) Orchard Bks Watts.

Roes, Ruth. Calculators, Number Patterns, & Magic. Bureloff, Morris & Johnson, Connie. (gr. 4-12). 1977. pap. text ed. 7.95 (0-918932-49-1) Activity Resources.

—Skeletons, Word Problems & Dinosaurs. new ed. Johnson, Connie. Roes, Ruth, ed. (gr. 9-12). 1978. pap. text ed. 7.95 (0-918932-53-X) Activity Resources.

Roessel, Monty, photos by. Kinaalda: A Navajo Girl Grows Up. Roessel, Monty & Dorris, Michaeltext by. LC 92-35204. 1993. 19.95 (0-8225-2655-7) Lerner Pubns.

Roever, Joan M. Snake Secrets. Roever, Joan M. LC 78-4318. (gr. 5 up). 1979. PLB 11.85 (0-8027-6333-2) Walker & Co.

Roffe, Michael, et al. Volcanoes & Earthquakes. Vrbova, Zuza. LC 89-20334. 32p. (gr. 4-6). 1990. PLB 11.59 (0-8167-1977-2); pap. text ed. 3.95 (0-8167-1978-0) Troll Assocs.

Roffey, Maureen. Bathtime. Roffey, Maureen. LC 89-18413. 32p. (ps). 1990. pap. 4.95 (0-689-70808-4, Aladdin) Macmillan Child Grp.

—Door to Door. Lodge, Bernard. LC 93-222003. 32p. (ps-12). 1993. smythe sewn reinforced 14.95 (1-879085-80-1) Whsprng Coyote Pr.

—The Grand Old Duke of York. rev. ed. Lodge, Bernard, contrib. by. LC 92-21339. 32p. (ps-12). 1993. 13.95 (1-879085-79-8) Whsprng Coyote Pr.

—Here, Kitty Kitty! Roffey, Maureen. 24p. (ps). 1991. 6.70 (0-395-57584-2, Sandpiper) HM.

—I Spy at the Zoo. Roffey, Maureen. LC 87-12116. 32p. (ps-2). 1988. SBE 12.95 (0-02-777150-4, Four Winds) Macmillan Child Grp.

—I Spy at the Zoo. Roffey, Maureen. LC 88-19360. 32p. (ps-2). 1989. pap. 3.95 (0-689-71227-8, Aladdin) Macmillan Child Grp.

—Let's Go. MacDonald, Amy. LC 92-46095. 1994. write for info. (1-56402-202-1) Candlewick Pr.

—Let's Make a Noise. MacDonald, Amy. LC 91-71837. 12p. (ps). 1992. bds. 4.95 (1-56402-025-8) Candlewick Pr.

—Let's Play. MacDonald, Amy. LC 91-71838. 12p. (ps). 1992. bds. 4.95 (1-56402-023-1) Candlewick Pr.

—Let's Pretend. MacDonald, Amy. LC 92-47373. 1994. write for info. (1-56402-233-1) Candlewick Pr.

—Let's Try. MacDonald, Amy. LC 91-71839. 12p. (ps). 1992. bds. 4.95 (1-56402-022-3) Candlewick Pr.

—Mealtime. Roffey, Maureen. LC 89-48006. 32p. (ps). 1990. pap. 4.95 (0-689-70809-2, Aladdin) Macmillan Child Grp.

—Quick, Catch Dan! Roffey, Maureen. 24p. (ps). 1991. 6.70 (0-395-57583-4, Sandpiper) HM.

—The Terrible Itch. Roddie, Shen. 24p. (ps-1). 1993. pap. 13.00 casebound (0-671-79169-9, S&S BFYR) S&S Trade.

Roffey, Maureen & Roffey, Maureen. Let's Do It. MacDonald, Amy. LC 91-71836. 12p. (ps). 1992. bds. 4.95 (1-56402-024-X) Candlewick Pr.

Rogasky, Barbara, photos by. Light & Shadow. Livingston, Myra C. LC 91-22355. 32p. (ps-3). 1992. reinforced bdg. 14.95 (0-8234-0931-7) Holiday.

Roger, Alan. Blue Tortoise. Roger, Alan. LC 90-9833. 16p. (ps-1). 1990. PLB 13.27 (0-8368-0404-X) Gareth Stevens Inc.

Roger, Marion. Caribbean ABC. Rogers, Marion. 26p. (Orig.). (ps-1). 1992. pap. 3.50 (0-935357-02-5) CRIC Prod.

Rogers, Alan. Green Bear. Rogers, Alan. LC 90-9831. (ps). 1990. PLB 13.27 (0-8368-0406-6) Gareth Stevens Inc.

—Little Giants, 4 vols. Rogers, Alan. 64p. (ps-1). 1990. Set. PLB 53.08 (0-8368-0434-1) Gareth Stevens Inc.

—Red Rhino. Rogers, Alan. LC 90-9830. 16p. (ps-1). 1990. PLB 13.27 (0-8368-0403-1) Gareth Stevens Inc.

—Yellow Hippo. Rogers, Alan. LC 90-9834. 16p. (ps-1). 1990. PLB 13.27 (0-8368-0405-8) Gareth Stevens Inc.

Rogers, Carl. Pioneers on Early Waterways. McCall, Edith. LC 61-10104. 128p. (gr. 3-10). 1980. PLB 15. 00 (0-516-03357-3) Childrens.

Rogers, Carol. Over the Mormon Trail. Jones, Helen H. LC 63-9706. 128p. (gr. 3-10). 1980. PLB 15.00 (0-516-03354-9) Childrens.

—Pioneering on the Plains. McCall, Edith. LC 62-15638. 128p. (gr. 3-10). 1980. PLB 15.00 (0-516-03358-1) Childrens.

—Settlers on a Strange Shore. McCall, Edith. LC 60-11154. 128p. (gr. 3-10). 1980. PLB 15.00 (0-516-03367-0) Childrens.

—Wagons Over the Mountains. McCall, Edith. LC 61-10101. 128p. (gr. 3-10). 1980. PLB 15.00 (0-516-03376-X) Childrens.

Rogers, Dennis. Presenting Ali Marie in Cabin Fever. Linsenman-Schuh, Norma. 32p. (Orig.). (gr. k-5). 1993. pap. 5.95 (1-884073-03-4); pap. 24.95 incl. doll (1-884073-00-X) Esteem Intl.

Rogers, Gregory. Great-Grandpa. McQuade, Susan. LC 92-27235. 1993. 3.75 (0-383-03622-4) SRA Schl Grp.

—Space Travelers. Wild, Margaret. LC 91-30252. 40p. (gr. 1-4). 1993. 14.95 (0-590-45598-2) Scholastic Inc.

Rogers, Jackie. The Marathon Race Mystery. McNear, Robert & Glassman, Bruce. LC 84-16395. 128p. (gr. 3-7). 1985. lib. bdg. 9.49 (0-8167-0444-9) Troll Assocs.

—The Missing Rock Star Caper. McVey, R. Parker. LC 84-8721. 128p. (gr. 3-7). 1985. lib. bdg. 9.49 (0-8167-0398-1); pap. text ed. 2.95 (0-8167-0399-X) Troll Assocs.

—Monkey See, Monkey Do. Gave, Marc. 32p. (ps-2). 1993. pap. 2.95 (0-590-45801-9) Scholastic Inc.

—Mystery at the Ball Game. McVey, R. Parker. LC 84-8486. 128p. (gr. 3-7). 1985. lib. bdg. 9.49 (0-8167-0336-1); pap. text ed. 2.95 (0-8167-0337-X) Troll Assocs.

—Mystery at the Bike Race. Topper, Frank. LC 84-16452. 128p. (gr. 3-7). 1985. lib. bdg. 9.49 (0-8167-0454-6); pap. text ed. 2.95 (0-8167-0455-4) Troll Assocs.

—William the Vehicle King. Newton, Laura P. LC 86-33412. 32p. (ps-2). 1987. RSBE 13.95 (0-02-768230-7, Bradbury Pr) Macmillan Child Grp.

Rogers, Jacqueline. A Blossom Promise. Byars, Betsy. 160p. (gr. k-6). 1989. pap. 2.95 (0-440-40137-2, YB) Dell.

—The Blossoms & the Green Phantom. Byars, Betsy. 160p. (gr. 4-6). 1987. pap. 14.95 (0-385-29533-2) Delacorte.

—The Blossoms & the Green Phantom. Byars, Betsy. 160p. (gr. k-6). 1988. pap. 2.95 (0-440-40069-4) Dell.

—Cosmic Kidnappers. Randall, E. T. LC 84-8579. 128p. (gr. 3-7). 1985. PLB 9.49 (0-8167-0328-0); pap. text ed. 2.95 (0-8167-0329-9) Troll Assocs.

—Crocodile Christmas: The Pet Lovers Club. Roos, Stephen. LC 91-47079. 128p. (gr. 3-6). 1992. 14.00 (0-385-30681-4) Delacorte.

—Dancing the Breeze. Shannon, George. LC 88-37598. 32p. (ps-1). 1991. RSBE 13.95 (0-02-782190-0, Bradbury Pr) Macmillan Child Grp.

—Emma & Freckles. Beales, Valerie. LC 91-20751. 208p. (gr. 5-9). 1992. pap. 13.00 jacketed, 3-pc. bdg. (0-671-74686-3, S&S BFYR) S&S Trade.

—Freddie & the Doctor. Steel, Danielle. 32p. (Orig.). (gr. 1-3). 1992. pap. 2.99 (0-440-40575-0, YB) Dell.

—Freddie's Accident. Steel, Danielle. 32p. (Orig.). (gr. 1-3). 1992. pap. 2.99 (0-440-40576-9, YB) Dell.

—Getting Rid of Krista. Hest, Amy. LC 87-23981. 80p. (gr. 2-5). 1988. 11.95 (0-688-07149-X) Morrow Jr Bks.

—Kenny & the Little Kickers. Marzollo, Claudio. 32p. 1992. pap. 2.95 (0-590-45417-X) Scholastic Inc.

—Martha's Best Friend. Steel, Danielle. (ps-2). 1989. 8.95 (0-385-29801-3) Delacorte.

—Martha's New Daddy. Steel, Danielle. (ps-2). 1989. 8.95 (0-385-29799-8) Delacorte.

—Martha's New School. Steel, Danielle. (ps-2). 1989. 8.95 (0-385-29800-5) Delacorte.

—Max & the Baby-Sitter. Steel, Danielle. (ps-2). 1989. 8.95 (0-385-29796-3) Delacorte.

—Max's Daddy Goes to the Hospital. Steel, Danielle. (ps-2). 1989. 8.95 (0-385-29797-1) Delacorte.

—Max's New Baby. Steel, Danielle. (ps-2). 1989. 8.95 (0-385-29798-X) Delacorte.

—My Mom Can't Read. Stanek, Muriel. Levine, Abby, ed. LC 86-1637. 32p. (gr. 1-4). 1986. 11.95 (0-8075-5343-3) A Whitman.

—Patrick's Day. O'Donnell, Elizabeth L. LC 92-27421. 1993. write for info. (0-688-07854-0); lib. bdg. write for info. (0-688-07854-0) Morrow Jr Bks.

—The Prince & the Princess: A Bohemian Fairy Tale. Mayer, Marianna. 64p. (gr. 3 up). 1989. 13.95 (0-553-05843-6) Bantam.

—Side Saddle Ballerina. Kirkland, Gelsey & Lawrence, Greg. LC 93-20355. 1993. pap. 14.95 (0-385-46978-0) Doubleday.

—Target: Earth. Randall, E. T. LC 84-2740. 128p. (gr. 3-7). 1985. PLB 9.49 (0-8167-0326-4); pap. text ed. 2.95 (0-8167-0327-2) Troll Assocs.

—Thieves from Space. Randall, E. T. LC 84-8538. 128p. (gr. 3-7). 1985. PLB 9.49 (0-8167-0330-2); pap. text ed. 2.95 (0-8167-0331-0) Troll Assocs.

—Town in Terror. Randall, E. T. LC 84-5617. 128p. (gr. 3-7). 1985. PLB 9.49 (0-8167-0332-9); pap. 2.95 (0-8167-0333-7) Troll Assocs.

—Willy Is My Brother. Parish, Peggy. (ps up). 1989. 12. 95 (0-385-29723-8) Delacorte.

—Winter Wonderland. Smith, Dick & Bernard, Felix. 32p. (ps-1). 1993. pap. 2.50 (0-590-46657-7, Cartwheel) Scholastic Inc.

Rogers, Jacqueline & Holub, Joan. The Scream Machine & other Scary Stories, No. 4. Razzi, Jim. LC 90-85301. (Orig.). (gr. 3-7). 1992. pap. 2.95 (0-448-41084-2, G&D) Putnam Pub Group.

Rogers, Kathy. Arbor Day. Burns, Diane L. 48p. (gr. k-4). 1989. 14.95 (0-87614-346-X) Carolrhoda Bks.

—The Children's ABC Christmas. McKissack, Patricia & McKissack, Frederick. LC 87-73525. 32p. (gr. 1-6). 1988. pap. 5.99 (0-8066-2356-X, 10-1046, Augsburg) Augsburg Fortress.

—God Is Here, I'm Not Afraid. Wade, Evelyn A. LC 88-83019. 32p. (Orig.). 1988. pap. 5.99 (0-8066-2382-9, 10-2646, Augsburg) Augsburg Fortress.

—A Surprise for Mrs. Dodds: A Little Boy's Friendship Changes a Lonely Woman's Life. Long, Kathy. LC 89-84939. 32p. (gr. 3-5). 1989. pap. 5.99 (0-8066-2437-X, 9-2437) Augsburg Fortress.

Rogers, Lynn. Bearman: Exploring the World of Black Bears. Pringle, Laurence. LC 89-5890. 48p. (gr. 5-7). 1989. 13.95 (0-684-19094-X, Scribners Young Read) Macmillan Child Grp.

—Wolf Magic for Kids. Wolpert, Tom. LC 90-50720. 48p. (gr. 2-3). 1991. PLB 18.60 (0-8368-0662-X) Gareth Stevens Inc.

Rogers, Lynn, photos by. The Wonder of Black Bears. Karpfinger, Beth, adapted by. LC 92-16944. 1992. PLB 18.60 (0-8368-0855-X) Gareth Stevens Inc.

Rogers, Nip. Kids & Computers. 2nd ed. Liebowitz, Jay & Zelde, Janet S. 70p. (gr. 3-6). 1989. write for info. (0-9623252-0-1); pap. write for info. (0-9623252-2-8) J Liebowitz.

Rogers, Stillman. South Africa. Rogers, Barbara R. LC 89-43188. 64p. (gr. 5-6). 1991. PLB 19.93 (0-8368-0247-0) Gareth Stevens Inc.

Rogers, Stillman, photos by. South Africa Is My Home. Daniel, Jamie, adapted by. LC 92-17722. 1992. PLB 18.60 (0-8368-0851-7) Gareth Stevens Inc.

—Zambia. Rogers, Barbara R. LC 89-43178. 64p. (gr. 5-6). 1991. PLB 19.93 (0-8368-0257-8) Gareth Stevens Inc.

Rogl, Manfred, photos by. Barn Owls. Epple, Wolfgang. 48p. (gr. 2-5). 1992. 19.95 (0-87614-742-2) Carolrhoda Bks.

Rohling, Claudia. Just Because I Am: A Child's Book of Affirmation. Payne, Lauren M. LC 93-30609. 1994. write for info. (0-915793-60-1) Free Spirit Pub.

Rohner, Thomas. Family Bear Pop-up Book. Van der Meer, Mara. 10p. (gr. k-3). 1994. bds. 9.95 (0-689-71766-0, Aladdin) Macmillan Child Grp.

Rojankovsky, Feodor. The Cabin Faced West. Fritz, Jean. (gr. 4-7). 1958. 13.95 (0-698-20016-0, Coward) Putnam Pub Group.

—Frog Went A-Courtin'. Langstaff, John & Rojankovsky, Feodor. LC 55-5237. 32p. 1955. 14.95 (0-15-230214-X, HB Juv Bks) HarBrace.

—Frog Went A-Courtin'. Langstaff, John & Rojankovsky, Feodor. LC 55-5237. 32p. (ps-3). 1972. pap. 4.95 (0-15-633900-5, Voyager Bks) HarBrace.

—Over in the Meadow. Langstaff, John & Rojankovsky, Feodor. LC 57-8587. (ps-3). 1957. 14.95 (0-15-258854-X, HB Juv Bks) HarBrace.

—Over in the Meadow. Langstaff, John & Rojankovsky, Feodor. LC 57-8587. 32p. (ps-3). 1973. pap. 3.95 (0-15-670500-1, Voyager Bks) HarBrace.
—Over in the Meadow. Langstaff, John. (ps-1). 1992. pap. 19.95 (0-15-258853-1) HarBrace.
—Tall Book of Mother Goose. Rojankovsky, Feodor. 120p. (ps up). 1942. 9.95 (0-06-025055-0) HarpC Child Bks.
—Tall Book of Nursery Tales. Rojankovsky, Feodor. LC 44-3881. 120p. (ps-3). 1944. 9.95 (0-06-025065-8) HarpC Child Bks.
—Three Best-Loved Tales: The Three Bears; The Cow Went over the Mountain; Hop, Little Kangaroo! 80p. (ps-2). 1992. write for info. (0-307-15631-1, 15631, Golden Pr) Western Pub.
Rojanovsky, Feodor. All Alone. Bishop, Claire H. 96p. (gr. 2-5). 1953. 15.00 (0-670-11336-0) Viking Child Bks.
—The Cabin Faced West. Fritz, Jean. (gr. 1-7). 1987. pap. 3.99 (0-14-032256-6, Puffin) Puffin Bks.
—The Double Life of Pocahantas. Fritz, Jean. (gr. 1-7). 1987. pap. 3.99 (0-14-032257-4, Puffin) Puffin Bks.
Rolland, Will. Echidna. Reilly, Pauline. 32p. (Orig.). 1993. pap. 5.95 saddlestitched (0-86417-285-0, Pub. by Kangaroo Pr AT) Seven Hills Bk Dists.
—Emu That Walks Toward Rain. Reilly, Pauline. 32p. (Orig.). 1993. pap. 5.95 saddlestitched (0-86417-059-9, Pub. by Kangaroo Pr AT) Seven Hills Bk Dists.
—Frillneck: An Australian Dragon. Reilly, Pauline. 32p. (Orig.). 1993. pap. 5.95 saddlestitched (0-86417-414-4, Pub. by Kangaroo Pr AT) Seven Hills Bk Dists.
—Galah. Reilly, Pauline. 32p. (Orig.). 1993. pap. 5.95 saddlestitched (0-86417-346-6, Pub. by Kangaroo Pr AT) Seven Hills Bk Dists.
—Kiwi. Reilly, Pauline. 32p. (Orig.). 1993. pap. 5.95 saddlestitched (0-86417-488-8, Pub. by Kangaroo Pr AT) Seven Hills Bk Dists.
—Koala. Reilly, Pauline. 32p. (Orig.). 1993. pap. 5.95 saddlestitched (0-86417-243-5, Pub. by Kangaroo Pr AT) Seven Hills Bk Dists.
—Kookabura That Helps at the Nest. Reilly, Pauline. 32p. (Orig.). 1993. pap. 5.95 saddlestitched (0-86417-119-6, Pub. by Kangaroo Pr AT) Seven Hills Bk Dists.
—Lyrebird That Is Too Busy to Dance. Reilly, Pauline. 32p. (Orig.). 1993. pap. 5.95 saddlestitched (0-86417-086-6, Pub. by Kangaroo Pr AT) Seven Hills Bk Dists.
—Mallefowl: The Incubator Bird. Reilly, Pauline. 32p. (Orig.). 1993. pap. 5.95 saddlestitched (0-86417-317-2, Pub. by Kangaroo Pr AT) Seven Hills Bk Dists.
—The Penguin That Walks at Night. Reilly, Pauline. 32p. (Orig.). 1993. pap. 5.95 saddlestitched (0-86417-034-3, Pub. by Kangaroo Pr AT) Seven Hills Bk Dists.
—Platypus. Reilly, Pauline. 32p. (Orig.). 1993. pap. 5.95 saddlestitched (0-86417-391-1, Pub. by Kangaroo Pr AT) Seven Hills Bk Dists.
—Tasmanian Devil. Reilly, Pauline. 32p. (Orig.). 1993. pap. 5.95 saddlestitched (0-86417-207-9, Pub. by Kangaroo Pr AT) Seven Hills Bk Dists.
—Wombat. Reilly, Pauline. 32p. (Orig.). 1993. pap. 5.95 saddlestitched (0-86417-148-X, Pub. by Kangaroo Pr AT) Seven Hills Bk Dists.
Rollins, Nancy O. Back Yard Attractions. Gaynor, Brigid. (ps). 1992. 15.95 (1-56828-018-1) Red Jacket Pr.
—Backyard Attractions. Gaynor, Brigid. (ps). 1993. Gift box set of bks., 12p. ea. incl. seed packs. bds. 14.95 (1-56828-043-2) Red Jacket Pr.
—The Flower Garden. Gaynor, Brigid. 12p. (ps). 1992. 4.95 (1-56828-014-9) Red Jacket Pr.
—The Home Zoo. Gaynor, Brigid. 12p. (ps). 1992. 4.95 (1-56828-017-3) Red Jacket Pr.
—Things to Do. Gaynor, Brigid. 12p. (ps). 1992. 4.95 (1-56828-015-7) Red Jacket Pr.
—The Vegetable Garden. Gaynor, Brigid. 12p. (ps). 1992. 4.95 (1-56828-016-5) Red Jacket Pr.
Rolph, Mic. Amazing Schemes within Your Genes. Balkwill, Fran. LC 92-42942. (gr. 3 up). 1993. 17.50 (0-87614-804-6) Carolrhoda Bks.
—Cell Wars. Balkwill, Fran. LC 92-6377. 1992. 17.50 (0-87614-761-9) Carolrhoda Bks.
—Cells Are Us. Balkwill, Fran. (gr. 3-6). 1993. 17.50 (0-87614-762-7) Carolrhoda Bks.
—DNA Is Here to Stay. Balkwill, Fran. 32p. (gr. 3-6). 1993. 17.50 (0-87614-763-5) Carolrhoda Bks.
Rom, Holly M. Mathematician & Computer Scientist. Caryn Navy. Verheyden-Hilliard, Mary E. LC 87-82595. 32p. (Orig.). (gr. 1-4). 1988. pap. 5.00 (0-932469-12-4) Equity Inst.
—Scientist & Activist. Phyllis Stearner. Verheyden-Hilliard, Mary E. LC 87-82597. 32p. (Orig.). (gr. 1-4). 1988. pap. 5.00 (0-932469-15-9) Equity Inst.
—Scientist & Strategist, June Rooks. Verheyden-Hilliard, Mary E. LC 87-82596. 32p. (Orig.). (gr. 1-4). 1988. pap. 5.00 (0-932469-14-0) Equity Inst.
—Scientist & Teacher, Anne Barrett Swanson. Verheyden-Hilliard, Mary E. LC 87-82598. 32p. (Orig.). (gr. 1-4). 1988. pap. 5.00 (0-932469-16-7) Equity Inst.
Rom, Holly M., jt. illus. see Biro, Scarlet.
Roman, Barbara. Jenny & the Grand Old Great-Aunts. Rodowsky, Colby. LC 90-42563. 40p. (gr. 1-4). 1992. RSBE 12.95 (0-02-777785-5, Bradbury Pr) Macmillan Child Grp.
Roman, Barbara J. Shoemaker & the Elves. Grimm, Jacob & Grimm, Wilhelm K. 32p. (ps-3). 1992. 6.95 (0-8362-4923-2) Andrews & McMeel.

Roman, Irena. The Voice from the Mendelsohns Maple. Ryan, Mary C. LC 89-31569. 132p. (gr. 5-7). 1990. 13.95 (0-316-76360-8) Little.
Romanelli, Serena. Fabian Youngpig Sails the World. Ostheeren, Ingrid. James, Alison, tr. from GER. LC 91-16531. 32p. (gr. k-3). 1992. 14.95 (1-55858-125-1); lib. bdg. 14.88 (1-55858-145-6) North-South Bks NYC.
Rombola, John. Counting Sheep. Archambault, John. LC 89-11163. 32p. (ps-2). 1989. 14.95 (0-8050-1135-8, Bks Young Read) H Holt & Co.
Ronan, Frank, jt. illus. see Meyerriecks, William.
Ronchi, Susanna. Where in the World Is Geo? A Child's First Atlas. 12p. (ps-4). 1991. bds. 14.95 (0-8120-6251-5) Barron.
Ronguillo, Resty. America Becomes a World Power, 1890-1920. Farr, Naunerle. Calhoun, D'Ann & Bloch, Lawrence W., eds. (gr. 4-12). 1977. pap. text ed. 2.95 (0-88301-199-9); student book 1.25 (0-88301-236-7) Pendulum Pr.
Ronniger, Mary S. Bach to Rock: An Introduction to Famous Composers & Their Music. 6th, rev. ed. Kennedy, Rosemary G. 161p. (gr. 4-9). 1989. pap. 14.95 (0-685-45404-5); audio cassette 16.95 (0-685-45405-3) Rosemary Corp.
Root, Barrett. April, Bubbles, Chocolate. Hopkins, Lee B., compiled by. LC 92-17100. 1994. pap. 15.00 (0-671-75911-6, S&S BFYR) S&S Trade.
—Someplace Else. Saul, Carol P. (gr. 4 up). 1995. pap. 14.00 (0-671-87283-4, S&S BFYR) S&S Trade.
Root, Barrett V. The Saint & the Circus. Piumini, Roberto. Holmes, Olivia, tr. from ITA. LC 90-23481. 32p. (ps-3). 1991. 14.95 (0-688-10377-4, Tambourine Bks); PLB 14.88 (0-688-10378-2, Tambourine Bks) Morrow.
Root, Barry. Alvah & Arvilla. Ray, Mary L. LC 93-31874. 1994. 16.95 (0-15-202655-X) HarBrace.
—The Araboolies of Liberty Street. Swope, Sam. LC 88-12687. 32p. (ps). 1989. 15.00 (0-517-56960-4, Clarkson Potter); PLB 15.99 (G-517-57411-X) Crown Bks Yng Read.
—Chinook! Tunnell, Michael O. LC 92-12711. 32p. (gr. k up). 1993. 14.00 (0-688-10869-5, Tambourine Bks); PLB 13.93 (0-688-10870-9, Tambourine Bks) Morrow.
—The Christmas Box. Wetzel, JoAnne S. LC 91-38911. 32p. (ps-3). 1992. 13.00 (0-679-81789-1); PLB 13.99 (0-679-91789-6) Knopf Bks Yng Read.
—Old Devil Wind. Martin, Bill, Jr LC 92-37908. 1993. 13.95 (0-15-257768-8) HarBrace.
—The Singing Fir Tree. Stone, Marti. 32p. (ps-3). 1992. 14.95 (0-399-22207-3, Putnam) Putnam Pub Group.
—Two Cool Cows. Speed, Toby. LC 93-34258. 1995. write for info. (0-399-22647-8, Putnam) Putnam Pub Group.
Root, Joseph. Further Adventures of Figaro. Eglsaer, Marie-Therese. Eglsaer, Robert J., ed. LC 89-61954. 108p. (Orig.). (gr. 8-10). 1989. pap. write for info. (0-88100-061-2) Natl Writ Pr.
Root, Kim. In a Messy, Messy Room: And Other Strange Stories. Gorog, Judith. 48p. (gr. 4-7). 1990. 14.95 (0-399-22218-9, Philomel Bks) Putnam Pub Group.
Root, Kimberly. Granny Will Your Dog Bite? And Other Mountain Rhymes. Milnes, Gerald. LC 88-27350. 48p. 1990. 14.95 (0-394-84749-0) Knopf Bks Yng Read.
—Granny Will Your Dog Bite? And Other Mountain Rhymes. Milnes, Gerald. Bird, Sonja, contrib. by. LC 88-27350. 48p. 1990. Incl. 40 min. cassette. slipcase 18.95 (0-394-85363-6) Knopf Bks Yng Read.
Root, Kimberly B. Beggars, Beasts & Easter Fire: Stories of Early Saints. Greene, Carol. Klausmeier, Robert, ed. LC 92-31408. 128p. (gr. 3-6). 1993. 15.95 (0-7459-2221-X) Lion USA.
—Billy Beg & His Bull: An Irish Tale. Greene, Ellin, retold by. LC 93-7730. 32p. (gr. 4-8). 1994. 15.95 (0-8234-1100-1) Holiday.
—Boots & His Brothers: A Tale from Norway. Kimmel, Eric A., retold by. LC 90-23659. 32p. (gr. k-3). 1992. reinforced bdg. 14.95 (0-8234-0886-8) Holiday.
—Hugh Can Do. Armstrong, Jennifer. LC 90-46275. 40p. (ps-4). 1992. 15.00 (0-517-58218-X); PLB 15.99 (0-517-58219-8) Crown Bks Yng Read.
—If I'd Known Then What I Know Now. Lindbergh, Reeve. LC 93-24058. 1994. write for info. (0-670-85351-8) Viking Child Bks.
—The Palace of Stars. Lakin, Patricia. LC 92-36796. 32p. (ps up). 1993. 15.00 (0-688-11176-9, Tambourine Bks); PLB 13.93 (0-688-11177-7, Tambourine Bks) Morrow.
—Papa's Bedtime Story. Donovan, Mary L. LC 91-27792. 40p. (ps-3). 1993. 15.00 (0-679-81790-5); PLB 15.99 (0-679-91790-X) Knopf Bks Yng Read.
Rorer, Abigail. Maybe I Will Do Something: Seven Coyote Tales. Ude, Wayne. LC 92-29392. 1993. 14.95 (0-395-65233-2) HM.
Rosa, Don, jt. illus. see Barks, Carl.
Rosado, Puig. Gentil Petit Diable et Autres Contes de la Rue Broca. Gripari, Pierre. (FRE). 157p. (gr. 5-10). 1988. pap. 7.95 (2-07-033451-1) Schoenhof.
—Sorciere de la Rue Mouffetard et Autres Contes de la Rue Broca. Gripari, Pierre. (FRE). 153p. (gr. 5-10). 1987. pap. 7.95 (2-07-033440-6) Schoenhof.
Rosales, Melodye. Addy Learns a Lesson. Porter, Connie. 70p. (gr. 2-5). 1993. PLB 12.95 (1-56247-078-7); pap. 5.95 (1-56247-077-9) Pleasant Co.
—Beans on the Roof. Byars, Betsy. 80p. (gr. k-3). 1988. pap. 13.95 (0-440-50055-9) Delacorte.

—Double Dutch & the Voodoo Shoes: An Urban Folktale. Rosales, Melodye. LC 91-13153. 32p. (ps-3). 1991. PLB 16.93 (0-516-05133-4); pap. 5.95 (0-516-45133-2) Childrens.
—The Good Witch. Wang, Mary L. LC 89-34415. 32p. (ps-2). 1989. PLB 11.93 (0-516-02368-3); pap. 3.95 (0-516-42368-1) Childrens.
—Jackson Jones & the Puddle of Thorns. Quattlebaum, Mary. LC 93-11433. (gr. 4-7). 1994. 13.95 (0-385-31165-6) Delacorte.
—Kwanzaa. Chocolate, Deborah M. LC 89-25418. 32p. (ps-3). 1990. PLB 15.00 (0-516-03991-1); pap. 3.95 (0-516-43991-X) Childrens.
—Meet Addy. Porter, Connie. 69p. (Orig.). (gr. 2-5). 1993. PLB 12.95 (1-56247-076-0); pap. 5.95 (1-56247-075-2) Pleasant Co.
—The Mystery of the Hard Luck Rodeo. Saunders, Susan. LC 88-37896. 64p. (Orig.). (gr. 2-4). 1989. PLB 6.99 (0-394-92344-8); pap. 1.95 (0-394-82344-3) Random Bks Yng Read.
—Thirty-Eight Weeks Till Summer Vacation. Kerby, Mona. 128p. (gr. 4-7). 1989. pap. 12.00 (0-670-82887-4) Viking Child Bks.
Rosamilia, Patricia. Little Big Girl. Horner, Althea J. 32p. (ps-3). 1982. 14.95 (0-89885-098-3); pap. 9.95 (0-89885-287-0) Human Sci Pr.
—Losing Your Best Friend. Bergstrom, Corinne. LC 79-20622. 32p. (ps-3). 1980. 16.95 (0-87705-471-1) Human Sci Pr.
Rosato, Amelia. The Lost Coin. O'Neal, Debbie T. & Rosato, Amelia. LC 92-46610. 14p. 1993. 7.00 (0-8170-1194-3) Judson.
—The Lost Sheep. O'Neal, Debbie T. & Rosato, Amelia. LC 92-46612. 14p. 1993. 7.00 (0-8170-1193-5) Judson.
Rosato, Amelio. Brer Anansi & the Boat Race: A Folk Tale from the Caribbean. Makhanlall, David. LC 88-925. 32p. (gr. k-3). 1988. PLB 14.95 (0-87226-184-0, Bedrick Blackie) P Bedrick Bks.
Rosborough, Thomas A. Moon Magic: Stories from Asia. Davison, Katherine. LC 92-44504. 1993. 18.95 (0-87614-751-1) Carolrhoda Bks.
Roschana. Korean Word Book. Pihl, Marshall R. LC 93-73161. (KOR & ENG.). 112p. (gr. k-6). 1993. 15.95 (1-880188-53-8); pap. 11.95 (1-880188-52-X) Bess Pr.
Rose, Ann C. Copasetic: Adventures of Bojangles Robinson. Pepper Bird Staff. 48p. (Orig.). (gr. 4-7). 1993. pap. 3.95 (1-56817-000-9) Pepper Bird.
—Frozen Fury: Adventures of Matthew Henson. Pepper Bird Staff. 48p. (Orig.). (gr. 4-7). 1993. pap. 4.95 (1-56817-001-7) Pepper Bird.
—Pea Island Rescue. Pepper Bird Staff. 48p. (Orig.). (gr. 4-7). 1993. pap. 4.95 (1-56817-002-5) Pepper Bird.
—Wild Frontier: Adventures of Jean Baptiste Du Sable. Pepper Bird Staff. 48p. (Orig.). (gr. 4-7). 1993. pap. 4.95 (1-56817-003-3) Pepper Bird.
Rose, Carl. The Blue-Nosed Witch. Embry, Margaret. 48p. (gr. 2-5). 1984. pap. 2.75 (0-553-15435-4) Bantam.
Rose, David. Dorothy & the Magic Belt. Saunders, Susan. LC 84-17946. 64p. (gr. 2-6). 1985. pap. 1.95 (0-394-87067-0) Random Bks Yng Read.
—Jed's Junior Space Patrol. Marzollo, Jean & Marzollo, Claudio. LC 81-12483. 56p. (ps-3). 1982. Dial Bks Young.
—The Teddy Bear Tree. Dillon, Barbara. MacDonald, Patricia, ed. 80p. (gr. 2-5). 1990. pap. 2.95 (0-671-68432-9, Minstrel Bks) PB.
—There's a Monster under My Bed. Howe, James. LC 89-18664. 32p. (gr. k-3). 1990. pap. 3.95 (0-689-71409-2, Aladdin) Macmillan Child Grp.
Rose, David S. Maynard's Dreams. Rose, David S. LC 92-43146. 32p. (ps-3). 1993. SBE 14.95 (0-689-31847-2, Atheneum Child Bk) Macmillan Child Grp.
—Teddy Bear's Scrapbook. Howe, Deborah & Howe, James. LC 87-1096. 80p. (gr. 2-6). 1988. pap. 3.50 (0-689-71168-9, Aladdin) Macmillan Child Grp.
—Teddy Bear's Scrapbook. 2nd ed. Howe, Deborah & Howe, James. 80p. (gr. 3-7). 1994. pap. 3.95 (0-689-71812-8, Aladdin) Macmillan Child Grp.
—There's a Dragon in My Sleeping Bag. Howe, James. LC 93-26572. 1994. 14.95 (0-689-31873-1, Atheneum Child Bk) Macmillan Child Grp.
—There's a Monster under My Bed. Howe, James. LC 85-20026. 32p. (ps-2). 1986. SBE 13.95 (0-689-31178-8, Atheneum Child Bk) Macmillan Child Grp.
Rose, Eve. Woody, Be Good! A First Book of Manners. Lundell, Margo. 24p. (ps-2). 1988. 3.95 (0-448-09288-3, G&D) Putnam Pub Group.
—Woody's First Dictionary. Kovacs, Deborah. 24p. (ps-2). 1988. 3.95 (0-448-09287-5, G&D) Putnam Pub Group.
Rose, Gerald. Laugh out Loud: More Funny Stories for Children. Corrin, Sara & Corrin, Stephen, eds. 116p. (gr. k-2). 1991. pap. 2.95 (0-571-14177-3) Faber & Faber.
Rose, Krystal. Recollections of a Mountain Boy Plus Stories of Sudden Death. Fleming, Red. Rose, Jennifer, ed. 112p. (Orig.). 1992. pap. 9.95 (0-930401-55-7) Artex Pub.
Rose, Mary K. The Children's Tarot: The Road Is a River. Rose, Mary K. 52p. (Orig.). (ps-8). 1993. pap. 18.95 incl. audio cass. & set of 24 cards (0-9636234-0-0) Wild Rose CO.

Rose, Mitchell. Getting Along: A Set of Fun-Filled Stories, Songs, & Activities to Help Children Work & Play Together. Page, Parker. LC 88-71899. 64p. (Orig.). (ps-5). 1989. 12.95 (0-929831-00-4) Childrens TV Resource.
Rose, Mitchell, jt. illus. see Young, Ruth.
Rose, Steve. Searching for Treasure Coloring Book. Elwell, Marty. 1992. 5.00 (0-923463-85-2) Noble Pub Assocs.
Rose, Ted. The Banshee Train. Bodkin, Odds. LC 93-39635. Date not set. write for info. (0-395-69426-4, Clarion Bks) HM.
Rosenberg, Amye. Five Little Kittens. Peters, Sharon. LC 81-2317. 32p. (gr. k-2). 1981. PLB 11.59 (0-89375-503-6); pap. 2.95 (0-89375-504-4) Troll Assocs.
—Jewels for Josephine. Rosenberg, Amye. 28p. (ps-2). 1993. 12.95 (0-448-40457-5, G&D) Putnam Pub Group.
—Maxwell Mouse. Gordon, Sharon. LC 81-4653. 32p. (gr. k-2). 1981. PLB 11.59 (0-89375-501-X); pap. 2.95 (0-89375-502-8) Troll Assocs.
—Nursery Rhymes. 24p. (ps-1). 1987. pap. 1.25 (0-7214-9550-8, S871-6) Ladybird Bks.
—The Pudgy Peek-a-Boo Book. 16p. (ps). 1983. pap. 2.95 (0-448-10205-6, G&D) Putnam Pub Group.
—Sam the Detective & the Alef Bet Mystery. Rosenberg, Amye & Mason, Patrice G. Rossel, Seymour, ed. 64p. (Orig.). (gr. 1-3). 1980. pap. text ed. 4.45 (0-87441-328-1) Behrman.
Rosenberg, Amye & Weihs, Erika. Exploring Our Living Past. Simms, Laura & Kozodoy, Ruth. Harlow, Jules, ed. (gr. k-2). 1978. pap. 7.95 (0-87441-309-5); tchr's guide 19.95x (0-87441-276-5) Behrman.
Rosenberry, Vera. Anne Frank: A Life in Hiding. Hurwitz, Johanna. 64p. (gr. 2-5). 1988. 12.95 (0-8276-0311-8) JPS Phila.
—Anne Frank: Life in Hiding. Hurwitz, Johanna. LC 92-29826. 64p. (gr. 4). 1993. pap. 3.95 (0-688-12405-4, Pub. by Beech Tree Bks) Morrow.
—Esther. Chaikin, Miriam. LC 86-20183. 32p. (gr. 2-6). 1987. 9.95 (0-8276-0272-3); pap. 7.95 (0-8276-0508-0) JPS Phila.
—Marc Chagall: Painter of Dreams. Bober, Natalie S. LC 91-25463. 124p. (gr. 4-8). 1991. 14.95 (0-8276-0379-7) JPS Phila.
—The Outside Inn. Lyon, George-Ella. LC 90-14285. 32p. (ps-1). 1991. 13.95 (0-531-05936-7); RLB 13.99 (0-531-08536-8) Orchard Bks Watts.
—Savitri: A Tale of Ancient India. Shepard, Aaron. Mathews, Judith, ed. LC 91-16591. 40p. (gr. 1-6). 1992. PLB 15.95 (0-8075-7251-9) A Whitman.
—Together. Lyon, George Ella. LC 89-2892. 32p. (ps-1). 1994. pap. 5.95 (0-531-07047-6) Orchard Bks Watts.
—William's Ninth Life. Jung, Minna. LC 92-44520. 32p. (ps-2). 1993. 14.95 (0-531-05492-6); PLB 14.99 (0-531-08642-9) Orchard Bks Watts.
Rosenblatt, Naomi. Virginia Woolf for Beginners. Rosenblatt, Aaron. (Orig.). (gr. 11 up). 1987. pap. 7.95 (0-86316-133-2) Writers & Readers.
Rosenbloom, Richard. How to Win a School Election. Dunnahoo, Terry. LC 88-30341. 96p. (gr. 10-12). 1990. 12.90 (0-531-10695-0) Watts.
Rosenbloom, Roger. The Old Synagogue. Rosenbloom, Richard. 32p. (gr. k-3). 1989. 12.95 (0-8276-0322-3) JPS Phila.
Rosenblum, R. My Synagogue. Weisser, M. 25p. (gr. k-5). 1984. pap. text ed. 4.25 (0-87441-386-9) Behrman.
Rosenblum, Richard. Brooklyn Dodger Days. Rosenblum, Richard. LC 90-36691. 32p. (gr. 1-5). 1991. SBE 12.95 (0-689-31512-0, Atheneum Child Bk) Macmillan Child Grp.
—Danger--Icebergs! Revised Edition of Icebergs. Gans, Roma. LC 87-45143. 32p. (ps-3). 1987. pap. 4.50 (0-06-445066-X, Trophy) HarpC Child Bks.
—Earthquakes. Branley, Franklyn M. LC 89-35424. 32p. (gr. k-4). 1990. 14.00 (0-690-04661-8, Crowell Jr Bks); PLB 13.89 (0-690-04663-4, Crowell Jr Bks) HarpC Child Bks.
—Journey to the Golden Land. Rosenblum, Richard. LC 91-44941. 32p. (gr. k-4). 1992. 14.95 (0-8276-0405-X) JPS Phila.
—My Land of Israel. Nover, Elizabeth Z. 35p. (Orig.). (gr. 1-2). 1987. pap. text ed. 4.25 (0-87441-447-4) Behrman.
Rosenfeld, Eileen. Rational Stories for Children. Waters, Virginia. 1980. pap. 8.95 (0-917476-18-2) Inst Rational-Emotive.
Rosenthal, David. What Can I Do? Asked the Kangaroo. Rosenthal, Ellie. 1993. 7.95 (0-533-10358-4) Vantage.
Rosenthal, Linda. Circles in the Sand. Macht, Philip. LC 84-90597. 64p. (gr. 7 up). 1985. 12.95 (0-930339-00-2) Maxrom Pr.
Rosenthal, Marc. Where on Earth: A Geografunny Guide to the Globe. Rosenthal, Paul. LC 92-1227. 112p. (Orig.). (gr. 3-7). 1992. 15.99 (0-679-80833-1); pap. 11.00 (0-679-80833-7) Knopf Bks Yng Read.
Rosinski, Bob, jt. photog. see Shahild, Wendy.
Rosinski, Grzegorz. The Legend of King Piast. Seidler, Babara. Kedron, Jane, tr. (gr. 2-8). 1977. pap. 1.00 (0-917004-08-6) Kosciuszko.
Rosner, Meryl. Ella of All-of-a-Kind Family. Taylor, Sydney. 133p. (gr. 4-8). 1988. Repr. of 1978 ed. 11.95 (0-929093-04-6) Taylor Prodns.
—The Tenement Writer: An Immigrant's Story. Sonder, Ben. LC 92-14400. 72p. (gr. 2-5). 1992. PLB 21.34 (0-8114-7235-3) Raintree Steck-V.

Rosner, Ruth. Arabba, Gah, Zee, Marissa & Me! Rosner, Ruth. Fay, Ann, ed. LC 86-15904. 32p. (ps-3). 1987. PLB 13.95 (0-8075-0442-4) A Whitman.
Ross, Alison. Daytime Baby: Baby Books. 8p. (ps). 1992. bds. 3.50 (0-7214-1515-6, S9212-4) Ladybird Bks.
—Hello Baby: Baby Books. 8p. (ps). 1992. bds. 3.50 (0-7214-1497-4, S9212-3) Ladybird Bks.
—Noisy Baby: Baby Books. 8p. (ps). 1992. bds. 3.50 (0-7214-1496-6, S9212-1) Ladybird Bks.
—Playtime Baby: Baby Books. 8p. (ps). 1992. bds. 3.50 (0-7214-1514-8, S9212-2) Ladybird Bks.

Ross, Andrea. Chester's Coloring Book. Ross, Andrea. 70p. (Orig.). (gr. k-2). 1992. 7.00 (1-56002-016-4, Univ Edtns) Aegina Pr.
CHESTER'S COLORING BOOK is a reading/coloring book. One page has the story/small picture...the next page has a larger version of small picture with coloring words but no text. 70 pages/$7 each. It is the story about Chester the little black earth ant. He lived in a beautiful valley, with grass & trees & sunlight & lots of other friendly ants. But Chester was so unhappy - none of the other ants were like him, & he did not like where he was. "STORY BOOK"...a children's television show created by Andrea Ross, won a P.A.L. Award for "BEST CHILDREN'S SHOW" on Paragon Cable in New York City. "CHESTER'S story is a real one & you've told it beautifully. He's unique & there should be other stories like: CHESTER Goes to Washington, CHESTER Goes to School..."--Andy Rooney/60 Minutes, CBS-TV. "CHESTER'S COLORING BOOK looks good. Thanks for passing it along. What a great little person Chester is. The children will adore him & all of his wonderful stories. My kids were thrilled."--Faith Daniels/NBC News Dept. "What a wonderful, happy book...CHESTER'S COLORING BOOK...You are a sensitive, courageous writer."--Dan Rather/CBS News Dept. "I am pleased about your success with CHESTER'S COLORING BOOK. It is a good learning tool. There's a magical, charismatic quality about Chester!"-- Bill Cosby/The Cosby Show.
Publisher Provided Annotation.

Ross, Bill. Crazy Christmas Characters. (Orig.). (ps-2). 1991. pap. 2.95 (0-8249-8522-2, Ideals Child) Hambleton-Hill.
—Easter Bunnyheads. 12p. (Orig.). (ps-2). 1992. pap. 2.95 (0-8249-8541-9, Ideals Child) Hambleton-Hill.
—Easter Eggheads. 12p. (Orig.). (ps-2). 1992. pap. 2.95 (0-8249-8540-0, Ideals Child) Hambleton-Hill.
Ross, Christine. Lily & the Present. Ross, Christine. LC 91-41134. 28p. (ps-3). 1992. 13.95 (0-395-61127-X) HM.
Ross, Connie. Betty Elizabeth Brown: A Keepsake Book. Larungu, Rute, as told by. 32p. (ps up). 1992. pap. 2.75 (1-878893-26-2) Telcraft Bks.
—Dearie Dot: A Keepsake Book. Larungu, Rute, as told by. 32p. (ps up). 1992. pap. 2.75 (1-878893-25-4) Telcraft Bks.
—Fun with Aesop, Vol. I. Tell, Paul. 32p. (gr. 2-6). 1991. pap. 2.25 (1-878893-06-8) Telcraft Bks.
—Fun with Aesop, Vol. II. Tell, Paul. 32p. (gr. 2-6). 1991. pap. 2.25 (1-878893-07-6) Telcraft Bks.
—Fun with Aesop, Vol. III. Tell, Paul. 32p. (gr. 2-6). 1991. pap. 2.25 (1-878893-08-4) Telcraft Bks.
—Fun with Aesop, 3 vols. Tell, Paul. 32p. (gr. 2-6). 1991. Set. pap. 6.75 (1-878893-09-2) Telcraft Bks.
—Fun with Aesop Reader. Tell, Paul. LC 91-90956. 96p. (gr. 2-6). 1991. 9.95 (1-878893-05-X); lib. bdg. 14.95 (1-878893-10-6); pap. 5.95 (1-878893-04-1) Telcraft Bks.
—The Pilgrims Thanksgiving: A Keepsake Book. Williams, Dianna. 32p. (gr. 2-6). 1992. pap. 2.75 (1-878893-27-0) Telcraft Bks.
—The Pilgrims Thanksgiving: With Thanksgiving Journal & Activities. Williams, Dianna. 32p. (gr. 2-6). 1991. pap. text ed. 1.95 (1-878893-16-5, Telecraft) Telcraft Bks.

Ross, Dave. A Book of Hugs. Ross, Dave. LC 79-7896. 32p. (gr. k up). 1991. pap. 3.95 (0-06-107418-7) HarpC Child Bks.
—Tiny Turtle's Thanksgiving. Ross, Dave. LC 86-5412. 32p. (ps-k). 1986. 12.95 (0-688-06440-X); lib. bdg. 12. 88 (0-688-06441-8, Morrow Jr Bks) Morrow Jr Bks.
Ross, David. Illustrated Soccer Dictionary for Young People. Gardner, James. 125p. (gr. 4 up). 1978. pap. 2.50 (0-13-451146-8, Pub. by Treehouse) P-H.
Ross, Jane. Little Eagle Lots of Owls. Edmiston, Jim. LC 92-22683. 32p. (gr. k-3). 1993. 13.95 (0-395-65564-1) HM.
Ross, Larry. C.L.U.T.Z. Wilkes, Marilyn. LC 81-68786. 128p. (gr. 3-7). 1982. 9.95 (0-8037-1157-3, 0966-290) Dial Bks Young.
—Hardie Gramatky's Little Toot. Ryder, Joanne, adapted by. 32p. (ps-2). 1988. pap. 2.25 (0-448-34301-0, Platt & Munk Pubs) Putnam Pub Group.
Ross, Richard. Guns for General Washington: The Impossible Journey. Reit, Seymour. 98p. (gr. 3-7). 1990. 15.95 (0-15-200466-1, Gulliver Bks) HarBrace.
Ross, Steve. Wildlife Rescue. Ford, Barbara. Tucker, Kathleen, ed. LC 87-6133. 48p. (gr. 3-7). 1987. PLB 11.95 (0-8075-9099-1) A Whitman.
Ross, Sueellen. Dachshund Tails Down the Yukon. Mosley, Marilyn C. 112p. (Orig.). (gr. 5). 1988. pap. 5.95 (0-9614850-2-7) M C Mosley.

Ross, Suzanne. What's in the Rainforest? One Hundred Six Answers from A to Z. Ross, Suzanne. LC 91-72682. 48p. (Orig.). (gr. 1-7). 1991. pap. 5.95 (0-9629895-0-9) Enchanted Rain Pr.
In this book you will find 106 interesting & sometimes startling examples of the many creatures that dwell in the world's tropical rainforests. "A well known organized dictionary of the rainforest & its inhabitants. An extensive introduction provides some background information, followed by brief descriptions of a select list of plants & animals. A map outlining the world's rainforests is provided. The climate is discussed, as are the three layers that make up its unique structure...drawings of some of the plants & animals break up the text."-- School Library Journal. "For those working to raise rainforest awareness, a new tool for reaching 7 to 12 year-olds...106 examples of flora & fauna from the world's rainforests...familiar terms like gorilla & orchid are accompanied by unusual words such as. ..rafflesia (a three-foot-wide leafless parasite plant), & agouti (a rodent that can jump about 6 1/2 feet, straight up) - that may add to parents' knowledge of the rainforest as well."--World Monitor Magazine. "A book that teaches the importance of the rainforest in a fun & creative way."--Rainforest Action Network. $5.95 plus postage. Enchanted Rainforest Press, Box 29885, L.A., CA 90029. (213) 663-3405. FAX (818) 766-2905.
Publisher Provided Annotation.

Ross, Tony. Alice's Adventures in Wonderland. Carroll, Lewis. LC 93-72323. 128p. (gr. 2 up). 1994. SBE 16. 95 (0-689-31864-2, Atheneum Child Bk) Macmillan Child Grp.
—Clement Aplati. Brown, Jeff. (FRE.). 79p. 1989. pap. 10.95 (2-07-031196-1) Schoenhof.
—Don't Do That! Ross, Tony. LC 91-9347. 32p. (ps-2). 1991. 12.00 (0-517-58575-8) Crown Bks Yng Read.
—Earth Mobiles, As Explained by Professor Xargle. Willis, Jeanne. LC 91-23500. 32p. (ps-2). 1992. 14.00 (0-525-44892-6, DCB) Dutton Child Bks.
—Earth Tigerlets, As Explained by Professor Xargle. Willis, Jeanne. LC 90-19346. 32p. (ps-2). 1991. 13.95 (0-525-44732-6, DCB) Dutton Child Bks.
—Earth Weather As Explained by Professor Xargle. Willis, Jeanne. LC 92-14067. 32p. (ps-2). 1993. Repr. of 1991 ed. 14.00 (0-525-45025-4, DCB) Dutton Child Bks.
—Earthlets, As Explained by Professor Xargle. Willis, Jeanne. LC 88-23692. 32p. (ps-2). 1989. 14.00 (0-525-44465-3, DCB) Dutton Child Bks.
—A Fairy Tale. Ross, Tony. 32p. (ps-3). 1992. cancelled 13.95 (0-316-75750-0) Little.
—Fantastique Maitre Renard. Dahl, Roald. (FRE.). 119p. (gr. 3-7). 1989. pap. 10.95 (2-07-031174-0) Schoenhof.

—Going Green: A Kid's Handbook to Saving the Planet. Elkington, John, et al. 96p. (gr. 3 up). 1990. 16.00 (0-670-83611-7) Viking Child Bks.
—Goldilocks & the Three Bears. Ross, Tony, retold by. 26p. (ps-3). 1992. 13.95 (0-87951-453-1) Overlook Pr.
—Hare & Badger Go to Town. Lewis, Naomi. 32p. (ps-1). 1987. 9.95 (0-905478-94-0, Pub. by Century UK) Trafalgar.
—If Cats Could Fly. large type ed. Westall, Robert. 1992. 13.95 (0-7451-1639-6, Galaxy Child Lrg Print) Chivers N Amer.
—Invasion of the Comet People: A Capers Book. Curtis, Philip. LC 82-9923. 128p. (gr. 3-5). 1983. lib. bdg. 5.99 (0-394-95490-4) Knopf Bks Yng Read.
—The Knight Who Was Afraid of the Dark. Hazen, Barbara S. LC 88-18149. 32p. (ps-3). 1989. 12.95 (0-8037-0667-7); PLB 12.89 (0-8037-0668-5) Dial Bks Young.
—The Knight Who Was Afraid of the Dark. Hazen, Barbara S. LC 88-18149. 32p. (ps-3). 1992. pap. 3.99 (0-14-054545-X, Puffin Pied Piper) Puffin Bks.
—The Magic Finger. Dahl, Roald. LC 92-31443. 64p. (gr. 2-6). 1993. pap. 3.99 (0-14-036303-3) Puffin Bks.
—Mallory Cox & His Interstellar Socks. Matthews, Andrew. 96p. (gr. 4-6). 1993. 18.95 (0-460-88126-4, Pub. by J M Dent & Sons) Trafalgar.
—Meanwhile Back at the Ranch. Noble, Trinka H. LC 86-11651. 32p. (ps-3). 1987. 13.95 (0-8037-0353-8); PLB 13.89 (0-8037-0354-6) Dial Bks Young.
—Meanwhile Back at the Ranch. Noble, Trinka H. 32p. (ps-3). 1992. pap. 3.99 (0-14-054564-6, Puffin Pied Piper) Puffin Bks.
—Michael. Bradman, Tony. LC 90-40523. 32p. (ps-2). 1991. SBE 13.95 (0-02-711850-9, Macmillan Child Bk) Macmillan Child Grp.
—Mrs. Goat & Her Seven Little Kids. Ross, Tony. LC 89-17933. 32p. (gr. 1-3). 1990. SBE 13.95 (0-689-31624-0, Atheneum Child Bk) Macmillan Child Grp.
—Reckless Ruby. Oram, Hiawyn. LC 91-20124. 32p. (ps-2). 1992. 12.00 (0-517-58744-0) Crown Bks Yng Read.
—Relativity, As Explained by Professor Xargle. Willis, Jeanne. LC 93-32606. (gr. 5 up). 1994. write for info. (0-525-45245-1, DCB) Dutton Child Bks.
—Through the Looking-Glass. abr. ed. Carroll, Lewis. 128p. (gr. 4-7). 1993. Repr. of 1993 ed. SBE 16.95 (0-689-31863-4, Atheneum Child Bk) Macmillan Child Grp.
—Towser & the Haunted House. Ross, Tony. 32p. (ps-1). 1987. 5.95 (0-86264-079-2, Pub. by Anderson Pr UK) Trafalgar.
—Towser & the Magic Apple. Ross, Tony. 32p. (ps-1). 1987. 5.95 (0-86264-078-4, Pub. by Anderson Pr UK) Trafalgar.
—Well, I Never! Eyles, Heather. 32p. (ps-3). 1990. 11.95 (0-87951-383-7) Overlook Pr.
Rossi, Richard. Don't Teach! Let Me Learn about Fantasy, Magic, Monkeys & Monsters. Crosby, Nina E. & Marten, Elizabeth H. 72p. (Orig.). (gr. 3-10). 1984. 8.95 (0-88047-045-3, 8410) DOK Pubs.
—Don't Teach Let Me Learn: About the F.B.I., Firefighters, Felines, Futures. Crosby, Nina E. & Marten, Elizabeth H. 72p. (gr. 3-6). 1983. tchr's. enrichment bk. 8.95 (0-88047-029-1, 8312) DOK Pubs.
—Don't Teach! Let Me Learn about World War II, Adventure, Dreams & Superstition. Crosby, Nina E. & Marten, Elizabeth H. 72p. (Orig.). (gr. 3-10). 1984. 8.95 (0-88047-044-5, 8411) DOK Pubs.
Roth, Harold, photos by. Harold Roth's Big Book of Horses. Lundell, Margo. 48p. (gr. 2-5). 1987. 7.95 (0-448-19203-9, G&D) Putnam Pub Group.
—Kidnap in San Juan. Reilly, Pat. 96p. (Orig.). (gr. 7 up). 1984. pap. 2.50 (0-440-94460-0, LFL) Dell.
Roth, Rob. Pearl Moscowitz's Last Stand. Levine, Arthur A. LC 91-10652. 32p. (ps-up). 1993. 14.00 (0-688-10753-2, Tambourine Bks); PLB 13.93 (0-688-10754-0, Tambourine Bks) Morrow.
Roth, Robert. And in the Beginning... Williams, Sheron. LC 90-43094. 40p. (gr. 1-5). 1992. SBE 13.95 (0-689-31650-X, Atheneum Child Bk) Macmillan Child Grp.
—Nobiah's Well: A Modern African Folk Tale. Guthrie, Donna. LC 93-586. 32p. (ps-2). 1993. 15.00 (0-8249-8631-8, Ideals Child); 14.95 (0-8249-8622-9) Hambleton-Hill.
—When the Monkeys Came Back. Franklin, Kristine L. LC 92-33684. 1994. text ed. 15.95 (0-689-31807-3, Atheneum) Macmillan.
Roth, Roger. The Giraffe That Walked to Paris. Milton, Nancy. LC 91-31767. 32p. (gr. k-4). 1992. 15.00 (0-517-58132-9); PLB 15.99 (0-517-58133-7) Crown Bks Yng Read.
—The Invisible Dog. King-Smith, Dick. LC 92-26978. 80p. (gr. 2-5). 1993. 14.00 (0-517-59424-2); PLB 14.99 (0-517-59425-0) Crown Bks Yng Read.
—The Sign Painter's Dream. Roth, Roger. LC 92-13041. 40p. (gr. k-4). 1993. 14.00 (0-517-58920-6); PLB 14.99 (0-517-58921-4) Crown Bks Yng Read.
Roth, Roger, jt. illus. see Vogelsang, Johanna.
Roth, Susan. Princess. Roth, Susan. LC 92-55042. 32p. (ps-3). 1993. 13.95 (1-56282-465-1); PLB 13.89 (1-56282-466-X) Hyprn Child.
Roth, Susan L. Another Christmas. Roth, Susan L. LC 91-33148. 32p. (gr. k). 1992. 15.00 (0-688-09942-4); PLB 14.93 (0-688-09943-2) Morrow Jr Bks.

—The Great Ball Game: A Muskogee Story. Bruchac, Joseph. LC 93-6269. 1994. write for info. (0-8037-1539-0); PLB write for info. (0-8037-1540-4) Dial Bks Young.
—Pass the Fritters, Critters. Chapman, Cheryl. LC 91-45055. 40p. (ps-k). 1993. RSBE 14.95 (0-02-717975-3, Four Winds) Macmillan Child Grp.
Rothero, Chris. Strawberry Fair. Williams, Sue, compiled by. 96p. (gr. 1-6). 1993. 14.95 (0-7136-2676-3, Pub. by A&C Black UK) Talman.
Rothman, Michael. Here is the Tropical Rainforest. Dunphy, Madeleine. LC 93-24850. 32p. (ps-3). 1994. 14.95 (1-56282-636-0); PLB 14.89 (1-56282-637-9) Hyprn Child.
—Lizard in the Sun. Ryder, Joanne. LC 89-33886. 32p. (gr. k up). 1990. 13.95 (0-688-07172-4); PLB 13.88 (0-688-07173-2, Morrow Jr Bks) Morrow Jr Bks.
—The Moon of the Alligators. new ed. George, Jean C. LC 90-38169. 48p. (gr. 3-7). 1991. 15.00 (0-06-022427-4); PLB 14.89 (0-06-022428-2) HarpC Child Bks.
—The Moon of the Moles. George, Jean C. LC 91-14535. 48p. (gr. 3-7). 1992. 15.00 (0-06-020258-0); PLB 14.89 (0-06-020259-9) HarpC Child Bks.
—Sea Elf. Ryder, Joanne, ed. LC 92-27608. 32p. (gr. k up). 1993. 15.00 (0-688-10060-0); PLB 14.93 (0-688-10061-9) Morrow Jr Bks.
—White Bear, Ice Bear. Ryder, Joanne. LC 87-36781. 32p. (gr. k-3). 1989. 13.95 (0-688-07174-0); PLB 13.88 (0-688-07175-9, Morrow Jr Bks) Morrow Jr Bks.
—Winter Whale. Ryder, Joanne. LC 90-19174. 32p. (gr. k up). 1991. 13.95 (0-688-07176-7); PLB 13.88 (0-688-07177-5) Morrow Jr Bks.
Rotman, Jeffrey L., photos by. Lobsters: Gangsters of the Sea. Cerullo, Mary M. LC 93-1288. 64p. (gr. 4 up). 1993. 15.95 (0-525-65153-5, Cobblehill Bks) Dutton Child Bks.
—Sharks: Challengers of the Deep. Cerullo, Mary M. LC 92-14206. 64p. (gr. 4 up). 1993. 15.00 (0-525-65100-4, Cobblehill Bks) Dutton Child Bks.
Rotner, Shelley. Ocean Day. Rotner, Shelley & Kreisler, Ken. LC 92-6114. 32p. (ps-1). 1993. RSBE 14.95 (0-02-777886-X, Macmillan Child Bk) Macmillan Child Grp.
Rotner, Shelley, photos by. Changes. Allen, Marjorie N. & Rotner, Shelley. LC 90-6601. 32p. (ps-1). 1991. RSBE 13.95 (0-02-700252-7, Macmillan Child Bk) Macmillan Child Grp.
—Citybook. Rotner, Shelley & Kreisler, Ken. LC 93-6350. 32p. (ps-1). 1994. 14.95 (0-531-06837-4); lib. bdg. 14.99 RLB (0-531-08687-5) Orchard Bks Watts.
Rotunno, Betsy. Dennis the Dinosaur Moves to Crystal Pond. Rotunno, Roccy & Roturno, Betsy. 12p. (gr. 2-6). 1992. Mixed Media Pkg. incls. stamp pad, stamps & box of 4 crayons. 7.00 (1-881980-03-0) Noteworthy.
—Little Bear's Best Birthday. Rotunno, Rocco & Rotunno, Betsy. 12p. (gr. 2-6). 1992. Mixed Media Pkg. incls. stamp pad, stamps & box of 4 crayons. 7.00 (1-881980-00-6) Noteworthy.
—Tessa Becomes a Ballerina. Rotunno, Rocco & Rotunno, Betsy. 12p. (gr. 2-6). 1992. Mixed Media Pkg. incls. stamp pad, stamps, box of 4 crayons. 7.00 (1-881980-01-4) Noteworthy.
—A Trick for Magic Bunny. Rotunno, Rocco & Rotunno, Betsy. 12p. (gr. 2-6). 1992. Mixed Media Pkg. incls. stamp pad, stamps & box of 4 crayons. 7.00 (1-881980-02-2) Noteworthy.
Rotzel, Spencer, jt. illus. see Grummer, Arnold.
Rougelot, Marilyn C. Mimi's First Mardi Gras. Couvillon, Alice & Moore, Elizabeth. LC 91-24006. 32p. (gr. 1-3). 1992. 17.95 (0-88289-840-X) Pelican.
Round. Computer Fun. Waters. 48p. (gr. 5-8). 1984. PLB 10.96 (0-88110-212-1); pap. 3.95 (0-86020-803-6) EDC.
—Computer Graphics. Tatchell. 48p. (gr. 6up). 1984. PLB 9.96 (0-88110-163-X); pap. 3.95 (0-86020-739-0) EDC.
Round, Graham. Bedtime: Stories for under Fives. Stimson, Joan. 44p. (ps-k). 1992. 3.50 (0-7214-1487-7) Ladybird Bks.
—Captain Ding, the Double-Decker Pirate. Cox, David. 32p. (ps-1). 1991. 17.95 (0-09-176365-7, Pub. by Hutchinson UK) Trafalgar.
—Practical Things to Do with a Microcomputer. Tatchell & Cutter, N. 48p. (gr. 6 up). 1983. pap. 3.95 (0-86020-731-5); PLB 10.96 (0-88110-140-0) EDC.
Round, Grahm. Creepy Computer Games. Tyler, Jenny. 16p. (gr. 6 up). 1984. pap. 2.95 (0-86020-780-3) EDC.
—Inside the Chip. Davies. (gr. 6 up) 1984. pap. 4.95 (0-86020-729-3) EDC.
Round, Jim & Johnson, Marc. Kirins: The Spell of No'an. Priest, James D. LC 90-90174. 470p. (Orig.). 1990. pap. 11.95 (0-9626225-4-0) Yellow Pr MN.
Rounds, Glen. The Blind Colt. Rounds, Glen, adapted by. LC 89-1779. 84p. (gr. 3-6). 1989. 15.95 (0-8234-0010-7); pap. 5.95 (0-8234-0758-6) Holiday.
—Charlie Drives the Stage. Kimmel, Eric A. LC 88-24558. 32p. (ps-3). 1989. reinforced bdg. 13.95 (0-8234-0738-1) Holiday.
—Cowboys. Rounds, Glen. LC 90-46501. 32p. (ps-3). 1991. reinforced 14.95 (0-8234-0867-1) Holiday.
—Cross Your Fingers, Spit in Your Hat: Superstitions & Other Beliefs. Schwartz, Alvin. LC 73-21912. 128p. (gr. 4-6). 1990. PLB 13.89 (0-397-32436-7, Lipp Jr Bks) HarpC Child Bks.

—Four Dollars & Fifty Cents. Kimmel, Eric A. LC 89-77515. 32p. (ps-3). 1990. reinforced 14.95 (0-8234-0817-5) Holiday.
—Four Dollars & Fifty Cents. Kimmel, Eric A. LC 89-77515. 1993. pap. 5.95 (0-8234-1024-2) Holiday.
—Hanna's Hog. Aylesworth, Jim. LC 87-11559. 32p. (gr. k-3). 1988. RSBE 13.95 (0-689-31367-5, Atheneum Child Bk) Macmillan Child Grp.
—I Know an Old Lady Who Swallowed a Fly. LC 89-46244. 32p. (ps-3). 1990. reinforced bdg. 14.95 (0-8234-0814-0) Holiday.
—I Know an Old Lady Who Swallowed a Fly. LC 89-46244. 32p. (ps-3). 1991. pap. 5.95 (0-8234-0908-2) Holiday.
—Kickle Snifters & Other Fearsome Critters. Schwartz, Alvin. LC 75-29048. 64p. (gr. 1-5). 1992. pap. 4.95 (0-06-446129-7, Trophy) HarpC Child Bks.
—Mike's Toads. Gage, Wilson. LC 88-34907. 96p. (gr. 3 up). 1990. 12.95 (0-688-08834-1) Greenwillow.
—Mike's Toads. Gage, Wilson. LC 88-34907. 96p. (gr. 4-6). 1991. pap. 3.95 (0-688-10977-2, Pub. by Beech Tree Bks) Morrow.
—Old MacDonald Had a Farm. Rounds, Glen. LC 88-24640. 32p. (ps-3). 1989. reinforced bdg. 14.95 (0-8234-0739-X); pap. 5.95 (0-8234-0846-9) Holiday.
—The Old Woman & the Jar of Ums. Wright, Jill. 32p. (ps-3). 1990. 14.95 (0-399-21736-3, Putnam) Putnam Pub Group.
—The Three Billy Goats Gruff. Rounds, Glen, retold by. LC 92-23951. 32p. (ps-3). 1993. reinforced bdg. 14.95 (0-8234-1015-3) Holiday.
—Three Little Pigs & the Big Bad Wolf. Rounds, Glen, retold by. LC 91-18173. 32p. (ps-3). 1992. reinforced bdg. 14.95 (0-8234-0923-6) Holiday.
—Tomfoolery: Trickery & Foolery with Words. Schwartz, Alvin. LC 72-12900. 128p. (gr. 4-6). 1990. PLB 14.89 (0-397-32437-5, Lipp Jr Bks) HarpC Child Bks.
—A Twister of Twists, a Tangler of Tongues. Schwartz, Alvin. LC 72-1434. 126p. (gr. 4 up). 1972. 14.00 (0-397-31387-X, Lipp Jr Bks) HarpC Child Bks.
—A Twister of Twists: A Tangler of Tongues. Schwartz, Alvin. LC 85-45372. 128p. (gr. 5 up). 1991. PLB 13.89 (0-397-32501-0, Lipp Jr Bks) HarpC Child Bks.
—Washday on Noah's Ark: A Story of Noah's Ark. Rounds, Glen, as told by. LC 91-4507. 32p. (ps-3). 1991. reinforced bdg. 14.95 (0-8234-0555-9); pap. 5.95 (0-8234-0880-9) Holiday.
—Whoppers: Tall Tales & Other Lies Collected from American Folklore. Schwartz, Alvin, ed. LC 74-32024. 128p. (gr. 4 up). 1990. pap. 3.95 (0-06-446091-6, Trophy) HarpC Child Bks.
—Wild Appaloosa. Rounds, Glen. LC 82-48751. 96p. (gr. 3-7). 1983. 13.95 (0-8234-0442-X) Holiday.
—Wild Horses. Rounds, Glen. 32p. (ps-3). 1993. reinforced bdg. 14.95 (0-8234-1019-6) Holiday.
—Wild Pill Hickok & Other Old West Riddles. Adler, David A. LC 88-6480. 64p. (gr. 1-4). 1988. reinforced bdg. 11.95 (0-8234-0718-7) Holiday.
Rounds, Glen & Truesdell, Sue. Witcracks: Jokes & Jests from American Folklore. Schwartz, Alvin. LC 73-7630. 128p. (gr. 5 up). 1993. 4.95 (0-06-446146-7, Trophy) HarpC Child Bks.
Roundtree, Katherine. A Carp for Kimiko. Kroll, Virginia L. LC 93-6940. 32p. 1993. 14.95 (0-88106-412-2); PLB 15.00 (0-88106-413-0) Charlesbridge Pub.
Rountree, Harry. The Adventures of Mabel. Peck, Harry T. Cabaniss, Anne M., intro. by. 236p. (gr. k-5). 1986. Repr. of 1896 ed. 19.95 (0-9616844-0-2) Greenhouse Pub.
Roussan, Irina. About Jazz Dance. Sanchez, Sharon S. 32p. (Orig.). 1991. pap. text ed. 5.95 (0-9626651-2-6) Dance Data.
Rousseau, May. The Counting Zoo: A Pop-up Number Book. Ruschak, Lynette. LC 91-42462. 24p. (ps-2). 1992. POB 13.95 (0-689-71619-2, Aladdin) Macmillan Child Grp.
Rousset, Francoise. Cool Calvin. Rocard, Ann. (ps-4). 1991. smythe sewn reinforced bdg. 9.95 (1-56182-030-X) Atomium Bks.
Routiaux, Claudine. Little Lost Fox Cub, on the Trail of Little Fox. Espinassous, Louis. LC 92-27116. 1993. PLB 18.60 (0-8368-0927-0) Gareth Stevens Inc.
Rouwntree, Julia, et al. The Christmas Collection. Nora, Clarke. 24p. (ps up) 1992. 9.95 (1-85697-833-8) Kingfisher Bks.
Rovetch, Lissa. Trigwater Did It. Rovetch, Lissa. LC 88-31791. 32p. (ps up). 1989. 12.95 (0-688-08057-X); PLB 12.88 (0-688-08058-8, Morrow Jr Bks) Morrow Jr Bks.
Rovetta, Ane. Exploring Pacific Coast Tide Pools. rev. & enl. ed. Brown, Vinson. 80p. (gr. 4 up). 1966. 16.95 (0-87961-216-9); pap. 8.95 (0-87961-217-7) Naturegraph.
—Life Cycle of the Pacific Gray Whale. Klobas, John. 32p. (gr. 6-9). 1993. 12.95 (0-89346-532-1) Heian Intl.
Rovira, Francesc. Ali Baba & the Forty Thieves: A Classic Tale. Jose, Eduard, adapted by Riehecky, Janet, tr. from SPA. LC 88-36871. 32p. (gr. 1-4). 1988. PLB 19.95 (0-89565-485-7); PLB 13.95s.p. (0-685-56049-X) Childs World.
—Alice in Wonderland: A Classic Tale. Carroll, Lewis. Jose, Eduard, adapted by Riehecky, Janet, tr. from SPA. LC 88-35309. 32p. (gr. 1-4). 1988. PLB 19.95 (0-89565-467-9); PLB 13.95s.p. (0-685-56033-3) Childs World.

—The Brave Little Tailor: A Classic Tale. Grimm, Jacob & Grimm, Wilhelm K. Jose, Eduard, adapted by. Moncure, Jane B., tr. LC 88-35311. 32p. (gr. 1-4). 1988. PLB 19.95 (0-89565-460-1); PLB 13.95s.p. (0-685-56032-5) Childs World.

—The Little Match Girl: A Classic Tale. Andersen, Hans Christian. Jose, Eduard, adapted by. Suire, Diane D., tr. LC 88-36868. 32p. (gr. 1-4). 1988. PLB 19.95 (0-89565-476-8); PLB 13.95s.p. (0-685-56046-5) Childs World.

—The Pied Piper of Hamelin: A Classic Tale. Browning, Robert. Jose, Eduard, adapted by. Suire, Diane D., tr. LC 88-35313. 32p. (gr. 1-4). 1988. PLB 19.95 (0-89565-471-7); PLB 13.95s.p. (0-685-56031-7) Childs World.

—The Princess & the Pea: A Classic Tale. Andersen, Hans Christian. Jose, Eduard, adapted by. Riehecky, Janet, tr. LC 88-35206. 32p. (gr. 1-4). 1988. PLB 19.95 (0-89565-486-5); PLB 13.95s.p. (0-685-56037-6) Childs World.

—Sinbad the Sailor: A Classic Tale. Jose, Eduard, adapted by. Riehecky, Janet, tr. from SPA. LC 88-36872. 32p. (gr. 1-4). 1988. PLB 19.95 (0-89565-472-5); PLB 13.95s.p. (0-685-56048-1) Childs World.

—Thumbelina: A Classic Tale. Andersen, Hans Christian. Jose, Eduard, adapted by. Riehecky, Janet, tr. LC 88-35307. 32p. (gr. 1-4). 1988. PLB 19.95 (0-89565-466-0); PLB 13.95s.p. (0-685-56022-8) Childs World.

—Till Eulenspiegel's Merry Pranks: A Classic Tale. Jose, Eduard, adapted by. Riehecky, Janet, tr. LC 88-36794. 32p. (gr. 1-4). 1988. PLB 19.95 (0-89565-475-X); PLB 13.95s.p. (0-685-56043-0) Childs World.

—Tom Thumb: A Classic Tale. Perrault, Charles. Jose, Eduard, adapted by. Riehecky, Janet, tr. from SPA. LC 88-35211. 32p. (gr. 1-4). 1988. PLB 19.95 (0-89565-462-8); PLB 13.95s.p. (0-685-56036-8) Childs World.

Rowan, N. R., photos by. Women in the Marines: The Book Camp Challenge. Rowan, N. R. LC 93-9706. 1993. deluxe ed. 22.95 (0-8225-1430-3) Lerner Pubns.

Rowand, Phyllis. Growing Story. Krauss, Ruth. LC 47-30688. (gr. k-3). 1947. 11.95i (0-06-023380-X) HarpC Child Bks.

—Monkey Day. Krauss, Ruth. 23p. (gr. k-5). 1973. pap. 8.00 (0-912846-05-4) Bookstore Pr.

Rowden, Rick. Mysteries. Winik, J. T. 48p. (gr. 5-9). 1985. pap. 5.95 (0-88625-094-3) Durkin Hayes Pub.

Rowden, Rick & Winik, J. T. Wild Animals. McKean, Barb. 32p. (gr. 3-7). 1985. pap. 3.50 (0-88625-117-6) Durkin Hayes Pub.

Rowden, Rick, jt. illus. see Bastien, Charles.

Rowden, Rick, et al. Kid's Party Cookbook. Stewart, Janet, ed. 32p. (gr. 2-6). 1988. PLB 14.65 (0-88625-201-6); pap. 5.95 (0-88625-200-8) Durkin Hayes Pub.

Rowe, Eric. Over Four Hundred & Fifty Years Ago: In the New World. Sauvain, Philip. LC 93-2649. 32p. (gr. 6 up). 1993. RSBE 13.95 (0-02-726327-4, New Discovery Bks) Macmillan Child Grp.

Rowe, Frank. The Famous Airplanes of Kansas. Rowe, Frank. Lickei, Elizabeth, ed. 64p. (Orig.). 1992. pap. 3.95 (1-880652-12-9) Wichita Eagle.

Rowe, Gavin. Abraham & Isaac. Storr, Catherine. LC 84-18076. 32p. (gr. k-4). 1985. PLB 14.65 (0-8172-1994-3) Raintree Steck-V.

—The Animals' Christmas. Gardam, Catharine. LC 90-5538. 32p. (gr. k-4). 1990. SBE 13.95 (0-689-50502-7, M K McElderry) Macmillan Child Grp.

—The Birth of Jesus. Storr, Catherine, retold by. LC 82-9048. 32p. (gr. k-4). 1982. PLB 14.65 (0-8172-1977-3) Raintree Steck-V.

—The Prodigal Son. Storr, Catherine, retold by. LC 82-23011. 32p. (gr. k-4). 1983. PLB 14.65 (0-8172-1982-X) Raintree Steck-V.

Rowe, John. Jack the Dog. Rowe, John. 28p. (gr. k up). 1993. 14.95 (0-88708-266-1) Picture Bk Studio.

—Rabbit Moon. Rowe, John. LC 92-6047. 28p. 1992. pap. 14.95 (0-88708-246-7) Picture Bk Studio.

Rowe, John A. The Sing-Song of Old Man Kangaroo. Kipling, Rudyard. LC 90-7382. 32p. (gr. k up). 1991. pap. 14.95 (0-88708-152-5) Picture Bk Studio.

Rowen, Amy. City, Sing, for Me: A Country Child Moves to the City. Jacobson, Jane. LC 77-11130. 32p. (gr. 1-5). 1978. 16.95 (0-87705-358-8) Human Sci Pr.

Rowes, Gavin. Stories for Christmas. Uttley, Alison. Lines, Kathleen, ed. 128p. (gr. 3-7). 1991. pap. 4.95 (0-571-16321-1) Faber & Faber.

Rowland, Jada. Heidi. Spyri, Johanna. Saunders, Susan, adapted by. LC 87-15466. 48p. (gr. 2-5). 1988. PLB 12.89 (0-8167-1215-8); pap. 3.95 (0-8167-1216-6) Troll Assocs.

—Miss Tizzy. Gray, Libba M. LC 92-8409. (ps-2). 1993. pap. 14.00 JRT (0-671-77590-1, S&S BFYR) S&S Trade.

Roxbury, David, et al. Jo Jo the Elf Meets Santa's Enemy. Sheppard, Dorothy M. & Sheppard, Jack G. 65p. (gr. 1-6). 1992. PLB 12.95 (0-9634300-1-7); pap. 7.95 (0-9634300-0-9) D & J Arts Pubs. JO JO THE ELF MEETS SANTA'S ENEMY, a children's fantasy, opens a new frontier for Santa & a loveable elf named Jo Jo. Jo Jo is a woods elf from the Black Forest of Germany who sails with Santa on Christmas Eve to protect him from an evil wizard named Natanzo. Natanzo is determined to steal Santa's bag, which has special magical powers that any wizard would crave to possess. Jo Jo battles giant birds, monsters, dragons, & Natanzo, Master of Evil in order to save Santa's bag, so toys can be delivered to all the children of the world. It's an adventure from start to finish, as Jo Jo fights to defeat evil. He not only wins his battles, but is guaranteed to win the hearts of all ages & emerge to become a new Christmas hero for all time. This exciting book, with 27 beautiful full-color illustrations, will encourage children to read. How to order info: P.O. Box 365, Sierra Vista, AZ 85636. *Publisher Provided Annotation.*

Roy, Cal. Bubble, the Birds, & the Noise. Roy, Cal. (gr. k-4). 1968. 8.95 (0-8392-3069-9) Astor-Honor.

—What Every Young Wizard Should Know. Roy, Cal. (gr. 2 up). 1963. 8.95 (0-8392-3043-5) Astor-Honor.

Roy, Doug. Los Seis Deseos de la Jirafa (Big Book) Ada, Alma F. (SPA). 16p. (Orig.). (gr. k-3). 1988. pap. text ed. 29.95 (0-917837-02-9) Hampton-Brown.

—Los Seis Deseos de la Jirafa (Small Book) Ada, Alma F. (SPA). 16p. (Orig.). (gr. k-3). 1992. pap. text ed. 6.00 (1-56334-078-X) Hampton-Brown.

Roy, Mike. Screaming Eagle. Deschaine, Scott. 296p. 1993. pap. 11.95 (1-878181-04-1) Discovery Comics.

Royall, Sandra. Every Day Can Feel Like Christmas: Color Your World with Love. Elliott, Paula. 32p. (Orig.). 1991. pap. 4.95 (1-879052-02-4) Planetary Pubns.

Royall, Sandy. The Crystal Lady. Rozman, Deborah. 72p. (gr. 1 up). 1991. 19.95 (1-879052-01-6, Planet Pubns) Planetary Pubns.

—Fluffy & Sparky: A Story about True Buddies. Elliott, Paula. 32p. (ps up). 1991. 12.95 (1-879052-00-8) Planetary Pubns.

Rozen, Yael. Alina: A Russian Girl Comes to Israel. Meir, Mira. Shapiro, Zeva, tr. from HEB. 48p. (gr. 2-4). 1982. 7.95 (0-8276-0208-1) JPS Phila.

Rozier, J. & Gaudriault, M. Quatre Filles du Docteur March. Alcott, Louisa May. (FRE.). (gr. 5-10). 1900. 10.95 (2-07-033413-9) Schoenhof.

Rozinsky, Bob, jt. photog. see Shattil, Wendy.

Rubel, Nicole. Batty Riddles. Hall, Katy & Eisenberg, Lisa. LC 91-20777. 48p. (ps-3). 1993. 11.99 (0-8037-1217-0); lib. bdg. 11.89 (0-8037-1218-9) Dial Bks Young.

—Bunny Riddles. Hall, Katy & Eisenberg, Lisa. LC 93-13241. (ps-4). 1995. write for info. (0-8037-1519-6); PLB write for info. (0-8037-1521-8) Dial Bks Young.

—The Ghost Family Meets Its Match. Rubel, Nicole. LC 91-10815. 32p. (ps-3). 1992. 14.00 (0-8037-1093-3); PLB 13.89 (0-8037-1094-1) Dial Bks Young.

—Goldie's Nap. Rubel, Nicole. LC 90-4401. 32p. (ps-2). 1991. PLB 14.89 (0-06-025107-7) HarpC Child Bks.

—Grizzly Riddles. Hall, Katy & Eisenberg, Lisa. LC 86-29275. 48p. (ps-3). 1992. pap. 3.99 (0-14-036116-2, Dial Easy to Read) Puffin Bks.

—Happy Birthday, Rotten Ralph. Gantos, Jack. 32p. (ps-3). 1990. 13.45 (0-395-53766-5) HM.

—It Came from the Swamp. Rubel, Nicole. LC 87-24653. 32p. (ps-3). 1988. 10.95 (0-8037-0513-1); PLB 10.89 (0-8037-0515-8) Dial Bks Young.

—Not So Rotten Ralph. Gantos, Jack. LC 93-759. (gr. 4 up). 1994. write for info. (0-395-62302-2) HM.

—Pirate Jupiter & the Moondogs. Rubel, Nicole. LC 84-13815. 32p. (ps-3). 1985. Dial Bks Young.

—Rotten Ralph. Gantos, Jack. LC 75-34101. 48p. (gr. k-3). 1976. 13.95 (0-395-24276-2); pap. 4.50 (0-685-02307-9) HM.

—Rotten Ralph. Gantos, Jack. (gr. k-3). 1980. pap. 4.80 (0-395-29202-6, Sandpiper) HM.

—Rotten Ralph. Gantos, Jack. 1988. Incl. cass. pap. 7.70 (0-395-48873-7) HM.

—Rotten Ralph's Rotten Christmas. Gantos, Jack. LC 84-664. 32p. (ps-3). 1984. 13.95 (0-395-35380-7); pap. 17.95 incl. doll (0-395-45346-1); pap. 4.80 (0-395-45685-1) HM.

—Rotten Ralph's Show & Tell. Gantos, Jack. 32p. (ps-3). 1989. 13.45 (0-395-44312-1) HM.

—Rotten Ralph's Show & Tell. Gantos, Jack. 32p. (gr. k-3). 1991. pap. 4.80 (0-395-60285-8, Sandpiper) HM.

—Rotten Ralph's Trick or Treat. Gantos, Jack. LC 86-7276. 32p. (gr. k-3). 1986. 13.45 (0-395-38943-7) HM.

—Rotten Ralph's Trick or Treat. Gantos, Jack. 32p. (gr. k-3). 1988. pap. 4.80 (0-395-48655-6, Sandpiper) HM.

—Worse Than Rotten, Ralph. Gantos, Jack. (gr. k-3). 1982. 13.95 (0-395-27106-1); pap. 5.70 (0-395-32919-1) HM.

Rubin, Caroline & Axeman, Lois. You Go Away. Corey, Dorothy. LC 75-33015. 32p. (ps-1). 1976. PLB 10.95 (0-8075-9441-5) A Whitman.

Rubin, Marvin. Color Your Way Through L. A. Los Angeles Children's Museum Staff. Polsky, Carol, ed. U. S.-Japan Cross Culture Center & Opinion Editors, trs. (ENG, SPA & JPN.). 56p. (Orig.). (gr. k up). 1983. 3.95 (0-914953-00-1) Los Angeles.

Rubin, Shannon. Book-Write: A Creative Bookmaking Guide for Young Authors. O'Brien-Palmer, Michelle. LC 91-68412. 128p. (gr. k-6). 1992. pap. 16.95 (1-879235-01-3) MicNik Pubns.

Rubin, Steffi. Ima on the Bima: My Mommy Is a Rabbi. Rabbi Mindy Avra Portnoy. LC 86-3023. 32p. (ps-4). 1986. 10.95 (0-930494-55-5); pap. 4.95 (0-930494-54-7) Kar Ben.

Ruble, Allison. Lani Goose Sings...for Hawaii's Children. Kahn, Elithe A. (Orig.). (ps up). 1988. pap. 14.95 incl. audio cassette (0-944264-03-4) Lani Goose Pubns.

Rucker, Patty L. Easter Fires. Wade, Mary D. 48p. (gr. k-4). 1985. 10.95 (0-89015-469-4, Pub. by Panda Bks) Eakin-Sunbelt.

Rucki, Ani. Turkey's Gift to the People. Rucki, Ani. LC 92-10764. 32p. (ps-4). 1992. 14.95 (0-87358-541-0) Northland AZ.

Rudegeair, Jean. Noah's Ark. Brown, Christopher, ed. 24p. (gr. 2-6). 1984. pap. 2.50 (0-89954-287-5) Antioch Pub Co.

—The Story of Christmas. Wolf, Jill. 24p. (gr. 3-7). 1986. pap. 2.50 (0-89954-459-2) Antioch Pub Co.

—Teddy Bears Night Before Christmas. Wolf, Jill & Moore, Clement C. 24p. (gr. 3-6). 1985. pap. 2.50 (0-89954-330-8) Antioch Pub Co.

Rudinski, Richard. Eric Needs Stitches. Marino, Barbara P. LC 84-40753. 32p. (gr. k-3). 1989. PLB 12.89 (0-397-32374-3, Lipp Jr Bks) HarpC Child Bks.

Rudkin, David, jt. illus. see Zabe, Michel.

Rudor, Tasha. Rosemary for Remembrance. Tudor, Tasha. 32p. (gr. 3-6). 1990. gift ed. 15.95 (0-399-21816-5, Philomel Bks) Putnam Pub Group.

Ruff, Donna. Grandma Moses: Painter of Rural America. O'Neal, Zibby. (gr. 2-6). pap. 3.50 (0-317-62289-7, Puffin) Puffin Bks.

—The Hanukkah of Great-Uncle Otto. Levoy, Myron. LC 84-12635. 48p. (gr. 3-7). 1984. 10.95 (0-8276-0242-1) JPS Phila.

—If Wishes Were Horses. Dana, Maggie. LC 87-16201. 128p. (gr. 4-8). 1988. PLB 9.89 (0-8167-1197-6); pap. text ed. 2.95 (0-8167-1198-4) Troll Assocs.

—Jumping into Trouble. Dana, Maggie. LC 87-16248. 128p. (gr. 4-8). 1988. PLB 9.89 (0-8167-1193-3); pap. text ed. 2.95 (0-8167-1194-1) Troll Assocs.

—Leave That Cricket Be, Alan Lee. Porte, Barbara A. LC 92-29401. 32p. (ps up). 1993. 14.00 (0-688-11793-7); PLB 13.93 (0-688-11794-5) Greenwillow.

—Molly Picon: A Gift of Laughter. Perl, Lila. 64p. (gr. 4-7). 1990. 12.95 (0-8276-0336-3) JPS Phila.

—No Time for Secrets. Dana, Maggie. LC 87-19027. 128p. (gr. 4-8). 1988. PLB 9.89 (0-8167-1191-7); pap. text ed. 2.95 (0-8167-1192-5) Troll Assocs.

—The Old Man & His Birds. Ginsburg, Mirra, adapted by. LC 93-26705. 1994. write for info. (0-688-04603-7); PLB write for info. (0-688-04604-5) Greenwillow.

—Our Golda: The Story of Golda Meir. Adler, David A. LC 83-16798. 64p. (gr. 3-7). 1984. pap. 11.95 (0-670-53107-3) Viking Child Bks.

—Our Golda: The Story of Golda Meir. Adler, David A. 64p. (gr. 2-6). 1986. pap. 4.50 (0-14-032104-7, Puffin) Puffin Bks.

—Racing for the Stars. Dana, Maggie. LC 87-16246. 128p. (gr. 4-8). 1988. PLB 9.89 (0-8167-1195-X); pap. text ed. 2.95 (0-8167-1196-8) Troll Assocs.

—Rowan. McKinley, Robin. LC 91-31809. 24p. (ps-4). 1992. 14.00 (0-688-10682-X); PLB 13.93 (0-688-10683-8) Greenwillow.

—Shirley Temple Black: Actress to Ambassador. Haskins, James S. 64p. (gr. 2-5). 1989. pap. 3.95 (0-14-032491-7, Puffin) Puffin Bks.

—Who Will Lead Kiddush? Pomerantz, Barbara. 32p. (Orig.). (gr. 1-3). 1985. pap. 6.00 (0-8074-0306-7, 102000) UAHC.

Ruff, Donna & Moses, Grandma. Grandma Moses: Painter of Rural. O'Neal, Zibby. LC 86-4071. 64p. (gr. 2-6). 1986. pap. 10.95 (0-670-80664-1) Viking Child Bks.

Ruff, Donna, photos by. Eleanor Roosevelt: First Lady of the World. Faber, Doris. LC 84-20861. 64p. (gr. 2-6). 1985. pap. 10.95 (0-670-80551-3) Viking Child Bks.

Ruff, Doris. Eleanor Roosevelt: First Lady of the World. Faber, Doris. 64p. (gr. 2-6). 1986. pap. 4.50 (0-14-032103-9, Puffin) Puffin Bks.

Ruffins, Reynold. Carnival. Burden-Patmon, Denise & Jones, Kathryn D. 32p. (gr. 2-5). 1993. pap. 4.95 (0-671-79840-5, S&S BYR) S&S Trade.

—Koi & the Kola Nuts. Gleeson, Brian. LC 92-7094. 40p. 1992. pap. 14.95 (0-88708-281-5, Rabbit Ears); pap. 19.95 incl. cass. (0-88708-282-3, Rabbit Ears) Picture Bk Studio.

—Misoso: Once Upon a Time Tales from Africa. Aardema, Verna, compiled by. LC 92-43288. (gr. 4 up). 1994. 18.00 (0-679-83430-3); lib. bdg. 18.99 (0-679-93430-8) Knopf.

—Words: A Book about the Origins of Every Day Words & Phrases. Sarnoff, Jane. LC 81-8943. 64p. (gr. 4-8). 1981. SBE 13.95 (0-684-16958-4, Scribners Young Read) Macmillan Child Grp.

Ruge, Don, Jr. Please Touch the Animals! McConnell, Nancy P. Gress, Jonna, ed. 12p. (ps-k). 1992. pap. text ed. 16.20 (0-944943-16-0) Current Inc.

Ruhlin, Roger. A Day in the Life of a Librarian. Paige, David. LC 84-8552. 32p. (gr. 4-8). 1985. PLB 11.79 (0-8167-0101-6); pap. text ed. 2.95 (0-8167-0102-4) Troll Assocs.

—A Day in the Life of a Sports Therapist. Paige, David. LC 84-2433. 32p. (gr. 4-8). 1985. PLB 11.79 (0-8167-0099-0); pap. text ed. 2.95 (0-8167-0100-8) Troll Assocs.

Ruhlin, Roger, photos by. A Day in the Life of a Marine Biologist. Paige, David. LC 80-54097. 32p. (gr. 4-8). 1981. PLB 11.79 (0-89375-447-3); pap. 2.95 (0-89375-447-1); cassette avail. Troll Assocs.

—A Day in the Life of a Police Detective. Paige, David. LC 80-54102. 32p. (gr. 4-8). 1981. PLB 11.79 (0-89375-442-0); cassette avail. Troll Assocs.

—A Day in the Life of a Rock Musician. Paige, David. LC 78-68808. 32p. (gr. 4-8). 1980. PLB 11.79 (0-89375-225-8); pap. 2.95 (0-89375-229-0) Troll Assocs.

Ruiz, Aristides. Beasty Bits: Cereal Box Joke Book. McNally, Bruce. LC 92-60580. 400p. (gr. 1-6). 1993. pap. 2.99 (0-679-83456-7) Random Bks Yng Read.

Ruiz, Art. Universal Monsters: Dracula. Teitelbaum, Mike. 96p. (gr. 3-7). 1992. pap. 2.95 (0-307-22331-0, 22331, Golden Pr) Western Pub.

—Universal Monsters: Frankenstein. Teitelbaum, Mike. 96p. (gr. 3-7). 1992. pap. 2.95 (0-307-22335-3, 22335, Golden Pr) Western Pub.

—Universal Monsters: The Mummy. Smith, Parker. 96p. (gr. 3-7). 1992. pap. 2.95 (0-307-22332-9, 22332, Golden Pr) Western Pub.

—Universal Monsters: The Wolf Man. Korman, Justine & Fontes, Ron. 96p. (gr. 3-7). 1992. pap. 2.95 (0-307-22336-1, 22336, Golden Pr) Western Pub.

—The Weirdest Fun Book, Ever! 1992. 7.95 (0-448-40503-2, G&D) Putnam Pub Group.

Rukstalis, Susan. How Many Steps Before the Queen? Rukstalis, Susan. Kopen, Dan F., intro. by. LC 92-60664. 32p. (ps-4). 1992. 14.95 (0-9628914-2-8) Padakami Pr.

Rullestad, Chris. The Official National Table Hockey League Handbook, Vol. 1. Phillips, Martin A. Phillips, Zoe A., ed. LC 89-91696. 66p. (Orig.). (gr. 12). 1989. write for info. (0-9623588-0-0); pap. write for info. (0-9623588-1-9) Gnu Wine Pr.

Rundell, Christopher. A Leash on Love: A Book for All Ages. Lipson, Greta B. LC 93-176359. 32p. 1992. 9.95 (0-9630637-0-7) Barclay Bks. Funny & insightful--a look at the enduring bond between humans & dogs as they walk the rocky road of life together, hand in paw. Strikes a chord in the hearts of all dedicated dog lovers. Thirty waggish illustrations. Written in doggerel by Greta B. Lipson, Associate Professor Emeritus of the University of Michigan where she taught Literature for Children & Young Adults. Honored by the Michigan Association of Governing Boards as distinguished Faculty Member for Extraordinary Contributions to Michigan Higher Education. Has authored & co-authored 15 books for teachers & parents: *THE SCOOP ON FROGS & PRINCES; Newspaper Commentaries; * AUDACIOUS POETRY: Reflections on Adolescence; * TALES WITH A TWIST: Ethical Dilemmas; * EVERYDAY LAW FOR YOUNG CITIZENS; * ROMEO & JULIET PLAINSPOKEN; * FAMOUS FABLES FOR LITTLE TROUPERS; * A BOOK FOR ALL SEASONS; * FAST IDEAS FOR BUSY TEACHERS; * ETHNIC PRIDE; * MIGHTY MYTH; * EXTRA! READ ALL ABOUT IT; * CALLIOPE; * FACT, FANTASY & FOLKLORE. Available Good Apple Publisher, Carthage, IL, 1-800-435-7234. Distributed by Publishers Distribution Service, Grawn, MI, 1-800-345-0096.
Publisher Provided Annotation.

Rundell, Wendi S. Research Pleasers. Petreshene, Susan S. Sussman, Ellen, ed. (Orig.). (gr. 3-6). 1982. pap. text ed. 5.95 (0-933606-19-2, MS-618) E Sussman Educ.

Runestrand, Meredith & Mayo, Steve. Marco the Manx Series, 3 bks. Roe, JoAnn. (gr. k-5). Set. write for info. (0-931551-06-4); Fisherman Cat, 1988. PLB 10.95 (0-931551-02-1); Alaska Cat. PLB 10.95 (0-931551-05-6); Castaway Cat. pap. 5.95 (0-931551-03-X); Fisherman Cat, 1988. pap. 6.95 (0-931551-01-3); Alaska Cat. pap. 6.95 (0-931551-04-8) Montevista Pr.

Rungius, Carl & Knight, C. W. Records of North American Big Game. 2nd ed. Gray, Prentiss N. 178p. (gr. 10 up). 1990. Repr. of 1932 ed. 39.95 (1-56416-011-4) Derrydale Pr.

Runnerstrom, Bengt-Arne. Save My Rainforest. Zak, Monica. LC 91-40179. 29p. 1992. 14.95 (0-912078-94-4) Volcano Pr.

Runyan, Merrilee. Plays & Puppets &cetera. 7th ed. Brooks, Courtaney. LC 81-68933. 100p. (Orig.). (gr. k up). 1981. pap. text ed. 14.95 (0-941274-00-4) Belnice Bks.
"Drama celebrates our differences & uses them. Plays draw out our individuality (which) is never wrong; it is ours--unique. We can all learn, for we're not like little cups waiting to be filled, but like lamps ready to be turned on." These excerpts sum up the philosophy that makes PLAYS & PUPPETS &CETERA much more powerful than the average how-to text. Brooks mixes a complete outlining of puppet & drama basics with a wonderfully positive attitude of respect & joy for life & its possibilities. Her explanations offer sufficient know-how to allow any teacher to carry a group through a show from start to curtain. "As a first time student teacher, I used the book to coordinate a play-project with six fourth-graders. One parent wrote a thank-you note telling us it was the first time she had heard her daughter speak above a whisper in public. I used the book again to help an adult troupe of Spanish-speaking novice players stage a Christmas story."--BREAKTHROUGH Winter/Summer 1990. (Illustrated sample plays; 7 sample plays for puppets or people actors with casts of 4 to 6, simple costuming such as ears for a dog or cat & props).
Publisher Provided Annotation.

Runyon, Anne & Brown, Jim. North Carolina Wild Places: A Closer Look. Earley, Lawrence S., intro. by. LC 92-81998. (Orig.). (gr. 8 up). 1993. pap. 8.50 (0-9628949-1-5) NC Wildlife.

Runyon, Linda. Wild Foods & Animals: Coloring Book. 2nd ed. Runyon, Linda. 16p. (gr. 1 up). 1986. pap. 1.99 (0-936699-01-9) Wild Foods Co.

Rupprecht, Maureen. Cabbage Patch Kids Jumbo Activity & Coloring Book. 128p. 1984. pap. 2.50 (0-910313-34-2) Parker Bros.

Rush, Ken. The Seltzer Man. Rush, Ken. LC 91-40905. 32p. (ps-3). 1993. RSBE 14.95 (0-02-777917-3, Macmillan Child Bk) Macmillan Child Grp.

—Some Things Never Change. Aldag, Kurt. LC 91-9907. 32p. (ps-3). 1992. RSBE 13.95 (0-02-700205-5, Macmillan Child Bk) Macmillan Child Grp.

Ruskin, Robert. Indians of the Tidewater Country: Of Maryland, Virginia, Delaware & North Carolina. Ruskin, Thelma. Buchanan, Carol & Ruskin, Robert, eds. Ruskin, Robert, intro. by. LC 85-73263. 132p. (gr. 4-5). 1986. casebound 15.00 (0-917882-20-2) MD Hist Pr.

Rusling, Albert. The Mouse & Mrs. Proudfoot. Rusling, Albert. LC 84-17871. 32p. (gr. k-3). 1985. 12.95 (0-13-604265-1) P-H.

Russell, Chris. Best Friends: Toddler's. Harker, Jillian. 26p. (ps). 1992. 3.50 (0-7214-1504-0) Ladybird Bks.

Russell, Chris, jt. illus. see Henley, Claire.

Russell, Dave. The Middlebatchers: Throw a Party for the Marriage of Hetty Wish & Lester Leg, Vol. 1. Barrett, Anna P. Darst, Shelia S., ed. 118p. (Orig.). (gr. 3-7). 1994. pap. 7.95 (0-89896-105-X) Larksdale.

Russell, Elizabeth A., jt. illus. see Gruelle, Justin C.

Russell, H. R. Thirteen Mississippi Ghosts & Jeffrey. Windham, Kathryn T. LC 74-15509. 152p. (gr. 6 up). 1987. pap. 9.50t (0-8173-0379-0) U of Ala Pr.

Russell, Jim. Moses of the Bullrushes: Retold by Catherine Storr. 32p. (gr. k-4). 1984. 14.65 (0-8172-1990-0, Raintree Children's Books Belitha Press Ltd. - London) Raintree Steck-V.

Russell, Judith. Dragons Are Lonely. Lewis, John R., Jr. 32p. (gr. 1-3). 1993. 14.95 (0-87797-239-7) Cherokee.

Russell, Katherine B. Guiding Children Through Grief: A Resource Manual of Recommended Books to Help Young Children Cope with Death, Dying & Grief. Russell, Katherine B. 48p. (Orig.). (ps up). 1989. pap. 5.25 (1-56123-036-7) Centering Corp.

Russell, Kerri G. Alphabet Tails. Erickson, Gina C. Foster, Kelli C., ed. 73p. (gr. k-4). 1989. pap. 6.95 (0-927971-00-3) OnTrack Inc.

—The Bug Club. Erickson, Gina C. & Foster, Kelli C. 24p. (ps-2). 1991. pap. 3.50 (0-8120-4730-3) Barron.

—Find Nat. Erickson, Gina C. & Foster, Kelli C. 24p. (ps-2). 1991. pap. 3.50 (0-8120-4678-1) Barron.

—Jake & the Snake. Erickson, Gina C. & Foster, Kelli C. 24p. (ps-3). 1993. pap. 3.50 (0-8120-1732-3) Barron.

—A Mop for Pop. Erickson, Gina C. & Foster, Kelli C. 24p. (ps-2). 1991. pap. 3.50 (0-8120-4680-3) Barron.

—Pip & Kip. Erickson, Gina C. & Foster, Kelli C. LC 92-29864. 24p. (ps-2). 1993. pap. 3.50 (0-8120-1454-5) Barron.

—The Sled Surprise. Erickson, Gina C. & Foster, Kelli C. 24p. (ps-2). 1991. pap. 3.50 (0-8120-4677-3) Barron.

—Sometimes I Wish. Erickson, Gina C. & Foster, Kelli C. 24p. (ps-2). 1991. pap. 3.50 (0-8120-4681-1) Barron.

—What a Day for Flying! Erickson, Gina C. & Foster, Kelli C. 92-42078. 32p. (ps-2). 1993. pap. 3.95 (0-8120-1557-6) Barron.

—Whiptale of Blackshale Trail. Erickson, Gina C. & Foster, Kelli C. 24p. (ps-3). 1993. pap. 3.50 (0-8120-1733-1) Barron.

Russell, Lynne. Api & the Boy Stranger: A Village Creation Tale. Roddy, Patricia. LC 93-8359. Date not set. 14.99 (0-8037-1221-9); PLB 14.89 (0-8037-1222-7) Dial Bks Young.

—One Smiling Grandma: A Caribbean Counting Book. Linden, Ann M. LC 91-30826. 32p. (ps-3). 1992. 15.00 (0-8037-1132-8) Dial Bks Young.

Russell, Marjorie H. The Glorious Presence. Fuller, Joy. Russell, Marjorie H., ed. LC 81-65753. 176p. (gr. 9-12). 1989. pap. 7.98x (0-9614745-1-3) Arcadia Corp.

Russell, Mary L. The Teddy Bear That Prowled at Night. Deihl, Edna G. 24p. (gr. k-3). 1991. pap. 7.95 (0-88138-079-2, Green Tiger) S&S Trade.

Russell, Naomi. The Stream. Russell, Naomi. LC 90-47497. 32p. (ps-1). 1991. 9.95 (0-525-44729-6, DCB) Dutton Child Bks.

Russell, Phillip K. A Day on a Shrimp Boat. Russell, Ching Y. Littlejohn, Beth, ed. 57p. (gr. 3-6). 1993. 13.95 (0-87844-120-4) Sandlapper Pub Co.
This book is written by Ching Yeung Russell, who grew up in China & Hong Kong. The story, both educational & entertaining is told through the eyes of her 12-year old son Jeremy. Although eating shrimp & other delicacies of the sea is a favorite pastime of people who visit & live in the South Carolina low country, few of us know what goes into bringing the shrimp to the table. The Russell family decided to find out. They hitched a ride with Captain Bob Upton of St. Helena Island & spent a day on his trawler the "Abbie R." A DAY ON A SHRIMP BOAT allows the reader to share in their experience. This book is written for young readers, aged 9 & up, but is suitable for kids of all ages. The book's black & white photographs are provided by the author's husband Phillip K. Russell.
Publisher Provided Annotation.

Russell-Arnot, Elizabeth. The Secrets of a Garden. Markham-David, Sally. LC 93-29003. 1994. 4.25 (0-383-03773-5) SRA Schl Grp.

Russo, Carol. Three-D Hidden Pictures Activity Book. 16p. 1991. pap. write for info. (1-56156-012-X) Kidsbks.

Russo, Marisabina. Easy-to-Make Spaceships That Really Fly. Blocksma, Dewey & Blocksma, Mary. LC 83-10986. 64p. (gr. 2-6). 1985. pap. 11.95 jacketed (0-671-66301-1, S&S BFYR); pap. 5.95 (0-671-66302-X, S&S BFYR) S&S Trade.

—Goodbye, House. Banks, Ann & Evans, Nancy. 64p. (gr. 2-6). 1988. pap. 7.95 (0-517-53907-1, Harmony) Crown Pub Group.

—It Begins with an A. Calmenson, Stephanie. LC 92-72016. 32p. (ps-2). 1993. 12.95 (1-56282-122-9); PLB 12.89 (1-56282-123-7) Hyprn Child.

—The Line-up Book. Russo, Marisabina. LC 85-24907. 24p. (ps-1). 1986. 11.75 (0-688-06204-0); PLB 11.88 (0-688-06205-9) Greenwillow.
—Vacation Time: Poems for Children. Giovanni, Nikki. LC 79-91643. 32p. (gr. 7 up). 1981. pap. 6.00 (0-688-00507-1, Quill) Morrow.
—A Week of Lullabies. Plotz, Helen. LC 86-18458. 32p. (ps-3). 1988. 11.95 (0-688-06652-6); lib. bdg. 11.88 (0-688-06653-4) Greenwillow.
—When Summer Ends. Fowler, Susi G. LC 87-14937. 32p. (ps up). 1989. 11.95 (0-688-07605-X); PLB 11.88 (0-688-07606-8) Greenwillow.
—When Summer Ends. Fowler, Susi G. 32p. (ps-3). 1992. pap. 4.50 (0-14-054472-0, Puffin) Puffin Bks.
—Why Do Grown-Ups Have All the Fun? Russo, Marisabina. LC 86-4644. 24p. (ps-3). 1987. 11.75 (0-688-06625-9); PLB 11.88 (0-688-06626-7) Greenwillow.
Russo, Susan. Eats. Adoff, Arnold. ALC Staff, ed. LC 79-11300. 48p. (gr. 2 up). 1992. pap. 3.95 (0-688-11695-7, Mulberry) Morrow.
—Eats: Poems. Adoff, Arnold. LC 79-11300. (gr. 4 up). 1979. 13.95 (0-688-41901-1); PLB 12.88 (0-688-51901-6) Lothrop.
Rust, Thomas O. U'n I Read a Note. Grasmick, Alta C. 68p. (gr. k-1). 1989. pap. 15.95 (0-9621909-0-X) A C Grasmick.
Ruten, Marlene L. High Holy Day Do It Yourself Dictionary. Friedman, Audrey M. & Zwerin, Raymond. 32p. (gr. k-3). 1983. pap. 5.00 (0-8074-0162-5, 101100) UAHC.
Ruth, Red. Zeke Hatfield & a Ghost Named Rocky. Barrett, John. (gr. k-10). 1978. 1.99 (0-686-22892-8) Silver Dollar.
Ruth, Rod. The Day the Toys Came to Silver Dollar City. Barrett, John. (gr. k-10). 1978. 1.99 (0-686-22891-X) Silver Dollar.
—Santa's Beard Is Soft & Warm. Ottum, Bob & Wood, JoAnne. (ps). 1974. write for info. (0-307-12148-8, Golden Bks) Western Pub.
—The Whale. Hogan, Paula Z. LC 79-13379. 32p. (gr. 1-4). 1979. PLB 17.96 (0-8172-1500-X); pap. 4.95 (0-8114-8180-8); pap. 9.95 incl. cassette (0-8114-8188-3) Raintree Steck-V.
Ruth, Susan, jt. illus. see Ruth, Trevor.
Ruth, Trevor. All about Bears. Ohanian, Susan. LC 93-28988. 1994. 4.25 (0-383-03735-2) SRA Schl Grp.
—The Big Brown Box. Drew, David. LC 92-30673. 1993. 2.50 (0-383-03619-4) SRA Schl Grp.
—Don't Cut down This Tree. Anderson, Honey & Reinholtd, Bill. LC 92-21446. 1993. 3.75 (0-383-03621-6) SRA Schl Grp.
—In the Forest. Ray, Stephen & Murdoch, Kathleen. LC 92-27266. 1993. 3.75 (0-383-03635-6) SRA Schl Grp.
—It Takes All Kinds. Markham-David, Sally. LC 93-21246. 1994. 4.25 (0-383-03753-0) SRA Schl Grp.
—Mouths & Noses. Markham-David, Sally. LC 93-29008. 1994. 4.25 (0-383-03764-6) SRA Schl Grp.
—Wolves. Ohanian, Susan. LC 93-28973. 1994. 4.25 (0-383-03742-5) SRA Schl Grp.
Ruth, Trevor & Ruth, Susan. Drawing My View. Ruth, Trevor & Ruth, Susan. LC 93-11827. 1994. 4.95 (0-383-03730-1) SRA Schl Grp.
Ruthen, Marlene L. A First Book of Jewish Holidays. Cedarbaum, Sophia. LC 85-105348. 80p. (gr. 1-3). 1984. pap. text ed. 6.95 (0-8074-0274-5, 301500) UAHC.
—I Learn about God. Bogot, Howard & Syme, Daniel B. 32p. (ps). 1982. pap. 4.00 (0-8074-0159-5, 101970) UAHC.
—Jewish Home Detectives. Syme, Deborah S. 32p. (gr. k-3). 1982. 4.00 (0-8074-0158-7, 101500) UAHC.
—Prayer Is Reaching. Bogot, Howard & Syme, Daniel. 32p. (ps). 1982. text ed. 4.00 (0-8074-0172-2, 101230) UAHC.
Rutherford, Donna. Prince. Van Susteren, Margery. 48p. 1991. pap. 7.95 (0-922510-05-9) Lucky Bks.
—Zonkey, the Donkey. Athey, Virginia. 20p. (ps-2). 1993. pap. 6.50 saddle stitch (0-922510-10-5) Lucky Bks.
Rutherford, Jenny. The Gift of the Pirate Queen. Giff, Patricia R. 160p. (gr. 4-8). 1983. pap. 3.25 (0-440-43046-1, Pub. by Yearling Classics) Dell.
—The Gift of the Pirate Queen. Giff, Patricia R. LC 82-70310. 160p. (gr. 4-6). 1982. 11.95 (0-385-28338-5); PLB 11.95 (0-385-28339-3) Delacorte.
—The Gift of the Pirate Queen. Giff, Patricia R. LC 82-70310. 160p. (gr. 4-8). 1982. 9.95 (0-440-02970-8); PLB 9.89 (0-440-02972-4) Delacorte.
—Invisible Lissa. Honeycutt, Natalie. LC 84-20466. 192p. (gr. 4-6). 1985. SBE 13.95 (0-02-744360-4, Bradbury Pr) Macmillan Child Grp.
—Mrs. Kiddy & the Moonbooms. Kibbe, Pat. LC 90-24406. 112p. (gr. 1-4). 1991. pap. 2.95 (0-689-71469-6, Aladdin) Macmillan Child Grp.
Rutherford, Meg. Big Panda, Little Panda. Stimson, Joan. LC 93-36235. 32p. (ps-2). 1994. 12.95 (0-8120-6404-6); pap. 4.95 (0-8120-1691-2) Barron.
—Hare's Choice. Hamley, Dennis. 96p. (gr. 5 up). 1992. pap. 3.25 (0-440-40698-6, YB) Dell.
—Picnic Pandemonium. Butler, M. Christina. LC 90-10148. 28p. (gr. 1-2). 1991. PLB 15.93 (0-8368-0433-3) Gareth Stevens Inc.
—Stanley in the Dark. Butler, M. Christina. 32p. (ps-1). 1990. with dust jacket 12.95 (0-8120-6158-6) Barron.
—Tigger & Friends. Hamley, Dennis. Briley, D., ed. LC 88-8385. (gr. k-3). 1989. 12.95 (0-688-08606-3); PLB 12.88 (0-688-08605-5) Lothrop.

—Tokoloshi: African Folktales Retold. Pitcher, Diana. 64p. (gr. 5 up). 1993. pap. write for info. (1-883672-03-1) Tricycle Pr.
Rutkovsky, Paul. Get. Rutkovsky, Paul. 72p. (Orig.). (gr. 9-12). 1987. pap. 8.95 (0-89822-048-3) Visual Studies.
Rutten, Nicole. The Great Invasion of the Stone Moles. Billiet, Daniel. Becker, Jane R., tr. from FRE. LC 89-26371. 32p. 1990. 13.95 (1-55670-153-5) Stewart Tabori & Chang.
—A Tale of Two Rats. Lager, Claude. 32p. (gr. k-3). 1991. 13.95 (1-55670-228-0) Stewart Tabori & Chang.
Ruyer, Francois. Robinson Crusoe. rev. & abr. ed. Defoe, Daniel. De Graaf, Anne, ed. 64p. (gr. 1-5). 1991. 8.95 (0-89107-601-8) Good News.
Ryan, Delores. Country Christmas. Marie, Nancy. 36p. (gr. k-5). 1979. 5.95 (0-941595-00-5) Heldreth Pub.
Ryan, Donna. Black Beauty. rev. ed. Currie, Quinn. 126p. (gr. k-8). 1990. pap. 10.95 (0-9623072-2-X) S Ink WA.
—Cousin Charlie, the Crow. Houts, Marshall. 84p. (Orig.). (gr. 2-8). 1992. pap. 10.95 (1-880812-00-2) S Ink WA.
—Lobo the Wolf: King of Currumpaw. rev. ed. Seton, Ernest T. 72p. (gr. 3-8). 1991. pap. 9.95 (0-9623072-4-6) S Ink WA.
—The Pacing Mustang. rev. ed. Seton, Ernest T. 72p. (gr. 3-8). 1991. pap. 9.95 (0-9623072-5-4) S Ink WA.
—William's Story. Duel, Debra. 72p. (Orig.). (gr. k-8). 1992. pap. 9.95 (1-880812-02-9) S Ink WA.
Ryan, John. Jonah, a Whale of a Tale. Ryan, John. 32p. (gr. 1-7). 1992. 11.95 (0-7459-2150-7) Lion USA.
—Mabel & the Tower of Babel. Ryan, John. 32p. (gr. 4-8). 1990. 9.99 (0-7459-1742-9) Lion USA.
—Pugwash & the Ghost Ship. Ryan, John. LC 68-23218. (gr. k-3). 1968. 21.95 (0-87599-146-7) S G Phillips.
Ryan, Ron, photos by. I'm Not a Bear. Burt, Denise. 32p. (gr. k-5). 1987. pap. 5.95 (0-944176-00-3) Terra Nova.
Ryan, Shea. Conklin's Atlas. Chadwick, Frank A. 80p. (Orig.). 1989. pap. 10.00 (1-55878-024-6) Game Designers.
Ryan, Susannah. Darcy & Gran Don't Like Babies. Cutler, Jane. LC 91-42214. 32p. (ps-2). 1993. 14.95 (0-590-44587-1, Scholastic Hardcover) Scholastic Inc.
—What's Missing. Yektai, Niki. LC 87-784. 32p. (ps-1). 1989. (Clarion Bks); pap. 4.95 (0-317-04349-8, Clarion Bks) HM.
—You Don't Need Words. Gross, Ruth B. 48p. 1991. 13. 95 (0-590-43897-2, Scholastic Hardcover) Scholastic Inc.
Ryan, Suzannah. What's Silly? Yektai, Niki. LC 88-22883. 32p. (gr. 2-4). 1989. 13.95 (0-89919-746-9, Clarion Bks) HM.
Ryden, Hope, photos by. Joey: The Story of a Baby Kangaroo. Ryden, Hope. LC 93-15419. 40p. 1994. 15. 00 (0-688-12744-4, Tambourine Bks); PLB 14.93 (0-688-12745-2, Tambourine Bks) Morrow.
—The Raggedy Red Squirrel. Ryden, Hope, text by. 48p. (gr. k-3). 1992. 16.00 (0-525-67400-4, Lodestar Bks) Dutton Child Bks.
—Wild Animals of America ABC. Ryden, Hope. LC 87-31127. (ps-3). 1988. 14.95 (0-525-67245-1, Lodestar Bks) Dutton Child Bks.
—Your Cat's Wild Cousins. Ryden, Hope, text by. 48p. (gr. 2-5). 1992. 16.00 (0-525-67354-7, Lodestar Bks) Dutton Child Bks.
—Your Dog's Wild Cousins. LC 93-26855. 1994. write for info. (0-525-67482-9, Lodestar Bks) Dutton Child Bks.
Rylands, Ljiljana. The Cinderella Rebus Book. Morris, Ann. LC 88-1451. 32p. (ps-3). 1989. 13.95 (0-531-05761-5); PLB 13.99 (0-531-08361-6) Orchard Bks Watts.
—The Little Red Riding Hood Rebus Book. Morris, Ann. LC 87-7696. 32p. (ps-3). 1987. 11.95 (0-531-05730-5); PLB 11.99 (0-531-08330-6) Orchard Bks Watts.
Rylant, Cynthia. The Everyday Books: Everyday Children. Rylant, Cynthia. LC 92-40932. 14p. (ps-k). 1993. bds. 4.95 with rounded corners (0-02-778022-8, Bradbury Pr) Macmillan Child Grp.
—The Everyday Books: Everyday Garden. Rylant, Cynthia. LC 92-40542. 14p. (ps-k). 1993. bds. 4.95 with rounded corners (0-02-778023-6, Bradbury Pr) Macmillan Child Grp.
—The Everyday Books: Everyday House. Rylant, Cynthia. LC 92-40943. 14p. (ps-k). 1993. bds. 4.95 with rounded corners (0-02-778024-4, Bradbury Pr) Macmillan Child Grp.
—The Everyday Books: Everyday Pets. Rylant, Cynthia. LC 92-40934. 14p. (ps-k). 1993. bds. 4.95 with rounded corners (0-02-778025-2, Bradbury Pr) Macmillan Child Grp.
—Everyday Town. Rylant, Cynthia. LC 92-40541. 14p. (ps-k). 1993. bds. 4.95 with rounded corners (0-02-778026-0, Bradbury Pr) Macmillan Child Grp.
Ryley, Chris. The Vikings: Fact & Fiction: Adventures of Young Vikings in Jorvik. Place, Robin. 52p. (gr. 2-8). 1987. pap. 7.50 (0-521-31572-7) Cambridge U Pr.
Rymer, Alta M. Captain Zomo. Rymer, Alta M. LC 79-67651. 48p. (Orig.). (gr. 4-6). 1985. pap. text ed. 12.50 (0-9600792-2-X) Rymer Bks.
—Hobart & Humbert Gruzzy. Rymer, Alta M. LC 85-61860. 28p. (Orig.). (gr. 4-6). 1988. pap. 12.50 (0-9600792-6-2) Rymer Bks.
—Oopletrump's Odyssey, Bk. 4. Rymer, Alta M. LC 85-61861. 38p. (Orig.). (gr. 4-6). 1987. pap. text ed. 12.50 (0-9600792-5-4) Rymer Bks.

—Stars of Obron: Chambo Returns. Rymer, Alta M. 48p. (Orig.). (gr. 4-6). 1987. pap. text ed. 12.50 (0-9600792-3-8) Rymer Bks.
—Up from Uzam. Rymer, Alta M. 28p. (Orig.). (gr. 2-4). 1987. pap. 11.50 (0-9600792-8-9) Rymer Bks.
Rytter, Peggy. Doing Things & Happenings. Kellogg, Mary G. LC 80-80271. 90p. (gr. 1-6). 1979. 6.95 (0-9603972-0-5); pap. 4.95 (0-9603972-1-3) Bks by Kellogg.

S

S, Svend O. The Man Who Kept House. Asbjornsen, P. C. & Moe, J. E. LC 91-37599. 32p. (gr. k-3). 1992. SBE 13.95 (0-689-50560-4, M K McElderry) Macmillan Child Grp.
Saahaddin, Anwar, et al. From the Young at Heart: A Student Anthology. Philadelphia Schools Students. Goodman, Sharon L., ed. 20p. (Orig.). (gr. 1-8). 1989. pap. write for info. (0-935369-19-8) In Tradition Pub.
Saba Designs, Inc. Staff. Safety Always Matters. Ahbe, Dottie & Pluta, Terry. Ahbe, S. 16p. (gr. 1-3). 1992. wkbk. 0.59 (0-9620584-1-6) Safety Always Matters.
—Safety Always Matters. Ahbe, Dottie & Pluta, Terry. Ahbe, S. 16p. (ps-k). 1992. wkbk. 0.59 (0-9620584-0-8) Safety Always Matters.
—Safety Always Matters. Ahbe, Dottie & Pluta, Terry. Ahbe, S. 16p. (gr. 4-6). 1992. wkbk. 0.59 (0-9620584-2-4) Safety Always Matters.
—Safety Always Matters. Ahbe, Dottie & Pluta, Terry. Ahbe, S. 32p. (ps-k). 1991. wkbk. 2.00 (0-9620584-3-2) Safety Always Matters.
—Safety Always Matters. Ahbe, Dottie & Pluta, Terry. Ahbe, S. 32p. (gr. 1-3). 1988. wkbk. 2.00 (0-9620584-4-0) Safety Always Matters.
—Safety Always Matters. Ahbe, Dottie & Pluta, Terry. Ahbe, S. 32p. (gr. 4-6). 1988. wkbk. 2.00 (0-9620584-5-9) Safety Always Matters.
Sabaka, Donna. Seashells in My Pocket: A Child's Nature Guide to Exploring the Atlantic Coast. 2nd ed. Hansen, Judith. LC 92-24397. 160p. (gr. 6 up). 1992. pap. 10.95 (1-878239-15-5) AMC Books.
—Secrets of Rivers & Streams. Swenson, Peter J. Jack, Susan, ed. 90p. (gr. 4-10). 1982. pap. 5.95 (0-930096-31-2) G Gannett.
Saban, Sonja. Johnny Egan of the Paintrock. Saban, Vera. LC 85-30958. 130p. (Orig.). (gr. 4-8). 1986. pap. 6.95 (0-914565-13-3, Timbertrails) Capstan Pubns.
Sabat, Jordi, jt. illus. see Segu, Jordi.
Sabatier, C. & Sabatier, R. Canard et la Panthere. Ayme, Marcel. (FRE). 63p. (gr. 1-5). 1991. pap. 9.95 (2-07-031128-7) Schoenhof.
—Mauvais Jars. Ayme, Marcel. (FRE). 72p. (gr. 1-5). 1990. pap. 10.95 (2-07-031236-4) Schoenhof.
—Paon. Ayme, Marcel. (FRE). 1985. pap. 8.95 (2-07-031087-6) Schoenhof.
Sabatier, R., jt. illus. see Sabatier, C.
Sabatier, Roland. Boites de Peinture. Ayme, Marcel. (FRE). 72p. (gr. 1-5). 1990. pap. 9.95 (2-07-031199-6) Schoenhof.
—Chien. Ayme, Marcel. (FRE). 72p. (gr. 1-5). 1990. pap. 9.95 (2-07-031201-1) Schoenhof.
—Cygnes. Ayme, Marcel. (FRE). 72p. (gr. 1-5). 1990. pap. 9.95 (2-07-031235-6) Schoenhof.
—Patte du Chat. Ayme, Marcel. (FRE). 72p. (gr. 1-5). 1990. pap. 9.95 (2-07-031200-3) Schoenhof.
—Probleme. Ayme, Marcel. (FRE). 71p. (ps-1). 1989. pap. 9.95 (2-07-031198-8) Schoenhof.
—Vaches. Ayme, Marcel. (FRE). 72p. (gr. 1-5). 1990. pap. 9.95 (2-07-031215-1) Schoenhof.
Sabatte, Frank. Where Is God? O'Leary, Daniel J. & Dalton, Kathleen. (gr. 4 up). 1991. pap. 2.95 (0-8091-6598-8) Paulist Pr.
Sabin, Francene. Autumn. Santrey, Louis. LC 82-19396. 32p. (gr. 4-7). 1983. lib. bdg. 10.79 (0-89375-905-8); pap. text ed. 2.95 (0-89375-906-6) Troll Assocs.
—Spring. Santrey, Louis. LC 82-19381. 32p. (gr. 4-7). 1983. lib. bdg. 10.79 (0-89375-909-0); pap. text ed. 2.95 (0-89375-910-4) Troll Assocs.
—Winter. Santrey, Louis. LC 82-19353. 32p. (gr. 4-7). 1983. lib. bdg. 10.79 (0-89375-907-4); pap. text ed. 2.95 (0-89375-908-2) Troll Assocs.
Sabuda, Robert. Earth Verses & Water Rhymes. Lewis, J. Patrick. LC 90-40709. 32p. (gr. 2-5). 1991. SBE 13.95 (0-689-31693-3, Atheneum Child Bk) Macmillan Child Grp.
—The Fiddler's Son. Coco, Eugene B. 32p. 1991. pap. 5.95 (0-88138-111-X, Green Tiger) S&S Trade.
—I Hear America Singing. Whitman, Walt. 32p. (ps-3). 1991. 14.95 (0-399-21808-4, Philomel) Putnam Pub Group.
—The Ibis & the Egret. Owen, Roy. LC 92-26220. 32p. (ps-3). 1993. 14.95 (0-399-22504-8, Philomel Bks) Putnam Pub Group.
—The Log of Christopher Columbus: The First Voyage: Spring, Summer & Fall, 1492. Columbus, Christopher. Lowe, Steve, ed. 32p. (ps-3). 1992. 14.95 (0-399-22139-5, Philomel Bks) Putnam Pub Group.
—Saint Valentine. Sabuda, Robert. LC 91-25012. 32p. (gr. 1-4). 1992. SBE 14.95 (0-689-31762-X, Atheneum Child Bk) Macmillan Child Grp.
—A Tree Place & Other Poems. Levy, Constance. LC 93-20586. 48p. (gr. k-5). 1994. SBE 13.95 (0-689-50599-X, M K McElderry) Macmillan Child Grp.

—Tutankhamen's Gift. Sabuda, Robert. LC 93-5401. 32p. (gr. 1-4). 1994. SBE 14.95 (0-689-31818-9, Atheneum Child Bk) Macmillan Child Grp.
—Walden. Thoreau, Henry David. Lowe, Steve, ed. 32p. 1990. 14.95 (0-399-22153-0, Philomel Bks) Putnam Pub Group.
—The Wishing Well. Coco, Eugene B. 36p. 1991. pap. 7.95 (0-88138-112-8, Green Tiger) S&S Trade.
Saccone, Vivian R. ABC's of What Is Black. Saccone, Vivian R. LC 92-84105. 44p. (ps-3). Date not set. pap. 5.95 (1-55523-583-2) Winston-Derek.
Sacre, Marie-Jose. Nobody Has Time for Me. Skutina, Vladimir. Klein, Zanvel, ed. Herrmann, Dagmar, tr. from CZE. LC 91-4457. 32p. (gr. k-3). 1991. 14.95 (0-922984-07-7) Wellington IL.
Sadowski, Wiktor. Grandma Essie's Covered Wagon. Williams, David. 48p. (ps-3). 1993. 16.00 (0-679-80253-3); PLB 16.99 (0-679-90253-8) Knopf Bks Yng Read.
Saekeres, Cyndy. Patsy Scarry's Big Bedtime Storybook. reissued ed. Scarry, Patsy. LC 79-5450. 72p. (ps-1). 1990. 9.95 (0-679-80756-X) Random Bks Yng Read.
Saelig, S. M. Moonhorse. Osborne, Mary P. LC 87-3818. 40p. (ps-3). 1991. 14.95 (0-394-88960-6); lib. bdg. 15.99 (0-394-98960-0) Knopf Bks Yng Read.
Saffioti, Lino. A History Mystery: The Disappearance of the Anasazi. Hubbard-Brown, Janet. 96p. (Orig.). 1992. pap. 3.50 (0-380-76845-3, Camelot) Avon.
—On Being Sarah. Helfman, Elizabeth. Mathews, Judith, ed. 144p. (gr. 5-9). 1992. 11.95g (0-8075-6068-5) A Whitman.
Safian, Elizabeth & Chernak, Judy. K'tonton in Israel, 3 bks. Weilerstein, Sadie R. (ps-6). 1988. Set of 3 bks. in zip loc bag. pap. 6.95 (0-944633-32-3); Set of 3 bks. & cassettes. pap. 29.95 (0-685-43967-4); pap. 2.95 ea. Bk. 1: A Visit with K'tonton & K'tonton on Kibbutz, 40p. Bk. 2: K'tonton in Jerusalem-I: Adventure on Yom Ha'atzma'ut, Israel's Independence Day, 32p. Bk. 3: K'tonton in Jerusalem-II: Adventure in the Old City, 36p. pap. 10.95 ea. bk. & cassette; cassette 8.95 ea. J Chernak.
Saflund, Birgitta. Reading to Matthew. Vivelo, Jackie. LC 93-84912. 40p. (gr. 3-8). 1993. 15.95 (1-879373-60-2) R Rinehart.
—Remember My Name. Banks, Sara H. LC 92-61905. 120p. (Orig.). (gr. 4-8). 1993. pap. 8.95 (1-879373-38-6) R Rinehart.

Sagan, Alexander. The Big Fish: An Alaskan Fairy Tale. Wakeland, Marcia A. 32p. (ps-4). 1993. 14.95 (0-9635083-1-8) Misty Mtn. THE BIG FISH recounts the story of Lena, an Alaskan native girl, who has a dream of catching the great King Salmon. She thinks that she will become someone special if she catches the big fish. After repeated attempts, she is about to give up on her dream when suddenly the King Salmon grabs her line & pulls her into the magic river. There he shows her the fish of his kingdom doing wonderful things because they believe they can. Lena finally understands that she is already special & that she can do anything if she believes in herself. Brilliant, splashy illustrations cover each of the 32 pages of this delightful book, that not only strives to affirm children just as they are, but to intrigue the reader with the beauty & grandeur of America's last frontier. Order from Misty Mountain Publishing, P.O. Box 773042, Eagle River, AK 99577 or phone/FAX orders at (907) 696-8166. Publisher Provided Annotation.

—Puffin: A Journey Home. Tilly, Jim. 32p. 1993. 14.95 (0-9635083-3-4) Misty Mtn.
Sagasti, Miriam. Bedtime. Lanton, Sandy. 32p. (ps-2). Date not set. 11.95 (1-56065-141-5) Capstone Pr. Postponed.
—I Am a Doctor. Benjamin, Cynthia. 24p. (ps). 1994. 8.95 (0-8120-6380-5) Barron.
—Number Fun. Baxter, Roberta. 32p. (ps-2). Date not set. 11.95 (1-56065-147-4) Capstone Pr. Postponed.
—The Shape of Your World. Baxter, Roberta. 32p. (ps-2). Date not set. 11.95 (1-56065-144-X) Capstone Pr. Postponed.
—Yo Soy un Medico. Benjamin, Cynthia. 24p. (ps). 1994. 8.95 (0-8120-6414-3) Barron.
Sagati, Miriam. Turn of the Seasons. Baxter, Roberta. 32p. (ps-2). Date not set. 11.95 (1-56065-146-6) Capstone Pr. Postponed.
Sage, Alison. Teddy Bears Cure a Cold. Gretz, Susanna. LC 84-4015. 40p. (gr. k-3). 1985. RSBE 13.95 (0-02-736960-9, Four Winds) Macmillan Child Grp.

—Teddy Bears Cure a Cold. Gretz, Susanna. 32p. (ps-2). 1986. pap. 3.95 (0-590-43495-0) Scholastic Inc.
Sage, Jacqueline I. Many Furs: A Grimm's Fairy Tale. LC 81-947. 32p. (gr. 1-4). 1990. 9.95 (0-89742-041-1) Celestial Arts.
Sagendorf, Kit. Country Antiques: A Child's Guide. Smith, Brad R. 64p. (Orig.). (gr. 1-3). 1987. pap. 11.95 (0-9618645-0-8) Sanford Hse Pr.
Sahlhoff, Carl. Friends in the Park. Bunnett, Rochelle. 32p. 1993. 7.95 (1-56288-347-X) Checkerboard.
Sahlin, Cliff. The Daligator. Sahlin, Cliff. LC 88-83575. 28p. (Orig.). (ps-3). 1988. pap. text ed. 4.95 (0-9621714-0-9) Gamin Pr.
Sahloff, Carl, jt. photog. see Brown, Matt.
St. George, Adrianne B. Enchanted Hike: Children's Adventure Story in Verse. Meet Magical Rabbit in California. Vickery, Eugene L. 20p. (Orig.). (gr. 1-8). 1987. pap. 3.95 (0-937775-04-5) Stonehaven Pubs.
—The Enchanted Mountain: Romantic & Science Fiction Story in Verse. Vickery, Eugene L. (Orig.). (gr. 1-8). 1987. pap. 3.95 (0-937775-05-3) Stonehaven Pubs.
St. George, Carolyn. Be Alive in Christ. Doolittle, Robert. Stamschror, Robert P., ed. 188p. (Orig.). (gr. 9-12). 1991. pap. 16.95 (0-88489-246-8) St Marys
—Create Community with Christ. Doolittle, Robert. Stamschror, Robert P., ed. 168p. (Orig.). (gr. 9-12). 1991. pap. 16.95 (0-88489-247-6) St Marys
—Growing in Christian Morality. Ahlers, Julia, et al. Nagel, Steve, ed. 304p. (Orig.). (gr. 10-11). 1992. pap. text ed. 13.50 (0-88489-260-3); 18.95 (0-88489-261-1) St Marys
—Vine & Branches, Vol. 1. Hakowski, Maryann. Stamschror, Robert P., ed. 168p. (gr. 7-12). 1992. spiral bdg. 22.95 (0-88489-255-7) St Marys
—Vine & Branches, Vol. 2. Hakowski, Maryann. Stamschror, Robert P., ed. 168p. (gr. 7-12). 1992. spiral bdg. 22.95 (0-88489-278-6) St Marys
St. James, Jim. Mystari. Northrop, Nancy. 16p. 1991. bds. 5.95 spiral bdg. (0-9627894-1-0) LNR Pubns.
St. James, Synthia. Snow on Snow on Snow. Chapman, Cheryl. 1994. write for info. (0-8037-1456-4); PLB write for info. (0-8037-1457-2) Dial Bks Young.
St. John, Maddie. A Story from Widg. St. John, Maddie, et al. LC 90-71987. 64p. (Orig.). (gr. k-3). 1992. pap. 6.00 (1-56002-047-4) Aegina Pr.
St. Marie, Janice. Kidding Around San Francisco: A Young Person's Guide to the City. Zibart, Rosemary. 64p. (Orig.). (gr. 3 up). 1989. pap. 9.95 (0-945465-23-8) John Muir.
St. Tamara. Asian Crafts. St. Tamara. LC 71-86983. (gr. 2-6). 1972. PLB 13.95 (0-87460-148-7) Lion Bks.
Saint-Exupery, Antoine de. Little Prince. Saint-Exupery, Antoine de. Woods, Katherine, tr. LC 67-1144. 91p. (gr. 3-7). 1943. 13.95 (0-15-246503-0, HB Juv Bks) HarBrace.
—Le Petit Prince. Saint-Exupery, Antoine de. LC 43-5812. (FRE.). 91p. (gr. 3-7). 1943. 14.95 (0-15-243818-1, HB Juv Bks) HarBrace.
Saito, Manabu. The Golden Carp, & Other Romantic Tales of Viet-Nam. Vuong, Lynette D. LC 92-38208. (gr. k-5). 1993. write for info. (0-688-12514-X) Lothrop.
Sakahara, Dick. How Honu the Turtle Got His Shell. McGuire-Turcotte, Casey A. 30p. (gr. k up). 1991. PLB 17.96 (0-8172-2783-0); pap. 3.95 (0-8114-4304-3) Raintree Steck-V.
—Huan Ching & the Golden Fish. Reeser, Michael. 32p. (gr. 2-4). 1988. PLB 17.96 (0-8172-2751-2); pap. 3.95 (0-685-58496-8) Raintree Steck-V.
Sakaka, Donna. Secrets of a Mountain. Ferriss, Lloyd. Jack, Susan, ed. 76p. (Orig.). (gr. 4-10). 1982. pap. 3.95 (0-930096-18-5) G Gannett.
Sakamoto, Dean, jt. illus. see Aguiar, Elithe.
Sakkal, Ma'moun. A Wicked Wazir. Simpson, Juwairiah J. 48p. (Orig.). (gr. 3-6). 1990. pap. 6.50 (0-89259-084-X) Am Trust Pubns.
Sakurai, Atsushi. Crabs. Johnson, Sylvia A. LC 82-10056. 48p. (gr. 4 up). 1982. PLB 19.95 (0-8225-1471-0) Lerner Pubns.
Saldutti, Denise. Feathers in the Wind. Chaikin, Miriam. LC 88-10978. 64p. (gr. 3-5). 1989. HarpC Child Bks.
—The Moon. Stevenson, Robert Louis. LC 83-47704. 32p. (ps-3). 1986. pap. 4.95 (0-06-443098-7, Trophy) HarpC Child Bks.
—Think of It. Killion, Bette. LC 89-26878. 32p. (ps-1). 1993. 12.00 (0-06-023257-9); PLB 11.89 (0-06-023258-7) HarpC Child Bks.
Sales, G. My First Visit to the Aquarium. Parramon, J. M. 32p. (ps). 1990. 5.95 (0-8120-4304-9) Barron.
—My First Visit to the Aviary. Parramon, J. M. 32p. (ps). 1990. pap. 4.95 (0-8120-4303-0) Barron.
—My First Visit to the Zoo. Parramon, J. M. 32p. (ps). 1990. pap. 5.95 (0-8120-4302-2) Barron.
Salinas, Ron. Cultural Pride Student Workbook. Matiella, Ana C. 96p. (Orig.). (gr. 5-8). 1988. pap. 7.95 (0-941816-68-0) ETR Assocs.
—La Familia Student Workbook. Matiella, Ana C. 96p. (Orig.). (gr. 5-8). 1988. pap. 7.95 (0-941816-70-2) ETR Assocs.
Salter, Heidi. Taddy McFinley & the Great Grey Grimly. Salter, Heidi. Thatch, Nancy R., ed. Melton, David, intro. by. LC 89-31820. 26p. (gr. 3-8). 1989. PLB 14.95 (0-933849-21-4) Landmark Edns.
Salter, Marsha C. Amerigo: The Amerigo Vespucci Story. Nilsen, Frances S. & Salter, James L. LC 92-93878. 253p. (gr. 10-12). 1992. 14.95 (0-9633937-6-6) Shamrock TN.

Salter, Safaya. Just So Stories. Kipling, Rudyard. LC 86-46271. 96p. (gr. 2-4). 1987. 16.95 (0-8050-0439-4, Bks Young Read) H Holt & Co.
Saltzberg, Barney. Jake & Jenny on the Town. Rojany, Lisa. 18p. (gr. k-3). 1993. 7.95 (0-8431-3584-0) Price Stern.
—Mrs. Morgan's Lawn. Saltzberg, Barney. 32p. (ps-2). 1993. write for info. (1-56282-423-6); PLB write for info. (1-56282-424-4) Hyprn Child.
—The No Barking at the Table Cookbook: Canine Recipes Most Begged For. Boyd-Smith, Wendy. 106p. (Orig.). 1991. pap. text ed. write for info. (0-9629459-0-0) Lip Smackers.
Saltzman, Yuri. Shabbat Can Be. Marcus, Audrey F. & Zwerin, Raymond A. Syme, Daniel B., ed. (gr. k-3). 1979. 10.95 (0-8074-0023-8) UAHC.
Salzman, Yuri. Chameleon's Rainbow. Walton, Marilyn J. LC 84-17760. 32p. (gr. 3-6). 1985. PLB 14.65 (0-940742-45-4); incl cassette 27.99 (0-8172-2285-5) Raintree Steck-V.
—The Three Bears. 24p. (gr. 2-5). 1987. pap. write for info. (0-307-10050-2, Pub. by Golden Bks) Western Pub.
—The Three Little Pigs. Salzman, Yuri, retold by. LC 87-81773. 24p. (ps-k). 1988. pap. write for info. (0-307-10099-5, Pub. by Golden Bks) Western Pub.
—The Three Wishes. Craig, M. Jean. 48p. (Orig.). (gr. k-3). 1986. pap. 2.50 (0-590-41744-4) Scholastic Inc.
Salzmann, Laurence, photos by. Family Passover. Rosen, Anne, et al. LC 79-89298. 64p. (gr. 2 up). 1980. 8.95 (0-8276-0169-7) JPS Phila.
Sam, Joe. The Invisible Hunters (Los cazadores invisibles) Rohmer, Harriet, et al, eds. LC 86-32658. (ENG & SPA.). (gr. 2-7). 1987. 13.95 (0-89239-031-X) Childrens Book Pr.
Samaha, MaryLou. Little Love's Color Corner: Color Me Book. Samaha, MaryLou. 16p. (ps-2). 1988. write for info. (0-9619988-0-6) Kenmar Ent.
Samapatti. Sing for Your Life. Kerr, Sandra, compiled by. 80p. (gr. 3 up). 12.95 (0-7136-5546-1, Pub. by A&C Black UK) Talman.
Sampson, Katharine. Dorothea L. Dix: Hospital Founder. Malone, Mary. 80p. (gr. 2-6). 1991. Repr. of 1968 ed. lib. bdg. 12.95 (0-7910-1436-3) Chelsea Hse.
Samton, Sheila W. Everyone Asked about You. Gross, Theodore F. 32p. (ps-3). 1990. 14.95 (0-399-21727-4, Philomel Bks) Putnam Pub Group.
—Moon to Sun: An Adding Book. Samton, Sheila W. LC 90-85729. 24p. (ps-1). 1991. 9.95 (1-878093-13-4) Boyds Mills Pr.
—My Haunted House: A Lift-the-Flap Book. Samton, Sheila W. 24p. (ps-k). 1992. bds. 12.95 (1-56397-093-7) Boyds Mills Pr.
—Oh No! A Naptime Adventure. Samton, Sheila W. 32p. (ps-1). 1993. RB 13.99 (0-670-84250-8) Viking Child Bks.
—On the River: An Adding Book. Samton, Sheila W. LC 90-85730. 24p. (ps-1). 1991. 9.95 (1-878093-14-2) Boyds Mills Pr.
—The World from My Window. Samton, Sheila W. LC 90-85732. 28p. (ps-2). 1991. Repr. 14.95 (1-878093-15-0) Boyds Mills Pr.
Samuel, A. Nupo. Iyabo of Nigeria. Johnston, Rhoda O. (gr. 5-12). 1973. pap. 5.00x (0-914522-01-9, 163808) Alpha Iota.
Samuels, Barbara. Baby Comes Home. Driscoll, Debbie. LC 91-2414. 40p. (gr. k-4). 1993. pap. 14.00 JRT (0-671-75540-4, S&S BFYR) S&S Trade.
—Duncan & Dolores. Samuels, Barbara. LC 85-17119. 32p. (ps-2). 1986. RSBE 13.95 (0-02-778210-7, Bradbury Pr) Macmillan Child Grp.
—Duncan & Dolores. Samuels, Barbara. LC 85-17119. 32p. (ps-3). 1989. pap. 3.95 (0-689-71294-4, Aladdin) Macmillan Child Grp.
—Faye & Dolores. Samuels, Barbara. LC 84-1612. 40p. (ps-2). 1985. RSBE 13.95 (0-02-778120-8, Bradbury Pr) Macmillan Child Grp.
—Faye & Dolores. Samuels, Barbara. LC 87-1419. 40p. (ps-3). 1987. pap. 4.95 (0-689-71154-9, Aladdin) Macmillan Child Grp.
—Someday Angeline. Sachar, Louis. 160p. (Orig.). (gr. 3-7). 1983. pap. 3.50 (0-380-83444-8, Camelot) Avon.
Samuels, Mark. Dumpy the Dump Truck. Dubowski, Cathy E. 24p. (Orig.). (gr. k-1). 1990. pap. 0.99 (1-878624-32-6) McClanahan Bk.
—Sammy the Steamroller. Coco, Eugene. 24p. (ps-2). 1993. pap. text ed. 0.99 (1-56293-347-7) McClanahan Bk.
Sanacore, Stephen, photos by. A Day in the Life of a Meteorologist. Witty, Margot & Witty, Ken. LC 80-54098. 32p. (gr. 4-8). 1981. PLB 11.79 (0-89375-450-1); pap. 2.95 (0-89375-451-X); cassettes avail. Troll Assocs.
—A Day in the Life of a TV News Reporter. Trainer, David. LC 78-68810. 32p. (gr. 4-8). 1980. PLB 11.79 (0-89375-228-2); pap. 2.95 (0-89375-232-0); cassettes avail. Troll Assocs.
—A Day in the Life of an Illustrator. Witty, Ken. LC 80-54100. 32p. (gr. 4-8). 1981. PLB 11.79 (0-89375-448-X); pap. 2.95 (0-89375-449-8); cassette avail. Troll Assocs.
Sancha, Sheila. Walter Dragun's Town: Crafts & Trade in the Middle Ages. Sancha, Sheila. LC 88-34066. 64p. (gr. 4 up). 1989. (Crowell Jr Bks); PLB 15.89 (0-690-04806-8, Crowell Jr Bks) HarpC Child Bks.

Sanchez, Bill. Book of the American Indians. Bovert, Howard E. & Baranzini, Marlene S. LC 93-3068. (gr. 1-8). 1993. 19.95 (*0-316-96921-4*); pap. 10.95 (*0-316-22208-9*) Little.
—Book of the American Revolution. Bovet, Howard E., et al. LC 93-21769. (gr. 9-12). 1994. 19.95 (*0-316-96922-2*) Little.
Sanchez, Carlos. Perez & Martina. Belpre, Pura. 64p. 1991. 15.95 (*0-670-84166-8*) Viking Child Bks.
Sanchez, Enrique O. Abuela's Weave. Castaneda, Omar S. LC 92-71927. 32p. (gr. k-3). 1993. 14.95 (*1-880000-00-8*) Lee & Low Bks.
—Amelia's Road. Altman, Linda J. LC 92-59982. 32p. (gr. k-3). 1993. 14.95 (*1-880000-04-0*) Lee & Low Bks.
Sanchez, Jesus A. Max Science & the Burned Out Bulb. Sanchez, Jesus A. Sanchez, Brenda L., ed. 24p. (gr. k-5). 1990. pap. 3.95 (*1-879350-00-9*) Max Sci Pub.
Sanchez, Jose R. Animals del Circo de Sonora. Bell, Clarisa. (SPA.). 24p. (Orig.). (gr. k-5). 1993. pap. 9.95x (*1-56492-081-X*) Laredo.
—At the Olympics. Bell, Clarisa. Kohen, Gabriela, tr. from SPA. 24p. (Orig.). (gr. 2-6). 1992. pap. 9.95x (*1-56492-007-0*) Laredo.

— El Circo. Bell, Clarisa. (SPA.). 24p. (Orig.). (gr. 2-6). 1992. PLB 9.95x (*1-56492-078-X*) Laredo.
A great artist & a fabulous author have combined efforts to provide an unusual view of circus people. Sparkling color & humor further enhance this book. In Spanish.
Publisher Provided Annotation.

—The Circus. Kohen, Gabriela. 24p. (Orig.). (gr. 2-6). 1992. pap. 9.95x (*1-56492-023-2*) Laredo.
—Circus Animals. Kohen, Gabriele. 24p. (Orig.). (gr. k-5). 1993. pap. 9.95x (*1-56492-026-7*) Laredo.
—The Circus: Big Book. Kohen, Gabriela. 24p. (gr. 2-6). 1992. pap. 19.95x (*1-56492-024-0*) Laredo.

— En Las Olimpidas. Bell, Clarisa. (SPA.). 24p. (Orig.). (gr. 2-6). 1992. PLB 9.95x (*1-56492-051-8*) Laredo.
Whoever expected to read about the Olympic games in rhyme...In this simple yet imaginative book, this topic is beautifully brought to life. In Spanish.
Publisher Provided Annotation.

—Games People Play. Bell, Clarisa. Kohen, Gabriela, tr. from SPA. 24p. (gr. 2-6). 1992. pap. 9.95x (*1-56492-004-6*) Laredo.
—Games People Play: Big Book. Bell, Clarisa. Kohen, Gabriela, tr. from SPA. 24p. (Orig.). (gr. 2-6). 1992. pap. 19.95x (*1-56492-005-4*) Laredo.
—El Rabo de Gato. Kohen, Clarita. (SPA.). 16p. (gr. k-3). 1993. pap. 7.50x (*1-56492-102-6*) Laredo.
—El Teatro. Bell, Clarisa. (SPA.). 24p. (gr. 2-6). 1992. pap. 9.95x (*1-56492-056-9*) Laredo.
—El Teatro: Big Book. Bell, Clarisa. (SPA.). 24p. (Orig.). (gr. 2-6). 1992. pap. 19.95x (*1-56492-057-7*) Laredo.
—The Theatre. Kohen, Gabriela. 24p. (Orig.). (gr. 2-6). 1992. pap. 9.95x (*1-56492-012-7*) Laredo.
—The Theatre: Big Book. Kohen, Gabriela. 24p. (Orig.). (gr. 2-6). 1992. pap. 19.95x (*1-56492-013-5*) Laredo.
—Vamos a Jugar. Bell, Clarisa. (SPA.). 24p. (Orig.). (gr. 2-6). 1992. pap. 9.95x (*1-56492-048-8*) Laredo.
—Vamos a Jugar: Big Book. Bell, Clarisa. (SPA.). 24p. (Orig.). (gr. 2-6). 1992. pap. 19.95x (*1-56492-049-6*) Laredo.
Sanchez, Larry M. Paul, the Shepherd Boy & the Birthday Sandals. LaGrange, Lynn M. 36p. (ps-6). 1990. lib. bdg. 10.95 (*1-878790-00-5*) Fables CO.
—Paul, the Shepherd Boy & the Birthday Sandals. LaGrange, Lynn M. 36p. (ps-6). 1990. pap. 6.95 (*1-878790-03-X*) Fables CO.
Sand, Maurice. Histoire du Veritable Gribouille. Sand, George. (FRE.). 122p. (gr. 5-10). 1978. pap. 7.95 (*2-07-033043-5*) Schoenhof.
Sandal, Maurice. Little Bear's Visit. Minarik, Else H. LC 61-11451. 64p. (gr. k-3). 1979. pap. 3.50 (*0-06-444023-0*, Trophy) HarpC Child Bks.
Sandberg, Lasse. Dusty Wants to Borrow Everything. Sandberg, Inger. Maurer, Judy A., tr. 32p. (ps up). 1988. 6.95 (*91-29-58782-4*, R & S Bks) FS&G.
—Dusty Wants to Help. Sandberg, Inger. Mauver, Judy A., tr. from SWE. 32p. (ps up). 1987. 6.95 (*91-29-58336-5*, Pub. by R & S Bks) FS&G.
Sandeen, Eileen. Jenna's Big Jump. Thureen, Faythe D. 112p. (gr. 2-5). 1993. SBE 12.95 (*0-689-31834-0*, Atheneum Child Bk) Macmillan Child Grp.
Sanders, Dave, Jr. Alligators, Monsters & Cool School Poems. Sanders, Addie M. 80p. (Orig.). (gr. 3-10). 1993. pap. 9.00 (*0-911943-36-6*) Leadership Pub.
Sanderson, Ruth. The Animal, the Vegetable, & John D. Jones. Byars, Betsy. 160p. (gr. 5 up). 1983. pap. 3.25 (*0-440-40356-1*, YB) Dell.
—Beauty & the Beast. Easton, Samantha. 32p. (ps-3). 1992. 6.95 (*0-8362-4919-4*) Andrews & McMeel.

—Bobbsey Twins: The Missing Pony Mystery. Hope, Laura L. 112p. (gr. 2-5). 1981. 7.95 (*0-671-42295-2*) S&S Trade.
—Don't Hurt Laurie! Roberts, Willo D. LC 76-46569. 176p. (gr. 4-6). 1977. SBE 14.95 (*0-689-30571-0*, Atheneum Child Bk) Macmillan Child Grp.
—Don't Hurt Laurie! Roberts, Willo D. LC 87-21742. 176p. (gr. 3-7). 1988. pap. 3.95 (*0-689-71206-5*, Aladdin) Macmillan Child Grp.
—Into the Dream. Sleator, William. LC 78-11825. 144p. (gr. 4-7). 1979. 13.95 (*0-525-32583-2*, DCB) Dutton Child Bks.
—The Mystery of Pony Hollow. Hall, Lynn. LC 91-29861. 64p. (Orig.). (gr. 2-4). 1992. PLB 6.99 (*0-679-93052-3*); pap. 2.50 (*0-679-83052-9*) Random Bks Yng Read.
—One of Us. Amdur, Nikki. LC 81-65847. (gr. 3-6). 1981. Dial Bks Young.
—The Pudgy Bunny Book. 16p. (gr. k). 1984. 2.95 (*0-448-10210-2*, G&D) Putnam Pub Group.
—Samantha on Stage. Farrar, Susan C. 164p. (gr. 3 up). 1990. pap. 3.95 (*0-14-034328-8*, Puffin) Puffin Bks.
—The Secret Garden. Burnett, Frances H. LC 86-46002. 240p. 1988. 18.95 (*0-394-55431-0*) Knopf Bks Yng Read.
Sandford, John. Argyle. Wallace, Brooks B. LC 91-76021. 32p. (ps-3). 1992. 13.95 (*1-56397-043-0*) Boyds Mills Pr.
—The Fox, the Bear, & the Fish. Bodnar, Judit Z., adapted by. & tr. LC 93-19046. 1995. write for info. (*0-688-12174-8*); lib. bdg. write for info. (*0-688-12175-6*) Lothrop.
—The Gum on the Drum. Gregorich, Barbara. Hoffman, Joan, ed. 16p. (Orig.). (gr. k-2). 1984. pap. 2.25 (*0-88743-004-X*, 06004) Sch Zone Pub Co.
—Nellie Lou's Hairdos. Sandford, John. 32p. 1990. pap. 9.95 (*1-55782-098-8*, Pub. by Warner Juvenile Bks) Little.
—Nine Men Chase a Hen. Gregorich, Barbara. Hoffman, Joan, ed. 16p. (Orig.). (gr. k-2). 1984. pap. 2.25 (*0-88743-009-0*, 06009) Sch Zone Pub Co.
—The Old Red Rocking Chair. Root, Phyllis. 32p. (ps-3). 1992. 14.95 (*1-55970-063-7*) Arcade Pub Inc.
—The Rinky-Dink Cafe. Davis, Maggie S. LC 87-35435. 32p. (ps-3). 1988. pap. 12.95 (*0-671-66408-5*) S&S Trade.
Sandford, John & Pape, Richard. The Raccoon on the Moon: Reading Workbook. Witty, Bruce & Gregorich, Barbara. Hoffman, Joan, ed. 32p. (Orig.). (gr. k-2). 1988. 1.99 (*0-88743-108-9*) Sch Zone Pub Co.
Sandin, J. Snowshoe Thompson. Levinson, Nancy S. LC 90-37401. 64p. (gr. k-3). 1992. 14.00 (*0-06-023801-1*); PLB 13.89 (*0-06-023802-X*) HarpC Child Bks.
Sandin, Joan. Always Wondering: Some Favorite Poems of Aileen Fisher. Fisher, Aileen. LC 90-23069. 96p. (gr. 2-6). 1991. 13.95 (*0-06-022851-2*); PLB 13.89 (*0-06-022858-X*) HarpC Child Bks.
—Clipper Ship. Lewis, Thomas P. LC 77-11858. 64p. (ps-3). 1978. 11.95 (*0-06-023808-9*); PLB 11.89 (*0-06-023809-7*) HarpC Child Bks.
—Clipper Ship. Lewis, Thomas P. LC 77-11858. 64p. (gr. k-3). 1992. pap. 3.50 (*0-06-444160-1*, Trophy) HarpC Child Bks.
—Daniel's Duck. Bulla, Clyde R. LC 77-25647. 64p. (gr. k-3). 1979. PLB 13.89 (*0-06-020909-7*) HarpC Child Bks.
—Daniel's Duck. Bulla, Clyde R. LC 78-22156. 64p. (gr. k-3). 1982. pap. 3.50 (*0-06-444031-1*, Trophy) HarpC Child Bks.
—From Anna. Little, Jean. LC 72-76505. 208p. (gr. 4-6). 1972. PLB 14.89 (*0-06-023912-3*) HarpC Child Bks.
—From Anna. Little, Jean. LC 72-76505. 208p. (gr. 4-6). 1973. pap. 3.95 (*0-06-440044-1*, Trophy) HarpC Child Bks.
—Hill of Fire. Lewis, Thomas P. LC 70-121802. 64p. (gr. k-3). 1971. PLB 13.89 (*0-06-023804-6*) HarpC Child Bks.
—Hill of Fire. Lewis, Thomas P. LC 70-121802. 64p. (gr. k-3). 1987. incl. cassette 5.98 (*0-694-00175-9*, Trophy); pap. 3.50 (*0-06-444040-0*, Trophy) HarpC Child Bks.
—The House of a Mouse. Fisher, Aileen. LC 87-24947. 32p. (ps-3). 1988. HarpC Child Bks.
—The Lemming Condition. Arkin, Alan. LC 75-6296. 64p. (gr. 4 up). 1976. 13.00 (*0-06-020133-9*) HarpC Child Bks.
—The Long Way to a New Land. Sandin, Joan. LC 80-8942. 64p. (gr. k-3). 1981. PLB 13.89 (*0-06-025194-8*) HarpC Child Bks.
—The Long Way to a New Land. Sandin, Joan. LC 80-8942. 64p. (gr. k-3). 1986. pap. 3.50 (*0-06-444100-8*, Trophy) HarpC Child Bks.
—The Long Way Westward. Sandin, Joan. LC 89-2024. 64p. (gr. k-3). 1989. 14.00 (*0-06-025206-5*); PLB 13.89 (*0-06-025207-3*) HarpC Child Bks.
—The Long Way Westward. Sandin, Joan. LC 89-2024. 64p. (gr. k-3). 1992. pap. 3.50 (*0-06-444198-9*, Trophy) HarpC Child Bks.
—Look Through My Window. Little, Jean. LC 71-105470. 270p. (gr. 4-7). 1970. PLB 14.89 (*0-06-023924-7*) HarpC Child Bks.
—Small Wolf. Benchley, Nathaniel. LC 70-183170. 64p. (gr. k-3). 1972. PLB 13.89 (*0-06-020492-3*) HarpC Child Bks.
—Small Wolf. Benchley, Nathaniel. 1994. write for info. (*0-06-444180-6*) HarpC Child Bks.

—Trouble at the Mines. Rappaport, Doreen. LC 84-45339. 96p. (gr. 3-7). 1987. (Crowell Jr Bks); PLB 13.89 (*0-690-04446-1*, Crowell Jr Bks) HarpC Child Bks.
Sandlain-Buchanan, Deborah. The Chocolate Tree: An African Folktale. Sandlain-Buchanan, Deborah. 16p. (Orig.). (gr. k-3). 1993. write for info. (*0-9639057-2-4*); lib. bdg. write for info. (*0-9639057-0-8*); 5.00 (*0-9639057-1-6*) Chocolate Tree.
Sandoval, Dolores. Be Patient, Abdul. Sandoval, Dolores. LC 93-34224. 1994. write for info. (*0-689-50607-4*, M K McElderry) Macmillan Child Grp.
Sandoval, Richard C. Miguel & the Santero. Guzzo, Sandra E. 32p. (Orig.). (gr. k-5). 1993. pap. text ed. 6.95 (*0-937206-30-X*) New Mexico Mag.
Sandoz, E. Greek Myths. Coolidge, Olivia. 256p. (gr. 7 up). 1949. 13.45 (*0-395-06721-9*) HM.
—Trojan War. Coolidge, Olivia E. (gr. 7-12). 1952. 16.95 (*0-395-06731-6*) HM.
Sandstrom, George. Starfish, Seashells, & Crabs. Fichter, George S. 36p. (gr. k-3). 1993. 4.95 (*0-307-11430-9*, 11430, Golden Pr) Western Pub.
Sandstrom, George F. Seashells of North America. Abbott, R. Tucker. Zim, Herbert S., ed. (gr. 9 up). 1969. (Golden Pr); pap. write for info (*0-307-13657-4*) Western Pub.
—Tropical Fish. Halstead, Bruce W. & Landa, Bonnie L. 160p. (gr. 7 up). 1975. pap. write for info. (*0-307-24361-3*, Golden Pr) Western Pub.
Sandstrom, George F. & Sandstrom, Marita. Seashells of the World. Rev. ed. Abbott, R. Tucker. Zim, Herbert S., ed. (gr. 9 up). 1985. pap. write for info. (*0-307-24410-5*, Golden Pr) Western Pub.
Sandstrom, Marita, jt. illus. see Sandstrom, George F.
Sandy, Percy T. Sun Journey: A Story of Zuni Pueblo. reissued ed. Clark, Ann N. LC 88-70955. 96p. (gr. 3 up). 1988. 19.95 (*0-941270-49-1*); pap. 9.95 (*0-941270-48-3*) Ancient City Pr.
Sanfilippo, Margaret. Tackle Without a Team. Christopher, Matt. LC 88-22644. 128p. (gr. 3-7). 1989. 14.95 (*0-316-14067-8*) Little.
—Takedown. Christopher, Matt. (gr. 3-7). 1990. 14.95 (*0-316-13930-0*) Little.
—Wonder Kid Meets the Evil Lunch Snatcher. Duncan, Lois. LC 87-26490. 76p. (gr. 7-10). 1988. 9.95 (*0-316-19558-8*) Little.
Sanford, James, Jr. & Bates, Dawn. Nuclear War Diary. Sanford, James, Jr. Alexander, Frank, ed. 186p. (gr. 7-12). 1989. pap. 6.95 (*0-915256-28-2*, 130) Front Row.
Sanford, John. The Gravity Company. Sandford, John. LC 88-10549. (gr. 2 up). 1988. 1.50 (*0-687-15686-6*) Abingdon.
—Mouse & Owl. Hoffman, Joan. Gregorich, Barbara, ed. 32p. (gr. k-2). 1987. wkbk. 1.99 (*0-88743-102-X*, 02602) Sch Zone Pub Co.
Sanford, Lloyd. Black Jack: Last of the Big Alligators. McClung, Robert M. LC 91-14387. 64p. (gr. 3-7). 1991. Repr. of 1967 ed. PLB 15.00 (*0-208-02326-7*, Linnet) Shoe String.
Sanford, Margaret L. The Teddy Bear ABC. Johnson, Laura R. LC 84-144481. 60p. (ps-2). 1991. pap. 7.95 (*0-914676-86-5*, Green Tiger) S&S Trade.
—The Teddy Bear ABC. Johnson, Laura R. LC 91-18207. 64p. (ps-2). 1992. 12.00 (*0-671-74979-X*, Green Tiger); pap. 7.95 (*0-671-75949-3*, Green Tiger) S&S Trade.
Sanor, Peggy. Poor Me & the Magic of Christmas. rev. ed. Crabtree, Cathy L. & Fowler, Joanne. LC 89-84463. 20p. (gr. 2-3). 1989. pap. text ed. 5.95 (*0-9622719-0-X*) Lavender Pr.
Sansome, Constance J. & Jefferson, Lisa E. Minnesota in Maps: A Trailblazer Atlas. Sansome, Constance J. 32p. (gr. 3 up). 1990. 17.95 (*0-9626025-0-7*); pap. 12.95 (*0-9626025-1-5*) Trailblazer Bks.
San Souci, Daniel. The Bedtime Book. LC 85-12898. 48p. (gr. k-3). 1985. PLB 11.79 (*0-685-42987-3*, J Messner) S&S Trade.
—Ceremony in the Circle of Life. White Deer of Autumn. 32p. (gr. 2-6). 1991. pap. 6.95 (*0-941831-68-X*) Beyond Words Pub.
—The Easter Treasures. Arico, Diane, compiled by. (ps-4). 1989. 8.95 (*0-385-24401-0*) Doubleday.
—Feathertop: Based on the Tale by Nathaniel Hawthorne. San Souci, Robert D. LC 91-10104. 32p. (gr. 1-5). 1992. map. 16.00 (*0-385-42044-7*) Doubleday.
—The Golden Deer. Hodges, Margaret, retold by. LC 90-42873. 32p. (gr. 1-3). 1992. SBE 14.95 (*0-684-19218-7*, Scribners Young Read) Macmillan Child Grp.
—Legend of Scarface. San Souci, Robert. LC 77-15170. 40p. (gr. k-3). 1987. 7.00 (*0-385-15874-2*, Pub. by Zephyr-BFYR) Doubleday.
—Legend of Sleepy Hollow. San Souci, Robert. LC 86-2064. 32p. (ps-3). 1986. 11.95 (*0-385-23396-5*, Zephyr-BFYR); PLB 11.95 (*0-385-23397-3*, Zephyr-BFYR) Doubleday.
—The Little Mermaid. Littledale, Freya, as told by. 40p. (Orig.). (gr. k-3). 1986. 3.95 (*0-590-44358-5*) Scholastic Inc.
—Muir of the Mountains. Douglas, William O. 112p. (gr. 4-7). Date not set. 15.95 (*0-87156-505-6*) Sierra.
—A Possible Tree. Aldridge, Josephine H. LC 92-13704. 32p. (gr. k-3). 1993. RSBE 14.95 (*0-02-700407-4*, Macmillan Child Bk) Macmillan Child Grp.
—Rip Van Winkle. Gipson, Morrell. LC 83-20624. 32p. (gr. k-3). 1987. pap. 4.95 (*0-385-23965-3*, Pub. by Zephyr-BFYR) Doubleday.

—A Season of Joy: Favorite Stories & Poems for Christmas. Arico, Diane, ed. LC 86-29059. 64p. (gr. k-3). 1987. Doubleday.

—The Ugly Duckling. Andersen, Hans Christian. Moore, Lilian, retold by. 48p. (ps-2). 1988. pap. 3.95 (0-590-43794-1); incl. cassette 5.95 (0-590-63231-0) Scholastic Inc.

—Vassilisa the Wise: A Tale of Medieval Russia. Sherman, Josepha, adapted by. LC 87-8563. 26p. (gr. k-3). 1988. 14.95 (0-15-293240-2) HarBrace.

Sant Bani School Children. Book of Jonah. LC 84-50924. (gr. 1-6). 1984. pap. 6.95 (0-89142-044-4) Sant Bani Ash.

Santilli, Marcos, photos by. Amazon: A Young Reader's Look at the Last Frontier. Lourie, Peter. LC 90-85720. 48p. (gr. 3-7). 1991. 17.95 (1-878093-00-2) Boyds Mills Pr.

Santini, Debrah. The Baby Who Would Not Come Down. Knight, Joan. LC 89-3987. 28p. (ps up) 1991. pap. 14.95 (0-88708-107-X) Picture Bk Studio.

—Santa's Secret Helper. Clements, Andrew. LC 90-8601. 32p. (gr. k up). 1991. pap. 14.95 (0-88708-136-3) Picture Bk Studio.

—Santa's Secret Helper. Clements, Andrew. LC 93-20119. (gr. 1-8). 1993. 4.95 (0-88708-325-0) Picture Bk Studio.

—Tulips. O'Callahan, Jay. LC 91-41704. 28p. (gr. k up). 1992. pap. 14.95 (0-88708-223-8) Picture Bk Studio.

Santore, Charles. Complete Tales of Peter Rabbit: And Other Favorite Stories. Potter, Beatrix. LC 86-10116. 36p. (gr. k up). 1986. 9.98 (0-89471-460-0) Courage Bks.

—The Complete Tales of Peter Rabbit: And Other Favorite Stories. Potter, Beatrix. LC 90-52736. 56p. (gr. 2 up). 1991. pap. 5.95 (0-89471-855-X) Running Pr.

—The Little Mermaid: The Original Story. Andersen, Hans Christian. LC 93-20375. 1993. 14.00 (0-517-06495-2) Outlet Bk Co.

—Tales of Peter Rabbit. Potter, Beatrix. LC 91-52695. 128p. 1991. 4.95 (1-56138-039-3) Running Pr.

—The Wizard of Oz. Baum, L. Frank. Hearn, Michael P., intro. by. 96p. 1991. 15.00 (0-517-69506-5, Pub. by Jellybean Pr); lib. bdg. 20.00 (0-517-06655-6, Pub. by Jellybean Pr) Outlet Bk Co.

Santoro, Chris. Lift a Rock, Find a Bug. LC 91-62580. 22p. (ps-k). 1993. 3.50 (0-679-80904-X) Random Bks Yng Read.

—Lift the Hood, Find a Motor. LC 91-62581. 22p. (ps-k). 1993. 3.50 (0-679-80903-1) Random Bks Yng Read.

—The Little Rabbit Who Wanted Red Wings. Bailey, Carolyn S. 32p. (ps-1). 1988. pap. 2.95 (0-448-19089-3, Platt & Munk); (Platt & Munk) Putnam Pub Group.

—Open the Barn Door, Find a Cow. LC 91-62579. 22p. (ps-k). 1993. 3.50 (0-679-80901-5) Random Bks Yng Read.

—Open the Box, Find a Prize. LC 91-62573. 22p. (ps-k). 1993. 3.50 (0-679-80902-3) Random Bks Yng Read.

—Your First Adventure: Little Goat's Big Brother, No. 12. Leonard, Marcia. 24p. (Orig.). 1987. pap. 2.50 (0-553-15503-2) Bantam.

Santoro, Christopher. Animals Build Amazing Homes. Nussbaum, Hedda. LC 79-11326. (gr. 2-5). 1979. 7.95 (0-394-83850-5) Random Bks Yng Read.

—The Big Golden Book of Dinosaurs. Elting, Mary. LC 87-81784. 64p. (gr. 3-6). pap. text ed. write for info. (0-307-15567-6, Golden Pr) Western Pub.

—Busy Bunnies. Benjamin, Alan. 16p. (ps). 1988. pap. 3.95 (0-671-64807-1, Little Simon) S&S Trade.

—Charlie the Caterpillar. DeLuise, Dom. LC 90-31557. 40p. (ps-1). 1990. pap. 13.95 jacketed (0-671-69358-1, S&S BFYR) S&S Trade.

—Charlie the Caterpillar. DeLuise, Dom. LC 90-31557. 40p. (ps-1). 1993. pap. 4.95 (0-671-79607-0, S&S BFYR) S&S Trade.

—Ducky's Easter Surprise. Benjamin, Alan. 16p. 1988. pap. 3.95 (0-671-64808-X, Little Simon) S&S Trade.

—A Garden for Miss Mouse. Muntean, Michaela. LC 82-2135. 48p. (ps-3). 1982. 5.95 (0-8193-1083-2); lib. bdg. 5.95 (0-8193-1084-0) Parents.

—Giraffes: The Sentinels of the Savannas. Sattler, Helen R. LC 89-2287. 80p. (gr. 3 up). 1990. 14.95 (0-688-08284-X); PLB 14.88 (0-688-08285-8) Lothrop.

—The Glow-in-the-Dark Book of Animal Skeletons. Kahney, Regina. LC 91-3810. 24p. (gr. 2-5). 1992. 14.00 (0-679-81080-3) Random Bks Yng Read.

—Here Comes Santa Claus. Hover, M. 14p. (ps) 1982. write for info. (0-307-12267-0, Golden Bks.) Western Pub.

—Hominids: A Look Back at Our Ancestors. Sattler, Helen R. LC 86-10624. (gr. 3 up) 1988. PLB 15.95 (0-688-06061-7) Lothrop.

—Make Way for Trucks: Big Machines on Wheels. Herman, Gail. LC 89-34458. 32p. (ps-2). 1990. lib. bdg. 10.99 (0-679-90110-8) Random Bks Yng Read.

—Peter Cottontail. Stephens, Amanda. 32p. (ps-3). 1994. pap. 2.50 (0-590-47761-7, Cartwheel) Scholastic Inc.

—Prehistoric Mammals. Miller, Susanne S. (ps-5). 1984. pap. 7.95 (0-671-47976-8, S&S BFYR) S&S Trade.

—Pterosaurs: The Flying Reptiles. Sattler, Helen R. LC 84-4428. 48p. (gr. 1-4). 1985. PLB 12.88 (0-688-03996-0) Lothrop.

—Rudolph the Red-Nosed Reindeer. LC 86-62550. 14p. (ps-1). 1987. 5.95 (0-394-88923-1) Random Bks Yng Read.

—Sharks. Berger, Gilda. LC 85-29327. 48p. (gr. k-4). 1987. pap. 10.95 (0-385-23418-X) Doubleday.

—Snakes & Other Reptiles. Elting, Mary. (gr. 3-7). 1987. pap. 8.95 (0-671-61835-0, S&S BFYR) S&S Trade.

Santoro, Christopher, et al. Bunnies, Bunnies, Bunnies. Retan, Walter, ed. LC 90-41486. 96p. (ps-2). 1991. pap. 14.95 (0-671-73221-8, S&S BYR); pap. 18.98 (0-671-73220-X) S&S Trade.

Santos, Duarte. The Frog in the Bog. Santos, Elsie S. 44p. (Orig.). (ps-2). 1986. pap. 3.95 (0-914151-04-5) Shawme Ent.

—The Mystery at Shawme Pond. Santos, Elsie S. Alvaro, Albert M., ed. 20p. (Orig.). (ps-1). 1983. pap. 3.95 (0-914151-01-0) Shawme Ent.

Santos, Duarte S. The Master of Song. Santos, Elsie S. 44p. (Orig.). (ps-1). 1984. pap. 3.95 (0-914151-02-9) Shawme Ent.

Sapaugh, Blaine. Amy Armadillo. Sargent, Dave & Sargent, Pat. 48p. (Orig.). (gr. k-8). 1993. text ed. 11.95 (1-56763-046-4); pap. text ed. 5.95 (1-56763-047-2) Ozark Pub.

—The Bandit. Sargent, Dave & Sargent, Pat. 48p. (Orig.). (gr. k-8). 1993. text ed. 11.95 (1-56763-048-0); pap. text ed. 5.95 (1-56763-049-9) Ozark Pub.

—Best Friends. Sargent, Dave. 48p. (Orig.). (gr. k-8). 1993. text ed. 11.95 (1-56763-056-1); pap. text ed. 5.95 (1-56763-057-X) Ozark Pub.

—Big Jake. Sargent, Dave & Sargent, Pat. 48p. (Orig.). (gr. k-8). 1993. text ed. 11.95 (1-56763-030-8); pap. text ed. 5.95 (1-56763-031-6) Ozark Pub.

—Buddy Badger. Sargent, Dave & Sargent, Pat. 48p. (Orig.). (gr. k-8). 1993. text ed. 11.95 (1-56763-036-7); pap. text ed. 5.95 (1-56763-037-5) Ozark Pub.

—Greta Groundhog. Sargent, Dave & Sargent, Pat. 48p. (Orig.). (gr. k-8). 1993. text ed. 11.95 (1-56763-040-5); pap. text ed. 5.95 (1-56763-041-3) Ozark Pub.

—Mad Jack. Sargent, Dave & Sargent, Pat. 48p. (Orig.). (gr. k-8). 1993. text ed. 11.95 (1-56763-034-0); pap. text ed. 5.95 (1-56763-035-9) Ozark Pub.

—Molly's Journey. Sargent, Dave & Sargent, Pat. 48p. (Orig.). (gr. k-8). 1993. text ed. 11.95 (1-56763-038-3); pap. text ed. 5.95 (1-56763-039-1) Ozark Pub.

—Peggy Porcupine. Sargent, Dave & Sargent, Pat. 48p. (Orig.). (gr. k-8). 1993. text ed. 11.95 (1-56763-044-8); pap. text ed. 5.95 (1-56763-045-6) Ozark Pub.

—Pokey Opossum. Sargent, Dave & Sargent, Pat. 48p. (Orig.). (gr. k-8). 1993. text ed. 11.95 (1-56763-042-1); pap. text ed. 5.95 (1-56763-043-X) Ozark Pub.

—Tunnel King. Sargent, Dave & Sargent, Pat. 48p. (Orig.). (gr. k-8). 1993. text ed. 11.95 (1-56763-032-4); pap. text ed. 5.95 (1-56763-033-2) Ozark Pub.

Sapaugh, Micah. Marlusk the Warrior. Sapaugh, Micah. Sargent, Dave, intro. by. 48p. (Orig.). (gr. k-8). 1993. text ed. 11.95 (1-56763-092-8); pap. text ed. 5.95 (1-56763-093-6) Ozark Pub.

Sapenter, Marcellus. I'll Make It Happen Without Drugs. Wingate, Rosalee M. 44p. (Orig.). (gr. 4-8). 1990. pap. 6.00 (0-9625391-0-4) R M Wingate.

Sapieha, Christine. Island of Cats. Fremantle, Anne. (gr. 1-4). 1964. 12.95 (0-8392-3011-7) Astor-Honor.

Sapp, Patt, jt. illus. see Birenbaum, Barbara.

Saprid, Pearle R. The Boy Who Looked Different. Bautista, Bezalie P. 24p. (Orig.). (gr. k-2). 1990. pap. 3.50x (971-10-0406-2, Pub. by New Day Pub PI) Cellar.

Sarasas, Claude. ABC's of Origami: Paper Folding for Children. Sarasas, Claude. LC 64-17160. (gr. 3-8). 1964. bds. 12.95 (0-8048-0000-6) C E Tuttle.

Sardar, Zahid. Celebration! Festivities for Reading. ESL ed. Haverson, Wayne W. & Haverson, Susan. Munch, Helen, ed. 340p. (gr. 3-12). 1987. pap. text ed. 9.00 (0-88084-241-5); Om ex. sheets & binder 79.95 (0-13-122086-1); poster set 102.60 (0-88084-240-7) Alemany Pr.

Sardo, Douglas. The Christmas Journey. Fisher, Sally. 40p. (ps-7). 1993. 19.99 (0-670-85039-X) Viking Child Bks.

Sarecky, Melody. Discover George Mason: Home, State, & Country: A Sampler of Lesson Plans, Activities, & Resources for Teachers of Students in Grades 3 Through 6. rev. ed. McHugh, Denise. vi, 101p. (gr. 3-6). 1993. pap. 9.50 (1-884085-02-4) Bd Regents.

—George Mason, Planter & Patriot: A Sampler of Lesson Plans Exploring Primary Sources for Teachers of Students in Grades 7 Through 12. McHugh, Denise. viii, 200p. (Orig.). (gr. 7-12). 1992. pap. 14.00 (1-884085-00-8) Bd Regents.

—One Dad, Two Dads, Brown Dad, Blue Dads. Valentine, Johnny. 32p. (gr. 2-6). 1994. 10.95 (1-55583-253-9, Alyson Wonderland) Alyson Pubns.

—Rainbow Collection, 1990: Stories & Poetry by Young People. Janger, Kathie, ed. Bush. Barbara, frwd. by. 176p. 1990. pap. 6.00 (0-929889-06-1) Young Writers Contest Found.

—Rainbow Collection, 1990-91: Stories & Poetry by Young People. Janger, Kathie, ed. DeVito, Danny, intro. by. 169p. (Orig.). (gr. 1-8). 1991. pap. 6.00 (0-929889-07-X) Young Writers Contest Found.

Sargent, Ben. How the Critters Created Texas. Abernethy, Francis E. LC 82-80440. 40p. (gr. 4-12). 1982. pap. 8.95 (0-936650-01-X) E C Temple.

Sargent, Heather & Gilliland, Hap. Sacajawea: A Native American Heroine. Bryant, Martha F. Gilliland, Hap, ed. 256p. (Orig.). 1989. 21.95 (0-89992-420-4); pap. 15.95 (0-89992-120-5) Coun India Ed.

Sargent, Patricia. Meher Baba Is Love. 2nd ed. Shifrin, Adah. 56p. (gr. 1-3). 1987. pap. 6.95 (0-913078-59-X) Sheriar Pr.

Sariola, Eulalia. Ibrahim. Sales, Francesc. Simont, Marc, tr. from CAT. LC 87-29382. 32p. (gr. k-3). 1989. (Lipp Jr Bks) HarpC Child Bks.

Sarmo, Tom. Orlanda & the Contest of Thieves. Cossi, Olga. LC 89-15107. 32p. (gr. 1-6). 1989. 14.95 (0-917665-32-5) Pelican.

Sarnoff, Arthur. The Black Swan & the Green See Saw. Greer, Blanche. LC 75-261399. (gr. 5 up) 1977. 4.50 (0-930422-07-4) Dennis-Landman.

Sarracino, William L. Mother Spider & Her Little Ones. 16p. (Orig.). (ps-7). 1982. pap. 3.75 (0-915347-11-3) Pueblo Acoma Pr.

Sarson, Peter & Bryan, Tony. Amphibious Techniques. Ladd, James D. LC 84-10003. 48p. (gr. 5 up). 1985. PLB 13.50 (0-8225-1379-X, First Ave Edns); pap. 4.95 (0-8225-9505-2, First Ave Edns) Lerner Pubns.

—Tanks. Hogg, Ian V. LC 84-9650. 48p. (gr. 5 up). 1985. PLB 14.95 (0-8225-1378-1, First Ave Edns); pap. 4.95 (0-8225-9507-9, First Ave Edns) Lerner Pubns.

Sarson, Peter, et al. Fighters. Lowe, Malcolm V. LC 84-7941. 48p. (gr. 5 up). 1985. PLB 13.50 (0-8225-1376-5, First Ave Edns); pap. 4.95 (0-8225-9506-0, First Ave Edns) Lerner Pubns.

Sasaki, Ellen J. Make Your Own...Videos, Commercials, Radio. Fun Group Staff. LC 90-86409. 96p. (gr. 2-6). 1992. pap. 2.95 (0-448-40201-7, G&D) Putnam Pub Group.

—The Riddle. Starkman, Neal. LC 89-25405. 50p. (Orig.). (gr. 2). 1989. pap. 11.00 (0-935529-13-6) Comprehen Health Educ.

—Yea, Hooray! The Son Came Home Today, & Other Bible Stories about Wisdom. Tangvald, Christine H. LC 93-9244. 1993. write for info. (0-7814-0927-6, Chariot Bks) Cook.

Sasaki, Joy, jt. illus. see Ellen, G.

Sasaki, Karen. Shiro in Love. Tokuda, Wendy & Hall, Richard. 32p. (gr. 1-3). 1989. 11.95 (0-89346-306-X) Heian Intl.

Sasaki, Kisa N. The Sioux Indians: Hunters & Warriors of the Plains. Bleeker, Sonia. LC 62-7713. 160p. (gr. 3-6). 1962. PLB 11.88 (0-688-31457-0) Morrow Jr Bks.

Sather, Kay. Soft Child. Hayes, Joe. LC 93-1641. 32p. (Orig.). (ps-3). 1993. pap. 8.95 (0-943173-89-3) Harbinger AZ.

Sato, Wakiko. Granny, Let Me In. Barnes, Jill & Sato, Wakiko. Rubin, Caroline, ed. Japan Foreign Rights Centre Staff, tr. from JPN. LC 90-37752. 40p. (gr. k-3). 1990. PLB 15.93 (0-944483-82-8) Garrett Ed Corp.

Sato, Yuko. Chirping Insects. Johnson, Sylvia A. LC 86-15380. 48p. (gr. 4 up). 1986. PLB 19.95 (0-8225-1486-9) Lerner Pubns.

—How Leaves Change. Johnson, Sylvia A. 48p. (gr. 4 up). 1986. PLB 19.95 (0-8225-1483-4, First Ave Edns); pap. 5.95 (0-8225-9513-3, First Ave Edns) Lerner Pubns.

—Ladybugs. Johnson, Sylvia A. LC 83-18777. 48p. (gr. 4 up). 1983. PLB 19.95 (0-8225-1481-8) Lerner Pubns.

—Morning Glories. Johnson, Sylvia A. 48p. (gr. 4-10). 1985. PLB 19.95 (0-8225-1462-1) Lerner Pubns.

Sato, Yuko, photos by. Grasshoppers. Dallinger, Jane. 48p. (gr. 4 up). pap. 5.95 (0-8225-9568-0) Lerner Pubns.

Satter, Denise. The Prince of Whales. Fisher, R. L. 160p. (gr. 3 up). 1987. pap. 2.50 (0-8125-6635-1) Tor Bks.

Satter, Leslie. Easter: Practical Activities for Teachers & Parents to Supplement Religious Instruction. Satter, Leslie. 85p. (Orig.). (gr. k-3). 1991. pap. text ed. 9.95 (1-879599-00-7) L Ross Pubns.

—Easter: Practical Activities for Teachers & Parents to Supplement Religious Instruction. Satter, Leslie. 86p. (Orig.). (gr. k-3). 1991. pap. text ed. 9.95 (1-879599-01-5) L Ross Pubns.

Sauber, Rob. Operation: Dump the Chump. Park, Barbara. LC 81-8147. 128p. (gr. 3-6). 1982. lib. bdg. 10.99 (0-394-95179-4) Knopf Bks Yng Read.

Sauber, Robert. The Gift of the Magi. O. Henry. LC 91-7313. 48p. (gr. 1-6). 1991. 9.95 (0-88101-116-9) Unicorn Pub.

—The Golden Swan. Mayer, Marianna. (gr. 3 up). 1990. 14.95 (0-553-07054-1, Skylark) Bantam.

—The Goose Girl: A Story from the Brothers Grimm. Kimmel, Eric A., retold by. LC 93-13138. 1994. write for info. (0-8234-1074-9) Holiday.

—Gray Fox. London, Jonathan. LC 92-20653. 32p. (gr. 3-8). 1993. 13.99 (0-670-84490-X) Viking Child Bks.

—I-Know-Not-What, I-Know-Not-Where: A Russian Tale. Kimmel, Eric A., adapted by. LC 92-32692. 64p. (gr. 6-10). 1994. 16.95 (0-8234-1020-X) Holiday.

—The Merry Adventures of Robin Hood. Pyle, Howard. Mattern, Joanne, ed. LC 92-12102. 48p. (gr. 3-6). 1992. PLB 12.89 (0-8167-2858-5); pap. text ed. 3.95 (0-8167-2859-3) Troll Assocs.

Saunders, Dave. Brave Jack. Saunders, Dave & Saunders, Julie. LC 92-23238. 32p. (ps-1). 1993. SBE 14.95 (0-02-781073-9, Bradbury Pr) Macmillan Child Grp.

—Snowtime. Saunders, Dave & Saunders, Julie. LC 90-42565. 32p. (ps-1). 1991. SBE 14.95 (0-02-781075-5, Bradbury Pr) Macmillan Child Grp.

Saunders, David, photos by. The Master Violinmaker. Fleisher, Paul. LC 92-28050. 1993. 14.95 (*0-395-65365-7*) HM.
Saunders, Dorothy. The Courtesy Book. Dunlea, Nancy. Hubalek, Linda K. & Rex, Margeryintro. by. LC 93-80030. 128p. (gr. 4-8). pap. 7.95 (*1-882420-07-1*) Hearth KS.
Saunders, Mike & Wright, David. The Simon & Schuster Young Readers' Atlas. Wright, Jill & Wright, David. Barish, Wendy, ed. 192p. 1984. pap. 7.95 (*0-671-50657-9*) S&S Trade.
Sautai, R., jt. illus. see Fuhr, U.
Savadier, Elivia. Billy & the Bad Teacher. Clements, Andrew. LC 92-6619. 28p. 1992. pap. 14.95 (*0-88708-244-0*) Picture Bk Studio.
—Hotter Than a Hot Dog! Calmenson, Stephanie. LC 93-313. (gr. 1-8). 1994. 14.95 (*0-316-12479-6*) Little.
—Treasure Nap. Havill, Juanita. 32p. (gr. k-3). 1992. 13.95 (*0-395-57817-5*) HM.
—The Uninvited Guest & Other Jewish Holiday Tales. Jaffe, Nina. LC 92-36308. 1993. write for info. (*0-590-44653-3*) Scholastic Inc.
Savage, Ann. Alarming Animals. Parker, Steve. LC 93-6651. 38p. (gr. 3-6). 1993. PLB 19.97 (*0-8114-0658-X*) Raintree Steck-V.
—Awesome Amphibians. Parker, Steve. LC 92-43196. 38p. (gr. 3-6). 1993. PLB 19.97 (*0-8114-0661-X*) Raintree Steck-V.
—Beastly Bugs. Parker, Steve. LC 92-43197. 38p. (gr. 3-6). 1993. PLB 19.97 (*0-8114-0689-X*) Raintree-Steck-V.
—Cunning Carnivores. Parker, Steve. LC 93-27256. 1993. write for info. (*0-8114-2347-6*) Raintree Steck-V.
—Fearsome Fish. Parker, Steve. LC 93-28905. 1993. write for info. (*0-8114-2346-8*) Raintree Steck-V.
—Revolting Reptiles. Parker, Steve. LC 92-43725. 38p. (gr. 3-6). 1992. PLB 19.97 (*0-8114-0692-X*) Raintree Steck-V.
—Scary Spiders. Parker, Steve. LC 93-27876. 1993. write for info. (*0-8114-2345-X*) Raintree Steck-V.
Savage, Beth. Artworks. Hodgson, Harriet. 64p. (gr. k-3). 1986. 6.95 (*0-912107-42-1*, Dist. by Good Apple) Monday Morning Bks.
Savage, Eileen D. Winning over Asthma. Savage, Eileen D. Plaut, Thomas F., intro. by. LC 89-50551. 32p. (gr. k-3). 1993. pap. 6.95 (*0-914625-09-8*) Pedipress.
Savage, Steele. The Adventures of Ulysses. Gottlieb, Gerald. LC 88-19232. xii, 170p. (gr. 6-12). 1988. Repr. of 1959 ed. lib. bdg. 16.50 (*0-208-02222-8*, Linnet) Shoe String.
—Mythology. Hamilton, Edith. (gr. 7 up). 1942. 21.95 (*0-316-34114-2*) Little.
Savage, Stephen. Ancient Greek Monuments to Make: The Parthenon & the Theatre of Dionysos. Savage, Stephen. Moon, Warren G., intro. by. 48p. (Orig.). (gr. 7 up). 1990. pap. 7.95 (*0-88045-096-7*) Stemmer Hse.
—Making Tracks: A Slide-&-See Book. Savage, Stephen. 10p. (gr. k-3). 1992. 10.00 (*0-525-67353-9*, Lodestar Bks) Dutton Child Bks.
Savee, Mark. Monster Gallery Color & Story Album. Waskey, Leah. 32p. 1973. pap. 4.50 (*0-8431-1728-1*) Price Stern.
Savitt, Sam. Lad: A Dog. Terhune, Albert P. LC 93-9365. 288p. (gr. 5 up). 1993. pap. 3.99 (*0-14-036474-9*, Puffin) Puffin Bks.
Sawyer, Barbara. Nightshade. Weininger, Rachel. LC 88-63135. 64p. (Orig.). (gr. 4-6). 1989. pap. 5.95 (*0-931093-11-2*) Red Hen Pr.
—An Owl Feather for Emily. Human, Gerrie. LC 91-26734. 32p. (Orig.). (gr. 2). 1992. pap. 4.95 (*0-931093-77-5*) Red Hen Pr.

Sawyer, Lori. Grandmother Five Baskets. Larrabee, Lisa. LC 93-10451. 64p. (gr. 3-7). 1993. 14.95 (*0-943173-86-8*); pap. 9.95 (*0-943173-90-6*) Harbinger AZ. Multi-cultural, Native American themes are the focus of three children's titles by Harbinger House of Tucson. These well-researched & sensitive presentations highlight family values, coming-of-age lessons, & respect for all. For beginning, middle & young adult readers, as noted. 1) GRANDMOTHER FIVE BASKETS. ISBN 0-943173-86-8 (hc), $14.95, ISBN 0-943173-90-6 (pb), $9.95. ages 8-12, by Lisa Larrabee, fully illustrated by Lori Sawyer. Authentic, multi-generational story of a contemporary American Indian woman who teaches the young girls of her tribe to make baskets in the traditional way. Interwoven are gentle lessons about life, love & the value of family. 2) SOFT CHILD: HOW RATTLESNAKE GOT ITS FANGS. ISBN 0-943173-89-2, $8.95, ages 4-8, retold by Joe Hayes, illustrated by

Kay Sather. Soft Child, a poor gentle snake, is defenseless in his desert environment until Sky God provides Soft Child with fangs. Adapted from Tohono O'odham (Papago) folklore. 3) SON-OF-THUNDER. ISBN 0-943173-88-4 (hc), $16.95, ISBN 0-943173-87-6, $10.95 (pb), by Stig Holmas, illustrated by John Hurford. The coming-of-age of a young Apache warrior. A straightforward, well-researched novel set in the time & homeland of Cochise & Geronimo, with new insights--from the Apache point of view--to balance conventional history. Order from Harbinger House, Inc., Books of Integrity or from your local distributor. *Publisher Provided Annotation.*

Say, Allen. The Bicycle Man. Say, Allen. 48p. (gr. k-3). 1982. 14.45 (*0-395-32254-5*); 11.95 (*0-685-05704-6*) HM.
—The Bicycle Man. Say, Allen. (ps-3). 1989. pap. 5.70 (*0-395-50652-2*, Sandpiper) HM.
—The Boy of the Three-Year Nap. Snyder, Diane, retold by. LC 87-30674. 32p. (ps-3). 1988. 15.45 (*0-395-44090-4*) HM.
—El Chino. Say, Allen. 32p. (gr. 2-8). 1990. 14.45 (*0-395-52023-1*) HM.
—How My Parents Learned to Eat. Friedman, Ina R. LC 84-18553. 32p. (gr. k-3). 1987. 13.45 (*0-395-35379-3*); pap. 4.80 (*0-395-44235-4*) HM.
—Lost Lake. Say, Allen. (gr. 1-4). 1989. 14.45 (*0-395-50933-5*) HM.
—The Lost Lake. Say, Allen. 32p. (gr. k-3). 1992. pap. 4.80 (*0-395-63036-3*, Sandpiper) HM.
—A River Dream. Say, Allen. 32p. (gr. k-3). 1988. 14.45 (*0-395-48294-1*) HM.
—A River Dream. Say, Allen. 32p. (gr. k-3). 1993. pap. 4.95 (*0-395-65749-0*) HM.
—Tree of Cranes. Say, Allen. 32p. (gr. k-3). 1991. 16.45 (*0-395-52024-X*, Sandpiper) HM.
Sayers, Fred. Where to Find the Best of Huntsville. 2nd ed. Kaylor, Mike. Easterling, Bill, intro. by. 150p. (Orig.). (gr. 9-12). 1985. pap. text ed. 4.95 (*0-916039-01-3*) Kaylor Christ Co.
Sayles, Elizabeth. Albie the Lifeguard. Borden, Louise. LC 91-11327. 32p. (ps-3). 1993. 14.95 (*0-590-44585-5*) Scholastic Inc.
—Bungalow Fungalow. Shea, Pegi D. 32p. (gr. k-3). 1991. 13.45 (*0-395-55387-3*, Clarion Bks) HM.
—Dribbles. Heckert, Connie. LC 92-24846. 1993. 14.45 (*0-395-62336-7*, Clarion Bks) HM.
—Molly & the Prince. Osborne, Mary P. LC 92-25305. 1993. write for info. (*0-679-81941-X*); PLB write for info. (*0-679-91941-4*) Knopf.
—Nettie's Gift. Tews, Susan. (gr. k-3). 1993. 14.95 (*0-395-59027-2*, Clarion Bks) HM.
—What Mary Jo Shared. Udry, Janice May. 32p. (ps-3). 1991. pap. 3.95 (*0-590-43757-7*) Scholastic Inc.
Saylor, Melissa. I Can Read Colors Big Book. Edge, Nellie. (ps). 1988. pap. text ed. 14.00 (*0-922053-03-0*) N Edge Res.
—I've Got a Cat Big Book. Edge, Nellie, adapted by. (ps-2). 1988. pap. text ed. 14.00 (*0-922053-13-8*) N Edge Res.
—Make Friends with Mother Goose, Vol. II. Edge, Nellie, compiled by. (ps-2). 1991. pap. text ed. 15.00 (*0-922053-24-3*) N Edge Res.
—Make Friends with Mother Goose Big Book, Vol. I. Edge, Nellie, compiled by. (ps-2). 1988. pap. text ed. 15.00 (*0-922053-11-1*) N Edge Res.
—Mary Wore Her Red Dress Big Book. (ps-2). 1988. pap. text ed. 14.00 (*0-922053-17-0*) N Edge Res.
—My Aunt Came Back Big Book. (ps-2). 1988. pap. text ed. 14.00 (*0-922053-12-X*) N Edge Res.
—Se Leer Colores. Edge, Nellie. Zamora-Pearson, Marissa, tr. from ENG. (SPA.) (ps-2). 1993. pap. text ed. 15.00 (*0-922053-28-6*) N Edge Res.
—Songs & Rhymes for a Rainy Day Big Book. Edge, Nellie, compiled by. (ps-2). 1988. pap. text ed. 15.00 (*0-922053-07-3*) N Edge Res.
—Yo Tengo un Gato. Edge, Nellie, adapted by. Zamora-Pearson, Marissa, tr. from ENG. (SPA.) (ps-2). 1993. pap. text ed. 15.00 (*0-922053-29-4*) N Edge Res.
Saypol, Judyth R. & Wikler, Madeline. My Very Own Simchat Torah. 24p. (gr. k-5). 1981. pap. 3.95 (*0-930494-11-3*) Kar Ben.
Scandia School. Secrets of Arhirit. Hughes-Calero, Heather. 176p. (Orig.). (gr. 5 up). pap. 8.95 (*0-932927-04-1*) Coastline Pub Co.
Scardova, Jaclyne. And Peter Said Goodbye. Farrington, Liz & Weil, Jennifer C. Farrington, Liz, created by. LC 92-35977. 40p. (gr. k-4). 1993. 14.95 (*1-56844-000-6*) Enchante Pub.
Scarpace, Frank, jt. illus. see Space, Peggy.
Scarry, Huck. Balloon Trip: A Sketchbook. Scarry, Huck. LC 82-23002. 68p. (gr. 3-7). 1983. 10.95 (*0-13-055939-3*) P-H.

—Life on a Barge: A Sketchbook. Scarry, Huck. 72p. (gr. 3-7). 1982. 10.95 (*0-13-535831-0*) P-H.
—My First Picture Dictionary. LC 76-24174. (ps-2). 1978. lib. bdg. 5.99 (*0-394-93486-5*); pap. 2.25 (*0-394-83486-0*) Random Bks Yng Read.
Scarry, Richard. Be Careful, Mr. Frumble! Scarry, Richard. LC 89-43154. 24p. (Orig.). (ps-2). 1990. pap. 2.25 (*0-679-80566-4*) Random Bks Yng Read.
—The Best Mistake Ever! A Step Two Book. Scarry, Richard. LC 84-2029. 48p. (ps-2). 1984. lib. bdg. 7.99 (*0-394-96816-6*); pap. 3.50 (*0-394-86816-1*) Random Bks Yng Read.
—Early Words. Scarry, Richard. LC 75-36466. 14p. (ps-1). 1976. 3.95 (*0-394-83238-8*) Random Bks Yng Read.
—Fun with Numbers: Grade One. Scarry, Richard. 32p. (ps-2). 1986. pap. 1.95 (*0-394-87665-2*) Random Bks Yng Read.
—Getting Ready for Writing. Scarry, Richard. 32p. (ps-k). 1987. pap. 1.95 (*0-394-89038-8*) Random Bks Yng Read.
—Golden Book of Three Hundred Sixty-Five Stories. Jackson, Kathryn. 1955. write for info. (*0-307-15557-9*, Golden Bks.) Western Pub.
—Huckle Cat's Busiest Day Ever. Scarry, Richard. LC 92-64139. 48p. (ps-2). 1993. 10.00 (*0-679-84188-1*) Random Bks Yng Read.
—I Am a Bunny. Scarry, Richard. 22p. (gr. k-2). 1967. write for info. (*0-307-12125-9*, Golden Bks.) Western Pub.
—Mr. Frumble's Worst Day Ever! Scarry, Richard. LC 91-62215. 48p. (ps-k). 1992. 10.00 (*0-679-81616-X*) Random Bks Yng Read.
—Richard Scarry Huckle's Book. Scarry, Richard. (ps). 1979. 2.95 (*0-394-84130-1*) Random Bks Yng Read.
—Richard Scarry's ABCs. Scarry, Richard. (ps-k). 1991. pap. 1.25 (*0-307-11515-1*, Golden Pr) Western Pub.
—Richard Scarry's Best Busy Year Ever. Scarry, Richard. (ps-1). 1991. 5.25 (*0-307-15748-2*, Golden Pr) Western Pub.
—Richard Scarry's Best Counting Book Ever. Scarry, Richard. LC 74-2544. 48p. (ps-2). 1975. 12.00 (*0-394-82924-7*); PLB 9.99 (*0-394-92924-1*) Random Bks Yng Read.
—Richard Scarry's Best First Book Ever. Scarry, Richard. LC 79-3900. (ps-1). 1979. 11.95 (*0-394-84250-2*); lib. bdg. 11.99 (*0-394-94250-7*) Random Bks Yng Read.
—Richard Scarry's Best Mother Goose Ever. (ps-1). 1970. write for info. (*0-307-15578-1*, Golden Bks) Western Pub.
—Richard Scarry's Best Story Book Ever. Scarry, Richard. (gr. 1-5). 1968. write for info. (*0-307-16548-5*, Golden Bks) Western Pub.
—Richard Scarry's Best Word Book Ever. Scarry, Richard. (ps-3). 1963. write for info. (*0-307-15510-2*, Golden Bks) Western Pub.
—Richard Scarry's Biggest Make-It Book Ever! Scarry, Richard. 256p. (Orig.). (ps-5). 1993. pap. 9.99 (*0-679-84767-7*) Random Bks Yng Read.
—Richard Scarry's Biggest Pop-up Book Ever! Scarry, Richard. 6p. (ps-3). 1992. write for info. (*0-307-12460-6*, 12460, Golden Pr) Western Pub.
—Richard Scarry's Biggest Word Book Ever! Scarry, Richard. 12p. (ps-1). 1985. bds. 29.95 (*0-394-87374-2*) Random Bks Yng Read.
—Richard Scarry's Busy Busy World. Scarry, Richard. (gr. k-5). write for info. (*0-307-15511-0*, Golden Bks) Western Pub.
—Richard Scarry's Cars & Trucks from A to Z. LC 89-64401. 22p. (ps). 1990. bds. 2.95 (*0-679-80663-6*) Random Bks Yng Read.
—Richard Scarry's Color Book. Scarry, Richard. LC 75-36465. 14p. (ps-1). 1976. 3.95 (*0-394-83237-X*) Random Bks Yng Read.
—Richard Scarry's Great Big Schoolhouse. Scarry, Richard. (ps-2). 1969. 9.99 (*0-394-80874-6*) Random Bks Yng Read.
—Richard Scarry's Just Right Word Book: (Just Right for 2's & 3's) Scarry, Richard. 48p. (gr. k-3). 1990. 6.00 (*0-679-80073-5*) Random Bks Yng Read.
—Richard Scarry's Lowly Worm Storybook. Scarry, Richard. LC 77-79842. 32p. (Orig.). (ps-1). 1989. pap. 2.25 (*0-394-88270-9*) Random Bks Yng Read.
—Richard Scarry's Lowly Worm Word Book. Scarry, Richard. LC 80-53103. 28p. (ps). 1981. pap. 2.95 board (*0-394-84728-8*) Random Bks Yng Read.
—Rudolph the Red-Nosed Reindeer. Hazen, Barbara S. 24p. (ps-1). 1985. Repr. of 1958 ed. write for info. (*0-307-10203-3*, Pub. by Golden Bks) Western Pub.
—Watch Your Step, Mr. Rabbit! Scarry, Richard. LC 90-34336. 24p. (ps-2). 1991. pap. 2.25 (*0-679-81072-2*) Random Bks Yng Read.
Schaar, John E. Portraits of Sedona. (Orig.). 1989. write for info. Canyon AZ.
Schachner, Judith B. Staying with Grandmother. Baker, Barbara. LC 93-13749. 48p. (gr. 1-4). 1994. 12.99 (*0-525-44603-6*, DCB) Dutton Child Bks.
Schade, Susan, jt. illus. see Buller, Jon.
Schaefer, Alex. The Wizard. Martin, Bill, Jr. LC 93-15521. 1994. write for info. (*0-15-298926-9*) HarBrace.
Schaeffer, Bob. Peppy Learns to Play Baseball. Heller, Pete. Kinsey, Thomas D., ed. 32p. (gr. k-5). pap. 3.95 (*0-932423-00-0*) Summa Bks.
Schaer, Miriam. Katie-Bo: An Adoption Story. Fisher, Iris L. (ps-3). 1988. 12.95 (*0-915361-91-4*) Modan-Adama Bks.

—Little Daniel & the Jewish Delicacies. Sidi, Smadar S. (ps-5). 1988. 9.95 (*1-55774-028-3*) Modan-Adama Bks.

Schaff, Joanne. Holidays & Celebrations: An Educational Activity Book. Schaff, Joanne. 48p. (ps-3). 1993. pap. 5.95 (*0-9619365-1-7*) Tree City Pr.

—What Am I? Schaff, Joanne. 38p. (Orig.). (ps-3). 1987. pap. 1.99 (*0-9619365-0-9*) Tree City Pr.

Schaffhausen, Suzanne. Morgan's Baby Sister: A Read-Aloud Book for Families Who Have Experienced the Death of a Newborn. Johnson, Patricia P. & Williams, Donna R. 64p. (Orig.). (ps-2). 1993. pap. 10.95 (*0-89390-257-8*) Resource Pubns.

Schanilec, Gaylord. A Box of Night Mirrors. Caddy, John. ed. 120p. (Orig.). 1980. pap. 5.00 (*0-927663-11-2*) COMPAS.

Schanzer, Rosalyn. All about Hanukkah. Groner, Judye & Wikler, Madeline. LC 88-13435. (gr. k-5). 1988. 10.95 (*0-930494-81-4*); pap. 4.95 (*0-930494-82-2*) Kar Ben.

—Ten Good Rules. Topek, Susan R. LC 91-32109. 24p. (ps-1). 1992. 12.95 (*0-929371-30-5*); pap. 5.95 (*0-929371-28-3*) Kar Ben.

Schanzer, Roz. A J.'s Mom Gets a New Job. Balter, Lawrence. 40p. (gr. 3-7). 1990. 5.95 (*0-8120-6151-9*) Barron.

—Alfred Goes to the Hospital. Balter, Lawrence. 40p. (gr. 3-7). 1990. 5.95 (*0-8120-6150-0*) Barron.

—Bible Heroes I Can Be. Eisenberg, Ann. LC 89-48188. 24p. (ps). 1990. 12.95 (*0-929371-09-7*); pap. 4.95 (*0-929371-10-0*) Kar Ben.

—A Funeral for Whiskers: Understanding Death. Balter, Lawrence. 40p. (gr. 3). 1991. 5.95 (*0-8120-6153-5*) Barron.

—I Can Celebrate. Eisenberg, Ann. LC 88-83567. 12p. (ps). 1989. bds. 4.95 (*0-930494-93-8*) Kar Ben.

—In the Synagogue. (ps). 1991. 4.95 (*0-929371-60-7*) Kar-Ben.

—It Happened in Shushan: A Purim Story. Feder, Harriet K. LC 88-2676. (Orig.). (ps-3). 1988. pap. 3.95 (*0-930494-75-X*) Kar Ben.

—Linda Saves the Day: Understanding Fear. Balter, Lawrence. 40p. (ps-2). 1989. 5.95 (*0-8120-6117-9*) Barron.

—My First Picture Dictionary. Nayer, Judy. 24p. (ps-2). 1992. pap. 9.99 (*1-56293-110-5*) McClanahan Bk.

—Phonics Consonants. Block, Arlene. Nayer, Judith E., ed. 32p. (gr. k-1). 1991. wkbk. 1.95 (*1-878624-64-4*) McClanahan Bk.

—Sue Lee Starts School: Adjusting to School. Balter, Lawrence. 40p. (ps-3). 1991. 5.95 (*0-8120-6152-7*) Barron.

—Sue Lee's New Neighborhood: Adjusting to a New Move. Balter, Lawrence. 40p. (ps-2). 1989. 5.95 (*0-8120-6116-0*) Barron.

—The Wedding: Adjusting to a Parent's Remarriage. Balter, Lawrence. 40p. (ps-2). 1989. 5.95 (*0-8120-6118-7*) Barron.

—What's the Matter with A J? Understanding Jealousy. Balter, Lawrence. 40p. (ps-2). 1989. 5.95 (*0-8120-6119-5*) Barron.

—Where is the Afikomen. Groner, Judye & Wikler, Madeline. LC 89-63254. 12p. (ps). 1989. bds. 4.95 (*0-929371-06-2*) Kar Ben.

Schar, Grant. Hieroglyphic Coloring Book. Schar, Grant. 48p. (gr. 1-12). 1992. pap. 4.95 (*0-912057-57-2*, 507440) AMORC.

Schatell, Brain. Gobs of Goo. Cobb, Vicki. LC 82-48457. 40p. (gr. 1-3). 1983. (Lipp Jr Bks); PLB 13.89 (*0-397-32022-1*) HarpC Child Bks.

Schatell, Brian. Farmer Goff & His Turkey Sam. Schatell, Brian. LC 81-47756. 32p. (gr. 1-3). 1982. PLB 13.89 (*0-397-31983-5*, Lipp Jr Bks) HarpC Child Bks.

—From Bed to Bus. Barbato, Juli. LC 84-20159. 32p. (ps-2). 1985. RSBE 13.95 (*0-02-708380-2*, Macmillan Child Bk) Macmillan Child Grp.

—Lots of Rot. Cobb, Vicki. LC 80-8726. 40p. (gr. 1-3). 1981. (Lipp Jr Bks); PLB 15.89 (*0-397-31939-8*) HarpC Child Bks.

—Two Crazy Pigs. Nagel, Karen. 32p. 1992. pap. 2.95 (*0-590-44972-9*, Cartwheel) Scholastic Inc.

Schecter, Ben. The Hating Book. Zolotow, Charlotte. LC 69-14444. 32p. (gr. k-3). 1989. pap. 3.95 (*0-06-443197-5*, Trophy) HarpC Child Bks.

Scheffer, Axel. Bottle Rabbit & Friends. McCabe, Bernard. 136p. (gr. 3-7). 1991. 14.95 (*0-571-15318-6*) Faber & Faber.

—Sam, Who Was Swallowed by a Shark. Root, Phyllis. LC 93-2884. 1994. write for info. (*1-56402-198-X*) Candlewick Pr.

—A Squash & a Squeeze. Donaldson, Julia. LC 92-16507. 32p. (ps-3). 1993. SBE 14.95 (*0-689-50571-X*, M K McElderry) Macmillan Child Grp.

Scheffler, Axel & Scheffler, Axel. Daley B. Blake, Jon. LC 91-58725. 32p. (ps up). 1992. 13.95 (*1-56402-078-9*) Candlewick Pr.

Scheid, Margaret. Discovering Acadia: A Guide for Young Naturalists. Scheid, Margaret. LC 86-71350. 80p. (ps-12). 1988. pap. 12.95 (*0-934745-04-8*) Acadia Pub Co.

Schein, Jonah. Forget-Me-Not. Schein, Jonah. 24p. 1988. 12.95 (*1-55037-001-4*, Pub. by Annick CN); pap. 4.95 (*1-55037-000-6*, Pub. by Annick CN) Firefly Bks Ltd.

Scheinberg, Shepsil. Chaimkel the Dreamer. Gottesman, Meir U. 157p. (gr. 3-5). 1987. 9.95 (*0-935063-26-9*); pap. 7.95 (*0-935063-27-7*) CIS Comm.

—The New York Express. Wicentowski, Deborah. 127p. (gr. 3-5). 1988. 8.95 (*0-935063-46-3*); pap. 6.95 (*0-935063-47-1*) CIS Comm.

—Operation C. H. E. S. E. D. & other Stories. Kohaine, Chayele. 139p. (gr. 2-5). 1989. 10.95 (*0-935063-81-1*); pap. text ed. 7.95 (*0-935063-82-X*) CIS Comm.

Scheiner, James B., jt. photog. see Scheiner, Martin.

Scheiner, Martin & Scheiner, James B., photos by. Night Dive. McGovern, Ann. LC 84-7163. 64p. (gr. 2-5). 1984. RSBE 14.95 (*0-02-765710-8*, Macmillan Child Bk) Macmillan Child Grp.

Schendle, Kathy A. Write That Down for Me Daddy. Addison, Harry W. LC 78-9028. 50p. (gr. 6-12). 1978. Repr. of 1974 ed. 4.95 (*0-88289-871-X*) Pelican.

Schepp, Warren & Dodson, Deborah. The Old El Toro Reader: A Guide to the Past. Osterman, Joe. Walker, Doris & Osterman, Tim, eds. LC 92-96902. 112p. 1992. pap. 9.95 (*1-881129-02-0*) Old El Toro Pr.

Scherer, Jeffrey. Wake Me in the Spring. Preller, James. LC 93-16787. 1994. pap. 2.95 (*0-590-47500-2*, Cartwheel) Scholastic Inc.

Schick, Alice, jt. illus. see Schick, Joel.

Schick, Eleanor. I Have Another Language: The Language Is Dance. Schick, Eleanor. LC 91-9485. 32p. (gr. k-6). 1992. RSBE 13.55 (*0-02-781209-X*, Macmillan Child Bk) Macmillan Child Grp.

Schick, Joel. How to Eat Fried Worms: And Other Plays. Rockwell, Thomas. LC 78-72854. (gr. 4-7). 1980. 9.95 (*0-440-03498-1*); PLB 9.89 (*0-440-03499-X*) Delacorte.

—Let's Get Dressed! Hooks, William A., et al. Bank Street College Media Group, ed. 32p. (Orig.). (ps). 1986. write for info. (*0-9617400-0-9*) Levi Strauss.

—My Robot Buddy. reissued ed. Slote, Alfred. LC 75-9922. 80p. (gr. 2-5). 1988. PLB 13.89 (*0-397-32505-3*, Lipp Jr Bks) HarpC Child Bks.

—Susannah & the Poison Green Halloween. Elmore, Patricia. LC 82-2493. 128p. (gr. 4-7). 1982. 9.95 (*0-525-44019-4*, DCB) Dutton Child Bks.

Schick, Joel & Schick, Alice. Bram Stoker's Dracula. Schick, Joel & Schick, Alice. LC 80-13619. 48p. (gr. 4-6). 1980. PLB 12.95 (*0-685-42954-7*); pap. 6.95 (*0-385-28141-2*) Delacorte.

—Mary Shelley's Frankenstein. Schick, Joel & Schick, Alice. LC 80-385. 48p. (gr. 4-6). 1981. PLB 11.95 (*0-385-28302-4*) Delacorte.

Schields, Gretchen. The Chinese Siamese Cat. Tan, Amy. LC 93-24008. 1994. write for info. (*0-02-788835-5*, Macmillan Child Bk) Macmillan Child Grp.

—The Moon Lady. Tan, Amy. LC 91-22321. 32p. (gr. 1 up). 1992. RSBE 16.95 (*0-02-788830-4*, Macmillan Child Bk) Macmillan Child Grp.

Schiller, Alexandra. The Raisin Eater. Schiller, Alexandra. Martin, John J. & Schiller, Alexandra, eds. 44p. (gr. 3-4). 1984. 5.00 (*0-9618682-0-1*) A Schiller. The dancing raisins illustrations created by the author for this publication were later adapted by the raisin industry for their animated caricature promotion of the tiny dried fruit. Although the text is at approximately a 3rd grade reading level, it is an enjoyable read-to story for younger children; & older readers may appreciate the subtle humor in the highly-imaginative & thoroughly amusing story about an 8 year old girl's fantasy adventure discovery of personified raisins. For all raisin lovers young at heart. "A darling book...really well done."--Pat Holt, Book Review Editor, San Francisco Chronicle. *Publisher Provided Annotation.*

Schiller, Juel K. Look at the Holidays. Poelker, Kathy. 64p. (ps-4). 1988. Repr. of 1980 ed. tchr's. ed. 7.95 (*0-317-91200-3*) LAM Co.

Schilling, Mickey E. Charlie the Shy Cowboy. Payne, Richard A. 36p. (gr. 1-9). 1993. pap. 4.95 (*0-9636186-2-8*) Blue Sky Grap.

Schimmel, Beth. Abigail's New Home. Taylor, Dorothy L. LC 82-238196. 20p. (gr. k-3). 7.50 (*0-9610640-0-5*) D L Taylor.

Schindelman, Joseph. Charlie & the Chocolate Factory. Dahl, Roald. (gr. 5 up). 1964. 15.00 (*0-394-81011-2*); PLB 15.99 (*0-394-91011-7*) Knopf Bks Yng Read.

—Charlie & the Great Glass Elevator: The Further Adventures of Charlie Bucket & Willie Wonka, the Chocolate-Maker Extraordinaire. Dahl, Roald. (gr. k-7). 1972. 15.00 (*0-394-82472-5*); lib. bdg. 15.99 (*0-394-92472-X*) Knopf Bks Yng Read.

Schindler, A. A. About the Splendid Macedonians: A Coloring Book & Much, Much More. Naumoff, Olga. 64p. 1982. pap. 4.95 (*0-941983-00-5*) Splendid Assocs.

Schindler, S. D. Big Pumpkin. Silverman, Erica. LC 91-14053. 32p. (ps-3). 1992. RSBE 14.95 (*0-02-782683-X*, Macmillan Child Bk) Macmillan Child Grp.

—The Big Race. Matthews, Morgan. LC 88-1287. 48p. (Orig.). (gr. 1-4). 1989. PLB 10.59 (*0-8167-1329-4*); pap. text ed. 3.50 (*0-8167-1330-8*) Troll Assocs.

—Catwings. Le Guin, Ursula K. LC 87-33104. 48p. (gr. 2-5). 1988. 11.95 (*0-531-05759-3*); PLB 11.99 (*0-531-08359-4*) Orchard Bks Watts.

—Catwings. LeGuin, Ursula K. 64p. (gr. 2-5). 1992. pap. 2.95 (*0-590-46072-2*) Scholastic Inc.

—Catwings Return. Le Guin, Ursula K. LC 88-17902. 56p. (gr. 2-5). 1989. 11.95 (*0-531-05803-4*); PLB 11.99 (*0-531-08403-5*) Orchard Bks Watts.

—Catwings Return. LeGuin, Ursula K. 64p. (gr. 2-5). 1992. pap. 2.95 (*0-590-46074-9*) Scholastic Inc.

—Children of Christmas: Stories for the Season. Rylant, Cynthia. LC 87-1690. 48p. (gr. 3 up). 1987. 13.95 (*0-531-05706-2*); PLB 13.99 (*0-531-08306-3*) Orchard Bks Watts.

—Children of Christmas: Stories for the Season. Rylant, Cynthia. LC 87-1690. 48p. (gr. 3 up). 1993. pap. 5.95 (*0-531-07042-5*) Orchard Bks Watts.

—Digging up the Past: The Story of an Archaeological Adventure. James, Carollyn. 64p. (gr. 5-8). 1990. PLB 11.90 (*0-531-10878-3*) Watts.

—The Earth Is Painted Green: A Garden of Poems about Our Planet. Brenner, Barbara, ed. LC 93-21466. 96p. 1993. 16.95 (*0-590-45134-0*) Scholastic Inc.

—Every Living Thing. Rylant, Cynthia. LC 88-19359. 96p. (gr. 5 up). 1988. pap. 3.50 (*0-689-71263-4*, Aladdin) Macmillan Child Grp.

—Favorite Fairy Tales Told Around the World. Haviland, Virginia, selected by. (ps-6). 1985. 24.95 (*0-316-35044-3*) Little.

—Floratorium. Oppenheim, Joanne. Eberbach, Catherine, intro. by. LC 92-17886. 1994. 15.95 (*0-553-09365-7*); PLB 9.95 (*0-553-37145-2*) Bantam.

—The Freeze-in-Place Contest. Silverman, Erica. LC 93-8707. 1994. write for info. (*0-02-782685-6*) Macmillan.

—The Great White Owl of Sissinghurst. Simmons, Dawn L. LC 91-17490. 32p. (ps-3). 1993. SBE 14.95g (*0-689-50522-1*, M K McElderry) Macmillan Child Grp.

—Gulliver's Travels. Swift, Jonathan. James, Raymond, ed. LC 89-33943. 48p. (gr. 3-6). 1990. PLB 12.89 (*0-8167-1865-2*); pap. text ed. 3.95 (*0-8167-1866-0*) Troll Assocs.

—I Love My Buzzard. Seymour, Tres. LC 93-4877. 1994. write for info. (*0-531-06819-6*); lib. bdg. write for info. (*0-531-08669-0*) Orchard Bks Watts.

—Is This a House for Hermit Crab? McDonald, Megan. LC 89-35653. 32p. (ps-1). 1990. 14.95 (*0-531-05855-7*); PLB 14.99 (*0-531-08455-8*) Orchard Bks Watts.

—Is This a House for Hermit Crab? McDonald, Megan. LC 89-35653. 32p. (ps-1). 1993. pap. 5.95 (*0-531-07041-7*) Orchard Bks Watts.

—Margery Williams "The Velveteen Rabbit" Williams, Margery. Eastman, David, ed. LC 87-11269. 32p. (gr. k-4). 1988. PLB 9.79 (*0-8167-1061-9*); pap. text ed. 1.95 (*0-8167-1062-7*) Troll Assocs.

—Moon. Santrey, Laurence. LC 84-8441. 32p. (gr. 3-6). 1985. PLB 9.49 (*0-8167-0252-7*); pap. text ed. 2.95 (*0-8167-0253-5*) Troll Assocs.

—Not the Piano, Mrs. Medley! Levine, Evan. LC 90-29085. 32p. (ps-2). 1991. 14.95 (*0-531-05956-1*); RLB 14.99 (*0-531-08556-2*) Orchard Bks Watts.

—Odds on Oliver. Greene, Constance C. LC 92-25932. 64p. (gr. 2-5). 1993. PLB 12.99 (*0-670-84549-3*) Viking Child Bks.

—Oh, What a Thanksgiving! Kroll, Steven. LC 88-1973. (gr. k-3). 1988. pap. 12.95 (*0-590-40613-2*, Scholastic Hardcover) Scholastic Inc.

—Penrod's Party. Christian, Mary B. LC 89-37203. 48p. (gr. 1-4). 1990. RSBE 11.95 (*0-02-718525-7*, Macmillan Child Bk) Macmillan Child Grp.

—Penrod's Picture. Christian, Mary B. LC 90-39808. 48p. (gr. 1-4). 1991. RSBE 11.95 (*0-02-718523-0*, Macmillan Child Bk) Macmillan Child Grp.

—The Pied Piper of Hamelin: A Step 2 Book. Hautzig, Deborah, retold by. LC 89-3968. 48p. (Orig.). (gr. 1-3). 1989. lib. bdg. 7.99 (*0-394-96579-5*); pap. 3.50 (*0-394-86579-0*) Random Bks Yng Read.

—The Stinky Book. Lukas, Noah. LC 92-22701. 24p. (ps up). 1993. 6.99 (*0-679-83619-5*) Random Bks Yng Read.

—The Three Little Pigs & the Fox. Hooks, William H. LC 88-29296. 32p. (gr. k-3). 1989. RSBE 13.95 (*0-02-744431-7*, Macmillan Child Bk) Macmillan Child Grp.

—Tiny Trolls' ABC. Lukas, Noah. LC 92-62940. 24p. (Orig.). (ps-k). 1993. pap. 1.50 (*0-679-84797-9*) Random Bks Yng Read.

—Tiny Trolls' 1, 2, 3. Lukas, Noah. LC 92-62939. 24p. (Orig.). (ps-k). 1993. pap. 1.50 (*0-679-84792-8*) Random Bks Yng Read.

—The Tree House Detective Club. Bolton, Elizabeth. LC 84-8762. 48p. (gr. 2-4). 1985. PLB 10.89 (*0-8167-0404-X*); pap. text ed. 3.50 (*0-8167-0405-8*) Troll Assocs.

—The Twelve Days of Christmas. LC 90-22389. 24p. (ps up). 1991. 2.95 (*0-694-00363-8*) HarpC Child Bks.

—Whoo-oo Is It? McDonald, Megan. LC 91-18494. 32p. (ps-1). 1992. 14.95 (*0-531-05974-X*); lib. bdg. 14.99 (*0-531-08574-0*) Orchard Bks Watts.

—Wonders of the Rain Forest. Craig, Janet. LC 89-5001. 32p. (gr. 2-4). 1990. PLB 11.59 (*0-8167-1763-X*); pap. text ed. 2.95 (*0-8167-1764-8*) Troll Assocs.

Schindler, Stephen. Bible Atlas: A First Reference Book. Wilson, Etta & Jones, Sally L. 24p. (gr. 3-5). 1993. text ed. 9.99 (0-7847-0080-X, 24-03620) Standard Pub.

—Bible Dictionary: A First Reference Book. Wilson, Etta & Jones, Sally L. 24p. (gr. 3-5). 1993. text ed. 9.99 (0-7847-0079-6, 24-03619) Standard Pub.

Schindler, Stephen D. As Old as the Hills. Berger, Melvin. LC 88-37403. 32p. (gr. k-4). 1989. PLB 12.90 (0-531-10699-3) Watts.

—Every Living Thing. Rylant, Cynthia. LC 85-7701. 96p. (gr. 5-7). 1985. SBE 12.95 (0-02-777200-4, Bradbury Pr) Macmillan Child Grp.

Schindler, Steve. Great Aunt Ida & Her Great Dane, Doc. Komaiko, Leah. LC 92-34196. 1994. 14.95 (0-385-30682-2) Doubleday.

Schindler, Steven. Night Creatures. Whayne, Susanne S. LC 91-24654. 48p. (gr. 2-7). 1993. pap. 15.00 JRT (0-671-73395-8, S&S BFYR) S&S Trade.

—Spooky Tricks. Wyler, Rose & Ames, Gerald. LC 92-47501. (ps-6). 1994. 14.00 (0-06-023025-8) HarpC Child Bks.

Schlatter, Becky. The White Stone. Weeks, Wilfred H. LC 85-51932. 37p. (Orig.). (gr. 4-9). 1990. pap. write for info (0-9615677-0-8) Three Riv Ctr.

Schlegel, Ralph A. I Heard Good News Today. Lehn, Cornelia. Oyer, Lora S., intro. by. LC 80-80401. 148p. (gr. 1-6). 1983. 12.95 (0-87303-073-7) Faith & Life.

Schlendorf, Lori. Kids Working with Computers: An Apple LOGO Manual. Kemnitz, Thomas M. & Mass, Lynne. 58p. (gr. 4-7). 1983. pap. 4.99 (0-89824-073-5) Trillium Pr.

—Kids Working with Computers: The Apple BASIC Manual. Kemnitz, Thomas M. & Mass, Lynne. 42p. (gr. 4-7). 1983. pap. 4.99 (0-89824-092-1) Trillium Pr.

—Kids Working with Computers: The Atari BASIC Manual. Kemnitz, Thomas M. & Mass, Lynne. 48p. (gr. 4-7). 1983. pap. 4.99 (0-89824-062-X) Trillium Pr.

—Kids Working with Computers: The Commodore BASIC Manual. Kemnitz, Thomas M. & Mass, Lynne. 48p. (gr. 4-7). 1983. pap. 4.99 (0-89824-060-3) Trillium Pr.

—Kids Working with Computers: The IBM BASIC Manual. Kemnitz, Thomas M. & Mass, Lynne. 48p. (gr. 4-7). 1983. pap. 4.99 (0-89824-063-8) Trillium Pr.

—Kids Working with Computers: The Texas Instruments BASIC Manual. Kemnitz, Thomas M. & Mass, Lynne. 48p. (gr. 4-7). 1983. pap. 4.99 (0-89824-059-X) Trillium Pr.

—Kids Working with Computers: The Texas Instruments LOGO Manual. Mass, Lynne. 64p. (gr. 4-7). 1983. pap. 4.99 (0-89824-074-3) Trillium Pr.

—Kids Working with Computers: The Timex-Sinclair BASIC Manual. Kemnitz, Thomas M. & Mass, Lynne. 48p. (gr. 4-7). 1983. pap. 4.99 (0-89824-058-1) Trillium Pr.

—Kids Working with Computers: TRS-80 BASIC Manual. Kemnitz, Thomas M. & Mass, Lynne. 44p. (gr. 4-7). 1983. pap. 4.99 (0-89824-055-7) Trillium Pr.

Schley, Cynthia. Wildwoods Dad. Oakland, Don. 220p. (Orig.). (gr. 5 up). 1987. pap. 6.95 (0-9615242-1-9) Oak Pr.

Schloss, Bevalee. Concepterms. Toomey, Marilyn M. Schloss, Bevalee, ed. 125p. (ps-5). 1986. vinyl binder 19.95 (0-923573-02-X) Circuit Pubns.

—Explanations: Level I. Toomey, Marilyn M. (gr. 2-6). 1988. cards & worksheets 27.50 (0-923573-05-4) Circuit Pubns.

—Explanations: Level II. Toomey, Marilyn M. (gr. 7-12). 1988. cards & worksheets 27.50 (0-923573-06-2) Circuit Pubns.

—Explanations: Primary. Toomey, Marilyn M. (ps-8). 1989. cards & worksheets 27.50 (0-923573-04-6) Circuit Pubns.

—Morph-Aid: A Source of Roots, Prefixes & Suffixes. 2nd ed. Toomey, Marilyn M. 124p. (gr. 4-10). 1989. pap. 15.95 (0-923573-03-8) Circuit Pubns.

—One Hundred One Categories. Toomey, Marilyn M. 106p. (ps-5). 1985. spiral bdg. 21.95 (0-923573-01-1) Circuit Pubns.

—Sounds All Around: Initial & Final Consonants. Toomey, Marilyn M. 384p. 1989. pap. 19.95 (0-923573-11-9) Circuit Pubns.

Schloss, E. Songs to the River. Rose B. (HEB & ENG.). 64p. (ps-5). 2.95x (0-8381-0720-6, 10-720) United Syn Bk.

Schlosser, Cy. My Own Book! Reading Is Fundamental (RIF) 20th Anniversary. Hammer, Roger A. LC 86-30410. 128p. (gr. 3-12). 1987. pap. 14.95 (0-932991-50-5) Place in the Woods.

Schlosser, Cy, et al. Hidden America: A Collection of Multi-Cultural Stories, 4 bks. rev. ed. Hammer, Roger A. (gr. 6 up). Set. pap. 29.95 (0-932991-00-9) Place in the Woods.

Schluter, Manfred. The Red Armchair. Broger, Achim. 28p. (ps-2). 1991. smythe sewn reinforced bdg. 9.95 (1-56182-034-2) Atomium Bks.

Schmacker, Pam. Count to the Stars. Tubbs, Beth. 28p. (ps). 1992. wiro-spiral bdg. 9.95 (0-9632993-4-4) Storytime Pub.

—Z Is for Zebra. Tubbs, Beth. 32p. (ps). 1992. 9.95 (0-9632993-3-6) Storytime Pub.

Schmid, Eleanor. Three Feathers. Grimm, Jacob & Grimm, Wilhelm K. 32p. (gr. 4 up). 1984. PLB 13.95s.p. (0-87191-941-9) Creative Ed.

Schmid, Eleanore. Story of Christmas. Schmid, Eleanore. LC 89-43724. 32p. (ps-3). 1990. 13.95 (1-55858-097-2) North-South Bks NYC.

—The Water's Journey. Schmid, Eleonore. LC 89-42872. 32p. (gr. k-3). 1990. 14.95 (1-55858-013-1) North-South Bks NYC.

Schmid, Eleonore. Farm Animals. Schmid, Eleonore. LC 85-63302. 12p. (ps-k). 1986. 3.95 (1-55858-045-X) North-South Bks NYC.

—The Lonely Wolf. De Marolles, Chantal. LC 86-2511. 32p. (gr. k-3). 1986. 14.95 (1-55858-073-5) North-South Bks NYC.

—Wake up, Dormouse, Santa Claus Is Here. Schmid, Eleonore. LC 89-42610. 32p. (gr. k-3). 1989. 14.95 (1-55858-020-4) North-South Bks NYC.

Schmid, Eleonore & James, J. Alison. The Air Around Us. Schmid, Eleonore. LC 92-9830. 32p. (gr. k-3). 1992. 14.95 (1-55858-165-0); PLB 14.88 (1-55858-166-9) North-South Bks NYC.

Schmid, Ross. Help! for Substitutes. Peterson, Sherrie. 80p. 1985. tchr's. wkbk. 5.95 (0-86653-277-3, GA 642) Good Apple.

Schmidt, Diane, photos by. I Am a Jesse White Tumbler. Schmidt, Diane. Tucker, Kathy, ed. LC 89-16590. 40p. (gr. 2-8). 1990. 13.95 (0-8075-3444-7) A Whitman.

—Where's Chimpy? Rabe, Berniece. Tucker, Kathleen, ed. LC 87-37259. 32p. (ps-2). 1988. PLB 13.95 (0-8075-8928-4); pap. 5.95 (0-8075-8927-6) A Whitman.

Schmidt, George. Just Like Max. Ackerman, Karen. LC 88-13214. 32p. (ps-3). 1990. PLB 13.99 (0-394-90176-2) Knopf Bks Yng Read.

Schmidt, Joseph K. The Children's Magic Kit: Sixteen Easy-to-Do Tricks Complete with Cardboard Cutouts. Fulves, Karl. 32p. (Orig.). (gr. 3-6). 1981. pap. 3.95 (0-486-24019-3) Dover.

—Easy-to-Do Magic Tricks for Children. Fulves, Karl. LC 93-9675. 48p. (Orig.). 1993. pap. 2.95 (0-486-27613-9) Dover.

—Self-Working Table Magic: Ninety-Seven Foolproof Tricks with Everyday Objects. Fulves, Karl. 128p. (Orig.). 1981. pap. 3.95 (0-486-24116-5) Dover.

Schmidt, Karen. Down by the Station. 1987. pap. 6.99 incl. audiocassette (0-553-45902-3) Bantam.

—The Gingerbread Man. 32p. (gr. k-2). 1985. pap. 2.50 (0-590-41056-3) Scholastic Inc.

—Little Red Riding Hood. Grimm, Jacob & Grimm, Wilhelm K. 32p. (Orig.). (gr. k-2). 1986. pap. 2.50 (0-590-41881-5) Scholastic Inc.

—Your First Adventure: Little Kitten Sleeps Over, No. 9. Leonard, Marcia, adapted by. 32p. (Orig.). 1987. pap. 2.50 (0-553-15472-9) Bantam.

Schmidt, Karen L. Bears, Bears, Bears. Osborne, Mary P., compiled by. 96p. (ps-2). 1990. pap. 14.95 (0-671-69631-9, S&S BYR); pap. 18.98 (0-671-69630-0) S&S Trade.

—Chicken Little. 18p. (ps). 1986. 3.95 (0-448-10223-4, G&D) Putnam Pub Group.

—The Little Red Hen. 16p. (ps). 1984. 3.95 (0-448-10218-8, G&D) Putnam Pub Group.

—My First Book of Baby Animals. LC 85-62639. 12p. (ps). 1986. 3.95 (0-448-10826-7, Platt & Munk) Putnam Pub Group.

—A Nickel Buys a Rhyme. Benjamin, Alan. LC 92-6475. 40p. (ps up). 1993. 15.00 (0-688-06698-4); PLB 14.93 (0-688-06699-2) Morrow Jr Bks.

—Pups Speak Up. Meltzer, Maxine. LC 92-33687. 32p. (ps-3). 1994. RSBE 13.95 (0-02-766710-3, Bradbury Pr) Macmillan Child Grp.

—Sleepytime for Baby Mouse. Hopkins, Margaret. 12p. (ps-3). 1985. 3.95 (0-448-40875-9, G&D) Putnam Pub Group.

—The Twelve Days of Summer. O'Donnell, Elizabeth L. LC 89-35161. 32p. (ps up). 1991. 13.95 (0-688-08202-5); PLB 13.88 (0-688-08203-3, Morrow Jr Bks) Morrow Jr Bks.

—Whiskerville Bake Shop. Barkan, Joanne. 12p. (ps-k). 1990. bds. 3.50 (0-448-19467-8, G&D) Putnam Pub Group.

—Whiskerville Firehouse. Barkan, Joanne. 12p. (ps-k). 1990. bds. 3.50 (0-448-19468-6, G&D) Putnam Pub Group.

—Whiskerville Post Office. Barkan, Joanne. 12p. (ps-k). 1990. bds. 3.50 (0-448-19466-X) Putnam Pub Group.

—Whiskerville School. Barkan, Joanne. 12p. (ps-k). 1990. bds. 3.50 (0-448-19465-1, G&D) Putnam Pub Group.

—You Be Good & I'll Be Night: Jump-on-the-Bed-Poems. Merriam, Eve. LC 87-24859. 40p. (ps-2). 1988. 13.95 (0-688-06742-5); PLB 13.88 (0-688-06743-3, Morrow Jr Bks) Morrow Jr Bks.

Schmidt, Karen L., jt. illus. see Upton, Pat.

Schmidt, Lynette. The Daddy Machine. Valentine, Johnny. 48p. (Orig.). (gr. k-4). 1992. pap. 6.95 (1-55583-107-9, Alyson Wonderland) Alyson Pubns.

—The Day They Put a Tax on Rainbows. Valentine, Johnny. 32p. (gr. k-5). 1992. 12.95 (1-55583-201-6, Alyson Wonderland) Alyson Pubns.

—The Duke Who Outlawed Jelly Beans & Other Stories. Valentine, Johnny. 32p. (gr. k-5). 1991. 12.95 (1-55583-199-0) Alyson Pubns.

—The Duke Who Outlawed Jelly Beans & Other Stories. Valentine, Johnny. 32p. (gr. k-4). 1993. pap. 8.95 (1-55583-219-9) Alyson Pubns.

Schmidt, Norman. Discover Aerodynamics with Paper Airplanes. Schmidt, Norman. 48p. (Orig.). (gr. 7-12). 1991. pap. 14.95 (0-920541-43-7) Peguis Pubs Ltd.

Schmidt, Ross. Friday Afternoon Fun. Bernstein, Bob. 64p. (gr. 2-6). 1984. wkbk. 7.95 (0-86653-206-4, GA 558) Good Apple.

Schmitt, Doug. Dinosaur ABC's Activity Book. rev. ed. Bliss, Richard B., ed. 32p. (gr. k-3). 1986. pap. 3.95 (0-89051-113-6) Master Bks.

Schmitt, Judy & Cooney, Cynthia D. Science Is Fun! For Families & Classroom Groups. Oppenheim, Carol. LC 92-35717. 198p. (Orig.). (ps up). 1993. pap. 14.95 (0-9633555-1-1) Cracom.

Schnatz, Grace. A Child's Introduction to a Garden. Schnatz, Grace. 33p. (gr. 4-8). 1984. PLB 4.75 (0-9614145-0-2) G Schnatz Pubns.

Schneck, Susan. Pandy's Rainbow. Plum, Carol T. 32p. (gr. k-3). 1991. 9.95 (0-87973-008-0, 8); pap. 5.95 (0-87973-009-9, 9) Our Sunday Visitor.

Schneider, Al. Research Challanges. Donovan, Melissa. 168p. (gr. 4-8). 1985. wkbk. 12.95 (0-86653-271-4, GA 660) Good Apple.

Schneider, Howie. The Amazing Amos & the Greatest Couch on Earth. Schneider, Howie & Seligson, Susan. 32p. (ps-3). 1989. 13.95 (0-316-78033-2, Joy St Bks) Little.

—Amos: The Story of an Old Dog & His Couch. Schneider, Howie & Seligson, Susan. LC 87-2813. 32p. (ps-3). 1987. 14.95 (0-316-77404-9) Little.

—Amos: The Story of an Old Dog & His Couch. Seligson, Susan. (ps-3). 1992. pap. 4.95 (0-316-78034-0, Joy St Bks) Little.

—Uncle Lester's Hat. Schneider, Howie. LC 92-20750. 32p. (ps-3). 1993. 14.95 (0-399-22439-4, Putnam) Putnam Pub Group.

Schneider, Jennifer. The Secret of the Ring in the Offering. Reinsma, Carol. 48p. (Orig.). (gr. 1-3). 1993. pap. 3.99 (0-7847-0094-X, 24-03944) Standard Pub.

Schneider, Josef, photos by. Aleksandra, Where Is Your Nose. Dubov, Christine. 12p. (ps). 1986. 3.95 (0-312-01719-7) St Martin.

Schneider, Rex. Caves. Brandt, Keith. LC 84-2573. 32p. (gr. 3-6). 1985. PLB 9.49 (0-8167-0142-3); pap. text ed. 2.95 (0-8167-0143-1) Troll Assocs.

—I Want a Pet. Gregorich, Barbara. Hoffman, Joan, ed. 16p. (Orig.). (gr. k-2). 1984. pap. 2.25 (0-88743-003-1, 06003) Sch Zone Pub Co.

—I'm Nobody! Who Are You? Poems of Emily Dickinson for Children. Dickinson, Emily. Sewall, Richard, intro. by. LC 78-6828. 96p. (gr. 1 up). 1978. 21.95 (0-916144-21-6); pap. 14.95 (0-916144-22-4) Stemmer Hse.

—Jog, Frog, Jog. Gregorich, Barbara. Hoffman, Joan, ed. 16p. (Orig.). (gr. k-2). 1984. pap. 2.25 (0-88743-006-6, 06006) Sch Zone Pub Co.

—Transportation. Brandt, Keith. LC 84-2584. 32p. (gr. 3-6). 1985. PLB 9.49 (0-8167-0172-5); pap. text ed. 2.95 (0-8167-0173-3) Troll Assocs.

—Wonders of Water. Dickinson, Jane. LC 82-17388. 32p. (gr. 3-6). 1983. PLB 10.59 (0-89375-874-4); pap. text ed. 2.95 (0-89375-875-2) Troll Assocs.

Schnell, Louise. Seasonal Art. Schnell, Louise. Evans, Carol, ed. 52p. (ps-3). 1988. wkbk. 5.95 (0-915505-01-0) Tchr Tested-Child.

Schnickel, Jacob, jt. illus. see Jesionowski, Mary.

Schnidler, S. D. Ants. Demuth, Patricia B. LC 93-1769. 1994. text ed. 14.95 (0-02-728467-0) MacMillan.

Schnieder, Josef, photos by. Aleksandra, Where Are Your Toes? Dubov, Christine. 14p. (ps). 1986. 3.95 (0-312-01717-0) St Martin.

Schoenherr, Ian. America Alive. Karl, Jean. LC 92-40539. 1994. write for info. (0-399-22013-5, Philomel Bks) Putnam Pub Group.

—Newf. Killilea, Marie. 32p. (ps up). 1992. PLB 14.95 (0-399-21875-0, Philomel Bks) Putnam Pub Group.

Schoenherr, John. Bear. Schoenherr, John. Thomas, Peter, narrated by. 32p. (ps-4). 1991. incl. audiocassette tape & plush stuffed bear toy 44.95 (0-924483-69-5); incl. audiocassette tape 17.95 (0-924483-34-2) Soundprints.

—Gentle Ben. Morey, Walt. LC 65-21290. 192p. (gr. 4 up). 1965. 12.95 (0-525-30429-0, DCB) Dutton Child Bks.

—Gentle Ben. Morey, Walt. 192p. (gr. 5 up). 1992. pap. 3.99 (0-14-036035-2, Puffin) Puffin Bks.

—The Grizzly Bear with the Golden Ears. George, Jean C. LC 80-7908. 32p. (gr. 3-5). 1982. PLB 13.89 (0-06-021966-1) HarpC Child Bks.

—Incident at Hawk's Hill. Eckert, Allan W. 173p. (gr. 7 up). 1971. 15.95 (0-316-20866-3) Little.

—Julie of the Wolves. George, Jean C. LC 72-76509. 180p. (gr. 7 up). 1974. 15.00i (0-06-021943-2); PLB 14.89 (0-06-021944-0); pap. 3.95 (0-06-440058-1) HarpC Child Bks.

—Kilroy & the Gull. Benchley, Nathaniel. LC 76-24309. (gr. 4-6). 1978. pap. 3.95 (0-06-440090-5, Trophy) HarpC Child Bks.

—Owl Moon. Yolen, Jane. (ps-1). 1987. 14.95 (0-399-21457-7, Philomel Bks) Putnam Pub Group.

—Rascal. North, Sterling. 192p. (ps up). 1990. pap. 3.99 (0-14-034445-4, Puffin) Puffin Bks.

—Wild Voices. Nelson, Drew. 96p. (gr. 3 up). 1991. 15.95 (0-399-21798-3, Philomel) Putnam Pub Group.

—The Wolfling. North, Sterling. 224p. (gr. 5-9). 1992. pap. 3.99 (0-14-036166-9, Puffin) Puffin Bks.

—The Wounded Wolf. George, Jean C. LC 76-58711. (ps-3). 1978. PLB 14.89 (0-06-021950-5) HarpC Child Bks.

Schoenherr, John & Mullins, Frank. Reader's Digest Best Loved Books for Young Readers: The Call of the Wild & Typhoon. London, Jack & Conrad, Joseph. Ogburn, Jackie, ed. 136p. (gr. 4-12). 1989. 3.99 (0-945260-28-8) Choice Pub NY.

Scholder, Fritz. ANPAO: An American Indian Odyssey. Highwater, Jamake. LC 77-9264. 256p. (gr. 7 up). 1992. pap. 6.95 (0-06-440437-4, Trophy) HarpC Child Bks.
—Anpao: An American Indian Odyssey. Highwater, Jamake. LC 77-9264. 256p. (gr. 7 up). 1993. PLB 14.89 (0-06-022878-4) HarpC Child Bks.
Scholefield, Ron, et al. Mickey Mouse in Let's Go...on a Beach Picnic. Guild, Anne V. 26p. (ps up). 1987. pap. 14.95 (1-55578-800-9) Worlds Wonder.
—Mickey Mouse in Let's Go...on a Camping Caper. Guild, Anne V. 26p. (ps up). 1987. pap. 14.95 (1-55578-803-3) Worlds Wonder.
—Mickey Mouse in Let's Go...to Disneyland. Guild, Anne V. 26p. (ps up). 1988. pap. 14.95 (1-55578-801-7) Worlds Wonder.
—Mickey Mouse in Let's Go...to the Zoo! Guild, Anne V. 26p. (ps up). 1987. pap. 14.95 (1-55578-802-5) Worlds Wonder.
Schongut, Emanuel. Hush Kitten. Schongut, Emanuel. Klimo, Kate, ed. 14p. 1983. 3.95 (0-671-46386-1) S&S Trade.
—The Private Nose. Taylor, Andrew. LC 92-53016. 96p. (gr. k-4). 1993. 13.95 (1-56402-135-1) Candlewick Pr.
Schoolcraft, Robert. Camping Basics. Armstrong, Wayne. LC 85-9407. 48p. (gr. 3-7). 1985. 10.95 (0-13-112657-1) P-H.
—Golf Basics. Schiffman, Roger. 48p. (gr. 3-7). 1986. 10.95 (0-13-357955-7) P-H.

Schooley, Joan. The Flood That Came to Grandma's House. Stallone, Linda. LC 91-33955. 21p. (ps-3). 1992. 9.95 (0-912975-02-4) Upshur Pr. Newsclips of hurricane disasters never tell the whole story. This year, more than ever, kids need to know about hurricanes & the entire process of recovery from destruction that forces thousands to flee their homes. THE FLOOD THAT CAME TO GRANDMA'S HOUSE has been reviewed enthusiastically by newspapers from Corning, New York down to St. Petersburg, Florida. "Teachers & parents find in its pages a way to explain to children what happens during a natural disaster." (Bloomsburg, PA Press Enterprise.) Used in hundreds of schools & loved by children or anyone who has experienced a flood, the book helps young children think through what could be traumatic or confusing. The story begins with the first days of rain from Hurricane Agnes & pulls the reader through the drama as the citizens attempt to sandbag the river, but are finally forced to evacuate. Humorous yet realistic illustrations show children exactly what happens inside a house that is filled with water & the mess left in its wake. A true story, simply told & lovingly illustrated. Captures a slice of history, while it helps young children understand why a flood isn't "fun" water. "Reassures how natural disasters are handled." "Satisfies curiosity of young readers." Order from: Upshur Press, P.O. Box 609, Dallas, PA 18612; or call 1-(800)-777-1461 or (717)-675-8835.
Publisher Provided Annotation.

Schoonover, Annette. My Trip. Nelson, Jackie & Halpern-Segal, Janice. 24p. (Orig.). (ps-3). 1989. pap. 6.95 (0-685-29177-4) Take Along Pubns.
Schoonover, Kevin. Makin Music! Patella, Chris & Oddo, Eileen. 75p. (Orig.). (gr. k-2). 1989. write for info. tchrs. ed. (0-944333-02-8); LP or Cassette avail. Musical Munchkins.
Schoonover, pat & Nelson, Anita. The Flopsy Bunnies. Potter, Beatrix, created by. 24p. (gr. 2-4). 1992. PLB 10.95 (1-56674-016-9, HTS Bks) Forest Hse.
—Jemima Puddle-Duck. Potter, Beatrix, created by. 24p. (gr. 2-4). 1992. PLB 10.95 (1-56674-018-5, HTS Bks) Forest Hse.
—Miss Moppet. Potter, Beatrix, created by. 24p. (gr. 2-4). 1992. PLB 10.95 (1-56674-020-7, HTS Bks) Forest Hse.

—Mr. Jeremy Fisher. Potter, Beatrix, created by. 24p. (gr. 2-4). 1992. PLB 10.95 (1-56674-019-3, HTS Bks) Forest Hse.
—Peter Rabbit. Potter, Beatrix, created by. 24p. (gr. 2-4). 1992. PLB 10.95 (1-56674-008-8, HTS Bks) Forest Hse.
—Squirrel Nutkin. Potter, Beatrix, created by. 24p. (gr. 2-4). 1992. PLB 10.95 (1-56674-009-6, HTS Bks) Forest Hse.
Schories, Pat. David & Goliath. Schorsch, Laurence, retold by. 24p. (ps-3). 1992. 4.95 (1-56288-221-X) Checkerboard.
—Noah's Ark. Schorsch, Laurence, retold by. 24p. (ps-3). 1992. 4.95 (1-56288-223-6) Checkerboard.
—Quiet As a Mouse. Roth, Carol. 32p. (ps-3). 1991. 6.95 (1-56288-121-3) Checkerboard.
—Tiny Star. Ginolfi, Arthur. 32p. 1989. 6.95 (1-56288-134-5) Checkerboard.
—Winter Barn. Ripley, Dorothy. LC 93-32420. 1994. write for info. (0-679-84472-4) Random Bks Yng Read.
—Young Abraham Lincoln, Log-Cabin President. Woods, Andrew. LC 91-26570. 32p. (gr. k-2). 1992. text ed. 11.59 (0-8167-2532-2); pap. text ed. 2.95 (0-8167-2533-0) Troll Assocs.
Schories, Patricia L. The Boo-Hoo Witch. Craig, Janet A. LC 93-2216. 32p. (gr. k-2). 1993. PLB 11.59 (0-8167-3186-1); pap. text ed. 2.95 (0-8167-3187-X) Troll Assocs.
Schornak, Mark, et al. Yesterday's River: The Archaeology of Ten Thousand Years along the Tennessee-Tombigbee Waterway. Brose, David S. 160p. (gr. 10). 1990. pap. 9.75 (1-878600-00-1) Cleve Mus Nat Hist.
Schott, Darlyne F. Pasitos Student Workbook, Libro 10. Schott, Darlyne F. (SPA.). 8p. (Orig.). (gr. k-1). 1991. pap. text ed. 1.25 (1-56537-131-3, 131) D F Schott Educ.
—Pasitos Student Workbook, Libro 6. Schott, Darlyne F. (SPA.). 8p. (Orig.). (gr. k-1). 1991. pap. text ed. 1.25 (1-56537-126-7, 126) D F Schott Educ.
—Pasitos Student Workbook, Libro 7. Schott, Darlyne F. (SPA.). 8p. (Orig.). (gr. k-1). 1991. pap. text ed. 1.25 (1-56537-127-5, 127) D F Schott Educ.
—Pasitos Student Workbook, Libro 8. Schott, Darlyne F. (SPA.). 8p. (Orig.). (gr. k-1). 1991. pap. text ed. 1.25 (1-56537-128-3, 128) D F Schott Educ.
—Pasitos Student Workbook, Libro 9. Schott, Darlyne F. (SPA.). 8p. (Orig.). (gr. k-1). 1991. pap. text ed. 1.25 (1-56537-129-1, 129) D F Schott Educ.
Schreiber, Jocelyn. How to Draw Zoo Animals. Schreiber, Jocelyn. LC 87-50427. 32p. (gr. 2-6). 1988. PLB 10.65 (0-8167-1004-X, Pub. by Watermill Pr); pap. text ed. 1.95 (0-8167-1005-8, Pub. by Watermill Pr) Troll Assocs.
Schreiber, Suzanne L. Yoga for the Fun of It! Hatha Yoga for Preschool Children. 4th ed. Schreiber, Suzanne L. Folan, Lilias, intro. by. 54p. (Orig.). (ps). 1991. pap. 9.00 (0-9608320-0-9) Sugar Marbel Pr.
Schrieber, Georges. The Light at Tern Rock. Sauer, Julia L. 64p. (gr. 3-7). 1994. pap. 3.99 (0-14-036857-4) Puffin Bks.
Schroeder, Binette. The Frog Prince. Grimm, Jacob & Grimm, Wilhelm K. Lewis, Naomi, tr. from GER. LC 89-42613. (GER.). 32p. (gr. k-3). 1989. 15.95 (1-55858-015-3) North-South Bks NYC.
—Der Froschkonig. Grimm, Jacob & Grimm, Wilhelm K. (GER.). 32p. (gr. k-3). 1992. 15.95 (3-314-00336-6) North-South Bks NYC.
—Le Prince Grenouille. Grimm, Jacob & Grimm, Wilhelm K. (FRE.). 32p. (gr. k-3). 1992. 15.95 (3-314-20666-6) North-South Bks NYC.
—The Wonderful Travels & Adventures of Baron Munchhausen: As Told by Himself in the Company of His Friends & Washed down by Many a Good Bottle of Wine - The Adventures on Land. Nickl, Peter. Taylor, Elizabeth B., tr. from GER. LC 91-16510. 32p. (gr. 5 up). 1992. 17.95 (1-55858-134-0) North-South Bks NYC.
Schroeder, Binnette. Crocodile, Crocodile. Nickl, Peter. Cutler, Ebbitt, tr. 32p. 1989. 11.95 (0-940793-33-4, Pub. by Crocodile Bks); pap. 6.95 (0-940793-32-6, Pub. by Crocodile Bks) Interlink Pub.
Schroeder, Ted. What Does a Witch Need? DeLage, Ida. 48p. (gr. k-4). 1991. Repr. of 1971 ed. PLB 12.95 (0-7910-1486-X) Chelsea Hse.
Schroeppel, Richard. The Hockey Machine. Christopher, Matt. (gr. 4 up). 1986. 14.95 (0-316-14055-4) Little.
Schubert, Annalee. I'll Do Better Tomorrow, I Promise. Adamek, Maurine R. LC 92-11169. 32p. 1992. pap. 6.99 (0-9628579-3-9) Vision WY.
Schubert, Dieter, jt. illus. see Schubert, Ingrid.
Schubert, Ingrid & Schubert, Dieter. Little Big Feet. Schubert, Ingrid & Schubert, Dieter. 32p. (ps-3). 1990. PLB 18.95 (0-87614-426-1) Carolrhoda Bks.
Schuett, Stacey. Beginnings: How Families Came to Be. Kroll, Virginia L. LC 93-29594. 1994. write for info. (0-8075-0602-8) A Whitman.
—I'll See You in My Dreams. Jukes, Mavis. LC 91-47605. 40p. (gr. k-5). 1993. 15.00 (0-679-82690-4); PLB 15.99 (0-679-92690-9) Knopf Bks Yng Read.
—Is It Dark? Is It Light? Lankford, Mary D. LC 90-21492. 32p. (ps-2). 1991. 13.00 (0-679-81579-1); lib. bdg. 13.99 (0-679-91579-6) Knopf Bks Yng Read.
—The Moon Comes Home. Salter, Mary J. LC 88-31735. 40p. (ps-2). 1989. 12.95 (0-394-99983-0); lib. bdg. 13.99 (0-394-99983-5) Knopf Bks Yng Read.

—Outside the Window. Smucker, Anna E. LC 92-33452. 1994. 15.00 (0-679-84023-0); PLB 15.99 (0-679-94023-5) Knopf Bks Yng Read.
—Watch Me. Mazer, Anne. LC 89-34920. 40p. (ps-k). 1990. lib. bdg. 13.99 (0-394-92946-2) Knopf Bks Yng Read.
—When Spring Comes. Kinsey-Warnock, Natalie. LC 92-14066. (ps-3). 1993. 14.99 (0-525-45008-4, DCB) Dutton Child Bks.
Schulke, Debra, jt. photog. see Schulke, Flip.
Schulke, Flip & Schulke, Debra, photos by. Your Future in Space: The U. S. Space Camp Training Program. McPhee, Penelope & McPhee, Raymond. McCandless, Bruce & Sullivan, Kathryn D.frwd. by, LC 86-9003. 128p. (gr. 7 up). 1986. pap. 14.95 (0-517-56418-1) Crown Bks Yng Read.
Schultz, Carolyn, jt. illus. see Pini, Wendy.
Schultz, Charles. Peanuts First Program Book. Edison, June. 30p. (Orig.). (gr. 1-6). 1989. pap. 5.50 (1-56516-044-4) Houston IN.
Schultz, Mark. Cadillacs & Dinosaurs. Chadwick, Frank S. 144p. (Orig.). (gr. 9-12). 1990. pap. 18.00 (1-55878-073-4) Game Designers.
—Cadillacs & Dinosaurs. Schultz, Mark. Schreiner, Davd, ed. Williamson, Al, intro. by. 152p. (gr. 3 up). 1994. pap. 14.95 (0-87816-261-5) Kitchen Sink.
Schultz, Patty. The Story of the Little Round Barn. Bright, Velma. LC 81-65540. 48p. (gr. 2-3). 1981. 10.00x (0-9605968-2-8); pap. 5.00 (0-9605968-3-6) Bright Bks.
—What Would You Like to Be? Bright, Velma. 32p. (gr. 1). 1976. PLB 10.00 (0-9605968-0-1) Bright Bks.
Schulz, Charles. Charlie Brown's Favorite Sunday School Songs. Bock, Fred. 24p. (Orig.). (gr. 1-6). 1992. pap. 7.95 (1-56516-012-6) Houston IN.
—Charlie Brown's Piano Album. Welch, John. 38p. (Orig.). (gr. 1-6). 1989. pap. 5.50 (1-56516-054-1) Houston IN.
—Clavinova Sampler Pack Software. Edison, June. 12p. (Orig.). (gr. 1-6). 1992. pap. 19.95 (1-56516-014-2) Houston IN.
—Kids Say the Darndest Things. Linkletter, Art. Disney, Walt, intro. by. LC 54-11661. 262p. (gr. 7 up). 1977. pap. 3.50 (0-89559-010-7, Dist. by National Book Network) Green Hill.
—Peanuts, Bk. 1. Edison, June. 40p. (Orig.). (gr. 1-6). 1989. pap. 5.50 (1-56516-038-X) Houston IN.
—Peanuts, Bk. 2. Edison, June. 38p. (Orig.). (gr. 1-6). 1989. pap. 5.50 (1-56516-039-8) Houston IN.
—Peanuts, Bk. 3. Edison, June. 40p. (Orig.). (gr. 1-6). 1989. pap. 5.50 (1-56516-040-1) Houston IN.
—Peanuts, Bk. 4. Edison, June. 40p. (Orig.). (gr. 1-6). 1989. pap. 5.50 (1-56516-041-X) Houston IN.
—Peanuts, Bk. 5. Edison, June. 38p. (Orig.). (gr. 1-6). 1989. pap. 5.50 (1-56516-042-8) Houston IN.
—Peanuts, Bk. 6. Edison, June. 38p. (Orig.). (gr. 1-6). 1989. pap. 5.50 (1-56516-043-6) Houston IN.
—Peanuts Christmas Album. Edison, June. 38p. (Orig.). (gr. 1-6). 1989. pap. 5.50 (1-56516-049-5) Houston IN.
—Peanuts First Program Book: Clavinova Software. Edison, June. 38p. (Orig.). (gr. 1-6). 1992. pap. 34.95 (1-56516-018-5) Houston IN.
—Peanuts Piano, Bk. 1: Clavinova Software. Edison, June. 40p. (Orig.). (gr. 1-6). 1992. pap. 34.95 (1-56516-015-0) Houston IN.
—Peanuts Piano, Bk. 2: Clavinova Software. Edison, June. 38p. (Orig.). (gr. 1-6). 1992. pap. 34.95 (1-56516-016-9) Houston IN.
—Peanuts Second Program Book. Edison, June. 36p. (Orig.). (gr. 1-6). 1989. pap. 5.50 (1-56516-045-2) Houston IN.
—Pet Snoopy. Determined Productions. (ps). 1983. pap. 4.95 (0-915696-72-X) Determined Prods.
—Schroeder's Favorite Classics, Vol. 1. Welch, John, ed. 38p. (Orig.). (gr. 1-6). 1989. pap. 5.50 (1-56516-047-9) Houston IN.
—Schroeder's Favorite Classics, Vol. 2. Welch, John, ed. 38p. (Orig.). (gr. 1-6). 1989. pap. 5.50 (1-56516-048-7) Houston IN.
—Schroeder's Favorite Classics, Vol. 1: Clavinova Software. Welch, John, ed. 38p. (Orig.). (gr. 1-6). 1992. pap. 34.95 (1-56516-021-5) Houston IN.
—Schroeder's First Recital. Welch, John, ed. 38p. (Orig.). (gr. 1-6). 1989. pap. 5.50 (1-56516-050-9) Houston IN.
—Schroeder's First Recital Encores. Welch, John, ed. 38p. (Orig.). (gr. 1-6). 1989. pap. 5.50 (1-56516-051-7) Houston IN.
—Snoopy's Easy Piano Album. Welch, John. 38p. (Orig.). (gr. 1-6). 1989. pap. 5.50 (1-56516-052-5) Houston IN.
—Snoopy's Favorite Piano Solos. Welch, John. 38p. (Orig.). (gr. 1-6). 1989. pap. 5.50 (1-56516-053-3) Houston IN.
—Snoopy's Very First Christmas Songs. Edison, June. 32p. (Orig.). (gr. 1-6). 1989. pap. 5.50 (1-56516-046-0) Houston IN.
—Snoopy's Very First Christmas Songs: Clavinova Software. Edison, June. 32p. (Orig.). (gr. 1-6). 1992. pap. 34.95 (1-56516-020-7) Houston IN.
Schulz, Janet. Will & Orv. Schulz, Walter A. 48p. 1991. lib. bdg. 14.95 (0-87614-669-8) Carolrhoda Bks.
Schumacher, Claire. A Big Chair for Little Bear. Schumacher, Claire. LC 89-10968. 32p. (Orig.). (ps-1). 1990. pap. 2.25 (0-679-80500-1) Random Bks Yng Read.

—Cat Games. Ziefert, Harriet. LC 87-25805. 32p. (Orig.). (ps-3). 1988. pap. 3.50 (0-14-050809-0, Puffin) Puffin Bks.

—Sam & Lucy. Ziefert, Harriet. LC 90-46963. 36p. (ps-1). 1992. PLB 14.89 (0-06-026974-X) HarpC Child Bks.

—The Story of Matt & Mary. Frost, Erica. LC 85-14011. 48p. (Orig.). (gr. 1-3). 1986. PLB 10.59 (0-8167-0602-6); pap. text ed. 3.50 (0-8167-0603-4) Troll Assocs.

—What Is Father's Day? Ziefert, Harriet. 16p. (ps-k). 1992. 5.95 (0-694-00383-2) HarpC Child Bks.

—What Is Halloween? Ziefert, Harriet. 16p. (ps) 1992. 5.95 (0-694-00381-6, Festival) HarpC Child Bks.

—What Is Mother's Day? Ziefert, Harriet. 16p. (ps-k). 1992. 5.95 (0-694-00382-4) HarpC Child Bks.

—What Is Thanksgiving? Ziefert, Harriet. 16p. (ps) 1992. 5.95 (0-694-00408-1, Festival) HarpC Child Bks.

—What Is Valentine's Day? Ziefert, Harriet. 16p. (ps-k). 1993. 5.95 (0-694-00413-8, Festival) HarpC Child Bks.

—What's a Birthday? Ziefert, Harriet. 16p. (ps-k). 1993. 5.95 (0-694-00380-8, Festival) HarpC Child Bks.

—What's a Vacation: A Lift-the Flap Bk. Ziefert, Harriet. 16p. (ps-k). 1993. 5.95 (0-694-00449-9, Festival) HarpC Child Bks.

—What's a Wedding? A Lift-the-Flap Bk. Ziefert, Harriet. 16p. (ps-k). 1993. 5.95 (0-694-00450-2, Festival) HarpC Child Bks.

—When Will Santa Come? Ziefert, Harriet. 16p. (ps-3). 1991. pap. 5.95 (0-06-107440-3) HarpC Child Bks.

—Who Can Boo the Loudest? Ziefert, Harriet. LC 90-4454. 36p. (ps-1). 1990. 13.95 (0-06-026898-0) HarpC Child Bks.

Schumacher, Sharon, jt. illus. see Megale, Marina.

Schumann, Peter. St. Francis Preaches to the Birds. Schumann, Peter. LC 92-7383. 36p. (gr. 3-10). 1992. Repr. of 1978 ed. 8.95 (0-8118-0222-1) Chronicle Bks.

Schuster, L. A. Outlaws of Ravenhurst. new ed. Wallace, M. Imelda, Sr. (gr. 6-10). 1950. 12.95 (0-910334-25-0); pap. 5.95 (0-910334-26-9) Cath Authors.

Schutzer, Dena. Erin's Voyage. Frank, John. LC 92-31783. 1994. pap. 14.00 (0-671-79585-6, S&S BFYR) S&S Trade.

—A Million Fish...More or Less. McKissack, Patricia C. LC 90-34322. 40p. (ps-3). 1992. 14.00 (0-679-80692-X); PLB 14.99 (0-679-90692-4) Knopf Bks Yng Read.

—Polka & Dot. Schutzer, Dena. LC 93-29935. 1994. 8.99 (0-679-84192-X); PLB 9.99 (0-679-94192-4) Knopf Bks Yng Read.

Schwartz, Amy. Albert Goes Hollywood. Schwartz, Henry. LC 91-18495. 32p. (ps-2). 1992. 14.95 (0-531-05980-4); lib. bdg. 14.99 (0-531-08580-5) Orchard Bks Watts.

—Bea & Mr. Jones. Schwartz, Amy. LC 81-18041. 32p. (ps-2). 1982. SBE 12.95 (0-02-781430-0, Bradbury Pr) Macmillan Child Grp.

—Bea & Mr. Jones. Schwartz, Amy. 30p. (ps-3). 1983. pap. 3.95 (0-14-050439-7, Puffin) Puffin Bks.

—Bea & Mr. Jones. Schwartz, Amy. LC 90-52752. 32p. (ps-3). 1994. pap. 3.95 (0-689-71796-2, Aladdin) Macmillan Child Grp.

—Because of Lozo Brown. King, Larry L. LC 88-3952. (ps-3). 1988. 11.95 (0-670-81031-2) Viking Child Bks.

—Begin at the Beginning. Schwartz, Amy. LC 84-48257. 32p. (ps-3). 1983. PLB 12.89 (0-06-025228-6) HarpC Child Bks.

—Blow Me a Kiss, Miss Lilly. Carlstrom, Nancy W. LC 89-34505. 32p. (ps-3). 1990. 13.00 (0-06-021012-5); PLB 12.89 (0-06-021013-3) HarpC Child Bks.

—The Crack of Dawn Walkers. Hest, Amy. LC 83-19557. 32p. (ps-2). 1984. RSBE 12.95 (0-02-743710-8, Macmillan Child Bk) Macmillan Child Grp.

—The Crack-of-Dawn Walkers. Hest, Amy. 32p. (Orig.). (ps-3). 1988. pap. 3.99 (0-14-050829-5, Puffin) Puffin Bks.

—How I Captured a Dinosaur. Schwartz, Henry. LC 88-1482. 32p. (ps-2). 1989. 14.95 (0-531-05770-4); PLB 14.99 (0-531-08370-5) Orchard Bks Watts.

—How I Captured a Dinosaur. Schwartz, Henry. LC 88-1482. 32p. (ps-2). 1993. pap. 5.95 (0-531-07028-X) Orchard Bks Watts.

—Jane Martin, Dog Detective. Bunting, Eve. 44p. (ps-3). 1988. pap. 3.95 (0-15-239587-3, Voyager Bks) HarBrace.

—The Lady Who Put Salt in Her Coffee. Hale, Lucretia. Schwartz, Amy, adapted by. 28p. (ps-3). 1989. 13.95 (0-15-243475-5) HarBrace.

—Maggie Doesn't Want to Move. O'Donnell, Elizabeth L. LC 86-23684. 32p. (gr. k-3). 1987. RSBE 13.95 (0-02-768830-5, Pub. by Four Winds Pr) Macmillan Child Grp.

—Magic Carpet. Brisson, Pat. LC 89-35993. 32p. (ps-3). 1991. RSBE 14.95 (0-02-714340-6, Bradbury Pr) Macmillan Child Grp.

—Mother Goose's Little Misfortunes. Schwartz, Amy & Marcus, Leonard S. LC 89-77425. 32p. 1990. SBE 15.95 (0-02-781431-9, Bradbury Pr) Macmillan Child Grp.

—Mrs. Moskowitz & the Sabbath Candlesticks. Schwartz, Amy. 32p. (gr. k-5). 1983. pap. 6.95t (0-8276-0231-6) JPS Phila.

—My Island Grandma. Lasky, Kathryn. LC 91-31000. 32p. (ps up). 1993. 15.00 (0-688-07946-6); PLB 14.93 (0-688-07948-2) Morrow Jr Bks.

—Nana's Birthday Party. Hest, Amy. LC 92-10260. 32p. (gr. k up). 1993. 15.00 (0-688-07497-9); PLB 14.93 (0-688-07498-7) Morrow Jr Bks.

—The Night Flight. Ryder, Joanne. LC 85-4482. 32p. (gr. k-3). 1985. RSBE 13.95 (0-02-778020-1, Four Winds) Macmillan Child Grp.

—The Purple Coat. Hest, Amy. LC 85-29186. 32p. (gr. k-3). 1986. RSBE 13.95 (0-02-743640-3, Four Winds) Macmillan Child Grp.

—The Purple Coat. Hest, Amy. LC 91-38499. 32p. (gr. k-3). 1992. pap. 4.95 (0-689-71634-6, Aladdin) Macmillan Child Grp.

—Wanted: Warm, Furry Friend. Calmenson, Stephanie. LC 88-13405. 32p. (gr. k-3). 1990. RSBE 13.95 (0-02-716390-3, Macmillan Child Bk) Macmillan Child Grp.

—The Witch Who Lives down the Hall. Guthrie, Donna. LC 85-887. 32p. (gr. k-3). 1985. 12.95 (0-15-298610-3, HB Juv Bks) HarBrace.

—Yossel Zissel & the Wisdom of Chelm. Schwartz, Amy. 32p. (gr. k-4). 9.95 (0-8276-0258-8) JPS Phila.

Schwartz, Carol. Goodnight to Annie. Merriam, Eve. LC 92-7111. 32p. (ps-1). 1992. Repr. of 1990 ed. 14.95 (1-56282-205-5); PLB 14.89 (1-56282-206-3) Hyprn Child.

—Hide & Seek Science: Where's That Reptile? Brenner, Barbara & Chardiet, Bernice. LC 92-20905. 1993. 10. 95 (0-590-45212-6) Scholastic Inc.

—Lee, the Rabbit with Epilepsy. Moss, Deborah. LC 88-40249. 32p. (gr. k-4). 1989. PLB 12.95 (0-933149-32-8) Woodbine House.

—One Small Fish. Ryder, Joanne. LC 92-21563. 32p. (gr. k up). 1993. 15.00 (0-688-07059-0); PLB 14.93 (0-688-07060-4) Morrow Jr Bks.

—Sea Squares. Hulme, Joy N. LC 91-71381. 32p. (ps-3). 1991. 13.95 (1-56282-079-6); PLB 13.89 (1-56282-080-X) Hyprn Child.

—Sea Squares. Hulme, Joy N. LC 91-71381. 32p. (ps-3). 1993. pap. 4.95 (1-56282-520-8) Hyprn Ppbks.

—Shelley, the Hyperactive Turtle. Moss, Deborah. LC 88-40248. 24p. (gr. k up). 1989. PLB 12.95 (0-933149-31-X) Woodbine House.

—Where's That Fish? Brenner, Barbara & Chardiet, Bernice. LC 93-2929. 32p. (ps-3). 1994. 10.95 (0-590-45214-2, Cartwheel) Scholastic Inc.

—Where's That Insect? Hide & Seek Science. Brenner, Barbara & Chardiet, Bernice. LC 92-20906. 32p. 1993. 10.95 (0-590-45210-X) Scholastic Inc.

Schwartz, Daniel. The House of Wings. Byars, Betsy C. 136p. (gr. 3-7). 1982. pap. 3.99 (0-14-031523-3, Puffin) Puffin Bks.

—The House of Wings. Byars, Betsy C. 160p. (gr. 4-6). 1972. pap. 14.95 (0-670-38025-3) Viking Child Bks.

Schwartz, Marc, photos by. A Collage of Crafts. Guerrier, Charlie. Colomb, Etienne, contrib. by. LC 93-24968. Date not set. 13.95 (0-395-68377-7) Ticknor & Fields.

—A Gallery of Games. Arnaud, Catherine M. Collomb, Etienne. LC 93-25053. (gr. 4 up). 1994. 13.95 (0-395-68379-3) Ticknor & Fields.

Schwartzfarb, Marilyn. Easy Writer Student Worksheets, 6 levels. Rothstein, Evelyn. Gess, Diane, ed. (Each level 35p.). (gr. 1-8). 1988. 14.95 ea. Level A Gr. 1-2 (0-9606172-5-6) Level B Gr. 2-3 (0-9606172-1-3) Level C Gr. 3-5 (0-9606172-2-1) Level D Gr. 4-6 (0-9606172-3-X) Level E Gr. 5-7 (0-9606172-4-8) Level F Gr. 6-8 (0-9606172-6-4) ERA-CCR.

Schwarz, Frank. Science Project Puzzlers: Starter Ideas for the Curious. Clark, John G. & Stone, Harris. 61p. (gr. 7 up). 1989. pap. 4.95 (0-13-795450-6, Pub. by Treehouse) P-H.

Schwarz, Jill K. The Monster That Grew Small. Grant, Joan. LC 86-15302. 32p. (ps-4). 1987. 12.95 (0-688-06808-1); PLB 12.88 (0-688-06809-X) Lothrop.

Schwarz, Marsha, photos by. Lolly Cochran: Veterinarian. Murrow, Liza K. LC 88-51682. 64p. (Orig.). (gr. 4-8). 1989. pap. text ed. 6.95 (0-9621820-0-1) Teachers Lab.

Schweitzer, Iris. About Learning. Cone, Molly. (Orig.). (gr. 1). 1972. pap. 6.00 (0-8074-0233-8, 101082) UAHC.

Schweitzer-Johnson, Betty. Lizards on the Wall. Buchanan, Ken & Buchanan, Debby. LC 92-13664. (gr. 1-4). 1992. 12.95 (0-943173-77-9) Harbinger AZ.

Schweninger, Ann. Amanda Pig & Her Big Brother Oliver. Van Leeuwen, Jean. LC 82-70188. 56p. (ps-3). 1982. pap. 4.95 (0-8037-0016-4) Dial Bks Young.

—Bedtime Story. Erskine, Jim. LC 81-3163. 32p. (ps-1). 1981. PLB 8.95 (0-517-54540-3) Crown Bks Yng Read.

—Christmas Secrets. Schweninger, Ann. 32p. (ps-1). 1986. pap. 4.99 (0-14-050577-6, Puffin) Puffin Bks.

—Halloween Surprises. Schweninger, Ann. 32p. (ps-1). 1986. pap. 3.99 (0-14-050634-9, Puffin) Puffin Bks.

—The Make-Something Club: Fun with Crafts, Food & Gifts. Zweifel, Frances. LC 93-2393. 32p. (ps-3). 1994. 13.99 (0-670-82361-9) Viking Child Bks.

—The Make-Something Club: Fun with Crafts, Food & Gifts. Zweifel, Frances. 32p. (ps-3). 1994. pap. 4.99 (0-14-050741-8) Puffin Bks.

—Mary Had a Little Lamb. 32p. (ps). 1992. bds. write for info. (0-307-06139-6, 6139) Western Pub.

—The Mother Goose Word Book. Donovan, Melanie, selected by. LC 86-81489. 22p. (ps). 1987. write for info. (0-307-12119-4, Pub. by Golden Bks) Western Pub.

—Oliver, Amanda & Grandmother Pig. Van Leeuwen, Jean. LC 86-243326. 56p. (ps-3). 1987. 9.95 (0-8037-0361-9); PLB 9.89 (0-8037-0362-7) Dial Bks Young.

—Oliver & Amanda's Christmas. Van Leeuwen, Jean. 9.95 (0-685-29542-7) Dial Bks Young.

—Oliver & Amanda's Christmas. Van Leeuwen, Jean. 56p. (ps-3). 1992. pap. 3.99 (0-14-054566-2, Dial Easy to Read) Puffin Bks.

—Oliver & Amanda's Halloween. Van Leeuwen, Jean. LC 91-30941. 48p. (ps-3). 1992. 11.00 (0-8037-1237-5); PLB 10.89 (0-8037-1238-3) Dial Bks Young.

—The Read-Aloud Treasury: Favorite Nursery Rhymes, Poems, Stories & More for the Very Young. Cole, Joanna & Calmenson, Stephanie, eds. 256p. 1988. pap. 18.95 (0-385-18560-X) Doubleday.

—Summertime. Schweninger, Ann. 32p. (ps-3). 1992. RB 13.50 (0-670-83610-9) Viking Child Bks.

—Tales of Amanda Pig. Van Leeuwen, Jean. LC 82-23545. 56p. (ps-3). 1983. pap. 4.95 (0-8037-8443-0) Dial Bks Young.

—Tales of Amanda Pig. Van Leeuwen, Jean. LC 93-25615. (ps-3). 1994. pap. 3.25 (0-14-036840-X, Puffin) Puffin Bks.

—The Teddy Bear Book. Marzollo, Jean. LC 87-24538. 32p. (ps-2). 1989. 11.95 (0-8037-0524-7); PLB 11.89 (0-8037-0632-4) Dial Bks Young.

—The Teddy Bear Book. Marzollo, Jean. LC 87-24538. 32p. (ps-2). 1992. pap. 3.99 (0-14-054546-8, Puffin Pied Piper) Puffin Bks.

—Thump & Plunk. Udry, Janice M. LC 80-8443. 32p. (ps-3). 1981. 14.00 (0-06-026149-8); PLB 13.89 (0-06-026150-1) HarpC Child Bks.

Schwier, Karin M. Keith Edward's Different Day. Schwier, Karin M. 36p. (Orig.). (gr. k-4). 1992. pap. 4.95 (0-915166-74-7) Impact Pubs Cal.

Schwinger, Larry. Ghostly Tales & Eerie Poems of Edgar Allan Poe. Poe, Edgar Allan. LC 92-30884. 256p. 1993. 13.95 (0-448-40533-4, G&D) Putnam Pub Group.

—Wild, Wild Wolves. Milton, Joyce. LC 90-8807. 48p. (Orig.). (gr. 1-3). 1992. PLB 7.99 (0-679-91052-2); pap. 3.50 (0-679-81052-8) Random Bks Yng Read.

Scoble, Lesley. Macbeth. Mulherin, Jennifer. LC 87-37225. 32p. (gr. 6-12). 1988. PLB 10.96 (0-382-09693-2) Silver Burdett Pr.

Scofield, Penrod. Isaac Bashevis Singer: The Story of a Storyteller. Kresh, Paul. LC 84-10271. 192p. (gr. 5 up). 1984. 13.95 (0-525-67156-0, Lodestar Bks) Dutton Child Bks.

Scott, Carlton. Grin's Message. Scott, Carlton. Marcus, Laurie R., ed. 32p. (gr. k-4). 1993. 9.95 (0-9636652-1-9); pap. cancelled (0-9636652-4-3) C T Scott.

Scott, Dennis. Let's Have a Party! Fritz, Ron. LC 92-28560. 32p. (gr. k-2). 1992. PLB 11.89 (0-8167-2984-0); pap. text ed. 3.95 (0-8167-2985-9) Troll Assocs.

Scott, Elaine. Young Scientists Explore: Seasons. Penn, Linda. 32p. (gr. k-3). 1983. wkbk. 5.95 (0-86653-123-8, GA 453) Good Apple.

Scott, Jonathan, photos by. The Leopard Family Book. Scott, Jonathan. LC 91-14578. 56p. (gr. k up). 1991. pap. 15.95 (0-88708-186-9) Picture Bk Studio.

Scott, Joseph & Scott, Lenore. Egyptian Hieroglyphs for Everyone: An Introduction to the Writing of Ancient Egypt. reissued ed. Scott, Joseph & Scott, Lenore. LC 68-13080. 96p. (gr. 7 up). 1990. PLB 14.89 (0-690-04753-3, Crowell Jr Bks) HarpC Child Bks.

Scott, Kay & Shouse, Lucille. Help Me Bear Shows You How to Call 911. Scott, Kay & Shouse, Lucille. Semingson, Roberta, tr. (ENG & SPA). 16p. (Orig.). (gr. k-4). 1988. write for info. text ed. (0-9620819-1-4); write for info. color bk. (0-9620819-0-6) L Shouse.

Scott, Lenore, jt. illus. see Scott, Joseph.

Scott, Margaret. A Child's First Book about Play Therapy. Nemiroff, Marc A. & Annunziata, Jane. LC 90-49954. 60p. (Orig.). 1990. 19.95 (1-55798-112-4, 4317180); pap. text ed. write for info. (1-55798-089-6, 4317200) Am Psychol.

Scott, R. Martin Luther King, Jr. Jones, Margaret. LC 68-9483. 36p. (gr. 2-4). 1968. PLB 14.60 (0-516-03524-8) Childrens.

Scott, Richard. A King Is Risen. St. John, Patricia. (gr. 2-7). 8.99 (0-8024-4576-4) Moody.

Scott, Ricky. Our Family Can Read, 2 bks. Oxendine, Reginald. 76p. (Orig.). (gr. k up). 1992. Set pap. text ed. 29.95 incl. audio cass. (0-944049-00-1); 29.95 (0-944049-01-3); 29.95 (0-944049-02-8) Arrow Pub NC.

Scott, Rita & Van Horn, Brian. A Boy Full of Joy. Van Horn, Brian & Van Horn, Chris. (ps-5). 1989. write for info. (1-877765-01-5) Lambgel Family.

—Lain Cain & Label Abel. Van Horn, Brian & Van Horn, Chris. (gr. k-5). 1989. write for info. (1-877765-02-3) Lambgel Family.

—Leve Eve Believes Werpent the Serpent in the Garden of Eden. Van Horn, Brian & Van Horn, Chris. (gr. k-5). 1989. write for info. (1-877765-03-1) Lambgel Family.

—Loah Noah & the Ark. Van Horn, Brian & Van Horn, Chris. (gr. k-5). 1989. write for info. (1-877765-04-X) Lambgel Family.

—Lordy Lamb & the Twelve Lisciples. Van Horn, Brian & Van Horn, Chris. Mowdy, Sharon, ed. 40p. (gr. k-5). 1989. 8.95 (1-877765-00-7) Lambgel Family.

—No Time in a Jam. Van Horn, Brian & Van Horn, Chris. (gr. 2-8). 1989. write for info. (*1-877765-05-8*) Lambgel Family.

Scrace, Carolyn. Rain Forest. Macdonald, Fiona. LC 93-24449. 1994. write for info. (*0-8114-9243-5*) Raintree Steck-V.

Scrace, Carolyn & Bergin, Mark. Seas & Oceans. Lambert, David. Salariya, David, created by. LC 93-6352. 1994. write for info. (*0-8114-9245-1*) Raintree Steck-V.

Scribbles, R. J. Back to School. Scribbles, R. J., pseud. 32p. (Orig.). (gr. 2-5). 1992. pap. 12.95 (*0-9632192-0-0*) R J Miller.

Scribner, Joanne. Noodle & Zeek Blast Off. Abbott, Tony. 1994. pap. write for info. (*0-06-440520-6*, Trophy) HarpC Child Bks.

Scribner, Toni. The Glo Friends' Good Night Book. LC 85-60757. (ps). 1986. 2.95 (*0-394-87797-7*) Random Bks Yng Read.

—Where's Baby? LC 86-43148. 14p. (ps). 1987. bds. 3.99 (*0-394-89071-X*) Random Bks Yng Read.

Scribner, Toni, jt. illus. see McCue, Lisa.

Scriven, Gill. Are You Asleep, Rabbit? Campbell, Alison & Barton, Julia. LC 89-12974. 32p. (ps-1). 1990. 12.95 (*0-688-09490-2*); lib. bdg. 12.88 (*0-688-09491-0*) Lothrop.

—Are You Asleep, Rabbit? Campbell, Alison & Barton, Julia. 32p. (ps-3). 1992. pap. 3.99 (*0-14-054495-X*) Puffin Bks.

—In the Night. Shipton, Jonathan. 32p. (ps-3). 1992. 14. 95 (*0-316-78586-5*) Little.

Scrofani, Joseph M. Lost in the Devil's Desert. Skurzynski, Glona. LC 92-45656. 96p. (gr. 5 up). 1993. pap. 3.95 (*0-688-04593-6*, Pub. by Beech Tree Bks) Morrow.

Scruton, Clive. It's a Go-to-the-Park Day. French, Vivian. LC 90-28506. 40p. (ps-1). 1992. jacketed 14.00 (*0-671-74477-1*, S&S BFYR) S&S Trade.

—The Secrets of Santa. Civardi, Annie. LC 91-130. 32p. (ps-1). 1991. pap. 13.95 jacketed (*0-671-74270-1*, S&S BFYR) S&S Trade.

Scruton, Clive & Falconer, Elizabeth. Super Motion. Watson, Philip. LC 82-80990. 48p. (gr. 3-6). 1983. PLB 11.88 (*0-688-00971-9*) Lothrop.

Scruton, Clive & Fenton, Ronald. Light Fantastic. Watson, Philip. LC 82-80989. 48p. (gr. 3-6). 1983. PLB 11.88 (*0-688-00969-7*) Lothrop.

Scudder, Barbara J. Of Butterflies & Buttercups. McCord, Catherine G. LC 85-61275. 64p. (gr. 5-12). 1985. 12.50 (*0-9614997-0-2*) Buttercup Bks.

Scull, Marie-Louise. Looking for Susie. Cook, Bernadine. LC 90-41001. 32p. (gr. 1-3). 1991. lib. bdg. 14.50 (*0-208-02241-4*, Pub. by Linnet) Shoe String.

Scullard, Sue. The Flyaway Pantaloons. Sharples, Joseph. 32p. (ps-4). 1990. PLB 18.95 (*0-87614-408-3*) Carolrhoda Bks.

—The Great Round-the-World Balloon Race. Scullard, Sue. LC 90-40590. 32p. (gr. 2-5). 1991. 12.95 (*0-525-44692-3*, DCB) Dutton Child Bks.

—Miss Fanshawe & the Great Dragon Adventure. Scullard, Sue. 32p. (ps-4). 1987. 9.95 (*0-312-00510-5*) St Martin.

Scwartz, Amy. Begin at the Beginning. Schwartz, Amy. LC 82-48257. 32p. (gr. k-3). 1984. pap. 3.95 (*0-06-443060-X*, Trophy) HarpC Child Bks.

Seaberg, Kurt. Snail Trails & Tadpole Tails: Nature Education for Young Children. Cohen, Richard, et al. Peterson, Roger T., intro. by. LC 93-5850. 96p. (Orig.). (ps-1). 1993. pap. text ed. 12.95 (*0-934140-78-2*) Redleaf Pr.

Seablom, Seth H. The Great Mukilteo to Friday Harbor Auto Race. Seablom, Seth H. LC 75-38037. (gr. 1-3). 1976. pap. 2.00 (*0-918800-00-5*) Seablom.

—Sailboat Coloring Guide: A Great Five Star Super Deluxe Coloring Book. Swolgaard, Carole. Seablom, Victoria, ed. 32p. (Orig.). (gr. 1-6). 1979. pap. 2.50 saddle stitched (*0-918800-07-2*) Seablom.

—Seattle Coloring Guide. Seablom, Seth H. (gr. 4-6). 1977. pap. 2.50 (*0-918800-01-3*) Seablom.

Seago, Robert. Come to Bethlehem: The Christmas Story. Cothen, Joe. LC 75-25503. 64p. (gr. 4 up). 1975. 7.95 (*0-88289-098-0*) Pelican.

Seal, Bob. Mr. Shanahan's Secret. Flanagan, Joan. LC 88-42914. 32p. (gr. 2-3). 1988. PLB 18.60 (*1-55532-930-6*) Gareth Stevens Inc.

Seale, Carl. Deaf Smith: The Eyes & Ears of the Texas Army. Seale, Jan. 30p. (gr. k-3). 1987. pap. 2.95 (*0-936927-20-8*) Knowing Pr.

—Dilue Rose: The Girl Who Saw Texas Independence. Seale, Jan. 30p. (gr. k-3). 1986. pap. 2.95 (*0-936927-21-6*) Knowing Pr.

—Juan Seguin: The Tejano Who Wouldn't Give Up. Seale, Jan. 28p. (gr. k-3). 1987. pap. 2.95 (*0-936927-19-4*) Knowing Pr.

—Kian Long: The Slave Girl Who Helped Start Texas. Seale, Jan. 30p. (gr. k-3). 1987. pap. 2.95 (*0-936927-18-6*) Knowing Pr.

—Madam Candelaria: The Nurse at the Alamo. Seale, Jan. 27p. (gr. k-3). 1987. pap. 2.95 (*0-936927-16-X*) Knowing Pr.

—William Goyens: The Texan Who Said No to Failure. Seale, Jan. 29p. (gr. k-3). 1987. pap. 2.95 (*0-936927-17-8*) Knowing Pr.

Seals, Elayne. The Opening Doors Series, 6 bks, Series 1. Barrows, Clifford, et al. Barenbaum, Ruth, ed. Lane, Barry, ed. Beckwith, Joel. (Orig.). (gr. 6 up). 1989. Set. pap. 22.95 (*1-877829-00-5*) Opening Doors.

Seals, Thelma, et al. A Very Special Day. Hershey, Katherine. 21p. (gr. k-6). 1980. 4.25 (*1-55976-131-8*) CEF Press.

Sealy, Kathy. Brown Eyes, Blue Eyes. McCullough, Mary F. 32p. (Orig.). (ps). 1986. pap. text ed. 3.95 (*0-936625-04-X*, New Hope AL) Womans Mission Union.

—God Made... Kizer, Kathryn. (Orig.). (ps) 1988. pap. 3.50 (*0-936625-43-0*, New Hope AL) Womans Mission Union.

—Matthew's Dad Is a Missionary. Strawn, Kathy. 32p. (Orig.). (gr. 1-3). 1988. pap. 2.95 (*0-936625-38-4*) Womans Mission Union.

—You Can Be a Musician & a Missionary, Too. Kent, Renee. McClain, Cindy, ed. 64p. (Orig.). (gr. 4-6). 1988. pap. 3.95 (*0-936625-37-6*, PZ7.K419Y) Womans Mission Union.

Search Press Studios Staff. Decorating Eggs: In the Style of Faberge. Purves, Pamela. Dace, Rosalind, ed. 96p. (Orig.). 1989. pap. 16.95 (*0-85532-644-1*, Pub. by Search Pr UK) A Schwartz & Co.

—Wool 'n Magic: Creative Uses of Yarn...Knitting, Crochet, Embroidery. Messent, Jan. Dawson, Pam, ed. 144p. 1989. 32.95 (*0-85532-614-X*, Pub. by Search Pr UK) A Schwartz & Co.

Sears, David. Tales from Reb Nachman: Parables Told by Rabbi Nachman of Breslov. Sears, David. 32p. (gr. k-6). 1987. 9.95 (*0-89906-808-1*); pap. 6.95 (*0-89906-809-X*) Mesorah Pubns.

Sears, David. The Captured Tzaddik: A Tale of the Baalshem Tov Father. Sears, David. 71p. (gr. 7-10). 1990. 9.00 (*0-940118-50-5*) Moznaim.

—The Children's Book of Jewish Holidays. Adler, David A. 48p. (gr. k-6). 1987. 11.95 (*0-89906-810-3*); pap. 7.95 (*0-89906-811-1*) Mesorah Pubns.

Sears, Lori. Celebrate: Holidays, Puppets & Creative Drama. Hunt, Tamara & Renfro, Nancy. Schwalb, Ann W., ed. 208p. (ps-4). 1987. 24.95 (*0-931044-09-X*); pap. 18.95 (*0-317-58474-X*) Renfro Studios.

—Imagination: At Play with Puppets & Creative Drama. Renfro, Nancy & Frazier, Nancy. Schwalb, Ann W., ed. 96p. (gr. 1-6). 1987. 16.95 (*0-931044-16-2*) Renfro Studios.

Sears, Nancy. Farm Animals. LC 77-70863. (ps-3). 1977. 8.99 (*0-394-83541-7*) Random Bks Yng Read.

Sears, Yvonne. Amber's Hallowe'er. Sears, Yvonne. LC 87-90131. 36p. (gr. 2-5). 1988. 12.95 (*0-9618803-0-9*) Y-Knot.

Secaur, Emiline. Andrew's Secret. Richardson, Arleta. Payne, Peggy & Yoder, Tamra, eds. 30p. (Orig.). (gr. 1-3). 1989. pap. 3.00 (*0-89367-143-6*) Light & Life.

Seckler, Judy & Shelly, Walt. Myth, Music & Dance of the American Indian. DeCesare, Ruth. Feldstein, Sandy, et al, eds. 80p. (gr. 4-12). 1988. tchr's. ed. 12. 50 (*0-88284-371-0*, 3518); student, 16p 3.95 (*0-88284-372-9*, 3520); Student Songbk., 24p 4.95 (*0-88284-373-7*, 3519); tchr's ed. with cassette 19.95 (*0-88284-383-4*, 3534) Alfred Pub.

Seed, Suzanne. Saturday's Child. Seed, Suzanne. LC 72-12599. (gr. 6-12). 1973. PLB 8.95 (*0-87955-803-2*); pap. 6.95 (*0-87955-203-4*) O'Hara.

Seeland, Rene K. RULES Phonological Evaluation. Webb, Jane C. & Duckett, Barbara. 140p. (ps-3). 1990. text ed. 49.95 (*0-937857-12-2*, 1577) Speech Bin.

Seeley, Laura L. Agatha's Feather Bed: Not Just Another Wild Goose Story. Deedy, Carmen A. 32p. (ps-5). 1991. 14.95 (*1-56145-008-1*) Peachtree Pubs.

—The Book of Shadowboxes: A Story of the ABC's. Seeley, Laura L. 64p. (ps-3). 1990. 16.95 (*0-934601-65-8*) Peachtree Pubs.

—Christmas & the Old House. Hall, Tom T. 48p. 1989. 13.95 (*0-934601-91-7*) Peachtree Pubs.

—The Four-Legged Ghosts. Hoffman, Mary. 96p. (gr. 2-6). 1993. 13.99 (*0-8037-1466-1*); lib. bdg. 13.89 (*0-8037-1645-1*) Dial Bks Young.

Seeman, Tina. Fun with Things Arcund the House. Hayes, Dympna & Lehman, Melanie. 32p. (gr. 2). 1987. PLB 14.97 (*0-88625-164-6*); pap. 2.95 (*0-88625-155-9*) Durkin Hayes Pub.

Segal, John. Little Mouse & Elephant: A Tale from Turkey. Yolen, Jane, retold by. LC 92-21748. 1994. 10.00 (*0-06-021502-X*, HarpT); PLB 9.89 (*0-06-021503-8*, HarpT) HarpC.

—The Musicians of Bremen. Yolen, Jane, retold by. LC 92-18695. 32p. (ps-2). 1995. 10.00 (*0-06-021498-8*); PLB 9.89 (*0-06-021499-6*) HarpC Child Bks.

—While Standing on One Foot: Puzzle Stories & Wisdom Tales from the Jewish Tradition. Jaffe, Nina & Zeitlin, Steve. 128p. (gr. 3-7). 1993. PLB 14.95 (*0-8050-2594-4*, Bks Young Read) H Holt & Co.

Segnit, Clare & Segnit, Jack. The Ugly Duckling: A Classic Pop-up Storybook. Segnit, Clare & Segnit, Jack. 12p. (ps-3). 1993. bds. 14.95 (*0-689-71722-9*, Aladdin) Macmillan Child Grp.

Segnit, Jack, jt. illus. see Segnit, Clare.

Segu, Jordi & Sabat, Jordi. Colored Pencils. Sanhez, Isidro. 48p. 1991. pap. 7.95 (*0-8120-4719-2*) Barron.

Seible, Bob. The Boston Tea Party. Charles, Carole. LC 75-33156. (gr. 2-6). 1992. PLB 21.95 (*0-913778-18-4*); pap. 14.95 (*0-685-57677-9*) Childs World.

—General George at Yorktown. Charles, Carole. LC 75-33158. 32p. (gr. 2-6). 1975. PLB 21.95 (*0-913778-23-0*); pap. 14.95 (*0-685-57679-5*) Childs World.

—John Paul Jones, Victory at Sea. Charles, Carole. LC 75-33157. 32p. (gr. 2-6). 1975. PLB 21.35 (*0-913778-21-4*); pap. 14.95 (*0-685-57680-9*) Childs World.

—Martha Helps the Rebel. Charles, Carole. LC 75-33126. (gr. 2-6). 1975. PLB 5.95 (*0-913778-22-2*) Childs World.

Seibold, J. Otto. Mr. Lunch Takes a Plane Ride. Walsh, Vivian & Seibold, J. Otto. 40p. (ps-3). 1993. RB 13.99 (*0-670-84775-5*) Viking Child Bks.

Seiden, Art. Bicycling Basics. Wilhelm, Tim & Wilhelm, Glenda. 48p. (gr. 3-7). 1985. pap. 4.95 (*0-13-077942-3*) P-H.

—Boating Basics. Halsted, Henry F. LC 85-9406. 48p. (gr. 4-9). 1985. 10.95 (*0-13-078502-4*) P-H.

—Computer Basics. Hellman, Hal. 48p. (gr. 3-7). 1986. pap. 5.95 (*0-13-165697-X*) P-H.

—Computer Graphics Basics. Stevens, Lawrence. LC 84-6826. 48p. (gr. 3-7). 1984. 9.95 (*0-13-164054-2*) P-H.

—Computer Programming Basics: An Introduction for Young People. Stevens, Lawrence. 48p. 1984. 9.95 (*0-13-164260-X*) P-H.

—Computer Software Basics. Laron, Carl. LC 84-22292. 48p. (gr. 4-9). 1985. 9.95 (*0-13-163858-0*) P-H.

—Diving Basics. Goldberg, Bob. 48p. (gr. 3-7). 1986. 10. 95 (*0-13-215963-5*) P-H.

—Easy-to-Make Water Toys That Really Work. Blocksma, Dewey & Blocksma, Mary. LC 84-24913. 64p. (gr. 2-6). 1988. pap. 5.95 (*0-671-66259-7*, S&S BFYR) S&S Trade.

—Fishing Basics. Randolph, John. 48p. (gr. 3-7). 1985. pap. 4.95 (*0-13-319732-8*) P-H.

—How on Earth Do We Recycle Glass? Rott, Joanna R. & Groves, Seli. LC 91-24241. 64p. (gr. 4-6). 1992. PLB 12.90 (*1-56294-141-0*) Millbrook Pr.

—How on Earth Do We Recycle Metal? Kouhoupt, Rudy & Marti, Donald B., Jr. LC 91-28953. 64p. (gr. 4-6). 1992. PLB 12.90 (*1-56294-142-9*) Millbrook Pr.

—How on Earth Do We Recycle Paper? Fletcher, Helen J. & Groves, Seli. LC 91-24404. 64p. (gr. 4-6). 1992. PLB 12.90 (*1-56294-140-2*) Millbrook Pr.

—Laser Basics. Stevens, Lawrence. 48p. (gr. 3-7). 1985. 10.95 (*0-13-523606-1*) P-H.

—Michael Shows off Baltimore. Seiden, Art. 32p. (gr. 1-5). 1982. 5.95 (*0-942806-01-8*) Outdoor Bks.

—Sailing Basics. Slocombe, Lorna. 48p. (gr. 3-7). 1982. 8.95 (*0-13-786053-6*) P-H.

—Soccer. Wilner, Barry. Photo Shoppe Staff, photos by. Charlton, Bobby, intro. by. LC 93-1525. 1993. write for info. (*0-8114-5777-X*) Raintree Steck-V.

—Track & Field Basics. McMane, Fred. LC 82-21458. 48p. (gr. 3-7). 1983. 9.95 (*0-13-925966-X*) P-H.

Seiger, Jamie. The Inheritance. Butts, W. E. 32p. (gr. 7-9). 1981. pap. 5.00 (*0-939622-27-0*) Four Zoas Night.

Seitz, Connie, jt. illus. see Horine, Billie.

Seitz, Eileen. The Message of the White Unicorn. Seitz, Eileen. LC 87-50260. 35p. (Orig.). (gr. 3-5). 1987. pap. 8.95 (*1-55523-057-1*) Winston-Derek.

Seitz, Jacqueline. The Angel's Quest. Thomas, Kathy. 32p. (gr. 2-6). 1983. casebound 9.95 (*0-914544-99-3*) Living Flame Pr.

Sekido, Isamu. Water & Light: Looking Through Lenses. Murata, Michinori. LC 92-19969. 1993. 17.50 (*0-8225-2904-1*) Lerner Pubns.

Sekido, Isamu, photos by. Fruit, Roots, & Fungi: Plants We Eat. Sekido, Isamu, text by. LC 92-19958. 1993. 17.50 (*0-8225-2902-5*) Lerner Pubns.

—Paws, Wings, & Hooves: Mammals on the Move. Yamashita, Keiko. LC 92-18506. 1993. 17.50 (*0-8225-2901-7*) Lerner Pubns.

—Snowflakes, Sugar, & Salt: Crystals up Close. Maki, Chu. LC 92-18538. 1993. 17.50 (*0-8225-2903-3*) Lerner Pubns.

Seligson, Judith. Seven Days of Creation. Aronow, Sara. 32p. (ps-2). 1985. 4.95 (*0-87203-119-5*) Hermon.

Sellers, Marci. Discovering Botany. Forsthoefel, John & Ransick, Gary. 84p. (gr. 3-6). 1982. 9.95 (*0-88047-005-4*, 8206) DOK Pubs.

—Quiz Bowl I. Lahey, Richard. 56p. (Orig.). (gr. 4-12). 1982. tchr's. manual 7.50 (*0-88047-012-7*, 8216) DOK Pubs.

—Quiz Bowl II. Lahey, Richard. 56p. (Orig.). (gr. 4-12). 1984. 7.50 (*0-88047-037-2*, 8408) DOK Pubs.

Sellon, Michael B. Treasures Beyond the Snows. Gouffe, Marie A. LC 77-95392. (gr. 3-9). 1970. 3.75 (*0-8356-0026-2*, Quest) Theos Pub Hse.

Seltzer, Isadore. The House I Live In: At Home in America. Seltzer, Isadore. LC 91-27469. 32p. (gr. 1-5). 1992. RSBE 14.95 (*0-02-781801-2*, Macmillan Child Bk) Macmillan Child Grp.

—The Man Who Tricked a Ghost. Yep, Laurence. LC 93-22202. 32p. (gr. k-4). 1993. PLB 15.95 (*0-8167-3030-X*); pap. text ed. write for info. (*0-8167-3031-8*) BrdgeWater.

—This Is the Bread I Baked for Ned. Dragonwagon, Crescent. LC 88-22619. 32p. (gr. k-3). 1989. RSBE 13.95 (*0-02-733220-9*, Macmillan Child Bk) Macmillan Child Grp.

—What's on My Plate? Gross, Ruth B. LC 87-22057. 32p. (gr. k-3). 1990. RSBE 13.95 (*0-02-737000-3*, Macmillan Child Bk) Macmillan Child Grp.

Seltzer, Meyer. Happy Holiday Riddles to You. Bernstein, Joanne E. & Cohen, Paul. Fay, Ann, ed. LC 85-717. 32p. (gr. 1-5). 1985. PLB 8.95 (*0-8075-3154-5*) A Whitman.

—Hide-&-Go Shriek Monster Riddles. Seltzer, Meyer. Levine, Abby, ed. LC 89-49379. 32p. (gr. 1-4). 1990. PLB 8.95 (*0-8075-3273-8*) A Whitman.

—Math-a-Magic: Number Tricks for Magicians. White, Laurence B., Jr. & Broekel, Ray. Mathews, Judith, ed. LC 89-35395. 48p. (gr. 3-6). 1990. 11.95 (*0-8075-4994-0*) A Whitman.

—Razzle Dazzle! Magic Tricks for You. White, Larry & Broekel, Ray. Fay, Ann, ed. LC 87-6114. 48p. (gr. 3-8). 1987. PLB 11.95 (*0-8075-6857-0*) A Whitman.

—Riddles to Tell Your Cat. Levine, Caroline. Grant, Christy, ed. 32p. (gr. 1-4). 1992. PLB 8.95 (*0-8075-7006-0*) A Whitman.

—Shazam! Simple Science Magic. White, Laurence B., Jr. & Broekel, Ray. Mathews, Judith, ed. LC 90-42441. 48p. (gr. 3-7). 1991. 11.95 (*0-8075-7332-9*) A Whitman.

—Unidentified Flying Riddles. Bernstein, Joanne & Cohen, Paul. Fay, Ann, ed. LC 83-17097. 32p. (gr. 1-5). 1983. PLB 8.95 (*0-8075-8329-4*) A Whitman.

Seltzer, Meyer, photos by. Here Comes the Recycling Truck! Seltzer, Meyer. Mathews, Judith, ed. LC 91-37927. 32p. (ps-2). 1992. PLB 13.95 (*0-8075-3235-5*) A Whitman.

Seltzer, Richard W., Jr. Now & Then & Other Tales from Ome. Seltzer, Richard W., Jr. LC 76-12138. (gr. 5). 1976. 4.50 (*0-915232-03-0*); pap. 1.95 (*0-915232-02-2*) B & R Samizdat.

Selway, Martina. Don't Forget to Write. Selway, Martina. 32p. (ps-2). 1992. 12.95 (*0-8249-8543-5*, Ideals Child) Hambleton-Hill.

Selwyn, Paul, jt. illus. see Christiansen, Lee.

Selzer, Isadore. The Golden Goose. Saunders, Susan. 32p. (gr. k-3). 1988. pap. 2.50 (*0-590-41715-0*) Scholastic Inc.

Selznick, Brian. Dollface Has a Party. Conrad, Pam. LC 93-33207. 1994. 15.00 (*0-06-024262-0*, Festival); PLB 14.89 (*0-06-024263-9*, Festival) HarpC Child Bks.

—The Houdini Box. Selznick, Brian. LC 90-5387. 64p. (gr. 1-6). 1991. 13.00 (*0-679-81429-9*); PLB 13.99 (*0-679-91429-3*) Knopf Bks Yng Read.

Sempe, Jean J., jt. illus. see MacLean, Robert.

Sempe, Jean J., jt. illus. see Moran, Patrick.

Sempe, Jean-Jacques. Catherine Certitude. Modiano, Patrick. 64p. (gr. 3 up). 1993. 17.95 (*0-87923-959-X*) Godine.

Sendak, Maurice. Alligators All Around. Sendak, Maurice. 32p. (ps-3). 1962. PLB 12.89 (*0-06-025530-7*) HarpC Child Bks.

—Alligators All Around: An Alphabet. Sendak, Maurice. LC 62-13315. 32p. (ps-3). 1991. pap. 3.95 (*0-06-443254-8*, Trophy) HarpC Child Bks.

—Along Came a Dog. DeJong, Meindert. LC 57-9265. 192p. (gr. 3-6). 1958. PLB 15.89 (*0-06-021421-X*) HarpC Child Bks.

—Along Came a Dog. DeJong, Meindert. LC 57-9265. 192p. (gr. 4-7). 1980. pap. 4.95 (*0-06-440114-6*, Trophy) HarpC Child Bks.

—The Animal Family. facsimile ed. Jarrell, Randall. LC 65-20659. 200p. (gr. 1 up). 1985. 16.95 (*0-394-81043-0*) Knopf Bks Yng Read.

—Bat-Poet. Jarrell, Randall. LC 64-16812. 44p. (gr. 3-6). 1964. RSBE 13.95 (*0-02-747640-5*, Macmillan Child Bk) Macmillan Child Grp.

—The Bee-Man of Orn. Stockton, Frank R. LC 85-45813. 48p. (ps up). 1987. Repr. of 1963 ed. 13.95 (*0-06-025818-7*); PLB 13.89 (*0-06-025819-5*) HarpC Child Bks.

—The Bee-Man of Orn. Stockton, Frank R. LC 85-45813. 48p. (gr. 2 up). 1987. pap. 4.95 (*0-06-443125-8*, Trophy) HarpC Child Bks.

—The Big Green Book. reissued ed. Graves, Robert. LC 84-42972. 64p. (gr. 1-4). 1985. RSBE 14.95 (*0-02-736810-6*, Macmillan Child Bk) Macmillan Child Grp.

—Birthday Party. Krauss, Ruth. (gr. k-3). 1978. PLB 11.89 (*0-06-023330-3*) HarpC Child Bks.

—Chicken Soup with Rice. Sendak, Maurice. 48p. (ps-3). 1962. PLB 12.89 (*0-06-025535-8*) HarpC Child Bks.

—Chicken Soup with Rice. Sendak, Maurice. 32p. (gr. k-3). 1986. Big book. 19.95 (*0-590-64645-1*); pap. 2.50 (*0-590-41033-4*) Scholastic Inc.

—Chicken Soup with Rice: A Book of Months. Sendak, Maurice. LC 62-13315. 32p. (ps-3). 1991. pap. 3.95 (*0-06-443253-X*, Trophy) HarpC Child Bks.

—Dear Mili. Grimm, Wilhelm K. Manheim, Ralph, tr. 40p. 1990. gift ed. 18.95 (*0-374-31766-6*); ltd. ed. 750.00 (*0-374-31763-1*); 1988 16.95, (*0-374-31762-3*) FS&G.

—Father Bear Comes Home. Minarik, Else H. LC 59-5794. 64p. (gr. k-3). 1959. 14.00 (*0-06-024230-2*); PLB 13.89 (*0-06-024231-0*) HarpC Child Bks.

—Father Bear Comes Home. Minarik, Else H. LC 59-5794. (ps-3). 1978. pap. 3.50 (*0-06-444014-1*, Trophy) HarpC Child Bks.

—Fly by Night. Jarrell, Randall. LC 76-27313. 40p. (ps up). 1985. 14.00 (*0-374-32348-8*); pap. 2.95, 1986 (*0-374-42350-4*) FS&G.

—The Golden Key. 2nd ed. MacDonald, George. Auden, W. H., afterword by. LC 67-6087. 96p. (gr. 1 up). 1984. 15.00 (*0-374-32706-8*); pap. 4.95 (*0-374-42590-6*) FS&G.

—The Griffin & the Minor Canon. Stockton, Frank R. LC 85-45827. 56p. (ps up). 1986. Repr. of 1964 ed. 13.95 (*0-06-025816-0*); PLB 13.89 (*0-06-025817-9*) HarpC Child Bks.

—The Griffin & the Minor Canon. Stockton, Frank R. LC 85-45827. 56p. (gr. 2 up). 1987. pap. 4.95 (*0-06-443126-6*, Trophy) HarpC Child Bks.

—Hector Protector & As I Went over the Water: Two Nursery Rhymes. Sendak, Maurice. LC 65-21388. 64p. (ps-1). 1990. pap. 5.95 (*0-06-443237-8*, Trophy) HarpC Child Bks.

—Higglety Pigglety Pop: Or, There Must Be More to Life. Sendak, Maurice. LC 67-18553. 80p. (gr. k-3). 1967. 15.00 (*0-06-025487-4*) HarpC Child Bks.

—A Hole Is to Dig. Krauss, Ruth. (gr. k-3). 1990. incl. cass. 19.95 (*0-87499-174-9*); pap. 12.95 incl. cass. (*0-87499-173-0*); Set; incl. 4 bks., cass., & guide. pap. 27.95 (*0-87499-175-7*) Live Oak Media.

—A Hole Is to Dig: A First Book of Definitions. Krauss, Ruth. LC 52-7731. 48p. (ps up). 1989. pap. 3.95 (*0-06-443205-X*, Trophy) HarpC Child Bks.

—Hole Is to Dig: A First Book of First Definitions. Krauss, Ruth. LC 52-7731. (ps-1). 1952. 14.00 (*0-06-023405-9*); PLB 13.89 (*0-06-023406-7*) HarpC Child Bks.

—House of Sixty Fathers. DeJong, Meindert. LC 56-8148. 192p. (gr. 5-8). 1956. PLB 13.89 (*0-06-021481-3*) HarpC Child Bks.

—The House of Sixty Fathers. DeJong, Meindert. LC 56-8148. 192p. (gr. 5-8). 1987. pap. 3.95 (*0-06-440200-2*, Trophy) HarpC Child Bks.

—Hurry Home, Candy. DeJong, Meindert. LC 53-8536. 224p. (gr. 4-7). 1953. PLB 14.89 (*0-06-021486-4*) HarpC Child Bks.

—I Saw Esau. Opie, Peter & Opie, Iona. LC 91-71845. 160p. (ps up). 1992. 19.95 (*1-56402-046-0*) Candlewick Pr.

—I'll Be You & You Be Me. Krauss, Ruth. LC 54-9214. (gr. k-3). 1954. PLB 12.89 (*0-06-023431-8*) HarpC Child Bks.

—I'll Be You-You Be Me. Krauss, Ruth. (gr. k-5). 1973. pap. 8.00 (*0-912846-14-3*) Bookstore Pr.

—In Grandpa's House. Sendak, Philip. Barofsky, Semour, tr. from YID. LC 85-42625. 48p. (ps up). 1985. 13.00 (*0-06-025462-9*); PLB 9.89 (*0-06-025463-7*) HarpC Child Bks.

—In the Night Kitchen. Sendak, Maurice. LC 70-105483. 48p. (ps-3). 1970. 16.00 (*0-06-025489-0*); PLB 15.89 (*0-06-025490-4*) HarpC Child Bks.

—In the Night Kitchen. Sendak, Maurice. LC 70-105483. 48p. (ps-3). 1985. pap. 5.95 (*0-06-443086-3*, Trophy) HarpC Child Bks.

—Kenny's Window. Sendak, Maurice. LC 56-5148. 64p. (ps up). 1989. pap. 4.95 (*0-06-443209-2*, Trophy) HarpC Child Bks.

—King Grisly-Beard. Grimm, Jacob & Grimm, Wilhelm K. Taylor, Edgar, tr. from GER. LC 73-77911. (ps-3). 1973. 14.00 (*0-374-34133-8*) FS&G.

—Kiss for Little Bear. Minarik, Else H. LC 57-9263. 32p. (gr. k-3). 1968. 14.00 (*0-06-024298-1*); PLB 13.89 (*0-06-024299-X*) HarpC Child Bks.

—A Kiss for Little Bear. Minarik, Else H. LC 68-16820. 32p. (ps-3). 1984. pap. 3.50 (*0-06-444050-8*, Trophy) HarpC Child Bks.

—A Kiss for Little Bear. unabr. ed. Minarik, Else H. (ps-3). 1991. pap. 6.95 incl. cassette (*1-55994-263-0*, Caedmon) HarperAudio.

—Let's Be Enemies. Udry, Janice M. LC 61-5777. 32p. (ps-1). 1961. 13.00 (*0-06-026130-7*); PLB 12.89 (*0-06-026131-5*) HarpC Child Bks.

—Let's Be Enemies. Udry, Janice M. LC 61-5777. 32p. (ps-2). 1988. pap. 4.50 (*0-06-443188-6*, Trophy) HarpC Child Bks.

—The Light Princess. rev. ed. MacDonald, George. LC 69-14981. 120p. (gr. 1 up). 1969. 15.00 (*0-374-34455-8*); pap. 4.95, 1984 (*0-374-44458-7*) FS&G.

—Little Bear. Minarik, Else H. 64p. (gr. k-3). 1957. 14.00i (*0-06-024240-X*); PLB 13.89 (*0-06-024241-8*) HarpC Child Bks.

—Little Bear. unabr. ed. Minarik, Else H. (ps-3). 1990. pap. 6.95 incl. cassette (*1-55994-234-7*, Caedmon) HarperAudio.

—Little Bear's Friend. Minarik, Else H. LC 60-6370. 64p. (gr. k-3). 1960. 14.00i (*0-06-024255-8*); PLB 13.89 (*0-06-024256-6*) HarpC Child Bks.

—Little Bear's Friend. Minarik, Else H. LC 60-6370. 64p. (ps-3). 1985. incl. cassette 5.98 (*0-694-00031-0*, Trophy); pap. 3.50 (*0-06-444051-6*, Trophy) HarpC Child Bks.

—Little Bear's Friend. unabr. ed. Minarik, Else H. (ps-3). 1990. pap. 6.95 incl. cassette (*1-55994-235-5*, Caedmon) HarperAudio.

—Little Bear's Visit. Minarik, Else H. LC 61-11451. 64p. (ps-3). 1961. 14.00 (*0-06-024265-5*); PLB 13.89 (*0-06-024266-3*) HarpC Child Bks.

—Little Bear's Visit. Minarik, Else H. LC 61-11451. 64p. (ps-3). 1985. incl. cassette 5.98 (*0-694-00032-9*, Trophy) HarpC Child Bks.

—Little Bear's Visit. unabr. ed. Minarik, Else H. (ps-3). 1990. pap. 6.95 incl. cassette (*1-55994-236-3*, Caedmon) HarperAudio.

—Lullabies & Night Songs. Engvick, William, ed. LC 65-22880. (ps-3). 1965. 26.00 (*0-06-021820-7*) HarpC Child Bks.

—Maurice Sendak Book & Poster Package: Where the Wild Things Are. Sendak, Maurice. LC 63-21253. 48p. (gr. k-3). 1991. incl. poster 21.95 (*0-06-025966-3*) HarpC Child Bks.

—Mister Rabbit & the Lovely Present. Zolotow, Charlotte. LC 62-7590. (gr. k-3). 1962. 14.00 (*0-06-026945-6*); PLB 13.89 (*0-06-026946-4*) HarpC Child Bks.

—Mr. Rabbit & the Lovely Present. Zolotow, Charlotte. LC 62-7590. 32p. (ps-3). 1977. pap. 4.50 (*0-06-443020-0*, Trophy) HarpC Child Bks.

—Mr. Rabbit & the Lovely Present. Zolotow, Charlotte. (gr. k-3). 1987. incl. cassette 19.95 (*0-87499-047-5*); pap. 12.95 incl. cassette (*0-87499-046-7*); 4 paperbacks, cassette & guide 27.95 (*0-87499-048-3*) Live Oak Media.

—Moon Jumpers. Udry, Janice M. 32p. (gr. k-2). 1959. 15.00 (*0-06-026145-5*) HarpC Child Bks.

—Mrs. Piggle-Wiggle's Farm. MacDonald, Betty. LC 54-7299. (gr. k-3). 1954. 14.00 (*0-397-31713-1*, Lipp Jr Bks) HarpC Child Bks.

—The Night Kitchen: (La Cocina de Noche) Sendak, Maurice. (SPA.). (gr. 1-6). 14.95 (*84-204-4570-3*) Santillana.

—No Fighting, No Biting! Minarik, Else H. LC 58-5293. 64p. (gr. k-3). 1958. 13.00 (*0-06-024290-6*); PLB 13.89 (*0-06-024291-4*) HarpC Child Bks.

—No Fighting, No Biting! Minarik, Else H. LC 58-5293. 64p. (ps-3). 1978. pap. 3.50 (*0-06-444015-X*, Trophy) HarpC Child Bks.

—The Nutcracker. Hoffmann, E. T. Manheim, Ralph, tr. 120p. 1991. pap. 16.00 (*0-517-58659-2*, Crown) Crown Pub Group.

—One Was Johnny: A Counting Book. Sendak, Maurice. 32p. (ps-3). 1962. PLB 12.89 (*0-06-025540-4*) HarpC Child Bks.

—One Was Johnny: A Counting Book. Sendak, Maurice. LC 62-13315. 48p. (ps-3). 1991. pap. 3.95 (*0-06-443251-3*, Trophy) HarpC Child Bks.

—Open House for Butterflies. reissued ed. Krauss, Ruth. LC 60-5782. 48p. (ps-3). 1990. 11.00 (*0-06-023445-8*); PLB 10.89 (*0-06-023446-6*) HarpC Child Bks.

—Outside Over There. Sendak, Maurice. LC 79-2682. 40p. (gr. k up). 1981. 20.00 (*0-06-025523-4*); PLB 19.89 (*0-06-025524-2*) HarpC Child Bks.

—Outside Over There. Sendak, Maurice. LC 79-2682. 40p. (ps up). 1989. pap. 7.95 (*0-06-443185-1*, Trophy) HarpC Child Bks.

—Pierre: A Cautionary Tale. Sendak, Maurice. LC 62-13315. 48p. (ps-3). 1991. pap. 3.95 (*0-06-443252-1*, Trophy) HarpC Child Bks.

—Pierre: A Cautionary Tale in Five Chapters & a Prologue. Sendak, Maurice. 48p. (ps-3). 1962. PLB 12.89 (*0-06-025965-5*) HarpC Child Bks.

—Pleasant Fieldmouse. Wahl, Jan. LC 64-14684. 80p. (gr. k-3). 1964. PLB 14.89 (*0-06-026331-8*) HarpC Child Bks.

—Pleasant Fieldmouse. Wahl, Jan. LC 64-14684. 72p. (gr. k-3). 1992. pap. 7.95 (*0-06-443226-2*, Trophy) HarpC Child Bks.

—Sarah's Room. Orgel, Doris. LC 63-13675. 48p. (ps-3). 1991. pap. 3.95 (*0-06-443238-6*, Trophy) HarpC Child Bks.

—Sarah's Room. reissued ed. Orgel, Doris. LC 63-13675. 48p. (gr. k-3). 1963. PLB 14.89 (*0-06-024606-5*) HarpC Child Bks.

—Seven Little Monsters. Sendak, Maurice. LC 76-18400. (gr. 1 up). 1977. PLB 13.89 (*0-06-025478-5*) HarpC Child Bks.

—Seven Tales by H. C. Andersen. Andersen, Hans Christian. Le Gallienne, Eva, retold by. LC 59-16151. 144p. (gr. k up). 1991. pap. 7.95 (*0-06-443172-X*, Trophy) HarpC Child Bks.

—Seven Tales by Hans Christian Andersen. reissued ed. Andersen, Hans Christian. Le Gallienne, Eva, tr. from DAN. LC 59-16151. 144p. (gr. 3 up). 1959. 13.95 (*0-06-023790-2*); PLB 13.89 (*0-06-023791-0*) HarpC Child Bks.

—Shadrach. DeJong, Meindert. LC 53-5250. 192p. (gr. 3-6). 1953. PLB 14.89 (*0-06-021546-1*) HarpC Child Bks.

—Shadrach. DeJong, Meindert. LC 53-5250. 192p. (gr. 3-6). 1980. pap. 3.95 (*0-06-440115-4*, Trophy) HarpC Child Bks.

—Sign on Rosie's Door. Sendak, Maurice. LC 60-9451. 48p. (gr. k-3). 1960. 14.00 (*0-06-025505-6*); PLB 13.89 (*0-06-025506-4*) HarpC Child Bks.

—Some Swell Pup or Are You Sure You Want a Dog? Sendak, Maurice & Margolis, Matthew. 32p. (ps up). 1989. pap. 4.95 (*0-374-46963-6*) FS&G.

—Somebody Else's Nut Tree & Other Tales from Children. Krauss, Ruth. LC 89-28056. 43p. (ps-5). 1990. Repr. of 1958 ed. lib. bdg. 14.00 (*0-208-02024-3*, Linnet) Shoe String.

—Very Far Away. Sendak, Maurice. LC 57-5356. (gr. k-3). 1962. 13.00 (*0-06-025514-5*); PLB 12.89 (*0-06-025515-3*) HarpC Child Bks.

—Very Special House. Krauss, Ruth. LC 53-7115. (ps-1). 1953. PLB 15.89 (*0-06-023456-3*) HarpC Child Bks.

—A Very Special House. Krauss, Ruth. LC 53-7115. 32p. (ps-1). 1990. pap. 4.95 (*0-06-443228-9*, Trophy) HarpC Child Bks.

—Visita de Osito: (La Visita de Osito) Minarik, Else H. (SPA.). (gr. 1-6). pap. 9.50 (*84-204-3051-X*) Santillana.

—We Are All in the Dumps with Jack & Guy. Sendak, Maurice. LC 93-77287. 56p. (ps up). 1993. 20.00 (*0-06-205014-1*); PLB 19.89 (*0-06-205015-X*) HarpC Child Bks.

—What Can You Do with a Shoe? De Regniers, Beatrice S. LC 55-6429. 32p. (ps-k). 1955. PLB 11.89 (*0-06-024850-5*) HarpC Child Bks.

—What Do You Do, Dear? Joslin, Sesyle. LC 84-43139. 48p. (ps-3). 1986. pap. 4.95 (0-06-443113-4, Trophy) HarpC Child Bks.
—What Do You Do, Dear? Joslin, Sesyle. LC 84-43139. 48p. 1958. 13.95 (0-201-09387-1); PLB 13.89 (0-06-023075-4) HarpC Child Bks.
—What Do You Say, Dear? Joslin, Sesyle. LC 84-43140. 48p. (ps-3). 1986. pap. 4.95 (0-06-443112-6, Trophy) HarpC Child Bks.
—What Do You Say, Dear? Joslin, Sesyle. LC 84-43140. 48p. 1958. 14.00 (0-201-09391-X); PLB 13.89 (0-06-023074-6) HarpC Child Bks.
—Wheel on the School. DeJong, Meindert. LC 54-8945. 256p. (gr. 4-7). 1954. 15.00 (0-06-021585-2); PLB 14. 89 (0-06-021586-0) HarpC Child Bks.
—Where the Wild Things Are. 25th anniversary ed. Sendak, Maurice. LC 63-21253. 48p. (ps up). 1988. 15.00 (0-06-025492-0); PLB 14.89 (0-06-025493-9) HarpC Child Bks.
—Where the Wild Things Are. new ed. Sendak, Maurice. LC 63-21253. 48p. (ps up). 1988. pap. 4.95 (0-06-443178-9, Trophy) HarpC Child Bks.
—Where the Wild Things Are: (Donde Viven los Monstruos) Sendak, Maurice. (SPA.). (gr. 1-6). 22.95 (84-204-3022-6) Santillana.
—Zlateh the Goat & Other Stories. Singer, Isaac Bashevis. LC 66-8114. (gr. 1-6). 1966. 16.00 (0-06-025698-2) HarpC Child Bks.
—Zlateh the Goat & Other Stories. Singer, Isaac Bashevis. Shub, Elizabeth, tr. LC 66-8114. 96p. (gr. 3-7). 1984. pap. 4.95 (0-06-440147-2, Trophy) HarpC Child Bks.
Senf, Richard L. The Triumphs of Trisha & Tripod: Tripod Finds a Home. White, James E. 22p. 1991. pap. 7.95 (0-9629102-0-1) Pyramid TX.
Senior, Helen. Butterfly. Chinery, Michael. Watts, Barrie, photos by. LC 90-10942. 32p. (gr. 4-6). 1991. lib. bdg. 11.59 (0-8167-2100-9); pap. text ed. 3.95 (0-8167-2101-7) Troll Assocs.
Senn, Steve. The Double Disappearance of Walter Fozbek. Senn, Steve. 128p. (gr. 3-5). 1983. pap. 2.50 (0-380-62737-X, 60064-1, Camelot) Avon.
Senungetuk, Joseph E. Green March Moons. TallMountain, Mary. LC 87-6018. 32p. (Orig.). (gr. 6 up). 1987. pap. 7.95 (0-938678-10-8) New Seed.
Serebriakov, Nikolai. Macbeth. Garfield, Leon, abridged by. LC 92-14521. 48p. (gr. 5 up). 1993. PLB 11.99 (0-679-93875-3); pap. 6.99 (0-679-83875-9) Knopf Bks Yng Read.
Seredy, Kate. White Stag. Seredy, Kate. (gr. 7 up). 1937. pap. 13.00 (0-670-76375-6) Viking Child Bks.
Seregny, Julie. Filling in the Blanks: A Guided Look at Growing up Adopted. Gabel, Susan. 160p. (gr. 5-10). 1988. pap. 15.00 (0-9609504-8-6) Perspect Indiana.
Sergio. How People Lived. Millard, Anne. LC 92-54315. 64p. (gr. 3-7). 1993. 12.95 (1-56458-237-X) Dorling Kindersley.
—Prehistoric Life. Parker, Steve. LC 92-54452. 64p. (gr. 3-7). 1993. 12.95 (1-56458-238-8) Dorling Kindersley.
—A Roman Soldier. Caselli, Giovanni. LC 86-4366. 32p. (gr. 3-6). 1991. PLB 12.95 (0-87226-106-9) P Bedrick Bks.
Serpico, Phil. Santa Fe Route to the Pacific. Serpico, Phil. LC 87-46360. 150p. (gr. 6 up). 1988. 25.00 (0-88418-000-X) Omni Hawthorne.
Servello, Joe. Daniel Discovers Daniel. Barrett, John. LC 79-17897. 32p. (gr. k-5). 1980. 16.95 (0-87705-423-1) Human Sci Pr.
—The Empty Notebook. Kotzwinkle, William. LC 89-46198. 96p. (gr. 4). 1990. 13.95 (0-87923-826-7) Godine.
—No Time for Me: Learning to Live with Busy Parents. Barrett, John M. LC 78-21257. 32p. (ps-3). 1985. 16. 95 (0-87705-385-5) Human Sci Pr.
—Trouble in Bugland: A Collection of Inspector Mantis Mysteries. Kotzwinkle, William. LC 82-49338. 160p. (gr. 5 up). 1986. pap. 12.95 (0-87923-555-1) Godine.
Servello, Joseph. Oscar, the Selfish Octopus. Barrett, John. LC 78-18760. 32p. (ps-3). 1978. 16.95 (0-87705-335-9) Human Sci Pr.
Serventy, Vincent, et al. Crocodile & Alligator. Serventy, Vincent. 24p. (gr. k-3). 1986. pap. 2.50 (0-590-44722-X) Scholastic Inc.
Setoda, C. Dodie. Seig the Magnificent. Gilbert, Ann. Martin, Jan, ed. 110p. (Orig.). (gr. 6-12). 1994. pap. 12.95 (0-944875-32-7) Doral Pub. Postponed.
Seton, Ernest T. Animal Heroes. rev. ed. Seton, Ernest T. LC 87-71143. 368p. (gr. 5 up). 1987. pap. 9.95 (0-88739-055-2) Creative Arts Bk.
—Wild Animals I Have Known. rev. ed. Seton, Ernest T. LC 87-71147. 368p. (gr. 5 up). 1987. pap. 9.95 (0-88739-053-6) Creative Arts Bk.
Setterlund, Donna J. Elephant, Please Go Back to the Zoo. Setterlund, Donna J. 30p. 1990. write for info. (0-9624342-3-X) Carriage Hse Studio Pubns.
Setzer, Debra, jt. illus. see Crask, Tammy.
Seuling, Barbara. The Teeny Tiny Woman: An Old English Ghost Tale. Seuling, Barbara. (gr. k-3). 1978. pap. 4.99 (0-14-050266-1, Puffin) Puffin Bks.
Sevaly, Karen. E-F Alphabook. Sevaly, Karen. Sevaly, Richard, et al, eds. 128p. (Orig.). (gr. k-4). 1993. pap. 10.95 tchr's ed. (0-943263-23-9, TF1803) Teachers Friend Pubns.
—G-H Alphabook. Sevaly, Karen. Sevaly, Richard, et al, eds. 128p. (Orig.). (gr. k-4). 1993. pap. 10.95 (0-943263-24-7, TF1804) Teachers Friend Pubns.

Severance, Lyn. Ben & Jerry...The Real Scoop! Older, Jules. 80p. (Orig.). (gr. 3-8). 1993. pap. 6.95 (1-881527-04-2) Chapters Pub.
Severe, Camille H. The Sex Education Dictionary for Today's Teens & Preteens. Hoch, Dean & Hoch, Nancy. LC 89-63577. 128p. (Orig.). (gr. 5-12). 1990. pap. 12.95 (0-9624209-0-5) Landmark ID.
Severn, Jeff. My First Book of Christmas Carols. Nayer, Judy, ed. 24p. (ps-2). 1991. pap. 0.99 (1-56293-117-2) McClanahan Bk.
Severn, Jeffrey. George & His Giant Shadow. Severn, Jeffrey. 32p. (ps-1). 1990. 12.95 (0-87701-634-8) Chronicle Bks.
Severs, Susan B. The Colorful Landis Brothers: Founders of the Landis Valley Museum. Reist, Linnaeus L. Severs, Susan B., ed. LC 87-90447. 100p. (Orig.). (gr. 11-12). 1987. pap. write for info. (0-9618501-0-8) S R Severs.
Sewall, M. The Golden Locket. Greene, C. 1992. 13.95 (0-15-231220-X, HB Juv Bks) HarBrace.
Sewall, Marcia. Animal Song. Sewall, Marcia. LC 87-4092. (ps-1). 1988. 14.95 (0-316-78191-6, Joy Street Bks) Little.
—The Birthday Tree. Fleischman, Paul. LC 78-22155. (gr. k-3). 1979. PLB 13.89 (0-06-021916-5) HarpC Child Bks.
—The Birthday Tree. Fleischman, Paul. LC 78-22155. 32p. (gr. k-3). 1991. pap. 4.50 (0-06-443246-7, Trophy) HarpC Child Bks.
—Captain Snap & the Children of Vinegar Lane. Schotter, Roni. LC 88-22489. 32p. (ps-3). 1989. 14.95 (0-531-05797-6); PLB 14.99 (0-531-08397-7) Orchard Bks Watts.
—Captain Snap & the Children of Vinegar Lane. Schotter, Roni. LC 88-22489. 32p. (ps-3). 1993. pap. 5.95 (0-531-07038-7) Orchard Bks Watts.
—Daisy's Taxi. Young, Ruth. LC 90-7735. 32p. (ps-1). 1991. 13.95 (0-531-05921-9); PLB 13.99 (0-531-08521-X) Orchard Bks Watts.
—Finzel the Farsighted. Fleischman, Paul. LC 83-1416. 48p. (gr. 1-5). 1983. 11.95 (0-525-44057-7, DCB) Dutton Child Bks.
—Jim Ugly. Fleischman, Sid. LC 91-14392. 144p. (gr. 3 up). 1992. 14.00 (0-688-10886-5) Greenwillow.
—John & the Fiddler. Foley, Patricia. LC 89-34514. 64p. (gr. 1-5). 1990. PLB 12.89 (0-06-021842-8) HarpC Child Bks.
—The Marzipan Moon. Willard, Nancy. LC 80-24221. 48p. (gr. 2-5). 1981. 9.95 (0-15-252962-4, HB Juv Bks) HarBrace.
—The Marzipan Moon. Willard, Nancy. LC 80-24221. 46p. (gr. 2-5). 1981. pap. 3.95 (0-15-252963-2, Voyager Bks) HarBrace.
—The Morning Chair. Joosse, Barbara M. LC 93-4870. Date not set. write for info. (0-395-62337-5, Clarion Bks) HM.
—Nobody's Cat. Joosse, Barbara M. LC 91-37619. 32p. (gr. k-3). 1992. 15.00 (0-06-020834-1); PLB 14.89 (0-06-020835-X) HarpC Child Bks.
—The Pilgrims of Plimoth. Sewall, Marcia. LC 86-3362. 48p. (gr. 2 up). 1986. 15.95 (0-689-31250-4, Atheneum Child Bk) Macmillan Child Grp.
—Saying Good-bye to Grandma. Thomas, Jane R. LC 87-20826. 40p. (gr. 1-4). 1988. 15.45 (0-89919-645-4, Clarion Bks) HM.
—Stone Fox. Gardiner, John R. LC 79-7895. 96p. (gr. 2-6). 1983. pap. 3.95 (0-06-440132-4, Trophy) HarpC Child Bks.
Sewall, Marcia A. People of the Breaking Day. Sewall, Marcia. LC 89-18194. 48p. (gr. 1 up). 1990. SBE 15. 95 (0-689-31407-8, Atheneum Child Bk) Macmillan Child Grp.
Sewalson, Don. Street Self-Defense. Sewalson, Don. 81p. (gr. 6-12). 1986. pap. 6.75 (0-938419-01-3) DM Pub.
—Street Self-Defense. Sewalson, Don. 63p. (gr. 6-12). 1986. pap. 6.75 (0-938419-03-X) DM Pub.
—Street Self-Defense. Sewalson, Don. 58p. (gr. 6-12). 1986. pap. 6.75 (0-938419-02-1) DM Pub.
—Street Self-Defense: Complete Edition. Sewalson, Don. 193p. (gr. 6-12). 1986. 27.00 (0-938419-04-8); pap. 16. 95 (0-938419-00-5) DM Pub.
Seward, James. Abraham Lincoln. Smith, Kathie B. LC 86-28060. 24p. (gr. 4-6). 1987. PLB 7.98 (0-671-64148-4, J Messner); PLB 5.99s.p. (0-685-18829-9) S&S Trade.
—Albert Einstein. Smith, Kathie B. Steltenpohl, Jane, ed. 24p. (gr. 4-6). 1989. lib. bdg. 7.98 (0-671-67514-1, J Messner); PLB 5.99s.p. (0-685-25426-7) S&S Trade.
—George Washington. Smith, Kathie B. 24p. (gr. 4-6). 1987. (J Messner); PLB 5.99s.p. (0-685-47101-2) S&S Trade.
—The Great Americans Series, 9 vols. Smith, Kathie B. 216p. (gr. 4-6). 1988. Set. PLB 71.82 (0-671-93118-0, J Messner); Set. PLB 53.91s.p. (0-685-54168-1) S&S Trade.
—Harriet Tubman. Smith, Kathie B. Steltenpohl, Jane, ed. 24p. (gr. 4-6). 1989. lib. bdg. 7.98 (0-671-67513-3, J Messner); PLB 5.99s.p. (0-685-25427-5) S&S Trade.
—John F. Kennedy. Smith, Kathie B. LC 86-33863. 24p. (gr. 4-6). 1987. lib. bdg. 7.98 (0-671-64602-8, J Messner); PLB 5.99s.p. (0-685-18831-0) S&S Trade.
—Martin Luther King, Jr. Smith, Kathie B. LC 86-28059. 24p. (gr. 4-6). 1987. lib. bdg. 7.98 (0-671-64149-2, J Messner); PLB 5.99s.p. (0-685-18830-2) S&S Trade.
—Men of the Constitution. Smith, Kathie B. & Bradbury, Pamela. 24p. (gr. 4-6). 1987. (J Messner); PLB 5. 99s.p. (0-685-54169-X) S&S Trade.

—Sitting Bull. Smith, Kathie B. LC 86-33888. 24p. (gr. 4-6). 1987. lib. bdg. 7.98 (0-671-64603-6, J Messner); PLB 5.99s.p. (0-685-47197-3) S&S Trade.
—Thomas Jefferson. Smith, Kathie B. Steltenpohl, Jane, ed. 24p. (gr. 4-6). 1989. lib. bdg. 7.98 (0-671-67512-5, J Messner); PLB 5.99s.p. (0-685-25428-3) S&S Trade.
Sewell, Helen. Baby Island. Brink, Carol R. LC 92-45577. 160p. (gr. 3-7). 1993. pap. 3.95 (0-689-71751-2, Aladdin) Macmillan Child Grp.
—The Bears on Hemlock Mountain. Dalgliesh, Alice. LC 89-27651. 64p. (gr. 1-4). 1990. Repr. of 1952 ed. RSBE 13.95 (0-684-19169-5, Scribners Young Read) Macmillan Child Grp.
—The Bears on Hemlock Mountain. 2nd ed. Dalgliesh, Alice. LC 91-40166. 64p. (gr. 1-3). 1992. pap. 3.95 (0-689-71604-4, Aladdin) Macmillan Child Grp.
—A Book of Myths. Bulfinch, Thomas & Sewell, H. LC 42-25450. 128p. (gr. 5-9). 1969. SBE 14.95 (0-02-782280-X, Macmillan Child Bk) Macmillan Child Grp.
—Dream Keeper. Hughes, Langston. (gr. 7-11). 1962. PLB 10.99 (0-394-91096-6) Knopf Bks Yng Read.
—The Thanksgiving Story. Dalgliesh, Alice. LC 87-11471. 32p. (gr. k-3). 1985. pap. 4.95 (0-689-71053-4, Aladdin) Macmillan Child Grp.
—The Thanksgiving Story. Dalgliesh, Alice. LC 88-4448. 32p. (gr. k-3). 1988. Repr. of 1954 ed. RSBE 13.95 (0-684-18999-2, Scribners Young Read) Macmillan Child Grp.
Shachat, Andrew. Mommy Doesn't Know My Name. Williams, Suzanne. 48p. (ps). 1990. 13.45 (0-395-54228-6) HM.
—The Simple People. Arnold, Tedd. LC 91-17697. 32p. (ps-3). 1992. 14.00 (0-8037-1012-7); PLB 13.89 (0-8037-1013-5) Dial Bks Young.
—Stop That Pickle! Armour, Peter. LC 92-903544. 1993. 14.95 (0-395-66375-X) HM.
—You Can't Catch Me! Oppenheim, Joanne F. LC 86-7211. 32p. (gr. k). 1986. 13.45 (0-395-41452-0) HM.
Shackelford, Bud. Draw Animals: Learn From Former Disney Artist Bud Shackelford. Shackelford, Bud. LC 92-96937. 64p. (Orig.). (gr. k-6). 1993. pap. 9.50 (0-9634693-0-4) B Shackelford.
Shackelford, Jean. Our Columbus Day Book. Moncure, Jane B. LC 86-6818. 32p. (ps-3). 1986. PLB 19.95 (0-89565-347-8); PLB 13.95s.p. (0-685-55829-0) Childs World.
Shackelford, Jeane, jt. illus. see Paris, Pat.
Shackell, Rodney. Enchantress from the Stars. Engdahl, Sylvia. 288p. (gr. 7 up). 1989. pap. 3.95 (0-02-043031-0, Collier Young Ad) Macmillan Child Grp.
Shafer, Mary A. Who Lives Here, Bk. 1. Brunke, Dawn B. Linder, Greg, ed. (Orig.). (gr. k-6). 1993. pap. 6.95 (1-55971-152-3) NorthWord.
—Who Lives Here, Bk. 2. Brunke, Dawn B. Linder, Greg, ed. (Orig.). (gr. k-6). 1993. pap. 6.95 (1-55971-153-1) NorthWord.
—Who Lives Here, Bk. 3. Brunke, Dawn B. Linder, Greg, ed. (Orig.). (gr. k-6). 1993. pap. 6.95 (1-55971-154-X) NorthWord.
—Who Lives Here, Bk. 4. Brunke, Dawn B. Linder, Greg, ed. (Orig.). (gr. k-6). 1993. pap. 6.95 (1-55971-155-8) NorthWord.
Shaffer, Dianna. The Green Jellybean. Case, Mary. 32p. (ps-8). 1989. pap. text ed. 4.95 (1-877995-01-0) Koala Pub Co.
—Katie Koala Bear, Vol. 1: What Will Katie Wear to School? Case, Mary. LC 89-83279. 28p. (gr. 2-4). 1989. pap. text ed. 4.95 (0-685-28857-9) Koala Pub Co.
—Katie Koala Bear, Vol. 2: Katie's Tree of Designs. Case, Mary. 28p. (gr. 2-4). 1989. pap. text ed. 4.95 (1-877995-00-2) Koala Pub Co.
—Katie Koala Bear, Vol. 3: Katie & Karla Make Pizza. Case, Mary. 28p. (gr. 2-4). 1989. pap. text ed. 4.95 (1-877995-05-3) Koala Pub Co.
—Katie Koala Bear, Vol. 4: Katie Loves Math. Case, Mary. 28p. (gr. 2-4). 1989. pap. text ed. 4.95 (1-877995-13-4) Koala Pub Co.
—Katie Koala Bear, Vol. 5: Katie Learns to Read. Case, Mary. 28p. (gr. 2-4). 1989. pap. text ed. 4.95 (1-877995-04-5) Koala Pub Co.
—The Man Who Loved Balloons. Shaffer, Dianna. 32p. (ps-8). 1989. pap. text ed. 4.95 (1-877995-02-9) Koala Pub Co.
Shaffer, Jim. Instant Recorder Package 2. Poffenberg, Nancy & Bane, Rosemary. 32p. (Orig.). (gr. 3-6). 1989. pap. write for info. incl. recorder (0-938293-17-6) Fun Pub OH.
Shaffer, Terea. The Old, Old Man & the Very Little Boy. Franklin, Kristine L. LC 91-2611. 32p. (ps-1). 1992. SBE 14.95 (0-689-31735-2, Atheneum Child Bk) Macmillan Child Grp.
Shaffer, Terea D. Come This Far to Freedom: A History of African Americans. Medearis, Angela S. LC 92-31251. 144p. (gr. 3-7). 1993. SBE 14.95 (0-689-31522-8, Atheneum Child Bk) Macmillan Child Grp.
Shahid, Wendy & Rosinski, Bob, photos by. The World of Eagles. Harrison, Virginia & Scott, Jim. LC 89-4459. 32p. (gr. 2-3). 1989. PLB 15.93 (0-8368-0138-5) Gareth Stevens Inc.
Shahn, Ben. Kay Kay Comes Home. Samstag, Nicholas. (gr. 5-7). 1962. 10.95 (0-8392-3015-X) Astor-Honor.

Shaker Almanac, 1886, NYS Library Staff. Fifteen Years a Shakeress. Shaver, Elizabeth, ed. Lee, Elizabeth. 105p. 1990. Repr. of 1872 ed. perfect bdg. 5.95 (*0-318-49991-6*) Shaker Her Soc.

Shakespeare, Sue. Minnie 'n Me: The Perfect Bow. Calder, Lyn. (ps-k). 1991. pap. write for info. (*0-307-10025-1*, Golden Pr) Western Pub.

Shand, Jim & Brown, Ron. The Hag of Halloween. Brown, Ron. LC 88-92081. 12p. (gr. 6). 1988. pap. 2.95 (*0-685-24339-7*) Deer Creek NY.

Shank, Will. Liking Myself. Palmer, Patricia. LC 77-88185. 80p. (gr. k-4). 1977. pap. 4.95 (*0-915166-41-0*) Impact Pubs Cal.

—The Mouse, the Monster & Me. Palmer, Patricia. LC 77-88186. 80p. (Orig.). (gr. 3-6). 1977. pap. 4.95 (*0-915166-43-7*) Impact Pubs Cal.

Shankar. Life with Grandfather. 9th ed. Shanjar. 54p. (Orig.). (gr. k-3). 1980. pap. 3.50 (*0-89744-212-1*, Pub. by Childrens Bk Trust IA) Auromere.

Shannon, D. Encounter. Yolen, Jane. 1992. 14.95 (*0-15-225962-7*, HB Juv Bks) HarBrace.

Shannon, David. The Boy Who Lived with Seals. Martin, Rafe. 32p. 1993. PLB 14.95 (*0-399-22413-0*, Putnam) Putnam Pub Group.

—Gawain & the Green Knight. Shannon, Mark. LC 93-13037. 1994. write for info. (*0-399-22446-7*, Putnam) Putnam Pub Group.

—How Many Spots Does a Leopard Have? & Other Tales. Lester, Julius. (gr. 2-6). 1989. pap. 14.95 (*0-590-41973-0*) Scholastic Inc.

—The Rough-Face Girl. Martin, Rafe. 32p. (ps-3). 1992. PLB 14.95 (*0-399-21859-9*, Putnam) Putnam Pub Group.

—Sacred Places. Yolen, Jane. LC 92-30323. 1994. write for info. (*0-15-269953-8*) HarBrace.

Shannon, Kenyon. Dinosaurs. Geis, Darlene. (Orig.). (gr. 4-6). 1960. pap. 2.95 (*0-8431-4250-2*) Wonder.

—Rocks & Minerals. Hyler, Nelson W. (gr. 4-6). pap. 2.95 (*0-8431-4274-X*) Wonder.

Shannon, Margaret. Elvira. Shannon, Margaret, text by. LC 92-39784. 1993. 13.45 (*0-395-66597-3*) Ticknor & Fields.

Shanower, Eric. The Forgotten Forest of Oz. Shanower, Eric. Oliver, Rick, ed. 48p. (Orig.). 1991. pap. 8.95 (*0-915419-44-0*) First Pub IL.

—The Ice King of Oz. Shanower, Eric. Oliver, Rick, ed. 48p. (Orig.). 1987. pap. 7.95 (*0-915419-25-4*) First Pub IL.

—The Secret Island of Oz. Shanower, Eric. Oliver, Rick, ed. 48p. (Orig.). 1988. pap. 7.95 (*0-915419-08-4*) First Pub IL.

Shao Wei Liu. The Magical Starfruit Tree. Wang, Rosalind. Livingston, Julie, ed. 32p. (gr. k-2). Date not set. 13.95 (*0-941831-89-2*) Beyond Words Pub.

—The Magical Starfruit Tree. Wang, Rosalind. LC 93-3656. 1993. 13.95 (*0-09-843189-7*) Beyond Words Pub.

Shapiro, Karen. Sometimes I Get So Mad. Hogan, Paula Z. Silverman, Manuel S., intro. by. LC 79-24057. 32p. (gr. k-6). 1980. PLB 17.96 (*0-8172-1359-7*) Raintree Steck-V.

Shapiro, Sara. Parshas Beshalach. Bernstein, David. (ENG & HEB.). 192p. (gr. 5-8). 1991. pap. text ed. 6.00 (*0-914131-96-4*) Torah Umesorah.

Shappell, Sherry. Bobbi, Father of the Finnish White Tailed Deer. Sharp, Mary & Niemi, Matt. LC 79-54100. (Orig.). (gr. 4-6). 1979. pap. 5.95 (*0-9603200-0-8*) Bobbi Ent.

Sharatt, Nick. Noisy Poems. Bennett, Jill. 32p. (gr. k-3). 1990. 10.95 (*0-19-276063-7*); pap. 4.95 (*0-19-278219-3*) OUP.

Shardin, Art. Wrongway Santa. Oetting, Rae. LC 90-62548. 32p. 1991. PLB 15.95 (*0-87873-254-4*) Oddo.

Shardin, Arthur. Whiskers, the Bank Mouse. Wells, Claudia E. LC 77-10823. (gr. 1-4). 1981. 4.50 (*0-930506-00-6*); pap. write for info. (*0-930506-01-4*) Popcorn Pubs.

Sharkey, J. Thomas. The Bluegreen Tree. Smith, Agnes. LC 76-50105. 180p. (Orig.). 1977. 9.00 (*0-87012-271-1*) Westwind Pr.

—An Edge of the Forest. Smith, Agnes. 207p. (gr. 7 up). 1974. 9.00 (*0-87012-171-5*) Westwind Pr.

Sharma, Mukesh. Bheesma. Narayana, T. R. (gr. 1-8). 1979. pap. 3.00 (*0-89744-151-6*) Auromere.

Sharma, P. N., photos by. Kashmir. Singh, Mala. (gr. 1-10). 1979. pap. 2.50 (*0-89744-177-X*) Auromere.

Sharp, Chris. The Best Day Ever: The Story of Jesus. Lashbrook, Marilyn. LC 90-63764. (gr. k-3). 1991. 5.95 (*0-86606-444-3*, 875) Roper Pr.

—The Fun Facts Dictionary: A World of Weird & Wonderful Words. Snyder, Bernadette M. 144p. (Orig.). (gr. 5-12). 1991. pap. text ed. 5.95 (*0-89243-348-5*) Liguori Pubns.

—God, Please Send Fire: Elijah & the Prophets of Baal. Lashbrook, Marilyn. LC 90-60458. 32p. (gr. k-3). 1990. 5.95 (*0-86606-440-0*, 871) Roper Pr.

—The Great Shake-Up: Miracles at Philippi. Lashbrook, Marilyn. LC 90-63768. 32p. (gr. k-3). 1991. 5.95 (*0-86606-445-1*, 876) Roper Pr.

—It's Not My Fault: Man's Big Mistake. Lashbrook, Marilyn. LC 90-60459. 32p. (gr. k-3). 1990. 5.95 (*0-86606-439-7*, 870) Roper Pr.

—Nothing to Fear: Jesus Walks on Water. Lashbrook, Marilyn. LC 90-61060. 32p. (gr. k-3). 1991. 5.95 (*0-86606-443-5*, 874) Roper Pr.

—One Hundred Fifty Fun Facts Found in the Bible: For Kids of All Ages. Snyder, Bernadette M. LC 90-70802. 144p. (gr. 1-6). 1990. pap. 5.95 (*0-89243-330-2*) Liguori Pubns.

—Too Bad, Ahab! Naboth's Vineyard. Lashbrook, Marilyn. LC 90-60457. 32p. (gr. k-3). 1990. 5.95 (*0-86606-441-9*, 872) Roper Pr.

—Two Lads & a Dad: The Prodigal Son. Lashbrook, Marilyn. LC 90-63769. (gr. k-3). 1991. 5.95 (*0-86606-446-X*, 877) Roper Pr.

—The Weak Strongman: Samson. Lashbrook, Marilyn. LC 90-60456. 32p. (gr. k-3). 1990. 5.95 (*0-86606-442-7*, 873) Roper Pr.

Sharp, Gene. Arriba y Abajo (Over-Under) Matthias, Catherine. LC 83-21005. (SPA.). 32p. (ps-2). 1989. PLB 11.93 (*0-516-32048-3*); pap. 2.95 (*0-516-52048-2*) Childrens.

—Demasiados Globos (Too Many Balloons) Matthias, Catherine. LC 81-15520. (SPA.). 32p. (ps-2). 1990. PLB 11.93 (*0-516-33633-9*); pap. 2.95 (*0-516-53633-8*) Childrens.

—Escuchame (Listen to Me) Neasi, Barbara J. LC 86-10665. (SPA.). 32p. (ps-2). 1988. PLB 11.93 (*0-516-32072-6*); PLB 30.60 big bk. (*0-516-59507-5*); pap. 2.95 (*0-516-52072-5*) Childrens.

—Hi, Clouds. Greene, Carol. LC 82-19854. 32p. (ps-2). 1983. PLB 11.93 (*0-516-02036-6*); pap. 2.95 (*0-516-42036-4*) Childrens.

—Listen to Me. Neasi, Barbara. LC 86-10664. 32p. (ps-2). 1986. PLB 11.93 (*0-516-02072-2*); pap. 2.95 (*0-516-42072-0*) Childrens.

—El Morado Es Parte del Arco Iris (Purple Is Part of a Rainbow) Kowalczyk, Carolyn. LC 85-11693. (SPA.). 32p. (ps-2). 1988. PLB 11.93 (*0-516-32068-8*); pap. 2.95 (*0-516-52068-7*) Childrens.

—Over-Under. Matthias, Catherine. LC 83-21005. 32p. (ps-2). 1984. lib. bdg. 11.93 (*0-516-02048-X*); pap. 2.95 (*0-516-42048-8*) Childrens.

—Purple Is Part of the Rainbow. Kowalczyk, Carolyn. LC 85-11693. 32p. (ps-2). 1985. PLB 11.93 (*0-516-02068-4*); pap. 2.95 (*0-516-42068-2*) Childrens.

—Shine, Sun! Greene, Carol. LC 82-19853. 32p. (ps-2). 1983. PLB 11.93 (*0-516-02038-2*); pap. 2.95 (*0-516-42038-0*) Childrens.

—Too Many Balloons. Matthias, Catherine. LC 81-15520. 32p. (ps-2). 1982. PLB 11.93 (*0-516-03633-5*); pap. text ed. 2.95 (*0-516-43633-3*) Childrens.

—Where Is It? Lillegard, Dee. LC 84-7005. 32p. (ps-2). 1984. lib. bdg. 11.93 (*0-516-02065-X*); pap. 2.95 (*0-516-42065-8*) Childrens.

Sharp, Paul. Hot Rod Harry. Petrie, Catherine. LC 81-15549. 32p. (ps-2). 1982. PLB 11.93 (*0-516-03493-6*); pap. text ed. 2.95 (*0-516-43493-4*) Childrens.

—Ice Is...Whee! Greene, Carol. LC 82-19855. 32p. (ps-2). 1983. PLB 11.93 (*0-516-02037-4*); pap. 2.95 (*0-516-42037-2*) Childrens.

—Ramon, el Lanzador (Paul the Pitcher) Sharp, Paul. LC 84-7071. (SPA.). 32p. (ps-2). 1990. PLB 11.93 (*0-516-32064-5*); pap. 2.95 (*0-516-52064-4*) Childrens.

Sharp, Shawn & McBride, Angus. Mouths of the Entwash. Staplehurst, Graham. Fenlon, Peter C., Jr., ed. 40p. (Orig.). (gr. 12). 1988. pap. 7.00 (*1-55806-010-3*, 8011) Iron Crown Ent Inc.

Sharp, William. Tall Book of Fairy Tales. reissued ed. Vance, Eleanor G. 128p. (ps-3). 1947. 9.95 (*0-06-025545-5*) HarpC Child Bks.

Sharpe, Alison, jt. illus. see Sharpe, Kate.

Sharpe, Jim. Great Book of Cryptograms. Moll, Louise B. LC 92-39447. 128p. (gr. 10-12). 1993. pap. 5.95 (*0-8069-8784-7*) Sterling.

—The World's Most Spine-Tingling True Ghost Stories. Barry, Sheila A. LC 92-19862. 96p. (gr. 3 up). 1992. 12.95 (*0-8069-8686-7*); pap. 3.95 (*0-8069-8687-5*) Sterling.

Sharpe, Kate & Sharpe, Alison. Spirit Quest. Sharpe, Susan. LC 91-4417. 128p. (gr. 4-6). 1991. SBE 13.95 (*0-02-782355-5*, Bradbury Pr) Macmillan Child Grp.

Sharpsteen, Linda. Famous Athletes Number Puzzles. Silvani, Harold. 28p. (gr. 4-6). 1975. wkbk. 6.95 (*1-878669-23-0*, 4161) Crea Tea Assocs.

Sharratt, Nick. The Green Queen. Sharratt, Nick. LC 91-58735. 24p. (ps up). 1992. 5.95 (*1-56402-093-2*) Candlewick Pr.

—I Look Like This. Sharratt, Nick. LC 91-71846. 32p. (ps). 1992. 9.95 (*1-56402-016-9*) Candlewick Pr.

—Look What I Found! Sharratt, Nick. LC 91-71833. 32p. (ps). 1992. 9.95 (*1-56402-017-7*) Candlewick Pr.

—Machine Poems. Bennett, Jill. 32p. (ps up) 1991. bds. 9.95 (*0-19-276094-7*) OUP.

—Machine Poems. Bennett, Jill, ed. 32p. 1993. pap. 5.95 (*0-19-276114-5*) OUP.

—Monday Run-Day. Sharratt, Nick. LC 91-58745. 24p. (ps up) 1992. 5.95 (*1-56402-092-4*) Candlewick Pr.

—People Poems. Bennett, Jill, ed. 28p. (gr. k up) 1990. bds. 11.00 laminated (*0-19-276086-6*) OUP.

—Tasty Poems. Bennett, Jill, ed. 28p. 1992. bds. 9.95 (*0-19-276109-9*) OUP.

Shattil, Wendy & Rozinsky, Bob, photos by. The Eagle in the Mountains. Scott, Jim. LC 89-4461. 32p. (gr. 4-6). 1989. PLB 15.93 (*0-8368-0113-X*) Gareth Stevens Inc.

Shattuck, William. Moonlight on the River. Kovacs, Deborah. LC 92-28377. (ps-3). 1993. 13.99 (*0-670-84463-2*) Viking Child Bks.

Shauck, Chuck. The Adventures of Phineous. Frick, Dumas F. 96p. (gr. 1-3). 1993. 21.95 (*1-56167-112-6*) Noble Hse MD.

—The Prince of Westmont. Haefli, Tom. 36p. 1993. write for info. saddle stitched (*1-56167-124-X*) Am Literary Pr.

Shaw, Annette. Understanding Cancer. Terkel, Susan N. & Brazz, Marlene L. 64p. (gr. k-4). 1993. PLB 12.40 (*0-531-11085-0*) Watts.

Shaw, Charles. After Pa Was Shot. Alter, Judy. LC 89-12176. 192p. (Orig.). (gr. 4-9). 1991. pap. 5.95 (*0-936650-12-5*) E C Temple.

—Billy Sunday: Homerun to Heaven. Allen, Robert A. Rock, Louise, ed. (gr. 3-7). 1985. pap. 6.95 (*0-88062-125-7*) Mott Media.

—Comanche Captive: You Are There. Milligan, Bryce. 156p. (gr. 5 up). 1989. pap. 3.95 (*0-87719-157-3*, Lone Star Bks) Gulf Pub.

—The Eagle & the Raven. Michener, James A. LC 90-9684. 228p. 1990. 19.95 (*0-938349-57-0*); ltd. ed. o.p. 100.00 (*0-938349-58-9*) State House Pr.

—Hanna, the Immigrant. Hart, Jan S. Roberts, Melissa, ed. 114p. (gr. 6-8). 1991. 12.95 (*0-89015-805-3*) Eakin-Sunbelt.

—The Hunchback of Notre Dame. Hugo, Victor. Stewart, Diana, adapted by. LC 81-5151. 48p. (gr. 4 up). 1983. PLB 18.64 (*0-8172-1671-5*) Raintree Steck-V.

—Jellybean Dreams. Kennedy, Joy. LC 92-46429. 120p. (gr. 6-12). 1993. 14.95 (*0-89015-864-9*) Eakin-Sunbelt.

—Little Johnny Raindrop. Chappell, James A. LC 88-2173. 32p. (ps-3). 1988. 12.95 (*0-938349-28-7*) State House Pr.

—Maggie & a Horse Named Devildust. Alter, Judy. LC 88-22815. 160p. (gr. 4-9). 1989. pap. 5.95 (*0-936650-08-7*) E C Temple.

—Maggie & Devildust Ridin' High. Alter, Judy. LC 89-2683. 176p. (Orig.). (gr. 4-9). 1990. pap. 5.95 (*0-936650-10-9*) E C Temple.

—Maggie & the Search for Devildust. Alter, Judy. LC 88-8019. 160p. (gr. 4-9). 1989. pap. 5.95 (*0-936650-09-5*) E C Temple.

—Molly Pitcher. Gleiter, Jan & Thompson, Kathleen. 32p. (gr. 2-5). 1987. PLB 17.96 (*0-8172-2652-4*) Raintree Steck-V.

—The Mountain Man & the President. Weitzman, David. LC 92-23040. 40p. (gr. 2-5). 1992. PLB 21.34 (*0-8114-7224-8*) Raintree Steck-V.

—The Pail of Nails. Savitz, Harriet M. & Syring, K. Michael. LC 88-7653. (gr. 3 up). 1990. 10.95 (*0-687-29974-8*) Abingdon.

—Picking Peas for a Penny. Medearis, Angela S. LC 89-49754. 36p. (gr. 1-4). 1990. 11.95 (*0-938349-54-6*) State House Pr.

—Picking Peas for a Penny. Medearis, Angela Shelf. 40p. (gr. 1-4). 1993. pap. 4.95 (*0-590-45942-2*) Scholastic Inc.

—The Red Badge of Courage. Crane, Stephen. Wright, Betty R., adapted by. LC 81-2611. 48p. (gr. 4 up). 1983. PLB 18.64 (*0-8172-1670-7*) Raintree Steck-V.

—Romeo & Juliet. Shakespeare, William. Stewart, Diana, adapted by. LC 79-24465. 48p. (gr. 4 up). 1983. PLB 18.64 (*0-8172-1653-7*) Raintree Steck-V.

—Stay Put, Robbie McAmis. Tunbo, Frances G. LC 87-18123. 160p. (gr. 4 up). 1988. PLB 15.95 (*0-87565-025-2*) Tex Christian.

—A Tale of Two Cities. Dickens, Charles. Krapesh, Patti, adapted by. LC 79-24746. (gr. 4 up). 1983. PLB 18.64 (*0-8172-1658-8*) Raintree Steck-V.

—Texas Forever!! The Paintings. Shaw, Charles, et al. 100p. (gr. 9 up). 1991. 39.95 (*0-9627589-0-6*) Oak Creek Pr.

—Texas Women - A Celebration of History: A Multicultural Guide. O'Keefe, Candace. 60p. (gr. 4 up). 1988. pap. 8.95 (*0-685-51123-5*) Hendrick-Long.

—That's How Love Is. Howes, Joan. LC 91-316. 32p. (gr. k-4). 1991. 12.95 (*0-938349-62-7*); pap. 6.95 (*0-938349-63-5*) State House Pr.

—The Turn of the Screw. James, Henry. Stewart, Diana, adapted by. LC 81-5217. 48p. (gr. 4 up). 1983. PLB 18.64 (*0-8172-1672-3*) Raintree Steck-V.

—A Vampire Named Fred. Crider, Bill. Alter, Judy, intro. by. LC 89-14524. 176p. (Orig.). (gr. 4-9). 1990. pap. 5.95 (*0-936650-11-7*) E C Temple.

—Volcanoes. Greenberg, Judith E. & Carey, Helen H. 32p. (gr. 2-4). 1990. 17.96 (*0-8172-3756-9*) Raintree Steck-V.

—You're an Orphan, Mollie Brown: A Novel. Penson, Mary. LC 92-23407. 122p. (gr. 5-8). 1993. pap. 9.95 (*0-87565-111-9*) Tex Christian.

Shaw, Charles G. It Looked Like Spilt Milk. Shaw, Charles G. LC 47-30767. 30p. (ps-2). 1947. 13.00 (*0-06-025566-8*); PLB 12.89 (*0-06-025565-X*) HarpC Child Bks.

—It Looked Like Spilt Milk. Shaw, Charles G. LC 47-30767. 32p. (ps-2). 1988. pap. 4.95 (*0-06-443159-2*, Trophy) HarpC Child Bks.

—It Looked Like Spilt Milk. Shaw, Charles G. (ps-2). 1988. pap. 19.95 incl. cassette (*0-87499-110-2*); bk. & cassette 12.95 (*0-87499-109-9*); 4 cassettes & guide 27.95 (*0-87499-111-0*) Live Oak Media.

—It Looked Like Spilt Milk Big Book. Shaw, Charles G. LC 47-30767. 32p. (ps-3). 1992. pap. 19.95 (*0-06-443312-9*, Trophy) HarpC Child Bks.

—It Looked Like Spilt Milk Board Book. Shaw, Charles G. LC 47-30767. 24p. (ps-1). 1993. 4.95 (*0-694-00491-X*, Festival) HarpC Child Bks.

—The Winter Noisy Book. new ed. Brown, Margaret W. LC 92-46880. 48p. (ps-1). 1986. 15.00 (*0-06-020865-1*); PLB 15.89 (*0-06-020866-X*) HarpC Child Bks.

Shaw, Charlie. Annie Oakley in the Wild West Extravaganza! Fontes, Ron & Korman, Justine. LC 93-70937. 80p. (gr. 1-4). 1993. PLB 12.89 (*1-56282-492-9*); pap. 2.95 (*1-56282-491-0*) Disney Pr.
—Davy Crockett Meets Death Hug. Fontes, Ron & Korman, Justine. LC 93-71032. 80p. (gr. 1-4). 1993. PLB 12.89 (*1-56282-496-1*); pap. 2.95 (*1-56282-495-3*) Disney Pr.
—The Iliad. Homer. Stewart, Diana, adapted By. LC 80-15669. 48p. (gr. 4 up). 1983. PLB 18.64 (*0-8172-1663-4*) Raintree Steck-V.
—Jane Eyre. Bronte, Charlotte. Stewart, Diana, adapted by. LC 80-14426. 48p. (gr. 4 up). 1983. PLB 18.64 (*0-8172-1661-8*) Raintree Steck-V.
—Julius Caesar. Shakespeare, William. Stewart, Diana, adapted by. LC 80-16406. 48p. (gr. 4 up). 1983. PLB 18.64 (*0-8172-1664-2*) Raintree Steck-V.
—Tales of Edgar Allan Poe. Poe, Edgar Allan. Stewart, Diana, adapted by. LC 80-14064. 48p. (gr. 4 up). 1980. PLB 18.64 (*0-8172-1662-6*) Raintree Steck-V.
—Tecumseh: One Nation for His People. Ingoglia, Gina. Bill Smith Studios Staff. LC 92-56162. 80p. (Orig.). (gr. 1-4). 1993. PLB 12.89 (*1-56282-490-2*); pap. 2.95 (*1-56282-489-9*) Disney Pr.
—Wild Bill Hickok & the Rebel Raiders. Fontes, Ron & Korman, Justine. Bill Smith Studios Staff. LC 92-56159. 80p. (Orig.). (gr. 1-4). 1993. PLB 12.89 (*1-56282-494-5*); pap. 2.95 (*1-56282-493-7*) Disney Pr.
Shaw, Peter. Dog Went for a Walk. Odgers, Sally F. LC 92-27100. (gr. 3 up). 1993. 2.50 (*0-383-03564-3*) SRA Schl Grp.
—Sarah Snail. Lowesdale School Children. LC 92-27084. 1993. 3.75 (*0-383-03592-9*) SRA Schl Grp.
Shea, Mikki. The Good Behavior Book. Martin, Michael. Harris, Stephen & Brower, Nancy, eds. (ps up). 1988. pap. 10.95 (*0-9621191-7-2*) Behavior Products.
Shearer, Hope. Plato's Fine Feathers. Slaughter, Hope. LC 84-4830. 32p. (ps-3). 1984. PLB 7.95 (*0-931093-00-7*); pap. 3.95 (*0-685-15364-9*) Red Hen Pr.
Shearer, Renee. The Water Bug Story. Britt, Dorothy. 10p. (Orig.). 1992. pap. 4.95 (*1-881809-32-3*) Gabriel TX.
Shecter, Ben. The Big Stew. Shecter, Ben. LC 90-46271. 32p. (ps-2). 1991. PLB 14.89 (*0-06-025610-9*) HarpC Child Bks.
—A Father Like That. Zolotow, Charlotte. LC 70-135778. (ps-3). 1971. PLB 12.89 (*0-06-026950-2*) HarpC Child Bks.
—Getting Something on Maggie Marmelstein. Sharmat, Marjorie W. LC 78-157895. 110p. (gr. 4-6). 1971. PLB 13.89 (*0-06-025552-8*) HarpC Child Bks.
—Ghost Named Fred. Benchley, Nathaniel. LC 68-24322. 64p. (gr. k-3). 1968. PLB 13.89 (*0-06-020474-5*) HarpC Child Bks.
—A Ghost Named Fred. Benchley, Nathaniel. LC 68-24322. 64p. (gr. k-3). 1979. pap. 3.50 (*0-06-444022-2*, Trophy) HarpC Child Bks.
—The Hating Book. Zolotow, Charlotte. LC 69-14444. 32p. (ps-3). 1969. 14.00 (*0-06-026923-5*); PLB 13.89 (*0-06-026924-3*) HarpC Child Bks.
—If It Weren't for You. Reissue. ed. Zolotow, Charlotte. LC 66-15682. 32p. (gr. k-3). 1966. HarpC Child Bks.
—Maggie Marmelstein for President. Sharmat, Marjorie W. LC 75-6300. 128p. (gr. 4-6). 1975. PLB 13.89 (*0-06-025555-2*) HarpC Child Bks.
—Merrily Comes Our Harvest In: Poems for Thanksgiving. Hopkins, Lee B. 32p. (gr. 2 up). 1993. 9.95 (*1-878093-57-6*, Wordsong) Boyds Mills Pr.
—Mooch the Messy. Sharmat, Marjorie W. LC 76-3842. 64p. (gr. k-3). 1976. PLB 13.89 (*0-06-025532-3*) HarpC Child Bks.
—My Friend John. Zolotow, Charlotte. LC 68-10209. (gr. k-3). 1968. (C Zolotow Bks); PLB 13.89 (*0-06-026948-0*, C Zolotow Bks) HarpC Child Bks.
—Mysteriously Yours, Maggie Marmelstein. Sharmat, Marjorie W. LC 81-48656. 160p. (gr. 3-6). 1984. pap. 3.95 (*0-06-440145-6*, Trophy) HarpC Child Bks.
—The Summer Night. Zolotow, Charlotte. LC 88-44522. 32p. (ps-3). 1991. PLB 13.89 (*0-06-026917-0*) HarpC Child Bks.
—When Will the Snow Trees Grow? Shecter, Ben. LC 92-32557. 32p. (gr. k-3). 1993. 14.00 (*0-06-022897-0*); PLB 13.89 (*0-06-022898-9*) HarpC Child Bks.
Shed, Greg. Casey over There. Rabin, Staton. LC 92-30322. 1994. write for info. (*0-15-253186-6*) HarBrace.
Sheean, Michael. Jackie Robinson. Sabin, Francene. LC 84-2603. 32p. (gr. 3-6). 1985. PLB 9.49 (*0-8167-0164-4*); pap. text ed. 2.95 (*0-8167-0165-2*) Troll Assocs.
Sheehan, Nancy. Families. 18p. (ps). 1993. bds. 4.95 (*0-448-40525-3*, G&D) Putnam Pub Group.
Sheehan, Nancy, photos by. What's That Sound? LC 90-83241. 24p. (ps). 1991. 2.50 (*0-448-40127-4*, G&D) Putnam Pub Group.
Sheehan, Pauline. God Hugs? Sheehan, Pauline. 20p. (Orig.). 1986. pap. 3.95 (*0-9617018-0-3*) Sheehan Indus.
Sheehan-Burke, Julia. Fencing Is for Me. Thomas, Art. LC 81-20716. 48p. (gr-2). 1982. PLB 13.50 (*0-8225-1129-0*) Lerner Pubns.
Sheehan-Burke, Julia, jt. illus. see Preston-Mauks, Susan.
Sheehan-Burke, Julia, jt. photog. see Francetic, Karl D.

Shefelman, Dan, et al. Spirit of Iron. Shefelman, Janice J. Eakin, Edwin M., ed. 136p. (gr. 4-7). 1987. 10.95 (*0-89015-636-0*, Pub. by Panda Bks); pap. 4.95 (*0-89015-624-7*) Eakin-Sunbelt.
Shefelman, Tom. A Mare for Young Wolf. Shefelman, Janice. LC 91-42749. 48p. (Orig.). (gr. 2-3). 1993. PLB 7.99 (*0-679-93445-6*); pap. 3.50 (*0-679-83445-1*) Random Bks Yng Read.
—A Peddler's Dream. Shefelman, Janice. LC 91-35285. 32p. (gr. 2-5). 1992. 14.45 (*0-395-60904-6*) HM.
—Victoria House. Shefelman, Janice. LC 86-33565. (ps-3). 1988. 12.95 (*0-15-200630-3*, Gulliver Bks) HarBrace.
Shefelman, Tom, jt. illus. see Karl, Dan.
Sheffield, Antoinette. Children, Today's Joy & Tomorrow's Hope, 8 bks, Set 2. Mylet, Trish. 224p. (ps-3). 1991. Set. pap. text ed. 16.00 (*0-945590-62-8*) Pals 1, Pals 2, Pals 3, Pals 4, Pals 5, Pals 6, Pals 7, Pals 8. Sizzy Bks.

—**Children, Today's Joy & Tomorrow's Hope Series, 19 bks. Mylet, Trish. 448p. (ps-3). 1991. Set 1 & 2. pap. text ed. 32.00 (*0-945590-74-1*) Set 1: Jan & Pam, The Van, Rex & Tex, The Bed, Siz & Liz, The Pit, Dod & Bob, The Box, Hun & Sun, The Hut, Pals. Set 2: Pals 1, Pals 2, Pals, 3, Pals 4, Pals 5, Pals, 6, Pals 7, Pals 8. Sizzy Bks. CHILDREN, TODAY'S JOY & TOMORROW'S HOPE SERIES: Set 1 & Set 2, 19 books. This SERIES consists of two Sets of books. Set 1 contains 11 beginning reader & activity books. Set 2 contains 8 books of short stories & activity books. The CHILDREN SERIES consists of positive global readers incorporating geography (the fifty United States & the District of Columbia), phonics (short & long vowels, blends & digraphs), number recognition & self expression & explores the areas of zoology, botany, history & global unity. Each pair of books in Set 1 & each story in Set 2 contain a state reference page with a dot-to-dot exercise in the shape of that state's outline. The first sixteen books include sentence completion exercises & that story's word list. In Set 2 at least one story in each book has an O. Henry-type ending in which the the child decides how the story ends. The SERIES includes a Reference Guide. Building on Set 1's themes of fun & fantasy, Set 2 expands & concludes with joy, fact & hope. This warmly written & illustrated series has been well received worldwide by Early Education, Special Education & English as a Second Language teachers, parents & most importantly, children. $32.00 (ISBN 0-945590-74-1). Trish Mylet, author. Antoinette Sheffield, illustrator. Sizzy Books. Write for brochure.**
Publisher Provided Annotation.

—Phonetic Readers for the Short Vowels, 11 bks, Set 1. Mylet, Trish. 224p. (ps-2). 1988 Set. pap. text ed. 16.00 (*0-945590-00-8*) Jan & Pam, The Van, Rex & Tex, The Bed, Siz & Liz, The Pit, Dod & Bob, The Box, Hun & Sun, The Hut, Pals. Sizzy Bks.
Shefts, Joelle. The Dancing Cats of Applesap. Lisle, Janet T. 1985. pap. 2.50 (*0-553-15348-X*, Skylark) Bantam.
—The Dancing Cats of Applesap. Lisle, Janet T. LC 92-1654. 176p. (gr. 3-7). 1993. pap. 3.95 (*0-689-71687-7*, Aladdin) Macmillan Child Grp.
Sheheen, Dennis. Children's Picture Dictionary: English-Chinese. (gr. k up). 9.95 (*0-685-18873-6*) Modan-Adama Bks.
—A Child's Picture English-Arabic Dictionary. LC 85-15658. (gr. k-2). 1985. 9.95 (*0-915361-30-2*) Modan-Adama Bks.
—A Child's Picture English-Chinese Dictionary. (gr. k-6). 1987. Repr. 9.95 (*1-55774-001-1*) Modan-Adama Bks.
—A Child's Picture English-German Dictionary. LC 86-13987. (gr. k-2). 1986. 9.95 (*0-915361-41-8*) Modan-Adama Bks.

—A Child's Picture English-Italian Dictionary. LC 86-14052. (gr. k-2). 1986. 9.95 (*0-915361-57-4*) Modan-Adama Bks.
—A Child's Picture English-Japanese Dictionary. (gr. k-6). 1987. 9.95 (*1-55774-000-3*) Modan-Adama Bks.
—A Child's Picture English-Spanish Dictionary. LC 84-71801. (gr. k-2). 1984. 9.95 (*0-915361-11-6*, 09407-3) Modan-Adama Bks.
—A Child's Picture English-Yiddish Dictionary. LC 85-15659. (gr. k-2). 1985. 9.95 (*0-915361-29-9*) Modan-Adama Bks.
Shein, Bob. Going Ape: Jokes from the Jungle. Phillips, Louis. 64p. (gr. 2-7). 1988. pap. 10.95 (*0-670-81520-9*) Viking Child Bks.
—Going Ape: Jokes from the Jungle. Phillips, Louis. 64p. (gr. 2 up). 1990. pap. 3.95 (*0-14-032263-9*, Puffin) Puffin Bks.
Shekerjian, Hiag & Shekerjian, Regina. The Well-Mannered Balloon. Willard, Nancy. D'Andrade, Diane, ed. 32p. (Orig.). (ps-3). 1991. pap. 3.95 (*0-15-294986-0*, HB Juv Bks) HarBrace.
Shekerjian, Regina, jt. illus. see Shekerjian, Hiag.
Shelia. Sheila's Show Biz Days. Allen, Adrianne T. 64p. (Orig.). (gr. k-6). 1993. pap. 9.95 (*0-685-65119-3*) Colonial Pr AL.
Shelley, Jeff. Disney Babies Goodnight Lullabies. LC 91-71345. 32p. (ps). 1991. 7.95 (*1-56282-054-0*) Disney Pr.
Shelley, John. The Mystery in the Bottle. Willis, Val. 32p. (gr. k-3). 1991. bds. 14.95 (*0-374-35194-5*) FS&G.
Shelly, Jeff. Somebody Loves You: Poems of Friendship & Love. Manushkin, Fran, compiled by. LC 92-53436. 32p. (ps-k). 1993. 9.95 (*1-56282-370-1*) Disney Pr.
Shelly, Walt, jt. illus. see Seckler, Judy.
Shelton, Caroline. Hopes, Prayers & Promises. Martinello, Marian, et al. 48p. (gr. k-8). 1986. 12.95 (*0-935857-05-2*); pap. write for info. (*0-935857-06-0*) Texart.
Shelton, Dean. Samuel: Prophet & Judge. Whaley, Richie. (gr. 1-6). 1979. 5.95 (*0-8054-4242-1*, 4242-42) Broadman.
Shemie, Bonnie. Houses of Bark: Tipi, Wigwam, & Longhouse. Shemie, Bonnie. LC 90-70130. 24p. (gr. 3-7). 1990. 13.95 (*0-88776-246-8*) Tundra Bks.
—Houses of Wood: The Northwest Coast. Shemie, Bonnie. LC 92-80415. 24p. (gr. 3-6). 1992. 13.95 (*0-88776-284-0*) Tundra Bks.
—Maisons D'Ecorce: Tipi, Wigwam et Longue Maison. Shemie, Bonnie. 24p. (gr. 3-7). 1990. 13.95 (*0-88776-256-5*) Tundra Bks.
—Mounds of Earth & Shell: Native Sites: the Southeast. Shemie, Bonnie. LC 93-60335. 24p. (gr. 3 up). 1993. 13.95 (*0-88776-318-9*) Tundra Bks.
Shemom, Mike. Bobbin Dustdobbin. Patron, Susan. LC 92-25099. 32p. (ps-2). 1993. 14.95 (*0-531-05468-3*); PLB 14.99 (*0-531-08618-6*) Orchard Bks Watts.
Shenks, Susie. That's What Happens When It's Spring. Good, Elaine W. LC 87-14964. 32p. (ps-1). 1987. 12.95 (*0-934672-53-9*) Good Bks PA.
Shenon, Mike. Burgoo Stew. Patron, Susan. LC 90-43791. 32p. (ps-1). 1991. 13.95 (*0-531-05916-2*); RLB 13.99 (*0-531-08516-3*) Orchard Bks Watts.
—Five Bad Boys, Billy Que, & the Dustdobbin. Patron, Susan. LC 91-736. 32p. (ps-1). 1992. 13.95 (*0-531-05989-8*); PLB 13.99 (*0-531-08589-9*) Orchard Bks Watts.
—Mr. Tall & Mr. Small. Brenner, Barbara. LC 93-8256. 1994. write for info. (*0-8050-2757-2*) H Holt & Co.
Shenton, Edward. On to Oregon. Morrow, Honore. (gr. 5-9). 1946. Repr. of 1926 ed. 16.00 (*0-688-21639-0*) Morrow Jr Bks.
—On to Oregon. Morrow, Honore. LC 26-16049. 240p. (gr. 4-6). 1991. pap. 4.95 (*0-688-10494-0*, Pub. by Beech Tree Bks) Morrow.
—Simon Kenton, Kentucky Scout. 2nd ed. Clark, Thomas D. Hay, Melba P., intro. by. 256p. (gr. 6-12). 17.95 (*0-945084-38-2*); pap. 8.95 (*0-945084-39-0*) J Stuart Found.
—The Yearling. 2nd ed. Rawlings, Marjorie K. LC 86-20743. 448p. (gr. 5 up). 1988. pap. 4.95 (*0-02-044931-3*, Collier Young Ad) Macmillan Child Grp.
Shepard, E. H. The Pooh Song Book. Milne, A. A. & Fraser-Simon, H. LC 61-1021. 154p. 1985. pap. 8.95 (*0-87923-557-8*) Godine.
Shepard, Ernest H. Christopher Robin Gives Pooh a Party. Milne, A. A. 32p. (ps up). 1992. incl. charm 13.95 (*0-525-44871-3*, DCB) Dutton Child Bks.
—Christopher Robin Gives Pooh a Party. Milne, A. A. 32p. 1993. 4.99 (*0-525-45144-7*, DCB) Dutton Child Bks.
—Christopher Robin Leads an Expotition. Milne, A. A. 32p. 1993. 4.99 (*0-525-45142-0*, DCB) Dutton Child Bks.
—Eeyore Loses a Tail. Milne, A. A. 32p. 1993. 4.99 (*0-525-45137-4*, DCB) Dutton Child Bks.
—Eeyore Loses a Tail. Milne, A. A. 32p. 1993. incl. charm 13.99 (*0-525-45045-9*, DCB) Dutton Child Bks.
—Eyeore Has a Birthday. Milne, A. A. 32p. 1993. 4.99 (*0-525-45043-2*, DCB) Dutton Child Bks.
—House at Pooh Corner. Milne, A. A. (gr. k up). 1985. 9.95 (*0-525-32302-3*, Dutton) NAL-Dutton.
—The House at Pooh Corner. Milne, A. A. 192p. (ps up). 1988. 9.95 (*0-525-44444-0*, DCB) Dutton Child Bks.
—The House at Pooh Corner. Milne, A. A. LC 91-29462. 192p. (ps up). 1991. Full-color Gift Edition. 20.00 (*0-525-44774-1*, DCB) Dutton Child Bks.

—The House at Pooh Corner. Milne, A. A. 192p. 1992. pap. 3.99 (*0-14-036122-7*, Puffin) Puffin Bks.
—Kanga & Baby Roo Come to the Forest. Milne, A. A. 32p. 1993. 4.99 (*0-525-45141-2*, DCB) Dutton Child Bks.
—Now We Are Six. Milne, A. A. 112p. (ps up). 1988. 9.95 (*0-525-44446-7*, DCB) Dutton Child Bks.
—Now We Are Six. Milne, A. A. 112p. 1992. pap. 3.99 (*0-14-036124-3*, Puffin) Puffin Bks.
—Piglet Is Entirely Surrounded by Water. Milne, A. A. 16p. (ps up). 1991. 7.95 (*0-525-44784-9*, DCB) Dutton Child Bks.
—Piglet Is Entirely Surrounded by Water. Milne, A. A. 32p. 1993. 4.99 (*0-525-45143-9*, DCB) Dutton Child Bks.
—Piglet Meets a Heffalump. Milne, A. A. 32p. 1993. 4.99 (*0-525-45042-4*, DCB) Dutton Child Bks.
—The Poems & Hums of Winnie-the-Pooh. Milne, A. A. 10p. (gr. 4-7). 1994. pap. 5.99 (*0-525-45205-2*, DCB) Dutton Child Bks.
—Pooh & Piglet Go Hunting. Milne, A. A. 32p. (ps up). 1992. incl. charm 13.95 (*0-525-44872-1*, DCB) Dutton Child Bks.
—Pooh & Piglet Go Hunting. Milne, A. A. 32p. 1993. 4.99 (*0-525-45136-6*, DCB) Dutton Child Bks.
—The Pooh Book of Quotations. Sibley, Brian, compiled by. LC 91-2628. 128p. (ps up). 1991. 12.50 (*0-525-44824-1*, DCB) Dutton Child Bks.
—Pooh Goes Visiting. Milne, A. A. 32p. 1993. 4.99 (*0-525-45040-8*, DCB) Dutton Child Bks.
—Pooh Invents a New Game. Milne, A. A. 16p. (ps up). 1991. 7.95 (*0-525-44783-0*, DCB) Dutton Child Bks.
—The Pooh Story Book. Milne, A. A. LC 65-19580. 80p. (gr. k-4). 1965. 13.00 (*0-525-37546-5*, DCB) Dutton Child Bks.
—Pooh's Birthday Book. Milne, A. A. 160p. (gr. 1-3). 1991. pap. 3.50 (*0-440-46934-1*, YB) Dell.
—Pooh's Library, 4 bks. Milne, A. A. (ps up). 1988. Set. 39.95 (*0-525-44451-3*, DCB) Dutton Child Bks.
—Pooh's Library, 4 bks. Milne, A. A. 1992. Set. pap. 16. 00 slipcased (*0-14-095560-7*, Puffin) Puffin Bks.
—Pooh's Pot O'Honey, 4 vols. Milne, A. A. (ps up). 1985. Boxed Set. 10.95 (*0-525-37518-X*, DCB) Dutton Child Bks.
—Reluctant Dragon. Grahame, Kenneth. LC 89-1658. 58p. (gr. 3-6). 1938. 12.95 (*0-8234-0093-X*); pap. 4.95 (*0-8234-0755-1*) Holiday.
—The Songs of Winnie-the-Pooh. Milne, A. A. 10p. (gr. 4-7). 1994. pap. 5.99 (*0-525-45206-0*, DCB) Dutton Child Bks.
—When We Were Very Young. Milne, A. A. 112p. (gr. 2-5). 1970. pap. 3.50 (*0-440-49485-0*, YB) Dell.
—When We Were Very Young. Milne, A. A. 112p. (ps up). 1988. 9.95 (*0-525-44445-9*, DCB) Dutton Child Bks.
—When We Were Very Young. Milne, A. A. 112p. 1992. pap. 3.99 (*0-14-036123-5*, Puffin) Puffin Bks.
—The Wind in the Willows. 75th Anniversary ed. Grahame, Kenneth. Hodges, Margaret, pref. by. LC 83-11573. 256p. (gr. 3 up). 1983. SBE 18.95 (*0-684-17957-1*, Scribners Young Read) Macmillan Child Grp.
—The Wind in the Willows. Grahame, Kenneth. LC 88-8046. 272p. (ps up). 1989. pap. 4.95 (*0-689-71310-X*, Aladdin) Macmillan Child Grp.
—The Wind in the Willows. Grahame, Kenneth. LC 90-64091. 264p. (gr. 8 up). 1991. SBE 24.95 (*0-684-19345-0*, Scribners Young Read) Macmillan Child Grp.
—Winnie-the-Pooh. Milne, A. A. (gr. 1-5). 1961. 9.95 (*0-525-43035-0*, Dutton) NAL-Dutton.
—Winnie-the-Pooh. Milne, A. A. 176p. (ps up). 1988. 9.95 (*0-525-44443-2*, DCB) Dutton Child Bks.
—Winnie-the-Pooh. Milne, A. A. LC 91-26203. 176p. (ps up). 1991. Full-color Gift Edition. 20.00 (*0-525-44776-8*, DCB) Dutton Child Bks.
—Winnie-the-Pooh. Milne, A. A. 176p. 1992. pap. 3.99 (*0-14-036121-9*, Puffin) Puffin Bks.
—Winnie the Pooh & Some Bees. Milne, A. A. 32p. 1993. incl. charm 13.99 (*0-525-45044-0*, DCB) Dutton Child Bks.
—The Winnie-the-Pooh Journal. Milne, A. A. 64p. (ps up). 1986. 7.99 (*0-525-44237-5*, DCB) Dutton Child Bks.
—Winnie-the-Pooh's Birthday Book. Milne, A. A., contrib. by. 128p. 1993. 11.99 (*0-525-45061-0*, DCB) Dutton Child Bks.
—Winnie-the-Pooh's Calendar Book 1987. Milne, A. A. (ps up). 1986. 4.95 (*0-525-44235-9*, Dutton) NAL-Dutton.
—Winnie-the-Pooh's Calendar Book 1988. Milne, A. A. (ps up). 1987. spiral bd. 4.95 (*0-525-44311-8*, Dutton) NAL-Dutton.
—Winnie-the-Pooh's Calendar Book 1989. Milne, A. A. 32p. (ps up). 1988. spiral bd. 5.95 (*0-525-44398-3*, Dutton) NAL-Dutton.
—Winnie-the-Pooh's Friendship Book. Milne, A. A. 48p. (gr. 4-7). 1994. 8.99 (*0-525-45204-4*, DCB) Dutton Child Bks.
—Winnie-the-Pooh's Little Book about Food. Milne, A. A. 10p. (ps up). 1992. 4.95 (*0-525-44875-6*, DCB) Dutton Child Bks.
—Winnie-the-Pooh's Little Book about Friends. Milne, A. A. 10p. (ps up). 1992. 4.95 (*0-525-44874-8*, DCB) Dutton Child Bks.
—Winnie-the-Pooh's Little Book about Parties. Milne, A. A. 10p. (ps up). 1992. 4.95 (*0-525-44876-4*, DCB) Dutton Child Bks.

—Winnie-the-Pooh's Little Book about Weather. Milne, A. A. 10p. (ps up). 1992. 4.95 (*0-525-44877-2*, DCB) Dutton Child Bks.
—Winnie-the-Pooh's Story Box, 10 bks. Milne, A. A. 1993. Set. 49.90 (*0-525-45168-4*, DCB) Dutton Child Bks.
—Winnie-the-Pooh's Teatime Cookbook. Milne, A. A. LC 92-35650. 64p. 1993. 9.99 (*0-525-45135-8*, DCB) Dutton Child Bks.
—The World of Christopher Robin. Milne, A. A. 256p. (ps up). 1988. 17.50 (*0-525-44448-3*, DCB) Dutton Child Bks.
—The World of Pooh. Milne, A. A. 320p. (ps up). 1988. 17.50 (*0-525-44447-5*, DCB) Dutton Child Bks.
—The World of Winnie-the-Pooh, 2 bks. Milne, A. A. (ps up). 1988. Set. 33.95 (*0-525-44452-1*, DCB) Dutton Child Bks.
Shepard, Mary. Mary Poppins & the House Next Door. Travers, Pamela L. (gr. 4 up) 1989. 12.95 (*0-385-29749-1*) Delacorte.
—Mary Poppins & the House Next Door. Travers, Pamela L. 96p. (gr. 4-7). 1992. pap. 3.50 (*0-440-40656-0*, YB) Dell.
—Mary Poppins from A to Z. Travers, Pamela L. LC 62-15629. (gr. 1-4). 1962. 10.95 (*0-15-252590-4*, HB Juv Bks) HarBrace.
—Mary Poppins in the Kitchen: A Cookery Book with a Story. Travers, Pamela L. & Moore-Betty, Maurice. LC 75-10131. 128p. (gr. k up). 1975. 6.95 (*0-15-252898-9*, HB Juv Bks) HarBrace.
Shepard, Roni. Third Grade Is Terrible. Baker, Barbara. MacDonald, Patricia, ed. 112p. 1991. pap. 2.99 (*0-671-70379-X*, Minstrel Bks) PB.
Shepard, Steve. Elvis Hornbill, International Business Bird. Shepard, Steve. LC 90-44052. 32p. (ps-2). 1991. 14.95 (*0-8050-1617-1*, Bks Young Read) H Holt & Co.
Shepard, Steven. Fogbound. Shepard, Steven. Thatch, Nancy R., ed. Melton, David, intro. by. LC 93-13422. 29p. (gr. 5-8). 1993. PLB 14.95 (*0-933849-43-5*) Landmark Edns.
Shepherd, Roni. Bronco Dogs. Cohen, Caron L. LC 90-47952. 32p. (ps-3). 1991. 12.95 (*0-525-44721-0*, DCB) Dutton Child Bks.
—The Match Between the Winds. Climo, Shirley. LC 90-1785. 32p. (ps-3). 1991. RSBE 13.95 (*0-02-719035-8*, Macmillan Child Bk) Macmillan Child Grp.
—Third Grade Is Terrible. Baker, Barbara. LC 88-3631. 80p. (gr. 2-5). 1989. 11.95 (*0-525-44425-4*, DCB) Dutton Child Bks.

Sheppard, Scott O. Another Fuzz Bugg Adventure. Jackson, Darcy. 40p. (gr. k-5). 1993. 15.95 (*1-883016-00-2*) Moonglow Pubns.
Imagine through the eyes of a child... Everywhere you look, there are Fuzz Buggs, Bojacks, pink porpoises & more. Travel to an island that is south of the border in your imagination. THE FUZZ BUGGS OF CABBAGE KEY are responsible for the antics of a lovable, but mischievous Captain Terry. Escape into the first of a delightful series of books illustrated & written for children of all ages. Created not only to entertain children, the Fuzz Buggs & their friends will exercise the imagination of adults as well. Scott O. Sheppard, award-winning commercial artist, illustrator, graphic designer & on a good day, all of the above, coupled with the writing talent of Darcy, form a dazzling team. Since both think on a level paralleled only by the brilliant imagination of a child, they are certain to entertain everyone. You will delight in Captain Terry's search for the very best shell. Please join us in our adventure.
Publisher Provided Annotation.

—William Willya & the Washing Machine. Masland, Skip. 40p. (gr. k-5). 1993. 15.95 (*1-883016-01-0*) Moonglow Pubns.
WILLIAM WILLYA & THE WASHING MACHINE, written by Skip Masland, illustrated by Scott Sheppard. What happens when a working mother asks her son to stay home & do the laundry on a Saturday morning & a mischievous little girl

stops by to give him a hand? Throw in a couple cupfuls of Spurt, his mother's white blouse & a checkerboard shirt & you'll have some good, clean fun with WILLIAM WILLYA & THE WASHING MACHINE. Scheduled to be published in June of 1993, WILLIAM WILLYA & THE WASHING MACHINE introduces a memorable new character to the ranks of classic children's literature: William Willya, an impressionable young lad with a heart of gold who always tries to do exactly what he's told but, quite often, manages to make a well-meaning mess of it all. WILLIAM WILLYA & THE WASHING MACHINE is delightfully illustrated by Scott Sheppard & written by Skip Masland in a lyrical rhythm reminiscent of the legendary Dr. Seuss. WILLIAM WILLYA & THE WASHING MACHINE - the first installment in the new William Willya series from Moonglow Publishing - is certain to become a favorite of children & parents alike.
Publisher Provided Annotation.

Shepperson, Bob. The Sandman. Shepperson, Bob. 32p. (ps-3). 1989. 13.95 (*0-374-36405-2*) FS&G.
—The Sandman. Shepperson, Bob. 32p. (ps-3). 1991. pap. 4.95 (*0-374-46450-2*) FS&G.
Shepperson, Claude, jt. illus. see Millar, H. R.
Sherentz, Michael & Horton, Terri. The Year That Santa Goofed & Other Short Stories. Black, Auguste R. 22p. (Orig.). (gr. 1-5). 1990. pap. 2.95 (*0-9628010-2-X*) A R Black.
Sherentz, Michael K. Miracles at the Inn. Black, Auguste R. 24p. (Orig.). (gr. 1-12). 1990. pap. 4.95 (*0-9628010-1-1*) A R Black.
Sheringham, George. Book of the Fly Rod. Sheringham, Hugh & Moore, John C., eds. 174p. (gr. 10 up). 1993. Repr. of 1921 ed. 42.90 (*1-56416-116-1*) Derrydale Pr.
Sherman, Ed, jt. illus. see Olugebefola, Ademola.

Sherman, Elizabeth. Alfie's Home. Cohen, Richard A. 30p. 1993. 14.95 (*0-9637058-0-6*) Intl Healing.
ALFIE'S HOME is the story of a young boy who thinks he's gay but finds out he's not. Written in simple language, it gives hope to children & adults of all ages who are struggling with their sexual orientation & choose not to be gay. ALFIE'S HOME is the first resource of its kind for teachers, students, parents, counselors, pastors-- anyone helping children heal their sexual identity. Alfie grows up in a dysfunctional family & experiences both abuse & neglect from a distant father, a dominating mother, & an abusive uncle. In his teen years he experiences feelings & attraction for other boys. A counselor explains to Alfie the meaning of his homosexual feelings & helps guide him to deeper healing. "Richard Cohen has hit upon the essential causal & curative themes of the homosexual condition. Many of my adult clients would not have needed psychotherapy today if their parents had read ALFIE'S HOME."--Joseph Nicolosi, Ph.D., Psychologist, Author, REPARATIVE THERAPY OF MALE HOMOSEXUALITY.
"ALFIE'S HOME is most definitely a vitally needed book for our children & for our school systems throughout America."--Dr. Thomas L. Brown, Indianapolis School Commissioner. To order contact: International Healing Foundation, P.O. Box 901, Bowie, MD

20718; phone: 301-773-5573.
Publisher Provided Annotation.

Sherman, Erin. My Jesus Pocketbook of ABC's. Fletcher, Cynthia H. LC 81-80218. 32p. (Orig.). (ps-3). 1981. pap. 0.69 (*0-937420-01-8*) Stirrup Assoc.
—My Jesus Pocketbook of Li'l Critters. Stirrup Associates, Inc. Staff. Phillips, Cheryl M., ed. LC 82-63139. 32p. (Orig.). (ps-3). 1983. pap. text ed. 17.50 spiral bdg. (*0-937420-05-0*) Stirrup Assoc.
—My Jesus Pocketbook of Manners. Stirrup Associates, Inc. Staff. Phillips, Cheryl M., ed. LC 82-63141. 32p. (ps-3). 1983. pap. 0.69 (*0-937420-06-9*) Stirrup Assoc.
—My Jesus Pocketbook of Nursery Rhymes. Fletcher, Cynthia H. LC 80-52041. 32p. (Orig.). (ps-3). 1980. pap. 0.69 (*0-937420-00-X*) Stirrup Assoc.
—My Jesus Pocketbook of Scripture Stories. Stirrup Associates, Inc. Staff. LC 82-80351. 32p. (Orig.). (ps-3). 1982. pap. 0.69 (*0-937420-02-6*) Stirrup Assoc.
Sherman, Ori. The Four Questions. Schwartz, Lynne S. LC 88-18881. 40p. (ps up). 1989. 15.95 (*0-8037-0600-6*); PLB 15.89 (*0-8037-0601-4*) Dial Bks Young.
—Story of Hanukkah. Ehrlich, Amy. (ps up). 1989. 14.95 (*0-8037-0615-4*); PLB 14.89 (*0-8037-0616-2*) Dial Bks Young.
Sherry, Helen J. Splashes. Sherry, Helen J. 36p. (Orig.). 1989. pap. 2.75 (*0-922273-00-6*) Chocho Bks.
Sherwood, Ed. Your Name & Colors: Secret Keys to Your Beauty, Personality, & Success, the Rolliett Letter-Color Theory. Rolliet, D. G. Reanult, Michael & Wolf, Jeannie, eds. LC 89-91991. 192p. (Orig.). 1990. pap. text ed. 12.95 (*0-9621693-0-7*) Spectra Pubns Hse.
Shetterly, Robert. Earthworms, Dirt, & Rotten Leaves. McLaughlin, Molly. 96p. 1990. pap. 3.50 (*0-380-71074-9*, Camelot) Avon.
—Earthworms, Dirt & Rotten Leaves: An Exploration in Ecology. Mclaughlin, Molly. LC 86-3318. 96p. (gr. 3-7). 1986. SBE 13.95 (*0-689-31215-6*, Atheneum Child Bk) Macmillan Child Grp.
—Muwin & the Magic Hare. Shetterly, Susan H. LC 91-2170. 32p. (gr-1). 1993. SBE 14.95 (*0-689-31699-2*, Atheneum Child Bk) Macmillan Child Grp.
—Project Panda Watch. Schlein, Miriam. LC 84-2914. 96p. (gr. 4 up). 1984. SBE 13.95 (*0-689-31071-4*, Atheneum Child Bk) Macmillan Child Grp.
—Raven's Light: A Myth from the People of the Northwest Coast. Shetterly, Susan H. LC 89-78183. 32p. (gr. 1-5). 1991. SBE 13.95 (*0-689-31629-1*, Atheneum Child Bk) Macmillan Child Grp.
—What's the Difference? A Guide to Some Familiar Animal Look-Alikes. Lacey, Elizabeth A. 80p. (gr. 4-7). 1993. 14.95 (*0-395-56182-5*, Clarion Bks) HM.
Shettly, Robert. Dwarf-Wizard of Uxmal. Shetterly, Susan H. LC 89-32864. 32p. (gr. k-3). 1990. SBE 13.95 (*0-689-31455-8*, Atheneum Child Bk) Macmillan Child Grp.
Shevett, Anita & Shevett, Steve, photos by. Baby's ABC. LC 85-62427. 28p. (ps). 1986. bds. 2.95 (*0-394-87870-1*) Random Bks Yng Read.
Shevett, Steve, jt. photog. see Shevett, Anita.
Shevis, Stell. The Story of Andre. Dietz, Lew. (gr. 2-3). 1979. pap. 9.95 (*0-89272-052-2*) Down East.
Shevo, Aharon. Story of Dona Gracia Mendes. Stadtler, Bea. LC 70-83166. (gr. 6-9). 1969. 4.50 (*0-8381-0734-6*) United Syn Bk.
Shi, Jihong. The Seal Prince. MacGill-Callahan, Sheila. LC 93-16248. 1995. 13.99 (*0-8037-1486-6*); PLB 13.89 (*0-8037-1487-4*) Dial Bks Young.
Shi Chen. How to Draw Prehistoric Animals. Murray, Linda. LC 93-23058. 32p. (gr. k-6). 1993. PLB 10.65 (*0-8167-3287-6*); pap. text ed. 1.95 (*0-8167-3288-4*) Troll Assocs.
Shields, Chris, jt. illus. see Jackson, Ian.
Shields, Sandra S. My Book of Bedtime Prayers. Wilkes, Paul. LC 92-70386. 32p. (ps-k). 1992. PLB 12.99 (*0-8066-2592-9*, 9-2592, Augsburg) Augsburg Fortress.
Shiffman, Lena. The Boy Toy. Johnson, Phyllis. 32p. (gr. k-3). 1988. pap. 5.95 (*0-914996-26-6*) Lollipop Power.
—Dancing with Manatees. McNulty, Faith. LC 93-7593. 48p. (ps-4). 1994. pap. 2.95 (*0-590-46401-9*) Scholastic Inc.
—First Grade King. Williams, Karen L. 112p. (gr. k-3). 1992. 13.95 (*0-395-58583-X*, Clarion Bks) HM.
—Keeping a Christmas Secret. Naylor, Phyllis R. LC 88-29277. 32p. (ps-2). 1989. RSBE 13.95 (*0-689-31447-7*, Atheneum Child Bk) Macmillan Child Grp.
—Keeping a Christmas Secret. Naylor, Phyllis R. LC 93-12248. 32p. (gr. k-2). 1993. pap. 4.95 (*0-689-71760-1*, Aladdin) Macmillan Child Grp.
—My First Book of Words. 64p. 1992. 10.95 (*0-590-45142-1*, Cartwheel) Scholastic Inc.
Shilstone, Arthur. Alfred Hitchcock's Daring Detectives. Hitchcock, Alfred, ed. LC 76-79077. (gr. 5 up). 1982. pap. 4.99 (*0-394-84902-7*) Random Bks Yng Read.
Shiman, Hedy. The Golden Gate. Gross, Sukey S. 172p. (gr. 5-8). 1989. 11.95 (*1-56062-002-1*); pap. 8.95 (*1-56062-003-X*) CIS Comm.
—The Silent Summer. Gross, Sukey S. 139p. (gr. 7-9). 1989. 10.95 (*1-56062-004-8*); pap. 7.95 (*1-56062-005-6*) CIS Comm.
—The Whispering Wind. Gross, Sukey. 128p. (gr. 6-8). 1991. 10.95 (*1-56062-068-4*); pap. 7.95 (*1-56062-069-2*) CIS Comm.
Shimin, Simeon. Young Kangaroo. Brown, Margaret W. 48p. (ps). 1992. pap. 3.99 (*0-440-40670-6*, YB) Dell.

Shimin, Symeon. Dance in the Desert. L'Engle, Madeleine. LC 68-29465. 64p. (ps up). 1969. 14.95 (*0-374-31684-8*) FS&G.
—Dance in the Desert. L'Engle, Madeleine. 56p. (ps up). 1988. pap. 4.95 (*0-374-44244-4*) FS&G.
—The Knee-Baby. Jarrell, Mary. 32p. (ps up). 1988. pap. 4.95 (*0-374-44244-4*) FS&G.
—Onion John. Krumgold, Joseph. LC 59-11395. 248p. (gr. 5 up). 1987. (Crowell Jr Bks); PLB 14.89 (*0-690-04698-7*, Crowell Jr Bks) HarpC Child Bks.
—Onion John. Krumgold, Joseph. LC 59-11395. 248p. (gr. 5 up). 1984. pap. 3.95 (*0-06-440144-8*, Trophy) HarpC Child Bks.
—Sam. Scott, Ann H. 40p. (ps-8). 1992. PLB 14.95 (*0-399-22104-2*, Philomel Bks) Putnam Pub Group.
—Zeely. Hamilton, Virginia. LC 67-10266. 128p. (gr. 5-7). 1967. SBE 13.95 (*0-02-742470-7*, Macmillan Child Bk) Macmillan Child Grp.
Shimono, Judy. The Gingerbread Kid. Warren, Jean. Cubley, Kathleen, ed. 8p. (Orig.). (ps-2). pap. 2.95 (*0-911019-83-9*) Warren Pub Hse.
—Goldilocks & the Three Bears. Warren, Jean. Cubley, Kathleen, ed. 8p. (Orig.). (ps-2). 1994. pap. 2.95 (*0-911019-85-5*) Warren Pub Hse.
—Henny Penny. Warren, Jean. Cubley, Kathleen, ed. 8p. (Orig.). (ps-2). 1994. pap. 2.95 (*0-911019-84-7*) Warren Pub Hse.
—Little Red Riding Hood. Warren, Jean. Cubley, Kathleen, ed. 8p. (Orig.). (ps-2). 1994. pap. 2.95 (*0-911019-88-X*) Warren Pub Hse.
—The Three Billy Goats. Warren, Jean. Cubley, Kathleen, ed. 8p. (Orig.). (ps-2). 1994. pap. 2.95 (*0-911019-91-X*) Warren Pub Hse.
—The Three Little Pigs. Warren, Jean. Cubley, Kathleen, ed. 8p. (Orig.). (ps-2). 1994. pap. 2.95 (*0-911019-89-8*) Warren Pub Hse.
Shinan, Devora. The Kingston Cast.e. Abrahamson, Ruth. 102p. (gr. 3-8). 1991. 10.95 (*0-922613-42-7*); pap. 8.95 (*0-922613-43-5*) Hachai Pubns.
Shine, Andrea. Danger at the Breaker. Welch, Catherine A. 48p. (gr-4). 1991. PLB 14.95 (*0-87614-693-0*) Carolrhoda Bks.
Shipman, Gary. Africa. Moore, Jo E. 16p. (gr. 3-6). 1993. pap. 5.95 (*1-55799-247-9*) Evan-Moor Corp.
—Antarctica. Moore, Jo E. 16p. (gr. 3-6). 1993. pap. 5.95 (*1-55799-246-0*) Evan-Moor Corp.
—Asia. Moore, Jo E. 16p. (gr. 3-6). 1993. pap. 5.95 (*1-55799-244-4*) Evan-Moor Corp.
—Australia. Moore, Jo E. 16p. (gr. 3-6). 1993. pap. 5.95 (*1-55799-243-6*) Evan-Moor Corp.
—Draw Animals Around the World. Evans, Joy. 36p. (gr. 2-6). 1992. pap. 7.95 (*1-55799-223-1*) Evan-Moor Corp.
—Europe. Moore, Jo E. 16p. (gr. 3-6). 1993. pap. 5.95 (*1-55799-245-2*) Evan-Moor Corp.
—North America. Moore, Jo E. 16p. (gr. 3-6). 1993. pap. 5.95 (*1-55799-241-X*) Evan-Moor Corp.
—South America. Moore, Jo E. 16p. (gr. 3-6). 1993. pap. 5.95 (*1-55799-242-8*) Evan-Moor Corp.
—Tinga Layo. 16p. (ps-2). 1992. pap. 14.95 (*1-55799-228-2*) Evan-Moor Corp.
Shirai, Shohei. Coral Reefs. Johnson, Sylvia A. LC 84-816. 48p. (gr-4). 1984. PLB 19.95 (*0-8225-1451-6*); pap. 5.95 (*0-8225-9545-1*) Lerner Pubns.
Shire, Ellen. Case of the Missing Cat. Palazzo-Craig, Janet. LC 81-7635. 48p. (gr. 2-4). 1982. PLB 10.89 (*0-89375-594-X*); pap. text ed. 3.50 (*0-89375-595-8*) Troll Assocs.
Shirkus, Lorraine. The Pocket Book: A Child's Activity Book. Colby, Sas & Shirkus, Lorraine. 10p. (ps-k). 1988. 39.95 (*0-922656-00-2*) Design Matters Inc.
Shishani, Ami. Ramadan Adventures of Fasfoose Mouse. Kezzeiz, Ediba. 36p. (Orig.). (gr. 1-6). 1991. pap. write for info. (*0-89259-117-X*) Am Trust Pubns.
—When I Grow up. Kezzeiz, Ediba. 17p. (Orig.). (ps-1). 1991. pap. write for info. (*0-89259-116-1*) Am Trust Pubns.
Shiu, Tom. Legends of Maui As Told by Lani Goose. Kahn, Elithe M. 20p. (gr. 6-9). 1989. pap. 8.95 incl. audiocassette (*0-944264-04-2*) Lani Goose Pubns.

Shles, Larry. The Adventure of the Squib Owl: Squib Ser. Shles, Larry. 1988. pap. 7.95 each (*0-915190-85-0*) Jalmar Pr.

Squib the Owl series, written & whimsically illustrated by Larry Shles, teaches self-esteem & personal & social responsibility as it entertains. The author uses the name Squib to personify the small vulnerable part of us all that struggles & at times feels helpless in an enormous world filled with emotions. This Series, five volumes, traces the adventures of this tiny owl as he struggles with his feelings searching at least for understanding. Each of the five titles explores a different vulnerability. MOTHS & MOTHERS, FEATHERS & FATHERS (explores feelings); HOOTS & TOOTS & HAIRY BRUTES (explores disabilities); ALIENS IN MY NEST (explores adolescent behavior); HUGS & SHRUGS (explores inner peace). The latest volume DO I HAVE TO GO TO SCHOOL TODAY? is great for the young reader who needs encouragement from teachers who accept him "just as he is". Brilliantly simple, yet realistically complex, Squib personifies each & every one of us. He is a reflection of what we are, & what we can become. Every reader who has struggled with life's limitations will recognize his own struggles & triumphs in the microcosm of Squib's forest world - in Squib we find a parable for all ages from 8-80.
Publisher Provided Annotation.

—Aliens in My Nest: Squib Meets the Teen Creature. Shles, Larry. Winch, Bradley L., ed. LC 88-80770. 80p. (Orig.). (gr. k up). 1988. pap. 7.95 (*0-915190-49-4*, JP9049-4) Jalmar Pr.
—Do I have to Go to School Today? Squib Measures Up. Shles, Larry. Winch, Bradley L., ed. 64p. (Orig.). (gr. k up). 1989. pap. 7.95 (*0-915190-62-1*, JP9062-1) Jalmar Pr.
—Hoots & Toots & Hairy Brutes, Vol. 2: The Continuing Adventures of Squib. 2nd ed. Shles, Larry. LC 89-83466. 72p. (gr. k-8). 1989. pap. 7.95 (*0-915190-56-7*, JP9056-7) Jalmar Pr.
—Hugs & Shrugs: The Continuing Saga of Squib. Shles, Larry. LC 87-82162. 72p. (gr. k up). 1987. pap. 7.95 (*0-915190-47-8*, JP9047-8) Jalmar Pr.
—Moths & Mothers, Feathers & Fathers, Vol. 1: A Story about a Tiny Owl Named Squib. 2nd ed. Shles, Larry. Winch, Bradley, ed. LC 89-83467. 72p. (gr. k-8). 1989. pap. 7.95 (*0-915190-57-5*, JP9057-5) Jalmar Pr.
Shles, Lawrence. Hoots & Toots & Hairy Brutes: Squib the Owl Saves the Day. Shles, Lawrence. 70p. (gr. k-3). 1984. 10.95 (*0-685-42996-2*); pap. 4.95 (*0-685-42997-0*) HM.
Shlomo, Bat. Meam Loez for Youth: Ruth. Touger, Malke. 47p. (gr. 6-9). 1988. 9.00 (*0-940118-27-0*) Moznaim.
Shoemaker, Katheryn. Oh, Brother! Oh, Sister! Halloran, Phyllis. McKissack, Patricia & McKissack, Fredrick, eds. LC 88-60392. 32p. (Orig.). (gr. 1-3). 1988. text ed. 8.95 (*0-88335-788-7*); pap. text ed. 4.95 (*0-88335-767-4*) Milliken Pub Co.
Shoemaker, Kathryn. The Mouse & the Mill & the Bottle Babies. Coon, Alma S. 44p. (ps-1). 1982. 5.95 (*0-87935-061-X*) Williamsburg.
Shoemaker, Kathryn E. All Paths Lead to Bethlehem. McKissack, Patricia & McKissack, Frederick. LC 87-70472. 32p. (Orig.). (ps-3). 1987. pap. 5.99 (*0-8066-2265-2*, 10-0220, Augsburg) Augsburg Fortress.
—I Love Spring. Kroll, Steven. LC 86-14844. 32p. (ps-3). 1987. reinforced bdg. 12.95 (*0-8234-0634-2*) Holiday.
Shoenherr, John. Rascal: A Memoir of a Better Era. North, Sterling. LC 63-13882. (gr. 4 up). 1984. 13.95 (*0-525-18839-8*, DCB) Dutton Child Bks.
Shohet, Marti. Recipes for Art & Craft Materials. rev. ed. Sattler, Helen R. LC 86-34271. 128p. (gr. 6 up). 1987. 13.95 (*0-688-07374-3*) Lothrop.
—Recipes for Art & Craft Materials. Sattler, Helen R. 144p. (gr. 5 up). 1994. pap. 3.95 (*0-688-13199-9*, Pub. by Beech Tree Bks) Morrow.
Shoji, Takashi. Zilya's Secret Plan. Schaffer, Ulrich. 32p. (ps-6). 1991. pap. 4.99 (*0-7459-1957-X*) Lion USA.
Shone, Karl, jt. illus. see Plomer, Martin.
Shone, Karl & Percival, Keith, photos by. Weather. Cosgrove, Brian. LC 90-4887. 64p. (gr. 5 up). 1991. 15.00 (*0-679-80784-5*); PLB 15.99 (*0-679-90784-X*) Knopf Bks Yng Read.
Shone, Rob. What Do We Know about the Aztecs? Defrates, Joanna. LC 92-16997. 40p. (gr. 3-6). 1993. 16.95 (*0-87226-357-6*) P Bedrick Bks.
Shone, Venice. My Activity Box. Shone, Venice. LC 93-3288. 20p. (ps). 1993. 2.99 (*0-525-67449-7*, Lodestar Bks) Dutton Child Bks.
—My Lunch Box. Shone, Venice. LC 93-3287. 20p. (ps). 1993. 2.99 (*0-525-67451-9*, Lodestar Bks) Dutton Child Bks.
—My Play Box. Shone, Venice. LC 93-3289. 20p. (ps). 1993. 2.99 (*0-525-67448-9*, Lodestar Bks) Dutton Child Bks.
—My Toy Box. Shone, Venice. LC 93-18682. 20p. (ps). 1993. 2.99 (*0-525-67450-0*, Lodestar Bks) Dutton Child Bks.
Short, John. Lives: One Hundred Thirteen Great Irishwomen & Irishmen. Byrne, Art & McMahon, Sean. 230p. (Orig.). (gr. 9-12). 1990. pap. 16.95 (*1-85371-094-6*, Pub. by Poolbeg Pr ER) Dufour.
Shortall, Leonard. Bully of Barkham Street. Stolz, Mary. LC 68-2661. 224p. (gr. 3-6). 1963. PLB 14.89 (*0-06-025821-7*) HarpC Child Bks.

—The Bully of Barkham Street. Stolz, Mary. LC 68-2661. 224p. (gr. 3-7). 1985. pap. 3.95 (*0-06-440159-6*, Trophy) HarpC Child Bks.

—Dog on Barkham Street. Stolz, Mary. LC 60-5787. 176p. (gr. 3-6). 1960. PLB 14.89 (*0-06-025841-1*) HarpC Child Bks.

—A Dog on Barkham Street. Stolz, Mary. LC 60-5787. 176p. (gr. 3-7). 1985. pap. 3.95 (*0-06-440160-X*, Trophy) HarpC Child Bks.

—The Magic Pizza. Major, Beverly. LC 77-26993. (gr. 2-5). 1978. 5.95 (*0-13-545202-3*) P-H.

—Mishmash. Cone, Molly. MacDonald, Patricia, ed. 128p. 1991. pap. 2.95 (*0-671-70937-2*, Minstrel Bks) PB.

—Mishmash & The Big Fat Problem. Cone, Molly. (gr. 2-5). 1982. 13.45 (*0-395-32078-X*) HM.

—Mishmash & The Sauerkraut Mystery. Cone, Molly. (gr. 4-6). 1974. pap. 0.95 (*0-395-18556-4*) HM.

—More Ballpoint Bananas. Keller, Charles, compiled by. LC 77-5356. (gr. 1-3). 1980. 7.95 (*0-13-600767-8*, Pub. by Treehouse) P-H.

—Old MacDonald Had a Farm. LC 84-60028. (ps up). 1984. 5.95 (*0-394-86797-1*) Random Bks Yng Read.

Shortall, Leonard & Brandi, Leonard. Encyclopedia Brown Takes the Case. Sobol, Donald J. LC 73-6443. 96p. (gr. 3-5). 1979. 12.50 (*0-525-66318-5*, Lodestar Bks) Dutton Child Bks.

Shortall, Leonard & Brandi, Lillian. Encyclopedia Brown & the Case of the Dead Eagles. Sobol, Donald J. LC 75-15911. 96p. (gr. 3-5). 1979. 12.50 (*0-525-67220-6*, Lodestar Bks) Dutton Child Bks.

—Encyclopedia Brown & the Case of the Secret Pitch. Sobol, Donald J. LC 65-199640. 96p. (gr. 3-5). 1979. 12.50 (*0-525-67202-8*, Lodestar Bks) Dutton Child Bks.

—Encyclopedia Brown, Boy Detective. Sobol, Donald J. LC 63-9632. 96p. (gr. 3-5). 1979. 12.95 (*0-525-67200-1*, Lodestar Bks) Dutton Child Bks.

—Encyclopedia Brown Finds the Clues. Sobol, Donald J. LC 66-10230. 96p. (gr. 3-5). 1979. 12.95 (*0-525-67204-4*, Lodestar Bks) Dutton Child Bks.

—Encyclopedia Brown Gets His Man. Sobol, Donald J. LC 67-24666. 96p. (gr. 3-5). 1979. 12.50 (*0-525-67206-0*, Lodestar Bks) Dutton Child Bks.

—Encyclopedia Brown Keeps the Peace. Sobol, Donald J. LC 73-82912. 96p. (gr. 3-5). 1979. 12.50 (*0-525-67208-7*, Lodestar Bks) Dutton Child Bks.

—Encyclopedia Brown Lends a Hand. Sobol, Donald J. LC 74-10281. 96p. (gr. 3-5). 1979. 13.00 (*0-525-67218-4*, Lodestar Bks) Dutton Child Bks.

—Encyclopedia Brown Saves the Day. Sobol, Donald J. LC 71-117149. 96p. (gr. 3-5). 1979. 12.50 (*0-525-67210-9*, Lodestar Bks) Dutton Child Bks.

—Encyclopedia Brown Solves Them All. Sobol, Donald J. LC 68-22746. 96p. (gr. 3-5). 1979. 12.50 (*0-525-67212-5*, Lodestar Bks) Dutton Child Bks.

—Encyclopedia Brown Tracks Them Down. Sobol, Donald J. LC 77-160147. 96p. (gr. 3-5). 1979. 12.95 (*0-525-67214-1*, Lodestar Bks) Dutton Child Bks.

Shortall, Leonard & Brandi, Shortall. Encyclopedia Brown Shows the Way. Sobol, Donald J. LC 72-2911. 96p. (gr. 3-5). 1979. 12.50 (*0-525-67216-8*, Lodestar Bks) Dutton Child Bks.

Shortall, Leonard, jt. illus. see Brandi, Lillian.

Shott, Stephen, photos by. Bathtime. LC 91-11121. 12p. (ps). 1991. bds. 4.95 (*0-525-44754-7*, DCB) Dutton Child Bks.

—Look at Me. LC 91-11162. 12p. (ps). 1991. bds. 4.95 (*0-525-44755-5*, DCB) Dutton Child Bks.

—Mealtime. LC 91-2600. 12p. (ps). 1991. bds. 4.95 (*0-525-44756-3*, DCB) Dutton Child Bks.

—El Mundo del Bebe. (SPA.). 48p. (ps). 1992. 14.95 (*0-525-44846-2*, DCB) Dutton Child Bks.

—Playtime. LC 91-2601. 12p. (ps). 1991. bds. 4.95 (*0-525-44757-1*, DCB) Dutton Child Bks.

Shott, Steven, photos by. Baby's World. LC 90-30587. 48p. (ps). 1990. 13.95 (*0-525-44617-6*, DCB) Dutton Child Bks.

Shouse, Lucille, jt. illus. see Scott, Kay.

Show, Michael. Child Abuse: Is It Happening to You? Wakcher, Bridget. 32p. (Orig.). (gr. 1 up). 1984. pap. 3.50 (*0-930363-00-0*) Teknek.

Shpakow, Tanya. On the Way to Christmas. Shpakow, Tanya. LC 90-5373. 40p. (ps-2). 1991. 15.00 (*0-679-81796-4*); lib. bdg. 15.99 (*0-679-91796-9*) Knopf Bks Yng Read.

Shpitalnik, Vladimir. Uncle Fedya, His Dog, & His Cat. Uspenski, Eduard. Heim, Michael, tr. from RUS. LC 92-44491. 144p. (gr. 1-5). 1993. 14.00 (*0-679-82064-7*) Knopf Bks Yng Read.

Shrader, Christine. Gluskabe & the Four Wishes. Bruchac, Joseph, retold by. LC 93-26924. 1995. write for info. (*0-525-65164-0*, Cobblehill Bks) Dutton Child Bks.

Shtainmets, Leon, jt. illus. see Lavallee, Barbara.

Shubert, Christiane. The Legacy of George Partridgeberry. Shubert, J. Lansing. Steele, Robert, ed. 381p. (Orig.). (gr. 9-12). 1990. pap. 12.95 (*0-9627015-0-5*) J L Shubert.

Shuett, Stacey. If You Want to Find Golden. Spinelli, Eileen. LC 93-12000. (gr. 1-3). 1993. 14.95 (*0-8075-3585-0*) A Whitman.

Shulevitz, Uri. Dawn. Shulevitz, Uri. LC 74-9761. 32p. (ps up). 1974. 16.00 (*0-374-31707-0*) FS&G.

—Dawn. Shulevitz, Uri. 32p. (ps up). 1988. 5.95 (*0-374-41689-3*) FS&G.

—The Diamond Tree: Jewish Tales from Around the World. Schwartz, Howard & Rush, Barbara. LC 90-32420. 120p. (gr. 2-5). 1991. 17.00 (*0-06-025239-1*); PLB 16.89 (*0-06-025243-X*) HarpC Child Bks.

—The Fool of the World & the Flying Ship: A Russian Tale. Ransome, Arthur. (ps up). 1987. pap. 5.95 (*0-374-42438-1*) FS&G.

—The Fool of the World & the Flying Ship. Ransome, Arthur. LC 68-54105. 48p. (ps-3). 1968. 16.00 (*0-374-32442-5*) FS&G.

—The Fools of Chelm & Their History. Singer, Isaac Bashevis. Shub, Elizabeth, tr. from YID. LC 73-81500. 64p. (gr. 3 up). 1973. 14.00 (*0-374-32444-1*) FS&G.

—Hanukah Money. Aleichem, Sholem. Shulevitz, Uri & Shub, Elizabeth, trs. LC 77-26693. 32p. (ps-3). 1991. pap. 3.95 (*0-688-10993-4*, Mulberry) Morrow.

—One Monday Morning. Shulevitz, Uri. LC 66-24483. 48p. (ps-4). 1974. SBE 14.95 (*0-684-13195-1*, Scribners Young Read) Macmillan Child Grp.

—Rain Rain Rivers. Shulevitz, Uri. LC 73-85370. 32p. (ps-3). 1969. 16.00 (*0-374-36171-1*) FS&G.

—Soldier & Tsar in the Forest: A Russian Tale. Shulevitz, Uri. Lourie, Richard, tr. from RUS. LC 72-188254. 32p. (ps-3). 1972. 16.00 (*0-374-37126-1*) FS&G.

—Tontimundo y el Barco Volador. Ransome, Arthur. Negroni, Maria, tr. (SPA.). 48p. (ps-3). 1991. 15.95 (*0-374-32443-3*) FS&G.

Shulist, Steve. Flight. Mackie, Dan. 32p. (gr. 5-9). 1985. pap. 5.95 (*0-88625-112-5*) Durkin Hayes Pub.

Shulvitz, Uri. The Treasure. Shulevitz, Uri. LC 78-12952. 32p. (ps-3). 1979. 15.95 (*0-374-37740-5*) FS&G.

Shuster, Dorarhye. The Sporting Way to Reading Comprehension. Oana, Katherine. Cooper, William H., ed. LC 84-51195. 68p. (Orig.). (gr. 3-8). 1984. 5.27 (*0-914127-17-9*) Univ Class.

Shute, Linda. Clever Tom & the Leprechaun. Shute, Linda. LC 87-29671. 32p. (gr. k-3). 1988. 12.95 (*0-688-07488-X*); PLB 12.88 (*0-688-07489-8*) Lothrop.

—How I Named the Baby. Shute, Linda. Grant, Christy, ed. LC 92-33292. 32p. (ps-3). 1993. PLB 13.95 (*0-8075-3417-X*) A Whitman.

—Jeremy Bean's St. Patrick's Day. Schertle, Alice. LC 86-7403. 32p. (ps-2). 1987. 12.95 (*0-688-04813-7*); PLB 12.88 (*0-688-04814-5*) Lothrop.

—Magic Fort. Havill, Juanita. LC 90-42012. 32p. (gr. k-3). 1991. 14.45 (*0-395-50067-2*) HM.

—The Other Emily. Davis, Gibbs. LC 83-18913. 32p. (gr. k-3). 1984. 14.45 (*0-395-35482-X*, 5-84351) HM.

—The Other Emily. Davis, Gibbs. 32p. (gr. k-3). 1990. pap. 4.95 (*0-395-54947-7*) HM.

—Princess Pooh. Muldoon, Kathleen M. Mathews, Judith, ed. LC 88-33978. 32p. (gr. 2-5). 1989. PLB 13.95 (*0-8075-6627-6*) A Whitman.

Shvo, Aaron. Once There Was a Hassid. Omer, Devorah. 28p. (gr. 4 up). 1987. 9.95 (*0-915361-73-6*) Modan-Adama Bks.

Sibbeck, John & Dew, Heather. Warriors, Gods & Spirits from Central & South American Mythology. Gifford, Douglas. LC 93-1013. 128p. (gr. 6 up). 1993. 22.50 (*0-87226-914-0*); pap. 14.95 sewn (*0-87226-915-9*) P Bedrick Bks.

Sibbick, John. Creatures of Long Ago: Dinosaurs, Vol. 1. (ps-3). 1993. 16.00 (*0-87044-723-8*) Natl Geog.

—Heroes, Gods & Emperors from Roman Mythology. Usher, Kerry. 132p. (gr. 6 up). 1992. 22.50 (*0-87226-909-4*) P Bedrick Bks.

—Spirits, Heroes & Hunters from North American Indian Mythology. Wood, Marion. LC 91-38954. 132p. (gr. 6 up). 1992. 22.50 (*0-87226-903-5*) P Bedrick Bks.

Sibbick, John, jt. illus. see O'Connor, David.

Siberell, Anne. Martin Luther King, Jr. The Story of a Dream. Behrens, June. LC 78-23873. 32p. (gr. k-4). 1979. PLB 15.93 (*0-516-08879-3*, Golden Gate) Childrens.

—Whale in the Sky. Siberell, Anne. LC 82-2483. 32p. (ps-3). 1985. 13.95 (*0-525-44021-6*, DCB); pap. 3.95 (*0-525-44197-2*, DCB) Dutton Child Bks.

Sibley, Don. Human Body. Sabin, Francene. LC 84-2591. 32p. (gr. 3-6). 1985. PLB 9.49 (*0-8167-0170-9*); pap. text ed. 2.95 (*0-8167-0171-7*) Troll Assocs.

Sibley, Norman & Krause, Robert. Sun & Moon: Fairy Tales from Korea. Seros, Kathleen, adapted by. LC 82-82510. 61p. (gr. 3-9). 1982. PLB 16.50x (*0-930878-25-6*) Hollym Intl.

Siculan, Dan. Feeling Frustrated. Anderson, Penny S. LC 82-19910. 32p. (gr. 1-2). 1983. PLB 21.35 (*0-89565-245-5*); PLB 14.95s.p. (*0-685-55660-3*) Childs World.

—Saying I'm Sorry. Alden, Laura. LC 82-19945. 32p. (gr. 1-2). 1983. PLB 21.35 (*0-89565-247-1*); PLB 14.95s.p. (*0-685-55663-8*) Childs World.

—UFOs. Riehecky, Janet. LC 88-25730. 100p. (gr. 3-7). 1989. PLB 21.35 (*0-89565-453-9*); PLB 14.95s.p. (*0-685-55995-5*) Childs World.

Siculan, Dan, jt. illus. see Halverson, Lydia.

Sidaras, Nanci. Willowby's World of Fluffits. Vrooman, Christine W. 56p. (Orig.). (gr. 2-6). 1984. pap. 8.95 with stickers incl. (*0-910349-02-8*) Cloud Ten.

—Willowby's World of Unicorns. Vrooman, Christine W. Kane, Sandy & Ogden, Peggy, eds. 56p. (gr. 2-6). 1982. pap. 8.95 with stickers incl. (*0-685-06580-4*) Cloud Ten.

Sidjakov, Nicholas. Baboushka & the Three Kings. Robbins, Ruth. LC 60-15036. (ps up). 1960. 13.45 (*0-395-27673-X*, Pub. by Parnassus) HM.

—Baboushka & the Three Kings. Robbins, Ruth. LC 60-15036. 32p. (ps-3). 1986. pap. 5.95 (*0-395-24647-2*) HM.

Siebel, Fritz. Amelia Bedelia. newly illus. ed. Parish, Peggy. LC 91-10163. 64p. (gr. k-3). 1992. 14.00 (*0-06-020186-X*); PLB 13.89 (*0-06-020187-8*) HarpC Child Bks.

—Amelia Bedelia. newly illus. ed. Parish, Peggy. LC 91-10164. 64p. (gr. k-3). 1992. pap. 3.50 (*0-06-444155-5*, Trophy) HarpC Child Bks.

—Amelia Bedelia & the Surprise Shower. Parish, Peggy. LC 66-18655. 64p. (gr. k-3). 1966. 14.00 (*0-06-024642-1*); PLB 13.89 (*0-06-024643-X*) HarpC Child Bks.

—Amelia Bedelia & the Surprise Shower. Parish, Peggy. LC 66-18655. 64p. (gr. k-3). 1979. pap. 3.50 (*0-06-444019-2*, Trophy) HarpC Child Bks.

—Amelia Bedelia & the Surprise Shower. Parish, Peggy. LC 66-18655. 64p. (gr. k-3). 1986. incl. cassette 5.98 (*0-694-00161-9*, Trophy) HarpC Child Bks.

—Cat & Dog. Minarik, Else H. LC 60-14998. 32p. (gr. k-2). 1960. PLB 13.89 (*0-06-024221-3*) HarpC Child Bks.

—Tell Me Some More. Bonsall, Crosby N. LC 61-5773. 64p. (gr. k-3). 1961. PLB 13.89 (*0-06-020601-2*) HarpC Child Bks.

—Thank You, Amelia Bedelia. Parish, Peggy. LC 64-11835. (gr. k-3). 1964. 13.00 (*0-06-024665-0*); PLB 12.89 (*0-06-024652-9*) HarpC Child Bks.

—Thank You, Amelia Bedelia. Parish, Peggy. LC 92-5746. 64p. (ps-3). 1993. pap. 3.50 (*0-06-444171-7*, Trophy) HarpC Child Bks.

—Who Took the Farmer's Hat? Nodset, Joan L. LC 62-17964. 32p. (gr. k-3). 1963. PLB 14.89 (*0-06-024566-2*) HarpC Child Bks.

—Who Took the Farmer's Hat? Nodset, Joan L. LC 62-17964. 32p. (ps-2). 1988. pap. 5.95 (*0-06-443174-6*, Trophy) HarpC Child Bks.

Sieck, Judyth, jt. illus. see Cline, Paul.

Sieck, Judythe. The Adventures of Little Red. Jones, J. David. Krull, Kathleen, ed. 64p. 1993. write for info. (*1-883088-01-1*) Source CA. THE ADVENTURES OF LITTLE RED is about an eight year old boy living out his fantasy of flying & adventure with his secret friend, a pilot named Buzz. Together they dive out of the sky over the coast of Malibu for a close-up look at a school of dolphin; fly so close to the Hollywood sign they can almost touch it; fly through the metropolitan downtown Los Angeles; cruise over the international airport as commercial airliners take off & land below them; fly in formation with the Good Year blimp over the Rose Bowl during a football game; discover a sinking boat & lead a Coast Guard helicopter to the scene for a dramatic rescue. Although Little Red assumes that his adventure has all been a fantastic dream, he soon learns that any dream can come true, as long as he believes in it & is willing to work hard to make it happen. These are just a few scenes from THE ADVENTURES OF LITTLE RED, illustrated with spectacular four-color ground & aerial photographs, directed by J. David Jones who has been stunt pilot & director in the motion picture industry for almost 30 years. Book store owners & librarians agree that this is a one of a kind book & a must! Available from Source Productions, 800-538-0603 or 818-990-6724. *Publisher Provided Annotation.*

—Ginger's Moon. Cline, Paul. (ps-8). 1990. 11.95 (*0-9625261-0-X*); PLB write for info. Medlicott Pr.

Siede, George & Preis, Donna, photos by. El Alfabeto: Mentes Activas. University of Mexico City Staff, tr. Schwager, Istar, contrib. by. (SPA.). 24p. (ps-8). 1992. PLB 11.95 (*1-56674-036-3*) Forest Hse.

—Alphabet: Active Minds. Schwager, Istar, contrib. by. 24p. (ps-3). 1992. PLB 9.95 (*1-56674-000-2*) Forest Hse.

—Colores: Mentes Activas. University of Mexico City Staff, tr. Schwager, Istar, contrib. by. (SPA.). 24p. (ps-8). 1992. PLB 11.95 (*1-56674-037-1*) Forest Hse.

—Colors: Active Minds. Schwager, Istar, contrib. by. 24p. (ps-3). 1992. PLB 9.95 (*1-56674-001-0*) Forest Hse.

—Counting. Schwager, Istar. 24p. (ps-3). 1993. PLB 12.95 (*1-56674-067-3*, HTS Bks) Forest Hse.

—Formas: Mentes Activas. University of Mexico City Staff, tr. Schwager, Istar, contrib. by. (SPA.). 24p. (ps-8). 1992. PLB 11.95 (*1-56674-041-X*) Forest Hse.
—Matching. Schwager, Istar. 24p. (ps-3). 1993. PLB 12.95 (*1-56674-068-1*, HTS Bks) Forest Hse.
—Mi Dia: Mentes Activas. University of Mexico City Staff, tr. Schwager, Istar, contrib. by. (SPA.). 24p. (ps-8). 1992. PLB 11.95 (*1-56674-038-X*) Forest Hse.
—My Day: Active Minds. Schwager, Istar, contrib. by. 24p. (ps-3). 1992. PLB 9.95 (*1-56674-002-9*) Forest Hse.
—Numbers: Active Minds. Schwager, Istar, contrib. by. 24p. (ps-3). 1992. PLB 9.95 (*1-56674-003-7*) Forest Hse.
—Numeros: Mentes Activas. University of Mexico City Staff, tr. Schwager, Istar, contrib. by. (SPA.). 24p. (ps-8). 1992. PLB 11.95 (*1-56674-039-8*) Forest Hse.
—Opposites: Active Minds. Schwager, Istar, contrib. by. 24p. (ps-3). 1992. PLB 9.95 (*1-56674-004-5*) Forest Hse.
—Opuestos: Mentes Activas. University of Mexico City Staff, tr. Schwager, Istar, contrib. by. (SPA.). 24p. (ps-8). 1992. PLB 11.95 (*1-56674-040-1*) Forest Hse.
—Shapes: Active Minds. Schwager, Istar, contrib. by. 24p. (ps-3). 1992. PLB 9.95 (*1-56674-005-3*) Forest Hse.
—Sorting. Schwager, Istar. 24p. (ps-3). 1993. PLB 12.95 (*1-56674-069-X*, HTS Bks) Forest Hse.
—What's Different? Schwager, Istar. 24p. (ps-3). 1993. PLB 12.95 (*1-56674-070-3*, HTS Bks) Forest Hse.
Sieff, Ben. Fire in My Heart - Ice in My Veins: A Journal for Teenager Experiencing a Loss. Traisman, Enid S. 64p. (Orig.). (gr. 7-12). 1992. wkbk. 8.95 (*1-56123-056-1*) Centering Corp.
Sieffert, Clare. Anne of Avonlea: An Anne of Green Gables Story. Montgomery, Lucy M. 320p. 1990. 13.95 (*0-448-40063-4*, G&D) Putnam Pub Group.
Siegel, Hal. That Was Then, This Is Now. Hinton, Susie E. 7 up) 1971. 13.95 (*0-670-69798-2*) Viking Child Bks.
Siegl, Helen. The Dancing Palm Tree: & Other Nigerian Folktales. Walker, Barbara K., retold by. LC 89-27748. 112p. (gr. 3 up). 1990. Repr. of 1968 ed. 19.95 (*0-89672-216-3*) Tex Tech Univ Pr.
Siegrist, Wes. Big Water: Flight to Okeechobee. Arnold, Eugene. LC 92-61845. 201p. (gr. 12). 1993. pap. 12.95 (*0-9628828-2-8*) Prospector Pr.
Siembieda, Kevin, jt. illus. see Long, Kevin.
Sieveking, Anthea. Rub a Dub Dub & Other Water Rhymes. 12p. (ps-3). 1991. bds. 5.95 (*0-8120-6219-1*) Barron.
—Twinkle, Twinkle, Little Star & Other Bedtime Rhymes. 12p. (ps-3). 1991. bds. 5.95 (*0-8120-6220-5*) Barron.
Sieveking, Anthea, photos by. The Baby's Book of Babies. Henderson, Kathy. LC 88-20428. 24p. (ps-k). 1989. 9.95 (*0-8037-0634-0*) Dial Bks Young.
—The Baby's Book of Babies. Henderson, Kathy. 24p. (ps-k). 1993. pap. 4.50 (*0-14-054882-3*, Puffin Pied Piper) Puffin Bks.
—Baby's First Year. MacKinnon, Debbie. LC 92-21830. 26p. (ps). 1993. 11.95 (*0-8120-6334-1*) Barron.
—How Many? MacKinnon, Debbie. LC 91-46720. 24p. (ps-k). 1992. 10.99 (*0-8037-1253-7*) Dial Bks Young.
—My First ABC. MacKinnon, Debbie. LC 92-11500. (ps). 1992. 11.95 (*0-8120-6331-7*) Barron.
—What Noise? MacKinnon, Debbie. LC 92-43651. (gr. 4 up). 1994. 10.99 (*0-8037-1510-2*) Dial Bks Young.
—What Shape? MacKinnon, Debbie. LC 91-34700. 24p. (ps-k). 1992. 10.99 (*0-8037-1244-8*) Dial Bks Young.
Sievert, Claus. The Lion & the Puppy. Tolstoy, Leo. Riordan, James, tr. from RUS. LC 87-28653. 80p. (gr. 1 up). 1988. 15.95 (*0-8050-0735-0*, Bks Young Read) H Holt & Co.
Sifen, Debra. Best of Storylines: Story for the Whole Family. Teller, Hanoch. 224p. (gr. 2-12). 1991. 14.95 (*0-9614772-9-6*) NYC Pub Co.
Signorino, Slug. How to Be Your Own Selfish Pig. Macaulay, Susan S. LC 81-70769. 1982. pap. 9.95 (*0-89191-530-3*) Cook.
—Touchdown Riddles. Bernstein, Joanne E. & Cohen, Paul. Levine, Abby, ed. LC 88-21761. 32p. (gr. 1-5). 1989. 8.95g (*0-8075-8036-8*) A Whitman.
Sikorski, Anne. Country Mouse & City Mouse. McKissack, Patricia & McKissack, Fredrick. LC 85-12759. (ps-2). 1985. PLB 11.93 (*0-516-02362-4*); pap. 3.95 (*0-516-42362-2*) Childrens.
Silberman, Miriam. Der Lichtiger Kuk Fin der Baal Shem. Silberman, Miriam. Scheiner, Mordecai, ed. 80p. (Orig.). (gr. 4-8). 1985. pap. text ed. 4.50 (*0-9618441-0-8*) Beth Chana.
Silbur, Stephanie. The Great Cover-Up: A Condom Compendium. Zimet, Susan & Goodman, Victor. LC 88-92769. 136p. (Orig.). (gr. 10 up). 1989. pap. text ed. 7.95 (*0-9621700-0-3*) Civan Inc.
Silk, Linda. Cites Endangered Species Coloring Book. rev. ed. Conservation Treaty Support Group Staff. Dollinger, Peter, ed. 72p. 1993. pap. 4.95 (*1-56002-281-7*) Aegina Pr.
Sill, John. About Birds: A Guide for Children. Sill, Cathryn. 40p. (gr. 4 up). 1991. 14.95 (*1-56145-028-6*) Peachtree Pubs.
Silva, Lou. Alligators: A Success Story. Lauber, Patricia. LC 93-3302. 64p. (gr. 2-4). 1993. PLB 14.95 (*0-8050-1909-X*, Bks Young Read) H Holt & Co.
Silver, Jody. Miss Mopp's Lucky Day. McGuire, Leslie. LC 81-4879. 48p. (ps-3). 1982. 5.95 (*0-8193-1061-1*); PLB 5.95 (*0-8193-1062-X*) Parents.

—Rupert, Polly & Daisy. Silver, Jody. LC 83-24979. 48p. (ps-3). 1984. 5.95 (*0-8193-1124-3*) Parents.
Silver, Maggie. Woods & Forests. Wood, John N. LC 93-22506. 22p. (gr. k-4). 1993. 13.00 (*0-679-83691-8*) Knopf Bks Yng Read.
Silver, Pattie. Halloween KidDoodles, No. 3. Boynton, Alice. 64p. (ps-2). 1992. pap. 0.99 (*1-56293-261-6*) McClanahan Bk.
—Halloween KidDoodles, No. 4. Lerner, Andy. 64p. (ps-2). 1992. pap. 0.99 (*1-56293-262-4*) McClanahan Bk.
Silverman, Burt. Lilies of the Field. Barrett, William E. LC 62-8085. (gr. 7 up). 1967. 3.95 (*0-685-01491-6*, Im); pap. 3.95 (*0-385-07246-5*, Im) Doubleday.
Silverstein, Cindy. Happy Birthday Books. (ps-k). 1993. Set, 8 mini-board bks., 6p. ea. bds. 12.95 (*1-56293-214-4*) McClanahan Bk.
—Hug a Cub. Rutman, Shereen. 16p. (ps). 1993. wkbk. 2.25 (*1-56293-323-X*) McClanahan Bk.
Silverstein, Don. House That Jack Built. Cutts, David, retold by. LC 78-18951. 32p. (gr. k-2). 1979. PLB 9.79 (*0-89375-127-8*); pap. 1.95 (*0-89375-105-7*) Troll Assocs.
—Sam the Scarecrow. Gordon, Sharon. 32p. (gr. k-2). 1980. PLB 7.89 (*0-89375-387-4*); pap. 1.95 (*0-89375-287-8*) Troll Assocs.
—Samuel el Espantapajaros. Gordon, Sharon. (SPA.). 32p. (gr. k-2). 1981. PLB 7.89 (*0-89375-556-7*); pap. 1.95 (*0-89375-958-9*) Troll Assocs.
—Stop That Rabbit. Peters, Sharon. 32p. (gr. k-2). 1980. PLB 7.89 (*0-89375-388-2*); pap. 1.95 (*0-89375-288-6*) Troll Assocs.
Silverstein, Shel. Giraffe & a Half. Silverstein, Shel. LC 64-19709. 48p. (gr. k-3). 1964. 15.00 (*0-06-025655-9*); PLB 14.89 (*0-06-025656-7*) HarpC Child Bks.
—Lafcadio, the Lion Who Shot Back. Silverstein, Shel. LC 62-13320. 112p. (gr. 3-6). 1963. 15.00 (*0-06-025675-3*); PLB 14.89 (*0-06-025676-1*) HarpC Child Bks.
—A Light in the Attic. Silverstein, Shel. LC 80-8453. 176p. 1981. 15.95 (*0-06-025673-7*); PLB 15.89 (*0-06-025674-5*) HarpC Child Bks.
—Where the Sidewalk Ends: Poems & Drawings. Silverstein, Shel. LC 70-105486. 176p. (gr. 4 up). 1974. 15.95 (*0-06-025667-2*); PLB 15.89 (*0-06-025668-0*) HarpC Child Bks.
Silverthorn, Tina. A New Sibling. 2nd ed. Hansen, Kathleen. 16p. (ps). 1989. color book 1.95x (*0-685-29408-0*) Time Grow Co.
Silverthorne, Sandy. All-Time Awesome Bible Search. Silverthorne, Sandy. 32p. (Orig.). (ps up) 1991. 11.99 (*0-89081-920-3*) Harvest Hse.
—The Great Bible Adventure. Silverthorne, Sandy. LC 90-36385. 32p. (Orig.). (ps-8). 1990. 11.99 (*0-89081-842-8*) Harvest Hse.
Simbrom, Janine C. Grandma's Teapot. Bobbi. 37p. 1992. pap. 3.95 (*0-9626608-3-3*) Magik NY.
—Matthew's Dream. Bobbi. 51p. 1993. pap. 5.95 (*0-9626608-6-8*) Magik NY.
Simeon, Michel. Charlie et la Chocolaterie. Dahl, Roald. (FRE.). 190p. (gr. 5-10). 1987. pap. 8.95 (*0-685-60279-6*) Schoenhof.
—James et la Grosse Peche. Dahl, Roald. (FRE.). 174p. (gr. 5-10). 1988. pap. 8.95 (*2-07-033517-8*) Schoenhof.

Simic, Tim. The Adventures of Spero the Orthodox Church Mouse: The Nativity of Our Lord Christ's Birth. Sarlas-Fontana, Jane. 20p. (ps-4). 1992. pap. 6.95 (*0-937032-91-3*) Light&Life Pub Co MN.
A delightful children's Christmas story & activity book. This book was designed for children ages 4 to 7 years old. Because children of these ages are active, curious, fun, joyful, mischievous, & full of energy...this book features some hands-on experiences & activities by which your children can grow...move...think...& learn! In this first ADVENTURES OF SPERO book, children will learn of the birth of Baby Jesus as seen through the eyes of Spero. Upon completing the storybook part the children may then complete the activity pages at the back of the book, & then once completed, cut them out & place them on the refrigerator door. Look for other ADVENTURES OF SPERO, THE ORTHODOX CHURCH MOUSE! (EASTER, MAKING THE SIGN OF THE CROSS & many others.) 8.5 X 11 inches. Softbound, $6.95. "Many years ago my grandmother told me of Spero - a special mouse who lived in the basement of an Orthodox church. Spero had many adventures in church & when you meet him, you will learn of the many teachings of the Holy Orthodox Church. Look for other adventures of Spero in the near future." --Jane Sarlas-Fontana, Author. *Publisher Provided Annotation.*

Simmonds, Posy. The Chocolate Wedding. Simmonds, Posy. LC 90-4932. 32p. (gr. k-5). 1991. 12.95 (*0-679-81447-7*) Knopf Bks Yng Read.
—Matilda: Who Told Such Dreadful Lies. Belloc, Hilaire. LC 91-15852. 32p. 1992. 15.00 (*0-679-82658-0*); PLB 15.99 (*0-679-92658-5*) Knopf Bks Yng Read.
Simmons, Bernadette. But She's Still My Grandma! Rappaport, Doreen. LC 81-13163. 32p. (gr. 1-5). 1982. 16.95 (*0-89885-072-X*) Human Sci Pr.
—It's a Shame about the Rain: The Bright Side of Disappointment. Hazen, Barbara S. LC 81-13163. 32p. (ps-3). 1982. 16.95 (*0-89885-050-9*) Human Sci Pr.
Simmons, Elly. The Magic Dogs of the Volcanoes (Los perros magicos de los volcanoes) Argueta, Manlio & Ross, Stacey. LC 90-2254. (SPA & ENG.). 32p. (gr. k-5). 1990. 13.95 (*0-89239-064-6*) Childrens Book Pr.
—There's Music in the Air. Reynolds, Malvina. LC 76-19261. 96p. (gr. 1-12). 1976. pap. 5.00 (*0-915620-05-7*) Schroder Music.
Simmons, Sheri. Ethnic Pride. Lipson, Greta & Romatowski, Jane. 152p. (gr. 4-9). 1983. wkbk. 12.95 (*0-86653-121-1*, GA 464) Good Apple.
Simmons, Shirley. The American Indian Coloring Book. Underwood, Thomas B. 20p. (gr. k-2). 1969. 3.50 (*0-935741-02-X*) Cherokee Pubns.
—The Magic Lake: A Mystical Healing Lake of the Cherokee. Underwood, Tom B. 20p. (gr. 1-3). 1982. 3.50 (*0-935741-08-9*) Cherokee Pubns.
Simon, Hilda. The Magic of Color. Simon, Hilda. LC 81-5044. 56p. (gr. 3 up). 1981. 12.95 (*0-688-00619-1*) Lothrop.
Simon, Seymour. Autumn Across America. Simon, Seymour. LC 92-55043. 32p. (gr. 1-5). 1993. 14.95 (*1-56282-467-8*); PLB 14.89 (*1-56282-468-6*) Hyprn Child.
—Big Cats. Simon, Seymour. LC 90-36374. 40p. (gr. k-3). 1991. 17.00 (*0-06-021646-8*); PLB 16.89 (*0-06-021647-6*) HarpC Child Bks.
—Snakes. Simon, Seymour. LC 91-15948. 32p. (gr. k-3). 1992. 16.00 (*0-06-022529-7*); PLB 15.89 (*0-06-022530-0*) HarpC Child Bks.
—Wolves. Simon, Seymour. LC 92-25924. 32p. (gr. k-3). 1993. 16.00 (*0-06-022531-9*); PLB 15.89 (*0-06-022534-3*) HarpC Child Bks.
Simons-Ailes, Sandra. Mrs. Ortiz Makes Fry Bread. 30p. (Orig.). 1979. pap. 3.00 (*0-915347-06-7*) Pueblo Acoma Pr.
Simont, Marac. Many Moons. Thurber, James. LC 89-36465. 48p. (gr. 3-7). 1990. 14.95 (*0-15-251872-X*) HarBrace.
Simont, Marc. Chasing after Annie. Sharmat, Marjorie W. LC 80-7906. 80p. (gr. 2-5). 1991. pap. 3.50 (*0-06-440351-3*, Trophy) HarpC Child Bks.
—The Dallas Titans Get Ready for Bed. Kuskin, Karla. LC 83-49470. 48p. (gr. k-3). 1986. 12.00 (*0-06-023562-4*); PLB 11.89 (*0-06-023563-2*) HarpC Child Bks.
—The Dallas Titans Get Ready for Bed. Kuskin, Karla. LC 83-49470. 48p. (ps-3). 1988. pap. 3.95 (*0-06-443180-0*, Trophy) HarpC Child Bks.
—The Elephant Who Couldn't Forget. Reissue. ed. McNulty, Faith. LC 79-2741. 64p. (gr. k-3). 1980. PLB 13.89 (*0-06-024146-2*) HarpC Child Bks.
—Every Time I Climb a Tree. McCord, David. LC 67-25611. 48p. (gr. k-3). 1985. pap. 4.95 (*0-316-55518-5*) Little.
—The First Christmas. rev. ed. Trent, Robbie. LC 89-29729. 32p. (ps-2). 1990. pap. 3.50 (*0-06-443249-1*, Trophy) HarpC Child Bks.
—First Christmas Board Book. Trent, Robbie. LC 89-29729. 26p. (ps). 1992. 4.95 (*0-694-00423-5*, Festival) HarpC Child Bks.
—Glaciers. rev. ed. Tangborn, Wendell V. LC 87-45306. 32p. (ps-3). 1988. pap. 4.50 (*0-06-445076-7*, Trophy) HarpC Child Bks.
—Glaciers. rev. ed. Tangborn, Wendell V. LC 87-47696. 32p. (ps-3). 1988. (Crowell Jr Bks); (Crowell Jr Bks) HarpC Child Bks.
—Glenda. Udry, Janice M. LC 69-14443. 64p. (gr. 1-5). 1991. pap. 3.95 (*0-06-440410-2*, Trophy) HarpC Child Bks.
—The Happy Day. Krauss, Ruth. LC 49-10568. 30p. (ps-3). 1949. PLB 14.89 (*0-06-023396-6*) HarpC Child Bks.
—The Happy Day. Krauss, Ruth. LC 49-10568. 36p. (gr. k-3). 1989. pap. 4.95 (*0-06-443191-6*, Trophy) HarpC Child Bks.
—How to Dig a Hole to the Other Side of the World. McNulty, Faith. LC 78-22479. 32p. (ps-3). 1979. PLB 14.89 (*0-06-024148-9*) HarpC Child Bks.
—How to Dig a Hole to the Other Side of the World. McNulty, Faith. LC 78-22479. 32p. (gr. k-3). 1990. pap. 4.95 (*0-06-443218-1*, Trophy) HarpC Child Bks.
—If You Listen. Reissue. ed. Zolotow, Charlotte. LC 79-2688. 32p. (gr. k-3). 1980. PLB 13.89 (*0-06-027050-0*) HarpC Child Bks.

—In the Year of the Boar & Jackie Robinson. Lord, Bette B. LC 83-48440. 176p. (gr. 3-7). 1984. PLB 13.89 (0-06-024004-0) HarpC Child Bks.
—In the Year of the Boar & Jackie Robinson. Lord, Betty B. LC 83-48440. 176p. (gr. 3-7). 1986. pap. 3.95 (0-06-440175-8, Trophy) HarpC Child Bks.
—Journey into a Black Hole. Branley, Franklyn M. LC 85-48249. 32p. (ps-3). 1986. PLB 13.89 (0-690-04544-1, Crowell Jr Bks) HarpC Child Bks.
—Journey into a Black Hole. Branley, Franklyn M. LC 85-48249. 32p. (gr. k-3). 1988. pap. 4.50 (0-06-445075-9, Trophy) HarpC Child Bks.
—Knight of the Golden Plain. Hunter, Mollie. LC 82-48747. 48p. (gr. k-4). 1983. 12.95 (0-06-022685-4) HarpC Child Bks.
—Martin's Hats. Blos, Joan W. LC 83-13389. 32p. (ps-3). 1984. 11.95 (0-688-02027-5); PLB 11.88 (0-688-02033-X, Morrow Jr Bks) Morrow Jr Bks.
—Nate the Great. Sharmat, Marjorie W. 48p. (gr. 1-4). 1986. 12.95 (0-698-20627-4, Coward) Putnam Pub Group.
—Nate the Great & the Boring Beach Bag. Sharmat, Marjorie W. 48p. (gr. 1-4). 1987. 13.95 (0-698-20631-2, Coward) Putnam Pub Group.
—Nate the Great & the Boring Beach Bag. Sharmat, Marjorie W. 48p. (gr. 1-4). 1989. pap. 3.25 (0-440-40168-2, YB) Dell.
—Nate the Great & the Lost List. Sharmat, Marjorie W. 48p. 1981. 3.25 (0-440-46282-7, YB) Dell.
—Nate the Great & the Missing Key. Sharmat, Marjorie W. 48p. (gr. 1-4). 1982. pap. 3.25 (0-440-46191-X, YB) Dell.
—Nate the Great & the Missing Key. Sharmat, Marjorie W. 48p. (gr. 1-4). 1981. 11.95 (0-698-20630-4, Coward) Putnam Pub Group.
—Nate the Great & the Mushy Valentine. Sharmat, Marjorie. LC 93-15488. 1994. 12.95 (0-385-31166-4) Delacorte.
—Nate the Great & the Musical Note. Sharmat, Marjorie W. & Sharmat, Craig. 48p. (gr. 1-4). 1990. 13.95 (0-698-20645-2, Coward) Putnam Pub Group.
—Nate the Great & the Phony Clue. Sharmat, Marjorie W. 48p. (gr. k-6). 1981. pap. 2.99 (0-440-46300-9, YB) Dell.
—Nate the Great & the Pillowcase. Sharmat, Marjorie W. & Weinman, Rosalind. LC 92-34405. 1993. 12.95 (0-385-31051-X) Delacorte.
—Nate the Great & The Snowy Trail. Sharmat, Marjorie W. 48p. (gr. 6-9). 1982. 11.95 (0-698-20628-2, Coward) Putnam Pub Group.
—Nate the Great & the Snowy Trail. Sharmat, Marjorie W. 48p. (gr. k-6). 1984. pap. 3.25 (0-440-46276-2, YB) Dell.
—Nate the Great & the Sticky Case. Sharmat, Marjorie W. (gr. k-6). 1981. pap. 3.25 (0-440-46289-4) Dell.
—Nate the Great & the Sticky Case. Sharmat, Marjorie W. (gr. 1-4). 1987. 11.95 (0-698-20629-0, Coward) Putnam Pub Group.
—Nate the Great: And the Stolen Base. Sharmat, Marjorie W. 48p. (gr. 1-4). 1992. 12.95 (0-698-20708-4, Coward) Putnam Pub Group.
—Nate the Great Goes Down in the Dumps. Sharmat, Marjorie W. 48p. (gr. 1-4). 1989. 13.95 (0-698-20636-3, Coward) Putnam Pub Group.
—Nate the Great Goes Undercover. Sharmat, Marjorie W. 48p. (gr. 1-4). 1989. 13.95 (0-698-20643-6, Coward); (Coward) Putnam Pub Group.
—Nate the Great Stalks Stupidweed. Sharmat, Marjorie W. LC 85-30161. 48p. (gr. 1-4). 1986. 11.95 (0-698-20626-6, Coward) Putnam Pub Group.
—Nate the Great Stalks Stupidweed. Sharmat, Marjorie W. 48p. (gr. 9-12). 1989. pap. 3.25 (0-440-40150-X, YB) Dell.
—No More Monsters for Me. Parish, Peggy. LC 81-47111. 64p. (gr. k-3). 1981. 14.00 (0-06-024657-X); PLB 13.89 (0-06-024658-8) HarpC Child Bks.
—No More Monsters for Me! Parish, Peggy. LC 81-47111. 64p. (gr. k-3). 1987. pap. 3.50 (0-06-444109-1, Trophy) HarpC Child Bks.
—The Philharmonic Gets Dressed. Kuskin, Karla. LC 81-48658. 48p. (ps-3). 1986. pap. 4.95 (0-06-443124-X, Trophy) HarpC Child Bks.
—The Quiet Mother & the Noisy Little Boy. Zolotow, Charlotte. LC 88-936. 32p. (ps-3). 1989. 13.00 (0-06-026978-2); PLB 12.89 (0-06-026979-0) HarpC Child Bks.
—Speak Up: More Rhymes of the Never Was & Always Is. McCord, David. 80p. (gr. 5 up). 1980. 13.95 (0-316-55517-7) Little.
—Ten Copycats in a Boat & Other Riddles. Schwartz, Alvin. LC 79-2811. 64p. (gr. k-3). 1985. pap. 3.50 (0-06-444076-1, Trophy) HarpC Child Bks.
—The Three-Day Enchantment. Hunter, Mollie. LC 84-48350. 64p. (gr. k-4). 1985. PLB 12.89 (0-06-022693-5) HarpC Child Bks.
—Top Secret. Gardiner, John R. 129p. (gr. 3-7). 1985. 15.95 (0-316-30368-2) Little.
—Tree Is Nice. Udry, Janice M. LC 56-5153. 32p. (ps-1). 1957. 14.00 (0-06-026155-2); PLB 13.89 (0-06-026156-0) HarpC Child Bks.
—A Tree Is Nice. Udry, Janice M. LC 56-5153. 32p. (ps-3). 1987. pap. 4.95 (0-06-443147-9, Trophy) HarpC Child Bks.
—Volcanoes. Branley, Franklyn M. LC 84-45344. 32p. (ps-3). 1985. (Crowell Jr Bks); PLB 13.89 (0-690-04431-3) HarpC Child Bks.

—Volcanoes. Branley, Franklyn M. LC 84-45344. 32p. (ps-3). 1986. pap. 4.50 (0-06-445059-7, Trophy) HarpC Child Bks.
—What Happened to the Dinosaurs? Branley, Franklyn M. LC 88-37626. 32p. (gr. k-3). 1989. (Crowell Jr Bks); PLB 13.89 (0-690-04749-5, Crowell Jr Bks) HarpC Child Bks.
—What Happened to the Dinosaurs? Branley, Franklyn M. LC 88-37626. 32p. (gr. k-4). 1991. pap. 4.50 (0-06-445105-4, Trophy) HarpC Child Bks.
Simont, Mark. The Elephant Who Couldn't Forget. McNulty, Faith. LC 79-2741. 64p. (gr. k-3). 1989. pap. 3.50 (0-06-444128-8, Trophy) HarpC Child Bks.
Simpson, Bill. Birds. Ricciuti, Edward. 64p. (gr. 4-8). 1993. jacketed 14.95 (1-56711-053-3) Blackbirch.
—Fish. Ricciuti, Edward. 64p. (gr. 4-8). 1993. jacketed 14.95 (1-56711-056-8) Blackbirch.
Simpson, Catherine. My Little Book of Nursery Rhymes. Simpson, Catherine. 32p. 1992. 5.95 (0-87226-502-1, Bedrick Blackie) P Bedrick Bks.
Simpson, Gretchen D. Gretchen's Abc. Simpson, Gretchen D. LC 90-19332. 32p. (ps up). 1991. 16.95 (0-06-025645-1); PLB 16.89 (0-06-025646-X) HarpC Child Bks.
Simpson, Lesley. The Hug. Simpson, Lesley. 24p. (ps-1). 1987. pap. 0.99 (0-920303-23-4, Pub. by Annick CN) Firefly Bks Ltd.
Simpson, Will. War Machine. Gibbons, Dave. Burton, Richard, ed. 80p. 1993. text ed. 14.95 (1-56862-018-7) Tundra MA.
Sims, Blanche. Adventure in the Haunted House. McBrier, Page. LC 85-8436. 96p. (gr. 3-6). 1986. PLB 9.89 (0-8167-0539-9); pap. text ed. 2.95 (0-8167-0540-2) Troll Assocs.
—Alex, the Kid with AIDS. Girard, Linda W. Levine, Abby, ed. LC 89-77592. 32p. (gr. 2-5). 1991. PLB 13.95 (0-8075-0245-6); pap. 5.95 (0-8075-0247-2) A Whitman.
—All about Asthma. Ostrow, William & Ostrow, Vivian. Levine, Abby, ed. LC 89-5254. 32p. (gr. 2-6). 1989. PLB 11.95 (0-8075-0276-6); pap. 4.95 (0-8075-0275-8) A Whitman.
—All about Stacy. Giff, Patricia R. 80p. (Orig.). (gr. k-6). 1988. pap. 3.25 (0-440-40088-0, YB) Dell.
—Beast & the Halloween Horror. Giff, Patricia R. (Orig.). (gr. k-6). 1990. pap. 2.99 (0-440-40335-9, YB) Dell.
—The Bunnysitters. Banks, Kate. LC 90-27441. 80p. (Orig.). (gr. 2-4). 1991. lib. bdg. 6.99 (0-679-91232-0); pap. 2.50 (0-679-81232-6) Random Bks Yng Read.
—Cannonball Chris. Marzollo, Jean. LC 86-31512. 48p. (gr. 2-3). 1987. lib. bdg. 6.99 (0-394-98512-5); pap. 3.50 (0-394-88512-0, Random Juv) Random Bks Yng Read.
—December Secrets. Giff, Patricia R. 80p. (gr. k-6). 1984. pap. 3.25 (0-440-41795-3, YB) Dell.
—Eddie, Incorporated. Naylor, Phyllis R. LC 79-22589. (gr. 4-6). 1980. SBE 12.95 (0-689-30754-3, Atheneum Child Bk) Macmillan Child Grp.
—Fish Face. Giff, Patricia R. 80p. (Orig.). (gr. 1-4). 1984. pap. 3.25 (0-440-42557-3, YB) Dell.
—Getting Oliver's Goat. McBrier, Michael. LC 87-13870. 96p. (gr. 3-6). 1988. PLB 9.89 (0-8167-1145-3); pap. text ed. 2.95 (0-8167-1146-1) Troll Assocs.
—Halloween Party. Feczko, Kathy. LC 84-8635. 32p. (gr. k-2). 1985. PLB 11.59 (0-8167-0354-X); pap. text ed. 2.95 (0-8167-0434-1) Troll Assocs.
—I Took My Frog to the Library. Kimmel, Eric A. 32p. (ps-3). 1990. pap. 13.00 (0-670-82418-6) Viking Child Bks.
—I Took My Frog to the Library. Kimmel, Eric A. 32p. (ps-3). 1992. pap. 3.99 (0-14-050916-X) Puffin Bks.
—In the Dinosaur's Paw. Giff, Patricia R. 80p. (gr. k-6). 1985. pap. 3.25 (0-440-44150-1, YB) Dell.
—Joey's Head. Cretan, Gladys. LC 90-41592. 48p. (gr. 2-4). 1991. pap. 13.95 jacketed (0-671-73201-3, S&S BFYR) S&S Trade.
—Joey's Head. Cretan, Gladys. LC 90-41592. 48p. (gr. 2-4). 1993. pap. 2.95 (0-671-86699-0, Half Moon Bks) S&S Trade.
—Lazy Lions, Lucky Lambs. Giff, Patricia R. 80p. (gr. k-6). 1985. pap. 3.25 (0-440-44640-6, YB) Dell.
—Mary Marony & the Snake. Kline, Suzy. LC 90-31071. 64p. (gr. 2-6). 1992. 12.95 (0-399-22044-5, Putnam) Putnam Pub Group.
—Mary Marony Hides Out. Kline, Suzy. LC 92-16064. 80p. (gr. 1-4). 1993. 13.95 (0-399-22433-5, Putnam) Putnam Pub Group.
—Mary Marony, Mummy Girl. Kline, Suzy. LC 93-14348. 1994. write for info. (0-399-22609-5, Putnam) Putnam Pub Group.
—Me & Katie (the Pest) Martin, Ann M. LC 85-5558. 160p. (gr. 4-7). 1985. 13.95 (0-8234-0580-X) Holiday.
—Mrs. Minetta's Car Pool. Spurr, Elizabeth. LC 84-20483. 32p. (ps-3). 1985. SBE 12.95 (0-689-31103-6, Atheneum Child Bk) Macmillan Child Grp.
—Mrs. Minetta's Car Pool. Spurr, Elizabeth. LC 90-35. 32p. (gr. k-3). 1990. pap. 3.95 (0-689-71430-0, Aladdin) Macmillan Child Grp.
—Mystery of the Disappearing Dogs. Brenner, Barbara. LC 82-186. 128p. (gr. k-3). 1982. pap. 1.95 (0-394-85162-5) Knopf Bks Yng Read.
—The Mystery of the Plumed Serpent. Brenner, Barbara. LC 80-17316. 128p. (gr. k-3). 1981. lib. bdg. 4.99 (0-394-94531-X) Knopf Bks Yng Read.
—Nurse Sally Ann. Dicks, Terrance. LC 92-22075. 1994. pap. 14.00 (0-671-79428-0, S&S BFYR) S&S Trade.

—Oliver & the Amazing Spy. McBrier, Michael. LC 87-13793. 96p. (gr. 3-6). 1988. PLB 9.89 (0-8167-1143-7); pap. text ed. 2.95 (0-8167-1144-5) Troll Assocs.
—Oliver & the Lucky Duck. McBrier, Page. LC 85-8417. 96p. (gr. 3-6). 1986. PLB 9.89 (0-8167-0541-0); pap. text ed. 2.95 (0-8167-0542-9) Troll Assocs.
—Oliver & the Runaway Alligator. McBrier, Michael. LC 86-7120. 96p. (Orig.). (gr. 3-6). 1987. PLB 9.89 (0-8167-0818-5); pap. text ed. 2.95 (0-8167-0819-3) Troll Assocs.
—Oliver Smells Trouble. McBrier, Michael. LC 87-13954. 96p. (gr. 3-6). 1988. PLB 9.89 (0-8167-1149-6); pap. text ed. 2.95 (0-8167-1150-X) Troll Assocs.
—Oliver's Back-Yard Circus. McBrier, Michael. LC 86-40378. 96p. (Orig.). (gr. 3-6). 1987. PLB 9.89 (0-8167-0822-3); pap. text ed. 2.95 (0-8167-0823-1) Troll Assocs.
—Oliver's Barnyard Blues. McBrier, Michael. LC 87-13864. 96p. (gr. 3-6). 1988. PLB 9.89 (0-8167-1147-X); pap. text ed. 2.95 (0-8167-1148-8) Troll Assocs.
—Oliver's High-Flying Adventure. McBrier, Michael. LC 86-16038. 96p. (Orig.). (gr. 3-6). 1987. PLB 9.89 (0-8167-0820-7); pap. text ed. 2.95 (0-8167-0821-5) Troll Assocs.
—Oliver's Lucky Day. McBrier, Page. LC 85-8437. 96p. (gr. 3-6). 1986. lib. bdg. 9.89 (0-8167-0537-2); pap. text ed. 2.95 (0-8167-0538-0) Troll Assocs.
—Pickle Puss. Giff, Patricia R. (ps-3). 1986. pap. 8.95 (0-385-29477-8) Delacorte.
—The Pizza Pie Slugger. Marzollo, Jean. LC 88-33379. 64p. (Orig.). (gr. 2-4). 1989. PLB 6.99 (0-394-92881-4); pap. 2.50 (0-394-82881-X) Random Bks Yng Read.
—Purple Climbing Days. Giff, Patricia R. 80p. (gr. 5 up). 1985. pap. 3.25 (0-440-47309-8, YB) Dell.
—Purple Climbing Days. Giff, Patricia R. (ps-3). 1986. pap. 8.95 (0-385-29500-6) Delacorte.
—Red Ribbon Rosie. Marzollo, Jean. LC 87-29641. 64p. (Orig.). (gr. 2-5). 1988. lib. bdg. 5.99 (0-394-99608-9); pap. 2.50 (0-394-89608-4) Random Bks Yng Read.
—Sally Ann & the Mystery Picnic. Dicks, Terrance. LC 92-22074. (gr. 1-3). 1993. pap. 14.00 (0-671-79427-2, S&S BFYR) S&S Trade.
—Sally Ann on Her Own. Dicks, Terrance. LC 91-15379. 64p. (gr. k-3). 1992. pap. 14.00 jacketed (0-671-74512-3, S&S BFYR) S&S Trade.
—Say "Cheese" Giff, Patricia R. (ps-3). 1986. pap. 8.95 (0-385-29501-4) Delacorte.
—Say "Cheese, No. 10. Giff, Patricia R. (gr. 6-9). 1985. pap. 3.25 (0-440-47639-9, YB) Dell.
—Secret of the Magic Potion. Bolton, Elizabeth. LC 84-8881. 48p. (gr. 2-4). 1985. PLB 10.89 (0-8167-0420-1); pap. text ed. 3.50 (0-8167-0421-X) Troll Assocs.
—Secret of the Missing Camel. McBrier, Page. LC 86-887. 96p. (Orig.). (gr. 3-6). 1987. PLB 9.89 (0-8167-0816-9); pap. text ed. 2.95 (0-8167-0817-7) Troll Assocs.
—Secret of the Old Garage. McBrier, Page. LC 85-16505. 96p. (gr. 3-6). 1986. PLB 9.89 (0-8167-0543-7); pap. text ed. 2.95 (0-8167-0544-5) Troll Assocs.
—Show Time at the Polk Street School: Plays You Can Do Yourself. Giff, Patricia R. LC 91-46163. 80p. (gr. 1-4). 1992. 14.00 (0-385-30794-2) Delacorte.
—A Smooth Move. Rabe, Berniece. Tucker, Kathleen, ed. LC 87-2099. (gr. 1-4). 1987. PLB 11.95 (0-8075-7486-4) A Whitman.
—Snaggle Doodles. Giff, Patricia R. 80p. (gr. 1-4). 1985. pap. 3.25 (0-440-48068-X, YB) Dell.
—Soccer Sam. Marzollo, Jean. LC 86-47533. 48p. (gr. 1-3). 1987. lib. bdg. 7.99 (0-394-98406-4); pap. 3.50 (0-394-88406-X) Random Bks Yng Read.
—Stacy Says Good-Bye. Giff, Patricia R. 80p. (gr. k-3). 1989. pap. 3.25 (0-440-40135-6, YB) Dell.
—Stage Fright. Martin, Ann M. LC 84-47834. 144p. (gr. 3-7). 1984. 13.95 (0-8234-0541-9) Holiday.
—Tu Puedes Decirles "No" A las Drogas! You Can Say "No" to Drugs! Super, Gretchen. (SPA.). 48p. (gr. k-4). 1991. PLB 21.27 (0-516-37372-2) Childrens.
—The Valentine Star. Giff, Patricia R. 80p. (Orig.). (gr. k-6). 1985. pap. 3.25 (0-440-49204-1, YB) Dell.
—Where Are the Stars During the Day? A Book about Stars. Berger, Melvin & Berger, Gilda. LC 92-18200. (gr. k-3). 1993. 12.00 (0-8249-8644-X, Ideals Child); pap. 3.95 (0-8249-8607-5) Hambleton-Hill.
—The World's Greatest Toe Show. Lamb, Nancy & Singer, Muff. LC 93-28440. 64p. (gr. 2-5). 1993. PLB 13.95 (0-8167-3322-8); pap. 3.95 (0-8167-3323-6) Troll Assocs.
Sims, Blanche C. Let Me off This Spaceship! Greer, Gery & Ruddick, Bob. LC 90-32045. 96p. (gr. 2-5). 1991. 12.95 (0-06-021605-0); PLB 12.89 (0-06-021606-9) HarpC Child Bks.
Sims, Blanche L. Jason & the Aliens down the Street. Greer, Gery & Ruddick, Bob. LC 90-47386. 96p. (gr. 2-5). 1991. 12.95 (0-06-021761-8); PLB 12.89 (0-06-021762-6) HarpC Child Bks.
—Jason & the Escape from Bat Planet. Greer, Gery & Ruddick, Bob. LC 92-44169. 96p. (gr. 2-5). 1993. 14.00 (0-06-021221-7); PLB 13.89 (0-06-021222-5) HarpC Child Bks.
—Jason & the Lizard Pirates. Greer, Gery & Ruddick, Robert. LC 91-14327. 96p. (gr. 2-5). 1992. 14.00 (0-06-022721-4); PLB 13.89 (0-06-022722-2) HarpC Child Bks.

—Jason & the Lizard Pirates. Greer, Gery & Ruddick, Bob. LC 91-14327. 96p. (gr. 2-5). 1993. pap. 3.95 (0-06-440481-1, Trophy) HarpC Child Bks.

—Let Me off This Spaceship! Greer, Gery & Ruddick, Bob. LC 90-47386. 80p. (gr. 2-5). 1992. pap. 3.95 (0-06-440436-6, Trophy) HarpC Child Bks.

—Valentine's Day: Stories & Poems. Bauer, Caroline F., ed. LC 91-37641. 96p. (gr. 2-5). 1993. 14.00 (0-06-020823-6); PLB 13.89 (0-06-020824-4) HarpC Child Bks.

Sims, Deborah. Christmas KidDoodles, Bk. 1. Herman, Emmi S. 64p. (Orig.). 1991. pap. 0.99 activity pad (1-56293-153-9) McClanahan Bk.

—Harold & the Dinosaur Mystery. new ed. Frost, Erica. LC 78-60123. 48p. (gr. 2-4). 1979. PLB 10.89 (0-89375-088-3); pap. 3.50 (0-89375-076-X) Troll Assocs.

—Mike's New Bike. Greydanus, Rose. 32p. (gr. k-2). 1980. PLB 7.89 (0-89375-382-3); pap. 1.95 (0-89375-282-7) Troll Assocs.

—Mud Pies. Grey, Judith. LC 81-4042. 32p. (gr. k-2). 1981. PLB 11.59 (0-89375-541-9); pap. 2.95 (0-89375-542-7) Troll Assocs.

—Three Little Witches. Gordon, Sharon. 32p. (gr. k-2). 1980. PLB 7.89 (0-89375-390-4); pap. 1.95 (0-89375-290-8) Troll Assocs.

—The Tooth Fairy. Peters, Sharon. LC 81-5100. 32p. (gr. k-2). 1981. PLB 11.59 (0-89375-519-2); pap. 2.95 (0-89375-520-6) Troll Assocs.

—What a Dog. Gordon, Sharon. 32p. (gr. k-2). 1980. PLB 7.89 (0-89375-393-9); pap. 1.95 (0-89375-293-2) Troll Assocs.

Sims, Deborah & Lustig, Loretta. Phonics Vowels. Wise, Beth A. & Block, Arlene. Nayer, Judith E., ed. 32p. (gr. k-1). 1991. wkbk. 1.95 (1-878624-65-2) McClanahan Bk.

Sinclair, Jeff. Go Ahead - Make Me Laugh. Berk, Meridith & Vavrus, Toni. 96p. (gr. 3-8). 1993. pap. 3.95 (0-8069-8443-0) Sterling.

—Kids' Funniest Jokes. Barry, Sheila A., ed. LC 93-23045. 96p. (gr. 2-10). 1993. 12.95 (0-8069-0449-6); pap. write for info. (0-8069-0448-8) Sterling.

—Mathemagic. Blum, Raymond. LC 91-22523. 128p. (gr. 4-11). 1991. 12.95 (0-8069-8354-X) Sterling.

—Mathemagic. Blum, Raymond. LC 91-22523. 128p. (gr. 8 up). 1992. pap. 4.95 (0-8069-8355-8) Sterling.

—On the Road: Fun Travel Games & Activities. Shea, George. 48p. (gr. 3-10). 1992. pap. 4.95 (0-8069-8228-4) Sterling.

—Super Silly Animal Riddles. Ertner, James D. LC 92-41919. 96p. 1993. 12.95 (0-8069-0333-3) Sterling.

—Super Silly Animal Riddles. Ertner, James D. 96p. (gr. 2-7). 1993. pap. 3.95 (0-8069-0334-1) Sterling.

—TV Jokes & Riddles. Bolton, Martha. LC 91-25297. 96p. 1992. pap. 3.95 (0-8069-7246-7) Sterling.

Sinetar, Marsha. Human Rights for Children. Amnesty International, Human Rights for Children Committee Staff. LC 92-35575. 80p. (Orig.). (gr. k-6). 1992. spiral bdg. 12.95 (0-89793-120-3); pap. 10.95 (0-89793-121-1) Hunter Hse.

Sineti, Don. The Whale Watchers' Guide. Gardner, Robert. LC 83-17425. 170p. (gr. 7 up). 1984. lib. bdg. 10.98 (0-671-45811-6, J Messner); pap. 5.95 (0-671-49807-X) S&S Trade.

Sineti, Donald. Grandiosas Criaturas del Mar: Una Introduccion al Mundo de las Ballenas y Otros Cetaceos. Barstow, Robbins. Accent, Inc. Staff, tr. from ENG. (SPA.). 46p. (Orig.). (gr. 7-12). 1988. pap. 5.00 (0-9618858-2-3) Cetacean Society.

—Meet the Great Ones: An Introduction to Whales & Other Cetaceans. Barstow, Robbins. LC 87-70553. 46p. (Orig.). (gr. 7-12). 1987. pap. 5.95 (0-9618858-1-5) Cetacean Society.

—Meet the Great Whales: An Illustrated Introduction to the Marvels of Cetaceans. 2nd ed. Barstow, Robbins. LC 87-70553. 56p. 1993. pap. 8.95 (0-685-67826-1) Parnassus Imprints.

Singer, Alan, jt. illus. see Singer, Arthur.

Singer, Alan D. Birds Do the Strangest Things. Hornblow, Leonora & Hornblow, Arthur. LC 90-8583. 64p. (gr. 2-4). 1991. pap. 3.95 (0-679-81159-1) Random Bks Yng Read.

Singer, Arthur. Families of Birds. Rev. ed. Austin, Oliver L., Jr. (gr. 9 up). 1985. pap. write for info. (0-307-13669-8); pap. write for info. (0-307-24015-0, Golden Pr) Western Pub.

Singer, Arthur & Singer, Alan. State Birds. Buckley, Virginia, text by. LC 86-2209. 64p. (gr. 4 up). 1986. 16.95 (0-525-67177-3, Lodestar Bks); pap. 5.95 (0-525-67314-8, Lodestar Bks) Dutton Child Bks.

Singer, Paula. David Decides about Thumbsucking: A Motivating Story for Children & an Informative Guide for Parents. Heitler, Susan M. LC 85-61019. 52p. (ps-3). 1985. PLB 17.95 (0-9614780-1-2); pap. 9.95 (0-9614780-0-4) Reading Matters.

Sioles, Anna M. & Boethner, Sandra. An Ethics Primer for Children, Honesty - Kindness - Respect: A Catalyst to Discussion. Sioles, Anna M. 83p. (Orig.). (gr. 1-7). 1989. pap. text ed. 7.95x (0-9620893-0-3) Agatha Pub Co.

Siow, Eric. Women in Society: Brazil. Winter, Jane K. LC 92-34403. 1993. Set. write for info. (1-85435-554-6); 22.95 (1-85435-558-9) Marshall Cavendish.

—Women in Society: Mexico. Dubois, Jill. LC 92-34402. 1993. 22.95 (1-85435-557-0); Set. write for info. Marshall Cavendish.

Siow, John. The Making of a Picture Book. Martin, Rodney. LC 88-42911. 32p. (gr. 3-4). 1989. PLB 18.60 (1-55532-958-6) Gareth Stevens Inc.

—Picasso the Green Tree Frog. Graham, Amanda. LC 86-42809. 1987p. (gr. 2-3). 1987. PLB 18.60 (1-55532-152-6) Gareth Stevens Inc.

—There's a Dinosaur in the Park! Martin, Rodney. LC 86-42811. 31p. (gr. 2-3). 1987. PLB 18.60 (1-55532-151-8) Gareth Stevens Inc.

Siracusa, Catherine. Beef Stew. Brenner, Barbara. LC 89-36769. 32p. (Orig.). (ps-1). 1990. lib. bdg. 7.99 (0-394-95046-1); pap. 3.50 (0-394-85046-7) Random Bks Yng Read.

—The Giant Zucchini. Siracusa, Catherine. LC 92-72018. 48p. (gr. k-3). 1993. 10.95 (1-56282-286-1); PLB 10. 89 (1-56282-287-X) Hyprn Child.

—Mike & Tony: Best Friends. Ziefert, Harriet. (ps-3). 1987. pap. 3.50 (0-14-050744-2, Puffin) Puffin Bks.

—Mike & Tony: Best Friends. Ziefert, Harriet. LC 93-25617. (ps-2). 1994. pap. 3.25 (0-14-036853-1, Puffin) Puffin Bks.

—No Mail for Mitchell: A Step 1 Book - Preschool-Gr. 1. Siracusa, Catherine. LC 89-7C010. 32p. (Orig.). (ps-1). 1990. lib. bdg. 7.99 (0-679-90476-X); pap. 2.95 (0-679-80476-5) Random Bks Yng Read.

—A Trip to the Dentist. Linn, Margot. LC 87-14884. 20p. (ps-k). 1988. HarpC Child Bks.

—A Trip to the Doctor. Linn, Margot. LC 87-15004. 20p. (ps-k). 1988. HarpC Child Bks.

Sis, Peter. After Good-Night. Mayper, Monica. LC 86-45766. 32p. (ps-3). 1987. HarpC Child Bks.

—Alphabet Soup. Banks, Kate. LC 87-3191. 32p. (ps-2). 1988. 12.95 (0-394-89151-1) Knopf Bks Yng Read.

—Beach Ball. Sis, Peter. LC 89-2076. 24p. (ps). 1990. 12. 95 (0-688-09181-4); PLB 12.88 (0-688-09182-2) Greenwillow.

—City Night. Rice, Eve. 24p. (ps-1). 1987. 11.75 (0-688-06856-1); PLB 11.88 (0-688-06857-X) Greenwillow.

—The Dragons Are Singing Tonight. Prelutsky, Jack. LC 92-29013. 40p. (ps up). 1993. 15.00 (0-688-09645-X); PLB 14.93 (0-688-12511-5) Greenwillow.

—Follow the Dream. Sis, Peter. LC 90-5392. 40p. (gr. k-5). 1991. 15.00 (0-679-80628-8); lib. bdg. 15.99 (0-679-90628-2) Knopf Bks Yng Read.

—The Ghost in the Noonday Sun. Fleischman, Sid. LC 88-11066. (gr. 5 up). 1989. 11.95 (0-688-08410-9) Greenwillow.

—Halloween: Stories & Poems. Bauer, Caroline F. LC 88-2675. 96p. (gr. 2-5). 1992. pap. 4.95 (0-06-446111-4, Trophy) HarpC Child Bks.

—The Midnight Horse. Fleischman, Sid. LC 89-23441. 84p. (gr. 3 up). 1990. 13.00 (0-688-09441-4) Greenwillow.

—More Stories to Solve. Shannon, George. 64p. (gr. 4 up). 1994. pap. 3.95 (0-688-12947-1, Pub. by Beech Tree Bks) Morrow.

—More Stories to Solve: Fifteen Folktales from Around the World. Shannon, George. LC 89-7413. 64p. (gr. k up). 1991. 12.95 (0-688-09161-X) Greenwillow.

—Rainbow Rhino. reissued ed. Sis, Peter. LC 88-2679. 40p. (ps-2). 1993. pap. 4.99 (0-679-85005-8) Knopf Bks Yng Read.

—Rumpelstiltskin. Noel, Christopher. LC 92-4592. 40p. (gr. k up). 1993. incl. cass. 19.95 (0-88708-280-7, Rabbit Ears); 14.95 (0-88708-279-3, Rabbit Ears) Picture Bk Studio.

—The Scarebird. Fleischman, Sid. LC 87-4099. 32p. (gr. k-3). 1988. 15.00 (0-688-07317-4); lib. bdg. 14.93 (0-688-07318-2) Greenwillow.

—The Scarebird. Fleischman, Sid. 32p. (ps up). 1994. pap. 4.95 (0-688-13105-0, Mulberry) Morrow.

—A Small, Tall Tale from the Far, Far North. Sis, Peter. LC 92-75906. 40p. (gr. k-5). 1993. 15.00 (0-679-84345-0); PLB 15.99 (0-679-94345-5) Knopf Bks Yng Read.

—Still More Stories to Solve: Fifteen Folktales from Around the World. Shannon, George, as told by. LC 93-26529. 1994. write for info. reinforced bdg. (0-688-04619-3) Greenwillow.

—Stories to Solve: Folktales from Around the World. Shannon, George. LC 84-18656. 56p. (gr. 3-5). 1985. 14.00 (0-688-04303-8); PLB 13.93 (0-688-04304-6) Greenwillow.

—Stories to Solve: Folktales from Around the World. Shannon, George. LC 84-18656. 53p. (gr. 4-6). 1991. pap. 4.95 (0-688-10496-7, Pub. by Beech Tree Bks) Morrow.

—The Whipping Boy. Fleischman, Sid. LC 85-17555. 96p. (gr. 2-6). 1986. PLB 15.00 (0-688-06216-4) Greenwillow.

—The Whipping Boy. Fleischman, Sid. (gr. 2-5). 1987. pap. 2.95 (0-8167-1038-4) Troll Assocs.

Sisco, Sam. Singing Fish & Flying Rhinos: Amazing Animal Habits. Owl Magazine Editors. 48p. (gr. 2 up). 1992. pap. 6.95 (0-920775-45-4, Fub. by Greey dePencier CN) Firefly Bks Ltd.

Sisson, Joan. Marigold. Sisson, Joan. 24p. (Orig.). (ps-5). 1988. pap. 4.00 (0-317-93622-0) J Sisson.

Sistare, Betty L. Minicomputer to the Rescue! Keagy, Denita. LC 87-62051. 36p. (gr. k-5). 1987. PLB 10.95 (0-944027-01-6) New Memories.

Sititra. Discovering the Whole You. Thiry, Joan. 64p. (Orig.). (gr. 5-6). 1991. pap. text ed. 6.00 (0-935046-05-4); tchr's. edition 14.00 (0-935046-06-2) Chateau Thierry.

Siu, Emma. Billy the Bean. Buria, Maria E. 36p. (Orig.). (ps-k). 1989. pap. 5.95 (1-878926-04-7) Colorful Lrngs.

Skalski, Margaret. Where Ravens Fly. Marzilli, Vincent, II. 64p. (Orig.). (gr. k-6). 1987. pap. 7.95 (0-9617809-0-8) Vincent Marzilli.

Skar, Cynthia S. Bobbi Saves Christmas! Sharp, Mary. 28p. (Orig.). (gr. 1-4). 1981. pap. 1.89 (0-9603200-1-6) Bobbi Ent.

Skeem, Jeanette. Genesis Fossil Booklet. Skeem, Kenneth A. (gr. 3-12). 1992. pap. text ed. 2.00 (0-9606782-1-2) Behemoth Pub.

Skeeter. The PMS Zone. Brown, Rose M. 80p. (Orig.). 1988. pap. 7.95 (0-9622109-0-0) Skeetoonies.

Skidd, David R. The Gladstone Lakes Mystery. Skidd, David R. 130p. (Orig.). (gr. 4-7). 1993. pap. write for info. (0-9636214-0-8) Midnight Ink.

—The Great Inukin Mystery. Skidd, David R. 142p. (Orig.). (gr. 4-7). 1993. pap. write for info. (0-9636214-1-6) Midnight Ink.

Skidmore, Joan L. You & the Cow. Rose, Phoebe E. LC 91-60008. 20p. (Orig.). (gr. k-6). 1991. pap. 8.50 (0-9630050-0-6) Oregon Info.

Skilbeck, Clare. Dinosaurs at the Supermarket. Camp, Lindsay. LC 92-16936. 32p. (gr. 3-8). 1993. 13.99 (0-670-84802-6) Viking Child Bks.

—Pie in the Sky. Balan, Bruce. 32p. (ps-3). 1993. 13.99 (0-670-85150-7) Viking Child Bks.

Skiles, Janet. Inventioneering. Stanish, Bob & Singletary, Carol. 64p. (gr. 3-9). 1987. pap. 7.95 (0-86653-402-4, GA 1019) Good Apple.

—Math America. Embry, Lynn & Bobo, Betty. 128p. (gr. 4-6). 1987. pap. 11.95 (0-86653-378-8, GA1015) Good Apple.

—Once upon a Felt Board. Chadwick, Roxane. 128p. (gr. k-4). 1986. wkbk. 10.95 (0-86653-338-9, GA 798) Good Apple.

Skivington, Janice. The Fourth Question: A Chinese Folktale. Hamada, Cheryl, retold by. LC 93-18237. 32p. (ps-3). 1993. PLB write for info. (0-516-05144-X) Childrens.

—The Free Pigs. Sanford, Monard G. Bookless, George, ed. LC 86-63205. 21p. (ps-5). 1987. PLB 13.00 (0-940273-00-4) Mill Creek Ent.

—The Girl from the Sky: An Inca Folktale from South America. LC 91-42163. 24p. (ps-3). 1992. PLB 16.93 (0-516-05138-5); pap. 5.95 (0-516-45138-3) Childrens.

—What's in a Box? Boivin, Kelly. LC 91-4062. 32p. (ps-2). 1991. PLB 11.93 (0-516-02010-2); pap. 2.95 (0-516-42010-0) Childrens.

Sklenitzka, Franz S. Ben & the Child of the Forest. Lobe, Mira. 96p. (gr. 3-4). 1988. pap. 2.95 (0-8120-3936-X) Barron.

—Caroline Moves In. Mayer-Skumanz, Lene. 96p. (gr. 1-3). 1988. pap. 2.95 (0-8120-3938-6) Barron.

Skoro, Martin. A Christmas Guest. La Rochelle, David. 32p. (ps-3). 1988. PLB 18.95 (0-87614-325-7); pap. 5.95 (0-87614-506-3) Carolrhoda Bks.

—A Christmas Guest. LaRochelle, David. 32p. (ps-3). 1989. pap. 5.95 (0-685-25636-7, First Ave Edns) Lerner Pubns.

—Count Your Way Through China. Haskins, Jim. 24p. (gr. 1-4). 1988. pap. 5.95 (0-87614-486-5, First Ave Edns) Lerner Pubns.

—Count Your Way Through the Arab World. Haskins, Jim. 24p. (gr. 1-4). 1988. pap. 5.95 (0-87614-487-3, First Ave Edns) Lerner Pubns.

Skrobisz, Jan. Ear Gear: A Student Workbook on Hearing & Hearing Aids. Simko, Carole B. 128p. (gr. 3-6). 1986. 7.95 (0-930323-15-7, Clerc Bks) Gallaudet Univ Pr.

—Wired for Sound: An Advanced Student Workbook on Hearing & Hearing Aids. Simko, Carole B. 149p. (gr. 8-12). 1986. wkbk. 7.95x (0-930323-16-5, Clerc Bks) Gallaudet Univ Pr.

Skurzynski, Gloria. Know the Score: Video Games in Your High-Tech World. Skurzynski, Gloria. LC 93-19470. 64p. (gr. 4 up). 1994. RSBE 16.95 (0-02-782922-7, Bradbury Pr) Macmillan Child Grp.

Slade, Catharine. Little Lost Rabbit. Cowley, Stewart. LC 92-60792. 22p. (ps). 1992. 6.99 (0-89577-445-3) RD Assn.

Slagle, Robert W. Tales of Joshua. 2nd ed. Slagle, Robert W. 230p. (gr. 3). 1992. 14.95 (0-9614218-2-7); pap. 9.95 (0-9614218-1-9) Family Relat.

Slater, Christopher. Big Snowy. Slater, Jim. LC 80-53066. (ps-3). 1981. pap. 1.25 (0-394-84736-9) Random Bks Yng Read.

Slavin, Bill. The Cat Came Back. Slavin, Bill & Tucker, Kathleen, eds. 32p. (gr. 1-6). 1992. 13.95g (0-8075-1097-1) A Whitman.

—Circles: Fun Ideas for Getting A-Round in Math. Ross, Catherine S. LC 92-40159. (gr. 4-7). 1993. pap. 9.57 (0-201-62268-8) Addison-Wesley.

—Extra! Extra! The Who, What, Where, When & Why of Newspapers. Granfield, Linda. LC 93-6929. 1994. write for info. (0-531-06833-1); lib. bdg. write for info. (0-531-08683-6) Orchard Bks Watts.

—How the Second Grade Got 8,205.50 to Visit the Statue of Liberty. Zimelman, Nathan. Mathews, Judith, ed. LC 92-996. 32p. (gr. k-3). 1992. 13.95g (0-8075-3431-5) A Whitman.

—Lemonade Parade. Brooks, Ben. Tucker, Kathleen, ed. LC 91-34870. 32p. (gr. k-3). 1992. PLB 13.95 (0-8075-4432-9) A Whitman.

—Sitting on the Farm. King, Bob. LC 91-17253. 32p. (ps-1). 1992. 13.95 (0-531-05985-5); lib. bdg. 13.99 (0-531-08585-0) Orchard Bks Watts.

Sleight, Katy. First Two Hundred Words in French. Alliance Francaise de Londres Staff, compiled by. LC 93-29562. 1994. 3.95 (*1-85697-954-7*) Kingfisher Bks.
—First Two Hundred Words in German. Khan, Christa. LC 93-29559. 1994. 3.95 (*1-85697-955-5*) Kingfisher Bks.
—First Two Hundred Words in Italian. Tite, Paola. LC 93-29560. 1994. write for info. (*1-85697-956-3*) Kingfisher Bks.
—Fun to Learn French. Grisewood, John. 48p. (gr. 2-5). 1992. 12.95 (*0-531-15241-3*, Warwick); PLB 12.90 (*0-531-19120-6*, Warwick) Watts.
—Fun to Learn Spanish. Grisewood, John. 48p. (gr. 2-5). 1992. 12.95 (*0-531-15242-1*, Warwick); PLB 12.90 (*0-531-19112-5*, Warwick) Watts.
Slifko, Fran, jt. illus. see Steffen, Ann T.
Sliwinska, Sara. Farm: First Readers. Harding, Jacqueline. 28p. (gr. k-1). 1992. 3.50 (*0-7214-1482-6*, 929-1) Ladybird Bks.
—Fun with Science: Practice at Home. Harker, Jillian. 24p. (Orig.). 1992. pap. 2.95 wkbk. (*0-7214-3239-5*, S9115-2) Ladybird Bks.
—The Snowman Flap Book. Briggs, Raymond. 16p. 1991. 7.00 (*0-679-81572-4*) Random Bks Yng Read.
Sloan, Ellen. The Old Witch & Her Magic Basket. DeLage, Ida. 48p. (gr. k-4). 1991. Repr. of 1978 ed. lib. bdg. 12.95 (*0-7910-1475-4*) Chelsea Hse.
—The Old Witch Gets a Surprise. DeLage, Ida. 48p. (gr. k-4). 1991. Repr. of 1981 ed. lib. bdg. 12.95 (*0-7910-1482-7*) Chelsea Hse.
Sloan, Robert, jt. illus. see Sloat, Teri.
Sloat, Teri. The Eye of the Needle. Sloat, Teri, as told by. 32p. (ps-3). 1993. pap. 4.99 (*0-14-054933-1*, Puffin Unicorn) Puffin Bks.
—The Eye of the Needle: Based on a Yupik Tale Told by Betty Huffman. Sloat, Teri, retold by. LC 89-49476. 32p. (ps-3). 1990. 13.95 (*0-525-44623-0*, DCB) Dutton Child Bks.
—From Letter to Letter. Sloat, Teri. LC 89-1135. 32p. (ps up) 1989. 13.95 (*0-525-44518-8*, DCB) Dutton Child Bks.
—From One to One Hundred. Sloat, Teri. LC 91-21948. 32p. 1991. 13.95 (*0-525-44764-4*, DCB) Dutton Child Bks.
Sloat, Teri & Sloat, Robert. The Hungry Giant of the Tundra. Sloat, Teri, retold by. LC 93-12166. 32p. (ps-3). 1993. 14.99 (*0-525-45126-9*, DCB) Dutton Child Bks.
Slobodkin, Louis. Los Cien Vestidos. Estes, Eleanor. 96p. (gr. 4). 1993. 13.95 (*1-880507-06-4*) Lectorum Pubns.
—Hundred Dresses. Estes, Eleanor. LC 44-8963. 32p. (gr. 1-5). 1944. 14.95 (*0-15-237374-8*, HB Juv Bks) HBrace.
—The Hundred Dresses. Estes, Eleanor. LC 73-12940. 80p. (gr. 1-5). 1974. pap. 4.95 (*0-15-642350-2*, Voyager Bks) HBrace.
—Many Moons. Thurber, James. LC 43-51250. (gr. 3-7). 1943. 14.95 (*0-15-251873-8*, HB Juv Bks) HBrace.
—Many Moons. Thurber, James. LC 43-51250. 46p. (gr. 3-7). 1973. pap. 5.95 (*0-15-656980-9*, Voyager Bks) HBrace.
—Moffats. Estes, Eleanor. LC 41-51893. 32p. (gr. 3-7). 1941. 14.95 (*0-15-255095-X*, HB Juv Bks) HBrace.
—Rufus M. Estes, Eleanor. LC 43-51239. (gr. 3-7). 1943. 15.95 (*0-15-269415-3*, HB Juv Bks) HBrace.
—The Space Ship Returns to the Apple Tree. Slobodkin, Louis. LC 93-10747. 128p. (gr. 3-7). 1994. pap. 3.95 (*0-689-71768-7*, Aladdin) Macmillan Child Grp.
—The Space Ship under the Apple Tree. 2nd ed. Slobodkin, Louis. LC 92-42712. 128p. (gr. 3-7). 1993. pap. 3.95 (*0-689-71741-5*, Aladdin) Macmillan Child Grp.
Slobodkina, Esphyr. Caps for Sale. Slobodkina, Esphyr. LC 84-43122. 1947. 13.00 (*0-201-09147-X*); PLB 12. 89 (*0-06-025778-4*) HarpC Child Bks.
—Caps for Sale. Slobodkina, Esphyr. LC 84-43122. 48p. (ps-2). 1987. pap. 3.95 (*0-06-443143-6*, Trophy) HarpC Child Bks.
—Caps for Sale. Slobodkina, Esphyr. (gr. k-3). 1987. incl. cassette 19.95 (*0-87499-059-9*); pap. 12.95 incl. cassette (*0-87499-058-0*); 4 paperbacks, cassette & guide 27.95 (*0-87499-060-2*) Live Oak Media.
—The Little Fireman. Brown, Margaret W. LC 84-43127. 40p. 1952. 11.95 (*0-201-09261-1*) HarpC Child Bks.
—The Little Fireman. new ed. Brown, Margaret W. LC 92-17571. 40p. (ps-3). 1993. 12.00 (*0-06-021476-7*); PLB 11.89 (*0-06-021477-5*) HarpC Child Bks.
Slonim, David, jt. illus. see Dugan, Terry.
Slote, Elizabeth. Nelly's Garden. Slote, Elizabeth. LC 90-33382. 32p. (ps-1). 1991. 13.95 (*0-688-10013-9*, Tambourine Bks); PLB 13.88 (*0-688-10014-7*, Tambourine Bks) Morrow.
—Nelly's Grannies. Slote, Elizabeth. LC 91-32600. 32p. (ps up) 1993. 14.00 (*0-688-11314-1*, Tambourine Bks); PLB 13.93 (*0-688-11315-X*, Tambourine Bks) Morrow.
Small, Carol B. Art Concepts for Children. Small, Carol B. LC 89-14917. 112p. (Orig.). (gr. 6 up). 1989. pap. 8.95 (*0-938267-04-3*) Bold Prodns.
—Handmade Christmas Gifts That Are Actually Usable. Brown, Ann. LC 87-31993. 75p. (Orig.). (gr. k-6). 1987. pap. 6.95 (*0-938267-03-5*) Bold Prodns.
—How to Improve Your Mind over Summer Vacation. Bold, Mary. 65p. (gr. 4-6). 1987. wkbk. 6.95 (*0-938267-05-1*) Bold Prodns.
—Publish Your Own Book: A Resource Book for Young Authors. Bold, Mary. LC 86-91615. 36p. (Orig.). (gr. 5 up). 1986. pap. 6.95 (*0-938267-02-7*) Bold Prodns.

—Travel-Ogs: The Do-It-Yourself Survival Kit for Traveling with Parents, Siblings, & Dirty Socks. Brown, Ann & Bold, Mary. 80p. (Orig.). (gr. 1-6). 1988. wkbk. 6.95 (*0-938267-06-X*) Bold Prodns.
Small, David. As: A Surfeit of Similes. Juster, Norton. LC 88-8449. 80p. 1989. 9.95 (*0-688-08139-8*); PLB 9.88 (*0-688-08140-1*, Morrow Jr Bks) Morrow Jr Bks.
—Box & Cox. Chetwin, Grace. LC 88-35337. 32p. (gr. k-3). 1990. SBE 13.95 (*0-02-718314-9*, Bradbury Pr) Macmillan Child Grp.
—The Christmas Box. Merriam, Eve. LC 85-5666. 32p. (ps-3). 1985. 12.95 (*0-688-05255-X*); lib. bdg. 12.88 (*0-688-05256-8*, Morrow Jr Bks) Morrow Jr Bks.
—Company's Coming. Yorinks, Arthur. LC 87-13579. (ps-3). 1988. 12.95 (*0-517-56751-2*) Crown Bks Yng Read.
—Company's Coming. Yorinks, Arthur. LC 87-13579. 32p. (ps-2). 1992. pap. 4.99 (*0-517-58858-7*) Crown Bks Yng Read.
—Fighting Words. Merriam, Eve. 32p. (gr. k up) 1992. 15.00 (*0-688-09676-X*); PLB 14.93 (*0-688-09677-8*) Morrow Jr Bks.
—Imogene's Antlers. Small, David. LC 84-12085. 32p. (ps-2). 1988. 12.95 (*0-517-55564-6*); pap. 3.95 (*0-517-56242-1*) Crown Bks Yng Read.
—The King Has Horse's Ears. Thomson, Peggy. (gr. 2 up). 1988. pap. 12.95 (*0-671-64953-1*, S&S BFYR) S&S Trade.
—The Money Tree. Stewart, Sarah. 32p. (gr. k up). 1991. 14.95 (*0-374-35014-0*) FS&G.
—Petey's Bedtime Story. Cleary, Beverly. LC 92-6184. 32p. (gr. k up). 1993. 15.00 (*0-688-10660-9*); PLB 14. 93 (*0-688-10661-7*) Morrow Jr Bks.
—Ruby Mae Has Something to Say. Small, David. LC 91-33785. 40p. (ps-4). 1992. 12.00 (*0-517-58248-1*); PLB 12.99 (*0-517-58249-X*) Crown Bks Yng Read.
Small, Terry. The Pied Piper of Hamelin. rev. ed. Browning, Robert. 47p. (gr. 1 up). 1988. 10.95 (*0-15-200566-8*, Gulliver Bks) HarBrace.
—Tails, Claws, Fangs & Paws: An Alpha Beast Caper. Small, Terry. 32p. (ps-3). 1990. 13.95 (*0-553-05852-5*) Bantam.
Smalley, Guy. My Very Own Book of ABCs. 32p. (ps-2). 1989. 9.95 (*0-929793-02-1*) Camex Bks Inc.
—My Very Own Book of Mother Goose Animals. 24p. (ps-2). 1989. 9.95 (*0-929793-01-3*) Camex Bks Inc.
—My Very Own Book of Numbers. 28p. (ps-2). 1989. 9.95 (*0-929793-00-5*) Camex Bks Inc.
—My Very Own Book of Sizes. 24p. (ps-2). 1989. 9.95 (*0-929793-04-8*) Camex Bks Inc.
—My Very Own Book of Toys. 24p. (ps-2). 1989. 9.95 (*0-929793-03-X*) Camex Bks Inc.
—My Very Own Book of What's for Lunch. 24p. (ps-2). 1989. 9.95 (*0-929793-05-6*) Camex Bks Inc.
Smallman, Steve. One to Ten. Randall, Ronne P. 24p. (ps). 1987. pap. 1.25 (*0-7214-9554-0*, S871-10) Ladybird Bks.
—Opposites. Randall, Ronne P. 24p. (ps). 1987. pap. 1.25 (*0-7214-9556-7*, S871) Ladybird Bks.
Smallwood, James. Map Rap: A Fun Way to Learn Geography Through Rap. Jones, Earl, Sr. Coleman, Booker T., intro. by. LC 90-84037. 60p. (Orig.). (gr. 2-12). 1990. pap. 12.75 (*0-935132-18-X*) C H Fairfax.
Smallwood, Laurie. Rhinoceros Success. 25th ed. Alexander, Scott. LC 80-51648. 123p. (Orig.). (gr. 1 up). 1985. pap. 7.95 (*0-937382-00-0*) Rhinos Pr.
Smallwood, Steve. Chrisgopher Columbus in Stowaway on the Santa Maria. Cecil, Terry & Cecil, Barbara. 32p. (Orig.). (gr. k-6). 1992. PLB 4.00 (*0-9633016-0-8*) Infiniti.
Smath, Jerry. But No Elephants. Smath, Jerry. LC 79-16136. 48p. (ps-3). 1979. 5.95 (*0-8193-1007-7*); PLB 5.95 (*0-8193-1008-5*) Parents.
—But No Elephants. Smath, Jerry. 48p. (ps-2). 1991. pap. 2.95 (*0-448-41078-8*, G&D) Putnam Pub Group.
—The Clown-Arounds. Cole, Joanna. LC 81-4662. 48p. (ps-3). 1981. 5.95 (*0-8193-1059-X*); PLB 5.95 (*0-8193-1060-3*) Parents.
—The Clown-Arounds. Cole, Joanna. 48p. (ps-2). 1992. pap. 2.95 (*0-448-40321-8*, G&D) Putnam Pub Group.
—The Clown-Arounds Go on Vacation. Cole, Joanna. LC 83-13480. 48p. (ps-3). 1984. 5.95 (*0-8193-1120-0*) Parents.
—The Clown-Arounds Go on Vacation. Cole, Joanna. LC 93-15471. 1993. write for info. (*0-8368-0966-1*) Gareth Stevens Inc.
—The Clown-Arounds Have a Party. Cole, Joanna. LC 82-2128. 48p. (ps-3). 1982. 5.95 (*0-8193-1085-9*); PLB 5.95 (*0-8193-1086-7*) Parents.
—The Country Mouse & the City Mouse: "Christmas Is Where the Heart Is" Fisher, Maxine P. LC 93-26488. 1994. write for info. (*0-679-84684-0*) Random Bks Yng Read.
—Double-Header. Herman, Gail. LC 92-34175. 32p. (ps-1). 1993. pap. 3.50 (*0-448-40157-6*, G&D) Putnam Pub Group.
—Elephant Goes to School. Smath, Jerry. LC 83-23823. 48p. (ps-3). 1984. 5.95 (*0-8193-1126-X*) Parents.
—Get Well, Clown-Arounds! Cole, Joanna. LC 82-8148. 48p. (ps-3). 1983. 5.95 (*0-8193-1095-6*); PLB 5.95 (*0-8193-1096-4*) Parents.
—Helicopters. 12p. (ps). 1992. bds. 3.95 (*0-448-41093-1*, G&D) Putnam Pub Group.
—The Housekeeper's Dog. Smath, Jerry. LC 80-10580. 48p. (ps-3). 1980. 5.95 (*0-8193-1023-9*); PLB 5.95 (*0-8193-1024-7*) Parents.
—Jumbo Jet. 12p. (ps). 1992. bds. 3.95 (*0-448-41094-X*, G&D) Putnam Pub Group.

—Never Mail an Elephant. Thaler, Mike. LC 93-14395. 32p. (ps-3). 1993. PLB 9.89 (*0-8167-3303-1*); pap. text ed. 2.95 (*0-8167-3304-X*) Troll Assocs.
—One Windy Day. Caraway, Jane. 24p. (ps-2). 1990. PLB 14.60 (*0-8172-3579-5*); PLB 10.95 3 bk. set (*0-685-67712-5*) Raintree Steck-V.
—Peek-a-Bug. LC 89-61381. 14p. (ps). 1990. pap. 3.99 (*0-679-80139-1*) Random Bks Yng Read.
—Pretzel & Pop's Closetful of Stories. Smath, Jerry. 64p. (gr. 1-3). 1991. 13.95 (*0-671-72232-8*); PLB 14.98 (*0-671-72231-X*) Silver Pr.
—Sing a Whale Song. Chapin, Tom & Forster, John. 32p. 1993. incl. cass. 14.00 (*0-679-83478-8*) Random Bks Yng Read.
—The Smallest Elf. Ingle, Annie. LC 90-30388. 32p. (Orig.). (ps-1). 1990. pap. 2.25 (*0-679-80846-9*) Random Bks Yng Read.
—The Smallest Elf's Big Surprise. Ingle, Annie. LC 91-67670. 22p. (ps-1). 1992. bds. 2.95 (*0-679-83380-3*) Random Bks Yng Read.
—Space Shuttle. 12p. (ps). 1992. bds. 3.95 (*0-448-41095-8*, G&D) Putnam Pub Group.
—Sweet Dreams, Clown-Arounds. Cole, Joanna. LC 85-6348. 48p. (ps-3). 1985. 5.95 (*0-8193-1138-3*) Parents.
—Sweet Dreams, Clown-Arounds. Cole, Joanna. LC 93-13038. 1994. PLB 13.27 (*0-8368-0976-9*) Gareth Stevens Inc.
—Uses for Mooses & Other Popular Pets. Thaler, Mike. LC 93-25542. 32p. (ps-3). 1993. PLB 9.89 (*0-8167-3301-5*); pap. text ed. 2.95 (*0-8167-3302-3*) Troll Assocs.
—Wheels on the Bus. Grosset & Dunlap Staff. 18p. (ps) 1991. bds. 2.95 (*0-448-40124-X*, G&D) Putnam Pub Group.
Smedley, Chris. Phantasmagoria. Umansky, Kaye. 64p. (gr. 2-6). 14.95 (*0-7136-3072-8*, Pub. by A&C Black UK) Talman.
Smee, Nicola. Down in the Woods. rev. ed. Smee, Nicola. 32p. (gr. k-2). 1989. Repr. of 1985 ed. lib. bdg. 10.50 (*1-878363-00-X*) Forest Hse.
—The Tusk Fairy. Smee, Nicola. LC 93-28444. 32p. (ps-2). 1993. PLB 14.95 (*0-8167-3311-2*); pap. 3.95 (*0-8167-3312-0*) Troll Assocs.
Smetana, Margaret. Marny's Ride with the Wind. McKay, Louise & McKay, George. (gr. k-3). 1979. 6.95 (*0-934986-00-2*) New Harbinger.
Smith, A. G. A Coloring Book of Stained Glass Windows from the Cathedral of St. John the Divine. Smith, A. G. (gr. 1-6). 1983. pap. 2.95 (*0-915075-00-8*) Cathedral Shop.
Smith, A. G. & Smith, A. G. Christopher Columbus. Rhodes, Bennie. LC 76-5788. (gr. 3-6). 1977. pap. 6.95 (*0-915134-26-8*) Mott Media.
Smith, Al, jt. illus. see Gurtzweiler, Michael.
Smith, Alvin. Mystery of the Fat Cat. Bonham, Frank. 160p. (gr. 5-9). 1971. pap. 1.25 (*0-440-46226-6*, YB) Dell.
Smith, Barry. A Child's Guide to Bad Behavior. Smith, Barry. 32p. (ps). 1991. 9.70 (*0-395-57435-8*, Sandpiper) HM.
—Cumberland Road. Smith, Barry. 32p. (gr. k-3). 1989. 9.70 (*0-395-51739-7*) HM.
—The First Voyage of Christopher Columbus. Smith, Barry. 32p. (ps-3). 1992. 12.95 (*0-670-84051-3*) Viking Child Bks.
—Minnie & Ginger: A Twentieth-Century Romance. Smith, Barry. LC 90-40330. 32p. (ps-3). 1991. 13.95 (*0-517-58253-8*, Clarkson Potter) Crown Bks Yng Read.
Smith, Bill, photos by. A Day in the Life of a School Basketball Coach. Paige, David. LC 80-54101. 32p. (gr. 4-8). 1981. PLB 11.79 (*0-89375-452-8*); cassettes avail. Troll Assocs.
Smith, Bron. Back to School in January. Carroll, Jeri, et al. 144p. (gr. k-5). 1989. wkbk. 11.95 (*0-86653-470-9*, GA1067) Good Apple.
Smith, Cat B. Angel & Me & the Bayside Bombers. Auch, Mary J. (gr. 2-4). 1991. pap. 2.95 (*0-316-05915-3*) Little.
—Chester the Out-of-Work Dog. Singer, Marilyn. LC 92-1141. 32p. (ps-3). 1992. 14.95 (*0-8050-1828-X*, Bks Young Read) H Holt & Co.
—The Closet Gorilla. Weller, Frances W. LC 90-40350. 32p. (gr. k-3). 1991. RSBE 13.95 (*0-02-792531-5*, Macmillan Child Bk) Macmillan Child Grp.
—Critter Sitters. Hiser, Constance. LC 91-23002. 96p. (gr. 3-7). 1992. 13.95 (*0-8234-0928-7*) Holiday.
—Feliciana Feydra LeRoux. Thomassie, Tynia. LC 93-30347. 1994. 14.95 (*0-316-84125-0*) Little.
—General Butterfingers. Gardiner, John R. LC 92-44487. 96p. (gr. 3-7). 1993. pap. 3.99 (*0-14-036355-6*, Puffin Bks.
—Ghosts in Fourth Grade. Hiser, Constance. LC 90-47564. 80p. (gr. 2-5). 1991. 13.95 (*0-8234-0865-5*) Holiday.
—Ghosts in the Fourth Grade. Hiser, Constance. MacDonald, Pat, ed. 80p. 1992. pap. 2.99 (*0-671-75880-2*, Minstrel Bks) PB.
—Good Night, Feet. Morgenstern, Constance. LC 90-42170. 32p. (ps-3). 1991. PLB 14.95 (*0-8050-1453-5*, Bks Young Read) H Holt & Co.
—Grandfather's Wheeliething. Ball, Duncan. LC 93-12524. 1994. pap. 14.00 (*0-671-79817-0*, S&S BFYR) S&S Trade.
—Great Rabbit & the Long-Tailed Wildcat. Gregg, Andy. Grant, Christy, ed. LC 92-22950. 32p. (gr. 1-5). 1993. PLB 13.95 (*0-8075-3047-6*) A Whitman.

—The Latch-Key Dog. Auch, Mary J. LC 93-18604. 1994. 13.95 (*0-316-05916-1*) Little.
—Matthew the Cowboy. Hooker, Ruth. Tucker, Kathy, ed. LC 89-21456. 32p. (ps-2). 1990. PLB 13.95 (*0-8075-4999-1*) A Whitman.
—Max Malone Makes a Million. Herman, Charlotte. LC 90-46373. 80p. (gr. 2-4). 1991. 13.95 (*0-8050-1374-1*, Redfeather BYR) H Holt & Co.
—Max Malone Makes a Million. Herman, Charlotte. LC 90-46373. 64p. (gr. 2-4). 1992. pap. 4.95 (*0-8050-2328-3*, Redfeather BYR) H Holt & Co.
—Max Malone, Superstar. Herman, Charlotte. LC 91-25191. 64p. (gr. 2-4). 1992. 14.95 (*0-8050-1375-X*, Redfeather BYR) H Holt & Co.
—Max Malone the Magnificent. Herman, Charlotte. LC 92-14123. 64p. (gr. 2-4). 1993. PLB 14.95 (*0-8050-2282-1*, Bks Young Read) H Holt & Co.
—Monkey Soup. Sachar, Louis. LC 91-15858. 32p. (ps-3). 1992. 12.00 (*0-679-80297-5*); PLB 13.99 (*0-679-90297-X*) Knopf Bks Yng Read.
—Peter's Trucks. Wolf, Sallie. Levine, Abby, ed. LC 91-19251. 24p. (ps-1). 1992. PLB 13.95 (*0-8075-6519-9*) A Whitman.
—Princess Bee & the Royal Good-Night Story. Asher, Sandy. Mathews, Judith, ed. LC 89-35790. 32p. (ps-1). 1990. 13.95 (*0-8075-6624-1*) A Whitman.
—Scoop Snoops. Hiser, Constance. LC 92-25922. 112p. (gr. 3-7). 1993. 13.95 (*0-8234-1011-0*) Holiday.
Smith, Catherine. Max Malone & the Great Cereal Rip-Off. Herman, Charlotte & Smith, Charlotte B. LC 89-26920. 64p. (gr. 2-4). 1991. 12.95 (*0-8050-1069-6*, Redfeather BYR); pap. 4.95 (*0-8050-1843-3*, Redfeather BYR) H Holt & Co.
Smith, Catherine B. General Butterfingers. Gardiner, John R. 96p. (gr. 3-7). 1986. 13.45 (*0-395-41853-4*) HM.
—My Friend the Doctor: A Read-Together Book for Parents & Children. rev. & updated ed. Watson, Jane W., et al. 32p. (ps up). 1987. pap. 3.50 (*0-517-56485-8*) Crown Bks Yng Read.
—Paul's Volcano. Gormley, Beatrice. LC 86-27543. (gr. 4-6). 1987. 13.95 (*0-395-43079-8*) HM.
Smith, Craig. The Emu Who Wanted to Be a Horse. Dugan, Michael. LC 93-11736. 1994. 4.25 (*0-383-03743-3*) SRA Schl Grp.
—Fat Cat Tompkin. Noonan, Diana. LC 92-34273. 1993. 3.75 (*0-383-03623-2*) SRA Schl Grp.
—Goodness Gracious! Cummings, Phil. LC 91-17473. 32p. (ps-1). 1992. 13.95 (*0-531-05967-7*); lib. bdg. 13.99 (*0-531-08567-8*) Orchard Bks Watts.
—I Know That. Loves, June. LC 92-34262. 1993. 4.25 (*0-383-03633-X*) SRA Schl Grp.
—Our Baby. McIlhenny, Robyn. LC 92-27268. 1993. 3.75 (*0-383-03646-1*) SRA Schl Grp.
—The Stick-Around Cloud. Vaughan, Marcia. LC 93-28962. 1994. 4.25 (*0-383-03777-8*) SRA Schl Grp.
—Trouble with Hairgrow. Watts, Margaret. LC 93-26298. 1994. 4.25 (*0-383-03782-4*) SRA Schl Grp.
Smith, Curtis W. Two Turtles of Paradise: A Love Story for Children & Adults. Logan, Joan S. 20p. (Orig.). 1988. pap. 1.95 (*0-944208-01-0*) Seventh-Wing Pubns.
Smith, Dale. Send Someone to Tell Me. Harner, Ruth. 16p. (gr. k-6). 1988. pap. text ed. 4.25 (*1-55976-135-0*) CEF Press.
Smith, Dan. The Second Dinosaur Action Set. Whyte, Malcolm. 24p. (gr. 7-11). 1988. 5.95 (*0-8431-1951-9*) Price Stern.
—The Story of Nicolet. Brandt, Betty. Nestingen, Jan, ed. 64p. (Orig.). (gr. 3-5). 1991. pap. 6.95 (*0-9622014-3-X*) Beaver Valley.
—Undersea Dinosaur Action Set. Whyte, Malcolm. 24p. (gr. 1 up). 1988. 5.95 (*0-8431-1954-3*) Price Stern.
Smith, Daniel. Dolphins & Whales Model Set. Whyte, Malcolm. 24p. (gr. 1 up). 1992. 5.95 (*0-8431-2993-X*) Price Stern.
Smith, Dennis. The Book of Comparing. Wassermann, Selma & Wassermann, Jack. 32p. (gr. k-3). 1990. lib. bdg. 12.85 (*0-8027-6944-6*); pap. 4.95 (*0-8027-9451-3*) Walker & Co.
—The Book of Deciding. Wassermann, Selma & Wassermann, Jack. LC 89-78073. (gr. k-3). 1990. lib. bdg. 12.85 (*0-8027-6952-7*); pap. 4.95 (*0-8027-9456-4*) Walker & Co.
—The Book of Hypotheses. Wassermann, Selma & Wassermann, Jack. LC 89-78082. 32p. (gr. k-3). 1990. PLB 12.85 (*0-8027-6946-2*); pap. 4.95 (*0-8027-9452-1*) Walker & Co.
—The Book of Imagining. Wassermann, Selma & Wassermann, Jack. LC 89-77869. 32p. (gr. k-3). 1990. PLB 12.85 (*0-8027-6948-9*); pap. 4.95 (*0-8027-9454-8*) Walker & Co.
—The Book of Judging. Wassermann, Selma & Wassermann, Jack. 32p. (gr. k-3). 1990. lib. bdg. 12.85 (*0-8027-6950-0*); pap. 4.95 (*0-8027-9455-6*) Walker & Co.
—The Book of Solving Problems. Wassermann, Selma & Wassermann, Jack. 32p. (gr. k-3). 1990. lib. bdg. 12.85 (*0-8027-6954-3*); pap. 4.95 (*0-8027-9457-2*) Walker & Co.
Smith, Duncan. Andrew McAndrew. Mac Laverty, Bernard. LC 92-52993. 80p. (gr. k-3). 1993. 13.95 (*1-56402-173-4*) Candlewick Pr.
Smith, E. Boyd. The Farm Book. Smith, E. Boyd. 64p. (gr. 3-5). 1982. 15.45 (*0-395-32951-5*) HM.
—The Farm Book. Smith, E. Boyd. 64p. (gr. up). 1990. pap. 6.70 (*0-395-54951-5*) HM.
—The Railroad Book. Smith, E. Boyd. 56p. (gr. 3-5). 1983. 16.45 (*0-395-34832-3*) HM.

—The Seashore Book. Smith, E. Boyd. LC 84-22483. 56p. (gr. k-12). 1985. Repr. of 1912 ed. 13.45 (*0-395-38015-4*) HM.
Smith, Edward J. Two's Company. Cavanna, Betty. 190p. (gr. 5-9). 1951. 7.00 (*0-664-32080-5*, Westminster) Westminster John Knox.
Smith, George W., Jr. & Edwards, Jason. Wall Framing. Chadwick, Charley G., et al. Harrington, Lois G., ed. 72p. (Orig.). (gr. 10-12). 1989. pap. text ed. 8.00 (*0-89606-266-X*, 701); tchr's. key 3.00 (*0-685-27030-0*, 701TK) Am Assn Voc Materials.
Smith, Gerald. Let Me Be the Boss. Bagert, Brod. LC 91-91408. 48p. (gr. 3-7). 1992. 14.95 (*1-56397-099-6*, Wordsong) Boyds Mills Pr.
Smith, Glen. The Not Like Any Other Children's Book, Book. Smith, Louisa & Smith, Glen, eds. 40p. (Orig.). (gr. 2 up). 1982. pap. 8.95 (*0-9609230-0-4*) Smith & Smith Pub.
Smith, Guy & Bull, Peter. Transportation. Mellet, Peter, et al. LC 89-11358. 48p. (gr. 4-5). 1989. PLB 17.27 (*0-8368-0134-2*) Gareth Stevens Inc.
Smith, Guy, et al. Future World. Hillman, Susan, et al. LC 89-42981. 48p. (gr. 4-5). 1989. PLB 17.27 (*0-8368-0015-X*) Gareth Stevens Inc.
Smith, J. A. Mine Will, Said John. Griffith, Helen V. LC 91-32476. 32p. (ps-8). 1992. 14.00 (*0-688-10957-8*); PLB 13.93 (*0-688-10958-6*) Greenwillow.
—Tales from the Jungle Book. Kipling, Rudyard. McKinley, Robin, adapted by. LC 84-11724. 64p. (gr. k-3). 1985. lib. bdg. 8.99 (*0-394-96940-5*) Random Bks Yng Read.
Smith, J. Gerard, photos by. Popcorn Park Zoo. Pfeffer, Wendy. LC 91-3273. 64p. (gr. 2-5). 1992. 14.95 (*0-671-74587-5*, J Messner); lib bdg. 16.98 (*0-671-74589-1*, J Messner) S&S Trade.
Smith, Jan. The Pirate Queen. MacDonald, Marianne. 32p. (ps-3). 1992. incl. dust jacket 12.95 (*0-8120-6288-4*); pap. 5.95 (*0-8120-4952-7*) Barron.
Smith, Jan H. America, I Hear You: A Story about George Gershwin. Mitchell, Barbara. 64p. (gr. 3-6). 1987. PLB 14.95 (*0-87614-309-5*) Carolrhoda Bks.
—Click! A Story about George Eastman. Mitchell, Barbara. (gr. 3-6). 1987. pap. 5.95 (*0-87614-472-5*, First Ave Edns) Lerner Pubns.
Smith, Jean P. Li'l Tuffy & His ABC's. Pajot-Smith, Jean. 64p. (ps-4). 1992. pap. 5.00 (*0-87485-063-0*) Johnson Chi.
Smith, Jesse W. An Old-Fashioned One Two Three Book. Ashton, Elizabeth A. 32p. (ps-3). 1991. 14.95 (*0-670-83499-8*) Viking Child Bks.
—Once upon a Time. Prince, Pamela. LC 87-33359. 48p. (ps up). 1988. 12.95 (*0-517-56832-2*, Harmony) Crown Pub Group.
—The Princess & the Goblin. MacDonald, George. Glassman, Peter, afterword by. LC 86-2532. 208p. (ps up). 1986. 17.95 (*0-688-06604-6*) Morrow Jr Bks.
Smith, Jessie W. At the Back of the North Wind. MacDonald, George. LC 88-63292. 352p. (gr. 5 up). 1989. 17.95 (*0-688-07808-7*) Morrow Jr Bks.
—A Child's Book of Country Stories. Skinner, Ada M. & Skinner, Eleanor L. 224p. (gr. 1-7). 1992. 12.99 (*0-517-69333-X*, Child Classics) Outlet Bk Co.
—A Child's Garden of Verses. Stevenson, Robert Louis. LC 85-12766. 120p. (ps-4). 1905. SBE 17.95 (*0-684-20949-7*, Scribners Young Read) Macmillan Child Grp.
—Little Women. Alcott, Louisa May. (gr. 7 up). 1968. 19.95 (*0-316-03095-3*) Little.
—An Old-Fashioned ABC Book. Ashton, Elizabeth A. 32p. (ps-3). 1990. pap. 14.95 (*0-670-83048-8*) Viking Child Bks.
—An Old-Fashioned ABC Book. Ashton, Elizabeth A. 32p. (ps-3). 1992. pap. 3.99 (*0-14-054189-6*) Puffin Bks.
—Twas the Night Before Christmas: A Visit from St. Nicholas. Moore, Clement C. (ps-2). 1912. 14.95 (*0-395-06952-1*) HM.
—The Water Babies. Kingsley, Charles. 256p. (gr. k-6). 1986. 10.99 (*0-517-61817-6*) Outlet Bk Co.
Smith, Jessie W. & Merrill, Frank. Little Women. Alcott, Louisa May. 400p. (gr. 2 up). 1988. 12.99 (*0-517-63489-9*) Outlet Bk Co.
Smith, Jessie Willcox. An Old-Fashned One Two Three Book. Ashton, Elizabeth Allen. LC 92-21109. 32p. (ps-3). 1993. pap. 4.99 (*0-14-054310-4*) Puffin Bks.
Smith, Jonathan. The Original Three Little Pigs Re-Told. Shearer, Marilyn J. LC 90-60398. 16p. (ps-6). 1990. 19.95 (*0-685-33065-6*); pap. 10.95 (*1-878389-03-3*) L Ashley & Joshua.
Smith, Jos A. The Adventures of King Midas. Banks, Lynne R. LC 92-3795. 160p. (gr. 3 up). 1992. 14.00 (*0-688-10894-6*) Morrow Jr Bks.
Smith, Jos. A. Matthew's Dragon. Cooper, Susan. LC 90-31532. 32p. (ps-3). 1991. SBE 13.95 (*0-689-50512-4*, M K McElderry) Macmillan Child Grp.
Smith, Joseph A. Benjamin Bigfoot. Serfozo, Mary. LC 92-321. 32p. (ps-3). 1993. SBE 14.95 (*0-689-50570-1*, M K McElderry) Macmillan Child Grp.
—Chipmunk! Haas, Jessie. LC 92-30080. 24p. (ps up). 1993. 14.00 (*0-688-11874-7*); PLB 13.93 (*0-688-11875-5*) Greenwillow.
—Danny & the Kings. Cooper, Susan. LC 92-22744. 32p. (ps-3). 1993. SBE 14.95 (*0-689-50577-9*, M K McElderry) Macmillan Child Grp.
—Hercules. Evslin, Bernard. LC 83-23834. 160p. (gr. 5up). 1984. 14.95 (*0-688-02748-2*) Morrow Jr Bks.
—Lady Daisy. King-Smith, Dick. LC 92-21834. 1993. 14. 00 (*0-385-30891-4*) Delacorte.

—Matthew's Dragon. Cooper, Susan. LC 93-26574. 32p. (gr. k-3). 1994. pap. 4.95 (*0-689-71794-6*, Aladdin) Macmillan Child Grp.
—Mowing. Haas, Jessie. LC 92-12240. 32p. (ps up). 1994. write for info. Greenwillow.
—Short Takes: A Collection of Short Stories. Segel, Elizabeth. 160p. (gr. 9 up). 1986. 12.95 (*0-688-06092-7*) Lothrop.
—Starshine & Sunglow. Levin, Betty. LC 93-26672. 1994. write for info. reinforced bdg. (*0-688-12806-8*) Greenwillow.
—Step by Step. Wolkstein, Diane. LC 93-14667. 1994. write for info. (*0-688-10315-4*); PLB write for info. (*0-688-10316-2*) Morrow Jr Bks.
Smith, Joseph A., photos by. Mowing. Haas, Jessie. LC 93-12240. 1994. write for info. (*0-688-11680-9*); lib. bdg. write for info. (*0-688-11681-7*) Greenwillow.
Smith, Juliet S., photos by. The Rocking Horse Secret. Godden, Rumer. (gr. 3-7). 1988. pap. 3.95 (*0-317-69650-5*, Puffin) Puffin Bks.
Smith, Kaitlin. Funny Things Happen. Smith, Kaitlin. 15p. (gr. k-3). 1993. pap. 12.95 (*1-56606-020-6*) Bradley Mann.
—Take a Walk with Me. Smith, Kaitlin. 12p. (gr. k-3). 1993. pap. 10.95 (*1-56606-019-2*) Bradley Mann.
Smith, Kaitlin M. Arizona Is Hot. Smith, Kaitlin M. 14p. (gr. k-3). 1992. pap. 10.95 (*1-895583-18-7*) MAYA Pubs.
—Big Monster Learns about Manners. Smith, Kaitlin M. 18p. (gr. 1-5). 1992. pap. 10.95 (*1-56606-006-0*) Bradley Mann.
—Counting with Buster Bear. Smith, Kaitlin M. 15p. (gr. k-3). 1992. pap. 12.95 (*1-895583-15-2*) MAYA Pubs.
—Going to the Hospital. Smith, Kaitlin M. 18p. (gr. k-3). 1992. pap. 13.95 (*1-895583-17-9*) MAYA Pubs.
—It's Time, Dad. Smith, Kaitlin M. 15p. (gr. k-3). 1992. pap. 15.95 (*1-895583-16-0*) MAYA Pubs.
—Sally Writes a Letter to Santa Claus. Smith, Kaitlin M. 15p. (gr. 1-4). 1992. pap. 10.95 (*1-56606-005-2*) Bradley Mann.
—Skating with Katie. Smith, Kaitlin M. 15p. (gr. k-3). 1992. pap. 11.95 (*1-895583-19-5*) MAYA Pubs.
Smith, Kenneth. The Rebus Bears: Level 1. Reit, Seymour V. 1989. 9.99 (*0-553-05822-3*) Bantam.
Smith, Lane. The Big Pets. Smith, Lane. 32p. (ps-3). 1991. 14.95 (*0-670-83378-9*) Viking Child Bks.
—Flying Jake. Smith, Lane. LC 87-25976. 32p. (ps-3). 1988. RSBE 14.95 (*0-02-785830-8*, Macmillan Child Bk) Macmillan Child Grp.
—The Good, the Bad, & the Goofy. Scieszka, Jon. 64p. (gr. 3-7). 1992. 11.00 (*0-670-84380-6*) Viking Child Bks.
—The Good, the Bad, & the Goofy. Scieszka, Jon. LC 93-15136. 80p. (gr. 2-5). 1993. pap. 3.50 (*0-14-036170-7*, Puffin) Puffin Bks.
—Halloween ABC. Merriam, Eve. LC 86-23772. 32p. (gr. k up). 1987. RSBE 14.95 (*0-02-766870-3*, Macmillan Child Bk) Macmillan Child Grp.
—The Happy Hocky Family. Smith, Lane. 64p. (ps-3). 1993. reinforced bdg. 13.99 (*0-670-85206-6*) Viking Child Bks.
—Knights of the Kitchen Table. Scieszka, Jon. 64p. (gr. 3-7). 1991. 11.00 (*0-670-83622-2*) Viking Child Bks.
—Knights of the Kitchen Table. Scieszka, Jon. 64p. (gr. 2-6). 1993. pap. 3.25 (*0-14-034603-1*, Puffin) Puffin Bks.
—The Not-So-Jolly-Roger. Scieszka, Jon. 64p. (gr. 3-7). 1991. 11.00 (*0-670-83754-7*) Viking Child Bks.
—The Not-So-Jolly Roger. Scieszka, Jon. 64p. (gr. 2-6). 1993. pap. 3.25 (*0-14-034684-8*, Puffin) Puffin Bks.
—The Stinky Cheese Man: And Other Fairly Stupid Tales. Scieszka, Jon. 56p. (gr. 1). 1992. 16.00 (*0-670-84487-X*) Viking Child Bks.
—The True Story of the Three Little Pigs. Scieszka, Jon. 32p. (ps-3). 1989. pap. 15.00 (*0-670-82759-2*) Viking Child Bks.
—The True Story of the Three Little Pigs Gift Set. Wolf, A. Scieszka, Jon & Scieszka, Jon, eds. 32p. (ps-3). 1992. incl. cass. 24.95 (*0-670-89779-5*) Viking Child Bks.
—Your Mother Was a Neanderthal. Scieszka, Jon. 64p. (gr. 2-6). 1993. PLB 10.99 (*0-670-84481-0*) Viking Child Bks.
Smith, Lawrence, photos by. Fishing a Trout Stream. 2nd ed. Connett, Eugene V. (gr. 10 up). 1989. Repr. of 1934 ed. 35.00 (*1-56416-006-8*) Derrydale Pr.
Smith, Lesley. All About Me. Rice, Melanie & Rice, Chris. LC 87-15498. 48p. (ps-3). 1988. PLB 11.99 (*0-385-24282-4*); pap. 10.95 (*0-385-24281-6*) Doubleday.
Smith, Lesley, et al. Start with Rhymes, Nos. 7-12: Little Miss Muffett; Baa Baa Black Sheep; 1, 2 Buckle My Shoe; Rain; In a Dark Dark Wood & Round the Moon, 6 bks. Warlow, Aidan, ed. 48p. (Orig.). (gr. k-1). 1988. Set. pap. text ed. 29.60 (*1-55624-518-1*) Wright Group.
Smith, Linda G. Gramma's Stories & Rhymes for Little Christians. Lang, Margaret A. 104p. (ps-5). 1982. 9.95 (*0-685-42235-6*) Lang Pubns.
Smith, Linda J. Three Little Kittens. Smith, Linda J. LC 90-5102. 32p. (ps-1). 1991. 13.95 (*0-8249-8490-0*, Ideals Child) Hambleton-Hill.
Smith, Louise. Where Indians Live: American Indian Houses. Nashone. 37p. (Orig.). (gr. k-6). 1989. pap. 6.95 (*0-940113-16-3*) Sierra Oaks Pub.

Smith, M. Kathryn. Ellie's Day. Conlin, Susan & Friedman, Susan L. Illsley-Clarke, Jean, intro. by. LC 89-60334. 32p. (Orig.). (ps-2) 1989. PLB 16.95 (0-943990-45-9); pap. 5.95 (0-943990-44-0) Parenting Pr.
—Nathan's Day. Conlin, Susan & Friedman, Susan L. LC 90-62679. 32p. (Orig.). (ps-k). 1991. lib. bdg. 16.95 (0-943990-61-0); pap. 5.95 (0-943990-60-2) Parenting Pr.
Smith, Marianne. The Old Witch & the Crows. DeLage, Ida. 48p. (gr. k-4). 1991. Repr. of 1983 ed. lib. bdg. 12.95 (0-7910-1476-2) Chelsea Hse.
Smith, Mark D. Bellyful of Ballet. Mallett, Jerry & Bartch, Marian. 56p. (gr. 2-5). 1986. PLB 7.35 (0-8479-9926-2, 027155) Perma-Bound.
—Close the Curtains. Mallett, Jerry & Bartch, Marian. 54p. (gr. 2-5). 1986. PLB 7.35 (0-8479-9927-0, 056115) Perma-Bound.
—First-Last Gravelsburg Elementary School Spelling Bee. Mallett, Jerry & Bartch, Marian. 55p. (gr. 2-5). 1986. PLB 7.35 (0-8479-9928-9, 101440) Perma-Bound.
—Goodbye to Camp Crumb. Mallett, Jerry & Bartch, Marian. 59p. (gr. 2-5). 1986. PLB 7.35 (0-8479-9929-7, 120950) Perma-Bound.
—The Mystery at Chung's Chinese Restaurant. Mallett, Jerry & Bartch, Marian. 61p. (gr. 4-7). 1987. PLB 7.65 (0-8000-1699-8, 207909) Perma-Bound.
—Mystery at Madame Darkle's Wax Museum. Mallett, Jerry & Bartch, Marian. 57p. (gr. 4-7). 1987. PLB 7.65 (0-8000-0506-6, 207916) Perma-Bound.
—Mystery at the Hollender Hotel. Mallett, Jerry & Bartch, Marian. 57p. (gr. 4-7). 1987. PLB 7.65 (0-8000-0507-4, 207918) Perma-Bound.
—Mystery at the Laff-a-Lott Amusement Park. Mallett, Jerry & Bartch, Marian. 59p. (gr. 4-7). 1987. PLB 7.65 (0-8000-0509-0, 207923) Perma-Bound.
—Mystery at the Seesaw Cinema Company. Mallett, Jerry & Bartch, Marian. 60p. (gr. 4-7). 1987. PLB 7.65 (0-8000-0508-2, 207922) Perma-Bound.
—On Your Mark...Get Set... Help! Mallett, Jerry & Bartch, Marian. 55p. (gr. 2-5). 1986. PLB 7.35 (0-8479-9931-9, 222340) Perma-Bound.
Smith, Martha. Arabella the Itchy Witch. Smith, Martha. Graves, Helen, ed. LC 85-40893. 86p. (gr. 3 up). 1986. 6.95 (1-55523-007-5) Winston-Derek.
Smith, Mary D., jt. illus. see Cracchiolo, Rachelle.
Smith, Mary D., jt. illus. see Crachiolo, Rachelle.
Smith, Matthew V. Billy Jean. Smith, Matthew V. 14p. (gr. k-3). 1993. pap. 9.95 (1-895583-57-8) MAYA Pubs.
—Clowns Are People Too. Smith, Matthew V. 12p. (gr. 1-3). 1992. pap. 11.95 (1-56606-010-9) Bradley Mann.
—Flip the Cat. Smith, Matthew V. 10p. (gr. k-3). 1993. pap. 10.95 (1-56606-013-3) Bradley Mann.
—Fun Time with Bonzo. Smith, Matthew V. 12p. (gr. k-3). 1992. pap. 11.95 (1-56606-014-1) Bradley Mann.
—Harold Gets a New Bike. Smith, Matthew V. 12p. (gr. k-3). 1993. pap. 11.95 (1-56606-014-1) Bradley Mann.
—Harvey Takes a Ride to the Park. Smith, Matthew V. 15p. (gr. k-3). 1992. pap. 10.95 (1-895583-05-5) MAYA Pubs.
—An Invitation to Sally's. Smith, Matthew V. 18p. (gr. k-3). 1992. pap. 12.95 (1-895583-07-1) MAYA Pubs.
—Jennie Learns to Drive. Smith, Matthew V. 15p. (gr. k-3). 1992. pap. 12.95 (1-895583-30-6) MAYA Pubs.
—A Penny for the Gum Machine. Smith, Matthew V. 12p. (gr. k-3). 1992. pap. 9.95 (1-895583-09-8) MAYA Pubs.
—Ralph's Funtime. Smith, Matthew V. 17p. (gr. k-3). 1992. pap. 19.95 (1-895583-08-X) MAYA Pubs.
—Shapes & Colours. Smith, Matthew V. 12p. 1992. pap. 4.95 (1-895583-03-9) MAYA Pubs.
—Time for Learning Colors. Smith, Matthew V. 12p. (gr. k-3). 1993. pap. 10.95 (1-895583-55-1) MAYA Pubs.
—Wake Up, Mommy. Smith, Matthew V. 15p. (gr. 1-3). 1992. pap. 10.95 (1-56606-009-5) Bradley Mann.
—What's a Right Turn. Smith, Matthew V. 13p. (gr. k-3). 1993. pap. 11.95 (1-895583-56-X) MAYA Pubs.
—When Not to Say Help. Smith, Matthew V. 16p. (gr. k-3). 1992. pap. 11.95 (1-895583-34-9) MAYA Pubs.
—When to Say Help. Smith, Matthew V. 18p. (gr. k-3). 1992. pap. 11.95 (1-895583-33-0) MAYA Pubs.
—Where Are All the Children. Smith, Matthew V. 10p. (gr. 1-2). 1992. pap. 12.95 (1-56606-002-8) Bradley Mann.
—Where Do We Go from Here? Smith, Matthew V. 15p. (gr. k-3). 1992. pap. 11.95 (1-895583-35-7) MAYA Pubs.
—Where Is All the Honey? Smith, Matthew V. 17p. (gr. k-3). 1992. pap. 13.95 (1-895583-31-4) MAYA Pubs.
—Why Do Clowns Smile? Smith, Matthew V. 14p. (gr. k-3). 1992. pap. 14.95 (1-895583-06-3) MAYA Pubs.
Smith, Mavis. Bob & Shirley: A Tale of Two Lobsters. Ziefert, Harriet. LC 90-43150. 32p. (gr. k-3). 1991. PLB 11.89 (0-06-026908-1); pap. 3.95 (0-06-107427-6) HarpC Child Bks.
—Can You Play: Stewart. Ziefert, Harriet. LC 88-24025. 24p. (Orig.). (ps-2). 1989. pap. 2.25 (0-394-82001-0) Random Bks Yng Read.
—Come out, Jessie! Ziefert, Harriet. LC 90-41880. 32p. (ps-1). 1991. pap. 4.95 (0-06-107414-4) HarpC Child Bks.
—Come Visit My House! Three Books Inside: My Mommy; My Daddy; My Puppy, 3 bks. Ziefert, Harriet. (ps-1). 1992. Set. bds. 12.00 (0-670-84485-3) Viking Child Bks.

—Dinner's Ready, Jessie! Ziefert, Harriet. LC 90-55149. 32p. (ps-1). 1991. pap. 4.95 (0-06-107402-0) HarpC Child Bks.
—Going on a Lion Hunt. Ziefert, Harriet. 20p. (ps). 1989. pap. 5.99 (0-14-054083-0, Puffin) Puffin Bks.
—Harry Gets Ready for School. Ziefert, Harriet. 32p. (ps-3). 1991. 8.95 (0-670-83861-6) Viking Child Bks.
—Harry Gets Ready for School. 32p. (ps-3). 1991. pap. 3.50 (0-14-054388-0, Puffin) Puffin Bks.
—Harry Gets Ready for School. Ziefert, Harriet. (ps-2). 1993. pap. 3.25 (0-14-036539-7, Puffin) Puffin Bks.
—Harry Goes to Day Camp. Ziefert, Harriet. 32p. (ps-3). 1990. pap. 3.50 (0-14-054223-X, Puffin) Puffin Bks.
—Harry Goes to Fun Land. Ziefert, Harriet. LC 88-62146. 32p. (ps-3). 1989. pap. 3.50 (0-14-050980-1, Puffin) Puffin Bks.
—Harry Takes a Bath. Ziefert, Harriet. (ps-3). 1987. pap. 8.95 (0-670-81721-X, Puffin); pap. 3.50 (0-14-050746-9, Puffin) Puffin Bks.
—Harry Takes a Bath. Ziefert, Harriet. LC 93-2718. (ps-2). 1993. pap. 3.25 (0-14-036537-0, Puffin) Puffin Bks.
—I Want to Sleep in Your Bed! Ziefert, Harriet. LC 90-4456. 36p. (ps-1). 1990. HarpC Child Bks.
—In a Scary Old House. Ziefert, Harriet. 20p. (ps). 1989. pap. 5.95 (0-14-054082-2, Puffin) Puffin Bks.
—It's about Time. Anastasio, Dina. 24p. (gr. k-3). 1993. 8.95 (0-448-40551-2, G&D) Putnam Pub Group.
—Let's Get a Pet. Ziefert, Harriet. 40p. (ps-5). 1993. PLB 13.50 (0-670-84550-7) Viking Child Bks.
—My Birthday Story Album. Ziefert, Harriet. 10p. (ps-2). 1993. 6.95 (0-694-00445-6, Festival) HarpC Child Bks.
—My Christmas Story Album. Ziefert, Harriet. 10p. (ps up). 1992. 6.95 (0-694-00430-8, Festival) HarpC Child Bks.
—My Getting-Ready-for-Bed Book. Ziefert, Harriet. LC 89-62012. 12p. (ps-1). 1990. 13.95 (0-694-00299-2) HarpC Child Bks.
—A Snake Mistake. Smith, Mavis. LC 90-43152. 32p. (gr. k-3). 1991. PLB 11.89 (0-06-026909-X); pap. 3.95 (0-06-107426-8) HarpC Child Bks.
—What Do I Taste: The Five Senses. Ziefert, Harriet. (ps-1). 1988. pap. 3.95 (0-317-69282-8) Bantam.
—When the TV Broke. Ziefert, Harriet. LC 92-47097. (ps-2). 1993. pap. 3.25 (0-14-036540-0, Puffin) Puffin Bks.
—You Can't Smell a Flower with Your Ear. Cole, Joanna. LC 93-27264. 1994. write for info. (0-448-40469-9, G&D); pap. write for info. (0-448-40470-2, G&D) Putnam Pub Group.
Smith, Merle. Los Dinosaurios Gigantes (Giant Dinosaurs) Rowe, Erna. Palacios, Argentina, tr. 32p. (ps-2). 1995. 3.95 (0-590-40647-7) Scholastic Inc.
—Giant Dinosaurs. Rowe, Erna. (gr. k-3). 1975. pap. 2.95 (0-590-40262-5) Scholastic Inc.
Smith, Nancy. The Chester Town Tea Party. Seabrooke, Brenda. 30p. (gr. k-5). 1991. 8.95 (0-87033-422-0) Tidewater.
Smith, Page. Florence the Goose: A True Story for Children of All Ages. Lee, Paul A. 47p. 1992. 14.95 (0-937011-51-7) Platonic Acad Pr.
Smith, Patti, jt. illus. see Menefee, Paige.
Smith, Patty. Mango Days: A Teen-Ager Facing Eternity Reflects on the Beauty of Life. Smith, Patty. Smith, Kit, intro. by. LC 92-10039. 135p. (Orig.). (gr. 9-12). 1992. lib. bdg. 17.95 (0-932727-59-X); pap. 11.95 (0-932727-58-1) Hope Pub Hse.
Smith, Pauline. The Risks of RO - Episode 4: Child's Play. Avery, Louisia. Wimberly, Potice & Andrews, Dianne, eds. 110p. (Orig.). 1988. pap. text ed. 5.95 (0-945779-03-8) Ethnic Role Model.
Smith, Phil. Cinderella. new ed. Perrault, Charles. LC 78-18067. 32p. (gr. k-3). 1979. PLB 9.79 (0-89375-120-0); pap. 1.95 (0-89375-098-0) Troll Assocs.
—No Need for Alarm. McKissack, Patricia & McKissack, Fredrick. LC 88-60388. 32p. (Orig.). (gr. 1-3). 1990. text ed. 8.95 (0-88335-783-6); pap. text ed. 4.95 (0-88335-795-X) Milliken Pub Co.
Smith, R. F. Just Lookin' Around. Wilkie, E. Cleve. Rogers, Dennis, intro. by. 224p. (Orig.). 1987. pap. 10. 00 (0-9617969-0-1) E C Wilkie.
Smith, Ralph L. Etienne Provost: Man of the Mountains. Tykal, Jack B. Smith, Monte, ed. Gowans, Fred, intro. by. 256p. (gr. 9 up). 1989. 15.95 (0-943604-24-9); pap. 9.95 perfect bdg. (0-943604-23-0) Eagles View.
Smith, Richard. Tilda's Treat: A New Way to Eat. Kelly, Karen & Hopkins, Joan. LC 74-15232. 128p. (gr. 6-12). 1975. pap. 2.95 (0-87983-091-3) Keats.
Smith, Rick. The Legend of the Cherokee Rose. Bailey, John B. Griffin, James D., Jr., ed. 10p. (Orig.). (gr. k-8). 1991. pap. 9.79 (0-9628023-1-X) J Laina Pub.
Smith, Robin A. Toot-in-Time Band: Introducing Children to the World of Music. Mercuri, Carmela. (Orig.). (gr. k-1). 1993. pap. 10.95 (0-935474-21-8) Carousel Pub Corp.
Smith, Roger. The Trickster's Handbook. Eldin, Peter. LC 89-32073. 96p. (gr. 3-10). 1991. pap. 3.95 (8069-5741-7) Sterling.
Smith, Ron & Murchison, Leon. Forty Acres; Little Jess & the Circus; Jubilee Day. 2nd ed. Shepard, Mary L. & Gaines, Edith. McCluskey, John A., ed. (gr. 4-7). 1993. pap. 3.00 (0-91367B-26-0) New Day Pr.
Smith, Sally. Grandfather Four Winds & Rising Moon. Chanin, Michael. LC 93-2689. 1994. 14.95 (0-915811-47-2) H J Kramer Inc.

Smith, Stephen J. Shy Vi. Lewison, Wendy C. LC 91-39658. 40p. (ps-2). 1993. pap. 9.99 14.00 JRT (0-671-76968-5, S&S BFYR) S&S Trade.
Smith, Ted. Hare & Bear. Frankel, Julie. McKissack, Patricia & McKissack, Fredrick, eds. LC 87-61647. 32p. (Orig.). (gr. 1-3). 1987. text ed. 8.95 (0-88335-724-0); pap. text ed. 4.95 (0-88335-744-5) Milliken Pub Co.
—Hare & Bear Go Shopping. Frankel, Julie. McKissack, Patricia & McKissack, Fredrick, eds. LC 88-60394. 32p. (Orig.). (gr. 1-3). 1990. text ed. 8.95 (0-88335-778-X); pap. text ed. 4.95 (0-88335-790-9) Milliken Pub Co.
Smith, Tom. Northwest Indian Coloring Book. Smith, Tom & Smith, Diane. 32p. (gr. 1-4). 1993. pap. 3.99 (0-8431-3491-7) Troubador Pr.
Smith, Tony. The Builder Through History. Wood, Richard. LC 93-24398. 48p. (gr. 5-8). 1994. 15.95 (1-56847-102-5) Thomson Lrning.
—The Farmer Through History. Chrisp, Peter. LC 92-38485. 48p. (gr. 5-8). 1993. 15.95 (1-56847-011-8) Thomson Lrning.
—The Great Pyramids & the Sphinx. 48p. (gr. 3-5). 1987. 7.95x (0-86685-454-1) Intl Bk Ctr.
—Roman Stories. Hull, Robert. LC 93-29996. 48p. (gr. 5-9). 1993. 15.95 (1-56847-105-X) Thomson Lrning.
—The Sailor Through History. Coote, Roger. LC 92-43640. 48p. (gr. 5-8). 1993. 15.95 (1-56847-012-6) Thomson Lrning.
—The Soldier Through History. Chrisp, Peter. LC 92-40639. 48p. (gr. 5-8). 1993. 15.95 (1-56847-010-X) Thomson Lrning.
—The Treasures of Tutankhamen. 48p. (gr. 3-5). 1987. 7. 95x (0-86685-453-3) Intl Bk Ctr.
—Viking Longboats. Mulvihill, Margaret. LC 89-31565. 32p. (gr. 3-6). 1989. PLB 12.40 (0-531-17168-X, Gloucester Pr) Watts.
Smith, Tony & Wheele, Steve. The Inventor Through History. Lafferty, Peter & Rowe, Julian. 48p. 1993. 15. 95 (1-56847-013-4) Thomson Lrning.
Smith, Wendy. The Blood-&-Thunder Adventure on Hurricane Peak. Mahy, Margaret. LC 89-8098. 144p. (gr. 4-7). 1989. SBE 13.95 (0-689-50488-8, M K McElderry) Macmillan Child Grp.
—The Blood-&-Thunder Adventure on Hurricane Peak. large type ed. Mahy, Margaret. 192p. (gr. 3-7). 1990. 13.95 (0-7451-1230-7, Galaxy Child Lrg Print) Chivers N Amer.
—Hector the Bully. Priestley, Dinah. 24p. (gr. 3-5). 1989. PLB 17.50 (0-87614-356-7) Carolrhoda Bks.
—Keeping House. Mahy, Margaret. LC 90-37591. 32p. (gr. k-4). 1991. SBE 13.95 (0-689-50515-9, M K McElderry) Macmillan Child Grp.
—The Mouse Butcher. King-Smith, Dick. 144p. (gr. 3-7). 1992. pap. 3.99 (0-14-031457-1) Puffin Bks.
—The Mouse Butcher. large type ed. King-Smith, Dick. 144p. (gr. 3-7). 1992. 13.95 (0-7451-1498-9, Galaxy Child Lrg Print) Chivers N Amer.
—Not in Here, Dad! Dutton, Cheryl. 32p. (ps-2). 1989. 10.95 (0-8120-6105-5) Barron.
—Tick Tock Tales. Mahy, Margaret. 96p. k-4). 1994. SBE 16.95 (0-689-50604-X, M K McElderry) Macmillan Child Grp.
Smith-Danell, Paula. Our Evergreen State Government: State & Local Government in Washington. Yates, Richard. 190p. 1989. 13.95 (0-911927-10-7) Info Oregon.
Smith-Griswold, Wendy. The Beetle. Mudd, Maria M. 14p. 1992. 14.95 (1-55670-255-8) Stewart Tabori & Chang.
—The Butterfly. Mudd, Maria M. 14p. (gr. 2 up). 1991. 12.95 (1-55670-219-1) Stewart Tabori & Chang.
Smith-Moore, J. J. Honor the Flag: A Guide to Its Care & Display. Radlauer, Ruth S. 48p. (gr. 2 up). 1992. PLB 12.95 (1-878363-61-1) Forest Hse.
—How Old Is Old? Combs, Ann. 32p. (ps-2). 1988. 8.95 (0-8431-2219-6) Price Stern.
Smithson, Colin. The Wonder of God's World: Air. Searle-Barnes, Bonita. LC 92-44575. 1993. 6.99 (0-7459-2021-7) Lion USA.
—The Wonder of God's World: Light. Searle-Barnes, Bonita. LC 92-44275. 1993. 6.99 (0-7459-2022-5) Lion USA.
—The Wonder of God's World: Sound. Searle-Barnes, Bonita. LC 92-44284. 1993. 6.99 (0-7459-2023-3) Lion USA.
—The Wonder of God's World: Water. Searle-Barnes, Bonita. LC 92-44274. 1993. 6.99 (0-7459-2024-1) Lion USA.
Smolinski, Dick. Abraham Lincoln. Bains, Rae. LC 84-2581. 32p. (gr. 3-6). 1985. PLB 9.49 (0-8167-0146-6); pap. text ed. 2.95 (0-8167-0147-4) Troll Assocs.
—Andrew Jackson, Frontier Patriot. Sabin, Louis. LC 85-1094. 48p. (gr. 4-6). 1986. lib. bdg. 10.79 (0-8167-0547-X); pap. text ed. 3.50 (0-8167-0548-8) Troll Assocs.
—Babe Ruth. Bains, Rae. LC 84-2595. 32p. (gr. 3-6). 1985. PLB 9.49 (0-8167-0144-X); pap. text ed. 2.95 (0-8167-0145-8) Troll Assocs.
—Children's Way of the Cross. Flanagan, Anne J. 39p. (Orig.). (gr. 2-6). 1992. pap. 1.50 (0-8198-6954-6) St Paul Bks.
—Christopher Columbus. Bains, Rae. LC 84-2585. 32p. (gr. 3-6). 1985. lib. bdg. 9.49 (0-8167-0150-4); pap. text ed. 2.95 (0-8167-0151-2) Troll Assocs.

—Frontier Dream: Life on the Great Plains. Chambers, Catherine E. LC 83-18282. 32p. (gr. 5-9). 1984. PLB 11.59 (0-8167-0039-7); pap. text ed. 2.95 (0-8167-0040-0) Troll Assocs.
—Frontier Village: A Town Is Born. Chambers, Catherine E. LC 83-18271. 32p. (gr. 5-9). 1984. PLB 11.59 (0-8167-0045-1); pap. text ed. 2.95 (0-8167-0046-X) Troll Assocs.
—Home Builder. Daniel, Kira. LC 88-10354. 32p. (gr. k-3). 1989. PLB 10.89 (0-8167-1420-7); pap. text ed. 2.95 (0-8167-1421-5) Troll Assocs.
—I Pray with Jesus. rev. ed. Daughters of St. Paul Staff. 177p. (gr. 1-5). 1991. deluxe ed. 8.50 white (0-8198-3630-3); deluxe ed. 8.50 black (0-8198-3631-1) St Paul Bks.
—John Adams, Brave Patriot. Santrey, Laurence. LC 85-1095. 48p. (gr. 4-6). 1986. lib. bdg. 10.79 (0-8167-0559-3); pap. text ed. 3.50 (0-8167-0560-7) Troll Assocs.
—Johnny Appleseed. Sabin, Louis. LC 84-2732. 32p. (gr. 3-6). 1985. PLB 9.49 (0-8167-0220-9); pap. text ed. 2.95 (0-8167-0221-7) Troll Assocs.
—Louis Pasteur. Bains, Rae. LC 84-2748. 32p. (gr. 3-6). 1985. PLB 9.49 (0-8167-0148-2); pap. text ed. 2.95 (0-8167-0149-0) Troll Assocs.
—Mystery of the Missing Fuzzy. Michaels, Ski. LC 85-14084. 48p. (Orig.). (gr. 1-3). 1986. PLB 10.59 (0-8167-0646-8); pap. text ed. 3.50 (0-8167-0647-6) Troll Assocs.
—Paul Bunyan. Sabin, Louis. LC 84-2747. 32p. (gr. 3-6). 1985. PLB 9.49 (0-8167-0254-3); pap. text ed. 2.95 (0-8167-0255-1) Troll Assocs.
—Prehistoric People. Santrey, Laurence. LC 84-8464. 32p. (gr. 3-6). 1985. PLB 9.49 (0-8167-0242-X); pap. text ed. 2.95 (0-8167-0243-8) Troll Assocs.
—Robert E. Lee: Brave Leader. Bains, Rae. LC 85-1092. 48p. (gr. 4-6). 1986. lib. bdg. 10.79 (0-8167-0545-3); pap. text ed. 3.50 (0-8167-0546-1) Troll Assocs.
—Secret of the Old Museum. Wandelmaier, Roy. LC 85-2533. 112p. (gr. 3-6). 1985. lib. bdg. 9.49 (0-8167-0531-3); pap. text ed. 2.95 (0-8167-0532-1) Troll Assocs.
—Wagons West: Off to Oregon. Chambers, Catherine E. LC 83-18276. 32p. (gr. 5-9). 1984. PLB 11.59 (0-8167-0043-5); pap. text ed. 2.95 (0-8167-0044-3) Troll Assocs.

Smollin, Michael. Laugh-Along Songs. 32p. (Orig.). (ps-2). 1990. pap. 6.95 incl. cass. (0-679-80305-X) Random Bks Yng Read.
Smollin, Michael J. Ernie & Bert Can...Can You. Sesame Street Staff. LC 81-83696. 28p. (ps). 1982. 2.95 (0-394-85150-1) Random Bks Yng Read.
—I Can Count to One Hundred...Can You? Howard, Katherine. LC 78-62700. (ps). 1979. pap. 2.25 (0-394-84090-9) Random Bks Yng Read.
—In & Out, Up & Down. Sesame Street Staff. LC 81-83697. 28p. (ps). 1982. bds. 2.95 (0-394-85151-X) Random Bks Yng Read.
—Maybe You Should Fly a Jet! Maybe You Should Be a Vet. Le Sieg, Theodore. LC 80-5084. 48p. (ps-3). 1980. lib. bdg. 9.99 (0-394-94448-8) Beginner.
—Tickle Yourself Again with Riddles. Electric Company Staff. LC 78-19699. (gr. 1-5). 1988. pap. 2.95 (0-394-84152-2) Random Bks Yng Read.
—Would You Like to Play Hide & Seek in This Book with Lovable, Furry Old Grover? Stone, Jon. LC 76-8120. (ps-1). 1976. pap. 2.25 (0-394-83292-2) Random Bks Yng Read.
—Your Friends from Sesame Street. Sesame Street Staff. (ps). 1979. 3.50 (0-394-84137-9) Random Bks Yng Read.
Smollin, Mike. Tickle Yourself with Riddles. Electric Company Staff. LC 77-90197. 96p. (gr. 1-5). 1988. pap. 2.99 (0-394-83783-5) Random Bks Yng Read.
Smothers, Mark. Lights! Camera! Love in Action! Fowler, Ruth. 64p. (Orig.). (gr. 4-6). 1989. pap. text ed. 3.95 (0-936625-68-6) Womans Mission Union.
Smyers, Carrie M. The Time a Cloud Came into the Cabin (A Mountain Tale for Boys) Smyers, Jacquelyn. LC 86-50627. 12p. (Orig.). (ps-6). 1986. pap. 3.98 (0-9615130-3-9) Very Idea.
—The Time a Cloud Came into the Cabin (A Mountain Tale for Girls) Smyers, Jacquelyn. LC 86-50626. 12p. (Orig.). (ps-6). 1986. pap. 3.98 (0-9615130-4-7) Very Idea.
Smyth, Dale. Trippy. Smyth, Virginia S. Walker, Erika D., ed. (Orig.). (gr. 1-3). 1989. pap. 5.00 (0-9624060-0-7) Mount Falcon.
Smyth, M. Jane. Billy & Our New Baby. Arnstein, Helene S. LC 73-7951. 32p. (gr. 3). 1973. 16.95x (0-87705-093-7) Human Sci Pr.
—One Little Girl. Fassler, Joan. LC 76-80120. 32p. (ps-3). 1969. 16.95 (0-87705-008-2) Human Sci Pr.
Smythe, Linda. The Bee & the Seed. Carratello, Patty. Spivak, Darlene, ed. 16p. (gr. k-2). 1987. wkbk. 1.95 (1-55734-381-0) Tchr Create Mat.
—Duke the Blue Mule. Carratello, Patty. Spivak, Darlene, ed. 16p. (gr. k-2). 1988. wkbk. 1.95 (1-55734-384-5) Tchr Create Mat.
—Hidden Pictures. Spivak, Darlene. 32p. (gr. k-2). 1988. wkbk. 4.95 (1-55734-120-6) Tchr Create Mat.
—Mice on Ice. Carratello, Patty. Spivak, Darlene, ed. 16p. (gr. k-2). 1988. wkbk. 1.95 (1-55734-382-9) Tchr Create Mat.
—My Cap. Carratello, Patty. Spivak, Darlene, ed. 16p. (gr. k-2). 1988. wkbk. 1.95 (1-55734-386-1) Tchr Create Mat.

—My Old Gold Boat. Carratello, Patty. Spivak, Darlene, ed. 16p. (gr. k-2). 1988. wkbk. 1.95 (1-55734-383-7) Tchr Create Mat.
—Skate, Kate, Skate. Carratello, Patty. Spivak, Darlene, ed. 16p. (gr. k-2). 1988. wkbk. 1.95 (1-55734-380-2) Tchr Create Mat.
Smythe, Linda, jt. illus. see Wright, Theresa.
Snader, Barbara. God's Power Versus Satan's Power: Christian Life Lessons. Norman, Louise. 64p. (Orig.). (gr. 1-8). 1985. pap. text ed. 11.50 (0-86508-062-3) BCM Pubn.
Snavely, Linda W. His Name Was David, Around the World: The Story of David & Goliath. Paxton, Lenore & Siadi, Phillip. 32p. (ps-4). Date not set. pap. 7.95 coloring bk.-cassette pkg. (1-880449-07-2) Wrldkids Pr.
Sneed, Brad. Grandpa's Song. Johnston, Tony. LC 90-43836. 32p. (ps-3). 1991. 12.95 (0-8037-0801-7); lib. bdg. 12.89 (0-8037-0802-5) Dial Bks Young.
—The Room. Peters, Lisa W. LC 92-39807. 1994. write for info. (0-8037-1431-9); PLB write for info. (0-8037-1432-7) Dial Bks Young.
—Turkey in the Straw. Hazen, Barbara S. LC 92-27516. 32p. (ps-3). 1993. 13.99 (0-8037-1298-7); PLB 13.89 (0-8037-1299-5) Dial Bks Young.
Sneider, Cary I. & Baker, Lisa H. The Magic of Electricity. Sneider, Cary I., et al. Bergman, Lincoln & Fairwell, Kay, eds. Sneider, Cary I., photos by. 50p. (Orig.). (gr. 3-6). 1985. pap. 10.00 (0-912511-52-4) Lawrence Science.
Snellenberger, Bonita, jt. illus. see Snellenberger, Earl.
Snellenberger, Earl & Snellenberger, Bonita. God Created Birds of the World. Snellenberger, Earl & Snellenberger, Bonita. 36p. (Orig.). (ps-6). 1989. pap. 4.95 (0-89051-152-7) Master Bks.
—God Created Sea Life of the World. Snellenberger, Earl & Snellenberger, Bonita. 36p. (Orig.). (ps-6). 1989. pap. 4.95 (0-89051-151-9) Master Bks.
—God Created the Dinosaurs of the World. Snellenberger, Earl & Snellenberger, Bonita. 36p. (Orig.). (ps-6). 1993. pap. 4.95 (0-89051-153-5) Master Bks.
—God Created the World & the Universe. Snellenberger, Earl & Snellenberger, Bonita. 36p. (Orig.). (ps-6). 1989. pap. 4.95 (0-89051-149-7) Master Bks.
Snow, Alan. Don't Climb out of the Window Tonight. McGilvray, Richard. LC 92-28136. (ps-2). 1993. 13.99 (0-8037-1373-8) Dial Bks Young.
—How to Deal with Babies. Powell, Richard. LC 91-3461. 24p. (gr. k-3). 1992. lib. bdg. 9.59 (0-8167-2420-2); pap. text ed. 2.95 (0-8167-2421-0) Troll Assocs.
—How to Deal with Friends. Powell, Richard. LC 91-15164. 24p. (gr. k-3). 1992. PLE 9.59 (0-8167-2422-9); pap. text ed. 2.95 (0-8167-2423-7) Troll Assocs.
—How to Deal with Monsters. Powell, Richard. LC 91-14975. 24p. (gr. k-3). 1992. PLE 9.59 (0-8167-2424-5); pap. text ed. 2.95 (0-8167-2425-3) Troll Assocs.
—How to Deal with Parents. Powell, Richard. LC 91-14997. 24p. (gr. k-3). 1992. lib. bdg. 9.59 (0-8167-2418-0); pap. text ed. 2.95 (0-8167-2419-9) Troll Assocs.
—The Monster Book of ABC Sounds. Snow, Alan. LC 90-39384. 32p. (ps-2). 1991. 12.95 (0-8037-0935-8) Dial Bks Young.
—My First Dictionary. Snow, Alan. LC 91-23485. 32p. (gr. k-3). 1992. PLB 12.79 (0-8167-2515-2); pap. text ed. 4.95 (0-8167-2516-0) Troll Assocs.
—My First Encyclopedia. Snow, Alan. LC 91-24320. 32p. (gr. k-3). 1992. PLB 12.79 (0-8167-2519-5); pap. 4.95 (0-8167-2520-9) Troll Assocs.
—Reader's Digest Children's Book of Poetry. Mathias, Beverly, selected by. (gr. k-5). 1992. 13.00 (0-89577-442-9, Readers Digest Kids) RD Assn.
—Stories from Hans Christian Andersen. Matthews, Andrew, retold by. LC 92-45627. 96p. (gr. 2-5). 1993. 18.95 (0-531-05463-2) Orchard Bks Watts.
Snow, Scott. Gandhi, Peaceful Warrior. Bains, Rae. LC 89-5101. 48p. (gr. 4-6). 1990. lib. bdg. 10.79 (0-8167-1767-2); pap. text ed. 3.50 (0-8167-1768-0) Troll Assocs.
—Lafayette, Hero of Two Nations. Brandt, Keith. LC 89-33981. 48p. (gr. 4-6). 1990. PLB 10.79 (0-8167-1771-0); pap. text ed. 3.50 (0-8167-1772-9) Troll Assocs.
—Maria Escapes. Avery, Gillian. LC 91-36730. 272p. (gr. 4-8). 1992. pap. 15.00 jacketed, 3-pc. bdg. (0-671-77074-8, S&S BFYR) S&S Trade.
—Maria's Italian Spring. Avery, Gillian. LC 92-16955. (gr. 4-8). 1993. pap. 15.00 JR3 (0-671-79582-1, S&S BFYR) S&S Trade.
Snowball, Peter. Grasslands. Catchpole, Clive. LC 83-27123. 32p. (gr. k-4). 1985. pap. 4.95 (0-8037-0083-0, 0481-140) Dial Bks Young.
Snowden, Linda & Horen, Michael. Arrogant Ari Learns a Lesson. Golding, Goldie. 32p. (gr. k-6). 1988. 6.95 (0-89906-500-7) Mesorah Pubns.
Snowdone, Linda. Uncle Moishy Visits Torah Island. Safran, Faigy. 32p. (gr. 2-8). 1987. incl. cassette 10.95 (0-318-32597-7); pap. 5.95 (0-89906-807-3) Mesorah Pubns.
Snyder, Carrie A. How to Draw Horses. Snyder, Carrie A. LC 84-51871. 32p. (gr. 2-6). 1985. PLB 10.65 (0-8167-0381-7, Pub. by Watermill Pr); pap. text ed. 1.95 (0-8167-0382-5) Troll Assocs.

—You Can Draw Funny Animals. Snyder, Carrie A. LC 81-69659. 32p. (gr. 2-6). 1981. PLB 10.65 (0-89375-689-X); pap. text ed. 1.95 (0-89375-409-9) Troll Assocs.
Snyder, Carrrie A. How to Draw Dogs. Snyder, Carrie A. LC 81-52120. 32p. (gr. 2-6). 1982. PLB 10.65 (0-89375-686-5); pap. text ed. 1.95 (0-89375-687-3) Troll Assocs.
Snyder, Dan. My Dad Sells Insurance. Shaw, Richard C. 40p. (ps-5). 1988. PLB write for info. (0-944900-00-3) Shaw & Co.
Snyder, Deborah, jt. illus. see Quinlivan, Mary.
Snyder, Jerome. Days to Remember. Lipkind, William. (gr. 3 up). 1961. 10.95 (0-8392-3006-0) Astor-Honor.
Snyder, Joel. Amazing World of Birds. Caitlin, Stephen. LC 89-4968. 32p. (gr. 2-4). 1990. PLB 11.59 (0-8167-1747-8); pap. text ed. 2.95 (0-8167-1748-6) Troll Assocs.
—Baby Animals. Kuchalla, Susan. LC 81-11434. 32p. (gr. k-2). 1982. lib. bdg. 11.59 (0-89375-666-0); pap. 2.95 (0-89375-667-9) Troll Assocs.
—Dinosaur Alphabet Book. Whitehead, Patricia. LC 84-8839. 32p. (gr. k-2). 1985. PLB 11.59 (0-8167-0363-9); pap. text ed. 2.95 (0-8167-0364-7) Troll Assocs.
—Discovering Electricity. Bains, Rae. LC 81-3339. 32p. (gr. 2-4). 1982. PLB 11.59 (0-89375-564-8); pap. text ed. 2.95 (0-89375-565-6) Troll Assocs.
—Forests & Jungles. Bains, Rae. LC 84-8641. 32p. (gr. 3-6). 1985. PLB 9.49 (0-8167-0312-4); pap. text ed. 2.95 (0-8167-0313-2) Troll Assocs.
—Horses. Greydanus, Rose. LC 82-20296. 32p. (gr. k-2). 1983. lib. bdg. 11.59 (0-89375-900-7); pap. 2.95 (0-8167-1479-7) Troll Assocs.
—I Can Read About Homonyms. Supraner, Robyn. LC 76-54442. (gr. 2-5). 1977. pap. 1.95 (0-89375-036-0) Troll Assocs.
—I Can Read About Paul Bunyan. Anderson, J. I. LC 76-54494. (gr. 2-5). 1977. pap. 1.95 (0-89375-041-7) Troll Assocs.
—Life in the Sea. Curran, Eileen. LC 84-16190. 32p. (gr. k-2). 1985. lib. bdg. 11.59 (0-8167-0448-1); pap. text ed. 2.95 (0-8167-0449-X) Troll Assocs.
—The Magic String. Sabin, Francene. LC 81-4076. 32p. (gr. k-2). 1981. PLB 11.59 (0-89375-547-8); pap. 2.95 (0-89375-548-6) Troll Assocs.
So, Meilo. Wishbones: A Folk Tale from China. Wilson, Barbara K. LC 92-26993. 32p. (ps-2). 1993. SBE 14.95 (0-02-793125-0, Bradbury Pr) Macmillan Child Grp.
Soasey, Beverly. Bright Beginnings Storybook: Building Self-Esteem Skills with Pumsy. Anderson, Jill. 42p. (gr. k-1). 1990. text ed. 3.95 (0-9608284-7-8); leader's guide 80.00 (0-9608284-6-X) Timberline Pr.
—Pumsy Storybook. Anderson, Jill. 40p. (Orig.). (gr. 1-4). 1990. pap. text ed. 3.95 (0-9608284-2-7) Timberline Pr.
Sobol, Richard, photos by. Seal Journey. Sobol, Richard & Sobol, Jonah. LC 92-25974. 32p. (gr. 1-5). 1993. 14.99 (0-525-65126-8, Cobblehill Bks) Dutton Child Bks.
Socias, Marcel. Our Planet: Earth. Estalella, Robert. LC 93-24597. (gr. 4-8). 1994. 12.95 (0-8120-6368-6); pap. write for info. (0-8120-1741-2) Barron.
Sodac, David. Amazing States. Burda, Margaret. 160p. (gr. 4-8). 1984. wkbk. 12.95 (0-86653-205-6, GA 546) Good Apple.
Soentpiet, Chris K. The Last Dragon. Nunes, Susan M. LC 93-30631. 1996. write for info. (0-395-67020-9, Clarion Bks) HM.
Sofilas, Mark. Black & White. Green, Robyn & Scarffe, Bronwen. LC 92-21393. (gr. 4 up). 1993. 2.50 (0-383-03555-4) SRA Schl Grp.
—There's a Bat on the Balcony. Caraher, Kim. LC 92-34260. 1993. 4.25 (0-383-03660-7) SRA Schl Grp.
—Wiz. Odgers, Sally F. LC 92-31952. 1993. 3.75 (0-383-03608-9) SRA Schl Grp.
Sogabe, Aki. Cinnamon, Mint, & Mothballs: A Visit to Grandmother's House. Tiller, Ruth. LC 92-32981. 1993. write for info. (0-15-276617-0) HarBrace.
Sokol, Bill. Time Cat. Alexander, Lloyd. (gr. 4-7). 16.25 (0-8446-6237-2) Peter Smith.
Sokoloff, David. Messy Activities & More. Morin, Virginia K. Jernberg, Ann M., intro. by. LC 92-41453. 144p. (Orig.). (ps-5). 1993. pap. 9.95 (1-55652-173-1) Chicago Review.
Solar, Dahna, jt. illus. see Kifer, Kathy.
Solbert, Ronni. Bronzeville Boys & Girls. Brooks, Gwendolyn. LC 56-8152. 48p. (gr. 3-6). 1967. PLB 13.89 (0-06-020651-9) HarpC Child Bks.
—The Pushcart War. Merrill, Jean. LC 84-43131. 224p. (gr. 5-8). 1992. PLB 14.89 (0-06-020822-8) HarpC Child Bks.

Sole, Carme. El Nino Gigante (The Giant Child) Garcia Sanchez, J. L. (SPA.). 32p. (gr. k-2). 1988. 9.95 (84-372-1346-0) Santillana.
An outstanding selection from the DERECHOS DEL NINO series (The Rights of Children). Each book portrays one of the rights of children declared by the United Nations General Assembly. In this selection, a young boy becomes separated from his parents. In searching for them, he

encounters a town of tiny people who abuse him until the children of the town come to his rescue. Young readers will enjoy this heartwarming story & its message. Simplistic illustrations by Carme Sole. To order: Santillana, 901 West Walnut, Compton, CA 90220. Telephone 1-310-763-0455. *Publisher Provided Annotation.*

Solis-Navarro, Kelly. Experiences with Plants for Young Children. Gale, Frank C. & Gale, Clarice W. Durett, Mary E., frwd. by. LC 78-88376. (ps-3). 1975. 12.95x (*0-87015-211-4*) Pacific Bks.

Solliday, Tim. Robert & the Balloon Machine. Darling, Benjamin. 32p. 1991. 11.95 (*0-88138-120-9*, Green Tiger) S&S Trade.

—Rover & Coo Coo. Hay, John. 32p. (gr. 3-6). 1991. 12.95 (*0-88138-078-4*, Green Tiger) S&S Trade.

Soloff-Levy, Barbara. How to Draw Forest Animals. Soloff-Levy, Barbara. LC 84-51873. 32p. (gr. 2-6). 1985. PLB 10.65 (*0-8167-0334-5*, Pub. by Watermill Pr); pap. text ed. 1.95 (*0-8167-0335-3*) Troll Assocs.

—How to Draw Ghosts, Goblins & Witches: And Other Spooky Characters. Soloff-Levy, Barbara. LC 81-52124. 32p. (gr. 2-6). 1982. PLB 10.65 (*0-89375-678-4*); pap. text ed. 1.95 (*0-89375-557-5*) Troll Assocs.

Solomon, Chuck, photos by. Major-League Batboy. Solomon, Chuck. LC 90-43275. 32p. (gr. 2-5). 1991. 11.95 (*0-517-58244-9*); PLB 12.99 (*0-517-58245-7*) Crown Bks Yng Read.

Solomon, Dorothy E. Color Bright. Solomon, Dorothy E. 32p. (gr. 3-7). 1990. 12.95 (*0-933813-02-3*); pap. 7.95 (*0-933813-04-X*) Mdsn Pub Assocs.

Solovic, Linda. Halloween KidDoodles, No. 1. Tuchman, Gail. 64p. (ps-2). 1992. pap. 0.99 (*1-56293-259-4*) McClanahan Bk.

Soman, David. The Leaving Morning. Johnson, Angela. LC 91-21123. 32p. (ps-2). 1992. 14.95 (*0-531-05992-8*); PLB 14.99 (*0-531-08592-9*) Orchard Bks Watts.

—Mommy's Office. Hazen, Barbara S. LC 91-25013. 32p. (ps-1). 1992. SBE 13.95 (*0-689-31601-1*, Atheneum Child Bk) Macmillan Child Grp.

—One of Three. Johnson, Angela. LC 90-29316. 32p. (ps-1). 1991. 14.95 (*0-531-05955-3*); RLB 14.99 (*0-531-08555-4*) Orchard Bks Watts.

—Tell Me a Story, Mama. Johnson, Angela. LC 88-17917. 32p. (ps-1). 1989. 14.95 (*0-531-05794-1*); PLB 14.99 (*0-531-08394-2*) Orchard Bks Watts.

—Tell Me a Story, Mama. Johnson, Angela. LC 88-17917. 32p. (ps-1). 1992. pap. 4.95 (*0-531-07032-8*) Orchard Bks Watts.

—When I Am Old with You. Johnson, Angela. LC 89-70928. 32p. (ps-2). 1990. 14.95 (*0-531-05884-0*); PLB 14.99 (*0-531-08484-1*) Orchard Bks Watts.

—When I Am Old with You. Johnson, Angela. LC 89-70928. 32p. (ps-2). 1993. pap. 4.95 (*0-531-07035-2*) Orchard Bks Watts.

Soman, David, photos by. Pole Dog. Seymour, Tres. LC 92-24174. 32p. (ps-1). 1993. 14.95 (*0-531-05470-5*); PLB 14.99 (*0-531-08620-8*) Orchard Bks Watts.

Somers, Stanley E. Learn from Everyone! Practical Guidelines to Living. Somers, Adele. 192p. (Orig.). (gr. 8 up). 1985. pap. 7.95 (*0-9615032-0-3*) World Relations Pr.

Somerville, Sheila. The Adventures of Walter the Weremouse. Dashney, John. 164p. (Orig.). (gr. 4-8). 1992. pap. 6.50x (*0-9633236-0-1*) J Dashney.
A boy by day--a mouse by night! WALTER THE WEREMOUSE runs through town (& the suburbs & countryside too)--pursued by packs of dogs, the police, organized crime, an ex-Roller Derby star & the telephone company! This first book by award-winning international storyteller John Dashney is now triumphantly into its second printing & like its author is gaining fans across America, Great Britain, Australia & New Zealand. "What fun to read about an underdog--or should I say, an under-weremouse--who finds a way to squeak his way to the top. A nice combination of fantasy & humor."--B.J. Quinlan, Youth Services Manager, Salem (OR) Public Library. "For children--& seekers--of all ages. This enchanting story will engage you from the start. Author/ storyteller John Dashney never lets you wander from Walter or the fabulous characters of his adventures."--Oregon State Library for the Blind. *Publisher Provided Annotation.*

—Five Little Pumpkins Big Book. (ps-2). 1988. pap. text ed. 14.00 (*0-922053-18-9*) N Edge Res.

—Osito, Osito. Edge, Nellie, adapted by. Zamora-Pearson, Marissa, tr. from ENG. (SPA.). (ps-2). 1993. pap. text ed. 15.00 (*0-922053-26-X*) N Edge Res.

—Over in the Meadow Big Book. (ps-2). 1988. pap. text ed. 14.00 (*0-922053-09-X*) N Edge Res.

—Teddy Bear, Teddy Bear Big Book. Edge, Nellie, adapted by. (ps-2). 1988. pap. text ed. 14.00 (*0-922053-04-9*) N Edge Res.

Somerville, Sheila & Muren, Nancy L. Finger Plays & Action Rhymes Big Book. (ps-2). 1988. pap. text ed. 15.00 (*0-922053-01-4*) N Edge Res.

Sommers, Linda. Magic Monsters Learn about Manners. Moncure, Jane B. LC 79-24528. (ps-3). 1980. PLB 21.35 (*0-89565-118-1*); PLB 14.95s.p. (*0-685-57682-5*) Childs World.

—Magic Monsters Learn about Space. Moncure, Jane B. LC 79-25765. (ps-3). 1980. PLB 21.35 (*0-89565-119-X*); PLB 14.95s.p. (*0-685-55500-3*) Childs World.

—My "b" Sound Box. Moncure, Jane B. LC 77-23588. (ps-2). 1977. PLB 21.35 (*0-913778-92-3*); PLB 14.95s.p. (*0-685-55506-2*) Childs World.

—My "c" Sound Box. Moncure, Jane B. LC 78-23638. (ps-2). 1979. PLB 21.35 (*0-89565-052-5*); PLB 14.95s.p. (*0-685-55507-0*) Child's World.

—My "d" Sound Box. Moncure, Jane B. LC 78-8450. (ps-2). 1978. PLB 21.35 (*0-89565-044-4*); PLB 14.95s.p. (*0-685-55508-9*) Childs World.

—My "f" Sound Box. Moncure, Jane B. LC 77-9377. (ps-2). 1977. PLB 21.35 (*0-913778-93-1*); PLB 14.95s.p. (*0-685-55509-7*); pap. 6.96 (*0-685-57684-1*) Childs World.

—My "g" Sound Box. Moncure, Jane B. LC 78-22037. (ps-2). 1979. PLB 21.35 (*0-89565-053-3*); PLB 14.95s.p. (*0-685-55510-0*) Childs World.

—My "h" Sound Box. Moncure, Jane B. LC 77-8977. (ps-2). 1977. PLB 21.35 (*0-913778-94-X*); PLB 14.95s.p. (*0-685-55511-9*) Childs World.

—My "j" Sound Box. Moncure, Jane B. LC 78-23178. (ps-2). 1979. PLB 21.35 (*0-89565-049-5*); PLB 14.95s.p. (*0-685-55512-7*) Childs World.

—My "k" Sound Box. Moncure, Jane B. LC 78-22034. (ps-2). 1979. PLB 21.35 (*0-89565-050-9*); PLB 14.95s.p. (*0-685-55513-5*) Childs World.

—My "l" Sound Box. Moncure, Jane B. LC 78-8373. (ps-2). 1978. PLB 21.35 (*0-89565-045-2*); PLB 14.95s.p. (*0-685-55514-3*) Childs World.

—My "m" Sound Box. Moncure, Jane B. LC 78-24458. (ps-2). 1979. PLB 21.35 (*0-89565-051-7*); PLB 14.95s.p. (*0-685-55515-1*) Childs World.

—My "n" Sound Box. Moncure, Jane B. LC 78-22053. (ps-2). 1979. PLB 21.35 (*0-89565-054-1*) Childs World.

—My "p" Sound Box. Moncure, Jane B. LC 78-7841. (ps-2). 1978. PLB 21.35 (*0-89565-047-9*); PLB 14.95s.p. (*0-685-55516-X*) Childs World.

—My "q" Sound Box. Moncure, Jane B. LC 79-13085. (ps-2). 1979. PLB 21.35 (*0-89565-100-9*); PLB 14.95s.p. (*0-685-55517-8*) Childs World.

—My "r" Sound Box. Moncure, Jane B. LC 78-7842. (ps-2). 1978. PLB 21.35 (*0-89565-048-7*); PLB 14.95s.p. (*0-685-55518-6*) Childs World.

—My "s" Sound Box. Moncure, Jane B. LC 77-8970. (ps-2). 1977. PLB 21.35 (*0-913778-95-8*); PLB 14.95s.p. (*0-685-55519-4*) Childs World.

—My Sound Parade. Moncure, Jane B. LC 79-15930. (ps-2). 1979. PLB 21.35 (*0-89565-103-3*); PLB 14.95s.p. (*0-685-55520-8*) Childs World.

—My Sound Parade. Moncure, Jane. 32p. (gr. k-2). 1993. pap. text ed. 5.95 (*1-56189-389-7*) Amer Educ Pub.

—My "t" Sound Box. Moncure, Jane B. LC 77-23587. (ps-2). 1977. PLB 21.35 (*0-913778-96-6*); PLB 14.95s.p. (*0-685-55521-6*) Childs World.

—My "v" Sound Box. Moncure, Jane B. LC 79-13084. (ps-2). 1979. PLB 21.35 (*0-89565-101-7*); PLB 14.95s.p. (*0-685-55522-4*) Childs World.

—My "w" Sound Box. Moncure, Jane B. LC 78-8614. (ps-2). 1978. PLB 21.35 (*0-89565-046-0*); PLB 14.95s.p. (*0-685-55523-2*) Childs World.

—My "x, y, z" Sound Box. Moncure, Jane B. LC 79-13086. (ps-2). 1979. PLB 21.35 (*0-89565-102-5*); PLB 14.95s.p. (*0-685-55524-0*) Childs World.

Song Nan Zhang. A Little Tiger in the Chinese Night. Song Nan Zhang. LC 93-60336. 48p. (gr. 6-9). 1993. 19.95 (*0-88776-320-0*) Tundra Bks.

Sonkaria, Gyan. Nala Damayanti. Shanta. (gr. 1-9). 1979. pap. 3.00 (*0-89744-158-3*) Auromere.

Sonkin, Susan. How to Draw Baby Animals. Sonkin, Susan. LC 81-52119. 32p. (gr. 2-6). 1982. PLB 10.65 (*0-89375-684-9*); pap. text ed. 1.95 (*0-89375-685-7*) Troll Assocs.

Sonnett, Barbie. It's a Great Day: The Story of Rusty, the Gunston Hall Fox. Turner, Louise. 45p. (Orig.). 1983. pap. 6.95 (*1-884085-04-0*) Bd Regents.

Sookikian, Charles J. Stranded! Bodie, Idella. LC 84-14098. 132p. (Orig.). (gr. 5-9). 1984. pap. 6.95 (*0-87844-060-7*) Sandlapper Pub Co.

Soper, Patrick. John Ross. Lowe, Felix C. Viola, Herman, intro. by. 32p. (gr. 3-6). 1990. PLB 17.96 (*0-8172-3407-1*); pap. 4.95 (*0-8114-4093-1*) Raintree Steck-V.

—The Night Thief. Allen, Valerie. LC 89-28459. 32p. (gr. k-3). 1990. 14.95 (*0-88289-774-8*) Pelican.

—Osceola, Patriot & Warrior. Jumper, Moses & Sonder, Ben. LC 92-25209. 76p. (gr. 2-5). 1992. PLB 21.34 (*0-8114-7225-6*) Raintree Steck-V.

Sopko, Eugen. The Falling Stars. Grimm, Jacob & Grimm, Wilhelm K. LC 85-7193. (gr. k-3). 1988. 14.95 (*1-55858-041-7*) North-South Bks NYC.

—The Miller, His Son & Their Donkey. Aesop. LC 85-7198. 32p. (gr. k-3). 1988. 14.95 (*1-55858-067-0*) North-South Bks NYC.

—The White Raven & the Black Sheep. Sopko, Eugen. Graves, Helen, tr. from GER. LC 91-7254. 32p. (gr. k-3). 1991. 14.95 (*1-55858-118-9*) North-South Bks NYC.

Sorel, Ed. Jack & the Beanstalk. Metaxas, Eric. LC 91-14176. 40p. (gr. k up). 1991. pap. 14.95 (*0-88708-188-6*, Rabbit Ears); incls. cassette 19.95 (*0-88708-189-4*, Rabbit Ears) Picture Bk Studio.

Sorensen, Henri. Deep River. Moore, Elaine. LC 93-23043. 1994. pap. 14.00 (*0-671-86534-X*, S&S BFYR) S&S Trade.

—I Know a Bridge. Sheppard, Jeff. LC 93-2656. 32p. (ps-k). 1993. RSBE 14.95 (*0-02-782457-8*, Macmillan Child Bk) Macmillan Child Grp.

—I Love You As Much... Melmed, Laura K. LC 92-27677. 1993. write for info. (*0-688-11718-X*); PLB write for info. (*0-688-11719-8*) Lothrop.

—River Day. Mason, Jane. LC 93-26573. 32p. (gr. k-3). 1994. RSBE 14.95 (*0-02-762869-8*, Macmillan Child Bk) Macmillan Child Grp.

—When the Rain Stops. Cole, Sheila. LC 90-19124. 32p. (ps up). 1991. 13.95 (*0-688-07654-8*); PLB 13.88 (*0-688-07655-6*) Lothrop.

Sorensen, Henry. What Does the Rain Play? Carlstrom, Nancy W. LC 91-47712. 32p. (ps-2). 1993. RSBE 14.95 (*0-02-717273-2*, Macmillan Child Bk) Macmillan Child Grp.

Sorenson, Reid. Conflict Resolution & Mediation for Peer Helpers. Sorenson, Don L. LC 92-70818. 128p. (Orig.). (gr. 8-12). 1992. pap. text ed. 8.95x (*0-932796-42-7*) Ed Media Corp.

Sorg, James M. Your Hospital Stay...It'll Be Okay. Rosenstock, Judith D. & Rosenstock, Harvey A. 36p. (Orig.). (gr. 1-5). 1988. pap. 4.95 (*0-9622172-0-4*) D Miller Fndtn.

Sorine, Daniel S. Our Ballet Class. Sorine, Stephanie R. LC 80-28927. 48p. (gr. k-3). 1981. lib. bdg. 8.99 (*0-394-94821-1*) Knopf Bks Yng Read.

Sornat, Czeslaw. First Math Dictionary. Dyches, Richard W. & Shaw, Jean M. LC 91-7527. 104p. (gr. k-4). 1991. 15.95 (*0-531-15238-3*); PLB 15.90 (*0-531-11111-3*) Watts.

—First Science Dictionary. Shaw, Jean M. & Dyches, Richard W. LC 91-7528. 104p. (gr. k-4). 1991. 15.95 (*0-531-15237-5*); PLB 15.90 (*0-531-11110-5*) Watts.

—Primer Diccionario de Ciencia. Shaw, Jean M. & Dyches, Richard W. (SPA.). 104p. (gr. k-4). 1991. 15.95 (*0-531-15235-9*); PLB 15.90 (*0-531-07925-2*) Watts.

—Primer Diccionario de Matematica. Dyches, Richard W. & Shaw, Jean M. (SPA.). 104p. (gr. k-4). 1991. 15.95 (*0-531-15236-7*); PLB 15.90 (*0-531-07926-0*) Watts.

Sorrels, Judith. Black Scientists of America. Donovan, Richard X. 134p. (gr. 6 up). 1990. pap. 10.95 (*0-89420-265-0*, 297000) Natl Book.

Sose, Bonnie. Designed by God So I Must Be Special. Sose, Bonnie. 24p. (ps-2). 1991. 10.95 (*0-9615279-6-X*); Afro-American version available. 10.95 (*0-9615279-4-3*) Character Builders.

Soto, Caroline. The Cat's Meow. Soto, Gary. LC 87-17982. 64p. (Orig.). 1987. pap. 4.95 (*0-89407-087-8*) Strawberry Hill.

Soto, Zachary & Bostick, Matthew. Surface Thoughts. Simmons, Aaron. Thornton, Don, intro. by. 48p. (Orig.). (gr. 6-12). 1993. pap. 7.50 (*1-882913-01-9*) Thornton LA.

Sott, Donna. Georgie the Jovial Giraffe. Grandma, Marian, pseud. LC 85-71331. 32p. (gr. 3 up). 1985. text ed. write for info. (*0-9614989-0-0*) Banmar Inc.

Soucie, Daniel S. Trapped in Slickrock Canyon. Skurzynski, Gloria. LC 83-14988. 128p. (gr. 4-6). 1984. 13.95 (*0-688-02688-5*) Lothrop.

Sours, Michael. Monstra vs. Irving. Manes, Stephen. LC 89-33423. 80p. (gr. 2-4). 1991. pap. 4.95 (*0-8050-1642-2*, Bks Young Read) H Holt & Co.

—The Twenty-Four Hour Genie. McGinnis, Lila S. LC 89-77786. 80p. (gr. 2-4). 1990. 12.95 (*0-8050-1303-2*, Redfeather BYR) H Holt & Co.

—The Twenty-Four Hour Genie. McGinnis, Lila S. LC 89-77786. 80p. (gr. 2-4). 1991. pap. 4.95 (*0-8050-1845-X*, Redfeather BYR) H Holt & Co.

Sousa, Joseph, jt. illus. See Pitz, Henry.

Southgate, Mark. The Princess & the Mirror. Alverson, Charles. 32p. (gr. k-3). 1989. 13.95 (*0-86264-174-8*, Pub. by Anderson Pr UK) Trafalgar.

Souza, Diana. Heather Has Two Mommies. Newman, Leslea. 38p. (ps-3). 1991. pap. 7.95 (*1-55583-180-X*) Alyson Pubns.

Sova, Mike & Sova, Mike. Kids in the Woods. McKelvy, Charles. LC 89-50591. 24p. (gr. 1-4). 1993. 14.95x (*0-944771-03-3*) Dunery Pr.

Soyer, Yitzhak. Hasefer Chelek Rishon, Pt. 1: Alef-Beis. Bachrach, Kalman. (HEB.). 68p. (gr. 1). 1941. pap. text ed. 2.25x (*1-878530-00-3*) K Bachrach Co.

Space, Peggy & Scarpace, Frank. A Trip on a Jet Plane: Photos & Fun for Boys & Girls. Space, Peggy. 32p. (gr. 3-7). 1981. pap. 2.50 (0-942772-00-8) Image Pubns.

Spahr, Kathy. Baby Kermit & the Magic Trunk. Gikow, Louise. 26p. (ps up). 1987. 12.95 (1-55578-601-4) Worlds Wonder.

Spalding, Tony. Snow White & the Dwarfs. Daniels, Patricia. LC 79-28431. 24p. (gr. k-5). 1980. PLB 14.64 (0-8393-0251-7) Raintree Steck-V.

Spanfeller, Jim. Twelve Iron Sandals: And other Czechoslovak Tales. Horejs, Vit. LC 84-22272. 128p. (gr. 4-6). 1985. 11.95 (0-13-934159-5) P-H.

Spangler, Melissa & Meyer, Lydia V. The Music of a Poet's Heart. Pitts, Teresa A. 147p. (Orig.). (gr. 7 up). 1987. pap. 10.00 (0-9618600-0-6) T A Pitts.

Spangler, Noel. Colors. Allington, Richard L. LC 79-19116. 32p. (gr. k-3). 1985. PLB 15.33 (0-8172-1280-9); pap. 3.95 (0-8114-8240-5) Raintree Steck-V.

Sparks, Barbara. Ganzy Remembers. Ketner, Mary G. LC 89-78261. 32p. (gr. k-3). 1991. SBE 13.95 (0-689-31610-0, Atheneum Child Bk) Macmillan Child Grp.

Sparks, Mary W. Taffy of Torpedo Junction. Wechter, Nell W. LC 57-9312. 134p. (gr. 5-9). 1990. pap. 7.95 (0-89587-076-2) Blair.

Sparr, Theanna, et al. Christian Mother Goose Big Book. Decker, Marjorie A. LC 92-60502. 304p. (ps-4). 1992. 14.99 (0-529-07315-3) World Bible.

Spavern, Marilyn. And Grandpa Sat on Friday. Marshall, Val & Tester, Bronwyn. LC 92-34159. 1993. 4.25 (0-383-03610-0) SRA Schl Grp.

Spear, Scott. Is Aetosaur a Dinosaur? Cole, Betsy. Hager, Michael, contrib. by. 64p. (Orig.). (gr. k-3). 1992. pap. 11.95 (0-9625801-4-7) VA Mus Natl Hist.

Spears, Diane S. Literature Activities for Young Children. Sullivan, Dianna. 96p. (ps-1). 1990. wkbk. 9.95 (1-55734-304-7) Tchr Create Mat.

Speed, jt. illus. see Ford, H. J.

Speed, Lancelot, jt. illus. see Ford, Henry J.

Speidel, Sandra. Clap Clap! Helldorfer, Mary C. 32p. (ps-2). 1993. reinforced bdg. 13.99 (0-670-85155-8) Viking Child Bks.

—Evan's Corner. Hill, Elizabeth S. LC 92-25334. 1993. pap. 4.99 (0-14-054406-2) Puffin Bks.

—Kelly in the Mirror. Vertreace, Martha. LC 92-22655. 1993. 13.95 (0-8075-4152-4) A Whitman.

—Louisa May Alcott, Young Writer. Santrey, Laurence. LC 85-1086. 48p. (gr. 4-6). 1986. lib. bdg. 10.79 (0-8167-0563-1); pap. text ed. 3.50 (0-8167-0564-X) Troll Assocs.

—Sing to the Stars. Barrett, Mary B. LC 92-41773. 1994. 14.95 (0-316-08224-4) Little.

—Songs for the Seasons. Highwater, Jamake. LC 93-8094. 1994. write for info. (0-688-10658-7); PLB write for info. (0-688-10659-5) Lothrop.

—Wind in the Long Grass: A Collection of Haiku. Higginson, William J., ed. LC 89-21804. 48p. (gr. 2-5). 1991. pap. 13.95 jacketed (0-671-67978-3, S&S BFYR) S&S Trade.

Speidel, Sandy. Happy Exercise: An Adventure into a Fit World. Jacobs, Don. LC 80-23547. 48p. (Orig.). (ps-5). 1980. pap. 4.95 (0-89037-170-9) Anderson World.

Speirs, Gill. I Can Draw Horses. Barish, Wendy, ed. 64p. (gr. 3-7). 1983. pap. 3.95 (0-671-46447-7, Little Simon) S&S Trade.

Speirs, John. The Bobbsey Twins: The Music Box Mystery. Hope, Laura L. Barish, Wendy, ed. 128p. (gr. 2-5). 1983. 8.95 (0-671-43588-4) S&S Trade.

—Carla the Carpenter. Dubowski, Cathy E. 28p. (ps-2). 1992. 3.95 (0-7214-5339-2) Ladybird Bks.

—Ernie the Electrician. Dubowski, Cathy E. 28p. (ps-2). 1992. 3.95 (0-7214-5340-6) Ladybird Bks.

—Give a Dog a Bone: Stories, Poems, Jokes, & Riddles about Dogs. Cole, Joanna & Calmenson, Stephanie, eds. LC 93-2536. 1994. write for info. (0-590-46374-8) Scholastic Inc.

—Key to the Playhouse. York, Carol B. LC 93-1800. 128p. (gr. 2-5). 1994. 13.95 (0-590-46258-X) Scholastic Inc.

—A Matter of Choice. Carl, Angela R. 32p. (gr. 1-3). 1990. PLB 19.95 (0-89565-699-X); PLB 13.95s.p. (0-685-56165-8) Childs World.

—Milo the Mechanic. Dubowski, Cathy E. 28p. (ps-2). 1992. 3.95 (0-7214-5341-4) Ladybird Bks.

—Paulina the Plummer. Dubowski, Cathy E. 28p. (ps-2). 1992. 3.95 (0-7214-5342-2) Ladybird Bks.

—The Quest for the Golden Mane. Speirs, John. LC 91-33894. 32p. 1991. 9.95 (0-89577-394-5, Reader's Digest Kids) RD Assn.

—The Twelve Days of Christmas. 24p. (Orig.). (ps-3). 1992. pap. 4.99 (0-679-82730-7) Random Bks Yng Read.

Spellman, Susan & Graves, Linda. Frosty's Snowy Day. Quattrocki, Carolyn. 24p. (ps-4). 1992. PLB 10.95 (1-56674-022-3) Forest Hse.

—The Little Drummer Boy. Quattrocki, Carolyn. 24p. (ps-4). 1992. PLB 10.95 (1-56674-023-1) Forest Hse.

—The Nutcracker. Quattrocki, Carolyn. 24p. (ps-4). 1992. PLB 10.95 (1-56674-024-X) Forest Hse.

—Rudolph's Adventure. Quattrocki, Carolyn. 24p. (ps-4). 1992. PLB 10.95 (1-56674-025-8) Forest Hse.

—Santa Claus Is Coming to Town. Quattrocki, Carolyn. 24p. (ps-4). 1992. PLB 10.95 (1-56674-026-6) Forest Hse.

—Twas the Night Before Christmas. Quattrocki, Carolyn. 24p. (ps-4). 1992. PLB 10.95 (1-56674-027-4) Forest Hse.

Spellman, Susan & Thiewes, Sam. Cinderella. Jerrard, Jane, adapted by. 24p. (gr. k-4). 1993. PLB 10.95 (1-56674-062-2, HTS Bks) Forest Hse.

—Jack & the Beanstalk. Jerrard, Jane, adapted by. 24p. (gr. k-4). 1993. PLB 10.95 (1-56674-064-9, HTS Bks) Forest Hse.

—Little Red Riding Hood. Jerrard, Jane, adapted by. 24p. (gr. k-4). 1993. PLB 10.95 (1-56674-065-7, HTS Bks) Forest Hse.

—The Ugly Duckling. Jerrard, Jane, adapted by. 24p. (gr. k-4). 1993. PLB 10.95 (1-56674-066-5, HTS Bks) Forest Hse.

Spence, Geraldine. Pakistani Twins. Shaw, Denis. (gr. 6-9). 1965. 12.95 (0-8023-1094-X) Dufour.

Spence, James. Fossils. Bell, Robert A. 24p. (gr. k-5). 1992. pap. write for info. blister pk., incl. 4 fossil specimens (0-307-12855-5, 12855, Golden Pr) Western Pub.

—The Golden Book of Monkeys, Apes, & Other Primates. Silverman, Maida. (gr. 3-6). 1991. 6.95 (0-307-15858-6, Golden Pr) Western Pub.

—Story of Joseph & a Dream Come True. Pingry, Patricia. 24p. (Orig.). (ps-3). 1988. pap. 3.95 (0-8249-8182-0, Ideals Child) Hambleton-Hill.

—Story of Joshua & the Bugles of Jericho. Pingry, Patricia. 24p. (Orig.). (ps-3). 1988. pap. 3.95 (0-8249-8178-2, Ideals Child) Hambleton-Hill.

Spence, Jim. Diana Ross: Star Supreme. Haskins, James S. 64p. (gr. 2-6). 1986. pap. 3.95 (0-14-032096-2, Puffin) Puffin Bks.

—Dracula. Stoker, Bram. Spinner, Stephanie, adapted by. LC 87-235417. 96p. (gr. 2-5). 1988. lib. bdg. 4.99 (0-394-94828-9); pap. 2.95 (0-394-84828-4) Random Bks Yng Read.

—Dracula. reissued ed. Stoker, Bram. Spinner, Stephanie, adapted by. 96p. (gr. 3-7). 1992. pap. 6.99 incl. cass. (0-679-82445-6) Random Bks Yng Read.

—Thunderbird. Sachs, Marilyn. LC 84-21252. 88p. (gr. 7 up). 1985. 10.95 (0-525-44163-3, 01063-320, DCB) Dutton Child Bks.

Spence, Jim, photos by. Diana Ross: Star Supreme. Haskins, James S. LC 84-21897. 64p. (gr. 2-6). 1985. pap. 10.95 (0-14-054814-9) Viking Child Bks.

Spence, Paula. Brett, My Pet. Carratello, Patty. Spivak, Darlene, ed. 16p. (gr. k-2). 1988. wkbk. 1.95 (1-55734-387-X) Tchr Create Mat.

—Holiday Crossword Puzzles. Nowlin, Susan S. 48p. (gr. 2-5). 1988. wkbk. 5.95 (1-55734-366-7) Tchr Create Mat.

—Literature Unit: The Witch of Blackbird Pond. Herweck, Dona. 48p. (Orig.). (gr. 5-8). 1992. pap. 5.95 wkbk. (1-55734-404-3) Tchr Create Mat.

—Patriotic Wordsearches, Codes & Crossword Puzzles. Sterling, Mary E. & Nowlin, Susan S. 48p. (gr. 2-5). 1988. wkbk. 5.95 (1-55734-367-5) Tchr Create Mat.

—Synonym-Antonym-Homonym Word Games. Sterling, Mary E. 48p. (gr. 2-5). 1988. wkbk. 5.95 (1-55734-368-3) Tchr Create Mat.

Spence, Paula & Wright, Terry. Crossword Puzzles. Sterling, Mary E. & Nowlin, Susan S. 48p. (gr. 2-5). 1988. wkbk. 5.95 (1-55734-365-9) Tchr Create Mat.

—Literature & Critical Thinking. Carratello, John & Carratello, Patty. 96p. (gr. 5-8). 1989. wkbk. 9.95 (1-55734-310-1) Tchr Create Mat.

Spence, Paula & Wright, Theresa. It's Easy to Punctuate. Carratello, Patty. 32p. (gr. 1-4). 1988. wkbk. 4.95 (1-55734-321-7) Tchr Create Mat.

Spence, Paula, jt. illus. see Apodaca, Blanqui.

Spence, Paula, jt. illus. see Wright, Terry.

Spence, Paula, jt. illus. see Wright, Theresa.

Spence, Paula, et al. December Monthly Activities. Sterling, Mary E. & Nowlin, Susan S. 80p. (gr. 1-5). 1989. wkbk. 7.95 (1-55734-154-0) Tchr Create Mat.

—Fall Time Savers. Nowlin, Susan S. 48p. (gr. k-6). 1989. wkbk. 5.95 (1-55734-123-0) Tchr Create Mat.

—Literature & Critical Thinking. Carratello, John & Carratello, Patty. 96p. (gr. 5-8). 1989. wkbk. 9.95 (1-55734-364-0) Tchr Create Mat.

—November Monthly Activities. Sterling, Mary E. & Nowlin, Susan S. 80p. (gr. 1-5). 1989. wkbk. 7.95 (1-55734-153-2) Tchr Create Mat.

—October Monthly Activities. Sterling, Mary E. & Nowlin, Susan S. 80p. (gr. 1-5). 1989. wkbk. 7.95 (1-55734-152-4) Tchr Create Mat.

—September Monthly Activities. Sterling, Mary E. & Nowlin, Susan S. 80p. (gr. 1-5). 1989. wkbk. 7.95 (1-55734-151-6) Tchr Create Mat.

—Spring Time Savers. Nowlin, Susan S. 48p. (gr. k-6). 1989. wkbk. 5.95 (1-55734-125-7) Tchr Create Mat.

—Winter Time Savers. Nowlin, Susan S. 48p. (gr. k-6). 1989. wkbk. 5.95 (1-55734-124-9) Tchr Create Mat.

—Year-Round Open Worksheets. Nowlin, Susan S. 48p. (gr. k-6). 1989. wkbk. 5.95 (1-55734-126-5) Tchr Create Mat.

Spenceley, Annabel. The Dragon, Giant & Monster Treasury. Royds, Caroline, selected by. 96p. 1988. 13.95 (0-399-21587-5, Putnam) Putnam Pub Group.

—The Ghost Story Treasury. Sonntag, Linda, ed. 96p. (gr. 7 up). 1987. 12.95 (0-399-21477-1, Putnam) Putnam Pub Group.

—Halloween Fun: Great Things to Make & Do. Willis, Abigail. LC 93-21712. 32p. (gr. 2-6). 1993. pap. 4.95 (1-85697-864-8) Kingfisher Bks.

—A Treasury of Animal Stories. Olliver, Jane, ed. LC 92-53110. 160p. (Orig.). (gr. k-5). 1992. pap. 5.95 (1-85697-831-1) Kingfisher Bks.

—A Treasury of Bedtime Stories. Clarke, Nora, compiled by. LC 92-43152. 160p. (gr. k-4). 1993. pap. 5.95 (1-85697-931-8) Kingfisher Bks.

—A Treasury of Giant & Monster Stories. Olliver, Jane, ed. LC 92-53112. 160p. (Orig.). (gr. k-5). 1992. pap. 5.95 (1-85697-832-X) Kingfisher Bks.

—A Treasury of Spooky Stories. Olliver, Jane, ed. LC 92-53111. 160p. (Orig.). (gr. k-5). 1992. pap. 5.95 (1-85697-830-3) Kingfisher Bks.

Spencely, Annabel. Daniel & the Lions' Den. Pipe, Rhona. LC 92-12073. 1993. 7.99 (0-8407-3422-0) Oliver-Nelson.

—The Easter Story. Pipe, Rhona. LC 92-13325. 1993. 7.99 (0-8407-3420-4) Oliver-Nelson.

Spencer, Pat. Bulletin Boards Through the Year. Spencer, Pat. 96p. (gr. k-4). 1988. wkbk. 9.95 (1-55734-062-5) Tchr Create Mat.

Spengler, Ken. How the Jackrabbit Got His Very Long Ears. Irbinskas, Heather. 32p. (gr. k up). 1994. 14.95 (0-87358-566-6) Northland AZ.

Sperling, Thomas. El Cuento de Ned y Su Nariz. Potash, Dorothy. (SPA.). 24p. (ps-4). 1993. PLB 13.95 (1-879567-24-5, Valeria Bks) Wonder Well.

—Evil Tales of Evil Things. Schorsch, Laurence, ed. 128p. (gr. 3 up). 1993. pap. 3.50 (1-56288-407-7) Checkerboard.

—The First Spell of Winnefred Broomstock. Blank, Peter. 32p. 1992. 7.95 (1-56288-273-2) Checkerboard.

—The Tale of Ned & His Nose. Potash, Dorothy. 24p. (gr. k-4). 1993. PLB 13.95 (1-879567-23-7, Valeria Bks) Wonder Well.

—Tales of the Living Dead. Schorsch, Laurence, ed. 128p. (gr. 3 up). 1993. pap. 3.50 (1-56288-406-9) Checkerboard.

Sperling, Tom. The Story of Joseph. Schorsch, Laurence, retold by. 24p. (ps-3). 1992. 4.95 (1-56288-224-4) Checkerboard.

—Three Ships for Columbus. Spencer, Eve. LC 92-14401. 32p. (gr. 2-5). 1992. PLB 21.34 (0-8114-7212-4) Raintree Steck-V.

Sperry, Angela. Purple Patches. Schultz, Betty K. 32p. (gr. k-3). 1991. write for info. (0-929568-01-X) Raspberry IL.

Sperry, Armstrong. Call It Courage. reissued ed. Sperry, Armstrong. LC 40-4229. 96p. (gr. 5-7). 1968. SBE 13.95 (0-02-786030-2, Macmillan Child Bk) Macmillan Child Grp.

Spier, John. A Treasury of Christmas Poems, Carols, & Games to Share. Wax, Wendy, compiled by. (ps-1). 1992. 10.00 (0-440-40731-1) Dell.

Spier, Nancy. Mr. Boffin. Schorsch, Laurence. 32p. (gr. k-3). 1993. 6.95 (1-56288-353-4) Checkerboard.

Spier, Peter. And So My Garden Grows. Spier, Peter. 48p. (ps-3). 1992. pap. 3.99 (0-440-40714-1, YB) Dell.

—Bored, Nothing to Do. Spier, Peter. LC 77-20726. 48p. (gr. 1-3). 1978. 11.95 (0-385-13177-1) Doubleday.

—Cow Who Fell in the Canal. Krasilovsky, Phyllis. LC 56-8236. 38p. (gr. k-1). 1985. pap. 11.95 (0-385-07585-5) Doubleday.

—Dreams. Spier, Peter. LC 85-13130. 32p. (ps-3). 1986. Doubleday.

—The Erie Canal. Spier, Peter. LC 70-102055. 36p. (gr. 1-3). 1990. pap. 10.95 (0-385-06777-1); pap. 5.95 (0-385-05234-0) Doubleday.

—Fast-Slow High-Low. Spier, Peter. LC 72-76207. 24p. (ps-k). 1988. 5.95 (0-385-24093-7) Doubleday.

—Fast-Slow High-Low: A Book of Opposites. Spier, Peter. LC 72-76207. 48p. (gr. k-3). 1972. pap. 10.95 (0-385-06781-X); pap. 10.95 (0-385-02876-8); pap. 2.95 (0-685-01490-8) Doubleday.

—Fox Went Out on a Chilly Night. Spier, Peter. LC 60-7139. 42p. (gr. k-3). 1961. pap. 11.95 (0-385-07990-7) Doubleday.

—Gobble, Growl, Grunt. Spier, Peter. LC 79-14430. 24p. (ps-1). 1988. 8.00 (0-385-24094-5) Doubleday.

—Hurrah, We're Outward Bound! Spier, Peter. 48p. (ps-3). 1992. pap. 9.99 (0-440-40715-X, YB) Dell.

—Last Hurdle. Brown, F. K. LC 87-29761. 202p. (gr. 3-9). 1988. Repr. of 1953 ed. 17.50 (0-208-02212-0, Linnet) Shoe String.

—The Little Riders. Shemin, Margaretha. 80p. (gr. 3-7). 1988. 12.95 (0-399-21462-3, Putnam) Putnam Pub Group.

—The Little Riders. Shemin, Margaretha. 80p. (gr. 4 up). 1993. pap. 3.95 (0-688-12499-2, Pub. by Beech Tree Bks) Morrow.

—London Bridge Is Falling Down. Spier, Peter. LC 67-17905. (ps). 1985. pap. 10.95 (0-385-08717-9) Doubleday.

—London Bridge Is Falling Down. Spier, Peter. 48p. (ps-3). 1992. pap. 3.99 (0-440-40710-9, YB) Dell.

—Noah's Ark. Spier, Peter. LC 76-43630. 44p. (gr. k-3). 1977. PLB 15.95 (0-385-09473-6) Doubleday.

—Noah's Ark. Spier, Peter. 48p. (ps-1). 1992. pap. 4.99 (0-440-40693-5, YB) Dell.

—Oh, Were They Ever Happy. Spier, Peter. LC 77-78144. 48p. (gr. k-3). 1978. 12.95 (0-385-13175-5); pap. 10.95 (0-385-13176-3) Doubleday.

—People. Spier, Peter. LC 78-19832. 48p. (gr. 1-3). 1980. PLB 15.00 (0-385-13181-X) Doubleday.

—Peter Spier's Christmas! Spier, Peter. LC 83-13184-4); pap. 14.95 (0-385-13183-6) Doubleday.

—Peter Spier's Christmas! Spier, Peter. 48p. (ps-5). 1992. 4.99 (0-440-40730-3, YB) Dell.

—Peter Spier's Circus! Spier, Peter. LC 90-23282. 48p.
(ps-3). 1992. pap. 16.00 (0-385-41969-4) Doubleday.
—Peter Spier's Little Animal Books, 4 bks. Spier, Peter.
(ps). 1987. Boxed Set. bds. 10.00 laminated
(0-385-19715-2) Doubleday.
—Peter Spier's Rain. Spier, Peter. LC 81-43506. 40p.
(ps-3). 1982. PLB 12.95 (0-385-15485-2, Zephyr-
BFYR) Doubleday.
—The Star-Spangled Banner. Spier, Peter. LC 73-79112.
48p. (gr. 1 up). 1973. 15.00 (0-385-09458-2); pap. 11.
95 (0-385-07746-7) Doubleday.
—Star-Spangled Banner. Spier, Peter. LC 73-79112. 48p.
(gr. 1 up). 1986. pap. 8.00 (0-385-23401-5, Pub. by
Zephyr-BFYR) Doubleday.
—Tin Lizzie. Spier, Peter. LC 74-1510. 48p. (gr. 3-5).
1990. 5.95 (0-385-13342-1); pap. 8.95 (0-385-09470-1)
Doubleday.
—To Market, to Market. Spier, Peter. LC 67-18664. 52p.
(gr. 1-3). 1967. 8.95a (0-385-08755-1); pap. 5.95
(0-385-09081-1) Doubleday.
—To Market! To Market! Spier, Peter. 48p. (ps-3). 1992.
pap. 3.99 (0-440-40713-3, YB) Dell.
—We the People: The Story of the U. S. Constitution.
Spier, Peter. LC 86-24205. 48p. (gr. k-3). 1987. PLB
16.00 (0-385-23589-5) Doubleday.
Spiers, John. Why Should I? Asks Jeremy. Venti, Pamela
R. 32p. (gr. 1-3). 1990. PLB 19.95 (0-89565-700-7);
PLB 13.95s.p. (0-685-56166-6) Childs World.
Spiess, Helga. If You Want to Scare Yourself. Sommer-
Bodenburg, Angela. Cafiero, Renee V., tr. from GER.
LC 87-45316. 112p. (gr. 2-5). 1989. (Lipp Jr Bks);
PLB 12.89 (0-397-32210-0, Lipp Jr Bks) HarpC Child
Bks.
Spillman, Fredericka. Angry Waters. Morey, Walt. (Orig.).
(gr. 5-9). 1990. Repr. 6.95 (0-936085-10-X) Blue
Heron OR.
Spillman, Fredrika. Death Walk. Morey, Walt. (gr. 5-12).
1991. 13.95 (0-936085-18-5) Blue Heron OR.
—Gloomy Gus. Morey, Walt. 192p. (gr. 4-8). 1989. pap.
6.95 (0-936085-17-7) Blue Heron OR.
—The Maybe Garden. Burke-Weiner, Kimberly. Roehm,
Michelle, ed. 36p. (gr. 1-4). 1992. 14.95
(0-941831-56-6); pap. 7.95 (0-941831-57-4) Beyond
Words Pub.
—Runaway Stallion. Morey, Walt. 176p. (gr. 4-8). 1989.
pap. 6.95 (0-936085-12-6) Blue Heron OR.
—Scrub Dog of Alaska. Morey, Walt. 160p. (gr. 4-9).
1989. pap. 6.95 (0-936085-13-4) Blue Heron OR.
—Year of the Black Pony. Morey, Walt. 160p. (gr. 4-8).
1989. pap. 6.95 (0-936085-14-2) Blue Heron OR.
Spina, Russell. Disney Babies Wake up & Play. LC 91-
71344. 32p. (ps). 1991. 7.95 (1-56282-055-9) Disney
Pr.
—Disney's Haunted Mansion Pop-up Book. 5p. 1993. 13.
95 (1-56282-499-6) Disney Pr.
Spirin, Gennady. Boots & the Glass Mountain. Martin,
Claire, retold by. LC 91-9724. 32p. (ps-3). 1992. 15.00
(0-8037-1110-7); PLB 14.89 (0-8037-1111-5) Dial Bks
Young.
—The Children of Lir. MacGill-Callahan, Sheila. LC 91-
2712. 32p. (ps-3). 1993. 14.99 (0-8037-1121-2); PLB
14.99 (0-8037-1122-0) Dial Bks Young.
—Fool & the Fish: A Tale from Russia. Afanasyev,
Alexander. Hort, Lenny, retold by. 32p. (ps-3). 1990.
12.95 (0-8037-0861-0) Dial Bks Young.
—The Frog Princess: A Russian Folktale. Lewis, Patrick,
retold by. LC 93-10827. 1994. write for info.
(0-8037-1623-0); lib. bdg. write for info.
(0-8037-1624-9) Dial Bks Young.
—Gulliver's Adventures in Lilliput. Swift, Jonathan.
Beneduce, Ann K., retold by. LC 92-26200. 32p. (ps).
1993. 15.95 (0-399-22021-6, Philomel Bks) Putnam
Pub Group.
—The Mysterious Tale of Gentle Jack & Lord
Bumblebee. Sand, George. LC 87-30490. 80p. (ps up).
1988. Dial Bks Young.
—Once There Was a Tree. Romanova, Natalia. LC 85-
6730. (ps up). 1989. pap. 4.99 (0-8037-0705-3) Dial
Bks Young.
—Rumpelstiltskin. Grimm, Jacob & Grimm, Wilhelm K.
Sage, Alison, retold by. 32p. (ps-3). 1991. 12.95
(0-8037-0908-0) Dial Bks Young.
—Snow White & Rose Red. Grimm, Jacob & Grimm,
Wilhelm K. 32p. (ps up). 1992. 14.95 (0-399-21873-4,
Philomel Bks) Putnam Pub Group.
—The Tale of the Unicorn. Preussler, Otfried. LC 88-
7141. 32p. (ps up) 1989. 12.95 (0-8037-0583-2) Dial
Bks Young.
—The Tale of the Unicorn. Preussler, Otfried. 32p. (ps
up). 1992. pap. 4.99 (0-14-054568-9, Puffin Pied
Piper) Puffin Bks.
—The White Cat. San Souci, Robert D. LC 88-19698.
32p. (ps-3). 1990. 15.95 (0-531-05809-3); PLB 15.99
(0-531-08409-4) Orchard Bks Watts.
Spivak, Darlene. Crossword Puzzles, Wordsearches &
Codes. Spivak, Darlene. 48p. (gr. 2-5). 1986. wkbk.
5.95 (1-55734-067-6) Tchr Create Mat.
Spivak, Darlene E. Scrambled Word Puzzles. Spivak,
Darlene E. 48p. (gr. 2-5). 1987. wkbk. 5.95
(1-55734-066-8) Tchr Create Mat.
Spivak, I. Howard, photos by. I Have Feelings. Berger,
Terry. LC 70-147123. 32p. 1971. 14.95
(0-87705-021-X); pap. 9.95 (0-89885-342-7) Human
Sci Pr.
Spivey, Elvera. The Little Computer. Mister Tom. 32p.
(gr. 2-4). 1978. write for info. Oddo.
—Messycat. Mister Tom. LC 77-85397. 36p. (gr. k-4).
1989. pap. 4.95 (0-925237-00-0) Ten Pubns.

—Queen Fussy. Mister Tom. 48p. (gr. 2-4). 1973.
Cassette. write for info. Oddo.
Spizzirri, Peter M. Paleozoic Life: An Educational
Coloring Book. Spizzirri Publishing Co. Staff. Spizzirri,
Linda, ed. 32p. (gr. 1-8). 1981. pap. 1.75
(0-86545-024-2) Spizzirri.
—Plains Indians: An Educational Coloring Book. Spizzirri
Publishing Co. Staff. Spizzirri, Linda, ed. 32p. (gr.
1-8). 1981. pap. 1.75 (0-86545-025-0) Spizzirri.
—Prehistoric Birds: An Educational Coloring Book.
Spizzirri Publishing Co. Staff. Spizzirri, Linda, ed. 32p.
(gr. 1-8). 1981. pap. 1.75 (0-86545-023-4) Spizzirri.
—Space Craft: An Educational Coloring Book. Spizzirri
Publishing Co. Staff. Spizzirri, Linda, ed. 32p. (gr.
1-8). 1981. pap. 1.75 (0-86545-036-6) Spizzirri.
—Space Explorers: An Educational Coloring Book.
Spizzirri Publishing Co. Staff. Spizzirri, Linda, ed. 32p.
(gr. 1-8). 1981. pap. 1.75 (0-86545-037-4) Spizzirri.
—Transportation: Educational Coloring Book. Spizzirri
Publishing Co. Staff. Spizzirri, Linda, ed. 32p. (gr.
1-8). 1981. pap. 1.75 (0-86545-038-2) Spizzirri.
Spizzirri, Peter M., jt. illus. see Fuller, Glenn.
Spizzirri, Peter M., jt. illus. see Goodman, Marlene.
Spizzirri, Peter M., et al. Mammals: An Educational
Coloring Book. Spizzirri Publishing Co. Staff. Spizzirri,
Linda, ed. 32p. (gr. 1-8). 1981. pap. 1.75
(0-86545-027-7) Spizzirri.
Splane, Lily & Duitsman, Penny. Understanding the
Horse. Duitsman, Dominique. 64p. (gr. 6-9). 1989.
pap. text ed. 8.95 (0-945962-02-9) Anaphase II.
Spoden, Dan, jt. illus. see Hohag, Linda.
Spohn, Cliff. Baseball's Best: Five True Stories. Gutelle,
Andrew. LC 89-35413. 48p. (Orig.). (gr. 2-4). 1990.
lib. bdg. 7.99 (0-394-90983-6); 3.50 (0-394-80983-1)
Random Bks Yng Read.
Spohn, Franz. Shoe Shine Shirley. Komaiko, Leah. LC
92-25816. 1993. 14.95 (0-385-30526-5) Doubleday.
Spohn, Kate. Christmas at Anna's. Spohn, Kate. 32p.
(ps-3). 1993. 13.99 (0-670-84895-6) Viking Child Bks.
—Hide-&-Seek in the Yellow House. Rose, Agatha. 32p.
(ps-1). 1992. PLB 14.00 (0-670-84383-0) Viking Child
Bks.
—Introducing Fanny. Spohn, Kate. LC 90-7736. 32p.
(ps-2). 1991. 14.95 (0-531-05920-0); PLB 14.99
(0-531-08520-1) Orchard Bks Watts.
—River. Staines, Bill. LC 93-27864. 1994. 13.99
(0-670-85353-4) Viking Child Bks.
—Ruth's Bake Shop. Spohn, Kate. LC 89-70930. 32p.
(ps-2). 1990. 13.95 (0-531-05889-1); PLB 13.99
(0-531-08489-2) Orchard Bks Watts.
Spong, Clive. Henry the Green Engine & the Tunnel.
Awdry, W. LC 91-67968. 12p. (ps-1). 1992. 3.99
(0-679-83451-6) Random Bks Yng Read.
—Percy the Small Engine Takes the Plunge. Awdry, W.
LC 91-67970. 12p. (ps-1). 1992. 3.99 (0-679-83453-2)
Random Bks Yng Read.
—Thomas the Tank Engine & the Tractor. Awdry, W.
LC 91-67969. 12p. (ps-1). 1992. 3.99 (0-679-83452-4)
Random Bks Yng Read.
—Thomas the Tank Engine Goes Fishing. Awdry, W. LC
91-67967. 12p. (ps-1). 1992. 3.99 (0-679-83450-8)
Random Bks Yng Read.
Spoon, Wilfred. My Friend the Manatee: An Ocean
Magic Book. Schneider, Jeff. LC 90-61576. 12p. (ps).
1991. 4.95g (1-877779-08-3) Schneider Educational.
—My Friend the Penguin: An Ocean Magic Book.
Schneider, Jeff. LC 90-61577. 12p. (ps). 1991. 4.95g
(1-877779-09-1) Schneider Educational.
—My Friend the Polar Bear: An Ocean Magic Book.
Schneider, Jeff. LC 90-61579. 12p. (ps). 1991. 4.95g
(1-877779-12-1) Schneider Educational.
—My Friend the Porpoise: An Ocean Magic Book.
Schneider, Jeff. LC 90-61572. 12p. (ps). 1991. 4.95g
(1-877779-07-5) Schneider Educational.
—My Friend the Sea Otter: An Ocean Magic Book.
Schneider, Jeff. LC 90-61578. 12p. (ps). 1991. 4.95g
(1-877779-10-5) Schneider Educational.
—My Friend the Walrus: An Ocean Magic Book.
Schneider, Jeff. LC 90-61581. 12p. (ps). 1991. 4.95g
(1-877779-11-3) Schneider Educational.
—Ocean Magic Book of Masks. Spoon, Wilfred. LC 90-
62142. (ps-1). 1991. incl. 6 punch-out hand-held face
masks - manatee 5¢, penguin, polar bear, porpoise,
sea otter, walrus (1-877779-13-X) Schneider
Educational.
—Ocean Magic "Press 'n Peel" Game Board. LC 90-
62146. (ps-1). 1991. incl. laminated ocean playboard,
18 vinyl stickers & storage guard for stickers 7.95
(1-877779-14-8) Schneider Educational.
Sporn, Michael. The Walt Disney Story. Fisher, Maxine
P. Rakos, Jennie, ed. 72p. (gr. 7 up). 1988. PLB 10.90
(0-531-10493-1) Watts.
Spowart, Robin. Latkes & Applesauce: A Hanukkah
Story. Manushkin, Fran. (ps-3). 1990. 12.95
(0-590-42261-8, Scholastic Hardcover) Scholastic Inc.
—Mama, If You Had a Wish. Modesitt, Jeanne. LC 91-
31354. 40p. (ps-1). 1993. JRT 14.00 (0-671-75437-8,
Green Tiger) S&S Trade.
—A Rose, a Bridge, & a Wild Black Horse. Zolotow,
Charlotte. LC 87-26840. 32p. (ps-1). 1987. PLB 12.89
(0-06-026939-1, C Zolotow Bks) HarpC Child Bks.
—The Star Grazers. Widman, Christine. LC 87-29377.
32p. (ps-3). 1989. HarpC Child Bks.
—To Rabbittown. Wayland, April H. (gr. 2-5). 1989. pap.
12.95 (0-590-40852-6) Scholastic Inc.
—To Rabbittown. Wayland, April H. 32p. 1992. pap. 3.95
(0-590-44777-7, Blue Ribbon Bks) Scholastic Inc.

—Vegetable Soup. Modesitt, Jeanne. LC 87-11169. 32p.
(ps-1). 1988. RSBE 13.95 (0-02-767630-7, Macmillan
Child Bk) Macmillan Child Grp.
—Vegetable Soup. Modesitt, Jeanne. LC 91-247. 32p.
(ps-3). 1991. pap. 4.50 (0-689-71523-4, Aladdin)
Macmillan Child Grp.
Spring, Grace J. The Fabulous House of Marcella Mouse.
Spring, Grace J. LC 85-7518. 24p. (gr. 1-6). 1985.
pap. 3.95 (0-317-39846-6) Andrew Mtn Pr.
—The Furry Wind. Boyd, Patricia R. 28p. (gr. 2-3). 1982.
pap. 2.25 (0-9603840-4-9) Andrew Mtn Pr.
Springer, Hariett. A First Look at Seashells. Selsam,
Millicent E. & Hunt, Joyce. LC 83-5876. 32p. (gr.
1-3). 1983. PLB 12.85 (0-8027-6503-3) Walker & Co.
Springer, Harriet. A First Look at Animals That Eat
Other Animals. Selsam, Millicent E. & Hunt, Joyce.
64p. (gr. 5 up). 1990. 11.95 (0-8027-6895-4); PLB 12.
85 (0-8027-6896-2) Walker & Co.
—A First Look at Animals with Backbones. Selsam,
Millicent E. & Hunt, Joyce. LC 78-4321. (gr. k-3).
1978. 6.95 (0-8027-6338-3); PLB 9.85
(0-8027-6339-1) Walker & Co.
—A First Look at Birds. Selsam, Millicent E. & Hunt,
Joyce. LC 73-81404. 32p. (gr. 2-4). 1973. PLB 12.85
(0-8027-6164-X) Walker & Co.
—A First Look at Ducks, Geese & Swans. Selsam,
Millicent E. & Hunt, Joyce. 32p. (gr. 1-4). 1990. 11.95
(0-8027-6975-6); lib. bdg. 12.85 (0-8027-6976-4)
Walker & Co.
—A First Look at Fish. Selsam, Millicent E. & Hunt,
Joyce. LC 72-81377. 32p. (gr. 2-4). 1972. 5.50
(0-8027-6119-4); PLB 9.85 (0-8027-6120-8) Walker &
Co.
—A First Look at Kangaroos, Kaolas & Other Animals
with Pouches. Selsam, Millicent E. & Hunt, Joyce. LC
85-3126. 32p. (gr. k-3). 1985. 9.95 (0-8027-6600-5);
PLB 12.85 (0-8027-6579-3) Walker & Co.
—A First Look at Owls, Eagles, & Other Hunters of the
Sky. Selsam, Millicent E. & Hunt, Joyce. 32p. (gr.
6-9). 1986. 10.95 (0-8027-6625-0); PLB 10.85
(0-8027-6642-0) Walker & Co.
—A First Look at Sharks. Selsam, Millicent E., et al. (gr.
k-3). 1979. PLB 12.85 (0-8027-6373-1) Walker & Co.
—A First Look at Snakes, Lizards & Other Reptiles.
Selsam, Millicent E. & Hunt, Joyce. LC 74-26315.
32p. (gr. 1-4). 1975. PLB 12.85 (0-8027-6211-5)
Walker & Co.
Springer, Harriett. A First Look at Animals with Horns.
Selsam, Millicent E. & Hunt, Joyce. (gr. 1 up). 1989.
10.95 (0-8027-6871-7); PLB 11.85 (0-8027-6872-5)
Walker & Co.
—A First Look at Animals Without Backbones. Selsam,
Millicent E. & Hunt, Joyce. LC 76-12056. (gr. 2-4).
1976. PLB 9.85 (0-8027-6269-7) Walker & Co.
—A First Look at Birds' Nest. Selsam, Millicent E., et al.
LC 84-15238. 32p. (gr. 1-4). 1984. lib. bdg. 9.85
(0-8027-6565-3) Walker & Co.
—First Look at Cats. Selsam, Millicent E. & Hunt, Joyce.
LC 80-7673. 32p. (gr. 1-4). 1981. 7.95
(0-8027-6398-7); PLB 9.85 (0-8027-6399-5) Walker &
Co.
—A First Look at Dinosaurs. Selsam, Millicent E. &
Hunt, Joyce. 32p. (gr. 1-4). 1982. 7.95
(0-8027-6454-1); PLB 12.85 (0-8027-6456-8) Walker
& Co.
—A First Look at Insects. Selsam, Millicent E. & Hunt,
Joyce. LC 73-92451. 32p. (gr. 2-4). 1974. PLB 12.85
(0-8027-6182-8) Walker & Co.
—A First Look at Leaves. Selsam, Millicent E. Selsam,
Millicent E. & Hunt, Joyce, eds. LC 72-81376. 32p.
(gr. 2-4). 1972. PLB 11.85 (0-8027-6118-6) Walker &
Co.
—A First Look at Monkeys & Apes. Selsam, Millicent E.
& Hunt, Joyce. LC 78-74164. (gr. 1-4). 1979. 7.95
(0-8027-6358-8); lib. bdg. 9.85 (0-8027-6359-6)
Walker & Co.
—A First Look at Seals, Sea Lions, & Walruses. Selsam,
Millicent E. & Hunt, Joyce. LC 87-29491. 36p. (ps-3).
1988. pap. 10.95 (0-8027-6787-7); pap. text ed. 11.85
(0-8027-6788-5) Walker & Co.
—A First Look at the World of Plants. Selsam, Millicent
E. & Hunt, Joyce. LC 77-78088. (gr. 1-4). 1978. PLB
9.85 (0-8027-6299-9) Walker & Co.
Springer, Sally. High Holiday Fun for Little Hands. 32p.
(ps). 1990. wkbk. 3.95 (0-929371-76-3) Kar Ben.
—A Holiday for Noah. Topek, Susan R. LC 89-48189.
24p. (ps). 1990. 10.95 (0-929371-07-0); pap. 4.95
(0-929371-08-9) Kar Ben.
—How the Weather Works. Seymour, Peter. 10p. (gr.
2-5). 1985. SBE 8.95 (0-02-782110-2, Macmillan
Child Bk) Macmillan Child Grp.
—Let's Make Latkes. LC 91-60403. 12p. (ps). 1991. bds.
4.95 (0-929371-58-5) Kar Ben.
—Let's Play Dreidel. Grossman, Roz & Gewirtz, Gladys.
LC 89-34892. 16p. (ps-3). 1989. incl. tape & dreidel
6.95 (0-929371-01-8) Kar Ben.
—Sukkot & Simchat Torah Fun for Little Hands. 32p.
(ps). 1990. wkbk. 3.95 (0-929371-77-1) Kar Ben.
—A Taste for Noah. Topek, Susan Remick. LC 92-39384.
(gr. k up). 1993. 12.95 (0-929371-39-9); pap. 4.95
(0-929371-40-2) Kar Ben.
—A Turn for Noah: A Hanukkah Story. Topek, Susan R.
LC 92-22958. 1992. 12.95 (0-929371-37-2); pap. 4.95
(0-929371-38-0) Kar Ben.
—What Can You Do with a Bagel? Feder, Harriet. LC
91-60591. 12p. (ps). 1992. bds. 4.95 (0-929371-59-3)
Kar Ben.

Springett, Martin. The Wise Old Woman. Uchida, Yoshiko, retold by. LC 92-46048. (gr. 4 up). 1994. write for info. (0-689-50582-5) Macmillan.

Sprock, Inge. The Land of Flop-Eared Piggies. Sprock, Inge & Biser, Len. 32p. (ps-3). 1992. write for info. (1-880015-30-7) Petra Pub Co.

Spunger, Harriett. A First Look at Frogs, Toads & Salamanders. Selsam, Millicent E. & Hunt, Joyce. 32p. (gr. 2-4). 1976. PLB 12.85 (0-8027-6244-1) Walker & Co.

Spurll, Barbara. The Flying Tortoise: An Igbo Tale. Mollel, Tololwa M., retold by. LC 94-14349. 1994. write for info. (0-395-68845-0) HM.

—Rhinos for Lunch & Elephants for Supper! Mollel, Tololwa M. 32p. (ps-3). 1992. 15.95 (0-395-60734-5, Clarion Bks) HM.

Squillace, Albert & Kuznetsov, Eugene. The Key to Music Making, Pt. I: Piano Method for Beginners. Bryansky, Faina. LC 88-50726. 48p. (gr. 1-5). 1988. pap. 8.00 (0-929571-00-2) White Lilac Pr.

Stack-Brison, Guy. Let's Learn the Alef Bet: Reading Readiness Book for the Hebrew Primer. Strauss, Ruby G. 94p. (gr. 4-7). 1987. pap. text ed. 4.45x (0-87441-439-3); tchr's. pamphlet avail. Behrman.

Stacy, Darryl. Missouri: Studies. Stacy, Darryl. 56p. (gr. 7-9). 1988. wkbk. 5.25 (0-911981-51-9) Cloud Pub.

—Missouri: Studies: Government & Constitution. Stacy, Darryl & Bimes, James D. 120p. (gr. 7-9). 1989. Repr. of 1988 ed. text ed. 15.95 (0-911981-50-0) Cloud Pub.

Stadler, John. The Adventures of Snail at School. Stadler, John. LC 91-45403. 64p. (gr. k-3). 1993. 14. 00 (0-06-021041-9); PLB 13.89 (0-06-021042-7) HarpC Child Bks.

—Cat at Bat. Stadler, John. LC 87-36400. 32p. (ps-2). 1988. 9.95 (0-525-44416-5, DCB) Dutton Child Bks.

—Cat is Back at Bat. Stadler, John. LC 90-24831. 32p. (ps-2). 1991. 10.95 (0-525-44762-8, DCB) Dutton Child Bks.

—Hooray for Snail! Stadler, John. LC 83-46164. 32p. (ps-2). 1985. pap. 5.95 (0-06-443075-8, Trophy) HarpC Child Bks.

—Jason & the Baseball Bear. Elish, Dan. LC 89-23102. 160p. (gr. 3-5). 1990. 13.95 (0-531-05868-9); PLB 13. 99 (0-531-08468-X) Orchard Bks Watts.

—Three Cheers for Hippo! Stadler, John. LC 87-497. 32p. (gr. k-3). 1990. pap. 3.95 (0-06-443220-3, Trophy) HarpC Child Bks.

—Words with Wrinkled Knees. Esbensen, Barbara J. LC 85-47886. 48p. (gr. 2-7). 1987. (Crowell Jr Bks); PLB 14.89 (0-690-04505-0, Crowell Jr Bks) HarpC Child Bks.

Staeck, Roy. Dreams Can Help: A Journal Guide to Understanding Your Dreams & Making Them Work for You. Kincher, Jonni. Morse, Mary & Espeland, Pamela, eds. LC 88-7630. 96p. (Orig.). (gr. 3-9). 1988. pap. 9.95 (0-915793-15-6) Free Spirit Pub.

Stafslien, Barbara. Moving Right Along. Sher, Barbara. 84p. (ps-3). 1985. pap. text ed. 6.95 (0-930681-03-7) Bright Baby.

Stair, Gobin. Old Tales for a New Day. 2nd ed. Fahs, Sophia L. & Cobb, Alice. 201p. (gr. 4-9). 1992. pap. 14.95 (0-87975-730-2) Prometheus Bks.

—Old Tales for a New Day: Early Answers to Life's Eternal Questions. Fahs, Sophia L. & Cobb, Alice. LC 80-84076. (gr. 3-9). 1980. 17.95 (0-87975-138-X); tchr's manual o.p. 9.95 (0-87975-131-2) Prometheus Bks.

STake, Fran. The Animals Talk to One Another: A Christmas Folktale Retold & Illustrated by Fran Stake. Stake, Fran. 20p. (ps). 1993. Set with painting. 1100. 00 (0-9619075-0-9) Stake Studio.

Stallings, Pat. Puzzling Your Way into Algebra. new ed. Stallings, Pat. (gr. 7-10). 1978. pap. text ed. 7.95 (0-918932-58-0) Activity Resources.

Stallings, Scott. Where in the World Did You Come From? Nichols, Paul. 32p. (ps up). 1993. 17.95g (1-884507-00-X) Boyer-Caswell.

Stamm, Gwen. Mystery at the Mall. Hostetler, Marian. LC 85-13951. 88p. (Orig.). (gr. 5-6). 1985. pap. 3.95 (0-8361-3401-X) Herald Pr.

Stammen, JoEllen M. Lobster for Lunch. Hartman, Bob. LC 91-77671. 32p. (gr. k-3). 1992. 14.95 (0-89272-302-5) Down East.

—Wild Fox: A True Story. Mason, Cherie. LC 92-74622. 32p. (gr. 2-5). 1993. 15.95 (0-89272-319-X) Down East.

Stamper, Silas. Bubbles, Rainbows & Worms: Science Experiments for Pre-School Children. Brown, Sam E. LC 80-84598. 105p. (ps-1). 1981. pap. 8.95 (0-87659-100-4) Gryphon Hse.

Stanger, Susan E. The Kaua'i Guide to Kaua'i Products & Speciality Shopping. Jobson, Joy. 64p. (Orig.). 1988. pap. 2.50 (0-942255-03-8, G2) Magic Fishes Pr.

Stanier, Linda. Scientist & Physician. Judith Pachciarz. Verheyden-Hilliard, Mary E. LC 87-82599. 32p. (Orig.). (gr. 1-4). 1988. pap. 5.00 (0-932469-13-2) Equity Inst.

Stanish, Bob. A Monster's Shoe & the Cat. Stanish, Bob. 44p. (gr. 1-4). 1983. pap. 9.95 tchr's. enrichment bk. (0-88047-018-6, 8303) DOK Pubs.

Stanish, Jon. Mindglow. Stanish, Bob. 96p. (gr. 3-12). 1986. wkbk. 9.95 (0-86653-346-X, GA 693) Good Apple.

Stanley, Diane. The Bard of Avon: The Story of William Shakespeare. Stanley, Diane & Vennema, Peter. LC 90-46564. 48p. (gr. 2 up). 1992. 15.00 (0-688-09108-3); PLB 14.93 (0-688-09109-1) Morrow Jr Bks.

—Birdsong Lullaby. Stanley, Diane. LC 85-5654. 32p. (ps-2). 1985. 12.95 (0-688-05804-3) Morrow Jr Bks.

—Captain Whiz-Bang. Stanley, Diane. LC 86-16432. 32p. (ps-2). 1987. 12.95 (0-688-06226-1); lib. bdg. 12.88 (0-688-06227-X, Morrow Jr Bks) Morrow Jr Bks.

—Charles Dickens: The Man Who Had Great Expectations. Stanley, Diane & Vennema, Peter. LC 91-41552. 48p. (gr. 2 up). 1993. 15.00 (0-688-09110-5); PLB 14.93 (0-688-09111-3) Morrow Jr Bks.

—Cleopatra. Vennema, Peter. LC 93-27032. (gr. 4 up). 1994. pap. write for info. (0-688-10413-4); PLB write for info. (0-688-10414-2) Morrow Jr Bks.

—The Conversation Club. Stanley, Diane. LC 83-739. 32p. (ps-2). 1983. RSBE 12.95 (0-02-786740-4, Macmillan Child Bk) Macmillan Child Grp.

—The Conversation Club. Stanley, Diane. LC 89-18665. 32p. (gr. k-2). 1990. pap. 3.95 (0-689-71401-7, Aladdin) Macmillan Child Grp.

—A Country Tale. Stanley, Diane. LC 84-14399. 32p. (gr. k-3). 1985. RSBE 12.95 (0-02-786780-3, Four Winds) Macmillan Child Grp.

—Fortune. Stanley, Diane. LC 88-13204. 32p. (ps-4). 1990. 12.95 (0-688-07210-0); PLB 12.88 (0-688-07211-9, Morrow Jr Bks) Morrow Jr Bks.

—Good Queen Bess: The Story of Queen Elizabeth I of England. Stanley, Diane & Vennema, Peter. LC 88-37501. 40p. (gr. 1-4). 1990. RSBE 15.95 (0-02-786810-9, Four Winds) Macmillan Child Grp.

—The Last Princess: The Story of Princess Ka'iulani of Hawai'i. Stanley, Fay. LC 89-11545. 40p. (gr. 1-4). 1991. RSBE 15.95 (0-02-786785-4, Four Winds) Macmillan Child Grp.

—The Month Brothers: A Slavic Tale. Marshak, Samuel. Whitney, Thomas P., tr. from RUS. LC 82-7927. 32p. (gr. k up). 1983. PLB 12.88 (0-688-01510-7) Morrow Jr Bks.

—Peter the Great. Stanley, Diane. LC 85-13060. 32p. (gr. k-3). 1986. RSBE 14.95 (0-02-786790-0, Four Winds) Macmillan Child Grp.

—Peter the Great. Stanley, Diane. LC 91-20089. 32p. (gr. 1-4). 1992. pap. 4.95 (0-689-71548-X, Aladdin) Macmillan Child Grp.

—Shaka: King of the Zulus. Stanley, Diane & Vennema, Peter. LC 93-11730. 32p. (gr. k up). 1994. pap. 4.95 (0-688-13114-X, Mulberry) Morrow.

Stanley, Stanley. Shaka, King of the Zulus. Stanley, Diane & Vennema, Peter. LC 87-27376. 40p. (gr. 1-4). 1988. 14.95 (0-688-07342-5); PLB 14.88 (0-688-07343-3, Morrow Jr Bks) Morrow Jr Bks.

Stan-Padilla, Viento. Dream Feather. Stan-Padilla, Viento. LC 87-17823. 60p. (Orig.). (gr. 7 up). 1987. pap. 10.95 (0-913990-51-4) Book Pub Co.

Stapler, Sarah. The Bear Next Door. Luttrell, Ida. LC 90-4153. 64p. (gr. k-3). 1991. 11.95 (0-06-024023-7); PLB 11.89 (0-06-024024-5) HarpC Child Bks.

—Waiting-for-Christmas Stories. Roberts, Bethany. LC 93-11480. Date not set. write for info. (0-395-67324-0) HM.

Stark, Steve. Let's Debate! Littlefield, Kathy M. & Littlefield, Robert S. 36p. (Orig.). (gr. 3-6). 1989. pap. text ed. 8.95 (1-879340-03-8, K0104) Kidspeak.

—Let's Work Together! Littlefield, Kathy M. & Littlefield, Robert S. 32p. (Orig.). (gr. 3-6). 1991. pap. text ed. 8.95 (1-879340-08-9, K0109) Kidspeak.

—Read to Me! Littlefield, Kathy M. & Littlefield, Robert S. 28p. (Orig.). (gr. 3-6). 1990. pap. text ed. 8.95 (1-879340-04-6, K0105) Kidspeak.

—Speak Up! Littlefield, Kathy M. & Littlefield, Robert S. 32p. (Orig.). (gr. 3-6). 1989. pap. text ed. 8.95 (1-879340-00-3, K0101) Kidspeak.

—Tell Me a Story! Littlefield, Kathy M. & Littlefield, Robert S. 32p. (Orig.). (gr. 3-6). 1989. pap. text ed. 8.95 (1-879340-02-X, K0103) Kidspeak.

—Tell Me the Way It Was... Littlefield, Robert S. & Ball, Jane A. 32p. (Orig.). (gr. 3-6). 1990. pap. text ed. 8.95 (1-879340-07-0, K0108) Kidspeak.

—What Did You Say? Littlefield, Kathy M. & Littlefield, Robert S. 32p. (Orig.). (gr. 3-6). 1989. pap. text ed. 8.95 (1-879340-01-1, K0102) Kidspeak.

—What's Your Point! Littlefield, Kathy M. & Littlefield, Robert S. 32p. (Orig.). (gr. 3-6). 1990. pap. text ed. 8.95 (1-879340-05-4, K0106) Kidspeak.

—Who Am I? Who Are They? Littlefield, Robert S. & Ball, Jane A. 28p. (Orig.). (gr. 3-6). 1990. pap. text ed. 8.95 (1-879340-06-2, K0107) Kidspeak.

Starr, Fiona. The Old Testament: Ten Plays for Readers' Theater. Davidson, Josephine. LC 92-90957. 189p. (Orig.). (gr. 6-8). 1992. pap. text ed. write for info. (0-9628252-1-2) Right Bk.

Starver, Randy, et al. Amazing Animal Facts. Fortson, Walter. LC 89-80109. 128p. (Orig.). (gr. 5). 1989. pap. 6.95 (0-685-29400-5) Fortson Pubs.

Stasiak, Krystyna. Cinco de Mayo. Riehecky, Janet. LC 93-13249. 1993. write for info. (0-516-00681-9) Childrens.

—Learning about Unicorns. Alden, Laura. LC 85-9926. 48p. (gr. 2-6). 1985. pap. 4.95 (0-516-46539-2) Childrens.

—Say Good Night. Gregorich, Barbara. Hoffman, Joan, ed. 16p. (Orig.). (gr. k-2). 1984. pap. 2.25 (0-87449-010-4, 06010) Sch Zone Pub Co.

Stasiak, Krystyna & Connelly, Gwen. Our Christmas Book. rev. ed. Moncure, Jane B. LC 85-29132. 32p. (ps-3). 1986. PLB 19.95 (0-89565-341-9); PLB 13. 95s.p. (0-685-55828-2) Childs World.

Stassburg, Brain. Maybe Yes, Maybe No: A Guide for Young Skeptics. Barker, Dan. 80p. (Orig.). (gr. 2-6). 1991. pap. 12.95 (0-87975-607-1) Prometheus Bks.

State of Being Staff. Some States of Being. State of Being Staff. 22p. (Orig.). (gr. 7 up). 1988. pap. 2.00 (0-929611-03-9) Plutonium Pr.

Staub, Frank. Yellowstone Park. Staub, Frank. LC 89-34371. 32p. (gr. 3-6). 1990. lib. bdg. 10.79 (0-8167-1737-0); pap. text ed. 2.95 (0-8167-1738-9) Troll Assocs.

Staub, Frank, photos by. A Day in the Life of a Ski Patroller. Staub, Frank. LC 90-37382. 32p. (gr. 4-8). 1991. lib. bdg. 11.79 (0-8167-2220-X); pap. text ed. 2.95 (0-8167-2221-8) Troll Assocs.

Staub, Frank J. An Ancient Forest. Spencer, Guy. LC 87-3487. 32p. (gr. 3-6). 1988. PLB 10.79 (0-8167-1167-4); pap. text ed. 2.95 (0-8167-1168-2) Troll Assocs.

Stauffer, P. Wayne. The Crystal Dragon. Stauffer, P. Wayne. Tunmore, Gary, ed. 47p. (gr. 3-5). 1991. 12.95 (0-924649-04-6); PLB 15.95 (0-924649-05-4); pap. 7.95 (0-924649-06-2) Scribblers Pub.

Staunton, James. Fifty Nifty Origami Crafts. Urton, Andrea. 80p. (Orig.). (gr. 3-7). 1993. pap. 3.95 (1-56565-011-5) Lowell Hse.

Steacy, Ken. Megapowers: Can Science Fact Defeat Science Fiction. Weyland, Jack. LC 92-5441. 1992. pap. 8.61 (0-201-58115-9) Addison-Wesley.

Steadman, Barbara. Fall. Webster, David. Steltenpohl, Jane, ed. 48p. (gr. 2-4). 1989. (J Messner); lib. bdg. 5.95 (0-671-65985-5, J Messner) S&S Trade.

—Spring. Webster, David. 48p. (gr. 2-4). 1990. lib. bdg. 10.98 (0-671-65858-1, J Messner); lib. bdg. 5.95 (0-671-65983-9) S&S Trade.

—Summer. Webster, David. 48p. (gr. 2-4). 1990. lib. bdg. 10.98 (0-671-65859-X, J Messner); pap. 5.95 (0-671-65984-7) S&S Trade.

—Winter. Webster, David. Steltenpohl, Jane, ed. 48p. (gr. 2-4). 1989. lib. bdg. 10.98 (0-671-65861-1, J Messner); lib. bdg. 5.95 (0-671-65986-3) S&S Trade.

Steadman, Ralph. The False Flamingoes. Damjan, Mischa. LC 70-105399. 32p. (ps-3). 7.95 (0-87592-016-0) Scroll Pr.

—The Jelly Book. Steadman, Ralph. LC 73-99918. 32p. (ps-3). 7.95 (0-685-04570-6) Scroll Pr.

—Quasimodo Mouse. Stone, Bernard. 32p. (gr. 1-4). 1987. 15.95 (0-86264-072-5, Pub. by Anderson Pr UK) Trafalgar.

Stebbing, Peter, jt. illus. see Milne, Annabel.

Stebbins, Pat. Boogins' Rainy Day. Loveland, Nicole. (ps-3). 1985. PLB 5.95 (0-917107-02-0) Cat-Tales Pr.

Stedman, Robert, photos by. Kalagas: The Wall Hangings of Southeast Asia. Stanislaw, Mary Anne. 64p. (Orig.). (gr. 7 up). 1987. pap. 12.50 (0-9618445-0-7) Ainslies.

Steele, Lawrence, jt. illus. see May, Lawrence.

Steele, Loren, jt. illus. see May, Lawrence.

Steele, Mark. A Bundle of Beasts. Hooper, Patrica. LC 86-34413. 64p. (gr. 3-7). 1987. 12.70 (0-395-44259-1) HM.

Steele, Martha. Jesus & Me. Jackson, Carol. Plunkett, Mark W., ed. 320p. (gr. 1-2). 1993. pap. 24.99 (0-87403-850-2, 13-42031) Standard Pub.

Steelhammer, Ilona. The Fine Family Farm. Cosgrove, Stephen. 24p. (gr. k-2). 1990. PLB 10.95 (1-878363-19-0) Forest Hse.

—The Kind & Gentle Ladies. Cosgrove, Stephen. 24p. (gr. k-2). 1990. PLB 10.95 (1-878363-20-4) Forest Hse.

—Lady Lonely. Cosgrove, Stephen. 24p. (gr. k-2). 1990. PLB 10.95 (1-878363-21-2) Forest Hse.

—The Nosey Birds. Cosgrove, Stephen. 24p. (gr. k-2). 1990. PLB 10.95 (1-878363-22-0) Forest Hse.

Steen, Bill, photos by. Children of Clay: A Family of Pueblo Potters. Swentzell, Rina. Dorris, Michael, frwd. by. LC 92-8680. 1992. 19.95 (0-8225-2654-9) Lerner Pubns.

Steen, Susan. Independence Hall. Steen, Susan. LC 93-5365. 72p. (gr. 4). 1994. RSBE 14.95 (0-87518-603-3, Dillon) Macmillan Child Grp.

Steere, Susan. Pangaea: The Mother Continent. Liptak, Karen. LC 89-15495. 36p. (Orig.). (gr. 4-6). 1989. pap. 8.95 (0-943173-42-6) Harbinger AZ.

—The Reef & the Wrasse. Steere, Susan & Ring, Kathryn M. LC 88-24528. 32p. (Orig.). (gr. 4-6). 1988. pap. 6.95 (0-943173-24-8) Harbinger AZ.

Stefano, Nancy Di. A Mayflower Adventure. McPherson, Betty. 32p. (ps-1). 1985. 6.00 (0-918823-00-5) Boyce-Pubns.

Steffan, Leonard. Down Came the Sun. Hall, Steven. Hall, Mary A. LC 72-176097. 64p. (gr. 3 up). 1972. 8.95 (0-87929-010-2) Barlenmir.

Steffans, Klaus. No Hero for the Kaiser. Frank, Rudolf. Crampton, Patricia, tr. from GER. 224p. (gr. 7 up). 1986. Repr. of 1931 ed. 13.00 (0-688-06093-5) Lothrop.

Steffen, Ann T. Adolescent Pregnancy & Prenatal Care. Poirier-Brode, Karen. Head, J. J., ed. LC 84-71144. 16p. (Orig.). (gr. 10 up). 1987. pap. text ed. 2.75 (0-89278-348-6, 45-9748) Carolina Biological.

—The Animal Cell. Moner, John G. Head, J. J., ed. LC 83-70597. 32p. (gr. 10 up). 1987. pap. text ed. 3.00 (0-89278-347-8, 45-9747) Carolina Biological.

—Cancer Therapy. Fingert, Howard J. Head, J. J., ed. LC 86-72194. 16p. (Orig.). (gr. 10 up). 1987. pap. text ed. 2.75 (0-89278-370-2, 45-9770) Carolina Biological.

—Energy & Life. Miller, Kenneth. Head, J. J., ed. LC 86-72192. 16p. (Orig.). (gr. 10 up). 1988. pap. text ed. 2.75 (0-89278-168-8, 45-9768) Carolina Biological.

—Enzymes: The Machines of Life. Breslow, Ronald. Head, J. J., ed. LC 84-45828. 16p. (Orig.). (gr. 10 up). 1986. pap. text ed. 2.75 (0-89278-155-6, 45-9755) Carolina Biological.

—From Genes to Proteins. Gerbi, Susan A. Head, J. J., ed. LC 84-45830. 16p. (Orig.). (gr. 10 up). 1993. pap. text ed. 2.75 (0-89278-358-3, 45-9758) Carolina Biological.

—The Greenhouse Effect. Wittwer, Sylvan H. Head, J. J., ed. LC 84-45833. 16p. (Orig.). (gr. 10 up). 1988. pap. text ed. 2.75 (0-89278-363-X, 45-9763) Carolina Biological.

—Mammalian Homeostasis. Smith, Robert E. Head, J. J., ed. LC 84-71146. 16p. (gr. 10 up). 1987. pap. text ed. 2.75 (0-89278-349-4, 45-9749) Carolina Biological.

—Photosynthesis. Nakatani, Herbert Y. Head, J. J., ed. LC 84-45838. 16p. (Orig.). (gr. 10 up). 1988. pap. text ed. 2.75 (0-89278-109-2, 45-9793) Carolina Biological.

—Pollution. Lo Pinto, Richard W. Head, J. J., ed. LC 86-72203. 16p. (Orig.). (gr. 10 up). 1987. pap. text ed. 2.75 (0-89278-392-3, 45-9792) Carolina Biological.

—Vision of Color & Pattern. Legge, Gordon E. & Campbell, Fergus W. Head, J. J., ed. LC 84-45835. 16p. (Orig.). (gr. 10 up). 1987. pap. text ed. 2.75 (0-89278-365-6, 45-9765) Carolina Biological.

Steffen, Ann T. & Slifko, Fran. Anorexia. Mallick, Joan. Head, J. J., ed. LC 86-72198. 16p. (Orig.). (gr. 10 up). 1987. pap. text ed. 2.75 (0-89278-373-7, 45-9773) Carolina Biological.

Steffen, Ann T. & Whitely, Derek. Genital Herpes. Felman, Yehudi M. Head, J. J., ed. LC 84-71142. 16p. (Orig.). (gr. 10 up). 1987. pap. text ed. 2.75 (0-89278-153-X, 45-9753) Carolina Biological.

Steffen, Ann T., jt. illus. see Johnson, Patricia.

Steffler, Shawn. Just One More Color. Silsbe, Brenda. 24p. (ps-3). 1991. PLB 14.95 (1-55037-133-9, Pub. by Annick CN); pap. 4.95 (1-55037-136-3, Pub. by Annick CN) Firefly Bks Ltd.

Stehr, Frederic. Quack-Quack. Stehr, Frederic. 28p. (ps up). 1988. pap. 3.95 (0-374-46141-4) FS&G.

Steig, William. Abel's Island. Steig, William. LC 75-35916. 128p. (gr. 1 up). 1976. 14.00 (0-374-30010-0) FS&G.

—Alpha Beta Chowder. Steig, Jeanne. LC 92-52641. 48p. (gr. k up). 1992. 15.00 (0-06-205006-0); PLB 14.89 (0-06-205007-9) HarpC Child Bks.

—The Amazing Bone. Steig, William. LC 76-26479. 32p. (ps-3). 1983. 17.00 (0-374-30248-0) FS&G.

—The Amazing Bone. Steig, William. 32p. (gr. 1-3). 1977. pap. 3.95 (0-14-050247-5, Puffin) Puffin Bks.

—Caleb & Katie. Steig, William. LC 77-4947. 32p. (ps-3). 1977. 16.00 (0-374-31016-5) FS&G.

—Caleb & Katie. Steig, William. 32p. (ps up). 1986. pap. 4.95 (0-374-41038-0) FS&G.

—Doctor De Soto Goes to Africa. Steig, William. LC 91-76414. 32p. (ps up). 1992. 15.00 (0-06-205002-8); PLB 14.89 (0-06-205003-6) HarpC Child Bks.

—The Real Thief. Steig, William. LC 73-77910. 64p. (ps up). 1976. 12.95 (0-374-36217-3) FS&G.

—Silvestre & la Piedrecita Magica. Steig, William. Mlawer, Teresa, tr. from ENG. 40p. (gr. 3). 1990. PLB 12.95 (0-9625162-0-1); pap. 5.95 (0-9625162-7-9) Lectorum Pubns.

—Solomon the Rusty Nail. Steig, William. 32p. (ps up). 1985. 16.00 (0-374-37131-8) FS&G.

—Sylvester & the Magic Pebble. Steig, William. 32p. (ps-1). 1988. Bk. & cassette. pap. 8.95 (0-671-67144-8, S&S BFYR) S&S Trade.

—Yellow & Pink. Steig, William. LC 84-80503. 32p. (ps up). 1984. 12.00 (0-374-38670-6) FS&G.

—The Zabajaba Jungle. Steig, William. LC 87-17690. (ps-4). 1987. 15.00 (0-374-38790-7) FS&G.

Stein, August. Ask Not for Victory. David, Ward S. Grant, Wilda L., ed. 234p. (Orig.). (gr. 8-12). 1991. pap. 9.95 (0-9630883-3-5) W S David.

Stein, Michele P. The Stained Glass Window. Stein, Charlotte M. Sakurai, Jennifer, ed. LC 88-70883. 150p. (Orig.). 1993. pap. 11.95 incl. wkbk. (0-916634-12-4) Double M Pr.

Stein, Sara. The Evolution Book. Stein, Sara. LC 84-40682. 400p. (Orig.). (gr. 5-9). 1986. pap. 12.95 (0-89480-927-X, 927) Workman Pub.

Steinbauer, S. Twelve Great Western Philosophers. Ozmon, H. LC 66-16403. 48p. (gr. 4 up). 1967. PLB 9.95 (0-87783-046-0); pap. 3.94 deluxe ed (0-87783-115-7) Oddo.

Steinberg, Chris. Su-Su, the Fremont School Panda. Eisemann, Henry. 22p. (gr. k-6). 1987. pap. 6.95 (0-938129-03-1) Emprise Pubns.

Steinberg, Lisa. Fun with Jewish Holiday Rhymes. Rouss, Sylvia A. LC 91-40931. (ps-1). 1992. 10.95 (0-8074-0463-2, 101981) UAHC.

Steinberger, Heidi. Bible Work & Play, Vol. 1. rev. ed. Fischman, Joyce. 80p. (Orig.). (gr. 1-3). 1985. pap. text ed. 5.00 (0-8074-0304-0, 103620) UAHC.

—God's Top Ten: The Meaning of the Ten Commandments. Osborn, Roberta L. 32p. (Orig.). (gr. 4-6). 1992. pap. text ed. 1.85 (0-933873-73-5) Torah Aura.

—Nineteen Out of Eighteen. Grishaver, Joel L. (Orig.). (gr. 5-8). 1991. pap. 5.95 wkbk. (0-685-50246-5) Torah Aura.

—Pesach: A Holiday Funtext. Bin-Nun, Judy & Cooper, Nancy. 32p. (gr. 1-3). 1983. pap. text ed. 5.00 (0-8074-0161-7, 101310) UAHC.

—Rosh Hashanah: A Holiday Funtext. Bin-Nun, Judy & Einhorn, Franne. (gr. 1-3). 1978. pap. 5.00 (0-8074-0230-3, 101300) UAHC.

—Shema & Company. rev. ed. Grishaver, Joel L. (gr. 5-8). 1991. wkbk. 5.95 (0-933873-62-X) Torah Aura.

Steiner, Connie. In Other Words. Walker, John C. 32p. 1993. lib. bdg. 14.95 (1-55037-309-9, Pub. by Annick CN); pap. 4.95 (1-55037-310-2, Pub. by Annick CN) Firefly Bks Ltd.

—Paul's New Ears. Steiner, Connie. 24p. (Orig.). (gr. k-3). 1991. pap. 9.95 (0-920541-44-5) Peguis Pubs Ltd.

Steiner, Pat. Erik of the Dragon Ships. Abraham, Norma J. LC 83-50987. 163p. (Orig.). (gr. 8-11). 1983. pap. 3.95 (0-912661-00-3) Woodsong Graph.

Steiner, Pat & Cozzolino, Sandra. Sleeping Beauty. Newby, Robert. 64p. (gr. k-3). 1992. PLB 15.95 (1-56674-035-5) Forest Hse.

—Sleeping Beauty: With Selected Sentences in American Sign Language. Newby, Robert. LC 91-29729. 64p. (gr. 1-7). 1992. 14.95 (0-930323-97-1, Pub. by K Green Pubns) video 29.95 (0-930323-98-X) Gallaudet Univ Pr.

Steinkraus, Edith. So, You Want to Be a Veterinarian. Wolfman, Melvin S. 38p. (Orig.). (gr. 3-12). 1993. pap. 15.00 (0-9629806-3-3) Benjamin OH. Wouldn't children love to read about a mule with a library card or a giraffe who wears a turtleneck sweater? They can with SO, YOU WANT TO BE A VETERINARIAN, written by Melvin S. Wolfman. The imagination is the limit in this interactive children's book. Thought provoking anecdotes allow children to provide their own solutions to unusual problems these many animals face; children actually share the writing credit with Mr. Wolfman. A bear wants to own a car repair shop so Mr. Wolfman gives the bear a screwdriver & then asks the reader "what would you do?" It is a wonderful tool for encouraging creativity. Illustrations are included & additional space is provided for the reader to draw his or her own pictures. SO, YOU WANT TO BE A VETERINARIAN is an outstanding introduction to the world of interactive media. *Publisher Provided Annotation.*

Steinmetz, Joseph J., photos by. The Circus Comes Home. Duncan, Lois. LC 92-7481. 1993. 16.95 (0-385-30689-X) Doubleday.

Steins, Deborah. The World of Young Herbert Hoover. Hilton, Suzanne. (gr. 5-8). 1987. 12.95 (0-8027-6708-7); PLB 13.85 (0-8027-6709-5) Walker & Co.

Stelson, Kim A. Safari. Stelson, Caren B. 40p. (gr. k-4). 1988. PLB 19.95 (0-87614-324-9) Carolrhoda Bks.

—Safari. Stelson, Caren B. 40p. (gr. k-4). 1989. pap. 5.95 (0-87614-512-8, First Ave Edns) Lerner Pubns.

Steltzer, Ulli. Building an Igloo. Steltzer, Ulli. 32p. (ps-2). 1991. pap. 4.95 (0-88899-118-5, Pub. by Groundwood-Douglas & McIntyre CN) Firefly Bks Ltd.

Stemple, Jason. A Letter from Phoenix Farm. Yolen, Jane. 32p. (gr. 2-5). 1992. 12.95 (1-878450-36-0) R Owen Pubs.

Stephan, Franck. Bears, Big & Little. Pfeffer, Pierre. Bogard, Vicki, tr. from FRE. LC 89-8883. 38p. (gr. k-5). 1989. 4.95 (0-944589-23-5, 023) Young Discovery Lib.

Stephen, Lib. The Animal Jiglets. Jolly, Christopher. (ps-1). 1994. 11.95 (1-870946-33-2, Pub. by Jolly Lrning UK) Am Intl Dist.

—Finger Phonics, 7 bks. Lloyd, Sue & Wernham, Sara. (ps-2). 1994. Set. 39.50 (1-870946-31-6, Pub. by Jolly Lrning UK) Am Intl Dist.

—Finger Phonics, Bk. 1: S, A, T, I, P, N. Lloyd, Sue & Wernham, Sara. 14p. (ps-2). 1994. 5.95 (1-870946-24-3, Pub. by Jolly Lrning UK) Am Intl Dist.

—Finger Phonics, Bk. 2: CK, E, H, R, M, D. Lloyd, Sue & Wernham, Sara. 14p. (ps-2). 1994. 5.95 (1-870946-25-1, Pub. by Jolly Lrning UK) Am Intl Dist.

—Finger Phonics, Bk. 3: G, O, U, L, F, B. Lloyd, Sue & Wernham, Sara. 14p. (ps-2). 1994. 5.95 (1-870946-26-X, Pub. by Jolly Lrning UK) Am Intl Dist.

—Finger Phonics, Bk. 4: AI, J, OA, IE, EE, OR. Lloyd, Sue & Wernham, Sara. 14p. (ps-2). 1994. 5.95 (1-870946-27-8, Pub. by Jolly Lrning UK) Am Intl Dist.

—Finger Phonics, Bk. 5: Z, W, NG, V, OO, OO. Lloyd, Sue & Wernham, Sara. 14p. (ps-2). 1994. 5.95 (1-870946-28-6, Pub. by Jolly Lrning UK) Am Intl Dist.

—Finger Phonics, Bk. 6: Y, X, CH, SH, TH, TH. Lloyd, Sue & Wernham, Sara. 14p. (ps-2). 1994. 5.95 (1-870946-29-4, Pub. by Jolly Lrning UK) Am Intl Dist.

—Finger Phonics, Bk. 7: QU, OU, OI, UE, ER, AR. Lloyd, Sue & Wernham, Sara. 14p. (ps-2). 1994. 5.95 (1-870946-30-8, Pub. by Jolly Lrning UK) Am Intl Dist.

—Phonic Wall Frieze. Lloyd, Sue & Wernham, Sara. (ps-2). 1994. 8.95 (1-870946-32-4, Pub. by Jolly Lrning UK) Am Intl Dist.

—The Phonics Handbook. Lloyd, Sue. 218p. (ps-3). 1993. pap. 19.95 (1-870946-08-1, Pub. by Jolly Lrning UK) Am Intl Dist.

—The Stencilets. Jolly, Christopher. (ps-1). 1994. 14.95 (1-870946-35-9, Pub. by Jolly Lrning UK) Am Intl Dist.

—The Vehicle Jiglets. Jolly, Christopher. (ps-1). 1994. 11.95 (1-870946-34-0, Pub. by Jolly Lrning UK) Am Intl Dist.

Stephens, Jacquelyn S. Robbie & the Raggedy Scarecrow. Oana, Katy D. LC 77-18349. (gr. k-2). 1978. PLB 5.95 (0-89508-065-6) Rainbow Bks.

—Shasta & the Shebang Machine. Oana, Katy D. LC 77-18350. (gr. k-2). 1978. PLB 5.95 (0-89508-066-4) Rainbow Bks.

Steptoe, John. All the Colors of the Race. Adoff, Arnold. LC 81-11777. 64p. (gr. 5 up). 1982. 13.95 (0-688-00879-8); PLB 13.88 (0-688-00880-1) Lothrop.

—All the Colors of the Race. Adoff, Arnold. LC 81-11777. 80p. 1992. pap. 4.95 (0-688-11496-2, Pub. by Beech Tree Bks) Morrow.

—Baby Says. Steptoe, John. LC 87-17296. 32p. (ps). 1988. 13.95 (0-688-07423-5); lib. bdg. 13.88 (0-688-07424-3) Lothrop.

—Birthday. Steptoe, John. LC 72-182782. 32p. (ps-2). 1991. 14.95 (0-8050-1849-2, Bks Young Read) H Holt & Co.

—Mother Crocodile: An Uncle Amadou Tale from Senegal. Guy, Rosa. LC 80-393. 32p. (ps-3). 1982. 8.89 (0-385-28455-1); pap. 8.95 (0-385-28454-3) Delacorte.

—Mufaro's Beautiful Daughters: An African Tale. Steptoe, John. LC 84-7158. 32p. (gr. k-3). 1987. 14.95 (0-688-04045-4); PLB 14.88 (0-688-04046-2) Lothrop.

—She Come Bringing Me That Little Baby Girl. Greenfield, Eloise. LC 74-8104. 32p. (gr. k-3). 1990. 14.00 (0-397-31586-4, Lipp Jr Bks); PLB 13.89 (0-397-32478-2) HarpC Child Bks.

—She Come Bringing Me That Little Baby Girl. Greenfield, Eloise. LC 74-8104. 32p. (gr. k-3). 1993. pap. 4.95 (0-06-443296-3, Trophy) HarpC Child Bks.

—Stevie. Steptoe, John. (gr. 1-4). 1987. incl. cassette 19.95 (0-87499-050-5); pap. 12.95 incl. cassette (0-87499-049-1); 4 paperbacks, cassette & guide 27.95 (0-87499-051-3) Live Oak Media.

—The Story of Jumping Mouse. Steptoe, John. LC 82-14848. 40p. (gr. k-3). 1984. 13.95 (0-688-01902-1); PLB 13.88 (0-688-01903-X) Lothrop.

Steptoe, John L. Stevie. Steptoe, John. LC 69-16700. 32p. (ps-3). 1969. PLB 12.89 (0-06-025764-4) HarpC Child Bks.

Steranko, James, jt. illus. see Gustovich, Mike.

Sterbenz, Carol E., et al. The Dog Album: A Pet Owner's Memory Book. Sterbenz, Carol E. 32p. (ps up). 1987. 11.95 (0-399-21460-7, Putnam) Putnam Pub Group.

Sterchele, Christina. Story Programs Activities for Older Children. Peterson, Carolyn S. (Orig.). (gr. 3-6). 1987. 20.00 (0-913545-11-2) Moonlight FL.

Sterchele, Christina L. Christmas Story Programs. Peterson, Carolyn S. & Fenton, Ann D. (ps-6). 1981. 10.00 (0-913545-01-5) Moonlight FL.

—A Hole in the Bottom of the Sea. (Orig.). (gr. k-6). 1984. pap. 3.50 (0-913545-09-0) Moonlight Fl.

—Ten Little Bunnies. Gawron, Marlene E. (ps-1). 1981. 3.50 (0-913545-06-6) Moonlight FL.

—Twelve Days of Christmas. (ps-6). 1981. 3.50 (0-913545-07-4) Moonlight FL.

Sterling, Suzanne. The Language Ladder, Bk. I. Childs, Phyllis. 76p. (ps-k). 1985. wkbk. 6.50 (0-931749-01-8) PJC Lrng Mtrls.

Sterling, Terry S. I Was Good to the Earth Today. Starr, Susan B. 32p. (ps-k). 1992. PLB 12.95 (0-9619556-0-0); pap. 5.95 (0-9619556-1-9) Starhse Pub.

Stermer, Dugald. Ghost Vision. Kortum, Jeanie. LC 83-4706. 160p. (gr. 5-9). 1983. 10.95 (0-394-86190-6, Pant Bks Young) Pantheon.

Stern, Ayala. The Man Who Rode with Eliyahu Haravi. Estrin, Leibel. 32p. (ps-3). 1990. 9.95 (0-922613-23-0); pap. 7.95 (0-922613-24-9) Hachai Pubns.

Stern, Fruma. The Place Where I Belong. Rotenberg, Abie. (ps-1). 1988. 9.95 (0-935063-43-9) CIS Comm.

Stern, Patti. Eating Ice Cream with a Werewolf. Green, Phyllis. LC 82-47727. 128p. (gr. 3-7). 1983. HarpC Child Bks.

Stern, Simon. Where Am I? Caveney, Sylvia & Giesen, Rosemary. LC 76-22476. 24p. (gr. k-3). 1977. PLB 7.95 (0-8225-1365-X) Lerner Pubns.

Steven, Janet. The Tortoise & the Hare: An Aesop Fable. Stevens, Janet. LC 83-18668. 32p. (ps-3). 1984. reinforced bdg. 14.95 (0-8234-0510-9); pap. 5.95 (0-8234-0564-8) Holiday.

Stevens, Barbara. Mortimer Meets Melody. Forelle, Helen. Leih, Janet, ed. 20p. (gr. 1-3). 1981. pap. 3.00 (1-877649-02-3) Tesseract SD.

Stevens, Bill. In Search of Energy. Durham, Jackie. Pennington, Celeste, ed. (Orig.). (gr. 4-6). 1984. pap. 1.75 (0-937170-27-5) Home Mission.

—Wanna Be Number One? Tiller, David. 40p. (Orig.). (gr. 4-6). pap. 2.00 (0-937170-32-1) Home Mission.

Stevens, Bill, jt. photog. see Swain, John.

Stevens, David. Stepping Stones Three. Stevens, Margaret M. 32p. (gr. 1-8). 1983. pap. 4.50 (0-87516-518-4) DeVorss.

Stevens, David S. Stepping Stones for Boys & Girls. Stevens, Margaret M. (gr. 5 up). 1977. pap. 4.50 (0-87516-248-7) DeVorss.

—Stepping Stones for Little Feet. Stevens, Margaret M. 31p. (gr. 4-6). 1975. pap. 4.50 (0-87516-202-9) DeVorss.

Stevens, Janet. Anansi & the Moss-Covered Rock. Kimmel, Eric A. LC 87-31766. (ps-3). 1988. reinforced bdg. 15.95 (0-8234-0689-X); pap. 5.95 (0-8234-0798-5) Holiday.

—Anansi Goes Fishing. Kimmel, Eric A., retold by. LC 91-17813. 32p. (ps-3). 1992. reinforced bdg. 15.95 (0-8234-0918-X) Holiday.

—Anansi Goes Fishing. Kimmel, Eric A., retold by. (ps-3). 1993. pap. 5.95 (0-8234-1022-6) Holiday.

—Androcles & the Lion. Stevens, Janet. LC 89-1953. 32p. (ps-3). 1989. reinforced bdg. 14.95 (0-8234-0768-3); pap. 5.95 (0-8234-0906-6) Holiday.

—Barry Bear & the Bad Guys. Cuyler, Margery. LC 92-11576. 1993. 14.45 (0-395-59939-3, Clarion Bks) HM.

—Big Bunny & the Easter Egg. Kroll, Steven. 32p. (gr. k-3). 1988. pap. 2.95 (0-590-41660-X) Scholastic Inc.

—The Big Bunny & the Magic Show. Kroll, Steven. LC 85-14147. 32p. (ps-3). 1986. reinforced bdg. 14.95 (0-8234-0589-3) Holiday.

—The Big Bunny & the Magic Show. Kroll, Steven. 32p. (ps-2). 1987. pap. 3.95 (0-590-44633-9) Holiday.

—The Bremen Town Musicians. Grimm, Jacob & Grimm, Wilhelm K. Stevens, Janet, retold by. LC 91-815. 32p. (ps-3). 1992. reinforced bdg. 15.95 (0-8234-0939-2) Holiday.

—The Cabbages Are Chasing the Rabbits. Adoff, Arnold. LC 85-893. 32p. (gr. k-3). 1985. 15.95 (0-15-213875-7, HB Juv Bks) HarBrace.

—Coyote Steals the Blanket: A Ute Tale. Stevens, Janet, retold by. LC 92-54415. 32p. (ps-3). 1993. reinforced bdg. 15.95 (0-8234-0996-1) Holiday.

—The Dog Who Had Kittens. Robertus, Polly. LC 90-39174. 32p. (ps-3). 1991. reinforced bdg. 14.95 (0-8234-0860-4); pap. 5.95 (0-8234-0974-0) Holiday.

—The Emperor's New Clothes: Adapted from Hans Christian Andersen. LC 85-728. 32p. (ps-3). 1985. reinforced 14.95 (0-8234-0566-4) Holiday.

—The House That Jack Built: A Mother Goose Nursery Rhyme. LC 84-15832. 32p. (ps-3). 1985. reinforced bdg. 14.95 (0-8234-0548-6) Holiday.

—I'm in the Zoo, Too. Ashabranner, Brent. LC 88-32662. (gr. k-4). 1989. 12.95 (0-525-65002-4, Cobblehill Bks) Dutton Child Bks.

—Nanny Goat & the Seven Little Kids. Kimmel, Eric A. LC 89-20058. 32p. (ps-3). 1990. reinforced bdg. 15.95 (0-8234-0789-6); pap. 5.95 (0-8234-0953-8) Holiday.

—The Owl & the Pussycat. rev. ed. Lear, Edward. LC 82-12092. 32p. (ps-3). 1983. reinforced bdg. 14.95 (0-8234-0474-9) Holiday.

—The Quangle Wangle's Hat. Lear, Edward. 32p. (ps-3). 1988. 12.95 (0-15-264450-4) HarBrace.

—The Three Billy Goats Gruff. Stevens, Janet. LC 86-33512. 40p. (ps-3). 1987. 12.95 (0-15-286396-6, HB Juv Bks) HarBrace.

—Tops & Bottoms. Stevens, Janet, adapted by. LC 93-19154. (ps-6). 1994. write for info. (0-15-292851-0) HarBrace.

—The Town Mouse & the Country Mouse. Stevens, Janet, adapted by. LC 86-14276. 32p. (ps-3). 1987. reinforced bdg. 14.95 (0-8234-0633-4); pap. 5.95 (0-8234-0733-0) Holiday.

—The Weighty Word Book. Levitt, Paul M., et al. 99p. (gr. 4-9). 1990. Repr. of 1985 ed. 17.95 (0-9627979-0-1) Manuscripts.

Stevens, Jill, jt. illus. see Boldway, John.

Stevens, Larry. Clown Games. Ziefert, Harriet. 32p. (ps-3). 1993. 9.00 (0-670-84652-X) Viking Child Bks.

—Clown Games. Ziefert, Harriet. 32p. (ps-3). 1993. pap. 3.50 (0-14-054581-6) Puffin Bks.

Stevens, LaVerne. Look & See H O T V or Letter E. Stevens, LaVerne. LC 91-75641. 32p. (ps-k). 1991. CIS cover 15 pt. with plastic comb binding 8.00 (0-9630441-0-9) B&B Pr.

Stevens, Mary. All-of-a-Kind Family Uptown. Taylor, Sydney. 160p. 1988. Repr. of 1958 ed. 11.95 (0-929093-03-8) Taylor Prodns.

—More All-of-a-Kind Family. Taylor, Sydney. 160p. (gr. 3-6). 1988. Repr. of 1954 ed. 11.95 (0-929093-02-X) Taylor Prodns.

—The Real Hole. rev. ed. Cleary, Beverly. LC 85-18815. 32p. (ps-1). 1986. 11.95 (0-688-05850-7); PLB 11.88 (0-688-05851-5) Morrow Jr Bks.

Stevens, Meg. Secret Brother & Other Poems. Jennings, Elizabeth. LC 69-14765. (gr. 1-5). 1966. 13.95 (0-8023-1194-6) Dufour.

Stevens, Wendelle C. UFO...Contact from the Pleiades: A Supplementary Investigation Report. Stevens, Wendelle C. 552p. (gr. 9-12). 1989. PLB 29.95 (0-9608558-4-X) UFO Photo.

Stevens, Wendelle C., et al. UFO...Contact from Reticulum, Update. Stevens, Wendelle C. 444p. (gr. 9-12). 1989. PLB 18.95 (0-934259-15-7) UFO Photo.

Stevenson, Anna. Blessed Is the Spot. Baha'u'llah. LC 58-8815. (gr. k-2). 1958. 14.50 (G-87743-014-4, 352-040) Bahai.

Stevenson, Harvey. As the Crow Flies: A First Book of Maps. Hartman, Gail. LC 90-33982. 32p. (ps-1). 1991. RSBE 12.95 (0-02-743005-7, Bradbury Pr) Macmillan Child Grp.

—As the Crow Flies: A First Book of Maps. Hartman, Gail. LC 93-22101. 32p. (ps-1). 1993. pap. 4.95 (0-689-71762-8, Aladdin) Macmillan Child Grp.

—The Bear Who Came To Stay. Woodman, Allen & Kirby, David. LC 92-7799. 32p. (ps-3). 1994. RSBE 14.95 (0-02-793397-0, Bradbury Pr) Macmillan Child Grp.

—Day Nights, Night Lights. Schoberle, Cecile. LC 93-18680. (gr. 4 up). 1994. pap. 14.00 (0-671-87439-X, S&S BFYR) S&S Trade.

—Elmer & the Chickens vs. the Big League. McConnachie, Brian. LC 91-2914. 32p. (ps-2). 1992. 14.00 (0-517-57616-3); PLB 14.99 (0-517-57617-1) Crown Bks Yng Read.

—Gone Fishing. Kroll, Steven. LC 89-22241. 48p. (ps-2). 1990. PLB 13.99 (0-517-57590-6) Crown Bks Yng Read.

—Good Books, Good Times. Hopkins, Lee B., ed. LC 89-49108. 32p. (gr. k-3). 1990. 14.00 (0-06-022527-0); PLB 13.89 (0-06-022528-9) HarpC Child Bks.

—Little Rabbit Goes to Sleep. Johnston, Tony. LC 92-8543. 32p. (ps-k). 1993. 15.00 (0-06-021239-X); PLB 14.89 (0-06-021241-1) HarpC Child Bks.

—New Feet for Old. Waller, Barrett. LC 90-21339. 32p. (gr. k-3). 1992. RSBE 13.95 (0-02-792371-1, Four Winds) Macmillan Child Grp.

—Violet's Finest Hour. Duggan, Alice. LC 91-52588. 64p. (gr. 1 up). 1991. text ed. 10.95 (0-688-09456-2) Lothrop.

—Weekend Girl. Hest, Amy. LC 92-9193. 32p. (gr. k up). 1993. 15.00 (0-688-09689-1); PLB 14.93 (0-688-09690-5) Morrow Jr Bks.

Stevenson, James. The Baby Uggs Are Hatching! Prelutsky, Jack. LC 81-7266. 32p. (gr. k-3). 1982. 13.95 (0-688-00922-0); PLB 13.88 (0-688-00923-9) Greenwillow.

—Could Be Worse! Stevenson, James. LC 76-28534. 32p. (gr. k-3). 1977. 13.95 (0-688-80075-0); PLB 13.88 (0-688-84075-2) Greenwillow.

—Cully Cully & the Bear. Gage, Wilson. LC 82-11715. (ps-3). 1988. pap. 7.95 incl. cassette (0-688-08401-X, Mulberry) Morrow.

—Emma. Stevenson, James. LC 84-4141. 32p. (gr. k-3). 1985. 11.75 (0-688-04020-9); PLB 11.88 (0-688-04021-7) Greenwillow.

—Fried Feathers for Thanksgiving. Stevenson, James. LC 86-3100. 32p. (gr. k-3). 1986. 13.95 (0-688-06675-5); PLB 13.88 (0-688-06676-3) Greenwillow.

—Georgia Music. Griffith, Helen. LC 85-24918. 24p. (gr. k-3). 1986. 13.95 (0-688-06071-4); PLB 13.88 (0-688-06072-2) Greenwillow.

—Georgia Music. Griffith, Helen V. LC 85-24918. 24p. (ps-2). 1990. pap. 3.95 (0-688-C9931-9, Mulberry) Morrow.

—Grandaddy & Janetta. Griffith, Helen V. LC 91-47707. 32p. (gr. k up). 1993. 14.00 (0-688-11226-9); PLB 13.93 (0-688-11227-7) Greenwillow.

—Grandaddy's Place. Griffith, Helen V. LC 86-19573. 40p. (gr. 1-4). 1987. 13.95 (0-688-06253-9); PLB 13.88 (0-688-06254-7) Greenwillow.

—Grandaddy's Place. Griffith, Helen V. LC 86-19573. 40p. (ps-3). 1991. pap. 4.95 (0-688-10491-6, Mulberry) Morrow.

—Grandpa's Great City Tour: An Alphabet Book. Stevenson, James. LC 83-1459. 48p. (gr. k-3). 1983. PLB 12.95 (0-688-02324-X); 12.88 (0-688-02323-1) Greenwillow.

—The Great Big Especially Beautiful Easter Egg. Stevenson, James. LC 82-11731. 32p. (gr. k-3). 1983. 15.88 (0-688-01789-4); PLB 13.88 (0-688-01791-6) Greenwillow.

—How Do You Get a Horse Out of the Bathtub? Profound Answers to Preposterous Questions. Phillips, Louis. 80p. (gr. 1 up). 1983. pap. 10.95 (0-670-38119-5) Viking Child Bks.

—How Do You Get a Horse Out of the Bathtub? Profound Answers to Preposterous Questions. Phillips, Louis. (gr. 4-6). 1983. pap. 4.95 (0-14-031618-3, Puffin Bks) Puffin Bks.

—I Am Not Going to Get up Today! Dr. Seuss. LC 87-11466. 48p. (gr. k-3). 1987. 6.95 (0-394-89217-8); lib. bdg. 7.99 (0-394-99217-2) Random Bks Yng Read.

—I Am Not Going to Get up Today! Dr. Seuss. 32p. (ps-1). 1990. pap. 6.95 (0-679-80307-6); cass. incl. Random Bks Yng Read.

—I Know a Lady. Zolotow, Charlotte. LC 83-25361. 24p. (gr. k-3). 1984. 14.95 (0-688-03837-9); PLB 14.88 (0-688-03838-7) Greenwillow.

—I Know a Lady. Zolotow, Charlotte. LC 83-25361. 24p. (ps up). 1992. pap. 4.95 (0-688-11519-5, Mulberry) Morrow.

—If I Owned a Candy Factory. Stevenson, James W. LC 87-37581. 32p. (ps up). 1989. 11.95 (0-688-08106-1); PLB 11.88 (0-688-08107-X) Greenwillow.

—July. Stevenson, James. LC 88-37584. (gr. k up). 1990. 12.95 (0-688-08822-8); PLB 12.88 (0-688-08823-6) Greenwillow.

—Loop the Loop. Dugan, Barbara. LC 90-21727. 32p. (gr. k up). 1992. 14.00 (0-688-09647-6); PLB 13.93 (0-688-09648-4) Greenwillow.

—Loop the Loop. Dugan, Barbara. LC 92-40168. 32p. (ps-3). 1993. pap. 4.99 (0-14-054904-8, Puffin) Puffin Bks.

—Monty. Stevenson, James. LC 78-11409. 32p. (ps up). 1992. pap. 4.95 (0-688-11288-9, Mulberry) Morrow.

—The New Kid on the Block. Prelutsky, Jack. LC 83-20621. 160p. (gr. 1 up). 1984. 15.00 (0-688-02271-5); PLB 14.88 (0-688-02272-3) Greenwillow.

—No Friends. Stevenson, James. LC 85-27247. 32p. (gr. k-3). 1986. 11.75 (0-688-06506-6); PLB 11.88 (0-688-06507-4) Greenwillow.

—No Need for Monty. Stevenson, James. LC 86-22818. 32p. (gr. k-3). 1987. 11.75 (0-688-07083-3); lib. bdg. 11.88 (0-688-07084-1) Greenwillow.

—Otto Is Different. Brandenberg, Franz. LC 84-13654. 24p. (gr. k-3). 1985. 11.75 (0-688-04253-8); PLB 11.88 (0-688-04254-6) Greenwillow.

—Percy the Five Houses. Minarik, Else H. LC 88-4804. 24p. (gr. k up). 1989. 11.95 (0-688-08104-5); PLB 11.88 (0-688-08105-3) Greenwillow.

—Say It! Zolotow, Charlotte. LC 78-25115. 24p. (gr. k-3). 1980. PLB 14.88 (0-688-84276-3) Greenwillow.

—Say It! Zolotow, Charlotte. ALC Staff, ed. LC 79-25115. 24p. (ps up). 1992. pap. 4.95 (0-688-11711-2, Mulberry) Morrow.

—Something Big Has Been Here. Prelutsky, Jack. LC 89-34773. 160p. (gr. k up). 1990. 15.95 (0-688-06434-5) Greenwillow.

—That Dreadful Day. Stevenson, James. LC 84-4164. 32p. (gr. k-3). 1985. 15.00 (0-688-04035-7); PLB 14.93 (0-688-04036-5) Greenwillow.

—There's Nothing to Do! Stevenson, James. LC 85-8104. 32p. (gr. k-3). 1986. 11.75 (0-688-04698-3); PLB 11.88 (0-688-04699-1) Greenwillow.

—Two Hundred Sixty-Three Brain Busters: Just How Smart Are You, Anyway? Phillips, Louis. LC 85-40446. 87p. (gr. 4-7). 1985. pap. 3.99 (0-14-031875-5, Puffin) Puffin Bks.

—What's under My Bed? Stevenson, James. LC 83-1454. 32p. (gr. k-3). 1983. 13.95 (0-688-02325-8); PLB 13.88 (0-688-02327-4) Greenwillow.

—When I Was Nine. Stevenson, James. LC 85-9777. 32p. (gr. k-3). 1986. 14.00 (0-688-05942-2); PLB 13.93 (0-688-05943-0) Greenwillow.

—Will You Please Feed Our Cat? Stevenson, James. LC 86-11927. 32p. (gr. k-3). 1987. 11.75 (0-688-06847-2); lib. bdg. 11.88 (0-688-06848-0) Greenwillow.

—The Wish Card Ran Out! Stevenson, James. LC 80-22139. 32p. (gr. k-4). 1981. 11.75 (0-688-80305-9) Greenwillow.

—Worse Than Willy! Stevenson, James. LC 83-14201. 32p. (gr. k-3). 1984. 10.25 (0-688-02596-X); PLB 10.88 (0-688-02597-8) Greenwillow.

—Yuck! Stevenson, James. LC 83-25421. 32p. (gr. k-3). 1984. 11.75 (0-688-03829-8); PLB 11.88 (0-688-03830-1) Greenwillow.

Stevenson, James, photos by. Volcano & Earthquake. Van Rose, Susanna. LC 92-4710. 64p. (gr. 5 up). 1992. 15.00 (0-679-81685-2); PLB 16.99 (0-679-91685-7) Knopf Bks Yng Read.

Stevenson, Jim. Explorer. Matthews, Rupert. LC 91-8428. 64p. (gr. 5 up). 1991. 15.00 (0-679-81460-4); lib. bdg. 15.99 (0-679-91460-9) Knopf Bks Yng Read.

Stevenson, Jim, photos by. Boat. Kentley, Eric. LC 91-53136. 64p. (gr. 5 up). 1992. 15.00 (0-679-81678-X); PLB 15.99 (0-679-91678-4) Knopf Bks Yng Read.

Stevenson, Nancy. Disney's Winnie the Pooh Helping Hands: Oh, Bother! Someone's Messy! Birney, Betty. 24p. (ps-3). 1992. pap. write for info. (0-307-12690-0, 12690, Golden Pr) Western Pub.

—Robby Visits the Doctor. Davidson, Martine. LC 91-30193. 32p. (Orig.). (ps-2). 1992. PLB 5.99 (0-679-91819-1); pap. 2.25 (0-679-81819-7) Random Bks Yng Read.

—Walt Disney's Winnie the Pooh Helping Hands: Oh, Bother! Someone Won't Share. Birney, Betty. 24p. (ps-3). 1993. pap. 1.95 (0-307-12766-4, 12766, Golden Pr) Western Pub.

Stevenson, Peter. Doubleday Children's Thesaurus. Bellamy, John. LC 86-16217. 192p. (gr. k-6). 1987. 15.00 (0-385-23833-9) Doubleday.

—Feel! A Fun Book of Touch. Morris, Neil. 32p. (ps-2). 1991. PLB 13.50 (0-87614-672-8) Carolrhoda Bks.

—Holly & Harry: A Fun Book of Sizes. Morris, Neil. 32p. (ps-2). 1991. PLB 13.50 (0-87614-673-6) Carolrhoda Bks.

—I'm Big: A Fun Book of Opposites. Morris, Neil. 32p. (ps-2). 1991. PLB 13.50 (0-87614-674-4) Carolrhoda Bks.

—Jump Along: A Fun Book of Movement. Morris, Neil. 32p. (ps-2). 1991. PLB 13.50 (0-87614-671-X) Carolrhoda Bks.

—The Kingfisher Book of Words: A-Z Guide to Quotations, Proverbs, Origins, Usage, & Idioms. Beal, George. LC 92-53105. 192p. (gr. 4 up). 1992. 10.95 (1-85697-805-2) Kingfisher Bks.

—Linda's Late: A Fun Book of Time. Morris, Neil. 32p. (ps-2). 1991. PLB 13.50 (0-87614-675-2) Carolrhoda Bks.

—Magic Monkey: A Fun Book of Numbers. Morris, Neil. 32p. (ps-2). 1991. PLB 13.50 (0-87614-677-9) Carolrhoda Bks.

—Picture Word Book Three. 28p. (ps). 1991. 3.50 (0-7214-1436-2, 916-3) Ladybird Bks.

—Picture Word Book Two. 28p. (ps). 1991. 3.50 (0-7214-1435-4, 916-2) Ladybird Bks.
—Raging Robots & Unruly Uncles. large type ed. Mahy, Margaret. 160p. 1992. 13.95 (0-7451-1526-8, Galaxy Child Lrg Print) Chivers N Amer.
—Raging Robots & Unruly Uncles. Mahy, Margaret. 94p. (gr. 3-7). 1993. 13.95 (0-87951-469-8) Overlook Pr.
—Rummage Sale: A Fun Book of Shapes & Colors. Morris, Neil. 32p. (ps-2). 1991. PLB 13.50 (0-87614-676-0) Carolrhoda Bks.
—What a Noise: A Fun Book of Sounds. Morris, Neil. 32p. (ps-2). 1991. PLB 13.50 (0-87614-670-1) Carolrhoda Bks.

Stevenson, Sucie. Baby-O. Carlstrom, Nancy W. 32p. (ps-3). 1992. 14.95 (0-316-12851-1) Little.
—Birthday Presents. Rylant, Cynthia. 32p. (ps-1). 1987. 13.95 (0-531-05705-4); PLB 13.99 (0-531-08305-5) Orchard Bks Watts.
—Christmas Eve. Stevenson, Sucie. 32p. (ps-2). 1992. pap. 3.99 (0-440-40729-X, YB) Dell.
—Crazy Clothes. Yektai, Niki. LC 93-19738. 32p. (gr. k-2). 1994. pap. 4.95 (0-689-71781-4, Aladdin) Macmillan Child Grp.
—Do I Have to Take Violet? Stevenson, Sucie. 32p. (ps-3). 1992. pap. 3.99 (0-440-40682-X, YB) Dell.
—Emily & Alice. Champion, Joyce. LC 92-13575. 1993. 13.95 (0-15-200588-9) HarBrace.
—Emily & Alice Again. Champion, Joyce. LC 93-5004. 1994. write for info. (0-15-200439-4, Gulliver Bks) HarBrace.
—Henry & Mudge & the Bedtime Thumps. Rylant, Cynthia. LC 89-49529. 40p. (gr. 1-3). 1991. RSBE 12.95 (0-02-778006-6, Bradbury Pr) Macmillan Child Grp.
—Henry & Mudge & the Careful Cousin: The Thirteenth Book of Their Adventures. Rylant, Cynthia. LC 92-12851. 48p. (gr. 1-3). 1994. RSBE 13.95 (0-02-778021-X, Bradbury Pr) Macmillan Child Grp.
—Henry & Mudge & the Forever Sea. Rylant, Cynthia. LC 92-28646. 48p. (gr. 1-3). 1993. pap. 3.95 (0-689-71701-6, Aladdin) Macmillan Child Grp.
—Henry & Mudge & the Forever Sea: The Sixth Book of Their Adventures. Rylant, Cynthia. LC 88-6130. 48p. (gr. 1-3). 1989. RSBE 12.95 (0-02-778007-4, Bradbury Pr) Macmillan Child Grp.
—Henry & Mudge & the Happy Cat. Rylant, Cynthia. LC 88-18855. 48p. (gr. 1-3). 1990. RSBE 12.95 (0-02-778008-2, Bradbury Pr) Macmillan Child Grp.
—Henry & Mudge & the Happy Cat: The Eighth Book of Their Adventures. Rylant, Cynthia. LC 93-10797. 48p. (gr. 1-3). 1994. pap. 3.95 (0-689-71791-1, Aladdin) Macmillan Child Grp.
—Henry & Mudge & the Long Weekend. Rylant, Cynthia. LC 90-26799. 40p. (gr. 1-3). 1992. RSBE 12.95 (0-02-778013-9, Bradbury Pr) Macmillan Child Grp.
—Henry & Mudge & the Wild Wind. Rylant, Cynthia. LC 91-12644. 40p. (gr. 1-3). 1993. RSBE 12.95 (0-02-778014-7, Bradbury Pr) Macmillan Child Grp.
—Henry & Mudge Get the Cold Shivers: The Seventh Book of Their Adventures. Rylant, Cynthia. LC 88-18854. 48p. (gr. 1-3). 1989. RSBE 12.95 (0-02-778011-2, Bradbury Pr) Macmillan Child Grp.
—Henry & Mudge in Puddle Trouble: The Second Book of Their Adventures. Rylant, Cynthia. LC 86-13616. 48p. (gr. 1-3). 1987. RSBE 12.95 (0-02-778002-3, Bradbury Pr) Macmillan Child Grp.
—Henry & Mudge in the Green Time. Rylant, Cynthia. LC 91-24942. 48p. (gr. 1-3). 1992. pap. 3.95 (0-689-71582-X, Aladdin) Macmillan Child Grp.
—Henry & Mudge in the Green Time: The Third Book of Their Adventures. Rylant, Cynthia. LC 86-26386. 48p. (gr. 1-3). 1987. RSBE 12.95 (0-02-778003-1, Bradbury Pr) Macmillan Child Grp.
—Henry & Mudge in the Sparkle Days: The Fifth Book of Their Adventures. Rylant, Cynthia. LC 86-23432. 40p. (gr. 1-3). 1988. RSBE 12.95 (0-02-778005-8, Bradbury Pr) Macmillan Child Grp.
—Henry & Mudge in the Sparkle Days: The Fifth Book of Their Adventures. Rylant, Cynthia. LC 92-42535. 48p. (gr. 1-3). 1993. pap. 3.95 (0-689-71752-0, Aladdin) Macmillan Child Grp.
—Henry & Mudge Take the Big Test: The Tenth Book of Their Adventures. Rylant, Cynthia. LC 90-35171. 40p. (gr. 1-3). 1991. RSBE 12.95 (0-02-778009-0, Bradbury Pr) Macmillan Child Grp.
—Henry & Mudge: The First Book. Rylant, Cynthia. LC 89-39809. 48p. (gr. 1-3). 1990. pap. 3.95 (0-689-71399-1, Aladdin) Macmillan Child Grp.
—Henry & Mudge under the Yellow Moon. Rylant, Cynthia. LC 91-23135. 48p. (gr. 1-3). 1992. pap. 3.95 (0-689-71580-3, Aladdin) Macmillan Child Grp.
—Henry & Mudge under the Yellow Moon: The Fourth Book of Their Adventures. Rylant, Cynthia. LC 86-26390. 48p. (gr. 1-3). 1987. RSBE 12.95 (0-02-778004-X, Bradbury Pr) Macmillan Child Grp.
—I Know I'm a Witch. Adler, David A. LC 86-33508. 32p. (ps-2). 1990. pap. 4.95 (0-8050-1480-2, Bks Young Read) H Holt & Co.
—The Princess & the Pea. Andersen, Hans Christian. Stevenson, Sucie, retold by. SO 3212. 32p. (gr. k-3). 1992. map. 15.00 (0-385-41375-0) Doubleday.
—Tubtime. Woodruff, Elvira. LC 89-36609. 32p. (ps-3). 1990. reinforced bdg. 14.95 (0-8234-0777-2) Holiday.

Stevenson, Suzie. Henry & Mudge: The First Book of Their Adventures. Rylant, Cynthia. LC 86-13615. 40p. (gr. 1-3). 1987. RSBE 12.95 (0-02-778001-5, Bradbury Pr) Macmillan Child Grp.

Stewart, Alan. The Kramurg. McCorkle, Beth. 32p. (Orig.). (gr. 1-8). 1991. pap. write for info. (0-9626729-1-2) Work Study Assn.
Stewart, Arvis. Bible Stories for Children. Horn, Geoffrey & Cavanaugh, Arthur. LC 79-27811. 336p. (gr. 1-5). 1980. SBE 13.95 (0-02-554060-2, Macmillan Child Bk) Macmillan Child Grp.
—Christopher Columbus. Young, Robert. Brook, Bonnie, ed. 32p. (gr. k-2). 1990. 6.95 (0-671-69110-4); PLB 10.98 (0-671-69104-X) Silver Pr.
—Felicia, the Critic. Conford, Ellen. (gr. 4-6). 1973. 14. 95 (0-316-15295-1) Little.
—A Gift of Magic. Duncan, Lois. (gr. 4-6). 1971. 15.95 (0-316-19545-6) Little.
—The Macmillan Book of Greek Gods & Heroes. Low, Alice. LC 85-7170. 192p. (gr. 2-6). 1985. SBE 16.95 (0-02-761390-9, Macmillan Child Bk) Macmillan Child Grp.
—Sage Smoke: Tales of the Shoshoni-Bannock Indians. Heady, Eleanor B. LC 92-46731. 94p. (gr. 4-6). 1993. PLB 12.98 (0-382-24361-7); 10.98 (0-382-24370-6) Silver Burdett Pr.
Stewart, Chantal. The Ant Nest. Ray, Stephen & Murdoch, Kathleen. LC 92-34254. 1993. 4.25 (0-383-03614-3) SRA Schl Grp.
—How Many Legs? Drew, David. LC 92-34268. 1993. 4.25 (0-383-03631-3) SRA Schl Grp.
Stewart, Charles. Path Through the Woods. Wilson, Barbara K. (gr. 7 up). 1958. 21.95 (0-685-40040-9) S G Phillips.
Stewart, Edgar. The Bird Alphabet Book. Pallotta, Jerry. 32p. (ps-3). 1989. 14.95 (0-88106-457-2); pap. 6.95 (0-88106-451-3) Charlesbridge Pub.
—Dirt Bike Runaway. Christopher, Matt. LC 83-13538. 160p. (gr. 4-6). 1989. pap. 3.95 (0-316-14002-3) Little.
—They Dance in the Sky. Guard, Jean & Williamson, Ray A. (gr. 6 up). 1987. 14.45 (0-395-39970-X) HM.
Stewart, Eve. Clown Plays. Waechter, F. K. & Campbell, Ken. Eyre, Richard, intro. by. 129p. 1992. pap. 11.95 (0-413-66550-X, A0661) Heinemann.
Stewart, Michael. Dinosaurs I Have Known. Polisar, Barry L. 48p. (Orig.). (gr. 2-6). 1988. 9.95 (0-938663-00-3); pap. 7.95 (0-938663-05-4) Rainbow Morn.
—Noises from under the Rug: The Barry Louis Polisar Songbook. Polisar, Barry L. 208p. (gr. 2-6). 1985. 18.98 (0-9615696-0-3); pap. 13.95 (0-9615696-1-1) Rainbow Morn.
Stewart, Pat. Jesus' Bethlehem Birthday. (ps-1). 1989. 9.99 (1-55513-814-4, Chariot Bks) Cook.
—Ouch! A Book about Cuts, Scratches, & Scrapes. Berger, Melvin. 32p. (gr. k-3). 1991. 12.95 (0-525-67323-7, Lodestar Bks) Dutton Child Bks.
—Science Fun Series, 6 vols. Wyler, Rose. 288p. (gr. 2-4). 1987. SET. PLB 88.28 (0-671-93016-8, J Messner); Set. PLB 51.24s.p. (0-685-47066-0); Set. pap. 29.70 (0-671-93018-4); Set. pap. 22.26s.p. (0-685-47067-9) S&S Trade.
—Science Fun with a Homemade Chemistry Set. Wyler, Rose. LC 86-21868. 48p. (gr. 2-4). 1987. lib. bdg. 11. 38 (0-671-55575-8, J Messner); lib. bdg. 4.95 (0-671-55570-7); PLB 8.54s.p. (0-685-47072-5); pap. 3.71s.p. (0-685-47073-3) S&S Trade.
—Science Fun with Drums, Bells, & Whistles. Wyler, Rose. LC 87-7838. 48p. (gr. 2-4). 1987. lib. bdg. 11.38 (0-671-63783-5, J Messner); lib. bdg. 4.95 (0-671-64760-1); PLB 8.54s.p. (0-685-47070-9); pap. 3.71s.p. (0-685-47071-7) S&S Trade.
—Science Fun With Mud & Dirt. Wyler, Rose. 48p. (gr. 3). 1987. pap. 4.95 (0-317-56794-2) S&S Trade.
—Science Fun with Mud & Dirt. Wyler, Rose. LC 86-8388. 48p. (gr. 2-4). 1986. lib. bdg. 11.38 (0-671-55569-3, J Messner); lib. bdg. 4.95 (0-671-62904-2); PLB 8.54s.p. (0-685-47076-8); pap. 3.71s.p. (0-685-47077-6) S&S Trade.
—Science Fun with Peanuts & Popcorn. Wyler, Rose. 48p. (gr. 2-4). 1986. lib. bdg. 11.38 (0-671-55572-3, J Messner); lib. bdg. 4.95 (0-671-62452-0); PLB 8.54s.p. (0-685-54164-9); pap. 3.71s.p. (0-685-54165-7) S&S Trade.
—Science Fun with Toy Boats & Planes. Wyler, Rose. 48p. (gr. 3). 1987. pap. 4.95 (0-317-56816-7) S&S Trade.
—Science Fun with Toy Boats & Planes. Wyler, Rose. LC 85-8842. 48p. (gr. 2-4). 1986. lib. bdg. 11.38 (0-671-55573-1, J Messner); lib. bdg. 4.95 (0-671-62453-9); PLB 8.54s.p. (0-685-47074-1); pap. 3.71s.p. (0-685-47075-X) S&S Trade.
—Science Fun with Toy Cars & Trucks. Wyler, Rose. LC 87-20326. 48p. (gr. 2-4). 1988. lib. bdg. 11.38 (0-671-63784-3, J Messner); lib. bdg. 4.95 (0-671-65854-9); PLB 8.54s.p. (0-685-47068-7); pap. 3.71s.p. (0-685-47069-5) S&S Trade.
—The Tale of Benjamin Bunny. Potter, Beatrix. LC 74-78812. 59p. (gr. 2 up). 1974. pap. 1.75 (0-486-21102-9) Dover.
Stewart, Roger, jt. illus. see Harris, Nick.
Stewart, Thomas R. & Kuller, Alison M. An Outward Bound School. Kuller, Alison M. LC 89-5169. 32p. (gr. 3-6). 1990. PLB 10.79 (0-8167-1731-1); pap. text ed. 2.95 (0-8167-1732-X) Troll Assocs.
Stickland, Paul. The Christmas Bear. Stickland, Henrietta. LC 93-10157. 32p. (ps-3). 1993. 15.99 (0-525-45062-9, DCB) Dutton Child Bks.
—Machines As Tall As Giants. Stickland, Paul. LC 88-34695. (gr. k-3). 1989. PLB 10.99 (0-394-95375-4) Random Bks Yng Read.

—Working Wheels. 14p. (ps). 1993. 3.50 (0-525-67457-8, Lodestar Bks) Dutton Child Bks.
Stiles, Andy. Breakfast with Jesus. Taylor, Mark A. 28p. (ps). 1993. PLB 4.99 (0-7847-0037-0, 24-03827) Standard Pub.
Still, Wayne A. Wilma Mankiller. Rand, Jacki T. LC 92-12813. 32p. (gr. 4-5). 1992. PLB 17.96 (0-8114-6576-4); pap. 4.95 (0-8114-4097-4) Raintree Steck-V.
Still, Wayne A. & Chandler, Alton. Conscious Choices of African-Americans During the American Revolution. Howell, Ann C. Ivery, Evelyn L., ed. Barboza, Maurice A., intro. by. 32p. (Orig.). (gr. 3-7). 1991. pap. text ed. 2.50 (1-877804-09-6) Chandler White.
Stillerman, Robbie. Case of the Missing Canary. new ed. Supraner, Robyn. LC 78-60122. 48p. (gr. 2-4). 1979. PLB 10.89 (0-89375-087-5); pap. 3.50 (0-89375-075-1) Troll Assocs.
Stillman, Peter. Paco y Ana Aprenden Acerca de la Amabilidad. Martinez, Carol. (SPA.). 32p. (Orig.). (gr. 2-4). 1988. pap. 1.50 (0-311-38590-7, Edit Mundo) Casa Bautista.
—Paco y Ana Aprenden Acerca de la Amistad. Martinez, Carol. (SPA., Orig.). (gr. 2-4). 1988. pap. 1.50 (0-311-38589-3, Edit Mundo) Casa Bautista.
—Paco y Ana Aprenden Acerca de la Honradez. Martinez, Carol. (SPA.). 32p. (Orig.). (gr. 2-4). 1988. pap. 1.50 (0-311-38587-7, Edit Mundo) Casa Bautista.
—Paco y Ana Aprenden Acerca de la Obediencia. Martinez, Carol. (SPA.). 32p. (Orig.). (gr. 2-4). 1988. pap. 1.50 (0-311-38588-5, Edit Mundo) Casa Bautista.
Stillman, Susan. Windsongs & Rainbows. Albert, Burton. LC 92-12012. (ps-3). 1993. map. 14.00 JRT (0-671-76004-1, S&S BFYR) S&S Trade.
Stillwater, Maitreya. Windows of Nature: A Story-Coloring Book. Stillwater, Maitreya. 40p. (Orig.). (ps-3). 1987. pap. 6.95 (07516-580-X) DeVorss.
Stillwell, Stella. Animal Colors. Bailey, Vanessa. 16p. (ps). 1991. 5.95 (0-8120-6245-0) Barron.
—Animal Sounds. Bailey, Vanessa. 16p. (ps). 1991. 5.95 (0-8120-6243-4) Barron.
—Egg! A Dozen Eggs, What Will They Be? Unfold Each Page & You Will See! Wood, A. J. LC 92-17930. 1993. 12.95 (0-316-81616-7) Little.
Stillwell, Stella & Ward, Helen. Living Fossils. Pope, Joyce. LC 91-13998. 48p. (gr. 4-8). 1992. PLB 19.92 (0-8114-3151-7); pap. 4.95 (0-8114-6256-0) Raintree Steck-V.
Stilwell, Alison. Chin Ling, the Chinese Cricket. Stilwell, Alison. LC 81-90045. 48p. (gr. 1-4). 1981. Repr. of 1947 ed. 12.95 (0-9605862-0-2) Stilwell Studio.
Stilwell, Stella & Ward, Helen. Two Lives. Pope, Joyce. LC 91-17460. 48p. (gr. 4-8). 1992. PLB 19.92 (0-8114-3153-3); pap. 4.95 (0-8114-6257-9) Raintree Steck-V.
Stinnett, Leia. Color Me One. Stinnett, Leia. 36p. (gr. 3 up). 1993. pap. text ed. 4.95 (1-880737-13-2) Crystal Jrns.
—The Twelve Universal Laws, Principles & Applications: A Workbook for Children of All Ages. Stinnett, Leia. 138p. 1993. wkbk. 18.95 (1-880737-14-0) Crystal Jrns.
Stirnweis, Shannon. The Last of the Mohicans. Cooper, James Fenimore. Martin, Les, adapted by. 96p. (Orig.). (gr. 2-7). 1993. PLB 5.99 (0-679-94706-X); pap. 2.95 (0-679-84706-5) Random Bks Yng Read.
Stites, Joe. Five Small Loaves & Two Small Fish. Stortz, Diane. 28p. (ps). 1992. 2.50 (0-87403-953-3, 24-03593) Standard Pub.
—I Like Sunday School! Keefer, Mikal. 28p. (ps-k). 1993. 4.99 (0-7847-0040-0, 24-03830) Standard Pub.
—Under Every Roof: A Kid's Study & Field Guide to the Architecture of American Houses. Glenn, Particia B. 112p. (gr. 3-6). 1993. 16.95 (0-89133-214-6) Preservation Pr.
Stitt, Sue & McCaig, Ron. Make This Model Castle. Ashman, Iain. (gr. 4-9). 1983. pap. 5.95 (0-13-545947-8, Pub. by Treehouse) P-H.
—Make This Model Village. Ashman, Iain. (gr. 4-9). 1983. pap. 5.95 (0-13-545954-0, Pub. by Treehouse) P-H.
Stobbs, William. Westward to Vinland. Treece, Henry. (gr. 8 up). 1967. 21.95 (0-87599-136-X) S G Phillips.
Stock, Catharine. Oh, Emma. Baker, Barbara. LC 91-2578. 96p. (gr. 2-5). 1991. 12.95 (0-525-44771-7, DCB) Dutton Child Bks.
Stock, Catherine. Alexander's Midnight Snack: A Little Elephant's ABC. Stock, Catherine. 88-2608. 40p. (ps-1). 1988. 13.95 (0-89919-512-1, Clarion Bks) HM.
—Bella Arabella. Fosburgh, Liza. 85-42809. 128p. (gr. 4-7). 1986. SBE 12.95 (0-02-735430-X, Four Winds) Macmillan Child Grp.
—The Birthday Present. Stock, Catherine. LC 90-1914. 32p. (ps-1). 1991. SBE 11.95 (0-02-788401-5, Bradbury Pr) Macmillan Child Grp.
—By the Dawn's Early Light: Al Amanecer. Ackerman, Karen. Ada, Alma F., tr. LC 92-35633. (ENG & SPA.). 40p. (gr-3). 1994. English ed. SBE 14.95 (0-689-31788-3, Atheneum Child Bk); Spanish ed. SBE 14.95 (0-689-31917-7) Macmillan Child Grp.
—A Christmas Angel Collection. Stock, Catherine. 32p. (gr. k up). 1988. 3.95 (0-394-80266-7) Random Bks Yng Read.
—Christmas Time. Stock, Catherine. LC 89-71249. 32p. (ps-1). 1990. SBE 11.95 (0-02-788403-1, Bradbury Pr) Macmillan Child Grp.
—Christmas Time. Stock, Catherine. LC 92-42225. 32p. (ps-1). 1993. pap. 3.95 (0-689-71725-3, Aladdin) Macmillan Child Grp.

—Easter Surprise. Stock, Catherine. LC 90-1915. 32p. (ps-1). 1991. SBE 11.95 (*0-02-788371-X*, Bradbury Pr) Macmillan Child Grp.

—Eddie's Friend Boodles. Haywood, Carolyn. LC 91-3212. (gr. 1 up). 1991. 12.95 (*0-688-09028-1*) Morrow Jr Bks.

—Emma's Dragon Hunt. Stock, Catherine. LC 83-25109. 32p. (gr. k up). 1984. 11.95 (*0-688-02696-6*); PLB 9.55 (*0-688-02698-2*) Lothrop.

—The Evening King. LaRochelle, David. LC 91-1970. 32p. (ps-3). 1993. SBE 14.95 (*0-689-31640-2*, Atheneum Child Bk) Macmillan Child Grp.

—Galimoto. Williams, Karen L. LC 89-2258. 32p. (gr. k-3). 1990. 13.95 (*0-688-08789-2*); lib. bdg. 13.88 (*0-688-08790-6*) Lothrop.

—Galimoto. Williams, Karen L. LC 89-2258. 32p. (ps-3). 1991. pap. 4.95 (*0-688-10991-8*, Mulberry) Morrow.

—Galimoto. Williams, Karen L. (gr. k-4). 1993. 13.95 (*0-685-64814-1*); audio cass. 11.00 (*1-882869-77-X*) Read Advent.

—Halloween Monster. Stock, Catherine. LC 89-49530. 32p. (ps-1). 1990. SBE 11.95 (*0-02-788404-X*, Bradbury Pr) Macmillan Child Grp.

—Halloween Monster. Stock, Catherine. LC 92-42987. 32p. (ps-1). 1993. pap. 3.95 (*0-689-71727-X*, Aladdin) Macmillan Child Grp.

—An Island Christmas. Joseph, Lynn. 32p. (ps-3). 1992. 14.45 (*0-395-58761-1*, Clarion Bks) HM.

—Justin & the Best Biscuits in the World. Walter, Mildred P. LC 86-7148. 128p. (gr. 3-7). 1986. 12.95 (*0-688-06645-3*) Lothrop.

—Mara in the Morning. Christiansen, C. B. LC 90-25049. 32p. (gr. k-3). 1991. RSBE 13.95 (*0-689-31616-X*, Atheneum Child Bk) Macmillan Child Grp.

—Midnight Snowman. Bauer, Caroline F. LC 86-26540. 32p. (ps-2). 1987. SBE 13.95 (*0-689-31294-6*, Atheneum Child Bk) Macmillan Child Grp.

—Miss Know-It-All & the Magic House. York, Carol B. (gr. 3-7). 1989. pap. 2.75 (*0-318-41641-7*, Skylark) Bantam.

—Oh, Emma. Baker, Barbara. LC 93-7767. 144p. (gr. 2-5). 1993. pap. 3.99 (*0-14-036357-2*, Puffin) Puffin Bks.

—Sea Swan. Lasky, Kathryn. LC 88-1444. 32p. (gr. k-3). 1988. RSBE 14.95 (*0-02-751700-4*, Macmillan Child Bk) Macmillan Child Grp.

—Secret Valentine. Stock, Catherine. LC 90-1916. 32p. (ps-1). 1991. SBE 11.95 (*0-02-788372-8*, Bradbury Pr) Macmillan Child Grp.

—Snowed In. Lucas, Barbara M. LC 92-39081. 32p. (ps-3). 1993. RSBE 14.95 (*0-02-761465-4*, Bradbury Pr) Macmillan Child Grp.

—Something is Going to Happen. Zolotow, Charlotte. LC 87-26661. 32p. (ps-3). 1988. PLB 13.89 (*0-06-027029-2*) HarpC Child Bks.

—Something is Going to Happen. Zolotow, Charlotte. LC 87-26661. 32p. (ps-3). 1991. pap. 4.95 (*0-06-443274-2*, Trophy) HarpC Child Bks.

—Taking Turns: Poetry to Share. Wolman, Bernice, compiled by. LC 90-46533. 32p. (gr. 1-4). 1992. SBE 13.95 (*0-689-31677-1*, Atheneum Child Bk) Macmillan Child Grp.

—Tap-Tap. Williams, Karen L. LC 93-13006. 1994. write for info. (*0-395-65617-6*, Clarion Bks) HM.

—Thanksgiving Treat. Stock, Catherine. LC 89-49528. 32p. (ps-1). 1990. SBE 11.95 (*0-02-788402-3*, Bradbury Pr) Macmillan Child Grp.

—A Tiger Called Thomas. rev. ed. Zolotow, Charlotte. LC 86-20878. 40p. (ps-3). 1988. 12.95 (*0-688-06786-8*); PLB 12.88 (*0-688-06697-6*) Lothrop.

—Timothy Tall Feather. Pomerantz, Charlotte. LC 85-24819. 32p. (gr. k-3). 1986. 11.75 (*0-688-04246-5*); PLB 11.88 (*0-688-04247-3*) Greenwillow.

—Too Far Away to Touch, Close Enough to See. Newman, Leslea. LC 93-30327. 1995. write for info. (*0-395-68968-6*, Clarion Bks) HM.

—Trot, Trot to Boston. Ra, Carol F. LC 86-7354. 32p. (ps). 1987. 12.95 (*0-688-06190-7*); PLB 12.88 (*0-688-06191-5*) Lothrop.

—Where Are You Going, Manyoni? Stock, Catherine. LC 92-29793. 48p. (ps up). 1993. 15.00 (*0-688-10352-9*); PLB 14.93 (*0-688-10353-7*) Morrow Jr Bks.

—The Willow Umbrella. Widman, Christine. LC 91-10989. 32p. (gr. k-3). 1993. RSBE 14.95 (*0-02-792760-1*, Macmillan Child Bk) Macmillan Child Grp.

Stock, Catherine & Stock, Catherine. Armien's Fishing Trip. Stock, Catherine. LC 89-3266. 40p. (gr. 1 up). 1990. 13.95 (*0-688-08395-1*); PLB 13.88 (*0-688-08396-X*, Morrow Jr Bks) Morrow Jr Bks.

Stock, Lois L. Sunny's Mittens: Learn to Knit - Lovikka Mittens. Hansen, Robin. LC 90-61410. 48p. (gr. 3-6). 1990. pap. 12.95 wire-o bdg. (*0-89272-290-8*) Down East.

Stockett, Thomas & Washington, Luther. I Am Somebody, I Am Me: A Black Child's Credo. Washington, Vivian E. 35p. (Orig.). (gr. 2-6). 1986. pap. 8.50 (*0-935132-07-4*) C H Fairfax.

Stockett, Thomas A. Black Mother Goose Book. 2nd ed. Oliver, Elizabeth M. LC 81-83427. 48p. (gr. 3-6). Repr. of 1981 ed. 12.95 (*0-912444-35-5*) DARE Bks.

Stockham, Leslie C. Divirtamonos Con el Abecedario. Stockham, Leslie C. 96p. (gr. k-2). 1993. wkbk. 8.95 (*0-9624096-2-6*) Bilingual Lang Mat.

Stockman, Jack. Gaal the Conqueror. White, John. LC 89-19821. 320p. (Orig.). (gr. 7-9). 1989. pap. 10.99 (*0-87784-591-3*, 591) InterVarsity.

Stoeke, Janet M. Hunky Dory Ate It. Evans, Katie. LC 91-13992. 32p. (ps-1). 1992. 13.50 (*0-525-44847-0*, DCB) Dutton Child Bks.

—Hunky Dory Found It. Evans, Katie. LC 93-15826. 32p. (ps-k). 1994. 13.99 (*0-525-45192-7*, DCB) Dutton Child Bks.

—Minerva Louise. Stoeke, Janet M. LC 87-24458. 24p. (ps-1). 1988. 12.00 (*0-525-44374-6*, 01063-320, DCB) Dutton Child Bks.

Stoffregen, Jill. Lucky Becomes a Frog. Petersen, Candyce A. LC 92-6417. Date not set. 11.95 (*1-56065-096-6*) Capstone Pr. Postponed.

Stoffregen, Jill A. Beauty the Butterfly. Petersen, Candyce A. 24p. (ps-3). Date not set. 11.95 (*1-56065-097-4*) Capstone Pr. Postponed.

—A Desert Cactus Comes to Life. Milios, Rita. LC 92-12895. 24p. (ps-3). Date not set. 11.95 (*1-56065-168-7*) Capstone Pr. Postponed.

—Eggbert the Robin. Petersen, Candyce A. LC 92-12894. 24p. (ps-3). Date not set. 11.95 (*1-56065-099-0*) Capstone Pr. Postponed.

—Silky the Spider. Petersen, Candyce A. 24p. (ps-3). Date not set. 11.95 (*1-56065-098-2*) Capstone Pr. Postponed.

Stoltz, David. Traffic Jam. Mendoza, George. LC 89-28597. 32p. 1990. PLB 14.95 (*1-55670-135-7*) Stewart Tabori & Chang.

Stone, Erika. About Phobias. Stein, Sara B. (ps-8). 1979. 10.95 (*0-8027-6348-0*) Walker & Co.

—The Adopted One. Stein, Sara B. (gr. k-6). 1979. 12.95 (*0-8027-6346-4*); pap. 7.95 (*0-8027-7224-2*) Walker & Co.

—Baby Talk. 18p. (ps). 1992. bds. 2.95 (*0-448-40312-9*, G&D) Putnam Pub Group.

—On Divorce. Stein, Sara B. 48p. 1979. 10.95 (*0-8027-6344-8*) Walker & Co.

Stone, Gary. Santa Plus Martha. Stone, Bev. 62p. (gr. k-6). 1992. pap. 12.95 (*0-9619791-1-9*) Stone Studios.

—The Secret of Santa Claus: Flower Blue & Snowie Elves Help Santa Meet His Brothers. Stone, Bev. 64p. (gr. k-6). 1987. pap. 12.95 (*0-9619791-0-0*) Stone Studios.

Stone, Helen. Little Witch. Bennett, Anna E. LC 52-13721. 128p. (gr. 3-5). 1981. pap. 3.95 (*0-06-440119-7*, Trophy) HarpC Child Bks.

Stone, L. Children's Hulas for Song Stories, Bk. 3. Roes, Carol & Kaiulani. 24p. (gr. 3-4). 1963. pap. 5.50 (*0-930932-08-0*); record incl. M Loke.

Stone, Lloyd. Children's Hulas from Hawaii, Bk. 1. Roes, Carol & Tuulikki. (gr. k). 1961. pap. text ed. 5.50 (*0-930932-05-6*, A516842); record incl. M Loke.

—Children's Songs from Hawaii. Roes, Carol. LC 81-670132. (ps-3). 1973. PLB 31.95 (*0-930932-01-3*, A875377) M Loke.

—Eight Children's Songs from Hawaii. Roes, Carol. (gr. 3-4). 1958. pap. text ed. 5.50 (*0-930932-06-4*, EP126127) M Loke.

—Keiki Songs of Hawaii. Roes, Carol. 26p. (gr. 6). 1966. pap. 5.50 (*0-930932-16-1*) M Loke.

—Song Stories of Hawaii. Roes, Carol. 24p. (gr. 1-8). 1959. pap. 5.50 (*0-930932-17-X*) M Loke.

Stone, Lynn M. Baby Animals. Mattern, Joanne. LC 91-40282. 24p. (gr. 4-7). 1993. pap. text ed. 1.95 (*0-8167-2958-1*) Troll Assocs.

—Lions & Tigers. Mattern, Joanne. LC 92-19053. 24p. (gr. 4-7). 1992. (Pub. by Watermill Pr); pap. 1.95 (*0-8167-2956-5*, Pub. by Watermill Pr) Troll Assocs.

—Reptiles & Amphibians. Mattern, Joanne. LC 92-20189. 24p. (gr. 4-7). 1992. pap. 1.95 (*0-8167-2954-9*, Pub. by Watermill Pr) Troll Assocs.

Stone, Rob. The Human Body & How It Works. Royston, Angela. LC 90-42978. 40p. (Orig.). (gr. 2-5). 1991. pap. 3.95 (*0-679-80860-4*) Random Bks Yng Read.

Stone, S. Callis. The Weeuns Journey of Two Cousins. Tallarico, Beatrice & Stone, S. Callis. 39p. (gr. 2-8). 1984. 12.95 (*0-936191-13-9*) Tallstone Pub.

Stoner, Laura M. Acts - a Story Color Book. Stoner, Laura M. Huskey, Freeda, ed. 80p. (Orig.). (gr. k-6). 1992. wkbk. 5.95 (*0-934426-46-5*) NAPSAC Reprods.

—Exodus: A Story Color Book. Stoner, Laura M. 90p. (Orig.). (gr. k-6). 1986. pap. 3.95 (*0-934426-11-2*) Napsac Reprods.

Storms, Robert. Buddy the Beaver. Storms, John. 24p. (Orig.). (gr. k-4). 1993. pap. 4.95 (*0-89346-529-1*) Heian Intl.

—Cory the Crocodile. Storms, John. 24p. (Orig.). (gr. k-4). 1993. pap. 4.95 (*0-89346-530-5*) Heian Intl.

—Sammy the Sea Otter. Storms, John. 24p. (gr. k-4). 1993. 4.95 (*0-89346-528-3*) Heian Intl.

—Tony the Tokay Gecko. Storms, John. 24p. (gr. k-4). 1993. pap. 4.95 (*0-89346-531-3*) Heian Intl.

Storms, Robert S. Hearing. Smith, Kathie B. & Crenson, Victoria. LC 87-5854. 24p. (gr. k-3). 1988. PLB 10.59 (*0-8167-1006-6*); pap. text ed. 2.50 (*0-8167-1007-4*) Troll Assocs.

—Seeing. Smith, Kathie B. & Crenson, Victoria. LC 87-5862. 24p. (gr. k-3). 1988. PLB 10.59 (*0-8167-1008-2*); pap. text ed. 2.50 (*0-8167-1009-0*) Troll Assocs.

—Smelling. Smith, Kathie B. & Crenson, Victoria. LC 87-5887. 24p. (gr. k-3). 1988. PLB 10.59 (*0-8167-1010-4*); pap. text ed. 2.50 (*0-8167-1011-2*) Troll Assocs.

—Thinking. Smith, Kathie B. & Crenson, Victoria. LC 87-5886. 24p. (gr. k-3). 1988. PLB 10.59 (*0-8167-1016-3*); pap. text ed. 2.50 (*0-8167-1017-1*) Troll Assocs.

—Touching. Smith, Kathie B. & Crenson, Victoria. LC 87-5885. 24p. (gr. k-3). 1988. PLB 10.59 (*0-8167-1012-0*); pap. text ed. 2.50 (*0-8167-1013-9*) Troll Assocs.

Storr, Sherman. The Ipswich Itinerants. Storr, Sherman, pseud. Wiegand, Betty, ed. Kern, W. C., intro. by. 258p. (Orig.). (gr. 9-12). 1988. pap. 8.00 (*0-9621380-0-2*) Alacran Pr Inc.

Story, Jim, jt. illus. see Williams, Don.

Story Rhyme Staff. Recipe Story Rhyme Cookbook. Story Rhyme Staff. 60p. (gr. 7-10). 1993. binder 21.95 (*1-56820-103-6*) Story Time.

—Recipe Story Rhyme: Greetings to Duplicate & Use. Story Rhyme Staff. 60p. (gr. 7-10). 1993. binder 29.95 (*1-56820-104-4*) Story Time.

—Self Esteem: Stories & Poetry. Story Rhyme Staff. 28p. (gr. 4-9). 1993. 8.95 (*1-56820-107-9*) Story Time.

—Story Rhyme Greetings: Directory of Story Letters for Birthdays, Celebrations, Holidays, Etcetera. Story Rhyme Staff. 60p. (gr. 7-9). 1993. notebk. 39.95 (*1-56820-106-0*) Story Time.

Story Time Staff. Home Schooling with Educational Story Rhymes. Story Time Staff. 50p. (gr. 6-9). 1993. binder 21.95 (*1-56820-108-7*) Story Time.

—Stories That Educate, Inform, Entertain & Rhyme: Kids Workshop Workbook I. Story Time Staff. 52p. 1992. GBC bdg. 29.95 (*1-56820-040-4*) Story Time.

—Stories That Educate, Inform, Entertain & Rhyme: Kids Workshop Workbook II. Story Time Staff. 52p. 1992. GBC bdg. 29.95 (*1-56820-041-2*) Story Time.

Story Time Stories That Rhyme Staff. Bean Sprouts: A How to Story Sample & Activity Pages. Story Time Stories That Rhyme Staff. 28p. (gr. 4-7). 1992. GBC bdg. 9.95 (*1-56820-009-9*) Story Time.

—Christmas Stories That Rhyme. Story Time Stories That Rhyme Staff. 39p. (gr. 4-7). 1992. binder 19.95 (*1-56820-015-3*) Story Time.

—Cowboy Boots: A Story Sample & Activity Pages. Story Time Stories That Rhyme Staff. 16p. (gr. 4-7). 1992. GBC bdg. 9.95 (*1-56820-008-0*) Story Time.

—Fables, Tales, & Stories That Rhyme. Story Time Stories That Rhyme Staff. 50p. (Orig.). (gr. 4-7). 1992. GBC bdg. 19.95 (*1-56820-016-1*) Story Time.

—Fish Convention: A Story Sample & Activity Pages. Story Time Stories That Rhyme Staff. 37p. (gr. 4-7). 1992. GBC bdg. 9.95 (*1-56820-011-0*) Story Time.

—Halloween Stories That Rhyme. Story Time Stories That Rhyme Staff. 38p. (Orig.). (gr. 4-7). 1992. GBC bdg. 15.95 (*1-56820-013-7*) Story Time.

—Math in Stories That Rhyme. Story Time Stories That Rhyme Staff. 50p. (Orig.). (gr. 4-7). 1992. GBC bdg. 19.95 (*1-56820-017-X*) Story Time.

—Mushrooms: A Story Sample & Activity Pages. Story Time Stories That Rhyme Staff. 20p. (gr. 4-7). 1992. GBC bdg. 9.95 (*1-56820-010-2*) Story Time.

—Seaweeds: A Story Sample & Activity Pages. Story Time Stories That Rhyme Staff. 17p. (gr. 4-7). 1992. GBC bdg. 9.95 (*1-56820-007-2*) Story Time.

—Story Habitat: Plant & Animal Stories. Story Time Stories That Rhyme Staff. 40p. (Orig.). (gr. 4-7). 1992. GBC bdg. 19.95 (*1-56820-014-5*) Story Time.

—Tennis Shoes: A Story Sample & Activity Pages. Story Time Stories That Rhyme Staff. 21p. (gr. 4-7). 1992. GBC bdg. 9.95 (*1-56820-012-9*) Story Time.

—Water World Convention: Stories & Word Mapping Activity Workbook. Story Time Stories That Rhyme Staff. 50p. (Orig.). (gr. 4-7). 1992. binder 25.95 (*1-56820-018-8*) Story Time.

Stott, Carol. Amazing Records. Ripley, Robert. 48p. (gr. 3-6). 1992. PLB 12.95 (*1-56065-124-5*) Capstone Pr.

—Clothing. Ripley, Robert L. 48p. (gr. 3-6). Date not set. PLB 12.95 (*1-56065-131-8*) Capstone Pr. Postponed.

—Incredible Journeys. Ripley, Robert L. 48p. (gr. 3-6). Date not set. PLB 12.95 (*1-56065-129-6*) Capstone Pr. Postponed.

—Inventions. Ripley, Robert L. 48p. (gr. 3-6). Date not set. PLB 12.95 (*1-56065-125-3*) Capstone Pr. Postponed.

—Literature. Ripley, Robert L. 48p. (gr. 3-6). 1992. PLB 12.95 (*1-56065-130-X*) Capstone Pr.

—Math & Science Facts. Ripley, Robert L. 48p. (gr. 3-6). 1992. PLB 12.95 (*1-56065-128-8*) Capstone Pr.

—The Psychic & Supernatural. Ripley, Robert L. 48p. (gr. 3-6). 1992. PLB 12.95 (*1-56065-127-X*) Capstone Pr.

—Puzzles. Ripley, Robert L. 48p. (gr. 3-6). Date not set. PLB 12.95 (*1-56065-126-1*) Capstone Pr. Postponed.

Stott, Dorothy. Baby Talk. Miranda, Anne. 16p. (ps). 1987. 9.95 (*0-525-44319-3*, 0772-230, DCB) Dutton Child Bks.

—Baby Walk. Miranda, Anne. 14p. (ps). 1988. 8.95 (*0-525-44421-1*, DCB) Dutton Child Bks.

—Little Duck's Bicycle Ride. Stott, Dorothy. LC 90-19425. 32p. (ps-k). 1991. 10.95 (*0-525-44728-8*, DCB) Dutton Child Bks.

—Zip, Whiz, Zoom! Calmenson, Stephanie. (ps-1). 1992. 13.95 (*0-316-12478-8*, Joy St Bks) Little.

Stott, Ken. Make Your Own Musical Instruments. McLean, Margaret. 32p. (gr. 4-7). 1988. PLB 14.95 (*0-8225-0895-8*, First Ave Edns); pap. 4.95 (*0-8225-9558-3*, First Ave Edns) Lerner Pubns.

—Tell the Time with Thomas. Awdry, Christopher. LC 91-67877. 32p. (ps-1). 1993. 7.99 (*0-679-83461-3*) Random Bks Yng Read.

—Thomas's Big Book of Words. Awdry, Christopher. LC 91-62681. 32p. (ps-1). 1992. 7.99 (*0-679-82778-1*) Random Bks Yng Read.

—Tracking Thomas the Tank Engine & His Friends: A Book with Finger Tabs. Awdry, W. LC 91-67876. 16p. (ps-1). 1992. bds. 7.99 (0-679-83458-3) Random Bks Yng Read.

Stotz, Gunther. Who Stole Travada? Brod, Alexandra. Lucke, Peggy, ed. 128p. (gr. 3-6). 1987. pap. 4.95 (0-940589-00-1) Adventure Pr.

Stoub, Paul. Decisions. 2nd ed. Roeda, Jack. Smith, Harvey A., intro. by. 80p. (gr. 9-12). 1992. pap. text ed. 6.50 (0-930265-96-3, 1240-4920); tchr's. manual 8.50 (1-56212-000-X, 1240-4940); session guides 4.95 (0-685-60757-7, 1240-4910) CRC Pubns.

—One Large Order of Faith to Go. Willingham, David. Smit, Harvey A., intro. by. 99p. (Orig.). (gr. 6-8). 1991. pap. text ed. 6.25 (1-56212-012-3, 1701-0480) CRC Pubns.

Stouffer, Deborah. The Eye & I. Wardlaw, Lee. LC 88-15664. 75p. (Orig.). (gr. 3-6). 1988. pap. 3.50 (0-931093-10-4) Red Hen Pr.

—Operation Rhinoceros. Wardlaw, Lee. LC 92-15933. 120p. (Orig.). (gr. 3-6). 1992. pap. 3.50 (0-931093-14-7) Red Hen Pr.

Stout, John W. The Tale of the Great Fruit Tree. Anderson, John W. 40p. 1992. 15.00 (0-9633296-0-X) Koinonia TX.

Stout, Robert T. Children's Favorite Story of Santa Claus. Stout, Robert T. 32p. (ps-6). 1982. 5.95 (0-911049-08-8); pap. 3.95 (0-911049-04-5) Yuletide Intl.

—The Noorps Are Coming. Stout, Robert T. 32p. (ps-6). 1982. 3.95 (0-911049-05-3) Yuletide Intl.

—The Original Story of Santa Claus. Stout, Robert T. 56p. (ps-8). 1981. 6.95 (0-911049-00-2) Yuletide Intl.

—The Secret of Halloween. Stout, Robert T. 24p. (Orig.). (ps-6). 1982. 3.50 (0-911049-02-9) Yuletide Intl.

Stover, Jo A. They Didn't Use Their Heads. Stover, Jo A. 45p. (ps). 1990. pap. 4.95 (0-89084-546-8) Bob Jones Univ Pr.

Stover, Jo Ann. If Everybody Did. Stover, Jo Ann. 48p. (Orig.). (gr. k-1). 1989. pap. 3.95 (0-89084-487-9) Bob Jones Univ Pr.

Stow, Jenny. The House That Jack Built. LC 91-23850. 32p. (ps-2). 1992. 14.00 (0-8037-1090-9) Dial Bks Young.

—The House That Jack Built. 32p. (ps-2). 1993. pap. 4.99 (0-14-054590-5, Puffin Pied Piper) Puffin Bks.

Stowell, Charlotte. The Kids Can Do It Book: Fun Things to Make and Do. Robins, Deri, et al. LC 92-43345. 80p. (gr. k-4). 1993. pap. 9.95 (1-85697-860-5) Kingfisher Bks.

Stowell, Gordon. Jesus Alimenta. Stowell, Gordon. De Martinez, Violeta S., tr. 24p. (ps). 1988. pap. 0.75 (0-311-38614-8) Casa Bautista.

—Jesus Ama. Stowell, Gordon. De Martinez, Violeta S., tr. from SPA. 24p. (ps). 1984. pap. 0.75 (0-311-38611-3) Casa Bautista.

—Jesus Cuenta. Stowell, Gordon. De Martinez, Violeta S., tr. from SPA. 24p. (ps). 1984. pap. 0.75 (0-311-38613-X) Casa Bautista.

—Jesus Ensena. Stowell, Gordon. De Martinez, Violeta S., tr. from SPA. 24p. (ps). 1984. pap. 0.75 (0-311-38609-1) Casa Bautista.

—Jesus Llama. Stowell, Gordon. De Martinez, Violeta S., tr. from SPA. 24p. (ps). 1984. pap. 0.75 (0-311-38612-1) Casa Bautista.

—Jesus Sana. Stowell, Gordon. De Martinez, Violeta S., tr. from ENG. 24p. (ps-1). 1984. pap. 0.75 (0-311-38610-5) Casa Bautista.

—Jesus Vive. Stowell, Gordon. De Martinez, Violeta S., tr. from SPA. 24p. (ps-1). 1984. pap. 0.75 (0-311-38615-6) Casa Bautista.

Stower, Adam & Robinson, Claire. Greek Stories. Hull, Robert. 48p. (gr. 5-9). 1994. 15.95 (1-56847-106-8) Thomson Lrning.

Stower, Adam, jt. illus. see Heap, Johnathan.

Strahan, Heather. All Dressed Up. Buckle, Mariette. LC 92-21447. 1993. 3.75 (0-383-03613-5) SRA Schl Grp.

—Molly's Bracelet. Bissett, Isabel. LC 92-34337. 1993. 3.75 (0-383-03641-0) SRA Schl Grp.

—Senses. Drew, David. LC 92-34162. 1993. 3.75 (0-383-03651-8) SRA Schl Grp.

—Taking Our Photo. Cartwright, Pauline. LC 92-31950. 1993. 3.75 (0-383-03595-3) SRA Schl Grp.

Strait, Barbara, jt. illus. see Ivins, Dorothy.

Strand, David. Gospel Duck. Mink, Len. 20p. (ps-5). 1988. pap. text ed. write for info. Mink Ministries.

—Gospel Duck Goes to School. Mink, Len. 24p. (ps-6). 1988. pap. text ed. write for info. Mink Ministries.

Strange, Florence. Brown Pelican at the Pond. O'Reilly, Edward. LC 78-58689. (gr. k-4). 1979. 7.95 (0-931644-01-1) Manzanita Pr.

Strassburg, Brian. Maybe Right, Maybe Wrong: A Guide for Young Thinkers. Barker, Dan. 72p. 1992. pap. 12. 95 (0-87975-731-0) Prometheus Bks.

Stratton, Helen. The Princess & Curdie. MacDonald, George. 332p. (gr. 5 up). 1993. Repr. of 1912 ed. 20. 00 (1-881084-15-9) Johannesen.

Stratton, Helen & Hughes. The Princess & the Goblin. MacDonald, George. 320p. (gr. 5 up). 1993. Repr. of 1911 ed. 20.00 (1-881084-14-0) Johannesen.

Strauss, Karen. Romanian Traditions & Customs. Gligor, Adrian & Strauss, Karen. 32p. (Orig.). (ps-4). 1993. pap. 11.95 (0-9634797-1-7) K Strauss & A Gligor.

Strawn, Susan. Butterflies East & West: A Book to Color. Opler, Paul. 96p. (Orig.). (gr. 1-6). 1993. pap. 8.95 (1-879373-45-9) R Rinehart.

—Butterflies of Eastern North America: A Coloring Album & Activity Book. Opler, Paul & Strawn, Susan. (gr. 1-6). 1989. pap. 4.95 (0-911797-53-X) R Rinehart.

—A Year at Elk Meadow. Gilmore, Jackie. 16p. (ps-3). 1986. pap. 4.95 (0-911797-24-6) R Rinehart.

Strecker, Rebekah. Bully on the Bus. Bosch, Carl. LC 88-42650. 64p. (Orig.). (gr. 2-5). 1988. PLB 16.95 (0-943990-43-2); pap. 5.95 (0-943990-42-4) Parenting Pr.

—Finders, Keepers. Crary, Elizabeth. LC 87-60369. 64p. (Orig.). (gr. 2-6). 1987. PLB 16.95 (0-943990-39-4); pap. 5.95 (0-943990-38-6) Parenting Pr.

—First Day Blues. Anderson, Peggy. LC 91-67808. 64p. (Orig.). (gr. 3-6). 1992. PLB 16.95 (0-943990-73-4); pap. 5.95 (0-943990-72-6) Parenting Pr.

—Making the Grade. Bosch, Carl W. LC 90-62674. 64p. (Orig.). (gr. 3). 1991. lib. bdg. 16.95 (0-943990-49-1); pap. 5.95 (0-943990-48-3) Parenting Pr.

—Under Whose Influence? Laik, Judy. LC 93-86233. 64p. 1994. lib. bdg. 16.95 (0-943990-98-X); pap. 5.95 (0-943990-97-1) Parenting Pr.

Strecker, Rebekah J. Peter Penguin & the Polar Sea. Obedin, Harry. LC 88-63171. 32p. (Orig.). (ps-4). 1989. pap. 4.95 (0-943990-54-8) Parenting Pr.

Streek, Tony. Illustrated World Atlas. Wright, Jill & Wright, David. Warwick Press, ed. 64p. (gr. 4-9). 1988. PLB 14.90 (0-531-19033-1, Warwick) Watts.

Street, Janet. Animal Fare: Zoological Nonsense Poems. Yolen, Jane. LC 92-44931. (gr. 4 up). 1994. write for info (0-15-203550-8) Harbrace.

—Dinosaur Dress Up. Sirois, Allen. LC 91-10583. 32p. (ps-3). 1992. 15.00 (0-688-10459-2, Tambourine Bks); PLB 14.93 (0-688-10460-6, Tambourine Bks) Morrow.

—The Gingham Dog & the Calico Cat. Field, Eugene. 32p. 1990. 14.95 (0-399-22151-4, Philomel Bks) Putnam Pub Group.

—The Gingham Dog & the Calico Cat. Field, Eugene. 32p. (gr. up). 1993. pap. 5.95 (0-399-22517-X, Philomel Bks) Putnam Pub Group.

—Good Night, Teddy Bear: A Book for Helping Get Ready for Bed, with Special Things to Touch, Smell, See & Do. Bertrand, Lynne. 24p. (ps). 1992. combbound 9.95 (0-9631591-1-9) Chapters Pub.

—Let's Go! Teddy Bear. Bertrand, Lynne. LC 93-71172. 24p. (ps). 1993. combbound 9.95 (1-881527-15-8) Chapters Pub.

—One Day, Two Dragons. Bertrand, Lynne. LC 91-32743. 32p. (ps-2). 1992. 14.00 (0-517-58411-5); PLB 14.99 (0-517-58413-1) Crown Bks Yng Read.

—One Little Chickadee. Burton, Marilee K. LC 93-27271. (gr. 2 up). write for info. (0-688-12651-0, Tamborine Bks); PLB write for info. (0-688-12652-9) Morrow.

Strekalovsky, Nicholas. Insect Pests. Fichter, George S. (gr. 5 up). 1966. pap. write for info. (0-307-24016-9, Golden Pr.) Western Pub.

—Spiders & Their Kin. rev. ed. Levi, Herbert W. & Levi, Lorna R. Zim, Herbert S. & Fichter, George S., eds. (gr. 9 up). 1969. pap. write for info. (0-307-24021-5, Golden Pr) Western Pub.

Stren, P. For Sale: One Brother. Stren, P. LC 91-73821. 32p. (gr. 1-4). 1993. 13.95 (1-56282-126-1); PLB 13. 89 (1-56282-127-X) Hyprn Child.

Stren, Patti. I Hate School! How to Hang In & When to Drop Out. Wirths, Claudine G. & Bowman-Kruhm, Mary. LC 85-48248. 128p. (gr. 7 up). 1986. pap. 7.95 (0-06-446054-1, Trophy) HarpC Child Bks.

—I Hate School! How to Hang In & When to Drop Out. Wirths, Claudine G. & Bowman-Kruhm, Mary. LC 85-48248. 128p. (gr. 7 up). 1986. 12.95 (0-690-04556-5, Crowell Jr Bks) (Crowell Jr Bks) HarpC Child Bks.

—Your New School. Wirths, Claudine G. & Bowman-Kruhm, Mary. LC 93-8513. (gr. 5-8). 1993. 14.95 (0-8050-2074-8) TFC Bks NY.

Stricklin, Patricia. Getting to Know Your Feelings. Dombrower, Jan. Johnson, Debbie, ed. 32p. (Orig.). (ps-3). 1990. pap. text ed. 5.95 (0-9626348-0-8) Heartwise Pr.

Strigens, Jerry. The Great Dinosaur Timescape. Kurokawa, Mitsuhiro. (gr. 4-5). 1989. PLB 22.60 (0-8368-0001-X) Gareth Stevens Inc.

Strigenz, Geri. Cross of Gold. Holmes, Mary Z. LC 91-37280. 48p. (gr. 4-5). 1992. PLB 20.70 (0-8114-3507-5); pap. write for info. (0-8114-6432-6) Raintree Steck-V.

—Dear Dad. Holmes, Mary Z. LC 91-37774. 48p. (gr. 4-5). 1992. PLB 20.70 (0-8114-3503-2); pap. write for info. (0-8114-6428-8) Raintree Steck-V.

—For Bread. Holmes, Mary Z. LC 91-37279. 48p. (gr. 4-5). 1992. PLB 20.70 (0-8114-3501-6); pap. write for info. (0-8114-6426-1) Raintree Steck-V.

—Thunder Foot. Holmes, Mary Z. LC 91-37548. 48p. (gr. 4-5). 1992. PLB 20.70 (0-8114-3500-8); pap. write for info. (0-8114-6425-3) Raintree Steck-V.

—Two Chimneys. Holmes, Mary Z. LC 91-35817. 48p. (gr. 4-5). 1992. PLB 20.70 (0-8114-3506-7); pap. write for info. (0-8114-6431-8) Raintree Steck-V.

—Year of the Sevens. Holmes, Mary Z. LC 91-33190. 48p. (gr. 4-5). 1992. PLB 20.70 (0-8114-3505-9); pap. write for info. (0-8114-6430-X) Raintree Steck-V.

Strigenz, Geri K. The Frog. Hogan, Paula Z. LC 78-21240. 32p. (gr. 1-4). 1979. PLB 17.96 (0-8172-1253-1); pap. 4.95 (0-8114-8175-1); pap. 9.95 incl. cassette (0-8114-8183-2) Raintree Steck-V.

—The Honeybee. Hogan, Paula Z. LC 78-21165. 32p. (gr. 1-4). 1979. PLB 17.96 (0-8172-1256-6); pap. 4.95 (0-8114-8179-4); pap. 9.95 incl. cassette (0-8114-8187-5) Raintree Steck-V.

—The Penguin. Hogan, Paula Z. LC 78-21225. 32p. (gr. 1-4). 1979. PLB 17.96 (0-8172-1257-4) Raintree Steck-V.

Stringenz, Geri. Dust of Life. Holmes, Mary Z. LC 91-34805. 48p. (gr. 4-5). 1992. PLB 20.70 (0-8114-3504-0); pap. write for info. (0-8114-6429-6) Raintree Steck-V.

Strock, Glen. Coyote Tales from the Indian Pueblos. Reed, Evelyn D. LC 86-14544. 96p. (gr. 4 up). 1988. pap. 8.95 (0-86534-094-3) Sunstone Pr.

—Kidding Around the National Parks of the Southwest: A Young Person's Guide. Lovett, Sarah. 108p. (Orig.). (gr. 3 up). 1990. pap. 12.95 (0-945465-72-6) John Muir.

Strode, William, photos by. Notre Dame: A Sense of Place. LC 92-80737. (gr. 9 up). 1992. pap. text ed. 21. 95 (0-268-01475-2) U of Notre Dame Pr.

Strogart, Alexander. Maxie, Rosie, & Earl...Partners in Grime. Park, Barbara. LC 89-28027. 128p. (gr. 3-7). 1990. 13.00 (0-679-80212-6); PLB 13.99 (0-679-90212-0) Random Bks Yng Read.

Strom, Yale. Uncertain Roads: Searching for the Gypsies. Strom, Yale. LC 93-21962. 112p. (gr. 4-7). 1993. pap. 19.95 SBE (0-02-788531-3, Four Winds) Macmillan Child Grp.

Stromoski, Rick. Trouble with School: A Family Story about Learning Disabilities. Dunn, Kathryn B. & Dunn, Allison B. 32p. (Orig.). (gr. 1-5). 1993. 9.95 (0-933149-57-3) Woodbine House.

Strong, Susan. S.T.A.R. Junior First Aid. Greeley, Sheila. 32p. (gr. k-5). 1989. write for info. spiral bdg. FAFCTPC.

Strop, Caroline, jt. illus. see Strop, John.

Strop, John & Strop, Caroline. Storytime for One Year Olds. Stimson, Joan. 28p. (ps). 1991. 3.50 (0-7214-1419-2, 887-7) Ladybird Bks.

Stroschin, Jane H. Sir Day the Knight. Marsano, Daniel T. 48p. (gr. k-6). 1993. 15.00 (1-883960-11-8) Henry Quill.

Stroyer, Paul. Cantankerous Crow. Hellsing, Lennart. (gr. k-3). 1962. 9.95 (0-8392-3002-8) Astor-Honor.

Strub, Susanne. My Cat & I. Strub, Susanne. LC 92-21839. 32p. (ps up). 1993. 14.00 (0-688-12008-3, Tambourine Bks); PLB 13.93 (0-688-12009-1, Tambourine Bks) Morrow.

—My Dog, My Sister, & I (Mon Chien, Ma Soeur, et Moi) Strub, Susanne. LC 92-22063. (ENG & FRE.). 32p. (ps up). 1993. 14.00 (0-688-12010-5, Tambourine Bks); PLB 13.93 (0-688-12011-3, Tambourine Bks) Morrow.

Strugnell, Ann. The Blue Whale. Kim, Melissa. 32p. (gr. 1-5). 1993. PLB 12.00 (0-8249-8614-8, Ideals Child); pap. 4.95 (0-8249-8628-8) Hambleton-Hill.

—Julian, Dream Doctor. Cameron, Ann. LC 89-37562. 64p. (Orig.). (gr. 2-4). 1993. PLB 6.99 (0-679-90524-3); pap. 2.50 (0-679-80524-9) Random Bks Yng Read.

—More Stories Julian Tells. Cameron, Ann. LC 84-10095. 96p. (gr. k-4). 1986. PLB 13.99 (0-394-96969-3) Knopf Bks Yng Read.

—More Stories Julian Tells. Cameron, Ann. LC 84-10095. 96p. (gr. k-3). 1989. pap. 2.99 (0-394-82454-7) Knopf Bks Yng Read.

—The Mountain Gorilla. Kim, Melissa. 32p. (gr. 1-5). 1993. PLB 12.00 (0-8249-8629-6, Ideals Child); pap. 4.95 (0-8249-8615-6) Hambleton-Hill.

—The Stories Julian Tells. Cameron, Ann. LC 80-18023. 88p. (gr. k-3). 1989. Repr. of 1981 ed. 3.25 (0-394-82892-5) Knopf Bks Yng Read.

Strugness, Ann. The Stories Julian Tells. Cameron, Ann. LC 80-18023. 96p. (gr. k-5). 1981. 8.95 (0-394-84301-0); lib. bdg. 10.99 (0-394-94301-5) Pantheon.

Strykowski, Joe. Manati: Un Libro Inicial. Corey, Donna. LC 92-64397. 48p. (ps-6). 1992. pap. 4.95 (1-879488-01-9) Sundiver.

Stuart, Dennis. Young Jackie Robinson, Baseball Hero. Farrell, Edward. LC 91-26480. 32p. (gr. k-2). 1992. text ed. 11.59 (0-8167-2536-5); pap. text ed. 2.95 (0-8167-2537-3) Troll Assocs.

—Young Orville & Wilbur Wright: First to Fly. Woods, Andrew. LC 91-26479. 32p. (gr. k-2). 1992. text ed. 11.59 (0-8167-2542-X); pap. text ed. 2.95 (0-8167-2543-8) Troll Assocs.

Stuart, Don. No Problem! Stortz, Diane. 28p. (ps). 1992. 2.50 (0-87403-954-1, 24-03594) Standard Pub.

Stuart, Edgar. The Furry Alphabet Book. Pallotta, Jerry. 32p. (Orig.). (ps-4). 1990. 14.95 (0-88106-465-3); pap. 6.95 (0-88106-464-5) Charlesbridge Pub.

Stuart, Sara B. Bellboy: A Muletrain Journey. McClain, Margaret S. LC 89-61681. 154p. (gr. 5 up). 1990. 14. 95 (0-9622468-1-6) NM Pub Co.

Stuart, Walten, jt. illus. see Hayward, Tim.

Stuart, Walter. Animal Wonders. Wildlife Education, Ltd. Staff. 20p. 1992. 13.95 (0-937934-74-7) Wildlife Educ.

—Night Animals. Wildlife Education, Ltd. Staff. 20p. (Orig.). (gr. 5 up). 1984. pap. 2.75 (0-937934-26-7) Wildlife Educ.

—Seals & Sea Lions. Wildlife Education, Ltd. Staff. 20p. (Orig.). (gr. 5 up). 1985. pap. 2.75 (0-937934-33-X) Wildlife Educ.

—Spiders. Wildlife Education, Ltd. Staff. 24p. 1992. 13. 95 (0-937934-88-7) Wildlife Educ.

Stuart, Walter & Boyer, Trevor. Penguins. Wildlife Education, Ltd. Staff. 20p. (gr. 5 up). 1983. pap. 2.75 (0-937934-17-8) Wildlife Educ.

Stuart, Walter & Hallett, Mark. Turtles. Wildlife Education, Ltd. Staff. 20p. (Orig.). (gr. 5 up). 1985. pap. 2.75 (0-937934-41-0) Wildlife Educ.
Stuart, Walter, jt. illus. see Bliss, Rebecca.
Stuart, Walter, jt. illus. see Francis, John.
Stuart, Walter, jt. illus. see Havlicek, Karel.
Stuart, Walter, jt. illus. see Hayward, Tim.
Stuart, Walter, jt. illus. see Orr, Richard.
Stuart, Walter, jt. illus. see Woods, Michael.
Stuart, Walter, et al. Cheetahs. Wildlife Education, Ltd. Staff. 24p. 1992. 13.95 (0-937934-77-1); pap. 2.75 (0-937934-67-4) Wildlife Educ.
—Spiders. Wildlife Education, Ltd. Staff. 20p. (Orig.). (gr. 5 up). 1985. pap. 2.75 (0-937934-39-9) Wildlife Educ.
Stubis, Talivaldis. Magic Secrets. Ames, Gerald & Wyler, Rose. LC 67-4229. 64p. (gr. k-3). 1967. PLB 10.89 (0-06-020069-3) HarpC Child Bks.
Stuchbury, Dianne. Listen! Stuchbury, Dianne. 24p. (ps-1). 1991. 4.99 (0-7459-2001-2) Lion USA.
—Look! Stuchbury, Dianne. 24p. (ps-1). 1991. 4.99 (0-7459-2000-4) Lion USA.
—Taste & Smell! Stuchbury, Dianne. 24p. (ps-1). 1991. 4.99 (0-7459-2003-9) Lion USA.
—Touch! Stuchbury, Dianne. 24p. (ps-1). 1991. 4.99 (0-7459-2002-0) Lion USA.
Stuckenschneider, Placid. The Ministry of Servers. Kwatera, Michael. 48p. (Orig.). (gr. 6-8). 1982. pap. 1.95 (0-8146-1300-4) Liturgical Pr.
Studio Illustratori Associati Boni Galante Staff. The Golden Atlas for Children. Morris, Neil. 48p. (gr. 1-6). 1992. 8.95 (0-307-17876-5, 17876, Golden Pr) Western Pub.
Stuker, Chris. Rooney Crooney's Second Chance. Miller, E. Lorraine. LC 77-88334. (ps-4). 1978. perfect bdg. 6. 50x (0-89566-351-1) Miller Ent.
Sturckler, Joe. Don't Teach Let Me Learn: About Nutrition, Chemistry, Medicine, Nursing. Crosby, Nina E. & Marten, Elizabeth H. 72p. (gr. 3-6). 1983. 8.95 (0-88047-030-5, 8313) DOK Pubs.
—Space. Dehnbostel, Nancy L. & Hartman, Mary E. 44p. (gr. 1-6). 1982. 6.50 (0-88047-010-0, 8205) DOK Pubs.
Sturm, Cathy. Whose Toes Are Those? Elias, Joyce. LC 92-8603. (ps). 1992. 11.95 (0-8120-6215-9) Barron.
Sturman, Sally. Chicken Soup: Thirty-Eight Easy Recipes from Classic to New. Zimmerman, Linda. LC 93-19280. (gr. 6 up). 1994. 12.00 (0-517-58622-3) Crown Bks Yng Read.
Sturms, Aina, jt. illus. see Graf, Heidi.
Sturrock, Walt. Aesop's Fables. 48p. (ps-3). 1992. 5.95 (0-88101-262-9) Unicorn Pub.
—A Christmas Carol. abr. ed. Dickens, Charles. Wendt, Michael & Pizar, Kathleen, eds. 80p. (gr. 2-5). 1988. 5.95 (0-88101-087-1) Unicorn Pub.
—Christmas Carol. Dickens, Charles. 1990. 11.95 (0-88101-108-8) Unicorn Pub.
—Ghosts. 160p. 1990. 14.95 (0-88101-269-6) Unicorn Pub.
Su, Lucy. Jinzi & Minzi Are Friends. Su, Lucy. LC 91-58738. 24p. (ps up). 1992. 5.95 (1-56402-051-7) Candlewick Pr.
—Jinzi & Minzi at the Playground. Su, Lucy. LC 91-58740. 24p. (ps up). 1992. 5.95 (1-56402-052-5) Candlewick Pr.
Suares, J. C. The Rough Gruff Goat Brothers. Chardiet, Jon. (gr. k-3). 1993. pap. 5.95 incl. cass. (0-590-69004-3) Scholastic Inc.
Suarez, Maribel. El Nino Maicero: The Corn Boy. Van Rhijn, Patricia. (SPA.). 35p. (gr. k-4). 1990. 7.95 (968-494-042-4) Donars.
Suba, Susanna. The Drugstore Cat. Petry, Ann. LC 88-3303. 96p. (gr. k-3). 1988. PLB 15.00 (0-318-35207-9, NL3); pap. 6.95 (0-8070-8309-7, BP801) Beacon Pr.
Suba, Sussanne. A Rocket in My Pocket: The Rhymes & Chants of Young Americans. Withers, Carl. LC 88-4881. 224p. (gr. 2-4). 1988. 14.95 (0-8050-0821-7, Bks Young Read); pap. 8.95 (0-8050-0804-7) H Holt & Co.
Suba, Suzanne. The Book of Jewish Holidays. Kozodoy, Ruth. Rossel, Seymour, ed. 192p. (Orig.). (gr. 4-5). 1981. pap. text ed. 7.95x (0-87441-334-6); tchr's. guide with duplicating masters by Moshe Ben-Aharon 12.50x (0-87441-367-2); By Morris J. Sugarman. student's activity bk. 4.25 (0-87441-338-9) Behrman.
Succot, Eliyah, jt. illus. see Succot, Miriam.
Succot, Miriam & Succot, Eliyah. The Fixer. Nachman of Breslov. Succot, Miriam & Succot, Eliyah, trs. from HEB. (gr. 3-12). 1977. pap. 1.50 (0-917246-04-7) Maimes.
Suckow, Will. Fifty Frightening Things to Do & Make. Bell, Alison. 64p. 1993. pap. 4.95 (1-56565-067-0) Lowell Hse.
—The Very Scary Almanac. Elfman, Eric. 80p. (Orig.). (gr. 4-7). 1993. pap. 4.99 (0-679-84401-5) Random Bks Yng Read.
Sugarman, S. Allan. The Heroes of Masada. Rosenfield, Geraldine. 38p. (gr. 6-10). pap. 1.50 (0-8381-0733-8, 10-732) United Syn Bk.
Suggs, Robert. Ideas Combo Edition 41-44, 4 bks. in 1. Rice, Wayne & McLaughlin, Tim, eds. 200p. (Orig.). 1988. pap. 19.95 (0-910125-35-X) Youth Special.
Sugita, Yataka. Good Morning-Sun's Up. Beach, Stewart. LC 70-108178. 32p. (ps-3). 8.95 (0-87592-021-7) Scroll Pr.
Sugita, Yutaka. Goodnight, One, Two, Three. Sugita, Yutaka. LC 76-149045. 32p. (ps-2). 9.95 (0-87592-022-5) Scroll Pub.

Sullivan, Barbara. Marvin Redpost: Alone in His Teacher's House. Sachar, Louis. LC 93-19791. Date not set. write for info. (0-679-81949-5); PLB write for info. (0-679-91949-X) Random.
—Marvin Redpost: Is He a Girl? Sachar, Louis. LC 92-40784. 1993. PLB 9.99 (0-679-91948-1); pap. 2.99 (0-679-81948-7) Random Bks Yng Read.
Sullivan, Dave. The Cardiff Giant. Shebar, Judith & Shebar, Sharon S. LC 83-13056. 64p. (gr. 7-11). 1983. lib. bdg. 9.29 (0-671-43851-4, J Messner) S&S Trade.
Sullivan, Dianna J. Holiday Art. Sullivan, Dianna J. 48p. (gr. k-3). 1985. wkbk. 5.95 (1-55734-007-2) Tchr Create Mat.
Sullivan, Jem. Flooty Hobbs & the Giggling Jolly Gollywobber. Sullivan, Jem & Dixon, Jim. 36p. (gr. k-2). 1991. 12.95 (1-880453-00-2) J Hefty Pub.
Sullivan, Leo. Afro-Classic Folk Tales, Bk. 3: Bro Rabbit. Sullivan, Leo & Norman, Floyd. Stewart, lyn, ed. 28p. (Orig.). (gr. 4-7). 1992. pap. 9.95 (1-881368-20-3) Vignette.
—Afro-Classic Folk Tales, Bk. 4: High John. Norman, Floyd. Stewart, lyn, ed. Sullivan, Leo, intro. by 28p. (Orig.). (gr. 4-7). 1992. pap. 9.95 (1-881368-21-1) Vignette.
—Afro-Classic Folk Tales, Bk. 5: Anancy's Riding Horse. Sullivan, Leo & Norman, Floyd. Stewart, Lyn, ed. 28p. (Orig.). (gr. 4-7). 1992. pap. 9.95 (1-881368-22-X) Vignette.
—Afro-Classic Folk Tales, Bk. 6: Work-Let-Me-See. Norman, Floyd & Sullivan, Leo. Stewart, Lyn, ed. 28p. (Orig.). (gr. 4-7). 1992. pap. 9.95 (1-881368-23-8) Vignette.
Sullivan, Linda. For Pete's Sake, Tell! Krause, Elaine. 54p. (Orig.). (gr. k-3). 1983. pap. text ed. 3.95 (0-930359-02-X) Krause Hse.
—Speak up, Say No! 3rd ed. Krause, Elaine. 40p. (ps-3). 1989. pap. text ed. 3.95 (0-930359-01-1) Krause Hse.
Sullivan, Steve. Who Really Discovered America? Krensky, Stephen. 64p. (Orig.). (gr. 4-6). 1987. pap. 2.50 (0-590-40854-2) Scholastic Inc.
—Who Really Discovered America? Krensky, Stephen. Donnelly, Judy, ed. 64p. (gr. 3-7). 1991. Repr. of 1987 ed. 12.95 (0-8038-9306-X) Raintree.
Sullivan, Suzanne. ComputerSleuths. Geehan, Wayne. (gr. 2-6). 1993. incl. puzzle 12.95 (0-922242-45-3) Lombard Mktg.
Sullivan, Tara. Tina's Science Adventures. DeCloux, Tina. Werges, Rosanne, ed. 80p. (ps-3). 1992. pap. 12. 95 spiral bdg. (0-9615903-3-5) Symbiosis Bks.
—Tina's Science Notebook. DeCloux, Tina & Werges, Rosanne. 80p. (gr. k-3). 1985. pap. 12.95 (0-9615903-0-0) Symbiosis Bks.
Sullivan, Tom & Leming, Ron. Terror Australis: Cthulhu down Under. Love, Penelope & Morrison, Mark. Willis, Lynn & Petersen, Sandy, eds. 136p. (Orig.). (gr. 12 up). 1987. pap. 17.95 (0-933635-40-0, 2319) Chaosium.
Sullivan-Szarek, Mary. The Library Experience: Sharing the Responsibility. Daniels, Lolee & Pollard, Rita. (gr. 6-8). 1987. Teacher's manual, 130pp. 64.95 (0-935637-08-7); Student workbook, 120pp. 11.99 (0-935637-09-5); Transparency Set. 85.00 (0-935637-10-9) Cambridge Strat.
Sullo, Lorraine T. Mrs. Pam Polar Bear. Grandma Marian, pseud. 32p. (gr. k-2). 1989. 7.95 (0-9614989-9-4) Banmar Inc.
Sumiko. My Summer Vacation. Sumiko. LC 89-43164. 32p. (ps-1). 1993. pap. 2.25 (0-679-80525-7) Random Bks Yng Read.
Sumile, Caridad. Hale-mano: A Legend of Hawai'i. Guard, David. Sumile, Caridad, intro. by. 92p. 1993. pap. 9.95 (1-883672-04-X) Tricycle Pr.
Summers, Leo. Danny Dunn & the Voice from Space. Williams, Jay & Abrashkin, Raymond. LC 67-22974. (gr. 4-6). 1982. pap. 1.95 (0-671-42684-2, Archway) PB.
Summers, Lesley. The Very Windy Day. MacDonald, Elizabeth. LC 91-690. 40p. (ps-3). 1992. 15.00 (0-688-11044-4, Tambourine Bks); PLB 14.93 (0-688-11045-2, Tambourine Bks) Morrow.
Summers, Wendy H. Mud Pies. Magorian, James. LC 91-70218. 24p. (gr. k-4). 1991. pap. 3.00 (0-930674-35-9) Black Oak.
Summy, Barbara L. Innovations in Cooking. 2nd ed. Elinsky, Stephen E. 85p. (gr. 7 up). 1988. pap. 17.95 (0-9620526-0-4) Elins Laboratories.
Sundstrom, Mary & Blakemore, Sally. Extremely Weird Sea Creatures. Lovett, Sarah. LC 92-18383. 48p. (Orig.). (gr. 3 up). Date not set. pap. 9.95 (1-56261-077-5) John Muir.
Sundstrom, Mary & Evans, Beth. Extremely Weird Insects. Lovett, Sarah. LC 92-20098. 48p. (gr. 3 up). Date not set. pap. 9.95 (1-56261-076-7) John Muir.
Sundstrom, Mary, jt. illus. see Blakemore, Sally.
Sunita-devi dosa. Gopal the Invincible. Yogesvara dosa-Jyotirmayi. Bhaktivedanta Swami Prabhupado, A. C., tr. 15p. (gr. 3 up). 1983. 7.95 (0-89647-017-2) Bala Bks.
Suomalaimen, Sami. Mud Puddle. Munsch, Robert. 32p. (gr. k-3). 1982. pap. 4.95 (0-920236-28-6, Pub. by Annick CN) Firefly Bks Ltd.
Suomalainen, Sami. The Dark. Munsch, Robert. 24p. (gr. k-3). 1984. pap. 4.95 (0-920236-85-5, Pub. by Annick CN) Firefly Bks Ltd.
—The Dark. Munsch, Robert. 24p. (ps-1). 1987. pap. 0.99 (0-920303-47-1, Pub. by Annick CN) Firefly Bks Ltd.

—Mud Puddle. Munsch, Robert. 24p. (ps-1). 1986. pap. 0.99 (0-920236-23-5, Pub. by Annick CN) Firefly Bks Ltd.
Supancich, Jo. Children Around the World-Writing Forms. Moore, Jo E. 48p. (gr. k-3). 1992. pap. 5.95 (1-55799-239-8) Evan-Moor Corp.
—Second Story Window. 16p. (ps-2). 1992. pap. 14.95 (1-55799-227-4) Evan-Moor Corp.
—Skip to My Lou. 16p. (ps-2). 1992. pap. 14.95 (1-55799-229-0) Evan-Moor Corp.
—Stories about Children from Many Lands. Moore, Jo E. 64p. (gr. k-2). 1993. pap. text ed. 11.95 (1-55799-248-7) Evan-Moor Corp.
Super, Terri. Animal Babies. LC 86-72426. 12p. (ps). 1988. pap. write for info. (0-307-06056-X, Pub. by Golden Bks) Western Pub.
—The Fast Rolling Little Engine That Could. Piper, Watty. LC 85-70661. 12p. (ps). 1985. 6.95 (0-448-09878-4, G&D) Putnam Pub Group.
—The Pudgy Pat-a-Cake. 16p. (ps). 1983. pap. 2.95 (0-448-10204-8, G&D) Putnam Pub Group.
—The Three Little Pigs. 16p. (ps-1). 1984. 3.95 (0-448-10214-5, G&D) Putnam Pub Group.
—What Do You Say When a Monkey Acts This Way? Moncure, Jane B. LC 87-11736. 32p. (ps-2). 1987. PLB 21.35 (0-89565-368-0); PLB 14.95s.p. (0-685-55878-9) Childs world.
Sushiela. The Ant & the Grasshopper: A Love Story. Sushiela. LC 89-92067. 129p. (Orig.). (gr. 5 up). 1990. pap. 15.95 (0-9623363-1-9) Running Water.
Sussman, Dee. Mis Primeros Cuentos. Ozaeta, Pablo. Frank, Marjorie & Lono, Luz P., eds. LC 75-16546. (gr. 4-8). 1975. pap. 6.60 student ed. (0-8325-9642-6, Natl Textbk); tchr's. ed. 10.60 (0-8325-9641-8, Natl Textbk); program pkg. (1 tchr's. ed. & 10 student wkbks). 76.60 (0-8325-9640-X, Natl Textbk) NTC Pub Grp.
Sustendal, Pat. The Care Bears' Party Cookbook. O'Connor, Jane. LC 84-18252. 48p. (gr. k-3). 1985. pap. 2.95 (0-394-87305-X) Random Bks Yng Read.
—The Popples' Pajama Party. George, Gail. LC 85-19403. 32p. (ps-3). 1986. pap. 1.95 (0-394-88041-2) Random Bks Yng Read.
—Sesame Street Farm Friends. 12p. (ps). 1985. 4.99 (0-394-87466-8) Random Bks Yng Read.
—Strawberry Shortcake & Pets on Parade. Daly, Kathleen N. 40p. (ps-3). 1983. cancelled 5.95 (0-910313-06-7) Parker Bros.
—Strawberry Shortcake & Sad Mister Sun. Lexau, Joan M. 40p. (ps-3). 1983. cancelled 5.95 (0-910313-10-5) Parker Bros.
—Strawberry Shortcake & the Big Balloon Race. Winthrop, Elizabeth. 40p. (ps-3). 1983. cancelled 5.95 (0-910313-08-3) Parker Bros.
—Strawberry Shortcake & the Birthday Surprise. Doyle, Elizabeth. 40p. (ps-3). 1983. cancelled 5.95 (0-910313-11-3) Parker Bros.
—Strawberry Shortcake & the Deep, Dark Woods. Rosenblatt, Arthur S. 40p. (ps-3). 1983. cancelled 5.95 (0-910313-07-5) Parker Bros.
—The Strawberryland Choo-Choo. Gondosch, Linda. 40p. (ps-3). 1984. cancelled 5.95 (0-910313-24-5) Parker Bros.
—A Surprise for Baby Blueberry Muffin. Poskanzer, Susan C. 40p. (ps-3). 1984. cancelled 5.95 (0-910313-23-7) Parker Bros.
Sustendal, Pat, jt. illus. see Ewers, Joe.
Sutcliffe, Justin, photos by. Rosie, a Visiting Dog's Story. Calmenson, Stephanie. LC 93-21243. 1994. write for info. (0-395-65477-7, Clarion Bks) HM.
Sutherland, David. Sesame Street Pop-up Riddle Book. Sesame Street Staff. LC 77-70852. (ps-3). 1977. bds. 8.99 (0-394-83546-8) Random Bks Yng Read.
Sutherland, Jackie, jt. illus. see Perez, George.
Sutter, Greg. Diving Is for Me. Briggs, Carole S. LC 82-17242. 48p. (gr. 2-5). 1983. PLB 13.50 (0-8225-1135-5) Lerner Pubns.
Sutter, Richard. The Sandlot Summit. Fishman, Richard A. LC 85-63032. 197p. (Orig.). (gr. 4-9). 1985. pap. 3.95 (0-9615884-0-3) Sunlakes Pub.
Suttie, A., jt. illus. see Jackson, I.
Sutton, Judith. Coat of Many Colors. Parton, Dolly. LC 93-3866. 1994. 14.00 (0-06-023413-X, HarpT); PLB 13.89 (0-06-023414-8) HarpC.
Sutton, Larry. Illustrated Football Dictionary for Young People. Olgin, Joseph. (gr. 4 up). 1978. pap. 2.50 (0-13-450874-2, Pub. by Treehouse) P-H.
Sutton, Scott E. The Family of Ree. Sutton, Scott E. 45p. (gr. 2-4). 1986. 13.95x (0-9617199-1-5) Sutton Pubns.
—The Legend of Snow Pookas. Sutton, Scott E. (gr. 2-4). 13.95x (0-9617199-6-6) Sutton Pubns.
—Look at the Size of That Long-Legged Ploot! Sutton, Scott E. 48p. (gr. 2-4). 1990. 13.95x (0-9617199-5-8) Sutton Pubns.
—Oh No! More Wizard Lessons! Sutton, Scott E. 35p. (gr. 2-4). 1986. 13.95x (0-9617199-2-3) Sutton Pubns.
Suvari, Mari-Ann, jt. illus. see Anthony, Stephen R.
Suyeoka, George. Urashima Taro. 2nd ed. Goodman, Robert & Spicer, Robert. 72p. Date not set. 15.95 (0-89610-276-9, 24019-000) Island Heritage.
Suzuki, Mamoru. Giant Tree & the Boy. Barnes, Jill & Tsurmi, Masao. Rubin, Caroline, ed. Japan Foreign Rights Centre Staff, tr. from JPN. LC 90-37751. 40p. (gr. k-4). 1990. PLB 15.93 (0-944483-80-1) Garrett Ed Corp.

—The Park Bench. Takeshita, Fumiko. Kanagy, Ruth A., tr. from JPN. 40p. (ps-3). 1988. 13.95 (0-916291-15-4) Kane-Miller Bk.
—The Park Bench. Takeshita, Fumiko. Kanagy, Ruth A., tr. from JPN. 40p. (gr. 3-8). 1989. pap. 6.95 (0-916291-21-9) Kane-Miller Bk.
Suzuki, Masaharu. Potatoes. Johnson, Sylvia A. 48p. (gr. 4 up). 1984. lib. bdg. 19.95 (0-8225-1459-1) Lerner Pubns.
—Wheat. Johnson, Sylvia A. 48p. (gr. 4 up). 1990. PLB 19.95 (0-8225-1490-7) Lerner Pubns.
Svenson, Borje. Adventures in the Solar System. Williams, Geoffrey & Regan, Dennis. 64p. 1986. bk. only 9.95x (0-8431-1552-1); incl. cass. 13.95x (0-8431-1553-X) Price stern.
Svensson, Borje. Discovering Our Past. Seymour, Peter. 10p. (gr. 2-5). 1987. 8.95 (0-02-782200-1, Macmillan Child Bk) Macmillan Child Grp.
—Lost in Dinosaur World. Williams, Geoffrey T. 32p. (gr. 6-11). 1987. incl. audiocassette 6.95 (0-8431-1885-7) Price Stern.
—The Nativity. Hecht, Johanna, notes by. LC 81-65400. (ps-3). 1981. pop-up bk. 9.95 (0-385-28713-5) Delacorte.
Swain, John & Stevens, Bill, photos by. Servant with a Smile. Barrett, Marsha. 40p. (Orig.). (gr. 1-3). 1985. pap. 2.00 (0-317-18029-0) Home Mission.
Swan, Kyle. The Recruiting Survival Guide: How to Be a Smart Recruit. Mooney, Chuck, III. Bucheit, Kelly S., ed. 84p. (Orig.). (gr. 11-12). 1991. pap. 9.95 (0-9630329-0-X) C Mooney.
Swan, Susan. Autumn Leaves. Ferguson, Virginia & Durkin, Peter. LC 92-34253. 1993. 3.75 (0-383-03615-1) SRA Schl Grp.
—John Paul Jones: Hero of the Seas. Brandt, Keith. LC 82-16045. 48p. (gr. 4-6). 1983. PLB 10.79 (0-89375-849-3); pap. text ed. 3.50 (0-89375-850-7) Troll Assocs.
—Louis Pasteur: Young Scientist. Sabin, Francene. LC 82-15924. 48p. (gr. 4-6). 1983. PLB 10.79 (0-89375-853-1); pap. text ed. 3.50 (0-89375-854-X) Troll Assocs.
—Who Can't Follow an Ant? Pellowski, Michael J. LC 85-14009. 48p. (Orig.). (gr. 1-3). 1986. PLB 10.59 (0-8167-0592-5); pap. text ed. 3.50 (0-8167-0593-3) Troll Assocs.
—Winter Fun. Schlachter, Rita. LC 85-14008. 48p. (Orig.). (gr. 1-3). 1986. PLB 10.59 (0-8167-0584-4); pap. text ed. 3.50 (0-8167-0585-2) Troll Assocs.
Swan, Susan E. The Twelve Days of Christmas. LC 80-28097. 32p. (gr. k-4). 1981. PLB 9.79 (0-89375-474-9); pap. text ed. 1.95 (0-89375-475-7) Troll Assocs.
Swanberg, Nancy & Anderson, L. Ancient Ireland. Stein, Wendy. (gr. k). 1978. pap. text ed. 3.95 (0-88388-060-1) Bellerophon Bks.
Swann, L. Marie. The Sacred Lake, 3 bks. Swann, L. Marie. (gr. 3-4). 1992. Set. pap. text ed. 25.00 (1-882156-05-6) Eye Of The Eagle.
Swanson, Harry. Easter Is Not for Bears. Swanson, Harry. 56p. (ps-6). 1989. pap. 5.00 (1-878200-04-6) SwanMark Bks.
—Eli Eagle Builds a Nest. Swanson, Harry. 52p. (Orig.). (ps-6). 1990. pap. 5.00 (1-878200-09-7) SwanMark Bks.
—Oscar Otter Meets the Mayor. Swanson, Harry. 48p. (Orig.). (ps-6). 1989. pap. 5.00 (1-878200-02-X) SwanMark Bks.
—Pets & Pathos. rev. ed. Swanson, Harry. 52p. (gr. 9-12). 1989. pap. 5.00 (1-878200-03-8) SwanMark Bks.
—Seagraham Seal's Perfect Gift. Swanson, Harry. 48p. (Orig.). (ps-6). 1989. pap. 5.00 (1-878200-05-4) Swanmark Bks.
Swanson, Karl. Carver. Radin, Ruth Y. LC 89-13413. 80p. (gr. 3-7). 1990. SBE 12.95 (0-02-775651-3, Macmillan Child Bk) Macmillan Child Grp.
—When Grampa Kissed His Elbow. DeFelice, Cynthia C. LC 90-6696. 32p. (gr. k-3). 1992. RSBE 13.95 (0-02-726455-6, Macmillan Child Bk) Macmillan Child Grp.
Swanson, Maggie. The American Heritage Picture Dictionary. Hillerich, Robert L. 144p. (gr. k-1). 1986. 9.70 (0-395-42531-X) HM.
—A Bird's Best Friend. Sommers, Tish. 32p. (ps-k). 1986. write for info. (0-307-12018-X, Pub. by Golden Bks) Western Pub.
—Grover Sleeps Over. Winthrop, Elizabeth. LC 83-83279. 32p. (ps). 1984. write for info. (0-307-12010-4, 12010, Golden Bks) Western Pub.
—My Name Is Big Bird. Allen, Constance. 24p. (ps-k). 1992. pap. write for info. (0-307-11533-X, 11533, Golden Pr) Western Pub.
—My Name Is Elmo. Allen, Constance. 24p. (ps-k). 1993. pap. 1.45 (0-307-11541-0, 11541, Golden Pr) Western Pub.
—My Name Is Ernie. Rabe, Tish. (ps-k). 1991. pap. write for info. (0-307-11513-5, Golden Pr) Western Pub.
—My Name Is Grover. Rabe, Tish. 24p. (ps-k). 1992. pap. write for info. (0-307-11534-8, 11534, Golden Pr) Western Pub.
—That Fat Hat. Barkan, Joanne. LC 92-7414. 1992. 2.95 (0-590-45643-1) Scholastic Inc.
Swanson, Maggie, jt. illus. see Wetzel, Rick.
Swearingen, Karen M. The Basket Counts. Christopher, Matt. (gr. 3-6). 1991. pap. 3.95 (0-316-14076-7) Little.
—When It Rains. Millicer, Jan. LC 92-31136. 1993. 2.50 (0-383-03667-4) SRA Schl Grp.

Sweat, Lynn. Amelia Bedelia & the Baby. Parish, Peggy. LC 80-22263. 64p. (gr. 1-3). 1981. 14.00 (0-688-00316-8); PLB 13.93 (0-688-00321-4) Greenwillow.
—Amelia Bedelia & the Baby. Parish, Peggy. 64p. (gr. k-3). 1982. pap. 3.99 (0-380-57067-X, Camelot) Avon.
—Amelia Bedelia Helps Out. Parish, Peggy. LC 79-11729. 64p. (gr. 1-3). 1979. 14.00 (0-688-80231-1); PLB 13.93 (0-688-84231-3) Greenwillow.
—Amelia Bedelia Helps Out. Parish, Peggy. 64p. (gr. k-3). 1981. pap. 3.99 (0-380-53405-3, Camelot) Avon.
—Amelia Bedelia's Family Album. Parish, Peggy. LC 87-15641. 48p. (gr. 3-9). 1988. 13.95 (0-688-07676-9); lib. bdg. 11.88 (0-688-07677-7) Greenwillow.
—A Breath of Air & a Breath of Smoke. Marr, John S. LC 70-161362. 48p. (gr. 3 up). 1970. 4.95 (0-87131-038-4) M Evans.
—The Cats' Burglar. Parish, Peggy. LC 82-11751. 64p. (gr. 1-3). 1983. 12.95 (0-688-01825-4); PLB 13.93 (0-688-01826-2) Greenwillow.
—Good Work, Amelia Bedelia. Parish, Peggy. LC 75-20360. 56p. (gr. 1-4). 1976. 14.00 (0-688-80022-X); PLB 13.93 (0-688-84022-1) Greenwillow.
—Good Work, Amelia Bedelia. Parish, Peggy. 164p. (gr. k-5). 1980. pap. 3.99 (0-380-49171-0, Camelot) Avon.
—Hidden Stories in Plants... Pellowski, Anne. LC 89-37166. 112p. (ps up). 1990. SBE 15.95 (0-02-770611-7, Macmillan Child Bk) Macmillan Child Grp.
—How Can I Help? rev. ed. Hazen, Barbara S. 32p. (gr. 2-4). 1990. Repr. of 1988 ed. PLB 9.95 (1-878363-13-1) Forest Hse.
—Let's Get a Pet. Greydanus, Rose. LC 87-10938. 32p. (gr. k-2). 1988. PLB 7.89 (0-8167-0986-6); pap. text ed. 1.95 (0-8167-0987-4) Troll Assocs.
—Merry Christmas, Amelia Bedelia. Parish, Peggy. LC 85-24919. 64p. (gr. 1-4). 1986. 13.00 (0-688-06101-X); PLB 12.93 (0-688-06102-8) Greenwillow.
—Merry Christmas, Amelia Bedelia. Parish, Peggy. 64p. 1987. pap. 3.99 (0-380-70325-4, Camelot) Avon.
—Rivers. Santrey, Laurence. LC 84-8818. 32p. (gr. 3-6). 1985. lib. bdg. 9.49 (0-8167-0210-1); pap. text ed. 2.95 (0-8167-0211-X) Troll Assocs.
—Secret Spaces, Imaginary Places: Creating Your Own Worlds for Play. McCoy, Elin. LC 85-23089. 80p. (gr. k-6). 1986. SBE 13.95 (0-02-765460-5) Macmillan Child Grp.
—The Smallest Stegosaurus. Sweat, Lynn & Phillips, Louis. 32p. (ps-k). 1993. PLB 13.99 (0-670-83865-9) Viking Child Bks.
—Sound. Brandt, Keith. LC 84-2632. 32p. (gr. 3-6). 1985. PLB 9.49 (0-8167-0128-8); pap. text ed. 2.95 (0-8167-0129-6) Troll Assocs.
—Sun. Brandt, Keith. LC 84-2715. 32p. (gr. 3-6). 1985. PLB 9.49 (0-8167-0190-3); pap. text ed. 2.95 (0-8167-0191-1) Troll Assocs.
—Teach Us, Amelia Bedelia. Parish, Peggy. LC 76-22663. 56p. (gr. 1-4). 1977. 12.95 (0-688-80069-6); PLB 12.88 (0-688-84069-8) Greenwillow.
—Teach Us, Amelia Bedelia. Parish, Peggy. 64p. (gr. k-3). 1987. pap. 2.95 (0-590-43345-8) Scholastic Inc.
—Wake up, Baby! Oppenheim, Joanne. (ps-3). 1990. PLB 9.99 (0-553-05907-6); pap. 3.50 (0-553-34914-7) Bantam.
—What Are Feelings? rev. ed. Hazen, Barbara S. 32p. (gr. 2-4). 1990. Repr. of 1988 ed. PLB 9.95 (1-878363-16-6) Forest Hse.
—What Is a Fish? Eastman, David. LC 81-11373. 32p. (gr. k-2). 1982. lib. bdg. 9.49 (0-89375-660-1); pap. text ed. 2.95 (0-89375-661-X) Troll Assocs.
—What's It Like to Be a Railroad Worker. Matthews, Morgan. LC 89-34389. 32p. (gr. k-3). 1989. lib. bdg. 10.89 (0-8167-1815-6); pap. text ed. 2.95 (0-8167-1816-4) Troll Assocs.
Swedberg, Jack, jt. photog. see Knight, Christopher G.
Sweeney, Hazel. Fit for the King. Martin, Bill. Haynes, Glenda, ed. 384p. (Orig.). (gr. 7 up). 1985. pap. 11.50 (0-89114-154-5) Baptist Pub Hse.
Sweeney, Phyllis. The Dog Who Didn't Know about Snow. Weingarten, Elaine. 58p. (ps-3). 1988. text ed. 13.50 (0-89777-703-4, 97005) Soc Issues.
—Kenny the Caterpillar. Weingarten, Elaine. 30p. (ps-3). 1988. text ed. 13.50 (0-89777-702-6, 97003) Soc Issues.
—Old Doctor Monkey. Weingarten, Elaine. 44p. (ps-3). 1988. text ed. 13.50 (0-89777-704-2, 97004) Soc Issues.
—One Duck. Weingarten, Elaine. 56p. (ps-3). 1988. text ed. 13.50 (0-89777-700-X, 97001) Soc Issues.
—The Robin Who Was Afraid to Fly. Weingarten, Elaine. 50p. (ps-3). 1988. text ed. 13.50 (0-89777-701-8, 97002) Soc Issues.
Sweeney, Toni. Spacedog's Best Friend. Sweeney, Toni. (Orig.). (gr. 5-12). 1989. pap. 6.95 (0-933025-13-0) Blue Bird Pub.
Sweeny, Raquel. Abraham's Great Discovery. Zlotowitz, Bernard M. & Maiben, Dina. 32p. 1991. 12.95t (0-911389-04-0) NightinGale Res.
Sweet, Darrell. Reader's Digest Best Loved Books for Young Readers: The Story of King Arthur & His Knights. Pyle, Howard. Ogburn, Jackie, ed. 208p. (gr. 4-12). 1989. 3.99 (0-945260-31-8) Choice Pub NY.
Sweet, Melissa. Blast Off! Poems about Space. Hopkins, Lee B., selected by. LC 93-24536. 1995. 14.00 (0-06-024260-4); PLB 13.89 (0-06-024261-2) HarpC Child Bks.

—Fiddle-I-Fee: A Farmyard Song for the Very Young. Sweet, Melissa, adapted by. 32p. (ps-1). 1992. 14.95 (0-316-82516-6, Joy St Bks) Little.
—Hippity-Hop. 18p. (ps). 1992. bds. 2.95 (0-448-40314-5) Putnam Pub Group.
—A House by the Sea. Ryder, Joanne. LC 93-22149. 1994. write for info. (0-688-12675-8); PLB write for info. (0-688-12676-6) Morrow Jr Bks.
—Little Chick. 24p. (ps). 1994. bds. 2.95 (0-448-40555-5, G&D) Putnam Pub Group.
—Pinky & Rex. Howe, James. 48p. (gr. 2). 1991. pap. 3.50 (0-380-71190-7, Pub. by Young Camelot) Avon.
—Pinky & Rex & the Mean Old Witch. Howe, James. LC 89-78204. 48p. (gr. k-3). 1991. SBE 11.95 (0-689-31617-8, Atheneum Child Bk) Macmillan Child Grp.
—Pinky & Rex & the New Baby. Howe, James. LC 91-39801. 48p. (gr. k-3). 1993. SBE 12.95 (0-689-31717-4, Atheneum Child Bk) Macmillan Child Grp.
—Pinky & Rex & the Spelling Bee. Howe, James. LC 89-78305. 48p. (gr. k-3). 1991. SBE 11.95 (0-689-31618-6, Atheneum Child Bk) Macmillan Child Grp.
—Pinky & Rex Get Married. Howe, James. LC 89-406. 48p. (gr. k-3). 1990. SBE 11.95 (0-685-58512-3, Atheneum Child Bk); 11.95 (0-689-31453-1, Atheneum Childrens Bks) Macmillan Child Grp.
—Pinky & Rex Go to Camp. Howe, James. LC 91-16123. 48p. (gr. k-3). 1992. SBE 11.95 (0-689-31718-2, Atheneum Child Bk) Macmillan Child Grp.
—Rosie & the Poor Rabbits. Macdonald, Maryann. LC 92-42766. 32p. (ps-2). 1994. SBE 13.95 (0-689-31832-4, Atheneum Child Bk) Macmillan Child Grp.
—Rosie Runs Away. Macdonald, Maryann. LC 89-27575. 32p. (ps-2). 1990. SBE 12.95 (0-689-31625-9, Atheneum Child Bk) Macmillan Child Grp.
—Rosie's Baby Tooth. Macdonald, Maryann. LC 90-35923. 32p. (ps-2). 1991. SBE 12.95 (0-689-31626-7, Atheneum Child Bk) Macmillan Child Grp.
—Sing Me a Window. O'Donnell, Elizabeth L. LC 92-10719. (ps up). 1993. 15.00 (0-688-09500-3); PLB 14.93 (0-688-09501-1) Morrow Jr Bks.
—Snippets: A Gathering of Poems, Pictures, & Possibilities... Zolotow, Charlotte. LC 91-37751. 48p. (ps-3). 1993. 16.00 (0-06-020818-X); PLB 15.89 (0-06-020819-8) HarpC Child Bks.
—Sycamore Street. Christiansen, C. B. LC 92-33685. 48p. (gr. 1-3). 1993. SBE 13.95 (0-689-31784-0, Atheneum Child Bk) Macmillan Child Grp.
Sweetland, Marsha L. Will Spring Ever Come to Gobbler's Knob? A Punxsutawney Phil Adventure Story. Moutran, Julia S. 64p. (ps-5). 1992. Incl. Phil's Field Guide to Woodland Animals. 15.95 (0-9617819-5-5); Incl. Phil's Field Guide to Woodland Animals. pap. 9.95 (0-9617819-4-7); audiocass. 10.95 (0-685-48131-X) Julia Res.
Sweetman, Daniel. The Cuckoo Clock Adventure. Lam, Roger. Gibb, George, ed. LC 82-99848. (Orig.). (gr. 5-12). 1983. pap. 2.25 (0-943310-01-6) Six Pr.
Swekel, Arnie, et al. Blood & Lust. Lockborn, Paul, et al. Shirley, Sam, ed. 128p. (Orig.). (gr. 7 up). 1991. pap. 18.95 (0-933635-84-2, 2711) Chaosium.
Swemba, Jeane. Rocks & Minerals. DeBruin, Jerry. 32p. (gr. 4 up). 1986. wkbk. 5.95 (0-86653-341-9, GA 689) Good Apple.
Swenson, Paula. Peervention: Training Peer Facilitators for Prevention Education. Myrick, Robert D. & Folk, Betsy E. LC 90-86235. 210p. (Orig.). (gr. 9-12). 1991. pap. text ed. 13.95x (0-932796-35-4) Ed Media Corp.
Swensson, Dale I. & Welles, T. Acadia Seacoast: A Guidebook for Appreciation. Haaland, Lynn. Mills, Louise & Johnson, Mercy, eds. 32p. (Orig.). (gr. k up). 1984. pap. 3.00 (0-915189-01-1) Oceanus.
Swiderska, Barbara. The Fisherman's Bride. Swiderska, Barbara. LC 78-148051. 32p. (ps-3). 8.95 (0-87592-018-7) Scroll Pr.
Swidor, M. J. Save the Haunted House. Wedell, Robert F. 124p. (Orig.). 1991. pap. 6.95 (0-962521-2-0) Milrob Pr.
Swisher, Elizabeth. Jesus for Children. Griffin, Henry W. 132p. 1986. 12.95 (0-685-43036-7); pap. 7.95 (0-86683-866-X) Harper SF.
—Oh, Happy, Happy Day! A Child's Easter in Story, Song, & Prayer. McKissack, Patricia & McKissack, Frederick. LC 88-83017. 32p. 1989. pap. 5.99 (0-8066-2394-2, 10-4733, Augsburg) Augsburg Fortress.
—The Tower of Babel. Jander, Martha. 24p. (Orig.). (gr. k-4). 1991. pap. 1.89 (0-570-09026-1) Concordia.
—Waiting for Christmas: Stories & Activities for Advent. Greene, Carol. LC 87-70474. 192p. (ps-5). 1987. pap. 5.99 (0-8066-2264-4, 10-6915, Augsburg) Augsburg Fortress.
Swofford, Jeanette. The Dawdlewalk. Tobias, Tobi. LC 81-21566. 32p. (ps-3). 1983. PLB 13.50 (0-87614-190-4) Carolrhoda Bks.
—Liza's Story: Neglect & the Police. Anderson, Deborah & Finne, Martha. LC 85-25379. 48p. (gr. 1-4). 1986. RSBE 11.95 (0-87518-323-9, Dillon) Macmillan Child Grp.
—Michael's Story: Emotional Abuse & Working with a Counselor. Anderson, Deborah & Finne, Martha. LC 85-25400. 48p. (gr. 1-4). 1986. RSBE 11.95 (0-87518-322-0, Dillon) Macmillan Child Grp.

—Robin's Story: Physical Abuse & Seeing the Doctor.
Anderson, Deborah & Finne, Martha. LC 85-25383.
48p. (gr. 1-4). 1986. RSBE 9.95 (0-87518-321-2,
Dillon) Macmillan Child Grp.
—The Stars: From Birth to Black Holes. Darling, David
J. LC 84-23067. 64p. (gr. 4 up). 1987. RSBE 12.95
(0-87518-284-4, Dillon) Macmillan Child Grp.
Swofford, Jeannette. Holiday Cooking Around the
World. Wolfe, Robert L. & Wolfe, Diane. 52p. (gr. 5
up). pap. 5.95 (0-8225-9573-7) Lerner Pubns.
Swope, Martha. Cynthia Gregory Dances Swan Lake.
Gregory, Cynthia. 48p. (gr. 3-7). 1990. pap. 14.95
jacketed (0-671-68786-7, S&S BFYR) S&S Trade.
Sydlik, Danilea & Campbell, Elisa L. Sunshine,
Rainbows & Friends. Beyl, Judith. LC 80-50828. 83p.
(Orig.). 1980. pap. 5.95 (0-933308-01-9)
Harper SF.
Sylvestre, Daniel. Just Me & My Dad, 6 titles. Gautier,
Bertrand. (gr. 2 up). 1993. Set. PLB 95.60
(0-8368-1006-6); PLB 15.93 ea. Gareth Stevens Inc.
—Zachary in Camping Out. Gauthier, Bertrand. LC 93-
15457. 1993. write for info. (0-8368-1012-0) Gareth
Stevens Inc.
—Zachary in I'm Zachary! Gauthier, Bertrand. LC 93-
1168. 1993. 21.27 (0-8368-1007-4) Gareth Stevens
Inc.
—Zachary in the Championship. Gauthier, Bertrand. LC
93-1169. 1993. 21.27 (0-8368-1008-2) Gareth Stevens
Inc.
—Zachary in the Present. Gauthier, Bertrand. LC 93-
7719. 1993. 21.27 (0-8368-1010-4) Gareth Stevens
Inc.
—Zachary in the Wawabongbong. Gauthier, Bertrand. LC
93-15456. 1993. write for info. (0-8368-1011-2)
Gareth Stevens Inc.
—Zachary in the Winner. Gauthier, Bertrand. LC 93-
7718. 1993. 21.27 (0-8368-1009-0) Gareth Stevens
Inc.
Sylvia, Dean. Awaken the Genius: Mind Technology for
the 21st Century. Porter, Patrick K. De Shazo, Jerry,
ed. 200p. (Orig.). 1994. aug. 14.98 (0-9637611-8-8)
Pure Light.
Szasz, Suzanne, photos by. Glenn Learns to Read. 2nd
ed. Appell, Clara & Appell, Morey. Appell, Clara T.,
intro. by. LC 87-62285. 64p. (ps-2). 1987. pap. 6.25
(0-943501-00-8) M L Appell.
—Love Songs for Our Children. Pennie. Siegel, Bernie S.,
intro. by. 40p. (Orig.). (ps up) 1989. pap. 13.95 incl.
cassette (0-9624135-1-8) Songs & Co.
Szekeres, Cyndy. ABC. Szekeres, Cyndy. LC 82-839989.
22p. (ps up). 1983. write for info. (0-307-12120-8,
12120, Golden Bks) Western Pub.
—Cyndy Szekeres' Colors. Szekeres, Cyndy. 24p. (ps-k).
1992. bds. write for info. (0-307-12167-4, 12167,
Golden Pr) Western Pub.
—Cyndy Szekeres' Teeny Mouse Counts Herself.
Szekeres, Cyndy. 12p. (ps). 1992. bds. write for info.
(0-307-06118-3, 6118, Golden Bks) Western Pub.
—Good Night, Sweet Mouse. Szekeres, Cyndy. LC 87-
81789. 20p. (ps). 1988. write for info. (0-307-12159-3)
Western Pub.
—Here's Pippa! Boegehold, Betty. LC 88-27256. 128p.
(gr. k-3). 1989. pap. 2.95 (0-394-82702-3) Knopf Bks
Yng Read.
—Honey Rabbit. Hopkins, Margo. 14p. (ps) 1982. write
for info. (0-307-12268-9, Golden Bks) Western Pub.
—I Am a Kitten. Risom, Ole. 26p. (ps). 1993. bds. 3.95
(0-307-12169-0, 12169, Golden Pr) Western Pub.
—Night Before Christmas. Moore, Clement C. (ps up)
1986. write for info. (0-307-13724-4, Golden Bks)
Western Pub.
—Pippa Pops Out! Boegehold, Betty D. 64p. (ps-3). 1980.
pap. 0.95 (0-440-46865-5, YB) Dell.
—Puppy Too Small. Szekeres, Cyndy. LC 83-83353. 18p.
(ps-k). 1992. bds. write for info. (0-307-12201-8,
12231, Golden Pr) Western Pub.
—Sammy's Special Day. Szekeres, Cyndy. LC 85-81986.
18p. (ps-k). 1992. bds. write for info. (0-307-12288-3,
12296, Golden Pr) Western Pub.
—The Tale of Peter Rabbit. Potter, Beatrix. 24p. (ps-3).
1993. 3.50 (0-307-12349-9, 12349, Golden Pr)
Western Pub.
—The Three Hundred Twenty-Ninth Friend. 2nd ed.
Sharmat, Marjorie W. LC 78-21770. 48p. (gr. k-3).
1992. RSBE 13.95 (0-02-782259-1, Four Winds)
Macmillan Child Grp.
—Thumpity Thump Gets Dressed. Szekeres, Cyndy. LC
83-83284. 16p. (ps-k). 1991. 4.95 (0-307-12203-4,
12233, Golden Bks) Western Pub.
—What Bunny Loves. Szekeres, Cyndy. (ps-1). 1990.
write for info. (Golden Pr) Western Pub.
—The Whispering Rabbit. Brown, Margaret W. 24p.
(ps-k). 1992. write for info. (0-307-00138-5, 312-03,
Golden Pr) Western Pub.
Szilagyi, Mary. The Apartment House Tree. Killion,
Bette. LC 88-35700. 32p. (ps-2). 1989. PLB 14.89
(0-06-023274-9) HarpC Child Bks.
—Basket. Lyon, George-Ella. LC 89-71011. 32p. (ps-2).
1990. 14.95 (0-531-05886-7); PLB 14.99
(0-531-08486-8) Orchard Bks Watts.
—Night in the Country. Rylant, Cynthia. LC 85-70963.
32p. (ps-1). 1986. RSBE 14.95 (0-02-777210-1,
Bradbury Pr) Macmillan Child Grp.
—Night in the Country. Rylant, Cynthia. LC 90-1043.
32p. (ps-2). 1991. pap. 4.95 (0-689-71473-4, Aladdin)
Macmillan Child Grp.

—This Year's Garden. Rylant, Cynthia. LC 84-10974.
32p. (gr. k-3). 1984. RSBE 13.95 (0-02-777970-X,
Bradbury Pr) Macmillan Child Grp.
—This Year's Garden. Rylant, Cynthia. LC 86-22224.
32p. (ps-3). 1987. pap. 4.95 (0-689-71122-0, Aladdin)
Macmillan Child Grp.
—Thunderstorm. Szilagyi, Mary. LC 84-24570. 32p.
(ps-2). 1985. RSBE 13.95 (0-02-788580-1, Bradbury
Pr) Macmillan Child Grp.

T

Taback, Simms. Buggy Riddles. Hall, Katy & Eisenberg,
Lisa. LC 85-1450. 48p. (ps-3). 1986. 9.95
(0-8037-0139-X); PLB 9.89 (0-8037-0140-3) Dial Bks
Young.
—Buggy Riddles. Hall, Katy & Eisenberg, Lisa. (gr. 2-5).
1989. bk. & cassette 19.95 (0-87499-118-8); bk. &
cassette 12.95 (0-87499-119-6); 4 cassettes & guide
27.95 (0-87499-120-X) Live Oak Media.
—Buggy Riddles. Hall, Katy & Eisenberg, Lisa. LC 85-
1450. 48p. (ps-3). 1988. pap. 4.95 (0-8037-0554-9)
Dial Bks Young.
—Buggy Riddles. Hall, Katy & Eisenberg, Lisa. LC 93-
6556. (gr. 1-4). 1993. pap. 3.25 (0-14-036543-5) Puffin
Bks.
—Fishy Riddles. Hall, Katy & Eisenberg, Lisa. (gr. 3-5).
1985. bk. & cassette 19.95 (0-941078-72-8); pap. 12.95
bk. & cassette (0-941078-70-1); cassette, 4 paperbacks
& guide 27.95 (0-941078-71-X) Live Oak Media.
—Fishy Riddles. Hall, Katy & Eisenberg, Lisa. LC 93-
6551. (gr. 1-4). 1993. pap. 3.25 (0-14-036546-X,
Puffin) Puffin Bks.
—Hands-On Science: Color & Light. Stine, Megan, et al.
LC 92-56889. 1993. PLB 18.60 (0-8368-0954-8)
Gareth Stevens Inc.
—Hands-On Science: Food & the Kitchen. Stine, Megan,
et al. LC 92-56890. 1993. PLB 18.60 (0-8368-0955-6)
Gareth Stevens Inc.
—Hands-On Science: Fun Machines. Stine, Megan, et al.
LC 92-56891. 1993. PLB 18.60 (0-8368-0956-4)
Gareth Stevens Inc.
—Hands-On Science: Games, Puzzles, & Toys. Stine,
Megan, et al. LC 92-56892. 1993. PLB 18.60
(0-8368-0957-2) Gareth Stevens Inc.
—Hands-On Science: Mystery & Magic. Stine, Megan, et
al. LC 92-56893. 1993. PLB 18.60 (0-8368-0958-0)
Gareth Stevens Inc.
—Hands-On Science: Things That Grow. Stine, Megan,
et al. LC 92-56894. 1993. PLB 18.60 (0-8368-0959-9)
Gareth Stevens Inc.
—Jason's Bus Ride. Ziefert, Harriet. (ps-3). 1987. pap.
8.95 (0-670-81718-X, Puffin); pap. 3.50
(0-14-050743-4, Puffin) Puffin Bks.
—Jason's Bus Ride. Ziefert, Harriet. LC 86-46224. 32p.
(gr. 4-8). 1987. pap. 2.95 (0-317-63655-3, Puffin)
Puffin Bks.
—Jason's Bus Ride. Ziefert, Harriet. (ps-2). 1993. pap.
3.25 (0-14-036536-2, Puffin) Puffin Bks.
—Laughing Together: Giggles & Grins from Around the
Globe. rev. ed. Walker, Barbara K. LC 91-43784.
128p. (Orig.). (gr. k up). 1992. pap. 12.95
(0-915793-37-7) Free Spirit Pub.
—Noisy Barn! Ziefert, Harriet. 16p. (ps-1). 1991. pap.
4.95 (0-06-107405-5) HarpC Child Bks.
—On Our Way to the Forest! Ziefert, Harriet. 16p.
(ps-1). 1993. pap. 4.95 (0-694-00458-8, Festival)
HarpC Child Bks.
—On Our Way to the Water! Ziefert, Harriet. 16p. (ps-1).
1993. pap. 4.95 (0-694-00459-6, Festival) HarpC Child
Bks.
—Snakey Riddles. Hall, Katy & Eisenberg, Lisa. 48p.
(ps-3). 1993. pap. 3.99 (0-14-054588-3) Puffin Bks.
—Too Much Noise. McGovern, Ann. 48p. (gr. k-3).
1992. pap. 4.80 (0-395-62985-3, Sandpiper) HM.
—Zoo Parade! Ziefert, Harriet. 16p. (ps-1). 1991. pap.
4.95 (0-06-107404-7) HarpC Child Bks.
Taber, Anthony. The Boy Who Stopped Time. Taber,
Anthony. LC 92-398. 32p. (ps-3). 1993. SBE 13.95
(0-689-50460-8, M K McElderry) Macmillan Child
Grp.
Taber, Ed. Beep, Beep. Gregorich, Barbara. Hoffman,
Joan, ed. 16p. (Orig.). (gr. k-2). 1984. pap. 2.25
(0-88743-007-4, 06007) Sch Zone Pub Co.
—The New Official Koosh Book. Cassidy, John &
Stillinger, Scott. 88p. 1992. perfect bdg., incl. 3 mini-
Koosh balls 9.95 (1-878257-30-7) Klutz Pr.
Tabesh, Delight. Look Ma, I'm Flying. Walters-Lucy,
Jean. Tabesh, Delight, ed. LC 92-13953. 48p. (Orig.).
(ps-5). 1992. pap. 6.95 perfect bdg. (0-941992-28-4)
Los Arboles Pub.
Tachiera, Andrea. Under the Sea. Greenberg, Judith E. &
Carey, Helen H. 32p. (gr. 2-4). 1990. 17.96
(0-8172-3755-0) Raintree Steck-V.
Tada, Joni E. The Great Alphabet Fight. Jensen, Steven
& Tada, Joni E. (ps-3). 1993. 12.99 (0-88070-572-8,
Gold & Honey) Questar Pubs.
Tadjo, Veronique. Lord of the Dance: An African
Retelling. Tadjo, Veronique. LC 89-2785. 32p. (gr.
1-4). 1989. (Lipp Jr Bks); PLB 12.89 (0-397-32352-2,
Lipp Jr Bks) HarpC Child Bks.
Tafuri, Lynn. Four Brave Sailors. Ginsburg, Mirra. LC
86-7555. 24p. (ps-1). 1987. 11.75 (0-688-06514-7);
PLB 11.88 (0-688-06515-5) Greenwillow.

Tafuri, Nancy. Across the Stream. Ginsburg, Mirra. LC
81-20306. 24p. (ps-1). 1982. 15.95 (0-688-01204-3);
PLB 15.88 (0-688-01206-X) Greenwillow.
—Across the Stream. Ginsburg, Mirra. LC 81-20306.
24p. (ps-1). 1991. pap. 3.95 (0-688-10477-0,
Mulberry) Morrow.
—All Year Long. Tafuri, Nancy. LC 82-9275. 32p. (gr.
k-2). 1983. PLB 13.88 (0-688-01416-X) Greenwillow.
—Asleep, Asleep. Ginsburg, Mirra. LC 91-14393. 24p.
(ps up). 1992. 14.00 (0-688-09153-9); PLB 13.93
(0-688-09154-7) Greenwillow.
—Early Morning in the Barn. Tafuri, Nancy. LC 83-
1436. 24p. (ps-1). 1983. 14.95 (0-688-02328-2); PLB
14.88 (0-688-02329-0) Greenwillow.
—Everything Has a Place. Lillie, Patricia. LC 90-23497.
24p. (ps up). 1993. 14.00 (0-688-10082-1); PLB 13.93
(0-688-10083-X) Greenwillow.
—Have You Seen My Duckling? Tafuri, Nancy. LC 83-
17196. 24p. (ps-1). 1984. 15.95 (0-688-02797-0); PLB
15.88 (0-688-02798-9) Greenwillow.
—Have You Seen My Duckling? Tafuri, Nancy. 32p.
(ps-k). 1986. pap. 3.95 (0-14-050532-6) Viking Child
Bks.
—If I Had a Paka: Poems in Eleven Languages.
Pomerantz, Charlotte. 32p. 1982. 11.75
(0-688-00836-4); PLB 11.88 (0-688-00837-2)
Greenwillow.
—In a Red House. Tafuri, Nancy. LC 86-27114. (ps).
1987. Board book. pap. 3.95 (0-688-07185-6)
Greenwillow.
—My Friends. Tafuri, Nancy. LC 86-29388. 12p. (ps).
1987. Board book. 3.95 (0-688-07187-2) Greenwillow.
—My Hands Can. Holzenthaler, Jean. 24p. 1978. 12.95
(0-525-35490-5, DCB) Dutton Child Bks.
—The Piney Woods Peddler. Shannon, George. LC 81-
2219. 32p. (gr. k-3). 1981. PLB 14.88 (0-688-84304-2)
Greenwillow.
—Rabbit's Morning. Tafuri, Nancy. LC 84-10229. 24p.
(ps-1). 1985. 13.95 (0-688-04063-2); PLB 13.88
(0-688-04064-0) Greenwillow.
—Who's Counting? Tafuri, Nancy. LC 85-17702. 24p.
(ps-1). 1986. 14.95 (0-688-06130-3); PLB 14.88
(0-688-06131-1) Greenwillow.
Tafuri, Nancy & Rice, Eve. If I Had a Paka: Poems in
Eleven Languages. Pomerantz, Charlotte. LC 92-
33088. 32p. (ps up). 1993. pap. 4.95 (0-688-12510-7,
Mulberry) Morrow.
Taggart, Tricia. Grandparents: A Special Kind of Love.
LeShan, Eda. LC 84-5673. 112p. (gr. 3-7). 1984. SBE
13.95 (0-02-756380-4, Macmillan Child Bk)
Macmillan Child Grp.
—How About A Hug. Holcomb, Nan. 32p. (Orig.).
1988. pap. 6.95 (0-944727-01-8) Jason & Nordic Pubs.
—How about a Hug. Holcomb, Nan. 32p. (ps-2). 1992.
Repr. of 1988 ed. 13.95 (0-944727-12-3) Jason &
Nordic Pubs.
Taina, Hannu. The Curious Fawn. Siekkinen, Raija. 32p.
(gr. k-4). 1990. PLB 18.95 (0-87614-379-6)
Carolrhoda Bks.
—Mister King. Siekkinen, Raija. Steffa, Tim, tr. 32p. (gr.
k-4). 1987. lib. bdg. 18.95 (0-87614-315-X)
Carolrhoda Bks.
Tait, Douglas. Sea & Cedar: How the Northwest Coast
Indians Lived. McConkey, Lois. 32p. (gr. 3-7). 1991.
pap. 8.95 (0-88894-371-7, Pub. by Groundwood-
Douglas & McIntyre CN) Firefly Bks Ltd.
—Thirty Indian Legends of Canada. Bemister, Margaret.
158p. (gr. 3-7). 1991. pap. 9.95 (0-88894-025-4, Pub.
by Groundwood-Douglas & McIntyre CN) Firefly Bks
Ltd.
Tait, Douglas & Twofeathers, Shannon. People of the
Buffalo: How the Plains Indians Lived. Campbell,
Maria. 48p. (gr. 3-7). 1992. pap. 7.95 (0-88894-329-6,
Pub. by Groundwood-Douglas & McIntyre CN)
Firefly Bks Ltd.
Taiwo. Adventures of Small Head, Square Head & Fat
Head. new ed. Sanchez, Sonia. 32p. (gr. 2-6). 1973.
11.95 (0-89388-094-9) Okpaku Communications.
Takahashi, Noriko. Action English Pictures. Frauman-
Prickel, Maxine. 120p. (gr. 7 up). 1985. pap. text ed.
19.95 (0-13-009077-8) Alemany Pr.
Taklender, Sharon. A Loving Guide to the World As a
Two Year-Old Says It. Field, Mary & Field, Elliot.
14p. (Orig.). 1983. pap. 5.95 (0-914445-00-6)
Palm Springs Pub.
Talbot, Eric, et al. Adventures in the Northern
Wilderness. Siembieda, Kevin, et al. Marciniszyn,
Alex, ed. 96p. (Orig.). (gr. 8 up). 1989. pap. 9.95
(0-916211-39-8, 456) Palladium Bks.
Talbot, Jim. Hide a Book: They Meet. Dott, A. Eric.
22p. (ps-1). 1987. PLB 5.95 (0-939871-00-9) Monarch
Toy.
Talbott, Hudson. Going Hollywood! A Dinosaur's
Dream. Talbott, Hudson. LC 89-1190. 32p. (ps-3).
1989. 12.95 (0-517-57354-7) Crown Bks Yng Read.
—Going Hollywood: A Dinosaur's Dream. Talbott,
Hudson. LC 89-1190. 32p. (ps-2). 1993. pap. 4.99
(0-517-58983-4) Crown Bks Yng Read.
—We're Back! A Dinosaur's Story. Talbott, Hudson. LC
87-5355. 32p. (ps-2). 1993. pap. 4.99 (0-517-58985-0)
Crown Bks Yng Read.
—Your Pet Dinosaur: An Owner's Manual. Talbott,
Hudson. LC 91-39762. 40p. (gr. 2 up). 1992. 15.00
(0-688-11337-0); PLB 14.93 (0-688-11338-9) Morrow
Jr Bks.
Talifero, Gerald. The Bridge Dancers. Saller, Carol. 40p.
(gr. 2-4). 1991. PLB 17.50 (0-87614-653-1)
Carolrhoda Bks.

—The Bridge Dancers. Saller, Carol. (gr. 2-4). 1993. pap. 5.95 (0-87614-579-9) Carolrhoda Bks.
Tallarico, A. Look & Look Again: Lost in the Haunted Mansion. Tropea, Maria. 24p. 1991. 2.98 (1-56156-044-8); pap. 1.95 (1-56156-050-2) Kidsbks.
—Look & Look Again: Missing Snowman. Tropea, Maria. 24p. 1991. 2.98 (1-56156-047-2); pap. 1.95 (1-56156-053-7) Kidsbks.
—Look & Look Again: Silly Schoolhouse. Tropea, Maria. 24p. 1991. pap. 1.95 (1-56156-051-0) Kidsbks.
—Look & Look Again: Silly Schoolhouse. Tropea, Maria. 24p. 1991. pap. 1.95 (1-56156-045-6) Kidsbks.
—Look & Look Again: Where's Benjy Bunny? Tropea, Maria. 24p. 1991. 2.98 (1-56156-046-4); pap. 1.95 (1-56156-052-9) Kidsbks.
Tallarico, Anthony. Find Freddie. Tallarico, Anthony. 24p. (gr. 2-6). 1990. lib. bdg. 10.59 (0-8167-1955-1); pap. 2.95 (0-685-44996-3) Troll Assocs.
—Hunt for Hector. Tallarico, Anthony. 24p. (gr. 2-6). 1990. lib. bdg. 10.59 (0-8167-1956-X); pap. 2.95 (0-685-44993-9) Troll Assocs.
—Look & Look Again, Lost in the Haunted Mansion. Tropea, Maria. 24p. (Orig.). (gr. 4-7). 1990. pap. 1.95 (1-878890-03-4) Palisades Prodns.
—Look for Lisa. Tallarico, Anthony. 24p. (gr. 2-6). 1990. lib. bdg. 10.59 (0-8167-1957-8); pap. 2.95 (0-685-44994-7) Troll Assocs.
—Search for Sam. Tallarico, Anthony. 24p. (gr. 2-6). 1990. lib. bdg. 10.59 (0-8167-1958-6); pap. 2.95 (0-685-44995-5) Troll Assocs.
—Stop & Find Maze Madness. Tallarico, Anthony. 12p. (Orig.). (gr. 4-7). 1990. pap. 1.95 (1-878890-00-X) Palisades Prodns.
Tallarico, Tony. A B C. 28p. (ps-1). 1988. bds. 2.95 (0-448-48817-5, Tuffy) Putnam Pub Group.
—Alphabet. 12p. (ps-1). 1987. bds. 3.95 (0-89828-317-5, Tuffy) Putnam Pub Group.
—At Home. 28p. (ps-1). 1984. bds. 2.95 (0-448-48818-3, Tuffy) Putnam Pub Group.
—Colors. Tallarico, Tony. 12p. (ps-1). 1982. bds. 3.95 (0-89828-304-3, Tuffy) Putnam Pub Group.
—Colors. 28p. (ps-1). 1988. bds. 2.95 (0-448-48819-1, Tuffy) Putnam Pub Group.
—Dinosaurs. 12p. (ps-1). 1988. bds. 3.95 (0-89828-318-3, Tuffy) Putnam Pub Group.
—Disney's Five Board Games to Go. 12p. (ps-5). 1990. bds. 16.95 (0-448-48815-9, Tuffy) Putnam Pub Group.
—Dolls, Dolls, Dolls. 12p. (ps-1). 1990. bds. 3.95 (0-89828-405-8, Tuffy) Putnam Pub Group.
—Finger Counting. 28p. (ps-1). 1984. bds. 2.95 (0-448-48820-5, Tuffy) Putnam Pub Group.
—Fire Engines. 12p. (ps-1). 1990. bds. 3.95 (0-448-40333-1, Tuffy) Putnam Pub Group.
—Five Wacky Games to Go. 12p. (ps-3). 1991. bds. 16.95 (0-448-48816-7, Tuffy) Putnam Pub Group.
—Happy Birthday. 12p. (ps-1). 1985. bds. 3.95 (0-89828-313-2, Tuffy) Putnam Pub Group.
—Haunted House. 12p. (ps-1). 1990. 3.95 (0-89828-402-3, Tuffy) Putnam Pub Group.
—Here We Go. 28p. (ps-1). 1988. bds. 2.95 (0-448-48821-3, Tuffy) Putnam Pub Group.
—How Many? 28p. (ps-1). 1984. bds. 2.95 (0-448-48822-1, Tuffy) Putnam Pub Group.
—I Love My Family. 12p. (ps-1). 1985. bds. 3.95 (0-89828-314-0, Tuffy) Putnam Pub Group.
—Let's Take a Trip. Tallarico, Tony. 12p. (ps-1). 1982. bds. 3.95 (0-89828-305-1, Tuffy) Putnam Pub Group.
—Little Engine That Could. 12p. (ps-1). 1990. bds. 3.95 (0-448-40334-X, Tuffy) Putnam Pub Group.
—Meet Peter Rabbit. 12p. (ps-1). 1988. bds. 3.95 (0-89828-321-3, Tuffy) Putnam Pub Group.
—Mr. Merlin's Puzzle & Game Book. Tallarico, Tony. Klimo, Kate. ed. 64p. (Orig.). (gr. 3-6). 1981. pap. 2.95 (0-671-44492-1) S&S Trade.
—More Preschool Can You Find Picture Book. Tallarico, Tony. (ps). 1991. 3.95 (0-448-48801-9, Tuffy) Putnam Pub Group.
—My First All about Cats Jigsaw Puzzle Book. Tallarico, Tony. (ps). 1991. 4.95 (0-448-48804-3, Tuffy) Putnam Pub Group.
—My First All about Circus Jigsaw Puzzle Book. Tallarico, Tony. (ps). 1991. 4.95 (0-448-48805-1, Tuffy) Putnam Pub Group.
—My First All about Dinosaurs Jigsaw Puzzle Book. Tallarico, Tony. (ps). 1991. 4.95 (0-448-48802-7, Tuffy) Putnam Pub Group.
—My First All about Dogs Jigsaw Puzzle Book. Tallarico, Tony. (ps). 1991. 4.95 (0-448-48803-5, Tuffy) Putnam Pub Group.
—Noah's Ark. Chariot Family Staff. 1987. plastic 6.47 (1-55513-653-2, 56531, Chariot Bks) Cook.
—Nursery Rhymes. 12p. (ps-1). 1988. bds. 3.95 (0-89828-320-5, Tuffy) Putnam Pub Group.
—Opposites. 12p. (ps-1). 1988. bds. 3.95 (0-89828-319-1, Tuffy) Putnam Pub Group.
—Peter Rabbit's Big Adventure. 12p. (ps-1). 1988. bds. 3.95 (0-89828-324-8, Tuffy) Putnam Pub Group.
—Peter Rabbit's Family. 12p. (ps-1). 1988. bds. 3.95 (0-89828-312-4, Tuffy) Putnam Pub Group.
—Pets. 12p. (ps-1). 1990. bds. 3.95 (0-89828-400-7, Tuffy) Putnam Pub Group.
—Preschool Can You Find Picture Book. Tallarico, Tony. (ps). 1991. 3.95 (0-448-48800-0, Tuffy) Putnam Pub Group.
—Shapes. 12p. (ps-1). 1985. bds. 3.95 (0-89828-315-9, Tuffy) Putnam Pub Group.
—Snowboy & Snowgirl. 12p. (ps-1). 1990. bds. 3.95 (0-448-40336-6, Tuffy) Putnam Pub Group.

—A Tale of Peter Rabbit. 12p. (ps-1). 1988. bds. 3.95 (0-89828-322-1, Tuffy) Putnam Pub Group.
—Time To... 28p. (ps-1). 1984. bds. 2.95 (0-448-48823-X, Tuffy) Putnam Pub Group.
—What's Opposite? 28p. (ps-1). 1984. bds. 2.95 (0-448-48824-8, Tuffy) Putnam Pub Group.
—Who Am I? 28p. (ps-1). 1984. bds. 2.95 (0-448-48825-6, Tuffy) Putnam Pub Group.
Tallon, Robert. ABCDEFGHIJKLMNOPQRSTUVWXYZ. LC 76-86987. (ENG & SPA.). 64p. (gr. k-2). 1969. PLB 14.95 (0-87460-131-2) Lion Bks.
Taloac, G., et al. The Best of Poe. new & abr. ed. Poe, Edgar Allan. Farr, Naunerle, ed. (gr. 4-12). 1977. pap. text ed. 2.95 (0-88301-269-3) Pendulum Pr.
Taloac, Gerry & Trinidad, Angel. Thomas Edison - Alexander Graham Bell. Farr, Naunerle C. (gr. 4-12). 1979. pap. text ed. 2.95 (0-88301-357-6); wkbk. 1.25 (0-88301-381-9) Pendulum Pr.
Tamblin, Treave. Night Creatures. Pope, Joyce. LC 91-45171. 32p. (gr. 3-6). 1993. PLB 11.59 (0-8167-2783-X); pap. text ed. 3.95 (0-8167-2784-8) Troll Assocs. Postponed.
Tamura, David. Mycca's Baby. Byers, Rinda M. LC 88-27320. 32p. (ps-2). 1990. 13.95 (0-531-05828-X); PLB 13.99 (0-531-08428-0) Orchard Bks Watts.
—When Justice Failed: The Fred Korematsu Story. Chin, Steven A. LC 92-18086. 105p. (gr. 2-5). 1992. PLB 21.34 (0-8114-7236-1) Raintree Steck-V.
Tanaka, Cliff. Let's Learn the Hawaiian Alphabet. Murray, Patricia A. 24p. (ps-k). 1987. 7.95 (0-89610-075-8) Island Heritage.
—Let's Learn the Hawaiian Alphabet. Murray, Patricia A. 24p. (ps-k). 1988. incls. cass. 11.95 (0-89610-079-0) Island Heritage.
—Let's Learn to Count in Hawaiian. Kawai'ae'a, Keiki C. 24p. (ps-k). 1988. 7.95 (0-89610-076-6) Island Heritage.
—Let's Learn to Count in Hawaiian. Kawai'ae'a, Keiki C. 24p. (ps-k). 1988. incl. cassette 11.95 (0-89610-080-4) Island Heritage.
Tang, Charles. The Pizza Mystery. Warner, Gertrude C., created by. LC 92-32263. 128p. (gr. 2-7). 1993. PLB 10.95 (0-8075-6534-2); pap. 3.50 (0-8075-6535-0) A Whitman.
Tang, You S. Almond Cookies & Dragon Well Tea. Chin-Lee, Cynthia. LC 92-21518. 36p. (gr. k-3). 1993. 12.95 (1-879965-03-8) Polychrome Pub.
Tanghal, Romeo & Bright, M. D. Green Lantern: Emerald Dawn (TPB) Giffen, Keith & Jones, Gerard. Dooley, Kevin, ed. & intro by. 144p. (Orig.). 1991. pap. 4.95 (0-930289-88-9) DC Comics.
Tanis, Joel E. The Dragon Pack Snack Attack. Tanis, Joel E. & Grooters, Jeff. LC 92-18433. 32p. (ps-2). 1993. RSBE 14.95 (0-02-788840-1, Four Winds) Macmillan Child Grp.
Tank, Darrel. The Carpenter: A Personal Look at Jesus. Holland, Kenneth J. & McFarland, Ken. 54p. (Orig.). (gr. 10). 1992. saddlestitch 3.95 (0-945460-15-5) Upward Way.
Tank, Darrel, et al. Uncle Arthur's Storytime, Vol. 1. Maxwell, Arthur S. & Holloway, Cheryl W. 128p. 1989. PLB 29.90 (1-877773-01-8) Family Media.
Tank-Richard, James. ABC's of Football. Hamilton, Jacklyn & Hamilton, Alfred T. 320p. (Orig.). 1992. pap. 12.00 (0-9635876-0-9) J&A Bks.
Tanner, Jane. Drac & the Gremlin. Baillie, Allan. LC 88-20275. 32p. (ps-3). 1989. 11.95 (0-8037-0628-6) Dial Bks Young.
—Drac & the Gremlin. Baillie, Allan. LC 88-20275. 32p. (ps-3). 1992. pap. 4.99 (0-14-054542-5, Puffin Pied Piper) Puffin Bks.
—The Wolf. Barbalet, Margaret. LC 91-25202. 32p. (gr. 1-4). 1992. 14.95 (0-02-711840-1, Macmillan Child Bk) Macmillan Child Grp.
Tanner, Suzy-Jane. Twelve Days of Christmas. Tanner, Suzy-Jane. 31p. (ps). 1993. Repr. 4.95 (1-882607-11-2) Merrybooks VA.
Tanner, Tim. Off the Map: The Journals of Lewis & Clark. Roop, Peter & Roop, Connie. LC 92-18340. 48p. (gr. 3-7). 1993. 14.95 (0-8027-8207-8); PLB 15.85 (0-8027-8208-6) Walker & Co.
Tanobe, Miyuki. Canada Je T'Aime - I Love You. Carrier, Roch. LC 90-70137. 72p. 1991. 29.95 (0-88776-253-0) Tundra Bks.
—Quebec, I Love You: Je t'Aime. Tanobe, Miyuki. 48p. (gr. 5 up). 1971. pap. 6.95 (0-88776-156-9) Tundra Bks.
Tanz, Freya. A Walk by the Seashore. Arnold, Caroline. Brook, Bonnie, ed. 32p. (ps-1). 1990. 5.95 (0-671-68666-6); lib. bdg. 9.98 (0-671-68662-3) Silver Pr.
—A Walk in the Desert. Arnold, Caroline. Brook, Bonnie, ed. 32p. (ps-1). 1990. 5.95 (0-671-68668-2); lib. bdg. 9.98 (0-671-68664-X) Silver Pr.
—A Walk in the Woods. Arnold, Caroline. Brook, Bonnie, ed. 32p. (ps-1). 1990. 5.95 (0-671-68665-8); lib. bdg. 9.98 (0-671-68661-5) Silver Pr.
—A Walk up a Mountain. Arnold, Caroline. Brook, Bonnie, ed. 32p. (ps-1). 1990. 5.95 (0-671-68667-4); lib. bdg. 9.98 (0-671-68663-1) Silver Pr.
Tappan, Eva M. Diary of Ruth Anna Hatch, Woods Hole, 1881. Smith, M. L., ed. 1992. text ed. write for info. (0-9611374-3-6) Woods Hole Hist.
Tardi, Jacques. The Enchanted Pig: Rumanian Fairy Tale. 32p. (gr. 6 up). 1984. PLB 13.95s.p. (0-87191-953-2) Creative Ed.

Tarlow, Phyllis. Bible Legends: An Introduction to Midrash, Vol. 2: Exodus. Freehof, Lillian S. Schwartz, Howard, ed. 160p. (gr. 4-6). 1988. pap. text ed. 6.95 (0-8074-0412-8, 123060) UAHC.
Tarrant, Carol. Shakespeare's Stories: Comedies. Birch, Beverly, retold by. LC 88-16947. 126p. (gr. 7-12). 1988. 12.95 (0-87226-191-3) P Bedrick Bks.
—Shakespeare's Stories: Comedies. Birch, Beverley, retold by. LC 88-16947. 126p. 1990. pap. 6.95 (0-87226-225-1) P Bedrick Bks.
—Shakespeare's Stories: Comedies. Birch, Beverley, retold by. LC 93-13366. 1993. 6.99 (0-517-09358-8) Outlet Bk Co.
—Sleeping Beauty. Daniels, Patricia. LC 79-26974. 24p. (gr. k-5). 1980. PLB 14.64 (0-8393-0254-1) Raintree Steck-V.
Tarrant, Valerie. Kirpal Singh: The Story of a Saint. 2nd ed. Scotti, Juliet & Linksman, Ricki. Zaffina, Bruno, intro. by. LC 77-79840. 96p. (gr. 1-7). 1982. pap. 12.95 (0-918224-05-5) Sawan Kirpal Pubns.
Tate, Carole. The Tale of the Spiteful Spirits: A Kampuchean Folk Tale. Tate, Carole. LC 90-41949. 32p. (gr. k-3). 1991. PLB 14.95 (0-87226-445-9, Bedrick Blackie) P Bedrick Bks.
Tauben, Carol. Integrating Arts & Crafts in the Jewish School, Vol. I. Tauben, Carol & Abrahams, Edith, eds. LC 79-15506. (gr. k-2). 1979. text ed. 14.95x (0-87441-288-9) Behrman.
Tausch, Cheryl C. Honey Bee Milly: Honey Bee - Apis Mellifera. Bernard, Eunice C. 72p. (Orig.). (gr. 4 up). 1994. pap. write for info. (0-9629950-5-3) Ashbrook Pr.
Tavonatti, Mia. Shivers & Shakes. Weinberg, Larry. LC 93-24445. 1993. pap. 2.95 (0-8167-3281-7) Troll Assocs.
Taylerson, Kareen. A Christmas Carol: A Changing Picture & Lift-the-Flap Book. Dickens, Charles. 32p. (ps-3). 1989. pap. 14.95 (0-670-82694-4) Viking Child Bks.
Taylor, Alice. Historic Denver for Kids. rev. ed. Smith, Barbara A. 90p. (Orig.). (gr. k up). 1982. pap. 5.00 (0-943804-25-6) U of Denver Teach.
Taylor, Anne. Math in Art. Taylor, Anne. (Orig.). (gr. 1-9). 1974. pap. 7.95 (0-918932-28-9) Activity Resources.
Taylor, B. K. One Hundred & One Silly Monster Jokes. Stine, Bob. 96p. (Orig.). (gr. 4-7). 1986. pap. 1.95 (0-590-33889-7) Scholastic Inc.
Taylor, C. J. Deux Plumes et la Solitude Disparue. Taylor, C. J. 24p. (gr. 1-5). 1990. 13.95 (0-88776-255-7) Tundra Bks.
—Geurrier-Solitaire et le Fantome: Native. Taylor, C. J. Boileau, Michele, tr. (FRE.). 24p. (gr. 1-5). 1991. 13.95 (0-88776-264-6) Tundra Bks.
—How Two-Feather Was Saved from Loneliness. Taylor, C. J. LC 90-70138. 24p. (gr. 1-5). 1990. 13.95 (0-88776-254-9) Tundra Bks.
—How We Saw the World: Nine Native Stories of Beginnings. Taylor, C. J. 32p. (gr. 1-5). 1993. 17.95 (0-88776-302-2) Tundra Bks.
—Little Water & the Gift of the Animals. Taylor, C. J. LC 92-8413. 24p. (gr. 1-5). 1992. PLB 13.95 (0-88776-285-9) Tundra Bks.
—Le Secret Du Bison Blanc: Taylor, C. J. Boileau, Michele, tr. from ENG. LC 93-60552. (FRE.). 24p. (gr. 3 up). 1993. 13.95 (0-88776-322-7) Tundra Bks.
—The Secret of the White Buffalo. Taylor, C. J. LC 93-60551. 24p. (gr. 3 up). 1993. 13.95 (0-88776-321-9) Tundra Bks.
Taylor, Cheryl. Guinea Pigs Don't Talk. Myers, Laurie. LC 93-39642. Date not set. write for info. (0-395-68967-8, Clarion Bks) HM.
Taylor, Christina. Teaching for Talent. Cline, Starr. Tannenbaum, A. J., intro. by. 56p. (Orig.). (gr. k-6). 1984. 6.50 (0-88047-040-2, 8406) DOK Pubs.
—Wings for Independent Thinking. Cochran, Belinda & Reid, Carol. 56p. (Orig.). (gr. 3). 1984. 6.50 (0-88047-038-0, 8403) DOK Pubs.
Taylor, Dave. Carl Lewis. Coffey, Wayne. 64p. (gr. 3-7). 1993. map 7.5 (1-56711-052-5) Blackbirch.
Taylor, David S. Who's on What? Basketball Trading Cards Reference Book, 1990-1991. Garrett, B. J. 100p. (Orig.). (gr. 3 up). 1993. pap. write for info. (1-882816-00-5) Eyes of August.
Taylor, Harriet P. Coyote Places the Stars. Taylor, Harriet P., retold by. LC 92-46431. 32p. (gr. k-2). 1993. RSBE 14.95 (0-02-788845-2, Bradbury Pr) Macmillan Child Grp.
Taylor, Jody. The Old Witch & the Ghost Parade. DeLage, Ida. 48p. (gr. k-4). 1991. Repr. of 1978 ed. lib. bdg. 12.95 (0-7910-1478-9) Chelsea Hse.
Taylor, Karen & Arkle, Dave. A Child's Guide to Computers, 4 vols. Stankowich, Mimi. 32p. (ps-3). 1984. 3.95 ea. Bk. 1 (0-916881-00-8, ALP701) Bk. 2 (0-916881-01-6, ALP702) Bk. 3 (0-916881-02-4, ALP703) Bk. 4 (0-916881-03-2, ALP704) Advan Learning.
Taylor, Kate. Animal Babies. Ganeri, Anita. 32p. (ps-1). 1991. 6.95 (0-8120-6241-8) Barron.
—Animal Behavior. Ganeri, Anita. 32p. (ps-1). 1992. 6.95 (0-8120-6301-5) Barron.
—Animal Camouflage. Ganeri, Anita. 32p. (ps-1). 1991. 6.95 (0-8120-6236-1) Barron.
—Animal Families. Ganeri, Anita. 32p. (ps-1). 1992. 6.95 (0-8120-6274-4) Barron.
—Animal Food. Ganeri, Anita. 32p. (ps-1). 1992. 6.95 (0-8120-6302-3) Barron.

—Animal Movements. Ganeri, Anita. 32p. (ps-1). 1991. 6.95 (*0-8120-6238-8*) Barron.
—Animal Records. Ganeri, Anita. 32p. (ps-1). 1992. 6.95 (*0-8120-6300-7*) Barron.
—Animal Talk. Ganeri, Anita. 32p. (ps-1). 1991. 6.95 (*0-8120-6239-6*) Barron.
—Colors Shapes & Numbers. Taylor, Kate. 14p. (gr. k-2). 1993. 7.95 (*0-87226-505-6*, Bedrick Blackie) P Bedrick Bks.
—What Do I Eat? Taylor, Kate. 16p. 1993. 6.95 (*0-87226-506-4*, Bedrick Blackie) P Bedrick Bks.
Taylor, Kim. Freckles the Rabbit. Burton, Jane. LC 89-11396. 32p. (gr. k-3). 1989. PLB 15.93 (*0-8368-0208-X*) Gareth Stevens Inc.
Taylor, Kim, jt. illus. see Burton, Jane.
Taylor, Kim, photos by. Forest Life. Taylor, Barbara. LC 92-53488. 32p. (gr. 2-5). 1993. 9.95 (*1-56458-210-8*) Dorling Kindersley.
—Tree Life. Greenway, Theresa. LC 92-52824. 32p. (gr. 2-5). 1992. 9.95 (*1-56458-132-2*) Dorling Kindersley.
Taylor, Kim & Burton, Jane, photos by. Meadow. Taylor, Barbara. LC 92-52821. 32p. (gr. 2-5). 1992. 9.95 (*1-56458-129-2*) Dorling Kindersley.
—See How They Grow: Frog. 24p. (gr. k-3). 1991. 6.95 (*0-525-67345-8*, Lodestar Bks) Dutton Child Bks.
—Swamp Life. Greenway, Theresa. LC 92-53489. 32p. (gr. 2-5). 1993. 9.95 (*1-56458-211-6*) Dorling Kindersley.
Taylor, Kim, jt. photog. see Burton, Jane.
Taylor, Leigh, jt. illus. see Dodd, John.
Taylor, Marie. Humphrey, Wimsey & Doo. Case, Elinor. 48p. (Orig.). (ps-6). 1984. pap. 5.95 (*0-910781-02-8*) G Whittell Mem.
Taylor, Marjorie. Cliffhanger. Press, Skip. Parker, Liz, ed. 45p. (Orig.). (gr. 6-12). 1992. pap. text ed. 2.95 (*1-56254-055-6*) Saddleback Pubns.
—Fraud, Fame, Alien Life Forms. Horton, Randy. Parker, Liz, ed. 45p. (Orig.). (gr. 6-12). 1992. pap. text ed. 2.95 (*1-56254-053-X*) Saddleback Pubns.
—Freeze Frame. Bricker, Sandra D. Parker, Liz, ed. 45p. (Orig.). (gr. 6-12). 1992. pap. text ed. 2.95 (*1-56254-050-5*) Saddleback Pubns.
—Mean Waters. Woodson, Frank. Parker, Liz, ed. 45p. (Orig.). (gr. 6-12). 1992. pap. text ed. 2.95 (*1-56254-059-9*) Saddleback Pubns.
—Nobody Lives in Apartment N-2. Schraff, Anne. Parker, Liz, ed. 45p. (Orig.). (gr. 6-12). 1992. pap. text ed. 2.95 (*1-56254-057-2*) Saddleback Pubns.
—The Return of the Eagle. Buchanan, Paul. Parker, Liz, ed. 45p. (Orig.). (gr. 6-12). 1992. pap. text ed. 2.95 (*1-56254-052-1*) Saddleback Pubns.
—The Seal Killers. Brin, Susannah. Parker, Liz, ed. 45p. (Orig.). (gr. 6-12). 1992. pap. text ed. 2.95 (*1-56254-051-3*) Saddleback Pubns.
—Stick Like Glue. Wells, Colin. Parker, Liz, ed. 45p. (Orig.). (gr. 6-12). 1992. pap. text ed. 2.95 (*1-56254-058-0*) Saddleback Pubns.
—Swamp Furies. Schraff, Anne. Parker, Liz, ed. 45p. (gr. 6-12). 1992. pap. text ed. 2.95 (*1-56254-056-4*) Saddleback Pubns.
—Touchdown. Steel, Richard. Parker, Liz, ed. 45p. (gr. 6-12). 1992. pap. text ed. 2.95 (*1-56254-054-8*) Saddleback Pubns.
Taylor, Michael. Kidding Around London: A Young Person's Guide to the City. Lovett, Sarah. 64p. (Orig.). (gr. 3 up). 1989. pap. 9.95 (*0-945465-24-6*) John Muir.
—Kidding Around the Hawaiian Islands: A Young Person's Guide to the Islands. Lovett, Sarah. 64p. (Orig.). (gr. 3 up). 1990. pap. 9.95 (*0-945465-37-8*) John Muir.
—New Medicine. rev. ed. Williams, Jeanne. 168p. 1993. write for info. (*0-937460-90-7*); pap. write for info. (*0-937460-93-1*) Hendrick-Long.
—Trails of Tears: American Indians Driven from Their Lands. rev. ed. Williams, Jeanne. LC 91-28849. 192p. (gr. 7 up). 1992. Repr. of 1972 ed. 15.95 (*0-937460-76-1*) Hendrick-Long.
Taylor, Nancy S. Dino Valentino. Taylor, Randy M. 33p. (gr. k-5). 1988. write for info. (*0-937745-05-7*) Traditions Pr.
Taylor, Neil. Back-Back & the Lima Bear. Weck, Thomas. Graves, Helen, ed. LC 85-51963. 64p. (gr. 1-6). 1986. 6.95 (*0-938232-97-5*) Winston-Derek.
—Farming Is OK. Stauffer, Patricia I. Mattingly, Jennie, ed. LC 87-50262. 44p. (gr. 1-3). 1987. 6.95 (*1-55523-077-6*) Winston-Derek.
—Kentucky Boy. Hines, Jane B. Graves, Helen, ed. LC 86-40281. 155p. (Orig.). (gr. 4-8). 1986. pap. 7.95 (*1-55523-033-4*) Winston-Derek.
—My Rainbow Friends. Hammond, Elizabeth. LC 87-51495. 44p. (ps). 1989. 5.95 (*1-55523-023-7*) Winston-Derek.
—Shelly from Rockytop Farm. Klusmeyer, Joann. 65p. (gr. 3-6). 1986. 5.95 (*1-55523-014-8*) Winston-Derek.
—The Space Twin. Davis, Natalie L. 112p. (gr. 4-8). 1987. 7.95 (*1-55523-037-7*) Winston-Derek.
—What Every Child Must Know about Grownups. Elbek, Gail. Jaworski, Jo, ed. LC 86-40333. 65p. (gr. k-4). 1990. 5.95 (*1-55523-015-6*) Winston-Derek.
Taylor, Pamela, jt. illus. see Greenough, Jackie.
Taylor, Richard. Dancing with the Times: What's a Young Adult to Believe! Evans, Pearl. 160p. (Orig.). (gr. 8 up). 1993. pap. 4.99 (*0-938453-05-X*) Small Helm Pr.
Taylor, Robert. Joan of Arc. Storr, Catherine. LC 84-18346. 32p. (gr. 2-5). 1985. PLB 17.96 (*0-8172-2111-5*) Raintree Steck-V.

Taylor, Scott. Fiesta! Behrens, June. LC 78-8468. 32p. (gr. k-4). 1978. PLB 15.00 (*0-516-08815-7*, Golden Gate); pap. 3.95 (*0-516-48815-5*) Childrens.
Taylor, Talus. Look out for Ghosts! Tison, Annette. LC 92-60790. 32p. (ps-3). 1992. 12.00 (*0-89577-438-0*) RD Assn.
Taylor, Tamar. How Georgina Drove the Car Very Carefully from Boston to New York. Bate, Lucy. LC 88-22861. 32p. (ps-1). 1993. pap. 4.99 (*0-517-59324-6*) Crown Bks Yng Read.
Teague, Mark. No Moon, No Milk! Babcock, Chris. LC 92-40697. 32p. (ps-2). 1993. 12.00 (*0-517-58779-3*); PLB 12.99 (*0-517-58780-7*) Crown Bks Yng Read.
Teague, Mark W. Any Kid Can Cook: A Kid Friendly Cookbook. Vincent, Richard J. Tanaka, Rita K. & Brandes, Mary J., eds. LC 93-94116. 160p. (Orig.). (gr. 2-8). Date not set. pap. write for info. (*0-9638354-0-8*) Vision Pr CA.
Teare, Brad. Will You Still Love Me? Walton, Rick. LC 92-341. 32p. (ps). 1992. 11.95 (*0-87579-582-X*) Deseret Bk.
Teasdale, Denise. The Moose in the Dress. Balan, Bruce. LC 90-86345. 32p. (ps-1). 1991. 14.00 (*0-517-58564-2*, Clarkson Potter) Crown Bks Yng Read.
—Mrs. Mary Malarky's Seven Cats. Hindley, Judy. LC 88-25873. 32p. (ps-2). 1990. 12.95 (*0-531-05822-0*); PLB 12.99 (*0-531-08422-1*) Orchard Bks Watts.
—Rob Goes A-Hunting. Turnbull, Ann. LC 90-30626. 32p. (ps-1). 1990. 13.95 (*0-531-05877-8*); PLB 13.99 (*0-531-08477-9*) Orchard Bks Watts.
—Walter's Magic Wand. Houghton, Eric. LC 89-35400. 32p. (ps-1). 1990. 13.95 (*0-531-05851-4*); PLB 13.99 (*0-531-08451-5*) Orchard Bks Watts.
Teason, James. Science. Allington, Richard L. & Krull, Kathleen. LC 82-101711. 32p. (gr. k-3). 1985. pap. 8.95 (*0-8172-2486-6*) Raintree Steck-V.
Technical Support Services Staff. Modems Made Easy. Brenner, Robert C. Brenner, Veronica L., ed. 270p. (Orig.). (gr. 9-12). 1991. pap. 19.95 (*0-929535-09-X*) Brenner Info Group.
Tedesco, Donna. Do You Know How Much I Love You? Tedesco, Donna. LC 92-7856. 32p. (ps-1). 1994. SBE 13.95 (*0-02-789120-8*, Bradbury Pr) Macmillan Child Grp.
Teeples, Lynn. The Son of the Day & the Daughter of the Night. MacDonald, George. LC 84-145155. 40p. (gr. 7-9). 1991. pap. 7.95 (*0-914676-45-8*, Green Tiger) S&S Trade.
Tegtmeyer, John. A Web of Good Manners: Grown-up Manners for Young People. Hillings, Phyllis. LC 92-85125. 96p. (gr. 3 up). 1993. 14.95 (*0-9634642-1-3*) Manhattan Pr.
Teichman, Mary. Color. Rossetti, Christina. LC 90-25588. 40p. (ps-1). 1992. 15.00 (*0-06-022626-9*); PLB 14.89 (*0-06-022650-1*) HarpC Child Bks.
—Merry Christmas: A Victorian Verse. LC 92-29870. 32p. (ps up). 1993. 10.00 (*0-06-022889-X*); PLB 9.89 (*0-06-022892-X*) HarpC Child Bks.
—Stars for Sarah. Turner, Ann. LC 89-26908. 32p. (ps-3). 1991. 13.95 (*0-06-026186-2*); PLB 13.89 (*0-06-026187-0*) HarpC Child Bks.
—Stars for Sarah. Turner, Ann. LC 89-36908. 32p. (ps-3). 1993. pap. 4.95 (*0-06-443344-7*, Trophy) HarpC Child Bks.
Teitelbaum, Michael. Sonic the Hedgehog. Teitelbaum, Michael. LC 93-14029. (gr. 2-4). 1993. pap. 2.50 (*0-8167-3199-3*) Troll Assocs.
Tejima, Keizaburo. The Bears' Autumn. Tejima, Keizaburo. Matsui, Susan, tr. from JPN. LC 91-17118. 42p. (gr. 1-4). 1991. 12.95 (*0-671-74981-1*, Green Tiger) S&S Trade.
—Fox's Dream. Tejima, Keizaburo. (ps-1). 1987. 14.95 (*0-399-21455-0*, Philomel Bks) Putnam Pub Group.
Telander, Todd. Exploring an Ocean Tide Pool. Bendick, Jeanne. LC 91-34572. 64p. (gr. 2-4). 1992. 14.95 (*0-8050-2043-8*, Bks Young Read) H Holt & Co.
Temple, Herbert. The Legend of Africania. Robinson, Dorothy. LC 74-4781. 32p. (gr. k-5). 1974. 10.95 (*0-87485-037-1*) Johnson Chi.
Templeton, Larry D. The Stars of Childsland. Templeton, Larry D. 22p. (gr. k-3). 1982. pap. 1.98 (*0-9608914-0-4*) Templeton.
Tenggren, Gustaf. The Poky Little Puppy. Lowrey, Janette S. 24p. (ps-k). 1992. Repr. of 1942 ed. write for info. (*0-307-10394-3*, 10394, Pub. by Golden Bks) Western Pub.
—The Shy Little Kitten. reissued ed. Schurr, Cathleen. 24p. (ps-k). 1992. write for info. (*0-307-00145-8*, 312-10, Golden Pr) Western Pub.
—Three Best-Loved Tales: Thumbelina; Tawny Scrawny Lion; The Poky Little Puppy. 80p. (ps-2). 1992. write for info. (*0-307-15630-3*, 15630, Golden Pr) Western Pub.
Tennent, Julie. The Three & Many Wishes of Jason Reid. Hutchins, Hazel. 96p. (gr. 1-4). 1990. pap. 3.95 (*0-14-032178-0*, Puffin) Puffin Bks.
Tenniel, John. Alice au Pays des Merveilles. Carroll, Lewis. (FRE.). 223p. (gr. 5-10). 1987. pap. 9.95 (*2-07-033437-6*) Schoenhof.
—Alice in Wonderland. Carroll, Lewis. 160p. (gr. 3-6). 1988. pap. 2.95 (*0-590-42035-6*, Apple Classics) Scholastic Inc.
—Alice in Wonderland & Through the Looking Glass. Carroll, Lewis. (gr. 4-6). 1963. 13.95 (*0-448-06004-3*, G&D) Putnam Pub Group.

—Alice's Adventures in Wonderland. Carroll, Lewis. LC 82-242973. (gr. 7 up). 1985. pap. 2.25 (*0-14-035038-1*, Puffin) Puffin Bks.
—Alice's Adventures in Wonderland. Carroll, Lewis. Glassman, Peter, intro. by. LC 91-31482. 208p. 1992. 15.00 (*0-688-11087-8*) Morrow Jr Bks.
—Alice's Adventures in Wonderland. Carroll, Lewis. LC 93-571. 240p. 1993. Repr. of 1866 ed. 6.00 (*1-56957-900-8*) Shambhala Pubns.
—Alice's Adventures in Wonderland & Through the Looking Glass. Carroll, Lewis. Cohen, Morton N., intro. by. 256p. 1984. pap. 2.75 (*0-553-21345-8*, Bantam Classics Spectra) Bantam.
—Alice's Adventures in Wonderland & Through the Looking Glass: And What Alice Found There. Carroll, Lewis. 416p. 1992. pap. 3.99 (*0-440-40743-5*, Pub. by Yearling Classics) Dell.
—Alice's Adventures in Wonderland & Through the Looking Glass. Carroll, Lewis. LC 92-53181. 336p. 1992. 12.95 (*0-679-41795-8*, Evrymans Lib Childs Class) Knopf.
—Alice's Adventures in Wonderland & Through the Looking-Glass, 2 bks. Carroll, Lewis. 1993. Boxed Set. 29.95 (*0-688-12050-4*) Morrow Jr Bks.
—Aventures D'Alice au Pays des Merveilles. Carroll, Lewis. Bue, Henri, tr. from ENG. Cohen, Morton N., intro. by. (FRE.). 196p. (gr. 4-8). 1972. pap. 4.95 (*0-486-22836-3*) Dover.
—The Little Alice Editions: Alice's Adventures in Wonderland; Through the Looking-Glass. Carroll, Lewis. 416p. (ps up). 1988. slipcased set 12.95 (*0-8037-0589-1*) Dial Bks Young.
—Reader's Digest Best Loved Books for Young Readers: Alice's Adventures in Wonderland & Through the Looking Glass. Carroll, Lewis. Ogburn, Jackie, ed. 192p. (gr. 4-12). 1989. 3.99 (*0-945260-21-0*) Choice Pub NY.
—Through the Looking Glass. Carroll, Lewis. 224p. 1977. Repr. 14.95 (*0-312-80374-5*) St Martin.
—Through the Looking Glass, & What Alice Found There. Carroll, Lewis. LC 84-60960. 184p. (gr. 2 up). 1984. Repr. of 1941 ed. 6.95 (*0-88088-991-8*, 889918) Peter Pauper.
—Through the Looking Glass & What Alice Found There. Carroll, Lewis. LC 92-20642. 240p. (gr. 1 up). 1993. 15.00 (*0-688-12049-0*) Morrow Jr Bks.
Tenniel, John, jt. illus. see Holiday, Henry.
Tennyson, Noel. Christmas Carols: A Treasury of Holiday Favorites with Words & Pictures. LC 83-60412. 24p. (gr. 1-5). 1983. 2.95 (*0-394-86125-6*) Random Bks Yng Read.
—The Lady's Chair & the Ottoman. Tennyson, Noel. LC 84-11196. 32p. (gr. k-3). 1987. PLB 12.88 (*0-688-04098-5*) Lothrop.
Tenorio, Greg. No Hang-Ups III: Funny Answering Machine Messages. Carfi, John & Carle, Cliff. 96p. (Orig.). 1988. pap. 3.95 (*0-918259-12-6*) CCC Pubns.
Tepley, Marilyn. Two Story Farmhouse. Schultz, Elva. (ps-3). 1986. write for info. (*0-9616431-0-2*) E Schultz.
Tepley, Marilyn M. Voyageur the Moose. Leagjeld, Ted. (Orig.). (gr. 4-8). Date not set. pap. write for info. (*0-9616127-0-3*) T Leagjeld.
Tepper, Elly. Aukele the Fearless. Thompson, Vivian L. LC 92-6126. 80p. (Orig.). (gr. k-5). 1992. pap. 9.95 (*0-8248-1445-2*) UH Pr.
Terpstra, Gwen. ChordTime Piano Hymns: Level 2 - I, IV, V7 Chords in Keys of C,G & F. Faber, Nancy & Faber, Randall. McLean, Edwin, ed. 24p. (gr. 2-4). 1988. pap. 4.95 (*0-929666-03-8*) FJH Music Co Inc.
—PlayTime Piano Christmas: Level 1 - Five Finger Melodies. Faber, Nancy & Faber, Randall. McLean, Edwin, ed. 24p. (gr. 1-3). 1988. pap. 4.95 (*0-929666-02-X*) FJH Music Co Inc.
—PlayTime Piano Hymns: Level One - Five Finger Melodies. Faber, Nancy & Faber, Randall. McLean, Edwin, ed. 24p. (gr. 1-3). 1988. pap. 4.95 (*0-929666-00-3*) FJH Music Co Inc.
—PlayTime Piano Popular: Level One - Five Finger Melodies. Faber, Nancy & Faber, Randall. McLean, Edwin, ed. 24p. (gr. 1-3). 1988. pap. 4.95 (*0-929666-01-1*) FJH Music Co Inc.
Terrill, Veronica. Learn & Grow from A to Z: Learning Centers & Activities for Young Children. Dunlavy, Kathy. 160p. (ps-2). 1992. Wkbk. 12.95 (*0-86653-682-5*, GA1416) Good Apple.
Terry, Hilda. Does God Eat Us? A Contemporary Response to Old Questions. Terry, Hilda. 271p. (Orig.). 1991. pap. 8.88 (*0-685-54234-3*) Art Ltd.
Terry, Phyllis D. Gingerbread & Friends. rev. ed. Nolan, Virginia J. & Terry, Phyllis D. 22p. 1987. pap. 3.50 (*0-9624497-0-9*) Planet Playmates.
Teskey, Donald. The Rebel Countess. Moriarty, Mary & Sweeney, Catherine. 80p. (Orig.). (gr. 1-7). 1992. pap. 8.95 (*0-86278-211-2*, Pub. by OBrien Pr EIRE) Dufour.
—The Tain: The Great Celtic Epic. MacUistin, Liam. 93p. (gr. 5-12). 1991. pap. 9.95 (*0-86278-238-4*, Pub. by OBrien Pr IE) Dufour.
—Under the Hawthorn Tree. Conlon-McKenna, Marita. LC 90-55097. 160p. (gr. 3-7). 1990. 13.95 (*0-8234-0838-8*) Holiday.
—Wildflower Girl. Conlon-McKenna, Marita. LC 92-52711. 176p. (gr. 5-9). 1992. 14.95 (*0-8234-0988-0*) Holiday.
Testa, Fulvio. Aesop's Fables. 48p. (gr. 2 up). 1989. incl. dust jacket 12.95 (*0-8120-5958-1*) Barron.

—If You Take a Paintbrush: A Book of Colors. Testa, Fulvio. LC 82-45512. 32p. (ps-2). 1986. pap. 4.95 (0-8037-0282-5) Dial Bks Young.
—Time to Get Out. Testa, Fulvio. LC 93-60218. 32p. (ps up). 1993. 14.00 (0-688-12907-2, Tambourine Bks); PLB 13.93 (0-688-12908-0, Tambourine Bks) Morrow.
—Wolf's Favor. Testa, Fulvio. LC 85-15934. 32p. (ps-3). 1986. 11.95 (0-8037-0244-2) Dial Bks Young.
Thamer, Katie. Black Horse. Mayer, Marianna. LC 83-25271. 42p. (ps-3). 1987. pap. 4.95 (0-8037-0181-0) Dial Bks Young.
Tharlet, Eve. Archibald the Great. Tharlet, Eve. Clements, Andrew, tr. from FRE. 28p. (gr. k up). 1993. 14.95 (0-88708-267-X) Picture Bk Studio.
—The Brave Little Tailor. Grimm, Jacob & Grimm, Wilhelm K. Bell, Anthea, tr. LC 88-33367. 28p. (ps up). 1991. pap. 14.95 (0-88708-091-X) Picture Bk Studio.
—Dizzy from Fools. Miller, M. L. LC 85-9390. 32p. (gr. 1 up). 1991. pap. 13.95 (0-88708-004-9) Picture Bk Studio.
—Jack in Luck. Grimm, Jacob & Grimm, Wilhelm K. Bell, Anthea, tr. LC 92-7102. 28p. (ps up). 1992. pap. 14.95 (0-88708-249-1) Picture Bk Studio.
—Little Pig, Big Trouble. Tharlet, Eve. Clements, Andrew, tr. LC 89-31369. (ps up). 1991. pap. 14.95 (0-88708-073-1) Picture Bk Studio.
—Little Pig, Big Trouble. Tharlet, Eve. Clements, Andrew, tr. LC 91-40637. 28p. (gr. k up). 1992. pap. 4.95 (0-88708-227-0) Picture Bk Studio.
—Little Pig, Bigger Trouble. Tharlet, Eve. Clements, Andrew, tr. LC 91-40637. 28p. (gr. k up). 1992. pap. 14.95 (0-88708-237-8) Picture Bk Studio.
—The Princess & the Pea. Andersen, Hans Christian. Bell, Anthea, tr. LC 87-13913. (ps up). 1991. pap. 13.95 (0-88708-052-9) Picture Bk Studio.
—The Princess & the Pea. Andersen, Hans Christian. Bell, Anthea, tr. from DAN. LC 90-25386. 28p. (gr. k up). 1991. pap. 4.95 (0-88708-170-3) Picture Bk Studio.
—Simon & the Holy Night. Tharlet, Eve. Clements, Andrew, adapted by. LC 93-306. 1993. 4.95 (0-88708-324-2) Picture Bk Studio.
Thatcher, Fran. The Adventures of Pussycat Wizzy Willums. Pearl, Lizzy. LC 92-9475. 26p. (ps-3). 1992. 13.95 (1-56566-020-X) Thomasson-Grant.
Thatcher, Fran & Williamson, Tracey. The Fantastic Fairy Tale Pop-up Book. Van Der Meer, Ron. LC 92-80742. 10p. (ps-3). 1993. 16.00 (0-679-83869-4) Random Bks Yng Read.
Thayer, Carolyn. The Rescue of Rusty Rabbit. Scherer, Bonnie L. Roberts, Mary & Hendricks, Janie, eds. LC 90-63371. 12p. (Orig.). (gr. 1-6). 1991. pap. text ed. write for info. (0-9622421-1-X) B Scherer.
Thelan, Mary. Abra-Ca-Dazzle: Easy Magic Tricks. Broekel, Ray & White, Laurence B., Jr. Fay, Ann, ed. LC 81-11578. 48p. (gr. 3 up). 1982. PLB 11.95 (0-8075-0121-2) A Whitman.
Thelen, Mary. Hocus Pocus: Magic You Can Do. Broekel, Ray & White, Laurence B., Jr. Fay, Anne, ed. LC 83-26096. 48p. (gr. 3 up). 1984. PLB 11.95 (0-8075-3350-5) A Whitman.
—The Hospital Scares Me. Hogan, Paula Z. & Hogan, Kirk. Wilson, Jerrian M., intro. by. LC 79-23886. 32p. (gr. k-6). 1980. PLB 17.96 (0-8172-1351-1) Raintree Steck-V.
Theobalds, Prue. For Teddy & Me. Theobalds, Prue. 30p. (gr. k-3). 1992. 14.95 (0-87226-470-X, Bedrick Blackie) P Bedrick Bks.
—The Miniature Old MacDonald Had a Farm. Theobalds, Prue. 28p. 1993. 5.95 (0-87226-503-X, Bedrick Blackie) P Bedrick Bks.
—The Miniature Teddy & Me. Theobalds, Prue. 30p. (gr. 4 up). 1993. 5.95 (0-87226-514-5, Bedrick Blackie) P Bedrick Bks.
—The Miniature Teddy Bear's Picnic. Kennedy, Jimmy. LC 86-32111. 32p. (gr. k-3). 1989. 5.95 (0-87226-417-3, Bedrick Blackie) P Bedrick Bks.
—Noah & the Animals. Theobalds, Prue. LC 92-45630. 34p. (gr. 4 up). 1993. 12.95 (0-87226-507-2, Bedrick Blackie) P Bedrick Bks.
—Old MacDonald Had a Farm. Theobalds, Prue. 32p. (ps-3). 1991. PLB 14.95 (0-87226-452-1, Bedrick Blackie) P Bedrick Bks.
—The Teddy Bears' Great Expedition. Theobalds, Prue. LC 89-77039. 32p. (gr. k-3). 1990. PLB 12.95 (0-87226-425-4, Bedrick Blackie) P Bedrick Bks.
—The Teddy Bears' Picnic. Kennedy, Jimmy. LC 86-32111. 32p. (ps-2). 1987. PLB 14.95 (0-87226-153-0, Bedrick Blackie); pap. 6.95 (0-685-67547-5) P Bedrick Bks.
—The Teddy Bears' Picnic. Kennedy, Jimmy. LC 86-32111. 32p. 1990. pap. 6.95 (0-87226-424-6, Bedrick Blackie) P Bedrick Bks.
—Ten Tired Teddies. Theobalds, Prue. 10p. 1992. 5.95 (0-87226-471-8, Bedrick Blackie) P Bedrick Bks.
Thewlis, Diana. Johnny Castleseed. Ormondroyd, Edward. LC 85-8189. 32p. (gr. k-3). 1988. 12.95 (0-395-38355-2); pap. 4.80 (0-395-47947-9) HM.
Thibault, Dominique. Cathedrals: Stone upon Stone. Gandiol-Coppin, Brigitte. Bogard, Vicki, tr. from FRE. LC 89-5361. 38p. (gr. k-5). 1989. 4.95 (0-944589-24-3, 024) Young Discovery Lib.
—Long Ago in a Castle. Farre, Marie. Matthews, Sarah, tr. from FRE. LC 87-33996. 38p. (gr. k-5). 1988. 4.95 (0-944589-06-5, 065) Young Discovery Lib.

Thien, Denis. Wait for Me: The Life of Junipero Serra. Helen, Mary. LC 88-13103. 100p. (gr. 4-8). 1988. 3.00 (0-8198-8232-1) St Paul Bks.
Thiesies, Darlene. Homework? My Locker Ate It! An Effective Method for Parents to Help Their Student Study at Home & Improve in School. Quackenbush, Ross & Gastineau, Jerrel. 143p. (Orig.). (gr. 6-12). 1988. pap. 19.95 (0-9621701-0-0) CWP.
Thiesing, Lisa. The Ghastly Gertie Swindle: With the Ghosts of Hungryhouse Lane. McBratney, Sam. 128p. (gr. 3-6). 1993. PLB 14.95 (0-8050-2614-2, Bks Young Read) H Holt & Co.
—The Ghosts of Hungryhouse Lane. McBratney, Sam. 128p. (gr. 4-6). 1989. 13.95 (0-8050-0985-X, Bks Young Read) H Holt & Co.
—Pudmuddles. York, Carol B. LC 91-23596. 48p. (gr. 2-5). 1993. 13.00 (0-06-020436-2); PLB 12.89 (0-06-020437-0) HarpC Child Bks.
—Rhymin' Simon & the Mystery of the Fat Cat. Apablasa, Bill. LC 90-21054. 64p. (gr. 2-5). 1991. 10.95 (0-525-44702-4, DCB) Dutton Child Bks.
—Two Silly Trolls. Jewell, Nancy. LC 90-4387. 64p. (gr. k-3). 1992. 14.00 (0-06-022829-6); PLB 13.89 (0-06-022830-X) HarpC Child Bks.
—Two Silly Trolls. Jewell, Nancy. LC 90-4387. 64p. (ps-3). 1994. pap. 3.50 (0-06-444173-3, Trophy) HarpC Child Bks.
Thiewes, Sam & Nelson, Anita. Ginger & Pickles. Potter, Beatrix, created by. 24p. (gr. 2-4). 1992. PLB 10.95 (1-56674-017-7, HTS Bks) Forest Hse.
—Pigling Bland. Potter, Beatrix, created by. 24p. (gr. 2-4). 1992. PLB 10.95 (1-56674-021-5, HTS Bks) Forest Hse.
Thiewes, Sam, jt. illus. see Nilles, Burgandy.
Thiewes, Sam, jt. illus. see Spellman, Susan.
Thiewes, Sam, et al. Benjamin Bunny. Potter, Beatrix, created by. 24p. (gr. 2-4). 1992. PLB 10.95 (1-56674-006-1, HTS Bks) Forest Hse.
—Mrs. Tiggy-Winkle. Potter, Beatrix, created by. 24p. (gr. 2-4). 1992. PLB 10.95 (1-56674-007-X, HTS Bks) Forest Hse.
Thill, Michael. The Adventures of Alice in Nutritionland: A Nutritional Storybook for Children. Thill, Larry. 31p. (Orig.). (gr. k-6). 1989. pap. 8.00 (0-317-93500-3) Impressive Pubns.
Thoenes, Michael. The Best Cook. Sikirycki, Igor. Knobbe, Czeslaw, ed. & tr. from POL. 26p. (gr. 1-6). 1993. text ed. 9.95 (0-9630328-2-8) SDPI.
Thollander, Earl. Cesar Chavez. Franchere, Ruth. LC 85-42999. 48p. (gr. 2-5). 1986. pap. 4.95 (0-06-446023-1, Trophy) HarpC Child Bks.
Thomas, Angela T. The Mighty Santa Fe. Hooks, William H. LC 92-17026. 32p. (gr. k-3). 1993. RSBE 14.95 (0-02-744432-5, Macmillan Child Bk) Macmillan Child Grp.
Thomas, Anika D. Life in the Ghetto. Thomas, Anika D. Thatch, Nancy R., ed. Melton, David, intro. by. LC 91-13944. 26p. (gr. 5 up). 1991. PLB 14.95 (0-933849-34-6) Landmark Edns.
Thomas, Art, photos by. Boxing Is for Me. Thomas, Art & Storms, Laura. LC 80-20086. 48p. (gr. 2-5). 1982. PLB 13.50 (0-8225-1133-9) Lerner Pubns.
Thomas, Avis T. God's Green Liniment. Rew, Lois J. LC 81-84183. 208p. (Orig.). (gr. 3-8). 1981. pap. 7.50 (0-938462-02-4) Green Leaf CA.
Thomas, Barbara. Thank You, Amelia Bedelia. newly illus ed. Parish, Peggy. LC 92-5746. 64p. (gr. k-3). 1993. 14.00 (0-06-022979-9); PLB 13.89 (0-06-022980-2) HarpC Child Bks.
Thomas, Charles & Robinson, W. Heath. Fairy Tales. Andersen, Hans Christian. Spink, Reginald, tr. LC 92-53178. 416p. 1992. 14.95 (0-679-41791-5, Evrymans Lib Childs Class) Knopf.

Thomas, Deborah. Arlie the Alligator. Warren, Sandra & Pfleger, Deborah B. LC 91-73758. 48p. (ps-3). Date not set. PLB 13.95 casebound (1-880175-13-4); bk. & cass. 19.90 (1-880175-11-8); audiocassette 5.95 (1-880175-12-6) Arlie Enter.

Arlie is a very curious alligator who longs to make friends with the strange creatures at the beach. Find out who the strange creatures are & what happens when he attempts to talk to them. The 10-minute audio cassette is fully produced with actors & actresses in mini-musical style. Four catchy tunes have children singing along the first time they listen. In beautiful color, this casebound, open-ended story book also includes a page about real alligators & sheet music. A creative use of fonts signals the change from song lyrics to dialogue. Non-readers enjoy the audio tape & pictures, while young readers & middle readers love to follow along, singing & reading, word-for-word, as the delightful story unfolds. Creative thinking is enhanced as children are encouraged to help Arlie find a way to communicate with the creatures. Unique in children's literature. ARLIE THE ALLIGATOR makes a great addition to the children's books-on-tape section of the library, elementary music libraries, elementary classrooms, in homes or for that long trip in the car. Activity guide also available, making that important classroom connection. *Publisher Provided Annotation.*

Thomas, DeVoe M. A Bird's-Eye View of Birds. Fugitt, Douglas & Fugitt, Elizabeth. 190p. (Orig.). (gr. 6). 1986. PLB 17.95 (0-9617159-0-1); pap. 11.95 (0-9617159-1-X) Willow Pr.
Thomas, Eric. The Children's Illustrated Bible. Hastings, Selina, retold by. LC 93-30814. 1994. write for info. (1-56458-472-0) Dorling Kindersley.
Thomas, Gary. Elijah McCoy, Inventor. Jackson, Garnet N. LC 92-28797. 1992. 56.50 (0-8136-5230-8); pap. 28.50 (0-8136-5703-2) Modern Curr.
Thomas, Ira. Jesus' Stocking. Crump, Patricia. 1990. 2.95 (0-8091-6591-0) Paulist Pr.
Thomas, Joan G. The Christmas Angel. Thomas, Joan G. 20p. (gr. 1-5). 1988. pap. 3.95 (0-8192-1429-9) Morehouse Pub.
—If Jesus Came to My House. Thomas, Joan G. 24p. (gr. k-3). 1951. 12.95 (0-688-40981-4) Lothrop.
Thomas, Linda. The Creepy Carousel. Avery, Lorraine. LC 89-20279. 96p. (gr. 4-6). 1990. PLB 9.89 (0-8167-1712-5); pap. text ed. 2.95 (0-8167-1713-3) Troll Assocs.
—Movie Madness. Avery, Lorraine. LC 89-20333. 96p. (gr. 4-6). 1990. PLB 9.89 (0-8167-1714-1); pap. text ed. 2.95 (0-8167-1715-X) Troll Assocs.
—The Runaway Winner. Avery, Lorraine. LC 89-34369. 96p. (gr. 4-6). 1990. PLB 9.89 (0-8167-1708-7); pap. text ed. 2.95 (0-8167-1709-5) Troll Assocs.
—Secret in the Lake. Avery, Lorraine. LC 89-5119. 96p. (gr. 4-6). 1990. PLB 9.89 (0-8167-1710-9); pap. text ed. 2.95 (0-8167-1711-7) Troll Assocs.
Thomas, Llewellyn. From a Railway Carriage. Stevenson, Robert Louis. 32p. (ps-3). 1993. 14.99 (0-670-84894-8) Viking Child Bks.
Thomas, Meredith. Hannah & Her Dad. Caisley, Raewyn. LC 93-28997. 1994. 4.25 (0-383-03787-5) SRA Schl Grp.
—Monday Came. Jenkins, Catherine. LC 93-28982. 1994. 4.25 (0-383-03762-X) SRA Schl Grp.
—Paper Shapes. Thomas, Meredith. LC 93-27994. 1994. 4.25 (0-383-03767-0) SRA Schl Grp.
Thomas, Steven N., photos by. A Child's Garden of Yoga. Hari Dass, Baba. Ault, Karuna, ed. LC 80-80299. 108p. (ps-7). 1980. pap. 9.95 (0-918100-02-X) Sri Rama.
Thomas, Susannah. A Red Rose for Francis: A Story of the Young Life of Francis Siedlisha. 2nd ed. Mohan, Claire J. (gr. 4-7). 1990. lib. bdg. write for info. (0-9621500-9-6) Young Sparrow Pr.

Thomas, Sylvia. Lighting Candles in the Dark. Clark, Marnie, et al, eds. 215p. (Orig.). 1992. pap. 9.50 (0-9620912-3-5) Friends Genl Conf.

LIGHTING CANDLES IN THE DARK is an illustrated anthology of 45 exciting stories about the courage of everyday people in the face of danger who use the power of love to save themselves & others. Divided into five sections "Courage & Nonviolence," "The Power of Love," "Acts of Loving Service," "Fairness & Equality," & "Belonging & Care of the Earth," the stories tell of characters dating from the 17th century to the present all over the world. The stories emphasize Quaker values of using love to heal ourselves, others, & our earth. Many stories have multicultural settings. From a recent review in FRIENDS JOURNAL: "How do we help our children choose love, courage, forgiveness, honesty, & fairness in a world saturated with violence, fear, selfishness, injustice & oppression? LIGHTING CANDLES IN THE DARK is a valuable resource in facing this awesome challenge....There's a good range of situations here, always something to catch a young reader's interest. The book looks bright & fresh, with appealing line drawings & open-looking typeface...this reader finds this book a welcome resource for kids, parents & teachers."--Margaret Springer. Friends General Conference, 1216 Arch Street 2B, Philadelphia, PA 19107. 800-966-4556, Libraries: 10% Bookstores: 40% actual postage. *Publisher Provided Annotation.*

Thomas, Tim & Zorn, Vic. Ghost of Black's Island: The Screenplay. Mulligan, Mark. 121p. (Orig.). (gr. 6-8). 1993. pap. 9.95x (*1-882444-01-9*) Blvd Bks FL.
—Manatee: The Screenplay. Mulligan, Mark. 121p. (Orig.). (gr. 9-12). 1993. pap. 9.95x (*1-882444-00-0*) Blvd Bks FL.
Thomas, Toni. A Donkey's Life: A Story for Children. Cheadle, J. A. LC 80-123421. iii, 88p. (Orig.). (gr. 2-6). 1979. pap. 3.50 (*0-9604244-0-7*) Heahstan Pr.
Thomas, Tony & Carlson, Bruce. How to Talk Midwestern. Thomas, Robert. Carlson, Bruce, ed. 109p. (Orig.). (gr. 9 up). 1990. pap. 7.95 (*1-878488-21-X*) Quixote Pr IA.
Thomas, Wendy. Percival the Piano. Perkins, Mary. (Orig.). (gr. k-4). 1990. pap. 5.75 (*0-85398-287-2*) G Ronald Pub.
Thomer, Susannah. Kaze's True Home: The Young Life of a Modern Day Saint, Mother Maria Kaupas. Mohan, Claire J. Xuzmickus, Marilyn, intro. by. LC 91-66722. 64p. (gr. 4-9). 1992. 8.95 (*0-9621500-5-3*) Young Sparrow Pr.
—A Red Rose for Frania: A Story of the Young Life of Francis Siedliska. Mohan, Claire J. (gr. 4-7). 1989. PLB 5.95 (*0-9621500-8-8*) Young Sparrow Pr.
Thomer, Susannah H. Am I Still a Big Sister? Weir, Audrey B. LC 92-35395. 1992. 4.95 (*0-9633243-0-6*) Fall Leaf Pr.
Thomes, Susannah H. Mother Teresa's Someday: The Young Life of Mother Teresa of Calcutta. Mohan, Claire J. Gallagher, Patricia C., ed. 60p. (Orig.). (gr. k-6). 1990. PLB 14.95 (*0-9621500-6-1*); pap. 6.95 (*0-9621500-7-X*) Young Sparrow Pr.
Tompkins, Kenny. The Disney Treasury of Princesses: Stories from the Films. Braybrooks, Ann & Rifkin, Mark. LC 92-56163. 80p. 1993. 14.95 (*1-56282-497-X*); PLB 14.89 (*1-56282-498-8*) Disney Pr.
Thompson, Brownlow L. The Sokokis: Native Americans of New Hampshire. Thompson, Dorothea M. 150p. (Orig.). (gr. 4). 1986. pap. 9.95x (*0-931947-50-2*) Thompson Pr.
—Will Stark & Boobear: Ranger Scouts, Vol. 2. 2nd ed. Thompson, Dorothea M. 150p. (gr. 5-10). pap. text ed. 9.95 (*0-931947-52-9*) Thompson Pr.
Thompson, Carol. Baby Days. Thompson, Carol. LC 90-28298. 48p. (ps). 1991. SBE 15.95 (*0-02-789325-1*, Macmillan Child Bk); pap. 4.95 counting frieze (*0-02-789215-X*) Macmillan Child Grp.
—Bounce, Bounce, Bounce. Henderson, Kathy. LC 93-3556. 1994. write for info. (*1-564023-11-7*) Candlewick Pr.
—Bumpety Bump. Henderson, Kathy. LC 93-3541. (ps). 1994. write for info. (*1-56402-312-5*) Candlewick Pr.
Thompson, Colin. The Paper Bag Prince. Thompson, Colin. LC 91-27453. 32p. (gr. 2-7). 1992. 15.00 (*0-679-83048-0*); PLB 15.99 (*0-679-93048-5*) Knopf Bks Yng Read.
Thompson, Dana. A Sheepful of Dollars. Hughes, Francine. LC 93-83722. 32p. (ps-3). 1993. pap. 2.25 (*0-679-85111-9*) Random Bks Yng Read.
—Very Like a Star. Watkins, Dawn L. 30p. (Orig.). (ps). 1990. pap. 4.95 (*0-89084-533-6*) Bob Jones Univ Pr.
Thompson, Dana, jt. illus. see Thompson, Del.
Thompson, Del. Wellsprings of Life: Understanding Proverbs. Orthner, Donald P. Minnick, Mark, pref. by. xii, 228p. (Orig.). (gr. 9 up). 1989. pap. 7.95 (*0-317-93833-9*) Adon Bks.
—Wetward, Whoa. Hughes, Francine. LC 93-83721. 32p. (Orig.). (ps-3). 1993. pap. 2.25 (*0-679-85281-6*) Random Bks Yng Read.
Thompson, Del & Thompson, Dana. The Myth of the Llama. Massi, Jeri. 118p. (Orig.). (gr. 6). 1989. pap. 5.95 (*1-877778-00-1*) Llama Bks.
Thompson, Del, et al. Tony Salerno's Good News Express. Salerno, Tony, et al. 64p. (Orig.). (gr. k-6). Date not set. pap. write for info. (*1-881597-00-8*) Magination CA.
Thompson, Eileen. Clues from the Past: A Resource Book on Archeology. Wheat, Pam & Whorton, Brenda, eds. LC 90-4991. 200p. (gr. 3 up). 1990. pap. 17.95 (*0-937460-65-6*) Hendrick-Long.
Thompson, Ellen. Choices. Scott, Elaine. LC 88-34537. 192p. (gr. 7 up). 1989. 12.95 (*0-688-07230-5*) Morrow Jr Bks.
—The Fighting Ground. Avi. LC 82-47719. 160p. (gr. 5 up). 1984. (Lipp Jr Bks); PLB 13.89 (*0-397-32074-4*, Lipp Jr Bks) HarpC Child Bks.
Thompson, Frances. Monterey Bay Aquarium Coloring Book. Thompson, Frances. Monterey Bay Aquarium Education Department Staff, ed. 16p. (Orig.). (gr. k-6). 1988. pap. 3.95 (*0-9604542-1-7*) Inkstone Books.

Thompson, George. As You Like It: Shakespeare for Everyone. Mulherin, Jennifer. LC 90-478. 32p. (gr. 3-7). 1990. PLB 12.95 (*0-87226-339-8*) P Bedrick Bks.
—Cobayos. Petty, Kate. LC 90-71412. (SPA). 24p. (gr. k-4). 1991. PLB 10.90 (*0-531-07914-7*) Watts.
—Gatos. Petty, Kate. LC 88-83087. (SPA). 24p. (gr. k-4). 1991. PLB 10.90 (*0-531-07916-3*) Watts.
—Hamsteres. Petty, Kate. LC 90-71413. (SPA). 24p. (gr. k-4). 1991. PLB 10.90 (*0-531-07913-9*) Watts.
—Hamsters. Petty, Kate. LC 89-50455. 32p. (gr. k-2). 1989. PLB 10.90 (*0-531-17159-0*, Gloucester Pr) Watts.
—Perros. Petty, Kate. (SPA). 24p. (gr. k-4). 1991. PLB 10.90 (*0-531-07915-5*) Watts.
—Romeo & Juliet. Mulherin, Jennifer. LC 87-37222. 32p. (gr. 6-12). 1988. 10.96 (*0-382-09688-6*) Silver Burdett Pr.
—Twelfth Night. Mulherin, Jennifer. 32p. (gr. 6-12). 1988. 10.96g (*0-382-09689-4*) Silver Burdett Pr.
Thompson, Gunnar. American Discovery: The Real Story. Thompson, Gunnar. 350p. (Orig.). (gr. 11). 1992. pap. 15.00 (*0-9621990-4-4*) Argonauts OTMI.
Thompson, Heidi. Reflections for Living Life Fully. Tully, Brock. 100p. (gr. 7 up). 1991. pap. 5.95 (*0-9693583-2-6*, Green Tiger) S&S Trade.
—Reflections for Sharing Dreams. Tully, Brock. 100p. (gr. 6 up). 1991. pap. 5.95 (*0-9693583-5-0*, Green Tiger) S&S Trade.
—Reflections for Someone Special. Tully, Brock. 100p. (gr. 6 up). 1991. 5.95 (*0-9693583-0-X*, Green Tiger) S&S Trade.
—Reflections for Touching Hearts. Tully, Brock. 100p. (gr. 6 up). 1991. pap. 5.95 (*0-9693583-3-4*, Green Tiger) S&S Trade.
Thompson, Jonathon. Witch Hazel's Whackey Adventures. Thompson, Jonathon J., Jr. 104p. (gr. 3-6). 1985. 5.95 (*0-933479-01-8*) Thompson.
Thompson, Judi. Honolulu Zoo Riddles. Johnson, Harriet. (ps-5). 1974. pap. 1.25 (*0-914916-07-6*) Topgallant.
Thompson, K. Dyble. My Name Is Maria Isabel. Ada, Alma F. Cerro, Ana M., tr. from SPA. LC 91-44910. 64p. (gr. 2-5). 1993. SBE 12.95 (*0-689-31517-1*, Atheneum Child Bk) Macmillan Child Grp.
Thompson, Karmen. Meet the Orchestra. Hayes, Ann. D'Andrade, Diane, ed. 32p. (ps-3). 1991. 13.95 (*0-15-200526-9*, Gulliver Bks) HarBrace.
Thompson, Mary. My Brother, Matthew. Thompson, Mary. LC 92-9858. 28p. (gr. k-6). 1992. 14.95 (*0-933149-47-6*) Woodbine House.
Thompson, Quentin, jt. illus. see Jones, Ken.
Thompson, Ralph. Chess-Dream in a Garden. Sutcliff, Rosemary. LC 92-54595. 48p. (ps up). 1993. 16.95 (*1-56402-192-0*) Candlewick Pr.
Thompson, Richard. Draw - & - Tell. Thompson, R. 88p. 1988. 19.95 (*1-55037-032-4*, Pub. by Annick CN) Firefly Bks Ltd.
—Frog's Riddle: And Other Draw-&-Tell Stories. Thompson, Richard. 96p. 1990. 19.95 (*1-55037-138-X*, Pub. by Annick CN) Firefly Bks Ltd.
Thompson, Sharon. Freya's Fantastic Surprise. Hathorn, Libby. 32p. (ps-3). 1989. 12.95 (*0-590-42442-4*, Scholastic Hardcover) Scholastic Inc.
Thompson, Timothy J. Figs & Nuts. Thompson, Timothy J. LC 80-83134. 15p. (Orig.). (ps-1). 1980. pap. text ed. 3.50 (*0-915676-03-6*) Ed Sys Pub.
—Ten Red Rods. Thompson, Timothy J. LC 80-83135. 16p. (Orig.). (ps-1). 1980. pap. text ed. 3.50 (*0-915676-02-8*) Ed Sys Pub.

Thompson, Tommy. Grandfather's Good Medicine. Walley, Deborah. Thorne, Kate & Callou, Nadia, eds. 72p. (Orig.). (gr. k up). 1993. pap. 9.95 (*0-9628329-6-0*) Thorne Enterprises. GRANDFATHER'S GOOD MEDICINE is a children's book for all ages; that is, a children's book that can be appreciated by adults as well as children. Its message is universal, its stories timeless & timely. It is a profound & poignant trilogy of stories containing an important message concerning man's relationship to his environment as seen through the Native American eye & expressed through the imagination of three non-native children. In each of the three parts, GRANDFATHER tells a story to a young person in modern times that parallels his or her current situation, taking us back to a time when white man was only a rumor & the people still roamed freely over the land. The highly entertaining & thought provoking stories are based on Native American folklore & the MEDICINE WHEEL WAY. Exquisitely illustrated by renowned Navajo artist Tommy

Thompson. This is a book to delight all ages. To order contact: THORNE ENTERPRISES, 149 Gambol Lane, Sedona, AZ 86336. (602) 282-7508. *Publisher Provided Annotation.*

Thomsen, Ernie. Good Grief! Good Grief! Nelson, JoAnne. LC 92-6685. 24p. (Orig.). (gr. k-2). 1993. pap. 5.95 (*0-935529-18-7*) Comprehen Health Educ.
—Our Friend, the Earth. Nelson, JoAnne. LC 92-37716. 1994. pap. 5.95 (*0-935529-59-4*) Comprehen Health Educ.
Thomson, Hugh. The Scarlet Letter. Hawthorne, Nathaniel. 312p. 1991. 9.99 (*0-517-64302-2*) Outlet Bk Co.
Thomson, Jenny. The Alice in Wonderland Pop-up. Carroll, Lewis. LC 80-7615. 12p. (gr. k-4). 1980. pap. 6.95 (*0-385-28038-6*) Delacorte.
Thornhill, Jan. Animal Legends. Thornhill, Jan, retold by. LC 93-20205. (gr. 1-3). 1993. pap. 15.00 (*0-671-87428-4*, S&S BFYR) S&S Trade.
Thornley, Jean, jt. illus. see Paris, Pat.
Thornton, John H. Mentor Wisdom: Requisites for Living. Mills-Thornton, Serena G. Allen, Sharon, ed. 31p. (Orig.). 1993. write for info. (*0-9614338-0-9*) Ideas.
Thornton, Peter. Daisy. Powell, E. Sandy. 40p. (gr. 1-4). 1991. PLB 13.50 (*0-87614-449-0*) Carolrhoda Bks.
—Everybody Cooks Rice. Dooley, Norah. 32p. (ps-3). 1991. PLB 18.95 (*0-87614-412-1*) Carolrhoda Bks.
—A Natural Man: The True Story of John Henry. Sanfield, Steve. LC 85-45965. 32p. (gr. 2-6). 1990. pap. 9.95 (*0-87923-844-5*) Godine.
Thornton, Shelley. Three Little Kittens. Marzollo, Jean. 32p. (Orig.). (ps-k). 1986. pap. 2.50 (*0-590-43713-5*) Scholastic Inc.
Thorpe, Jean J. Kirtpatrick's Kritters. Thorpe, Jean J. 50p. (gr. k-6). 1988. pap. 7.95 (*0-317-93347-7*) Art & Earth.
Thorpe, Karen E. Life after Survival: A Therapeutic Approach for Adult Children of Alcoholics. Mansmann, Patricia A. & Neuhausel, Patricia A. Bowden, Julie & Gravitz, Herbertfrwd. by. 56p. (gr. 9 up). 1986. pap. text ed. 6.95 (*0-940967-00-6*) Genesis Pub PA.
Thrall, Mary. Reading Stories, Grades 3-4. Hoffman, James. Hoffman, Joan, ed. 32p. (gr. 3-4). 1979. wkbk. 1.99 (*0-938256-13-0*) Sch Zone Pub Co.
Thrall, Sidney. Computers & Children, Bk. I. Singletary, Helen P. & Glover, Zebrena M. 81p. (Orig.). 1991. pap. text ed. 20.00 (*1-880850-01-X*) Comp Trng Clinic.
Threadgall, Colin. Dinosaur Fright. Threadgall, Colin. LC 91-40049. 32p. (ps up). 1993. 15.00 (*0-688-11733-3*, Tambourine Bks); PLB 14.93 (*0-688-11734-1*, Tambourine Bks) Morrow.
Thrun, Rick. Talking. Allington, Richard L. & Krull, Kathleen. LC 80-17021. 32p. (ps-2). 1985. pap. 3.95 (*0-8114-8234-0*) Raintree Steck-V.
Tiano, Bethoven. Si Wayt at Ang Kanyang Mga Kaibigan. Bayles, Miriam. (TAG.). 35p. (Orig.). (gr. k-2). 1990. pap. 4.00x (*971-10-0416-X*, Pub. by New Day Pub PI) Cellar.
Tibo, Gilles. The Beast. Bartels, Alice. 32p. (ps-2). 1990. 14.95 (*1-55037-101-0*, Pub. by Annick CN); pap. 5.95 (*1-55037-102-9*, Pub. by Annick CN) Firefly Bks Ltd.
—Giant. Munsch, Robert. 32p. (gr. k-3). 1989. PLB 15.95 (*1-550370-71-5*, Pub. by Annick CN); pap. 5.95 (*1-550370-70-7*, Pub. by Annick CN) Firefly Bks Ltd.
—Maria Chapdelaine. Hemon, Louis. Brown, Alan, tr. from FRE. Carrier, Roch, intro. by. LC 89-50775. 96p. (gr. 6 up). 1989. Repr. of 1914 ed. 29.95 (*0-88776-236-0*) Tundra Bks.
—Maria Chapdelaine. Hemon, Louis. LC 89-50775. 192p. 1991. pap. 9.95 (*0-88776-242-5*) Tundra Bks.
—Paper Nights. Tibo, Gilles. 32p. 1992. PLB 15.95 (*1-55037-225-4*, Pub. by Annick CN); pap. 5.95 (*1-55037-224-6*, Pub. by Annick CN) Firefly Bks Ltd.
—Pikolo: Le Secret du Garde-Robe (Paper Nights in French) Tibo, Gilles. (FRE.). 32p. (Orig.). (ps-6). 1992. PLB 15.95 (*1-55037-227-0*, Pub. by Annick CN); pap. 5.95 (*1-55037-226-2*, Pub. by Annick CN) Firefly Bks Ltd.
—Simon & the Boxes. Tibo, Gilles. LC 92-80416. 24p. (gr. k-4). 1992. PLB 10.95 (*0-88776-287-5*) Tundra Bks.
—Simon & the Snowflakes. Tibo, Gilles. LC 88-50259. 24p. (ps-4). 1991. pap. 4.95 (*0-88776-274-3*) Tundra Bks.
—Simon & the Wind. Tibo, Gilles. LC 89-50777. 24p. (gr. k-4). 1989. 10.95 (*0-88776-234-4*) Tundra Bks.
—Simon & the Wind. Tibo, Gilles. LC 89-50776. 24p. (ps-4). 1991. pap. 4.95 (*0-88776-276-X*) Tundra Bks.
—Simon Au Clair De Lune. Tibo, Gilles. LC 93-60333. 24p. (gr. k up). 1993. 10.95 (*0-88776-317-0*) Tundra Bks.
—Simon Celebra la Primavera (Simon Welcomes Spring) Tibo, Gilles. Salazar, Arturo, tr. from ENG. LC 92-85471. (SPA.). 24p. (Orig.). (gr. k-3). 1993. pap. 5.95 (*0-88776-297-2*) Tundra Bks.
—Simon en Verano. Tibo, Gilles. Salazar, Arturo, tr. from ENG. LC 92-85470. (SPA.). 24p. (Orig.). (gr. k-3). Date not set. pap. 5.95 (*0-88776-298-0*) Tundra Bks.
—Simon et le Vent d'Automne. Tibo, Gilles. LC 89-50776. (FRE.). 24p. (gr. k-4). 1989. 10.95 (*0-88776-235-2*) Tundra Bks.

—Simon in the Moonlight. Tibo, Gilles. LC 93-60334. 24p. (gr. k up). 1993. 10.95 (*0-88776-316-2*) Tundra Bks.

—Simon Welcomes Spring. Tibo, Gilles. LC 90-70132. 24p. (gr. k-4). 1990. 10.95 (*0-88776-247-6*) Tundra Bks.

Tiefenthal, Colleen. Martian Goo. Salem, Lynn & Stewart, Josie. 8p. (gr. 1). 1993. pap. 3.50 (*1-880612-13-5*) Seedling Pubns.

Tiegreen. Pat-a-Cake & Other Play Rhymes. Cole, Joanna & Calmenson, Stephanie. ALC Staff, ed. LC 91-32264. 48p. (ps up). 1992. pap. 6.95 (*0-688-11533-0*, Mulberry) Morrow.

Tiegreen, Alan. The Beezus & Ramona Diary. Cleary, Beverly. 224p. (gr. 5-7). 1986. pap. 9.95 (*0-688-06353-5*, Pub. by Beech Tree Bks) Morrow.

—Bobby Baseball. Smith, Robert K. (gr. 3-7). 1989. 13.95 (*0-385-29807-2*) Delacorte.

—Crazy Eights & Other Card Games. Cole, Joanna & Calmenson, Stephanie. LC 93-5427. 1994. write for info. (*0-688-12199-3*); PLB write for info. (*0-688-12200-0*); pap. write for info. (*0-688-12201-9*) Morrow Jr Bks.

—Grounded for Life? Simmons, Alex. DeMasco, Steve, created by. LC 93-22061. 64p. (gr. 1-4). 1993. PLB 9.59t (*0-8167-3102-0*); pap. 2.50 (*0-8167-3103-9*) Troll Assocs.

—Hello Huckleberry Heights. Delton, Judy. (Orig.). 1990. pap. 2.95 (*0-440-40304-9*) Dell.

—Kelly's Creek. Smith, Doris B. LC 75-6761. 80p. (gr. 4-6). 1989. PLB 13.89 (*0-690-04774-6*, Crowell Jr Bks) HarpC Child Bks.

—Lights, Action, Land-Ho! Delton, Judy. 80p. (Orig.). (gr. 1-4). 1992. pap. 3.25 (*0-440-40732-X*, YB) Dell.

—Merry Merry Huckleberry. Delton, Judy. (Orig.). 1990. pap. 2.95 (*0-440-40365-0*, Pub. by Yearling Classics) Dell.

—Pat a Cake: And Other Play Phymes. Cole, Joanna & Calmenson, Stephanie. LC 91-32264. 48p. (ps). 1992. 14.00 (*0-688-11038-X*); PLB 13.93 (*0-688-11039-8*) Morrow Jr Bks.

—Pee Wees on Parade. Delton, Judy. 80p. (ps-3). 1992. pap. 2.99 (*0-440-40461-4*, YB) Dell.

—Pin the Tail on the Donkey & Other Party Games. Cole, Joanna & Calmenson, Stephanie. LC 92-29786. 48p. (ps up). 1993. 15.00 (*0-688-11891-7*); PLB 14.93 (*0-688-11892-5*); pap. 6.95 (*0-688-12521-2*) Morrow Jr Bks.

—The Pooped Troop. Delton, Judy. 80p. (ps-3). 1989. pap. 3.25 (*0-440-40184-4*, YB) Dell.

—Ramona & Her Father. Cleary, Beverly. LC 77-1614. 192p. (gr. 3-7). 1977. 13.95 (*0-688-22114-9*); PLB 13.88 (*0-688-32114-3*) Morrow Jr Bks.

—Ramona, Forever. Cleary, Beverly. LC 84-704. 192p. (gr. 3-7). 1984. 13.95 (*0-688-03785-2*); PLB 13.88 (*0-688-03786-0*, Morrow Jr Bks) Morrow Jr Bks.

—Ramona Quimby, Age Eight. Cleary, Beverly. LC 80-28425. 192p. (gr. 4-6). 1981. 13.95 (*0-688-00477-6*); PLB 13.88 (*0-688-00478-4*) Morrow Jr Bks.

—Ramona Quimby, Age Eight. Cleary, Beverly. 192p. (gr. 3-7). 1982. pap. 3.25 (*0-440-47350-0*, YB) Dell.

—Ramona Quimby, Age 8. large type ed. Cleary, Beverly. 142p. (gr. 2-6). 1987. Repr. of 1981 ed. lib. bdg. 14.95 (*1-55736-000-6*, Crnrstn Bks) BDD LT Grp.

—The Ramona Quimby Diary. Cleary, Beverly. 160p. (gr. 3-7). 1984. pap. 10.95 spiral bdg. (*0-688-03883-2*, Pub. by Beech Tree Bks) Morrow.

—Ramona the Brave. Cleary, Beverly. LC 74-16494. 192p. (gr. 3-7). 1975. 13.95 (*0-688-22015-0*); PLB 13.88 (*0-688-32015-5*) Morrow Jr Bks.

—Ramona the Brave. Cleary, Beverly. 192p. (gr. k-6). 1984. pap. 3.25 (*0-440-47351-9*, YB) Dell.

—Rosy Noses, Freezing Toes. Delton, Judy. (Orig.). 1990. pap. 2.99 (*0-440-40384-7*, YB) Dell.

—Scary, Scary Huckleberry. Delton, Judy. (Orig.). (gr. k-6). 1990. pap. 2.95 (*0-440-40336-7*, YB) Dell.

—Silver Woven in My Hair. Murphy, Shirley R. LC 91-23144. 128p. (gr. 3-7). 1992. pap. 3.95 (*0-689-71525-0*, Aladdin) Macmillan Child Grp.

—Six Sick Sheep: One Hundred One Tongue Twisters. Cole, Joanna & Calmenson, Stephanie. LC 92-5715. 64p. (gr. 3 up). 1993. 15.00 (*0-688-11139-4*); PLB 14.93 (*0-688-11140-8*) Morrow Jr Bks.

—Spring Sprouts. Delton, Judy. 80p. (Orig.). (gr. k-6). 1989. pap. 3.25 (*0-440-40160-7*, YB) Dell.

—Summer Showdown. Delton, Judy. (Orig.). 1990. pap. 2.95 (*0-440-40307-3*) Dell.

—We Want to Win! De Masco, Steve & Simmons, Alex. LC 91-40935. 64p. (gr. 1-4). 1993. text ed. 9.59 (*0-8167-3100-4*); tchr's. ed. 2.50 (*0-8167-3101-2*) Troll Assocs.

Tieman, Peggy. Seven Ears of Corn. Harman, Betty & Meador, Nancy, eds. 149p. (gr. 5-9). 1991. pap. 6.00 (*0-9630661-0-2*) Harman & Meador.

Tien. The Night Before Christmas. Moore, Clement C. 32p. (ps-1). 1986. pap. 5.95 (*0-671-62209-9*, Little Simon) S&S Trade.

Tikka, Saara. The Journey of Pietari & His Wolf. Helakisa, Kaarina. Rollerson, Michael, tr. from SWE. LC 84-80571. 72p. (gr. 7-12). 1991. pap. 12.95 (*0-88138-043-1*, Green Tiger) S&S Trade.

Till, Tom. Troll's Christmas. Wolf, Jill. 24p. (gr. 3-7). 1981. pap. 2.50 (*0-89954-460-6*) Antioch Pub Co.

Time-Life Books Staff. Barnyard Babies: Oink, Baa, Moo, Meow, Neigh, Peep. Time-Life Books Editors. Marshall, Blaine, ed. 6p. (ps). 1993. 16.95 (*0-8094-6692-9*) Time-Life.

Timmins, Harry L. & Gardner, Donald. The Pickering Collection: Neighbors Have My Ducks, Merry Xmas, Mr. Williams Dog Days on Trout Waters & Angling of the Test. Pickering, H. G. 189p. (gr. 10 up). 1993. Repr. of 1933 ed. 40.00 (*1-56416-047-5*) Derrydale Pr.

Timmons, Bonnie. Professor Curious & the Mystery of the Hiking Dinosaurs. Gil, Yvonne. LC 90-42592. 24p. (gr. 1-5). 1991. 13.95 (*0-517-58025-X*, Clarkson Potter); PLB 14.99 (*0-517-58178-7*, C N Potter Bks) Crown Bks Yng Read.

Timms, Diann. Matty's Midnight Monster. Kemp, Gene. 32p. (ps up). 1991. bds. 14.95 (*0-571-14336-9*) Faber & Faber.

Timyan, Janis. A Happy Day for Ramona & Other Missionary Stories for Children. LC 87-71018. (Orig.). (gr. 1-5). 1987. pap. 3.99 (*0-87509-392-2*) Chr Pubns.

—The Pink & Green Church & Other Missionary Stories for Children. LC 87-71019. (gr. 1-5). 1988. pap. 3.99 (*0-87509-393-0*) Chr Pubns.

Tindal, Pauline. Say Another One about How I Feel. Pendergast, Kathleen. LC 81-90678. 54p. (org.). (gr. k-6). 1982. pap. 6.95 (*0-942178-00-9*) Madison Park Pr.

—Say Another One about My Family. Pendergast, Kathleen. LC 82-61139. 54p. (gr. k-6). 1982. pap. 6.95 (*0-942178-01-7*) Madison Park Pr.

Tinkelman, Murray. Sharks. McGovern, Ann. 48p. (gr. k-3). 1987. pap. 2.50 (*0-590-41360-0*) Scholastic Inc.

Tinkleman, Murray. Dinosaurs. Hopkins, Lee B. 47p. (ps-3). 1987. 12.95 (*0-15-223495-0*) HarBrace.

Tiritilli, Jerry. The Pagemaster. Kirschner, David. 128p. (gr. 4 up). 1993. 19.95 (*1-878685-43-0*) Turner Pub GA.

Tirtitilli, Jerry. King Arthur. Pyle, Howard. Hinkle, Don, ed. LC 87-15461. 48p. (gr. 3-6). 1988. PLB 12.89 (*0-8167-1213-1*); pap. 3.95 (*0-8167-1214-X*) Troll Assocs.

Tisserand, Rose-Ann & Huculak, Greg. The Weirdest, Wackiest, Craziest Practical Joke Book in the Universe. Messerly, Laura. LC 90-24598. 96p. (gr. 2-10). 1991. pap. 3.95 (*0-8069-8258-6*) Sterling.

Titherington, Jeanne. Big World, Small World. Titherington, Jeanne. LC 84-4140. 24p. (ps-1). 1985. 11.75 (*0-688-04022-5*); PLB 11.88 (*0-688-04023-3*) GreenWillow.

—Child's Prayer. Titherington, Jeanne. LC 88-16566. 24p. (ps up). 1989. 13.95 (*0-688-08317-X*); PLB 13.88 (*0-688-08318-8*) Greenwillow.

—It's Snowing! It's Snowing! Prelutsky, Jack. LC 83-16583. 48p. (gr. 1-3). 1984. 12.95 (*0-688-01512-3*); PLB 14.93 (*0-688-01513-1*) Greenwillow.

—A Place for Ben. Titherington, Jeanne. LC 86-7656. 24p. (ps-3). 1987. 11.95 (*0-688-06493-0*); PLB 11.88 (*0-688-06494-9*) Greenwillow.

—Pumpkin, Pumpkin. Titherington, Jeanne. LC 84-25334. 24p. (ps-1). 1986. 13.95 (*0-688-05695-4*); PLB 13.88 (*0-688-05696-2*) Greenwillow.

Titolo, Nancy. Confessions for Kids. Harrison House Staff. 29p. (Orig.). (gr. 1-3). 1984. pap. 0.98 (*0-89274-322-0*) Harrison Hse.

—God Are You Really Real? Burgess, Beverly C. 30p. (Orig.). (gr. 1-3). 1985. pap. 1.98 (*0-89274-309-3*) Harrison Hse.

—Is Easter Just for Bunnies? Burgess, Beverly C. 30p. (Orig.). (gr. 1-3). 1985. pap. 1.98 (*0-89274-310-7*) Harrison Hse.

Titra, Stephen. Harvest: A Faithful Approach to Life Issues for Junior High People. Ristow, Kate S. & Comeaux, Maureen N. 167p. (gr. 6-8). 1984. pap. 24.50 (*0-940634-20-1*) Puissance Pubns.

Tjong Khing. The Big Fish. Kordon, Klaus. Hattery-Beyer, Lynn, tr. from GER. LC 91-28467. 32p. (ps-3). 1992. 13.95 (*0-02-750945-1*, Macmillan Child Bk) Macmillan Child Grp.

Tobias, Jerry J. Imma Drug. Tobias, Jerry J. 70p. (ps-6). Date not set. pap. write for info. (*1-880017-12-1*) Teddy Bear Pr.

—Imma Fish: And Other Related Poems. Tobias, Jerry J. (Orig.). (ps-6). 1993. pap. 5.95 (*1-880017-13-X*) Teddy Bear Pr.

Tobin, Patricia. Good Sports: Plain Talk about Health & Fitness for Teens. Simon, Nissa. LC 89-78556. 128p. (gr. 7 up). 1990. 13.95 (*0-690-04902-1*, Crowell Jr Bks); PLB 13.89 (*0-690-04904-8*, Crowell Jr Bks) HarpC Child Bks.

—The Riddle of the Rosetta Stone. Giblin, James. LC 89-29289. 96p. (gr. 3-7). 1993. pap. 5.95 (*0-06-446137-8*, Trophy) HarpC Child Bks.

Todd, Amy. Wonders of Water. Silvani, Harold. 43p. (gr. 4-12). 1988. wkbk. 6.95 (*1-878669-29-X*, CTA-6552) Crea Tea Assocs.

Todd, Barbara. Ballet Dancer. Craig, Janet. LC 88-10043. 32p. (gr. k-3). 1989. PLB 10.89 (*0-8167-1434-7*); pap. text ed. 2.95 (*0-8167-1435-5*) Troll Assocs.

—What Is Loving? McCaw, Mabel. 12p. (ps). 1987. 3.25 (*0-8378-5208-0*) Gibson.

Todd, Frank S., photos by. The Sea World Book of Penguins. Todd, Frank S. LC 80-25588. 96p. (gr. 4-7). 1984. pap. 9.95 (*0-15-271951-2*, Voyager Bks) HarBrace.

Todd, Janette. My Pet Crocodile: And Other Slightly Outrageous Verse. Billings, John. LC 93-72718. 128p. (gr. k-12). 1993. 16.95 (*1-884035-55-8*) Chokecherry.

Todd, Justin. Alice's Adventures in Wonderland. Carroll, Lewis. LC 82-242973. 160p. (gr. 3 up). 1984. 3.99 (*0-517-55591-3*) Outlet Bk Co.

—The Owl & the Pussy Cat. Lear, Edward. 32p. 1992. 15.95 (*0-575-04709-7*, Pub. by Gollancz UK) Trafalgar.

Todd, Justin, photos by. The Starlight Cloak. Nimmo, Jenny, retold by. LC 92-26186. (ps-3). 1993. 14.99 (*0-8037-1508-0*) Dial Bks Young.

Todd, Linda. The Marin Mountain Bike Guide. 2nd ed. Todd, Armor. 80p. (gr. 9-12). 1989. pap. 8.95t (*0-9623537-0-1*) A Todd.

Todd, Robert. Wilderness Pioneer: Stephen F. Austin of Texas. Hoff, Carol. LC 55-7501. 192p. (gr. 4-8). 1987. Repr. of 1955 ed. PLB 13.95 (*0-937460-25-7*) Hendrick-Long.

Todd, Thomas. Stanley, the Talking Parrot. Robinson, Ronald W. LC 89-60801. 22p. (Orig.). (gr. 3-4). 1989. Incl. cassette & filmstrip pkg. 12.95 (*0-9622692-2-0*); Incl. cassette pkg. 8.95 (*0-9622692-1-2*); pap. 4.95 (*0-9622692-0-4*) R W Robinson.

Toddy, Irving. Uncegila's Seventh Spot: A Dakota Legend. Rubalcaba, Jill, retold by. LC 93-33350. 1995. write for info. (*0-395-68970-8*, Clarion Bks) HM.

Toft, Lis. Girl Wonder & the Terrific Twins. Blackman, Malorie. LC 92-27667. (gr. 2-5). 1993. 12.99 (*0-525-45065-3*, DCB) Dutton Child Bks.

Tofts, Hannah. The Party Book. James, Diane. LC 93-21219. 48p. (gr. 4-8). 1994. 16.95 (*1-56847-135-1*) Thomson Lrning.

Tofts, Hannah & Barnes, Jon. Do-It-Yourself. Watts, Clare, et al. LC 93-21218. 48p. (gr. 3-7). 1994. 16.95 (*1-56847-147-5*) Thomson Lrning.

Toht, Don. I Like Being Alone. Wright, Betty R. Okun, Barbara F., intro. by. LC 80-25513. 32p. (gr. k-6). 1981. PLB 17.96 (*0-8172-1367-8*) Raintree Steck-V.

—Sherlock Holmes. Doyle, Arthur Conan. Stewart, Diana, adapted by. LC 79-24106. 48p. (gr. 4 up). 1983. PLB 18.64 (*0-8172-1657-X*) Raintree Steck-V.

Tolenen, Susan. Noises in the Night. Turk, Ruth. LC 93-1167. 1993. write for info. (*0-8368-0673-5*) Time-Life.

Tolford, Joshua. Singing Games & Playparty Games. Chase, Richard. 63p. (gr. 1-4). 1949. pap. 2.50 (*0-486-21785-X*) Dover.

—Singing Games & Playparty Games. Chase, Richard. Rufty, Hilton, contrib. by. (gr. 4-8). 16.50 (*0-8446-4721-7*) Peter Smith.

Tolley, Lynn & Olds, Tom. Sugar Princess. Katherine, Sharon. Wood, Paul, ed. 31p. 1989. pap. 8.95 (*0-685-68779-1*) Jungle Pr. On a lush tropical island, a lonely voice cries out. Here in this one spot, the land has become parched, cracked & barren. The forces of nature gather around -- the wind, the water, the plants & animals -- & they listen to the lonely voice calling. She cannot come out & play, for she has no "Self." In sympathy, all natural elements work together, each contributing a gift to the lonely voice. The flowers give their colors, the mountain its strength, the moon its brilliance, & so on. In the end, the little voice steps forth in her true condition, a beautiful Sugar Princess! This brilliantly illustrated read-aloud story, which includes a color-it-yourself poster, is the first in a series of "Sharon Katherine" books by author Sharon Morneau. (Jungle Press, P.O. Box 1058, Makawao, HI 96768. (808) 572-3453. FAX: (808) 572-4886.) In this simple tale of transformation, children see the forces of nature working together to create beauty. They learn about cooperation & respect for the environment. By means of the book's glossary, they also learn a few Hawaiian words & the names of various tropical plants & animals. *Publisher Provided Annotation.*

Tolpo, Lily. Frontier Adventures: Stories in Verse of Young People in Kentucky & the South West. Vickery, Eugene L. Vickery, Millie M., ed. 40p. (Orig.). (gr. 1-8). 1987. pap. 4.95 perfect bdg. (*0-937775-06-1*) Stonehaven Pubs.

—New Friends in a New World: Thanksgiving Story of Children with New Friends. Vickery, Eugene L. 20p. (Orig.). (gr. k-8). 1986. pap. 1.95 (*0-937775-03-7*) Stonehaven Pubs.

—The Ramiluk Stories: Adventures of an Eskimo Family in the Prehistoric Arctic. Vickery, Eugene L. 124p. (Orig.). (gr. 5 up). 1989. 16.00 (*0-937775-11-8*); pap. 10.95 (*0-937775-10-X*) Stonehaven Pubs.

Tom, Darcy. Choosing. Sanders, Corinne. 64p. (gr. 3-8). 1985. wkbk. 7.95 (*0-86653-333-8*, GA 677) Good Apple.
—Cooperating. McElmurry, Mary A. 64p. (gr. 3-8). 1985. wkbk. 7.95 (*0-86653-334-6*, GA 680) Good Apple.
—Living. Carswell, Evelyn & Bisignano, Judy. 64p. (gr. 3-8). 1985. wkbk. 7.95 (*0-86653-332-X*, GA 679) Good Apple.
—Practical Math Skills - Intermediate Level. Duncan, Jim. 64p. (gr. 4-6). 1989. wkbk. 7.95 (*0-86653-465-2*, GA1070) Good Apple.
—Practical Math Skills - Junior High Level. Duncan, Jim. 64p. (gr. 7-9). 1989. wkbk. 7.95 (*0-86653-466-0*, GA1071) Good Apple.
—Practical Math Skills - Primary Level. Duncan, Jim. 64p. (gr. 1-3). 1989. wkbk. 7.95 (*0-86653-464-4*, GA1069) Good Apple.
—Relating. Bisignano, Judy. 64p. (gr. 3-8). 1985. wkbk. 7.95 (*0-86653-331-1*, GA 678) Good Apple.
Tom, Linda, jt. illus. see Peters, Patricia.
Tom, Linda C. Fire Fighter Brown. Bornstein, Harry. 16p. (ps). 1976. pap. 3.50 (*0-913580-50-3*, Pub. by K Green Pubns) Gallaudet Univ Pr.
Tom, Linda C., jt. illus. see Peters, Patricia.
Tom, Tiana. Creative Writing Patterns. Smith, Mary D. & Smith, Brad. 48p. (gr. k-4). 1983. wkbk. 5.95 (*1-55734-130-3*) Tchr Create Mat.

Tomblin, Gill. Cenicienta (Cinderella) Hayes, Sarah. Puncel, Maria, tr. from ENG. (SPA.). 32p. (gr. 2-4). 1990. Incl. cass. 11.95 (*84-372-8055-9*) Santillana. Beautifully illustrated version of the traditional story in Spanish. A cassette with original music & dramatic narrations presented by Alma Flor Ada & Suni Paz accompanies the storybook. Two other stories are also included in the collection: JUAN EL VAGO (Lazy Jack) & LA REINA DE LAS ABEJAS (Queen Bee). To order: Santillana, 901 W. Walnut, Compton, CA 90220. Telephone: 1-310-763-0455. *Publisher Provided Annotation.*

—Make Your Own Coral Reef: Includes Giant Three-Dimensional Press-Out Model. Wells, Sue. Johnston, Damian, designed by. 18p. (gr. 3-7). 1994. 13.99 (*0-525-67461-6*, Lodestar Bks) Dutton Child Bks.
—Make Your Own Rain Forest. Johnston, Damian, concept by. & contrib. by. 18p. (gr. 3-7). 1993. incl. kit 12.95 (*0-525-67409-8*, Lodestar Bks) Dutton Child Bks.
—Small & Furry Animals: A Watercolor Sketchbook of Mammals in the Wild. Tomblin, Gill. 64p. (gr. 2-5). 1992. 14.95 (*0-399-22122-0*, Putnam) Putnam Pub Group.
Tomei, Lorna. Jungle Safari. Packard, Edward. 51p. (gr. 4). 1983. pap. 2.25 (*0-553-15403-6*) Bantam.
—Just Between Us. Pfeffer, Susan B. LC 79-53606. 128p. (gr. 4-6). 1980. pap. 9.89 (*0-385-28594-9*) Delacorte.
—Rosie & Michael. Viorst, Judith. LC 74-75571. 40p. (gr. 1-4). 1974. SBE 13.95 (*0-689-30439-0*, Atheneum Child Bk) Macmillan Child Grp.
—Rosie & Michael. 2nd ed. Viorst, Judith. LC 86-13969. 40p. (gr. 1-4). 1988. pap. 3.95 (*0-689-71272-3*, Aladdin) Macmillan Child Grp.
—What Do You Do When Your Mouth Won't Open? Pfeffer, Susan B. LC 80-68731. 160p. (gr. 4-6). 1981. 8.95 (*0-440-09471-2*); pap. 9.89 (*0-385-29140-X*) Delacorte.
Tomes, Margot. And Then What Happened, Paul Revere? Fritz, Jean. 48p. (gr. 2-6). 1973. 13.95 (*0-698-20274-0*, Coward); pap. 6.95 (*0-698-20541-3*) Putnam Pub Group.
—Anna, Grandpa & the Big Storm. Stevens, Carla. 48p. (gr. 6-9). 1982. 13.45 (*0-89919-066-9*, Clarion Bks) HM.
—Anna, Grandpa, & the Big Storm. Stevens, Carla. 64p. (gr. 1-4). 1986. (Puffin); pap. 3.99 (*0-14-031705-8*, Puffin) Puffin Bks.
—Birthday Poems. Livingston, Myra C. LC 89-2114. 32p. (ps-3). 1989. reinforced bdg. 13.95 (*0-8234-0783-7*) Holiday.
—By George, Bloomers! St. George, Judith. LC 89-17898. 48p. (gr. 1-4). 1989. pap. 5.95 (*1-55870-135-4*) Shoe Tree Pr.
—Chimney Sweeps. Giblin, James C. LC 81-43878. 64p. (gr. 4-8). 1982. (Crowell Jr Bks) (Crowell Jr Bks) HarpC Child Bks.
—Chimney Sweeps: Yesterday & Today. Giblin, James C. LC 81-43878. 64p. (gr. 4-7). 1987. pap. 5.95 (*0-06-446061-4*, Trophy) HarpC Child Bks.
—Everything Glistens & Everything Sings. Zolotow, Charlotte. LC 86-31917. 96p. (ps-3). 1987. 11.95 (*0-15-226488-4*, HB Juv Bks) HarBrace.
—The Fisherman & His Wife. Stewig, John W., retold by. LC 88-1698. 32p. (ps-3). 1988. reinforced bdg. 13.95 (*0-8234-0714-4*) Holiday.
—Homesick: My Own Story. Fritz, Jean. 160p. (gr. 3-7). 1982. 14.95 (*0-399-20933-6*, Putnam) Putnam Pub Group.

—The Lap-Time Song & Play Book. Yolen, Jane, compiled by. Stemple, Adam, contrib. by. 28p. (p up). 1989. 15.95 (*0-15-243588-3*) HarBrace.
—Little Sister & the Month Brothers. De Regniers, Beatrice S. LC 75-4594. 48p. (ps-3). 1976. 8.95 (*0-8164-3147-7*, Clarion Bks) HM.
—New Year's Poems. Livingston, Myra C., selected by. LC 86-22885. 32p. (ps-3). 1987. reinforced bdg. 12.95 (*0-8234-0641-5*) Holiday.
—A Norse Lullaby. Van Vorst, M. L. LC 87-31058. 32p. (ps-1). 1988. 12.95 (*0-688-05812-4*); PLB 12.88 (*0-688-05813-2*) Lothrop.
—The Secret of the Sachem's Tree. Monjo, F. N. 64p. (gr. 1-5). 1973. pap. 0.75 (*0-440-47634-8*, Yearling) Dell.
—The Shadowmaker. Hansen, Ron. LC 85-45272. 80p. (gr. 2-6). 1987. PLB 10.89 (*0-06-022203-4*) HarpC Child Bks.
—The Shadowmaker. Hansen, Ron. LC 85-45272. 80p. (gr. 2-6). 1990. pap. 3.95 (*0-06-440287-8*, Trophy) HarpC Child Bks.
—Snowy Day: Stories & Poems. Bauer, Caroline F., ed. LC 85-45858. 80p. (gr. 2-5). 1986. (Lipp Jr Bks); PLB 13.89 (*0-397-32177-5*) HarpC Child Bks.
—Snowy Day: Stories & Poems. Bauer, Caroline F., ed. LC 85-45858. 80p. (gr. 2-5). 1992. pap. 3.95 (*0-06-446123-8*, Trophy) HarpC Child Bks.
—A Song I Sang to You: A Selection of Poems. Livingston, Myra C. LC 84-4585. 84p. (ps-3). 1984. 12.95 (*0-15-277105-0*, HB Juv Bks) HarBrace.
—Stone Soup. Stewig, John W., retold by. LC 90-46502. 32p. (ps-3). 1991. reinforced 14.95 (*0-8234-0863-9*) Holiday.
—This Time, Tempe Wick? Gauch, Patricia L. 48p. (gr. 1-4). 1992. 12.95 (*0-399-21880-7*, Putnam) Putnam Pub Group.
—Ty's One-Man Band. Walter, Mildred P. 48p. (gr. k-3). 1984. pap. 3.95 (*0-590-40178-5*) Scholastic Inc.
—Ty's One-Man Band. Walter, Mildred P. LC 80-11224. 32p. (gr. k-3). 1987. Repr. of 1980 ed. RSBE 14.95 (*0-02-792300-2*, Pub. by Four Winds Pr) Macmillan Child Grp.
—Where Do You Think You're Going, Christopher Columbus? Fritz, Jean. 80p. (gr. 3-7). 1981. (Putnam); pap. 7.95 (*0-399-20734-1*, Putnam) Putnam Pub Group.
—Where Was Patrick Henry on the 29th of May? Fritz, Jean. 48p. (gr. 3-5). 1982. 13.95 (*0-698-20307-0*, Coward); pap. 6.95 (*0-698-20544-8*, Coward) Putnam Pub Group.
—Witch Hazel. Schertle, Alice. LC 90-39630. 32p. (gr. k-4). 1991. 15.00 (*0-06-025140-9*); PLB 14.89 (*0-06-025141-7*) HarpC Child Bks.
Tomkins, Jasper. My Cousin Has Eight Legs. Tomkins, Jasper. 40p. (Orig.). 1992. pap. 9.95 (*0-912365-68-4*) Sasquatch Bks.
Tomlinson, Albert. Talk to God... I'll Get the Message: Catholic Version. Geller, Norman. 23p. (gr. 1-4). 1983. pap. 4.95 (*0-915753-03-0*) N Geller Pub.
Tomlinson, Albert J. I Don't Want to Visit Grandma Anymore. Geller, Norman. 28p. (gr. 1-4). 1984. pap. 4.95 (*0-915753-05-7*) N Geller Pub.
—Talk to God... I'll Get the Message: Black Version. Geller, Norman. 23p. (gr. 1-4). 1985. pap. 4.95 (*0-915753-08-1*) N Geller Pub.
—Talk to God... I'll Get the Message: Jewish Version. Geller, Norman. 23p. (gr. 1-4). 1983. pap. 4.95 (*0-915753-02-2*) N Geller Pub.
—Talk to God... I'll Get the Message: Protestant Version. Geller, Norman. 23p. (gr. 1-4). 1983. pap. 4.95 (*0-915753-04-9*) N Geller Pub.
—Talk to God... I'll Get the Message: Spanish Version. Geller, Norman. Galway, Bonnie, tr. from ENG. 23p. (gr. 1-4). 1985. pap. 4.95 (*0-915753-07-3*) N Geller Pub.
Tomoko. A Peek at Japan: A Lighthearted Look at Japan's Language & Culture. 2nd, rev. ed. Metcalf, Florence E. 133p. (gr. 1-5). 1992. pap. text ed. 14.95 (*0-9631684-3-6*) Metco Pub.
Tomonari, Itsuko. Counting. Jonson, Liz & Silliman, Emery. Nayer, Judith E., ed. 32p. (gr. k-1). 1991. wkbk. 1.95 (*1-878624-54-7*) McClanahan Bk.
Tomova, Veselina. A Dozen Silk Diapers. Kajpust, Melissa. 32-41937. 32p. (ps-2). 1993. 13.95 (*1-56282-456-2*); PLB 13.89 (*1-56282-457-0*) Hyprn Child.
Tompkins, Ptolemy. Big Cats, Little Cats. American Society for the Prevention of Cruelty to Animals Staff. 48p. (Orig.). (gr. k-4). 1991. stapled bdg. 4.95 (*1-879326-09-4*) Living Planet Pr.
Tongier, Steve. There Still Are Buffalo. Clark, Ann N. Beatty, Willard W., ed. LC 90-85645. 40p. (gr. 1-4). 1992. pap. 8.95 (*0-941270-67-X*) Ancient City Pr.
Tonra, Ian. Martin Luther King, Jr. & Our January 15th Holiday for Children. Cauper, Eunice. 32p. (Orig.). (gr. k-3). 1991. pap. text ed. 6.00 (*0-9617551-3-X*) E Cauper.
Tony Productions Staff. Flags of the African People: Benderas of the African Diaspora, 2 vols. Banks, Valerie J. Tyler, Brian. (Orig.). (gr. k-8). 1990. pap. 9.95 (*0-9622340-9-5*) Sala Enterp.
Tootill, Ginger. The Cat Who Conducted with His Tail. Radke, Martha E. LC 81-90803. 28p. (Orig.). (ps-3). 1982. pap. 1.95 (*0-9607994-0-0*) G E Radke.
Topolski, Diane F. The Rainier Ice Caves & Other Northwest Stories. Silver, Jeffrey H. 32p. (gr. 5 up). 1983. pap. 4.00 (*0-910867-01-1*) Silver Seal Bks.

Topolski, Feliks. Lonesome Boy. Bontemps, Arna. LC 88-3434. 32p. (gr. k-3). 1988. pap. 4.95 (*0-8070-8307-0*, NL 2) Beacon Pr.
Topor, Roland. Snow White & Rose Red. Grimm, Jacob & Grimm, Wilhelm K. 32p. (gr. 6 up). 1984. PLB 13.95s.p. (*0-87191-938-9*) Creative Ed.
Torah Aura Staff, photos by. Building Jewish Life: Siddur Commentary. Grishaver, Joel L. 48p. (Orig.). (gr. 2-4). 1992. pap. text ed. 2.45 (*0-933873-74-3*) Torah Aura.
Torbit, Stephen C. Large Mammals of the Central Rockies: A Guide to Their Locations & Ecology. Torbit, Stephen C. 72p. (gr. 12). 1987. pap. 7.95 (*0-9618450-0-7*) Bennet Creek.
Tornqvist, Marit. A Calf for Christmas. Lindgren, Astrid. Lucas, Barbara, tr. 32p. (ps up). 1991. bds. 13.95 (*91-29-59920-2*, Pub. by R & S Bks) FS&G.
—The Christmas Carp. Tornqvist, Rita. Kilburn, Greta, tr. 32p. (gr. k-3). 1990. 13.95 (*91-29-59784-6*, Pub. by R & S Bks) FS&G.
—The Old Musician. Tornqvist, Rita. LC 93-664. 1993. Repr. 13.00 (*91-29-62244-1*, Pub. by R & S Bks) FS&G.
Torrecilla, Pablo. Barquitos de Papel. Ada, Alma F. (SPA.). 24p. (gr. 3-9). 1993. 16.95x (*1-56492-118-2*) Laredo.
—Barrilets. Ada, Alma F. (SPA.). 24p. (gr. 3-9). 1993. 16.95x (*1-56492-126-3*) Laredo.

—**Caperucita Roja y la Luna de Papel.** Marcuse, Aida E. (SPA.). 24p. (Orig.). (gr. k-6). 1993. PLB 9.95x (*1-56492-103-4*) Laredo. A modern adaptation of the original Little Red Riding Hood through rhyme. Rich illustrations & text will entertain young & older readers alike. Written in play format in Spanish. *Publisher Provided Annotation.*

—Dias de Circo. Ada, Alma F. (SPA.). 24p. (gr. 3-9). 1993. 16.95x (*1-56492-127-1*) Laredo.
—Pajaritos. Kohen, Clarita. 24p. (Orig.). (gr. k-3). 1993. pap. 7.50x (*1-56492-104-2*) Laredo.
—Pin, Pin, Sarabin. Ada, Alma F. (SPA.). 24p. (gr. 3-9). 1993. 16.95x (*1-56492-130-1*) Laredo.

—**Pregones.** Ada, Alma F. (SPA.). 24p. (gr. 3-8). 1993. PLB 16.95x (*1-56492-110-7*) Laredo. The author remembers the everyday sights & sounds of the street vendors who came to her house & the important lesson she learned as a child about the value of being fair & honest. Rich descriptions of "vendor cries" & beautiful color illustrations. Text in Spanish. *Publisher Provided Annotation.*

Torrence, Susan. The California Alphabet Book. Torrence, Susan. Torrence, Charles, ed. LC 86-51505. 32p. (gr. k-3). 1987. pap. 6.95 (*0-914281-48-8*) Torrence Pubns.
—A Cozy Place. Slaughter, Hope. LC 90-49715. 32p. (ps-2). 1990. 15.95 (*0-931093-13-9*) Red Hen Pr.
—Extraordinary Chester. Wilde, Susie. LC 88-11441. 32p. (Orig.). (ps-2). 1988. 14.95 (*0-931093-09-0*); pap. 6.95 (*0-931093-08-2*) Red Hen Pr.
—The Oregon Alphabet Book. 2nd ed. Torrence, Susan & Polansky, Leslie. 32p. (ps-6). 1983. 5.95 (*0-914281-00-3*) Torrence Pubns.
Torres, Margot. The Little Jewel Box. Mayer, Marianna. (ps-3). 1990. pap. 3.95 (*0-8037-0737-1*, Dial Pied Piper) Puffin Bks.
Torriani, Graziella. Baby Birds. Bonsignori, Martina. 18p. (ps-k). 1992. Set of 3 bks. bds. 11.95 (*1-56397-158-5*); bds. 3.95 (*1-56397-153-4*) Boyds Mills Pr.
Torudd, Cecilia. The Big Sister. Widerberg, Siv. Sjogren, Birgitta, tr. from SWE. 1989. 9.95 (*91-29-59186-4*, Pub. by R&S Bks) FS&G.
Torvik, Brian. Little Tree. Stiles, Louise. 32p. (gr. 3 up). 1987. pap. 5.95 (*0-88144-051-5*) Christian Pub.
Torvik, Sharon. Ancient Forests. Field, Nancy, et al. 40p. (Orig.). (gr. 3-6). 1994. pap. 4.95 (*0-941042-14-6*) Dog Eared Pubns.
Torvik, Sharon, jt. illus. see Machlis, Sally.
Tosti, Selma. Spinning with Gold: Poems for Young & Old. Raemsch, Dorothy C. 32p. 1991. pap. 7.50 (*0-9605398-2-4*) D C Raemsch.
Totten, Bob. Beth: The Little Girl of Pine Knoll. Hausman, Gerald. LC 74-82228. 32p. (gr. 6 up). 1974. 15.00 (*0-912846-08-9*) Bookstore Pr.
Totten, Robert. The Phantom Hand. Harter, Walter. 128p. (gr. 4 up). 1976. pap. 5.96 (*0-13-661843-X*, Pub. by Treehouse) P-H.
Touchstone, Samuel J. How to Build: Mud Chimney, Water Grist Mill, Brush Arbor, Charcoal-Tar Kiln, Wooden Rake, Lard Squeezer, No. 1. Touchstone, Samuel J. LC 87-80814. 60p. (Orig.). (gr. 6 up). 1987. pap. 3.95 (*0-914917-01-3*) Folk-Life.

Toulmin-Rothe, Ann. The Cask of Amontillado. Poe, Edgar Allan. Cutts, David E., adapted by. LC 81-15997. 32p. (gr. 5-10). 1982. PLB 10.79 (*0-89375-622-9*); pap. text ed. 2.95 (*0-89375-623-7*); cassettes avail. Troll Assocs.
—Haunted House Tales. Denan, Corinne. LC 79-66335. 48p. (gr. 5-7). 1980. PLB 9.89 (*0-89375-336-X*); pap. text ed. 2.95 (*0-89375-335-1*); cassette avail. Troll Assocs.
—Nightmare Ship. Crawford, F. Marion. Richardson, I. M., adapted by. LC 81-21805. 32p. (gr. 5-10). 1982. PLB 10.79 (*0-89375-632-6*); pap. text ed. 2.95 (*0-89375-633-4*) Troll Assocs.
Tounsi, Corinne. Legs & Bizou. Cherry, Frances. 36p. (ps-8). 1986. 7.95 (*0-920806-60-0*, Pub. by Penumbra Pr CN) U of Toronto Pr.
Tourillotte, Barb, jt. illus. see Connelly, Gwen.
Tourret, Gwen. Baby Forest Animals. Randall, Ronne P. 24p. (ps-k). 1987. pap. 1.25 (*0-7214-9546-X*, S871-2) Ladybird Bks.
Tourtillotte, Barb. Object Rhymes: Reproducible Pre-Reading Books for Young Children. Warren, Jean. Bittinger, Gayle, ed. 160p. (Orig.). (ps-1). 1990. pap. text ed. 14.95 (*0-911019-33-2*) Warren Pub Hse.
Tourtillotte, Barb, jt. illus. see Isaacs, Jean.
Tourtillotte, Barbara. The Wishing Fish: A Totline Teaching Tale. Warren, Jean. Cubley, Kathleen, ed. LC 93-12523. 32p. (Orig.). (ps-2). 1994. 12.95 (*0-911019-73-1*); pap. 5.95 (*0-911019-74-X*) Warren Pub Hse.
Townsend, Tony, jt. illus. see Donohoe, Bill.
Tozuka, Takako, photos by. Children of the World: Turkey. Tozuks, Takako. Reitci, Rita & Sherwood, Rhoda I., eds. LC 88-32745. 64p. (gr. 5-6). 1989. PLB 19.93 (*1-55532-851-2*) Gareth Stevens Inc.
Traba, Henry & Faigin, Cecilia. Slippers & Wraparound Wraps. Jensen, Kent W. 41p. (ps-2). 1988. pap. 7.95 (*0-9621024-0-7*) K Jensen.
Trachsler, Don. How to Make School Fun. Smith, Allan H., ed. LC 84-90227. 200p. (Orig.). (gr. 6-12). 1984. pap. 10.00 (*0-931113-03-2*) Success Publ.
—Teenage Money Making Guide. Smith, Allan H., ed. LC 84-90126. 281p. (Orig.). (ps-12). 1984. pap. 10.00 (*0-931113-00-8*) Success Publ.
Tracy, Libba. Building a Bridge. Begaye, Lisa S. LC 92-82138. 32p. (gr. k). 1993. 14.95 (*0-87358-557-7*) Northland AZ.
—It Rained on the Desert Today. Buchanan, Ken & Buchanan, Debby. 32p. (ps up). 1994. 14.95 (*0-87358-575-5*) Northland AZ.
—This House Is Made of Mud. Buchanan, Ken. LC 90-53589. 32p. (ps-k). 1991. 14.95 (*0-87358-518-6*) Northland AZ.
Trafton, Mary. High Mountain Challenge: A Guide for Young Mountaineers. Allen, Linda B. LC 89-16. 224p. (Orig.). (gr. 6-12). 1989. pap. 9.95 (*0-910146-98-5*) AMC Books.
Trammel, Kim. You, God & Your Sexuality. McAllister, Dawson & Altman, Tim. Peterson, Wayne, ed. (gr. 5-12). 1988. pap. 3.95 (*0-923417-01-X*) Shepherd Minst.
Transue, David. The Enchanted Unicorn. Cissom, Joan. 20p. (Orig.). 1989. pap. 3.95 (*0-929560-01-9*) Southern Rose Prodns.
Trapani, Iza. I Am Three - I Am Four. Steed, Alice. 32p. (ps-k). 1993. bds. 3.95 (*1-879085-78-X*) Whsprng Coyote Pr.
—The Itsy-Bitsy Spider. Trapani, Iza, retold by. LC 92-25150. 32p. (ps-12). 1993. smythe sewn reinforced 14.95 (*1-879085-77-1*) Whsprng Coyote Pr.
—What Am I? An Animal Guessing Game. Trapani, Iza. LC 92-15029. 32p. (ps-8). 1992. smythe sewn reinforced 13.95 (*1-879085-76-3*) Whsprng Coyote Pr.

Travis-Keene, Gayle. The World Turned Upside Down: Children of 1776. Jensen, Ann D. 32p. (Orig.). (gr. 4-5). 1993. pap. 5.95 (*0-9638113-0-4*) Sands Hse.
THE WORLD TURNED UPSIDE DOWN opens in Annapolis, Maryland on the eve of the American Revolution. Young readers meet the Sands family: parents John & Ann, & their 5 children; Will, 18; Nan, 15; Johnny, 12; Sarah, 7; & Joseph, 6. They were a real family & their home still stands in Annapolis. In reading about this family children learn what it was like to live during the Revolutionary War, & how the world of families like the Sands really was turned upside down. A section of thumbnail sketches of the day-to-day life of the story's main characters help youngsters to further understand how children lived during this critical time in American history. Here is a real life story of the Revolutionary War & of people, neither rich nor famous, who gave their lives & contributed in other significant ways to the cause of liberty. The book includes an extensive glossary, as well as a map & brief description of Maryland's capital city as it was in 1776.
Publisher Provided Annotation.

Traynor, Pete. Cigarettes, Cigarettes. Traynor, Pete. Reynolds, Patrick, frwd. by. LC 92-31033. 24p. 1993. 14.95 (*0-9629978-7-0*) Sights Prods.
This landmark children's book, with a foreword by Patrick Reynolds, tells a cautionary story that casts cigarette smoking in a most unfavorable light. The tale follows the afternoon adventure of four children, one of whom is a smoker & the object of unfortunate circumstances. As the book unfolds, the reader sees the danger of cigarettes themselves as well as the advertising tactics practiced by tobacco companies to market cigarettes to children. Through an allegorical narrative, the long-term danger of smoking takes on an immediacy that makes it easy to understand, & the advertising images that are so attractive to youth are strongly satirized. The book also features an illustrated section of factual information about smoking & health & an expose of the tobacco industry. Additionally, there is an interactive question & answer section to allow adults & children to discuss the book & reinforce its anti-smoking message. CIGARETTES, CIGARETTES paves the way for its coming companion volume, CRACK, CRACK which similarly warns children about the dangers of crack-cocaine. Volume discounts available from the publisher. ISBN 0-9629978-7-0, $14.95. SIGHTS PRODUCTIONS, P.O. Box, Mt. Airy, MD 21771, (410) 795-4582; FAX (301) 829-2585.
Publisher Provided Annotation.

Trebing, Tom. My Play a Tune Book: Children's Songs. Ellis, John S. & Leary, Mary B., eds. 26p. (ps up). 1985. 14.95 (*0-938971-00-X*) JTG Nashville.
Trebor Eugol. Space Needle Journey to Mars. Idore. 38p. (gr. k-3). 1991. pap. 4.95 (*0-926060-07-4*) Anschell Pub Co.
Treherne, Katie T. The Little Mermaid. Andersen, Hans Christian. Treherne, Katie T., adapted by. LC 89-31602. 42p. (gr. k-3). 1989. 15.95 (*0-15-246320-8*) HarBrace.
—Tatsinda. Enright, Elizabeth. Johnston, Allyn, ed. 65p. (gr. k-5). 1991. 16.95 (*0-15-284280-2*) HarBrace.
Treherne, Katie T. & Bodecker, N. M. Half Magic. Eager, Edward. 192p. (gr. 3-7). 1989. pap. 4.95 (*0-15-233081-X*, Odyssey) HarBrace.
—Knight's Castle. Eager, Edward. 198p. (gr. 3-7). 1989. pap. 3.95 (*0-15-243105-5*, Odyssey) HarBrace.
—Magic by the Lake. Eager, Edward. 190p. (gr. 3-7). 1989. pap. 3.95 (*0-15-250444-3*, Odyssey) HarBrace.
—Magic or Not? Eager, Edward. 197p. (gr. 3-7). 1989. pap. 3.95 (*0-15-251160-1*, Odyssey) HarBrace.
—Seven-Day Magic. Eager, Edward. 190p. (gr. 3-7). 1989. pap. 3.95 (*0-15-272916-X*, Odyssey) HarBrace.
—The Time Garden. Eager, Edward. 193p. (gr. 3-7). 1990. pap. 4.95 (*0-15-288193-X*, Odyssey) HarBrace.
—The Well Wishers. Eager, Edward. 220p. (gr. 3-7). 1990. pap. 4.95 (*0-15-294994-1*, Odyssey) HarBrace.
Treherne, Katie T., jt. illus. see McKinley, Robin.
Trella, Phyllis. Butterflies Have Grandparents, Too. Trella, Phyllis. LC 82-73691. 48p. (gr. 2-6). write for info. (*0-914201-02-6*) Cheeruppet.
—Les Duit at the Olympics...& Be a Strong. Trella, Phyllis. 48p. (gr. 2-6). write for info. (*0-914201-01-8*) Cheeruppet.
—Jodee's Closet. Trella, Phyllis. LC 82-73689. 48p. (gr. 2-6). write for info. (*0-914201-04-2*) Cheeruppet.
—A Peek at Occupations. Trella, Phyllis. LC 82-73692. 48p. (gr. 2-6). write for info. (*0-914201-03-4*) Cheeruppet.

Treman, Terry. Intermission: Breaking Away with God. Schaap, James C. Smith, Harvey A., intro. by. LC 85-4156. 221p. (Orig.). (gr. 9-12). 1987. pap. 11.50 (*0-930265-06-8*, 1701-5000) CRC Pubns.
Tremblay, Martin. The E-waa, Vol. 1. Davis, Robert C. LC 91-61838. 28p. (Orig.). 1991. pap. 5.50g (*0-9629949-0-1*) Across the Road.
Tremblay, Ruth. Far Away Gramma. Kerensky, Elaine. 24p. (Orig.). (gr. k-3). 1990. pap. text ed. write for info. (*0-9627228-0-4*) Far Away Fam Playhse.
Treog-Hill, Vicki. La Llorona. Hayes, Joe. 32p. (Orig.). (gr. 1-9). 1986. pap. 4.95 (*0-938317-02-4*) Cinco Puntos.
Trexler, Richard. Victor's Place. Sherman, Eileen. 598p. (Orig.). (gr. 10-12). 1989. pap. write for info. (*0-9604382-2-X*) Cornerstone Pr.
Trezzo-Braren Studio Staff. Kids Make Music! Clapping & Tapping from Bach to Rock. Hart, Avery & Mantell, Paul. 160p. (Orig.). (ps-4). 1993. pap. 12.95 (*0-913589-69-1*) Williamson Pub Co.
—The Kids' Multicultural Art Book: Art & Craft Experiences from Around the World. Terzian, Alexandra. 160p. (Orig.). (ps-4). 1993. pap. 12.95 (*0-913589-72-1*) Williamson Pub Co.
Trezzo, Loretta. Kids Cook! Fabulous Food for the Whole Family. Williamson, Sarah & Williamson, Zachary. Williamson, Susan, ed. LC 91-38513. 160p. (Orig.). (gr. 2-12). 1992. pap. 12.95 (*0-913589-61-6*) Williamson Pub Co.
Trimby, Elisa. The Night Before Christmas. Moore, Clement C. LC 77-71994. (gr. 1 up). 1977. pap. 5.95 (*0-385-13615-3*) Doubleday.
Trinidad, Angel & Guitierez, Domy. The House of the Seven Gables. abr. ed. Hawthorne, Nathaniel. Farr, Naunerle, ed. (gr. 4-12). 1977. pap. text ed. 2.95 (*0-88301-265-0*) Pendulum Pr.
Trinidad, Angel, jt. illus. see Taloac, Gerry.

Tripp, Charles. Super ABC's of the Human Body. Wrenn, Romel. 56p. (gr. k-4). 1993. Wkbk. write for info. (*0-9637869-0-3*) Chldrns Med.
SUPER ABC'S OF THE HUMAN BODY is a MULTISENSORY tool. Its educational features include: Alphabet Chart, Printing Workbook, Human Anatomy, Alphabet Rhyme, Coloring Book. A is for ANKLE. I am Talus by name. I connect the leg & foot: that is my game. B is for BACK & Spine is my label. I can carry the load, because I am strong & able. Each alphabet has a super hero pointing to the appropriate part of the body. The opposing page has an anatomically correct illustration of the body part. These are line drawings which may be colored by the students. Space is provided for printing of upper/lower case alphabets. Children ages 2-10 years are the target audience. The author, Dr. Romel C. Wrenn, M.D., has made this first of a planned series of books to be used for health education in primary school. SUPER ABC'S retails for $4.95. It may be obtained for $3.50 at quantities above 100. For more information, telephone Dr. Romel C. Wrenn at 318-445-9931/ 318-443-5524 or Ms. Theresa Rose at 318-445-3658. Mail inquiries to Children's Medical World, P.O. Drawer 8238, Alexandria, LA 71306.
Publisher Provided Annotation.

Tripp, Ned. They Reached for the Stars. Turk, Ruth. (gr. 5-9). 1990. pap. 11.95 (*0-933025-20-3*) Blue Bird Pub.
Tripp, Wallace. Amelia Bedelia & the Surprise Shower. unabr. ed. Parish, Peggy. (ps-3). 1990. pap. 6.95 incl. cassette (*1-55994-216-9*, Caedmon) HarperAudio.
—The Bad Child's Book of Beasts. rev. ed. Belloc, Hilaire. 48p. (Orig.). (gr. 7 up). 1982. pap. 4.95 (*0-9605776-3-7*) Sparhawk.
—Casey at the Bat. Thayer, Ernest L. 32p. (Orig.). (ps-2). 1989. pap. 1.95 (*0-448-19112-1*, Platt & Munk Pubs) Putnam Pub Group.
—Casey at the Bat: A Ballad of the Republic, Sung in the Year 1888. Thayer, Ernest L. LC 77-21199. (gr. k-5). 1980. 14.95 (*0-399-21585-9*, Putnam); pap. 1.95 (*0-698-20486-7*, Putnam) Putnam Pub Group.
—Come Back, Amelia Bedelia. Parish, Peggy. LC 73-121799. 64p. (ps-3). 1971. 14.00 (*0-06-024667-7*); PLB 13.89 (*0-06-024668-5*) HarpC Child Bks.

—Come Back, Amelia Bedelia. Parish, Peggy. LC 73-121799. 64p. (gr. k-3). 1986. incl. cassette 5.98 (0-694-00112-0, Trophy); pap. 3.50 (0-06-444016-8, Trophy) HarperC Child Bks.

—Come Back, Amelia Bedelia. unabr. ed. Parish, Peggy. (ps-3). 1990. pap. 6.95 incl. cassette (1-55994-225-8, Caedmon) HarperAudio.

—Granfa' Grig Had a Pig & Other Rhymes Without Reason from Mother Goose. Tripp, Wallace. 96p. (gr. 4-12). 1976. 19.95 (0-316-85282-1); pap. 10.95 (0-316-85284-8) Little.

—No Flying in the House. Brock, Betty. LC 79-104755. 144p. (gr. 2-5). 1982. pap. 3.95 (0-06-440130-8, Trophy) HarperC Child Bks.

—Play Ball, Amelia Bedelia. Parish, Peggy. LC 71-85028. 64p. (gr. k-3). 1972. 14.00 (0-06-024655-3); PLB 13.89 (0-06-024656-1) HarperC Child Bks.

—Play Ball, Amelia Bedelia. Parish, Peggy. LC 71-85028. 64p. (ps-3). 1985. (Trophy); pap. 3.50 (0-06-444005-2, Trophy) HarperC Child Bks.

—Play Ball, Amelia Bedelia. unabr. ed. Parish, Peggy. (ps-3). 1990. pap. 6.95 incl. cassette (1-55994-241-X, Caedmon) HarperAudio.

—Stand Back, Said the Elephant, I'm Going to Sneeze! Thomas, Patricia. LC 89-43215. 32p. (ps-2). 1990. 13.95 (0-688-09338-8); lib. bdg. 13.88 (0-688-09339-6) Lothrop.

Trisler, Alana & Cardiel, Patrice H. Words I Use When I Write. Trisler, Alana & Cardiel, Patrice H. 36p. (Orig.). (gr. k-3). 1989. pap. text ed. 2.50 (0-935493-93-8) Programs Educ.

Triva, Irene. Nannies for Hire. Hest, Amy. LC 93-7040. 1994. write for info. (0-688-12527-1); PLB write for info. (0-688-12528-X) Morrow Jr Bks.

Trivas, Irene. Alone at Home. Hazen, Barbara S. LC 91-15878. 64p. (gr. 2-4). 1992. SBE 13.95 (0-689-31691-7, Atheneum Child Bk) Macmillan Child Grp.

—Black, White, Just Right. Davol, Marguerite. LC 93-19932. 1993. write for info. (0-8075-0785-7) A Whitman.

—Emily's Snowball: The World's Biggest. Keown, Elizabeth. LC 90-1181. 32p. (ps-3). 1992. SBE 13.95 (0-689-31518-X, Atheneum Child Bk) Macmillan Child Grp.

—The Fourth Floor Twins & the Fish Snitch Mystery. Adler, David A. 64p. (gr. 1-4). 1986. pap. 3.99 (0-14-032082-2, Puffin) Puffin Bks.

—The Fourth Floor Twins & the Fortune Cookie Chase. Adler, David A. 64p. (gr. 1-4). 1986. pap. 3.95 (0-14-032083-0, Puffin) Puffin Bks.

—The Fourth Floor Twins & the Sand Castle Contest. Adler, David A. (gr. 2-5). 1988. 9.95 (0-318-37432-3) Viking Child Bks.

—The Fourth Floor Twins & the Silver Ghost Express. Adler, David A. (gr. 2-5). 1987. pap. 4.99 (0-14-032215-9, Puffin) Puffin Bks.

—Fun at Camp. Peters, Sharon. 32p. (gr. k-2). 1980. PLB 7.89 (0-89375-378-5); pap. 1.95 (0-89375-278-9) Troll Assocs.

—The Great Easter Egg Mystery. Sabin, Fran & Sabin, Lou. LC 81-7610. 48p. (gr. 2-4). 1982. PLB 10.89 (0-89375-604-0); pap. text ed. 3.50 (0-89375-605-9) Troll Assocs.

—The Great Santa Claus Mystery. Sabin, Fran & Sabin, Lou. LC 81-7530. 48p. (gr. 2-4). 1982. PLB 10.89 (0-89375-602-4); pap. text ed. 3.50 (0-89375-603-2) Troll Assocs.

—Listos, En Sus Marcas, Adelante! Peters, Sharon. (SPA.). 32p. (gr. k-2). 1981. PLB 7.89 (0-89375-550-8); pap. 1.95 (0-89375-957-0) Troll Assocs.

—Lottie's Circus. Blos, Joan W. LC 88-39035. 32p. (ps up). 1989. 13.95 (0-688-06746-8); PLB 13.88 (0-688-06747-6, Morrow Jr Bks) Morrow Jr Bks.

—The Marching Band Mystery. Peters, Sharon. LC 84-8783. 48p. (gr. 2-4). 1985. PLB 10.89 (0-8167-0406-6); pap. text ed. 3.50 (0-8167-0407-4) Troll Assocs.

—Meredith's Mother Takes the Train. Rose, Deborah L. Levine, Abby, ed. LC 90-12756. 24p. (ps-k). 1991. 11.95 (0-8075-5061-2) A Whitman.

—Messy Mark. Peters, Sharon. 32p. (gr. k-2). 1980. PLB 7.89 (0-89375-381-5); pap. 1.95 (0-89375-281-9) Troll Assocs.

—My Mother's House, My Father's House. Christiansen, C. B. LC 88-16802. 32p. (gr. k-3). 1989. SBE 13.95 (0-689-31394-2, Atheneum Child Bk) Macmillan Child Grp.

—Mystery at the Jellybean Factory. Sabin, Fran & Sabin, Lou. LC 81-10388. 48p. (gr. 2-4). 1982. PLB 10.89 (0-89375-600-8); pap. text ed. 3.50 (0-89375-601-6) Troll Assocs.

—No Room for a Sneeze! Supraner, Robyn. LC 85-14164. 48p. (Orig.). (gr. 1-3). 1986. PLB 10.59 (0-8167-0656-5); pap. text ed. 3.50 (0-8167-0657-3) Troll Assocs.

—Not Yet, Yvette. Ketteman, Helen. Mathews, Judith, ed. LC 91-19608. 24p. (ps-2). 1992. PLB 11.95 (0-8075-5771-4) A Whitman.

—One-Eyed Cat. Fox, Paula. LC 84-10964. 192p. (gr. 6-8). 1984. SBE 14.95 (0-02-735540-3, Bradbury Pr) Macmillan Child Grp.

—The One in the Middle Is the Green Kangaroo. 2nd ed. Blume, Judy. LC 80-29664. 32p. (gr. k-2). 1991. Repr. of 1981 ed. 13.95 (0-02-711055-9, Bradbury Pr) Macmillan Child Grp.

—The One in the Middle is the Green Kangaroo. Blume, Judy. (ps-3). 1992. pap. 3.99 (0-440-40668-4, YB) Dell.

—The Pain & the Great One. Blume, Judy. LC 84-11009. 32p. (gr. k-3). 1984. RSBE 13.95 (0-02-711100-8, Bradbury Pr) Macmillan Child Grp.

—Pajama Party. Hest, Amy. LC 91-13676. 48p. (gr. 2 up). 1992. 14.00 (0-688-07866-4); PLB 13.93 (0-688-07870-2) Morrow Jr Bks.

—Pajama Party. Hest, Amy. 48p. (gr. 3 up). 1994. pap. 4.95 (0-688-12949-8, Pub. by Beech Tree Bks) Morrow.

—Potluck. Shelby, Anne. LC 90-7757. 32p. (ps-1). 1991. 14.95 (0-531-05919-7); PLB 14.99 (0-531-08519-8) Orchard Bks Watts.

—Potluck. Shelby, Anne. LC 90-7757. 32p. (ps-2). 1994. pap. 5.95 (0-531-07045-X) Orchard Bks Watts.

—Ready, Get Set, Go! Peters, Sharon. 32p. (gr. k-2). 1980. PLB 7.89 (0-89375-386-6); pap. 1.95 (0-89375-285-1) Troll Assocs.

—Secret of the Haunted Chimney. Robert, Adrian. LC 84-8763. 48p. (gr. 2-4). 1985. PLB 10.89 (0-8167-0408-2); pap. text ed. 3.50 (0-8167-0409-0) Troll Assocs.

—Secret of the Haunted House. Sabin, Fran & Sabin, Lou. LC 81-8751. 48p. (gr. 2-4). 1982. PLB 10.89 (0-89375-598-2); pap. text ed. 3.50 (0-89375-599-0) Troll Assocs.

—Stars. Wandelmaier, Roy. LC 84-8642. 32p. (gr. k-2). 1985. PLB 11.59 (0-8167-0339-6); pap. text ed. 2.95 (0-8167-0442-2) Troll Assocs.

—Trees. Gordon, Sharon. LC 82-20291. 32p. (gr. k-2). 1983. lib. bdg. 11.59 (0-89375-901-5); pap. text ed. 2.95 (0-89375-879-7) Troll Assocs.

—What to Do about Pollution. Shelby, Anne. LC 92-24173. 32p. (ps-1). 1993. 14.95 (0-531-05471-3); PLB 14.99 (0-531-08621-6) Orchard Bks Watts.

—Who Will Pick Me up When I Fall? Molnar, Dorothy E. & Fenton, Stephen H. Mathews, Judith, ed. LC 90-28250. 32p. (ps-2). 1991. 13.95 (0-8075-9072-X) A Whitman.

—Winter Book. Webster, Harriet. LC 88-4371. 128p. (gr. 3-7). 1988. SBE 13.95 (0-684-18891-0, Scribners Young Read) Macmillan Child Grp.

Trivedi, Kartik. Kartik Trivedi, Contemporary Impressionist. Beauzile, Anthony L. & Beauzile, Gerard, Jr. Fairhall, Winnifred, ed. (Orig.). (gr. 10-12). 1992. 59.95g (0-9633124-1-3); pap. 34.95g (0-685-62455-2) T&T Dyno-Srvs.

Troshkov, Andrei. Prince Ivan & the Firebird. Gilchrist, Cherry, retold by. 1994. 15.00 (1-56957-920-2) Barefoot Bks.

Trotter, Stuart. Building: First Readers. Harding, Jacqueline. (ps-k). 1992. 3.50 (0-7214-1491-5) Ladybird Bks.

—A Busy Day. Grace, John. 28p. (ps-1). 1991. 3.95 (0-7214-5333-3, S914-2) Ladybird Bks.

—Exploring Science: Practice at Home Science Activity. Hurt, Roger. 24p. (Orig.). (gr. 2-5). 1992. pap. 2.95 wkbk. (0-7214-3246-8) Ladybird Bks.

—A Quiet Walk. Grace, John. 28p. (ps-1). 1991. 3.95 (0-7214-5332-5, S914-1 SER.) Ladybird Bks.

—Reader's Digest Children's Book of Animals. Grindley, Sally. LC 92-15234. 48p. 1992. 13.00 (0-89577-443-7, Readers Digest Kids) RD Assn.

—What Am I Made Of? Bennett, David. LC 91-278. 32p. (gr. k-3). 1991. POB 5.95 (0-689-71490-4, Aladdin) Macmillan Child Grp.

—Why Do I Eat? Wright, Rachel. LC 91-26683. 32p. (ps-2). 1992. pap. 5.95 (0-689-71588-9, Aladdin) Macmillan Child Grp.

Trottier, Maxine. The Big Heart. McDowell, Margaret & Trottier, Maxine. 32p. (ps-2). 1991. pap. 29.50 (1-55037-186-X, Pub. by Annick CN) Firefly Bks Ltd.

Troughton, Joanna. How Night Came: A Folk Tale from the Amazon. Troughton, Joanna, retold by. LC 86-10917. 32p. (gr. k-3). 1986. PLB 14.95 (0-87226-093-3, Bedrick Blackie) P Bedrick Bks.

—How Rabbit Stole the Fire: A North American Indian Folk Tale. Troughton, Joanna, retold by. LC 85-15629. 32p. (gr. k-3). 1986. PLB 14.95 (0-87226-040-2, Bedrick Blackie) P Bedrick Bks.

—How the Birds Changed Their Feathers: A South American Folk Tale. Troughton, Joanna, retold by. LC 86-1251. 32p. (gr. k-3). 1986. PLB 14.95 (0-87226-080-1, Bedrick Blackie) P Bedrick Bks.

—How the Seasons Came: A North American Indian Folk Tale. Troughton, Joanna, retold by. LC 91-40499. 32p. (gr. k-3). 1992. PLB 14.95 (0-87226-464-5, Bedrick Blackie) P Bedrick Bks.

—The Magic Mill: A Finnish Folk Tale from the Kalevala. Troughton, Joanna, retold by. LC 88-24170. 32p. 1989. PLB 14.95 (0-87226-405-X, Bedrick Blackie) P Bedrick Bks.

—Make-Believe Tales: A Folk Tale from Burma. Troughton, Joanna. LC 90-48962. 32p. (gr. k-3). 1991. PLB 14.95 (0-87226-451-3, Bedrick Blackie) P Bedrick Bks.

—Mouse-Deer's Market: A Folk Tale from Borneo. Troughton, Joanna. LC 84-11049. 32p. (gr. k-3). 1984. PLB 14.95 (0-911745-63-7, Bedrick Blackie) P Bedrick Bks.

—Pilgrim's Progress. Reeves, James, retold by. LC 86-25902. 160p. (gr. 4 up). 1987. 12.95 (0-87226-147-6, Bedrick Blackie) P Bedrick Bks.

—The Quail's Egg: A Folk Tale from Sri Lanka. Troughton, Joanna, retold by. LC 87-33376. 32p. (gr. k-3). 1988. PLB 14.95 (0-87226-185-9, Bedrick Blackie) P Bedrick Bks.

—Whale's Canoe: A Folk Tale from Australia. Troughton, Joanna, retold by. LC 92-43616. 32p. (gr. k-3). 1993. 14.95 (0-87226-509-9) P Bedrick Bks.

—What Made Tiddalik Laugh: An Australian Aborigine Folk Tale. Troughton, Joanna, retold by. LC 86-1234. 32p. (gr. k-3). 1986. PLB 14.95 (0-87226-081-X, Bedrick Blackie) P Bedrick Bks.

—Who Will Be the Sun? A North American Indian Folk Tale. Troughton, Joanna, retold by. LC 85-15074. 32p. (gr. k-3). 1986. PLB 14.95 (0-87226-038-0, Bedrick Blackie) P Bedrick Bks.

—The Wizard Punchkin: A Folk Tale from India. Troughton, Joanna. LC 87-11517. 32p. (gr. k-3). 1988. PLB 14.95 (0-87226-162-X, Bedrick Blackie) P Bedrick Bks.

Troughton, Joannna. Tortoise's Dream: An African Folk Tale. Troughton, Joanna, retold by. LC 85-15065. 28p. (ps-2). 1986. PLB 14.95 (0-87226-039-9, Bedrick Blackie) P Bedrick Bks.

Troupe, Connie. Four Chinese Children's Stories. Ramos, Lindsey. 1991. 14.95 (0-9628563-0-4) Lttle Peop Pr.

Trout, Cary M. The World of Small: Nature Explorations with a Hand Lens. Ross, Michael E. Medley, Steven P., ed. 64p. (gr. k-6). 1993. wire-o bdg., incl. magnification lens 15.95t (0-939666-62-6) Yosemite Assn.

Truax, Nancy. Annie's Birthday Party: Learning Colors & Shapes. Shearer, Marilyn J. 16p. (Orig.). (ps-6). 1989. 19.95 (0-685-30095-1); pap. 10.95 (0-685-30096-X) L Ashley & Joshua.

True, Stephanie. Renegade in the Hills. Thomson, Andy. Moore, Rebecca, ed. 135p. (Orig.). (gr. 5-8). 1989. pap. 4.95 (0-89084-444-1) Bob Jones Univ Pr.

Truesdell, Sue. Addie Meets Max. Robins, Joan. LC 84-48329. 32p. (ps-3). 1985. PLB 13.89 (0-06-025064-X) HarperC Child Bks.

—Addie Meets Max. Robins, Joan. LC 84-48329. 32p. (ps-2). 1988. pap. 3.50 (0-06-444116-4, Trophy) HarperC Child Bks.

—Addie Runs Away. Robins, Joan. LC 88-24350. 32p. (ps-2). 1989. PLB 10.89 (0-06-025081-X) HarperC Child Bks.

—Addie Runs Away. Robins, Joan. LC 88-24350. 32p. (ps-2). 1991. pap. 3.50 (0-06-444147-4, Trophy) HarperC Child Bks.

—Addie's Bad Day. Robins, Joan. LC 92-13101. 32p. (ps-2). 1993. 14.00 (0-06-021297-7); PLB 13.89 (0-06-021298-5) HarperC Child Bks.

—And the Green Grass Grew All Around: Folk Poetry from Everyone. Schwartz, Alvin. LC 89-26722. 208p. (gr. 1-7). 1992. 15.00 (0-06-022757-5); PLB 14.89 (0-06-022758-3) HarperC Child Bks.

—Dabble Duck. Ellis, Anne L. LC 83-47692. 32p. (ps-2). 1984. 13.00i (0-06-021817-7); PLB 12.89 (0-06-021818-5) HarperC Child Bks.

—Dabble Duck. Ellis, Anne L. LC 83-47692. 32p. (ps-3). 1984. pap. 3.95 (0-06-443153-3, Trophy) HarperC Child Bks.

—Donna O'Neeshuck Was Chased by Some Cows. Grossman, Bill. LC 85-45823. 40p. (gr. k-3). 1988. PLB 12.89 (0-06-022159-3) HarperC Child Bks.

—Donna O'Neeshuck Was Chased by Some Cows. Grossman, Bill. LC 85-45823. 40p. (ps-3). 1991. pap. 5.95 (0-06-443255-6, Trophy) HarperC Child Bks.

—The Golly Sisters Go West. Byars, Betsy. LC 84-48474. 64p. (gr. k-3). 1986. PLB 13.89 (0-06-020884-8) HarperC Child Bks.

—Hey, World, Here I Am! Little, Jean. LC 88-10987. 96p. (gr. 3-7). 1989. 13.00i (0-06-023989-1); PLB 12.89 (0-06-024006-7) HarperC Child Bks.

—Hey World, Here I Am! Little, Jean. LC 88-10987. 96p. (gr. 4 up). 1990. pap. 3.95 (0-06-440384-X, Trophy) HarperC Child Bks.

—Hooray for the Golly Sisters! Byars, Betsy. LC 89-48147. 64p. (gr. k-3). 1990. 14.00 (0-06-020898-8); PLB 13.89 (0-06-020899-6) HarperC Child Bks.

—Lily & the Runaway Baby. Shreve, Susan. LC 87-4684. 64p. (gr. 2-4). 1987. 2.50 (0-394-89104-X, Random Juv) Random Bks Yng Read.

—Look Out, Look Out, It's Coming! Geringer, Laura. LC 91-4707. 40p. (ps-2). 1992. 15.00 (0-06-021711-1); PLB 14.89 (0-06-021712-X) HarperC Child Bks.

—The Losers Fight Back. Joosse, Barbara M. LC 92-40783. 1994. write for info. (0-395-62335-9, Clarion Bks) HM.

—O'Diddy. Stevenson, Jocelyn. LC 87-22676. 64p. (Orig.). (gr. 2-4). 1988. lib. bdg. 6.99 (0-394-99609-7); pap. 1.95 (0-394-89609-2) Random Bks Yng Read.

—The Pirate Who Tried to Capture the Moon. new ed. Haseley, Dennis. LC 82-47734. 64p. (gr. k-4). 1992. pap. 3.95 (0-06-440420-X, Trophy) HarperC Child Bks.

—Travel Tips from Harry: A Guide to Family Vacations in the Sun. Hest, Amy. LC 88-39887. 64p. (gr. 2 up). 1989. 11.95 (0-688-07972-5); PLB 11.88 (0-688-09291-8, Morrow Jr Bks) Morrow Jr Bks.

—Unriddling. Schwartz, Alvin. LC 82-48778. 128p. (gr. 4 up). 1983. PLB 13.89 (0-397-32030-2, Lipp Jr Bks) HarperC Child Bks.

—Unriddling: All Sorts of Riddles to Puzzle Your Guessary. Schwartz, Alvin. LC 82-48778. 128p. (gr. 4 up). 1987. pap. 4.95 (0-06-446057-6, Trophy) HarperC Child Bks.

—Wild Willie & King Kyle Detectives. Joosse, Barbara. LC 92-9816. 80p. (gr. 2-5). 1993. 12.95 (*0-395-64338-4*, Clarion Bks) HM.
Truesdell, Sue, jt. illus. see Rounds, Glen.
Truesdell, Sue, photos by. The Golly Sisters Ride Again. Byars, Betsy. LC 92-23394. 1994. 13.00 (*0-06-021563-1*); PLB 12.89 (*0-06-021564-X*) HarpC Child Bks.
Tryon, Leslie. Albert's Alphabet. Tryon, Leslie. LC 90-38883. 40p. (ps-1). 1991. SBE 13.95 (*0-689-31642-9*, Atheneum Child Bk) Macmillan Child Grp.
—Albert's Field Trip. Tryon, Leslie. LC 92-43686. 32p. (gr. k-3). 1993. SBE 14.95 (*0-689-31821-9*, Atheneum Child Bk) Macmillan Child Grp.
—Albert's Play. Tryon, Leslie. LC 91-23145. 32p. (gr. k-3). 1992. SBE 13.95 (*0-689-31525-2*, Atheneum Child Bk) Macmillan Child Grp.
—Dear Peter Rabbit: Querido Pedrin. Ada, Alma F. Zubizarreta, Rosa, tr. LC 93-8459. 40p. (ps-3). 1994. English ed. SBE 14.95 (*0-689-31850-2*, Atheneum Child Bk); Spanish ed. SBE 14.95 (*0-689-31915-0*, Atheneum Child Bk) Macmillan Child Grp.
—One Gaping Wide-Mouthed Hopping Frog. Tryon, Leslie. LC 92-11368. 32p. (ps-1). 1993. SBE 14.95 (*0-689-31785-9*, Atheneum Child Bk) Macmillan Child Grp.
—Toohy & Wood. Monsell, Mary E. LC 91-38217. 64p. (gr. 2-5). 1992. SBE 12.95 (*0-689-31721-2*, Atheneum Child Bk) Macmillan Child Grp.
Tsao, Alex. Wind in the Willows. Grahame, Kenneth. Ellman, M., intro. by. 224p. (Orig.). (RL 4). 1989. pap. 2.95 (*0-451-52164-1*, Sig Classics) NAL-Dutton.
Tseng, Jean & Mou-sien Tseng. Seven Chinese Brothers. Mahy, Margaret. (gr-3). 1990. pap. 13.95 (*0-590-42055-0*) Scholastic Inc.
—Tales from the Bamboo Grove. Watkins, Yoko K. LC 91-38218. 64p. (gr. 4-11). 1992. SBE 14.95 (*0-02-792525-0*, Bradbury Pr) Macmillan Child Grp.
Tseng, Jean & Tseng, Mou-Sien. The Boy Who Swallowed Snakes. Yep, Laurence, et al. LC 93-21822. 32p. (gr. 5 up). 1994. 14.95 (*0-590-46168-0*) Scholastic Inc.
—The River Dragon. Pattison, Darcy. LC 90-49931. 32p. (gr. k up). 1991. 13.95 (*0-688-10426-6*); PLB 13.88 (*0-688-10427-4*) Lothrop.
—Three Strong Women. Stamm, Claus. 32p. (gr. 2-5). 1990. pap. 12.95 (*0-670-83323-1*) Viking Child Bks.
—Three Strong Women. Stamm, Claus & Mizumura, Kazue. LC 92-25331. 1993. pap. 4.99 (*0-14-054530-1*) Puffin Bks.
—Why Ducks Sleep on One Leg. Garland, Sherry. LC 92-9709. 32p. (ps-3). 1993. 14.95 (*0-590-45697-0*) Scholastic Inc.
Tseng, Mou-Sien. Dragon Parade: A Chinese New Year Story. Chin, Steven A. LC 92-18079. 32p. (gr. 2-5). 1992. PLB 21.34 (*0-8114-7215-9*) Raintree Steck-V.
Tseng, Mou-sien, jt. illus. see Tseng, Jean.
Tseng, Mou-Sien, jt. illus. see Tseng, Jean.
Tseng, Mou-Sien, jt. illus. see Tseng, Jean.
Tseng, Mou-Sien, jt. illus. see Tseng, Jean.
Tsuchida, Yoshiharu. Rise & Shine, Mariko-Chan! Tomioka, Chiyoko. 32p. (ps-1). 1992. pap. 3.95 (*0-590-45507-9*) Scholastic Inc.
Tsui, George. The Clue That Flew Away. Hope, Laura L. (gr. 2-4). 1987. pap. 2.95 (*0-671-62653-1*, Minstrel Bks) PB.
—The Secret of Jungle Park. Hope, Laura L. (gr. 2-4). 1987. pap. 2.95 (*0-671-62651-5*, Minstrel Bks) PB.
Tubbs, Orrin. Spike Mosquito & the Flying Ants. Wilkinson, Jack & Tubbs, Orrin. Haigis, Debbie, ed. (Orig.). (gr. 1-6). 1991. pap. write for info. (*0-9629543-0-6*) Maine Heritage.
Tucker, Ezra, jt. illus. see Henry, Marguerite.
Tucker, Harry. Your Book of Vintage Cars. Coleman, John. (gr. 7 up). 1969. 7.95 (*0-571-08276-9*) Transatl Arts.
Tucker, Sian. The Shapes Game. Rogers, Paul. LC 89-19957. 32p. (ps-2). 1990. 12.95 (*0-8050-1280-X*, Bks Young Read) H Holt & Co.
Tudor, Tash. The Real Pretend. Donaldson, Joan. 32p. (ps-3). 1992. 12.95 (*1-56288-158-2*) Checkerboard.
Tudor, Tasha. A Is for Annabelle. Tudor, Tasha. LC 60-15911. 64p. (ps-1). 1988. pap. 5.95 (*0-02-688534-4*, Aladdin) Macmillan Child Grp.
—All for Love. Tudor, Tasha, ed. LC 83-21959. 96p. (gr. 6-8). 1984. 16.95 (*0-399-21012-1*, Philomel) Putnam Pub Group.
—Amy's Goose. reissued ed. Holmes, Efner T. LC 85-45391. 32p. (ps-3). 1986. pap. 5.95 (*0-06-443091-X*, Trophy) HarpC Child Bks.
—And It Was So: Words from the Scripture. 2nd, rev. ed. LC 87-16130. 48p. (ps up). 1988. 12.00 (*0-664-32724-9*, Westminster) Westminster John Knox.
—Becky's Christmas. Tudor, Tasha. LC 91-61679. 46p. (gr. 3 up). with autograph 25.00 (*0-9621753-5-8*) Jenny Wren Pr.
—A Brighter Garden. Dickinson, Emily. Ackerman, Karen, compiled by. 63p. 1990. 17.95 (*0-399-21490-9*, Philomel Bks) Putnam Pub Group.
—A Child's Garden of Verses. Stevenson, Robert Louis. LC 85-12766. 72p. (ps up). 1988. SBE 13.95 (*0-02-788365-5*) Macmillan Child Grp.
—Christmas Cat. Holmes, Efner T. LC 80-8432. 32p. (ps-3). 1989. pap. 4.95 (*0-06-443208-4*, Trophy) HarpC Child Bks.

—Corgiville Fair. Tudor, Tasha. LC 72-154042. 56p. (ps-3). 1991. pap. 5.95 (*0-06-443236-X*, Trophy) HarpC Child Bks.
—Dolls' Christmas. Tudor, Tasha. LC 59-12744. (gr. k-3). 1979. 6.95 (*0-8098-1026-3*); pap. 4.95 (*0-8098-2912-6*) McKay.
—First Delights: A Book About the Five Senses. Tudor, Tasha. 32p. (ps-1). 1988. 8.95 (*0-448-09327-8*, G&D) Putnam Pub Group.
—First Graces. Tudor, Tasha. LC 59-12017. (gr. k-3). 1978. pap. 6.95 (*0-8098-1953-8*) McKay.
—First Poems of Childhood. 32p. (ps-1). 1990. 9.95 (*0-448-09326-X*, G&D) Putnam Pub Group.
—First Prayers. Tudor, Tasha. LC 59-9631. (gr. k-3). 1978. protestant ed. 6.95 (*0-8098-1952-X*) McKay.
—The Jenny Wren Book of Valentines. Tudor, Tasha. Wren, Jenny, intro. by. LC 88-51832. 16p. (Orig.). (gr. k up). 1989. pap. 6.95 (*0-9621753-1-5*) Jenny Wren Pr.
—Little Princess. Burnett, Frances H. LC 63-15435. (gr. 4-6). 1963. 15.00 (*0-397-30693-8*, Lipp Jr Bks); PLB 14.89 (*0-397-31339-X*, Lipp Jr Bks) HarpC Child Bks.
—A Little Princess. Burnett, Frances H. LC 63-15435. 240p. (gr. 4-8). 1987. pap. 3.95 (*0-06-440187-1*, Trophy) HarpC Child Bks.
—The Lord Is My Shepherd: The Twenty-Third Psalm. LC 79-27134. 32p. (gr. 2 up). 1989. 9.95 (*0-399-20756-2*, Philomel) Putnam Pub Group.
—Mother Goose. Tudor, Tasha. LC 58-58523. (gr. k-3). 1980. 9.95 (*0-8098-1901-5*) McKay.
—Mouse Mills Catalogue for Spring. Tudor, Tasha. Mouse, Timothy D., tr. LC 89-50061. 40p. (gr. k up). 1989. pap. text ed. 6.95 (*0-9621753-2-3*) Jenny Wren Pr.
—One Is One. Tudor, Tasha. LC 56-11381. (ps-1). 1988. pap. 4.95 (*0-02-688535-2*, Aladdin) Macmillan Child Grp.
—Pumpkin Moonshine. Tudor, Tasha. LC 89-3543. 40p. (ps-2). 1989. pap. 5.95 (*0-394-84588-9*) Random Bks Yng Read.
—Seasons of Delight: A Year on an Old-Fashioned Farm. Tudor, Tasha. 12p. (gr. 1 up). 1986. 14.95 (*0-399-21308-2*, Philomel) Putnam Pub Group.
—The Secret Garden. Burnett, Frances H. LC 62-17457. 256p. (gr. 4-8). 1987. pap. 3.50 (*0-06-440188-X*, Trophy) HarpC Child Bks.
—The Springs of Joy. Tudor, Tasha. LC 79-66708. 64p. (ps up). 1988. SBE 12.95 (*0-02-689092-5*) Macmillan Child Grp.
—Take Joy: The Tasha Tudor Christmas Book. Tudor, Tasha. LC 66-10645. (gr. k up). 1980. 18.95 (*0-399-20766-X*, Philomel) Putnam Pub Group.
—Tale for Easter. Tudor, Tasha. LC 62-8626. (gr. k-3). 1985. 6.95 (*0-8098-1008-5*); pap. 4.95 (*0-8098-1807-8*) McKay.
—A Tasha Tudor's Sampler: A Tale for Easter, Pumpkin Moonshine, The Dolls' Christmas. Tudor, Tasha. (gr. k-3). 1977. 9.95 (*0-679-20412-1*) McKay.
Tullier, Debra L. Flags of Tennessee. Cannon, Devereaux D., Jr. LC 90-7679. 112p. (gr. 6-8). 1990. 14.95 (*0-88289-794-2*) Pelican.
Tulloch, Coral. Ah, Treasure! Drew, David. LC 92-21455. 1993. 3.75 (*0-383-03611-9*) SRA Schl Grp.
—Lunch for Three. Vandine, JoAnn. LC 92-31954. 1993. 4.25 (*0-383-03582-1*) SRA Schl Grp.
—That's Dangerous. Bissett, Isabel. LC 92-31947. 1993. 3.75 (*0-383-03596-1*) SRA Schl Grp.
Tully, Carol & Rizzuto, Joe. Decisions, 5 Vols. Westfall, Tanja & Miles, Patrick. Karch, Cheri, ed. 160p. (gr. 4-7). 1989. Set. text ed. 38.95 (*1-877618-00-4*) APIX Intl.
—Decisions: Building Bricks - Crystal, Vol 3. Westfall, Tanja & Miles, Patrick. Karch, Cheri, ed. 32p. (gr. 4-7). 1989. text ed. 7.79 (*1-877618-03-9*) APIX Intl.
—Decisions: Struggle in the Willow Tree, Vol. 1. Westfall, Tanja & Miles, Patrick. Karch, Cheri, ed. 32p. (gr. 4-7). 1989. text ed. 7.79 (*1-877618-01-2*) APIX Intl.
—Decisions: The Edge - LSD, Vol. 5. Westfall, Tanja & Miles, Patrick. Karch, Cheri, ed. 32p. (gr. 4-7). 1989. text ed. 7.79 ea. (*1-877618-05-5*) APIX Intl.
—Decisions: The Pit, Vol. 2. Westfall, Tanja & Miles, Patrick. Karch, Cheri, ed. 32p. (gr. 4-7). 1989. text ed. 7.79 (*1-877618-02-0*) APIX Intl.
—Decisions: The Survivor, Vol. 4. Westfall, Tanja & Miles, Patrick. Karch, Cheri, ed. 32p. (gr. 4-7). 1989. text ed. 7.84 (*1-877618-04-7*) APIX Intl.
Tuma-Church, Deb. The Storytime Handbook. Tuma-Church, Deb. 73p. (ps-5). 1988. wkbk. spiral bdg. 7.95 (*0-939644-37-1*) Media Pub.
Tuminell, jt. illus. see Maclean.
Tunis, Edwin. Colonial Craftsmen: The Beginnings of American Industry. Tunis, Edwin. LC 75-29612. 160p. (gr. 7 up). 1976. 25.00 (*0-690-01062-1*, Crowell Jr Bks) HarpC Child Bks.
—Colonial Living. Tunis, Edwin. LC 75-29611. 160p. (gr. 7 up). 1976. 25.00 (*0-690-01063-X*, Crowell Jr Bks) HarpC Child Bks.
—Frontier Living. Tunis, Edwin. LC 75-29639. 168p. (gr. 7 up). 1976. 26.00 (*0-690-01064-8*, Crowell Jr Bks) HarpC Child Bks.
—Indians. rev. ed. Tunis, Edwin. LC 78-60175. 160p. (gr. 5 up). 1979. Repr. of 1959 ed. PLB 24.89 (*0-690-01283-7*, Crowell Jr Bks) HarpC Child Bks.
—Oars, Sails & Steam: A Picture Book of Ships. Tunis, Edwin. LC 76-25453. (gr. 6 up). 1977. 25.00i (*0-690-01284-5*, Crowell Jr Bks) HarpC Child Bks.
Tunis, Edwin, jt. illus. see Baruffa, Joanne.

Tunney, Linda. How Do Ants Know When You're Having A Picnic? (And Other Questions Kids Ask about Insects & Other Crawly Things) Settel, Joanne & Baggett, Nancy. LC 86-3353. 112p. (gr. 3-7). 1986. SBE 13.95 (*0-689-31268-7*, Atheneum Childrens Bk) Macmillan Child Grp.
—Why Do Cats' Eyes Glow in the Dark? (And Other Questions Kids Ask about Animals) Settel, Joanne & Baggett, Nancy. LC 87-13708. 112p. (gr. 3-7). 1988. SBE 13.95 (*0-689-31267-9*, Atheneum Child Bk) Macmillan Child Grp.
—Why Does My Nose Run? (And Other Questions Kids Ask about Their Bodies) Settel, Joanne & Baggett, Nancy. LC 84-21549. 80p. (gr. 4-6). 1985. SBE 12.95 (*0-689-31078-1*, Atheneum Child Bk) Macmillan Child Grp.
—Your Two Brains. Stafford, Patricia. LC 85-28575. 96p. (gr. 3-7). 1986. SBE 13.95 (*0-689-31142-7*, Atheneum Child Bk) Macmillan Child Grp.

Turechek, Lou. African-American Cultures: Myths & Legends from Ghana for Children. Larungu, Rute. LC 92-81116. 96p. (gr. 3 up). 1992. lib. bdg. 14.95 (*1-878893-21-1*); pap. 8.95 (*1-878893-20-3*) Telcraft Bks. KIRKUS REVIEWS: "'A story, a story, let it go, let it come.' Three Hausa & five Ashanti tales...one can almost hear the teller's voice." BOOKLIST: "In an insightful, interactive manner, this collection provides a range of fast-paced tales... these stories should be read aloud, perhaps even dramatized, to be fully appreciated." SCHOOL LIBRARY JOURNAL: "...free verse...a fuller background to West African folklore than single-story books." To order: Quality Books, Inc. (libraries); Baker & Taylor (all). *Publisher Provided Annotation.*

Turgenieff, Assja. And There Was Light. Streit, Jacob. Piening, Ekkehard, tr. from GER. 112p. (gr. 3-4). 1976. pap. 13.00 (*0-88010-034-6*, Pub. by Verlag Walter Keller Switzerland) Anthroposophic.
Turk, Hanne. Rabbit & Chicken Count Eggs. Landa, Norbert. LC 90-33436. (ps). 1992. bds. 4.95 (*0-688-09971-8*, Tambourine Bks) Morrow.
—Rabbit & Chicken Find a Box. Landa, Norbert. LC 90-33379. (ps). 1992. bds. 4.95 (*0-688-09968-8*, Tambourine Bks) Morrow.
—Rabbit & Chicken Play Hide & Seek. Landa, Norbert. LC 90-33484. (ps). 1992. bds. 4.95 (*0-688-09970-X*, Tambourine Bks) Morrow.
—Rabbit & Chicken Play with Colors. Landa, Norbert. LC 90-33485. (ps). 1992. bds. 4.95 (*0-688-09969-6*, Tambourine Bks) Morrow.
Turkle, Brinton. The Boy Who Didn't Believe in Spring. Clifton, Lucille. (gr. 3-4). 1973. 13.95 (*0-525-27145-7*, DCB); pap. 1.95 (*0-525-45038-6*, DCB) Dutton Child Bks.
—The Boy Who Didn't Believe in Spring. Clifton, Lucille. LC 87-21745. 32p. (ps-3). 1988. pap. 4.95 (*0-525-44365-7*, 0383-120, DCB) Dutton Child Bks.
—Do Not Open. Turkle, Brinton. LC 80-10289. 32p. (ps-2). 1981. pap. 13.95 (*0-525-28785-X*, 01258-370, DCB) Dutton Child Bks.
—Do Not Open. Turkle, Brinton. LC 80-10289. 32p. (ps-2). 1985. pap. 3.95 (*0-525-44224-3*, DCB) Dutton Child Bks.
—If You Grew up with Abraham Lincoln. McGovern, Ann. 64p. 1992. pap. 3.95 (*0-590-45154-5*) Scholastic Inc.
—If You Lived in Colonial Times. 1992. pap. 4.95 (*0-590-45160-X*) Scholastic Inc.
—Obadiah the Bold. Turkle, Brinton. LC 65-13350. (gr. k-3). 1977. 3.95 (*0-14-050233-5*, Puffin) Puffin Bks.
—Over the River & Through the Wood. Child, Lydia Maria. 32p. (gr. k-3). 1987. pap. 3.95 (*0-590-41190-X*, Blue Ribbons Bks) Scholastic Inc.
—Rachel & Obadiah. Turkle, Brinton. LC 77-15661. (gr. k-3). 1978. 15.00 (*0-525-38020-5*, DCB) Dutton Child Bks.
—Rachel & Obadiah. Turkle, Brinton. (gr. 1-3). 1987. pap. 4.95 (*0-525-44303-7*, DCB) Dutton Child Bks.
Turnbaugh, Paul. The Journey of Wishes. Bibee, John. LC 93-8173. 192p. (Orig.). (gr. 4-8). 1993. pap. 6.99 (*0-8308-1207-5*, 1207) InterVarsity.
—The Only Game in Town. Bibee, John. LC 88-9369. 209p. (ps-6). 1988. pap. 6.99 (*0-8308-1202-4*, 1202) InterVarsity.
—The Runaway Parents: A Parable of Problem Parents. Bibee, John. LC 91-22762. 204p. (gr. 3-8). 1991. pap. 6.99 (*0-8308-1205-9*, 1205) InterVarsity.
—The Spirit Flyers Series, 4 bks, Set A. Bibee, John. (Orig.). 1992. Boxed Set. pap. 24.99 (*0-8308-1208-3*, 1208) InterVarsity.

—The Spirit Flyers Series, 4 bks, Set B. Bibee, John. (Orig.). 1993. Set. pap. 24.99 boxed (*0-8308-1289-X*, 1289) InterVarsity.
—The Toy Campaign. Bibee, John. LC 87-3261. 225p. (Orig.). (gr. 4 up). 1987. pap. 6.99 (*0-8308-1201-6*, 1201) InterVarsity.
Turnbull, Jean. School Makes Sense...Sometimes. Gatch, Jean. LC 80-10281. 32p. (gr. k-5). 1980. 16.95 (*0-87705-494-0*) Human Sci Pr.
Turner, Corinne. Golden Spears & Other Fairy Tales. Leamy, Edmund. LC 76-9902. (gr. 4-6). 1976. Repr. of 1928 ed. 15.00x (*0-8486-0211-0*) Roth Pub Inc.
Turner, Elizabeth, jt. illus. see Bissex, Thelma.
Turner, Erin. What Will the Weather Be?, No. 1: A Folk Weather Calendar. Davis, Hubert J. LC 88-17869. 40p. (Orig.). (gr. k-12). 1988. pap. 4.95 (*0-936015-11-X*) Pocahontas Pr.
—What Will the Weather Be?, No. 2: Animal Signs. Davis, Hubert J. LC 90-22327. 56p. (Orig.). (gr. k-12). 1991. pap. 5.95 (*0-936015-12-8*) Pocahontas Pr.
Turner, Gwenda. Opposites. Turner, Gwenda. 24p. (ps-k). 1993. 9.99 (*0-670-84813-1*) Viking Child Bks.
Turner, James. Colonel Neverfail's Christmas. Coltharp, Barbara. Sandifer, Shannon & Woolfolk, Doug, eds. (Orig.). (gr. 1-3). 1981. 7.95 (*0-86518-019-9*) Moran Pub Corp.
Turner, Jeanne. Grilled Cheese at Four O'Clock in the Morning. American Diabetes Association Staff. 90p. (gr. 3-7). 1988. pap. 5.95 (*0-945448-02-3*, CCHGC) Am Diabetes.
Turner, Joseph R., III. Jessie J: Red Rock Ranch Detective: A Literary Adventure for Gifted Students. Schuyler, Royce. Kester, Ellen S., ed. 190p. (Orig.). (gr. 3-6). 1989. pap. 6.95 (*0-685-26280-4*); tchr's. manual 35.00 (*0-685-26281-2*) Pickwick Pubs.
—Word Magic: Shakespeare's Rhetoric for Gifted Students: Elementary & Secondary Shakespearian Excerpts. 2nd ed. Kester, Ellen S. 194p. 1989. pap. text ed. 35.00 (*0-685-26279-0*) Pickwick Pubs.
Turner, Peggy. ABC Career Book for Girls: Introducing the Career Pals. Turner, Peggy & Brewer, Linda S. Hollis, Myrlys, ed. Lincoln, Rebecca, intro. by. 32p. (gr. 1-4). 1992. pap. 6.95 (*0-9622514-2-9*) Columbia Sacramento.
Turner, William. Sex for Straights: A Call for Critical Thinking by Teenagers Who Oppose Sexual Perversion. Knot, Madonna. Rachner, Mary J., intro. by. 34p. (gr. 7-12). 1993. PLB 49.95 (*0-9623133-5-1*) Oxner Inst.
Turska, Krystyna. The Gondolier's Cat. Corlett, William. 32p. (ps-1). 1994. 19.95 (*0-340-54165-2*, Pub. by Hodder & Stoughton UK) Trafalgar.
Turtiainen, Tuomas. Rainbow Collection, 1988: Stories & Poetry by Young People. Janger, Kathie, ed. Valenti, Jack, intro. by. 160p. (gr. 1-8). 1988. pap. 6.00 (*0-929889-03-7*) Young Writers Contest Found.
Tusa, Tricia. Chicken. Tusa, Tricia. LC 85-10591. 32p. (gr. k-3). 1986. RSBE 13.95 (*0-02-789320-0*, Macmillan Child Bk) Macmillan Child Grp.
—Maebelle's Suitcase. Tusa, Tricia. LC 86-12434. 32p. (gr. k-3). 1987. SBE 13.95 (*0-02-789250-6*, Macmillan Child Bk) Macmillan Child Grp.
—Maebelle's Suitcase. Tusa, Tricia. LC 90-40678. 32p. (gr. k-3). 1991. pap. 4.95 (*0-689-71444-0*, Aladdin) Macmillan Child Grp.
—Stay Away from the Junkyard! Tusa, Tricia. LC 87-15274. 32p. (gr. k-3). 1988. RSBE 14.95 (*0-02-789541-6*, Macmillan Child Bk) Macmillan Child Grp.
—Stay Away from the Junkyard! Tusa, Tricia. LC 91-38498. 32p. (gr. k-3). 1992. pap. 4.95 (*0-689-71626-5*, Aladdin) Macmillan Child Grp.
Tusan, Stan L. The Worst Show-and-Tell Ever. Walsh, Rita A. LC 93-24844. 32p. (gr. 2-4). 1993. PLB 9.89 (*0-8167-3176-4*); pap. text ed. 2.95 (*0-8167-3177-2*) Troll Assocs.
Tusken, Dee. Wee Taste & See: A Story Book - Cook Book - Coloring Book. Sage, Margaret A. 32p. (Orig.). (gr. 1-3). 1992. pap. 9.95 (*0-9631988-1-5*) Taste & See.
Tuttle, Merlin D. Batman: Exploring the World of Bats. Pringle, Laurence. LC 90-8679. 48p. (gr. 4-6). 1991. SBE 14.95 (*0-684-19232-2*, Scribners Young Read) Macmillan Child Grp.
Tvaryanas, Alphonse. Computer Basics. Hellman, Hal. LC 82-21483. 48p. (gr. 3-7). 1983. 9.95 (*0-13-164574-9*) P-H.
Twachtman, J. Alden. Col. Weatherford & His Friends. Grand, Gordon. 242p. (gr. 10 up). 1991. Repr. of 1933 ed. 40.00 (*1-56416-026-2*) Derrydale Pr.
—Silver Horn: And Other Sporting Tales of John Weatherford. Grand, Gordon. 200p. (gr. 10 up). 1991. Repr. of 1932 ed. 40.00 (*1-56416-025-4*) Derrydale Pr.
Twede, jt. illus. see Clarkson.
Twede, Evan. Brite Dreams. Brady, Janeen & Woolley, Diane. 32p. (Orig.). (ps). 1988. pap. 2.25 (*0-944803-79-2*); pap. 9.95 incl. cassette (*0-944803-80-6*) Brite Intl.
—My Body Machine. Brady, Janeen. (ps-6). 1989. songbook 45p. 7.95 (*0-944803-71-7*); activity bk. 2.25 (*0-944803-65-2*); cassette & activity bk. 9.95 (*0-944803-66-0*) Brite Intl.
—Safety Kids Personal Safety, Vol. 1. Brady, Janeen. 14p. (gr. k-6). 1983. Set of 20. wkbk. 12.00 (*0-944803-20-2*) Brite Intl.
—Safety Kids Play it Smart: Stay Safe from Drugs, Vol. 2. Brady, Janeen. 14p. (gr. k-6). 1985. Set of 20. wkbk. 12.00 (*0-944803-25-3*) Brite Intl.

—Safety Kids Play It Smart, Vol. 2: Stay Safe from Drugs. Brady, Janeen. (Orig.). (gr. k-6). 1985. pap. text ed. 5.95 songbook (*0-944803-21-0*); pap. text ed. 1.25 dialogue bk., 1985, 16pgs. (*0-944803-24-5*); act. bk. 2.25 (*0-944803-22-9*); cassette & bk. 9.95 (*0-944803-23-7*); video avail. (*0-944803-72-5*) Brite Intl.
—Safety Kids, Vol. 3: Protect Their Minds. Brady, Janeen J. 32p. (Orig.). (gr. k-6). 1992. pap. 2.25 (*0-944803-78-4*); pap. 9.95 incl. cassette (*0-944803-77-6*) Brite Intl.
Twede, Evan & Nelson, Eloise. Watch Me Sing, Vol. 2. Brady, Janeen. 30p. (ps-2). 1986. pap. text ed. 5.95 songbk. (*0-944803-11-3*); cassette 7.95 (*0-944803-12-1*) Brite Intl.
Twinn, Colin. Jeremy Fisher. Potter, Beatrix. 10p. (ps-5). 1992. 5.99 (*0-7232-3999-1*) Warne.
—Peter Rabbit. Potter, Beatrix. 10p. (ps-5). 1992. 5.99 (*0-7232-3997-5*) Warne.
—Where's Peter Rabbit? Potter, Beatrix. (ps-3). 1988. 6.95 (*0-7232-3519-8*) Warne.
—The World of Peter Rabbit Sticker Book. Potter, Beatrix. 32p. (ps-3). 1990. pap. 6.95 (*0-7232-3645-3*) Warne.
Twinney, Dick. Nibblers & Gnawers. Carwardine, Mark. Young, Richard G., ed. LC 89-32807. 45p. (gr. 3-5). 1989. PLB 14.60 (*0-944483-29-1*) Garrett Ed Corp.
Twins, Ahbleza. I Am the Power. Rizer, Arden, Jr. 87p. (Orig.). (gr. 7-12). 1992. pap. 10.00x (*0-939795-46-9*) Amer Spirit.
Twofeathers, Shannon, jt. illus. see Tait, Douglas.
Tyler, Barbara. Plugly, the Horse That Could Do Everything. McClung, Cooky. 48p. 1993. 16.95 (*0-939481-32-4*) Half Halt Pr.
Tyler, D. D. Bears in the Wild. Graham, Ada & Graham, Frank. LC 80-68732. 128p. (gr. 4-7). 1981. 8.95 (*0-440-00532-9*); PLB 8.44 (*0-440-00538-8*) Delacorte.
—Bears in the Wild. Graham, Ada & Graham, Frank. 176p. (gr. 4-8). 1983. pap. 2.25 (*0-440-40897-0*, YB) Dell.
—Whale Watch. Graham, Ada & Graham, Frank. LC 77-20531. 32p. (gr. 5 up). 1978. 7.95 (*0-440-09505-0*); pap. 6.46 (*0-440-09506-9*) Delacorte.
Tyler, Gillian. The Good Little Christmas Tree. Williams, Ursula M. LC 90-4498. 48p. 1991. 14.95 (*0-679-81060-9*) Knopf Bks Yng Read.
Tyree, Michael. I Want to Know. Starr, Aloa. (Orig.). (ps-6). 1990. pap. 7.00 (*0-929686-02-0*, Dist. by Aloa Starr) Temple Golden Pubns.
Tyrrell, Frances. Huron Carol. De Brebeuf, Jean. LC 91-35965. 32p. (ps-6). 1992. 15.00 (*0-525-44909-4*, DCB) Dutton Child Bks.
—Joy to the World! Forrester, Maureen, selected by. Heller, Charles, contrib. by. 32p. 1993. reinforced bdg. 14.99 (*0-525-45169-2*, DCB) Dutton Child Bks.
Tyrrell, Robert A., photos by. Hummingbirds: Jewels in the Sky. Tyrrell, Esther Q. LC 91-40857. 36p. (gr. 1-5). 1992. 14.00 (*0-517-58390-9*); PLB 14.99 (*0-517-58391-7*) Crown Bks Yng Read.

U

Uchida, Yoshiko. The Magic Listening Cap. Uchida, Yoshiko. 160p. (Orig.). 1987. pap. 7.95 (*0-88739-016-1*) Creative Arts Bk.
Uderzo. Asterix & Cleopatra. De Goscinny, Rene. 1976. pap. 9.95 (*0-340-17220-7*) Intl Lang.
—Asterix & the Big Fight. De Goscinny, Rene. 1976. pap. 9.95 (*0-340-19167-8*) Intl Lang.
—Asterix & the Cauldron. De Goscinny, Rene. 1976. pap. 9.95 (*0-340-22711-7*) Intl Lang.
—Asterix & the Golden Sickle. De Goscinny, Rene. 1976. pap. 9.95 (*0-340-21209-8*) Intl Lang.
—Asterix & the Goths. De Goscinny, Rene. 1976. pap. 9.95 (*0-917201-54-X*) Intl Lang.
—Asterix & the Great Crossing. De Goscinny, Rene. 1976. pap. 9.95 (*0-340-21589-5*) Intl Lang.
—Asterix & the Laurel Wreath. De Goscinny, Rene. 1976. pap. 9.95 (*0-340-20699-3*) Intl Lang.
—Asterix & the Roman Agent. De Goscinny, Rene. 1976. pap. 9.95 (*0-340-19168-6*) Intl Lang.
—Asterix & the Soothsayer. De Goscinny, Rene. 1976. pap. 9.95 (*0-340-20697-7*) Intl Lang.
—Asterix at the Olympic Games. De Goscinny, Rene. 1976. pap. 9.95 (*0-340-19169-4*) Intl Lang.
—Asterix in Britain. De Goscinny, Rene. 1976. pap. 9.95 (*0-340-17221-5*) Intl Lang.
—Asterix in Spain. De Goscinny, Rene. 1976. pap. 9.95 (*0-340-18326-8*) Intl Lang.
—Asterix in Switzerland. De Goscinny, Rene. 1976. pap. 9.95 (*0-340-19270-4*) Intl Lang.
—Asterix the Gladiator. De Goscinny, Rene. 1976. pap. 9.95 (*0-340-18320-9*) Intl Lang.
—Asterix the Legionary. De Goscinny, Rene. 1976. pap. 9.95 (*0-340-18321-7*) Intl Lang.
—The Mansion of the Gods. De Goscinny, Rene. 1976. pap. 9.95 (*0-340-19269-0*) Intl Lang.
Udry, Leslie. The Lost Bellybutton. Gullette, Margaret M. LC 76-26377. 32p. (Orig.). (ps-2). 1976. pap. 4.95 (*0-914996-11-8*) Lollipop Power.
Uggla, Goran. The Car Book. LC 93-4422. 1993. spiral bdg. 17.95 (*0-8118-0514-X*) Chronicle Bks.
Uhler, Kimanne. Always Gramma. Nelson, Vaunda M. 32p. (ps-3). 1988. PLB 14.95 (*0-399-21542-5*, Putnam) Putnam Pub Group.

Ulan, Helen C. Science Magic Tricks: Over 50 Fun Tricks That Mystify & Dazzle. Shalit, Nathan. LC 79-18645. 128p. (gr. 6 up). 1981. (Bks Young Read); pap. 5.95 (*0-8050-0234-0*) H Holt & Co.
Ullom, A. Thomas. Come Aboard Boats: Ship-Shape 3-D Activities. Ullom, A. Thomas. Art In-Forms Staff, ed. 20p. (Orig.). 1983. pap. 8.95 wkbk. (*0-911835-00-8*) Art In-Forms.
Ulm, Robert. Alaska: In Words & Pictures. Fradin, Dennis. LC 77-4353. 48p. (gr. 2-5). 1977. PLB 17.27 (*0-516-03902-4*) Childrens.
—California: In Words & Pictures. Fradin, Dennis. LC 76-50600. 48p. (gr. 2-5). 1977. PLB 17.27 (*0-516-03905-9*) Childrens.
—Ohio: In Words & Pictures. Fradin, Dennis. LC 76-46941. 48p. (gr. 2-5). 1977. PLB 17.27 (*0-516-03935-0*); pap. 3.95 (*0-516-43935-9*) Childrens.
—Wisconsin: In Words & Pictures. Fradin, Dennis. LC 77-5330. 48p. (gr. 2-5). 1977. PLB 17.27 (*0-516-03948-2*) Childrens.
Ulrich, George. The American Heritage First Dictionary. Krensky, Stephen, ed. LC 86-7363. (gr. 1-2). 1986. 12.70 (*0-395-42530-1*) HM.
—Babe Ruth & the Home Run Derby. Mooser, Stephen. 80p. (Orig.). (gr. 2-5). 1992. pap. 3.25 (*0-440-40486-X*, YB) Dell.
—Climb Aboard. Greydanus, Rose. LC 87-19150. 32p. (gr. k-2). 1988. PLB 11.59 (*0-8167-1099-6*); pap. text ed. 2.95 (*0-8167-1100-3*) Troll Assocs.
—Dairy Farmer. Poskanzer, Susan C. LC 88-10040. 32p. (gr. k-3). 1989. PLB 10.89 (*0-8167-1426-6*); pap. text ed. 2.95 (*0-8167-1427-4*) Troll Assocs.
—Emily Eyefinger. Ball, Duncan. LC 91-20751. 96p. (gr. 2-5). 1992. 13.00 jacketed (*0-671-74618-9*, S&S BFYR) S&S Trade.
—Emily Eyefinger & the Lost Treasure. Ball, Duncan. LC 93-39648. Date not set. write for info. (*0-671-86535-8*, S&S BFYR) S&S Trade.
—Emily Eyefinger, Secret Agent. Ball, Duncan. LC 92-30518. 96p. (gr. 2-5). 1993. pap. 13.00 JRT (*0-671-79827-8*, S&S BFYR) S&S Trade.
—First Dictionary. Houghton Mifflin Company Staff, ed. LC 78-27760. 864p. (gr. 3-6). 1979. text ed. 11.95 (*0-685-07955-4*) HM.
—Forest Ranger. Pellowski, Michael J. LC 88-10355. 32p. (gr. 1-3). 1989. PLB 10.89 (*0-8167-1422-3*); pap. text ed. 2.95 (*0-8167-1423-1*) Troll Assocs.
—Gorgonzola Zombies in the Park. Levy, Elizabeth. LC 92-11353. 96p. (gr. 2-5). 1993. 14.00 (*0-06-021461-9*); PLB 13.89 (*0-06-021460-0*) HarpC Child Bks.
—The Headless Snowman. Mooser, Stephen. 80p. (Orig.). (gr. 2-5). 1992. pap. 3.25 (*0-440-40542-4*, YB) Dell.
—Jim Thorpe: Young Athlete. Santrey, Laurence. LC 82-15982. 48p. (gr. 4-6). 1983. PLB 10.79 (*0-89375-845-0*); pap. text ed. 3.50 (*0-89375-846-9*) Troll Assocs.
—Make Four Million Dollars by Next Thursday! Manes, Stephen. (gr. 3-7). 1992. pap. 3.50 (*0-553-15908-9*, Skylark) Bantam.
—A New Friend for Me. Hollander, Cass. 24p. (ps-2). 1992. pap. 0.99 (*1-56293-108-3*) McClanahan Bk.
—Rainy Day Fun. Palazzo, Janet. LC 87-10842. 32p. (gr. k-2). 1988. PLB 11.59 (*0-8167-1095-3*); pap. text ed. 2.95 (*0-8167-1096-1*) Troll Assocs.
—Scary Scraped-up Skaters. Mooser, Stephen. 80p. (Orig.). (gr. 2-5). 1992. pap. 3.25 (*0-440-40488-6*, YB) Dell.
—School Spirit Sabotage: Brian & Pea Brain Mystery. Levy, Elizabeth. LC 93-23029. 1994. write for info. (*0-06-023407-5*); PLB write for info. (*0-06-023408-3*) HarpC Child Bks.
—The Snow Bowl. Mooser, Stephen. 80p. (gr. 2-5). 1992. pap. 3.25 (*0-440-40563-7*, YB) Dell.
—The Spy on Third Base. Christopher, Matt. LC 88-8914. (gr. 2-4). 1988. 12.95 (*0-316-13996-3*) Little.
—The Terrible Tickler. Mooser, Stephen. 80p. (Orig.). (gr. 2-5). 1992. pap. 3.25 (*0-440-40487-8*, YB) Dell.
—Thomas Alva Edison: Young Inventor. Sabin, Louis. LC 82-15889. 48p. (gr. 4-6). 1983. PLB 10.79 (*0-89375-841-8*); pap. text ed. 3.50 (*0-89375-842-6*) Troll Assocs.
—Truck Driver. Stamper, Judith B. LC 88-10039. 32p. (gr. k-3). 1989. PLB 10.89 (*0-8167-1424-X*); pap. text ed. 2.95 (*0-8167-1425-8*) Troll Assocs.
Unada. The Old Witch & the Dragon. DeLage, Ida. 48p. (gr. k-4). 1991. Repr. of 1979 ed. lib. bdg. 12.95 (*0-7910-1477-0*) Chelsea Hse.
—Rosalie. Hamilton, Dorothy. LC 76-39961. 128p. (gr. 3-10). 1977. pap. text ed. 3.95 (*0-8361-1807-3*) Herald Pr.
Uncle Hyggly. Tad Gonopolis & His Adventures in the Slumberyard, No. 3. Uncle Hyggly, pseud. 48p. (gr. 3-6). 1987. pap. 8.95 (*0-935583-03-3*) Wounded Coot.
Underhill, Graham. Animals Underground. Ruffault, Charlotte. Matthews, Sarah, tr. from FRE. LC 87-34616. 38p. (gr. k-5). 1988. 4.95 (*0-944589-03-0*, 030) Young Discovery Lib.
—Seashore Life. Lazier, Christine. Bogard, Vicki, tr. from FRE. LC 90-50781. 38p. (gr. k-5). 1991. 4.95 (*0-944589-39-1*, 391) Young Discovery Lib.
Underhill, Liz. The Lucky Coin. Greaves, Margaret. LC 89-19718. 12p. 1990. 14.95 (*1-55670-129-2*) Stewart Tabori & Chang.
—One, Two, Tie Up My Shoe: A New Look at an Old Nursery Rhyme. Underhill, Liz. LC 89-28587. 32p. 1990. PLB 12.95 (*1-55670-142-X*) Stewart Tabori & Chang.

Ungerer, Tomi. The Beast of Monsieur Racine. Ungerer, Tomi. LC 74-149216. 32p. (ps-3). 1971. 15.95 (0-374-30640-0) FS&G.
—Christmas Eve at the Mellops. Ungerer, Tomi. 32p. (gr. k-3). 1992. pap. 3.99 (0-440-40728-1, YB) Dell.
—Crictor. Ungerer, Tomi. LC 58-5288. 32p. (ps-3). 1958. 13.00 (0-06-026180-3); PLB 12.89 (0-06-026181-1) HarpC Child Bks.
—Emile. Ungerer, Tomi. 32p. (ps-2). 1992. pap. 3.99 (0-440-40593-9, YB) Dell.
—Flat Stanley. Brown, Jeff. LC 63-17525. 64p. (gr. 1-5). 1964. PLB 13.89 (0-06-020681-0) HarpC Child Bks.
—Flat Stanley. Brown, Jeff. LC 63-17525. 48p. (gr. 2-5). 1989. pap. 4.95 (0-06-440293-2, Trophy) HarpC Child Bks.
—I Am Papa Snap & These Are My Favorite No Such Stories. Ungerer, Tomi. (gr. k-3). 1992. 15.00 (0-385-30653-9) Delacorte.
—The Mellops Go Spelunking. Ungerer, Tomi. 32p. (gr. k-3). 1992. pap. 3.99 (0-440-40727-3, YB) Dell.
—Oh, How Silly! Cole, William. 80p. (gr. 2 up). 1990. pap. 3.95 (0-14-034441-1, Puffin) Puffin Bks.
—Oh, That's Ridiculous! Cole, William, selected by. 80p. (gr. 1-4). 1988. pap. 3.95 (0-14-032857-2, Puffin) Puffin Bks.
—Oh, What Nonsense. Cole, William. 80p. (gr. 2 up). 1990. pap. 3.95 (0-14-034442-X, Puffin) Puffin Bks.
—The Three Robbers. Ungerer, Tomi. LC 87-11549. 32p. (ps-3). 1987. Repr. of 1962 ed. SBE 14.95 (0-689-31391-8, Atheneum Child Bk) Macmillan Child Grp.
—The Three Robbers. 2nd ed. Ungerer, Tomi. LC 91-246. 40p. (gr. k-3). 1991. pap. 4.95 (0-689-71511-0, Aladdin) Macmillan Child Grp.
—Tomi Ungerer's Heidi: The Classic Novel. Spyri, Johanna. Dole, Helen B., tr. Githens, John, contrib. by. (gr. 3-6). 1990. 19.95 (0-385-30244-4) Delacorte.
—Los Tres Bandidos - The Three Robbers. Ungerer, Tomi. Azaola, Miguel, tr. (SPA.). 36p. (gr. 2-4). 1990. pap. write for info. (84-204-5084-7) Santillana.
Unruh, Arch. Lenka of Emma Creek. Unruh, Sophia. Shelly, Maynard, ed. LC 89-81282. 32p. (Orig.). (ps-7). 1989. pap. 9.95 (0-87303-136-9) Faith & Life.
Unson, Ria. Nene & the Horrible Math Monster. Villanueva, Marie. LC 92-35425. 36p. (gr. 2-4). 1993. 12.95 (1-879965-02-X) Polychrome Pub.
Unwin, Nora S. Amos Fortune, Free Man. Yates, Elizabeth. (gr. 7 up). 1967. 15.00 (0-525-25570-2, DCB) Dutton Child Bks.
—Amos Fortune, Free Man. Yates, Elizabeth. 192p. (gr. 3-7). 1989. pap. 3.99 (0-14-034158-7, Puffin) Puffin Bks.
—The Lighted Heart. Yates, Elizabeth. (gr. 7 up). 1974. pap. 8.95 (0-87233-027-3) Bauhan.
—Mountain Born. Yates, Elizabeth. LC 92-40545. 128p. (gr. 3-7). 1993. pap. 6.95 (0-8027-7402-4) Walker & Co.
Unwin, Pippa. Herbie Hamster, Where Are You? Blacker, Terence. LC 90-8053. 32p. (ps-3). 1990. 10.95 (0-679-80838-8) Random Bks Yng Read.
Unzner-Fischer, Christa. Annie's Dancing Day. Moers, Hermann. Lanning, Rosemary, tr. from GER. LC 92-3612. 32p. (gr. k-3). 1992. 14.95 (1-55858-160-X); PLB 14.88 (1-55858-161-8) North-South Bks NYC.
—Loretta & the Little Fairy. Scheidl, Gerda M. James, J. Alison, tr. from GER. LC 92-33832. 32p. (gr. 2-3). 1993. 13.95 (1-55858-185-5); PLB 13.88 (1-55858-186-3) North-South Bks NYC.
Updike, David, photos by. A Helpful Alphabet of Friendly Objects. Updike, John. LC 93-29922. Date not set. write for info. (0-679-84324-8); PLB write for info. (0-679-94324-2) Knopf.
Upitis, Alvis. Extra Cheese, Please! Mozzarella's Journey from Cow to Pizza. Peterson, Cris. 32p. (ps-3). 1994. 13.95 (1-56397-177-1) Boyds Mills Pr.
Upman, Michael. Sylvan: The Magic Tree. Burbank, Linda. Van Treese, James B., ed. 30p. 1993. pap. 7.95 (1-56901-201-6) NW Pub.
Upton, Pat & Schmidt, Karen L. Who Lives in the Woods? Upton, Pat. LC 90-85721. 32p. (ps-1). 1991. 7.95 (1-878093-19-3) Boyds Mills Pr.
Uptton, Clive. Egermeier's Bible Story Book. 5th ed. Egermeier, Elsie E. LC 68-23397. (gr. k-6). 1969. 14.95 (0-87162-006-5, D2005); deluxe ed. 15.95 (0-87162-007-3, D2006); pap. 8.95 (0-87162-229-7, D2008) Warner Pr.
Urbahn, Clara. The Good Bad Wolf. Horowitz, Lynn R. LC 89-63141. 26p. (Orig.). (ps-1). 1989. pap. 7.95 spiral bdg. (0-938678-12-4) New Seed.

—Lulu Turns Four. Horwitz, Lynn. 32p. (ps-k). 1993. 13.95 (0-9625620-5-X) DOT Garnet.
A little chimp named Lulu is about to celebrate her fourth birthday, & like every small person in the process of getting bigger, she wonders if she'll master the challenges: standing by herself all the time; going to the doctor without feeling afraid; sharing happily with her little sister; eating bugs & green leaves like the grownups. Release from her fears comes in the form of a

birthday present from her mother, a helpless kitten who needs Lulu to help her grow up, in this charming book about the responsibilities--& the pleasures--of birthdays. LYNN HOROWITZ, a Yale graduate with a Masters in education, is the author of two previous books for young readers, THE GOOD BAD WOLF & MANOS A LA OBRA. She lives in Berkeley, California. CLARA URBAHN, an artist & illustrator of children's books, lives in Nantucket, Massachusetts. To order: Talman Company, 131 Spring St., New York, NY 10012. (212) 431-7175; FAX (212) 431-7215.
Publisher Provided Annotation.

Urbanovic, Jacki. Ot La-Ba'ot, 5 bks. Gordon, Yosi. 120p. (gr. 3-4). 1991. Set. wkbk. 6.95 (0-933873-54-9) Torah Aura.
Urbanovic, Jackie. The Best Trade of All. Bourque, Nina. LC 83-7352. 32p. (gr. 3-6). 1984. PLB 27.99 incl. cassette (0-8172-2280-4); cassette only 14.00 (0-317-19659-6) Raintree Steck-V.
—Do Cats Have Nine Lives? The Strange Things People Say about Animals Around the House. Dennard, Deborah. LC 92-10353. 1992. 19.95 (0-87614-773-2) Carolrhoda Bks.
—Gifted Kids Speak Out: Hundreds of Kids Ages 6-13 Talk about School, Friends, Their Families & the Future. Delisle, James R. Espeland, Pamela, ed. LC 87-25139. 120p. (Orig.). (gr. 2-7). 1987. pap. 9.95 (0-915793-10-5) Free Spirit Pub.
—It's All in Your Head: A Guide to Understanding Your Brain & Boosting Your Brain Power. rev. ed. Barrett, Susan L. Espeland, Pamela, ed. LC 18-18090. 160p. (gr. 3-7). 1992. pap. 9.95 (0-915793-45-8) Free Spirit Pub.
—Mah la'Asot: What Should I Do? A Book of Ethical Problems & Jewish Responses. Alper, Janis & Grishaver, Joel. 64p. (Orig.). (gr. 4-8). 1992. pap. text ed. 4.95 (0-933873-69-7) Torah Aura.
—The Survival Guide for Kids with LD: Learning Differences. Fisher, Gary & Cummings, Rhoda. Nielsen, Nancy, ed. LC 89-37084. 104p. (Orig.). (gr. 2 up). 1990. pap. 16.95 incl. audiocassette (0-915793-21-0); pap. 9.95 (0-915793-18-0); audiocassette 10.00 (0-915793-20-2) Free Spirit Pub.
Urberuaga, Emilio. Paper Bird. Lobato, Arcadio. LC 93-24469. 1994. 18.95 (0-87614-817-8) Carolrhoda Bks.
Utton, Peter. Shhh! A Lift the Flap Book. Grindley, Sally. 32p. (ps-3). 1992. 13.95 (0-316-32899-5, Joy St Bks) Little.
—Uncle Harold & the Green Hat. Hindley, Judy. 26p. (ps-3). 1991. bds. 13.95 (0-374-38030-9) FS&G.
Uzanus, Phil. Charles Caterpillar. Haas, James. Kendzia, Mary C., ed. 32p. (Orig.). 1992. pap. 4.95 (0-89622-530-5) Twenty-Third.

V

Va, Leong. A Letter to the King. Va, Leong. Anderson, James, tr. from CHI. LC 91-9469. 32p. (gr. k-3). 1991. 14.95 (0-06-020079-0); PLB 14.89 (0-06-020070-7) HarpC Child Bks.
Vaccaro Associates, Inc. Staff. Minnie 'n Me: Lemonade for Sale. Calder, Lyn. 24p. (ps-k). 1992. pap. write for info. (0-307-11649-2, 11649, Golden Pr) Western Pub.
—Minnie 'n Me: That's What Friends Are For. Calder, Lyn. 24p. (ps-k). 1992. pap. write for info. (0-307-11629-8, 11629, Golden Pr) Western Pub.
Vaccaro Associates Staff. Winnie the Pooh's Halloween. Talkington, Bruce. LC 93-70934. 32p. (ps-4). 1993. 11.95 (1-56282-540-2) Disney Pr.
Vaccaro, Garparo. Aladdin: The Magic Carpet Ride. Lampl, Cathy, ed. LC 92-54878. 10p. (ps-k). 1993. 4.95 (1-56282-396-5) Disney Pr.
Vachio, Tony. My Secret. Boulden, Jim. 32p. (Orig.). (gr. 1-7). 1991. pap. 4.95 (1-878076-13-2) Boulden Pub.
Vaes, Alain. Puss in Boots. Kirstein, Lincoln, retold by. 32p. (ps-3). 1992. 15.95 (0-316-89506-7) Little.
Vagin, Vladimir. Insects from Outer Space. Asch, Frank & Vagin, Vladimir. LC 93-26876. 1994. 14.95 (0-590-45489-7) Scholastic Inc.
—The King's Equal. Paterson, Katherine. LC 90-30527. 64p. (gr. 2-5). 1992. 17.00 (0-06-022496-7); PLB 16.89 (0-06-022497-5) HarpC Child Bks.
Vagin, Vladimir & Asch, Frank. Here Comes the Cat! Vagin, Vladimir & Asch, Frank. LC 88-3083. (gr. k-3). 1989. pap. 11.95 (0-590-41859-9) Scholastic Inc.
Vaing, Jocelang. Trip Through Cambodia. Diep, Bridgette. LC 73-159478. 32p. (ps-3). 8.95 (0-87592-054-3) Scroll Pr.
Vainio, Pirkko. Josie Smith. Nabb, Magdalen. LC 88-8301. 80p. (gr. 1-4). 1989. SBE 12.95 (0-689-50485-3, M K McElderry) Macmillan Child Grp.
—Josie Smith. large type ed. Nabb, Magdalen. 88p. 1993. 13.95 (0-7451-1673-6, Galaxy Child Lrg Print) Chivers N Amer.
—Josie Smith & Eileen. Nabb, Magdalen. LC 91-31848. 96p. (gr. 1-5). 1992. SBE 12.95 (0-689-50534-5, M K McElderry) Macmillan Child Grp.
—Josie Smith at School. Nabb, Magdalen. LC 91-10970. 112p. (gr. 1-5). 1992. SBE 12.95 (0-689-50533-7, M K McElderry) Macmillan Child Grp.
—Josie Smith at the Seashore. Nabb, Magdalen. LC 89-8168. 96p. (gr. 1-5). 1990. SBE 12.95 (0-689-50492-6, M K McElderry) Macmillan Child Grp.
—Josie Smith at the Seaside. large type ed. Nabb, Magdalen. 1993. 15.95 (0-7451-1808-9, Galaxy Child Lrg Print) Chivers N Amer.
—The Snow Goose. Vainio, Pirkko. James, J. Alison, tr. from GER. LC 92-31330. 32p. (gr. k-3). 1993. 14.95 (1-55858-194-4); lib. bdg. 14.88 (1-55858-195-2) North-South Bks NYC.
Valat, P. M. & Perols, S. Couleur. (FRE.). (ps-1). 1989. 17.95 (2-07-035706-6) Schoenhof.
Valat, P. M. & Perols, Sylvie. Colors. De Bourgoing, Pascale. 1991. pap. 10.95 (0-590-45236-3, Cartwheel) Scholastic Inc.
—Egg. De Bourgoing, Pascale. 24p. 1992. pap. 10.95 (0-590-45266-5, Cartwheel) Scholastic Inc.
—Tree. De Bourgoing, Pascale. 24p. 1992. pap. 10.95 (0-590-45265-7, Cartwheel) Scholastic Inc.
Valat, Pierre-Marie. Australia: On the Other Side of the World. Stanley-Baker, Penny. LC 87-34523. 38p. (gr. k-5). 1988. 4.95 (0-944589-15-4, 154) Young Discovery Lib.
—The Camera: Snapshots, Movies, Videos, & Cartoons. Jeunesse, Gallimard, et al, eds. LC 92-41412. 1993. 11.95 (0-590-47129-5) Scholastic Inc.
—Pomme. (FRE.). (ps-1). 1989. 14.95 (2-07-035702-3) Schoenhof.
—Teeth, Tusks & Fangs. Dievart, Roger. Bogard, Vicki, tr. from FRE. LC 90-50778. 38p. (gr. k-5). 1991. 4.95 (0-944589-35-9, 359) Young Discovery Lib.
Valdivia, Rochelle. Time for Rhyme: Stories, Poems, Games, Art Projects, Fun Sheets. 64p. (ps-k). 1988. pap. text ed. 8.95 (0-943129-02-8) Chatterbox Pr.
Valens, Amy. Danilo the Fruit Man. Valens, Amy. LC 91-46893. 32p. (ps-3). 1993. 12.99 (0-8037-1151-4); PLB 12.89 (0-8037-1152-2) Dial Bks Young.
Valenzuela, Walter V. Molecular Ramjet: And Other Bedtime Stories... Carlson, Larry G. 212p. (gr. 7-9). 1989. pap. 4.95 (0-929301-01-3) TadAlex Bks.
Vallet, Cedric. Almost Finished. Vallet, Cedric. 18p. (gr. k-3). 1992. pap. 11.95 (1-895583-28-4) MAYA Pubs.
—Mother, Where Is New York? Vallet, Cedric. 11p. (gr. k-3). 1992. pap. 13.95 (1-895583-27-6) MAYA Pubs.
—Now Is the Time. Vallet, Cedric. 16p. (gr. k-3). 1992. pap. 14.95 (1-895583-25-X) MAYA Pubs.
—A Trip to Paris. Vallet, Cedric. 17p. (gr. k-3). 1992. pap. 15.95 (1-895583-26-8) MAYA Pubs.
—Where Is Here? Vallet, Cedric. 19p. (gr. k-3). 1992. pap. 12.95 (1-895583-29-2) MAYA Pubs.
Vallet, Muriel. Camping Is Exciting. Vallet, Muriel. 19p. (gr. k-3). 1992. pap. 13.95 (1-895583-48-9) MAYA Pubs.
—Chantal Takes Her First Steps. Vallet, Muriel. 11p. (gr. k-3). 1992. pap. 6.95 (1-895583-50-0) MAYA Pubs.
—Dad, Can We Go Camping Tonight? Vallet, Muriel. 16p. (gr. 1-6). 1992. pap. 13.95 (1-56606-003-6) Bradley Mann.
—How Many Times? Vallet, Muriel. 13p. (gr. k-3). 1992. pap. 6.95 (1-895583-47-0) MAYA Pubs.
—Let's Take Turns. Vallet, Muriel. 15p. (gr. k-3). 1993. pap. 10.95 (1-895583-58-6) MAYA Pubs.
—My Turn. Vallet, Muriel. 17p. (gr. k-3). 1992. pap. 12.95 (1-895583-46-2) MAYA Pubs.
—Pinky Saves the Forest. Vallet, Muriel. 12p. (gr. 1-3). 1992. pap. 6.95 (1-895583-01-2) MAYA Pubs.
—Take the Plane. Vallet, Muriel. 10p. (gr. k-3). 1993. pap. 10.95 (1-895583-59-4) MAYA Pubs.
—Where on Earth Is Jean? Vallet, Muriel. 17p. (gr. k-3). 1992. pap. 8.95 (1-895583-49-7) MAYA Pubs.
Vallet, Roxanne. The Balloon Book. Vallet, Roxanne. 15p. (gr. 1-4). 1992. pap. 11.95 (1-56606-008-7) Bradley Mann.
—Children Can Be Scarry. Vallet, Roxanne. 14p. (gr. k-3). 1993. pap. 12.95 (1-56606-018-4) Bradley Mann.
—Geography Is Fun. Vallet, Roxanne. 13p. (gr. k-3). 1992. pap. 10.95 (1-895583-37-3) MAYA Pubs.
—Horses. Vallet, Roxanne. 19p. (gr. k-3). 1992. pap. 10.95 (1-895583-40-3) MAYA Pubs.
—How Tall Is Too Tall? Vallet, Roxanne. 12p. (gr. 1-3). 1992. pap. 10.95 (1-56606-007-9) Bradley Mann.
—Minochet. Vallet, Roxanne. 19p. (gr. k-3). 1992. pap. 10.95 (1-895583-36-5) MAYA Pubs.
—Ralph Gets a Prize. Vallet, Roxanne. 12p. (gr. k-3). 1993. pap. text ed. 12.95 (1-56606-017-6) Bradley Mann.
—Thinking. Vallet, Roxanne. 14p. 1992. pap. 10.95 (1-895583-39-X) MAYA Pubs.
—Vacation to Marsailles. Vallet, Roxanne. 15p. (gr. k-3). 1992. pap. 13.95 (1-895583-38-1) MAYA Pubs.
Vallier, Jean. King, the Mice & the Cheese. Gurney, Nancy & Gurney, Eric. LC 89-8463. 72p. (gr. k-3). 1965. 6.95 (0-394-80039-7); lib. bdg. 7.99 (0-394-90039-1) Random Bks Yng Read.
Van Allsburg, Chris. Jumanji. Van Allsburg, Chris. (gr. 3 up). 1981. 15.95 (0-395-30448-2) HM.
—Polar Express. Van Allsburg, Chris. LC 85-10907. 32p. (gr. 2 up). 1985. 17.45 (0-395-38949-6) HM.

—The Stranger. Van Allsburg, Chris. LC 86-15235. 32p. (gr. 2-4). 1986. 16.45 (0-395-42331-7) HM.
—Swan Lake. Helprin, Mark, as told by. (gr. 1-8). 1989. 19.45 (0-395-49858-9) HM.
—Swan Lake. Helprin, Mark. 112p. (gr. 4-7). 1992. pap. 12.95 (0-395-64647-2) HM.
—The Sweetest Fig. Van Allsburg, Chris. LC 93-12692. (gr. 4 up). 1993. 17.95 (0-395-67346-1) HM.
—Two Bad Ants. Van Allsburg, Chris. 32p. (ps up). 1988. 17.45 (0-395-48668-8) HM.
—The Wreck of the Zephyr. Van Allsburg, Chris. LC 82-23371. 32p. (ps up). 1983. 16.45 (0-395-33075-0) HM.
—The Wretched Stone. Van Allsburg, Chris. 32p. 1991. 17.45 (0-395-53307-4, Sandpiper) HM.
—The Z Was Zapped: A Play in Twenty-Six Acts. Van Allsburg, Chris. 56p. (ps up). 1987. 16.45 (0-395-44612-0, Clarion Bks) HM.
Van Bergen, Jamie. Jamestown Journey. Kay, Alan N. 56p. (gr. 4-7). 1992. pap. 4.95 (0-939631-52-0) Thomas Publications.
Van Bilsen, Rita. The Best Gift of All. Wilkeshuis, Cornelis. LC 89-38122. 28p. (gr. k-2). 1989. 8.95 (0-8198-1126-2) St Paul Bks.
Van Brunt, Jon. Skeletons in the Closet: A Collection of Short Stories. Vollaro, Joseph. Paretta, Joseph, ed. 208p. (Orig.). (gr. 9-12). 1993. pap. 13.95 (0-9633309-3-4) Rightway Educ.
Van Buren, Bobby. Kwanzaa. Porter, A. P. 48p. (gr. k-4). 1991. PLB 14.95 (0-87614-668-X); pap. 5.95 (0-87614-545-4) Carolrhoda Bks.
Van Buuren, John. Legend of Sleepy Hollow. Irving, Washington. Hitchner, Earle, adapted by. LC 89-33942. 48p. (gr. k-4). 1990. PLB 12.89 (0-8167-1869-5); pap. text ed. 3.95 (0-8167-1870-9) Troll Assocs.
Vance, R. Scott. How Do You Feel? Nelson, JoAnne. LC 91-36336. 24p. (Orig.). (gr. k-2). 1993. pap. write for info. (0-935529-15-2) Comprehen Health Educ.
Van Demark, Paul. Cricket. Hamilton, Dorothy. LC 74-30421. 80p. (gr. 3-7). 1975. pap. 3.95 (0-8361-1761-1) Herald Pr.
Vanden Broeck, Fabricio. Ah Bak's Strange New Crop. Goldman, Judy, adapted by. LC 92-11322. 1994. text ed. 14.95 (0-02-775657-2) Macmillan.
—The Mouse Bride: A Mayan Folktale. Dupre, Judith. LC 92-15275. (ps-3). 1993. 8.99 (0-679-83273-4); PLB 9.99 (0-679-93273-9) Knopf Bks Yng Read.
—The Witch's Face: A Mexican Tale. Kimmel, Eric A. LC 92-44380. 32p. (gr. 3). 1993. reinforced bdg. 15.95 (0-8234-1038-2) Holiday.
Van Den Hurk, Nicolle. Donde Esta Springer? De Wijs, Ivo. (SPA.). 32p. (ps-2). 1993. pap. 5.95 (0-8120-1747-1) Barron.
—Where Is Springer? De Wijs, Ivo. 32p. (ps-2). 1993. 12. 95 (0-8120-6360-0); pap. 4.95 (0-8120-1728-5) Barron.
Van der Beek, Debbie. The Bad Babies' Book of Colors. Bradman, Tony. Schulman, Janet, ed. Greenstein, Mina, designed by. LC 86-27860. 32p. (ps-2). 1987. 5.95 (0-394-89046-9) Knopf Bks Yng Read.
—The Bad Babies' Counting Book. Bradman, Tony. LC 86-71. 32p. (ps-2). 1986. Set. 4.95 (0-394-88352-7) Knopf Bks Yng Read.
Vanderlinden, Kathy. The Sound of Money: A Musical Adventure about Economics & the Building of Community. Mueller, Tobin J. (ps-8). Audio tape incl. pap. 14.95 (1-56213-031-5) Ctr Stage Prodns.
Van Der Meer, Altie, jt. illus. see Van der Meer, Ron.
Van Der Meer, Atie, jt. illus. see Van Der Meer, Ron.
Van der Meer, Atie, jt. illus. see Van der Meer, Ron.
Van der Meer, Ron. The Birthday Cake: A Lift-the-Flap Pop-up Book. Van der Meer, Ron. LC 91-62464. 14p. (ps-1). 1993. 8.99 (0-679-82849-4) Random Bks Yng Read.
—The World's First Ever Pop-Up Games Book. Van der Meer, Ron. 8p. (gr. k-3). 1982. 9.95 (0-440-06943-2) Delacorte.
Van der Meer, Ron & Van der Meer, Altie. Funny Shoes. Van der Meer, Ron & Van der Meer, Altie. 14p. (ps-k). 1994. bds. 9.95 (0-689-71823-3, Aladdin) Macmillan Child Grp.
Van der Meer, Ron & Van der Meer, Atie. Funny Hats: A Lift-the-Flap Book. Van der Meer, Ron & Van der Meer, Atie. LC 91-62463. 16p. (ps). 1992. 7.99 (0-679-82850-8) Random Bks Yng Read.
—Your Amazing Senses: Thirty-Six Games, Puzzles & Tricks to Show How Your Senses Work. Van Der Meer, Ron & Van Der Meer, Atie. 12p. (gr. 4-7). 1987. pap. 6.95 (0-689-71184-0, Aladdin) Macmillan Child Grp.
Van der Plas, Rob. Roadside Bicycle Repairs: The Simple Guide to Fixing Your Bike. 2nd ed. Van der Plas, Rob. LC 89-81203. 128p. 1990. pap. 4.95 (0-933201-27-3) Bicycle Books.
Van Don, Pham. Tuan. Boholm-Olsson, Eva. Jonasson, Dianne, tr. 32p. (gr. up). 1988. 11.95 (91-29-58766-2, R & S Bks) FS&G.
Van Dun, Anke. Another Tortoise & a Different Hare. Cole, Judith. 32p. (gr. k-6). 1993. 12.95 (0-918080-31-2) Treasure Chest.
Vane, Mitch. Here Comes Annette! Bissett, Isabel. LC 92-27267. 1993. 3.75 (0-383-03628-3) SRA Schl Grp.
—Hurry Up! Gleeson, Libby. LC 92-21448. 1993. 3.75 (0-383-03632-1) SRA Schl Grp.
—Rocks. Tuer, Judy. LC 92-30670. 1993. 2.50 (0-383-03649-6) SRA Schl Grp.
Van Fleet, Matthew. Match It: A Fold-the-Flap Book. 10p. (ps-3). 1993. 11.95 (0-8037-1379-7) Dial Bks Young.

Van Heusen, Drew. Danish Fairy Tales. Grundtvig, Sven. Cramer, J. Grant, tr. from DAN. vii, 115p. (gr. k-5). 1972. pap. 4.95 (0-486-22891-6) Dover.
Van Horn, Brian, jt. illus. see Scott, Rita.
Van Horn, Donald. Poley Morgan, Son of a Texas Scalawag: (A Historical Novel) Smyrl, Frank M. vi, 63p. 1990. 2.00 (0-910779-00-7) Tex St Hist Assn.
Van Horn, George, photos by. Boas Constrictoras. Bargar, Sherie & Johnson, Linda. Palacios, Argentina, tr. from ENG. LC 93-8391. (SPA.). 1993. write for info. (0-86593-333-2) Rourke Corp.
Van Horn, William. Celebrate Valentine's Day. Butler, Elvie. 48p. (gr. 1-4). 1989. pap. 2.95 (0-590-42052-6) Scholastic Inc.
—This Is the Place for Me. Cole, Joanna. 32p. (Orig.). (gr. k-3). 1986. pap. 2.50 (0-590-33996-6) Scholastic Inc.
Van Horne, Carmon. The Three Big Pigs. Van Horne, Carmon. LC 92-91035. 48p. (Orig.). (ps-3). 1993. incl. computer coloring disk 23.95 (1-882643-02-X); pap. 18.95 incl. computer coloring disk (1-882643-03-8); 12.95 (1-882643-00-3); pap. 7.95 (1-882643-01-1) V H Visionarts.
—The Three Big Pigs. Van Horne, Carmon. LC 92-91035. 32p. (ps-3). 1993. PLB 13.95 (1-882643-04-6) V H Visionarts.
Van Kampen, Vlasta. Animal Hours. Manning, Linda. 32p. (ps-2). 1991. bds. 13.95 (0-19-540771-7) OUP.
—Dinosaur Days. Manning, Linda. LC 93-28443. 32p. (ps-2). 1993. PLB 12.95 (0-8167-3315-5); pap. 3.95 (0-8167-3316-3) Troll Assocs.
—My Dad Takes Care of Me. Quinlan, Patricia. 24p. (ps-3). 1987. PLB 14.95 (0-920303-79-X, Pub. by Annick CN); pap. 4.95 (0-920303-76-5, Pub. by Annick CN) Firefly Bks Ltd.
Van Kanegan, Jeff. Bible Christmas Puzzles. Schlegl, William. 48p. (gr. 3 up). 1987. pap. 6.95 (0-86653-409-1, SS 884, Shining Star Pubns) Good Apple.
Van Kleeck, Cynthia. Sierra Summers: Fireside Tales to Share with Young & Old. Trussell, Margaret E. Trussell, Margaret E., et al, photos by. Bechtol, Bruce, intro. by. LC 89-51208. 200p. (Orig.). (gr. 8-9). 1989. pap. 10.95 (0-9624235-1-3) Talking Mtn.
Van Loon, Roland. The Adventures of Kalakoa: A Hawaiian Rainbow Fantasy. Masuda, Akiko. 32p. (gr. k-7). 1991. 7.95 (0-9629842-1-3) Stew & Rice.
Van Munching, Paul. Dr. Jekyll & Mr. Hyde. Stevenson, Robert Louis. McMullan, Kate, ed. LC 83-15972. 96p. (gr. 3-7). 1988. pap. 2.95 (0-394-86365-8) Random Bks Yng Read.
—King Kong. Lovelace, Delos W. Conaway, Judith, ed. LC 87-28354. 96p. (gr. 3-7). 1988. pap. 2.95 (0-394-89789-7) Random Bks Yng Read.
Vanner, Vera. Ketivoni Chelek Chamishi, Pt. 5. Bachrach, Kalman & Axelrod, Herman. (HEB.). 64p. (gr. 6). 1972. pap. text ed. 3.50x (1-878530-06-2) K Bachrach Co.
—Ketivoni Chelek R'Viyi, Pt. 4. Bachrach, Kalman & Axelrod, Herman. (HEB.). 55p. (gr. 5). 1972. pap. text ed. 3.50x (1-878530-05-4) K Bachrach Co.
Van Nutt, Robert. The Emperor's New Clothes. Andersen, Hans Christian. Metaxas, Eric, tr. LC 90-25376. 32p. (gr. k up). 1991. pap. 14.95 (0-88708-160-6, Rabbit Ears); pap. 19.95 incl. cassette (0-88708-161-4, Rabbit Ears) Picture Bk Studio.
—The Legend of Sleepy Hollow. Irving, Washington. Van Nutt, Robert, adapted by. LC 88-33375. 32p. (ps up). 1991. pap. 14.95 (0-88708-088-X, Rabbit Ears); incl. cassette 19.95 (0-88708-089-8, Rabbit Ears) Picture Bk Studio.
—The Legend of Sleepy Hollow. Irving, Washington. Close, Glenn, read by. Story, Tim, contrib. by. 32p. (ps up). 1992. pap. write for info. slipcase pkg., incl. cassette (0-307-14326-0, 14326, Golden Pr) Western Pub.
—The Legend of Sleepy Hollow: Minibook Edition. Irving, Washington. LC 93-12153. 1993. incl. cass. 9.95 (0-88708-321-8, Rabbit Ears) Picture Bk Studio.
—The Savior Is Born. Gleeson, Brian. LC 92-4577. 40p. 1992. pap. 14.95 (0-88708-283-1, Rabbit Ears); pap. 19.95 incl. cass. (0-88708-284-X, Rabbit Ears) Picture Bk Studio.
—The Ugly Duckling. Andersen, Hans Christian. LC 86-185. 48p. (gr. k up). 1986. 12.95 (0-394-88403-5); incl. cassette 15.95 (0-394-88298-9) Knopf Bks Yng Read.
Van Patten, Michele. Grandfather's Orchard. Ghazi, Abidullah. Ghazi, Tasneema, et al, eds. 15p. Date not set. text ed. 15.x (1-56316-307-1) Iqra Intl Ed Fdtn.
Van Ronzelen, George & Oberste, Kenneth. TiL: A Book of Puzzles. 88-70805. 264p. (Orig.). (gr. 6 up). 1988. pap. 13.00 (0-934426-18-X) NAPSAC Reprods.
VanRoon, Terry & Kielesinski, Chris. Proverbs for Kids from the Book. Osborne, Richard, compiled by. 240p. (gr. k). 1987. 12.95 (0-8423-4975-8) Tyndale.
Van Rynbach, Iris. Keeping Time. Branley, Franklyn. LC 92-6783. 1993. 13.95 (0-395-47777-8) HM.
—Over the River & Through the Wood. Child, Lydia M. ALC Staff, ed. LC 88-4712. 32p. (ps up). 1992. pap. 3.95 (0-688-11839-9, Mulberry) Morrow.
—Over the River & Through the Wood, Vol. 1. Child, Lydia Maria. 1989. 15.95 (0-316-13873-8) Little.
Vansant, Jo. Amanda's Tree. Jones, Jo. (gr. 3-6). 1977. pap. 3.50 (0-9602266-0-5) Jo-Jo Pubns.
—That Hardhead Cinnamon. Jones, Jo. LC 89-92753. 36p. (Orig.). (gr. 2-5). 1989. pap. 6.95 (0-9602266-1-3) Jo-Jo Pubns.

Van Santvoord, George & Coolidge, Archibald C. Favorite Uncle Remus. Harris, Joel C. Van Santvoord, George & Coolidge, Archibald C., eds. 320p. (gr. 4-8). 1973. 17.45 (0-395-06800-2) HM.
Van Sciver, Ethan. Are You a Critter? Tom, Mister. Neely, David, ed. 77p. (gr. 4-6). 1993. pap. 6.95 spiral bdg. (0-925237-10-8) Ten Pubns.
Van Seversen, Joe. Francis Scott Key. Collins, David. 113p. (gr. 3-6). 1982. pap. 6.95 (0-915134-91-8) Mott Media.
—George Washington Carver. Collins, David. 131p. (gr. 3-6). 1981. pap. 6.95 (0-915134-90-X) Mott Media.
Van Someron, Terry. Speaking in Tongues: Is That All There Is? Cook, Bob. 48p. (gr. 9-12). 1982. pap. text ed. 1.50 (0-88243-932-4, 02-0932); leader's guide 3.95 (0-88243-935-9, 02-0935) Gospel Pub.
Van Swearingen, E. C., jt. illus. see Price, Norman.
Vantage Art Staff. Inks, Food Colors, & Papers. Zubrowski, Bernie. 80p. (gr. 5-8). 1993. pap. text ed. 10.95 (0-685-68097-5) Cuisenaire.
Van Way Hampton, Cindy. Diggy Armadillo Goes to Fort Worth Stock Show & Rodeo, Bk. 2: Further Adventures. Pugh, Ann, et al. Bold, Mary, ed. 68p. (gr. 3-6). 1993. staple bdg. 7.95 (1-879465-02-7) Diggy & Assocs.
Van Wright, Cornelius. First Facts, 12 bks. Calder, S. J. (ps-1). 1989. Set, 32p. ea. write for info. (0-671-94108-9, J Messner); Set, 32p. ea. lib. bdg. write for info. (0-671-94107-0) S&S Trade.
—If You Were a Bird. Calder, S. J. Brook, Bonnie, ed. 32p. (ps-1). 1989. 5.95 (0-671-68599-6); PLB 9.98 (0-671-68595-3) Silver Pr.
—If You Were a Cat. Calder, S. J. Brook, Bonnie, ed. 32p. (ps-1). 1989. 5.95 (0-671-68604-6); PLB 9.98 (0-671-68598-8) Silver Pr.
—If You Were an Ant. Calder, S. J. Brook, Bonnie, ed. 32p. (ps-1). 1989. 5.95 (0-671-68603-8); PLB 9.98 (0-671-68798-0) Silver Pr.
—Jeff Rides a Spaceship. Cohen, Della. 24p. (ps-2). 1992. pap. 0.99 (1-56293-107-5) McClanahan Bk.
—The Little Policeman. McClanahan, Frank. 24p. (Orig.). (gr. k-1). 1990. pap. 0.99 (1-878624-38-5) McClanahan Bk.
Van Wright, Cornelius & Ying-Hwa Hu. Poems to Share. Paton, Kathleen, ed. 24p. (ps-3). 1990. 4.95 (1-56288-050-0) Checkerboard.
Van Zale, Jon. The Eyes of Grey Wolf. London, Jonathan. LC 92-35987. (gr. 4 up). 1993. 13.95 (0-8118-0285-X) Chronicle Bks.
Van Zandt, William. Rick Tees Off. Walker, David. Wright, Malcolm, ed. Nicklaus, Jack, frwd. by. 112p. (Orig.). (gr. 4-9). 1985. pap. text ed. 3.95 (0-9614856-0-4) Pro Golfers.
Vanzet, Gaston. The Great Big, Enormous, Gigantic Cardboard Box. Brook, Leeanne. LC 92-29957. (gr. 3 up). 1993. 14.00 (0-383-03571-6) SRA Schl Grp.
Van Zyle, Jon. A Caribou Journey. Miller, Debbie S. LC 93-9777. (gr. 2-5). 1995. 14.95 (0-316-57380-9) Little.
Vargo, Kurt. The Tiger & the Brahmin. Gleeson, Brian. 40p. (gr. k up). 1992. pap. 14.95 (0-88708-232-7, Rabbit Ears); incl. cass. 19.95 (0-88708-233-5, Rabbit Ears) Picture Bk Studio.
Vargas, Jane A. Ashmouse & the Wrong Side of the Bed. Vargus, Jane A. LC 92-61365. 44p. 1993. pap. 5.95 (1-55523-557-3) Winston-Derek.
Varley, Jeanne. The Monster Bed. Willis, Jeanne. LC 86-10366. 32p. (ps-2). 1987. 12.95 (0-688-06804-9); PLB 12.88 (0-688-06805-7) Lothrop.
Varley, Susan. After Dark. Baum, Louis. LC 89-16123. 32p. (ps-3). 1990. 11.95 (0-87951-382-9) Overlook Pr.
—Badger's Parting Gifts. Varley, Susan. LC 83-17500. 32p. (ps-3). 1984. 13.95 (0-688-02699-0); lib. bdg. 13.88 (0-688-02703-2) Lothrop.
—Jack & the Monster. Graham, Richard. (ps-3). 1989. 13.45 (0-395-49680-2) HM.
—Lollopy. Dunbar, Joyce. LC 91-26212. 32p. (ps-1). 1992. SBE 14.95 (0-02-733195-4, Macmillan Child Bk) Macmillan Child Grp.
Varner, Charles. Who Are You, God? McAllister, Dawson & Miller, Rich. (gr. 5-12). 1988. pap. 7.95 (0-923417-11-7) Shepherd Minst.
Varno, John. Katrina & Elishia Teach about the Aura. Bennett, Geraldine M. Rider, Tracy & Sheil, Audrey, eds. LC 92-83809. 32p. (gr. 3-8). 1993. pap. 7.98 (0-9630718-9-0) New Dawn NY.
—Katrina Tells Jamie about John's Invisible Lesson. Bennett, Geraldine M. Rider, Tracy & Sheil, Audrey, eds. 42p. (gr. 3-8). 1993. pap. 7.98 (0-9630718-8-2) New Dawn NY.
—Rebecca Tells of a Miracle of Life: A Special Belief in the Healing Power of Love. Bennett, Gerald M. Rider, Tracy & Sheil, Audrey, eds. LC 92-83744. 42p. (Orig.). (gr. 3-8). 1993. pap. 7.98 (0-9630718-4-X) New Dawn NY.
Varvasovszky, Laszlo. Henry in Shadowland. Varvasovszky, Laszlo. 32p. (gr. 2-7). 1989. 17.95 (0-87923-785-6) Godine.
Vasconcelles, Keith. Birds: A Thematic Unit. Hollis, Barbara. Goldfluss, Karen, ed. 80p. (Orig.). (gr. 1-3). 1992. pap. 7.95 wkbk. (1-55734-256-3) Tchr Create Mat.
—Clothespin Games. Sterling, Mary E. 28p. (ps-k). 1989. wkbk 7.95 (1-55734-172-9) Tchr Create Mat.
—Dragonwings. Robbins, Mary L. 48p. 1993. wkbk. 5.95 (1-55734-429-9) Tchr Create Mat.
—File Folder Games. Sterling, Mary E. 28p. (ps-k). 1989. wkbk 7.95 (1-55734-171-0) Tchr Create Mat.

—Patterns for Big Books. Sterling, Mary E. 80p. (ps-3). 1991. wkbk. 7.95 (1-55734-132-X) Tchr Create Mat.
—Readiness Manipulatives: Counting. Levin, Ina M. & Sterling, Mary E. 28p. (Orig.). (ps-1). 1992. wkbk. 7.95 (1-55734-179-6) Tchr Create Mat.
—Readiness Manipulatives: Shapes. Levin, Ina M. & Sterling, Mary E. 28p. (Orig.). (ps-1). 1992. wkbk. 7.95 (1-55734-180-X) Tchr Create Mat.
—Transcontinental Railroad: A Thematic Unit. Sterling, Mary E. 80p. (gr. 5-8). 1993. wkbk. 7.95 (1-55734-295-4) Tchr Create Mat.
—Wheel Games. Sterling, Mary E. 28p. (ps-k). 1989. wkbk 7.95 (1-55734-170-2) Tchr Create Mat.
Vasconcelles, Keith & Fullam, Sue. Whole Language Units for Math. Merrick, Sandra. 144p. (ps-1). 1993. wkbk. 12.95 (1-55734-200-8) Tchr Create Mat.
Vasconcelles, Keith, jt. illus. see Apodaca, Blanca.
Vasconcelles, Keith, jt. illus. see Apodaca, Blanqui.
Vasconcelles, Keith, jt. illus. see Fullam, Sue.
Vasconcelles, Keith, et al. Inventions. Goldfluss, Karen J. & Sima, Patricia M. 80p. (gr. 4-6). 1993. wkbk. 7.95 (1-55734-232-6) Tchr Create Mat.
Vasconcellos, Daniel. The Dog That Pitched a No-Hitter. Christopher, Matt. (gr. 1-3). 1988. 11.95 (0-316-14057-0) Little.
—The Dog That Stole Home. Christopher, Matt. LC 92-15613. 1993. 12.95 (0-316-14082-1) Little.
Vasiliev, Valery. Dreamsong. McLerran, Alice. LC 91-32622. 32p. (gr. k up). 1992. 14.00 (0-688-10105-4, Tambourine Bks); PLB 13.93 (0-688-10106-2, Tambourine Bks) Morrow.
—The Whittler's Tale. Armstrong, Jennifer. LC 93-14749. 1994. write for info. (0-688-10751-6, Tambourine Bks); PLB write for info. (0-688-10752-4) Morrow.
Vasiliy. Cheaper by the Dozen. rev. ed. Gilbreth, Frank B. & Carey, Ernestine G. LC 63-20411. 256p. (gr. 7 up). 1963. 20.00 (0-690-18632-0, Crowell Jr Bks) HarpC.
Vasquez, Gina. It's Easy to Say Crepidula! A Phonetic Guide to Pronunciation of the Scientific Names of Sea Shells. Cate, Jean M. & Raskin, Selma. 158p. (Orig.). (gr. 5-7). 1986. pap. 19.95 (0-938509-00-4) Pretty Penny Pr.
Vaughan, Mike. Deadly Animals! Holmes, Martha. LC 90-26903. 32p. (gr. k-3). 1991. SBE 13.95 (0-689-31737-9, Atheneum Child Bk) Macmillan Child Grp.
Vaughn, Jimmy. A Little One's Draw a Story Drawing Book. Vaughn, Salle W. 120p. (ps-5). 1990. wkbk. incl. protective envelope & rainbow drawing pencil 35.00 (0-9625832-0-0) Crystal TX.

Veal, Janice. Adventures in Greater Puget Sound: An Educational Guide Exploring the Marine Environment of Greater Puget Sound. Ashbach, Dawn & Veal, Janice. 56p. (Orig.). (gr. 3-9). 1991. 7.95 (0-9629778-0-2) NW Island. ADVENTURES IN GREATER PUGET SOUND captures the magic of marine life in this unique region. An educational guide & activity book, it is designed for 8 to 12 year olds, but adults are tempted to try their hands at a variety of challenges ranging from hidden pictures to crossword puzzles & decoding the "Captain's Secret Message." The rich green waters of Greater Puget Sound are the hub for a multitude of marine activities. Colorful sea anemones & shy octopuses undulate their tentacles on the sea floor, while orca whales breach & yachts & ferry boats wend their watery ways at the surface. ADVENTURES IN GREATER PUGET SOUND includes concise & definitive information on a host of creatures & boats from wrinkled whelks to eagles, to oil freighters. The activities are designed to reinforce text information. The book is illustrated with more than 150 pen & ink drawings. To order: Northwest Island Associates, 444 Guemes Island Road, Anacortes, WA 98221; (206) 293-3721.
Publisher Provided Annotation.

Veara, Kevin. Thumpy's Story: A Story of Love & Grief Shared. Dodge, Nancy C. LC 84-61293. 24p. (gr. k-12). 1985. pap. 5.95 (0-918533-00-7) Prairie Lark.
Vecchio, Tony. How I Feel: Feelings Activity Book. Boulden, Jim. 32p. (Orig.). (gr. 1-7). Date not set. pap. 4.95 (1-878076-21-3) Boulden Pub.

Vecchione, Glen. World's Best Street & Yard Games. Vecchione, Glen. LC 88-38273. 128p. (gr. 2-8). 1990. pap. 4.95 (0-8069-5762-X) Sterling.
Vegh, Toby. Is It Shabbos Yet? Emerman, Ellen. 32p. (ps-1). 1990. 8.95 (0-922613-21-4); pap. 6.95 (0-922613-22-2) Hachai Pubns.
Vehslage, Cynthia. The Alphabet of Civility. Clarkson, Virginia C. LC 93-16585. 1993. write for info. (0-913515-86-8) Starrhill Pr.
Velasquez, Eric. Chain of Fire. Naidoo, Beverley. LC 89-27551. 256p. (gr. 6 up). 1990. 14.00 (0-397-32426-X, Lipp Jr Bks); PLB 13.89 (0-397-32427-8, Lipp Jr Bks) HarpC Child Bks.
—Journey to Jo'burg: A South African Story. reissued ed. Naidoo, Beverley. LC 85-45508. 96p. (gr. 4-7). 1986. 14.00 (0-397-32168-6, Lipp Jr Bks); PLB 13.89 (0-397-32169-4) HarpC Child Bks.
—Journey to Jo'burg: A South African Story. Naidoo, Beverley. LC 85-45508. 96p. (gr. 4-7). 1988. pap. 3.95 (0-06-440237-1, Trophy) HarpC Child Bks.
—The Shirt. Soto, Gary. LC 91-26145. 64p. (gr. 2-5). 1992. 14.00 (0-385-30665-2) Delacorte.
—Tanya & the Tobo Man: A Story for Children Entering Therapy. Koplow, Lesley. LC 92-56875. 1993. PLB 17.26 (0-8368-0936-X) Gareth Stevens Inc.
Velez, Waller & Martin, Ellisa. The Durandrium Find. LaDell, Leo. Amthor, Terry K., ed. 32p. (Orig.). (gr. 12). 1989. pap. 6.00 (1-55806-021-9, 9105) Iron Crown Ent Inc.
Velez, Waller & Waltrip, Jason. War on a Distant Moon. Foley, Tod. LaDell, Leo, ed. 32p. (Orig.). (gr. 12). 1988. pap. 6.00 (1-55806-020-0, 9104) Iron Crown Ent Inc.
Velez, Walter. RoleMaster Companion II. Khanna & Ridley. 112p. (Orig.). (gr. 10-12). 1987. pap. 12.00 (0-915795-97-3, 1600) Iron Crown Ent Inc.
Velthuijs, Max. A Birthday Cake for Little Bear. Velthuijs, Max. Lanning, Rosemary, tr. LC 87-73270. 32p. (gr. k-3). 1988. 9.95 (1-55858-046-8) North-South Bks NYC.
—Frog & the Stranger. Velthuijs, Max. LC 93-26401. 32p. 1994. 14.00 (0-688-13267-7, Tambourine Bks); PLB 13.93 (0-688-13268-5, Tambourine Bks) Morrow.
—Frog in Winter. Velthuijs, Max. LC 92-20545. 32p. (ps up). 1993. 14.00 (0-688-12306-6, Tambourine Bks); PLB 13.93 (0-688-12307-4, Tambourine Bks) Morrow.
Venable, James, et al. Food: A Salute to Black Inventors. rev. ed. Howell, Ann C. Ivery, Evelyn L., ed. Chndler, Alton, intro. by. 24p. (gr. 3-7). 1992. pap. text ed. 1.50 (1-877804-01-0) Chandler White.
—Black Science Communications: Coloring - Learning Activities. Howell, Ann C. & Massey, Grace C. Ivery, Evelyn, ed. Chandler, Alton, intro. by. (Orig.). (gr. 1-6). 1987. pap. text ed. 1.50 (0-685-26060-7) Chandler White.
—Black Science Food: Coloring - Learning Activities. Howell, Ann C. & Massey, Grace C. Ivery, Evelyn L., ed. Chandler, Alton H., intro. by. (Orig.). (gr. 1-6). 1987. pap. text ed. 1.50 (0-685-26061-5) Chandler White.
—Black Science Oldwest: Coloring - Learning Activities. Howell, Ann C. & Massey, Grace C. Ivery, Evelyn L., ed. Chandler, Alton H., intro. by. (Orig.). (gr. 1-6). 1987. pap. text ed. 1.50 (0-685-26062-3) Chandler White.
—Black Science Safety: Coloring - Learning Activities. Howell, Ann C. & Massey, Grace C. Ivery, Evelyn L., ed. Chandler, Alton H., intro. by. (Orig.). (gr. 1-6). 1987. pap. text ed. 1.50 (0-685-26059-3) Chandler White.
—Black Science Transportation: Coloring - Learning Activities. Howell, Ann C. & Massey, Grace C. Ivery, Evelyn L., ed. Chandler, Alton H., intro. by. (Orig.). (gr. 1-6). 1987. pap. text ed. 1.50 (0-685-26063-1) Chandler White.
—Transportation: A Salute to Black Inventors. rev. ed. Howell, Ann C. Ivery, Evelyn L., ed. Chandler, Alton, intro. by. 24p. (gr. 3-7). 1992. pap. text ed. 1.50 (1-877804-00-2) Chandler White.
Vendrell, Carme S. A Bear in the Air. Williams, Leslie. LC 80-10290. 28p. (gr. k up). 1980. 7.95 (0-916144-54-2) Stemmer Hse.
—Brush. Calders, Pere. Feitlowitz, Marguerite, tr. from SPA. LC 85-23873. 32p. (ps-3). 1986. 10.95 (0-916291-05-7) Kane-Miller Bk.
—Brush. Calders, Pere. Feitlowitz, Marguerite, tr. from SPA. 32p. (ps-3). 1988. pap. 6.95 (0-916291-16-2) Kane-Miller Bk.
—Pigs Can't Fly. Gray, Nigel. 32p. (ps-1). 1991. 15.95 (0-86264-272-8, Pub. by Andersen Pr UK) Trafalgar.

Venema, Jon R. What Do You Do with a Cardboard Box on a Day When the Rain's Pourin' Down? Sandling, R. Harris. Carter, Mary C., ed. 50p. (gr. 3 up). 1993. write for info. (1-883194-00-8) Emerald Hummngbrd. "I'm Bored! There's nothing to do!" So begins a great adventure for Justin. He doesn't know it, yet, but the wonder of his imagination is about to be unleashed. From an impromptu parade to barn-storming planes that fight the Red Baron & fly to the moon, Justin begins his great adventure. His guides are none other than Dad, Grandmom & good old Grandad, "whose ideas are always rad!" From these three Justin learns about a valuable set of keys that open mysterious doors to great treasures. The trick is discovering the whereabouts of the keys & knowing how to unlock the doors. Does Justin do it? What about the barn-storming plane? How do Dad, Grandmom & good old Grandad know about these mysterious keys? Where will this adventure lead Justin? Here is a delightfully charming story that all children, be they nine or ninety, will have great fun with! Justin's story is the story of every child that has lived since the beginning of time. WHAT DO YOU DO WITH A CARDBOARD BOX ON A DAY WHEN THE RAIN'S POURIN' DOWN? is rich with warmth, silliness & pearls of love & wisdom. This reading is a must for every individual who has known & experienced the boredom of a rainy afternoon. For pre-publication order & general information: Write: Emerald Hummingbird Productions, P.O. Box 577438, Modesto, CA 95355-7438. USA. Phone: 209-527-1771.
Publisher Provided Annotation.

Venezia, Mike. Botticelli. Venezia, Mike. LC 90-21645. 32p. (ps-4). 1991. PLB 15.00 (0-516-02291-1); pap. 4.95 (0-516-42291-X) Childrens.
—Come los Guisantes, Cuanto Antes: (Eat Your Peas, Louise!) Snow, Pegeen. LC 84-27445. (ENG & SPA.). 32p. (ps-2). 1989. PLB 11.93 (0-516-32067-X); pap. 2.95 (0-516-52067-9) Childrens.
—Da Vinci. Venezia, Mike. LC 88-37715. 32p. (ps-4). 1989. PLB 15.00 (0-516-02275-X); pap. 4.95 (0-516-42275-8) Childrens.
—Eat Your Peas, Louise! Snow, Pegeen. LC 84-27445. 32p. (ps-2). 1985. PLB 11.93 (0-516-02067-6); pap. 2.95 (0-516-42067-4); pap. 30.60 big bk. (0-516-49452-X) Childrens.
—Edward Hopper. Venezia, Mike. LC 90-2166. 32p. (ps-4). 1990. PLB 15.00 (0-516-02277-6); pap. 4.95 (0-516-42277-4) Childrens.
—For Sale: One Sister--Cheap! Adler, Katie & McBride, Rachael. LC 86-11723. 32p. (ps-3). 1986. PLB 13.93 (0-516-03476-6); pap. 3.95 (0-516-43476-4) Childrens.
—Francisco Goya. Venezia, Mike. LC 90-20887. 32p. (ps-4). 1991. PLB 15.00 (0-516-02292-X); pap. 4.95 (0-516-42292-8) Childrens.
—Georgia O'Keeffe. Venezia, Mike. 32p. (ps-4). 1993. PLB 16.60 (0-516-02297-0) Childrens.
—How to Be an Older Brother or Sister. Venezia, Mike. LC 85-27977. 32p. (ps-3). 1986. PLB 13.93 (0-516-03494-4); pap. 3.95 (0-516-43494-2) Childrens.
—Mary Cassatt. Venezia, Mike. LC 90-2165. 32p. (ps-4). 1990. PLB 15.00 (0-516-02278-4); pap. 4.95 (0-516-42278-2) Childrens.
—Mice! Frankel, Julie E. LC 86-1008. 32p. (ps-2). 1986. PLB 11.93 (0-516-02070-6); pap. 2.95 (0-516-42070-4) Childrens.
—Michelangelo. Venezia, Mike. LC 91-555. 32p. (ps-4). 1991. PLB 15.00 (0-516-02293-8); pap. 4.95 (0-516-42293-6) Childrens.
—Monet. Venezia, Mike. LC 89-25452. 32p. (ps-4). 1990. PLB 15.00 (0-516-02276-8); pap. 4.95 (0-516-42276-6) Childrens.
—Paul Gauguin. Venezia, Mike. LC 91-35054. 32p. (ps-4). PLB 15.00, Apr. 1992 (0-516-02295-4); pap. 4.95, Jul. 1992 (0-516-42295-2) Childrens.
—Paul Klee. Venezia, Mike. LC 91-12554. 32p. (gr. 4). 1991. PLB 15.00 (0-516-02294-6); pap. 4.95 (0-516-42294-4) Childrens.
—Picasso. Venezia, Mike. LC 87-33023. 32p. (ps-4). 1988. PLB 15.00 (0-516-02271-7); pap. 4.95 (0-516-42271-5) Childrens.
—Pieter Bruegel. Venezia, Mike. LC 92-4810. 32p. (ps-4). 1992. PLB 15.00 (0-516-02279-2) Childrens.
—Pieter Bruegel. Venezia, Mike. LC 92-4810. 32p. 1993. pap. 4.95 (0-516-42279-0) Childrens.
—Rembrandt. Venezia, Mike. LC 87-33014. 32p. (ps-4). 1988. PLB 15.00 (0-516-02272-5); pap. 4.95 (0-516-42272-3) Childrens.
—Salvador Dali. Venezia, Mike. LC 92-35053. 32p. (ps-4). 1993. PLB 15.00 (0-516-02296-2); pap. 4.95 (0-516-42296-0) Childrens.
—Van Gogh. Venezia, Mike. LC 88-11842. 32p. (ps-4). 1988. PLB 15.00 (0-516-02274-1); pap. 4.95 (0-516-42274-X) Childrens.

—What If the Teacher Calls on Me? Gross, Alan. LC 79-18560. 32p. (ps-3). 1980. pap. 3.95 (0-516-43671-6) Childrens.

Venice. A Mouse in My Roof. Edwards, Richard. (ps up). 1990. write for info. Delacorte.

Venkatakrishnan, Rames. Roadside Geology of Virginia. Frye, Keith. Alt, David & Hyndman, Donald, eds. Milici, Robert C., frwd. by. LC 86-8755. 256p. (Orig.). (gr. 5 up). 1986. pap. 12.00 (0-87842-199-8) Mountain Pr.

Venning, Sue. The Muppet Babies in Let's Imagine...What Happened in the Nursery. Barkan, Joanne, et al. (ps up). 1987. pap. 14.95 (1-55578-808-4) Worlds Wonder.

Veno, Joe. What Do You Think I Am... Crazy? Farmer, Patti. 32p. (ps-3). 1991. 10.95 (0-8120-5979-4) Barron.

Veno, Joseph. Agriculture. Sabin, Louis. LC 84-2710. 32p. (gr. 3-6). 1985. PLB 9.49 (0-8167-0204-7); pap. text ed. 2.95 (0-8167-0205-5) Troll Assocs.

—All about Mountains & Volcanoes. Marcus, Elizabeth. LC 83-4834. 32p. (gr. 3-6). 1984. lib. bdg. 10.59 (0-89375-969-4); pap. text ed. 2.95 (0-89375-970-8) Troll Assocs.

—All about Ponds. Rockwell, Jane. LC 83-4835. 32p. (gr. 3-6). 1984. lib. bdg. 10.59 (0-89375-971-6); pap. text ed. 2.95 (0-89375-972-4) Troll Assocs.

—All about Stars. Jefferies, Lawrence. LC 82-20027. 32p. (gr. 3-6). 1983. PLB 10.59 (0-89375-888-4); pap. text ed. 2.95 (0-89375-889-2) Troll Assocs.

—Computers. Sabin, Francene. LC 84-2708. 32p. (gr. 3-6). 1985. PLB 9.49 (0-8167-0314-0); pap. text ed. 2.95 (0-8167-0315-9) Troll Assocs.

—Magnets. Santrey, Laurence. LC 84-2597. 32p. (gr. 3-6). 1985. PLB 9.49 (0-8167-0140-7); pap. text ed. 2.95 (0-8167-0141-5) Troll Assocs.

—Mammals. Sabin, Francene. LC 84-2658. 32p. (gr. 3-6). 1985. PLB 9.49 (0-8167-0208-X); pap. text ed. 2.95 (0-8167-0209-8) Troll Assocs.

—Our Amazing Ocean. Adler, David. LC 82-17373. 32p. (gr. 3-6). 1983. PLB 10.59 (0-89375-882-5); pap. text ed. 2.95 (0-89375-883-3) Troll Assocs.

—Planets & the Solar System. Brandt, Keith. LC 84-2714. 32p. (gr. 3-6). 1985. PLB 9.49 (0-8167-0300-0); pap. text ed. 2.95 (0-8167-0301-9) Troll Assocs.

—Simples Machines. Bains, Rae. LC 84-2607. 32p. (gr. 3-6). 1985. PLB 9.49 (0-8167-0166-0); pap. text ed. 2.95 (0-8167-0167-9) Troll Assocs.

—Television & Radio. Sabin, Louis. LC 84-8446. 32p. (gr. 3-6). 1985. PLB 9.49 (0-8167-0310-8); pap. text ed. 2.95 (0-8167-0311-6) Troll Assocs.

—Weather. Sabin, Louis. LC 84-2706. 32p. (gr. 3-6). 1985. PLB 9.49 (0-8167-0200-4); pap. text ed. 2.95 (0-8167-0201-2) Troll Assocs.

Venters, Steve. ASW Forms. Miller, Marc W. 49p. (Orig.). 1990. pap. 8.00 (1-55878-057-2) Game Designers.

—Data Annex Upgrade. Bond, Larry. 136p. (Orig.). 1990. pap. 10.00 (1-55878-053-X) Game Designers.

—Infantry Weapons of the World. Wiseman, Loren K. 104p. (Orig.). (gr. 9-12). 1991. pap. 12.00 (1-55878-068-8) Game Designers.

—Soviet Combat Vehicle Handbook. Wiseman, Loren K. 104p. (Orig.). (gr. 9-12). 1990. pap. 12.00 (1-55878-067-X) Game Designers.

—Sub Forms. Miller, Marc W. 49p. (Orig.). 1989. pap. 8.00 (1-55878-019-X) Game Designers.

Venters, Steve & Knutson, Dana. Mechwarrior. 2nd ed. Nystul, Mike & Smith, Lester. Ippolito, Donna & Mullvihill, Sharon T., eds. 167p. (Orig.). (gr. 7 up). 1991. pap. 15.00 (1-55560-129-4) FASA Corp.

Venti, Anthony B. Around the World in a Hundred Years: Henry the Navigator - Magellan. Fritz, Jean. LC 92-27042. 128p. (gr. 2-6). 1994. 17.95 (0-399-22527-7, Putnam) Putnam Pub Group.

Ventura, Marisa, jt. illus. see Ventura, Piero.

Ventura, Piero. Great Composers. Ventura, Piero. 128p. 1989. 24.95 (0-399-21746-0, Putnam) Putnam Pub Group.

—Great Painters. Ventura, Piero. LC 84-3423. 160p. (gr. 5 up). 1984. 24.95 (0-399-21115-2, Putnam) Putnam Pub Group.

—Michelangelo's World. Ventura, Piero. 48p. (gr. 9-12). 1989. 13.95 (0-399-21593-X, Putnam) Putnam Pub Group.

Ventura, Piero & Ventura, Marisa. The Painter's Trick. Ventura, Piero & Ventura, Marisa. LC 76-54411. (gr. k-2). 1977. lib. bdg. 6.99 (0-394-93320-6) Random Bks Yng Read.

Venturi-Pickett, Stacy. Christmas Activity Book. Venturi-Pickett, Stacy. 24p. (ps-3). 1992. pap. 4.95 (0-8249-8621-0, Ideals Child) Hambleton-Hill.

—The Halloween Activity Book. 24p. (ps-3). 1992. pap. 4.95 (0-8249-8573-7, Ideals Child) Hambleton-Hill.

—Story of Johan & the Big Fish. Pingry, Patricia. 24p. (Orig.). (ps-3). 1988. pap. 3.95 (0-8249-8181-2, Ideals Child) Hambleton-Hill.

Venus, Joanna. Fun with Fabric. Bawden, Juliet. Johnson, David, photos by. LC 92-51070. 48p. (gr. 1-5). 1993. 6.99 (0-679-83494-X); PLB 9.99 (0-679-93494-4) Random Bks Yng Read.

Venus, Joanna & Kerr, Elizabeth. Fun with Paint. Butterfield, Moira. 48p. (gr. 1-5). 1993. 6.99 (0-679-83492-3); PLB 9.99 (0-679-93492-8) Random Bks Yng Read.

Verbeck, Frank. Donegal Fairy Stories. MacManus, Seumas, ed. xii, 256p. (gr. 4-6). 1968. pap. 5.95 (0-486-21971-2) Dover.

Ver Beck, Frank. Surprising Adventures of the Magical Monarch of Mo & His People. Baum, L. Frank. (ps-4). 1968. pap. 6.95 (0-486-21892-9) Dover.

Verheijn, Jan. Mary's Little Donkey: A Christmas Story for Young Children. Sehlin, Gunhild. Latham, Hugh & Mackan, Donald, trs. (SWE.). 157p. (gr. 3-6). 1992. pap. 10.95 (0-86315-064-0, Pub. by Floris Bks UK) Gryphon Hse.

Vermeulen, Leon. Desert December. Haarhoff, Dorian. 32p. (ps-3). 1992. 13.95 (0-395-61300-0, Clarion Bks) HM.

Veronique. La Aventura de la Vida (The Adventure of Life) LeLoeuff, Jean. Puebla, Luis M., tr. (SPA.). 96p. (gr. 4 up). 1992. PLB 15.90 (1-56294-177-1) Millbrook Pr.

Verreaux, V. Carlin. The Hallelujah Corn Cobs. George, Linda C. LC 90-71549. 41p. (Orig.). (gr. k-6). 1991. pap. 4.95 (1-56002-027-X) Aegina Pr.

Verrier, Claude. Tobey: A Tale of Transition. Acker, Toni. 40p. (gr. 7-12). 1987. pap. 5.95 (0-942953-00-2) Wonder Works Studio.

Verrier, Suzy. Titus Tidewater. Verrier, Suzy. LC 70-112636. 48p. (gr. 2-4). 1990. Repr. of 1970 ed. 12.95 (0-89272-289-4) Down East.

Versel, Lauren. Creative Food Experiences for Children. 2nd rev. ed. Goodwin, Mary T. & Pollen, Gerry. 256p. (gr. k-6). 1980. pap. 7.95 (0-89329-027-0) Ctr Sci Public.

Verstraete, Elaine. Games to Play. 32p. (ps-3). 1990. 4.95 (1-56288-051-9) Checkerboard.

—The Littlest Christmas Tree. Hollander, Cass. 24p. (Orig.). (gr. k-1). 1990. pap. 0.99 (1-878624-44-X) McClanahan Bk.

—My Mommy Has Cancer. Parkinson, Carolyn S. 20p. (ps-4). 1991. pap. 8.95 (0-9630287-0-7) Solace Pub.

Vesey, Amanda. Hector's New Sneakers. Vesey, Amanda. 32p. (ps-3). 1993. 13.50 (0-670-84882-4) Viking Child Bks.

Vicatan. Amelia Earhart - Charles Lindbergh. Farr, Naunerle C. & Fago, John N. (gr. 4-12). 1979. pap. text ed. 2.95 (0-88301-349-5); wkbk. 1.25 (0-88301-373-8) Pendulum Pr.

Vickery, Diane. A Christmas Trilogy. Parker, Ann N. (gr. k-4). 1988. pap. 3.95 (0-943487-14-5) Sevgo Pr.

—Home Is Where the Shade Tree Is. Parker, Ann N. 18p. (gr. k-4). 1988. pap. 3.95 (0-943487-13-7) Sevgo Pr.

Victor, Ymonne. Icky, Sticky Gloop. Matthews, Morgan. LC 85-14013. 48p. (Orig.). (gr. 1-3). 1986. lib. bdg. 10.59 (0-8167-0616-6); pap. text ed. 3.50 (0-8167-0617-4) Troll Assocs.

Vidal, Beatriz. Bringing the Rain to Kapiti Plain. Aardema, Verna. LC 80-25886. 32p. (ps). 1981. 14.95 (0-8037-0809-2); PLB 13.89 (0-8037-0807-6) Dial Bks Young.

—Bringing the Rain to Kapiti Plain. Aardema, Verna. 32p. (ps-2). 1983. pap. 3.95 (0-8037-0904-8, Dial Pied Piper) Puffin Bks.

—Bringing the Rain to Kapiti Plain: A Nandi Tale. Aardema, Verna. (ps-3). 1993. pap. 6.99 incl. cassette (0-14-095052-4, Puffin) Puffin Bks.

—The Legend of El Dorado. Van Laan, Nancy. LC 89-7998. 40p. (ps-4). 1991. 16.00 (0-679-80136-7); lib. bdg. 15.99 (0-679-90136-1) Knopf Bks Yng Read.

—A Promise to the Sun: A Story of Africa. Mollel, Tololwa M. 32p. (ps-3). 1992. 15.95 (0-316-57813-4, Joy St Bks) Little.

—Rainbow Crow. Van Laan, Nancy. LC 88-12967. 40p. (ps-3). 1989. PLB 13.99 (0-394-99577-5) Knopf Bks Yng Read.

Vienneau, Jim. A Child's Gift of Lullabyes. Brown, J. Aaron, ed. 14p. (ps). 1987. Book packaged with cassette. 12.95 (0-927945-01-0) Someday Baby.

—Un Regalo de Arrullos Para Ninos. Brown, J. Aaron, ed. Pineda, Sysy, tr. (SPA.). 14p. (ps). 1988. Book with cassette. 12.95 (0-927945-02-9) Someday Baby.

—The Rock-a-Bye Collection. Brown, J. Aaron, ed. 12p. (Orig.). (ps). 1989. lyric bk. of lullabies & cassette 9.95 (0-927945-00-2) Someday Baby.

—The Rock-a-Bye Collection, Vols. 1 & 2. rev. ed. Brown, J. Aaron, ed. 14p. (ps). 1990. incl. cassette 12. 95 ea. Vol. 1 (0-927945-03-7) Vol. 2 (0-927945-04-5) Someday Baby.

—Snuggle Up: A Gift of Songs for Sweet Dreams. Brown, J. Aaron, ed. 14p. (ps). 1992. incl. cass. tape 12.95 (0-927945-05-3) Someday Baby.

Vienneau, Larry. A Cycle of Myths: Native Legends from Southeast Alaska. Smelcer, John E., ed. 116p. (Orig.). (gr. 7 up). 1993. pap. 12.95 (0-9634000-2-9) Salmon Run.

View-Master International, jt. photog. see Barrett, John E.

Vigna, Judith. Black Like Kyra, White Like Me. Vigna, Judith. Tucker, Kathleen, ed. LC 92-1203. 32p. (gr. 2-6). 1992. 13.95g (0-8075-0778-4) A Whitman.

—Boot Weather. Vigna, Judith. Fay, Ann, ed. LC 88-20563. 32p. (ps-2). 1989. 13.95 (0-8075-0837-3) A Whitman.

—Grandma Without Me. Vigna, Judith. Tucker, Kathleen, ed. LC 83-26031. 32p. (ps-3). 1984. PLB 13. 95 (0-8075-3030-1) A Whitman.

—Mommy & Me by Ourselves Again. Vigna, Judith. Fay, Ann, ed. LC 87-2059. 32p. (ps-3). 1987. PLB 13.95 (0-8075-5232-1) A Whitman.

—My Big Sister Takes Drugs. Vigna, Judith. Mathews, Judith, ed. LC 89-70736. 32p. (gr. k-3). 1990. PLB 13. 95 (0-8075-5317-4) A Whitman.

—Nobody Wants a Nuclear War. Vigna, Judith. Tucker, Kathleen, ed. LC 86-1654. 40p. (gr. 1-4). 1986. 13.95 (0-8075-5739-0) A Whitman.

—Saying Goodbye to Daddy. Vigna, Judith. Levine, Abby, ed. LC 90-12757. 32p. (gr. k-2). 1991. 13.95 (0-8075-7253-5) A Whitman.

—She's Not My Real Mother. Vigna, Judith. Fay, Ann, ed. LC 80-19073. 32p. (gr. 1-3). 1980. PLB 13.95 (0-8075-7340-X) A Whitman.

Vignazia, Franco. The First Sacraments. Biffi, Inos. Walsh, Kevin, tr. from ITA. Martini, Carlo, intro. by. LC 88-80658. 94p. (gr. 4-9). 1989. 15.95 (0-89870-206-2) Ignatius Pr.

—Prayer. Biffi, Inos. LC 93-41090. 1994. write for info. (0-8028-3759-X) Eerdmans.

—The Story of the Eucharist. Biffi, Inos. Drury, John, tr. from ITA. LC 85-82173. 125p. (gr. 5 up). 1986. 16.95 (0-89870-089-2) Ignatius Pr.

Vignes, Denise S. English-Korean Picture Dictionary. Koh, Frances M., ed. LC 87-83309. 49p. (Orig.). (ps up). 1987. pap. 7.95 (0-9606090-3-2) EastWest Pr.

Vilas, Anil. Chanakya. Ghosh, A. (gr. 1-8). 1979. pap. 3.00 (0-89744-152-4) Auromere.

Villagran, Ricardo, jt. illus. see Purcell, Gordon.

Villalpando, Eleanor. Coping. Sanders, Corine & Turner, Cynthia. 64p. (gr. 2-8). 1983. wkbk. 7.95 (0-9607366-2-X, GA 494) Good Apple.

Villegas, Carene. Mama Llama's Pajamas. Shine, Michael. 45p. (Orig.). (ps-3). 1990. pap. 8.95 (0-945265-32-8) Accord Comm.

Vincent, Ben. Vocabulary Mastery. Bornstein, Scott. 272p. (gr. 9-12). 1982. 22.50 (0-9602610-1-X); pap. 14.95 (0-9602610-2-8) Bornstein Memory.

Vincent, Eric. Clovis Crawfish & the Orphan Zo Zo. Fontenot, Mary A. LC 81-17740. 32p. (ps-3). 1983. 12.95 (0-88289-312-2) Pelican.

—Clovis Crawfish & the Singing Cigales. Fontenot, Mary A. LC 81-5608. 32p. (ps-3). 1981. 12.95 (0-88289-270-3) Pelican.

Vincent, Francois. TV & Films: Behind the Scenes. Limousin, Odile & Neumann, Daniele. Bogard, Vicki, tr. from FRE. LC 92-966. (gr. k-5). 1992. 4.95 (0-944589-36-7) Young Discovery Lib.

—TV & Films: Behind the Scenes. Limousin, Odile & Neumann, Daniele. 40p. (gr. k-5). 1993. PLB 9.95 (1-56674-073-8, HTS Bks) Forest Hse.

Vincent, Gabrielle. Ernest & Celestine's Patchwork Quilt. Vincent, Gabrielle. LC 84-25891. 16p. (ps-1). 1985. 5.25 (0-688-04557-X) Greenwillow.

—Ernest & Celestine's Picnic. Vincent, Gabrielle. LC 82-2909. 24p. (gr. k-3). 1982. 15.95 (0-688-01250-7); PLB 15.88 (0-688-01252-3) Greenwillow.

—Halfway to Your House. Pomerantz, Charlotte. LC 92-30083. 32p. (ps up). 1993. 14.00 (0-688-11804-6); PLB 13.93 (0-688-11805-4) Greenwillow.

—Merry Christmas, Ernest & Celestine. Vincent, Gabrielle. LC 83-14155. 32p. (gr. k-3). 1984. PLB 11. 88 (0-688-02605-2); 12.00 (0-688-02606-0) Greenwillow.

—Threadbear. Gallaz, Christophe. 40p. (ps-3). 1993. 14. 95 (1-56846-085-6) Creat Editions.

—Threadbear. Gallaz, Christophe. Sokolinsky, Martin, tr. from FRE. LC 93-14581. 1993. 14.95 (0-88682-630-6) Creative Ed.

—Where Are You, Ernest & Celestine? Vincent, Gabrielle. LC 85-17595. 28p. (gr. k-3). 1986. 11.75 (0-688-06234-2); PLB 14.93 (0-688-06235-0) Greenwillow.

Vincente. The Case of the Dancing Dinosaur. Estes, Rose. LC 83-63444. 128p. (gr. 4-7). 1985. pap. 2.95 (0-394-86431-X) Random Bks Yng Read.

Vincente, Gonzalez. The Young Indiana Jones Chronicles: Safari in Africa. Bell, Sally. 48p. (gr. 2-4). 1992. pap. write for info. (0-307-11470-8, 11470, Golden Pr) Western Pub.

Vincer, Carole. Beds & Bedding. Watson, Mary G. 24p. (Orig.). (gr. 3 up). 1988. pap. 10.00 (0-901366-27-7, Pub. by Threshold Bks) Half Halt Pr.

—Feeds & Feeding. Watson, Mary G. 24p. (Orig.). (gr. 3 up). 1988. pap. 10.00 (0-901366-37-4, Pub. by Threshold Bks) Half Halt Pr.

—Fields & Fencing. Watson, Mary G. 24p. (Orig.). (gr. 3 up). 1988. pap. 10.00 (0-901366-66-8, Pub. by Threshold Bks) Half Halt Pr.

—First Aid. Holderness-Roddam, Jane. 24p. (Orig.). (gr. 3 up). 1989. pap. 10.00 (0-901366-98-6, Pub. by Threshold Bks) Half Halt Pr.

—Herbs for Horses, No. 27: Threshold Picture Guide. Morgan, Jenny. 24p. (Orig.). 1993. pap. 12.00 (1-872082-46-7, Pub. by Kenilworth Pr UK) Half Halt Pr.

—Making Your Own Jumps. Watson, Mary G. 24p. (Orig.). (gr. 3 up). 1988. pap. 10.00 (0-901366-76-5, Pub. by Threshold Bks) Half Halt Pr.

—Poles & Gridwork, No. 26: Threshold Picture Guide. Wallace, Jane. 24p. (Orig.). 1993. pap. 12.00 (1-872082-44-0, Pub. by Kenilworth Pr UK) Half Halt Pr.

—Preparing for a Show. Holderness-Roddam, Jane. 24p. (gr. 3 up). 1989. pap. 10.00 (0-901366-09-9, Pub. by Threshold Bks) Half Halt Pr.

—Solving Flatwork Problems, No. 25: Threshold Picture Guide. Wallace, Jane. 24p. (Orig.). 1993. pap. 12.00 (1-872082-43-2, Pub. by Kenilworth Pr UK) Half Halt Pr.

Viner, Carole & Giesen, Rosemary. Bones & Skeletons. Thompson, Brenda & Giesen, Rosemary. LC 76-22420. (gr. k-3). 1977. PLB 7.95 (*0-8225-1352-8*) Lerner Pubns.

Vinik, Michael. Math Games for the Young Child. Azzolino, Agnes. (Orig.). (ps-2). 1987. pap. text ed. 8.40 (*0-9623593-1-9*) Mathematical.

Vinvent, Benjamin. Bluebonnet at Dinosaur Valley State Park. Casad, Mary B. LC 90-7338. 32p. (gr. k-3). 1990. 13.95 (*0-88289-776-4*) Pelican.

Vishniac, Roman, photos by. A Day of Pleasure: Stories of a Boy Growing up in Warsaw. Singer, Isaac Bashevis. LC 70-95461. 160p. (gr. 3 up). 1986. pap. 5.95 (*0-374-41696-6*, Sunburst) FS&G.

Vissell, Rami. Rami's Book: The Inner Life of a Child. Vissell, Rami. Vissell, Barry, intro. by. LC 88-91345. 56p. 1990. 13.95 (*0-9612720-4-X*, 104) Ramira Pub.

Vista III Design. Plesiosaurus: The Swimming Reptile. Sandell, Elizabeth. Oelerich, Marjorie & Schroeder, Howard, eds. LC 88-962. 32p. (gr. k-5). 1988. lib. bdg. 12.95 (*0-944280-04-8*); pap. 5.95 (*0-944280-10-2*) Bancroft-Sage.

—Pteranodon: The Flying Reptile. Sandell, Elizabeth. Oelerich, Marjorie & Schroeder, Howard, eds. LC 88-953. 32p. 1988. lib. bdg. 12.95 (*0-944280-05-6*); pap. 5.95 (*0-944280-11-0*) Bancroft-Sage.

—Seismasaurus: The Longest Dinosaur. Sandell, Elizabeth. Oelerich, Marjorie & Schroeder, Howard, eds. LC 88-963. 32p. (gr. k-5). 1988. lib. bdg. 12.95 (*0-944280-03-X*); pap. 5.95 (*0-944280-09-9*) Bancroft-Sage.

—Stegosaurus: The Dinosaur with the Smallest Brain. Sandell, Elizabeth. Oelerich, Marjorie & Schroeder, Howard, eds. LC 88-995. 32p. (gr. k-5). 1988. lib. bdg. 12.95 (*0-944280-02-1*); pap. 5.95 (*0-944280-08-0*) Bancroft-Sage.

—Triceratops: The Last Dinosaur. Sandell, Elizabeth. Oelerich, Marjorie & Schroeder, Howard, eds. LC 88-952. 32p. (gr. k-5). 1988. lib. bdg. 12.95 (*0-944280-01-3*); pap. 5.95 (*0-944280-07-2*) Bancroft-Sage.

—Tyrannsasaurus Rex: The Fierce Dinosaur. Sandell, Elizabeth. Oelerich, Marjorie & Schroeder, Howard, eds. LC 88-958. 32p. (gr. k-5). 1988. lib. bdg. 12.95 (*0-944280-00-5*); pap. 5.95 (*0-944280-06-4*) Bancroft-Sage.

Vista III Design Staff. Ankylosaurus: The Armored Dinosaur. Sandell, Elizabeth. Oelerich, Marjorie & Hansen, Harlan S., eds. LC 88-39806. 32p. (gr. k-5). 1989. PLB 12.95 (*0-944280-16-1*); pap. text ed. 5.95 (*0-944280-22-6*) Bancroft-Sage.

—Apatosaurus: The Deceptive Dinosaur. Sandell, Elizabeth. Oelerich, Marjorie & Hansen, Harlan S., eds. LC 88-39805. 32p. (gr. k-5). 1989. PLB 12.95 (*0-944280-12-9*); pap. text ed. 5.95 (*0-944280-18-8*) Bancroft-Sage.

—Archaeopteryx: The First Bird. Sandell, Elizabeth. Oelerich, Marjorie & Hansen, Harlan S., eds. LC 88-39803. 32p. (gr. k-5). 1989. PLB 12.95 (*0-944280-13-7*); pap. text ed. 5.95 (*0-944280-19-6*) Bancroft-Sage.

—Compsognathus: The Smallest Dinosaur. Sandell, Elizabeth. Oelerich, Marjorie & Hansen, Harlan S., eds. LC 88-39801. 32p. (gr. k-5). 1989. PLB 12.95 (*0-944280-14-5*); pap. text ed. 5.95 (*0-944280-20-X*) Bancroft-Sage.

—Dimetrodon: The Sail-Backed Dinosaur. Sandell, Elizabeth. Oelerich, Marjorie & Hansen, Harlan S., eds. LC 88-39802. 32p. (gr. k-5). 1989. PLB 12.95 (*0-944280-15-3*); pap. text ed. 5.95 (*0-944280-21-8*) Bancroft-Sage.

—Maiasaura: The Good Mother Dinosaur. Sandell, Elizabeth. Oelerich, Marjorie & Hansen, Harlan S., eds. LC 88-39799. 32p. (gr. k-5). 1989. lib. bdg. 12.95 (*0-944280-17-X*); pap. text ed. 5.95 (*0-944280-23-4*) Bancroft-Sage.

Vista Three Design Staff. Environmental Awareness: Acid Rain. Snodgrass, M. E. James, Jody, ed. LC 90-26255. 48p. (gr. 4 up). 1991. lib. bdg. 14.95 (*0-944280-30-7*) Bancroft-Sage.

—Environmental Awareness: Air Pollution. Snodgrass, M. E. James, Jody, ed. LC 90-25726. 48p. (gr. 4 up). 1991. lib. bdg. 14.95 (*0-944280-31-5*) Bancroft-Sage.

—Environmental Awareness: Land Pollution. Snodgrass, M. E. James, Jody, ed. LC 91-8303. 48p. (gr. 4 up). 1991. lib. bdg. 14.95 (*0-944280-29-3*) Bancroft-Sage.

—Environmental Awareness: Solid Waste. Snodgrass, M. E. James, Jody, ed. LC 90-20950. 48p. (gr. 4 up). 1991. PLB 14.95 (*0-944280-28-5*) Bancroft-Sage.

—Environmental Awareness: Toxic Waste. Snodgrass, M. E. James, Jody, ed. LC 91-7427. 48p. (gr. 4 up). 1991. lib. bdg. 14.95 (*0-944280-27-7*) Bancroft-Sage.

—Environmental Awareness: Water Pollution. Snodgrass, M. E. James, Jody, ed. LC 90-20949. 48p. (gr. 4 up). 1991. PLB 14.95 (*0-944280-26-9*) Bancroft-Sage.

Vitale, Stefano. The Folks in the Valley: A Pennsylvania Dutch ABC. Aylesworth, Jim. LC 91-12451. 32p. (ps-3). 1992. 15.00 (*0-06-021672-7*); PLB 14.89 (*0-06-021929-7*) HarpC Child Bks.

—Nursery Tales Around the World. Sierra, Judy, ed. LC 93-2068. Date not set. write for info. (*0-395-67894-3*, Clarion Bks) HM.

Vittitow, Mary L. Fun Things for Kids at Christmastime. Vittitow, Mary L. & Liu, Sarah. 64p. (gr. 1-4). 1991. pap. 7.99 wkbk. (*0-87403-843-X*, 28-03063) Standard Pub.

Vivas, Julia. The Nativity. Vivas, Julie. 34p. (ps up). 1988. 13.95 (*0-15-200535-8*, Gulliver Bks) HarBrace.

Vivas, Julie. I Went Walking. Williams, Sue. 30p. (ps-2). 1990. 13.95 (*0-15-200471-8*, Gulliver Bks) HarBrace.

—I Went Walking. Williams, Sue. 32p. (ps-2). 1991. pap. 19.95 (*0-15-238010-8*) HarBrace.

—Let the Celebrations Begin! Wild, Margaret. LC 90-21606. 32p. (ps-1). 1991. 14.95 (*0-531-05937-5*); RLB 14.99 (*0-531-08537-6*) Orchard Bks Watts.

—Nurse Lugton's Curtain. Woolf, Virginia. Van Doren, Liz, ed. 32p. (gr. 2 up). 1991. 14.95 (*0-15-200545-5*, Gulliver Bks) HarBrace.

—Our Granny. Wild, Margaret. LC 93-11950. 1994. 14. 95 (*0-395-67023-3*) Ticknor & Fields.

—Possum Magic. Fox, Mem. 32p. (ps-2). 1990. 13.95 (*0-15-200572-2*, Gulliver Bks) HarBrace.

—Stories from Our House. Tulloch, Richard. 32p. (ps-3). 1987. 11.95 (*0-521-33485-3*) Cambridge U Pr.

—Stories from Our Street. Tulloch, Richard. 32p. 1990. 11.95 (*0-521-36603-8*) Cambridge U Pr.

—The Tram to Bondi Beach. Hathorn, Elizabeth. 32p. (gr. 4-8). 1989. 12.95 (*0-916291-20-0*) Kane-Miller Bk.

—The Very Best of Friends. Wild, Margaret. 30p. (ps-3). 1990. 13.95 (*0-15-200625-7*, Gulliver Bks) HarBrace.

—Wilfrid Gordon McDonald Partridge. Fox, Mem. LC 85-14720. 32p. (gr. k-5). 1985. 13.95 (*0-916291-04-9*) Kane Miller Bk.

—Wilfrid Gordon McDonald Partridge. Fox, Mem. 32p. (gr. k-4). 1989. pap. 7.95 (*0-916291-26-X*) Kane-Miller Bk.

Vivian, E. Charles. Adventures of Robin Hood. Vivian, E. Charles. (gr. 5 up). 1965. Apr. 1.75 (*0-8049-0067-1*, CL-67) Airmont.

Vladimir, Vagin, jt. illus. see Asch, Frank.

Vlakos, Jon. Ladle Rat Rotten Hut. 6th ed. 12p. 1988. pap. 2.00 (*0-934714-05-3*) Swamp Pr.

Vo, Dinh M. The Brocaded Slipper & Other Vietnamese Tales. Vuong, Lynette D. LC 84-40746. 96p. (gr. 3-7). 1992. PLB 13.89 (*0-397-32508-8*, Lipp Jr Bks) HarpC Child Bks.

Voake, Charlotte. Caterpillar, Caterpillar. French, Vivian. LC 92-544006. 32p. (ps up). 1993. 14.95 (*1-56402-206-4*) Candlewick Pr.

—Mrs. Goose's Baby. Voake, Charlotte. 24p. (ps-1). 1989. 12.95 (*0-316-90511-9*, Joy St Bks) Little.

—Over the Moon: A Book of Nursery Rhymes. LC 91-71826. 128p. (ps up). 1992. 19.95 (*1-56402-018-X*) Candlewick Pr.

—The Three Little Pigs & Other Favorite Nursery Stories. Voake, Charlotte, retold by. LC 91-58759. 96p. (ps up). 1992. 18.95 (*1-56402-181-1*) Candlewick Pr.

Voce, Louise. Hello, Goodbye. Lloyd, David. LC 87-17110. (ps-1). 1988. 12.95 (*0-688-07698-X*); lib. bdg. 12.88 (*0-688-07699-8*) Lothrop.

—The Owl & the Pussy-Cat. Lear, Edward. LC 90-39673. 32p. (ps up). 1991. 13.95 (*0-688-09536-4*); PLB 13.88 (*0-688-09537-2*) Lothrop.

Vo-Dinh, Mai. The Land I Lost. Huynh Quang Nhuong. LC 80-8437. 128p. (gr. 4-7). 1986. pap. 3.95 (*0-06-440183-9*, Trophy) HarpC Child Bks.

—Tet: The New Year. Tran, Kim-Lan. 32p. (gr. 2-5). 1993. pap. 4.95 (*0-671-79843-X*, S&S BYR) S&S Trade.

Vo-Dinh Mai. The Brocaded Slipper & Other Vietnamese Tales. Vuong, Lynette D. LC 81-19139. 128p. (gr. 2-5). 1992. pap. 3.95 (*0-06-440440-4*, Trophy) HarpC Child Bks.

—Sky Legends of Vietnam. Vuong, Lynette D. LC 92-38345. 96p. (gr. 4 up). 1993. 14.00 (*0-06-023000-2*); PLB 13.89 (*0-06-023001-0*) HarpC Child Bks.

Vogel, Nathaele. Huckleberry Finn. Twain, Mark, pseud. (FRE.). 380p. (gr. 5-10). 1990. pap. 9.95 (*2-07-033230-6*) Schoenhof.

Vogelsang, Johanna. Music! Words! Opera, 4 vols, Level 2. Brooks, Clifford, et al. Fowler, Charles, frwd. by. LC 91-45210. (gr. 3-5). 1991. One vol., 460p. tchr's. manual 82.50 (*0-918812-66-6*); Three vols., 48p. ea. wkbk. 4.95 (*0-918812-68-2*) MMB Music.

Vogelsang, Johanna & Roth, Roger. Music! Words! Opera, 4 vols, Level 1. Purrington, Sandra, et al. Fowler, Charles, frwd. by. LC 90-19274. 264p. (gr. k-2). 1990. One vol., 24p. tchr's. manual 65.00 (*0-918812-65-8*, SE0694); Three vols., 24p. ea. wkbk. 3.50 (*0-918812-67-4*, SE0695, SE0696, SE0697) MMB Music.

Voigt, Erna. Peter & the Wolf. Prokofiev, Sergei. LC 79-92902. 32p. 1987. 15.95 (*0-87923-331-1*) Godine.

Vojtech, Anna. Blow Away Soon. James, Betsy. LC 93-27135. 1995. write for info. (*0-399-22648-6*, Putnam) Putnam Pub Group.

—The First Strawberries: A Cherokee Story. Bruchac, Joseph, retold by. LC 91-31058. 32p. (ps-3). 1993. 13. 99 (*0-8037-1331-2*); lib. bdg. 13.89 (*0-8037-1332-0*) Dial Bks Young.

Volkmer, Jame A. Song of Chirimia - La Musica de la Chirimia: A Guatemalan Folktale - Folklore Guatemalteco. Volkmer, Jane A. (SPA & ENG.). 40p. (ps-4). 1990. PLB 18.95 (*0-87614-423-7*) Carolrhoda Bks.

Vollmer, Dennis. Joshua Disobeys. Vollmer, Dennis. LC 88-9464. 26p. (gr. k-3). 1988. PLB 14.95 (*0-933849-12-5*) Landmark Edns.

Volpe, Nancee. The Good Apple Guide to Learning Centers. Borba, Craig & Borba, Michele. 208p. (gr. k-6). 1978. 14.95 (*0-916456-33-1*, GA86) Good Apple.

Von Konigslow, Andrea W. Toilet Tales. Von Konigslow, Andrea W. 24p. (ps-2). 1989. pap. 0.99 (*0-920303-81-1*, Pub. by Annick CN) Firefly Bks Ltd.

Von Mason, Stephen. Brother Anansi & the Cattle Ranch: (El Hermano Anansi y el Rancho) De Sauza, James, as told by. Zubizarreta, Rosalma, tr. Rohmer, Harriet, adapted by. LC 88-37091. (SPA & ENG.). 32p. (ps-7). 1989. 13.95 (*0-89239-044-1*) Childrens Book Pr.

Von Ohlen, Nick, photos by. A Beekeeper's Year. Johnson, Sylvia A. LC 93-10199. Date not set. 14.95 (*0-316-46745-6*) Little.

Von Olfers, Sibylle. The Story of the Root Children. Von Olfers, Sibylle. (GER.). 32p. (ps-3). 1992. Repr. of 1906 ed. 12.95 (*0-86315-106-X*, Pub. by Floris Bks UK) Gryphon Hse.

—When the Root Children Wake Up. Fish, Helen D. LC 91-22577. 24p. 1991. Repr. of 1906 ed. 12.95 (*0-671-75216-2*, Green Tiger) S&S Trade.

Von Roesnberg, Marjorie. Elisabet Ney: Sculptor of American Heroes. Von Rosenberg, Marjorie. 64p. (gr. 4-7). 1990. 10.95 (*0-89015-747-2*) Eakin-Sunbelt.

Von Rosenberg, Marjorie. Cowboy Bob's Critters Visit Texas Heroes. Von Rosenberg, Marjorie. LC 93-2908. 80p. (gr. 2-5). 1993. 12.95 (*0-89015-905-X*) Eakin-Sunbelt.

Von Schmidt, Eric. By the Great Horn Spoon. Fleischman, Sid. (gr. 4-6). 1988. 15.95 (*0-316-28577-3*, Joy St Bks); pap. 4.95 (*0-316-28612-5*, Joy St Bks) Little.

—Chancy & the Grand Rascal. Fleischman, Sid. 190p. (gr. 3-7). 1989. 14.95 (*0-316-28575-7*, Joy St Bks); pap. 4.95 (*0-316-26012-6*, Joy St Bks) Little.

—The Ghost on Saturday Night. Fleischman, Sid. 64p. (gr. 4-6). 1974. 14.95 (*0-316-28583-8*, Joy St Bks) Little.

—Humbug Mountain. Fleischman, Sid. (gr. 3-7). 1988. pap. 4.95 (*0-316-28613-3*, Joy St Bks) Little.

Von Strohe, Patricia. The School That Was: A School Marm's Tale. Tennis, Rose H. LC 90-70254. 80p. (Orig.). 1990. pap. text ed. 6.95 (*0-923568-08-5*) Wilderness Adventure Bks.

Von Trutzschler, Wolf. Amanda. Von Trutzschler, Wolf. LC 89-82473. 48p. (ps-2). 1990. Repr. of 1941 ed. 14. 95 (*0-944439-19-5*) Clark City Pr.

Vorhand, Rachel. Oh, Zalmy! Or, Tales of Two Esthers, Bk. 3. Kleinbard, Gitel. (gr. 1-4). 1979. pap. 3.95 (*0-917274-05-9*) Mah Tov Pubns.

Vukovich, Charles. Fourth Wise Man. Atiyeh, Wadeeha. (gr. 4 up). 1959. pap. 3.00 (*0-8315-0038-7*) Speller.

Vulliamy, Clara. Ellen & Penguin. Vulliamy, Clara. LC 92-54590. 32p. (ps up). 1993. 13.95 (*1-56402-193-9*) Candlewick Pr.

—Poor Monty. Fine, Anne. 32p. (ps-1). 1992. 14.45 (*0-395-60472-9*, Clarion Bks) HM.

Vu Viet Dung, photos by. Vietnam. Nurland, Patricia. LC 89-43178. 64p. (gr. 5-6). 1991. PLB 19.93 (*0-8368-0230-6*) Gareth Stevens Inc.

Vyas, Anil. The Seven Queens. Shankar, Alaka. 16p. (Orig.). (gr. k-3). 1980. pap. 2.50 (*0-89744-217-2*, Pub. by Childrens Bk Trust IA) Auromere.

—Treasury of Indian Tales: Book II. Shankar. (gr. 8-12). 1979. 4.95 (*0-89744-171-0*) Auromere.

Vyner, Tim. Arctic Spring. Vyner, Sue. LC 92-32280. (ps-3). 1993. 13.99 (*0-670-84934-0*) Viking Child Bks.

—The Stolen Egg. Vyner, Sue. 32p. (ps-3). 1992. 14.00 (*0-670-84460-8*) Viking Child Bks.

W

Waas, Uli. Where's Molly? Waas, Uli. Lanning, Rosemary, tr. from GER. 32p. (gr. k-3). 1993. 12.95 (*1-55858-229-0*); lib. bdg. 12.88 (*1-55858-230-4*) North-South Bks NYC.

Wabbes, Marie. Happy Birthday, Little Rabbit. Wabbes, Marie. 24p. (ps-k). 1987. pap. 4.95 (*0-87113-129-3*, Joy St Bks) Little.

—It's Snowing, Little Rabbit. Wabbes, Marie. 24p. (ps-k). 1987. pap. 4.95 (*0-87113-128-5*, Joy St Bks) Little.

Waber, Bernard. Anteater Named Arthur. Waber, Bernard. LC 67-20374. 48p. (gr. k-3). 1977. 13.95 (*0-395-20336-8*); pap. 5.70 (*0-395-25936-3*) HM.

—Bernard. Waber, Bernard. 48p. (gr. k-3). 1986. 13.45 (*0-395-31865-3*); pap. 5.70 (*0-395-42648-0*) HM.

—But Names Will Never Hurt Me. Waber, Bernard. LC 75-40473. 32p. (gr. k-3). 1976. 14.45 (*0-395-24383-1*) HM.

—Funny, Funny Lyle. Waber, Bernard. LC 86-27772. 40p. (gr. k-3). 1987. 13.45 (*0-395-43619-2*) HM.

—Funny, Funny Lyle. Waber, Bernard. 40p. (gr. k-3). 1991. pap. 4.80 (*0-395-60287-4*, Sandpiper) HM.

—The House on East Eighty-Eighth Street. Waber, Bernard. LC 62-8144. 48p. (gr. k-4). 1975. pap. 4.80 (*0-395-19970-0*, Sandpiper) HM.

—The House on East Eighty-Eighth Street. Waber, Bernard. (ps up). 1993. pap. 7.95 incl. cass. (*0-395-48878-8*) HM.

—I Was All Thumbs. Waber, Bernard. LC 75-11689. 48p. (gr. k-3). 1975. pap. 4.80 (*0-395-53969-2*) HM.

—Ira Sleeps Over. Waber, Bernard. LC 72-75605. 48p. (gr. k-3). 1973. 13.45 (*0-395-13893-0*) HM.

—Ira Sleeps Over. Waber, Bernard. (gr. k-3). 1975. pap. 4.80 (*0-395-20503-4*, Sandpiper) HM.

—Lyle Finds His Mother. Waber, Bernard. (gr. k-3). 1978. pap. 5.95 (*0-395-27398-6*) HM.

—Nobody Is Perfick. Waber, Bernard. 128p. (gr. k-3). 1991. pap. write for info. (0-395-60288-2, Sandpiper) HM.
—The Snake: A Very Long Love Story. Waber, Bernard. (ps-1). 1978. PLB 7.95 (0-685-02310-9) HM.
Wacker, Kay. Arizona A to Z. Weaver, Dorothy H. 32p. (Orig.). (gr. k up). 1994. pap. 7.95 (0-87358-564-X) Northland AZ.
Wade, Gini. The Wonderful Bag: An Arabian Tale from the "Thousand & One Nights" Wade, Gini, retold by. LC 92-43615. 32p. (gr. k-3). 1993. 14.95 (0-87226-508-0) P Bedrick Bks.

Wade, John. Twas the Night Before Jesus. Heise, Robert F. 28p. (gr. 3-6). 1990. smyth-sewn 12.95 (0-9627049-0-3) Dogwood NC. This new family-oriented book promises to be a fast & steady seller with wide appeal for both Christian & general audiences. Based loosely on the time-honored Christmas classic, "The Night Before Christmas," Bud Heise has created a Christmas tale that will delight both children & their parents, as the story of the Christ Child's birth is retold in rhyme & striking full color illustrations. 'TWAS THE NIGHT BEFORE JESUS is a 8 1/2" X 11" hardcover book, beautifully bound in a durable, washable cloth which will make reading aloud with a child or grandchild on one knee a family strengthening pleasure for the Holidays. Christian parents especially will appreciate the instructive value as well as the aesthetic appeal of this unique book. 'TWAS THE NIGHT BEFORE JESUS returns to the true meaning of Christmas. It promises to become a classic in years to come. Order now in time for the Christmas season.
Publisher Provided Annotation.

Wade, Tony. Rosa Parks: Hero of Our Time. Jackson, Garnet N. LC 92-28583. 1992. write for info. (0-8136-5232-4); pap. write for info. (0-8136-5705-9) Modern Curr.
Wadsworth, Elaine. Fights over Rights. Deegan, Paul. Abbott, Phyllis, et al, eds. LC 87-71091. 48p. (gr. 4). 1987. lib. bdg. 10.95 (0-939179-21-0) Abdo & Dghtrs.
—A Revolutionary Idea. Deegan, Paul. Abbott, Phyllis, et al, eds. LC 87-71092. 48p. (gr. 4). 1987. lib. bdg. 10. 95 (0-939179-20-2) Abdo & Dghtrs.
—Right to Bear Arms. Deegan, Paul. Abbott, Phyllis, et al, eds. LC 87-71088. 32p. (gr. 4). 1987. lib. bdg. 10. 95 (0-939179-24-5) Abdo & Dghtrs.
—Search & Seizure. Deegan, Paul. Abbott, Phyllis, et al, eds. LC 87-71090. 32p. (gr. 4). 1987. lib. bdg. 10.95 (0-939179-23-7) Abdo & Dghtrs.
Wagenman, Mark A. Aloha Bear ABC: Coloring & Activity Book. Wagenman, Mark A. 24p. (ps-k). 1989. pap. 2.95 (0-89610-146-0) Island Heritage.
—Aloha Bear & Maui the Whale (the Adventures of) Wagenman, Mark A. 28p. (ps-2). 1989. 7.95 (0-89610-148-7) Island Heritage.
—Aloha Bear: Color & Activity Book. Wagenman, Mark A. 24p. (ps-k). 1988. pap. 2.95 (0-89610-023-5) Island Heritage.
—Atlantis the Submarine: Coloring & Activity Book. Wagenman, Mark A. 24p. (ps-k). 1990. pap. 2.95 (0-89610-168-1) Island Heritage.
Wagner, David. In My Own Backyard. Kurjian, Judi. LC 93-18472. 32p. (ps-8). 1993. 14.95 (0-88106-442-4); PLB 15.00 (0-88106-443-2) Charlesbridge Pub.
Wagner, E. Vernel. Dinosaurs & Prehistoric Animals Coloring Book. Wagner, E. Vernel. 64p. (gr. 3-5). 1988. pap. 3.00 (0-941875-05-9) Wolverine Gallery.
—Rodeo, America's Number One Sport. 2nd ed. Bryant, Thomas A. 64p. (gr. 3-5). 1986. pap. 3.00 (0-941875-00-8) Wolverine Gallery.
Wagner, Jane T. Some Brief Cases of Inspector Alec Stuart of Scotland Yard. Wagner, Archibald C. 69p. (Orig.). 1992. pap. 12.95 (1-880664-01-1) E M Pr.
Wagner, Matt & Rankin, Rich. Grendel, No. 4. Wagner, Matt, et al. 48p. (gr. 9-12). 1986. 29.95 (0-936211-02-4); pap. 5.95 (0-938695-01-0) Graphitti Designs.
Wagner, Pete. Get off My Brain: A Survival Guide for Lazy Students. McCutcheon, Randall J. LC 84-82166. 120p. (gr. 9 up). 1985. pap. 8.95 (0-915793-02-4) Free Spirit Pub.

Wagstaff Advertising Design Staff. Bring Me What I Ask: A Hawaiian Story about Numbers. Kaopuiki, Stacey S. Despins, Cindy R., ed. Kaopuiki, Stacey S. 32p. (ps-3). 1991. 10.95 (1-878498-03-7) Hawaiian Isl Concepts.
—The Secret of the Hawaiian Rainbow: A Hawaiian Story about Colors. Kaopuiki, Stacey S. Despins, Cindy R., ed. Wagstaff, Bob. 32p. (ps-3). 1991. 10.95 (1-878498-02-9) Hawaiian Isl Concepts.
Wagstaff, Bob. To Tell the Truth. Ogawa, Brian K., et al. LC 88-51256. 40p. (gr. 4-6). 1988. text ed. write for info. (0-9621260-0-4) VWAP.
Wahl, Diana. Beyond the Magpie: A Selection of Winning Entries from Four Years - 1987, 1988, 1989, 1990 - of the West Virginia Writers, Inc. Annual Awards Competition. West Virginia Writers, Inc., Staff & McClure, Patricia. Carper, Helen, ed. Love, Patrick, contrib. by. (Orig.). 1991. pap. 9.40 (0-941092-23-2) Mtn St Pr.
Wahl, Dick. Basic Bible Dictionary. Matthews, Velda & Beard, Ray. Korth, Bob, ed. 128p. (Orig.). (gr. 4-12). 1984. pap. 12.99 (0-87239-720-3, 2770) Standard Pub.
Wahl, Len. Rhode Island: In Words & Pictures. Fradin, Dennis. LC 80-22497. 48p. (gr. 2-5). 1981. PLB 17.27 (0-516-03939-3) Childrens.
Wahl, Richard. Alabama: In Words & Pictures. Fradin, Dennis. LC 80-15135. 48p. (gr. 2-5). 1980. PLB 17.27 (0-516-03901-6) Childrens.
—Arkansas: In Words & Pictures. Fradin, Dennis. LC 80-11995. 48p. (gr. 2-5). 1980. PLB 17.27 (0-516-03904-0) Childrens.
—Colorado: In Words & Pictures. Fradin, Dennis. LC 80-15778. 48p. (gr. k-4). 1980. PLB 17.27 (0-516-03906-7); pap. 4.95 (0-516-43906-5) Childrens.
—District of Columbia: In Words & Pictures. Lumley, Katherine W. LC 80-39645. 48p. (gr. 2-5). 1981. PLB 17.27 (0-516-03951-2) Childrens.
—Florida: In Words & Pictures. Fradin, Dennis. LC 80-16681. 48p. (gr. 2-5). 1980. PLB 17.27 (0-516-03909-1) Childrens.
—Georgia: In Words & Pictures. Fradin, Dennis. LC 80-26768. 48p. (gr. 2-5). 1981. PLB 17.27 (0-516-03910-5) Childrens.
—Kansas: In Words & Pictures. Fradin, Dennis. LC 80-12576. 48p. (gr. 2-5). 1980. PLB 17.27 (0-516-03916-4) Childrens.
—Kentucky: In Words & Pictures. Fradin, Dennis. LC 80-25810. 48p. (gr. 2-5). 1981. PLB 17.27 (0-516-03917-2) Childrens.
—Louisiana: In Words & Pictures. Fradin, Dennis. LC 80-28609. 48p. (gr. 2-5). 1981. PLB 17.27 (0-516-03918-0); pap. 3.95 (0-516-43918-9) Childrens.
—Massachusetts: In Words & Pictures. Fradin, Dennis. LC 80-26161. 48p. (gr. 2-5). 1981. PLB 17.27 (0-516-03921-0) Childrens.
—Mississippi: In Words & Pictures. Fradin, Dennis. LC 80-36855. 48p. (gr. 2-5). 1980. PLB 17.27 (0-516-03924-5) Childrens.
—Missouri: In Words & Pictures. Fradin, Dennis. LC 80-12249. 48p. (gr. 2-5). 1980. PLB 17.27 (0-516-03925-3) Childrens.
—Montana: In Words & Pictures. Fradin, Dennis. LC 80-25023. 48p. (gr. 2-5). 1981. PLB 17.27 (0-516-03926-1) Childrens.
—Nevada: In Words & Pictures. Fradin, Dennis. LC 80-24179. 48p. (gr. 2-6). 1981. PLB 17.27 (0-516-03928-8) Childrens.
—New Hampshire: In Words & Pictures. Fradin, Dennis. LC 80-25421. 48p. (gr. 2-5). 1981. PLB 17.27 (0-516-03929-6) Childrens.
—New Jersey: In Words & Pictures. Fradin, Dennis. LC 80-19688. 48p. (gr. 2-5). 1980. PLB 17.27 (0-516-03930-X) Childrens.
—New Mexico: In Words & Pictures. Fradin, Dennis. LC 81-298. 48p. (gr. 2-5). 1981. PLB 17.27 (0-516-03931-8) Childrens.
—New York: In Words & Pictures. Fradin, Dennis. LC 81-28366. 48p. (gr. 2-5). 1981. PLB 17.27 (0-516-03932-6) Childrens.
—North Dakota: In Words & Pictures. Fradin, Dennis. LC 80-26480. 48p. (gr. 2-5). 1981. PLB 17.27 (0-516-03934-2) Childrens.
—Oklahoma: In Words & Pictures. Fradin, Dennis. LC 80-26961. 48p. (gr. 2-5). 1981. PLB 17.27 (0-516-03936-9) Childrens.
—Oregon: In Words & Pictures. Fradin, Dennis. LC 80-15183. 48p. (gr. 3-8). 1980. PLB 17.27 (0-516-03937-7) Childrens.
—South Dakota: In Words & Pictures. Fradin, Dennis. LC 80-25349. 48p. (gr. 2-5). 1981. PLB 17.27 (0-516-03941-5) Childrens.
—The Story of the Chicago Fire. Stein, R. Conrad. LC 81-15543. 32p. (gr. 3-6). 1982. pap. 3.95 (0-516-44633-9) Childrens.
—Texas: In Words & Pictures. Fradin, Dennis. LC 80-27497. 48p. (gr. 2-5). 1981. PLB 17.27 (0-516-03943-1); pap. 3.95 (0-516-43943-X) Childrens.
—Washington: In Words & Pictures. Fradin, Dennis. LC 80-14745. 48p. (gr. 2-5). 1980. PLB 17.27 (0-516-03947-4) Childrens.
—West Virginia: In Words & Pictures. Fradin, Dennis. LC 80-12133. 48p. (gr. 2-5). 1980. PLB 17.27 (0-516-03949-0) Childrens.
Wahl, Richard & Meents, Len. Connecticut: In Words & Pictures. Fradin, Dennis. LC 79-23292. 48p. (gr. 2-5). 1980. PLB 17.27 (0-516-03907-5) Childrens.

Waite, Mitchell. The Lost Dutchman & Superstition Mountain Who's Who. Waite, Mitchell. LC 93-83367. 150p. (Orig.). 1993. pap. text ed. 9.95 (1-881260-07-0) Southwest Pubns.
Wakeman, Diana. Disney's Aladdin. LC 91-58974. 12p. (ps-3). 1993. 11.95 (1-56282-242-X) Disney Pr.
Wakeman, Diana, jt. illus. see Langley, Bill.
Wakeman, Diana, jt. illus. see Martin, Kerry.
Wakeman, Diana, jt. illus. see Ortiz, Phil.
Wakeman, Diana, jt. illus. see Pacheco, Dave.
Wakeman, Diana, jt. illus. see Pacheco, David.
Wakeraw, Diana, jt. illus. see Langley, Bill.
Wakiyama, Hanako. Humphrey: The Lost Whale. Tokuda, Wendy & Hall, Richard. 32p. (gr. k-4). 1986. 11.95 (0-89346-270-5) Heian Intl.
—Humphrey, the Lost Whale: A True Story. Tokuda, Wendy & Hall, Richard. 32p. (gr. k-6). 1992. pap. 5.95 (0-89346-346-9) Heian Intl.
Waldherr, Kris. Persephone & the Pomegranate: A Myth from Greece. Waldherr, Kris. LC 92-21349. 32p. (ps-3). 1993. 14.99 (0-8037-1191-3); PLB 14.89 (0-8037-1192-1) Dial Bks Young.
—Rapunzel. Ehrlich, Amy. LC 88-25918. 32p. (ps-3). 1989. 12.95 (0-8037-0654-5); PLB 12.89 (0-8037-0655-3) Dial Bks Young.
Waldman, Bryna. Aladdin & the Wonderful Lamp. Eastman, David, adapted by. LC 87-13756. 32p. (gr. 1-4). 1988. PLB 9.79 (0-8167-1073-2); pap. text ed. 1.95 (0-8167-1074-0) Troll Assocs.
—Anansi Finds a Fool. Aardema, Verna. LC 91-21127. 32p. (ps-3). 1992. 14.00 (0-8037-1164-6); PLB 13.89 (0-8037-1165-4) Dial Bks Young.
—Christmas Countdown: A Story a Day for 25 Days for Everyone Who Just Can't Wait 'til Christmas. Englehart, Steve. 64p. (Orig.). 1992. pap. 5.99 (0-380-76842-9, Camelot Young) Avon.
—The First Christmas. 48p. 1992. 9.95 (0-88101-229-7) Unicorn Pub.
—The First Christmas. 48p. 1992. 12.95 (0-88101-239-4) Unicorn Pub.
—King Leopard's Gift: And Other Legends of the Animal World. Kerven, Rosalind. 32p. 1990. 14.95 (0-521-36180-X) Cambridge U Pr.
—The Three Riddles: A Jewish Folktale. Jaffe, Nina. (ps-3). 1989. incl. cassette 7.95 (0-553-45910-4) Bantam.
—The Three Riddles: A Jewish Folktale. Jaffe, Nina. (ps-3). 1989. pap. 3.95 (0-553-34649-0) Bantam.
—The Very First Americans. Ashrose, Cara. LC 92-38076. 32p. (ps-3). 1993. pap. 2.25 (0-448-40169-X, G&D); (G&D) Putnam Pub Group.
Waldman, Neil. America the Beautiful. Bates, Katherine L. LC 92-46199. 32p. 1993. SBE 14.95 (0-689-31861-8, Atheneum Child Bk) Macmillan Child Grp.
—Best True Ghost Stories of the Twentieth Century. Knight, David C. LC 83-23075. 64p. (gr. 3-7). 1984. pap. 11.95 jacketed (0-671-66556-1) S&S Trade.
—Bring Back the Deer. Prusski, Jeffrey. 32p. (ps-3). 1988. 13.95 (0-15-200418-1, Gulliver Bks) HarBrace.
—The Gold Coin. Ada, Alma F. LC 90-32806. 32p. (gr. k-3). 1991. SBE 13.95 (0-689-31633-X, Atheneum Child Bk) Macmillan Child Grp.
—The Gold Coin. Ada, Alma F. Randall, Bernice, tr. from SPA. LC 93-14403. 32p. (gr. k-3). 1994. pap. 4.95 (0-689-71793-8, Aladdin) Macmillan Child Grp.
—The Headless Ghost: True Tales of the Unexplained. Warren, William E. LC 85-28214. 144p. (gr. 6 up). 1986. pap. 12.95 jacketed (0-671-67710-1, Little Simon) S&S Trade.
—Highwayman. Noyes, Alfred. 28p. (ps-3). 1990. 14.95 (0-15-234340-7) HarBrace.
—Mother Earth. Luenn, Nancy. LC 90-19134. 32p. (ps-3). 1992. SBE 13.95 (0-689-31668-2, Atheneum Child Bk) Macmillan Child Grp.
—Nessa's Fish. Luenn, Nancy. LC 89-10548. 32p. (gr. k-3). 1990. SBE 13.95 (0-689-31477-9, Atheneum Child Bk) Macmillan Child Grp.
—Nessa's Fish. Luenn, Nancy. (gr. k-4). 1993. 13.95 (0-685-64812-5); audio cass. 11.00 (1-882869-81-8) Read Advent.
—Nessa's Story: El Cuento de Nessa. Luenn, Nancy. Ada, Alma F., tr. LC 92-16984. (ENG & SPA). 32p. (ps-3). 1994. English ed. SBE 14.95 (0-689-31782-4, Atheneum Child Bk); Spanish ed. SBE 14.95 (0-689-31919-3, Atheneum Child Bk) Macmillan Child Grp.
—The Passover Journey: A Seder Companion. Goldin, Barbara D. LC 93-5133. 64p. 1994. 15.99 (0-670-82421-6) Viking Child Bks.
—The Screaming Skull: True Tales of the Unexplained. Warren, William E. LC 87-6909. 144p. (gr. 5 up). 1987. pap. 11.95 jacketed (0-671-66809-9, S&S BFYR) S&S Trade.
—The Sea Lion. Kesey, Ken. 48p. (ps up). 1991. 14.95 (0-670-83916-7) Viking Child Bks.
—Tales of Terror: Ten Short Stories. Poe, Edgar Allan. LC 84-22290. 208p. (gr. 5 up). 1985. 12.95 (0-13-884214-0) P-H.
—The Tyger. Blake, William. LC 92-23378. 1993. 15.95 (0-15-292375-6) HarBrace.
Waldman, Selma. Pathblazers: Eight People Who Made a Difference. Fullen, M. K. 64p. (Orig.). (gr. 3-10). 1992. 12.95 (0-940880-35-0); pap. 6.95 (0-940880-36-9) Open Hand.
Waldron, Sarah M. Can You Dig It? Richardson, Delores. 20p. (gr. 3-7). 1990. write for info. (0-9619482-9-9) Little Spirit.

Waldron, Shirley, jt. illus. see Wolf, Barbara.
Wales, Johnny. Chung Lee Loves Lobsters. MacDonald, High. 24p. (gr. k-3). 1992. PLB 14.95 (*1-55037-217-3*, Pub. by Annick CN); pap. 4.95 (*1-55037-214-9*, Pub. by Annick CN) Firefly Bks Ltd.
—The Toronto Story. MacKay, Claire. 112p. (Orig.). (gr. 5 up). 1991. 34.95 (*1-55037-137-1*, Pub. by Annick CN); pap. 24.95 (*1-55037-135-5*, Pub. by Annick CN) Firefly Bks Ltd.
Walhood, Darlene. Christmas Activities from Around the World. Sullivan, Dianna. 48p. (gr. 1-4). 1985. wkbk. 5.95 (*1-55734-008-0*) Tchr Create Mat.
—Patriotic Holidays. Sullivan, Dianna J. 48p. (gr. 1-5). 1986. wkbk. 5.95 (*1-55734-115-X*) Tchr Create Mat.
Walker, Barbara. More of Magic. Blaisdell, Frank. Dawson, Steve, ed. iv, 97p. (gr. 8). 1980. 10.00 (*0-915926-48-2*) Magic Ltd.
—The Weather Cat. rev. ed. Cresswall, Helen. 32p. (gr. k-2). 1990. Repr. of 1989 ed. PLB 10.50 (*1-878363-06-9*) Forest Hse.
Walker, Brian. Adventure Stories. King, Clive, ed. LC 92-26452. 1993. pap. 6.95 (*1-85697-882-6*) Kingfisher Bks.
Walker, C. Henry Clay. Kelly, Regina Z. (gr. 4-6). 1960. (Piper) pap. 2.44 (*0-395-01717-3*) HM.
Walker, Cora. One - Two - Three Books. Warren, Jean. Bittinger, Gayle, ed. LC 89-50120. 80p. (Orig.). (ps-1). 1989. pap. text ed. 7.95 (*0-911019-23-5*) Warren Pub Hse.
—One-Two-Three Murals: Simple Murals to Make Using Children's Open-Ended Art. Warren, Jean. Bittinger, Gayle, ed. LC 89-50121. 80p. (Orig.). (ps-1). 1989. pap. 7.95 (*0-911019-22-7*) Warren Pub Hse.
—One-Two-Three Puppets: Simple Puppets to Make for Working with Young Children. Warren, Jean. Bittinger, Gayle, ed. LC 89-50122. 80p. (Orig.). (ps-1). 1989. pap. 7.95 (*0-911019-21-9*) Warren Pub Hse.
Walker, Cora L. Theme-A-Saurus: The Great Big Book of Mini Teaching Topics. Warren, Jean. Bittinger, Gayle, ed. LC 88-51450. 280p. (Orig.). (ps-1). 1989. pap. text ed. 19.95 (*0-911019-20-0*) Warren Pub Hse.
Walker, Galen B., photos by. What Is a Bird? Hirschi, Ron. (ps-4). 1987. 10.95 (*0-8027-6720-6*); PLB 11.85 (*0-8027-6721-4*) Walker & Co.
—Where Do Birds Live? Hirschi, Ron. (ps-4). 1987. 10.95 (*0-8027-6722-2*); PLB 11.85 (*0-8027-6723-0*) Walker & Co.
Walker, Jan, jt. illus. see Delany, Dan.
Walker, Karen. How to Draw Funny Faces. 32p. 1991. 3.98 (*1-56156-020-0*); pap. 2.95 (*1-56156-065-0*) Kidsbks.
—Make-a-Face: Monster Faces. 24p. (Orig.). 1990. pap. 1.95 (*0-942025-98-9*) Kidsbks.
—White Fang: Illustrated Classics. London, Jack. Arneson, D. J., ed. 128p. (Orig.). 1990. pap. 2.95 (*0-942025-84-9*) Kidsbks.
Walker, Larry. The Nubian Princess. Shearer, Marilyn J. 16p. (Orig.). (ps-6). 1989. 19.95 (*0-685-30091-9*); pap. 10.95 (*0-685-30092-7*) L Ashley & Joshua.
—Sleeping Beauty. Shearer, Marilyn J. 16p. (ps-6). 1989. 19.95 (*0-685-30099-4*); pap. 10.95 (*0-685-30100-1*) L Ashley & Joshua.
Walker, Malcolm. Projects for Spring & Holiday Activities. McInnes, Celia. Young, Richard G., ed. LC 88-33514. 32p. (gr. 3-5). 1989. PLB 15.93 (*0-944483-40-2*) Garrett Ed Corp.
Walker, Roger. The Student's Activity Atlas. Morris, Neil. 48p. (gr. 3 up). 1993. PLB 19.93 (*0-8368-1041-4*) Gareth Stevens Inc.
Walker, Sylvia. Land of the Four Winds. Ellis, Veronica F. LC 92-72001. 32p. (gr. 1-4). 1993. 14.95 (*0-940975-38-6*); pap. 6.95 (*0-940975-39-4*) Just Us Bks.
Walker, Timothy. Darby's Rainbow. McCoy, James C. Davenport, May, intro. by. LC 88-70551. 32p. (gr. k-3). 1990. pap. 3.50x (*0-943864-52-6*) Davenport.
Walker, Timothy, et al. Comic Tales Anthology, No. 2. 2nd ed. McCoy, James C., et al. Davenport, May, intro. by. LC 88-70551. 100p. (Orig.). (gr. 7-12). 1988. pap. 6.95x (*0-943864-53-4*) Davenport.
Walker, Walt. Little Yummy & the Basketball. Sealy, Adrienne V. (gr. 2-6). 1980. 3.50x (*0-9602670-4-2*) Assn Family Living.
Walker-Carleson, Cora. Alphabet & Number Rhymes. Warren, Jean. Bittinger, Gayle, ed. 160p. (Orig.). (ps-1). 1989. pap. text ed. 14.95 (*0-911019-27-8*) Warren Pub Hse.
—Color, Shape & Season Rhymes: Reproducible Pre-Reading Books for Young Children. Warren, Jean. Bittinger, Gayle, ed. 160p. (Orig.). (ps-1). 1989. pap. text ed. 14.95 (*0-911019-28-6*) Warren Pub Hse.
—Theme-A-Saurus II: The Great Big Book of More Teaching Units. Warren, Jean. Bittinger, Gayle, ed. LC 89-51179. 280p. (Orig.). (ps-1). 1990. pap. text ed. 19.95 (*0-911019-26-X*) Warren Pub Hse.

Wallace, Dan. The Room Parent's Party Planner: How to Host Great Parties in Your Child's Classroom. Basow, Lynn. Marsh, Chuck, ed. 56p. (Orig.). 1993. pap. 9.95 (*0-9638975-0-0*) Inverness Pr. Busy parents of grade-schoolers will love this warm, wonderful guidebook that shows them how to be heroes to their kids - & their kid's teachers &

---

classmates - by helping with classroom parties. Full of practical advice, specific examples & encouragement, THE ROOM PARENT'S PARTY PLANNER is perfect for busy parents who want hands-on participation in their children's education. Lynn Basow, a working mother of two, shares a decade of classroom party planning with tips on organizing a parents' team to spread the word & the work; involving kids in party planning; pacing & controlling the party to keep everyone involved; planning snacks, crafts & games; keeping plans flexible & ready for the unexpected, & building on successes as kids progress through school. With help from THE ROOM PARENT'S PARTY PLANNER, parents don't have to spend a lot of time or money to have a lot of fun - & show their commitment to their children's education. Single copy price: $9.95 plus $3.00 shipping & handling. Quantity discounts available. Order directly from Inverness Press, P.O. Box 1174, Lawrence, KS 66044 or FAX 913-843-2640. *Publisher Provided Annotation.*

Wallace, Dorathye. Spacebear Lands on Earth. Oana, Katherine. Baird, Tate, ed. LC 86-51210. 16p. (Orig.). (ps up). 1988. pap. 3.72 (*0-914127-26-8*) Univ Class.
Wallace, Dorathye B. Learning the Words of Color. Oana, Katherine. Baird, Tate, ed. LC 86-50866. 32p. (Orig.). (ps-1). 1986. pap. 2.65 (*0-914127-79-9*) Univ Class.
Wallace, Edwin B. The Cornhusk Doll. Minshull, Evelyn. LC 86-27125. 72p. (ps). 1987. 14.95 (*0-8361-3431-1*) Herald Pr.
Wallace, Ian. Builder of the Moon. Wynne-Jones, Tim. LC 88-12703. (ps-3). 1989. SBE 14.95 (*0-689-50472-1*, M K McElderry) Macmillan Child Grp.
—Morgan the Magnificent. Wallace, Ian. LC 87-15482. 32p. (gr. k-4). 1988. SBE 13.95 (*0-689-50441-1*, M K McElderry) Macmillan Child Grp.
—The Name of the Tree: A Bantu Folktale. Lottridge, Celia B., retold by. LC 89-2430. 36p. (gr. 1-5). 1990. SBE 14.95 (*0-689-50490-X*, M K McElderry) Macmillan Child Grp.
—Very Last First Time. Andrews, Jan. LC 85-71606. 32p. (gr. k-4). 1986. SBE 14.95 (*0-689-50388-1*, M K McElderry) Macmillan Child Grp.
—The Year of Fire. Jam, Teddy. LC 92-2882. 48p. (gr. 1-5). 1993. SBE 14.95 (*0-689-50566-3*, M K McElderry) Macmillan Child Grp.
Wallace, Joan. The Mystery of Horseshoe Mountain. Sanborn, Laura & Sanborn, Jane. 108p. (Orig.). (gr. 4-12). 1988. 4.95x (*0-910715-01-7*) Search Public.
Wallace, Mary. How to Make Great Stuff for Your Room. Wallace, Mary. 88p. 1992. pap. 8.95 (*0-920775-85-3*, Pub. by Greey de Pencier CN) Firefly Bks Ltd.
Wallace, Michael, photos by. On the Brink of Extinction: The California Condor. Arnold, Caroline. LC 92-14914. 1993. write for info. (*0-15-257990-7*) HarBrace.
Wallace, Shawn, jt. illus. see Harbo, Gary.
Waller, Nancy G. Primary Passages Plus: Favorite Songs & Hymns Arranged for Newcomers to the Piano. Hammond, Vicky L. & Dalby, Judy N. 32p. (Orig.). 1989. pap. 5.95 (*0-9624262-3-7*) Hammond Dalby Music.
Walles, Dwight. Halloween, Is It For Real? Myra, Harold. LC 82-6323. 32p. (gr. 2-4). 1982. 8.99 (*0-8407-5268-7*) Nelson.
—My Friend Jesus. Lindvall, Ella K. 32p. (Orig.). (gr. 1-3). 1989. pap. 2.99 (*0-8024-5949-8*) Moody.
—My Hospital Book. Coleman, William L. LC 81-10094. 96p. (Orig.). (gr. 2-7). 1981. pap. 5.99 (*0-87123-354-1*) Bethany Hse.
—My Teacher Jesus. Lindvall, Ella K. (ps-2). 1991. pap. 2.99 (*0-8024-5946-3*) Moody.
—Second Ark Book of Riddles. Shofner, Myra. (gr. 3-7). 1981. pap. 3.99 (*0-89191-531-1*, 55319, Chariot Bks) Cook.
Wallis, Diz. Crocodiles & Alligators. Farre, Marie. Matthews, Sarah, tr. from FRE. LC 87-31804. 38p. (gr. k-5). 1988. 4.95 (*0-944589-01-4*, 014) Young Discovery Lib.
—A Jar Full of Mice. Wallis, Diz. LC 90-85919. 24p. 1991. 5.95 (*1-878093-14-6*) Boyds Mills Pr.
—Monkeys, Apes & Other Primates. Bogard, Vicki, tr. from FRE. LC 89-5378. 38p. (gr. k-5). 1989. 4.95 (*0-944589-26-X*, 026) Young Discovery Lib.
—Pip's Adventure. Wallis, Diz. LC 90-85917. 24p. (ps up). 1991. 5.95 (*1-878093-43-6*) Boyds Mills Pr.
—Something Nasty in the Cabbages. Wallis, Diz. LC 90-84007. 32p. 1991. 15.95 (*1-878093-10-X*); poster avail. (*1-56397-000-7*, Caroline Hse) Boyds Mills Pr.
Wallner, Alexandra. Alice Meets the Aliens. Slater, Teddy. 24p. (ps-1). 1994. 15.95 (*0-671-72980-2*); lib. bdg. 9.98 (*0-671-72979-9*) Silver Pr.
—Betsy Ross. Wallner, Alexandra. LC 93-3559. 32p. (gr. 4-8). 1994. 15.95 (*0-8234-1071-4*) Holiday.
—Ghoulish Giggles & Monster Riddles. Wallner, Alexandra. Tucker, Kathy, ed. LC 82-10969. 32p. (gr. 1-5). 1983. PLB 8.95 (*0-8075-2863-3*) A Whitman.
—Glitter Glow-Deck the Halls. Wallner, Alexandra. 1989. 4.95 (*1-55782-317-0*, Pub. by Warner Juvenile Bks) Little.
—King Lionheart's Castle. Leonard, Marcia. 24p. (ps-1). 1992. 5.95 (*0-382-72974-9*); PLB 9.98 (*0-382-72973-0*) Silver.
Wallner, Alexandra, jt. illus. see Wallner, John.
Wallner, J. Min-Yo & the Moon Dragon. Hillman, E. 1992. 14.95 (*0-15-254230-2*, HB Juv Bks) HarBrace.
Wallner, John. Aldo Applesauce. Hurwitz, Johanna. LC 79-16200. 128p. (gr. 4-6). 1979. 12.95 (*0-688-22199-8*); PLB 12.88 (*0-688-32199-2*, Morrow Jr Bks) Morrow Jr Bks.
—Aldo Applesauce. Hurwitz, Johanna. 128p. (gr. 3-5). 1989. pap. 3.99 (*0-14-034083-1*, Puffin Puffin Bks.
—Aldo Ice Cream. Hurwitz, Johanna. LC 80-24371. 128p. (gr. 4-6). 1981. 13.95 (*0-688-00375-3*); PLB 13.88 (*0-688-00374-5*, Morrow Jr Bks) Morrow Jr Bks.
—Aldo Ice Cream. Hurwitz, Johanna. 128p. (gr. 3-7). 1989. pap. 3.99 (*0-14-034084-X*, Puffin) Puffin Bks.
—Animal Mixups. Selsam, Millicent & Hunt, Joyce. LC 91-16114. 32p. (ps-2). 1992. RSBE 13.95 (*0-02-778081-3*, Macmillan Child Bk) Macmillan Child Grp.
—Birthday in a Bathtub. Leonard, Marcia. Brook, Bonnie, ed. 24p. (gr-1). 1989. 5.95 (*0-671-68592-9*); PLB 9.98 (*0-671-68588-0*) Silver Pr.
—Case of the Missing Dinosaur. Brandt, Keith. LC 81-7620. 48p. (gr. 2-4). 1982. PLB 10.89 (*0-89375-586-9*); pap. text ed. 3.50 (*0-89375-587-7*) Troll Assocs.
—City Mouse - Country Mouse & Two More Tales from Aesop. Wallner, John. 32p. (Orig.). (gr. k-3). 1987. pap. 2.50 (*0-590-41155-1*) Scholastic Inc.
—A Colonial Williamsburg Activities Book: Fun Activities for Young Visitors. Fortunato, Pat. 48p. (Orig.). (gr. 1-4). 1982. pap. 3.95 (*0-87935-062-8*) Williamsburg.
—Easter Poems. Livingston, Myra C., ed. LC 84-15866. 32p. (ps-3). 1985. reinforced bdg. 13.95 (*0-8234-0546-X*) Holiday.
—Good King Wenceslas. 32p. 1990. 14.95 (*0-399-21620-0*, Philomel Bks) Putnam Pub Group.
—Hailstones & Halibut Bones: Adventures in Color. O'Neill, Mary. 1989. 12.95 (*0-385-24484-3*) Doubleday.
—Harvey, the Beer Can King. Gilson, Jamie. LC 78-1807. 128p. (gr. 4-6). 1983. 13.95 (*0-688-02382-7*) Lothrop.
—Hello, My Name Is Scrambled Eggs. Gilson, Jamie. LC 84-10075. 160p. (gr. 4-6). 1985. 12.95 (*0-688-04095-0*) Lothrop.
—Hello, My Name Is Scrambled Eggs. Gilson, Jamie. (gr. 3-6). 1991. pap. 2.99 (*0-671-74104-7*, Minstrel Bks) PB.
—Henry & the Haunted House. Slater, Teddy. 24p. (ps-1). 1992. 5.95 (*0-671-72978-0*); lib. bdg. 9.98 (*0-671-72977-2*) Silver Pr.
—Hooray for Father's Day. Sharmat, Marjorie W. LC 86-15037. 32p. (ps-3). 1987. reinforced bdg. 14.95 (*0-8234-0637-7*) Holiday.
—Hooray for Mother's Day! Sharmat, Marjorie W. LC 85-14146. 32p. (ps-3). 1986. reinforced bdg. 14.95 (*0-8234-0588-5*) Holiday.
—Lizzie Lies a Lot. Levy, Elizabeth. LC 75-32914. 80p. (gr. 4-6). 1976. 6.95 (*0-440-04919-9*); PLB 6.46 (*0-440-04920-2*) Delacorte.
—The Macmillan Picture Wordbook. Daly, Kathleen N. LC 82-6619. 80p. (ps-1). 1982. 7.95 (*0-02-725600-6*) Macmillan.
—Mrs. Claus's Crazy Christmas. Kroll, Steven. LC 84-25218. 32p. (ps-3). 1985. reinforced bdg. 14.95 (*0-8234-0563-X*) Holiday.
—Much Ado about Aldo. Hurwitz, Johanna. LC 78-5434. 96p. (gr. 4-6). 1978. PLB 13.88 (*0-688-32160-7*) Morrow Jr Bks.
—Much Ado about Aldo. Hurwitz, Johanna. 96p. (gr. 3-7). 1989. pap. 3.99 (*0-14-034082-3*, Puffin) Puffin Bks.
—My Favorite Time of Year. Pearson, Susan. LC 87-45296. 32p. (ps-3). 1988. PLB 12.89 (*0-06-024682-0*) HarpC Child Bks.
—One Tough Turkey. Kroll, Steven. LC 82-2925. 32p. (ps-3). 1982. reinforced bdg. 14.95 (*0-8234-0457-9*) Holiday.
—Remember Betsy Floss & Other Colonial American Riddles. Adler, David A. LC 87-45333. 64p. (gr. 1-4). 1987. reinforced bdg. 11.95 (*0-8234-0664-4*) Holiday.
—Ring of Earth: A Child's Book of Seasons. Yolen, Jane. LC 86-4800. 32p. (ps-1). 1986. 14.95 (*0-15-267140-4*, HB Juv Bks) HarBrace.
—Rumpelstiltskin. Wallner, John. LC 83-19100. 32p. 1984. 10.95 (*0-13-783747-X*) P-H.
—Snow White & Rose Red. Grimm, Jacob & Grimm, Wilhelm K. LC 84-4910. 32p. (gr. k-3). 1984. 10.95 (*0-13-815234-9*) P-H.

—Swimming in the Sand. Leonard, Marcia. Brook, Bonnie, ed. 24p. (ps-1). 1989. 5.95 (0-671-68593-7); PLB 9.98 (0-671-68589-9) Silver Pr.
—A Teacher on Roller Skates & Other School Riddles. Adler, David A. LC 89-1929. 64p. (gr. 1-4). 1989. reinforced bdg. 11.95 (0-8234-0775-6) Holiday.
—The Terrible Thing That Happened at Our House. Blaine, Marge. LC 86-4827. 40p. (ps-3). 1984. Repr. of 1975 ed. RSBE 13.95 (0-02-710720-5, Four Winds) Macmillan Child Grp.
—Things That Go Zoom! Rojany, Lisa. 18p. (gr. k-3). 1993. 6.95 (0-8431-3605-7) Price Stern.
—To the Zoo: Animal Poems. Hopkins, Lee B., compiled by. LC 89-12559. 32p. (ps-3). 1992. 14.95 (0-316-37273-0) Little.
—Violet & the Pirates. Leonard, Marcia. 24p. (ps-1). 1992. 5.95 (0-671-72976-4); lib. bdg. 9.98 (0-671-72975-6) Silver Pr.
—When the Dark Comes Dancing: A Bedtime Poetry Book. Larrick, Nancy. LC 81-428. (ps-2). 1983. 17.95 (0-399-20807-0, Philomel) Putnam Pub Group.
—Where Is the Bear? Nims, Bonnie L. Fay, Ann, ed. LC 87-25321. 24p. (ps-2). 1988. PLB 11.95 (0-8075-8933-0) A Whitman.
—Where's That Pig? Rojany, Lisa. 24p. (gr. k-3). 1993. 6.95 (0-8431-3604-9) Price Stern.
—Winter. Allington, Richard L. & Krull, Kathleen. LC 80-25115. 32p. (gr. k-3). 1985. PLB 15.95 (0-8172-1340-6); pap. 3.95 (0-8114-8243-X) Raintree Steck-V.
—You're Going Out There a Kid, but You're Coming Back a Star. Hirsch, Linda. 128p. (Orig.). (gr. 3-7). 1984. pap. 2.25 (0-553-15272-6, Skylark) Bantam.
Wallner, John & Wallner, Alexandra. Un Libro Ilustrado sobre Abraham Lincoln. Adler, David A. Mlawer, Teresa, tr. from ENG. (SPA.). 32p. (ps-3). 1992. reinforced bdg. 14.95 (0-8234-0980-5); pap. 5.95 (0-8234-0989-9) Holiday.
—Un Libro Ilustrado Sobre Cristobal Colon. Adler, David A. Mlawer, Teresa, tr. from ENG. (SPA.). 32p. (ps-3). 1992. reinforced bdg. 14.95 (0-8234-0981-3); pap. 5.95 (0-8234-0990-2) Holiday.
—A Picture Book of Benjamin Franklin. Adler, David A. LC 89-20059. 32p. (ps-3). 1990. reinforced bdg. 14.95 (0-8234-0792-6); pap. 5.95 (0-8234-0882-5) Holiday.
—A Picture Book of Christopher Columbus. Adler, David A. LC 90-39211. 32p. (ps-3). 1991. reinforced 14.95 (0-8234-0857-0) Holiday.
—A Picture Book of Christopher Columbus. Adler, David A. pap. 5.95 (0-8234-0949-X) Holiday.
—A Picture Book of Florence Nightingale. Adler, David A. LC 91-43388. 32p. (ps-3). 1992. reinforced bdg. 14. 95 (0-8234-0965-1) Holiday.
—A Picture Book of George Washington. Adler, David A. LC 88-16384. 32p. (ps-3). 1989. reinforced bdg. 14. 95 (0-8234-0732-2); pap. 5.95 (0-8234-0800-0) Holiday.
—A Picture Book of Helen Keller. Adler, David A. LC 89-77510. 32p. (ps-3). 1990. reinforced 14.95 (0-8234-0818-3) Holiday.
—A Picture Book of Helen Keller. Adler, David A. LC 89-77510. pap. 5.95 (0-8234-0950-3) Holiday.
—A Picture Book of Robert E. Lee. Adler, David A. LC 93-22998. 32p. (gr. 4-8). 1994. 15.95 (0-8234-1111-7) Holiday.
—A Picture Book of Thomas Jefferson. Adler, David A. LC 89-20076. 32p. (ps-3). 1990. reinforced bdg. 14.95 (0-8234-0791-8); pap. 5.95 (0-8234-0881-7) Holiday.
Wallner, John, jt. illus. see Himmelman, John.
Wallner, John C. The Terrible Thing That Happened at Our House. Marge, Marge. 32p. (gr. 1-4). 1991. pap. 3.95 (0-590-42371-1) Scholastic Inc.
Wallner, Susan. A Colonial Williamsburg Activities Book: Fun Things to Do for Children 4 & Up. Bethell, Jean & Axtell, Susan. 40p. (ps). 1984. pap. 3.95 (0-87935-068-7) Williamsburg.
Wallower, Lucille. All about Pennsylvania. Wallower, Lucille. Wholey, Ellen J., ed. (gr. 3-4). 1984. pap. 4.55 (0-931992-05-2) Penns Valley.
Walner, Hari. English Experiences. Gonzalez-Mena, Janet. LC 75-5307. (ps). 1975. Program Package Set. 87.25 (0-685-02507-1, Natl Textbk); wkbk. 6.60 (0-8325-0684-6, Natl Textbk); tchr's. manual 21.25 (0-8325-0681-8, Natl Textbk); Spanish. wkbk. 6.60 (0-8325-9639-6, Natl Textbk); Spanish. tchr's. manual 21.25 (0-8325-9638-8, Natl Textbk) NTC Pub Grp.
Walsh, Amanda. The Buried Moon. Walsh, Amanda. 32p. 1991. 14.45 (0-395-59349-2, Sandpiper) HM.
Walsh, Ellen S. Mouse Count. Walsh, Ellen S. D'Andrade, Diane, ed. 32p. (ps-1). 1991. 11.95 (0-15-256023-8) HarBrace.
—Mouse Paint. Walsh, Ellen S. 32p. (ps-1). 1989. 11.95 (0-15-256025-4) HarBrace.
Walsh, Janice. Fun Times Growing Up. Collins, Doris. 24p. (Orig.). (gr. k-3). 1988. pap. 7.95 (0-9621650-0-X) Periwinkle MA.
Walsh, Karen J. How to Cope with an Artichoke & other Mannerly Mishaps. Thiry, Joan. 40p. (gr. 7-12). 1982. pap. 4.95 (0-935046-04-6) Chateau Thierry.
—How to Entertain a Gnu & Not Disturb Your Family. Thiry, Joan. 40p. (gr. k-3). 1982. pap. 4.95 (0-935046-02-X) Chateau Thierry.
—How to Make a Courtesy Butter Sandwich & Serve it Properly. Thiry, Joan. 40p. (Orig.). (gr. 4-6). 1982. pap. 4.95 (0-935046-03-8) Chateau Thierry.
Walsh, Lloyd. The Return of Sinta Claus: A Family Winter Solstice Tale. Porter-Chase, Mary. (Orig.). (gr. 3-12). 1991. pap. 6.00 (0-9630798-0-8) Samary Pr.

Walsh, Michael S. Jack in the Beanstalk. Greenburg, Joanne. 48p. (gr. 3 up). 1980. 16.50 (0-8299-1033-6) West Pub.
Walston, Dennis. The Education of an Egg. Walston, Mark. 48p. (Orig.). (gr. 7 up). 1982. pap. 6.95 (0-9605776-2-9) Sparhawk.
Walt Disney Company Staff. Reindeer Round-Up: A Merry Christmas at the North Pole. Walt Disney Company Staff. 26p. (up). 1988. 19.95 (1-55578-313-9) Worlds Wonder.
Walt Disney Music Co. Staff. Disney Afternoon Songbook. 80p. (Orig.). 1991. pap. 12.95 (0-7935-0346-9, 00490518) H Leonard Pub.
Walt Disney Studios Staff. Walt Disney's Pinocchio. Collodi, Carlo. 80p. 1989. 19.95 (0-8109-1467-0) Abrams.
Walter, Eugene. Mobile Mardi Gras Annual 1948, Vol. 1, No. 2. Walter, Eugene. Plummer, Cameron, ed. 32p. (gr. 7 up). 1948. pap. 10.00 (0-940882-05-1) HB Pubns.
Walter, Marion. Make a Bigger Puddle, Make a Smaller Worm. Walter, Marion. LC 70-186593. 32p. (ps-3). 1970. 5.95 (0-87131-073-2) M Evans.
Walter, Mary W. How Many. McQueen, Priscilla L. (gr. k). 1968. pap. 2.54 (0-685-16725-9) McQueen.
—What Kind. McQueen, Priscilla L. (gr. k). 1968. pap. 2.07 (0-685-16726-7) McQueen.
—Which One. McQueen, Priscilla L. (gr. k). 1968. pap. 6.15 (0-685-16727-5) McQueen.
Walter, Nancy L., photos by. Inside of Me Series. Walter, Nancy L. 48p. (gr. k-2). 1993. pap. 18.95 (0-9635127-9-X) Naturally by Nan.
Walter, Paul. Why Am I Going to the Hospital? Livingston, Carole & Ciliotta, Claire. (gr. 1 up). 1981. 12.00 (0-8184-0316-0) Carol Pub Group.
Walter, Paul & Robins, Arthur. What's Happening to Me? Mayle, Peter. LC 75-14410. 56p. (gr. 3 up). 1975. 12.00 (0-8184-0221-0); pap. 6.95 (0-8184-0312-8) Carol Pub Group.
Walter, Paul, jt. illus. see Robbins, Arthur.
Walters, Catherine. The Dog Who Found Christmas. Jennings, Linda. 40p. (ps-2). 1993. 11.99 (0-525-45155-2, DCB) Dutton Child Bks.
Walters, Mary C. The Ant & the Dove. Wang, Mary L. LC 89-34414. 32p. (ps-2). 1989. PLB 11.93 (0-516-02367-5); pap. 3.95 (0-516-42367-3) Childrens.
—The Hungry Billy Goat. Milios, Rita. LC 88-673. 32p. (ps-2). 1989. PLB 11.93 (0-516-02090-0); pap. 2.95 (0-516-42090-9) Childrens.
Walther, Tom. Make Mine Music. Walther, Tom. 128p. (Orig.). (gr. 3 up). 1981. pap. 9.95 (0-316-92112-2) Little.
Walton, Garry. Shipwrecks: A Three-Dimensional Exploration. Hawcock, David. 24p. (gr. k-2). 1993. 15. 95 (0-694-00452-9, Festival) HarpC Child Bks.
Walton, Richard K. & Morrison, Gordon. A Field Guide to Endangered Wildlife Coloring Book. Walton, Richard K. & Morrison, Gordon. 64p. 1991. pap. 4.80 (0-395-57324-6) HM.
Waltrip, Jason, jt. illus. see Ridge, Jeff.
Waltrip, Jason, jt. illus. see Velez, Waller.
Waltz, Catherine. The Dragon, the Winds & the Witches. Waltz, Marjorie. LC 86-72867. 64p. (Orig.). (gr. k-2). 1987. pap. 5.00 (0-916383-14-8) Aegina Pr.
Waltz, Dick. Mickey Mouse & His Boat. Hughes, Alice. LC 87-83494. 40p. (gr. k-2). 1988. write for info. (0-307-11692-1) Western Pub.
Walz, Richard. A Baby Sister for Herry. Kingsley, Emily P. LC 83-83280. 24p. (ps). 1984. write for info. (0-307-12011-2, 12011, Golden Bks) Western Pub.
—Boxcar. Barkan, Joanne. 12p. (ps-k). 1992. POB 3.50 (0-689-71573-0, Aladdin) Macmillan Child Grp.
—Caboose. Barkan, Joanne. 12p. (ps-k). 1992. POB 3.50 (0-689-71574-9, Aladdin) Macmillan Child Grp.
—The Emperor's New Clothes. Andersen, Hans Christian. Easton, Samantha, retold by. 1991. 6.95 (0-8362-4928-3) Andrews & McMeel.
—The Little Engine That Could. Piper, Watty. LC 99-44044. 12p. (ps-2). 1984. 8.95 (0-448-18963-1, Platt & Munk) Putnam Pub Group.
—Locomotive. Barkan, Joanne. 12p. (ps-k). 1992. bds. 3.50 (0-689-71576-5, Aladdin) Macmillan Child Grp.
—Passenger Car. Barkan, Joanne. 12p. (ps-k). 1992. bds. 3.50 (0-689-71575-7, Aladdin) Macmillan Child Grp.
—The Pudgy Book of Mother Goose. 16p. (gr. k). 1984. 2.95 (0-448-10212-9, G&D) Putnam Pub Group.
Warburton, Bartt. The Very Scary Dictionary: Who's Who in Fright. Welch, R. C. 64p. 1993. pap. 4.95 (1-56565-072-7) Lowell Hse.
Warburton, Nick. Mr. Tite's Belongings. Warburton, Nick. 32p. (ps-3). 1992. 13.95 (0-670-84155-2) Viking Child Bks.
Ward, Bryan. Ant & Bee: Alphabetical Story for Tiny Tots. Banner, Angela. 96p. (ps-1). 1991. 6.95 (0-434-92966-2, Pub. by W Heinemann Ltd) Trafalgar.
—Ant & Bee & Kind Dog. Banner, Angela. 96p. (ps-1). 1992. 6.95 (0-434-92960-3, Pub. by W Heinemann Ltd) Trafalgar.
—Ant & Bee & the Doctor. Banner, Angela. 96p. (ps-1). 1992. 6.95 (0-434-92968-9, Pub. by W. Heinemann Ltd) Trafalgar.
—Ant & Bee & the Rainbow. Banner, Angela. 96p. (ps-1). 1992. 6.95 (0-434-92972-7, Pub. by W. Heinemann Ltd) Trafalgar.
—Ant & Bee Go Shopping. Banner, Angela. 96p. (ps-1). 1992. 6.95 (0-434-92970-0, Pub. by W Heinemann Ltd) Trafalgar.
Ward, Fredrick, jt. illus. see Kennan, Elaine.

Ward, Helen. Amazing Animals. Wood, A. J. LC 90-85906. 24p. (ps-1). 1991. 8.95 (1-878093-46-0) Boyds Mills Pr.
—Beautiful Birds. Wood, A. J. LC 90-85907. 24p. (ps-1). 1991. 8.95 (1-878093-47-9) Boyds Mills Pr.
—The Golden Pear. Ward, Helen. LC 91-9102. 40p. (ps-3). 1991. 14.95 (0-8249-8471-4, Ideals Child) Hambleton-Hill.
—The Golden Pear. Ward, Helen. 40p. (ps-3). 1993. pap. 4.95 (0-8249-8639-3, Ideals Child) Hambleton-Hill.
Ward, Helen, jt. illus. see Stillwell, Stella.
Ward, Helen, jt. illus. see Stilwell, Stella.
Ward, John. The Adventures of High John the Conqueror. Sanfield, Steve. LC 88-17946. 128p. (gr. 3 up). 1989. 12.95 (0-531-05807-7); PLB 12.99 (0-531-08407-8) Orchard Bks Watts.
—The Car Washing Street. Patrick, Denise L. LC 92-9229. 32p. (ps up). 1993. 14.00 (0-688-11452-0, Tambourine Bks); PLB 13.93 (0-688-11453-9, Tambourine Bks) Morrow.
—The Christmas Riddle. Medearis, Angela S., adapted by. LC 93-10713. (gr. 2 up). 1994. write for info. (0-525-67469-1, Lodestar Bks) Dutton Child Bks.
—We Keep a Store. Shelby, Anne. LC 89-35105. 32p. (ps-2). 1990. 14.95 (0-531-05856-5); PLB 14.99 (0-531-08456-6) Orchard Bks Watts.
Ward, Keith. Black Stallion. Farley, Walter. LC 85-19927. (gr. 3-7). 1977. 3.95 (0-394-80601-8); lib. bdg. 11.99 (0-394-90601-2); pap. 3.95 (0-394-83609-X) Random Bks Yng Read.
Ward, Ken. Twelve Kids One Cow: Ken Ward's World. Ward, Ken. 36p. 1989. pap. 4.95 (1-55037-076-6, Pub. by Annick CN) Firefly Bks Ltd.
Ward, Lynd. America's Paul Revere. Forbes, Esther. 48p. (gr. 3-5). 1990. pap. 5.70 (0-395-24907-4) HM.
—The Biggest Bear. Ward, Lynd. LC 52-8730. 80p. (gr. k-3). 1973. pap. 5.70 (0-395-15024-8, Sandpiper) HM.
—Brady. Fritz, Jean. (gr. 5-9). 1987. pap. 4.99 (0-14-032258-2, Puffin Bks.
—The Cat Who Went to Heaven. reissued ed. Coatsworth, Elizabeth. LC 58-10917. 72p. (gr. 4-6). 1967. RSBE 13.95 (0-02-719710-7, Macmillan Child Bk) Macmillan Child Grp.
—Early Thunder. Fritz, Jean. (gr. 5-9). 1987. pap. 4.99 (0-14-032259-0, Puffin) Puffin Bks.
—Fog Magic. Sauer, Julia. 128p. (gr. 5-9). 1986. pap. 3.99 (0-14-032163-2, Puffin) Puffin Bks.
—Johnny Tremain. Forbes, Esther. 272p. (gr. k-6). 1969. pap. 3.99 (0-440-94250-0, YB) Dell.
—Johnny Tremain. Forbes, Esther. (gr. 7-9). 1943. 13.45 (0-395-06766-9) HM.
—Little Red Lighthouse & the Great Gray Bridge. Swift, Hildegarde H. & Ward, Lynd. LC 42-36286. (ps-3). 1942. 15.95 (0-15-247040-9, HB Juv Bks) HarBrace.
—Robinson Crusoe. Defoe, Daniel. (gr. 4-6). 1952-63. 13. 95 (0-448-06021-3, G&D) Putnam Pub Group.
—The Silver Pony: A Story in Pictures. Ward, Lynd. LC 72-5402. 192p. (gr. k-3). 1973. 17.95 (0-395-14753-0) HM.
Ward, Lynd & Gregori, Lee. Swiss Family Robinson. Wyss, Johann. (gr. 4-6). 1949. 14.95 (0-448-06022-1, G&D) Putnam Pub Group.
Ward, Lynd & Jael. The Cat Who Went to Heaven. rev. ed. Coatsworth, Elizabeth. LC 90-175. 80p. (gr. 3-7). 1990. pap. 3.95 (0-689-71433-5, Aladdin) Macmillan Child Grp.
Ward, Rebecca, jt. photog. see Mear, Roger.
Ward, Sally. Laney's Lost Momma. Hamm, Diane J. Mathews, Judith, ed. LC 90-26824. 32p. (ps-1). 1991. 13.95 (0-8075-4340-3) A Whitman.
Ward, Sally G. Keep Your Socks on, Albert! Glaser, Linda. LC 91-19387. 48p. (ps-2). 1992. 11.00 (0-525-44838-1, DCB) Dutton Child Bks.
Warde, Ann. Lark's Magic. Pastore, Michael. LC 89-51204. 113p. (gr. 4-12). 1990. pap. 10.00 (0-927379-36-8, ZP36) Zorba Pr.
Warhola, James. The Brave Little Tailor. Thomson, Peggy, retold by. LC 91-20982. 48p. (ps-3). 1992. pap. 15.00 jacketed, 3-pc. bdg. (0-671-73736-8, S&S BFYR) S&S Trade.
—Hurricane City. Weeks, Sarah. LC 92-23389. 32p. (ps-1). 1993. 15.00 (0-06-021572-0); PLB 14.89 (0-06-021573-9) HarpC Child Bks.
—Jack & the Beanstalk. Pearson, Susan, retold by. (ps-3). 1989. pap. 13.95 (0-671-67196-0, S&S BFYR) S&S Trade.
—The Pumpkinville Mystery. Cole, Bruce. (gr. 1-4). 1987. 10.95 (0-13-741620-2) P-H.
—The Pumpkinville Mystery. LC 87-2533. 32p. (gr. 1-4). 1987. PLB 10.95 (0-671-66905-2); pap. 5.95 (0-671-66906-0) S&S Trade.
—The Pumpkinville Mystery. Cole, Bruce. LC 87-2533. 32p. (gr. 1-4). 1991. pap. 3.95 (0-671-74199-3, Little Simon) S&S Trade.
—Rodgers & Hammerstein's My Favorite Things. Hammerstein, Oscar, II & Rodgers, Richard. LC 93-26116. 1994. write for info. (0-671-79547-4, S&S BFYR) S&S Trade.
—Rodgers & Hammerstein's "The Surrey with the Fringe on Top" Hammerstein, Oscar, II, contrib. by. LC 92-2462. 1993. pap. 14.00 (0-671-79456-6, S&S BFYR) S&S Trade.
—Well, I Never! Pearson, Susan. LC 89-48016. 40p. (ps-1). 1990. pap. 13.95 (0-671-69199-6, S&S BFYR) S&S Trade.

Warlick, Cal. In-Laws, Out-Laws & Other Theories of Relativity. Alpern, Lynne & Blumenfeld, Esther. 128p. (Orig.). 1990. pap. 6.95 (0-934601-94-1) Peachtree Pubs.
—Out of My Head. Powell, Leroy. LC 89-28418. 240p. 1990. 15.95 (0-934601-95-X) Peachtree Pubs.
Warner Bros. Studios Staff. Special Delivery Symphony. Hill, Stephanie. 24p. 1993. pap. 7.98 incl. 20 min. cassette (0-943351-58-8, XL1001) Astor Bks.
—What's Opera Doc? Hill, Stephanie. 24p. 1993. pap. 7.95 (0-943351-59-6, XL1002) Astor Bks.
Warner, Rita. Cats & Kittens Coloring Album. Kunic, Debbie. 32p. 1977. pap. 4.50 (0-8431-1720-6, 80-9) Price Stern.
—North American Indians Color & Story Album. 32p. (Orig.). 1978. pap. 4.50 (0-8431-1727-3) Price Stern.
Warners, Sheila B. Rolf the Green Ghost. Wedell, Robert F. 69p. (Orig.). (ps-8). 1988. pap. 4.95 (0-685-30435-3) Milrob Pr.
Warnick, Kelly & Hall, Leo D. B'tween: Messages from Michael. Hall, Leo D. 180p. (Orig.). (gr. 6-12). 1992. pap. 8.75 (0-914107-03-8) Lion House Pr.
Warp, Eric & Elley, Charles. Nebraska: Our Pioneer Heritage. Manley, Robert N. 197p. (gr. 4-6). 1981. text ed. 7.50 (0-939644-00-2); tchr's. guide 50 pgs. 4.00 (0-939644-01-0) Media Pub.
Warr, Debra H. The Horrible, Homemade Halloween Costume. Masters, Nanvy R. 32p. (gr. 2-4). 1993. 14.95 (0-9623563-3-6) J R Matthews.
Warren, B. Story of the Liberty Bell. Miller, Natalie. LC 65-12215. 32p. (gr. 2-5). 1965. PLB 13.27 (0-516-04622-5) Childrens.
Warren, Betsy. Indians Who Lived in Texas. Warren, Betsy. LC 71-76607. 48p. (gr. 2 up). 1981. Repr. of 1970 ed. lib. bdg. 10.95 (0-937460-02-8) Hendrick-Long.
—Let's Look Inside a Tepee. Warren, Betsy. 28p. (Orig.). (gr. 4 up). 1989. pap. 3.50 (0-9618660-2-0) Ranch Gate Bks.
—Let's Remember When Texas Belonged to Spain. Warren, Betsy. 32p. (gr. 3-7). 1982. pap. 5.95 (0-937460-04-4) Hendrick-Long.
—Let's Remember When Texas Was a Republic. Warren, Betsy. 32p. (gr. 3-7). 1983. pap. 5.95 (0-937460-09-5) Hendrick-Long.
—Let's Remember...Indians of Texas. Warren, Betsy. 32p. (gr. 3-7). 1981. pap. 5.95 (0-937460-03-6) Hendrick-Long.
—The Story of Texas: A History Picture Book. Warren, Betsy. 46p. (gr. 3 up). 1988. pap. 3.50 (0-9618660-1-2) Ranch Gate Bks.
—Texas in Historic Sites & Symbols. Warren, Betsy. 28p. (gr. k-3). 1982. pap. 5.50 (0-937460-05-2) Hendrick-Long.
—Wilderness Walkers: Naturalists in Early Texas. Warren, Betsy. La Freniere, Annette, ed. LC 55-7501. 112p. (gr. 4-8). 1987. PLB 12.95 (0-937460-26-5) Hendrick-Long.
Warren, Harry. Ashkii & His Grandfather. Garaway, Margaret K. LC 89-50604. 32p. (Orig.). (gr. k-6). 1989. pap. 5.95 (0-918080-41-X) Treasure Chest.
Warren, Paul. The Erl King's Daughter. Aiken, Joan. 42p. (gr. 2-4). 1989. 3.95 (0-8120-6137-3) Barron.
Warren, Scott S. Cities in the Sand: The Ancient Civilizations of the Southwest. Warren, Scott S. 64p. (gr. 4-8). 1991. 10.95 (0-8118-0012-1) Chronicle Bks.
Warshaw, Jerry. Code Busters! Albert, Burton, Jr. Levine, Abby, ed. LC 84-2935. 32p. (gr. 3-6). 1985. 11.95 (0-8075-1235-4) A Whitman.
—Joshua James Likes Trucks. Petrie, Catherine. LC 81-17076. 32p. (ps-2). 1982. PLB 11.93 (0-516-03525-8); pap. text ed. 2.95 (0-516-43525-6) Childrens.
—A Pedro Perez le Gustan los Camiones (Joshua James Likes Trucks) Petrie, Catherine. LC 81-17076. (SPA.). 32p. (ps-2). 1988. PLB 11.93 (0-516-33525-1); pap. 2.95 (0-516-53525-0) Childrens.
—Polly Wants a Cracker. Hamsa, Bobbie. LC 85-30000. 32p. (ps-2). 1986. PLB 11.93 (0-516-02071-4); pap. 2.95 (0-516-42071-2) Childrens.
—Riddle Ages! Bishop, Ann. Rubin, Caroline, ed. LC 77-12828. (gr. 1-4). 1977. PLB 8.95 (0-8075-6965-8) A Whitman.
—Top Secret! Codes to Crack. Albert, Burton, Jr. Levine, Abby, ed. LC 87-2146. 32p. (gr. 4-7). 1987. PLB 11.95 (0-8075-8027-9) A Whitman.
Warshaw, Johanna. Chameleon. Kaplan, Shelley. LC 92-70212. 24p. 1992. 15.00 (0-9631833-0-3) Kaplan IL.
Warshaw, Mal, photos by. The Hospital Book. Howe, James. LC 93-15701. (gr. 1-8). 1994. write for info. (0-688-12734-7); pap. write for info. (0-688-12734-7) Morrow Jr Bks.
Warter, Fred. Annie Oakley. Kunstler, James H. LC 93-19246. 1993. 14.95 (0-88708-338-2, Rabbit Ears); pap. 19.95 incl. cassette (0-88708-337-4, Rabbit Ears) Picture Bk Studio.
Warter, Fred, jt. illus. see French, Marty.
Washington, Bill. Chocolate Wildcat. Hawthorne, Dorothy. LC 87-72602. (gr. 4-6). 1988. pap. 5.95 (0-931722-65-9) Corona Pub.
Washington, Burl. Have Gun - Need Bullets. Tolliver, Ruby C. LC 90-49363. 120p. (gr. 4 up). 1991. 15.95 (0-87565-085-6); pap. 10.95 (0-87565-089-9) Tex Christian.
Washington, Helen. My Island: A Picture Storybook. Joseph, Lorraine F. 23p. (Orig.). (gr. k-3). 1985. pap. 2.95 (0-935357-00-9) Cric Prod.
Washington, Luther, jt. illus. see Stockett, Thomas.

Washington, Mariama K., jt. illus. see Williams, Vanessa R.
Washington, Ruby, jt. photog. see George, Anthony.
Wasmer, Kristina. Down by the Christmas Stream. Bowen, Sally. 38p. 1992. pap. 10.95 (0-9633546-0-4, Dist. by BookWorld Services, Inc.) Bowen & Assocs.
—Down by the Enchanted Stream. Bowen, Sally. 38p. 1992. pap. 10.95 (0-9633546-1-2, Dist. by BookWorld Services, Inc.) Bowen & Assocs.
Watanabe, Yuichi. Wally the Whale Who Loved Balloons. Watanabe, Yuichi. Ooka, D. T., tr. from JPN. 32p. (ps-4). 1982. 11.95 (0-89346-150-4) Heian Intl.
Waterline, Wendy. A Look over the Edge. Creedon, Sharon. 16p. (gr. k-4). 1987. pap. 5.95 (0-9620446-0-1) Sunset Mktg.
Waterlow, Julia, photos by. The Amazon. Waterlow, Julia. LC 92-25446. 48p. (gr. 5-6). 1993. PLB 22.80 (0-8114-3101-0) Raintree Steck-V.
—The Nile. Waterlow, Julia. LC 92-39951. 48p. (gr. 5-6). 1993. PLB 22.80 (0-8114-3100-2) Raintree Steck-V.

Waters, Robyn & Ipina, David. Protectors of the Land: An Environmental Journey to Understanding the Conservation Ethic. Burrill, Richard. Macias, Regina, ed. 300p. (gr. 3-12). 1993. pap. text ed. 22.95 (1-878464-02-7); write for info. (1-878464-03-5) Anthro Co.

An environmental survival guide about "belongingness" for students, teachers & parents. For thousands of years, the native Californians lived in harmony with the Earth. Their wise elders understand a 'conservation ethic' that all things are connected in one giant web & that our rightful place as human beings is to preserve it. The California Indians respect that elders are the link to the past & the children are the hope for the future. PROTECTORS OF THE LAND calls young people --& all of us-- to environmental action. Grizzly Bear Heart, a fictional Maidu medicine man, prepares us to become protectors of the land. In the first section of the book, he takes us on an environmental journey to understanding the conservation ethic. We fly above the Sacramento Valley to observe the dying Sacramento River & the brown smog from automobiles. We witness the devastating impacts of clear cut logging & overgrazing in the Sierra Nevada rangeland & mountains. We visit Auburn RANCHERIA to learn about energy & fire making from a Maidu-Nisenan elder. The Sierra Mewuk from Yosemite Valley share with us their story of TOO-TAUK-A NOOLAH, the inchworm -- a story that reminds us we make a difference in the world no matter how small we are. In the Cooperative Games & Songs section, we learn more about the Indian cultural ways through activities that instill the values of cooperation & sharing. Maps & charts, Indian storytelling & wisdom words, 'stepping outdoor' environmental activities, & discussion questions also are included. Volume discount available from the publisher, The Anthro Company. Post Office Box 661765, Sacramento, CA 95866-1765. Telephone: 916-971-1675. Resource book for parents & teachers of 4th & 5th grade. Students will want to read & use the book themselves. *Publisher Provided Annotation.*

Waters, Tony. Just One Blade. Wright, Lynn F. 32p. (gr. 1-4). 1993. 11.95 (1-881519-00-7) WorryWart.
Watkinson, Brent. Land of the Thundering Herds. Denzel, Justin. LC 92-26222. 176p. (gr. 5 up). 1993. 14.95 (0-399-21894-7, Philomel Bks) Putnam Pub Group.

Watling, James. Along the Santa Fe Trail: Marion Russell's Own Story. Wadsworth, Ginger, retold by. (gr. 2-6). 1993. 16.95 (0-8075-0295-2) A Whitman.
—Deserts. Brandt, Keith. LC 84-8623. 32p. (gr. 3-6). 1985. PLB 9.49 (0-8167-0262-4); pap. text ed. 2.95 (0-8167-0263-2) Troll Assocs.
—Discovering Prehistoric Animals. Craig, Janet. LC 89-4973. 32p. (gr. 2-4). 1990. PLB 11.59 (0-8167-1755-9); pap. text ed. 2.95 (0-8167-1756-7) Troll Assocs.
—Discovering the Stars. Santrey, Laurence. LC 81-7489. 32p. (gr. 2-4). 1982. PLB 11.59 (0-89375-568-0); pap. text ed. 2.95 (0-89375-569-9); cassette 9.95 (0-685-04946-9) Troll Assocs.
—Emperor & the Nightingale. Andersen, Hans Christian. LC 78-18065. 32p. (gr. k-4). 1979. PLB 9.79 (0-89375-134-0); pap. 1.95 (0-89375-112-X) Troll Assocs.
—Fire! The Beginnings of the Labor Movement. Goldin, Barbara D. 64p. (gr. 2-6). 1992. RB 13.00 (0-670-84475-6) Viking Child Bks.
—The First Thanksgiving. reissue ed. Hayward, Linda. 48p. (gr. k-4). 1992. pap. 6.99 incl. cass. (0-679-83058-8) Random Bks Yng Read.
—The First Thanksgiving: A Step 2 Book - Grades 1-3. Hayward, Linda. LC 90-52517. 48p. (Orig.). (gr. k-3). 1990. lib. bdg. 7.99 (0-679-90218-X); pap. 2.95 (0-679-80218-5) Random Bks Yng Read.
—Grasslands. Sabin, Louis. LC 84-2661. 32p. (gr. 3-6). 1985. PLB 9.49 (0-8167-0214-4); pap. text ed. 2.95 (0-8167-0215-2) Troll Assocs.
—Hard Times: A Story of the Great Depression. Antle, Nancy. 64p. (gr. 2-6). 1993. RB 12.99 (0-670-84665-1) Viking Child Bks.
—King of the Golden Mountain. Bros. Grimm. Cutts, David, ed. LC 87-11262. 32p. (gr. 2-4). 1988. PLB 9.79 (0-8167-1055-4); pap. text ed. 1.95 (0-8167-1056-2) Troll Assocs.
—Life in the Meadow. Curran, Eileen. LC 84-12384. 32p. (gr. k-2). 1985. PLB 11.59 (0-8167-0343-4); pap. 2.95 (0-8167-0344-2) Troll Assocs.
—Mountains & Volcanoes. Curran, Eileen. LC 84-8638. 32p. (gr. k-2). 1985. PLB 11.59 (0-8167-0347-7); pap. text ed. 2.95 (0-8167-0348-5) Troll Assocs.
—Night Bird: A Story of the Seminole Indians. Kudlinski, Kathleen V. LC 92-25935. 64p. (gr. 2-6). 1990. PLB 12.99 (0-670-83157-3) Viking Child Bks.
—The Planets. Jackson, Kim. LC 84-16451. 32p. (gr. k-2). 1985. lib. bdg. 11.59 (0-8167-0450-3); pap. text ed. 2.95 (0-8167-0451-1) Troll Assocs.
—The Roanoke Missing Persons Case. Larsen, Anita. LC 91-19524. 48p. (gr. 5 up). 1992. RSBE 11.95 (0-89686-619-X, Crestwood Hse) Macmillan Child Grp.
—Samuel's Choice. Berleth, Richard. Mathews, Judith, ed. LC 89-77186. 40p. (gr. 3-6). 1990. PLB 14.95 (0-8075-7218-7) A Whitman.
—Scenes along the Santa Fe Trail. Wadsworth, Ginger. LC 93-6491. 1993. write for info. (0-8075-7258-6) A Whitman.
—Tales of Magic & Spells. Denan, Corinne. LC 79-66325. 48p. (gr. 3-6). 1980. PLB 9.89 (0-89375-318-1); pap. text ed. 2.95 (0-89375-317-3); cassette avail. Troll Assocs.
—Tut's Mummy: Lost & Found. Donnelly, Judy. LC 87-20790. (Orig.). (gr. 2-3). 1988. lib. bdg. 7.99 (0-394-99189-3); pap. 2.95 (0-394-89189-9) Random Bks Yng Read.
—Witch Hunt: It Happened in Salem Village. Krensky, Stephen. LC 88-42865. 48p. (Orig.). (gr. 2-4). 1989. PLB 7.99 (0-394-91923-8); pap. 2.95 (0-394-81923-3) Random Bks Yng Read.
—Wonders of Swamps & Marshes. Caitlin, Stephen. LC 89-4967. 32p. (gr. 2-4). 1990. PLB 11.59 (0-8167-1765-6); pap. text ed. 2.95 (0-8167-1766-4) Troll Assocs.
—Wonders of the Seasons. Brandt, Keith. LC 81-7411. 32p. (gr. 2-4). 1982. PLB 11.59 (0-89375-580-X); pap. text ed. 2.95 (0-89375-581-8) Troll Assocs.
Watson, Aldren. Gulliver's Travels. Swift, Jonathan. LC 47-31082. 352p. (gr. 4-6). 1947. 13.95 (0-448-05461-2, G&D) Putnam Pub Group.
Watson, John. We're the Noisy Dinosaurs. Watson, John. LC 91-58764. 32p. (ps up). 1992. 14.95 (1-56402-089-4) Candlewick Pr.
Watson, Mary. The Market Lady & the Mango Tree. Watson, Pete. LC 93-7725. 32p. 1994. 14.00 (0-688-12970-6, Tambourine Bks); PLB 13.93 (0-688-12971-4, Tambourine Bks) Morrow.
Watson, N. Cameron. The Little Pigs' First Cookbook. Watson, N. Cameron. 48p. (gr. 1-3). 1987. 12.95 (0-316-92467-9) Little.
—Mister Toad. Watson, Clyde. LC 91-24208. 32p. (gr. k-3). 1992. RSBE 13.95 (0-02-792527-7, Macmillan Child Bk) Macmillan Child Grp.
—The Weeds & the Weather. Stolz, Mary. LC 93-240. 40p. (gr. k up). 1994. write for info. (0-688-12289-2); PLB write for info. (0-688-12290-6) Greenwillow.
Watson, Richard J. Bronwen, the Traw, & the Shape-Shifter. Dickey, James. LC 85-27082. 32p. (gr. k-3). 1986. 13.95 (0-15-212580-9, HB Juv Bks) HarBrace.
—The Dream Stair. James, Betsy. LC 89-36420. 32p. (gr. k-2). 1990. PLB 13.89 (0-06-022788-5) HarpC Child Bks.
—High Rise Glorious Skittle Skat Roarious Sky Pie Angel Food Cake. Willard, Nancy. 54p. (gr. 3 up). 1990. 15.95 (0-15-234332-6) HarBrace.

Watson, Wendy. A, B, C, D, Tummy, Toes, Hands, Knees. Hennessy, B. G. 32p. (ps-1). 1989. pap. 13.95 (0-670-81703-1) Viking Child Bks.
—A, B, C, D, Tummy, Toes, Hands, Knees. Hennessy, B. G. 32p. (ps-1). 1991. pap. 4.50 (0-14-050739-6, Puffin) Puffin Bks.
—Applebet: An ABC. Watson, Clyde. 32p. (ps up). 1987. pap. 3.95 (0-374-40427-5) FS&G.
—Belinda's Hurricane. Winthrop, Elizabeth. LC 84-8028. 64p. (gr. 1-4). 1984. 10.95 (0-525-44106-9, DCB) Dutton Child Bks.
—Belinda's Hurricane. Winthrop, Elizabeth. 64p. (gr. 2-6). 1989. pap. 3.95 (0-14-032985-4, Puffin) Puffin Bks.
—Binary Numbers. Watson, Clyde. LC 75-29161. 40p. (gr. 1-4). 1977. PLB 12.89 (0-690-00993-3, Crowell Jr Bks) HarpC Child Bks.
—Boo! It's Halloween. Watson, Wendy. 32p. (ps-3). 1992. 14.45 (0-395-53628-6, Clarion Bks) HM.
—Catch Me & Kiss Me & Say It Again. Watson, Clyde. LC 78-17644. 64p. (gr. 1-12). 1983. (Philomel); pap. 7.95 (0-399-20954-9) Putnam Pub Group.
—The Cruise of the Aardvark. Nash, Ogden. LC 67-27296. 48p. (ps up). 1989. pap. 5.95 (0-87131-570-X) M Evans.
—Doctor Coyote: A Native American Aesop's Fables. Bierhorst, John. LC 86-8669. 48p. (gr. 2-5). 1987. SBE 15.95 (0-02-709780-3, Macmillan Child Bk) Macmillan Child Grp.
—Father Fox's Feast of Songs. Watson, Clyde. 32p. 1992. PLB 14.95 (1-878093-84-3) Boyds Mills Pr.
—Father Fox's Pennyrhymes. Watson, Clyde. LC 71-146291. 56p. (ps-3). 1987. pap. 5.95 (0-06-443137-1, Trophy) HarpC Child Bks.
—Happy Easter Day! Watson, Wendy. 32p. (ps-1). 1993. 14.45 (0-395-53629-4, Clarion Bks) HM.
—How Brown Mouse Kept Christmas. Watson, Clyde. LC 80-18532. 32p. (ps-3). 1980. 10.00 (0-374-33494-3) FS&G.
—Hurray for the Fourth of July. Watson, Wendy. 32p. (ps-1). 1992. 14.45 (0-395-53627-8, Clarion Bks) HM.
—I Love My Baby Sister: Most of the Time. Edelman, Elaine. LC 85-574. 24p. (ps-3). 1985. pap. 3.95 (0-14-050547-4, Puffin) Puffin Bks.
—Is My Friend at Home? Pueblo Fireside Tales. Bierhorst, John. LC 93-14249. 1994. text ed. 14.95 (0-02-709733-1) Macmillan.
—The Night Before Christmas. Moore, Clement C. 32p. (ps-1). 1990. 13.95 (0-395-53624-3, Clarion Bks) HM.
—Sleep Is for Everyone. Showers, Paul. LC 72-83785. 40p. (ps-3). 1974. PLB 13.89 (0-690-01118-0, Crowell Jr Bks) HarpC Child Bks.
—Thanksgiving at Our House. Watson, Wendy. 32p. (ps-1). 1991. 14.45 (0-395-53626-X, Clarion Bks) HM.
—Tom Fox & the Apple Pie. Watson, Clyde. LC 74-171010. 32p. (ps-3). 1972. (Crowell Jr Bks) HarpC Child Bks.
—Upside Down & Inside Out: Poems for All Your Pockets. Katz, Bobbi. 48p. (ps-3). 1992. PLB 14.95 (1-56397-122-4) Boyds Mills Pr.
—A Valentine for You. Watson, Wendy. Briley, Dorothy, ed. 32p. (ps-1). 1991. 14.45 (0-395-53625-1, Clarion Bks) HM.
—A Valentine for You. Watson, Wendy. 32p. (gr. k-3). 1993. pap. 5.95 (0-395-66411-X, Clarion Bks) HM.
—The Valentine Foxes. Watson, Clyde. LC 88-22392. 32p. (ps-3). 1989. 13.95 (0-531-05800-X); PLB 13.99 (0-531-08400-0) Orchard Bks Watts.
—Valentine Foxes. Watson, Clyde. LC 88-22392. 32p. (ps-3). 1992. pap. 5.95 (0-531-07033-6) Orchard Bks Watts.
—Wendy Watson's Frog Went A-Courting. Watson, Wendy. LC 89-63022. 32p. (ps-3). 1990. 13.95 (0-688-06539-2); lib. bdg. 13.88 (0-688-06540-6) Lothrop.

Watterson, Bill. The Essential Calvin & Hobbes: A Calvin & Hobbes Treasury. Watterson, Bill. Schulz, Charles. 256p. 1988. 19.95 (0-8362-1809-4); pap. 12.95 (0-8362-1805-1) Andrews & McMeel.

Watts, Barrie, photos by. Ants. Watts, Barrie. 32p. (gr. k-4). 1991. PLB 11.40 (0-531-14042-3); pap. 4.95 (0-531-15615-X) Watts.
—Frog. Chinery, Michael. Camm, Martin. LC 90-10962. 32p. (gr. 4-6). 1991. lib. bdg. 11.59 (0-8167-2102-5); pap. text ed. 3.95 (0-8167-2103-3) Troll Assocs.
—Ladybugs. Watts, Barrie. 32p. (gr. k-4). 1991. PLB 11.40 (0-531-14043-1); pap. 4.95 (0-531-15616-8) Watts.
—Mouse. 24p. (gr. k-3). 1992. 6.95 (0-525-67357-1, Lodestar Bks) Dutton Child Bks.
—Rabbit. 24p. (gr. k-3). 1992. 6.95 (0-525-67356-3, Lodestar Bks) Dutton Child Bks.
—See How They Grow: Duck. 24p. (gr. k-3). 1991. 6.95 (0-525-67346-6, Lodestar Bks) Dutton Child Bks.
—Stick Insects. Watts, Barrie. Kline, Marjory, ed. 32p. (gr. k-4). 1992. PLB 11.40 (0-531-14220-5) Watts.
—Twenty-Four Hours in a Game Reserve. Watts, Barrie. Kline, Marjory, ed. 48p. (gr. 5-7). 1992. PLB 12.90 (0-531-14173-X) Watts.
—Wood Lice & Millipedes. Watts, Barrie. Kline, Marjory, ed. 32p. (gr. k-4). 1992. PLB 11.40 (0-531-14162-4) Watts.

Watts, Bernadette. The Bremen Town Musicians. Grimm, Jacob & Grimm, Wilhelm K. Bell, Anthea, tr. from GER. LC 91-30375. 32p. (gr. k-3). 1992. 14.95 (1-55858-140-5); lib. bdg. 14.88 (1-55858-148-0) North-South Bks NYC.
—The Elves & the Shoemaker. Grimm, Jacob & Grimm, Wilhelm K. LC 85-63306. 32p. (gr. k-2). 1986. 14.95 (1-55858-035-2) North-South Bks NYC.
—Fir Tree. Andersen, Hans Christian. LC 89-43730. (ps-3). 1990. 14.95 (1-55858-093-X) North-South Bks NYC.
—Fly Away, Fly Away over the Sea. Rossetti, Christina. LC 90-42738. 32p. (ps-k). 1991. 14.95 (1-55858-101-4) North-South Bks NYC.
—The Four Good Friends. Curle, Jock. LC 86-62520. 32p. (gr. k-3). 1987. 14.95 (1-55858-062-X) North-South Bks NYC.
—Goldilocks & the Three Bears. Watts, Bernadette. LC 85-7192. (gr. k-3). 1985. 13.95 (1-55858-039-5); pap. 3.95 (1-55858-040-9) North-South Bks NYC.
—The Little Donkey. Scheidl, Gerda M. LC 87-73271. 32p. (gr. k-3). 1988. 13.95 (1-55858-026-3) North-South Bks NYC.
—Les Nains. Grimm, Jacob & Grimm, Wilhelm K. (FRE.). (gr. k-3). 1992. 14.95 (3-85539-581-0) North-South Bks NYC.
—Ragamuffins. Grimm, Jacob & Grimm, Wilhelm K. LC 89-42609. 32p. (gr. k-3). 1989. 13.95 (1-55858-014-X) North-South Bks NYC.
—La Reine Des Neiges. Andersen, Hans Christian. (FRE.). (gr. k-3). 1992. 14.95 (3-85539-629-9) North-South Bks NYC.
—Rumpelstiltskin: A Fairy Tale. Grimm, Jacob & Grimm, Wilhelm K. Bell, Anthea, tr. LC 92-31331. 32p. (gr. k-3). 1993. 14.95 (1-55858-188-X); PLB 14.88 (1-55858-189-8) North-South Bks NYC.
—Die Schneekonigin. Andersen, Hans Christian. (GER.). 32p. (gr. k-3). 1992. 14.95 (3-85825-292-1) North-South Bks NYC.
—Shoemaker Martin. Tolstoy, Leo. Hanhart, Brigitte, adapted by. LC 86-60489. 32p. (gr. k-3). 1986. 14.95 (1-55858-044-1) North-South Bks NYC.
—The Snow Queen. Andersen, Hans Christian. Bell, Anthea, adapted by. LC 87-1518. 32p. (gr. k-3). 1987. 14.95 (1-55858-053-0) North-South Bks NYC.
—Snow White & Rose Red. Grimm, Jacob & Grimm, Wilhelm K. LC 87-72036. 32p. (gr. k-3). 1988. 14.95 (1-55858-054-9) North-South Bks NYC.
—Tattercoats. Watts, Bernadette. LC 87-30198. 32p. (gr. k-3). 1989. 13.95 (1-55858-002-6) North-South Bks NYC.
—Trouble at Christmas. Johnson, Russell. LC 90-28988. 32p. (gr. k-3). 1991. 14.95 (1-55858-116-2) North-South Bks NYC.
—Die Wichtelmanner. Grimm, Jacob & Grimm, Wilhelm K. (GER.). 32p. (gr. k-3). 1992. 14.95 (3-85825-256-5) North-South Bks NYC.
—The Wind & the Sun. Aesop. LC 92-2653. 32p. (gr. k-3). 1992. 14.95 (1-55858-162-6); PLB 14.88 (1-55858-163-4) North-South Bks NYC.

Watts, James. Back in the Beforetime: Tales of the California Indians. Curry, Jane L. LC 86-21339. 144p. (gr. 3-7). 1987. SBE 13.95 (0-689-50410-1, M K McElderry) Macmillan Child Grp.
—Best Friends. Hopkins, Lee B., ed. LC 85-45257. 48p. (gr. k-4). 1986. PLB 14.89 (0-06-022562-9) HarpC Child Bks.
—Brats. Kennedy, X. J. LC 85-20018. 48p. (gr. 3 up). 1986. SBE 12.95 (0-689-50392-X, M K McElderry) Macmillan Child Grp.
—Bridget Goes to School. Mozelle, Shirley. LC 92-29871. 1994. 13.00 (0-06-022887-3); PLB 12.89 (0-06-022888-1) HarpC Child Bks.
—Drat These Brats! Kennedy, X. J. LC 92-33686. 48p. (gr. 3 up). 1993. SBE 12.95 (0-689-50589-2, M K McElderry) Macmillan Child Grp.
—Fresh Brats. Kennedy, X. J. LC 89-38031. 48p. (gr. 3-5). 1990. SBE 12.95 (0-689-50499-3, M K McElderry) Macmillan Child Grp.
—Good Hunting, Blue Sky. Parish, Peggy. LC 84-43143. 64p. (gr. k-3). 1988. 14.00 (0-06-024661-8); PLB 13.89 (0-06-024662-6) HarpC Child Bks.
—Good Hunting, Blue Sky. Parish, Peggy. LC 84-43143. 64p. (gr. k-3). 1991. pap. 3.50 (0-06-444148-2, Trophy) HarpC Child Bks.
—How Raven Brought Light to People. Dixon, Ann, retold by. LC 90-28948. 32p. (gr. k-4). 1992. SBE 13.95 (0-689-50536-1, M K McElderry) Macmillan Child Grp.
—I'll Meet You Halfway. Schindel, John. LC 91-44019. 32p. (ps-2). 1993. SBE 14.95 (0-689-50564-7, M K McElderry) Macmillan Child Grp.
—The Trouble on Janus. Slote, Alfred. LC 85-40099. 192p. (gr. 3-6). 1985. PLB 13.89 (0-397-32159-7, Lipp Jr Bks) HarpC Child Bks.
—The Trouble on Janus. Slote, Alfred. LC 85-40099. 192p. (gr. 3-6). 1988. pap. 3.50 (0-06-440216-9, Trophy) HarpC Child Bks.
—The Wedding of the Rat Family. Kendall, Carol. LC 88-2197. 32p. (gr. 2-5). 1988. SBE 13.95 (0-689-50450-0, M K McElderry) Macmillan Child Grp.
—Who Are You? Schindel, John. LC 90-39850. 32p. (ps-3). 1991. SBE 13.95 (0-689-50523-X, M K McElderry) Macmillan Child Grp.
—Zack's Alligator. Mozelle, Shirley. LC 88-32069. 64p. (gr. k-3). 1989. 14.00 (0-06-024309-0); PLB 13.89 (0-06-024310-4) HarpC Child Bks.

Watts, John. When Sea & Sky Are Blue. Parr, Letitia. LC 78-151272. 32p. (ps-3). 1978. 7.95 (0-87592-059-4) Scroll Pr.

Watts, Marjorie-Ann. Clever Polly & the Stupid Wolf. large type ed. Storr, Catherine. 117p. 1992. 13.95 (0-7451-1623-X, Galaxy Child Lrg Print) Chivers N Amer.

Watts, Melissah. The Mudpies Activity Book: Recipes for Invention. Blakey, Nancy. 144p. (ps-6). 1989. pap. 7.95 (0-89815-576-2) Ten Speed Pr.

Watts, S. A., photos by. Science Experiments & Amusements for Children. Vivian, Charles. LC 67-28142. (ps-6). 1967. pap. 2.95 (0-486-21856-2) Dover.

Waura, Grace M. The First Families of West Virginia. Waura, Grace. LC 90-70666. 70p. (gr. 3-6). 1991. pap. 6.00 (1-56002-007-5) Aegina Pr.

Wawiorka, Matthew. The White Elephant: Modern Expressions & the Ancient Stories Behind Them. Klausner, Janet. LC 93-4753. 1994. 16.00 (0-06-023564-0); PLB 15.89 (0-06-023565-9) HarpC Child Bks.

Way, Marrilee. Eight Steps to Choral Reading. Brooks, Courtaney. (Orig.). (gr. 1 up). 1983. text ed. 3.00x (0-941274-01-2) Belnice Bks.

Way, Merrilee. The Case of the Stolen Dinosaur: A Play in Two Versions: Stage & Radio. Brooks, Courtaney. 26p. (Orig.). (gr. 4 up). 1983. pap. text ed. 4.00x (0-941274-02-0) Belnice Bks.
—Little Red & the Wolf: A Puppet Play. Brooks, Courtaney. (gr. k up). 1983. pap. text ed. 2.50x (0-941274-04-7) Belnice Bks.
—Pardner & Freddie: A Puppet Play. Brooks, Courtaney. (gr. k up). 1983. pap. text ed. 2.50x (0-941274-03-9) Belnice Bks.

Wayman, Joe. Don't Burn down the Birthday Cake. Wayman, Joe. 90p. (gr. k up). 1989. 13.95 (0-945799-00-4) Audio cassette 12.95. Pieces of Lrning.
—Let's Talk about It! Wayman, Joe. 96p. (gr. 1-8). 1986. wkbk. 9.95 (0-86653-372-9, GA 799) Good Apple.

Wayson, Catherine. Supergranny, No. 1: The Mystery of the Shrunken Heads. Van Hook, Beverly. 96p. (gr. 3-7). 1985. lib. bdg. 7.95 (0-916761-11-8); pap. 2.95 (0-916761-10-X) Holderby & Bierce.
—Supergranny, No. 2: The Case of the Riverboat Riverbelle. Van Hook, Beverly. 112p. (gr. 3-7). 1986. lib. bdg. 7.95 (0-916761-09-6); pap. 2.95 (0-916761-08-8) Holderby & Bierce.
—Supergranny, No. 3: The Ghost of Heidelberg Castle. Van Hook, Beverly. 112p. (gr. 3-7). 1987. lib. bdg. 7.95 (0-916761-07-X); pap. 2.95 (0-916761-06-1) Holderby & Bierce.
—Supergranny, No. 5: Character Who Came to Life. Van Hook, Beverly. Nelken, Andrea, ed. 112p. (Orig.). (gr. 3-6). 1989. lib. bdg. 7.95 (0-916761-13-4); pap. 2.95 (0-916761-12-6) Holderby & Bierce.
—Supergranny: Secret of Devil Mountain. Van Hook, Beverly. Nelken, Andrea, ed. 112p. (Orig.). (gr. 3-6). 1988. lib. bdg. 7.95 (0-916761-05-3); pap. 2.95 (0-916761-04-5) Holderby & Bierce.
—Supergranny 6: The Great College Caper, 6 bks. Van Hook, Beverly. Nelken, Andrea, ed. 112p. (gr. 3-7). 1991. Set. 53.00 (0-916761-15-0); 8.95 ea.; Set. pap. 17.70 (0-916761-14-2); pap. 3.25 ea. Holderby & Bierce.

Wazejewski, Don, et al. Dinosaurs & Other Prehistoric Animals. Wright, Robin. LC 90-38028. 96p. (gr. 3-6). 1991. lib. bdg. 14.89 (0-8167-2232-3); pap. text ed. 6.95 (0-8167-2233-1) Troll Assocs.

Weare, Phil. Animal Journeys. Pope, Joyce. LC 91-45379. 32p. (gr. 3-6). 1993. PLB 11.59 (0-8167-2777-5); pap. text ed. 3.95 (0-8167-2778-3) Troll Assocs. Postponed.
—Seashores. Pope, Joyce. LC 89-20318. 32p. (gr. 3-6). 1990. PLB 11.59 (0-8167-1965-9); pap. text ed. 3.95 (0-8167-1966-7) Troll Assocs.

Weatherby, Mark A. The Call of the Wolves. Murphy, Jim. 32p. (gr. k-3). 1989. pap. 13.95 (0-590-41941-2) Scholastic Inc.
—The Last Dinosaur. Murphy, Jim. LC 87-3008. 32p. (gr. 1-3). 1988. pap. 14.95 (0-590-41097-0, Scholastic Hardcover) Scholastic Inc.
—The Last Dinosaur. Murphy, Jim. 1991. pap. 3.95 (0-590-44875-7, Blue Ribbon Bks) Scholastic Inc.
—When the Root Children Wake Up. Wood, Audrey, retold by. LC 93-32737. 1995. Repr. of 1906 ed. 14.95 (0-590-42517-X) Scholastic Inc.

Weatherlow, Regina. Dr. Ed: The Story of General Edward Hand. Shelley, Mary V. LC 78-10331. 36p. (gr. 4-7). 1978. 5.75 (0-915010-24-0) Sutter House.

Weathers, Susan, et al. The Whole World Kit: American Dream Activity Cards. Schreiner, Nikki B., et al. 60p. (gr. 4-8). 1990. pap. text ed. 215.00 (1-879218-29-1) Touch & See Educ.

Weaver, Duane, jt. illus. see Wolters, Ronald.

Webb, Allice. Global Primer - Skills for a Changing World. rev. ed. Collins, Thomas & Czarra, Fred. 293p. (gr. k-8). 1991. pap. 26.95 (0-943804-60-4) U of Denver Teach.

Webb, Gary A. Who Helps. Palmer, Bernard & Palmer, Marjorie. 32p. (Orig.). (ps-k). 1982. pap. 3.99 (0-934998-08-6) Bethel Pub.
—Who Shows. Palmer, Bernard & Palmer, Marjorie. 32p. (Orig.). (ps-k). 1982. pap. 3.99 (0-934998-09-4) Bethel Pub.

Webb, Jim. Monica Made Me Promise. Cousins, Linda. 32p. (gr. 5-8). Date not set. pap. 3.99 (0-912444-39-8) DARE Bks.

Webb, Kathy. Yurok Tales. Bell, Rosemary. 90p. (Orig.). (gr. 4-8). 1992. pap. 9.95 (1-880922-01-0) Bell Bks CA.

Webb, Philip. Farmer Schnuck. Parkes, Brenda. LC 92-31078. 1993. 4.25 (*0-383-03568-6*) SRA Schl Grp.
—The Real Cinderella Rap. Trussell-Cullen, Alan. LC 93-24528. 1994. 4.25 (*0-383-03771-9*) SRA Schl Grp.
—Sandy's Suitcase. Edwards, Elsy. LC 92-34269. 1993. 14.00 (*0-383-03650-X*) SRA Schl Grp.
—What a Haircut! Gray, Patricia. LC 93-26931. 1994. 4.25 (*0-383-03783-2*) SRA Schl Grp.
Webb, Phillip. What Happened to Aunt Cordelia? Best, Elizabeth. LC 93-167. 1994. write for info. (*0-383-03725-5*) SRA Schl Grp.
Webb, Roger. Sinbad the Sailor. Daniels, Patricia. LC 79-28588. 24p. (gr. k-5). 1980. PLB 14.64 (*0-8393-0256-8*) Raintree Steck-V.
Webb, William. I've Been Working on the Subway: The Folklore & Oral History of Transit. New York Transit Museum Staff. 54p. (Orig.). (gr. 5-10). 1991. pap. 5.00 incl. curriculum guide (*0-9637492-9-3*) NY Transit Mus.
Webber, Helen. Good Night, Night. Webber, Helen. (gr. k-6). 1968. 8.95 (*0-8392-3054-0*) Astor-Honor.
—How Long Is Long Ago & Other Poems. Webber, Helen. (gr. k-6). 1968. 8.95 (*0-8392-3068-0*) Astor-Honor.
—My Kite Is the Magic Me. Webber, Helen. (gr. k-6). 1968. 8.95 (*0-8392-3055-9*) Astor-Honor.
—Summer Sun. Webber, Helen. (gr. k-6). 1968. 8.95 (*0-8392-3056-7*) Astor-Honor.
Webber, Irma E. It Looks Like This. Webber, Irma E. LC 76-43571. (ps up). 1976. text ed. 7.00x (*0-918970-21-0*) Intl Gen Semantics.
Weber, Bernard. Ira Says Goodbye. Weber, Bernard. 40p. (ps-3). 1988. 13.45 (*0-395-48315-8*) HM.
Weber, Debora. Last Names First..& Some First Names too. Lee, Mary P. & Lee, Richard S. LC 84-20860. 119p. (gr. 5-9). 1985. 12.00 (*0-664-32719-2*, Westminster) Westminster John Knox.
Weber, Deborah. Know about AIDS. rev. ed. Hyde, Margaret O. & Forsyth, Elizabeth. 102p. (gr. 3-7). 1990. 12.95 (*0-8027-6920-9*); lib. bdg. (*0-8027-6921-7*) Walker & Co.
Weber, Jill. The Penny Whistle Christmas Party Book: Including Hanukkah, New Year's, & Twelfth Night Family Parties. Brokaw, Meredith & Gilbar, Annie. 128p. (Orig.). 1991. (Fireside); pap. 12.00 (*0-671-73794-5*, Fireside) S&S Trade.
Weber, June Kern. Warm-Up to Creativity. Eberle, Bob. 64p. (gr. 5 up). 1985. wkbk. 7.95 (*0-86653-275-7*, GA 667) Good Apple.
Weber, Susan M. The Golden Monster. Knief, William. 32p. (Orig.). 1971. pap. 1.00 staple bound (*0-685-30030-7*) Cottonwood KS.
Webster, Carroll. Pebbles in the Wind. Baldner, Jean V. 52p. (Orig.). (gr. 7 up). pap. 5.95 (*0-9615317-0-3*) Baldner J V.
Webster, Genevieve. Buster's Echo. Scamell, Ragnhild. LC 92-9868. 32p. (ps-2). 1993. 14.00 (*0-06-022883-0*); PLB 13.89 (*0-06-022884-9*) HarpC Child Bks.
Weedn, Flavia. Flavia & the Dream Maker. Weedn, Flavia. 56p. 1988. 14.95 (*0-929632-00-1*) deluxe limited 24.95 (*0-929632-02-8*) Applause Inc.
Weekly Reader Staff. Be an Inventor. Taylor, Barbara. 74p. (gr. 3-7). 1987. 11.95 (*0-15-205950-4*, Voyager Bks); pap. 7.95 (*0-15-205951-2*, Voyager Bks) HarBrace.
Wees, Dick. Fanny the Fanciful Frog - Coloring Book. Wees, Marty. Joyce, Susan, ed. Wees, Dick, intro. by. 30p. (gr. k-2). 1989. pap. write for info. Richmar Prodns.
Weevers, Peter. The Hare & the Tortoise. Castle, Caroline. LC 84-9569. 32p. (ps-3). 1985. 10.95 (*0-8037-0138-1*) Dial Bks Young.
—Hare & the Tortoise. Castle, Caroline, retold by. LC 84-9569. 32p. (ps-3). 1987. pap. 4.95 (*0-8037-0147-0*) Dial Bks Young.
Wegman, William. Cinderella. Wegman, William. LC 92-72028. 40p. 1993. 16.95 (*1-56282-348-5*); PLB 16.89 (*1-56282-349-3*) Hyprn Child.
—Little Red Riding Hood. Wegman, William. LC 92-54874. 40p. 1993. 16.95 (*1-56282-416-3*); PLB 16.89 (*1-56282-417-1*) Hyprn Child.
Wegner, Fritz. The Sneeze. Lloyd, David. LC 85-46022. 32p. (ps-2). 1986. PLB 11.89 (*0-685-12397-9*, Lipp Jr Bks) HarpC Child Bks.
—Woof! Ahlberg, Allan. LC 86-40009. 155p. (gr. 3-7). 1986. pap. 11.95 (*0-670-80832-6*) Viking Child Bks.
—Woof! Ahlberg, Allan. (gr. 3-7). 1988. pap. 3.99 (*0-14-031996-4*, Puffin) Puffin Bks.
Wegrzecki, Lester L. Christmas Decoration: Eggshell-Wydmuski. Wegrzecki, Lester L. Chrypinski, Anna, intro. by. 88p. (gr. 4 up). 1987. 9.50x (*0-317-90582-1*) L L Wegrzecki.
Weidenaar, Reynold H. Bird Life in Wington: Practical Parables for Young People. Reid, John C. 142p. (gr. 1-4). 1990. pap. 8.99 (*0-8028-4062-0*) Eerdmans.
Weidner, Bea. Signs of God's Love: Baptism & Communion. Fogle, Jeanne S. Duckert, Mary J. & Lane, W. Ben, eds. 32p. (Orig.). (gr. 3-8). 1984. pap. 7.99 (*0-664-24636-2*, Geneva Pr) Westminster John Knox.
—Symbols of God's Love: Codes & Passwords. Fogle, Jeanne S. Ducket, Mary Jean & Lane, W. Ben, eds. LC 86-12014. 32p. (Orig.). (gr. k-3). 1986. pap. 7.99 (*0-664-24050-X*, Westminster) Westminster John Knox.

Weidner, Teri. Helen the Fish. Kroll, Virginia L. Mathews, Judith, ed. LC 91-17230. 32p. (gr. k-3). 1992. PLB 13.95 (*0-8075-3194-4*) A Whitman.
Weihs, Erika. Cakes & Miracles: A Purim Tale. Goldin, Barbara D. LC 92-25848. 1993. pap. 4.99 (*0-14-054871-8*) Puffin Bks.
—Cakes & Miracles: A Purim Tale. Goldin, Barbara D. (ps-3). 1991. 15.00 (*0-670-83047-X*) Viking Child Bks.
—Days of Awe: Stories for Rosh Hashanah & Yom Kippur. Kimmel, Eric A. LC 93-583. 48p. (gr. 3-7). pap. 4.99 (*0-14-050271-8*, Puffin) Puffin Bks.
—How a Shirt Grew in the Field. Ushinsky, Konstantin. Rudolph, Marguerita, adapted by. 32p. (ps-3). 1992. 13.45 (*0-395-59761-7*, Clarion Bks) HM.
—Menorahs, Mezuzas, & Other Jewish Symbols. Chaikin, Miriam. 96p. (gr. 5 up). 1990. 14.95 (*0-89919-856-2*, Clarion Bks) HM.
—Mummies, Tombs, & Treasure: Secrets of Ancient Egypt. Perl, Lila. LC 86-17646. 128p. (gr. 4 up). 1987. 15.45 (*0-89919-407-9*, Clarion Bks) HM.
—Mummies, Tombs, & Treasure: Secrets of Ancient Egypt. Perl, Lila. LC 86-17646. 128p. (gr. 2-5). 1990. pap. 5.70 (*0-395-54796-2*, Clarion Bks) HM.
—Sound the Shofar: The Story & Meaning of Rosh HaShanah & Yom Kippur. Chaikin, Miriam. LC 86-2651. 96p. (gr. 3-7). 1986. (Clarion Bks); pap. 4.95 (*0-89919-427-3*, Clarion Bks) HM.
—Stories from Our Living Past. new ed. Prose, Francine. Harlow, Jules, ed. LC 74-8514. 128p. (gr. 3-4). 1974. 7.95 (*0-87441-081-9*); wkbk. 1 2.95 (*0-87441-083-5*); wkbk. 2 2.95 (*0-87441-084-3*); tchr's guide 14.95 (*0-87441-082-7*) Behrman.
—The Story of Religion. Maestro, Betsy. LC 92-38980. 1994. write for info (*0-395-62364-2*, Clarion Bks) HM.
—Theodor Herzl: The Road to Israel. Gurko, Miriam. 96p. (gr. 3-7). 1988. 14.95 (*0-8276-0312-6*) JPS Phila.
—When a Jew Celebrates. Gersh, Harry. LC 70-116678. 256p. (gr. 5-6). 1971. pap. text ed. 7.95x (*0-87441-001-0*); tchr's guide 14.95 (*0-685-41997-5*); student activity bk. 3.95 (*0-685-41998-3*); tchr's cassette 5.95 (*0-685-00740-5*) Behrman.
Weihs, Erika, jt. illus. see Rosenberg, Amye.
Weikel, Cheryl. Every Perfect Gift. Nye, Julie. Vogt, Carla, ed. 201p. (Orig.). (gr. 9 up). 1990. pap. 4.95 (*0-89084-499-2*) Bob Jones Univ Pr.
—Great Expectations. rev. ed. Dickens, Charles. Klischer, Beth, ed. 587p. (Orig.). (gr. 10 up). 1989. pap. 6.95 (*0-89084-504-2*) Bob Jones Univ Pr.
Weil, Lisl. Let's Go to the Circus. Weil, Lisl. LC 87-25201. 32p. (ps-3). 1988. reinforced bdg. 13.95 (*0-8234-0693-8*) Holiday.
—Let's Go to the Library. Weil, Lisl. LC 90-55105. 32p. (ps-3). 1990. reinforced 13.95 (*0-8234-0829-9*) Holiday.
—Let's Go to the Museum. Weil, Lisl. LC 89-2078. 32p. (ps-3). 1989. reinforced 13.95 (*0-8234-0784-5*) Holiday.
—The Magic of Music. Weil, Lisl. LC 88-21362. 32p. (ps-3). 1989. reinforced bdg. 13.95 (*0-8234-0735-7*) Holiday.
—Santa Claus Around the World. Weil, Lisl. LC 87-45334. 32p. (ps-3). 1987. reinforced 13.95 (*0-8234-0665-2*) Holiday.
—What Makes Me Feel This Way? Growing up with Human Emotions. LeShan, Eda. LC 71-165573. 128p. (gr. 3-6). 1972. SBE 13.95 (*0-02-757320-6*, Macmillan Child Bk); pap. 3.95 (*0-02-044340-4*, Aladdin) Macmillan Child Grp.
—Wolferl: The First Six Years in the Life of Wolfgang Amadeus Mozart. Weil, Lisl. LC 90-47684. 33p. (ps-3). 1991. reinforced 14.95 (*0-8234-0876-0*) Holiday.
Weiler, Milton. Big Stony. Walden, Howard T., II. 401p. (gr. 10 up). 1993. Repr. of 1972 ed. 40.00 (*1-56416-045-9*) Derrydale Pr.
—Tall Tales & Short. 2nd ed. Smith, Edmund W. 187p. (gr. 10 up). 1991. Repr. of 1938 ed. 35.00 (*1-56416-020-3*) Derrydale Pr.
—Upstream & Down. Walden, Howard T., II. 367p. (gr. 10 up). 1993. Repr. of 1972 ed. 40.00 (*1-56416-044-0*) Derrydale Pr.
Weiman, Jon. Let the Balloon Go. reissue ed. Southall, Ivan. LC 84-5984. 144p. (gr. 4-6). 1985. SBE 12.95 (*0-02-786220-8*, Bradbury Pr) Macmillan Child Grp.
Wein, Charlotte E. Maybe Tomorrow I'll Have a Good Time. Soderstrom, Mary. LC 80-25357. 32p. (ps-3). 1981. 16.95 (*0-89885-012-6*) Human Sci Pr.
Weinberg, Kay. The Horrible Terrible Dragon: A Folktale. Weinberg, Michael A. 10p. (gr. 1-3). 1949. pap. 1.00 (*0-9601014-3-8*) Weinberg.
Weinberg, Lisa F. Animals of the National Zoological Park Coloring Book. Lumpkin, Susan & Weinberg, Susan. 24p. (Orig.). (ps-4). 1989. pap. 3.95 (*0-9622062-1-0*) Friends Natl Zoo.
Weinberger, Tanya. The Littlest Spruce. Jerris, Tony. 20p. (Orig.). (ps up) 1991. pap. 9.95 (*0-9630107-1-9*) Little Spruce.
Weiner, Beth L. The Pudgy Book of Here We Go. 16p. (gr. k). 1984. pap. 2.95 (*0-448-10208-0*, G&D) Putnam Pub Group.
Weiner, Sally E. Born to Shine. Schaefer, Susan E. 36p. 1993. 14.95 (*0-9638908-4-0*) Blink Bks.
Weinhaus, Karen. Poem Stew. Cole, William, ed. LC 81-47106. 96p. (gr. 3-6). 1981. (Lipp Jr Bks); PLB 12.89 (*0-397-31964-9*) HarpC Child Bks.
—Poem Stew. Cole, William, ed. LC 81-47106. 96p. (gr. 2-6). 1983. pap. 4.95 (*0-06-440136-7*, Trophy) HarpC Child Bks.

Weinhaus, Karen A. All of Our Noses Are Here & Other Noodle Tales. Schwartz, Alvin. LC 84-48330. 64p. (gr. k-3). 1985. PLB 13.89 (*0-06-025288-X*) HarpC Child Bks.
—All of Our Noses Are Here & Other Noodle Tales. Schwartz, Alvin. LC 84-48330. 64p. (gr. k-3). 1987. pap. 3.50 (*0-06-444108-3*, Trophy) HarpC Child Bks.
—Knock at a Star: A Child's Introduction to Poetry. Kennedy, X. J. & Kennedy, Dorothy M. 160p. (gr. 2-6). 1985. pap. 8.95 (*0-316-48854-2*) Little.
—The Perfect Christmas Picture. Manushkin, Fran. LC 79-2678. 64p. (ps-3). 1987. pap. 3.50 (*0-06-444112-1*, Trophy) HarpC Child Bks.
—There Is a Carrot in My Ear & Other Noodle Tales. Schwartz, Alvin. LC 80-8442. 64p. (gr. k-3). 1982. PLB 13.89 (*0-06-025234-0*) HarpC Child Bks.
—There Is a Carrot in My Ear & Other Noodle Tales. Schwartz, Alvin. LC 80-8442. 64p. (gr. k-3). 1986. pap. 3.50 (*0-06-444103-2*, Trophy) HarpC Child Bks.
Weinhaus, Karen T. Music for Ones & Twos: Songs & Games for the Very Young Child. Glazer, Tom. LC 82-45199. 96p. (ps). 1983. pap. 12.00 (*0-385-14252-8*, Pub. by Zephyr-BFYR) Doubleday.
Weir, Wendy. Panther Dream: A Story of the African Rainforest. Weir, Bob & Weir, Wendy. LC 91-71385. 40p. (gr. k-5). 1991. PLB 14.89 (*1-56282-075-3*); PLB 19.95 incl. cassette (*1-56282-076-1*) Hyprn Child.
—Panther Dream: A Story of the African Rainforest. Weir, Bob & Weir, Wendy. LC 91-71385. 40p. (gr. k-5). 1993. pap. 4.95 (*1-56282-525-9*); incl. cassette 8.95 (*1-56282-591-7*); Incl. tchr's. guide, 12 bks. & 1 cassette. classroom pkg. 32.95 (*1-56282-548-8*) Hyprn Ppbks.
Weisbecker, Gene. Pup Pup & Murray Find a New Home. Stoneback, Jean C. 45p. (Orig.). (ps). 1984. pap. 4.00 (*0-931440-09-2*) Stoneback Pub.
Weisberg, Lynette, jt. illus. see Deschaine, Scott.
Weisgard, Leonard. The Courage of Sarah Noble. Dalgliesh, Alice. LC 54-5922. 64p. (gr. 1-5). 1987. Repr. of 1954 ed. SBE 13.95 (*0-684-18830-9*, Scribners Young Read) Macmillan Child Grp.
—The Courage of Sarah Noble. 2nd ed. Dalgliesh, Alice. LC 91-15531. 64p. (gr. 1-5). 1991. pap. 3.95 (*0-689-71540-4*, Aladdin) Macmillan Child Grp.
—Favorite Poems Old & New. Ferris, Helen, ed. LC 57-11418. 598p. (gr. 3-7). 1957. pap. 19.95 (*0-385-07696-7*) Doubleday.
—Growing Time. Warburg, Sandol S. LC 69-14729. (gr. k-3). 1975. 13.95 (*0-395-16966-6*) HM.
—Growing Time. Warburg, Sandol S. 48p. (gr. k-3). 1975. pap. 1.50 (*0-395-19971-9*, Sandpiper) HM.
—Growing Time. Warburg, Sandol S. (ps-3). 1989. pap. 4.80 (*0-395-51009-0*, Sandpiper) HM.
—Important Book. Brown, Margaret W. LC 49-9133. 22p. (ps-1). 1949. 13.00 (*0-06-020720-5*); PLB 12.89 (*0-06-020721-3*) HarpC Child Bks.
—The Important Book. Brown, Margaret W. LC 49-9133. 24p. (gr. k-3). 1990. pap. 4.95 (*0-06-443227-0*, Trophy) HarpC Child Bks.
—The Indoor Noisy Book. new ed. Brown, Margaret Wise. LC 92-46879. (ps-1). 1986. 15.00 (*0-06-020820-1*); PLB 15.89 (*0-06-020821-X*) HarpC Child Bks.
—Indoor Noisy Book. new ed. Brown, Margaret W. LC 92-46879. 48p. (ps-3). 1976. pap. 4.95 (*0-06-443003-0*, Trophy) HarpC Child Bks.
—Little Chicken. Brown, Margaret W. LC 43-16942. 32p. (ps-3). 1943. 13.00 (*0-06-020739-6*); PLB 12.89 (*0-06-020740-X*) HarpC Child Bks.
—Nannabah's Friend. Perrine, Mary. 32p. (gr. k-3). 1989. pap. 4.80 (*0-395-52020-7*) HM.
—Nibble Nibble: Poems for Children. Brown, Margaret W. LC 84-43128. 64p. (ps-3). 1959. PLB 13.89 (*0-201-09291-3*) HarpC Child Bks.
—The Noisy Book. new ed. Brown, Margaret W. LC 92-8322. 48p. (ps-1). 1939. 15.00 (*0-06-020830-9*); PLB 14.89 (*0-06-020831-7*) HarpC Child Bks.
—The Noisy Book. new ed. Brown, Margaret W. LC 92-8322. 48p. (ps-1). 1939. pap. 4.95 (*0-06-443001-4*, Trophy) HarpC Child Bks.
—The Quiet Noisy Book. new ed. Brown, Margaret W. LC 92-8320. 40p. (ps-1). 1993. 15.00 (*0-06-020845-7*); PLB 14.89 (*0-06-021220-9*) HarpC Child Bks.
—The Quiet Noisy Book. new ed. Brown, Margaret W. LC 92-8320. 40p. (ps-1). 1993. pap. 4.95 (*0-06-443215-7*, Trophy) HarpC Child Bks.
—Rain Drop Splash. Tresselt, Alvin. LC 46-11878. 28p. (ps-3). 1990. pap. 3.95 (*0-688-09352-3*, Mulberry) Morrow.
—Red Light, Green Light. Brown, Margaret W. 40p. 1992. 14.95 (*0-590-44558-8*, Scholastic Hardcover) Scholastic Inc.
—The Seashore Noisy Book. new ed. Brown, Margaret W. LC 92-31433. 48p. (ps-1). 1993. 15.00 (*0-06-020840-6*); PLB 15.89 (*0-06-020841-4*) HarpC Child Bks.
—Seashore Noisy Book. Wise Brown, Margaret. LC 92-31433. 48p. (ps-1). 1993. pap. 4.95 (*0-06-443329-3*, Trophy) HarpC Child Bks.
—The Secret River. 3rd, facsimile ed. Rawlings, Marjorie K. Bigham, Julia S., intro. by. 57p. (gr. 3-6). 1987. Repr. of 1955 ed. PLB 12.95 (*0-935259-02-3*) San Marco Bk.
—The Summer Noisy Book. new ed. Brown, Margaret W. LC 92-31435. 40p. (ps-1). 1993. 15.00 (*0-06-020855-4*); PLB 15.89 (*0-06-020856-2*) HarpC Child Bks.

—Summer Noisy Book. new ed. Brown, Margaret W. LC 92-31435. 40p. (ps-1). 1993. pap. 4.95 (0-06-443328-5, Trophy) HarpC Child Bks.
—The Winter Noisy Book. new ed. Brown, Margaret W. LC 92-46880. 48p. (ps-1). 1976. pap. 4.95 (0-06-443004-9, Trophy) HarpC Child Bks.
Weisgard, Leonard, photos by. The Country Noisy Book. Brown, Margaret Wise. LC 93-4755. 1988. 15.00 (0-06-020810-4, Festival); PLB 14.89 (0-06-020811-2) HarpC Child Bks.
Weismuller, Dieter. Pernix: The Adventures of a Small Dinosaur. Wiesmuller, Dieter. LC 92-39419. 44p. (gr. 3-6). 1993. 14.99 (0-525-65127-6, Cobblehill Bks) Dutton Child Bks.
Weiss, Ellen. Baby Dot: A Dinosaur Story. Cuyler, Margery. 32p. (ps-1). 1990. 13.45 (0-395-51934-9, Clarion Bks) HM.
—For Sand Castles or Seashells. Hartman, Gail. LC 89-35994. 32p. (ps-1). 1990. RSBE 13.95 (0-02-743091-X, Bradbury Pr) Macmillan Child Grp.
—Hanukkah. Chaikin, Miriam. LC 89-77512. 32p. (ps-3). 1990. reinforced bdg. 15.95 (0-8234-0816-7) Holiday.
—Hanukkah. Chaikin, Miriam. LC 89-77512. 32p. (ps-3). 1991. pap. 5.95 (0-8234-0905-8) Holiday.
—My Teacher Sleeps in School. Weiss, Leatie. LC 85-40449. 32p. (ps-3). 1985. pap. 4.50 (0-14-050559-8, Puffin) Puffin Bks.
—Shadow's Baby. Cuyler, Margery. LC 88-35257. 32p. (ps-1). 1989. 13.45 (0-89919-831-7, Clarion Bks) HM.
—So Many Cats. De Regniers, Beatrice S. LC 85-3739. 32p. (ps-3). 1985. (Clarion Bks); pap. 4.95 (0-89919-700-0, Clarion Bks) HM.
—Tuscanini. Propp, Jim. LC 91-240. 32p. (ps-1). 1992. RSBE 13.95 (0-02-774911-8, Bradbury Pr) Macmillan Child Grp.
—The Vingananee & the Tree Toad. Aardema, Verna. (gr. 3-8). 1988. pap. 4.99 (0-14-050890-2, Puffin) Puffin Bks.
—Who Said Meow? Polushkin, Maria. LC 87-28073. 32p. (ps). 1988. RSBE 13.95 (0-02-774770-0, Bradbury Pr) Macmillan Child Grp.
Weiss, Emil. D. J.'s Worst Enemy: A Novel by Robert Burch. Burch, Robert. LC 92-44783. 144p. (gr. 4-6). 1993. Repr. of 1965 ed. 19.95 (0-8203-1554-0) U of Ga Pr.
—It's Like This, Cat. Neville, Emily C. LC 62-21292. 192p. (gr. 5-9). 1964. 15.00 (0-06-024390-2); PLB 14.89 (0-06-024391-0) HarpC Child Bks.
—It's Like This, Cat. Neville, Emily C. LC 62-21292. 192p. (gr. 5-9). 1975. pap. 3.95 (0-06-440073-5, Trophy) HarpC Child Bks.
Weiss, Harvey. Every Friday Night. Simon, Norma. (ps-k). plastic cover 4.50 (0-8381-0708-7) United Syn Bk.
—Maps: Getting from Here to There. Weiss, Harvey. 64p. (gr. 2-5). 1991. 14.45 (0-395-56264-3, Sandpiper) HM.
—My Family Seder. Simon, Norma. (ps-k). 1961. plastic cover 4.50 (0-8381-0710-9, 10-710) United Syn Bk.
—Shelters: From Tepee to Igloo. Weiss, Harvey. LC 87-47698. 80p. (gr. 5-8). 1988. (Crowell Jr Bks); PLB 12.89 (0-690-04555-7, Crowell Jr Bks) HarpC Child Bks.
—Submarines & Other Underwater Craft. Weiss, Harvey. LC 89-37614. 64p. (gr. 3-7). 1990. (Crowell Jr Bks); PLB 12.89 (0-690-04761-4, Crowell Jr Bks) HarpC Child Bks.
—Tu Bishvat. Simon, Norma. (ps-k). 1961. plastic cover 4.50 (0-8381-0709-5) United Syn Bk.
Weiss, Nicki. A Family Story. Weiss, Nicki. LC 85-27231. 24p. (ps-3). 1987. 11.75 (0-688-06504-X); PLB 11.88 (0-688-06505-8) Greenwillow.
—Maude & Sally. Weiss, Nicki. LC 82-12003. 32p. (gr. k-3). 1983. 13.95 (0-688-01859-9); PLB 13.88 (0-688-01861-0) Greenwillow.
—On a Hot, Hot Day. Weiss, Nicki. 32p. (ps-1). 1992. PLB 13.95 (0-399-22119-0, Putnam) Putnam Pub Group.
—Princess Pearl. Weiss, Nicki. LC 85-17699. 24p. (gr. k-3). 1986. 11.75 (0-688-05894-9); PLB 11.88 (0-688-05895-7) Greenwillow.
Weissman, Bari. Celebrate: A Book of Jewish Holidays. Gross, Judith. 32p. (gr. k-3). 1992. PLB 7.99 (0-448-40303-X, Platt & Munk Pubs); pap. 2.25 (0-448-40302-1, Platt & Munk Pubs) Putnam Pub Group.
—Golly Gump Swallowed a Fly. Cole, Joanna. LC 81-11072. 48p. (ps-3). 1982. 5.95 (0-8193-1069-7); lib. bdg. 5.95 (0-8193-1070-0) Parents.
—The Hippo's Adventure. Jones, Sally L. 8p. (ps). 1993. vinyl 8.49 (0-7847-0049-4, 24-03687) Standard Pub.
—Noisy Neighbors: A Book about Animal Sounds. Leonard, Marcia. LC 89-4959. 24p. (gr. k-2). 1990. PLB 9.59 (0-8167-1726-5); pap. text ed. 1.95 (0-8167-1727-3) Troll Assocs.
—The Old Man & the Afternoon Cat. Muntean, Michaela. LC 81-11047. 48p. (ps-3). 1982. 5.95 (0-8193-1071-9); PLB 5.95 (0-8193-1072-7) Parents.
—Teddy Toast & Twelve Other Yummy Easy Recipes You Can Make Yourself: With a Little Help from a Grownup & a Very Special Cookie Cutter! Wermert, Rosie & McClurg, Marie. 24p. (ps-2). 1994. 7.99 plastic comb bdg. (0-679-80745-4) Random Bks Yng Read.
—Three Special Journeys, 3 bks. Jones, Sally L. (ps). 1993. Set. 9.99 (0-7847-0075-3, 24-03645) Standard Pub.
—The Whale's Tale. Jones, Sally L. 8p. (ps). 1993. vinyl 8.49 (0-7847-0048-6, 24-03686) Standard Pub.

Weissman, Bari & Garcia, T. R. Valentine Holiday Grab Bag. Stamper, Judith. LC 92-13225. 48p. (gr. 2-5). 1992. PLB 11.89 (0-8167-2910-7); pap. text ed. 3.95 (0-8167-2911-5) Troll Assocs.
Weissman, Bari, jt. illus. see Kalish, Lionel.
Weissman, Barry. The Squire Takes a Wife. Feldman, Eve. 24p. (ps-2). 1990. PLB 14.60 (0-8172-3580-9); PLB 10.95 pkg. of 3 (0-685-58551-4) Raintree Steck-V.
Weissman, Sam Q. Last, First, Middle & Nick: All About Names. Hazen, Barbara S. (gr. 1-4). 1979. 7.95 (0-13-523944-3) P-H.
—Put Your Foot in Your Mouth & Other Silly Sayings. Cox, James A. LC 80-12877. 72p. (gr. 2-5). 1980. bds. 3.95 (0-394-84503-X) Random Bks Yng Read.
—School Daze. Keller, Charles. (gr. 2-5). 1981. pap. 3.95 (0-13-793612-5, Pub. by Treehouse) P-H.
—Sports Riddles. Rosenbloom, Joseph. LC 81-7232. 64p. (gr. 6 up). 1982. 8.95 (0-15-277994-9, HB Juv Bks) HarBrace.
Weissmann, Joe. The Paper Book & Paper Maker. Levine, Shar. LC 92-72021. 32p. (gr. k-5). 1993. 12.95 (1-56282-235-7) Hyprn Child.
Welch, Rose. Guatemala. Cummins, Ronnie. LC 89-40246. 64p. (gr. 5-6). 1990. PLB 19.93 (0-8368-0120-2) Gareth Stevens Inc.
Welch, Rose, photos by. Children of the World: Costa Rica. Cummins, Ronnie & Weber, Valerie. LC 89-43138. 64p. (gr. 5-6). 1990. PLB 19.93 (0-8368-0222-5) Gareth Stevens Inc.
—Children of the World: El Salvador. Cummins, Ronnie & Welch, Rose. LC 89-43137. 64p. (gr. 5-6). 1990. PLB 19.93 (0-8368-0220-9) Gareth Stevens Inc.
—Costa Rica Is My Home. Foran, Eileen, adapted by. LC 92-17727. 1992. PLB 18.60 (0-8368-0847-9) Gareth Stevens Inc.
—El Salvador Is My Home. Foran, Eileen, adapted by. LC 92-17724. 1992. PLB 18.60 (0-8368-0849-5) Gareth Stevens Inc.
—Nicaragua Is My Home. Daniel, Jamie, adapted by. LC 92-17723. 1992. PLB 18.60 (0-8368-0850-9) Gareth Stevens Inc.
Welch, Sandy. Immigration: A Thematic Unit. Sima, Patricia, et al. 80p. (gr. 3-5). 1993. wkbk. 7.95 (1-55734-234-2) Tchr Create Mat.
Welch, Sheila K. Don't Call Me Marda. Welch, Sheila K. 138p. (gr. 4 up). 1990. 16.95 (0-9611872-3-9); pap. 12.95 (0-9611872-4-7) Our Child Pr.
—Is That Your Sister? A True Story of Adoption. Bunin, Catherine & Bunin, Sherry. 32p. (gr. 2-6). 1992. Repr. of 1976 ed. 14.95 (0-9611872-6-3) Our Child Pr.
Welcher, Rosalind. My Brother Says There's a Monster Living in Our Toilet. Welcher, Rosalind. 96p. (Orig.). 1987. pap. 6.95 (0-939775-01-8) West Hill Pr.
Weller, Don. Martin the Cavebine. Nickerson, Sara. LC 88-71369. 28p. (Orig.). (gr. 1-4). 1989. pap. 8.00 (0-935529-06-3) Comprehen Health Educ.
—Professor Fergus Fahrenheit & His Wonderful Weather Machine. Fleming, Candace. LC 93-4432. 1994. pap. 14.00 (0-671-87047-5, S&S BFYR) S&S Trade.
Weller, Linda. Jason Goes to Show & Tell. Sutherland, Colleen. 32p. (ps-k). 1992. bds. 9.95 (1-878093-89-4) Boyds Mills Pr.
—Quiet Time. Rosen, Gary & Shontz, Bill. 24p. (ps-1). 1990. pap. 9.95 incl. cassette (0-679-80801-9) Random Bks Yng Read.
Welles, Laura. Will & Grandmother Change the Seashore. Welles, Laura & Welles, Ted. McCloskey, Maris, ed. LC 92-62260. 40p. (Orig.). (gr. k-7). 1992. pap. 7.95 (0-915189-07-0) Oceanus.
—Will & Grandmother Change the Seashore. Welles, Laura & Welles, Ted. McCloskey, Maris, ed. LC 92-62260. 40p. (Orig.). (gr. k-7). 1993. text ed. 24.00 (0-915189-08-9) Oceanus.
Welles, T., jt. illus. see Swensson, Dale I.
Wellington, Monica. All My Little Ducklings. Wellington, Monica. LC 88-22841. 32p. (ps-k). 1989. 11.95 (0-525-44459-9, DCB) Dutton Child Bks.
—The Sheep Follow. Wellington, Monica. LC 91-3420. 32p. (ps-k). 1992. 13.00 (0-525-44837-3, DCB) Dutton Child Bks.
—What Is Your Language? Leventhal, Debra. LC 93-10156. 32p. (ps-1). 1994. 12.99 (0-525-45133-1, DCB) Dutton Child Bks.
—Who Is Tapping at My Window? Deming, A. G. 24p. (ps). 1994. pap. 4.99 (0-14-054553-0, Puffin Unicorn) Puffin Bks.
—Who Is Tapping at My Window? Deming, A. G. 24p. (ps). 1994. pap. 17.99 giant format (0-14-050303-X) Puffin Bks.
—Who Says That? Shapiro, Arnold L. LC 90-3996. 32p. (ps). 1991. 13.95 (0-525-44698-2, DCB) Dutton Child Bks.
Welliver, Norma. This Is My Trunk. Harris, Steven M. LC 85-74621. 32p. (ps-4). 1985. SBE 13.95 (0-689-31128-1, Atheneum Child Bk) Macmillan Child Grp.
Wells, Chrissie. I'm Growing Up! Things I Can Do by Myself. Nash, Corey. (ps-5). 1990. 4.95 (1-55782-028-7, Pub. by Warner Juvenile Bks) Little.
Wells, Gregory. Frank & Sam's Summer at Aramoana. Farry, Liane. LC 93-11733. 1994. 4.25 (0-383-03744-1) SRA Schl Grp.
Wells, Haru. The Master Puppeteer. Paterson, Katherine. 180p. (gr. 5 up). 1981. pap. 2.95 (0-380-53322-7, Camelot) Avon.

—The Master Puppeteer. Paterson, Katherine. LC 75-8614. 192p. (gr. 6 up). 1976. 15.00 (0-690-00913-5, Crowell Jr Bks) HarpC Child Bks.
—The Master Puppeteer. Paterson, Katherine. LC 75-8614. 192p. (gr. 4 up). 1989. pap. 3.95 (0-06-440281-9, Trophy) HarpC Child Bks.
—Of Nightingales That Weep. Paterson, Katherine. LC 74-8294. 192p. (gr. 4 up). 1989. pap. 3.95 (0-06-440282-7, Trophy) HarpC Child Bks.
Wells, Jesse. Little Blaze & the Buffalo Jump. Roop, Peter. 28p. (Orig.). (gr. 3-8). 1984. pap. 2.45 (0-89992-089-6) Coun India Ed.
Wells, Rosemary. Benjamin & Tulip. Wells, Rosemary. LC 73-6018. 32p. (ps-2). 1977. 12.00 (0-8037-1808-X); PLB 9.89 (0-8037-2057-2); pap. 4.50 (0-8037-0545-X) Dial Bks Young.
—First Tomato. Wells, Rosemary. LC 91-41599. 32p. (ps-3). 1992. PLB 12.89 (0-8037-1175-1) Dial Bks Young.
—Good Night, Fred. Wells, Rosemary. LC 81-65849. 32p. (ps-3). 1981. Dial Bks Young.
—Hazel's Amazing Mother. Wells, Rosemary. LC 85-1447. 32p. (ps-2). 1985. 13.95 (0-8037-0209-4); PLB 13.89 (0-8037-0210-8) Dial Bks Young.
—Hazel's Amazing Mother. Wells, Rosemary. LC 85-1447. (ps-2). 1989. 3.95 (0-8037-0703-7) Dial Bks Young.
—Hooray for Max. Wells, Rosemary. (ps). 1986. Max doll 8.95 (0-8037-0203-5) Dial Bks Young.
—The Island Light. Wells, Rosemary. LC 91-41598. 32p. (ps-3). 1992. PLB 12.89 (0-8037-1178-6) Dial Bks Young.
—A Lion for Lewis. Wells, Rosemary. 32p. (ps-2). 1984. pap. 3.95 (0-8037-0096-2, Dial Pied Piper) Puffin Bks.
—Max & Ruby's First Greek Myth. Wells, Rosemary. LC 92-30332. 32p. (ps-3). 1993. 11.99 (0-8037-1524-2); PLB 11.89 (0-8037-1525-0) Dial Bks Young.
—Max's Bath. Wells, Rosemary. LC 84-14969. 12p. (ps-k). 1985. bds. 3.95 (0-8037-0162-4) Dial Bks Young.
—Max's Bedtime. Well, Rosemary. LC 84-14968. 12p. (ps-k). 1985. bds. 3.95 (0-8037-0160-8) Dial Bks Young.
—Max's Birthday. Wells, Rosemary. LC 84-14970. 12p. (ps-k). 1985. bds. 4.50 (0-8037-0163-2) Dial Bks Young.
—Max's Breakfast. Wells, Rosemary. LC 84-14968. 12p. (ps-k). 1985. bds. 3.95 (0-8037-0161-6) Dial Bks Young.
—Max's Chocolate Chicken. Wells, Rosemary. LC 88-14954. 32p. (ps-2). 1989. 9.95 (0-8037-0585-9); PLB 9.89 (0-8037-0586-7) Dial Bks Young.
—Max's Christmas. Wells, Rosemary. LC 85-27547. 32p. (ps-2). 1986. 9.95 (0-8037-0289-2); PLB 9.89 (0-8037-0290-6) Dial Bks Young.
—Max's Dragon Shirt. Wells, Rosemary. LC 90-43755. 32p. (ps-2). 1991. 12.00 (0-8037-0944-7); lib. bdg. 10.89 (0-8037-0945-5) Dial Bks Young.
—Max's First Word. Wells, Rosemary. LC 79-59745. (ps-k). 1979. bds. 4.50 (0-8037-6066-3) Dial Bks Young.
—Max's New Suit. Wells, Rosemary. LC 79-50747. (ps-k). 1979. bds. 3.95 (0-8037-6065-5) Dial Bks Young.
—Max's Ride. Wells, Rosemary. LC 79-50746. (ps-k). 1979. bds. 3.95 (0-8037-6069-8) Dial Bks Young.
—Max's Toys: A Counting Book. Wells, Rosemary. LC 79-50748. (ps-k). 1979. bds. 4.50 (0-8037-6068-X) Dial Bks Young.
—Morris's Disappearing Bag. Wells, Rosemary. 1975. 9.95 (0-8037-5441-8) Dial Bks Young.
—Moss Pillows. Wells, Rosemary. LC 91-41600. 32p. (ps-3). 1992. PLB 12.89 (0-8037-1177-8) Dial Bks Young.
—Noisy Nora. Wells, Rosemary. LC 72-6068. 40p. (ps-2). 1973. 10.95 (0-8037-6638-6); PLB 10.89 (0-8037-6639-4) Dial Bks Young.
—Noisy Nora. Wells, Rosemary. 40p. (ps-2). 1980. pap. 3.99 (0-8037-6193-7) Dial Bks Young.
—Shy Charles. Wells, Rosemary. LC 87-27247. 32p. (ps-3). 1988. 11.95 (0-8037-0563-8); PLB 11.89 (0-8037-0564-6) Dial Bks Young.
—Stanley & Rhoda. Wells, Rosemary. LC 78-51874. 40p. (ps-2). 1981. pap. 4.95 (0-8037-7995-X, 0383-120) Dial Bks Young.
—Tell Me a Trudy. Segal, Lore. LC 77-24123. 40p. (ps-3). 1977. 15.00 (0-374-37395-7) FS&G.
—Tell Me a Trudy. Segal, Lore. (ps up) 1989. pap. 4.95 (0-374-47504-0) FS&G.
—Timothy Goes to School. Wells, Rosemary. LC 80-20785. 32p. (ps-2). 1981. 13.95 (0-8037-8948-3); PLB 11.89 (0-8037-8949-1) Dial Bks Young.
—Unfortunately Harriet. Wells, Rosemary. LC 76-181786. 32p. (ps-3). 1972. Dial Bks Young.
—Voyage to the Bunny Planet: First Tomato, Moss Pillows, the Island Light, 3 bks. Wells, Rosemary. 32p. (ps-3). 1992. Boxed Set, 32p. ea. 13.00 (0-8037-1174-3) Dial Bks Young.
Wells, Sarah. A Day in the Life of a Carpenter. Martin, John H. LC 84-2420. 32p. (gr. 4-8). 1985. PLB 11.79 (0-8167-0093-1); pap. text ed. 2.95 (0-8167-0094-X) Troll Assocs.
Wells, Tony. The Naughty Lamb. Blanchard, Arlene. LC 88-4098. 32p. (ps-1). 1989. 9.95 (0-8037-0577-8) Dial Bks Young.
—Out in Space. Wood, Tim. LC 91-7483. 32p. (gr. k-3). 1991. pap. 5.95 (0-689-71491-2, Aladdin) Macmillan Child Grp.

Wells, William S., jt. illus. see Allison, Linda.
Welply, Michael. The Magic Toyshop. Seymour, Peter. (gr. 3 up). 1988. pap. 14.95 (0-671-66907-9, S&S BFYR) S&S Trade.
—The Nutcracker. Hoffman, E. T. Angus, Fay, adapted by. (gr. 2 up). 1989. pap. 16.95 casebound, pop-up (0-671-68617-8, Little Simon) S&S Trade.
—The Rise of Major Religions. Makhlouf, Georgia. Moeller, Walter O., tr. from FRE. 77p. (gr. 7 up). 1988. 17.98 (0-382-09482-4) Silver Burdett Pr.
Wenger, Rachelle & Wenger, Renee. Word of God, Priceless Treasure. Wenger, Rachelle & Wenger, Renee. Wenger, Ray M., ed. 64p. (Orig.). (gr. 3-6). 1993. pap. 5.99 (0-9634616-1-3) Plumb Line Pr.
Wenger, Renee, jt. illus. see Wenger, Rachelle.
Wenger, Susie J. Fall Is Here! I Love It! Good, Elaine W. LC 90-71115. 32p. (ps-1). 1990. text ed. 12.95 (1-56148-007-X) Good Bks PA.
—White Wonderful Winter. Good, Elaine W. LC 91-74052. 32p. (ps-1). 1991. 12.95 (1-56148-018-5) Good Bks PA.
Wenger-Marsh, Beth. The Great Balloon Game Book & More Balloon Activities. Grummer, Arnold E. 112p. (gr. 2 up). 1987. 12.95 (0-938251-00-7) G Markim.
Wennekes, Ron. Losing Uncle Tim. Jordan, MaryKate. Levine, Abby, ed. LC 89-5280. 32p. (gr. 2-6). 1989. PLB 13.95 (0-8075-4756-5); pap. 5.95 (0-8075-4758-1) A Whitman.

Wensell, Uliises. La Nina Invisible (The Invisible Girl) Sanchez, J. L. & Pacheco, M. A. (SPA.). 42p. (gr. k-2). 1988. write for info. (84-372-1829-2) Santillana.
An outstanding selection from the DERECHOS DEL NINO series (The Rights of Children). Each book portrays one of the rights of children declared by the United Nations General Assembly. In this selection, a young girl named Maria is friendless. She lives in an area between the Green City & the Blue City. The children from the two cities despise each other & Maria belongs to neither. Maria grows so lonely & miserable that one day she simply becomes invisible. But in this new state she is able to bring about amazing changes in the two cities. Young readers will enjoy this heartwarming story & its message. Simplistic illustrations by Ulises Wendell add to the charm. To order: Santillana, 901 West Walnut, Compton, CA 90220. Telephone 1-310-763-0455. *Publisher Provided Annotation.*

Wensell, Ulises. Paul & Sebastian. Escudie, Rene. Townley, Roderick, tr. from FRE. LC 88-12768. 32p. (ps-3). 1988. 11.95 (0-916291-19-7) Kane-Miller Bk.
—Paul & Sebastian. Escudie, Rene. Townley, Roderick, tr. (FRE.). 32p. (ps-3). 1994. pap. 6.95 (0-916291-49-9) Kane-Miller Bk.
—They Followed a Bright Star. LC 93-6065. 1994. write for info. (0-399-22706-7, Putnam) Putnam Pub Group.
Wentworth, Elaine. The Lighthouse Keeper's Daughter. Olson, Arielle N. 32p. (ps-3). 1987. 14.95 (0-316-65057-9) Little.
Wentworth, Janet. Cady. Eige, Lillian. LC 85-45818. 192p. (gr. 3-7). 1987. HarpC Child Bks.
—Rondo in C. Fleischman, Paul. LC 87-29375. 32p. (gr. k-3). 1988. PLB 13.89 (0-06-021857-6) HarpC Child Bks.
Wenzel, David. Backyard Dragon. Sterman, Betsy & Sterman, Samuel. LC 92-26292. 192p. (gr. 3-7). 1993. 14.00 (0-06-020783-3); PLB 13.89 (0-06-020784-1) HarpC Child Bks.
—Boston Tea Party, Rebellion in the Colonies. Knight, James E. LC 81-23077. 32p. (gr. 5-9). 1982. PLB 11.59 (0-89375-734-9); pap. text ed. 2.95 (0-89375-735-7) Troll Assocs.
—Hauntings: Ghosts & Ghouls from Around the World. Hodges, Margaret, retold by. (gr. 3-7). 1991. 16.95 (0-316-36796-6) Little.
—Jamestown, New World Adventure. Knight, James E. LC 81-23086. 32p. (gr. 5-9). 1982. PLB 11.59 (0-89375-724-1); pap. text ed. 2.95 (0-89375-725-X) Troll Assocs.
—Pilgrims & Thanksgiving. Bains, Rae. LC 84-2686. 32p. (gr. 3-6). 1985. PLB 9.49 (0-8167-0222-5); pap. text ed. 2.95 (0-8167-0223-3) Troll Assocs.
—Pocahontas. Santrey, Laurence. LC 84-8443. 32p. (gr. 3-6). 1985. PLB 9.49 (0-8167-0276-4); pap. text ed. 2.95 (0-8167-0277-2) Troll Assocs.
—Salem Days, Life in a Colonial Seaport. Knight, James E. LC 81-23076. 32p. (gr. 5-9). 1982. PLB 11.59 (0-89375-732-2); pap. text ed. 2.95 (0-89375-733-0) Troll Assocs.

—The Wizard's Tale, Bk. 1. Busiek, Kurt. Yronwode, Catherine & Adair, Lynn, eds. 42p. (Orig.). (gr. 1-4). 1993. pap. 4.95t (1-56060-206-6) Eclipse Bks.
—The Wizard's Tale, Bk. 2. Busiek, Kurt. Yronwode, Catherine & Adair, Lynn, eds. 42p. (Orig.). (gr. 1-4). 1993. pap. 4.95t (1-56060-207-4) Eclipse Bks.
—The Wizard's Tale, Bk. 3. Busiek, Kurt. Yronwode, Catherine & Adair, Lynn, eds. 42p. (Orig.). (gr. 1-4). 1994. pap. 4.95t (1-56060-208-2) Eclipse Bks.
—The Wizard's Tale, Collection, 3 bks. Busiek, Kurt. Yronwode, Catherine & Adair, Lynn, eds. 42p. (Orig.). (gr. 1-4). Date not set. write for info. (1-56060-210-4); pap. write for info. (1-56060-209-0) Eclipse Bks.
Wenzel, Greg. The Monsters Who Died: A Mystery about Dinosaurs. Cobb, Vicki. 64p. (gr. 3-6). 1983. 13.95 (0-698-20571-5, Coward) Putnam Pub Group.
Wenzel, Gregory C. More about Dinosaurs. Cutts, David. LC 81-11432. 32p. (gr. k-2). 1982. PLB 11.59 (0-89375-668-7); pap. text ed. 2.95 (0-89375-669-5) Troll Assocs.
Wenzel, Paul. A Wall of Names: The Story of the Vietnam Veterans Memorial A Step 4 Book - Grades 2-4. Donnelly, Judy. LC 90-30275. 48p. (Orig.). (gr. 2-4). 1991. PLB 7.99 (0-679-90169-8); pap. 2.95 (0-679-80169-3) Random Bks Yng Read.
Wenzel, Rick. Bert's Little Bedtime Story: A Sesame Street Book. Ross, K. K. LC 89-64283. 28p. (ps). 1991. bds. 2.95 (0-679-80757-8) Random Bks Yng Read.
Wenz-Vietor, Ilse. Sweet Dreams for Little Ones. Pappas, Michael G. 64p. (Orig.). 1985. pap. 10.00 (0-86683-641-1, AY8156) Harper SF.
Wepplo, Mike. Davy Crockett & the Creek Indians. Korman, Justine. LC 91-71357. 80p. (gr. 1-4). 1991. PLB 12.89 (1-56282-004-4); pap. 2.95 (1-56282-005-2) Disney Pr.
—Davy Crockett & the King of the River. Singer, A. L. LC 91-71356. 80p. (gr. 1-4). 1991. PLB 12.89 (1-56282-006-0); pap. 2.95 (1-56282-007-9) Disney Pr.
—Davy Crockett & the Pirates at Cave-in Rock. Singer, A. L. LC 91-71355. 80p. (gr. 1-4). 1991. PLB 12.89 (1-56282-002-8); pap. 2.95 (1-56282-003-6) Disney Pr.
—Davy Crockett at the Alamo. Korman, Justine. LC 91-71350. 80p. (gr. 1-4). 1991. PLB 12.89 (1-56282-008-7); pap. 2.95 (1-56282-009-5) Disney Pr.
Weren, James. Snow White & Rose Red. Grimm, Jacob & Grimm, Wilhelm K. LC 78-18074. 32p. (gr. k-3). 1979. PLB 9.79 (0-89375-136-7); pap. 1.95 (0-89375-114-6) Troll Assocs.
Werner, Marlene H. The Moon of the Salamanders. new ed. George, Jean C. LC 90-25591. 48p. (gr. 3-7). 1992. 15.00 (0-06-022609-9); PLB 14.89 (0-06-022694-3) HarpC Child Bks.
Werth, Kurt. Thing at the Foot of the Bed. Leach, Maria. LC 59-6658. 128p. (gr. 3-5). 1987. PLB 12.95 (0-399-21496-8, Philomel) Putnam Pub Group.
West, Colin. The Beginner's Book of Bad Behaviour. West, Colin. 96p. (gr. 4-7). 1988. 13.95 (0-09-172120-2, Pub. by Hutchinson UK) Trafalgar.
—Go Tell It to the Toucan. West, Colin. (ps-3). 1990. PLB 8.95 (0-553-05889-4, Little Rooster) Bantam.
—Have You Seen the Crocodile? West, Colin. LC 85-45748. 24p. (ps-2). 1986. pap. 4.95 (0-06-443101-0, Trophy) HarpC Child Bks.
—Pardon? Said the Giraffe. West, Colin. LC 85-45747. 24p. (ps-2). 1986. pap. 4.95 (0-06-443102-9, Trophy) HarpC Child Bks.
—Shape Up, Monty! West, Colin. LC 91-20316. 64p. (gr. 2-5). 1991. 10.95 (0-525-44777-6, DCB) Dutton Child Bks.
West, David. Biggest & Smallest: Questions & Answers about Record Breakers. Ganeri, Anita. LC 92-12497. (ps-3). 1992. 6.95 (0-8120-6291-4) Barron.
—Fastest & Slowest: Questions & Answers about Record Breakers. Ganeri, Anita. LC 92-10077. (ps-3). 1992. 6.95 (0-8120-6290-6) Barron.
West, James A. Discovering Genetics. Higgins, Jane H. 48p. (Orig.). (gr. 4-12). 1983. pap. text ed. 9.95 tchr's. enrichment bk. (0-88047-033-X, 8315) DOK Pubs.
—Extending U. S. History & Geography. Schroeder, Mary. 32p. (Orig.). (gr. 3-6). 1984. 6.50 (0-88047-041-0, 8404) DOK Pubs.
—Know Your State. Crosby, Nina E. & Marten, Elizabeth H. 32p. (Orig.). (gr. 4-7). 1984. pap. 5.95 (0-88047-036-4, 8401) DOK Pubs.
West, Joanne. Rosie, the Rosedown Rabbit: A Storybook to Color. Sundeen, Poppy. West, Joanne, ed. 26p. (Orig.). 1988. pap. text ed. 5.95 (0-929317-00-9) Rosedown Plantation.
West, Keith. Keeper. Durrell, Gerald. LC 90-55612. 32p. (gr. 1-4). 1991. 13.95 (1-55970-122-6) Arcade Pub Inc.
—Toby the Tortoise. Durrell, Gerald. 32p. (ps-3). 1991. 14.95 (1-55970-145-5) Arcade Pub Inc.
West, Linnea F. The First Adventure of Peter Nelson Panda. Dowell, Olivia S. 16p. (gr. 2-4). 1986. pap. 5.95 (0-9617624-0-3) Bear Tracks Pub.
West Side High School Students. Love Is Like. Warwick, Catherine A. Iscaro, Nancy L., ed. 33p. (Orig.). (gr. 10-12). 1989. pap. text ed. write for info. West Side Pubns.
—My Life. Fernandez, Brenda. Iscaro, Nancy L., ed. 50p. (Orig.). (gr. 10-12). 1989. pap. text ed. write for info. West Side Pubns.
—My Life in the City. Beane, Kelly D. Iscaro, Nancy L., frwd. by. 48p. (Orig.). (gr. 10-12). 1989. pap. text ed. write for info. West Side Pubns.

—Quiet Thoughts. Garay, Julio. Cohen, Mel & Iscaro, Nancy L., eds. 38p. (Orig.). (gr. 10-12). 1989. pap. text ed. write for info. West Side Pubns.
Westcott, Nadine B. Dinner at the Panda Palace. Calmenson, Stephanie. LC 90-33720. 32p. (ps-3). 1991. 15.00 (0-06-021010-9); PLB 14.89 (0-06-021011-7) HarpC Child Bks.
—Down by the Bay. Raffi. 32p. (ps-2). 1988. PLB 14.00 (0-517-56644-3) Crown Bks Yng Read.
—Down by the Bay. Raffi. LC 87-750291. 32p. (ps-2). 1988. pap. 3.99 (0-517-56645-1) Crown Bks Yng Read.
—The Emperor's New Clothes. Andersen, Hans Christian. (ps-3). 1984. pap. 5.95 (0-316-93124-1) Little.
—Even Little Kids Get Diabetes. Pirner, Connie. Tucker, Kathy, ed. LC 90-12738. 24p. (ps-2). 1991. 10.95 (0-8075-2158-2) A Whitman.
—Famous Seaweed Soup. Martin, Antoinette T. Mathews, Judith, ed. LC 92-31612. 32p. (ps-2). 1993. PLB 13.95 (0-8075-2263-5) A Whitman.
—Getting Up. Westcott, Nadine B. LC 86-28721. (ps). 1987. pap. 4.95 (0-316-93131-4, Joy St Bks) Little.
—Going to Bed. Westcott, Nadine B. LC 86-28767. (ps). 1987. pap. 4.95 (0-316-93132-2, Joy St Bks) Little.
—The Hippopotamus Song: A Muddy Love Story. Flanders, Michael & Swann, Donald. (ps-3). 1991. 14.95 (0-316-28557-9) Little.
—How to Grow a Picket Fence. Cuneo, Mary L. LC 91-36444. 32p. (ps-3). 1993. 15.00 (0-06-020863-5); PLB 14.89 (0-06-020864-3) HarpC Child Bks.
—I Can Tell by Touching. Otto, Carolyn. LC 93-18630. (gr. 4 up). 1994. 14.00 (0-06-023324-9); PLB 13.89 (0-06-023325-7) HarpC Child Bks.
—I Know an Old Lady Who Swallowed a Fly. Westcott, Nadine B. 32p. (gr. k-3). 1980. lib. bdg. 14.95 (0-316-93128-4, Joy St Bks); pap. 5.95 (0-316-93127-6) Little.
—Kathy's Hats: A Story of Hope. Krisher, Trudy. Levine, Abby, ed. LC 92-2659. 32p. (gr. 1-5). 1992. 13.95g (0-8075-4116-8) A Whitman.
—The Lady with the Alligator Purse. Westcott, Nadine B., adapted by. LC 87-21368. (ps-3). 1988. 13.95 (0-316-93135-7, Joy St Bks) Little.
—The Lion Who Had Asthma. Lion, Jonathan. Levine, Abby, ed. LC 91-16553. 32p. (ps-1). 1992. PLB 13.95 (0-8075-4559-7) A Whitman.
—Never Take a Pig to Lunch: And Other Poems about the Fun of Eating. Westcott, Nadine B., ed. LC 93-11801. 64p. 1994. 16.95 (0-531-06834-X); lib. bdg. 16.99 RLB (0-531-08684-4) Orchard Bks Watts.
—Over the River & Through the Wood. Child, Lydia M. LC 92-14979. 32p. (gr. 1-5). 1993. 14.00 (0-06-021303-5); PLB 13.89 (0-06-021304-3) HarpC Child Bks.
—Peanut Butter & Jelly: A Play Rhyme. LC 86-32889. 32p. (ps-k). 1987. 13.00 (0-525-44317-7, DCB) Dutton Child Bks.
—Peanut Butter & Jelly: A Play Rhyme. LC 86-32889. 24p. (ps-k). 1992. pap. 3.99 (0-525-44885-3, DCB) Dutton Child Bks.
—Peanut Butter & Jelly: A Play Rhyme. giant ed. 24p. (ps-k). 1993. pap. 17.99 (0-14-054850-5) Puffin Bks.
—Peanut Butter & Jelly: A Play Rhyme. (ps-3). 1994. pap. 6.99 incl. cassette (0-14-095142-3, Puffin) Puffin Bks.
—Peanut Butter & Jelly Read-Aloud Set. (ps-k). 1993. Set incls. 1 Giant copy, 6 paperbacks, giant-sized bookmark & tchr's. guide in a free- standing easel. pap. 41.93 (0-14-778975-3) Puffin Bks.
—People, People, Everywhere! Van Laan, Nancy. LC 90-5303. 40p. (ps-2). 1992. 13.00 (0-679-81063-3); PLB 13.99 (0-679-91063-8) Knopf Bks Yng Read.
—Raffi's Christmas Treasury: 14 Illustrated Songs & Musical Arrangements. (ps up). 1988. PLB 17.95 (0-517-56806-3) Crown Bks Yng Read.
—A Real Nice Clambake. Rodgers, Richard & Hammerstein, Oscar, II. 32p. (ps-3). 1992. 14.95 (0-316-75422-6, Joy St Bks) Little.
—Skip to My Lou. Westcott, Nadine B., adapted by. 32p. (ps-3). 1989. 12.95 (0-316-93137-3, Joy St Bks) Little.
—Skip to My Lou. Westcott, Nadine B., adapted by. 32p. (ps-3). 1992. pap. 4.95 (0-316-93140-3, Joy St Bks) Little.
—Thanksgiving: Stories & Poems. Bauer, Caroline F., ed. LC 93-18631. (gr. 4 up). 1994. 14.00 (0-06-023326-5); PLB 13.89 (0-06-023327-3) HarpC Child Bks.
—There's a Hole in the Bucket. Westcott, Nadine B. LC 89-34538. 32p. (ps). 1990. 14.00 (0-06-026422-5); PLB 13.89 (0-06-026423-3) HarpC Child Bks.
—There's a Hole in the Bucket. Westcott, Nadine B. LC 89-34538. 32p. (ps-2). 1993. pap. 4.95 (0-06-443195-9, Trophy) HarpC Child Bks.
Westerman, Johanna. The Christmas Snowman. Cuyler, Margery. 32p. (ps-3). 1992. 14.95 (1-55970-066-1) Arcade Pub Inc.
—Maggie Mab & the Bogey Beast. Carey, Valerie S. 32p. (ps-3). 1992. 14.95 (1-55970-155-2) Arcade Pub Inc.
Westman, Barbara. Dancing Dogs: Charlotte & Emilio at the Circus. Westman, Barbara. LC 90-23070. 32p. (ps-3). 1991. PLB 14.89 (0-06-022460-6) HarpC Child Bks.
—I Like the Music. Komaiko, Leah. LC 87-170. 32p. (ps-3). 1987. HarpC Child Bks.
—I Like the Music. Komaiko, Leah. LC 87-170. 32p. (ps-3). 1989. pap. 5.95 (0-06-443189-4, Trophy) HarpC Child Bks.

—My Perfect Neighborhood. Komaiko, Leah. LC 89-37871. 32p. (ps-3). 1990. PLB 13.89 (0-06-023288-9) HarpC Child Bks.
Westman, David. Absolute Barbeque. Kansas City Barbeque Inner Circle Staff. Venable, Bill, et al, eds. 176p. (Orig.). 1993. pap. 9.95 (1-882907-04-3) Old Market.
Weston, Martha. Bea's Four Bears. Weston, Martha. 32p. (ps-k). 1992. 9.70 (0-395-57791-8, Clarion Bks) HM.
—Bet You Can't! Science Impossibilities to Fool You. Cobb, Vicki & Darling, Kathy. LC 79-9254. 128p. (gr. 5 up). 1980. 12.95 (0-688-41905-4); PLB 12.88 (0-688-51905-9) Lothrop.
—Bet You Can't: Science Impossibilities to Fool You. Cobb, Vicki & Darling, Kathy. 128p. (gr. 3-7). 1983. pap. 3.50 (0-380-54502-0, Camelot) Avon.
—The Big Beast Book: Dinosaurs & How They Got That Way. Booth, Jerry. LC 87-36206. (gr. 3-7). 1988. 14.95 (0-316-10263-6); pap. 9.95 (0-316-10266-0) Little.
—The Book of Think: Or How to Solve Problems Twice Your Size. Burns, Marilyn. (gr. 5 up). 1976. 15.95 (0-316-11742-0); pap. 9.95 (0-316-11743-9) Little.
—Do You Wanna Bet? Your Chance to Find Out about Probability. Cushman, Jean. 112p. (gr. 3-7). 1991. 14.45 (0-395-56516-2, Clarion Bks) HM.
—The Hanukkah Book. Burns, Marilyn. LC 80-27935. 128p. (gr. 3-7). 1981. SBE 13.95 (0-02-716140-4, Four Winds) Macmillan Child Grp.
—The Hooples' Haunted House. Manes, Stephen. LC 81-2216. 128p. (gr. 4-6). 1981. pap. 11.95 (0-385-28416-0) Delacorte.
—The Hooples' Haunted House. Manes, Stephen. 112p. (gr. 3-7). 1983. pap. 2.25 (0-440-43794-6, YB) Dell.
—Lizzie & Harold. Winthrop, Elizabeth. LC 83-14858. 32p. (gr. k-3). 1985. 12.95 (0-688-02711-3); PLB 12.88 (0-688-02712-1) Lothrop.
—The Long Ago Lake. Wilkins, Marne. 160p. (gr. 4 up). 1990. pap. 7.95 (0-87701-632-1) Chronicle Bks.
—Lucky Me! An Adoption Story. Fairbank, Anna. LC 88-60649. 32p. (Orig.). (ps-1). 1988. pap. 8.95 (0-945436-01-7) Mariah Pr.
—Make It Special: Cards, Decorations, & Party Favors for Holiday & Other Celebrations. Hautzig, Esther. LC 86-8616. 96p. (gr. 3-7). 1986. SBE 13.95 (0-02-743370-6, Macmillan Child Bk) Macmillan Child Grp.
—Math for Smarty Pants: Or Who Says Mathematicians Have Little Pig Eyes. Burns, Marilyn. 140p. (gr. 7 up). 1982. 15.95 (0-316-11738-2); pap. 9.95 (0-316-11739-0) Little.
—The One Dollar Word Riddle Book. Burns, Marilyn. 48p. (Orig.). (gr. 3-8). 1990. pap. 6.95 (0-938587-29-3) Cuisenaire.
—Should You Shut Your Eyes When You Kiss? Or, How to Survive "The Best Years of Your Life" Wallace, Carol M. LC 83-5458. 112p. (gr. 7 up). 1983. 13.45i (0-316-91998-5) Little.
—The Sierra Club Kid's Guide to Planet Care & Repair. McVey, Vicki. LC 91-30307. 96p. (gr. 4-7). 1993. 16.95 (0-87156-567-6) Sierra.
—The Sierra Club Wayfinding Book. McVey, Vicki. 96p. (gr. 4-7). 1991. 14.95 (0-316-56340-4); pap. 7.95 (0-316-56342-0) Little.
—Something for Mom. Sawicki, Norma J. LC 86-34421. 32p. (ps-1). 1987. PLB 12.88 (0-688-05590-7) Lothrop.
—Take a Hike! The Sierra Club Beginner's Guide to Hiking & Backpacking. Foster, Lynne. (gr. 4-7). 1990. write for info. Sierra.
—This Book Is about Time. Burns, Marilyn. LC 78-6614. (gr. 5 up). 1978. pap. 9.95 (0-316-11750-1) Little.
—What Big Teeth You Have! Lauber, Patricia. LC 85-47902. 64p. (gr. 2-6). 1986. (Crowell Jr Bks); PLB 13.89 (0-690-04507-7, Crowell Jr Bks) HarpC Child Bks.
—Word Works: Why the Alphabet Is a Kid's Best Friend. Kaye, Catherine B. 128p. (gr. 4 up). 1985. 14.95 (0-316-48376-1); pap. 7.95 (0-316-48375-3) Little.
Weston, Steve, jt. illus. see Lings, Steve.
Wetmore, Gordon, et al. Love, Dating & Marriage. Eager, George B. LC 86-90552. 136p. (Orig.). (gr. 6-12). 1987. pap. 6.95 (0-9603752-5-2) Mailbox.
Wetzel, JoAnne, jt. photog. see Huberman, Caryn.
Wetzel, Rick. What Do You Eat? Wetzel, Rick. LC 92-61623. 6p. (ps-1). 1993. 3.99 (0-679-83844-9) Random Bks Yng Read.
—What Do You Say? Wetzel, Rick. LC 91-61624. 6p. (ps-1). 1993. 3.99 (0-679-83845-7) Random Bks Yng Read.
Wetzel, Rick & Swanson, Maggie. Big Bird's Bedtime Story. Wetzel, Rick & Swanson, Maggie. LC 87-4764. 32p. (ps-1). 1987. lib. bdg. 5.99 (0-394-99126-5); 2.25 (0-394-89126-0) Random Bks Yng Read.
—Un Cuento Para la Hora De Dormir De Big Bird. Wetzel, Rick & Swanson, Maggie. Guibert, Rita, tr. from ENG. LC 92-3815. (SPA). 32p. (ps-3). 1992. pap. 2.25 (0-679-83500-8) Random Bks Yng Read.
Wexler, Jerome. A Bird's Body. Cole, Joanna. LC 82-6446. 48p. (gr. k-3). 1982. 12.95 (0-688-01470-4); lib. bdg. 12.88 (0-688-01471-2, Morrow Jr Bks) Morrow Jr Bks.
—A Cat's Body. Cole, Joanna. LC 81-22386. 48p. (gr. k-3). 1982. lib. bdg. 12.88 (0-688-01054-7, Morrow Jr Bks) Morrow Jr Bks.
—Cotton. Selsam, Millicent E. LC 82-6496. 48p. (gr. k-3). 1982. 12.95 (0-688-01499-2); lib. bdg. 14.88 (0-688-01500-X, Morrow Jr Bks) Morrow Jr Bks.

—A Dog's Body. Cole, Joanna. LC 85-25885. 48p. (ps-3). 1986. 12.95 (0-688-04153-1); lib. bdg. 12.88 (0-688-04154-X, Morrow Jr Bks) Morrow Jr Bks.
—A Frog's Body. Cole, Joanna. LC 80-10705. 48p. (gr. k-3). 1980. PLB 12.88 (0-688-32228-X, Morrow Jr Bks) Morrow Jr Bks.
—Jack-in-the-Pulpit. Wexler, Jerome. 40p. (gr. 2-6). 1993. 14.99 (0-525-45073-4, DCB) Dutton Child Bks.
Wexler, Jerome, photos by. From Flower to Flower: Animals & Pollination. Lauber, Patricia. (gr. 3-6). 1987. 13.95 (0-517-55539-5) Crown Bks Yng Read.
—A Horse's Body. Cole, Joanna. LC 80-28147. 48p. (gr. k-3). 1981. 13.95 (0-688-00362-1); PLB 13.88 (0-688-00363-X, Morrow Jr Bks) Morrow Jr Bks.
—Mushrooms. Selsam, Millicent E. LC 85-18953. 48p. (gr. 2-5). 1986. 12.95 (0-688-06248-2); (Morrow Jr Bks) Morrow Jr Bks.
—Pet Hamsters. Wexler, Jerome. Tucker, Kathleen, ed. 48p. (gr. 2-6). 1992. PLB 14.95 (0-8075-6525-3) A Whitman.
—Seeds: Pop Stick Glide. Lauber, Patricia. LC 80-14553. 64p. (gr. 2-4). 1988. 12.95 (0-517-54165-3) Crown Bks Yng Read.
—Seeds: Pop Stick Glide. Lauber, Patricia. LC 80-14553. 64p. (gr. 2-4). 1991. lib. bdg. 14.99 (0-517-58554-5) Crown Bks Yng Read.
—A Snake's Body. Cole, Joanna. LC 81-9443. 48p. (gr. k-3). 1981. 12.95 (0-688-00702-3); 12.88 (0-688-00703-1, Morrow Jr Bks) Morrow Jr Bks.
—What Do You See? Lauber, Patricia. LC 93-2388. 1994. 15.00 (0-517-59390-4); PLB 15.99 (0-517-59391-2) Crown Bks Yng Read.
—Wonderful Pussy Willows. Wexler, Jerome. LC 91-32262. 32p. (ps-3). 1992. 14.50 (0-525-44867-5, DCB) Dutton Child Bks.
Wexler, Jerome & Mendez, Raymond A., photos by. An Insect's Body. Cole, Joanna. LC 83-22027. 48p. (ps-3). 1984. 13.95 (0-688-02771-7); PLB 13.88 (0-688-02772-5, Morrow Jr Bks) Morrow Jr Bks.
Weyl, Nancy. Let's Do Fingerplays. Grayson, Marion. LC 62-10217. (ps-3). 1962. 12 95 (0-88331-003-1) Luce.
Wezyk, Joanna. Marushka's Egg. Rael, Elsa O. LC 92-303. 40p. (gr. k-4). 1993. RSBE 14.95 (0-02-775655-6, Four Winds) Macmillan Child Grp.
Wharton, Jennifer H. Broken Wings Will Fly. Blackistone, Mick. 32p. (gr. 2-5). 1992. 10.95 (0-87033-439-5) Tidewater.
—First Sail. Henderson, Richard. 42p. (gr. 3-8). 1993. bds. 15.95 (0-87033-442-5) Tidewater.
Wheaton, Jaya. Harishchandra. Dutta, S. & Hemalata. (gr. 1-8). 1979. pap. 3.00 (0-85744-155-9) Auromere.
—Savitri & Satyavan. Savitri. (gr. 1-9). 1979. pap. 2.75 (0-89744-160-5) Auromere.
Wheele, Stephen. Projects for Autumn & Holiday Activities. Jones, Joan. Young, Richard G., ed. LC 89-17008. 32p. (gr. 3-5). 1989. PLB 15.93 (0-944483-42-9) Garrett Ed Corp.
—Projects for Summer & Holiday Activities. McInnes, Celia. Young, Richard G., ed. LC 89-11791. 32p. (gr. 3-5). 1989. PLB 15.93 (0-944483-39-9) Garrett Ed Corp.
Wheele, Steve, jt. illus. see Smith, Tony.
Wheeler, Cindy. Rose. Wheeler, Cindy. LC 83-19985. 32p. (ps-1). 1985. lib. bdg. 10.99 (0-394-96233-8) Knopf Bks Yng Read.
—That Olive! Schertle, Alice. LC 84-10025. 32p. (ps-1). 1986. PLB 11.88 (0-688-04091-8) Lothrop.
Wheeler, Jodie. A Very Scary Haunted House. Barkan, Joanne. 24p. 1991. pap. 3.95 (0-590-44497-2) Scholastic Inc.
—The Very Scary Jack'O Lantern. Barkan, Joanne. 24p. 1991. pap. 3.95 (0-590-44496-4) Scholastic Inc.
Wheeler, Jody. The City Mouse & the Country Mouse. Aesop. LC 85-70290. 18p. (ps) 1985. 3.95 (0-448-10226-9, G&D) Putnam Pub Group.
—The First Noel. LC 92-14438. 32p. 1992. 13.95 (0-8249-8565-6, Ideals Child) Hambleton-Hill.
—Gift of the Magi. O. Henry. 24p. (ps-3). 1989. pap. 2.95 (0-8249-8388-2, Ideals Child) Hambleton-Hill.
—Home for a Puppy. Gordon, Sharon. LC 86-30853. 32p. (gr. k-2). 1988. PLB 7.89 (0-8167-0978-5); pap. text ed. 1.95 (0-8167-0979-3) Troll Assocs.
—An Old Fashioned Thanksgiving. adpt. ed. Alcott, Louisa May, adapted by. LC 93-20352. 40p. (ps-3). 1993. PLB 14.00 (0-8249-8630-X, Ideals Child); pap. 13.95 (0-8249-8620-2) Hambleton-Hill.
—The Tea Party Book. Penner, Lucille R. LC 91-52093. 48p. (ps-4). 1993. 10.00 (0-679-92440-5); PLB 10.99 (0-679-92440-X) Random Bks Yng Read.
—What a Teddy Bear Needs. Kaye, Marilyn. 26p. 1993. 2.95 (0-7214-3510-6) Ladybird Bks.
—Wild Weather: Tornadoes! Hopping, Lorraine J. LC 92-27947. 48p. (ps-4). 1994. pap. 3.50 (0-590-46338-1) Scholastic Inc.
Wheelhouse, A. V. & Houghes. Ranald Bannerman's Boyhood. MacDonald, George. 347p. (gr. 5 up). 1993. Repr. of 1911 ed. 20.00 (1-881084-13-2) Johannesen.
Wheeling, Darren. Alyndoria: Tales of Inner Magic. Maglione, Robin S. 71p. (Orig.). (gr. k-12). 1986. pap. 12.00 (0-910609-11-X) Gifted Educ Pr.
Wheelwright, Rowland, jt. illus. see Rhead, Louis.
Wheelwright, Sidnee, photos by. Come Back, Salmon: How a Group of Dedicated Kids Adopted a Stream & Brought It Back to Life. Cone, Molly. 48p. (gr. 2-6). 1992. 16.95 (0-87156-572-2) Sierra.

Whelan, Michael, et al. Stormbringer: Fantasy Roleplaying in the World of Elric. 4th ed. St. Andre, Ken & Perrin, Steve. Monroe, John B., ed. 208p. (gr. 8 up). 1990. pap. 21.95 (0-933635-66-4, 2110) Chaosium.
Whipple, Catherine, photos by. Shannon: An Ojibway Dancer. King, Sandra. Dorris, Michael, frwd. by. LC 92-27261. 1993. PLB 19.95 (0-8225-2652-2) Lerner Pubns.
Whipple, Rick. Christopher Columbus. Gleiter, Jan & Thompson, Kathleen. 32p. (gr. 2-5). 1986. PLB 17.96 (0-8172-2643-5); pap. text ed. 9.27 (0-8172-2647-8) Raintree Steck-V.
—Hole-in-the-Day. Kvasnicka, Robert M. Viola, Herman, intro. by. 32p. (gr. 3-6). 1990. PLB 17.96 (0-8172-3405-5); pap. 4.95 (0-8114-4091-5) Raintree Steck-V.
—Kit Carson. Gleiter, Jan & Thompson, Kathleen. 32p. (gr. 2-5). 1987. PLB 17.96 (0-8172-2650-8) Raintree Steck-V.
—Maria Tallchief. Erdrich, Heidi E. LC 92-12256. 32p. (gr. 3-6). 1992. PLB 17.96 (0-8114-6577-2); pap. 4.95 (0-8114-4099-0) Raintree Steck-V.
—Queen Isabella the First. Codye, Corinn. De Varona, Frank, intro. by. (SPA & ENG.). 32p. (gr. 3-6). 1990. PLB 15.96 (0-8172-3380-6); pap. 4.95 (0-8114-6758-9) Raintree Steck-V.
—See You in Heaven. Holmes, Mary Z. LC 91-37283. 48p. (gr. 4-5). 1992. PLB 20.70 (0-8114-3502-4); pap. write for info. (0-8114-6427-X) Raintree Steck-V.
Whitaker, Angela. A Father's Love. Young, David C. 24p. 1993. 14.00 (0-9638833-0-5) Yng & Yng Prods.
Whitaker, Arleen. The Little People. McDowell, Mildred. Harman, Sandra L., intro. by. LC 72-133255. 44p. (gr. 1-2). 1971. 2.50 (0-87884-002-8) Unicorn Ent.
Whitaker, Kate. The Moongift. Higa, Mandy. Weinberger, Jane, ed. 40p. (ps-4). 1994. pap. 9.95 (0-932433-69-3) Windswept Hse.
White, Craig. Clockwise, Vol. One: Quotes on Life. Young, Woody. 50p. (Orig.). 1984. pap. text ed. 4.95 (0-939513-01-3) Joy Pub SJC.
—Clockwise, Vol. Two: Learn to Tell Time. Young, Woody. 48p. (Orig.). 1985. pap. text ed. 4.95 (0-939513-02-1) Joy Pub SJC.
—Moneywise. Young, Woody. 48p. (Orig.). (gr. 1-5). 1986. pap. text ed. 4.95 (0-939513-30-7) Joy Pub SJC.
—One Hundred Plus Craft & Gift Ideas: Fun & Easy Ideas for Any Occasion. Stuart, Sally E. & Young, Woody C. 96p. (Orig.). (gr. 1 up). 1990. pap. 9.95 (0-939513-62-5) Joy Pub SJC.
—One-Hundred Plus Party Games. Stuart, Sally E. & Young, Woody. Dongarra, Kathryn, ed. 96p. (Orig.). 1988. pap. text ed. 7.95 (0-939513-61-7) Joy Pub SJC.
—Smile Wise. Young, Woody. 48p. (Orig.). 1986. pap. text ed. 4.95 (0-939513-21-8) Joy Pub SJC.
—Song Wise, Three: Battle Hymn of the Republic. Young, Woody. 24p. (Orig.). 1986. pap. text ed. 2.95 (0-939513-13-7) Joy Pub SJC.
—Song Wise, Vol. Four: America. Young, Woody. 24p. (Orig.). 1986. pap. text ed. 2.95 (0-939513-14-5) Joy Pub SJC.
—Song Wise, Vol. One: The Star Spangled Banner. Young, Woody. 24p. (Orig.). 1986. pap. text ed. 2.95 (0-939513-11-0) Joy Pub SJC.
—Song Wise, Vol. Two: America the Beautiful. Young, Woody. 24p. (Orig.). 1986. pap. text ed. 2.95 (0-939513-12-9) Joy Pub SJC.
White, Dan. The Flight of the Nez Perce. rev. ed. Schneider, Bill. LC 88-80227. 32p. 1993. pap. 5.95 (0-937959-39-1) Falcon Pr MT.
White, David O. Black Fairy Tales. Berger, Terry, ed. LC 70-75517. (gr. 3-7). 1974. (Atheneum Childrens Bk); pap. 3.95 (0-689-70402-X) Macmillan Child Grp.
White, Flora & Bedford, F. D. Peter Pan. Barrie, James. 304p. (gr. k-5). 1988. Repr. of 1911 ed. 12.99 (0-517-63222-5) Outlet Bk Co.
White, Kenneth R. There Are Trolls. rev. ed. Green, John F. 24p. (gr. k-3). 1975. 7.95 (0-919566-38-3) Peguis Pubs Ltd.
White, Kim, jt. illus. see Herron, Sandra.
White, Lorrain. Trouble Next Door. Apps, Roy. 80p. (ps-2). 1992. 13.95 (0-09-173975-6, Pub. by Hutchinson UK) Trafalgar.
White, Martin & Wright, Joseph. A Second Poetry Book. Foster, John & Curless, Alan. 128p. (gr. 4-6). 1987. 11.95 (0-19-918137-3); pap. 5.95 (0-19-918136-5) OUP.
White, Monica. How the Robin Got Its Red Breast. Green, Belva. Beitler, Stanley, ed. LC 90-80399. 32p. (ps-3). 1990. 12.95 (0-945740-01-8) Indp Pubs.
White, Robert. Wei Wei & Other Friends. Simpson, Louis. 24p. 1990. pap. 25.00x (0-930126-30-0) Typographeum.
White, Susan. Nursery Rhymes in Meher's Time. Irani, Meheru. (gr. 3 up). 1977. pap. text ed. 5.95 (0-913078-29-8) Sheriar Pr.

White, Trevor. Choosing Your Children's Books: Beginning Readers 5 to 8 Years Old. White, Valerie. 32p. (Orig.). (gr. k-3). 1993. pap. 4.95 (1-882726-00-6) Bayley & Musgrave. CHOOSING YOUR CHILDREN'S BOOKS is a series of INEXPENSIVE, EASY-TO-USE guides to the best in children's literature, intended for teachers, parents, grandparents & children. **BEGINNING READERS** is the first in the series, & selects over 100 of the best books ever, for 5 to 8 year-olds. Selections are arranged in themes, such as **EASY READERS, EVERYDAY LIFE & HUMOROUS,** each lightly illustrated. Chosen from the classics, award winners & modern stories for today, each book is identified by title, author, publisher & ISBN number for loan request or purchase. Major awards such as Newbery & Caldecott are identified, & a brief outline of the story is given to help the reader choose. A full author & title index is provided. "A fabulous, concise guide...I am most impressed with the scope - from brand new titles to children's classics. Many multi-cultural authors & stories are included."--KATHLEEN SHELNUTT, Elementary School Media Specialist. "This book makes shopping for books a joy - many great classics, & so easy to find! A great resource."--ANNETTE SAVAGE, Owner of the National Award-winning store THE TOY SCHOOL, Atlanta, GA. Bayley & Musgrave, 4949 Trailridge Pass, Atlanta, GA 30338. (404) 668-9738 or Baker & Taylor. *Publisher Provided Annotation.*

Whitefeather, Willy. Willy Whitefeather's Outdoor Survival Handbook for Kids. Whitefeather, Willy. LC 89-26929. 104p. (Orig.). (gr. 3 up). 1990. pap. 9.95 (*0-943173-47-7*) Harbinger AZ.
—Willy Whitefeather's River Book for Kids. Whitefeather, Willy. 88p. (Orig.). (gr. 1-8). 1994. pap. write for info. (*0-943173-94-9*) Harbinger AZ.

Whitehead, Barbara. Letters to Oma, a Young German Girl's Account of Her First Year in Texas, 1847. Gurasich, Marj. LC 88-38747. 162p. (gr. 4-8). 1989. pap. 9.95 (*0-87565-037-6*) Tex Christian.

Whitehead, S. B. Red Foley's Cartoon History of Baseball. Foley, Red. 96p. (gr. 3 up). 1992. pap. 8.95 (*0-671-73627-2*, Little Simon) S&S Trade.

Whitehead, Sam. Basketball Super Stars. Gowdey, David. 64p. (gr. 1-4). 1994. pap. 8.95 (*0-448-40542-3*, G&D) Putnam Pub Group.

Whitehorse, David. Grandfather's Story of Navajo Monsters. Red Hawk, Richard. (gr.-7). 1988. pap. 6.95 (*0-940113-11-2*) Sierra Oaks Pub.

Whitely, Derek, jt. illus. see Steffen, Ann T.

Whiteside, Rita, jt. illus. see Whiteside, Saundra.

Whiteside, Saundra & Whiteside, Rita. Primary Writing Fun. Whiteside, Sandra & Whiteside, Rita G. 80p. (gr. 1-3). 1983. wkbk. 8.95 (*0-86653-101-7*, GA 461) Good Apple.

Whitethorne, Baje. Monster Birds: A Navajo Folktale. Browne, Vee. LC 92-82139. 32p. (gr. 2 up). 1993. 14.95 (*0-87358-558-5*) Northland AZ.
—Monster Slayer: A Navajo Folktale. Browne, Vee. LC 91-52603. 32p. (gr. k-6). 1991. 14.95 (*0-87358-525-9*) Northland AZ.

Whitfield, Karen. I Didn't Know Cops Did Things Like That. Whitfield, Karen & Tackett, Eric. Hunsinger, Ruth A., ed. 20p. (gr. k up). 1988. PLB 2.95 (*0-943155-03-7*) Laser Tech.

Whiting, Carl. Dizzy Doctor Riddles. Bernstein, Joanne E. & Cohen, Paul. Tucker, Kathy, ed. LC 89-35392. 32p. (gr. 1-5). 1989. 8.95 (*0-8075-1648-1*) A Whitman.
—Oh, How Waffle! Riddles You Can Eat. Mathews, Judith & Robinson, Fay. Levine, Abby, ed. LC 92-13478. 32p. (gr. 1-4). 1992. 8.95g (*0-8075-5907-5*) A Whitman.
—Why Didn't the Dinosaur Cross the Road? And Other Prehistoric Riddles. Bernstein, Joanne E. & Cohen, Paul. Tucker, Kathy, ed. LC 90-12726. 32p. (gr. 2-5). 1990. 8.95 (*0-8075-9077-0*) A Whitman.

Whiting, William T. Wings of Love. Bernet, Elizabeth C. 40p. (ps). 1991. 11.95 (*0-88138-109-8*, Green Tiger) S&S Trade.

Whitlatch, Issac. Me & My Veggies. Whitlatch, Issac. LC 87-2920. 24p. (gr. 1-7). 1987. PLB 14.95 (*0-933849-16-8*) Landmark Edns.

Whitman, Rick, photos by. More Cheers & Chants. rev. ed. Haller, Lynda. 39p. (Orig.). (gr. 3-12). 1988. pap. text ed. 8.00 (*0-685-22930-0*); cassette 6.00 (*0-9614174-5-5*) Cheertime USA.

Whitman, Shirley. Indians in New York State. Job, Kenneth. Whitman, Bernard, ed. 48p. (Orig.). (gr. 4-7). 1989. pap. text ed. 5.00 (*0-918433-01-0*) In Educ.
—New York State Map Skills Resource Guide. Whitman, Bernard. 85p. (Orig.). (gr. 4-7). 1984. tchr's. ed. 18.00 (*0-918433-00-2*) In Educ.

Whitmore, Janice N. A Treasure in the Enchanted Forest. Hughes, Deborah L. Robertson-Boudreaux, Jane, ed. 30p. (Orig.). (gr. 2-4). 1991. pap. 6.95g (*1-879203-03-0*) Metagnosis.

Whitney, Dick. Madugu. Beck, Margaret. 26p. (gr. k-6). 1987. pap. text ed. 5.50 (*1-55976-052-4*) CEF Press.

Whitney, George G. Penn. Vining, Elizabeth J. LC 86-63992. 298p. (gr. 8-12). 1986. pap. 9.00 (*0-941308-06-5*) Phila Yrly Mtg RSOF.

Whitney, Jean. I'm Excited. Crary, Elizabeth. LC 93-85378. 32p. (ps-4). 1993. lib. bdg. 16.95 (*0-943990-92-0*); pap. 5.95 (*0-943990-91-2*) Parenting Pr.
—I'm Furious. Crary, Elizabeth. LC 93-79529. 32p. (ps-4). 1993. lib. bdg. 16.95 (*0-943990-94-7*); pap. 5.95 (*0-943990-93-9*) Parenting Pr.
—I'm Scared. Crary, Elizabeth. LC 93-85377. 32p. (Orig.). (ps-4). 1993. lib. bdg. 16.95 (*0-943990-90-4*); pap. 5.95 (*0-943990-89-0*) Parenting Pr.
—Joe's Earthday Birthday. Scovel, Karen & Hunter, Ted. 32p. (Orig.). (gr. 2-4). 1992. PLB 16.95 (*0-943990-85-8*); pap. 5.95 (*0-943990-84-X*) Parenting Pr.
—What Is a Feeling? Kreuger, David. 32p. (ps-3). 1993. lib. bdg. 16.95 (*0-943990-76-9*); pap. 5.95 (*0-943990-75-0*) Parenting Pr.

Whitney, Roger. A Walk with Christ Through the Resurrection. McAllister, Dawson. (gr. 5-12). 1981. pap. 8.95 (*0-923417-14-1*) Shepherd Minst.
—A Walk with Christ to the Cross. McAllister, Dawson. (gr. 5-12). 1980. pap. 8.95 (*0-923417-09-5*) Shepherd Minst.

Whitney, William S. Microcosm of the Platte: A Guide to Bader Memorial Park Natural Area. Prairie-Plains Resource Institute Staff & Whitney, William S. Whitney, Jan & Twedt, Curt, eds. 140p. (Orig.). (gr. 10-12). 1988. pap. text ed. 10.00 (*0-945614-00-4*) Prairie Plains Res Inst.

Whittaker, Jessica L., jt. illus. see DeLapp, Tom.

Whitten, Jessie. All the Way to China. Pyne, K. D. 16p. (ps). 1993. saddle-stitch 4.95 (*1-882185-06-4*) Crnrstone Pub.

Whitten, Leesa. Gifted & Talented Language Arts. Amerikaner, Susan. 96p. (gr. 1-3). 1993. pap. 3.95 (*1-56565-064-6*) Lowell Hse.
—Gifted & Talented Math Workbook. Spancer, Cookie. 96p. (ps-3). 1992. pap. 3.95 (*0-929923-82-0*) Lowell Hse.
—The Gifted & Talented Math Workbook. Casolaro, Nancy. 96p. (gr. 1-3). 1993. pap. 3.95 (*1-56565-039-5*) Lowell Hse.
—Gifted & Talented Puzzles & Games for Reading & Math. Furlong, Kaye & Casolaro, Nancy. 96p. (gr. 1-3). 1993. pap. 3.95 (*1-56565-065-4*) Lowell Hse.
—Gifted & Talented Reading Workbook. Amerikaner, Susan. 96p. (ps-3). 1992. pap. 3.95 (*0-929923-83-9*) Lowell Hse.
—The Gifted & Talented Reading Workbook. Amerikaner, Susan. 96p. (gr. 1-3). 1993. pap. 3.95 (*1-56565-040-9*) Lowell Hse.

Whittington, Julianne S. Sleep & Dreams. Hobson, J. Allan. Head, J. J., ed. 16p. (Orig.). (gr. 10 up). 1992. pap. text ed. 2.75 (*0-89278-117-3*, 45-9617) Carolina Biological.

Whyte, Mal. North American Wildlife Color & Story Album. Whyte, Mal. 32p. 1972. pap. 4.50 (*0-8431-1735-4*) Price Stern.

Whyte, Mary. Boomer's Big Day. McGeorge, Constance W. LC 93-27273. 1994. 12.95 (*0-8118-0526-3*) Chronicle Bks.

Wiberg, Harald. Christmas in the Stable. Lindgren, Astrid. 32p. 1991. 5.95 (*0-698-20677-0*, Sandcastle Bks) Putnam Pub Group.
—The Tomten. Lindgren, Astrid. LC 61-10658. (gr. 1-3). 1979. 14.95 (*0-698-20147-7*, Coward) (Coward) Putnam Pub Group.
—The Tomten & the Fox. Lindgren, Astrid. 32p. (ps-3). 1989. pap. 5.95 (*0-698-20644-4*, Sandcastle Bks) Putnam Pub Group.

Wiberg, Harold. The Tomten. Lindgren, Astrid. 32p. (ps-3). 1990. pap. 5.95 (*0-698-20680-0*, Coward) Putnam Pub Group.

Wibright, Betsy. I Don't Care. Tauber, Debra. 16p. (Orig.). (gr. 1). 1993. pap. write for info. (*1-882225-14-7*) Tott Pubns.
—We Can Play. McFann, Julia B. 13p. (Orig.). (gr. 1). 1993. pap. text ed. write for info. (*1-882225-15-5*) Tott Pubns.

Wick, Walter. I Spy: A Book of Picture Riddles. Marzollo, Jean & Carson, Carol D. 48p. 1992. 12.95 (*0-590-45087-5*, Cartwheel) Scholastic Inc.

Wick, Walter, photos by. I Spy Funhouse. Marzollo, Jean. Carson, Carol D., designed by. LC 92-16425. 40p. 1993. 12.95 (*0-590-46293-8*) Scholastic Inc.
—I Spy, Mystery: A Book of Picture Riddles. Marzollo, Jean. LC 92-40863. 1993. 12.95 (*0-590-46294-6*) Scholastic Inc.

Wickstrom, Sylvie. Armadillo. Monsell, Mary E. LC 90-19135. 32p. (ps-1). 1991. SBE 13.95 (*0-689-31676-3*, Atheneum Child Bk) Macmillan Child Grp.

—The Christmas Coat. Bulla, Clyde R. LC 89-2380. 48p. (gr. 2-4). 1990. 13.95 (*0-394-89385-9*); PLB 14.99 (*0-394-99385-3*) Knopf Bks Yng Read.
—Five Silly Fishermen: A Step One Book. Edwards, Roberta, retold by. LC 89-42508. 32p. (Orig.). (ps-1). 1989. PLB 7.99 (*0-679-90092-6*); pap. 3.50 (*0-679-80092-1*) Random Bks Yng Read.
—This Old House. Ackerman, Karen. LC 91-20449. 40p. (ps-1). 1992. SBE 14.95 (*0-689-31741-7*, Atheneum Child Bk) Macmillan Child Grp.

Wickstrom, Sylvie K. Wheels on the Bus. 32p. (ps-2). 1988. PLB 11.00 (*0-517-56784-9*) Crown Bks Yng Read.
—Wheels on the Bus. Raffi. LC 87-30126. 32p. (ps-2). 1990. pap. 3.99 (*0-517-57645-7*) Crown Bks Yng Read.

Wickstrom, Thor. The Big Night Out. Wickstrom, Thor. LC 91-46563. 32p. (ps-3). 1993. 13.99 (*0-8037-1170-0*); PLB 13.89 (*0-8037-1171-9*) Dial Bks Young.
—The Carey Street Cat. Hendry, Diana. LC 91-52852. 48p. (gr. 1 up). 1991. text ed. 10.95 (*0-688-10289-1*) Lothrop.
—I'm Not Moving, Mama! Carlstrom, Nancy W. LC 89-38151. 32p. (ps-1). 1990. RSBE 13.95 (*0-02-717286-4*, Macmillan Child Bk) Macmillan Child Grp.
—Kiss Your Sister, Rose Marie! Carlstrom, Nancy W. LC 90-48671. 32p. (ps-1). 1992. RSBE 13.95 (*0-02-717271-6*, Macmillan Child Bk) Macmillan Child Grp.
—Millie & the Mud Hole. Reddix, Valerie. Bodnar, Judit Z., ed. LC 90-21147. 32p. (ps-3). 1992. 14.00 (*0-688-10212-3*); PLB 13.93 (*0-688-10213-1*) Lothrop.
—The Rainbow Watchers. Hendry, Diana. LC 91-52853. 48p. (gr. 1 up). 1991. text ed. 10.95 (*0-688-10305-7*) Lothrop.
—The Rooster Who Lost His Crow. Lewison, Wendy C. LC 93-28059. 1994. write for info. (*0-8037-1545-5*); PLB write for info. (*0-8037-1546-3*) Dial Bks Young.
—When Crocodiles Clean Up. Schotter, Roni. LC 92-10808. 32p. (gr. 1-3). 1993. RSBE 14.95 (*0-02-781297-9*, Macmillan Child Bk) Macmillan Child Grp.

Widdowson, Kay. Brantub the Dancing Bear. Norton, Margaret. 32p. (ps-2). 1992. 15.95 (*0-370-31409-3*, Pub. by Bodley Head UK) Trafalgar.
—Minibeasts: Poems about Little Creatures. Fisher, Robert, ed. 96p. (gr. 2 up). 1992. 13.95 (*0-571-16511-7*) Faber & Faber.

Widener, Bea. Seasons of God's Love: The Church Year. Fogle, Jeanne S. Duckert, Mary J. & Lane, Ben, eds. LC 88-6414. 32p. 1988. pap. 7.99 (*0-664-25032-7*, Geneva Pr) Westminster John Knox.

Wiese, Kurt. Daughter of the Mountains. Rankin, Louise. LC 92-26793. 192p. (gr. 5 up). 1993. pap. 4.99 (*0-14-036335-1*) Puffin Bks.
—The Five Chinese Brothers. Bishop, Claire H. 64p. (ps-3). 1989. pap. 4.95 (*0-698-20642-8*, Sandcastle Bks) Putnam Pub Group.
—The Story about Ping. Flack, Marjorie. (gr. k-2). 1977. pap. 3.99 (*0-14-050241-6*, Puffin) Puffin Bks.
—Story about Ping. Flack, Marjorie. LC 33-29356. (ps-2). 1933. pap. 14.00 (*0-670-67223-8*) Viking Child Bks.

Wiese, Kurt, jt. illus. see Morrill, Leslie.

Wiesner, David. Hurricane. Wiesner, David. (gr. k-3). 1990. 14.95 (*0-395-54382-7*, Clarion Bks) HM.
—June 29, 1999. Wiesner, David. 32p. (ps-3). 1992. 15.95 (*0-395-59762-5*, Clarion Bks) HM.
—Kite Flier. Haseley, Dennis. LC 92-22721. 32p. (ps-3). 1993. pap. 4.95 (*0-689-71668-0*, Aladdin) Macmillan Child Grp.
—Man from the Sky. Avi. LC 92-389. 96p. 1992. 14.00 (*0-688-11896-8*) Morrow Jr Bks.
—Night of the Gargoyles. Bunting, Eve. LC 93-8160. 1994. write for info. (*0-395-66553-1*, Clarion Bks) HM.
—The Rainbow People. Yep, Laurence. LC 88-21203. 208p. (gr. 3-7). 1989. 16.00 (*0-06-026760-7*); PLB 15.89 (*0-06-026761-5*) HarpC Child Bks.
—The Rainbow People. Yep, Laurence. LC 89-21203. 208p. (gr. 3-7). 1992. pap. 3.95 (*0-06-440441-2*, Trophy) HarpC Child Bks.
—The Sorcerer's Apprentice: A Greek Fable. Mayer, Marianna. (gr. 3 up). 1989. 13.95 (*0-553-05844-4*) Bantam.
—Tongues of Jade. Yep, Laurence. LC 91-2119. 208p. (gr. 3-7). 1991. 14.95 (*0-06-022470-3*); PLB 14.89 (*0-06-022471-1*) HarpC Child Bks.
—Tuesday. Wiesner, David. Briley, Dorothy, ed. 32p. (gr. k up). 1991. 15.45 (*0-395-55113-7*, Clarion Bks) HM.

Wiesner, William. Gunniwolf. Harper, Wilhelmina, ed. LC 67-22387. 32p. (ps-3). 1970. 13.00 (*0-525-31139-4*, DCB) Dutton Child Bks.

Wiethorn, Randall J. Rock Finds a Friend. Wiethorn, Randall J. 32p. 1991. pap. 5.95 (*0-88138-110-1*, Green Tiger) S&S Trade.

Wiggins, D. Kevin. The Adventure of Christian Fast. Oakley, Don. LC 88-8001. 279p. (Orig.). (gr. 9 up). 1989. 12.95 (*0-9619465-1-2*); pap. 8.95 (*0-9619465-2-0*) Eyrie Pr.

Wigglesworth, Sheila. Rite Easy from A to Z. Robinson, Lafayette. Gonzalez, Inez, tr. (SPA & ENG.). 48p. (gr. 1-3). 1993. lib. bdg. write for info. (*0-9621081-0-3*) Educ Graphics.

Wijngaard, Juan. Bear. Wijngaard, Juan. LC 90-81897. 12p. (ps). 1991. bds. 3.95 (*0-517-58201-5*) Crown Bks Yng Read.

—Dog. Wijngaard, Juan. LC 90-81895. 12p. (ps). 1991. bds. 3.95 (0-517-58203-1) Crown Bks Yng Read.
—Duck. Wijngaard, Juan. LC 90-81896. 12p. (ps). 1991. bds. 3.95 (0-517-58204-X) Crown Bks Yng Read.
—Emma Bean. Van Leeuwen, Jean. LC 92-29035. 40p. (ps-3). 1993. 13.99 (0-8037-1392-4); PLB 13.89 (0-8037-1393-2) Dial Bks Young.
—Going to Sleep on the Farm. Lewison, Wendy C. LC 91-3737. 32p. (ps-2). 1992. 13.00 (0-8037-1096-8); PLB 12.89 (0-8037-1097-6) Dial Bks Young.
—Hanukkah: The Festival of Lights. Koralek, Jenny. LC 89-8064. 32p. (gr. k-4). 1990. 13.95 (0-688-09329-9); lib. bdg. 13.88 (0-688-09330-2) Lothrop.
—The Nativity. LC 90-5309. 29p. (gr. k up). 1990. write for info. (0-7445-1260-3) Lothrop.
—The Nativity: King James Bible Text. 32p. 1990. 13.95 (0-688-09870-3); PLB 13.88 (0-688-09871-1) Lothrop.
—Sir Gawain & the Green Knight. Hastings, Selina. LC 80-85379. 32p. (gr. 3-7). 1981. 12.95 (0-688-00592-6) Lothrop.
—Sir Gawain & the Loathly Lady. Hastings, Selina, retold by. LC 85-63. 32p. (ps-3). 1987. pap. 4.95 (0-688-07046-9, Mulberry) Morrow.
—Thunderstorm! Tripp, Nathaniel. LC 93-4612. Date not set. write for info. (0-8037-1365-7); PLB write for info. (0-8037-1366-5) Dial Bks Young.
Wik, Lars, photos by. Baby's First Words. LC 84-60700. 28p. (ps). 1985. 2.95 (0-394-86945-1) Random Bks Yng Read.
Wikland, Ilon. The Children on Troublemaker Street. Lindgren, Astrid. LC 91-15647. 112p. (gr. 1-4). 1991. pap. 3.50 (0-689-71515-3, Aladdin) Macmillan Child Grp.
—I Don't Want to Go to Bed. Lindgren, Astrid. Lucas, Barbara, tr. from SWE. 32p. (ps up). 1988. 12.95 (91-29-59066-3, R & S Bks) FS&G.
—I Want a Brother or Sister. Lindgren, Astrid. Bibb, Eric, tr. 32p. (ps up). 1988. 10.95 (91-29-58778-6, R & S Bks) FS&G.
—Lotta's Christmas Surprise. Lindgren, Astrid. 32p. (ps-3). 1990. 13.95 (91-29-59782-X, Pub. by R & S Bks) FS&G.
—Lotta's Easter Surprise. Lindgren, Astrid. Lucas, Barbara, tr. 32p. (ps up). 1991. bds. 13.95 (91-29-59862-1, Pub. by R&S Bks) FS&G.
—The Runaway Sleigh Ride. Lindgren, Astrid. LC 83-23347. 32p. (ps-3). 1984. pap. 11.95 (0-670-40454-3) Viking Child Bks.
Wikland, Ilon, photos by. Mio My Son. Lindgren, Astrid. (gr. 3-7). 1988. pap. 4.99 (0-14-032608-1, Puffin) Puffin Bks.
Wikland, Llon. I Want to Go to School, Too! Lindgren, Astrid. Lucas, Barbara, tr. from SWE. 32p. (ps up). 1987. 10.95 (91-29-58328-4, Pub. by R & S Bks) FS&G.
—Springtime in Noisy Village. Lindgren, Astrid. LC 66-15648. 32p. (ps-3). 1988. pap. 11.95 (0-670-82185-3) Viking Child Bks.
Wikler, Madeline. My Very Own Sukkot Book. Saypol, Judyth R. & Wikler, Madeline. LC 83-26738. 40p. (gr. k-5). 1980. pap. 3.95 (0-930494-09-1) Kar Ben.
Wikler, Madeline & Fishman, Tamar. My Very Own Shavuot Book. Saypol, Judyth R. & Wikler, Madeline. 28p. (gr. k-6). 1982. pap. 2.95 (0-930494-15-6) Kar Ben.
Wikler, Madeline, jt. illus. see Saypol, Judyth R.
Wilber, Ron. Dan Turner, Hollywood Detective: Lights! Camera! Murder! Bellem, Robert L. Mason, Tom, ed. 62p. 1990. pap. 7.95 (0-944735-65-7) Malibu Graphics.
Wilburn, Kathy. Babies. Calmenson, Stephanie. LC 86-81490. 22p. (ps). 1987. write for info. (0-307-12118-6, Golden Bks) Western Pub.
—Bear's New House. Cobb, Annie. 32p. (gr. k-3). 1991. 6.95 (0-671-70397-8); PLB 10.98 (0-671-70393-5) Silver Pr.
—Detective Duckworth to the Rescue. Cobb, Annie. 32p. (gr. k-3). 1991. 6.95 (0-671-70398-6); PLB 10.98 (0-671-70394-3) Silver Pr.
—Going Places Series, 4 vols. Cobb, Annie. (gr. k-3). 1991. Set, 32p. ea. 27.80 (0-671-31248-0); Set, 32p. ea. lib. bdg. 43.92 (0-671-31247-2) Silver Pr.
—Mouse's Birthday Party. Cobb, Annie. 32p. (gr. k-3). 1991. 6.95 (0-671-70396-X); PLB 10.98 (0-671-70392-7) Silver Pr.
—My Favorite Christmas Carols. LC 90-22390. 24p. (ps up). 1991. 2.95 (0-694-00366-2) HarpC Child Bks.
—The Night Before Christmas. Moore, Clement C. 24p. (ps-1). 1985. write for info. (0-307-10202-5, Pub. by Golden Bks) Western Pub.
—Peek-a-Boo! I See You! Phillips, Joan. (ps). 1983. 4.95 (0-448-03092-6, G&D) Putnam Pub Group.
—The Pudgy Book of Babies. 16p. (gr. k). 1984. pap. 2.95 (0-448-10207-2, G&D) Putnam Pub Group.
—Pudgy Pals. 16p. (ps). 1983. pap. 2.95 (0-448-10203-X, G&D) Putnam Pub Group.
—The Pudgy Rock-a-Bye Book. 16p. (ps). 1983. pap. 2.95 (0-448-10206-4, G&D) Putnam Pub Group.
—Squirrel's Treasure Hunt. Cobb, Annie. 32p. (gr. k-3). 1991. PLB 10.98 (0-671-70391-9); 6.95 (0-671-70395-1) Silver Pr.
—Two-Minute Bedtime Stories. Packard, Mary. LC 87-83202. 36p. (ps-1). 1988. write for info. (0-307-12183-6) Western Pub.
Wilcox, Cathy. Andrew Jessup. Hilton, Nette. LC 92-39799. 1993. 13.45 (0-395-66900-6) Ticknor & Fields.

—Boris & Borsch. Klein, Robin. 32p. (Orig.). (gr. k-4). 1993. 16.95 (0-04-442266-0, Pub. by Allen & Unwin Aust Pty AT); pap. 6.95 (1-86373-048-6, Pub. by Allen & Unwin Aust Pty AT) IPG Chicago.
—Emma's Rat-Tastic Adventure. Bernardson, Derek. 96p. (Orig.). (gr. k-4). 1993. pap. 6.95 (0-04-442345-4, Pub. by Allen & Unwin Aust Pty AT) IPG Chicago.
—In the Old Gum Tree: Nursery Rhymes & Verse for Little Kids. Wilcox, Cathy. 48p. (ps-3). 1993. pap. 6.95 (0-04-442216-4, Pub. by Allen & Unwin Aust Pty AT) IPG Chicago.
—A Proper Little Lady. Hilton, Nette. LC 89-35399. 32p. (ps-1). 1990. 12.95 (0-531-05860-3); PLB 12.99 (0-531-08460-4) Orchard Bks Watts.
—The Weird Things in Nanna's House. Mason, Ann M. LC 91-16208. 32p. (ps-1). 1992. 13.95 (0-531-05970-7); lib. bdg. 13.99 (0-531-08570-8) Orchard Bks Watts.
Wilcox, Kelly K. Winnie, the Humpback Whale & Her Second Tale. LaGrange, Lynn M. 40p. (ps-3). 1990. lib. bdg. 10.95 (1-878790-01-3) Fables CO.
—Winnie, the Humpback Whale & Her Second Tale. LaGrange, Lynn M. 38p. (ps-3). 1990. pap. 6.95 (1-878790-04-8) Fables CO.
Wild, Jocelyn. The Animal Parade. King-Smith, Dick. LC 91-30332. 96p. (gr. 1-8). 1992. 16.00 (0-688-11375-3, Tambourine Bks) Morrow.
—No Trouble at All. Thomson, Pat. 28p. (gr. 1-4). 1990. 13.95 (0-575-04577-9, Pub. by Gollancz UK) Trafalgar.
Wilda, Fred. The Rubbers Bros. Comics, Vol. 1, No. 3. Mozeleski, Peter A. Mozeleski, Paul M. & Pinatti, Gloria J., eds. Pagan, Margarita, tr. 16p. (Orig.). (gr. 6-12). 1992. pap. text ed. 0.85 ea. English (1-880058-03-0) Spanish (1-880058-15-4) Rubbers Bros Comics.
Wilde, Carol. The Bells of Freedom. Butters, Dorothy G. (gr. 4-8). 1984. 15.50 (0-8446-6162-7) Peter Smith.
Wilde, G. Story of the Star-Spangled Banner. Miller, Natalie. LC 65-1221. (gr. 2-5). 1965. pap. 3.95 (0-516-44636-3) Childrens.
Wilde, Irma. Baby's Farm Animals. 20p. (ps-1). 1986. bds. 4.95 (0-448-03094-2, G&D) Putnam Pub Group.
Wildman, George. Funny Faces Tracing Fun. Sperling, Anita, et al. 24p. (gr. k-3). 1987. pap. 1.95 (0-590-40889-5) Scholastic Inc.
Wildsmith, Brian. Animal Games. Wildsmith, Brian. (ps-3). 1980. 9.95 (0-19-279731-X) OUP.
—Animal Homes. Wildsmith, Brian. (ps-3). 1980. 9.95 (0-19-279732-8) OUP.
—Animal Shapes. Wildsmith, Brian. (ps-3). 1981. 9.95 (0-19-279733-6) OUP.
—Animal Tricks. Wildsmith, Brian. (ps-3). 1981. 9.95 (0-19-279743-3) OUP.
—Bear's Adventure. Wildsmith, Brian. LC 81-18814. 32p. (ps-2). 1982. 9.95 (0-394-85295-8); pap. 16.99 (0-394-95295-2) Pantheon.
—The Bible Story. Turner, Philip. 142p. 1987. 19.95 (0-19-273104-1) OUP.
—Bible Story. Turner, Philip. 142p. (gr. k up). 1989. pap. 9.95 (0-19-273160-2) OUP.
—The Cherry Tree. Ikeda, Daisaku. McCaughrean, Geraldine, tr. LC 91-22148. 32p. (ps-3). 1992. 15.00 (0-679-82669-6); PLB 15.99 (0-679-92669-0) Knopf Bks Yng Read.
—A Child's Garden of Verses. Stevenson, Robert Louis. 96p. (gr. 1-4). 16.00 (0-19-276032-7); pap. 10.95 (0-19-276065-3) OUP.
—A Christmas Story. Wildsmith, Brian. LC 89-7959. 32p. (ps-3). 1989. 15.95 (0-679-80074-3) Knopf Bks Yng Read.
—A Christmas Story. Wildsmith, Brian. LC 89-7959. (ps-3). 1993. 6.99 (0-679-84726-X) Knopf Bks Yng Read.
—An Easter Story. Wildsmith, Brian. LC 93-25097. 40p. (ps-3). 1994. 15.00 (0-679-84727-8) Knopf Bks Yng Read.
—Goat's Trail. Wildsmith, Brian. LC 86-2731. 40p. (gr. k-3). 1986. 10.95 (0-394-88275-8); lib. bdg. 12.99 (0-394-98276-2) Knopf Bks Yng Read.
—The Hare & the Tortoise. La Fontaine. 32p. 1987. 16.00 (0-19-279625-9); pap. 7.50 (0-19-272126-7) OUP.
—The Hunter & His Dog. Wildsmith, Brian. 32p. (ps-2). 1979. 16.00 (0-19-279725-5); pap. 7.50 (0-19-272147-X) OUP.
—The Lion & the Rat. La Fontaine. 32p. 1987. 16.00 (0-19-279607-0); pap. 7.50 (0-19-272167-4) OUP.
—The Miller, the Boy & the Donkey. Wildsmith, Brian. 32p. (ps-1). 1987. 16.00 (0-19-279652-6); pap. 7.50 (0-19-272114-3) OUP.
—Myths of the Norsemen. Green, Richard L. (gr. 4-6). 1970. pap. 3.50 (0-14-030464-7) Viking Child Bks.
—The North Wind & the Sun. La Fontaine. 32p. 1987. 16.00 (0-19-279610-0); pap. 7.50 (0-19-272168-2) OUP.
—Over the Deep Blue Sea. Ikeda, Daisaku. McCaughrean, Geraldine, tr. from JPN. LC 92-22557. 32p. (ps-3). 1993. 16.00 (0-679-84184-9); PLB 15.99 (0-679-94184-3) Knopf Bks Yng Read.
—Oxford Book of Poetry for Children. Blishen, Edward, ed. 168p. (gr. k-5). 1987. 16.95 (0-19-276031-9) OUP.
—Pelican. Wildsmith, Brian. LC 82-12431. 64p. (ps-2). 1983. lib. bdg. 10.99 (0-394-95668-0) Pantheon.
—The Princess & the Moon. Ikeda, Daisaku. McCaughrean, Geraldine, tr. from JPN. LC 92-148. 32p. (ps-3). 1992. 15.00 (0-679-83620-9); PLB 15.99 (0-679-93620-3) Knopf Bks Yng Read.

—Professor Noah's Spaceship. Wildsmith, Brian. 32p. (ps-3). 1980. 16.00 (0-19-279741-7); pap. 7.50 (0-19-272149-6) OUP.
—Seasons. Wildsmith, Brian. (ps-3). 1980. 9.95 (0-19-279730-1) OUP.
—The Snow Country Prince. Ikeda, Daisaku. McCaughrean, Geraldine, tr. LC 90-24908. 32p. (ps-3). 1991. 15.00 (0-679-81965-7); lib. bdg. 15.99 (0-679-91965-1) Knopf Bks Yng Read.
—What the Moon Saw. Wildsmith, Brian. 32p. (ps-3). 1978. 16.00 (0-19-279724-7); pap. 7.50 (0-19-272157-7) OUP.
Wilgus, David. Here There Be Dragons. Yolen, Jane. LC 92-23194. 1993. 16.95 (0-15-209888-7) HarBrace.
Wilhelm, Hans. Blackberry Ink. Merriam, Eve. LC 84-16633. 40p. (ps-2). 1985. 12.95 (0-688-04150-7); PLB 12.88 (0-688-04151-5, Morrow Jr Bks) Morrow Jr Bks.
—Buzz Said the Bee. Lewison, Wendy. 32p. 1992. pap. 2.95 (0-590-44185-X, Cartwheel) Scholastic Inc.
—David & the Giant. Little, Emily. LC 86-22079. 48p. (ps-1). 1987. lib. bdg. 7.99 (0-394-98867-1); pap. 3.50 (0-394-88867-7) Random Bks Yng Read.
—Don't Give Up, Josephine! Wilhelm, Hans. LC 84-24849. 40p. (ps-3). 1985. lib. bdg. 7.99 (0-394-97244-9) Random Bks Yng Read.
—Funniest Dinosaur Book Ever. Rosenbloom, Joseph. LC 87-7098. 24p. (gr. 1-6). 1987. 12.95 (0-8069-6624-6) Sterling.
—Funniest Haunted House Book Ever! Rosenbloom, Joseph. LC 89-38605. 24p. (gr. 1-7). 1989. 12.95 (0-8069-6818-4); PLB 15.69 (0-8069-6819-2) Sterling.
—Funniest Joke Book Ever! Rosenbloom, Joseph. LC 85-27859. 24p. (gr. k-6). 1986. 12.95 (0-8069-4724-1); PLB 15.69 (0-8069-4725-X) Sterling.
—The Funniest Riddle Book Ever! Rosenbloom, Joseph. LC 84-16192. 24p. (ps up). 1985. 12.95 (0-8069-4698-9); lib. bdg. 15.69 (0-8069-4699-7) Sterling.
—Higgle Wiggle. Merriam, Eve. LC 92-29795. 1994. write for info. (0-688-11948-4); PLB write for info. (0-688-11949-2) Morrow Jr Bks.
—I'll Always Love You. Wilhelm, Hans. LC 84-20060. 32p. (ps up). 1988. 15.00 (0-517-55648-0); pap. 3.99 (0-517-57265-6) Crown Bks Yng Read.
—I'm Tyrannosaurus! A Book of Dinosaur Rhymes. Marzollo, Jean. 32p. (ps-3). 1993. pap. 2.50 (0-590-44641-X, Cartwheel) Scholastic Inc.
—Pancake Pie. Nordqvist, Sven. LC 84-16640. 32p. (ps-3). 1985. 11.95 (0-688-04141-8); PLB 11.88 (0-688-04142-6, Morrow Jr Bks) Morrow Jr Bks.
—Pirates Ahoy! Wilhelm, Hans. LC 87-30197. 40p. (ps-3). 1987. 5.95 (0-8193-1162-6) Parents.
—Pirates Ahoy. Wilhelm, Hans. 48p. (ps-2). 1990. pap. 2.95 (0-448-04340-8, G&D) Putnam Pub Group.
—Ten Little Bunnies. Karin, Nurit. LC 93-13450. 1994. pap. 14.00 (0-671-88026-8, S&S BFYR) S&S Trade.
—Tyrone the Double Dirty Rotten Cheater. Wilhelm, Hans. 32p. (gr. 1-3). 1991. 12.95 (0-590-44079-9, Scholastic Hardcover) Scholastic Inc.
—Wake up! Sun! Harrison, David. LC 85-30053. 32p. (ps-1). 1986. lib. bdg. 7.99 (0-394-98256-8); 3.50 (0-394-88256-3) Random Bks Yng Read.
—Waldo, Tell Me about Christ. Wilhelm, Hans. 40p. (gr. 3 up). 1988. 4.95 (0-8378-1812-5) Gibson.
—Waldo, Tell Me about God. Wilhelm, Hans. 40p. (gr. 3 up). 1988. 4.95 (0-8378-1809-5) Gibson.
—Waldo, Tell Me about Guardian Angels. Wilhelm, Hans. 40p. (gr. 3 up). 1988. 4.95 (0-8378-1811-7) Gibson.
—Waldo, Tell Me about Me. Wilhelm, Hans. 40p. (gr. 3 up). 1988. 4.95 (0-8378-1810-9) Gibson.
Wilhelm, Pamela, jt. illus. see Albertson, Rebecca.
Wilken, Mark. Comprendiendo el SIDA. Lerner, Ethan A. (SPA.). 64p. (gr. 3-6). 1988. 15.95 (0-8225-2000-1) Lerner Pubns.
—The Country Artist: A Story about Beatrix Potter. Collins, David R. 56p. (gr. 3-6). 1989. 14.95 (0-87614-344-3); pap. 5.95 (0-87614-509-8) Carolrhoda Bks.
Wilkensen, Diane. Empowering Teens to Build Self-Esteem. Harrill, Suzanne E. 80p. (Orig.). (gr. 5-12). 1993. pap. 8.95 (1-883648-00-9) Innerworks Pub.
Wilker, Debbie A. Deadly Drugs: An Informative Coloring Book. Wilker, Debbie A. (Orig.). (ps-3). 1990. pap. 5.95 (1-878282-10-7) St Johann Pr.
Wilkerson, Napoleon. The Great Encounter: A Special Meeting Before Columbus. Piercy, Patricia A. 47p. (gr. 1-7). 1991. pap. 5.95 (0-913543-26-8) African Am Imag.
Wilkes, Larry. Fairy Tales from Eastern Europe. Philip, Neil, compiled by. & retold by. 160p. (gr. 4 up). 1991. 19.45 (0-395-57456-0, Clarion Bks) HM.
—Find the White Horse. large type ed. King-Smith, Dick. 1993. 15.95 (0-7451-1804-6, Galaxy Child Lrg Print) Chivers N Amer.
—The King's Egg Dance. Wilkes, Larry. 32p. (gr. k-4). 1990. PLB 18.95 (0-87614-446-6) Carolrhoda Bks.
Wilkin, Eloise. Baby's First Christmas. LC 80-80710. 14p. (ps). 1980. 3.95 (0-394-84575-7) Random Bks Yng Read.
—How Many Kisses Goodnight: Just Right for 2's & 3's. Monrad, Jean. LC 88-6453. 24p. (ps). 1986. 6.00 (0-394-88253-9) Random Bks Yng Read.
—My Goodnight Book. 14p. (ps-k). 1981. write for info. (0-307-12258-1, Golden Bks.) Western Pub.

—My Puppy. reissued ed. Scarry, Patsy. 24p. (ps-k). 1992. write for info. (*0-307-00147-4*, 312-11, Golden Pr) Western Pub.
—Nursery Rhymes. LC 78-64606. (ps). 1979. bds. 3.95 (*0-394-84129-8*) Random Bks Yng Read.
—Poems to Read to the Very Young. Frank, Josette, ed. LC 82-518. 48p. (ps-3). 1982. 7.95 (*0-394-85188-9*) Random Bks Yng Read.
—Rock-a-Bye Baby. LC 84-60029. (ps up). 1984. 5.95 (*0-394-86798-X*) Random Bks Yng Read.
—Three Best-Loved Tales: Play with Me; So Big; The Boy with a Drum. 80p. (ps-2). 1992. write for info. (*0-307-15632-X*, 15632, Golden Pr) Western Pub.
Wilkin, Mike. I Remember When. Aldridge, Ruth. LC 93-26926. 1994. 4.25 (*0-383-03750-6*) SRA Schl Grp.
—My Own Place. Bosworth, Michael. LC 93-27058. 1994. 4.25 (*0-383-03766-2*) SRA Schl Grp.
Wilkins, Janet. Bertha's Garden. Dyjak, Elisabeth. LC 93-28594. 1994. write for info. (*0-395-68715-2*) HM.
Wilkins, Sarah & Mennella, Roxanna. Dolls. Wilkins, Sarah & Mennella, Roxanna. Fisher, Barbara, ed. 27p. (Orig.). (gr. 4-6). 1984. pap. 2.00 (*0-934830-34-7*) Ten Penny.
Wilkinson, Barry. Abena & the Rock: A Story from Ghana. Wilkins, Verna & McLean, Gill, eds. Ramamurthy, Sita, contrib. by. LC 93-12122. 1993. 7.95 (*1-870516-08-7*) Childs Play.
—Five Things to Find: A Story from Tunisia. Wilkins, Verna & McLean, Gill, eds. LC 93-12121. 1993. 7.95 (*1-870516-07-9*) Childs Play.
—Just a Pile of Rice: A Story from China. Wilkins, Verna & McLean, Gill, eds. LC 93-6645. 1993. 7.95 (*1-870516-06-0*) Childs Play.
—The Snowball Rent: A Story from Scotland. Wilkins, Verna & McLean, Gill, eds. LC 93-16156. 1993. 7.95 (*1-870516-09-5*) Childs Play.
Wilkinson, Gerald. Hovercraft. Croome, Angela. (gr. 5 up). 1962. 14.95 (*0-8392-3008-7*) Astor-Honor.
Wilkinson, Sue. Harvey the Hiccupping Hippopotamus. Baker, Tanya & Holm, Carlton. 32p. (ps-k). 1992. lib. bdg. 10.95 with dust jacket (*0-8120-6248-5*); pap. 5.95 (*0-8120-4927-6*) Barron.
—Where Did the Dinosaurs Go? Cast, C. Vance. 40p. (ps-2). 1994. 4.95 (*0-8120-1573-8*) Barron.
—Where Does Electricity Come From? Cast, C. Vance. 40p. (ps-2). 1992. pap. 5.95 (*0-8120-4835-0*) Barron.
—Where Does Oil Come From? Cast, C. Vance. 40p. (ps-2). 1993. pap. 4.95 (*0-8120-1467-7*) Barron.
—Where Does Paper Come From? Cast, C. Vance. 40p. (ps-2). 1993. pap. 4.95 (*0-8120-1468-5*) Barron.
—Where Does Pollution Come From? Cast, C. Vance. 40p. (ps-2). 1994. pap. 4.95 (*0-8120-1571-1*) Barron.
—Where Does Water Come From? Cast, C. Vance. 40p. (ps-2). 1992. pap. 5.95 (*0-8120-4642-0*) Barron.
Wilkon, Josef. Atuk. Damjan, Mischa. LC 89-43728. 32p. (ps-3). 1990. 13.95 (*1-55858-091-3*) North-South Bks NYC.
Wilkon, Jozef. Bonko. Schnell, Robert W. LC 77-99446. 28p. (ps-3). 8.95 (*0-87592-008-X*) Scroll Pr.
—The Brave Little Kittens. Wilkon, Piotr. Graves, Helen, tr. from GER. LC 90-44095. 32p. (ps-k). 1991. 14.95 (*1-55858-103-0*) North-South Bks NYC.
—Flowers for the Snowman. Scheidl, Gerda M. Lanning, Rosemary, tr. LC 88-42532. 32p. (gr. k-3). 1988. 13.95 (*1-55858-068-9*) North-South Bks NYC.
—Hugo's Baby Brother. Moers, Hermann. Lanning, Rosemary, tr. from GER. LC 91-7775. 32p. (gr. k-3). 1992. 14.95 (*1-55858-137-5*); lib. bdg. 14.88 (*1-55858-146-4*) North-South Bks NYC.
—Katzenausflug. Wilkon, Piotr. (GER.). 32p. (gr. k-3). 1992. 14.95 (*3-314-00536-9*) North-South Bks NYC.
—Lullaby for a Newborn King. Wilkon, Jozef & Moers, Hermann. Lanning, Rosemary, tr. from GER. LC 91-11684. 32p. (gr. k-3). 1991. 14.95 (*1-55858-123-5*) North-South Bks NYC.
—Noah's Ark. Wilkon, Piotr. LC 92-2687. 32p. (gr. k-3). 1992. 14.95 (*1-55858-158-8*); PLB 14.88 (*1-55858-159-6*) North-South Bks NYC.
—The Story of the Kind Wolf. Nickl, Peter. LC 87-42923. 32p. (gr. k-3). 1988. 13.95 (*1-55858-066-2*); pap. 4.95 (*1-55858-058-1*) North-South Bks NYC.
—The Tale of the Vanishing Rainbow. Rupprecht, Siegfried P. Lewis, Naomi, tr. from GER. LC 88-43120. 32p. (gr. k-3). 1989. 14.95 (*1-55858-001-8*) North-South Bks NYC.
—Three Little Bears. Bolliger, Max. (ps-3). 1987. 12.95 (*1-55774-006-2*) Modan-Adama Bks.
—Tim, the Peacemaker. Friesel, Uwe. LC 72-145822. 32p. (ps-3). 8.95 (*0-87592-052-7*) Scroll Pr.
—Trois Chatons Intrepides. Wilkon, Piotr. (FRE.). 32p. (gr. k-3). 1992. 14.95 (*3-314-20735-2*) North-South Bks NYC.
—Wipe Your Feet, Santa Claus. Richter, Konrad. LC 85-7246. 24p. (gr. k-2). 1985. 14.95 (*1-55858-016-6*) North-South Bks NYC.
Wilks, Mike. The Ultimate Noah's Ark: Perfect Puzzle for All Ages. Wilks, Mike. LC 93-4021. 80p. (gr. 7 up). 1993. 24.95 (*0-8050-2802-1*) H Holt & Co.
Willard, Michael. Wonders of the Forest. Sabin, Francene. LC 81-7401. 32p. (gr. 2-4). 1982. PLB 11.59 (*0-89375-572-9*); pap. text ed. 2.95 (*0-89375-573-7*) Troll Assocs.
Willard, Nancy. Firebrat. Willard, Nancy. 1992. pap. 3.50 (*0-553-15985-2*) Bantam.
—The Octopus Who Wanted to Juggle. Pack, Robert. (Orig.). (ps-7). 1990. text ed. 13.95 (*0-913123-26-9*) Galileo.

Willard-Chang, Nancy. A Southern Yarn. Richards, R. W. Bogart, Jeffrey, ed. LC 89-92811. (Orig.). 1990. pap. write for info. (*0-9625502-0-5*) Rokarn Pubns.
Willey, Lynne. Time to Get Up. McLean, Gill. LC 93-18114. 1993. 7.95 (*1-870516-11-7*) Childs Play.
—Touch...What Do You Feel? Wood, Nicholas. LC 90-10925. 32p. (gr. k-3). 1991. PLB 11.59 (*0-8167-2126-2*); pap. text ed. 3.95 (*0-8167-2127-0*) Troll Assocs.
Willgoss, Brigitte. Fish Fish Fish. Adams, Georgie. LC 91-43748. 32p. (ps-2). 1993. 13.00 (*0-8037-1208-1*) Dial Bks Young.
Willhoite, Michael. Belinda's Bouquet. Newman, Leslea. 24p. (gr. k-3). 1991. pamphlet 6.95 (*1-55583-154-0*) Alyson Pubns.
—Daddy's Roommate. Willhoite, Michael. 32p. (ps). 1990. 14.95 (*1-55583-178-8*) Alyson Pubns.
—Daddy's Roommate. Willhoite, Michael. 32p. (ps-2). 1991. pap. 8.95 (*1-55583-118-4*) Alyson Pubns.
—Families: A Coloring Book. Willhoite, Michael. 32p. (Orig.). (ps-1). 1991. pap. 2.95 saddle-stitched (*1-55583-192-3*) Alyson Pubns.

Williams, Aaron. Cracks in the Sidewalk: Children's Daily Adventures. Bowman, Crystal. Hartman, Alan G., ed. 128p. (Orig.). (gr. k-8). 1993. 12.00 (*0-9636050-1-1*); pap. 6.00 (*0-9636050-0-3*) Cygnet Pub.
Crystal Bowman is a homemaker, lyricist, & freelance writer. She especially enjoys writing for children & draws from her experience as a mother & former school teacher. When Crystal began sharing her poems with students in the local schools, the response was so positive that she wanted to make her poems available to the students. CRACKS IN THE SIDEWALK is a wonderful collection of these poems that children of all ages & backgrounds will enjoy. These poems address everyday issues such as the hiccups, mosquito bites, vegetables, & bubble gum. The reader will have an opportunity to meet such characters as Charles with snarles, messy Bess, Walter who hates his name, & a unique set of twins named Marilyn May & Mike. CRACKS IN THE SIDEWALK allows the reader to observe life through the eyes of an innocent child. It is warm, sensitive, humorous, & thought provoking. The poems are cleverly written in precise rhythm & rhyme, often with delightful endings. The poems are richly enhanced by outstanding illustrations. The illustrator, a fourteen year old boy, beautifully captures the warmth, humor, & emotions in unique & refreshing drawings. This book will appeal to all children, regardless of age, race or creed. To order: Cygnet Publishing Co., 2153 Wealthy Street, SE #238. East Grand Rapids, MI 49506. *Publisher Provided Annotation.*

Williams, Abbie. Little Talks with God. Dumelle, Grace & Stong, Susantext by. LC 93-2782. 1993. write for info. (*0-937739-17-0*) Roman IL.
—The Lord's Prayer: Explained for Little Ones. Dumelle, Grace. 24p. (Orig.). 1990. pap. text ed. 4.95 (*0-937739-08-1*) Roman IL.
Williams, Bill. Winnie-the-Pooh All Year Long. 14p. (ps). 1981. write for info. (*0-307-12260-3*, Golden Bks) Western Pub.
Williams, Don. Walt Disney's Snow White & the Seven Dwarfs. Balducci, Rita, adapted by. 24p. (ps-k). 1992. pap. write for info. laminated covers (*0-307-10037-5*, 10037, Golden Pr) Western Pub.
Williams, Don & Bailey, Cathy. Disney's Beauty & the Beast: Belle Explores the Castle. LC 92-52971. 18p. (ps-1). 1992. 9.95 (*1-56282-271-3*) Disney Pr.
Williams, Don & Story, Jim. Walt Disney's Cinderella. Grimes, Nikki, retold by. 24p. (ps-3). 1993. pap. 1.95 (*0-307-12684-6*, 12684, Golden Pr) Western Pub.
Williams, Exin R. The Enchanted Cowboy. Findlay, Lois P. Roberts, Anne F., ed. 99p. (Orig.). (gr. 1 up). 1988. pap. 5.00 (*0-317-89520-6*) Libr Commns Servs.

Williams, Garth. Amigo. Baylor, Byrd. 48p. (gr. 1-3). 1989. pap. 4.95 (*0-689-71299-5*, Aladdin) Macmillan Child Grp.
—Bedtime for Frances. Hoban, Russell. LC 60-8347. 32p. (gr. k-3). 1960. 14.00 (*0-06-022350-2*); PLB 13.89 (*0-06-022351-0*) HarpC Child Bks.
—Bedtime for Frances. Hoban, Russell. LC 60-8347. (ps-2). 1976. pap. 4.95 (*0-06-443005-7*, Trophy) HarpC Child Bks.
—Beneath a Blue Umbrella. Prelutsky, Jack. LC 86-19406. 64p. (ps up) 1990. 15.95 (*0-688-06429-9*) Greenwillow.
—By the Shores of Silver Lake. rev. ed. Wilder, Laura I. LC 52-7529. 292p. (gr. 3-7). 1961. 15.00 (*0-06-026416-0*); PLB 14.89 (*0-06-026417-9*) HarpC Child Bks.
—Charlotte's Web. White, E. B. LC 52-9760. (gr. 2-6). 1952. 15.00 (*0-06-026385-7*); PLB 12.89 (*0-06-026386-5*) HarpC Child Bks.
—Chester Cricket's New Home. Selden, George. LC 82-24206. 144p. (gr. 4 up). 1983. 15.00 (*0-374-31240-0*) FS&G.
—Chester Cricket's Pigeon Ride. Selden, George. 80p. (gr. 2-6). 1983. pap. 3.25 (*0-440-41389-3*, YB) Dell.
—Cricket in Times Square. Selden, George. (gr. 2-7). 1970. pap. 3.99 (*0-440-41563-2*, YB) Dell.
—The Cricket in Times Square. Selden, George. LC 60-12640. 160p. (gr. 4 up). 1960. 15.00 (*0-374-31650-3*) FS&G.
—Do You Know What I'll Do? Zolotow, Charlotte. LC 58-7755. 32p. (ps-1). 1958. PLB 13.89 (*0-06-026940-5*) HarpC Child Bks.
—Emmett's Pig. Stolz, Mary. LC 58-7763. 64p. (gr. k-3). 1959. PLB 13.89 (*0-06-025856-X*) HarpC Child Bks.
—Family under the Bridge. Carlson, Natalie S. LC 58-5292. 112p. (gr. 3-7). 1958. PLB 14.89 (*0-06-020991-7*) HarpC Child Bks.
—The Family under the Bridge. Carlson, Natalie S. LC 58-5292. 112p. (gr. 2-5). 1989. pap. 3.95 (*0-06-440250-9*, Trophy) HarpC Child Bks.
—Farmer Boy. rev. ed. Wilder, Laura I. LC 52-7527. (gr. 3-7). 1961. 15.00 (*0-06-026425-X*); PLB 14.89 (*0-06-026421-7*) HarpC Child Bks.
—First Four Years. Wilder, Laura I. Macbride, R. L., intro. by. LC 76-135774. (gr. 3-7). 1971. 15.00 (*0-06-026426-8*); PLB 14.89 (*0-06-026427-6*) HarpC Child Bks.
—El Grillo en Times Square: The Cricket in Times Square. Selden, George. Longshaw, Robin, tr. (SPA.). 160p. (gr. 3-7). 1992. 15.00 (*0-374-32790-4*, Mirasol) FS&G.
—Harry Cat's Pet Puppy. Selden, George. LC 74-12436. 160p. (gr. 3 up). 1974. 15.00 (*0-374-32856-0*) FS&G.
—Harry Kitten & Tucker Mouse. Selden, George. LC 83-16530. 64p. (gr. 2-5). 1986. 14.00 (*0-374-32860-9*) FS&G.
—King Emmett the Second. Stolz, Mary. LC 89-77506. 56p. (gr. 2 up). 1991. 12.95 (*0-688-09520-8*) Greenwillow.
—The Laura Ingalls Wilder Songbook: Favorite Songs from the "Little House" Books. reissued ed. Garson, Eugenia, ed. LC 68-24327. 160p. (gr. 4 up). 1968. 19.00 (*0-06-021933-5*); PLB 18.89 (*0-06-021934-3*) HarpC Child Bks.
—Little Fur Family. special rel. ed. Brown, Margaret W. LC 51-11657. 32p. (ps-3). 1951. 14.00 (*0-06-020745-0*); PLB 13.89 (*0-06-020746-9*) HarpC Child Bks.
—Little House, Boxed set of 5 bks. Wilder, Laura I. (gr. 3-7). 1993. pap. 19.75 (*0-06-440476-5*, Trophy) HarpC Child Bks.
—Little House Christmas Trees: Christmas Stories from the Little House Books. Wilder, Laura I. LC 93-24537. 1994. 14.00 (*0-06-024269-8*, Festival); PLB 13.89 (*0-06-024270-1*, Festival) HarpC Child Bks.
—The Little House Cookbook: Frontier Foods from Laura Ingalls Wilder's Classic Stories. Walker, Barbara. LC 76-58733. 256p. (gr. 4 up). 1979. 15.00 (*0-06-026418-7*); PLB 14.89 (*0-06-026419-5*) HarpC Child Bks.
—Little House in the Big Woods. rev. ed. Wilder, Laura I. LC 52-7525. (gr. 3-7). 1961. 15.00 (*0-06-026430-6*); PLB 14.89 (*0-06-026431-4*) HarpC Child Bks.
—Little House on the Prairie. rev. ed. Wilder, Laura I. LC 52-7526. 336p. (gr. 3-7). 1961. 15.00 (*0-06-026445-4*); PLB 14.89 (*0-06-026446-2*) HarpC Child Bks.
—The Little Silver House. Lindquist, Jennie D. (gr. 2-6). 15.50 (*0-8446-6190-2*) Peter Smith.
—Little Town on the Prairie. rev. ed. Wilder, Laura I. LC 52-7531. 308p. (gr. 3-7). 1961. 15.00 (*0-06-026450-0*); PLB 14.89 (*0-06-026451-9*) HarpC Child Bks.
—The Long Winter. rev. ed. Wilder, Laura I. LC 52-7530. 334p. (gr. 3-7). 1961. 15.00 (*0-06-026460-8*); PLB 14.89 (*0-06-026461-6*) HarpC Child Bks.
—Miss Bianca. Sharp, Margery. (gr. 2-4). 1923. 0.95 (*0-440-45761-0*, YB) Dell.
—The Old Meadow. Selden, George. 192p. (gr. 3-7). 1987. 15.00 (*0-374-35616-5*) FS&G.
—On the Banks of Plum Creek. rev. ed. Wilder, Laura I. LC 52-7528. 340p. (gr. 3-7). 1961. 15.00 (*0-06-026470-5*); PLB 14.89 (*0-06-026471-3*) HarpC Child Bks.
—Over & Over. Zolotow, Charlotte. LC 56-8149. (gr. k-2). 1957. HarpC Child Bks.
—Over & Over. Reissue. ed. Zolotow, Charlotte. LC 56-8149. 32p. (ps-3). 1987. PLB 14.89 (*0-06-026956-1*) HarpC Child Bks.

—Rabbits' Wedding. Williams, Garth. LC 58-5285. 30p. (ps-1). 1958. 15.00 (0-06-026495-0) HarpC Child Bks.
—Ride a Purple Pelican. Prelutsky, Jack. LC 84-6024. 64p. (ps up). 1986. 15.95 (0-688-04031-4) Greenwillow.
—The Sailor Dog. reissued ed. Brown, Margaret W. 24p. (ps-k). 1992. write for info. (0-307-00143-1, 312-08, Golden Pr) Western Pub.
—The Sky Was Blue. Zolotow, Charlotte. LC 62-13328. (gr. k-3). 1963. PLB 14.89 (0-06-027001-2) HarpC Child Bks.
—Stuart Little. White, E. B. LC 45-9585. 132p. (gr. 3-6). 1945. 13.00 (0-06-026395-4); PLB 12.89 (0-06-026396-2) HarpC Child Bks.
—Tela Charlottae. White, E. B. Fox, Bernice, tr. LC 90-55691. (LAT.). 256p. (gr. 2 up). 1991. 18.95 (0-06-026401-2) HarpC Child Bks.
—These Happy Golden Years. rev. ed. Wilder, Laura I. LC 52-7532. 289p. (gr. 5-9). 1961. 15.00 (0-06-026480-2); PLB 14.89 (0-06-026481-0) HarpC Child Bks.
—Three Best-Loved Tales: The Kitten Who Thought He Was a Mouse; My First Counting Book; Home for a Bunny. 80p. (ps-2). 1992. write for info. (0-307-15635-4, 15635, Golden Pr) Western Pub.
—Tucker's Countryside. Selden, George. LC 69-14975. 176p. (gr. 3 up). 1969. 16.00 (0-374-37854-1) FS&G.
—Wait Till the Moon Is Full. Brown, Margaret W. LC 48-9278. 32p. (ps-1). 1948. 15.00 (0-06-020800-7); PLB 14.89 (0-06-020801-5) HarpC Child Bks.
Williams, Harland. Chuckle Mountain. Hunter, Tammy. 64p. (Orig.). (gr. 3-6). 1992. pap. 2.95 (0-88625-280-6) Durkin Hayes Pub.
—My Birthday Book. Vowles, Andrew & Illingworth, Lynn. 32p. (gr. 1-5). 1985. pap. 2.95 (0-88625-061-7) Durkin Hayes Pub.
Williams, Harland & O'Halloran, Tim. My Travel Book. Vowles, Andrew. 32p. (gr. 1-5). 1985. pap. 2.95 (0-88625-063-3) Durkin Hayes Pub.
Williams, Herb. Little Red Hen: La Pequena Gallina Roja. Williams, Letty. LC 78-75684. (ENG & SPA.). (ps-3). 1969. (Pub. by Treehouse); pap. 3.95 (0-13-537894-X) P-H.
Williams, Jack. The Ghosts, Witches & Vampires Quiz Book. Liebman, Arthur. LC 91-23371. 128p. (gr. 3-10). 1992. pap. 4.95 (0-8069-8409-0) Sterling.
—Merlin Book of Logic Puzzles. Edmiston, Margaret C. LC 91-24019. 128p. (gr. 8 up). 1992. pap. 4.95 (0-8069-8221-7) Sterling.
Williams, Jane S. Super Duck: A True Story. Williams, Jane S. Pruett, Robert H., ed. 61p. (Orig.). (ps-4). 1990. pap. 9.95 (0-9627635-0-0) Brandylane.
Williams, Jennie. The Gingerbread Boy. Kassirer, Sue. 24p. (Orig.). (ps-k). 1993. pap. 1.50 (0-679-84795-2) Random Bks Yng Read.
—Jack & the Beanstalk. Lee, Sharon. 24p. (Orig.). (ps-k). 1993. pap. 1.50 (0-679-84794-4) Random Bks Yng Read.
—Ugly Duckling. Andersen, Hans Christian. LC 78-18059. 32p. (gr. k-2). 1979. PLB 9.79 (0-89375-128-6); pap. 1.95 (0-89375-106-5) Troll Assocs.
Williams, Jennifer & Williams, Vera B. Stringbean's Trip to The Shining Sea. Williams, Vera B. LC 86-29502. 48p. (gr. k-3). 1988. 13.95 (0-688-07161-9); lib. bdg. 13.88 (0-688-07162-7) Greenwillow.
Williams, Jennifer H. Scaredy Ghost. Packard, Mary. LC 93-24845. 24p. (gr. k-2). 1993. pap. text ed. 1.50 (0-8167-3246-9) Troll Assocs.
Williams, Jenny. A Bad Week for the Three Bears. Bradman, Tony. LC 91-41871. 32p. (Orig.). (ps-1). 1993. pap. 2.25 (0-679-83379-X) Random Bks Yng Read.
—The Boy with Two Shadows. Mahy, Margaret. LC 87-17160. 32p. (ps-3). 1988. (Lipp Jr Bks) HarpC Child Bks.
—The First Christmas: Bible Stories. Bradbury, Lynne. 28p. (ps-2). 1989. 3.95 (0-7214-5197-7, S846-1 SER.) Ladybird Bks.
—Hugging. Dellinger, Annetta E. LC 84-21505. 32p. (gr. k-3). 1985. PLB 21.35 (0-89565-301-X); PLB 14.95s.p. (0-685-57947-6) Childs World.
—A Lion in the Meadow. Mahy, Margaret. 32p. (ps-3). 1992. 13.95 (0-87951-446-9) Overlook Pr.
—Mousekin's Special Day. Moncure, Jane B. LC 87-11750. 32p. (ps-2). 1987. PLB 21.35 (0-89565-366-4); PLB 14.95s.p. (0-685-67590-4) Childs World.
—Mouse's Adventure in Alphabet Town. McDonnell, Janet. LC 91-47717. 32p. (ps-2). 1992. PLB 14.60 (0-516-05413-9) Childrens.
—Penguin's Adventure in Alphabet Town. Alden, Laura. LC 92-1068. 32p. (ps-2). 1992. PLB 14.60 (0-516-05416-3) Childrens.
—Staying at Sam's. Hessell, Jenny. LC 89-14561. 32p. (ps-3). 1990. (Lipp Jr Bks); (Lipp Jr Bks) HarpC Child Bks.
—Step into Spring: A New Season. Moncure, Jane B. LC 90-30375. 32p. (ps-2). 1990. PLB 19.95 (0-89565-571-3); PLB 13.95s.p. (0-685-56187-9) Childs World.
—This Little Baby. Bradman, Tony. 32p. (ps-k). 1990. 13.95 (0-399-22202-2, Putnam) Putnam Pub Group.
—Understanding. Ziegler, Sandra. LC 88-23745. 32p. (gr. k-3). 1989. PLB 21.35 (0-89565-452-0); PLB 14.95s.p. (0-685-55991-2) Childs World.

—What's So Special about Lauren? She's My Baby Sister. Moncure, Jane B. LC 87-21927. 32p. (ps-2). 1987. PLB 21.35 (0-89565-413-X); PLB 14.95s.p. (0-685-55942-4) Childs World.
—What's So Special about This Fall? I'm Going to School: I'm Going to School. Moncure, Jane B. LC 88-2868. 32p. (ps-2). 1988. PLB 21.35 (0-89565-420-2); PLB 14.95s.p. (0-685-55941-6) Childs World.
—What's So Special about Today? It's My Birthday. Moncure, Jane B. LC 87-21907. 32p. (ps-2). 1987. PLB 21.35 (0-89565-414-8); PLB 14.95s.p. (0-685-55944-0) Childs World.
Williams, Joanna. Picture Word Book Four. 28p. (ps). 1991. 3.50 (0-7214-1437-0, 916-4) Ladybird Bks.
—Picture Word Book One. 28p. (ps). 1991. 3.50 (0-7214-1434-6, 916-1) Ladybird Bks.
Williams, Julie S. Made in Hawaii. Abernethy, Jane F. & Tune, Suelyn C. LC 83-4895. 140p. (gr. 3-12). 1983. pap. 7.95 (0-8248-0870-3) UH Pr.
Williams, Karin. Followers of Jesus. Odor, Ruth S. LC 91-67210. 32p. (gr. 5-7). 1992. saddle-stitch 5.99 (0-87403-393-9, 24-03563) Standard Pub.
—I Heard It from a Little Bird. Shapiro, Arnold. Dudley, Dick, designed by. 12p. (ps). 1991. 12.95 (0-8120-6204-3) Barron.
—Mr. Popper's Penguins: A Pop-Up Book. Atwater, Richard & Atwater, Florence. LC 92-53195. 1993. 16.95 (0-316-05844-0) Little.
Williams, Karin, jt. illus. see Paris, Pat.
Williams, Kent. Getting Your Period: A Book about Menstruation. Marzollo, Jean. Storch, Marcia, intro. by. LC 88-3986. 112p. (gr. 4 up). 1989. 13.95 (0-8037-0355-4); 6.95 (0-8037-0356-2) Dial Bks Young.
Williams, Marcia. Don Quixote. Williams, Marcia, adapted by. LC 92-52995. 32p. (gr. 3-6). 1993. 13.95 (1-56402-174-2) Candlewick Pr.
—The First Christmas. Williams, Marcia. LC 88-1961. 32p. (Orig.). (ps-1). 1988. 4.95 (0-394-80434-1) Random Bks Yng Read.
—Greek Myths for Young Children. Williams, Marcia. LC 91-58733. 40p. (ps up). 1992. 17.95 (1-56402-115-7) Candlewick Pr.
—Joseph & His Magnificent Coat of Many Colors. Williams, Marcia. LC 91-71843. 32p. (ps up). 1992. 13.95 (1-56402-019-3) Candlewick Pr.
Williams, Mark. Enemies. Peterson, Steve & McDonald, George, eds. 24p. (gr. 10-12). 1986. pap. 6.00 (0-915795-51-5, 02) Iron Crown Ent Inc.
Williams, Mark, jt. illus. see Hunter, Marjorie B.
Williams, Mary L. Aaron Goes to the Shelter: A Story & Workbook Guide about Abuse, Placement & Protective Services. Nasta, Phyllis. 37p. (Orig.). (gr. k-6). 1992. pap. text ed. 5.95 (1-880702-00-2) Whole Child.
Williams, Mauri. The Rainbow People. Sims, Claudette E. (Orig.). (ps-5). 1992. pap. 6.95x (0-9616121-1-8) Impressions TX.
Williams, Maya. Empty Masks. Henshall, Barbara E. 32p. (gr. 3-6). 1986. pap. 3.50 (0-936983-00-0) Safari Museum Pr.
Williams, Michele, jt. illus. see Hall, Nancy.
Williams, Richard. The Ghost in Tent Nineteen. O'Connor, Jane & O'Connor, Jim. LC 87-82372. 64p. (Orig.). (gr. 2-4). 1988. lib. bdg. 6.99 (0-394-99800-6); pap. 2.50 (0-394-89800-1) Random Bks Yng Read.
—Herbie Jones. Kline, Suzy. LC 84-24915. 96p. (gr. 2-6). 1985. 13.95 (0-399-21183-7, Putnam) Putnam Pub Group.
—Herbie Jones. Kline, Suzy. 96p. (gr. 3-7). 1986. pap. 3.95 (0-14-032071-7, Puffin) Puffin Bks.
—Herbie Jones & Hamburger Head. Kline, Suzy. 112p. (gr. 2-6). 1989. 13.95 (0-399-21748-7, Putnam) Putnam Pub Group.
—Herbie Jones & the Class Gift. Kline, Suzy. 96p. (gr. 2-6). 1987. 12.95 (0-399-21452-6, Putnam) Putnam Pub Group.
—Herbie Jones & the Class Gift. Kline, Suzy. 96p. (gr. 3-7). 1989. pap. 3.99 (0-14-032723-1, Puffin) Puffin Bks.
—Herbie Jones & the Dark Attic. Kline, Suzy. 112p. (gr. 2-6). 1992. 14.95 (0-399-21838-5, Putnam) Putnam Pub Group.
—Herbie Jones & the Monster Ball. Kline, Suzy. 112p. (gr. 2-6). 1988. 12.95 (0-399-21569-7, Putnam) Putnam Pub Group.
—Herbie Jones & the Monster Ball. Kline, Suzy. 128p. (gr. 3 up). 1990. pap. 3.99 (0-14-034170-6, Puffin) Puffin Bks.
—The Herbie Jones Reader's Theater. Kline, Suzy. 160p. (gr. 2-6). 1992. pap. 8.95 (0-399-22120-4, Putnam) Putnam Pub Group.
—If You Lived at the Time of the Great San Francisco Earthquake. Levine, Ellen. 64p. 1992. pap. 4.95 (0-590-45157-X) Scholastic Inc.
—Lewis & Clark: Explorers of the Far West. Kroll, Steven. LC 92-40427. (gr. 3-7). 1994. write for info. (0-8234-1034-X) Holiday.
—Oh Honestly, Angela! Robinson, Nancy K. 128p. 1991. pap. 2.95 (0-590-44902-8, Apple Paperbacks) Scholastic Inc.
—What's the Matter with Herbie Jones? Kline, Suzy. (gr. 3-7). pap. 3.95 (0-317-62246-3, Puffin) Puffin Bks.
Williams, Robert M. Friends of Frederick Douglass. Gibbs, Carrol R. 23p. (Orig.). (gr. 5-12). 1992. pap. 5.00 (1-877835-50-1); pap. text ed. 3.75 (1-877835-51-X) TD Pub.

Williams, Roger, jt. illus. see Neel, Jennifer.
Williams, Sarah. FACTS & Reasons. Fuller, Rose, et al. 70p. (gr. 10-11). 1993. wkbk. 3.50 (1-880220-07-5) NW Family Srvs.
Williams, Shan. Quacker Meets Mrs. Moo: In Tales from a Duck Named Quacker. Van Shelton, Ricky. 32p. (Orig.). Date not set. pap. write for info. (0-9634257-1-4) RVS Bks.
Williams, Sophy. Moving. Rosen, Michael. 32p. (ps-1). 1993. 12.99 (0-670-84865-4) Viking Child Bks.
—Nana's Garden. Williams, Sophy. 32p. (ps-1). 1994. 14.99 (0-670-85287-2) Viking Child Bks.
—When Grandma Came. Walsh, Jill P. 32p. (ps-3). 1992. 13.00 (0-670-83581-1) Viking Child Bks.
Williams, Sue. Bringing Back the Animals. Kennedy, Teresa. 32p. (gr. 3 up). 1991. lib. bdg. 15.95 incl. dust jacket (0-944256-06-6) Amethyst Bks.
—Tales for Telling: From Around the World. Medlicott, Mary, ed. LC 92-53095. 96p. (gr. k-5). 1992. 16.95 (1-85697-824-9) Kingfisher Bks.
Williams, Tim, et al. The Reading Carnival. Schwartz, Linda. 150p. (gr. 1). 1993. 29.95 (1-884126-01-4); software 49.95 (1-884126-00-6) Digital Theater.
Williams, Travis. Changes. Williams, Travis. Thatch, Nancy R., ed. Melton, David, intro. by. LC 93-13420. 29p. (gr. 6-9). 1993. PLB 14.95 (0-933849-44-3) Landmark Edns.
Williams, Vanessa R. & Washington, Mariama K. Smarty's New Friend. Dennie, Joseph & Weathers, Joseph. Bonnette, Charlotte A., ed. 22p. (Orig.). (gr. k-3). 1993. pap. 6.95 (1-877971-11-1) Mid Atl Reg Pr.
Williams, Vera. A Chair for My Mother. Williams, Vera. Marcuse, Aida, tr. from ENG. (SPA.). 32p. (ps up). 1994. pap. 4.95 (0-688-13200-6, Mulberry) Morrow.
—Home: A Collaboration of Thirty Authors & Illustrators of Children's Books to Aid the Homeless. Rosen, Michael J., ed. LC 91-29125. 32p. (ps-3). 1992. 16.00 (0-06-021788-X); PLB 15.89 (0-06-021789-8) HarpC Child Bks.
Williams, Vera B. A Chair for My Mother. Williams, Vera B. LC 81-7010. 32p. (gr. k-3). 1982. 16.00 (0-688-00914-X); PLB 15.93 (0-688-00915-8) Greenwillow.
—A Chair for My Mother. enl. ed. Williams, Vera B. 32p. (ps). 1993. pap. 18.95 (0-688-12612-X, Mulberry) Morrow.
—Cherries & Cherry Pits. Williams, Vera B. LC 85-17156. 40p. (ps up). 1986. 13.95 (0-688-05145-6); PLB 13.88 (0-688-05146-4) Greenwillow.
—Music, Music for Everyone. Williams, Vera B. LC 83-14196. 32p. (gr. k-3). 1984. 14.95 (0-688-02603-6); PLB 14.93 (0-688-02604-4) Greenwillow.
—Something Special for Me. Williams, Vera B. LC 82-11884. 32p. (gr. k-3). 1983. 16.00 (0-688-01806-8); PLB 15.93 (0-688-01807-6) Greenwillow.
Williams, Vera B., jt. illus. see Williams, Jennifer.
Williamson, Kevin. Heaven How to Get There. 6p. (gr. k-6). 1964. pap. text ed. 2.65 (1-55976-125-3) CEF Press.
Williamson, Kevin, jt. illus. see Bates, Stephen.
Williamson, Tracey. A Child's Book of Prayers. Yeatman, Linda, ed. LC 91-37706. 93p. 1992. 19.95 (1-55670-251-5) Stewart Tabori & Chang.
Williamson, Tracey, jt. illus. see Thatcher, Fran.
Willie, Gutta P., jt. illus. see Hughes, Arthur.
Williges, Mel. Days of Courage: The Little Rock Story. Kelso, Richard. LC 92-12805. 88p. (gr. 2-5). 1992. PLB 21.34 (0-8114-7230-2) Raintree Steck-V.
Willis, Christine. First Day of Spring. Gordon, Sharon. LC 81-2750. 32p. (gr. k-2). 1981. PLB 11.59 (0-89375-531-1); pap. text ed. 2.95 (0-89375-532-X) Troll Assocs.
Willis, Jan. Children's Atlas of World Wildlife. Rand McNally Staff. Fagan, Elizabeth, ed. 96p. (gr. 3-7). 1990. 14.95 (0-528-83409-6) Rand McNally.
Willock, Harry. The Human Body. Miller, Jonathan. Pelham, David, ed. LC 83-80311. 1983. pap. 22.50 (0-670-38605-7, Studio) Viking Child Bks.
Willow. Babies' Hotel. Hoffman, Mary. 32p. (ps-1). 1993. pap. 8.95 (0-460-88091-8, Pub. by J M Dent & Sons) Trafalgar.
—Happy Birthday: Nine Birthday Stories. Fleetwood, Jennie. 96p. (gr. 2-4). 1993. 16.95 (0-460-88050-0, Pub. by J M Dent & Sons) Trafalgar.
Wills, Jan. Rand McNally Children's Atlas of World Wildlife. Fagan, Elizabeth G. LC 93-503. 1993. write for info. (0-528-83581-5) Rand McNally.
Wilsdorf, Anne. Jack & the Beanstalk: Retold in Verse for Boys & Girls to Read Themselves. De Regniers, Beatrice S. LC 89-18663. 48p. (ps-2). 1990. pap. 4.95 (0-689-71421-1, Aladdin) Macmillan Child Grp.
—Jack the Giant Killer. De Regniers, Beatrice S. LC 86-3606. 32p. (gr. k-3). 1987. 13.95 (0-689-31218-0, Atheneum Child Bk) Macmillan Child Grp.
—Woodcutter's Coat. Wolff, Ferida. (ps-3). 1992. 15.95 (0-316-95048-3, Joy St Bks) Little.
Wilson, Ann. Baby Fozzie Goes Camping. Muntean, Michaela. 26p. (ps up). 1987. 12.95 (1-55578-604-9) Worlds Wonder.
—The Fox in the Farmyard. Katz, Bobbi & Moseley, Keith. 14p. (ps-3). 1986. 5.95 (0-394-87428-5) Random Bks Yng Read.
—The Muppet Babies in Let's Imagine...The Missing Toy's Adventure. Barkan, Joanne, et al. 26p. (ps up). 1987. pap. 14.95 (1-55578-805-X) Worlds Wonder.
Wilson, Ann, jt. illus. see Kennedy, Anne.

Wilson, April. Look Again! The Second Ultimate Spot-the-Difference Book. Wood, A. J., notes by. LC 91-31214. 40p. (gr. 1 up). 1992. 13.00 (*0-8037-0958-7*) Dial Bks Young.
—Look! The Ultimate Spot-the-Difference Book. Wood, A. J. 40p. (gr. 1 up). 1993. pap. 4.99 (*0-14-054879-3*, Puffin Pied Piper) Puffin Bks.
Wilson, Bennett. The Magic Feather: An Adventure in Navajo Land. Wilson, Bennett. 42p. (Orig.). (gr. 1-6). 1989. pap. 5.00 (*0-918080-48-7*) Treasure Chest.
Wilson, Bill. If I Were a Boston Celtic. D'Andrea, Joseph C. 24p. (Orig.). (gr. k-5). Date not set. pap. 5.95 (*1-878338-45-5*) Picture Me Bks.
—If I Were a Buffalo Bill. D'Andrea, Joseph C. 24p. (Orig.). 1993. pap. 5.95 (*1-878338-51-X*) Picture Me Bks.
—If I Were a Charlotte Hornet. D'Andrea, Joseph C. 24p. (Orig.). (ps-5). Date not set. pap. 5.95 (*1-878338-49-8*) Picture Me Bks.
—If I Were a Chicago Bull. D'Andrea, Joseph C. 24p. (Orig.). (ps-5). Date not set. pap. 5.95 (*1-878338-42-0*) Picture Me Bks.
—If I Were a Chicago Cub. D'Andrea, Joseph C. 28p. (ps-5). pap. 5.95 (*1-878338-14-5*) Picture Me Bks.
—If I Were a Chicago White Sox. D'Andrea, Joseph C. 28p. (ps-5). pap. 5.95 (*1-878338-15-3*) Picture Me Bks.
—If I Were a Cleveland Cavalier. D'Andrea, Joseph C. 24p. (Orig.). (ps-5). Date not set. pap. 5.95 (*1-878338-50-1*) Picture Me Bks.
—If I Were a Colorado Rockie. D'Andrea, Joseph C. 28p. (ps-5). pap. 5.95 (*1-878338-20-X*) Picture Me Bks.
—If I Were a Florida Marlin. D'Andrea, Joseph C. 28p. (ps-5). pap. 5.95 (*1-878338-21-8*) Picture Me Bks.
—If I Were a Kansas City Chief. D'Andrea, Joseph C. 24p. (Orig.). (ps-5). 1993. pap. 5.95 (*1-878338-52-8*) Picture Me Bks.
—If I Were a Los Angeles Dodger. D'Andrea, Joseph C. 28p. (ps-5). pap. 5.95 (*1-878338-16-1*) Picture Me Bks.
—If I Were a Los Angeles Laker. D'Andrea, Joseph C. 24p. (Orig.). (ps-5). Date not set. pap. 5.95 (*1-878338-44-7*) Picture Me Bks.
—If I Were a New York Knick. D'Andrea, Joseph C. 24p. (Orig.). (ps-5). Date not set. pap. 5.95 (*1-878338-43-9*) Picture Me Bks.
—If I Were a New York Yankee. D'Andrea, Joseph C. 28p. (ps-5). pap. 5.95 (*1-878338-18-8*) Picture Me Bks.
—If I Were a Phoenix Sun. D'Andrea, Joseph C. 24p. (Orig.). (ps-5). Date not set. pap. 5.95 (*1-878338-46-3*) Picture Me Bks.
—If I Were a San Antonio Spur. D'Andrea, Joseph C. 24p. (Orig.). (ps-5). Date not set. pap. 5.95 (*1-878338-48-X*) Picture Me Bks.
—If I Were a Toronto Blue Jay. D'Andrea, Joseph C. 28p. (ps-5). pap. 5.95 (*1-878338-25-0*) Picture Me Bks.
—If I Were an Atlanta Brave. D'Andrea, Joseph C. 28p. (ps-5). pap. 5.95 (*1-878338-17-X*) Picture Me Bks.
—If I Were an Oakland Athletic. D'Andrea, Joseph C. 28p. (ps-5). pap. 5.95 (*1-878338-19-6*) Picture Me Bks.
—If I Were an Orlando Magic. D'Andrea, Joseph C. 24p. (Orig.). (ps-5). Date not set. pap. 5.95 (*1-878338-47-1*) Picture Me Bks.
Wilson, Craig, jt. illus. see Pegoda, Dan.
Wilson, Dagmar. Gertie the Duck. Georgiady, Nicholas P. & Romano, Louis G. (gr. 1-3). 1982. lib. ed. 2.97 (*0-695-43363-6*); pap. 1.50 (*0-685-10942-9*) Follett Pr.
Wilson, Dagmar W. Casey, the Utterly Impossible Horse. Feagles, Anita. LC 88-13871. 96p. (gr. 3-7). 1989. Repr. of 1960 ed. lib. bdg. 16.00 (*0-208-02239-2*, Linnet) Shoe String.
—Poems to Read to the Very Young. Frank, Josette, ed. LC 87-23234. 32p. (in-p.). 1988. pap. 2.25 (*0-394-89768-4*) Random Bks Yng Read.
—Trudi La Cane. Georgiady, Nicholas P. & Romano, Louis G. Thorne, Patrice, tr. 32p. (gr. 1-4). 1982. pap. 5.00 (*0-317-05572-0*) Argee Pubs.
—Trudi La Cane. Georgiady, Nicholas P. & Romano, Louis G. Thorne, Patrice, tr. from ENG. (FRE.). 27p. (gr. k-4). pap. 5.00 (*0-317-03037-X*) Argee Pubs.
—Tulita la Patita. Georgiady, Nicholas P. & Romano, Louis G. De Ninojosa, Ida N., tr. 32p. (gr. 1-4). 1984. pap. 3.00 (*0-317-03352-2*) Argee Pubs.
Wilson, Deborah. Grandfather Woo Goes to School. Collins, David R. McKissack, Patricia & McKissack, Fredrick, eds. LC 88-60389. 32p. (Orig.). (gr. 1-3). 1990. text ed. 8.95 (*0-88335-784-4*); pap. text ed. 4.95 (*0-88335-796-8*) Milliken Pub Co.
—The Locked-In Friend. Fryar, Jane. 32p. (ps-2). 1991. 7.99 (*0-570-04195-3*) Concordia.
—Lost at the Mall: Morris the Mouse Adventure Ser. Fryar, Jane. 32p. (ps-1). 1991. 7.99 (*0-570-04196-1*, 56-1655) Concordia.
—The Wisest Answer. Collins, David R. McKissack, Patricia & McKissack, Fredrick, eds. LC 87-61640. 32p. (Orig.). (gr. 1-3). text ed. 8.95 (*0-88335-731-3*); pap. text ed. 4.95 (*0-88335-751-8*) Milliken Pub Co.
Wilson, Deborah G. Danger for Old Ruff. Seek, Vesta. 32p. (ps-2). 1991. pap. 4.49 (*1-55513-360-6*, 33605, Chariot Bks) Cook.
—Old Ruff & the Mother Bird. Seek, Vesta. 32p. (ps-2). 1991. pap. 4.49 (*1-55513-361-4*, 33613, Chariot Bks) Cook.

Wilson, Dick. What Am I Doing in a Step-Family? Berman, Claire G. 48p. (gr. 2 up). 1982. 12.00 (*0-8184-0325-X*) Carol Pub Group.
—What Am I Doing in a Stepfamily? Berman, Claire. (gr. k-7). 1992. pap. 8.95 (*0-8184-0563-5*, L Stuart) Carol Pub Group.
—Why Am I Going to the Hospital? Ciliotta, Claire & Livingston, Carole. (gr. k-7). 1992. pap. 8.95 (*0-8184-0568-6*, L Stuart) Carol Pub Group.
Wilson, Forrest. What It Feels Like to Be a Building. rev. ed. Wilson, Forrest. LC 88-22382. 80p. (gr. 2 up). 1988. pap. 10.95 (*0-89133-147-6*) Preservation Pr.
Wilson, Grant. Standin' Tall Courage. Brady, Janeen. 22p. (Orig.). (ps-6). 1982. pap. text ed. 1.50 activity bk. (*0-944803-43-1*); cassette & bk. 8.95 (*0-944803-45-8*) Brite Intl.
—Standin' Tall Gratitude. Brady, Janeen & Woolley, Diane. 22p. (Orig.). (ps-6). 1982. pap. text ed. 1.50 activity bk. (*0-944803-48-2*); cassette & bk. 8.95 (*0-944803-49-0*) Brite Intl.
—Standin' Tall Happiness. Brady, Janeen & Woolley, Diane. 22p. (Orig.). (ps-6). 1982. pap. text ed. 1.50 activity bk. (*0-944803-46-6*); cassette & bk. 8.95 (*0-944803-47-4*) Brite Intl.
—Standin' Tall Love. Brady, Janeen & Woolley, Diane. 22p. (Orig.). (ps-6). 1982. pap. text ed. 1.50 activity bk. (*0-944803-50-4*); cassette & bk. 8.95 (*0-944803-51-2*) Brite Intl.
—Standin' Tall Self-Esteem. Brady, Janeen & Woolley, Diane. 22p. (Orig.). (ps-6). 1984. pap. text ed. 1.50 activity bk. (*0-944803-56-3*); cassette & bk. 8.95 (*0-944803-57-1*) Brite Intl.
—Standin' Tall Service. Brady, Janeen & Woolley, Diane. 22p. (Orig.). (ps-6). 1984. pap. text ed. 1.50 activity bk. (*0-944803-52-0*); cassette & bk. 8.95 (*0-944803-53-9*) Brite Intl.
Wilson, Grant & Galloway, Neil. Standin' Tall Forgiveness. Brady, Janeen. 22p. (Orig.). (ps-6). 1981. pap. text ed. 1.50 activity bk. (*0-944803-39-3*); cassette & bk. 8.95 (*0-944803-40-7*) Brite Intl.
—Standin' Tall Honesty. Brady, Janeen. 22p. (Orig.). (ps-6). 1981. pap. text ed. 1.50 activity bk. (*0-944803-37-7*); cassette & bk. 8.95 (*0-944803-38-5*) Brite Intl.
—Standin' Tall Obedience. Brady, Janeen. 22p. (Orig.). (ps-6). 1981. pap. text ed. 1.50 activity bk. (*0-944803-35-0*); cassette & bk. 8.95 (*0-944803-36-9*) Brite Intl.
—Standin' Tall Work. Brady, Janeen. 22p. (Orig.). (ps-6). 1981. pap. text ed. 1.50 activity bk. (*0-944803-41-5*); cassette & bk. 8.95 (*0-944803-42-3*) Brite Intl.
Wilson, J. Kay. Brian Robertson's Favorite Texas Tales. Robertson, Brian. LC 92-17115. 112p. (gr. 4-7). 1992. 12.95 (*0-89015-862-2*) Eakin-Sunbelt.
Wilson, James P. The Hardest Thing about Going to School. Winston, Barbara F. (Orig.). (gr. k-5). 1987. pap. text ed. 3.95 (*0-9622810-0-X*) B Winston.
Wilson, Janet. Benny & the No-Good Teacher. Zach, Cheryl. LC 91-30588. 80p. (gr. 2-6). 1992. SBE 12.95 (*0-02-793706-2*, Bradbury Pr) Macmillan Child Grp.
—Daniel's Dog. Bogart, Jo-Ellen. 1992. pap. 3.95 (*0-590-43401-2*, Blue Ribbon Bks) Scholastic Inc.
—Gopher Takes Heart. Scribner, Virginia. LC 92-25939. 128p. (gr. 3-7). 1993. 13.99 (*0-670-84839-5*) Viking Child Bks.
—How to Be Cool in the Third Grade. Duffey, Betsy. 80p. (gr. 2-5). 1993. 12.99 (*0-670-84798-4*) Viking Child Bks.
—Jess Was the Brave One. Little, Jean. 32p. (ps-3). 1992. 13.95 (*0-670-83495-5*) Viking Child Bks.
—The Math Wiz. Duffey, Betsy. 80p. (gr. 2-5). 1993. pap. 3.99 (*0-14-034477-2*) Puffin Bks.
—The Nightingale: European Folk Tales. Andersen, Hans Christian. (ps-2). 1992. pap. 3.50 (*0-88625-284-9*) Durkin Hayes Pub.
—Revenge of the Small Small. Little, Jean. 32p. (ps-3). 1993. 14.00 (*0-670-84471-3*) Viking Child Bks.
—Tiger Flowers. Quinlan, Patricia. LC 93-15214. Date not set. write for info. (*0-8037-1407-6*); PLB write for info. (*0-8037-1408-4*) Dial Bks Young.
Wilson, Jo K. Sarah's Flag for Texas. Knapik, Jane A. LC 93-16117. (gr. 3-6). 1993. 12.95 (*0-89015-900-9*) Eakin-Sunbelt.
Wilson, John. Malcolm X. Adoff, Arnold. LC 85-42974. 40p. (gr. 2-5). 1985. pap. 5.95 (*0-06-446015-0*, Trophy) HarpC Child Bks.
—Malcolm X. Adoff, Arnold. LC 70-94787. 48p. (gr. 2-5). 1970. PLB 14.89 (*0-690-51414-X*, Crowell Jr Bks) HarpC Child Bks.
Wilson, Karen. Story Clay. Murphy, Lois. 8p. (gr. 1-8). 1990. pap. write for info. (*0-9620672-0-2*) Dragon Studio.

Wilson, Kathleen A. The Rebellion of Humans. Anderson, David A. & Sankofa. 32p. 1993. 18.95 (*0-9629978-6-2*) Sights Prods.
This book, the second in a trilogy of African creation & early mythology, starts where the 1992 African Studies Association African Children's Book Award Winner, THE ORIGIN OF LIFE ON EARTH ends. The narrative tells of humankind's loss of respect for

---

life & its responsibilities, & of the calamities that befall civilization as a result. The story centers on the struggle of one Yoruban individual who attains awareness & ponders how to transmit his knowledge to others. This volume continues the ORIGIN OF LIFE ON EARTH's (ISBN 0-9629978-5-4, $18.95) focus, about which the SCHOOL LIBRARY JOURNAL said, "This story's themes of determination, effort, generosity & the sacredness of life, as well as the attractive art, extend its appeal beyond myth, religion or ethnic collections." Volume discounts available from the publisher. ISBN 0-9629978-6-2, $18.95, SIGHTS PRODUCTIONS, P.O. Box 101, Mt. Airy, MD 21771. Telephone: 410-795-4582; FAX: 301-829-2585. *Publisher Provided Annotation.*

Wilson, Kay. The Many Adventures of Minnie. Hart, Jan S. LC 92-17740. 96p. (gr. 4-7). 1992. 12.95 (*0-89015-859-2*) Eakin-Sunbelt.
Wilson, Krista. Mr. Farmer & His Animals. Mason, Judy S. Scoggan, Nita, ed. Shaw, Gwen, intro. by. 52p. (Orig.). (gr. 3 up). 1987. pap. 3.95 (*0-910487-11-1*) Royalty Pub.
Wilson, Lillian. Daniel Hale Williams: Surgeon. Thompson-Peters, Flossie E. 32p. (Orig.). (gr. 3-9). 1988. pap. 4.70 (*1-880784-05-X*) Atlas Pr.
Wilson, Lillian M. Harriet Tubman: Freedom Fighter. Thompson-Peters, Flossie E. 32p. (Orig.). (gr. 3-9). 1988. pap. 4.70 (*1-880784-04-1*) Atlas Pr.
Wilson, Lynn, et al. I Can Do Gymnastics: Essential Skills for Beginning Gymnasts. United States Gymnastics Federation Staff. Feeney, Rik, intro. by. LC 92-2441. 144p. (Orig.). (gr. 1-5). 1993. pap. 14.95 (*0-940279-51-7*) Masters Pr IN.
Wilson, Mark. The Bone Tree. Bacon, Ron. LC 93-20806. 1994. 4.25 (*0-383-03738-7*) SRA Schl Grp.
Wilson, Mike. Black Wallstreet Children's Storybook: A Black City Made of Gold! Wallace, Latressia & Wilson, Annette. Wilson, Jay J. & Wallace, Ron, eds. 32p. (Orig.). (ps-5). 1993. pap. text ed. 8.95 (*1-884265-02-2*) Black Wallst.
Wilson, Patricia. Animal Stories. DeGroat, Florence. 88p. (gr. 2-6). 1983. pap. 2.95 (*0-87516-509-5*) DeVorss.
—A Fairy's Workday. Degroat, Florence. 65p. (gr. 1-6). 1983. pap. 2.25 (*0-87516-508-7*) DeVorss.
Wilson, Phil. Disney's the Prince & the Pauper. Slater, Teddy. LC 92-56165. 48p. 1993. 12.95 (*1-56282-511-9*); PLB 12.89 (*1-56282-512-7*) Disney Pr.
—Walt Disney's Mickey & the Beanstalk. Slater, Teddy, adapted by. 48p. 1993. 12.95 (*1-56282-385-X*); PLB 12.89 (*1-56282-386-8*) Disney Pr.

Wilson, Richard C. Caz & His Cat: Now We Like the Night. Wilson, Jean A. 32p. 1994. 14.95 (*0-685-68122-X*) Wahr.
What does a 4-year old think about in bed after the lights are out? Watch this observant 4-year old with his cat (apparent at first only by a tail sticking out from under the bed) use a bed & a window to come up with the solution to his fears of the night. In her third book of verses for young children, Jean A. Wilson introduces Caz & his cat & takes the reader into the mind of a young child who uses what he calls his "thinking time" after he's in bed to solve being afraid in the dark. His progress is echoed by the gradual emergence of the cat until both cat & child are fully apparent to the reader, led by Ms. Wilson's sensitive verses. Both Jean Wilson, who writes the verses, & her husband Richard Wilson, who illustrated the book, know their 4-year olds, & deal with Caz's fears with knowledge, warmth & humor, allowing him to come up with his own answer to his problem. He does, with brilliance-- no pun intended. Watch Caz deal with what's in the room, what's "out there,"

until he's comfortable with his own solution. And so is the cat. From George Wahr Publishing Company, 304-1/2 S. State, Ann Arbor, MI 48104, (313) 668-6097/(800) 805-2497. *Publisher Provided Annotation.*

Wilson, Roberta. Patrick's Tree House. Kroll, Steven. LC 93-4571. 64p. (gr. 2-5). 1994. RSBE 13.95 (0-02-751005-0, Macmillan Child Bk) Macmillan Child Grp.

Wilson, Roger B. Going Bananas: Jokes for Kids. Keller, Charles, compiled by. (gr. 2-5). 1977. 8.95 (0-13-357772-4, Pub. by Treehouse); pap. 3.95 (0-13-357780-5) P-H.

Wilson, Rosemary. Stickybeak. Edwards, Hazel. Sherwood, Rhoda, ed. LC 88-42915. 32p. (gr. 2-3). 1988. PLB 18.60 (1-55532-932-2) Gareth Stevens Inc.

Wilson, Sarah. Beware the Dragons! Wilson, Sarah. LC 85-42164. 32p. (ps-3). 1988. pap. 4.95 (0-06-443186-X, Trophy) HarpC Child Bks.

—Muskrat, Muskrat, Eat Your Peas! Wilson, Sarah. LC 88-29742. (ps). 1992. pap. 13.95 jacketed (0-671-67515-X, S&S BFYR); pap. 3.95 (0-671-77822-6, S&S BFYR) S&S Trade.

—Sledding. Winthrop, Elizabeth. LC 89-1761. 32p. (ps-2). 1989. PLB 13.89 (0-06-026566-3) HarpC Child Bks.

Wilson, Shelby. Jenny Giraffe Discovers the French Quarter. Dartez, Cecilia C. LC 90-48720. 32p. (ps-8). 1991. 12.95 (0-88289-819-1) Pelican.

Wilson, Tom. Ziggy's Christmas Book Level 1. Smith, Lani. 32p. (gr. 1). 1991. pap. 5.95 (0-89328-112-3) Lorenz Corp.

—Ziggy's Christmas Book Level 2. Smith, Lani. 32p. (Orig.). 1991. pap. 5.95 (0-89328-113-1) Lorenz Corp.

Wilson, Towana E. Sam, a Cocker: Sam & His Country Home. Wilson, Towana E. LC 90-87585. (Orig.). (gr. 7 up). 1990. pap. 5.00 (0-9623607-1-6) BRAT Pubns.

—Sam, a Cocker: Sam & the Periwinkles. Wilson, Towana E. LC 90-83106. (Orig.). (gr. 7 up). 1990. pap. 5.00 (0-9623607-2-4) BRAT Pubns.

—Sam a Cocker: Same Goes Home. Wilson, Towana E. LC 89-92115. 24p. (Orig.). (gr. 5 up). 1989. pap. 5.00 (0-9623607-0-8) BRAT Pubns.

Wilson-Heaney, Kathyrn. Teddy Bear's Are Special Friends: Little Treasure Book. Wolf, Jill. 24p. (gr. 3-7). 1985. pap. 2.50 (0-89954-466-5) Antioch Pub Co.

Wimer, Rodney. Adventures of Blaze. Tell, Paul. LC 92-80452. 64p. (gr. 2-6). 1992. PLB 12.95 (1-878893-19-X); pap. 5.95 (1-878893-18-1) Telcraft Bks.

—African Tales: Folklore of the Central African Republic. Strong, Polly. Strong, Polly, tr. from SAG. LC 91-66693. 96p. (gr. 2 up). 1992. 10.95 (1-878893-15-7); pap. 6.95 (1-878893-14-9) Telcraft Bks.

Wimmer, Chuck. Doubletalk: Codes, Signs & Symbols. Hovanec, Helene. (gr. 7-10). 1993. pap. 1.25 (0-553-37218-1) Bantam.

Wimmer, Jan. Twenty-Six More Object Talks: For Children's Worship. Van Seters, Virginia A. 48p. (gr. k-2). 1990. pap. 3.99 (0-87403-653-4, 14-02864) Standard Pub.

Wimmer, Mike. All the Places to Love. MacLachlan, Patricia. LC 92-794. 32p. (gr. 1 up). 1994. 15.00 (0-06-021098-2); PLB 14.89 (0-06-021099-0) HarpC Child Bks.

—Flight: The Journey of Charles Lindbergh. Burleigh, Bob. 32p. (ps-3). 1991. 14.95 (0-399-22272-3, Philomel) Putnam Pub Group.

—Seven Silly Circles. Conrad, Pam. LC 85-45835. 64p. (gr. 2-5). 1987. HarpC Child Bks.

—Staying Nine. Conrad, Pam. LC 87-45862. 80p. (gr. 2-5). 1988. 13.00 (0-06-021319-1); PLB 12.89 (0-06-021320-5) HarpC Child Bks.

—A Taste of Blackberries. Smith, Doris B. LC 88-45077. 64p. (gr. 3-6). 1988. pap. 3.95 (0-06-440238-X, Trophy) HarpC Child Bks.

—Train Song. Siebert, Diane. LC 88-389. 32p. (ps-3). 1990. 15.00 (0-690-04726-6, Crowell Jr Bks); PLB 14.89 (0-690-04728-2, Crowell Jr Bks) HarpC Child Bks.

—Train Song. Siebert, Diane. LC 88-389. 32p. (gr. k-3). 1993. pap. 5.95 (0-06-443340-4, Trophy) HarpC Child Bks.

Wimmer, Sandy. Bible Learning Games. Gambill, Hentietta D. 16p. (gr. 1-7). 1993. 8.99 (9-5032-0569-7, 14-02259) Standard Pub.

Winants, Jean-Marie. Animal Bandits. Henno, Robert. LC 93-31750. 1993. 14.95 (0-88106-672-9) Charlesbridge Pub.

—Birds of the Night. De Sart, Jean. LC 93-31749. 1994. 14.95 (0-88106-671-0) Charlesbridge Pub.

—Scary Animals. De Sart, Jean. LC 93-20963. 1994. 14.95 (0-88106-674-5) Charlesbridge Pub.

Winborn, Marsha. Bert's New Collection: A Story about What Belongs Together. Stevenson, Jocelyn. LC 87-83489. 32p. (ps-1). 1988. write for info. (0-307-13109-2) Western Pub.

—Digby & Kate. Baker, Barbara. LC 87-24455. 48p. (ps-2). 1988. 9.95 (0-525-44370-3, 0966-290, DCB) Dutton Child Bks.

—Digby & Kate Again. Baker, Barbara. LC 88-25677. 48p. (ps-2). 1989. 9.95 (0-525-44477-7, DCB) Dutton Child Bks.

—Freckles & Willie: A Valentine's Day Story. Cuyler, Margery. LC 85-8646. 32p. (ps-2). 1986. 12.95 (0-03-003772-7, Bks Young Read) H Holt & Co.

—Freckles & Willie: A Valentine's Day Story. Cuyler, Margery. LC 85-8646. 32p. (ps-2). 1989. pap. 4.95 (0-8050-0949-3, Bks Young Read) H Holt & Co.

—I Like It When... Auster, Benjamin. 24p. (ps-2). 1990. PLB 14.60 (0-8172-3578-7); PLB 10.95 pkg. of 3 (0-8114-2933-4) Raintree Steck-V.

—Inside Sesame Street. 22p. (ps) 1986. write for info. (0-307-12142-9, Pub. by Golden Bks.) Western Pub.

—Let's Pretend. Greydanus, Rose. LC 81-2357. 32p. (gr. k-2). 1981. PLB 11.59 (0-89375-545-1); pap. text ed. 2.95 (0-89375-546-X) Troll Assocs.

—Mystery of the Lost Ring (with Two Hearts) Supraner, Robyn. LC 81-7520. 48p. (gr. 2-4). 1982. PLB 10.89 (0-89375-596-6); pap. text ed. 3.50 (0-89375-597-4); cassette 9.95 (0-685-04951-5) Troll Assocs.

—Sir William & the Pumpkin Monster. Cuyler, Margery. LC 84-610. 32p. (ps-2). 1989. pap. 4.95 (0-8050-1017-3, Bks Young Read) H Holt & Co.

Winch, Madeleine. Come by Chance. Winch, Madeleine. LC 89-22157. 32p. (ps-2). 1990. PLB 11.99 (0-517-57667-8) Crown Bks Yng Read.

Winchell, Karl. The Leopard Speaks about Changes in Life. Avent, Barbara P. Alston. Nelson G., ed. 64p. (Orig.). 1993. pap. 9.95 (0-9632202-1-7) Alpha Bk Pr.

Wind, B. Most Wonderful King. Hill, Dave. (gr. 3-4). 1968. laminated bdg. 1.89 (0-570-06032-X, 59-1145) Concordia.

Wind, Betty. Eric's Discovery. Hamilton, Dorothy. LC 79-18537. 120p. (gr. 4-9). 1979. pap. 3.95 (0-8361-1903-7) Herald Pr.

Windborn, Marsha. Digby & Kate. Baker, Barbara. LC 93-6555. (gr. k-3). 1993. pap. 3.25 (0-14-036547-8, Puffin) Puffin Bks.

Wine, Jeanine M. Gladdys Makes Peace. Hogan, Jan. 22p. (gr. 1-5). 1985. 9.95 (0-87178-313-4) Brethren.

—Mattie Loves All. Grimley, Mildred H. 22p. (gr. 1-5). 1985. 5.95 (0-87178-552-8) Brethren.

Wines, James. Edward Lear's Nonsense. LC 93-20461. 1994. write for info. (0-8478-1682-6) Rizzoli Intl.

Winfrey, Buford A. An Easter Parade of Verse. 24p. (Orig.). 1991. pap. 3.95 (0-8249-8504-4, Ideals Child) Hambleton-Hill.

—When Santa Was Late. Leet, Frank R. 32p. (ps-4). 1990. 3.95 (0-8249-8483-8, Ideals Child) Hambleton-Hill.

Wingfield, Ken, Jr. Where Did Papa Go: Looking at Death from a Young Child's Perspective. Laufer, Judy E. 32p. (Orig.). (ps-2). 1991. pap. 9.95 (1-881669-00-9) Little Egg Pub

Wingham, Peter. Activity Picture Dictionary. Ridout, Ronald. 48p. (gr. 1 up). 1987. 9.95 (0-8120-5844-5) Barron.

—And Now...the Weather. Ganeri, Anita. LC 91-26682. 32p. (ps-2). 1992. pap. 5.95 (0-689-71583-8, Aladdin) Macmillan Child Grp.

Wingrad, Deborah. Why Winter Comes. Simons, Scott & Simons, Jamie. 32p. (gr. 2-5). 1992. incl. jacket 13.95 (0-671-69123-6); lib. bdg. 14.98 (0-671-69119-8) Silver Pr.

Winik, J. T. Fun with Numbers. Winik, J. T. 32p. (ps-k). 1985. pap. 2.95 (0-88625-104-4) Durkin Hayes Pub.

Winik, J. T. & Pashuk, Lauren. Fun from A-Z. Winik, J. T. & Pashuk, Lauren. 32p. (ps-k). 1985. pap. 2.95 (0-88625-105-2) Durkin Hayes Pub.

Winik, J. T., jt. illus. see Rowden, Rick.

Winkler, Chris. Anatomy of a Male Slut: PO Box 61564. Shields, Bill. 16p. (Orig.). (gr. 10 up). 1988. pap. 2.00 saddle stapled (0-929611-02-0) Plutonium Pr.

Winkowski, Fred. Einstein Anderson Goes to Bat. Simon, Seymour. (gr. 3-7). 1987. pap. 3.99 (0-14-032303-1, Puffin) Puffin Bks.

—Einstein Anderson Lights up the Sky. Simon, Seymour. (gr. 3-7). pap. 3.95 (0-317-62300-1, Puffin) Puffin Bks.

—Einstein Anderson Makes Up for Lost Time. Simon, Seymour. 80p. (gr. 3-7). 1986. pap. 3.95 (0-14-032100-4, Puffin) Puffin Bks.

—Einstein Anderson, Science Sleuth. Simon, Seymour. 80p. (gr. 3-7). 1986. pap. 3.99 (0-14-032098-9, Puffin) Puffin Bks.

—Einstein Anderson Sees Through the Invisible Man. Simon, Seymour. (gr. 3-7). 1987. pap. 3.95 (0-14-032306-6, Puffin) Puffin Bks.

—Einstein Anderson Shocks His Friends. Simon, Seymour. 80p. (gr. 3-7). 1986. pap. 3.95 (0-14-032099-7, Puffin) Puffin Bks.

—Einstein Anderson Tells a Comet's Tale. Simon, Seymour. (gr. 3-7). 1987. pap. 3.95 (0-14-032302-3, Puffin) Puffin Bks.

Winkowski, Frederic. The Book of Foolish Machinery. Pape, Donna L. 32p. (gr. 2-5). 1988. pap. 2.50 (0-590-40907-7) Scholastic Inc.

Winn, Leslie. A Boy Learns to Write: Beginning Writing (Boy's Version) Leachman, Clara G. 28p. (gr. k-1). 1990. pap. text ed. write for info. (0-9618517-2-4) C Leachman.

—A Girl Learns to Write: Beginning Writing (Girl's Version) Leachman, Clara G. 28p (gr. k-1). 1990. pap. text ed. write for info. (0-9618517-1-6) C Leachman.

—Julie Learns to Write. Leachman, Clara G. 22p. (gr. k-1). 1987. pap. 5.50 (0-9618517-0-8) C Leachman.

Winn-Lederer, Ilene. Kind Little Rivka. Rosenfeld, Dina. Englin, A., tr. from ENG. (RUS.). 32p. (ps-1). 1993. write for info. (0-922613-29-X) Hachai Pubns.

Winograd, Deborah. The Gods of Olympus Series, 4 vols. Simons, Scott & Simons, Jamie. (gr. 2-5). 1992. Set, 32p. ea. incl. jacket 51.80 (0-671-31229-4); Set, 32p. ea. lib. bdg. 59.92 (0-671-31228-6) Silver Pr.

—My Color Is Panda. Winograd, Deborah. LC 92-17423. 32p. (ps-1). 1993. JRT 13.00 (0-671-79152-4, Green Tiger) S&S Trade.

—Why Dolphins Call: A Story of Dionysus. Simons, Scott & Simons, Jamie. 32p. (gr. 2-5). 1992. 13.95 (0-671-69125-2); PLB 14.98 (0-671-69121-X) Silver Pr.

—Why Seashells Sing. Simons, Scott & Simons, Jamie. 32p. (gr. 2-5). 1992. incl. jacket 13.95 (0-382-69122-9); PLB 14.98 (0-382-69118-0) Silver.

—Why Spiders Spin: A Story of Arachne. Simons, Scott & Simons, Jamie. 32p. (gr. 2-5). 1992. 13.95 (0-671-69124-4); PLB 14.98 (0-671-69120-1) Silver Pr.

Wint, Florence. Cowboy Ed. Grossman, Bill. LC 92-23393. 32p. (ps-2). 1993. 15.00 (0-06-021570-4); PLB 14.89 (0-06-021571-2) HarpC Child Bks.

Winter, Donna. Patterns for the Flannel Board. 32p. (ps-2). Date not set. 11.95 (1-56065-167-9) Capstone Pr. Postponed.

Winter, Ginny L. Ballet Book. Winter, Ginny L. (gr. 1-5). 1962. 8.95 (0-8392-3001-X) Astor-Honor.

—Riding Book. Winter, Ginny L. (gr. k-3). 1963. 8.95 (0-8392-3031-1) Astor-Honor.

—Skating Book. Winter, Ginny L. (gr. k-3). 1963. 8.95 (0-8392-3035-4) Astor-Honor.

—Swimming Book. Winter, Ginny L. (gr. k-3). 1964. 8.95 (0-8392-3037-0) Astor-Honor.

—What's in My Tree. Winter, Ginny L. (gr. k-1). 1962. 8.95 (0-8392-3044-3) Astor-Honor.

Winter, Jeanette. The Changeling. Lagerlof, Selma. Stevens, Susanna, tr. from SWE. LC 90-45277. 48p. (gr. k-5). 1992. 15.00 (0-679-81035-8); PLB 15.99 (0-679-91035-2) Knopf Bks Yng Read.

—Cotton Mill Town. Hershey, Kathleen. LC 92-7379. (ps-2). 1993. 12.99 (0-525-44966-3, DCB) Dutton Child Bks.

—Diego. Winter, Jonah. Prince, Amy, tr. LC 90-25923. (ENG & SPA.). 40p. (gr. k-4). 1991. 14.00 (0-679-81987-8); PLB 14.99 (0-679-91987-2) Knopf Bks Yng Read.

—Eight Hands Round: A Patchwork Alphabet. Paul, Ann W. LC 88-745. 32p. (gr. 3 up). 1991. 15.00 (0-06-024689-8); PLB 14.89 (0-06-024704-5) HarpC Child Bks.

—Klara's New World. Winter, Jeanette. LC 91-30212. 48p. (gr. 2-7). 1992. 15.00 (0-679-80626-1); PLB 15.99 (0-679-90626-6) Knopf Bks Yng Read.

—More Witch, Goblin & Ghost Stories. Alexander, Sue. LC 78-3280. (gr. 1-4). 1978. 6.95 (0-394-83933-1) Pantheon.

—Shaker Boy. Ray, Mary L. LC 93-1333. 1994. write for info. (0-15-276921-8) HarBrace.

—Sleepy River. Bandes, Hanna. LC 92-26198. 32p. (ps). 1993. 14.95 (0-399-22349-5, Philomel Bks) Putnam Pub Group.

—Witch, Goblin, & Ghost Are Back. Alexander, Sue. LC 83-22157. 62p. (gr. 1-4). 1985. 6.95 (0-394-86296-1, Pant Bks Young); lib. bdg. 9.99 (0-394-96296-6) Pantheon.

—Witch, Goblin & Ghost in the Haunted Woods. Alexander, Sue. LC 80-20863. 72p. (gr. 1-4). 1981. 6.95 (0-394-84443-2); lib. bdg. 7.99 (0-394-94443-7) Pantheon.

—Witch, Goblin, & Sometimes Ghost: Six Read-Alone Stories. Alexander, Sue. LC 76-8657. (ps-3). 1976. 6.95 (0-394-83216-7) Pantheon.

Winter, Jeanette, photos by. A Fruit & Vegetable Man. Schotter, Roni. LC 92-17555. 1993. 15.95 (0-316-77467-7, Joy St Bks) Little.

Winter, Judeanne. The Tree of Life: The Wonders of Evolution. Jackson, Ellen. 40p. (gr. k-3). 1993. 14.95 (0-87975-819-8) Prometheus Bks.

Winter, Milo. Aesop for Children. Aesop. LC 86-73175. 96p. (gr. 2 up). 1984. Repr. of 1919 ed. 12.95 (1-56288-039-X) Checkerboard.

Winter, Nilo. The Aesop for Children. large type ed. Aesop. Clauss, J., intro. by. (gr. 1-12). 1976. lib. bdg. 20.95x (0-88411-991-2, Pub. by Aeonian Pr) Amereon Ltd.

Winter, Paula. The Bear & the Fly. Winter, Paula. LC 76-2479. (ps-1). 1987. PLB 12.95 (0-517-52605-0) Crown Bks Yng Read.

Winter, Peter. Feelings & Faces: Feelings Activity Book. Boulden, Jim. 32p. (Orig.). (gr. 1-7). 1993. pap. 4.95 (1-878076-20-5) Boulden Pub.

—Mom & Me. Boulden, Jim & Boulden, Joan. 32p. (Orig.). (gr. 1-6). 1993. pap. 4.95 (1-878076-25-6) Boulden Pub.

—Secrets That Hurt. Boulden, Jim & Boulden, Joan. 32p. (Orig.). (gr. 1-6). 1993. pap. 4.95 (1-878076-28-0) Boulden Pub.

—Uncle Jerry Has AIDS. Boulden, Jim. 32p. (Orig.). (gr. 3-7). 1992. pap. 3.95 (1-878076-18-3) Boulden Pub.

Winter, Susan. Bon Appetit, Bertie! Knight, Joan. LC 92-54319. 32p. (ps-1). 1993. 13.95 (1-56458-195-0) Dorling Kindersley.

—Henry's Baby. Hoffman, Mary. LC 92-53485. 32p. (gr. 1-4). 1993. 13.95 (1-56458-196-9) Dorling Kindersley.

—I Can. Winter, Susan. LC 92-54384. 24p. (ps-1). 1993. 9.95 (1-56458-197-7) Dorling Kindersley.

—Me, Too. Winter, Susan. LC 92-54383. 24p. (ps-1). 1993. 9.95 (1-56458-198-5) Dorling Kindersley.

Winters, Nina. Carrot Holes & Frisbee Trees. Bodecker, N. M. LC 83-2799. 48p. (gr. 3-5). 1983. SBE 12.95 (0-689-50097-1, M K McElderry) Macmillan Child Grp.

Winton, Andrea. A Teenager's Guide How to Manipulate Your Way to Happiness: Thirty-Seven Easy Steps in the Care & Feeding of Your Parents. Denny, Kevin M. LC 92-81556. 240p. (Orig.). (gr. 8-12). 1992. pap. 13.95 (0-9633108-0-1) Warthog Pub.

Winton, Ian. The Big Green Book. Pearce, Fred. LC 90-84673. 32p. (gr. 2-5). 1991. 13.95 (0-448-40142-8, G&D) Putnam Pub Group.

Wirth, Pascale. A Home for Little Turtle. Chottin, Ariane. LC 91-40650. 22p. (ps). 1992. 6.99 (0-89577-420-8, Readers Digest Kids) RD Assn.
—Little Goat's New Horns. Chottin, Ariane. Jensen, Patricia, adapted by. LC 93-4241. 1993. write for info. (0-89577-544-1, Readers Digest Kids) RD Assn.

Wise, Caroline. Strong & Safe: A Children's Guide to Self Protection. Elias, Susan C. 60p. (Orig.). (gr. 1-3). 1989. pap. 8.95 (0-317-93904-1) Womansource.

Wise, Joyce. Ann's Pans & Cans. Wise, Francis H. & Wise, Joyce M. 20p. (ps-1). 1974. pap. text ed. 1.50 (0-915766-28-0) Wise Pub.

Wise, Joyce M. Ann. Wise, Francis H. Wise, Joyce M., ed. 21p. (ps-1). 1983. pap. 1.50 (0-915766-60-4) Wise Pub.
—The Beach. Wise, Francis H. Wise, Joyce M., ed. 21p. (ps-1). 1983. pap. 1.50 (0-915766-63-9) Wise Pub.
—Black Crow. Wise, Francis H. Wise, Joyce M., ed. 21p. (gr. k-1). 1983. pap. 1.50 (0-915766-62-0) Wise Pub.
—Ed's Red Bed. Wise, Francis H. & Wise, Joyce M. 20p. (ps). 1974. pap. 1.50 (0-915766-27-2) Wise Pub.
—Fun in the Sun. Wise, Francis H. & Wise, Joyce M. 21p. (ps-1). 1975. pap. 1.50 (0-915766-30-2) Wise Pub.
—Jay's Fat Cat. Wise, Francis H. & Wise, Joyce M. 20p. (ps-1). 1974. pap. text ed. 1.50 (0-915766-29-9) Wise Pub.
—Park the Car. Wise, Francis H. & Wise, Joyce M. (ps-1). 1975. pap. text ed. 1.50 (0-915766-32-9) Wise Pub.
—Play Ball. Wise, Francis H. & Wise, Joyce M. (ps-1). 1975. pap. text ed. 1.50 (0-915766-31-0) Wise Pub.
—Sit By Me. Wise, Francis H. & Wise, Joyce M. (ps-1). 1975. pap. text ed. 1.50 (0-915766-33-7) Wise Pub.
—Snowman. Wise, Francis H. & Wise, Joyce M. (gr. 1). 1976. pap. 1.50 (0-915766-37-X) Wise Pub.
—Youth & Drugs. Wise, Francis H. (gr. 10 up). Date not set. 4.95 (0-686-86911-7) Wise Pub.

Wise, Lu Celia. Alli Gator Gets a Bump on His Nose. Searcy, Margaret Z. LC 78-61369. (gr. 2-4). 1978. 7.50 (0-916620-20-4) Portals Pr.
—Tiny Bat & the Ball Game. Searcy, Margaret Z. LC 78-61367. (gr. 2-4). 1978. 7.50 (0-916620-19-0) Portals Pr.

Wisegard, Leonard. The Golden Egg Book. Brown, Margaret W. 32p. (ps-1). 1976. write for info. (0-307-12045-7, Golden Pr); PLB 9.15 (0-685-05367-9) Western Pub.

Wiseman, Ann. Making Musical Things: Improvised Instruments. Wiseman, Ann. LC 79-4474. 64p. (gr. 3 up). 1979. SBE 14.95 (0-684-16114-1, Scribners Young Read) Macmillan Child Grp.
—Making Things: The Hand Book of Creative Discovery. Wiseman, Ann. 192p. (gr. 4 up). 1973. pap. 14.95 (0-316-94849-7) Little.

Wiseman, Ann S., et al. Nightmare Help: A Guide for Adults & Children. Wiseman, Ann S. 137p. (Orig.). (gr. 1-12). 1986. pap. text ed. 9.00 (0-937369-00-4) Ansayre Pr.

Wiseman, Bernard. Barber Bear. Wiseman, Bernard. LC 86-27594. 48p. (gr. 1-3). 1987. pap. 11.95 (0-316-94859-4) Little.
—Cats! Cats! Cats! Wiseman, Bernard. LC 83-27288. 48p. (ps-3). 1984. 5.95 (0-8193-1127-8) Parents.
—Christmas with Morris & Boris. Wiseman, Bernard. LC 83-11962. 44p. (gr. 1-3). 1983. 12.95 (0-316-94855-1) Little.
—George's Store. Asch, Frank. LC 82-22298. 48p. (ps-3). 1983. 5.95 (0-8193-1101-4); PLB 5.95 (0-8193-1102-2) Parents.
—Morris & Boris at the Circus. Wiseman, Bernard. LC 87-45682. 64p. (gr. k-3). 1988. 14.00 (0-06-026477-2); PLB 13.89 (0-06-026478-0) HarpC Child Bks.
—Morris & Boris at the Circus. Wiseman, Bernard. LC 87-45682. 64p. (gr. k-3). 1990. pap. 3.50 (0-06-444143-1, Trophy) HarpC Child Bks.
—Morris Goes to School. Wiseman, Bernard. LC 75-77944. 64p. (gr. k-3). 1970. PLB 13.89 (0-06-026548-5) HarpC Child Bks.
—Morris the Moose. rev. ed. Wiseman, Bernard. LC 87-33485. 32p. (gr. ps-2). 1989. PLB 13.89 (0-06-026476-4) HarpC Child Bks.
—Morris the Moose. rev. ed. Wiseman, Bernard. LC 87-33485. 32p. (gr. ps-2). 1991. pap. 3.50 (0-06-444146-6, Trophy) HarpC Child Bks.
—The Very Bumpy Bus Ride. Muntean, Michaela. LC 81-16905. 48p. (ps-3). 1982. 5.95 (0-8193-1079-4); 5.95 (0-8193-1080-8) Parents.
—The Very Bumpy Bus Ride. Muntean, Michaela. 48p. (gr. 3-7). 1990. pap. 2.95 (0-448-04337-8, G&D) Putnam Pub Group.
—The Very Bumpy Bus Ride. Muntean, Michaela. LC 93-13042. 1993. PLB 13.27 (0-8368-0980-7) Gareth Stevens Inc.

Wisenfeld, Alison. The Tree. Hindley, Judy. LC 89-16105. 32p. (gr. k-3). 1990. 13.95 (0-517-57630-9, Crown); PLB 14.99 (0-517-57669-4) Crown Pub Group.

Wiskur, Darrell. Forts in the Wilderness. McCall, Edith. LC 68-24378. 128p. (gr. 3-10). 1980. PLB 15.00 (0-516-03324-7) Childrens.
—Silver Dollar City's ABC Words & Rhymes. Wiskur, Darrell. Silver Dollar City, Inc. Staff, ed. (ps-1). 1977. 1.99g (0-686-19127-7) Silver Dollar.
—The Story of the Capitol. Prolman, Marilyn. LC 69-14681. 32p. (gr. 3-6). 1969. pap. 3.95 (0-516-44604-5) Childrens.
—The Story of the Mayflower Compact. Richards, Norman. LC 67-22901. 32p. (gr. 3-6). 1967. pap. 3.95 (0-516-44625-8) Childrens.

Wisniewski, David. Rain Player. Wisiniewski, David. 32p. (gr. k-4). 1991. 15.45 (0-395-55112-9, Clarion Bks) HM.
—Sundiata: Lion King of Mali. Wisniewski, David. 32p. (gr. k-4). 1992. 15.95 (0-395-61302-7, Clarion Bks) HM.

Wisniewski, Dennis, photos by. Play. Shapiro, Mary S. 14p. (ps-k). 1985. 3.95 (0-934361-02-9); Set. write for info. Kinder Read.

Wissmann, Joyce. Meet Me at the Fair: A "Choose Your Own Adventure" that lets You Explore the Exciting Treasures of the 1904 St. Louis World's Fair. McDonough, Barbara. 64p. (Orig.). (gr. 4-6). 1988. pap. 4.50 (0-931821-43-6) Info Res Cons.

Witalis-Burke Agency Staff. Lionel Trains: Standard of the World, 1900-1943. 2nd ed. National TCA Book Committee Staff, et al. 256p. 1989. Repr. of 1976 ed. 34.95 (0-917896-02-5); prepub. 24.95 (0-317-93968-8) TCA PA.

Witcomb, Gerald. The Moon. 32p. (gr. 3-5). 1985. 7.95x (0-86685-448-7) Intl Bk Ctr.

Witcombmsia, Gerald. Paper. 32p. (gr. 3-5). 1985. 7.95x (0-86685-450-9) Intl Bk Ctr.

Witt, Dick. Let's Look at Animals. Becker & Mayer. 12p. 1993. 5.95 (0-590-45700-4) Scholastic Inc.
—Let's Look at My World. Becker & Mayer. 12p. 1993. 5.95 (0-590-45699-7) Scholastic Inc.

Witt, Linda A. Let's Go to the Arctic: A Story & Activities Book about Arctic People & Animals. Mateer, Charlotte F. 64p. (gr. 4-6). 1993. pap. text ed. 7.95 (1-879373-24-6) R Rinehart.

Witte, Michael. Otter Nonsense. Juster, Norman. LC 93-22041. (gr. 3 up). 1994. write for info. (0-688-12283-5); PLB write for info. (0-688-12283-3) Morrow Jr Bks.

Witte, Sue. Murder at Sun Valley. Thorburn, James W. LC 86-50305. 304p. (Orig.). (gr. 6). 1986. 8.99 (0-938191-00-4) Woodside Pr ID.

Witte, Suzanne. Grace Delight & Tricksey. Blank, Grace W. LC 91-75093. 111p. (gr. k-3). 1992. 8.95 (1-55523-459-3) Winston-Derek.

Witte-Barrett, Suzanne. Jennie & Sue Visit a Kentucky Farm. Blank, Grace W. 70p. (gr. 3-6). Date not set. write for info. (0-9634122-5-6) Feather Fables.

Wittenborn, Sally. On Halloween Night. Barth, Nancy & Wittenborn, Sally. 12p. (Orig.). (ps-1). 1987. pap. 4.95 (0-942565-00-2) Country Schl Pubns.

Wittles, Harriet & Greisman, Joan. How to Spell It: A Dictionary of Commonly Misspelled Words. Wittles, Harriet & Greisman, Joan. 336p. (gr. 4 up). 1982. pap. 10.95 (0-448-14756-4, G&D) Putnam Pub Group.

Witwer, Julia. Gesar! The Wondrous Adventures of King Gesar of Tibet. Wallace, Zara & Cook, Elizabeth, eds. LC 91-35260. 190p. (Orig.). (gr. 10-12). 1991. pap. 11.95 (0-89800-223-0) Dharma Pub.
—Hero of the Land of Snow. Gretchen, Sylvia, ed. & tr. from TIB. LC 89-25603. vi, 32p. (gr. 5-8). 1990. 14.95 (0-89800-201-X); pap. 7.95 (0-89800-202-8) Dharma Pub.

Witwer, Julia, jt. illus. see Clemmons, Bradley.

Woe, Jonathan. The Longneck Bird of Longboat Key: One of the Privileged Class. Woe, Jonathan. 32p. 1992. 14.95 (0-9627946-6-X) Hawk FL.
—The Wing'ed Whale from Woefully. Woe, Jonathan. Constantine, R., ed. 32p. 1992. 14.95 (0-9627946-3-5) Hawk FL.

Woell, J. Fred. Gloucester: College Life Between Classes. Woell, J. Fred. 144p. (Orig.). pap. 15.00x (0-9626935-2-9) Turtle Gal Edit.

Woessner, Circe. David David. Todd, Cynthia & Ziemann, Debbie. 23p. (gr. k-6). 1990. PLB 7.95 (1-879056-01-1) Alpenhorn Pr.
—Heidelberg Castle. Todd, Cynthia & Ziemann, Debbie. 28p. (gr. k-6). 1990. PLB 9.95 (1-879056-00-3) Alpenhorn Pr.
—Mother Earth. Todd, Cynthia & Ziemann, Debbie. 24p. Date not set. pap. 9.95 (1-879056-03-8) Alpenhorn Pr.
—Nessie. 2nd ed. Todd, Cynthia & Ziemann, Debbie. 9p. (gr. k-6). 1990. PLB 9.95 (1-879056-02-X) Alpenhorn Pr.
—People from Outer Space. Todd, Cynthia & Ziemann, Debbie. 9p. 1991. PLB 9.95 (0-685-51627-X) Alpenhorn Pr.
—Take One Hand. Todd, Cynthia & Ziemann, Debbie. 25p. (gr. k-6). 1990. PLB 9.95 (1-879056-05-4) Alpenhorn Pr.

Wofford, Roberta A. Sidney & Sally: The Danger of Strangers. Wofford, Roberta A. 38p. (gr. k-4). 1987. pap. text ed. 1.85 (0-9616198-0-5) Pt Orchard Spec.

Woggon, Bill. Yes! Jesus Loves Me. Sparks, Judy, ed. 24p. (ps-2). 1985. 2.50 (0-87239-882-X, 3682) Standard Pub.

Wohlberg, Meg. Night Before Christmas - in Texas, That Is. Harris, Leon. (gr. k-7). 1977. Repr. of 1952 ed. 9.95 (0-88289-175-8) Pelican.

Wolde, Gunilla. Betsy's Fixing Day. Wolde, Gunilla. LC 78-50056. 24p. (ps). 1990. 4.95 (0-394-83781-9) Random Bks Yng Read.
—This Is Betsy. Wolde, Gunilla. LC 75-7566. 24p. (ps). 1990. 4.95 (0-394-83161-6) Random Bks Yng Read.

Woldin, Beth W. Call for Mr. Sniff. Lewis, Thomas P. LC 79-2679. 64p. (gr. k-3). 1981. HarpC Child Bks.

Wolf, Alexander. Valentino. Wolf, Andrea. Bradford, Elizabeth, ed. Verlag, Mangold, tr. from GER. LC 91-21301. 32p. (gr. k-3). 1991. PLB 14.60 (1-56074-030-2) Garrett Ed Corp.

Wolf, Barbara & Waldron, Shirley. Dear Mr. Rainbows, 1994. Goldberg, Larry. LC 93-72611. 112p. (Orig.). (gr. 2-6). 1993. pap. 9.95 (0-9638457-0-5) Blue-Black.

Wolf, Bernard, photos by. Beneath the Stone: A Mexican Zapotec Tale. Wolf, Bernard. LC 92-27103. 48p. (gr. k-6). 1994. 15.95 (0-531-06835-8); lib. bdg. 15.99 RLB (0-531-08685-2) Orchard Bks Watts.

Wolf, Billy. California State Capitol Time Machine Coloring Book. Donnelly, Loraine B. 23p. (Orig.). (gr. 4-9). 1989. pap. text ed. 3.50 (0-9626304-0-3) Capital Enter.

Wolf, Dennis, photos by. Kids in Jail. Hjelmeland, Andy. 40p. (gr. 4-8). 1992. PLB 17.50 (0-8225-2552-6) Lerner Pubns.

Wolf, Elizabeth. Your Balance Sense. Loomar, Jane & Friedman, Barbara. 20p. (ps-3). 1992. pap. text ed. 11.00 (0-910317-88-7) Am Occup Therapy.
—Your Muscle Senses. Loomar, Jane & Friedman, Barbara. 16p. (ps-3). 1992. pap. text ed. 11.00 (0-910317-89-5) Am Occup Therapy.

Wolf, Gerald, jt. illus. see Rajpar, Shamin.

Wolf, Janet. Rosie & the Yellow Ribbon. DePaolo, Paula. 32p. (ps-3). 1992. 14.95 (0-316-18100-5, Joy St Bks) Little.

Wolfe, Art. Hiding Out: Camouflage in the Wild. Martin, James. LC 92-38211. 32p. (gr. 2-6). 1993. 13.00 (0-517-59392-0); PLB 13.99 (0-517-59393-9) Crown Bks Yng Read.

Wolfe, Art, photos by. Chameleons: Dragons in the Trees. Martin, James. LC 91-8736. 36p. (gr. 1-5). 1991. 13.00 (0-517-58388-7); lib. bdg. 13.99 (0-517-58389-5) Crown Bks Yng Read.

Wolfe, Bob & Wolfe, Diane. Dinosaur Discoveries: How to Create Your Own Prehistoric World. West, Robin. 72p. (gr. 1-5). 1989. PLB 19.95 (0-87614-351-6) Carolrhoda Bks.
—Lessons from the Samurai: Ancient Self-Defense Strategies & Techniques. Neff, Fred. 96p. (gr. 5 up). 1987. PLB 14.95 (0-8225-1161-4, First Ave Edns); pap. 4.95 (0-8225-9531-1, First Ave Edns) Lerner Pubns.
—Lessons from the Western Warriors: Dynamic Self-Defense Techniques. Neff, Fred. 96p. (gr. 5 up). 1987. PLB 14.95 (0-8225-1159-2, First Ave Edns); pap. 4.95 (0-8225-9533-8, First Ave Edns) Lerner Pubns.
—Rock Climbing Is for Me. Hyden, Tom & Anderson, Tim. LC 84-2906. 48p. (gr. 2-5). 1984. PLB 13.50 (0-8225-1147-9) Lerner Pubns.

Wolfe, Bob, photos by. Far Out: How to Create Your Own Star World. West, Robin. 72p. (gr. k-4). 1987. lib. bdg. 19.95 (0-87614-279-X); pap. 5.95 (0-87614-463-6) Carolrhoda Bks.

Wolfe, Bob & Wolfe, Diane, photos by. Cooking the Australian Way. Germaine, Elizabeth & Burckhardt, Ann. 48p. (gr. 5 up). 1990. PLB 14.95 (0-8225-0923-7) Lerner Pubns.
—Cooking the Austrian Way. Hughes, Helga. 48p. (gr. 5 up). 1990. PLB 14.95 (0-8225-0924-5) Lerner Pubns.
—Holiday Cooking Around the World. Swofford, Jeannette. 52p. (gr. 5 up). 1988. 15.95 (0-8225-0922-9) Lerner Pubns.
—Lessons from the Art of Kempo: Subtle & Effective Self-Defense. Neff, Fred. 96p. (gr. 5 up). 1987. PLB 14.95 (0-8225-1160-6, First Ave Edns); pap. 4.95 (0-8225-9532-X, First Ave Edns) Lerner Pubns.

Wolfe, Bob, et al. Cooking the Israeli Way. Bacon, Josephine. LC 85-18059. 48p. (gr. 5 up). 1986. PLB 14.95 (0-8225-0912-1) Lerner Pubns.

Wolfe, Debra. Pen Pals Series, No. 1. Gunn, Jeffrey. (Orig.). (gr. 1). 1991. pap. write for info. (1-879146-00-2) Knowldg Pub.
—Pen Pals, Vol. 10: Facts about Nicotine. Gunn, Jeffrey. (Orig.). 1990. pap. write for info. (1-879146-10-X) Knowldg Pub.
—Pen Pals, Vol. 11: Facts about Alcohol. Gunn, Jeffrey. (Orig.). 1990. pap. write for info. (1-879146-11-8) Knowldg Pub.
—Pen Pals, Vol. 2: Facts about Cocaine. Gunn, Jeffrey. (Orig.). 1990. pap. write for info. (1-879146-02-9) Knowldg Pub.
—Pen Pals, Vol. 3: Facts about Heroin. Gunn, Jeffrey. (Orig.). 1990. pap. write for info. (1-879146-03-7) Knowldg Pub.
—Pen Pals, Vol. 4: Facts about Pot. Gunn, Jeffrey. (Orig.). 1990. pap. write for info. (1-879146-04-5) Knowldg Pub.
—Pen Pals, Vol. 6: Facts about Speed. Gunn, Jeffrey. (Orig.). (gr. 3). 1990. pap. write for info. (1-879146-06-1) Knowldg Pub.
—Pen Pals, Vol. 7: Facts about Downers. Gunn, Jeffrey. (Orig.). (gr. 3). 1990. pap. write for info. (1-879146-07-X) Knowldg Pub.

—Pen Pals, Vol. 8: Facts about Acid. Gunn, Jeffrey. (Orig.). (gr. 3). 1990. pap. write for info. (1-879146-08-8) Knowldg Pub.
—Pen Pals, Vol. 9: Facts about Crack. Gunn, Jeffrey. (Orig.). (gr. 3). 1990. pap. write for info. (1-879146-09-6) Knowldg Pub.
Wolfe, Diane, jt. illus. see Wolfe, Bob.
Wolfe, Diane, jt. photog. see Wolfe, Bob.
Wolfe, Diane, jt. photog. see Wolfe, Robert.
Wolfe, Diane, jt. photog. see Wolfe, Robert L.
Wolfe, Robert & Wolfe, Diane, photos by. How to Cook a Gooseberry Fool: Unusual Recipes from Around the World. Vaughan, Marcia. LC 93-9117. 1993. 14.95 (0-8225-0928-8) Lerner Pubns.
Wolfe, Robert, et al. Cooking the Polish Way. Zamojska-Hutchins, Danuta. LC 84-11226. 52p. (gr. 5 up). 1984. PLB 14.95 (0-8225-0909-1) Lerner Pubns.
Wolfe, Robert L. Bowling Is for Me. Lerner, Mark. LC 81-12433. 48p. (gr. 2-5). 1981. PLB 13.50 (0-8225-1099-5) Lerner Pubns.
—Canoeing Is for Me. Moran, Tom. LC 83-19957. 48p. (gr. 2-5). 1984. PLB 13.50 (0-8225-1142-8) Lerner Pubns.
—Racquetball Is for Me. Lerner, Mark. LC 83-13611. 48p. (gr. 2-5). 1983. PLB 13.50 (0-8225-1144-4) Lerner Pubns.
Wolfe, Robert L. & Wolfe, Diane, photos by. Desserts Around the World. 56p. (gr. 5 up). 1991. PLB 14.95 (0-8225-0926-1) Lerner Pubns.
—Ethnic Cooking the Microwave Way. Cappelloni, Nancy. LC 93-29543. (gr. 6 up). 1994. 14.95 (0-8225-0929-6) Lerner Pubns.
—My Very Own Valentine's Day: A Book of Cooking & Crafts. West, Robin. Burke, Susan S. LC 92-22254. 1993. 19.95 (0-87614-724-4) Carolrhoda Bks.
—Vegetarian Cooking Around the World. 52p. (gr. 5-12). 1992. PLB 14.95 (0-8225-0927-X) Lerner Pubns.
Wolfe, Robert L., et al. Cooking the Greek Way. Villios, Lynne W. 52p. (gr. 5 up). 1984. PLB 14.95 (0-8225-0910-5) Lerner Pubns.
Wolff. Who Is Coming to Our House? Slate. 32p. 1991. pap. 5.95 (0-399-21790-8, Sandcastle Bks) Putnam Pub Group.
Wolff, Ashley. Baby Beluga. Raffi. LC 89-49367. 32p. (ps-2). 1990. 13.00 (0-517-57839-5); PLB 11.99 (0-517-57840-9) Crown Bks Yng Read.
—Baby Beluga. Raffi. LC 89-49367. 32p. (ps-2). 1992. pap. 3.99 (0-517-58362-3) Crown Bks Yng Read.
—Block City. Stevenson, Robert Louis. LC 87-33397. 32p. (ps-2). 1988. 12.95 (0-525-44399-1, DCB) Dutton Child Bks.
—Block City. Stevenson, Robert Louis. 32p. (ps-2). 1992. pap. 3.99 (0-14-054551-4, Puffin Unicorn) Puffin Bks.
—A Garden Alphabet. Wilner, Isabel. LC 90-19619. 32p. (ps-2). 1991. 12.95 (0-525-44731-8, DCB) Dutton Child Bks.
—I Love My Daddy Because... Porter-Gaylord, Laurel. LC 90-2865. 24p. (ps). 1991. 5.95 (0-525-44624-9, DCB) Dutton Child Bks.
—I Love My Mommy Because... Porter-Gaylord, Laurel. LC 90-2792. 24p. (ps). 1991. 5.95 (0-525-44625-7, DCB) Dutton Child Bks.
—Stella & Roy. Wolff, Ashley. LC 92-27005. 32p. (ps-k). 1993. 12.99 (0-525-45081-5, DCB) Dutton Child Bks.
—Who Is Coming to Our House? Slate, Joseph. LC 87-7319. 32p. (ps-1). 1988. PLB 14.95 (0-399-21537-9, Putnam) Putnam Pub Group.
—A Year of Beasts. Wolff, Ashley. LC 85-27419. 32p. (ps-1). 1986. 11.95 (0-525-44240-5, DCB) Dutton Child Bks.
Wolff, Barbara. Egg to Chick. rev. ed. Selsam, Millicent E. LC 74-85034. 64p. (ps-3). 1970. PLB 13.89 (0-06-025290-1) HarpC Child Bks.
—Egg to Chick. Selsam, Millicent E. LC 74-85034. 64p. (gr. k-3). 1987. pap. 3.50 (0-06-444113-X, Trophy) HarpC Child Bks.
Wolff, Barbara M. Mi Abuelito y Yo. Wolff, Barbara M. (SPA.). 16p. (ps-1). 1992. PLB 13.95 (1-879567-12-1, Valeria Bks) Wonder Well.
—My Family & Me. Wolff, Barbara M. 16p. (ps-1). 1993. PLB 13.95 (0-685-59697-4, Valeria Bks) Wonder Well.
—Odisea. Sands, Stella. (SPA.). 32p. (gr. k-4). 1992. PLB 13.95 (1-879567-18-0, Valeria Bks) Wonder Well.
—Odyssea. Sands, Stella. 32p. (gr. k-4). 1991. PLB 13.95 (1-879567-04-0, Valeria Bks); pap. text ed. 7.95 (1-879567-03-2) Wonder Well.
—Pappa & Me. Wolff, Barbara M. 16p. (ps-1). 1991. PLB 13.95 (1-879567-11-3, Valeria Bks) Wonder Well.
Wolff, Mark R. The Illustrated Math Book on Animalcules. Wolff, Mark R. 83p. (Orig.). (gr. 6-12). 1994. pap. text ed. 7.00 (0-9637132-0-5) M R Wolff.
Wolgamott, Elizabeth. Sam's Stamp Store. Stevenson, Ralph L., Jr. O'Neil, Greg, intro. by. 28p. (Orig.). (ps-2). 1983. pap. 3.50 (0-9610762-0-8) Sirius Leag.
Wolters, Ronald & Weaver, Duane. Luther's Catechism. Kuske, David P. 383p. (gr. 7-8). 1982. text ed. 7.50 (0-938272-11-X); pap. 2.50 catechism aid bklet. (0-938272-13-6) WELS Board.
Wolverton, Lock. Drugs - a Dead End Street: The Dangers of Substance Abuse. Enns, Peter. 40p. (Orig.). (ps-6). 1992. pap. 5.98 incl. cassette (0-943593-98-0) Kids Intl Inc.
—The Pollution Solution: Keeping Earth a Beautiful Place. Enns, Peter. 40p. (Orig.). (ps-6). 1992. pap. 5.98 incl. cassette (0-943593-76-X) Kids Intl Inc.
—Putting the Brakes on AIDS: The Story of Macho McKar. Enns, Peter. 40p. (Orig.). (ps-6). 1992. pap. 5.98 incl. cassette (0-943593-97-2) Kids Intl Inc.

—Street Smarts! The Rewards of a Good Education. Enns, Peter. 40p. (Orig.). (ps-6). 1992. pap. 5.98 incl. cassette (0-943593-75-1) Kids Intl Inc.
Womack, Fred. Johnnie Ollie Carri III & His Friend. Wakeman, Cheryl A. 32p. (ps-3). 1985. 5.95 (0-9614819-0-0) R E Moen.
Wong, David. The Landing: A Night of Birds. Scholes, Katherine. 72p. (gr. 4 up). 1989. 12.95 (0-385-26191-8, Zephyr-BFYR) Doubleday.
Wong, Vera M. Memories of the Pasque & Prairie. Ames, Mary. Thornley, Phyllis, intro. by. 79p. (gr. 9-12). 1987. 13.95 (0-9619407-0-0) Country Messenger Inc.
Wood, Audrey. Balloonia. Wood, Audrey. LC 90-46602. 32p. (ps-2). 1981. 7.95 (0-85953-122-8, Pub. by Child's Play England); pap. 3.95 (0-85953-320-4, Pub. by Child's Play England) Childs Play.
—Magic Shoelaces. Wood, Audrey. LC 90-49097. 32p. (ps-2). 1989. 7.95 (0-85953-109-0); pap. 3.95 (0-85953-321-2) Childs Play.
—Orlando's Littlewhile Friends. Wood, Audrey. LC 90-45723. (ps-2). 1989. 11.95 (0-85953-111-2); pap. 5.95 (0-85953-106-6) Childs Play.
—Princess & the Dragon. Wood, Audrey. LC 90-49098. 32p. (ps-2). 1989. 7.95 (0-85953-150-3); pap. 3.95 (0-85953-013-2) Childs Play.
—Scaredy Cats. Wood, Audrey. LC 90-46913. 32p. (ps-2). 1989. 7.95 (0-85953-110-4); pap. 3.95 (0-85953-323-9) Childs Play.
—Twenty-Four Robbers. Wood, Audrey. LC 90-46182. 32p. (ps-2). 1989. 7.95 (0-85953-100-7); pap. 3.95 (0-85953-324-7) Childs Play.
—Weird Parents. Wood, Audrey. Fogelman, Phyllis J., ed. LC 88-25742. 32p. (ps-3). 1990. 12.99 (0-8037-0648-0); PLB 11.89 (0-8037-0649-9) Dial Bks Young.
Wood, Audrey & Wood, Don. Elbert's Bad Word. Wood, Audrey. LC 86-7557. 32p. (ps-3). 1988. 13.95 (0-15-225320-3, HB Juv Bks) HarBrace.
Wood, Bill. My House. Drew, David. LC 92-30424. 1993. 2.50 (0-383-03586-4) SRA Schl Grp.
—Wheels. Bissett, Isabel. LC 92-21399. 1993. 3.75 (0-383-03605-4) SRA Schl Grp.
Wood, Bruce J. Pip: The Adventures of a Deer Mouse. Woods, Shirley E. 80p. (Orig.). (gr. 3). 1992. pap. 6.95 (0-921054-98-X, Pub. by Nimbus Publishing Ltd CN) Chelsea Green Pub.
Wood, Carol, jt. illus. see Fadden, John K.
Wood, David & Wood, Vivian B. You're a Very Special Person. Wood, Vivian B. 38p. (Orig.). (gr. 1). 1988. pap. 5.95 (0-9621567-0-1) V B Wood.
Wood, Don. Heckedy Peg. Wood, Audrey. LC 86-33639. 32p. (ps-3). 1987. 14.95 (0-15-233678-8, HB Juv Bks) HarBrace.
—Into the Napping House. Wood, Audrey. Shaylen, Carl, contrib. by. (ps-2). 1990. Incl. cassette. 19.95 (0-15-256709-7) HarBrace.
—King Bidgood's in the Bathtub. Wood, Audrey. LC 85-5472. 32p. (ps-3). 1985. 14.95 (0-15-242730-9, HB Juv Bks) HarBrace.
—Moonflute. Wood, Audrey. LC 86-4666. 25p. (ps-3). 1986. 14.95 (0-15-255337-1) HarBrace.
—The Napping House. Wood, Audrey. LC 83-13035. 32p. (ps-3). 1984. 13.95 (0-15-255708-9, HB Juv Bks) HarBrace.
—The Napping House. Wood, Audrey. 32p. (ps-3). 1991. pap. 19.95 (0-15-256711-9) HarBrace.
—Tugford Wanted to Be Bad. Wood, Audrey. LC 83-318. 32p. (ps-3). 1983. pap. 4.95 (0-15-291084-0, Voyager Bks) HarBrace.
Wood, Don, jt. illus. see Wood, Audrey.
Wood, Elizabeth & Fenton, Ronald. Liquid Magic. Watson, Philip. LC 82-80988. 48p. (gr. 3-6). 1983. PLB 11.88 (0-688-00967-0) Lothrop.
Wood, Gerald. The French Revolution. Mulvihill, Margaret. LC 88-31564. 32p. (gr. 3-6). 1989. PLB 12.40 (0-531-17167-1, Gloucester Pr) Watts.
—Planet Earth. Jessop, Joanne. LC 93-28339. 1994. write for info. (0-8114-9244-3) Raintree Steck-V.
—A Roman Fort. Macdonald, Fiona. LC 93-16397. 48p. (gr. 5 up). 1993. 17.95 (0-87226-370-3); pap. 8.95 sewn (0-87226-259-6) P Bedrick Bks.
Wood, Gerry. The Story of Money. Kain, Carolyn. LC 91-38898. 32p. (gr. 3-6). 1993. PLB 11.89 (0-8167-2711-2); pap. text ed. 3.95 (0-8167-2712-0) Troll Assocs. Postponed.
Wood, Ivor. Paddington Takes to TV. Bond, Michael. 128p. (gr. 1-5). 1974. 14.45 (0-395-19881-X) HM.
Wood, Jakki. Animal Parade. Wood, Jakki. LC 92-22826. 32p. (ps-k). 1993. SBE 14.95 (0-02-793394-6, Bradbury Pr) Macmillan Child Grp.
—Deserts. Petty, Kate. 32p. (gr. 2-4). 1993. pap. 5.95 (0-8120-1762-5) Barron.
—Fiddle-I-Fee. Wood, Jakki. LC 93-72322. 32p. (ps-1). 1994. SBE 14.95 (0-02-793396-2, Bradbury Pr) Macmillan Child Grp.
—Into Space. Petty, Kate. 32p. (gr. 2-4). 1993. pap. 5.95 (0-8120-1761-7) Barron.
—My Cat Buster. Bryant, Donna. 20p. (ps-3). 1991. 8.95 (0-8120-6211-6) Barron.
—My Dog Jessie. Bryant, Donna. 20p. (ps-3). 1991. 8.95 (0-8120-6212-4) Barron.
—My Guinea Pigs Pip & Gus. Bryant, Donna. 20p. (ps-3). 1991. 8.95 (0-8120-6213-2) Barron.
—My Rabbit Roberta. Bryant, Donna. 20p. (ps-3). 1991. 8.95 (0-8120-6210-8) Barron.
—One Bear with Bees in His Hair. Wood, Jakki. LC 90-43211. 32p. (ps-1). 1991. 13.95 (0-525-44695-8, DCB) Dutton Child Bks.

—Rainforests. Petty, Kate. 32p. (gr. 2-4). 1993. pap. 5.95 (0-8120-1760-9) Barron.
—Under the Sea. Petty, Kate. 32p. (gr. 2-4). 1993. pap. 5.95 (0-8120-1759-5) Barron.
Wood, John N. & Dean, Kevin. Nature Hide & Seek: Rivers & Lake. Wood, John N. LC 93-22501. (gr. 1-4). 1993. 13.00 (0-679-83690-X) Knopf Bks Yng Read.
Wood, Marce. The Ragged Heart. Dittberner-Jax, Norita, ed. 164p. (Orig.). 1989. pap. 8.00 (0-927663-14-7) COMPAS.
Wood, Marina. Crayon Creations. Wood, Marina. 40p. (Orig.). (gr. 4-8). 1984. pap. 6.00 (0-932946-12-7) Burdett CA.
Wood, Tanya, photos by. They Dreamed of Horses: Careers for Horse Lovers. Frydenborg, Kay. LC 93-33023. 1994. write for info. (0-8027-8283-3); PLB write for info. (0-8027-8284-1) Walker & Co.
Wood, Ted, photos by. In the Village of the Elephants. Schmidt, Jeremy. LC 93-8545. 1994. 15.95 (0-8027-8226-4); PLB 16.85 (0-8027-8227-2) Walker & Co.
Wood, Vivian B., jt. illus. see Wood, David.
Wood, Wallace. Henry Ford: Young Man with Ideas. Aird, Hazel B. & Ruddiman, Catherine. LC 86-10756. 192p. (gr. 2-6). 1986. pap. 3.95 (0-02-041910-4, Aladdin) Macmillan Child Grp.
Woodaman, W. Mikey Goes Whale Watching. Allen, Joseph. Trout, M. D., ed. 50p. (Orig.). (gr. 1-5). 1986. PLB 13.50 (0-917071-05-0); pap. 8.95 (0-917071-04-2) Ocean Allen Pub.
Woodard, Chris. The Year Christmas Almost Stopped. 1st. ed. Kreysa, Francis J. 106p. (gr. 4-7). 1982. pap. 3.00 (0-9611398-0-3) Kreysa.
Woodbury Graphics Design Staff. School Records: Kindergarten - 12th Grade. Cox, Tom & Cox, Sherri. 27p. (gr. k-12). 1990. comb. processing 9.95 (0-9626932-0-0) TCA Pub.
Woodcock, John, jt. illus. see End, Simone.
Wooden, Bryan. Followers of the North Star: Rhymes about African American Heroes, Heroines, & Historical Times. Altman, Susan & Lechner, Susan. LC 93-797. 1993. write for info. (0-516-05151-2) Childrens.
Woodfin, James. Is He the One? Aderman, James. Fischer, William E., ed. 64p. (gr. 9-12). 1985. pap. 3.95 leader's guide (0-938272-21-7); pap. 3.25 student's guide (0-938272-20-9) WELS Board.
—Living As a Winner. Stadler, Richard H. Fischer, William E., ed. 64p. (gr. 9-12). 1985. pap. 2.95 leaders guide (0-938272-23-3); pap. 2.95 students guide (0-938272-22-5) WELS Board.
Wooding, Sharon. I'll Meet You at the Cucumbers. Moore, Lilian. LC 87-15195. 72p. (gr. 2-6). 1988. SBE 12.95 (0-689-31243-1, Atheneum Child Bk) Macmillan Child Grp.
—I'll Meet You at the Cucumbers. Moore, Lilian. (gr. 1-4). 1989. pap. 2.75 (0-553-15705-1, Skylark) Bantam.
—Tania's Trolls. Peters, Lisa W. 64p. (gr. 2-4). 1989. 10.95 (1-55970-040-8) Arcade Pub Inc.
Woodman, Nancy. Alpha Books. Warren, Vic & Reasoner, Charles. (ps-1). 1991. miniature board books in a tray 14.95 (1-878624-66-0) McClanahan Bk.
—Alpha-Books & Count with Us. Warren, Vic & Reasoner, Charles. (ps-1). 1991. miniature board books in a tray 19.95 (1-878624-83-0) McClanahan Bk.
—Consonants. 6p. (gr. k-1). 1992. bds. 3.95 (1-56293-184-9) McClanahan Bk.
—Count with Us. Warren, Vic & Reasoner, Charles. (ps-1). 1991. miniature board books in a tray 9.95 (1-878624-67-9) McClanahan Bk.
Woodroffe, Patrick. Balook. Anthony, Piers. 200p. 1990. 24.95 (0-88733-069-X); signed ed. 75.00 (0-685-53972-5) Underwood-Miller.
Woodruff, Mark. Travel Games for the Family. Boatness, Marie E. Westheimer, Mary, ed. LC 93-90005. 144p. (Orig.). (gr. 1-8). 1993. pap. 9.95 (0-9635619-0-1) Canyon Creek.
Woodruff, Thomas R. Great Lakes & Great Ships: An Illustrated History for Children. Mitchell, John C. 52p. (gr. 2-7). 1991. 15.95 (0-9621466-1-7) Suttons Bay Pubns.
Woodrutt, Thomas R. Michigan: An Illustrated History for Children. 2nd ed. Mitchell, John C. 52p. (gr. 1-6). 1987. Repr. 14.95 (0-9621466-0-9) Suttons Bay Pubns.
Woods, Dan. Marco Polo. Reynolds, Kathy, ed. LC 86-6678. 32p. (gr. 2-5). 1986. PLB 17.96 (0-8172-2627-3) Raintree Steck-V.
Woods Hole Oceanographic Institution Staff, photos by. Susan Humphris: Geologist. Murrow, Liza K. LC 88-51681. 64p. (Orig.). (gr. 4-8). 1989. pap. text ed. 6.95 (0-9621820-1-X) Teachers Lab.
Woods, Michael & Stuart, Walter. Polar Bears. Wildlife Education, Ltd. Staff. 24p. 1992. 13.95 (0-937934-85-2) Wildlife Educ.
Woods, Michael, et al. Rhinos. Wildlife Education, Ltd. Staff. 20p. (Orig.). (gr. 1-8). 1985. pap. 2.75 (0-937934-29-1) Wildlife Educ.
Woods, Michael J. Bambi. Salten, Felix. LC 90-26533. 160p. (ps up). 1992. pap. 18.00 jacketed, three-piece bdg (0-671-73937-9, S&S BFYR) S&S Trade.
Woodward, Alice B. The Study of Peter Pan. unabr., slightly altered ed. Barrie, James M. O'Connor, Daniel, adapted by. Kliros, Thea, contrib. by. LC 92-18641. 96p. 1992. Repr. 1.00 (0-486-27294-X) Dover.

Woodworth, Viki. Amazing Coin Tricks. Charles, Kirk. LC 93-29259. 1994. write for info. (*1-56766-084-3*) Childs World.
—Amazing String Tricks. Charles, Kirk. LC 93-35866. 1994. write for info. (*1-56766-085-1*, Pub. by Childs World) Standard Pub.
—Animal Jokes. Rothaus, Jim. (gr. 1-8). 1992. PLB 13.95 (*0-89565-861-5*); Resale. 19.95 (*0-685-60962-6*) Childs World.
—Bug Riddles. Rothaus, Jim. (gr. 1-8). 1992. PLB 13.95 (*0-89565-864-X*); Resale. 19.95 (*0-685-60959-6*) Childs World.
—Can You Grow a Popsicle? Woodworth, Viki. (gr. 1-8). 1992. PLB 18.50 (*0-89565-820-8*); Resale. 12.95 (*0-685-60958-8*) Childs World.
—Fairy Tale Jokes. Rothaus, Jim. (gr. 1-8). 1992. PLB 13.95 (*0-89565-862-3*); Resale. 19.95 (*0-685-60961-8*) Childs World.
—Fish Jokes. Woodworth, Viki. LC 92-34646. Date not set. write for info. (*1-56766-065-7*) Childs World. Postponed.
—Food Riddles. Woodworth, Viki. LC 92-38579. Date not set. write for info. (*1-56766-064-9*) Childs World. Postponed.
—Have You Heard a Kangaroo Buzz? Woodworth, Viki. (gr. 1-8). 1992. PLB 12.95 (*0-89565-822-4*); Resale. 18.50 (*0-685-60956-1*) Childs World.
—Have You Seen a Green Gorilla? Woodworth, Viki. (gr. 1-8). 1992. PLB 12.95 (*0-89565-825-9*); Resale. 18.50 (*0-685-60953-7*) Childs World.
—Have You Seen an Elephant's Nest? Woodworth, Viki. (gr. 1-8). 1992. PLB 12.95 (*0-89565-824-0*); Resale. 18.50 (*0-685-60954-5*) Childs World.
—Jungle Safari Jokes. Woodworth, Viki. LC 92-38581. Date not set. write for info. (*1-56766-062-2*) Childs World. Postponed.
—Mix & Match Jokes. Woodworth, Viki. LC 92-38580. Date not set. write for info. (*1-56766-063-0*) Childs World. Postponed.
—Monster Riddles. Rothaus, Jim. (gr. 1-8). 1992. PLB 13.95 (*0-89565-863-1*); Resale. 19.95 (*0-685-60960-X*) Childs World.
—Would You Spread a Turtle on Toast? Woodworth, Viki. (gr. 1-8). 1992. PLB 12.95 (*0-89565-823-2*); Resale. 18.50 (*0-685-60957-X*) Childs World.
—Would You Wear a Snake? Woodworth, Viki. (gr. 1-8). 1992. PLB 12.95 (*0-89565-821-6*); Resale. 18.50 (*0-685-60955-3*) Childs World.
Woofenden, Louise. Rainbow Colors in the Word: An Activity Book with Puzzles & Pictures to Color. Woofenden, Louise. Hill, Betty, ed. 32p. (Orig.). 1992. pap. text ed. 2.50 (*0-917426-08-8*) Am New Church Sunday.
Wook, Wallace. Thomas A. Edison: Young Inventor. Guthridge, Sue. LC 86-10862. 192p. (gr. 2-6). 1986. pap. 3.95 (*0-02-041850-7*, Aladdin) Macmillan Child Grp.
Wool, David. How Did We Find Out about Antarctica? Asimov, Isaac. (gr. 5-8). 1979. PLB 11.85 (*0-8027-6371-5*) Walker & Co.
—How Did We Find Out about Black Holes? Asimov, Isaac. LC 73-4320. (gr. 5 up). 1978. PLB 12.85 reinforced (*0-8027-6337-5*) Walker & Co.
—How Did We Find Out about Comets? Asimov, Isaac. LC 74-78115. 64p. (gr. 5-8). 1975. lib. bdg. 10.85 (*0-8027-6204-2*) Walker & Co.
—How Did We Find Out about Computers? Asimov, Isaac. LC 83-40401. 64p. (gr. 5 up). 1984. lib. bdg. 11.85 (*0-8027-6533-5*) Walker & Co.
—How Did We Find Out about DNA? Asimov, Isaac. LC 85-15589. 61p. (gr. 9 up). 1985. 9.95 (*0-8027-6596-3*); PLB 10.85 (*0-8027-6604-8*) Walker & Co.
—How Did We Find Out about Earthquakes? Asimov, Isaac. LC 77-78984. (gr. 6 up). 1978. PLB 12.85 (*0-8027-6306-5*) Walker & Co.
—How Did We Find Out about Germs. Asimov, Isaac. LC 73-81402. 64p. (gr. 5-8). 1973. PLB 10.85 (*0-8027-6166-6*) Walker & Co.
—How Did We Find Out about Life in the Deep Sea? Asimov, Isaac. (gr. 4-7). 1981. lib. bdg. 10.85 (*0-8027-6428-2*) Walker & Co.
—How Did We Find Out about Oil? Asimov, Isaac. 64p. (gr. 5-8). 1980. PLB 10.85 (*0-8027-6381-2*) Walker & Co.
—How Did We Find Out about Our Genes? Asimov, Isaac. LC 83-1211. 64p. (gr. 5-8). 1983. PLB 10.85 (*0-8027-6500-9*) Walker & Co.
—How Did We Find Out about Our Human Roots? Asimov, Isaac. (gr. 4-8). 1979. PLB 10.85 (*0-8027-6361-8*) Walker & Co.
—How Did We Find Out about Robots? Asimov, Isaac. 64p. (gr. 4-7). 1984. PLB 10.85 (*0-8027-6563-7*) Walker & Co.
—How Did We Find Out about Solar Power? Asimov, Isaac. 64p. (gr. 4-7). 1983. PLB 12.85 (*0-8027-6423-1*) Walker & Co.
—How Did We Find Out about the Beginning of Life? Asimov, Isaac. LC 81-71196. 64p. (gr. 4-7). 1982. PLB 10.85 (*0-8027-6448-7*) Walker & Co.
—How Did We Find Out about the Speed of Light? Asimov, Isaac. LC 86-4085. 64p. (gr. 5 up). 1986. 10.95 (*0-8027-6637-4*); PLB 11.85 (*0-8027-6613-7*) Walker & Co.
—How Did We Find Out about the Universe? Asimov, Isaac. LC 82-42531. 64p. (gr. 5-8). 1983. PLB 12.85 (*0-8027-6477-0*) Walker & Co.

—How Did We Find Out About Vitamins? Asimov, Isaac. LC 73-92453. 64p. (gr. 5-8). 1974. PLB 11.85 (*0-8027-6184-4*) Walker & Co.
—How Did We Find Out about Volcanoes? Asimov, Isaac. 64p. (gr. 4-7). 1981. PLB 12.85 (*0-8027-6412-6*) Walker & Co.
—People, Love, Sex & Families. Johnson, Eric W. 144p. (gr. 4 up). 1985. PLB 14.85 (*0-8027-6605-6*) Walker & Co.
Wooley, Kim. Getting to Know Britain: People, Places. Butterfield, Moira & Wright, Nicola. LC 93-29716. (gr. 3-7). 1994. 12.95 (*0-8120-6392-9*); pap. 5.95 (*0-8120-1854-0*) Barron.
—Getting to Know France. Wright, Nicola. 32p. (gr. 3-7). 1993. pap. 12.95 incl. 60 min. cassette (*0-8120-8125-0*) Barron.
—Getting to Know: France & French. Wright, Nicola. 32p. (gr. 3-7). 1993. 12.95 (*0-8120-6336-8*); pap. 5.95 (*0-8120-1532-0*) Barron.
—Getting to Know: Germany & German. Wright, Nicola. 32p. (gr. 3-7). 1993. 12.95 (*0-8120-6337-6*); pap. 5.95 (*0-8120-1533-9*) Barron.
—Getting to Know: Italy & Italian. Wright, Nicola. 32p. (gr. 3-7). 1993. 12.95 (*0-8120-6338-4*); pap. 5.95 (*0-8120-1534-7*) Barron.
—Getting to Know Spain. De Saules, Janet. 32p. (gr. 3-7). 1993. pap. 12.95 incl. 60 min. cassette (*0-8120-8127-7*) Barron.
—Getting to Know: Spain & Spanish. Wright, Nicola. 32p. (gr. 3-7). 1993. 12.95 (*0-8120-6339-2*); pap. 5.95 (*0-8120-1535-5*) Barron.
Woolf, Marie W. We Are Family. Nelson, JoAnne. LC 93-12176. 1994. 5.95 (*0-935529-60-8*) Comprehen Health Educ.
Woon, Kay. The Manmade Bear. Saunders, Kathleen. 33p. (gr. 2-5). 1980. pap. 2.95 (*0-939666-11-1*) Yosemite Assn.
Wormell, Christopher. Mowgli's Brothers. Kipling, Rudyard. (gr. 5 up). 1992. PLB 19.95 (*0-88682-488-5*) Creative Ed.
Worth, Jo & Knight, Ann. Look at Trees. rev. ed. Kirkpatrick, Rena K. LC 84-26225. 32p. (gr. 2-4). 1985. PLB 17.28 (*0-8172-2359-2*); pap. 4.95 (*0-8114-6905-0*) Raintree Steck-V.
Wosmek, Frances. Neighbors. Wosmek, Frances. LC 93-5079. 32p. (ps). 1993. 14.95 (*1-883280-01-X*); pap. 6.95 (*1-883280-02-8*) Font & Ctr Pr.
Wouters, Anne. This Book Is for Us. Wouters, Anne. LC 91-23742. 32p. (ps-1). 1992. 8.95 (*0-525-44882-9*, DCB) Dutton Child Bks.
—This Book Is Too Small. Wouters, Anne. LC 91-23743. 32p. (ps-1). 1992. 8.95 (*0-525-44881-0*, DCB) Dutton Child Bks.
Wozniak, Patricia. Tutu Kane & Granpa. Mower, Nancy. 32p. (ps). 1989. 7.95 (*0-916630-66-8*) Pr Pacifica.
Wozniak, Patricia A. Hawaiian Legends of Tricksters & Riddlers. Thompson, Vivian L. LC 90-44432. 112p. (Orig.). (gr. 4-8). 1990. pap. 8.50 (*0-8248-1302-2*, Kolowalu Bk) UH Pr.
—I Visit My Tutu & Grandma. Mower, Nancy A. LC 84-3280. (ps). 1984. 7.95 (*0-916630-41-2*) Pr Pacifica.
—Kawelo, Roving Chief. Thompson, Vivian L. LC 91-13651. 96p. (gr. 4-6). 1991. 14.95 (*0-8248-1339-1*, Kolowalu Bk) UH Pr.
Wray, Kit. Hidden Picture Fairy Tales: Rapunzel. Wray, Kit, retold by. LC 90-85901. 32p. (gr. k-5). 1991. 7.95 (*1-878093-25-8*) Boyds Mills Pr.
—Hidden Picture Fairy Tales: Snow White. Wray, Kit, retold by. LC 90-85902. 32p. (gr. k-5). 1991. 7.95 (*1-878093-26-6*) Boyds Mills Pr.
—King Arthur: A Hidden Picture Story. Wray, Kit, as told by. LC 91-76019. 32p. (ps-5). 1992. 7.95 (*1-56397-018-X*) Boyds Mills Pr.
—Robin Hood: A Hidden Picture Story. Wray, Kit, retold by. LC 91-72976. 32p. (ps-3). 1992. 7.95 (*1-56397-020-1*) Boyds Mills Pr.
Wren. At the Beach. Wren & Maile. (ENG & HAW.). 10p. (ps). 1992. bds. 3.95 (*1-880188-04-X*) Bess Pr.
—Flowers of Hawaii Coloring Book. Wren. 32p. (ps-2). 1992. pap. 3.95 (*1-880188-42-2*) Bess Pr.
—Local Colors. Wren & Maile. (ENG & HAW.). 10p. (ps). 1992. bds. 3.95 (*1-880188-02-3*) Bess Pr.
—Na Holoholona Maoli: Native Animals. Wren & Maile. (ENG & HAW.). 10p. (ps). 1992. bds. 3.95 (*1-880188-27-9*) Bess Pr.
—Na Mea Kanu: Plants. Wren & Maile. (ENG & HAW.). 10p. (ps). 1992. bds. 3.95 (*1-880188-28-7*) Bess Pr.
—Na 'Olelo Hawaii: Words. Wren & Maile. (ENG & HAW.). 10p. (ps). 1992. bds. 3.95 (*1-880188-29-5*) Bess Pr.
—One-Two-Three Counting Locally. Wren & Maile. (ENG & HAW.). 10p. (ps). 1992. bds. 3.95 (*1-880188-01-5*) Bess Pr.
—Pi'a'pa: Alphabet. Wren & Maile. (ENG & HAW.). 10p. (ps). 1992. bds. 3.95 (*1-880188-30-9*) Bess Pr.
—Say It in Hawaiian: My Body. Wren & Maile. (ENG & HAW.). 10p. (ps). 1992. bds. 3.95 (*1-880188-03-1*) Bess Pr.
Wren, James E. & MacMillan, Marilyn. Understanding Microcomputers. Ashworth, Dennis. Hylton, Richard M., ed. 32p. (Orig.). (gr. 9-12). 1987. pap. text ed. 6.50 (*0-89606-215-5*, 801) Am Assn Voc Materials.
Wright, Beth. The Boy Who Knew the Language of the Birds. Wetterer, Margaret K. 48p. (gr. k-4). 1991. PLB 17.50 (*0-87614-652-3*) Carolrhoda Bks.

—Count Your Way Through Italy. Haskins, Jim. 24p. (gr. 1-4). 1990. PLB 17.50 (*0-87614-406-7*) Carolrhoda Bks.
Wright, Blanche F. Miniature Mother Goose. Running Press Staff, ed. LC 91-50783. 128p. 1992. 4.95 (*1-56138-105-5*) Running Pr.
—Original Mother Goose. Running Press Staff, ed. LC 91-51057. 136p. 1992. 14.95 (*1-56138-113-6*) Running Pr.
—The Real Mother Goose, 4 bks. 96p. (ps-2). Set Incl. cassettes. pap. 16.98 (*1-55886-018-5*) Smarty Pants.
—The Real Mother Goose, Vol. I. 24p. (ps-2). Incl. cassettes. pap. 5.98 (*1-55886-012-6*) Smarty Pants.
—The Real Mother Goose, Vol. II. 24p. (ps-2). Incl. cassettes. pap. 5.98 (*1-55886-013-4*) Smarty Pants.
—The Real Mother Goose, Vol. III. 24p. (ps-2). Incl. cassettes. pap. 5.98 (*1-55886-014-2*) Smarty Pants.
—The Real Mother Goose, Vol. IV. 24p. (ps-2). Incl. cassettes. pap. 5.98 (*1-55886-015-0*) Smarty Pants.
—Real Mother Goose. 128p. (ps-1). 1991. Repr. 12.95 (*1-56288-041-1*) Checkerboard.
Wright, Curt, photos by. Changing Bodies, Changing Goals & Other Youth Soccer Stories. Russman, Penny & Wright, Sheila. Woog, Dan, ed. LC 84-71345. 96p. (Orig.). (gr. 5-9). 1984. pap. 5.95 (*0-9613538-0-5*) Ascot Pr.
Wright, David. Desert Animals. Chinery, Michael. LC 91-53146. 40p. (Orig.). (gr. 2-5). 1992. PLB 8.99 (*0-679-92048-X*); pap. 4.99 (*0-679-82048-5*) Random Bks Yng Read.
Wright, David, jt. illus. see Saunders, Mike.
Wright, David, photos by. Canada Is My Home. Wright, David, adapted by. LC 92-17726. 1992. PLB 18.60 (*0-8368-0846-0*) Gareth Stevens Inc.
Wright, David K., photos by. Canada. Wright, David K. LC 89-43197. 64p. (gr. 5-6). 1991. PLB 19.93 (*0-8368-0256-X*) Gareth Stevens Inc.
Wright, Evelyn M. Who Is Who at the Zoo. Graner, Carl E. Long, J. O., ed. (gr. k-1). 1989. pap. text ed. 3.95 (*0-685-27226-5*) Word & Image Pr.
Wright, Freire. Noah's Ark. Hayward, Linda. LC 86-17790. 32p. (ps-1). 1987. lib. bdg. 6.99 (*0-394-98716-0*); pap. 3.50 (*0-394-88716-6*) Random Bks Yng Read.
Wright, Freire & Foreman, Michael. The Nightingale & the Rose. Wilde, Oscar. (gr. 4 up). 1981. 14.95 (*0-19-520231-7*) OUP.
Wright, Freire & Foreman, Michael. Seven in One Blow. Wright, Freire & Foreman, Michael. 32p. (ps-3). 1981. lib. bdg. 4.99 (*0-394-93805-4*) Random Bks Yng Read.
Wright, Joan R. Frogs, Toads, Lizards & Salamanders. Parker, Nancy W. (gr. 1 up). 1990. 15.00 (*0-688-08680-2*); PLB 13.93 (*0-688-08681-0*) Greenwillow.
Wright, Joe. Rain & Shine. Lynn, Sara & James, Diane. LC 93-36420. 32p. (gr. k-2). 1994. 15.95 (*1-56847-142-4*) Thomson Lrning.
—What We Eat. James, Sara L. & James, Diane. LC 93-35627. 32p. (gr. k-2). 1994. 15.95 (*1-56847-141-6*) Thomson Lrning.
Wright, Joseph. Little Dracula at the Seashore. Waddell, Martin. LC 91-71835. 32p. (ps up). 1992. pap. 3.95 (*1-56402-026-6*) Candlewick Pr.
—Little Dracula Goes to School. Waddell, Martin. LC 91-71834. 32p. (ps up). 1992. pap. 3.95 (*1-56402-027-4*) Candlewick Pr.
—Little Dracula's Christmas. Waddell, Martin. 32p. (gr. k up). 1986. pap. 3.95 (*0-14-050658-6*) Viking Child Bks.
—Little Dracula's First Bite. Waddell, Martin. 32p. (gr. k up). 1986. pap. 3.95 (*0-14-050657-8*) Viking Child Bks.
Wright, Joseph, jt. illus. see White, Martin.
Wright, Meg. Our Bodies: Learning to Use Them to Please God. Brena, Brena. 20p. (gr. 1-8). 1983. pap. 3.95 (*0-86508-157-3*) BCM Pubn.
—Three Stories from India. (gr. 1-8). 1984. pap. text ed. 9.50 (*0-86508-166-2*) BCM Pubn.
Wright, Orville & Wright, Wilbur, photos by. The Wright Brothers: How They Invented the Airplane. Freedman, Russell. LC 90-48440. 132p. (gr. 5 up). 1991. 18.95 (*0-8234-0875-2*) Holiday.
Wright, Paul, et al. The Voyages of Columbus. Hills, Ken. LC 91-7580. 32p. (gr. 3-7). 1991. 9.00 (*0-679-82185-6*); lib. bdg. 12.99 (*0-679-92185-0*) Random Bks Yng Read.
Wright, Terry. Hands on Science: Animals. Carratello, John & Carratello, Patty. 32p. (gr. 2-5). 1988. wkbk. 4.95 (*1-55734-225-3*) Tchr Create Mat.
—Hands on Science: Our Changing Earth. Carratello, John & Carratello, Patty. 32p. (gr. 2-5). 1988. wkbk. 4.95 (*1-55734-226-1*) Tchr Create Mat.
—Hands on Science: Plants. Carratello, John & Carratello, Patty. 32p. (gr. 2-5). 1988. wkbk. 4.95 (*1-55734-224-5*) Tchr Create Mat.
—Think & Do Bulletin Boards. Nowlin, Susan & Sterling, Mary E. 96p. (gr. k-4). 1988. wkbk. 9.95 (*1-55734-063-3*) Tchr Create Mat.
Wright, Terry & Spence, Paula. Hands on Science: Simple Machines. Carratello, John & Carratello, Patty. 32p. (gr. 2-5). 1988. wkbk. 4.95 (*1-55734-227-X*) Tchr Create Mat.
Wright, Terry, jt. illus. see Spence, Paula.
Wright, Theresa. All about Cooperative Learning. Brown, Marzella. 48p. (gr. 2-5). 1990. wkbk. 5.95 (*1-55734-107-9*) Tchr Create Mat.
—Body Basics. Carratello, Patty. 48p. (gr. 1-5). 1987. wkbk. 5.95 (*1-55734-220-2*) Tchr Create Mat.

—It's Easy to Capitalize. Carratello, Patty. 32p. (gr. 1-4). 1988. 4.95 (1-55734-322-5) Tchr Create Mat.
—It's Easy to Write a Paragraph. Carratello, Patty. 32p. (gr. 1-4). 1988. wkbk. 4.95 (1-55734-324-1) Tchr Create Mat.
—Literature & Critical Thinking. Carratello, John & Carratello, Patty. 96p. (gr. 3-5). 1987. wkbk. 9.95 (1-55734-355-1) Tchr Create Mat.
—Literature & Critical Thinking, CB. Carratello, John & Carratello, Patty. 96p. (gr. k-3). 1987. wkbk. 9.95 (1-55734-356-X) Tchr Create Mat.
—Nutrition & Me. Carratello, Patty. 48p. (gr. 1-5). 1987. wkbk. 5.95 (1-55734-222-9) Tchr Create Mat.
—Sequence Fun. Spivak, Darlene. 32p. (gr. k-2). 1988. wkbk. 4.95 (1-55734-121-4) Tchr Create Mat.
Wright, Theresa & Smythe, Linda. Literature & Critical Thinking. Carratello, John & Carratello, Patty. 96p. (gr. k-3). 1988. wkbk. 9.95 (1-55734-357-8) Tchr Create Mat.
Wright, Theresa & Spence, Paula. Literature & Critical Thinking. Carratello, John & Carratello, Patty. Spivak, Darlene. ed. 96p. (gr. k-3). 1989. wkbk. 9.95 (1-55734-311-X) Tchr Create Mat.
—Valentine's Day Activities. Spivak, Darlene & Sterling, Mary E. 48p. (gr. 1-4). 1989. wkbk. 5.95 (1-55734-009-9) Tchr Create Mat.
Wright, Theresa, jt. illus. see Apodaca, Blanqui.
Wright, Theresa, jt. illus. see Fullam, Sue.
Wright, Theresa, jt. illus. see Spence, Paula.
Wright, Theresa, et al. Literature & Critical Thinking. Carratello, Patty. 96p. (gr. 3-5). 1988. wkbk. 9.95 (1-55734-358-6) Tchr Create Mat.
—Literature & Critical Thinking. Carratello, Patty. 96p. (gr. 3-5). 1988. wkbk. 9.95 (1-55734-359-4) Tchr Create Mat.
—Literature & Critical Thinking. Carratello, Patty. 96p. (gr. 5-8). 1988. wkbk. 9.95 (1-55734-360-8) Tchr Create Mat.
—Literature & Critical Thinking. Carratello, John & Carratello, Patty. 96p. (gr. 3-5). 1989. wkbk. 9.95 (1-55734-313-6) Tchr Create Mat.
Wright, Theresa M. D'Aulaires Book of Greek Myths. Ross, Cynthia. 48p. 1993. wkbk. 5.95 (1-55734-423-X) Tchr Create Mat.
—Farmer Boy. Swinwood, Laurie. 48p. 1993. wkbk. 5.95 (1-55734-428-0) Tchr Create Mat.
Wright, Theresa M., jt. illus. see Apodaca-LaBounty, Blanca.
Wright, Theresa N. Graph Art Puzzles. Spivak, Darlene E. 48p. (gr. 2-5). 1987. wkbk. 5.95 (1-55734-068-4) Tchr Create Mat.
Wright, Wilbur, jt. photog. see Wright, Orville.
Wright-Frierson, Virginia. Down at the Bottom of the Deep Dark Sea. Jones, Rebecca C. LC 90-33981. 40p. (ps-k). 1991. RSBE 14.95 (0-02-747901-3, Bradbury Pr) Macmillan Child Grp.
—Flowers for You: Blooms for Every Month. Holmes, Anita. LC 91-9482. 48p. (gr. 2-5). 1993. SBE 16.95 (0-02-744280-2, Bradbury Pr) Macmillan Child Grp.
—We're Growing Together. Ransom, Candice F. LC 92-7424. 32p. (ps-2). 1993. RSBE 14.95 (0-02-775666-1, Bradbury Pr) Macmillan Child Grp.
—When the Tide Is Low. Cole, Sheila. LC 84-10023. 32p. (ps-1). 1985. 12.95 (0-688-04066-7); PLB 12.88 (0-688-04067-5) Lothrop.
Wrightson, Bernie. Batman: The Cult. Starlin, Jim. Thorsland, Dan & O'Neil, Dennis, eds. Starlin, Jim, intro. by. 208p. (Orig.). 1991. pap. 14.95 (0-930289-85-4) DC Comics.
Wu, Marshall. A Child's Walk Through Asia. Levine, Bobbie & Lichter, Carolyn. 25p. (gr. 2-6). 1984. spiral bdg. 1.50 (0-912303-31-X) Michigan Mus.
Wu, Norbert. Beneath the Waves: Exploring the World of the Kelp Forest. Wu, Norbert. (gr. 3-7). 1992. 12.95 (0-87701-835-9) Chronicle Bks.
Wu, Shan M. The Mending of the Sky & Other Chinese Myths. Li, Xiao M., tr. from CHI. Buckley, Cicely, intro. by. 54p. (Orig.). (gr. 5 up). 1989. pap. 9.00 (0-9617481-3-3) Oyster River Pr.
Wuest, Gerard. The Cow. Benedict, Kitty. Soutter-Perrot, Andrienne, contrib. by. LC 92-14456. 32p. (gr. 5 up). 1992. PLB 10.95 (0-88682-567-9) Creative Ed.
Wulf, Barbara L. I Want to Be a Missionary. Hibschman, Barbara. 24p. (Orig.). (gr. 1-6). 1990. pap. 3.99 (0-87509-436-8) Chr Pubns.
Wummer, Amy. The Jellybean Principal. Morrow, Catherine. LC 93-26537. (gr. 3 up). 1994. write for info. (0-679-94743-4); pap. write for info. (0-679-84743-X) Random Bks Yng Read.
Wunderlin, Linda W. Celebrations. Bauman, Toni & Zinkgraf, June. 240p. (gr. k-6). 1985. wkbk. 14.95 (0-86653-330-3, GA 666) Good Apple.
Wunsch, Marjory. The Answered Prayer: And Other Yemenite Folktales. Gold, Sharlya & Caspi, Mishael M. 80p. (gr. 3-5). 1990. 13.95 (0-8276-0354-1) JPS Phila.
—Junkyard Dog. Ruch, Sandi B. LC 89-35652. 96p. (gr. 2-4). 1990. 14.95 (0-531-05842-5); PLB 14.99 (0-531-08442-6) Orchard Bks Watts.
Wurmfeld, Hope H. Trucker. Wurmfeld, Hope H. LC 89-13296. 64p. (gr. 3 up). 1990. RSBE 14.95 (0-02-793581-7, Macmillan Child Bk) Macmillan Child Grp.
Wyatt, Mildred. Julie Finds a Friend: Julie's Journey. Schenk, Julie W. Johnson, Sherry M., ed. 36p. (Orig.). (gr. 1-6). 1993. pap. write for info. (0-9635637-0-X) Amer Design.

Wyatt, Tracey. My Friend Jesus. Wyatt, Margaret. LC 86-90051. 20p. (Orig.). (ps-12). 1986. pap. 2.25 (0-9616117-0-7) M Wyatt.
Wyeth, N. C. The Boy's King Arthur. reissued ed. Lanier, Sidney. LC 73-13451. 336p. 1989. SBE 24.95 (0-684-19111-3, Scribners Young Read); deluxe ed. 75.00 (0-684-19118-0, Scribner) Macmillan Child Grp.
—The Deerslayer: or The First War-Path. Cooper, James Fenimore. LC 90-34326. 480p. 1990. SBE 24.95 (0-684-19224-1, Scribners Young Read); (Scribner) Macmillan Child Grp.
—Kidnapped. Stevenson, Robert Louis. 304p. 1989. 12.99 (0-517-68783-6) Outlet Bk Co.
—Kidnapped. Stevenson, Robert Louis. LC 89-43033. 290p. (gr. 6 up). 1993. Repr. of 1989 ed. 16.95 (1-56138-262-0) Running Pr.
—The Last of the Mohicans. reissue ed. Cooper, James Fenimore. LC 86-17694. 376p. 1986. SBE 24.95 (0-684-18711-6, Scribners Young Read); deluxe ed. 75.00 (0-684-18716-7, Scribner) Macmillan Child Grp.
—The Mysterious Island. reissued ed. Verne, Jules. LC 88-3167. 512p. 1988. SBE 25.95 (0-684-18957-7, Scribners Young Read); deluxe ed. 100.00 limited ed. (0-684-18991-7, Scribner) Macmillan Child Grp.
—N. C. Wyeth's Pilgrims. San Souci, Robert. 40p. (gr. 3-7). 1991. 13.95 (0-87701-806-5) Chronicle Bks.
—Reader's Digest Best Loved Books for Young Readers: Kidnapped - The Adventures of David Balfour. Stevenson, Robert Louis. Ogburn, Jackie, ed. 136p. (gr. 4-12). 1989. 3.99 (0-945260-32-6) Choice Pub NY.
—Rip Van Winkle. Irving, Washington. Glassman, Peter, afterword by. LC 87-60720. 110p. (ps up). 1987. 15.00 (0-688-07459-6) Morrow Jr Bks.
—Robin Hood. Creswick, Paul. LC 92-50796. 376p. (gr. 6 up). 1993. 16.95 (1-56138-265-5) Running Pr.
—Robinson Crusoe. Defoe, Daniel. LC 90-84707. 370p. (gr. 7 up). 1993. Repr. of 1990 ed. 16.95 (1-56138-263-9) Running Pr.
—Treasure Island. Stevenson, Robert Louis. LC 81-8788. 273p. (gr. 3 up). 1981. SBE 24.95 (0-684-17160-0, Scribners Young Read) Macmillan Child Grp.
—Treasure Island. Stevenson, Robert Louis. 274p. (gr. 5 up). 1992. Repr. of 1911 ed. 24.95 (1-879329-07-7) Time Warner Libraries.
—Treasure Island. Stevenson, Robert Louis. LC 89-43034. 274p. (gr. 5 up). 1993. Repr. of 1989 ed. 16.95 (1-56138-264-7) Running Pr.
—Westward Ho! reissue ed. Kingsley, Charles. LC 20-18930. 432p. (gr. 7 up). 1992. deluxe, limited ed. 75.00 (0-684-19443-0, Scribners Young Read); SBE 26.95 (0-684-19444-9, Scribners Young Read) Macmillan Child Grp.
—The White Company. Doyle, Arthur Conan. Glassman, Peter, afterword by. LC 87-62625. 362p. (ps up). 1988. 17.00 (0-688-07817-6) Morrow Jr Bks.
—The Yearling. Rawlings, Marjorie K. LC 85-40301. 416p. 1985. SBE 24.95 (0-684-18461-3, Scribners Young Read); deluxe, limited ed. o.s.i. 75.00 (0-684-18508-3, Scribners) Macmillan Child Grp.
Wyeth, N. C. & Murtagh, Mark. Rip Van Winkle: The Mountain Top Edition. rev. ed. Irving, Washington. Oakes, Donald T., ed. Hommel, Justine L., contrib. by. LC 89-62869. 92p. (gr. 9). 1989. pap. write for info. (0-9624216-0-X) MTH Soc Inc.
Wylie, David. Un Cuento Curioso de Colores. Wylie, Joanne. Kratky, Lada, tr. from ENG. LC 83-7448. (SPA.). 32p. (ps-2). 1984. PLB 15.00 (0-516-32983-9); pap. 3.95 (0-516-52983-8) Childrens.
—Un Cuento de Peces y Sus Formas (A Fishy Shape Story) Wylie, Joanne. Kratky, Lada, tr. LC 85-23264. (SPA.). 32p. (ps-2). 1986. PLB 15.00 (0-516-32985-5); pap. 3.95 (0-516-52985-4) Childrens.
—Un Cuento de un Pez Grande (A Big Fish Story) Wylie, Joanne. Kratky, Lada, tr. from ENG. LC 83-7449. (SPA.). 32p. (ps-2). 1984. PLB 15.00 (0-516-32982-0); pap. 3.95 (0-516-52982-X) Childrens.
—A Fishy Shape Story. Wylie, Joanne & Wylie, David. LC 83-25222. 32p. (ps-2). 1984. pap. 3.95 (0-516-42985-X) Childrens.
—A Funny Fish Story. Wylie, Joanne & Wylie, David. LC 83-24058. 32p. (ps-2). 1984. pap. 3.95 (0-516-42986-8) Childrens.
—A More or Less Fish Story. Wylie, Joanne & Wylie, David. LC 83-25223. 32p. (ps-2). 1984. pap. 3.95 (0-516-42984-1) Childrens.
—Sabes Donde Esta Tu Monstruo Esta Noche? Wylie, Joanne. Kratky, Lada, tr. LC 85-31423. (SPA.). 32p. (ps-2). 1986. PLB 15.00 (0-516-34491-9); pap. 3.95 (0-516-54491-8) Childrens.
Wyman, Cherie R. Hush, Puppies. Mitchell, Barbara. LC 82-4465. 48p. (gr. k-4). 1983. PLB 14.95 (0-87614-201-3) Carolrhoda Bks.
—Labor Day. Scott, Geoffrey. LC 81-15485. 48p. (gr. k-4). 1982. PLB 14.95 (0-87614-178-5) Carolrhoda Bks.
Wyman, Helen B. Millie Milkweed Seed Meets the Genny Geranium Gang. Cernobous, Wayne J. 46p. (Orig.). (gr. k-5). 1984. pap. 5.95 (0-9615065-0-4) Kinnickinnic Pr.
Wynne, Diana. My Brother & I Like Cookies. 2nd. ed. Carlson, Anna L. & Wynne, Diana. LC 80-81624. 96p. (Orig.). (gr. 1-7). 1983. pap. 4.95 (0-939938-00-6) Karwyn Ent.
—Stories to Treasure. Carlson, Anna L. 24p. (Orig.). (ps-5). 1984. pap. 62.40 (0-939938-06-5) Karwyn Ent.

Wynne, Dianna. Homer Bear's Secret. 1st. ed. Carlson, Anna L. 24p. (Orig.). (gr. k-4). 1983. pap. 1.95 (0-939938-05-7) Karwyn Ent.
Wynne, Patricia. The Animal ABC. LC 77-74470. 14p. (ps-k). 1977. bds. 3.95 (0-394-83589-1) Random Bks Yng Read.
—The Animal World: From Single-Cell Creatures to Giants of the Land & Sea. Silver, Donald M. LC 86-3894. 112p. (gr. 5 up). 1987. lib. bdg. 9.99 (0-394-96650-3); (BYR) Random Bks Yng Read.
—The Human Body. Bruun, Ruth D. & Bruun, Bertel. LC 82-5210. 96p. (gr. 5 up). 1982. lib. bdg. 12.99 (0-394-94424-0); pap. 11.95 smythe-sewn (0-394-84424-6) Random Bks Yng Read.
—Hungry, Hungry Sharks: A Step Two Book. Cole, Joanna. LC 85-2218. 48p. (gr. 1-3). 1986. lib. bdg. 7.99 (0-394-97471-9); pap. 3.50 (0-394-87471-4) Random Bks Yng Read.
—Life on Earth: Biology Today. Silver, Donald M. 96p. (gr. 5 up). 1983. lib. bdg. 7.99 (0-394-95971-X) Random Bks Yng Read.
—Why Save the Rain Forest? Silver, Donald. LC 93-22313. 1993. lib. bdg. 12.98 (0-671-86609-5, Messner); lib. bdg. 6.95 (0-671-86610-9, Messner) S&S Trade.
Wynne, Patricia J. The Checkerboard Press Nature Encyclopedia. Silver, Donald M. LC 89-48801. 128p. (gr. 3-7). 1990. 12.95 (1-56288-001-2) Checkerboard.
—Earth: The Ever-Changing Planet. Silver, Donald M. LC 88-11331. 96p. (Orig.). (gr. 5 up). 1989. lib. bdg. 12.99 (0-394-99195-8) Random Bks Yng Read.
—Extinction Is Forever. Silver, Donald. LC 93-32567. 1994. write for info. (0-671-86769-5, J Messner); pap. write for info. (0-671-86770-9, J Messner) S&S Trade.
—One Small Square Backyard. Silver, Donald M. LC 93-18353. (gr. 4 up). 1993. 14.95 (0-7167-6510-1, Sci Am Yng Rdrs) W H Freeman.
Wynne, Patrick. Fish Soup. Le Guin, Ursula K. LC 91-29740. 40p. (gr. 2-4). 1992. SBE 13.95 (0-689-31733-6, Atheneum Child Bk) Macmillan Child Grp.
Wyrick, Monica. God's Promise. Graham, Bill. 18p. (ps). 1991. 9.95 (1-879680-11-4) About You.
Wyss, Manspeter. King for One Day. Brenner, Peter. LC 74-151271. 36p. (ps-3). 7.95 (0-87592-027-6) Scroll Pr.

X

Xiao Jun Li. Nekane, the Lamina & the Bear: A Tale of the Basque Pyrenees. Araujo, Frank P. LC 93-84620. 32p. 1993. 16.95 (1-877810-01-0) Rayve Prodns.
Xieu-Lin, Li. The Fox Borrows the Tiger's Awe. Jwing-Ming Yang. Dougall, Alan, ed. 54p. (gr. 4 up). 1990. 4.95 (0-940871-12-2) Yangs Martial Arts.
—The Mask of the King. Ywing-Ming Yang. Dougall, Alan, ed. 52p. (gr. 4 up). 1990. 4.95 (0-940871-11-4) Yangs Martial Arts.

Y

Yaccarino, Dan. Big Brother Mike. Yaccarino, Dan. LC 92-72017. 32p. (ps-2). 1993. 13.95 (1-56282-329-9); PLB 13.89 (1-56282-330-2) Hyprn Child.
Yacoba. Ready for Something New. Keefer, Mikal. 48p. (Orig.). (gr. 1-3). 1993. pap. text ed. 3.99 (0-7847-0097-4, 24-03947) Standard Pub.
Yaffa. Shabbat Shalom. Groner, Judye & Wikler, Madeline. LC 88-83568. 12p. (ps). 1989. bds. 4.95 (0-930494-91-1) Kar Ben.
Yakovetic. Barney Wigglesworth & the Birthday Surprise. Murphy, Elspeth C. LC 88-4346. 32p. (ps-2). 1988. 7.99 (1-55513-696-6, Chariot Bks) Cook.
—Barney Wigglesworth & the Church Flood. Murphy, Elspeth C. LC 88-5008. 32p. (ps-2). 1988. 7.99 (1-55513-685-0, Chariot Bks) Cook.
—Barney Wigglesworth & the Party That Almost Wasn't. Murphy, Elspeth C. LC 88-4342. 32p. (ps-2). 1988. 7.99 (1-55513-684-2, Chariot Bks) Cook.
—Barney Wigglesworth & the Smallest Christmas Pageant. Murphy, Elspeth C. LC 88-5009. 32p. (ps-2). 1989. 7.99 (1-55513-686-9, Chariot Bks) Cook.
—Sir Lacksalot & the Two Headed Dragon. Thomas, Lenerd & Thomas, Janis. (gr. k-6). 1990. 16.95 (1-879480-00-X) L T Pub.
—Sir Lacksalot & the Two Headed Dragon Meet the Savage Sea Serpent. Thomas, Janis & Thomas, Lenerd. LC 91-61114. 48p. (gr. k-5). 1991. 16.95 (1-879480-01-8) L T Pub.
Yakovetic, Joe, jt. illus. see Haywood, Carolyn.
Yalowitz, Paul. Big, Bigger, Biggest Adventure. Banks, Kate. LC 89-34919. 40p. (ps-3). 1990. 12.95 (0-394-89857-5); lib. bdg. 13.99 (0-394-99857-X) Knopf Bks Yng Read.
—Boy, Can He Dance! Spinelli, Eileen. LC 92-12929. 32p. (ps-2). 1993. RSBE 14.95 (0-02-786350-6, Four Winds) Macmillan Child Grp.
—Fee Fiddle Foo What Should We Do? Rayburn, Cherie. Gress, Jonna, ed. LC 92-76154. 14p. (ps-3). 1993. pap. 11.40 (0-944943-23-3, 20588-8) Current Inc.

—Hurricane Music. Bottner, Barbara. LC 92-43697. 1994. write for info. (0-399-22544-7, Putnam) Putnam Pub Group.
—Somebody Loves You, Mr. Hatch. Spinelli, Eileen. LC 90-33016. 32p. (ps-2). 1992. RSBE 13.95 (0-02-786015-9, Bradbury Pr) Macmillan Child Grp.
—The Spooky Eerie Night Noise. Reeves, Mona R. LC 89-447. 32p. (ps-2). 1989. RSBE 12.95 (0-02-775732-3, Bradbury Pr) Macmillan Child Grp.
Yamaguchi, Marianne. The Miracle Tree. Mattingley, Christobel. LC 86-4541. 28p. (gr. 3 up). 1986. 11.95 (0-15-200530-7, Gulliver Bks) HarBrace.
Yamamoto, Joyce. The Raffi Singable Songbook. Raffi. 104p. (ps up). 1988. spiral bdg. 18.00 (0-517-56638-9) Crown Bks Yng Read.
Yamamoto, Neal. The Curious Carnival Caper. Woo, Diane. 64p. (Orig.). (gr. 2-6). 1992. pap. 3.95 (1-56288-217-1) Checkerboard.
—Fifty Nifty Magic Tricks. Wood, Elizabeth. 64p. (ps-3). 1992. pap. 2.95 (0-929923-93-6) Lowell Hse.
—Fifty Nifty Science Experiments. Melton, Lisa & Ladizinsky, Eric. 64p. (ps-3). 1992. pap. 3.95 (0-929923-92-8) Lowell Hse.
—The Mystery of Cavanaugh's Mansion. Woo, Diane. 64p. (Orig.). (gr. 2-6). 1992. pap. 3.95 (1-56288-219-8) Checkerboard.
—The Riddle of Rattlesnake Gulch. Woo, Diane. 64p. (Orig.). (gr. 2-6). 1992. pap. 3.95 (1-56288-216-3) Checkerboard.
—The Secret of the S. S. Crimson. Woo, Diane. 64p. (Orig.). (gr. 2-6). 1992. pap. 3.95 (1-56288-218-X) Checkerboard.
Yamashita, Mina. Done in the Sun: Solar Projects for Children. Hillerman, Anne. LC 83-638. 48p. (Orig.). (gr. 3-5). 1983. pap. 6.95 (0-86534-018-8) Sunstone Pr.
—Galisteo Legend. Atwood, Marjorie, Jr. Smith, James C., ed. LC 91-41394. 48p. (Orig.). 1992. pap. 6.95 (0-86534-154-0) Sunstone Pr.
—Learning to Color with Rhymes. Page, Burdys. 32p. (Orig.). 1990. pap. 6.95 (0-86534-146-X) Sunstone Pr.
Yamazaki, Sanae. Ooka the Wise: Tales of Old Japan. Edmonds, I. G. 96p. (gr. 3 up). 1994. Repr. of 1961 ed. PLB 14.95 (0-208-02379-8, Pub. by Linnet) Shoe String.
Yancey, Louise. The Mystery of the Pirate's Treasure. Bodie, Idella. LC 72-94930. 136p. (gr. 5-9). 1984. pap. 6.95 (0-87844-059-3) Sandlapper Pub Co.
Yancy, Louise. The Secret of Telfair Inn. Bodie, Idella. LC 79-177909. 98p. (gr. 5-9). 1983. pap. 6.95 (0-87844-050-X) Sandlapper Pub Co.
Yanez, Juan, jt. illus. see Katz, David A.
Yang Ming-Yi. The Long-Haired Girl: A Chinese Legend. Rappaport, Doreen, retold by. LC 93-28626. 1995. write for info. (0-8037-1411-4); PLB write for info. (0-8037-1412-2) Dial Bks Young.
—Peach Blossom Spring. Bordewich, Fergus M. LC 92-19676. 1994. 15.00 (0-671-78710-1, Green Tiger) S&S Trade.
Yardley, Joanna. Appleblossom. Oppenheim, Shulamith L. Yolen, Jane, ed. 28p. (gr. 1-7). 1991. 14.95 (0-15-203750-0, HB Juv Bks) HarBrace.
—The Bracelet. Uchida, Yoshiko. LC 92-26196. 32p. (ps-3). 1993. 14.95 (0-399-22503-X, Philomel Bks) Putnam Pub Group.
—The Red Ball. Yardley, Joanna. Yolen, Jane, ed. 32p. (ps-3). 1991. 14.95 (0-15-200894-2, J Yolen Bks) HarBrace.
Yaroslava. Holiday Treats. Hautzig, Esther. LC 83-9347. 96p. (gr. 3 up). 1983. SBE 13.95 (0-02-743350-1, Macmillan Child Bk) Macmillan Child Grp.
Yashima, T. Crow Boy. Yashima, Taro. (gr. k-3). 1955. pap. 14.99 (0-670-24931-9) Viking Child Bks.
—Umbrella. Yashima, Taro. (ps-1). 1958. pap. 15.99 (0-670-73858-1) Viking Child Bks.
Yashima, Taro. Momo's Kitten. Yashima, Mitsu & Yashima, Taro. (gr. k-2). 1977. pap. 4.99 (0-14-050200-9, Puffin) Puffin Bks.
—Umbrella. Yashima, Taro. (ps-1). 1977. pap. 3.99 (0-14-050240-8, Puffin) Puffin Bks.
Yasuki, Meredith. The Apple. Starkman, Neal. LC 91-16800. 44p. (Orig.). (gr. 7-9). 1991. pap. 7.00 (0-935529-29-2) Comprehen Health Educ.
Yasu Osawa. Northwest Coast Indian Art Series, 3 bks. rev. ed. McNutt, Nan. 118p. (gr. k-8). 1992. Set. pap. text ed. 29.95 (0-9614534-5-1) N McNutt Assocs.
Yates, John. Bread. Turner, Dorothy. 32p. (gr. 1-4). 1989. PLB 14.95 (0-87614-359-1) Carolrhoda Bks.
—Eggs. Turner, Dorothy. 32p. (gr. 1-4). 1989. PLB 14.95 (0-87614-360-5) Carolrhoda Bks.
—Milk. Turner, Dorothy. 32p. (gr. 1-4). 1989. PLB 14.95 (0-87614-361-3) Carolrhoda Bks.
—The Plant Cycle. Morgan, Nina. LC 93-977. 32p. (gr. 2-5). 1993. 12.95 (1-56847-091-6) Thomson Lrning.
—Potatoes. Turner, Dorothy. 32p. (gr. 1-4). 1989. PLB 14.95 (0-87614-362-1) Carolrhoda Bks.
Yazzie, Johnson. Witch Watch. Higgins, Betty. Sun Star Publications Staff, ed. August, Clara & Schatt, Paulintro. by. 24p. (Orig.). (gr. 3-8). 1986. pap. 2.95 (0-937787-05-1) Sun Star Pubns.
Yazzie, William P. Look up Look Down Look All Around Canyon de Chelly National Monument. Hallett, Bill & Hallett, Jane. 32p. (Orig.). (gr. 3-8). 1990. activity bk. 3.95 (1-877827-05-3) Look & See.
—Look up Look Down Look All Around Hubbell Trading Post. Hallett, Bill & Hallett, Jane. 16p. (Orig.). (gr. 3-8). 1990. write for info. activity bk. (1-877827-06-1) Look & See.

—Look up, Look down, Look All Around Mesa Verde National Park. Hallett, Bill & Hallett, Jane. 32p. (Orig.). (gr. 3-8). 1990. pap. 3.95 activity bk. (1-877827-04-5) Look & See.
Yealdhall, Gary. A Koosa for the Kids. Johnson, Ward. (ps-3). 1985. pap. 0.99 (0-87372-007-5) Parker Bros.
—The Magical Train. Rosenblatt, Arthur. 32p. (ps-3). 1985. pap. 0.99 (0-87372-008-3) Parker Bros.
Yeats, John. Beans & Peas. Miller, Susanna. 32p. (gr. 1-4). 1990. PLB 14.95 (0-87614-428-8) Carolrhoda Bks.
—Butter. Wake, Susan. 32p. (gr. 1-4). 1990. PLB 14.95 (0-87614-427-X) Carolrhoda Bks.
—Rice. Merrison, Lynne. 32p. (gr. 1-4). 1990. PLB 13.50 (0-87614-417-2) Carolrhoda Bks.
—Sugar. Nottridge, Rhoda. 32p. (gr. 1-4). 1990. PLB 14.95 (0-87614-418-0) Carolrhoda Bks.
Yee, Wong H. Big Black Bear. Yee, Wong H. LC 92-40862. 1993. 14.95 (0-395-66359-8) HM.
Yell, Vonett & Bergmann, Melvin. Jesus & Caesar Augustus: A Legend. Yzermans, Vincent A. LC 89-50566. 180p. (Orig.). (gr. 7-12). 1989. pap. 7.95 (0-89622-396-5) Twenty-Third.
Yen, Wenche. Goodbye Rune. Kaldhol, Marit. Crosby-Jones, Michael, tr. from NOR. (NOR). 32p. (ps-5). 1987. 13.95 (0-916291-11-1) Kane-Miller Bk.
Yencho, Mike. The First Step - Humility. Hipp, Earl. 30p. (gr. 9-12). 1992. pap. 2.50 (0-89486-624-9) Hazelden.
—The Second Step - Hope. Hipp, Earl. 28p. (gr. 9-12). 1992. pap. 2.50 (0-89486-642-7) Hazelden.
—The Third Step - POWER. Hipp, Earl. 35p. (gr. 9-12). 1992. pap. 2.50 (0-89486-643-5) Hazelden.
Yepsen, Roger. City Trains: Moving Through America's Cities by Rail. Yepsen, Roger. LC 92-2395. 96p. (gr. 3-7). 1993. SBE 14.95 (0-02-793675-9, Macmillan Child Bk) Macmillan Child Grp.
—Humanpower: Cars, Planes, & Boats with Muscles for Motors. Yepsen, Roger. LC 91-17575. 96p. (gr. 3-7). 1992. SBE 14.95 (0-02-793615-5, Macmillan Child Bk) Macmillan Child Grp.
Yerkes, Lane. The Birth of a New Tradition. Asmar, Ramsey. LC 92-35284. 32p. (gr. 4-6). 1992. PLB 17.96 (0-8114-3583-0) Raintree Steck-V.
—La Gallinita, el Gallo y el Frijol (Big Book) Kratky, Lada J. (SPA.). 24p. (Orig.). (gr. k-3). 1988. pap. text ed. 29.95 (0-917837-05-3) Hampton-Brown.
—La Gallinita, el Gallo y el Frijol (Small Book) Kratky, Lada J. (SPA.). 24p. (Orig.). (gr. k-3). 1992. pap. text ed. 6.00 (1-56334-081-X) Hampton-Brown.
—Muriel & Ruth: A Book about Friendship. Gordon, Jeffie R. LC 91-728718. 24p. (ps-3). 1992. 8.95 (1-878093-18-5) Boyds Mills Pr.
—Veo, Veo, Que Veo? (Big Book) Kratky, Lada J. (SPA.). 16p. (Orig.). (gr. k-3). 1990. pap. text ed. 29. 95 (0-917837-57-6) Hampton-Brown.
—Veo, Veo, Que Veo? (Small Book) Kratky, Lada J. (SPA.). 16p. (Orig.). (gr. k-3). 1992. pap. text ed. 6.00 (1-56334-082-8) Hampton-Brown.
Ying-Hwa Hu, jt. illus. see Van Wright, Cornelius.
Ylla, photos by. Sleepy Little Lion. Brown, Margaret W. LC 47-11482. 24p. (gr. k-3). 1947. PLB 12.89 (0-06-020771-X) HarpC Child Bks.
Yoder, Dot. Andy Finds a Turtle. Holcomb, Nan. 32p. (Orig.). (ps-2). 1988. pap. 6.95 (0-944727-02-6) Jason & Nordic Pubs.
—Andy Finds a Turtle. Holcomb, Nan. 32p. (ps-2). 1992. Repr. of 1988 ed. 13.95 (0-944727-13-1) Jason & Nordic Pubs.
—Andy Opens Wide. Holcomb, Nan. 32p. (ps-2). 1990. pap. 6.95 (0-944727-06-9) Jason & Nordic Pubs.
—Andy Opens Wide. Holcomb, Nan. 32p. (ps-2). 1992. Repr. of 1990 ed. 13.95 (0-944727-17-4) Jason & Nordic Pubs.
—Fair & Square. Holcomb, Nan. 32p. (ps-2). 1992. pap. 6.95 (0-944727-09-3) Jason & Nordic Pubs.
—Fair & Square. Holcomb, Nan. 32p. (ps-2). 1992. 13.95 (0-944727-10-7) Jason & Nordic Pubs.
—Patrick & Emma Lou. Holcomb, Nan. 32p. (ps-2). 1989. pap. 6.95 (0-944727-03-4) Jason & Nordic Pubs.
—Patrick & Emma Lou. Holcomb, Nan. 32p. (ps-2). 1992. Repr. of 1989 ed. 13.95 (0-944727-14-X) Jason & Nordic Pubs.
—Sarah's Surprise. Holcomb, Nan. 32p. (ps-2). 1990. pap. 6.95 (0-944727-07-7) Jason & Nordic Pubs.
—Sarah's Surprise. Holcomb, Nan. 32p. (ps-3). 1992. Repr. of 1990 ed. 13.95 (0-944727-18-2) Jason & Nordic Pubs.
—A Smile from Andy. Holcomb, Nan. 32p. (ps-2). 1989. pap. 6.95 (0-944727-04-2) Jason & Nordic Pubs.
—A Smile from Andy. Holcomb, Nan. 32p. (ps-3). 1992. Repr. of 1989 ed. 13.95 (0-944727-15-8) Jason & Nordic Pubs.
Yoe, Craig. The Secret of the Gifts. Flucke, Paul. LC 92-5679. 32p. 1992. 11.99 (0-8308-1841-3, 1841) InterVarsity.
Yolla Bolly Press Staff. Big Bugs. Yolla Bolly Press Staff. LC 93-27516. 1994. write for info. (0-15-200693-1, Gulliver Bks) HarBrace.
—Nightprowlers. Yolla Bolly Press Staff. LC 93-27547. 1994. write for info. (0-15-200694-X, Gulliver Bks) HarBrace.
Yoon, Hak-Jung. The Birth of Tangun: The Legend of Korea's First King. Ilyon. Adams, Edward B., tr. from KOR. 28p. (gr. 5). 1986. 7.50 (0-685-17153-1, Pub. by Seoul Intl Tourist SK) C E Tuttle.

—The Death of Echadon: How Buddhism Came to Silla. Ilyon. Adams, Edward B., tr. 28p. (gr. 5). 1986. 7.50 (0-685-17155-8, Pub. by Seoul Intl Tourist SK) C E Tuttle.
—King Munmu of Silla: A Korean Ruler Who United His Country. Ilyon. Adams, Edward B., tr. 28p. (gr. 5). 1986. 7.50 (0-685-17157-4, Pub. by Seoul Intl Tourist SK) C E Tuttle.
—The Three Good Events. Ilyon. Adams, Edward B., tr. from KOR. 28p. (gr. 5). 1986. 7.50 (0-685-17156-6, Pub. by Seoul Intl Tourist SK) C E Tuttle.
Yoshi. A to Zen - A Book of Japanese Culture. Wells, Ruth. LC 91-14183. 28p. (gr. k up). 1992. pap. 15.95 (0-88708-175-4) Picture Bk Studio.
—Big Al. Clements, Andrew. LC 88-15129. 28p. (ps up). 1991. pap. 14.95 (0-88708-075-8) Picture Bk Studio.
—Big Al. 2nd ed. Clements, Andrew. LC 88-15129. 32p. (gr. k up). 1991. pap. 4.95 (0-88708-154-1) Picture Bk Studio.
—Big Al. Clements, Andrew. 1991. pap. 3.95 (0-590-44455-7, Blue Ribbon Bks) Scholastic Inc.
—The Butterfly Hunt. Yoshi. LC 90-7361. 32p. (gr. k up). 1991. pap. 14.95 (0-88708-137-1) Picture Bk Studio.
—The Butterfly Hunt. Yoshi. LC 92-6631. 28p. (gr. k). 1993. Repr. Mini-bk. 4.95 (0-88708-270-X) Picture Bk Studio.
—Magical Hands. Barker, Marjorie. LC 89-31373. 32p. (ps up). 1991. pap. 14.95 (0-88708-103-7) Picture Bk Studio.
—One, Two, Three. Yoshi. LC 90-23918. 28p. (gr. k up). 1991. pap. 15.95 (0-88708-159-2) Picture Bk Studio.
—The Poor God: A Japanese Folktale. Wells, Ruth, retold by. LC 93-18236. 1993. 15.95 (0-88708-330-7) Picture Bk Studio.
—Who's Hiding Here? Yoshi. LC 92-6631. 32p. (ps up). 1992. pap. 4.95 minibk. (0-88708-277-7) Picture Bk Studio.
Yoshida, Toshi. Elephant Crossing. Yoshida, Toshi. 40p. (gr. k-4). 1989. 14.95 (0-399-21745-2, Philomel Bks) Putnam Pub Group.
—Young Lions. Yoshida, Toshi. 40p. (gr. 1-5). 1989. 14. 95 (0-399-21546-8, Philomel Bks) Putnam Pub Group.
—Young Lions. Yoshida, Toshi. 32p. (ps-3). 1992. pap. 5.95 (0-399-21886-6, Sandcastle Bks) Putnam Pub Group.
Yoshiko, Fujita. Move Like the Animals. Rosenholtz, Stephen. LC 91-66970. 32p. (ps-3). 1992. incl. cassette 19.95 (0-9630979-1-1); pap. 14.95 incl. cassette (0-9630979-0-3) Rosewood Pub.
Yoshi Miyake. The Pegasus Club & Mr. Beck, Amanda. LC 91-38330. 32p. (gr. 2-6). 1992. PLB 17.96 (0-8114-3577-6) Raintree Steck-V.
Yoshimura, Fumio. Sh-Ko & His Eight Wicked Brothers. Bryan, Ashley. LC 88-892. 32p. (ps-3). 1988. SBE 13. 95 (0-689-31446-9, Atheneum Child Bk) Macmillan Child Grp.
Yoshino, Shin. Cats. Overbeck, Cynthia. LC 83-17530. 48p. (gr. 4 up). 1983. PLB 19.95 (0-8225-1480-X) Lerner Pubns.
Young, Debby. Don't Do That: A Child's Guide to Bad Manners, Ridiculous Rules & Inadequate Etiquette. Polisar, Barry L. 64p. (Orig.). (gr. 3-6). 1989. 9.95 (0-938663-01-1); pap. 7.95 (0-938663-10-0) Rainbow Morn.
—Squeak the Dinosaur. Donnely, Marcus. 32p. (ps-2). 1987. 9.00 (0-938715-02-X) Toy Works Pr.
Young, Ed. All of You Was Singing. Lewis, Richard. LC 89-18263. 32p. 1991. SBE 13.95 (0-689-31596-1, Atheneum Child Bk) Macmillan Child Grp.
—Bicycle Rider. Scioscia, Mary. LC 82-47702. 48p. (gr. 2-6). 1983. PLB 13.89 (0-06-025223-5) HarpC Child Bks.
—Bicycle Rider. Scioscia, Mary. LC 82-47702. 48p. (gr. 2-6). 1993. pap. 3.95 (0-06-443295-5, Trophy) HarpC Child Bks.
—Birches. Frost, Robert. LC 87-46359. 32p. (gr. 2-4). 1988. 13.95 (0-8050-0570-6, Bks Young Read) H Holt & Co.
—Cats Are Cats. Larrick, Nancy, compiled by. 80p. (gr. 1 up). 1988. 17.95 (0-399-21517-4, Philomel Bks) Putnam Pub Group.
—Chinese Mother Goose Rhymes. Wyndham, Robert. 48p. (ps-k). 1989. (Sandcastle Bks); pap. 5.95 (0-399-21718-5) Putnam Pub Group.
—Dreamcatcher. Osofsky, Audrey. LC 91-20029. 32p. (ps-2). 1992. 14.95 (0-531-05988-X); lib. bdg. 14.99 (0-531-08588-0) Orchard Bks Watts.
—The Emperor & the Kite. Yolen, Jane. 32p. (ps-2). 1988. 15.95 (0-399-21499-2, Philomel Bks) Putnam Pub Group.
—Emperor & the Kite. Yolen, Jane. 32p. (ps up) 1992. pap. 5.95 (0-399-22512-9, Philomel Bks) Putnam Pub Group.
—Eyes of the Dragon. Leaf, Margaret. LC 85-11670. 32p. (ps-2). 1987. 14.95 (0-688-06155-9); PLB 14.88 (0-688-06156-7) Lothrop.
—Foolish Rabbit's Big Mistake. Martin, Rafe, rev. by. LC 84-11665. 32p. (gr. k-3). 1985. 14.95 (0-399-21178-0, Putnam) Putnam Pub Group.
—The Girl Who Loved the Wind. Yolen, Jane. LC 71-171012. 32p. (ps-3). 1982. (Crowell Jr Bks); PLB 14. 89 (0-690-33101-0, Crowell Jr Bks) HarpC Child Bks.
—The Girl Who Loved the Wind. reissue ed. Yolen, Jane. LC 71-171012. 32p. (ps-3). 1987. pap. 5.95 (0-06-443088-X, Trophy) HarpC Child Bks.
—Goodbye Geese. Carlstrom, Nancy. 32p. (ps-3). 1991. 14.95 (0-399-21832-7, Philomel) Putnam Pub Group.

—The Happy Prince. Wilde, Oscar. LC 88-29694. (gr. 1-3). 1992. pap. 14.95 jacketed (*0-671-67754-3*, S&S BFYR); pap. 5.95 (*0-671-77819-6*, S&S BFYR) S&S Trade.

—High in the Mountains. Radin, Ruth Y. LC 88-13395. 32p. (gr. k-4). 1989. RSBE 13.95 (*0-02-775650-5*, Macmillan Child Bk) Macmillan Child Grp.

—I Wish I Were a Butterfly. Howe, James. LC 86-33635. 28p. (ps-3). 1987. 15.95 (*0-15-200470-X*, Gulliver Bks) HarBrace.

—Iblis: An Islamic Tale. Oppenheim, Shulamith. LC 92-15060. 1993. write for info. (*0-15-238016-7*) HarBrace.

—In the Night, Still Dark. Lewis, Richard. LC 87-11538. 32p. 1988. RSBE 13.95 (*0-689-31310-1*, Atheneum Child Bk) Macmillan Child Grp.

—Lon Po Po: A Red Riding Hood Story from China. Young, Ed, tr. from CHI. 32p. (gr. k-4). 1989. 14.95 (*0-399-21619-7*, Philomel Bks) Putnam Pub Group.

—Mice Are Nice. Larrick, Nancy, ed. 48p. 1990. 15.95 (*0-399-21495-X*, Philomel Bks) Putnam Pub Group.

—Moon Tiger. Root, Phyllis. LC 85-7572. 32p. (ps-2). 1988. pap. 3.95 (*0-8050-0803-9*, Bks Young Read) H Holt & Co.

—The Other Bone. Young, Ed. LC 83-47706. 32p. (ps-3). 1984. PLB 14.89 (*0-06-026871-9*) HarpC Child Bks.

—The Rime of the Ancient Mariner. Coleridge, Samuel Taylor. LC 90-20403. 64p. (ps up) 1992. SBE 16.95 (*0-689-31613-5*, Atheneum Child Bk) Macmillan Child Grp.

—Sadako. Coerr, Eleanor. LC 92-41483. 48p. (gr. 1-4). 1993. TLB 16.95 (*0-399-21771-1*, Putnam) Putnam Pub Group.

—Seven Blind Mice. Young, Ed. 40p. (ps-6). 1992. PLB 16.95 (*0-399-22261-8*, Philomel Bks) Putnam Pub Group.

—The Turkey Girl: A Zuni Cinderella. Pollock, Penny, retold by. LC 93-28947. 1995. 15.95 (*0-316-71314-7*) Little.

—Up a Tree: A Wordless Picture Book. Young, Ed. LC 82-47733. 32p. (ps-3). 1983. PLB 14.89 (*0-06-026814-X*) HarpC Child Bks.

—Whale Song. Johnston, Tony. 32p. (ps-3). 1987. 14.95 (*0-399-21402-X*, Putnam) Putnam Pub Group.

—Whale Song. Johnston, Tony. 32p. (ps-3). 1992. pap. 5.95 (*0-399-22408-4*, Putnam) Putnam Pub Group.

—What Comes in Spring? Horton, Barbara S. LC 89-39695. 40p. (ps-1). 1992. 14.00 (*0-679-80268-1*); PLB 14.99 (*0-679-90268-6*) Knopf Bks Yng Read.

—While I Sleep. Calhoun, Mary. LC 90-25488. 32p. (ps up). 1992. 14.00 (*0-688-08200-9*); PLB 13.93 (*0-688-08201-7*) Morrow Jr Bks.

—White Wave: A Chinese Tale. Wolkstein, Diane. LC 78-4781. (gr. 2 up). 1979. (Crowell Jr Bks) HarpC Child Bks.

—Yeh Shen: A Cinderella Story from China. Louie, Ai-Ling. 32p. (ps-2). 1990. 14.95 (*0-399-20900-X*, Philomel) Putnam Pub Group.

—Yeh-Shen: A Cinderella Story from China. Ai-Ling, Louie, retold by. (ps-3). 1988. pap. 5.95 (*0-399-21594-8*, Sandcastle Bks) Putnam Pub Group.

—Young Fu of the Upper Yangtze. new ed. Lewis, Elizabeth F. LC 72-91654. 268p. (gr. 4-6). 1973. 18.95 (*0-8050-0549-8*, Bks Young Read) H Holt & Co.

Young, Elaine, et al. Poetry for Wee Folks. Hill, Charlotte M. Hill, Fred D., ed. LC 88-70281. 31p. (gr. k-3). 1988. 11.95 (*0-9620182-0-1*); pap. 6.95 (*0-9620182-2-8*) Charill Pubs.

Young, Ellan. Red Pandas: A Natural History. MacClintock, Dorcas. LC 88-3528. 112p. (gr. 7 up). 1988. SBE 14.95 (*0-684-18677-2*, Scribners Young Read) Macmillan Child Grp.

Young, James. Everyone Loves the Moon. Young. 32p. (ps-3). 1992. 14.95 (*0-316-97130-8*) Little.

—Penelope & the Pirates. Young, James. 32p. (ps-2). 1990. text ed. 12.95 (*1-55970-074-2*) Arcade Pub Inc.

Young, Janet. Easy Going Games. Sher, Barbara. LC 87-70022. 78p. (ps-6). 1987. pap. 8.00 (*0-930681-04-5*) Bright Baby.

Young, Jerry. Amazing Beetles. Still, John. LC 91-6516. 32p. (Orig.). (gr. 1-5). 1991. lib. bdg. 9.99 (*0-679-91519-2*); pap. 6.95 (*0-679-81519-8*) Knopf Bks Yng Read.

Young, Jerry, photos by. Amazing Animal Disguises. Sowler, Sandie. LC 91-53141. 32p. (Orig.). (gr. 1-5). 1992. PLB 9.99 (*0-679-92768-9*); pap. 6.95 (*0-679-82768-4*) Knopf Bks Yng Read.

—Amazing Armored Animals. Sowler, Sandie. LC 91-53140. 32p. (Orig.). (gr. 1-5). 1992. PLB 9.99 (*0-679-92767-0*); pap. 6.95 (*0-679-82767-6*) Knopf Bks Yng Read.

—Amazing Butterflies & Moths. Still, John. LC 90-19234. 32p. (Orig.). (gr. 1-5). 1991. PLB 9.99 (*0-679-91515-X*); pap. 6.95 (*0-679-81515-5*) Knopf Bks Yng Read.

—Amazing Cats. Parsons, Alexandra. LC 90-31885. 32p. (Orig.). (gr. 1-5). 1990. lib. bdg. 9.99 (*0-679-90690-8*); pap. 7.99 (*0-679-80690-3*) Knopf Bks Yng Read.

—Amazing Crocodiles & Other Reptiles. Ling, Mary. LC 90-19239. 32p. (Orig.). (gr. 1-5). 1991. PLB 9.99 (*0-679-90689-4*); pap. 7.99 (*0-679-80689-X*) Knopf Bks Yng Read.

—Amazing Fish. Ling, Mary. LC 90-49651. 32p. (Orig.). (gr. 1-5). 1991. PLB 9.99 (*0-679-91516-8*); pap. 7.99 (*0-679-81516-3*) Knopf Bks Yng Read.

—Amazing Frogs & Toads. Clarke, Barry. LC 90-31882. 32p. (Orig.). (gr. 1-5). 1990. lib. bdg. 9.99 (*0-679-90688-6*); pap. 7.99 (*0-679-80688-1*) Knopf Bks Yng Read.

—Amazing Lizards. Smith, Trevor. LC 90-31884. 32p. (Orig.). (gr. 1-5). 1990. lib. bdg. 9.99 (*0-679-90819-6*); pap. 7.99 (*0-679-80819-1*) Knopf Bks Yng Read.

—Amazing Mammals. Parsons, Alexandra. LC 89-38831. 32p. (gr. 1-5). 1990. 6.95 (*0-679-80224-X*); PLB 9.99 (*0-679-90224-4*) Random Bks Yng Read.

—Amazing Monkeys. Steedman, Scott. LC 90-19238. 32p. (Orig.). (gr. 1-5). 1991. PLB 9.99 (*0-679-91517-6*); pap. 6.95 (*0-679-81517-1*) Knopf Bks Yng Read.

—Amazing Poisonous Animals. Parsons, Alexandra. LC 90-31883. 32p. (Orig.). (gr. 1-5). 1990. lib. bdg. 9.99 (*0-679-90699-1*); pap. 6.95 (*0-679-80699-7*) Knopf Bks Yng Read.

—Amazing Snakes. Parsons, Alexandra. LC 89-38944. 32p. (gr. 1-5). 1990. 7.99 (*0-679-80225-8*); PLB 9.99 (*0-679-90225-2*) Random Bks Yng Read.

—Amazing Spiders. Parsons, Alexandra. LC 89-38833. 32p. (gr. 1-5). 1990. 7.99 (*0-679-80226-6*); PLB 9.99 (*0-679-90226-0*) Random Bks Yng Read.

—Amazing Tropical Birds. Legg, Gerald. LC 91-6515. 32p. (Orig.). (gr. 1-5). 1991. lib. bdg. 9.99 (*0-679-91520-6*); pap. 6.95 (*0-679-81520-1*) Knopf Bks Yng Read.

—Amazing Wolves, Dogs, & Foxes. Ling, Mary. LC 91-6514. 32p. (Orig.). (gr. 1-5). 1991. lib. bdg. 9.99 (*0-679-91521-4*); pap. 7.99 (*0-679-81521-X*) Knopf Bks Yng Read.

—Dog. Clutton-Brock, Juliet. LC 91-10135. 64p. (gr. 5 up). 1991. 15.00 (*0-679-81459-0*); lib. bdg. 15.99 (*0-679-91459-5*) Knopf Bks Yng Read.

—Horse. Clutton-Brock, Juliet. LC 91-53132. 64p. (gr. 5 up). 1992. 15.00 (*0-679-81681-X*); PLB 15.99 (*0-679-91681-4*) Knopf Bks Yng Read.

Young, Jerry & Greenaway, Frank, photos by. Amazing Bats. Greenaway, Frank. LC 91-6517. 32p. (Orig.). (gr. 1-5). 1991. lib. bdg. 9.99 (*0-679-91518-4*); pap. 7.99 (*0-679-81518-X*) Knopf Bks Yng Read.

Young, Karen. Mitchell D. Fardle. Taylor, Lucinda. LC 93-28987. 1994. 4.25 (*0-383-03761-1*) SRA Schl Grp.

Young, Kathy O. Once upon a Princess & a Pea. Campbell, Ann. LC 92-30526. 32p. 1993. 13.95 (*1-55670-289-2*) Stewart Tabori & Chang.

Young, Marian. A Fortune Branches Out. Mahy, Margaret. LC 93-11441. 1994. 13.95 (*0-385-32037-X*) Delacorte.

—Penny & the Four Questions. Krulik, Nancy E. 32p. (gr. 1-3). 1993. pap. 2.50 (*0-590-46339-X*) Scholastic Inc.

Young, Marion. A Fortunate Name. Mahy, Margaret. LC 93-560. 1993. 13.95 (*0-385-31135-4*) Delacorte.

—The Good Fortunes Gang. Mahy, Margaret. LC 92-38784. (gr. 5 up). 1993. 13.95 (*0-385-31015-3*) Delacorte.

Young, Mary M. Bear with Me: Story & Coloring Book Adjusting to Life with a New Baby. 16p. (ps-3). 1989. pap. 7.95 (*0-943114-20-9*, CB100) Childbirth Graphics.

Young, Mary O. The Moon Is Following Me. Heckman, Philip. LC 89-14921. 32p. (ps-1). 1991. SBE 13.95 (*0-689-31565-1*, Atheneum Child Bk) Macmillan Child Grp.

—Sea, Salt, & Air. Bat-Ami, Miriam. LC 91-34140. 32p. (gr. 1-5). 1993. RSBE 14.95 (*0-02-708495-7*, Macmillan Child Bk) Macmillan Child Grp.

Young, Noela. The Best Kept Secret. Rodda, Emily. 112p. (gr. 2-4). 1990. 14.95 (*0-8050-0936-1*, Bks Young Read) H Holt & Co.

—Finders Keepers. Rodda, Emily. LC 92-43776. 192p. (gr. 5 up). 1993. pap. 3.95 (*0-688-11846-1*, Pub. by Beech Tree Bks) Morrow.

—Moon-Dark. Wrightson, Patricia. LC 87-3903. 176p. (gr. 4-7). 1988. SBE 14.95 (*0-689-50451-9*, M K McElderry) Macmillan Child Grp.

—The Pigs Are Flying! Rodda, Emily. LC 88-2449. 160p. (gr. 4-6). 1988. Repr. of 1986 ed. 13.95 (*0-688-08130-4*) Greenwillow.

—Something Special. Rodda, Emily. 80p. (gr. 2-4). 1991. pap. 4.95 (*0-8050-1641-4*, Bks Young Read) H Holt & Co.

—The Timekeeper. Rodda, Emily. LC 92-31512. 160p. (gr. 5 up). 1993. 14.00 (*0-688-12448-8*) Greenwillow.

—Toby. Wild, Margaret. LC 93-14394. Date not set. write for info. (*0-395-67024-1*) Ticknor & Fields.

Young, Norman. People. Langley, Andrew & Butterfield, Moira. LC 89-42986. 48p. (gr. 5-6). 1989. PLB 17.27 (*0-8368-0132-6*) Gareth Stevens Inc.

Young, Ruth. One Crow: A Counting Rhyme. Aylesworth, Jim. LC 85-45856. 32p. (ps-1). 1988. (Lipp Jr Bks); PLB 12.89 (*0-397-32175-9*) HarpC Child Bks.

—One Crow: A Counting Rhyme. Aylesworth, Jim. LC 85-45856. 32p. (ps-1). 1990. pap. 5.95 (*0-06-443242-4*, Trophy) HarpC Child Bks.

Young, Ruth & Rose, Mitchell. Bear Magic. Cahill, Chris. LC 89-61636. 12p. (ps-1). 1990. bds. 5.95 incl. finger puppet (*1-877779-00-8*) Schneider Educational.

—Bunny Magic. Cahill, Chris. LC 89-61633. 12p. (ps-1). 1990. bds. 5.95 incl. finger puppet (*1-877779-02-4*) Schneider Educational.

—Spider Magic. LC 89-61632. 12p. (ps-1). 1990. bds. 5.95 incl. finger puppet (*1-877779-03-2*) Schneider Educational.

—Turtle Magic. LC 89-61634. 12p. (ps-1). 1990. bds. 5.95 incl. finger puppet (*1-877779-01-6*) Schneider Educational.

Young, Selina. Maybe It's a Pirate. Hindley, Judy. LC 92-7261. 32p. (ps-3). 1992. 14.95 (*1-56566-016-1*) Thomasson-Grant.

—Nanny Fox. Adams, Georgie. LC 93-72433. 32p. (ps-2). 1994. SBE 13.95 (*0-689-31920-7*, Atheneum Child Bk) Macmillan Child Grp.

—Whistling in the Woods. Young, Selina. LC 93-23765. 32p. 1994. 14.00 (*0-688-13073-9*, Tambourine Bks) Morrow.

Youngblood, Paul. She Made Many Rich: Sister Emma Francis of the Virgin Islands. Herzel, Catherine B. 24p. (gr. 6 up). 1990. pap. 4.50 (*0-935357-06-8*) CRIC Prod.

Younker, Linda Q. What Is a Cat? Hirschi, Ron. 32p. (gr. 1-3). 1991. 13.95 (*0-8027-8122-5*); PLB 14.85 (*0-8027-8123-3*) Walker & Co.

—Where Do Cats Live? Hirschi, Ron. 32p. (gr. 1-3). 1991. 13.95 (*0-8027-8109-8*); PLB 14.85 (*0-8027-8110-1*) Walker & Co.

Younker, Linda Q., photos by. What Is a Horse? Hirschi, Ron. 32p. (ps-4). 1989. 11.95 (*0-8027-6876-8*); PLB 12.85 (*0-8027-6877-6*) Walker & Co.

Youra, Dan. Oswald Hoot: The Owl Who Was Scared of the Dark. Gullander, Elizabeth. 64p. (ps-6). 1982. PLB 7.95 (*0-940828-06-5*); pap. 4.95 (*0-940828-05-7*) Olympic Pub.

Yourell, Pamela. The Friendship Tree & Other Stories for Children by Children. Graf, Virginia, ed. (Orig.). (gr. 3-8). Date not set. pap. 9.50 (*1-882788-03-6*) VanGar Pubs.

Youth Specialities Clip Art Staff. Creative Activities for Small Youth Groups. Rice, Wayne & Yaconelli, Mike. Stamschror, Robert P., ed. 101p. (gr. 7-12). 1991. pap. 12.95 (*0-88489-264-6*) St Marys.

Youth Specialties Clip Art Staff. Creative Communication & Discussion Activities. Rice, Wayne & Yaconelli, Mike. Stamschror, Robert P., ed. 96p. (gr. 7-12). 1991. pap. 12.95 (*0-88489-266-2*) St Marys.

—Creative Crowdbreakers, Mixers, & Games. Rice, Wayne & Yaconelli, Mike. Stamschror, Robert P., ed. 96p. (gr. 7-12). 1991. pap. 12.95 (*0-88489-265-4*) St Marys.

Yuditskaya, Tatyana. The Black Hen: or The Underground Inhabitants. Pogorelsky, Antony. Hamilton, Morse, retold by. LC 92-28599. 32p. (gr. 2-5). 1994. 14.99 (*0-525-65133-0*, Cobblehill Bks) Dutton Child Bks.

—The Four Gallant Sisters. Kimmel, Eric A., ed. LC 91-28231. 32p. (gr. 1-4). 1992. 15.95 (*0-8050-1901-4*, Bks Young Read) H Holt & Co.

Yue, David. Christopher Columbus: How He Did It. Yue, Charlotte & Yue, David. 144p. (gr. 3-6). 1992. 13.95 (*0-395-52100-9*) HM.

—The Tipi: A Center of Native American Life. Yue, Charlotte. LC 83-19529. 96p. (gr. 4-7). 1984. PLB 11.99 (*0-394-96177-3*) Knopf Bks Yng Read.

Z

Zabar, Abbie. Alphabet Soup. Zabar, Abbie. 32p. 1990. 14.95 (*1-55670-154-3*) Stewart Tabori & Chang.

—A Perfectly Irregular Christmas Tree. Zabar, Abbie. 40p. 1991. 14.00 (*0-517-58608-8*, C Potter Bks) Crown Pub Group.

Zabe, Michel & Rudkin, David. Aztec, Inca, & Maya. Baquedano, Elizabeth. 64p. (gr. 5 up). 1993. 15.00 (*0-679-83883-X*); PLB 15.99 (*0-679-93883-4*) Knopf Bks Yng Read.

Zabroski, Patricia. My Friend Has Asthma. Casterline, Charlotte L. 24p. (Orig.). (ps-6). 1985. pap. 4.95 (*0-9617218-0-4*) Info All Bk.

Zady, Mary. Tyrannosaurus Tex. Greenberg, Robert B. LC 89-4225. 64p. (gr. k-4). 1989. pap. 5.95 (*0-938349-38-4*) State House Pr.

Zafuto, Charles. Lone Woman of Ghalas-hat. Oliver, Rice D. 32p. (gr. 4-8). 1993. PLB 12.00 (*0-936778-52-0*); pap. 6.00 (*0-936778-51-2*) Calif Weekly.

Zagone, Arlene T. The Adventures of Micki Microbe. Guymon, Maurine B. 88p. (gr. 2-5). 1987. 15.00 (*0-9618650-0-8*) MoDel Pubs.

Zahn, Ellsworth E. Dudley. Zahn, Ellsworth E. 40p. (Orig.). Date not set. pap. text ed. 14.95 (*0-9637308-0-0*) L E Zahn.

Zahradka, Miroslav. The Un-Terrible Tiger. Zahradka, Miroslav. LC 78-155815. 32p. (ps-3). 7.95 (*0-87592-056-X*) Scroll Pr.

Zak, Drahos. Murgatroyd's Garden. Zavos, Judy. 32p. (gr. k-3). 1988. 9.95 (*0-312-01629-8*) St Martin.

Zala, Emma. Staying with Grandma Norma. Salem, Lynn & Stewart, Josie. 16p. (gr. 1). 1993. pap. 3.50 (*1-880612-08-9*) Seedling Pubns.

Zalben, Jane B. All in the Woodland Early: An ABC Book. Yolen, Jane. LC 91-70415. 32p. (ps-3). 1991. Repr. 14.95 (*1-878093-62-2*) Boyds Mills Pr.

—Beni's First Chanukah. Zalben, Jane B. LC 86-33634. 32p. (gr. k-3). 1988. 12.95 (*0-8050-0479-3*, Bks Young Read) H Holt & Co.

—Buster Gets Braces. Zalben, Jane B. LC 91-13967. 32p. (ps-2). 1992. 15.95 (*0-8050-1682-1*, Bks Young Read) H Holt & Co.

—Earth to Andrew O. Blechman. Zalben, Jane B. (gr. 3-7). 1989. 14.00 (0-374-31916-2) FS&G.
—Happy Passover, Rosie. Zalben, Jane B. LC 89-19979. 32p. (ps-2). 1990. 13.95 (0-8050-1221-4, Bks Young Read) H Holt & Co.
—Inner Chimes: Poems on Poetry. Goldstein, Bobbye S., ed. 32p. (ps-7). 1992. PLB 14.95 (1-56397-040-6) Boyds Mills Pr.
—An Invitation to the Butterfly Ball: A Counting Rhyme. Yolen, Jane. LC 91-70416. 32p. (ps-3). 1991. 14.95 (1-878093-61-4) Boyds Mills Pr.
—Leo & Blossom's Sukkah. Zalben, Jane B. LC 89-24596. 32p. (ps-2). 1990. 13.95 (0-8050-1226-5, Bks Young Read) H Holt & Co.
—Lewis Carroll's Jabberwocky. reissue ed. Carroll, Lewis. Humpty Dumpty, annotations by. 32p. 1992. PLB 14. 95 (1-56397-080-5) Boyds Mills Pr.
—The Walrus & the Carpenter. Carroll, Lewis. LC 85-7591. 32p. (gr. 2-4). 1986. 13.95 (0-8050-0071-2, Bks Young Read) H Holt & Co.
—The Walrus & the Carpenter. Carroll, Lewis. LC 85-7591. 32p. (gr. 2-4). 1990. pap. 4.95 (0-8050-1482-9, Owlet BYR) H Holt & Co.
Zalben, Jane B., photos by. Happy New Year, Beni. Zalben, Jane B. LC 92-25013. 32p. (gr. k-3). 1993. PLB 13.95 (0-8050-1961-8, Bks Young Read) H Holt & Co.
Zallinger, Jean. Oliver Twist. abridged ed. Dickens, Charles. Martin, Les, adapted by. LC 89-24279. 96p. (Orig.). (gr. 2-6). 1990. PLB 5.99 (0-679-90391-7); pap. 2.95 (0-679-80391-2) Random Bks Yng Read.
—Peter Pan. Barrie, J. M. Dubowski, Cathy, adapted by. LC 90-23077. 96p. (Orig.). (gr. 2-7). 1991. lib. bdg. 5.99 (0-679-91044-1); pap. 2.95 (0-679-81044-7) Random Bks Yng Read.
—Poems for Brothers, Poems for Sisters. Livingston, Myra C., selected by. LC 90-44463. 32p. (ps-3). 1991. reinforced 12.95 (0-8234-0861-2) Holiday.
—Weeds. Martin, Alexander C. 160p. (gr. 7 up). 1973. pap. write for info. (0-307-24353-2, Golden Pr) Western Pub.
Zallinger, Jean D. Baby Dinosaurs. Sattler, Helen R. LC 83-25631. 40p. (ps-3). 1984. 12.95 (0-688-03817-4); PLB 12.88 (0-688-03818-2) Lothrop.
—The Earliest Americans. Sattler, Helen R. 128p. (gr. 4-7). 1993. 16.45 (0-395-54996-5, Clarion Bks) HM.
—Sea Creatures Do Amazing Things. Myers, Arthur. LC 80-20089. 72p. (gr. 2-5). 1981. 7.95 (0-394-84487-4); lib. bdg. 8.99 (0-394-94487-9) Random Bks Yng Read.
—Sharks, the Super Fish. Sattler, Helen R. LC 84-4381. 96p. (gr. 9 up). 1985. 15.95 (0-688-03993-6) Lothrop.
—Whales, the Nomads of the Sea. Sattler, Helen R. LC 86-10397. 128p. (gr. 3 up). 1987. 15.00 (0-688-05587-7) Lothrop.
Zallinger, Peter. Dinosaurs. Zallinger, Peter. LC 76-24178. (ps-1). 1977. pap. 2.25 (0-394-83485-2) Random Bks Yng Read.
—Dinosaurs & Other Archosaurs. Zallinger, Peter. Risom, Ole & Luke, Melinda, eds. LC 85-42930. 96p. (gr. 5 up). 1986. lib. bdg. 9.99 (0-394-94421-6) Random Bks Yng Read.
—Prehistoric Animals. Zallinger, Peter. 32p. (ps-3). 1981. 2.25 (0-394-83737-1) Random Bks Yng Read.
Zander, Hans. Tunafish Sandwiches. Wolcott, Patty. LC 91-13496. 32p. (ps-2). 1991. 3.50 (0-679-81927-4); PLB 6.99 (0-679-91927-9) Random Bks Yng Read.
Zane, John. American Women: Four Centuries of Progress. 2nd, rev. ed. Zane, Polly & Zane, John. (gr. 7 up). 1989. write for info. (0-935070-03-6) Proof Pr.
Zangari, Rose M. Folk Tales of Connecticut, Vol. I. White, Glenn E. 61p. (Orig.). (gr. k-12). 1977. pap. 6.50 (0-9611926-0-7) GEF White.
—Folk Tales of Connecticut, Vol. II. White, Glenn E. 62p. (gr. k-12). 1981. pap. 6.50 (0-9611926-1-5) GEF White.
Zapel, Michelle. Acting & Stage Movement. White, Edwin C., et al. Wolfit, Donald, intro. by. LC 85-60573. 193p. (gr. 11-12). 1985. pap. text net 9.95 (0-916260-30-5, B187) Meriwether Pub.
Zarchy, Harry. Let's Go Camping: A Guide to Outdoor Living. Zarchy, Harry. (gr. 2 up). 1964. lib. bdg. 5.69 (0-394-91328-0) Knopf Bks Yng Read.
Zarins, Joyce A. The Go-Around Dollar. Adams, Barbara J. LC 90-26269. 32p. (gr. 1-4). 1992. RSBE 13.95 (0-02-700031-1, Four Winds) Macmillan Child Grp.
—How to Survive Third Grade. Lawlor, Laurie. (gr. 2-4). 1991. pap. 2.99 (0-671-67713-6, Minstrel Bks) PB.
Zarins, Joyce A. & Porter, Coni. The Struggle for Freedom: Plays on the American Revolution, 1762-1788. Baker, Charles F., III. Yoder, Carolyn P., ed. 144p. (Orig.). (gr. 4-9). 1990. pap. 15.95 (0-942389-05-0) Cobblestone Pub.
Zaunders, Bo. Max, the Bad-Talking Parrot. Demuth, Patricia B. LC 89-26015. 32p. (gr. k-4). 1990. 12.95 (0-525-44613-3, DCB); pap. 3.95 (0-525-44595-1, DCB) Dutton Child Bks.
Zavrel, Stepan. Vodnik. Zavrel, Stepan. LC 72-121796. 32p. (ps-3). 8.95 (0-87592-058-6) Scroll Pr.
Zehrfuss, D. Aventure de Choura. Modiano, Patrick. (FRE.). 36p. 1986. 24.95 (2-07-056294-8) Schoenhof.
Zelcer, Amir. All about Us. Rosenfeld, Dina. 32p. (ps-1). 1989. 8.95 (0-922613-02-8); pap. 6.95 (0-922613-03-6) Hachai Pubns.
—The Story of Danny Three Times. Estrin, Leibel. 32p. (ps-1). 1989. 8.95 (0-922613-10-9); pap. 6.95 (0-922613-11-7) Hachai Pubns.

—Take Care of Me. Jacobs, Chana R. Rosenfeld, Dina, ed. 32p. (ps-1). 1989. 8.95 (0-922613-06-0); pap. 6.95 (0-922613-07-9) Hachai Pubns.
Zeldich, Arieh. Always, Always. Dragonwagon, Crescent. LC 83-22199. 32p. (gr. 1-4). 1984. RSBE 12.95 (0-02-733080-X, Macmillan Child Bk) Macmillan Child Grp.
Zeldis, Malcah. Eve & Her Sisters: Women of the Old Testament. McDonough, Yona Z. LC 93-9378. 32p. (gr. k up). 1994. write for info. (0-688-12512-3); PLB write for info. (0-688-12513-1) Greenwillow.
—A Fine Fat Pig: And Other Animal Poems. Hoberman, Mary Ann. LC 90-37403. 32p. (ps-2). 1991. PLB 14. 89 (0-06-022426-6) HarpC Child Bks.
—Honest Abe. Kunhardt, Edith, photos by. LC 91-47191. 32p. (gr-3). 1993. 15.00 (0-688-11189-0); PLB 14. 93 (0-688-11190-4) Greenwillow.
Zeleznik, et al. Compendium of Contemporary Weapons. Siembieda, Kevin & Siembieda, Maryann. Marciniszyn, Alex, et al, eds. 176p. (Orig.). (gr. 8 up). 1993. pap. 19.95 (0-916211-65-7, 415) Palladium Bks.
Zelinsky, Paul. Emily Upham's Revenge. Avi. ALC Staff, ed. 176p. (gr. 5-12). 1992. pap. 3.95 (0-688-11899-2, Pub. by Beech Tree Bks) Morrow.
—More Rootabagas. Sandburg, Carl. LC 92-14930. 96p. (ps up). 1993. 18.00 (0-679-80070-0); PLB 18.99 (0-679-90070-5) Knopf Bks Yng Read.
—The Story of Mrs. Lovewright & Purrless Her Cat. reissued ed. Segal, Lore. LC 84-25011. 40p. (ps up). 1993. 14.00 (0-394-86817-X) Knopf Bks Yng Read.
Zelinsky, Paul O. Dear Mr. Henshaw. Cleary, Beverly. LC 83-5372. 144p. (gr. 3-7). 1983. 12.95 (0-688-02405-X); PLB 12.88 (0-688-02406-8, Morrow Jr Bks) Morrow Jr Bks.
—Dear Mr. Henshaw. Cleary, Beverly. 144p. (gr. k-6). 1984. pap. 3.99 (0-440-41794-5, YB) Dell.
—Dear Mr. Henshaw. large type ed. Cleary, Beverly. 141p. (gr. 2-6). 1987. Repr. of 1983 ed. lib. bdg. 14.95 (1-55736-001-4, Crnrstn Bks) BDD LT Grp.
—Emily Upham's Revenge, or, How Deadwood Dick Saved the Banker's Niece: Massachusetts Adventure. Avi. LC 92-390. 192p. 1992. 14.00 (0-688-11898-4) Morrow Jr Bks.
—Enano Saltarin. Zelinsky, Paul O., retold by. (SPA.). 40p. (gr. k-6). 1992. 15.00 (0-525-44903-5, DCB) Dutton Child Bks.
—The Enchanted Castle. Nesbit, E. Glassman, Peter, afterword by. LC 91-46267. 304p. 1992. 20.00 (0-688-05435-8) Morrow Jr Bks.
—Hansel & Gretel. Lesser, Rika, retold by. 48p. (ps-3). 1989. pap. 6.95 (0-399-21725-8, Sandcastle Bks) Putnam Pub Group.
—The Lion & the Stoat. Zelinsky, Paul O. LC 83-16326. 40p. (gr. 1-3). 1984. PLB 10.88 (0-688-02563-3) Greenwillow.
—The Maid & the Mouse & the Odd-Shaped House. Zelinsky, Paul O., adapted by. 32p. (ps-2). 1993. pap. 4.99 (0-14-054946-3, Puffin Unicorn) Puffin Bks.
—The Maid & the Mouse & the Odd-Shaped House. Zelinsky, Paul O., adapted by. 32p. (ps-2). 1993. 14.99 (0-525-45095-5, DCB) Dutton Child Bks.
—Ralph S. Mouse. Cleary, Beverly. LC 82-3516. 160p. (gr. 4-6). 1982. 14.95 (0-688-01452-6); lib. bdg. 14.88 (0-688-01455-0) Morrow Jr Bks.
—Ralph S. Mouse. Cleary, Beverly. 144p. (gr. 2-6). 1983. pap. 3.25 (0-440-47582-1, YB) Dell.
—The Random House Book of Humor for Children. Pollack, Pamela, compiled by. LC 86-31478. 320p. (gr. 2-6). 1988. 15.95 (0-394-88049-8); lib. bdg. 16.99 (0-394-98049-2) Random Bks Yng Read.
—Rumpelstiltskin. Grimm, Jacob & Grimm, Wilhelm K. Zelinsky, Paul O., retold by. LC 86-4482. 40p. (gr. k up). 1986. 14.00 (0-525-44265-0, DCB) Dutton Child Bks.
—Strider. Cleary, Beverly. LC 90-6608. 192p. (gr. 3 up). 1991. 13.95 (0-688-09900-9); PLB 13.88 (0-688-09901-7) Morrow Jr Bks.
—The Sun's Asleep Behind the Hill. Ginsburg, Mirra. LC 81-6615. 32p. (ps-1). 1982. 12.95 (0-688-00824-0); PLB 12.88 (0-688-00825-9) Greenwillow.
—Zoo Doings: Animal Poems. Prelutsky, Jack. LC 82-11996. 80p. (gr. 1-3). 1983. 13.00 (0-688-01782-7); PLB 12.93 (0-688-01784-3) Greenwillow.
Zellers, Toby. Rainbow Dragon: Lessons in Basic Values. Sells, Carole G. Guese, Raymond F., intro. by. 34p. (Orig.). (ps-6). 1988. pap. 3.95 (0-926739-00-X) Sells Pub.
Zemach, Margot. All God's Critters Got a Place in the Choir. Staines, Bill. LC 88-31696. 32p. (ps-2). 1989. 13.95 (0-525-44469-6, DCB) Dutton Child Bks.
—All God's Critters Got a Place in the Choir. Staines, Bill. 32p. (ps-2). 1993. pap. 4.99 (0-14-054838-6) Puffin Bks.
—The Cat's Elbow: & Other Secret Languages. Schwartz, Alvin. LC 81-5513. 96p. (gr. 3 up). 1982. 15.00 (0-374-31224-9) FS&G.
—The Chinese Mirror. Ginsburg, Mirra, ed. LC 86-22940. 26p. (ps-3). 1988. 15.95 (0-15-200420-3, Gulliver Bks) HarBrace.
—Duffy & the Devil. Zemach, Harve. LC 72-81491. 40p. (ps up). 1973. 17.00 (0-374-31887-5); pap. 4.95, 1986 (0-374-41897-7, Sunburst) FS&G.
—The Enchanted Umbrella: With a Short History of the Umbrella. Meyers, Odette. 28p. (ps-3). 1988. 13.95 (0-15-200448-3, Gulliver Bks) HarBrace.
—The Fisherman & His Wife. Grimm, Jacob & Grimm, Wilhelm K. Jarrell, Randall, tr. from GER. 32p. (ps up). 1987. pap. 4.95 (0-374-42326-1) FS&G.

—Jake & Honeybunch Go to Heaven. Zemach, Margot. 40p. (ps up). 1987. pap. 4.95 (0-374-43714-9, Sunburst) FS&G.
—The Judge: An Untrue Tale. Zemach, Harve. LC 79-87209. 48p. (ps-3). 1969. 17.00 (0-374-33960-0) FS&G.
—The Judge: An Untrue Tale. Zemach, Harve. 48p. (ps up). 1988. pap. 5.95 (0-374-43962-1, Sunburst) FS&G.
—The Little Red Hen: An Old Story. Zemach, Margot. LC 83-14159. 32p. (ps-3). 1983. 14.00 (0-374-34621-6) FS&G.
—Mommy, Buy Me a China Doll. Zemach, Harve. 32p. (ps up). 1989. pap. 4.95 (0-374-45286-5, Sunburst) FS&G.
—Naftali, the Storyteller & His Horse, Sus. Singer, Isaac Bashevis. (gr. 3 up). 1987. pap. 3.50 (0-374-45487-6) FS&G.
—A Penny a Look. Zemach, Harve. 48p. (ps up). 1989. pap. 4.95 (0-374-45758-1, Sunburst) FS&G.
—A Penny a Look: An Old Story. Zemach, Harve. LC 71-161373. 48p. (ps-3). 1971. 16.00 (0-374-35793-5) FS&G.
—The Princess & Froggie. Zemach, Harve & Zemach, Kaethe. (ps-3). 1992. pap. 4.95 (0-374-46011-6, Sunburst) FS&G.
—The Three Wishes: An Old Story. Zemach, Margot. LC 86-30956. 32p. (ps up). 1986. 16.00 (0-374-37529-1) FS&G.
—When Shlemiel Went to Warsaw & Other Stories. Singer, Isaac Bashevis. 161p. (gr. 3-7). 1986. pap. 4.95 (0-374-48365-5) FS&G.
Zeman, Ludmila. Gilgamesh the King, Bk. 1. Zeman, Ludmila. LC 91-67565. 24p. (gr. 3 up). 1992. 19.95 (0-88776-283-2) Tundra Bks.
—The Revenge of Ishtar, Bk. II: Gilgamesh the King. Zeman, Ludmila. LC 93-60332. 24p. (gr. 3 up). Date not set. 19.95 (0-88776-315-4) Tundra Bks.
—Le Roi Gilgamesh. Zeman, Ludmila. Boileau, Michele, tr. from ENG. LC 91-67565. (FRE.). 24p. (gr. 3 up). 1993. 19.95 (0-88776-288-3) Tundra Bks.
Zemke, Deborah. Shadow of Matilda Hunt. Zemke, Deborah. LC 90-46140. 32p. (gr. k-3). 1991. 14.45 (0-395-55334-2) HM.
—The Terrible Fight. St. Germain, Sharon. 32p. (gr. k-3). 1990. 13.45 (0-395-50069-9) HM.
Zemsky, Jessica. A Child's Introduction to Torah. Newman, Shirley. Newman, Louis, ed. 128p. (Orig.). (gr. 4). 1972. pap. text ed. 12.50 (0-87441-067-3) Behrman.
Zeringue, Dona. I Am I. Zeringue, Dona. Thornton, Don, intro. by. 32p. (Orig.). (gr. 6-12). Date not set. pap. 7.50 (1-882913-02-7) Thornton LA.
Zerner, Amy. Zen ABC. LC 92-22940. 1993. 14.95 (0-8048-1806-1) C E Tuttle.
Zerner, Amy & Drake, Charles. Astro-Dome Book: 3-D Map of the Night Sky. Hunig, Klaus. Solensten, Lori, ed. Himelfarb, Donna, intro. by. 68p. (Orig.). (gr. 4 up). 1983. pap. 9.95 incl. Constellation Handbook (0-913319-00-7) Sunstone Pubns.
Zerner, Jesse. Astro-Dots: Find the Constellations. 64p. (Orig.). (gr. 7). 1985. pap. 3.95 (0-913319-01-5) Sunstone Pubns.
Zhan, Tong. Legends of Ten Chinese Traditional Festivals. Li Shufen, ed. 54p. (gr. 1-3). 1992. pap. 8.95 (0-8351-2560-2) China Bks.
Zharkova, Olga. We Three Kings. LC 92-38571. 1993. 14.95 (0-590-46433-7) Scholastic Inc.
Zhou, Hoda D. The Awakening. Kaaki, Lisa. 30p. (Orig.). (gr. 1-4). 1991. pap. 3.50 (0-89259-118-8) Am Trust Pubns.
Ziba Design Staff. Strange Planes: A Collection of Unusual Paper Airplanes. Forcier, Mitchell D. 32p. (Orig.). (gr. k up). 1989. pap. 5.95 (0-9618419-4-X) Paper Press.
Zickefoose, Julie. Backyard Birds. Pine, Jonathan. LC 91-45184. 48p. (gr. 2-5). 1993. 12.00 (0-06-021039-7); PLB 11.89 (0-06-021040-0) HarpC Child Bks.
—Backyard Birds. Pine, Jonathan. LC 91-45184. 48p. (gr. 2-5). 1993. pap. 7.95 (0-06-446150-5, Trophy) HarpC Child Bks.
Zickefoose, Julie, et al. El Sur de Mexico: Cruce de Caminos para las Pajaros Migratorios: Southern Mexico: Crossroads for Migratory Birds. Greenberg, Russell. (ENG & SPA.). 32p. 1990. pap. 3.00 (1-881230-01-5) Smiths Migratory.
Zickefooser, Julie. Birds over Troubled Forests. Greenberg, Russell & Lumpkin, Susan. 32p. (Orig.). 1991. pap. 5.00 (1-881230-00-7) Smiths Migratory.
Ziebel, Peter, photos by. Greening the City Streets: The Story of Community Gardens. Huff, Barbara A. 80p. (gr. 3-7). 1990. 15.45 (0-89919-741-8, Clarion Bks) HM.
Ziegler, Jack. Annie's Pet: Level 2. Brenner, Barbara A. (ps-3). 1989. 9.99 (0-553-05833-9); pap. 3.50 (0-553-34693-8) Bantam.
—Eli & the Dimplemeyers. Kornblatt, Marc. LC 92-36793. 32p. (gr. k-3). 1994. RSBE 14.95 (0-02-750947-8, Macmillan Child Bk) Macmillan Child Grp.
—Mr. Knocky. Ziegler, Jack. LC 91-34145. 32p. (ps-3). 1993. RSBE 14.95 (0-02-793725-9, Macmillan Child Bk) Macmillan Child Grp.
Ziegler, Judy. My Silly Book of ABC's. Amerikaner, Susan. Brook, Bonnie, ed. 32p. (ps-1). 1989. 5.95 (0-671-68119-2); PLB 8.98 (0-671-68363-2) Silver Pr.
—My Silly Book of Colors. Amerikaner, Susan. Brook, Bonnie, ed. 32p. (ps-1). 1989. 5.95 (0-671-68120-6); PLB 8.98 (0-671-68364-0) Silver Pr.

—My Silly Book of Counting. Amerikaner, Susan. Brook, Bonnie, ed. 32p. (ps-1). 1989. 5.95 (0-671-68121-4); PLB 8.98 (0-671-68365-9) Silver Pr.
—My Silly Book of Opposites. Amerikaner, Susan. Brook, Bonnie, ed. 32p. (ps-1). 1989. 5.90 (0-671-68122-2); PLB 8.98 (0-671-68366-7) Silver Pr.
—Silly Me! Books, 4 bks. Amerikaner, Susan. (ps-1). 1990. Set, 24p. ea. 19.80 (0-671-93116-4, J Messner); Set, 24p. ea. lib. bdg. 35.92 (0-671-93137-7) S&S Trade.
Ziese, Mark. Unicorns for Everyone. large type ed. Riddle, Marilyn R. 24p. (Orig.). 1980. pap. 5.00 (0-9603748-1-7) Sandpiper OR.
Ziesler, Gunter. The Lion Family Book. Hofer, Angelika. LC 88-15139. 52p. (gr. k up). 1991. pap. 15.95 (0-88708-070-7) Picture Bk Studio.
Ziffer, Louise. Jake Finds a Penny. Sobel, Barbara. LC 86-81370. 32p. (gr. k-2). 1986. PLB 7.59 (0-87386-019-5); pap. 1.95 (0-87386-015-2) Jan Prods.
Zilka, Pat. Peter & His Pick-up Truck: A Southwestern Children's Tale. Nasta, Cynthia V. LC 89-80351. 24p. (ps-8). 1989. pap. 6.95 (0-9622064-0-7) Little Buckaroo.
—Peter & His Pick-up Truck: An Arizona Children's Tale. Nasta, Cynthia V. LC 89-80352. 24p. (ps-8). 1989. PLB 6.95 (0-9622064-1-5); pap. 6.95 (0-9622064-2-3) Little Buckaroo.
**Zilliox, Don't Teach Let Me Learn: About Mysteries, Mythology, Fairy Tales, Fables, Legends, the Supernatural. Crosby, Nina E. & Marten, Elizabeth H. 72p. (gr. 3-6). 1978. 8.95 (0-88047-006-2, 8209) DOK Pubs.
—Don't Teach Let Me Learn: About Opera, Ballet, American Theatre, Cinema. Crosby, Nina E. & Marten, Elizabeth H. 72p. (gr. 3-6). 1983. 8.95 (0-88047-008-9, 8210) DOK Pubs.
Zilliox, Elaine. Utilizing Problem Solving in Math. Forsthoefel, John. 40p. (Orig.). (gr. 3-8). 1984. 5.95 (0-88047-039-9, 8405) DOK Pubs.
—Who Lives in the Igloo? Lund, Coby, et al. 52p. (Orig.). (gr. 4-9). 1984. 6.95 (0-88047-046-1, 8402) DOK Pubs.
Zillmer, Rolf. Haleakala National Park. updated ed. Radlauer, Ruth. LC 79-10500. 48p. (gr. 3 up). 1987. PLB 17.27 (0-516-07499-7); pap. 4.95 (0-516-47499-5) Childrens.
Zillmer, Rolf, photos by. Great Smoky Mountains National Park. updated ed. Radlauer, Ruth. LC 76-9839. 48p. (gr. 3 up). 1985. pap. 4.95 (0-516-47489-8) Childrens.
—Mesa Verde National Park. updated ed. Radlauer, Ruth. LC 76-27350. 48p. (gr. 3 up). 1984. pap. 4.95 (0-516-47490-1) Childrens.
—Yosemite National Park. updated ed. Radlauer, Ruth S. LC 75-2160. 48p. (gr. 3 up). 1984. PLB 17.27 (0-516-07486-5) Childrens.
Zimdars, Berta. A Christmas Tree for Lydia. Enright, Elizabeth. 32p. (gr. 4 up). 1986. PLB 13.95s.p. (0-88682-063-4) Creative Ed.
—The Circus. Saroyan, William. 32p. (gr. 4 up). 1986. PLB 13.95s.p. (0-88682-066-9) Creative Ed.
—Fresh. Pearce, Phillippa. 64p. 1987. PLB 13.95s.p. (0-88682-125-8) Creative Ed.
Zimmer, Dirk. The Adventures of Ratman. Weiss, Ellen & Friedman, Mel. LC 89-10869. 64p. (Orig.). (gr. 2-4). 1990. pap. 2.50 (0-679-80531-1) Random Bks Yng Read.
—Bony-Legs. Cole, Joanna. LC 85-5070. 48p. (ps-3). 1984. RSBE 13.95 (0-02-722970-X, Four Winds) Macmillan Child Grp.
—Bony-Legs. Cole, Joanna. 48p. (ps-2). 1986. pap. 2.95 (0-590-40516-0) Scholastic Inc.
—Buster Loves Buttons! Manushkin, Fran. LC 84-48332. 64p. (gr. k-3). 1985. HarpC Child Bks.
—The Cow Is Mooing Anyhow. Geringer, Laura. LC 85-45251. 40p. (ps-4). 1991. PLB 14.89 (0-06-021987-4) HarpC Child Bks.
—The Cow Is Mooing Anyhow. Geringer, Laura. LC 85-45251. 40p. (ps-4). 1993. pap. 4.95 (0-06-443332-3, Trophy) HarpC Child Bks.
—The Curse of the Squirrel. Yep, Laurence. LC 87-4612. 64p. (gr. 2-4). 1987. lib. bdg. 6.99 (0-394-98200-2); pap. 1.95 (0-394-88200-8, Random Juv) Random Bks Yng Read.
—Esteban & the Ghost. Hancock, Sibyl. LC 82-22125. 32p. (ps-3). 1983. PLB 10.89 (0-8037-2411-X) Dial Bks Young.
—Goody Sherman's Pig. Christian, Mary B. LC 90-35181. 48p. (gr. 2-6). 1991. RSBE 12.95 (0-02-718251-7, Macmillan Child Bk) Macmillan Child Grp.
—In a Dark, Dark Room & Other Scary Stories. Schwartz, Alvin. LC 83-47699. 64p. (gr. k-3). 1984. 14.00 (0-06-025271-5); PLB 13.89 (0-06-025274-X) HarpC Child Bks.
—The Iron Giant: A Story in Five Nights. Hughes, Ted. LC 87-45089. 64p. (gr. 3-7). 1988. PLB 11.89 (0-06-022639-0) HarpC Child Bks.
—The Iron Giant: A Story in Five Nights. Hughes, Ted. LC 87-45089. 64p. (gr. 3-7). 1988. pap. 4.95 (0-06-440214-2, Trophy) HarpC Child Bks.
—John Tabor's Ride. Day, Edward C. LC 88-9065. 40p. (ps-3). 1989. PLB 13.99 (0-394-98577-X) Knopf Bks Yng Read.
—Ma & Pa Dracula. Martin, Ann M. LC 89-2081. 128p. (gr. 3-7). 1989. 13.95 (0-8234-0781-0) Holiday.
—Mean Jake & the Devils. Hooks, William H. LC 81-65846. 64p. (gr. 3-6). 1981. Dial Bks Young.

—The Moonbow of Mr. B. Bones. Lewis, J. Patrick. LC 88-37107. 40p. (ps-4). 1992. 16.00 (0-394-85365-2); PLB 16.99 (0-394-95365-7) Knopf Bks Yng Read.
—The Naked Bear: Folktales of the Iroquois. Bierhorst, John, ed. LC 86-21836. 144p. (gr. 3 up). 1987. 14.95 (0-688-06422-1) Morrow Jr Bks.
—The One That Got Away. Everett, Percival. 32p. (gr. 1-4). 1992. PLB 14.95 (0-685-52550-3, Clarion Bks) HM.
—The One That Got Away. Everett, Percival. (gr. 1-4). 1992. 14.45 (0-395-56437-9, Clarion Bks) HM.
—Perrywinkle & the Book of Magic Spells. Madsen, Ross M. LC 85-15932. 48p. (ps-3). 1988. pap. 4.95 (0-8037-0501-8) Dial Bks Young.
—Poor Gertie. Bograd, Larry. LC 86-3091. 96p. (gr. 3-6). 1986. pap. 12.95 (0-385-29487-5) Delacorte.
—The Sky Is Full of Song. Hopkins, Lee B., ed. LC 82-48263. 48p. (gr. 3-7). 1983. PLB 13.89 (0-06-022583-1) HarpC Child Bks.
—The Sky Is Full of Song. Hopkins, Lee B. LC 82-48263. 48p. (gr. k-3). 1987. pap. 4.95 (0-06-446064-9, Trophy) HarpC Child Bks.
—Some Fine Grampa! Arkin, Alan. LC 92-24436. 32p. (gr. k-3). 1994. 14.00 (0-06-021533-X); PLB 13.89 (0-06-021534-8) HarpC Child Bks.
—Tsugele's Broom. Carey, Valerie S. LC 92-9873. 48p. (gr. k-3). 1993. 15.00 (0-06-020986-0); PLB 14.89 (0-06-020987-9) HarpC Child Bks.
—Weird Wolf. Cuyler, Margery. LC 89-7541. 80p. (gr. 2-4). 1989. 12.95 (0-8050-0835-7, Bks Young Read) H Holt & Co.
—Weird Wolf. Cuyler, Margery. LC 89-1541. 80p. (gr. 2-4). 1991. pap. 4.95 (0-8050-1643-0, Bks Young Read) H Holt & Co.
—Windy Day: Stories & Poems. Bauer, Caroline F., ed. LC 86-42994. 96p. (gr. 2-5). 1988. (Lipp Jr Bks); PLB 13.89 (0-397-32208-9) HarpC Child Bks.
Zimmer, Ronald. The Key to Understanding Global Studies: A Regents-RCT Review Book. Killoran, James, et al. LC 89-92425. 362p. (Orig.). (gr. 9-10). 1990. pap. text ed. 5.95 (0-9624723-0-1) Jarrett Pub.
Zimmerman, Jerry. Frosty the Snowman: Book & Cookie Cutter Set. Nelson, Steve & Rollins, Jack. 17p. (ps-2). 1993. Incl. 2 cookie cutters. pap. 3.95 (0-590-69016-7, Cartwheel) Scholastic Inc.
—Think Fast: Nickelodeon's Brain-Bending Games & Puzzles. Hovanec, Helene. LC 90-86410. 96p. (Orig.). (gr. 2-6). 1992. pap. 2.95 (0-448-40200-9, G&D) Putnam Pub Group.
Zimmerman, Paul & Dearth, D. L. Mackinac Island for Kids-on-the-Go. Jolliffe, Susan D. & McVeigh, Amy. 32p. (Orig.). (ps-7). 1993. pap. 5.00 (0-9623213-2-X) Mackinac Pub.
Zimmerman, Robert. Blame It on the Wolf & Be Kind to Your Mother (Earth): Two Original Plays. Love, Douglas. LC 92-4624. 80p. (gr. 5 up). 1993. PLB 13.89 (0-06-021106-7) HarpC Child Bks.
—Holiday in the Rain Forest & Kabuki Gift: Two Plays. Love, Douglas. 112p. (gr. 4 up). 1994. PLB 13.89 (0-06-024276-0) HarpC Child Bks.
—Holiday in the Rain Forest: Theater Kit. Love, Douglas. (gr. 5 up). 1993. 14.95 (0-694-00561-4, Festival) HarpC Child Bks.
—Kabuki Gift: Theater Kit. Love, Douglas. 32p. (gr. 5 up). 1993. 14.95 (0-694-00562-2, Festival) HarpC Child Bks.
—So You Want to Be a Star. Love, Douglas. 32p. (gr. 5 up). 1993. 18.95 (0-694-00428-6, Festival) HarpC Child Bks.
Zink-White, Nancy. Health & Hygiene. Bains, Rae. LC 84-2627. 32p. (gr. 3-6). 1985. PLB 9.49 (0-8167-0180-6); pap. text ed. 2.95 (0-8167-0181-4) Troll Assocs.
—Reptiles & Amphibians. Sabin, Louis. LC 84-8445. 32p. (gr. 3-6). 1985. PLB 9.49 (0-8167-0294-2); pap. text ed. 2.95 (0-8167-0295-0) Troll Assocs.
Zistel, Era. Wintertime Cat. rev. ed. Zistel, Era. 64p. 1988. pap. 5.95 (0-9617426-4-X) J N Townsend.
Zmolek, Sandy D. Froggie Kicks & Duck Dives: A Child's Primer for Beginning Swimming. Kolbisen, Irene M. Reiter, John, ed. Graves, Steve, intro. by. (ps). 1990. 12.95 (1-877863-02-5); pap. 8.95 (0-685-26751-2) I Think I Can.
—Starfish Floats & Motorboats: A Child's Primer for Beginning Swimming. Kolbisen, Irene M. Reiter, John, ed. Graves, Steve, intro. by. 20p. (ps). 1990. 12.95g (1-877863-01-7); pap. 8.95g (0-685-26750-4) I Think I Can.
—Wiggle-Butts & Up-Faces: A Child's Primer for Beginning Swimming. Kolbisen, Irene M. Reiter, John, ed. Graves, Steve, intro. by. 32p. (ps). 1989. PLB 14.95 (1-877863-00-9) I Think I Can.
Zokeisha. Firehouse. Zokeisha. Klimo, Kate, ed. 16p. (ps-k). 1983. pap. 3.50 (0-671-46128-1, Little Simon) S&S Trade.
—A Little Book of Baby Animals. Zokeisha. Klimo, Kate, ed. 16p. 1982. pap. 2.95 (0-671-44840-4, Little Simon) S&S Trade.
—A Little Book of Colors. Zokeisha. Klimo, Kate, ed. 16p. 1982. pap. 2.95 (0-671-45570-2, Little Simon) S&S Trade.
—Mother Goose House. Zokeisha. Klimo, Kate, ed. 16p. (ps-k). 1983. pap. 3.50 (0-671-46127-3, Little Simon) S&S Trade.
—Mouse House. Zokeisha. Klimo, Kate, ed. 16p. 1983. pap. 2.95 (0-671-46129-X, Little Simon) S&S Trade.
Zorn, Vic, jt. illus. see Thomas, Tim.

Zornes, Rocky. A Penny's Worth of Character. Stuart, Jesse. Miller, Jim W., et al, eds. 62p. (gr. 3-6). 1988. 10.00 (0-945084-03-X) J Stuart Found.
—A Penny's Worth of Character. 3rd ed. Stuart, Jesse. Miller, Jim W. & Herndon, Jerry A., eds. LC 92-31438. 62p. (gr. 3-6). 1993. pap. 3.00 (0-945084-32-3) J Stuart Found.
—A Ride with Huey the Engineer. 3rd ed. Stuart, Jesse. Gifford, James M., intro. by. 112p. (gr. 3 up). 1988. 12.00 (0-945084-11-0); pap. 6.00 (0-945084-10-2) J Stuart Found.
Zudeck, Darryl. Prairie Visions: The Life & Times of Solomon Butcher. Conrad, Pam. LC 90-38658. 96p. (gr. 5 up). 1991. 17.00 (0-06-021373-6); PLB 16.89 (0-06-021375-2) HarpC Child Bks.
Zudeck, Darryl S. Prairie Songs. reissue ed. Conrad, Pam. LC 85-42633. 176p. (gr. 5 up). 1987. pap. 3.95 (0-06-440206-1, Trophy) HarpC Child Bks.
Zuniga, A. de. The Story of My Life: Student Activity Book. Sohl, Marcia & Dackerman, Gerald. (gr. 4-10). 1976. wkbk 1.25 (0-88301-195-6) Pendulum Pr.
Zuraw, Stephen, et al. Smile: Be True to Your Teeth & They'll Never be False to You. rev. ed. Rauch, Robert S. 105p. 1991. pap. text ed. 4.95 (0-9624076-0-7) R S Rauch.
Zvorykin, Boris. Golden Cockerel & Other Fairy Tales. Pushkin, Aleksandr. Wood, Jessie, tr. Nureyev, Rudolf, intro. by. 1990. 24.95 (0-385-26252-3) Doubleday.
Zweger, Lisbeth. The Strange Child. Hoffmann, E. T. LC 84-8404. 28p. (gr. 3 up). 1991. pap. 16.95 (0-907234-60-7) Picture Bk Studio.
Zweifel, Frances. Amazing Science Experiments with Everyday Materials. Churchill, E. Richard. LC 90-20641. 128p. (gr. 4-12). 1992. 12.95 (0-8069-7372-2); pap. 4.95 (0-8069-7371-4) Sterling.
—Simple Physics Experiments with Everyday Materials. Breckenridge, Judy. LC 92-25312. 128p. (gr. 4 up). 1993. 12.95 (0-8069-8606-9) Sterling.
—Simple Physics Experiments with Everyday Materials. Breckenridge, Judy. 128p. (gr. 4-10). 1993. pap. 4.95 (0-8069-8607-7) Sterling.
—Simple Weather Experiments with Everyday Materials. Mandell, Muriel. LC 90-37915. 128p. (gr. 4 up). 1991. pap. 4.95 (0-8069-7295-5) Sterling.
Zweifel, Frances W. Simple Science Experiments with Everyday Materials. Mandell, Muriel. LC 88-31201. 128p. (gr. 4-10). 1989. 12.95 (0-8069-6794-3) Sterling.
Zweiger, Jackie. Coyote Tales: How the Sandbur Came to West Texas. Johnson, Frances. 32p. (gr. 1-3). 1992. 11.95 (0-89015-866-5) Eakin-Sunbelt.
Zwerger, Lisbeth. Aesop's Fables. (ps up). 1991. pap. 15.95 (0-88708-108-8); pap. 4.95 (0-88708-179-7) Picture Bk Studio.
—The Canterville Ghost. Wilde, Oscar. LC 86-8179. (gr. 4 up). 1991. pap. 15.95 (0-88708-027-8) Picture Bk Studio.
—A Christmas Carol. Dickens, Charles. LC 88-15161. 60p. (gr. 5 up). 1991. pap. 19.95 (0-88708-069-3) Picture Bk Studio.
—The Deliverers of Their Country. Nesbit, Edith. LC 85-9389. 32p. (gr. 3-5). 1991. pap. 15.95 (0-88708-005-7) Picture Bk Studio.
—The Gift of the Magi. O. Henry. LC 92-6632. 28p. 1992. pap. 5.95 (0-88708-276-9) Picture Bk Studio.
—Hans Christian Andersen Fairy Tales. Andersen, Hans Christian. Zwerger, Lisbeth, selected by. Bell, Anthea, tr. from DAN. LC 91-13132. 68p. (gr. up). 1992. 19.95 (0-88708-182-7) Picture Bk Studio.
—Hansel & Gretel. Grimm, Jacob & Grimm, Wilhelm K. 32p. (ps-2). 1991. pap. 3.95 (0-590-44459-X, Blue Ribbon Bks) Scholastic Inc.
—The Legend of Rosepetal. Brentano, Clemens. LC 84-27386. 32p. (gr. 2-6). 1991. pap. 16.95 (0-907234-71-2) Picture Bk Studio.
—Little Red Cap. Grimm, Jacob & Grimm, Wilhelm K. Crawford, Elizabeth D., tr. from GER. LC 82-14211. 24p. (ps-3). 1983. PLB 11.88 (0-688-01716-9) Morrow Jr Bks.
—The Nightingale. Andersen, Hans Christian. LC 84-9492. (gr. 1 up). 1991. pap. 14.95 (0-907234-57-7) Picture Bk Studio.
—The Nightingale. Andersen, Hans Christian. Bell, Anthea, tr. from DAN. LC 92-6632. 28p. (gr. 4 up). 1993. Repr. Mini-bk. 4.95 (0-88708-269-6) Picture Bk Studio.
—The Nutcracker. Hoffmann, E. T. Bell, Anthea, adapted by. LC 87-15249. (gr. 1 up). 1991. pap. 14.95 (0-88708-051-0) Picture Bk Studio.
—The Nutcracker. 2nd, abr. ed. Hoffmann, E. T. Bell, Anthea, tr. LC 87-15249. 28p. (gr. k up). 1991. pap. 4.95 (0-88708-156-8) Picture Bk Studio.
—The Selfish Giant. Wilde, Oscar. LC 83-24930. 28p. (gr. 1 up). 1991. pap. 15.95 (0-907234-30-5) Picture Bk Studio.
—The Selfish Giant. Wilde, Oscar. 1991. pap. 4.95 (0-590-44459-X) Scholastic Inc.
—The Seven Ravens. Grimm, Jacob & Grimm, Wilhelm K. LC 83-61777. 28p. (gr. k up). 1991. pap. 14.95 (0-88708-092-8); pap. 5.95 (0-685-24951-4) Picture Bk Studio.
—The Seven Ravens. Grimm, Jacob & Grimm, Wilhelm K. Bell, Anthea, tr. LC 93-20122. (ps-8). 1993. 4.95 (0-88708-326-9) Picture Bk Studio.
—Thumbeline. Andersen, Hans Christian. LC 85-12062. 28p. (gr. 1 up). 1991. pap. 14.95 (0-88708-006-5) Picture Bk Studio.

—Thumbeline. abr. ed. Andersen, Hans Christian. Bell,
Anthea, tr. from DAN. LC 90-25387. 28p. (gr. k up).
1991. pap. 4.95 (*0-88708-171-1*) Picture Bk Studio.
—Till Eulenspiegel's Merry Pranks. Janisch, Heinz. Bell,
Anthea, tr. from GER. LC 90-7168. 32p. (gr. 3 up).
1991. pap. 15.95 (*0-88708-150-9*) Picture Bk Studio.